The

CHARLES F. STANLEY

LIFE PRINCIPLES BIBLE

IS PRESENTED TO:

BY:

ON:

A LIFE PRINCIPLES RESOURCE

THE
CHARLES F. STANLEY
LIFE PRINCIPLES
BIBLE

THE CHARLES F. STANLEY LIFE PRINCIPLES BIBLE

CHARLES F. STANLEY
GENERAL EDITOR

NKJV
NEW KING JAMES VERSION®
Build Your Life On It.™

NELSON BIBLES
A Division of Thomas Nelson Publishers
Since 1798
www.thomasnelson.com

THE CHARLES F. STANLEY LIFE PRINCIPLES BIBLE

Printed in the United States of America

3 4 5 6 7 8 9 – 11 10 09 08 07 06

TABLE OF CONTENTS

OLD TESTAMENT

NEW TESTAMENT

ABBREVIATIONS

Book abbreviations used in the notes and articles:

OT = Old Testament
NT = New Testament

Abbr.	Book	Testament	Page
1 Chr.	1 Chronicles	OT	464
1 Cor.	1 Corinthians	NT	1330
1 John	1 John	NT	1479
1 Kin.	1 Kings	OT	389
1 Pet.	1 Peter	NT	1467
1 Sam.	1 Samuel	OT	310
1 Thess.	1 Thessalonians	NT	1404
1 Tim.	1 Timothy	NT	1417
2 Chr.	2 Chronicles	OT	497
2 Cor.	2 Corinthians	NT	1350
2 John	2 John	NT	1486
2 Kin.	2 Kings	OT	427
2 Pet.	2 Peter	NT	1474
2 Sam.	2 Samuel	OT	354
2 Thess.	2 Thessalonians	NT	1411
2 Tim.	2 Timothy	NT	1424
3 John	3 John	NT	1487
Acts	Acts	NT	1264
Amos	Amos	OT	1041
Col.	Colossians	NT	1397
Dan.	Daniel	OT	995
Deut.	Deuteronomy	OT	195
Eccl.	Ecclesiastes	OT	756
Eph.	Ephesians	NT	1377
Esth.	Esther	OT	573
Ex.	Exodus	OT	64
Ezek.	Ezekiel	OT	937
Ezra	Ezra	OT	539
Gal.	Galatians	NT	1366
Gen.	Genesis	OT	1
Hab.	Habakkuk	OT	1072
Hag.	Haggai	OT	1084
Heb.	Hebrews	NT	1438
Hos.	Hosea	OT	1018
Is.	Isaiah	OT	780
James	James	NT	1457
Jer.	Jeremiah	OT	854
Job	Job	OT	584
Joel	Joel	OT	1034
John	John	NT	1229
Jon.	Jonah	OT	1055
Josh.	Joshua	OT	240
Jude	Jude	NT	1488
Judg.	Judges	OT	272
Lam.	Lamentations	OT	928
Lev.	Leviticus	OT	114
Luke	Luke	NT	1183
Mal.	Malachi	OT	1102
Mark	Mark	NT	1156
Matt.	Matthew	NT	1111
Mic.	Micah	OT	1060
Nah.	Nahum	OT	1068
Neh.	Nehemiah	OT	553
Num.	Numbers	OT	147
Obad.	Obadiah	OT	1052
Phil.	Philippians	NT	1388
Philem.	Philemon	NT	1435
Prov.	Proverbs	OT	723
Ps.	Psalms	OT	622
Rev.	Revelation	NT	1491
Rom.	Romans	NT	1308
Ruth	Ruth	OT	304
Song	Song of Solomon	OT	770
Titus	Titus	NT	1431
Zech.	Zechariah	OT	1089
Zeph.	Zephaniah	OT	1079

SYMBOLS

➤ A pointer next to the Bible text indicates that there is a corresponding Life Lesson at the foot of the page.

✳ An asterisk next to highlighted Bible text indicates a Bible promise. (Some of these include a Life Lesson.) See the Promises Index on p. xxxix.

Welcome to *The Charles F. Stanley Life Principles Bible*

Dear Friend,

The Christian life is an adventure, full of twists and turns, good times and challenges. In the midst of those changes, you and I must seek God's wisdom to lead and guide us in the right direction. To find His wisdom, there is simply no substitute for spending uninterrupted time alone with the Lord in prayerful, Spirit-soaked interaction with His Word.

In *The Charles F. Stanley Life Principles Bible,* I have attempted to distill the most powerful insights God has granted me in more than fifty years of ministry to help you mine the riches of His Word for yourself. The various features and helps included here are not intended to substitute for or stand on an equal footing with the riches of His divine wisdom; instead, they are meant as signposts to help you travel safely to the delightful destination of His best for you. I see this resource, and my whole ministry, as standing in the great biblical tradition of Ezra the scribe and his assistants, who "read distinctly from the book, in the Law of God; and they gave the sense, and helped them to understand the reading" (Neh. 8:8).

God has graciously given us hundreds of timeless life principles to help us become everything He designed us to be. In this new resource, I have tried to highlight many of the most crucial ones so that you and I might grow into whole and mature people-body, mind, and spirit. By learning and putting into practice the life principles God has given us, we can set ourselves up for a lifetime of spiritual success, and avoid the traps that would sentence us to a lifetime of ineffectiveness and spiritual misery.

Throughout this resource you'll find several features designed to help you get the most out of your time in God's Word:

- **Book introductions** to each of Scripture's 66 books offer helpful background information and alert you to some of the most crucial Life Principles found in each book.
- **Life Principles** articles highlight thirty of the Bible's most critical principles for successful Christian living. They focus on such crucial topics as building intimacy with God, prayer, obedience, dealing with adversity, and more.
- **What the Bible Says About** articles bring scriptural insight to bear on a wide variety of topics of special concern to all believers in Christ: the Holy Spirit's guidance, the process of spiritual growth, experiencing forgiveness, listening to God, and much more.
- **Answers to Life's Questions** focus on the many challenges we face in our Christian faith as we try to live for God in a world often hostile to our growth in grace. How do we deal with jealousy or bitterness, or how do we gain God's mind in a tough situation? You'll find those kinds of questions answered here.

- **Life Examples** briefly consider the lives of scores of God's choice servants spotlighted in the Bible, with a special eye toward discerning how their experience can encourage and help us.
- **Life Lessons** offer more than 2,500 insights into individual Bible verses and passages, emphasizing the practical and personal nature of God's Word to us.
- **God's Promises** highlight more than 300 of the Lord's promises to His people-promises meant to encourage, strengthen, and fill us with hope.
- **The Life Principles Indexes** and **the Promises Index,** located in the front of the Bible, give you a convenient way to study God's principles and promises throughout the Old and New Testaments.

As you read God's holy Word, I encourage you to do so with a notebook and a pen nearby. Record the date and time of your interaction. As God shows you fresh truths, write them down. If He gives you a moment of conviction, write your prayer confessing that particular sin. If He gives you a moment of joy, praise Him in writing. If you have questions, ask the Holy Spirit to teach you. Don't fear to use additional study helps, like Bible dictionaries and commentaries, to shed light on difficult passages. Don't try to read large portions of the Bible at one time; sit and meditate on one verse or one portion of a verse. Ask the Holy Spirit what that verse means to you—how to make a practical application of that verse *today.*

If you find a promise, a provision, a requirement or a commandment, record it in your notebook. If you will do this faithfully, day after day, you will begin to use the mind of Christ, which the Bible says you have (1 Cor. 2:16). You will begin to see things from God's point of view. God will bless you abundantly as you seek to know Him more through the riches of His Word.

Of course, there is no pat formula for discovering the richness of His truth. But by following principles of obedience, you'll be on the road to the fresh, liberated life He designed for you. Always when you obey God, you can anticipate that He will reveal exciting new things to you. Never forget that the key to crossing the bridge between *belief* and *experience* is *obedience.* You must take the step of faith and do what He says (John 14:21). The act of understanding His Word and obeying what He says comes *before* the growth of intimacy with the Lord. He will increasingly show Himself to you as you increasingly and joyfully obey Him.

That's part of what makes the journey into His truth so exciting. You have the guarantee that the Lord will reveal more of Himself and His goodness to you as you mature in your relationship with Him. As you obey, God will pour out His blessings and you will gain a greater understanding of His awesome character. God wants you to place your absolute trust in Him!

Yes, the Christian journey is often difficult and filled with challenges. But as you learn and put into practice crucial principles of how to live triumphantly in your walk with the Lord, you will begin to enjoy the abundant life that Jesus so earnestly desires for you (John 10:10).

Charles F. Stanley

Preface to the New King James Version®

In the preface to the 1611 edition, the translators of the Authorized Version, known popularly as the King James Bible, state that it was not their purpose "to make a new translation . . . but to make a good one better." Indebted to the earlier work of William Tyndale and others, they saw their best contribution to consist in revising and enhancing the excellence of the English versions which had sprung from the Reformation of the sixteenth century. In harmony with the purpose of the King James scholars, the translators and editors of the present work have not pursued a goal of innovation. They have perceived the Holy Bible, New King James Version, as a continuation of the labors of the earlier translators, thus unlocking for today's readers the spiritual treasures found especially in the Authorized Version of the Holy Scriptures.

A Living Legacy

For nearly four hundred years, and throughout several revisions of its English form, the King James Bible has been deeply revered among the English-speaking peoples of the world. The precision of translation for which it is historically renowned, and its majesty of style, have enabled that monumental version of the word of God to become the mainspring of the religion, language, and legal foundations of our civilization.

Although the Elizabethan period and our own era share in zeal for technical advance, the former period was more aggressively devoted to classical learning. Along with this awakened concern for the classics came a flourishing companion interest in the Scriptures, an interest that was enlivened by the conviction that the manuscripts were providentially handed down and were a trustworthy record of the inspired Word of God. The King James translators were committed to producing an English Bible that would be a precise translation, and by no means a paraphrase or a broadly approximate rendering. On the one hand, the scholars were almost as familiar with the original languages of the Bible as with their native English. On the other hand, their reverence for the divine Author and His Word assured a translation of the Scriptures in which only a principle of utmost accuracy could be accepted.

In 1786 Catholic scholar Alexander Geddes said of the King James Bible, "If accuracy and strictest attention to the letter of the text be supposed to constitute an excellent version, this is of all versions the most excellent." George Bernard Shaw became a literary legend in our century because of his severe and often humorous criticisms of our most cherished values. Surprisingly, however, Shaw pays the following tribute to the scholars commissioned by King James: "The translation was extraordinarily well done because to the translators what they were translating was not merely a curious collection of ancient books written by different authors in different stages of culture, but the Word of God divinely revealed through His chosen and expressly inspired scribes. In this conviction they carried out their work with boundless reverence and care and achieved a beautifully artistic result." History agrees with these estimates. Therefore, while seeking to unveil the excellent *form* of the traditional English Bible, special care has also been taken in the present edition to preserve the work of *precision* which is the legacy of the 1611 translators.

Complete Equivalence in Translation

Where new translation has been necessary in the New King James Version, the most complete representation of the original has been rendered by considering the history of usage and etymology of words in their contexts. This principle of complete equivalence seeks to preserve *all* of the information in the text, while presenting it in good literary form. Dynamic equivalence, a recent procedure in Bible translation, commonly results in paraphrasing where a more literal rendering is needed to reflect a specific and vital sense. For example, complete equivalence truly renders the original text in expressions such as "lifted her voice and wept" (Gen. 21:16); "I gave you cleanness of teeth" (Amos 4:6); "Jesus met them, saying, 'Rejoice!'" (Matt. 28:9); and "Woman, what does your concern have to do with Me?" (John 2:4). Complete equivalence translates fully, in order to provide an English text that is both accurate and readable.

In keeping with the principle of complete equivalence, it is the policy to translate interjections which are commonly omitted in modern language renderings of the Bible. As an example, the interjection *behold,* in the older King James editions, continues to have a place in English usage, especially in dramatically calling attention to a spectacular scene, or an event of profound importance such as the Immanuel prophecy of Isaiah 7:14. Consequently, *behold* is retained for these occasions in the present edition. However, the Hebrew and Greek originals for this word can be translated variously, depending on the circumstances in the passage. Therefore, in addition to *behold,* words such as *indeed, look, see,* and *surely* are also rendered to convey the appropriate sense suggested by the context in each case.

In faithfulness to God and to our readers, it was deemed appropriate that all participating scholars sign a statement affirming their belief in the verbal and plenary inspiration of Scripture, and in the inerrancy of the original autographs.

Devotional Quality

The King James scholars readily appreciated the intrinsic beauty of divine revelation. They accordingly disciplined their talents to render well-chosen English words of their time, as well as a graceful, often musical arrangement of language, which has stirred the hearts of Bible readers through the years. The translators, the committees, and the editors of the present edition, while sensitive to the late-twentieth-century English idiom, and while adhering faithfully to the Hebrew, Aramaic, and Greek texts, have sought to maintain those lyrical and devotional qualities that are so highly regarded in the Authorized Version. This devotional quality is especially apparent in the poetic and prophetic books, although even the relatively plain style of the Gospels and Epistles cannot strictly be likened, as sometimes suggested, to modern newspaper style. The Koine Greek of the New Testament is influenced by the Hebrew background of the writers, for whom even the gospel narratives were not merely flat utterance, but often song in various degrees of rhythm.

The Style

Students of the Bible applaud the timeless devotional character of our historic Bible. Yet it is also universally understood that our language, like all living languages, has undergone profound change since 1611. Subsequent revisions of the King James Bible have sought to keep abreast of changes in

English speech. The present work is a further step toward this objective. Where obsolescence and other reading difficulties exist, present-day vocabulary, punctuation, and grammar have been carefully integrated. Words representing ancient objects, such as *chariot* and *phylactery,* have no modern substitutes and are therefore retained.

A special feature of the New King James Version is its conformity to the thought flow of the 1611 Bible. The reader discovers that the sequence and selection of words, phrases, and clauses of the new edition, while much clearer, are so close to the traditional that there is remarkable ease in listening to the reading of either edition while following with the other.

In the discipline of translating biblical and other ancient languages, a standard method of transliteration, that is, the English spelling of untranslated words, such as names of persons and places, has never been commonly adopted. In keeping with the design of the present work, the King James spelling of untranslated words is retained, although made uniform throughout. For example, instead of the spellings *Isaiah* and *Elijah* in the Old Testament, and *Esaias* and *Elias* in the New Testament, *Isaiah* and *Elijah* now appear in both Testaments.

King James doctrinal and theological terms, for example, *propitiation, justification,* and *sanctification,* are generally familiar to English-speaking peoples. Such terms have been retained except where the original language indicates need for a more precise translation.

Readers of the Authorized Version will immediately be struck by the absence of several pronouns: *thee, thou,* and *ye* are replaced by the simple *you,* while *your* and *yours* are substituted for *thy* and *thine* as applicable. *Thee, thou, thy* and *thine* were once forms of address to express a special relationship to human as well as divine persons. These pronouns are no longer part of our language. However, reverence for God in the present work is preserved by capitalizing pronouns, including *You, Your,* and *Yours,* which refer to Him. Additionally, capitalization of these pronouns benefits the reader by clearly distinguishing divine and human persons referred to in a passage. Without such capitalization the distinction is often obscure, because the antecedent of a pronoun is not always clear in the English translation.

In addition to the pronoun usages of the seventeenth century, the *-eth* and *-est* verb endings, so familiar in the earlier King James editions, are now obsolete. Unless a speaker is schooled in these verb endings, there is common difficulty in selecting the correct form to be used with a given subject of the verb in vocal prayer. That is, should we use *love, loveth,* or *lovest? do, doeth, doest,* or *dost? have, hath,* or *hast?* Because these forms are obsolete, contemporary English usage has been substituted for the previous verb endings.

In older editions of the King James Version, the frequency of the connective *and* far exceeded the limits of present English usage. Also, biblical linguists agree that the Hebrew and Greek original words for this conjunction may commonly be translated otherwise, depending on the immediate context. Therefore, instead of *and,* alternatives such as *also, but, however, now, so, then,* and *thus* are accordingly rendered in the present edition, when the original language permits.

The real character of the Authorized Version does not reside in its archaic pronouns or verbs or other grammatical forms of the seventeenth century, but rather in the care taken by its scholars to impart the letter and spirit of the original text in a majestic and reverent style.

The Format

The format of the New King James Version is designed to enhance the vividness and devotional quality of the Holy Scriptures:

- Subject headings assist the reader to identify topics and transitions in the biblical content.
- Words or phrases in *italics* indicate expressions in the original language which require clarification by additional English words, as also done throughout the history of the King James Bible.
- *Oblique type* in the New Testament indicates a quotation from the Old Testament.
- Verse numbers in **bold type** indicate the beginning of a paragraph.
- Prose is divided into paragraphs to indicate the structure of thought.
- Poetry is structured as contemporary verse to reflect the poetic form and beauty of the passage in the original language.
- The covenant name of God was usually translated from the Hebrew as LORD or GOD (using capital letters as shown) in the King James Old Testament. This tradition is maintained. In the present edition the name is so capitalized whenever the covenant name is quoted in the New Testament from a passage in the Old Testament.

The Old Testament Text

The Hebrew Bible has come down to us through the scrupulous care of ancient scribes who copied the original text in successive generations. By the sixth century A.D. the scribes were succeeded by a group known as the Masoretes, who continued to preserve the sacred Scriptures for another five hundred years in a form known as the Masoretic Text. Babylonia, Palestine, and Tiberias were the main centers of Masoretic activity; but by the tenth century A.D. the Masoretes of Tiberias, led by the family of ben Asher, gained the ascendancy. Through subsequent editions, the ben Asher text became in the twelfth century the only recognized form of the Hebrew Scriptures.

Daniel Bomberg printed the first Rabbinic Bible in 1516–17; that work was followed in 1524–25 by a second edition prepared by Jacob ben Chayyim and also published by Bomberg. The text of ben Chayyim was adopted in most subsequent Hebrew Bibles, including those used by the King James translators. The ben Chayyim text was also used for the first two editions of Rudolph Kittel's *Biblia Hebraica* of 1906 and 1912. In 1937 Paul Kahle published a third edition of *Biblia Hebraica*. This edition was based on the oldest dated manuscript of the ben Asher text, the Leningrad Manuscript B19a (A.D. 1008), which Kahle regarded as superior to that used by ben Chayyim.

For the New King James Version the text used was the 1967/1977 Stuttgart edition of the *Biblia Hebraica*, with frequent comparisons being made with the Bomberg edition of 1524–5. The Septuagint (Greek) Version of the Old Testament and the Latin Vulgate also were consulted. In addition to referring to a variety of ancient versions of the Hebrew Scriptures, the New King James Version draws on the resources of relevant manuscripts from the Dead Sea caves. In the few places where the Hebrew was so obscure that the 1611 King James was compelled to follow one of the versions, but where information is now available to resolve the problems, the New King James Version follows the Hebrew text.

Significant variations are recorded in the New King James translators' notes.

The New Testament Text

There is more manuscript support for the New Testament than for any other body of ancient literature. Over five thousand Greek, eight thousand Latin, and many more manuscripts in other languages attest the integrity of the New Testament. There is only one basic New Testament used by Protestants, Roman Catholics, and Orthodox, by conservatives and liberals. Minor variations in hand copying have appeared through the centuries, before mechanical printing began about A.D. 1450.

Some variations exist in the spelling of Greek words, in word order, and in similar details. These ordinarily do not show up in translation and do not affect the sense of the text in any way.

Other manuscript differences such as omission or inclusion of a word or a clause, and two paragraphs in the Gospels, should not overshadow the overwhelming degree of *agreement* which exists among the ancient records. Bible readers may be assured that the most important differences in English New Testaments of today are due, not to manuscript divergence, but to the way in which translators view the task of translation: How literally should the text be rendered? How does the translator view the matter of biblical inspiration? Does the translator adopt a paraphrase when a literal rendering would be quite clear and more to the point? The New King James Version follows the historic precedent of the Authorized Version in maintaining a literal approach to translation, except where the idiom of the original language cannot be translated directly into our tongue.

The King James New Testament was based on the traditional text of the Greek-speaking churches, first published in 1516, and later called the Textus Receptus or Received Text. Although based on the relatively few available manuscripts, these were representative of many more which existed at the time but only became known later. In the late nineteenth century, B. Westcott and F. Hort taught that this text had been officially edited by the fourth-century church, but a total lack of historical evidence for this event has forced a revision of the theory. It is now widely held that the Byzantine Text that largely supports the Textus Receptus has as much right as the Alexandrian or any other tradition to be weighed in determining the text of the New Testament.

Since the 1880s most contemporary translations of the New Testament have relied upon a relatively few manuscripts discovered chiefly in the late nineteenth and early twentieth centuries. Such translations depend primarily on two manuscripts, Codex Vaticanus and Codex Sinaiticus, because of their greater age. The Greek text obtained by using these sources and the related papyri (our most ancient manuscripts) is known as the Alexandrian Text. However, some scholars have grounds for doubting the faithfulness of Vaticanus and Sinaiticus, since they often disagree with one another, and Sinaiticus exhibits excessive omission.

A third viewpoint of New Testament scholarship holds that the best text is based on the consensus of the majority of existing Greek manuscripts. This text is called the Majority Text. Most of these manuscripts are in substantial agreement. Even though many are late, and none is earlier than the fifth century, usually their readings are verified by papyri, ancient versions, quotations from the early church fathers, or a combination of these. The Majority Text is similar to the Textus

Receptus, but it corrects those readings which have little or no support in the Greek manuscript tradition.

Today, scholars agree that the science of New Testament textual criticism is in a state of flux. Very few scholars still favor the Textus Receptus as such, and then often for its historical prestige as the text of Luther, Calvin, Tyndale, and the King James Version. For about a century most have followed a Critical Text (so called because it is edited according to specific principles of textual criticism) which depends heavily upon the Alexandrian type of text. More recently many have abandoned this Critical Text (which is quite similar to the one edited by Westcott and Hort) for one that is more eclectic. Finally, a small but growing number of scholars prefer the Majority Text, which is close to the traditional text except in the Revelation.

In light of these facts, and also because the New King James Version is the fifth revision of a historic document translated from specific Greek texts, the editors decided to retain the traditional text in the body of the New Testament and to indicate major Critical and Majority Text variant readings in the translators' notes. Although these variations are duly indicated in the translators' notes of the present edition, it is most important to emphasize that fully eighty-five percent of the New Testament text is the same in the Textus Receptus, the Alexandrian Text, and the Majority Text.

New King James Translators' Notes

Significant textual explanations, alternate translations, and New Testament citations of Old Testament passages are supplied in the New King James translators' notes.

Important textual variants in the Old Testament are identified in a standard form.

The textual notes in the present edition of the New Testament make no evaluation of readings, but do clearly indicate the manuscript sources of readings. They objectively present the facts without such tendentious remarks as "the best manuscripts omit" or "the most reliable manuscripts read." Such notes are value judgments that differ according to varying viewpoints on the text. By giving a clearly defined set of variants the New King James Version benefits readers of all textual persuasions.

Where significant variations occur in the New Testament Greek manuscripts, textual notes are classified as follows:

NU-Text

These variations from the traditional text generally represent the Alexandrian or Egyptian type of text described previously in "The New Testament Text." They are found in the Critical Text published in the twenty-seventh edition of the Nestle-Aland Greek New Testament (N) and in the United Bible Societies' fourth edition (U), hence the acronym, "NU-Text."

M-Text

This symbol indicates points of variation in the Majority Text from the traditional text, as also previously discussed in "The New Testament Text." It should be noted that M stands for whatever reading is printed in the published *Greek New Testament According to the Majority Text,* whether supported by overwhelming, strong, or only a divided majority textual tradition.

The textual notes reflect the scholarship of the past two centuries and will assist the reader to observe the variations between the different manuscript traditions of the New Testament. Such information is generally not available in English translations of the New Testament.

LIFE PRINCIPLES INDEX

LIFE PRINCIPLE 1

Our intimacy with God—His highest priority for our lives—determines the impact of our lives. Gen. 1:26, p. 4

WHAT THE BIBLE SAYS ABOUT

ANSWERS TO LIFE'S QUESTIONS

LIFE EXAMPLES

continued on next page

LIFE PRINCIPLE 1

continued from previous page

LIFE LESSONS

- Gen. 1:16
- Gen. 2:18
- Gen. 2:25
- Gen. 3:7
- Gen. 3:8
- Gen. 3:15
- Gen. 4:16
- Gen. 4:26
- Gen. 5:24
- Gen. 8:20
- Gen. 24:63
- Gen. 29:35
- Gen. 35:2
- Ex. 20:3
- Lev. 20:26
- Lev. 26:12
- Deut. 4:24
- Deut. 7:4
- Deut. 32:36
- Judg. 17:3
- 1 Sam. 2:17
- 1 Sam. 7:3
- 1 Sam. 12:21
- 2 Sam. 6:22
- 1 Kin. 8:10
- 1 Kin. 8:43
- 1 Kin. 12:33
- 2 Kin. 17:33
- 1 Chr. 16:7
- 1 Chr. 28:9
- 2 Chr. 26:5
- Ezra 7:10
- Neh. 13:26
- Job 31:4
- Job 42:5, 6
- Ps. 37:3
- Ps. 42:1
- Ps. 63:1
- Ps. 84:10
- Ps. 92:2
- Ps. 103:1
- Eccl. 1:18
- Song 2:13
- Song 5:16
- Song 8:6
- Is. 17:7
- Is. 57:15
- Jer. 2:32
- Jer. 13:11
- Jer. 24:7
- Dan. 11:32
- Hos. 2:16
- Nah. 1:2
- Nah. 3:19
- Zeph. 3:9
- Zech. 7:5
- Zech. 12:10
- Matt. 4:23
- Matt. 14:23
- Mark 1:35
- Mark 6:46
- Mark 15:38
- Luke 2:47
- Luke 3:11
- Luke 5:16
- Luke 14:23
- Luke 15:32
- Luke 19:10
- John 4:23
- John 7:37
- Acts 3:19
- 2 Cor. 5:19
- Gal. 4:6
- Gal. 6:2
- Eph. 2:13
- 1 John 1:3
- Rev. 2:4

LIFE PRINCIPLE 2

Obey God and leave all the consequences to Him. Ex. 19:5, p. 86

WHAT THE BIBLE SAYS ABOUT

ANSWERS TO LIFE'S QUESTIONS

continued on next page

LIFE PRINCIPLE 2

continued from previous page

LIFE EXAMPLES

LIFE LESSONS

LIFE PRINCIPLE 3

God's Word is an immovable anchor in times of storm. Num. 23:19, p. 178

WHAT THE BIBLE SAYS ABOUT

ANSWERS TO LIFE'S QUESTIONS

LIFE EXAMPLES

continued on next page

LIFE PRINCIPLE 3

continued from previous page

LIFE LESSONS

- Gen. 8:22
- Gen. 12:10
- Gen. 21:33
- Gen. 28:15
- Gen. 46:4
- Ex. 3:2
- Ex. 33:19
- Num. 7:89
- Num. 13:31
- Num. 14:9
- Deut. 17:19
- Deut. 26:7
- Deut. 27:2, 3
- Deut. 32:31
- Josh. 1:8
- Judg. 19:25
- Judg. 20:46
- 1 Sam. 8:6
- 1 Sam. 28:19
- 1 Kin. 12:15
- 2 Kin. 22:10
- 2 Chr. 6:15
- Ezra 5:1, 2
- Neh. 6:2
- Esth. 7:9
- Job 23:12
- Job 38:1
- Ps. 4:8
- Ps. 9:10
- Ps. 12:6
- Ps. 31:3
- Ps. 43:3
- Ps. 46:1, 2
- Ps. 61:2
- Ps. 109:4
- Ps. 111:2
- Ps. 117:2
- Ps. 119:11
- Ps. 119:28
- Ps. 119:67
- Ps. 119:105
- Ps. 119:125
- Ps. 119:162
- Ps. 138:2
- Prov. 6:23
- Prov. 18:10
- Is. 40:8
- Is. 41:10
- Jer. 25:11
- Ezek. 12:25
- Joel 2:11
- Amos 2:4
- Matt. 4:4, 7, 10
- Matt. 28:18, 19
- John 12:16
- Acts 4:29
- Acts 6:4
- Col. 3:16
- 1 Thess. 1:6
- 2 Tim. 3:16, 17
- Titus 1:9
- Heb. 4:12

LIFE PRINCIPLE 4

The awareness of God's presence energizes us for our work. Deut. 20:1, p. 222

WHAT THE BIBLE SAYS ABOUT

The Value of Hard Work, Gen. 39:2–6, p. 48
Enjoying God's Presence, Eccl. 2:26, p. 759
The Value of Diligence, Eccl. 11:6, p. 768
God's Empowering Presence, Jer. 1:6–10, p. 856

ANSWERS TO LIFE'S QUESTIONS

How can I find courage in times of adversity?
Josh. 1:6–9, p. 242

How does my relationship with the Lord affect what and how I hear from Him?
Ps. 79:13, p. 678

How can I find fulfillment in my work?
Eccl. 9:10, p. 765

How do I deal with burnout? Is. 40:28–31, p. 822

How can I feel secure in the Lord during troubled times? Hag. 2:4, p. 1087

When and how am I filled with the Holy Spirit?
Acts 2:4, p. 1266

How can I cope with feelings of loneliness?
2 Tim. 4:13, 17, 21, p. 1430

How can God use an imperfect person like me?
1 John 1:9, p. 1481

LIFE EXAMPLES

Elijah: Responding to Stress,
1 Kin. 19:3, p. 419

Micaiah: Bold Servant of God,
2 Chr. 18:13, p. 513

Isaiah: A Life-Changing Encounter,
Is. 6:1–7, p. 789

Zacchaeus: A Life That Counts,
Luke 19:1–10, p. 1217

Martha: Worship as You Work,
John 11:19–44, p. 1247

John Mark: Learning to End Well,
Col. 4:10, p. 1402

Luke: Laboring in the Background,
2 Tim. 4:11, p. 1429

LIFE LESSONS

- Gen. 2:15
- Ex. 28:3
- Deut. 3:20
- Deut. 7:17, 18
- Deut. 8:18
- Josh. 3:10
- 2 Kin. 1:10
- 2 Kin. 2:21
- 1 Chr. 15:26
- Ps. 100:2
- Prov. 16:3
- Eccl. 9:10
- Eccl. 10:18
- Hag. 2:4
- Acts 1:5
- Acts 1:8
- 1 Cor. 15:10

PRINCIPLE 5

God does not require us to understand His will, just obey it, even if it seems unreasonable. Josh. 3:8, p. 244

WHAT THE BIBLE SAYS ABOUT

How to Control Our Anger, Is. 64:9, p. 851

ANSWERS TO LIFE'S QUESTIONS

What does it mean to be set free in Christ?
John 8:31, 32, p. 1243

Why is it so important to forgive others?
Eph. 4:31, 32, p. 1385

LIFE EXAMPLES

Gideon: Circumstances Convey Confirmation,
Judg. 6:36–40, p. 286

Mary: Woman of Faith, Luke 1:31–38, p. 1185

Simeon: Whole in the Arms of God,
Luke 2:25–35, p. 1188

LIFE LESSONS

- Gen. 3:1
- Gen. 3:5
- Gen. 12:7
- Gen. 15:6
- Gen. 17:23
- Gen. 18:14
- Gen. 22:5
- Ex. 2:8–10
- Ex. 4:12
- Ex. 8:15
- Ex. 10:11
- Ex. 16:4
- Ex. 16:8
- Ex. 16:18
- Ex. 30:9
- Lev. 1:17
- Lev. 15:31
- Num. 2:2
- Num. 9:23
- Deut. 19:5
- Josh. 6:5
- Josh. 8:2
- Josh. 17:4
- Josh. 23:13
- 1 Sam. 1:5
- 1 Sam. 1:18
- 1 Sam. 10:22
- 1 Sam. 10:27
- 1 Sam. 15:9
- 1 Sam. 24:6
- 1 Sam. 26:10
- 1 Kin. 8:18, 19
- 1 Kin. 17:9
- 2 Kin. 3:7
- 2 Kin. 5:14
- Job 26:7
- Job 40:8
- Job 42:10
- Ps. 13:1
- Jer. 13:1
- Mark 13:13
- Luke 24:31
- John 4:10
- John 7:17
- John 16:33
- John 18:11
- 2 Cor. 5:7
- Rev. 2:10

LIFE PRINCIPLE 6

You reap what you sow, more than you sow, and later than you sow. Judg. 2:1–4, p. 276

WHAT THE BIBLE SAYS ABOUT

The Forbidden Practice of the Occult,
Deut. 18, p. 218

The Deadliness of Anger,
1 Sam. 18:7, 8, p. 336

How God Judges and Rewards Our Work,
Rev. 22:12, p. 1512

ANSWERS TO LIFE'S QUESTIONS

Why does God tell us to "flee from evil"?
Deut. 19:19, 20, p. 220

How important is it to set goals?
Phil. 3:11–14, p. 1394

Will God really meet all my needs?
Phil. 4:19, p. 1395

continued on next page

LIFE PRINCIPLE 6

continued from previous page

LIFE EXAMPLES

David: Competent over Time,
1 Sam. 17:48–51, p. 335

Nebuchadnezzar: A Lesson in Humility,
Dan. 4:30–37, p. 1003

Tychicus: Beloved Messenger,
Eph. 6:21, p. 1387

LIFE LESSONS

- Gen. 2:20
- Gen. 3:16–19
- Gen. 4:11, 12
- Gen. 4:23
- Gen. 8:1
- Gen. 17:5
- Gen. 19:9
- Gen. 19:29
- Gen. 19:36
- Gen. 25:18
- Num. 11:34
- Num. 12:14
- Num. 15:30
- 1 Sam. 25:21
- 1 Sam. 30:6
- 2 Sam. 16:21
- 2 Sam. 19:4
- 2 Sam. 21:1
- 1 Kin. 2:32
- 1 Kin. 12:1
- 1 Chr. 9:1
- 1 Chr. 21:14
- 2 Chr. 21:19
- 2 Chr. 24:21
- Esth. 2:10
- Job 21:7
- Job 36:11
- Is. 14:24
- Dan. 7:25
- Hos. 8:7
- Hag. 2:19
- Matt. 7:12
- Luke 20:47
- 1 Cor. 5:5
- 1 Cor. 5:11
- 2 John 8
- Rev. 2:23

LIFE PRINCIPLE 7

The dark moments of our life will last only so long as is necessary for God to accomplish His purpose in us. 1 Sam. 30:1–6, p. 350

WHAT THE BIBLE SAYS ABOUT

God's Limitations on Adversity,
2 Chr. 20:29, p. 520

How God Limits Our Adversity,
Job 1:12–2:6, p. 586

The Process of Spiritual Growth,
Jer. 18:1–6, p. 881

ANSWERS TO LIFE'S QUESTIONS

How can a good God allow suffering in a believer's life? Joel 1:19, p. 1036

How does God deal with our disobedience?
Jon. 3:1, p. 1058

How does God teach me patience?
2 Thess. 3:5, p. 1416

How do I handle a difficult trial not of my own doing? 1 Pet. 1:6, 7, p. 1468

LIFE EXAMPLES

Joseph: Waiting and Trusting,
Gen. 40:23, p. 51

Moses: God's Pattern for Success,
Ex. 3:1–4, p. 67

Ezekiel: Watching Dead Bones Come Alive,
Ezek. 37:14, p. 981

LIFE LESSONS

- Gen. 6:18
- Gen. 12:10
- Gen. 21:16
- Gen. 22:1
- Gen. 32:31
- Gen. 39:2
- Gen. 39:21
- Gen. 41:1
- Gen. 41:46
- Gen. 42:5
- Gen. 50:20
- Ex. 5:9
- Ex. 5:22
- Ex. 13:21
- Ex. 14:2
- Ex. 15:18
- Ex. 17:7
- Ex. 33:19
- Lev. 14:33, 34
- Num. 21:2
- Num. 35:10, 11
- Deut. 2:7
- Deut. 8:2
- Deut. 8:16
- Josh. 11:23
- Judg. 2:22
- Ruth 1:21
- 1 Sam. 1:18
- 1 Sam. 9:16
- 1 Sam. 30:1, 2
- 1 Sam. 31:2
- 1 Kin. 14:5
- 1 Kin. 19:18
- 2 Kin. 11:17
- 1 Chr. 21:16
- 2 Chr. 26:16
- Esth. 9:22
- Job 5:7
- Job 7:11
- Job 16:9
- Job 29:2
- Job 34:12
- Job 36:15
- Job 42:8
- Job 42:12
- Ps. 10:1
- Ps. 13:1
- Ps. 18:18
- Ps. 22:1
- Ps. 43:3
- Ps. 44:22
- Ps. 55:6
- Ps. 66:10
- Ps. 119:105
- Eccl. 7:14
- Song 2:3
- Is. 10:25
- Is. 41:17
- Is. 43:20
- Is. 45:15
- Is. 49:15
- Is. 50:10
- Mic. 7:8
- Luke 12:6
- John 11:37
- Acts 27:20
- Rom. 5:3, 4
- 1 Cor. 7:11
- 2 Cor. 1:3, 4
- 2 Cor. 1:9
- James 1:2, 3

LIFE PRINCIPLE 8

Fight all your battles on your knees and you win every time. 2 Sam. 15:31, p. 376

WHAT THE BIBLE SAYS ABOUT

Asking God for Specific Things,
1 Kin. 3:5, p. 395

Effectively Tackling a Prayer Burden,
Neh 1:4–6, p. 555

Binding Satan, Matt. 16:19, p. 1136

The Many Faces of Prayer,
Col. 1:9–12, p. 1399

Principles for Effective Intercession,
James 5:15, 16, p. 1463

ANSWERS TO LIFE'S QUESTIONS

How can I find courage in the face of stiff challenges? 1 Sam. 17:12–54, p. 332

What role does faith play in doing great things for God? 1 Sam. 17:26, p. 334

What can I do to help change the spiritual and moral climate of my nation?
2 Chr. 7:14, p. 504

How can I deal with the anger or bitterness of another? Prov. 14:10, p. 737

How can I deal with discouragement?
Jer. 29:11, p. 894

How can I make my prayer life fresh and new?
Jer. 33:1–3, p. 901

How can I become a godly influence on others?
Ezek. 22:30, p. 961

How can I learn to pray effectively?
Dan. 9:2, p. 1012

What tools has God provided to help me share my faith?
Mark 16:15, p. 1181

How do I handle nagging doubt?
Luke 24:38, p. 1227

What does it mean to "pray without ceasing"?
1 Thess. 5:17, p. 1409

How can I combat my fears?
2 Tim. 1:7, p. 1425

LIFE EXAMPLES

Jacob: Wrestling with God,
Gen. 32:24–32, p. 41

Hannah: Asking in Faith,
1 Sam. 1:10, 11, p. 311

Elisha: Enjoying a Hedge of Angels,
2 Kin. 6:18, p. 438

David: The Joy of Forgiveness,
Ps. 32:1–11, p. 644

Daniel: A Man of Prayer,
Dan. 6:10, p. 1005

Rhoda: Joy in Prayer,
Acts 12:12–17, p. 1285

LIFE LESSONS

- Gen. 20:17
- Gen. 24:12
- Gen. 30:2
- Num. 14:19
- Deut. 4:7
- Josh. 10:12, 13
- Judg. 5:13
- 1 Sam. 1:10
- 2 Sam. 12:4
- 2 Kin. 19:20
- 1 Chr. 5:20
- 2 Chr. 14:11
- 2 Chr. 16:12
- Ezra 8:31
- Neh. 4:4
- Job 26:14
- Ps. 20:7
- Ps. 115:3
- Matt. 7:7
- Matt. 18:20
- Mark 14:35
- Luke 21:36
- Acts 4:31
- Acts 16:25
- Eph. 6:18
- Heb. 4:16
- Heb. 5:7

LIFE PRINCIPLE 9

Trusting God means looking beyond what we can see to what God sees. 2 Kin. 6:17, p. 436

WHAT THE BIBLE SAYS ABOUT

The Origin, Work, and Destiny of Satan,
Ezek. 28:12–19, p. 970

How Adversity Reveals Our Level of Faith,
Mark 4:35, p. 1163

Growing in Our Faith,
Luke 18:1–8, p. 1215

The Grace in Which We Stand,
Rom. 5:2, p. 1315

continued on next page

LIFE PRINCIPLE 9

continued from previous page

ANSWERS TO LIFE'S QUESTIONS

LIFE EXAMPLES

LIFE LESSONS

LIFE PRINCIPLE 10

If necessary, God will move heaven and earth to show us His will.
2 Chr. 20:12, p. 518

WHAT THE BIBLE SAYS ABOUT

The Importance of Developing a Discerning Spirit, Deut. 6:6, p. 205

Seeking God's Guidance, Ps. 27:14, p. 641

How the Holy Spirit Guides Us, John 16:13, p. 1255

ANSWERS TO LIFE'S QUESTIONS

What good does fasting do us? Neh. 1:4, p. 554

Why do I sometimes fail to hear God when He speaks? Jer. 22:21, p. 886

How can I rightly comprehend God's truth? 1 Cor. 2:9, 10, p. 1333

LIFE EXAMPLES

John the Baptist: A Man of Discernment, Mark 6:14–29, p. 1165

LIFE LESSONS

- Gen. 3:15
- Gen. 6:22
- Gen. 8:1
- Gen. 15:1
- Ex. 2:8–10
- Ex. 9:16
- Lev. 24:12
- Num. 8:4
- Num. 17:8
- Deut. 32:36
- Josh. 14:9, 10
- 1 Sam. 3:7
- 1 Sam. 23:13
- 2 Kin. 4:2
- 2 Kin. 4:17
- 2 Kin. 8:5
- 1 Chr. 10:14
- Esth. 8:8
- Ps. 148:8
- Eccl. 8:5
- Is. 20:2
- Is. 45:19
- Matt. 1:20
- Acts 4:31
- Acts 5:19, 20
- Acts 9:4
- Acts 12:9
- Rom. 12:2
- Titus 2:11, 12

LIFE PRINCIPLE 11

God assumes full responsibility for our needs when we obey Him.
Job 42:7–17, p. 620

WHAT THE BIBLE SAYS ABOUT

Gagging on Financial Indebtedness, 2 Kin. 4:1, p. 432

The Thrilling Adventure of Obedience, Is. 30:21, p. 812

Finding Confidence in God, Lam. 3:23, 24, p. 933

ANSWERS TO LIFE'S QUESTIONS

Can I really trust God to provide what I need? Ex. 16:1–3, p. 82

What place should money take in my life? Ex. 20:2, 3, p. 90

How should I respond to failure or setbacks? Josh. 7:6–15, p. 252

Why do I sometimes fail to hear God when He speaks? Jer. 22:21, p. 886

What role does obedience play in a mature Christian's life? Jer. 42:1–6, p. 911

How can I overcome anxiety? Matt. 6:25–34, p. 1121

How can I learn to feel content? 1 Tim. 6:7, 8, p. 1422

LIFE EXAMPLES

Naomi: Sowing in the Midst of Suffering, Ruth 1:18–22, p. 307

The Preacher: Rich Doesn't Mean Expensive, Eccl. 2:4, p. 758

John the Baptist: A Man of Discernment, Mark 6:14–29, p. 1165

continued on next page

LIFE PRINCIPLE 11

continued from previous page

LIFE LESSONS

- Gen. 2:20
- Gen. 3:1
- Gen. 3:5
- Gen. 3:7
- Gen. 17:23
- Gen. 22:5
- Ex. 1:20
- Ex. 4:12
- Ex. 5:22
- Ex. 8:15
- Ex. 9:12
- Ex. 10:11
- Ex. 16:4
- Ex. 16:8
- Ex. 16:18
- Ex. 23:22
- Lev. 1:17
- Lev. 9:24
- Num. 11:1
- Num. 14:24
- Num. 33:55
- Deut. 19:5
- Josh. 5:12
- Josh. 23:13
- 1 Sam. 10:22
- 1 Sam. 15:9
- 2 Sam. 15:25
- 2 Kin. 11:2
- 1 Chr. 22:13
- Job 42:10
- Job 42:12
- Ps. 1:3
- Ps. 5:4
- Ps. 112:2
- Matt. 6:4
- Matt. 10:42
- John 7:17
- Acts 18:9, 10
- Phil. 4:6
- James 4:3
- Rev. 2:3

LIFE PRINCIPLE 12

Peace with God is the fruit of oneness with God. Ps. 4:8, p. 626

WHAT THE BIBLE SAYS ABOUT

The Cover-Up, Lev. 6:6, 7, p. 120

Confidence in Times of Distress, Ps. 46:1–11, p. 656

God as Our Comforter, Jer. 8:18, p. 868

Your Identity in Christ, Heb. 3:1, p. 1441

ANSWERS TO LIFE'S QUESTIONS

What should I do when I feel distant from God? Judg. 6:6, p. 282

What does the Bible say to lonely people? 1 Sam 12:22, p. 324

How can I find renewal and restoration? Ps. 23:2–4, p. 638

What does God's love look like? Song 6:4, p. 777

How can I have God's peace? Is. 26:3, p. 805

How can I get to *really* know God? Hos. 6:6, p. 1027

How can I endure in my faith during hard times? Zeph. 3:17, p. 1083

How can I know if my worship pleases God? John 4:23, 24, p. 1235

What does God really think of me? Rom. 3:24, p. 1313

Is there a limit to God's forgiveness? 1 Cor. 6:9–11, p. 1336

LIFE EXAMPLES

The Wise Men: Giving Passionate Praise, Matt. 2:1–12, p. 1114

Jesus: Example or Sacrifice? Matt. 26:39, p. 1150

Nicodemus: Unclean but Unblemished, John 3:1–21, p. 1232

Mary of Bethany: A Life Devoted to God, John 12:1–8, p. 1249

LIFE LESSONS

- Gen. 2:25
- Gen. 4:26
- Deut. 12:18
- Josh. 21:44
- 2 Kin. 6:15
- 1 Chr. 22:9
- Job 23:12
- Job 25:4
- Ps. 4:8
- Ps. 17:8
- Ps. 92:2
- Is. 26:12
- Is. 57:21
- Jer. 6:14
- John 14:27
- Rom. 5:1
- Heb. 13:20, 21

LIFE PRINCIPLE 13

Listening to God is essential to walking with God. Ps. 81:8, p. 680

WHAT THE BIBLE SAYS ABOUT

ANSWERS TO LIFE'S QUESTIONS

LIFE EXAMPLES

LIFE LESSONS

- Gen. 5:24
- Gen. 6:8
- Ex. 3:2
- Num. 1:1
- Num. 7:89
- Num. 9:8
- Deut. 5:24
- Josh. 1:1
- Judg. 1:1
- 2 Sam. 2:1
- 2 Sam. 5:19
- 2 Sam. 5:23
- 2 Sam. 13:32
- 2 Sam. 15:8
- 1 Kin. 8:58
- 2 Kin. 14:10
- 2 Kin. 20:17
- 2 Chr. 33:10
- 2 Chr. 35:22
- Esth. 3:4
- Job 33:14
- Job 38:1
- Ps. 16:7
- Ps. 31:3
- Ps. 77:10
- Ps. 143:8
- Is. 28:29
- Jer. 22:21
- Jer. 33:3
- Lam. 3:25
- Luke 5:16
- John 6:38
- Acts 10:20
- 1 Thess. 4:3

LIFE PRINCIPLE 14

God acts on behalf of those who wait for Him. Is. 64:4, p. 848

WHAT THE BIBLE SAYS ABOUT

ANSWERS TO LIFE'S QUESTIONS

continued on next page

LIFE PRINCIPLE 14

continued from previous page

LIFE EXAMPLES

Abraham: The Man of Endurance, Gen. 21:1–3, p. 26

Joseph: Waiting and Trusting, Gen. 40:23, p. 51

Simeon: Whole in the Arms of God, Luke 2:25–35, p. 1188

LIFE LESSONS

- Gen. 2:20
- Gen. 8:1
- Gen. 17:5
- Gen. 17:17
- Gen. 22:14
- Gen. 41:1
- Ex. 2:23
- Ex. 8:23
- Deut. 1:30
- Judg. 1:8
- Ruth 3:18
- 1 Sam. 1:10
- 1 Sam. 13:8
- 1 Sam. 22:2
- 1 Sam. 26:10
- 2 Sam. 3:1
- 2 Sam. 5:23
- 1 Kin. 9:3
- 1 Kin. 16:30
- 1 Kin. 18:43
- 2 Kin. 6:33
- 2 Kin. 24:20
- Esth. 8:12
- Esth. 9:1
- Job 30:20
- Job 42:8
- Ps. 25:4, 5
- Ps. 36:5
- Ps. 40:1
- Ps. 46:10
- Ps. 62:5
- Ps. 77:10
- Ps. 123:2
- Ps. 130:5
- Eccl. 3:1, 2
- Is. 25:9
- Is. 38:14
- Is. 64:4
- Ezek. 39:22
- Dan. 10:13
- Hag. 2:19
- Matt. 28:4, 5
- Rom. 4:20
- James 5:7
- 2 Pet. 3:8

LIFE PRINCIPLE 15

Brokenness is God's requirement for maximum usefulness. Jer. 15:19, p. 878

WHAT THE BIBLE SAYS ABOUT

The Benefits of Prayer and Fasting, Esth. 4:16, p. 579

God's Hatred of Human Pride, Prov. 16:18, p. 741

How to Handle Feelings of Guilt, Is. 44:9–11, p. 828

God as Our Comforter, Jer. 8:18, p. 868

Brokenness, the Way to Blessing, Joel 2:12–20, p. 1038

How God Uses Adversity to Get Our Attention, Acts 9:1–20, p. 1277

ANSWERS TO LIFE'S QUESTIONS

How can I rid myself of guilt? Lev. 5:5, p. 118

How should I respond to failure or setbacks? Josh. 7:6–15, p. 252

What should I do when I feel distant from God? Judg. 6:6, p. 282

What can I do to help change the spiritual and moral climate of my nation? 2 Chr. 7:14, p. 504

How can I help to restore someone to fellowship with God? Ezek. 36:16–38, p. 980

How does God deal with our disobedience? Jon. 3:1, p. 1058

What does it mean to do spiritual battle? Rom. 7:15–25, p. 1318

LIFE EXAMPLES

David: A Case Study in Repentance, 2 Sam. 12:13, p. 369

Uzziah: The Downfall of Pride, 2 Chr. 26:16–23, p. 526

David: The Joy of Forgiveness, Ps. 32:1–11, p. 644

Isaiah: A Life-Changing Encounter, Is. 6:1–7, p. 786

Gomer: What Did She Want? Hos. 2:14, p. 1020

Martha: Worship as You Work, John 11:19–44, p. 1247

Paul: Strength in Weakness, 2 Cor. 12:7, p. 1363

John Mark: Learning to End Well, Col. 4:10, p. 1402

continued on next page

LIFE PRINCIPLE 15

continued from previous page

LIFE LESSONS

- Gen. 12:10
- Gen. 21:16
- Gen. 25:21
- Gen. 39:2
- Ex. 5:9
- Josh. 13:1
- Judg. 13:3
- Ruth 1:21
- 1 Sam. 1:10
- 1 Sam. 1:18
- 1 Sam. 9:16
- 1 Sam. 30:1, 2
- 2 Chr. 26:16
- Job 42:17
- Ps. 113:7, 8
- Ps. 126:5
- Is. 40:29
- Is. 41:17
- Is. 64:8
- Jer. 18:6
- Zech. 1:17
- Acts 8:4
- Acts 9:4
- James 1:2, 3
- James 4:10

LIFE PRINCIPLE 16

Whatever you acquire outside of God's will eventually turns to ashes. Ezek. 25:6, 7, p. 966

WHAT THE BIBLE SAYS ABOUT

The Deadliness of Anger,
1 Sam. 18:7, 8, p. 336

Gagging on Financial Indebtedness,
2 Kin. 4:1, p. 432

ANSWERS TO LIFE'S QUESTIONS

How does God define sin?
Jer. 2:13, p. 858

How can I learn to feel content?
1 Tim. 6:7, 8, p. 1422

LIFE EXAMPLES

Pharaoh: A Bad Case of a Hard Heart,
Ex. 3:19, 20, p. 69

LIFE LESSONS

- Gen. 3:1
- Gen. 3:5
- Gen. 3:12
- Gen. 6:18
- Gen. 11:4
- Gen. 16:4
- Gen. 19:24
- Gen. 19:36
- Gen. 25:34
- Gen. 41:16
- Ex. 3:11, 12
- Num. 11:34
- Num. 12:2
- Judg. 7:2
- 1 Sam. 4:13
- 1 Sam. 12:21
- 1 Sam. 18:8
- 1 Sam. 22:8
- 2 Sam. 2:10
- 2 Sam. 16:3
- 2 Sam. 18:18
- 1 Kin. 1:5
- 2 Kin. 8:18
- 2 Chr. 20:37
- Ps. 49:20
- Ps. 106:15
- Ps. 107:9
- Prov. 23:4, 5
- Eccl. 2:11
- Eccl. 2:17
- Jer. 2:11
- Jer. 8:9
- Mark 14:10
- Acts 12:23
- 2 Cor. 3:5
- 3 John 9

LIFE PRINCIPLE 17

We stand tallest and strongest on our knees. Dan. 6:10, 11, p. 1006

WHAT THE BIBLE SAYS ABOUT

How to Pray with Authority,
1 Kin. 18:20–40, p. 418

Effectively Tackling a Prayer Burden,
Neh 1:4–6, p. 555

The Many Faces of Prayer,
Col. 1:9–12, p. 1399

continued on next page

LIFE PRINCIPLE 17

continued from previous page

ANSWERS TO LIFE'S QUESTIONS

Why doesn't God answer my prayers sooner?
Gen. 45:25–46:4, p. 58

What is our authority in prayer?
2 Chr. 20:3, p. 515

How does my relationship with the Lord affect what and how I hear from Him?
Ps. 79:13, p. 678

How can I make my prayer life fresh and new?
Jer. 33:1–3, p. 901

How can I learn to pray effectively?
Dan. 9:2, p. 1012

What does it mean to "pray without ceasing"?
1 Thess. 5:17, p. 1409

LIFE EXAMPLES

Stephen: Echoing His Savior,
Acts 7:59, 60, p. 1275

Silas: Singing for Victory,
Acts 16:24–34, p. 1291

LIFE LESSONS

- Gen. 30:2
- Num. 14:19
- Deut. 4:7
- Josh. 10:12, 13
- Judg. 5:13
- 1 Sam. 1:10
- 1 Sam. 7:8
- 2 Kin. 19:20
- 1 Chr. 5:20
- 2 Chr. 14:11
- 2 Chr. 16:12
- Neh. 4:4
- Job 26:14
- Ps. 115:3
- Dan. 9:18
- Matt. 7:7
- Matt. 14:23
- Matt. 18:20
- Luke 6:12
- Luke 21:36
- Acts 4:31
- Acts 12:5
- Eph. 6:18
- Phil. 4:6
- Heb. 4:16

LIFE PRINCIPLE 18

As children of a sovereign God, we are never victims of our circumstances. Hos. 3:4, 5, p. 1024

WHAT THE BIBLE SAYS ABOUT

God's Desire to Communicate with Us,
Ps. 139:1–24, p. 716

The Origin, Work, and Destiny of Satan,
Ezek. 28:12–19, p. 970

ANSWERS TO LIFE'S QUESTIONS

Does God bring us adversity? Gen. 39:20, p. 50

How can I find courage in the face of stiff challenges? 1 Sam. 17:12–54, p. 332

What role does faith play in doing great things for God? 1 Sam. 17:26, p. 334

How can I find the strength to endure when I face spiritual opposition?
Ezra 4:1–24, p. 544

How can I endure in my faith during hard times?
Zeph. 3:17, p. 1083

LIFE EXAMPLES

Sarah: Laughing All the Way to the Crib,
Gen. 18:9–15, p. 22

Cyrus: An Instrument of God, Ezra 1:1, p. 540

Job's Friends: Adamant, but Wrong,
Job 42:7–9, p. 619

Jonah: No Fleeing the God of Everywhere,
Jon. 1:3, p. 1056

Rhoda: Joy in Prayer,
Acts 12:12–17, p. 1285

LIFE LESSONS

- Gen. 4:16
- Gen. 12:10
- Gen. 16:9
- Gen. 32:31
- Gen. 39:21
- Gen. 41:46
- Gen. 50:20
- Num. 11:14
- Num. 13:28
- Num. 14:18
- Num. 20:21
- Deut. 1:27
- Ruth 1:21
- 1 Sam. 1:10
- 1 Sam. 1:18
- 1 Sam. 30:1, 2
- 1 Sam. 31:2
- 2 Chr. 13:18
- Ezra 6:12
- Job 4:17
- Job 20:4, 5
- Job 29:2
- Ps. 31:15
- Ps. 42:11
- Luke 13:3
- Acts 2:23
- Rom. 8:28
- Rom. 11:33
- Phil. 1:6, 12, 29
- 1 Pet. 1:3

LIFE PRINCIPLE 19

Anything you hold too tightly you will lose. Amos 6:6, 7, p. 1048

WHAT THE BIBLE SAYS ABOUT

Gagging on Financial Indebtedness, 2 Kin. 4:1, p. 432

Brokenness, the Way to Blessing, Joel 2:12–20, p. 1038

ANSWERS TO LIFE'S QUESTIONS

What place should money take in my life? Ex. 20:2, 3, p. 90

How do I deal with the temptation toward pride? 1 Chr. 28:9, p. 493

How do I deal with burnout? Is. 40:28–31, p. 822

How does God teach me patience? 2 Thess. 3:5, p. 1416

LIFE EXAMPLES

David: A Case Study in Repentance, 2 Sam. 12:13, p. 369

Uzziah: The Downfall of Pride, 2 Chr. 26:16–23, p. 526

Nebuchadnezzar: A Lesson in Humility, Dan. 4:30–37, p. 1003

Gomer: What Did She Want? Hos. 2:14, p. 1020

LIFE LESSONS

- Gen. 3:1
- Gen. 3:5
- Gen. 3:12
- Gen. 6:18
- Gen. 11:4
- Gen. 16:4
- Gen. 19:36
- Gen. 41:16
- Ex. 3:11, 12
- Num. 11:5
- Num. 11:34
- Num. 12:2
- Judg. 7:2
- 1 Sam. 2:29
- 1 Sam. 4:13
- 1 Sam. 18:8
- 1 Sam. 22:8
- 2 Sam. 3:9
- Ezra 1:6
- Prov. 23:4, 5
- Eccl. 2:11
- Eccl. 5:15
- Matt. 6:21
- Matt. 6:24
- 1 Tim. 6:9

LIFE PRINCIPLE 20

Disappointments are inevitable; discouragement is a choice. Hab. 3:17–19, p. 1076

WHAT THE BIBLE SAYS ABOUT

Your Identity in Christ, Heb. 3:1, p. 1441

ANSWERS TO LIFE'S QUESTIONS

How can I deal with discouragement? Jer. 29:11, p. 894

How can I praise God when life doesn't go well? Lam. 3:40, p. 934

Why doesn't God keep us from tests and trials? Dan. 6:16, p. 1008

LIFE EXAMPLES

Joshua: The Need for Courage, Josh. 3:5–17, p. 246

Job: Choosing to Trust, Job 19:25, 26, p. 602

Ezekiel: Watching Dead Bones Come Alive, Ezek. 37:14, p. 981

LIFE LESSONS

- Gen. 12:10
- Gen. 39:2
- Gen. 41:46
- Ex. 5:9
- Ex. 6:9
- Num. 13:28
- Ruth 1:21
- Ezra 3:3
- Ps. 42:11
- 1 Cor. 16:9
- 2 Cor. 2:14
- 2 Tim. 3:12

LIFE PRINCIPLE 21

Obedience always brings blessing. Luke 11:28, p. 1204

WHAT THE BIBLE SAYS ABOUT

The Forbidden Practice of the Occult,
Deut. 18, p. 218

The Thrilling Adventure of Obedience,
Is. 30:21, p. 812

Grieving the Holy Spirit,
Eph. 4:30, p. 1384

How God Judges and Rewards Our Work,
Rev. 22:12, p. 1512

ANSWERS TO LIFE'S QUESTIONS

How can I become a more obedient child of God? Gen. 12:1, p. 16

What can I do to earn a more spiritually responsible role? Ex. 3:3–9, p. 68

How do I keep my focus on God and not on the obstacles in my life? Num. 14:8, 9, p. 166

What should I do during times of adversity?
1 Chr. 22:13, p. 487

What role does obedience play in a mature Christian's life? Jer. 42:1–6, p. 911

How can I become a more obedient Christian?
Dan. 1:4–16, p. 996

Should I tithe when I am struggling financially?
Mal. 3:8–12, p. 1106

Do I have a role to play in communicating God's truth to others?
Matt. 28:19, 20, p. 1154

What does it mean to be set free in Christ?
John 8:31, 32, p. 1243

How can I be the kind of faithful person God honors?
Heb. 6:11, 12, p. 1445

How can I claim God's promises?
Heb. 10:23, p. 1449

LIFE EXAMPLES

Pharaoh: A Bad Case of a Hard Heart,
Ex. 3:19, 20, p. 69

Deborah: A Mother in Israel,
Judg. 5:7, p. 280

Josiah: Committed to Following the Lord,
2 Kin. 23:25, p. 461

Mordecai: Bowing Before No Man,
Esth. 3:2, p. 576

Baruch: Given His Life as a Prize,
Jer. 45:1–5, p. 915

Peter: Willing to Change,
Matt. 16:18, p. 1135

LIFE LESSONS

- Gen. 2:20
- Gen. 3:1
- Gen. 3:5
- Gen. 4:7
- Gen. 12:1
- Gen. 12:7
- Gen. 17:23
- Gen. 18:19
- Gen. 22:18
- Gen. 24:1
- Gen. 24:7
- Gen. 28:9
- Ex. 1:20
- Ex. 4:12
- Ex. 5:22
- Ex. 8:15
- Ex. 16:4
- Ex. 16:18
- Ex. 19:5
- Ex. 20:12
- Lev. 1:17
- Lev. 8:35
- Lev. 25:21
- Num. 9:23
- Num. 11:1
- Num. 11:28
- Num. 14:24
- Num. 15:39
- Num. 16:28
- Num. 20:12
- Num. 22:12
- Num. 33:55
- Deut. 5:24
- Deut. 5:29
- Deut. 5:33
- Deut. 6:5
- Deut. 6:18
- Deut. 11:13,14
- Deut. 23:12,13
- Deut. 28:3, 4
- Deut. 30:1–3
- Josh. 5:8
- Josh. 11:11
- Josh. 23:13
- Josh. 24:24
- Judg. 9:4
- Judg. 13:23
- Judg. 16:20
- Judg. 17:13
- Ruth 3:10
- Ruth 4:15
- 1 Sam. 1:20
- 1 Sam. 2:35
- 1 Sam. 22:18
- 1 Sam. 26:10
- 1 Sam. 30:20
- 2 Sam. 6:3
- 2 Sam. 6:13
- 2 Sam. 7:21
- 1 Kin. 17:17
- 2 Kin. 4:2
- 2 Kin. 4:17
- 2 Kin. 5:14
- 2 Kin. 6:31
- 2 Kin. 18:7
- 1 Chr. 5:26
- 1 Chr. 14:12
- 1 Chr. 15:13
- 2 Chr. 15:7
- 2 Chr. 20:25
- 2 Chr. 31:21
- Neh. 3:5
- Neh. 8:17
- Esth. 2:10
- Esth. 8:8
- Job 1:10
- Job 36:11
- Job 42:12
- Ps. 1:3
- Ps. 66:18
- Ps. 72:17
- Ps. 81:10
- Ps. 81:13, 16
- Ps. 88:3
- Ps. 112:2
- Is. 1:5
- Is. 3:10
- Is. 28:29
- Is. 55:2
- Jer. 5:12
- Jer. 23:3
- Jer. 38:20
- Nah. 1:9
- Nah. 2:13
- Hab. 1:13
- Mal. 3:16
- Matt. 10:42
- Luke 1:45
- John 6:38
- John 13:17
- Acts 7:9, 10
- Heb. 12:11
- 1 John 1:4
- 2 John 8
- Rev. 2:10

LIFE PRINCIPLE 22

To walk in the Spirit is to obey the initial promptings of the Spirit. Acts 10:19, p. 1282

WHAT THE BIBLE SAYS ABOUT

How the Holy Spirit Guides Us, John 16:13, p. 1255

Grieving the Holy Spirit, Eph. 4:30, p. 1384

ANSWERS TO LIFE'S QUESTIONS

How can I become a more obedient child of God? Gen. 12:1, p. 16

What are the characteristics of a godly man? Matt. 1:20, 21, p. 1113

How does my conscience differ from the guidance of the Holy Spirit? Rom. 2:14, 15, p. 1311

How can I partner with the Holy Spirit in my life? Col. 2:6, 7, p. 1400

LIFE EXAMPLES

King Ahasuerus: A Restless Spirit, Esth. 6:1, p. 580

Tychicus: Beloved Messenger, Eph. 6:21, p. 1387

LIFE LESSONS

- Gen. 3:12
- Gen. 12:7
- Gen. 17:23
- Gen. 35:5
- Ex. 4:12
- Ex. 8:15
- Ex. 10:10, 11
- Ex. 16:4
- Ex. 16:18
- Lev. 1:17
- Lev. 8:35
- Num. 1:1
- Num. 7:89
- Num. 9:23
- Num. 11:28
- Num. 16:28
- Deut. 5:24
- Josh. 7:21
- Josh. 23:13
- 1 Sam. 3:7
- 1 Sam. 10:22
- 1 Sam. 16:3
- 1 Kin. 8:58
- 1 Kin. 17:9
- 1 Chr. 12:18
- Ezra 1:5
- Neh. 2:12
- Neh. 7:5
- Job 33:14
- Job 40:8
- Ps. 63:6
- Jer. 26:2
- Mark 2:22
- Luke 4:1, 14
- Luke 24:31
- Acts 1:8
- Acts 16:6, 7
- Rom. 3:23
- 1 Cor. 2:12
- Heb. 13:20, 21
- 2 John 8

LIFE PRINCIPLE 23

You can never outgive God. 2 Cor. 9:8, p. 1360

WHAT THE BIBLE SAYS ABOUT

How God Defines Wealth, 1 Chr. 29:12, p. 495

Spiritual Shortsightedness in Giving, Hag. 1:2–11, p. 1086

Tithing and Giving, Mal. 3:8–12, p. 1107

ANSWERS TO LIFE'S QUESTIONS

Does God consider loyalty an important trait in His people? Ruth 1:16, 17, p. 306

Should I tithe when I am struggling financially? Mal. 3:8–12, p. 1106

LIFE EXAMPLES

Matthew: Leaving It All Behind, Matt. 9:9–17, p. 1124

Zacchaeus: A Life That Counts, Luke 19:1–10, p. 1217

LIFE LESSONS

- Gen. 11:4
- Gen. 13:8
- Gen. 31:42
- Gen. 48:11
- Num. 14:11
- Num. 18:20
- Deut. 15:7
- Deut. 15:11
- Deut. 16:17
- Judg. 11:24
- 1 Sam. 2:21
- 2 Sam. 7:8
- 2 Sam. 7:11
- 2 Sam. 9:7
- 1 Chr. 17:1
- 1 Chr. 29:9
- 1 Chr. 29:14
- 2 Chr. 25:9
- Ezra 2:69
- Neh. 10:38
- Ps. 108:12
- Ps. 109:27
- Matt. 6:4
- Matt. 6:32
- Luke 14:14
- 2 Cor. 9:7
- 2 Cor. 9:8
- 2 Cor. 9:15

LIFE PRINCIPLE 24

To live the Christian life is to allow Jesus to live His life in and through us. Gal. 2:20, p. 1370

WHAT THE BIBLE SAYS ABOUT

Adversity as a Revealer of Our Strengths and Weaknesses, Judg. 6:12, 13, p. 283

How to Control Our Anger, Is. 64:9, p. 851

True Religion, Mic. 6:8, p. 1065

Loving the Unlovable, Matt. 5:45, p. 1119

Growing in Our Faith, Luke 18:1–8, p. 1215

Spiritual Growth, 2 Pet. 3:18, p. 1477

ANSWERS TO LIFE'S QUESTIONS

What does it mean to live in "the fear of the Lord"? Lev. 25:36, p. 143

How can I deal effectively with jealousy? Ps. 37:4, p. 648

How can I confront a believer who has fallen spiritually? Ezek. 16:2, p. 951

How can I avoid burnout in doing God's work? Zech. 4:6, 7, p. 1092

When and how am I filled with the Holy Spirit? Acts 2:4, p. 1266

What does it mean to do spiritual battle? Rom. 7:15–25, p. 1318

What value could there possibly be in weakness? 2 Cor. 12:9, p. 1364

Why do I still have the impulse to sin? Gal. 2:20, p. 1369

What is the fruit of the Spirit and how does it grow in me? Gal. 5:22, 23, p. 1374

How can I cope with feelings of loneliness? 2 Tim. 4:13, 17, 21, p. 1430

LIFE EXAMPLES

Jeremiah: Sorrowful Compassion, Jer. 14:17, p. 874

Jesus: Example or Sacrifice? Matt. 26:39, p. 1150

Judas: Rabbi Is Not Enough, John 18:3, p. 1257

Stephen: Echoing His Savior, Acts 7:59, 60, p. 1275

LIFE LESSONS

- Gen. 2:25
- Gen. 6:22
- Ex. 7:5
- Ex. 21:36
- Ex. 22:28
- Lev. 8:35
- Lev. 18:4
- Lev. 19:9, 10
- Lev. 22:21
- Gal. 2:20
- Col. 2:6
- Col. 3:2

LIFE PRINCIPLE 25

God blesses us so that we might bless others. Eph. 4:28, p. 1382

WHAT THE BIBLE SAYS ABOUT

How God Defines Wealth, 1 Chr. 29:12, p. 495

The Benefits of Prayer and Fasting, Esth. 4:16, p. 579

The Best Friend You Will Ever Have, Song 5:16, p. 776

Accountability Relationships, 2 Cor. 5:10, p. 1355

ANSWERS TO LIFE'S QUESTIONS

What does God's love look like? Song 6:4, p. 777

Do I have a role to play in communicating God's truth to others? Matt. 28:19, 20, p. 1154

What tools has God provided to help me share my faith? Mark 16:15, p. 1181

continued on next page

Life Principle 25

continued from previous page

Life Examples

Barnabas: Always an Encouraging Word, 1 Cor. 9:6, p. 1339

Life Lessons

- Gen. 1:22
- Gen. 30:27
- Gen. 33:11
- Ex. 25:2
- Num. 10:29
- Num. 22:12
- Deut. 15:7
- Deut. 15:11
- Ruth 2:15
- 1 Sam. 30:6
- 1 Kin. 2:6, 9
- Ps. 37:3
- Ps. 70:4
- Ps. 106:3
- Prov. 3:27
- Prov. 17:5
- Eccl. 4:9, 10
- Eccl. 5:19
- Is. 58:6
- Jer. 38:20
- Ezek. 22:30
- Matt. 10:8
- Luke 12:48
- Acts 9:4
- Acts 11:29
- Acts 27:25
- 1 Tim. 6:18
- 2 Tim. 1:6

Life Principle 26

Adversity is a bridge to a deeper relationship with God. Phil. 3:10, 11, p. 1392

What the Bible Says About

God's Limitations on Adversity, 2 Chr. 20:29, p. 520

How God Uses Adversity to Get Our Attention, Acts 9:1–20, p. 1277

Answers to Life's Questions

Does God bring us adversity? Gen. 39:20, p. 50

How can I find courage in times of adversity? Josh. 1:6–9, p. 242

What role does Satan play in our adversity? Job 2:4–7, p. 587

Where is God when I'm in pain? Is. 63:9, p. 847

Why doesn't God keep us from tests and trials? Dan. 6:16, p. 1008

Is there a limit to God's forgiveness? 1 Cor. 6:9–11, p. 1336

How do I handle a difficult trial not of my own doing? 1 Pet. 1:6, 7, p. 1468

Life Examples

Joel: Prophet of Revival, Joel 2:13, p. 1037

Paul: Strength in Weakness, 2 Cor. 12:7, p. 1363

Life Lessons

- Gen. 6:18
- Gen. 12:10
- Gen. 22:1
- Gen. 32:31
- Gen. 39:2
- Gen. 41:46
- Gen. 42:5
- Gen. 50:20
- Ex. 5:9
- Ex. 14:2
- Ex. 17:7
- Ex. 33:19
- Lev. 14:33, 34
- Num. 13:31
- Num. 14:9
- Num. 21:2
- Num. 35:10, 11
- Deut. 8:2
- Deut. 8:16
- Josh. 1:9
- Josh. 11:23
- Judg. 2:22
- Ruth 1:21
- 1 Sam. 1:18
- 1 Sam. 8:6
- 1 Sam. 9:16
- 1 Sam. 30:1, 2
- 2 Sam. 4:9
- 2 Sam. 10:12
- 1 Kin. 19:18
- 2 Kin. 11:17
- 2 Chr. 26:16
- 2 Chr. 28:22
- Ezra 4:23
- Esth. 9:22
- Job 1:20
- Job 5:7
- Job 10:20
- Job 12:13
- Job 16:9
- Job 29:2
- Job 36:15
- Job 42:8
- Job 42:12
- Ps. 10:1
- Ps. 13:1
- Ps. 35:27
- Ps. 57:1
- Ps. 66:10
- Ps. 107:19
- Ps. 119:67
- Eccl. 7:14
- Is. 9:13
- Is. 29:24
- Is. 38:17
- Is. 41:17
- Is. 51:12
- Jer. 31:14
- Lam. 3:31, 32
- Lam. 4:17
- Mark 13:13
- Luke 12:6
- John 11:37
- Acts 27:20
- Rom. 5:3, 4
- 2 Cor. 1:3, 4
- 2 Cor. 1:9
- James 5:11
- Rev. 2:10

LIFE PRINCIPLE 27

Prayer is life's greatest time saver. 2 Thess. 3:1, p. 1414

WHAT THE BIBLE SAYS ABOUT

Asking God for Specific Things, 1 Kin. 3:5, p. 395

Seeking God's Guidance, Ps. 27:14, p. 641

The Many Faces of Prayer, Col. 1:9–12, p. 1399

ANSWERS TO LIFE'S QUESTIONS

What does it mean to "sit before the Lord"? 2 Sam. 7:18, p. 362

What steps can I take when I really need to hear from God? 2 Kin. 7:1, p. 439

What good does fasting do us? Neh. 1:4, p. 554

How can I deal with the anger or bitterness of another? Prov. 14:10, p. 737

Will God really meet all my needs? Phil. 4:19, p. 1395

What does it mean to "pray without ceasing"? 1 Thess. 5:17, p. 1409

LIFE LESSONS

- Gen. 13:4
- Gen. 19:29
- Josh. 7:5
- Josh. 9:14
- 1 Sam. 7:8
- 2 Sam. 12:4
- 2 Kin. 20:5
- 1 Chr. 4:10
- Ezra 8:21
- Ezra 8:31
- Job 26:14
- Ps. 115:3
- Matt. 7:7
- Mark 9:24
- James 4:2

LIFE PRINCIPLE 28

No Christian has ever been called to "go it alone" in his or her walk of faith. Heb. 10:24, 25, p. 1450

WHAT THE BIBLE SAYS ABOUT

The Need for Christian Friendship, 1 Sam. 20:42, p. 338

Loving the Unlovable, Matt. 5:45, p. 1119

Accountability Relationships, 2 Cor. 5:10, p. 1355

Bearing One Another's Burdens, Gal. 6:1–3, p. 1375

The Making of an Encourager, 1 Thess. 3:1–10, p. 1407

ANSWERS TO LIFE'S QUESTIONS

Does God consider loyalty an important trait in His people? Ruth 1:16, 17, p. 306

How can I find the strength to endure when I face spiritual opposition? Ezra 4:1–24, p. 544

LIFE EXAMPLES

Ruth: Loyal to the End, Ruth 4:13–22, p. 309

Nathan: The Value of Godly Counsel, 2 Sam 12, p. 368

Barnabas: Always an Encouraging Word, 1 Cor. 9:6, p. 1339

continued on next page

Life Principle 28

continued from previous page

Life Lessons

- Gen. 2:18
- Gen. 2:20
- Ex. 17:12
- Ex. 18:8
- Ex. 18:23
- Lev. 23:2
- Num. 13:31
- Deut. 1:13
- Deut. 1:38
- Deut. 3:20
- Deut. 7:17, 18
- Deut. 31:6
- Deut. 33:27
- Josh. 1:9
- Josh. 23:6
- Judg. 5:13
- Judg. 6:16
- Ruth 1:6
- 1 Sam. 12:23
- 1 Sam. 18:1
- 1 Sam. 20:12, 13
- 1 Sam. 23:16
- 1 Sam. 30:6
- 2 Sam. 1:26
- 1 Kin. 2:3
- 1 Kin. 8:66
- 1 Kin. 19:18
- 1 Chr. 22:19
- Neh. 2:18
- Job 2:11
- Job 10:20
- Ps. 3:2
- Ps. 9:10
- Ps. 10:14
- Ps. 26:12
- Ps. 43:3
- Ps. 104:4
- Ps. 122:1
- Ps. 124:1, 3
- Prov. 15:22
- Eccl. 4:9, 10
- Song 1:4
- Is. 37:4
- Acts 2:42
- Acts 4:31
- Acts 11:29
- Acts 13:2
- Acts 27:25
- Rom. 15:2
- Rom. 15:30
- 1 Cor. 1:10
- 1 Cor. 12:7
- 1 Cor. 13:9
- 1 Cor. 14:12
- Eph. 6:18
- Col. 3:16
- 2 Thess. 1:3
- James 5:16

Life Principle 29

We learn more in our valley experiences than on our mountaintops.
James 5:10, p. 1464

What the Bible Says About

Adversity as a Revealer of Our Strengths and Weaknesses, Judg. 6:12, 13, p. 283

How Adversity Reveals Our Level of Faith, Mark 4:35, p. 1163

Answers to Life's Questions

How can I handle criticism during times of adversity? Job 2:10, p. 588

Does Satan cause all of our adversity? Job 16:11, p. 599

Where is God when I'm in pain? Is. 63:9, p. 847

How can I help to restore someone to fellowship with God? Ezek. 36:16–38, p. 980

How can a good God allow suffering in a believer's life? Joel 1:19, p. 1036

What can I do when my feelings go from discouraged to hopeless? Hab. 3:17–19, p. 1078

What value could there possibly be in weakness? 2 Cor. 12:9, p. 1364

Life Examples

Moses: God's Pattern for Success, Ex. 3:1–4, p. 67

Life Lessons

- Gen. 12:10
- Gen. 21:16
- Gen. 32:31
- Gen. 39:2
- Gen. 41:1
- Gen. 41:46
- Gen. 42:5
- Gen. 50:20
- Ex. 5:9
- Ex. 14:2
- Ex. 17:7
- Lev. 14:33, 34
- Num. 13:31
- Num. 14:9
- Num. 21:2
- Deut. 2:7
- Deut. 8:2
- Deut. 8:16
- Josh. 11:23
- Judg. 2:22
- Ruth 1:21
- 1 Sam. 1:18
- 1 Sam. 9:16
- 1 Sam. 17:37
- 1 Sam. 30:1, 2
- 1 Sam. 30:20
- 2 Sam. 4:9
- 1 Kin. 19:18
- 2 Kin. 11:17
- 2 Chr. 26:16
- 2 Chr. 28:22
- Ezra 4:23
- Job 5:7
- Job 16:9
- Job 23:10
- Job 29:2
- Job 36:15
- Job 42:12
- Ps. 66:10
- Eccl. 7:14
- Is. 29:24
- Is. 41:17
- Is. 43:20
- Is. 49:15
- Luke 12:6
- Luke 22:31
- John 11:37
- Acts 27:20
- Rom. 5:3, 4
- 2 Cor. 1:3, 4
- 2 Cor. 1:9
- Rev. 2:10

LIFE PRINCIPLE 30

An eager anticipation of the Lord's return keeps us living productively.
Rev. 22:12, p. 1514

WHAT THE BIBLE SAYS ABOUT

The Value of Diligence,
Eccl. 11:6, p. 768

How God Judges and Rewards Our Work,
Rev. 22:12, p. 1512

ANSWERS TO LIFE'S QUESTIONS

How can I find fulfillment in my work?
Eccl. 9:10, p. 765

LIFE EXAMPLES

Timothy: A Man Who Honored God,
1 Tim. 1:2, 18, p. 1418

Luke: Laboring in the Background,
2 Tim. 4:11, p. 1429

Titus: Serving God with Abandon,
Titus 1:4, p. 1432

LIFE LESSONS

- Gen. 45:7
- Ex. 28:3
- Deut. 3:20
- Eccl. 9:10
- Matt. 25:13
- Luke 21:34
- 1 Thess. 5:6
- 2 Thess. 3:5
- 1 Tim. 6:12
- Heb. 6:12
- Rev. 19:16
- Rev. 22:7
- Rev. 22:20

* Promises Index

Hundreds of Bible promises are highlighted and marked with an asterisk in the Bible text. The following index will help you locate these promises by topic.

Promises for Your Family

... FOR YOUR DESCENDANTS

Genesis 22:17, 18
Deuteronomy 1:11

... FOR YOUR CHILDREN

Joshua 14:9

... FOR AN INHERITANCE

Joshua 14:9

Promises for Provision

... FOR OUR NEEDS

Matthew 6:33
Matthew 7:11
Philippians 4:19

... THROUGH SEEDTIME AND HARVEST

Genesis 8:22
Leviticus 26:3, 4
Psalms 126:5, 6
Ecclesiastes 11:1
Isaiah 61:11
Ezekiel 37:26
Ezekiel 47:12
Amos 9:13
Matthew 19:29
2 Corinthians 9:6
Galatians 6:9

Promises for Obeying

... GOD'S VOICE

Genesis 22:17, 18
Exodus 15:26

... GOD'S WRITTEN WORD

Leviticus 26:3, 4
Deuteronomy 7:9
Joshua 1:8
Joshua 14:9
1 Kings 2:2, 3
1 Chronicles 22:13
Psalm 119:165
Isaiah 1:19
Isaiah 66:2
1 John 3:22
Revelation 1:3

... WITH LOYALTY

2 Chronicles 16:9
Psalm 37:4
Matthew 6:33
Ephesians 6:2, 3

... WITH A PURE HEART

Psalm 84:11
Luke 6:35

... IN TURNING FROM SIN

2 Chronicles 7:14
1 John 2:17

Promises for Salvation

... THROUGH DELIVERANCE

Genesis 45:7, 8
Numbers 21:8
2 Samuel 22:26-28
Psalm 72:4
Ezekiel 34:12
Romans 8:32
Romans 11:26, 27

... THROUGH CHRIST

Exodus 12:13
Leviticus 17:11
1 Samuel 14:6
1 Chronicles 28:9
Isaiah 43:25
Isaiah 45:22
Jeremiah 3:22
Ezekiel 11:19, 20
Hosea 14:4
Joel 2:32
Zechariah 9:16
Matthew 1:21
Matthew 10:32
Matthew 16:18
Matthew 16:25
Mark 8:35
Luke 5:32
Luke 9:56
Luke 11:9
John 3:16
John 4:14
John 5:24
John 6:37
John 7:38, 39
John 8:36
John 10:10
John 10:27, 28
Romans 5:10
Romans 6:23
Romans 10:9
2 Corinthians 5:17
Ephesians 5:14
1 Thessalonians 5:9
Hebrews 7:25
Hebrews 9:28
1 Peter 2:6
1 John 1:7
1 John 1:9
1 John 5:4

... FROM OUR ENEMIES

Deuteronomy 28:7
1 Samuel 17:47
Isaiah 51:7, 8

Promises for Salvation *continued*

... THROUGH GOD'S DEFENSE
Joshua 23:10
Job 5:15, 16
Psalm 20:6
Isaiah 35:4
Zechariah 8:13

... THROUGH GOD'S MERCY
2 Chronicles 30:9
Zephaniah 3:17
Mark 13:20

... FROM EVIL
Psalm 121:7
Malachi 3:6

... IN ADVERSITY
Isaiah 41:10
Isaiah 43:2

... THROUGH FAITH
Habakkuk 2:4
Mark 8:35
Luke 18:17
John 1:12
John 11:25, 26
John 12:46
Acts 10:43
1 Timothy 2:15
James 5:15

... THROUGH REPENTANCE
Luke 15:7
2 Chronicles 7:14
2 Peter 3:9

Promises for Deliverance

... IN ADVERSITY
Genesis 45:7, 8
Esther 4:14
Psalm 41:1
Psalm 50:15
Psalm 65:3
Isaiah 41:10
Isaiah 43:1
Isaiah 43:2
Jeremiah 15:11

... IN THE WILDERNESS
Exodus 2:24, 25
Judges 3:9

... FROM YOUR ENEMIES
2 Kings 17:39
Esther 9:1
Psalm 34:19
Psalm 72:4
Jeremiah 1:8
Jeremiah 15:11

... THROUGH SALVATION
Psalm 91:14
Hosea 13:14
1 Thessalonians 1:10

... THROUGH RIGHTEOUSNESS
Ezekiel 3:21
Daniel 6:16
Obadiah 17

Promises of God's Presence

... ALWAYS ABIDING
Exodus 33:14
Numbers 6:24, 26
Isaiah 24:23
Isaiah 41:10
Isaiah 43:1
Isaiah 43:2
Habakkuk 2:14
Haggai 1:13
Haggai 2:5
Zechariah 2:10
Matthew 28:20
Luke 24:49
Hebrews 13:5
James 4:8

... THROUGH INTIMACY
Deuteronomy 32:36
1 Chronicles 28:9
Song of Solomon 2:16
Song of Solomon 7:10
Song of Solomon 8:7
Hosea 2:19

... AS OUR FATHER
1 Samuel 12:22
1 Chronicles 28:9

... WHEN WE SEEK HIM
1 Chronicles 28:9
Ezra 8:22
Psalm 145:18
Hebrews 11:6

... WHEN HE HEARS US
Exodus 2:24, 25
Psalm 4:3
Psalm 10:17
Psalm 145:18
Isaiah 65:24
1 John 5:15

Promises for Peace

... IN GOD'S PRESENCE
Numbers 6:24, 26

... IN STRENGTH
1 Chronicles 12:18
Psalm 29:11

... IN OBEYING GOD'S WORD
Psalm 119:165
Isaiah 32:17
Philippians 4:9

... IN TRUSTING GOD
Isaiah 26:3
Jeremiah 29:11
Ezekiel 37:26

... FOR HEALING
Isaiah 57:19

Promises of God's Blessings

... TO GENERATIONS
Genesis 22:17, 18
Deuteronomy 1:11
Psalm 67:7

... WITH PEACE
Numbers 6:24, 26

... IN ADVERSITY
Judges 5:31
Luke 6:35
1 Peter 4:14

... IN ABUNDANCE FOR LIFE
Malachi 3:10
Psalm 37:4
Proverbs 10:22
2 Samuel 7:28
Matthew 6:33
Matthew 7:11
John 15:7

... IN HEALING
Malachi 4:2

Promises to Preserve

... WITH LIFE
Job 10:12
Psalm 16:11
Psalm 138:7
Proverbs 19:23
Ecclesiastes 7:17
Isaiah 25:8
Isaiah 26:19
Amos 5:14

... WITH PROTECTION
Deuteronomy 28:7
Psalm 5:12
Psalm 48:14
Isaiah 41:10
Isaiah 43:1
Isaiah 43:2
Joel 3:16
Ephesians 6:13
2 Thessalonians 3:3

... WITH HEALING
Exodus 15:26
2 Chronicles 7:14
Psalm 34:19
Isaiah 57:19
Hosea 6:1
James 5:15

... THROUGH HOPE
Job 5:15, 16
Psalms 31:24
Psalm 48:14
Psalm 55:22
Jeremiah 29:11

... THROUGH REST
Exodus 33:14
Judges 5:31
Ruth 2:12
1 Kings 8:56
Jeremiah 6:16
Matthew 11:28
2 Thessalonians 1:6, 7
Hebrews 4:9

... WITH GRACE
2 Chronicles 30:9
Nehemiah 9:17
Psalm 84:11

... THROUGH RESTORATION
Deuteronomy 32:36
2 Samuel 16:12
2 Chronicles 7:14
Job 19:25, 26
Isaiah 25:8
Isaiah 65:17
Joel 2:25
Jonah 2:6
Zephaniah 3:9
Mark 4:22

... THROUGH MERCY
Ezra 4:11
Nehemiah 9:17
Isaiah 49:13
Lamentations 3:22, 23
Lamentations 3:31, 32
Hosea 2:19
Hosea 10:12
Joel 2:13
Jonah 2:6
Micah 7:18, 19
Luke 1:50

... THROUGH JOY
Psalm 16:11
Psalms 126:5, 6
Ecclesiastes 2:26

... THROUGH FAVOR
Job 10:12
Psalm 5:12
Psalm 84:11

... THROUGH COMFORT
Isaiah 49:13
Hebrews 2:16

Promises for Success

... THROUGH PROSPERITY
Joshua 1:8
1 Chronicles 22:13
Nehemiah 2:20

... IN OBEDIENCE
Joshua 1:8
1 Kings 2:2-3

... THROUGH REWARD
Ruth 2:12
Psalm 37:4
1 Corinthians 3:14
1 Peter 5:4
Revelation 22:12

... WITH WEALTH
1 Samuel 2:7-8

Promises When Waiting

... for mercy
Isaiah 30:18
Isaiah 64:4
Hebrews 9:28

... for strength
Isaiah 40:31
Nahum 1:7

Promises for Strength

... to His children
2 Chronicles 16:9
Psalm 20:6
Psalm 29:11
Micah 5:4
Habakkuk 3:19

... in adversity
Psalms 31:24
Psalm 41:1
Psalm 50:15
Psalm 138:7
Isaiah 35:4
Nahum 1:7
Mark 10:27
2 Corinthians 12:9

... when we wait
Isaiah 40:31

Promises of God's Word

... He will do it
Numbers 23:19
Matthew 24:35
Hebrews 12:26
2 Corinthians 1:20

... He blesses
2 Samuel 7:28
1 Kings 8:56

... He will not harm
Hosea 11:9

... He will protect
Hebrews 13:5

Promises of Christ

... we have a Shepherd
2 Corinthians 6:16

... we have a Savior
Luke 1:31, 32

... salvation
Exodus 12:13
Leviticus 17:11
1 Samuel 14:6
1 Chronicles 28:9
Isaiah 43:25
Isaiah 45:22
Jeremiah 3:22
Ezekiel 11:19, 20
Hosea 14:4
Joel 2:32
Zechariah 9:16
Matthew 1:21
Matthew 10:32
Matthew 16:18
Matthew 16:25
Mark 8:35
Luke 5:32
Luke 9:56
Luke 11:9
John 3:16
John 4:14
John 5:24
John 6:37
John 7:38, 39
John 8:36
John 10:10
John 10:27, 28
Romans 5:10
Romans 6:23
Romans 10:9
2 Corinthians 5:17
Ephesians 5:14
1 Thessalonians 5:9
Hebrews 7:25
Hebrews 9:28
1 Peter 2:6
1 John 1:7
1 John 1:9
1 John 5:4

... in serving Christ
2 Timothy 1:12

... through sanctification
Daniel 11:35
Philippians 1:6
Colossians 1:21, 22
1 Thessalonians 5:24
Hebrews 12:10

... of Christ's return
Matthew 26:64
Matthew 28:20
John 14:2, 3
Acts 1:11
James 5:8
1 Peter 5:4
Micah 4:3
Revelation 22:12

... eternal life in Heaven
1 Corinthians 9:25
1 Corinthians 13:12
Galatians 3:29
Galatians 6:8
Philippians 3:20, 21
Colossians 3:4
1 Thessalonians 4:14
1 Timothy 4:18
2 Timothy 2:11-13
Hebrews 11:16
2 Peter 1:4
2 Peter 3:13
1 John 2:17
1 John 2:25
Revelation 2:7
Revelation 3:5
Revelation 7:16
Revelation 14:13
Revelation 20:6
Revelation 21:4

Promises of the Holy Spirit

... When Walking in the Spirit
Romans 8:1
Galatians 5:16
Galatians 6:8
2 Corinthians 4:16

... For Direction
Psalm 18:28
Psalm 48:14
Proverbs 3:5, 6
Proverbs 16:9
Mark 1:17
John 8:12
John 16:13

... When We Pray in the Spirit
Romans 8:26

... When We Are Filled with the Spirit
Ezekiel 36:27
Ezekiel 39:29
Joel 2:28
Haggai 2:5
Luke 24:49
Acts 2:38
Ezekiel 43:7

... In Wisdom, Knowledge, and Revelation
Ecclesiastes 2:26
Daniel 2:20, 21, 22
Daniel 12:3
Amos 3:7
Luke 21:15
Philippians 3:15
James 1:5

Promises for Temptation

... When We Are Tempted
1 Corinthians 6:14
1 Corinthians 10:13
Galatians 5:16
James 1:12
James 4:7
2 Peter 1:4
2 Peter 1:10
2 Peter 2:9

... When We Overcome
Revelation 2:7
Revelation 3:5

Promises of Faith

... When We Believe
Jeremiah 17:7, 8
Matthew 17:20
Matthew 18:19
Mark 9:23
Mark 11:24
Luke 17:6
John 14:12
John 20:29
Acts 10:43
1 John 5:4

... In Adversity
Jeremiah 31:16
Matthew 17:20

... As a Child
Mark 10:15
Luke 18:17

... To the Humble
Isaiah 66:2
Matthew 23:12
Mark 10:15
1 Peter 5:6

Promises of Justice

... For Salvation
Psalm 65:3

... For the Afflicted
Psalm 72:4
Psalm 140:12

... For His People
Psalm 96:10
Zephaniah 2:3
Zephaniah 3:5
Hebrews 6:10
Isaiah 30:18

... On the Wicked
Proverbs 3:33
Ecclesiastes 12:14
Nahum 1:3
1 Samuel 2:30
Romans 16:20

... Through Christ
Isaiah 9:7
Isaiah 16:5
Jeremiah 23:5

... On the World
Acts 17:31

Promises for God's Protection

... As Our Defense
Joshua 23:10
1 Samuel 14:6
1 Samuel 17:47
2 Samuel 22:26-28
2 Kings 6:16
Psalm 5:12
1 Corinthians 1:7, 8
Proverbs 30:5, 6
Jeremiah 20:11
Ephesians 6:13

... As Our Refuge
Ruth 2:12
Psalm 9:9
Isaiah 11:10
Isaiah 41:10
Isaiah 43:1
Isaiah 43:2

... As Our Security
2 Samuel 7:10
Psalm 48:14
Psalm 55:22
Psalm 119:165

OLD TESTAMENT

THE FIRST BOOK OF MOSES CALLED

GENESIS

The Greek word *Genesis* means "origin," "source," "generation," or "beginning." The original Hebrew title, *Bereshith*, means, "In the beginning." So Genesis tells us about the beginnings of many things, including the physical universe, mankind, sin, and death, and God's amazing plan to redeem it all.

The first part of Genesis focuses on the beginning and spread of sin in the world, culminating in a devastating flood. In this section of the book we see God creating, again and again, by speaking various aspects of our universe into existence. Then God "defines" what He has created, again by speaking his word. By naming things, God gives them an identity, a purpose, and a definition. Finally, God establishes and blesses what He has made, sealing the truth of His creation through His spoken word.

So what does this mean for you and me today? It means that God made you for a special purpose. He spoke you into existence long before you were conceived in your mother's womb. He "called" you—He defined you and gave you specific talents, gifts, and dreams. All your life, He has continued to call you, giving you guidance, direction, and protection. This is the truth about who you are as His beloved child who is born again and saved by His grace forever.

The second part of Genesis focuses on God's dealings with one man, Abraham, through whom He promises to bring salvation and blessing to the world. Abraham and his descendants learn firsthand that it is always best to trust in the Lord in times of famine and feasting, blessing and bondage. From Abraham to Isaac to Jacob to Joseph, God's promises begin to manifest to a great nation that would possess a great land.

Theme: Genesis provides a solid framework for understanding the big picture of the Bible. This book of beginnings introduces us to God and His holiness, righteousness, grace, and mercy, to His creation, man's sin, and God's plan of redemption as it began to unfold through Abraham and his descendants.

Author: Moses.

Time: Genesis begins with the creation story and ends with the death of Joseph, which probably occurred around the nineteenth century B.C.

Structure: The literary structure of Genesis is built around eleven distinct units, each signaled by the presence of the word "genealogy." The eleven sections include: (1) Introduction to the genealogies (1:1—2:3); (2) Heaven and Earth (2:4—4:26); (3) Adam (5:1—6:8); (4) Noah (6:9—9:29); (5) Sons of Noah (10:1—11:9); (6) Shem (11:10–26); (7) Terah (11:27—25:11); (8) Ishmael (25:12–18); (9) Isaac (25:19—35:29); (10) Esau (36:1—37:1); (11) Jacob (37:2—50:26).

As you read Genesis, watch for several life principles that play an important role in this book:

1. **Our intimacy with God—His highest priority for our lives—determines the impact of our lives.** *See Genesis 1:26; 15:1–6; pages 2, 19.*

9. **Trusting God means looking beyond what we can see to what God sees.** *See Genesis 22:1–14; page 27.*

26. **Adversity is a bridge to a deeper relationship with God.** *See Genesis 50:20, 21; page 63.*

The History of Creation
1 In the beginning God created the heavens
and the earth.
2 The earth was without form, and void; and
darkness *was*[a] on the face of the deep. And
the Spirit of God was hovering over the face
of the waters.
3 Then God said, "Let there be light"; and
there was light.
4 And God saw the light, that *it was* good;
and God divided the light from the darkness.
5 God called the light Day, and the darkness
He called Night. So the evening and the
morning were the first day.
6 Then God said, "Let there be a firmament
in the midst of the waters, and let it divide the
waters from the waters."
7 Thus God made the firmament, and divided the waters which *were* under the firmament from the waters which *were* above the
firmament; and it was so.
8 And God called the firmament Heaven. So
the evening and the morning were the second
day.
9 Then God said, "Let the waters under
the heavens be gathered together into one
place, and let the dry *land* appear"; and it
was so.
10 And God called the dry *land* Earth, and
the gathering together of the waters He called
Seas. And God saw that *it was* good.
11 Then God said, "Let the earth bring forth
grass, the herb *that* yields seed, *and* the fruit
tree *that* yields fruit according to its kind,
whose seed *is* in itself, on the earth"; and it
was so.
12 And the earth brought forth grass, the
herb *that* yields seed according to its kind,
and the tree *that* yields fruit, whose seed *is* in
itself according to its kind. And God saw that
it was good.
13 So the evening and the morning were the
third day.
14 Then God said, "Let there be lights in the
firmament of the heavens to divide the day
from the night; and let them be for signs and
seasons, and for days and years;
15 "and let them be for lights in the firmament of the heavens to give light on the
earth"; and it was so.
16 Then God made two great lights: the
greater light to rule the day, and the lesser
light to rule the night. *He made* the stars also.
17 God set them in the firmament of the
heavens to give light on the earth,
18 and to rule over the day and over the
night, and to divide the light from the darkness. And God saw that *it was* good.
19 So the evening and the morning were the
fourth day.
20 Then God said, "Let the waters abound
with an abundance of living creatures, and let
birds fly above the earth across the face of the
firmament of the heavens."
21 So God created great sea creatures and
every living thing that moves, with which the
waters abounded, according to their kind, and
every winged bird according to its kind. And
God saw that *it was* good.
22 And God blessed them, saying, "Be fruitful
and multiply, and fill the waters in the seas,
and let birds multiply on the earth."
23 So the evening and the morning were the
fifth day.
24 Then God said, "Let the earth bring forth
the living creature according to its kind: cattle and creeping thing and beast of the earth,
each according to its kind"; and it was so.
25 And God made the beast of the earth according to its kind, cattle according to its
kind, and everything that creeps on the earth
according to its kind. And God saw that *it was*
good.
26 Then God said, "Let Us make man in Our
image, according to Our likeness; let them
have dominion over the fish of the sea, over
the birds of the air, and over the cattle, over
all[a] the earth and over every creeping thing
that creeps on the earth."
27 So God created man in His *own* image; in
the image of God He created him; male and
female He created them.

1:2 [a]Words in italic type have been added for clarity. They are not found in the original Hebrew or Aramaic. **1:26** [a]Syriac reads *all the wild animals of.*

LIFE LESSONS

➤ **1:16 — *Then God made two great lights: the greater light to rule the day, and the lesser light to rule the night. He made the stars also.***

Many ancient peoples worshiped the sun and moon; but God's Word makes it clear that these celestial bodies are only "lights," one "greater" and one "lesser." We were made for an intimate relationship with God, not to worship inanimate objects!

➤ **1:22 — *And God blessed them, saying, "Be fruitful and multiply, and fill the waters in the seas, and let birds multiply on the earth."***

It is God's nature to "bless" the living creatures He makes. He always wants their—and our—best.

➤ **1:26 — *Then God said, "Let Us make man in Our image, according to Our likeness; let them have dominion over the fish of the sea, over the birds of the air, and over the cattle, over all the earth and over every creeping thing that creeps on the earth."***

When God created us, He made us like Himself; therefore we have the capacity for close, personal fellowship with Him.

WHAT THE BIBLE SAYS ABOUT **THE HOLY SPIRIT AND THE TRINITY**

Gen. 1:1, 2

Look closely at Genesis 1:1, 2, and you'll notice the Bible refers to "God" and "the Spirit of God" without making the slightest distinction between the two. It uses the two terms interchangeably. Have you ever wondered why?

It's because the two are one! This is the first allusion to the doctrine of the Trinity in Scripture.

A little later in the creation story we find a second reference to the Trinity: "Then God said, 'Let Us make man in Our image, according to Our likeness'" (Gen. 1:26). Now, to whom was God speaking? Whoever He meant, he (or they) clearly played a crucial part in the creation process: "Let *Us* make man." So who was this mysterious "Us"? The only other beings then alive were animals and angels, and the Bible gives no indication that either group played any role in the creation process.

Fortunately, in the very next verse God clarifies who He meant: "And God created man in His own image, in the image of God He created him; male and female He created them" (Gen. 1:27). God did not create Adam and Eve in the image of animals or angels; He created them in the image of God. Therefore, the "Us" in Genesis 1:26 *must* refer to God alone, that is, to God the Father, God the Son, and God the Spirit.

He created us in His image.

Within the eternal fellowship of the Trinity, the members of the Godhead have always enjoyed a deep and rich and unbroken relationship of love with one another. When God created us, He wanted us to share in some measure of that fellowship; that's why He created us in His image. By creating us to reflect His own nature, He made it possible for us to develop a deep and intimate relationship with Himself.

In this truth we come to the heart of who God made us to be. Our intimacy with God—His highest priority for our lives—determines the impact of our lives! So the closer we grow to Him, the more positive and lasting impact we can have on this world.

See the Life Principles Index for further study:

1. Our intimacy with God—His highest priority for our lives—determines the impact of our lives.

LIFE PRINCIPLE 1

OUR INTIMACY WITH GOD—HIS HIGHEST PRIORITY FOR OUR LIVES—DETERMINES THE IMPACT OF OUR LIVES.

GEN. 1:26

One of our greatest needs is to know that we are loved. Each one of us has to feel certain, deep down in our hearts, that someone loves us, cares for us, and has our best interests at heart.

That is how God designed us. He wants us to know that He loves every one of us with a passionate intensity too deep for words.

God created human beings with fellowship in mind—first with Himself, and then with others. But we cannot fully love one another until we have ourselves experienced the love of God. We experience His love when we willingly surrender to His call to be our Savior, Lord, and Friend.

There are at least three reasons God seeks our surrender:

- *He loves us and desires our fellowship and worship.*

So long as we hold something back from God, we cannot know Him completely or fully experience His love. When we surrender to Him, we get all of Him.

- *He wants our service for Him to be effective and fruitful.*

The more we get to know and love Jesus, the more effective our service will be. The closer we draw to God, the more impact our lives will have. The more energetically we nurture our relationship with the Lord, the greater the positive mark we will leave behind.

- *He waits for the freedom to bless us.*

God is omnipotent but will not violate His own principles. He draws us to Himself so we can experience His love and forgiveness. He asks for our willing surrender so that He can give us the best blessings He has to offer.

So why do we resist? With all this in mind, why does anyone resist surrendering to God?

Pride is the key reason most people resist surrender. They think they know better than God and that they can handle their life better than He can, so they keep Him at arm's distance.

Others do not surrender because

God created human beings with fellowship in mind.

they fear what God will do (or not do) for them. They think that if they give Him control, He'll make them do exactly what will make them most miserable.

Still others refuse to surrender to Christ because they believe Satan's lie, which tells them that God is judgmental and will punish them for their mistakes.

All of this is completely false! God *always* has our best in mind. He will refuse us no good thing when we gladly submit to His will (Rom. 8:32). He tells us, "For I know the thoughts that I think toward you, says the LORD, thoughts of peace and not of evil, to give you a future and a hope" (Jer. 29:11).

It only makes sense to surrender to God, because when we do, we grow close to Him—His highest priority for us—and we begin to have an impact on our world.

Fulfill your destiny. Anne Graham Lotz once told an interviewer about the many trials she had faced over the previous few years, including her parents' serious illnesses and her son's battle with cancer. She finally came to the point where all she wanted was Jesus. "Just give me Jesus," she declared.

Pray that He would draw you near once more.

Anne realized that if she had a personal, intimate relationship with the Savior of this universe, then whatever problems she faced, He would face them with her and He would bring a sweet resolve and a peace to her heart.

Is this the cry of your heart? Do you want to know the Savior and live in the fullness of His blessing each day? You can. David wrote, "those who seek the LORD shall not lack any good thing" (Ps. 34:10).

When you accepted Jesus Christ as your Savior, He not only forgave you but also made you into a new creature, no longer standing at a distance from God, but able to draw near to Him.

If you have drifted in your devotion to the Savior and feel as though you grow more distant each day in your relationship to Him, then pray that He would draw you near once more. He knows your weaknesses, and if you will tell Him that you want Him to take control of your life, He will come to you in a mighty way and bring hope and light to your situation, no matter how dark and hopeless it may feel (Is. 55:6, 7).

See the Life Principles Index for further study.

28 Then God blessed them, and God said to
them, "Be fruitful and multiply; fill the earth
and subdue it; have dominion over the fish of
the sea, over the birds of the air, and over
every living thing that moves on the earth."
29 And God said, "See, I have given you every
herb *that* yields seed which *is* on the face of
all the earth, and every tree whose fruit yields
seed; to you it shall be for food.
30 "Also, to every beast of the earth, to every
bird of the air, and to everything that creeps
on the earth, in which *there is* life, *I have given*
every green herb for food"; and it was so.
➤ 31 Then God saw everything that He had
made, and indeed *it was* very good. So the
evening and the morning were the sixth day.
2 Thus the heavens and the earth, and all
the host of them, were finished.
➤ 2 And on the seventh day God ended His
work which He had done, and He rested on
the seventh day from all His work which He
had done.
3 Then God blessed the seventh day and
sanctified it, because in it He rested from all
His work which God had created and made.
4 This *is* the history[a] of the heavens and the
earth when they were created, in the day that
the LORD God made the earth and the heavens,
5 before any plant of the field was in the
earth and before any herb of the field had
grown. For the LORD God had not caused it to
rain on the earth, and *there was* no man to till
the ground;
6 but a mist went up from the earth and watered the whole face of the ground.
7 And the LORD God formed man *of* the dust
of the ground, and breathed into his nostrils
the breath of life; and man became a living
being.

Life in God's Garden

8 The LORD God planted a garden eastward
in Eden, and there He put the man whom He
had formed.
9 And out of the ground the LORD God made
every tree grow that is pleasant to the sight
and good for food. The tree of life *was* also in
the midst of the garden, and the tree of the
knowledge of good and evil.
10 Now a river went out of Eden to water the
garden, and from there it parted and became
four riverheads.
11 The name of the first *is* Pishon; it *is* the
one which skirts the whole land of Havilah,
where *there is* gold.
12 And the gold of that land *is* good. Bdellium and the onyx stone *are* there.
13 The name of the second river *is* Gihon; it
is the one which goes around the whole land
of Cush.
14 The name of the third river *is* Hiddekel;[a] it
is the one which goes toward the east of Assyria. The fourth river *is* the Euphrates.
15 Then the LORD God took the man and put ➤
him in the garden of Eden to tend and keep it.
16 And the LORD God commanded the man,
saying, "Of every tree of the garden you may
freely eat;
17 but of the tree of the knowledge of good
and evil you shall not eat, for in the day that
you eat of it you shall surely die."
18 And the LORD God said, "*It is* not good ➤
that man should be alone; I will make him a
helper comparable to him."
19 Out of the ground the LORD God formed
every beast of the field and every bird of the
air, and brought *them* to Adam to see what he
would call them. And whatever Adam called
each living creature, that *was* its name.
20 So Adam gave names to all cattle, to the ➤
birds of the air, and to every beast of the field.
But for Adam there was not found a helper
comparable to him.
21 And the LORD God caused a deep sleep to
fall on Adam, and he slept; and He took one
of his ribs, and closed up the flesh in its place.

2:4 [a]Hebrew *toledoth,* literally *generations* **2:14** [a]Or *Tigris*

LIFE LESSONS

➤ 1:31 — *Then God saw everything that He had made, and indeed it was very good. So the evening and the morning were the sixth day.*

Everything that God made was not only "good," but "very good." All the good we see around us is nothing but an overflow of the goodness that flows out of God's generous heart (see James 1:17).

➤ 2:2 — *And on the seventh day God ended His work which He had done, and He rested on the seventh day from all His work which He had done.*

God did not "rest" from His work because He felt tired and needed to recoup His strength, but because He had finished His creation and He wanted to give us a model to follow. Rest is part of His blessing.

➤ 2:15 — *Then the LORD God took the man and put him in the garden of Eden to tend and keep it.*

God gave the man work to do long before sin entered the world. Adam felt energized in his work because he knew God was present—exactly the same as with us.

➤ 2:18 — *And the LORD God said, "It is not good that man should be alone; I will make him a helper comparable to him."*

God made us for fellowship, both with Himself and with other people. We can count on Him to meet our need for deep personal connection.

22 Then the rib which the LORD God had
taken from man He made into a woman, and
He brought her to the man.
23 And Adam said:

"This *is* now bone of my bones
And flesh of my flesh;
She shall be called Woman,
Because she was taken out of Man."

24 Therefore a man shall leave his father and
mother and be joined to his wife, and they
shall become one flesh.
➤ 25 And they were both naked, the man and
his wife, and were not ashamed.

The Temptation and Fall of Man

➤ 3 Now the serpent was more cunning than
any beast of the field which the LORD God
had made. And he said to the woman, "Has
God indeed said, 'You shall not eat of every
tree of the garden'?"
2 And the woman said to the serpent, "We
may eat the fruit of the trees of the garden;
3 "but of the fruit of the tree which *is* in the
midst of the garden, God has said, 'You shall
not eat it, nor shall you touch it, lest you
die.'"
4 Then the serpent said to the woman, "You
will not surely die.
➤ 5 "For God knows that in the day you eat of
it your eyes will be opened, and you will be
like God, knowing good and evil."
6 So when the woman saw that the tree *was*
good for food, that it *was* pleasant to the eyes,
and a tree desirable to make *one* wise, she
took of its fruit and ate. She also gave to her
husband with her, and he ate.
7 Then the eyes of both of them were ◄
opened, and they knew that they *were* naked;
and they sewed fig leaves together and made
themselves coverings.
8 And they heard the sound of the LORD God ◄
walking in the garden in the cool of the day,
and Adam and his wife hid themselves from
the presence of the LORD God among the trees
of the garden.
9 Then the LORD God called to Adam and
said to him, "Where *are* you?"
10 So he said, "I heard Your voice in the gar- ◄
den, and I was afraid because I was naked;
and I hid myself."
11 And He said, "Who told you that you *were*
naked? Have you eaten from the tree of
which I commanded you that you should not
eat?"
12 Then the man said, "The woman whom ◄
You gave *to be* with me, she gave me of the
tree, and I ate."
13 And the LORD God said to the woman,
"What *is* this you have done?"

LIFE LESSONS

➤ 2:20 — *So Adam gave names to all cattle, to the birds of the air, and to every beast of the field. But for Adam there was not found a helper comparable to him.*

A significant delay occurred between the time God said He would make a "helper" for Adam and the time He actually made Eve. We may have to wait for God's blessing, but it's always worth it!

➤ 2:25 — *And they were both naked, the man and his wife, and were not ashamed.*

God's intention for us has always been a deep, unrestricted intimacy with Him, with no walls between us. Sin has injured that intimacy, but when we see Jesus it will be completely restored (see 1 John 3:2).

➤ 3:1 — . . . *And he said to the woman, "Has God indeed said, 'You shall not eat of every tree of the garden'?"*

Satan often begins his temptations by questioning God's commands and suggesting that obedience is not really necessary.

➤ 3:5 — *"For God knows that in the day you eat of it your eyes will be opened, and you will be like God, knowing good and evil."*

We do ourselves great harm when we believe that we will find greater blessing in doing our own thing than in obeying God.

➤ 3:7 — *Then the eyes of both of them were opened, and they knew that they were naked; and they sewed fig leaves together and made themselves coverings.*

Sin fractures the relationship between God and us and between others and us. It also creates a painful emotional distance and destroys the close fellowship God intended for us to enjoy.

➤ 3:8 — *And they heard the sound of the LORD God walking in the garden in the cool of the day, and Adam and his wife hid themselves from the presence of the LORD God among the trees of the garden.*

God created us to interact with Him in an intimate friendship, even on a face-to-face basis. God desires that we walk with him daily, enjoying the rich fellowship that He offers.

➤ 3:10 — *So he said, "I heard Your voice in the garden, and I was afraid because I was naked; and I hid myself."*

Before he sinned, Adam loved to hear the voice of the Lord; after he sinned, that same voice made him afraid and prompted him to try to hide himself. But there is no hiding from God (Hebrews 4:13).

➤ 3:12 — *Then the man said, "The woman whom You gave to be with me, she gave me of the tree, and I ate."*

Sin impels us to blame others for our disobedience and folly, but God holds us personally accountable for what we do.

The woman said, "The serpent deceived me, and I ate."
14 So the LORD God said to the serpent:

"Because you have done this,
You *are* cursed more than all cattle,
And more than every beast of the field;
On your belly you shall go,
And you shall eat dust
All the days of your life.
15 And I will put enmity
Between you and the woman,
And between your seed and her Seed;
He shall bruise your head,
And you shall bruise His heel."

16 To the woman He said:

"I will greatly multiply your sorrow and your conception;
In pain you shall bring forth children;
Your desire *shall be* for your husband,
And he shall rule over you."

17 Then to Adam He said, "Because you have heeded the voice of your wife, and have eaten from the tree of which I commanded you, saying, 'You shall not eat of it':

"Cursed *is* the ground for your sake;
In toil you shall eat *of* it
All the days of your life.
18 Both thorns and thistles it shall bring forth for you,
And you shall eat the herb of the field.
19 In the sweat of your face you shall eat bread
Till you return to the ground,
For out of it you were taken;
For dust you *are*,
And to dust you shall return."

20 And Adam called his wife's name Eve, because she was the mother of all living.
21 Also for Adam and his wife the LORD God made tunics of skin, and clothed them.
22 Then the LORD God said, "Behold, the man has become like one of Us, to know good and evil. And now, lest he put out his hand and take also of the tree of life, and eat, and live forever"—
23 therefore the LORD God sent him out of the garden of Eden to till the ground from which he was taken.
24 So He drove out the man; and He placed cherubim at the east of the garden of Eden, and a flaming sword which turned every way, to guard the way to the tree of life.

Cain Murders Abel

4 Now Adam knew Eve his wife, and she
conceived and bore Cain, and said, "I have
acquired a man from the LORD."
2 Then she bore again, this time his brother
Abel. Now Abel was a keeper of sheep, but
Cain was a tiller of the ground.
3 And in the process of time it came to pass
that Cain brought an offering of the fruit of
the ground to the LORD.
4 Abel also brought of the firstborn of his
flock and of their fat. And the LORD respected
Abel and his offering,
5 but He did not respect Cain and his offering. And Cain was very angry, and his countenance fell.
6 So the LORD said to Cain, "Why are you
angry? And why has your countenance
fallen?
7 "If you do well, will you not be accepted?
And if you do not do well, sin lies at the door.
And its desire *is* for you, but you should rule
over it."
8 Now Cain talked with Abel his brother;[a]
and it came to pass, when they were in the
field, that Cain rose up against Abel his
brother and killed him.
9 Then the LORD said to Cain, "Where *is*
Abel your brother?" He said, "I do not know.
Am I my brother's keeper?"
10 And He said, "What have you done? The
voice of your brother's blood cries out to Me
from the ground.
11 "So now you *are* cursed from the earth,
which has opened its mouth to receive your
brother's blood from your hand.

4:8 [a]Samaritan Pentateuch, Septuagint, Syriac, and Vulgate add *"Let us go out to the field."*

LIFE LESSONS

➢ 3:15 — *"And I will put enmity between you and the woman, and between your seed and her Seed; He shall bruise your head, and you shall bruise His heel."*

Our God has a plan. From the very beginning of time, He moved history toward a colossal event that would restore sinful humans like us to rich fellowship with Himself.

➢ 3:16–19 — *To the woman He said . . . . Then to Adam He said . . . .*

Adam and Eve quickly found out that we reap what we sow, more than we sow, and later than we sow. God always follows through on both His promises and His threats.

➢ 4:7 — *"If you do well, will you not be accepted? And if you do not do well, sin lies at the door. And its desire is for you, but you should rule over it."*

God told Cain that obedience always brings blessing, but Cain allowed his anger to lead him into terrible sin.

➢ 4:11, 12 — *"So now you are cursed from the earth, which has opened its mouth to receive your brother's blood from your hand. When you till the*

12 "When you till the ground, it shall no
longer yield its strength to you. A fugitive and
a vagabond you shall be on the earth."
13 And Cain said to the LORD, "My punishment *is* greater than I can bear!
14 "Surely You have driven me out this day
from the face of the ground; I shall be hidden
from Your face; I shall be a fugitive and a
vagabond on the earth, and it will happen
that anyone who finds me will kill me."
15 And the LORD said to him, "Therefore,[a]
whoever kills Cain, vengeance shall be taken
on him sevenfold." And the LORD set a mark
on Cain, lest anyone finding him should kill
him.

The Family of Cain

➤ **16** Then Cain went out from the presence of
the LORD and dwelt in the land of Nod on the
east of Eden.
17 And Cain knew his wife, and she conceived and bore Enoch. And he built a city,
and called the name of the city after the name
of his son—Enoch.
18 To Enoch was born Irad; and Irad begot
Mehujael, and Mehujael begot Methushael,
and Methushael begot Lamech.
19 Then Lamech took for himself two wives:
the name of one *was* Adah, and the name of
the second *was* Zillah.
20 And Adah bore Jabal. He was the father
of those who dwell in tents and have livestock.
21 His brother's name *was* Jubal. He was the
father of all those who play the harp and
flute.
22 And as for Zillah, she also bore Tubal-
Cain, an instructor of every craftsman in
bronze and iron. And the sister of Tubal-Cain
was Naamah.
➤ 23 Then Lamech said to his wives:

"Adah and Zillah, hear my voice;
Wives of Lamech, listen to my speech!
For I have killed a man for wounding me,
Even a young man for hurting me.
24 If Cain shall be avenged sevenfold,
Then Lamech seventy-sevenfold."

A New Son

25 And Adam knew his wife again, and she
bore a son and named him Seth, "For God has
appointed another seed for me instead of
Abel, whom Cain killed."
26 And as for Seth, to him also a son was ➤
born; and he named him Enosh.[a] Then *men*
began to call on the name of the LORD.

The Family of Adam

5 This is the book of the genealogy of
Adam. In the day that God created man,
He made him in the likeness of God.
2 He created them male and female, and
blessed them and called them Mankind in the
day they were created.
3 And Adam lived one hundred and thirty
years, and begot *a son* in his own likeness,
after his image, and named him Seth.
4 After he begot Seth, the days of Adam
were eight hundred years; and he had sons
and daughters.
5 So all the days that Adam lived were nine
hundred and thirty years; and he died.
6 Seth lived one hundred and five years, and
begot Enosh.
7 After he begot Enosh, Seth lived eight
hundred and seven years, and had sons and
daughters.
8 So all the days of Seth were nine hundred
and twelve years; and he died.
9 Enosh lived ninety years, and begot
Cainan.[a]
10 After he begot Cainan, Enosh lived eight
hundred and fifteen years, and had sons and
daughters.
11 So all the days of Enosh were nine hundred and five years; and he died.
12 Cainan lived seventy years, and begot Mahalalel.
13 After he begot Mahalalel, Cainan lived
eight hundred and forty years, and had sons
and daughters.

4:15 [a]Following Masoretic Text and Targum; Septuagint, Syriac, and Vulgate read *Not so.* **4:26** [a]Greek *Enos* **5:9** [a]Hebrew *Qenan*

LIFE LESSONS

ground, it shall no longer yield its strength to you. A fugitive and a vagabond you shall be on the earth."

Cain, like his parents before him, learned the hard way that you reap what you sow, more than you sow, and later than you sow.

➤ **4:16 — *Then Cain went out from the presence of the LORD and dwelt in the land of Nod on the east of Eden.***

What a sad note that Cain "went out from the presence of the LORD"! Although we were made to live in the presence of God, we can choose, as Cain did, to go our own way, out of fellowship with the Lord.

➤ **4:23 — *"For I have killed a man for wounding me, even a young man for hurting me."***

Bad things happen when we refuse to repent of our sin. Adam and Eve's sin led to a murderous son; Cain's descendant, Lamech, killed a man merely for hurting him—and Lamech celebrated instead of repenting.

➤ **4:26 — *And as for Seth, to him also a son was born; and he named him Enosh. Then men began to call on the name of the LORD.***

God wants us to call on Him throughout the day, not only to ask Him for things, but even more simply to spend time with Him.

14 So all the days of Cainan were nine hundred and ten years; and he died.
15 Mahalalel lived sixty-five years, and begot
Jared.
16 After he begot Jared, Mahalalel lived eight
hundred and thirty years, and had sons and
daughters.
17 So all the days of Mahalalel were eight
hundred and ninety-five years; and he died.
18 Jared lived one hundred and sixty-two
years, and begot Enoch.
19 After he begot Enoch, Jared lived eight
hundred years, and had sons and daughters.
20 So all the days of Jared were nine hundred
and sixty-two years; and he died.
21 Enoch lived sixty-five years, and begot
Methuselah.
22 After he begot Methuselah, Enoch walked
with God three hundred years, and had sons
and daughters.
23 So all the days of Enoch were three hundred and sixty-five years.
➤ 24 And Enoch walked with God; and he *was*
not, for God took him.
25 Methuselah lived one hundred and eighty-
seven years, and begot Lamech.
26 After he begot Lamech, Methuselah lived
seven hundred and eighty-two years, and had
sons and daughters.
27 So all the days of Methuselah were nine
hundred and sixty-nine years; and he died.
28 Lamech lived one hundred and eighty-two
years, and had a son.
29 And he called his name Noah, saying,
"This *one* will comfort us concerning our
work and the toil of our hands, because of the
ground which the LORD has cursed."
30 After he begot Noah, Lamech lived five
hundred and ninety-five years, and had sons
and daughters.
31 So all the days of Lamech were seven hundred and seventy-seven years; and he died.
32 And Noah was five hundred years old, and
Noah begot Shem, Ham, and Japheth.

The Wickedness and Judgment of Man

6 Now it came to pass, when men began to
multiply on the face of the earth, and
daughters were born to them,
2 that the sons of God saw the daughters of
men, that they *were* beautiful; and they took
wives for themselves of all whom they chose.
3 And the LORD said, "My Spirit shall not
strive[a] with man forever, for he *is* indeed
flesh; yet his days shall be one hundred and
twenty years."
4 There were giants on the earth in those
days, and also afterward, when the sons of
God came in to the daughters of men and they
bore *children* to them. Those *were* the mighty
men who *were* of old, men of renown.
5 Then the LORD[a] saw that the wickedness
of man *was* great in the earth, and *that* every
intent of the thoughts of his heart *was* only
evil continually.
6 And the LORD was sorry that He had made ≺
man on the earth, and He was grieved in His
heart.
7 So the LORD said, "I will destroy man
whom I have created from the face of the
earth, both man and beast, creeping thing and
birds of the air, for I am sorry that I have
made them."
8 But Noah found grace in the eyes of the ≺
LORD.

Noah Pleases God

9 This is the genealogy of Noah. Noah was a
just man, perfect in his generations. Noah
walked with God.
10 And Noah begot three sons: Shem, Ham,
and Japheth.
11 The earth also was corrupt before God,
and the earth was filled with violence.
12 So God looked upon the earth, and indeed
it was corrupt; for all flesh had corrupted
their way on the earth.

The Ark Prepared

13 And God said to Noah, "The end of all
flesh has come before Me, for the earth is
filled with violence through them; and behold, I will destroy them with the earth.
14 "Make yourself an ark of gopherwood;
make rooms in the ark, and cover it inside
and outside with pitch.

6:3 [a]Septuagint, Syriac, Targum, and Vulgate read *abide.*
6:5 [a]Following Masoretic Text and Targum; Vulgate reads *God;* Septuagint reads *LORD God.*

LIFE LESSONS

➤ 5:24 — *Enoch walked with God; and he was not, for God took him.*

Enoch walked with God for 300 years, and then rather than dying, he moved directly into God's presence. Why? Because he "pleased God" (Hebrews 11:5)—just as all of us can.

➤ 6:6 — *And the LORD was sorry that He had made man on the earth, and He was grieved in His heart.*

Our sin pains the Creator who made us because it stands against His very nature. God will always judge sin; He cannot merely ignore it.

➤ 6:8 — *But Noah found grace in the eyes of the LORD.*

Why did Noah find "grace" in the eyes of the Lord? The next verse tells us: he was a "just man, perfect in his generations. Noah walked with God." We can find favor in the same way.

15 "And this is how you shall make it: The
length of the ark *shall be* three hundred cubits, its width fifty cubits, and its height thirty
cubits.
16 "You shall make a window for the ark, and
you shall finish it to a cubit from above;
and set the door of the ark in its side. You
shall make it *with* lower, second, and third
decks.
17 "And behold, I Myself am bringing
floodwaters on the earth, to destroy from
under heaven all flesh in which *is* the breath
of life; everything that *is* on the earth shall
die.
➤ 18 "But I will establish My covenant with you;
and you shall go into the ark—you, your sons,
your wife, and your sons' wives with you.
19 "And of every living thing of all flesh you
shall bring two of every *sort* into the ark, to
keep *them* alive with you; they shall be male
and female.
20 "Of the birds after their kind, of animals
after their kind, and of every creeping thing
of the earth after its kind, two of every *kind*
will come to you to keep *them* alive.
21 "And you shall take for yourself of all food
that is eaten, and you shall gather *it* to yourself; and it shall be food for you and for
them."
➤ **22** Thus Noah did; according to all that God
commanded him, so he did.

The Great Flood

7 Then the LORD said to Noah, "Come into
the ark, you and all your household, because I have seen *that* you *are* righteous before Me in this generation.
2 "You shall take with you seven each of
every clean animal, a male and his female;
two each of animals that *are* unclean, a male
and his female;
3 "also seven each of birds of the air, male
and female, to keep the species alive on the
face of all the earth.
4 "For after seven more days I will cause it
to rain on the earth forty days and forty
nights, and I will destroy from the face of the
earth all living things that I have made."
5 And Noah did according to all that the
LORD commanded him.
6 Noah *was* six hundred years old when the
floodwaters were on the earth.
7 So Noah, with his sons, his wife, and his
sons' wives, went into the ark because of the
waters of the flood.
8 Of clean animals, of animals that *are* unclean, of birds, and of everything that creeps
on the earth,
9 two by two they went into the ark to Noah,
male and female, as God had commanded
Noah.
10 And it came to pass after seven days that
the waters of the flood were on the earth.
11 In the six hundredth year of Noah's life, in

Life Examples:

NOAH

Obedient and Dry

GEN. 6:22

Nothing indicated an approaching storm. Still, since Noah believed God, he prepared for the downpour God promised. His friends must have mocked him, but he built an ark (Gen. 6).

Obedience is the cornerstone to our faith in God. While Noah's obedience led to God's blessing and reward, the disobedience of his contemporaries led to their destruction. At the time of the flood, the physical salvation of mankind fell to Noah and his willingness to be used by God.

The ark merely foreshadowed the eternal salvation from sin that is ours through Jesus Christ. Just as Noah's faith saved him and his family, so our faith saves us today. We are saved by grace through faith and not by good deeds. Building the ark did not bring Noah any closer to the Lord—but his obedience and faith in God did. And it kept him safe and dry.

See the Life Principles Index for further study:
2. Obey God and leave all the consequences to Him.

LIFE LESSONS

➤ 6:18 — *"But I will establish My covenant with you; and you shall go into the ark—you, your sons, your wife, and your sons' wives with you."*

Even in judgment, God displays His mercy. He acts in grace to save life even when He must act in holiness to take away life.

➤ 6:22 — *Thus Noah did; according to all that God commanded him, so he did.*

Noah displayed his righteous character by doing exactly as God had commanded him—even though building the ark must have seemed ridiculous to his neighbors. And his obedience saved his life.

the second month, the seventeenth day of the
month, on that day all the fountains of the
great deep were broken up, and the windows
of heaven were opened.
12 And the rain was on the earth forty days
and forty nights.
13 On the very same day Noah and Noah's
sons, Shem, Ham, and Japheth, and Noah's
wife and the three wives of his sons with
them, entered the ark—
14 they and every beast after its kind, all cattle after their kind, every creeping thing that
creeps on the earth after its kind, and every
bird after its kind, every bird of every sort.
15 And they went into the ark to Noah, two
by two, of all flesh in which *is* the breath of
life.
16 So those that entered, male and female of
all flesh, went in as God had commanded
him; and the LORD shut him in.
17 Now the flood was on the earth forty days.
The waters increased and lifted up the ark,
and it rose high above the earth.
18 The waters prevailed and greatly increased on the earth, and the ark moved
about on the surface of the waters.
19 And the waters prevailed exceedingly on
the earth, and all the high hills under the
whole heaven were covered.
20 The waters prevailed fifteen cubits upward, and the mountains were covered.
21 And all flesh died that moved on the earth:
birds and cattle and beasts and every creeping thing that creeps on the earth, and every
man.
22 All in whose nostrils *was* the breath of the
spirit[a] of life, all that *was* on the dry *land*,
died.
23 So He destroyed all living things which
were on the face of the ground: both man and
cattle, creeping thing and bird of the air. They
were destroyed from the earth. Only Noah
and those who *were* with him in the ark remained *alive*.
24 And the waters prevailed on the earth one
hundred and fifty days.

Noah's Deliverance

➤ **8** Then God remembered Noah, and every
living thing, and all the animals that *were*
with him in the ark. And God made a wind to
pass over the earth, and the waters subsided.
2 The fountains of the deep and the windows of heaven were also stopped, and the
rain from heaven was restrained.
3 And the waters receded continually from
the earth. At the end of the hundred and fifty
days the waters decreased.
4 Then the ark rested in the seventh month,
the seventeenth day of the month, on the
mountains of Ararat.
5 And the waters decreased continually
until the tenth month. In the tenth *month*, on
the first *day* of the month, the tops of the
mountains were seen.
6 So it came to pass, at the end of forty days,
that Noah opened the window of the ark
which he had made.
7 Then he sent out a raven, which kept
going to and fro until the waters had dried up
from the earth.
8 He also sent out from himself a dove, to
see if the waters had receded from the face of
the ground.
9 But the dove found no resting place for the
sole of her foot, and she returned into the ark
to him, for the waters *were* on the face of the
whole earth. So he put out his hand and took
her, and drew her into the ark to himself.
10 And he waited yet another seven days,
and again he sent the dove out from the ark.
11 Then the dove came to him in the evening,
and behold, a freshly plucked olive leaf *was*
in her mouth; and Noah knew that the waters
had receded from the earth.
12 So he waited yet another seven days and
sent out the dove, which did not return again
to him anymore.
13 And it came to pass in the six hundred and
first year, in the first *month*, the first *day* of
the month, that the waters were dried up from
the earth; and Noah removed the covering
of the ark and looked, and indeed the surface
of the ground was dry.
14 And in the second month, on the twenty-
seventh day of the month, the earth was
dried.
15 Then God spoke to Noah, saying,
16 "Go out of the ark, you and your wife, and
your sons and your sons' wives with you.
17 "Bring out with you every living thing of
all flesh that *is* with you: birds and cattle and
every creeping thing that creeps on the earth,
so that they may abound on the earth, and be
fruitful and multiply on the earth."
18 So Noah went out, and his sons and his
wife and his sons' wives with him.

7:22 [a]Septuagint and Vulgate omit *of the spirit.*

LIFE LESSONS

➤ ***8:1 — Then God remembered Noah, and every living thing, and all the animals that were with him in the ark. And God made a wind to pass over the earth, and the waters subsided.***

God always "remembers" His people, not merely to recall their existence or names, but to act in grace toward them . . . even if they must wait for Him to act.

19 Every animal, every creeping thing, every
bird, *and* whatever creeps on the earth, according to their families, went out of the ark.

God's Covenant with Creation

➤ 20 Then Noah built an altar to the LORD, and
took of every clean animal and of every clean
bird, and offered burnt offerings on the altar.
21 And the LORD smelled a soothing aroma.
Then the LORD said in His heart, "I will never
again curse the ground for man's sake, although the imagination of man's heart *is* evil
from his youth; nor will I again destroy every
living thing as I have done.

✳ 22 "While the earth remains,
➤ Seedtime and harvest,
Cold and heat,
Winter and summer,
And day and night
Shall not cease."

God's Promise to Noah

9 So God blessed Noah and his sons, and
said to them: "Be fruitful and multiply, and
fill the earth.[a]
2 "And the fear of you and the dread of you
shall be on every beast of the earth, on every
bird of the air, on all that move *on* the earth,
and on all the fish of the sea. They are given
into your hand.
3 "Every moving thing that lives shall be
food for you. I have given you all things, even
as the green herbs.
4 "But you shall not eat flesh with its life,
that is, its blood.
5 "Surely for your lifeblood I will demand *a
reckoning;* from the hand of every beast I will
require it, and from the hand of man. From
the hand of every man's brother I will require
the life of man.

➤ 6 "Whoever sheds man's blood,
By man his blood shall be shed;
For in the image of God
He made man.
7 And as for you, be fruitful and multiply;
Bring forth abundantly in the earth
And multiply in it."

8 Then God spoke to Noah and to his sons
with him, saying:
9 "And as for Me, behold, I establish My
covenant with you and with your descendants[a] after you,
10 "and with every living creature that *is* with
you: the birds, the cattle, and every beast of
the earth with you, of all that go out of the
ark, every beast of the earth.
11 "Thus I establish My covenant with you:
Never again shall all flesh be cut off by the
waters of the flood; never again shall there be
a flood to destroy the earth."
12 And God said: "This *is* the sign of the cov- ➤
enant which I make between Me and you, and
every living creature that *is* with you, for perpetual generations:
13 "I set My rainbow in the cloud, and it shall
be for the sign of the covenant between Me
and the earth.
14 "It shall be, when I bring a cloud over the
earth, that the rainbow shall be seen in the
cloud;
15 "and I will remember My covenant which
is between Me and you and every living creature of all flesh; the waters shall never again
become a flood to destroy all flesh.
16 "The rainbow shall be in the cloud, and I
will look on it to remember the everlasting
covenant between God and every living creature of all flesh that *is* on the earth."
17 And God said to Noah, "This *is* the sign of
the covenant which I have established between Me and all flesh that *is* on the earth."

Noah and His Sons

18 Now the sons of Noah who went out of the
ark were Shem, Ham, and Japheth. And Ham
was the father of Canaan.
19 These three *were* the sons of Noah, and
from these the whole earth was populated.

9:1 [a]Compare Genesis 1:28 **9:9** [a]Literally *seed*

LIFE LESSONS

➤ 8:20 — *Then Noah built an altar to the LORD, and took of every clean animal and of every clean bird, and offered burnt offerings on the altar.*

The first thing Noah did after leaving the ark was to prepare for worship. If we want to grow our relationship with the Lord, we too must make worship a priority.

➤ 8:22 — *"While the earth remains, seedtime and harvest, cold and heat, winter and summer, and day and night shall not cease."*

God's promises mean the difference between life and death. Even when things look darkest, we can rely on His trustworthy Word.

➤ 9:6 — *"Whoever sheds man's blood, by man his blood shall be shed; for in the image of God He made man."*

Murder is a terrible crime because God made human beings in His image. Murder therefore shows an utter contempt for God—as does treating others disdainfully, as Jesus would later say (Matthew 5:22).

➤ 9:12 — *And God said: "This is the sign of the covenant which I make between Me and you, and every living creature that is with you, for perpetual generations . . . ."*

When God makes a promise, He does not want us to forget it. Therefore He often gives us some tangible sign or pledge to memorialize His promise.

20 And Noah began *to be* a farmer, and he
planted a vineyard.
➤ 21 Then he drank of the wine and was drunk,
and became uncovered in his tent.
22 And Ham, the father of Canaan, saw the
nakedness of his father, and told his two
brothers outside.
23 But Shem and Japheth took a garment,
laid *it* on both their shoulders, and went
backward and covered the nakedness of
their father. Their faces *were* turned away,
and they did not see their father's nakedness.
24 So Noah awoke from his wine, and knew
what his younger son had done to him.
25 Then he said:

"Cursed *be* Canaan;
A servant of servants
He shall be to his brethren."

26 And he said:

"Blessed *be* the LORD,
The God of Shem,
And may Canaan be his servant.
27 May God enlarge Japheth,
And may he dwell in the tents of Shem;
And may Canaan be his servant."

28 And Noah lived after the flood three hundred and fifty years.
29 So all the days of Noah were nine hundred
and fifty years; and he died.

Nations Descended from Noah

10 Now this *is* the genealogy of the sons of
Noah: Shem, Ham, and Japheth. And
sons were born to them after the flood.
2 The sons of Japheth *were* Gomer, Magog,
Madai, Javan, Tubal, Meshech, and Tiras.
3 The sons of Gomer *were* Ashkenaz,
Riphath,[a] and Togarmah.
4 The sons of Javan *were* Elishah, Tarshish,
Kittim, and Dodanim.[a]
5 From these the coastland *peoples* of the
Gentiles were separated into their lands,
everyone according to his language, according to their families, into their nations.
6 The sons of Ham *were* Cush, Mizraim,
Put,[a] and Canaan.
7 The sons of Cush *were* Seba, Havilah,
Sabtah, Raamah, and Sabtechah; and the
sons of Raamah *were* Sheba and Dedan.
8 Cush begot Nimrod; he began to be a
mighty one on the earth.
9 He was a mighty hunter before the LORD;
therefore it is said, "Like Nimrod the mighty
hunter before the LORD."
10 And the beginning of his kingdom was
Babel, Erech, Accad, and Calneh, in the land
of Shinar.
11 From that land he went to Assyria and
built Nineveh, Rehoboth Ir, Calah,
12 and Resen between Nineveh and Calah
(that *is* the principal city).
13 Mizraim begot Ludim, Anamim, Lehabim,
Naphtuhim,
14 Pathrusim, and Casluhim (from whom
came the Philistines and Caphtorim).
15 Canaan begot Sidon his firstborn, and
Heth;
16 the Jebusite, the Amorite, and the Girgashite;
17 the Hivite, the Arkite, and the Sinite;
18 the Arvadite, the Zemarite, and the
Hamathite. Afterward the families of the
Canaanites were dispersed.
19 And the border of the Canaanites was
from Sidon as you go toward Gerar, as far
as Gaza; then as you go toward Sodom, Gomorrah, Admah, and Zeboiim, as far as
Lasha.
20 These *were* the sons of Ham, according to
their families, according to their languages, in
their lands *and* in their nations.
21 And *children* were born also to Shem, the
father of all the children of Eber, the brother
of Japheth the elder.
22 The sons of Shem *were* Elam, Asshur,
Arphaxad, Lud, and Aram.
23 The sons of Aram *were* Uz, Hul, Gether,
and Mash.[a]
24 Arphaxad begot Salah,[a] and Salah begot
Eber.
25 To Eber were born two sons: the name of
one *was* Peleg, for in his days the earth was
divided; and his brother's name *was* Joktan.
26 Joktan begot Almodad, Sheleph, Hazarmaveth, Jerah,
27 Hadoram, Uzal, Diklah,
28 Obal,[a] Abimael, Sheba,
29 Ophir, Havilah, and Jobab. All these *were*
the sons of Joktan.

10:3 [a]Spelled *Diphath* in 1 Chronicles 1:6 **10:4** [a]Spelled *Rodanim* in Samaritan Pentateuch and 1 Chronicles 1:7 **10:6** [a]Or *Phut* **10:23** [a]Called *Meshech* in Septuagint and 1 Chronicles 1:17 **10:24** [a]Following Masoretic Text, Vulgate, and Targum; Septuagint reads *Arphaxad begot Cainan, and Cainan begot Salah* (compare Luke 3:35, 36). **10:28** [a]Spelled *Ebal* in 1 Chronicles 1:22

LIFE LESSONS

➤ 9:21 — *Then he drank of the wine and was drunk, and became uncovered in his tent.*

Even righteous and blameless people, like Noah, do foolish things and fall into sin. But God is so gracious that He calls us to repentance, so that we might once more enjoy the fullness of His blessing.

30 And their dwelling place was from Mesha
as you go toward Sephar, the mountain of the
east.
31 These *were* the sons of Shem, according to
their families, according to their languages, in
their lands, according to their nations.
32 These *were* the families of the sons of
Noah, according to their generations, in their
nations; and from these the nations were divided on the earth after the flood.

The Tower of Babel

11 Now the whole earth had one language
and one speech.
2 And it came to pass, as they journeyed
from the east, that they found a plain in the
land of Shinar, and they dwelt there.
3 Then they said to one another, "Come, let
us make bricks and bake *them* thoroughly."
They had brick for stone, and they had asphalt for mortar.
➤4 And they said, "Come, let us build ourselves a city, and a tower whose top *is* in the
heavens; let us make a name for ourselves,
lest we be scattered abroad over the face of
the whole earth."
5 But the LORD came down to see the city
and the tower which the sons of men had
built.
6 And the LORD said, "Indeed the people *are*
one and they all have one language, and this
is what they begin to do; now nothing that
they propose to do will be withheld from
them.
7 "Come, let Us go down and there confuse
their language, that they may not understand
one another's speech."
8 So the LORD scattered them abroad from
there over the face of all the earth, and they
ceased building the city.
9 Therefore its name is called Babel, because there the LORD confused the language
of all the earth; and from there the LORD scattered them abroad over the face of all the
earth.

Shem's Descendants

10 This *is* the genealogy of Shem: Shem *was*
one hundred years old, and begot Arphaxad
two years after the flood.
11 After he begot Arphaxad, Shem lived five
hundred years, and begot sons and daughters.
12 Arphaxad lived thirty-five years, and
begot Salah.
13 After he begot Salah, Arphaxad lived four
hundred and three years, and begot sons and
daughters.
14 Salah lived thirty years, and begot Eber.
15 After he begot Eber, Salah lived four hundred and three years, and begot sons and
daughters.
16 Eber lived thirty-four years, and begot
Peleg.
17 After he begot Peleg, Eber lived four hundred and thirty years, and begot sons and
daughters.
18 Peleg lived thirty years, and begot Reu.
19 After he begot Reu, Peleg lived two hundred and nine years, and begot sons and
daughters.
20 Reu lived thirty-two years, and begot
Serug.
21 After he begot Serug, Reu lived two hundred and seven years, and begot sons and
daughters.
22 Serug lived thirty years, and begot Nahor.
23 After he begot Nahor, Serug lived two
hundred years, and begot sons and daughters.
24 Nahor lived twenty-nine years, and begot
Terah.
25 After he begot Terah, Nahor lived one
hundred and nineteen years, and begot sons
and daughters.
26 Now Terah lived seventy years, and begot
Abram, Nahor, and Haran.

Terah's Descendants

27 This *is* the genealogy of Terah: Terah
begot Abram, Nahor, and Haran. Haran begot
Lot.
28 And Haran died before his father Terah in
his native land, in Ur of the Chaldeans.
29 Then Abram and Nahor took wives: the
name of Abram's wife *was* Sarai, and the
name of Nahor's wife, Milcah, the daughter of
Haran the father of Milcah and the father of
Iscah.
30 But Sarai was barren; she had no child.
31 And Terah took his son Abram and
his grandson Lot, the son of Haran, and
his daughter-in-law Sarai, his son Abram's
wife, and they went out with them from Ur
of the Chaldeans to go to the land of Canaan; and they came to Haran and dwelt
there.
32 So the days of Terah were two hundred
and five years, and Terah died in Haran.

LIFE LESSONS

➤ **11:4 — *And they said, "Come, let us build ourselves a city, and a tower whose top is in the heavens; let us make a name for ourselves, lest we be scattered abroad over the face of the whole earth."***

God always opposes pride wherever it raises its head. If we want to advance in God's kingdom, we must not strive to make a name for ourselves, but rather humble ourselves before the Lord (1 Pet. 5:6).

ANSWERS TO LIFE'S QUESTIONS

How can I become a more obedient child of God?

GEN. 12:1

Obedience is a major characteristic of a person mighty in spirit. Generally speaking, obedience characterized the faith of Abraham from his first encounter with God until his death.

❶ ***All obedience begins with faith in the sovereignty of God.***
If we fail to believe in God's sovereignty, we will find it difficult to obey Him. Abraham based his relationship with God on his confidence that God would do what He had promised (Rom. 4:20, 21). Until we study and meditate on God's Word, we will never learn to trust Him. Faith comes by hearing the Word of God and responding in confident trust (Rom. 10:17).

❷ ***We grow in obedience by waiting for God's timing.***
God is very time conscious—not in terms of minutes and seconds, but in regard to our acting in obedience according to His schedule. Throughout the Scriptures we find Him moving "in the fullness of time" (see Galatians 4:4). He is neither early nor late. Ever.

❸ ***We continue to grow in obedience by refusing to subject God's plan to "common sense" or the reasoning of the world.***
Some things that God requires look ridiculous from a human perspective. God told Abraham he would have a son through whom He would bless the entire world. Yet He allowed Abraham's obedience to be severely tested—first by requiring him to wait nearly a quarter of a century before providing the promised provision, and later by requiring him to offer Isaac as a sacrifice. When God saw the obedience of Abraham's heart, He provided a ram in Isaac's place.

❹ ***The final step: prompt obedience.***
If you long to obey God, you will not hesitate when He tells you to do something. Many times we fail to obey God because we fear the consequences. Yet He never requires us to do anything outside His will for our lives. Our only responsibility is to obey; God's responsibility is to take care of the consequences of our obedience.

Our sensitivity to God's will increases as we obey Him. Along the way, He provides glimpses of the blessings waiting for us. God always blesses obedience. You can trust Him, obey Him, and be blessed. Or you can disobey Him and spend the rest of your life wondering what He would have done had you obeyed Him. Once you glimpse the blessings of obedience, however, the consequences no longer matter.

See the Life Principles Index for further study:
21. Obedience always brings blessing.
22. To walk in the Spirit is to obey the initial promptings of the Spirit.

Promises to Abram

12 Now the LORD had said to Abram:
"Get out of your country,
From your family
And from your father's house,
To a land that I will show you.
2 I will make you a great nation;
I will bless you
And make your name great;
And you shall be a blessing.
3 I will bless those who bless you,
And I will curse him who curses you;
And in you all the families of the earth
shall be blessed."

4 So Abram departed as the LORD had spoken to him, and Lot went with him. And
Abram *was* seventy-five years old when he
departed from Haran.
5 Then Abram took Sarai his wife and Lot
his brother's son, and all their possessions
that they had gathered, and the people whom
they had acquired in Haran, and they departed to go to the land of Canaan. So they
came to the land of Canaan.
6 Abram passed through the land to the
place of Shechem, as far as the terebinth tree
of Moreh.[a] And the Canaanites *were* then in
the land.
7 Then the LORD appeared to Abram and
said, "To your descendants I will give this
land." And there he built an altar to the LORD,
who had appeared to him.
8 And he moved from there to the mountain
east of Bethel, and he pitched his tent *with*
Bethel on the west and Ai on the east; there
he built an altar to the LORD and called on the
name of the LORD.

12:6 [a]Hebrew *Alon Moreh*

9 So Abram journeyed, going on still toward
the South.[a]

Abram in Egypt

➤ 10 Now there was a famine in the land, and
Abram went down to Egypt to dwell there, for
the famine *was* severe in the land.
11 And it came to pass, when he was close to
entering Egypt, that he said to Sarai his wife,
"Indeed I know that you *are* a woman of
beautiful countenance.
12 "Therefore it will happen, when the Egyptians see you, that they will say, 'This *is* his
wife'; and they will kill me, but they will let
you live.
13 "Please say you *are* my sister, that it may
be well with me for your sake, and that I[a] may
live because of you."
14 So it was, when Abram came into Egypt,
that the Egyptians saw the woman, that she
was very beautiful.
15 The princes of Pharaoh also saw her and
commended her to Pharaoh. And the woman
was taken to Pharaoh's house.
16 He treated Abram well for her sake. He
had sheep, oxen, male donkeys, male and female servants, female donkeys, and camels.
17 But the LORD plagued Pharaoh and his
house with great plagues because of Sarai,
Abram's wife.
➤ 18 And Pharaoh called Abram and said,
"What *is* this you have done to me? Why did
you not tell me that she *was* your wife?
19 "Why did you say, 'She *is* my sister'? I
might have taken her as my wife. Now therefore, here is your wife; take *her* and go your
way."
20 So Pharaoh commanded *his* men concerning him; and they sent him away, with his wife
and all that he had.

Abram Inherits Canaan

13 Then Abram went up from Egypt, he
and his wife and all that he had, and
Lot with him, to the South.[a]
2 Abram *was* very rich in livestock, in silver,
and in gold.
3 And he went on his journey from the
South as far as Bethel, to the place where his
tent had been at the beginning, between
Bethel and Ai,
4 to the place of the altar which he had ➤
made there at first. And there Abram called
on the name of the LORD.
5 Lot also, who went with Abram, had
flocks and herds and tents.
6 Now the land was not able to support
them, that they might dwell together, for their
possessions were so great that they could not
dwell together.
7 And there was strife between the herdsmen of Abram's livestock and the herdsmen
of Lot's livestock. The Canaanites and the
Perizzites then dwelt in the land.
8 So Abram said to Lot, "Please let there be ➤
no strife between you and me, and between
my herdsmen and your herdsmen; for we *are*
brethren.
9 "*Is* not the whole land before you? Please
separate from me. If *you take* the left, then I
will go to the right; or, if *you go* to the right,
then I will go to the left."
10 And Lot lifted his eyes and saw all the
plain of Jordan, that it *was* well watered
everywhere (before the LORD destroyed
Sodom and Gomorrah) like the garden of the
LORD, like the land of Egypt as you go toward
Zoar.

12:9 [a]Hebrew *Negev* **12:13** [a]Literally *my soul* **13:1** [a]Hebrew *Negev*

LIFE LESSONS

➤ 12:1 — *"Get out of your country, from your family and from your father's house, to a land that I will show you . . . ."*

God always connects obedience with blessing, even when He does not sketch out the full details of what that blessing may be.

➤ 12:7 — *Then the LORD appeared to Abram and said, "To your descendants I will give this land." And there he built an altar to the LORD, who had appeared to him.*

The Lord "appeared" to Abram only after Abram obeyed His voice by moving to Canaan. As Abram's faith grew, so did the details of God's promise to him.

➤ 12:10 — *Now there was a famine in the land, and Abram went down to Egypt to dwell there, for the famine was severe in the land.*

Men and women of faith must endure hardship, just like anyone else. But God wants to use adversity to deepen and strengthen our relationship with Him.

➤ 12:18 — *". . . Why did you not tell me that she was your wife? . . ."*

Abram had to learn that trusting God means looking beyond what we can see to what God sees. God does not need our half-truths and lies in order to protect and bless us.

➤ 13:4 — *. . . And there Abram called on the name of the LORD.*

We have no record that Abram "called on the name of the Lord" while in Egypt, where he got into trouble. How much better off we would be if we would learn that prayer is life's greatest time saver!

➤ 13:8 — *So Abram said to Lot, "Please let there be no strife between you and me, and between my herdsmen and your herdsmen; for we are brethren.*

Abram counted a good relationship with his nephew as more important than his own material prosperity. Apparently he didn't worry much about his possessions, because he had seen that no one can ever out give God.

11 Then Lot chose for himself all the plain of
Jordan, and Lot journeyed east. And they separated from each other.
12 Abram dwelt in the land of Canaan, and
Lot dwelt in the cities of the plain and pitched
his tent even as far as Sodom.
13 But the men of Sodom *were* exceedingly
wicked and sinful against the LORD.
14 And the LORD said to Abram, after Lot had
separated from him: "Lift your eyes now and
look from the place where you are—northward, southward, eastward, and westward;
15 "for all the land which you see I give to
you and your descendants[a] forever.
16 "And I will make your descendants as the
dust of the earth; so that if a man could number the dust of the earth, *then* your descendants also could be numbered.
17 "Arise, walk in the land through its length
and its width, for I give it to you."
18 Then Abram moved *his* tent, and went and
dwelt by the terebinth trees of Mamre,[a] which
are in Hebron, and built an altar there to the
LORD.

Lot's Captivity and Rescue

14 And it came to pass in the days of
Amraphel king of Shinar, Arioch king
of Ellasar, Chedorlaomer king of Elam, and
Tidal king of nations,[a]
2 *that* they made war with Bera king of
Sodom, Birsha king of Gomorrah, Shinab
king of Admah, Shemeber king of Zeboiim,
and the king of Bela (that is, Zoar).
3 All these joined together in the Valley of
Siddim (that is, the Salt Sea).
4 Twelve years they served Chedorlaomer,
and in the thirteenth year they rebelled.
5 In the fourteenth year Chedorlaomer and
the kings that *were* with him came and attacked the Rephaim in Ashteroth Karnaim,
the Zuzim in Ham, the Emim in Shaveh
Kiriathaim,
6 and the Horites in their mountain of Seir,
as far as El Paran, which *is* by the wilderness.
7 Then they turned back and came to En
Mishpat (that *is,* Kadesh), and attacked all the
country of the Amalekites, and also the
Amorites who dwelt in Hazezon Tamar.
8 And the king of Sodom, the king of Gomorrah, the king of Admah, the king of Zeboiim, and the king of Bela (that *is,* Zoar)
went out and joined together in battle in the
Valley of Siddim
9 against Chedorlaomer king of Elam, Tidal
king of nations,[a] Amraphel king of Shinar,
and Arioch king of Ellasar—four kings
against five.
10 Now the Valley of Siddim *was full of* asphalt pits; and the kings of Sodom and Gomorrah fled; *some* fell there, and the
remainder fled to the mountains.
11 Then they took all the goods of Sodom
and Gomorrah, and all their provisions, and
went their way.
12 They also took Lot, Abram's brother's son
who dwelt in Sodom, and his goods, and departed.
13 Then one who had escaped came and told
Abram the Hebrew, for he dwelt by the terebinth trees of Mamre[a] the Amorite, brother of
Eshcol and brother of Aner; and they *were* allies with Abram.
14 Now when Abram heard that his brother
was taken captive, he armed his three hundred and eighteen trained *servants* who were
born in his own house, and went in pursuit as
far as Dan.
15 He divided his forces against them by
night, and he and his servants attacked them
and pursued them as far as Hobah, which *is*
north of Damascus.
16 So he brought back all the goods, and also
brought back his brother Lot and his goods,
as well as the women and the people.
17 And the king of Sodom went out to meet
him at the Valley of Shaveh (that *is,* the King's
Valley), after his return from the defeat of
Chedorlaomer and the kings who *were* with
him.

Abram and Melchizedek

18 Then Melchizedek king of Salem brought
out bread and wine; he *was* the priest of God
Most High.
19 And he blessed him and said:

"Blessed be Abram of God Most High,
Possessor of heaven and earth;
20 And blessed be God Most High,
Who has delivered your enemies into
your hand."

And he gave him a tithe of all.
21 Now the king of Sodom said to Abram,

13:15 [a]Literally *seed,* and so throughout the book
13:18 [a]Hebrew *Alon Mamre* **14:1** [a]Hebrew *goyim*
14:9 [a]Hebrew *goyim* **14:13** [a]Hebrew *Alon Mamre*

LIFE LESSONS

➤ 14:20 — *"And blessed be God Most High, who has delivered your enemies into your hand."*

The mysterious priest Melchizedek reminded Abram that God had delivered Abram's enemies into his hand, even though it was Abram's men that did the fight-ing. God is the author of all blessings.

"Give me the persons, and take the goods for
yourself."
22 But Abram said to the king of Sodom, "I
have raised my hand to the LORD, God Most
High, the Possessor of heaven and earth,
23 "that I *will take* nothing, from a thread to
a sandal strap, and that I will not take anything that *is* yours, lest you should say, 'I have
made Abram rich'—
24 "except only what the young men have
eaten, and the portion of the men who went
with me: Aner, Eshcol, and Mamre; let them
take their portion."

God's Covenant with Abram

15 After these things the word of the LORD
came to Abram in a vision, saying, "Do
not be afraid, Abram. I *am* your shield, your
exceedingly great reward."
2 But Abram said, "Lord GOD, what will You
give me, seeing I go childless, and the heir of
my house *is* Eliezer of Damascus?"
3 Then Abram said, "Look, You have given
me no offspring; indeed one born in my house
is my heir!"
4 And behold, the word of the LORD *came* to
him, saying, "This one shall not be your heir,
but one who will come from your own body
shall be your heir."
5 Then He brought him outside and said,
"Look now toward heaven, and count the
stars if you are able to number them." And
He said to him, "So shall your descendants
be."
6 And he believed in the LORD, and He accounted it to him for righteousness.
7 Then He said to him, "I *am* the LORD, who
brought you out of Ur of the Chaldeans, to
give you this land to inherit it."
8 And he said, "Lord GOD, how shall I know
that I will inherit it?"
9 So He said to him, "Bring Me a three-year-
old heifer, a three-year-old female goat, a
three-year-old ram, a turtledove, and a young
pigeon."
10 Then he brought all these to Him and cut
them in two, down the middle, and placed
each piece opposite the other; but he did not
cut the birds in two.
11 And when the vultures came down on the
carcasses, Abram drove them away.
12 Now when the sun was going down, a
deep sleep fell upon Abram; and behold, horror *and* great darkness fell upon him.
13 Then He said to Abram: "Know certainly
that your descendants will be strangers in
a land *that is* not theirs, and will serve
them, and they will afflict them four hundred
years.
14 "And also the nation whom they serve I
will judge; afterward they shall come out with
great possessions.
15 "Now as for you, you shall go to your fathers in peace; you shall be buried at a good
old age.
16 "But in the fourth generation they shall return here, for the iniquity of the Amorites *is*
not yet complete."
17 And it came to pass, when the sun went
down and it was dark, that behold, there appeared a smoking oven and a burning torch
that passed between those pieces.
18 On the same day the LORD made a covenant with Abram, saying:

"To your descendants I have given this
land, from the river of Egypt to the great
river, the River Euphrates—

19 "the Kenites, the Kenezzites, the Kad-
monites,
20 "the Hittites, the Perizzites, the Rephaim,
21 "the Amorites, the Canaanites, the Girgashites, and the Jebusites."

Hagar and Ishmael

16 Now Sarai, Abram's wife, had borne
him no *children.* And she had an
Egyptian maidservant whose name was
Hagar.
2 So Sarai said to Abram, "See now, the
LORD has restrained me from bearing *children.* Please, go in to my maid; perhaps I shall
obtain children by her." And Abram heeded
the voice of Sarai.
3 Then Sarai, Abram's wife, took Hagar

LIFE LESSONS

➤ 15:1 — *After these things the word of the LORD came to Abram in a vision, saying, "Do not be afraid, Abram. I am your shield, your exceedingly great reward."*

Sometimes God "spoke" to Abram, sometimes He "appeared to" him, and here He communicated His will through a vision. God will do whatever it takes to show us His will!

➤ 15:6 — *And he believed in the LORD, and He accounted it to him for righteousness.*

Even when Abram did not see how God could fulfill His gracious promise to him regarding an heir, he trusted the Lord anyway. He looked beyond what he could see to what God could see.

➤ 15:16 — *"But in the fourth generation they shall return here, for the iniquity of the Amorites is not yet complete."*

God is more patient than we can imagine. He would wait over 400 years to give the land of promise to His people, because the wicked Canaanites had not yet reached the point of no return (see 2 Peter 3:9).

her maid, the Egyptian, and gave her to her
husband Abram to be his wife, after Abram
had dwelt ten years in the land of Canaan.
➤ 4 So he went in to Hagar, and she conceived. And when she saw that she had conceived, her mistress became despised in her
eyes.
5 Then Sarai said to Abram, "My wrong *be*
upon you! I gave my maid into your embrace;
and when she saw that she had conceived, I
became despised in her eyes. The LORD judge
between you and me."
6 So Abram said to Sarai, "Indeed your
maid *is* in your hand; do to her as you please."
And when Sarai dealt harshly with her, she
fled from her presence.
7 Now the Angel of the LORD found her by a
spring of water in the wilderness, by the
spring on the way to Shur.
8 And He said, "Hagar, Sarai's maid, where
have you come from, and where are you
going?" She said, "I am fleeing from the presence of my mistress Sarai."
➤ 9 The Angel of the LORD said to her, "Return
to your mistress, and submit yourself under
her hand."
10 Then the Angel of the LORD said to her, "I
will multiply your descendants exceedingly,
so that they shall not be counted for multitude."
11 And the Angel of the LORD said to her:

"Behold, you *are* with child,
And you shall bear a son.
You shall call his name Ishmael,
Because the LORD has heard your
affliction.
12 He shall be a wild man;
His hand *shall be* against every man,
And every man's hand against him.
And he shall dwell in the presence of all
his brethren."

13 Then she called the name of the LORD who
spoke to her, You-Are-the-God-Who-Sees; for
she said, "Have I also here seen Him who sees
me?"
14 Therefore the well was called Beer Lahai
Roi;[a] observe, *it is* between Kadesh and
Bered.
15 So Hagar bore Abram a son; and Abram
named his son, whom Hagar bore, Ishmael.
16 Abram *was* eighty-six years old when
Hagar bore Ishmael to Abram.

The Sign of the Covenant

17 When Abram was ninety-nine years
old, the LORD appeared to Abram and
said to him, "I *am* Almighty God; walk before
Me and be blameless.
2 "And I will make My covenant between Me
and you, and will multiply you exceedingly."
3 Then Abram fell on his face, and God
talked with him, saying:
4 "As for Me, behold, My covenant is with
you, and you shall be a father of many nations.
5 "No longer shall your name be called ➤
Abram, but your name shall be Abraham; for
I have made you a father of many nations.
6 "I will make you exceedingly fruitful; and
I will make nations of you, and kings shall
come from you.
7 "And I will establish My covenant between
Me and you and your descendants after you
in their generations, for an everlasting covenant, to be God to you and your descendants
after you.
8 "Also I give to you and your descendants
after you the land in which you are a stranger,
all the land of Canaan, as an everlasting possession; and I will be their God."
9 And God said to Abraham: "As for you,
you shall keep My covenant, you and your descendants after you throughout their generations.
10 "This *is* My covenant which you shall
keep, between Me and you and your descendants after you: Every male child among you
shall be circumcised;
11 "and you shall be circumcised in the flesh
of your foreskins, and it shall be a sign of the
covenant between Me and you.

16:14 [a]Literally *Well of the One Who Lives and Sees Me*

LIFE LESSONS

➤ **16:4 — *So he went in to Hagar, and she conceived. And when she saw that she had conceived, her mistress became despised in her eyes.***

Sarai found out the hard way that whatever we acquire outside of God's will often turns to ashes. Her plan to raise a family through Hagar misfired badly.

➤ **16:9 — *The Angel of the LORD said to her, "Return to your mistress, and submit yourself under her hand."***

Hagar had to learn that as children of a sovereign God, we are never victims of our circumstances. God does not want us to run away from our problems, but to face them with His help.

➤ **17:5 — *"No longer shall your name be called Abram, but your name shall be Abraham; for I have made you a father of many nations."***

Even before God fulfilled His promise to Abraham to give him a son through Sarai, He said, "I *have made* you a father of many nations." God's promises are so solid that He can speak of their future fulfillment in the past tense!

12 "He who is eight days old among you shall be circumcised, every male child in your generations, he who is born in your house or bought with money from any foreigner who is not your descendant.
13 "He who is born in your house and he who is bought with your money must be circumcised, and My covenant shall be in your flesh for an everlasting covenant.
14 "And the uncircumcised male child, who is not circumcised in the flesh of his foreskin, that person shall be cut off from his people; he has broken My covenant."
15 Then God said to Abraham, "As for Sarai your wife, you shall not call her name Sarai, but Sarah *shall be* her name.
16 "And I will bless her and also give you a son by her; then I will bless her, and she shall be *a mother of* nations; kings of peoples shall be from her."
➤ 17 Then Abraham fell on his face and laughed, and said in his heart, "Shall *a child* be born to a man who is one hundred years old? And shall Sarah, who is ninety years old, bear *a child*?"
18 And Abraham said to God, "Oh, that Ishmael might live before You!"
19 Then God said: "No, Sarah your wife shall bear you a son, and you shall call his name Isaac; I will establish My covenant with him for an everlasting covenant, *and* with his descendants after him.
20 "And as for Ishmael, I have heard you. Behold, I have blessed him, and will make him fruitful, and will multiply him exceedingly. He shall beget twelve princes, and I will make him a great nation.
21 "But My covenant I will establish with Isaac, whom Sarah shall bear to you at this set time next year."
22 Then He finished talking with him, and God went up from Abraham.
➤ **23** So Abraham took Ishmael his son, all who were born in his house and all who were bought with his money, every male among the men of Abraham's house, and circumcised the flesh of their foreskins that very same day, as God had said to him.
24 Abraham *was* ninety-nine years old when he was circumcised in the flesh of his foreskin.
25 And Ishmael his son *was* thirteen years old when he was circumcised in the flesh of his foreskin.
26 That very same day Abraham was circumcised, and his son Ishmael;
27 and all the men of his house, born in the house or bought with money from a foreigner, were circumcised with him.

The Son of Promise

18 Then the LORD appeared to him by the terebinth trees of Mamre,[a] as he was sitting in the tent door in the heat of the day.
2 So he lifted his eyes and looked, and behold, three men were standing by him; and when he saw *them,* he ran from the tent door to meet them, and bowed himself to the ground,
3 and said, "My Lord, if I have now found favor in Your sight, do not pass on by Your servant.
4 "Please let a little water be brought, and wash your feet, and rest yourselves under the tree.
5 "And I will bring a morsel of bread, that you may refresh your hearts. After that you may pass by, inasmuch as you have come to your servant." They said, "Do as you have said."
6 So Abraham hurried into the tent to Sarah and said, "Quickly, make ready three measures of fine meal; knead *it* and make cakes."
7 And Abraham ran to the herd, took a tender and good calf, gave *it* to a young man, and he hastened to prepare it.
8 So he took butter and milk and the calf which he had prepared, and set *it* before them; and he stood by them under the tree as they ate.
9 Then they said to him, "Where *is* Sarah your wife?" So he said, "Here, in the tent."
10 And He said, "I will certainly return to you according to the time of life, and behold, Sarah your wife shall have a son." (Sarah was listening in the tent door which *was* behind him.)
11 Now Abraham and Sarah were old, well advanced in age; *and* Sarah had passed the age of childbearing.[a]

18:1 [a]Hebrew *Alon Mamre* **18:11** [a]Literally *the manner of women had ceased to be with Sarah*

LIFE LESSONS

➤ 17:17 — *Then Abraham fell on his face and laughed, and said in his heart, "Shall a child be born to a man who is one hundred years old? And shall Sarah, who is ninety years old, bear a child?"*

God promised Abraham at age 75 (Gen. 12:4) that He would make him into a great nation—and then made him wait a quarter of a century to fulfill that promise. But God acts on behalf of those who wait for Him!

➤ 17:23 — *So Abraham took Ishmael his son, all who were born in his house and all who were bought with his money, every male among the men of Abraham's house, and circumcised the flesh of their foreskins that very same day, as God had said to him.*

Abraham obeyed God, even when it caused him personal discomfort, even when it caused pain to his family. Because he believed God, he obeyed God.

Life Examples:

SARAH

Laughing All the Way to the Crib

GEN. 18:9–15

Sarah smirked as the words of her husband rang in her ears. How could she believe the outlandish story? "God spoke to me!" he had said. "He promised to make me the head of many nations—*me*! A man of 99 years! And He is going to do it through you!"

Sarah reacted to the news much as her dear husband had earlier—she hit the ground laughing. "I am 90 years old; I am no longer capable of giving you children. There must be some mistake!"

But there had been no mistake. God challenged Sarah with the words, "Is anything too hard for the Lord?" (Gen. 18:14). Ninths months later, the birth of a baby boy provided the answer.

Sarah's story represents something much greater than one woman's experience. It demonstrates God's unrelenting pursuit of each of us. Despite her faults and persistent lack of faith, Sarah witnessed God turn the "impossible" into reality. So can we.

See the Life Principles Index for further study:
9. Trusting God means looking beyond what we can see to what God sees.
18. As children of a sovereign God, we are never victims of our circumstances.

12 Therefore Sarah laughed within herself,
saying, "After I have grown old, shall I have
pleasure, my lord being old also?"
13 And the LORD said to Abraham, "Why did
Sarah laugh, saying, 'Shall I surely bear *a
child,* since I am old?'
14 "Is anything too hard for the LORD? At ➤
the appointed time I will return to you, according to the time of life, and Sarah shall
have a son."
15 But Sarah denied *it,* saying, "I did not
laugh," for she was afraid.
And He said, "No, but you did laugh!"

Abraham Intercedes for Sodom
16 Then the men rose from there and looked
toward Sodom, and Abraham went with them
to send them on the way.
17 And the LORD said, "Shall I hide from
Abraham what I am doing,
18 "since Abraham shall surely become a
great and mighty nation, and all the nations
of the earth shall be blessed in him?
19 "For I have known him, in order that he ➤
may command his children and his household after him, that they keep the way of the
LORD, to do righteousness and justice, that the
LORD may bring to Abraham what He has
spoken to him."
20 And the LORD said, "Because the outcry
against Sodom and Gomorrah is great, and
because their sin is very grave,
21 "I will go down now and see whether they
have done altogether according to the outcry
against it that has come to Me; and if not, I
will know."
22 Then the men turned away from there and
went toward Sodom, but Abraham still stood
before the LORD.
23 And Abraham came near and said,
"Would You also destroy the righteous with
the wicked?
24 "Suppose there were fifty righteous within
the city; would You also destroy the place and
not spare *it* for the fifty righteous that were in
it?
25 "Far be it from You to do such a thing as ➤
this, to slay the righteous with the wicked, so

LIFE LESSONS

➤ 18:14 — *"Is anything too hard for the LORD? At the appointed time I will return to you, according to the time of life, and Sarah shall have a son."*

Things that we humans find impossible to do, God finds very easy. That is why we can trust all of His promises. We do not have to understand how He will fulfill them; we have only to believe that He will.

➤ 18:19 — *"For I have known him, in order that he may command his children and his household after him, that they keep the way of the LORD, to do righteousness and justice, that the LORD may bring to Abraham what He has spoken to him."*

The "way of the LORD" is to do "righteousness and justice." When we walk the Lord's path, He blesses us with the delightful benefits of His promises.

➤ 18:25 — *"Far be it from You to do such a thing as this, to slay the righteous with the wicked, so that the righteous should be as the wicked; far be it from You! Shall not the Judge of all the earth do right?"*

We can rest assured that God, "the Judge of all the earth," will always do exactly what is right. We

that the righteous should be as the wicked;
far be it from You! Shall not the Judge of all
the earth do right?"
26 So the LORD said, "If I find in Sodom fifty
righteous within the city, then I will spare all
the place for their sakes."
27 Then Abraham answered and said, "Indeed now, I who *am but* dust and ashes
have taken it upon myself to speak to the
Lord:
28 "Suppose there were five less than the
fifty righteous; would You destroy all of the
city for *lack of* five?" So He said, "If I find
there forty-five, I will not destroy *it*."
29 And he spoke to Him yet again and said,
"Suppose there should be forty found there?"
So He said, "I will not do *it* for the sake of
forty."
30 Then he said, "Let not the Lord be angry,
and I will speak: Suppose thirty should be
found there?" So He said, "I will not do *it* if I
find thirty there."
31 And he said, "Indeed now, I have taken
it upon myself to speak to the Lord: Suppose twenty should be found there?" So He
said, "I will not destroy *it* for the sake of
twenty."
32 Then he said, "Let not the Lord be angry,
and I will speak but once more: Suppose ten
should be found there?" And He said, "I will
not destroy *it* for the sake of ten."
33 So the LORD went His way as soon as He
had finished speaking with Abraham; and
Abraham returned to his place.

Sodom's Depravity

19 Now the two angels came to Sodom in
the evening, and Lot was sitting in the
gate of Sodom. When Lot saw *them*, he rose
to meet them, and he bowed himself with his
face toward the ground.
2 And he said, "Here now, my lords, please
turn in to your servant's house and spend the
night, and wash your feet; then you may rise
early and go on your way." And they said,
"No, but we will spend the night in the open
square."
3 But he insisted strongly; so they turned in
to him and entered his house. Then he made
them a feast, and baked unleavened bread,
and they ate.
4 Now before they lay down, the men of the
city, the men of Sodom, both old and young,
all the people from every quarter, surrounded
the house.
5 And they called to Lot and said to him,
"Where are the men who came to you
tonight? Bring them out to us that we may
know them *carnally*."
6 So Lot went out to them through the doorway, shut the door behind him,
7 and said, "Please, my brethren, do not do
so wickedly!
8 "See now, I have two daughters who have
not known a man; please, let me bring them
out to you, and you may do to them as you
wish; only do nothing to these men, since this
is the reason they have come under the
shadow of my roof."
9 And they said, "Stand back!" Then they
said, "This one came in to stay *here*, and he
keeps acting as a judge; now we will deal
worse with you than with them." So they
pressed hard against the man Lot, and came
near to break down the door.
10 But the men reached out their hands and
pulled Lot into the house with them, and shut
the door.
11 And they struck the men who *were* at the
doorway of the house with blindness, both
small and great, so that they became weary
trying to find the door.

Sodom and Gomorrah Destroyed

12 Then the men said to Lot, "Have you anyone else here? Son-in-law, your sons, your
daughters, and whomever you have in the
city—take *them* out of this place!
13 "For we will destroy this place, because
the outcry against them has grown great before the face of the LORD, and the LORD has
sent us to destroy it."
14 So Lot went out and spoke to his sons-in-
law, who had married his daughters, and said,
"Get up, get out of this place; for the LORD will
destroy this city!" But to his sons-in-law he
seemed to be joking.
15 When the morning dawned, the angels
urged Lot to hurry, saying, "Arise, take your
wife and your two daughters who are here,
lest you be consumed in the punishment of
the city."
16 And while he lingered, the men took hold
of his hand, his wife's hand, and the hands of
his two daughters, the LORD being merciful to
him, and they brought him out and set him
outside the city.

LIFE LESSONS

never have to fear that He will make a mistake or suffer a lapse in judgment.

➤ **19:9** — ***. . . Then they said, "This one came in to stay here, and he keeps acting as a judge; now we will deal worse with you than with them." So they pressed hard against the man Lot, and came near to break down the door.***

When we refuse to repent of our sin, we tend to get self-righteous and easily offended when someone suggests we are in the wrong. But if we sow to our flesh, we will reap nothing but judgment and destruction.

17 So it came to pass, when they had brought them outside, that he[a] said, “Escape for your life! Do not look behind you nor stay anywhere in the plain. Escape to the mountains, lest you be destroyed.”

18 Then Lot said to them, “Please, no, my lords!

19 “Indeed now, your servant has found favor in your sight, and you have increased your mercy which you have shown me by saving my life; but I cannot escape to the mountains, lest some evil overtake me and I die.

20 “See now, this city *is* near *enough* to flee to, and it *is* a little one; please let me escape there (*is* it not a little one?) and my soul shall live.”

21 And he said to him, “See, I have favored you concerning this thing also, in that I will not overthrow this city for which you have spoken.

22 “Hurry, escape there. For I cannot do anything until you arrive there.” Therefore the name of the city was called Zoar.

23 The sun had risen upon the earth when Lot entered Zoar.

➤ 24 Then the LORD rained brimstone and fire on Sodom and Gomorrah, from the LORD out of the heavens.

25 So He overthrew those cities, all the plain, all the inhabitants of the cities, and what grew on the ground.

26 But his wife looked back behind him, and she became a pillar of salt.

27 And Abraham went early in the morning to the place where he had stood before the LORD.

28 Then he looked toward Sodom and Gomorrah, and toward all the land of the plain; and he saw, and behold, the smoke of the land which went up like the smoke of a furnace.

➤ **29** And it came to pass, when God destroyed the cities of the plain, that God remembered Abraham, and sent Lot out of the midst of the overthrow, when He overthrew the cities in which Lot had dwelt.

The Descendants of Lot

30 Then Lot went up out of Zoar and dwelt in the mountains, and his two daughters were with him; for he was afraid to dwell in Zoar. And he and his two daughters dwelt in a cave.

31 Now the firstborn said to the younger, “Our father *is* old, and *there is* no man on the earth to come in to us as is the custom of all the earth.

32 “Come, let us make our father drink wine, and we will lie with him, that we may preserve the lineage of our father.”

33 So they made their father drink wine that night. And the firstborn went in and lay with her father, and he did not know when she lay down or when she arose.

34 It happened on the next day that the firstborn said to the younger, “Indeed I lay with my father last night; let us make him drink wine tonight also, and you go in *and* lie with him, that we may preserve the lineage of our father.”

35 Then they made their father drink wine that night also. And the younger arose and lay with him, and he did not know when she lay down or when she arose.

36 Thus both the daughters of Lot were with child by their father. ➤

37 The firstborn bore a son and called his name Moab; he *is* the father of the Moabites to this day.

38 And the younger, she also bore a son and called his name Ben-Ammi; he *is* the father of the people of Ammon to this day.

Abraham and Abimelech

20 And Abraham journeyed from there to the South, and dwelt between Kadesh and Shur, and stayed in Gerar.

2 Now Abraham said of Sarah his wife, “She *is* my sister.” And Abimelech king of Gerar sent and took Sarah.

3 But God came to Abimelech in a dream by night, and said to him, “Indeed you *are* a dead man because of the woman whom you have taken, for she *is* a man’s wife.”

4 But Abimelech had not come near her; and he said, “Lord, will You slay a righteous nation also?

5 “Did he not say to me, ‘She *is* my sister’? And she, even she herself said, ‘He *is* my brother.’ In the integrity of my heart and innocence of my hands I have done this.”

19:17 [a]Septuagint, Syriac, and Vulgate read *they.*

LIFE LESSONS

➤ **19:24 — *Then the LORD rained brimstone and fire on Sodom and Gomorrah . . . .***

Everything Lot had gained during his time in Sodom, he lost in an instant. What we gain outside of God’s blessing is not worth having, and eventually goes up in smoke.

➤ **19:29 — *And it came to pass, when God destroyed the cities of the plain, that God remembered Abraham, and sent Lot out of the midst of the overthrow . . . .***

God spared Lot’s life because of the request of righteous Abraham. Our prayers bring mightier results than we will ever know.

➤ **19:36 — *Thus both the daughters of Lot were with child by their father . . . .***

The sinful plan of Lot’s daughters failed even as it succeeded. They did manage to preserve their father’s family line, but in so doing they created two peoples who became vicious enemies of God’s people.

6 And God said to him in a dream, "Yes, I
know that you did this in the integrity of your
heart. For I also withheld you from sinning
against Me; therefore I did not let you touch
her.
7 "Now therefore, restore the man's wife;
for he *is* a prophet, and he will pray for you
and you shall live. But if you do not restore
her, know that you shall surely die, you and
all who *are* yours."
8 So Abimelech rose early in the morning,
called all his servants, and told all these
things in their hearing; and the men were
very much afraid.
➤ 9 And Abimelech called Abraham and said
to him, "What have you done to us? How have
I offended you, that you have brought on me
and on my kingdom a great sin? You have
done deeds to me that ought not to be done."
10 Then Abimelech said to Abraham, "What
did you have in view, that you have done this
thing?"
11 And Abraham said, "Because I thought,
surely the fear of God *is* not in this place; and
they will kill me on account of my wife.
12 "But indeed *she is* truly my sister. She *is*
the daughter of my father, but not the daughter of my mother; and she became my wife.
13 And it came to pass, when God caused me
to wander from my father's house, that I said
to her, 'This *is* your kindness that you should
do for me: in every place, wherever we go, say
of me, "He *is* my brother." ' "
14 Then Abimelech took sheep, oxen, and
male and female servants, and gave *them* to
Abraham; and he restored Sarah his wife to
him.
15 And Abimelech said, "See, my land *is* before you; dwell where it pleases you."
16 Then to Sarah he said, "Behold, I have
given your brother a thousand *pieces* of silver; indeed this vindicates you[a] before all who
are with you and before everybody." Thus she
was rebuked.
➤ **17** So Abraham prayed to God; and God
healed Abimelech, his wife, and his female
servants. Then they bore *children;*
18 for the LORD had closed up all the wombs
of the house of Abimelech because of Sarah,
Abraham's wife.

Isaac Is Born

21 And the LORD visited Sarah as He had ➤
said, and the LORD did for Sarah as He
had spoken.
2 For Sarah conceived and bore Abraham a
son in his old age, at the set time of which
God had spoken to him.
3 And Abraham called the name of his son
who was born to him—whom Sarah bore to
him—Isaac.
4 Then Abraham circumcised his son Isaac
when he was eight days old, as God had commanded him.
5 Now Abraham was one hundred years old
when his son Isaac was born to him.
6 And Sarah said, "God has made me laugh, ➤
and all who hear will laugh with me."
7 She also said, "Who would have said to
Abraham that Sarah would nurse children?
For I have borne *him* a son in his old age."

Hagar and Ishmael Depart

8 So the child grew and was weaned. And
Abraham made a great feast on the same day
that Isaac was weaned.
9 And Sarah saw the son of Hagar the Egyptian, whom she had borne to Abraham, scoffing.
10 Therefore she said to Abraham, "Cast out
this bondwoman and her son; for the son of
this bondwoman shall not be heir with my
son, *namely* with Isaac."
11 And the matter was very displeasing in
Abraham's sight because of his son.
12 But God said to Abraham, "Do not let it be
displeasing in your sight because of the lad or
because of your bondwoman. Whatever Sarah has said to you, listen to her voice; for in
Isaac your seed shall be called.

20:16 [a]Literally *it is a covering of the eyes for you*

LIFE LESSONS

➤ 20:9 — *And Abimelech called Abraham and said to him, " . . . You have done deeds to me that ought not to be done."*

Sometimes God uses the ungodly to rebuke and correct His own people. He does so to remind us that we can trust Him in all circumstances, however dangerous they may seem.

➤ 20:17 — *So Abraham prayed to God; and God healed Abimelech, his wife, and his female servants . . . .*

The only time Abraham stands tall in this story is when he gets on his knees in prayer.

➤ 21:1 — *And the LORD visited Sarah as He had said, and the LORD did for Sarah as He had spoken.*

God always keeps His promises, no matter how impossible their fulfillment may seem. And every promise He keeps is an expression of His grace.

➤ 21:6 — *And Sarah said, "God has made me laugh, and all who hear will laugh with me."*

The name "Isaac" means "he laughs"—a reference not only to the skeptical laughter of both Abraham and Sarah in response to God's promise of a son, but also to their joyful laughter at Isaac's birth.

Life Examples:

ABRAHAM

The Man of Endurance

GEN. 21:1–3

Call Abraham not only a man of faith (Gal. 3:9), but a man of endurance.

The starting gun sounded when God promised Abraham a son in his old age, and Abraham "believed in the LORD" (Gen. 15:5, 6). But a year came and went, and no child arrived.

Abraham kept running.

Two years flashed by, and still no child.

Still Abraham kept running.

Despite a stumble at mid-race (see Gen. 16), Abraham kept running. For 25 *years* he kept running, until at last, at age 100, he and his wife, age 99, had a son (Gen. 21:1–3).

Why the long wait? Apparently, God wanted Abraham (and us!) to learn the connection between waiting, trust, and hope (Ps. 33:20). And that hope, the apostle Paul reminds us, prompts us to wait on God "with perseverance" (Rom. 8:25).

Even if that means running the longest marathon of our life.

See the Life Principles Index for further study:
14. God acts on behalf of those who wait for Him.

13 "Yet I will also make a nation of the son
of the bondwoman, because he *is* your
seed."
14 So Abraham rose early in the morning,
and took bread and a skin of water; and putting *it* on her shoulder, he gave *it* and the boy
to Hagar, and sent her away. Then she departed and wandered in the Wilderness of
Beersheba.
15 And the water in the skin was used up,
and she placed the boy under one of the
shrubs.
16 Then she went and sat down across from ➤
him at a distance of about a bowshot; for she
said to herself, "Let me not see the death of
the boy." So she sat opposite *him,* and lifted
her voice and wept.
17 And God heard the voice of the lad. Then
the angel of God called to Hagar out of
heaven, and said to her, "What ails you,
Hagar? Fear not, for God has heard the voice
of the lad where he *is.*
18 "Arise, lift up the lad and hold him with
your hand, for I will make him a great nation."
19 Then God opened her eyes, and she saw a
well of water. And she went and filled the skin
with water, and gave the lad a drink.
20 So God was with the lad; and he grew and
dwelt in the wilderness, and became an
archer.
21 He dwelt in the Wilderness of Paran; and
his mother took a wife for him from the land
of Egypt.

A Covenant with Abimelech

22 And it came to pass at that time that
Abimelech and Phichol, the commander of
his army, spoke to Abraham, saying, "God *is*
with you in all that you do.
23 "Now therefore, swear to me by God that
you will not deal falsely with me, with my offspring, or with my posterity; but that according to the kindness that I have done to you,
you will do to me and to the land in which you
have dwelt."
24 And Abraham said, "I will swear."
25 Then Abraham rebuked Abimelech because of a well of water which Abimelech's
servants had seized.
26 And Abimelech said, "I do not know who
has done this thing; you did not tell me, nor
had I heard *of it* until today."
27 So Abraham took sheep and oxen and
gave them to Abimelech, and the two of them
made a covenant.
28 And Abraham set seven ewe lambs of the
flock by themselves.
29 Then Abimelech asked Abraham, "What *is*
the meaning of these seven ewe lambs which
you have set by themselves?"
30 And he said, "You will take *these* seven
ewe lambs from my hand, that they may be
my witness that I have dug this well."

LIFE LESSONS

➤ **21:16 — *. . . She said to herself, "Let me not see the death of the boy." So she sat opposite him, and lifted her voice and wept.***

Hagar discovered that we learn more in our valley experiences than on our mountaintops. Only when it seemed as though all hope was lost, did she find her ultimate hope in God.

31 Therefore he called that place Beersheba,[a]
because the two of them swore an oath there.
32 Thus they made a covenant at Beersheba.
So Abimelech rose with Phichol, the commander of his army, and they returned to the
land of the Philistines.
➤ 33 Then *Abraham* planted a tamarisk tree in
Beersheba, and there called on the name of
the LORD, the Everlasting God.
34 And Abraham stayed in the land of the
Philistines many days.

Abraham's Faith Confirmed

➤ 22 Now it came to pass after these things
that God tested Abraham, and said to
him, "Abraham!" And he said, "Here I am."
2 Then He said, "Take now your son, your
only *son* Isaac, whom you love, and go to the
land of Moriah, and offer him there as a burnt
offering on one of the mountains of which I
shall tell you."
3 So Abraham rose early in the morning
and saddled his donkey, and took two of his
young men with him, and Isaac his son; and
he split the wood for the burnt offering, and
arose and went to the place of which God had
told him.
4 Then on the third day Abraham lifted his
eyes and saw the place afar off.
➤ 5 And Abraham said to his young men,
"Stay here with the donkey; the lad[a] and I will
go yonder and worship, and we will come
back to you."
6 So Abraham took the wood of the burnt
offering and laid *it* on Isaac his son; and he
took the fire in his hand, and a knife, and the
two of them went together.
7 But Isaac spoke to Abraham his father
and said, "My father!" And he said, "Here I
am, my son." Then he said, "Look, the fire and
the wood, but where *is* the lamb for a burnt
offering?"
8 And Abraham said, "My son, God will provide for Himself the lamb for a burnt offering." So the two of them went together.
9 Then they came to the place of which God
had told him. And Abraham built an altar
there and placed the wood in order; and he
bound Isaac his son and laid him on the altar,
upon the wood.
10 And Abraham stretched out his hand and
took the knife to slay his son.
11 But the Angel of the LORD called to him
from heaven and said, "Abraham, Abraham!"
So he said, "Here I am."
12 And He said, "Do not lay your hand on the
lad, or do anything to him; for now I know
that you fear God, since you have not withheld your son, your only *son,* from Me."
13 Then Abraham lifted his eyes and looked,
and there behind *him was* a ram caught in a
thicket by its horns. So Abraham went and
took the ram, and offered it up for a burnt offering instead of his son.
14 And Abraham called the name of the
place, The-LORD-Will-Provide;[a] as it is said *to*
this day, "In the Mount of the LORD it shall be
provided."
15 Then the Angel of the LORD called to Abraham a second time out of heaven,
16 and said: "By Myself I have sworn, says
the LORD, because you have done this thing,
and have not withheld your son, your only
son—
17 "blessing I will bless you, and multiplying
I will multiply your descendants as the stars
of the heaven and as the sand which *is* on the
seashore; and your descendants shall possess
the gate of their enemies.
18 "In your seed all the nations of the earth
shall be blessed, because you have obeyed My
voice."

21:31 [a]Literally *Well of the Oath* or *Well of the Seven* **22:5** [a]Or *young man* **22:14** [a]Hebrew *YHWH Yireh*

LIFE LESSONS

➤ 21:33 — *Then Abraham planted a tamarisk tree in Beersheba, and there called on the name of the LORD, the Everlasting God.*

Abraham knew the Lord as "the Everlasting God," a title found only here. We can count on God to keep all His promises because, as He says, "I am the LORD, I do not change" (Mal. 3:6).

➤ 22:1 — *Now it came to pass after these things that God tested Abraham . . . .*

God permits testing for all of His children, including His own Son, Jesus Christ (Matt. 4:1). For Abraham, this had to be a dark time—but it lasted only so long as was necessary for God to accomplish His purpose in Abraham's life.

➤ 22:5 — *And Abraham said to his young men, "Stay here with the donkey; the lad and I will go yonder and worship, and we will come back to you."*

Abraham expressed confidence that both he and Isaac would return alive to the servants, even though he intended to obey God's command to sacrifice his son. Abraham obeyed and trusted, though he did not understand (Heb. 11:17–19).

➤ 22:14 — *And Abraham called the name of the place, The-LORD-Will-Provide; as it is said to this day, "In the Mount of the LORD it shall be provided."*

The Lord will provide—*always.* He may surprise us, He may perplex us, He may make us wait. But He will *always* provide exactly what we need, when we need it.

➤ 22:18 — *". . . In your seed all the nations of the earth shall be blessed, because you have obeyed My voice."*

God always blesses obedience, and obedience always follows genuine faith. If we do not obey, it is because we do not believe (see Heb. 3:18-19).

19 So Abraham returned to his young men,
and they rose and went together to Beersheba; and Abraham dwelt at Beersheba.

The Family of Nahor

20 Now it came to pass after these things that
it was told Abraham, saying, "Indeed Milcah
also has borne children to your brother
Nahor:
21 "Huz his firstborn, Buz his brother, Kemuel the father of Aram,
22 "Chesed, Hazo, Pildash, Jidlaph, and
Bethuel."
23 And Bethuel begot Rebekah.[a] These eight
Milcah bore to Nahor, Abraham's brother.
24 His concubine, whose name was Reumah,
also bore Tebah, Gaham, Thahash, and Maachah.

Sarah's Death and Burial

23 Sarah lived one hundred and twenty-
seven years; *these were* the years of the
life of Sarah.
2 So Sarah died in Kirjath Arba (that *is*, Hebron) in the land of Canaan, and Abraham
came to mourn for Sarah and to weep for her.
3 Then Abraham stood up from before his
dead, and spoke to the sons of Heth, saying,
4 "I *am* a foreigner and a visitor among you.
Give me property for a burial place among
you, that I may bury my dead out of my sight."
5 And the sons of Heth answered Abraham,
saying to him,
6 "Hear us, my lord: You *are* a mighty prince
among us; bury your dead in the choicest of
our burial places. None of us will withhold
from you his burial place, that you may bury
your dead."
7 Then Abraham stood up and bowed himself to the people of the land, the sons of Heth.
8 And he spoke with them, saying, "If it is
your wish that I bury my dead out of my sight,
hear me, and meet with Ephron the son of
Zohar for me,
9 "that he may give me the cave of Machpelah which he has, which *is* at the end of his
field. Let him give it to me at the full price, as
property for a burial place among you."
10 Now Ephron dwelt among the sons of
Heth; and Ephron the Hittite answered Abraham in the presence of the sons of Heth, all
who entered at the gate of his city, saying,
11 "No, my lord, hear me: I give you the field
and the cave that *is* in it; I give it to you in the
presence of the sons of my people. I give it to
you. Bury your dead!"
12 Then Abraham bowed himself down before the people of the land;
13 and he spoke to Ephron in the hearing of
the people of the land, saying, "If you *will give
it*, please hear me. I will give you money for
the field; take *it* from me and I will bury my
dead there."
14 And Ephron answered Abraham, saying
to him,
15 "My lord, listen to me; the land *is worth*
four hundred shekels of silver. What *is*
that between you and me? So bury your
dead."
16 And Abraham listened to Ephron; and
Abraham weighed out the silver for Ephron
which he had named in the hearing of the
sons of Heth, four hundred shekels of silver,
currency of the merchants.
17 So the field of Ephron which *was* in Machpelah, which *was* before Mamre, the field and
the cave which *was* in it, and all the trees that
were in the field, which *were* within all the
surrounding borders, were deeded
18 to Abraham as a possession in the presence of the sons of Heth, before all who went
in at the gate of his city.
19 And after this, Abraham buried Sarah his
wife in the cave of the field of Machpelah, before Mamre (that *is*, Hebron) in the land of
Canaan.
20 So the field and the cave that *is* in it were
deeded to Abraham by the sons of Heth as
property for a burial place.

A Bride for Isaac

24 Now Abraham was old, well advanced
in age; and the LORD had blessed Abraham in all things.
2 So Abraham said to the oldest servant of
his house, who ruled over all that he had,
"Please, put your hand under my thigh,
3 "and I will make you swear by the LORD,
the God of heaven and the God of the earth,
that you will not take a wife for my son from
the daughters of the Canaanites, among
whom I dwell;
4 "but you shall go to my country and to my
family, and take a wife for my son Isaac."
5 And the servant said to him, "Perhaps the
woman will not be willing to follow me to this
land. Must I take your son back to the land
from which you came?"
6 But Abraham said to him, "Beware that
you do not take my son back there.

22:23 [a]Spelled *Rebecca* in Romans 9:10

LIFE LESSONS

➤ **24:1 — *Now Abraham was old, well advanced in age; and the LORD had blessed Abraham in all things.***

Would you like to be blessed "in all things," as Abraham was? Then you must follow Abraham's example of trust and obedience, for that is the way to great blessing.

➤ 7 "The LORD God of heaven, who took me
from my father's house and from the land of
my family, and who spoke to me and swore to
me, saying, 'To your descendants[a] I give this
land,' He will send His angel before you, and
you shall take a wife for my son from there.
8 "And if the woman is not willing to follow
you, then you will be released from this oath;
only do not take my son back there."
9 So the servant put his hand under the
thigh of Abraham his master, and swore to
him concerning this matter.
10 Then the servant took ten of his master's
camels and departed, for all his master's
goods *were in* his hand. And he arose and
went to Mesopotamia, to the city of Nahor.
11 And he made his camels kneel down outside the city by a well of water at evening time,
the time when women go out to draw *water*.
➤ 12 Then he said, "O LORD God of my master
Abraham, please give me success this day,
and show kindness to my master Abraham.
13 "Behold, *here* I stand by the well of water,
and the daughters of the men of the city are
coming out to draw water.
14 "Now let it be that the young woman to
whom I say, 'Please let down your pitcher that
I may drink,' and she says, 'Drink, and I will
also give your camels a drink'—*let* her *be the
one* You have appointed for Your servant
Isaac. And by this I will know that You have
shown kindness to my master."
15 And it happened, before he had finished
speaking, that behold, Rebekah, who was
born to Bethuel, son of Milcah, the wife of
Nahor, Abraham's brother, came out with her
pitcher on her shoulder.
16 Now the young woman *was* very beautiful
to behold, a virgin; no man had known her.
And she went down to the well, filled her
pitcher, and came up.
17 And the servant ran to meet her and said,
"Please let me drink a little water from your
pitcher."
18 So she said, "Drink, my lord." Then she
quickly let her pitcher down to her hand, and
gave him a drink.
19 And when she had finished giving him a
drink, she said, "I will draw *water* for your
camels also, until they have finished drinking."
20 Then she quickly emptied her pitcher into
the trough, ran back to the well to draw *water*, and drew for all his camels.
21 And the man, wondering at her, remained
silent so as to know whether the LORD had
made his journey prosperous or not.
22 So it was, when the camels had finished
drinking, that the man took a golden nose
ring weighing half a shekel, and two bracelets
for her wrists weighing ten *shekels* of gold,
23 and said, "Whose daughter *are* you? Tell
me, please, is there room *in* your father's
house for us to lodge?"
24 So she said to him, "I *am* the daughter of
Bethuel, Milcah's son, whom she bore to
Nahor."
25 Moreover she said to him, "We have both
straw and feed enough, and room to lodge."
26 Then the man bowed down his head and ➤
worshiped the LORD.
27 And he said, "Blessed *be* the LORD God of
my master Abraham, who has not forsaken
His mercy and His truth toward my master.
As for me, being on the way, the LORD led me
to the house of my master's brethren."
28 So the young woman ran and told her
mother's household these things.
29 Now Rebekah had a brother whose name
was Laban, and Laban ran out to the man by
the well.
30 So it came to pass, when he saw the nose
ring, and the bracelets on his sister's wrists,
and when he heard the words of his sister Rebekah, saying, "Thus the man spoke to me,"
that he went to the man. And there he stood
by the camels at the well.
31 And he said, "Come in, O blessed of the
LORD! Why do you stand outside? For I have
prepared the house, and a place for the
camels."
32 Then the man came to the house. And he
unloaded the camels, and provided straw and
feed for the camels, and water to wash his feet
and the feet of the men who *were* with him.
33 *Food* was set before him to eat, but he
said, "I will not eat until I have told about my
errand." And he said, "Speak on."

24:7 [a]Literally *seed*

LIFE LESSONS

➤ **24:7 — *"The LORD God . . . will send His angel before you, and you shall take a wife for my son from there."***

When we walk in faith and obedience, God sends His angels ahead of us to make sure we arrive at a place of blessing.

➤ **24:12 — *Then he said, "O LORD God of my master Abraham, please give me success this day, and show kindness to my master Abraham."***

The servant of Abraham fought his greatest battle on his knees, and in doing so he won a great victory even before he opened his eyes. God loves to answer the selfless prayers of His people!

➤ **24:26 — *Then the man bowed down his head and worshiped the LORD.***

When God answers our prayers, worship is the only proper response.

34 So he said, "I *am* Abraham's servant.
35 "The LORD has blessed my master greatly,
and he has become great; and He has given
him flocks and herds, silver and gold, male
and female servants, and camels and donkeys.
36 "And Sarah my master's wife bore a son to
my master when she was old; and to him he
has given all that he has.
37 "Now my master made me swear, saying,
'You shall not take a wife for my son from the
daughters of the Canaanites, in whose land I
dwell;
38 "but you shall go to my father's house and
to my family, and take a wife for my son.'
39 "And I said to my master, 'Perhaps the
woman will not follow me.'
➤ 40 "But he said to me, 'The LORD, before
whom I walk, will send His angel with you
and prosper your way; and you shall take a
wife for my son from my family and from my
father's house.
41 "You will be clear from this oath when you
arrive among my family; for if they will not
give *her* to you, then you will be released from
my oath.'
42 "And this day I came to the well and said,
'O LORD God of my master Abraham, if You
will now prosper the way in which I go,
43 "behold, I stand by the well of water; and
it shall come to pass that when the virgin
comes out to draw *water,* and I say to her,
"Please give me a little water from your
pitcher to drink,"
44 "and she says to me, "Drink, and I will
draw for your camels also,"—*let* her *be* the
woman whom the LORD has appointed for my
master's son.'
45 "But before I had finished speaking in my
heart, there was Rebekah, coming out with
her pitcher on her shoulder; and she went
down to the well and drew *water.* And I said
to her, 'Please let me drink.'
46 "And she made haste and let her pitcher
down from her *shoulder,* and said, 'Drink, and
I will give your camels a drink also.' So I
drank, and she gave the camels a drink also.
47 "Then I asked her, and said, 'Whose
daughter *are* you?' And she said, 'The daughter of Bethuel, Nahor's son, whom Milcah
bore to him.' So I put the nose ring on her
nose and the bracelets on her wrists.
48 "And I bowed my head and worshiped the
LORD, and blessed the LORD God of my master
Abraham, who had led me in the way of truth
to take the daughter of my master's brother
for his son.
49 "Now if you will deal kindly and truly with
my master, tell me. And if not, tell me, that I
may turn to the right hand or to the left."
50 Then Laban and Bethuel answered and ➤
said, "The thing comes from the LORD; we
cannot speak to you either bad or good.
51 "Here *is* Rebekah before you; take *her* and
go, and let her be your master's son's wife, as
the LORD has spoken."
52 And it came to pass, when Abraham's servant heard their words, that he worshiped the
LORD, *bowing himself* to the earth.
53 Then the servant brought out jewelry
of silver, jewelry of gold, and clothing,
and gave *them* to Rebekah. He also gave
precious things to her brother and to her
mother.
54 And he and the men who *were* with him
ate and drank and stayed all night. Then they
arose in the morning, and he said, "Send me
away to my master."
55 But her brother and her mother said, "Let
the young woman stay with us *a few* days, at
least ten; after that she may go."
56 And he said to them, "Do not hinder me,
since the LORD has prospered my way; send
me away so that I may go to my master."
57 So they said, "We will call the young
woman and ask her personally."
58 Then they called Rebekah and said to her,
"Will you go with this man?" And she said, "I
will go."
59 So they sent away Rebekah their sister
and her nurse, and Abraham's servant and
his men.
60 And they blessed Rebekah and said to
her:

"Our sister, *may* you *become*
The mother of thousands of ten
thousands;
And may your descendants possess
The gates of those who hate them."

61 Then Rebekah and her maids arose, and
they rode on the camels and followed the
man. So the servant took Rebekah and departed.

LIFE LESSONS

➤ 24:40 — *"But he said to me, 'The LORD, before whom I walk, will send His angel with you and prosper your way . . . .'"*

Abraham saw his relationship with God as a long walk—slow, steady, full of twists and turns, but ending up at a wonderful destination. We should see our relationship with the Lord in the same way.

➤ 24:50 — *Then Laban and Bethuel answered and said, "The thing comes from the LORD; we cannot speak to you either bad or good."*

When we see a direct answer to prayer, we are wise to get out of the way and allow the Lord to finish His good work.

62 Now Isaac came from the way of Beer
Lahai Roi, for he dwelt in the South.
➤ 63 And Isaac went out to meditate in the
field in the evening; and he lifted his eyes
and looked, and there, the camels *were* coming.
64 Then Rebekah lifted her eyes, and when
she saw Isaac she dismounted from her
camel;
65 for she had said to the servant, "Who *is*
this man walking in the field to meet us?" The
servant said, "It *is* my master." So she took a
veil and covered herself.
66 And the servant told Isaac all the things
that he had done.
67 Then Isaac brought her into his mother
Sarah's tent; and he took Rebekah and she
became his wife, and he loved her. So Isaac
was comforted after his mother's *death*.

Abraham and Keturah

25 Abraham again took a wife, and her
name *was* Keturah.
2 And she bore him Zimran, Jokshan,
Medan, Midian, Ishbak, and Shuah.
3 Jokshan begot Sheba and Dedan. And the
sons of Dedan were Asshurim, Letushim, and
Leummim.
4 And the sons of Midian *were* Ephah,
Epher, Hanoch, Abidah, and Eldaah. All these
were the children of Keturah.
5 And Abraham gave all that he had to
Isaac.
6 But Abraham gave gifts to the sons of the
concubines which Abraham had; and while
he was still living he sent them eastward,
away from Isaac his son, to the country of the
east.

Abraham's Death and Burial

7 This *is* the sum of the years of Abraham's
life which he lived: one hundred and seventy-
five years.
8 Then Abraham breathed his last and died
in a good old age, an old man and full *of
years*, and was gathered to his people.
9 And his sons Isaac and Ishmael buried
him in the cave of Machpelah, which *is* before
Mamre, in the field of Ephron the son of
Zohar the Hittite,
10 the field which Abraham purchased from
the sons of Heth. There Abraham was buried,
and Sarah his wife.
11 And it came to pass, after the death of
Abraham, that God blessed his son Isaac. And
Isaac dwelt at Beer Lahai Roi.

The Families of Ishmael and Isaac

12 Now this *is* the genealogy of Ishmael,
Abraham's son, whom Hagar the Egyptian,
Sarah's maidservant, bore to Abraham.
13 And these *were* the names of the sons of
Ishmael, by their names, according to their
generations: The firstborn of Ishmael, Nebajoth; then Kedar, Adbeel, Mibsam,
14 Mishma, Dumah, Massa,
15 Hadar,[a] Tema, Jetur, Naphish, and
Kedemah.
16 These *were* the sons of Ishmael and these
were their names, by their towns and their
settlements, twelve princes according to
their nations.
17 These *were* the years of the life of Ishmael: one hundred and thirty-seven years;
and he breathed his last and died, and was
gathered to his people.
18 (They dwelt from Havilah as far as Shur, ➤
which *is* east of Egypt as you go toward Assyria.) He died in the presence of all his
brethren.
19 This *is* the genealogy of Isaac, Abraham's
son. Abraham begot Isaac.
20 Isaac was forty years old when he took
Rebekah as wife, the daughter of Bethuel the
Syrian of Padan Aram, the sister of Laban the
Syrian.
21 Now Isaac pleaded with the LORD for his ➤
wife, because she *was* barren; and the LORD
granted his plea, and Rebekah his wife conceived.
22 But the children struggled together within

25:15 [a]Masoretic Text reads *Hadad*.

LIFE LESSONS

➤ 24:63 — *And Isaac went out to meditate in the field in the evening; and he lifted his eyes and looked, and there, the camels were coming.*

Isaac must have learned the value of meditation from his godly father, Abraham, who clearly taught his son that intimacy with God was life's highest priority.

➤ 25:18 — *(They dwelt from Havilah as far as Shur, which is east of Egypt as you go toward Assyria.) He died in the presence of all his brethren.*

The promises of God always come true, whether those promises concern delightful or unpleasant things. Genesis 16:12 predicted this very outcome.

➤ 25:21 — *Now Isaac pleaded with the LORD for his wife, because she was barren; and the LORD granted his plea, and Rebekah his wife conceived.*

At many key points in Scripture, God grants a childless woman a family, often in response to prayer. Why saddle His people with such a difficult burden? Perhaps because brokenness is God's requirement for maximum usefulness.

her; and she said, "If *all is* well, why *am I like*
this?" So she went to inquire of the LORD.
23 And the LORD said to her:

"Two nations *are* in your womb,
Two peoples shall be separated from your body;
One people shall be stronger than the other,
And the older shall serve the younger."

24 So when her days were fulfilled *for her* to
give birth, indeed *there were* twins in her
womb.
25 And the first came out red. *He was* like a
hairy garment all over; so they called his
name Esau.[a]
26 Afterward his brother came out, and his
hand took hold of Esau's heel; so his name
was called Jacob.[a] Isaac *was* sixty years old
when she bore them.
27 So the boys grew. And Esau was a skillful
hunter, a man of the field; but Jacob was a
mild man, dwelling in tents.
28 And Isaac loved Esau because he ate *of his*
game, but Rebekah loved Jacob.

Esau Sells His Birthright

29 Now Jacob cooked a stew; and Esau came
in from the field, and he *was* weary.
30 And Esau said to Jacob, "Please feed me
with that same red *stew,* for I *am* weary."
Therefore his name was called Edom.[a]
31 But Jacob said, "Sell me your birthright as
of this day."
32 And Esau said, "Look, I *am* about to die;
so what *is* this birthright to me?"
33 Then Jacob said, "Swear to me as of this
day." So he swore to him, and sold his
birthright to Jacob.
➤ 34 And Jacob gave Esau bread and stew of
lentils; then he ate and drank, arose, and went
his way. Thus Esau despised *his* birthright.

Isaac and Abimelech

26 There was a famine in the land, besides
the first famine that was in the days of
Abraham. And Isaac went to Abimelech king
of the Philistines, in Gerar.
2 Then the LORD appeared to him and said:
"Do not go down to Egypt; live in the land of
which I shall tell you.
3 "Dwell in this land, and I will be with you
and bless you; for to you and your descendants I give all these lands, and I will perform
the oath which I swore to Abraham your father.
4 "And I will make your descendants multiply as the stars of heaven; I will give to
your descendants all these lands; and in your
seed all the nations of the earth shall be
blessed;
5 "because Abraham obeyed My voice and ➤
kept My charge, My commandments, My
statutes, and My laws."
6 So Isaac dwelt in Gerar.
7 And the men of the place asked about his ➤
wife. And he said, "She *is* my sister"; for he
was afraid to say, "*She is* my wife," *because he
thought,* "lest the men of the place kill me for
Rebekah, because she *is* beautiful to behold."
8 Now it came to pass, when he had been
there a long time, that Abimelech king of the
Philistines looked through a window, and
saw, and there was Isaac, showing endearment to Rebekah his wife.
9 Then Abimelech called Isaac and said,
"Quite obviously she *is* your wife; so how
could you say, 'She *is* my sister'?" Isaac said to
him, "Because I said, 'Lest I die on account of
her.'"
10 And Abimelech said, "What *is* this you
have done to us? One of the people might
soon have lain with your wife, and you would
have brought guilt on us."
11 So Abimelech charged all *his* people, saying, "He who touches this man or his wife
shall surely be put to death."
12 Then Isaac sowed in that land, and reaped
in the same year a hundredfold; and the LORD
blessed him.
13 The man began to prosper, and continued
prospering until he became very prosperous;
14 for he had possessions of flocks and possessions of herds and a great number of servants. So the Philistines envied him.

25:25 [a]Literally *Hairy* **25:26** [a]Literally *Supplanter*
25:30 [a]Literally *Red*

LIFE LESSONS

➤ 25:34 — *And Jacob gave Esau bread and stew of lentils; then he ate and drank, arose, and went his way. Thus Esau despised his birthright.*

In "despising" his birthright, Esau proved himself "profane" (Hebrews 12:16) because he considered filling his empty stomach more important than the spiritual promises of God to Abraham.

➤ 26:5 — *". . . because Abraham obeyed My voice and kept My charge, My commandments, My statutes, and My laws."*

God remembered Abraham as one who obeyed Him—and therefore Abraham provided his descendants with the greatest possible legacy.

➤ 26:7 — *And he said, "She is my sister"; for he was afraid to say, "She is my wife" . . . .*

Our children learn from us not only our wise habits, but also our foolish ones (see Genesis 12, 20). We spare them much heartache when we model for them a consistent life of faith.

15 Now the Philistines had stopped up all the
wells which his father's servants had dug in
the days of Abraham his father, and they had
filled them with earth.
16 And Abimelech said to Isaac, "Go away
from us, for you are much mightier than we."
17 Then Isaac departed from there and
pitched his tent in the Valley of Gerar, and
dwelt there.
18 And Isaac dug again the wells of water
which they had dug in the days of Abraham
his father, for the Philistines had stopped
them up after the death of Abraham. He
called them by the names which his father
had called them.
19 Also Isaac's servants dug in the valley,
and found a well of running water there.
20 But the herdsmen of Gerar quarreled with
Isaac's herdsmen, saying, "The water *is* ours."
So he called the name of the well Esek,[a] because they quarreled with him.
21 Then they dug another well, and they
quarreled over that *one* also. So he called its
name Sitnah.[a]
22 And he moved from there and dug another well, and they did not quarrel over it. So
he called its name Rehoboth,[a] because he
said, "For now the LORD has made room for
us, and we shall be fruitful in the land."
23 Then he went up from there to Beersheba.
24 And the LORD appeared to him the same
night and said, "I *am* the God of your father
Abraham; do not fear, for I *am* with you. I will
bless you and multiply your descendants for
My servant Abraham's sake."
25 So he built an altar there and called on the
name of the LORD, and he pitched his tent
there; and there Isaac's servants dug a well.
26 Then Abimelech came to him from Gerar
with Ahuzzath, one of his friends, and Phichol the commander of his army.
27 And Isaac said to them, "Why have you
come to me, since you hate me and have sent
me away from you?"
➤ 28 But they said, "We have certainly seen that
the LORD is with you. So we said, 'Let there
now be an oath between us, between you and
us; and let us make a covenant with you,
29 "that you will do us no harm, since we
have not touched you, and since we have done
nothing to you but good and have sent you
away in peace. You *are* now the blessed of the
LORD.'"
30 So he made them a feast, and they ate and
drank.
31 Then they arose early in the morning and
swore an oath with one another; and Isaac
sent them away, and they departed from him
in peace.
32 It came to pass the same day that Isaac's
servants came and told him about the well
which they had dug, and said to him, "We
have found water."
33 So he called it Shebah.[a] Therefore the
name of the city *is* Beersheba[b] to this day.
34 When Esau was forty years old, he took as
wives Judith the daughter of Beeri the Hittite,
and Basemath the daughter of Elon the Hittite.
35 And they were a grief of mind to Isaac and ➤
Rebekah.

Isaac Blesses Jacob

27 Now it came to pass, when Isaac was
old and his eyes were so dim that he
could not see, that he called Esau his older
son and said to him, "My son." And he answered him, "Here I am."
2 Then he said, "Behold now, I am old. I do
not know the day of my death.
3 "Now therefore, please take your
weapons, your quiver and your bow, and go
out to the field and hunt game for me.
4 "And make me savory food, such as I love,
and bring *it* to me that I may eat, that my soul
may bless you before I die."
5 Now Rebekah was listening when Isaac
spoke to Esau his son. And Esau went to the
field to hunt game and to bring *it*.
6 So Rebekah spoke to Jacob her son, saying, "Indeed I heard your father speak to Esau
your brother, saying,
7 'Bring me game and make savory food for
me, that I may eat it and bless you in the presence of the LORD before my death.'
8 "Now therefore, my son, obey my voice according to what I command you.
9 "Go now to the flock and bring me from

26:20 [a]Literally *Quarrel* **26:21** [a]Literally *Enmity* **26:22** [a]Literally *Spaciousness* **26:33** [a]Literally *Oath* or *Seven* [b]Literally *Well of the Oath* or *Well of the Seven*

LIFE LESSONS

➤ **26:28 — *But they said, "We have certainly seen that the LORD is with you. So we said, 'Let there now be an oath between us, between you and us; and let us make a covenant with you . . . .'"***

When God blesses His children, sometimes even the ungodly can clearly see it (see Proverbs 16:7). When we live in a way that invites the blessing of the Lord, that blessing can spill over to our neighbors.

➤ **26:35 — *. . . And they were a grief of mind to Isaac and Rebekah.***

God's people are not to be unequally yoked with unbelievers (see 2 Corinthians 6:14). Disobedience to this command causes tremendous and unnecessary heartache.

there two choice kids of the goats, and I will
make savory food from them for your father,
such as he loves.
10 "Then you shall take *it* to your father, that
he may eat *it*, and that he may bless you before his death."
11 And Jacob said to Rebekah his mother,
"Look, Esau my brother *is* a hairy man, and I
am a smooth-*skinned* man.
12 "Perhaps my father will feel me, and I
shall seem to be a deceiver to him; and I
shall bring a curse on myself and not a blessing."
13 But his mother said to him, "*Let* your
curse *be* on me, my son; only obey my voice,
and go, get *them* for me."
14 And he went and got *them* and brought
them to his mother, and his mother made savory food, such as his father loved.
15 Then Rebekah took the choice clothes of
her elder son Esau, which *were* with her in
the house, and put them on Jacob her
younger son.
16 And she put the skins of the kids of the
goats on his hands and on the smooth part of
his neck.
17 Then she gave the savory food and the
bread, which she had prepared, into the hand
of her son Jacob.
18 So he went to his father and said, "My father." And he said, "Here I am. Who *are* you,
my son?"
19 Jacob said to his father, "I *am* Esau your
firstborn; I have done just as you told me;
please arise, sit and eat of my game, that your
soul may bless me."
20 But Isaac said to his son, "How *is it* that
you have found *it* so quickly, my son?" And he
said, "Because the LORD your God brought *it*
to me."
21 Isaac said to Jacob, "Please come near,
that I may feel you, my son, whether you *are*
really my son Esau or not."
22 So Jacob went near to Isaac his father, and
he felt him and said, "The voice *is* Jacob's
voice, but the hands *are* the hands of Esau."
23 And he did not recognize him, because his
hands were hairy like his brother Esau's
hands; so he blessed him.
24 Then he said, "*Are* you really my son
Esau?" He said, "I *am*."
25 He said, "Bring *it* near to me, and I will
eat of my son's game, so that my soul may
bless you." So he brought *it* near to him, and
he ate; and he brought him wine, and he
drank.
26 Then his father Isaac said to him, "Come
near now and kiss me, my son."
27 And he came near and kissed him; and he
smelled the smell of his clothing, and blessed
him and said:

"Surely, the smell of my son
Is like the smell of a field
Which the LORD has blessed.
28 Therefore may God give you
Of the dew of heaven,
Of the fatness of the earth,
And plenty of grain and wine.
29 Let peoples serve you,
And nations bow down to you.
Be master over your brethren,
And let your mother's sons bow down to
you.
Cursed *be* everyone who curses you,
And blessed *be* those who bless you!"

Esau's Lost Hope

30 Now it happened, as soon as Isaac had finished blessing Jacob, and Jacob had scarcely
gone out from the presence of Isaac his father, that Esau his brother came in from his
hunting.
31 He also had made savory food, and
brought it to his father, and said to his father,
"Let my father arise and eat of his son's
game, that your soul may bless me."
32 And his father Isaac said to him, "Who *are*
you?" So he said, "I *am* your son, your firstborn, Esau."
33 Then Isaac trembled exceedingly, and
said, "Who? Where *is* the one who hunted
game and brought *it* to me? I ate all *of it* before you came, and I have blessed him—*and*
indeed he shall be blessed."
34 When Esau heard the words of his father,
he cried with an exceedingly great and bitter
cry, and said to his father, "Bless me—me
also, O my father!"
35 But he said, "Your brother came with deceit and has taken away your blessing."
36 And *Esau* said, "Is he not rightly named
Jacob? For he has supplanted me these two
times. He took away my birthright, and now
look, he has taken away my blessing!" And he
said, "Have you not reserved a blessing for
me?"
37 Then Isaac answered and said to Esau,
"Indeed I have made him your master, and all
his brethren I have given to him as servants;
with grain and wine I have sustained him.
What shall I do now for you, my son?"
38 And Esau said to his father, "Have you
only one blessing, my father? Bless me—me
also, O my father!" And Esau lifted up his
voice and wept.
39 Then Isaac his father answered and said
to him:

"Behold, your dwelling shall be of the
fatness of the earth,
And of the dew of heaven from
above.

40 By your sword you shall live,
And you shall serve your brother;
And it shall come to pass, when you
become restless,

That you shall break his yoke from your
neck."

Jacob Escapes from Esau

41 So Esau hated Jacob because of the blessing with which his father blessed him, and
Esau said in his heart, "The days of mourning
for my father are at hand; then I will kill my
brother Jacob."
42 And the words of Esau her older son were
told to Rebekah. So she sent and called Jacob
her younger son, and said to him, "Surely
your brother Esau comforts himself concerning you *by intending* to kill you.
43 "Now therefore, my son, obey my voice:
arise, flee to my brother Laban in Haran.
44 "And stay with him a few days, until your
brother's fury turns away,
45 "until your brother's anger turns away
from you, and he forgets what you have done
to him; then I will send and bring you from
there. Why should I be bereaved also of you
both in one day?"
46 And Rebekah said to Isaac, "I am weary of
my life because of the daughters of Heth; if
Jacob takes a wife of the daughters of Heth,
like these *who are* the daughters of the land,
what good will my life be to me?"

28 Then Isaac called Jacob and blessed
him, and charged him, and said to him:
"You shall not take a wife from the daughters
of Canaan.
2 "Arise, go to Padan Aram, to the house of
Bethuel your mother's father; and take yourself a wife from there of the daughters of
Laban your mother's brother.

3 "May God Almighty bless you,
And make you fruitful and multiply you,
That you may be an assembly of peoples;
4 And give you the blessing of Abraham,
To you and your descendants with you,
That you may inherit the land
In which you are a stranger,
Which God gave to Abraham."

5 So Isaac sent Jacob away, and he went to
Padan Aram, to Laban the son of Bethuel the
Syrian, the brother of Rebekah, the mother of
Jacob and Esau.

Esau Marries Mahalath

6 Esau saw that Isaac had blessed Jacob
and sent him away to Padan Aram to take
himself a wife from there, *and that* as he
blessed him he gave him a charge, saying,
"You shall not take a wife from the daughters
of Canaan,"
7 and that Jacob had obeyed his father and
his mother and had gone to Padan Aram.
8 Also Esau saw that the daughters of
Canaan did not please his father Isaac.
9 So Esau went to Ishmael and took Mahalath the daughter of Ishmael, Abraham's son,
the sister of Nebajoth, to be his wife in addition to the wives he had.

Jacob's Vow at Bethel

10 Now Jacob went out from Beersheba and
went toward Haran.
11 So he came to a certain place and stayed
there all night, because the sun had set. And
he took one of the stones of that place and put
it at his head, and he lay down in that place to
sleep.
12 Then he dreamed, and behold, a ladder
was set up on the earth, and its top reached to
heaven; and there the angels of God were ascending and descending on it.
13 And behold, the LORD stood above it and
said: "I *am* the LORD God of Abraham your father and the God of Isaac; the land on which
you lie I will give to you and your descendants.
14 "Also your descendants shall be as the
dust of the earth; you shall spread abroad to
the west and the east, to the north and the
south; and in you and in your seed all the
families of the earth shall be blessed.
15 "Behold, I *am* with you and will keep you
wherever you go, and will bring you back to
this land; for I will not leave you until I have
done what I have spoken to you."
16 Then Jacob awoke from his sleep and
said, "Surely the LORD is in this place, and I
did not know *it*."
17 And he was afraid and said, "How awesome *is* this place! This *is* none other than
the house of God, and this *is* the gate of
heaven!"
18 Then Jacob rose early in the morning, and

LIFE LESSONS

➤ 27:41 — *So Esau hated Jacob because the blessing with which his father blessed him . . . .*

Jacob knew little peace in his life until he learned not to *use* God to get a blessing (Gen. 27:20), but to *obey* God to receive a blessing.

➤ 28:9 — *So Esau went to Ishmael and took Mahalath the daughter of Ishmael . . . .*

By his several marriages, Esau demonstrated that there is a world of difference between outward compliance to gain favor, and inward desire to do what is right.

➤ 28:15 — *"Behold, I am with you and will keep you wherever you go, and will bring you back to this land; for I will not leave you until I have done what I have spoken to you."*

God will always stay with us and keep all His promises to us, even when we go through the storms of life. When we wonder if He's really there—He is!

took the stone that he had put at his head, set
it up as a pillar, and poured oil on top of it.
19 And he called the name of that place
Bethel;[a] but the name of that city had been
Luz previously.
20 Then Jacob made a vow, saying, "If God
will be with me, and keep me in this way that
I am going, and give me bread to eat and
clothing to put on,
21 "so that I come back to my father's house
in peace, then the LORD shall be my God.
22 "And this stone which I have set as a pillar
shall be God's house, and of all that You give
me I will surely give a tenth to You."

Jacob Meets Rachel

29 So Jacob went on his journey and came
to the land of the people of the East.
2 And he looked, and saw a well in the field;
and behold, there *were* three flocks of sheep
lying by it; for out of that well they watered
the flocks. A large stone *was* on the well's
mouth.
3 Now all the flocks would be gathered
there; and they would roll the stone from the
well's mouth, water the sheep, and put the
stone back in its place on the well's mouth.
4 And Jacob said to them, "My brethren,
where *are* you from?" And they said, "We *are*
from Haran."
5 Then he said to them, "Do you know
Laban the son of Nahor?" And they said, "We
know him."
6 So he said to them, "Is he well?" And they
said, "*He is* well. And look, his daughter Rachel is coming with the sheep."
7 Then he said, "Look, *it is* still high day; *it*
is not time for the cattle to be gathered together. Water the sheep, and go and feed
them."
8 But they said, "We cannot until all the
flocks are gathered together, and they have
rolled the stone from the well's mouth; then
we water the sheep."
9 Now while he was still speaking with
them, Rachel came with her father's sheep,
for she was a shepherdess.
10 And it came to pass, when Jacob saw Rachel the daughter of Laban his mother's
brother, and the sheep of Laban his mother's
brother, that Jacob went near and rolled the
stone from the well's mouth, and watered the
flock of Laban his mother's brother.
11 Then Jacob kissed Rachel, and lifted up
his voice and wept.
12 And Jacob told Rachel that he *was* her father's relative and that he *was* Rebekah's son.
So she ran and told her father.
13 Then it came to pass, when Laban heard
the report about Jacob his sister's son, that he
ran to meet him, and embraced him and
kissed him, and brought him to his house. So
he told Laban all these things.
14 And Laban said to him, "Surely you *are*
my bone and my flesh." And he stayed with
him for a month.

Jacob Marries Leah and Rachel

15 Then Laban said to Jacob, "Because you
are my relative, should you therefore serve
me for nothing? Tell me, what *should* your
wages *be*?"
16 Now Laban had two daughters: the name
of the elder *was* Leah, and the name of the
younger *was* Rachel.
17 Leah's eyes *were* delicate, but Rachel was
beautiful of form and appearance.
18 Now Jacob loved Rachel; so he said, "I will
serve you seven years for Rachel your
younger daughter."
19 And Laban said, "*It is* better that I give her
to you than that I should give her to another
man. Stay with me."
20 So Jacob served seven years for Rachel,
and they seemed *only* a few days to him because of the love he had for her.
21 Then Jacob said to Laban, "Give *me* my
wife, for my days are fulfilled, that I may go in
to her."
22 And Laban gathered together all the men
of the place and made a feast.
23 Now it came to pass in the evening, that he
took Leah his daughter and brought her to Jacob; and he went in to her.
24 And Laban gave his maid Zilpah to his
daughter Leah *as* a maid.
25 So it came to pass in the morning, that behold, it *was* Leah. And he said to Laban,
"What is this you have done to me? Was it not
for Rachel that I served you? Why then have
you deceived me?"
26 And Laban said, "It must not be done so in
our country, to give the younger before the
firstborn.
27 "Fulfill her week, and we will give you this
one also for the service which you will serve
with me still another seven years."
28 Then Jacob did so and fulfilled her week.
So he gave him his daughter Rachel as wife
also.
29 And Laban gave his maid Bilhah to his
daughter Rachel as a maid.
30 Then *Jacob* also went in to Rachel, and
he also loved Rachel more than Leah. And
he served with Laban still another seven
years.

The Children of Jacob

31 When the LORD saw that Leah *was* unloved, He opened her womb; but Rachel *was*
barren.
32 So Leah conceived and bore a son, and
she called his name Reuben;[a] for she said,
"The LORD has surely looked on my affliction.
Now therefore, my husband will love me."

28:19 [a]Literally *House of God* **29:32** [a]Literally *See, a Son*

33 Then she conceived again and bore a
son, and said, "Because the LORD has heard
that I *am* unloved, He has therefore given me
this *son* also." And she called his name
Simeon.[a]
34 She conceived again and bore a son, and
said, "Now this time my husband will become
attached to me, because I have borne him
three sons." Therefore his name was called
Levi.[a]
➤ 35 And she conceived again and bore a son,
and said, "Now I will praise the LORD." Therefore she called his name Judah.[a] Then she
stopped bearing.
30 Now when Rachel saw that she bore
Jacob no children, Rachel envied her
sister, and said to Jacob, "Give me children, or
else I die!"
➤ 2 And Jacob's anger was aroused against
Rachel, and he said, "*Am* I in the place of
God, who has withheld from you the fruit of
the womb?"
3 So she said, "Here is my maid Bilhah;
go in to her, and she will bear *a child* on
my knees, that I also may have children by
her."
4 Then she gave him Bilhah her maid as
wife, and Jacob went in to her.
5 And Bilhah conceived and bore Jacob a
son.
6 Then Rachel said, "God has judged my
case; and He has also heard my voice and
given me a son." Therefore she called his
name Dan.[a]
7 And Rachel's maid Bilhah conceived
again and bore Jacob a second son.
8 Then Rachel said, "With great wrestlings I
have wrestled with my sister, *and* indeed I
have prevailed." So she called his name
Naphtali.[a]
9 When Leah saw that she had stopped
bearing, she took Zilpah her maid and gave
her to Jacob as wife.
10 And Leah's maid Zilpah bore Jacob a son.
11 Then Leah said, "A troop comes!"[a] So she
called his name Gad.[b]
12 And Leah's maid Zilpah bore Jacob a second son.
13 Then Leah said, "I am happy, for the
daughters will call me blessed." So she called
his name Asher.[a]
14 Now Reuben went in the days of wheat
harvest and found mandrakes in the field,
and brought them to his mother Leah. Then
Rachel said to Leah, "Please give me *some* of
your son's mandrakes."
15 But she said to her, "*Is it* a small matter
that you have taken away my husband?
Would you take away my son's mandrakes
also?" And Rachel said, "Therefore he will
lie with you tonight for your son's mandrakes."
16 When Jacob came out of the field in the
evening, Leah went out to meet him and said,
"You must come in to me, for I have surely
hired you with my son's mandrakes." And he
lay with her that night.
17 And God listened to Leah, and she conceived and bore Jacob a fifth son.
18 Leah said, "God has given me my wages,
because I have given my maid to my husband." So she called his name Issachar.[a]
19 Then Leah conceived again and bore Jacob a sixth son.
20 And Leah said, "God has endowed me
with a good endowment; now my husband
will dwell with me, because I have borne
him six sons." So she called his name Zebulun.[a]
21 Afterward she bore a daughter, and called
her name Dinah.
22 Then God remembered Rachel, and God
listened to her and opened her womb.
23 And she conceived and bore a son, and
said, "God has taken away my reproach."
24 So she called his name Joseph,[a] and said,
"The LORD shall add to me another son."

Jacob's Agreement with Laban

25 And it came to pass, when Rachel had
borne Joseph, that Jacob said to Laban, "Send
me away, that I may go to my own place and
to my country.
26 "Give *me* my wives and my children for
whom I have served you, and let me go; for
you know my service which I have done
for you."

29:33 [a]Literally *Heard* **29:34** [a]Literally *Attached* **29:35** [a]Literally *Praise* **30:6** [a]Literally *Judge* **30:8** [a]Literally *My Wrestling* **30:11** [a]Following Qere, Syriac, and Targum; Kethib, Septuagint, and Vulgate read *in fortune*. [b]Literally *Troop* or *Fortune* **30:13** [a]Literally *Happy* **30:18** [a]Literally *Wages* **30:20** [a]Literally *Dwelling* **30:24** [a]Literally *He Will Add*

LIFE LESSONS

➤ 29:35 — *And she conceived again and bore a son, and said, "Now I will praise the LORD." Therefore she called his name Judah . . . .*

Leah hoped to find happiness, first in the love of her husband, then in the blessing of sons. But in the end she began to see that lasting contentment can be found only in an intimate relationship with God.

➤ 30:2 — *And Jacob's anger was aroused against Rachel, and he said, "Am I in the place of God, who has withheld from you the fruit of the womb?"*

When Rebekah tried and failed to have children, her husband, Isaac, prayed for her (Gen. 25:21). Abraham had done the same for Abimelech's household (Gen. 20:17). But Jacob had not yet learned to stand tall on his knees in prayer.

➤ 27 And Laban said to him, "Please *stay*, if I
have found favor in your eyes, *for* I have
learned by experience that the LORD has
blessed me for your sake."
28 Then he said, "Name me your wages, and
I will give *it*."
29 So *Jacob* said to him, "You know how I
have served you and how your livestock has
been with me.
30 "For what you had before I *came was* little,
and it has increased to a great amount; the LORD
has blessed you since my coming. And now,
when shall I also provide for my own house?"
31 So he said, "What shall I give you?" And
Jacob said, "You shall not give me anything. If
you will do this thing for me, I will again feed
and keep your flocks:
32 "Let me pass through all your flock today,
removing from there all the speckled and
spotted sheep, and all the brown ones among
the lambs, and the spotted and speckled
among the goats; and *these* shall be my wages.
33 "So my righteousness will answer for me
in time to come, when the subject of my
wages comes before you: every one that *is* not
speckled and spotted among the goats, and
brown among the lambs, will be considered
stolen, if *it is* with me."
34 And Laban said, "Oh, that it were according to your word!"
35 So he removed that day the male goats
that were speckled and spotted, all the female
goats that were speckled and spotted, every
one that had *some* white in it, and all the
brown ones among the lambs, and gave *them*
into the hand of his sons.
36 Then he put three days' journey between
himself and Jacob, and Jacob fed the rest of
Laban's flocks.
37 Now Jacob took for himself rods of green
poplar and of the almond and chestnut trees,
peeled white strips in them, and exposed the
white which *was* in the rods.
38 And the rods which he had peeled, he set
before the flocks in the gutters, in the watering troughs where the flocks came to drink,
so that they should conceive when they came
to drink.
39 So the flocks conceived before the rods,
and the flocks brought forth streaked, speckled, and spotted.
40 Then Jacob separated the lambs, and
made the flocks face toward the streaked and
all the brown in the flock of Laban; but he put
his own flocks by themselves and did not put
them with Laban's flock.
41 And it came to pass, whenever the
stronger livestock conceived, that Jacob
placed the rods before the eyes of the livestock in the gutters, that they might conceive
among the rods.
42 But when the flocks were feeble, he did
not put *them* in; so the feebler were Laban's
and the stronger Jacob's.
43 Thus the man became exceedingly prosperous, and had large flocks, female and male
servants, and camels and donkeys.

Jacob Flees from Laban

31 Now *Jacob* heard the words of Laban's
sons, saying, "Jacob has taken away all
that was our father's, and from what was our
father's he has acquired all this wealth."
2 And Jacob saw the countenance of Laban,
and indeed it *was* not *favorable* toward him
as before.
3 Then the LORD said to Jacob, "Return to
the land of your fathers and to your family,
and I will be with you."
4 So Jacob sent and called Rachel and Leah
to the field, to his flock,
5 and said to them, "I see your father's countenance, that it *is* not *favorable* toward me as
before; but the God of my father has been
with me.
6 "And you know that with all my might I
have served your father.
7 "Yet your father has deceived me and
changed my wages ten times, but God did not
allow him to hurt me.
8 "If he said thus: 'The speckled shall be
your wages,' then all the flocks bore speckled.
And if he said thus: 'The streaked shall be
your wages,' then all the flocks bore streaked.
9 "So God has taken away the livestock of
your father and given *them* to me.
10 "And it happened, at the time when the
flocks conceived, that I lifted my eyes and
saw in a dream, and behold, the rams which
leaped upon the flocks *were* streaked, speckled, and gray-spotted.
11 "Then the Angel of God spoke to me in a
dream, saying, 'Jacob.' And I said, 'Here I am.'
12 "And He said, 'Lift your eyes now and see,
all the rams which leap on the flocks *are*
streaked, speckled, and gray-spotted; for I
have seen all that Laban is doing to you.
13 "I *am* the God of Bethel, where you
anointed the pillar *and* where you made a
vow to Me. Now arise, get out of this land, and
return to the land of your family.'"
14 Then Rachel and Leah answered and said

LIFE LESSONS

➤ **30:27 — *And Laban said to him, "Please stay, if I have found favor in your eyes, for I have learned by experience that the LORD has blessed me for your sake."***

The blessing of God has a way of spilling over to touch others.

to him, "Is there still any portion or inheritance for us in our father's house?
15 "Are we not considered strangers by him? For he has sold us, and also completely consumed our money.
16 "For all these riches which God has taken from our father are *really* ours and our children's; now then, whatever God has said to you, do it."
17 Then Jacob rose and set his sons and his wives on camels.
18 And he carried away all his livestock and all his possessions which he had gained, his acquired livestock which he had gained in Padan Aram, to go to his father Isaac in the land of Canaan.
19 Now Laban had gone to shear his sheep, and Rachel had stolen the household idols that were her father's.
20 And Jacob stole away, unknown to Laban the Syrian, in that he did not tell him that he intended to flee.
21 So he fled with all that he had. He arose and crossed the river, and headed toward the mountains of Gilead.

Laban Pursues Jacob

22 And Laban was told on the third day that Jacob had fled.
23 Then he took his brethren with him and pursued him for seven days' journey, and he overtook him in the mountains of Gilead.
24 But God had come to Laban the Syrian in a dream by night, and said to him, "Be careful that you speak to Jacob neither good nor bad."
25 So Laban overtook Jacob. Now Jacob had pitched his tent in the mountains, and Laban with his brethren pitched in the mountains of Gilead.
26 And Laban said to Jacob: "What have you done, that you have stolen away unknown to me, and carried away my daughters like captives *taken* with the sword?
27 "Why did you flee away secretly, and steal away from me, and not tell me; for I might have sent you away with joy and songs, with timbrel and harp?
28 "And you did not allow me to kiss my sons and my daughters. Now you have done foolishly in so doing.
➤ 29 "It is in my power to do you harm, but the God of your father spoke to me last night, saying, 'Be careful that you speak to Jacob neither good nor bad.'
30 "And now you have surely gone because you greatly long for your father's house, *but* why did you steal my gods?"
31 Then Jacob answered and said to Laban, "Because I was afraid, for I said, 'Perhaps you would take your daughters from me by force.'
32 "With whomever you find your gods, do not let him live. In the presence of our brethren, identify what I have of yours and take *it* with you." For Jacob did not know that Rachel had stolen them.
33 And Laban went into Jacob's tent, into Leah's tent, and into the two maids' tents, but he did not find *them*. Then he went out of Leah's tent and entered Rachel's tent.
34 Now Rachel had taken the household idols, put them in the camel's saddle, and sat on them. And Laban searched all about the tent but did not find *them*.
35 And she said to her father, "Let it not displease my lord that I cannot rise before you, for the manner of women *is* with me." And he searched but did not find the household idols.
36 Then Jacob was angry and rebuked Laban, and Jacob answered and said to Laban: "What *is* my trespass? What *is* my sin, that you have so hotly pursued me?
37 "Although you have searched all my things, what part of your household things have you found? Set *it* here before my brethren and your brethren, that they may judge between us both!
38 "These twenty years I *have been* with you; your ewes and your female goats have not miscarried their young, and I have not eaten the rams of your flock.
39 "That which was torn *by beasts* I did not bring to you; I bore the loss of it. You required it from my hand, *whether* stolen by day or stolen by night.
40 "*There* I was! In the day the drought consumed me, and the frost by night, and my sleep departed from my eyes.
41 "Thus I have been in your house twenty years; I served you fourteen years for your two daughters, and six years for your flock, and you have changed my wages ten times.
42 "Unless the God of my father, the God of ➤

LIFE LESSONS

➤ 31:29 — *"It is in my power to do you harm, but the God of your father spoke to me last night, saying, 'Be careful that you speak to Jacob neither good nor bad.'"*

Laban did not know the Lord—he knew him only as the God of Isaac's father—and yet the Lord protected Jacob from the harm Laban wanted to do to him. We serve a sovereign God!

➤ 31:42 — *"Unless the God of my father, the God of Abraham and the Fear of Isaac, had been with me, surely now you would have sent me away empty-handed. God has seen my affliction and the labor of my hands, and rebuked you last night."*

Jacob was finally beginning to understand that scheming for blessings cannot compete with God-given blessings.

Abraham and the Fear of Isaac, had been with
me, surely now you would have sent me away
empty-handed. God has seen my affliction
and the labor of my hands, and rebuked *you*
last night."

Laban's Covenant with Jacob

43 And Laban answered and said to Jacob,
"*These* daughters *are* my daughters, and
these children *are* my children, and *this* flock
is my flock; all that you see *is* mine. But what
can I do this day to these my daughters or to
their children whom they have borne?
44 "Now therefore, come, let us make a covenant, you and I, and let it be a witness between you and me."
45 So Jacob took a stone and set it up *as* a
pillar.
46 Then Jacob said to his brethren, "Gather
stones." And they took stones and made a
heap, and they ate there on the heap.
47 Laban called it Jegar Sahadutha,[a] but Jacob called it Galeed.[b]
48 And Laban said, "This heap *is* a witness
between you and me this day." Therefore its
name was called Galeed,
49 also Mizpah,[a] because he said, "May the
LORD watch between you and me when we
are absent one from another.
50 "If you afflict my daughters, or if you take
other wives besides my daughters, *although*
no man *is* with us—see, God *is* witness between you and me!"
51 Then Laban said to Jacob, "Here is this
heap and here is *this* pillar, which I have
placed between you and me.
52 "This heap *is* a witness, and *this* pillar *is* a
witness, that I will not pass beyond this heap
to you, and you will not pass beyond this heap
and this pillar to me, for harm.
➤ 53 "The God of Abraham, the God of Nahor,
and the God of their father judge between us."
And Jacob swore by the Fear of his father
Isaac.
54 Then Jacob offered a sacrifice on the
mountain, and called his brethren to eat
bread. And they ate bread and stayed all night
on the mountain.
55 And early in the morning Laban arose,
and kissed his sons and daughters and
blessed them. Then Laban departed and returned to his place.

Esau Comes to Meet Jacob

32 So Jacob went on his way, and the
angels of God met him.
2 When Jacob saw them, he said, "This *is*
God's camp." And he called the name of that
place Mahanaim.[a]
3 Then Jacob sent messengers before him to
Esau his brother in the land of Seir, the country of Edom.
4 And he commanded them, saying, "Speak
thus to my lord Esau, 'Thus your servant Jacob says: "I have dwelt with Laban and stayed
there until now.
5 "I have oxen, donkeys, flocks, and male
and female servants; and I have sent to tell
my lord, that I may find favor in your sight." ' "
6 Then the messengers returned to Jacob,
saying, "We came to your brother Esau, and
he also is coming to meet you, and four hundred men *are* with him."
7 So Jacob was greatly afraid and distressed; and he divided the people that *were*
with him, and the flocks and herds and
camels, into two companies.
8 And he said, "If Esau comes to the one
company and attacks it, then the other company which is left will escape."
9 Then Jacob said, "O God of my father ➤
Abraham and God of my father Isaac, the
LORD who said to me, 'Return to your country
and to your family, and I will deal well with
you':
10 "I am not worthy of the least of all the
mercies and of all the truth which You have
shown Your servant; for I crossed over this
Jordan with my staff, and now I have become
two companies.
11 "Deliver me, I pray, from the hand of my
brother, from the hand of Esau; for I fear him,
lest he come and attack me *and* the mother
with the children.
12 "For You said, 'I will surely treat you well,
and make your descendants as the sand of the
sea, which cannot be numbered for multitude.' "
13 So he lodged there that same night, and
took what came to his hand as a present for
Esau his brother:

31:47 [a]Literally, in Aramaic, *Heap of Witness* [b]Literally, in Hebrew, *Heap of Witness* **31:49** [a]Literally *Watch* **32:2** [a]Literally *Double Camp*

LIFE LESSONS

➤ ***31:53 — The God of Abraham, the God of Nahor, and the God of their father judge between us." And Jacob swore by the Fear of his father Isaac.***

When the passage calls God "the fear of Isaac" (see also Gen. 31:42), it declares that God is not only loving, but just; not only gentle, but strong—what Romans 11:22 calls the "goodness and severity" of God.

➤ ***32:9 — Then Jacob said, "O God of my father Abraham and God of my father Isaac, the LORD who said to me . . . ."***

Jacob had learned to pray effectively by basing his petitions on the promises of God. He knew he could win this battle only through prayer.

14 two hundred female goats and twenty male goats, two hundred ewes and twenty rams,
15 thirty milk camels with their colts, forty cows and ten bulls, twenty female donkeys and ten foals.
16 Then he delivered *them* to the hand of his servants, every drove by itself, and said to his servants, "Pass over before me, and put some distance between successive droves."
17 And he commanded the first one, saying, "When Esau my brother meets you and asks you, saying, 'To whom do you belong, and where are you going? Whose *are* these in front of you?'
18 "then you shall say, 'They *are* your servant Jacob's. It *is* a present sent to my lord Esau; and behold, he also *is* behind us.'"
19 So he commanded the second, the third, and all who followed the droves, saying, "In this manner you shall speak to Esau when you find him;
20 "and also say, 'Behold, your servant Jacob *is* behind us.'" For he said, "I will appease him with the present that goes before me, and afterward I will see his face; perhaps he will accept me."
21 So the present went on over before him, but he himself lodged that night in the camp.

Wrestling with God
22 And he arose that night and took his two wives, his two female servants, and his eleven sons, and crossed over the ford of Jabbok.
23 He took them, sent them over the brook, and sent over what he had.
24 Then Jacob was left alone; and a Man wrestled with him until the breaking of day.
25 Now when He saw that He did not prevail against him, He touched the socket of his hip; and the socket of Jacob's hip was out of joint as He wrestled with him.
26 And He said, "Let Me go, for the day breaks." But he said, "I will not let You go unless You bless me!"
27 So He said to him, "What *is* your name?" He said, "Jacob."
28 And He said, "Your name shall no longer be called Jacob, but Israel;[a] for you have struggled with God and with men, and have prevailed."
29 Then Jacob asked, saying, "Tell *me* Your name, I pray." And He said, "Why *is* it *that* you ask about My name?" And He blessed him there.

Life Examples:

JACOB

Wrestling with God

GEN. 32:24–32

The story of Jacob alternately comforts and confounds. For while we could look upon many of his decisions with contempt—and even wonder why God would so favor such a man—it equally reassures us to realize that the God who extended grace to Jacob also extends it to us.

In a famous episode described in Genesis 32, Jacob wrestles with a powerful stranger that he later concludes is God. Some scholars believe that Jacob wrestled with the pre-incarnate Christ; others consider the opponent an angel. Still others suggest that Jacob wrangled with God only in prayer. In any event, the nation Israel received its name from Jacob, whom God renamed "Israel," meaning, "he struggles with God."

Despite his many failings, weaknesses, and subsequent sorrows, Jacob was elected and loved of God (Mal. 1:2; Rom. 9:10–13). And through his strange wrestling match, he provides us with a model of the effort required for effective prayer (Col. 4:12).

See the Life Principles Index for further study:
8. Fight all your battles on your knees and you win every time.

30 So Jacob called the name of the place Peniel:[a] "For I have seen God face to face, and my life is preserved."
31 Just as he crossed over Penuel[a] the sun rose on him, and he limped on his hip.
32 Therefore to this day the children of Israel

32:28 [a]Literally *Prince with God* **32:30** [a]Literally *Face of God*
32:31 [a]Same as *Peniel,* verse 30

LIFE LESSONS

➤ ***32:31 — Just as he crossed over Penuel the sun rose on him, and he limped on his hip.***

Jacob's wrestling match left him with a painful limp, but also with a better understanding of God. God renamed him Israel, meaning "he struggles with God," or perhaps "a prince with God," and because of this painful encounter, Jacob took a great spiritual leap forward.

do not eat the muscle that shrank, which *is* on
the hip socket, because He touched the socket
of Jacob's hip in the muscle that shrank.

Jacob and Esau Meet

33 Now Jacob lifted his eyes and looked,
and there, Esau was coming, and with
him were four hundred men. So he divided
the children among Leah, Rachel, and the two
maidservants.
2 And he put the maidservants and their
children in front, Leah and her children behind, and Rachel and Joseph last.
3 Then he crossed over before them and
bowed himself to the ground seven times,
until he came near to his brother.
4 But Esau ran to meet him, and embraced
him, and fell on his neck and kissed him, and
they wept.
5 And he lifted his eyes and saw the women
and children, and said, "Who *are* these with
you?" So he said, "The children whom God
has graciously given your servant."
6 Then the maidservants came near, they
and their children, and bowed down.
7 And Leah also came near with her children, and they bowed down. Afterward Joseph and Rachel came near, and they bowed
down.
8 Then Esau said, "What *do* you *mean by* all
this company which I met?" And he said,
"*These are* to find favor in the sight of my
lord."
9 But Esau said, "I have enough, my brother;
keep what you have for yourself."
10 And Jacob said, "No, please, if I have
now found favor in your sight, then receive
my present from my hand, inasmuch as I
have seen your face as though I had seen
the face of God, and you were pleased with
me.
➤ 11 "Please, take my blessing that is brought
to you, because God has dealt graciously with
me, and because I have enough." So he urged
him, and he took *it*.
12 Then Esau said, "Let us take our journey;
let us go, and I will go before you."
13 But Jacob said to him, "My lord knows
that the children *are* weak, and the flocks and
herds which are nursing *are* with me. And if
the men should drive them hard one day, all
the flock will die.
14 "Please let my lord go on ahead before his
servant. I will lead on slowly at a pace which
the livestock that go before me, and the children, are able to endure, until I come to my
lord in Seir."
15 And Esau said, "Now let me leave with
you *some* of the people who *are* with me."
But he said, "What need is there? Let me find
favor in the sight of my lord."
16 So Esau returned that day on his way to
Seir.
17 And Jacob journeyed to Succoth, built
himself a house, and made booths for his livestock. Therefore the name of the place is
called Succoth.[a]

Jacob Comes to Canaan

18 Then Jacob came safely to the city of
Shechem, which *is* in the land of Canaan,
when he came from Padan Aram; and he
pitched his tent before the city.
19 And he bought the parcel of land, where
he had pitched his tent, from the children of
Hamor, Shechem's father, for one hundred
pieces of money.
20 Then he erected an altar there and called
it El Elohe Israel.[a]

The Dinah Incident

34 Now Dinah the daughter of Leah,
whom she had borne to Jacob, went out
to see the daughters of the land.
2 And when Shechem the son of Hamor the
Hivite, prince of the country, saw her, he took
her and lay with her, and violated her.
3 His soul was strongly attracted to Dinah
the daughter of Jacob, and he loved the young
woman and spoke kindly to the young
woman.
4 So Shechem spoke to his father Hamor,
saying, "Get me this young woman as a wife."
5 And Jacob heard that he had defiled
Dinah his daughter. Now his sons were with
his livestock in the field; so Jacob held his
peace until they came.
6 Then Hamor the father of Shechem went
out to Jacob to speak with him.
7 And the sons of Jacob came in from the
field when they heard *it*; and the men were
grieved and very angry, because he had done
a disgraceful thing in Israel by lying with Jacob's daughter, a thing which ought not to be
done.
8 But Hamor spoke with them, saying, "The
soul of my son Shechem longs for your
daughter. Please give her to him as a wife.

33:17 [a]Literally *Booths* **33:20** [a]Literally *God, the God of Israel*

LIFE LESSONS

➤ 33:11 — *"Please, take my blessing that is brought to you, because God has dealt graciously with me, and because I have enough." So he urged him, and he took it.*

We should be glad that God does not deal with us on the basis of our own righteousness, but on the basis of His boundless grace. He blesses us because of who He is, not who we are.

9 "And make marriages with us; give your
daughters to us, and take our daughters to
yourselves.
10 "So you shall dwell with us, and the land
shall be before you. Dwell and trade in it, and
acquire possessions for yourselves in it."
11 Then Shechem said to her father and her
brothers, "Let me find favor in your eyes, and
whatever you say to me I will give.
12 "Ask me ever so much dowry and gift, and
I will give according to what you say to me;
but give me the young woman as a wife."
13 But the sons of Jacob answered Shechem
and Hamor his father, and spoke deceitfully,
because he had defiled Dinah their sister.
14 And they said to them, "We cannot do this
thing, to give our sister to one who is uncircumcised, for that *would be* a reproach to us.
15 "But on this *condition* we will consent to
you: If you will become as we *are,* if every
male of you is circumcised,
16 "then we will give our daughters to you,
and we will take your daughters to us; and we
will dwell with you, and we will become one
people.
17 "But if you will not heed us and be circumcised, then we will take our daughter and
be gone."
18 And their words pleased Hamor and
Shechem, Hamor's son.
19 So the young man did not delay to do the
thing, because he delighted in Jacob's daughter. He *was* more honorable than all the
household of his father.
20 And Hamor and Shechem his son came to
the gate of their city, and spoke with the men
of their city, saying:
21 "These men *are* at peace with us. Therefore let them dwell in the land and trade in it.
For indeed the land *is* large enough for them.
Let us take their daughters to us as wives, and
let us give them our daughters.
22 "Only on this *condition* will the men consent to dwell with us, to be one people: if
every male among us is circumcised as they
are circumcised.
23 "*Will* not their livestock, their property,
and every animal of theirs *be* ours? Only
let us consent to them, and they will dwell
with us."
24 And all who went out of the gate of his city
heeded Hamor and Shechem his son; every
male was circumcised, all who went out of the
gate of his city.
25 Now it came to pass on the third day,
when they were in pain, that two of the sons
of Jacob, Simeon and Levi, Dinah's brothers,
each took his sword and came boldly upon
the city and killed all the males.
26 And they killed Hamor and Shechem his
son with the edge of the sword, and took
Dinah from Shechem's house, and went out.
27 The sons of Jacob came upon the slain,
and plundered the city, because their sister
had been defiled.
28 They took their sheep, their oxen, and
their donkeys, what *was* in the city and what
was in the field,
29 and all their wealth. All their little ones
and their wives they took captive; and they
plundered even all that *was* in the houses.
30 Then Jacob said to Simeon and Levi, "You
have troubled me by making me obnoxious
among the inhabitants of the land, among the
Canaanites and the Perizzites; and since I *am*
few in number, they will gather themselves
together against me and kill me. I shall be destroyed, my household and I."
31 But they said, "Should he treat our sister
like a harlot?"

Jacob's Return to Bethel

35 Then God said to Jacob, "Arise, go up
to Bethel and dwell there; and make an
altar there to God, who appeared to you
when you fled from the face of Esau your
brother."
2 And Jacob said to his household and to all
who *were* with him, "Put away the foreign
gods that *are* among you, purify yourselves,
and change your garments.
3 "Then let us arise and go up to Bethel; and
I will make an altar there to God, who answered me in the day of my distress and has
been with me in the way which I have gone."
4 So they gave Jacob all the foreign gods
which *were* in their hands, and the earrings
which *were* in their ears; and Jacob hid them
under the terebinth tree which *was* by
Shechem.
5 And they journeyed, and the terror of God
was upon the cities that *were* all around them,
and they did not pursue the sons of Jacob.
6 So Jacob came to Luz (that *is,* Bethel),

LIFE LESSONS

➤ 35:2 — ***And Jacob said to his household and to all who were with him, "Put away the foreign gods that are among you, purify yourselves, and change your garments.***

God calls for our exclusive allegiance, not allegiance to God *and* something or someone else, but allegiance to God alone. He will accept no other kind of loyalty.

➤ 35:5 — ***And they journeyed, and the terror of God was upon the cities that were all around them, and they did not pursue the sons of Jacob.***

God knows how to use even a feeling of terror to protect His people.

which *is* in the land of Canaan, he and all the
people who *were* with him.
7 And he built an altar there and called the
place El Bethel,[a] because there God appeared
to him when he fled from the face of his
brother.
8 Now Deborah, Rebekah's nurse, died, and
she was buried below Bethel under the terebinth tree. So the name of it was called Allon
Bachuth.[a]
9 Then God appeared to Jacob again, when
he came from Padan Aram, and blessed him.
10 And God said to him, "Your name *is* Jacob;
your name shall not be called Jacob anymore,
but Israel shall be your name." So He called
his name Israel.
11 Also God said to him: "I *am* God Almighty.
Be fruitful and multiply; a nation and a company of nations shall proceed from you, and
kings shall come from your body.
12 "The land which I gave Abraham and
Isaac I give to you; and to your descendants
after you I give this land."
13 Then God went up from him in the place
where He talked with him.
14 So Jacob set up a pillar in the place where
He talked with him, a pillar of stone; and he
poured a drink offering on it, and he poured
oil on it.
15 And Jacob called the name of the place
where God spoke with him, Bethel.

Death of Rachel

16 Then they journeyed from Bethel. And
when there was but a little distance to go to
Ephrath, Rachel labored *in childbirth,* and
she had hard labor.
17 Now it came to pass, when she was in
hard labor, that the midwife said to her, "Do
not fear; you will have this son also."
18 And so it was, as her soul was departing
(for she died), that she called his name Ben-
Oni;[a] but his father called him Benjamin.[b]
19 So Rachel died and was buried on the way
to Ephrath (that *is,* Bethlehem).
20 And Jacob set a pillar on her grave, which
is the pillar of Rachel's grave to this day.
21 Then Israel journeyed and pitched his tent
beyond the tower of Eder.
22 And it happened, when Israel dwelt in
that land, that Reuben went and lay with Bilhah his father's concubine; and Israel heard
about it.

Jacob's Twelve Sons

Now the sons of Jacob were twelve:
23 the sons of Leah *were* Reuben, Jacob's
firstborn, and Simeon, Levi, Judah, Issachar,
and Zebulun;
24 the sons of Rachel *were* Joseph and Benjamin;
25 the sons of Bilhah, Rachel's maidservant,
were Dan and Naphtali;
26 and the sons of Zilpah, Leah's maidservant, *were* Gad and Asher. These *were* the
sons of Jacob who were born to him in Padan
Aram.

Death of Isaac

27 Then Jacob came to his father Isaac at
Mamre, or Kirjath Arba[a] (that *is,* Hebron),
where Abraham and Isaac had dwelt.
28 Now the days of Isaac were one hundred
and eighty years.
29 So Isaac breathed his last and died, and
was gathered to his people, *being* old and full
of days. And his sons Esau and Jacob buried
him.

The Family of Esau

36 Now this *is* the genealogy of Esau, who
is Edom.
2 Esau took his wives from the daughters of
Canaan: Adah the daughter of Elon the Hittite; Aholibamah the daughter of Anah, the
daughter of Zibeon the Hivite;
3 and Basemath, Ishmael's daughter, sister
of Nebajoth.
4 Now Adah bore Eliphaz to Esau, and
Basemath bore Reuel.
5 And Aholibamah bore Jeush, Jaalam, and
Korah. These *were* the sons of Esau who were
born to him in the land of Canaan.
6 Then Esau took his wives, his sons, his
daughters, and all the persons of his household, his cattle and all his animals, and all his
goods which he had gained in the land of
Canaan, and went to a country away from the
presence of his brother Jacob.
7 For their possessions were too great for
them to dwell together, and the land where
they were strangers could not support them
because of their livestock.
8 So Esau dwelt in Mount Seir. Esau *is*
Edom.
9 And this *is* the genealogy of Esau the father of the Edomites in Mount Seir.
10 These *were* the names of Esau's sons:
Eliphaz the son of Adah the wife of Esau, and
Reuel the son of Basemath the wife of Esau.
11 And the sons of Eliphaz were Teman,
Omar, Zepho,[a] Gatam, and Kenaz.
12 Now Timna was the concubine of Eliphaz,
Esau's son, and she bore Amalek to Eliphaz.
These *were* the sons of Adah, Esau's wife.
13 These *were* the sons of Reuel: Nahath,
Zerah, Shammah, and Mizzah. These were
the sons of Basemath, Esau's wife.
14 These were the sons of Aholibamah,
Esau's wife, the daughter of Anah, the daugh-
ter of Zibeon. And she bore to Esau: Jeush,
Jaalam, and Korah.

35:7 [a]Literally *God of the House of God* **35:8** [a]Literally *Terebinth of Weeping* **35:18** [a]Literally *Son of My Sorrow* [b]Literally *Son of the Right Hand* **35:27** [a]Literally *Town of Arba* **36:11** [a]Spelled *Zephi* in 1 Chronicles 1:36

The Chiefs of Edom

15 These *were* the chiefs of the sons of Esau. The sons of Eliphaz, the firstborn *son* of Esau, were Chief Teman, Chief Omar, Chief Zepho, Chief Kenaz,
16 Chief Korah,[a] Chief Gatam, *and* Chief Amalek. These *were* the chiefs of Eliphaz in the land of Edom. They *were* the sons of Adah.
17 These *were* the sons of Reuel, Esau's son: Chief Nahath, Chief Zerah, Chief Shammah, and Chief Mizzah. These *were* the chiefs of Reuel in the land of Edom. These *were* the sons of Basemath, Esau's wife.
18 And these *were* the sons of Aholibamah, Esau's wife: Chief Jeush, Chief Jaalam, and Chief Korah. These *were* the chiefs *who descended* from Aholibamah, Esau's wife, the daughter of Anah.
19 These *were* the sons of Esau, who is Edom, and these *were* their chiefs.

The Sons of Seir

20 These *were* the sons of Seir the Horite who inhabited the land: Lotan, Shobal, Zibeon, Anah,
21 Dishon, Ezer, and Dishan. These *were* the chiefs of the Horites, the sons of Seir, in the land of Edom.
22 And the sons of Lotan were Hori and Hemam.[a] Lotan's sister *was* Timna.
23 These *were* the sons of Shobal: Alvan,[a] Manahath, Ebal, Shepho,[b] and Onam.
24 These *were* the sons of Zibeon: both Ajah and Anah. This *was the* Anah who found the water[a] in the wilderness as he pastured the donkeys of his father Zibeon.
25 These *were* the children of Anah: Dishon and Aholibamah the daughter of Anah.
26 These *were* the sons of Dishon:[a] Hemdan,[b] Eshban, Ithran, and Cheran.
27 These *were* the sons of Ezer: Bilhan, Zaavan, and Akan.[a]
28 These *were* the sons of Dishan: Uz and Aran.
29 These *were* the chiefs of the Horites: Chief Lotan, Chief Shobal, Chief Zibeon, Chief Anah,
30 Chief Dishon, Chief Ezer, and Chief Dishan. These *were* the chiefs of the Horites, according to their chiefs in the land of Seir.

The Kings of Edom

31 Now these *were* the kings who reigned in the land of Edom before any king reigned over the children of Israel:
32 Bela the son of Beor reigned in Edom, and the name of his city *was* Dinhabah.
33 And when Bela died, Jobab the son of Zerah of Bozrah reigned in his place.
34 When Jobab died, Husham of the land of the Temanites reigned in his place.
35 And when Husham died, Hadad the son of Bedad, who attacked Midian in the field of Moab, reigned in his place. And the name of his city *was* Avith.
36 When Hadad died, Samlah of Masrekah reigned in his place.
37 And when Samlah died, Saul of Rehoboth-*by*-the-River reigned in his place.
38 When Saul died, Baal-Hanan the son of Achbor reigned in his place.
39 And when Baal-Hanan the son of Achbor died, Hadar[a] reigned in his place; and the name of his city *was* Pau.[b] His wife's name *was* Mehetabel, the daughter of Matred, the daughter of Mezahab.

The Chiefs of Esau

40 And these *were* the names of the chiefs of Esau, according to their families and their places, by their names: Chief Timnah, Chief Alvah,[a] Chief Jetheth,
41 Chief Aholibamah, Chief Elah, Chief Pinon,
42 Chief Kenaz, Chief Teman, Chief Mibzar,
43 Chief Magdiel, and Chief Iram. These *were* the chiefs of Edom, according to their dwelling places in the land of their possession. Esau *was* the father of the Edomites.

Joseph Dreams of Greatness

37 Now Jacob dwelt in the land where his father was a stranger, in the land of Canaan.
2 This *is* the history of Jacob. Joseph, *being* seventeen years old, was feeding the flock with his brothers. And the lad *was* with the sons of Bilhah and the sons of Zilpah, his father's wives; and Joseph brought a bad report of them to his father.
3 Now Israel loved Joseph more than all his children, because he *was* the son of his old age. Also he made him a tunic of *many* colors.
4 But when his brothers saw that their father loved him more than all his brothers, they hated him and could not speak peaceably to him.
5 Now Joseph had a dream, and he told *it* to his brothers; and they hated him even more.
6 So he said to them, "Please hear this dream which I have dreamed:
7 "There we were, binding sheaves in the field. Then behold, my sheaf arose and also stood upright; and indeed your sheaves stood all around and bowed down to my sheaf."
8 And his brothers said to him, "Shall you

36:16 [a]Samaritan Pentateuch omits *Chief Korah.* **36:22** [a]Spelled *Homam* in 1 Chronicles 1:39 **36:23** [a]Spelled *Alian* in 1 Chronicles 1:40 [b]Spelled *Shephi* in 1 Chronicles 1:40
36:24 [a]Following Masoretic Text and Vulgate (*hot springs*); Septuagint reads *Jamin;* Targum reads *mighty men;* Talmud interprets as *mules.* **36:26** [a]Hebrew *Dishan* [b]Spelled *Hamran* in 1 Chronicles 1:41 **36:27** [a]Spelled *Jaakan* in 1 Chronicles 1:42
36:39 [a]Spelled *Hadad* in Samaritan Pentateuch, Syriac, and 1 Chronicles 1:50 [b]Spelled *Pai* in 1 Chronicles 1:50
36:40 [a]Spelled *Aliah* in 1 Chronicles 1:51

indeed reign over us? Or shall you indeed
have dominion over us?" So they hated him
even more for his dreams and for his words.
9 Then he dreamed still another dream and
told it to his brothers, and said, "Look, I have
dreamed another dream. And this time, the
sun, the moon, and the eleven stars bowed
down to me."
10 So he told *it* to his father and his brothers;
and his father rebuked him and said to him,
"What *is* this dream that you have dreamed?
Shall your mother and I and your brothers indeed come to bow down to the earth before
you?"
11 And his brothers envied him, but his father kept the matter *in mind.*

Joseph Sold by His Brothers

12 Then his brothers went to feed their father's flock in Shechem.
13 And Israel said to Joseph, "Are not your
brothers feeding *the flock* in Shechem?
Come, I will send you to them." So he said to
him, "Here I am."
14 Then he said to him, "Please go and see if
it is well with your brothers and well with the
flocks, and bring back word to me." So he
sent him out of the Valley of Hebron, and he
went to Shechem.
15 Now a certain man found him, and there
he was, wandering in the field. And the man
asked him, saying, "What are you seeking?"
16 So he said, "I am seeking my brothers.
Please tell me where they are feeding *their
flocks.*"
17 And the man said, "They have departed
from here, for I heard them say, 'Let us go to
Dothan.'" So Joseph went after his brothers
and found them in Dothan.
18 Now when they saw him afar off, even before he came near them, they conspired
against him to kill him.
19 Then they said to one another, "Look, this
dreamer is coming!
20 "Come therefore, let us now kill him and
cast him into some pit; and we shall say,
'Some wild beast has devoured him.' We shall
see what will become of his dreams!"
21 But Reuben heard *it,* and he delivered him
out of their hands, and said, "Let us not kill
him."
22 And Reuben said to them, "Shed no blood,
but cast him into this pit which *is* in the
wilderness, and do not lay a hand on him"—
that he might deliver him out of their hands,
and bring him back to his father.
23 So it came to pass, when Joseph had come
to his brothers, that they stripped Joseph *of*
his tunic, the tunic of *many* colors that *was* on
him.
24 Then they took him and cast him into a
pit. And the pit *was* empty; *there was* no
water in it.
25 And they sat down to eat a meal. Then
they lifted their eyes and looked, and there
was a company of Ishmaelites, coming from
Gilead with their camels, bearing spices,
balm, and myrrh, on their way to carry *them*
down to Egypt.
26 So Judah said to his brothers, "What profit
is there if we kill our brother and conceal his
blood?
27 "Come and let us sell him to the Ishmaelites, and let not our hand be upon him,
for he *is* our brother *and* our flesh." And his
brothers listened.
28 Then Midianite traders passed by; so *the
brothers* pulled Joseph up and lifted him out
of the pit, and sold him to the Ishmaelites for
twenty *shekels* of silver. And they took Joseph
to Egypt.
29 Then Reuben returned to the pit, and indeed Joseph *was* not in the pit; and he tore his
clothes.
30 And he returned to his brothers and said,
"The lad *is* no *more;* and I, where shall I go?"
31 So they took Joseph's tunic, killed a kid of
the goats, and dipped the tunic in the blood.
32 Then they sent the tunic of *many* colors,
and they brought *it* to their father and said,
"We have found this. Do you know whether it
is your son's tunic or not?"
33 And he recognized it and said, "*It is* my
son's tunic. A wild beast has devoured him.
Without doubt Joseph is torn to pieces."
34 Then Jacob tore his clothes, put sackcloth
on his waist, and mourned for his son many
days.
35 And all his sons and all his daughters
arose to comfort him; but he refused to be
comforted, and he said, "For I shall go down
into the grave to my son in mourning." Thus
his father wept for him.
36 Now the Midianites[a] had sold him in
Egypt to Potiphar, an officer of Pharaoh *and*
captain of the guard.

Judah and Tamar

38 It came to pass at that time that Judah
departed from his brothers, and visited
a certain Adullamite whose name *was* Hirah.
2 And Judah saw there a daughter of a certain Canaanite whose name *was* Shua, and he
married her and went in to her.
3 So she conceived and bore a son, and he
called his name Er.
4 She conceived again and bore a son, and
she called his name Onan.
5 And she conceived yet again and bore a
son, and called his name Shelah. He was at
Chezib when she bore him.
6 Then Judah took a wife for Er his firstborn, and her name *was* Tamar.
7 But Er, Judah's firstborn, was wicked in
the sight of the LORD, and the LORD killed
him.

37:36 [a]Masoretic Text reads *Medanites.*

8 And Judah said to Onan, “Go in to your brother’s wife and marry her, and raise up an heir to your brother.”

9 But Onan knew that the heir would not be his; and it came to pass, when he went in to his brother’s wife, that he emitted on the ground, lest he should give an heir to his brother.

➤ 10 And the thing which he did displeased the LORD; therefore He killed him also.

11 Then Judah said to Tamar his daughter-in-law, “Remain a widow in your father’s house till my son Shelah is grown.” For he said, “Lest he also die like his brothers.” And Tamar went and dwelt in her father’s house.

12 Now in the process of time the daughter of Shua, Judah’s wife, died; and Judah was comforted, and went up to his sheepshearers at Timnah, he and his friend Hirah the Adullamite.

13 And it was told Tamar, saying, “Look, your father-in-law is going up to Timnah to shear his sheep.”

14 So she took off her widow’s garments, covered *herself* with a veil and wrapped herself, and sat in an open place which *was* on the way to Timnah; for she saw that Shelah was grown, and she was not given to him as a wife.

15 When Judah saw her, he thought she *was* a harlot, because she had covered her face.

16 Then he turned to her by the way, and said, “Please let me come in to you”; for he did not know that she *was* his daughter-in-law.
So she said, “What will you give me, that you may come in to me?”

17 And he said, “I will send a young goat from the flock.”
So she said, “Will you give *me* a pledge till you send *it?*”

18 Then he said, “What pledge shall I give you?”
So she said, “Your signet and cord, and your staff that *is* in your hand.” Then he gave *them* to her, and went in to her, and she conceived by him.

19 So she arose and went away, and laid aside her veil and put on the garments of her widowhood.

20 And Judah sent the young goat by the hand of his friend the Adullamite, to receive *his* pledge from the woman’s hand, but he did not find her.

21 Then he asked the men of that place, saying, “Where is the harlot who *was* openly by the roadside?”
And they said, “There was no harlot in this *place.*”

22 So he returned to Judah and said, “I cannot find her. Also, the men of the place said there was no harlot in this *place.*”

23 Then Judah said, “Let her take *them* for herself, lest we be shamed; for I sent this young goat and you have not found her.”

24 And it came to pass, about three months after, that Judah was told, saying, “Tamar your daughter-in-law has played the harlot; furthermore she *is* with child by harlotry.”
So Judah said, “Bring her out and let her be burned!”

25 When she *was* brought out, she sent to her father-in-law, saying, “By the man to whom these belong, I *am* with child.” And she said, “Please determine whose these *are*—the signet and cord, and staff.”

26 So Judah acknowledged *them* and said, “She has been more righteous than I, because I did not give her to Shelah my son.” And he never knew her again.

27 Now it came to pass, at the time for giving birth, that behold, twins *were* in her womb.

28 And so it was, when she was giving birth, that *the one* put out *his* hand; and the midwife took a scarlet *thread* and bound it on his hand, saying, “This one came out first.”

29 Then it happened, as he drew back his hand, that his brother came out unexpectedly; and she said, “How did you break through? *This* breach *be* upon you!” Therefore his name was called Perez.[a]

30 Afterward his brother came out who had the scarlet *thread* on his hand. And his name was called Zerah.

Joseph a Slave in Egypt

39 Now Joseph had been taken down to Egypt. And Potiphar, an officer of Pharaoh, captain of the guard, an Egyptian, bought him from the Ishmaelites who had taken him down there.

2 The LORD was with Joseph, and he was a successful man; and he was in the house of his master the Egyptian. ➤

3 And his master saw that the LORD *was* with him and that the LORD made all he did to prosper in his hand.

38:29 [a]Literally *Breach* or *Breakthrough*

LIFE LESSONS

➤ **38:10 — . . . *And the thing which he did displeased the LORD; therefore He killed him also.***

If we ever doubt that we serve a holy and righteous God who hates sin, we should remember Er and Onan, the wicked sons of Judah (Gen. 38:6–9).

➤ **39:2 — *The LORD was with Joseph, and he was a successful man; and he was in the house of his master the Egyptian.***

Joseph is a prime illustration of the truth that adversity is a setback from which we take our greatest leaps forward.

WHAT THE BIBLE SAYS ABOUT THE VALUE OF HARD WORK

Gen. 39:2–6

While God requires that we work, at the same time, He leads others to fairly pay us for our work. We find a marvelous example of good compensation for hard work in the life of Joseph, the eleventh son of Jacob. Joseph's spiteful brothers sold him into slavery to some passing merchants, and eventually the young man wound up the property of a powerful Egyptian official. Yet despite Joseph's slavery, "The Lord was with Joseph, and he was a successful man . . . . And his master saw that the Lord was with him and that the Lord made all he did to prosper in his hand. So Joseph found favor in his sight, and served him. Then he made him overseer of his house, and all that he had he put under his authority. So . . . the Lord blessed the Egyptian's house for Joseph's sake . . . . Thus he left all that he had in Joseph's hand" (Gen. 39:2–6).

Joseph owned none of the large Egyptian estate he managed, yet he had the full run of it. So he lived well, ate well, and dressed well. He had all of his material needs met—why? Because the Lord caused his master to deal with him favorably.

If you are giving your best effort at work and are trusting God to give you wisdom in all of your endeavors, then watch for the ways in which the Lord will cause others to bless *you*.

Second, the Egyptian received blessing in return. He had no worries or concerns while Joseph managed his household. Joseph had proven himself worthy of his trust.

God calls you to give maximum effort in your work and to do all you can to earn the trust of those who work with you or who supervise you. How can you motivate yourself to reach this high standard? The best way is to consciously acknowledge God's presence in every area of your work. The knowledge that God is with me as I work energizes me every day!

See the Life Principles Index for further study:
4. The awareness of God's presence energizes us for our work.

Acknowledge God's presence in every area of your work.

4 So Joseph found favor in his sight, and
served him. Then he made him overseer of his
house, and all *that* he had he put under his
authority.
5 So it was, from the time *that* he had made
him overseer of his house and all that he had,
that the LORD blessed the Egyptian's house
for Joseph's sake; and the blessing of the
LORD was on all that he had in the house and
in the field.
6 Thus he left all that he had in Joseph's
hand, and he did not know what he had
except for the bread which he ate. Now
Joseph was handsome in form and appearance.
7 And it came to pass after these things that
his master's wife cast longing eyes on Joseph,
and she said, "Lie with me."
8 But he refused and said to his master's
wife, "Look, my master does not know what *is*
with me in the house, and he has committed
all that he has to my hand.
➤ 9 "*There is* no one greater in this house than
I, nor has he kept back anything from me but
you, because you *are* his wife. How then can I
do this great wickedness, and sin against
God?"
10 So it was, as she spoke to Joseph day by
day, that he did not heed her, to lie with her *or*
to be with her.
11 But it happened about this time, when Joseph went into the house to do his work, and
none of the men of the house *was* inside,
12 that she caught him by his garment, saying, "Lie with me." But he left his garment in
her hand, and fled and ran outside.
13 And so it was, when she saw that he had
left his garment in her hand and fled outside,
14 that she called to the men of her house
and spoke to them, saying, "See, he has
brought in to us a Hebrew to mock us. He
came in to me to lie with me, and I cried out
with a loud voice.
15 "And it happened, when he heard that I
lifted my voice and cried out, that he left his
garment with me, and fled and went outside."
16 So she kept his garment with her until his
master came home.
17 Then she spoke to him with words like
these, saying, "The Hebrew servant whom
you brought to us came in to me to mock me;
18 "so it happened, as I lifted my voice and
cried out, that he left his garment with me and
fled outside."
19 So it was, when his master heard the
words which his wife spoke to him, saying,
"Your servant did to me after this manner,"
that his anger was aroused.
20 Then Joseph's master took him and put
him into the prison, a place where the king's
prisoners *were* confined. And he was there in
the prison.
21 But the LORD was with Joseph and showed ➤
him mercy, and He gave him favor in the sight
of the keeper of the prison.
22 And the keeper of the prison committed to
Joseph's hand all the prisoners who *were* in
the prison; whatever they did there, it was his
doing.
23 The keeper of the prison did not look into
anything *that was* under *Joseph's* authority,[a]
because the LORD was with him; and whatever he did, the LORD made *it* prosper.

The Prisoners' Dreams

40 It came to pass after these things *that*
the butler and the baker of the king of
Egypt offended their lord, the king of Egypt.
2 And Pharaoh was angry with his two officers, the chief butler and the chief baker.
3 So he put them in custody in the house of
the captain of the guard, in the prison, the
place where Joseph *was* confined.
4 And the captain of the guard charged Joseph with them, and he served them; so they
were in custody for a while.
5 Then the butler and the baker of the king
of Egypt, who *were* confined in the prison,
had a dream, both of them, each man's dream
in one night *and* each man's dream with its
own interpretation.
6 And Joseph came in to them in the morning and looked at them, and saw that they
were sad.
7 So he asked Pharaoh's officers who *were*
with him in the custody of his lord's house,
saying, "Why do you look so sad today?"
8 And they said to him, "We each have had
a dream, and *there is* no interpreter of it."
So Joseph said to them, "Do not interpretations belong to God? Tell *them* to me, please."

39:23 [a]Literally *his hand*

LIFE LESSONS

➤ **39:9 — *"There is no one greater in this house than I, nor has he kept back anything from me but you, because you are his wife. How then can I do this great wickedness, and sin against God?"***

Joseph understood that any sin we commit is really an offense against God. Our sins may harm and defraud others, but God is always the one most aggrieved.

➤ **39:21 — *But the LORD was with Joseph and showed him mercy, and He gave him favor in the sight of the keeper of the prison.***

Even when Joseph was thrown into prison for doing nothing wrong, God was with him and blessed him even in that dark place. So the young man learned not to think of himself as a victim, but as a child of God.

ANSWERS TO LIFE'S QUESTIONS

Does God bring us adversity?

GEN. 39:20

The life story of Joseph clearly illustrates that God sometimes grants permission for adversity to enter our lives so that He might accomplish an ultimate good.

Jacob didn't try to hide his lopsided love for Joseph, his son by his favorite wife, Rachel. So when Joseph shared two dreams with his brothers—dreams in which Joseph took center stage and his brothers bowed low to serve him—they started looking for a way to destroy him.

One day, Joseph's brothers secretly sold him into slavery. Eventually he wound up as the slave of Potiphar, an officer of Pharaoh. Joseph quickly rose to prominence in his new position, but when Potiphar's wife falsely accused Joseph of rape, the beleaguered young man got tossed into prison.

Even there, he rose to a position of leadership. When he correctly interpreted the dream of a royal servant, Joseph hoped that his fortunes were about to change. But the man promptly forgot him for two long years. Not until Pharaoh himself needed someone to interpret a troubling dream did the man mention Joseph (Gen. 39–40).

At the right time, God reversed Joseph's adversity.

After Joseph correctly interpreted the dream, Pharaoh put him in charge of the nation's harvest. Later, Joseph used his new authority as prime minister to help his family through a severe famine.

After Jacob's death, Joseph's brothers feared that he might try to "pay them back." But Joseph said to them, "Do not be afraid, for am I in the place of God? But as for you, you meant evil against me; but God meant it for good, in order to bring it about as it is this day, to save many people alive" (Gen. 50:19, 20).

In looking back over his life—even the dark and painful events—Joseph realized that God had been in charge all the time. Nothing had happened to him apart from God's will and divine plan.

In the same way, when you belong to the Lord, any adversity you may experience remains subject to the Lord's power and grace. He never stops being in charge of your life. He never loses authority over you or over the circumstances that affect you. God is *always* in control.

Therefore, you must realize that, on occasion, the Lord permits adversity to enter your life. He uses adversity to fulfill His purposes in you and through you.

See the Life Principles Index for further study:

7. The dark moments of our life will last only so long as is necessary for God to accomplish His purpose in us.

18. As children of a sovereign God, we are never victims of our circumstances.

9 Then the chief butler told his dream to Joseph, and said to him, "Behold, in my dream a
vine *was* before me,
10 "and in the vine *were* three branches; it
was as though it budded, its blossoms shot
forth, and its clusters brought forth ripe
grapes.
11 "Then Pharaoh's cup *was* in my hand; and
I took the grapes and pressed them into
Pharaoh's cup, and placed the cup in
Pharaoh's hand."
12 And Joseph said to him, "This *is* the interpretation of it: The three branches *are* three
days.
13 "Now within three days Pharaoh will lift
up your head and restore you to your place,
and you will put Pharaoh's cup in his hand
according to the former manner, when you
were his butler.
14 "But remember me when it is well with
you, and please show kindness to me; make
mention of me to Pharaoh, and get me out of
this house.
15 "For indeed I was stolen away from the
land of the Hebrews; and also I have done
nothing here that they should put me into the
dungeon."
16 When the chief baker saw that the interpretation was good, he said to Joseph, "I also
was in my dream, and there *were* three white
baskets on my head.
17 "In the uppermost basket *were* all kinds of
baked goods for Pharaoh, and the birds ate
them out of the basket on my head."
18 So Joseph answered and said, "This *is* the
interpretation of it: The three baskets *are*
three days.
19 "Within three days Pharaoh will lift off
your head from you and hang you on a
tree; and the birds will eat your flesh from
you."

20 Now it came to pass on the third day,
which was Pharaoh's birthday, that he made a
feast for all his servants; and he lifted up the
head of the chief butler and of the chief baker
among his servants.
21 Then he restored the chief butler to his
butlership again, and he placed the cup in
Pharaoh's hand.
22 But he hanged the chief baker, as Joseph
had interpreted to them.
23 Yet the chief butler did not remember Joseph, but forgot him.

Pharaoh's Dreams

➤ 41 Then it came to pass, at the end of two
full years, that Pharaoh had a dream;
and behold, he stood by the river.
2 Suddenly there came up out of the river
seven cows, fine looking and fat; and they fed
in the meadow.
3 Then behold, seven other cows came up
after them out of the river, ugly and gaunt,
and stood by the *other* cows on the bank of
the river.
4 And the ugly and gaunt cows ate up the
seven fine looking and fat cows. So Pharaoh
awoke.
5 He slept and dreamed a second time; and
suddenly seven heads of grain came up on
one stalk, plump and good.
6 Then behold, seven thin heads, blighted by
the east wind, sprang up after them.
7 And the seven thin heads devoured the
seven plump and full heads. So Pharaoh
awoke, and indeed, *it was* a dream.
8 Now it came to pass in the morning that
his spirit was troubled, and he sent and called
for all the magicians of Egypt and all its wise
men. And Pharaoh told them his dreams, but
there was no one who could interpret them
for Pharaoh.
9 Then the chief butler spoke to Pharaoh,
saying: "I remember my faults this day.
10 "When Pharaoh was angry with his servants, and put me in custody in the house of
the captain of the guard, *both* me and the
chief baker,
11 "we each had a dream in one night, he and
I. Each of us dreamed according to the interpretation of his *own* dream.
12 "Now there *was* a young Hebrew man
with us there, a servant of the captain of the
guard. And we told him, and he interpreted
our dreams for us; to each man he interpreted
according to his *own* dream.
13 "And it came to pass, just as he interpreted
for us, so it happened. He restored me to my
office, and he hanged him."
14 Then Pharaoh sent and called Joseph, and
they brought him quickly out of the dungeon;
and he shaved, changed his clothing, and
came to Pharaoh.
15 And Pharaoh said to Joseph, "I have had a
dream, and *there is* no one who can interpret
it. But I have heard it said of you *that* you can
understand a dream, to interpret it."

Life Examples:

JOSEPH

Waiting and Trusting

GEN. 40:23

God doesn't always meet our needs immediately or in a way that completely satisfies us. Why not? Because often He is redirecting us or preparing us for something new. The life of Joseph in the Old Testament provides a perfect example of this.

During his life Joseph had many critical needs. Once, he needed to be released from a deep pit. Later, he needed to be released from a dark prison. Still later, he needed to be remembered and rescued.

So why did God delay so long before meeting such crucial needs? Answer: So that a greater purpose might be accomplished, namely the meeting of the needs of Joseph's entire family.

In a similar way, while God is in the process of redirecting our lives, sometimes He delays meeting certain needs. Why? So that His greater plan for us—and for others—might be accomplished.

See the Life Principles Index for further study:

14. God acts on behalf of those who wait for Him.

7. The dark moments of our life will last only so long as is necessary for God to accomplish His purpose in us.

LIFE LESSONS

➤ 41:1 — *Then it came to pass, at the end of two full years, that Pharaoh had a dream; and behold, he stood by the river.*

Joseph languished in prison for two full years before he gained his freedom. Yet he did not blame God, but continued to serve him. He learned, as we must, that God acts on behalf of those who wait for Him.

➤ 16 So Joseph answered Pharaoh, saying, "*It*
is not in me; God will give Pharaoh an answer
of peace."
17 Then Pharaoh said to Joseph: "Behold, in
my dream I stood on the bank of the river.
18 "Suddenly seven cows came up out of the
river, fine looking and fat; and they fed in the
meadow.
19 "Then behold, seven other cows came up
after them, poor and very ugly and gaunt,
such ugliness as I have never seen in all the
land of Egypt.
20 "And the gaunt and ugly cows ate up the
first seven, the fat cows.
21 "When they had eaten them up, no one
would have known that they had eaten them,
for they *were* just as ugly as at the beginning.
So I awoke.
22 "Also I saw in my dream, and suddenly
seven heads came up on one stalk, full and
good.
23 "Then behold, seven heads, withered, thin,
and blighted by the east wind, sprang up after
them.
24 "And the thin heads devoured the seven
good heads. So I told *this* to the magicians,
but *there was* no one who could explain *it* to
me."
25 Then Joseph said to Pharaoh, "The
dreams of Pharaoh *are* one; God has shown
Pharaoh what He *is* about to do:
26 "The seven good cows *are* seven years,
and the seven good heads *are* seven years; the
dreams *are* one.
27 "And the seven thin and ugly cows which
came up after them *are* seven years, and the
seven empty heads blighted by the east wind
are seven years of famine.
28 "This *is* the thing which I have spoken to
Pharaoh. God has shown Pharaoh what He *is*
about to do.
29 "Indeed seven years of great plenty will
come throughout all the land of Egypt;
30 "but after them seven years of famine will
arise, and all the plenty will be forgotten in
the land of Egypt; and the famine will deplete
the land.
31 "So the plenty will not be known in the
land because of the famine following, for it
will be very severe.
32 "And the dream was repeated to Pharaoh
twice because the thing *is* established by God,
and God will shortly bring it to pass.
33 "Now therefore, let Pharaoh select a discerning and wise man, and set him over the
land of Egypt.
34 "Let Pharaoh do *this*, and let him appoint
officers over the land, to collect one-fifth *of*
the produce of the land of Egypt in the seven
plentiful years.
35 "And let them gather all the food of those
good years that are coming, and store up
grain under the authority of Pharaoh, and let
them keep food in the cities.
36 "Then that food shall be as a reserve for
the land for the seven years of famine which
shall be in the land of Egypt, that the land
may not perish during the famine."

Joseph's Rise to Power

37 So the advice was good in the eyes of
Pharaoh and in the eyes of all his servants.
38 And Pharaoh said to his servants, "Can we
find *such a one* as this, a man in whom *is* the
Spirit of God?"
39 Then Pharaoh said to Joseph, "Inasmuch
as God has shown you all this, *there is* no one
as discerning and wise as you.
40 "You shall be over my house, and all my
people shall be ruled according to your word;
only in regard to the throne will I be greater
than you."
41 And Pharaoh said to Joseph, "See, I have
set you over all the land of Egypt."
42 Then Pharaoh took his signet ring off his
hand and put it on Joseph's hand; and he
clothed him in garments of fine linen and put
a gold chain around his neck.
43 And he had him ride in the second chariot
which he had; and they cried out before him,
"Bow the knee!" So he set him over all the
land of Egypt.
44 Pharaoh also said to Joseph, "I *am*
Pharaoh, and without your consent no man
may lift his hand or foot in all the land of
Egypt."
45 And Pharaoh called Joseph's name Zaph-
nath-Paaneah. And he gave him as a wife
Asenath, the daughter of Poti-Pherah priest of
On. So Joseph went out over *all* the land of
Egypt.
46 Joseph was thirty years old when he stood ➤

LIFE LESSONS

➤ 41:16 — *So Joseph answered Pharaoh, saying, "It is not in me; God will give Pharaoh an answer of peace."*

We never truly advance our interests by shining the spotlight on ourselves. Godly men and women realize and eagerly declare that God is the true source of all wisdom.

➤ 41:46 — *Joseph was thirty years old when he stood before Pharaoh king of Egypt. And Joseph went out from the presence of Pharaoh, and went throughout all the land of Egypt.*

By the time Joseph rose to power in Egypt, he was 30 years old—perhaps a dozen or more years after his brothers sold him into slavery. No doubt he felt disappointed during those years, but he never chose to feel discouraged.

before Pharaoh king of Egypt. And Joseph
went out from the presence of Pharaoh, and
went throughout all the land of Egypt.
47 Now in the seven plentiful years the
ground brought forth abundantly.
48 So he gathered up all the food of the seven
years which were in the land of Egypt, and
laid up the food in the cities; he laid up in
every city the food of the fields which surrounded them.
49 Joseph gathered very much grain, as the
sand of the sea, until he stopped counting, for
it was immeasurable.
50 And to Joseph were born two sons before
the years of famine came, whom Asenath, the
daughter of Poti-Pherah priest of On, bore to
him.
51 Joseph called the name of the firstborn
Manasseh:[a] "For God has made me forget all
my toil and all my father's house."
52 And the name of the second he called
Ephraim:[a] "For God has caused me to be fruitful in the land of my affliction."
53 Then the seven years of plenty which were
in the land of Egypt ended,
54 and the seven years of famine began to
come, as Joseph had said. The famine was in
all lands, but in all the land of Egypt there
was bread.
55 So when all the land of Egypt was famished, the people cried to Pharaoh for bread.
Then Pharaoh said to all the Egyptians, "Go
to Joseph; whatever he says to you, do."
56 The famine was over all the face of the
earth, and Joseph opened all the storehouses[a]
and sold to the Egyptians. And the famine became severe in the land of Egypt.
57 So all countries came to Joseph in Egypt
to buy *grain,* because the famine was severe
in all lands.

Joseph's Brothers Go to Egypt

42 When Jacob saw that there was grain
in Egypt, Jacob said to his sons, "Why
do you look at one another?"
2 And he said, "Indeed I have heard that
there is grain in Egypt; go down to that place
and buy for us there, that we may live and not
die."
3 So Joseph's ten brothers went down to
buy grain in Egypt.
4 But Jacob did not send Joseph's brother
Benjamin with his brothers, for he said, "Lest
some calamity befall him."
➤ 5 And the sons of Israel went to buy *grain*
among those who journeyed, for the famine
was in the land of Canaan.
6 Now Joseph *was* governor over the land;
and it was he who sold to all the people of
the land. And Joseph's brothers came and
bowed down before him with *their* faces to
the earth.
7 Joseph saw his brothers and recognized
them, but he acted as a stranger to them and
spoke roughly to them. Then he said to them,
"Where do you come from?" And they said,
"From the land of Canaan to buy food."
8 So Joseph recognized his brothers, but
they did not recognize him.
9 Then Joseph remembered the dreams
which he had dreamed about them, and said
to them, "You *are* spies! You have come to see
the nakedness of the land!"
10 And they said to him, "No, my lord, but
your servants have come to buy food.
11 "We *are* all one man's sons; we *are* honest
men; your servants are not spies."
12 But he said to them, "No, but you have
come to see the nakedness of the land."
13 And they said, "Your servants *are* twelve
brothers, the sons of one man in the land of
Canaan; and in fact, the youngest *is* with our
father today, and one *is* no more."
14 But Joseph said to them, "It *is* as I spoke to
you, saying, 'You *are* spies!'
15 "In this *manner* you shall be tested: By
the life of Pharaoh, you shall not leave this
place unless your youngest brother comes
here.
16 "Send one of you, and let him bring your
brother; and you shall be kept in prison, that
your words may be tested to see whether
there is any truth in you; or else, by the life of
Pharaoh, surely you *are* spies!"
17 So he put them all together in prison three
days.
18 Then Joseph said to them the third day,
"Do this and live, *for* I fear God:
19 "If you *are* honest *men,* let one of your
brothers be confined to your prison house;
but you, go and carry grain for the famine of
your houses.
20 "And bring your youngest brother to me;
so your words will be verified, and you shall
not die." And they did so.
21 Then they said to one another, "We *are*
truly guilty concerning our brother, for we
saw the anguish of his soul when he pleaded
with us, and we would not hear; therefore this
distress has come upon us."
22 And Reuben answered them, saying, "Did

41:51 [a]Literally *Making Forgetful* **41:52** [a]Literally *Fruitfulness*
41:56 [a]Literally *all that was in them*

LIFE LESSONS

➤ ***42:5 — And the sons of Israel went to buy grain among those who journeyed, for the famine was in the land of Canaan.***

God used a famine to bring together the fractured family of Jacob. What we see as disasters, God can use for good.

I not speak to you, saying, 'Do not sin against
the boy'; and you would not listen? Therefore
behold, his blood is now required of us."
23 But they did not know that Joseph understood *them,* for he spoke to them through an
interpreter.
24 And he turned himself away from them
and wept. Then he returned to them again,
and talked with them. And he took Simeon
from them and bound him before their eyes.

The Brothers Return to Canaan

25 Then Joseph gave a command to fill their
sacks with grain, to restore every man's
money to his sack, and to give them provisions for the journey. Thus he did for them.
26 So they loaded their donkeys with the
grain and departed from there.
27 But as one *of them* opened his sack to give
his donkey feed at the encampment, he saw
his money; and there it was, in the mouth of
his sack.
28 So he said to his brothers, "My money has
been restored, and there it is, in my sack!"
Then their hearts failed *them* and they were
afraid, saying to one another, "What *is* this
that God has done to us?"
29 Then they went to Jacob their father in the
land of Canaan and told him all that had happened to them, saying:
30 "The man *who is* lord of the land spoke
roughly to us, and took us for spies of the
country.
31 "But we said to him, 'We *are* honest *men;*
we are not spies.
32 "We *are* twelve brothers, sons of our father; one *is* no *more,* and the youngest *is* with
our father this day in the land of Canaan.'
33 "Then the man, the lord of the country,
said to us, 'By this I will know that you *are*
honest *men:* Leave one of your brothers *here*
with me, take *food for* the famine of your
households, and be gone.
34 'And bring your youngest brother to me;
so I shall know that you *are* not spies, but *that*
you *are* honest *men.* I will grant your brother
to you, and you may trade in the land.'"
35 Then it happened as they emptied their
sacks, that surprisingly each man's bundle of
money *was* in his sack; and when they and
their father saw the bundles of money, they
were afraid.
36 And Jacob their father said to them, "You
have bereaved me: Joseph is no *more,* Simeon
is no *more,* and you want to take Benjamin.
All these things are against me."
37 Then Reuben spoke to his father, saying,
"Kill my two sons if I do not bring him *back*
to you; put him in my hands, and I will bring
him back to you."
38 But he said, "My son shall not go down
with you, for his brother is dead, and he is left
alone. If any calamity should befall him along
the way in which you go, then you would
bring down my gray hair with sorrow to the
grave."

Joseph's Brothers Return with Benjamin

43 Now the famine *was* severe in the
land.
2 And it came to pass, when they had eaten
up the grain which they had brought from
Egypt, that their father said to them, "Go
back, buy us a little food."
3 But Judah spoke to him, saying, "The man
solemnly warned us, saying, 'You shall not
see my face unless your brother *is* with you.'
4 "If you send our brother with us, we will
go down and buy you food.
5 "But if you will not send *him,* we will not
go down; for the man said to us, 'You shall not
see my face unless your brother *is* with you.'"
6 And Israel said, "Why did you deal *so*
wrongfully with me *as* to tell the man
whether you had still *another* brother?"
7 But they said, "The man asked us pointedly about ourselves and our family, saying,
'*Is* your father still alive? Have you *another*
brother?' And we told him according to these
words. Could we possibly have known that he
would say, 'Bring your brother down'?"
8 Then Judah said to Israel his father, "Send
the lad with me, and we will arise and go, that
we may live and not die, both we and you *and*
also our little ones.
9 "I myself will be surety for him; from my
hand you shall require him. If I do not bring
him *back* to you and set him before you, then
let me bear the blame forever.
10 "For if we had not lingered, surely by now
we would have returned this second time."
11 And their father Israel said to them, "If *it*
must be so, then do this: Take some of the
best fruits of the land in your vessels and
carry down a present for the man—a little
balm and a little honey, spices and myrrh, pis-
tachio nuts and almonds.
12 "Take double money in your hand, and
take back in your hand the money that was
returned in the mouth of your sacks; perhaps
it was an oversight.
13 "Take your brother also, and arise, go
back to the man.
14 "And may God Almighty give you mercy
before the man, that he may release your
other brother and Benjamin. If I am bereaved,
I am bereaved!"
15 So the men took that present and Benjamin, and they took double money in their
hand, and arose and went down to Egypt; and
they stood before Joseph.
16 When Joseph saw Benjamin with them, he
said to the steward of his house, "Take *these*
men to my home, and slaughter an animal
and make ready; for *these* men will dine with
me at noon."
17 Then the man did as Joseph ordered, and
the man brought the men into Joseph's house.

18 Now the men were afraid because they
were brought into Joseph's house; and they
said, "*It is* because of the money, which was
returned in our sacks the first time, that we
are brought in, so that he may make a case
against us and seize us, to take us as slaves
with our donkeys."
19 When they drew near to the steward of Joseph's house, they talked with him at the door
of the house,
20 and said, "O sir, we indeed came down the
first time to buy food;
21 "but it happened, when we came to the encampment, that we opened our sacks, and
there, *each* man's money *was* in the mouth of
his sack, our money in full weight; so we have
brought it back in our hand.
22 "And we have brought down other money
in our hands to buy food. We do not know
who put our money in our sacks."
23 But he said, "Peace *be* with you, do not be
afraid. Your God and the God of your father
has given you treasure in your sacks; I had
your money." Then he brought Simeon out to
them.
24 So the man brought the men into Joseph's
house and gave *them* water, and they washed
their feet; and he gave their donkeys feed.
25 Then they made the present ready for Joseph's coming at noon, for they heard that
they would eat bread there.
26 And when Joseph came home, they
brought him the present which *was* in their
hand into the house, and bowed down before
him to the earth.
27 Then he asked them about *their* well-being, and said, "*Is* your father well, the old man
of whom you spoke? *Is* he still alive?"
28 And they answered, "Your servant our father *is* in good health; he *is* still alive." And
they bowed their heads down and prostrated
themselves.
29 Then he lifted his eyes and saw his brother
Benjamin, his mother's son, and said, "*Is* this
your younger brother of whom you spoke to
me?" And he said, "God be gracious to you,
my son."
30 Now his heart yearned for his brother; so
Joseph made haste and sought *somewhere* to
weep. And he went into *his* chamber and wept
there.
31 Then he washed his face and came out;
and he restrained himself, and said, "Serve
the bread."
32 So they set him a place by himself, and
them by themselves, and the Egyptians who
ate with him by themselves; because the
Egyptians could not eat food with the Hebrews, for that *is* an abomination to the Egyptians.
33 And they sat before him, the firstborn according to his birthright and the youngest according to his youth; and the men looked in
astonishment at one another.
34 Then he took servings to them from before him, but Benjamin's serving was five
times as much as any of theirs. So they drank
and were merry with him.

Joseph's Cup

44 And he commanded the steward of his
house, saying, "Fill the men's sacks
with food, as much as they can carry, and
put each man's money in the mouth of his
sack.
2 "Also put my cup, the silver cup, in the
mouth of the sack of the youngest, and his
grain money." So he did according to the
word that Joseph had spoken.
3 As soon as the morning dawned, the men
were sent away, they and their donkeys.
4 When they had gone out of the city, *and*
were not *yet* far off, Joseph said to his steward, "Get up, follow the men; and when you
overtake them, say to them, 'Why have you
repaid evil for good?
5 *Is* not this *the one* from which my lord
drinks, and with which he indeed practices
divination? You have done evil in so doing.'"
6 So he overtook them, and he spoke to
them these same words.
7 And they said to him, "Why does my lord
say these words? Far be it from us that your
servants should do such a thing.
8 "Look, we brought back to you from the
land of Canaan the money which we found in
the mouth of our sacks. How then could we
steal silver or gold from your lord's house?
9 "With whomever of your servants it is
found, let him die, and we also will be my
lord's slaves."
10 And he said, "Now also *let* it *be* according
to your words; he with whom it is found shall
be my slave, and you shall be blameless."
11 Then each man speedily let down his sack
to the ground, and each opened his sack.
12 So he searched. He began with the oldest
and left off with the youngest; and the cup
was found in Benjamin's sack.
13 Then they tore their clothes, and each man
loaded his donkey and returned to the city.
14 So Judah and his brothers came to Joseph's house, and he *was* still there; and they
fell before him on the ground.
15 And Joseph said to them, "What deed *is*
this you have done? Did you not know that
such a man as I can certainly practice divination?"
16 Then Judah said, "What shall we say to
my lord? What shall we speak? Or how shall
we clear ourselves? God has found out the iniquity of your servants; here we are, my lord's
slaves, both we and *he* also with whom the
cup was found."
17 But he said, "Far be it from me that I
should do so; the man in whose hand the cup
was found, he shall be my slave. And as for
you, go up in peace to your father."

Judah Intercedes for Benjamin
18 Then Judah came near to him and said: "O
my lord, please let your servant speak a word
in my lord's hearing, and do not let your
anger burn against your servant; for you *are*
even like Pharaoh.
19 "My lord asked his servants, saying, 'Have
you a father or a brother?'
20 "And we said to my lord, 'We have a father,
an old man, and a child of *his* old age, *who is*
young; his brother is dead, and he alone is left
of his mother's children, and his father loves
him.'
21 "Then you said to your servants, 'Bring him
down to me, that I may set my eyes on him.'
22 "And we said to my lord, 'The lad cannot
leave his father, for *if* he should leave his father, *his father* would die.'
23 "But you said to your servants, 'Unless
your youngest brother comes down with you,
you shall see my face no more.'
24 "So it was, when we went up to your servant my father, that we told him the words of
my lord.
25 "And our father said, 'Go back *and* buy us
a little food.'
26 "But we said, 'We cannot go down; if our
youngest brother is with us, then we will go
down; for we may not see the man's face unless our youngest brother *is* with us.'
27 "Then your servant my father said to us,
'You know that my wife bore me two sons;
28 "and the one went out from me, and I said,
"Surely he is torn to pieces"; and I have not
seen him since.
29 But if you take this one also from me, and
calamity befalls him, you shall bring down
my gray hair with sorrow to the grave.'
30 "Now therefore, when I come to your servant my father, and the lad *is* not with us,
since his life is bound up in the lad's life,
31 "it will happen, when he sees that the lad
is not *with us*, that he will die. So your servants will bring down the gray hair of your
servant our father with sorrow to the grave.
32 "For your servant became surety for the
lad to my father, saying, 'If I do not bring him
back to you, then I shall bear the blame before my father forever.'
33 "Now therefore, please let your servant remain instead of the lad as a slave to my lord,
and let the lad go up with his brothers.
34 "For how shall I go up to my father if the
lad *is* not with me, lest perhaps I see the evil
that would come upon my father?"

Joseph Revealed to His Brothers
45 Then Joseph could not restrain himself
before all those who stood by him, and
he cried out, "Make everyone go out from
me!" So no one stood with him while Joseph
made himself known to his brothers.
2 And he wept aloud, and the Egyptians and
the house of Pharaoh heard *it*.
3 Then Joseph said to his brothers, "I *am* Joseph; does my father still live?" But his brothers could not answer him, for they were
dismayed in his presence.
4 And Joseph said to his brothers, "Please
come near to me." So they came near. Then he
said: "I *am* Joseph your brother, whom you
sold into Egypt.
5 "But now, do not therefore be grieved or
angry with yourselves because you sold me
here; for God sent me before you to preserve
life.
6 "For these two years the famine *has been*
in the land, and *there are* still five years in
which *there will be* neither plowing nor har-
vesting.
7 "And God sent me before you to preserve
a posterity for you in the earth, and to save
your lives by a great deliverance.
8 "So now *it was* not you *who* sent me here,
but God; and He has made me a father to
Pharaoh, and lord of all his house, and a ruler
throughout all the land of Egypt.
9 "Hurry and go up to my father, and say to
him, 'Thus says your son Joseph: "God has
made me lord of all Egypt; come down to me,
do not tarry.
10 "You shall dwell in the land of Goshen,
and you shall be near to me, you and your
children, your children's children, your flocks
and your herds, and all that you have.
11 "There I will provide for you, lest you and
your household, and all that you have, come
to poverty; for *there are* still five years of
famine."'
12 "And behold, your eyes and the eyes of my
brother Benjamin see that *it is* my mouth that
speaks to you.
13 "So you shall tell my father of all my glory
in Egypt, and of all that you have seen; and

LIFE LESSONS

➤ 45:4, 5 — *And Joseph said to his brothers, ". . . Do not therefore be grieved or angry with yourselves because you sold me here; for God sent me before you to preserve life.*

God calls us to have a forgiving spirit. Knowing that God remains in control of all that happens to us releases us to forgive others.

➤ 45:7 — *"And God sent me before you to preserve a posterity for you in the earth, and to save your lives by a great deliverance . . ."*

God never asks any of us to sit down and wait idly for Him to vault us into success. He asks us to trust and obey Him day by day and to learn the lessons He sets before us.

you shall hurry and bring my father down
here."
14 Then he fell on his brother Benjamin's
neck and wept, and Benjamin wept on his
neck.
15 Moreover he kissed all his brothers and
wept over them, and after that his brothers
talked with him.
16 Now the report of it was heard in
Pharaoh's house, saying, "Joseph's brothers
have come." So it pleased Pharaoh and his
servants well.
17 And Pharaoh said to Joseph, "Say to your
brothers, 'Do this: Load your animals and depart; go to the land of Canaan.
18 'Bring your father and your households
and come to me; I will give you the best of the
land of Egypt, and you will eat the fat of the
land.
19 'Now you are commanded—do this: Take
carts out of the land of Egypt for your little
ones and your wives; bring your father and
come.
20 'Also do not be concerned about your
goods, for the best of all the land of Egypt *is*
yours.'"
21 Then the sons of Israel did so; and Joseph
gave them carts, according to the command
of Pharaoh, and he gave them provisions for
the journey.
22 He gave to all of them, to each man,
changes of garments; but to Benjamin he
gave three hundred *pieces* of silver and five
changes of garments.
23 And he sent to his father these *things:* ten
donkeys loaded with the good things of
Egypt, and ten female donkeys loaded with
grain, bread, and food for his father for the
journey.
24 So he sent his brothers away, and they departed; and he said to them, "See that you do
not become troubled along the way."
25 Then they went up out of Egypt, and
came to the land of Canaan to Jacob their father.
26 And they told him, saying, "Joseph *is* still
alive, and he *is* governor over all the land of
Egypt." And Jacob's heart stood still, because
he did not believe them.
27 But when they told him all the words
which Joseph had said to them, and when
he saw the carts which Joseph had sent to
carry him, the spirit of Jacob their father revived.
28 Then Israel said, "*It is* enough. Joseph my
son *is* still alive. I will go and see him before I
die."

Jacob's Journey to Egypt

46 So Israel took his journey with all that
he had, and came to Beersheba, and
offered sacrifices to the God of his father
Isaac.
2 Then God spoke to Israel in the visions of
the night, and said, "Jacob, Jacob!"
And he said, "Here I am."
3 So He said, "I *am* God, the God of your father; do not fear to go down to Egypt, for I
will make of you a great nation there.
4 "I will go down with you to Egypt, and I ➤
will also surely bring you up *again;* and Joseph will put his hand on your eyes."
5 Then Jacob arose from Beersheba; and
the sons of Israel carried their father Jacob,
their little ones, and their wives, in the carts
which Pharaoh had sent to carry him.
6 So they took their livestock and their
goods, which they had acquired in the land of
Canaan, and went to Egypt, Jacob and all his
descendants with him.
7 His sons and his sons' sons, his daughters
and his sons' daughters, and all his descendants he brought with him to Egypt.
8 Now these *were* the names of the children
of Israel, Jacob and his sons, who went to
Egypt: Reuben *was* Jacob's firstborn.
9 The sons of Reuben *were* Hanoch, Pallu,
Hezron, and Carmi.
10 The sons of Simeon *were* Jemuel,[a] Jamin,
Ohad, Jachin,[b] Zohar,[c] and Shaul, the son of a
Canaanite woman.
11 The sons of Levi *were* Gershon, Kohath,
and Merari.
12 The sons of Judah *were* Er, Onan, Shelah,
Perez, and Zerah (but Er and Onan died in the
land of Canaan). The sons of Perez were
Hezron and Hamul.
13 The sons of Issachar *were* Tola, Puvah,[a]
Job,[b] and Shimron.
14 The sons of Zebulun *were* Sered, Elon,
and Jahleel.
15 These *were* the sons of Leah, whom she
bore to Jacob in Padan Aram, with his daughter Dinah. All the persons, his sons and his
daughters, *were* thirty-three.
16 The sons of Gad *were* Ziphion,[a] Haggi,
Shuni, Ezbon,[b] Eri, Arodi,[c] and Areli.
17 The sons of Asher *were* Jimnah, Ishuah,

46:10 [a]Spelled *Nemuel* in 1 Chronicles 4:24 [b]Called *Jarib* in 1 Chronicles 4:24 [c]Called *Zerah* in 1 Chronicles 4:24
46:13 [a]Spelled *Puah* in 1 Chronicles 7:1 [b]Same as *Jashub* in Numbers 26:24 and 1 Chronicles 7:1 **46:16** [a]Spelled *Zephon* in Samaritan Pentateuch, Septuagint, and Numbers 26:15 [b]Called *Ozni* in Numbers 26:16 [c]Spelled *Arod* in Numbers 26:17

LIFE LESSONS

➤ ***46:4 — "I will go down with you to Egypt, and I will also surely bring you up again . . . ."***

Israel found strength to do even a difficult thing once he heard God's promise, for God's Word is an immovable anchor in times of storm.

ANSWERS TO LIFE'S QUESTIONS

Why doesn't God answer my prayers sooner?

GEN. 45:25—46:4

If God hears our requests and loves us so much that He sent His own Son, Jesus Christ, to die for us, then why does it appear to take Him so long to respond to some of our most urgent requests? Carefully consider the following ten reasons. The delay may be caused by:

❶ ***Our disobedience***
Our sin can prompt God to withhold His gracious hand (Ps. 81:10–12). When we disobey His commands and refuse to repent, He sometimes stops His ears from hearing our requests.

❷ ***Our doubt***
Without faith, no one who asks *anything* of God will receive what he requests (James 1:5–8). But with faith, all things are possible (Mark 9:23).

❸ ***Our attempts at manipulation***
If we try to control or manipulate God, we should not expect answers to our prayers (1 Sam. 13:9–14). He is the Master; we are the servants.

❹ ***Wrong motivation***
Neither self-centered requests nor those tinged with evil intent will receive an answer (James 4:3). God refuses to partner with our lusts or our schemes.

❺ ***Our lack of responsibility***
God cannot be expected to compensate for a lazy or negligent person (Prov. 19:15). The Lord has His work to do; we have ours.

❻ ***An illegitimate "need"***
Is this thing you want really a need, or is it something that you have illegitimately come to expect? Often we have bigger eyes than stomachs (Jer. 45:1–5).

❼ ***Rejecting God's method***
Don't turn away a means of supply merely because it doesn't fit your expectations or criteria (see Joshua 6). A man named Naaman almost made this mistake—and it would have cost him his health (2 Kin. 5:8–14).

❽ ***God's redirection***
Sometimes God is in the process of redirecting us or preparing us for something new (see Gen. 37, 39–50). God loves to do fresh, exciting things with His people (Is. 43:19).

❾ ***God's desire to teach us***
God may want us to focus on our spiritual and eternal needs so that we will learn to trust Him in all things and for all things (Is. 48:18).

❿ ***God's desire to bring us to repentance***
God may want us to own up to our sin, confess it, and repent of it (see Luke 15:11–31).

And even when God delays His answers, He instructs us to keep on praying (Luke 18:1-8). Prayer is life's greatest time saver, even when it doesn't seem like it.

See the Life Principles Index for further study:
17. We stand tallest and strongest on our knees.
9. Trusting God means looking beyond what we can see to what God sees.

Isui, Beriah, and Serah, their sister. And the sons of Beriah *were* Heber and Malchiel.
18 These *were* the sons of Zilpah, whom Laban gave to Leah his daughter; and these she bore to Jacob: sixteen persons.
19 The sons of Rachel, Jacob's wife, *were* Joseph and Benjamin.
20 And to Joseph in the land of Egypt were born Manasseh and Ephraim, whom Asenath, the daughter of Poti-Pherah priest of On, bore to him.
21 The sons of Benjamin *were* Belah, Becher, Ashbel, Gera, Naaman, Ehi, Rosh, Muppim, Huppim,[a] and Ard.
22 These *were* the sons of Rachel, who were born to Jacob: fourteen persons in all.
23 The son of Dan *was* Hushim.[a]
24 The sons of Naphtali *were* Jahzeel,[a] Guni, Jezer, and Shillem.[b]
25 These *were* the sons of Bilhah, whom Laban gave to Rachel his daughter, and she bore these to Jacob: seven persons in all.
26 All the persons who went with Jacob to Egypt, who came from his body, besides Jacob's sons' wives, *were* sixty-six persons in all.
27 And the sons of Joseph who were born to him in Egypt *were* two persons. All the persons of the house of Jacob who went to Egypt were seventy.

46:21 [a]Called *Hupham* in Numbers 26:39 **46:23** [a]Called *Shuham* in Numbers 26:42 **46:24** [a]Spelled *Jahziel* in 1 Chronicles 7:13 [b]Spelled *Shallum* in 1 Chronicles 7:13

Jacob Settles in Goshen
28 Then he sent Judah before him to Joseph,
to point out before him *the way* to Goshen.
And they came to the land of Goshen.
29 So Joseph made ready his chariot and
went up to Goshen to meet his father Israel;
and he presented himself to him, and fell on
his neck and wept on his neck a good while.
30 And Israel said to Joseph, "Now let me
die, since I have seen your face, because you
are still alive."
31 Then Joseph said to his brothers and to
his father's household, "I will go up and tell
Pharaoh, and say to him, 'My brothers and
those of my father's house, who *were* in the
land of Canaan, have come to me.
32 'And the men *are* shepherds, for their occupation has been to feed livestock; and they
have brought their flocks, their herds, and all
that they have.'
33 "So it shall be, when Pharaoh calls you
and says, 'What is your occupation?'
34 "that you shall say, 'Your servants' occupation has been with livestock from our youth
even till now, both we *and* also our fathers,'
that you may dwell in the land of Goshen; for
every shepherd *is* an abomination to the
Egyptians."
47 Then Joseph went and told Pharaoh,
and said, "My father and my brothers,
their flocks and their herds and all that they
possess, have come from the land of Canaan;
and indeed they *are* in the land of Goshen."
2 And he took five men from among his
brothers and presented them to Pharaoh.
3 Then Pharaoh said to his brothers, "What
is your occupation?"
And they said to Pharaoh, "Your servants *are*
shepherds, both we *and* also our fathers."
4 And they said to Pharaoh, "We have come
to dwell in the land, because your servants
have no pasture for their flocks, for the
famine *is* severe in the land of Canaan. Now
therefore, please let your servants dwell in
the land of Goshen."
5 Then Pharaoh spoke to Joseph, saying,
"Your father and your brothers have come to
you.
6 "The land of Egypt *is* before you. Have
your father and brothers dwell in the best of
the land; let them dwell in the land of Goshen.
And if you know *any* competent men among
them, then make them chief herdsmen over
my livestock."
7 Then Joseph brought in his father Jacob
and set him before Pharaoh; and Jacob
blessed Pharaoh.
8 Pharaoh said to Jacob, "How old *are* you?"
9 And Jacob said to Pharaoh, "The days of
the years of my pilgrimage *are* one hundred
and thirty years; few and evil have been the
days of the years of my life, and they have not
attained to the days of the years of the life of
my fathers in the days of their pilgrimage."
10 So Jacob blessed Pharaoh, and went out
from before Pharaoh.
11 And Joseph situated his father and his
brothers, and gave them a possession in the
land of Egypt, in the best of the land, in the
land of Rameses, as Pharaoh had commanded.
12 Then Joseph provided his father, his
brothers, and all his father's household with
bread, according to the number in *their* families.

Joseph Deals with the Famine
13 Now *there was* no bread in all the land;
for the famine *was* very severe, so that the
land of Egypt and the land of Canaan languished because of the famine.
14 And Joseph gathered up all the money
that was found in the land of Egypt and in the
land of Canaan, for the grain which they
bought; and Joseph brought the money into
Pharaoh's house.
15 So when the money failed in the land of
Egypt and in the land of Canaan, all the Egyptians came to Joseph and said, "Give us
bread, for why should we die in your presence? For the money has failed."
16 Then Joseph said, "Give your livestock,
and I will give you *bread* for your livestock, if
the money is gone."
17 So they brought their livestock to Joseph,
and Joseph gave them bread *in exchange* for
the horses, the flocks, the cattle of the herds,
and for the donkeys. Thus he fed them with
bread *in exchange* for all their livestock that
year.
18 When that year had ended, they came to
him the next year and said to him, "We will
not hide from my lord that our money is gone;
my lord also has our herds of livestock. There
is nothing left in the sight of my lord but our
bodies and our lands.
19 "Why should we die before your eyes, both
we and our land? Buy us and our land for
bread, and we and our land will be servants of
Pharaoh; give *us* seed, that we may live and
not die, that the land may not be desolate."
20 Then Joseph bought all the land of Egypt
for Pharaoh; for every man of the Egyptians
sold his field, because the famine was severe
upon them. So the land became Pharaoh's.
21 And as for the people, he moved them into
the cities,[a] from *one* end of the borders of
Egypt to the *other* end.
22 Only the land of the priests he did not buy;
for the priests had rations *allotted to them* by
Pharaoh, and they ate their rations which
Pharaoh gave them; therefore they did not
sell their lands.
23 Then Joseph said to the people, "Indeed I

47:21 [a]Following Masoretic Text and Targum; Samaritan Pentateuch, Septuagint, and Vulgate read *made the people virtual slaves.*

have bought you and your land this day for Pharaoh. Look, *here is* seed for you, and you shall sow the land.

24 "And it shall come to pass in the harvest that you shall give one-fifth to Pharaoh. Four-fifths shall be your own, as seed for the field and for your food, for those of your households and as food for your little ones."

25 So they said, "You have saved our lives; let us find favor in the sight of my lord, and we will be Pharaoh's servants."

26 And Joseph made it a law over the land of Egypt to this day, *that* Pharaoh should have one-fifth, except for the land of the priests only, *which* did not become Pharaoh's.

Joseph's Vow to Jacob

27 So Israel dwelt in the land of Egypt, in the country of Goshen; and they had possessions there and grew and multiplied exceedingly.

28 And Jacob lived in the land of Egypt seventeen years. So the length of Jacob's life was one hundred and forty-seven years.

29 When the time drew near that Israel must die, he called his son Joseph and said to him, "Now if I have found favor in your sight, please put your hand under my thigh, and deal kindly and truly with me. Please do not bury me in Egypt,

30 "but let me lie with my fathers; you shall carry me out of Egypt and bury me in their burial place." And he said, "I will do as you have said."

31 Then he said, "Swear to me." And he swore to him. So Israel bowed himself on the head of the bed.

Jacob Blesses Joseph's Sons

48 Now it came to pass after these things that Joseph was told, "Indeed your father *is* sick"; and he took with him his two sons, Manasseh and Ephraim.

2 And Jacob was told, "Look, your son Joseph is coming to you"; and Israel strengthened himself and sat up on the bed.

3 Then Jacob said to Joseph: "God Almighty appeared to me at Luz in the land of Canaan and blessed me,

4 "and said to me, 'Behold, I will make you fruitful and multiply you, and I will make of you a multitude of people, and give this land to your descendants after you *as* an everlasting possession.'

5 "And now your two sons, Ephraim and Manasseh, who were born to you in the land of Egypt before I came to you in Egypt, *are* mine; as Reuben and Simeon, they shall be mine.

6 "Your offspring whom you beget after them shall be yours; they will be called by the name of their brothers in their inheritance.

7 "But as for me, when I came from Padan, Rachel died beside me in the land of Canaan on the way, when *there was* but a little distance to go to Ephrath; and I buried her there on the way to Ephrath (that is, Bethlehem)."

8 Then Israel saw Joseph's sons, and said, "Who *are* these?"

9 Joseph said to his father, "They *are* my sons, whom God has given me in this *place.*" And he said, "Please bring them to me, and I will bless them."

10 Now the eyes of Israel were dim with age, *so that* he could not see. Then Joseph brought them near him, and he kissed them and embraced them.

11 And Israel said to Joseph, "I had not thought to see your face; but in fact, God has also shown me your offspring!"

12 So Joseph brought them from beside his knees, and he bowed down with his face to the earth.

13 And Joseph took them both, Ephraim with his right hand toward Israel's left hand, and Manasseh with his left hand toward Israel's right hand, and brought *them* near him.

14 Then Israel stretched out his right hand and laid *it* on Ephraim's head, who *was* the younger, and his left hand on Manasseh's head, guiding his hands knowingly, for Manasseh *was* the firstborn.

15 And he blessed Joseph, and said:

"God, before whom my fathers Abraham
and Isaac walked,
The God who has fed me all my life long
to this day,
16 The Angel who has redeemed me from
all evil,
Bless the lads;
Let my name be named upon them,
And the name of my fathers Abraham
and Isaac;
And let them grow into a multitude in the
midst of the earth."

LIFE LESSONS

➤ ***48:11 — And Israel said to Joseph, "I had not thought to see your face; but in fact, God has also shown me your offspring!"***

God often blesses us in ways far beyond anything we can imagine. We hope for "A," and He gives us the whole alphabet!

➤ ***48:15 — And he blessed Joseph, and said: "God, before whom my fathers Abraham and Isaac walked, the God who has fed me all my life long to this day . . . ."***

When Israel called God, "the God who has fed me all my life long to this day," he proclaimed that every good thing we have comes from the hand and grace of God.

17 Now when Joseph saw that his father laid
his right hand on the head of Ephraim, it displeased him; so he took hold of his father's
hand to remove it from Ephraim's head to
Manasseh's head.
18 And Joseph said to his father, "Not so, my
father, for this *one is* the firstborn; put your
right hand on his head."
19 But his father refused and said, "I know,
my son, I know. He also shall become a people, and he also shall be great; but truly his
younger brother shall be greater than he,
and his descendants shall become a multitude
of nations."
20 So he blessed them that day, saying, "By
you Israel will bless, saying, 'May God make
you as Ephraim and as Manasseh!'" And thus
he set Ephraim before Manasseh.
21 Then Israel said to Joseph, "Behold, I am
dying, but God will be with you and bring you
back to the land of your fathers.
22 "Moreover I have given to you one portion
above your brothers, which I took from the
hand of the Amorite with my sword and my
bow."

Jacob's Last Words to His Sons

49 And Jacob called his sons and said,
"Gather together, that I may tell you
what shall befall you in the last days:

2 "Gather together and hear, you sons of Jacob,
And listen to Israel your father.

3 "Reuben, you are my firstborn,
My might and the beginning of my strength,
The excellency of dignity and the excellency of power.
4 Unstable as water, you shall not excel,
Because you went up to your father's bed;
Then you defiled *it*—
He went up to my couch.

5 "Simeon and Levi *are* brothers;
Instruments of cruelty *are in* their dwelling place.
6 Let not my soul enter their council;
Let not my honor be united to their assembly;
For in their anger they slew a man,
And in their self-will they hamstrung an ox.
7 Cursed *be* their anger, for *it is* fierce;
And their wrath, for it is cruel!
I will divide them in Jacob
And scatter them in Israel.

8 "Judah, you *are he* whom your brothers shall praise;
Your hand *shall be* on the neck of your enemies;
Your father's children shall bow down before you.
9 Judah *is* a lion's whelp;
From the prey, my son, you have gone up.
He bows down, he lies down as a lion;
And as a lion, who shall rouse him?
10 The scepter shall not depart from Judah,
Nor a lawgiver from between his feet,
Until Shiloh comes;
And to Him *shall be* the obedience of the people.
11 Binding his donkey to the vine,
And his donkey's colt to the choice vine,
He washed his garments in wine,
And his clothes in the blood of grapes.
12 His eyes *are* darker than wine,
And his teeth whiter than milk.

13 "Zebulun shall dwell by the haven of the sea;
He *shall become* a haven for ships,
And his border shall adjoin Sidon.

14 "Issachar is a strong donkey,
Lying down between two burdens;
15 He saw that rest *was* good,
And that the land *was* pleasant;
He bowed his shoulder to bear *a burden*,
And became a band of slaves.

16 "Dan shall judge his people
As one of the tribes of Israel.
17 Dan shall be a serpent by the way,
A viper by the path,
That bites the horse's heels
So that its rider shall fall backward.
18 I have waited for your salvation, O LORD!

19 "Gad, a troop shall tramp upon him,
But he shall triumph at last.

LIFE LESSONS

➤ **49:10 — *"The scepter shall not depart from Judah, nor a lawgiver from between his feet, until Shiloh comes; and to Him shall be the obedience of the people."***

Israel foresaw that the Messiah, Jesus, would come through the line of Judah, and that He would be both the King and the Judge of the whole earth.

20"Bread from Asher *shall be* rich,
And he shall yield royal dainties.

21"Naphtali *is* a deer let loose;
He uses beautiful words.

22"Joseph *is* a fruitful bough,
A fruitful bough by a well;
His branches run over the wall.
23 The archers have bitterly grieved him,
Shot *at him* and hated him.
24 But his bow remained in strength,
And the arms of his hands were made strong
By the hands of the Mighty *God* of Jacob
(From there *is* the Shepherd, the Stone of Israel),
25 By the God of your father who will help you,
And by the Almighty who will bless you
With blessings of heaven above,
Blessings of the deep that lies beneath,
Blessings of the breasts and of the womb.
26 The blessings of your father
Have excelled the blessings of my ancestors,
Up to the utmost bound of the everlasting hills.
They shall be on the head of Joseph,
And on the crown of the head of him who was separate from his brothers.

27"Benjamin is a ravenous wolf;
In the morning he shall devour the prey,
And at night he shall divide the spoil."

28 All these *are* the twelve tribes of Israel,
and this *is* what their father spoke to them.
And he blessed them; he blessed each one according to his own blessing.

Jacob's Death and Burial

29 Then he charged them and said to them: "I
am to be gathered to my people; bury me with
my fathers in the cave that *is* in the field of
Ephron the Hittite,
30 "in the cave that *is* in the field of Machpelah, which *is* before Mamre in the land of
Canaan, which Abraham bought with the
field of Ephron the Hittite as a possession for
a burial place.
31 "There they buried Abraham and Sarah
his wife, there they buried Isaac and Rebekah
his wife, and there I buried Leah.
32 "The field and the cave that *is* there *were*
purchased from the sons of Heth."
33 And when Jacob had finished commanding his sons, he drew his feet up into the bed
and breathed his last, and was gathered to his
people.

50 Then Joseph fell on his father's face
and wept over him, and kissed him.
2 And Joseph commanded his servants the
physicians to embalm his father. So the physicians embalmed Israel.
3 Forty days were required for him, for such
are the days required for those who are embalmed; and the Egyptians mourned for him
seventy days.
4 Now when the days of his mourning were
past, Joseph spoke to the household of
Pharaoh, saying, "If now I have found favor in
your eyes, please speak in the hearing of
Pharaoh, saying,
5 'My father made me swear, saying, "Behold, I am dying; in my grave which I dug
for myself in the land of Canaan, there you
shall bury me." Now therefore, please let me
go up and bury my father, and I will come
back.'"
6 And Pharaoh said, "Go up and bury your
father, as he made you swear."
7 So Joseph went up to bury his father; and
with him went up all the servants of Pharaoh,
the elders of his house, and all the elders of
the land of Egypt,
8 as well as all the house of Joseph, his
brothers, and his father's house. Only their
little ones, their flocks, and their herds they
left in the land of Goshen.
9 And there went up with him both chariots
and horsemen, and it was a very great gathering.
10 Then they came to the threshing floor of
Atad, which *is* beyond the Jordan, and they
mourned there with a great and very solemn
lamentation. He observed seven days of
mourning for his father.
11 And when the inhabitants of the land, the
Canaanites, saw the mourning at the threshing floor of Atad, they said, "This *is* a deep
mourning of the Egyptians." Therefore its
name was called Abel Mizraim,[a] which *is* beyond the Jordan.
12 So his sons did for him just as he had commanded them.
13 For his sons carried him to the land
of Canaan, and buried him in the cave of
the field of Machpelah, before Mamre, which
Abraham bought with the field from Ephron
the Hittite as property for a burial place.
14 And after he had buried his father, Joseph
returned to Egypt, he and his brothers and all
who went up with him to bury his father.

Joseph Reassures His Brothers

15 When Joseph's brothers saw that their father was dead, they said, "Perhaps Joseph will
hate us, and may actually repay us for all the
evil which we did to him."
16 So they sent *messengers* to Joseph, saying, "Before your father died he commanded,
saying,

50:11 [a]Literally *Mourning of Egypt*

17 'Thus you shall say to Joseph: "I beg you,
please forgive the trespass of your brothers
and their sin; for they did evil to you."' Now,
please, forgive the trespass of the servants of
the God of your father." And Joseph wept
when they spoke to him.
18 Then his brothers also went and fell down
before his face, and they said, "Behold, we *are*
your servants."
19 Joseph said to them, "Do not be afraid, for
am I in the place of God?
➤ 20 "But as for you, you meant evil against me;
but God meant it for good, in order to bring it
about as *it is* this day, to save many people
alive.
21 "Now therefore, do not be afraid; I will
provide for you and your little ones." And
he comforted them and spoke kindly to
them.

Death of Joseph

22 So Joseph dwelt in Egypt, he and his father's household. And Joseph lived one hundred and ten years.
23 Joseph saw Ephraim's children to the
third *generation.* The children of Machir, the
son of Manasseh, were also brought up on Joseph's knees.
24 And Joseph said to his brethren, "I am
dying; but God will surely visit you, and bring
you out of this land to the land of which He
swore to Abraham, to Isaac, and to Jacob."
25 Then Joseph took an oath from the children of Israel, saying, "God will surely visit
you, and you shall carry up my bones from
here."
26 So Joseph died, *being* one hundred and
ten years old; and they embalmed him, and he
was put in a coffin in Egypt.

LIFE LESSONS

➤ 50:20 — *"But as for you, you meant evil against me; but God meant it for good, in order to bring it about as it is this day, to save many people alive."*

Sometimes God allows us to go through difficult times, even as a result of the wicked actions of others. Yet whatever we have to endure, no matter how unfair or unjust, we can be sure that God will use it for good.

THE SECOND BOOK OF MOSES CALLED

EXODUS

"Exodus" is a Greek word that literally means "exit," "departure," or "going out." The Septuagint (an ancient Greek translation of the Old Testament) uses this word to describe the book by its key event (see 19:1, "gone out"). In Luke 9:31 and in 2 Peter 1:15, the word *exodus* speaks of physical death (of both Jesus and Peter), thus echoing Exodus's theme of redemption through death.

Exodus records Israel's birth as a nation. During their time in Egypt, one Hebrew family of seventy persons rapidly multiplies. At the right time and accompanied by severe birth pains, an infant nation numbering between two and three million persons comes into the world, where God protects, feeds, and nurtures it.

The key figure in the Book of Exodus is Moses, a man who greatly doubted his ability to lead God's people but who nevertheless remained steadfast in his commitment to God. Although Moses was born into the home of a Levite couple, he grew up in an Egyptian household with all the advantages of royalty. After a failed attempt to deliver God's people from Egyptian bondage by his own strength, he spent forty years in a wilderness exile, where he received a thorough divine education.

To show Moses the seriousness of His plan, God called him from the midst of a burning bush that somehow did not burn up. In that remarkable encounter, God tasked a reluctant Moses with delivering His people from the Egyptians. So in Exodus, Moses sets out to fulfill his special calling: to lead the people of God out of harsh bondage.

Theme: The Book of Exodus demonstrates twin themes of divine redemption and deliverance. These themes are wonderfully demonstrated in Moses' calling to lead the people of Israel and in the ten plagues sent upon Egypt when Pharaoh refused to set the Israelites free (7–11).

Author: Moses

Time: The Book of Exodus covers a period from the birth of Moses (about 1525 B.C.) to the construction of the tabernacle, about 1446 B.C. Most scholars date the Exodus from Egypt to around 1447 B.C.

Structure: The Book of Exodus begins with an account of Egyptian oppression (1:7–22), then moves to the early years of Moses' life (2:1–21), followed by Moses' calling and his demand to Pharaoh to release his people from captivity (3:1—12:30), then describes the exodus from Egypt and the Israelites' journey to Mount Sinai (12:31—18:27). The remainder of the book covers the giving of the Law and the establishment of Hebrew culture.

As you read Exodus, watch for several life principles that play an important role in this book:

5. God does not require us to understand His will, just obey it, even if it seems unreasonable. *See Exodus 12:1–28, page 77.*

11. God assumes full responsibility for our needs when we obey Him. *See Exodus 14:1–31, page 79.*

13. Listening to God is essential to walking with God. *See Exodus 15:26, page 82.*

2. Obey God and leave all the consequences to Him. *See Exodus 19:5, page 88.*

Israel's Suffering in Egypt

1 Now these *are* the names of the children of Israel who came to Egypt; each man and his household came with Jacob:
2 Reuben, Simeon, Levi, and Judah;
3 Issachar, Zebulun, and Benjamin;
4 Dan, Naphtali, Gad, and Asher.
5 All those who were descendants[a] of Jacob were seventy[b] persons (for Joseph was in Egypt *already*).
6 And Joseph died, all his brothers, and all that generation.
7 But the children of Israel were fruitful and increased abundantly, multiplied and grew exceedingly mighty; and the land was filled with them.
8 Now there arose a new king over Egypt, who did not know Joseph.
9 And he said to his people, "Look, the people of the children of Israel *are* more and mightier than we;
10 "come, let us deal shrewdly with them, lest they multiply, and it happen, in the event of war, that they also join our enemies and fight against us, and *so* go up out of the land."
11 Therefore they set taskmasters over them to afflict them with their burdens. And they built for Pharaoh supply cities, Pithom and Raamses.
12 But the more they afflicted them, the more they multiplied and grew. And they were in dread of the children of Israel.
13 So the Egyptians made the children of Israel serve with rigor.
14 And they made their lives bitter with hard bondage—in mortar, in brick, and in all manner of service in the field. All their service in which they made them serve *was* with rigor.
15 Then the king of Egypt spoke to the Hebrew midwives, of whom the name of one *was* Shiphrah and the name of the other Puah;
16 and he said, "When you do the duties of a midwife for the Hebrew women, and see *them* on the birthstools, if it *is* a son, then you shall kill him; but if it *is* a daughter, then she shall live."
➤ 17 But the midwives feared God, and did not do as the king of Egypt commanded them, but saved the male children alive.
18 So the king of Egypt called for the midwives and said to them, "Why have you done this thing, and saved the male children alive?"
19 And the midwives said to Pharaoh, "Because the Hebrew women *are* not like the Egyptian women; for they *are* lively and give birth before the midwives come to them."
20 Therefore God dealt well with the midwives, and the people multiplied and grew very mighty. ➤
21 And so it was, because the midwives feared God, that He provided households for them.
22 So Pharaoh commanded all his people, saying, "Every son who is born[a] you shall cast into the river, and every daughter you shall save alive."

Moses Is Born

2 And a man of the house of Levi went and took *as wife* a daughter of Levi.
2 So the woman conceived and bore a son. And when she saw that he *was* a beautiful *child,* she hid him three months.
3 But when she could no longer hide him, she took an ark of bulrushes for him, daubed it with asphalt and pitch, put the child in it, and laid *it* in the reeds by the river's bank.
4 And his sister stood afar off, to know what would be done to him.
5 Then the daughter of Pharaoh came down to bathe at the river. And her maidens walked along the riverside; and when she saw the ark among the reeds, she sent her maid to get it.
6 And when she opened *it,* she saw the child, and behold, the baby wept. So she had compassion on him, and said, "This is one of the Hebrews' children."
7 Then his sister said to Pharaoh's daughter, "Shall I go and call a nurse for you from the Hebrew women, that she may nurse the child for you?"
8 And Pharaoh's daughter said to her, "Go." ➤
So the maiden went and called the child's mother.

1:5 [a]Literally *who came from the loins of* [b]Dead Sea Scrolls and Septuagint read *seventy-five* (compare Acts 7:14).
1:22 [a]Samaritan Pentateuch, Septuagint, and Targum add *to the Hebrews.*

LIFE LESSONS

➤ **1:17 — *But the midwives feared God, and did not do as the king of Egypt commanded them, but saved the male children alive.***

When we fear God more than we fear anyone or anything else, God can do mighty things through us.

➤ **1:20 — *Therefore God dealt well with the midwives, and the people multiplied and grew very mighty.***

God blessed the midwives for their courageous actions. He always blesses wholehearted obedience!

➤ **2:8–10 — *. . . So the maiden went and called the child's mother . . . . So the woman took the child and nursed him. And the child grew, and she brought him to Pharaoh's daughter, and he became her son . . . .***

The Lord delights in taking the evil of men and using it for good. Here, God took an Egyptian edict meant to kill Hebrew boys and used it to rear a Hebrew deliverer in Pharaoh's own household!

9 Then Pharaoh's daughter said to her, "Take this child away and nurse him for me, and I will give *you* your wages." So the woman took the child and nursed him.
10 And the child grew, and she brought him to Pharaoh's daughter, and he became her son. So she called his name Moses,[a] saying, "Because I drew him out of the water."

Moses Flees to Midian

11 Now it came to pass in those days, when Moses was grown, that he went out to his brethren and looked at their burdens. And he saw an Egyptian beating a Hebrew, one of his brethren.
➤ 12 So he looked this way and that way, and when he saw no one, he killed the Egyptian and hid him in the sand.
13 And when he went out the second day, behold, two Hebrew men were fighting, and he said to the one who did the wrong, "Why are you striking your companion?"
14 Then he said, "Who made you a prince and a judge over us? Do you intend to kill me as you killed the Egyptian?" So Moses feared and said, "Surely this thing is known!"
15 When Pharaoh heard of this matter, he sought to kill Moses. But Moses fled from the face of Pharaoh and dwelt in the land of Midian; and he sat down by a well.
16 Now the priest of Midian had seven daughters. And they came and drew water, and they filled the troughs to water their father's flock.
17 Then the shepherds came and drove them away; but Moses stood up and helped them, and watered their flock.
18 When they came to Reuel their father, he said, "How *is it that* you have come so soon today?"
19 And they said, "An Egyptian delivered us from the hand of the shepherds, and he also drew enough water for us and watered the flock."
20 So he said to his daughters, "And where *is* he? Why *is* it *that* you have left the man? Call him, that he may eat bread."
21 Then Moses was content to live with the man, and he gave Zipporah his daughter to Moses.
22 And she bore *him* a son. He called his name Gershom,[a] for he said, "I have been a stranger in a foreign land."
23 Now it happened in the process of time ➤ that the king of Egypt died. Then the children of Israel groaned because of the bondage, and they cried out; and their cry came up to God because of the bondage.
24 So God heard their groaning, and God remembered His covenant with Abraham, with Isaac, and with Jacob. ✳
25 And God looked upon the children of Israel, and God acknowledged *them.*

Moses at the Burning Bush

3 Now Moses was tending the flock of Jethro his father-in-law, the priest of Midian. And he led the flock to the back of the desert, and came to Horeb, the mountain of God.
2 And the Angel of the LORD appeared to ➤ him in a flame of fire from the midst of a bush. So he looked, and behold, the bush was burning with fire, but the bush *was* not consumed.
3 Then Moses said, "I will now turn aside and see this great sight, why the bush does not burn."
4 So when the LORD saw that he turned aside to look, God called to him from the midst of the bush and said, "Moses, Moses!" And he said, "Here I am."
5 Then He said, "Do not draw near this place. Take your sandals off your feet, for the place where you stand *is* holy ground."
6 Moreover He said, "I *am* the God of your father—the God of Abraham, the God of Isaac, and the God of Jacob." And Moses hid his face, for he was afraid to look upon God.
7 And the LORD said: "I have surely seen the oppression of My people who *are* in Egypt, and have heard their cry because of their taskmasters, for I know their sorrows.

2:10 [a]Literally *Drawn Out* **2:22** [a]Literally *Stranger There*

LIFE LESSONS

➤ 2:12 — *So he looked this way and that way, and when he saw no one, he killed the Egyptian and hid him in the sand.*

Moses looked this way and that way, but he failed to look up. If he had brought God into his deliberations, he would not have become a murderer.

➤ 2:23 — *Now it happened in the process of time that the king of Egypt died. Then the children of Israel groaned because of the bondage, and they cried out; and their cry came up to God because of the bondage.*

God heard the cries and groans of the enslaved Hebrews and moved to act for their deliverance long before they knew anything about it. God is at work on our behalf even when He appears silent.

➤ 3:2 — *. . . So he looked, and behold, the bush was burning with fire, but the bush was not consumed.*

God often speaks to us through unusual circumstances. When we find ourselves in the midst of confusing times that we can't understand, we should slow down and listen. God just might be trying to tell us something.

8 "So I have come down to deliver them out
of the hand of the Egyptians, and to bring
them up from that land to a good and large
land, to a land flowing with milk and honey,
to the place of the Canaanites and the Hittites
and the Amorites and the Perizzites and the
Hivites and the Jebusites.
➤ 9 "Now therefore, behold, the cry of the children of Israel has come to Me, and I have also
seen the oppression with which the Egyptians
oppress them.
10 "Come now, therefore, and I will send you
to Pharaoh that you may bring My people, the
children of Israel, out of Egypt."
➤ 11 But Moses said to God, "Who *am* I that I
should go to Pharaoh, and that I should bring
the children of Israel out of Egypt?"
12 So He said, "I will certainly be with you.
And this *shall be* a sign to you that I have sent
you: When you have brought the people out of
Egypt, you shall serve God on this mountain."
13 Then Moses said to God, "Indeed, *when* I
come to the children of Israel and say to
them, 'The God of your fathers has sent me to
you,' and they say to me, 'What *is* His name?'
what shall I say to them?"
➤ 14 And God said to Moses, "I AM WHO I
AM." And He said, "Thus you shall say to the
children of Israel, 'I AM has sent me to you.'"
15 Moreover God said to Moses, "Thus you
shall say to the children of Israel: 'The LORD
God of your fathers, the God of Abraham, the
God of Isaac, and the God of Jacob, has sent
me to you. This *is* My name forever, and this
is My memorial to all generations.'
16 "Go and gather the elders of Israel together, and say to them, 'The LORD God of
your fathers, the God of Abraham, of Isaac,
and of Jacob, appeared to me, saying, "I have
surely visited you and *seen* what is done to
you in Egypt;
17 "and I have said I will bring you up out of
the affliction of Egypt to the land of the
Canaanites and the Hittites and the Amorites
and the Perizzites and the Hivites and the Jebusites, to a land flowing with milk and
honey."'
18 "Then they will heed your voice; and you
shall come, you and the elders of Israel, to the
king of Egypt; and you shall say to him, 'The
LORD God of the Hebrews has met with us;
and now, please, let us go three days' journey

Life Examples:

MOSES

God's Pattern for Success

EX. 3:1–4

One of the greatest differences between the world's message about success and God's is this: The world seeks a single formula to produce one set of results for all people, while God's plan is far more creative, far more individualized, and far more personal.

Moses did not have a vision for success early in his life, although as an adopted son of Pharaoh he enjoyed a certain degree of privilege. After murdering an Egyptian, however, he ran for his life and then spent forty years tending sheep. But one day the Lord revealed Himself to Moses and gave him a specific life mission.

Many of us go through difficult and even devastating experiences, and then one day come face-to-face with the reality of God. Is this the pattern that God seems to be implementing in your life? If so, stick with His plan, regardless of how unorthodox it may seem—the Promised Land lies in that direction!

See the Life Principles Index for further study:

7. The dark moments of our life will last only so long as is necessary for God to accomplish His purpose in us.

29. We learn more in our valley experiences than on our mountaintops.

LIFE LESSONS

➤ 3:9 — *"Now therefore, behold, the cry of the children of Israel has come to Me, and I have also seen the oppression with which the Egyptians oppress them."*

God hears our cries and sees our troubles, and in His sovereign way moves to deliver us from our oppressors. But He does His work in His time, not ours.

➤ 3:11, 12 — *But Moses said to God, "Who am I that I should go to Pharaoh, and that I should bring the children of Israel out of Egypt?" So He said, "I will certainly be with you . . . ."*

We are qualified to do God's work, not because of our own talents or abilities or training, but because God is with us. And if He is not with us, then no amount of skill or experience will make us qualified.

➤ 3:14 — *And God said to Moses, "I AM WHO I AM." And He said, "Thus you shall say to the children of Israel, 'I AM has sent me to you.'"*

We serve the God who is alive, who is present, who is here right now and who gives life and breath to everything that lives (see Acts 17:25). He IS, whether anything else remains or not.

ANSWERS TO LIFE'S QUESTIONS

What can I do to earn a more spiritually responsible role?

EX. 3:3–9

Few men ever had a greater responsibility placed on their shoulders than Moses, whom God tasked with leading the nation of Israel out of Egyptian bondage and into the Promised Land.

Responsibility requires a spirit of faithfulness, dependability, and the refusal to give up when times get rough. Moses had these qualities, and God chose him as His special human representative.

It took years, however, to prepare Moses for the enormous job. He began life as an impetuous, hotheaded, and stubborn young man. When he witnessed the suffering of God's people in Egypt, immediately he sought to deliver them through his own human strength. And neither he nor his people benefited from his hasty actions.

God always clarifies our responsibility so we can respond in obedience. He never leaves us alone; He promises to shoulder the responsibility with us. If He didn't, we would become easily discouraged and would fail to understand the significance of our calling.

God uses various events and circumstances to prepare us for increasing levels of spiritual responsibility. He used a burning bush to gain Moses' attention (Ex. 3:3–9): This was the man's moment of calling. By this time, Moses' heart had become receptive and his spirit primed for greater spiritual responsibility.

God always equips us for the responsibilities He gives us. He provided Aaron as a friend and spokesman for Moses. Even the staff God gave Moses was amazingly useful as a symbol of His power.

God also always prepares us for the responsibility He assigns us. Throughout Moses' life, God had been preparing him to lead the nation of Israel.

Anytime God calls us to fulfill a certain responsibility, we enter a period of waiting. Moses tried to take a shortcut but failed, and he spent forty years in the desert as a result. Yet in these times of waiting, God molds and shapes us. The *only* way to meet the challenge of responsibility is to be willing to wait on God's timing in every situation.

Three words characterize a responsible person: *confidence* in God's calling and ability; the *courage* to obey regardless of the cost; and a *commitment* to Jesus Christ.

God gives us limitless opportunities, but we must assume responsibility and obey His call. As you pray, ask God to expand your world of opportunities and give you the desire to become responsible, like Moses, and willing to obey regardless of the cost.

See the Life Principles Index for further study:
21. Obedience always brings blessing.
14. God acts on behalf of those who wait for Him.

into the wilderness, that we may sacrifice to
the LORD our God.'
19 "But I am sure that the king of Egypt ➤
will not let you go, no, not even by a mighty
hand.
20 "So I will stretch out My hand and strike
Egypt with all My wonders which I will do in
its midst; and after that he will let you go.
21 "And I will give this people favor in the
sight of the Egyptians; and it shall be, when
you go, that you shall not go empty-handed.
22 "But every woman shall ask of her neighbor, namely, of her who dwells near her
house, articles of silver, articles of gold, and
clothing; and you shall put *them* on your sons
and on your daughters. So you shall plunder
the Egyptians."

Miraculous Signs for Pharaoh

4 Then Moses answered and said, "But suppose they will not believe me or listen to
my voice; suppose they say, 'The LORD has not
appeared to you.'"
2 So the LORD said to him, "What *is* that in ➤
your hand?" He said, "A rod."
3 And He said, "Cast it on the ground." So
he cast it on the ground, and it became a serpent; and Moses fled from it.
4 Then the LORD said to Moses, "Reach out
your hand and take *it* by the tail" (and he
reached out his hand and caught it, and it became a rod in his hand),
5 "that they may believe that the LORD God
of their fathers, the God of Abraham, the God
of Isaac, and the God of Jacob, has appeared
to you."
6 Furthermore the LORD said to him, "Now
put your hand in your bosom." And he put his

hand in his bosom, and when he took it out,
behold, his hand *was* leprous, like snow.
7 And He said, "Put your hand in your
bosom again." So he put his hand in his bosom
again, and drew it out of his bosom, and behold,
it was restored like his *other* flesh.
8 "Then it will be, if they do not believe you,
nor heed the message of the first sign, that
they may believe the message of the latter
sign.
9 "And it shall be, if they do not believe even
these two signs, or listen to your voice, that
you shall take water from the river[a] and pour
it on the dry *land*. The water which you take
from the river will become blood on the dry
land."
10 Then Moses said to the LORD, "O my Lord,
I *am* not eloquent, neither before nor since
You have spoken to Your servant; but I *am*
slow of speech and slow of tongue."
11 So the LORD said to him, "Who has made
man's mouth? Or who makes the mute, the
deaf, the seeing, or the blind? *Have* not I, the
LORD?
➤ 12 "Now therefore, go, and I will be with your
mouth and teach you what you shall say."
13 But he said, "O my Lord, please send by
the hand of whomever *else* You may send."
14 So the anger of the LORD was kindled
against Moses, and He said: "Is not Aaron the
Levite your brother? I know that he can speak
well. And look, he is also coming out to meet
you. When he sees you, he will be glad in his
heart.
15 "Now you shall speak to him and put the
words in his mouth. And I will be with your
mouth and with his mouth, and I will teach
you what you shall do.
16 "So he shall be your spokesman to the
people. And he himself shall be as a mouth
for you, and you shall be to him as God.
17 "And you shall take this rod in your hand,
with which you shall do the signs."

Moses Goes to Egypt

18 So Moses went and returned to Jethro his
father-in-law, and said to him, "Please let me
go and return to my brethren who *are* in
Egypt, and see whether they are still alive."
And Jethro said to Moses, "Go in peace."
19 Now the LORD said to Moses in Midian,
"Go, return to Egypt; for all the men who
sought your life are dead."
20 Then Moses took his wife and his sons
and set them on a donkey, and he returned to

Life Examples:

PHARAOH

A Bad Case of a Hard Heart

EX. 3:19, 20

Pharaoh is probably the best illustration in the Bible of a person with a hard heart. He thus provides a blueprint for what happens when a person refuses to accept and bend his or her will to the truth of God.

Pharaoh received overwhelming evidence—plague after plague, sign after sign, miracle after miracle—and still refused to let the Israelites go. Even when faced with undeniable evidence of his error, Pharaoh refused to acknowledge that another was greater than he. In the end, his pride and hard-heartedness cost him his army and almost his kingdom.

All of us have stubbornly desired to have things the way we want them, even when our way opposes God's way. Every time we say no to God, we skirt the edges of rebelling once too often. If we repeatedly say no to God, then like Pharaoh we may develop a hard heart that leads to destruction.

See the Life Principles Index for further study:
21. Obedience always brings blessing.
16. Whatever you acquire outside of God's will eventually turns to ashes.

4:9 [a]That is, the Nile

LIFE LESSONS

➤ 3:19 — *"But I am sure that the king of Egypt will not let you go, no, not even by a mighty hand."*

We can have confidence in our prayer lives because we serve the God who knows the end from the beginning. Just as the Lord knew how Pharaoh would respond to Moses, so He knows exactly what lies ahead of us.

➤ 4:2 — *So the LORD said to him, "What is that in your hand?" He said, "A rod."*

What is in *your* hand? It may not seem like much to you—maybe it's just a stick—but if you allow God to use both you and it, He can accomplish mighty things in your world.

➤ 4:12 — *"Now therefore, go, and I will be with your mouth and teach you what you shall say."*

If we submit ourselves to God and obey His Word to us, He will make us competent for whatever task He gives us.

the land of Egypt. And Moses took the rod of
God in his hand.
21 And the LORD said to Moses, "When you
go back to Egypt, see that you do all those
wonders before Pharaoh which I have put in
your hand. But I will harden his heart, so that
he will not let the people go.
22 "Then you shall say to Pharaoh, 'Thus
says the LORD: "Israel *is* My son, My firstborn.
23 "So I say to you, let My son go that he may
serve Me. But if you refuse to let him go, indeed I will kill your son, your firstborn."'"
24 And it came to pass on the way, at the encampment, that the LORD met him and sought
to kill him.
25 Then Zipporah took a sharp stone and cut
off the foreskin of her son and cast *it* at *Moses'*[a] feet, and said, "Surely you *are* a husband
of blood to me!"
26 So He let him go. Then she said, "*You are*
a husband of blood!"—because of the circumcision.
27 And the LORD said to Aaron, "Go into the
wilderness to meet Moses." So he went and
met him on the mountain of God, and kissed
him.
28 So Moses told Aaron all the words of the
LORD who had sent him, and all the signs
which He had commanded him.
29 Then Moses and Aaron went and gathered
together all the elders of the children of Israel.
30 And Aaron spoke all the words which the
LORD had spoken to Moses. Then he did the
signs in the sight of the people.
➤ 31 So the people believed; and when they
heard that the LORD had visited the children
of Israel and that He had looked on their affliction, then they bowed their heads and worshiped.

First Encounter with Pharaoh

5 Afterward Moses and Aaron went in and
told Pharaoh, "Thus says the LORD God of
Israel: 'Let My people go, that they may hold
a feast to Me in the wilderness.'"
2 And Pharaoh said, "Who *is* the LORD, that
I should obey His voice to let Israel go? I do
not know the LORD, nor will I let Israel go."
3 So they said, "The God of the Hebrews has
met with us. Please, let us go three days' journey into the desert and sacrifice to the LORD
our God, lest He fall upon us with pestilence
or with the sword."
4 Then the king of Egypt said to them, "Moses and Aaron, why do you take the people
from their work? Get *back* to your labor."
5 And Pharaoh said, "Look, the people of
the land *are* many now, and you make them
rest from their labor!"
6 So the same day Pharaoh commanded the
taskmasters of the people and their officers,
saying,
7 "You shall no longer give the people straw
to make brick as before. Let them go and
gather straw for themselves.
8 "And you shall lay on them the quota of
bricks which they made before. You shall not
reduce it. For they are idle; therefore they cry
out, saying, 'Let us go *and* sacrifice to our
God.'
9 "Let more work be laid on the men, that ➤
they may labor in it, and let them not regard
false words."
10 And the taskmasters of the people and
their officers went out and spoke to the people, saying, "Thus says Pharaoh: 'I will not
give you straw.
11 'Go, get yourselves straw where you can
find it; yet none of your work will be reduced.'"
12 So the people were scattered abroad
throughout all the land of Egypt to gather
stubble instead of straw.
13 And the taskmasters forced *them* to hurry,
saying, "Fulfill your work, *your* daily quota,
as when there was straw."
14 Also the officers of the children of Israel,
whom Pharaoh's taskmasters had set over
them, were beaten *and* were asked, "Why
have you not fulfilled your task in making
brick both yesterday and today, as before?"
15 Then the officers of the children of Israel
came and cried out to Pharaoh, saying, "Why
are you dealing thus with your servants?
16 There is no straw given to your servants,
and they say to us, 'Make brick!' And indeed
your servants *are* beaten, but the fault *is* in
your *own* people."
17 But he said, "You *are* idle! Idle! Therefore
you say, 'Let us go *and* sacrifice to the LORD.'
18 Therefore go now *and* work; for no straw

4:25 [a]Literally *his*

LIFE LESSONS

➤ **4:31 — *So the people believed; and when they heard that the LORD had visited the children of Israel and that He had looked on their affliction, then they bowed their heads and worshiped.***

When we know that the Lord has heard our cries and responded in grace to our prayers, worship ought to flow naturally out of our mouths and hearts.

➤ **5:9 — *"Let more work be laid on the men, that they may labor in it, and let them not regard false words."***

When God begins to move in power on our behalf, sometimes our situation can actually grow worse before it gets better. Yet adversity is a setback from which we take our greatest leaps forward.

shall be given you, yet you shall deliver the
quota of bricks."
19 And the officers of the children of Israel
saw *that* they *were* in trouble after it was
said, "You shall not reduce *any* bricks from
your daily quota."
20 Then, as they came out from Pharaoh,
they met Moses and Aaron who stood there to
meet them.
21 And they said to them, "Let the LORD look
on you and judge, because you have made us
abhorrent in the sight of Pharaoh and in the
sight of his servants, to put a sword in their
hand to kill us."

Israel's Deliverance Assured

➤ **22** So Moses returned to the LORD and said,
"Lord, why have You brought trouble on this
people? Why *is* it You have sent me?
23 "For since I came to Pharaoh to speak in
Your name, he has done evil to this people;
neither have You delivered Your people at all."
6 Then the LORD said to Moses, "Now you
shall see what I will do to Pharaoh. For
with a strong hand he will let them go, and
with a strong hand he will drive them out of
his land."
2 And God spoke to Moses and said to him:
"I *am* the LORD.
3 "I appeared to Abraham, to Isaac, and to
Jacob, as God Almighty, but *by* My name
LORD[a] I was not known to them.
4 "I have also established My covenant with
them, to give them the land of Canaan, the
land of their pilgrimage, in which they were
strangers.
5 "And I have also heard the groaning of the
children of Israel whom the Egyptians keep
in bondage, and I have remembered My covenant.
6 "Therefore say to the children of Israel: 'I
am the LORD; I will bring you out from under
the burdens of the Egyptians, I will rescue
you from their bondage, and I will redeem
you with an outstretched arm and with great
judgments.
7 'I will take you as My people, and I will be
your God. Then you shall know that I *am* the
LORD your God who brings you out from
under the burdens of the Egyptians.
8 'And I will bring you into the land which I
swore to give to Abraham, Isaac, and Jacob;
and I will give it to you *as* a heritage: I *am* the
LORD.'"
9 So Moses spoke thus to the children of Is- ➤
rael; but they did not heed Moses, because of
anguish of spirit and cruel bondage.
10 And the LORD spoke to Moses, saying,
11 "Go in, tell Pharaoh king of Egypt to let
the children of Israel go out of his land."
12 And Moses spoke before the LORD, saying,
"The children of Israel have not heeded me.
How then shall Pharaoh heed me, for I *am* of
uncircumcised lips?"
13 Then the LORD spoke to Moses and Aaron,
and gave them a command for the children of
Israel and for Pharaoh king of Egypt, to bring
the children of Israel out of the land of Egypt.

The Family of Moses and Aaron

14 These *are* the heads of their fathers'
houses: The sons of Reuben, the firstborn of
Israel, *were* Hanoch, Pallu, Hezron, and
Carmi. These are the families of Reuben.
15 And the sons of Simeon *were* Jemuel,[a]
Jamin, Ohad, Jachin, Zohar, and Shaul the
son of a Canaanite woman. These *are* the
families of Simeon.
16 These *are* the names of the sons of Levi
according to their generations: Gershon, Kohath, and Merari. And the years of the life of
Levi *were* one hundred and thirty-seven.
17 The sons of Gershon *were* Libni and
Shimi according to their families.
18 And the sons of Kohath *were* Amram,
Izhar, Hebron, and Uzziel. And the years of
the life of Kohath *were* one hundred and
thirty-three.
19 The sons of Merari *were* Mahli and Mushi.
These *are* the families of Levi according to
their generations.
20 Now Amram took for himself Jochebed,
his father's sister, as wife; and she bore him
Aaron and Moses. And the years of the life of
Amram *were* one hundred and thirty-seven.
21 The sons of Izhar *were* Korah, Nepheg,
and Zichri.
22 And the sons of Uzziel *were* Mishael,
Elzaphan, and Zithri.
23 Aaron took to himself Elisheba, daughter
of Amminadab, sister of Nahshon, as wife;

6:3 [a]Hebrew *YHWH,* traditionally *Jehovah* **6:15** [a]Spelled *Nemuel* in Numbers 26:12

LIFE LESSONS

➤ **5:22 — *So Moses returned to the LORD and said, "Lord, why have You brought trouble on this people? . . ."***

Sometimes we obey God, expecting a certain result—and the opposite happens. Then we wonder if God has made a mistake. But He never does; we simply have to wait until He finishes the story.

➤ **6:9 — *So Moses spoke thus to the children of Israel; but they did not heed Moses, because of anguish of spirit and cruel bondage.***

When we feel oppressed and our spirit groans, it is difficult for us to believe the good promises of God regarding our welfare. But disappointments are inevitable; discouragement is a choice.

and she bore him Nadab, Abihu, Eleazar, and Ithamar.

24 And the sons of Korah *were* Assir, Elkanah, and Abiasaph. These are the families of the Korahites.

25 Eleazar, Aaron's son, took for himself one of the daughters of Putiel as wife; and she bore him Phinehas. These *are* the heads of the fathers' houses of the Levites according to their families.

26 These *are the same* Aaron and Moses to whom the LORD said, "Bring out the children of Israel from the land of Egypt according to their armies."

27 These *are* the ones who spoke to Pharaoh king of Egypt, to bring out the children of Israel from Egypt. These *are the same* Moses and Aaron.

Aaron Is Moses' Spokesman

28 And it came to pass, on the day the LORD spoke to Moses in the land of Egypt,

29 that the LORD spoke to Moses, saying, "I *am* the LORD. Speak to Pharaoh king of Egypt all that I say to you."

30 But Moses said before the LORD, "Behold, I *am* of uncircumcised lips, and how shall Pharaoh heed me?"

7 So the LORD said to Moses: "See, I have made you *as* God to Pharaoh, and Aaron your brother shall be your prophet.

2 "You shall speak all that I command you. And Aaron your brother shall tell Pharaoh to send the children of Israel out of his land.

3 "And I will harden Pharaoh's heart, and multiply My signs and My wonders in the land of Egypt.

4 "But Pharaoh will not heed you, so that I may lay My hand on Egypt and bring My armies *and* My people, the children of Israel, out of the land of Egypt by great judgments.

➤ 5 "And the Egyptians shall know that I *am* the LORD, when I stretch out My hand on Egypt and bring out the children of Israel from among them."

6 Then Moses and Aaron did *so;* just as the LORD commanded them, so they did.

7 And Moses *was* eighty years old and Aaron eighty-three years old when they spoke to Pharaoh.

Aaron's Miraculous Rod

8 Then the LORD spoke to Moses and Aaron, saying,

9 "When Pharaoh speaks to you, saying, 'Show a miracle for yourselves,' then you shall say to Aaron, 'Take your rod and cast *it* before Pharaoh, *and* let it become a serpent.'"

10 So Moses and Aaron went in to Pharaoh, and they did so, just as the LORD commanded. And Aaron cast down his rod before Pharaoh and before his servants, and it became a serpent.

11 But Pharaoh also called the wise men and the sorcerers; so the magicians of Egypt, they also did in like manner with their enchantments. ➤

12 For every man threw down his rod, and they became serpents. But Aaron's rod swallowed up their rods.

13 And Pharaoh's heart grew hard, and he did not heed them, as the LORD had said.

The First Plague: Waters Become Blood

14 So the LORD said to Moses: "Pharaoh's heart *is* hard; he refuses to let the people go.

15 "Go to Pharaoh in the morning, when he goes out to the water, and you shall stand by the river's bank to meet him; and the rod which was turned to a serpent you shall take in your hand.

16 "And you shall say to him, 'The LORD God of the Hebrews has sent me to you, saying, "Let My people go, that they may serve Me in the wilderness"; but indeed, until now you would not hear!

17 'Thus says the LORD: "By this you shall know that I *am* the LORD. Behold, I will strike the waters which *are* in the river with the rod that *is* in my hand, and they shall be turned to blood.

18 "And the fish that *are* in the river shall die, the river shall stink, and the Egyptians will loathe to drink the water of the river."'"

19 Then the LORD spoke to Moses, "Say to Aaron, 'Take your rod and stretch out your hand over the waters of Egypt, over their streams, over their rivers, over their ponds, and over all their pools of water, that they may become blood. And there shall be blood throughout all the land of Egypt, both in *buckets of* wood and *pitchers of* stone.'"

20 And Moses and Aaron did so, just as the

LIFE LESSONS

➤ ***7:5 — "And the Egyptians shall know that I am the LORD, when I stretch out My hand on Egypt and bring out the children of Israel from among them."***

The Lord wants all the peoples of the earth to know Him—His power and glory and love and grace and justice. And He wants to show the world who He is through what He does in our lives.

➤ ***7:11 — But Pharaoh also called the wise men and the sorcerers; so the magicians of Egypt, they also did in like manner with their enchantments.***

The devil is fully capable of counterfeiting some of God's miraculous works, and so blinds many people to the truth (Matt. 24:24). This is why we must stay alert (2 Cor. 2:11; 1 Pet. 5:8).

LORD commanded. So he lifted up the rod and
struck the waters that *were* in the river, in the
sight of Pharaoh and in the sight of his servants. And all the waters that *were* in the
river were turned to blood.
21 The fish that *were* in the river died, the
river stank, and the Egyptians could not drink
the water of the river. So there was blood
throughout all the land of Egypt.
22 Then the magicians of Egypt did so with
their enchantments; and Pharaoh's heart
grew hard, and he did not heed them, as the
LORD had said.
23 And Pharaoh turned and went into his
house. Neither was his heart moved by this.
24 So all the Egyptians dug all around the
river for water to drink, because they could
not drink the water of the river.
25 And seven days passed after the LORD had
struck the river.

The Second Plague: Frogs

8 And the LORD spoke to Moses, "Go to
Pharaoh and say to him, 'Thus says the
LORD: "Let My people go, that they may serve
Me.
2 "But if you refuse to let *them* go, behold, I
will smite all your territory with frogs.
3 "So the river shall bring forth frogs abundantly, which shall go up and come into your
house, into your bedroom, on your bed, into
the houses of your servants, on your people,
into your ovens, and into your kneading
bowls.
4 "And the frogs shall come up on you, on
your people, and on all your servants."'"
5 Then the LORD spoke to Moses, "Say to
Aaron, 'Stretch out your hand with your rod
over the streams, over the rivers, and over the
ponds, and cause frogs to come up on the
land of Egypt.'"
6 So Aaron stretched out his hand over the
waters of Egypt, and the frogs came up and
covered the land of Egypt.
7 And the magicians did so with their enchantments, and brought up frogs on the land
of Egypt.
8 Then Pharaoh called for Moses and
Aaron, and said, "Entreat the LORD that He
may take away the frogs from me and from
my people; and I will let the people go, that
they may sacrifice to the LORD."
9 And Moses said to Pharaoh, "Accept the
honor of saying when I shall intercede for
you, for your servants, and for your people, to
destroy the frogs from you and your houses,
that they may remain in the river only."
10 So he said, "Tomorrow." And he said, "*Let
it be* according to your word, that you may
know that *there is* no one like the LORD our
God.
11 "And the frogs shall depart from you, from
your houses, from your servants, and from
your people. They shall remain in the river
only."
12 Then Moses and Aaron went out from
Pharaoh. And Moses cried out to the LORD
concerning the frogs which He had brought
against Pharaoh.
13 So the LORD did according to the word
of Moses. And the frogs died out of the
houses, out of the courtyards, and out of
the fields.
14 They gathered them together in heaps,
and the land stank.
15 But when Pharaoh saw that there was relief, he hardened his heart and did not heed
them, as the LORD had said.

The Third Plague: Lice

16 So the LORD said to Moses, "Say to Aaron,
'Stretch out your rod, and strike the dust of
the land, so that it may become lice throughout all the land of Egypt.'"
17 And they did so. For Aaron stretched out
his hand with his rod and struck the dust of
the earth, and it became lice on man and
beast. All the dust of the land became lice
throughout all the land of Egypt.
18 Now the magicians so worked with their
enchantments to bring forth lice, but they
could not. So there were lice on man and
beast.
19 Then the magicians said to Pharaoh, "This
is the finger of God." But Pharaoh's heart
grew hard, and he did not heed them, just as
the LORD had said.

The Fourth Plague: Flies

20 And the LORD said to Moses, "Rise early in
the morning and stand before Pharaoh as he
comes out to the water. Then say to him, 'Thus
says the LORD: "Let My people go, that they
may serve Me.
21 "Or else, if you will not let My people go,
behold, I will send swarms *of flies* on you and
your servants, on your people and into your
houses. The houses of the Egyptians shall be

LIFE LESSONS

➤ 8:15 — *But when Pharaoh saw that there was relief, he hardened his heart and did not heed them, as the LORD had said.*

"Foxhole Christians" are like Pharaoh: They acknowledge God and promise to obey so long as some trouble continues, but once relief arrives, they return to their old ways. But such a foolish lifestyle has serious consequences.

full of swarms *of flies*, and also the ground on
which they *stand*.
22 "And in that day I will set apart the land of
Goshen, in which My people dwell, that no
swarms *of flies* shall be there, in order that
you may know that I *am* the LORD in the midst
of the land.
23 "I will make a difference[a] between My
people and your people. Tomorrow this sign
shall be." ' "
24 And the LORD did so. Thick swarms *of flies*
came into the house of Pharaoh, *into* his servants' houses, and into all the land of Egypt.
The land was corrupted because of the
swarms *of flies*.
25 Then Pharaoh called for Moses and
Aaron, and said, "Go, sacrifice to your God in
the land."
26 And Moses said, "It is not right to do so,
for we would be sacrificing the abomination
of the Egyptians to the LORD our God. If we
sacrifice the abomination of the Egyptians
before their eyes, then will they not stone us?
27 "We will go three days' journey into the
wilderness and sacrifice to the LORD our God
as He will command us."
28 So Pharaoh said, "I will let you go, that
you may sacrifice to the LORD your God in the
wilderness; only you shall not go very far
away. Intercede for me."
29 Then Moses said, "Indeed I am going out
from you, and I will entreat the LORD, that the
swarms *of flies* may depart tomorrow from
Pharaoh, from his servants, and from his people. But let Pharaoh not deal deceitfully anymore in not letting the people go to sacrifice
to the LORD."
30 So Moses went out from Pharaoh and entreated the LORD.
31 And the LORD did according to the word of
Moses; He removed the swarms *of flies* from
Pharaoh, from his servants, and from his people. Not one remained.
32 But Pharaoh hardened his heart at this
time also; neither would he let the people go.

The Fifth Plague: Livestock Diseased

9 Then the LORD said to Moses, "Go in to
Pharaoh and tell him, 'Thus says the LORD
God of the Hebrews: "Let My people go, that
they may serve Me.
2 "For if you refuse to let *them* go, and still
hold them,
3 "behold, the hand of the LORD will be on
your cattle in the field, on the horses, on the
donkeys, on the camels, on the oxen, and on
the sheep—a very severe pestilence.
4 "And the LORD will make a difference between the livestock of Israel and the livestock
of Egypt. So nothing shall die of all *that* belongs to the children of Israel." ' "
5 Then the LORD appointed a set time, saying, "Tomorrow the LORD will do this thing in
the land."
6 So the LORD did this thing on the next day,
and all the livestock of Egypt died; but of the
livestock of the children of Israel, not one died.
7 Then Pharaoh sent, and indeed, not even
one of the livestock of the Israelites was dead.
But the heart of Pharaoh became hard, and he
did not let the people go.

The Sixth Plague: Boils

8 So the LORD said to Moses and Aaron,
"Take for yourselves handfuls of ashes from a
furnace, and let Moses scatter it toward the
heavens in the sight of Pharaoh.
9 "And it will become fine dust in all the
land of Egypt, and it will cause boils that
break out in sores on man and beast throughout all the land of Egypt."
10 Then they took ashes from the furnace
and stood before Pharaoh, and Moses scattered *them* toward heaven. And *they* caused
boils that break out in sores on man and
beast.
11 And the magicians could not stand before
Moses because of the boils, for the boils were
on the magicians and on all the Egyptians.
12 But the LORD hardened the heart of
Pharaoh; and he did not heed them, just as
the LORD had spoken to Moses.

The Seventh Plague: Hail

13 Then the LORD said to Moses, "Rise early
in the morning and stand before Pharaoh,
and say to him, 'Thus says the LORD God of
the Hebrews: "Let My people go, that they
may serve Me,
14 "for at this time I will send all My plagues
to your very heart, and on your servants and
on your people, that you may know that *there
is* none like Me in all the earth.

8:23 [a]Literally *set a ransom* (compare Exodus 9:4 and 11:7)

LIFE LESSONS

➤ 8:23 — *"I will make a difference between My people and your people. Tomorrow this sign shall be."*

Although Christians suffer troubles and hardships like anyone else, yet the Lord does make a difference between His people and those who do not believe. We may have to wait to see it, but it will come.

➤ 9:12 — *But the LORD hardened the heart of Pharaoh; and he did not heed them, just as the LORD had spoken to Moses.*

To this point in the story, Pharaoh had hardened his own heart. But now, *God* hardens his heart. Willful disobedience can reach a point of no return.

15 "Now if I had stretched out My hand and struck you and your people with pestilence, then you would have been cut off from the earth.
➤ 16 "But indeed for this *purpose* I have raised you up, that I may show My power *in* you, and that My name may be declared in all the earth.
17 "As yet you exalt yourself against My people in that you will not let them go.
18 "Behold, tomorrow about this time I will cause very heavy hail to rain down, such as has not been in Egypt since its founding until now.
19 "Therefore send now *and* gather your livestock and all that you have in the field, for the hail shall come down on every man and every animal which is found in the field and is not brought home; and they shall die."'"
20 He who feared the word of the LORD among the servants of Pharaoh made his servants and his livestock flee to the houses.
21 But he who did not regard the word of the LORD left his servants and his livestock in the field.
22 Then the LORD said to Moses, "Stretch out your hand toward heaven, that there may be hail in all the land of Egypt—on man, on beast, and on every herb of the field, throughout the land of Egypt."
23 And Moses stretched out his rod toward heaven; and the LORD sent thunder and hail, and fire darted to the ground. And the LORD rained hail on the land of Egypt.
24 So there was hail, and fire mingled with the hail, so very heavy that there was none like it in all the land of Egypt since it became a nation.
25 And the hail struck throughout the whole land of Egypt, all that *was* in the field, both man and beast; and the hail struck every herb of the field and broke every tree of the field.
26 Only in the land of Goshen, where the children of Israel *were*, there was no hail.
27 And Pharaoh sent and called for Moses and Aaron, and said to them, "I have sinned this time. The LORD *is* righteous, and my people and I *are* wicked.
28 "Entreat the LORD, that there may be no *more* mighty thundering and hail, for *it is* enough. I will let you go, and you shall stay no longer."
29 So Moses said to him, "As soon as I have gone out of the city, I will spread out my hands to the LORD; the thunder will cease, and there will be no more hail, that you may know that the earth *is* the LORD's.
30 "But as for you and your servants, I know that you will not yet fear the LORD God."
31 Now the flax and the barley were struck, for the barley *was* in the head and the flax *was* in bud.
32 But the wheat and the spelt were not struck, for they *are* late crops.
33 So Moses went out of the city from Pharaoh and spread out his hands to the LORD; then the thunder and the hail ceased, and the rain was not poured on the earth.
34 And when Pharaoh saw that the rain, the hail, and the thunder had ceased, he sinned yet more; and he hardened his heart, he and his servants.
35 So the heart of Pharaoh was hard; neither would he let the children of Israel go, as the LORD had spoken by Moses.

The Eighth Plague: Locusts

10 Now the LORD said to Moses, "Go in to Pharaoh; for I have hardened his heart and the hearts of his servants, that I may show these signs of Mine before him,
2 "and that you may tell in the hearing of ➤
your son and your son's son the mighty things I have done in Egypt, and My signs which I have done among them, that you may know that I *am* the LORD."
3 So Moses and Aaron came in to Pharaoh and said to him, "Thus says the LORD God of the Hebrews: 'How long will you refuse to humble yourself before Me? Let My people go, that they may serve Me.
4 'Or else, if you refuse to let My people go, behold, tomorrow I will bring locusts into your territory.
5 'And they shall cover the face of the earth, so that no one will be able to see the earth; and they shall eat the residue of what is left, which remains to you from the hail, and they shall eat every tree which grows up for you out of the field.
6 'They shall fill your houses, the houses of all your servants, and the houses of all the Egyptians—which neither your fathers nor your fathers' fathers have seen, since the day

LIFE LESSONS

➤ 9:16 — *"But indeed for this purpose I have raised you up, that I may show My power in you, and that My name may be declared in all the earth."*

God is so sovereign and rules with such a mighty hand that He raises up even adversaries in order to demonstrate to the world His glory and might.

➤ 10:2 — *". . . and that you may tell in the hearing of your son and your son's son the mighty things I have done in Egypt, and My signs which I have done among them, that you may know that I am the LORD."*

God works His wonders not only so that unbelievers might see His power and repent and believe, but also so that His own people might remember His glory and so remain loyal to Him.

that they were on the earth to this day.'" And
he turned and went out from Pharaoh.
7 Then Pharaoh's servants said to him,
"How long shall this man be a snare to us? Let
the men go, that they may serve the LORD
their God. Do you not yet know that Egypt is
destroyed?"
8 So Moses and Aaron were brought again
to Pharaoh, and he said to them, "Go, serve
the LORD your God. Who *are* the ones that are
going?"
9 And Moses said, "We will go with our
young and our old; with our sons and our
daughters, with our flocks and our herds we
will go, for we must hold a feast to the LORD."
10 Then he said to them, "The LORD had better be with you when I let you and your little
ones go! Beware, for evil is ahead of you.
➤ 11 "Not so! Go now, you *who are* men, and
serve the LORD, for that is what you desired."
And they were driven out from Pharaoh's
presence.
12 Then the LORD said to Moses, "Stretch out
your hand over the land of Egypt for the locusts, that they may come upon the land of
Egypt, and eat every herb of the land—all that
the hail has left."
13 So Moses stretched out his rod over the
land of Egypt, and the LORD brought an east
wind on the land all that day and all *that*
night. When it was morning, the east wind
brought the locusts.
14 And the locusts went up over all the land
of Egypt and rested on all the territory of
Egypt. *They were* very severe; previously
there had been no such locusts as they, nor
shall there be such after them.
15 For they covered the face of the whole
earth, so that the land was darkened; and
they ate every herb of the land and all the
fruit of the trees which the hail had left. So
there remained nothing green on the trees or
on the plants of the field throughout all the
land of Egypt.
16 Then Pharaoh called for Moses and Aaron
in haste, and said, "I have sinned against the
LORD your God and against you.
17 "Now therefore, please forgive my sin only
this once, and entreat the LORD your God,
that He may take away from me this death
only."
18 So he went out from Pharaoh and entreated the LORD.
19 And the LORD turned a very strong
west wind, which took the locusts away
and blew them into the Red Sea. There remained not one locust in all the territory of
Egypt.
20 But the LORD hardened Pharaoh's heart,
and he did not let the children of Israel go.

The Ninth Plague: Darkness

21 Then the LORD said to Moses, "Stretch out
your hand toward heaven, that there may be
darkness over the land of Egypt, darkness
which may even be felt."
22 So Moses stretched out his hand toward
heaven, and there was thick darkness in all
the land of Egypt three days.
23 They did not see one another; nor did anyone rise from his place for three days. But all
the children of Israel had light in their
dwellings.
24 Then Pharaoh called to Moses and said,
"Go, serve the LORD; only let your flocks and
your herds be kept back. Let your little ones
also go with you."
25 But Moses said, "You must also give us
sacrifices and burnt offerings, that we may
sacrifice to the LORD our God.
26 "Our livestock also shall go with us; not a
hoof shall be left behind. For we must take
some of them to serve the LORD our God, and
even we do not know with what we must
serve the LORD until we arrive there."
27 But the LORD hardened Pharaoh's heart,
and he would not let them go.
28 Then Pharaoh said to him, "Get away from
me! Take heed to yourself and see my face no
more! For in the day you see my face you
shall die!"
29 So Moses said, "You have spoken well. I
will never see your face again."

Death of the Firstborn Announced

11 And the LORD said to Moses, "I will
bring one more plague on Pharaoh and
on Egypt. Afterward he will let you go from
here. When he lets *you* go, he will surely drive
you out of here altogether.
2 "Speak now in the hearing of the people,
and let every man ask from his neighbor and
every woman from her neighbor, articles of
silver and articles of gold."
3 And the LORD gave the people favor in the ◄
sight of the Egyptians. Moreover the man Mo-

LIFE LESSONS

➤ 10:11 — *". . . Go now, you who are men, and serve the LORD, for that is what you desired." And they were driven out from Pharaoh's presence.*

Partial obedience is no obedience at all. If we are to walk with God, we must listen to what He says—*all* of what He says.

➤ 11:3 — *". . . Moreover the man Moses was very great in the land of Egypt, in the sight of Pharaoh's servants and in the sight of the people.*

When we do what the Lord requires of us, God takes pleasure in causing even our enemies to show us favor.

ses *was* very great in the land of Egypt, in the
sight of Pharaoh's servants and in the sight of
the people.
4 Then Moses said, "Thus says the LORD:
'About midnight I will go out into the midst of
Egypt;
5 'and all the firstborn in the land of Egypt
shall die, from the firstborn of Pharaoh who
sits on his throne, even to the firstborn of the
female servant who *is* behind the handmill,
and all the firstborn of the animals.
6 'Then there shall be a great cry throughout all the land of Egypt, such as was not like
it *before*, nor shall be like it again.
7 'But against none of the children of Israel
shall a dog move its tongue, against man or
beast, that you may know that the LORD does
make a difference between the Egyptians and
Israel.'
8 "And all these your servants shall come
down to me and bow down to me, saying, 'Get
out, and all the people who follow you!' After
that I will go out." Then he went out from
Pharaoh in great anger.
9 But the LORD said to Moses, "Pharaoh will
not heed you, so that My wonders may be
multiplied in the land of Egypt."
10 So Moses and Aaron did all these wonders
before Pharaoh; and the LORD hardened
Pharaoh's heart, and he did not let the children of Israel go out of his land.

The Passover Instituted

12 Now the LORD spoke to Moses and
Aaron in the land of Egypt, saying,
2 "This month *shall be* your beginning of
months; it *shall be* the first month of the year
to you.
3 "Speak to all the congregation of Israel,
saying: 'On the tenth of this month every man
shall take for himself a lamb, according to
the house of *his* father, a lamb for a household.
4 'And if the household is too small for the
lamb, let him and his neighbor next to his
house take *it* according to the number of the
persons; according to each man's need you
shall make your count for the lamb.
5 'Your lamb shall be without blemish, a
male of the first year. You may take *it* from the
sheep or from the goats.
6 'Now you shall keep it until the fourteenth
day of the same month. Then the whole assembly of the congregation of Israel shall kill
it at twilight.
7 'And they shall take *some* of the blood and
put *it* on the two doorposts and on the lintel
of the houses where they eat it.
8 'Then they shall eat the flesh on that night;
roasted in fire, with unleavened bread *and*
with bitter *herbs* they shall eat it.
9 'Do not eat it raw, nor boiled at all with
water, but roasted in fire—its head with its
legs and its entrails.
10 'You shall let none of it remain until morning, and what remains of it until morning you
shall burn with fire.
11 'And thus you shall eat it: *with* a belt on
your waist, your sandals on your feet, and
your staff in your hand. So you shall eat it in
haste. It *is* the LORD's Passover.
12 'For I will pass through the land of Egypt
on that night, and will strike all the firstborn
in the land of Egypt, both man and beast; and
against all the gods of Egypt I will execute
judgment: I *am* the LORD.
13 'Now the blood shall be a sign for you on
the houses where you *are*. And when I see the
blood, I will pass over you; and the plague
shall not be on you to destroy *you* when I
strike the land of Egypt.
14 'So this day shall be to you a memorial;
and you shall keep it as a feast to the LORD
throughout your generations. You shall keep it
as a feast by an everlasting ordinance.
15 'Seven days you shall eat unleavened
bread. On the first day you shall remove
leaven from your houses. For whoever eats
leavened bread from the first day until the
seventh day, that person shall be cut off from
Israel.
16 'On the first day *there shall be* a holy convocation, and on the seventh day there shall
be a holy convocation for you. No manner of
work shall be done on them; but *that* which
everyone must eat—that only may be prepared by you.
17 'So you shall observe *the Feast of* Unleavened Bread, for on this same day I will have
brought your armies out of the land of Egypt.
Therefore you shall observe this day throughout your generations as an everlasting ordinance.
18 'In the first *month*, on the fourteenth day
of the month at evening, you shall eat unleavened bread, until the twenty-first day of the
month at evening.
19 'For seven days no leaven shall be found in
your houses, since whoever eats what is leavened, that same person shall be cut off from

LIFE LESSONS

12:5, 6, 11 — *". . . Your lamb shall be without blemish, a male of the first year . . . . Then the whole assembly of the congregation of Israel shall kill it at twilight . . . . It is the LORD's Passover."*

The Passover lamb symbolized the work that Jesus Christ would finish in His death on the cross and resurrection from the grave. So the apostle Paul writes, ". . . Christ, our Passover, was sacrificed for us" (1 Cor. 5:7).

the congregation of Israel, whether *he is* a
stranger or a native of the land.
20 'You shall eat nothing leavened; in all your
dwellings you shall eat unleavened bread.'"
21 Then Moses called for all the elders of Israel and said to them, "Pick out and take
lambs for yourselves according to your families, and kill the Passover *lamb.*
22 "And you shall take a bunch of hyssop, dip
it in the blood that *is* in the basin, and strike
the lintel and the two doorposts with the
blood that *is* in the basin. And none of you
shall go out of the door of his house until
morning.
23 "For the LORD will pass through to strike
the Egyptians; and when He sees the blood on
the lintel and on the two doorposts, the LORD
will pass over the door and not allow the destroyer to come into your houses to strike
you.
24 "And you shall observe this thing as an ordinance for you and your sons forever.
25 "It will come to pass when you come to
the land which the LORD will give you, just
as He promised, that you shall keep this service.
26 "And it shall be, when your children say to
you, 'What do you mean by this service?'
27 "that you shall say, 'It *is* the Passover sacrifice of the LORD, who passed over the
houses of the children of Israel in Egypt when
He struck the Egyptians and delivered our
households.'" So the people bowed their
heads and worshiped.
28 Then the children of Israel went away and
did *so;* just as the LORD had commanded Moses and Aaron, so they did.

The Tenth Plague: Death of the Firstborn

29 And it came to pass at midnight that the
LORD struck all the firstborn in the land of
Egypt, from the firstborn of Pharaoh who sat
on his throne to the firstborn of the captive
who *was* in the dungeon, and all the firstborn
of livestock.
30 So Pharaoh rose in the night, he, all his
servants, and all the Egyptians; and there was
a great cry in Egypt, for *there was* not a house
where *there was* not one dead.

The Exodus

31 Then he called for Moses and Aaron by
night, and said, "Rise, go out from among my
people, both you and the children of Israel.
And go, serve the LORD as you have said.
32 "Also take your flocks and your herds, as
you have said, and be gone; and bless me
also."
33 And the Egyptians urged the people, that
they might send them out of the land in haste.
For they said, "We *shall* all *be* dead."
34 So the people took their dough before it
was leavened, having their kneading bowls
bound up in their clothes on their shoulders.
35 Now the children of Israel had done according to the word of Moses, and they had
asked from the Egyptians articles of silver, articles of gold, and clothing.
36 And the LORD had given the people favor
in the sight of the Egyptians, so that they
granted them *what they requested.* Thus they
plundered the Egyptians.
37 Then the children of Israel journeyed from
Rameses to Succoth, about six hundred thousand men on foot, besides children.
38 A mixed multitude went up with them
also, and flocks and herds—a great deal of
livestock.
39 And they baked unleavened cakes of the
dough which they had brought out of Egypt;
for it was not leavened, because they were
driven out of Egypt and could not wait,
nor had they prepared provisions for themselves.
40 Now the sojourn of the children of Israel
who lived in Egypt[a] *was* four hundred and
thirty years.
41 And it came to pass at the end of the four
hundred and thirty years—on that very same
day—it came to pass that all the armies of the
LORD went out from the land of Egypt.
42 It *is* a night of solemn observance to the
LORD for bringing them out of the land of
Egypt. This *is* that night of the LORD, a solemn
observance for all the children of Israel
throughout their generations.

Passover Regulations

43 And the LORD said to Moses and Aaron,
"This *is* the ordinance of the Passover: No foreigner shall eat it.
44 "But every man's servant who is bought
for money, when you have circumcised him,
then he may eat it.
45 "A sojourner and a hired servant shall not
eat it.
46 "In one house it shall be eaten; you shall
not carry any of the flesh outside the house,
nor shall you break one of its bones.
47 "All the congregation of Israel shall keep it.
48 "And when a stranger dwells with you *and*
wants to keep the Passover to the LORD, let all
his males be circumcised, and then let him
come near and keep it; and he shall be as a
native of the land. For no uncircumcised person shall eat it.
49 "One law shall be for the native-born and
for the stranger who dwells among you."
50 Thus all the children of Israel did; as the
LORD commanded Moses and Aaron, so they
did.
51 And it came to pass, on that very same
day, that the LORD brought the children of Israel out of the land of Egypt according to
their armies.

12:40 [a]Samaritan Pentateuch and Septuagint read *Egypt and Canaan.*

The Firstborn Consecrated

13 Then the LORD spoke to Moses, saying,
2 "Consecrate to Me all the firstborn, whatever opens the womb among the children of
Israel, *both* of man and beast; it is Mine."

The Feast of Unleavened Bread

3 And Moses said to the people: "Remember
this day in which you went out of Egypt, out
of the house of bondage; for by strength of
hand the LORD brought you out of this *place.*
No leavened bread shall be eaten.
4 "On this day you are going out, in the
month Abib.
5 "And it shall be, when the LORD brings you
into the land of the Canaanites and the Hittites and the Amorites and the Hivites and the
Jebusites, which He swore to your fathers to
give you, a land flowing with milk and honey,
that you shall keep this service in this month.
6 "Seven days you shall eat unleavened
bread, and on the seventh day *there shall be* a
feast to the LORD.
7 "Unleavened bread shall be eaten seven
days. And no leavened bread shall be seen
among you, nor shall leaven be seen among
you in all your quarters.
8 "And you shall tell your son in that day,
saying, '*This is done* because of what the
LORD did for me when I came up from Egypt.'
9 "It shall be as a sign to you on your hand
and as a memorial between your eyes, that
the LORD's law may be in your mouth; for
with a strong hand the LORD has brought you
out of Egypt.
10 "You shall therefore keep this ordinance
in its season from year to year.

The Law of the Firstborn

11 "And it shall be, when the LORD brings you
into the land of the Canaanites, as He swore
to you and your fathers, and gives it to you,
12 "that you shall set apart to the LORD all
that open the womb, that is, every firstborn
that comes from an animal which you have;
the males *shall be* the LORD's.
13 "But every firstborn of a donkey you shall
redeem with a lamb; and if you will not redeem *it,* then you shall break its neck. And all
the firstborn of man among your sons you
shall redeem.
14 "So it shall be, when your son asks you in
time to come, saying, 'What *is* this?' that you
shall say to him, 'By strength of hand the
LORD brought us out of Egypt, out of the
house of bondage.
15 'And it came to pass, when Pharaoh was
stubborn about letting us go, that the LORD
killed all the firstborn in the land of Egypt,
both the firstborn of man and the firstborn of
beast. Therefore I sacrifice to the LORD all
males that open the womb, but all the firstborn of my sons I redeem.'
16 "It shall be as a sign on your hand and as
frontlets between your eyes, for by strength of
hand the LORD brought us out of Egypt."

The Wilderness Way

17 Then it came to pass, when Pharaoh had
let the people go, that God did not lead them
by way of the land of the Philistines, although
that *was* near; for God said, "Lest perhaps the
people change their minds when they see
war, and return to Egypt."
18 So God led the people around *by* way of
the wilderness of the Red Sea. And the children of Israel went up in orderly ranks out of
the land of Egypt.
19 And Moses took the bones of Joseph with
him, for he had placed the children of Israel
under solemn oath, saying, "God will surely
visit you, and you shall carry up my bones
from here with you."[a]
20 So they took their journey from Succoth
and camped in Etham at the edge of the
wilderness.
21 And the LORD went before them by day in
a pillar of cloud to lead the way, and by night
in a pillar of fire to give them light, so as to go
by day and night.
22 He did not take away the pillar of cloud by
day or the pillar of fire by night *from* before
the people.

The Red Sea Crossing

14 Now the LORD spoke to Moses, saying:
2 "Speak to the children of Israel, that they
turn and camp before Pi Hahiroth, between
Migdol and the sea, opposite Baal Zephon;
you shall camp before it by the sea.

13:19 [a]Genesis 50:25

LIFE LESSONS

➤ **13:17 — . . . *God did not lead them by way of the land of the Philistines, although that was near; for God said, "Lest perhaps the people change their minds when they see war, and return to Egypt."***

Our God is a practical God, and He deals with us according to our nature. So He will always lead us in a way appropriate to us.

➤ **13:21 — *And the LORD went before them by day in a pillar of cloud to lead the way, and by night in a pillar of fire to give them light, so as to go by day and night.***

When we personally know the Lord, we never need to feel "in the dark" in how we follow Him. God provides everything we need for life in Him, and that includes illumination of the path before us.

3 "For Pharaoh will say of the children of Israel, 'They *are* bewildered by the land; the
wilderness has closed them in.'
4 "Then I will harden Pharaoh's heart, so
that he will pursue them; and I will gain
honor over Pharaoh and over all his army,
that the Egyptians may know that I *am* the
LORD." And they did so.
5 Now it was told the king of Egypt that the
people had fled, and the heart of Pharaoh and
his servants was turned against the people;
and they said, "Why have we done this, that
we have let Israel go from serving us?"
6 So he made ready his chariot and took his
people with him.
7 Also, he took six hundred choice chariots,
and all the chariots of Egypt with captains
over every one of them.
8 And the LORD hardened the heart of
Pharaoh king of Egypt, and he pursued the
children of Israel; and the children of Israel
went out with boldness.
9 So the Egyptians pursued them, all the
horses *and* chariots of Pharaoh, his horsemen
and his army, and overtook them camping by
the sea beside Pi Hahiroth, before Baal
Zephon.
10 And when Pharaoh drew near, the children of Israel lifted their eyes, and behold, the
Egyptians marched after them. So they were
very afraid, and the children of Israel cried
out to the LORD.
11 Then they said to Moses, "Because *there
were* no graves in Egypt, have you taken us
away to die in the wilderness? Why have you
so dealt with us, to bring us up out of Egypt?
12 "*Is* this not the word that we told you in
Egypt, saying, 'Let us alone that we may serve
the Egyptians'? For *it would have been* better
for us to serve the Egyptians than that we
should die in the wilderness."
➤ 13 And Moses said to the people, "Do not be
afraid. Stand still, and see the salvation of the
LORD, which He will accomplish for you
today. For the Egyptians whom you see today,
you shall see again no more forever.
14 "The LORD will fight for you, and you shall
hold your peace."
15 And the LORD said to Moses, "Why do you
cry to Me? Tell the children of Israel to go forward.
16 "But lift up your rod, and stretch out your
hand over the sea and divide it. And the children of Israel shall go on dry *ground* through
the midst of the sea.
17 "And I indeed will harden the hearts of the
Egyptians, and they shall follow them. So I
will gain honor over Pharaoh and over all his
army, his chariots, and his horsemen.
18 "Then the Egyptians shall know that I *am*
the LORD, when I have gained honor for Myself over Pharaoh, his chariots, and his horsemen."
19 And the Angel of God, who went before
the camp of Israel, moved and went behind
them; and the pillar of cloud went from before
them and stood behind them.
20 So it came between the camp of the Egyptians and the camp of Israel. Thus it was a
cloud and darkness *to the one,* and it gave
light by night *to the other,* so that the one did
not come near the other all that night.
21 Then Moses stretched out his hand over
the sea; and the LORD caused the sea to go
back by a strong east wind all that night, and
made the sea into dry *land,* and the waters
were divided.
22 So the children of Israel went into the
midst of the sea on the dry *ground,* and the
waters *were* a wall to them on their right
hand and on their left.
23 And the Egyptians pursued and went after
them into the midst of the sea, all Pharaoh's
horses, his chariots, and his horsemen.
24 Now it came to pass, in the morning
watch, that the LORD looked down upon the
army of the Egyptians through the pillar of
fire and cloud, and He troubled the army of
the Egyptians.
25 And He took off[a] their chariot wheels, so
that they drove them with difficulty; and the
Egyptians said, "Let us flee from the face of
Israel, for the LORD fights for them against the
Egyptians."
26 Then the LORD said to Moses, "Stretch out
your hand over the sea, that the waters may
come back upon the Egyptians, on their chariots, and on their horsemen."
27 And Moses stretched out his hand over

14:25 [a]Samaritan Pentateuch, Septuagint, and Syriac read *bound.*

LIFE LESSONS

➤ **14:2 — *"Speak to the children of Israel, that they turn and camp before Pi Hahiroth, between Migdol and the sea, opposite Baal Zephon; you shall camp before it by the sea."***

Sometimes the Lord purposefully leads us into situations that look like dead-ends, not only to test our faith, but also to show His power and complete control over all situations. Wherever He leads, we must follow.

➤ **14:13 — *And Moses said to the people, "Do not be afraid. Stand still, and see the salvation of the LORD, which He will accomplish for you today. For the Egyptians whom you see today, you shall see again no more forever."***

Throughout the Scriptures we read the phrase, "Do not be afraid." It is God's refrain to His people, whatever their circumstances, for He has promised to save and deliver us.

the sea; and when the morning appeared, the sea returned to its full depth, while the Egyptians were fleeing into it. So the LORD overthrew the Egyptians in the midst of the sea.
28 Then the waters returned and covered the chariots, the horsemen, *and* all the army of Pharaoh that came into the sea after them. Not so much as one of them remained.
29 But the children of Israel had walked on dry *land* in the midst of the sea, and the waters *were* a wall to them on their right hand and on their left.
30 So the LORD saved Israel that day out of the hand of the Egyptians, and Israel saw the Egyptians dead on the seashore.
31 Thus Israel saw the great work which the LORD had done in Egypt; so the people feared the LORD, and believed the LORD and His servant Moses.

The Song of Moses

15 Then Moses and the children of Israel sang this song to the LORD, and spoke, saying:

"I will sing to the LORD,
For He has triumphed gloriously!
The horse and its rider
He has thrown into the sea!
2 The LORD *is* my strength and song,
And He has become my salvation;
He *is* my God, and I will praise Him;
My father's God, and I will exalt Him.
3 The LORD *is* a man of war;
The LORD *is* His name.
4 Pharaoh's chariots and his army He has cast into the sea;
His chosen captains also are drowned in the Red Sea.
5 The depths have covered them;
They sank to the bottom like a stone.

6 "Your right hand, O LORD, has become glorious in power;
Your right hand, O LORD, has dashed the enemy in pieces.
7 And in the greatness of Your excellence
You have overthrown those who rose against You;
You sent forth Your wrath;
It consumed them like stubble.
8 And with the blast of Your nostrils
The waters were gathered together;
The floods stood upright like a heap;
The depths congealed in the heart of the sea.
9 The enemy said, 'I will pursue,
I will overtake,
I will divide the spoil;
My desire shall be satisfied on them.
I will draw my sword,
My hand shall destroy them.'
10 You blew with Your wind,
The sea covered them;
They sank like lead in the mighty waters.

11 "Who *is* like You, O LORD, among the gods?
Who *is* like You, glorious in holiness,
Fearful in praises, doing wonders?
12 You stretched out Your right hand;
The earth swallowed them.
13 You in Your mercy have led forth
The people whom You have redeemed;
You have guided *them* in Your strength
To Your holy habitation.

14 "The people will hear *and* be afraid;
Sorrow will take hold of the inhabitants of Philistia.
15 Then the chiefs of Edom will be dismayed;
The mighty men of Moab,
Trembling will take hold of them;
All the inhabitants of Canaan will melt away.
16 Fear and dread will fall on them;
By the greatness of Your arm
They will be *as* still as a stone,
Till Your people pass over, O LORD,
Till the people pass over
Whom You have purchased.
17 You will bring them in and plant them
In the mountain of Your inheritance,
In the place, O LORD, *which* You have made
For Your own dwelling,
The sanctuary, O Lord, *which* Your hands have established.

18 "The LORD shall reign forever and ever."

19 For the horses of Pharaoh went with his chariots and his horsemen into the sea, and the LORD brought back the waters of the sea upon them. But the children of Israel went on dry *land* in the midst of the sea.

The Song of Miriam

20 Then Miriam the prophetess, the sister of Aaron, took the timbrel in her hand; and all the women went out after her with timbrels and with dances.
21 And Miriam answered them:

LIFE LESSONS

➤ 15:18 — *"The LORD shall reign forever and ever."*

We can find great comfort during times of difficulty in knowing that God has promised that He was, is, and always will be in control—not only over world events, but also over all events in our own lives.

ANSWERS TO LIFE'S QUESTIONS

Can I really trust God to provide what I need?

EX. 16:1–3

From cover to cover, the Bible brims over with God's promises to provide for our needs. Our heavenly Father always gives, always loves, always remains generous toward His children.

In the first few chapters of Genesis, the Lord gives the first man and woman a perfect garden. In Revelation, we read about our ultimate home, a perfect and eternal heaven. In all the books between, we read how God delights in blessing His people. At the very outset of the New Testament, we read how God sent His Son, Jesus Christ, as His ultimate gift of blessing to provide what we need most of all: forgiveness of sin and restored fellowship with God.

When you limit yourself to your own ability and resources, you run out of both commodities very quickly. But when you focus your faith on what God can do for you, you discover an infinite supply that cannot be measured or depleted. God's resources are 100 percent inflation-proof and recession-proof.

The very nature of God gives you assurance of His abundant provision. God is:

- Omniscient—the Lord knows your need. He knows it even better than you do and before you do (Matt. 6:8).
- Omnipotent—the Lord has all power to supply to you whatever you need (Phil. 4:19).
- Omnipresent—the Lord is at work even now to meet your needs (Ps. 34:7, 8).

Not only do you have the character of God as your assurance that He is going to provide for you, but you also have the testimony of God's past performance in providing for His people. The Scriptures repeatedly point to Him as a faithful Source of life. Consider just a few examples from the Book of Exodus:

- He made a way for His people to cross the Red Sea and find deliverance from their enemies.
- He provided manna for the people to eat in the wilderness.
- He caused water to gush forth from a rock to quench the people's thirst.
- He gave His commandments to His people, even when they lacked moral fiber.
- He healed His people when poisonous snakes struck them.

As the Israelites left behind the only "home" they had ever known, in Egypt, God provided for all their needs. He provided for their protection, their basic physical necessities (food and water), spiritual grounding, and healing. He does the same for us today!

See the Life Principles Index for further study:
11. God assumes full responsibility for our needs when we obey Him.
9. Trusting God means looking beyond what we can see to what God sees.

"Sing to the LORD,
For He has triumphed gloriously!
The horse and its rider
He has thrown into the sea!"

Bitter Waters Made Sweet

22 So Moses brought Israel from the Red
Sea; then they went out into the Wilderness of
Shur. And they went three days in the wilderness and found no water.
23 Now when they came to Marah, they
could not drink the waters of Marah, for they
were bitter. Therefore the name of it was
called Marah.[a]
24 And the people complained against Moses, saying, "What shall we drink?"
25 So he cried out to the LORD, and the LORD
showed him a tree. When he cast *it* into the
waters, the waters were made sweet. There
He made a statute and an ordinance for them,
and there He tested them,
26 and said, "If you diligently heed the voice
of the LORD your God and do what is right in
His sight, give ear to His commandments and
keep all His statutes, I will put none of the diseases on you which I have brought on the
Egyptians. For I *am* the LORD who heals you."
27 Then they came to Elim, where there *were*
twelve wells of water and seventy palm trees;
so they camped there by the waters.

Bread from Heaven

16 And they journeyed from Elim, and all
the congregation of the children of Israel came to the Wilderness of Sin, which is

15:23 [a]Literally *Bitter*

between Elim and Sinai, on the fifteenth day of the second month after they departed from the land of Egypt.

2 Then the whole congregation of the children of Israel complained against Moses and Aaron in the wilderness.

3 And the children of Israel said to them, "Oh, that we had died by the hand of the LORD in the land of Egypt, when we sat by the pots of meat *and* when we ate bread to the full! For you have brought us out into this wilderness to kill this whole assembly with hunger."

➤ **4** Then the LORD said to Moses, "Behold, I will rain bread from heaven for you. And the people shall go out and gather a certain quota every day, that I may test them, whether they will walk in My law or not.

5 "And it shall be on the sixth day that they shall prepare what they bring in, and it shall be twice as much as they gather daily."

6 Then Moses and Aaron said to all the children of Israel, "At evening you shall know that the LORD has brought you out of the land of Egypt.

7 "And in the morning you shall see the glory of the LORD; for He hears your complaints against the LORD. But what *are* we, that you complain against us?"

➤ 8 Also Moses said, "*This shall be seen* when the LORD gives you meat to eat in the evening, and in the morning bread to the full; for the LORD hears your complaints which you make against Him. And what *are* we? Your complaints *are* not against us but against the LORD."

9 Then Moses spoke to Aaron, "Say to all the congregation of the children of Israel, 'Come near before the LORD, for He has heard your complaints.'"

10 Now it came to pass, as Aaron spoke to the whole congregation of the children of Israel, that they looked toward the wilderness, and behold, the glory of the LORD appeared in the cloud.

11 And the LORD spoke to Moses, saying,

12 "I have heard the complaints of the children of Israel. Speak to them, saying, 'At twilight you shall eat meat, and in the morning you shall be filled with bread. And you shall know that I *am* the LORD your God.'"

13 So it was that quails came up at evening and covered the camp, and in the morning the dew lay all around the camp.

14 And when the layer of dew lifted, there, on the surface of the wilderness, was a small round substance, *as* fine as frost on the ground.

15 So when the children of Israel saw *it,* they said to one another, "What is it?" For they did not know what it *was.* And Moses said to them, "This *is* the bread which the LORD has given you to eat.

16 "This is the thing which the LORD has commanded: 'Let every man gather it according to each one's need, one omer for each person, *according to the* number of persons; let every man take for *those* who *are* in his tent.'"

17 Then the children of Israel did so and gathered, some more, some less.

18 So when they measured *it* by omers, he who gathered much had nothing left over, and he who gathered little had no lack. Every man had gathered according to each one's need. ➤

19 And Moses said, "Let no one leave any of it till morning."

20 Notwithstanding they did not heed Moses. But some of them left part of it until morning, and it bred worms and stank. And Moses was angry with them.

21 So they gathered it every morning, every man according to his need. And when the sun became hot, it melted.

22 And so it was, on the sixth day, *that* they gathered twice as much bread, two omers for each one. And all the rulers of the congregation came and told Moses.

23 Then he said to them, "This *is what* the

LIFE LESSONS

➤ **15:22, 23 — *. . . And they went three days in the wilderness and found no water. Now when they came to Marah, they could not drink the waters of Marah, for they were bitter . . . .***

Immediately after the miraculous triumph at the Red Sea, God led Israel for three days on a route devoid of water. Why? The Lord trains us to trust Him by letting us experience both need and abundance.

➤ **16:4 — *Then the LORD said to Moses, "Behold, I will rain bread from heaven for you. And the people shall go out and gather a certain quota every day, that I may test them, whether they will walk in My law or not."***

The Lord provides regular tests to see whether we will obey Him, whether we fully understand the reasons for His commandments or not. But obedience always brings blessing.

➤ **16:8 — *Also Moses said, ". . . Your complaints are not against us but against the LORD."***

When we complain about our circumstances and blame others, in fact we're complaining against the Lord, who exercises complete control over our circumstances.

➤ **16:18 — *So when they measured it by omers, he who gathered much had nothing left over, and he who gathered little had no lack. Every man had gathered according to each one's need.***

When we obey the Lord, He assumes full responsibility for our needs.

LORD has said: 'Tomorrow *is* a Sabbath rest, a holy Sabbath to the LORD. Bake what you will bake *today,* and boil what you will boil; and lay up for yourselves all that remains, to be kept until morning.'"

24 So they laid it up till morning, as Moses commanded; and it did not stink, nor were there any worms in it.

25 Then Moses said, "Eat that today, for today *is* a Sabbath to the LORD; today you will not find it in the field.

26 "Six days you shall gather it, but on the seventh day, the Sabbath, there will be none."

27 Now it happened *that some* of the people went out on the seventh day to gather, but they found none.

28 And the LORD said to Moses, "How long do you refuse to keep My commandments and My laws?

29 "See! For the LORD has given you the Sabbath; therefore He gives you on the sixth day bread for two days. Let every man remain in his place; let no man go out of his place on the seventh day."

30 So the people rested on the seventh day.

31 And the house of Israel called its name Manna.[a] And it *was* like white coriander seed, and the taste of it *was* like wafers *made* with honey.

32 Then Moses said, "This *is* the thing which the LORD has commanded: 'Fill an omer with it, to be kept for your generations, that they may see the bread with which I fed you in the wilderness, when I brought you out of the land of Egypt.'"

33 And Moses said to Aaron, "Take a pot and put an omer of manna in it, and lay it up before the LORD, to be kept for your generations."

34 As the LORD commanded Moses, so Aaron laid it up before the Testimony, to be kept.

35 And the children of Israel ate manna forty years, until they came to an inhabited land; they ate manna until they came to the border of the land of Canaan.

36 Now an omer *is* one-tenth of an ephah.

Water from the Rock

17 Then all the congregation of the children of Israel set out on their journey from the Wilderness of Sin, according to the commandment of the LORD, and camped in Rephidim; but *there was* no water for the people to drink.

2 Therefore the people contended with Moses, and said, "Give us water, that we may drink." So Moses said to them, "Why do you contend with me? Why do you tempt the LORD?"

3 And the people thirsted there for water, and the people complained against Moses, and said, "Why *is* it you have brought us up out of Egypt, to kill us and our children and our livestock with thirst?"

4 So Moses cried out to the LORD, saying, "What shall I do with this people? They are almost ready to stone me!"

5 And the LORD said to Moses, "Go on before the people, and take with you some of the elders of Israel. Also take in your hand your rod with which you struck the river, and go.

6 "Behold, I will stand before you there on the rock in Horeb; and you shall strike the rock, and water will come out of it, that the people may drink." And Moses did so in the sight of the elders of Israel.

7 So he called the name of the place Massah[a] and Meribah,[b] because of the contention of the children of Israel, and because they tempted the LORD, saying, "Is the LORD among us or not?"

Victory over the Amalekites

8 Now Amalek came and fought with Israel in Rephidim.

9 And Moses said to Joshua, "Choose us some men and go out, fight with Amalek. Tomorrow I will stand on the top of the hill with the rod of God in my hand."

10 So Joshua did as Moses said to him, and fought with Amalek. And Moses, Aaron, and Hur went up to the top of the hill.

11 And so it was, when Moses held up his hand, that Israel prevailed; and when he let down his hand, Amalek prevailed.

12 But Moses' hands *became* heavy; so they took a stone and put *it* under him, and he sat on it. And Aaron and Hur supported his hands, one on one side, and the other on the side; and his hands were steady until the going down of the sun.

16:31 [a]Literally *What?* (compare Exodus 16:15) **17:7** [a]Literally *Tempted* [b]Literally *Contention*

LIFE LESSONS

➤ **17:7 — *So he called the name of the place Massah and Meribah, because of the contention of the children of Israel, and because they tempted the LORD, saying, "Is the Lord among us or not?"***

In times of difficulty, it is easy to start wondering, "Is the LORD among us or not?" If we have placed our faith in Him, however, He has promised to be with us—so the question actually casts doubt on His truthfulness.

➤ **17:12 — *But Moses' hands became heavy; so they took a stone and put it under him, and he sat on it. And Aaron and Hur supported his hands . . . .***

In order to succeed in the Christian life, we need the help and support of others. No believer has ever been called to "go it alone" in his or her walk of faith.

13 So Joshua defeated Amalek and his people with the edge of the sword.

14 Then the LORD said to Moses, "Write this *for* a memorial in the book and recount *it* in the hearing of Joshua, that I will utterly blot out the remembrance of Amalek from under heaven."

15 And Moses built an altar and called its name, The-LORD-Is-My-Banner;[a]

16 for he said, "Because the LORD has sworn: the LORD *will have* war with Amalek from generation to generation."

Jethro's Advice

18 And Jethro, the priest of Midian, Moses' father-in-law, heard of all that God had done for Moses and for Israel His people—that the LORD had brought Israel out of Egypt.

2 Then Jethro, Moses' father-in-law, took Zipporah, Moses' wife, after he had sent her back,

3 with her two sons, of whom the name of one *was* Gershom (for he said, "I have been a stranger in a foreign land")[a]

4 and the name of the other *was* Eliezer[a] (for *he said,* "The God of my father *was* my help, and delivered me from the sword of Pharaoh");

5 and Jethro, Moses' father-in-law, came with his sons and his wife to Moses in the wilderness, where he was encamped at the mountain of God.

6 Now he had said to Moses, "I, your father-in-law Jethro, am coming to you with your wife and her two sons with her."

7 So Moses went out to meet his father-in-law, bowed down, and kissed him. And they asked each other about *their* well-being, and they went into the tent.

➢ 8 And Moses told his father-in-law all that the LORD had done to Pharaoh and to the Egyptians for Israel's sake, all the hardship that had come upon them on the way, and *how* the LORD had delivered them.

9 Then Jethro rejoiced for all the good which the LORD had done for Israel, whom He had delivered out of the hand of the Egyptians.

10 And Jethro said, "Blessed *be* the LORD, who has delivered you out of the hand of the Egyptians and out of the hand of Pharaoh, *and* who has delivered the people from under the hand of the Egyptians.

11 "Now I know that the LORD *is* greater than all the gods; for in the very thing in which they behaved proudly, *He was* above them."

12 Then Jethro, Moses' father-in-law, took[a] a burnt offering and *other* sacrifices *to offer* to God. And Aaron came with all the elders of Israel to eat bread with Moses' father-in-law before God.

13 And so it was, on the next day, that Moses sat to judge the people; and the people stood before Moses from morning until evening.

14 So when Moses' father-in-law saw all that he did for the people, he said, "What *is* this thing that you are doing for the people? Why do you alone sit, and all the people stand before you from morning until evening?"

15 And Moses said to his father-in-law, "Because the people come to me to inquire of God.

16 "When they have a difficulty, they come to me, and I judge between one and another; and I make known the statutes of God and His laws."

17 So Moses' father-in-law said to him, "The thing that you do *is* not good.

18 "Both you and these people who *are* with you will surely wear yourselves out. For this thing *is* too much for you; you are not able to perform it by yourself.

19 "Listen now to my voice; I will give you counsel, and God will be with you: Stand before God for the people, so that you may bring the difficulties to God.

20 "And you shall teach them the statutes and the laws, and show them the way in which they must walk and the work they must do.

21 "Moreover you shall select from all the people able men, such as fear God, men of truth, hating covetousness; and place *such* over them *to be* rulers of thousands, rulers of hundreds, rulers of fifties, and rulers of tens.

22 "And let them judge the people at all times. Then it will be *that* every great matter they shall bring to you, but every small matter they themselves shall judge. So it will be easier for you, for they will bear *the burden* with you.

23 "If you do this thing, and God *so* commands ➢

17:15 [a]Hebrew *YHWH Nissi* **18:3** [a]Compare Exodus 2:22
18:4 [a]Literally *My God Is Help* **18:12** [a]Following Masoretic Text and Septuagint; Syriac, Targum, and Vulgate read *offered.*

LIFE LESSONS

➢ **18:8 — *And Moses told his father-in-law all that the LORD had done to Pharaoh and to the Egyptians for Israel's sake, all the hardship that had come upon them on the way, and how the LORD had delivered them.***

It helps us to discuss with others what God has been doing in our lives, both the triumphs and the challenges. Faithful involvement with other believers glorifies God and blesses us.

➢ **18:23 — *"If you do this thing, and God so commands you, then you will be able to endure, and all this people will also go to their place in peace."***

God often uses the advice of wise counselors to help us find His will for our lives. Any helpful counsel has to line up with the Word of God and usually leads to peace.

LIFE PRINCIPLE 2

OBEY GOD AND LEAVE ALL THE CONSEQUENCES TO HIM.

EX. 19:5

Obedience can be a challenge, especially when we feel tempted to believe that we stand to lose more through our obedience than we might gain. Obeying God is essential to pleasing Him, however, not just in times of temptation, but at all times.

When God commands us to obey Him, He is giving us a principle by which to live. He is also setting a framework around our lives that forms a hedge of protection from evil.

Can you remember the last time you felt tempted to do the opposite of what you knew God desired you to do? A struggle erupted within your heart. The question arose: *Will obeying God cost me more than disobeying Him? Can I experience greater happiness by committing this sin than I would by obeying God?*

When we choose to obey God, we choose the way of wisdom. His promises of blessing for obedience far outweigh any possible consequences. He asks us to obey Him and leave whatever happens to Him.

As we grow in our walk with the Lord, obedience becomes a cornerstone to fellowship with God. If we obey Him, He pulls us closer to Himself and teaches us more about His precepts and His love.

Disobedience sends a message to the Lord, declaring that we know better than He does when it comes to our lives and the circumstances surrounding them.

God loves us and is committed to us. He commands our obedience, not because He is a strict taskmaster, but because He knows the devastating effect that disobedience and sin will have on our lives.

Satan, however, has another goal in mind. He seeks to tempt believers to disobey God, usually by telling them that God's promises cannot be trusted and that we can enjoy life more through disobedience than by our obedience.

Remember, disobedience always has fierce repercussions—feelings of guilt, shame, and worthlessness, broken lives, destroyed marriages, and bitter disputes, among them. While sin can never change God's eternal love for His children, it certainly disrupts our fellowship with the Savior and alienates us from God's blessings. In times of disobedience, we become spiritually weak and unable to discern right from wrong. We sink deeper into sin's grasp and find it impossible to reverse our sinfulness on our own.

Obeying God is essential to pleasing Him.

As we begin to apply the following principles to our lives, we will begin to obey God with confidence and joy, knowing that He can be fully trusted to keep all His promises:

- *Trust God with your life and all that concerns you.*

There is no way to go wrong if you place your hope and trust in God. He created you and He loves you with an eternal love. Therefore, you are His greatest concern and the apple of His eye.

- *Wait on the Lord for an answer to your problem or situation.*

When in doubt, refuse to move ahead unless you know that God is leading you.

- *Meditate on God's Word.*

When you saturate your mind with the Word of God, you gain God's viewpoint. When a temptation comes, you will know right from wrong and can act accordingly.

- *Listen to the Holy Spirit.*

God continues to speak to His people today. He speaks to us through His Word, the Holy Spirit, and through the words of a pastor or trusted Christian friend. We become sensitive to the Spirit of God by seeking Him through His Word and by spending time with Him—praying and studying the principles in Scripture.

- *Be willing to wait or walk away when the way before you is unclear.*

If you desire to please God above all others, obedience to God will require you to remain firm. If you do not sense clear guidance in your situation, ask God to confirm His will to you in His Word. He will never contradict Scripture. His will for your life always lines up perfectly with what the Bible says.

- *Be willing to endure conflict.*

When Israel entered the Promised Land at God's direction, it had to face strong enemy opposition. God rarely empties our lives of trouble and conflict. If He did, our dependence on Him would fade. He allows enough difficulty to keep us turned toward Him.

- *Leave the consequences to God.*

Obedience may not be viewed as popular, but it will always put you in a favorable position before God. Therefore, stay on the path of obedience and leave the rest to Him.

Disobedience always has fierce repercussions.

See the Life Principles Index for further study.

you, then you will be able to endure, and all this people will also go to their place in peace."
24 So Moses heeded the voice of his father-in-law and did all that he had said.
25 And Moses chose able men out of all Israel, and made them heads over the people: rulers of thousands, rulers of hundreds, rulers of fifties, and rulers of tens.
26 So they judged the people at all times; the hard cases they brought to Moses, but they judged every small case themselves.
27 Then Moses let his father-in-law depart, and he went his way to his own land.

Israel at Mount Sinai

19 In the third month after the children of Israel had gone out of the land of Egypt, on the same day, they came *to* the Wilderness of Sinai.
2 For they had departed from Rephidim, had come *to* the Wilderness of Sinai, and camped in the wilderness. So Israel camped there before the mountain.
3 And Moses went up to God, and the LORD called to him from the mountain, saying, "Thus you shall say to the house of Jacob, and tell the children of Israel:
4 'You have seen what I did to the Egyptians, and *how* I bore you on eagles' wings and brought you to Myself.
➤ 5 'Now therefore, if you will indeed obey My voice and keep My covenant, then you shall be a special treasure to Me above all people; for all the earth *is* Mine.
6 'And you shall be to Me a kingdom of priests and a holy nation.' These *are* the words which you shall speak to the children of Israel."
7 So Moses came and called for the elders of the people, and laid before them all these words which the LORD commanded him.
8 Then all the people answered together and said, "All that the LORD has spoken we will do." So Moses brought back the words of the people to the LORD.
9 And the LORD said to Moses, "Behold, I come to you in the thick cloud, that the people may hear when I speak with you, and believe you forever." So Moses told the words of the people to the LORD.
10 Then the LORD said to Moses, "Go to the people and consecrate them today and tomorrow, and let them wash their clothes.
11 "And let them be ready for the third day. For on the third day the LORD will come down upon Mount Sinai in the sight of all the people.
12 "You shall set bounds for the people all around, saying, 'Take heed to yourselves *that* you do *not* go up to the mountain or touch its base. Whoever touches the mountain shall surely be put to death.
13 'Not a hand shall touch him, but he shall surely be stoned or shot *with an arrow;* whether man or beast, he shall not live.' When the trumpet sounds long, they shall come near the mountain."
14 So Moses went down from the mountain to the people and sanctified the people, and they washed their clothes.
15 And he said to the people, "Be ready for the third day; do not come near *your* wives."
16 Then it came to pass on the third day, in the morning, that there were thunderings and lightnings, and a thick cloud on the mountain; and the sound of the trumpet was very loud, so that all the people who *were* in the camp trembled. ➤
17 And Moses brought the people out of the camp to meet with God, and they stood at the foot of the mountain.
18 Now Mount Sinai *was* completely in smoke, because the LORD descended upon it in fire. Its smoke ascended like the smoke of a furnace, and the whole mountain[a] quaked greatly.
19 And when the blast of the trumpet sounded long and became louder and louder, Moses spoke, and God answered him by voice.
20 Then the LORD came down upon Mount Sinai, on the top of the mountain. And the LORD called Moses to the top of the mountain, and Moses went up.

19:18 [a]Septuagint reads *all the people.*

LIFE LESSONS

➤ 19:5 — *"Now therefore, if you will indeed obey My voice and keep My covenant, then you shall be a special treasure to Me above all people; for all the earth is Mine."*

What an amazing thing to be called the "special treasure" of God! Obedience always brings blessing, and far more than we can imagine.

➤ 19:16 — *Then it came to pass on the third day, in the morning, that there were thunderings and lightnings, and a thick cloud on the mountain; and the sound of the trumpet was very loud, so that all the people who were in the camp trembled.*

For good reason the people trembled at the manifested presence of God on Mount Sinai. The Bible reminds us that we must serve God "with reverence and godly fear" since "our God is a consuming fire" (Heb. 12:28, 29).

21 And the LORD said to Moses, "Go down and warn the people, lest they break through to gaze at the LORD, and many of them perish.
22 "Also let the priests who come near the LORD consecrate themselves, lest the LORD break out against them."
23 But Moses said to the LORD, "The people cannot come up to Mount Sinai; for You warned us, saying, 'Set bounds around the mountain and consecrate it.'"
24 Then the LORD said to him, "Away! Get down and then come up, you and Aaron with you. But do not let the priests and the people break through to come up to the LORD, lest He break out against them."
25 So Moses went down to the people and spoke to them.

The Ten Commandments

20 And God spoke all these words, saying:
2 "I *am* the LORD your God, who brought you out of the land of Egypt, out of the house of bondage.
➤ 3 "You shall have no other gods before Me.
4 "You shall not make for yourself a carved image—any likeness *of anything* that *is* in heaven above, or that *is* in the earth beneath, or that *is* in the water under the earth;
5 you shall not bow down to them nor serve them. For I, the LORD your God, *am* a jealous God, visiting the iniquity of the fathers upon the children to the third and fourth *generations* of those who hate Me,
6 but showing mercy to thousands, to those who love Me and keep My commandments.
7 "You shall not take the name of the LORD your God in vain, for the LORD will not hold *him* guiltless who takes His name in vain.
8 "Remember the Sabbath day, to keep it holy.
9 Six days you shall labor and do all your work,
10 but the seventh day *is* the Sabbath of the LORD your God. *In it* you shall do no work: you, nor your son, nor your daughter, nor your male servant, nor your female servant, nor your cattle, nor your stranger who *is* within your gates.
11 For *in* six days the LORD made the heavens and the earth, the sea, and all that *is* in them, and rested the seventh day. Therefore the LORD blessed the Sabbath day and hallowed it.
12 "Honor your father and your mother, that your days may be long upon the land which the LORD your God is giving you. ➤
13 "You shall not murder.
14 "You shall not commit adultery.
15 "You shall not steal.
16 "You shall not bear false witness against your neighbor.
17 "You shall not covet your neighbor's house; you shall not covet your neighbor's wife, nor his male servant, nor his female servant, nor his ox, nor his donkey, nor anything that *is* your neighbor's."

The People Afraid of God's Presence

18 Now all the people witnessed the thunderings, the lightning flashes, the sound of the trumpet, and the mountain smoking; and when the people saw *it*, they trembled and stood afar off.
19 Then they said to Moses, "You speak with us, and we will hear; but let not God speak with us, lest we die."
20 And Moses said to the people, "Do not fear; for God has come to test you, and that His fear may be before you, so that you may not sin."
21 So the people stood afar off, but Moses drew near the thick darkness where God *was*.

The Law of the Altar

22 Then the LORD said to Moses, "Thus you shall say to the children of Israel: 'You have seen that I have talked with you from heaven.
23 'You shall not make *anything to be* with Me—gods of silver or gods of gold you shall not make for yourselves.
24 'An altar of earth you shall make for Me, and you shall sacrifice on it your burnt offerings and your peace offerings, your sheep and your oxen. In every place where I record My name I will come to you, and I will bless you.
25 'And if you make Me an altar of stone, you

LIFE LESSONS

➤ 20:3 — *"You shall have no other gods before Me."*

The First Commandment is first for a reason. God must be first in everything we do, for intimacy with God is His highest priority for our life.

➤ 20:12 — *"Honor your father and your mother, that your days may be long upon the land which the LORD your God is giving you."*

With every divine commandment comes not merely a curse for disobedience, but a blessing for obedience. God does not give us commandments because He wants to control us; His commandments prepare us for His blessings.

ANSWERS TO LIFE'S QUESTIONS

What place should money take in my life?

EX. 20:2, 3

For some, money becomes central. They worship money, which means that they devote most of their time, energy, and attention to its gain and use. They regard money as the key to power and prestige.

"Oh, I'd never worship the idol of finance," you may say. But ask yourself these questions:

- How much time do I spend every day thinking about my financial life—my income, my bills, my past and upcoming purchases, my investments? In comparison, how much time do I spend meditating upon God's Word?
- How much time do I spend every week working, shopping, or dealing with money? (Be sure to include trips to automatic teller machines and the bank, discussion with your spouse about budgets or spending plans and habits, and the time you spend paying bills and balancing your checking account.) In comparison, how much time do I spend in prayer, reading my Bible, or participating in church-related activities and outreaches?
- Am I more likely to discuss with my family and friends a hot stock tip, the cost of an item, or a new business opportunity . . . or an insight I have into God's Word, the major truths of last Sunday's sermon, or a way in which the Holy Spirit has helped me during the day? Which conversation is more likely to attract a greater amount of my energy, enthusiasm, or concern?

You may say that you trust God in every area of your life—but do you ever conduct business transactions, make purchases and investments, and enter into money-making opportunities without asking God's opinion or seeking God's wisdom? When you leave God out of your financial life, you are in grave danger of making money your idol.

So how can you make sure you don't fall into such a deadly trap? You could begin by focusing on Philippians 4:19, where God promises to supply all your need. All of us have very specific needs: emotional, physical, material, mental, and spiritual. God knows that our needs must be met (Matt. 6:32) if we are to carry out the complete life plan He has ordained for us. By making intimacy with God your number one priority in life, you can be assured that He will meet all those needs. Jesus said it like this: "Seek first the kingdom of God and His righteousness, and all these things shall be added to you" (Matt. 6:33).

See the Life Principles Index for further study:
19. Anything you hold too tightly you will lose.
11. God assumes full responsibility for our needs when we obey Him.

shall not build it of hewn stone; for if you use
your tool on it, you have profaned it.
26 'Nor shall you go up by steps to My altar,
that your nakedness may not be exposed
on it.'

The Law Concerning Servants

21 "Now these *are* the judgments which
you shall set before them:
2 "If you buy a Hebrew servant, he shall
serve six years; and in the seventh he shall go
out free and pay nothing.
3 "If he comes in by himself, he shall go out
by himself; if he *comes in* married, then his
wife shall go out with him.
4 "If his master has given him a wife, and
she has borne him sons or daughters, the wife
and her children shall be her master's, and he
shall go out by himself.
5 "But if the servant plainly says, 'I love my
master, my wife, and my children; I will not
go out free,'
6 "then his master shall bring him to the
judges. He shall also bring him to the door, or
to the doorpost, and his master shall pierce
his ear with an awl; and he shall serve him
forever.
7 "And if a man sells his daughter to be a female slave, she shall not go out as the male
slaves do.
8 "If she does not please her master, who
has betrothed her to himself, then he shall let
her be redeemed. He shall have no right to
sell her to a foreign people, since he has dealt
deceitfully with her.
9 "And if he has betrothed her to his son, he
shall deal with her according to the custom of
daughters.
10 "If he takes another *wife*, he shall not diminish her food, her clothing, and her marriage rights.
11 "And if he does not do these three for her,
then she shall go out free, without *paying*
money.

The Law Concerning Violence
12 "He who strikes a man so that he dies
shall surely be put to death.
13 However, if he did not lie in wait, but God
delivered *him* into his hand, then I will appoint for you a place where he may flee.
14 "But if a man acts with premeditation
against his neighbor, to kill him by treachery,
you shall take him from My altar, that he may
die.
15 "And he who strikes his father or his
mother shall surely be put to death.
16 "He who kidnaps a man and sells him, or
if he is found in his hand, shall surely be put
to death.
17 "And he who curses his father or his
mother shall surely be put to death.
18 "If men contend with each other, and one
strikes the other with a stone or with *his* fist,
and he does not die but is confined to *his* bed,
19 "if he rises again and walks about outside
with his staff, then he who struck *him* shall be
acquitted. He shall only pay *for* the loss of his
time, and shall provide *for him* to be thoroughly healed.
20 "And if a man beats his male or female
servant with a rod, so that he dies under his
hand, he shall surely be punished.
21 "Notwithstanding, if he remains alive a
day or two, he shall not be punished; for he *is*
his property.
22 "If men fight, and hurt a woman with child,
so that she gives birth prematurely, yet no
harm follows, he shall surely be punished accordingly as the woman's husband imposes on
him; and he shall pay as the judges *determine.*
23 "But if *any* harm follows, then you shall
give life for life,
24 "eye for eye, tooth for tooth, hand for
hand, foot for foot,
25 "burn for burn, wound for wound, stripe
for stripe.
26 "If a man strikes the eye of his male or female servant, and destroys it, he shall let him
go free for the sake of his eye.
27 "And if he knocks out the tooth of his male
or female servant, he shall let him go free for
the sake of his tooth.

Animal Control Laws
28 "If an ox gores a man or a woman to
death, then the ox shall surely be stoned, and
its flesh shall not be eaten; but the owner of
the ox *shall be* acquitted.
29 "But if the ox tended to thrust with its
horn in times past, and it has been made
known to his owner, and he has not kept it
confined, so that it has killed a man or a
woman, the ox shall be stoned and its owner
also shall be put to death.
30 "If there is imposed on him a sum of
money, then he shall pay to redeem his life,
whatever is imposed on him.
31 "Whether it has gored a son or gored a
daughter, according to this judgment it shall
be done to him.
32 "If the ox gores a male or female servant,
he shall give to their master thirty shekels of
silver, and the ox shall be stoned.
33 "And if a man opens a pit, or if a man digs
a pit and does not cover it, and an ox or a donkey falls in it,
34 "the owner of the pit shall make *it* good;
he shall give money to their owner, but the
dead *animal* shall be his.
35 "If one man's ox hurts another's, so that it
dies, then they shall sell the live ox and divide
the money from it; and the dead *ox* they shall
also divide.
36 "Or if it was known that the ox tended to
thrust in time past, and its owner has not kept
it confined, he shall surely pay ox for ox, and
the dead animal shall be his own.

Responsibility for Property
22 "If a man steals an ox or a sheep, and
slaughters it or sells it, he shall restore
five oxen for an ox and four sheep for a
sheep.
2 "If the thief is found breaking in, and he is
struck so that he dies, *there shall be* no guilt
for his bloodshed.
3 "If the sun has risen on him, *there shall be*
guilt for his bloodshed. He should make full
restitution; if he has nothing, then he shall be
sold for his theft.
4 "If the theft is certainly found alive in his
hand, whether it is an ox or donkey or sheep,
he shall restore double.
5 "If a man causes a field or vineyard to be
grazed, and lets loose his animal, and it feeds
in another man's field, he shall make restitution from the best of his own field and the
best of his own vineyard.

LIFE LESSONS

➢ 21:33 — *"And if a man opens a pit, or if a man digs a pit and does not cover it, and an ox or a donkey falls in it . . . ."*

Even in a world ruled by a sovereign God, "accidents" happen. We live on a fallen planet, and although God has the power to prevent every accident, He does not. Instead, He asks us to trust Him whatever happens.

➢ 21:36 — *"Or if it was known that the ox tended to thrust in time past, and its owner has not kept it confined, he shall surely pay ox for ox, and the dead animal shall be his own."*

God expects His people to act in a responsible manner and to use sound judgment in the way they conduct their affairs. And He holds us accountable for our inaction as well as for our actions.

6 "If fire breaks out and catches in thorns,
so that stacked grain, standing grain, or the
field is consumed, he who kindled the fire
shall surely make restitution.
7 "If a man delivers to his neighbor money
or articles to keep, and it is stolen out of the
man's house, if the thief is found, he shall pay
double.
8 "If the thief is not found, then the master
of the house shall be brought to the judges *to
see* whether he has put his hand into his
neighbor's goods.
9 "For any kind of trespass, *whether it concerns* an ox, a donkey, a sheep, or clothing, *or*
for any kind of lost thing which *another*
claims to be his, the cause of both parties
shall come before the judges; *and* whomever
the judges condemn shall pay double to his
neighbor.
10 "If a man delivers to his neighbor a donkey, an ox, a sheep, or any animal to keep, and
it dies, is hurt, or driven away, no one seeing *it*,
11 "*then* an oath of the LORD shall be between
them both, that he has not put his hand into
his neighbor's goods; and the owner of it shall
accept *that*, and he shall not make *it* good.
12 "But if, in fact, it is stolen from him, he
shall make restitution to the owner of it.
13 "If it is torn to pieces *by a beast, then* he
shall bring it as evidence, *and* he shall not
make good what was torn.
14 "And if a man borrows *anything* from his
neighbor, and it becomes injured or dies, the
owner of it not *being* with it, he shall surely
make *it* good.
15 "If its owner *was* with it, he shall not make
it good; if it *was* hired, it came for its hire.

Moral and Ceremonial Principles

16 "If a man entices a virgin who is not betrothed, and lies with her, he shall surely pay
the bride-price for her *to be* his wife.
17 "If her father utterly refuses to give her to
him, he shall pay money according to the
bride-price of virgins.
18 "You shall not permit a sorceress to live.
19 "Whoever lies with an animal shall surely
be put to death.
20 "He who sacrifices to *any* god, except to
the LORD only, he shall be utterly destroyed.
21 "You shall neither mistreat a stranger nor
oppress him, for you were strangers in the
land of Egypt.
22 "You shall not afflict any widow or fatherless child.
23 "If you afflict them in any way, *and* they
cry at all to Me, I will surely hear their cry;
24 "and My wrath will become hot, and I will
kill you with the sword; your wives shall be
widows, and your children fatherless.
25 "If you lend money to *any of* My people
who are poor among you, you shall not be like
a moneylender to him; you shall not charge
him interest.
26 "If you ever take your neighbor's garment
as a pledge, you shall return it to him before
the sun goes down.
27 "For that *is* his only covering, it *is* his garment for his skin. What will he sleep in? And
it will be that when he cries to Me, I will hear,
for I *am* gracious.
28 "You shall not revile God, nor curse a ruler
of your people.
29 "You shall not delay *to offer* the first of
your ripe produce and your juices. The firstborn of your sons you shall give to Me.
30 "Likewise you shall do with your oxen *and*
your sheep. It shall be with its mother seven
days; on the eighth day you shall give it to Me.
31 "And you shall be holy men to Me: you
shall not eat meat torn *by beasts* in the field;
you shall throw it to the dogs.

Justice for All

23 "You shall not circulate a false report.
Do not put your hand with the wicked
to be an unrighteous witness.
2 "You shall not follow a crowd to do evil;
nor shall you testify in a dispute so as to turn
aside after many to pervert *justice*.
3 "You shall not show partiality to a poor
man in his dispute.
4 "If you meet your enemy's ox or his donkey going astray, you shall surely bring it
back to him again.
5 "If you see the donkey of one who hates
you lying under its burden, and you would refrain from helping it, you shall surely help
him with it.
6 "You shall not pervert the judgment of
your poor in his dispute.
7 "Keep yourself far from a false matter; do
not kill the innocent and righteous. For I will
not justify the wicked.
8 "And you shall take no bribe, for a bribe
blinds the discerning and perverts the words
of the righteous.
9 "Also you shall not oppress a stranger, for
you know the heart of a stranger, because you
were strangers in the land of Egypt.

LIFE LESSONS

➤ 22:28 — *"You shall not revile God, nor curse a ruler of your people."*

Followers of Christ are to honor their leaders, regardless of whether they agree with their politics. God places leaders in their roles (Dan. 4:17) and calls us to pray for them, not revile them (1 Tim. 2:1, 2).

The Law of Sabbaths
10 "Six years you shall sow your land and
gather in its produce,
11 "but the seventh *year* you shall let it rest
and lie fallow, that the poor of your people
may eat; and what they leave, the beasts of
the field may eat. In like manner you shall do
with your vineyard *and* your olive grove.
12 "Six days you shall do your work, and on
the seventh day you shall rest, that your ox
and your donkey may rest, and the son of
your female servant and the stranger may be
refreshed.
13 "And in all that I have said to you, be circumspect and make no mention of the name
of other gods, nor let it be heard from your
mouth.

Three Annual Feasts
14 "Three times you shall keep a feast to Me
in the year:
15 "You shall keep the Feast of Unleavened
Bread (you shall eat unleavened bread seven
days, as I commanded you, at the time appointed in the month of Abib, for in it you
came out of Egypt; none shall appear before
Me empty);
16 "and the Feast of Harvest, the firstfruits of
your labors which you have sown in the field;
and the Feast of Ingathering at the end of the
year, when you have gathered in *the fruit of*
your labors from the field.
17 "Three times in the year all your males
shall appear before the Lord GOD.[a]
18 "You shall not offer the blood of My sacrifice with leavened bread; nor shall the fat of
My sacrifice remain until morning.
19 "The first of the firstfruits of your land you
shall bring into the house of the LORD your
God. You shall not boil a young goat in its
mother's milk.

The Angel and the Promises
20 "Behold, I send an Angel before you to
keep you in the way and to bring you into the
place which I have prepared.
21 "Beware of Him and obey His voice; do
not provoke Him, for He will not pardon your
transgressions; for My name *is* in Him.
➤ 22 "But if you indeed obey His voice and do
all that I speak, then I will be an enemy to
your enemies and an adversary to your adversaries.
23 "For My Angel will go before you and
bring you in to the Amorites and the Hittites
and the Perizzites and the Canaanites and the
Hivites and the Jebusites; and I will cut them
off.
24 "You shall not bow down to their gods,
nor serve them, nor do according to their
works; but you shall utterly overthrow them
and completely break down their *sacred*
pillars.
25 "So you shall serve the LORD your God,
and He will bless your bread and your water.
And I will take sickness away from the midst
of you.
26 "No one shall suffer miscarriage or be
barren in your land; I will fulfill the number
of your days.
27 "I will send My fear before you, I will
cause confusion among all the people to
whom you come, and will make all your enemies turn *their* backs to you.
28 "And I will send hornets before you, which
shall drive out the Hivite, the Canaanite, and
the Hittite from before you.
29 "I will not drive them out from before you
in one year, lest the land become desolate and
the beasts of the field become too numerous
for you.
30 "Little by little I will drive them out from
before you, until you have increased, and you
inherit the land.
31 "And I will set your bounds from the Red
Sea to the sea, Philistia, and from the desert
to the River.[a] For I will deliver the inhabitants
of the land into your hand, and you shall drive
them out before you.
32 "You shall make no covenant with them,
nor with their gods.
33 "They shall not dwell in your land, lest
they make you sin against Me. For *if* you serve
their gods, it will surely be a snare to you."

Israel Affirms the Covenant
24 Now He said to Moses, "Come up to the
LORD, you and Aaron, Nadab and
Abihu, and seventy of the elders of Israel, and
worship from afar.
2 "And Moses alone shall come near the
LORD, but they shall not come near; nor shall
the people go up with him."
3 So Moses came and told the people all the
words of the LORD and all the judgments. And

23:17 [a]Hebrew *YHWH,* usually translated *LORD* **23:31** [a]Hebrew *Nahar,* the Euphrates

LIFE LESSONS

➤ **23:22 — *"But if you indeed obey His voice and do all that I speak, then I will be an enemy to your enemies and an adversary to your adversaries."***

As we travel the journey of life, it comforts and empowers us to know that our God gives us His loyalty and protection against the spiritual enemies and pitfalls we are sure to encounter.

all the people answered with one voice and said, "All the words which the LORD has said we will do."

4 And Moses wrote all the words of the LORD. And he rose early in the morning, and built an altar at the foot of the mountain, and twelve pillars according to the twelve tribes of Israel.

5 Then he sent young men of the children of Israel, who offered burnt offerings and sacrificed peace offerings of oxen to the LORD.

6 And Moses took half the blood and put *it* in basins, and half the blood he sprinkled on the altar.

7 Then he took the Book of the Covenant and read in the hearing of the people. And they said, "All that the LORD has said we will do, and be obedient."

8 And Moses took the blood, sprinkled *it* on the people, and said, "This is the blood of the covenant which the LORD has made with you according to all these words."

On the Mountain with God

9 Then Moses went up, also Aaron, Nadab, and Abihu, and seventy of the elders of Israel,

➤ 10 and they saw the God of Israel. And *there was* under His feet as it were a paved work of sapphire stone, and it was like the very heavens in *its* clarity.

11 But on the nobles of the children of Israel He did not lay His hand. So they saw God, and they ate and drank.

12 Then the LORD said to Moses, "Come up to Me on the mountain and be there; and I will give you tablets of stone, and the law and commandments which I have written, that you may teach them."

13 So Moses arose with his assistant Joshua, and Moses went up to the mountain of God.

14 And he said to the elders, "Wait here for us until we come back to you. Indeed, Aaron and Hur *are* with you. If any man has a difficulty, let him go to them."

15 Then Moses went up into the mountain, and a cloud covered the mountain.

16 Now the glory of the LORD rested on Mount Sinai, and the cloud covered it six days. And on the seventh day He called to Moses out of the midst of the cloud.

17 The sight of the glory of the LORD *was* like a consuming fire on the top of the mountain in the eyes of the children of Israel.

18 So Moses went into the midst of the cloud and went up into the mountain. And Moses was on the mountain forty days and forty nights.

Offerings for the Sanctuary

25 Then the LORD spoke to Moses, saying:

2 "Speak to the children of Israel, that they bring Me an offering. From everyone who gives it willingly with his heart you shall take My offering. ➤

3 "And this *is* the offering which you shall take from them: gold, silver, and bronze;

4 "blue, purple, and scarlet *thread,* fine linen, and goats' *hair;*

5 "ram skins dyed red, badger skins, and acacia wood;

6 "oil for the light, and spices for the anointing oil and for the sweet incense;

7 "onyx stones, and stones to be set in the ephod and in the breastplate.

8 "And let them make Me a sanctuary, that I may dwell among them.

9 "According to all that I show you, *that is,* the pattern of the tabernacle and the pattern of all its furnishings, just so you shall make *it.*

The Ark of the Testimony

10 "And they shall make an ark of acacia wood; two and a half cubits *shall be* its length, a cubit and a half its width, and a cubit and a half its height.

11 "And you shall overlay it with pure gold, inside and out you shall overlay it, and shall make on it a molding of gold all around.

12 "You shall cast four rings of gold for it, and put *them* in its four corners; two rings *shall be* on one side, and two rings on the other side.

13 "And you shall make poles of acacia wood, and overlay them with gold.

14 "You shall put the poles into the rings on the sides of the ark, that the ark may be carried by them.

15 "The poles shall be in the rings of the ark; they shall not be taken from it.

16 "And you shall put into the ark the Testimony which I will give you.

LIFE LESSONS

➤ 24:10 — *. . . and they saw the God of Israel. And there was under His feet as it were a paved work of sapphire stone, and it was like the very heavens in its clarity.*

Biblical descriptions of God tend to focus more on the surroundings of God than on the Lord Himself, primarily because He is beyond description. But what a wonder that this majestic God calls us His own!

➤ 25:2 — *"Speak to the children of Israel, that they bring Me an offering. From everyone who gives it willingly with his heart you shall take My offering."*

The kind of offering God most desires from us is a willing one given out of a grateful heart. But even when we give in this joyful way, we can never out give God.

17 "You shall make a mercy seat of pure gold; two and a half cubits *shall be* its length and a cubit and a half its width.

18 "And you shall make two cherubim of gold; of hammered work you shall make them at the two ends of the mercy seat.

19 "Make one cherub at one end, and the other cherub at the other end; you shall make the cherubim at the two ends of it *of one piece* with the mercy seat.

20 "And the cherubim shall stretch out *their* wings above, covering the mercy seat with their wings, and they shall face one another; the faces of the cherubim *shall be* toward the mercy seat.

21 "You shall put the mercy seat on top of the ark, and in the ark you shall put the Testimony that I will give you.

22 "And there I will meet with you, and I will speak with you from above the mercy seat, from between the two cherubim which *are* on the ark of the Testimony, about everything which I will give you in commandment to the children of Israel.

The Table for the Showbread

23 "You shall also make a table of acacia wood; two cubits *shall be* its length, a cubit its width, and a cubit and a half its height.

24 "And you shall overlay it with pure gold, and make a molding of gold all around.

25 "You shall make for it a frame of a handbreadth all around, and you shall make a gold molding for the frame all around.

26 "And you shall make for it four rings of gold, and put the rings on the four corners that *are* at its four legs.

27 "The rings shall be close to the frame, as holders for the poles to bear the table.

28 "And you shall make the poles of acacia wood, and overlay them with gold, that the table may be carried with them.

29 "You shall make its dishes, its pans, its pitchers, and its bowls for pouring. You shall make them of pure gold.

30 "And you shall set the showbread on the table before Me always.

The Gold Lampstand

31 "You shall also make a lampstand of pure gold; the lampstand shall be of hammered work. Its shaft, its branches, its bowls, its *ornamental* knobs, and flowers shall be *of one piece*.

32 "And six branches shall come out of its sides: three branches of the lampstand out of one side, and three branches of the lampstand out of the other side.

33 "Three bowls *shall be* made like almond *blossoms* on one branch, *with* an *ornamental* knob and a flower, and three bowls made like almond *blossoms* on the other branch, *with* an *ornamental* knob and a flower—and so for the six branches that come out of the lampstand.

34 "On the lampstand itself four bowls *shall be* made like almond *blossoms, each with* its *ornamental* knob and flower.

35 "And *there shall be* a knob under the *first* two branches of the same, a knob under the *second* two branches of the same, and a knob under the *third* two branches of the same, according to the six branches that extend from the lampstand.

36 "Their knobs and their branches *shall be of one piece;* all of it *shall be* one hammered piece of pure gold.

37 "You shall make seven lamps for it, and they shall arrange its lamps so that they give light in front of it.

38 "And its wick-trimmers and their trays *shall be* of pure gold.

39 "It shall be made of a talent of pure gold, with all these utensils.

40 "And see to it that you make *them* according to the pattern which was shown you on the mountain.

The Tabernacle

26 "Moreover you shall make the tabernacle *with* ten curtains *of* fine woven linen and blue, purple, and scarlet *thread;* with artistic designs of cherubim you shall weave them.

2 "The length of each curtain *shall be* twenty-eight cubits, and the width of each curtain four cubits. And every one of the curtains shall have the same measurements.

3 "Five curtains shall be coupled to one another, and *the other* five curtains *shall be* coupled to one another.

4 "And you shall make loops of blue *yarn* on the edge of the curtain on the selvedge of *one* set, and likewise you shall do on the outer edge of *the other* curtain of the second set.

5 "Fifty loops you shall make in the one curtain, and fifty loops you shall make on the edge of the curtain that *is* on the end of the second set, that the loops may be clasped to one another.

6 "And you shall make fifty clasps of gold, and couple the curtains together with the clasps, so that it may be one tabernacle.

7 "You shall also make curtains of goats' *hair,* to be a tent over the tabernacle. You shall make eleven curtains.

8 "The length of each curtain *shall be* thirty cubits, and the width of each curtain four cubits; and the eleven curtains shall all have the same measurements.

9 "And you shall couple five curtains by themselves and six curtains by themselves, and you shall double over the sixth curtain at the forefront of the tent.

10 "You shall make fifty loops on the edge of the curtain that is outermost in *one* set, and

fifty loops on the edge of the curtain of the
second set.
11 "And you shall make fifty bronze clasps,
put the clasps into the loops, and couple the
tent together, that it may be one.
12 "The remnant that remains of the curtains
of the tent, the half curtain that remains, shall
hang over the back of the tabernacle.
13 "And a cubit on one side and a cubit on the
other side, of what remains of the length of
the curtains of the tent, shall hang over the
sides of the tabernacle, on this side and on
that side, to cover it.
14 "You shall also make a covering of ram
skins dyed red for the tent, and a covering of
badger skins above that.
15 "And for the tabernacle you shall make
the boards of acacia wood, standing upright.
16 "Ten cubits *shall be* the length of a board,
and a cubit and a half *shall be* the width of
each board.
17 "Two tenons *shall be* in each board for
binding one to another. Thus you shall make
for all the boards of the tabernacle.
18 "And you shall make the boards for the
tabernacle, twenty boards for the south side.
19 "You shall make forty sockets of silver
under the twenty boards: two sockets under
each of the boards for its two tenons.
20 "And for the second side of the tabernacle,
the north side, *there shall be* twenty boards
21 "and their forty sockets of silver: two
sockets under each of the boards.
22 "For the far side of the tabernacle, westward, you shall make six boards.
23 "And you shall also make two boards for
the two back corners of the tabernacle.
24 "They shall be coupled together at the bottom and they shall be coupled together at the
top by one ring. Thus it shall be for both of
them. They shall be for the two corners.
25 "So there shall be eight boards with their
sockets of silver—sixteen sockets—two sockets under each of the boards.
26 "And you shall make bars of acacia wood:
five for the boards on one side of the tabernacle,
27 "five bars for the boards on the other side
of the tabernacle, and five bars for the boards
of the side of the tabernacle, for the far side
westward.
28 "The middle bar shall pass through the
midst of the boards from end to end.
29 "You shall overlay the boards with gold,
make their rings of gold *as* holders for the
bars, and overlay the bars with gold.
30 "And you shall raise up the tabernacle according to its pattern which you were shown
on the mountain.
31 "You shall make a veil woven of blue, purple, and scarlet *thread,* and fine woven linen.
It shall be woven with an artistic design of
cherubim.
32 "You shall hang it upon the four pillars of
acacia *wood* overlaid with gold. Their hooks
shall be gold, upon four sockets of silver.
33 "And you shall hang the veil from the
clasps. Then you shall bring the ark of the
Testimony in there, behind the veil. The veil
shall be a divider for you between the holy
place and the Most Holy.
34 "You shall put the mercy seat upon the ark
of the Testimony in the Most Holy.
35 "You shall set the table outside the veil,
and the lampstand across from the table on
the side of the tabernacle toward the south;
and you shall put the table on the north side.
36 "You shall make a screen for the door of
the tabernacle, *woven of* blue, purple, and
scarlet *thread,* and fine woven linen, made by
a weaver.
37 "And you shall make for the screen five
pillars of acacia *wood,* and overlay them with
gold; their hooks *shall be* gold, and you shall
cast five sockets of bronze for them.

The Altar of Burnt Offering

27 "You shall make an altar of acacia
wood, five cubits long and five cubits
wide—the altar shall be square—and its
height *shall be* three cubits.
2 "You shall make its horns on its four corners; its horns shall be of one piece with it.
And you shall overlay it with bronze.
3 "Also you shall make its pans to receive its
ashes, and its shovels and its basins and its
forks and its firepans; you shall make all its
utensils of bronze.
4 "You shall make a grate for it, a network
of bronze; and on the network you shall make
four bronze rings at its four corners.
5 "You shall put it under the rim of the altar
beneath, that the network may be midway up
the altar.
6 "And you shall make poles for the altar,
poles of acacia wood, and overlay them with
bronze.
7 "The poles shall be put in the rings, and
the poles shall be on the two sides of the altar
to bear it.
8 "You shall make it hollow with boards; as
it was shown you on the mountain, so shall
they make *it.*

The Court of the Tabernacle

9 "You shall also make the court of the tabernacle. For the south side *there shall be*
hangings for the court *made of* fine woven
linen, one hundred cubits long for one side.
10 "And its twenty pillars and their twenty
sockets *shall be* bronze. The hooks of the pillars and their bands *shall be* silver.
11 "Likewise along the length of the north
side *there shall be* hangings one hundred *cubits* long, with its twenty pillars and their
twenty sockets of bronze, and the hooks of
the pillars and their bands of silver.
12 "And along the width of the court on the

west side *shall be* hangings of fifty cubits, with their ten pillars and their ten sockets.
13 "The width of the court on the east side *shall be* fifty cubits.
14 "The hangings on *one* side *of the gate shall be* fifteen cubits, *with* their three pillars and their three sockets.
15 "And on the other side *shall be* hangings of fifteen *cubits, with* their three pillars and their three sockets.
16 "For the gate of the court *there shall be* a screen twenty cubits long, *woven of* blue, purple, and scarlet *thread,* and fine woven linen, made by a weaver. It *shall have* four pillars and four sockets.
17 "All the pillars around the court shall have bands of silver; their hooks *shall be* of silver and their sockets of bronze.
18 "The length of the court *shall be* one hundred cubits, the width fifty throughout, and the height five cubits, *made of* fine woven linen, and its sockets of bronze.
19 "All the utensils of the tabernacle for all its service, all its pegs, and all the pegs of the court, *shall be* of bronze.

The Care of the Lampstand

20 "And you shall command the children of Israel that they bring you pure oil of pressed olives for the light, to cause the lamp to burn continually.
21 "In the tabernacle of meeting, outside the veil which *is* before the Testimony, Aaron and his sons shall tend it from evening until morning before the LORD. *It shall be* a statute forever to their generations on behalf of the children of Israel.

Garments for the Priesthood

28 "Now take Aaron your brother, and his sons with him, from among the children of Israel, that he may minister to Me as priest, Aaron *and* Aaron's sons: Nadab, Abihu, Eleazar, and Ithamar.
2 "And you shall make holy garments for Aaron your brother, for glory and for beauty.
➤ 3 "So you shall speak to all *who are* gifted artisans, whom I have filled with the spirit of wisdom, that they may make Aaron's garments, to consecrate him, that he may minister to Me as priest.
4 "And these *are* the garments which they shall make: a breastplate, an ephod,[a] a robe, a skillfully woven tunic, a turban, and a sash. So they shall make holy garments for Aaron your brother and his sons, that he may minister to Me as priest.

The Ephod

5 "They shall take the gold, blue, purple, and scarlet *thread,* and the fine linen,
6 "and they shall make the ephod of gold, blue, purple, *and* scarlet *thread,* and fine woven linen, artistically worked.
7 "It shall have two shoulder straps joined at its two edges, and *so* it shall be joined together.
8 "And the intricately woven band of the ephod, which *is* on it, shall be of the same workmanship, *made of* gold, blue, purple, and scarlet *thread,* and fine woven linen.
9 "Then you shall take two onyx stones and engrave on them the names of the sons of Israel:
10 "six of their names on one stone and six names on the other stone, in order of their birth.
11 "With the work of an engraver in stone, *like* the engravings of a signet, you shall engrave the two stones with the names of the sons of Israel. You shall set them in settings of gold.
12 "And you shall put the two stones on the shoulders of the ephod *as* memorial stones for the sons of Israel. So Aaron shall bear their names before the LORD on his two shoulders as a memorial.
13 "You shall also make settings of gold,
14 "and you shall make two chains of pure gold like braided cords, and fasten the braided chains to the settings.

The Breastplate

15 "You shall make the breastplate of judgment. Artistically woven according to the workmanship of the ephod you shall make it: of gold, blue, purple, and scarlet *thread,* and fine woven linen, you shall make it.
16 "It shall be doubled into a square: a span *shall be* its length, and a span *shall be* its width.
17 "And you shall put settings of stones in it, four rows of stones: *The first* row *shall be* a sardius, a topaz, and an emerald; *this shall be* the first row;
18 "the second row *shall be* a turquoise, a sapphire, and a diamond;

28:4 [a]That is, an ornamented vest

LIFE LESSONS

➤ 28:3 — *"So you shall speak to all who are gifted artisans, whom I have filled with the spirit of wisdom, that they may make Aaron's garments, to consecrate him, that he may minister to Me as priest."*

God commissions and equips for His service, not merely "religious" individuals such as pastors and evangelists, but men and women whom He gifts in many ways. If you answer phones, do so as unto the Lord!

19 "the third row, a jacinth, an agate, and an amethyst;
20 "and the fourth row, a beryl, an onyx, and a jasper. They shall be set in gold settings.
21 "And the stones shall have the names of the sons of Israel, twelve according to their names, *like* the engravings of a signet, each one with its own name; they shall be according to the twelve tribes.
22 "You shall make chains for the breastplate at the end, like braided cords of pure gold.
23 "And you shall make two rings of gold for the breastplate, and put the two rings on the two ends of the breastplate.
24 "Then you shall put the two braided *chains* of gold in the two rings which are on the ends of the breastplate;
25 "and the *other* two ends of the two braided *chains* you shall fasten to the two settings, and put them on the shoulder straps of the ephod in the front.
26 "You shall make two rings of gold, and put them on the two ends of the breastplate, on the edge of it, which is on the inner side of the ephod.
27 "And two *other* rings of gold you shall make, and put them on the two shoulder straps, underneath the ephod toward its front, right at the seam above the intricately woven band of the ephod.
28 "They shall bind the breastplate by means of its rings to the rings of the ephod, using a blue cord, so that it is above the intricately woven band of the ephod, and so that the breastplate does not come loose from the ephod.
29 "So Aaron shall bear the names of the sons of Israel on the breastplate of judgment over his heart, when he goes into the holy *place*, as a memorial before the LORD continually.
30 "And you shall put in the breastplate of judgment the Urim and the Thummim,[a] and they shall be over Aaron's heart when he goes in before the LORD. So Aaron shall bear the judgment of the children of Israel over his heart before the LORD continually.

Other Priestly Garments

31 "You shall make the robe of the ephod all of blue.
32 "There shall be an opening for his head in the middle of it; it shall have a woven binding all around its opening, like the opening in a coat of mail, so that it does not tear.
33 "And upon its hem you shall make pomegranates of blue, purple, and scarlet, all around its hem, and bells of gold between them all around:
34 "a golden bell and a pomegranate, a golden bell and a pomegranate, upon the hem of the robe all around.
35 "And it shall be upon Aaron when he ministers, and its sound will be heard when he goes into the holy *place* before the LORD and when he comes out, that he may not die.
36 "You shall also make a plate of pure gold and engrave on it, *like* the engraving of a signet:

HOLINESS TO THE LORD.

37 "And you shall put it on a blue cord, that it may be on the turban; it shall be on the front of the turban.
38 "So it shall be on Aaron's forehead, that Aaron may bear the iniquity of the holy things which the children of Israel hallow in all their holy gifts; and it shall always be on his forehead, that they may be accepted before the LORD.
39 "You shall skillfully weave the tunic of fine linen *thread*, you shall make the turban of fine linen, and you shall make the sash of woven work.
40 "For Aaron's sons you shall make tunics, and you shall make sashes for them. And you shall make hats for them, for glory and beauty.
41 "So you shall put them on Aaron your brother and on his sons with him. You shall anoint them, consecrate them, and sanctify them, that they may minister to Me as priests.
42 "And you shall make for them linen trousers to cover their nakedness; they shall reach from the waist to the thighs.
43 "They shall be on Aaron and on his sons when they come into the tabernacle of meeting, or when they come near the altar to minister in the holy *place*, that they do not incur iniquity and die. *It shall be* a statute forever to him and his descendants after him.

Aaron and His Sons Consecrated

29 "And this is what you shall do to them to hallow them for ministering to Me as priests: Take one young bull and two rams without blemish,
2 "and unleavened bread, unleavened cakes mixed with oil, and unleavened wafers anointed with oil (you shall make them of wheat flour).
3 "You shall put them in one basket and bring them in the basket, with the bull and the two rams.
4 "And Aaron and his sons you shall bring to the door of the tabernacle of meeting, and you shall wash them with water.
5 "Then you shall take the garments, put the tunic on Aaron, and the robe of the ephod, the ephod, and the breastplate, and gird him with the intricately woven band of the ephod.
6 "You shall put the turban on his head, and put the holy crown on the turban.
7 "And you shall take the anointing oil, pour *it* on his head, and anoint him.

28:30 [a]Literally *the Lights and the Perfections* (compare Leviticus 8:8)

8 "Then you shall bring his sons and put tunics on them.
9 "And you shall gird them with sashes,
Aaron and his sons, and put the hats on them.
The priesthood shall be theirs for a perpetual
statute. So you shall consecrate Aaron and his
sons.
10 "You shall also have the bull brought before the tabernacle of meeting, and Aaron
and his sons shall put their hands on the head
of the bull.
11 "Then you shall kill the bull before the
LORD, *by* the door of the tabernacle of meeting.
12 "You shall take *some* of the blood of the
bull and put *it* on the horns of the altar with
your finger, and pour all the blood beside the
base of the altar.
13 "And you shall take all the fat that covers
the entrails, the fatty lobe *attached* to the
liver, and the two kidneys and the fat that *is*
on them, and burn *them* on the altar.
14 "But the flesh of the bull, with its skin and
its offal, you shall burn with fire outside the
camp. It *is* a sin offering.
15 "You shall also take one ram, and Aaron
and his sons shall put their hands on the head
of the ram;
16 "and you shall kill the ram, and you shall
take its blood and sprinkle *it* all around on
the altar.
17 "Then you shall cut the ram in pieces,
wash its entrails and its legs, and put *them*
with its pieces and with its head.
18 "And you shall burn the whole ram on the
altar. It *is* a burnt offering to the LORD; it *is* a
sweet aroma, an offering made by fire to the
LORD.
19 "You shall also take the other ram, and
Aaron and his sons shall put their hands on
the head of the ram.
20 "Then you shall kill the ram, and take
some of its blood and put *it* on the tip of the
right ear of Aaron and on the tip of the right
ear of his sons, on the thumb of their right
hand and on the big toe of their right foot, and
sprinkle the blood all around on the altar.
21 "And you shall take some of the blood that
is on the altar, and some of the anointing oil,
and sprinkle *it* on Aaron and on his garments, on his sons and on the garments of his
sons with him; and he and his garments shall
be hallowed, and his sons and his sons' garments with him.
22 "Also you shall take the fat of the ram, the
fat tail, the fat that covers the entrails, the
fatty lobe *attached to* the liver, the two kidneys and the fat on them, the right thigh (for
it *is* a ram of consecration),
23 "one loaf of bread, one cake *made with* oil,
and one wafer from the basket of the unleavened bread that *is* before the LORD;
24 "and you shall put all these in the hands of
Aaron and in the hands of his sons, and you
shall wave them *as* a wave offering before the
LORD.
25 "You shall receive them back from their
hands and burn *them* on the altar as a burnt
offering, as a sweet aroma before the LORD. It
is an offering made by fire to the LORD.
26 "Then you shall take the breast of the ram
of Aaron's consecration and wave it *as* a wave
offering before the LORD; and it shall be your
portion.
27 "And from the ram of the consecration you
shall consecrate the breast of the wave offering which is waved, and the thigh of the heave
offering which is raised, of *that* which *is* for
Aaron and of *that* which is for his sons.
28 "It shall be from the children of Israel *for*
Aaron and his sons by a statute forever. For it
is a heave offering; it shall be a heave offering
from the children of Israel from the sacrifices
of their peace offerings, *that is,* their heave
offering to the LORD.
29 "And the holy garments of Aaron shall be
his sons' after him, to be anointed in them
and to be consecrated in them.
30 "That son who becomes priest in his place
shall put them on for seven days, when he enters the tabernacle of meeting to minister in
the holy *place.*
31 "And you shall take the ram of the consecration and boil its flesh in the holy place.
32 "Then Aaron and his sons shall eat the
flesh of the ram, and the bread that *is* in the
basket, *by* the door of the tabernacle of meeting.
33 "They shall eat those things with which
the atonement was made, to consecrate *and*
to sanctify them; but an outsider shall not eat
them, because they *are* holy.
34 "And if any of the flesh of the consecration
offerings, or of the bread, remains until the
morning, then you shall burn the remainder
with fire. It shall not be eaten, because it *is*
holy.
35 "Thus you shall do to Aaron and his sons,
according to all that I have commanded you.
Seven days you shall consecrate them.

LIFE LESSONS

➤ **29:4 — *"And Aaron and his sons you shall bring to the door of the tabernacle of meeting, and you shall wash them with water."***

We must be clean in order to come before the Holy One of Israel. Under the new covenant, we do this by making sure we have "a true heart in full assurance of faith" (Heb. 10:22).

36 "And you shall offer a bull every day *as* a
sin offering for atonement. You shall cleanse
the altar when you make atonement for it,
and you shall anoint it to sanctify it.
37 "Seven days you shall make atonement for
the altar and sanctify it. And the altar shall be
most holy. Whatever touches the altar must be
holy.[a]

The Daily Offerings

38 "Now this *is* what you shall offer on the
altar: two lambs of the first year, day by day
continually.
39 "One lamb you shall offer in the morning,
and the other lamb you shall offer at twilight.
40 "With the one lamb shall be one-tenth *of
an ephah* of flour mixed with one-fourth of a
hin of pressed oil, and one-fourth of a hin of
wine *as* a drink offering.
41 "And the other lamb you shall offer at twilight; and you shall offer with it the grain offering and the drink offering, as in the
morning, for a sweet aroma, an offering made
by fire to the LORD.
42 "*This shall be* a continual burnt offering
throughout your generations *at* the door of
the tabernacle of meeting before the LORD,
where I will meet you to speak with you.
43 "And there I will meet with the children of
Israel, and *the tabernacle* shall be sanctified
by My glory.
44 "So I will consecrate the tabernacle of
meeting and the altar. I will also consecrate
both Aaron and his sons to minister to Me as
priests.
45 "I will dwell among the children of Israel
and will be their God.
46 "And they shall know that I *am* the LORD
their God, who brought them up out of the
land of Egypt, that I may dwell among them. I
am the LORD their God.

The Altar of Incense

30 "You shall make an altar to burn incense on; you shall make it of acacia
wood.
2 "A cubit *shall be* its length and a cubit its
width—it shall be square—and two cubits
shall be its height. Its horns *shall be* of one
piece with it.
3 "And you shall overlay its top, its sides all
around, and its horns with pure gold; and
you shall make for it a molding of gold all
around.
4 "Two gold rings you shall make for it,
under the molding on both its sides. You shall
place *them* on its two sides, and they will be
holders for the poles with which to bear it.
5 "You shall make the poles of acacia wood,
and overlay them with gold.
6 "And you shall put it before the veil that *is*
before the ark of the Testimony, before the
mercy seat that *is* over the Testimony, where I
will meet with you.
7 "Aaron shall burn on it sweet incense
every morning; when he tends the lamps, he
shall burn incense on it.
8 "And when Aaron lights the lamps at twilight, he shall burn incense on it, a perpetual
incense before the LORD throughout your generations.
9 "You shall not offer strange incense on it, ➤
or a burnt offering, or a grain offering; nor
shall you pour a drink offering on it.
10 "And Aaron shall make atonement upon
its horns once a year with the blood of the sin
offering of atonement; once a year he shall
make atonement upon it throughout your
generations. It *is* most holy to the LORD."

The Ransom Money

11 Then the LORD spoke to Moses, saying:
12 "When you take the census of the children
of Israel for their number, then every man
shall give a ransom for himself to the LORD,
when you number them, that there may be no
plague among them when *you* number them.
13 "This is what everyone among those who
are numbered shall give: half a shekel according to the shekel of the sanctuary (a
shekel *is* twenty gerahs). The half-shekel
shall be an offering to the LORD.
14 "Everyone included among those who are
numbered, from twenty years old and above,
shall give an offering to the LORD.
15 "The rich shall not give more and the poor
shall not give less than half a shekel, when
you give an offering to the LORD, to make
atonement for yourselves.
16 "And you shall take the atonement money
of the children of Israel, and shall appoint it
for the service of the tabernacle of meeting,
that it may be a memorial for the children of
Israel before the LORD, to make atonement for
yourselves."

29:37 [a]Compare Numbers 4:15 and Haggai 2:11–13

LIFE LESSONS

➤ **30:9 — *"You shall not offer strange incense on it, or a burnt offering, or a grain offering; nor shall you pour a drink offering on it."***

When Aaron's sons, Nadab and Abihu, transgressed this command, the Lord destroyed them in fire (Lev. 10:1, 2). God does not require us to understand His will, just obey it, even if it seems unreasonable.

The Bronze Laver

17 Then the LORD spoke to Moses, saying:
18 "You shall also make a laver of bronze, with its base also of bronze, for washing. You shall put it between the tabernacle of meeting and the altar. And you shall put water in it,
19 "for Aaron and his sons shall wash their hands and their feet in water from it.
20 "When they go into the tabernacle of meeting, or when they come near the altar to minister, to burn an offering made by fire to the LORD, they shall wash with water, lest they die.
21 "So they shall wash their hands and their feet, lest they die. And it shall be a statute forever to them—to him and his descendants throughout their generations."

The Holy Anointing Oil

22 Moreover the LORD spoke to Moses, saying:
23 "Also take for yourself quality spices—five hundred *shekels* of liquid myrrh, half as much sweet-smelling cinnamon (two hundred and fifty *shekels*), two hundred and fifty *shekels* of sweet-smelling cane,
24 "five hundred *shekels* of cassia, according to the shekel of the sanctuary, and a hin of olive oil.
25 "And you shall make from these a holy anointing oil, an ointment compounded according to the art of the perfumer. It shall be a holy anointing oil.
26 "With it you shall anoint the tabernacle of meeting and the ark of the Testimony;
27 "the table and all its utensils, the lampstand and its utensils, and the altar of incense;
28 "the altar of burnt offering with all its utensils, and the laver and its base.
29 "You shall consecrate them, that they may be most holy; whatever touches them must be holy.[a]
30 "And you shall anoint Aaron and his sons, and consecrate them, that *they* may minister to Me as priests.
31 "And you shall speak to the children of Israel, saying: 'This shall be a holy anointing oil to Me throughout your generations.
32 'It shall not be poured on man's flesh; nor shall you make *any other* like it, according to its composition. It *is* holy, *and* it shall be holy to you.
33 'Whoever compounds *any* like it, or whoever puts *any* of it on an outsider, shall be cut off from his people.'"

The Incense

34 And the LORD said to Moses: "Take sweet spices, stacte and onycha and galbanum, and pure frankincense with *these* sweet spices; there shall be equal amounts of each.
35 "You shall make of these an incense, a compound according to the art of the perfumer, salted, pure, *and* holy.
36 "And you shall beat *some* of it very fine, and put some of it before the Testimony in the tabernacle of meeting where I will meet with you. It shall be most holy to you.
37 "But *as for* the incense which you shall make, you shall not make any for yourselves, according to its composition. It shall be to you holy for the LORD.
38 "Whoever makes *any* like it, to smell it, he shall be cut off from his people."

Artisans for Building the Tabernacle

31 Then the LORD spoke to Moses, saying:
2 "See, I have called by name Bezalel the son of Uri, the son of Hur, of the tribe of Judah.
3 "And I have filled him with the Spirit of God, in wisdom, in understanding, in knowledge, and in all *manner of* workmanship,
4 "to design artistic works, to work in gold, in silver, in bronze,
5 "in cutting jewels for setting, in carving wood, and to work in all *manner of* workmanship.
6 "And I, indeed I, have appointed with him Aholiab the son of Ahisamach, of the tribe of Dan; and I have put wisdom in the hearts of all the gifted artisans, that they may make all that I have commanded you:
7 "the tabernacle of meeting, the ark of the Testimony and the mercy seat that *is* on it, and all the furniture of the tabernacle—
8 "the table and its utensils, the pure *gold* lampstand with all its utensils, the altar of incense,
9 "the altar of burnt offering with all its utensils, and the laver and its base—
10 "the garments of ministry,[a] the holy garments for Aaron the priest and the garments of his sons, to minister as priests,
11 "and the anointing oil and sweet incense for the holy *place*. According to all that I have commanded you they shall do."

The Sabbath Law

12 And the LORD spoke to Moses, saying,
13 "Speak also to the children of Israel, saying: 'Surely My Sabbaths you shall keep, for it *is* a sign between Me and you throughout your generations, that *you* may know that I *am* the LORD who sanctifies you.
14 'You shall keep the Sabbath, therefore, for *it is* holy to you. Everyone who profanes it shall surely be put to death; for whoever does *any* work on it, that person shall be cut off from among his people.
15 'Work shall be done for six days, but the seventh *is* the Sabbath of rest, holy to the LORD. Whoever does *any* work on the Sabbath day, he shall surely be put to death.

30:29 [a]Compare Numbers 4:15 and Haggai 2:11–13 **31:10** [a]Or *woven garments*

16 'Therefore the children of Israel shall keep the Sabbath, to observe the Sabbath throughout their generations *as* a perpetual covenant.

17 'It *is* a sign between Me and the children of Israel forever; for *in* six days the LORD made the heavens and the earth, and on the seventh day He rested and was refreshed.'"

18 And when He had made an end of speaking with him on Mount Sinai, He gave Moses two tablets of the Testimony, tablets of stone, written with the finger of God.

The Gold Calf

32 Now when the people saw that Moses delayed coming down from the mountain, the people gathered together to Aaron, and said to him, "Come, make us gods that shall go before us; for *as for* this Moses, the man who brought us up out of the land of Egypt, we do not know what has become of him."

2 And Aaron said to them, "Break off the golden earrings which *are* in the ears of your wives, your sons, and your daughters, and bring *them* to me."

3 So all the people broke off the golden earrings which *were* in their ears, and brought *them* to Aaron.

4 And he received *the gold* from their hand, and he fashioned it with an engraving tool, and made a molded calf. Then they said, "This *is* your god, O Israel, that brought you out of the land of Egypt!"

5 So when Aaron saw *it*, he built an altar before it. And Aaron made a proclamation and said, "Tomorrow *is* a feast to the LORD."

6 Then they rose early on the next day, offered burnt offerings, and brought peace offerings; and the people sat down to eat and drink, and rose up to play.

7 And the LORD said to Moses, "Go, get down! For your people whom you brought out of the land of Egypt have corrupted *themselves*.

8 "They have turned aside quickly out of the way which I commanded them. They have made themselves a molded calf, and worshiped it and sacrificed to it, and said, 'This *is* your god, O Israel, that brought you out of the land of Egypt!'"

9 And the LORD said to Moses, "I have seen this people, and indeed it *is* a stiff-necked people!

10 "Now therefore, let Me alone, that My wrath may burn hot against them and I may consume them. And I will make of you a great nation."

11 Then Moses pleaded with the LORD his God, and said: "LORD, why does Your wrath burn hot against Your people whom You have brought out of the land of Egypt with great power and with a mighty hand?

12 "Why should the Egyptians speak, and say, 'He brought them out to harm them, to kill them in the mountains, and to consume them from the face of the earth'? Turn from Your fierce wrath, and relent from this harm to Your people.

13 "Remember Abraham, Isaac, and Israel, Your servants, to whom You swore by Your own self, and said to them, 'I will multiply your descendants as the stars of heaven; and all this land that I have spoken of I give to your descendants, and they shall inherit *it* forever.'"[a]

14 So the LORD relented from the harm which He said He would do to His people.

15 And Moses turned and went down from the mountain, and the two tablets of the Testimony *were* in his hand. The tablets *were* written on both sides; on the one *side* and on the other they were written.

16 Now the tablets *were* the work of God, and the writing *was* the writing of God engraved on the tablets.

17 And when Joshua heard the noise of the people as they shouted, he said to Moses, "*There is* a noise of war in the camp."

18 But he said:

"*It is* not the noise of the shout of victory,
Nor the noise of the cry of defeat,
But the sound of singing I hear."

19 So it was, as soon as he came near the camp, that he saw the calf *and* the dancing. So Moses' anger became hot, and he cast the tablets out of his hands and broke them at the foot of the mountain.

20 Then he took the calf which they had

32:13 [a]Genesis 13:15 and 22:17

LIFE LESSONS

➤ 31:18 — *And when He had made an end of speaking with him on Mount Sinai, He gave Moses two tablets of the Testimony, tablets of stone, written with the finger of God.*

Since God does not want His people to wonder what He has said, He has committed His words to written form. We can depend upon that Word no matter what happens around us.

➤ 32:13 — *"Remember Abraham, Isaac, and Israel, Your servants, to whom You swore by Your own self . . . ."*

Powerful prayer finds its support in the promises of God. When we base our prayers on what God has pledged Himself to do, we stand on unshakeable ground.

WHAT THE BIBLE SAYS ABOUT HOW GOD SPEAKS TO US

Ex. 31:18

Through the ages, God has used a variety of ways to speak to His people. He spoke directly with Adam and Eve in the Garden of Eden, meeting them in the cool of the day (Gen. 3:8). After God expelled the disobedient pair from the garden, He turned to other forms of communication. These forms have included direct revelation, dreams and visions, the words of prophets, and others. Today, God's primary (though not only) form of communication with His people is the written Word, the Bible.

We read in Exodus 31:18: "And when He had made an end of speaking with him [Moses] on Mount Sinai, He gave Moses two tablets of the Testimony, tablets of stone, written with the finger of God."

God has always placed great value on the written Word. In fact, the Hebrew people were among the first on earth to have an alphabet that allowed them to record documents. The reading of the Torah (the first five books of the Old Testament) has remained a mainstay in synagogue services through the centuries.

Behind the written Word of God always stands the inspiration of God.

The early church received God's counsel through both spoken and written means. The Gospel accounts document the life and words of Jesus, while much of the rest of the New Testament consists of letters from the apostles to various groups of believers.

Behind the written Word of God always stands the inspiration of God. We read in 2 Timothy 3:16: "All Scripture is given by inspiration of God, and is profitable for doctrine, for reproof, for correction, for instruction in righteousness, that the man of God may be complete, thoroughly equipped for every good work."

The psalmist acknowledged the importance of knowing and obeying the word of God when he wrote, "Your word is a lamp to my feet and a light to my path" (Ps. 119:105). Centuries later, the apostle Paul referred to the written Word as a weapon to be used in spiritual battle: "Take the . . . sword of the Spirit, which is the word of God" (Eph. 6:17). God's Word really is an immovable anchor in times of storm!

See the Life Principles Index for further study:

3. God's Word is an immovable anchor in times of storm.

13. Listening to God is essential to walking with God.

made, burned *it* in the fire, and ground *it* to
powder; and he scattered *it* on the water and
made the children of Israel drink *it*.
21 And Moses said to Aaron, "What did this
people do to you that you have brought *so*
great a sin upon them?"
22 So Aaron said, "Do not let the anger of my
lord become hot. You know the people, that
they *are set* on evil.
23 "For they said to me, 'Make us gods that
shall go before us; *as for* this Moses, the man
who brought us out of the land of Egypt, we
do not know what has become of him.'
24 "And I said to them, 'Whoever has any
gold, let them break *it* off.' So they gave *it* to
me, and I cast it into the fire, and this calf
came out."
25 Now when Moses saw that the people
were unrestrained (for Aaron had not restrained them, to *their* shame among their enemies),
26 then Moses stood in the entrance of the
camp, and said, "Whoever *is* on the LORD's
side—*come* to me!" And all the sons of Levi
gathered themselves together to him.
27 And he said to them, "Thus says the LORD
God of Israel: 'Let every man put his sword on
his side, and go in and out from entrance to
entrance throughout the camp, and let every
man kill his brother, every man his companion, and every man his neighbor.'"
28 So the sons of Levi did according to the
word of Moses. And about three thousand
men of the people fell that day.
29 Then Moses said, "Consecrate yourselves
today to the LORD, that He may bestow on you
a blessing this day, for every man has opposed his son and his brother."
30 Now it came to pass on the next day that
Moses said to the people, "You have committed a great sin. So now I will go up to the
LORD; perhaps I can make atonement for your
sin."
31 Then Moses returned to the LORD and
said, "Oh, these people have committed a
great sin, and have made for themselves a god
of gold!
32 "Yet now, if You will forgive their sin—but
if not, I pray, blot me out of Your book which
You have written."
33 And the LORD said to Moses, "Whoever
has sinned against Me, I will blot him out of
My book.
➤ 34 "Now therefore, go, lead the people to *the*
place of which I have spoken to you. Behold,
My Angel shall go before you. Nevertheless,
in the day when I visit for punishment, I will
visit punishment upon them for their sin."
35 So the LORD plagued the people because
of what they did with the calf which Aaron
made.

The Command to Leave Sinai

33 Then the LORD said to Moses, "Depart
and go up from here, you and the people whom you have brought out of the land of
Egypt, to the land of which I swore to Abraham, Isaac, and Jacob, saying, 'To your descendants I will give it.'
2 "And I will send *My* Angel before you, and
I will drive out the Canaanite and the Amorite and the Hittite and the Perizzite and the
Hivite and the Jebusite.
3 "*Go up* to a land flowing with milk and
honey; for I will not go up in your midst, lest
I consume you on the way, for you *are* a stiff-
necked people."
4 And when the people heard this bad news,
they mourned, and no one put on his ornaments.
5 For the LORD had said to Moses, "Say to
the children of Israel, 'You *are* a stiff-necked
people. I could come up into your midst in one
moment and consume you. Now therefore,
take off your ornaments, that I may know
what to do to you.'"
6 So the children of Israel stripped themselves of their ornaments by Mount Horeb.

Moses Meets with the LORD

7 Moses took his tent and pitched it outside
the camp, far from the camp, and called it the
tabernacle of meeting. And it came to pass
that everyone who sought the LORD went out
to the tabernacle of meeting which *was* outside the camp.
8 So it was, whenever Moses went out to the
tabernacle, *that* all the people rose, and each
man stood *at* his tent door and watched Moses until he had gone into the tabernacle.
9 And it came to pass, when Moses entered
the tabernacle, that the pillar of cloud descended and stood *at* the door of the tabernacle, and *the LORD* talked with Moses.
10 All the people saw the pillar of cloud
standing *at* the tabernacle door, and all the
people rose and worshiped, each man *in* his
tent door.

LIFE LESSONS

➤ 32:34 — ". . . Nevertheless, in the day when I visit for punishment, I will visit punishment upon them for their sin."

God forgives sin and wickedness when we repent and come to Him in faith, but He does not always prevent us from experiencing the consequences of our wicked behavior.

11 So the LORD spoke to Moses face to face, as a man speaks to his friend. And he would return to the camp, but his servant Joshua the son of Nun, a young man, did not depart from the tabernacle.

The Promise of God's Presence

12 Then Moses said to the LORD, "See, You say to me, 'Bring up this people.' But You have not let me know whom You will send with me. Yet You have said, 'I know you by name, and you have also found grace in My sight.'

➤ 13 "Now therefore, I pray, if I have found grace in Your sight, [R]show me now Your way, that I may know You and that I may find grace in Your sight. And consider that this nation *is* Your people."

✳ 14 And He said, "My Presence will go *with you*, and I will give you rest."

15 Then he said to Him, "If Your Presence does not go *with us*, do not bring us up from here.

16 "For how then will it be known that Your people and I have found grace in Your sight, except You go with us? So we shall be separate, Your people and I, from all the people who *are* upon the face of the earth."

➤ **17** So the LORD said to Moses, "I will also do this thing that you have spoken; for you have found grace in My sight, and I know you by name."

18 And he said, "Please, show me Your glory."

➤ 19 Then He said, "I will make all My goodness pass before you, and I will proclaim the name of the LORD before you. I will be gracious to whom I will be gracious, and I will have compassion on whom I will have compassion."

20 But He said, "You cannot see My face; for no man shall see Me, and live."

21 And the LORD said, "Here is a place by Me, and you shall stand on the rock.

22 "So it shall be, while My glory passes by, that I will put you in the cleft of the rock, and will cover you with My hand while I pass by.

23 "Then I will take away My hand, and you shall see My back; but My face shall not be seen."

Moses Makes New Tablets

34 And the LORD said to Moses, "Cut two tablets of stone like the first *ones*, and I will write on *these* tablets the words that were on the first tablets which you broke.

2 "So be ready in the morning, and come up in the morning to Mount Sinai, and present yourself to Me there on the top of the mountain.

3 "And no man shall come up with you, and let no man be seen throughout all the mountain; let neither flocks nor herds feed before that mountain."

4 So he cut two tablets of stone like the first *ones*. Then Moses rose early in the morning and went up Mount Sinai, as the LORD had commanded him; and he took in his hand the two tablets of stone.

5 Now the LORD descended in the cloud and stood with him there, and proclaimed the name of the LORD.

6 And the LORD passed before him and proclaimed, "The LORD, the LORD God, merciful and gracious, longsuffering, and abounding in goodness and truth,

7 "keeping mercy for thousands, forgiving iniquity and transgression and sin, by no means clearing *the guilty*, visiting the iniquity of the fathers upon the children and the children's children to the third and the fourth generation."

8 So Moses made haste and bowed his head toward the earth, and worshiped.

9 Then he said, "If now I have found grace in ◄ Your sight, O Lord, let my Lord, I pray, go among us, even though we *are* a stiff-necked people; and pardon our iniquity and our sin, and take us as Your inheritance."

The Covenant Renewed

10 And He said: "Behold, I make a covenant. Before all your people I will do marvels such

LIFE LESSONS

➤ 33:13 — *"Now therefore, I pray, if I have found grace in Your sight, show me now Your way, that I may know You and that I may find grace in Your sight. And consider that this nation is Your people."*

As children of God, we have received the Lord's unmerited and unending favor. But as we get to know Him better through such things as prayer, fasting, and study of His Word, He extends us even more favor!

➤ 33:17 — *So the LORD said to Moses, "I will also do this thing that you have spoken; for you have found grace in My sight, and I know you by name."*

Nothing comforts and empowers us more than knowing that God promises to grant our requests . . . and that He knows each of His own personally and by name.

➤ 33:19 — *". . . I will be gracious to whom I will be gracious, and I will have compassion on whom I will have compassion."*

God consistently reveals Himself as a God of grace and compassion—something that greatly comforts us during difficult times or when we sin or make errors in judgment. It's a promise we can always count on.

➤ 34:9 — *"If now I have found grace in Your sight, O Lord, let my Lord, I pray, go among us, even though we are a stiff-necked people; and pardon our iniquity and our sin, and take us as Your inheritance."*

Only by grace has anyone ever been able to establish, develop, and enjoy an intimate relationship with the God of glory. Moses and his people did not earn their standing before God any more than we do.

as have not been done in all the earth, nor
in any nation; and all the people among
whom you *are* shall see the work of the LORD.
For it *is* an awesome thing that I will do with
you.
11 "Observe what I command you this day.
Behold, I am driving out from before you the
Amorite and the Canaanite and the Hittite
and the Perizzite and the Hivite and the Jebusite.
12 "Take heed to yourself, lest you make a covenant with the inhabitants of the land where
you are going, lest it be a snare in your midst.
13 "But you shall destroy their altars, break
their *sacred* pillars, and cut down their
wooden images
➤ 14 "(for you shall worship no other god, for
the LORD, whose name *is* Jealous, *is* a jealous
God),
15 "lest you make a covenant with the inhabitants of the land, and they play the harlot
with their gods and make sacrifice to their
gods, and *one of them* invites you and you eat
of his sacrifice,
16 "and you take of his daughters for your
sons, and his daughters play the harlot with
their gods and make your sons play the harlot
with their gods.
17 "You shall make no molded gods for yourselves.
18 "The Feast of Unleavened Bread you shall
keep. Seven days you shall eat unleavened
bread, as I commanded you, in the appointed
time of the month of Abib; for in the month of
Abib you came out from Egypt.
19 "All that open the womb *are* Mine, and
every male firstborn among your livestock,
whether ox or sheep.
20 "But the firstborn of a donkey you shall
redeem with a lamb. And if you will not redeem *him*, then you shall break his neck. All
the firstborn of your sons you shall redeem.
"And none shall appear before Me empty-
handed.
21 "Six days you shall work, but on the seventh day you shall rest; in plowing time and
in harvest you shall rest.
22 "And you shall observe the Feast of Weeks,
of the firstfruits of wheat harvest, and the
Feast of Ingathering at the year's end.
23 "Three times in the year all your men shall
appear before the Lord, the LORD God of Israel.
24 "For I will cast out the nations before you
and enlarge your borders; neither will any
man covet your land when you go up to appear before the LORD your God three times in
the year.
25 "You shall not offer the blood of My sacrifice with leaven, nor shall the sacrifice of the
Feast of the Passover be left until morning.
26 "The first of the firstfruits of your land you
shall bring to the house of the LORD your God.
You shall not boil a young goat in its mother's
milk."
27 Then the LORD said to Moses, "Write these
words, for according to the tenor of these
words I have made a covenant with you and
with Israel."
28 So he was there with the LORD forty days
and forty nights; he neither ate bread nor
drank water. And He wrote on the tablets the
words of the covenant, the Ten Commandments.[a]

The Shining Face of Moses

29 Now it was so, when Moses came down
from Mount Sinai (and the two tablets of the
Testimony *were* in Moses' hand when he
came down from the mountain), that Moses
did not know that the skin of his face shone
while he talked with Him.
30 So when Aaron and all the children of Israel saw Moses, behold, the skin of his face
shone, and they were afraid to come near
him.
31 Then Moses called to them, and Aaron
and all the rulers of the congregation returned to him; and Moses talked with them.
32 Afterward all the children of Israel came
near, and he gave them as commandments all
that the LORD had spoken with him on Mount
Sinai.
33 And when Moses had finished speaking
with them, he put a veil on his face.
34 But whenever Moses went in before the
LORD to speak with Him, he would take the
veil off until he came out; and he would come
out and speak to the children of Israel whatever he had been commanded.
35 And whenever the children of Israel saw
the face of Moses, that the skin of Moses' face
shone, then Moses would put the veil on his
face again, until he went in to speak with
Him.

34:28 [a]Literally *Ten Words*

LIFE LESSONS

➤ ***34:14 — " . . . for you shall worship no other god, for the LORD, whose name is Jealous, is a jealous God . . . "***

God made us for a relationship with Himself, and He will never stand idly by while a rival tries to replace Him in our hearts. Giving our hearts to anyone else arouses His jealousy—a dangerous proposition (1 Cor. 10:22).

Sabbath Regulations

35 Then Moses gathered all the congregation of the children of Israel together,
and said to them, "These *are* the words which
the LORD has commanded *you* to do:
2 "Work shall be done for six days, but the
seventh day shall be a holy day for you, a
Sabbath of rest to the LORD. Whoever does
any work on it shall be put to death.
3 "You shall kindle no fire throughout your
dwellings on the Sabbath day."

Offerings for the Tabernacle

4 And Moses spoke to all the congregation
of the children of Israel, saying, "This *is* the
thing which the LORD commanded, saying:
5 'Take from among you an offering to the
LORD. Whoever *is* of a willing heart, let him
bring it as an offering to the LORD: gold, silver, and bronze;
6 "blue, purple, and scarlet *thread,* fine
linen, and goats' *hair;*
7 "ram skins dyed red, badger skins, and
acacia wood;
8 "oil for the light, and spices for the anointing oil and for the sweet incense;
9 "onyx stones, and stones to be set in the
ephod and in the breastplate.

Articles of the Tabernacle

10 'All *who are* gifted artisans among you
shall come and make all that the LORD has
commanded:
11 "the tabernacle, its tent, its covering, its
clasps, its boards, its bars, its pillars, and its
sockets;
12 "the ark and its poles, *with* the mercy seat,
and the veil of the covering;
13 "the table and its poles, all its utensils, and
the showbread;
14 "also the lampstand for the light, its utensils, its lamps, and the oil for the light;
15 "the incense altar, its poles, the anointing
oil, the sweet incense, and the screen for the
door at the entrance of the tabernacle;
16 "the altar of burnt offering with its bronze
grating, its poles, all its utensils, *and* the laver
and its base;
17 "the hangings of the court, its pillars, their
sockets, and the screen for the gate of the
court;
18 "the pegs of the tabernacle, the pegs of the
court, and their cords;
19 "the garments of ministry,[a] for ministering
in the holy *place*—the holy garments for
Aaron the priest and the garments of his
sons, to minister as priests.'"

The Tabernacle Offerings Presented

20 And all the congregation of the children of
Israel departed from the presence of Moses.
21 Then everyone came whose heart was
stirred, and everyone whose spirit was willing, *and* they brought the LORD's offering for
the work of the tabernacle of meeting, for all
its service, and for the holy garments.
22 They came, both men and women, as
many as had a willing heart, *and* brought earrings and nose rings, rings and necklaces, all
jewelry of gold, that is, every man who *made*
an offering of gold to the LORD.
23 And every man, with whom was found
blue, purple, and scarlet *thread,* fine linen,
goats' *hair,* red skins of rams, and badger
skins, brought *them.*
24 Everyone who offered an offering of silver
or bronze brought the LORD's offering. And
everyone with whom was found acacia wood
for any work of the service, brought *it.*
25 All the women *who were* gifted artisans
spun yarn with their hands, and brought what
they had spun, of blue, purple, *and* scarlet,
and fine linen.
26 And all the women whose hearts stirred
with wisdom spun yarn of goats' *hair.*
27 The rulers brought onyx stones, and the
stones to be set in the ephod and in the
breastplate,
28 and spices and oil for the light, for the
anointing oil, and for the sweet incense.
29 The children of Israel brought a freewill
offering to the LORD, all the men and women
whose hearts were willing to bring *material*
for all kinds of work which the LORD, by
the hand of Moses, had commanded to be
done.

The Artisans Called by God

30 And Moses said to the children of Israel,
"See, the LORD has called by name Bezalel the
son of Uri, the son of Hur, of the tribe of Judah;
31 "and He has filled him with the Spirit of
God, in wisdom and understanding, in knowledge and all manner of workmanship,

35:19 [a]Or *woven garments*

LIFE LESSONS

➤ **35:21 — *Then everyone came whose heart was stirred, and everyone whose spirit was willing, and they brought the LORD's offering . . . .***

God loves cheerful, willing, and self-motivated giving because it demonstrates a genuine devotion to and a vibrant connection with Him. Regular giving breaks money's hold over us and deepens our devotion to God.

32 "to design artistic works, to work in gold
and silver and bronze,
33 "in cutting jewels for setting, in carving
wood, and to work in all manner of artistic
workmanship.
34 "And He has put in his heart the ability to
teach, *in* him and Aholiab the son of Ahisamach, of the tribe of Dan.
35 "He has filled them with skill to do all
manner of work of the engraver and the designer and the tapestry maker, in blue, purple,
and scarlet *thread,* and fine linen, and of the
weaver—those who do every work and those
who design artistic works.

➤ **36** "And Bezalel and Aholiab, and every
gifted artisan in whom the LORD has
put wisdom and understanding, to know how
to do all manner of work for the service of the
sanctuary, shall do according to all that the
LORD has commanded."

The People Give More than Enough

2 Then Moses called Bezalel and Aholiab,
and every gifted artisan in whose heart the
LORD had put wisdom, everyone whose heart
was stirred, to come and do the work.
3 And they received from Moses all the offering which the children of Israel had
brought for the work of the service of making
the sanctuary. So they continued bringing to
him freewill offerings every morning.
4 Then all the craftsmen who were doing all
the work of the sanctuary came, each from
the work he was doing,
5 and they spoke to Moses, saying, "The
people bring much more than enough for the
service of the work which the LORD commanded *us* to do."
6 So Moses gave a commandment, and they
caused it to be proclaimed throughout the
camp, saying, "Let neither man nor woman do
any more work for the offering of the sanctuary." And the people were restrained from
bringing,
7 for the material they had was sufficient
for all the work to be done—indeed too much.

Building the Tabernacle

8 Then all the gifted artisans among them
who worked on the tabernacle made ten curtains woven of fine linen, and of blue, purple,
and scarlet thread; *with* artistic designs of
cherubim they made them.
9 The length of each curtain *was* twenty-
eight cubits, and the width of each curtain four
cubits; the curtains *were* all the same size.
10 And he coupled five curtains to one another, and *the other* five curtains he coupled
to one another.
11 He made loops of blue *yarn* on the edge of
the curtain on the selvedge of one set; likewise he did on the outer edge of *the other* curtain of the second set.
12 Fifty loops he made on one curtain, and
fifty loops he made on the edge of the curtain
on the end of the second set; the loops held
one *curtain* to another.
13 And he made fifty clasps of gold, and coupled the curtains to one another with the
clasps, that it might be one tabernacle.
14 He made curtains of goats' *hair* for the
tent over the tabernacle; he made eleven curtains.
15 The length of each curtain *was* thirty cubits, and the width of each curtain four cubits;
the eleven curtains *were* the same size.
16 He coupled five curtains by themselves
and six curtains by themselves.
17 And he made fifty loops on the edge of the
curtain that is outermost in one set, and fifty
loops he made on the edge of the curtain of
the second set.
18 He also made fifty bronze clasps to couple
the tent together, that it might be one.
19 Then he made a covering for the tent of
ram skins dyed red, and a covering of badger
skins above *that.*
20 For the tabernacle he made boards of acacia wood, standing upright.
21 The length of each board *was* ten cubits,
and the width of each board a cubit and a
half.
22 Each board had two tenons for binding
one to another. Thus he made for all the
boards of the tabernacle.
23 And he made boards for the tabernacle,
twenty boards for the south side.
24 Forty sockets of silver he made to go
under the twenty boards: two sockets under
each of the boards for its two tenons.
25 And for the other side of the tabernacle,
the north side, he made twenty boards
26 and their forty sockets of silver: two sockets under each of the boards.
27 For the west side of the tabernacle he
made six boards.
28 He also made two boards for the two back
corners of the tabernacle.

LIFE LESSONS

➤ 36:1 — *"And Bezalel and Aholiab, and every gifted artisan in whom the LORD has put wisdom and understanding . . . ."*

The gifts we normally call spiritual gifts differ from natural gifts in that the Lord gives the former at the moment of conversion (1 Cor. 12:7). But both kinds of gifts come from Him and may be used for His glory.

29 And they were coupled at the bottom and
coupled together at the top by one ring. Thus
he made both of them for the two corners.
30 So there were eight boards and their sockets—sixteen sockets of silver—two sockets
under each of the boards.
31 And he made bars of acacia wood: five for
the boards on one side of the tabernacle,
32 five bars for the boards on the other side
of the tabernacle, and five bars for the boards
of the tabernacle on the far side westward.
33 And he made the middle bar to pass
through the boards from one end to the other.
34 He overlaid the boards with gold, made
their rings of gold *to be* holders for the bars,
and overlaid the bars with gold.
35 And he made a veil of blue, purple,
and scarlet *thread,* and fine woven linen; it
was worked *with* an artistic design of cherubim.
36 He made for it four pillars of acacia *wood,*
and overlaid them with gold, with their hooks
of gold; and he cast four sockets of silver for
them.
37 He also made a screen for the tabernacle
door, of blue, purple, and scarlet *thread,* and
fine woven linen, made by a weaver,
38 and its five pillars with their hooks. And
he overlaid their capitals and their rings with
gold, but their five sockets *were* bronze.

Making the Ark of the Testimony

➤ **37** Then Bezalel made the ark of acacia
wood; two and a half cubits *was* its
length, a cubit and a half its width, and a cubit
and a half its height.
2 He overlaid it with pure gold inside and
outside, and made a molding of gold all
around it.
3 And he cast for it four rings of gold *to be*
set in its four corners: two rings on one side,
and two rings on the other side of it.
4 He made poles of acacia wood, and overlaid them with gold.
5 And he put the poles into the rings at the
sides of the ark, to bear the ark.
6 He also made the mercy seat of pure gold;
two and a half cubits *was* its length and a
cubit and a half its width.
7 He made two cherubim of beaten gold; he
made them of one piece at the two ends of the
mercy seat:
8 one cherub at one end on this side, and the
other cherub at the *other* end on that side. He
made the cherubim at the two ends *of one*
piece with the mercy seat.
9 The cherubim spread out *their* wings
above, *and* covered the mercy seat with their
wings. They faced one another; the faces of
the cherubim were toward the mercy seat.

Making the Table for the Showbread

10 He made the table of acacia wood; two cubits *was* its length, a cubit its width, and a
cubit and a half its height.
11 And he overlaid it with pure gold, and
made a molding of gold all around it.
12 Also he made a frame of a handbreadth all
around it, and made a molding of gold for the
frame all around it.
13 And he cast for it four rings of gold, and
put the rings on the four corners that *were* at
its four legs.
14 The rings were close to the frame, as holders for the poles to bear the table.
15 And he made the poles of acacia wood to
bear the table, and overlaid them with gold.
16 He made of pure gold the utensils which
were on the table: its dishes, its cups, its
bowls, and its pitchers for pouring.

Making the Gold Lampstand

17 He also made the lampstand of pure gold;
of hammered work he made the lampstand.
Its shaft, its branches, its bowls, its *orna-*
mental knobs, and its flowers were of the
same piece.
18 And six branches came out of its sides:
three branches of the lampstand out of one
side, and three branches of the lampstand out
of the other side.
19 There were three bowls made like almond
blossoms on one branch, with an *ornamental*
knob and a flower, and three bowls made like
almond *blossoms* on the other branch, with
an *ornamental* knob and a flower—and so for
the six branches coming out of the lampstand.
20 And on the lampstand itself *were* four
bowls made like almond *blossoms, each with*
its *ornamental* knob and flower.
21 *There was* a knob under the *first* two
branches of the same, a knob under the *sec-*
ond two branches of the same, and a knob
under the *third* two branches of the same, according to the six branches extending from it.
22 Their knobs and their branches were of
one piece; all of it *was* one hammered piece of
pure gold.

LIFE LESSONS

➤ 37:1 — *Then Bezalel made the ark of acacia wood; two and a half cubits was its length, a cubit and a half its width, and a cubit and a half its height.*

The ark of the covenant was essentially a wooden chest, covered with pure gold, that contained the law of God. It disappears from the biblical record before the Babylonian captivity. Whether it was hidden or destroyed is not generally known.

23 And he made its seven lamps, its wick-
trimmers, and its trays of pure gold.
24 Of a talent of pure gold he made it, with all
its utensils.

Making the Altar of Incense

25 He made the incense altar of acacia wood.
Its length *was* a cubit and its width a cubit—
it was square—and two cubits *was* its height.
Its horns were *of one piece* with it.
26 And he overlaid it with pure gold: its top,
its sides all around, and its horns. He also
made for it a molding of gold all around it.
27 He made two rings of gold for it under
its molding, by its two corners on both
sides, as holders for the poles with which to
bear it.
28 And he made the poles of acacia wood,
and overlaid them with gold.

Making the Anointing Oil and the Incense

29 He also made the holy anointing oil and
the pure incense of sweet spices, according to
the work of the perfumer.

Making the Altar of Burnt Offering

38 He made the altar of burnt offering of
acacia wood; five cubits *was* its length
and five cubits its width—*it was* square—and
its height *was* three cubits.
2 He made its horns on its four corners; the
horns were *of one piece* with it. And he overlaid it with bronze.
3 He made all the utensils for the altar: the
pans, the shovels, the basins, the forks, and
the firepans; all its utensils he made of
bronze.
4 And he made a grate of bronze network
for the altar, under its rim, midway from the
bottom.
5 He cast four rings for the four corners
of the bronze grating, *as* holders for the
poles.
6 And he made the poles of acacia wood,
and overlaid them with bronze.
7 Then he put the poles into the rings on the
sides of the altar, with which to bear it. He
made the altar hollow with boards.

Making the Bronze Laver

8 He made the laver of bronze and its base
of bronze, from the bronze mirrors of the
serving women who assembled at the door of
the tabernacle of meeting.

Making the Court of the Tabernacle

9 Then he made the court on the south side;
the hangings of the court *were of* fine woven
linen, one hundred cubits long.
10 There *were* twenty pillars for them, with
twenty bronze sockets. The hooks of the pillars and their bands *were* silver.
11 On the north side *the hangings were* one
hundred cubits *long,* with twenty pillars and
their twenty bronze sockets. The hooks of the
pillars and their bands *were* silver.
12 And on the west side *there were* hangings
of fifty cubits, with ten pillars and their ten
sockets. The hooks of the pillars and their
bands *were* silver.
13 For the east side *the hangings were* fifty
cubits.
14 The hangings of one side *of the gate were*
fifteen cubits *long, with* their three pillars and
their three sockets,
15 and the same for the other side of the
court gate; on this side and that *were* hangings of fifteen cubits, *with* their three pillars
and their three sockets.
16 All the hangings of the court all around
were of fine woven linen.
17 The sockets for the pillars *were* bronze,
the hooks of the pillars and their bands *were*
silver, and the overlay of their capitals *was*
silver; and all the pillars of the court had
bands of silver.
18 The screen for the gate of the court *was*
woven of blue, purple, and scarlet *thread,* and
of fine woven linen. The length *was* twenty
cubits, and the height along its width *was* five
cubits, corresponding to the hangings of the
court.
19 And *there were* four pillars *with* their four
sockets of bronze; their hooks *were* silver,
and the overlay of their capitals and their
bands *was* silver.
20 All the pegs of the tabernacle, and of the
court all around, *were* bronze.

Materials of the Tabernacle

21 This is the inventory of the tabernacle, the ➤
tabernacle of the Testimony, which was
counted according to the commandment of
Moses, for the service of the Levites, by the
hand of Ithamar, son of Aaron the priest.
22 Bezalel the son of Uri, the son of Hur, of
the tribe of Judah, made all that the LORD had
commanded Moses.
23 And with him *was* Aholiab the son of

LIFE LESSONS

➤ **38:21 — *This is the inventory of the tabernacle, the tabernacle of the Testimony, which was counted according to the commandment of Moses . . . .***

God has always taken an acute interest in the offerings and gifts and items of material worth that help His people to effectively worship in a corporate setting. Jesus carefully observed what went into the temple treasury (Mark 12:41).

Ahisamach, of the tribe of Dan, an engraver and designer, a weaver of blue, purple, and scarlet *thread,* and of fine linen.

24 All the gold that was used in all the work of the holy *place,* that is, the gold of the offering, was twenty-nine talents and seven hundred and thirty shekels, according to the shekel of the sanctuary.

25 And the silver from those who were numbered of the congregation *was* one hundred talents and one thousand seven hundred and seventy-five shekels, according to the shekel of the sanctuary:

26 a bekah for each man (*that is,* half a shekel, according to the shekel of the sanctuary), for everyone included in the numbering from twenty years old and above, for six hundred and three thousand, five hundred and fifty *men.*

27 And from the hundred talents of silver were cast the sockets of the sanctuary and the bases of the veil: one hundred sockets from the hundred talents, one talent for each socket.

28 Then from the one thousand seven hundred and seventy-five *shekels* he made hooks for the pillars, overlaid their capitals, and made bands for them.

29 The offering of bronze *was* seventy talents and two thousand four hundred shekels.

30 And with it he made the sockets for the door of the tabernacle of meeting, the bronze altar, the bronze grating for it, and all the utensils for the altar,

31 the sockets for the court all around, the bases for the court gate, all the pegs for the tabernacle, and all the pegs for the court all around.

Making the Garments of the Priesthood

39 Of the blue, purple, and scarlet *thread* they made garments of ministry,[a] for ministering in the holy *place,* and made the holy garments for Aaron, as the LORD had commanded Moses.

Making the Ephod

2 He made the ephod of gold, blue, purple, and scarlet *thread,* and of fine woven linen.

3 And they beat the gold into thin sheets and cut *it into* threads, to work *it* in *with* the blue, purple, and scarlet *thread,* and the fine linen, *into* artistic designs.

4 They made shoulder straps for it to couple *it* together; it was coupled together at its two edges.

5 And the intricately woven band of his ephod that *was* on it *was* of the same workmanship, *woven of* gold, blue, purple, and scarlet *thread,* and of fine woven linen, as the LORD had commanded Moses.

6 And they set onyx stones, enclosed in settings of gold; they were engraved, as signets are engraved, with the names of the sons of Israel.

7 He put them on the shoulders of the ephod *as* memorial stones for the sons of Israel, as the LORD had commanded Moses.

Making the Breastplate

8 And he made the breastplate, artistically woven like the workmanship of the ephod, of gold, blue, purple, and scarlet *thread,* and of fine woven linen.

9 They made the breastplate square by doubling it; a span *was* its length and a span its width when doubled.

10 And they set in it four rows of stones: a row with a sardius, a topaz, and an emerald was the first row;

11 the second row, a turquoise, a sapphire, and a diamond;

12 the third row, a jacinth, an agate, and an amethyst;

13 the fourth row, a beryl, an onyx, and a jasper. *They were* enclosed in settings of gold in their mountings.

14 *There were* twelve stones according to the names of the sons of Israel: according to their names, *engraved like* a signet, each one with its own name according to the twelve tribes.

15 And they made chains for the breastplate at the ends, like braided cords of pure gold.

16 They also made two settings of gold and two gold rings, and put the two rings on the two ends of the breastplate.

17 And they put the two braided *chains* of gold in the two rings on the ends of the breastplate.

18 The two ends of the two braided *chains* they fastened in the two settings, and put them on the shoulder straps of the ephod in the front.

19 And they made two rings of gold and put *them* on the two ends of the breastplate, on the edge of it, which *was* on the inward side of the ephod.

20 They made two *other* gold rings and put them on the two shoulder straps, underneath the ephod toward its front, right at the seam above the intricately woven band of the ephod.

21 And they bound the breastplate by means of its rings to the rings of the ephod with a blue cord, so that it would be above the intricately woven band of the ephod, and that the breastplate would not come loose from the ephod, as the LORD had commanded Moses.

Making the Other Priestly Garments

22 He made the robe of the ephod of woven work, all of blue.

23 And *there was* an opening in the middle of the robe, like the opening in a coat of mail, *with* a woven binding all around the opening, so that it would not tear.

39:1 [a]Or *woven garments*

24 They made on the hem of the robe pomegranates of blue, purple, and scarlet, and of fine woven *linen.*
25 And they made bells of pure gold, and put the bells between the pomegranates on the hem of the robe all around between the pomegranates:
26 a bell and a pomegranate, a bell and a pomegranate, all around the hem of the robe to minister in, as the LORD had commanded Moses.
27 They made tunics, artistically woven of fine linen, for Aaron and his sons,
28 a turban of fine linen, exquisite hats of fine linen, short trousers of fine woven linen,
29 and a sash of fine woven linen with blue, purple, and scarlet *thread,* made by a weaver, as the LORD had commanded Moses.
30 Then they made the plate of the holy crown of pure gold, and wrote on it an inscription *like* the engraving of a signet:

HOLINESS TO THE LORD.

31 And they tied to it a blue cord, to fasten *it* above on the turban, as the LORD had commanded Moses.

The Work Completed

32 Thus all the work of the tabernacle of the tent of meeting was finished. And the children of Israel did according to all that the LORD had commanded Moses; so they did.
33 And they brought the tabernacle to Moses, the tent and all its furnishings: its clasps, its boards, its bars, its pillars, and its sockets;
34 the covering of ram skins dyed red, the covering of badger skins, and the veil of the covering;
35 the ark of the Testimony with its poles, and the mercy seat;
36 the table, all its utensils, and the showbread;
37 the pure *gold* lampstand with its lamps (the lamps set in order), all its utensils, and the oil for light;
38 the gold altar, the anointing oil, and the sweet incense; the screen for the tabernacle door;
39 the bronze altar, its grate of bronze, its poles, and all its utensils; the laver with its base;
40 the hangings of the court, its pillars and its sockets, the screen for the court gate, its cords, and its pegs; all the utensils for the service of the tabernacle, for the tent of meeting;
41 and the garments of ministry,[a] to minister in the holy *place:* the holy garments for Aaron the priest, and his sons' garments, to minister as priests.
42 According to all that the LORD had commanded Moses, so the children of Israel did all the work.
43 Then Moses looked over all the work, and indeed they had done it; as the LORD had commanded, just so they had done it. And Moses blessed them.

The Tabernacle Erected and Arranged

40 Then the LORD spoke to Moses, saying:
2 "On the first day of the first month you shall set up the tabernacle of the tent of meeting.
3 "You shall put in it the ark of the Testimony, and partition off the ark with the veil.
4 "You shall bring in the table and arrange the things that are to be set in order on it; and you shall bring in the lampstand and light its lamps.
5 "You shall also set the altar of gold for the incense before the ark of the Testimony, and put up the screen for the door of the tabernacle.
6 "Then you shall set the altar of the burnt offering before the door of the tabernacle of the tent of meeting.
7 "And you shall set the laver between the tabernacle of meeting and the altar, and put water in it.
8 "You shall set up the court all around, and hang up the screen at the court gate.
9 "And you shall take the anointing oil, and anoint the tabernacle and all that *is* in it; and you shall hallow it and all its utensils, and it shall be holy.
10 "You shall anoint the altar of the burnt offering and all its utensils, and consecrate the altar. The altar shall be most holy.
11 "And you shall anoint the laver and its base, and consecrate it.
12 "Then you shall bring Aaron and his sons to the door of the tabernacle of meeting and wash them with water.
13 "You shall put the holy garments on

39:41 [a]Or *woven garments*

LIFE LESSONS

➤ 39:42 — *According to all that the LORD had commanded Moses, so the children of Israel did all the work.*

God calls us to obey Him in all things, whether we understand all of His commands or not. The people carefully carried out all of Moses' instructions, even down to little details that might not have seemed crucial to them.

Aaron, and anoint him and consecrate him,
that he may minister to Me as priest.
14 "And you shall bring his sons and clothe
them with tunics.
15 "You shall anoint them, as you anointed
their father, that they may minister to Me as
priests; for their anointing shall surely be an
everlasting priesthood throughout their generations."
16 Thus Moses did; according to all that the
LORD had commanded him, so he did.
17 And it came to pass in the first month of
the second year, on the first *day* of the month,
that the tabernacle was raised up.
18 So Moses raised up the tabernacle, fastened its sockets, set up its boards, put in its
bars, and raised up its pillars.
19 And he spread out the tent over the
tabernacle and put the covering of the tent
on top of it, as the LORD had commanded
Moses.
20 He took the Testimony and put *it* into the
ark, inserted the poles through the rings of
the ark, and put the mercy seat on top of the
ark.
21 And he brought the ark into the tabernacle, hung up the veil of the covering, and par-
titioned off the ark of the Testimony, as the
LORD had commanded Moses.
22 He put the table in the tabernacle of meeting, on the north side of the tabernacle, outside the veil;
23 and he set the bread in order upon it before the LORD, as the LORD had commanded
Moses.
24 He put the lampstand in the tabernacle of
meeting, across from the table, on the south
side of the tabernacle;
25 and he lit the lamps before the LORD, as
the LORD had commanded Moses.
26 He put the gold altar in the tabernacle of
meeting in front of the veil;
27 and he burned sweet incense on it, as the
LORD had commanded Moses.
28 He hung up the screen *at* the door of the
tabernacle.
29 And he put the altar of burnt offering *be-*
fore the door of the tabernacle of the tent of
meeting, and offered upon it the burnt offering and the grain offering, as the LORD had
commanded Moses.
30 He set the laver between the tabernacle of
meeting and the altar, and put water there for
washing;
31 and Moses, Aaron, and his sons would
wash their hands and their feet *with water*
from it.
32 Whenever they went into the tabernacle of
meeting, and when they came near the altar,
they washed, as the LORD had commanded
Moses.
33 And he raised up the court all around the
tabernacle and the altar, and hung up the
screen of the court gate. So Moses finished
the work.

The Cloud and the Glory

34 Then the cloud covered the tabernacle of
meeting, and the glory of the LORD filled the
tabernacle.
35 And Moses was not able to enter the tabernacle of meeting, because the cloud rested
above it, and the glory of the LORD filled the
tabernacle.
36 Whenever the cloud was taken up from
above the tabernacle, the children of Israel
would go onward in all their journeys.
37 But if the cloud was not taken up, then
they did not journey till the day that it was
taken up.
38 For the cloud of the LORD *was* above the
tabernacle by day, and fire was over it by
night, in the sight of all the house of Israel,
throughout all their journeys.

LIFE LESSONS

➢ 40:35 — *And Moses was not able to enter the tabernacle of meeting, because the cloud rested above it, and the glory of the LORD filled the tabernacle.*

A similar phenomenon occurred when Solomon dedicated the temple in Jerusalem (1 Kin. 8:10, 11). God wanted to leave no doubt among His people that He would be with them as promised (Is. 6:4; Rev. 8:4).

➢ 40:38 — *For the cloud of the LORD was above the tabernacle by day, and fire was over it by night, in the sight of all the house of Israel, throughout all their journeys.*

With such a continuous and obvious sign of the Lord's guiding presence, we might wonder why the Israelites ever doubted His leading. Yet we have His Spirit within us, and how many of us ever doubt His guidance?

THE THIRD BOOK OF MOSES CALLED

LEVITICUS

The Talmud, an ancient Jewish commentary, refers to the Book of Leviticus as the "Law of the priests" and the "law of the offerings." The Septuagint gives the book the title *Leuitikon*, which means, "that which pertains to the Levites." From this word, the Latin Vulgate derived the title *Leviticus*, the name that appears in all English translations.

Leviticus is God's guidebook for his newly redeemed people, showing them how to worship, serve, and obey God. The book highlights the awesome holiness of the Lord of Israel by detailing the kind of sacrifice and obedience necessary to enjoy fellowship with Him. Indeed, "you shall be holy, for I the LORD your God am holy" (19:2).

Leviticus focuses on the worship and spiritual walk of the nation of God and spells out in great detail the laws regulating sacrificial offerings, the appointment of the priesthood, as well as personal, cultural, and priestly purity. It also describes how to celebrate eight national feasts.

The laws regarding sacrificial offerings beautifully illustrate God's desire to enjoy fellowship with men and women. To us, the instructions seem complex; it almost looks as though God went out of His way to make it difficult for His people to get to Him. But the whole sacrificial system—fulfilled and culminated in the sacrifice of Jesus Christ on the cross—actually pictures God's grace, since through it He provided a way for His people to get to Him.

God designed this system to allow sinful men and women to carry on a relationship with their sinless Creator. God, of course, was under no obligation to provide such a system. Yet He had such a strong desire for fellowship that He willingly went to great lengths to make such fellowship possible.

Theme: Leviticus focuses on holiness—the prerequisite for sinful people to have fellowship with a holy God. The Hebrew people achieved a kind of "temporary holiness" through animal sacrifice and by obedience to God's Word. Obedience always brings a blessing!

Author: Moses

Time: God delivered the Book of Leviticus to Moses on Mount Sinai, shortly after the exodus from Egypt, around 1447 B.C.

Structure: Leviticus opens with the laws surrounding sacrifices and offerings (1–7), followed by the lawful duties and requirements of the priests (8–10), then by laws regarding personal and national cleanliness and holiness (11–22), followed by laws regarding feasts (23). The laws of the final four chapters of Leviticus include God's promises for keeping the Law and His warnings for violating it.

As you read Leviticus, watch for several life principles that play an important role in this book:

5. God does not require us to understand His will, just obey it, even if it seems unreasonable. *See Leviticus 10:1–7; page 124.*

21. Obedience always brings blessing. *See Leviticus 25:18; page 141.*

13. Listening to God is essential to walking with God. *See Leviticus 26:14–30; page 144.*

The Burnt Offering

1 Now the LORD called to Moses, and spoke
to him from the tabernacle of meeting,
saying,
2 "Speak to the children of Israel, and say
to them: 'When any one of you brings an offering to the LORD, you shall bring your
offering of the livestock—of the herd and of
the flock.
➤ **3** 'If his offering *is* a burnt sacrifice of the
herd, let him offer a male without blemish;
he shall offer it of his own free will at the
door of the tabernacle of meeting before the
LORD.
4 'Then he shall put his hand on the head of
the burnt offering, and it will be accepted on
his behalf to make atonement for him.
5 'He shall kill the bull before the LORD; and
the priests, Aaron's sons, shall bring the
blood and sprinkle the blood all around on
the altar that *is by* the door of the tabernacle
of meeting.
6 'And he shall skin the burnt offering and
cut it into its pieces.
7 'The sons of Aaron the priest shall put fire
on the altar, and lay the wood in order on the
fire.
8 'Then the priests, Aaron's sons, shall lay
the parts, the head, and the fat in order on the
wood that *is* on the fire upon the altar;
9 'but he shall wash its entrails and its legs
with water. And the priest shall burn all on
the altar as a burnt sacrifice, an offering
made by fire, a sweet aroma to the LORD.
10 'If his offering *is* of the flocks—of the
sheep or of the goats—as a burnt sacrifice, he
shall bring a male without blemish.
11 'He shall kill it on the north side of the
altar before the LORD; and the priests, Aaron's
sons, shall sprinkle its blood all around on the
altar.
12 'And he shall cut it into its pieces, with its
head and its fat; and the priest shall lay them
in order on the wood that *is* on the fire upon
the altar;
13 'but he shall wash the entrails and the legs
with water. Then the priest shall bring *it* all
and burn *it* on the altar; it *is* a burnt sacrifice,
an offering made by fire, a sweet aroma to the
LORD.
14 'And if the burnt sacrifice of his offering to
the LORD *is* of birds, then he shall bring his offering of turtledoves or young pigeons.
15 'The priest shall bring it to the altar, wring
off its head, and burn *it* on the altar; its blood
shall be drained out at the side of the altar.
16 'And he shall remove its crop with its
feathers and cast it beside the altar on the
east side, into the place for ashes.
17 'Then he shall split it at its wings, *but* shall ➤
not divide *it* completely; and the priest shall
burn it on the altar, on the wood that *is* on the
fire. It *is* a burnt sacrifice, an offering made
by fire, a sweet aroma to the LORD.

The Grain Offering

2 'When anyone offers a grain offering to
the LORD, his offering shall be *of* fine flour.
And he shall pour oil on it, and put frankincense on it.
2 'He shall bring it to Aaron's sons, the
priests, one of whom shall take from it his
handful of fine flour and oil with all the
frankincense. And the priest shall burn *it as* a
memorial on the altar, an offering made by
fire, a sweet aroma to the LORD.
3 'The rest of the grain offering *shall be* Aaron's and his sons'. *It is* most holy of the offerings to the LORD made by fire.
4 'And if you bring as an offering a grain offering baked in the oven, *it shall be* unleavened cakes of fine flour mixed with oil, or
unleavened wafers anointed with oil.
5 'But if your offering *is* a grain offering
baked in a pan, *it shall be of* fine flour, unleavened, mixed with oil.
6 'You shall break it in pieces and pour oil
on it; it *is* a grain offering.
7 'If your offering *is* a grain offering *baked*
in a covered pan, it shall be made *of* fine flour
with oil.
8 'You shall bring the grain offering that is
made of these things to the LORD. And when it
is presented to the priest, he shall bring it to
the altar.
9 'Then the priest shall take from the grain
offering a memorial portion, and burn *it* on
the altar. *It is* an offering made by fire, a
sweet aroma to the LORD.
10 'And what is left of the grain offering *shall
be* Aaron's and his sons'. *It is* most holy of the
offerings to the LORD made by fire.

LIFE LESSONS

➤ **1:3 — *"If his offering is a burnt sacrifice of the herd, let him offer a male without blemish; he shall offer it of his own free will at the door of the tabernacle of meeting before the LORD."***

Willing offerings to the Lord demonstrate where the desires of our heart truly lie.

➤ **1:17 — *"Then he shall split it at its wings, but shall not divide it completely; and the priest shall burn it on the altar, on the wood that is on the fire. It is a burnt sacrifice, an offering made by fire, a sweet aroma to the LORD."***

Eager obedience is a sweet aroma to the Lord. Christ lived to obey His Father, and when we follow His example, we too become a sweet aroma to the Lord—the aroma of Christ Himself (2 Cor. 2:15).

➤ 11 'No grain offering which you bring to the
LORD shall be made with leaven, for you shall
burn no leaven nor any honey in any offering
to the LORD made by fire.
12 'As for the offering of the firstfruits, you
shall offer them to the LORD, but they shall
not be burned on the altar for a sweet aroma.
➤ 13 'And every offering of your grain offering
you shall season with salt; you shall not allow
the salt of the covenant of your God to be
lacking from your grain offering. With all
your offerings you shall offer salt.
14 'If you offer a grain offering of your firstfruits to the LORD, you shall offer for the grain
offering of your firstfruits green heads of
grain roasted on the fire, grain beaten from
full heads.
15 'And you shall put oil on it, and lay frankincense on it. It *is* a grain offering.
16 'Then the priest shall burn the memorial
portion: *part* of its beaten grain and *part* of its
oil, with all the frankincense, as an offering
made by fire to the LORD.

The Peace Offering

3 'When his offering *is* a sacrifice of a peace
offering, if he offers *it* of the herd, whether
male or female, he shall offer it without blemish before the LORD.
2 'And he shall lay his hand on the head of
his offering, and kill it *at* the door of the tabernacle of meeting; and Aaron's sons, the
priests, shall sprinkle the blood all around on
the altar.
3 'Then he shall offer from the sacrifice of
the peace offering an offering made by fire to
the LORD. The fat that covers the entrails and
all the fat that *is* on the entrails,
4 'the two kidneys and the fat that *is* on them
by the flanks, and the fatty lobe *attached* to
the liver above the kidneys, he shall remove;
5 'and Aaron's sons shall burn it on the altar
upon the burnt sacrifice, which *is* on the wood
that *is* on the fire, *as* an offering made by fire,
a sweet aroma to the LORD.
6 'If his offering as a sacrifice of a peace offering to the LORD *is* of the flock, *whether*
male or female, he shall offer it without blemish.
7 'If he offers a lamb as his offering, then he
shall offer it before the LORD.
8 'And he shall lay his hand on the head of
his offering, and kill it before the tabernacle
of meeting; and Aaron's sons shall sprinkle
its blood all around on the altar.
9 'Then he shall offer from the sacrifice of
the peace offering, as an offering made by fire
to the LORD, its fat *and* the whole fat tail
which he shall remove close to the backbone.
And the fat that covers the entrails and all the
fat that *is* on the entrails,
10 'the two kidneys and the fat that *is* on them
by the flanks, and the fatty lobe *attached* to
the liver above the kidneys, he shall remove;
11 'and the priest shall burn *them* on the altar
as food, an offering made by fire to the LORD.
12 'And if his offering *is* a goat, then he shall
offer it before the LORD.
13 'He shall lay his hand on its head and kill
it before the tabernacle of meeting; and the
sons of Aaron shall sprinkle its blood all
around on the altar.
14 'Then he shall offer from it his offering, as
an offering made by fire to the LORD. The fat
that covers the entrails and all the fat that *is*
on the entrails,
15 'the two kidneys and the fat that *is* on them
by the flanks, and the fatty lobe *attached* to
the liver above the kidneys, he shall remove;
16 'and the priest shall burn them on the
altar *as* food, an offering made by fire for a
sweet aroma; all the fat *is* the LORD's.
17 '*This shall be* a perpetual statute throughout your generations in all your dwellings:
you shall eat neither fat nor blood.'"

The Sin Offering

4 Now the LORD spoke to Moses, saying,
2 "Speak to the children of Israel, saying: ➤
'If a person sins unintentionally against any
of the commandments of the LORD *in anything* which ought not to be done, and does
any of them,
3 'if the anointed priest sins, bringing guilt

LIFE LESSONS

➤ 2:11 — *"No grain offering which you bring to the LORD shall be made with leaven, for you shall burn no leaven nor any honey in any offering to the LORD made by fire."*

The Bible often uses "leaven" or "yeast" as a picture of sin (see Matt. 16:6). It was not to be offered on the altar, just as sin is not to be allowed to dominate the life of the believer.

➤ 2:13 — *"And every offering of your grain offering you shall season with salt; you shall not allow the salt of the covenant of your God to be lacking from your grain offering. With all your offerings you shall offer salt."*

Salt is here used to symbolize God's covenant with His people. Just as salt is necessary to sustain life, so is God's continual relationship with us necessary to sustain and enjoy life everlasting.

➤ 4:2 — *"Speak to the children of Israel, saying: 'If a person sins unintentionally against any of the commandments of the LORD in anything which ought not to be done, and does any of them . . . .'"*

To sin "unintentionally" is better understood as to sin "unthinkingly," something we all do. Yet God is gracious; He not only reveals our sin to us, but He also offers us His forgiveness.

on the people, then let him offer to the LORD
for his sin which he has sinned a young bull
without blemish as a sin offering.
4 'He shall bring the bull to the door of the
tabernacle of meeting before the LORD, lay his
hand on the bull's head, and kill the bull before the LORD.
5 'Then the anointed priest shall take some
of the bull's blood and bring it to the tabernacle of meeting.
6 'The priest shall dip his finger in the blood
and sprinkle some of the blood seven times
before the LORD, in front of the veil of the
sanctuary.
7 'And the priest shall put some of the blood
on the horns of the altar of sweet incense before the LORD, which is in the tabernacle of
meeting; and he shall pour the remaining
blood of the bull at the base of the altar of the
burnt offering, which is at the door of the tabernacle of meeting.
8 'He shall take from it all the fat of the bull
as the sin offering. The fat that covers the entrails and all the fat which *is* on the entrails,
9 'the two kidneys and the fat that *is* on them
by the flanks, and the fatty lobe *attached* to
the liver above the kidneys, he shall remove,
10 'as it was taken from the bull of the sacrifice of the peace offering; and the priest shall
burn them on the altar of the burnt offering.
11 'But the bull's hide and all its flesh, with
its head and legs, its entrails and offal—
12 'the whole bull he shall carry outside the
camp to a clean place, where the ashes are
poured out, and burn it on wood with fire;
where the ashes are poured out it shall be
burned.
13 'Now if the whole congregation of Israel
sins unintentionally, and the thing is hidden
from the eyes of the assembly, and they have
done *something against* any of the commandments of the LORD *in anything* which
should not be done, and are guilty;
14 'when the sin which they have committed
becomes known, then the assembly shall
offer a young bull for the sin, and bring it before the tabernacle of meeting.
15 'And the elders of the congregation shall
lay their hands on the head of the bull before
the LORD. Then the bull shall be killed before
the LORD.
16 'The anointed priest shall bring some of
the bull's blood to the tabernacle of meeting.
17 'Then the priest shall dip his finger in the
blood and sprinkle *it* seven times before the
LORD, in front of the veil.
18 'And he shall put *some* of the blood on the
horns of the altar which *is* before the LORD,
which *is* in the tabernacle of meeting; and he
shall pour the remaining blood at the base of
the altar of burnt offering, which is at the
door of the tabernacle of meeting.
19 'He shall take all the fat from it and burn
it on the altar.
20 'And he shall do with the bull as he did
with the bull as a sin offering; thus he shall do
with it. So the priest shall make atonement
for them, and it shall be forgiven them.
21 'Then he shall carry the bull outside the
camp, and burn it as he burned the first bull.
It *is* a sin offering for the assembly.
22 'When a ruler has sinned, and done *something* unintentionally *against* any of the commandments of the LORD his God *in anything*
which should not be done, and is guilty,
23 'or if his sin which he has committed
comes to his knowledge, he shall bring as his
offering a kid of the goats, a male without
blemish.
24 'And he shall lay his hand on the head of
the goat, and kill it at the place where they
kill the burnt offering before the LORD. It *is* a
sin offering.
25 'The priest shall take some of the blood of
the sin offering with his finger, put *it* on the
horns of the altar of burnt offering, and pour
its blood at the base of the altar of burnt offering.
26 'And he shall burn all its fat on the altar,
like the fat of the sacrifice of the peace offering. So the priest shall make atonement for
him concerning his sin, and it shall be forgiven him.
27 'If anyone of the common people sins
unintentionally by doing *something against*
any of the commandments of the LORD *in anything* which ought not to be done, and is
guilty,
28 'or if his sin which he has committed
comes to his knowledge, then he shall bring
as his offering a kid of the goats, a female
without blemish, for his sin which he has
committed.
29 'And he shall lay his hand on the head of
the sin offering, and kill the sin offering at the
place of the burnt offering.
30 'Then the priest shall take *some* of its
blood with his finger, put *it* on the horns of
the altar of burnt offering, and pour all *the remaining* blood at the base of the altar.
31 'He shall remove all its fat, as fat is removed from the sacrifice of the peace offering; and the priest shall burn it on the altar
for a sweet aroma to the LORD. So the priest
shall make atonement for him, and it shall be
forgiven him.
32 'If he brings a lamb as his sin offering, he
shall bring a female without blemish.
33 'Then he shall lay his hand on the head of
the sin offering, and kill it as a sin offering at
the place where they kill the burnt offering.
34 'The priest shall take *some* of the blood of
the sin offering with his finger, put *it* on the
horns of the altar of burnt offering, and pour
all *the remaining* blood at the base of the
altar.
35 'He shall remove all its fat, as the fat of the
lamb is removed from the sacrifice of the

ANSWERS TO LIFE'S QUESTIONS

How can I rid myself of guilt?

LEV. 5:5

Consider several key steps required to get free of guilt, all under the banner of forgiveness:

❶ ***Admit to the sin that created your guilt.***
Repent of your sin to God. If you have sinned against another person, confess to that person. Also, in facing your sin, make certain that it is a sin before God. The "sin" you think you have committed may have been merely a mistake or error or someone else's sin. On the other hand, remember that our society is quick to accept some sinful behaviors as normal. The Bible presents a very clear picture of what is sin and isn't. If you have any doubt about whether you have sinned, consult the Scriptures.

When you confess to God or a person that you have sinned, don't try to justify what you did. Simply state your sin or error. Then ask God or the person to forgive you.

❷ ***Make amends.***
If you have wronged another person, don't try to substitute a request for forgiveness by doing kind deeds for that person. This same principle holds for your relationship with God—don't try to substitute works for genuine forgiveness.

In seeking to make amends for a wrong committed against another person, you may be wise to ask the person what she would consider fair payment for the hurt or injury, or you may want to offer satisfaction of some type. The best repayment may be a genuine change in your life (which may involve counseling or professional help or therapy). Ask God to give you wisdom in identifying appropriate amends. Also ask Him to give you the courage and the fortitude to follow through on your commitment to the offended person.

❸ ***Accept Forgiveness.***
If you have sinned against God and have repented, you can be assured that He forgives you. His Word promises that He will pardon you—and God always keeps His Word. If you have sinned against another person and he forgives you, accept his words of forgiveness at face value. Don't try to second-guess his sincerity or motives.

What happens if you confess a sin against another person and the person refuses to forgive you? That person bears the responsibility for failing to forgive; you don't. You have done what the Lord requires of you, and you stand clear before the Lord.

See the Life Principles Index for further study:
15. Brokenness is God's requirement for maximum usefulness.
2. Obey God and leave all the consequences to Him.

peace offering. Then the priest shall burn it
on the altar, according to the offerings made
by fire to the LORD. So the priest shall make
atonement for his sin that he has committed,
and it shall be forgiven him.

The Trespass Offering

5 'If a person sins in hearing the utterance
of an oath, and *is* a witness, whether he
has seen or known *of the matter*—if he does
not tell *it*, he bears guilt.
2 'Or if a person touches any unclean thing,
whether *it is* the carcass of an unclean beast,
or the carcass of unclean livestock, or the carcass
of unclean creeping things, and he is unaware
of it, he also shall be unclean and
guilty.
3 'Or if he touches human uncleanness—
whatever uncleanness with which a man may
be defiled, and he is unaware of it—when he
realizes *it*, then he shall be guilty.
4 'Or if a person swears, speaking thoughtlessly
with *his* lips to do evil or to do good,
whatever *it is* that a man may pronounce by
an oath, and he is unaware of it—when he realizes
it, then he shall be guilty in any of
these *matters*.
5 'And it shall be, when he is guilty in any of
these *matters*, that he shall confess that he
has sinned in that *thing*;
6 'and he shall bring his trespass offering to
the LORD for his sin which he has committed,
a female from the flock, a lamb or a kid of the
goats as a sin offering. So the priest shall
make atonement for him concerning his sin.
7 'If he is not able to bring a lamb, then he
shall bring to the LORD, for his trespass which
he has committed, two turtledoves or two
young pigeons: one as a sin offering and the
other as a burnt offering.
8 'And he shall bring them to the priest, who
shall offer *that* which *is* for the sin offering

first, and wring off its head from its neck, but
shall not divide *it* completely.
9 'Then he shall sprinkle *some* of the blood
of the sin offering on the side of the altar, and
the rest of the blood shall be drained out at
the base of the altar. It *is* a sin offering.
10 'And he shall offer the second *as* a burnt
offering according to the prescribed manner.
So the priest shall make atonement on his behalf for his sin which he has committed, and
it shall be forgiven him.
11 'But if he is not able to bring two turtledoves or two young pigeons, then he who
sinned shall bring for his offering one-tenth
of an ephah of fine flour as a sin offering. He
shall put no oil on it, nor shall he put frankincense on it, for it *is* a sin offering.
12 'Then he shall bring it to the priest, and
the priest shall take his handful of it as a memorial portion, and burn *it* on the altar according to the offerings made by fire to the
LORD. It *is* a sin offering.
13 'The priest shall make atonement for him,
for his sin that he has committed in any of
these matters; and it shall be forgiven him.
The rest shall be the priest's as a grain offering.' "

Offerings with Restitution
14 Then the LORD spoke to Moses, saying:
15 "If a person commits a trespass, and sins
unintentionally in regard to the holy things of
the LORD, then he shall bring to the LORD as
his trespass offering a ram without blemish
from the flocks, with your valuation in
shekels of silver according to the shekel of
the sanctuary, as a trespass offering.
16 "And he shall make restitution for the
harm that he has done in regard to the holy
thing, and shall add one-fifth to it and give it
to the priest. So the priest shall make atonement for him with the ram of the trespass offering, and it shall be forgiven him.
➤ **17** "If a person sins, and commits any of
these things which are forbidden to be done
by the commandments of the LORD, though he
does not know *it*, yet he is guilty and shall
bear his iniquity.
18 "And he shall bring to the priest a ram
without blemish from the flock, with your valuation, as a trespass offering. So the priest
shall make atonement for him regarding his
ignorance in which he erred and did not
know *it*, and it shall be forgiven him.
19 "It is a trespass offering; he has certainly
trespassed against the LORD."
6 And the LORD spoke to Moses, saying:
2 "If a person sins and commits a trespass against the LORD by lying to his neighbor
about what was delivered to him for
safekeeping, or about a pledge, or about a
robbery, or if he has extorted from his neighbor,
3 "or if he has found what was lost and lies
concerning it, and swears falsely—in any one
of these things that a man may do in which he
sins:
4 "then it shall be, because he has sinned
and is guilty, that he shall restore what he has
stolen, or the thing which he has extorted, or
what was delivered to him for safekeeping, or
the lost thing which he found,
5 "or all that about which he has sworn ➤
falsely. He shall restore its full value, add one-
fifth more to it, *and* give it to whomever it belongs, on the day of his trespass offering.
6 "And he shall bring his trespass offering
to the LORD, a ram without blemish from the
flock, with your valuation, as a trespass offering, to the priest.
7 "So the priest shall make atonement for
him before the LORD, and he shall be forgiven
for any one of these things that he may have
done in which he trespasses."

The Law of the Burnt Offering
8 Then the LORD spoke to Moses, saying,
9 "Command Aaron and his sons, saying,
'This *is* the law of the burnt offering: The
burnt offering *shall be* on the hearth upon the
altar all night until morning, and the fire of
the altar shall be kept burning on it.
10 'And the priest shall put on his linen garment, and his linen trousers he shall put on
his body, and take up the ashes of the burnt
offering which the fire has consumed on the
altar, and he shall put them beside the altar.
11 'Then he shall take off his garments, put
on other garments, and carry the ashes outside the camp to a clean place.
12 'And the fire on the altar shall be kept
burning on it; it shall not be put out. And the
priest shall burn wood on it every morning,
and lay the burnt offering in order on it; and

LIFE LESSONS

➤ 5:17 — *"If a person sins, and commits any of these things which are forbidden to be done by the commandments of the LORD, though he does not know it, yet he is guilty and shall bear his iniquity."*

Guilt is real, not merely a feeling. Hardened sinners may feel no guilt, but in fact bear great guilt. This is why we need the blood of Christ to cleanse us from *all* sin (1 John 1:7).

➤ 6:5 — *". . . or all that about which he has sworn falsely. He shall restore its full value, add one-fifth more to it, and give it to whomever it belongs, on the day of his trespass offering."*

When we have defrauded or hurt someone, genuine repentance requires restitution. It is not enough to say, "I'm sorry," or "please forgive me." We are to put right what we have done wrong (see Luke 19:8).

WHAT THE BIBLE SAYS ABOUT THE COVER-UP

Lev. 6:6, 7

The Old Testament uses an interesting word, "atonement," in connection with the forgiveness of God. Leviticus tells sinful Hebrews to bring a guilt offering to the priest, who "shall make atonement for him before the LORD, and he shall be forgiven for any one of these things that he may have done in which he trespasses" (6:7).

Atonement means "to cover." It is the same Hebrew word translated "to coat" in Genesis 6:14, where God instructs Noah how to build the ark: "Make yourself an ark of gopherwood, make rooms in the ark, and cover it inside and outside with pitch."

While the sacrificial system functioned adequately for a time, it was temporary in nature. The sins of those living under the Levitical system were *covered* but not *forgiven* in the absolute sense. Why? Because the blood of animals can never pay the whole debt incurred by sinners: "But in those sacrifices there is a reminder of sins every year. For it is not possible that the blood of bulls and goats could take away sins" (Heb. 10:3, 4).

God wants something more than retribution.

In God's economy, sin creates a deficit. Whenever sin occurs, something is taken or demanded from the sinner. Ultimately, God requires death as payment for sin. So Paul writes, ". . . through one man sin entered the world, and death through sin, and thus death spread to all men, because all sinned" (Rom. 5:12).

So if the penalty for sin is death, then why did God not immediately snuff out the lives of Adam and Eve? Did He not say that on the "day" they sinned, they would "surely die" (Gen. 2:17)? Why does He not do the same for all sinners? Why provide a system through which fellowship could be restored if sin ultimately results in death?

The answer is simple, yet life-changing. God wants something more than retribution. He desires something more than getting paid back for the disrespect shown Him. *God wants fellowship with us.* And He willingly put His own system of justice on hold while He made final provision for the rescue of sinful men and women.

See the Life Principles Index for further study:
12. *Peace with God is the fruit of oneness with God.*
1. *Our intimacy with God—His highest priority for our lives—determines the impact of our lives.*

he shall burn on it the fat of the peace offerings.
13 'A fire shall always be burning on the altar; it shall never go out.

The Law of the Grain Offering
14 'This *is* the law of the grain offering: The sons of Aaron shall offer it on the altar before the LORD.
15 'He shall take from it his handful of the fine flour of the grain offering, with its oil, and all the frankincense which *is* on the grain offering, and shall burn *it* on the altar *for* a sweet aroma, as a memorial to the LORD.
16 'And the remainder of it Aaron and his sons shall eat; with unleavened bread it shall be eaten in a holy place; in the court of the tabernacle of meeting they shall eat it.
17 'It shall not be baked with leaven. I have given it *as* their portion of My offerings made by fire; it *is* most holy, like the sin offering and the trespass offering.
18 'All the males among the children of Aaron may eat it. *It shall be* a statute forever in your generations concerning the offerings made by fire to the LORD. Everyone who touches them must be holy.' "[a]
19 And the LORD spoke to Moses, saying,
20 "This *is* the offering of Aaron and his sons, which they shall offer to the LORD, *beginning* on the day when he is anointed: one-tenth of an ephah of fine flour as a daily grain offering, half of it in the morning and half of it at night.
21 "It shall be made in a pan with oil. *When it is* mixed, you shall bring it in. The baked pieces of the grain offering you shall offer *for* a sweet aroma to the LORD.
22 "The priest from among his sons, who is anointed in his place, shall offer it. *It is* a statute forever to the LORD. It shall be wholly burned.
23 "For every grain offering for the priest shall be wholly burned. It shall not be eaten."

The Law of the Sin Offering
24 Also the LORD spoke to Moses, saying,
25 "Speak to Aaron and to his sons, saying, 'This *is* the law of the sin offering: In the place where the burnt offering is killed, the sin offering shall be killed before the LORD. It *is* most holy.
26 'The priest who offers it for sin shall eat it. In a holy place it shall be eaten, in the court of the tabernacle of meeting.
27 'Everyone who touches its flesh must be holy.[a] And when its blood is sprinkled on any garment, you shall wash that on which it was sprinkled, in a holy place.
28 'But the earthen vessel in which it is boiled shall be broken. And if it is boiled in a bronze pot, it shall be both scoured and rinsed in water.
29 'All the males among the priests may eat it. It *is* most holy.
30 'But no sin offering from which *any* of the blood is brought into the tabernacle of meeting, to make atonement in the holy *place*,[a] shall be eaten. It shall be burned in the fire.

The Law of the Trespass Offering
7 'Likewise this *is* the law of the trespass offering (it *is* most holy):
2 'In the place where they kill the burnt offering they shall kill the trespass offering. And its blood he shall sprinkle all around on the altar.
3 'And he shall offer from it all its fat. The fat tail and the fat that covers the entrails,
4 'the two kidneys and the fat that *is* on them by the flanks, and the fatty lobe *attached* to the liver above the kidneys, he shall remove;
5 'and the priest shall burn them on the altar *as* an offering made by fire to the LORD. It *is* a trespass offering.
6 'Every male among the priests may eat it. It shall be eaten in a holy place. It *is* most holy.
7 'The trespass offering *is* like the sin offering; *there is* one law for them both: the priest who makes atonement with it shall have *it*.
8 'And the priest who offers anyone's burnt offering, that priest shall have for himself the skin of the burnt offering which he has offered.
9 'Also every grain offering that is baked in the oven and all that is prepared in the covered pan, or in a pan, shall be the priest's who offers it.
10 'Every grain offering, *whether* mixed with oil or dry, shall belong to all the sons of Aaron, to one *as much* as the other.

The Law of Peace Offerings
11 'This *is* the law of the sacrifice of peace offerings which he shall offer to the LORD:
12 'If he offers it for a thanksgiving, then he shall offer, with the sacrifice of thanksgiving, unleavened cakes mixed with oil, unleavened wafers anointed with oil, or cakes of blended flour mixed with oil.
13 'Besides the cakes, *as* his offering he shall offer leavened bread with the sacrifice of thanksgiving of his peace offering.
14 'And from it he shall offer one cake from each offering *as* a heave offering to the LORD. It shall belong to the priest who sprinkles the blood of the peace offering.
15 'The flesh of the sacrifice of his peace offering for thanksgiving shall be eaten the same day it is offered. He shall not leave any of it until morning.
16 'But if the sacrifice of his offering *is* a vow or a voluntary offering, it shall be eaten the same day that he offers his sacrifice; but on the next day the remainder of it also may be eaten;

6:18 [a]Compare Numbers 4:15 and Haggai 2:11–13
6:27 [a]Compare Numbers 4:15 and Haggai 2:11–13
6:30 [a]The Most Holy Place when capitalized

Life Examples:

AARON

A Fatal Compromise

LEV. 8:2, 3

Aaron—Moses' older brother, right-hand man, and spokesman during the time of the Exodus—received a very high diving calling: to serve as priest for the liberated nation (Lev. 8:1–36). Because this enormous task also carried great responsibility, such a man had to live in a manner beyond reproach.

Aaron, unfortunately, had a weakness for unwise compromise. At a crucial time when Moses and his people needed him to stand strong, he gave in to the clamoring of the Israelites and forged a golden calf for them to worship. Through his failure he missed out on God's very best for himself and doomed a number of Israelites to a fatal encounter with a holy God. Aaron's compromise led to the deaths of three thousand of his fellow Hebrews (Ex. 32:28).

Aaron reminds us that God requires full obedience to His Word, no matter how tempting it may feel to compromise.

See the Life Principles Index for further study:
2. Obey God and leave all the consequences to Him.

17 'the remainder of the flesh of the sacrifice
on the third day must be burned with fire.
18 'And if *any* of the flesh of the sacrifice of
his peace offering is eaten at all on the third
day, it shall not be accepted, nor shall it be imputed to him; it shall be an abomination *to*
him who offers it, and the person who eats of
it shall bear guilt.
19 'The flesh that touches any unclean thing
shall not be eaten. It shall be burned with fire.
And as for the *clean* flesh, all who are clean
may eat of it.
20 'But the person who eats the flesh of the
sacrifice of the peace offering that *belongs* to
the LORD, while he is unclean, that person
shall be cut off from his people.
21 'Moreover the person who touches any
unclean thing, *such as* human uncleanness,
an unclean animal, or any abominable unclean thing,[a] and who eats the flesh of the
sacrifice of the peace offering that *belongs* to
the LORD, that person shall be cut off from his
people.' "

Fat and Blood May Not Be Eaten
22 And the LORD spoke to Moses, saying,
23 "Speak to the children of Israel, saying:
'You shall not eat any fat, of ox or sheep or
goat.
24 'And the fat of an animal that dies *naturally,* and the fat of what is torn by wild
beasts, may be used in any other way; but you
shall by no means eat it.
25 'For whoever eats the fat of the animal of
which men offer an offering made by fire to
the LORD, the person who eats *it* shall be cut
off from his people.
26 'Moreover you shall not eat any blood in
any of your dwellings, *whether* of bird or
beast.
27 'Whoever eats any blood, that person shall
be cut off from his people.' "

The Portion of Aaron and His Sons
28 Then the LORD spoke to Moses, saying,
29 "Speak to the children of Israel, saying:
'He who offers the sacrifice of his peace offering to the LORD shall bring his offering to
the LORD from the sacrifice of his peace offering.
30 'His own hands shall bring the offerings
made by fire to the LORD. The fat with the
breast he shall bring, that the breast may be
waved *as* a wave offering before the LORD.
31 'And the priest shall burn the fat on the
altar, but the breast shall be Aaron's and his
sons'.
32 'Also the right thigh you shall give to the
priest *as* a heave offering from the sacrifices
of your peace offerings.
33 'He among the sons of Aaron, who offers
the blood of the peace offering and the fat,
shall have the right thigh for *his* part.
34 'For the breast of the wave offering and
the thigh of the heave offering I have taken
from the children of Israel, from the sacrifices
of their peace offerings, and I have given
them to Aaron the priest and to his sons from
the children of Israel by a statute forever.' "
35 This *is* the consecrated portion for Aaron
and his sons, from the offerings made by fire
to the LORD, on the day when *Moses* presented them to minister to the LORD as
priests.
36 The LORD commanded this to be given to
them by the children of Israel, on the day that
He anointed them, *by* a statute forever
throughout their generations.
37 This *is* the law of the burnt offering, the
grain offering, the sin offering, the trespass
offering, the consecrations, and the sacrifice
of the peace offering,
38 which the LORD commanded Moses on
Mount Sinai, on the day when He com-

7:21 [a]Following Masoretic Text, Septuagint, and Vulgate; Samaritan Pentateuch, Syriac, and Targum read *swarming thing* (compare 5:2).

manded the children of Israel to offer their offerings to the LORD in the Wilderness of Sinai.

Aaron and His Sons Consecrated

8 And the LORD spoke to Moses, saying:
2 "Take Aaron and his sons with him,
and the garments, the anointing oil, a bull as
the sin offering, two rams, and a basket of unleavened bread;
3 "and gather all the congregation together
at the door of the tabernacle of meeting."
4 So Moses did as the LORD commanded
him. And the congregation was gathered together at the door of the tabernacle of meeting.
5 And Moses said to the congregation, "This
is what the LORD commanded to be done."
6 Then Moses brought Aaron and his sons
and washed them with water.
7 And he put the tunic on him, girded him
with the sash, clothed him with the robe, and
put the ephod on him; and he girded him with
the intricately woven band of the ephod, and
with it tied *the ephod* on him.
8 Then he put the breastplate on him, and
he put the Urim and the Thummim[a] in the
breastplate.
9 And he put the turban on his head. Also
on the turban, on its front, he put the golden
plate, the holy crown, as the LORD had commanded Moses.
10 Also Moses took the anointing oil, and
anointed the tabernacle and all that *was* in it,
and consecrated them.
11 He sprinkled some of it on the altar seven
times, anointed the altar and all its utensils,
and the laver and its base, to consecrate
them.
12 And he poured some of the anointing oil
on Aaron's head and anointed him, to consecrate him.
13 Then Moses brought Aaron's sons and put
tunics on them, girded them with sashes, and
put hats on them, as the LORD had commanded Moses.
14 And he brought the bull for the sin offering. Then Aaron and his sons laid their hands
on the head of the bull for the sin offering,
15 and Moses killed *it*. Then he took the
blood, and put *some* on the horns of the altar
all around with his finger, and purified the
altar. And he poured the blood at the base of
the altar, and consecrated it, to make atonement for it.
16 Then he took all the fat that *was* on the entrails, the fatty lobe *attached to* the liver, and
the two kidneys with their fat, and Moses
burned *them* on the altar.
17 But the bull, its hide, its flesh, and its offal,
he burned with fire outside the camp, as the
LORD had commanded Moses.
18 Then he brought the ram as the burnt offering. And Aaron and his sons laid their
hands on the head of the ram,
19 and Moses killed *it*. Then he sprinkled the
blood all around on the altar.
20 And he cut the ram into pieces; and Moses
burned the head, the pieces, and the fat.
21 Then he washed the entrails and the legs
in water. And Moses burned the whole ram on
the altar. It *was* a burnt sacrifice for a sweet
aroma, an offering made by fire to the LORD,
as the LORD had commanded Moses.
22 And he brought the second ram, the ram
of consecration. Then Aaron and his sons laid
their hands on the head of the ram,
23 and Moses killed *it*. Also he took *some* of
its blood and put it on the tip of Aaron's right
ear, on the thumb of his right hand, and on
the big toe of his right foot.
24 Then he brought Aaron's sons. And Moses
put *some* of the blood on the tips of their right
ears, on the thumbs of their right hands, and
on the big toes of their right feet. And Moses
sprinkled the blood all around on the altar.
25 Then he took the fat and the fat tail, all the
fat that *was* on the entrails, the fatty lobe *attached to* the liver, the two kidneys and their
fat, and the right thigh;
26 and from the basket of unleavened bread
that was before the LORD he took one unleavened cake, a cake of bread *anointed with* oil,
and one wafer, and put *them* on the fat and on
the right thigh;
27 and he put all *these* in Aaron's hands and
in his sons' hands, and waved them *as* a wave
offering before the LORD.
28 Then Moses took them from their hands
and burned *them* on the altar, on the burnt offering. They *were* consecration offerings for a
sweet aroma. That *was* an offering made by
fire to the LORD.
29 And Moses took the breast and waved it
as a wave offering before the LORD. It was
Moses' part of the ram of consecration, as the
LORD had commanded Moses.
30 Then Moses took some of the anointing oil
and some of the blood which *was* on the altar,
and sprinkled *it* on Aaron, on his garments,
on his sons, and on the garments of his sons
with him; and he consecrated Aaron, his garments, his sons, and the garments of his sons
with him.
31 And Moses said to Aaron and his sons,
"Boil the flesh *at* the door of the tabernacle of
meeting, and eat it there with the bread that *is*
in the basket of consecration offerings, as I
commanded, saying, 'Aaron and his sons
shall eat it.'
32 "What remains of the flesh and of the
bread you shall burn with fire.
33 "And you shall not go outside the door of
the tabernacle of meeting *for* seven days, until
the days of your consecration are ended. For
seven days he shall consecrate you.

8:8 [a]Literally *the Lights and the Perfections* (compare Exodus 28:30)

34 "As he has done this day, *so* the LORD has
commanded to do, to make atonement for
you.
➤ 35 "Therefore you shall stay *at* the door of
the tabernacle of meeting day and night for
seven days, and keep the charge of the LORD,
so that you may not die; for so I have been
commanded."
36 So Aaron and his sons did all the things
that the LORD had commanded by the hand of
Moses.

The Priestly Ministry Begins

9 It came to pass on the eighth day that
Moses called Aaron and his sons and the
elders of Israel.
2 And he said to Aaron, "Take for yourself a
young bull as a sin offering and a ram as a
burnt offering, without blemish, and offer
them before the LORD.
3 "And to the children of Israel you shall
speak, saying, 'Take a kid of the goats as a sin
offering, and a calf and a lamb, *both* of the
first year, without blemish, as a burnt offering,
4 'also a bull and a ram as peace offerings,
to sacrifice before the LORD, and a grain offering mixed with oil; for today the LORD will
appear to you.'"
5 So they brought what Moses commanded
before the tabernacle of meeting. And all the
congregation drew near and stood before the
LORD.
6 Then Moses said, "This *is* the thing which
the LORD commanded you to do, and the glory
of the LORD will appear to you."
7 And Moses said to Aaron, "Go to the altar,
offer your sin offering and your burnt offering, and make atonement for yourself and for
the people. Offer the offering of the people,
and make atonement for them, as the LORD
commanded."
8 Aaron therefore went to the altar and
killed the calf of the sin offering, which *was*
for himself.
9 Then the sons of Aaron brought the blood
to him. And he dipped his finger in the blood,
put *it* on the horns of the altar, and poured the
blood at the base of the altar.
10 But the fat, the kidneys, and the fatty lobe
from the liver of the sin offering he burned on
the altar, as the LORD had commanded Moses.
11 The flesh and the hide he burned with fire
outside the camp.
12 And he killed the burnt offering; and Aaron's sons presented to him the blood, which
he sprinkled all around on the altar.
13 Then they presented the burnt offering to
him, with its pieces and head, and he burned
them on the altar.
14 And he washed the entrails and the legs,
and burned *them* with the burnt offering on
the altar.
15 Then he brought the people's offering, and
took the goat, which *was* the sin offering for
the people, and killed it and offered it for sin,
like the first one.
16 And he brought the burnt offering and offered it according to the prescribed manner.
17 Then he brought the grain offering, took a
handful of it, and burned *it* on the altar, besides the burnt sacrifice of the morning.
18 He also killed the bull and the ram *as* sacrifices of peace offerings, which *were* for the
people. And Aaron's sons presented to him
the blood, which he sprinkled all around on
the altar,
19 and the fat from the bull and the ram—the
fatty tail, what covers *the entrails* and
the kidneys, and the fatty lobe *attached to*
the liver;
20 and they put the fat on the breasts. Then
he burned the fat on the altar;
21 but the breasts and the right thigh Aaron
waved *as* a wave offering before the LORD, as
Moses had commanded.
22 Then Aaron lifted his hand toward the
people, blessed them, and came down from
offering the sin offering, the burnt offering,
and peace offerings.
23 And Moses and Aaron went into the tabernacle of meeting, and came out and blessed
the people. Then the glory of the LORD appeared to all the people,
24 and fire came out from before the LORD ◄
and consumed the burnt offering and the fat
on the altar. When all the people saw *it,* they
shouted and fell on their faces.

The Profane Fire of Nadab and Abihu

10 Then Nadab and Abihu, the sons of
Aaron, each took his censer and put
fire in it, put incense on it, and offered profane fire before the LORD, which He had not
commanded them.
2 So fire went out from the LORD and devoured them, and they died before the LORD.

LIFE LESSONS

➤ 8:35 — *"Therefore you shall stay at the door of the tabernacle of meeting day and night for seven days, and keep the charge of the LORD, so that you may not die; for so I have been commanded."*

Even in worship, Moses did only what God had commanded him. God takes the lead; we are to follow.

➤ 9:24 — *". . . and fire came out from before the LORD and consumed the burnt offering and the fat on the altar. When all the people saw it, they shouted and fell on their faces."*

When we do our part, God does His part—what we could never do.

➤ 3 And Moses said to Aaron, "This is what the LORD spoke, saying:

'By those who come near Me
I must be regarded as holy;
And before all the people
I must be glorified.'"

So Aaron held his peace.

4 Then Moses called Mishael and Elzaphan, the sons of Uzziel the uncle of Aaron, and said to them, "Come near, carry your brethren from before the sanctuary out of the camp."

5 So they went near and carried them by their tunics out of the camp, as Moses had said.

6 And Moses said to Aaron, and to Eleazar and Ithamar, his sons, "Do not uncover your heads nor tear your clothes, lest you die, and wrath come upon all the people. But let your brethren, the whole house of Israel, bewail the burning which the LORD has kindled.

7 "You shall not go out from the door of the tabernacle of meeting, lest you die, for the anointing oil of the LORD *is* upon you." And they did according to the word of Moses.

Conduct Prescribed for Priests

8 Then the LORD spoke to Aaron, saying:

9 "Do not drink wine or intoxicating drink, you, nor your sons with you, when you go into the tabernacle of meeting, lest you die. *It shall be* a statute forever throughout your generations,

10 "that you may distinguish between holy and unholy, and between unclean and clean,

11 "and that you may teach the children of Israel all the statutes which the LORD has spoken to them by the hand of Moses."

12 And Moses spoke to Aaron, and to Eleazar and Ithamar, his sons who were left: "Take the grain offering that remains of the offerings made by fire to the LORD, and eat it without leaven beside the altar; for it *is* most holy.

13 "You shall eat it in a holy place, because it *is* your due and your sons' due, of the sacrifices made by fire to the LORD; for so I have been commanded.

14 "The breast of the wave offering and the thigh of the heave offering you shall eat in a clean place, you, your sons, and your daughters with you; for *they are* your due and your sons' due, *which* are given from the sacrifices of peace offerings of the children of Israel.

15 "The thigh of the heave offering and the breast of the wave offering they shall bring with the offerings of fat made by fire, to offer *as* a wave offering before the LORD. And it shall be yours and your sons' with you, by a statute forever, as the LORD has commanded."

16 Then Moses made careful inquiry about the goat of the sin offering, and there it was—burned up. And he was angry with Eleazar and Ithamar, the sons of Aaron *who were* left, saying,

17 "Why have you not eaten the sin offering in a holy place, since it *is* most holy, and *God* has given it to you to bear the guilt of the congregation, to make atonement for them before the LORD?

18 "See! Its blood was not brought inside the holy *place*;[a] indeed you should have eaten it in a holy *place*, as I commanded."

19 And Aaron said to Moses, "Look, this day they have offered their sin offering and their burnt offering before the LORD, and such things have befallen me! *If* I had eaten the sin offering today, would it have been accepted in the sight of the LORD?" ◄

20 So when Moses heard *that*, he was content.

Foods Permitted and Forbidden

11 Now the LORD spoke to Moses and Aaron, saying to them,

2 "Speak to the children of Israel, saying, 'These *are* the animals which you may eat among all the animals that *are* on the earth:

3 'Among the animals, whatever divides the hoof, having cloven hooves *and* chewing the cud—that you may eat.

4 'Nevertheless these you shall not eat among those that chew the cud or those that have cloven hooves: the camel, because it chews the cud but does not have cloven hooves, is unclean to you;

5 'the rock hyrax, because it chews the cud but does not have cloven hooves, *is* unclean to you;

6 'the hare, because it chews the cud but does not have cloven hooves, *is* unclean to you;

10:18 [a]The Most Holy Place when capitalized

LIFE LESSONS

➤ 10:3 — *And Moses said to Aaron, "This is what the LORD spoke, saying: 'By those who come near Me I must be regarded as holy; And before all the people I must be glorified.'" So Aaron held his peace.*

While we no longer live under the Mosaic Law, God's nature has not changed. We can never forget that we serve a holy God, who insists on being treated as holy.

➤ 10:19 — *". . . If I had eaten the sin offering today, would it have been accepted in the sight of the LORD?"*

God is holy, and yet He is also merciful. We should never forget His holiness, and never take for granted His mercy.

7 'and the swine, though it divides the hoof,
having cloven hooves, yet does not chew the
cud, *is* unclean to you.
8 'Their flesh you shall not eat, and their
carcasses you shall not touch. They *are* unclean to you.
9 'These you may eat of all that *are* in the
water: whatever in the water has fins and
scales, whether in the seas or in the rivers—
that you may eat.
10 'But all in the seas or in the rivers that do
not have fins and scales, all that move in the
water or any living thing which *is* in the
water, they *are* an abomination to you.
11 'They shall be an abomination to you; you
shall not eat their flesh, but you shall regard
their carcasses as an abomination.
12 'Whatever in the water does not have fins
or scales—that *shall be* an abomination to
you.
13 'And these you shall regard as an
abomination among the birds; they shall not
be eaten, they *are* an abomination: the eagle,
the vulture, the buzzard,
14 'the kite, and the falcon after its kind;
15 'every raven after its kind,
16 'the ostrich, the short-eared owl, the sea
gull, and the hawk after its kind;
17 'the little owl, the fisher owl, and the
screech owl;
18 'the white owl, the jackdaw, and the carrion vulture;
19 'the stork, the heron after its kind, the
hoopoe, and the bat.
20 'All flying insects that creep on *all* fours
shall be an abomination to you.
21 'Yet these you may eat of every flying in-
sect that creeps on *all* fours: those which have
jointed legs above their feet with which to
leap on the earth.
22 'These you may eat: the locust after its
kind, the destroying locust after its kind, the
cricket after its kind, and the grasshopper
after its kind.
23 'But all *other* flying insects which have
four feet *shall be* an abomination to you.

Unclean Animals

24 'By these you shall become unclean; whoever touches the carcass of any of them shall
be unclean until evening;
25 'whoever carries part of the carcass of any
of them shall wash his clothes and be unclean
until evening:
26 '*The carcass* of any animal which divides
the foot, but is not cloven-hoofed or does not
chew the cud, *is* unclean to you. Everyone
who touches it shall be unclean.
27 'And whatever goes on its paws, among
all kinds of animals that go on *all* fours,
those *are* unclean to you. Whoever touches
any such carcass shall be unclean until
evening.
28 'Whoever carries *any such* carcass shall
wash his clothes and be unclean until
evening. It *is* unclean to you.
29 'These also *shall be* unclean to you among
the creeping things that creep on the earth:
the mole, the mouse, and the large lizard after
its kind;
30 'the gecko, the monitor lizard, the sand
reptile, the sand lizard, and the chameleon.
31 'These *are* unclean to you among all that
creep. Whoever touches them when they are
dead shall be unclean until evening.
32 'Anything on which *any* of them falls,
when they are dead shall be unclean, whether
it is any item of wood or clothing or skin or
sack, whatever item *it is,* in which *any* work
is done, it must be put in water. And it shall
be unclean until evening; then it shall be
clean.
33 'Any earthen vessel into which *any* of
them falls you shall break; and whatever *is* in
it shall be unclean:
34 'in such a vessel, any edible food upon
which water falls becomes unclean, and any
drink that may be drunk from it becomes unclean.
35 'And everything on which *a part* of *any
such* carcass falls shall be unclean; *whether it
is* an oven or cooking stove, it shall be broken
down; *for* they *are* unclean, and shall be unclean to you.
36 'Nevertheless a spring or a cistern, *in
which there is* plenty of water, shall be clean,
but whatever touches any such carcass becomes unclean.
37 'And if a part of *any such* carcass falls on
any planting seed which is to be sown, it *remains* clean.
38 'But if water is put on the seed, and if *a
part* of *any such* carcass falls on it, it *becomes*
unclean to you.
39 'And if any animal which you may eat
dies, he who touches its carcass shall be unclean until evening.
40 'He who eats of its carcass shall wash his
clothes and be unclean until evening. He also
who carries its carcass shall wash his clothes
and be unclean until evening.
41 'And every creeping thing that creeps on
the earth *shall be* an abomination. It shall not
be eaten.
42 'Whatever crawls on its belly, whatever
goes on *all* fours, or whatever has many feet
among all creeping things that creep on the
earth—these you shall not eat, for they *are* an
abomination.
43 'You shall not make yourselves abominable with any creeping thing that creeps; nor
shall you make yourselves unclean with
them, lest you be defiled by them.
44 'For I *am* the LORD your God. You shall
therefore consecrate yourselves, and you
shall be holy; for I *am* holy. Neither shall you
defile yourselves with any creeping thing that
creeps on the earth.

➤ 45 'For I *am* the LORD who brings you up out
of the land of Egypt, to be your God. You shall
therefore be holy, for I *am* holy.
46 'This *is* the law of the animals and the
birds and every living creature that moves in
the waters, and of every creature that creeps
on the earth,
47 'to distinguish between the unclean and
the clean, and between the animal that may
be eaten and the animal that may not be
eaten.'"

The Ritual After Childbirth

12 Then the LORD spoke to Moses, saying,
2 "Speak to the children of Israel, saying: 'If a woman has conceived, and borne a
male child, then she shall be unclean seven
days; as in the days of her customary impurity she shall be unclean.
3 'And on the eighth day the flesh of his
foreskin shall be circumcised.
4 'She shall then continue in the blood of
her purification thirty-three days. She shall
not touch any hallowed thing, nor come into
the sanctuary until the days of her purification are fulfilled.
5 'But if she bears a female child, then she
shall be unclean two weeks, as in her customary impurity, and she shall continue in the
blood of *her* purification sixty-six days.
6 'When the days of her purification are fulfilled, whether for a son or a daughter, she
shall bring to the priest a lamb of the first
year as a burnt offering, and a young pigeon
or a turtledove as a sin offering, to the door of
the tabernacle of meeting.
7 'Then he shall offer it before the LORD, and
make atonement for her. And she shall be
clean from the flow of her blood. This *is* the
law for her who has borne a male or a female.
8 'And if she is not able to bring a lamb, then
she may bring two turtledoves or two young
pigeons—one as a burnt offering and the other
as a sin offering. So the priest shall make
atonement for her, and she will be clean.'"

The Law Concerning Leprosy

13 And the LORD spoke to Moses and
Aaron, saying:
2 "When a man has on the skin of his body
a swelling, a scab, or a bright spot, and it becomes on the skin of his body *like* a leprous[a]
sore, then he shall be brought to Aaron the
priest or to one of his sons the priests.
3 "The priest shall examine the sore on the
skin of the body; and if the hair on the sore
has turned white, and the sore appears *to be*
deeper than the skin of his body, it *is* a leprous sore. Then the priest shall examine him,
and pronounce him unclean.
4 "But if the bright spot *is* white on the skin
of his body, and does not appear *to be* deeper
than the skin, and its hair has not turned
white, then the priest shall isolate *the one*
who has the sore seven days.
5 "And the priest shall examine him on the
seventh day; and indeed *if* the sore appears to
be as it was, *and* the sore has not spread on
the skin, then the priest shall isolate him another seven days.
6 "Then the priest shall examine him again
on the seventh day; and indeed *if* the sore has
faded, *and* the sore has not spread on the
skin, then the priest shall pronounce him
clean; it *is only* a scab, and he shall wash his
clothes and be clean.
7 "But if the scab should at all spread over
the skin, after he has been seen by the priest
for his cleansing, he shall be seen by the
priest again.
8 "And *if* the priest sees that the scab has indeed spread on the skin, then the priest shall
pronounce him unclean. It *is* leprosy.
9 "When the leprous sore is on a person,
then he shall be brought to the priest.
10 "And the priest shall examine *him;* and indeed *if* the swelling on the skin *is* white, and
it has turned the hair white, and *there is* a
spot of raw flesh in the swelling,
11 "it *is* an old leprosy on the skin of his body.
The priest shall pronounce him unclean, and
shall not isolate him, for he *is* unclean.
12 "And if leprosy breaks out all over the
skin, and the leprosy covers all the skin of *the*
one who has the sore, from his head to his
foot, wherever the priest looks,
13 "then the priest shall consider; and indeed
if the leprosy has covered all his body, he
shall pronounce *him* clean *who has* the sore.
It has all turned white. He *is* clean.
14 "But when raw flesh appears on him, he
shall be unclean.
15 "And the priest shall examine the raw
flesh and pronounce him to be unclean; *for*
the raw flesh *is* unclean. It *is* leprosy.
16 "Or if the raw flesh changes and turns
white again, he shall come to the priest.
17 "And the priest shall examine him; and indeed *if* the sore has turned white, then the
priest shall pronounce *him* clean *who has* the
sore. He *is* clean.

13:2 [a]Hebrew *saraath,* disfiguring skin diseases, including leprosy, and so in verses 2–46 and 14:2–32

LIFE LESSONS

➤ **11:45 — *"For I am the LORD who brings you up out of the land of Egypt, to be your God. You shall therefore be holy, for I am holy."***

God created us to be holy, as He is holy. He makes us holy when we place our faith in Christ, and we live out that holiness when we depend on the power of His Spirit.

18 "If the body develops a boil in the skin,
and it is healed,
19 "and in the place of the boil there comes a
white swelling or a bright spot, reddish-white,
then it shall be shown to the priest;
20 "and *if*, when the priest sees it, it indeed
appears deeper than the skin, and its hair has
turned white, the priest shall pronounce him
unclean. It *is* a leprous sore which has broken
out of the boil.
21 "But if the priest examines it, and indeed
there are no white hairs in it, and it *is* not
deeper than the skin, but has faded, then the
priest shall isolate him seven days;
22 "and if it should at all spread over the
skin, then the priest shall pronounce him unclean. It *is* a leprous sore.
23 "But if the bright spot stays in one place,
and has not spread, it *is* the scar of the boil;
and the priest shall pronounce him clean.
24 "Or if the body receives a burn on its skin
by fire, and the raw *flesh* of the burn becomes
a bright spot, reddish-white or white,
25 "then the priest shall examine it; and indeed *if* the hair of the bright spot has turned
white, and it appears deeper than the skin, it
is leprosy broken out in the burn. Therefore
the priest shall pronounce him unclean. It *is* a
leprous sore.
26 "But if the priest examines it, and indeed
there are no white hairs in the bright spot,
and it *is* not deeper than the skin, but has
faded, then the priest shall isolate him seven
days.
27 "And the priest shall examine him on the
seventh day. If it has at all spread over the
skin, then the priest shall pronounce him unclean. It *is* a leprous sore.
28 "But if the bright spot stays in one place,
and has not spread on the skin, but has faded,
it *is* a swelling from the burn. The priest shall
pronounce him clean, for it *is* the scar from
the burn.
29 "If a man or woman has a sore on the head
or the beard,
30 "then the priest shall examine the sore;
and indeed if it appears deeper than the skin,
and there is in it thin yellow hair, then the
priest shall pronounce him unclean. It *is* a
scaly leprosy of the head or beard.
31 "But if the priest examines the scaly sore,
and indeed it does not appear deeper than the
skin, and *there is* no black hair in it, then the
priest shall isolate *the one who has* the scale
seven days.
32 "And on the seventh day the priest shall examine the sore; and indeed *if* the scale has not
spread, and there is no yellow hair in it, and
the scale does not appear deeper than the skin,
33 "he shall shave himself, but the scale he
shall not shave. And the priest shall isolate
the one who has the scale another seven days.
34 "On the seventh day the priest shall examine the scale; and indeed *if* the scale has not
spread over the skin, and does not appear
deeper than the skin, then the priest shall pronounce him clean. He shall wash his clothes
and be clean.
35 "But if the scale should at all spread over
the skin after his cleansing,
36 "then the priest shall examine him; and indeed *if* the scale has spread over the skin, the
priest need not seek for yellow hair. He *is* unclean.
37 "But if the scale appears to be at a standstill, and there is black hair grown up in it, the
scale has healed. He *is* clean, and the priest
shall pronounce him clean.
38 "If a man or a woman has bright spots on
the skin of the body, *specifically* white bright
spots,
39 "then the priest shall look; and indeed *if*
the bright spots on the skin of the body *are*
dull white, it *is* a white spot *that* grows on the
skin. He *is* clean.
40 "As for the man whose hair has fallen
from his head, he *is* bald, *but* he *is* clean.
41 "He whose hair has fallen from his forehead, he *is* bald on the forehead, *but* he *is*
clean.
42 "And if there is on the bald head or bald
forehead a reddish-white sore, it *is* leprosy
breaking out on his bald head or his bald
forehead.
43 "Then the priest shall examine it; and indeed *if* the swelling of the sore *is* reddish-
white on his bald head or on his bald
forehead, as the appearance of leprosy on the
skin of the body,
44 "he is a leprous man. He *is* unclean. The
priest shall surely pronounce him unclean;
his sore *is* on his head.
45 "Now the leper on whom the sore *is*, his
clothes shall be torn and his head bare; and
he shall cover his mustache, and cry, 'Unclean! Unclean!'
46 "He shall be unclean. All the days he has
the sore he shall be unclean. He *is* unclean,
and he shall dwell alone; his dwelling *shall be*
outside the camp.

The Law Concerning Leprous Garments

47 "Also, if a garment has a leprous plague[a]
in it, *whether it is* a woolen garment or a
linen garment,
48 "whether *it is* in the warp or woof of linen
or wool, whether in leather or in anything
made of leather,
49 "and if the plague is greenish or reddish in
the garment or in the leather, whether in the
warp or in the woof, or in anything made of
leather, it *is* a leprous plague and shall be
shown to the priest.
50 "The priest shall examine the plague and
isolate *that which has* the plague seven days.

13:47 [a]A mold, fungus, or similar infestation, and so in verses 47–59

51 "And he shall examine the plague on the seventh day. If the plague has spread in the garment, either in the warp or in the woof, in the leather *or* in anything made of leather, the plague *is* an active leprosy. It *is* unclean.

52 "He shall therefore burn that garment in which is the plague, whether warp or woof, in wool or in linen, or anything of leather, for it *is* an active leprosy; *the garment* shall be burned in the fire.

53 "But if the priest examines *it,* and indeed the plague has not spread in the garment, either in the warp or in the woof, or in anything made of leather,

54 "then the priest shall command that they wash *the thing* in which *is* the plague; and he shall isolate it another seven days.

55 "Then the priest shall examine the plague after it has been washed; and indeed *if* the plague has not changed its color, though the plague has not spread, it *is* unclean, and you shall burn it in the fire; it continues eating away, *whether* the damage *is* outside or inside.

56 "If the priest examines *it,* and indeed the plague has faded after washing it, then he shall tear it out of the garment, whether out of the warp or out of the woof, or out of the leather.

57 "But if it appears again in the garment, either in the warp or in the woof, or in anything made of leather, it *is* a spreading *plague;* you shall burn with fire that in which is the plague.

58 "And if you wash the garment, either warp or woof, or whatever is made of leather, if the plague has disappeared from it, then it shall be washed a second time, and shall be clean.

59 "This *is* the law of the leprous plague in a garment of wool or linen, either in the warp or woof, or in anything made of leather, to pronounce it clean or to pronounce it unclean."

The Ritual for Cleansing Healed Lepers

14 Then the LORD spoke to Moses, saying,

2 "This shall be the law of the leper for the day of his cleansing: He shall be brought to the priest.

3 "And the priest shall go out of the camp, and the priest shall examine *him;* and indeed, *if* the leprosy is healed in the leper,

4 "then the priest shall command to take for him who is to be cleansed two living *and* clean birds, cedar wood, scarlet, and hyssop.

5 "And the priest shall command that one of the birds be killed in an earthen vessel over running water.

6 "As for the living bird, he shall take it, the cedar wood and the scarlet and the hyssop, and dip them and the living bird in the blood of the bird *that was* killed over the running water.

7 "And he shall sprinkle it seven times on him who is to be cleansed from the leprosy, and shall pronounce him clean, and shall let the living bird loose in the open field.

8 "He who is to be cleansed shall wash his clothes, shave off all his hair, and wash himself in water, that he may be clean. After that he shall come into the camp, and shall stay outside his tent seven days.

9 "But on the seventh day he shall shave all the hair off his head and his beard and his eyebrows—all his hair he shall shave off. He shall wash his clothes and wash his body in water, and he shall be clean.

10 "And on the eighth day he shall take two male lambs without blemish, one ewe lamb of the first year without blemish, three-tenths *of an ephah* of fine flour mixed with oil as a grain offering, and one log of oil.

11 "Then the priest who makes *him* clean shall present the man who is to be made clean, and those things, before the LORD, *at* the door of the tabernacle of meeting.

12 "And the priest shall take one male lamb and offer it as a trespass offering, and the log of oil, and wave them *as* a wave offering before the LORD.

13 "Then he shall kill the lamb in the place where he kills the sin offering and the burnt offering, in a holy place; for as the sin offering *is* the priest's, so *is* the trespass offering. It *is* most holy.

14 "The priest shall take *some* of the blood of the trespass offering, and the priest shall put *it* on the tip of the right ear of him who is to be cleansed, on the thumb of his right hand, and on the big toe of his right foot.

15 "And the priest shall take *some* of the log of oil, and pour *it* into the palm of his own left hand.

16 "Then the priest shall dip his right finger in the oil that *is* in his left hand, and shall sprinkle some of the oil with his finger seven times before the LORD.

17 "And of the rest of the oil in his hand, the priest shall put *some* on the tip of the right ear of him who is to be cleansed, on the thumb of his right hand, and on the big toe of his right foot, on the blood of the trespass offering.

18 "The rest of the oil that *is* in the priest's hand he shall put on the head of him who is to be cleansed. So the priest shall make atonement for him before the LORD.

19 "Then the priest shall offer the sin offering, and make atonement for him who is to be cleansed from his uncleanness. Afterward he shall kill the burnt offering.

20 "And the priest shall offer the burnt offering and the grain offering on the altar. So the priest shall make atonement for him, and he shall be clean.

21 "But if he *is* poor and cannot afford it, then he shall take one male lamb *as* a trespass offering to be waved, to make atonement for

him, one-tenth *of an ephah* of fine flour mixed with oil as a grain offering, a log of oil,
22 "and two turtledoves or two young pigeons, such as he is able to afford: one shall be a sin offering and the other a burnt offering.
23 "He shall bring them to the priest on the eighth day for his cleansing, to the door of the tabernacle of meeting, before the LORD.
24 "And the priest shall take the lamb of the trespass offering and the log of oil, and the priest shall wave them *as* a wave offering before the LORD.
25 "Then he shall kill the lamb of the trespass offering, and the priest shall take *some* of the blood of the trespass offering and put *it* on the tip of the right ear of him who is to be cleansed, on the thumb of his right hand, and on the big toe of his right foot.
26 "And the priest shall pour some of the oil into the palm of his own left hand.
27 "Then the priest shall sprinkle with his right finger *some* of the oil that *is* in his left hand seven times before the LORD.
28 "And the priest shall put *some* of the oil that *is* in his hand on the tip of the right ear of him who is to be cleansed, on the thumb of the right hand, and on the big toe of his right foot, on the place of the blood of the trespass offering.
29 "The rest of the oil that *is* in the priest's hand he shall put on the head of him who is to be cleansed, to make atonement for him before the LORD.
30 "And he shall offer one of the turtledoves or young pigeons, such as he can afford—
31 "such as he is able to afford, the one *as* a sin offering and the other *as* a burnt offering, with the grain offering. So the priest shall make atonement for him who is to be cleansed before the LORD.
32 "This *is* the law *for one* who had a leprous sore, who cannot afford the usual cleansing."

The Law Concerning Leprous Houses

➤ **33** And the LORD spoke to Moses and Aaron, saying:
34 "When you have come into the land of Canaan, which I give you as a possession, and I put the leprous plague[a] in a house in the land of your possession,
35 "and he who owns the house comes and tells the priest, saying, 'It seems to me that *there is* some plague in the house,'
36 "then the priest shall command that they empty the house, before the priest goes *into it* to examine the plague, that all that *is* in the house may not be made unclean; and afterward the priest shall go in to examine the house.
37 "And he shall examine the plague; and indeed *if* the plague *is* on the walls of the house with ingrained streaks, greenish or reddish, which appear to be deep in the wall,
38 "then the priest shall go out of the house, to the door of the house, and shut up the house seven days.
39 "And the priest shall come again on the seventh day and look; and indeed *if* the plague has spread on the walls of the house,
40 "then the priest shall command that they take away the stones in which *is* the plague, and they shall cast them into an unclean place outside the city.
41 "And he shall cause the house to be scraped inside, all around, and the dust that they scrape off they shall pour out in an unclean place outside the city.
42 "Then they shall take other stones and put *them* in the place of *those* stones, and he shall take other mortar and plaster the house.
43 "Now if the plague comes back and breaks out in the house, after he has taken away the stones, after he has scraped the house, and after it is plastered,
44 "then the priest shall come and look; and indeed *if* the plague has spread in the house, it *is* an active leprosy in the house. It *is* unclean.
45 "And he shall break down the house, its stones, its timber, and all the plaster of the house, and he shall carry *them* outside the city to an unclean place.
46 "Moreover he who goes into the house at all while it is shut up shall be unclean until evening.
47 "And he who lies down in the house shall wash his clothes, and he who eats in the house shall wash his clothes.
48 "But if the priest comes in and examines *it,* and indeed the plague has not spread in the house after the house was plastered, then the priest shall pronounce the house clean, because the plague is healed.
49 "And he shall take, to cleanse the house, two birds, cedar wood, scarlet, and hyssop.
50 "Then he shall kill one of the birds in an earthen vessel over running water;

14:34 [a]Decomposition by mildew, mold, dry rot, etc., and so in verses 34–53

LIFE LESSONS

➤ **14:33, 34 — *And the LORD spoke to Moses and Aaron, saying: "When you have come into the land of Canaan, which I give you as a possession, and I put the leprous plague in a house in the land of your possession . . . ."***

God is sovereign. Just as the Lord would bring His people into the Promised Land, so would He afflict some houses in the land with mildew and mold. Why? Perhaps so we will trust Him regardless.

51 "and he shall take the cedar wood, the
hyssop, the scarlet, and the living bird, and
dip them in the blood of the slain bird and in
the running water, and sprinkle the house
seven times.
52 "And he shall cleanse the house with the
blood of the bird and the running water and
the living bird, with the cedar wood, the hyssop, and the scarlet.
53 "Then he shall let the living bird loose outside the city in the open field, and make
atonement for the house, and it shall be clean.
54 "This *is* the law for any leprous sore and
scale,
55 "for the leprosy of a garment and of a
house,
56 "for a swelling and a scab and a bright
spot,
57 "to teach when *it is* unclean and when *it is*
clean. This *is* the law of leprosy."

The Law Concerning Bodily Discharges

15 And the LORD spoke to Moses and
Aaron, saying,
2 "Speak to the children of Israel, and say to
them: 'When any man has a discharge from
his body, his discharge *is* unclean.
3 'And this shall be his uncleanness in regard to his discharge—whether his body runs
with his discharge, or his body is stopped up
by his discharge, it *is* his uncleanness.
4 'Every bed is unclean on which he who
has the discharge lies, and everything on
which he sits shall be unclean.
5 'And whoever touches his bed shall wash
his clothes and bathe in water, and be unclean
until evening.
6 'He who sits on anything on which he who
has the discharge sat shall wash his clothes
and bathe in water, and be unclean until
evening.
7 'And he who touches the body of him who
has the discharge shall wash his clothes and
bathe in water, and be unclean until evening.
8 'If he who has the discharge spits on him
who is clean, then he shall wash his clothes
and bathe in water, and be unclean until
evening.
9 'Any saddle on which he who has the discharge rides shall be unclean.
10 'Whoever touches anything that was
under him shall be unclean until evening. He
who carries *any of* those things shall wash his
clothes and bathe in water, and be unclean
until evening.
11 'And whomever the one who has the discharge touches, and has not rinsed his hands
in water, he shall wash his clothes and bathe
in water, and be unclean until evening.
12 'The vessel of earth that he who has the
discharge touches shall be broken, and every
vessel of wood shall be rinsed in water.
13 'And when he who has a discharge is
cleansed of his discharge, then he shall count
for himself seven days for his cleansing, wash
his clothes, and bathe his body in running
water; then he shall be clean.
14 'On the eighth day he shall take for himself two turtledoves or two young pigeons,
and come before the LORD, to the door of the
tabernacle of meeting, and give them to the
priest.
15 'Then the priest shall offer them, the one
as a sin offering and the other *as* a burnt offering. So the priest shall make atonement for
him before the LORD because of his discharge.
16 'If any man has an emission of semen,
then he shall wash all his body in water, and
be unclean until evening.
17 'And any garment and any leather on
which there is semen, it shall be washed with
water, and be unclean until evening.
18 'Also, when a woman lies with a man, and
there is an emission of semen, they shall
bathe in water, and be unclean until evening.
19 'If a woman has a discharge, *and* the discharge from her body is blood, she shall be
set apart seven days; and whoever touches
her shall be unclean until evening.
20 'Everything that she lies on during her impurity shall be unclean; also everything that
she sits on shall be unclean.
21 'Whoever touches her bed shall wash his
clothes and bathe in water, and be unclean
until evening.
22 'And whoever touches anything that she
sat on shall wash his clothes and bathe in
water, and be unclean until evening.
23 'If *anything* is on *her* bed or on anything
on which she sits, when he touches it, he shall
be unclean until evening.
24 'And if any man lies with her at all, so that
her impurity is on him, he shall be unclean
seven days; and every bed on which he lies
shall be unclean.
25 'If a woman has a discharge of blood for
many days, other than at the time of her *customary* impurity, or if it runs beyond her
usual time of impurity, all the days of her unclean discharge shall be as the days of her
customary impurity. She *shall be* unclean.
26 'Every bed on which she lies all the days of
her discharge shall be to her as the bed of her
impurity; and whatever she sits on shall be
unclean, as the uncleanness of her impurity.
27 'Whoever touches those things shall be
unclean; he shall wash his clothes and bathe
in water, and be unclean until evening.
28 'But if she is cleansed of her discharge,
then she shall count for herself seven days,
and after that she shall be clean.
29 'And on the eighth day she shall take for
herself two turtledoves or two young pigeons,
and bring them to the priest, to the door of the
tabernacle of meeting.
30 'Then the priest shall offer the one *as* a sin
offering and the other *as* a burnt offering, and
the priest shall make atonement for her be-

fore the LORD for the discharge of her
uncleanness.
➤ **31** 'Thus you shall separate the children of Israel from their uncleanness, lest they die in
their uncleanness when they defile My tabernacle that *is* among them.
32 'This *is* the law for one who has a discharge, and *for him* who emits semen and is
unclean thereby,
33 'and for her who is indisposed because of
her *customary* impurity, and for one who has
a discharge, either man or woman, and for
him who lies with her who is unclean.'"

The Day of Atonement

16 Now the LORD spoke to Moses after the
death of the two sons of Aaron, when
they offered *profane fire* before the LORD, and
died;
➤ 2 and the LORD said to Moses: "Tell Aaron
your brother not to come at *just* any time into
the Holy *Place* inside the veil, before the
mercy seat which *is* on the ark, lest he die; for
I will appear in the cloud above the mercy
seat.
3 "Thus Aaron shall come into the Holy
Place: with *the blood of* a young bull as a sin
offering, and *of* a ram as a burnt offering.
4 "He shall put the holy linen tunic and the
linen trousers on his body; he shall be girded
with a linen sash, and with the linen turban
he shall be attired. These *are* holy garments.
Therefore he shall wash his body in water,
and put them on.
5 "And he shall take from the congregation
of the children of Israel two kids of the goats
as a sin offering, and one ram as a burnt offering.
6 "Aaron shall offer the bull as a sin offering, which *is* for himself, and make atonement for himself and for his house.
7 "He shall take the two goats and present
them before the LORD *at* the door of the tabernacle of meeting.
8 "Then Aaron shall cast lots for the two
goats: one lot for the LORD and the other lot
for the scapegoat.
9 "And Aaron shall bring the goat on which
the LORD's lot fell, and offer it *as* a sin offering.
10 "But the goat on which the lot fell to be the
scapegoat shall be presented alive before the
LORD, to make atonement upon it, *and* to let it
go as the scapegoat into the wilderness.
11 "And Aaron shall bring the bull of the sin
offering, which is for himself, and make
atonement for himself and for his house, and
shall kill the bull as the sin offering which *is*
for himself.
12 "Then he shall take a censer full of burning coals of fire from the altar before the
LORD, with his hands full of sweet incense
beaten fine, and bring *it* inside the veil.
13 "And he shall put the incense on the fire
before the LORD, that the cloud of incense
may cover the mercy seat that *is* on the Testimony, lest he die.
14 "He shall take some of the blood of the
bull and sprinkle *it* with his finger on the
mercy seat on the east *side;* and before the
mercy seat he shall sprinkle some of the
blood with his finger seven times.
15 "Then he shall kill the goat of the sin offering, which *is* for the people, bring its blood
inside the veil, do with that blood as he did
with the blood of the bull, and sprinkle it on
the mercy seat and before the mercy seat.
16 "So he shall make atonement for the Holy
Place, because of the uncleanness of the children of Israel, and because of their transgressions, for all their sins; and so he shall do for
the tabernacle of meeting which remains
among them in the midst of their uncleanness.
17 "There shall be no man in the tabernacle of
meeting when he goes in to make atonement
in the Holy *Place,* until he comes out, that he
may make atonement for himself, for his
household, and for all the assembly of Israel.
18 "And he shall go out to the altar that *is* before the LORD, and make atonement for it, and
shall take some of the blood of the bull and
some of the blood of the goat, and put it on
the horns of the altar all around.
19 "Then he shall sprinkle some of the blood
on it with his finger seven times, cleanse it,
and consecrate it from the uncleanness of the
children of Israel.
20 "And when he has made an end of atoning
for the Holy *Place,* the tabernacle of meeting,
and the altar, he shall bring the live goat.
21 "Aaron shall lay both his hands on the

LIFE LESSONS

➤ 15:31 — *"Thus you shall separate the children of Israel from their uncleanness, lest they die in their uncleanness when they defile My tabernacle that is among them."*

We may wonder at all of the rules and regulations given to Moses, but it comes down to this: Will we trust God, that He knows best, even when something makes no sense to us?

➤ 16:2 — *. . . and the LORD said to Moses: "Tell Aaron your brother not to come at just any time into the Holy Place inside the veil, before the mercy seat which is on the ark, lest he die; for I will appear in the cloud above the mercy seat."*

It is a holy thing to come into the presence of the Lord. We should never treat it casually or flippantly, as Aaron learned.

head of the live goat, confess over it all the iniquities of the children of Israel, and all their
transgressions, concerning all their sins, putting them on the head of the goat, and shall
send *it* away into the wilderness by the hand
of a suitable man.
22 "The goat shall bear on itself all their iniquities to an uninhabited land; and he shall release the goat in the wilderness.
23 "Then Aaron shall come into the tabernacle of meeting, shall take off the linen garments which he put on when he went into the
Holy *Place,* and shall leave them there.
24 "And he shall wash his body with water in
a holy place, put on his garments, come out
and offer his burnt offering and the burnt offering of the people, and make atonement for
himself and for the people.
25 "The fat of the sin offering he shall burn
on the altar.
26 "And he who released the goat as the
scapegoat shall wash his clothes and bathe
his body in water, and afterward he may come
into the camp.
27 "The bull *for* the sin offering and the goat
for the sin offering, whose blood was brought
in to make atonement in the Holy *Place,* shall
be carried outside the camp. And they shall
burn in the fire their skins, their flesh, and
their offal.
28 "Then he who burns them shall wash his
clothes and bathe his body in water, and afterward he may come into the camp.
➤ **29** "*This* shall be a statute forever for you: In
the seventh month, on the tenth *day* of the
month, you shall afflict your souls, and do no
work at all, *whether* a native of your own
country or a stranger who dwells among you.
30 "For on that day *the priest* shall make
atonement for you, to cleanse you, *that* you
may be clean from all your sins before the
LORD.
31 "It *is* a sabbath of solemn rest for you, and
you shall afflict your souls. *It is* a statute forever.
32 "And the priest, who is anointed and consecrated to minister as priest in his father's
place, shall make atonement, and put on the
linen clothes, the holy garments;
33 "then he shall make atonement for the
Holy Sanctuary,[a] and he shall make atonement for the tabernacle of meeting and for
the altar, and he shall make atonement for the
priests and for all the people of the assembly.
34 "This shall be an everlasting statute for
you, to make atonement for the children of Israel, for all their sins, once a year." And he did
as the LORD commanded Moses.

The Sanctity of Blood

17 And the LORD spoke to Moses, saying,
2 "Speak to Aaron, to his sons, and to
all the children of Israel, and say to them,
'This *is* the thing which the LORD has commanded, saying:
3 "Whatever man of the house of Israel who
kills an ox or lamb or goat in the camp, or
who kills *it* outside the camp,
4 "and does not bring it to the door of the
tabernacle of meeting to offer an offering to
the LORD before the tabernacle of the LORD,
the guilt of bloodshed shall be imputed to that
man. He has shed blood; and that man shall
be cut off from among his people,
5 "to the end that the children of Israel may
bring their sacrifices which they offer in the
open field, that they may bring them to the
LORD at the door of the tabernacle of meeting,
to the priest, and offer them *as* peace offerings to the LORD.
6 "And the priest shall sprinkle the blood on
the altar of the LORD *at* the door of the tabernacle of meeting, and burn the fat for a sweet
aroma to the LORD.
7 "They shall no more offer their sacrifices ◄
to demons, after whom they have played the
harlot. This shall be a statute forever for them
throughout their generations."'
8 "Also you shall say to them: 'Whatever
man of the house of Israel, or of the strangers
who dwell among you, who offers a burnt offering or sacrifice,
9 'and does not bring it to the door of the
tabernacle of meeting, to offer it to the LORD,
that man shall be cut off from among his people.
10 'And whatever man of the house of Israel,

16:33 [a]That is, the Most Holy Place

LIFE LESSONS

➤ **16:29 — *"This shall be a statute forever for you: In the seventh month, on the tenth day of the month, you shall afflict your souls, and do no work at all, whether a native of your own country or a stranger who dwells among you."***

Only on the Day of Atonement was the whole nation of Israel commanded to fast ("afflict your souls"). Fasting helps us to focus not only on the seriousness of our sin, but even more on the treasure of God's forgiveness.

➤ **17:7 — *"They shall no more offer their sacrifices to demons, after whom they have played the harlot. This shall be a statute forever for them throughout their generations."***

To serve and worship other gods is described as spiritual adultery—a detestable unfaithfulness both then and now. As adultery rouses an offended spouse's wrath, so idolatry rouses the anger of God.

or of the strangers who dwell among you, who eats any blood, I will set My face against that person who eats blood, and will cut him off from among his people.

11 'For the life of the flesh *is* in the blood, and I have given it to you upon the altar to make atonement for your souls; for it *is* the blood *that* makes atonement for the soul.'

12 "Therefore I said to the children of Israel, 'No one among you shall eat blood, nor shall any stranger who dwells among you eat blood.'

13 "Whatever man of the children of Israel, or of the strangers who dwell among you, who hunts and catches any animal or bird that may be eaten, he shall pour out its blood and cover it with dust;

14 "for *it is* the life of all flesh. Its blood sustains its life. Therefore I said to the children of Israel, 'You shall not eat the blood of any flesh, for the life of all flesh is its blood. Whoever eats it shall be cut off.'

15 "And every person who eats what died *naturally* or what was torn *by beasts, whether he is* a native of your own country or a stranger, he shall both wash his clothes and bathe in water, and be unclean until evening. Then he shall be clean.

16 "But if he does not wash *them* or bathe his body, then he shall bear his guilt."

Laws of Sexual Morality

18 Then the LORD spoke to Moses, saying, 2 "Speak to the children of Israel, and say to them: 'I am the LORD your God.

3 'According to the doings of the land of Egypt, where you dwelt, you shall not do; and according to the doings of the land of Canaan, where I am bringing you, you shall not do; nor shall you walk in their ordinances.

4 'You shall observe My judgments and keep My ordinances, to walk in them: I *am* the LORD your God.

5 'You shall therefore keep My statutes and My judgments, which if a man does, he shall live by them: I *am* the LORD.

6 'None of you shall approach anyone who is near of kin to him, to uncover his nakedness: I *am* the LORD.

7 'The nakedness of your father or the nakedness of your mother you shall not uncover. She *is* your mother; you shall not uncover her nakedness.

8 'The nakedness of your father's wife you shall not uncover; it *is* your father's nakedness.

9 'The nakedness of your sister, the daughter of your father, or the daughter of your mother, *whether* born at home or elsewhere, their nakedness you shall not uncover.

10 'The nakedness of your son's daughter or your daughter's daughter, their nakedness you shall not uncover; for theirs *is* your own nakedness.

11 'The nakedness of your father's wife's daughter, begotten by your father—she *is* your sister—you shall not uncover her nakedness.

12 'You shall not uncover the nakedness of your father's sister; she *is* near of kin to your father.

13 'You shall not uncover the nakedness of your mother's sister, for she *is* near of kin to your mother.

14 'You shall not uncover the nakedness of your father's brother. You shall not approach his wife; she *is* your aunt.

15 'You shall not uncover the nakedness of your daughter-in-law—she *is* your son's wife—you shall not uncover her nakedness.

16 'You shall not uncover the nakedness of your brother's wife; it *is* your brother's nakedness.

17 'You shall not uncover the nakedness of a woman and her daughter, nor shall you take her son's daughter or her daughter's daughter, to uncover her nakedness. They *are* near of kin to her. It *is* wickedness.

18 'Nor shall you take a woman as a rival to her sister, to uncover her nakedness while the other is alive.

19 'Also you shall not approach a woman to uncover her nakedness as long as she is in her *customary* impurity.

20 'Moreover you shall not lie carnally with your neighbor's wife, to defile yourself with her.

21 'And you shall not let any of your descendants pass through *the fire* to Molech, nor shall you profane the name of your God: I *am* the LORD.

22 'You shall not lie with a male as with a woman. It *is* an abomination.

LIFE LESSONS

➤ 17:11 — *"For the life of the flesh is in the blood, and I have given it to you upon the altar to make atonement for your souls; for it is the blood that makes atonement for the soul."*

Blood was sacred, since it stood for the life of human beings made in God's image. So Christ's blood had to be shed for the salvation of the world (see Rom. 3:25; 5:9; Eph. 1:7).

➤ 18:4 — *"You shall observe My judgments and keep My ordinances, to walk in them: I am the LORD your God."*

We are to be a distinct people who follow the ways of God rather than the ways of the ungodly. When we allow Jesus to live His life through us, we live in the holy way God requires.

23 'Nor shall you mate with any animal, to
defile yourself with it. Nor shall any woman
stand before an animal to mate with it. It *is*
perversion.
24 'Do not defile yourselves with any of these
things; for by all these the nations are defiled,
which I am casting out before you.
25 'For the land is defiled; therefore I visit the
punishment of its iniquity upon it, and the
land vomits out its inhabitants.
26 'You shall therefore keep My statutes and
My judgments, and shall not commit *any* of
these abominations, *either* any of your own
nation or any stranger who dwells among you
27 '(for all these abominations the men of the
land have done, who *were* before you, and
thus the land is defiled),
28 'lest the land vomit you out also when you
defile it, as it vomited out the nations that
were before you.
29 'For whoever commits any of these
abominations, the persons who commit *them*
shall be cut off from among their people.
30 'Therefore you shall keep My ordinance,
so that *you* do not commit *any* of these abominable customs which were committed before
you, and that you do not defile yourselves by
them: I *am* the LORD your God.' "

Moral and Ceremonial Laws

19 And the LORD spoke to Moses, saying,
2 "Speak to all the congregation of
the children of Israel, and say to them: 'You
shall be holy, for I the LORD your God *am*
holy.
3 'Every one of you shall revere his mother
and his father, and keep My Sabbaths: I *am*
the LORD your God.
4 'Do not turn to idols, nor make for yourselves molded gods: I *am* the LORD your God.
5 'And if you offer a sacrifice of a peace offering to the LORD, you shall offer it of your
own free will.
6 'It shall be eaten the same day you offer *it*,
and on the next day. And if any remains until
the third day, it shall be burned in the fire.
7 'And if it is eaten at all on the third day, it
is an abomination. It shall not be accepted.
8 'Therefore *everyone* who eats it shall bear
his iniquity, because he has profaned the hallowed *offering* of the LORD; and that person
shall be cut off from his people.
➤ **9** 'When you reap the harvest of your land,
you shall not wholly reap the corners of your
field, nor shall you gather the gleanings of
your harvest.
10 'And you shall not glean your vineyard,
nor shall you gather *every* grape of your vineyard; you shall leave them for the poor and
the stranger: I *am* the LORD your God.
11 'You shall not steal, nor deal falsely, nor lie
to one another.
12 'And you shall not swear by My name
falsely, nor shall you profane the name of
your God: I *am* the LORD.
13 'You shall not cheat your neighbor, nor
rob *him*. The wages of him who is hired shall
not remain with you all night until morning.
14 'You shall not curse the deaf, nor put a
stumbling block before the blind, but shall
fear your God: I *am* the LORD.
15 'You shall do no injustice in judgment. You
shall not be partial to the poor, nor honor the
person of the mighty. In righteousness you
shall judge your neighbor.
16 'You shall not go about *as* a talebearer
among your people; nor shall you take a
stand against the life of your neighbor: I *am*
the LORD.
17 'You shall not hate your brother in your
heart. You shall surely rebuke your neighbor,
and not bear sin because of him.
18 'You shall not take vengeance, nor bear
any grudge against the children of your people, but you shall love your neighbor as yourself: I *am* the LORD.
19 'You shall keep My statutes. You shall not
let your livestock breed with another kind.
You shall not sow your field with mixed seed.
Nor shall a garment of mixed linen and wool
come upon you.
20 'Whoever lies carnally with a woman who
is betrothed to a man as a concubine, and
who has not at all been redeemed nor given
her freedom, for this there shall be scourging;
but they shall not be put to death, because she
was not free.
21 'And he shall bring his trespass offering to
the LORD, to the door of the tabernacle of
meeting, a ram as a trespass offering.
22 'The priest shall make atonement for him
with the ram of the trespass offering before
the LORD for his sin which he has committed.
And the sin which he has committed shall be
forgiven him.
23 'When you come into the land, and have
planted all kinds of trees for food, then you
shall count their fruit as uncircumcised.

LIFE LESSONS

➤ 19:9, 10 — *"When you reap the harvest of your land, you shall not wholly reap the corners of your field, nor shall you gather the gleanings of your harvest. And you shall not glean your vineyard, nor shall you gather every grape of your vineyard; you shall leave them for the poor and the stranger: I am the LORD your God."*

God has a special concern for the poor and the disadvantaged, and His people are to share His concern for them. The more we become like God, the more we share His concerns.

Three years it shall be as uncircumcised to
you. *It* shall not be eaten.
24 'But in the fourth year all its fruit shall be
holy, a praise to the LORD.
25 'And in the fifth year you may eat its fruit,
that it may yield to you its increase: I *am* the
LORD your God.
26 'You shall not eat *anything* with the blood,
nor shall you practice divination or soothsaying.
27 'You shall not shave around the sides of
your head, nor shall you disfigure the edges
of your beard.
28 'You shall not make any cuttings in your
flesh for the dead, nor tattoo any marks on
you: I *am* the LORD.
29 'Do not prostitute your daughter, to cause
her to be a harlot, lest the land fall into harlotry,
and the land become full of wickedness.
30 'You shall keep My Sabbaths and reverence
My sanctuary: I *am* the LORD.
31 'Give no regard to mediums and familiar
spirits; do not seek after them, to be defiled by
them: I *am* the LORD your God.
➤ **32** 'You shall rise before the gray headed and
honor the presence of an old man, and fear
your God: I *am* the LORD.
33 'And if a stranger dwells with you in your
land, you shall not mistreat him.
34 'The stranger who dwells among you shall
be to you as one born among you, and you shall
love him as yourself; for you were strangers in
the land of Egypt: I *am* the LORD your God.
35 'You shall do no injustice in judgment, in
measurement of length, weight, or volume.
36 'You shall have honest scales, honest
weights, an honest ephah, and an honest hin:
I *am* the LORD your God, who brought you out
of the land of Egypt.
37 'Therefore you shall observe all My
statutes and all My judgments, and perform
them: I *am* the LORD.' "

Penalties for Breaking the Law

20 Then the LORD spoke to Moses, saying,
2 "Again, you shall say to the children
of Israel: 'Whoever of the children of Israel, or
of the strangers who dwell in Israel, who
gives *any* of his descendants to Molech, he
shall surely be put to death. The people of the
land shall stone him with stones.
3 'I will set My face against that man, and
will cut him off from his people, because he
has given *some* of his descendants to Molech,
to defile My sanctuary and profane My holy
name.
4 'And if the people of the land should in
any way hide their eyes from the man, when
he gives *some* of his descendants to Molech,
and they do not kill him,
5 'then I will set My face against that man
and against his family; and I will cut him off
from his people, and all who prostitute themselves
with him to commit harlotry with Molech.
6 'And the person who turns to mediums
and familiar spirits, to prostitute himself with
them, I will set My face against that person
and cut him off from his people.
7 'Consecrate yourselves therefore, and be
holy, for I *am* the LORD your God.
8 'And you shall keep My statutes, and perform
them: I *am* the LORD who sanctifies you.
9 'For everyone who curses his father or his
mother shall surely be put to death. He has
cursed his father or his mother. His blood
shall be upon him.
10 'The man who commits adultery with *another*
man's wife, *he* who commits adultery
with his neighbor's wife, the adulterer and
the adulteress, shall surely be put to death.
11 'The man who lies with his father's wife
has uncovered his father's nakedness; both of
them shall surely be put to death. Their blood
shall be upon them.
12 'If a man lies with his daughter-in-law,
both of them shall surely be put to death.
They have committed perversion. Their blood
shall be upon them.
13 'If a man lies with a male as he lies with a
woman, both of them have committed an
abomination. They shall surely be put to
death. Their blood *shall be* upon them.
14 'If a man marries a woman and her
mother, it *is* wickedness. They shall be burned
with fire, both he and they, that there may be
no wickedness among you.
15 'If a man mates with an animal, he shall
surely be put to death, and you shall kill the
animal.
16 'If a woman approaches any animal and
mates with it, you shall kill the woman and
the animal. They shall surely be put to death.
Their blood *is* upon them.
17 'If a man takes his sister, his father's
daughter or his mother's daughter, and sees
her nakedness and she sees his nakedness, it
is a wicked thing. And they shall be cut off in
the sight of their people. He has uncovered
his sister's nakedness. He shall bear his guilt.
18 'If a man lies with a woman during her
sickness and uncovers her nakedness, he has

LIFE LESSONS

➤ 19:32 — *"You shall rise before the gray headed and honor the presence of an old man, and fear your God: I am the LORD."*

God connects fear of the Lord with honoring the elderly. Those who disrespect the aged in fact slander the Lord.

exposed her flow, and she has uncovered the flow of her blood. Both of them shall be cut off from their people.
19 'You shall not uncover the nakedness of your mother's sister nor of your father's sister, for that would uncover his near of kin. They shall bear their guilt.
20 'If a man lies with his uncle's wife, he has uncovered his uncle's nakedness. They shall bear their sin; they shall die childless.
21 'If a man takes his brother's wife, it *is* an unclean thing. He has uncovered his brother's nakedness. They shall be childless.
22 'You shall therefore keep all My statutes and all My judgments, and perform them, that the land where I am bringing you to dwell may not vomit you out.
23 'And you shall not walk in the statutes of the nation which I am casting out before you; for they commit all these things, and therefore I abhor them.
24 'But I have said to you, "You shall inherit their land, and I will give it to you to possess, a land flowing with milk and honey." I *am* the LORD your God, who has separated you from the peoples.
25 'You shall therefore distinguish between clean animals and unclean, between unclean birds and clean, and you shall not make yourselves abominable by beast or by bird, or by any kind of living thing that creeps on the ground, which I have separated from you as unclean.
➤ 26 'And you shall be holy to Me, for I the LORD *am* holy, and have separated you from the peoples, that you should be Mine.
27 'A man or a woman who is a medium, or who has familiar spirits, shall surely be put to death; they shall stone them with stones. Their blood *shall be* upon them.'"

Regulations for Conduct of Priests

21 And the LORD said to Moses, "Speak to the priests, the sons of Aaron, and say to them: 'None shall defile himself for the dead among his people,
2 'except for his relatives who are nearest to him: his mother, his father, his son, his daughter, and his brother;
3 'also his virgin sister who is near to him, who has had no husband, for her he may defile himself.
4 '*Otherwise* he shall not defile himself, *being* a chief man among his people, to profane himself.
5 'They shall not make any bald *place* on their heads, nor shall they shave the edges of their beards nor make any cuttings in their flesh.
6 'They shall be holy to their God and not profane the name of their God, for they offer the offerings of the LORD made by fire, *and* the bread of their God; therefore they shall be holy.
7 'They shall not take a wife *who is* a harlot or a defiled woman, nor shall they take a woman divorced from her husband; for *the priest*[a] is holy to his God.
8 'Therefore you shall consecrate him, for he offers the bread of your God. He shall be holy to you, for I the LORD, who sanctify you, *am* holy.
9 'The daughter of any priest, if she profanes herself by playing the harlot, she profanes her father. She shall be burned with fire.
10 '*He who is* the high priest among his brethren, on whose head the anointing oil was poured and who is consecrated to wear the garments, shall not uncover his head nor tear his clothes;
11 'nor shall he go near any dead body, nor defile himself for his father or his mother;
12 'nor shall he go out of the sanctuary, nor profane the sanctuary of his God; for the consecration of the anointing oil of his God *is* upon him: I *am* the LORD.
13 'And he shall take a wife in her virginity.
14 'A widow or a divorced woman or a defiled woman *or* a harlot—these he shall not marry; but he shall take a virgin of his own people as wife.
15 'Nor shall he profane his posterity among his people, for I the LORD sanctify him.'"
16 And the LORD spoke to Moses, saying,
17 "Speak to Aaron, saying: 'No man of your descendants in *succeeding* generations, who has *any* defect, may approach to offer the bread of his God.
18 'For any man who has a defect shall not approach: a man blind or lame, who has a marred *face* or any *limb* too long,
19 'a man who has a broken foot or broken hand,
20 'or is a hunchback or a dwarf, or *a man* who has a defect in his eye, or eczema or scab, or is a eunuch.
21 'No man of the descendants of Aaron the priest, who has a defect, shall come near to offer the offerings made by fire to the LORD.

21:7 [a]Literally *he*

LIFE LESSONS

➤ 20:26 — *"And you shall be holy to Me, for I the LORD am holy, and have separated you from the peoples, that you should be Mine."*

It is both a great privilege and an enormous responsibility to belong to the Lord. We cannot have an intimate relationship with God without reflecting His holiness, and intimacy with Him is our highest calling.

He has a defect; he shall not come near to offer the bread of his God.
22 'He may eat the bread of his God, *both* the most holy and the holy;
23 'only he shall not go near the veil or approach the altar, because he has a defect, lest he profane My sanctuaries; for I the LORD sanctify them.'"
24 'And Moses told *it* to Aaron and his sons, and to all the children of Israel.

22 Then the LORD spoke to Moses, saying,
2 "Speak to Aaron and his sons, that they separate themselves from the holy things of the children of Israel, and that they do not profane My holy name *by* what they dedicate to Me: I *am* the LORD.
3 "Say to them: 'Whoever of all your descendants throughout your generations, who goes near the holy things which the children of Israel dedicate to the LORD, while he has uncleanness upon him, that person shall be cut off from My presence: I *am* the LORD.
4 'Whatever man of the descendants of Aaron, who *is* a leper or has a discharge, shall not eat the holy offerings until he is clean. And whoever touches anything made unclean *by* a corpse, or a man who has had an emission of semen,
5 'or whoever touches any creeping thing by which he would be made unclean, or any person by whom he would become unclean, whatever his uncleanness may be—
6 'the person who has touched any such thing shall be unclean until evening, and shall not eat the holy *offerings* unless he washes his body with water.
7 'And when the sun goes down he shall be clean; and afterward he may eat the holy *offerings*, because it *is* his food.
8 'Whatever dies *naturally* or is torn *by beasts* he shall not eat, to defile himself with it: I *am* the LORD.
9 'They shall therefore keep My ordinance, lest they bear sin for it and die thereby, if they profane it: I the LORD sanctify them.
10 'No outsider shall eat the holy *offering*; one who dwells with the priest, or a hired servant, shall not eat the holy thing.
11 'But if the priest buys a person with his money, he may eat it; and one who is born in his house may eat his food.
12 'If the priest's daughter is married to an outsider, she may not eat of the holy offerings.
13 'But if the priest's daughter is a widow or divorced, and has no child, and has returned to her father's house as in her youth, she may eat her father's food; but no outsider shall eat it.
14 'And if a man eats the holy *offering* unintentionally, then he shall restore a holy *offering* to the priest, and add one-fifth to it.
15 'They shall not profane the holy *offerings* of the children of Israel, which they offer to the LORD,
16 'or allow them to bear the guilt of trespass when they eat their holy *offerings*; for I the LORD sanctify them.'"

Offerings Accepted and Not Accepted

17 And the LORD spoke to Moses, saying,
18 "Speak to Aaron and his sons, and to all the children of Israel, and say to them: 'Whatever man of the house of Israel, or of the strangers in Israel, who offers his sacrifice for any of his vows or for any of his freewill offerings, which they offer to the LORD as a burnt offering—
19 '*you shall offer* of your own free will a male without blemish from the cattle, from the sheep, or from the goats.
20 'Whatever has a defect, you shall not offer, for it shall not be acceptable on your behalf.
21 'And whoever offers a sacrifice of a peace offering to the LORD, to fulfill *his* vow, or a freewill offering from the cattle or the sheep, it must be perfect to be accepted; there shall be no defect in it.
22 'Those *that are* blind or broken or maimed, or have an ulcer or eczema or scabs, you shall not offer to the LORD, nor make an offering by fire of them on the altar to the LORD.
23 'Either a bull or a lamb that has any limb too long or too short you may offer *as* a freewill offering, but for a vow it shall not be accepted.
24 'You shall not offer to the LORD what is bruised or crushed, or torn or cut; nor shall you make *any offering of them* in your land.
25 'Nor from a foreigner's hand shall you offer any of these as the bread of your God, because their corruption *is* in them, *and* defects *are* in them. They shall not be accepted on your behalf.'"
26 And the LORD spoke to Moses, saying:
27 "When a bull or a sheep or a goat is born, it shall be seven days with its mother; and from the eighth day and thereafter it shall be accepted as an offering made by fire to the LORD.

LIFE LESSONS

➤ 22:21 — *". . . it must be perfect to be accepted; there shall be no defect in it."*

We are to give our best to the Lord, not our leftovers. We reveal what the Lord means to us by what we freely offer to him. Most of all, He wants our hearts—and in return, He gives us Himself.

28 "*Whether it is* a cow or ewe, do not kill both her and her young on the same day.
29 "And when you offer a sacrifice of thanksgiving to the LORD, offer *it* of your own free will.
30 "On the same day it shall be eaten; you shall leave none of it until morning: I *am* the LORD.
31 "Therefore you shall keep My commandments, and perform them: I *am* the LORD.
32 "You shall not profane My holy name, but I will be hallowed among the children of Israel. I *am* the LORD who sanctifies you,
33 "who brought you out of the land of Egypt, to be your God: I *am* the LORD."

Feasts of the LORD

➤**23** And the LORD spoke to Moses, saying,
2 "Speak to the children of Israel, and say to them: 'The feasts of the LORD, which you shall proclaim *to be* holy convocations, these *are* My feasts.

The Sabbath

3 'Six days shall work be done, but the seventh day *is* a Sabbath of solemn rest, a holy convocation. You shall do no work *on it;* it *is* the Sabbath of the LORD in all your dwellings.

The Passover and Unleavened Bread

4 'These *are* the feasts of the LORD, holy convocations which you shall proclaim at their appointed times.
5 'On the fourteenth *day* of the first month at twilight *is* the LORD's Passover.
6 'And on the fifteenth day of the same month *is* the Feast of Unleavened Bread to the LORD; seven days you must eat unleavened bread.
7 'On the first day you shall have a holy convocation; you shall do no customary work on it.
8 'But you shall offer an offering made by fire to the LORD for seven days. The seventh day *shall be* a holy convocation; you shall do no customary work *on it.*' "

The Feast of Firstfruits

9 And the LORD spoke to Moses, saying,
10 "Speak to the children of Israel, and say to them: 'When you come into the land which I give to you, and reap its harvest, then you shall bring a sheaf of the firstfruits of your harvest to the priest.
11 'He shall wave the sheaf before the LORD, to be accepted on your behalf; on the day after the Sabbath the priest shall wave it.
12 'And you shall offer on that day, when you wave the sheaf, a male lamb of the first year, without blemish, as a burnt offering to the LORD.
13 'Its grain offering *shall be* two-tenths *of an ephah* of fine flour mixed with oil, an offering made by fire to the LORD, for a sweet aroma; and its drink offering *shall be* of wine, one-fourth of a hin.
14 'You shall eat neither bread nor parched grain nor fresh grain until the same day that you have brought an offering to your God; *it shall be* a statute forever throughout your generations in all your dwellings.

The Feast of Weeks

15 'And you shall count for yourselves from the day after the Sabbath, from the day that you brought the sheaf of the wave offering: seven Sabbaths shall be completed.
16 'Count fifty days to the day after the seventh Sabbath; then you shall offer a new grain offering to the LORD.
17 'You shall bring from your dwellings two wave *loaves* of two-tenths *of an ephah.* They shall be of fine flour; they shall be baked with leaven. *They are* the firstfruits to the LORD.
18 'And you shall offer with the bread seven lambs of the first year, without blemish, one young bull, and two rams. They shall be *as* a burnt offering to the LORD, with their grain offering and their drink offerings, an offering made by fire for a sweet aroma to the LORD.
19 'Then you shall sacrifice one kid of the goats as a sin offering, and two male lambs of the first year as a sacrifice of a peace offering.
20 'The priest shall wave them with the bread of the firstfruits *as* a wave offering before the LORD, with the two lambs. They shall be holy to the LORD for the priest.
21 'And you shall proclaim on the same day *that* it is a holy convocation to you. You shall do no customary work *on it. It shall be* a statute forever in all your dwellings throughout your generations.
22 'When you reap the harvest of your land, you shall not wholly reap the corners of your field when you reap, nor shall you gather any gleaning from your harvest. You shall leave them for the poor and for the stranger: I *am* the LORD your God.' "

The Feast of Trumpets

23 Then the LORD spoke to Moses, saying,
24 "Speak to the children of Israel, saying: 'In the seventh month, on the first *day* of the

LIFE LESSONS

➤ 23:2 — *"Speak to the children of Israel, and say to them: 'The feasts of the LORD, which you shall proclaim to be holy convocations, these are My feasts.'"*

It is important to God that His people regularly come together to celebrate His goodness and provision. Something happens in community that cannot happen in solitude.

month, you shall have a sabbath-*rest*, a memorial of blowing of trumpets, a holy convocation.
25 'You shall do no customary work *on it;* and you shall offer an offering made by fire to the LORD.'"

The Day of Atonement
26 And the LORD spoke to Moses, saying:
27 "Also the tenth *day* of this seventh month *shall be* the Day of Atonement. It shall be a holy convocation for you; you shall afflict your souls, and offer an offering made by fire to the LORD.
28 "And you shall do no work on that same day, for it *is* the Day of Atonement, to make atonement for you before the LORD your God.
29 "For any person who is not afflicted *in soul* on that same day shall be cut off from his people.
30 "And any person who does any work on that same day, that person I will destroy from among his people.
31 "You shall do no manner of work; *it shall be* a statute forever throughout your generations in all your dwellings.
32 "It *shall be* to you a sabbath of *solemn* rest, and you shall afflict your souls; on the ninth *day* of the month at evening, from evening to evening, you shall celebrate your sabbath."

The Feast of Tabernacles
33 Then the LORD spoke to Moses, saying,
34 "Speak to the children of Israel, saying: 'The fifteenth day of this seventh month *shall be* the Feast of Tabernacles *for* seven days to the LORD.
35 'On the first day *there shall be* a holy convocation. You shall do no customary work *on it.*
36 '*For* seven days you shall offer an offering made by fire to the LORD. On the eighth day you shall have a holy convocation, and you shall offer an offering made by fire to the LORD. It *is* a sacred assembly, *and* you shall do no customary work *on it.*
37 'These *are* the feasts of the LORD which you shall proclaim *to be* holy convocations, to offer an offering made by fire to the LORD, a burnt offering and a grain offering, a sacrifice and drink offerings, everything on its day—
38 'besides the Sabbaths of the LORD, besides your gifts, besides all your vows, and besides all your freewill offerings which you give to the LORD.
39 'Also on the fifteenth day of the seventh month, when you have gathered in the fruit of the land, you shall keep the feast of the LORD *for* seven days; on the first day *there shall be* a sabbath-*rest*, and on the eighth day a sabbath-*rest*.
40 'And you shall take for yourselves on the first day the fruit of beautiful trees, branches of palm trees, the boughs of leafy trees, and willows of the brook; and you shall rejoice before the LORD your God for seven days.
41 'You shall keep it as a feast to the LORD for seven days in the year. *It shall be* a statute forever in your generations. You shall celebrate it in the seventh month.
42 'You shall dwell in booths for seven days. All who are native Israelites shall dwell in booths,
43 'that your generations may know that I made the children of Israel dwell in booths when I brought them out of the land of Egypt: I *am* the LORD your God.'"
44 So Moses declared to the children of Israel the feasts of the LORD.

Care of the Tabernacle Lamps
24 Then the LORD spoke to Moses, saying:
2 "Command the children of Israel that they bring to you pure oil of pressed olives for the light, to make the lamps burn continually.
3 "Outside the veil of the Testimony, in the tabernacle of meeting, Aaron shall be in charge of it from evening until morning before the LORD continually; *it shall be* a statute forever in your generations.
4 "He shall be in charge of the lamps on the pure *gold* lampstand before the LORD continually.

The Bread of the Tabernacle
5 "And you shall take fine flour and bake twelve cakes with it. Two-tenths *of an ephah* shall be in each cake.
6 "You shall set them in two rows, six in a row, on the pure *gold* table before the LORD.
7 "And you shall put pure frankincense on *each* row, that it may be on the bread for a memorial, an offering made by fire to the LORD.
8 "Every Sabbath he shall set it in order before the LORD continually, *being taken* from the children of Israel by an everlasting covenant.
9 "And it shall be for Aaron and his sons, and they shall eat it in a holy place; for it *is* most holy to him from the offerings of the LORD made by fire, by a perpetual statute."

The Penalty for Blasphemy
10 Now the son of an Israelite woman, whose father *was* an Egyptian, went out among the children of Israel; and this Israelite *woman's* son and a man of Israel fought each other in the camp.
11 And the Israelite woman's son blasphemed the name *of the LORD* and cursed; and so they brought him to Moses. (His mother's name *was* Shelomith the daughter of Dibri, of the tribe of Dan.)

➤ 12 Then they put him in custody, that the mind of the LORD might be shown to them.
13 And the LORD spoke to Moses, saying,
14 "Take outside the camp him who has cursed; then let all who heard *him* lay their hands on his head, and let all the congregation stone him.
15 "Then you shall speak to the children of Israel, saying: 'Whoever curses his God shall bear his sin.
16 'And whoever blasphemes the name of the LORD shall surely be put to death. All the congregation shall certainly stone him, the stranger as well as him who is born in the land. When he blasphemes the name *of the LORD*, he shall be put to death.
17 'Whoever kills any man shall surely be put to death.
18 'Whoever kills an animal shall make it good, animal for animal.
19 'If a man causes disfigurement of his neighbor, as he has done, so shall it be done to him—
20 'fracture for fracture, eye for eye, tooth for tooth; as he has caused disfigurement of a man, so shall it be done to him.
21 'And whoever kills an animal shall restore it; but whoever kills a man shall be put to death.
22 'You shall have the same law for the stranger and for one from your own country; for I *am* the LORD your God.'"
23 Then Moses spoke to the children of Israel; and they took outside the camp him who had cursed, and stoned him with stones. So the children of Israel did as the LORD commanded Moses.

The Sabbath of the Seventh Year

25 And the LORD spoke to Moses on Mount Sinai, saying,
2 "Speak to the children of Israel, and say to them: 'When you come into the land which I give you, then the land shall keep a sabbath to the LORD.
3 'Six years you shall sow your field, and six years you shall prune your vineyard, and gather its fruit;
4 'but in the seventh year there shall be a sabbath of solemn rest for the land, a sabbath to the LORD. You shall neither sow your field nor prune your vineyard.
5 'What grows of its own accord of your harvest you shall not reap, nor gather the grapes of your untended vine, *for* it is a year of rest for the land.
6 'And the sabbath *produce* of the land shall be food for you: for you, your male and female servants, your hired man, and the stranger who dwells with you,
7 'for your livestock and the beasts that *are* in your land—all its produce shall be for food.

The Year of Jubilee

8 'And you shall count seven sabbaths of years for yourself, seven times seven years; and the time of the seven sabbaths of years shall be to you forty-nine years.
9 'Then you shall cause the trumpet of the Jubilee to sound on the tenth *day* of the seventh month; on the Day of Atonement you shall make the trumpet to sound throughout all your land.
10 'And you shall consecrate the fiftieth year, and proclaim liberty throughout *all* the land to all its inhabitants. It shall be a Jubilee for you; and each of you shall return to his possession, and each of you shall return to his family.
11 'That fiftieth year shall be a Jubilee to you; in it you shall neither sow nor reap what grows of its own accord, nor gather *the grapes* of your untended vine.
12 'For it *is* the Jubilee; it shall be holy to you; you shall eat its produce from the field.
13 'In this Year of Jubilee, each of you shall return to his possession.
14 'And if you sell anything to your neighbor or buy from your neighbor's hand, you shall not oppress one another.
15 'According to the number of years after the Jubilee you shall buy from your neighbor, and according to the number of years of crops he shall sell to you.
16 'According to the multitude of years you shall increase its price, and according to the fewer number of years you shall diminish its price; for he sells to you *according* to the number *of the years* of the crops.
17 'Therefore you shall not oppress one another, but you shall fear your God; for I *am* the LORD your God.

Provisions for the Seventh Year

18 'So you shall observe My statutes and keep My judgments, and perform them; and you will dwell in the land in safety.
19 'Then the land will yield its fruit, and you will eat your fill, and dwell there in safety.
20 'And if you say, "What shall we eat in the seventh year, since we shall not sow nor gather in our produce?"

LIFE LESSONS

➤ 24:12 — *Then they put him in custody, that the mind of the LORD might be shown to them.*

It is always wise to wait to act until we can learn the mind of the Lord. If we truly want to know God's will, He will move heaven and earth to show it to us.

➤ 21 'Then I will command My blessing on you
in the sixth year, and it will bring forth produce enough for three years.
22 'And you shall sow in the eighth year, and
eat old produce until the ninth year; until its
produce comes in, you shall eat *of* the old *har-*
vest.

Redemption of Property

23 'The land shall not be sold permanently,
for the land *is* Mine; for you *are* strangers and
sojourners with Me.
24 'And in all the land of your possession you
shall grant redemption of the land.
25 'If one of your brethren becomes poor, and
has sold *some* of his possession, and if his redeeming relative comes to redeem it, then he
may redeem what his brother sold.
26 'Or if the man has no one to redeem it, but
he himself becomes able to redeem it,
27 'then let him count the years since its sale,
and restore the remainder to the man to
whom he sold it, that he may return to his
possession.
28 'But if he is not able to have *it* restored
to himself, then what was sold shall remain
in the hand of him who bought it until the
Year of Jubilee; and in the Jubilee it shall be
released, and he shall return to his possession.
29 'If a man sells a house in a walled city,
then he may redeem it within a whole year
after it is sold; *within* a full year he may redeem it.
30 'But if it is not redeemed within the space
of a full year, then the house in the walled city
shall belong permanently to him who bought
it, throughout his generations. It shall not be
released in the Jubilee.
31 'However the houses of villages which
have no wall around them shall be counted as
the fields of the country. They may be redeemed, and they shall be released in the Jubilee.
32 'Nevertheless the cities of the Levites, *and*
the houses in the cities of their possession,
the Levites may redeem at any time.
33 'And if a man purchases a house from the
Levites, then the house that was sold in
the city of his possession shall be released in
the Jubilee; for the houses in the cities of the
Levites *are* their possession among the children of Israel.
34 'But the field of the common-land of their
cities may not be sold, for it *is* their perpetual
possession.

Lending to the Poor

35 'If one of your brethren becomes poor, and
falls into poverty among you, then you shall
help him, like a stranger or a sojourner, that
he may live with you.
36 'Take no usury or interest from him; but
fear your God, that your brother may live
with you.
37 'You shall not lend him your money for
usury, nor lend him your food at a profit.
38 'I *am* the LORD your God, who brought you
out of the land of Egypt, to give you the land
of Canaan *and* to be your God.

The Law Concerning Slavery

39 'And if *one of* your brethren *who dwells* by
you becomes poor, and sells himself to you,
you shall not compel him to serve as a slave.
40 'As a hired servant *and* a sojourner he
shall be with you, *and* shall serve you until
the Year of Jubilee.
41 'And *then* he shall depart from you—he
and his children with him—and shall return
to his own family. He shall return to the possession of his fathers.
42 'For they *are* My servants, whom I brought
out of the land of Egypt; they shall not be sold
as slaves.
43 'You shall not rule over him with rigor, but
you shall fear your God.
44 'And as for your male and female slaves
whom you may have—from the nations that
are around you, from them you may buy male
and female slaves.
45 'Moreover you may buy the children of the
strangers who dwell among you, and their
families who are with you, which they beget
in your land; and they shall become your
property.
46 'And you may take them as an inheritance
for your children after you, to inherit *them as*
a possession; they shall be your permanent
slaves. But regarding your brethren, the children of Israel, you shall not rule over one another with rigor.
47 'Now if a sojourner or stranger close to
you becomes rich, and *one of* your brethren
who dwells by him becomes poor, and sells
himself to the stranger *or* sojourner close to
you, or to a member of the stranger's family,
48 'after he is sold he may be redeemed
again. One of his brothers may redeem him;
49 'or his uncle or his uncle's son may redeem him; or *anyone* who is near of kin to
him in his family may redeem him; or if he is
able he may redeem himself.

LIFE LESSONS

➤ ***25:21 — "Then I will command My blessing on you in the sixth year, and it will bring forth produce enough for three years."***

The Lord commands His blessing to descend on those who choose to obey Him.

ANSWERS TO LIFE'S QUESTIONS

What does it mean to live in "the fear of the Lord"?

LEV. 25:36

There are several practical manifestations of a life lived in "the fear of the Lord."

1. ***Obedience to God's commandments***
   The Lord has given us very specific commandments in his Word, and He expects us to keep those commandments *without regard to circumstances or situations.* No matter what others may say in offering us an alluring, good-sounding "alternative plan" to God's commandments, we must never choose to follow their advice. Plans or schemes of man's design may seem prudent and wise, but God tells us, "There is a way that seems right to a man, but its end is the way of death" (Prov. 14:12). God's Word is very clear. The problem most Christians have is not that they do not *understand* God's standards for right and wrong, but that they choose not to *obey* what He has said.
2. ***A desire to be like Jesus***
   Those who truly love Jesus as their Savior and Lord will want to be like Him. How did Jesus live? Jesus lived in complete obedience to His Father. He did only what the Father instructed Him to do; He spoke only what the Father prompted Him to say. What Jesus did, we are to do—not to the "best of our ability," but to the best of the Holy Spirit's ability within us! The Holy Spirit empowers us to live as Jesus lived. It is our responsibility to ask the Holy Spirit to guide, help, counsel, and give us the ability to obey. The more we allow the Holy Spirit to work in us and through us, the more we gain the ability to live like Jesus.
3. ***A life of courage***
   Those who fear mankind and natural disaster suffer a panic that paralyzes. Those who fear the Lord with a holy awe, on the other hand, find a courage that mobilizes them to act. God challenges His people to live in confidence and to respond boldly and courageously to life. Such "heroes of the faith" as Moses, Joshua, and the apostles Peter and Paul faced incredible challenges, yet they succeeded because of their God-given courage. They learned the same lesson that emboldened Ezra to say, ". . . So I was encouraged, as the hand of the LORD my God was upon me . . ." (Ezra 7:28).

See the Life Principles Index for further study:
2. Obey God and leave all the consequences to Him.
24. To live the Christian life is to allow Jesus to live His life in and through us.

50 'Thus he shall reckon with him who bought him: The price of his release shall be according to the number of years, from the year that he was sold to him until the Year of Jubilee; *it shall be* according to the time of a hired servant for him.
51 'If *there are* still many years *remaining,* according to them he shall repay the price of his redemption from the money with which he was bought.
52 'And if there remain but a few years until the Year of Jubilee, then he shall reckon with him, *and* according to his years he shall repay him the price of his redemption.
53 'He shall be with him as a yearly hired servant, and he shall not rule with rigor over him in your sight.
54 'And if he is not redeemed in these *years,* then he shall be released in the Year of Jubilee—he and his children with him.
55 'For the children of Israel *are* servants to ➤
Me; they *are* My servants whom I brought out of the land of Egypt: I *am* the LORD your God.

Promise of Blessing and Retribution

26 'You shall not make idols for yourselves;
neither a carved image nor a *sacred* pillar shall you rear up for yourselves;
nor shall you set up an engraved stone in your land, to bow down to it;
for I *am* the LORD your God.
2 You shall keep My Sabbaths and reverence My sanctuary:
I *am* the LORD.

LIFE LESSONS

➤ 25:55 — *"For the children of Israel are servants to Me; they are My servants whom I brought out of the land of Egypt: I am the LORD your God."*

We are not only children of God, we are His servants. The one speaks of privilege, the other of duty. Both are ours in Christ.

✳ **3** 'If you walk in My statutes and keep My
commandments, and perform them,
4 then I will give you rain in its season, the
land shall yield its produce, and the
trees of the field shall yield their fruit.
5 Your threshing shall last till the time of
vintage, and the vintage shall last till
the time of sowing;
you shall eat your bread to the full, and
dwell in your land safely.
6 I will give peace in the land, and you
shall lie down, and none will make
you afraid;
I will rid the land of evil beasts,
and the sword will not go through your
land.
7 You will chase your enemies, and they
shall fall by the sword before you.
8 Five of you shall chase a hundred, and a
hundred of you shall put ten thousand
to flight;
your enemies shall fall by the sword
before you.
9 'For I will look on you favorably and
make you fruitful, multiply you and
confirm My covenant with you.
10 You shall eat the old harvest, and clear
out the old because of the new.
11 I will set My tabernacle among you, and
My soul shall not abhor you.
➤ 12 I will walk among you and be your God,
and you shall be My people.
13 I *am* the LORD your God, who brought
you out of the land of Egypt, that *you*
should not be their slaves;
I have broken the bands of your yoke and
made you walk upright.

14 'But if you do not obey Me, and do not
observe all these commandments,
15 and if you despise My statutes, or if your
soul abhors My judgments, so that
you do not perform all My
commandments, *but* break My
covenant,
16 I also will do this to you:
I will even appoint terror over you,
wasting disease and fever which shall
consume the eyes and cause sorrow of
heart.
And you shall sow your seed in vain, for
your enemies shall eat it.
17 I will set My face against you, and you
shall be defeated by your enemies.
Those who hate you shall reign over you,
and you shall flee when no one
pursues you.

18 'And after all this, if you do not obey Me,
then I will punish you seven times
more for your sins.
19 I will break the pride of your power;
I will make your heavens like iron and
your earth like bronze.
20 And your strength shall be spent in vain;
for your land shall not yield its produce,
nor shall the trees of the land yield
their fruit.

21 'Then, if you walk contrary to Me, and
are not willing to obey Me, I will
bring on you seven times more
plagues, according to your sins.
22 I will also send wild beasts among you,
which shall rob you of your children,
destroy your livestock, and make you
few in number;
and your highways shall be desolate.

23 'And if by these things you are not reformed by Me, but walk contrary to Me,
24 then I also will walk contrary to you, and
I will punish you yet seven times for
your sins.
25 And I will bring a sword against you that
will execute the vengeance of the
covenant;
when you are gathered together within
your cities I will send pestilence
among you;
and you shall be delivered into the hand
of the enemy.
26 When I have cut off your supply of bread,
ten women shall bake your bread in
one oven, and they shall bring back
your bread by weight, and you shall
eat and not be satisfied.

27 'And after all this, if you do not obey Me,
but walk contrary to Me,
28 then I also will walk contrary to you in
fury;
and I, even I, will chastise you seven
times for your sins.
29 You shall eat the flesh of your sons, and
you shall eat the flesh of your
daughters.
30 I will destroy your high places, cut down
your incense altars, and cast your
carcasses on the lifeless forms of your
idols;
and My soul shall abhor you.

LIFE LESSONS

➤ **26:12 — *"I will walk among you and be your God, and you shall be My people."***

God's greatest desire since the beginning of creation is to be with us, His people, and to bless us. God not only desires to be in the closest, most intimate relationship possible with His people, but He promises to do so.

31 I will lay your cities waste and bring your
sanctuaries to desolation, and I will
not smell the fragrance of your sweet
aromas.
32 I will bring the land to desolation, and
your enemies who dwell in it shall be
astonished at it.
33 I will scatter you among the nations and
draw out a sword after you;
your land shall be desolate and your
cities waste.
34 Then the land shall enjoy its sabbaths as
long as it lies desolate and you *are* in
your enemies' land;
then the land shall rest and enjoy its
sabbaths.
35 As long as *it* lies desolate it shall rest—
for the time it did not rest on your
sabbaths when you dwelt in it.

36 'And as for those of you who are left, I
will send faintness into their hearts in
the lands of their enemies;
the sound of a shaken leaf shall cause
them to flee;
they shall flee as though fleeing from a
sword, and they shall fall when no
one pursues.
37 They shall stumble over one another, as it
were before a sword, when no one
pursues;
and you shall have no *power* to stand
before your enemies.
38 You shall perish among the nations, and
the land of your enemies shall eat you
up.
39 And those of you who are left shall waste
away in their iniquity in your
enemies' lands;
also in their fathers' iniquities, which are
with them, they shall waste away.

40 '*But* if they confess their iniquity and the
iniquity of their fathers, with their
unfaithfulness in which they were
unfaithful to Me, and that they also
have walked contrary to Me,
41 and *that* I also have walked contrary to
them and have brought them into the
land of their enemies;
if their uncircumcised hearts are humbled,
and they accept their guilt—
42 then I will remember My covenant with
Jacob, and My covenant with Isaac
and My covenant with Abraham I will
remember;
I will remember the land.
43 The land also shall be left empty by
them, and will enjoy its sabbaths
while it lies desolate without them;
they will accept their guilt, because they
despised My judgments and because
their soul abhorred My statutes.
44 Yet for all that, when they are in the land
of their enemies, I will not cast them
away, nor shall I abhor them, to
utterly destroy them and break My
covenant with them;
for I *am* the LORD their God.
45 But for their sake I will remember the
covenant of their ancestors, whom I
brought out of the land of Egypt in
the sight of the nations, that I might
be their God:
I *am* the LORD.'"

46 These *are* the statutes and judgments and
laws which the LORD made between Himself
and the children of Israel on Mount Sinai by
the hand of Moses.

Redeeming Persons and Property Dedicated to God

27 Now the LORD spoke to Moses, saying,
2 "Speak to the children of Israel, and
say to them: 'When a man consecrates by a
vow certain persons to the LORD, according to
your valuation,
3 'if your valuation is of a male from twenty
years old up to sixty years old, then your valuation shall be fifty shekels of silver, according to the shekel of the sanctuary.
4 'If it *is* a female, then your valuation shall
be thirty shekels;
5 'and if from five years old up to twenty
years old, then your valuation for a male shall
be twenty shekels, and for a female ten
shekels;
6 'and if from a month old up to five years
old, then your valuation for a male shall be
five shekels of silver, and for a female your
valuation shall be three shekels of silver;
7 'and if from sixty years old and above, if *it
is* a male, then your valuation shall be fifteen
shekels, and for a female ten shekels.
8 'But if he is too poor to pay your valuation,
then he shall present himself before the
priest, and the priest shall set a value for him;
according to the ability of him who vowed,
the priest shall value him.
9 'If *it is* an animal that men may bring as
an offering to the LORD, all that *anyone* gives
to the LORD shall be holy.
10 'He shall not substitute it or exchange it,
good for bad or bad for good; and if he at all
exchanges animal for animal, then both it and
the one exchanged for it shall be holy.
11 'If *it is* an unclean animal which they do
not offer as a sacrifice to the LORD, then he
shall present the animal before the priest;
12 'and the priest shall set a value for it,
whether it is good or bad; as you, the priest,
value it, so it shall be.
13 'But if he *wants* at all *to* redeem it, then he
must add one-fifth to your valuation.
14 'And when a man dedicates his house *to
be* holy to the LORD, then the priest shall set a
value for it, whether it is good or bad; as the
priest values it, so it shall stand.

15 'If he who dedicated it *wants to* redeem his house, then he must add one-fifth of the money of your valuation to it, and it shall be his.
16 'If a man dedicates to the LORD *part* of a field of his possession, then your valuation shall be according to the seed for it. A homer of barley seed *shall be valued* at fifty shekels of silver.
17 'If he dedicates his field from the Year of Jubilee, according to your valuation it shall stand.
18 'But if he dedicates his field after the Jubilee, then the priest shall reckon to him the money due according to the years that remain till the Year of Jubilee, and it shall be deducted from your valuation.
19 'And if he who dedicates the field ever wishes to redeem it, then he must add one-fifth of the money of your valuation to it, and it shall belong to him.
20 'But if he does not want to redeem the field, or if he has sold the field to another man, it shall not be redeemed anymore;
21 'but the field, when it is released in the Jubilee, shall be holy to the LORD, as a devoted field; it shall be the possession of the priest.
22 'And if a man dedicates to the LORD a field which he has bought, which is not the field of his possession,
23 'then the priest shall reckon to him the worth of your valuation, up to the Year of Jubilee, and he shall give your valuation on that day *as* a holy *offering* to the LORD.
24 'In the Year of Jubilee the field shall return to him from whom it was bought, to the one who *owned* the land as a possession.
25 'And all your valuations shall be according to the shekel of the sanctuary: twenty gerahs to the shekel.
26 'But the firstborn of the animals, which should be the LORD's firstborn, no man shall dedicate; whether *it is* an ox or sheep, it *is* the LORD's.
27 'And if *it is* an unclean animal, then he shall redeem *it* according to your valuation, and shall add one-fifth to it; or if it is not redeemed, then it shall be sold according to your valuation.
28 'Nevertheless no devoted *offering* that a man may devote to the LORD of all that he has, *both* man and beast, or the field of his possession, shall be sold or redeemed; every devoted *offering is* most holy to the LORD.
29 'No person under the ban, who may become doomed to destruction among men, shall be redeemed, *but* shall surely be put to death.
30 'And all the tithe of the land, *whether* of the seed of the land *or* of the fruit of the tree, *is* the LORD's. It *is* holy to the LORD.
31 'If a man wants at all to redeem *any* of his tithes, he shall add one-fifth to it.
32 'And concerning the tithe of the herd or the flock, of whatever passes under the rod, the tenth one shall be holy to the LORD.
33 'He shall not inquire whether it is good or bad, nor shall he exchange it; and if he exchanges it at all, then both it and the one exchanged for it shall be holy; it shall not be redeemed.' "
34 These *are* the commandments which the LORD commanded Moses for the children of Israel on Mount Sinai.

THE FOURTH BOOK OF MOSES CALLED

NUMBERS

The title of Numbers comes from the Greek name given to it in the Septuagint, *Arithmoi* ("Numbers"). The Latin Vulgate followed this title and translated it *Liber Numeri*, "Book of Numbers." These titles are based on the two numberings of the Israelites described in the book—the first at Mount Sinai (Num. 1) and the second on the plains of Moab (Num. 26). Numbers also has been called the "Book of the Journeyings," the "Book of the Murmurings," and the "Fourth Book of Moses."

Most of the book describes Israel's experience as the contentious people wander in the wilderness. What originally was to be an eleven-day journey for Israel became a forty-year agony. Thus the book provides a clear lesson: While it may be necessary to pass through the wilderness, you do not have to live there.

Numbers teaches us that God will allow us to go through prolonged wilderness experiences, not only in order to get our attention, but also to change our thinking or behavior. It isn't enough merely to engage in self-examination. We can see a problem and know ourselves thoroughly, but unless we change our response to God in some way, we will never benefit fully from our wilderness experiences or grow as a result of them.

If, on the other hand, we are willing to allow God to use our wilderness experiences to surface the inner rubbish of our lives, and if we are willing to change what needs to be changed, we will emerge from the desert much closer to our heavenly Father, more mature as His child, and with far greater potential to reflect the love of God to the world around us. This is the great lesson of the Book of Numbers.

Theme: Numbers demonstrates that wrong choices bring specific consequences, some of them very painful. When the first generation of Israelites that left Egypt rebelled against God and sinned against His law, its members were forced to spend years wandering in the wilderness—though God intended for His obedient people to spend those years in the Promised Land.

Author: Moses

Time: The events recorded in the Book of Numbers began about one year after the exodus from Egypt (c. 1446 B.C.).

Structure: The first ten chapters of Numbers contain legal instructions and record a census (or "numbering") of the people of Israel. The remainder of the book records the Israelites' wandering in the wilderness, as well as their complaints and rebellion against God and their leader, Moses.

As you read Numbers, watch for several life principles that play an important part in this book:

5. God does not require us to understand His will, just obey it, even if it seems unreasonable. *See Numbers 11:10–23; page 161.*

9. Trusting God means looking beyond what we can see to what God sees. *See Numbers 13:1–30; page 163.*

21. Obedience always brings blessing. *See Numbers 14:18–24; page 165.*

6. You reap what you sow, more than you sow, and later than you sow. *See Numbers 14:26–38; page 166.*

3. God's Word is an immovable anchor in times of storm. *See Numbers 23:19; page 177.*

The First Census of Israel

1 Now the LORD spoke to Moses in the
Wilderness of Sinai, in the tabernacle of
meeting, on the first *day* of the second month,
in the second year after they had come out of
the land of Egypt, saying:
2 "Take a census of all the congregation of
the children of Israel, by their families, by
their fathers' houses, according to the number of names, every male individually,
3 "from twenty years old and above—all
who *are able to* go to war in Israel. You and
Aaron shall number them by their armies.
4 "And with you there shall be a man from
every tribe, each one the head of his father's
house.
5 "These are the names of the men who
shall stand with you: from Reuben, Elizur the
son of Shedeur;
6 "from Simeon, Shelumiel the son of Zurishaddai;
7 "from Judah, Nahshon the son of Amminadab;
8 "from Issachar, Nethanel the son of Zuar;
9 "from Zebulun, Eliab the son of Helon;
10 "from the sons of Joseph: from Ephraim,
Elishama the son of Ammihud; from Manasseh, Gamaliel the son of Pedahzur;
11 "from Benjamin, Abidan the son of
Gideoni;
12 "from Dan, Ahiezer the son of Ammishaddai;
13 "from Asher, Pagiel the son of Ocran;
14 "from Gad, Eliasaph the son of Deuel;[a]
15 "from Naphtali, Ahira the son of Enan."
16 These *were* chosen from the congregation,
leaders of their fathers' tribes, heads of the
divisions in Israel.
17 Then Moses and Aaron took these men
who had been mentioned by name,
18 and they assembled all the congregation
together on the first *day* of the second month;
and they recited their ancestry by families, by
their fathers' houses, according to the number of names, from twenty years old and
above, each one individually.
19 As the LORD commanded Moses, so he
numbered them in the Wilderness of Sinai.
20 Now the children of Reuben, Israel's oldest son, their genealogies by their families, by
their fathers' house, according to the number
of names, every male individually, from
twenty years old and above, all who *were able
to* go to war:
21 those who were numbered of the tribe of
Reuben *were* forty-six thousand five hundred.
22 From the children of Simeon, their genealogies by their families, by their fathers'
house, of those who were numbered, according to the number of names, every male individually, from twenty years old and above, all
who *were able to* go to war:
23 those who were numbered of the tribe of
Simeon *were* fifty-nine thousand three hundred.
24 From the children of Gad, their genealogies by their families, by their fathers' house,
according to the number of names, from
twenty years old and above, all who *were able
to* go to war:
25 those who were numbered of the tribe of
Gad *were* forty-five thousand six hundred
and fifty.
26 From the children of Judah, their genealogies by their families, by their fathers' house,
according to the number of names, from
twenty years old and above, all who *were able
to* go to war:
27 those who were numbered of the tribe of
Judah *were* seventy-four thousand six hundred.
28 From the children of Issachar, their genealogies by their families, by their fathers'
house, according to the number of names,
from twenty years old and above, all who
were able to go to war:
29 those who were numbered of the tribe of
Issachar *were* fifty-four thousand four hundred.
30 From the children of Zebulun, their genealogies by their families, by their fathers'
house, according to the number of names,
from twenty years old and above, all who
were able to go to war:
31 those who were numbered of the tribe of
Zebulun *were* fifty-seven thousand four hundred.
32 From the sons of Joseph, the children of
Ephraim, their genealogies by their families,
by their fathers' house, according to the num-

1:14 [a]Spelled *Reuel* in 2:14

LIFE LESSONS

➤ 1:1 — *Now the LORD spoke to Moses in the Wilderness of Sinai, in the tabernacle of meeting, on the first day of the second month, in the second year after they had come out of the land of Egypt . . . .*

God speaks to us at specific times, in specific places, about specific things. Listening to what He says is essential to walking with Him.

➤ 1:17 — *. . . Moses and Aaron took these men who had been mentioned by name . . . .*

God calls us *by name* into His service. He knows the gifts, abilities and backgrounds of each one of us, and by His Spirit He places us in exactly the right spots to serve Him best.

ber of names, from twenty years old and above, all who *were able to* go to war:

33 those who were numbered of the tribe of Ephraim *were* forty thousand five hundred.

34 From the children of Manasseh, their genealogies by their families, by their fathers' house, according to the number of names, from twenty years old and above, all who *were able to* go to war:

35 those who were numbered of the tribe of Manasseh *were* thirty-two thousand two hundred.

36 From the children of Benjamin, their genealogies by their families, by their fathers' house, according to the number of names, from twenty years old and above, all who *were able to* go to war:

37 those who were numbered of the tribe of Benjamin *were* thirty-five thousand four hundred.

38 From the children of Dan, their genealogies by their families, by their fathers' house, according to the number of names, from twenty years old and above, all who *were able to* go to war:

39 those who were numbered of the tribe of Dan *were* sixty-two thousand seven hundred.

40 From the children of Asher, their genealogies by their families, by their fathers' house, according to the number of names, from twenty years old and above, all who *were able to* go to war:

41 those who were numbered of the tribe of Asher *were* forty-one thousand five hundred.

42 From the children of Naphtali, their genealogies by their families, by their fathers' house, according to the number of names, from twenty years old and above, all who *were able to* go to war:

43 those who were numbered of the tribe of Naphtali *were* fifty-three thousand four hundred.

44 These are the ones who were numbered, whom Moses and Aaron numbered, with the leaders of Israel, twelve men, each one representing his father's house.

45 So all who were numbered of the children of Israel, by their fathers' houses, from twenty years old and above, all who *were able to* go to war in Israel—

46 all who were numbered were six hundred and three thousand five hundred and fifty.

47 But the Levites were not numbered among them by their fathers' tribe;

48 for the LORD had spoken to Moses, saying:

49 "Only the tribe of Levi you shall not number, nor take a census of them among the children of Israel;

50 "but you shall appoint the Levites over the tabernacle of the Testimony, over all its furnishings, and over all things that belong to it; they shall carry the tabernacle and all its furnishings; they shall attend to it and camp around the tabernacle.

51 "And when the tabernacle is to go forward, the Levites shall take it down; and when the tabernacle is to be set up, the Levites shall set it up. The outsider who comes near shall be put to death.

52 "The children of Israel shall pitch their tents, everyone by his own camp, everyone by his own standard, according to their armies;

53 "but the Levites shall camp around the tabernacle of the Testimony, that there may be no wrath on the congregation of the children of Israel; and the Levites shall keep charge of the tabernacle of the Testimony."

54 Thus the children of Israel did; according to all that the LORD commanded Moses, so they did.

The Tribes and Leaders by Armies

2 And the LORD spoke to Moses and Aaron, saying:

2 "Everyone of the children of Israel shall camp by his own standard, beside the emblems of his father's house; they shall camp some distance from the tabernacle of meeting.

3 "On the east side, toward the rising of the sun, those of the standard of the forces with Judah shall camp according to their armies; and Nahshon the son of Amminadab *shall be* the leader of the children of Judah."

4 And his army was numbered at seventy-four thousand six hundred.

5 "Those who camp next to him *shall be* the tribe of Issachar, and Nethanel the son of Zuar *shall be* the leader of the children of Issachar."

6 And his army was numbered at fifty-four thousand four hundred.

7 "Then *comes* the tribe of Zebulun, and Eliab the son of Helon *shall be* the leader of the children of Zebulun."

8 And his army was numbered at fifty-seven thousand four hundred.

9 "All who were numbered according to their armies of the forces with Judah, one hundred and eighty-six thousand four hundred—these shall break camp first.

LIFE LESSONS

➢ 2:2 — *"Everyone of the children of Israel shall camp by his own standard, beside the emblems of his father's house; they shall camp some distance from the tabernacle of meeting."*

God directed each of the tribes of Israel to camp in specific locations. Why? He does not say. But God does not require us to understand His will, just obey it.

10 "On the south side *shall be* the standard of
the forces with Reuben according to their
armies, and the leader of the children of Reuben *shall be* Elizur the son of Shedeur."
11 And his army was numbered at forty-six
thousand five hundred.
12 "Those who camp next to him *shall be* the
tribe of Simeon, and the leader of the children
of Simeon *shall be* Shelumiel the son of Zurishaddai."
13 And his army was numbered at fifty-nine
thousand three hundred.
14 "Then *comes* the tribe of Gad, and the
leader of the children of Gad *shall be* Eliasaph the son of Reuel."[a]
15 And his army was numbered at forty-five
thousand six hundred and fifty.
16 "All who were numbered according to
their armies of the forces with Reuben, one
hundred and fifty-one thousand four hundred
and fifty—they shall be the second to break
camp.
17 "And the tabernacle of meeting shall move
out with the camp of the Levites in the middle
of the camps; as they camp, so they shall
move out, everyone in his place, by their standards.
18 "On the west side *shall be* the standard of
the forces with Ephraim according to their
armies, and the leader of the children of
Ephraim *shall be* Elishama the son of Ammihud."
19 And his army was numbered at forty thousand five hundred.
20 "Next to him *comes* the tribe of Manasseh,
and the leader of the children of Manasseh
shall be Gamaliel the son of Pedahzur."
21 And his army was numbered at thirty-two
thousand two hundred.
22 "Then *comes* the tribe of Benjamin, and
the leader of the children of Benjamin *shall
be* Abidan the son of Gideoni."
23 And his army was numbered at thirty-five
thousand four hundred.
24 "All who were numbered according to
their armies of the forces with Ephraim, one
hundred and eight thousand one hundred—
they shall be the third to break camp.
25 "The standard of the forces with Dan *shall
be* on the north side according to their
armies, and the leader of the children of Dan
shall be Ahiezer the son of Ammishaddai."
26 And his army was numbered at sixty-two
thousand seven hundred.
27 "Those who camp next to him *shall be* the
tribe of Asher, and the leader of the children
of Asher *shall be* Pagiel the son of Ocran."
28 And his army was numbered at forty-one
thousand five hundred.
29 "Then *comes* the tribe of Naphtali, and the
leader of the children of Naphtali *shall be*
Ahira the son of Enan."
30 And his army was numbered at fifty-three
thousand four hundred.
31 "All who were numbered of the forces
with Dan, one hundred and fifty-seven thousand six hundred—they shall break camp
last, with their standards."
32 These *are* the ones who were numbered of
the children of Israel by their fathers' houses.
All who were numbered according to their
armies of the forces *were* six hundred and
three thousand five hundred and fifty.
33 But the Levites were not numbered among
the children of Israel, just as the LORD commanded Moses.
34 Thus the children of Israel did according
to all that the LORD commanded Moses; so
they camped by their standards and so they
broke camp, each one by his family, according to their fathers' houses.

The Sons of Aaron

3 Now these *are* the records of Aaron and
Moses when the LORD spoke with Moses
on Mount Sinai.
2 And these *are* the names of the sons of
Aaron: Nadab, the firstborn, and Abihu,
Eleazar, and Ithamar.
3 These *are* the names of the sons of Aaron,
the anointed priests, whom he consecrated to
minister as priests.
4 Nadab and Abihu had died before the
LORD when they offered profane fire before
the LORD in the Wilderness of Sinai; and they
had no children. So Eleazar and Ithamar ministered as priests in the presence of Aaron
their father.

The Levites Serve in the Tabernacle

5 And the LORD spoke to Moses, saying:
6 "Bring the tribe of Levi near, and present
them before Aaron the priest, that they may
serve him.
7 "And they shall attend to his needs and the
needs of the whole congregation before the
tabernacle of meeting, to do the work of the
tabernacle.
8 "Also they shall attend to all the furnishings of the tabernacle of meeting, and to the
needs of the children of Israel, to do the work
of the tabernacle.
9 "And you shall give the Levites to Aaron
and his sons; they *are* given entirely to him[a]
from among the children of Israel.
10 "So you shall appoint Aaron and his sons,
and they shall attend to their priesthood; but
the outsider who comes near shall be put to
death."
11 Then the LORD spoke to Moses, saying:
12 "Now behold, I Myself have taken the
Levites from among the children of Israel instead of every firstborn who opens the womb
among the children of Israel. Therefore the
Levites shall be Mine,

2:14 [a]Spelled *Deuel* in 1:14 and 7:42 **3:9** [a]Samaritan Pentateuch and Septuagint read *Me*.

13 "because all the firstborn *are* Mine. On the day that I struck all the firstborn in the land of Egypt, I sanctified to Myself all the firstborn in Israel, both man and beast. They shall be Mine: I *am* the LORD."

Census of the Levites Commanded

14 Then the LORD spoke to Moses in the Wilderness of Sinai, saying:

15 "Number the children of Levi by their fathers' houses, by their families; you shall number every male from a month old and above."

16 So Moses numbered them according to the word of the LORD, as he was commanded.

17 These were the sons of Levi by their names: Gershon, Kohath, and Merari.

18 And these *are* the names of the sons of Gershon by their families: Libni and Shimei.

19 And the sons of Kohath by their families: Amram, Izehar, Hebron, and Uzziel.

20 And the sons of Merari by their families: Mahli and Mushi. These *are* the families of the Levites by their fathers' houses.

21 From Gershon *came* the family of the Libnites and the family of the Shimites; these *were* the families of the Gershonites.

22 Those who were numbered, according to the number of all the males from a month old and above—of those who were numbered *there were* seven thousand five hundred.

23 The families of the Gershonites were to camp behind the tabernacle westward.

24 And the leader of the father's house of the Gershonites *was* Eliasaph the son of Lael.

25 The duties of the children of Gershon in the tabernacle of meeting *included* the tabernacle, the tent with its covering, the screen for the door of the tabernacle of meeting,

26 the screen for the door of the court, the hangings of the court which *are* around the tabernacle and the altar, and their cords, according to all the work relating to them.

27 From Kohath *came* the family of the Amramites, the family of the Izharites, the family of the Hebronites, and the family of the Uzzielites; these *were* the families of the Kohathites.

28 According to the number of all the males, from a month old and above, *there were* eight thousand six[a] hundred keeping charge of the sanctuary.

29 The families of the children of Kohath were to camp on the south side of the tabernacle.

30 And the leader of the fathers' house of the families of the Kohathites *was* Elizaphan the son of Uzziel.

31 Their duty *included* the ark, the table, the lampstand, the altars, the utensils of the sanctuary with which they ministered, the screen, and all the work relating to them.

32 And Eleazar the son of Aaron the priest *was to be* chief over the leaders of the Levites, *with* oversight of those who kept charge of the sanctuary.

33 From Merari *came* the family of the Mahlites and the family of the Mushites; these *were* the families of Merari.

34 And those who were numbered, according to the number of all the males from a month old and above, *were* six thousand two hundred.

35 The leader of the fathers' house of the families of Merari *was* Zuriel the son of Abihail. These *were* to camp on the north side of the tabernacle.

36 And the appointed duty of the children of Merari *included* the boards of the tabernacle, its bars, its pillars, its sockets, its utensils, all the work relating to them,

37 and the pillars of the court all around, with their sockets, their pegs, and their cords.

38 Moreover those who were to camp before the tabernacle on the east, before the tabernacle of meeting, *were* Moses, Aaron, and his sons, keeping charge of the sanctuary, to meet the needs of the children of Israel; but the outsider who came near was to be put to death.

39 All who were numbered of the Levites, whom Moses and Aaron numbered at the commandment of the LORD, by their families, all the males from a month old and above, *were* twenty-two thousand.

Levites Dedicated Instead of the Firstborn

40 Then the LORD said to Moses: "Number all the firstborn males of the children of Israel from a month old and above, and take the number of their names.

41 "And you shall take the Levites for Me—I *am* the LORD—instead of all the firstborn among the children of Israel, and the livestock of the Levites instead of all the firstborn among the livestock of the children of Israel."

3:28 [a]Some manuscripts of the Septuagint read *three.*

LIFE LESSONS

➤ **3:10 — *"So you shall appoint Aaron and his sons, and they shall attend to their priesthood; but the outsider who comes near shall be put to death."***

While God invites all of us to approach Him, we must approach Him in the way He has appointed. Today, we draw near to God through faith in Jesus. Nothing else will be accepted.

42 So Moses numbered all the firstborn
among the children of Israel, as the LORD
commanded him.
43 And all the firstborn males, according to
the number of names from a month old and
above, of those who were numbered of them,
were twenty-two thousand two hundred and
seventy-three.
44 Then the LORD spoke to Moses, saying:
45 "Take the Levites instead of all the firstborn among the children of Israel, and the
livestock of the Levites instead of their livestock. The Levites shall be Mine: I *am* the
LORD.
46 "And for the redemption of the two hundred and seventy-three of the firstborn of the
children of Israel, who are more than the
number of the Levites,
47 "you shall take five shekels for each one
individually; you shall take *them* in the currency of the shekel of the sanctuary, the
shekel of twenty gerahs.
48 "And you shall give the money, with which
the excess number of them is redeemed, to
Aaron and his sons."
49 So Moses took the redemption money
from those who were over and above those
who were redeemed by the Levites.
50 From the firstborn of the children of Israel
he took the money, one thousand three hundred and sixty-five *shekels,* according to the
shekel of the sanctuary.
51 And Moses gave their redemption money
to Aaron and his sons, according to the word
of the LORD, as the LORD commanded Moses.

Duties of the Sons of Kohath

4 Then the LORD spoke to Moses and Aaron,
saying:
2 "Take a census of the sons of Kohath from
among the children of Levi, by their families,
by their fathers' house,
3 "from thirty years old and above, even to
fifty years old, all who enter the service to do
the work in the tabernacle of meeting.
4 "This *is* the service of the sons of Kohath
in the tabernacle of meeting, *relating to* the
most holy things:
5 "When the camp prepares to journey,
Aaron and his sons shall come, and they shall
take down the covering veil and cover the ark
of the Testimony with it.
6 "Then they shall put on it a covering of
badger skins, and spread over *that* a cloth entirely of blue; and they shall insert its poles.
7 "On the table of showbread they shall
spread a blue cloth, and put on it the dishes,
the pans, the bowls, and the pitchers for pouring; and the showbread[a] shall be on it.
8 "They shall spread over them a scarlet
cloth, and cover the same with a covering of
badger skins; and they shall insert its poles.
9 "And they shall take a blue cloth and cover
the lampstand of the light, with its lamps, its
wick-trimmers, its trays, and all its oil vessels,
with which they service it.
10 "Then they shall put it with all its utensils
in a covering of badger skins, and put *it* on a
carrying beam.
11 "Over the golden altar they shall spread a
blue cloth, and cover it with a covering of
badger skins; and they shall insert its poles.
12 "Then they shall take all the utensils of
service with which they minister in the sanctuary, put *them* in a blue cloth, cover them
with a covering of badger skins, and put *them*
on a carrying beam.
13 "Also they shall take away the ashes from
the altar, and spread a purple cloth over it.
14 "They shall put on it all its implements with
which they minister there—the firepans, the
forks, the shovels, the basins, and all the utensils of the altar—and they shall spread on it a
covering of badger skins, and insert its poles.
15 "And when Aaron and his sons have finished covering the sanctuary and all the furnishings of the sanctuary, when the camp is
set to go, then the sons of Kohath shall come
to carry *them;* but they shall not touch any
holy thing, lest they die. "These *are* the things
in the tabernacle of meeting which the sons of
Kohath are to carry.
16 "The appointed duty of Eleazar the son of
Aaron the priest *is* the oil for the light, the
sweet incense, the daily grain offering, the
anointing oil, the oversight of all the tabernacle, of all that *is* in it, with the sanctuary and
its furnishings."
17 Then the LORD spoke to Moses and Aaron,
saying:
18 "Do not cut off the tribe of the families of
the Kohathites from among the Levites;
19 "but do this in regard to them, that they
may live and not die when they approach the
most holy things: Aaron and his sons shall go
in and appoint each of them to his service and
his task.
20 "But they shall not go in to watch while
the holy things are being covered, lest they
die."

Duties of the Sons of Gershon

21 Then the LORD spoke to Moses, saying:
22 "Also take a census of the sons of Gershon, by their fathers' house, by their families.
23 "From thirty years old and above, even to
fifty years old, you shall number them, all
who enter to perform the service, to do the
work in the tabernacle of meeting.
24 "This *is* the service of the families of the
Gershonites, in serving and carrying:
25 "They shall carry the curtains of the tabernacle and the tabernacle of meeting *with* its
covering, the covering of badger skins that *is*

4:7 [a]Literally *the continual bread*

on it, the screen for the door of the tabernacle of meeting,
26 "the screen for the door of the gate of the court, the hangings of the court which *are* around the tabernacle and altar, and their cords, all the furnishings for their service and all that is made for these things: so shall they serve.
27 "Aaron and his sons shall assign all the service of the sons of the Gershonites, all their tasks and all their service. And you shall appoint to them all their tasks as their duty.
28 "This *is* the service of the families of the sons of Gershon in the tabernacle of meeting. And their duties *shall be* under the authority[a] of Ithamar the son of Aaron the priest.

Duties of the Sons of Merari

29 "*As for* the sons of Merari, you shall number them by their families and by their fathers' house.
30 "From thirty years old and above, even to fifty years old, you shall number them, everyone who enters the service to do the work of the tabernacle of meeting.
31 "And this *is* what they must carry as all their service for the tabernacle of meeting: the boards of the tabernacle, its bars, its pillars, its sockets,
➤ 32 "and the pillars around the court with their sockets, pegs, and cords, with all their furnishings and all their service; and you shall assign *to each man* by name the items he must carry.
33 "This *is* the service of the families of the sons of Merari, as all their service for the tabernacle of meeting, under the authority[a] of Ithamar the son of Aaron the priest."

Census of the Levites

34 And Moses, Aaron, and the leaders of the congregation numbered the sons of the Kohathites by their families and by their fathers' house,
35 from thirty years old and above, even to fifty years old, everyone who entered the service for work in the tabernacle of meeting;
36 and those who were numbered by their families were two thousand seven hundred and fifty.
37 These *were* the ones who were numbered of the families of the Kohathites, all who might serve in the tabernacle of meeting, whom Moses and Aaron numbered according to the commandment of the LORD by the hand of Moses.
38 And those who were numbered of the sons of Gershon, by their families and by their fathers' house,
39 from thirty years old and above, even to fifty years old, everyone who entered the service for work in the tabernacle of meeting—
40 those who were numbered by their families, by their fathers' house, were two thousand six hundred and thirty.
41 These *are* the ones who were numbered of the families of the sons of Gershon, of all who might serve in the tabernacle of meeting, whom Moses and Aaron numbered according to the commandment of the LORD.
42 Those of the families of the sons of Merari who were numbered, by their families, by their fathers' house,
43 from thirty years old and above, even to fifty years old, everyone who entered the service for work in the tabernacle of meeting—
44 those who were numbered by their families were three thousand two hundred.
45 These *are* the ones who were numbered of the families of the sons of Merari, whom Moses and Aaron numbered according to the word of the LORD by the hand of Moses.
46 All who were numbered of the Levites, whom Moses, Aaron, and the leaders of Israel numbered, by their families and by their fathers' houses,
47 from thirty years old and above, even to fifty years old, everyone who came to do the work of service and the work of bearing burdens in the tabernacle of meeting—
48 those who were numbered were eight thousand five hundred and eighty.
49 According to the commandment of the LORD they were numbered by the hand of Moses, each according to his service and according to his task; thus were they numbered by him, as the LORD commanded Moses.

Ceremonially Unclean Persons Isolated

5 And the LORD spoke to Moses, saying:
2 "Command the children of Israel that they put out of the camp every leper, everyone who has a discharge, and whoever becomes defiled by a corpse.

4:28 [a]Literally *hand* **4:33** [a]Literally *hand*

LIFE LESSONS

➤ **4:32 — *". . . and the pillars around the court with their sockets, pegs, and cords, with all their furnishings and all their service; and you shall assign to each man by name the items he must carry."***

Our service is important to God, regardless of what that service is. He calls us individually to particular ministries and kinds of service. And He knows us by name!

3 You shall put out both male and female;
you shall put them outside the camp, that they
may not defile their camps in the midst of
which I dwell."
4 And the children of Israel did so, and put
them outside the camp; as the LORD spoke to
Moses, so the children of Israel did.

Confession and Restitution

5 Then the LORD spoke to Moses, saying,
6 "Speak to the children of Israel: 'When a
man or woman commits any sin that men
commit in unfaithfulness against the LORD,
and that person is guilty,
➤ 7 'then he shall confess the sin which he has
committed. He shall make restitution for his
trespass in full, plus one-fifth of it, and give *it*
to the one he has wronged.
8 'But if the man has no relative to whom
restitution may be made for the wrong, the
restitution for the wrong *must go* to the LORD
for the priest, in addition to the ram of the
atonement with which atonement is made for
him.
9 'Every offering of all the holy things of the
children of Israel, which they bring to the
priest, shall be his.
10 'And every man's holy things shall be his;
whatever any man gives the priest shall be
his.'"

Concerning Unfaithful Wives

11 And the LORD spoke to Moses, saying,
12 "Speak to the children of Israel, and say to
them: 'If any man's wife goes astray and behaves unfaithfully toward him,
13 'and a man lies with her carnally, and it is
hidden from the eyes of her husband, and it is
concealed that she has defiled herself, and
there was no witness against her, nor was she
caught—
14 'if the spirit of jealousy comes upon him
and he becomes jealous of his wife, who has
defiled herself; or if the spirit of jealousy
comes upon him and he becomes jealous of
his wife, although she has not defiled herself—
15 'then the man shall bring his wife to the
priest. He shall bring the offering required for
her, one-tenth of an ephah of barley meal; he
shall pour no oil on it and put no frankincense on it, because it *is* a grain offering of
jealousy, an offering for remembering, for
bringing iniquity to remembrance.
16 'And the priest shall bring her near, and
set her before the LORD.
17 'The priest shall take holy water in an
earthen vessel, and take some of the dust that
is on the floor of the tabernacle and put *it* into
the water.
18 'Then the priest shall stand the woman before the LORD, uncover the woman's head,
and put the offering for remembering in her
hands, which *is* the grain offering of jealousy.
And the priest shall have in his hand the bitter water that brings a curse.
19 'And the priest shall put her under oath,
and say to the woman, "If no man has lain
with you, and if you have not gone astray to
uncleanness *while* under your husband's *authority,* be free from this bitter water that
brings a curse.
20 "But if you have gone astray *while* under
your husband's *authority,* and if you have defiled yourself and some man other than your
husband has lain with you"—
21 "then the priest shall put the woman under
the oath of the curse, and he shall say to the
woman—"the LORD make you a curse and an
oath among your people, when the LORD
makes your thigh rot and your belly swell;
22 "and may this water that causes the curse
go into your stomach, and make *your* belly
swell and *your* thigh rot." Then the woman
shall say, "Amen, so be it."
23 'Then the priest shall write these curses in
a book, and he shall scrape *them* off into the
bitter water.
24 'And he shall make the woman drink the
bitter water that brings a curse, and the water
that brings the curse shall enter her *to become* bitter.
25 'Then the priest shall take the grain offering of jealousy from the woman's hand, shall
wave the offering before the LORD, and bring
it to the altar;
26 'and the priest shall take a handful of the
offering, as its memorial portion, burn *it* on
the altar, and afterward make the woman
drink the water.
27 'When he has made her drink the water,
then it shall be, if she has defiled herself and
behaved unfaithfully toward her husband,
that the water that brings a curse will enter
her *and become* bitter, and her belly will
swell, her thigh will rot, and the woman will
become a curse among her people.
28 'But if the woman has not defiled herself,
and is clean, then she shall be free and may
conceive children.
29 'This *is* the law of jealousy, when a wife,

LIFE LESSONS

➤ 5:7 — ". . . then he shall confess the sin which he has committed. He shall make restitution for his trespass . . . ."

Confession of sin is a prerequisite for re-establishing close fellowship with the Lord. Since all sin is unfaithfulness to God, we must admit to Him how we have been unfaithful.

while under her husband's *authority,* goes
astray and defiles herself,
30 'or when the spirit of jealousy comes upon
a man, and he becomes jealous of his wife;
then he shall stand the woman before the
LORD, and the priest shall execute all this law
upon her.
31 'Then the man shall be free from iniquity,
but that woman shall bear her guilt.'"

The Law of the Nazirite

6 Then the LORD spoke to Moses, saying,
2 "Speak to the children of Israel, and
say to them: 'When either a man or woman
consecrates an offering to take the vow of a
Nazirite, to separate himself to the LORD,
3 'he shall separate himself from wine and
similar drink; he shall drink neither vinegar
made from wine nor vinegar made from *similar* drink; neither shall he drink any grape
juice, nor eat fresh grapes or raisins.
4 'All the days of his separation he shall eat
nothing that is produced by the grapevine,
from seed to skin.
5 'All the days of the vow of his separation
no razor shall come upon his head; until the
days are fulfilled for which he separated himself to the LORD, he shall be holy. *Then* he
shall let the locks of the hair of his head grow.
6 'All the days that he separates himself to
the LORD he shall not go near a dead body.
7 'He shall not make himself unclean even
for his father or his mother, for his brother or
his sister, when they die, because his separation to God *is* on his head.
8 'All the days of his separation he shall be
holy to the LORD.
9 'And if anyone dies very suddenly beside
him, and he defiles his consecrated head, then
he shall shave his head on the day of his
cleansing; on the seventh day he shall shave it.
10 'Then on the eighth day he shall bring two
turtledoves or two young pigeons to the
priest, to the door of the tabernacle of meeting;
11 'and the priest shall offer one as a sin offering and *the* other as a burnt offering, and
make atonement for him, because he sinned
in regard to the corpse; and he shall sanctify
his head that same day.
12 'He shall consecrate to the LORD the days
of his separation, and bring a male lamb in its
first year as a trespass offering; but the former days shall be lost, because his separation
was defiled.
13 'Now this *is* the law of the Nazirite: When
the days of his separation are fulfilled, he
shall be brought to the door of the tabernacle
of meeting.
14 'And he shall present his offering to the
LORD: one male lamb in its first year without
blemish as a burnt offering, one ewe lamb in
its first year without blemish as a sin offering,
one ram without blemish as a peace offering,
15 'a basket of unleavened bread, cakes of
fine flour mixed with oil, unleavened wafers
anointed with oil, and their grain offering
with their drink offerings.
16 'Then the priest shall bring *them* before
the LORD and offer his sin offering and his
burnt offering;
17 'and he shall offer the ram as a sacrifice
of a peace offering to the LORD, with the
basket of unleavened bread; the priest shall
also offer its grain offering and its drink offering.
18 'Then the Nazirite shall shave his consecrated head *at* the door of the tabernacle of
meeting, and shall take the hair from his consecrated head and put *it* on the fire which is
under the sacrifice of the peace offering.
19 'And the priest shall take the boiled shoulder of the ram, one unleavened cake from the
basket, and one unleavened wafer, and put
them upon the hands of the Nazirite after he
has shaved his consecrated *hair,*
20 'and the priest shall wave them as a wave
offering before the LORD; they *are* holy for the
priest, together with the breast of the wave offering and the thigh of the heave offering.
After that the Nazirite may drink wine.'
21 "This is the law of the Nazirite who vows
to the LORD the offering for his separation,
and besides that, whatever else his hand is
able to provide; according to the vow which
he takes, so he must do according to the law
of his separation."

The Priestly Blessing

22 And the LORD spoke to Moses, saying:
23 "Speak to Aaron and his sons, saying,
'This is the way you shall bless the children of
Israel. Say to them:

24 "The LORD bless you and keep you;
25 The LORD make His face shine upon you,
And be gracious to you;
26 The LORD lift up His countenance upon
you,
And give you peace."'

LIFE LESSONS

➤ 6:26 — *"The LORD lift up His countenance upon you, And give you peace."*

God loves to bless His people, to show them grace and favor and peace. And the greatest blessing of all is that He blesses them with His very presence.

27 "So they shall put My name on the children of Israel, and I will bless them."

Offerings of the Leaders

7 Now it came to pass, when Moses had finished setting up the tabernacle, that he
anointed it and consecrated it and all its furnishings, and the altar and all its utensils; so
he anointed them and consecrated them.
2 Then the leaders of Israel, the heads of
their fathers' houses, who *were* the leaders of
the tribes and over those who were numbered, made an offering.
3 And they brought their offering before the
LORD, six covered carts and twelve oxen, a
cart for *every* two of the leaders, and for each
one an ox; and they presented them before
the tabernacle.
4 Then the LORD spoke to Moses, saying,
5 "Accept *these* from them, that they may be
used in doing the work of the tabernacle of
meeting; and you shall give them to the
Levites, *to* every man according to his service."
6 So Moses took the carts and the oxen, and
gave them to the Levites.
7 Two carts and four oxen he gave to the
sons of Gershon, according to their service;
8 and four carts and eight oxen he gave to
the sons of Merari, according to their service,
under the authority[a] of Ithamar the son of
Aaron the priest.
9 But to the sons of Kohath he gave none,
because theirs *was* the service of the holy
things, *which* they carried on their shoulders.
10 Now the leaders offered the dedication *offering* for the altar when it was anointed; so
the leaders offered their offering before the
altar.
11 For the LORD said to Moses, "They shall
offer their offering, one leader each day, for
the dedication of the altar."
12 And the one who offered his offering on
the first day *was* Nahshon the son of Amminadab, from the tribe of Judah.
13 His offering *was* one silver platter, the
weight of which *was* one hundred and thirty
shekels, and one silver bowl of seventy
shekels, according to the shekel of the sanctuary, both of them full of fine flour mixed
with oil as a grain offering;
14 one gold pan of ten *shekels,* full of incense;
15 one young bull, one ram, and one male
lamb in its first year, as a burnt offering;
16 one kid of the goats as a sin offering;
17 and for the sacrifice of peace offerings:
two oxen, five rams, five male goats, and five
male lambs in their first year. This *was* the offering of Nahshon the son of Amminadab.
18 On the second day Nethanel the son of
Zuar, leader of Issachar, presented *an offering.*
19 *For* his offering he offered one silver platter, the weight of which *was* one hundred and
thirty *shekels,* and one silver bowl of seventy
shekels, according to the shekel of the sanctuary, both of them full of fine flour mixed
with oil as a grain offering;
20 one gold pan of ten *shekels,* full of incense;
21 one young bull, one ram, and one male
lamb in its first year, as a burnt offering;
22 one kid of the goats as a sin offering;
23 and as the sacrifice of peace offerings: two
oxen, five rams, five male goats, and five male
lambs in their first year. This *was* the offering
of Nethanel the son of Zuar.
24 On the third day Eliab the son of Helon,
leader of the children of Zebulun, *presented
an offering.*
25 His offering *was* one silver platter, the
weight of which *was* one hundred and thirty
shekels, and one silver bowl of seventy
shekels, according to the shekel of the sanctuary, both of them full of fine flour mixed
with oil as a grain offering;
26 one gold pan of ten *shekels,* full of incense;
27 one young bull, one ram, and one male
lamb in its first year, as a burnt offering;
28 one kid of the goats as a sin offering;
29 and for the sacrifice of peace offerings:
two oxen, five rams, five male goats, and five
male lambs in their first year. This *was* the offering of Eliab the son of Helon.
30 On the fourth day Elizur the son of
Shedeur, leader of the children of Reuben,
presented an offering.
31 His offering *was* one silver platter, the
weight of which *was* one hundred and thirty
shekels, and one silver bowl of seventy
shekels, according to the shekel of the sanctuary, both of them full of fine flour mixed
with oil as a grain offering;
32 one gold pan of ten *shekels,* full of incense;
33 one young bull, one ram, and one male
lamb in its first year, as a burnt offering;
34 one kid of the goats as a sin offering;
35 and as the sacrifice of peace offerings: two
oxen, five rams, five male goats, and five male
lambs in their first year. This *was* the offering
of Elizur the son of Shedeur.
36 On the fifth day Shelumiel the son of Zurishaddai, leader of the children of Simeon,
presented an offering.
37 His offering *was* one silver platter, the
weight of which *was* one hundred and thirty
shekels, and one silver bowl of seventy
shekels, according to the shekel of the sanctuary, both of them full of fine flour mixed
with oil as a grain offering;
38 one gold pan of ten *shekels,* full of incense;

7:8 [a]Literally *hand*

39 one young bull, one ram, and one male
lamb in its first year, as a burnt offering;
40 one kid of the goats as a sin offering;
41 and as the sacrifice of peace offerings: two
oxen, five rams, five male goats, and five male
lambs in their first year. This *was* the offering
of Shelumiel the son of Zurishaddai.
42 On the sixth day Eliasaph the son of
Deuel,[a] leader of the children of Gad, *presented an offering.*
43 His offering *was* one silver platter, the
weight of which *was* one hundred and thirty
shekels, and one silver bowl of seventy
shekels, according to the shekel of the sanctuary, both of them full of fine flour mixed
with oil as a grain offering;
44 one gold pan of ten *shekels,* full of incense;
45 one young bull, one ram, and one male
lamb in its first year, as a burnt offering;
46 one kid of the goats as a sin offering;
47 and as the sacrifice of peace offerings: two
oxen, five rams, five male goats, and five male
lambs in their first year. This *was* the offering
of Eliasaph the son of Deuel.
48 On the seventh day Elishama the son of
Ammihud, leader of the children of Ephraim,
presented an offering.
49 His offering *was* one silver platter, the
weight of which *was* one hundred and thirty
shekels, and one silver bowl of seventy
shekels, according to the shekel of the sanctuary, both of them full of fine flour mixed
with oil as a grain offering;
50 one gold pan of ten *shekels,* full of incense;
51 one young bull, one ram, and one male
lamb in its first year, as a burnt offering;
52 one kid of the goats as a sin offering;
53 and as the sacrifice of peace offerings: two
oxen, five rams, five male goats, and five male
lambs in their first year. This *was* the offering
of Elishama the son of Ammihud.
54 On the eighth day Gamaliel the son of
Pedahzur, leader of the children of Manasseh,
presented an offering.
55 His offering *was* one silver platter, the
weight of which *was* one hundred and thirty
shekels, and one silver bowl of seventy
shekels, according to the shekel of the sanctuary, both of them full of fine flour mixed
with oil as a grain offering;
56 one gold pan of ten *shekels,* full of incense;
57 one young bull, one ram, and one male
lamb in its first year, as a burnt offering;
58 one kid of the goats as a sin offering;
59 and as the sacrifice of peace offerings: two
oxen, five rams, five male goats, and five male
lambs in their first year. This *was* the offering
of Gamaliel the son of Pedahzur.
60 On the ninth day Abidan the son of
Gideoni, leader of the children of Benjamin,
presented an offering.
61 His offering *was* one silver platter, the
weight of which *was* one hundred and thirty
shekels, and one silver bowl of seventy
shekels, according to the shekel of the sanctuary, both of them full of fine flour mixed
with oil as a grain offering;
62 one gold pan of ten *shekels,* full of incense;
63 one young bull, one ram, and one male
lamb in its first year, as a burnt offering;
64 one kid of the goats as a sin offering;
65 and as the sacrifice of peace offerings: two
oxen, five rams, five male goats, and five male
lambs in their first year. This *was* the offering
of Abidan the son of Gideoni.
66 On the tenth day Ahiezer the son of Ammishaddai, leader of the children of Dan, *presented an offering.*
67 His offering *was* one silver platter, the
weight of which *was* one hundred and thirty
shekels, and one silver bowl of seventy
shekels, according to the shekel of the sanctuary, both of them full of fine flour mixed
with oil as a grain offering;
68 one gold pan of ten *shekels,* full of incense;
69 one young bull, one ram, and one male
lamb in its first year, as a burnt offering;
70 one kid of the goats as a sin offering;
71 and as the sacrifice of peace offerings: two
oxen, five rams, five male goats, and five male
lambs in their first year. This *was* the offering
of Ahiezer the son of Ammishaddai.
72 On the eleventh day Pagiel the son of
Ocran, leader of the children of Asher, *presented an offering.*
73 His offering *was* one silver platter, the
weight of which *was* one hundred and thirty
shekels, and one silver bowl of seventy
shekels, according to the shekel of the sanctuary, both of them full of fine flour mixed
with oil as a grain offering;
74 one gold pan of ten *shekels,* full of incense;
75 one young bull, one ram, and one male
lamb in its first year, as a burnt offering;
76 one kid of the goats as a sin offering;
77 and as the sacrifice of peace offerings: two
oxen, five rams, five male goats, and five male
lambs in their first year. This *was* the offering
of Pagiel the son of Ocran.
78 On the twelfth day Ahira the son of Enan,
leader of the children of Naphtali, *presented
an offering.*
79 His offering *was* one silver platter, the
weight of which *was* one hundred and thirty
shekels, and one silver bowl of seventy
shekels, according to the shekel of the sanctuary, both of them full of fine flour mixed
with oil as a grain offering;
80 one gold pan of ten *shekels,* full of incense;

7:42 [a]Spelled *Reuel* in 2:14

81 one young bull, one ram, and one male
lamb in its first year, as a burnt offering;
82 one kid of the goats as a sin offering;
83 and as the sacrifice of peace offerings: two
oxen, five rams, five male goats, and five male
lambs in their first year. This *was* the offering
of Ahira the son of Enan.
84 This *was* the dedication *offering* for the
altar from the leaders of Israel, when it was
anointed: twelve silver platters, twelve silver
bowls, and twelve gold pans.
85 Each silver platter *weighed* one hundred
and thirty *shekels* and each bowl seventy
shekels. All the silver of the vessels *weighed*
two thousand four hundred *shekels*, according to the shekel of the sanctuary.
86 The twelve gold pans full of incense
weighed ten *shekels* apiece, according to the
shekel of the sanctuary; all the gold of the
pans *weighed* one hundred and twenty
shekels.
87 All the oxen for the burnt offering *were*
twelve young bulls, the rams twelve, the male
lambs in their first year twelve, with their
grain offering, and the kids of the goats as a
sin offering twelve.
88 And all the oxen for the sacrifice of peace
offerings were twenty-four bulls, the rams
sixty, the male goats sixty, and the lambs in
their first year sixty. This *was* the dedication
offering for the altar after it was anointed.
➤ **89** Now when Moses went into the tabernacle
of meeting to speak with Him, he heard the
voice of One speaking to him from above the
mercy seat that *was* on the ark of the Testimony, from between the two cherubim; thus
He spoke to him.

Arrangement of the Lamps

8 And the LORD spoke to Moses, saying:
2 "Speak to Aaron, and say to him,
'When you arrange the lamps, the seven
lamps shall give light in front of the lampstand.'"
3 And Aaron did so; he arranged the lamps
to face toward the front of the lampstand, as
the LORD commanded Moses.
➤ 4 Now this workmanship of the lampstand
was hammered gold; from its shaft to its flowers it *was* hammered work. According to the
pattern which the LORD had shown Moses, so
he made the lampstand.

Cleansing and Dedication of the Levites

5 Then the LORD spoke to Moses, saying:
6 "Take the Levites from among the children of Israel and cleanse them *ceremonially*.
7 "Thus you shall do to them to cleanse
them: Sprinkle water of purification on them,
and let them shave all their body, and let them
wash their clothes, and *so* make themselves
clean.
8 "Then let them take a young bull with its
grain offering of fine flour mixed with oil, and
you shall take another young bull as a sin offering.
9 "And you shall bring the Levites before
the tabernacle of meeting, and you shall
gather together the whole congregation of the
children of Israel.
10 "So you shall bring the Levites before the
LORD, and the children of Israel shall lay their
hands on the Levites;
11 "and Aaron shall offer the Levites before
the LORD *like* a wave offering from the children of Israel, that they may perform the
work of the LORD.
12 "Then the Levites shall lay their hands on
the heads of the young bulls, and you shall
offer one as a sin offering and the other as a
burnt offering to the LORD, to make atonement for the Levites.
13 "And you shall stand the Levites before
Aaron and his sons, and then offer them *like*
a wave offering to the LORD.
14 "Thus you shall separate the Levites from
among the children of Israel, and the Levites
shall be Mine.
15 "After that the Levites shall go in to service the tabernacle of meeting. So you shall
cleanse them and offer them *like* a wave offering.
16 "For they *are* wholly given to Me from
among the children of Israel; I have taken
them for Myself instead of all who open the
womb, the firstborn of all the children of Israel.
17 "For all the firstborn among the children
of Israel *are* Mine, *both* man and beast; on the
day that I struck all the firstborn in the land
of Egypt I sanctified them to Myself.
18 "I have taken the Levites instead of all the
firstborn of the children of Israel.
19 "And I have given the Levites as a gift to
Aaron and his sons from among the children

LIFE LESSONS

➤ 7:89 — *Now when Moses went into the tabernacle of meeting to speak with Him, he heard the voice of One speaking to him from above the mercy seat . . . .*

Moses heard the voice of the Lord speaking to him from above the ark of the covenant, but did not see His face. He did not need to; neither do we. We listen for His voice and follow His word.

➤ 8:4 — *. . . According to the pattern which the LORD had shown Moses, so he made the lampstand.*

The Lord "showed" Moses a particular pattern that needed to be followed. How did He show him? We do not know. But we do know that God will use whatever means necessary to show us His will.

of Israel, to do the work for the children of Israel in the tabernacle of meeting, and to make atonement for the children of Israel, that there be no plague among the children of Israel when the children of Israel come near the sanctuary."

20 Thus Moses and Aaron and all the congregation of the children of Israel did to the Levites; according to all that the LORD commanded Moses concerning the Levites, so the children of Israel did to them.

21 And the Levites purified themselves and washed their clothes; then Aaron presented them *like* a wave offering before the LORD, and Aaron made atonement for them to cleanse them.

22 After that the Levites went in to do their work in the tabernacle of meeting before Aaron and his sons; as the LORD commanded Moses concerning the Levites, so they did to them.

23 Then the LORD spoke to Moses, saying,

24 "This *is* what *pertains* to the Levites: From twenty-five years old and above one may enter to perform service in the work of the tabernacle of meeting;

25 "and at the age of fifty years they must cease performing this work, and shall work no more.

26 "They may minister with their brethren in the tabernacle of meeting, to attend to needs, but they *themselves* shall do no work. Thus you shall do to the Levites regarding their duties."

The Second Passover

9 Now the LORD spoke to Moses in the Wilderness of Sinai, in the first month of the second year after they had come out of the land of Egypt, saying:

2 "Let the children of Israel keep the Passover at its appointed time.

3 "On the fourteenth day of this month, at twilight, you shall keep it at its appointed time. According to all its rites and ceremonies you shall keep it."

4 So Moses told the children of Israel that they should keep the Passover.

5 And they kept the Passover on the fourteenth day of the first month, at twilight, in the Wilderness of Sinai; according to all that the LORD commanded Moses, so the children of Israel did.

6 Now there were *certain* men who were defiled by a human corpse, so that they could not keep the Passover on that day; and they came before Moses and Aaron that day.

7 And those men said to him, "We *became* defiled by a human corpse. Why are we kept from presenting the offering of the LORD at its appointed time among the children of Israel?"

8 And Moses said to them, "Stand still, that I may hear what the LORD will command concerning you."

9 Then the LORD spoke to Moses, saying,

10 "Speak to the children of Israel, saying: 'If anyone of you or your posterity is unclean because of a corpse, or *is* far away on a journey, he may still keep the LORD's Passover.

11 'On the fourteenth day of the second month, at twilight, they may keep it. They shall eat it with unleavened bread and bitter herbs.

12 'They shall leave none of it until morning, nor break one of its bones. According to all the ordinances of the Passover they shall keep it.

13 'But the man who *is* clean and is not on a journey, and ceases to keep the Passover, that same person shall be cut off from among his people, because he did not bring the offering of the LORD at its appointed time; that man shall bear his sin.

14 'And if a stranger dwells among you, and would keep the LORD's Passover, he must do so according to the rite of the Passover and according to its ceremony; you shall have one ordinance, both for the stranger and the native of the land.'"

The Cloud and the Fire

15 Now on the day that the tabernacle was raised up, the cloud covered the tabernacle, the tent of the Testimony; from evening until morning it was above the tabernacle like the appearance of fire.

16 So it was always: the cloud covered it *by day,* and the appearance of fire by night.

17 Whenever the cloud was taken up from above the tabernacle, after that the children of Israel would journey; and in the place where the cloud settled, there the children of Israel would pitch their tents.

18 At the command of the LORD the children of Israel would journey, and at the command of the LORD they would camp; as long as the cloud stayed above the tabernacle they remained encamped.

LIFE LESSONS

➤ 9:8 — *And Moses said to them, "Stand still, that I may hear what the LORD will command concerning you."*

Despite his exalted leadership position, Moses did not presume to speak for the Lord when the Lord had not spoken to him. He, like all of us, must continually listen for the voice of God.

19 Even when the cloud continued long,
many days above the tabernacle, the children
of Israel kept the charge of the LORD and did
not journey.
20 So it was, when the cloud was above the
tabernacle a few days: according to the command of the LORD they would remain encamped, and according to the command of
the LORD they would journey.
21 So it was, when the cloud remained only
from evening until morning: when the cloud
was taken up in the morning, then they would
journey; whether by day or by night, whenever the cloud was taken up, they would journey.
22 *Whether it was* two days, a month, or a
year that the cloud remained above the tabernacle, the children of Israel would remain encamped and not journey; but when it was
taken up, they would journey.
➤ 23 At the command of the LORD they remained encamped, and at the command of
the LORD they journeyed; they kept the charge
of the LORD, at the command of the LORD by
the hand of Moses.

Two Silver Trumpets

10 And the LORD spoke to Moses, saying:
2 "Make two silver trumpets for yourself;
you shall make them of hammered work; you
shall use them for calling the congregation
and for directing the movement of the camps.
3 "When they blow both of them, all the
congregation shall gather before you at the
door of the tabernacle of meeting.
4 "But if they blow *only* one, then the leaders, the heads of the divisions of Israel, shall
gather to you.
5 "When you sound the advance, the camps
that lie on the east side shall then begin their
journey.
6 "When you sound the advance the second
time, then the camps that lie on the south side
shall begin their journey; they shall sound the
call for them to begin their journeys.
7 "And when the assembly is to be gathered
together, you shall blow, but not sound the advance.
8 "The sons of Aaron, the priests, shall blow
the trumpets; and these shall be to you as an
ordinance forever throughout your generations.
9 "When you go to war in your land against
the enemy who oppresses you, then you shall
sound an alarm with the trumpets, and you
will be remembered before the LORD your
God, and you will be saved from your enemies.
10 "Also in the day of your gladness, in your ◄
appointed feasts, and at the beginning of your
months, you shall blow the trumpets over
your burnt offerings and over the sacrifices of
your peace offerings; and they shall be a memorial for you before your God: I *am* the
LORD your God."

Departure from Sinai

11 Now it came to pass on the twentieth *day*
of the second month, in the second year, that
the cloud was taken up from above the tabernacle of the Testimony.
12 And the children of Israel set out from the
Wilderness of Sinai on their journeys; then
the cloud settled down in the Wilderness of
Paran.
13 So they started out for the first time according to the command of the LORD by the
hand of Moses.
14 The standard of the camp of the children
of Judah set out first according to their
armies; over their army was Nahshon the son
of Amminadab.
15 Over the army of the tribe of the children
of Issachar *was* Nethanel the son of Zuar.
16 And over the army of the tribe of the children of Zebulun *was* Eliab the son of Helon.
17 Then the tabernacle was taken down; and
the sons of Gershon and the sons of Merari
set out, carrying the tabernacle.
18 And the standard of the camp of Reuben
set out according to their armies; over their
army *was* Elizur the son of Shedeur.
19 Over the army of the tribe of the children
of Simeon *was* Shelumiel the son of Zurishaddai.
20 And over the army of the tribe of the children of Gad *was* Eliasaph the son of Deuel.
21 Then the Kohathites set out, carrying the
holy things. (The tabernacle would be prepared for their arrival.)
22 And the standard of the camp of the children of Ephraim set out according to their
armies; over their army *was* Elishama the son
of Ammihud.
23 Over the army of the tribe of the children

LIFE LESSONS

➤ **9:23 — *At the command of the LORD they remained encamped, and at the command of the LORD they journeyed . . . .***

How blessed we would be if we would go when the Lord told us to go and stay when the Lord told us to stay! Obedience always brings blessing.

➤ **10:10 — *"Also in the day of your gladness, in your appointed feasts, and at the beginning of your months, you shall blow the trumpets over your burnt offerings and over the sacrifices . . . ."***

A close relationship with God always brings gladness. We must take care that we do not so focus on duty that we overlook the equal call to joy.

of Manasseh *was* Gamaliel the son of Pedahzur.
24 And over the army of the tribe of the children of Benjamin *was* Abidan the son of
Gideoni.
25 Then the standard of the camp of the children of Dan (the rear guard of all the camps)
set out according to their armies; over their
army *was* Ahiezer the son of Ammishaddai.
26 Over the army of the tribe of the children
of Asher *was* Pagiel the son of Ocran.
27 And over the army of the tribe of the children of Naphtali *was* Ahira the son of Enan.
28 Thus *was* the order of march of the children of Israel, according to their armies,
when they began their journey.
➤ **29** Now Moses said to Hobab the son of
Reuel[a] the Midianite, Moses' father-in-law,
"We are setting out for the place of which the
LORD said, 'I will give it to you.' Come with us,
and we will treat you well; for the LORD has
promised good things to Israel."
30 And he said to him, "I will not go, but I
will depart to my *own* land and to my relatives."
31 So *Moses* said, "Please do not leave, inasmuch as you know how we are to camp in the
wilderness, and you can be our eyes.
32 "And it shall be, if you go with us—indeed
it shall be—that whatever good the LORD will
do to us, the same we will do to you."
33 So they departed from the mountain of the
LORD on a journey of three days; and the ark
of the covenant of the LORD went before them
for the three days' journey, to search out a
resting place for them.
34 And the cloud of the LORD *was* above
them by day when they went out from the
camp.
35 So it was, whenever the ark set out, that
Moses said:

"Rise up, O LORD!
Let Your enemies be scattered,
And let those who hate You flee before
You."

36 And when it rested, he said:

"Return, O LORD,
To the many thousands of Israel."

The People Complain

11 Now *when* the people complained, it
displeased the LORD; for the LORD
heard *it,* and His anger was aroused. So the
fire of the LORD burned among them, and consumed *some* in the outskirts of the camp.
2 Then the people cried out to Moses, and
when Moses prayed to the LORD, the fire was
quenched.
3 So he called the name of the place
Taberah,[a] because the fire of the LORD had
burned among them.
4 Now the mixed multitude who were
among them yielded to intense craving; so the
children of Israel also wept again and said:
"Who will give us meat to eat?
5 "We remember the fish which we ate
freely in Egypt, the cucumbers, the melons,
the leeks, the onions, and the garlic;
6 "but now our whole being *is* dried up;
there is nothing at all except this manna *before* our eyes!"
7 Now the manna *was* like coriander seed,
and its color like the color of bdellium.
8 The people went about and gathered *it,*
ground *it* on millstones or beat *it* in the mortar, cooked *it* in pans, and made cakes of it;
and its taste was like the taste of pastry prepared with oil.
9 And when the dew fell on the camp in the
night, the manna fell on it.
10 Then Moses heard the people weeping
throughout their families, everyone at the
door of his tent; and the anger of the LORD
was greatly aroused; Moses also was displeased.
11 So Moses said to the LORD, "Why have You
afflicted Your servant? And why have I not
found favor in Your sight, that You have laid
the burden of all these people on me?
12 "Did I conceive all these people? Did I
beget them, that You should say to me, 'Carry
them in your bosom, as a guardian carries a
nursing child,' to the land which You swore to
their fathers?
13 "Where am I to get meat to give to all

10:29 [a]Septuagint reads *Raguel* (compare Exodus 2:18).
11:3 [a]Literally *Burning*

LIFE LESSONS

➤ 10:29 — *". . . Come with us, and we will treat you well; for the LORD has promised good things to Israel."*

Generosity of spirit always accompanies a mature saint of God. Godly believers understand that God blesses them so that they might bless others (see 2 Cor. 9:11).

➤ 11:1 — *Now when the people complained, it displeased the LORD; for the LORD heard it, and His anger was aroused.*

Just as God always blesses an obedient spirit, so He always judges a complaining spirit (see 1 Cor. 10:10). No one can grumble and honor God at the same time.

➤ 11:5 — *"We remember the fish which we ate freely in Egypt, the cucumbers, the melons, the leeks, the onions, and the garlic . . . ."*

When we focus on what we do not have rather than on what we do have, we tend to forget the hardships from which God already has delivered us. Israel remembered the food, but forgot the slavery.

these people? For they weep all over me, saying, 'Give us meat, that we may eat.'
➤ 14 "I am not able to bear all these people
alone, because the burden *is* too heavy for me.
15 "If You treat me like this, please kill me
here and now—if I have found favor in Your
sight—and do not let me see my wretched-
ness!"

The Seventy Elders

16 So the LORD said to Moses: "Gather to Me
seventy men of the elders of Israel, whom you
know to be the elders of the people and officers over them; bring them to the tabernacle
of meeting, that they may stand there with
you.
17 "Then I will come down and talk with you
there. I will take of the Spirit that *is* upon you
and will put *the same* upon them; and they
shall bear the burden of the people with you,
that you may not bear *it* yourself alone.
18 "Then you shall say to the people, 'Consecrate yourselves for tomorrow, and you shall
eat meat; for you have wept in the hearing of
the LORD, saying, "Who will give us meat to
eat? For *it was* well with us in Egypt." Therefore the LORD will give you meat, and you
shall eat.
19 'You shall eat, not one day, nor two days,
nor five days, nor ten days, nor twenty days,
➤ 20 'but *for* a whole month, until it comes out of
your nostrils and becomes loathsome to you,
because you have despised the LORD who is
among you, and have wept before Him, saying,
"Why did we ever come up out of Egypt?" ' "
21 And Moses said, "The people whom I *am*
among *are* six hundred thousand men on
foot; yet You have said, 'I will give them meat,
that they may eat *for* a whole month.'
22 "Shall flocks and herds be slaughtered for
them, to provide enough for them? Or shall all
the fish of the sea be gathered together for
them, to provide enough for them?"
➤ 23 And the LORD said to Moses, "Has the
LORD's arm been shortened? Now you shall
see whether what I say will happen to you or
not."
24 So Moses went out and told the people the
words of the LORD, and he gathered the seventy men of the elders of the people and
placed them around the tabernacle.
25 Then the LORD came down in the cloud,
and spoke to him, and took of the Spirit that
was upon him, and placed *the same* upon the
seventy elders; and it happened, when the
Spirit rested upon them, that they prophesied,
although they never did *so* again.[a]
26 But two men had remained in the camp:
the name of one *was* Eldad, and the name of
the other Medad. And the Spirit rested upon
them. Now they *were* among those listed, but
who had not gone out to the tabernacle; yet
they prophesied in the camp.
27 And a young man ran and told Moses, and
said, "Eldad and Medad are prophesying in
the camp."
28 So Joshua the son of Nun, Moses' assis- ➤
tant, *one* of his choice men, answered and
said, "Moses my lord, forbid them!"
29 Then Moses said to him, "Are you zealous
for my sake? Oh, that all the LORD's people
were prophets *and* that the LORD would put
His Spirit upon them!"
30 And Moses returned to the camp, *both* he
and the elders of Israel.

The LORD Sends Quail

31 Now a wind went out from the LORD, and
it brought quail from the sea and left *them*
fluttering near the camp, about a day's journey on this side and about a day's journey on
the other side, all around the camp, and about
two cubits above the surface of the ground.
32 And the people stayed up all that day, all
night, and all the next day, and gathered the
quail (he who gathered least gathered ten homers); and they spread *them* out for themselves all around the camp.

11:25 [a]Targum and Vulgate read *did not cease*.

LIFE LESSONS

➤ 11:14 — *"I am not able to bear all these people alone, because the burden is too heavy for me."*

Depending on how we react to our circumstances, we are able to make the work of those who lead the church either a joy or a chore. God wants it to be a joy (see Heb. 13:17).

➤ 11:20 — *". . . but for a whole month, until it comes out of your nostrils and becomes loathsome to you, because you have despised the LORD who is among you . . . ."*

We "despise" the Lord, who lives among us, when we declare His provision insufficient and His plan defective. How much better to praise the Lord for who He is than to complain about what we don't have!

➤ 11:23 — *. . . "Has the LORD's arm been shortened? Now you shall see whether what I say will happen to you or not."*

Frustration can make us doubt the Lord's power and wisdom. But God is sovereign and almighty and fully able to fulfill all of His promises.

➤ 11:28 — *So Joshua the son of Nun, Moses' assistant, one of his choice men, answered and said, "Moses my lord, forbid them!"*

The Spirit of the Lord often moves in ways that we do not expect, and sometimes in ways that offend us. Yet we are wise—and blessed—if we are careful to follow His promptings.

33 But while the meat *was* still between their
teeth, before it was chewed, the wrath of the
LORD was aroused against the people, and
the LORD struck the people with a very great
plague.
➤ 34 So he called the name of that place Kibroth Hattaavah,[a] because there they buried
the people who had yielded to craving.
35 From Kibroth Hattaavah the people
moved to Hazeroth, and camped at Hazeroth.

Dissension of Aaron and Miriam

12 Then Miriam and Aaron spoke against
Moses because of the Ethiopian
woman whom he had married; for he had
married an Ethiopian woman.
➤ 2 So they said, "Has the LORD indeed spoken
only through Moses? Has He not spoken
through us also?" And the LORD heard *it.*
3 (Now the man Moses *was* very humble,
more than all men who *were* on the face of
the earth.)
4 Suddenly the LORD said to Moses, Aaron,
and Miriam, "Come out, you three, to the tabernacle of meeting!" So the three came out.
5 Then the LORD came down in the pillar of
cloud and stood *in* the door of the tabernacle,
and called Aaron and Miriam. And they both
went forward.
6 Then He said,

"Hear now My words:
If there is a prophet among you,
I, the LORD, make Myself known to him
in a vision;
I speak to him in a dream.
7 Not so with My servant Moses;
He *is* faithful in all My house.
8 I speak with him face to face,
Even plainly, and not in dark sayings;
And he sees the form of the LORD.
Why then were you not afraid
To speak against My servant Moses?"

9 So the anger of the LORD was aroused
against them, and He departed.
10 And when the cloud departed from above
the tabernacle, suddenly Miriam *became* leprous, as *white as* snow. Then Aaron turned toward Miriam, and there she was, a leper.
11 So Aaron said to Moses, "Oh, my lord!
Please do not lay *this* sin on us, in which we
have done foolishly and in which we have
sinned.
12 "Please do not let her be as one dead,
whose flesh is half consumed when he comes
out of his mother's womb!"
13 So Moses cried out to the LORD, saying,
"Please heal her, O God, I pray!"
14 Then the LORD said to Moses, "If her fa- ➤
ther had but spit in her face, would she not be
shamed seven days? Let her be shut out of the
camp seven days, and afterward she may be
received *again.*"
15 So Miriam was shut out of the camp seven
days, and the people did not journey till Miriam was brought in *again.*
16 And afterward the people moved from
Hazeroth and camped in the Wilderness of
Paran.

Spies Sent into Canaan

13 And the LORD spoke to Moses, saying,
2 "Send men to spy out the land of Canaan, ➤
which I am giving to the children of Israel;
from each tribe of their fathers you shall send
a man, every one a leader among them."
3 So Moses sent them from the Wilderness
of Paran according to the command of the
LORD, all of them men who *were* heads of the
children of Israel.
4 Now these *were* their names: from the
tribe of Reuben, Shammua the son of Zaccur;
5 from the tribe of Simeon, Shaphat the son
of Hori;
6 from the tribe of Judah, Caleb the son of
Jephunneh;
7 from the tribe of Issachar, Igal the son of
Joseph;
8 from the tribe of Ephraim, Hoshea[a] the
son of Nun;

11:34 [a]Literally *Graves of Craving* **13:8** [a]Septuagint and Vulgate read *Oshea.*

LIFE LESSONS

➤ **11:34 — *So he called the name of that place Kibroth Hattaavah, because there they buried the people who had yielded to craving.***

It is always a dangerous thing to give in to the cravings of the flesh, for "he who sows to his flesh will of the flesh reap corruption" (Gal. 6:8).

➤ **12:2 — *So they said, "Has the LORD indeed spoken only through Moses? Has He not spoken through us also?" . . .***

We are to be content with the place of service and leadership that the Lord assigns to us. Self-promotion may bring serious consequences.

➤ **12:14 — *Then the LORD said to Moses, ". . . Let her be shut out of the camp seven days, and afterward she may be received again."***

God is gracious, but He will not be mocked. Sin remains sin, whoever commits it, and God will respond to it. Forgiveness of sin does not necessarily mean removal of all consequences of sin.

➤ **13:2 — *"Send men to spy out the land of Canaan, which I am giving to the children of Israel . . . ."***

The Lord had said that He was sending His people into a good land, and now He directs them to send spies ahead to confirm His words. He could have sent them in blindly, but instead graciously gave them a preview.

9 from the tribe of Benjamin, Palti the son of
Raphu;
10 from the tribe of Zebulun, Gaddiel the son
of Sodi;
11 from the tribe of Joseph, *that is,* from the
tribe of Manasseh, Gaddi the son of Susi;
12 from the tribe of Dan, Ammiel the son of
Gemalli;
13 from the tribe of Asher, Sethur the son of
Michael;
14 from the tribe of Naphtali, Nahbi the son
of Vophsi;
15 from the tribe of Gad, Geuel the son of
Machi.
16 These *are* the names of the men whom
Moses sent to spy out the land. And Moses
called Hoshea[a] the son of Nun, Joshua.
17 Then Moses sent them to spy out the land
of Canaan, and said to them, "Go up this *way*
into the South, and go up to the mountains,
18 "and see what the land is like: whether the
people who dwell in it *are* strong or weak, few
or many;
19 "whether the land they dwell in *is* good or
bad; whether the cities they inhabit *are* like
camps or strongholds;
20 "whether the land *is* rich or poor; and
whether there are forests there or not. Be of
good courage. And bring some of the fruit of
the land." Now the time *was* the season of the
first ripe grapes.
21 So they went up and spied out the land
from the Wilderness of Zin as far as Rehob,
near the entrance of Hamath.
22 And they went up through the South and
came to Hebron; Ahiman, Sheshai, and Talmai, the descendants of Anak, *were* there.
(Now Hebron was built seven years before
Zoan in Egypt.)
23 Then they came to the Valley of Eshcol,
and there cut down a branch with one cluster
of grapes; they carried it between two of them
on a pole. *They* also *brought* some of the
pomegranates and figs.
24 The place was called the Valley of Eshcol,[a]
because of the cluster which the men of Israel
cut down there.
25 And they returned from spying out the
land after forty days.
26 Now they departed and came back to Moses and Aaron and all the congregation of the
children of Israel in the Wilderness of Paran,
at Kadesh; they brought back word to them
and to all the congregation, and showed them
the fruit of the land.
27 Then they told him, and said: "We went to
the land where you sent us. It truly flows with
milk and honey, and this *is* its fruit.
28 "Nevertheless the people who dwell in the
land *are* strong; the cities *are* fortified *and*
very large; moreover we saw the descendants
of Anak there.
29 "The Amalekites dwell in the land of
the South; the Hittites, the Jebusites, and
the Amorites dwell in the mountains; and the
Canaanites dwell by the sea and along the
banks of the Jordan."
30 Then Caleb quieted the people before Moses, and said, "Let us go up at once and take
possession, for we are well able to overcome
it."
31 But the men who had gone up with him
said, "We are not able to go up against the
people, for they *are* stronger than we."
32 And they gave the children of Israel a bad
report of the land which they had spied out,
saying, "The land through which we have
gone as spies *is* a land that devours its inhabitants, and all the people whom we saw in it
are men of *great* stature.
33 "There we saw the giants[a] (the descendants of Anak came from the giants); and we
were like grasshoppers in our own sight, and
so we were in their sight."

Israel Refuses to Enter Canaan

14 So all the congregation lifted up their
voices and cried, and the people wept
that night.
2 And all the children of Israel complained
against Moses and Aaron, and the whole congregation said to them, "If only we had died in
the land of Egypt! Or if only we had died in
this wilderness!
3 "Why has the LORD brought us to this land

13:16 [a]Septuagint and Vulgate read *Oshea.* **13:24** [a]Literally *Cluster* **13:33** [a]Hebrew *nephilim*

LIFE LESSONS

➤ 13:28 — *"Nevertheless the people who dwell in the land are strong; the cities are fortified and very large . . . ."*

It is always spiritually foolish to focus our attention on the very things that the Lord ignores. The Lord had emphasized the goodness of the land; ten spies focused on the strength of the opposition.

➤ 13:31 — *But the men who had gone up with him said, "We are not able to go up against the people, for they are stronger than we."*

The point is never whether our spiritual opponents are stronger than us; most often, they are. But they are *never* stronger than the Lord, and that's the point we must not forget.

➤ 14:3 — *" . . . Would it not be better for us to return to Egypt?"*

At times it might seem better and easier to return to a place of spiritual bondage, but we never move toward blessing by returning to slavery. God had told the people to move forward, not back.

to fall by the sword, that our wives and children should become victims? Would it not be
better for us to return to Egypt?"
4 So they said to one another, "Let us select
a leader and return to Egypt."
5 Then Moses and Aaron fell on their faces
before all the assembly of the congregation of
the children of Israel.
6 But Joshua the son of Nun and Caleb the
son of Jephunneh, *who were* among those
who had spied out the land, tore their clothes;
7 and they spoke to all the congregation of
the children of Israel, saying: "The land we
passed through to spy out *is* an exceedingly
good land.
8 "If the LORD delights in us, then He will
bring us into this land and give it to us, 'a land
which flows with milk and honey.'[a]
➤ 9 "Only do not rebel against the LORD, nor
fear the people of the land, for they *are* our
bread; their protection has departed from
them, and the LORD *is* with us. Do not fear
them."
10 And all the congregation said to stone
them with stones. Now the glory of the LORD
appeared in the tabernacle of meeting before
all the children of Israel.

Moses Intercedes for the People

➤ **11** Then the LORD said to Moses: "How long
will these people reject Me? And how long
will they not believe Me, with all the signs
which I have performed among them?
12 "I will strike them with the pestilence and
disinherit them, and I will make of you a nation greater and mightier than they."
13 And Moses said to the LORD: "Then the
Egyptians will hear *it*, for by Your might You
brought these people up from among them,
14 "and they will tell *it* to the inhabitants of
this land. They have heard that You, LORD, *are*
among these people; that You, LORD, are seen
face to face and Your cloud stands above
them, and You go before them in a pillar of
cloud by day and in a pillar of fire by night.
15 "Now *if* You kill these people as one man,
then the nations which have heard of Your
fame will speak, saying,
16 'Because the LORD was not able to bring
this people to the land which He swore to give
them, therefore He killed them in the wilderness.'
17 "And now, I pray, let the power of my Lord
be great, just as You have spoken, saying,
18 'The LORD is longsuffering and abundant ➤
in mercy, forgiving iniquity and transgression; but He by no means clears *the guilty*,
visiting the iniquity of the fathers on the children to the third and fourth *generation*.'[a]
19 "Pardon the iniquity of this people, I pray, ➤
according to the greatness of Your mercy, just
as You have forgiven this people, from Egypt
even until now."
20 Then the LORD said: "I have pardoned, according to your word;
21 "but truly, as I live, all the earth shall be
filled with the glory of the LORD—
22 "because all these men who have seen My
glory and the signs which I did in Egypt and
in the wilderness, and have put Me to the test
now these ten times, and have not heeded My
voice,
23 "they certainly shall not see the land of
which I swore to their fathers, nor shall any of
those who rejected Me see it.
24 "But My servant Caleb, because he has a ➤

14:8 [a]Exodus 3:8 **14:18** [a]Exodus 34:6, 7

LIFE LESSONS

➤ 14:9 — *"Only do not rebel against the LORD, nor fear the people of the land . . . . the LORD is with us . . . ."*

When we allow fear to drive us to spiritual rebellion, we take a step toward devastation, not preservation. Perfect love in God drives out fear—and preserves our lives (see 1 John 4:18).

➤ 14:11 — *" . . . And how long will they not believe Me, with all the signs which I have performed among them?"*

How easily we forget the many "signs" of God's love and protection! One great way to drive out unbelief from our hearts is to regularly count the blessings that God has showered upon us. When did you last do this?

➤ 14:18 — *"The LORD is longsuffering and abundant in mercy, forgiving iniquity and transgression; but He by no means clears the guilty, visiting the iniquity of the fathers on the children to the third and fourth generation."*

When God speaks, do we hear a forgiving or demanding Father, intimate or distant Friend, patient or intolerant Teacher, gentle or angry Guide, understanding or insensitive Counselor, generous or reluctant Provider, or a faithful or inconsistent Sustainer?

➤ 14:19 — *"Pardon the iniquity of this people, I pray, according to the greatness of Your mercy, just as You have forgiven this people, from Egypt even until now."*

Moses appeals to the Lord on behalf of His people on the basis of God's name—that is, His reputation, attributes and fame. Moses won this battle because he fought it on his knees.

➤ 14:24 — *"But My servant Caleb, because he has a different spirit in him and has followed Me fully, I will bring into the land where he went, and his descendants shall inherit it."*

God promised to do for Caleb what He refused to do for the rebels. Why? Because Caleb followed his Lord "fully." God assumes full responsibility for our needs when we obey Him wholeheartedly.

ANSWERS TO LIFE'S QUESTIONS

How do I keep my focus on God and not on the obstacles in my life?

NUM. 14:8, 9

Fear can paralyze the stoutest of hearts. When we perceive a threat to our well-being or an obstacle standing between us and our goals, we often fear that the overall plan for our lives is in serious jeopardy.

In those times we need to remember the promises of God.

When the Israelite spies set out on a reconnaissance mission to assess the land of Canaan, they had no idea what they would encounter. It was a great honor to be chosen by Moses for such an assignment, and Moses selected the top leader from each of the twelve tribes for the job.

Yet all their training and leadership experience did not prepare them for something so overwhelming. Who had ever heard of a grape cluster so huge that it had to be carried on a pole lifted by two men? Who could possibly be prepared for Canaanite warriors so massive they dwarfed the best of Israel's army? It is no wonder these spies felt a whirling mix of emotions as they headed back to their commander-in-chief to give a full report.

You can imagine the scene. Moses and Aaron (Moses' brother) gathered the people to hear the news. The spies confirmed that the Promised Land was indeed everything God said it was—but they focused on what they saw as the obstacles to their taking the land, namely the giants who lived there. They gave an accurate report, but they failed to give the whole story. Only Joshua and Caleb spoke the truth.

These faithful men recounted what they had seen and then reiterated, in their own words, the promises of God that had brought them to his point: "If the LORD delights in us, then He will bring us into this land and give it to us, a land which flows with milk and honey. Only do not rebel against the LORD, nor fear the people of the land, for they are our bread; their protection has departed from them, and the LORD is with us. Do not fear them" (Num. 14:8, 9). Joshua and Caleb lived to see the Promised Land, but only because they focused on the goal God had laid out for them and not on the obstacles standing in the way.

The blessings God has in store for you are just as rich! Never allow shortsighted vision—especially one focused on obstacles—to block the far-reaching plan of the Lord.

See the Life Principles Index for further study:
21. Obedience always brings blessing.
9. Trusting God means looking beyond what we can see to what God sees.

different spirit in him and has followed Me
fully, I will bring into the land where he went,
and his descendants shall inherit it.
25 "Now the Amalekites and the Canaanites
dwell in the valley; tomorrow turn and move
out into the wilderness by the Way of the Red
Sea."

Death Sentence on the Rebels

26 And the LORD spoke to Moses and Aaron,
saying,
27 "How long *shall I bear with* this evil congregation
who complain against Me? I have
heard the complaints which the children of Israel
make against Me.
28 "Say to them, 'As I live,' says the LORD,
'just as you have spoken in My hearing, so I
will do to you:
29 'The carcasses of you who have complained
against Me shall fall in this wilderness,
all of you who were numbered,
according to your entire number, from twenty
years old and above.
30 'Except for Caleb the son of Jephunneh
and Joshua the son of Nun, you shall by no
means enter the land which I swore I would
make you dwell in.
31 'But your little ones, whom you said would
be victims, I will bring in, and they shall know
the land which you have despised.
32 'But *as for* you, your carcasses shall fall in
this wilderness.
33 'And your sons shall be shepherds in the
wilderness forty years, and bear the brunt of
your infidelity, until your carcasses are consumed
in the wilderness.
34 'According to the number of the days in
which you spied out the land, forty days, for
each day you shall bear your guilt one year,
namely forty years, and you shall know My
rejection.
35 'I the LORD have spoken this. I will surely
do so to all this evil congregation who are
gathered together against Me. In this wilderness
they shall be consumed, and there they
shall die.'"

36 Now the men whom Moses sent to spy out
the land, who returned and made all the congregation complain against him by bringing a
bad report of the land,
37 those very men who brought the evil report about the land, died by the plague before
the LORD.
38 But Joshua the son of Nun and Caleb the
son of Jephunneh remained alive, of the men
who went to spy out the land.

A Futile Invasion Attempt

39 Then Moses told these words to all the
children of Israel, and the people mourned
greatly.
40 And they rose early in the morning and
went up to the top of the mountain, saying,
"Here we are, and we will go up to the place
which the LORD has promised, for we have
sinned!"
41 And Moses said, "Now why do you transgress the command of the LORD? For this will
not succeed.
➤ 42 "Do not go up, lest you be defeated by
your enemies, for the LORD *is* not among you.
43 "For the Amalekites and the Canaanites
are there before you, and you shall fall by the
sword; because you have turned away from
the LORD, the LORD will not be with you."
44 But they presumed to go up to the mountaintop. Nevertheless, neither the ark of the
covenant of the LORD nor Moses departed
from the camp.
45 Then the Amalekites and the Canaanites
who dwelt in that mountain came down and
attacked them, and drove them back as far as
Hormah.

Laws of Grain and Drink Offerings

15 And the LORD spoke to Moses, saying,
2 "Speak to the children of Israel, and say to
them: 'When you have come into the land you
are to inhabit, which I am giving to you,
3 'and you make an offering by fire to the
LORD, a burnt offering or a sacrifice, to fulfill
a vow or as a freewill offering or in your appointed feasts, to make a sweet aroma to the
LORD, from the herd or the flock,
4 'then he who presents his offering to the
LORD shall bring a grain offering of one-tenth
of an ephah of fine flour mixed with one-
fourth of a hin of oil;
5 'and one-fourth of a hin of wine as a drink
offering you shall prepare with the burnt offering or the sacrifice, for each lamb.
6 'Or for a ram you shall prepare as a grain
offering two-tenths *of an ephah* of fine flour
mixed with one-third of a hin of oil;
7 'and as a drink offering you shall offer
one-third of a hin of wine as a sweet aroma to
the LORD.
8 'And when you prepare a young bull as a
burnt offering, or as a sacrifice to fulfill a
vow, or as a peace offering to the LORD,
9 'then shall be offered with the young bull
a grain offering of three-tenths *of an ephah* of
fine flour mixed with half a hin of oil;
10 'and you shall bring as the drink offering
half a hin of wine as an offering made by fire,
a sweet aroma to the LORD.
11 'Thus it shall be done for each young bull,
for each ram, or for each lamb or young goat.
12 'According to the number that you prepare, so you shall do with everyone according
to their number.
13 'All who are native-born shall do these
things in this manner, in presenting an offering made by fire, a sweet aroma to the LORD.
14 'And if a stranger dwells with you, or whoever *is* among you throughout your generations, and would present an offering made by
fire, a sweet aroma to the LORD, just as you
do, so shall he do.
15 'One ordinance *shall be* for you of the assembly and for the stranger who dwells *with
you,* an ordinance forever throughout your
generations; as you are, so shall the stranger
be before the LORD.
16 'One law and one custom shall be for you
and for the stranger who dwells with you.'"[a]
17 Again the LORD spoke to Moses, saying,
18 "Speak to the children of Israel, and say to
them: 'When you come into the land to which
I bring you,
19 'then it will be, when you eat of the bread
of the land, that you shall offer up a heave offering to the LORD.
20 'You shall offer up a cake of the first of
your ground meal *as* a heave offering; as a
heave offering of the threshing floor, so shall
you offer it up.
21 'Of the first of your ground meal you shall

15:16 [a]Compare Exodus 12:49

LIFE LESSONS

➤ ***14:28 — Say to them, "As I live," says the LORD, "just as you have spoken in My hearing, so I will do to you . . . "***

The Lord hears every word we say, whether in praise or complaint. Jesus told us that we will give an account for every "idle word" we speak (Matt. 12:36).

➤ ***14:42 — "Do not go up, lest you be defeated by your enemies, for the LORD is not among you."***

The difference between success and failure comes down to the answer to one question: Is the Lord with you?

give to the LORD a heave offering throughout
your generations.

Laws Concerning Unintentional Sin

22 'If you sin unintentionally, and do not observe all these commandments which the LORD has spoken to Moses—
23 'all that the LORD has commanded you by the hand of Moses, from the day the LORD gave commandment and onward throughout your generations—
24 'then it will be, if it is unintentionally committed, without the knowledge of the congregation, that the whole congregation shall offer one young bull as a burnt offering, as a sweet aroma to the LORD, with its grain offering and its drink offering, according to the ordinance, and one kid of the goats as a sin offering.
25 'So the priest shall make atonement for the whole congregation of the children of Israel, and it shall be forgiven them, for it was unintentional; they shall bring their offering, an offering made by fire to the LORD, and their sin offering before the LORD, for their unintended sin.
26 'It shall be forgiven the whole congregation of the children of Israel and the stranger who dwells among them, because all the people *did it* unintentionally.
27 'And if a person sins unintentionally, then he shall bring a female goat in its first year as a sin offering.
28 'So the priest shall make atonement for the person who sins unintentionally, when he sins unintentionally before the LORD, to make atonement for him; and it shall be forgiven him.
29 'You shall have one law for him who sins unintentionally, *for* him who is native-born among the children of Israel and for the stranger who dwells among them.

Law Concerning Presumptuous Sin

➤ **30** 'But the person who does *anything* presumptuously, *whether he is* native-born or a stranger, that one brings reproach on the LORD, and he shall be cut off from among his people.
31 'Because he has despised the word of the LORD, and has broken His commandment, that person shall be completely cut off; his guilt *shall be* upon him.'"

Penalty for Violating the Sabbath

32 Now while the children of Israel were in the wilderness, they found a man gathering sticks on the Sabbath day.
33 And those who found him gathering sticks brought him to Moses and Aaron, and to all the congregation.
34 They put him under guard, because it had not been explained what should be done to him.
35 Then the LORD said to Moses, "The man must surely be put to death; all the congregation shall stone him with stones outside the camp."
36 So, as the LORD commanded Moses, all the congregation brought him outside the camp and stoned him with stones, and he died.

Tassels on Garments

37 Again the LORD spoke to Moses, saying,
38 "Speak to the children of Israel: Tell them to make tassels on the corners of their garments throughout their generations, and to put a blue thread in the tassels of the corners.
39 "And you shall have the tassel, that you ◄
may look upon it and remember all the commandments of the LORD and do them, and that you *may* not follow the harlotry to which your own heart and your own eyes are inclined,
40 "and that you may remember and do all My commandments, and be holy for your God.
41 "I *am* the LORD your God, who brought you out of the land of Egypt, to be your God: I *am* the LORD your God."

Rebellion Against Moses and Aaron

16 Now Korah the son of Izhar, the son of Kohath, the son of Levi, with Dathan and Abiram the sons of Eliab, and On the son of Peleth, sons of Reuben, took *men;*
2 and they rose up before Moses with some of the children of Israel, two hundred and fifty leaders of the congregation, representatives of the congregation, men of renown.

LIFE LESSONS

➤ 15:30 — *"But the person who does anything presumptuously, whether he is native-born or a stranger, that one brings reproach on the LORD, and he shall be cut off from among his people."*

All sin separates us from God, but some sins bring a harsher judgment than others. Presumptuous sins—brazen, knowing, defiant, arrogant, premeditated sins—carry a heavy penalty. Only fools plan to sin and ask forgiveness later.

➤ 15:39 — *"And you shall have the tassel, that you may look upon it and remember all the commandments of the LORD and do them . . . ."*

It pays to place around yourself practical, physical reminders of who God is, what He requires of you, and how He promises to bless your obedience. Some things we can't afford to forget!

➤ 3 They gathered together against Moses
and Aaron, and said to them, "*You take* too
much upon yourselves, for all the congregation *is* holy, every one of them, and the LORD
is among them. Why then do you exalt yourselves above the assembly of the LORD?"
4 So when Moses heard *it*, he fell on his
face;
5 and he spoke to Korah and all his company, saying, "Tomorrow morning the LORD
will show who *is* His and *who is* holy, and will
cause *him* to come near to Him. That one
whom He chooses He will cause to come near
to Him.
6 "Do this: Take censers, Korah and all your
company;
7 "put fire in them and put incense in them
before the LORD tomorrow, and it shall be
that the man whom the LORD chooses *is* the
holy one. *You take* too much upon yourselves,
you sons of Levi!"
8 Then Moses said to Korah, "Hear now, you
sons of Levi:
9 "*Is it* a small thing to you that the God of Israel has separated you from the congregation
of Israel, to bring you near to Himself, to do
the work of the tabernacle of the LORD, and to
stand before the congregation to serve them;
10 "and that He has brought you near *to
Himself*, you and all your brethren, the sons
of Levi, with you? And are you seeking the
priesthood also?
➤ 11 "Therefore you and all your company *are*
gathered together against the LORD. And what
is Aaron that you complain against him?"
12 And Moses sent to call Dathan and Abiram the sons of Eliab, but they said, "We will
not come up!
13 "*Is it* a small thing that you have brought
us up out of a land flowing with milk and
honey, to kill us in the wilderness, that you
should keep acting like a prince over us?
14 "Moreover you have not brought us into a
land flowing with milk and honey, nor given
us inheritance of fields and vineyards. Will
you put out the eyes of these men? We will not
come up!"
15 Then Moses was very angry, and said to
the LORD, "Do not respect their offering. I
have not taken one donkey from them, nor
have I hurt one of them."
16 And Moses said to Korah, "Tomorrow, you
and all your company be present before the
LORD—you and they, as well as Aaron.
17 "Let each take his censer and put incense
in it, and each of you bring his censer before
the LORD, two hundred and fifty censers; both
you and Aaron, each *with* his censer."
18 So every man took his censer, put fire in it,
laid incense on it, and stood at the door of the
tabernacle of meeting with Moses and Aaron.
19 And Korah gathered all the congregation
against them at the door of the tabernacle of
meeting. Then the glory of the LORD appeared
to all the congregation.
20 And the LORD spoke to Moses and Aaron,
saying,
21 "Separate yourselves from among this
congregation, that I may consume them in a
moment."
22 Then they fell on their faces, and said,
"O God, the God of the spirits of all flesh,
shall one man sin, and You be angry with all
the congregation?"
23 So the LORD spoke to Moses, saying,
24 "Speak to the congregation, saying, 'Get
away from the tents of Korah, Dathan, and
Abiram.'"
25 Then Moses rose and went to Dathan and
Abiram, and the elders of Israel followed him.
26 And he spoke to the congregation, saying,
"Depart now from the tents of these wicked
men! Touch nothing of theirs, lest you be consumed in all their sins."
27 So they got away from around the tents of
Korah, Dathan, and Abiram; and Dathan and
Abiram came out and stood at the door of
their tents, with their wives, their sons, and
their little children.
28 And Moses said: "By this you shall know ➤
that the LORD has sent me to do all these
works, for *I have* not *done them* of my own
will.
29 "If these men die naturally like all men, or
if they are visited by the common fate of all
men, *then* the LORD has not sent me.
30 "But if the LORD creates a new thing, and
the earth opens its mouth and swallows them

LIFE LESSONS

➤ 16:3 — *They gathered together against Moses and Aaron, and said to them, ". . . Why then do you exalt yourselves above the assembly of the LORD?"*

Why didn't Korah and his entourage learn from what happened to Miriam and Aaron when they challenged Moses' special place of leadership (Num. 12)? God honors humility, not pride.

➤ 16:11 — *"Therefore you and all your company are gathered together against the LORD. And what is Aaron that you complain against him?"*

Moses reminded the rebels that God places whomever He wills wherever He wants them; we have no right to claim for ourselves a place of authority. As servants of God, we should delight in whatever place He gives us.

➤ 16:28 — *And Moses said: "By this you shall know that the LORD has sent me to do all these works, for I have not done them of my own will."*

Moses did only what God sent him to do. Centuries later, Jesus said, "I do nothing of Myself; but as My Father taught Me, I speak these things . . . for I always do those things that please Him" (John 8:28, 29).

up with all that belongs to them, and they go
down alive into the pit, then you will understand that these men have rejected the LORD."
31 Now it came to pass, as he finished speaking all these words, that the ground split apart
under them,
32 and the earth opened its mouth and swallowed them up, with their households and all
the men with Korah, with all *their* goods.
33 So they and all those with them went
down alive into the pit; the earth closed over
them, and they perished from among the assembly.
34 Then all Israel who *were* around them fled
at their cry, for they said, "Lest the earth swallow us up *also!*"
35 And a fire came out from the LORD and
consumed the two hundred and fifty men who
were offering incense.
36 Then the LORD spoke to Moses, saying:
37 "Tell Eleazar, the son of Aaron the priest,
to pick up the censers out of the blaze, for
they are holy, and scatter the fire some distance away.
38 "The censers of these men who sinned
against their own souls, let them be made into
hammered plates as a covering for the altar.
Because they presented them before the
LORD, therefore they are holy; and they shall
be a sign to the children of Israel."
39 So Eleazar the priest took the bronze
censers, which those who were burned up
had presented, and they were hammered out
as a covering on the altar,
40 *to be* a memorial to the children of Israel
that no outsider, who *is* not a descendant of
Aaron, should come near to offer incense before the LORD, that he might not become like
Korah and his companions, just as the LORD
had said to him through Moses.

Complaints of the People

41 On the next day all the congregation of
the children of Israel complained against Moses and Aaron, saying, "You have killed the
people of the LORD."
42 Now it happened, when the congregation
had gathered against Moses and Aaron, that
they turned toward the tabernacle of meeting;
and suddenly the cloud covered it, and the
glory of the LORD appeared.
43 Then Moses and Aaron came before the
tabernacle of meeting.
44 And the LORD spoke to Moses, saying,
45 "Get away from among this congregation,
that I may consume them in a moment." And
they fell on their faces.
46 So Moses said to Aaron, "Take a censer
and put fire in it from the altar, put incense *on*
it, and take it quickly to the congregation and
make atonement for them; for wrath has gone
out from the LORD. The plague has begun."
47 Then Aaron took *it* as Moses commanded,
and ran into the midst of the assembly; and
already the plague had begun among the people. So he put in the incense and made atonement for the people.
48 And he stood between the dead and the
living; so the plague was stopped.
49 Now those who died in the plague were
fourteen thousand seven hundred, besides
those who died in the Korah incident.
50 So Aaron returned to Moses at the door of
the tabernacle of meeting, for the plague had
stopped.

The Budding of Aaron's Rod

17 And the LORD spoke to Moses, saying:
2 "Speak to the children of Israel, and get
from them a rod from each father's house, all
their leaders according to their fathers'
houses—twelve rods. Write each man's name
on his rod.
3 "And you shall write Aaron's name on the
rod of Levi. For there shall be one rod for the
head of *each* father's house.
4 "Then you shall place them in the tabernacle of meeting before the Testimony, where
I meet with you.
5 "And it shall be *that* the rod of the man
whom I choose will blossom; thus I will rid
Myself of the complaints of the children of Israel, which they make against you."
6 So Moses spoke to the children of Israel,
and each of their leaders gave him a rod
apiece, for each leader according to their fathers' houses, twelve rods; and the rod of
Aaron *was* among their rods.
7 And Moses placed the rods before the
LORD in the tabernacle of witness.
8 Now it came to pass on the next day that
Moses went into the tabernacle of witness,
and behold, the rod of Aaron, of the house of
Levi, had sprouted and put forth buds, had
produced blossoms and yielded ripe almonds.

LIFE LESSONS

➤ ***16:48 — And he stood between the dead and the living; so the plague was stopped.***

As ambassadors of Christ (see 2 Cor. 5:20), we also stand between the living and the dead, calling the spiritually dead to new life in Jesus.

➤ ***17:8 — Now it came to pass on the next day that Moses went into the tabernacle of witness, and behold, the rod of Aaron, of the house of Levi, had sprouted and put forth buds, had produced blossoms and yielded ripe almonds.***

The Lord will go to great lengths to show us and confirm to us His perfect will.

9 Then Moses brought out all the rods from
before the LORD to all the children of Israel;
and they looked, and each man took his rod.
10 And the LORD said to Moses, "Bring Aaron's rod back before the Testimony, to be kept
as a sign against the rebels, that you may put
their complaints away from Me, lest they die."
11 Thus did Moses; just as the LORD had
commanded him, so he did.
12 So the children of Israel spoke to Moses,
saying, "Surely we die, we perish, we all perish!
13 "Whoever even comes near the tabernacle
of the LORD must die. Shall we all utterly die?"

Duties of Priests and Levites

18 Then the LORD said to Aaron: "You and
your sons and your father's house with
you shall bear the iniquity *related to* the
sanctuary, and you and your sons with you
shall bear the iniquity *associated with* your
priesthood.
2 "Also bring with you your brethren of the
tribe of Levi, the tribe of your father, that they
may be joined with you and serve you while
you and your sons *are* with you before the
tabernacle of witness.
3 "They shall attend to your needs and all
the needs of the tabernacle; but they shall not
come near the articles of the sanctuary and
the altar, lest they die—they and you also.
4 "They shall be joined with you and attend
to the needs of the tabernacle of meeting, for
all the work of the tabernacle; but an outsider
shall not come near you.
5 "And you shall attend to the duties of the
sanctuary and the duties of the altar, that
there *may* be no more wrath on the children
of Israel.
6 "Behold, I Myself have taken your brethren
the Levites from among the children of Israel;
they are a gift to you, given by the LORD, to do
the work of the tabernacle of meeting.
7 "Therefore you and your sons with you
shall attend to your priesthood for everything
at the altar and behind the veil; and you shall
serve. I give your priesthood *to you* as a gift
for service, but the outsider who comes near
shall be put to death."

Offerings for Support of the Priests

8 And the LORD spoke to Aaron: "Here, I
Myself have also given you charge of My
heave offerings, all the holy gifts of the children of Israel; I have given them as a portion
to you and your sons, as an ordinance forever.
9 "This shall be yours of the most holy
things *reserved* from the fire: every offering
of theirs, every grain offering and every sin
offering and every trespass offering which
they render to Me, *shall be* most holy for you
and your sons.
10 "In a most holy *place* you shall eat it;
every male shall eat it. It shall be holy to you.
11 "This also *is* yours: the heave offering of
their gift, with all the wave offerings of the
children of Israel; I have given them to you,
and your sons and daughters with you, as an
ordinance forever. everyone who is clean in
your house may eat it.
12 "All the best of the oil, all the best of the
new wine and the grain, their firstfruits which
they offer to the LORD, I have given them to
you.
13 "Whatever first ripe fruit is in their land,
which they bring to the LORD, shall be yours.
Everyone who is clean in your house may eat
it.
14 "Every devoted thing in Israel shall be
yours.
15 "Everything that first opens the womb of
all flesh, which they bring to the LORD,
whether man or beast, shall be yours; nevertheless the firstborn of man you shall surely
redeem, and the firstborn of unclean animals
you shall redeem.
16 "And those redeemed of the devoted
things you shall redeem when one month old,
according to your valuation, for five shekels
of silver, according to the shekel of the sanctuary, which *is* twenty gerahs.
17 "But the firstborn of a cow, the firstborn of
a sheep, or the firstborn of a goat you shall
not redeem; they *are* holy. You shall sprinkle
their blood on the altar, and burn their fat *as*
an offering made by fire for a sweet aroma to
the LORD.
18 "And their flesh shall be yours, just as the
wave breast and the right thigh are yours.
19 "All the heave offerings of the holy things,
which the children of Israel offer to the LORD,
I have given to you and your sons and daughters with you as an ordinance forever; it *is* a
covenant of salt forever before the LORD with
you and your descendants with you."
20 Then the LORD said to Aaron: "You shall ➤
have no inheritance in their land, nor shall
you have any portion among them; I *am* your
portion and your inheritance among the children of Israel.

LIFE LESSONS

➤ **18:20 — *". . . I am your portion and your inheritance among the children of Israel."***

Aaron had no terrestrial property, but God gave him Himself as Aaron's portion and inheritance. When we find our treasure in God, we gain a rich store of salvation and wisdom and knowledge (see Is. 33:6).

Tithes for Support of the Levites

21 "Behold, I have given the children of Levi all the tithes in Israel as an inheritance in return for the work which they perform, the work of the tabernacle of meeting.

22 "Hereafter the children of Israel shall not come near the tabernacle of meeting, lest they bear sin and die.

23 "But the Levites shall perform the work of the tabernacle of meeting, and they shall bear their iniquity; *it shall be* a statute forever, throughout your generations, that among the children of Israel they shall have no inheritance.

24 "For the tithes of the children of Israel, which they offer up *as* a heave offering to the LORD, I have given to the Levites as an inheritance; therefore I have said to them, 'Among the children of Israel they shall have no inheritance.' "

The Tithe of the Levites

25 Then the LORD spoke to Moses, saying,

26 "Speak thus to the Levites, and say to them: 'When you take from the children of Israel the tithes which I have given you from them as your inheritance, then you shall offer up a heave offering of it to the LORD, a tenth of the tithe.

27 'And your heave offering shall be reckoned to you as though *it were* the grain of the threshing floor and as the fullness of the winepress.

28 'Thus you shall also offer a heave offering to the LORD from all your tithes which you receive from the children of Israel, and you shall give the LORD's heave offering from it to Aaron the priest.

29 'Of all your gifts you shall offer up every heave offering due to the LORD, from all the best of them, the consecrated part of them.'

30 'Therefore you shall say to them: 'When you have lifted up the best of it, then *the rest* shall be accounted to the Levites as the produce of the threshing floor and as the produce of the winepress.

31 'You may eat it in any place, you and your households, for it *is* your reward for your work in the tabernacle of meeting.

32 'And you shall bear no sin because of it, when you have lifted up the best of it. But you shall not profane the holy gifts of the children of Israel, lest you die.' "

Laws of Purification

19 Now the LORD spoke to Moses and Aaron, saying,

2 "This *is* the ordinance of the law which the LORD has commanded, saying: 'Speak to the children of Israel, that they bring you a red heifer without blemish, in which there *is* no defect *and* on which a yoke has never come.

3 'You shall give it to Eleazar the priest, that he may take it outside the camp, and it shall be slaughtered before him;

4 'and Eleazar the priest shall take some of its blood with his finger, and sprinkle some of its blood seven times directly in front of the tabernacle of meeting.

5 'Then the heifer shall be burned in his sight: its hide, its flesh, its blood, and its offal shall be burned.

6 'And the priest shall take cedar wood and hyssop and scarlet, and cast *them* into the midst of the fire burning the heifer.

7 'Then the priest shall wash his clothes, he shall bathe in water, and afterward he shall come into the camp; the priest shall be unclean until evening.

8 'And the one who burns it shall wash his clothes in water, bathe in water, and shall be unclean until evening.

9 'Then a man *who is* clean shall gather up the ashes of the heifer, and store *them* outside the camp in a clean place; and they shall be kept for the congregation of the children of Israel for the water of purification;[a] it *is* for purifying from sin.

10 'And the one who gathers the ashes of the heifer shall wash his clothes, and be unclean until evening. It shall be a statute forever to the children of Israel and to the stranger who dwells among them.

11 'He who touches the dead body of anyone shall be unclean seven days.

12 'He shall purify himself with the water on the third day and on the seventh day; *then* he will be clean. But if he does not purify himself on the third day and on the seventh day, he will not be clean.

13 'Whoever touches the body of anyone who has died, and does not purify himself, defiles the tabernacle of the LORD. That person shall be cut off from Israel. He shall be unclean, because the water of purification was not sprinkled on him; his uncleanness *is* still on him.

14 'This *is* the law when a man dies in a tent: All who come into the tent and all who *are* in the tent shall be unclean seven days;

15 'and every open vessel, which has no cover fastened on it, *is* unclean.

16 'Whoever in the open field touches one who is slain by a sword or who has died, or a bone of a man, or a grave, shall be unclean seven days.

17 'And for an unclean *person* they shall take some of the ashes of the heifer burnt for purification from sin, and running water shall be put on them in a vessel.

18 'A clean person shall take hyssop and dip *it* in the water, sprinkle *it* on the tent, on all the vessels, on the persons who were there, or on the one who touched a bone, the slain, the dead, or a grave.

19:9 [a]Literally *impurity*

19 'The clean *person* shall sprinkle the unclean on the third day and on the seventh day; and on the seventh day he shall purify himself, wash his clothes, and bathe in water; and at evening he shall be clean.
20 'But the man who is unclean and does not purify himself, that person shall be cut off from among the assembly, because he has defiled the sanctuary of the LORD. The water of purification has not been sprinkled on him; he *is* unclean.
21 'It shall be a perpetual statute for them. He who sprinkles the water of purification shall wash his clothes; and he who touches the water of purification shall be unclean until evening.
22 'Whatever the unclean *person* touches shall be unclean; and the person who touches *it* shall be unclean until evening.'"

Moses' Error at Kadesh

20 Then the children of Israel, the whole congregation, came into the Wilderness of Zin in the first month, and the people stayed in Kadesh; and Miriam died there and was buried there.
2 Now there was no water for the congregation; so they gathered together against Moses and Aaron.
3 And the people contended with Moses and spoke, saying: "If only we had died when our brethren died before the LORD!
4 "Why have you brought up the assembly of the LORD into this wilderness, that we and our animals should die here?
5 "And why have you made us come up out of Egypt, to bring us to this evil place? It *is* not a place of grain or figs or vines or pomegranates; nor *is* there any water to drink."
6 So Moses and Aaron went from the presence of the assembly to the door of the tabernacle of meeting, and they fell on their faces. And the glory of the LORD appeared to them.
7 Then the LORD spoke to Moses, saying,
8 "Take the rod; you and your brother Aaron gather the congregation together. Speak to the rock before their eyes, and it will yield its water; thus you shall bring water for them out of the rock, and give drink to the congregation and their animals."
9 So Moses took the rod from before the LORD as He commanded him.
10 And Moses and Aaron gathered the assembly together before the rock; and he said to them, "Hear now, you rebels! Must we bring water for you out of this rock?"
11 Then Moses lifted his hand and struck the rock twice with his rod; and water came out abundantly, and the congregation and their animals drank.
12 Then the LORD spoke to Moses and Aaron, "Because you did not believe Me, to hallow Me in the eyes of the children of Israel, therefore you shall not bring this assembly into the land which I have given them."
13 This *was* the water of Meribah,[a] because the children of Israel contended with the LORD, and He was hallowed among them.

Passage Through Edom Refused

14 Now Moses sent messengers from Kadesh to the king of Edom. "Thus says your brother Israel: 'You know all the hardship that has befallen us,
15 'how our fathers went down to Egypt, and we dwelt in Egypt a long time, and the Egyptians afflicted us and our fathers.
16 'When we cried out to the LORD, He heard our voice and sent the Angel and brought us up out of Egypt; now here we are in Kadesh, a city on the edge of your border.
17 'Please let us pass through your country. We will not pass through fields or vineyards, nor will we drink water from wells; we will go along the King's Highway; we will not turn aside to the right hand or to the left until we have passed through your territory.'"
18 Then Edom said to him, "You shall not pass through my *land*, lest I come out against you with the sword."
19 So the children of Israel said to him, "We will go by the Highway, and if I or my livestock drink any of your water, then I will pay for it; let me only pass through on foot, nothing *more*."
20 Then he said, "You shall not pass through." So Edom came out against them with many men and with a strong hand.
21 Thus Edom refused to give Israel passage through his territory; so Israel turned away from him.

20:13 [a]Literally *Contention*

LIFE LESSONS

➤ 20:12 — *Then the LORD spoke to Moses and Aaron, "Because you did not believe Me, to hallow Me in the eyes of the children of Israel, therefore you shall not bring this assembly into the land which I have given them."*

God is no respecter of persons; obedience always brings blessing, as disobedience brings consequences. Moses allowed his anger and frustration to goad him into an ugly display of the flesh.

➤ 20:21 — *Thus Edom refused to give Israel passage through his territory; so Israel turned away from him.*

It may have confused Israel why the Lord allowed the Edomites to refuse them passage. But as children of a sovereign God, we are never victims of our circumstances.

Death of Aaron

22 Now the children of Israel, the whole congregation, journeyed from Kadesh and came to Mount Hor.

23 And the LORD spoke to Moses and Aaron in Mount Hor by the border of the land of Edom, saying:

24 "Aaron shall be gathered to his people, for he shall not enter the land which I have given to the children of Israel, because you rebelled against My word at the water of Meribah.

25 "Take Aaron and Eleazar his son, and bring them up to Mount Hor;

26 "and strip Aaron of his garments and put them on Eleazar his son; for Aaron shall be gathered *to his people* and die there."

27 So Moses did just as the LORD commanded, and they went up to Mount Hor in the sight of all the congregation.

28 Moses stripped Aaron of his garments and put them on Eleazar his son; and Aaron died there on the top of the mountain. Then Moses and Eleazar came down from the mountain.

29 Now when all the congregation saw that Aaron was dead, all the house of Israel mourned for Aaron thirty days.

Canaanites Defeated at Hormah

21 The king of Arad, the Canaanite, who dwelt in the South, heard that Israel was coming on the road to Atharim. Then he fought against Israel and took *some* of them prisoners.

➤ 2 So Israel made a vow to the LORD, and said, "If You will indeed deliver this people into my hand, then I will utterly destroy their cities."

3 And the LORD listened to the voice of Israel and delivered up the Canaanites, and they utterly destroyed them and their cities. So the name of that place was called Hormah.[a]

The Bronze Serpent

4 Then they journeyed from Mount Hor by the Way of the Red Sea, to go around the land of Edom; and the soul of the people became very discouraged on the way.

5 And the people spoke against God and against Moses: "Why have you brought us up out of Egypt to die in the wilderness? For *there is* no food and no water, and our soul loathes this worthless bread."

6 So the LORD sent fiery serpents among the people, and they bit the people; and many of the people of Israel died.

7 Therefore the people came to Moses, and said, "We have sinned, for we have spoken against the LORD and against you; pray to the LORD that He take away the serpents from us." So Moses prayed for the people.

8 Then the LORD said to Moses, "Make a fiery *serpent,* and set it on a pole; and it shall be that everyone who is bitten, when he looks at it, shall live."

9 So Moses made a bronze serpent, and put it on a pole; and so it was, if a serpent had bitten anyone, when he looked at the bronze serpent, he lived.

From Mount Hor to Moab

10 Now the children of Israel moved on and camped in Oboth.

11 And they journeyed from Oboth and camped at Ije Abarim, in the wilderness which *is* east of Moab, toward the sunrise.

12 From there they moved and camped in the Valley of Zered.

13 From there they moved and camped on the other side of the Arnon, which *is* in the wilderness that extends from the border of the Amorites; for the Arnon *is* the border of Moab, between Moab and the Amorites.

14 Therefore it is said in the Book of the Wars of the LORD:

"Waheb in Suphah,[a]
The brooks of the Arnon,
15 And the slope of the brooks
That reaches to the dwelling of Ar,
And lies on the border of Moab."

16 From there *they went* to Beer, which *is* the well where the LORD said to Moses, "Gather the people together, and I will give them water."

17 Then Israel sang this song:

"Spring up, O well!
All of you sing to it—
18 The well the leaders sank,
Dug by the nation's nobles,
By the lawgiver, with their staves."

21:3 [a]Literally *Utter Destruction* **21:14** [a]Ancient unknown places; Vulgate reads *What He did in the Red Sea.*

LIFE LESSONS

➤ 21:2 — *So Israel made a vow to the LORD, and said, "If You will indeed deliver this people into my hand, then I will utterly destroy their cities."*

God allowed a pagan king to take some Israelites captive in battle. But when we serve God, momentary defeats give way to ultimate victory. Adversity is a setback from which we take our greatest leaps forward.

➤ 21:9 — *So Moses made a bronze serpent, and put it on a pole; and so it was, if a serpent had bitten anyone, when he looked at the bronze serpent, he lived.*

The bronze serpent that Moses made in the desert foreshadowed the ultimate work of salvation that Jesus accomplished for us on the cross (see John 3:14-16).

And from the wilderness *they went* to Mattanah,
19 from Mattanah to Nahaliel, from Nahaliel to Bamoth,
20 and from Bamoth, *in* the valley that *is* in the country of Moab, to the top of Pisgah which looks down on the wasteland.[a]

King Sihon Defeated

21 Then Israel sent messengers to Sihon king of the Amorites, saying,
22 "Let me pass through your land. We will not turn aside into fields or vineyards; we will not drink water from wells. We will go by the King's Highway until we have passed through your territory."
23 But Sihon would not allow Israel to pass through his territory. So Sihon gathered all his people together and went out against Israel in the wilderness, and he came to Jahaz and fought against Israel.
➤ 24 Then Israel defeated him with the edge of the sword, and took possession of his land from the Arnon to the Jabbok, as far as the people of Ammon; for the border of the people of Ammon *was* fortified.
25 So Israel took all these cities, and Israel dwelt in all the cities of the Amorites, in Heshbon and in all its villages.
26 For Heshbon *was* the city of Sihon king of the Amorites, who had fought against the former king of Moab, and had taken all his land from his hand as far as the Arnon.
27 Therefore those who speak in proverbs say:

"Come to Heshbon, let it be built;
Let the city of Sihon be repaired.

28 "For fire went out from Heshbon,
A flame from the city of Sihon;
It consumed Ar of Moab,
The lords of the heights of the Arnon.
29 Woe to you, Moab!
You have perished, O people of Chemosh!
He has given his sons as fugitives,
And his daughters into captivity,
To Sihon king of the Amorites.

30 "But we have shot at them;
Heshbon has perished as far as Dibon.
Then we laid waste as far as Nophah,
Which *reaches* to Medeba."

31 Thus Israel dwelt in the land of the Amorites.
32 Then Moses sent to spy out Jazer; and they took its villages and drove out the Amorites who *were* there.

King Og Defeated

33 And they turned and went up by the way to Bashan. So Og king of Bashan went out against them, he and all his people, to battle at Edrei.
34 Then the LORD said to Moses, "Do not fear him, for I have delivered him into your hand, with all his people and his land; and you shall do to him as you did to Sihon king of the Amorites, who dwelt at Heshbon."
35 So they defeated him, his sons, and all his people, until there was no survivor left him; and they took possession of his land.

Balak Sends for Balaam

22 Then the children of Israel moved, and camped in the plains of Moab on the side of the Jordan *across from* Jericho.
2 Now Balak the son of Zippor saw all that Israel had done to the Amorites.
3 And Moab was exceedingly afraid of the people because they *were* many, and Moab was sick with dread because of the children of Israel.
4 So Moab said to the elders of Midian, "Now this company will lick up everything around us, as an ox licks up the grass of the field." And Balak the son of Zippor *was* king of the Moabites at that time.
5 Then he sent messengers to Balaam the son of Beor at Pethor, which *is* near the River[a] in the land of the sons of his people,[b] to call him, saying: "Look, a people has come from Egypt. See, they cover the face of the earth, and are settling next to me!
6 "Therefore please come at once, curse this people for me, for they *are* too mighty for me. Perhaps I shall be able to defeat them and drive them out of the land, for I know that he whom you bless *is* blessed, and he whom you curse is cursed."
7 So the elders of Moab and the elders of Midian departed with the diviner's fee in their hand, and they came to Balaam and spoke to him the words of Balak.
8 And he said to them, "Lodge here tonight, and I will bring back word to you, as the LORD

21:20 [a]Hebrew *Jeshimon* **22:5** [a]That is, the Euphrates [b]Or *the people of Amau*

LIFE LESSONS

➤ **21:24 — *Then Israel defeated him with the edge of the sword, and took possession of his land from the Arnon to the Jabbok . . . .***

In years to come, Israel often remembered the victories God had given them over Sihon and Og (see Deut. 31:4; Josh. 2:10; Judg. 11:21; Ps. 135:10, 11; Neh. 9:22). It helps us move forward to commemorate spiritual victories!

speaks to me." So the princes of Moab stayed
with Balaam.
9 Then God came to Balaam and said, "Who
are these men with you?"
10 So Balaam said to God, "Balak the son of
Zippor, king of Moab, has sent to me, *saying,*
11 'Look, a people has come out of Egypt,
and they cover the face of the earth. Come
now, curse them for me; perhaps I shall be
able to overpower them and drive them out.'"
➤ 12 And God said to Balaam, "You shall not go
with them; you shall not curse the people, for
they *are* blessed."
13 So Balaam rose in the morning and said to
the princes of Balak, "Go back to your land,
for the LORD has refused to give me permission to go with you."
14 And the princes of Moab rose and went to
Balak, and said, "Balaam refuses to come
with us."
15 Then Balak again sent princes, more numerous and more honorable than they.
16 And they came to Balaam and said to him,
"Thus says Balak the son of Zippor: 'Please
let nothing hinder you from coming to me;
17 'for I will certainly honor you greatly, and
I will do whatever you say to me. Therefore
please come, curse this people for me.'"
18 Then Balaam answered and said to the
servants of Balak, "Though Balak were to
give me his house full of silver and gold, I
could not go beyond the word of the LORD my
God, to do less or more.
19 "Now therefore, please, you also stay here
tonight, that I may know what more the LORD
will say to me."
20 And God came to Balaam at night and
said to him, "If the men come to call you, rise
and go with them; but only the word which I
speak to you—that you shall do."
21 So Balaam rose in the morning, saddled
his donkey, and went with the princes of
Moab.

Balaam, the Donkey, and the Angel

22 Then God's anger was aroused because he
went, and the Angel of the LORD took His
stand in the way as an adversary against him.
And he was riding on his donkey, and his two
servants *were* with him.
23 Now the donkey saw the Angel of the
LORD standing in the way with His drawn
sword in His hand, and the donkey turned
aside out of the way and went into the field.
So Balaam struck the donkey to turn her back
onto the road.
24 Then the Angel of the LORD stood in a narrow path between the vineyards, *with* a wall
on this side and a wall on that side.
25 And when the donkey saw the Angel of
the LORD, she pushed herself against the wall
and crushed Balaam's foot against the wall;
so he struck her again.
26 Then the Angel of the LORD went further,
and stood in a narrow place where there *was*
no way to turn either to the right hand or to
the left.
27 And when the donkey saw the Angel of
the LORD, she lay down under Balaam; so Balaam's anger was aroused, and he struck the
donkey with his staff.
28 Then the LORD opened the mouth of the
donkey, and she said to Balaam, "What have I
done to you, that you have struck me these
three times?"
29 And Balaam said to the donkey, "Because
you have abused me. I wish there were a
sword in my hand, for now I would kill you!"
30 So the donkey said to Balaam, "*Am* I
not your donkey on which you have ridden,
ever since *I became* yours, to this day? Was I
ever disposed to do this to you?" And he said,
"No."
31 Then the LORD opened Balaam's eyes, and
he saw the Angel of the LORD standing in the
way with His drawn sword in His hand; and
he bowed his head and fell flat on his face.
32 And the Angel of the LORD said to him, ➤
"Why have you struck your donkey these
three times? Behold, I have come out to stand
against you, because *your* way is perverse before Me.
33 "The donkey saw Me and turned aside
from Me these three times. If she had not
turned aside from Me, surely I would also
have killed you by now, and let her live."
34 And Balaam said to the Angel of the LORD,
"I have sinned, for I did not know You stood in
the way against me. Now therefore, if it displeases You, I will turn back."
35 Then the Angel of the LORD said to Balaam, "Go with the men, but only the word that
I speak to you, that you shall speak." So Balaam went with the princes of Balak.

LIFE LESSONS

➤ **22:12 — *And God said to Balaam, "You shall not go with them; you shall not curse the people, for they are blessed."***

Those whom the Lord blesses cannot be cursed. And those in Christ have been blessed "with every spiritual blessing in the heavenly places in Christ" (Eph. 1:3)!

➤ **22:32 — *And the Angel of the LORD said to him, "Why have you struck your donkey these three times? Behold, I have come out to stand against you, because your way is perverse before Me."***

Why was Balaam's way "perverse" before God? Because despite his good words, he harbored ill will against God's people—and eventually he died because of it (see Num. 31:8). God wants a right heart, not nice words.

36 Now when Balak heard that Balaam was
coming, he went out to meet him at the city of
Moab, which *is* on the border at the Arnon,
the boundary of the territory.
37 Then Balak said to Balaam, "Did I not
earnestly send to you, calling for you? Why
did you not come to me? Am I not able to
honor you?"
38 And Balaam said to Balak, "Look, I have
come to you! Now, have I any power at all to
say anything? The word that God puts in my
mouth, that I must speak."
39 So Balaam went with Balak, and they
came to Kirjath Huzoth.
40 Then Balak offered oxen and sheep, and
he sent *some* to Balaam and to the princes
who *were* with him.

Balaam's First Prophecy

41 So it was, the next day, that Balak took
Balaam and brought him up to the high
places of Baal, that from there he might observe the extent of the people.

23 Then Balaam said to Balak, "Build
seven altars for me here, and prepare
for me here seven bulls and seven rams."
2 And Balak did just as Balaam had spoken,
and Balak and Balaam offered a bull and a
ram on *each* altar.
3 Then Balaam said to Balak, "Stand by
your burnt offering, and I will go; perhaps the
LORD will come to meet me, and whatever He
shows me I will tell you." So he went to a desolate height.
4 And God met Balaam, and he said to Him,
"I have prepared the seven altars, and I have
offered on *each* altar a bull and a ram."
5 Then the LORD put a word in Balaam's
mouth, and said, "Return to Balak, and thus
you shall speak."
6 So he returned to him, and there he was,
standing by his burnt offering, he and all the
princes of Moab.
7 And he took up his oracle and said:

"Balak the king of Moab has brought me
from Aram,
From the mountains of the east.
'Come, curse Jacob for me,
And come, denounce Israel!'

8 "How shall I curse whom God has not
cursed?
And how shall I denounce *whom* the
LORD has not denounced?
9 For from the top of the rocks I see him,
And from the hills I behold him;
There! A people dwelling alone,
Not reckoning itself among the
nations.

10 "Who can count the dust[a] of Jacob,
Or number one-fourth of Israel?
Let me die the death of the righteous,
And let my end be like his!"

11 Then Balak said to Balaam, "What have
you done to me? I took you to curse my enemies, and look, you have blessed *them* bountifully!"
12 So he answered and said, "Must I not take
heed to speak what the LORD has put in my
mouth?"

Balaam's Second Prophecy

13 Then Balak said to him, "Please come with
me to another place from which you may see
them; you shall see only the outer part of
them, and shall not see them all; curse them
for me from there."
14 So he brought him to the field of Zophim,
to the top of Pisgah, and built seven altars,
and offered a bull and a ram on *each* altar.
15 And he said to Balak, "Stand here by your
burnt offering while I meet[a] *the LORD* over
there."
16 Then the LORD met Balaam, and put a
word in his mouth, and said, "Go back to
Balak, and thus you shall speak."
17 So he came to him, and there he was,
standing by his burnt offering, and the
princes of Moab were with him. And Balak
said to him, "What has the LORD spoken?"
18 Then he took up his oracle and said:

"Rise up, Balak, and hear!
Listen to me, son of Zippor!

19 "God *is* not a man, that He should lie,
Nor a son of man, that He should repent.
Has He said, and will He not do?
Or has He spoken, and will He not make
it good?
20 Behold, I have received *a command* to
bless;
He has blessed, and I cannot reverse it.

21 "He has not observed iniquity in Jacob,
Nor has He seen wickedness in Israel.
The LORD his God *is* with him,
And the shout of a King *is* among them.
22 God brings them out of Egypt;
He has strength like a wild ox.

23 "For *there is* no sorcery against Jacob,
Nor any divination against Israel.
It now must be said of Jacob
And of Israel, 'Oh, what God has done!'
24 Look, a people rises like a lioness,
And lifts itself up like a lion;
It shall not lie down until it devours the
prey,
And drinks the blood of the slain."

25 Then Balak said to Balaam, "Neither curse
them at all, nor bless them at all!"
26 So Balaam answered and said to Balak,
"Did I not tell you, saying, 'All that the LORD
speaks, that I must do'?"

23:10 [a]Or *dust cloud* **23:15** [a]Following Masoretic Text, Targum, and Vulgate; Syriac reads *call;* Septuagint reads *go and ask God.*

LIFE PRINCIPLE 3

GOD'S WORD IS AN IMMOVABLE ANCHOR IN TIMES OF STORM.

NUM. 23:19

The words of King Darius echoed through Daniel's mind as servants lowered him into the lion's den. "Your God whom you constantly serve will Himself deliver you" (Dan. 6:16). Workers then laid a heavy stone over the opening to the underground chamber.

Even after assessing his dire situation, Daniel did not waver in his faith. The next morning, King Darius found Daniel untouched and proclaiming, "O king, live forever! My God sent His angel to shut the lions' mouths, and they have not harmed me" (vv. 21, 22).

How did Daniel survive? Were the lions not hungry? Historians tell us animals used for such planned executions went unfed for days in an effort to ensure the death of the accused. But Daniel's fate was never in the hands of men. His life belonged to God, and therein lies the victory. Daniel survived by placing his trust in God and his faith in God's promises.

Each of us can remember times when we wished we had a sure word from God—something we could cling to when doubts and fears arose. God knows when we need encouragement, guidance, and hope. This is why He provides specific promises in His Word, that we might understand His nature and trust Him. In emotionally devastating times, God's promises are essential to our spiritual welfare.

God's Word is therefore a compass, a guide, and an instruction book to life. Just as we use instruction manuals at work or in the kitchen, we are to use God's Word as our resource for wisdom and truth. No one would think of baking a cake without a recipe, nor would a mechanic rebuild a car engine without a manual.

Some of God's promises are conditional (see "How can I claim God's promises?" placed near Heb. 10:23), but we can stand in faith on the vast majority of them. It's not a matter of naming and claiming a promise, however; promises should be coupled with prayer and an earnestness to know God's will for our lives. While God wants each of us to experience His best, He also wants us to know and enjoy His presence in a personal way that best expresses His sufficiency. Claiming a promise without leadership from His Holy Spirit will lead to disappointment, disillusionment, and frustration.

At times God brings a specific scripture to mind that ministers His hope and reassurance to our hearts. At other times He challenges us to pray and seek His wisdom on a certain issue.

God's promises are essential to our spiritual welfare.

When King David sought God's heart regarding his desire to build the temple, the Bible says: "Then king David went in and sat before the LORD" (2 Sam. 7:18). David didn't order his men to begin construction. He waited for God's leadership—and it was a good thing he did, because God wanted David's son Solomon to do the job instead.

God honored David's attitude, however, and gave him a wonderful promise: "Your house and your kingdom shall be established forever before you. Your throne shall be established forever" (2 Sam. 7:16). God always honors our desire to seek His guidance and wisdom. If we will come to God expecting Him to answer, He will never disappoint us.

In Daniel's day, God spoke through visions, dreams, and sometimes audibly. Today, He speaks primarily through His Word, since He never wants us involved in anything that contradicts Scripture. Any verse can be taken out of context and twisted. But if we are true to God's Word and interpret Scripture within its context, then we will find God's promises rewarding.

He never wants us involved in anything that contradicts Scripture.

When we look to God in faith, He will lead us according to His will. Of course, this may not happen overnight! Many times God wants us to meditate on a certain scripture over a period of time before He gives His guidance.

Instead of being emotionally blown one way and then another, we learn to stand firm in our commitment and trust in Christ. Consider God's promises your spiritual anchors. Once you learn to follow Him, pursue His lead wherever He goes.

God never fails to keep a promise He makes. He wants us to get in His Word and listen for His voice. This is where our responsibility comes in.

God gives promises, but we must be willing to patiently wait for Him to fulfill them. Never try putting God in a time box! Instead, leave room for Him to bring everything together according to His plan and His timing. You'll be glad you did.

See the Life Principles Index for further study.

Balaam's Third Prophecy

27 Then Balak said to Balaam, "Please come,
I will take you to another place; perhaps it
will please God that you may curse them for
me from there."
28 So Balak took Balaam to the top of Peor,
that overlooks the wasteland.[a]
29 Then Balaam said to Balak, "Build for me
here seven altars, and prepare for me here
seven bulls and seven rams."
30 And Balak did as Balaam had said, and offered a bull and a ram on *every* altar.

24 Now when Balaam saw that it pleased
the LORD to bless Israel, he did not go
as at other times, to seek to use sorcery, but
he set his face toward the wilderness.
2 And Balaam raised his eyes, and saw Israel encamped according to their tribes; and
the Spirit of God came upon him.
3 Then he took up his oracle and said:

"The utterance of Balaam the son of
Beor,
The utterance of the man whose eyes are
opened,
4 The utterance of him who hears the
words of God,
Who sees the vision of the Almighty,
Who falls down, with eyes wide open:

5 "How lovely are your tents, O Jacob!
Your dwellings, O Israel!
6 Like valleys that stretch out,
Like gardens by the riverside,
Like aloes planted by the LORD,
Like cedars beside the waters.
7 He shall pour water from his buckets,
And his seed *shall be* in many waters.

"His king shall be higher than Agag,
And his kingdom shall be exalted.

8 "God brings him out of Egypt;
He has strength like a wild ox;
He shall consume the nations, his
enemies;
He shall break their bones
And pierce *them* with his arrows.
9 'He bows down, he lies down as a lion;
And as a lion, who shall rouse him?'[a]

"Blessed *is* he who blesses you,
And cursed *is* he who curses you."

10 Then Balak's anger was aroused against
Balaam, and he struck his hands together;
and Balak said to Balaam, "I called you to
curse my enemies, and look, you have bountifully blessed *them* these three times!
11 "Now therefore, flee to your place. I said I
would greatly honor you, but in fact, the LORD
has kept you back from honor."
12 So Balaam said to Balak, "Did I not also
speak to your messengers whom you sent to
me, saying,
13 'If Balak were to give me his house full of
silver and gold, I could not go beyond the
word of the LORD, to do good or bad of my
own will. What the LORD says, that I must
speak'?
14 "And now, indeed, I am going to my peo- ➤
ple. Come, I will advise you what this people
will do to your people in the latter days."

Balaam's Fourth Prophecy

15 So he took up his oracle and said:

"The utterance of Balaam the son of Beor,
And the utterance of the man whose eyes
are opened;
16 The utterance of him who hears the
words of God,
And has the knowledge of the Most High,
Who sees the vision of the Almighty,
Who falls down, with eyes wide open:

17 "I see Him, but not now;
I behold Him, but not near;
A Star shall come out of Jacob;
A Scepter shall rise out of Israel,
And batter the brow of Moab,
And destroy all the sons of tumult.[a]

18 "And Edom shall be a possession;
Seir also, his enemies, shall be a
possession,
While Israel does valiantly.
19 Out of Jacob One shall have dominion,
And destroy the remains of the city."

20 Then he looked on Amalek, and he took
up his oracle and said:

"Amalek *was* first among the nations,
But *shall be* last until he perishes."

21 Then he looked on the Kenites, and he
took up his oracle and said:

"Firm is your dwelling place,
And your nest is set in the rock;

23:28 [a]Hebrew *Jeshimon* **24:9** [a]Genesis 49:9 **24:17** [a]Hebrew *Sheth* (compare Jeremiah 48:45)

LIFE LESSONS

➤ ***24:14 — "And now, indeed, I am going to my people. Come, I will advise you what this people will do to your people in the latter days."***

Balaam not only advised Balak what Israel would do to his nation "in the latter days." Apparently he also advised him how to get Israel to sin and so lose the favor of God (Num. 31:16; Rev. 2:14).

22 Nevertheless Kain shall be burned.
How long until Asshur carries you away captive?"

23 Then he took up his oracle and said:

"Alas! Who shall live when God does this?
24 But ships *shall come* from the coasts of Cyprus,[a]
And they shall afflict Asshur and afflict Eber,
And so shall *Amalek*,[b] until he perishes."

25 So Balaam rose and departed and returned to his place; Balak also went his way.

Israel's Harlotry in Moab

25 Now Israel remained in Acacia Grove,[a] and the people began to commit harlotry with the women of Moab.
➤ 2 They invited the people to the sacrifices of their gods, and the people ate and bowed down to their gods.
3 So Israel was joined to Baal of Peor, and the anger of the LORD was aroused against Israel.
4 Then the LORD said to Moses, "Take all the leaders of the people and hang the offenders before the LORD, out in the sun, that the fierce anger of the LORD may turn away from Israel."
5 So Moses said to the judges of Israel, "Every one of you kill his men who were joined to Baal of Peor."
6 And indeed, one of the children of Israel came and presented to his brethren a Midianite woman in the sight of Moses and in the sight of all the congregation of the children of Israel, who *were* weeping at the door of the tabernacle of meeting.
7 Now when Phinehas the son of Eleazar, the son of Aaron the priest, saw *it*, he rose from among the congregation and took a javelin in his hand;
8 and he went after the man of Israel into the tent and thrust both of them through, the man of Israel, and the woman through her body. So the plague was stopped among the children of Israel.
9 And those who died in the plague were twenty-four thousand.
10 Then the LORD spoke to Moses, saying:
11 "Phinehas the son of Eleazar, the son of Aaron the priest, has turned back My wrath from the children of Israel, because he was zealous with My zeal among them, so that I did not consume the children of Israel in My zeal.
12 "Therefore say, 'Behold, I give to him My covenant of peace;
13 'and it shall be to him and his descendants after him a covenant of an everlasting priesthood, because he was zealous for his God, and made atonement for the children of Israel.'"

Life Examples:

PHINEHAS

A Man with a Zeal for God

NUM. 25:12, 13

Phinehas, the son of Eleazar and the grandson of the high priest Aaron, was a man noted by God for his zeal. God highly esteemed him and gave him a remarkable promise because of his passion (Num. 25:12, 13).

And how did Phinehas earn such favor? He took a javelin in hand and executed a wicked Israelite who had brazenly committed adultery with a pagan woman in full sight of the nation. The quick action of Phinehas stopped a divine plague that took the lives of 24 thousand sinning Israelites. And the Lord lauded him for his godly zeal.

As believers, we are to have a passion for God. Today, the word "passion" often carries a sexual connotation; but the true meaning of the word is "an overwhelming, strong desire," which can be a strong desire for matters of the spirit. Like Phinehas, believers are to have an urgency, a fervor, a zealous desire for the Lord and everything related to Him.

See the Life Principles Index for further study:
1. *Our intimacy with God—His highest priority for our lives—determines the impact of our lives.*

24:24 [a]Hebrew *Kittim* [b]Literally *he* or *that one* **25:1** [a]Hebrew *Shittim*

LIFE LESSONS

➤ ***25:2 — They invited the people to the sacrifices of their gods, and the people ate and bowed down to their gods.***

Even a polite invitation to worship any god other than the Lord ought to be immediately and firmly rejected. We are to serve God alone—no exceptions.

14 Now the name of the Israelite who was
killed, who was killed with the Midianite
woman, *was* Zimri the son of Salu, a leader of
a father's house among the Simeonites.
15 And the name of the Midianite woman
who was killed *was* Cozbi the daughter of
Zur; he *was* head of the people of a father's
house in Midian.
16 Then the LORD spoke to Moses, saying:
17 "Harass the Midianites, and attack them;
➤ 18 "for they harassed you with their schemes
by which they seduced you in the matter of
Peor and in the matter of Cozbi, the daughter
of a leader of Midian, their sister, who was
killed in the day of the plague because of
Peor."

The Second Census of Israel

26 And it came to pass, after the plague,
that the LORD spoke to Moses and
Eleazar the son of Aaron the priest, saying:
2 "Take a census of all the congregation of
the children of Israel from twenty years old
and above, by their fathers' houses, all who
are able to go to war in Israel."
3 So Moses and Eleazar the priest spoke
with them in the plains of Moab by the Jordan, *across from* Jericho, saying:
4 "*Take a census of the people* from twenty
years old and above, just as the LORD commanded Moses and the children of Israel who
came out of the land of Egypt."
5 Reuben *was* the firstborn of Israel. The
children of Reuben *were: of* Hanoch, the family of the Hanochites; *of* Pallu, the family of
the Palluites;
6 *of* Hezron, the family of the Hezronites; *of*
Carmi, the family of the Carmites.
7 These *are* the families of the Reubenites:
those who were numbered of them were
forty-three thousand seven hundred and
thirty.
8 And the son of Pallu *was* Eliab.
9 The sons of Eliab *were* Nemuel, Dathan,
and Abiram. These *are* the Dathan and Abiram, representatives of the congregation, who
contended against Moses and Aaron in the
company of Korah, when they contended
against the LORD;
10 and the earth opened its mouth and swallowed them up together with Korah when that
company died, when the fire devoured two
hundred and fifty men; and they became a
sign.
11 Nevertheless the children of Korah did not
die.
12 The sons of Simeon according to their
families *were: of* Nemuel,[a] the family of the
Nemuelites; *of* Jamin, the family of the
Jaminites; *of* Jachin,[b] the family of the Ja-
chinites;
13 *of* Zerah,[a] the family of the Zarhites; *of*
Shaul, the family of the Shaulites.
14 These *are* the families of the Simeonites:
twenty-two thousand two hundred.
15 The sons of Gad according to their families *were: of* Zephon,[a] the family of the Ze-
phonites; *of* Haggi, the family of the Haggites;
of Shuni, the family of the Shunites;
16 *of* Ozni,[a] the family of the Oznites; *of* Eri,
the family of the Erites;
17 *of* Arod,[a] the family of the Arodites; *of*
Areli, the family of the Arelites.
18 These *are* the families of the sons of Gad
according to those who were numbered of
them: forty thousand five hundred.
19 The sons of Judah *were* Er and Onan; and
Er and Onan died in the land of Canaan.
20 And the sons of Judah according to their
families were: *of* Shelah, the family of the
Shelanites; *of* Perez, the family of the
Parzites; *of* Zerah, the family of the Zarhites.
21 And the sons of Perez were: *of* Hezron, the
family of the Hezronites; *of* Hamul, the family
of the Hamulites.
22 These *are* the families of Judah according
to those who were numbered of them: sev-
enty-six thousand five hundred.
23 The sons of Issachar according to their
families *were: of* Tola, the family of the To-
laites; of Puah,[a] the family of the Punites;[b]
24 of Jashub, the family of the Jashubites; of
Shimron, the family of the Shimronites.
25 These *are* the families of Issachar according to those who were numbered of them:
sixty-four thousand three hundred.
26 The sons of Zebulun according to their
families *were:* of Sered, the family of the

26:12 [a]Spelled *Jemuel* in Genesis 46:10 and Exodus 6:15 [b]Called *Jarib* in 1 Chronicles 4:24 **26:13** [a]Called *Zohar* in Genesis 46:10 **26:15** [a]Called *Ziphion* in Genesis 46:16 **26:16** [a]Called *Ezbon* in Genesis 46:16 **26:17** [a]Spelled *Arodi* in Samaritan Pentateuch, Syriac, and Genesis 46:16 **26:23** [a]Hebrew *Puvah* (compare Genesis 46:13 and 1 Chronicles 7:1); Samaritan Pentateuch, Septuagint, Syriac, and Vulgate read *Puah.* [b]Samaritan Pentateuch, Septuagint, Syriac, and Vulgate read *Puaites.*

LIFE LESSONS

➤ 25:18 — *". . . for they harassed you with their schemes by which they seduced you in the matter of Peor and in the matter of Cozbi . . . ."*

Satan has his own people, who scheme to seduce God's people into sin. We must remain aware of their traps and escape from them by knowing God's Word and depending on God's power.

Sardites; of Elon, the family of the Elonites; of
Jahleel, the family of the Jahleelites.
27 These *are* the families of the Zebulunites
according to those who were numbered of
them: sixty thousand five hundred.
28 The sons of Joseph according to their families, by Manasseh and Ephraim, *were:*
29 The sons of Manasseh: of Machir, the
family of the Machirites; and Machir begot Gilead; of Gilead, the family of the Gileadites.
30 These *are* the sons of Gilead: *of* Jeezer,[a]
the family of the Jeezerites; of Helek, the family of the Helekites;
31 *of* Asriel, the family of the Asrielites; *of*
Shechem, the family of the Shechemites;
32 *of* Shemida, the family of the Shemidaites;
of Hepher, the family of the Hepherites.
33 Now Zelophehad the son of Hepher had
no sons, but daughters; and the names of the
daughters of Zelophehad *were* Mahlah,
Noah, Hoglah, Milcah, and Tirzah.
34 These *are* the families of Manasseh; and
those who were numbered of them *were* fifty-
two thousand seven hundred.
35 These *are* the sons of Ephraim according
to their families: of Shuthelah, the family of
the Shuthalhites; of Becher,[a] the family of the
Bachrites; of Tahan, the family of the Tahan-
ites.
36 And these *are* the sons of Shuthelah: of
Eran, the family of the Eranites.
37 These *are* the families of the sons of
Ephraim according to those who were numbered of them: thirty-two thousand five hundred. These *are* the sons of Joseph according
to their families.
38 The sons of Benjamin according to
their families were: of Bela, the family of
the Belaites; of Ashbel, the family of the Ash-
belites; of Ahiram, the family of the Ahi-
ramites;
39 of Shupham,[a] the family of the Shupha-
mites; of Hupham,[b] the family of the Hupha-
mites.
40 And the sons of Bela were Ard[a] and Naaman: *of Ard,* the family of the Ardites; of Naaman, the family of the Naamites.
41 These *are* the sons of Benjamin according
to their families; and those who were numbered of them *were* forty-five thousand six
hundred.
42 These *are* the sons of Dan according to
their families: of Shuham,[a] the family of the
Shuhamites. These *are* the families of Dan according to their families.
43 All the families of the Shuhamites, according to those who were numbered of them,
were sixty-four thousand four hundred.
44 The sons of Asher according to their families *were:* of Jimna, the family of the
Jimnites; of Jesui, the family of the Jesuites;
of Beriah, the family of the Beriites.
45 Of the sons of Beriah: of Heber, the family
of the Heberites; of Malchiel, the family of the
Malchielites.
46 And the name of the daughter of Asher
was Serah.
47 These *are* the families of the sons of Asher
according to those who were numbered of
them: fifty-three thousand four hundred.
48 The sons of Naphtali according to their
families *were:* of Jahzeel,[a] the family of the
Jahzeelites; of Guni, the family of the Gu-
nites;
49 of Jezer, the family of the Jezerites; of
Shillem, the family of the Shillemites.
50 These *are* the families of Naphtali according to their families; and those who were
numbered of them *were* forty-five thousand
four hundred.
51 These *are* those who were numbered of
the children of Israel: six hundred and one
thousand seven hundred and thirty.
52 Then the LORD spoke to Moses, saying:
53 "To these the land shall be divided as an
inheritance, according to the number of
names.
54 "To a large *tribe* you shall give a larger inheritance, and to a small *tribe* you shall give
a smaller inheritance. Each shall be given its
inheritance according to those who were
numbered of them.
55 "But the land shall be divided by lot; they
shall inherit according to the names of the
tribes of their fathers.
56 "According to the lot their inheritance
shall be divided between the larger and the
smaller."
57 And these *are* those who were numbered
of the Levites according to their families: of
Gershon, the family of the Gershonites; of Kohath, the family of the Kohathites; of Merari,
the family of the Merarites.
58 These *are* the families of the Levites: the
family of the Libnites, the family of the Hebronites, the family of the Mahlites, the family of the Mushites, and the family of the
Korathites. And Kohath begot Amram.
59 The name of Amram's wife *was* Jochebed
the daughter of Levi, who was born to Levi in
Egypt; and to Amram she bore Aaron and
Moses and their sister Miriam.
60 To Aaron were born Nadab and Abihu,
Eleazar and Ithamar.
61 And Nadab and Abihu died when they offered profane fire before the LORD.
62 Now those who were numbered of them
were twenty-three thousand, every male from
a month old and above; for they were not
numbered among the other children of Israel,

26:30 [a]Called *Abiezer* in Joshua 17:2 **26:35** [a]Called *Bered* in 1 Chronicles 7:20 **26:39** [a]Masoretic Text reads *Shephupham,* spelled *Shephuphan* in 1 Chronicles 8:5. [b]Called *Huppim* in Genesis 46:21 **26:40** [a]Called *Addar* in 1 Chronicles 8:3 **26:42** [a]Called *Hushim* in Genesis 46:23 **26:48** [a]Spelled *Jahziel* in 1 Chronicles 7:13

because there was no inheritance given to
them among the children of Israel.
63 These *are* those who were numbered by
Moses and Eleazar the priest, who numbered
the children of Israel in the plains of Moab by
the Jordan, *across from* Jericho.
64 But among these there was not a man
of those who were numbered by Moses
and Aaron the priest when they numbered
the children of Israel in the Wilderness of Sinai.
➤ 65 For the LORD had said of them, "They shall
surely die in the wilderness." So there was not
left a man of them, except Caleb the son of Jephunneh and Joshua the son of Nun.

Inheritance Laws

27 Then came the daughters of Zelophehad the son of Hepher, the son of
Gilead, the son of Machir, the son of Manasseh, from the families of Manasseh the son
of Joseph; and these *were* the names of his
daughters: Mahlah, Noah, Hoglah, Milcah,
and Tirzah.
2 And they stood before Moses, before
Eleazar the priest, and before the leaders and
all the congregation, *by* the doorway of the
tabernacle of meeting, saying:
3 "Our father died in the wilderness; but he
was not in the company of those who gathered together against the LORD, in company
with Korah, but he died in his own sin; and he
had no sons.
4 "Why should the name of our father be removed from among his family because he had
no son? Give us a possession among our father's brothers."
5 So Moses brought their case before the
LORD.
6 And the LORD spoke to Moses, saying:
7 "The daughters of Zelophehad speak
what is right; you shall surely give them a
possession of inheritance among their father's brothers, and cause the inheritance of
their father to pass to them.
8 "And you shall speak to the children of Israel, saying: 'If a man dies and has no son,
then you shall cause his inheritance to pass to
his daughter.
9 'If he has no daughter, then you shall give
his inheritance to his brothers.
10 'If he has no brothers, then you shall give
his inheritance to his father's brothers.
11 'And if his father has no brothers, then you
shall give his inheritance to the relative closest to him in his family, and he shall possess
it.'" And it shall be to the children of Israel a
statute of judgment, just as the LORD commanded Moses.

Joshua the Next Leader of Israel

12 Now the LORD said to Moses: "Go up into ➤
this Mount Abarim, and see the land which I
have given to the children of Israel.
13 "And when you have seen it, you also shall
be gathered to your people, as Aaron your
brother was gathered.
14 "For in the Wilderness of Zin, during the
strife of the congregation, you rebelled
against My command to hallow Me at the waters before their eyes." (These *are* the waters
of Meribah, at Kadesh in the Wilderness of
Zin.)
15 "Then Moses spoke to the LORD, saying:
16 "Let the LORD, the God of the spirits of all
flesh, set a man over the congregation,
17 "who may go out before them and go in
before them, who may lead them out and
bring them in, that the congregation of the
LORD may not be like sheep which have no
shepherd."
18 And the LORD said to Moses: "Take Joshua ➤
the son of Nun with you, a man in whom *is*
the Spirit, and lay your hand on him;
19 "set him before Eleazar the priest and before all the congregation, and inaugurate him
in their sight.
20 "And you shall give *some* of your authority to him, that all the congregation of the
children of Israel may be obedient.
21 "He shall stand before Eleazar the priest,
who shall inquire before the LORD for him by
the judgment of the Urim. At his word they
shall go out, and at his word they shall come
in, he and all the children of Israel with him—
all the congregation."
22 So Moses did as the LORD commanded
him. He took Joshua and set him before

LIFE LESSONS

➤ 26:65 — *For the LORD had said of them, "They shall surely die in the wilderness." So there was not left a man of them, except Caleb the son of Jephunneh and Joshua the son of Nun.*

God had said that all those who had accepted the spies' report and refused to enter Canaan would die in the wilderness, and His word came true. It always does.

➤ 27:12 — *Now the LORD said to Moses: "Go up into this Mount Abarim, and see the land which I have given to the children of Israel."*

God would not allow Moses to enter the Promised Land because of his public disobedience at the waters of Meribah, but in His grace He did allow him to view the land from a distance. Even in judgment, God is merciful.

➤ 27:18 — *And the LORD said to Moses: "Take Joshua the son of Nun with you, a man in whom is the Spirit, and lay your hand on him . . . ."*

God authorized Moses to make Joshua, "a man in whom is the Spirit," the next leader of Israel. Spirit-filled leadership is the only kind of leadership worth following.

Eleazar the priest and before all the congregation.
23 And he laid his hands on him and inaugurated him, just as the LORD commanded by
the hand of Moses.

Daily Offerings

28 Now the LORD spoke to Moses, saying,
2 "Command the children of Israel, and say
to them, 'My offering, My food for My offerings made by fire as a sweet aroma to Me, you
shall be careful to offer to Me at their appointed time.'
3 "And you shall say to them, 'This *is* the offering made by fire which you shall offer to
the LORD: two male lambs in their first year
without blemish, day by day, as a regular
burnt offering.
4 'The one lamb you shall offer in the morning, the other lamb you shall offer in the
evening,
5 'and one-tenth of an ephah of fine flour as
a grain offering mixed with one-fourth of a
hin of pressed oil.
6 '*It is* a regular burnt offering which was
ordained at Mount Sinai for a sweet aroma,
an offering made by fire to the LORD.
7 'And its drink offering *shall be* one-fourth
of a hin for each lamb; in a holy *place* you
shall pour out the drink to the LORD as an offering.
8 'The other lamb you shall offer in the
evening; as the morning grain offering and its
drink offering, you shall offer *it* as an offering
made by fire, a sweet aroma to the LORD.

Sabbath Offerings

9 'And on the Sabbath day two lambs in
their first year, without blemish, and two-
tenths *of an ephah* of fine flour as a grain offering, mixed with oil, with its drink
offering—
10 '*this is* the burnt offering for every Sabbath, besides the regular burnt offering with
its drink offering.

Monthly Offerings

11 'At the beginnings of your months you
shall present a burnt offering to the LORD: two
young bulls, one ram, and seven lambs in
their first year, without blemish;
12 'three-tenths *of an ephah* of fine flour as
a grain offering, mixed with oil, for each
bull; two-tenths *of an ephah* of fine flour as a
grain offering, mixed with oil, for the one
ram;
13 'and one-tenth *of an ephah* of fine flour,
mixed with oil, as a grain offering for each
lamb, as a burnt offering of sweet aroma, an
offering made by fire to the LORD.
14 'Their drink offering shall be half a hin of
wine for a bull, one-third of a hin for a ram,
and one-fourth of a hin for a lamb; this *is* the
burnt offering for each month throughout the
months of the year.
15 'Also one kid of the goats as a sin offering
to the LORD shall be offered, besides the regular burnt offering and its drink offering.

Offerings at Passover

16 'On the fourteenth day of the first month
is the Passover of the LORD.
17 'And on the fifteenth day of this month *is*
the feast; unleavened bread shall be eaten for
seven days.
18 'On the first day *you shall have* a holy convocation. You shall do no customary work.
19 'And you shall present an offering made
by fire as a burnt offering to the LORD: two
young bulls, one ram, and seven lambs in
their first year. Be sure they are without blemish.
20 'Their grain offering shall be of fine flour
mixed with oil: three-tenths *of an ephah* you
shall offer for a bull, and two-tenths for a
ram;
21 'you shall offer one-tenth *of an ephah* for
each of the seven lambs;
22 'also one goat *as* a sin offering, to make
atonement for you.
23 'You shall offer these besides the burnt offering of the morning, which *is* for a regular
burnt offering.
24 'In this manner you shall offer the food of
the offering made by fire daily for seven days,
as a sweet aroma to the LORD; it shall be offered besides the regular burnt offering and
its drink offering.
25 'And on the seventh day you shall have a
holy convocation. You shall do no customary
work.

Offerings at the Feast of Weeks

26 'Also on the day of the firstfruits, when
you bring a new grain offering to the LORD at
your *Feast of* Weeks, you shall have a holy
convocation. You shall do no customary work.
27 'You shall present a burnt offering as a
sweet aroma to the LORD: two young bulls,
one ram, and seven lambs in their first year,
28 'with their grain offering of fine flour
mixed with oil: three-tenths *of an ephah* for
each bull, two-tenths for the one ram,
29 'and one-tenth for each of the seven lambs;
30 '*also* one kid of the goats, to make atonement for you.
31 'Be sure they are without blemish. You
shall present *them* with their drink offerings,
besides the regular burnt offering with its
grain offering.

Offerings at the Feast of Trumpets

29 'And in the seventh month, on the first
day of the month, you shall have a
holy convocation. You shall do no customary
work. For you it is a day of blowing the trumpets.

2 'You shall offer a burnt offering as a sweet
aroma to the LORD: one young bull, one ram,
and seven lambs in their first year, without
blemish.
3 'Their grain offering *shall be* fine flour
mixed with oil: three-tenths *of an ephah* for
the bull, two-tenths for the ram,
4 'and one-tenth for each of the seven lambs;
5 'also one kid of the goats *as* a sin offering,
to make atonement for you;
6 'besides the burnt offering with its grain
offering for the New Moon, the regular burnt
offering with its grain offering, and their
drink offerings, according to their ordinance,
as a sweet aroma, an offering made by fire to
the LORD.

Offerings on the Day of Atonement

7 'On the tenth *day* of this seventh month
you shall have a holy convocation. You shall
afflict your souls; you shall not do any work.
8 'You shall present a burnt offering to the
LORD *as* a sweet aroma: one young bull, one
ram, *and* seven lambs in their first year. Be
sure they are without blemish.
9 'Their grain offering *shall be of* fine flour
mixed with oil: three-tenths *of an ephah* for
the bull, two-tenths for the one ram,
10 'and one-tenth for each of the seven lambs;
11 'also one kid of the goats *as* a sin offering,
besides the sin offering for atonement, the
regular burnt offering with its grain offering,
and their drink offerings.

Offerings at the Feast of Tabernacles

12 'On the fifteenth day of the seventh month
you shall have a holy convocation. You shall
do no customary work, and you shall keep a
feast to the LORD seven days.
13 'You shall present a burnt offering, an offering made by fire as a sweet aroma to the
LORD: thirteen young bulls, two rams, *and*
fourteen lambs in their first year. They shall
be without blemish.
14 'Their grain offering *shall be of* fine flour
mixed with oil: three-tenths *of an ephah* for
each of the thirteen bulls, two-tenths for each
of the two rams,
15 'and one-tenth for each of the fourteen
lambs;
16 'also one kid of the goats *as* a sin offering,
besides the regular burnt offering, its grain
offering, and its drink offering.
17 'On the second day *present* twelve young
bulls, two rams, fourteen lambs in their first
year without blemish,
18 'and their grain offering and their drink
offerings for the bulls, for the rams, and for
the lambs, by their number, according to the
ordinance;
19 'also one kid of the goats *as* a sin offering,
besides the regular burnt offering with its
grain offering, and their drink offerings.
20 'On the third day *present* eleven bulls, two
rams, fourteen lambs in their first year without blemish,
21 'and their grain offering and their drink
offerings for the bulls, for the rams, and for
the lambs, by their number, according to the
ordinance;
22 'also one goat *as* a sin offering, besides the
regular burnt offering, its grain offering, and
its drink offering.
23 'On the fourth day *present* ten bulls, two
rams, *and* fourteen lambs in their first year,
without blemish,
24 'and their grain offering and their drink
offerings for the bulls, for the rams, and for
the lambs, by their number, according to the
ordinance;
25 'also one kid of the goats *as* a sin offering,
besides the regular burnt offering, its grain
offering, and its drink offering.
26 'On the fifth day *present* nine bulls, two
rams, *and* fourteen lambs in their first year
without blemish,
27 'and their grain offering and their drink
offerings for the bulls, for the rams, and for
the lambs, by their number, according to the
ordinance;
28 'also one goat *as* a sin offering, besides the
regular burnt offering, its grain offering, and
its drink offering.
29 'On the sixth day *present* eight bulls, two
rams, *and* fourteen lambs in their first year
without blemish,
30 'and their grain offering and their drink
offerings for the bulls, for the rams, and for
the lambs, by their number, according to the
ordinance;
31 'also one goat *as* a sin offering, besides the
regular burnt offering, its grain offering, and
its drink offering.
32 'On the seventh day *present* seven bulls,
two rams, *and* fourteen lambs in their first
year without blemish,
33 'and their grain offering and their drink
offerings for the bulls, for the rams, and for
the lambs, by their number, according to the
ordinance;
34 'also one goat *as* a sin offering, besides the
regular burnt offering, its grain offering, and
its drink offering.
35 'On the eighth day you shall have a sacred
assembly. You shall do no customary work.
36 'You shall present a burnt offering, an offering made by fire as a sweet aroma to the
LORD: one bull, one ram, seven lambs in their
first year without blemish,
37 'and their grain offering and their drink
offerings for the bull, for the ram, and for the
lambs, by their number, according to the ordinance;
38 'also one goat *as* a sin offering, besides the
regular burnt offering, its grain offering, and
its drink offering.
39 'These you shall present to the LORD at your
appointed feasts (besides your vowed offer-

ings and your freewill offerings) as your burnt offerings and your grain offerings, as your drink offerings and your peace offerings.'"

40 So Moses told the children of Israel everything, just as the LORD commanded Moses.

The Law Concerning Vows

30 Then Moses spoke to the heads of the tribes concerning the children of Israel, saying, "This *is* the thing which the LORD has commanded:

➤ 2 "If a man makes a vow to the LORD, or swears an oath to bind himself by some agreement, he shall not break his word; he shall do according to all that proceeds out of his mouth.

3 "Or if a woman makes a vow to the LORD, and binds *herself* by some agreement while in her father's house in her youth,

4 "and her father hears her vow and the agreement by which she has bound herself, and her father holds his peace, then all her vows shall stand, and every agreement with which she has bound herself shall stand.

5 "But if her father overrules her on the day that he hears, then none of her vows nor her agreements by which she has bound herself shall stand; and the LORD will release her, because her father overruled her.

6 "If indeed she takes a husband, while bound by her vows or by a rash utterance from her lips by which she bound herself,

7 "and her husband hears *it*, and makes no response to her on the day that he hears, then her vows shall stand, and her agreements by which she bound herself shall stand.

8 "But if her husband overrules her on the day that he hears *it*, he shall make void her vow which she took and what she uttered with her lips, by which she bound herself, and the LORD will release her.

9 "Also any vow of a widow or a divorced woman, by which she has bound herself, shall stand against her.

10 "If she vowed in her husband's house, or bound herself by an agreement with an oath,

11 "and her husband heard *it*, and made no response to her *and* did not overrule her, then all her vows shall stand, and every agreement by which she bound herself shall stand.

12 "But if her husband truly made them void on the day he heard *them*, then whatever proceeded from her lips concerning her vows or concerning the agreement binding her, it shall not stand; her husband has made them void, and the LORD will release her.

13 "Every vow and every binding oath to afflict her soul, her husband may confirm it, or her husband may make it void.

14 "Now if her husband makes no response whatever to her from day to day, then he confirms all her vows or all the agreements that bind her; he confirms them, because he made no response to her on the day that he heard *them*.

15 "But if he does make them void after he has heard *them*, then he shall bear her guilt."

16 These *are* the statutes which the LORD commanded Moses, between a man and his wife, and between a father and his daughter in her youth in her father's house.

Vengeance on the Midianites

31 And the LORD spoke to Moses, saying:

2 "Take vengeance on the Midianites for the children of Israel. Afterward you shall be gathered to your people."

3 So Moses spoke to the people, saying, "Arm some of yourselves for war, and let them go against the Midianites to take vengeance for the LORD on Midian.

4 "A thousand from each tribe of all the tribes of Israel you shall send to the war."

5 So there were recruited from the divisions of Israel one thousand from *each* tribe, twelve thousand armed for war.

6 Then Moses sent them to the war, one thousand from *each* tribe; he sent them to the war with Phinehas the son of Eleazar the priest, with the holy articles and the signal trumpets in his hand.

7 And they warred against the Midianites, just as the LORD commanded Moses, and they killed all the males.

8 They killed the kings of Midian with *the rest of* those who were killed—Evi, Rekem, Zur, Hur, and Reba, the five kings of Midian. Balaam the son of Beor they also killed with the sword.

9 And the children of Israel took the women of Midian captive, with their little ones, and took as spoil all their cattle, all their flocks, and all their goods.

10 They also burned with fire all the cities where they dwelt, and all their forts.

11 And they took all the spoil and all the booty—of man and beast.

LIFE LESSONS

➤ **30:2 — *"If a man makes a vow to the LORD . . . he shall do according to all that proceeds out of his mouth."***

If we make a vow to God, we are not to violate it or "take it back." Jesus tells us, however, that it is better not to make a vow at all, but rather to always speak forthrightly (Matt. 5:33-37).

Return from the War
12 Then they brought the captives, the booty,
and the spoil to Moses, to Eleazar the priest,
and to the congregation of the children of Israel, to the camp in the plains of Moab by the
Jordan, *across from* Jericho.
13 And Moses, Eleazar the priest, and all the
leaders of the congregation, went to meet
them outside the camp.
14 But Moses was angry with the officers of
the army, *with* the captains over thousands
and captains over hundreds, who had come
from the battle.
15 And Moses said to them: "Have you kept
all the women alive?
16 "Look, these *women* caused the children
of Israel, through the counsel of Balaam, to
trespass against the LORD in the incident of
Peor, and there was a plague among the congregation of the LORD.
17 "Now therefore, kill every male among the
little ones, and kill every woman who has
known a man intimately.
18 "But keep alive for yourselves all the young
girls who have not known a man intimately.
19 "And as for you, remain outside the camp
seven days; whoever has killed any person,
and whoever has touched any slain, purify
yourselves and your captives on the third day
and on the seventh day.
20 "Purify every garment, everything made
of leather, everything woven of goats' *hair,*
and everything made of wood."
21 Then Eleazar the priest said to the men of
war who had gone to the battle, "This *is* the
ordinance of the law which the LORD commanded Moses:
22 "Only the gold, the silver, the bronze, the
iron, the tin, and the lead,
23 "everything that can endure fire, you shall
put through the fire, and it shall be clean; and
it shall be purified with the water of purification. But all that cannot endure fire you shall
put through water.
24 "And you shall wash your clothes on the
seventh day and be clean, and afterward you
may come into the camp."

Division of the Plunder
25 Now the LORD spoke to Moses, saying:
26 "Count up the plunder that was taken—of
man and beast—you and Eleazar the priest
and the chief fathers of the congregation;
27 "and divide the plunder into two parts, between those who took part in the war, who
went out to battle, and all the congregation.
28 "And levy a tribute for the LORD on the
men of war who went out to battle: one of
every five hundred of the persons, the cattle,
the donkeys, and the sheep;
29 "take *it* from their half, and give *it* to
Eleazar the priest as a heave offering to the
LORD.
30 "And from the children of Israel's half you
shall take one of every fifty, drawn from the
persons, the cattle, the donkeys, and the
sheep, from all the livestock, and give them to
the Levites who keep charge of the tabernacle
of the LORD."
31 So Moses and Eleazar the priest did as the
LORD commanded Moses.
32 The booty remaining from the plunder,
which the men of war had taken, was six hundred and seventy-five thousand sheep,
33 seventy-two thousand cattle,
34 sixty-one thousand donkeys,
35 and thirty-two thousand persons in all, of
women who had not known a man intimately.
36 And the half, the portion for those who
had gone out to war, was in number three
hundred and thirty-seven thousand five hundred sheep;
37 and the LORD's tribute of the sheep was six
hundred and seventy-five.
38 The cattle *were* thirty-six thousand, of
which the LORD's tribute *was* seventy-two.
39 The donkeys *were* thirty thousand five
hundred, of which the LORD's tribute *was*
sixty-one.
40 The persons *were* sixteen thousand, of
which the LORD's tribute *was* thirty-two persons.
41 So Moses gave the tribute *which was* the
LORD's heave offering to Eleazar the priest, as
the LORD commanded Moses.
42 And from the children of Israel's half,
which Moses separated from the men who
fought—
43 now the half belonging to the congregation was three hundred and thirty-seven thousand five hundred sheep,
44 thirty-six thousand cattle,
45 thirty thousand five hundred donkeys,
46 and sixteen thousand persons—
47 and from the children of Israel's half Moses took one of every fifty, drawn from man
and beast, and gave them to the Levites, who
kept charge of the tabernacle of the LORD, as
the LORD commanded Moses.
48 Then the officers who *were* over thousands of the army, the captains of thousands
and captains of hundreds, came near to Moses;
49 and they said to Moses, "Your servants
have taken a count of the men of war who *are*
under our command, and not a man of us is
missing.
50 "Therefore we have brought an offering
for the LORD, what every man found of ornaments of gold: armlets and bracelets and
signet rings and earrings and necklaces, to
make atonement for ourselves before the
LORD."
51 So Moses and Eleazar the priest received
the gold from them, all the fashioned ornaments.
52 And all the gold of the offering that they
offered to the LORD, from the captains of

thousands and captains of hundreds, was sixteen thousand seven hundred and fifty shekels.
53 (The men of war had taken spoil, every man for himself.)
54 And Moses and Eleazar the priest received the gold from the captains of thousands and of hundreds, and brought it into the tabernacle of meeting as a memorial for the children of Israel before the LORD.

The Tribes Settling East of the Jordan

32 Now the children of Reuben and the children of Gad had a very great multitude of livestock; and when they saw the land of Jazer and the land of Gilead, that indeed the region *was* a place for livestock,
2 the children of Gad and the children of Reuben came and spoke to Moses, to Eleazar the priest, and to the leaders of the congregation, saying,
3 "Ataroth, Dibon, Jazer, Nimrah, Heshbon, Elealeh, Shebam, Nebo, and Beon,
4 "the country which the LORD defeated before the congregation of Israel, *is* a land for livestock, and your servants have livestock."
5 Therefore they said, "If we have found favor in your sight, let this land be given to your servants as a possession. Do not take us over the Jordan."
6 And Moses said to the children of Gad and to the children of Reuben: "Shall your brethren go to war while you sit here?
7 "Now why will you discourage the heart of the children of Israel from going over into the land which the LORD has given them?
8 "Thus your fathers did when I sent them away from Kadesh Barnea to see the land.
9 "For when they went up to the Valley of Eshcol and saw the land, they discouraged the heart of the children of Israel, so that they did not go into the land which the LORD had given them.
10 "So the LORD's anger was aroused on that day, and He swore an oath, saying,
11 'Surely none of the men who came up from Egypt, from twenty years old and above, shall see the land of which I swore to Abraham, Isaac, and Jacob, because they have not wholly followed Me,
12 'except Caleb the son of Jephunneh, the Kenizzite, and Joshua the son of Nun, for they have wholly followed the LORD.'
13 "So the LORD's anger was aroused against Israel, and He made them wander in the wilderness forty years, until all the generation that had done evil in the sight of the LORD was gone.
14 "And look! You have risen in your fathers' place, a brood of sinful men, to increase still more the fierce anger of the LORD against Israel.
15 "For if you turn away from following Him, He will once again leave them in the wilderness, and you will destroy all these people."
16 Then they came near to him and said: "We will build sheepfolds here for our livestock, and cities for our little ones,
17 "but we ourselves will be armed, ready *to go* before the children of Israel until we have brought them to their place; and our little ones will dwell in the fortified cities because of the inhabitants of the land.
18 "We will not return to our homes until every one of the children of Israel has received his inheritance.
19 "For we will not inherit with them on the other side of the Jordan and beyond, because our inheritance has fallen to us on this eastern side of the Jordan."
20 Then Moses said to them: "If you do this thing, if you arm yourselves before the LORD for the war,
21 "and all your armed men cross over the Jordan before the LORD until He has driven out His enemies from before Him,
22 "and the land is subdued before the LORD, then afterward you may return and be blameless before the LORD and before Israel; and this land shall be your possession before the LORD.
23 "But if you do not do so, then take note, you have sinned against the LORD; and be sure your sin will find you out.
24 "Build cities for your little ones and folds for your sheep, and do what has proceeded out of your mouth."
25 And the children of Gad and the children of Reuben spoke to Moses, saying: "Your servants will do as my lord commands.
26 "Our little ones, our wives, our flocks, and all our livestock will be there in the cities of Gilead;
27 "but your servants will cross over, every man armed for war, before the LORD to battle, just as my lord says."
28 So Moses gave command concerning them to Eleazar the priest, to Joshua the son of Nun, and to the chief fathers of the tribes of the children of Israel.
29 And Moses said to them: "If the children of Gad and the children of Reuben cross over the Jordan with you, every man armed for battle before the LORD, and the land is subdued before you, then you shall give them the land of Gilead as a possession.
30 "But if they do not cross over armed with you, they shall have possessions among you in the land of Canaan."
31 Then the children of Gad and the children of Reuben answered, saying: "As the LORD has said to your servants, so we will do.
32 "We will cross over armed before the LORD into the land of Canaan, but the possession of our inheritance *shall remain* with us on this side of the Jordan."
33 So Moses gave to the children of Gad, to the children of Reuben, and to half the tribe

of Manasseh the son of Joseph, the kingdom of Sihon king of the Amorites and the kingdom of Og king of Bashan, the land with its cities within the borders, the cities of the surrounding country.

34 And the children of Gad built Dibon and Ataroth and Aroer,

35 Atroth and Shophan and Jazer and Jogbehah,

36 Beth Nimrah and Beth Haran, fortified cities, and folds for sheep.

37 And the children of Reuben built Heshbon and Elealeh and Kirjathaim,

38 Nebo and Baal Meon (*their* names being changed) and Shibmah; and they gave *other* names to the cities which they built.

39 And the children of Machir the son of Manasseh went to Gilead and took it, and dispossessed the Amorites who *were* in it.

40 So Moses gave Gilead to Machir the son of Manasseh, and he dwelt in it.

41 Also Jair the son of Manasseh went and took its small towns, and called them Havoth Jair.[a]

42 Then Nobah went and took Kenath and its villages, and he called it Nobah, after his own name.

Israel's Journey from Egypt Reviewed

33 These *are* the journeys of the children of Israel, who went out of the land of Egypt by their armies under the hand of Moses and Aaron.

2 Now Moses wrote down the starting points of their journeys at the command of the LORD. And these *are* their journeys according to their starting points:

3 They departed from Rameses in the first month, on the fifteenth day of the first month; on the day after the Passover the children of Israel went out with boldness in the sight of all the Egyptians.

4 For the Egyptians were burying all *their* firstborn, whom the LORD had killed among them. Also on their gods the LORD had executed judgments.

5 Then the children of Israel moved from Rameses and camped at Succoth.

6 They departed from Succoth and camped at Etham, which *is* on the edge of the wilderness.

7 They moved from Etham and turned back to Pi Hahiroth, which *is* east of Baal Zephon; and they camped near Migdol.

8 They departed from before Hahiroth[a] and passed through the midst of the sea into the wilderness, went three days' journey in the Wilderness of Etham, and camped at Marah.

9 They moved from Marah and came to Elim. At Elim *were* twelve springs of water and seventy palm trees; so they camped there.

10 They moved from Elim and camped by the Red Sea.

11 They moved from the Red Sea and camped in the Wilderness of Sin.

12 They journeyed from the Wilderness of Sin and camped at Dophkah.

13 They departed from Dophkah and camped at Alush.

14 They moved from Alush and camped at Rephidim, where there was no water for the people to drink.

15 They departed from Rephidim and camped in the Wilderness of Sinai.

16 They moved from the Wilderness of Sinai and camped at Kibroth Hattaavah.

17 They departed from Kibroth Hattaavah and camped at Hazeroth.

18 They departed from Hazeroth and camped at Rithmah.

19 They departed from Rithmah and camped at Rimmon Perez.

20 They departed from Rimmon Perez and camped at Libnah.

21 They moved from Libnah and camped at Rissah.

22 They journeyed from Rissah and camped at Kehelathah.

23 They went from Kehelathah and camped at Mount Shepher.

24 They moved from Mount Shepher and camped at Haradah.

25 They moved from Haradah and camped at Makheloth.

26 They moved from Makheloth and camped at Tahath.

27 They departed from Tahath and camped at Terah.

28 They moved from Terah and camped at Mithkah.

29 They went from Mithkah and camped at Hashmonah.

30 They departed from Hashmonah and camped at Moseroth.

31 They departed from Moseroth and camped at Bene Jaakan.

32 They moved from Bene Jaakan and camped at Hor Hagidgad.

33 They went from Hor Hagidgad and camped at Jotbathah.

34 They moved from Jotbathah and camped at Abronah.

35 They departed from Abronah and camped at Ezion Geber.

36 They moved from Ezion Geber and camped in the Wilderness of Zin, which *is* Kadesh.

37 They moved from Kadesh and camped at Mount Hor, on the boundary of the land of Edom.

38 Then Aaron the priest went up to Mount Hor at the command of the LORD, and died there in the fortieth year after the children of

---

32:41 [a]Literally *Towns of Jair* **33:8** [a]Many Hebrew manuscripts, Samaritan Pentateuch, Syriac, Targum, and Vulgate read *from Pi Hahiroth* (compare verse 7).

Israel had come out of the land of Egypt, on
the first *day* of the fifth month.
39 Aaron *was* one hundred and twenty-three
years old when he died on Mount Hor.
40 Now the king of Arad, the Canaanite, who
dwelt in the South in the land of Canaan,
heard of the coming of the children of Israel.
41 So they departed from Mount Hor and
camped at Zalmonah.
42 They departed from Zalmonah and
camped at Punon.
43 They departed from Punon and camped at
Oboth.
44 They departed from Oboth and camped at
Ije Abarim, at the border of Moab.
45 They departed from Ijim[a] and camped at
Dibon Gad.
46 They moved from Dibon Gad and camped
at Almon Diblathaim.
47 They moved from Almon Diblathaim and
camped in the mountains of Abarim, before
Nebo.
48 They departed from the mountains of
Abarim and camped in the plains of Moab by
the Jordan, *across from* Jericho.
49 They camped by the Jordan, from Beth
Jesimoth as far as the Abel Acacia Grove[a] in
the plains of Moab.

Instructions for the Conquest of Canaan

50 Now the LORD spoke to Moses in the
plains of Moab by the Jordan, *across from*
Jericho, saying,
51 "Speak to the children of Israel, and say to
them: 'When you have crossed the Jordan
into the land of Canaan,
52 'then you shall drive out all the inhabitants of the land from before you, destroy all
their engraved stones, destroy all their
molded images, and demolish all their high
places;
53 'you shall dispossess *the inhabitants of*
the land and dwell in it, for I have given you
the land to possess.
54 'And you shall divide the land by lot as an
inheritance among your families; to the
larger you shall give a larger inheritance, and
to the smaller you shall give a smaller inheritance; there everyone's *inheritance* shall be
whatever falls to him by lot. You shall inherit
according to the tribes of your fathers.
➤ 55 'But if you do not drive out the inhabitants
of the land from before you, then it shall be
that those whom you let remain *shall be* irritants in your eyes and thorns in your sides,
and they shall harass you in the land where
you dwell.
56 'Moreover it shall be *that* I will do to you
as I thought to do to them.'"

The Appointed Boundaries of Canaan

34 Then the LORD spoke to Moses, saying,
2 "Command the children of Israel, and say
to them: 'When you come into the land of
Canaan, this *is* the land that shall fall to you
as an inheritance—the land of Canaan to its
boundaries.
3 'Your southern border shall be from the
Wilderness of Zin along the border of Edom;
then your southern border shall extend eastward to the end of the Salt Sea;
4 'your border shall turn from the southern
side of the Ascent of Akrabbim, continue to
Zin, and be on the south of Kadesh Barnea;
then it shall go on to Hazar Addar, and continue to Azmon;
5 'the border shall turn from Azmon to the
Brook of Egypt, and it shall end at the Sea.
6 'As for the western border, you shall have
the Great Sea for a border; this shall be your
western border.
7 'And this shall be your northern border:
From the Great Sea you shall mark out your
border line to Mount Hor;
8 'from Mount Hor you shall mark out *your
border* to the entrance of Hamath; then the direction of the border shall be toward Zedad;
9 'the border shall proceed to Ziphron, and
it shall end at Hazar Enan. This shall be your
northern border.
10 'You shall mark out your eastern border
from Hazar Enan to Shepham;
11 'the border shall go down from Shepham
to Riblah on the east side of Ain; the border
shall go down and reach to the eastern side of
the Sea of Chinnereth;
12 'the border shall go down along the Jordan, and it shall end at the Salt Sea. This shall
be your land with its surrounding boundaries.'"
13 Then Moses commanded the children of
Israel, saying: "This *is* the land which you
shall inherit by lot, which the LORD has commanded to give to the nine tribes and to the
half-tribe.
14 "For the tribe of the children of Reuben ac-

33:45 [a]Same as *Ije Abarim,* verse 44 **33:49** [a]Hebrew *Abel Shittim*

LIFE LESSONS

➤ **33:55 — *"But if you do not drive out the inhabitants of the land from before you, then it shall be that those whom you let remain shall be irritants in your eyes and thorns in your sides, and they shall harass you in the land where you dwell."***

The Lord warned Israel what would happen if they failed to drive out *all* the inhabitants of the land, as He had commanded. And in this too His Word proved true (Judg. 2:11, 12).

cording to the house of their fathers, and the
tribe of the children of Gad according to the
house of their fathers, have received *their inheritance;* and the half-tribe of Manasseh has
received its inheritance.
15 "The two tribes and the half-tribe have received their inheritance on this side of the
Jordan, *across from* Jericho eastward, toward
the sunrise."

The Leaders Appointed to Divide the Land
16 And the LORD spoke to Moses, saying,
17 "These *are* the names of the men who
shall divide the land among you as an inheritance: Eleazar the priest and Joshua the son
of Nun.
18 "And you shall take one leader of every
tribe to divide the land for the inheritance.
19 "These *are* the names of the men: from the
tribe of Judah, Caleb the son of Jephunneh;
20 "from the tribe of the children of Simeon,
Shemuel the son of Ammihud;
21 "from the tribe of Benjamin, Elidad the
son of Chislon;
22 "a leader from the tribe of the children of
Dan, Bukki the son of Jogli;
23 "from the sons of Joseph: a leader from
the tribe of the children of Manasseh, Hanniel
the son of Ephod,
24 "and a leader from the tribe of the children of Ephraim, Kemuel the son of Shiphtan;
25 "a leader from the tribe of the children of
Zebulun, Elizaphan the son of Parnach;
26 "a leader from the tribe of the children of
Issachar, Paltiel the son of Azzan;
27 "a leader from the tribe of the children of
Asher, Ahihud the son of Shelomi;
28 "and a leader from the tribe of the children
of Naphtali, Pedahel the son of Ammihud."
29 These *are* the ones the LORD commanded
to divide the inheritance among the children
of Israel in the land of Canaan.

Cities for the Levites
35 And the LORD spoke to Moses in the
plains of Moab by the Jordan *across
from* Jericho, saying:
2 "Command the children of Israel that they
give the Levites cities to dwell in from the inheritance of their possession, and you shall
also give the Levites common-land around
the cities.
3 "They shall have the cities to dwell in; and
their common-land shall be for their cattle,
for their herds, and for all their animals.
4 "The common-land of the cities which you
will give the Levites *shall extend* from the
wall of the city outward a thousand cubits all
around.
5 "And you shall measure outside the city on
the east side two thousand cubits, on the
south side two thousand cubits, on the west
side two thousand cubits, and on the north
side two thousand cubits. The city *shall be* in
the middle. This shall belong to them as common-land for the cities.
6 "Now among the cities which you will give
to the Levites *you shall appoint* six cities of
refuge, to which a manslayer may flee. And to
these you shall add forty-two cities.
7 "So all the cities you will give to the
Levites *shall be* forty-eight; these *you shall
give* with their common-land.
8 "And the cities which you will give *shall be*
from the possession of the children of Israel;
from the larger *tribe* you shall give many,
from the smaller you shall give few. Each
shall give some of its cities to the Levites, in
proportion to the inheritance that each receives."

Cities of Refuge
9 Then the LORD spoke to Moses, saying,
10 "Speak to the children of Israel, and say to
them: 'When you cross the Jordan into the
land of Canaan,
11 'then you shall appoint cities to be cities of ➤
refuge for you, that the manslayer who kills
any person accidentally may flee there.
12 'They shall be cities of refuge for you from
the avenger, that the manslayer may not die
until he stands before the congregation in
judgment.
13 'And of the cities which you give, you shall
have six cities of refuge.
14 'You shall appoint three cities on this side
of the Jordan, and three cities you shall appoint in the land of Canaan, *which* will be
cities of refuge.
15 'These six cities shall be for refuge for the
children of Israel, for the stranger, and for the
sojourner among them, that anyone who kills
a person accidentally may flee there.
16 'But if he strikes him with an iron implement, so that he dies, he *is* a murderer; the
murderer shall surely be put to death.
17 'And if he strikes him with a stone in the
hand, by which one could die, and he does
die, he *is* a murderer; the murderer shall
surely be put to death.
18 'Or *if* he strikes him with a wooden hand
weapon, by which one could die, and he does

LIFE LESSONS

➤ 35:11 — *". . . then you shall appoint cities to be cities of refuge for you, that the manslayer who kills any person accidentally may flee there."*

Why doesn't a sovereign God stop fatal accidents from happening? We can only guess. But in His grace He does make provision for the surviving party of the accident.

die, he *is* a murderer; the murderer shall
surely be put to death.
19 'The avenger of blood himself shall put the
murderer to death; when he meets him, he
shall put him to death.
20 'If he pushes him out of hatred or, while
lying in wait, hurls something at him so that
he dies,
21 'or in enmity he strikes him with his hand
so that he dies, the one who struck *him* shall
surely be put to death. He *is* a murderer. The
avenger of blood shall put the murderer to
death when he meets him.
22 'However, if he pushes him suddenly without enmity, or throws anything at him without
lying in wait,
23 'or uses a stone, by which a man could die,
throwing *it* at him without seeing *him*, so that
he dies, while he was not his enemy or seeking his harm,
24 'then the congregation shall judge between the manslayer and the avenger of
blood according to these judgments.
25 'So the congregation shall deliver the
manslayer from the hand of the avenger of
blood, and the congregation shall return him
to the city of refuge where he had fled, and he
shall remain there until the death of the high
priest who was anointed with the holy oil.
26 'But if the manslayer at any time goes outside the limits of the city of refuge where he
fled,
27 'and the avenger of blood finds him outside the limits of his city of refuge, and the
avenger of blood kills the manslayer, he shall
not be guilty of blood,
28 'because he should have remained in his
city of refuge until the death of the high
priest. But after the death of the high priest
the manslayer may return to the land of his
possession.
29 'And these *things* shall be a statute of
judgment to you throughout your generations
in all your dwellings.
30 'Whoever kills a person, the murderer
shall be put to death on the testimony of witnesses; but one witness is not *sufficient* testimony against a person for the death *penalty*.
31 'Moreover you shall take no ransom for
the life of a murderer who *is* guilty of death,
but he shall surely be put to death.
32 'And you shall take no ransom for him
who has fled to his city of refuge, that he may
return to dwell in the land before the death of
the priest.
33 'So you shall not pollute the land where
you *are*; for blood defiles the land, and no
atonement can be made for the land, for the
blood that is shed on it, except by the blood of
him who shed it.
34 'Therefore do not defile the land which you
inhabit, in the midst of which I dwell; for I the
LORD dwell among the children of Israel.' "

Marriage of Female Heirs

36 Now the chief fathers of the families of
the children of Gilead the son of
Machir, the son of Manasseh, of the families
of the sons of Joseph, came near and spoke
before Moses and before the leaders, the chief
fathers of the children of Israel.
2 And they said: "The LORD commanded my
lord *Moses* to give the land as an inheritance
by lot to the children of Israel, and my lord
was commanded by the LORD to give the inheritance of our brother Zelophehad to his
daughters.
3 "Now if they are married to any of the
sons of the *other* tribes of the children of Israel, then their inheritance will be taken from
the inheritance of our fathers, and it will be
added to the inheritance of the tribe into
which they marry; so it will be taken from the
lot of our inheritance.
4 "And when the Jubilee of the children of
Israel comes, then their inheritance will be
added to the inheritance of the tribe into
which they marry; so their inheritance will be
taken away from the inheritance of the tribe
of our fathers."
5 Then Moses commanded the children of
Israel according to the word of the LORD, saying: "What the tribe of the sons of Joseph
speaks is right.
6 "This *is* what the LORD commands concerning the daughters of Zelophehad, saying,
'Let them marry whom they think best, but
they may marry only within the family of
their father's tribe.'
7 "So the inheritance of the children of Israel shall not change hands from tribe to tribe,
for every one of the children of Israel shall
keep the inheritance of the tribe of his fathers.
8 "And every daughter who possesses an inheritance in any tribe of the children of Israel
shall be the wife of one of the family of her father's tribe, so that the children of Israel each
may possess the inheritance of his fathers.
9 "Thus no inheritance shall change hands
from *one* tribe to another, but every tribe of
the children of Israel shall keep its own inheritance."

LIFE LESSONS

➤ **35:34 — *"Therefore do not defile the land which you inhabit, in the midst of which I dwell; for I the LORD dwell among the children of Israel."***

We are never to forget that a holy God lives among us. That knowledge alone should shape the way we live.

10 Just as the LORD commanded Moses, so
did the daughters of Zelophehad;
11 for Mahlah, Tirzah, Hoglah, Milcah, and
Noah, the daughters of Zelophehad, were
married to the sons of their father's brothers.
12 They were married into the families of the
children of Manasseh the son of Joseph, and
their inheritance remained in the tribe of
their father's family.
13 These *are* the commandments and the
judgments which the LORD commanded the
children of Israel by the hand of Moses in the
plains of Moab by the Jordan, *across from*
Jericho.

THE FIFTH BOOK OF MOSES CALLED

DEUTERONOMY

Deuteronomy, Moses' "Upper Desert Discourse," consists of a series of farewell messages by Israel's 120-year-old leader. He addressed his words to the new generation destined to possess the Land of Promise—those who survived the forty years of wilderness wandering.

Deuteronomy has been called "five-fifths of the Law" since it completes the five books of Moses. The Jewish people also have called it *Mishneh Hattorah*, which means "Repetition of the Law." The Septuagint gave it the name, *To Deuteronomion Touto*, "This Second Law." The English title comes from the Greek word *Deuteronomion*, which means "Second Law." Deuteronomy is really not a second law, however, but an adaptation and expansion of much of the original law given on Mount Sinai.

Deuteronomy opens with a review of Israel's forty years of wandering in the desert on her way to the Promised Land. Moses didn't want the people to forget the importance of obeying their God, and he didn't want them to forget that disobedience caused a whole generation of Israelites—men and women who had personally experienced a spectacular and miraculous deliverance from the hands of the Egyptians—to miss out on entering the land God had promised them.

Like Leviticus, Deuteronomy contains a vast amount of legal detail, but it emphasizes the layman rather than the priest. Moses reminds the new generation that their parents all died in the wilderness without receiving God's promises, because they refused to obey.

The Book of Deuteronomy contains an invaluable lesson for each of us. God wants us to remember our walk with Him—the highs and lows, the triumphs and the failures, the run-of-the-mill and the out-of-the-ordinary. He wants us to remember that even in the difficult times, when we may have believed Him far from us, He was always right there, encouraging us, giving us strength and motivation to change what needed to change, and blessing us every step of the way.

Theme: The key word in this book is "remember." Deuteronomy has been appropriately called the "Book of Remembrance." God wants us to remember that every blessing we receive depends on our remembering not just what He's done for us, but also His laws and principles regarding life on this earth.

Author: Moses.

Time: Delivered shortly before Moses' death, sometime around 1407 B.C.

Structure: Deuteronomy breaks down into four sections, starting with Moses' review of the Israelites' history (1:1—4:43); moving through a review of the Law (4:44—26:19); and the covenant (27:1—30:20); and ending with Moses' final words for the Israelites as he prepares to leave them (31—34).

As you read Deuteronomy, watch for several life principles that play an important role in this book:

21. Obedience always brings blessing. *See Deuteronomy 4:40; page 202.*

1. Our intimacy with God—His highest priority for our lives—determines the impact of our lives. *See Deuteronomy 7:6–8; page 206.*

3. God's Word is an immovable anchor in times of storm. *See Deuteronomy 8:3; page 207.*

29. We learn more in our valley experiences than on our mountaintops. *See Deuteronomy 9:7–29; page 208.*

4. The awareness of God's presence energizes us for our work. *See Deuteronomy 20:1; page 220.*

The Previous Command to Enter Canaan

1 These *are* the words which Moses spoke
to all Israel on this side of the Jordan in
the wilderness, in the plain[a] opposite Suph,[b]
between Paran, Tophel, Laban, Hazeroth, and
Dizahab.
2 *It is* eleven days' *journey* from Horeb by
way of Mount Seir to Kadesh Barnea.
3 Now it came to pass in the fortieth year, in
the eleventh month, on the first *day* of the
month, *that* Moses spoke to the children of Israel according to all that the LORD had given
him as commandments to them,
4 after he had killed Sihon king of the
Amorites, who dwelt in Heshbon, and Og
king of Bashan, who dwelt at Ashtaroth in[a]
Edrei.
➤ 5 On this side of the Jordan in the land of
Moab, Moses began to explain this law, saying,
6 "The LORD our God spoke to us in Horeb,
saying: 'You have dwelt long enough at this
mountain.
7 'Turn and take your journey, and go to the
mountains of the Amorites, to all the neighboring *places* in the plain,[a] in the mountains
and in the lowland, in the South and on the
seacoast, to the land of the Canaanites and to
Lebanon, as far as the great river, the River
Euphrates.
8 'See, I have set the land before you; go in
and possess the land which the LORD swore to
your fathers—to Abraham, Isaac, and Jacob—
to give to them and their descendants after
them.'

Tribal Leaders Appointed

9 "And I spoke to you at that time, saying: 'I
alone am not able to bear you.
10 'The LORD your God has multiplied you,
and here you *are* today, as the stars of heaven
in multitude.
✳ 11 'May the LORD God of your fathers make
you a thousand times more numerous than
you are, and bless you as He has promised
you!
12 'How can I alone bear your problems and
your burdens and your complaints?
➤ 13 'Choose wise, understanding, and knowledgeable men from among your tribes, and I
will make them heads over you.'
14 "And you answered me and said, 'The
thing which you have told *us* to do *is* good.'
15 "So I took the heads of your tribes, wise
and knowledgeable men, and made them
heads over you, leaders of thousands, leaders
of hundreds, leaders of fifties, leaders of tens,
and officers for your tribes.
16 "Then I commanded your judges at that
time, saying, 'Hear *the cases* between your
brethren, and judge righteously between a
man and his brother or the stranger who is
with him.
17 'You shall not show partiality in judgment; you shall hear the small as well as the
great; you shall not be afraid in any man's
presence, for the judgment *is* God's. The case
that is too hard for you, bring to me, and I
will hear it.'
18 "And I commanded you at that time all the
things which you should do.

Israel's Refusal to Enter the Land

19 "So we departed from Horeb, and went
through all that great and terrible wilderness
which you saw on the way to the mountains
of the Amorites, as the LORD our God had
commanded us. Then we came to Kadesh
Barnea.
20 "And I said to you, 'You have come to the
mountains of the Amorites, which the LORD
our God is giving us.
21 'Look, the LORD your God has set the land
before you; go up *and* possess *it*, as the LORD
God of your fathers has spoken to you; do not
fear or be discouraged.'
22 "And every one of you came near to me
and said, 'Let us send men before us, and let
them search out the land for us, and bring
back word to us of the way by which we
should go up, and of the cities into which we
shall come.'
23 "The plan pleased me well; so I took
twelve of your men, one man from *each* tribe.
24 "And they departed and went up into the
mountains, and came to the Valley of Eshcol,
and spied it out.
25 "They also took *some* of the fruit of the
land in their hands and brought *it* down to us;
and they brought back word to us, saying, '*It
is* a good land which the LORD our God is giving us.'

1:1 [a]Hebrew *arabah* [b]One manuscript of the Septuagint, also Targum and Vulgate, read *Red Sea.* **1:4** [a]Septuagint, Syriac, and Vulgate read *and* (compare Joshua 12:4). **1:7** [a]Hebrew *arabah*

LIFE LESSONS

➤ 1:5 — *On this side of the Jordan in the land of Moab, Moses began to explain this law . . . .*

Many times it helps to have a wise, mature believer explain what God says in His Word. Today, this most often happens in church. Are you regularly attending a Christ-centered church where the Bible has a central role?

➤ 1:13 — *"Choose wise, understanding, and knowledgeable men from among your tribes, and I will make them heads over you."*

The kingdom of God cannot advance as it should without wise, understanding and knowledgeable leaders, filled with the Spirit of God. We do not move forward in godliness alone; we need each other.

26 "Nevertheless you would not go up, but rebelled against the command of the LORD your God;
➤ 27 "and you complained in your tents, and said, 'Because the LORD hates us, He has brought us out of the land of Egypt to deliver us into the hand of the Amorites, to destroy us.
28 'Where can we go up? Our brethren have discouraged our hearts, saying, "The people *are* greater and taller than we; the cities *are* great and fortified up to heaven; moreover we have seen the sons of the Anakim there." '
29 "Then I said to you, 'Do not be terrified, or afraid of them.
➤ 30 'The LORD your God, who goes before you, He will fight for you, according to all He did for you in Egypt before your eyes,
31 'and in the wilderness where you saw how the LORD your God carried you, as a man carries his son, in all the way that you went until you came to this place.'
32 "Yet, for all that, you did not believe the LORD your God,
33 "who went in the way before you to search out a place for you to pitch your tents, to show you the way you should go, in the fire by night and in the cloud by day.

The Penalty for Israel's Rebellion

34 "And the LORD heard the sound of your words, and was angry, and took an oath, saying,
35 'Surely not one of these men of this evil generation shall see that good land of which I swore to give to your fathers,
36 'except Caleb the son of Jephunneh; he shall see it, and to him and his children I am giving the land on which he walked, because he wholly followed the LORD.'
37 "The LORD was also angry with me for your sakes, saying, 'Even you shall not go in there.
➤ 38 'Joshua the son of Nun, who stands before you, he shall go in there. Encourage him, for he shall cause Israel to inherit it.
39 'Moreover your little ones and your children, who you say will be victims, who today have no knowledge of good and evil, they shall go in there; to them I will give it, and they shall possess it.
40 'But *as for* you, turn and take your journey into the wilderness by the Way of the Red Sea.'
41 "Then you answered and said to me, 'We have sinned against the LORD; we will go up and fight, just as the LORD our God commanded us.' And when everyone of you had girded on his weapons of war, you were ready to go up into the mountain.
42 "And the LORD said to me, 'Tell them, "Do not go up nor fight, for I *am* not among you; lest you be defeated before your enemies." '
43 "So I spoke to you; yet you would not listen, but rebelled against the command of the LORD, and presumptuously went up into the mountain.
44 "And the Amorites who dwelt in that mountain came out against you and chased you as bees do, and drove you back from Seir to Hormah.
45 "Then you returned and wept before the LORD, but the LORD would not listen to your voice nor give ear to you.
46 "So you remained in Kadesh many days, according to the days that you spent *there.*

The Desert Years

2 "Then we turned and journeyed into the wilderness of the Way of the Red Sea, as the LORD spoke to me, and we skirted Mount Seir for many days.
2 "And the LORD spoke to me, saying:
3 'You have skirted this mountain long enough; turn northward.
4 'And command the people, saying, "You *are about to* pass through the territory of your brethren, the descendants of Esau, who live in Seir; and they will be afraid of you. Therefore watch yourselves carefully.
5 "Do not meddle with them, for I will not give you *any* of their land, no, not so much as one footstep, because I have given Mount Seir to Esau *as* a possession.
6 "You shall buy food from them with money, that you may eat; and you shall also buy water from them with money, that you may drink.

LIFE LESSONS

➤ 1:27 — *". . . and you complained in your tents, and said, 'Because the LORD hates us, He has brought us out of the land of Egypt to deliver us into the hand of the Amorites, to destroy us.'"*

Ever since the Garden of Eden, one of Satan's most successful tactics has been to get God's people to believe that the Lord is not really loving and gracious.

➤ 1:30 — *"The LORD your God, who goes before you, He will fight for you, according to all He did for you in Egypt before your eyes . . . ."*

The Lord is not only with us; He also goes ahead of us, to prepare our way and give us success.

➤ 1:38 — *"Joshua the son of Nun, who stands before you, he shall go in there. Encourage him, for he shall cause Israel to inherit it."*

Because we are in this together, God directs us to encourage one another. He never enlists "Lone Rangers" in His service.

➤ 7 "For the LORD your God has blessed you in
all the work of your hand. He knows your
trudging through this great wilderness. These
forty years the LORD your God *has been* with
you; you have lacked nothing."'
8 "And when we passed beyond our
brethren, the descendants of Esau who dwell
in Seir, away from the road of the plain, away
from Elath and Ezion Geber, we turned and
passed by way of the Wilderness of Moab.
9 "Then the LORD said to me, 'Do not harass
Moab, nor contend with them in battle, for I
will not give you *any* of their land *as* a possession, because I have given Ar to the descendants of Lot *as* a possession.'"
➤ 10 (The Emim had dwelt there in times past,
a people as great and numerous and tall as
the Anakim.
11 They were also regarded as giants,[a] like
the Anakim, but the Moabites call them
Emim.
12 The Horites formerly dwelt in Seir, but the
descendants of Esau dispossessed them and
destroyed them from before them, and dwelt
in their place, just as Israel did to the land of
their possession which the LORD gave them.)
13 "'Now rise and cross over the Valley of the
Zered.' So we crossed over the Valley of the
Zered.
14 "And the time we took to come from
Kadesh Barnea until we crossed over the Valley of the Zered *was* thirty-eight years, until
all the generation of the men of war was consumed from the midst of the camp, just as the
LORD had sworn to them.
15 "For indeed the hand of the LORD was
against them, to destroy them from the midst
of the camp until they were consumed.
16 "So it was, when all the men of war had finally perished from among the people,
17 "that the LORD spoke to me, saying:
18 'This day you are to cross over at Ar, the
boundary of Moab.
19 'And *when* you come near the people of
Ammon, do not harass them or meddle with
them, for I will not give you *any* of the land of
the people of Ammon *as* a possession, because I have given it to the descendants of Lot
as a possession.'"
20 (That was also regarded as a land of giants;[a] giants formerly dwelt there. But the
Ammonites call them Zamzummim,
21 a people as great and numerous and tall as
the Anakim. But the LORD destroyed them before them, and they dispossessed them and
dwelt in their place,
22 just as He had done for the descendants of
Esau, who dwelt in Seir, when He destroyed
the Horites from before them. They dispossessed them and dwelt in their place, even to
this day.
23 And the Avim, who dwelt in villages as far
as Gaza—the Caphtorim, who came from
Caphtor, destroyed them and dwelt in their
place.)
24 "'Rise, take your journey, and cross over
the River Arnon. Look, I have given into your
hand Sihon the Amorite, king of Heshbon,
and his land. Begin to possess *it*, and engage
him in battle.
25 'This day I will begin to put the dread and
fear of you upon the nations under the whole
heaven, who shall hear the report of you, and
shall tremble and be in anguish because of you.'

King Sihon Defeated

26 "And I sent messengers from the Wilderness of Kedemoth to Sihon king of Heshbon,
with words of peace, saying,
27 'Let me pass through your land; I will
keep strictly to the road, and I will turn neither to the right nor to the left.
28 'You shall sell me food for money, that I
may eat, and give me water for money, that I
may drink; only let me pass through on foot,
29 'just as the descendants of Esau who dwell
in Seir and the Moabites who dwell in Ar did
for me, until I cross the Jordan to the land
which the LORD our God is giving us.'
30 "But Sihon king of Heshbon would not let ➤
us pass through, for the LORD your God hard-

2:11 [a]Hebrew *rephaim* **2:20** [a]Hebrew *rephaim*

LIFE LESSONS

➤ 2:7 — *"For the LORD your God has blessed you in all the work of your hand. He knows your trudging through this great wilderness. These forty years the LORD your God has been with you; you have lacked nothing."*

Even though Israel ended up in the wilderness because of her disobedience, even there God blessed His people and gave them everything they needed. He tempers even His justice with grace.

➤ 2:10 — *(The Emim had dwelt there in times past, a people as great and numerous and tall as the Anakim.)*

Moses reminds this new generation that other descendants of Abraham had earlier encountered giants—and had defeated them and taken possession of their land. How much more could God's people inherit the land God had promised them!

➤ 2:30 — *"But Sihon king of Heshbon would not let us pass through, for the LORD your God hardened his spirit and made his heart obstinate, that He might deliver him into your hand, as it is this day."*

Sometimes the people of God encounter stiff opposition so that the Lord might permanently remove that opposition. And so what looks like a bad thing makes way for a very good thing.

ened his spirit and made his heart obstinate, that He might deliver him into your hand, as *it is* this day.

31 "And the LORD said to me, 'See, I have begun to give Sihon and his land over to you. Begin to possess *it*, that you may inherit his land.'

32 "Then Sihon and all his people came out against us to fight at Jahaz.

33 "And the LORD our God delivered him over to us; so we defeated him, his sons, and all his people.

34 "We took all his cities at that time, and we utterly destroyed the men, women, and little ones of every city; we left none remaining.

35 "We took only the livestock as plunder for ourselves, with the spoil of the cities which we took.

36 "From Aroer, which *is* on the bank of the River Arnon, and *from* the city that *is* in the ravine, as far as Gilead, there was not one city too strong for us; the LORD our God delivered all to us.

37 "Only you did not go near the land of the people of Ammon—anywhere along the River Jabbok, or to the cities of the mountains, or wherever the LORD our God had forbidden us.

King Og Defeated

3 "Then we turned and went up the road to Bashan; and Og king of Bashan came out against us, he and all his people, to battle at Edrei.

2 "And the LORD said to me, 'Do not fear him, for I have delivered him and all his people and his land into your hand; you shall do to him as you did to Sihon king of the Amorites, who dwelt at Heshbon.'

3 "So the LORD our God also delivered into our hands Og king of Bashan, with all his people, and we attacked him until he had no survivors remaining.

4 "And we took all his cities at that time; there was not a city which we did not take from them: sixty cities, all the region of Argob, the kingdom of Og in Bashan.

5 "All these cities *were* fortified with high walls, gates, and bars, besides a great many rural towns.

6 "And we utterly destroyed them, as we did to Sihon king of Heshbon, utterly destroying the men, women, and children of every city.

7 "But all the livestock and the spoil of the cities we took as booty for ourselves.

8 "And at that time we took the land from the hand of the two kings of the Amorites who *were* on this side of the Jordan, from the River Arnon to Mount Hermon

9 "(the Sidonians call Hermon Sirion, and the Amorites call it Senir),

10 "all the cities of the plain, all Gilead, and all Bashan, as far as Salcah and Edrei, cities of the kingdom of Og in Bashan.

11 "For only Og king of Bashan remained of the remnant of the giants.[a] Indeed his bedstead *was* an iron bedstead. (*Is* it not in Rabbah of the people of Ammon?) Nine cubits *is* its length and four cubits its width, according to the standard cubit.

The Land East of the Jordan Divided

12 "And this land, *which* we possessed at that time, from Aroer, which *is* by the River Arnon, and half the mountains of Gilead and its cities, I gave to the Reubenites and the Gadites.

13 "The rest of Gilead, and all Bashan, the kingdom of Og, I gave to half the tribe of Manasseh. (All the region of Argob, with all Bashan, was called the land of the giants.[a]

14 "Jair the son of Manasseh took all the region of Argob, as far as the border of the Geshurites and the Maachathites, and called Bashan after his own name, Havoth Jair,[a] to this day.)

15 "Also I gave Gilead to Machir.

16 "And to the Reubenites and the Gadites I gave from Gilead as far as the River Arnon, the middle of the river as *the* border, as far as the River Jabbok, the border of the people of Ammon;

17 "the plain also, with the Jordan as *the* border, from Chinnereth as far as the east side of the Sea of the Arabah (the Salt Sea), below the slopes of Pisgah.

18 "Then I commanded you at that time, saying: 'The LORD your God has given you this land to possess. All you men of valor shall cross over armed before your brethren, the children of Israel.

19 'But your wives, your little ones, and your livestock (I know that you have much livestock) shall stay in your cities which I have given you,

20 'until the LORD has given rest to your brethren as to you, and they also possess the land which the LORD your God is giving them

3:11 [a]Hebrew *rephaim* **3:13** [a]Hebrew *rephaim* **3:14** [a]Literally *Towns of Jair*

LIFE LESSONS

➤ 3:20 — ***" . . . until the LORD has given rest to your brethren as to you, and they also possess the land which the LORD your God is giving them beyond the Jordan. Then each of you may return to his possession which I have given you."***

God's plan calls for His people to work together to achieve the goals He sets for them. We are both to work together and to rest together (see Rom. 12:15).

beyond the Jordan. Then each of you may return to his possession which I have given
you.'
21 "And I commanded Joshua at that time,
saying, 'Your eyes have seen all that the LORD
your God has done to these two kings; so will
the LORD do to all the kingdoms through
which you pass.
22 'You must not fear them, for the LORD your
God Himself fights for you.'

Moses Forbidden to Enter the Land

23 "Then I pleaded with the LORD at that
time, saying:
24 'O Lord GOD, You have begun to show Your
servant Your greatness and Your mighty hand,
for what god *is there* in heaven or on earth
who can do *anything* like Your works and
Your mighty *deeds?*
25 'I pray, let me cross over and see the good
land beyond the Jordan, those pleasant
mountains, and Lebanon.'
➤ 26 "But the LORD was angry with me on your
account, and would not listen to me. So the
LORD said to me: 'Enough of that! Speak no
more to Me of this matter.
27 'Go up to the top of Pisgah, and lift your
eyes toward the west, the north, the south,
and the east; behold *it* with your eyes, for you
shall not cross over this Jordan.
28 'But command Joshua, and encourage him
and strengthen him; for he shall go over before this people, and he shall cause them to
inherit the land which you will see.'
29 "So we stayed in the valley opposite Beth
Peor.

Moses Commands Obedience

4 "Now, O Israel, listen to the statutes and
the judgments which I teach you to observe, that you may live, and go in and possess the land which the LORD God of your
fathers is giving you.
➤ 2 "You shall not add to the word which I
command you, nor take from it, that you may
keep the commandments of the LORD your
God which I command you.
3 "Your eyes have seen what the LORD did at
Baal Peor; for the LORD your God has destroyed from among you all the men who followed Baal of Peor.
4 "But you who held fast to the LORD your
God *are* alive today, every one of you.
5 "Surely I have taught you statutes and
judgments, just as the LORD my God commanded me, that you should act according to
them in the land which you go to possess.
6 "Therefore be careful to observe *them;* for
this *is* your wisdom and your understanding
in the sight of the peoples who will hear all
these statutes, and say, 'Surely this great nation *is* a wise and understanding people.'
7 "For what great nation *is there* that has ◄
God *so* near to it, as the LORD our God *is* to us,
for whatever *reason* we may call upon Him?
8 "And what great nation *is there* that has
such statutes and righteous judgments as are
in all this law which I set before you this day?
9 "Only take heed to yourself, and diligently ◄
keep yourself, lest you forget the things your
eyes have seen, and lest they depart from your
heart all the days of your life. And teach them
to your children and your grandchildren,
10 "*especially concerning* the day you stood
before the LORD your God in Horeb, when the
LORD said to me, 'Gather the people to Me,
and I will let them hear My words, that they
may learn to fear Me all the days they live on
the earth, and *that* they may teach their children.'
11 "Then you came near and stood at the foot
of the mountain, and the mountain burned
with fire to the midst of heaven, with darkness, cloud, and thick darkness.
12 "And the LORD spoke to you out of the
midst of the fire. You heard the sound of the
words, but saw no form; *you* only *heard* a
voice.

LIFE LESSONS

➤ 3:26 — *"But the LORD was angry with me on your account, and would not listen to me. So the LORD said to me: 'Enough of that! Speak no more to Me of this matter.'"*

The Bible teaches us to pray and keep on praying, and not to give up (Luke 18:1). Yet there may come times when the Lord lets us know it is time to stop praying for a particular thing.

➤ 4:2 — *"You shall not add to the word which I command you, nor take from it, that you may keep the commandments of the LORD your God which I command you."*

The Word of God is sufficient for us. We are not to add to or subtract from it, for it contains all we need for life and godliness (see Rev. 22:18, 19).

➤ 4:7 — *"For what great nation is there that has God so near to it, as the LORD our God is to us, for whatever reason we may call upon Him?"*

We may call upon God for *any* reason, at *any* time, regarding *any* problem or difficulty or challenge. When we fight our battles on our knees, we win every time.

➤ 4:9 — *"Only take heed to yourself, and diligently keep yourself, lest you forget the things your eyes have seen . . . . And teach them to your children and your grandchildren . . . ."*

To keep your children on your team, you must keep your testimony intact—be sure you model faithfulness to God, admit when you are wrong, and fulfill your proper role.

13 "So He declared to you His covenant
which He commanded you to perform, the
Ten Commandments; and He wrote them on
two tablets of stone.
14 "And the LORD commanded me at that
time to teach you statutes and judgments, that
you might observe them in the land which
you cross over to possess.

Beware of Idolatry

15 "Take careful heed to yourselves, for you
saw no form when the LORD spoke to you at
Horeb out of the midst of the fire,
16 "lest you act corruptly and make for yourselves a carved image in the form of any figure: the likeness of male or female,
17 "the likeness of any animal that *is* on the
earth or the likeness of any winged bird that
flies in the air,
18 "the likeness of anything that creeps on
the ground or the likeness of any fish that *is*
in the water beneath the earth.
19 "And *take heed,* lest you lift your eyes to
heaven, and *when* you see the sun, the moon,
and the stars, all the host of heaven, you feel
driven to worship them and serve them,
which the LORD your God has given to all the
peoples under the whole heaven as a heritage.
20 "But the LORD has taken you and brought
you out of the iron furnace, out of Egypt, to be
His people, an inheritance, as you are this day.
21 "Furthermore the LORD was angry with
me for your sakes, and swore that I would not
cross over the Jordan, and that I would not
enter the good land which the LORD your God
is giving you as an inheritance.
22 "But I must die in this land, I must not
cross over the Jordan; but you shall cross
over and possess that good land.
23 "Take heed to yourselves, lest you forget
the covenant of the LORD your God which He
made with you, and make for yourselves a
carved image in the form of anything which
the LORD your God has forbidden you.
➤ 24 "For the LORD your God *is* a consuming
fire, a jealous God.
25 "When you beget children and grandchildren and have grown old in the land, and act
corruptly and make a carved image in the
form of anything, and do evil in the sight of
the LORD your God to provoke Him to anger,
26 "I call heaven and earth to witness against
you this day, that you will soon utterly perish
from the land which you cross over the Jordan to possess; you will not prolong *your*
days in it, but will be utterly destroyed.
27 "And the LORD will scatter you among the
peoples, and you will be left few in number
among the nations where the LORD will drive
you.
28 "And there you will serve gods, the work
of men's hands, wood and stone, which neither see nor hear nor eat nor smell.
29 "But from there you will seek the LORD
your God, and you will find *Him* if you seek
Him with all your heart and with all your
soul.
30 "When you are in distress, and all these
things come upon you in the latter days, when
you turn to the LORD your God and obey His
voice
31 "(for the LORD your God *is* a merciful ➤
God), He will not forsake you nor destroy
you, nor forget the covenant of your fathers
which He swore to them.
32 "For ask now concerning the days that are
past, which were before you, since the day
that God created man on the earth, and *ask*
from one end of heaven to the other, whether
any great *thing* like this has happened, or
anything like it has been heard.
33 "Did *any* people *ever* hear the voice of
God speaking out of the midst of the fire, as
you have heard, and live?
34 "Or did God *ever* try to go *and* take for
Himself a nation from the midst of *another*
nation, by trials, by signs, by wonders, by war,
by a mighty hand and an outstretched arm,
and by great terrors, according to all that the
LORD your God did for you in Egypt before
your eyes?
35 "To you it was shown, that you might
know that the LORD Himself *is* God; *there is*
none other besides Him.
36 "Out of heaven He let you hear His voice,
that He might instruct you; on earth He
showed you His great fire, and you heard His
words out of the midst of the fire.
37 "And because He loved your fathers,
therefore He chose their descendants after
them; and He brought you out of Egypt with
His Presence, with His mighty power,
38 "driving out from before you nations

LIFE LESSONS

➤ 4:24 — *"For the LORD your God is a consuming fire, a jealous God."*

The Lord is jealous in the sense that He will not share the hearts of His people with anyone or anything else. We belong to Him alone. Intimacy with God is His highest priority for our lives.

➤ 4:31 — *". . . (for the LORD your God is a merciful God), He will not forsake you nor destroy you, nor forget the covenant of your fathers which He swore to them."*

We serve a God who is powerful, awesome, mighty, loving, compassionate . . . and fully worthy of our trust. The Lord never makes a promise He can't keep, and He never forgets the promises He has made.

ANSWERS TO LIFE'S QUESTIONS

How does God get our attention?

DEUT. 4:42–44

A whistle can get our attention quickly. We use it to control unruly behavior, signal the start or finish of an event, or interrupt the action in a game. Regardless of who blows it, a whistle tells us to stop and learn why it was blown.

What does God use to get our attention? Sometimes He uses the tool of a restless spirit, which might appear as some vague dissatisfaction with life. Other times, God uses another person's words to help us recognize that He is speaking to us. Sometimes He uses the method of unusual blessing (Rom. 2:4). In each case, we are to stop and ask, "Lord, are You trying to say something to me?"

God sometimes allows our prayers to remain unanswered in order to prompt us to sharpen our focus on Him. Or He may say "no" to our request in order to gain our attention. He occasionally uses disappointments, difficulties, and failures for the same reason. If we are wise, we will quickly seek Him out. In tragedies, financial reversals, and physical affliction, God wants to see if we will turn to Him and ask, "God, are you speaking to me?"

What does it take for the Lord to get our attention? Will a restless spirit cause us to seek godly counsel? Do we listen when God sends someone to point out His way? When blessings come, do we turn to God and ask how He would like us to use them? Do we seek God when our prayers go unanswered? How long does it take us to get past our emotions over disappointments, difficulties, and failures to listen to what our heavenly Father has to say? In times of great financial crisis, tragedy, and sickness, do our eyes and minds lift heavenward to seek God's love and wisdom? God deserves our undivided attention . . . but we get preoccupied. He waits to speak with us . . . but we keep looking at our circumstances.

Allow the events of your life—both the pleasant and the painful—to prompt you to turn to God and ask, "Lord, are You asking for my attention?"

Don't allow yourself to miss what the Lord wants to tell you. Begin *now* to train yourself to give Him your full attention. Allow what happens in your day to draw you to Him. He is waiting for you.

See the Life Principles Index for further study:
13. Listening to God is essential to walking with God.

greater and mightier than you, to bring you
in, to give you their land *as* an inheritance, as
it is this day.
39 "Therefore know this day, and consider *it*
in your heart, that the LORD Himself *is* God in
heaven above and on the earth beneath; *there*
is no other.
40 "You shall therefore keep His statutes and
His commandments which I command you
today, that it may go well with you and with
your children after you, and that you may
prolong *your* days in the land which the LORD
your God is giving you for all time."

Cities of Refuge East of the Jordan
41 Then Moses set apart three cities on this
side of the Jordan, toward the rising of the
sun,
42 that the manslayer might flee there, who
kills his neighbor unintentionally, without
having hated him in time past, and that by
fleeing to one of these cities he might live:
43 Bezer in the wilderness on the plateau for
the Reubenites, Ramoth in Gilead for the
Gadites, and Golan in Bashan for the Manassites.

Introduction to God's Law
44 Now this *is* the law which Moses set before the children of Israel.
45 These *are* the testimonies, the statutes,
and the judgments which Moses spoke to the
children of Israel after they came out of
Egypt,
46 on this side of the Jordan, in the valley opposite Beth Peor, in the land of Sihon king of
the Amorites, who dwelt at Heshbon, whom
Moses and the children of Israel defeated
after they came out of Egypt.
47 And they took possession of his land and
the land of Og king of Bashan, two kings of
the Amorites, who *were* on this side of the
Jordan, toward the rising of the sun,
48 from Aroer, which *is* on the bank of the
River Arnon, even to Mount Sion[a] (that is,
Hermon),
49 and all the plain on the east side of the
Jordan as far as the Sea of the Arabah, below
the slopes of Pisgah.

4:48 [a]Syriac reads *Sirion* (compare 3:9).

The Ten Commandments Reviewed

5 And Moses called all Israel, and said to them: "Hear, O Israel, the statutes and judgments which I speak in your hearing today, that you may learn them and be careful to observe them.

2 "The LORD our God made a covenant with us in Horeb.

3 "The LORD did not make this covenant with our fathers, but with us, those who *are* here today, all of us who *are* alive.

4 "The LORD talked with you face to face on the mountain from the midst of the fire.

5 "I stood between the LORD and you at that time, to declare to you the word of the LORD; for you were afraid because of the fire, and you did not go up the mountain. *He* said:

6 'I *am* the LORD your God who brought you out of the land of Egypt, out of the house of bondage.

7 'You shall have no other gods before Me.

8 'You shall not make for yourself a carved image—any likeness *of anything* that *is* in heaven above, or that *is* in the earth beneath, or that *is* in the water under the earth;

9 you shall not bow down to them nor serve them. For I, the LORD your God, *am* a jealous God, visiting the iniquity of the fathers upon the children to the third and fourth *generations* of those who hate Me,

10 but showing mercy to thousands, to those who love Me and keep My commandments.

11 'You shall not take the name of the LORD your God in vain, for the LORD will not hold *him* guiltless who takes His name in vain.

12 'Observe the Sabbath day, to keep it holy, as the LORD your God commanded you.

13 Six days you shall labor and do all your work,

14 but the seventh day *is* the Sabbath of the LORD your God. *In it* you shall do no work: you, nor your son, nor your daughter, nor your male servant, nor your female servant, nor your ox, nor your donkey, nor any of your cattle, nor your stranger who *is* within your gates, that your male servant and your female servant may rest as well as you.

15 And remember that you were a slave in the land of Egypt, and the LORD your God brought you out from there by a mighty hand and by an outstretched arm; therefore the LORD your God commanded you to keep the Sabbath day.

16 'Honor your father and your mother, as the LORD your God has commanded you, that your days may be long, and that it may be well with you in the land which the LORD your God is giving you.

17 'You shall not murder.

18 'You shall not commit adultery.

19 'You shall not steal.

20 'You shall not bear false witness against your neighbor.

21 'You shall not covet your neighbor's wife; and you shall not desire your neighbor's house, his field, his male servant, his female servant, his ox, his donkey, or anything that *is* your neighbor's.'

22 "These words the LORD spoke to all your assembly, in the mountain from the midst of the fire, the cloud, and the thick darkness, with a loud voice; and He added no more. And He wrote them on two tablets of stone and gave them to me.

The People Afraid of God's Presence

23 "So it was, when you heard the voice from the midst of the darkness, while the mountain was burning with fire, that you came near to me, all the heads of your tribes and your elders.

24 "And you said: 'Surely the LORD our God has shown us His glory and His greatness, and we have heard His voice from the midst of the fire. We have seen this day that God speaks with man; yet he *still* lives.

25 'Now therefore, why should we die? For this great fire will consume us; if we hear the voice of the LORD our God anymore, then we shall die.

26 'For who *is there* of all flesh who has heard the voice of the living God speaking from the midst of the fire, as we *have,* and lived?

27 'You go near and hear all that the LORD our God may say, and tell us all that the LORD our God says to you, and we will hear and do *it.*'

28 "Then the LORD heard the voice of your words when you spoke to me, and the LORD

LIFE LESSONS

➤ 5:24 — *"Surely the LORD our God has shown us His glory and His greatness, and we have heard His voice from the midst of the fire . . . ."*

God shows us both His glory and His greatness—what greater blessing could we enjoy? It is this: He also speaks to us. Our job is to listen for His voice and to obey gladly.

said to me: 'I have heard the voice of the words of this people which they have spoken to you. They are right *in* all that they have spoken.

➤ 29 'Oh, that they had such a heart in them that they would fear Me and always keep all My commandments, that it might be well with them and with their children forever!

30 'Go and say to them, "Return to your tents."

31 'But as for you, stand here by Me, and I will speak to you all the commandments, the statutes, and the judgments which you shall teach them, that they may observe *them* in the land which I am giving them to possess.'

32 "Therefore you shall be careful to do as the LORD your God has commanded you; you shall not turn aside to the right hand or to the left.

➤ 33 "You shall walk in all the ways which the LORD your God has commanded you, that you may live and *that it may be* well with you, and *that* you may prolong *your* days in the land which you shall possess.

The Greatest Commandment

6 "Now this *is* the commandment, *and these are* the statutes and judgments which the LORD your God has commanded to teach you, that you may observe *them* in the land which you are crossing over to possess,

2 "that you may fear the LORD your God, to keep all His statutes and His commandments which I command you, you and your son and your grandson, all the days of your life, and that your days may be prolonged.

3 "Therefore hear, O Israel, and be careful to observe *it*, that it may be well with you, and that you may multiply greatly as the LORD God of your fathers has promised you—'a land flowing with milk and honey.'[a]

4 "Hear, O Israel: The LORD our God, the LORD *is* one![a]

➤ 5 "You shall love the LORD your God with all your heart, with all your soul, and with all your strength.

6 "And these words which I command you today shall be in your heart.

7 "You shall teach them diligently to your children, and shall talk of them when you sit in your house, when you walk by the way, when you lie down, and when you rise up.

8 "You shall bind them as a sign on your hand, and they shall be as frontlets between your eyes.

9 "You shall write them on the doorposts of your house and on your gates.

Caution Against Disobedience

10 "So it shall be, when the LORD your God brings you into the land of which He swore to your fathers, to Abraham, Isaac, and Jacob, to give you large and beautiful cities which you did not build,

11 "houses full of all good things, which you did not fill, hewn-out wells which you did not dig, vineyards and olive trees which you did not plant—when you have eaten and are full—

12 "*then* beware, lest you forget the LORD who brought you out of the land of Egypt, from the house of bondage.

13 "You shall fear the LORD your God and serve Him, and shall take oaths in His name.

14 "You shall not go after other gods, the gods of the peoples who *are* all around you

15 "(for the LORD your God *is* a jealous God among you), lest the anger of the LORD your God be aroused against you and destroy you from the face of the earth.

16 "You shall not tempt the LORD your God as you tempted *Him* in Massah.

17 "You shall diligently keep the commandments of the LORD your God, His testimonies, and His statutes which He has commanded you.

18 "And you shall do *what is* right and good in the sight of the LORD, that it may be well with you, and that you may go in and possess the good land of which the LORD swore to your fathers, ◄

19 "to cast out all your enemies from before you, as the LORD has spoken.

6:3 [a]Exodus 3:8 6:4 [a]Or *The LORD is our God, the LORD alone* (that is, the only one)

LIFE LESSONS

➤ 5:29 — *"Oh, that they had such a heart in them that they would fear Me and always keep all My commandments, that it might be well with them and with their children forever!"*

Here God states the desire of His own heart. He longs that a godly fear of Him would prompt us to eagerly keep His commandments, so that He could bless us and our descendants *forever*. That is a gracious God!

➤ 5:33 — *"You shall walk in all the ways which the LORD your God has commanded you, that you may live and that it may be well with you, and that you may prolong your days in the land which you shall possess."*

God gives us His commandments for our good. By keeping them His people gain not only life, but a *successful* life and a *long* life.

➤ 6:5 — *"You shall love the LORD your God with all your heart, with all your soul, and with all your strength."*

Of all God's commandments, this is the central and most important one. When we love God first and foremost, obedience follows as a natural result and ceases to be a chore (see John 14:15; 1 John 5:3).

WHAT THE BIBLE SAYS ABOUT THE IMPORTANCE OF DEVELOPING A DISCERNING SPIRIT

Deut. 6:6

Many of God's people get into trouble because they lack a discerning spirit. They walk right into Satan's traps and never even know what hit them. "I can't imagine what went wrong," they might say. But a person with a discerning spirit will be quick to explain, "Here's the trap Satan set, and here's how you fell into it."

Each of us needs to develop a discerning spirit, rooted in the knowledge of right and wrong, and to teach our children how to do the same. The time to begin teaching them discernment is not when they reach adulthood; we teach it to them from the time they are very young. Moses told the Israelites they must thoroughly train their children in God's commandments:

> These words which I command you today shall be in your heart. You shall teach them diligently to your children, and shall talk of them when you sit in your house, when you walk by the way, when you lie down, and when you rise up. You shall bind them as a sign on your hand, and they shall be as frontlets between your eyes. You shall write them on the doorposts of your house and on your gates. (Deut. 6:6–9)

We must know right from wrong, not only in theory but in practice.

We must know right from wrong, not only in theory but in practice. We must know how to apply God's truth to our lives and how to live in obedience to His commandments. That's why Moses instructed us to teach our children God's commandments throughout the day, not just in a half-hour Sunday school lesson. We are to say plainly to them, "This is right behavior; this is wrong behavior. This is God's commandment. This is the consequence for breaking God's commandment." An education in right and wrong must occur twenty-four hours a day, every day of the year.

A child thoroughly trained in God's commandments, who knows right from wrong, has very little trouble discerning Satan at work. He quickly picks up signals that tell him when things are askew; his conscience remains alive and sensitive. So he avoids becoming a slow-moving target for the enemy.

See the Life Principles Index for further study:
10. If necessary, God will move heaven and earth to show us His will.
3. God's Word is an immovable anchor in times of storm.

20 "When your son asks you in time to come,
saying, 'What *is the meaning of* the testimonies, the statutes, and the judgments
which the LORD our God has commanded
you?'
21 "then you shall say to your son: 'We were
slaves of Pharaoh in Egypt, and the LORD
brought us out of Egypt with a mighty hand;
22 'and the LORD showed signs and wonders
before our eyes, great and severe, against
Egypt, Pharaoh, and all his household.
23 'Then He brought us out from there, that
He might bring us in, to give us the land of
which He swore to our fathers.
24 'And the LORD commanded us to observe
all these statutes, to fear the LORD our God,
for our good always, that He might preserve
us alive, as *it is* this day.
25 'Then it will be righteousness for us, if we
are careful to observe all these commandments before the LORD our God, as He has
commanded us.'

A Chosen People

7 "When the LORD your God brings you into
the land which you go to possess, and has
cast out many nations before you, the Hittites
and the Girgashites and the Amorites and the
Canaanites and the Perizzites and the Hivites
and the Jebusites, seven nations greater and
mightier than you,
2 "and when the LORD your God delivers
them over to you, you shall conquer them *and*
utterly destroy them. You shall make no covenant with them nor show mercy to them.
3 "Nor shall you make marriages with them.
You shall not give your daughter to their son,
nor take their daughter for your son.
➤ 4 "For they will turn your sons away from
following Me, to serve other gods; so the
anger of the LORD will be aroused against you
and destroy you suddenly.
5 "But thus you shall deal with them: you
shall destroy their altars, and break down
their *sacred* pillars, and cut down their
wooden images,[a] and burn their carved images with fire.
6 "For you *are* a holy people to the LORD
your God; the LORD your God has chosen you
to be a people for Himself, a special treasure
above all the peoples on the face of the earth.
7 "The LORD did not set His love on you nor ➤
choose you because you were more in number than any other people, for you were the
least of all peoples;
8 "but because the LORD loves you, and because He would keep the oath which He
swore to your fathers, the LORD has brought
you out with a mighty hand, and redeemed
you from the house of bondage, from the
hand of Pharaoh king of Egypt.
9 "Therefore know that the LORD your God, ✳
He *is* God, the faithful God who keeps cov- ➤
enant and mercy for a thousand generations
with those who love Him and keep His commandments;
10 "and He repays those who hate Him to
their face, to destroy them. He will not be
slack with him who hates Him; He will repay
him to his face.
11 "Therefore you shall keep the commandment, the statutes, and the judgments which I
command you today, to observe them.

Blessings of Obedience

12 "Then it shall come to pass, because you
listen to these judgments, and keep and do
them, that the LORD your God will keep with
you the covenant and the mercy which He
swore to your fathers.
13 "And He will love you and bless you and
multiply you; He will also bless the fruit of
your womb and the fruit of your land, your

7:5 [a]Hebrew *Asherim,* Canaanite deities

LIFE LESSONS

➤ 6:18 — *"And you shall do what is right and good in the sight of the LORD, that it may be well with you, and that you may go in and possess the good land of which the LORD swore to your fathers . . . ."*

God's promises often come with conditions. Here He promises His people that if they will only do what He says is good and right, then they will surely receive His blessings.

➤ 7:4 — *"For they will turn your sons away from following Me, to serve other gods; so the anger of the LORD will be aroused against you and destroy you suddenly."*

Since intimacy with God is His highest priority for our lives, no greater sin exists than to turn someone's heart away from the one true God.

➤ 7:7, 8 — *"The LORD did not set His love on you nor choose you because you were more in number than any other people, for you were the least of all peoples; but because the LORD loves you . . . ."*

God does not love us because we're so loveable; He loves us because He loves us, and because of His promise to Abraham. We owe our very salvation to the love of God, and nothing else.

➤ 7:9 — *"Therefore know that the LORD your God, He is God, the faithful God who keeps covenant and mercy for a thousand generations with those who love Him and keep His commandments . . . ."*

The apostle Paul in Romans 8:35 rhetorically asks what could separate us from the love of God. The answer: Absolutely nothing! Even before God's chosen people entered the Promised Land, God assured them of His everlasting love.

grain and your new wine and your oil, the increase of your cattle and the offspring of your
flock, in the land of which He swore to your
fathers to give you.
14 "You shall be blessed above all peoples;
there shall not be a male or female barren
among you or among your livestock.
15 "And the LORD will take away from you all
sickness, and will afflict you with none of the
terrible diseases of Egypt which you have
known, but will lay *them* on all those who
hate you.
16 "Also you shall destroy all the peoples
whom the LORD your God delivers over to
you; your eye shall have no pity on them; nor
shall you serve their gods, for that *will be* a
snare to you.
➤ 17 "If you should say in your heart, 'These
nations are greater than I; how can I dispossess them?'—
18 "you shall not be afraid of them, *but* you
shall remember well what the LORD your God
did to Pharaoh and to all Egypt:
19 "the great trials which your eyes saw, the
signs and the wonders, the mighty hand and
the outstretched arm, by which the LORD your
God brought you out. So shall the LORD your
God do to all the peoples of whom you are
afraid.
20 "Moreover the LORD your God will send the
hornet among them until those who are left,
who hide themselves from you, are destroyed.
➤ 21 "You shall not be terrified of them; for the
LORD your God, the great and awesome God,
is among you.
22 "And the LORD your God will drive out
those nations before you little by little; you
will be unable to destroy them at once, lest
the beasts of the field become *too* numerous
for you.
23 "But the LORD your God will deliver them
over to you, and will inflict defeat upon them
until they are destroyed.
24 "And He will deliver their kings into your
hand, and you will destroy their name from
under heaven; no one shall be able to stand
against you until you have destroyed them.
25 "You shall burn the carved images of their
gods with fire; you shall not covet the silver or
gold *that is* on them, nor take *it* for yourselves, lest you be snared by it; for it *is* an
abomination to the LORD your God.
26 "Nor shall you bring an abomination into
your house, lest you be doomed to destruction
like it. You shall utterly detest it and utterly
abhor it, for it *is* an accursed thing.

Remember the LORD Your God

8 "Every commandment which I command
you today you must be careful to observe,
that you may live and multiply, and go in and
possess the land of which the LORD swore to
your fathers.
2 "And you shall remember that the LORD ➤
your God led you all the way these forty years
in the wilderness, to humble you *and* test you,
to know what *was* in your heart, whether you
would keep His commandments or not.
3 "So He humbled you, allowed you to
hunger, and fed you with manna which you
did not know nor did your fathers know, that
He might make you know that man shall not
live by bread alone; but man lives by every
word that proceeds from the mouth of the
LORD.
4 "Your garments did not wear out on you,
nor did your foot swell these forty years.
5 "You should know in your heart that as a
man chastens his son, *so* the LORD your God
chastens you.
6 "Therefore you shall keep the commandments of the LORD your God, to walk in His
ways and to fear Him.
7 "For the LORD your God is bringing you
into a good land, a land of brooks of water, of
fountains and springs, that flow out of valleys
and hills;
8 "a land of wheat and barley, of vines and
fig trees and pomegranates, a land of olive oil
and honey;

LIFE LESSONS

➤ 7:17, 18 — *"If you should say in your heart, 'These nations are greater than I; how can I dispossess them?'—you shall not be afraid of them, but you shall remember well what the LORD your God did to Pharaoh . . . ."*

When God calls us to some intimidating work, we are not to focus on our own abilities and strengths, but on His limitless power and grace. We succeed only when we align ourselves with Him.

➤ 7:21 — *"You shall not be terrified of them; for the LORD your God, the great and awesome God, is among you."*

Our God really is both great and awesome—and He is with us! Today, not only is He with us, He is *in* us in the Person of the Holy Spirit. So what do we have to fear?

➤ 8:2 — *"And you shall remember that the LORD your God led you all the way these forty years in the wilderness, to humble you and test you, to know what was in your heart, whether you would keep His commandments or not."*

God promises to lead us, even when we walk through the wilderness. There He humbles us and tests us, to see whether we will obey Him, even when things get difficult.

9 "a land in which you will eat bread without scarcity, in which you will lack nothing; a land whose stones *are* iron and out of whose hills you can dig copper.
10 "When you have eaten and are full, then you shall bless the LORD your God for the good land which He has given you.
11 "Beware that you do not forget the LORD your God by not keeping His commandments, His judgments, and His statutes which I command you today,
12 "lest—*when* you have eaten and are full, and have built beautiful houses and dwell *in them;*
13 "and *when* your herds and your flocks multiply, and your silver and your gold are multiplied, and all that you have is multiplied;
14 "when your heart is lifted up, and you forget the LORD your God who brought you out of the land of Egypt, from the house of bondage;
15 "who led you through that great and terrible wilderness, *in which were* fiery serpents and scorpions and thirsty land where there was no water; who brought water for you out of the flinty rock;
➤ 16 "who fed you in the wilderness with manna, which your fathers did not know, that He might humble you and that He might test you, to do you good in the end—
17 "then you say in your heart, 'My power and the might of my hand have gained me this wealth.'
➤ 18 "And you shall remember the LORD your God, for *it is* He who gives you power to get wealth, that He may establish His covenant which He swore to your fathers, as *it is* this day.
19 "Then it shall be, if you by any means forget the LORD your God, and follow other gods, and serve them and worship them, I testify against you this day that you shall surely perish.
20 "As the nations which the LORD destroys before you, so you shall perish, because you would not be obedient to the voice of the LORD your God.

Israel's Rebellions Reviewed

9 "Hear, O Israel: You *are* to cross over the Jordan today, and go in to dispossess nations greater and mightier than yourself, cities great and fortified up to heaven,
2 "a people great and tall, the descendants of the Anakim, whom you know, and *of whom* you heard *it said,* 'Who can stand before the descendants of Anak?'
3 "Therefore understand today that the LORD your God *is* He who goes over before you *as* a consuming fire. He will destroy them and bring them down before you; so you shall drive them out and destroy them quickly, as the LORD has said to you.
4 "Do not think in your heart, after the LORD your God has cast them out before you, saying, 'Because of my righteousness the LORD has brought me in to possess this land'; but *it is* because of the wickedness of these nations *that* the LORD is driving them out from before you.
5 "*It is* not because of your righteousness or the uprightness of your heart *that* you go in to possess their land, but because of the wickedness of these nations *that* the LORD your God drives them out from before you, and that He may fulfill the word which the LORD swore to your fathers, to Abraham, Isaac, and Jacob.
6 "Therefore understand that the LORD your God is not giving you this good land to possess because of your righteousness, for you *are* a stiff-necked people. ➤
7 "Remember! Do not forget how you provoked the LORD your God to wrath in the wilderness. From the day that you departed from the land of Egypt until you came to this place, you have been rebellious against the LORD.
8 "Also in Horeb you provoked the LORD to wrath, so that the LORD was angry *enough* with you to have destroyed you.
9 "When I went up into the mountain to receive the tablets of stone, the tablets of the covenant which the LORD made with you, then I stayed on the mountain forty days and

LIFE LESSONS

➤ 8:16 — *". . . who fed you in the wilderness with manna, which your fathers did not know, that He might humble you and that He might test you, to do you good in the end . . . ."*

God may allow us to go through tough times, but He does all this to do us "good in the end." We may not see that good right away, but if we will trust Him, He will bless us in His time.

➤ 8:18 — *"And you shall remember the LORD your God, for it is He who gives you power to get wealth, that He may establish His covenant which He swore to your fathers . . . ."*

Nothing in the Bible condemns hard work in the acquisition of material wealth. God wants us to remember, however, that our ability to earn wealth comes from Him and Him alone.

➤ 9:6 — *"Therefore understand that the LORD your God is not giving you this good land to possess because of your righteousness, for you are a stiff-necked people."*

The Lord does not shower us with His love because we deserve it, but because He is gracious and loving. "God demonstrates His own love toward us, in that while we were still sinners, Christ died for us" (Rom. 5:8).

forty nights. I neither ate bread nor drank water.

10 "Then the LORD delivered to me two tablets of stone written with the finger of God, and on them *were* all the words which the LORD had spoken to you on the mountain from the midst of the fire in the day of the assembly.

11 "And it came to pass, at the end of forty days and forty nights, *that* the LORD gave me the two tablets of stone, the tablets of the covenant.

12 "Then the LORD said to me, 'Arise, go down quickly from here, for your people whom you brought out of Egypt have acted corruptly; they have quickly turned aside from the way which I commanded them; they have made themselves a molded image.'

13 "Furthermore the LORD spoke to me, saying, 'I have seen this people, and indeed they are a stiff-necked people.

14 'Let Me alone, that I may destroy them and blot out their name from under heaven; and I will make of you a nation mightier and greater than they.'

15 "So I turned and came down from the mountain, and the mountain burned with fire; and the two tablets of the covenant *were* in my two hands.

16 "And I looked, and behold, you had sinned against the LORD your God—had made for yourselves a molded calf! You had turned aside quickly from the way which the LORD had commanded you.

17 "Then I took the two tablets and threw them out of my two hands and broke them before your eyes.

18 "And I fell down before the LORD, as at the first, forty days and forty nights; I neither ate bread nor drank water, because of all your sin which you committed in doing wickedly in the sight of the LORD, to provoke Him to anger.

19 "For I was afraid of the anger and hot displeasure with which the LORD was angry with you, to destroy you. But the LORD listened to me at that time also.

20 "And the LORD was very angry with Aaron *and* would have destroyed him; so I prayed for Aaron also at the same time.

21 "Then I took your sin, the calf which you had made, and burned it with fire and crushed it *and* ground *it* very small, until it was as fine as dust; and I threw its dust into the brook that descended from the mountain.

22 "Also at Taberah and Massah and Kibroth Hattaavah you provoked the LORD to wrath.

23 "Likewise, when the LORD sent you from Kadesh Barnea, saying, 'Go up and possess the land which I have given you,' then you rebelled against the commandment of the LORD your God, and you did not believe Him nor obey His voice.

24 "You have been rebellious against the LORD from the day that I knew you.

25 "Thus I prostrated myself before the LORD; forty days and forty nights I kept prostrating myself, because the LORD had said He would destroy you.

26 "Therefore I prayed to the LORD, and said: 'O Lord GOD, do not destroy Your people and Your inheritance whom You have redeemed through Your greatness, whom You have brought out of Egypt with a mighty hand.

27 'Remember Your servants, Abraham, Isaac, and Jacob; do not look on the stubbornness of this people, or on their wickedness or their sin,

28 'lest the land from which You brought us should say, "Because the LORD was not able to bring them to the land which He promised them, and because He hated them, He has brought them out to kill them in the wilderness."

29 'Yet they *are* Your people and Your inheritance, whom You brought out by Your mighty power and by Your outstretched arm.'

The Second Pair of Tablets

10 "At that time the LORD said to me, 'Hew for yourself two tablets of stone like the first, and come up to Me on the mountain and make yourself an ark of wood.

2 'And I will write on the tablets the words that were on the first tablets, which you broke; and you shall put them in the ark.'

3 "So I made an ark of acacia wood, hewed two tablets of stone like the first, and went up the mountain, having the two tablets in my hand.

4 "And He wrote on the tablets according to the first writing, the Ten Commandments, which the LORD had spoken to you in the mountain from the midst of the fire in the day of the assembly; and the LORD gave them to me.

5 "Then I turned and came down from the mountain, and put the tablets in the ark which I had made; and there they are, just as the LORD commanded me."

6 (Now the children of Israel journeyed from the wells of Bene Jaakan to Moserah, where Aaron died, and where he was buried; and Eleazar his son ministered as priest in his stead.

7 From there they journeyed to Gudgodah, and from Gudgodah to Jotbathah, a land of rivers of water.

8 At that time the LORD separated the tribe of Levi to bear the ark of the covenant of the LORD, to stand before the LORD to minister to Him and to bless in His name, to this day.

9 Therefore Levi has no portion nor inheritance with his brethren; the LORD *is* his inheritance, just as the LORD your God promised him.)

10 'As at the first time, I stayed in the mountain forty days and forty nights; the LORD also

heard me at that time, *and* the LORD chose not
to destroy you.
11 "Then the LORD said to me, 'Arise, begin
your journey before the people, that they may
go in and possess the land which I swore to
their fathers to give them.'

The Essence of the Law

➤ **12** "And now, Israel, what does the LORD your
God require of you, but to fear the LORD your
God, to walk in all His ways and to love Him,
to serve the LORD your God with all your
heart and with all your soul,
13 "*and* to keep the commandments of the
LORD and His statutes which I command you
today for your good?
14 "Indeed heaven and the highest heavens
belong to the LORD your God, *also* the earth
with all that *is* in it.
15 "The LORD delighted only in your fathers,
to love them; and He chose their descendants
after them, you above all peoples, as *it is* this
day.
16 "Therefore circumcise the foreskin of your
heart, and be stiff-necked no longer.
17 "For the LORD your God *is* God of gods and
Lord of lords, the great God, mighty and awesome, who shows no partiality nor takes a
bribe.
18 "He administers justice for the fatherless
and the widow, and loves the stranger, giving
him food and clothing.
19 "Therefore love the stranger, for you were
strangers in the land of Egypt.
20 "You shall fear the LORD your God; you
shall serve Him, and to Him you shall hold
fast, and take oaths in His name.
21 "He *is* your praise, and He *is* your God,
who has done for you these great and awesome things which your eyes have seen.
22 "Your fathers went down to Egypt with seventy persons, and now the LORD your God has
made you as the stars of heaven in multitude.

Love and Obedience Rewarded

11 "Therefore you shall love the LORD
your God, and keep His charge, His
statutes, His judgments, and His commandments always.
2 "Know today that *I do* not *speak* with your
children, who have not known and who have
not seen the chastening of the LORD your
God, His greatness and His mighty hand and
His outstretched arm—
3 "His signs and His acts which He did in
the midst of Egypt, to Pharaoh king of Egypt,
and to all his land;
4 "what He did to the army of Egypt, to their
horses and their chariots: how He made the
waters of the Red Sea overflow them as they
pursued you, and *how* the LORD has destroyed
them to this day;
5 "what He did for you in the wilderness
until you came to this place;
6 "and what He did to Dathan and Abiram
the sons of Eliab, the son of Reuben: how the
earth opened its mouth and swallowed them
up, their households, their tents, and all the
substance that *was* in their possession, in the
midst of all Israel—
7 "but your eyes have seen every great act of
the LORD which He did.
8 "Therefore you shall keep every commandment which I command you today, that
you may be strong, and go in and possess the
land which you cross over to possess,
9 "and that you may prolong *your* days in
the land which the LORD swore to give your
fathers, to them and their descendants, 'a
land flowing with milk and honey.'[a]
10 "For the land which you go to possess *is*
not like the land of Egypt from which you
have come, where you sowed your seed and
watered *it* by foot, as a vegetable garden;
11 "but the land which you cross over to possess *is* a land of hills and valleys, which
drinks water from the rain of heaven,
12 "a land for which the LORD your God
cares; the eyes of the LORD your God *are* always on it, from the beginning of the year to
the very end of the year.
13 'And it shall be that if you earnestly obey ◄
My commandments which I command you
today, to love the LORD your God and serve
Him with all your heart and with all your
soul,
14 "then I[a] will give *you* the rain for your land

11:9 [a]Exodus 3:8 **11:14** [a]Following Masoretic Text and Targum; Samaritan Pentateuch, Septuagint, and Vulgate read *He*.

LIFE LESSONS

➤ 10:12 — *"And now, Israel, what does the LORD your God require of you, but to fear the LORD your God, to walk in all His ways and to love Him, to serve the LORD your God with all your heart and with all your soul . . . ."*

Moses gives a condensed version of the law: (1) fear God; (2) walk in God's ways; (3) love God; (4) serve God wholeheartedly; (5) obey God. God promises to bless all those who live like this.

➤ 11:13, 14 — *"And it shall be that if you earnestly obey My commandments which I command you today . . . then I will give you the rain for your land in its season, the early rain and the latter rain . . . ."*

Our God provides for those who love Him and who obey His commandments. In today's uncertain world, it's good to be in the hands of a loving God who knows what we need before we even ask Him for it.

in its season, the early rain and the latter rain,
that you may gather in your grain, your new
wine, and your oil.
15 'And I will send grass in your fields for
your livestock, that you may eat and be filled.'
➤ 16 "Take heed to yourselves, lest your heart
be deceived, and you turn aside and serve
other gods and worship them,
17 "lest the LORD's anger be aroused against
you, and He shut up the heavens so that there
be no rain, and the land yield no produce, and
you perish quickly from the good land which
the LORD is giving you.
18 "Therefore you shall lay up these words of
mine in your heart and in your soul, and bind
them as a sign on your hand, and they shall
be as frontlets between your eyes.
19 "You shall teach them to your children,
speaking of them when you sit in your house,
when you walk by the way, when you lie
down, and when you rise up.
20 "And you shall write them on the doorposts of your house and on your gates,
21 "that your days and the days of your children may be multiplied in the land of which
the LORD swore to your fathers to give them,
like the days of the heavens above the earth.
22 "For if you carefully keep all these commandments which I command you to do—to
love the LORD your God, to walk in all His
ways, and to hold fast to Him—
23 "then the LORD will drive out all these nations from before you, and you will dispossess greater and mightier nations than
yourselves.
24 "Every place on which the sole of your
foot treads shall be yours: from the wilderness and Lebanon, from the river, the River
Euphrates, even to the Western Sea,[a] shall be
your territory.
25 "No man shall be able to stand against
you; the LORD your God will put the dread of
you and the fear of you upon all the land
where you tread, just as He has said to you.
26 "Behold, I set before you today a blessing
and a curse:
27 "the blessing, if you obey the commandments of the LORD your God which I command you today;
28 "and the curse, if you do not obey the commandments of the LORD your God, but turn
aside from the way which I command you
today, to go after other gods which you have
not known.
29 "Now it shall be, when the LORD your God
has brought you into the land which you go to
possess, that you shall put the blessing on
Mount Gerizim and the curse on Mount Ebal.
30 "*Are* they not on the other side of the Jordan, toward the setting sun, in the land of the
Canaanites who dwell in the plain opposite
Gilgal, beside the terebinth trees of Moreh?
31 "For you will cross over the Jordan and go
in to possess the land which the LORD your
God is giving you, and you will possess it and
dwell in it.
32 "And you shall be careful to observe all
the statutes and judgments which I set before
you today.

A Prescribed Place of Worship

12 "These *are* the statutes and judgments
which you shall be careful to observe in
the land which the LORD God of your fathers
is giving you to possess, all the days that you
live on the earth.
2 "You shall utterly destroy all the places
where the nations which you shall dispossess
served their gods, on the high mountains and
on the hills and under every green tree.
3 "And you shall destroy their altars, break
their *sacred* pillars, and burn their wooden
images with fire; you shall cut down the
carved images of their gods and destroy their
names from that place.
4 "You shall not worship the LORD your God ➤
with such *things*.
5 "But you shall seek the place where the
LORD your God chooses, out of all your tribes,
to put His name for His dwelling place; and
there you shall go.
6 "There you shall take your burnt offerings, your sacrifices, your tithes, the heave offerings of your hand, your vowed offerings,
your freewill offerings, and the firstborn of
your herds and flocks.
7 "And there you shall eat before the LORD
your God, and you shall rejoice in all to which
you have put your hand, you and your households, in which the LORD your God has
blessed you.

11:24 [a]That is, the Mediterranean

LIFE LESSONS

➤ **11:16 — *"Take heed to yourselves, lest your heart be deceived, and you turn aside and serve other gods and worship them . . . ."***

Most people do not simply wake up one day and decide to abandon God. Deception usually plays a large role—just as it did in Eden, just as it will at the end of time (see Gen. 3:13; Matt. 24:5).

➤ **12:4 — *"You shall not worship the LORD your God with such things."***

All worship is not godly worship. God calls us to worship Him in Spirit and in truth, and not all forms of worship fit this criteria.

8 "You shall not at all do as we are doing
here today—every man doing whatever *is*
right in his own eyes—
9 "for as yet you have not come to the rest
and the inheritance which the LORD your God
is giving you.
10 "But *when* you cross over the Jordan and
dwell in the land which the LORD your God is
giving you to inherit, and He gives you rest
from all your enemies round about, so that
you dwell in safety,
11 "then there will be the place where the
LORD your God chooses to make His name
abide. There you shall bring all that I command you: your burnt offerings, your sacrifices, your tithes, the heave offerings of your
hand, and all your choice offerings which you
vow to the LORD.
12 "And you shall rejoice before the LORD
your God, you and your sons and your daughters, your male and female servants, and the
Levite who *is* within your gates, since he has
no portion nor inheritance with you.
13 "Take heed to yourself that you do not
offer your burnt offerings in every place that
you see;
14 "but in the place which the LORD chooses,
in one of your tribes, there you shall offer
your burnt offerings, and there you shall do
all that I command you.
15 "However, you may slaughter and eat
meat within all your gates, whatever your
heart desires, according to the blessing of
the LORD your God which He has given you;
the unclean and the clean may eat of it, of the
gazelle and the deer alike.
16 "Only you shall not eat the blood; you
shall pour it on the earth like water.
17 "You may not eat within your gates the
tithe of your grain or your new wine or your
oil, of the firstborn of your herd or your flock,
of any of your offerings which you vow, of
your freewill offerings, or of the heave offering of your hand.
➤ 18 "But you must eat them before the LORD
your God in the place which the LORD your
God chooses, you and your son and your
daughter, your male servant and your female
servant, and the Levite who *is* within your
gates; and you shall rejoice before the LORD
your God in all to which you put your hands.
19 "Take heed to yourself that you do not forsake the Levite as long as you live in your
land.
20 "When the LORD your God enlarges your
border as He has promised you, and you say,
'Let me eat meat,' because you long to eat
meat, you may eat as much meat as your
heart desires.
21 "If the place where the LORD your God
chooses to put His name is too far from you,
then you may slaughter from your herd and
from your flock which the LORD has given
you, just as I have commanded you, and you
may eat within your gates as much as your
heart desires.
22 "Just as the gazelle and the deer are eaten,
so you may eat them; the unclean and the
clean alike may eat them.
23 "Only be sure that you do not eat the
blood, for the blood *is* the life; you may not
eat the life with the meat.
24 "You shall not eat it; you shall pour it on
the earth like water.
25 "You shall not eat it, that it may go well
with you and your children after you, when
you do *what is* right in the sight of the LORD.
26 "Only the holy things which you have, and
your vowed offerings, you shall take and go
to the place which the LORD chooses.
27 "And you shall offer your burnt offerings,
the meat and the blood, on the altar of the
LORD your God; and the blood of your sacrifices shall be poured out on the altar of the
LORD your God, and you shall eat the meat.
28 "Observe and obey all these words which
I command you, that it may go well with you
and your children after you forever, when you
do *what is* good and right in the sight of the
LORD your God.

Beware of False Gods

29 "When the LORD your God cuts off from
before you the nations which you go to
dispossess, and you displace them and dwell
in their land,
30 "take heed to yourself that you are not ensnared to follow them, after they are destroyed from before you, and that you do not
inquire after their gods, saying, 'How did
these nations serve their gods? I also will do
likewise.'
31 "You shall not worship the LORD your God
in that way; for every abomination to the
LORD which He hates they have done to their
gods; for they burn even their sons and
daughters in the fire to their gods.
32 "Whatever I command you, be careful to
observe it; you shall not add to it nor take
away from it.

LIFE LESSONS

➤ 12:18 — *". . . you shall rejoice before the LORD your God in all to which you put your hands."*

God wants a happy people who rejoice in all they do, not a dour company of saints who focus on all the evil in the world. Oneness with God produces peace and joy, not chaos and grumbling.

Punishment of Apostates

13 "If there arises among you a prophet or a dreamer of dreams, and he gives you a sign or a wonder,

2 "and the sign or the wonder comes to pass, of which he spoke to you, saying, 'Let us go after other gods'—which you have not known—'and let us serve them,'

➤ 3 "you shall not listen to the words of that prophet or that dreamer of dreams, for the LORD your God is testing you to know whether you love the LORD your God with all your heart and with all your soul.

4 "You shall walk after the LORD your God and fear Him, and keep His commandments and obey His voice; you shall serve Him and hold fast to Him.

5 "But that prophet or that dreamer of dreams shall be put to death, because he has spoken in order to turn *you* away from the LORD your God, who brought you out of the land of Egypt and redeemed you from the house of bondage, to entice you from the way in which the LORD your God commanded you to walk. So you shall put away the evil from your midst.

6 "If your brother, the son of your mother, your son or your daughter, the wife of your bosom, or your friend who is as your own soul, secretly entices you, saying, 'Let us go and serve other gods,' which you have not known, neither you nor your fathers,

7 "of the gods of the people which *are* all around you, near to you or far off from you, from *one* end of the earth to the *other* end of the earth,

8 "you shall not consent to him or listen to him, nor shall your eye pity him, nor shall you spare him or conceal him;

9 "but you shall surely kill him; your hand shall be first against him to put him to death, and afterward the hand of all the people.

10 "And you shall stone him with stones until he dies, because he sought to entice you away from the LORD your God, who brought you out of the land of Egypt, from the house of bondage.

11 "So all Israel shall hear and fear, and not again do such wickedness as this among you.

12 "If you hear someone in one of your cities, which the LORD your God gives you to dwell in, saying,

13 'Corrupt men have gone out from among you and enticed the inhabitants of their city, saying, "Let us go and serve other gods"'—which you have not known—

14 "then you shall inquire, search out, and ask diligently. And *if it is* indeed true *and* certain *that* such an abomination was committed among you,

15 "you shall surely strike the inhabitants of that city with the edge of the sword, utterly destroying it, all that is in it and its livestock—with the edge of the sword.

16 "And you shall gather all its plunder into the middle of the street, and completely burn with fire the city and all its plunder, for the LORD your God. It shall be a heap forever; it shall not be built again.

17 "So none of the accursed things shall remain in your hand, that the LORD may turn from the fierceness of His anger and show you mercy, have compassion on you and multiply you, just as He swore to your fathers,

18 "because you have listened to the voice of the LORD your God, to keep all His commandments which I command you today, to do *what is* right in the eyes of the LORD your God.

Improper Mourning

14 "You *are* the children of the LORD your God; you shall not cut yourselves nor shave the front of your head for the dead.

2 "For you *are* a holy people to the LORD your God, and the LORD has chosen you to be a people for Himself, a special treasure above all the peoples who *are* on the face of the earth.

Clean and Unclean Meat

3 "You shall not eat any detestable thing.

4 "These *are* the animals which you may eat: the ox, the sheep, the goat,

5 "the deer, the gazelle, the roe deer, the wild goat, the mountain goat,[a] the antelope, and the mountain sheep.

6 "And you may eat every animal with cloven hooves, having the hoof split into two parts, *and that* chews the cud, among the animals.

7 "Nevertheless, of those that chew the cud or have cloven hooves, you shall not eat, *such as* these: the camel, the hare, and the rock hyrax; for they chew the cud but do not have cloven hooves; they *are* unclean for you.

14:5 [a]Or *addax*

LIFE LESSONS

➤ 13:3 — *". . . you shall not listen to the words of that prophet or that dreamer of dreams, for the LORD your God is testing you to know whether you love the LORD your God with all your heart and with all your soul."*

A miracle is no proof of God's involvement. Pharaoh's magicians reproduced some of God's plagues (see Gen. 7:11, 22), and similar things will happen in the future (2 Thess. 2:9). The real test is: does it honor God?

8 “Also the swine is unclean for you, because it has cloven hooves, yet *does* not *chew*
the cud; you shall not eat their flesh or touch
their dead carcasses.
9 “These you may eat of all that *are* in the
waters: you may eat all that have fins and
scales.
10 “And whatever does not have fins and
scales you shall not eat; it *is* unclean for you.
11 “All clean birds you may eat.
12 “But these you shall not eat: the eagle, the
vulture, the buzzard,
13 “the red kite, the falcon, and the kite after
their kinds;
14 “every raven after its kind;
15 “the ostrich, the short-eared owl, the sea
gull, and the hawk after their kinds;
16 “the little owl, the screech owl, the white
owl,
17 “the jackdaw, the carrion vulture, the
fisher owl,
18 “the stork, the heron after its kind, and the
hoopoe and the bat.
19 “Also every creeping thing that flies is unclean for you; they shall not be eaten.
20 “You may eat all clean birds.
21 “You shall not eat anything that dies *of itself;* you may give it to the alien who *is* within
your gates, that he may eat it, or you may sell
it to a foreigner; for you *are* a holy people to
the LORD your God. “You shall not boil a
young goat in its mother’s milk.

Tithing Principles

22 “You shall truly tithe all the increase of
your grain that the field produces year by
year.
23 “And you shall eat before the LORD your
God, in the place where He chooses to
make His name abide, the tithe of your grain
and your new wine and your oil, of the
firstborn of your herds and your flocks, that
you may learn to fear the LORD your God always.
24 “But if the journey is too long for you, so
that you are not able to carry *the tithe, or* if
the place where the LORD your God chooses
to put His name is too far from you, when the
LORD your God has blessed you,
25 “then you shall exchange *it* for money,
take the money in your hand, and go to the
place which the LORD your God chooses.
26 “And you shall spend that money for
whatever your heart desires: for oxen or
sheep, for wine or similar drink, for whatever
your heart desires; you shall eat there before
the LORD your God, and you shall rejoice, you
and your household.
27 “You shall not forsake the Levite who *is*
within your gates, for he has no part nor inheritance with you.
28 “At the end of *every* third year you shall
bring out the tithe of your produce of that
year and store *it* up within your gates.
29 “And the Levite, because he has no portion
nor inheritance with you, and the stranger
and the fatherless and the widow who *are*
within your gates, may come and eat and
be satisfied, that the LORD your God may
bless you in all the work of your hand which
you do.

Debts Canceled Every Seven Years

15 “At the end of *every* seven years you
shall grant a release *of debts.*
2 “And this *is* the form of the release: Every
creditor who has lent *anything* to his neighbor shall release *it;* he shall not require *it* of
his neighbor or his brother, because it is
called the LORD’s release.
3 “Of a foreigner you may require *it;* but you
shall give up your claim to what is owed by
your brother,
4 “except when there may be no poor
among you; for the LORD will greatly bless
you in the land which the LORD your God is
giving you to possess *as* an inheritance—
5 “only if you carefully obey the voice of the
LORD your God, to observe with care all these
commandments which I command you today.
6 “For the LORD your God will bless you just
as He promised you; you shall lend to many
nations, but you shall not borrow; you shall
reign over many nations, but they shall not
reign over you.

Generosity to the Poor

7 “If there is among you a poor man of your
brethren, within any of the gates in your land
which the LORD your God is giving you, you
shall not harden your heart nor shut your
hand from your poor brother,
8 “but you shall open your hand wide to him
and willingly lend him sufficient for his need,
whatever he needs.
9 “Beware lest there be a wicked thought in
your heart, saying, ‘The seventh year, the year
of release, is at hand,’ and your eye be evil
against your poor brother and you give him
nothing, and he cry out to the LORD against
you, and it become sin among you.
10 “You shall surely give to him, and your

LIFE LESSONS

➢ 15:7 — *“If there is among you a poor man of your brethren . . . you shall not harden your heart nor shut your hand from your poor brother . . . .”*

As children of a God who loves to give, the Lord instructs us and encourages us to give generously to the poor. He blesses us so that we might bless others.

heart should not be grieved when you give to him, because for this thing the LORD your God will bless you in all your works and in all to which you put your hand.

➤ 11 "For the poor will never cease from the land; therefore I command you, saying, 'You shall open your hand wide to your brother, to your poor and your needy, in your land.'

The Law Concerning Bondservants

12 "If your brother, a Hebrew man, or a Hebrew woman, is sold to you and serves you six years, then in the seventh year you shall let him go free from you.

13 "And when you send him away free from you, you shall not let him go away empty-handed;

14 "you shall supply him liberally from your flock, from your threshing floor, and from your winepress. *From what* the LORD your God has blessed you with, you shall give to him.

15 "You shall remember that you were a slave in the land of Egypt, and the LORD your God redeemed you; therefore I command you this thing today.

16 "And if it happens that he says to you, 'I will not go away from you,' because he loves you and your house, since he prospers with you,

17 "then you shall take an awl and thrust *it* through his ear to the door, and he shall be your servant forever. Also to your female servant you shall do likewise.

18 "It shall not seem hard to you when you send him away free from you; for he has been worth a double hired servant in serving you six years. Then the LORD your God will bless you in all that you do.

The Law Concerning Firstborn Animals

19 "All the firstborn males that come from your herd and your flock you shall sanctify to the LORD your God; you shall do no work with the firstborn of your herd, nor shear the firstborn of your flock.

20 "You and your household shall eat *it* before the LORD your God year by year in the place which the LORD chooses.

21 "But if there is a defect in it, *if it is* lame or blind *or has* any serious defect, you shall not sacrifice it to the LORD your God.

22 "You may eat it within your gates; the unclean and the clean *person* alike *may eat it*, as *if it were* a gazelle or a deer.

23 "Only you shall not eat its blood; you shall pour it on the ground like water.

The Passover Reviewed

16 "Observe the month of Abib, and keep the Passover to the LORD your God, for in the month of Abib the LORD your God brought you out of Egypt by night.

2 "Therefore you shall sacrifice the Passover to the LORD your God, from the flock and the herd, in the place where the LORD chooses to put His name.

3 "You shall eat no leavened bread with it; seven days you shall eat unleavened bread with it, *that is*, the bread of affliction (for you came out of the land of Egypt in haste), that you may remember the day in which you came out of the land of Egypt all the days of your life.

4 "And no leaven shall be seen among you in all your territory for seven days, nor shall *any* of the meat which you sacrifice the first day at twilight remain overnight until morning.

5 "You may not sacrifice the Passover within any of your gates which the LORD your God gives you;

6 "but at the place where the LORD your God chooses to make His name abide, there you shall sacrifice the Passover at twilight, at the going down of the sun, at the time you came out of Egypt.

7 "And you shall roast and eat *it* in the place which the LORD your God chooses, and in the morning you shall turn and go to your tents.

8 "Six days you shall eat unleavened bread, and on the seventh day there *shall be* a sacred assembly to the LORD your God. You shall do no work *on it*.

The Feast of Weeks Reviewed

9 "You shall count seven weeks for yourself; begin to count the seven weeks from *the time* you begin *to put* the sickle to the grain.

10 "Then you shall keep the Feast of Weeks to the LORD your God with the tribute of a freewill offering from your hand, which you shall give as the LORD your God blesses you.

11 "You shall rejoice before the LORD your God, you and your son and your daughter, your male servant and your female servant, the Levite who *is* within your gates, the stranger and the fatherless and the widow who *are* among you, at the place where the LORD your God chooses to make His name abide.

12 "And you shall remember that you were a slave in Egypt, and you shall be careful to observe these statutes.

LIFE LESSONS

➤ **15:11 — *"For the poor will never cease from the land; therefore I command you, saying, 'You shall open your hand wide to your brother . . . .'"***

Both Moses and Jesus told us that the poor would always live among us (see Matt. 26:11). Therefore we are always to remain generous.

The Feast of Tabernacles Reviewed
13 "You shall observe the Feast of Tabernacles seven days, when you have gathered
from your threshing floor and from your
winepress.
14 "And you shall rejoice in your feast, you
and your son and your daughter, your male
servant and your female servant and the
Levite, the stranger and the fatherless and the
widow, who *are* within your gates.
15 "Seven days you shall keep a sacred feast
to the LORD your God in the place which the
LORD chooses, because the LORD your God
will bless you in all your produce and in all
the work of your hands, so that you surely rejoice.
16 "Three times a year all your males shall
appear before the LORD your God in the place
which He chooses: at the Feast of Unleavened
Bread, at the Feast of Weeks, and at the Feast
of Tabernacles; and they shall not appear before the LORD empty-handed.
➤ 17 "Every man *shall give* as he is able, according to the blessing of the LORD your God
which He has given you.

Justice Must Be Administered
18 "You shall appoint judges and officers in
all your gates, which the LORD your God gives
you, according to your tribes, and they shall
judge the people with just judgment.
19 "You shall not pervert justice; you shall
not show partiality, nor take a bribe, for a
bribe blinds the eyes of the wise and twists
the words of the righteous.
20 "You shall follow what is altogether just,
that you may live and inherit the land which
the LORD your God is giving you.
21 "You shall not plant for yourself any tree,
as a wooden image, near the altar which you
build for yourself to the LORD your God.
22 "You shall not set up a *sacred* pillar, which
the LORD your God hates.
17 "You shall not sacrifice to the LORD
your God a bull or sheep which has any
blemish *or* defect, for that *is* an abomination
to the LORD your God.
2 "If there is found among you, within any
of your gates which the LORD your God gives
you, a man or a woman who has been wicked
in the sight of the LORD your God, in transgressing His covenant,
3 "who has gone and served other gods and
worshiped them, either the sun or moon or
any of the host of heaven, which I have not
commanded,
4 "and it is told you, and you hear *of it,* then
you shall inquire diligently. And if *it is* indeed
true *and* certain that such an abomination has
been committed in Israel,
5 "then you shall bring out to your gates
that man or woman who has committed that
wicked thing, and shall stone to death that
man or woman with stones.
6 "Whoever is deserving of death shall be
put to death on the testimony of two or three
witnesses; he shall not be put to death on the
testimony of one witness.
7 "The hands of the witnesses shall be the
first against him to put him to death, and afterward the hands of all the people. So you
shall put away the evil from among you.
8 "If a matter arises which is too hard for
you to judge, between degrees of guilt for
bloodshed, between one judgment or another,
or between one punishment or another, matters of controversy within your gates, then
you shall arise and go up to the place which
the LORD your God chooses.
9 "And you shall come to the priests, the
Levites, and to the judge *there* in those days,
and inquire *of them;* they shall pronounce
upon you the sentence of judgment.
10 "You shall do according to the sentence
which they pronounce upon you in that place
which the LORD chooses. And you shall be
careful to do according to all that they order
you.
11 "According to the sentence of the law in
which they instruct you, according to the
judgment which they tell you, you shall do;
you shall not turn aside *to* the right hand or
to the left from the sentence which they pronounce upon you.
12 "Now the man who acts presumptuously
and will not heed the priest who stands to
minister there before the LORD your God, or
the judge, that man shall die. So you shall put
away the evil from Israel.
13 "And all the people shall hear and fear,
and no longer act presumptuously.

Principles Governing Kings
14 "When you come to the land which the
LORD your God is giving you, and possess it
and dwell in it, and say, 'I will set a king over
me like all the nations that *are* around me,'
15 "you shall surely set a king over you whom

LIFE LESSONS

➤ 16:17 — *"Every man shall give as he is able, according to the blessing of the LORD your God which He has given you."*

In both the Old and New Testaments, God instructs His people to give back to the Lord a proportionate amount, as He had blessed them (see 2 Cor. 8:12). And no one ever out gives God!

the LORD your God chooses; *one* from among
your brethren you shall set as king over you;
you may not set a foreigner over you, who *is*
not your brother.
➤ 16 "But he shall not multiply horses for himself, nor cause the people to return to Egypt to
multiply horses, for the LORD has said to you,
'You shall not return that way again.'
17 "Neither shall he multiply wives for himself, lest his heart turn away; nor shall he
greatly multiply silver and gold for himself.
18 "Also it shall be, when he sits on the
throne of his kingdom, that he shall write for
himself a copy of this law in a book, from *the*
one before the priests, the Levites.
➤ 19 "And it shall be with him, and he shall
read it all the days of his life, that he may
learn to fear the LORD his God and be careful
to observe all the words of this law and these
statutes,
20 "that his heart may not be lifted above his
brethren, that he may not turn aside from the
commandment *to* the right hand or *to* the left,
and that he may prolong *his* days in his kingdom, he and his children in the midst of Israel.

The Portion of the Priests and Levites

18 "The priests, the Levites—all the tribe
of Levi—shall have no part nor inheritance with Israel; they shall eat the offerings
of the LORD made by fire, and His portion.
2 "Therefore they shall have no inheritance
among their brethren; the LORD is their inheritance, as He said to them.
3 "And this shall be the priest's due from the
people, from those who offer a sacrifice,
whether *it is* bull or sheep: they shall give to
the priest the shoulder, the cheeks, and the
stomach.
4 "The firstfruits of your grain and your new
wine and your oil, and the first of the fleece of
your sheep, you shall give him.
5 "For the LORD your God has chosen him
out of all your tribes to stand to minister in the
name of the LORD, him and his sons forever.
6 "So if a Levite comes from any of your
gates, from where he dwells among all Israel,
and comes with all the desire of his mind to
the place which the LORD chooses,
7 "then he may serve in the name of the
LORD his God as all his brethren the Levites
do, who stand there before the LORD.
8 "They shall have equal portions to eat, besides what comes from the sale of his inheritance.

Avoid Wicked Customs

9 "When you come into the land which the
LORD your God is giving you, you shall not
learn to follow the abominations of those nations.
10 "There shall not be found among you *any-*
one who makes his son or his daughter pass
through the fire, *or one* who practices witchcraft, *or* a soothsayer, or one who interprets
omens, or a sorcerer,
11 "or one who conjures spells, or a medium,
or a spiritist, or one who calls up the dead.
12 "For all who do these things *are* an
abomination to the LORD, and because of
these abominations the LORD your God drives
them out from before you.
13 "You shall be blameless before the LORD
your God.
14 "For these nations which you will dispossess listened to soothsayers and diviners; but
as for you, the LORD your God has not appointed such for you.

A New Prophet Like Moses

15 "The LORD your God will raise up for you
a Prophet like me from your midst, from your
brethren. Him you shall hear,
16 "according to all you desired of the LORD
your God in Horeb in the day of the assembly,
saying, 'Let me not hear again the voice of the
LORD my God, nor let me see this great fire
anymore, lest I die.'
17 "And the LORD said to me: 'What they have
spoken is good.
18 'I will raise up for them a Prophet like you ➤
from among their brethren, and will put My
words in His mouth, and He shall speak to
them all that I command Him.
19 'And it shall be *that* whoever will not hear

LIFE LESSONS

➤ **17:16, 17 — *"But he shall not multiply horses for himself . . . . Neither shall he multiply wives for himself, lest his heart turn away; nor shall he greatly multiply silver and gold for himself.***

All the things God told Israel's future kings *not* to do, Solomon did. Despite his wisdom, Solomon neglected the wisdom of God—and his nation paid dearly for it.

➤ **17:19 — *"And it shall be with him, and he shall read it all the days of his life, that he may learn to fear the LORD his God . . . ."***

Daily Bible study helps us to fear God and obey His commands, keeps us humble, and lengthens life. And during times of storm, it gives us an immovable anchor.

➤ **18:18 — *"I will raise up for them a Prophet like you from among their brethren, and will put My words in His mouth . . . ."***

Jesus Christ fulfilled this prophecy during His earthly ministry (John 1:21–27; 6:14; 7:40). So it was appropriate that Moses appeared with Jesus at the Transfiguration (Matt. 17:1–3).

WHAT THE BIBLE SAYS ABOUT THE FORBIDDEN PRACTICE OF THE OCCULT

Deut. 18

Most believers readily recognize that the Bible forbids the occult practices of Satan worship and witchcraft. They might not, however, so quickly identify other practices as satanic or occult.

While the Bible forbids and rebukes practice of astrology, including the use of horoscopes and predicting events by the alignment of planets (see Deut. 18:10; Is. 47:12, 13), many Christians consider it harmless fun to consult their horoscopes in the daily newspaper. God says it's not.

Another practice, divination (fortune-telling), is forbidden in many places (Lev. 20:27; Deut. 18:9-14; Is. 44:25; Jer. 27:9; Ezek. 13:8). Other Scriptures could be included, but the Scripture makes it abundantly clear that the practice of fortune-telling is occultic in nature and therefore forbidden.

The Bible also condemns other practices, such as enchantments (sometimes referred to as incantations, spells, or charming; see Deut. 18:11 and Is. 19:3). God forbids the practice of magic (Ex. 7:11, 12). Of course, there is a considerable difference between one who practices magic by tapping into supernatural forces, and those who perform acts of illusion that depend on sleight of hand, not supernatural powers. A friend of mine is a master illusionist. He is great at doing tricks, but he explains to his audience that his tricks are just that—tricks, illusions—and that they have nothing to do with magic or supernatural powers. His ministry enables him to talk about the occult, but he makes it clear that what he does is sleight of hand, no matter how amazing it appears to the onlooker.

Probably you have enjoyed an illusion or trick performed in a show and never considered it dangerous. As children, many had their "fortunes" told at Halloween parties at school. Some consider the use of Ouija boards a harmless form of entertainment, in no way connected to supernatural powers—but we need to remember that the practice of attempting to contact the dead through the use of a medium is strictly forbidden in the Bible (Deut. 10:10–12; 2 Kin. 21:6; Lev. 19:31). No believer should ever play with the occult.

No believer should ever play with the occult.

See the Life Principles Index for further study:
21. Obedience always brings blessing.
6. You reap what you sow, more than you sow, and later than you sow.

My words, which He speaks in My name, I will require *it* of him.
20 'But the prophet who presumes to speak a word in My name, which I have not commanded him to speak, or who speaks in the name of other gods, that prophet shall die.'
21 "And if you say in your heart, 'How shall we know the word which the LORD has not spoken?'—
➤ 22 "when a prophet speaks in the name of the LORD, if the thing does not happen or come to pass, that *is* the thing which the LORD has not spoken; the prophet has spoken it presumptuously; you shall not be afraid of him.

Three Cities of Refuge

19 "When the LORD your God has cut off the nations whose land the LORD your God is giving you, and you dispossess them and dwell in their cities and in their houses,
2 "you shall separate three cities for yourself in the midst of your land which the LORD your God is giving you to possess.
3 "You shall prepare roads for yourself, and divide into three parts the territory of your land which the LORD your God is giving you to inherit, that any manslayer may flee there.
4 "And this *is* the case of the manslayer who flees there, that he may live: Whoever kills his neighbor unintentionally, not having hated him in time past—
➤ 5 "as when *a man* goes to the woods with his neighbor to cut timber, and his hand swings a stroke with the ax to cut down the tree, and the head slips from the handle and strikes his neighbor so that he dies—he shall flee to one of these cities and live;
6 "lest the avenger of blood, while his anger is hot, pursue the manslayer and overtake him, because the way is long, and kill him, though he *was* not deserving of death, since he had not hated the victim in time past.
7 "Therefore I command you, saying, 'You shall separate three cities for yourself.'
8 "Now if the LORD your God enlarges your territory, as He swore to your fathers, and gives you the land which He promised to give to your fathers,
9 "and if you keep all these commandments and do them, which I command you today, to love the LORD your God and to walk always in His ways, then you shall add three more cities for yourself besides these three,
10 "lest innocent blood be shed in the midst of your land which the LORD your God is giving you *as* an inheritance, and *thus* guilt of bloodshed be upon you.
11 "But if anyone hates his neighbor, lies in wait for him, rises against him and strikes him mortally, so that he dies, and he flees to one of these cities,
12 "then the elders of his city shall send and bring him from there, and deliver him over to the hand of the avenger of blood, that he may die.
13 "Your eye shall not pity him, but you shall put away *the guilt* of innocent blood from Israel, that it may go well with you.

Property Boundaries

14 "You shall not remove your neighbor's landmark, which the men of old have set, in your inheritance which you will inherit in the land that the LORD your God is giving you to possess.

The Law Concerning Witnesses

15 "One witness shall not rise against a man concerning any iniquity or any sin that he commits; by the mouth of two or three witnesses the matter shall be established.
16 "If a false witness rises against any man to testify against him of wrongdoing,
17 "then both men in the controversy shall stand before the LORD, before the priests and the judges who serve in those days.
18 "And the judges shall make careful inquiry, and indeed, *if* the witness *is* a false witness, who has testified falsely against his brother,
19 "then you shall do to him as he thought to have done to his brother; so you shall put away the evil from among you.
20 "And those who remain shall hear and fear, and hereafter they shall not again commit such evil among you.
21 "Your eye shall not pity: life *shall be* for life, eye for eye, tooth for tooth, hand for hand, foot for foot.

LIFE LESSONS

➤ 18:22 — ". . . when a prophet speaks in the name of the LORD, if the thing does not happen or come to pass, that is the thing which the LORD has not spoken . . . ."

Since God always keeps His promises and always fulfills His word, any prophecy or prediction that fails to come true has a source other than God.

➤ 19:5 — ". . . he shall flee to one of these cities and live . . . ."

Accidents and tragedies occur in a fallen world, and God rarely tells us why. He does, however, instruct us how to respond—and He assumes full responsibility for our needs when we obey Him.

ANSWERS TO LIFE'S QUESTIONS

Why does God tell us to "flee from evil"?

DEUT. 19:19, 20

Those who hope that God will tolerate a little sinfulness also tend to tolerate sinfulness in themselves—to the point that they do nothing about their sin even though they recognize it as wrong.

"But we are all sinful," you protest. "We all fall short of perfection." True enough. Romans 3:23 says plainly, "All have sinned and fall short of the glory of God."

But recognizing our sin should compel us to do something about it. When we understand that we have sinned, we need to come to the Father and say, "I need Your forgiveness. Please wash me and make me clean in Your sight." When we recognize we have committed a trespass against our neighbors, or that we have sinned against God, we should not casually brush aside our offense as if to say, "Well, that's just my human nature!" Rather, we need to come to God and say, "I have sinned. Have mercy upon me. Transform me, Lord, into the likeness of Christ so that I won't desire to do this again!"

Deuteronomy 19:19–20 states, ". . . You shall put away the evil from among you. And those who remain shall hear and fear, and hereafter they shall not again commit such evil among you." Centuries later, Jesus told a woman caught in the act of blatant sin, "Go and sin no more" (John 8:11).

Facing the fact that we are sinful creatures is not the same as tolerating sin in our lives. The Scriptures teach us that God desires for us to hate sin and its consequences and to turn from evil at every opportunity.

We are not to imitate evil.

We are not to embrace evil.

We are not to flirt with evi

We are not to be curious about evil.

Rather, we are to turn our backs on it and run from it at full speed.

Why does God want you to flee from evil? Because He desires to protect you from sin's terrible consequences! The Lord can look into the future and see what you will reap when you sow sinfulness. Remember, you never receive only what you sow as a seed of sin. That seed produces a harvest of sinful consequences—anguish, trials, heartaches, adversity. You will receive from your sinful deed a negative consequence, with compounding interest. Sinful seed multiplies, just as good seed multiplies.

See the Life Principles Index for further study:

2. Obey God and leave all the consequences to Him.

6. Your reap what you sow, more than you sow, and later than you sow.

Principles Governing Warfare

20 "When you go out to battle against
your enemies, and see horses and chariots *and* people more numerous than you, do
not be afraid of them; for the LORD your God
is with you, who brought you up from the
land of Egypt.
2 "So it shall be, when you are on the verge
of battle, that the priest shall approach and
speak to the people.
3 "And he shall say to them, 'Hear, O Israel:
Today you are on the verge of battle with your
enemies. Do not let your heart faint, do not be
afraid, and do not tremble or be terrified because of them;
4 'for the LORD your God *is* He who goes
with you, to fight for you against your enemies, to save you.'
5 "Then the officers shall speak to the people, saying: 'What man *is there* who has built
a new house and has not dedicated it? Let him
go and return to his house, lest he die in the
battle and another man dedicate it.
6 'Also what man *is there* who has planted a
vineyard and has not eaten of it? Let him go
and return to his house, lest he die in the battle and another man eat of it.
7 'And what man *is there* who is betrothed
to a woman and has not married her? Let him
go and return to his house, lest he die in the
battle and another man marry her.'
8 "The officers shall speak further to the
people, and say, 'What man *is there who is*
fearful and fainthearted? Let him go and return to his house, lest the heart of his
brethren faint[a] like his heart.'
9 "And so it shall be, when the officers have
finished speaking to the people, that they

20:8 [a]Following Masoretic Text and Targum; Samaritan Pentateuch, Septuagint, Syriac, and Vulgate read *lest he make his brother's heart faint.*

shall make captains of the armies to lead the
people.
10 "When you go near a city to fight against
it, then proclaim an offer of peace to it.
11 "And it shall be that if they accept your
offer of peace, and open to you, then all the
people *who are* found in it shall be placed
under tribute to you, and serve you.
12 "Now if *the city* will not make peace with
you, but war against you, then you shall besiege it.
13 "And when the LORD your God delivers it
into your hands, you shall strike every male
in it with the edge of the sword.
14 "But the women, the little ones, the livestock, and all that is in the city, all its spoil,
you shall plunder for yourself; and you shall
eat the enemies' plunder which the LORD your
God gives you.
15 "Thus you shall do to all the cities *which
are* very far from you, which *are* not of the
cities of these nations.
16 "But of the cities of these peoples which
the LORD your God gives you *as* an inheritance, you shall let nothing that breathes remain alive,
17 "but you shall utterly destroy them: the
Hittite and the Amorite and the Canaanite
and the Perizzite and the Hivite and the Jebusite, just as the LORD your God has commanded you,
18 "lest they teach you to do according to all
their abominations which they have done for
their gods, and you sin against the LORD your
God.
19 "When you besiege a city for a long time,
while making war against it to take it, you
shall not destroy its trees by wielding an ax
against them; if you can eat of them, do not
cut them down to use in the siege, for the tree
of the field *is* man's *food.*
20 "Only the trees which you know *are* not
trees for food you may destroy and cut down,
to build siegeworks against the city that
makes war with you, until it is subdued.

The Law Concerning Unsolved Murder

21 "If *anyone* is found slain, lying in the
field in the land which the LORD your
God is giving you to possess, *and* it is not
known who killed him,
2 "then your elders and your judges shall go
out and measure *the distance* from the slain
man to the surrounding cities.
3 "And it shall be *that* the elders of the city
nearest to the slain man will take a heifer
which has not been worked *and* which has
not pulled with a yoke.
4 "The elders of that city shall bring the
heifer down to a valley with flowing water,
which is neither plowed nor sown, and they
shall break the heifer's neck there in the valley.
5 "Then the priests, the sons of Levi, shall
come near, for the LORD your God has chosen
them to minister to Him and to bless in the
name of the LORD; by their word every controversy and every assault shall be *settled.*
6 "And all the elders of that city nearest to
the slain *man* shall wash their hands over
the heifer whose neck was broken in the valley.
7 "Then they shall answer and say, 'Our
hands have not shed this blood, nor have our
eyes seen *it.*
8 'Provide atonement, O LORD, for Your people Israel, whom You have redeemed, and do
not lay innocent blood to the charge of Your
people Israel.' And atonement shall be provided on their behalf for the blood.
9 "So you shall put away the *guilt of* innocent blood from among you when you do
what is right in the sight of the LORD.

Female Captives

10 "When you go out to war against your enemies, and the LORD your God delivers them
into your hand, and you take them captive,
11 "and you see among the captives a beautiful woman, and desire her and would take her
for your wife,
12 "then you shall bring her home to your
house, and she shall shave her head and trim
her nails.
13 "She shall put off the clothes of her captivity, remain in your house, and mourn her
father and her mother a full month; after that
you may go in to her and be her husband, and
she shall be your wife.
14 "And it shall be, if you have no delight in
her, then you shall set her free, but you certainly shall not sell her for money; you shall
not treat her brutally, because you have humbled her.

LIFE LESSONS

➤ 20:1 — *"When you go out to battle against your enemies . . . do not be afraid of them; for the LORD your God is with you, who brought you up from the land of Egypt."*

The number, strength, and hostility of our enemies matter little when the Lord is with us. As He delivered Israel from Egypt, so He can deliver us from our enemies.

➤ 20:7 — *" . . . Let him go and return to his house, lest he die in the battle and another man marry her."*

The Lord did not promise His people that they would suffer no casualties when they followed Him into battle, only that they would surely triumph.

LIFE PRINCIPLE 4

THE AWARENESS OF GOD'S PRESENCE ENERGIZES US FOR OUR WORK.

DEUT. 20:1

How can you get the most out of your work? Let me offer three suggestions.

1. View yourself as a servant.

Jesus came to earth not to be served, but to serve—and He instructed us to adopt the same attitude (Matt. 20:25–28). Paul wrote, "Bondservants, obey in all things your masters according to the flesh, not with eyeservice, as men-pleasers, but in sincerity of heart, fearing God" (Col. 3:22).

If Paul told slaves to do their work heartily (and they received no paycheck), then what about the rest of us who *do* get paid? "Well, they don't pay me nearly enough," you say. Okay, you may not get paid adequately—but taking longer lunch hours, clocking out early, or coming in late is not the way to even things out. If you are paid for eight hours, you need to give eight full hours. Why? Because you are a servant, and good servants do good work.

Besides, the best pathway to promotion is servanthood. Whoever wants to be a leader must adopt the attitude of a servant. A prideful employee is seldom seen as a "promotion possibility." It is the humble worker who diligently labors with a godly attitude that management sees as leadership material. Never doubt the impact of your attitude on everyone around you—the boss included!

But who's your real employer? That leads us to our second suggestion.

2. Realize that you work for the Lord Himself.

Your employer exercises supervisory authority over you, but Jesus Christ is your Lord. You work for *Him*: "And whatever you do, do it heartily, as to the Lord and not to men" (Col. 3:23).

If you are a Christian, Jesus Christ is the supervisor at your place of work—and He not only watches you from afar, He's right there with you. You and I need to give a full day's labor regardless of whether we think management is fair, because Jesus is ultimately the employer, and He's always on site. You and I should do our very best because the Holy Spirit is present, equipping and energizing us.

We make a terrible mistake by segmenting life! We may think that Monday through Friday we go to work, Saturday we play, and Sunday we worship. God has not designed life that way. If Jesus

Good servants do good work.

Christ is our Savior, we can't exclude Him from *any* part of life. It isn't right to teach a Sunday school class with everything we have, but meander into work the rest of the week. We won't be tempted to do our work merely to be seen by men if we remind ourselves that Jesus is our real Boss.

Do I mean that your mundane Monday job is also the Lord's work? Yes! *Ministry is not just what you do at church.* You worship God every day of the week, Sunday through Sunday. On Sunday, you worship Him in church; on Monday through Friday, you worship Him by doing a good job at work. Your exalted status as a child of God dignifies your work. That's why your office or place of employment should never be the same because *you* work there.

You serve the Lord Jesus Christ (Col. 3:24). Do you have a good testimony in the marketplace for Him? Are you one of your company's most faithful employees because you serve Him? Does your attitude reflect the joy you have in seeing His name on the door as the *real* CEO?

God will much more than equalize everything in the Judgment.

3. Realize your pay comes both now and hereafter.

Paul wrote, " . . . knowing that from the Lord you will receive the reward of the inheritance" (Col. 3:24).

Of course, you must get paid now to take care of your household expenses. But if you have done your very best and given all you have, you will never really get paid all you are worth. The wonderful thing to remember is this: you may get insufficient wages down here, but you will get rewarded beyond all reason up there! God will much more than equalize everything in the Judgment. The Boss who has watched you all these years will reward you justly.

Do you see yourself as a servant? Do you consider Him your real Boss and work "as unto the Lord," no matter how menial or boring your job might seem? Have you realized that you have a tremendous reward coming later for faithful labor performed now?

If so, you are getting the most out of your work.

See the Life Principles Index for further study.

Firstborn Inheritance Rights
15 "If a man has two wives, one loved and the other unloved, and they have borne him children, *both* the loved and the unloved, and *if* the firstborn son is of her who is unloved,
16 "then it shall be, on the day he bequeaths his possessions to his sons, *that* he must not bestow firstborn status on the son of the loved wife in preference to the son of the unloved, the *true* firstborn.
17 "But he shall acknowledge the son of the unloved wife *as* the firstborn by giving him a double portion of all that he has, for he *is* the beginning of his strength; the right of the firstborn *is* his.

The Rebellious Son
18 "If a man has a stubborn and rebellious son who will not obey the voice of his father or the voice of his mother, and *who,* when they have chastened him, will not heed them,
19 "then his father and his mother shall take hold of him and bring him out to the elders of his city, to the gate of his city.
20 "And they shall say to the elders of his city, 'This son of ours is stubborn and rebellious; he will not obey our voice; he is a glutton and a drunkard.'
21 "Then all the men of his city shall stone him to death with stones; so you shall put away the evil from among you, and all Israel shall hear and fear.

Miscellaneous Laws
22 "If a man has committed a sin deserving of death, and he is put to death, and you hang him on a tree,
➤ 23 "his body shall not remain overnight on the tree, but you shall surely bury him that day, so that you do not defile the land which the LORD your God is giving you *as* an inheritance; for he who is hanged *is* accursed of God.

22 "You shall not see your brother's ox or his sheep going astray, and hide yourself from them; you shall certainly bring them back to your brother.
2 "And if your brother *is* not near you, or if you do not know him, then you shall bring it to your own house, and it shall remain with you until your brother seeks it; then you shall restore it to him.
3 "You shall do the same with his donkey, and so shall you do with his garment; with any lost thing of your brother's, which he has lost and you have found, you shall do likewise; you must not hide yourself.
4 "You shall not see your brother's donkey or his ox fall down along the road, and hide yourself from them; you shall surely help him lift *them* up again.
5 "A woman shall not wear anything that pertains to a man, nor shall a man put on a woman's garment, for all who do so *are* an abomination to the LORD your God.
6 "If a bird's nest happens to be before you along the way, in any tree or on the ground, with young ones or eggs, with the mother sitting on the young or on the eggs, you shall not take the mother with the young;
7 "you shall surely let the mother go, and take the young for yourself, that it may be well with you and *that* you may prolong *your* days.
8 "When you build a new house, then you shall make a parapet for your roof, that you may not bring guilt of bloodshed on your household if anyone falls from it.
9 "You shall not sow your vineyard with different kinds of seed, lest the yield of the seed which you have sown and the fruit of your vineyard be defiled.
10 "You shall not plow with an ox and a donkey together.
11 "You shall not wear a garment of different sorts, *such as* wool and linen mixed together.
12 "You shall make tassels on the four corners of the clothing with which you cover *yourself.*

Laws of Sexual Morality
13 "If any man takes a wife, and goes in to her, and detests her,
14 "and charges her with shameful conduct, and brings a bad name on her, and says, 'I took this woman, and when I came to her I found she *was* not a virgin,'
15 "then the father and mother of the young woman shall take and bring out *the evidence of* the young woman's virginity to the elders of the city at the gate.
16 "And the young woman's father shall say to the elders, 'I gave my daughter to this man as wife, and he detests her.
17 "Now he has charged her with shameful conduct, saying, "I found your daughter *was* not a virgin," and yet these *are the evidences of* my daughter's virginity.' And they shall spread the cloth before the elders of the city.

LIFE LESSONS

➤ 21:23 — ". . . his body shall not remain overnight on the tree, but you shall surely bury him that day, so that you do not defile the land . . . for he who is hanged is accursed of God."

When Jesus hung on the cross to pay the penalty for our sins, He became a curse for us, in fulfillment of this verse (see Gal. 3:13). How amazing that God can use even His curses for our blessing!

18 "Then the elders of that city shall take that man and punish him;
19 "and they shall fine him one hundred *shekels* of silver and give *them* to the father of the young woman, because he has brought a bad name on a virgin of Israel. And she shall be his wife; he cannot divorce her all his days.
20 "But if the thing is true, *and evidences of* virginity are not found for the young woman,
21 "then they shall bring out the young woman to the door of her father's house, and the men of her city shall stone her to death with stones, because she has done a disgraceful thing in Israel, to play the harlot in her father's house. So you shall put away the evil from among you.
22 "If a man is found lying with a woman married to a husband, then both of them shall die—the man that lay with the woman, and the woman; so you shall put away the evil from Israel.
23 "If a young woman *who is* a virgin is betrothed to a husband, and a man finds her in the city and lies with her,
24 "then you shall bring them both out to the gate of that city, and you shall stone them to death with stones, the young woman because she did not cry out in the city, and the man because he humbled his neighbor's wife; so you shall put away the evil from among you.
25 "But if a man finds a betrothed young woman in the countryside, and the man forces her and lies with her, then only the man who lay with her shall die.
26 "But you shall do nothing to the young woman; *there is* in the young woman no sin *deserving* of death, for just as when a man rises against his neighbor and kills him, even so *is* this matter.
27 "For he found her in the countryside, *and* the betrothed young woman cried out, but *there was* no one to save her.
28 "If a man finds a young woman *who is* a virgin, who is not betrothed, and he seizes her and lies with her, and they are found out,
29 "then the man who lay with her shall give to the young woman's father fifty *shekels* of silver, and she shall be his wife because he has humbled her; he shall not be permitted to divorce her all his days.
30 "A man shall not take his father's wife, nor uncover his father's bed.

Those Excluded from the Congregation

23 "He who is emasculated by crushing or mutilation shall not enter the assembly of the LORD.
2 "One of illegitimate birth shall not enter the assembly of the LORD; even to the tenth generation none of his *descendants* shall enter the assembly of the LORD.
3 "An Ammonite or Moabite shall not enter the assembly of the LORD; even to the tenth generation none of his *descendants* shall enter the assembly of the LORD forever,
4 "because they did not meet you with bread and water on the road when you came out of Egypt, and because they hired against you Balaam the son of Beor from Pethor of Mesopotamia,[a] to curse you.
5 "Nevertheless the LORD your God would not listen to Balaam, but the LORD your God turned the curse into a blessing for you, because the LORD your God loves you.
6 "You shall not seek their peace nor their prosperity all your days forever.
7 "You shall not abhor an Edomite, for he *is* your brother. You shall not abhor an Egyptian, because you were an alien in his land.
8 "The children of the third generation born to them may enter the assembly of the LORD.

Cleanliness of the Campsite

9 "When the army goes out against your enemies, then keep yourself from every wicked thing.
10 "If there is any man among you who becomes unclean by some occurrence in the night, then he shall go outside the camp; he shall not come inside the camp.
11 "But it shall be, when evening comes, that he shall wash with water; and when the sun sets, he may come into the camp.
12 "Also you shall have a place outside the camp, where you may go out;
13 "and you shall have an implement among your equipment, and when you sit down outside, you shall dig with it and turn and cover your refuse.
14 "For the LORD your God walks in the midst of your camp, to deliver you and give your enemies over to you; therefore your camp shall be holy, that He may see no unclean thing among you, and turn away from you.

23:4 [a]Hebrew *Aram Naharaim*

LIFE LESSONS

➤ 23:12, 13 — *"Also you shall have a place outside the camp . . . and you shall have an implement among your equipment, and when you sit down outside, you shall dig with it and turn and cover your refuse."*

Long before humankind knew anything about the connection between personal hygiene and good health, God gave His people commands to keep them physically healthy. Obedience always brings blessing!

Miscellaneous Laws

15 "You shall not give back to his master the slave who has escaped from his master to you.
16 "He may dwell with you in your midst, in the place which he chooses within one of your gates, where it seems best to him; you shall not oppress him.
17 "There shall be no *ritual* harlot[a] of the daughters of Israel, or a perverted[b] one of the sons of Israel.
18 "You shall not bring the wages of a harlot or the price of a dog to the house of the LORD your God for any vowed offering, for both of these *are* an abomination to the LORD your God.
19 "You shall not charge interest to your brother—interest on money *or* food *or* anything that is lent out at interest.
20 "To a foreigner you may charge interest, but to your brother you shall not charge interest, that the LORD your God may bless you in all to which you set your hand in the land which you are entering to possess.
21 "When you make a vow to the LORD your God, you shall not delay to pay it; for the LORD your God will surely require it of you, and it would be sin to you.
22 "But if you abstain from vowing, it shall not be sin to you.
23 "That which has gone from your lips you shall keep and perform, for you voluntarily vowed to the LORD your God what you have promised with your mouth.
24 "When you come into your neighbor's vineyard, you may eat your fill of grapes at your pleasure, but you shall not put *any* in your container.
25 "When you come into your neighbor's standing grain, you may pluck the heads with your hand, but you shall not use a sickle on your neighbor's standing grain.

Law Concerning Divorce

24 "When a man takes a wife and marries her, and it happens that she finds no favor in his eyes because he has found some uncleanness in her, and he writes her a certificate of divorce, puts *it* in her hand, and sends her out of his house,
2 "when she has departed from his house, and goes and becomes another man's *wife*,
3 "*if* the latter husband detests her and writes her a certificate of divorce, puts *it* in her hand, and sends her out of his house, or if the latter husband dies who took her as his wife,
4 "*then* her former husband who divorced her must not take her back to be his wife after she has been defiled; for that *is* an abomination before the LORD, and you shall not bring sin on the land which the LORD your God is giving you *as* an inheritance.

Miscellaneous Laws

5 "When a man has taken a new wife, he shall not go out to war or be charged with any business; he shall be free at home one year, and bring happiness to his wife whom he has taken.
6 "No man shall take the lower or the upper millstone in pledge, for he takes *one's* living in pledge.
7 "If a man is found kidnapping any of his brethren of the children of Israel, and mistreats him or sells him, then that kidnapper shall die; and you shall put away the evil from among you.
8 "Take heed in an outbreak of leprosy, that you carefully observe and do according to all that the priests, the Levites, shall teach you; just as I commanded them, *so* you shall be careful to do.
9 "Remember what the LORD your God did to Miriam on the way when you came out of Egypt!
10 "When you lend your brother anything, you shall not go into his house to get his pledge.
11 "You shall stand outside, and the man to whom you lend shall bring the pledge out to you.
12 "And if the man *is* poor, you shall not keep his pledge overnight.
13 "You shall in any case return the pledge to him again when the sun goes down, that he may sleep in his own garment and bless you; and it shall be righteousness to you before the LORD your God.
14 "You shall not oppress a hired servant *who is* poor and needy, *whether* one of your brethren or one of the aliens who *is* in your land within your gates.
15 "Each day you shall give *him* his wages, and not let the sun go down on it, for he *is* poor and has set his heart on it; lest he cry out against you to the LORD, and it be sin to you.

23:17 [a]Hebrew *qedeshah,* feminine of *qadesh* (see note *b*)
[b]Hebrew *qadesh,* that is, one practicing sodomy and prostitution in religious rituals

LIFE LESSONS

➤ 24:5 — *"When a man has taken a new wife, he shall not go out to war or be charged with any business; he shall be free at home one year, and bring happiness to his wife whom he has taken."*

God is most concerned about our holiness, but He is not unconcerned about our happiness, as this verse demonstrates.

➤ 16 "Fathers shall not be put to death for *their*
children, nor shall children be put to death for
their fathers; a person shall be put to death
for his own sin.
17 "You shall not pervert justice due the
stranger or the fatherless, nor take a widow's
garment as a pledge.
18 "But you shall remember that you were a
slave in Egypt, and the LORD your God redeemed you from there; therefore I command
you to do this thing.
19 "When you reap your harvest in your
field, and forget a sheaf in the field, you shall
not go back to get it; it shall be for the stranger, the fatherless, and the widow, that the
LORD your God may bless you in all the work
of your hands.
20 "When you beat your olive trees, you shall
not go over the boughs again; it shall be for
the stranger, the fatherless, and the widow.
21 "When you gather the grapes of your vineyard, you shall not glean *it* afterward; it shall
be for the stranger, the fatherless, and the
widow.
➤ 22 "And you shall remember that you were a
slave in the land of Egypt; therefore I command you to do this thing.
25 "If there is a dispute between men, and
they come to court, that *the judges* may
judge them, and they justify the righteous and
condemn the wicked,
2 "then it shall be, if the wicked man deserves to be beaten, that the judge will cause
him to lie down and be beaten in his presence, according to his guilt, with a certain
number of blows.
3 "Forty blows he may give him *and* no
more, lest he should exceed this and beat him
with many blows above these, and your
brother be humiliated in your sight.
➤ **4** "You shall not muzzle an ox while it treads
out *the grain.*

Marriage Duty of the Surviving Brother
5 "If brothers dwell together, and one of
them dies and has no son, the widow of the
dead man shall not be *married* to a stranger
outside *the family;* her husband's brother
shall go in to her, take her as his wife, and
perform the duty of a husband's brother to
her.
6 "And it shall be *that* the firstborn son
which she bears will succeed to the name of
his dead brother, that his name may not be
blotted out of Israel.
7 "But if the man does not want to take his
brother's wife, then let his brother's wife go
up to the gate to the elders, and say, 'My husband's brother refuses to raise up a name to
his brother in Israel; he will not perform the
duty of my husband's brother.'
8 "Then the elders of his city shall call him
and speak to him. But *if* he stands firm and
says, 'I do not want to take her,'
9 "then his brother's wife shall come to him
in the presence of the elders, remove his sandal from his foot, spit in his face, and answer
and say, 'So shall it be done to the man who
will not build up his brother's house.'
10 "And his name shall be called in Israel,
'The house of him who had his sandal removed.'

Miscellaneous Laws
11 "If *two* men fight together, and the wife of
one draws near to rescue her husband from
the hand of the one attacking him, and
puts out her hand and seizes him by the gen-
itals,
12 "then you shall cut off her hand; your eye
shall not pity *her.*
13 "You shall not have in your bag differing
weights, a heavy and a light.
14 "You shall not have in your house differ- ➤
ing measures, a large and a small.
15 "You shall have a perfect and just weight,
a perfect and just measure, that your days
may be lengthened in the land which the
LORD your God is giving you.
16 "For all who do such things, all who behave unrighteously, *are* an abomination to the
LORD your God.

LIFE LESSONS

➤ 24:16 — *"Fathers shall not be put to death for their children, nor shall children be put to death for their fathers; a person shall be put to death for his own sin."*

Each of us is responsible to God for our own lives. We do not "accrue" the righteousness of our ancestors, nor must we pay for the sins of our forebears. God judges each person individually.

➤ 24:22 — *"And you shall remember that you were a slave in the land of Egypt . . . ."*

God often reminded Israel that they had been slaves in Egypt. Why? To foster compassion in them for the downtrodden. Likewise, He reminds us that we once were estranged from Him (Eph. 2:12). We are to be a compassionate people.

➤ 25:4 — *"You shall not muzzle an ox while it treads out the grain."*

Paul uses this verse about cattle to make a point about materially honoring faithful servants of God (see 1 Cor. 9:7-12; 1 Tim. 5:18). He thus shows the value of mining Scripture for its core principles.

➤ 25:14 — *"You shall not have in your house differing measures, a large and a small."*

God is concerned about every aspect of our lives—not only our "religious" duties, but our civic ones as well. We are to live all of our life for His glory (1 Cor. 10:31).

Destroy the Amalekites
17 "Remember what Amalek did to you on the way as you were coming out of Egypt,
18 "how he met you on the way and attacked your rear ranks, all the stragglers at your rear, when you *were* tired and weary; and he did not fear God.
19 "Therefore it shall be, when the LORD your God has given you rest from your enemies all around, in the land which the LORD your God is giving you to possess *as* an inheritance, *that* you will blot out the remembrance of Amalek from under heaven. You shall not forget.

Offerings of Firstfruits and Tithes
26 "And it shall be, when you come into the land which the LORD your God is giving you *as* an inheritance, and you possess it and dwell in it,
2 "that you shall take some of the first of all the produce of the ground, which you shall bring from your land that the LORD your God is giving you, and put *it* in a basket and go to the place where the LORD your God chooses to make His name abide.
3 "And you shall go to the one who is priest in those days, and say to him, 'I declare today to the LORD your[a] God that I have come to the country which the LORD swore to our fathers to give us.'
4 "Then the priest shall take the basket out of your hand and set it down before the altar of the LORD your God.
5 "And you shall answer and say before the LORD your God: 'My father *was* a Syrian,[a] about to perish, and he went down to Egypt and dwelt there, few in number; and there he became a nation, great, mighty, and populous.
6 'But the Egyptians mistreated us, afflicted us, and laid hard bondage on us.
➤ 7 'Then we cried out to the LORD God of our fathers, and the LORD heard our voice and looked on our affliction and our labor and our oppression.
8 'So the LORD brought us out of Egypt with a mighty hand and with an outstretched arm, with great terror and with signs and wonders.
9 'He has brought us to this place and has given us this land, "a land flowing with milk and honey";[a]
10 'and now, behold, I have brought the firstfruits of the land which you, O LORD, have given me.' "Then you shall set it before the LORD your God, and worship before the LORD your God.
11 "So you shall rejoice in every good *thing* ➤
which the LORD your God has given to you and your house, you and the Levite and the stranger who *is* among you.
12 "When you have finished laying aside all the tithe of your increase in the third year—the year of tithing—and have given *it* to the Levite, the stranger, the fatherless, and the widow, so that they may eat within your gates and be filled,
13 "then you shall say before the LORD your God: 'I have removed the holy *tithe* from *my* house, and also have given them to the Levite, the stranger, the fatherless, and the widow, according to all Your commandments which You have commanded me; I have not transgressed Your commandments, nor have I forgotten *them.*
14 'I have not eaten any of it when in mourning, nor have I removed *any* of it for an unclean *use,* nor given *any* of it for the dead. I have obeyed the voice of the LORD my God, and have done according to all that You have commanded me.
15 'Look down from Your holy habitation, from heaven, and bless Your people Israel and the land which You have given us, just as You swore to our fathers, "a land flowing with milk and honey." '[a]

A Special People of God
16 "This day the LORD your God commands you to observe these statutes and judgments; therefore you shall be careful to observe them with all your heart and with all your soul.
17 "Today you have proclaimed the LORD to be your God, and that you will walk in His ways and keep His statutes, His commandments, and His judgments, and that you will obey His voice.
18 "Also today the LORD has proclaimed you to be His special people, just as He promised you, that *you* should keep all His commandments,

26:3 [a]Septuagint reads *my.* **26:5** [a]Or *Aramean*
26:9 [a]Exodus 3:8 **26:15** [a]Exodus 3:8

LIFE LESSONS

➤ 26:7 — *"Then we cried out to the LORD God of our fathers, and the LORD heard our voice and looked on our affliction and our labor and our oppression."*

It is good to remember and to declare to others how the Lord has rescued us in times past. These remembrances strengthen our faith and give us the courage to endure in difficult times.

➤ 26:11 — *"So you shall rejoice in every good thing which the LORD your God has given to you and your house, you and the Levite and the stranger who is among you."*

Why is it so important to "rejoice in every good thing which the LORD your God has given you"? Rejoicing in God is a powerful way to draw close to Him, which is the very reason He created us.

19 "and that He will set you high above all
nations which He has made, in praise, in
name, and in honor, and that you may be a
holy people to the LORD your God, just as He
has spoken."

The Law Inscribed on Stones

27 Now Moses, with the elders of Israel,
commanded the people, saying: "Keep
all the commandments which I command you
today.
➤2 "And it shall be, on the day when you
cross over the Jordan to the land which the
LORD your God is giving you, that you shall
set up for yourselves large stones, and whitewash them with lime.
3 "You shall write on them all the words of
this law, when you have crossed over, that you
may enter the land which the LORD your God
is giving you, 'a land flowing with milk and
honey,'[a] just as the LORD God of your fathers
promised you.
4 "Therefore it shall be, when you have
crossed over the Jordan, *that* on Mount Ebal
you shall set up these stones, which I command you today, and you shall whitewash
them with lime.
5 "And there you shall build an altar to the
LORD your God, an altar of stones; you shall
not use an iron *tool* on them.
6 "You shall build with whole stones the
altar of the LORD your God, and offer burnt
offerings on it to the LORD your God.
7 "You shall offer peace offerings, and shall
eat there, and rejoice before the LORD your
God.
8 "And you shall write very plainly on the
stones all the words of this law."
9 Then Moses and the priests, the Levites,
spoke to all Israel, saying, "Take heed and listen, O Israel: This day you have become the
people of the LORD your God.
10 "Therefore you shall obey the voice of the
LORD your God, and observe His commandments and His statutes which I command you
today."

Curses Pronounced from Mount Ebal

11 And Moses commanded the people on the
same day, saying,
12 "These shall stand on Mount Gerizim to
bless the people, when you have crossed over
the Jordan: Simeon, Levi, Judah, Issachar, Joseph, and Benjamin;
13 "and these shall stand on Mount Ebal to
curse: Reuben, Gad, Asher, Zebulun, Dan, and
Naphtali.
14 "And the Levites shall speak with a loud
voice and say to all the men of Israel:
15 'Cursed *is* the one who makes a carved or ➤
molded image, an abomination to the LORD,
the work of the hands of the craftsman, and
sets *it* up in secret.'
"And all the people shall answer and say,
'Amen!'
16 'Cursed *is* the one who treats his father or
his mother with contempt.'
"And all the people shall say, 'Amen!'
17 'Cursed *is* the one who moves his neighbor's landmark.'
"And all the people shall say, 'Amen!'
18 'Cursed *is* the one who makes the blind to
wander off the road.'
"And all the people shall say, 'Amen!'
19 'Cursed *is* the one who perverts the justice
due the stranger, the fatherless, and widow.'
"And all the people shall say, 'Amen!'
20 'Cursed *is* the one who lies with his father's wife, because he has uncovered his father's bed.'
"And all the people shall say, 'Amen!'
21 'Cursed *is* the one who lies with any kind
of animal.'
"And all the people shall say, 'Amen!'
22 'Cursed *is* the one who lies with his sister,
the daughter of his father or the daughter of
his mother.'
"And all the people shall say, 'Amen!'
23 'Cursed *is* the one who lies with his
mother-in-law.'
"And all the people shall say, 'Amen!'
24 'Cursed *is* the one who attacks his neighbor secretly.'
"And all the people shall say, 'Amen!'
25 'Cursed *is* the one who takes a bribe to
slay an innocent person.'
"And all the people shall say, 'Amen!'
26 'Cursed *is* the one who does not confirm *all* the words of this law by observing
them.'
"And all the people shall say, 'Amen!'"

27:3 [a]Exodus 3:8

LIFE LESSONS

➤ 27:2, 3 — *". . . you shall set up for yourselves large stones, and whitewash them with lime. You shall write on them all the words of this law . . . ."*

This may be the first billboard in history. God did not want His people to forget His Law, so He commanded them to put it in full public view. How do you remind yourself to remember God's Word?

➤ 27:15 — *"And all the people shall answer and say, 'Amen!'"*

Congregational response is a powerful way to cement in our minds the requirements and words of God. Our faith is never a solitary business, but is meant to grow in community.

Blessings on Obedience

28 "Now it shall come to pass, if you diligently obey the voice of the LORD your God, to observe carefully all His commandments which I command you today, that the LORD your God will set you high above all nations of the earth.

2 "And all these blessings shall come upon you and overtake you, because you obey the voice of the LORD your God:

➤ 3 "Blessed *shall* you *be* in the city, and blessed *shall* you *be* in the country.

4 "Blessed *shall be* the fruit of your body, the produce of your ground and the increase of your herds, the increase of your cattle and the offspring of your flocks.

5 "Blessed *shall be* your basket and your kneading bowl.

6 "Blessed *shall* you *be* when you come in, and blessed *shall* you *be* when you go out.

✳ **7** "The LORD will cause your enemies who ➤ rise against you to be defeated before your face; they shall come out against you one way and flee before you seven ways.

8 "The LORD will command the blessing on you in your storehouses and in all to which you set your hand, and He will bless you in the land which the LORD your God is giving you.

9 "The LORD will establish you as a holy people to Himself, just as He has sworn to you, if you keep the commandments of the LORD your God and walk in His ways.

10 "Then all peoples of the earth shall see that you are called by the name of the LORD, and they shall be afraid of you.

11 "And the LORD will grant you plenty of goods, in the fruit of your body, in the increase of your livestock, and in the produce of your ground, in the land of which the LORD swore to your fathers to give you.

12 "The LORD will open to you His good treasure, the heavens, to give the rain to your land in its season, and to bless all the work of your hand. You shall lend to many nations, but you shall not borrow.

13 "And the LORD will make you the head and not the tail; you shall be above only, and not be beneath, if you heed the commandments of the LORD your God, which I command you today, and are careful to observe *them.*

14 "So you shall not turn aside from any of the words which I command you this day, *to* the right or the left, to go after other gods to serve them.

Curses on Disobedience

15 "But it shall come to pass, if you do not obey the voice of the LORD your God, to observe carefully all His commandments and His statutes which I command you today, that all these curses will come upon you and overtake you:

16 "Cursed *shall* you *be* in the city, and cursed *shall* you *be* in the country.

17 "Cursed *shall be* your basket and your kneading bowl.

18 "Cursed *shall be* the fruit of your body and the produce of your land, the increase of your cattle and the offspring of your flocks.

19 "Cursed *shall* you *be* when you come in, and cursed *shall* you *be* when you go out.

20 "The LORD will send on you cursing, confusion, and rebuke in all that you set your hand to do, until you are destroyed and until you perish quickly, because of the wickedness of your doings in which you have forsaken Me.

21 "The LORD will make the plague cling to you until He has consumed you from the land which you are going to possess.

22 "The LORD will strike you with consumption, with fever, with inflammation, with severe burning fever, with the sword, with scorching, and with mildew; they shall pursue you until you perish.

23 "And your heavens which *are* over your head shall be bronze, and the earth which is under you *shall be* iron.

24 "The LORD will change the rain of your land to powder and dust; from the heaven it shall come down on you until you are destroyed.

25 "The LORD will cause you to be defeated before your enemies; you shall go out one way against them and flee seven ways before them; and you shall become troublesome to all the kingdoms of the earth.

26 "Your carcasses shall be food for all the birds of the air and the beasts of the earth, and no one shall frighten *them* away.

27 "The LORD will strike you with the boils of

LIFE LESSONS

➤ 28:3, 4 — *"Blessed shall you be in the city, and blessed shall you be in the country. Blessed shall be the fruit of your body, the produce of your ground and the increase of your herds . . . ."*

God left no doubt about the kinds of blessings in store for those who obey Him. No matter where we live, what we do, or where we go, if we obey God's commandments, we can be assured of His blessing.

➤ 28:7 — *"The LORD will cause your enemies who rise against you to be defeated before your face; they shall come out against you one way and flee before you seven ways."*

God spoke these words to a people about to learn about the danger of enemies. Yet He assured them—and us today—that no enemy can withstand His passion in standing up for those who belong to Him.

Egypt, with tumors, with the scab, and with
the itch, from which you cannot be healed.
28 "The LORD will strike you with madness
and blindness and confusion of heart.
29 "And you shall grope at noonday, as a
blind man gropes in darkness; you shall not
prosper in your ways; you shall be only oppressed and plundered continually, and no
one shall save *you.*
30 "You shall betroth a wife, but another man
shall lie with her; you shall build a house, but
you shall not dwell in it; you shall plant a
vineyard, but shall not gather its grapes.
31 "Your ox *shall be* slaughtered before your
eyes, but you shall not eat of it; your donkey
shall be violently taken away from before
you, and shall not be restored to you; your
sheep *shall be* given to your enemies, and you
shall have no one to rescue *them.*
32 "Your sons and your daughters *shall be*
given to another people, and your eyes shall
look and fail *with longing* for them all day long;
and *there shall be* no strength in your hand.
33 "A nation whom you have not known shall
eat the fruit of your land and the produce of
your labor, and you shall be only oppressed
and crushed continually.
34 "So you shall be driven mad because of
the sight which your eyes see.
35 "The LORD will strike you in the knees and
on the legs with severe boils which cannot be
healed, and from the sole of your foot to the
top of your head.
36 "The LORD will bring you and the king
whom you set over you to a nation which neither you nor your fathers have known, and
there you shall serve other gods—wood and
stone.
37 "And you shall become an astonishment, a
proverb, and a byword among all nations
where the LORD will drive you.
38 "You shall carry much seed out to the field
but gather little in, for the locust shall consume it.
39 "You shall plant vineyards and tend *them,*
but you shall neither drink *of* the wine nor
gather the *grapes;* for the worms shall eat
them.
40 "You shall have olive trees throughout all
your territory, but you shall not anoint *yourself* with the oil; for your olives shall drop off.
41 "You shall beget sons and daughters, but
they shall not be yours; for they shall go into
captivity.
42 "Locusts shall consume all your trees and
the produce of your land.
43 "The alien who *is* among you shall rise
higher and higher above you, and you shall
come down lower and lower.
44 "He shall lend to you, but you shall not
lend to him; he shall be the head, and you
shall be the tail.
45 "Moreover all these curses shall come
upon you and pursue and overtake you, until
you are destroyed, because you did not obey
the voice of the LORD your God, to keep His
commandments and His statutes which He
commanded you.
46 "And they shall be upon you for a sign and
a wonder, and on your descendants forever.
47 "Because you did not serve the LORD your
God with joy and gladness of heart, for the
abundance of everything,
48 "therefore you shall serve your enemies,
whom the LORD will send against you, in hunger, in thirst, in nakedness, and in need of
everything; and He will put a yoke of iron on
your neck until He has destroyed you.
49 "The LORD will bring a nation against you
from afar, from the end of the earth, *as swift*
as the eagle flies, a nation whose language
you will not understand,
50 "a nation of fierce countenance, which
does not respect the elderly nor show favor to
the young.
51 "And they shall eat the increase of your
livestock and the produce of your land, until
you are destroyed; they shall not leave you
grain or new wine or oil, *or* the increase of
your cattle or the offspring of your flocks,
until they have destroyed you.
52 "They shall besiege you at all your gates
until your high and fortified walls, in which
you trust, come down throughout all your
land; and they shall besiege you at all your
gates throughout all your land which the
LORD your God has given you.
53 "You shall eat the fruit of your own body,
the flesh of your sons and your daughters
whom the LORD your God has given you, in
the siege and desperate straits in which your
enemy shall distress you.
54 "The sensitive and very refined man
among you will be hostile toward his brother,
toward the wife of his bosom, and toward the
rest of his children whom he leaves behind,
55 "so that he will not give any of them the
flesh of his children whom he will eat, because he has nothing left in the siege and desperate straits in which your enemy shall
distress you at all your gates.
56 "The tender and delicate woman among
you, who would not venture to set the sole of
her foot on the ground because of her deli-
cateness and sensitivity, will refuse[a] to the
husband of her bosom, and to her son and her
daughter,
57 "her placenta which comes out from between her feet and her children whom she
bears; for she will eat them secretly for lack
of everything in the siege and desperate
straits in which your enemy shall distress you
at all your gates.
58 "If you do not carefully observe all the
words of this law that are written in this book,

28:56 [a]Literally *her eye shall be evil toward*

that you may fear this glorious and awesome
name, THE LORD YOUR GOD,
59 "then the LORD will bring upon you and
your descendants extraordinary plagues—
great and prolonged plagues—and serious
and prolonged sicknesses.
60 "Moreover He will bring back on you all
the diseases of Egypt, of which you were
afraid, and they shall cling to you.
61 "Also every sickness and every plague,
which *is* not written in this Book of the Law,
will the LORD bring upon you until you are destroyed.
62 "You shall be left few in number, whereas
you were as the stars of heaven in multitude,
because you would not obey the voice of the
LORD your God.
63 "And it shall be, *that* just as the LORD rejoiced over you to do you good and multiply
you, so the LORD will rejoice over you to destroy you and bring you to nothing; and you
shall be plucked from off the land which you
go to possess.
64 "Then the LORD will scatter you among all
peoples, from one end of the earth to the
other, and there you shall serve other gods,
which neither you nor your fathers have
known—wood and stone.
65 "And among those nations you shall find
no rest, nor shall the sole of your foot have a
resting place; but there the LORD will give you
a trembling heart, failing eyes, and anguish of
soul.
66 "Your life shall hang in doubt before you;
you shall fear day and night, and have no assurance of life.
67 "In the morning you shall say, 'Oh, that it
were evening!' And at evening you shall say,
'Oh, that it were morning!' because of the fear
which terrifies your heart, and because of the
sight which your eyes see.
68 "And the LORD will take you back to Egypt
in ships, by the way of which I said to you,
'You shall never see it again.' And there you
shall be offered for sale to your enemies as
male and female slaves, but no one will buy
you."

The Covenant Renewed in Moab

29 These *are* the words of the covenant
which the LORD commanded Moses to
make with the children of Israel in the land of
Moab, besides the covenant which He made
with them in Horeb.
2 Now Moses called all Israel and said to
them: "You have seen all that the LORD did before your eyes in the land of Egypt, to
Pharaoh and to all his servants and to all his
land—
3 "the great trials which your eyes have
seen, the signs, and those great wonders.
4 "Yet the LORD has not given you a heart to
perceive and eyes to see and ears to hear, to
this *very* day.
5 "And I have led you forty years in the
wilderness. Your clothes have not worn out on
you, and your sandals have not worn out on
your feet.
6 "You have not eaten bread, nor have you
drunk wine or *similar* drink, that you may
know that I *am* the LORD your God.
7 "And when you came to this place, Sihon
king of Heshbon and Og king of Bashan came
out against us to battle, and we conquered
them.
8 "We took their land and gave it as an inheritance to the Reubenites, to the Gadites,
and to half the tribe of Manasseh.
9 "Therefore keep the words of this covenant, and do them, that you may prosper in
all that you do.
10 "All of you stand today before the LORD
your God: your leaders and your tribes and
your elders and your officers, all the men of
Israel,
11 "your little ones and your wives—also the
stranger who *is* in your camp, from the one
who cuts your wood to the one who draws
your water—
12 "that you may enter into covenant with the
LORD your God, and into His oath, which the
LORD your God makes with you today,
13 "that He may establish you today as a people for Himself, and *that* He may be God to
you, just as He has spoken to you, and just as
He has sworn to your fathers, to Abraham,
Isaac, and Jacob.
14 "I make this covenant and this oath, not
with you alone,
15 "but with *him* who stands here with us
today before the LORD our God, as well as
with *him* who *is* not here with us today
16 (for you know that we dwelt in the land of
Egypt and that we came through the nations
which you passed by,
17 and you saw their abominations and their
idols which *were* among them—wood and
stone and silver and gold);
18 "so that there may not be among you man
or woman or family or tribe, whose heart
turns away today from the LORD our God, to
go *and* serve the gods of these nations, and

LIFE LESSONS

➤ ***29:4 — "Yet the LORD has not given you a heart to perceive and eyes to see and ears to hear, to this very day."***

What the Lord had not given to His people Israel, He has given to members of the church, to those in whom the Spirit of God dwells (Ezek. 36:26; Eph. 1:18).

that there may not be among you a root bearing bitterness or wormwood;
➤ 19 "and so it may not happen, when he hears the words of this curse, that he blesses himself in his heart, saying, 'I shall have peace, even though I follow the dictates[a] of my heart'—as though the drunkard could be included with the sober.
20 "The LORD would not spare him; for then the anger of the LORD and His jealousy would burn against that man, and every curse that is written in this book would settle on him, and the LORD would blot out his name from under heaven.
21 "And the LORD would separate him from all the tribes of Israel for adversity, according to all the curses of the covenant that are written in this Book of the Law,
22 "so that the coming generation of your children who rise up after you, and the foreigner who comes from a far land, would say, when they see the plagues of that land and the sicknesses which the LORD has laid on it:
23 'The whole land *is* brimstone, salt, and burning; it is not sown, nor does it bear, nor does any grass grow there, like the overthrow of Sodom and Gomorrah, Admah, and Zeboiim, which the LORD overthrew in His anger and His wrath.'
24 "All nations would say, 'Why has the LORD done so to this land? What does the heat of this great anger mean?'
25 "Then *people* would say: 'Because they have forsaken the covenant of the LORD God of their fathers, which He made with them when He brought them out of the land of Egypt;
26 'for they went and served other gods and worshiped them, gods that they did not know and that He had not given to them.
27 'Then the anger of the LORD was aroused against this land, to bring on it every curse that is written in this book.
28 'And the LORD uprooted them from their land in anger, in wrath, and in great indignation, and cast them into another land, as *it is* this day.'
29 "The secret *things belong* to the LORD our God, but those *things which are* revealed *belong* to us and to our children forever, that *we* may do all the words of this law. ◄

The Blessing of Returning to God

30 "Now it shall come to pass, when all these things come upon you, the blessing and the curse which I have set before you, and you call *them* to mind among all the nations where the LORD your God drives you, ◄
2 "and you return to the LORD your God and obey His voice, according to all that I command you today, you and your children, with all your heart and with all your soul,
3 "that the LORD your God will bring you back from captivity, and have compassion on you, and gather you again from all the nations where the LORD your God has scattered you.
4 "If *any* of you are driven out to the farthest *parts* under heaven, from there the LORD your God will gather you, and from there He will bring you.
5 "Then the LORD your God will bring you to the land which your fathers possessed, and you shall possess it. He will prosper you and multiply you more than your fathers.
6 "And the LORD your God will circumcise your heart and the heart of your descendants, to love the LORD your God with all your heart and with all your soul, that you may live.
7 "Also the LORD your God will put all these curses on your enemies and on those who hate you, who persecuted you.
8 "And you will again obey the voice of the LORD and do all His commandments which I command you today.
9 "The LORD your God will make you ◄

29:19 [a]Or *stubbornness*

LIFE LESSONS

➤ 29:19 — *"... and so it may not happen, when he hears the words of this curse, that he blesses himself in his heart, saying, 'I shall have peace, even though I follow the dictates of my heart'...."*

Obedience matters. God must judge sin, and believers are not exempt in this world (see Acts 5:1–6; 1 Pet. 4:17). God saves us, not so that we can sin with impunity, but so that we can obey with joy.

➤ 29:29 — *"The secret things belong to the LORD our God, but those things which are revealed belong to us and to our children forever, that we may do all the words of this law."*

God withholds many pieces of information from us—that is His right—but He reveals everything we need to know in order for us to live holy and joy-filled lives.

➤ 30:1–3 — *"Now it shall come to pass, when . . . you return to the LORD your God and obey His voice . . . the LORD your God will bring you back from captivity, and have compassion on you . . . ."*

In these few verses God lays out in brief the entire history of Israel. It comes down to this: Obedience brings blessing, while rebellion brings judgment.

➤ 30:9 — *"The LORD your God will make you abound . . . . For the LORD will again rejoice over you for good as He rejoiced over your fathers . . . ."*

The Lord loves to rejoice over His people for good, not to pronounce curses over them for their punishment. Whether we receive the blessing or the judgment of God is up to us.

abound in all the work of your hand, in the
fruit of your body, in the increase of your livestock, and in the produce of your land for
good. For the LORD will again rejoice over you
for good as He rejoiced over your fathers,
10 "if you obey the voice of the LORD your
God, to keep His commandments and His
statutes which are written in this Book of the
Law, *and* if you turn to the LORD your God
with all your heart and with all your soul.

The Choice of Life or Death

11 "For this commandment which I command you today *is* not *too* mysterious for you,
nor *is* it far off.
12 "It *is* not in heaven, that you should say,
'Who will ascend into heaven for us and bring
it to us, that we may hear it and do it?'
13 "Nor *is* it beyond the sea, that you should
say, 'Who will go over the sea for us and bring
it to us, that we may hear it and do it?'
14 "But the word *is* very near you, in your
mouth and in your heart, that you may do it.
15 "See, I have set before you today life and
good, death and evil,
16 "in that I command you today to love the
LORD your God, to walk in His ways, and to
keep His commandments, His statutes, and
His judgments, that you may live and multiply; and the LORD your God will bless you in
the land which you go to possess.
17 "But if your heart turns away so that you
do not hear, and are drawn away, and worship
other gods and serve them,
18 "I announce to you today that you shall
surely perish; you shall not prolong *your* days
in the land which you cross over the Jordan to
go in and possess.
19 "I call heaven and earth as witnesses
today against you, *that* I have set before you
life and death, blessing and cursing; therefore
choose life, that both you and your descendants may live;
20 "that you may love the LORD your God, that
you may obey His voice, and that you may
cling to Him, for He *is* your life and the length
of your days; and that you may dwell in the
land which the LORD swore to your fathers, to
Abraham, Isaac, and Jacob, to give them."

Joshua the New Leader of Israel

31 Then Moses went and spoke these
words to all Israel.
2 And he said to them: "I *am* one hundred
and twenty years old today. I can no longer go
out and come in. Also the LORD has said to
me, 'You shall not cross over this Jordan.'
3 "The LORD your God Himself crosses over
before you; He will destroy these nations
from before you, and you shall dispossess
them. Joshua himself crosses over before you,
just as the LORD has said.
4 "And the LORD will do to them as He did to
Sihon and Og, the kings of the Amorites and
their land, when He destroyed them.
5 "The LORD will give them over to you, that
you may do to them according to every commandment which I have commanded you.
6 "Be strong and of good courage, do not
fear nor be afraid of them; for the LORD your
God, He *is* the One who goes with you. He will
not leave you nor forsake you."
7 Then Moses called Joshua and said to him
in the sight of all Israel, "Be strong and of
good courage, for you must go with this people to the land which the LORD has sworn to
their fathers to give them, and you shall cause
them to inherit it.
8 "And the LORD, He *is* the One who goes before you. He will be with you, He will not
leave you nor forsake you; do not fear nor be
dismayed."

The Law to Be Read Every Seven Years

9 So Moses wrote this law and delivered it
to the priests, the sons of Levi, who bore the
ark of the covenant of the LORD, and to all the
elders of Israel.
10 And Moses commanded them, saying: "At
the end of *every* seven years, at the appointed
time in the year of release, at the Feast of
Tabernacles,
11 "when all Israel comes to appear before
the LORD your God in the place which He
chooses, you shall read this law before all Israel in their hearing.
12 "Gather the people together, men and
women and little ones, and the stranger who
is within your gates, that they may hear and
that they may learn to fear the LORD your God
and carefully observe all the words of this
law,
13 "and *that* their children, who have not
known it, may hear and learn to fear the LORD
your God as long as you live in the land which
you cross the Jordan to possess."

Prediction of Israel's Rebellion

14 Then the LORD said to Moses, "Behold, the
days approach when you must die; call

LIFE LESSONS

➤ **31:6 — *"Be strong and of good courage, do not fear nor be afraid of them; for the LORD your God, He is the One who goes with you. He will not leave you nor forsake you."***

Could anything feel more disconcerting or frightening than having to face a terrible trial *all by yourself*? God tells us that those who know Him never have to worry about that. He's right there with us, in the easiest and most difficult of times.

Joshua, and present yourselves in the tabernacle of meeting, that I may inaugurate him." So Moses and Joshua went and presented themselves in the tabernacle of meeting.
15 Now the LORD appeared at the tabernacle in a pillar of cloud, and the pillar of cloud stood above the door of the tabernacle.
16 And the LORD said to Moses: "Behold, you will rest with your fathers; and this people will rise and play the harlot with the gods of the foreigners of the land, where they go *to be* among them, and they will forsake Me and break My covenant which I have made with them.
17 "Then My anger shall be aroused against them in that day, and I will forsake them, and I will hide My face from them, and they shall be devoured. And many evils and troubles shall befall them, so that they will say in that day, 'Have not these evils come upon us because our God *is* not among us?'
18 "And I will surely hide My face in that day because of all the evil which they have done, in that they have turned to other gods.
19 "Now therefore, write down this song for yourselves, and teach it to the children of Israel; put it in their mouths, that this song may be a witness for Me against the children of Israel.
20 "When I have brought them to the land flowing with milk and honey, of which I swore to their fathers, and they have eaten and filled themselves and grown fat, then they will turn to other gods and serve them; and they will provoke Me and break My covenant.
21 "Then it shall be, when many evils and troubles have come upon them, that this song will testify against them as a witness; for it will not be forgotten in the mouths of their descendants, for I know the inclination of their behavior today, even before I have brought them to the land of which I swore *to give them.*"
22 Therefore Moses wrote this song the same day, and taught it to the children of Israel.
23 Then He inaugurated Joshua the son of Nun, and said, "Be strong and of good courage; for you shall bring the children of Israel into the land of which I swore to them, and I will be with you."
24 So it was, when Moses had completed writing the words of this law in a book, when they were finished,
25 that Moses commanded the Levites, who bore the ark of the covenant of the LORD, saying:
26 "Take this Book of the Law, and put it beside the ark of the covenant of the LORD your God, that it may be there as a witness against you;
27 "for I know your rebellion and your stiff neck. *If* today, while I am yet alive with you, you have been rebellious against the LORD, then how much more after my death?
28 "Gather to me all the elders of your tribes, and your officers, that I may speak these words in their hearing and call heaven and earth to witness against them.
29 "For I know that after my death you will become utterly corrupt, and turn aside from the way which I have commanded you. And evil will befall you in the latter days, because you will do evil in the sight of the LORD, to provoke Him to anger through the work of your hands."

The Song of Moses

30 Then Moses spoke in the hearing of all the assembly of Israel the words of this song until they were ended:

32 "Give ear, O heavens, and I will speak;
And hear, O earth, the words of my mouth.
2 Let my teaching drop as the rain,
My speech distill as the dew,
As raindrops on the tender herb,
And as showers on the grass.
3 For I proclaim the name of the LORD:
Ascribe greatness to our God.
4 *He is* the Rock, His work *is* perfect;
For all His ways *are* justice,
A God of truth and without injustice;
Righteous and upright *is* He.

5 "They have corrupted themselves;
They are not His children,
Because of their blemish:
A perverse and crooked generation.
6 Do you thus deal with the LORD,
O foolish and unwise people?
Is He not your Father, *who* bought you?
Has He not made you and established you?

7 "Remember the days of old,
Consider the years of many generations.
Ask your father, and he will show you;
Your elders, and they will tell you:
8 When the Most High divided their inheritance to the nations,
When He separated the sons of Adam,
He set the boundaries of the peoples
According to the number of the children of Israel.

LIFE LESSONS

➤ 32:4 — *"He is the Rock, His work is perfect; for all His ways are justice, a God of truth and without injustice; righteous and upright is He."*

When we feel afraid or uncertain about the future, it lifts our spirits and strengthens our faith to remind ourselves of the glorious character of God.

9 For the LORD's portion *is* His people;
Jacob *is* the place of His inheritance.
10 "He found him in a desert land
And in the wasteland, a howling
wilderness;
He encircled him, He instructed him,
He kept him as the apple of His eye.
11 As an eagle stirs up its nest,
Hovers over its young,
Spreading out its wings, taking them up,
Carrying them on its wings,
12 *So* the LORD alone led him,
And *there was* no foreign god with him.

13 "He made him ride in the heights of the
earth,
That he might eat the produce of the
fields;
He made him draw honey from the
rock,
And oil from the flinty rock;
14 Curds from the cattle, and milk of the
flock,
With fat of lambs;
And rams of the breed of Bashan, and
goats,
With the choicest wheat;
And you drank wine, the blood of the
grapes.

15 "But Jeshurun grew fat and kicked;
You grew fat, you grew thick,
You are obese!
Then he forsook God *who* made him,
And scornfully esteemed the Rock of his
salvation.
16 They provoked Him to jealousy with
foreign *gods;*
With abominations they provoked Him to
anger.
17 They sacrificed to demons, not to God,
To gods they did not know,
To new *gods,* new arrivals
That your fathers did not fear.
18 Of the Rock *who* begot you, you are
unmindful,
And have forgotten the God who fathered
you.

19 "And when the LORD saw *it,* He spurned
them,
Because of the provocation of His sons
and His daughters.
20 And He said: 'I will hide My face from
them,
I will see what their end *will be,*
For they *are* a perverse generation,
Children in whom *is* no faith.
21 They have provoked Me to jealousy by
what is not God;
They have moved Me to anger by their
foolish idols.
But I will provoke them to jealousy by
those who are not a nation;
I will move them to anger by a foolish
nation.
22 For a fire is kindled in My anger,
And shall burn to the lowest hell;
It shall consume the earth with her
increase,
And set on fire the foundations of the
mountains.

23 'I will heap disasters on them;
I will spend My arrows on them.
24 *They shall be* wasted with hunger,
Devoured by pestilence and bitter
destruction;
I will also send against them the teeth of
beasts,
With the poison of serpents of the dust.
25 The sword shall destroy outside;
There shall be terror within
For the young man and virgin,
The nursing child with the man of gray
hairs.
26 I would have said, "I will dash them in
pieces,
I will make the memory of them to cease
from among men,"
27 Had I not feared the wrath of the enemy,
Lest their adversaries should
misunderstand,
Lest they should say, "Our hand *is* high;
And it is not the LORD who has done all
this." '

28 "For they *are* a nation void of counsel,
Nor *is there any* understanding in them.
29 Oh, that they were wise, *that* they
understood this,
That they would consider their latter
end!
30 How could one chase a thousand,
And two put ten thousand to flight,
Unless their Rock had sold them,
And the LORD had surrendered them?
31 For their rock *is* not like our Rock, ◄
Even our enemies themselves *being*
judges.
32 For their vine *is* of the vine of Sodom
And of the fields of Gomorrah;
Their grapes *are* grapes of gall,
Their clusters *are* bitter.
33 Their wine *is* the poison of serpents,
And the cruel venom of cobras.

LIFE LESSONS

➤ ***32:31 — "For their rock is not like our Rock, even our enemies themselves being judges."***

There is no Rock like the God of Abraham. When push comes to shove, only the God of Israel remains standing and immovable. And He is *our* God!

34 'Is this not laid up in store with Me,
Sealed up among My treasures?
35 Vengeance is Mine, and recompense;
Their foot shall slip in *due* time;
For the day of their calamity *is* at hand,
And the things to come hasten upon them.'

36 "For the LORD will judge His people
And have compassion on His servants,
When He sees that *their* power is gone,
And *there is* no one *remaining*, bond or free.
37 He will say: 'Where *are* their gods,
The rock in which they sought refuge?
38 Who ate the fat of their sacrifices,
And drank the wine of their drink offering?
Let them rise and help you,
And be your refuge.

39 'Now see that I, *even* I, *am* He,
And *there is* no God besides Me;
I kill and I make alive;
I wound and I heal;
Nor *is there any* who can deliver from My hand.
40 For I raise My hand to heaven,
And say, "As I live forever,
41 If I whet My glittering sword,
And My hand takes hold on judgment,
I will render vengeance to My enemies,
And repay those who hate Me.
42 I will make My arrows drunk with blood,
And My sword shall devour flesh,
With the blood of the slain and the captives,
From the heads of the leaders of the enemy."'

43 "Rejoice, O Gentiles, *with* His people;[a]
For He will avenge the blood of His servants,
And render vengeance to His adversaries;
He will provide atonement for His land
and His people."

44 So Moses came with Joshua[a] the son of Nun and spoke all the words of this song in the hearing of the people.
45 Moses finished speaking all these words
to all Israel,
46 and he said to them: "Set your hearts on
all the words which I testify among you today,
which you shall command your children to be
careful to observe—all the words of this law.
47 "For it *is* not a futile thing for you, because
it *is* your life, and by this word you shall prolong *your* days in the land which you cross over the Jordan to possess."

Moses to Die on Mount Nebo

48 Then the LORD spoke to Moses that very
same day, saying:
49 "Go up this mountain of the Abarim,
Mount Nebo, which *is* in the land of Moab, across from Jericho; view the land of Canaan, which I give to the children of Israel as a possession;
50 "and die on the mountain which you ascend, and be gathered to your people, just as Aaron your brother died on Mount Hor and was gathered to his people;
51 "because you trespassed against Me among the children of Israel at the waters of Meribah Kadesh, in the Wilderness of Zin, because you did not hallow Me in the midst of the children of Israel.
52 "Yet you shall see the land before *you*, though you shall not go there, into the land which I am giving to the children of Israel."

Moses' Final Blessing on Israel

33 Now this *is* the blessing with which Moses the man of God blessed the children of Israel before his death.
2 And he said:

"The LORD came from Sinai,
And dawned on them from Seir;
He shone forth from Mount Paran,
And He came with ten thousands of saints;
From His right hand
Came a fiery law for them.
3 Yes, He loves the people;
All His saints *are* in Your hand;
They sit down at Your feet;
Everyone receives Your words.
4 Moses commanded a law for us,
A heritage of the congregation of Jacob.
5 And He was King in Jeshurun,
When the leaders of the people were gathered,
All the tribes of Israel together.

6 "Let Reuben live, and not die,
Nor let his men be few."

32:43 [a]A Dead Sea Scroll fragment adds *And let all the gods (angels) worship Him* (compare Septuagint and Hebrews 1:6).
32:44 [a]Hebrew *Hoshea* (compare Numbers 13:8, 16)

LIFE LESSONS

➤ 32:36 — *"For the LORD will judge His people and have compassion on His servants, when He sees that their power is gone, and there is no one remaining, bond or free."*

God both judges and restores His people. He loves us too much to allow us to stay disconnected from His love. He will move to restore the intimacy He desires with us, no matter what it takes.

7 And this he said of Judah:

"Hear, LORD, the voice of Judah,
And bring him to his people;
Let his hands be sufficient for him,
And may You be a help against his enemies."

8 And of Levi he said:

"*Let* Your Thummim and Your Urim *be* with Your holy one,
Whom You tested at Massah,
And with whom You contended at the waters of Meribah,
9 Who says of his father and mother,
'I have not seen them';
Nor did he acknowledge his brothers,
Or know his own children;
For they have observed Your word
And kept Your covenant.
10 They shall teach Jacob Your judgments,
And Israel Your law.
They shall put incense before You,
And a whole burnt sacrifice on Your altar.
11 Bless his substance, LORD,
And accept the work of his hands;
Strike the loins of those who rise against him,
And of those who hate him, that they rise not again."

12 Of Benjamin he said:

"The beloved of the LORD shall dwell in safety by Him,
Who shelters him all the day long;
And he shall dwell between His shoulders."

13 And of Joseph he said:

"Blessed of the LORD *is* his land,
With the precious things of heaven, with the dew,
And the deep lying beneath,
14 With the precious fruits of the sun,
With the precious produce of the months,
15 With the best things of the ancient mountains,
With the precious things of the everlasting hills,
16 With the precious things of the earth and its fullness,
And the favor of Him who dwelt in the bush.
Let *the blessing* come 'on the head of Joseph,
And on the crown of the head of him *who was* separate from his brothers.'[a]
17 His glory *is like* a firstborn bull,
And his horns *like* the horns of the wild ox;
Together with them
He shall push the peoples
To the ends of the earth;
They *are* the ten thousands of Ephraim,
And they *are* the thousands of Manasseh."

18 And of Zebulun he said:

"Rejoice, Zebulun, in your going out,
And Issachar in your tents!
19 They shall call the peoples *to* the mountain;
There they shall offer sacrifices of righteousness;
For they shall partake *of* the abundance of the seas
And *of* treasures hidden in the sand."

20 And of Gad he said:

"Blessed *is* he who enlarges Gad;
He dwells as a lion,
And tears the arm and the crown of his head.
21 He provided the first *part* for himself,
Because a lawgiver's portion was reserved there.
He came *with* the heads of the people;
He administered the justice of the LORD,
And His judgments with Israel."

22 And of Dan he said:

"Dan *is* a lion's whelp;
He shall leap from Bashan."

23 And of Naphtali he said:

"O Naphtali, satisfied with favor,
And full of the blessing of the LORD,
Possess the west and the south."

24 And of Asher he said:

"Asher *is* most blessed of sons;
Let him be favored by his brothers,
And let him dip his foot in oil.
25 Your sandals *shall be* iron and bronze;
As your days, *so shall* your strength *be*.

26 "*There is* no one like the God of Jeshurun,
Who rides the heavens to help you,
And in His excellency on the clouds.
27 The eternal God *is your* refuge,
And underneath *are* the everlasting arms;

33:16 [a]Genesis 49:26

LIFE LESSONS

➤ **33:27 — *"The eternal God is your refuge, and underneath are the everlasting arms; He will thrust out the enemy from before you, and will say, 'Destroy!'"***

Can we have a better friend than one who is infinitely strong and mighty, yet at the same time loving and gentle? Our God tenderly loves us and protects us, yet has defeated all our spiritual enemies, including the devil.

He will thrust out the enemy from before
you,
And will say, 'Destroy!'
28 Then Israel shall dwell in safety,
The fountain of Jacob alone,
In a land of grain and new wine;
His heavens shall also drop dew.
29 Happy *are* you, O Israel!
Who *is* like you, a people saved by the
LORD,
The shield of your help
And the sword of your majesty!
Your enemies shall submit to you,
And you shall tread down their high
places."

Moses Dies on Mount Nebo

34 Then Moses went up from the plains of
Moab to Mount Nebo, to the top of Pisgah, which is across from Jericho. And the
LORD showed him all the land of Gilead as far
as Dan,
2 all Naphtali and the land of Ephraim and
Manasseh, all the land of Judah as far as the
Western Sea,[a]
3 the South, and the plain of the Valley of
Jericho, the city of palm trees, as far as Zoar.
4 Then the LORD said to him, "This *is* the
land of which I swore to give Abraham, Isaac,
and Jacob, saying, 'I will give it to your descendants.' I have caused you to see *it* with
your eyes, but you shall not cross over there."
5 So Moses the servant of the LORD died
there in the land of Moab, according to the
word of the LORD.
6 And He buried him in a valley in the land ➤
of Moab, opposite Beth Peor; but no one
knows his grave to this day.
7 Moses *was* one hundred and twenty years
old when he died. His eyes were not dim nor
his natural vigor diminished.
8 And the children of Israel wept for Moses
in the plains of Moab thirty days. So the days
of weeping *and* mourning for Moses ended.
9 Now Joshua the son of Nun was full of the
spirit of wisdom, for Moses had laid his hands
on him; so the children of Israel heeded him,
and did as the LORD had commanded Moses.
10 But since then there has not arisen in Israel a prophet like Moses, whom the LORD
knew face to face,
11 in all the signs and wonders which the
LORD sent him to do in the land of Egypt, before Pharaoh, before all his servants, and in
all his land,
12 and by all that mighty power and all the
great terror which Moses performed in the
sight of all Israel.

34:2 [a]That is, the Mediterranean

LIFE LESSONS

➤ **34:6 — *And He buried him in a valley in the land of Moab, opposite Beth Peor; but no one knows his grave to this day.***

God buried Moses in a grave He kept secret. As great as Moses was, he was only a man, and God did not want anyone to remember him as anything but a man.

THE BOOK OF JOSHUA

Joshua, the first of the twelve historical books (Joshua—Esther), forges a link between the days of Moses and the remainder of Israel's history. Through three major military campaigns involving more than thirty enemy armies, the people of Israel learn a crucial lesson under Joshua's capable leadership: Victory comes through faith in God and obedience to His word, rather than through military might or numerical superiority.

The events narrated in Joshua take place over a period of about fifty years. In that span of time Israel goes from a group of squabbling refugees to a cooperative nation comprised of twelve distinct tribes that work together to claim the land God has given them.

Unlike the previous generation, this group of Israelites obeys God's word to cross the Jordan River. They do so partly in response to the Lord's word to Joshua at the beginning of the book: "As I was with Moses, so I will be with you. I will not leave you nor forsake you" (1:5). As if to bring home that message, through a miracle the Lord allows the nation to cross into the Promised Land on dry ground (3).

The book does not record an unbroken string of military successes and conquests, but instead chronicles both the high and low points of the nation's growing possession of Canaan. By the end of the book, Joshua has become an old man—and yet his faithful, God-honoring spirit remains as strong as ever as he tells his people, "choose for yourselves this day whom you will serve, whether the gods which your fathers served that were on the other side of the River, or the gods of the Amorites, in whose land you dwell. But as for me and my house, we will serve the LORD" (24:15).

Theme: Listening to God is essential to walking with God. God told Joshua to be brave and to trust Him. Joshua obeyed, and the rest is history.

Author: Probably Joshua himself (Josh. 24:26).

Time: Moses died about 1407 B.C., at which time Joshua assumed command and led the Israelites in the occupation of Canaan. The Book of Joshua closes with Joshua's farewell address and his death.

Structure: Chapters 1–12 of the Book of Joshua cover the invasion and conquest of Canaan; chapters 13–22 tell of the division of the territories among the tribes of Israel; chapters 23–24 record Joshua's farewell address to his people.

As you read Joshua, watch for several life principles that play an important role in this book:

4. The awareness of God's presence energizes us for our work. *See Joshua 1:5; 3:7; pages 241; 243.*

9. Trusting God means looking beyond what we can see to what God sees. *See Joshua 2:1–13; page 241.*

5. God does not require us to understand His will, just obey it, even if it seems unreasonable. *See Joshua 3:8; 6:1–20; pages 246; 248.*

26. Adversity is a bridge to a deeper relationship with God. *See Joshua 7:10–26; page 248.*

God's Commission to Joshua

➤ 1 After the death of Moses the servant of the
LORD, it came to pass that the LORD spoke
to Joshua the son of Nun, Moses' assistant,
saying:
2 "Moses My servant is dead. Now therefore, arise, go over this Jordan, you and all
this people, to the land which I am giving to
them—the children of Israel.
3 "Every place that the sole of your foot will
tread upon I have given you, as I said to Moses.
4 "From the wilderness and this Lebanon as
far as the great river, the River Euphrates, all
the land of the Hittites, and to the Great Sea
toward the going down of the sun, shall be
your territory.
➤ 5 "No man shall *be able to* stand before you
all the days of your life; as I was with Moses,
so I will be with you. I will not leave you nor
forsake you.
6 "Be strong and of good courage, for to this
people you shall divide as an inheritance the
land which I swore to their fathers to give
them.
7 "Only be strong and very courageous, that
you may observe to do according to all the
law which Moses My servant commanded
you; do not turn from it to the right hand or to
the left, that you may prosper wherever you
go.
✳ 8 "This Book of the Law shall not depart
➤ from your mouth, but you shall meditate in it
day and night, that you may observe to do according to all that is written in it. For then you
will make your way prosperous, and then you
will have good success.
➤ 9 "Have I not commanded you? Be strong
and of good courage; do not be afraid, nor be
dismayed, for the LORD your God *is* with you
wherever you go."

The Order to Cross the Jordan

10 Then Joshua commanded the officers of
the people, saying,
11 "Pass through the camp and command the
people, saying, 'Prepare provisions for yourselves, for within three days you will cross
over this Jordan, to go in to possess the land
which the LORD your God is giving you to possess.'"
12 And to the Reubenites, the Gadites, and
half the tribe of Manasseh Joshua spoke, saying,
13 "Remember the word which Moses the
servant of the LORD commanded you, saying,
'The LORD your God is giving you rest and is
giving you this land.'
14 "Your wives, your little ones, and your
livestock shall remain in the land which
Moses gave you on this side of the Jordan.
But you shall pass before your brethren
armed, all your mighty men of valor, and help
them,
15 "until the LORD has given your brethren
rest, as He *gave* you, and they also have
taken possession of the land which the LORD
your God is giving them. Then you shall return to the land of your possession and enjoy
it, which Moses the LORD's servant gave you
on this side of the Jordan toward the sunrise."
16 So they answered Joshua, saying, "All that
you command us we will do, and wherever
you send us we will go.
17 "Just as we heeded Moses in all things, so
we will heed you. Only the LORD your God be
with you, as He was with Moses.
18 "Whoever rebels against your command
and does not heed your words, in all that you
command him, shall be put to death. Only be
strong and of good courage."

Rahab Hides the Spies

2 Now Joshua the son of Nun sent out two
men from Acacia Grove[a] to spy secretly,
saying, "Go, view the land, especially Jericho."

2:1 [a]Hebrew *Shittim*

LIFE LESSONS

➤ 1:1 — *"After the death of Moses the servant of the LORD, it came to pass that the LORD spoke to Joshua the son of Nun, Moses' assistant . . . ."*

Before Joshua gave his first order or made his first move as the new leader of Israel, he listened for the voice of God. Listening to God is essential to walking with God and securing His blessings.

➤ 1:5 — *"No man shall be able to stand before you all the days of your life; as I was with Moses, so I will be with you. I will not leave you nor forsake you."*

When we do God's will in God's way with God's help, no one and nothing can stand in the way of our success. The key is the presence of the Lord.

➤ 1:8 — *"This Book of the Law shall not depart from your mouth, but you shall meditate in it day and night, that you may observe to do according to all that is written in it . . . ."*

The Lord gave Joshua the same command he issued to future Israelite kings in Deuteronomy 17:19—he was to meditate on the Word of God every day. Knowledge of God's will is crucial to doing it.

➤ 1:9 — *"Have I not commanded you? Be strong and of good courage; do not be afraid, nor be dismayed, for the LORD your God is with you wherever you go."*

It's easy to focus on our problems, which we can see, and not on God, whom we can't. As Joshua discovered, God is with us no matter where we are or how big our problems seem.

ANSWERS TO LIFE'S QUESTIONS

How can I find courage in times of adversity?

JOSH. 1:6–9

In many ways, adversity is like boot camp; it is rigorous, painful, and challenging. Adversity causes us to adopt new routines and habits, to develop aspects of our being—physical, mental, emotional, or spiritual—that might not have developed as they should. Adversity can put us under the authority of people who affect our lives in ways foreign to us.

In all these areas, we need courage to keep our balance. We need courage as we get hit by many new feelings, facts, restrictions, limitations, obstacles, challenges, and offerings of advice and help. We need courage not only to endure times of adversity, but also to make the changes that adversity compels us to make.

In any case, we can trust the Holy Spirit to help us in times of adversity and to grow and change so that we can live in keeping with the example set by Jesus Christ.

Joshua knew all about adversity. Without question, forty years of wandering in the wilderness had qualified him to understand hardship, trials, and troubles—physical, relational, spiritual, and no doubt emotional and mental. Joshua also knew that the Lord was with him and his people. As a close associate of Moses, Joshua had grown in his faith and leadership abilities. When the time came for the people of God to cross the Jordan River and inhabit the land of promise, God named Joshua as the leader to succeed Moses.

At three specific times, the Lord spoke to Joshua about courage:

> Be strong and of good courage, for to this people you shall divide as an inheritance the land which I swore to their fathers to give them (Josh. 1:6).
>
> Only be strong and very courageous, that you may observe to do according to all the law which Moses My servant commanded you . . . . (Josh. 1:7).
>
> Have I not commanded you? Be strong and of good courage; do not be afraid, nor be dismayed, for the LORD your God is with you wherever you go (Josh. 1:9).

Note the three things that required courage of Joshua: (1) to make decisions that affected other people under his leadership; (2) to keep the laws and commandments, even as changes occurred; and (3) to remember continually that the Lord was with him, despite what circumstances might indicate to the contrary.

Every one of us needs courage in exactly the same three areas of our lives as we face adversity.

See the Life Principles Index for further study:
26 Adversity is a bridge to a deeper relation ship with God.
4. The awareness of God's presence energizes us for our work.

So they went, and came to the house of a harlot named Rahab, and lodged there.
2 And it was told the king of Jericho, saying, "Behold, men have come here tonight from the children of Israel to search out the country."
3 So the king of Jericho sent to Rahab, saying, "Bring out the men who have come to you, who have entered your house, for they have come to search out all the country."
4 Then the woman took the two men and hid them. So she said, "Yes, the men came to me, but I did not know where they *were* from.
5 And it happened as the gate was being shut, when it was dark, that the men went out. Where the men went I do not know; pursue them quickly, for you may overtake them."
6 (But she had brought them up to the roof and hidden them with the stalks of flax, which she had laid in order on the roof.)
7 Then the men pursued them by the road to the Jordan, to the fords. And as soon as those who pursued them had gone out, they shut the gate.
8 Now before they lay down, she came up to them on the roof,
9 and said to the men: "I know that the LORD has given you the land, that the terror of you has fallen on us, and that all the inhabitants of the land are fainthearted because of you.
10 "For we have heard how the LORD dried up the water of the Red Sea for you when you came out of Egypt, and what you did to the two kings of the Amorites who *were* on the other side of the Jordan, Sihon and Og, whom you utterly destroyed.
11 "And as soon as we heard *these things,* our hearts melted; neither did there remain any

more courage in anyone because of you, for
the LORD your God, He *is* God in heaven
above and on earth beneath.
12 "Now therefore, I beg you, swear to me by
the LORD, since I have shown you kindness,
that you also will show kindness to my father's house, and give me a true token,
13 "and spare my father, my mother, my
brothers, my sisters, and all that they have,
and deliver our lives from death."
14 So the men answered her, "Our lives for
yours, if none of you tell this business of ours.
And it shall be, when the LORD has given us
the land, that we will deal kindly and truly
with you."
15 Then she let them down by a rope through
the window, for her house *was* on the city
wall; she dwelt on the wall.
16 And she said to them, "Get to the mountain, lest the pursuers meet you. Hide there
three days, until the pursuers have returned.
Afterward you may go your way."
17 So the men said to her: "We *will be* blameless of this oath of yours which you have
made us swear,
18 "unless, *when* we come into the land, you
bind this line of scarlet cord in the window
through which you let us down, and unless
you bring your father, your mother, your
brothers, and all your father's household to
your own home.
19 "So it shall be *that* whoever goes outside
the doors of your house into the street, his
blood *shall be* on his own head, and we *will be*
guiltless. And whoever is with you in the
house, his blood *shall be* on our head if a
hand is laid on him.
20 "And if you tell this business of ours, then
we will be free from your oath which you
made us swear."
21 Then she said, "According to your words,
so *be* it." And she sent them away, and they
departed. And she bound the scarlet cord in
the window.
22 They departed and went to the mountain,
and stayed there three days until the pursuers
returned. The pursuers sought *them* all along
the way, but did not find *them*.
23 So the two men returned, descended from
the mountain, and crossed over; and they
came to Joshua the son of Nun, and told him
all that had befallen them.
24 And they said to Joshua, "Truly the LORD
has delivered all the land into our hands, for
indeed all the inhabitants of the country are
fainthearted because of us."

Israel Crosses the Jordan

3 Then Joshua rose early in the morning;
and they set out from Acacia Grove[a] and
came to the Jordan, he and all the children of
Israel, and lodged there before they crossed
over.
2 So it was, after three days, that the officers
went through the camp;
3 and they commanded the people, saying,
"When you see the ark of the covenant of the
LORD your God, and the priests, the Levites,
bearing it, then you shall set out from your
place and go after it.
4 "Yet there shall be a space between you
and it, about two thousand cubits by measure.
Do not come near it, that you may know the
way by which you must go, for you have not
passed *this* way before."
5 And Joshua said to the people, "Sanctify
yourselves, for tomorrow the LORD will do
wonders among you."
6 Then Joshua spoke to the priests, saying,
"Take up the ark of the covenant and cross
over before the people." So they took up the
ark of the covenant and went before the people.
7 And the LORD said to Joshua, "This day I
will begin to exalt you in the sight of all Israel,

3:1 [a]Hebrew *Shittim*

LIFE LESSONS

➤ 2:4 — *Then the woman took the two men and hid them. So she said, "Yes, the men came to me, but I did not know where they were from."*

Sometimes the Lord works miracles on our behalf to bless us; sometimes He uses less spectacular means, as here. But always it is the Lord blessing us.

➤ 2:11 — *"And as soon as we heard these things, our hearts melted; neither did there remain any more courage in anyone because of you, for the LORD your God, He is God in heaven above and on earth beneath."*

Genuine faith can take root in the unlikeliest of soils, as it did in the heart of the pagan prostitute Rahab. She had heard enough to believe—and the Lord saved her (see Heb. 11:31).

➤ 2:24 — *And they said to Joshua, "Truly the LORD has delivered all the land into our hands, for indeed all the inhabitants of the country are fainthearted because of us."*

God always follows through on His promises—but it encourages us greatly when, in His grace, He gives us a foretaste of that fulfilled promise.

➤ 3:4 — *". . . Do not come near it, that you may know the way by which you must go, for you have not passed this way before."*

Since the Israelites had never traveled this path before, they wisely chose to follow the lead of God, in this case by trailing the ark of the covenant. God leads, we are to follow.

LIFE PRINCIPLE 5

GOD DOES NOT REQUIRE US TO UNDERSTAND HIS WILL, JUST OBEY IT, EVEN IF IT SEEMS UNREASONABLE.

JOSH. 3:8

Do you often find yourself wondering why God doesn't answer your prayers, or why, despite all your best efforts, the circumstances of your life still don't work out? The answer could lie in your level of obedience to God.

If you have received Jesus Christ as your Savior and are still experiencing great spiritual frustration, there may be an area of disobedience in your life that you have not dealt with. Perhaps God has asked something of you, and in response, you have either ignored His words or done only part of what He asked. True obedience to God means doing what God says, when He says it, how He says it should be done, as long as He says to do it—regardless of whether you understand the reasons for it—until what He says is accomplished.

Before you try to make a list of everything God has ever asked you to do or not do, consider this: Is there one particular area of your life in which you struggle to obey God's Word? As you read the Scriptures, does He continually bring a specific sin to your attention? When you go to Him in prayer, does the same issue surface repeatedly? If the Lord is bringing something to your mind right now, consider this: It could be that you have been living in the same uncomfortable situation for years because at some point, you chose to do things your way instead of God's way.

Understanding this key distinction between your way and God's way can make a tremendous difference in your life. You must place obedience at the top of your priority list. But to do so, I think you need to see why obedience plays such an important role in your relationship with God—and there may be no better biblical example to illustrate the point than Noah, a man who obeyed God, even when what God asked him to do didn't seem to make much sense. God called this man to do something extraordinary—something that seemed both impossible and illogical—and Noah complied without asking questions (Gen. 6–9).

Noah obeyed God despite what other people thought of him. When we choose the path of obedience, we also

You must place obedience at the top of your priority list.

must be prepared for the negative responses we will undoubtedly receive.

Will it always be popular to obey God? No. Will people criticize you? Probably. Will they think you do some ridiculous things? No doubt. Will they laugh at you? Yes. But think about this: Noah chose to walk with God in the midst of a corrupt society. In fact, it had grown so wicked that God determined to destroy every living human being on the face of this earth, with the exception of one family—Noah's. We can only imagine what those evil people must have said to Noah as they watched him day after day.

But soon after the raindrops started falling, all the mocking dried up.

We can deduce an important key to obedience from the life of Noah: when God tells us to do something, we must not focus on the things or the persons who try to distract us from doing it. If Noah had begun to listen to his critics, he would not have built the ark and he would have been swept away with everyone else. Instead, he chose to obey God regardless of any misgivings he might have had.

The Holy Spirit enables you to walk obediently before God.

The Holy Spirit enables us to obey every one of God's commandments. If this were not possible, God would not be a just God. Therefore, whatever He requires of us—whether it be painful or joyful, profitable or costly, reasonable or peculiar—our heavenly Father will help us to obey Him.

Obedience must be a priority in every believer's life. It is the only way you will ever become the person God wants you to be, and the only way you will ever achieve the things in life that He has so wonderfully prepared for you. The Holy Spirit enables you to walk obediently before God, in His strength and His power.

My prayer for you—my petition to God on your behalf—is that you will choose to obey Him, even if you don't understand why He asks you to do something. That way, you can become the person He wants you to be, do the work He desires of you, bear the fruit He enables you to bear, and receive the blessings He has prepared for you.

See the Life Principles Index for further study.

Life Examples:
JOSHUA

The Need for Courage

JOSH. 3:5–17

Any time you take a risk for God, you are going to need courage. Joshua certainly understood this requirement.

The Lord challenged Joshua with the mission of getting a multitude of Israelites across the Jordan River so they might claim the Land of Promise. Before sending the people across the river, the Lord exhorted Joshua three times to have courage, telling him to remember the promises He had made to his forefathers, reminding him to obey the Law of Moses, and promising Joshua He would be with him every step of the way.

Fear and discouragement are subject to your will. Through faith in God, you can rule over them, not them over you. Remind yourself daily of what you heard God say in His Word, stay close to Him, and refuse to allow yourself to give in to fear and discouragement.

See the Life Principles Index for further study:
20. Disappointments are inevitable; discouragement is a choice.

that they may know that, as I was with Moses,
so I will be with you.
8 "You shall command the priests who bear
the ark of the covenant, saying, 'When you
have come to the edge of the water of the Jordan, you shall stand in the Jordan.'"
9 So Joshua said to the children of Israel,
"Come here, and hear the words of the LORD
your God."
➤ 10 And Joshua said, "By this you shall know
that the living God *is* among you, and *that* He
will without fail drive out from before you the
Canaanites and the Hittites and the Hivites
and the Perizzites and the Girgashites and the
Amorites and the Jebusites:
11 "Behold, the ark of the covenant of the
Lord of all the earth is crossing over before
you into the Jordan.
12 "Now therefore, take for yourselves
twelve men from the tribes of Israel, one man
from every tribe.
13 "And it shall come to pass, as soon as the
soles of the feet of the priests who bear the
ark of the LORD, the Lord of all the earth, shall
rest in the waters of the Jordan, *that* the waters of the Jordan shall be cut off, the waters
that come down from upstream, and they
shall stand as a heap."
14 So it was, when the people set out from
their camp to cross over the Jordan, with the
priests bearing the ark of the covenant before
the people,
15 and as those who bore the ark came to the
Jordan, and the feet of the priests who bore
the ark dipped in the edge of the water (for
the Jordan overflows all its banks during the
whole time of harvest),
16 that the waters which came down from
upstream stood *still, and* rose in a heap very
far away at Adam, the city that *is* beside Zaretan. So the waters that went down into the
Sea of the Arabah, the Salt Sea, failed, *and*
were cut off; and the people crossed over opposite Jericho.
17 Then the priests who bore the ark of the
covenant of the LORD stood firm on dry
ground in the midst of the Jordan; and all Israel crossed over on dry ground, until all the
people had crossed completely over the Jordan.

The Memorial Stones

4 And it came to pass, when all the people
had completely crossed over the Jordan,
that the LORD spoke to Joshua, saying:
2 "Take for yourselves twelve men from the
people, one man from every tribe,
3 and command them, saying, 'Take for
yourselves twelve stones from here, out of the
midst of the Jordan, from the place where the
priests' feet stood firm. You shall carry them
over with you and leave them in the lodging
place where you lodge tonight.'"
4 Then Joshua called the twelve men whom
he had appointed from the children of Israel,
one man from every tribe;
5 and Joshua said to them: "Cross over before the ark of the LORD your God into the
midst of the Jordan, and each one of you take
up a stone on his shoulder, according to the

LIFE LESSONS

➤ **3:10 — *And Joshua said, "By this you shall know that the living God is among you, and that He will without fail drive out from before you the Canaanites . . . ."***

When the living God is among us, no problem is insurmountable. The awareness of God's presence energizes us for our work.

number of the tribes of the children of Israel,
6 "that this may be a sign among you when your children ask in time to come, saying, 'What do these stones *mean* to you?'
➤ 7 "Then you shall answer them that the waters of the Jordan were cut off before the ark of the covenant of the LORD; when it crossed over the Jordan, the waters of the Jordan were cut off. And these stones shall be for a memorial to the children of Israel forever."
8 And the children of Israel did so, just as Joshua commanded, and took up twelve stones from the midst of the Jordan, as the LORD had spoken to Joshua, according to the number of the tribes of the children of Israel, and carried them over with them to the place where they lodged, and laid them down there.
9 Then Joshua set up twelve stones in the midst of the Jordan, in the place where the feet of the priests who bore the ark of the covenant stood; and they are there to this day.
10 So the priests who bore the ark stood in the midst of the Jordan until everything was finished that the LORD had commanded Joshua to speak to the people, according to all that Moses had commanded Joshua; and the people hurried and crossed over.
11 Then it came to pass, when all the people had completely crossed over, that the ark of the LORD and the priests crossed over in the presence of the people.
12 And the men of Reuben, the men of Gad, and half the tribe of Manasseh crossed over armed before the children of Israel, as Moses had spoken to them.
13 About forty thousand prepared for war crossed over before the LORD for battle, to the plains of Jericho.
14 On that day the LORD exalted Joshua in the sight of all Israel; and they feared him, as they had feared Moses, all the days of his life.
15 Then the LORD spoke to Joshua, saying,
16 "Command the priests who bear the ark of the Testimony to come up from the Jordan."
17 Joshua therefore commanded the priests, saying, "Come up from the Jordan."
18 And it came to pass, when the priests who bore the ark of the covenant of the LORD had come from the midst of the Jordan, *and* the soles of the priests' feet touched the dry land, that the waters of the Jordan returned to their place and overflowed all its banks as before.
19 Now the people came up from the Jordan on the tenth *day* of the first month, and they camped in Gilgal on the east border of Jericho.
20 And those twelve stones which they took out of the Jordan, Joshua set up in Gilgal.
21 Then he spoke to the children of Israel, saying: "When your children ask their fathers in time to come, saying, 'What *are* these stones?'
22 "then you shall let your children know, saying, 'Israel crossed over this Jordan on dry land';
23 "for the LORD your God dried up the waters of the Jordan before you until you had crossed over, as the LORD your God did to the Red Sea, which He dried up before us until we had crossed over,
24 "that all the peoples of the earth may ➤
know the hand of the LORD, that it *is* mighty, that you may fear the LORD your God forever."

The Second Generation Circumcised

5 So it was, when all the kings of the Amorites who *were* on the west side of the Jordan, and all the kings of the Canaanites who *were* by the sea, heard that the LORD had dried up the waters of the Jordan from before the children of Israel until we[a] had crossed over, that their heart melted; and there was no spirit in them any longer because of the children of Israel.
2 At that time the LORD said to Joshua, "Make flint knives for yourself, and circumcise the sons of Israel again the second time."
3 So Joshua made flint knives for himself, and circumcised the sons of Israel at the hill of the foreskins.[a]
4 And this *is* the reason why Joshua circumcised them: All the people who came out of Egypt *who were* males, all the men of war, had died in the wilderness on the way, after they had come out of Egypt.
5 For all the people who came out had been circumcised, but all the people born in the

5:1 [a]Following Kethib; Qere, some Hebrew manuscripts and editions, Septuagint, Syriac, Targum, and Vulgate read *they*.
5:3 [a]Hebrew *Gibeath Haaraloth*

LIFE LESSONS

➤ 4:7 — *"Then you shall answer them that the waters of the Jordan were cut off before the ark of the covenant of the LORD . . . . And these stones shall be for a memorial to the children of Israel forever."*

For years after Israel had defeated Jericho, the people could look at the stones taken from the Jordan's dry riverbed and remember God's work on their behalf. What "memorial stones" remind you of God's work in your own life?

➤ 4:24 — *". . . that all the peoples of the earth may know the hand of the LORD, that it is mighty, that you may fear the LORD your God forever."*

What happens to God's people has ramifications far beyond their own lives. The Lord wants the whole world to know Him, and He "advertises" His activity through us.

wilderness, on the way as they came out of Egypt, had not been circumcised.
6 For the children of Israel walked forty years in the wilderness, till all the people *who were* men of war, who came out of Egypt, were consumed, because they did not obey the voice of the LORD—to whom the LORD swore that He would not show them the land which the LORD had sworn to their fathers that He would give us, "a land flowing with milk and honey."[a]
7 Then Joshua circumcised their sons *whom* He raised up in their place; for they were uncircumcised, because they had not been circumcised on the way.
➤ 8 So it was, when they had finished circumcising all the people, that they stayed in their places in the camp till they were healed.
9 Then the LORD said to Joshua, "This day I have rolled away the reproach of Egypt from you." Therefore the name of the place is called Gilgal[a] to this day.
10 Now the children of Israel camped in Gilgal, and kept the Passover on the fourteenth day of the month at twilight on the plains of Jericho.
11 And they ate of the produce of the land on the day after the Passover, unleavened bread and parched grain, on the very same day.
➤ 12 Then the manna ceased on the day after they had eaten the produce of the land; and the children of Israel no longer had manna, but they ate the food of the land of Canaan that year.

The Commander of the Army of the LORD

13 And it came to pass, when Joshua was by Jericho, that he lifted his eyes and looked, and behold, a Man stood opposite him with His sword drawn in His hand. And Joshua went to Him and said to Him, "*Are* You for us or for our adversaries?"
➤ 14 So He said, "No, but *as* Commander of the army of the LORD I have now come." And Joshua fell on his face to the earth and worshiped, and said to Him, "What does my Lord say to His servant?"
15 Then the Commander of the LORD's army said to Joshua, "Take your sandal off your foot, for the place where you stand *is* holy." And Joshua did so.

The Destruction of Jericho

6 Now Jericho was securely shut up because of the children of Israel; none went out, and none came in.
2 And the LORD said to Joshua: "See! I have given Jericho into your hand, its king, *and* the mighty men of valor.
3 "You shall march around the city, all *you* men of war; you shall go all around the city once. This you shall do six days.
4 "And seven priests shall bear seven trumpets of rams' horns before the ark. But the seventh day you shall march around the city seven times, and the priests shall blow the trumpets.
5 "It shall come to pass, when they make a long *blast* with the ram's horn, *and* when you hear the sound of the trumpet, that all the people shall shout with a great shout; then the wall of the city will fall down flat. And the people shall go up every man straight before him." ➤
6 Then Joshua the son of Nun called the priests and said to them, "Take up the ark of the covenant, and let seven priests bear seven trumpets of rams' horns before the ark of the LORD."
7 And he said to the people, "Proceed, and march around the city, and let him who is armed advance before the ark of the LORD."
8 So it was, when Joshua had spoken to the people, that the seven priests bearing the seven trumpets of rams' horns before the LORD advanced and blew the trumpets, and the ark of the covenant of the LORD followed them.

5:6 [a]Exodus 3:8 **5:9** [a]Literally *Rolling*

LIFE LESSONS

➤ 5:8 — *So it was, when they had finished circumcising all the people, that they stayed in their places in the camp till they were healed.*

While the men healed from their painful circumcisions, they remained vulnerable to attack from hostile forces (see Gen. 34:1–29). Yet our sovereign God protected them even then (Josh. 5:1). Obedience always brings blessing!

➤ 5:12 — *. . . and the children of Israel no longer had manna, but they ate the food of the land of Canaan that year.*

God provides exactly what we need, when we need it. In fact, He assumes full responsibility for our needs when we obey Him.

➤ 5:14 — *So He said, "No, but as Commander of the army of the LORD I have now come."*

The question is never "is God on our side," but rather "are we on God's side?" God does not choose sides, but He invites us to choose His side.

➤ 6:5 — *". . . when you hear the sound of the trumpet . . . all the people shall shout with a great shout; then the wall of the city will fall down flat . . . ."*

As a soldier, Joshua must have seen these instructions as very strange. Yet as a man of God, he immediately obeyed. God does not require us to understand His will, just obey it, whether it "makes sense" or not.

9 The armed men went before the priests
who blew the trumpets, and the rear guard
came after the ark, while *the priests* continued blowing the trumpets.
10 Now Joshua had commanded the people,
saying, "You shall not shout or make any
noise with your voice, nor shall a word proceed out of your mouth, until the day I say to
you, 'Shout!' Then you shall shout."
11 So he had the ark of the LORD circle the
city, going around *it* once. Then they came
into the camp and lodged in the camp.
12 And Joshua rose early in the morning, and
the priests took up the ark of the LORD.
13 Then seven priests bearing seven trumpets of rams' horns before the ark of the LORD
went on continually and blew with the trumpets. And the armed men went before them.
But the rear guard came after the ark of the
LORD, while *the priests* continued blowing the
trumpets.
14 And the second day they marched around
the city once and returned to the camp. So
they did six days.
15 But it came to pass on the seventh day that
they rose early, about the dawning of the day,
and marched around the city seven times in
the same manner. On that day only they
marched around the city seven times.
16 And the seventh time it happened, when
the priests blew the trumpets, that Joshua
said to the people: "Shout, for the LORD has
given you the city!
17 "Now the city shall be doomed by the
LORD to destruction, it and all who *are* in it.
Only Rahab the harlot shall live, she and all
who *are* with her in the house, because she
hid the messengers that we sent.
18 "And you, by all means abstain from
the accursed things, lest you become accursed when you take of the accursed things,
and make the camp of Israel a curse, and
trouble it.
19 "But all the silver and gold, and vessels of
bronze and iron, *are* consecrated to the LORD;
they shall come into the treasury of the
LORD."
20 So the people shouted when *the priests*
blew the trumpets. And it happened when the
people heard the sound of the trumpet, and
the people shouted with a great shout, that
the wall fell down flat. Then the people went
up into the city, every man straight before
him, and they took the city.
21 And they utterly destroyed all that *was* in
the city, both man and woman, young and old,
ox and sheep and donkey, with the edge of the
sword.
22 But Joshua had said to the two men who
had spied out the country, "Go into the harlot's house, and from there bring out the
woman and all that she has, as you swore to
her."
23 And the young men who had been spies
went in and brought out Rahab, her father,
her mother, her brothers, and all that she had.
So they brought out all her relatives and left
them outside the camp of Israel.
24 But they burned the city and all that *was*
in it with fire. Only the silver and gold, and
the vessels of bronze and iron, they put into
the treasury of the house of the LORD.
25 And Joshua spared Rahab the harlot, her
father's household, and all that she had. So
she dwells in Israel to this day, because she
hid the messengers whom Joshua sent to spy
out Jericho.
26 Then Joshua charged *them* at that time,
saying, "Cursed *be* the man before the LORD
who rises up and builds this city Jericho;
he shall lay its foundation with his firstborn,
and with his youngest he shall set up its
gates."
27 So the LORD was with Joshua, and his
fame spread throughout all the country.

Defeat at Ai

7 But the children of Israel committed a
trespass regarding the accursed things,
for Achan the son of Carmi, the son of Zabdi,[a]
the son of Zerah, of the tribe of Judah, took
of the accursed things; so the anger of
the LORD burned against the children of Israel.
2 Now Joshua sent men from Jericho to Ai,
which *is* beside Beth Aven, on the east side of
Bethel, and spoke to them, saying, "Go up and
spy out the country." So the men went up and
spied out Ai.
3 And they returned to Joshua and said to
him, "Do not let all the people go up, but let
about two or three thousand men go up and
attack Ai. Do not weary all the people there,
for *the people of Ai are* few."
4 So about three thousand men went up
there from the people, but they fled before the
men of Ai.

7:1 [a]Called *Zimri* in 1 Chronicles 2:6

LIFE LESSONS

➤ 6:26 — *"Cursed be the man before the LORD who rises up and builds this city Jericho; he shall lay its foundation with his firstborn, and with his youngest he shall set up its gates."*

The curse of Joshua on Jericho came into force many centuries later in the time of King Ahab, when a man named Hiel rebuilt it—at the very cost prophesied by Joshua (1 Kin. 16:34).

WHAT THE BIBLE SAYS ABOUT **HOW LISTENING SPARES US PAIN**

Josh. 7:1–13

Listening well does more than give us necessary information. Sometimes it spells the difference between success and failure, joy and sorrow, pleasure and pain. The failure to listen can cause us a great deal of heartache.

A good example of this is found in Joshua 7:1–13. Immediately after God gave the Israelites a great victory at Jericho, Joshua sent some men to spy out the little town of Ai, and then sent a small force to take it. Although Ai paled in size to Jericho, the Israelites were soundly defeated in a serious setback that caused grief and fear throughout the Israelite camp.

What differed in the two campaigns?

First, God gave Joshua an order to defeat Jericho and promised that He would give the city into Joshua's hand. Second, God gave Joshua the military strategy by which the victory could be won (see Josh. 6). The victory was God's, and He received full glory for it.

The failure to listen can cause us a great deal of heartache.

God no doubt had a battle plan for Ai, but Joshua didn't ask to hear it. Instead he sent out spies, and when they came back with a report that Ai could easily be taken, he dispatched a few thousand men without consulting God. He relied solely on human opinion.

In addition, God had commanded that the people not touch the "accursed things" of Jericho—items considered unclean according to the Law, including various personal effects. They were to take only the silver, gold, bronze, and iron vessels for the house of the Lord, and burn the rest (Josh. 6:18). A man named Achan did not obey. He brought accursed things into the camp, including a beautiful Babylonian garment. He also took two hundred shekels of silver and wedges of gold for himself, burying them in the ground beneath his tent.

Had Joshua listened for the Lord's counsel before moving against Ai, no doubt God would have revealed to him Achan's sin. The problem could have and should have been resolved before the assault on Ai. If it had been, no doubt the Israelites would have enjoyed another great success, again without any loss of Israelite life.

See the Life Principles Index for further study:
13. Listening to God is essential to walking with God.

➤ 5 And the men of Ai struck down about
thirty-six men, for they chased them *from* before the gate as far as Shebarim, and struck
them down on the descent; therefore the hearts
of the people melted and became like water.
6 Then Joshua tore his clothes, and fell to
the earth on his face before the ark of the
LORD until evening, he and the elders of Israel; and they put dust on their heads.
7 And Joshua said, "Alas, Lord GOD, why
have You brought this people over the Jordan
at all—to deliver us into the hand of the
Amorites, to destroy us? Oh, that we had been
content, and dwelt on the other side of the
Jordan!
8 "O Lord, what shall I say when Israel turns
its back before its enemies?
9 For the Canaanites and all the inhabitants
of the land will hear *it*, and surround us, and
cut off our name from the earth. Then what
will You do for Your great name?"

The Sin of Achan
10 So the LORD said to Joshua: "Get up! Why
do you lie thus on your face?
11 "Israel has sinned, and they have also
transgressed My covenant which I commanded them. For they have even taken some
of the accursed things, and have both stolen
and deceived; and they have also put *it*
among their own stuff.
12 "Therefore the children of Israel could not
stand before their enemies, *but* turned *their*
backs before their enemies, because they
have become doomed to destruction. Neither
will I be with you anymore, unless you destroy the accursed from among you.
➤ 13 "Get up, sanctify the people, and say, 'Sanctify yourselves for tomorrow, because thus
says the LORD God of Israel: "*There is* an accursed thing in your midst, O Israel; you cannot stand before your enemies until you take
away the accursed thing from among you."
14 "In the morning therefore you shall be
brought according to your tribes. And it shall
be *that* the tribe which the LORD takes shall
come according to families; and the family
which the LORD takes shall come by households; and the household which the LORD
takes shall come man by man.
15 Then it shall be *that* he who is taken with
the accursed thing shall be burned with fire,
he and all that he has, because he has transgressed the covenant of the LORD, and because he has done a disgraceful thing in
Israel.'"
16 So Joshua rose early in the morning and
brought Israel by their tribes, and the tribe of
Judah was taken.
17 He brought the clan of Judah, and he took
the family of the Zarhites; and he brought the
family of the Zarhites man by man, and Zabdi
was taken.
18 Then he brought his household man by
man, and Achan the son of Carmi, the son of
Zabdi, the son of Zerah, of the tribe of Judah,
was taken.
19 Now Joshua said to Achan, "My son, I beg
you, give glory to the LORD God of Israel, and
make confession to Him, and tell me now
what you have done; do not hide *it* from me."
20 And Achan answered Joshua and said,
"Indeed I have sinned against the LORD God
of Israel, and this is what I have done:
21 "When I saw among the spoils a beautiful ◄
Babylonian garment, two hundred shekels of
silver, and a wedge of gold weighing fifty
shekels, I coveted them and took them. And
there they are, hidden in the earth in the
midst of my tent, with the silver under it."
22 So Joshua sent messengers, and they ran
to the tent; and there it was, hidden in his
tent, with the silver under it.
23 And they took them from the midst of the
tent, brought them to Joshua and to all the
children of Israel, and laid them out before
the LORD.
24 Then Joshua, and all Israel with him, took ◄

LIFE LESSONS

➤ 7:5 — *And the men of Ai struck down about thirty-six men . . . therefore the hearts of the people melted and became like water.*

Thirty-six soldiers of Israel died in a failed attack on the little town of Ai because the people had not inquired of the Lord before they acted. Prayer is life's greatest time saver—and often a life saver as well.

➤ 7:13 — *"Sanctify yourselves for tomorrow, because thus says the LORD God of Israel: 'There is an accursed thing in your midst, O Israel . . . .'"*

There is a time for prayer, and there is a time for action. Because Joshua missed his time of prayer, God required him to take swift, decisive, and sobering action to rid the camp of sin.

➤ 7:21 — *"When I saw among the spoils a beautiful Babylonian garment, two hundred shekels of silver, and a wedge of gold weighing fifty shekels, I coveted them and took them . . . ."*

Sin begins in the heart. Achan's problems began when he broke the last commandment about coveting, the very sin the apostle Paul noted in himself (Rom. 7:7). It takes God's Spirit within us to create a new, obedient heart.

➤ 7:24 — *Then Joshua, and all Israel with him, took Achan the son of Zerah, the silver, the garment, the wedge of gold, his sons, his daughters . . . and all that he had, and they brought them to the Valley of Achor.*

If God punishes each man for his own sins, then why did Israel execute Achan's whole family? Apparently his family knew about his illicit acquisitions, but they kept quiet and so shared his guilt.

ANSWERS TO LIFE'S QUESTIONS

How should I respond to failure or setbacks?

JOSH. 7:6–15

When the men of Israel returned in defeat at Ai, Joshua needed some answers and so turned immediately to prayer. He tore his garments, an act of grief, and fell on his face in humiliation before the ark of the covenant until nightfall. All of the elders joined him. Joshua cried out to God, "Why did You do this to us?"

Joshua asked the wrong question—a question many of us ask when unexpected trouble strikes. Our first impulse is often to blame God for the tragedy or problem that overwhelms us. We cry out, "Why me? What did I do to deserve this? Why did You allow me to get in this mess?" Usually, these are exactly the wrong questions to ask. Consider a few more appropriate questions: "What may I have done wrong? What can I do to correct this situation?"

Sometimes we need to change a habit or correct a bad attitude. We may need to confront our own sin and errors. God is usually far from the cause of our trouble. We human beings are at fault, either collectively or individually.

When Joshua ceased pouring out his hurt, frustration, and questions, God said, "Get up! Why are you lying on your face? Israel has sinned and that is the reason for your defeat."

When we go to God in prayer, we must be willing to hear what He says. Often, we never stop to listen to Him. We must learn to wait when we voice our petitions, to hear His response.

This is especially true when we pray in the aftermath of a setback or defeat. It is also vitally important that we do this anytime we find ourselves blaming God for our troubles. We must be willing to listen for His explanation, which often includes a correction.

Once the Lord reveals to us what we need to do, the time for prayer has ended. Nothing more needs to be said—no excuses, no attempts to justify what we have done. We must accept what the Lord says and immediately move to obey Him. Our obedience may include asking Him to forgive us and to help us to obey Him in the future. But our obedience must follow quickly. Usually this requires that we make amends or take specific actions that will help right the wrong.

See the Life Principles Index for further study:

11. God assumes full responsibility for our needs when we obey Him.

15. Brokenness is God's requirement for maximum usefulness.

Achan the son of Zerah, the silver, the garment, the wedge of gold, his sons, his daughters, his oxen, his donkeys, his sheep, his tent, and all that he had, and they brought them to the Valley of Achor.
25 And Joshua said, "Why have you troubled us? The LORD will trouble you this day." So all Israel stoned him with stones; and they burned them with fire after they had stoned them with stones.
26 Then they raised over him a great heap of stones, still there to this day. So the LORD turned from the fierceness of His anger. Therefore the name of that place has been called the Valley of Achor[a] to this day.

The Fall of Ai

8 Now the LORD said to Joshua: "Do not be afraid, nor be dismayed; take all the people of war with you, and arise, go up to Ai. See, I have given into your hand the king of Ai, his people, his city, and his land.
2 "And you shall do to Ai and its king as you did to Jericho and its king. Only its spoil and its cattle you shall take as booty for yourselves. Lay an ambush for the city behind it."
3 So Joshua arose, and all the people of war, to go up against Ai; and Joshua chose thirty thousand mighty men of valor and sent them away by night.
4 And he commanded them, saying: "Behold, you shall lie in ambush against the city, behind the city. Do not go very far from the city, but all of you be ready.
5 "Then I and all the people who *are* with me will approach the city; and it will come about, when they come out against us as at the first, that we shall flee before them.
6 "For they will come out after us till we have drawn them from the city, for they will say, '*They are* fleeing before us as at the first.' Therefore we will flee before them.
7 "Then you shall rise from the ambush and seize the city, for the LORD your God will deliver it into your hand.

7:26 [a]Literally *Trouble*

8 And it will be, when you have taken the city, *that* you shall set the city on fire. According to the commandment of the LORD you shall do. See, I have commanded you."
9 Joshua therefore sent them out; and they went to lie in ambush, and stayed between Bethel and Ai, on the west side of Ai; but Joshua lodged that night among the people.
10 Then Joshua rose up early in the morning and mustered the people, and went up, he and the elders of Israel, before the people to Ai.
11 And all the people of war who *were* with him went up and drew near; and they came before the city and camped on the north side of Ai. Now a valley *lay* between them and Ai.
12 So he took about five thousand men and set them in ambush between Bethel and Ai, on the west side of the city.
13 And when they had set the people, all the army that *was* on the north of the city, and its rear guard on the west of the city, Joshua went that night into the midst of the valley.
14 Now it happened, when the king of Ai saw *it,* that the men of the city hurried and rose early and went out against Israel to battle, he and all his people, at an appointed place before the plain. But he did not know that *there was* an ambush against him behind the city.
15 And Joshua and all Israel made as if they were beaten before them, and fled by the way of the wilderness.
16 So all the people who *were* in Ai were called together to pursue them. And they pursued Joshua and were drawn away from the city.
17 There was not a man left in Ai or Bethel who did not go out after Israel. So they left the city open and pursued Israel.
18 Then the LORD said to Joshua, "Stretch out the spear that *is* in your hand toward Ai, for I will give it into your hand." And Joshua stretched out the spear that *was* in his hand toward the city.
19 So *those in* ambush arose quickly out of their place; they ran as soon as he had stretched out his hand, and they entered the city and took it, and hurried to set the city on fire.
20 And when the men of Ai looked behind them, they saw, and behold, the smoke of the city ascended to heaven. So they had no power to flee this way or that way, and the people who had fled to the wilderness turned back on the pursuers.
21 Now when Joshua and all Israel saw that the ambush had taken the city and that the smoke of the city ascended, they turned back and struck down the men of Ai.
22 Then the others came out of the city against them; so they were *caught* in the midst of Israel, some on this side and some on that side. And they struck them down, so that they let none of them remain or escape.
23 But the king of Ai they took alive, and brought him to Joshua.
24 And it came to pass when Israel had made an end of slaying all the inhabitants of Ai in the field, in the wilderness where they pursued them, and when they all had fallen by the edge of the sword until they were consumed, that all the Israelites returned to Ai and struck it with the edge of the sword.
25 So it was *that* all who fell that day, both men and women, *were* twelve thousand—all the people of Ai.
26 For Joshua did not draw back his hand, with which he stretched out the spear, until he had utterly destroyed all the inhabitants of Ai.
27 Only the livestock and the spoil of that city Israel took as booty for themselves, according to the word of the LORD which He had commanded Joshua.
28 So Joshua burned Ai and made it a heap forever, a desolation to this day.
29 And the king of Ai he hanged on a tree until evening. And as soon as the sun was down, Joshua commanded that they should take his corpse down from the tree, cast it at the entrance of the gate of the city, and raise over it a great heap of stones *that remains* to this day.

Joshua Renews the Covenant

30 Now Joshua built an altar to the LORD God of Israel in Mount Ebal,
31 as Moses the servant of the LORD had commanded the children of Israel, as it is written in the Book of the Law of Moses: "an altar of whole stones over which no man has wielded an iron *tool.*"[a] And they offered on it burnt offerings to the LORD, and sacrificed peace offerings.
32 And there, in the presence of the children of Israel, he wrote on the stones a copy of the law of Moses, which he had written.
33 Then all Israel, with their elders and officers and judges, stood on either side of the

8:31 [a]Deuteronomy 27:5, 6

LIFE LESSONS

➤ ***8:2 — And you shall do to Ai and its king as you did to Jericho and its king. Only its spoil and its cattle you shall take as booty for yourselves. Lay an ambush for the city behind it.***

The divine plan to take Ai looked quite different from the one to capture Jericho. God guides us along various paths—our job is to listen for His voice and to obey whatever He tells us.

ark before the priests, the Levites, who bore
the ark of the covenant of the LORD, the stranger as well as he who was born among them.
Half of them *were* in front of Mount Gerizim
and half of them in front of Mount Ebal, as
Moses the servant of the LORD had commanded before, that they should bless the
people of Israel.
34 And afterward he read all the words of the
law, the blessings and the cursings, according
to all that is written in the Book of the Law.
➤ 35 There was not a word of all that Moses
had commanded which Joshua did not read
before all the assembly of Israel, with the
women, the little ones, and the strangers who
were living among them.

The Treaty with the Gibeonites

9 And it came to pass when all the kings
who *were* on this side of the Jordan, in the
hills and in the lowland and in all the coasts
of the Great Sea toward Lebanon—the Hittite,
the Amorite, the Canaanite, the Perizzite, the
Hivite, and the Jebusite—heard *about it,*
2 that they gathered together to fight with
Joshua and Israel with one accord.
3 But when the inhabitants of Gibeon heard
what Joshua had done to Jericho and Ai,
4 they worked craftily, and went and pretended to be ambassadors. And they took old
sacks on their donkeys, old wineskins torn
and mended,
5 old and patched sandals on their feet, and
old garments on themselves; and all the bread
of their provision was dry *and* moldy.
6 And they went to Joshua, to the camp at
Gilgal, and said to him and to the men of Israel, "We have come from a far country; now
therefore, make a covenant with us."
7 Then the men of Israel said to the Hivites,
"Perhaps you dwell among us; so how can we
make a covenant with you?"
8 But they said to Joshua, "We *are* your servants." And Joshua said to them, "Who *are*
you, and where do you come from?"
9 So they said to him: "From a very far
country your servants have come, because of
the name of the LORD your God; for we have
heard of His fame, and all that He did in
Egypt,
10 "and all that He did to the two kings of the
Amorites who *were* beyond the Jordan—to
Sihon king of Heshbon, and Og king of
Bashan, who was at Ashtaroth.
11 "Therefore our elders and all the inhabitants of our country spoke to us, saying, 'Take
provisions with you for the journey, and go to
meet them, and say to them, "We *are* your servants; now therefore, make a covenant with
us." '
12 "This bread of ours we took hot *for* our
provision from our houses on the day we departed to come to you. But now look, it is dry
and moldy.
13 And these wineskins which we filled *were*
new, and see, they are torn; and these our garments and our sandals have become old because of the very long journey."
14 Then the men of Israel took some of their ➤
provisions; but they did not ask counsel of the
LORD.
15 So Joshua made peace with them, and
made a covenant with them to let them live;
and the rulers of the congregation swore to
them.
16 And it happened at the end of three days,
after they had made a covenant with them,
that they heard that they *were* their neighbors
who dwelt near them.
17 Then the children of Israel journeyed and
came to their cities on the third day. Now
their cities *were* Gibeon, Chephirah, Beeroth,
and Kirjath Jearim.
18 But the children of Israel did not attack
them, because the rulers of the congregation
had sworn to them by the LORD God of Israel.
And all the congregation complained against
the rulers.
19 Then all the rulers said to all the congre- ➤
gation, "We have sworn to them by the LORD
God of Israel; now therefore, we may not
touch them.
20 "This we will do to them: We will let them
live, lest wrath be upon us because of the oath
which we swore to them."
21 And the rulers said to them, "Let them
live, but let them be woodcutters and water
carriers for all the congregation, as the rulers
had promised them."
22 Then Joshua called for them, and he

LIFE LESSONS

➤ **8:35 — *There was not a word of all that Moses had commanded which Joshua did not read before all the assembly of Israel, with the women, the little ones, and the strangers who were living among them.***

Every word of God is precious and important and worthy of our attention (see Matt. 5:18). We are to pay attention to "the whole counsel of God" (Acts 20:27).

➤ **9:14 — *Then the men of Israel took some of their provisions; but they did not ask counsel of the LORD.***

How often do we get ourselves into trouble because we fail to "ask counsel of the LORD"? Prayer is life's greatest time saver—and trouble saver!

➤ **9:19 — *Then all the rulers said to all the congregation, "We have sworn to them by the LORD God of Israel; now therefore, we may not touch them."***

Israel's leaders erred in failing to ask God about the Gibeonites, but they did right in recognizing the serious and solemn act of taking an oath in God's name. God does not take lightly His reputation, and neither should we.

spoke to them, saying, "Why have you deceived us, saying, 'We *are* very far from you,'
when you dwell near us?
23 "Now therefore, you *are* cursed, and none
of you shall be freed from being slaves—
woodcutters and water carriers for the house
of my God."
24 So they answered Joshua and said, "Because your servants were clearly told that the
LORD your God commanded His servant Moses to give you all the land, and to destroy all
the inhabitants of the land from before you;
therefore we were very much afraid for our
lives because of you, and have done this
thing.
25 And now, here we are, in your hands; do
with us as it seems good and right to do to us."
26 So he did to them, and delivered them out
of the hand of the children of Israel, so that
they did not kill them.
27 And that day Joshua made them woodcutters and water carriers for the congregation
and for the altar of the LORD, in the place
which He would choose, even to this day.

The Sun Stands Still

10 Now it came to pass when Adoni-
Zedek king of Jerusalem heard how
Joshua had taken Ai and had utterly destroyed it—as he had done to Jericho and its
king, so he had done to Ai and its king—and
how the inhabitants of Gibeon had made
peace with Israel and were among them,
2 that they feared greatly, because Gibeon
was a great city, like one of the royal cities,
and because it *was* greater than Ai, and all its
men *were* mighty.
3 Therefore Adoni-Zedek king of Jerusalem
sent to Hoham king of Hebron, Piram king of
Jarmuth, Japhia king of Lachish, and Debir
king of Eglon, saying,
4 "Come up to me and help me, that we may
attack Gibeon, for it has made peace with
Joshua and with the children of Israel."
5 Therefore the five kings of the Amorites,
the king of Jerusalem, the king of Hebron, the
king of Jarmuth, the king of Lachish, *and* the
king of Eglon, gathered together and went up,
they and all their armies, and camped before
Gibeon and made war against it.
6 And the men of Gibeon sent to Joshua at
the camp at Gilgal, saying, "Do not forsake
your servants; come up to us quickly, save us
and help us, for all the kings of the Amorites
who dwell in the mountains have gathered together against us."
7 So Joshua ascended from Gilgal, he and
all the people of war with him, and all the
mighty men of valor.
8 And the LORD said to Joshua, "Do not fear
them, for I have delivered them into your
hand; not a man of them shall stand before
you."
9 Joshua therefore came upon them suddenly, having marched all night from Gilgal.
10 So the LORD routed them before Israel,
killed them with a great slaughter at Gibeon,
chased them along the road that goes to Beth
Horon, and struck them down as far as
Azekah and Makkedah.
11 And it happened, as they fled before Israel
and were on the descent of Beth Horon, that
the LORD cast down large hailstones from
heaven on them as far as Azekah, and they
died. *There were* more who died from the
hailstones than the children of Israel killed
with the sword.
12 Then Joshua spoke to the LORD in the day
when the LORD delivered up the Amorites before the children of Israel, and he said in the
sight of Israel:

"Sun, stand still over Gibeon;
And Moon, in the Valley of Aijalon."
13 So the sun stood still,
And the moon stopped,
Till the people had revenge
Upon their enemies.

Is this not written in the Book of Jasher? So
the sun stood still in the midst of heaven, and
did not hasten to go *down* for about a whole
day.
14 And there has been no day like that, before it or after it, that the LORD heeded the
voice of a man; for the LORD fought for Israel.
15 Then Joshua returned, and all Israel with
him, to the camp at Gilgal.

The Amorite Kings Executed

16 But these five kings had fled and hidden
themselves in a cave at Makkedah.
17 And it was told Joshua, saying, "The five
kings have been found hidden in the cave at
Makkedah."

LIFE LESSONS

➤ 10:11 — *. . . the LORD cast down large hailstones from heaven on them as far as Azekah, and they died. There were more who died from the hailstones than the children of Israel killed with the sword.*

God invites us to partner with Him in the work of His kingdom, but we must never forget that we are very much the junior partners.

➤ 10:12, 13 — *Then Joshua spoke to the LORD . . . and he said in the sight of Israel: "Sun, stand still over Gibeon; and Moon, in the Valley of Aijalon."*

We do not know how God accomplished this great miracle; we know only that He did it in response to believing prayer. When we fight our battles on our knees, we win every time.

18 So Joshua said, "Roll large stones against
the mouth of the cave, and set men by it to
guard them.
19 "And do not stay *there* yourselves, *but*
pursue your enemies, and attack their rear
guard. Do not allow them to enter their cities,
for the LORD your God has delivered them
into your hand."
20 Then it happened, while Joshua and the
children of Israel made an end of slaying
them with a very great slaughter, till they had
finished, that those who escaped entered fortified cities.
21 And all the people returned to the camp, to
Joshua at Makkedah, in peace. No one moved
his tongue against any of the children of Israel.
22 Then Joshua said, "Open the mouth of the
cave, and bring out those five kings to me
from the cave."
23 And they did so, and brought out those five
kings to him from the cave: the king of Jerusalem, the king of Hebron, the king of Jarmuth,
the king of Lachish, *and* the king of Eglon.
24 So it was, when they brought out those
kings to Joshua, that Joshua called for all the
men of Israel, and said to the captains of the
men of war who went with him, "Come near,
put your feet on the necks of these kings."
And they drew near and put their feet on their
necks.
➤ 25 Then Joshua said to them, "Do not be
afraid, nor be dismayed; be strong and of
good courage, for thus the LORD will do to all
your enemies against whom you fight."
26 And afterward Joshua struck them and
killed them, and hanged them on five trees;
and they were hanging on the trees until
evening.
27 So it was at the time of the going down of
the sun *that* Joshua commanded, and they
took them down from the trees, cast them into
the cave where they had been hidden, and
laid large stones against the cave's mouth,
which remain until this very day.

Conquest of the Southland

28 On that day Joshua took Makkedah, and
struck it and its king with the edge of the
sword. He utterly destroyed them[a]—all the
people who *were* in it. He let none remain. He
also did to the king of Makkedah as he had
done to the king of Jericho.
29 Then Joshua passed from Makkedah, and
all Israel with him, to Libnah; and they fought
against Libnah.
30 And the LORD also delivered it and its king
into the hand of Israel; he struck it and all the
people who *were* in it with the edge of the
sword. He let none remain in it, but did to its
king as he had done to the king of Jericho.
31 Then Joshua passed from Libnah, and all
Israel with him, to Lachish; and they encamped against it and fought against it.
32 And the LORD delivered Lachish into the
hand of Israel, who took it on the second day,
and struck it and all the people who *were* in it
with the edge of the sword, according to all
that he had done to Libnah.
33 Then Horam king of Gezer came up to
help Lachish; and Joshua struck him and his
people, until he left him none remaining.
34 From Lachish Joshua passed to Eglon,
and all Israel with him; and they encamped
against it and fought against it.
35 They took it on that day and struck it with
the edge of the sword; all the people who
were in it he utterly destroyed that day, according to all that he had done to Lachish.
36 So Joshua went up from Eglon, and all Israel with him, to Hebron; and they fought
against it.
37 And they took it and struck it with the
edge of the sword—its king, all its cities, and
all the people who *were* in it; he left none remaining, according to all that he had done to
Eglon, but utterly destroyed it and all the people who *were* in it.
38 Then Joshua returned, and all Israel with
him, to Debir; and they fought against it.
39 And he took it and its king and all its
cities; they struck them with the edge of the
sword and utterly destroyed all the people
who *were* in it. He left none remaining; as he
had done to Hebron, so he did to Debir and its
king, as he had done also to Libnah and its
king.
40 So Joshua conquered all the land: the ◄

10:28 [a]Following Masoretic Text and most authorities; many Hebrew manuscripts, some manuscripts of the Septuagint, and some manuscripts of the Targum read *it.*

LIFE LESSONS

➤ **10:25 — *Then Joshua said to them, "Do not be afraid, nor be dismayed; be strong and of good courage, for thus the LORD will do to all your enemies against whom you fight."***

At the beginning of his military career, Joshua needed to be encouraged by his people (see Josh. 1:18). Now he returns the favor and encourages them. We need each other more than we know.

➤ **10:40 — *So Joshua conquered all the land . . . and all their kings; he left none remaining, but utterly destroyed all that breathed, as the LORD God of Israel had commanded.***

A story like the annihilation of the Canaanites often makes us wince, but it illustrates God's implacable hatred of sin. God destroyed those nations due to sin (Gen. 15:16; Deut. 9:5). Sin always brings His wrath.

mountain country and the South[a] and the
lowland and the wilderness slopes, and all
their kings; he left none remaining, but utterly destroyed all that breathed, as the LORD
God of Israel had commanded.
41 And Joshua conquered them from Kadesh
Barnea as far as Gaza, and all the country of
Goshen, even as far as Gibeon.
42 All these kings and their land Joshua took
at one time, because the LORD God of Israel
fought for Israel.
43 Then Joshua returned, and all Israel with
him, to the camp at Gilgal.

The Northern Conquest

11 And it came to pass, when Jabin king
of Hazor heard *these things,* that he
sent to Jobab king of Madon, to the king of
Shimron, to the king of Achshaph,
2 and to the kings who *were* from the north,
in the mountains, in the plain south of Chinneroth, in the lowland, and in the heights of
Dor on the west,
3 to the Canaanites in the east and in the
west, the Amorite, the Hittite, the Perizzite,
the Jebusite in the mountains, and the Hivite
below Hermon in the land of Mizpah.
4 So they went out, they and all their armies
with them, *as* many people *as* the sand that *is*
on the seashore in multitude, with very many
horses and chariots.
5 And when all these kings had met together, they came and camped together at the
waters of Merom to fight against Israel.
6 But the LORD said to Joshua, "Do not be
afraid because of them, for tomorrow about
this time I will deliver all of them slain before
Israel. You shall hamstring their horses and
burn their chariots with fire."
7 So Joshua and all the people of war with
him came against them suddenly by the waters of Merom, and they attacked them.
8 And the LORD delivered them into the
hand of Israel, who defeated them and chased
them to Greater Sidon, to the Brook Misrephoth,[a] and to the Valley of Mizpah eastward; they attacked them until they left none
of them remaining.
9 So Joshua did to them as the LORD had
told him: he hamstrung their horses and
burned their chariots with fire.
10 Joshua turned back at that time and took
Hazor, and struck its king with the sword; for
Hazor was formerly the head of all those
kingdoms.
11 And they struck all the people who *were*
in it with the edge of the sword, utterly destroying *them.* There was none left breathing.
Then he burned Hazor with fire.
12 So all the cities of those kings, and all
their kings, Joshua took and struck with the
edge of the sword. He utterly destroyed them,
as Moses the servant of the LORD had commanded.
13 But *as for* the cities that stood on their
mounds,[a] Israel burned none of them, except
Hazor only, *which* Joshua burned.
14 And all the spoil of these cities and the
livestock, the children of Israel took as booty
for themselves; but they struck every man
with the edge of the sword until they had destroyed them, and they left none breathing.
15 As the LORD had commanded Moses his
servant, so Moses commanded Joshua, and so
Joshua did. He left nothing undone of all that
the LORD had commanded Moses.

Summary of Joshua's Conquests

16 Thus Joshua took all this land: the mountain country, all the South, all the land of
Goshen, the lowland, and the Jordan plain[a]—
the mountains of Israel and its lowlands,
17 from Mount Halak and the ascent to Seir,
even as far as Baal Gad in the Valley of Lebanon below Mount Hermon. He captured all
their kings, and struck them down and killed
them.
18 Joshua made war a long time with all
those kings.
19 There was not a city that made peace with
the children of Israel, except the Hivites, the
inhabitants of Gibeon. All *the others* they
took in battle.
20 For it was of the LORD to harden their
hearts, that they should come against Israel in
battle, that He might utterly destroy them,
and that they might receive no mercy, but that
He might destroy them, as the LORD had commanded Moses.
21 And at that time Joshua came and cut off
the Anakim from the mountains: from Hebron, from Debir, from Anab, from all the

10:40 [a]Hebrew *Negev,* and so throughout this book
11:8 [a]Hebrew *Misrephoth Maim* **11:13** [a]Hebrew *tel,* a heap of successive city ruins **11:16** [a]Hebrew *arabah*

LIFE LESSONS

➤ **11:11 — *And they struck all the people who were in it with the edge of the sword, utterly destroying them. There was none left breathing. Then he burned Hazor with fire.***

Unreserved and total obedience leads to unreserved and total blessing. See verse 23.

➤ **11:20 — *For it was of the LORD to harden their hearts, that they should come against Israel in battle, that He might utterly destroy them . . . .***

Our sovereign God hardens the hearts of some so that He might execute His judgment on them. He can take even opposition and use it for His glory and our benefit.

mountains of Judah, and from all the mountains of Israel; Joshua utterly destroyed them
with their cities.
22 None of the Anakim were left in the land
of the children of Israel; they remained only
in Gaza, in Gath, and in Ashdod.
➤ 23 So Joshua took the whole land, according
to all that the LORD had said to Moses; and
Joshua gave it as an inheritance to Israel according to their divisions by their tribes. Then
the land rested from war.

The Kings Conquered by Moses

12 These *are* the kings of the land whom
the children of Israel defeated, and
whose land they possessed on the other side
of the Jordan toward the rising of the sun,
from the River Arnon to Mount Hermon, and
all the eastern Jordan plain:
2 *One king was* Sihon king of the Amorites,
who dwelt in Heshbon *and* ruled half of
Gilead, from Aroer, which is on the bank of
the River Arnon, from the middle of that river,
even as far as the River Jabbok, *which is* the
border of the Ammonites,
3 and the eastern Jordan plain from the Sea
of Chinneroth as far as the Sea of the Arabah
(the Salt Sea), the road to Beth Jeshimoth,
and southward below the slopes of Pisgah.
4 *The other king was* Og king of Bashan and
his territory, *who was* of the remnant of the giants, who dwelt at Ashtaroth and at Edrei,
5 and reigned over Mount Hermon, over
Salcah, over all Bashan, as far as the border
of the Geshurites and the Maachathites, and
over half of Gilead *to* the border of Sihon
king of Heshbon.
➤ 6 These Moses the servant of the LORD and
the children of Israel had conquered; and Moses the servant of the LORD had given it *as* a
possession to the Reubenites, the Gadites,
and half the tribe of Manasseh.

The Kings Conquered by Joshua

7 And these *are* the kings of the country
which Joshua and the children of Israel conquered on this side of the Jordan, on the west,
from Baal Gad in the Valley of Lebanon as far
as Mount Halak and the ascent to Seir, which
Joshua gave to the tribes of Israel *as* a possession according to their divisions,
8 in the mountain country, in the lowlands,
in the *Jordan* plain, in the slopes, in the
wilderness, and in the South—the Hittites,
the Amorites, the Canaanites, the Perizzites,
the Hivites, and the Jebusites:
9 the king of Jericho, one; the king of Ai,
which *is* beside Bethel, one;
10 the king of Jerusalem, one; the king of
Hebron, one;
11 the king of Jarmuth, one; the king of Lachish, one;
12 the king of Eglon, one; the king of Gezer,
one;
13 the king of Debir, one; the king of Geder,
one;
14 the king of Hormah, one; the king of Arad,
one;
15 the king of Libnah, one; the king of Adullam, one;
16 the king of Makkedah, one; the king of
Bethel, one;
17 the king of Tappuah, one; the king of Hepher, one;
18 the king of Aphek, one; the king of
Lasharon, one;
19 the king of Madon, one; the king of Hazor,
one;
20 the king of Shimron Meron, one; the king
of Achshaph, one;
21 the king of Taanach, one; the king of
Megiddo, one;
22 the king of Kedesh, one; the king of
Jokneam in Carmel, one;
23 the king of Dor in the heights of Dor, one;
the king of the people of Gilgal, one;
24 the king of Tirzah, one—all the kings,
thirty-one.

Remaining Land to Be Conquered

13 Now Joshua was old, advanced in ◄
years. And the LORD said to him: "You
are old, advanced in years, and there remains
very much land yet to be possessed.

LIFE LESSONS

➤ 11:23 — *So Joshua took the whole land, according to all that the LORD had said to Moses; and Joshua gave it as an inheritance to Israel according to their divisions by their tribes . . . .*

Sometimes God doesn't keep His promises when or how we thought He would. God told Moses that Israel would take possession of the Promised Land, and that's just what happened—in God's way and in God's timing.

➤ 12:6 — *These Moses the servant of the LORD and the children of Israel had conquered; and Moses the servant of the LORD had given it as a possession to the Reubenites, the Gadites, and half the tribe of Manasseh.*

It is wise to rehearse the spiritual victories God gives us. We do well to periodically remind ourselves of the truth we already know, so that we do not forget and act foolishly (see 2 Pet. 1:12).

➤ 13:1 — *. . . And the LORD said to him: "You are old, advanced in years, and there remains very much land yet to be possessed."*

We may sometimes try to paint God in sentimental hues, but He remains as forthright, honest and unsentimental as always. He tells us the truth, not to hurt us, but to ground us in reality.

2 "This is the land that yet remains: all the
territory of the Philistines and all *that of* the
Geshurites,
3 "from Sihor, which *is* east of Egypt, as far
as the border of Ekron northward (*which* is
counted as Canaanite); the five lords of the
Philistines—the Gazites, the Ashdodites, the
Ashkelonites, the Gittites, and the Ekronites;
also the Avites;
4 "from the south, all the land of the
Canaanites, and Mearah that belongs to the
Sidonians as far as Aphek, to the border of
the Amorites;
5 "the land of the Gebalites,[a] and all Lebanon, toward the sunrise, from Baal Gad below
Mount Hermon as far as the entrance to
Hamath;
6 "all the inhabitants of the mountains from
Lebanon as far as the Brook Misrephoth,[a] *and*
all the Sidonians—them I will drive out from
before the children of Israel; only divide it by
lot to Israel as an inheritance, as I have commanded you.
7 "Now therefore, divide this land as an inheritance to the nine tribes and half the tribe
of Manasseh."

The Land Divided East of the Jordan

8 With the other half-tribe the Reubenites
and the Gadites received their inheritance,
which Moses had given them, beyond the Jordan eastward, as Moses the servant of the
LORD had given them:
9 from Aroer which *is* on the bank of the
River Arnon, and the town that *is* in the midst
of the ravine, and all the plain of Medeba as
far as Dibon;
10 all the cities of Sihon king of the Amorites,
who reigned in Heshbon, as far as the border
of the children of Ammon;
11 Gilead, and the border of the Geshurites
and Maachathites, all Mount Hermon, and all
Bashan as far as Salcah;
12 all the kingdom of Og in Bashan, who
reigned in Ashtaroth and Edrei, who remained of the remnant of the giants; for Moses had defeated and cast out these.
13 Nevertheless the children of Israel did not
drive out the Geshurites or the Maachathites,
but the Geshurites and the Maachathites
dwell among the Israelites until this day.
14 Only to the tribe of Levi he had given no
inheritance; the sacrifices of the LORD God of
Israel made by fire *are* their inheritance, as
He said to them.

The Land of Reuben

15 And Moses had given to the tribe of the
children of Reuben *an inheritance* according
to their families.
16 Their territory was from Aroer, which *is*
on the bank of the River Arnon, and the city
that *is* in the midst of the ravine, and all the
plain by Medeba;
17 Heshbon and all its cities that *are* in the
plain: Dibon, Bamoth Baal, Beth Baal Meon,
18 Jahaza, Kedemoth, Mephaath,
19 Kirjathaim, Sibmah, Zereth Shahar on the
mountain of the valley,
20 Beth Peor, the slopes of Pisgah, and Beth
Jeshimoth—
21 all the cities of the plain and all the kingdom of Sihon king of the Amorites, who
reigned in Heshbon, whom Moses had struck
with the princes of Midian: Evi, Rekem, Zur,
Hur, and Reba, who *were* princes of Sihon
dwelling in the country.
22 The children of Israel also killed with the ➤
sword Balaam the son of Beor, the soothsayer,
among those who were killed by them.
23 And the border of the children of Reuben
was the bank of the Jordan. This *was* the inheritance of the children of Reuben according
to their families, the cities and their villages.

The Land of Gad

24 Moses also had given *an inheritance* to
the tribe of Gad, to the children of Gad according to their families.
25 Their territory was Jazer, and all the cities
of Gilead, and half the land of the Ammonites
as far as Aroer, which *is* before Rabbah,
26 and from Heshbon to Ramath Mizpah and
Betonim, and from Mahanaim to the border
of Debir,
27 and in the valley Beth Haram, Beth Nimrah, Succoth, and Zaphon, the rest of the
kingdom of Sihon king of Heshbon, with
the Jordan as *its* border, as far as the edge of
the Sea of Chinnereth, on the other side of the
Jordan eastward.
28 This *is* the inheritance of the children of
Gad according to their families, the cities and
their villages.

Half the Tribe of Manasseh (East)

29 Moses also had given *an inheritance* to
half the tribe of Manasseh; it was for half the

13:5 [a]Or *Giblites* **13:6** [a]Hebrew *Misrephoth Maim*

LIFE LESSONS

➤ **13:22 — *The children of Israel also killed with the sword Balaam the son of Beor, the soothsayer . . . .***

Balaam spoke many positive, true, insightful, and even flattering things about God and Israel (see Num. 23–25). Yet as a "soothsayer," he demonstrated his wickedness. We cannot pick and choose which commands of God we will obey.

Life Examples:

CALEB

A Profile in Boldness

JOSH. 14:6–12

When ten Hebrew spies warned their countrymen to steer clear of Canaan, only two others, Joshua and Caleb, urged them to advance with God.

The name Caleb can mean, "bold, impetuous," and Joshua's friend certainly had boldness. Caleb had a faith so full that even the fearsome giants living on Hebron did not deter him (Josh. 14:6–12). He believed the Lord when few others did. He claimed the promises of God and did not allow four harsh decades in the wilderness to erode his belief. He had wanted to take possession of Canaan forty-five years earlier, and he hadn't changed his mind. Truly, Caleb was all heart—for he obeyed the Spirit of God.

All of us would do well to follow suit. First let's make sure we have a full faith, and then a surrendered heart. Only then can we face the foreboding giants before us.

See the Life Principles Index for further study:
9. Trusting God means looking beyond what we can see to what God sees.

tribe of the children of Manasseh according
to their families:
30 Their territory was from Mahanaim, all
Bashan, all the kingdom of Og king of
Bashan, and all the towns of Jair which are
in Bashan, sixty cities;
31 half of Gilead, and Ashtaroth and Edrei,
cities of the kingdom of Og in Bashan, *were*
for the children of Machir the son of Manasseh,
for half of the children of Machir according to their families.
32 These *are the areas* which Moses had distributed
as an inheritance in the plains of
Moab on the other side of the Jordan, by Jericho eastward.
33 But to the tribe of Levi Moses had given
no inheritance; the LORD God of Israel *was*
their inheritance, as He had said to them.

The Land Divided West of the Jordan

14 These *are the areas* which the children
of Israel inherited in the land of
Canaan, which Eleazar the priest, Joshua the
son of Nun, and the heads of the fathers of the
tribes of the children of Israel distributed as
an inheritance to them.
2 Their inheritance *was* by lot, as the LORD
had commanded by the hand of Moses, for
the nine tribes and the half-tribe.
3 For Moses had given the inheritance of the
two tribes and the half-tribe on the other side
of the Jordan; but to the Levites he had given
no inheritance among them.
4 For the children of Joseph were two tribes:
Manasseh and Ephraim. And they gave no
part to the Levites in the land, except cities to
dwell *in,* with their common-lands for their
livestock and their property.
5 As the LORD had commanded Moses, so
the children of Israel did; and they divided the
land.

Caleb Inherits Hebron

6 Then the children of Judah came to
Joshua in Gilgal. And Caleb the son of Jephunneh
the Kenizzite said to him: "You
know the word which the LORD said to Moses
the man of God concerning you and me in
Kadesh Barnea.
7 "I *was* forty years old when Moses the
servant of the LORD sent me from Kadesh
Barnea to spy out the land, and I brought
back word to him as *it was* in my heart.
8 "Nevertheless my brethren who went up
with me made the heart of the people melt,
but I wholly followed the LORD my God.
9 "So Moses swore on that day, saying, ✳
'Surely the land where your foot has trodden ➤
shall be your inheritance and your children's
forever, because you have wholly followed
the LORD my God.'
10 "And now, behold, the LORD has kept me
alive, as He said, these forty-five years, ever
since the LORD spoke this word to Moses
while Israel wandered in the wilderness;
and now, here I am this day, eighty-five years
old.
11 "As yet I *am as* strong this day as on the
day that Moses sent me; just as my strength
was then, so now *is* my strength for war, both
for going out and for coming in.
12 "Now therefore, give me this mountain of

LIFE LESSONS

➤ **14:9 — *"So Moses swore on that day, saying, 'Surely the land where your foot has trodden shall be your inheritance and your children's forever, because you have wholly followed the LORD my God . . . .'"***

When we choose to "wholly follow" the Lord, He will move heaven and earth, if necessary, to fulfill His good promises to us.

which the LORD spoke in that day; for you heard in that day how the Anakim *were* there, and *that* the cities *were* great *and* fortified. It may be that the LORD *will be* with me, and I shall be able to drive them out as the LORD said."

13 And Joshua blessed him, and gave Hebron to Caleb the son of Jephunneh as an inheritance.

14 Hebron therefore became the inheritance of Caleb the son of Jephunneh the Kenizzite to this day, because he wholly followed the LORD God of Israel.

15 And the name of Hebron formerly was Kirjath Arba (*Arba was* the greatest man among the Anakim). Then the land had rest from war.

The Land of Judah

15 So *this* was the lot of the tribe of the children of Judah according to their families: The border of Edom at the Wilderness of Zin southward *was* the extreme southern boundary.

2 And their southern border began at the shore of the Salt Sea, from the bay that faces southward.

3 Then it went out to the southern side of the Ascent of Akrabbim, passed along to Zin, ascended on the south side of Kadesh Barnea, passed along to Hezron, went up to Adar, and went around to Karkaa.

4 *From there* it passed toward Azmon and went out to the Brook of Egypt; and the border ended at the sea. This shall be your southern border.

5 The east border *was* the Salt Sea as far as the mouth of the Jordan. And the border on the northern quarter *began* at the bay of the sea at the mouth of the Jordan.

6 The border went up to Beth Hoglah and passed north of Beth Arabah; and the border went up to the stone of Bohan the son of Reuben.

7 Then the border went up toward Debir from the Valley of Achor, and it turned northward toward Gilgal, which *is* before the Ascent of Adummim, which *is* on the south side of the valley. The border continued toward the waters of En Shemesh and ended at En Rogel.

8 And the border went up by the Valley of the Son of Hinnom to the southern slope of the Jebusite *city* (which *is* Jerusalem). The border went up to the top of the mountain that *lies* before the Valley of Hinnom westward, which *is* at the end of the Valley of Rephaim[a] northward.

9 Then the border went around from the top of the hill to the fountain of the water of Nephtoah, and extended to the cities of Mount Ephron. And the border went around to Baalah (which *is* Kirjath Jearim).

10 Then the border turned westward from Baalah to Mount Seir, passed along to the side of Mount Jearim on the north (which *is* Chesalon), went down to Beth Shemesh, and passed on to Timnah.

11 And the border went out to the side of Ekron northward. Then the border went around to Shicron, passed along to Mount Baalah, and extended to Jabneel; and the border ended at the sea.

12 The west border *was* the coastline of the Great Sea. This *is* the boundary of the children of Judah all around according to their families.

Caleb Occupies Hebron and Debir

13 Now to Caleb the son of Jephunneh he gave a share among the children of Judah, according to the commandment of the LORD to Joshua, *namely,* Kirjath Arba, which *is* Hebron (*Arba was* the father of Anak).

14 Caleb drove out the three sons of Anak from there: Sheshai, Ahiman, and Talmai, the children of Anak.

15 Then he went up from there to the inhabitants of Debir (formerly the name of Debir *was* Kirjath Sepher).

16 And Caleb said, "He who attacks Kirjath Sepher and takes it, to him I will give Achsah my daughter as wife."

17 So Othniel the son of Kenaz, the brother of Caleb, took it; and he gave him Achsah his daughter as wife.

18 Now it was so, when she came *to him,* that she persuaded him to ask her father for a field. So she dismounted from *her* donkey, and Caleb said to her, "What do you wish?"

19 She answered, "Give me a blessing; since you have given me land in the South, give me also springs of water." So he gave her the upper springs and the lower springs.

15:8 [a]Literally *Giants*

LIFE LESSONS

➤ 15:19 — *She answered, "Give me a blessing; since you have given me land in the South, give me also springs of water." So he gave her the upper springs and the lower springs.*

It is no surprise that a courageous man of faith like Caleb would raise a bold daughter like Achsah. Genuine fear of God is more "caught" than "taught," especially in families.

The Cities of Judah

20 This *was* the inheritance of the tribe of the children of Judah according to their families:
21 The cities at the limits of the tribe of the children of Judah, toward the border of Edom in the South, were Kabzeel, Eder, Jagur,
22 Kinah, Dimonah, Adadah,
23 Kedesh, Hazor, Ithnan,
24 Ziph, Telem, Bealoth,
25 Hazor, Hadattah, Kerioth, Hezron (which *is* Hazor),
26 Amam, Shema, Moladah,
27 Hazar Gaddah, Heshmon, Beth Pelet,
28 Hazar Shual, Beersheba, Bizjothjah,
29 Baalah, Ijim, Ezem,
30 Eltolad, Chesil, Hormah,
31 Ziklag, Madmannah, Sansannah,
32 Lebaoth, Shilhim, Ain, and Rimmon: all the cities *are* twenty-nine, with their villages.
33 In the lowland: Eshtaol, Zorah, Ashnah,
34 Zanoah, En Gannim, Tappuah, Enam,
35 Jarmuth, Adullam, Socoh, Azekah,
36 Sharaim, Adithaim, Gederah, and Gederothaim: fourteen cities with their villages;
37 Zenan, Hadashah, Migdal Gad,
38 Dilean, Mizpah, Joktheel,
39 Lachish, Bozkath, Eglon,
40 Cabbon, Lahmas,[a] Kithlish,
41 Gederoth, Beth Dagon, Naamah, and Makkedah: sixteen cities with their villages;
42 Libnah, Ether, Ashan,
43 Jiphtah, Ashnah, Nezib,
44 Keilah, Achzib, and Mareshah: nine cities with their villages;
45 Ekron, with its towns and villages;
46 from Ekron to the sea, all that *lay* near Ashdod, with their villages;
47 Ashdod with its towns and villages, Gaza with its towns and villages—as far as the Brook of Egypt and the Great Sea with *its* coastline.
48 And in the mountain country: Shamir, Jattir, Sochoh,
49 Dannah, Kirjath Sannah (which *is* Debir),
50 Anab, Eshtemoh, Anim,
51 Goshen, Holon, and Giloh: eleven cities with their villages;
52 Arab, Dumah, Eshean,
53 Janum, Beth Tappuah, Aphekah,
54 Humtah, Kirjath Arba (which *is* Hebron), and Zior: nine cities with their villages;
55 Maon, Carmel, Ziph, Juttah,
56 Jezreel, Jokdeam, Zanoah,
57 Kain, Gibeah, and Timnah: ten cities with their villages;
58 Halhul, Beth Zur, Gedor,
59 Maarath, Beth Anoth, and Eltekon: six cities with their villages;
60 Kirjath Baal (which *is* Kirjath Jearim) and Rabbah: two cities with their villages.
61 In the wilderness: Beth Arabah, Middin, Secacah,
62 Nibshan, the City of Salt, and En Gedi: six cities with their villages.
63 As for the Jebusites, the inhabitants of Jerusalem, the children of Judah could not drive them out; but the Jebusites dwell with the children of Judah at Jerusalem to this day.

Ephraim and West Manasseh

16 The lot fell to the children of Joseph from the Jordan, by Jericho, to the waters of Jericho on the east, to the wilderness that goes up from Jericho through the mountains to Bethel,
2 then went out from Bethel to Luz,[a] passed along to the border of the Archites at Ataroth,
3 and went down westward to the boundary of the Japhletites, as far as the boundary of Lower Beth Horon to Gezer; and it ended at the sea.
4 So the children of Joseph, Manasseh and Ephraim, took their inheritance.

The Land of Ephraim

5 The border of the children of Ephraim, according to their families, was *thus:* The border of their inheritance on the east side was Ataroth Addar as far as Upper Beth Horon.
6 And the border went out toward the sea on the north side of Michmethath; then the border went around eastward to Taanath Shiloh, and passed by it on the east of Janohah.
7 Then it went down from Janohah to Ataroth and Naarah,[a] reached to Jericho, and came out at the Jordan.
8 The border went out from Tappuah westward to the Brook Kanah, and it ended at the sea. This *was* the inheritance of the tribe of the children of Ephraim according to their families.
9 The separate cities for the children of Ephraim *were* among the inheritance of the children of Manasseh, all the cities with their villages.
10 And they did not drive out the Canaanites

15:40 [a]Or *Lahmam* **16:2** [a]Septuagint reads *Bethel* (that is, Luz).
16:7 [a]Or *Naaran* (compare 1 Chronicles 7:28)

LIFE LESSONS

➤ ***15:63 — As for the Jebusites, the inhabitants of Jerusalem, the children of Judah could not drive them out; but the Jebusites dwell with the children of Judah at Jerusalem to this day.***

The Jebusite city of Jerusalem did not fall to the Israelites until the time of David (see 2 Sam. 5:6, 7). Sometimes God waits to fulfill His promises; but He always keeps His word in the end.

who dwelt in Gezer; but the Canaanites dwell among the Ephraimites to this day and have become forced laborers.

The Other Half-Tribe of Manasseh (West)

17 There was also a lot for the tribe of Manasseh, for he *was* the firstborn of Joseph: *namely* for Machir the firstborn of Manasseh, the father of Gilead, because he was a man of war; therefore he was given Gilead and Bashan.
2 And there was *a lot* for the rest of the children of Manasseh according to their families: for the children of Abiezer,[a] the children of Helek, the children of Asriel, the children of Shechem, the children of Hepher, and the children of Shemida; these *were* the male children of Manasseh the son of Joseph according to their families.
3 But Zelophehad the son of Hepher, the son of Gilead, the son of Machir, the son of Manasseh, had no sons, but only daughters. And these *are* the names of his daughters: Mahlah, Noah, Hoglah, Milcah, and Tirzah.
➤ 4 And they came near before Eleazar the priest, before Joshua the son of Nun, and before the rulers, saying, "The LORD commanded Moses to give us an inheritance among our brothers." Therefore, according to the commandment of the LORD, he gave them an inheritance among their father's brothers.
5 Ten shares fell to Manasseh, besides the land of Gilead and Bashan, which *were* on the other side of the Jordan,
6 because the daughters of Manasseh received an inheritance among his sons; and the rest of Manasseh's sons had the land of Gilead.
7 And the territory of Manasseh was from Asher to Michmethath, that *lies* east of Shechem; and the border went along south to the inhabitants of En Tappuah.
8 Manasseh had the land of Tappuah, but Tappuah on the border of Manasseh *belonged* to the children of Ephraim.
9 And the border descended to the Brook Kanah, southward to the brook. These cities of Ephraim *are* among the cities of Manasseh. The border of Manasseh *was* on the north side of the brook; and it ended at the sea.
10 Southward *it was* Ephraim's, northward *it was* Manasseh's, and the sea was its border. Manasseh's territory was adjoining Asher on the north and Issachar on the east.
11 And in Issachar and in Asher, Manasseh had Beth Shean and its towns, Ibleam and its towns, the inhabitants of Dor and its towns, the inhabitants of En Dor and its towns, the inhabitants of Taanach and its towns, and the inhabitants of Megiddo and its towns—three hilly regions.
12 Yet the children of Manasseh could not drive out *the inhabitants of* those cities, but the Canaanites were determined to dwell in that land.
13 And it happened, when the children of Israel grew strong, that they put the Canaanites to forced labor, but did not utterly drive them out.

More Land for Ephraim and Manasseh

14 Then the children of Joseph spoke to Joshua, saying, "Why have you given us *only* one lot and one share to inherit, since we *are* a great people, inasmuch as the LORD has blessed us until now?"
15 So Joshua answered them, "If you *are* a great people, *then* go up to the forest *country* and clear a place for yourself there in the land of the Perizzites and the giants, since the mountains of Ephraim are too confined for you."
16 But the children of Joseph said, "The mountain country is not enough for us; and all the Canaanites who dwell in the land of the valley have chariots of iron, *both those* who *are* of Beth Shean and its towns and *those* who *are* of the Valley of Jezreel."
17 And Joshua spoke to the house of Joseph—to Ephraim and Manasseh—saying, "You *are* a great people and have great power; you shall not have *only* one lot,
18 "but the mountain country shall be yours. ➤
Although it *is* wooded, you shall cut it down, and its farthest extent shall be yours; for you shall drive out the Canaanites, though they have iron chariots *and* are strong."

17:2 [a]Called *Jeezer* in Numbers 26:30

LIFE LESSONS

➤ 17:4 — *And they came near . . . saying, "The LORD commanded Moses to give us an inheritance among our brothers." Therefore, according to the commandment of the LORD, he gave them an inheritance . . . .*

We should never hesitate to come before the Lord and ask Him to do what He has promised, even if it seems out of the ordinary. James tells us, " . . . You do not have because you do not ask" (James 4:2).

➤ 17:18 — *" . . . but the mountain country shall be yours. Although it is wooded, you shall cut it down, and its farthest extent shall be yours; for you shall drive out the Canaanites . . . ."*

If we are to fully benefit from the promises of God, we have our own work to do. God requires His people to put forth great effort in their lives of faith (see 1 Cor. 4:12).

The Remainder of the Land Divided

18 Now the whole congregation of the children of Israel assembled together at Shiloh, and set up the tabernacle of meeting there. And the land was subdued before them.

2 But there remained among the children of Israel seven tribes which had not yet received their inheritance.

➤ 3 Then Joshua said to the children of Israel: "How long will you neglect to go and possess the land which the LORD God of your fathers has given you?

4 "Pick out from among you three men for *each* tribe, and I will send them; they shall rise and go through the land, survey it according to their inheritance, and come *back* to me.

5 "And they shall divide it into seven parts. Judah shall remain in their territory on the south, and the house of Joseph shall remain in their territory on the north.

6 "You shall therefore survey the land in seven parts and bring *the survey* here to me, that I may cast lots for you here before the LORD our God.

7 "But the Levites have no part among you, for the priesthood of the LORD *is* their inheritance. And Gad, Reuben, and half the tribe of Manasseh have received their inheritance beyond the Jordan on the east, which Moses the servant of the LORD gave them."

8 Then the men arose to go away; and Joshua charged those who went to survey the land, saying, "Go, walk through the land, survey it, and come back to me, that I may cast lots for you here before the LORD in Shiloh."

9 So the men went, passed through the land, and wrote the survey in a book in seven parts by cities; and they came to Joshua at the camp in Shiloh.

10 Then Joshua cast lots for them in Shiloh before the LORD, and there Joshua divided the land to the children of Israel according to their divisions.

The Land of Benjamin

11 Now the lot of the tribe of the children of Benjamin came up according to their families, and the territory of their lot came out between the children of Judah and the children of Joseph.

12 Their border on the north side began at the Jordan, and the border went up to the side of Jericho on the north, and went up through the mountains westward; it ended at the Wilderness of Beth Aven.

13 The border went over from there toward Luz, to the side of Luz (which *is* Bethel) southward; and the border descended to Ataroth Addar, near the hill that *lies* on the south side of Lower Beth Horon.

14 Then the border extended around the west side to the south, from the hill that *lies* before Beth Horon southward; and it ended at Kirjath Baal (which *is* Kirjath Jearim), a city of the children of Judah. This *was* the west side.

15 The south side *began* at the end of Kirjath Jearim, and the border extended on the west and went out to the spring of the waters of Nephtoah.

16 Then the border came down to the end of the mountain that *lies* before the Valley of the Son of Hinnom, which *is* in the Valley of the Rephaim[a] on the north, descended to the Valley of Hinnom, to the side of the Jebusite *city* on the south, and descended to En Rogel.

17 And it went around from the north, went out to En Shemesh, and extended toward Geliloth, which is before the Ascent of Adummim, and descended to the stone of Bohan the son of Reuben.

18 Then it passed along toward the north side of Arabah,[a] and went down to Arabah.

19 And the border passed along to the north side of Beth Hoglah; then the border ended at the north bay at the Salt Sea, at the south end of the Jordan. This *was* the southern boundary.

20 The Jordan was its border on the east side. This *was* the inheritance of the children of Benjamin, according to its boundaries all around, according to their families.

21 Now the cities of the tribe of the children of Benjamin, according to their families, were Jericho, Beth Hoglah, Emek Keziz,

22 Beth Arabah, Zemaraim, Bethel,

23 Avim, Parah, Ophrah,

24 Chephar Haammoni, Ophni, and Gaba: twelve cities with their villages;

25 Gibeon, Ramah, Beeroth,

26 Mizpah, Chephirah, Mozah,

27 Rekem, Irpeel, Taralah,

28 Zelah, Eleph, Jebus (which *is* Jerusalem), Gibeath, *and* Kirjath: fourteen cities with their villages. This was the inheritance of the

18:16 [a]Literally *Giants* **18:18** [a]Or *Beth Arabah* (compare 15:6 and 18:22)

LIFE LESSONS

➤ 18:3 — *Then Joshua said to the children of Israel: "How long will you neglect to go and possess the land which the LORD God of your fathers has given you?"*

What keeps you from claiming the "territory" that God wants to give you? What is holding you back from acting on His promises? How long will you "neglect to possess the land" which God has given to you?

children of Benjamin according to their families.

Simeon's Inheritance with Judah

19 The second lot came out for Simeon, for the tribe of the children of Simeon according to their families. And their inheritance was within the inheritance of the children of Judah.
2 They had in their inheritance Beersheba (Sheba), Moladah,
3 Hazar Shual, Balah, Ezem,
4 Eltolad, Bethul, Hormah,
5 Ziklag, Beth Marcaboth, Hazar Susah,
6 Beth Lebaoth, and Sharuhen: thirteen cities and their villages;
7 Ain, Rimmon, Ether, and Ashan: four cities and their villages;
8 and all the villages that *were* all around these cities as far as Baalath Beer, Ramah of the South. This *was* the inheritance of the tribe of the children of Simeon according to their families.
9 The inheritance of the children of Simeon *was included* in the share of the children of Judah, for the share of the children of Judah was too much for them. Therefore the children of Simeon had *their* inheritance within the inheritance of that people.

The Land of Zebulun

10 The third lot came out for the children of Zebulun according to their families, and the border of their inheritance was as far as Sarid.
11 Their border went toward the west and to Maralah, went to Dabbasheth, and extended along the brook that is east of Jokneam.
12 Then from Sarid it went eastward toward the sunrise along the border of Chisloth Tabor, and went out toward Daberath, bypassing Japhia.
13 And from there it passed along on the east of Gath Hepher, toward Eth Kazin, and extended to Rimmon, which borders on Neah.
14 Then the border went around it on the north side of Hannathon, and it ended in the Valley of Jiphthah El.
15 Included were Kattath, Nahallal, Shimron, Idalah, and Bethlehem: twelve cities with their villages.
16 This *was* the inheritance of the children of Zebulun according to their families, these cities with their villages.

The Land of Issachar

17 The fourth lot came out to Issachar, for the children of Issachar according to their families.
18 And their territory went to Jezreel, and *included* Chesulloth, Shunem,
19 Haphraim, Shion, Anaharath,
20 Rabbith, Kishion, Abez,
21 Remeth, En Gannim, En Haddah, and Beth Pazzez.
22 And the border reached to Tabor, Shahazimah, and Beth Shemesh; their border ended at the Jordan: sixteen cities with their villages.
23 This *was* the inheritance of the tribe of the children of Issachar according to their families, the cities and their villages.

The Land of Asher

24 The fifth lot came out for the tribe of the children of Asher according to their families.
25 And their territory included Helkath, Hali, Beten, Achshaph,
26 Alammelech, Amad, and Mishal; it reached to Mount Carmel westward, along *the Brook* Shihor Libnath.
27 It turned toward the sunrise to Beth Dagon; and it reached to Zebulun and to the Valley of Jiphthah El, then northward beyond Beth Emek and Neiel, bypassing Cabul *which was* on the left,
28 including Ebron,[a] Rehob, Hammon, and Kanah, as far as Greater Sidon.
29 And the border turned to Ramah and to the fortified city of Tyre; then the border turned to Hosah, and ended at the sea by the region of Achzib.
30 Also Ummah, Aphek, and Rehob *were included:* twenty-two cities with their villages.
31 This *was* the inheritance of the tribe of the children of Asher according to their families, these cities with their villages.

The Land of Naphtali

32 The sixth lot came out to the children of Naphtali, for the children of Naphtali according to their families.
33 And their border began at Heleph, enclosing the territory from the terebinth tree in Zaanannim, Adami Nekeb, and Jabneel, as far as Lakkum; it ended at the Jordan.
34 From Heleph the border extended westward to Aznoth Tabor, and went out from there toward Hukkok; it adjoined Zebulun on the south side and Asher on the west side, and ended at Judah by the Jordan toward the sunrise.
35 And the fortified cities *are* Ziddim, Zer, Hammath, Rakkath, Chinnereth,
36 Adamah, Ramah, Hazor,
37 Kedesh, Edrei, En Hazor,
38 Iron, Migdal El, Horem, Beth Anath, and Beth Shemesh: nineteen cities with their villages.
39 This *was* the inheritance of the tribe of the children of Naphtali according to their families, the cities and their villages.

19:28 [a]Following Masoretic Text, Targum, and Vulgate; a few Hebrew manuscripts read *Abdon* (compare 21:30 and 1 Chronicles 6:74).

The Land of Dan
40 The seventh lot came out for the tribe of the children of Dan according to their families.
41 And the territory of their inheritance was Zorah, Eshtaol, Ir Shemesh,
42 Shaalabbin, Aijalon, Jethlah,
43 Elon, Timnah, Ekron,
44 Eltekeh, Gibbethon, Baalath,
45 Jehud, Bene Berak, Gath Rimmon,
46 Me Jarkon, and Rakkon, with the region near Joppa.
47 And the border of the children of Dan went beyond these, because the children of Dan went up to fight against Leshem and took it; and they struck it with the edge of the sword, took possession of it, and dwelt in it. They called Leshem, Dan, after the name of Dan their father.
48 This *is* the inheritance of the tribe of the children of Dan according to their families, these cities with their villages.

Joshua's Inheritance
49 When they had made an end of dividing the land as an inheritance according to their borders, the children of Israel gave an inheritance among them to Joshua the son of Nun.
50 According to the word of the LORD they gave him the city which he asked for, Timnath Serah in the mountains of Ephraim; and he built the city and dwelt in it.
➤ 51 These *were* the inheritances which Eleazar the priest, Joshua the son of Nun, and the heads of the fathers of the tribes of the children of Israel divided as an inheritance by lot in Shiloh before the LORD, at the door of the tabernacle of meeting. So they made an end of dividing the country.

The Cities of Refuge
20 The LORD also spoke to Joshua, saying,
2 "Speak to the children of Israel, saying: 'Appoint for yourselves cities of refuge, of which I spoke to you through Moses,
3 'that the slayer who kills a person accidentally *or* unintentionally may flee there; and they shall be your refuge from the avenger of blood.
4 'And when he flees to one of those cities, and stands at the entrance of the gate of the city, and declares his case in the hearing of the elders of that city, they shall take him into the city as one of them, and give him a place, that he may dwell among them.
5 'Then if the avenger of blood pursues him, they shall not deliver the slayer into his hand, because he struck his neighbor unintentionally, but did not hate him beforehand.
6 'And he shall dwell in that city until he stands before the congregation for judgment, *and* until the death of the one who is high priest in those days. Then the slayer may return and come to his own city and his own house, to the city from which he fled.'"
7 So they appointed Kedesh in Galilee, in the mountains of Naphtali, Shechem in the mountains of Ephraim, and Kirjath Arba (which *is* Hebron) in the mountains of Judah.
8 And on the other side of the Jordan, by Jericho eastward, they assigned Bezer in the wilderness on the plain, from the tribe of Reuben, Ramoth in Gilead, from the tribe of Gad, and Golan in Bashan, from the tribe of Manasseh.
9 These were the cities appointed for all the children of Israel and for the stranger who dwelt among them, that whoever killed a person accidentally might flee there, and not die by the hand of the avenger of blood until he stood before the congregation.

Cities of the Levites
21 Then the heads of the fathers' *houses* of the Levites came near to Eleazar the priest, to Joshua the son of Nun, and to the heads of the fathers' *houses* of the tribes of the children of Israel.
2 And they spoke to them at Shiloh in the land of Canaan, saying, "The LORD commanded through Moses to give us cities to dwell in, with their common-lands for our livestock."
3 So the children of Israel gave to the Levites from their inheritance, at the commandment of the LORD, these cities and their common-lands:
4 Now the lot came out for the families of the Kohathites. And the children of Aaron the priest, *who were* of the Levites, had thirteen cities by lot from the tribe of Judah, from the tribe of Simeon, and from the tribe of Benjamin.
5 The rest of the children of Kohath had ten cities by lot from the families of the tribe of Ephraim, from the tribe of Dan, and from the half-tribe of Manasseh.

LIFE LESSONS

➤ **19:51** — ***These were the inheritances which Eleazar the priest, Joshua the son of Nun, and the heads of the fathers of the tribes of the children of Israel divided as an inheritance by lot in Shiloh before the LORD . . . .***

Everything we do ought to be done "as unto the Lord" and before the Lord. Where we live, who we marry, how we make a living—all these things are proper issues to bring before the Lord in prayer.

6 And the children of Gershon had thirteen
cities by lot from the families of the tribe of Issachar, from the tribe of Asher, from the tribe of Naphtali, and from the half-tribe of Manasseh in Bashan.
7 The children of Merari according to their
families had twelve cities from the tribe of Reuben, from the tribe of Gad, and from the tribe of Zebulun.
8 And the children of Israel gave these cities
with their common-lands by lot to the Levites, as the LORD had commanded by the hand of Moses.
9 So they gave from the tribe of the children
of Judah and from the tribe of the children of Simeon these cities which are designated by name,
10 which were for the children of Aaron, one
of the families of the Kohathites, *who were* of the children of Levi; for the lot was theirs first.
11 And they gave them Kirjath Arba (*Arba*
was the father of Anak), which *is* Hebron, in the mountains of Judah, with the common-land surrounding it.
12 But the fields of the city and its villages
they gave to Caleb the son of Jephunneh as his possession.
13 Thus to the children of Aaron the priest
they gave Hebron with its common-land (a city of refuge for the slayer), Libnah with its common-land,
14 Jattir with its common-land, Eshtemoa
with its common-land,
15 Holon with its common-land, Debir with
its common-land,
16 Ain with its common-land, Juttah with its
common-land, and Beth Shemesh with its common-land: nine cities from those two tribes;
17 and from the tribe of Benjamin, Gibeon
with its common-land, Geba with its common-land,
18 Anathoth with its common-land, and
Almon with its common-land: four cities.
19 All the cities of the children of Aaron, the
priests, *were* thirteen cities with their common-lands.
20 And the families of the children of Ko-
hath, the Levites, the rest of the children of Kohath, even they had the cities of their lot from the tribe of Ephraim.
21 For they gave them Shechem with its com-
mon-land in the mountains of Ephraim (a city of refuge for the slayer), Gezer with its common-land,
22 Kibzaim with its common-land, and Beth
Horon with its common-land: four cities;
23 and from the tribe of Dan, Eltekeh with its
common-land, Gibbethon with its common-land,
24 Aijalon with its common-land, *and* Gath
Rimmon with its common-land: four cities;
25 and from the half-tribe of Manasseh,
Tanach with its common-land and Gath Rimmon with its common-land: two cities.
26 All the ten cities with their common-lands
were for the rest of the families of the children of Kohath.
27 Also to the children of Gershon, of the
families of the Levites, from the *other* half-tribe of Manasseh, *they gave* Golan in Bashan with its common-land (a city of refuge for the slayer), and Be Eshterah with its common-land: two cities;
28 and from the tribe of Issachar, Kishion
with its common-land, Daberath with its common-land,
29 Jarmuth with its common-land, *and* En
Gannim with its common-land: four cities;
30 and from the tribe of Asher, Mishal with
its common-land, Abdon with its common-land,
31 Helkath with its common-land, and Rehob
with its common-land: four cities;
32 and from the tribe of Naphtali, Kedesh in
Galilee with its common-land (a city of refuge for the slayer), Hammoth Dor with its common-land, and Kartan with its common-land: three cities.
33 All the cities of the Gershonites according
to their families *were* thirteen cities with their common-lands.
34 And to the families of the children of Me-
rari, the rest of the Levites, from the tribe of Zebulun, Jokneam with its common-land, Kartah with its common-land,
35 Dimnah with its common-land, *and* Naha-
lal with its common-land: four cities;
36 and from the tribe of Reuben, Bezer with
its common-land, Jahaz with its common-land,
37 Kedemoth with its common-land, and
Mephaath with its common-land: four cities;[a]
38 and from the tribe of Gad, Ramoth in
Gilead with its common-land (a city of refuge for the slayer), Mahanaim with its common-land,
39 Heshbon with its common-land, *and* Jazer
with its common-land: four cities in all.
40 So all the cities for the children of Merari
according to their families, the rest of the families of the Levites, were *by* their lot twelve cities.
41 All the cities of the Levites within the pos-
session of the children of Israel *were* forty-eight cities with their common-lands.
42 Every one of these cities had its common-
land surrounding it; thus *were* all these cities.

The Promise Fulfilled

43 So the LORD gave to Israel all the land of
which He had sworn to give to their fathers, and they took possession of it and dwelt in it.

21:37 [a]Following Septuagint and Vulgate (compare 1 Chronicles 6:78, 79); Masoretic Text, Bomberg, and Targum omit verses 36 and 37.

➤ 44 The LORD gave them rest all around, according to all that He had sworn to their fathers. And not a man of all their enemies stood against them; the LORD delivered all their enemies into their hand.
45 Not a word failed of any good thing which the LORD had spoken to the house of Israel. All came to pass.

Eastern Tribes Return to Their Lands

22 Then Joshua called the Reubenites, the Gadites, and half the tribe of Manasseh,
2 and said to them: "You have kept all that Moses the servant of the LORD commanded you, and have obeyed my voice in all that I commanded you.
3 "You have not left your brethren these many days, up to this day, but have kept the charge of the commandment of the LORD your God.
4 "And now the LORD your God has given rest to your brethren, as He promised them; now therefore, return and go to your tents *and* to the land of your possession, which Moses the servant of the LORD gave you on the other side of the Jordan.
➤ 5 "But take careful heed to do the commandment and the law which Moses the servant of the LORD commanded you, to love the LORD your God, to walk in all His ways, to keep His commandments, to hold fast to Him, and to serve Him with all your heart and with all your soul."
6 So Joshua blessed them and sent them away, and they went to their tents.
7 Now to half the tribe of Manasseh Moses had given a possession in Bashan, but to the *other* half of it Joshua gave *a possession* among their brethren on this side of the Jordan, westward. And indeed, when Joshua sent them away to their tents, he blessed them,
8 and spoke to them, saying, "Return with much riches to your tents, with very much livestock, with silver, with gold, with bronze, with iron, and with very much clothing. Divide the spoil of your enemies with your brethren."
9 So the children of Reuben, the children of Gad, and half the tribe of Manasseh returned, and departed from the children of Israel at Shiloh, which *is* in the land of Canaan, to go to the country of Gilead, to the land of their possession, which they had obtained according to the word of the LORD by the hand of Moses.

An Altar by the Jordan

10 And when they came to the region of the Jordan which *is* in the land of Canaan, the children of Reuben, the children of Gad, and half the tribe of Manasseh built an altar there by the Jordan—a great, impressive altar.
11 Now the children of Israel heard *someone* say, "Behold, the children of Reuben, the children of Gad, and half the tribe of Manasseh have built an altar on the frontier of the land of Canaan, in the region of the Jordan—on the children of Israel's side."
12 And when the children of Israel heard *of it,* the whole congregation of the children of Israel gathered together at Shiloh to go to war against them.
13 Then the children of Israel sent Phinehas the son of Eleazar the priest to the children of Reuben, to the children of Gad, and to half the tribe of Manasseh, into the land of Gilead,
14 and with him ten rulers, one ruler each from the chief house of every tribe of Israel; and each one *was* the head of the house of his father among the divisions[a] of Israel.
15 Then they came to the children of Reuben, to the children of Gad, and to half the tribe of Manasseh, to the land of Gilead, and they spoke with them, saying,
16 "Thus says the whole congregation of the LORD: 'What treachery *is* this that you have committed against the God of Israel, to turn away this day from following the LORD, in that you have built for yourselves an altar, that you might rebel this day against the LORD?
17 '*Is* the iniquity of Peor not enough for us, from which we are not cleansed till this day, although there was a plague in the congregation of the LORD,
18 'but that you must turn away this day from following the LORD? And it shall be, if you rebel today against the LORD, that tomorrow He will be angry with the whole congregation of Israel.

22:14 [a]Literally *thousands*

LIFE LESSONS

➤ 21:44 — *The LORD gave them rest all around, according to all that He had sworn to their fathers. And not a man of all their enemies stood against them; the LORD delivered all their enemies into their hand.*

God's good promises ultimately lead to peace and rest. God tells us that in "rest you shall be saved; in quietness and confidence shall be your strength" (Is. 30:15).

➤ 22:5 — *"But take careful heed to do the commandment and the law which Moses the servant of the LORD commanded you, to love the LORD your God, to walk in all His ways, to keep His commandments, to hold fast to Him, and to serve Him with all your heart and with all your soul."*

What Joshua told the eastern tribes still holds true today. We will surely succeed if we: (1) love God; (2) walk in God's ways; (3) keep God's commandments; (4) hold fast to God; (5) serve God wholeheartedly.

19 'Nevertheless, if the land of your possession *is* unclean, *then* cross over to the land of the possession of the LORD, where the LORD's tabernacle stands, and take possession among us; but do not rebel against the LORD, nor rebel against us, by building yourselves an altar besides the altar of the LORD our God.
20 'Did not Achan the son of Zerah commit a trespass in the accursed thing, and wrath fell on all the congregation of Israel? And that man did not perish alone in his iniquity.'"
21 Then the children of Reuben, the children of Gad, and half the tribe of Manasseh answered and said to the heads of the divisions[a] of Israel:
➤ 22 "The LORD God of gods, the LORD God of gods, He knows, and let Israel itself know—if *it is* in rebellion, or if in treachery against the LORD, do not save us this day.
23 "If we have built ourselves an altar to turn from following the LORD, or if to offer on it burnt offerings or grain offerings, or if to offer peace offerings on it, let the LORD Himself require *an account.*
24 "But in fact we have done it for fear, for a reason, saying, 'In time to come your descendants may speak to our descendants, saying, "What have you to do with the LORD God of Israel?
25 "For the LORD has made the Jordan a border between you and us, *you* children of Reuben and children of Gad. You have no part in the LORD." So your descendants would make our descendants cease fearing the LORD.'
26 "Therefore we said, 'Let us now prepare to build ourselves an altar, not for burnt offering nor for sacrifice,
27 'but *that* it *may be* a witness between you and us and our generations after us, that we may perform the service of the LORD before Him with our burnt offerings, with our sacrifices, and with our peace offerings; that your descendants may not say to our descendants in time to come, "You have no part in the LORD."'
28 "Therefore we said that it will be, when they say *this* to us or to our generations in time to come, that we may say, 'Here is the replica of the altar of the LORD which our fathers made, though not for burnt offerings nor for sacrifices; but it *is* a witness between you and us.'
29 "Far be it from us that we should rebel against the LORD, and turn from following the LORD this day, to build an altar for burnt offerings, for grain offerings, or for sacrifices, besides the altar of the LORD our God which *is* before His tabernacle."
30 Now when Phinehas the priest and the rulers of the congregation, the heads of the divisions[a] of Israel who *were* with him, heard the words that the children of Reuben, the children of Gad, and the children of Manasseh spoke, it pleased them.
31 Then Phinehas the son of Eleazar the priest said to the children of Reuben, the children of Gad, and the children of Manasseh, "This day we perceive that the LORD *is* among us, because you have not committed this treachery against the LORD. Now you have delivered the children of Israel out of the hand of the LORD."
32 And Phinehas the son of Eleazar the priest, and the rulers, returned from the children of Reuben and the children of Gad, from the land of Gilead to the land of Canaan, to the children of Israel, and brought back word to them.
33 So the thing pleased the children of Israel, ➤ and the children of Israel blessed God; they spoke no more of going against them in battle, to destroy the land where the children of Reuben and Gad dwelt.
34 The children of Reuben and the children of Gad[a] called the altar, *Witness,* "For *it is* a witness between us that the LORD *is* God."

Joshua's Farewell Address

23 Now it came to pass, a long time after the LORD had given rest to Israel from all their enemies round about, that Joshua was old, advanced in age.
2 And Joshua called for all Israel, for their elders, for their heads, for their judges, and for their officers, and said to them: "I am old, advanced in age.
3 "You have seen all that the LORD your God has done to all these nations because of you, for the LORD your God *is* He who has fought for you.
4 "See, I have divided to you by lot these nations that remain, to be an inheritance for your tribes, from the Jordan, with all the na-

22:21 [a]Literally *thousands* **22:30** [a]Literally *thousands*
22:34 [a]Septuagint adds *and half the tribe of Manasseh.*

LIFE LESSONS

➤ ***22:22 — "The LORD God of gods . . . He knows, and let Israel itself know—if it is in rebellion, or if in treachery against the LORD, do not save us this day."***

People may misunderstand our actions or expressions of devotion, but if we keep a clean conscience and take care to obey God in all things, the Lord will vindicate us in the end.

➤ ***22:33 — So the thing pleased the children of Israel, and the children of Israel blessed God . . . .***

God loves to bless His children, but it is also appropriate for His children to bless Him. How? With the only thing we have to give: a "sacrifice of praise" (Heb. 13:15).

tions that I have cut off, as far as the Great
Sea westward.
5 "And the LORD your God will expel them
from before you and drive them out of your
sight. So you shall possess their land, as the
LORD your God promised you.
➤6 "Therefore be very courageous to keep
and to do all that is written in the Book of the
Law of Moses, lest you turn aside from it to
the right hand or to the left,
7 "*and* lest you go among these nations,
these who remain among you. You shall not
make mention of the name of their gods, nor
cause *anyone* to swear *by them;* you shall not
serve them nor bow down to them,
8 "but you shall hold fast to the LORD your
God, as you have done to this day.
9 "For the LORD has driven out from before
you great and strong nations; but *as for* you,
no one has been able to stand against you to
this day.
✳10 "One man of you shall chase a thousand,
for the LORD your God *is* He who fights for
you, as He promised you.
11 "Therefore take careful heed to yourselves, that you love the LORD your God.
12 "Or else, if indeed you do go back, and
cling to the remnant of these nations—these
that remain among you—and make marriages with them, and go in to them and they
to you,
➤13 "know for certain that the LORD your God
will no longer drive out these nations from
before you. But they shall be snares and traps
to you, and scourges on your sides and thorns
in your eyes, until you perish from this good
land which the LORD your God has given you.
14 "Behold, this day I *am* going the way of all
the earth. And you know in all your hearts
and in all your souls that not one thing has
failed of all the good things which the LORD
your God spoke concerning you. All have
come to pass for you; not one word of them
has failed.
15 "Therefore it shall come to pass, that as all
the good things have come upon you which
the LORD your God promised you, so the LORD
will bring upon you all harmful things, until
He has destroyed you from this good land
which the LORD your God has given you.
16 "When you have transgressed the covenant of the LORD your God, which He commanded you, and have gone and served other
gods, and bowed down to them, then the anger of the LORD will burn against you, and you
shall perish quickly from the good land which
He has given you."

The Covenant at Shechem

24 Then Joshua gathered all the tribes of
Israel to Shechem and called for the
elders of Israel, for their heads, for their
judges, and for their officers; and they presented themselves before God.
2 And Joshua said to all the people, "Thus
says the LORD God of Israel: 'Your fathers, *including* Terah, the father of Abraham and the
father of Nahor, dwelt on the other side of the
River[a] in old times; and they served other
gods.
3 'Then I took your father Abraham from
the other side of the River, led him throughout
all the land of Canaan, and multiplied his descendants and gave him Isaac.
4 'To Isaac I gave Jacob and Esau. To Esau I
gave the mountains of Seir to possess, but Jacob and his children went down to Egypt.
5 'Also I sent Moses and Aaron, and I
plagued Egypt, according to what I did
among them. Afterward I brought you out.
6 'Then I brought your fathers out of Egypt,
and you came to the sea; and the Egyptians
pursued your fathers with chariots and horsemen to the Red Sea.
7 'So they cried out to the LORD; and He put
darkness between you and the Egyptians,
brought the sea upon them, and covered
them. And your eyes saw what I did in Egypt.
Then you dwelt in the wilderness a long time.
8 'And I brought you into the land of the
Amorites, who dwelt on the other side of the
Jordan, and they fought with you. But I gave
them into your hand, that you might possess
their land, and I destroyed them from before
you.
9 'Then Balak the son of Zippor, king of
Moab, arose to make war against Israel, and
sent and called Balaam the son of Beor to
curse you.
10 'But I would not listen to Balaam; there- ◀
fore he continued to bless you. So I delivered
you out of his hand.
11 'Then you went over the Jordan and came

24:2 [a]Hebrew *Nahar,* the Euphrates, and so in verses 3, 14, and 15

LIFE LESSONS

➤ 23:6 — ***Therefore be very courageous to keep and to do all that is written in the Book of the Law of Moses, lest you turn aside from it to the right hand or to the left . . . .***

It takes courage to obey God, and as His people we need to encourage one another daily, "lest any of you be hardened through the deceitfulness of sin" (Heb. 3:13).

➤ 23:13 — ***". . . But they shall be snares and traps to you, and scourges on your sides and thorns in your eyes, until you perish from this good land which the LORD your God has given you."***

When God tells us that we need to rid our lives of certain things, we are wise to obey. Bad things happen when we give the devil a foothold (see Eph. 4:27).

to Jericho. And the men of Jericho fought
against you—*also* the Amorites, the Perizzites, the Canaanites, the Hittites, the Girgashites, the Hivites, and the Jebusites. But I
delivered them into your hand.
➤ 12 'I sent the hornet before you which drove
them out from before you, *also* the two kings
of the Amorites, *but* not with your sword or
with your bow.
13 'I have given you a land for which you did
not labor, and cities which you did not build,
and you dwell in them; you eat of the vineyards and olive groves which you did not
plant.'
14 "Now therefore, fear the LORD, serve Him
in sincerity and in truth, and put away the
gods which your fathers served on the other
side of the River and in Egypt. Serve the
LORD!
15 "And if it seems evil to you to serve the
LORD, choose for yourselves this day whom
you will serve, whether the gods which your
fathers served that *were* on the other side of
the River, or the gods of the Amorites, in
whose land you dwell. But as for me and my
house, we will serve the LORD."
16 So the people answered and said: "Far be
it from us that we should forsake the LORD to
serve other gods;
17 "for the LORD our God *is* He who brought
us and our fathers up out of the land of Egypt,
from the house of bondage, who did those
great signs in our sight, and preserved us in
all the way that we went and among all the
people through whom we passed.
18 "And the LORD drove out from before us all
the people, including the Amorites who dwelt
in the land. We also will serve the LORD, for
He *is* our God."
19 But Joshua said to the people, "You cannot
serve the LORD, for He *is* a holy God. He *is* a
jealous God; He will not forgive your transgressions nor your sins.
20 "If you forsake the LORD and serve foreign
gods, then He will turn and do you harm
and consume you, after He has done you
good."
21 And the people said to Joshua, "No, but we
will serve the LORD!"
22 So Joshua said to the people, "You *are* witnesses against yourselves that you have chosen the LORD for yourselves, to serve Him."
And they said, "*We are* witnesses!"
23 "Now therefore," *he said*, "put away the
foreign gods which *are* among you, and incline your heart to the LORD God of Israel."
24 And the people said to Joshua, "The LORD ➤
our God we will serve, and His voice we will
obey!"
25 So Joshua made a covenant with the people that day, and made for them a statute and
an ordinance in Shechem.
26 Then Joshua wrote these words in the
Book of the Law of God. And he took a large
stone, and set it up there under the oak that
was by the sanctuary of the LORD.
27 And Joshua said to all the people, "Behold, this stone shall be a witness to us, for it
has heard all the words of the LORD which He
spoke to us. It shall therefore be a witness to
you, lest you deny your God."
28 So Joshua let the people depart, each to
his own inheritance.

Death of Joshua and Eleazar

29 Now it came to pass after these things that
Joshua the son of Nun, the servant of the
LORD, died, *being* one hundred and ten years
old.
30 And they buried him within the border of
his inheritance at Timnath Serah, which *is* in
the mountains of Ephraim, on the north side
of Mount Gaash.
31 Israel served the LORD all the days of
Joshua, and all the days of the elders who outlived Joshua, who had known all the works of
the LORD which He had done for Israel.
32 The bones of Joseph, which the children
of Israel had brought up out of Egypt, they
buried at Shechem, in the plot of ground
which Jacob had bought from the sons of
Hamor the father of Shechem for one hundred pieces of silver, and which had become
an inheritance of the children of Joseph.
33 And Eleazar the son of Aaron died. They
buried him in a hill *belonging to* Phinehas his
son, which was given to him in the mountains
of Ephraim.

LIFE LESSONS

➤ 24:10 — *"But I would not listen to Balaam; therefore he continued to bless you. So I delivered you out of his hand."*

When God sets His favor upon someone, He causes even the enemies of that person to speak blessings rather than curses.

➤ 24:12 — *"I sent the hornet before you which drove them out from before you, also the two kings of the Amorites, but not with your sword or with your bow."*

Our sovereign God can use even wild creatures to bring about His will and bless His people. *Nothing* is beyond His control, and *everything* can be a mighty tool in His hand.

➤ 24:24 — *And the people said to Joshua, "The LORD our God we will serve, and His voice we will obey!"*

What a motto for success! When we make the Lord our own, choose to serve Him, and open our ears to hear His Word and obey Him—then our own Promised Land opens wide before us.

THE BOOK OF

JUDGES

The Hebrew title of the Book of Judges is *Shophetim*, meaning "judges," "rulers," "deliverers," or "saviors." *Shophet* suggests not only the idea of maintaining justice and settling disputes, but it also can mean "liberating" and "delivering." First the judges delivered the people; then they ruled and administered justice.

The Book of Judges records the history of Israel from the death of Joshua, the successor of Moses as leader of the Jewish people, to shortly before the beginning of the monarchy under Saul, Israel's first king. It records the history of the government of Israel under fourteen judges who ruled Israel before the nation had a king.

The Book of Judges stands in stark contrast to the Book of Joshua. In Joshua, an obedient and faithful people, under the leadership of a godly man, conquered the land through trust in the power of God. In Judges, however, a disobedient and idolatrous people suffer defeat time and again because of their rebellion against God.

In seven distinct cycles of sin to salvation, Judges shows how Israel set aside God's law and in its place every man did "what was right in his own eyes" (21:25). The result was corruption from within and oppression from without.

During the more than three centuries spanned by this book, God raised up military champions to throw off the yoke of bondage and to restore the nation to pure worship. But all too soon the "sin cycle" repeated itself as the nation's spiritual temperature grew steadily colder. Yet it also reminds us that our God is a merciful and gracious Lord who is willing to restore us and bless us when we fall.

Themes: God is ever patient and always willing to extend grace and mercy to His people, even when they engage in a centuries-long cycle of apostasy and judgment then repentance. Obedience always brings blessing.

Author: Unknown, but tradition ascribes the book to Samuel.

Time: The period of the judges began after the conquest of Canaan and lasted for a little more than three hundred years, until the establishment of the monarchy under King Saul, which began around 1043 B.C.

Structure: The Book of Judges can be divided into three sections. First, Judges 1–2 chronicles Israel's increasing difficulty in her battles with the Canaanites, followed by her apostasy subsequent to the death of Joshua. Second, Judges 3–16 records a series of seven apostasies, followed by oppression from outside forces, then national repentance. Third, Judges 17–21 tells us of a terrible time of idolatry and moral decline.

As you read Judges, watch for several life principles that play an important role in this book:

6. You reap what you sow, more than you sow, and later than you sow. *See Judges 2:1–4; page 274.*

7. The dark moments of our life will last only so long as is necessary for God to accomplish His purpose in us. *See Judges 3:7–11; page 275.*

11. God assumes full responsibility for our needs when we obey Him. *See Judges 7:1–9; page 285.*

16. Whatever you acquire outside of God's will eventually turns to ashes. *See Judges 8:22–35; page 288.*

The Continuing Conquest of Canaan

➤ 1 Now after the death of Joshua it came to pass that the children of Israel asked the LORD, saying, "Who shall be first to go up for us against the Canaanites to fight against them?"

2 And the LORD said, "Judah shall go up. Indeed I have delivered the land into his hand."

3 So Judah said to Simeon his brother, "Come up with me to my allotted territory, that we may fight against the Canaanites; and I will likewise go with you to your allotted territory." And Simeon went with him.

4 Then Judah went up, and the LORD delivered the Canaanites and the Perizzites into their hand; and they killed ten thousand men at Bezek.

5 And they found Adoni-Bezek in Bezek, and fought against him; and they defeated the Canaanites and the Perizzites.

6 Then Adoni-Bezek fled, and they pursued him and caught him and cut off his thumbs and big toes.

7 And Adoni-Bezek said, "Seventy kings with their thumbs and big toes cut off used to gather *scraps* under my table; as I have done, so God has repaid me." Then they brought him to Jerusalem, and there he died.

➤ 8 Now the children of Judah fought against Jerusalem and took it; they struck it with the edge of the sword and set the city on fire.

9 And afterward the children of Judah went down to fight against the Canaanites who dwelt in the mountains, in the South,[a] and in the lowland.

10 Then Judah went against the Canaanites who dwelt in Hebron. (Now the name of Hebron *was* formerly Kirjath Arba.) And they killed Sheshai, Ahiman, and Talmai.

11 From there they went against the inhabitants of Debir. (The name of Debir *was* formerly Kirjath Sepher.)

12 Then Caleb said, "Whoever attacks Kirjath Sepher and takes it, to him I will give my daughter Achsah as wife."

13 And Othniel the son of Kenaz, Caleb's younger brother, took it; so he gave him his daughter Achsah as wife.

14 Now it happened, when she came *to him*, that she urged him[a] to ask her father for a field. And she dismounted from *her* donkey, and Caleb said to her, "What do you wish?"

15 So she said to him, "Give me a blessing; since you have given me land in the South, give me also springs of water." And Caleb gave her the upper springs and the lower springs.

16 Now the children of the Kenite, Moses' father-in-law, went up from the City of Palms with the children of Judah into the Wilderness of Judah, which *lies* in the South *near* Arad; and they went and dwelt among the people.

17 And Judah went with his brother Simeon, and they attacked the Canaanites who inhabited Zephath, and utterly destroyed it. So the name of the city was called Hormah.

18 Also Judah took Gaza with its territory, Ashkelon with its territory, and Ekron with its territory.

19 So the LORD was with Judah. And they drove out the mountaineers, but they could not drive out the inhabitants of the lowland, because they had chariots of iron.

20 And they gave Hebron to Caleb, as Moses had said. Then he expelled from there the three sons of Anak.

21 But the children of Benjamin did not drive out the Jebusites who inhabited Jerusalem; so the Jebusites dwell with the children of Benjamin in Jerusalem to this day.

22 And the house of Joseph also went up against Bethel, and the LORD *was* with them.

23 So the house of Joseph sent men to spy out Bethel. (The name of the city *was* formerly Luz.)

24 And when the spies saw a man coming out of the city, they said to him, "Please show us the entrance to the city, and we will show you mercy."

25 So he showed them the entrance to the city, and they struck the city with the edge of the sword; but they let the man and all his family go.

26 And the man went to the land of the Hittites, built a city, and called its name Luz, which *is* its name to this day.

1:9 [a]Hebrew *Negev,* and so throughout this book
1:14 [a]Septuagint and Vulgate read *he urged her.*

LIFE LESSONS

➤ 1:1 — *Now after the death of Joshua it came to pass that the children of Israel asked the LORD, saying, "Who shall be first to go up for us against the Canaanites to fight against them?"*

The Book of Judges begins well, with the successors to Joshua asking the Lord for His guidance and direction. Joshua had taught them to listen to God, and as a result they enjoyed a successful walk with God.

➤ 1:8 — *Now the children of Judah fought against Jerusalem and took it; they struck it with the edge of the sword and set the city on fire.*

The men of Judah did not capture all of Jerusalem (see Judg. 1:21); not until much later did David take the Jebusite inner citadel (see 2 Sam. 5:7). Sometimes we have to wait for God to give us final victory.

Incomplete Conquest of the Land

27 However, Manasseh did not drive out *the inhabitants of* Beth Shean and its villages, or Taanach and its villages, or the inhabitants of Dor and its villages, or the inhabitants of Ibleam and its villages, or the inhabitants of Megiddo and its villages; for the Canaanites were determined to dwell in that land.

28 And it came to pass, when Israel was strong, that they put the Canaanites under tribute, but did not completely drive them out.

29 Nor did Ephraim drive out the Canaanites who dwelt in Gezer; so the Canaanites dwelt in Gezer among them.

30 Nor did Zebulun drive out the inhabitants of Kitron or the inhabitants of Nahalol; so the Canaanites dwelt among them, and were put under tribute.

31 Nor did Asher drive out the inhabitants of Acco or the inhabitants of Sidon, or of Ahlab, Achzib, Helbah, Aphik, or Rehob.

32 So the Asherites dwelt among the Canaanites, the inhabitants of the land; for they did not drive them out.

33 Nor did Naphtali drive out the inhabitants of Beth Shemesh or the inhabitants of Beth Anath; but they dwelt among the Canaanites, the inhabitants of the land. Nevertheless the inhabitants of Beth Shemesh and Beth Anath were put under tribute to them.

34 And the Amorites forced the children of Dan into the mountains, for they would not allow them to come down to the valley;

35 and the Amorites were determined to dwell in Mount Heres, in Aijalon, and in Shaalbim;[a] yet when the strength of the house of Joseph became greater, they were put under tribute.

36 Now the boundary of the Amorites *was* from the Ascent of Akrabbim, from Sela, and upward.

Israel's Disobedience

2 Then the Angel of the LORD came up from Gilgal to Bochim, and said: "I led you up from Egypt and brought you to the land of which I swore to your fathers; and I said, 'I will never break My covenant with you.

2 'And you shall make no covenant with the inhabitants of this land; you shall tear down their altars.' But you have not obeyed My voice. Why have you done this?

3 "Therefore I also said, 'I will not drive them out before you; but they shall be *thorns* in your side,[a] and their gods shall be a snare to you.'"

4 So it was, when the Angel of the LORD spoke these words to all the children of Israel, that the people lifted up their voices and wept.

5 Then they called the name of that place Bochim;[a] and they sacrificed there to the LORD.

6 And when Joshua had dismissed the people, the children of Israel went each to his own inheritance to possess the land.

Death of Joshua

7 So the people served the LORD all the days of Joshua, and all the days of the elders who outlived Joshua, who had seen all the great works of the LORD which He had done for Israel.

8 Now Joshua the son of Nun, the servant of the LORD, died *when he was* one hundred and ten years old.

9 And they buried him within the border of his inheritance at Timnath Heres, in the mountains of Ephraim, on the north side of Mount Gaash.

10 When all that generation had been gathered to their fathers, another generation arose after them who did not know the LORD nor the work which He had done for Israel.

Israel's Unfaithfulness

11 Then the children of Israel did evil in the sight of the LORD, and served the Baals;

12 and they forsook the LORD God of their fathers, who had brought them out of the land of Egypt; and they followed other gods from *among* the gods of the people who *were* all

---

1:35 [a]Spelled *Shaalabbin* in Joshua 19:42 **2:3** [a]Septuagint, Targum, and Vulgate read *enemies to you.* **2:5** [a]Literally *Weeping*

LIFE LESSONS

➤ 2:2-3 — *". . . you have not obeyed My voice. Why have you done this? Therefore I also said, 'I will not drive them out before you; but they shall be thorns in your side, and their gods shall be a snare to you.'"*

Incomplete obedience has dire consequences. Will we continue to trust the Lord and obey His Word when the going gets tough? Our answer will determine whether we ultimately succeed or fail.

➤ 2:10 — *When all that generation had been gathered to their fathers, another generation arose after them who did not know the LORD nor the work which He had done for Israel.*

There is no such thing as hand-me-down faith. Each person and generation must come to know God personally and make their faith their own.

➤ 2:12 — *. . . and they forsook the LORD God of their fathers . . . and they followed other gods . . . and they bowed down to them; and they provoked the LORD to anger.*

The Lord predicted that if the people did not completely remove the pagan influence from their land, they would eventually serve pagan gods (Judg. 2:3). His Word always comes true, for blessing or for judgment.

around them, and they bowed down to them; and they provoked the LORD to anger.
13 They forsook the LORD and served Baal and the Ashtoreths.[a]
14 And the anger of the LORD was hot against Israel. So He delivered them into the hands of plunderers who despoiled them; and He sold them into the hands of their enemies all around, so that they could no longer stand before their enemies.
15 Wherever they went out, the hand of the LORD was against them for calamity, as the LORD had said, and as the LORD had sworn to them. And they were greatly distressed.
16 Nevertheless, the LORD raised up judges who delivered them out of the hand of those who plundered them.
17 Yet they would not listen to their judges, but they played the harlot with other gods, and bowed down to them. They turned quickly from the way in which their fathers walked, in obeying the commandments of the LORD; they did not do so.
➤ 18 And when the LORD raised up judges for them, the LORD was with the judge and delivered them out of the hand of their enemies all the days of the judge; for the LORD was moved to pity by their groaning because of those who oppressed them and harassed them.
19 And it came to pass, when the judge was dead, that they reverted and behaved more corruptly than their fathers, by following other gods, to serve them and bow down to them. They did not cease from their own doings nor from their stubborn way.
20 Then the anger of the LORD was hot against Israel; and He said, "Because this nation has transgressed My covenant which I commanded their fathers, and has not heeded My voice,
21 "I also will no longer drive out before them any of the nations which Joshua left when he died,
➤ 22 "so that through them I may test Israel, whether they will keep the ways of the LORD, to walk in them as their fathers kept *them,* or not."
23 Therefore the LORD left those nations, without driving them out immediately; nor did He deliver them into the hand of Joshua.

The Nations Remaining in the Land

3 Now these *are* the nations which the LORD left, that He might test Israel by them, *that is,* all who had not known any of the wars in Canaan
2 (*this was* only so that the generations of the children of Israel might be taught to know war, at least those who had not formerly known it),
3 *namely,* five lords of the Philistines, all the Canaanites, the Sidonians, and the Hivites who dwelt in Mount Lebanon, from Mount Baal Hermon to the entrance of Hamath.
4 And they were *left, that He might* test Israel by them, to know whether they would obey the commandments of the LORD, which He had commanded their fathers by the hand of Moses.
5 Thus the children of Israel dwelt among the Canaanites, the Hittites, the Amorites, the Perizzites, the Hivites, and the Jebusites.
6 And they took their daughters to be their wives, and gave their daughters to their sons; and they served their gods. ➤

Othniel

7 So the children of Israel did evil in the sight of the LORD. They forgot the LORD their God, and served the Baals and Asherahs.[a]
8 Therefore the anger of the LORD was hot against Israel, and He sold them into the hand of Cushan-Rishathaim king of Mesopotamia; and the children of Israel served Cushan-Rishathaim eight years.
9 When the children of Israel cried out to the LORD, the LORD raised up a deliverer for the children of Israel, who delivered them: Othniel the son of Kenaz, Caleb's younger brother. ✳
10 The Spirit of the LORD came upon him, and he judged Israel. He went out to war, and the LORD delivered Cushan-Rishathaim king of Mesopotamia into his hand; and his hand prevailed over Cushan-Rishathaim.
11 So the land had rest for forty years. Then Othniel the son of Kenaz died.

2:13 [a]Canaanite goddesses **3:7** [a]Name or symbol for Canaanite goddesses

LIFE LESSONS

➤ **2:18 — . . . *the LORD was moved to pity by their groaning because of those who oppressed them and harassed them.***

Where would we be if the Lord did not temper His judgment with mercy? He is a holy God with a loving heart—and for that reason we continue to live and breathe.

➤ **2:22 — *". . . so that through them I may test Israel, whether they will keep the ways of the LORD, to walk in them as their fathers kept them, or not."***

God often uses difficulties and hardships to test us, to see whether we will continue to trust Him and obey Him "no matter what."

➤ **3:6 — *And they took their daughters to be their wives, and gave their daughters to their sons; and they served their gods.***

Marriage can make or break one's faith. Judges declares that Israel fell into idolatry by marrying into it, just as King Solomon would many years later (1 Kin. 11:4). Christians are not to marry unbelievers—period (2 Cor. 6:14).

LIFE PRINCIPLE 6

YOU REAP WHAT YOU SOW, MORE THAN YOU SOW, AND LATER THAN YOU SOW.

JUDG. 2:1–4

Today is the father of tomorrow. What we are today is the result of what we have been thinking and the way we have lived in the past. Those who save wisely today will have plenty tomorrow. Those who spend everything they have today will have little or nothing in the future. It is a shortsighted person who thinks only of the now, doing as little as possible, for on payday he will have no way to avoid the poor quality and small quantity of his rewards.

God has given us in Scripture a principle that serves both as a warning and an encouragement: "Do not be deceived, God is not mocked; for whatever a man sows, that he will also reap" (Gal. 6:7). This is an unalterable law that affects everyone in every area of life, family, work, and pleasure.

Every farmer understands the hidden meaning in this principle: we reap what we sow, more than we sow, and later than we sow. Let's look at each part of the principle to make sure we understand its full implications.

1. The principle applies to everyone, both Christians and non-Christians.

This principle is irrevocable; there is no escape, either for the believer or for the unbeliever. It is a law of life.

Did you notice how Galatians 6:7 begins? It says, "Do not be deceived, God is not mocked." Herein lies the root cause of the careless and indulgent lifestyle of many believers. They *are* deceived. They either do not believe the truth, or they think they will somehow be the exceptions to God's laws.

To mock God is to turn up one's nose at Him, to hope to outwit Him—a foolish thought, as 2 Corinthians 5:10 reveals: "For we must all appear before the judgment seat of Christ, that each one may receive the things done in the body, according to what he has done, whether good or bad."

If you were required to appear before the judgment seat of Christ in the next five minutes, what kind of crops would you be able to show?

2. We reap what we sow.

The fact that we reap what we sow is good news for those who sow good habits, but a frightening thought for those currently involved in ungodly activities such as promiscuity, drug and alco-

"Whatever a man sows, that he will also reap."

hol abuse, neglect of family or mistreatment of others in order to climb the ladder of success. We cannot sow crabgrass and expect to reap pineapples. We cannot sow disobedience to God and expect to reap His blessing. What we sow, we reap. Let us not deceive ourselves: we *will* reap the harvest of our lives.

3. We reap more than we sow.

Why do farmers plant their seed? Because they expect to harvest a great deal more than they sow. A single seed that sprouts can yield dozens, scores, even hundreds of seeds. It is the same way with both sin and righteousness—a small decision to do either good or bad reaps a much bigger crop, for either joy or sorrow.

Jesus used the picture of a sprouting seed to show that when we allow God's Word to produce good things in us, the results multiply: "He who received seed on the good ground is he who hears the word and understands it, who indeed bears fruit and produces: some a hundredfold, some sixty, some thirty" (Matt. 13:23). On the other side of the ledger, the prophet Hosea describes what awaits those who choose to sow seeds of wickedness: "They sow the wind, and reap the whirlwind" (Hos. 8:7).

4. We reap later than we sow.

Some are deceived because their present seed does not appear to be producing an immediate crop. So they continue down their course, mistakenly believing that there will never be a harvest. But unlike the crops of the field, which get harvested at approximately the same time each year, there is no regular timetable for the harvest of life. Some crops we reap quickly; others take a long time. But do not be deceived—their season *will* come. And by going the second mile now and giving more than is required, we will reap rich dividends later.

"For whatever a man sows, that he will also reap." What a comforting and assuring thought to those who faithfully labor under difficult circumstances! Faithfulness in such situations *will* produce a rich harvest in the future, for our heavenly Father always keeps His promises.

See the Life Principles Index for further study.

Some crops we reap quickly; others take a long time.

Ehud

➤ **12** And the children of Israel again did evil in
the sight of the LORD. So the LORD strengthened Eglon king of Moab against Israel, because they had done evil in the sight of the
LORD.
13 Then he gathered to himself the people of
Ammon and Amalek, went and defeated Israel, and took possession of the City of
Palms.
14 So the children of Israel served Eglon king
of Moab eighteen years.
15 But when the children of Israel cried out
to the LORD, the LORD raised up a deliverer for
them: Ehud the son of Gera, the Benjamite, a
left-handed man. By him the children of Israel sent tribute to Eglon king of Moab.
16 Now Ehud made himself a dagger (it
was double-edged and a cubit in length) and
fastened it under his clothes on his right
thigh.
17 So he brought the tribute to Eglon king of
Moab. (Now Eglon *was* a very fat man.)
18 And when he had finished presenting the
tribute, he sent away the people who had carried the tribute.
19 But he himself turned back from the stone
images that *were* at Gilgal, and said, "I have a
secret message for you, O king." He said,
"Keep silence!" And all who attended him
went out from him.
20 So Ehud came to him (now he was sitting
upstairs in his cool private chamber). Then
Ehud said, "I have a message from God for
you." So he arose from *his* seat.
21 Then Ehud reached with his left hand,
took the dagger from his right thigh, and
thrust it into his belly.
22 Even the hilt went in after the blade, and
the fat closed over the blade, for he did not
draw the dagger out of his belly; and his entrails came out.
23 Then Ehud went out through the porch
and shut the doors of the upper room behind
him and locked them.
24 When he had gone out, *Eglon's*[a] servants
came to look, and *to their* surprise, the doors
of the upper room were locked. So they said,
"He is probably attending to his needs in the
cool chamber."
25 So they waited till they were embarrassed,
and still he had not opened the doors of the
upper room. Therefore they took the key and
opened *them*. And there was their master,
fallen dead on the floor.
26 But Ehud had escaped while they delayed,
and passed beyond the stone images and escaped to Seirah.
27 And it happened, when he arrived, that he
blew the trumpet in the mountains of
Ephraim, and the children of Israel went
down with him from the mountains; and he
led them.
28 Then he said to them, "Follow *me*, for the
LORD has delivered your enemies the
Moabites into your hand." So they went down
after him, seized the fords of the Jordan leading to Moab, and did not allow anyone to
cross over.
29 And at that time they killed about ten
thousand men of Moab, all stout men of valor;
not a man escaped.
30 So Moab was subdued that day under the
hand of Israel. And the land had rest for
eighty years.

Shamgar

31 After him was Shamgar the son of Anath,
who killed six hundred men of the Philistines with an ox goad; and he also delivered
Israel.

Deborah

4 When Ehud was dead, the children of
Israel again did evil in the sight of the
LORD.
2 So the LORD sold them into the hand of
Jabin king of Canaan, who reigned in Hazor.
The commander of his army *was* Sisera, who
dwelt in Harosheth Hagoyim.
3 And the children of Israel cried out to the
LORD; for Jabin had nine hundred chariots of
iron, and for twenty years he had harshly oppressed the children of Israel.
4 Now Deborah, a prophetess, the wife of
Lapidoth, was judging Israel at that time.
5 And she would sit under the palm tree of
Deborah between Ramah and Bethel in the
mountains of Ephraim. And the children of Israel came up to her for judgment.
6 Then she sent and called for Barak the
son of Abinoam from Kedesh in Naphtali,
and said to him, "Has not the LORD God of Israel commanded, 'Go and deploy *troops* at
Mount Tabor; take with you ten thousand
men of the sons of Naphtali and of the sons of
Zebulun;

3:24 [a]Literally *his*

LIFE LESSONS

➤ **3:12 — . . . *So the LORD strengthened Eglon king of Moab against Israel, because they had done evil in the sight of the LORD.***

When we make it a habit to disobey Him, God may take an active role in increasing the power of our enemies. He does this so we will repent and return to Him, not to destroy us.

➤ 7 'and against you I will deploy Sisera, the commander of Jabin's army, with his chariots and his multitude at the River Kishon; and I will deliver him into your hand'?"

8 And Barak said to her, "If you will go with me, then I will go; but if you will not go with me, I will not go!"

9 So she said, "I will surely go with you; nevertheless there will be no glory for you in the journey you are taking, for the LORD will sell Sisera into the hand of a woman." Then Deborah arose and went with Barak to Kedesh.

10 And Barak called Zebulun and Naphtali to Kedesh; he went up with ten thousand men under his command,[a] and Deborah went up with him.

11 Now Heber the Kenite, of the children of Hobab the father-in-law of Moses, had separated himself from the Kenites and pitched his tent near the terebinth tree at Zaanaim, which *is* beside Kedesh.

12 And they reported to Sisera that Barak the son of Abinoam had gone up to Mount Tabor.

13 So Sisera gathered together all his chariots, nine hundred chariots of iron, and all the people who *were* with him, from Harosheth Hagoyim to the River Kishon.

14 Then Deborah said to Barak, "Up! For this *is* the day in which the LORD has delivered Sisera into your hand. Has not the LORD gone out before you?" So Barak went down from Mount Tabor with ten thousand men following him.

➤ 15 And the LORD routed Sisera and all *his* chariots and all *his* army with the edge of the sword before Barak; and Sisera alighted from *his* chariot and fled away on foot.

16 But Barak pursued the chariots and the army as far as Harosheth Hagoyim, and all the army of Sisera fell by the edge of the sword; not a man was left.

17 However, Sisera had fled away on foot to the tent of Jael, the wife of Heber the Kenite; for *there was* peace between Jabin king of Hazor and the house of Heber the Kenite.

18 And Jael went out to meet Sisera, and said to him, "Turn aside, my lord, turn aside to me; do not fear." And when he had turned aside with her into the tent, she covered him with a blanket.

19 Then he said to her, "Please give me a little water to drink, for I am thirsty." So she opened a jug of milk, gave him a drink, and covered him.

20 And he said to her, "Stand at the door of the tent, and if any man comes and inquires of you, and says, 'Is there any man here?' you shall say, 'No.'"

21 Then Jael, Heber's wife, took a tent peg and took a hammer in her hand, and went softly to him and drove the peg into his temple, and it went down into the ground; for he was fast asleep and weary. So he died.

22 And then, as Barak pursued Sisera, Jael came out to meet him, and said to him, "Come, I will show you the man whom you seek." And when he went into her *tent*, there lay Sisera, dead with the peg in his temple.

23 So on that day God subdued Jabin king of Canaan in the presence of the children of Israel.

24 And the hand of the children of Israel grew stronger and stronger against Jabin king of Canaan, until they had destroyed Jabin king of Canaan.

The Song of Deborah

5 Then Deborah and Barak the son of Abinoam sang on that day, saying:

2 "When leaders lead in Israel,
When the people willingly offer
themselves,
Bless the LORD!

3 "Hear, O kings! Give ear, O princes!
I, *even* I, will sing to the LORD;
I will sing praise to the LORD God of Israel.

4 "LORD, when You went out from Seir,
When You marched from the field of
Edom,
The earth trembled and the heavens
poured,
The clouds also poured water;
5 The mountains gushed before the LORD,
This Sinai, before the LORD God of Israel.

6 "In the days of Shamgar, son of Anath,
In the days of Jael,

4:10 [a]Literally *at his feet*

LIFE LESSONS

➤ 4:7 — *". . . against you I will deploy Sisera, the commander of Jabin's army, with his chariots and his multitude at the River Kishon . . . ."*

Note that the Lord says, "*I* will deploy Sisera," the enemy commander. God is sovereign! Even the movement of enemy troops is subject to His rule.

➤ 4:15 — *And the LORD routed Sisera and all his chariots and all his army with the edge of the sword before Barak . . . .*

The Bible declares that *the Lord* routed Sisera; the sword of Barak and his men were only secondary. As David said years later, "the LORD does not save with sword and spear; for the battle is the LORD's" (1 Sam. 17:47).

Life Examples:

DEBORAH

A Mother in Israel

JUDG. 5:7

The Bible doesn't tell us much about Deborah other than to call her a prophetess, a highly esteemed judge of Israel, and the wife of Lappidoth. We don't know if Scripture's description of her as "a mother in Israel" (Judg. 5:7) means that she had children or that she cared for Israel as only a loving mother could. We do not know why God chose Deborah to become a judge; that seems strange in a culture generally ruled by men.

We do know that Deborah loved God and served Him faithfully. We do know the people trusted her, and that even the commander of the army, Barak, respected her leadership.

Deborah's example indicates that it doesn't take a certain set of credentials to become an effective servant of God. The Lord uses the person who listens to Him and obeys. Deborah made herself available to God, and God made her victorious.

See the Life Principles Index for further study:
21. Obedience always brings blessing.
1. Our intimacy with God—His highest priority for our lives—determines the impact of our lives.

The highways were deserted,
And the travelers walked along the byways.
7 Village life ceased, it ceased in Israel,
Until I, Deborah, arose,
Arose a mother in Israel.
8 They chose new gods;
Then *there was* war in the gates;
Not a shield or spear was seen among forty thousand in Israel.
9 My heart *is* with the rulers of Israel
Who offered themselves willingly with the people.
Bless the LORD!

10 "Speak, you who ride on white donkeys,
Who sit in judges' attire,
And who walk along the road.
11 Far from the noise of the archers, among the watering places,
There they shall recount the righteous acts of the LORD,
The righteous acts *for* His villagers in Israel;
Then the people of the LORD shall go down to the gates.

12 "Awake, awake, Deborah!
Awake, awake, sing a song!
Arise, Barak, and lead your captives away,
O son of Abinoam!

13 "Then the survivors came down, the people against the nobles;
The LORD came down for me against the mighty.
14 From Ephraim *were* those whose roots were in Amalek.
After you, Benjamin, with your peoples,
From Machir rulers came down,
And from Zebulun those who bear the recruiter's staff.
15 And the princes of Issachar[a] *were* with Deborah;
As Issachar, so *was* Barak
Sent into the valley under his command;[b]
Among the divisions of Reuben
There were great resolves of heart.
16 Why did you sit among the sheepfolds,
To hear the pipings for the flocks?
The divisions of Reuben have great searchings of heart.
17 Gilead stayed beyond the Jordan,
And why did Dan remain on ships?[a]
Asher continued at the seashore,
And stayed by his inlets.
18 Zebulun *is* a people *who* jeopardized their lives to the point of death,
Naphtali also, on the heights of the battlefield.

19 "The kings came *and* fought,
Then the kings of Canaan fought

5:15 [a]Following Septuagint, Syriac, Targum, and Vulgate; Masoretic Text reads *And my princes in Issachar.* [b]Literally *at his feet* 5:17 [a]Or *at ease*

LIFE LESSONS

➤ 5:13 — "... The LORD came down for me against the mighty."

When we face off against the mighty, we need the Lord to help us. If we want to win, then we will get on our knees in prayer.

In Taanach, by the waters of Megiddo;
They took no spoils of silver.
20 They fought from the heavens;
The stars from their courses fought
against Sisera.
21 The torrent of Kishon swept them away,
That ancient torrent, the torrent of
Kishon.
O my soul, march on in strength!
22 Then the horses' hooves pounded,
The galloping, galloping of his steeds.
23 'Curse Meroz,' said the angel[a] of the
LORD,
'Curse its inhabitants bitterly,
Because they did not come to the help of
the LORD,
To the help of the LORD against the
mighty.'

24 "Most blessed among women is Jael,
The wife of Heber the Kenite;
Blessed is she among women in tents.
25 He asked for water, she gave milk;
She brought out cream in a lordly
bowl.
26 She stretched her hand to the tent
peg,
Her right hand to the workmen's
hammer;
She pounded Sisera, she pierced his
head,
She split and struck through his temple.
27 At her feet he sank, he fell, he lay still;
At her feet he sank, he fell;
Where he sank, there he fell dead.

28 "The mother of Sisera looked through the
window,
And cried out through the lattice,
'Why is his chariot *so* long in coming?
Why tarries the clatter of his chariots?'
29 Her wisest ladies answered her,
Yes, she answered herself,
30 'Are they not finding and dividing the
spoil:
To every man a girl *or* two;
For Sisera, plunder of dyed garments,
Plunder of garments embroidered and
dyed,
Two pieces of dyed embroidery for the
neck of the looter?'

✳ 31 "Thus let all Your enemies perish,
O LORD!
But *let* those who love Him *be* like the
sun
When it comes out in full strength."

So the land had rest for forty years.

Midianites Oppress Israel

6 Then the children of Israel did evil in the
sight of the LORD. So the LORD delivered
them into the hand of Midian for seven
years,
2 and the hand of Midian prevailed against
Israel. Because of the Midianites, the children
of Israel made for themselves the dens, the
caves, and the strongholds which *are* in the
mountains.
3 So it was, whenever Israel had sown, Midianites would come up; also Amalekites and
the people of the East would come up against
them.
4 Then they would encamp against them
and destroy the produce of the earth as far as
Gaza, and leave no sustenance for Israel, neither sheep nor ox nor donkey.
5 For they would come up with their livestock and their tents, coming in as numerous
as locusts; both they and their camels were
without number; and they would enter the
land to destroy it.
6 So Israel was greatly impoverished because of the Midianites, and the children of
Israel cried out to the LORD.
7 And it came to pass, when the children of
Israel cried out to the LORD because of the
Midianites,
8 that the LORD sent a prophet to the children of Israel, who said to them, "Thus says
the LORD God of Israel: 'I brought you up from
Egypt and brought you out of the house of
bondage;
9 and I delivered you out of the hand of the
Egyptians and out of the hand of all who oppressed you, and drove them out before you
and gave you their land.
10 Also I said to you, "I *am* the LORD your ➤
God; do not fear the gods of the Amorites, in
whose land you dwell." But you have not
obeyed My voice.'"

Gideon

11 Now the Angel of the LORD came and sat
under the terebinth tree which *was* in
Ophrah, which *belonged* to Joash the
Abiezrite, while his son Gideon threshed

5:23 [a]Or *Angel*

LIFE LESSONS

➤ **6:10 — *"Also I said to you, 'I am the LORD your God; do not fear the gods of the Amorites, in whose land you dwell.' But you have not obeyed My voice."***

God intends all of His words for our benefit, although not all of them bring us comfort. When the Lord rebukes or admonishes us, He does so out of love, desiring that we return to Him, the source of life.

ANSWERS TO LIFE'S QUESTIONS

What should I do when I feel distant from God?

JUDG. 6:6

It's safe to say that not a believer alive today has avoided those "desert" times when he or she just didn't feel the presence of God. It's a problem that all of us have to confront at some point along the way.

Many factors can make us feel distant from our heavenly Father. Sometimes, it's a matter of our accuser, the devil, whispering in our ears and speaking his deception. At other times, these "distant" times turn out to be seasons when God is trying to bring us closer to Himself. But sometimes it's a matter of our need to do some inner "housecleaning."

Nothing can make us feel more distant from God than our own unconfessed sin. While our stumbles don't make God love us one bit less, they do drive a wedge between us and Him, much like some offense can drive a wedge between even the most loving and devoted husband and wife.

Throughout the Book of Judges, we read how Israel had sinned and drifted in its devotion to God. Many times when our hearts become entangled with sin and the things of this world, God allows us to experience a feeling of distance between Him and us. This is exactly what Israel felt in those dark days.

Israel should have recognized the Lord's coolness and lack of nearness. Instead, the people of God continued to worship Baal without regard for God's intimate love for them. Therefore, God allowed them to experience a time of testing. In Judges 6 we read that "Israel was greatly impoverished because of the Midianites, and the children of Israel cried out to the LORD" (v. 6). Here we see at work an important principle regarding repentance and regaining favor with the Lord.

When we realize our error and cry out to God, He comes to us. He never comes, however, as if being summoned by a superior. He comes when our hearts have been broken and when at last we realize our need for Him. When we humbly confess our sins and our dependence on Him, He hears our prayers and brings deliverance from sin (Judg. 6:11).

If you are experiencing a time of coolness in your devotion to God, don't hesitate to turn to Him in prayer. Confess any known sin, and ask Him to restore the sweetness of His fellowship to your heart.

See the Life Principles Index for further study:

12. Peace with God is the fruit of oneness with God.

15. Brokenness is God's requirement for maximum usefulness.

wheat in the winepress, in order to hide *it* from the Midianites.
12 And the Angel of the LORD appeared to him, and said to him, "The LORD *is* with you, you mighty man of valor!"
13 Gideon said to Him, "O my lord,[a] if the LORD is with us, why then has all this happened to us? And where *are* all His miracles which our fathers told us about, saying, 'Did not the LORD bring us up from Egypt?' But now the LORD has forsaken us and delivered us into the hands of the Midianites."
14 Then the LORD turned to him and said, "Go in this might of yours, and you shall save Israel from the hand of the Midianites. Have I not sent you?"
15 So he said to Him, "O my Lord,[a] how can I save Israel? Indeed my clan *is* the weakest in Manasseh, and I *am* the least in my father's house."

6:13 [a]Hebrew *adoni,* used of man **6:15** [a]Hebrew *Adonai,* used of God

LIFE LESSONS

➤ ***6:12 — And the Angel of the LORD appeared to him, and said to him, "The LORD is with you, you mighty man of valor!"***

The Lord's estimation of us often differs from our own. God saw Gideon as a "mighty man of valor." Gideon saw himself as weak and little (Judg. 6:15). When we believe God and not ourselves, we become what He says we are.

What the Bible Says About Adversity as a Revealer of Our Strengths and Weaknesses

Judg. 6:12, 13

When adversity strikes, we find out what we are made of. Perhaps you've said in the aftermath of some hardship, "Before this happened, I never would have thought that I could deal with something like this."

Gideon had that type of understanding. When the angel of the Lord said to him, "The LORD is with you, you mighty man of valor!" Gideon automatically responded, "O my lord, if the LORD is with us, why then has all this happened to us? . . . The LORD has forsaken us" (Judg. 6:12, 13). Gideon saw himself and his people as weak and unworthy. The Lord replied almost as if He hadn't heard him: "Go in this might of yours, and you shall save Israel from the hand of the Midianites. Have I not sent you?" (v. 14).

Again, Gideon replied with an extremely low view of himself: "O my Lord, how can I save Israel? Indeed my clan is the weakest in Manasseh, and I am the least in my father's house" (v. 15). Once more the Lord encouraged Gideon, "Surely I will be with you, and you shall defeat the Midianites as one man" (v. 16).

Our strength lies in the Lord and not in ourselves.

Friend, when the Lord calls you strong, don't declare yourself weak!

When the Lord says you are forgiven, don't dwell on your sins!

When the Lord says you are righteous, don't see yourself as guilty!

Never try to cope with adversity on your own. You need the Lord's help. We cannot help ourselves at any time. We need the Lord's help every hour of every day of every year. And He is our ever-present help.

Our strength lies in the Lord and not in ourselves. There is no comparison between the might and ability of God and of humankind. He is infinite; we are finite. When we rely on the Lord, we have access to his unlimited power and wisdom, and therefore, we will not end up as failures. When we attempt to rely on ourselves, however, usually we fail miserably . . . and often suffer even more adversity. Don't make that mistake!

See the Life Principles Index for further study:
24. To live the Christian life is to allow Jesus to live His life in and through us.
29. We learn more in our valley experiences than on our mountaintops.

➤ 16 And the LORD said to him, "Surely I will be
with you, and you shall defeat the Midianites
as one man."
17 Then he said to Him, "If now I have found
favor in Your sight, then show me a sign that
it is You who talk with me.
18 "Do not depart from here, I pray, until I
come to You and bring out my offering and set
it before You." And He said, "I will wait until
you come back."
19 So Gideon went in and prepared a young
goat, and unleavened bread from an ephah of
flour. The meat he put in a basket, and he put
the broth in a pot; and he brought *them* out to
Him under the terebinth tree and presented
them.
20 The Angel of God said to him, "Take the
meat and the unleavened bread and lay *them*
on this rock, and pour out the broth." And he
did so.
21 Then the Angel of the LORD put out the
end of the staff that *was* in His hand, and
touched the meat and the unleavened bread;
and fire rose out of the rock and consumed
the meat and the unleavened bread. And
the Angel of the LORD departed out of his
sight.
22 Now Gideon perceived that He *was* the
Angel of the LORD. So Gideon said, "Alas, O
Lord GOD! For I have seen the Angel of the
LORD face to face."
23 Then the LORD said to him, "Peace *be* with
you; do not fear, you shall not die."
24 So Gideon built an altar there to the LORD,
and called it The-LORD-*Is*-Peace.[a] To this day
it *is* still in Ophrah of the Abiezrites.
25 Now it came to pass the same night that
the LORD said to him, "Take your father's
young bull, the second bull of seven years old,
and tear down the altar of Baal that your father has, and cut down the wooden image[a]
that *is* beside it;
26 "and build an altar to the LORD your God
on top of this rock in the proper arrangement,
and take the second bull and offer a burnt
sacrifice with the wood of the image which
you shall cut down."
27 So Gideon took ten men from among his
servants and did as the LORD had said to him.
But because he feared his father's household
and the men of the city too much to do *it* by
day, he did *it* by night.

Gideon Destroys the Altar of Baal

28 And when the men of the city arose early
in the morning, there was the altar of Baal,
torn down; and the wooden image that *was*
beside it was cut down, and the second bull
was being offered on the altar *which had been*
built.
29 So they said to one another, "Who has
done this thing?" And when they had inquired
and asked, they said, "Gideon the son of
Joash has done this thing."
30 Then the men of the city said to Joash,
"Bring out your son, that he may die, because
he has torn down the altar of Baal, and because he has cut down the wooden image that
was beside it."
31 But Joash said to all who stood against
him, "Would you plead for Baal? Would you
save him? Let the one who would plead for
him be put to death by morning! If he *is* a god,
let him plead for himself, because his altar
has been torn down!"
32 Therefore on that day he called him Jerubbaal,[a] saying, "Let Baal plead against him, because he has torn down his altar."
33 Then all the Midianites and Amalekites,
the people of the East, gathered together; and
they crossed over and encamped in the Valley
of Jezreel.
34 But the Spirit of the LORD came upon Gid- ➤
eon; then he blew the trumpet, and the
Abiezrites gathered behind him.
35 And he sent messengers throughout all
Manasseh, who also gathered behind him. He
also sent messengers to Asher, Zebulun, and
Naphtali; and they came up to meet them.

The Sign of the Fleece

36 So Gideon said to God, "If You will save Israel by my hand as You have said—
37 look, I shall put a fleece of wool on the
threshing floor; if there is dew on the fleece
only, and *it is* dry on all the ground, then I
shall know that You will save Israel by my
hand, as You have said."
38 And it was so. When he rose early the next
morning and squeezed the fleece together, he
wrung the dew out of the fleece, a bowlful of
water.

6:24 [a]Hebrew *YHWH Shalom* **6:25** [a]Hebrew *Asherah*, a Canaanite goddess **6:32** [a]Literally *Let Baal Plead*

LIFE LESSONS

➤ 6:16 — *And the LORD said to him, "Surely I will be with you, and you shall defeat the Midianites as one man."*

The secret to success remains the same throughout the Bible: the presence of God. When He is with us—or more accurately, when we are with Him—success naturally follows.

➤ 6:34 — *But the Spirit of the LORD came upon Gideon; then he blew the trumpet, and the Abiezrites gathered behind him.*

When the Spirit of the living God fills us, "impossibilities" become possible. As Paul writes, "For God has not given us a spirit of fear, but of power and of love and of a sound mind" (2 Tim. 1:7).

ANSWERS TO LIFE'S QUESTIONS

Is "fleece throwing" a good way to discover the will of God?

JUDG. 6:36–40

Some try to determine God's will by "throwing fleeces." We say, "If X happens, then I'll do one thing; but if Z happens, then I'll do another." But how does such a strategy differ from treating the will of God like a coin toss and basing our decisions on whether it falls heads or tails? In most cases, putting out a fleece demonstrates not a robust faith in God, but an unhealthy suspicion that He doesn't have our best interests at heart and that He really can't be trusted to fulfill His Word.

We find the act of fleece throwing in the Book of Judges, when God calls Gideon to fight the Midianites (Judg. 6:36–40). Gideon doesn't feel so sure about the divine assignment and puts out his fleece, not to discover the will of God, but to try to gain some confidence that he will enjoy success. Notice three things about this questionable practice.

First, the fleece throwing was Gideon's idea, not God's. Nowhere in Scripture does God authorize such a practice or call it a desirable method for knowing His purposes.

Second, only here in Scripture is this method used. No one else employs it.

Third, Gideon did not perform the fleece-throwing to know God's will, but to gain confidence in the outcome that God had promised. Gideon already knew with certainty that God wanted him to lead the people into battle against the Midianites. The armies had already gathered for battle! Gideon knew he was the leader. He simply wanted an extraordinary sign from God that he and the Israelites would succeed.

Repeatedly in Scripture, God calls us to remain faithful to Him without regard to whether we will succeed. Genuine trust in God means that we follow Him wherever He leads and do whatever He directs, without any concern for the outcome. Job had the right idea: "Though He slay me, yet will I trust Him" (Job 13:15).

Gideon's fleece throwing indicated that he didn't really trust God. Likewise today, many people who use "fleece throwing" reveal that they don't really trust God to remain true to His word. But God calls us to a different path, laid out by the psalmist: "God is our refuge and strength, a very present help in trouble. Therefore we will not fear, even though the earth be removed, and though the mountains be carried into the midst of the sea" (Ps. 46:1–2).

See the Life Principles Index for further study:

9. Trusting God means looking beyond what we can see to what God sees.

2. Obey God and leave all the consequences to Him.

39 Then Gideon said to God, "Do not be angry with me, but let me speak just once more: Let me test, I pray, just once more with the fleece; let it now be dry only on the fleece, but on all the ground let there be dew."
40 And God did so that night. It was dry on the fleece only, but there was dew on all the ground.

Gideon's Valiant Three Hundred

7 Then Jerubbaal (that *is,* Gideon) and all the people who *were* with him rose early and encamped beside the well of Harod, so that the camp of the Midianites was on the north side of them by the hill of Moreh in the valley.
2 And the LORD said to Gideon, "The people who *are* with you *are* too many for Me to give the Midianites into their hands, lest Israel claim glory for itself against Me, saying, 'My own hand has saved me.'
3 "Now therefore, proclaim in the hearing of the people, saying, 'Whoever *is* fearful and afraid, let him turn and depart at once from Mount Gilead.'" And twenty-two thousand of

LIFE LESSONS

➤ 7:2 — *And the LORD said to Gideon, "The people who are with you are too many for Me to give the Midianites into their hands, lest Israel claim glory for itself against Me, saying, 'My own hand has saved me.'"*

When God wants to do a mighty thing in our lives, He may first reduce our physical resources in order to demonstrate that He accomplishes the feat and not we ourselves.

Life Examples:

GIDEON

Circumstances Convey Confirmation

JUDG. 6:36–40

Sometimes God uses natural phenomena to confirm His guidance. Gideon provides a notable example of this.

Unsure that he had heard God clearly—and feeling more than a little fearful—Gideon asked God to confirm that he was to lead his people into battle. So one evening he laid out a fleece and asked that God make it soaking wet by the following morning, while the ground around it remained dry. And that's what happened. Still unsure, he asked for the fleece to remain dry in the midst of wet grass. And again God granted his request (Judg. 6:36–40).

While I never recommend that a person stipulate the way, means, or method that God should use to confirm His word—we are to trust Him and take Him at His word—I believe we can ask God to confirm His will to us. But we must leave the methodology up to Him!

See the Life Principles Index for further study:
5. God does not require us to understand His will, just obey it, even if it seems unreasonable.

the people returned, and ten thousand remained.
4 But the LORD said to Gideon, "The people
are still *too* many; bring them down to the
water, and I will test them for you there. Then
it will be, *that* of whom I say to you, 'This one
shall go with you,' the same shall go with you;
and of whomever I say to you, 'This one shall
not go with you,' the same shall not go."
5 So he brought the people down to the
water. And the LORD said to Gideon, "Everyone who laps from the water with his tongue,
as a dog laps, you shall set apart by himself;
likewise everyone who gets down on his
knees to drink."
6 And the number of those who lapped,
putting their hand to their mouth, was three
hundred men; but all the rest of the people got
down on their knees to drink water.
7 Then the LORD said to Gideon, "By the ➤
three hundred men who lapped I will save
you, and deliver the Midianites into your
hand. Let all the *other* people go, every man
to his place."
8 So the people took provisions and their
trumpets in their hands. And he sent away all
the rest of Israel, every man to his tent, and
retained those three hundred men. Now the
camp of Midian was below him in the valley.
9 It happened on the same night that the
LORD said to him, "Arise, go down against the
camp, for I have delivered it into your hand.
10 "But if you are afraid to go down, go down
to the camp with Purah your servant,
11 "and you shall hear what they say; and afterward your hands shall be strengthened to
go down against the camp." Then he went
down with Purah his servant to the outpost of
the armed men who *were* in the camp.
12 Now the Midianites and Amalekites, all
the people of the East, were lying in the valley
as numerous as locusts; and their camels
were without number, as the sand by the
seashore in multitude.
13 And when Gideon had come, there was a
man telling a dream to his companion. He
said, "I have had a dream: *To my* surprise, a
loaf of barley bread tumbled into the camp of
Midian; it came to a tent and struck it so that
it fell and overturned, and the tent collapsed."
14 Then his companion answered and said,
"This *is* nothing else but the sword of Gideon
the son of Joash, a man of Israel! Into his
hand God has delivered Midian and the
whole camp."
15 And so it was, when Gideon heard the
telling of the dream and its interpretation,
that he worshiped. He returned to the camp of
Israel, and said, "Arise, for the LORD has delivered the camp of Midian into your hand."
16 Then he divided the three hundred men
into three companies, and he put a trumpet
into every man's hand, with empty pitchers,
and torches inside the pitchers.
17 And he said to them, "Look at me and do
likewise; watch, and when I come to the edge
of the camp you shall do as I do:
18 "When I blow the trumpet, I and all who

LIFE LESSONS

➤ ***7:7 — Then the LORD said to Gideon, "By the three hundred men who lapped I will save you, and deliver the Midianites into your hand. Let all the other people go, every man to his place."***

On hearing these odd instructions for battle, Gideon may have felt as Joshua no doubt did many years before at Jericho. But both men obeyed, and both men won a great victory.

are with me, then you also blow the trumpets
on every side of the whole camp, and say, '*The
sword of* the LORD and of Gideon!'"
19 So Gideon and the hundred men who
were with him came to the outpost of the
camp at the beginning of the middle watch,
just as they had posted the watch; and they
blew the trumpets and broke the pitchers that
were in their hands.
20 Then the three companies blew the trumpets and broke the pitchers—they held the
torches in their left hands and the trumpets in
their right hands for blowing—and they cried,
"The sword of the LORD and of Gideon!"
21 And every man stood in his place all
around the camp; and the whole army ran
and cried out and fled.
22 When the three hundred blew the trumpets, the LORD set every man's sword against
his companion throughout the whole camp;
and the army fled to Beth Acacia,[a] toward
Zererah, as far as the border of Abel Meholah, by Tabbath.
23 And the men of Israel gathered together
from Naphtali, Asher, and all Manasseh, and
pursued the Midianites.
24 Then Gideon sent messengers throughout
all the mountains of Ephraim, saying, "Come
down against the Midianites, and seize from
them the watering places as far as Beth Barah
and the Jordan." Then all the men of Ephraim
gathered together and seized the watering
places as far as Beth Barah and the Jordan.
25 And they captured two princes of the Midianites, Oreb and Zeeb. They killed Oreb at
the rock of Oreb, and Zeeb they killed at the
winepress of Zeeb. They pursued Midian and
brought the heads of Oreb and Zeeb to Gideon on the other side of the Jordan.

Gideon Subdues the Midianites

8 Now the men of Ephraim said to him,
"Why have you done this to us by not calling us when you went to fight with the Midianites?" And they reprimanded him sharply.
2 So he said to them, "What have I done
now in comparison with you? *Is* not the
gleaning *of the grapes* of Ephraim better than
the vintage of Abiezer?
3 "God has delivered into your hands the
princes of Midian, Oreb and Zeeb. And what
was I able to do in comparison with you?"
Then their anger toward him subsided when
he said that.
4 When Gideon came to the Jordan, he and
the three hundred men who *were* with him
crossed over, exhausted but still in pursuit.
5 Then he said to the men of Succoth,
"Please give loaves of bread to the people
who follow me, for they are exhausted, and I
am pursuing Zebah and Zalmunna, kings of
Midian."
6 And the leaders of Succoth said, "*Are* the
hands of Zebah and Zalmunna now in your
hand, that we should give bread to your
army?"
7 So Gideon said, "For this cause, when the
LORD has delivered Zebah and Zalmunna into
my hand, then I will tear your flesh with the
thorns of the wilderness and with briers!"
8 Then he went up from there to Penuel and
spoke to them in the same way. And the men
of Penuel answered him as the men of Succoth had answered.
9 So he also spoke to the men of Penuel,
saying, "When I come back in peace, I will
tear down this tower!"
10 Now Zebah and Zalmunna *were* at
Karkor, and their armies with them, about fifteen thousand, all who were left of all the
army of the people of the East; for one hundred and twenty thousand men who drew the
sword had fallen.
11 Then Gideon went up by the road of those
who dwell in tents on the east of Nobah and
Jogbehah; and he attacked the army while the
camp felt secure.
12 When Zebah and Zalmunna fled, he pursued them; and he took the two kings of Midian, Zebah and Zalmunna, and routed the
whole army.
13 Then Gideon the son of Joash returned
from battle, from the Ascent of Heres.
14 And he caught a young man of the men of
Succoth and interrogated him; and he wrote
down for him the leaders of Succoth and its
elders, seventy-seven men.
15 Then he came to the men of Succoth and
said, "Here are Zebah and Zalmunna, about
whom you ridiculed me, saying, '*Are* the
hands of Zebah and Zalmunna now in your
hand, that we should give bread to your
weary men?'"
16 And he took the elders of the city, and
thorns of the wilderness and briers, and with
them he taught the men of Succoth.
17 Then he tore down the tower of Penuel
and killed the men of the city.
18 And he said to Zebah and Zalmunna,
"What kind of men *were they* whom you
killed at Tabor?" So they answered, "As you
are, so *were* they; each one resembled the son
of a king."
19 Then he said, "They *were* my brothers, the
sons of my mother. *As* the LORD lives, if you
had let them live, I would not kill you."
20 And he said to Jether his firstborn, "Rise,
kill them!" But the youth would not draw his
sword; for he was afraid, because he *was* still
a youth.
21 So Zebah and Zalmunna said, "Rise yourself, and kill us; for as a man *is, so is* his
strength." So Gideon arose and killed Zebah
and Zalmunna, and took the crescent ornaments that *were* on their camels' necks.

7:22 [a]Hebrew *Beth Shittah*

Gideon's Ephod

22 Then the men of Israel said to Gideon, "Rule over us, both you and your son, and your grandson also; for you have delivered us from the hand of Midian."

23 But Gideon said to them, "I will not rule over you, nor shall my son rule over you; the LORD shall rule over you."

24 Then Gideon said to them, "I would like to make a request of you, that each of you would give me the earrings from his plunder." For they had golden earrings, because they *were* Ishmaelites.

25 So they answered, "We will gladly give *them.*" And they spread out a garment, and each man threw into it the earrings from his plunder.

26 Now the weight of the gold earrings that he requested was one thousand seven hundred *shekels* of gold, besides the crescent ornaments, pendants, and purple robes which *were* on the kings of Midian, and besides the chains that *were* around their camels' necks.

27 Then Gideon made it into an ephod and set it up in his city, Ophrah. And all Israel played the harlot with it there. It became a snare to Gideon and to his house.

28 Thus Midian was subdued before the children of Israel, so that they lifted their heads no more. And the country was quiet for forty years in the days of Gideon.

Death of Gideon

29 Then Jerubbaal the son of Joash went and dwelt in his own house.

30 Gideon had seventy sons who were his own offspring, for he had many wives.

31 And his concubine who *was* in Shechem also bore him a son, whose name he called Abimelech.

32 Now Gideon the son of Joash died at a good old age, and was buried in the tomb of Joash his father, in Ophrah of the Abiezrites.

33 So it was, as soon as Gideon was dead, that the children of Israel again played the harlot with the Baals, and made Baal-Berith their god.

34 Thus the children of Israel did not remember the LORD their God, who had delivered them from the hands of all their enemies on every side;

35 nor did they show kindness to the house of Jerubbaal (Gideon) in accordance with the good he had done for Israel.

Abimelech's Conspiracy

9 Then Abimelech the son of Jerubbaal went to Shechem, to his mother's brothers, and spoke with them and with all the family of the house of his mother's father, saying,

2 "Please speak in the hearing of all the men of Shechem: 'Which is better for you, that all seventy of the sons of Jerubbaal reign over you, or that one reign over you?' Remember that I *am* your own flesh and bone."

3 And his mother's brothers spoke all these words concerning him in the hearing of all the men of Shechem; and their heart was inclined to follow Abimelech, for they said, "He is our brother."

4 So they gave him seventy *shekels* of silver ➤
from the temple of Baal-Berith, with which Abimelech hired worthless and reckless men; and they followed him.

5 Then he went to his father's house at Ophrah and killed his brothers, the seventy sons of Jerubbaal, on one stone. But Jotham the youngest son of Jerubbaal was left, because he hid himself.

6 And all the men of Shechem gathered together, all of Beth Millo, and they went and made Abimelech king beside the terebinth tree at the pillar that *was* in Shechem.

The Parable of the Trees

7 Now when they told Jotham, he went and stood on top of Mount Gerizim, and lifted his voice and cried out. And he said to them:

"Listen to me, you men of Shechem,
That God may listen to you!

8 "The trees once went forth to anoint a king over them.
And they said to the olive tree,
'Reign over us!'
9 But the olive tree said to them,
'Should I cease giving my oil,
With which they honor God and men,
And go to sway over trees?'

10 "Then the trees said to the fig tree,
'You come *and* reign over us!'
11 But the fig tree said to them,
'Should I cease my sweetness and my good fruit,
And go to sway over trees?'

12 "Then the trees said to the vine,
'You come *and* reign over us!'

LIFE LESSONS

➤ 9:4 — *So they gave him seventy shekels of silver from the temple of Baal-Berith, with which Abimelech hired worthless and reckless men; and they followed him.*

God may allow "worthless and reckless men" to assume power for a time, but in the end, their evil deeds catch up with them. Just as God blesses obedience, so He judges disobedience.

13 But the vine said to them,
'Should I cease my new wine,
Which cheers *both* God and men,
And go to sway over trees?'

14"Then all the trees said to the bramble,
'You come *and* reign over us!'
15 And the bramble said to the trees,
'If in truth you anoint me as king over you,
Then come *and* take shelter in my shade;
But if not, let fire come out of the bramble
And devour the cedars of Lebanon!'

16 "Now therefore, if you have acted in truth
and sincerity in making Abimelech king, and
if you have dealt well with Jerubbaal and his
house, and have done to him as he deserves—
17 "for my father fought for you, risked his
life, and delivered you out of the hand of Midian;
18 "but you have risen up against my father's
house this day, and killed his seventy sons on
one stone, and made Abimelech, the son of
his female servant, king over the men of
Shechem, because he is your brother—
19 "if then you have acted in truth and sincerity
with Jerubbaal and with his house this
day, *then* rejoice in Abimelech, and let him
also rejoice in you.
20 "But if not, let fire come from Abimelech
and devour the men of Shechem and Beth
Millo; and let fire come from the men of
Shechem and from Beth Millo and devour
Abimelech!"
21 And Jotham ran away and fled; and he
went to Beer and dwelt there, for fear of
Abimelech his brother.

Downfall of Abimelech

22 After Abimelech had reigned over Israel
three years,
23 God sent a spirit of ill will between Abimelech
and the men of Shechem; and the men
of Shechem dealt treacherously with Abimelech,
24 that the crime *done* to the seventy sons of
Jerubbaal might be settled and their blood be
laid on Abimelech their brother, who killed
them, and on the men of Shechem, who aided
him in the killing of his brothers.
25 And the men of Shechem set men in ambush
against him on the tops of the mountains,
and they robbed all who passed by
them along that way; and it was told Abimelech.
26 Now Gaal the son of Ebed came with his
brothers and went over to Shechem; and the
men of Shechem put their confidence in
him.
27 So they went out into the fields, and gathered
grapes from their vineyards and trod
them, and made merry. And they went into
the house of their god, and ate and drank, and
cursed Abimelech.
28 Then Gaal the son of Ebed said, "Who *is*
Abimelech, and who *is* Shechem, that we
should serve him? *Is he* not the son of Jerubbaal,
and *is not* Zebul his officer? Serve the
men of Hamor the father of Shechem; but
why should we serve him?
29 "If only this people were under my authority![a]
Then I would remove Abimelech." So he[b]
said to Abimelech, "Increase your army and
come out!"
30 When Zebul, the ruler of the city, heard
the words of Gaal the son of Ebed, his anger
was aroused.
31 And he sent messengers to Abimelech secretly,
saying, "Take note! Gaal the son of
Ebed and his brothers have come to
Shechem; and here they are, fortifying the
city against you.
32 "Now therefore, get up by night, you and
the people who *are* with you, and lie in wait in
the field.
33 "And it shall be, as soon as the sun is up in
the morning, *that* you shall rise early and
rush upon the city; and *when* he and the people
who are with him come out against you,
you may then do to them as you find opportunity."
34 So Abimelech and all the people who *were*
with him rose by night, and lay in wait
against Shechem in four companies.
35 When Gaal the son of Ebed went out and
stood in the entrance to the city gate, Abimelech
and the people who *were* with him rose
from lying in wait.
36 And when Gaal saw the people, he said to
Zebul, "Look, people are coming down from
the tops of the mountains!" But Zebul said to
him, "You see the shadows of the mountains
as *if they were* men."
37 So Gaal spoke again and said, "See, people
are coming down from the center of the
land, and another company is coming from
the Diviners'[a] Terebinth Tree."
38 Then Zebul said to him, "Where indeed *is*
your mouth now, with which you said, 'Who
is Abimelech, that we should serve him?'
Are not these the people whom you despised?
Go out, if you will, and fight with
them now."
39 So Gaal went out, leading the men of
Shechem, and fought with Abimelech.
40 And Abimelech chased him, and he fled
from him; and many fell wounded, to the *very*
entrance of the gate.
41 Then Abimelech dwelt at Arumah, and
Zebul drove out Gaal and his brothers, so that
they would not dwell in Shechem.

9:29 [a]Literally *hand* [b]Following Masoretic Text and Targum; Dead Sea Scrolls read *they;* Septuagint reads *I.* **9:37** [a]Hebrew *Meonenim*

42 And it came about on the next day that the people went out into the field, and they told Abimelech.

43 So he took his people, divided them into three companies, and lay in wait in the field. And he looked, and there were the people, coming out of the city; and he rose against them and attacked them.

44 Then Abimelech and the company that *was* with him rushed forward and stood at the entrance of the gate of the city; and the *other* two companies rushed upon all who *were* in the fields and killed them.

45 So Abimelech fought against the city all that day; he took the city and killed the people who *were* in it; and he demolished the city and sowed it with salt.

46 Now when all the men of the tower of Shechem had heard *that,* they entered the stronghold of the temple of the god Berith.

47 And it was told Abimelech that all the men of the tower of Shechem were gathered together.

48 Then Abimelech went up to Mount Zalmon, he and all the people who *were* with him. And Abimelech took an ax in his hand and cut down a bough from the trees, and took it and laid *it* on his shoulder; then he said to the people who were with him, "What you have seen me do, make haste *and* do as I *have done.*"

49 So each of the people likewise cut down his own bough and followed Abimelech, put *them* against the stronghold, and set the stronghold on fire above them, so that all the people of the tower of Shechem died, about a thousand men and women.

50 Then Abimelech went to Thebez, and he encamped against Thebez and took it.

51 But there was a strong tower in the city, and all the men and women—all the people of the city—fled there and shut themselves in; then they went up to the top of the tower.

52 So Abimelech came as far as the tower and fought against it; and he drew near the door of the tower to burn it with fire.

53 But a certain woman dropped an upper millstone on Abimelech's head and crushed his skull.

54 Then he called quickly to the young man, his armorbearer, and said to him, "Draw your sword and kill me, lest men say of me, 'A woman killed him.'" So his young man thrust him through, and he died.

55 And when the men of Israel saw that Abimelech was dead, they departed, every man to his place.

56 Thus God repaid the wickedness of Abimelech, which he had done to his father by killing his seventy brothers.

57 And all the evil of the men of Shechem God returned on their own heads, and on them came the curse of Jotham the son of Jerubbaal.

Tola

10 After Abimelech there arose to save Israel Tola the son of Puah, the son of Dodo, a man of Issachar; and he dwelt in Shamir in the mountains of Ephraim.

2 He judged Israel twenty-three years; and he died and was buried in Shamir.

Jair

3 After him arose Jair, a Gileadite; and he judged Israel twenty-two years.

4 Now he had thirty sons who rode on thirty donkeys; they also had thirty towns, which are called "Havoth Jair"[a] to this day, which *are* in the land of Gilead.

5 And Jair died and was buried in Camon.

Israel Oppressed Again

6 Then the children of Israel again did evil in the sight of the LORD, and served the Baals and the Ashtoreths, the gods of Syria, the gods of Sidon, the gods of Moab, the gods of the people of Ammon, and the gods of the Philistines; and they forsook the LORD and did not serve Him.

7 So the anger of the LORD was hot against Israel; and He sold them into the hands of the Philistines and into the hands of the people of Ammon.

8 From that year they harassed and oppressed the children of Israel for eighteen years—all the children of Israel who *were* on the other side of the Jordan in the land of the Amorites, in Gilead.

9 Moreover the people of Ammon crossed over the Jordan to fight against Judah also, against Benjamin, and against the house of Ephraim, so that Israel was severely distressed.

10 And the children of Israel cried out to the LORD, saying, "We have sinned against You, because we have both forsaken our God and served the Baals!"

11 So the LORD said to the children of Israel, "*Did I* not *deliver you* from the Egyptians and from the Amorites and from the people of Ammon and from the Philistines?

12 "Also the Sidonians and Amalekites and Maonites[a] oppressed you; and you cried out to Me, and I delivered you from their hand.

13 "Yet you have forsaken Me and served other gods. Therefore I will deliver you no more.

14 "Go and cry out to the gods which you have chosen; let them deliver you in your time of distress."

15 And the children of Israel said to the LORD, "We have sinned! Do to us whatever seems best to You; only deliver us this day, we pray."

10:4 [a]Literally *Towns of Jair* (compare Numbers 32:41 and Deuteronomy 3:14) **10:12** [a]Some Septuagint manuscripts read *Midianites.*

➤ 16 So they put away the foreign gods from
among them and served the LORD. And His
soul could no longer endure the misery of Israel.
17 Then the people of Ammon gathered together and encamped in Gilead. And the children of Israel assembled together and
encamped in Mizpah.
18 And the people, the leaders of Gilead, said
to one another, "Who *is* the man who will
begin the fight against the people of Ammon?
He shall be head over all the inhabitants of
Gilead."

Jephthah

11 Now Jephthah the Gileadite was a
mighty man of valor, but he *was* the
son of a harlot; and Gilead begot Jephthah.
2 Gilead's wife bore sons; and when his
wife's sons grew up, they drove Jephthah out,
and said to him, "You shall have no inheritance in our father's house, for you *are* the
son of another woman."
3 Then Jephthah fled from his brothers and
dwelt in the land of Tob; and worthless men
banded together with Jephthah and went out
raiding with him.
4 It came to pass after a time that the people
of Ammon made war against Israel.
5 And so it was, when the people of Ammon
made war against Israel, that the elders of
Gilead went to get Jephthah from the land of
Tob.
6 Then they said to Jephthah, "Come and be
our commander, that we may fight against the
people of Ammon."
7 So Jephthah said to the elders of Gilead,
"Did you not hate me, and expel me from my
father's house? Why have you come to me
now when you are in distress?"
8 And the elders of Gilead said to Jephthah,
"That is why we have turned again to you
now, that you may go with us and fight
against the people of Ammon, and be our
head over all the inhabitants of Gilead."
9 So Jephthah said to the elders of Gilead,
"If you take me back home to fight against the
people of Ammon, and the LORD delivers
them to me, shall I be your head?"
10 And the elders of Gilead said to Jephthah,
"The LORD will be a witness between us, if we
do not do according to your words."
11 Then Jephthah went with the elders of
Gilead, and the people made him head and
commander over them; and Jephthah spoke
all his words before the LORD in Mizpah.
12 Now Jephthah sent messengers to the
king of the people of Ammon, saying, "What
do you have against me, that you have come
to fight against me in my land?"
13 And the king of the people of Ammon answered the messengers of Jephthah, "Because
Israel took away my land when they came up
out of Egypt, from the Arnon as far as the
Jabbok, and to the Jordan. Now therefore, restore those *lands* peaceably."
14 So Jephthah again sent messengers to the
king of the people of Ammon,
15 and said to him, "Thus says Jephthah: 'Israel did not take away the land of Moab, nor
the land of the people of Ammon;
16 'for when Israel came up from Egypt, they
walked through the wilderness as far as the
Red Sea and came to Kadesh.
17 'Then Israel sent messengers to the king
of Edom, saying, "Please let me pass through
your land." But the king of Edom would not
heed. And in like manner they sent to the king
of Moab, but he would not *consent*. So Israel
remained in Kadesh.
18 'And they went along through the wilderness and bypassed the land of Edom and the
land of Moab, came to the east side of the
land of Moab, and encamped on the other
side of the Arnon. But they did not enter the
border of Moab, for the Arnon *was* the border
of Moab.
19 'Then Israel sent messengers to Sihon
king of the Amorites, king of Heshbon; and
Israel said to him, "Please let us pass through
your land into our place."
20 'But Sihon did not trust Israel to pass
through his territory. So Sihon gathered all
his people together, encamped in Jahaz, and
fought against Israel.
21 'And the LORD God of Israel delivered
Sihon and all his people into the hand of Israel, and they defeated them. Thus Israel
gained possession of all the land of the Amorites, who inhabited that country.
22 'They took possession of all the territory
of the Amorites, from the Arnon to the Jabbok and from the wilderness to the Jordan.
23 'And now the LORD God of Israel has dispossessed the Amorites from before His people Israel; should you then possess it?
24 'Will you not possess whatever Chemosh ◄
your god gives you to possess? So whatever

LIFE LESSONS

➤ 10:16 — *So they put away the foreign gods from among them and served the LORD. And His soul could no longer endure the misery of Israel.*

God will always judge sin, but He longs to show mercy. His first inclination, always, is to redeem and rescue.

➤ 11:24 — *". . . So whatever the LORD our God takes possession of before us, we will possess."*

It is quite a statement: we will possess whatever the Lord possesses before us. Can you make the same statement? Are you possessing every spiritual blessing that God has gone ahead of you to possess?

the LORD our God takes possession of before
us, we will possess.
25 'And now, *are* you any better than Balak
the son of Zippor, king of Moab? Did he ever
strive against Israel? Did he ever fight against
them?
26 'While Israel dwelt in Heshbon and its villages, in Aroer and its villages, and in all the
cities along the banks of the Arnon, for three
hundred years, why did you not recover *them*
within that time?
27 'Therefore I have not sinned against you,
but you wronged me by fighting against me.
May the LORD, the Judge, render judgment
this day between the children of Israel and
the people of Ammon.'"
28 However, the king of the people of
Ammon did not heed the words which Jephthah sent him.

Jephthah's Vow and Victory

29 Then the Spirit of the LORD came upon
Jephthah, and he passed through Gilead and
Manasseh, and passed through Mizpah of
Gilead; and from Mizpah of Gilead he advanced *toward* the people of Ammon.
30 And Jephthah made a vow to the LORD,
and said, "If You will indeed deliver the people
of Ammon into my hands,
31 "then it will be that whatever comes out of
the doors of my house to meet me, when I return in peace from the people of Ammon,
shall surely be the LORD's, and I will offer it
up as a burnt offering."
32 So Jephthah advanced toward the people
of Ammon to fight against them, and the
LORD delivered them into his hands.
33 And he defeated them from Aroer as far as
Minnith—twenty cities—and to Abel
Keramim,[a] with a very great slaughter. Thus
the people of Ammon were subdued before
the children of Israel.

Jephthah's Daughter

34 When Jephthah came to his house at Mizpah, there was his daughter, coming out to
meet him with timbrels and dancing; and she
was his only child. Besides her he had neither
son nor daughter.
35 And it came to pass, when he saw her, that
he tore his clothes, and said, "Alas, my daughter! You have brought me very low! You are
among those who trouble me! For I have
given my word to the LORD, and I cannot go
back on it."
36 So she said to him, "My father, *if* you have
given your word to the LORD, do to me according to what has gone out of your mouth,
because the LORD has avenged you of your
enemies, the people of Ammon."
37 Then she said to her father, "Let this thing
be done for me: let me alone for two months,
that I may go and wander on the mountains
and bewail my virginity, my friends and I."
38 So he said, "Go." And he sent her away *for*
two months; and she went with her friends,
and bewailed her virginity on the mountains.
39 And it was so at the end of two months
that she returned to her father, and he carried
out his vow with her which he had vowed.
She knew no man. And it became a custom in
Israel
40 *that* the daughters of Israel went four
days each year to lament the daughter of
Jephthah the Gileadite.

Jephthah's Conflict with Ephraim

12 Then the men of Ephraim gathered
together, crossed over toward Zaphon,
and said to Jephthah, "Why did you cross
over to fight against the people of Ammon,
and did not call us to go with you? We will
burn your house down on you with fire!"
2 And Jephthah said to them, "My people
and I were in a great struggle with the people
of Ammon; and when I called you, you did not
deliver me out of their hands.
3 "So when I saw that you would not deliver ➤
me, I took my life in my hands and crossed
over against the people of Ammon; and the
LORD delivered them into my hand. Why then
have you come up to me this day to fight
against me?"
4 Now Jephthah gathered together all the
men of Gilead and fought against Ephraim.
And the men of Gilead defeated Ephraim, because they said, "You Gileadites *are* fugitives
of Ephraim among the Ephraimites *and*
among the Manassites."
5 The Gileadites seized the fords of the Jordan before the Ephraimites *arrived*. And when
any Ephraimite who escaped said, "Let me
cross over," the men of Gilead would say to
him, "*Are* you an Ephraimite?" If he said, "No,"
6 then they would say to him, "Then say,
'Shibboleth'!" And he would say, "Sibboleth,"
for he could not pronounce *it* right. Then they
would take him and kill him at the fords of

11:33 [a]Literally *Plain of Vineyards*

LIFE LESSONS

➤ **12:3 — *"So when I saw that you would not deliver me, I took my life in my hands and crossed over against the people of Ammon; and the LORD delivered them into my hand . . . ."***

When in faith and obedience we take our life in our hands to do what God has called us to do, He does for us what we cannot do for ourselves. God takes care of our needs when we obey Him.

the Jordan. There fell at that time forty-two thousand Ephraimites.

7 And Jephthah judged Israel six years. Then Jephthah the Gileadite died and was buried among the cities of Gilead.

Ibzan, Elon, and Abdon

8 After him, Ibzan of Bethlehem judged Israel.

9 He had thirty sons. And he gave away thirty daughters in marriage, and brought in thirty daughters from elsewhere for his sons. He judged Israel seven years.

10 Then Ibzan died and was buried at Bethlehem.

11 After him, Elon the Zebulunite judged Israel. He judged Israel ten years.

12 And Elon the Zebulunite died and was buried at Aijalon in the country of Zebulun.

13 After him, Abdon the son of Hillel the Pirathonite judged Israel.

14 He had forty sons and thirty grandsons, who rode on seventy young donkeys. He judged Israel eight years.

15 Then Abdon the son of Hillel the Pirathonite died and was buried in Pirathon in the land of Ephraim, in the mountains of the Amalekites.

The Birth of Samson

13 Again the children of Israel did evil in the sight of the LORD, and the LORD delivered them into the hand of the Philistines for forty years.

2 Now there was a certain man from Zorah, of the family of the Danites, whose name *was* Manoah; and his wife *was* barren and had no children.

➤ 3 And the Angel of the LORD appeared to the woman and said to her, "Indeed now, you are barren and have borne no children, but you shall conceive and bear a son.

4 "Now therefore, please be careful not to drink wine or *similar* drink, and not to eat anything unclean.

5 "For behold, you shall conceive and bear a son. And no razor shall come upon his head, for the child shall be a Nazirite to God from the womb; and he shall begin to deliver Israel out of the hand of the Philistines."

6 So the woman came and told her husband, saying, "A Man of God came to me, and His countenance *was* like the countenance of the Angel of God, very awesome; but I did not ask Him where He *was* from, and He did not tell me His name.

7 "And He said to me, 'Behold, you shall conceive and bear a son. Now drink no wine or *similar* drink, nor eat anything unclean, for the child shall be a Nazirite to God from the womb to the day of his death.'"

8 Then Manoah prayed to the LORD, and said, "O my Lord, please let the Man of God whom You sent come to us again and teach us what we shall do for the child who will be born." ➤

9 And God listened to the voice of Manoah, and the Angel of God came to the woman again as she was sitting in the field; but Manoah her husband *was* not with her.

10 Then the woman ran in haste and told her husband, and said to him, "Look, the Man who came to me the *other* day has just now appeared to me!"

11 So Manoah arose and followed his wife. When he came to the Man, he said to Him, "Are You the Man who spoke to this woman?" And He said, "I *am.*"

12 Manoah said, "Now let Your words come *to pass!* What will be the boy's rule of life, and his work?"

13 So the Angel of the LORD said to Manoah, "Of all that I said to the woman let her be careful.

14 "She may not eat anything that comes from the vine, nor may she drink wine or *similar* drink, nor eat anything unclean. All that I commanded her let her observe."

15 Then Manoah said to the Angel of the LORD, "Please let us detain You, and we will prepare a young goat for You."

16 And the Angel of the LORD said to Manoah, "Though you detain Me, I will not eat your food. But if you offer a burnt offering, you must offer it to the LORD." (For Manoah did not know He *was* the Angel of the LORD.) ➤

17 Then Manoah said to the Angel of the LORD, "What *is* Your name, that when Your words come *to pass* we may honor You?"

LIFE LESSONS

➤ 13:3 — *And the Angel of the LORD appeared to the woman and said to her, "Indeed now, you are barren and have borne no children, but you shall conceive and bear a son."*

Why does God so often choose a childless woman to give birth to someone of great spiritual importance? Perhaps because such people are broken, and brokenness is God's requirement for maximum usefulness.

➤ 13:8 — *Then Manoah prayed to the LORD, and said, "O my Lord, please let the Man of God whom You sent come to us again and teach us what we shall do for the child who will be born."*

In the midst of a disobedient nation, Manoah and his wife stand out as faithful people of God. They sought God's counsel on how to rear their child in difficult times, and God answered their prayers.

➤ 13:16 — *(For Manoah did not know He was the Angel of the LORD.)*

How many of our "ordinary" encounters are actually appointments with God's heavenly ambassadors? We will never know, this side of heaven; that is one reason why we must treat every encounter as a divine appointment (Heb. 13:2).

18 And the Angel of the LORD said to him,
"Why do you ask My name, seeing it *is* wonderful?"
19 So Manoah took the young goat with the
grain offering, and offered it upon the rock to
the LORD. And He did a wondrous thing while
Manoah and his wife looked on—
20 it happened as the flame went up toward
heaven from the altar—the Angel of the LORD
ascended in the flame of the altar! When
Manoah and his wife saw *this*, they fell on
their faces to the ground.
21 When the Angel of the LORD appeared
no more to Manoah and his wife, then
Manoah knew that He *was* the Angel of the
LORD.
22 And Manoah said to his wife, "We shall
surely die, because we have seen God!"
➤ 23 But his wife said to him, "If the LORD had
desired to kill us, He would not have accepted
a burnt offering and a grain offering from our
hands, nor would He have shown us all these
things, nor would He have told us *such things*
as these at this time."
24 So the woman bore a son and called his
name Samson; and the child grew, and the
LORD blessed him.
25 And the Spirit of the LORD began to move
upon him at Mahaneh Dan[a] between Zorah
and Eshtaol.

Samson's Philistine Wife

14 Now Samson went down to Timnah,
and saw a woman in Timnah of the
daughters of the Philistines.
2 So he went up and told his father and
mother, saying, "I have seen a woman in Timnah of the daughters of the Philistines; now
therefore, get her for me as a wife."
3 Then his father and mother said to him,
"*Is there* no woman among the daughters of
your brethren, or among all my people, that
you must go and get a wife from the uncircumcised Philistines?" And Samson said to
his father, "Get her for me, for she pleases me
well."
➤ 4 But his father and mother did not know
that it was of the LORD—that He was seeking
an occasion to move against the Philistines.
For at that time the Philistines had dominion
over Israel.
5 So Samson went down to Timnah with his
father and mother, and came to the vineyards
of Timnah. Now *to his* surprise, a young lion
came roaring against him.
6 And the Spirit of the LORD came mightily
upon him, and he tore the lion apart as
one would have torn apart a young goat,
though *he had* nothing in his hand. But he did
not tell his father or his mother what he had
done.
7 Then he went down and talked with the
woman; and she pleased Samson well.
8 After some time, when he returned to get
her, he turned aside to see the carcass of the
lion. And behold, a swarm of bees and honey
were in the carcass of the lion.
9 He took some of it in his hands and went
along, eating. When he came to his father and
mother, he gave *some* to them, and they also
ate. But he did not tell them that he had taken
the honey out of the carcass of the lion.
10 So his father went down to the woman.
And Samson gave a feast there, for young
men used to do so.
11 And it happened, when they saw him, that
they brought thirty companions to be with him.
12 Then Samson said to them, "Let me pose a
riddle to you. If you can correctly solve and
explain it to me within the seven days of the
feast, then I will give you thirty linen garments and thirty changes of clothing.
13 "But if you cannot explain *it* to me, then
you shall give me thirty linen garments
and thirty changes of clothing." And they said
to him, "Pose your riddle, that we may hear
it."
14 So he said to them:

"Out of the eater came something to eat,
And out of the strong came something
sweet."

Now for three days they could not explain the
riddle.
15 But it came to pass on the seventh[a] day
that they said to Samson's wife, "Entice your
husband, that he may explain the riddle to us,
or else we will burn you and your father's
house with fire. Have you invited us in order
to take what is ours? *Is that* not *so*?"

13:25 [a]Literally *Camp of Dan* (compare 18:12) **14:15** [a]Following Masoretic Text, Targum, and Vulgate; Septuagint and Syriac read *fourth.*

LIFE LESSONS

➤ **13:23 — *But his wife said to him, "If the LORD had desired to kill us, He would not have accepted a burnt offering and a grain offering from our hands, nor would He have shown us all these things, nor would He have told us such things as these at this time."***

The Lord does not desire to kill us but to bless us. And He will bless us if we will take to heart His gracious promises and obey His word by the power of His Spirit.

➤ **14:4 — *But his father and mother did not know that it was of the LORD—that He was seeking an occasion to move against the Philistines.***

Samson's desire for a Philistine wife clearly transgressed God's law (Deut. 7:3, 4), yet God used even his disobedience for the good of His people. Note, however, that Samson himself never received a blessing for his rebellious choice.

16 Then Samson's wife wept on him, and
said, "You only hate me! You do not love me!
You have posed a riddle to the sons of my
people, but you have not explained *it* to me."
And he said to her, "Look, I have not explained *it* to my father or my mother; so
should I explain *it* to you?"
17 Now she had wept on him the seven days
while their feast lasted. And it happened on
the seventh day that he told her, because she
pressed him so much. Then she explained the
riddle to the sons of her people.
18 So the men of the city said to him on the
seventh day before the sun went down:

"What *is* sweeter than honey?
And what *is* stronger than a lion?"

And he said to them:

"If you had not plowed with my heifer,
You would not have solved my riddle!"

19 Then the Spirit of the LORD came upon
him mightily, and he went down to Ashkelon
and killed thirty of their men, took their apparel, and gave the changes *of clothing* to
those who had explained the riddle. So his
anger was aroused, and he went back up to
his father's house.
20 And Samson's wife was *given* to his companion, who had been his best man.

Samson Defeats the Philistines

15 After a while, in the time of wheat
harvest, it happened that Samson visited his wife with a young goat. And he said,
"Let me go in to my wife, into *her* room." But
her father would not permit him to go in.
2 Her father said, "I really thought that you
thoroughly hated her; therefore I gave her to
your companion. *Is* not her younger sister
better than she? Please, take her instead."
3 And Samson said to them, "This time I
shall be blameless regarding the Philistines if
I harm them!"
4 Then Samson went and caught three hundred foxes; and he took torches, turned *the foxes* tail to tail, and put a torch between each
pair of tails.
5 When he had set the torches on fire, he let
the foxes go into the standing grain of the
Philistines, and burned up both the shocks
and the standing grain, as well as the vineyards *and* olive groves.
6 Then the Philistines said, "Who has done
this?" And they answered, "Samson, the son-in-law of the Timnite, because he has taken
his wife and given her to his companion." So
the Philistines came up and burned her and
her father with fire.
7 Samson said to them, "Since you would do
a thing like this, I will surely take revenge on
you, and after that I will cease."
8 So he attacked them hip and thigh with a
great slaughter; then he went down and dwelt
in the cleft of the rock of Etam.
9 Now the Philistines went up, encamped
in Judah, and deployed themselves against
Lehi.
10 And the men of Judah said, "Why have
you come up against us?" So they answered,
"We have come up to arrest Samson, to do to
him as he has done to us."
11 Then three thousand men of Judah went
down to the cleft of the rock of Etam, and said
to Samson, "Do you not know that the Philistines rule over us? What *is* this you have done
to us?" And he said to them, "As they did to
me, so I have done to them."
12 But they said to him, "We have come down
to arrest you, that we may deliver you into the
hand of the Philistines." Then Samson said to
them, "Swear to me that you will not kill me
yourselves."
13 So they spoke to him, saying, "No, but we
will tie you securely and deliver you into their
hand; but we will surely not kill you." And
they bound him with two new ropes and
brought him up from the rock.
14 When he came to Lehi, the Philistines
came shouting against him. Then the Spirit of
the LORD came mightily upon him; and the
ropes that *were* on his arms became like flax
that is burned with fire, and his bonds broke
loose from his hands.
15 He found a fresh jawbone of a donkey,
reached out his hand and took it, and killed a
thousand men with it.
16 Then Samson said:

"With the jawbone of a donkey,
Heaps upon heaps,
With the jawbone of a donkey
I have slain a thousand men!"

17 And so it was, when he had finished
speaking, that he threw the jawbone from his
hand, and called that place Ramath Lehi.[a]
18 Then he became very thirsty; so he cried ➤

15:17 [a]Literally *Jawbone Height*

LIFE LESSONS

➤ ***15:18 — Then he became very thirsty; so he cried out to the LORD and said, "You have given this great deliverance by the hand of Your servant; and now shall I die of thirst and fall into the hand of the uncircumcised?"***

Although Samson had many serious character flaws, he is included in the "hall of faith" (Heb.13:32) and God listened to his pleas for help. But imagine what God could have done through a wholeheartedly obedient Samson!

out to the LORD and said, "You have given this
great deliverance by the hand of Your servant;
and now shall I die of thirst and fall into the
hand of the uncircumcised?"
19 So God split the hollow place that *is* in
Lehi,[a] and water came out, and he drank; and
his spirit returned, and he revived. Therefore
he called its name En Hakkore,[b] which is in
Lehi to this day.
20 And he judged Israel twenty years in the
days of the Philistines.

Samson and Delilah

16 Now Samson went to Gaza and saw a
harlot there, and went in to her.
2 *When* the Gazites *were told,* "Samson has
come here!" they surrounded *the place* and
lay in wait for him all night at the gate of the
city. They were quiet all night, saying, "In the
morning, when it is daylight, we will kill him."
3 And Samson lay *low* till midnight; then he
arose at midnight, took hold of the doors of
the gate of the city and the two gateposts,
pulled them up, bar and all, put *them* on his
shoulders, and carried them to the top of the
hill that faces Hebron.
4 Afterward it happened that he loved a
woman in the Valley of Sorek, whose name
was Delilah.
5 And the lords of the Philistines came up to
her and said to her, "Entice him, and find out
where his great strength *lies,* and by what
means we may overpower him, that we may
bind him to afflict him; and every one of us
will give you eleven hundred *pieces* of silver."
6 So Delilah said to Samson, "Please tell me
where your great strength *lies,* and with what
you may be bound to afflict you."
7 And Samson said to her, "If they bind me
with seven fresh bowstrings, not yet dried,
then I shall become weak, and be like any
other man."
8 So the lords of the Philistines brought up
to her seven fresh bowstrings, not yet dried,
and she bound him with them.
9 Now *men were* lying in wait, staying with
her in the room. And she said to him, "The
Philistines *are* upon you, Samson!" But he
broke the bowstrings as a strand of yarn
breaks when it touches fire. So the secret of
his strength was not known.
10 Then Delilah said to Samson, "Look,
you have mocked me and told me lies.
Now, please tell me what you may be bound
with."
11 So he said to her, "If they bind me securely
with new ropes that have never been used,
then I shall become weak, and be like any
other man."
12 Therefore Delilah took new ropes and
bound him with them, and said to him, "The
Philistines *are* upon you, Samson!" And *men
were* lying in wait, staying in the room. But he
broke them off his arms like a thread.
13 Delilah said to Samson, "Until now you
have mocked me and told me lies. Tell me
what you may be bound with." And he said to
her, "If you weave the seven locks of my head
into the web of the loom"—
14 So she wove *it* tightly with the batten of
the loom, and said to him, "The Philistines *are*
upon you, Samson!" But he awoke from his
sleep, and pulled out the batten and the web
from the loom.
15 Then she said to him, "How can you say,
'I love you,' when your heart *is* not with me?
You have mocked me these three times, and
have not told me where your great strength
lies."
16 And it came to pass, when she pestered
him daily with her words and pressed him, *so*
that his soul was vexed to death,
17 that he told her all his heart, and said to
her, "No razor has ever come upon my head,
for I *have been* a Nazirite to God from my
mother's womb. If I am shaven, then my
strength will leave me, and I shall become
weak, and be like any *other* man."
18 When Delilah saw that he had told her all
his heart, she sent and called for the lords of
the Philistines, saying, "Come up once more,
for he has told me all his heart." So the lords
of the Philistines came up to her and brought
the money in their hand.
19 Then she lulled him to sleep on her knees,
and called for a man and had him shave off
the seven locks of his head. Then she began to
torment him,[a] and his strength left him.

15:19 [a]Literally *Jawbone* (compare verse 14) [b]Literally *Spring of the Caller* **16:19** [a]Following Masoretic Text, Targum, and Vulgate; Septuagint reads *he began to be weak.*

LIFE LESSONS

➤ 16:15 — *Then she said to him, "How can you say, 'I love you,' when your heart is not with me? You have mocked me these three times, and have not told me where your great strength lies."*

It is easy to say, "I love you," but real love always wants the best for the other. Samson did not want the best for Delilah, nor did she want the best for him. Lust is a very poor substitute for love.

➤ 16:19 — *Then she lulled him to sleep on her knees, and called for a man and had him shave off the seven locks of his head. Then she began to torment him, and his strength left him.*

How quickly some "love" turns to "torment"! Spent lust often generates feelings of hatred more potent than the earlier feelings of "love" (see 2 Sam. 13:15).

➤ 20 And she said, "The Philistines *are* upon you, Samson!" So he awoke from his sleep, and said, "I will go out as before, at other times, and shake myself free!" But he did not know that the LORD had departed from him.
21 Then the Philistines took him and put out his eyes, and brought him down to Gaza. They bound him with bronze fetters, and he became a grinder in the prison.
22 However, the hair of his head began to grow again after it had been shaven.

Samson Dies with the Philistines

23 Now the lords of the Philistines gathered together to offer a great sacrifice to Dagon their god, and to rejoice. And they said:

> "Our god has delivered into our hands
> Samson our enemy!"

24 When the people saw him, they praised their god; for they said:

> "Our god has delivered into our hands our enemy,
> The destroyer of our land,
> And the one who multiplied our dead."

25 So it happened, when their hearts were merry, that they said, "Call for Samson, that he may perform for us." So they called for Samson from the prison, and he performed for them. And they stationed him between the pillars.
26 Then Samson said to the lad who held him by the hand, "Let me feel the pillars which support the temple, so that I can lean on them."
27 Now the temple was full of men and women. All the lords of the Philistines *were* there—about three thousand men and women on the roof watching while Samson performed.
28 Then Samson called to the LORD, saying, "O Lord GOD, remember me, I pray! Strengthen me, I pray, just this once, O God, that I may with one *blow* take vengeance on the Philistines for my two eyes!"
29 And Samson took hold of the two middle pillars which supported the temple, and he braced himself against them, one on his right and the other on his left.
30 Then Samson said, "Let me die with the Philistines!" And he pushed with *all his* might, and the temple fell on the lords and all the people who *were* in it. So the dead that he killed at his death were more than he had killed in his life.
31 And his brothers and all his father's household came down and took him, and brought *him* up and buried him between Zorah and Eshtaol in the tomb of his father Manoah. He had judged Israel twenty years.

Micah's Idolatry

17 Now there was a man from the mountains of Ephraim, whose name *was* Micah.
2 And he said to his mother, "The eleven hundred *shekels* of silver that were taken from you, and on which you put a curse, even saying it in my ears—here *is* the silver with me; I took it." And his mother said, "*May you be* blessed by the LORD, my son!"
3 So when he had returned the eleven hundred *shekels* of silver to his mother, his ◄
mother said, "I had wholly dedicated the silver from my hand to the LORD for my son, to make a carved image and a molded image; now therefore, I will return it to you."
4 Thus he returned the silver to his mother. Then his mother took two hundred *shekels* of silver and gave them to the silversmith, and he made it into a carved image and a molded image; and they were in the house of Micah.
5 The man Micah had a shrine, and made an ephod and household idols;[a] and he consecrated one of his sons, who became his priest.
6 In those days *there was* no king in Israel; ◄
everyone did *what was* right in his own eyes.
7 Now there was a young man from Bethlehem in Judah, of the family of Judah; he *was* a Levite, and was staying there.
8 The man departed from the city of Bethlehem in Judah to stay wherever he could find *a place*. Then he came to the mountains of Ephraim, to the house of Micah, as he journeyed.

17:5 [a]Hebrew *teraphim*

LIFE LESSONS

➤ 16:20 — *. . . But he did not know that the LORD had departed from him.*

Samson had fallen so low spiritually that he could not tell the difference between the Lord's presence and His absence. While God's Spirit will never leave believers in Christ, His blessings may. That hinges on our obedience.

➤ 17:3 — *". . . I had wholly dedicated the silver from my hand to the LORD for my son, to make a carved image and a molded image . . . ."*

This woman tried to wed idolatry with worship of the true God. But we cannot serve God *and* anything else. We cannot worship God *and* something else. The Lord deserves our exclusive devotion (see Matt. 6:24).

➤ 17:6 — *In those days there was no king in Israel; everyone did what was right in his own eyes.*

Moses had warned against "every man doing whatever is right in his own eyes" (Deut. 12:8). But when God's people refuse to obey Him, that is exactly what starts to happen. And the result is chaos, as Judges proves.

9 And Micah said to him, "Where do you
come from?" So he said to him, "I *am* a Levite
from Bethlehem in Judah, and I am on my
way to find *a place* to stay."
10 Micah said to him, "Dwell with me, and
be a father and a priest to me, and I will give
you ten *shekels* of silver per year, a suit of
clothes, and your sustenance." So the Levite
went in.
11 Then the Levite was content to dwell with
the man; and the young man became like one
of his sons to him.
12 So Micah consecrated the Levite, and the
young man became his priest, and lived in the
house of Micah.
➤ 13 Then Micah said, "Now I know that the
LORD will be good to me, since I have a Levite
as priest!"

The Danites Adopt Micah's Idolatry

18 In those days *there was* no king in
Israel. And in those days the tribe of
the Danites was seeking an inheritance for itself to dwell in; for until that day *their* inheritance among the tribes of Israel had not fallen
to them.
2 So the children of Dan sent five men of
their family from their territory, men of valor
from Zorah and Eshtaol, to spy out the land
and search it. They said to them, "Go, search
the land." So they went to the mountains of
Ephraim, to the house of Micah, and lodged
there.
3 While they *were* at the house of Micah,
they recognized the voice of the young Levite.
They turned aside and said to him, "Who
brought you here? What are you doing in this
place? What do you have here?"
4 He said to them, "Thus and so Micah did
for me. He has hired me, and I have become
his priest."
5 So they said to him, "Please inquire of
God, that we may know whether the journey
on which we go will be prosperous."
6 And the priest said to them, "Go in peace.
The presence of the LORD *be* with you on your
way."
7 So the five men departed and went to
Laish. They saw the people who *were* there,
how they dwelt safely, in the manner of the
Sidonians, quiet and secure. *There were* no
rulers in the land who might put *them* to
shame for anything. They *were* far from the
Sidonians, and they had no ties with anyone.[a]
8 Then *the spies* came back to their
brethren at Zorah and Eshtaol, and their
brethren said to them, "What *is* your *report?*"
9 So they said, "Arise, let us go up against
them. For we have seen the land, and indeed
it *is* very good. *Would* you *do* nothing? Do not
hesitate to go, *and* enter to possess the land.
10 When you go, you will come to a secure
people and a large land. For God has given it
into your hands, a place where *there is* no
lack of anything that *is* on the earth."
11 And six hundred men of the family of the
Danites went from there, from Zorah and
Eshtaol, armed with weapons of war.
12 Then they went up and encamped in Kirjath Jearim in Judah. (Therefore they call that
place Mahaneh Dan[a] to this day. There *it is,*
west of Kirjath Jearim.)
13 And they passed from there to the mountains of Ephraim, and came to the house of
Micah.
14 Then the five men who had gone to spy
out the country of Laish answered and said to
their brethren, "Do you know that there are in
these houses an ephod, household idols, a
carved image, and a molded image? Now
therefore, consider what you should do."
15 So they turned aside there, and came to
the house of the young Levite man—to the
house of Micah—and greeted him.
16 The six hundred men armed with their
weapons of war, who *were* of the children of
Dan, stood by the entrance of the gate.
17 Then the five men who had gone to spy
out the land went up. Entering there, they
took the carved image, the ephod, the household idols, and the molded image. The priest
stood at the entrance of the gate with the six
hundred men *who were* armed with weapons
of war.
18 When these went into Micah's house and
took the carved image, the ephod, the household idols, and the molded image, the priest
said to them, "What are you doing?"
19 And they said to him, "Be quiet, put your
hand over your mouth, and come with us; be
a father and a priest to us. *Is it* better for you
to be a priest to the household of one man, or
that you be a priest to a tribe and a family in
Israel?"
20 So the priest's heart was glad; and he took
the ephod, the household idols, and the carved
image, and took his place among the people.
21 Then they turned and departed, and put
the little ones, the livestock, and the goods in
front of them.

18:7 [a]Following Masoretic Text, Targum, and Vulgate; Septuagint reads *with Syria.* **18:12** [a]Literally *Camp of Dan*

LIFE LESSONS

➤ 17:13 — *Then Micah said, "Now I know that the LORD will be good to me, since I have a Levite as priest!"*

The Word of God makes clear that God's blessing does not come because of proper ritual or special connection to religious people. God's blessing comes on those who obey Him.

22 When they were a good way from the
house of Micah, the men who *were* in the
houses near Micah's house gathered together
and overtook the children of Dan.
23 And they called out to the children of Dan.
So they turned around and said to Micah,
"What ails you, that you have gathered such a
company?"
24 So he said, "You have taken away my gods
which I made, and the priest, and you have
gone away. Now what more do I have? How
can you say to me, 'What ails you?'"
25 And the children of Dan said to him, "Do
not let your voice be heard among us, lest angry men fall upon you, and you lose your life,
with the lives of your household!"
26 Then the children of Dan went their way.
And when Micah saw that they *were* too
strong for him, he turned and went back to
his house.

Danites Settle in Laish

27 So they took *the things* Micah had made,
and the priest who had belonged to him, and
went to Laish, to a people quiet and secure;
and they struck them with the edge of the
sword and burned the city with fire.
28 *There was* no deliverer, because it *was* far
from Sidon, and they had no ties with anyone.
It was in the valley that belongs to Beth
Rehob. So they rebuilt the city and dwelt
there.
29 And they called the name of the city Dan,
after the name of Dan their father, who was
born to Israel. However, the name of the city
formerly *was* Laish.
➤ **30** Then the children of Dan set up for themselves the carved image; and Jonathan the
son of Gershom, the son of Manasseh,[a] and
his sons were priests to the tribe of Dan until
the day of the captivity of the land.
31 So they set up for themselves Micah's
carved image which he made, all the time that
the house of God was in Shiloh.

The Levite's Concubine

19 And it came to pass in those days,
when *there was* no king in Israel, that
there was a certain Levite staying in the remote mountains of Ephraim. He took for himself a concubine from Bethlehem in Judah.
2 But his concubine played the harlot
against him, and went away from him to her
father's house at Bethlehem in Judah, and
was there four whole months.
3 Then her husband arose and went after
her, to speak kindly to her *and* bring her
back, having his servant and a couple of donkeys with him. So she brought him into her
father's house; and when the father of the
young woman saw him, he was glad to meet
him.
4 Now his father-in-law, the young woman's
father, detained him; and he stayed with him
three days. So they ate and drank and lodged
there.
5 Then it came to pass on the fourth day
that they arose early in the morning, and he
stood to depart; but the young woman's father said to his son-in-law, "Refresh your
heart with a morsel of bread, and afterward
go your way."
6 So they sat down, and the two of them ate
and drank together. Then the young woman's
father said to the man, "Please be content to
stay all night, and let your heart be merry."
7 And when the man stood to depart, his father-in-law urged him; so he lodged there
again.
8 Then he arose early in the morning on the
fifth day to depart, but the young woman's father said, "Please refresh your heart." So they
delayed until afternoon; and both of them ate.
9 And when the man stood to depart—he
and his concubine and his servant—his father-in-law, the young woman's father, said to
him, "Look, the day is now drawing toward
evening; please spend the night. See, the day
is coming to an end; lodge here, that your
heart may be merry. Tomorrow go your way
early, so that you may get home."
10 However, the man was not willing to
spend that night; so he rose and departed, and
came opposite Jebus (that *is*, Jerusalem). With
him were the two saddled donkeys; his concubine *was* also with him.
11 They *were* near Jebus, and the day was far
spent; and the servant said to his master,
"Come, please, and let us turn aside into this
city of the Jebusites and lodge in it."
12 But his master said to him, "We will not
turn aside here into a city of foreigners, who
are not of the children of Israel; we will go on
to Gibeah."
13 So he said to his servant, "Come, let us
draw near to one of these places, and spend
the night in Gibeah or in Ramah."

18:30 [a]Septuagint and Vulgate read *Moses.*

LIFE LESSONS

➤ ***18:30 — Then the children of Dan set up for themselves the carved image; and Jonathan . . . and his sons were priests to the tribe of Dan until the day of the captivity of the land.***

The tribe of Dan held fast to its idolatry all the way until the exile. God patiently waited centuries for them to repent, but they never did. This may explain why Dan is missing from the list of tribes in Revelation 7:4–8.

14 And they passed by and went their way; and the sun went down on them near Gibeah, which belongs to Benjamin.
15 They turned aside there to go in to lodge in Gibeah. And when he went in, he sat down in the open square of the city, for no one would take them into *his* house to spend the night.
16 Just then an old man came in from his work in the field at evening, who also *was* from the mountains of Ephraim; he was staying in Gibeah, whereas the men of the place *were* Benjamites.
17 And when he raised his eyes, he saw the traveler in the open square of the city; and the old man said, "Where are you going, and where do you come from?"
18 So he said to him, "We *are* passing from Bethlehem in Judah toward the remote mountains of Ephraim; I *am* from there. I went to Bethlehem in Judah; *now* I am going to the house of the LORD. But there *is* no one who will take me into his house,
19 although we have both straw and fodder for our donkeys, and bread and wine for myself, for your female servant, and for the young man *who is* with your servant; *there is* no lack of anything."
20 And the old man said, "Peace *be* with you! However, *let* all your needs *be* my responsibility; only do not spend the night in the open square."
21 So he brought him into his house, and gave fodder to the donkeys. And they washed their feet, and ate and drank.

Gibeah's Crime

22 As they were enjoying themselves, suddenly certain men of the city, perverted men,[a] surrounded the house *and* beat on the door. They spoke to the master of the house, the old man, saying, "Bring out the man who came to your house, that we may know him *carnally!*"
23 But the man, the master of the house, went out to them and said to them, "No, my brethren! I beg you, do not act *so* wickedly! Seeing this man has come into my house, do not commit this outrage.
24 Look, *here is* my virgin daughter and *the man's*[a] concubine; let me bring them out now. Humble them, and do with them as you please; but to this man do not do such a vile thing!"
➤ 25 But the men would not heed him. So the man took his concubine and brought *her* out to them. And they knew her and abused her all night until morning; and when the day began to break, they let her go.
26 Then the woman came as the day was dawning, and fell down at the door of the man's house where her master *was,* till it was light.
27 When her master arose in the morning, and opened the doors of the house and went out to go his way, there was his concubine, fallen *at* the door of the house with her hands on the threshold.
28 And he said to her, "Get up and let us be going." But there was no answer. So the man lifted her onto the donkey; and the man got up and went to his place.
29 When he entered his house he took a knife, laid hold of his concubine, and divided her into twelve pieces, limb by limb,[a] and sent her throughout all the territory of Israel.
30 And so it was that all who saw it said, "No such deed has been done or seen from the day that the children of Israel came up from the land of Egypt until this day. Consider it, confer, and speak up!"

Israel's War with the Benjamites

20 So all the children of Israel came out, from Dan to Beersheba, as well as from the land of Gilead, and the congregation gathered together as one man before the LORD at Mizpah.
2 And the leaders of all the people, all the tribes of Israel, presented themselves in the assembly of the people of God, four hundred thousand foot soldiers who drew the sword.
3 (Now the children of Benjamin heard that the children of Israel had gone up to Mizpah.) Then the children of Israel said, "Tell *us,* how did this wicked deed happen?"
4 So the Levite, the husband of the woman who was murdered, answered and said, "My concubine and I went into Gibeah, which belongs to Benjamin, to spend the night.
5 And the men of Gibeah rose against me, and surrounded the house at night because of me. They intended to kill me, but instead they ravished my concubine so that she died.
6 So I took hold of my concubine, cut her in pieces, and sent her throughout all the territory of the inheritance of Israel, because they committed lewdness and outrage in Israel.

19:22 [a]Literally *sons of Belial* **19:24** [a]Literally *his*
19:29 [a]Literally *with her bones*

LIFE LESSONS

➤ 19:25 — *. . . So the man took his concubine and brought her out to them. And they knew her and abused her all night until morning; and when the day began to break, they let her go.*

When everyone does what is right in his own eyes, before long moral conditions sink to the perverted level of Sodom (see Gen. 19:1–8). We need the Word of God to show us the right way.

7 Look! All of you *are* children of Israel;
give your advice and counsel here and now!"
8 So all the people arose as one man, saying, "None *of us* will go to his tent, nor will
any turn back to his house;
9 "but now this *is* the thing which we will do
to Gibeah: *We will go up* against it by lot.
10 "We will take ten men out of *every* hundred throughout all the tribes of Israel, a hundred out of *every* thousand, and a thousand
out of *every* ten thousand, to make provisions
for the people, that when they come to Gibeah
in Benjamin, they may repay all the vileness
that they have done in Israel."
11 So all the men of Israel were gathered
against the city, united together as one man.
12 Then the tribes of Israel sent men through
all the tribe of Benjamin, saying, "What *is* this
wickedness that has occurred among you?
13 "Now therefore, deliver up the men, the
perverted men[a] who *are* in Gibeah, that we
may put them to death and remove the evil
from Israel!" But the children of Benjamin
would not listen to the voice of their brethren,
the children of Israel.
14 Instead, the children of Benjamin gathered together from their cities to Gibeah, to
go to battle against the children of Israel.
15 And from their cities at that time the children of Benjamin numbered twenty-six thousand men who drew the sword, besides the
inhabitants of Gibeah, who numbered seven
hundred select men.
16 Among all this people *were* seven hundred select men *who were* left-handed; every
one could sling a stone at a hair's *breadth* and
not miss.
17 Now besides Benjamin, the men of Israel
numbered four hundred thousand men
who drew the sword; all of these *were* men of
war.
18 Then the children of Israel arose and went
up to the house of God[a] to inquire of God.
They said, "Which of us shall go up first to
battle against the children of Benjamin?" The
LORD said, "Judah first!"
19 So the children of Israel rose in the morning and encamped against Gibeah.
20 And the men of Israel went out to battle
against Benjamin, and the men of Israel put
themselves in battle array to fight against
them at Gibeah.
21 Then the children of Benjamin came out
of Gibeah, and on that day cut down to the
ground twenty-two thousand men of the Israelites.
22 And the people, that is, the men of Israel,
encouraged themselves and again formed the
battle line at the place where they had put
themselves in array on the first day.
23 Then the children of Israel went up and
wept before the LORD until evening, and
asked counsel of the LORD, saying, "Shall I
again draw near for battle against the children of my brother Benjamin?" And the LORD
said, "Go up against him."
24 So the children of Israel approached the
children of Benjamin on the second day.
25 And Benjamin went out against them
from Gibeah on the second day, and cut down
to the ground eighteen thousand more of the
children of Israel; all these drew the sword.
26 Then all the children of Israel, that is, all
the people, went up and came to the house of
God[a] and wept. They sat there before the
LORD and fasted that day until evening; and
they offered burnt offerings and peace offerings before the LORD.
27 So the children of Israel inquired of the
LORD (the ark of the covenant of God *was*
there in those days,
28 and Phinehas the son of Eleazar, the son
of Aaron, stood before it in those days),
saying, "Shall I yet again go out to battle
against the children of my brother Benjamin,
or shall I cease?" And the LORD said, "Go up,
for tomorrow I will deliver them into your
hand."
29 Then Israel set men in ambush all around
Gibeah.
30 And the children of Israel went up against
the children of Benjamin on the third day, and
put themselves in battle array against Gibeah
as at the other times.
31 So the children of Benjamin went out
against the people, *and* were drawn away
from the city. They began to strike down *and*
kill some of the people, as at the other times,
in the highways (one of which goes up to
Bethel and the other to Gibeah) and in the
field, about thirty men of Israel.
32 And the children of Benjamin said, "They
are defeated before us, as at first." But the
children of Israel said, "Let us flee and draw
them away from the city to the highways."
33 So all the men of Israel rose from their
place and put themselves in battle array at
Baal Tamar. Then Israel's men in ambush
burst forth from their position in the plain of
Geba.
34 And ten thousand select men from all Israel came against Gibeah, and the battle was
fierce. But *the Benjamites*[a] did not know that
disaster *was* upon them.
35 The LORD defeated Benjamin before Israel. And the children of Israel destroyed that
day twenty-five thousand one hundred Benjamites; all these drew the sword.
36 So the children of Benjamin saw that they
were defeated. The men of Israel had given
ground to the Benjamites, because they relied
on the men in ambush whom they had set
against Gibeah.
37 And the men in ambush quickly rushed
upon Gibeah; the men in ambush spread out

20:13 [a]Literally *sons of Belial* **20:18** [a]Or *Bethel* **20:26** [a]Or *Bethel*
20:34 [a]Literally *they*

and struck the whole city with the edge of the sword.

38 Now the appointed signal between the men of Israel and the men in ambush was that they would make a great cloud of smoke rise up from the city,

39 whereupon the men of Israel would turn in battle. Now Benjamin had begun to strike *and* kill about thirty of the men of Israel. For they said, "Surely they are defeated before us, as *in* the first battle."

40 But when the cloud began to rise from the city in a column of smoke, the Benjamites looked behind them, and there was the whole city going up *in smoke* to heaven.

41 And when the men of Israel turned back, the men of Benjamin panicked, for they saw that disaster had come upon them.

42 Therefore they turned *their backs* before the men of Israel in the direction of the wilderness; but the battle overtook them, and whoever *came* out of the cities they destroyed in their midst.

43 They surrounded the Benjamites, chased them, *and* easily trampled them down as far as the front of Gibeah toward the east.

44 And eighteen thousand men of Benjamin fell; all these *were* men of valor.

45 Then they[a] turned and fled toward the wilderness to the rock of Rimmon; and they cut down five thousand of them on the highways. Then they pursued them relentlessly up to Gidom, and killed two thousand of them.

➤ 46 So all who fell of Benjamin that day were twenty-five thousand men who drew the sword; all these *were* men of valor.

47 But six hundred men turned and fled toward the wilderness to the rock of Rimmon, and they stayed at the rock of Rimmon for four months.

48 And the men of Israel turned back against the children of Benjamin, and struck them down with the edge of the sword—from *every* city, men and beasts, all who were found. They also set fire to all the cities they came to.

Wives Provided for the Benjamites

21 Now the men of Israel had sworn an oath at Mizpah, saying, "None of us shall give his daughter to Benjamin as a wife."

2 Then the people came to the house of God,[a] and remained there before God till evening. They lifted up their voices and wept bitterly,

3 and said, "O LORD God of Israel, why has this come to pass in Israel, that today there should be one tribe *missing* in Israel?"

4 So it was, on the next morning, that the people rose early and built an altar there, and offered burnt offerings and peace offerings.

5 The children of Israel said, "Who *is there* among all the tribes of Israel who did not come up with the assembly to the LORD?" For they had made a great oath concerning anyone who had not come up to the LORD at Mizpah, saying, "He shall surely be put to death."

6 And the children of Israel grieved for Benjamin their brother, and said, "One tribe is cut off from Israel today.

7 "What shall we do for wives for those who remain, seeing we have sworn by the LORD that we will not give them our daughters as wives?"

8 And they said, "What one *is there* from the tribes of Israel who did not come up to Mizpah to the LORD?" And, in fact, no one had come to the camp from Jabesh Gilead to the assembly.

9 For when the people were counted, indeed, not one of the inhabitants of Jabesh Gilead *was* there.

10 So the congregation sent out there twelve thousand of their most valiant men, and commanded them, saying, "Go and strike the inhabitants of Jabesh Gilead with the edge of the sword, including the women and children.

11 "And this *is* the thing that you shall do: You shall utterly destroy every male, and every woman who has known a man intimately."

12 So they found among the inhabitants of Jabesh Gilead four hundred young virgins who had not known a man intimately; and they brought them to the camp at Shiloh, which is in the land of Canaan.

13 Then the whole congregation sent *word* to the children of Benjamin who *were* at the rock of Rimmon, and announced peace to them.

14 So Benjamin came back at that time, and they gave them the women whom they had saved alive of the women of Jabesh Gilead; and yet they had not found enough for them.

15 And the people grieved for Benjamin, because the LORD had made a void in the tribes of Israel.

16 Then the elders of the congregation said, "What shall we do for wives for those who re-

20:45 [a]Septuagint reads *the rest.* **21:2** [a]Or *Bethel*

LIFE LESSONS

➤ ***20:46 — So all who fell of Benjamin that day were twenty-five thousand men who drew the sword; all these were men of valor.***

The tribe of Benjamin lost more than 25 thousand men in battle, while Israel lost over 40 thousand of its men—a bloody civil war that didn't need to happen. When we lose connection to God's Word, we lose our senses.

main, since the women of Benjamin have
been destroyed?"
17 And they said, "*There must be* an inheritance for the survivors of Benjamin, that a
tribe may not be destroyed from Israel.
18 "However, we cannot give them wives
from our daughters, for the children of Israel
have sworn an oath, saying, 'Cursed *be* the
one who gives a wife to Benjamin.'"
19 Then they said, "In fact, *there is* a yearly
feast of the LORD in Shiloh, which *is* north of
Bethel, on the east side of the highway that
goes up from Bethel to Shechem, and south of
Lebonah."
20 Therefore they instructed the children of
Benjamin, saying, "Go, lie in wait in the vineyards,
21 "and watch; and just when the daughters
of Shiloh come out to perform their dances,
then come out from the vineyards, and every
man catch a wife for himself from the daughters of Shiloh; then go to the land of Benjamin.
22 "Then it shall be, when their fathers or
their brothers come to us to complain, that we
will say to them, 'Be kind to them for our
sakes, because we did not take a wife for any
of them in the war; for *it is* not *as though* you
have given the *women* to them at this time,
making yourselves guilty of your oath.'"
23 And the children of Benjamin did so; they
took enough wives for their number from
those who danced, whom they caught. Then
they went and returned to their inheritance,
and they rebuilt the cities and dwelt in them.
24 So the children of Israel departed from
there at that time, every man to his tribe and
family; they went out from there, every man
to his inheritance.
25 In those days *there was* no king in Israel;
everyone did *what was* right in his own eyes.

THE BOOK OF RUTH

Ruth is a cameo story of love, devotion, and redemption set in the dark context of the days of the judges. It tells the story of a Moabite woman who forsakes her pagan heritage in order to cling to the people and the God of Israel. Because of her faithfulness in a time of national unfaithfulness, God rewards her by giving her a new husband (Boaz), a son (Obed), and a privileged position in the lineage of Christ (as the great-grandmother of David).

Ruth had married one of Naomi's sons, but when all of the men of the family died, the two women found themselves alone. Naomi decided to return home to Bethlehem. In a moving demonstration of loyalty, Ruth insisted on staying with Naomi, even though it meant becoming a stranger in someone else's land. Yet Ruth declared, "Your people shall be my people, and your God, my God" (1:16).

After arriving in Bethlehem, Ruth began gleaning in the fields because she had no other source of support. She needed a deliverer, a savior—but what did she have to offer? Ruth did not know that the field where she worked belonged to a wealthy man named Boaz, who noticed her hard at work. He approached and graciously offered her a safe haven on his property, complete with all the food and water she desired.

When Ruth expressed her gratitude, Boaz responded, "The LORD repay your work, and a full reward be given you by the LORD God of Israel, under whose wings you have come for refuge" (2:12). Boaz could not have known that he was about to become the living representation of God's salvation as Ruth's kinsman redeemer. The two eventually married and all the townspeople rejoiced with them in God's provision.

The story of Ruth teaches us many things, especially the value of trusting God in our circumstances. But her story also pictures God's redemptive love for us in Jesus Christ.

Theme: Faithfulness to God, even in times and places of unfaithfulness, will bring God's blessing.

Author: Unknown, possibly Samuel.

Time: The events of Ruth take place during the period of the judges, which began following Joshua's death and lasted about three hundred years, to the beginning of King Saul's reign, around 1043 B.C.

Structure: A simple four-chapter narrative that functions as the spiritual biography of a young Moabite widow whose faith and devotion to her family led to a blessing like few in history would enjoy.

As you read Ruth, watch for several life principles that play an important role in this book:

22. To walk in the Spirit is to obey the initial promptings of the Holy Spirit. *See Ruth 1:15–18; page 305.*

18. As children of a sovereign God, we are never victims of our circumstances. *See Ruth 1:20, 21; 4:14, 15; pages 305; 309.*

6. You reap what you sow, more than you sow, and later than you sow. *See Ruth 4:13–17; page 309.*

Elimelech's Family Goes to Moab

1 Now it came to pass, in the days when the
judges ruled, that there was a famine in
the land. And a certain man of Bethlehem, Judah, went to dwell in the country of Moab, he
and his wife and his two sons.
2 The name of the man *was* Elimelech, the
name of his wife *was* Naomi, and the names of
his two sons *were* Mahlon and Chilion—Eph-
rathites of Bethlehem, Judah. And they went to
the country of Moab and remained there.
3 Then Elimelech, Naomi's husband, died;
and she was left, and her two sons.
4 Now they took wives of the women of
Moab: the name of the one *was* Orpah, and
the name of the other Ruth. And they dwelt
there about ten years.
5 Then both Mahlon and Chilion also died;
so the woman survived her two sons and her
husband.

Naomi Returns with Ruth

➤ **6** Then she arose with her daughters-in-law
that she might return from the country of
Moab, for she had heard in the country of
Moab that the LORD had visited His people by
giving them bread.
7 Therefore she went out from the place
where she was, and her two daughters-in-law
with her; and they went on the way to return
to the land of Judah.
8 And Naomi said to her two daughters-in-
law, "Go, return each to her mother's house.
The LORD deal kindly with you, as you have
dealt with the dead and with me.
9 "The LORD grant that you may find rest,
each in the house of her husband." So she
kissed them, and they lifted up their voices
and wept.
10 And they said to her, "Surely we will return with you to your people."
11 But Naomi said, "Turn back, my daughters;
why will you go with me? *Are* there still sons
in my womb, that they may be your husbands?
12 "Turn back, my daughters, go—for I am
too old to have a husband. If I should say I
have hope, *if* I should have a husband tonight
and should also bear sons,
13 "would you wait for them till they were
grown? Would you restrain yourselves from
having husbands? No, my daughters; for it
grieves me very much for your sakes that the
hand of the LORD has gone out against me!"
14 Then they lifted up their voices and wept
again; and Orpah kissed her mother-in-law,
but Ruth clung to her.
15 And she said, "Look, your sister-in-law
has gone back to her people and to her gods;
return after your sister-in-law."
16 But Ruth said:

"Entreat me not to leave you,
Or to turn back from following after you;
For wherever you go, I will go;
And wherever you lodge, I will lodge;
Your people *shall be* my people,
And your God, my God.
17 Where you die, I will die,
And there will I be buried.
The LORD do so to me, and more also,
If *anything but* death parts you and me."

18 When she saw that she was determined to
go with her, she stopped speaking to her.
19 Now the two of them went until they came
to Bethlehem. And it happened, when they
had come to Bethlehem, that all the city was
excited because of them; and the women said,
"*Is* this Naomi?"
20 But she said to them, "Do not call me
Naomi;[a] call me Mara,[b] for the Almighty has
dealt very bitterly with me.
21 "I went out full, and the LORD has brought ➤
me home again empty. Why do you call me
Naomi, since the LORD has testified against
me, and the Almighty has afflicted me?"
22 So Naomi returned, and Ruth the
Moabitess her daughter-in-law with her, who
returned from the country of Moab. Now they
came to Bethlehem at the beginning of barley
harvest.

Ruth Meets Boaz

2 There was a relative of Naomi's husband, ➤
a man of great wealth, of the family of
Elimelech. His name *was* Boaz.

1:20 [a]Literally *Pleasant* [b]Literally *Bitter*

LIFE LESSONS

➤ 1:6 — *Then she arose with her daughters-in-law that she might return from the country of Moab, for she had heard in the country of Moab that the LORD had visited His people by giving them bread.*

Wondrous indeed is the grace of our God, who never forsakes the wanderer, but draws and restores with cords of love.

➤ 1:21 — *"I went out full, and the LORD has brought me home again empty. Why do you call me Naomi, since the LORD has testified against me, and the Almighty has afflicted me?"*

Hardship has a way of prompting us to believe that God has turned against us, even though we can see no reason for it. But God is good, and He knows how to turn sad stories into joyful ones.

➤ 2:1 — *There was a relative of Naomi's husband, a man of great wealth, of the family of Elimelech. His name was Boaz.*

Boaz had wealth but no wife; Ruth had poverty and no husband. Both demonstrated their commitment to God by their lives. And for such people, God loves to take deficits and turn them into unbelievable assets.

ANSWERS TO LIFE'S QUESTIONS

Does God consider loyalty an important trait in His people?

RUTH 1:16, 17

Our relationship with God usually gets reflected in our relationships with other people. The more loyal we are to God, the more loyal we tend to be with friends and family members. That's no accident.

God considers loyalty an important trait. David thought it so important that he prayed, "give my son Solomon a loyal heart to keep Your commandments and Your testimonies and Your statutes" (1 Chr. 29:19). God wants us to remain loyal to Him, and He wants us to remain loyal to the people He puts in our lives.

Perhaps this helps to explain why we find so many beautiful pictures of loyalty in the Bible. For example, Jonathan remained loyal to David, even at the risk of his own health and safety (1 Sam. 18:4; 19:2). In the New Testament, we see a bond of loyalty between the apostle Paul and Barnabas, two men who helped change the course of the world for Christ, even though they couldn't always agree.

But perhaps the most beautiful picture of loyalty in all of the Scriptures is that of Ruth for her mother-in-law, Naomi. Many people have inscribed her words on bracelets and pendants that they carry with them everywhere: "For wherever you go, I will go, and wherever you lodge, I will lodge. Your people shall be my people, and your God, my God. Where you die, I will die, and there I will be buried. The LORD do so to me, and more also, if anything but death parts you and me" (Ruth 1:16, 17).

A loyal person remains steadfast. Loyalty comes from the heart. It is motivated by love and wants the best for the other person. You never have to beg the support of a loyal friend or co-worker.

Loyalty also demands trust. It leaves no room for deception or mistrust. As a result, individuals loyal to one another relate at much deeper levels than others.

A loyal person makes for a reliable messenger. Disloyalty causes division, especially among Christians. Loyal friends defend the other person and refuse to listen to gossip. Loyalty speaks the truth. A loyal person has a strong sense of responsibility.

Genuine loyalty is not built around circumstances, environment, popularity, or convenience. True loyalty is built on devotion to God and love to others.

Last, God always rewards those who remain loyal to Him and to the people He places in our lives. You can never out give God, even in loyalty!

See the Life Principles Index for further study:
28. No Christian has ever been called to "go it alone" in his or her walk of faith.
23. You can never out give God.

2 So Ruth the Moabitess said to Naomi,
"Please let me go to the field, and glean
heads of grain after *him* in whose sight I may
find favor." And she said to her, "Go, my
daughter."
3 Then she left, and went and gleaned in the
field after the reapers. And she happened to
come to the part of the field *belonging* to
Boaz, who *was* of the family of Elimelech.
4 Now behold, Boaz came from Bethlehem,
and said to the reapers, "The LORD *be* with
you!" And they answered him, "The LORD
bless you!"
5 Then Boaz said to his servant who was in
charge of the reapers, "Whose young woman
is this?"
6 So the servant who was in charge of the
reapers answered and said, "It *is* the young
Moabite woman who came back with Naomi
from the country of Moab.
7 "And she said, 'Please let me glean and
gather after the reapers among the sheaves.'
So she came and has continued from morning
until now, though she rested a little in the
house."
8 Then Boaz said to Ruth, "You will listen,
my daughter, will you not? Do not go to glean
in another field, nor go from here, but stay
close by my young women.
9 "*Let* your eyes *be* on the field which they
reap, and go after them. Have I not commanded the young men not to touch you?
And when you are thirsty, go to the vessels
and drink from what the young men have
drawn."
10 So she fell on her face, bowed down to the
ground, and said to him, "Why have I found
favor in your eyes, that you should take notice
of me, since I *am* a foreigner?"
11 And Boaz answered and said to her, "It
has been fully reported to me, all that you
have done for your mother-in-law since the
death of your husband, and *how* you have left
your father and your mother and the land of

your birth, and have come to a people whom
you did not know before.
✻ 12 "The LORD repay your work, and a full reward be given you by the LORD God of Israel, under whose wings you have come for refuge."
13 Then she said, "Let me find favor in your sight, my lord; for you have comforted me, and have spoken kindly to your maidservant, though I am not like one of your maidservants."
14 Now Boaz said to her at mealtime, "Come here, and eat of the bread, and dip your piece of bread in the vinegar." So she sat beside the reapers, and he passed parched *grain* to her; and she ate and was satisfied, and kept some back.
➤ 15 And when she rose up to glean, Boaz commanded his young men, saying, "Let her glean even among the sheaves, and do not reproach her.
16 "Also let *grain* from the bundles fall purposely for her; leave *it* that she may glean, and do not rebuke her."
17 So she gleaned in the field until evening, and beat out what she had gleaned, and it was about an ephah of barley.
18 Then she took *it* up and went into the city, and her mother-in-law saw what she had gleaned. So she brought out and gave to her what she had kept back after she had been satisfied.
19 And her mother-in-law said to her, "Where have you gleaned today? And where did you work? Blessed be the one who took notice of you."

So she told her mother-in-law with whom she had worked, and said, "The man's name with whom I worked today *is* Boaz."
➤ 20 Then Naomi said to her daughter-in-law, "Blessed *be* he of the LORD, who has not forsaken His kindness to the living and the dead!" And Naomi said to her, "This man *is* a relation of ours, one of our close relatives."
21 Ruth the Moabitess said, "He also said to me, 'You shall stay close by my young men until they have finished all my harvest.'"
22 And Naomi said to Ruth her daughter-in-law, "*It is* good, my daughter, that you go out with his young women, and that people do not meet you in any other field."
23 So she stayed close by the young women of Boaz, to glean until the end of barley harvest and wheat harvest; and she dwelt with her mother-in-law.

Life Examples:

NAOMI

Sowing in the Midst of Suffering

RUTH 1:18–22

As Naomi looked at the shambles of her life, she could see only a barren field of sorrow—yet she clung to the roots of hope. *Even though my sons and husband are gone*, she may have thought, *perhaps I may yet see fruitfulness in my life.*

But God had not abandoned her, and in time Naomi reaped a rich, unexpected yield of love. Her daughter-in-law, Ruth, looked tenderly into Naomi's face and declared her firm commitment to stay with her, even all the way to death (Ruth 1:16-17). Naomi placed her faith in the Lord, and He provided for her.

Whatever situation you face, the Lord is with you and can sustain you. Though there may be no fruit now, the grains of love and faithfulness you have scattered will produce a rich harvest. Will you persevere as Naomi did, and sow in the midst of suffering?

See the Life Principles Index for further study:
11. God assumes full responsibility for our needs when we obey Him.

Ruth's Redemption Assured

3 Then Naomi her mother-in-law said to her, "My daughter, shall I not seek security for you, that it may be well with you?
2 "Now Boaz, whose young women you were with, *is he* not our relative? In fact, he is winnowing barley tonight at the threshing floor.

LIFE LESSONS

➤ 2:15 — *And when she rose up to glean, Boaz commanded his young men, saying, "Let her glean even among the sheaves, and do not reproach her."*

Boaz did not act so generously to Ruth because he knew what was coming. He acted generously because he had made generosity a habit. "He who has a generous eye will be blessed . . ." (Prov. 22:9).

➤ 2:20 — *Then Naomi said to her daughter-in-law, "Blessed be he of the LORD, who has not forsaken His kindness to the living and the dead!"*

Although a discouraged believer may say foolish and rash things while in pain, God's grace within remains and erupts into praise when He once more shows His favor. Even this shows His goodness.

3 "Therefore wash yourself and anoint
yourself, put on your *best* garment and go
down to the threshing floor; *but* do not make
yourself known to the man until he has finished eating and drinking.
4 "Then it shall be, when he lies down, that
you shall notice the place where he lies; and
you shall go in, uncover his feet, and lie down;
and he will tell you what you should do."
5 And she said to her, "All that you say to me
I will do."
6 So she went down to the threshing floor
and did according to all that her mother-in-
law instructed her.
7 And after Boaz had eaten and drunk, and
his heart was cheerful, he went to lie down at
the end of the heap of grain; and she came
softly, uncovered his feet, and lay down.
8 Now it happened at midnight that the man
was startled, and turned himself; and there, a
woman was lying at his feet.
9 And he said, "Who *are* you?" So she answered, "I *am* Ruth, your maidservant. Take
your maidservant under your wing,[a] for you
are a close relative."
➤ 10 Then he said, "Blessed *are* you of the
LORD, my daughter! For you have shown more
kindness at the end than at the beginning, in
that you did not go after young men, whether
poor or rich.
11 "And now, my daughter, do not fear. I will
do for you all that you request, for all the people of my town know that you *are* a virtuous
woman.
12 "Now it is true that I *am* a close relative;
however, there is a relative closer than I.
13 "Stay this night, and in the morning it
shall be *that* if he will perform the duty of a
close relative for you—good; let him do it. But
if he does not want to perform the duty for
you, then I will perform the duty for you, *as*
the LORD lives! Lie down until morning."
14 So she lay at his feet until morning, and
she arose before one could recognize another.
Then he said, "Do not let it be known that the
woman came to the threshing floor."
15 Also he said, "Bring the shawl that *is* on
you and hold it." And when she held it, he
measured six *ephahs* of barley, and laid *it* on
her. Then she[a] went into the city.
16 When she came to her mother-in-law, she
said, "*Is* that you, my daughter?" Then she
told her all that the man had done for her.
17 And she said, "These six *ephahs* of barley
he gave me; for he said to me, 'Do not go
empty-handed to your mother-in-law.'"
18 Then she said, "Sit still, my daughter, until ➤
you know how the matter will turn out; for
the man will not rest until he has concluded
the matter this day."

Boaz Redeems Ruth

4 Now Boaz went up to the gate and sat
down there; and behold, the close relative
of whom Boaz had spoken came by. So Boaz
said, "Come aside, friend,[a] sit down here." So
he came aside and sat down.
2 And he took ten men of the elders of the
city, and said, "Sit down here." So they sat
down.
3 Then he said to the close relative, "Naomi,
who has come back from the country of
Moab, sold the piece of land which *belonged*
to our brother Elimelech.
4 "And I thought to inform you, saying, 'Buy
it back in the presence of the inhabitants and
the elders of my people. If you will redeem *it*,
redeem *it;* but if you[a] will not redeem *it*, *then*
tell me, that I may know; for *there is* no one
but you to redeem *it*, and I *am* next after you.'"
And he said, "I will redeem *it*."
5 Then Boaz said, "On the day you buy the
field from the hand of Naomi, you must also
buy *it* from Ruth the Moabitess, the wife of
the dead, to perpetuate[a] the name of the dead
through his inheritance."
6 And the close relative said, "I cannot redeem *it* for myself, lest I ruin my own inheritance. You redeem my right of redemption for
yourself, for I cannot redeem *it*."
7 Now this *was the custom* in former times
in Israel concerning redeeming and exchang-
ing, to confirm anything: one man took off his
sandal and gave *it* to the other, and this *was* a
confirmation in Israel.

3:9 [a]Or *Spread the corner of your garment over your maidservant* **3:15** [a]Many Hebrew manuscripts, Syriac, and Vulgate read *she;* Masoretic Text, Septuagint, and Targum read *he.* **4:1** [a]Hebrew *peloni almoni;* literally *so and so* **4:4** [a]Following many Hebrew manuscripts, Septuagint, Syriac, Targum, and Vulgate; Masoretic Text reads *he.* **4:5** [a]Literally *raise up*

LIFE LESSONS

➤ **3:10 — *Then he said, "Blessed are you of the LORD, my daughter! For you have shown more kindness at the end than at the beginning, in that you did not go after young men, whether poor or rich."***

Apparently, it had never entered Boaz's head that such a beautiful and faithful young woman as Ruth could show a personal interest in him. God loves to shower His obedient people with amazing surprises!

➤ **3:18 — *Then she said, "Sit still, my daughter, until you know how the matter will turn out; for the man will not rest until he has concluded the matter this day."***

There is a time to act, and there is a time to wait. When we have done what we should do, we must wait to see what God will do.

8 Therefore the close relative said to Boaz, "Buy *it* for yourself." So he took off his sandal.
9 And Boaz said to the elders and all the people, "You *are* witnesses this day that I have bought all that was Elimelech's, and all that *was* Chilion's and Mahlon's, from the hand of Naomi.
10 Moreover, Ruth the Moabitess, the widow of Mahlon, I have acquired as my wife, to perpetuate the name of the dead through his inheritance, that the name of the dead may not be cut off from among his brethren and from his position at the gate.[a] You *are* witnesses this day."
➤ 11 And all the people who *were* at the gate, and the elders, said, "*We are* witnesses. The LORD make the woman who is coming to your house like Rachel and Leah, the two who built the house of Israel; and may you prosper in Ephrathah and be famous in Bethlehem.
12 "May your house be like the house of Perez, whom Tamar bore to Judah, because of the offspring which the LORD will give you from this young woman."

Descendants of Boaz and Ruth

13 So Boaz took Ruth and she became his wife; and when he went in to her, the LORD gave her conception, and she bore a son.
14 Then the women said to Naomi, "Blessed *be* the LORD, who has not left you this day without a close relative; and may his name be famous in Israel!
➤ 15 "And may he be to you a restorer of life and a nourisher of your old age; for your daughter-in-law, who loves you, who is better to you than seven sons, has borne him."
16 Then Naomi took the child and laid him on her bosom, and became a nurse to him.
17 Also the neighbor women gave him a name, saying, "There is a son born to Naomi." And they called his name Obed. He *is* the father of Jesse, the father of David.
18 Now this *is* the genealogy of Perez: Perez begot Hezron;
19 Hezron begot Ram, and Ram begot Amminadab;
20 Amminadab begot Nahshon, and Nahshon begot Salmon;[a]
21 Salmon begot Boaz, and Boaz begot Obed;
22 Obed begot Jesse, and Jesse begot David.

4:10 [a]Probably his civic office 4:20 [a]Hebrew *Salmah*

Life Examples:

RUTH

Loyal to the End

RUTH 4:13–22

After the death of her Hebrew husband, Ruth could have remained in her own culture—the expected and easier route—but instead chose to travel with Naomi, her mother-in-law, back to Bethlehem, a place totally foreign to her. Why? Because Ruth felt a fierce loyalty to this bereaved woman.

Loyalty ties individuals together. True loyalty is seldom easy. It takes both patience and a willingness to be inconvenienced. Genuinely loyal people adjust their schedules to meet the needs of those they serve. Loyalty often comes at a price. Ruth, for example, made a tremendous sacrifice by leaving her family and friends behind in order to serve Naomi.

Ultimately, however, godly loyalty tends to pay big dividends. God saw Ruth's deep, abiding loyalty and rewarded her by giving her a loving husband, a beautiful son—and most of all, by placing her in the family line of Jesus Christ.

See the Life Principles Index for further study:
28. No Christian has ever been called to "go it alone" in his or her walk of faith.

LIFE LESSONS

➤ 4:11 — *"The LORD make the woman who is coming to your house like Rachel and Leah, the two who built the house of Israel; and may you prosper in Ephrathah and be famous in Bethlehem."*

The elders of Bethlehem had no way of knowing that the blessing they pronounced upon Boaz would come abundantly true, for the child to come of this new couple would be an ancestor of Jesus Christ.

➤ 4:15 — *"And may he be to you a restorer of life and a nourisher of your old age; for your daughter-in-law, who loves you, who is better to you than seven sons, has borne him."*

Naomi had lost two sons, but in a devoted and virtuous daughter-in-law she found someone better than seven sons—and in the end, a grandson who gave her great joy in her old age. God loves to bless His faithful people!

THE FIRST BOOK OF SAMUEL

The Book of First Samuel describes the transition of leadership in Israel from judges to kings. Three characters take prominent roles in the book: Samuel, the last judge and first prophet; Saul, the first king; and David, who had been anointed but not yet recognized as Saul's successor.

God had chosen the nation of Israel to greatly bless the world, and His plan to do that involved putting David (His choice) and not Saul (the people's choice) on the throne as king. While David many times faced what appeared to be certain death, God kept him from permanent harm, allowing him to take a storied place in Israel's history and gain a vital place in bringing to pass God's ultimate plan for the salvation of all humankind.

The books of 1 and 2 Samuel—named for the prophet who anointed both Saul and David as king—originally formed one book in the Hebrew Bible, known as the "Book of Samuel." This name has been variously translated "The Name of God," "His Name Is God," "Heard of God," and "Asked of God." The Septuagint divided Samuel into two books, even though this division artificially breaks up the history of David. The Greek title for Samuel is "Books of the kingdoms" and refers to the later kingdoms of Israel and Judah. The Latin Vulgate originally called the books of Samuel and Kings, "Books of the Kings." Later, it combined the Hebrew and Greek titles for the first of these books, calling it the "First Book of Samuel."

Themes: God is faithful and sovereign in keeping His promises to His people, even in the face of human mistakes, sin, and rebellion. First Samuel demonstrates that God protects and empowers those He has chosen and called for a specific purpose.

Author: Unknown

Time: First Samuel covers a period of about ninety-four years, beginning at the time of Samuel (around 1100 B.C.), Israel's final judge; moving through the ascension of Saul to the throne as the first king of Israel (1050 B.C.); continuing through David's anointing as king and the persecution by Saul that followed; and ending with the final years of Saul's reign and his suicide (around 1015 B.C.).

Structure: First Samuel gives a history of Israel, centered around three key characters: Samuel, the last of the Judges; Saul, Israel's first king and one who rebelled against God; and David, whom God had appointed to become Israel's greatest king.

As you read 1 Samuel, watch for several life principles that play an important role in this book:

8. Fight all your battles on your knees and you win every time. *See 1 Samuel 1:10-27; page 311.*

1. Our intimacy with God—His highest priority for our lives—determines the impact of our lives. *See 1 Samuel 13:14; page 326.*

10. If necessary, God will move heaven and earth to show us His will. *See 1 Samuel 16:3; page 330.*

7. The dark moments of our life will last only so long as is necessary for God to accomplish His purpose in us. *See 1 Samuel 30:1-6; page 349.*

The Family of Elkanah

1 Now there was a certain man of Rama-
thaim Zophim, of the mountains of
Ephraim, and his name *was* Elkanah the son
of Jeroham, the son of Elihu,[a] the son of
Tohu,[b] the son of Zuph, an Ephraimite.
2 And he had two wives: the name of one
was Hannah, and the name of the other Peninnah. Peninnah had children, but Hannah
had no children.
3 This man went up from his city yearly to
worship and sacrifice to the LORD of hosts in
Shiloh. Also the two sons of Eli, Hophni and
Phinehas, the priests of the LORD, *were* there.
4 And whenever the time came for Elkanah
to make an offering, he would give portions to
Peninnah his wife and to all her sons and
daughters.
➤ 5 But to Hannah he would give a double
portion, for he loved Hannah, although the
LORD had closed her womb.
6 And her rival also provoked her severely,
to make her miserable, because the LORD had
closed her womb.
7 So it was, year by year, when she went up
to the house of the LORD, that she provoked
her; therefore she wept and did not eat.

Hannah's Vow

8 Then Elkanah her husband said to her,
"Hannah, why do you weep? Why do you not
eat? And why is your heart grieved? *Am* I not
better to you than ten sons?"
9 So Hannah arose after they had finished
eating and drinking in Shiloh. Now Eli the
priest was sitting on the seat by the doorpost
of the tabernacle[a] of the LORD.
➤ 10 And she *was* in bitterness of soul, and
prayed to the LORD and wept in anguish.
11 Then she made a vow and said, "O LORD of
hosts, if You will indeed look on the affliction
of Your maidservant and remember me, and
not forget Your maidservant, but will give
Your maidservant a male child, then I will
give him to the LORD all the days of his life,
and no razor shall come upon his head."
12 And it happened, as she continued praying before the LORD, that Eli watched her
mouth.
13 Now Hannah spoke in her heart; only her
lips moved, but her voice was not heard.
Therefore Eli thought she was drunk.
14 So Eli said to her, "How long will you be
drunk? Put your wine away from you!"

Life Examples:

HANNAH

Asking in Faith

1 SAM. 1:10, 11

Hannah is an excellent biblical example of asking in faith. She had married a man named Elkanah—and so had someone else. Through the years, Elkanah's second wife, Peninnah, bore several sons and daughters to him, while Hannah remained barren. Hannah longed for a baby of her own.

Finally, one year Hannah went to the doorway of the tabernacle and wept and prayed to the Lord in great anguish, asking for a son and vowing to give him to the Lord. The Lord heard Hannah's request and answered it. Nine months later she bore a son named Samuel, who grew up to become the prophet and judge of all Israel.

Would Samuel have been born if Hannah had not asked God to give her a son? The Bible seems to answer, "No." Samuel appeared on the scene in direct response to Hannah's heartfelt request.

See the Life Principles Index for further study:
8. Fight all your battles on your knees and you win every time.

15 But Hannah answered and said, "No, my
lord, I *am* a woman of sorrowful spirit. I have
drunk neither wine nor intoxicating drink,
but have poured out my soul before the LORD.
16 "Do not consider your maidservant a
wicked woman,[a] for out of the abundance of
my complaint and grief I have spoken until
now."
17 Then Eli answered and said, "Go in peace,

1:1 [a]Spelled *Eliel* in 1 Chronicles 6:34 [b]Spelled *Toah* in 1 Chronicles 6:34 **1:9** [a]Hebrew *heykal,* palace or temple **1:16** [a]Literally *daughter of Belial*

LIFE LESSONS

➤ 1:5 — *. . . although the LORD had closed her womb.*

The Lord closed Hannah's womb—not Satan, not an accident, not nature. He is sovereign and "He does according to His will" (Dan. 4:35). God used Hannah's grief to bring forth Samuel—and give her great joy.

➤ 1:10 — *And she was in bitterness of soul, and prayed to the LORD and wept in anguish.*

Hannah faced a battle she could not win on her own. When she finally fought that battle on her knees, she won a great victory. So can we.

and the God of Israel grant your petition
which you have asked of Him."
➤ 18 And she said, "Let your maidservant find
favor in your sight." So the woman went her
way and ate, and her face was no longer *sad.*

Samuel Is Born and Dedicated

19 Then they rose early in the morning and
worshiped before the LORD, and returned and
came to their house at Ramah. And Elkanah
knew Hannah his wife, and the LORD remembered her.
➤ 20 So it came to pass in the process of time
that Hannah conceived and bore a son, and
called his name Samuel,[a] *saying,* "Because I
have asked for him from the LORD."
21 Now the man Elkanah and all his house
went up to offer to the LORD the yearly sacrifice and his vow.
22 But Hannah did not go up, for she said to
her husband, "*Not* until the child is weaned;
then I will take him, that he may appear before the LORD and remain there forever."
23 So Elkanah her husband said to her, "Do
what seems best to you; wait until you have
weaned him. Only let the LORD establish His[a]
word." Then the woman stayed and nursed
her son until she had weaned him.
24 Now when she had weaned him, she took
him up with her, with three bulls,[a] one ephah
of flour, and a skin of wine, and brought him
to the house of the LORD in Shiloh. And the
child *was* young.
25 Then they slaughtered a bull, and brought
the child to Eli.
26 And she said, "O my lord! As your soul
lives, my lord, I *am* the woman who stood by
you here, praying to the LORD.
27 "For this child I prayed, and the LORD has
granted me my petition which I asked of
Him.
28 "Therefore I also have lent him to the
LORD; as long as he lives he shall be lent to
the LORD." So they worshiped the LORD there.

Hannah's Prayer

2 And Hannah prayed and said:

"My heart rejoices in the LORD;
My horn[a] is exalted in the LORD.
I smile at my enemies,
Because I rejoice in Your salvation.

2 "No one is holy like the LORD,
For *there is* none besides You,
Nor *is there* any rock like our God.

3 "Talk no more so very proudly;
Let no arrogance come from your mouth,
For the LORD *is* the God of knowledge;
And by Him actions are weighed.

4 "The bows of the mighty men *are* broken,
And those who stumbled are girded with
strength.
5 *Those who were* full have hired
themselves out for bread,
And the hungry have ceased *to hunger.*
Even the barren has borne seven,
And she who has many children has
become feeble.

6 "The LORD kills and makes alive;
He brings down to the grave and brings
up.
7 The LORD makes poor and makes rich;
He brings low and lifts up.
8 He raises the poor from the dust
And lifts the beggar from the ash heap,
To set *them* among princes
And make them inherit the throne of
glory.

"For the pillars of the earth *are* the LORD's,
And He has set the world upon them.
9 He will guard the feet of His saints,

1:20 [a]Literally *Heard by God* **1:23** [a]Following Masoretic Text, Targum, and Vulgate; Dead Sea Scrolls, Septuagint, and Syriac read *your.* **1:24** [a]Dead Sea Scrolls, Septuagint, and Syriac read *a three-year-old bull.* **2:1** [a]That is, strength

LIFE LESSONS

➤ 1:18 — *And she said, "Let your maidservant find favor in your sight." So the woman went her way and ate, and her face was no longer sad.*

Hannah left behind her grief, not when her circumstances changed—they hadn't—but after she poured out her soul to the Lord. Because of her grief, she connected with the Lord on a level she had never known.

➤ 1:20 — *So it came to pass in the process of time that Hannah conceived and bore a son, and called his name Samuel, saying, "Because I have asked for him from the LORD."*

The name Samuel means, "Heard by God." No doubt Hannah told her son the story of his birth time after time. Samuel grew up knowing that God loves to answer the prayers of His obedient people.

➤ 2:1 — *And Hannah prayed and said: "My heart rejoices in the LORD; my horn is exalted in the LORD. I smile at my enemies, because I rejoice in Your salvation.*

We can smile at our enemies when we remember that we serve a God who takes great delight in saving and redeeming us. When we rejoice in the Lord, and not merely in His blessings, we find a joy known nowhere else.

➤ 2:9 — *"He will guard the feet of His saints . . . . "*

If you are a believer in Christ, then you are a "saint," and the Lord promises to guard your feet—to give you direction, counsel, guidance, and protection on the life road ahead of you.

But the wicked shall be silent in
darkness.
"For by strength no man shall prevail.
10 The adversaries of the LORD shall be
broken in pieces;
From heaven He will thunder against
them.
The LORD will judge the ends of the
earth.
"He will give strength to His king,
And exalt the horn of His anointed."
11 Then Elkanah went to his house at
Ramah. But the child ministered to the LORD
before Eli the priest.

The Wicked Sons of Eli

➤ **12** Now the sons of Eli *were* corrupt;[a] they
did not know the LORD.
13 And the priests' custom with the people
was that when any man offered a sacrifice,
the priest's servant would come with a three-pronged fleshhook in his hand while the meat
was boiling.
14 Then he would thrust *it* into the pan, or
kettle, or caldron, or pot; and the priest would
take for himself all that the fleshhook
brought up. So they did in Shiloh to all the Israelites who came there.
15 Also, before they burned the fat, the
priest's servant would come and say to the
man who sacrificed, "Give meat for roasting
to the priest, for he will not take boiled meat
from you, but raw."
16 And *if* the man said to him, "They should
really burn the fat first; *then* you may take *as
much* as your heart desires," he would then
answer him, "No, but you must give *it* now;
and if not, I will take *it* by force."
➤ 17 Therefore the sin of the young men was
very great before the LORD, for men abhorred
the offering of the LORD.

Samuel's Childhood Ministry

18 But Samuel ministered before the LORD,
even as a child, wearing a linen ephod.
19 Moreover his mother used to make him a
little robe, and bring *it* to him year by year
when she came up with her husband to offer
the yearly sacrifice.
20 And Eli would bless Elkanah and his wife,
and say, "The LORD give you descendants
from this woman for the loan that was given
to the LORD." Then they would go to their own
home.
21 And the LORD visited Hannah, so that she ◄
conceived and bore three sons and two
daughters. Meanwhile the child Samuel grew
before the LORD.

Prophecy Against Eli's Household

22 Now Eli was very old; and he heard everything his sons did to all Israel,[a] and how they
lay with the women who assembled at the
door of the tabernacle of meeting.
23 So he said to them, "Why do you do such ◄
things? For I hear of your evil dealings from
all the people.
24 "No, my sons! For *it is* not a good report
that I hear. You make the LORD's people transgress.
25 "If one man sins against another, God will
judge him. But if a man sins against the LORD,
who will intercede for him?" Nevertheless
they did not heed the voice of their father, because the LORD desired to kill them.
26 And the child Samuel grew in stature, and
in favor both with the LORD and men.
27 Then a man of God came to Eli and said to
him, "Thus says the LORD: 'Did I not clearly
reveal Myself to the house of your father
when they were in Egypt in Pharaoh's house?
28 'Did I not choose him out of all the tribes
of Israel *to be* My priest, to offer upon My
altar, to burn incense, and to wear an ephod
before Me? And did I not give to the house of
your father all the offerings of the children of
Israel made by fire?

2:12 [a]Literally *sons of Belial* **2:22** [a]Following Masoretic Text, Targum, and Vulgate; Dead Sea Scrolls and Septuagint omit the rest of this verse.

LIFE LESSONS

➤ 2:12 — *Now the sons of Eli were corrupt; they did not know the LORD.*

The two sons of Eli served as priests for a long time, even though "they did not know the LORD." It is easy to go to church and even serve in leadership capacities there without ever making the Lord *your* Lord.

➤ 2:17 — *Therefore the sin of the young men was very great before the LORD, for men abhorred the offering of the LORD.*

God takes it very seriously when leaders, by their evil conduct, make it hard for people to worship in spirit and in truth. He wants a close relationship with us, and He will move against anything that stands in the way.

➤ 2:21 — *And the LORD visited Hannah, so that she conceived and bore three sons and two daughters.*

You can never out give the Lord. Hannah "loaned" to God her firstborn, Samuel, and in response the Lord gave this formerly childless woman three more sons and two daughters.

➤ 2:23 — *So he said to them, "Why do you do such things? For I hear of your evil dealings from all the people."*

Eli heard "everything" that his wicked sons had been doing (1 Sam. 2:22), but he took no action, other than to mildly rebuke them. We should never allow our love for our children to keep us from disciplining them as God directs.

Life Examples:

SAMUEL

Learning to Hear God's Voice

1 SAM. 3:1–10

As one of the mightiest prophets of the Old Testament, it's no coincidence that Samuel's first divine assignment called for him to learn how to hear God's voice, to recognize it for what it was.

As 1 Samuel 3:1–10 tells us, a young Samuel, entrusted to the care of Eli the priest, was lying down one evening when the Lord spoke. At first, Samuel didn't know who he was hearing; he thought Eli was calling him. But finally, after Eli told Samuel three times that he hadn't called, Eli realized that it was the Lord. So he instructed the boy to respond, "Speak, LORD, for Your servant hears."

Isn't that a beautiful way to answer God? "Speak, LORD, for Your servant hears." Eli taught Samuel how to listen to God—and if we are going to be men and women of God, we too must learn how to recognize God's efforts to speak to us.

See the Life Principles Index for further study:
13. Listening to God is essential to walking with God.

➤ 29 'Why do you kick at My sacrifice and My
offering which I have commanded *in My*
dwelling place, and honor your sons more
than Me, to make yourselves fat with the best
of all the offerings of Israel My people?'
✳ 30 "Therefore the LORD God of Israel says: 'I
said indeed *that* your house and the house of
your father would walk before Me forever.'
But now the LORD says: 'Far be it from Me; for
those who honor Me I will honor, and those
who despise Me shall be lightly esteemed.
31 'Behold, the days are coming that I will cut
off your arm and the arm of your father's
house, so that there will not be an old man in
your house.
32 'And you will see an enemy *in My* dwelling
place, *despite* all the good which God does for
Israel. And there shall not be an old man in
your house forever.
33 'But any of your men *whom* I do not cut off
from My altar shall consume your eyes and
grieve your heart. And all the descendants of
your house shall die in the flower of their
age.
34 'Now this *shall be* a sign to you that will
come upon your two sons, on Hophni and
Phinehas: in one day they shall die, both of
them.
35 'Then I will raise up for Myself a faithful
priest *who* shall do according to what *is* in My
heart and in My mind. I will build him a sure
house, and he shall walk before My anointed
forever.
36 'And it shall come to pass that everyone
who is left in your house will come *and* bow
down to him for a piece of silver and a morsel
of bread, and say, "Please, put me in one of
the priestly positions, that I may eat a piece of
bread."'"

Samuel's First Prophecy

3 Now the boy Samuel ministered to the
LORD before Eli. And the word of the LORD
was rare in those days; *there was* no widespread revelation.
2 And it came to pass at that time, while Eli
was lying down in his place, and when his
eyes had begun to grow so dim that he could
not see,
3 and before the lamp of God went out in
the tabernacle[a] of the LORD where the ark of
God *was,* and while Samuel was lying down,
4 that the LORD called Samuel. And he answered, "Here I am!"
5 So he ran to Eli and said, "Here I am, for ➤
you called me." And he said, "I did not call; lie
down again." And he went and lay down.
6 Then the LORD called yet again, "Samuel!"
So Samuel arose and went to Eli, and said,

3:3 [a]Hebrew *heykal,* palace or temple

LIFE LESSONS

➤ 2:29 — *"Why do you . . . honor your sons more than Me, to make yourselves fat with the best of all the offerings of Israel My people?"*

Parents must beware of honoring their children more than they honor the Lord. Eli put his sons first—and lost them because of it. Anything we hold too tightly, we will lose.

➤ 3:5 — *So he ran to Eli and said, "Here I am, for you called me." And he said, "I did not call; lie down again." And he went and lay down.*

Early in life Samuel learned to obey, even though at the beginning he did not understand the process. If early on we teach our children to obey God, we set them up to mature into godly men and women of spiritual understanding.

"Here I am, for you called me." He answered,
"I did not call, my son; lie down again."
➤ 7 (Now Samuel did not yet know the LORD,
nor was the word of the LORD yet revealed to
him.)
8 And the LORD called Samuel again the
third time. So he arose and went to Eli,
and said, "Here I am, for you did call me."
Then Eli perceived that the LORD had called
the boy.
9 Therefore Eli said to Samuel, "Go, lie
down; and it shall be, if He calls you, that you
must say, 'Speak, LORD, for Your servant
hears.'" So Samuel went and lay down in his
place.
10 Now the LORD came and stood and called
as at other times, "Samuel! Samuel!" And
Samuel answered, "Speak, for Your servant
hears."
11 Then the LORD said to Samuel: "Behold, I
will do something in Israel at which both ears
of everyone who hears it will tingle.
12 "In that day I will perform against Eli all
that I have spoken concerning his house, from
beginning to end.
13 "For I have told him that I will judge his
house forever for the iniquity which he
knows, because his sons made themselves
vile, and he did not restrain them.
14 "And therefore I have sworn to the house
of Eli that the iniquity of Eli's house shall not
be atoned for by sacrifice or offering forever."
15 So Samuel lay down until morning,[a] and
opened the doors of the house of the LORD.
And Samuel was afraid to tell Eli the vision.
16 Then Eli called Samuel and said, "Samuel,
my son!" He answered, "Here I am."
17 And he said, "What *is* the word that *the
LORD* spoke to you? Please do not hide *it* from
me. God do so to you, and more also, if you
hide anything from me of all the things that
He said to you."
➤ 18 Then Samuel told him everything, and
hid nothing from him. And he said, "It *is*
the LORD. Let Him do what seems good to
Him."
19 So Samuel grew, and the LORD was with
him and let none of his words fall to the
ground.
20 And all Israel from Dan to Beersheba
knew that Samuel *had been* established as a
prophet of the LORD.
21 Then the LORD appeared again in Shiloh.
For the LORD revealed Himself to Samuel in
Shiloh by the word of the LORD.
4 And the word of Samuel came to all
Israel.[a]

The Ark of God Captured

Now Israel went out to battle against the
Philistines, and encamped beside Ebenezer;
and the Philistines encamped in Aphek.
2 Then the Philistines put themselves in battle array against Israel. And when they joined
battle, Israel was defeated by the Philistines,
who killed about four thousand men of the
army in the field.
3 And when the people had come into the ➤
camp, the elders of Israel said, "Why has the
LORD defeated us today before the Philistines? Let us bring the ark of the covenant of
the LORD from Shiloh to us, that when it
comes among us it may save us from the hand
of our enemies."
4 So the people sent to Shiloh, that they
might bring from there the ark of the covenant of the LORD of hosts, who dwells *between* the cherubim. And the two sons of Eli,
Hophni and Phinehas, *were* there with the
ark of the covenant of God.
5 And when the ark of the covenant of the
LORD came into the camp, all Israel shouted
so loudly that the earth shook.
6 Now when the Philistines heard the noise
of the shout, they said, "What *does* the sound
of this great shout in the camp of the Hebrews
mean?" Then they understood that the ark of
the LORD had come into the camp.
7 So the Philistines were afraid, for they
said, "God has come into the camp!" And they
said, "Woe to us! For such a thing has never
happened before.
8 "Woe to us! Who will deliver us from the
hand of these mighty gods? These *are* the

3:15 [a]Following Masoretic Text, Targum, and Vulgate; Septuagint adds *and he arose in the morning.* **4:1** [a]Following Masoretic Text and Targum; Septuagint and Vulgate add *And it came to pass in those days that the Philistines gathered themselves together to fight;* Septuagint adds further *against Israel.*

LIFE LESSONS

➤ 3:7 — *(Now Samuel did not yet know the LORD, nor was the word of the LORD yet revealed to him.)*

When God first spoke to Samuel, the boy didn't yet know His voice—but he learned to hear it. God desires that we enjoy a close relationship with Him, and He will do everything necessary to make it possible.

➤ 3:18 — *Then Samuel told him everything, and hid nothing from him. And he said, "It is the LORD. Let Him do what seems good to Him."*

While it is good to endorse the work of God, Eli again showed an unwise passivity in regard to his sons. He simply was not willing to "restrain" them (1 Sam. 3:13). But God must be first in *everything.*

➤ 4:3 — *"Let us bring the ark of the covenant of the LORD from Shiloh to us, that when it comes among us it may save us from the hand of our enemies."*

No religious artifact or ceremony, no matter how sacred, can rescue us. Israel's leaders thought that the ark of the covenant could save them, but it had no power to do so. God alone rescues.

ANSWERS TO LIFE'S QUESTIONS

How can I know it's God's voice I hear and not something else?

1 SAM. 3:19, 20

The book of 1 Samuel describes how the boy Samuel came to hear and understand the spoken word of God. The Bible records that the word of the Lord was rare in those days; Samuel, therefore, had to learn how to recognize the voice of God and not get it mixed up with ideas that conflicted with the Lord's true character.

Samuel not only learned to clearly hear the words of God, he also came to speak them with authority. So the Bible says of him, "the LORD was with him and let none of his words fall to the ground. And all Israel from Dan to Beersheba knew that Samuel had been established as a prophet of the LORD" (1 Sam. 3:19, 20).

We sometimes let our preconceptions about God influence what we think we hear from Him. If, for instance, we think of God as a wise and caring counselor, we will be open to the love He has for us in the midst of calamities brought on by our own foolishness. If, however, we think of God as a vindictive judge, we will expect to hear words of condemnation and harsh punishment when we act foolishly.

Our relationship with God influences how we hear God. If we approach God as His saved children living under His grace, then we come with the assurance that He will speak the words we really need—even if they are not what we want to hear. When we know Him as an infinitely loving God, then we can believe everything He says.

This same problem occurs in any area where our ideas of God's character conflict with Scripture. We may think of Him as a generous provider or a stingy one. We may view Him as a faithful, trustworthy guide or a fair-weather friend.

Too many Christians fall for twisted conceptions of God that misrepresent our gracious, consistent, patient, trustworthy Father. We have all heard too many unbiblical ideas offered as if they were gospel truth—and such error can lead us into horrible emotional and spiritual bondage.

Our view of God must remain correct and biblically informed. By knowing Him as the God of love (1 John 4:8) who wants us to approach the throne of grace boldly (Heb. 4:16), we will trust more completely whatever He tells us. Take the advice of 1 Thessalonians 5:21, and test whatever you hear against the truth of Scripture.

See the Life Principles Index for further study:

13. Listening to God is essential to walking with God.

3. God's Word is an immovable anchor in times of storm.

gods who struck the Egyptians with all the
plagues in the wilderness.
9 "Be strong and conduct yourselves like
men, you Philistines, that you do not become
servants of the Hebrews, as they have been to
you. Conduct yourselves like men, and fight!"
10 So the Philistines fought, and Israel was
defeated, and every man fled to his tent.
There was a very great slaughter, and there
fell of Israel thirty thousand foot soldiers.
11 Also the ark of God was captured; and the
two sons of Eli, Hophni and Phinehas, died.

Death of Eli

12 Then a man of Benjamin ran from the battle line the same day, and came to Shiloh with
his clothes torn and dirt on his head.
13 Now when he came, there was Eli, sitting
on a seat by the wayside watching,[a] for his
heart trembled for the ark of God. And when
the man came into the city and told *it*, all the
city cried out.
14 When Eli heard the noise of the outcry, he
said, "What *does* the sound of this tumult
mean?" And the man came quickly and told
Eli.
15 Eli was ninety-eight years old, and his
eyes were so dim that he could not see.
16 Then the man said to Eli, "I *am* he who
came from the battle. And I fled today from
the battle line." And he said, "What happened,
my son?"
17 So the messenger answered and said, "Israel has fled before the Philistines, and there
has been a great slaughter among the people.
Also your two sons, Hophni and Phinehas,
are dead; and the ark of God has been captured."
18 Then it happened, when he made mention
of the ark of God, that Eli fell off the seat
backward by the side of the gate; and his neck

4:13 [a]Following Masoretic Text and Vulgate; Septuagint reads *beside the gate watching the road.*

was broken and he died, for the man was old
and heavy. And he had judged Israel forty
years.

Ichabod

19 Now his daughter-in-law, Phinehas' wife,
was with child, *due* to be delivered; and when
she heard the news that the ark of God was
captured, and that her father-in-law and her
husband were dead, she bowed herself and
gave birth, for her labor pains came upon her.
20 And about the time of her death the
women who stood by her said to her, "Do not
fear, for you have borne a son." But she did
not answer, nor did she regard *it*.
21 Then she named the child Ichabod,[a] saying, "The glory has departed from Israel!" because the ark of God had been captured and
because of her father-in-law and her husband.
22 And she said, "The glory has departed
from Israel, for the ark of God has been captured."

The Philistines and the Ark

5 Then the Philistines took the ark of God
and brought it from Ebenezer to Ashdod.
➤ 2 When the Philistines took the ark of God,
they brought it into the house of Dagon[a] and
set it by Dagon.
3 And when the people of Ashdod arose
early in the morning, there was Dagon, fallen
on its face to the earth before the ark of the
LORD. So they took Dagon and set it in its
place again.
4 And when they arose early the next
morning, there was Dagon, fallen on its face
to the ground before the ark of the LORD. The
head of Dagon and both the palms of its
hands *were* broken off on the threshold; only
Dagon's *torso*[a] was left of it.
5 Therefore neither the priests of Dagon nor
any who come into Dagon's house tread on
the threshold of Dagon in Ashdod to this day.
6 But the hand of the LORD was heavy on the
people of Ashdod, and He ravaged them and
struck them with tumors,[a] *both* Ashdod and
its territory.
7 And when the men of Ashdod saw how *it*
was, they said, "The ark of the God of Israel
must not remain with us, for His hand is
harsh toward us and Dagon our god."
8 Therefore they sent and gathered to
themselves all the lords of the Philistines,
and said, "What shall we do with the ark of
the God of Israel?" And they answered, "Let
the ark of the God of Israel be carried away
to Gath." So they carried the ark of the God
of Israel away.
9 So it was, after they had carried it away, ➤
that the hand of the LORD was against the city
with a very great destruction; and He struck
the men of the city, both small and great, and
tumors broke out on them.
10 Therefore they sent the ark of God to
Ekron. So it was, as the ark of God came to
Ekron, that the Ekronites cried out, saying,
"They have brought the ark of the God of Israel to us, to kill us and our people!"
11 So they sent and gathered together all the
lords of the Philistines, and said, "Send away
the ark of the God of Israel, and let it go back
to its own place, so that it does not kill us and
our people." For there was a deadly destruction throughout all the city; the hand of God
was very heavy there.
12 And the men who did not die were stricken
with the tumors, and the cry of the city went
up to heaven.

The Ark Returned to Israel

6 Now the ark of the LORD was in the
country of the Philistines seven months.
2 And the Philistines called for the priests
and the diviners, saying, "What shall we do
with the ark of the LORD? Tell us how we
should send it to its place."
3 So they said, "If you send away the ark of
the God of Israel, do not send it empty; but by

4:21 [a]Literally *Inglorious* **5:2** [a]A Philistine idol **5:4** [a]Following Septuagint, Syriac, Targum, and Vulgate; Masoretic Text reads *Dagon*. **5:6** [a]Probably bubonic plague. Septuagint and Vulgate add here *And in the midst of their land rats sprang up, and there was a great death panic in the city.*

LIFE LESSONS

➤ **4:13 — *Now when he came, there was Eli, sitting on a seat by the wayside watching, for his heart trembled for the ark of God.***

Eli was a good man who feared the Lord—but not enough. He allowed other things to weaken his devotion to God, and eventually that failure cost him not only his family, but his life.

➤ **5:2 — *When the Philistines took the ark of God, they brought it into the temple of Dagon and set it by Dagon.***

The Philistines placed the ark of the covenant in the temple of Dagon to show that their god had triumphed over Israel's God. But even in an apparent "weakness," God shows Himself fantastically strong (1 Cor. 1:25).

➤ **5:9 — *So it was, after they had carried it away, that the hand of the LORD was against the city with a very great destruction; and He struck the men of the city, both small and great, and tumors broke out on them.***

The Lord wanted the Philistines to know that what had happened did not occur by chance, but that He had been behind it all. God desires that the whole world acknowledge His glory—and He wants to use us to display it.

all means return *it* to Him *with* a trespass offering. Then you will be healed, and it will be
known to you why His hand is not removed
from you."
4 Then they said, "What *is* the trespass offering which we shall return to Him?" They
answered, "Five golden tumors and five
golden rats, *according to* the number of the
lords of the Philistines. For the same plague
was on all of you and on your lords.
5 "Therefore you shall make images of your
tumors and images of your rats that ravage
the land, and you shall give glory to the God
of Israel; perhaps He will lighten His hand
from you, from your gods, and from your
land.
6 "Why then do you harden your hearts as
the Egyptians and Pharaoh hardened their
hearts? When He did mighty things among
them, did they not let the people go, that they
might depart?
7 "Now therefore, make a new cart, take two
milk cows which have never been yoked, and
hitch the cows to the cart; and take their
calves home, away from them.
8 "Then take the ark of the LORD and set it
on the cart; and put the articles of gold which
you are returning to Him *as* a trespass offering in a chest by its side. Then send it away,
and let it go.
9 "And watch: if it goes up the road to its
own territory, to Beth Shemesh, *then* He has
done us this great evil. But if not, then we
shall know that *it is* not His hand *that* struck
us—it happened to us by chance."
10 Then the men did so; they took two milk
cows and hitched them to the cart, and shut
up their calves at home.
11 And they set the ark of the LORD on the
cart, and the chest with the gold rats and
the images of their tumors.
12 Then the cows headed straight for the
road to Beth Shemesh, *and* went along the
highway, lowing as they went, and did not
turn aside to the right hand or the left. And
the lords of the Philistines went after them to
the border of Beth Shemesh.
13 Now *the people of* Beth Shemesh *were*
reaping their wheat harvest in the valley; and
they lifted their eyes and saw the ark, and rejoiced to see *it*.
14 Then the cart came into the field of Joshua
of Beth Shemesh, and stood there; a large
stone *was* there. So they split the wood of the
cart and offered the cows as a burnt offering
to the LORD.
15 The Levites took down the ark of the LORD
and the chest that *was* with it, in which *were*
the articles of gold, and put *them* on the large
stone. Then the men of Beth Shemesh offered
burnt offerings and made sacrifices the same
day to the LORD.
16 So when the five lords of the Philistines had
seen *it*, they returned to Ekron the same day.
17 These *are* the golden tumors which the
Philistines returned *as* a trespass offering to
the LORD: one for Ashdod, one for Gaza, one
for Ashkelon, one for Gath, one for Ekron;
18 and the golden rats, *according to* the number of all the cities of the Philistines *belonging*
to the five lords, *both* fortified cities and country villages, even as far as the large *stone* of
Abel on which they set the ark of the LORD,
which stone remains to this day in the field of
Joshua of Beth Shemesh.
19 Then He struck the men of Beth Shemesh,
because they had looked into the ark of the
LORD. He struck fifty thousand and seventy
men[a] of the people, and the people lamented
because the LORD had struck the people with
a great slaughter.

The Ark at Kirjath Jearim

20 And the men of Beth Shemesh said, "Who
is able to stand before this holy LORD God?
And to whom shall it go up from us?"
21 So they sent messengers to the inhabitants of Kirjath Jearim, saying, "The Philistines have brought back the ark of the LORD;
come down *and* take it up with you."

7 Then the men of Kirjath Jearim came and
took the ark of the LORD, and brought it
into the house of Abinadab on the hill, and
consecrated Eleazar his son to keep the ark of
the LORD.

Samuel Judges Israel

2 So it was that the ark remained in Kirjath
Jearim a long time; it was there twenty years.
And all the house of Israel lamented after the
LORD.
3 Then Samuel spoke to all the house of Israel, saying, "If you return to the LORD with all
your hearts, *then* put away the foreign gods
and the Ashtoreths[a] from among you, and

6:19 [a]Or *He struck seventy men of the people and fifty oxen of a man* **7:3** [a]Canaanite goddesses

LIFE LESSONS

➤ ***6:19 — Then He struck the men of Beth Shemesh, because they had looked into the ark of the LORD . . . .***

In His grace, God brought the ark back to Israel. But in His holiness, He struck down some Israelites who treated the ark as a curiosity rather than as a symbol of God's glory.

➤ ***7:3 — "If you return to the LORD with all your hearts, then put away the foreign gods and the Ashtoreths from among you, and prepare your hearts for the LORD, and serve Him only . . . ."***

God demands and deserves our exclusive loyalty and love. He made us for Himself, and we have no higher calling than to draw near to Him.

prepare your hearts for the LORD, and serve
Him only; and He will deliver you from the
hand of the Philistines."
4 So the children of Israel put away the
Baals and the Ashtoreths,[a] and served the LORD
only.
5 And Samuel said, "Gather all Israel to
Mizpah, and I will pray to the LORD for you."
6 So they gathered together at Mizpah, drew
water, and poured *it* out before the LORD. And
they fasted that day, and said there, "We have
sinned against the LORD." And Samuel judged
the children of Israel at Mizpah.
7 Now when the Philistines heard that the
children of Israel had gathered together at
Mizpah, the lords of the Philistines went up
against Israel. And when the children of Israel heard *of it,* they were afraid of the Philistines.
➤ 8 So the children of Israel said to Samuel,
"Do not cease to cry out to the LORD our God
for us, that He may save us from the hand of
the Philistines."
9 And Samuel took a suckling lamb and offered *it as* a whole burnt offering to the LORD.
Then Samuel cried out to the LORD for Israel,
and the LORD answered him.
10 Now as Samuel was offering up the burnt
offering, the Philistines drew near to battle
against Israel. But the LORD thundered with a
loud thunder upon the Philistines that day,
and so confused them that they were overcome before Israel.
11 And the men of Israel went out of Mizpah
and pursued the Philistines, and drove them
back as far as below Beth Car.
12 Then Samuel took a stone and set *it* up between Mizpah and Shen, and called its name
Ebenezer,[a] saying, "Thus far the LORD has
helped us."
13 So the Philistines were subdued, and they
did not come anymore into the territory of Israel. And the hand of the LORD was against
the Philistines all the days of Samuel.
14 Then the cities which the Philistines had
taken from Israel were restored to Israel,
from Ekron to Gath; and Israel recovered its
territory from the hands of the Philistines.
Also there was peace between Israel and the
Amorites.
15 And Samuel judged Israel all the days of
his life.
16 He went from year to year on a circuit to
Bethel, Gilgal, and Mizpah, and judged Israel
in all those places.
17 But he always returned to Ramah, for his
home *was* there. There he judged Israel, and
there he built an altar to the LORD.

Israel Demands a King

8 Now it came to pass when Samuel was old
that he made his sons judges over Israel.
2 The name of his firstborn was Joel, and
the name of his second, Abijah; *they were*
judges in Beersheba.
3 But his sons did not walk in his ways; they ◄
turned aside after dishonest gain, took bribes,
and perverted justice.
4 Then all the elders of Israel gathered together and came to Samuel at Ramah,
5 and said to him, "Look, you are old, and
your sons do not walk in your ways. Now
make us a king to judge us like all the nations."
6 But the thing displeased Samuel when they ◄
said, "Give us a king to judge us." So Samuel
prayed to the LORD.
7 And the LORD said to Samuel, "Heed the
voice of the people in all that they say to you;
for they have not rejected you, but they have
rejected Me, that I should not reign over them.
8 "According to all the works which they
have done since the day that I brought them up
out of Egypt, even to this day—with which they
have forsaken Me and served other gods—so
they are doing to you also.
9 "Now therefore, heed their voice. However, you shall solemnly forewarn them, and
show them the behavior of the king who will
reign over them."
10 So Samuel told all the words of the LORD
to the people who asked him for a king.
11 And he said, "This will be the behavior of
the king who will reign over you: He will take

7:4 [a]Canaanite goddesses **7:12** [a]Literally *Stone of Help*

LIFE LESSONS

➤ 7:8 — *So the children of Israel said to Samuel, "Do not cease to cry out to the LORD our God for us, that He may save us from the hand of the Philistines."*

You win every time when you fight your battles on your knees.

➤ 8:3 — *But his sons did not walk in his ways; they turned aside after dishonest gain, took bribes, and perverted justice.*

As great and as godly as Samuel was, he did not do a much better job as father than did Eli. Regardless of how involved in ministry we are, we cannot afford to neglect the spiritual training of our children.

➤ 8:6 — *But the thing displeased Samuel when they said, "Give us a king to judge us." So Samuel prayed to the LORD.*

Even in his old age, Samuel sought to hear the voice of God when confronted with a challenge. He didn't think he "knew it all"; he went to the Lord for guidance. So should we.

your sons and appoint *them* for his own chariots and *to be* his horsemen, and *some* will
run before his chariots.
12 "He will appoint captains over his thousands and captains over his fifties, *will set*
some to plow his ground and reap his harvest,
and *some* to make his weapons of war and
equipment for his chariots.
13 "He will take your daughters *to be* perfumers, cooks, and bakers.
14 "And he will take the best of your fields,
your vineyards, and your olive groves, and
give *them* to his servants.
15 "He will take a tenth of your grain and your
vintage, and give it to his officers and servants.
16 "And he will take your male servants, your
female servants, your finest young men,[a] and
your donkeys, and put *them* to his work.
17 "He will take a tenth of your sheep. And
you will be his servants.
18 "And you will cry out in that day because
of your king whom you have chosen for yourselves, and the LORD will not hear you in that
day."
➤ **19** Nevertheless the people refused to obey
the voice of Samuel; and they said, "No, but
we will have a king over us,
20 "that we also may be like all the nations,
and that our king may judge us and go out before us and fight our battles."
21 And Samuel heard all the words of the
people, and he repeated them in the hearing
of the LORD.
22 So the LORD said to Samuel, "Heed their
voice, and make them a king." And Samuel
said to the men of Israel, "Every man go to his
city."

Saul Chosen to Be King

9 There was a man of Benjamin whose
name *was* Kish the son of Abiel, the son of
Zeror, the son of Bechorath, the son of
Aphiah, a Benjamite, a mighty man of power.
2 And he had a choice and handsome son
whose name *was* Saul. *There was* not a more
handsome person than he among the children
of Israel. From his shoulders upward *he was*
taller than any of the people.
3 Now the donkeys of Kish, Saul's father,
were lost. And Kish said to his son Saul,
"Please take one of the servants with you, and
arise, go and look for the donkeys."
4 So he passed through the mountains of
Ephraim and through the land of Shalisha,
but they did not find *them*. Then they passed
through the land of Shaalim, and *they were*
not *there*. Then he passed through the land of
the Benjamites, but they did not find *them*.
5 When they had come to the land of Zuph,
Saul said to his servant who *was* with him,
"Come, let us return, lest my father cease *car-*
ing about the donkeys and become worried
about us."
6 And he said to him, "Look now, *there is* in
this city a man of God, and *he is* an honorable
man; all that he says surely comes to pass. So
let us go there; perhaps he can show us the
way that we should go."
7 Then Saul said to his servant, "But look, *if*
we go, what shall we bring the man? For the
bread in our vessels is all gone, and *there is*
no present to bring to the man of God. What
do we have?"
8 And the servant answered Saul again and
said, "Look, I have here at hand one-fourth of
a shekel of silver. I will give *that* to the man
of God, to tell us our way."
9 (Formerly in Israel, when a man went to
inquire of God, he spoke thus: "Come, let us
go to the seer"; for *he who is* now *called* a
prophet was formerly called a seer.)
10 Then Saul said to his servant, "Well said;
come, let us go." So they went to the city
where the man of God *was*.
11 As they went up the hill to the city, they
met some young women going out to draw
water, and said to them, "Is the seer here?"
12 And they answered them and said, "Yes,
there he is, just ahead of you. Hurry now; for
today he came to this city, because there is a
sacrifice of the people today on the high place.
13 "As soon as you come into the city, you
will surely find him before he goes up to the
high place to eat. For the people will not eat
until he comes, because he must bless the sacrifice; afterward those who are invited will
eat. Now therefore, go up, for about this time
you will find him."
14 So they went up to the city. As they were
coming into the city, there was Samuel, coming out toward them on his way up to the high
place.
15 Now the LORD had told Samuel in his ear
the day before Saul came, saying,

8:16 [a]Septuagint reads *cattle*.

LIFE LESSONS

➤ **8:19, 20 — *. . . and they said, "No, but we will have a king over us, that we also may be like all the nations . . . ."***

In every culture and time God's people feel a tug to be like those around them, to conform to the customs of their unbelieving neighbors. But Jesus tells us, "do not be like them" (Matt. 6:8).

➤ **9:16 — *"Tomorrow about this time I will send you a man from the land of Benjamin, and you shall anoint him commander over My people Israel . . . ."***

God often uses misfortune to bring us to the very place where He will show us His will. The dark moments of life will last only so long as is necessary for God to accomplish His purpose in us.

➤ 16 "Tomorrow about this time I will send
you a man from the land of Benjamin, and
you shall anoint him commander over My
people Israel, that he may save My people
from the hand of the Philistines; for I have
looked upon My people, because their cry has
come to Me."
17 So when Samuel saw Saul, the LORD said
to him, "There he is, the man of whom I spoke
to you. This one shall reign over My people."
18 Then Saul drew near to Samuel in the
gate, and said, "Please tell me, where *is* the
seer's house?"
19 Samuel answered Saul and said, "I *am* the
seer. Go up before me to the high place, for
you shall eat with me today; and tomorrow I
will let you go and will tell you all that *is* in
your heart.
20 "But as for your donkeys that were lost
three days ago, do not be anxious about them,
for they have been found. And on whom *is* all
the desire of Israel? *Is it* not on you and on all
your father's house?"
➤ 21 And Saul answered and said, "*Am* I not a
Benjamite, of the smallest of the tribes of Israel, and my family the least of all the families of the tribe[a] of Benjamin? Why then do
you speak like this to me?"
22 Now Samuel took Saul and his servant
and brought them into the hall, and had
them sit in the place of honor among those
who were invited; there *were* about thirty
persons.
23 And Samuel said to the cook, "Bring the
portion which I gave you, of which I said to
you, 'Set it apart.'"
24 So the cook took up the thigh with its
upper part and set *it* before Saul. And *Samuel*
said, "Here it is, what was kept back. *It* was
set apart for you. Eat; for until this time it has
been kept for you, since I said I invited the
people." So Saul ate with Samuel that day.
25 When they had come down from the high
place into the city, *Samuel* spoke with Saul on
the top of the house.[a]
26 They arose early; and it was about the
dawning of the day that Samuel called to Saul
on the top of the house, saying, "Get up, that I
may send you on your way." And Saul arose,
and both of them went outside, he and Samuel.

Saul Anointed King

27 As they were going down to the outskirts
of the city, Samuel said to Saul, "Tell the servant to go on ahead of us." And he went on.
"But you stand here awhile, that I may announce to you the word of God."
10 Then Samuel took a flask of oil and
poured *it* on his head, and kissed him
and said: "*Is it* not because the LORD has
anointed you commander over His inheritance?[a]
2 "When you have departed from me today,
you will find two men by Rachel's tomb in the
territory of Benjamin at Zelzah; and they will
say to you, 'The donkeys which you went to
look for have been found. And now your father has ceased caring about the donkeys and
is worrying about you, saying, "What shall I
do about my son?"'
3 "Then you shall go on forward from there
and come to the terebinth tree of Tabor. There
three men going up to God at Bethel will meet
you, one carrying three young goats, another
carrying three loaves of bread, and another
carrying a skin of wine.
4 "And they will greet you and give you two
loaves of bread, which you shall receive from
their hands.
5 "After that you shall come to the hill of God
where the Philistine garrison *is*. And it will
happen, when you have come there to the city,
that you will meet a group of prophets coming
down from the high place with a stringed instrument, a tambourine, a flute, and a harp
before them; and they will be prophesying.
6 "Then the Spirit of the LORD will come ➤
upon you, and you will prophesy with them
and be turned into another man.
7 "And let it be, when these signs come to
you, *that* you do as the occasion demands; for
God *is* with you.

9:21 [a]Literally *tribes* **9:25** [a]Following Masoretic Text and Targum; Septuagint omits *He spoke with Saul on the top of the house;* Septuagint and Vulgate add *And he prepared a bed for Saul on the top of the house, and he slept.* **10:1** [a]Following Masoretic Text, Targum, and Vulgate; Septuagint reads *His people Israel; and you shall rule the people of the Lord;* Septuagint and Vulgate add *And you shall deliver His people from the hands of their enemies all around them. And this shall be a sign to you, that God has anointed you to be a prince.*

LIFE LESSONS

➤ 9:21 — *And Saul answered and said, "Am I not a Benjamite, of the smallest of the tribes of Israel, and my family the least of all the families of the tribe of Benjamin?"*

Like Gideon before him, Saul thought of himself as small, unimportant, and powerless. But God loves to use "the weak things of the world to put to shame the things which are mighty" (1 Cor. 1:27).

➤ 10:6 — *"Then the Spirit of the LORD will come upon you, and you will prophesy with them and be turned into another man."*

It takes the Spirit of the living God to turn us into other men and women, to transform us into the likeness of Christ. But such a transformation is God's will for every one of us (Rom. 12:2).

8 "You shall go down before me to Gilgal;
and surely I will come down to you to offer
burnt offerings *and* make sacrifices of peace
offerings. Seven days you shall wait, till I
come to you and show you what you should
do."
➤ 9 So it was, when he had turned his back to
go from Samuel, that God gave him another
heart; and all those signs came to pass that
day.
10 When they came there to the hill, there
was a group of prophets to meet him; then the
Spirit of God came upon him, and he prophesied among them.
11 And it happened, when all who knew him
formerly saw that he indeed prophesied
among the prophets, that the people said to
one another, "What *is* this *that* has come
upon the son of Kish? *Is* Saul also among the
prophets?"
12 Then a man from there answered and
said, "But who *is* their father?" Therefore it
became a proverb: "*Is* Saul also among the
prophets?"
13 And when he had finished prophesying,
he went to the high place.
14 Then Saul's uncle said to him and his servant, "Where did you go?" So he said, "To
look for the donkeys. When we saw that *they
were* nowhere *to be found,* we went to Samuel."
15 And Saul's uncle said, "Tell me, please,
what Samuel said to you."
16 So Saul said to his uncle, "He told us
plainly that the donkeys had been found." But
about the matter of the kingdom, he did not
tell him what Samuel had said.

Saul Proclaimed King

17 Then Samuel called the people together to
the LORD at Mizpah,
18 and said to the children of Israel, "Thus
says the LORD God of Israel: 'I brought up Israel out of Egypt, and delivered you from the
hand of the Egyptians *and* from the hand of
all kingdoms and from those who oppressed
you.'
19 "But you have today rejected your God,
who Himself saved you from all your adversities and your tribulations; and you have said
to Him, 'No, set a king over us!' Now therefore, present yourselves before the LORD by
your tribes and by your clans."[a]
20 And when Samuel had caused all the
tribes of Israel to come near, the tribe of Benjamin was chosen.
21 When he had caused the tribe of Benjamin
to come near by their families, the family of
Matri was chosen. And Saul the son of Kish
was chosen. But when they sought him, he
could not be found.
22 Therefore they inquired of the LORD further, "Has the man come here yet?" And the
LORD answered, "There he is, hidden among
the equipment."
23 So they ran and brought him from there;
and when he stood among the people, he was
taller than any of the people from his shoulders upward.
24 And Samuel said to all the people, "Do
you see him whom the LORD has chosen, that
there is no one like him among all the people?" So all the people shouted and said,
"Long live the king!"
25 Then Samuel explained to the people the
behavior of royalty, and wrote *it* in a book
and laid *it* up before the LORD. And Samuel
sent all the people away, every man to his
house.
26 And Saul also went home to Gibeah; and
valiant *men* went with him, whose hearts God
had touched.
27 But some rebels said, "How can this man
save us?" So they despised him, and brought
him no presents. But he held his peace.

Saul Saves Jabesh Gilead

11 Then Nahash the Ammonite came up
and encamped against Jabesh Gilead;
and all the men of Jabesh said to Nahash,
"Make a covenant with us, and we will serve
you."
2 And Nahash the Ammonite answered
them, "On this *condition* I will make *a cov-*

10:19 [a]Literally *thousands*

LIFE LESSONS

➤ 10:9 — *So it was, when he had turned his back to go from Samuel, that God gave him another heart . . . .*

We should pray that God would give us another heart, a heart that loves Him and wants to serve Him and obey Him. Only with such a new heart will we be able to live the new life He calls us to.

➤ 10:22 — *Therefore they inquired of the LORD further, "Has the man come here yet?" And the LORD answered, "There he is, hidden among the equipment."*

Saul knew that God had chosen him to be king, and yet he tried to avoid God's will by running away. Throughout his rule he let fear keep him from obeying God—and in the end, it cost him everything.

➤ 10:27 — *But some rebels said, "How can this man save us?" So they despised him, and brought him no presents . . . .*

God's will looks neither impressive nor reasonable to some people. Yet God does not require us to understand His will, just obey it, even if it seems unreasonable.

enant with you, that I may put out all your
right eyes, and bring reproach on all Israel."
3 Then the elders of Jabesh said to him,
"Hold off for seven days, that we may send
messengers to all the territory of Israel. And
then, if *there is* no one to save us, we will
come out to you."
4 So the messengers came to Gibeah of Saul
and told the news in the hearing of the people. And all the people lifted up their voices
and wept.
5 Now there was Saul, coming behind the
herd from the field; and Saul said, "What
troubles the people, that they weep?" And
they told him the words of the men of Jabesh.
➤ 6 Then the Spirit of God came upon Saul
when he heard this news, and his anger was
greatly aroused.
7 So he took a yoke of oxen and cut them in
pieces, and sent *them* throughout all the territory of Israel by the hands of messengers,
saying, "Whoever does not go out with Saul
and Samuel to battle, so it shall be done to
his oxen." And the fear of the LORD fell on
the people, and they came out with one consent.
8 When he numbered them in Bezek, the
children of Israel were three hundred thousand, and the men of Judah thirty thousand.
9 And they said to the messengers who
came, "Thus you shall say to the men of Jabesh
Gilead: 'Tomorrow, by *the time* the sun is hot,
you shall have help.'" Then the messengers
came and reported *it* to the men of Jabesh, and
they were glad.
10 Therefore the men of Jabesh said, "Tomorrow we will come out to you, and you may do
with us whatever seems good to you."
11 So it was, on the next day, that Saul put
the people in three companies; and they came
into the midst of the camp in the morning
watch, and killed Ammonites until the heat of
the day. And it happened that those who survived were scattered, so that no two of them
were left together.
12 Then the people said to Samuel, "Who *is*
he who said, 'Shall Saul reign over us?' Bring
the men, that we may put them to death."
➤ 13 But Saul said, "Not a man shall be put to
death this day, for today the LORD has accomplished salvation in Israel."
14 Then Samuel said to the people, "Come,
let us go to Gilgal and renew the kingdom
there."
15 So all the people went to Gilgal, and there
they made Saul king before the LORD in Gilgal. There they made sacrifices of peace offerings before the LORD, and there Saul and
all the men of Israel rejoiced greatly.

Samuel's Address at Saul's Coronation

12 Now Samuel said to all Israel: "Indeed
I have heeded your voice in all that
you said to me, and have made a king over
you.
2 "And now here is the king, walking before
you; and I am old and grayheaded, and look,
my sons *are* with you. I have walked before
you from my childhood to this day.
3 "Here I am. Witness against me before the ➤
LORD and before His anointed: Whose ox have
I taken, or whose donkey have I taken, or
whom have I cheated? Whom have I oppressed, or from whose hand have I received
any bribe with which to blind my eyes? I will
restore *it* to you."
4 And they said, "You have not cheated us or
oppressed us, nor have you taken anything
from any man's hand."
5 Then he said to them, "The LORD *is* witness against you, and His anointed *is* witness
this day, that you have not found anything in
my hand." And they answered, "*He is* witness."
6 Then Samuel said to the people, "*It is* the
LORD who raised up Moses and Aaron, and
who brought your fathers up from the land of
Egypt.
7 "Now therefore, stand still, that I may reason with you before the LORD concerning all
the righteous acts of the LORD which He did to
you and your fathers:
8 "When Jacob had gone into Egypt,[a] and
your fathers cried out to the LORD, then the
LORD sent Moses and Aaron, who brought

12:8 [a]Following Masoretic Text, Targum, and Vulgate; Septuagint adds *and the Egyptians afflicted them.*

LIFE LESSONS

➤ 11:6 — *Then the Spirit of God came upon Saul when he heard this news, and his anger was greatly aroused.*

Saul did great things for God only when the Spirit of God empowered him and directed him. God can use us to do mighty things when we choose to be filled with His Spirit (Eph. 5:18).

➤ 11:13 — *But Saul said, "Not a man shall be put to death this day, for today the LORD has accomplished salvation in Israel."*

When Saul honored the Lord and put Him first, he enjoyed a successful and prosperous rule. Only when he allowed his eyes to drift did he begin his swift and steep decline.

➤ 12:3 — *"Whose ox have I taken, or whose donkey have I taken, or whom have I cheated?"*

Integrity—the consuming desire to acknowledge and obey the Father in conjunction with a readiness to confess and repent of sin—testifies to our private and public behavior. Integrity leaves no ground for accusation.

ANSWERS TO LIFE'S QUESTIONS

What does the Bible say to lonely people?

1 SAM 12:22

Time and again throughout the Old Testament, we find the Lord reaching out to His people, revealing Himself to them, desiring to be with them and to communicate with them. In 1 Samuel 12:22, we find this promise of God: "For the LORD will not forsake His people, for His great name's sake, because it has pleased the LORD to make you His people." God desires companionship, fellowship, and communion with those who will reciprocate His expressions of friendship.

We can count on the close communion of the Lord, even if everyone else abandons us. We see this in the life of Jesus. On the very night He was arrested and put on trial—trial that led to His crucifixion—He said to His disciples, "Indeed the hour is coming, yes, has now come, that you will be scattered, each to his own, and will leave Me alone." Can you hear the pain in that statement? Jesus knew what it was to be lonely! But then He said, "And yet I am not alone, because the Father is with Me" (John 16:32). Jesus knew what it was to be comforted even in the face of abandonment.

When loneliness engulfs us, the first thing we must do is to turn our focus away from what we don't have to what we do have. What do we have?

God Himself!

You can never be alone once you have trusted in Jesus Christ as your Savior. He promises that He dwells within you when you have received Him into your life and that He is connected to you, just as a vine and a branch are connected. In the same way that sap flows through a vine and its branches, so too the love of Christ flows in you and through you. He abides in you, and you abide in Him. You are one being with Christ. You share with him the most intimate relationship possible—an eternal, spiritual intimacy (see John 15:1–9).

The depth of that intimacy, to a great extent, is up to you. How much do you desire that intimacy with the Lord? How much do you allow Him to fill you up with His presence? How willing are you for Him to reveal Himself to you? Even so, you can never totally isolate yourself from the Lord. He is always there, desiring to move ever closer to you.

See the Life Principles Index for further study:

1. Our intimacy with God—His highest priority for our lives—determines the impact of our lives.

12. Peace with God is the fruit of oneness with God.

your fathers out of Egypt and made them
dwell in this place.
9 "And when they forgot the LORD their God,
He sold them into the hand of Sisera, commander of the army of Hazor, into the hand of
the Philistines, and into the hand of the king
of Moab; and they fought against them.
10 "Then they cried out to the LORD, and said,
'We have sinned, because we have forsaken
the LORD and served the Baals and Ashtoreths;[a] but now deliver us from the hand of
our enemies, and we will serve You.'
11 "And the LORD sent Jerubbaal,[a] Bedan,[b]
Jephthah, and Samuel,[c] and delivered you out
of the hand of your enemies on every side;
and you dwelt in safety.
12 "And when you saw that Nahash king of
the Ammonites came against you, you said to
me, 'No, but a king shall reign over us,' when
the LORD your God *was* your king.
13 "Now therefore, here is the king whom you
have chosen *and* whom you have desired. And
take note, the LORD has set a king over you.
14 "If you fear the LORD and serve Him and
obey His voice, and do not rebel against the
commandment of the LORD, then both you
and the king who reigns over you will continue following the LORD your God.
15 "However, if you do not obey the voice of
the LORD, but rebel against the commandment of the LORD, then the hand of the LORD
will be against you, as *it was* against your fathers.
16 "Now therefore, stand and see this great
thing which the LORD will do before your
eyes:
17 "*Is* today not the wheat harvest? I will call
to the LORD, and He will send thunder and
rain, that you may perceive and see that your
wickedness *is* great, which you have done in
the sight of the LORD, in asking a king for
yourselves."

12:10 [a]Canaanite goddesses **12:11** [a]Syriac reads *Deborah;* Targum reads *Gideon.* [b]Septuagint and Syriac read *Barak;* Targum reads *Simson.* [c]Syriac reads *Simson.*

18 So Samuel called to the LORD, and the
LORD sent thunder and rain that day; and all
the people greatly feared the LORD and Samuel.
19 And all the people said to Samuel, "Pray
for your servants to the LORD your God, that
we may not die; for we have added to all our
sins the evil of asking a king for ourselves."
20 Then Samuel said to the people, "Do not
fear. You have done all this wickedness; yet do
not turn aside from following the LORD, but
serve the LORD with all your heart.
➤ 21 "And do not turn aside; for *then you would
go* after empty things which cannot profit or
deliver, for they *are* nothing.
✳ 22 "For the LORD will not forsake His people,
➤ for His great name's sake, because it has
pleased the LORD to make you His people.
➤ 23 "Moreover, as for me, far be it from me
that I should sin against the LORD in ceasing
to pray for you; but I will teach you the good
and the right way.
24 "Only fear the LORD, and serve Him in
truth with all your heart; for consider what
great things He has done for you.
25 "But if you still do wickedly, you shall be
swept away, both you and your king."

Saul's Unlawful Sacrifice

13 Saul reigned one year; and when he
had reigned two years over Israel,[a]
2 Saul chose for himself three thousand
men of Israel. Two thousand were with Saul in
Michmash and in the mountains of Bethel,
and a thousand were with Jonathan in
Gibeah of Benjamin. The rest of the people he
sent away, every man to his tent.
3 And Jonathan attacked the garrison of the
Philistines that *was* in Geba, and the Philistines heard *of it*. Then Saul blew the trumpet
throughout all the land, saying, "Let the Hebrews hear!"
4 Now all Israel heard it said *that* Saul had
attacked a garrison of the Philistines, and
that Israel had also become an abomination
to the Philistines. And the people were called
together to Saul at Gilgal.
5 Then the Philistines gathered together to
fight with Israel, thirty[a] thousand chariots
and six thousand horsemen, and people as
the sand which *is* on the seashore in multitude. And they came up and encamped in
Michmash, to the east of Beth Aven.
6 When the men of Israel saw that they were
in danger (for the people were distressed),
then the people hid in caves, in thickets, in
rocks, in holes, and in pits.
7 And *some of* the Hebrews crossed over the
Jordan to the land of Gad and Gilead. As for
Saul, he *was* still in Gilgal, and all the people
followed him trembling.
8 Then he waited seven days, according to ➤
the time set by Samuel. But Samuel did not
come to Gilgal; and the people were scattered
from him.
9 So Saul said, "Bring a burnt offering and
peace offerings here to me." And he offered
the burnt offering.
10 Now it happened, as soon as he had finished presenting the burnt offering, that Samuel came; and Saul went out to meet him, that
he might greet him.
11 And Samuel said, "What have you done?"
Saul said, "When I saw that the people were
scattered from me, and *that* you did not come
within the days appointed, and *that* the Philistines gathered together at Michmash,
12 "then I said, 'The Philistines will now
come down on me at Gilgal, and I have not
made supplication to the LORD.' Therefore I
felt compelled, and offered a burnt offering."
13 And Samuel said to Saul, "You have done
foolishly. You have not kept the commandment

13:1 [a]The Hebrew is difficult (compare 2 Samuel 5:4; 2 Kings 14:2; see also 2 Samuel 2:10; Acts 13:21).
13:5 [a]Following Masoretic Text, Septuagint, Targum, and Vulgate; Syriac and some manuscripts of the Septuagint read *three*.

LIFE LESSONS

➤ 12:21 — *"And do not turn aside; for then you would go after empty things which cannot profit or deliver, for they are nothing."*

How often do we go after "empty things" that can neither bless nor deliver us? Even if we get these things, we end up with precisely nothing. Intimacy with God is always His highest priority for our lives.

➤ 12:22 — *"For the LORD will not forsake His people, for His great name's sake, because it has pleased the LORD to make you His people."*

Throughout the Bible, we find the Lord reaching out to His people, revealing Himself to them, desiring to be with them and to communicate with them. He promises never to forsake those who respond to Him in the same way.

➤ 12:23 — *"Moreover, as for me, far be it from me that I should sin against the LORD in ceasing to pray for you . . . ."*

Samuel considered it a sin against the Lord if he should stop praying for his fellow Israelites. We are all in this together; we need each other, especially in prayer (Col. 4:3; Heb. 13:18).

➤ 13:8 — *Then he waited seven days, according to the time set by Samuel. But Samuel did not come to Gilgal; and the people were scattered from him.*

God delights in rescuing His people at the last moment. We are to wait, even if it seems as though He may not act in time. God acts on behalf of those who trust Him enough to wait for Him.

of the LORD your God, which He commanded you. For now the LORD would have established your kingdom over Israel forever.

➤ 14 “But now your kingdom shall not continue. The LORD has sought for Himself a man after His own heart, and the LORD has commanded him *to be* commander over His people, because you have not kept what the LORD commanded you.”

15 Then Samuel arose and went up from Gilgal to Gibeah of Benjamin.[a] And Saul numbered the people present with him, about six hundred men.

No Weapons for the Army

16 Saul, Jonathan his son, and the people present with them remained in Gibeah of Benjamin. But the Philistines encamped in Michmash.

17 Then raiders came out of the camp of the Philistines in three companies. One company turned onto the road to Ophrah, to the land of Shual,

18 another company turned to the road *to* Beth Horon, and another company turned *to* the road of the border that overlooks the Valley of Zeboim toward the wilderness.

19 Now there was no blacksmith to be found throughout all the land of Israel, for the Philistines said, “Lest the Hebrews make swords or spears.”

20 But all the Israelites would go down to the Philistines to sharpen each man’s plowshare, his mattock, his ax, and his sickle;

21 and the charge for a sharpening was a pim[a] for the plowshares, the mattocks, the forks, and the axes, and to set the points of the goads.

22 So it came about, on the day of battle, that there was neither sword nor spear found in the hand of any of the people who *were* with Saul and Jonathan. But they were found with Saul and Jonathan his son.

23 And the garrison of the Philistines went out to the pass of Michmash.

Jonathan Defeats the Philistines

14 Now it happened one day that Jonathan the son of Saul said to the young man who bore his armor, “Come, let us go over to the Philistines’ garrison that *is* on the other side.” But he did not tell his father.

2 And Saul was sitting in the outskirts of Gibeah under a pomegranate tree which *is* in Migron. The people who *were* with him *were* about six hundred men.

3 Ahijah the son of Ahitub, Ichabod’s brother, the son of Phinehas, the son of Eli, the LORD’s priest in Shiloh, was wearing an ephod. But the people did not know that Jonathan had gone.

4 Between the passes, by which Jonathan sought to go over to the Philistines’ garrison, *there was* a sharp rock on one side and a sharp rock on the other side. And the name of one *was* Bozez, and the name of the other Seneh.

5 The front of one faced northward opposite Michmash, and the other southward opposite Gibeah.

6 Then Jonathan said to the young man who bore his armor, “Come, let us go over to the garrison of these uncircumcised; it may be that the LORD will work for us. For nothing restrains the LORD from saving by many or by few.”

7 So his armorbearer said to him, “Do all that is in your heart. Go then; here I am with you, according to your heart.”

8 Then Jonathan said, “Very well, let us cross over to *these* men, and we will show ourselves to them.

9 “If they say thus to us, ‘Wait until we come to you,’ then we will stand still in our place and not go up to them.

10 “But if they say thus, ‘Come up to us,’ then we will go up. For the LORD has delivered them into our hand, and this *will be* a sign to us.”

11 So both of them showed themselves to the garrison of the Philistines. And the Philistines said, “Look, the Hebrews are coming out of the holes where they have hidden.”

12 Then the men of the garrison called to Jonathan and his armorbearer, and said, “Come up to us, and we will show you something.” Jonathan said to his armorbearer, “Come up after me, for the LORD has delivered them into the hand of Israel.”

13 And Jonathan climbed up on his hands and knees with his armorbearer after him;

13:15 [a]Following Masoretic Text and Targum; Septuagint and Vulgate add *And the rest of the people went up after Saul to meet the people who fought against them, going from Gilgal to Gibeah in the hill of Benjamin.* **13:21** [a]About two-thirds shekel weight

LIFE LESSONS

➤ 13:14 — *“. . . The LORD has sought for Himself a man after His own heart, and the LORD has commanded him to be commander over His people . . . .”*

Even before Samuel had anointed David as the next king of Israel—even before Samuel had met the boy—the Lord had “commanded” David to lead Israel. God has a plan for us, long before we see it.

➤ 14:6 — *“. . . For nothing restrains the LORD from saving by many or by few.”*

Jonathan had a spirit very different from that of his father. Saul feared men; Jonathan feared God. And so the Lord did mighty things through Jonathan.

and they fell before Jonathan. And as he
came after him, his armorbearer killed them.
14 That first slaughter which Jonathan and
his armorbearer made was about twenty men
within about half an acre of land.[a]
15 And there was trembling in the camp, in
the field, and among all the people. The garrison and the raiders also trembled; and the
earth quaked, so that it was a very great trembling.
16 Now the watchmen of Saul in Gibeah of
Benjamin looked, and *there* was the multitude,
melting away; and they went here and there.
17 Then Saul said to the people who *were*
with him, "Now call the roll and see who has
gone from us." And when they had called the
roll, surprisingly, Jonathan and his armorbearer *were* not *there.*
18 And Saul said to Ahijah, "Bring the ark[a] of
God here" (for at that time the ark[b] of God
was with the children of Israel).
19 Now it happened, while Saul talked to the
priest, that the noise which *was* in the camp
of the Philistines continued to increase; so
Saul said to the priest, "Withdraw your hand."
20 Then Saul and all the people who *were*
with him assembled, and they went to the battle; and indeed every man's sword was against
his neighbor, *and there was* very great confusion.
21 Moreover the Hebrews *who* were with the
Philistines before that time, who went up with
them into the camp *from the* surrounding
country, they also joined the Israelites who
were with Saul and Jonathan.
22 Likewise all the men of Israel who had
hidden in the mountains of Ephraim, *when*
they heard that the Philistines fled, they also
followed hard after them in the battle.
➤ 23 So the LORD saved Israel that day, and the
battle shifted to Beth Aven.

Saul's Rash Oath

➤ **24** And the men of Israel were distressed that
day, for Saul had placed the people under oath,
saying, "Cursed *is* the man who eats *any* food
until evening, before I have taken vengeance
on my enemies." So none of the people tasted
food.
25 Now all *the people* of the land came to a
forest; and there was honey on the ground.
26 And when the people had come into the
woods, there was the honey, dripping; but no
one put his hand to his mouth, for the people
feared the oath.
27 But Jonathan had not heard his father
charge the people with the oath; therefore he
stretched out the end of the rod that *was* in
his hand and dipped it in a honeycomb, and
put his hand to his mouth; and his countenance brightened.
28 Then one of the people said, "Your father
strictly charged the people with an oath, saying, 'Cursed *is* the man who eats food this
day.'" And the people were faint.
29 But Jonathan said, "My father has troubled the land. Look now, how my countenance has brightened because I tasted a little
of this honey.
30 How much better if the people had eaten
freely today of the spoil of their enemies
which they found! For now would there not
have been a much greater slaughter among
the Philistines?"
31 Now they had driven back the Philistines
that day from Michmash to Aijalon. So the
people were very faint.
32 And the people rushed on the spoil, and
took sheep, oxen, and calves, and slaughtered
them on the ground; and the people ate *them*
with the blood.
33 Then they told Saul, saying, "Look, the
people are sinning against the LORD by eating
with the blood!" So he said, "You have dealt
treacherously; roll a large stone to me this
day."
34 Then Saul said, "Disperse yourselves
among the people, and say to them, 'Bring
me here every man's ox and every man's
sheep, slaughter *them* here, and eat; and do
not sin against the LORD by eating with the
blood.'" So every one of the people brought
his ox with him that night, and slaughtered *it*
there.
35 Then Saul built an altar to the LORD. This
was the first altar that he built to the LORD.
36 Now Saul said, "Let us go down after the
Philistines by night, and plunder them until

14:14 [a]Literally *half the area plowed by a yoke* (of oxen in a day)
14:18 [a]Following Masoretic Text, Targum, and Vulgate; Septuagint reads *ephod.* [b]Following Masoretic Text, Targum, and Vulgate; Septuagint reads *ephod.*

LIFE LESSONS

➤ **14:23 — *So the LORD saved Israel that day, and the battle shifted to Beth Aven.***

Jonathan had no idea how God would validate the words he had spoken (1 Sam. 14:6). When we move ahead in faith, we likewise have no idea how God may move in power on our behalf (see Eph. 3:20).

➤ **14:24 — *And the men of Israel were distressed that day, for Saul had placed the people under oath, saying, "Cursed is the man who eats any food until evening, before I have taken vengeance on my enemies." So none of the people tasted food.***

Saul pronounced this oath, not to honor God, but to honor himself. He said, "before *I* have taken vengeance." Through his selfishness he nearly cost his son his life, and did allow many of his enemies to escape (1 Sam. 17:30).

the morning light; and let us not leave a man
of them." And they said, "Do whatever seems
good to you." Then the priest said, "Let us
draw near to God here."
37 So Saul asked counsel of God, "Shall I go
down after the Philistines? Will You deliver
them into the hand of Israel?" But He did not
answer him that day.
38 And Saul said, "Come over here, all you
chiefs of the people, and know and see what
this sin was today.
39 "For *as* the LORD lives, who saves Israel,
though it be in Jonathan my son, he shall
surely die." But not a man among all the people answered him.
40 Then he said to all Israel, "You be on one
side, and my son Jonathan and I will be on the
other side." And the people said to Saul, "Do
what seems good to you."
41 Therefore Saul said to the LORD God of Israel, "Give a perfect *lot*."[a] So Saul and Jonathan were taken, but the people escaped.
42 And Saul said, "Cast *lots* between my son
Jonathan and me." So Jonathan was taken.
43 Then Saul said to Jonathan, "Tell me what
you have done." And Jonathan told him, and
said, "I only tasted a little honey with the end
of the rod that *was* in my hand. So now I must
die!"
44 Saul answered, "God do so and more also;
for you shall surely die, Jonathan."
45 But the people said to Saul, "Shall Jonathan die, who has accomplished this great deliverance in Israel? Certainly not! *As* the
LORD lives, not one hair of his head shall fall
to the ground, for he has worked with God
this day." So the people rescued Jonathan,
and he did not die.
46 Then Saul returned from pursuing the
Philistines, and the Philistines went to their
own place.

Saul's Continuing Wars

47 So Saul established his sovereignty over
Israel, and fought against all his enemies on
every side, against Moab, against the people
of Ammon, against Edom, against the kings
of Zobah, and against the Philistines. Wherever he turned, he harassed *them*.[a]
48 And he gathered an army and attacked
the Amalekites, and delivered Israel from the
hands of those who plundered them.
49 The sons of Saul were Jonathan, Jishui,[a]
and Malchishua. And the names of his two
daughters *were these:* the name of the firstborn Merab, and the name of the younger
Michal.
50 The name of Saul's wife *was* Ahinoam the
daughter of Ahimaaz. And the name of the
commander of his army *was* Abner the son of
Ner, Saul's uncle.
51 Kish *was* the father of Saul, and Ner the
father of Abner *was* the son of Abiel.
52 Now there was fierce war with the Philistines all the days of Saul. And when Saul saw
any strong man or any valiant man, he took
him for himself.

Saul Spares King Agag

15 Samuel also said to Saul, "The LORD
sent me to anoint you king over His
people, over Israel. Now therefore, heed the
voice of the words of the LORD.
2 "Thus says the LORD of hosts: 'I will punish Amalek *for* what he did to Israel, how he
ambushed him on the way when he came up
from Egypt.
3 'Now go and attack Amalek, and utterly
destroy all that they have, and do not spare
them. But kill both man and woman, infant
and nursing child, ox and sheep, camel and
donkey.'"
4 So Saul gathered the people together and
numbered them in Telaim, two hundred thousand foot soldiers and ten thousand men of
Judah.
5 And Saul came to a city of Amalek, and
lay in wait in the valley.
6 Then Saul said to the Kenites, "Go, depart,
get down from among the Amalekites, lest I
destroy you with them. For you showed kindness to all the children of Israel when they
came up out of Egypt." So the Kenites departed from among the Amalekites.
7 And Saul attacked the Amalekites, from
Havilah all the way to Shur, which is east of
Egypt.
8 He also took Agag king of the Amalekites
alive, and utterly destroyed all the people
with the edge of the sword.
9 But Saul and the people spared Agag and ➤
the best of the sheep, the oxen, the fatlings,
the lambs, and all *that was* good, and were
unwilling to utterly destroy them. But every-

14:41 [a]Following Masoretic Text and Targum; Septuagint and Vulgate read *Why do You not answer Your servant today? If the injustice is with me or Jonathan my son, O LORD God of Israel, give proof; and if You say it is with Your people Israel, give holiness.* **14:47** [a]Septuagint and Vulgate read *prospered.* **14:49** [a]Called *Abinadab* in 1 Chronicles 8:33 and 9:39

LIFE LESSONS

➤ **15:9 — *But Saul and the people spared Agag and the best of the sheep, the oxen, the fatlings, the lambs, and all that was good, and were unwilling to utterly destroy them . . . .***

God tells us to obey His commands—all of them—not merely the ones we like, understand, or make us comfortable. Incomplete obedience is arrogant disobedience.

thing despised and worthless, that they utterly destroyed.

Saul Rejected as King

10 Now the word of the LORD came to Samuel, saying,
11 "I greatly regret that I have set up Saul *as*
king, for he has turned back from following
Me, and has not performed My commandments." And it grieved Samuel, and he cried
out to the LORD all night.
12 So when Samuel rose early in the morning to meet Saul, it was told Samuel, saying, "Saul went to Carmel, and indeed, he set
up a monument for himself; and he has gone
on around, passed by, and gone down to Gilgal."
13 Then Samuel went to Saul, and Saul said
to him, "Blessed *are* you of the LORD! I have
performed the commandment of the LORD."
14 But Samuel said, "What then *is* this bleat-
ing of the sheep in my ears, and the lowing of
the oxen which I hear?"
15 And Saul said, "They have brought them
from the Amalekites; for the people spared
the best of the sheep and the oxen, to sacrifice
to the LORD your God; and the rest we have
utterly destroyed."
16 Then Samuel said to Saul, "Be quiet! And
I will tell you what the LORD said to me last
night." And he said to him, "Speak on."
17 So Samuel said, "When you *were* little in
your own eyes, *were* you not head of the
tribes of Israel? And did not the LORD anoint
you king over Israel?
18 "Now the LORD sent you on a mission, and
said, 'Go, and utterly destroy the sinners, the
Amalekites, and fight against them until they
are consumed.'
19 "Why then did you not obey the voice of
the LORD? Why did you swoop down on the
spoil, and do evil in the sight of the LORD?"
20 And Saul said to Samuel, "But I have
obeyed the voice of the LORD, and gone on the
mission on which the LORD sent me, and
brought back Agag king of Amalek; I have utterly destroyed the Amalekites.
21 But the people took of the plunder, sheep
and oxen, the best of the things which should
have been utterly destroyed, to sacrifice to the
LORD your God in Gilgal."
22 So Samuel said:

"Has the LORD *as great* delight in burnt
offerings and sacrifices,
As in obeying the voice of the LORD?
Behold, to obey is better than sacrifice,
And to heed than the fat of rams.
23 For rebellion *is as* the sin of witchcraft,
And stubbornness *is as* iniquity and
idolatry.
Because you have rejected the word of
the LORD,
He also has rejected you from *being*
king."

24 Then Saul said to Samuel, "I have sinned,
for I have transgressed the commandment of
the LORD and your words, because I feared
the people and obeyed their voice.
25 "Now therefore, please pardon my sin, and
return with me, that I may worship the LORD."
26 But Samuel said to Saul, "I will not return
with you, for you have rejected the word of
the LORD, and the LORD has rejected you from
being king over Israel."
27 And as Samuel turned around to go away,
Saul seized the edge of his robe, and it tore.
28 So Samuel said to him, "The LORD has
torn the kingdom of Israel from you today,
and has given it to a neighbor of yours, *who is*
better than you.
29 "And also the Strength of Israel will not lie
nor relent. For He *is* not a man, that He should
relent."
30 Then he said, "I have sinned; *yet* honor me
now, please, before the elders of my people
and before Israel, and return with me, that I
may worship the LORD your God."
31 So Samuel turned back after Saul, and
Saul worshiped the LORD.
32 Then Samuel said, "Bring Agag king of
the Amalekites here to me." So Agag came to
him cautiously. And Agag said, "Surely the
bitterness of death is past."

LIFE LESSONS

➤ 15:12 — *"Saul went to Carmel, and indeed, he set up a monument for himself . . . ."*

The young man who once thought of himself as small has now set up a monument to honor himself. When we cease to follow the Lord wholeheartedly, we follow our prideful hearts to our own destruction.

➤ 15:22 — *"Has the LORD as great delight in burnt offerings and sacrifices, as in obeying the voice of the LORD? Behold, to obey is better than sacrifice, and to heed than the fat of rams."*

Our heavenly Father places a high value on obedience, preferring it even to outward expressions of worship. In fact, our obedience is the ultimate expression of worship and service.

➤ 15:24 — *Then Saul said to Samuel, "I have sinned, for I have transgressed the commandment of the LORD and your words, because I feared the people and obeyed their voice."*

Saul recognized fear as a real problem in his life, but he did nothing about it. The best way to deal with our fear of people is to nurture a greater fear and love of God by meditating on His works and words.

33 But Samuel said, "As your sword has made
women childless, so shall your mother be
childless among women." And Samuel hacked
Agag in pieces before the LORD in Gilgal.
34 Then Samuel went to Ramah, and Saul
went up to his house at Gibeah of Saul.
35 And Samuel went no more to see Saul
until the day of his death. Nevertheless Samuel mourned for Saul, and the LORD regretted
that He had made Saul king over Israel.

David Anointed King

➤ 16 Now the LORD said to Samuel, "How
long will you mourn for Saul, seeing I
have rejected him from reigning over Israel?
Fill your horn with oil, and go; I am sending
you to Jesse the Bethlehemite. For I have provided Myself a king among his sons."
2 And Samuel said, "How can I go? If Saul
hears *it,* he will kill me." But the LORD said,
"Take a heifer with you, and say, 'I have come
to sacrifice to the LORD.'
➤ 3 "Then invite Jesse to the sacrifice, and I
will show you what you shall do; you shall
anoint for Me the one I name to you."
4 So Samuel did what the LORD said, and
went to Bethlehem. And the elders of the
town trembled at his coming, and said, "Do
you come peaceably?"
5 And he said, "Peaceably; I have come to
sacrifice to the LORD. Sanctify yourselves, and
come with me to the sacrifice." Then he consecrated Jesse and his sons, and invited them
to the sacrifice.
6 So it was, when they came, that he looked
at Eliab and said, "Surely the LORD's anointed
is before Him!"
➤ 7 But the LORD said to Samuel, "Do not look
at his appearance or at his physical stature,
because I have refused him. For *the LORD does*
not *see* as man sees;[a] for man looks at the
outward appearance, but the LORD looks at the
heart."
8 So Jesse called Abinadab, and made him
pass before Samuel. And he said, "Neither
has the LORD chosen this one."
9 Then Jesse made Shammah pass by. And
he said, "Neither has the LORD chosen this one."
10 Thus Jesse made seven of his sons pass
before Samuel. And Samuel said to Jesse,
"The LORD has not chosen these."
11 And Samuel said to Jesse, "Are all the
young men here?" Then he said, "There remains yet the youngest, and there he is, keeping the sheep." And Samuel said to Jesse,
"Send and bring him. For we will not sit
down[a] till he comes here."
12 So he sent and brought him in. Now he
was ruddy, with bright eyes, and good-looking. And the LORD said, "Arise, anoint him; for
this *is* the one!"
13 Then Samuel took the horn of oil and
anointed him in the midst of his brothers; and ➤
the Spirit of the LORD came upon David from
that day forward. So Samuel arose and went
to Ramah.

A Distressing Spirit Troubles Saul

14 But the Spirit of the LORD departed from
Saul, and a distressing spirit from the LORD
troubled him.
15 And Saul's servants said to him, "Surely,
a distressing spirit from God is troubling
you.
16 "Let our master now command your servants, *who are* before you, to seek out a man
who is a skillful player on the harp. And it
shall be that he will play it with his hand
when the distressing spirit from God is upon
you, and you shall be well."

16:7 [a]Septuagint reads *For God does not see as man sees;* Targum reads *It is not by the appearance of a man;* Vulgate reads *Nor do I judge according to the looks of a man.*
16:11 [a]Following Septuagint and Vulgate; Masoretic Text reads *turn around;* Targum and Syriac read *turn away.*

LIFE LESSONS

➤ 16:1 — *Now the LORD said to Samuel, "How long will you mourn for Saul, seeing I have rejected him from reigning over Israel?"*

God is not the "softie" we sometimes think He is. While He regretted making Saul king (1 Sam. 15:11, 35), He did not allow grief to paralyze Him. Samuel did; so God had to shake the prophet out of his mourning.

➤ 16:3 — *"Then invite Jesse to the sacrifice, and I will show you what you shall do; you shall anoint for Me the one I name to you."*

God could have told Samuel ahead of time what to do and who to anoint, but He didn't. Instead He leads us one step at a time, teaching us to trust Him and to continually listen for His voice.

➤ 16:7 — *But the LORD said to Samuel, "Do not look at his appearance or at his physical stature, because I have refused him. For the LORD does not see as man sees; for man looks at the outward appearance, but the LORD looks at the heart."*

Even a godly man like Samuel couldn't help but judge a man's character by his appearance. This is why we must continually go to the Lord for His wisdom; only He sees the heart.

➤ 16:13 — *Then Samuel took the horn of oil and anointed him in the midst of his brothers; and the Spirit of the LORD came upon David from that day forward.*

David could not succeed without the Spirit of the Lord any more than Saul could. We will enjoy true success only when we cooperate with the Lord by allowing His Spirit to fill us.

17 So Saul said to his servants, "Provide me
now a man who can play well, and bring *him*
to me."
18 Then one of the servants answered and
said, "Look, I have seen a son of Jesse the
Bethlehemite, *who is* skillful in playing, a
mighty man of valor, a man of war, prudent in
speech, and a handsome person; and the
LORD *is* with him."
➤ **19** Therefore Saul sent messengers to Jesse,
and said, "Send me your son David, who *is*
with the sheep."
20 And Jesse took a donkey *loaded with*
bread, a skin of wine, and a young goat, and
sent *them* by his son David to Saul.
21 So David came to Saul and stood before
him. And he loved him greatly, and he became
his armorbearer.
22 Then Saul sent to Jesse, saying, "Please let
David stand before me, for he has found favor
in my sight."
23 And so it was, whenever the spirit from
God was upon Saul, that David would take a
harp and play *it* with his hand. Then Saul
would become refreshed and well, and the
distressing spirit would depart from him.

David and Goliath

17 Now the Philistines gathered their
armies together to battle, and were
gathered at Sochoh, which *belongs* to Judah;
they encamped between Sochoh and Azekah,
in Ephes Dammim.
2 And Saul and the men of Israel were gathered together, and they encamped in the Valley
of Elah, and drew up in battle array against the
Philistines.
3 The Philistines stood on a mountain on
one side, and Israel stood on a mountain on
the other side, with a valley between them.
4 And a champion went out from the camp
of the Philistines, named Goliath, from Gath,
whose height *was* six cubits and a span.
5 *He had* a bronze helmet on his head, and
he *was* armed with a coat of mail, and the
weight of the coat *was* five thousand shekels
of bronze.
6 And *he had* bronze armor on his legs and
a bronze javelin between his shoulders.
7 Now the staff of his spear *was* like a
weaver's beam, and his iron spearhead
weighed six hundred shekels; and a shield-
bearer went before him.
8 Then he stood and cried out to the armies
of Israel, and said to them, "Why have you
come out to line up for battle? *Am* I not a Philistine, and you the servants of Saul? Choose
a man for yourselves, and let him come down
to me.
9 "If he is able to fight with me and kill me,
then we will be your servants. But if I prevail
against him and kill him, then you shall be
our servants and serve us."
10 And the Philistine said, "I defy the armies
of Israel this day; give me a man, that we may
fight together."
11 When Saul and all Israel heard these ➤
words of the Philistine, they were dismayed
and greatly afraid.
12 Now David *was* the son of that Ephrathite
of Bethlehem Judah, whose name *was* Jesse,
and who had eight sons. And the man was
old, advanced *in years*, in the days of Saul.
13 The three oldest sons of Jesse had gone to
follow Saul to the battle. The names of his
three sons who went to the battle *were* Eliab
the firstborn, next to him Abinadab, and the
third Shammah.
14 David *was* the youngest. And the three
oldest followed Saul.
15 But David occasionally went and returned
from Saul to feed his father's sheep at Bethlehem.
16 And the Philistine drew near and presented himself forty days, morning and evening.
17 Then Jesse said to his son David, "Take
now for your brothers an ephah of this dried
grain and these ten loaves, and run to your
brothers at the camp.
18 "And carry these ten cheeses to the captain of *their* thousand, and see how your
brothers fare, and bring back news of them."
19 Now Saul and they and all the men of Israel *were* in the Valley of Elah, fighting with
the Philistines.
20 So David rose early in the morning, left
the sheep with a keeper, and took *the things*
and went as Jesse had commanded him. And
he came to the camp as the army was going
out to the fight and shouting for the battle.
21 For Israel and the Philistines had drawn
up in battle array, army against army.
22 And David left his supplies in the hand of
the supply keeper, ran to the army, and came
and greeted his brothers.

LIFE LESSONS

➤ 16:19 — *Therefore Saul sent messengers to Jesse, and said, "Send me your son David, who is with the sheep."*

As God sent Moses into the household of Pharaoh to train him for the future, so He sent David into Saul's palace to train him for the future. God will always equip us for the tasks He gives us.

➤ 17:11 — *When Saul and all Israel heard these words of the Philistine, they were dismayed and greatly afraid.*

Once again, Saul allows his fear of men to eclipse a godly fear of the Lord. Fear, left unchecked, can ruin us both spiritually and physically.

ANSWERS TO LIFE'S QUESTIONS

How can I find courage in the face of stiff challenges?

1 SAM. 17:12–54

Any time God requires us to face trials and tribulations, He always provides the courage to meet the demand. David was a man of great courage—not merely human courage, but courage rooted in the sovereignty of God. In 1 Samuel 17 we see God's supernatural strength in action in the life of David.

Defeat is never a viable option for the person of courage. As David faced his battle with Goliath, he never considered defeat an option. People of courage refuse to look for ways of escape. They set their gaze on advancement and victory. Never go into battle entertaining thoughts of defeat; you will lose every time. Men and women of courage know their success lies with an unshakable God.

Courageous people recall past victories and God's faithfulness. At times David had faced enemies just as vicious as Goliath. In the moments before the battle, David recalled how God had strengthened him in the past to kill both a lion and a bear. He expected the same sort of help to strengthen him against Goliath.

Courage is a result of having the right attitude. David realized he could not win in his own strength. He knew God had to be with him or he would suffer defeat.

Courageous people look to God and trust His guidance. David's brothers mocked him. Saul pacified him. Goliath made fun of him. But their negative talk did not affect David. Every time God calls you to follow Him, expect opposition, even from surprising sources.

Genuine courage is not chilled by inner fears or outward difficulties. The attributes and characteristics of courage turn a deaf ear to those who refuse to believe God. Take time to study God's Word and apply His principles to your life. You can always face your enemies head on when you stand on the promises of God's Word.

A courageous person applies resources at hand in creative ways. David chose five smooth stones and a slingshot as his weapons instead of the bulky armor of Saul. He faced Goliath clothed in the strong faith of the living God. And mere men cannot penetrate nor defeat God-centered faith!

A person with the attribute of courage confronts an opponent with confidence that he will ultimately succeed. When we face life's trials as David did, by faith, we become men and women of courage—and the victory is always ours.

See the Life Principles Index for further study:
8. Fight all your battles on your knees and you win every time.
18. As children of a sovereign God, we are never victims of our circumstances.

23 Then as he talked with them, there was the champion, the Philistine of Gath, Goliath by name, coming up from the armies of the Philistines; and he spoke according to the same words. So David heard *them.*
24 And all the men of Israel, when they saw the man, fled from him and were dreadfully afraid.
25 So the men of Israel said, "Have you seen this man who has come up? Surely he has come up to defy Israel; and it shall be *that* the man who kills him the king will enrich with great riches, will give him his daughter, and give his father's house exemption *from taxes* in Israel."
26 Then David spoke to the men who stood by him, saying, "What shall be done for the man who kills this Philistine and takes away the reproach from Israel? For who *is* this uncircumcised Philistine, that he should defy the armies of the living God?"
27 And the people answered him in this manner, saying, "So shall it be done for the man who kills him."
28 Now Eliab his oldest brother heard when he spoke to the men; and Eliab's anger was aroused against David, and he said, "Why did you come down here? And with whom have you left those few sheep in the wilderness? I know your pride and the insolence of your heart, for you have come down to see the battle."
29 And David said, "What have I done now? *Is there* not a cause?"
30 Then he turned from him toward another and said the same thing; and these people answered him as the first ones *did.*
31 Now when the words which David spoke were heard, they reported *them* to Saul; and he sent for him.
32 Then David said to Saul, "Let no man's heart fail because of him; your servant will go and fight with this Philistine."

➤ 33 And Saul said to David, "You are not able
to go against this Philistine to fight with him;
for you *are* a youth, and he a man of war from
his youth."
34 But David said to Saul, "Your servant used
to keep his father's sheep, and when a lion
or a bear came and took a lamb out of the
flock,
35 "I went out after it and struck it, and delivered *the lamb* from its mouth; and when it
arose against me, I caught *it* by its beard, and
struck and killed it.
36 "Your servant has killed both lion and
bear; and this uncircumcised Philistine will
be like one of them, seeing he has defied the
armies of the living God."
➤ 37 Moreover David said, "The LORD, who delivered me from the paw of the lion and from
the paw of the bear, He will deliver me from
the hand of this Philistine." And Saul said to
David, "Go, and the LORD be with you!"
38 So Saul clothed David with his armor, and
he put a bronze helmet on his head; he also
clothed him with a coat of mail.
39 David fastened his sword to his armor and
tried to walk, for he had not tested *them*. And
David said to Saul, "I cannot walk with these,
for I have not tested *them*." So David took
them off.
40 Then he took his staff in his hand; and he
chose for himself five smooth stones from the
brook, and put them in a shepherd's bag, in a
pouch which he had, and his sling was in his
hand. And he drew near to the Philistine.
41 So the Philistine came, and began drawing near to David, and the man who bore the
shield *went* before him.
42 And when the Philistine looked about and
saw David, he disdained him; for he was *only*
a youth, ruddy and good-looking.
43 So the Philistine said to David, "*Am* I a
dog, that you come to me with sticks?" And
the Philistine cursed David by his gods.
44 And the Philistine said to David, "Come to
me, and I will give your flesh to the birds of
the air and the beasts of the field!"
45 Then David said to the Philistine, "You ➤
come to me with a sword, with a spear, and
with a javelin. But I come to you in the name
of the LORD of hosts, the God of the armies of
Israel, whom you have defied.
46 "This day the LORD will deliver you into
my hand, and I will strike you and take your
head from you. And this day I will give the
carcasses of the camp of the Philistines to the
birds of the air and the wild beasts of the
earth, that all the earth may know that there
is a God in Israel.
47 "Then all this assembly shall know that *
the LORD does not save with sword and spear;
for the battle *is* the LORD's, and He will give
you into our hands."
48 So it was, when the Philistine arose and
came and drew near to meet David, that David hurried and ran toward the army to meet
the Philistine.
49 Then David put his hand in his bag and
took out a stone; and he slung *it* and struck
the Philistine in his forehead, so that the
stone sank into his forehead, and he fell on
his face to the earth.
50 So David prevailed over the Philistine
with a sling and a stone, and struck the Philistine and killed him. But *there was* no sword
in the hand of David.
51 Therefore David ran and stood over the ➤
Philistine, took his sword and drew it out of
its sheath and killed him, and cut off his head
with it.
And when the Philistines saw that their
champion was dead, they fled.
52 Now the men of Israel and Judah arose

LIFE LESSONS

➤ 17:26 — *"For who is this uncircumcised Philistine, that he should defy the armies of the living God?"*

Why did David not allow Goliath to frighten him, as the giant had all the others in Israel's army? Because he feared and loved God more than he feared anything else. That is the key to success.

➤ 17:33 — *And Saul said to David, "You are not able to go against this Philistine to fight with him; for you are a youth, and he a man of war from his youth."*

Saul had trained himself to look at things only through the eyes of the flesh; he had no idea how to see with eyes of faith. But trusting God means looking beyond what we can see to what God sees.

➤ 17:37 — *Moreover David said, "The LORD, who delivered me from the paw of the lion and from the paw of the bear, He will deliver me from the hand of this Philistine."*

Faith is the Holy Spirit's signal to go into action. David activated his faith before he activated his will. Before he began his walk into the valley, he exercised his faith in the Lord.

➤ 17:45 — *Then David said to the Philistine, "You come to me with a sword, with a spear, and with a javelin. But I come to you in the name of the LORD of hosts, the God of the armies of Israel, whom you have defied."*

A sword, a spear, and a javelin are no match for a living faith in the Lord of hosts. David knew God was with him, and already he had seen what His presence can accomplish.

➤ 17:51 — *Therefore David ran and stood over the Philistine, took his sword and drew it out of its sheath and killed him, and cut off his head with it . . . .*

After David felled Goliath with his sling, he used the giant's own sword to cut off his head. God took something intended for his harm and used it for his good.

ANSWERS TO LIFE'S QUESTIONS

What role does faith play in doing great things for God?

1 SAM. 17:26

Faith is *believing that God will do as He has promised.* Faith is not a power. It's not something we have to drum up inside ourselves. Faith is trusting that God will honor His promises. That is all there is to it.

The famous story of David and Goliath illustrates this as well as any. The armies of Israel had lined up on one side of the valley, while the Philistines had lined up on the other. Every day the giant warrior Goliath would walk down into the valley and taunt the armies of Israel.

One day young David arrived on the scene with a fresh outlook. Notice what he said when he heard Goliath's arrogant threats: "Who is this uncircumcised Philistine, that he should taunt the armies of the living God?" (1 Sam. 17:26).

David didn't see Goliath as merely the enemy of Israel. He saw him as *God's* enemy—and David knew that God could take Goliath out of the picture with no problem. So David acted on his faith.

Hundreds, maybe even thousands, of Israelite soldiers had greater training to do battle with Goliath than David. But they responded to the giant's threats with paralyzing fear, stress and anxious frustration. David, on the other hand, didn't seem upset at all. Why not? Because he knew it was God's battle, not his. Apart from the Lord, he knew he didn't stand a chance. But with the help of the Lord, he knew that everything would turn out all right.

Neither David nor the soldiers of Israel had the natural ability to defeat the giant. But while one party focused on its inability—and therefore panicked—the other party focused on God's provision—and therefore remained confident. The only difference was focus.

David did e*xactly what he knew how to do, while trusting God to do the rest.* That is what living by faith boils down to: living in the confidence that God is supremely faithful to keep His word. So David gathered a few stones, walked down into the valley, carried on a short but heated exchange with Goliath, loaded, and then fired. He had taken those actions countless times before; nothing out of the ordinary there.

But once that first stone left its sling, God stepped in to do what only He could do. And Goliath went down.

That's faith. And that's where great things originate.

See the Life Principles Index for further study:
9. Trusting God means looking beyond what we can see to what God sees.

and shouted, and pursued the Philistines as
far as the entrance of the valley[a] and to the
gates of Ekron. And the wounded of the Philistines fell along the road to Shaaraim, even
as far as Gath and Ekron.
53 Then the children of Israel returned from
chasing the Philistines, and they plundered
their tents.
54 And David took the head of the Philistine
and brought it to Jerusalem, but he put his
armor in his tent.
55 When Saul saw David going out against
the Philistine, he said to Abner, the commander of the army, "Abner, whose son *is* this
youth?" And Abner said, "As your soul lives,
O king, I do not know."
56 So the king said, "Inquire whose son this
young man *is*."
57 Then, as David returned from the slaughter of the Philistine, Abner took him and
brought him before Saul with the head of the
Philistine in his hand.
58 And Saul said to him, "Whose son *are*
you, young man?" So David answered, "*I am*
the son of your servant Jesse the Bethlehemite."

Saul Resents David

18 Now when he had finished speaking to
Saul, the soul of Jonathan was knit to
the soul of David, and Jonathan loved him as
his own soul.
2 Saul took him that day, and would not let
him go home to his father's house anymore.
3 Then Jonathan and David made a covenant, because he loved him as his own soul.
4 And Jonathan took off the robe that *was*
on him and gave it to David, with his armor,
even to his sword and his bow and his belt.
5 So David went out wherever Saul sent

17:52 [a]Following Masoretic Text, Syriac, Targum, and Vulgate; Septuagint reads *Gath*.

him, *and* behaved wisely. And Saul set him
over the men of war, and he was accepted in
the sight of all the people and also in the sight
of Saul's servants.
6 Now it had happened as they were coming
home, when David was returning from the
slaughter of the Philistine, that the women
had come out of all the cities of Israel, singing
and dancing, to meet King Saul, with tambourines, with joy, and with musical instruments.
7 So the women sang as they danced, and
said:

"Saul has slain his thousands,
And David his ten thousands."

➤ 8 Then Saul was very angry, and the saying
displeased him; and he said, "They have ascribed to David ten thousands, and to me they
have ascribed *only* thousands. Now *what*
more can he have but the kingdom?"
9 So Saul eyed David from that day forward.
10 And it happened on the next day that the
distressing spirit from God came upon Saul,
and he prophesied inside the house. So David
played *music* with his hand, as at other times;
but *there was* a spear in Saul's hand.
11 And Saul cast the spear, for he said, "I will
pin David to the wall!" But David escaped his
presence twice.
➤ **12** Now Saul was afraid of David, because
the LORD was with him, but had departed from
Saul.
13 Therefore Saul removed him from his
presence, and made him his captain over a
thousand; and he went out and came in before the people.
14 And David behaved wisely in all his ways,
and the LORD *was* with him.
15 Therefore, when Saul saw that he behaved
very wisely, he was afraid of him.
16 But all Israel and Judah loved David, because he went out and came in before them.

David Marries Michal

17 Then Saul said to David, "Here is my older
daughter Merab; I will give her to you as a
wife. Only be valiant for me, and fight the
LORD's battles." For Saul thought, "Let my

Life Examples:

DAVID

Competent over Time

1 SAM. 17:48–51

Often we want too much, too soon. This is often true in our desire to become highly competent. But skills take time to fully develop. We acquire wisdom over time and build character slowly.

David knew about the development of competency over time. Samuel anointed David as king of Israel fairly early in his life, probably when he was a teenager. Yet David did not automatically become king.

In the military realm, few people experienced as much success as David. Yet David slew a bear and a lion long before he encountered Goliath. God was working in David during his shepherd days, giving him experiences that would build his courage. David's faith grew as he saw the Lord's presence in his life during memorable experiences.

And so it is with our competency. The Lord works in us over time, helping us to develop and hone certain skills, in the end making us effective and successful.

See the Life Principles Index for further study:
6. You reap what you sow, more than you sow, and later than you sow.

hand not be against him, but let the hand of
the Philistines be against him."
18 So David said to Saul, "Who *am* I, and
what *is* my life *or* my father's family in Israel,
that I should be son-in-law to the king?"

LIFE LESSONS

➤ 18:1 — *Now when he had finished speaking to Saul, the soul of Jonathan was knit to the soul of David, and Jonathan loved him as his own soul.*

Jonathan recognized in David a kindred spirit, a man who loved the Lord wholeheartedly, as he did. Their close friendship blessed not only themselves, but eventually all of Israel. We need each other to move forward in faith.

➤ 18:8 — *Then Saul was very angry, and the saying displeased him; and he said, "They have ascribed to David ten thousands, and to me they have ascribed only thousands. Now what more can he have but the kingdom?"*

Instead of dwelling on the great deliverance that God had just brought about through David, Saul focused on what he considered a slight to himself. This self-focus eventually destroyed him.

➤ 18:12 — *Now Saul was afraid of David, because the LORD was with him, but had departed from Saul.*

Saul continued to fear the one he should not fear—in this case, David—because he did not fear the one he should have feared—God.

WHAT THE BIBLE SAYS ABOUT THE DEADLINESS OF ANGER

1 Sam. 18:7, 8

Few people in the Scriptures exhibited as much anger as did King Saul. Saul's anger seemed to erupt when David returned from battle and the women greeted him with this song: "Saul has slain his thousands, and David his ten thousands." The Scriptures tell us, "Saul was very angry, and the saying displeased him" (1 Sam. 18:7-8).

In his anger and jealousy, Saul:

- twice threw his spear at David, trying to pin David to the wall (1 Sam. 18:10–11; 19:9–10).
- put David in a position of authority, hoping that David would fail to lead wisely and thus be discredited (1 Sam. 18:12–15).
- required that David kill one hundred Philistines before he would give him his daughter in marriage, hoping that David would die while fighting the Philistines (1 Sam. 18:25–29).
- pursued David continually for more than a decade, forcing David to live in exile and move frequently from hiding place to hiding place (1 Sam. 24; 26).

It is far more difficult to recognize anger in ourselves.

Not only did Saul pursue David without mercy, but he ordered the murder of those who helped David. He even turned on his own son with murderous intent (see 1 Sam. 20:30). Saul's anger had no end.

It is easy to see anger at work in a person such as Saul. Violent outbursts lead to a boiling rage that manifests itself repeatedly over time. The angry person often has visible changes in physical appearance, such as dilated eyes and tense muscles. Internally, blood pressure rises, and the stomach feels tied in knots.

It is far more difficult to recognize anger in ourselves. We tend to tolerate a great deal of anger in our personal lives. Some even see anger as a sign of strength or power.

God's Word, however, forbids such an ungodly tolerance for anger. That kind of anger damages emotional health and well-being and hampers spiritual growth and witness. God closely links "wrath" with the work of the evil one in our lives. So the Scriptures admonish us clearly: "Do not let the sun go down on your wrath, nor give place to the devil" (Eph. 4:26, 27).

See the Life Principles Index for further study:
6. *You reap what you sow, more than you sow, and later than you sow.*
16. *Whatever you acquire outside of God's will eventually turns to ashes.*

19 But it happened at the time when Merab,
Saul's daughter, should have been given to
David, that she was given to Adriel the Meholathite as a wife.
20 Now Michal, Saul's daughter, loved David.
And they told Saul, and the thing pleased him.
21 So Saul said, "I will give her to him, that
she may be a snare to him, and that the hand
of the Philistines may be against him." Therefore Saul said to David a second time, "You
shall be my son-in-law today."
22 And Saul commanded his servants, "Communicate with David secretly, and say, 'Look,
the king has delight in you, and all his servants love you. Now therefore, become the
king's son-in-law.'"
23 So Saul's servants spoke those words in
the hearing of David. And David said, "Does it
seem to you *a* light *thing* to be a king's son-in-
law, seeing I *am* a poor and lightly esteemed
man?"
24 And the servants of Saul told him, saying,
"In this manner David spoke."
25 Then Saul said, "Thus you shall say to David: 'The king does not desire any dowry but
one hundred foreskins of the Philistines, to
take vengeance on the king's enemies.'" But
Saul thought to make David fall by the hand
of the Philistines.
26 So when his servants told David these
words, it pleased David well to become the
king's son-in-law. Now the days had not expired;
27 therefore David arose and went, he and
his men, and killed two hundred men of the
Philistines. And David brought their foreskins, and they gave them in full count to the
king, that he might become the king's son-in-
law. Then Saul gave him Michal his daughter
as a wife.
➤ **28** Thus Saul saw and knew that the LORD *was*
with David, and *that* Michal, Saul's daughter,
loved him;
29 and Saul was still more afraid of David. So
Saul became David's enemy continually.
30 Then the princes of the Philistines went
out *to war.* And so it was, whenever they went
out, *that* David behaved more wisely than all
the servants of Saul, so that his name became
highly esteemed.

Saul Persecutes David

19 Now Saul spoke to Jonathan his son
and to all his servants, that they should
kill David; but Jonathan, Saul's son, delighted
greatly in David.
2 So Jonathan told David, saying, "My father Saul seeks to kill you. Therefore please
be on your guard until morning, and stay in a
secret *place* and hide.
3 "And I will go out and stand beside my father in the field where you *are,* and I will
speak with my father about you. Then what I
observe, I will tell you."
4 Thus Jonathan spoke well of David to
Saul his father, and said to him, "Let not the
king sin against his servant, against David,
because he has not sinned against you, and
because his works *have been* very good toward you.
5 "For he took his life in his hands and killed
the Philistine, and the LORD brought about a
great deliverance for all Israel. You saw *it* and
rejoiced. Why then will you sin against innocent blood, to kill David without a cause?"
6 So Saul heeded the voice of Jonathan, and
Saul swore, "*As* the LORD lives, he shall not be
killed."
7 Then Jonathan called David, and Jonathan told him all these things. So Jonathan
brought David to Saul, and he was in his presence as in times past.
8 And there was war again; and David went
out and fought with the Philistines, and
struck them with a mighty blow, and they fled
from him.
9 Now the distressing spirit from the LORD
came upon Saul as he sat in his house with
his spear in his hand. And David was playing
music with *his* hand.
10 Then Saul sought to pin David to the wall
with the spear, but he slipped away from
Saul's presence; and he drove the spear into
the wall. So David fled and escaped that night.
11 Saul also sent messengers to David's house
to watch him and to kill him in the morning.
And Michal, David's wife, told him, saying, "If
you do not save your life tonight, tomorrow
you will be killed."
12 So Michal let David down through a window. And he went and fled and escaped.
13 And Michal took an image and laid *it* in
the bed, put a cover of goats' *hair* for his head,
and covered *it* with clothes.
14 So when Saul sent messengers to take David, she said, "He *is* sick."
15 Then Saul sent the messengers *back* to
see David, saying, "Bring him up to me in the
bed, that I may kill him."
16 And when the messengers had come in,
there was the image in the bed, with a cover
of goats' *hair* for his head.

LIFE LESSONS

➤ 18:28, 29 — *Thus Saul saw and knew that the LORD was with David, and that Michal, Saul's daughter, loved him; and Saul was still more afraid of David. So Saul became David's enemy continually.*

Why did Saul become David's enemy when he recognized that the Lord was with David? Because he feared for his future, and he would not trust that future to the Lord. We never win by failing to trust.

WHAT THE BIBLE SAYS ABOUT THE NEED FOR CHRISTIAN FRIENDSHIP

1 Sam. 20:42

Adversity often brings us face-to-face with our need to associate with a different set of people. Perhaps we need new friends. Perhaps we need to sever ties with others. Perhaps we need to align ourselves more closely with Christian believers.

God made us for fellowship and communication with other human beings and with Himself. None of us were designed to go it alone. We need other people, and they need us.

At times, however, we make unwise associations. We choose the wrong friend or employer or partner or employee. And inevitably, our bad choices bring us adversity.

David and Jonathan provide us with a very good model for true friendship. Jonathan's love for his friend caused him to act in several specific ways:

- He warned David of possible danger (1 Sam. 19:1–3).
- He spoke well of David, even to a person who considered David an enemy and who was angry with Jonathan for having David as a friend (1 Sam. 19:4).
- He sought to do what David needed him to do (1 Sam. 20:4).
- He risked his life in defending David (1 Sam. 20:32–33).
- He helped David to escape death (1 Sam. 20:35–41).

Friendships are divine blessings in our lives.

Jonathan voiced one of the greatest statements of friendship in the Bible when he said to David, "Go in peace, since we have both sworn in the name of the LORD, saying, 'May the LORD be between you and me, and between your descendants and my descendants, forever'" (1 Sam. 20:42). Now, *that's* friendship!

Paul describes Christian friendship in what we have come to call the love chapter of the Bible, 1 Corinthians 13. He describes Christian friendship as: patient, kind, and humble (v. 4), polite, selfless, unruffled, and positive (v. 5), magnanimous and rooted in truth (v. 6), and supportive, hopeful, and enduring (v. 7).

Such love, Paul said, never fails. And such friendships are divine blessings in our lives, God's rich rewards to us on this earth.

See the Life Principles Index for further study:
28. No Christian has ever been called to "go it alone" in his or her walk of faith.

17 Then Saul said to Michal, "Why have you deceived me like this, and sent my enemy away, so that he has escaped?" And Michal answered Saul, "He said to me, 'Let me go! Why should I kill you?'"
18 So David fled and escaped, and went to Samuel at Ramah, and told him all that Saul had done to him. And he and Samuel went and stayed in Naioth.
19 Now it was told Saul, saying, "Take note, David *is* at Naioth in Ramah!"
➤ 20 Then Saul sent messengers to take David. And when they saw the group of prophets prophesying, and Samuel standing *as* leader over them, the Spirit of God came upon the messengers of Saul, and they also prophesied.
21 And when Saul was told, he sent other messengers, and they prophesied likewise. Then Saul sent messengers again the third time, and they prophesied also.
22 Then he also went to Ramah, and came to the great well that *is* at Sechu. So he asked, and said, "Where *are* Samuel and David?" And *someone* said, "Indeed *they are* at Naioth in Ramah."
23 So he went there to Naioth in Ramah. Then the Spirit of God was upon him also, and he went on and prophesied until he came to Naioth in Ramah.
24 And he also stripped off his clothes and prophesied before Samuel in like manner, and lay down naked all that day and all that night. Therefore they say, "*Is* Saul also among the prophets?"[a]

Jonathan's Loyalty to David

20 Then David fled from Naioth in Ramah, and went and said to Jonathan, "What have I done? What *is* my iniquity, and what *is* my sin before your father, that he seeks my life?"
2 So Jonathan said to him, "By no means! You shall not die! Indeed, my father will do nothing either great or small without first telling me. And why should my father hide this thing from me? It *is* not *so!*"
3 Then David took an oath again, and said, "Your father certainly knows that I have found favor in your eyes, and he has said, 'Do not let Jonathan know this, lest he be grieved.' But truly, *as* the LORD lives and *as* your soul lives, *there is* but a step between me and death."
4 So Jonathan said to David, "Whatever you yourself desire, I will do *it* for you."
5 And David said to Jonathan, "Indeed tomorrow *is* the New Moon, and I should not fail to sit with the king to eat. But let me go, that I may hide in the field until the third *day* at evening.
6 "If your father misses me at all, then say, 'David earnestly asked *permission* of me that he might run over to Bethlehem, his city, for *there is* a yearly sacrifice there for all the family.'
7 "If he says thus: '*It is* well,' your servant will be safe. But if he is very angry, be sure that evil is determined by him.
8 "Therefore you shall deal kindly with your servant, for you have brought your servant into a covenant of the LORD with you. Nevertheless, if there is iniquity in me, kill me yourself, for why should you bring me to your father?"
9 But Jonathan said, "Far be it from you! For if I knew certainly that evil was determined by my father to come upon you, then would I not tell you?"
10 Then David said to Jonathan, "Who will tell me, or what *if* your father answers you roughly?"
11 And Jonathan said to David, "Come, let us go out into the field." So both of them went out into the field.
12 Then Jonathan said to David: "The LORD ◄
God of Israel *is witness!* When I have sounded out my father sometime tomorrow, *or* the third *day,* and indeed *there is* good toward David, and I do not send to you and tell you,
13 "may the LORD do so and much more to Jonathan. But if it pleases my father *to do* you evil, then I will report it to you and send you away, that you may go in safety. And the LORD be with you as He has been with my father.
14 "And you shall not only show me the kindness of the LORD while I still live, that I may not die;
15 "but you shall not cut off your kindness

19:24 [a]Compare 1 Samuel 10:12

LIFE LESSONS

➤ **19:20 — *Then Saul sent messengers to take David. And when they saw the group of prophets prophesying, and Samuel standing* as *leader over them, the Spirit of God came upon the messengers of Saul, and they also prophesied.***

God can protect His children in the most unorthodox of ways. He does not need weapons of war or fast horses; He can cause even our mortal enemies to act in ways contrary to their nature. He is sovereign!

➤ **20:12, 13 — *Then Jonathan said to David: "The LORD God of Israel is witness! . . . And the LORD be with you as He has been with my father."***

Jonathan cast his whole friendship with David in spiritual terms, making the Lord the centerpiece of their relationship. That is always the way to the closest and best of friendships.

from my house forever, no, not when the LORD
has cut off every one of the enemies of David
from the face of the earth."
16 So Jonathan made *a covenant* with the
house of David, *saying*, "Let the LORD require
it at the hand of David's enemies."
17 Now Jonathan again caused David to vow,
because he loved him; for he loved him as he
loved his own soul.
18 Then Jonathan said to David, "Tomorrow
is the New Moon; and you will be missed, because your seat will be empty.
19 "And *when* you have stayed three days, go
down quickly and come to the place where
you hid on the day of the deed; and remain by
the stone Ezel.
20 "Then I will shoot three arrows to the side,
as though I shot at a target;
21 "and there I will send a lad, *saying*, 'Go,
find the arrows.' If I expressly say to the lad,
'Look, the arrows *are* on this side of you; get
them and come'—then, as the LORD lives,
there is safety for you and no harm.
22 "But if I say thus to the young man, 'Look,
the arrows *are* beyond you'—go your way, for
the LORD has sent you away.
23 "And as for the matter which you and I
have spoken of, indeed the LORD *be* between
you and me forever."
24 Then David hid in the field. And when the
New Moon had come, the king sat down to
eat the feast.
25 Now the king sat on his seat, as at other
times, on a seat by the wall. And Jonathan
arose,[a] and Abner sat by Saul's side, but David's place was empty.
26 Nevertheless Saul did not say anything
that day, for he thought, "Something has happened to him; he *is* unclean, surely he *is* unclean."
27 And it happened the next day, the second
day of the month, that David's place was
empty. And Saul said to Jonathan his son,
"Why has the son of Jesse not come to eat, either yesterday or today?"
28 So Jonathan answered Saul, "David
earnestly asked *permission* of me *to go* to
Bethlehem.
29 "And he said, 'Please let me go, for our
family has a sacrifice in the city, and my
brother has commanded me *to be there*. And
now, if I have found favor in your eyes, please
let me get away and see my brothers.' Therefore he has not come to the king's table."
30 Then Saul's anger was aroused against
Jonathan, and he said to him, "You son of a
perverse, rebellious *woman!* Do I not know
that you have chosen the son of Jesse to your
own shame and to the shame of your mother's
nakedness?
31 "For as long as the son of Jesse lives on
the earth, you shall not be established, nor
your kingdom. Now therefore, send and bring
him to me, for he shall surely die."
32 And Jonathan answered Saul his father,
and said to him, "Why should he be killed?
What has he done?"
33 Then Saul cast a spear at him to kill him,
by which Jonathan knew that it was determined by his father to kill David.
34 So Jonathan arose from the table in fierce
anger, and ate no food the second day of the
month, for he was grieved for David, because
his father had treated him shamefully.
35 And so it was, in the morning, that Jonathan went out into the field at the time appointed with David, and a little lad *was* with
him.
36 Then he said to his lad, "Now run, find the
arrows which I shoot." As the lad ran, he shot
an arrow beyond him.
37 When the lad had come to the place where
the arrow was which Jonathan had shot, Jonathan cried out after the lad and said, "*Is* not
the arrow beyond you?"
38 And Jonathan cried out after the lad, "Make
haste, hurry, do not delay!" So Jonathan's lad
gathered up the arrows and came back to his
master.
39 But the lad did not know anything. Only
Jonathan and David knew of the matter.
40 Then Jonathan gave his weapons to his
lad, and said to him, "Go, carry *them* to the
city."
41 As soon as the lad had gone, David arose
from *a place* toward the south, fell on his face
to the ground, and bowed down three times.
And they kissed one another; and they wept
together, but David more so.
42 Then Jonathan said to David, "Go in
peace, since we have both sworn in the name
of the LORD, saying, 'May the LORD be between you and me, and between your descendants and my descendants, forever.'" So he
arose and departed, and Jonathan went into
the city.

David and the Holy Bread

21 Now David came to Nob, to Ahimelech
the priest. And Ahimelech was afraid
when he met David, and said to him, "Why
are you alone, and no one is with you?"
2 So David said to Ahimelech the priest,
"The king has ordered me on some business,
and said to me, 'Do not let anyone know anything about the business on which I send you,
or what I have commanded you.' And I have
directed *my* young men to such and such a
place.
3 "Now therefore, what have you on hand?
Give *me* five *loaves of* bread in my hand, or
whatever can be found."
4 And the priest answered David and said,
"*There is* no common bread on hand; but

20:25 [a]Following Masoretic Text, Syriac, Targum, and Vulgate; Septuagint reads *he sat across from Jonathan*.

there is holy bread, if the young men have at
least kept themselves from women."
5 Then David answered the priest, and said
to him, "Truly, women *have been* kept from us
about three days since I came out. And the
vessels of the young men are holy, and *the
bread is* in effect common, even though it was
consecrated in the vessel this day."
6 So the priest gave him holy *bread;* for
there was no bread there but the showbread
which had been taken from before the LORD,
in order to put hot bread *in its place* on the
day when it was taken away.
7 Now a certain man of the servants of Saul
was there that day, detained before the LORD.
And his name *was* Doeg, an Edomite, the
chief of the herdsmen who *belonged* to Saul.
8 And David said to Ahimelech, "Is there not
here on hand a spear or a sword? For I have
brought neither my sword nor my weapons
with me, because the king's business required
haste."
9 So the priest said, "The sword of Goliath
the Philistine, whom you killed in the Valley of
Elah, there it is, wrapped in a cloth behind the
ephod. If you will take that, take *it*. For *there
is* no other except that one here." And David
said, "*There is* none like it; give it to me."

David Flees to Gath

10 Then David arose and fled that day from
before Saul, and went to Achish the king of
Gath.
11 And the servants of Achish said to him, "*Is*
this not David the king of the land? Did they
not sing of him to one another in dances, saying:

'Saul has slain his thousands,
And David his ten thousands'?"[a]

12 Now David took these words to heart, and
was very much afraid of Achish the king of
Gath.
13 So he changed his behavior before them,
pretended madness in their hands, scratched
on the doors of the gate, and let his saliva fall
down on his beard.
14 Then Achish said to his servants, "Look,
you see the man is insane. Why have you
brought him to me?
15 Have I need of madmen, that you have
brought this *fellow* to play the madman in my
presence? Shall this *fellow* come into my
house?"

David's Four Hundred Men

22 David therefore departed from there
and escaped to the cave of Adullam. So
when his brothers and all his father's house
heard *it*, they went down there to him.
2 And everyone *who was* in distress, everyone who *was* in debt, and everyone *who was*
discontented gathered to him. So he became
captain over them. And there were about four
hundred men with him.
3 Then David went from there to Mizpah of
Moab; and he said to the king of Moab,
"Please let my father and mother come here
with you, till I know what God will do for me."
4 So he brought them before the king of
Moab, and they dwelt with him all the time
that David was in the stronghold.
5 Now the prophet Gad said to David, "Do
not stay in the stronghold; depart, and go to
the land of Judah." So David departed and
went into the forest of Hereth.

Saul Murders the Priests

6 When Saul heard that David and the men
who *were* with him had been discovered—now
Saul was staying in Gibeah under a tamarisk
tree in Ramah, with his spear in his hand, and
all his servants standing about him—
7 then Saul said to his servants who stood
about him, "Hear now, you Benjamites! Will
the son of Jesse give every one of you fields
and vineyards, *and* make you all captains of
thousands and captains of hundreds?
8 "All of you have conspired against me, and
there is no one who reveals to me that my son

21:11 [a]Compare 1 Samuel 18:7

LIFE LESSONS

➤ **22:2 — *And everyone who was in distress, everyone who was in debt, and everyone who was discontented gathered to him. So he became captain over them.***

David's first "army" consisted of the distressed, the debtors, and the discontented. Hardly a picture of the blessing of God! Yet God would bless David, as He had said. But David had to wait to see it.

➤ **22:3 — *Then David went from there to Mizpah of Moab; and he said to the king of Moab, "Please let my father and mother come here with you, till I know what God will do for me."***

While David had the anointing of God, he did not have a detailed map of his future. So he trusted God for what he could not do, and acted wisely in regard to the things he could do.

➤ **22:8 — *"All of you have conspired against me, and there is no one who reveals to me that my son has made a covenant with the son of Jesse; and there is not one of you who is sorry for me . . . ."***

When we turn from the Lord, life becomes "all about us." And a self-focused life plants the seeds of its own destruction.

has made a covenant with the son of Jesse;
and *there is* not one of you who is sorry for
me or reveals to me that my son has stirred up
my servant against me, to lie in wait, as *it is*
this day."
9 Then answered Doeg the Edomite, who
was set over the servants of Saul, and said, "I
saw the son of Jesse going to Nob, to Ahimelech the son of Ahitub.
10 "And he inquired of the LORD for him, gave
him provisions, and gave him the sword of
Goliath the Philistine."
11 So the king sent to call Ahimelech the
priest, the son of Ahitub, and all his father's
house, the priests who *were* in Nob. And they
all came to the king.
12 And Saul said, "Hear now, son of Ahitub!"
He answered, "Here I am, my lord."
13 Then Saul said to him, "Why have you
conspired against me, you and the son of
Jesse, in that you have given him bread and a
sword, and have inquired of God for him, that
he should rise against me, to lie in wait, as it
is this day?"
14 So Ahimelech answered the king and said,
"And who among all your servants *is as* faithful as David, who is the king's son-in-law,
who goes at your bidding, and is honorable in
your house?
15 "Did I then begin to inquire of God for
him? Far be it from me! Let not the king impute anything to his servant, *or* to any in the
house of my father. For your servant knew
nothing of all this, little or much."
16 And the king said, "You shall surely die,
Ahimelech, you and all your father's house!"
17 Then the king said to the guards who
stood about him, "Turn and kill the priests of
the LORD, because their hand also *is* with David, and because they knew when he fled and
did not tell it to me." But the servants of the
king would not lift their hands to strike the
priests of the LORD.
➤ 18 And the king said to Doeg, "You turn and
kill the priests!" So Doeg the Edomite turned
and struck the priests, and killed on that day
eighty-five men who wore a linen ephod.
19 Also Nob, the city of the priests, he struck
with the edge of the sword, both men and
women, children and nursing infants, oxen
and donkeys and sheep—with the edge of the
sword.
20 Now one of the sons of Ahimelech the son
of Ahitub, named Abiathar, escaped and fled
after David.
21 And Abiathar told David that Saul had
killed the LORD's priests.
22 So David said to Abiathar, "I knew that
day, when Doeg the Edomite *was* there, that
he would surely tell Saul. I have caused *the*
death of all the persons of your father's house.
23 "Stay with me; do not fear. For he who
seeks my life seeks your life, but with me you
shall be safe."

David Saves the City of Keilah

23 Then they told David, saying, "Look,
the Philistines are fighting against
Keilah, and they are robbing the threshing
floors."
2 Therefore David inquired of the LORD,
saying, "Shall I go and attack these Philistines?" And the LORD said to David, "Go and
attack the Philistines, and save Keilah."
3 But David's men said to him, "Look, we
are afraid here in Judah. How much more
then if we go to Keilah against the armies of
the Philistines?"
4 Then David inquired of the LORD once
again. And the LORD answered him and said,
"Arise, go down to Keilah. For I will deliver
the Philistines into your hand."
5 And David and his men went to Keilah
and fought with the Philistines, struck them
with a mighty blow, and took away their
livestock. So David saved the inhabitants of
Keilah.
6 Now it happened, when Abiathar the son
of Ahimelech fled to David at Keilah, *that* he
went down *with* an ephod in his hand.
7 And Saul was told that David had gone
to Keilah. So Saul said, "God has delivered
him into my hand, for he has shut himself
in by entering a town that has gates and
bars."
8 Then Saul called all the people together
for war, to go down to Keilah to besiege David and his men.
9 When David knew that Saul plotted evil
against him, he said to Abiathar the priest,
"Bring the ephod here."
10 Then David said, "O LORD God of Israel,
Your servant has certainly heard that Saul
seeks to come to Keilah to destroy the city for
my sake.
11 "Will the men of Keilah deliver me into his
hand? Will Saul come down, as Your servant
has heard? O LORD God of Israel, I pray, tell
Your servant." And the LORD said, "He will
come down."

LIFE LESSONS

➤ 22:18 — *And the king said to Doeg, "You turn and kill the priests!" So Doeg the Edomite turned and struck the priests, and killed on that day eighty-five men who wore a linen ephod.*

God never hides the fact that there may be a high price to pay for doing what is right. But He also promises to reward us for doing what is good (Eph. 6:8), even if that reward comes in heaven.

12 Then David said, "Will the men of Keilah deliver me and my men into the hand of Saul?" And the LORD said, "They will deliver *you.*"
➤ 13 So David and his men, about six hundred, arose and departed from Keilah and went wherever they could go. Then it was told Saul that David had escaped from Keilah; so he halted the expedition.

David in Wilderness Strongholds

14 And David stayed in strongholds in the wilderness, and remained in the mountains in the Wilderness of Ziph. Saul sought him every day, but God did not deliver him into his hand.
15 So David saw that Saul had come out to seek his life. And David *was* in the Wilderness of Ziph in a forest.[a]
➤ 16 Then Jonathan, Saul's son, arose and went to David in the woods and strengthened his hand in God.
17 And he said to him, "Do not fear, for the hand of Saul my father shall not find you. You shall be king over Israel, and I shall be next to you. Even my father Saul knows that."
18 So the two of them made a covenant before the LORD. And David stayed in the woods, and Jonathan went to his own house.
19 Then the Ziphites came up to Saul at Gibeah, saying, "Is David not hiding with us in strongholds in the woods, in the hill of Hachilah, which *is* on the south of Jeshimon?
20 "Now therefore, O king, come down according to all the desire of your soul to come down; and our part *shall be* to deliver him into the king's hand."
➤ 21 And Saul said, "Blessed *are* you of the LORD, for you have compassion on me.
22 "Please go and find out for sure, and see the place where his hideout is, *and* who has seen him there. For I am told he is very crafty.
23 "See therefore, and take knowledge of all the lurking places where he hides; and come back to me with certainty, and I will go with you. And it shall be, if he is in the land, that I will search for him throughout all the clans[a] of Judah."
24 So they arose and went to Ziph before Saul. But David and his men *were* in the Wilderness of Maon, in the plain on the south of Jeshimon.
25 When Saul and his men went to seek *him,* they told David. Therefore he went down to the rock, and stayed in the Wilderness of Maon. And when Saul heard *that,* he pursued David in the Wilderness of Maon.
26 Then Saul went on one side of the mountain, and David and his men on the other side of the mountain. So David made haste to get away from Saul, for Saul and his men were encircling David and his men to take them.
27 But a messenger came to Saul, saying, "Hurry and come, for the Philistines have invaded the land!" ➤
28 Therefore Saul returned from pursuing David, and went against the Philistines; so they called that place the Rock of Escape.[a]
29 Then David went up from there and dwelt in strongholds at En Gedi.

David Spares Saul

24 Now it happened, when Saul had returned from following the Philistines, that it was told him, saying, "Take note! David *is* in the Wilderness of En Gedi."
2 Then Saul took three thousand chosen men from all Israel, and went to seek David and his men on the Rocks of the Wild Goats.
3 So he came to the sheepfolds by the road, where there *was* a cave; and Saul went in to attend to his needs. (David and his men were staying in the recesses of the cave.)
4 Then the men of David said to him, "This

23:15 [a]Or *in Horesh* **23:23** [a]Literally *thousands* **23:28** [a]Hebrew *Sela Hammahlekoth*

LIFE LESSONS

➤ 23:13 — *So David and his men, about six hundred, arose and departed from Keilah and went wherever they could go. Then it was told Saul that David had escaped from Keilah; so he halted the expedition.*

Abiathar came to David only because of a tragedy, but God used him to guide David and keep him safe. The Lord will move heaven and earth, if necessary, to show us His will.

➤ 23:16 — *Then Jonathan, Saul's son, arose and went to David in the woods and strengthened his hand in God.*

We all need friends who will "strengthen our hands in God," to encourage us in our faith and give us the help and support we need to continue. None of us is in this alone.

➤ 23:21 — *And Saul said, "Blessed are you of the LORD, for you have compassion on me."*

Anyone can use religious verbiage and try to appear deeply spiritual by the phrases he uses. But God is not impressed, and neither should we be. Nor should we be fooled (2 Cor. 11:14, 15).

➤ 23:27 — *But a messenger came to Saul, saying, "Hasten and come, for the Philistines have invaded the land!"*

During this time in Israel's history, the Philistines were the primary oppressors and enemies of God's people. But in His sovereignty, God used even them to rescue His servant David. So he can do for us.

is the day of which the LORD said to you, 'Behold, I will deliver your enemy into your hand, that you may do to him as it seems good to you.'" And David arose and secretly cut off a corner of Saul's robe.
5 Now it happened afterward that David's heart troubled him because he had cut Saul's robe.
➤6 And he said to his men, "The LORD forbid that I should do this thing to my master, the LORD's anointed, to stretch out my hand against him, seeing he *is* the anointed of the LORD."
7 So David restrained his servants with *these* words, and did not allow them to rise against Saul. And Saul got up from the cave and went on *his* way.
8 David also arose afterward, went out of the cave, and called out to Saul, saying, "My lord the king!" And when Saul looked behind him, David stooped with his face to the earth, and bowed down.
9 And David said to Saul: "Why do you listen to the words of men who say, 'Indeed David seeks your harm'?
10 "Look, this day your eyes have seen that the LORD delivered you today into my hand in the cave, and *someone* urged *me* to kill you. But *my eye* spared you, and I said, 'I will not stretch out my hand against my lord, for he *is* the LORD's anointed.'
11 "Moreover, my father, see! Yes, see the corner of your robe in my hand! For in that I cut off the corner of your robe, and did not kill you, know and see that *there is* neither evil nor rebellion in my hand, and I have not sinned against you. Yet you hunt my life to take it.
➤12 "Let the LORD judge between you and me, and let the LORD avenge me on you. But my hand shall not be against you.
13 "As the proverb of the ancients says, 'Wickedness proceeds from the wicked.' But my hand shall not be against you.
14 "After whom has the king of Israel come out? Whom do you pursue? A dead dog? A flea?
15 "Therefore let the LORD be judge, and judge between you and me, and see and plead my case, and deliver me out of your hand."
16 So it was, when David had finished speaking these words to Saul, that Saul said, "*Is* this your voice, my son David?" And Saul lifted up his voice and wept.
17 Then he said to David: "You *are* more righteous than I; for you have rewarded me with good, whereas I have rewarded you with evil.
18 "And you have shown this day how you have dealt well with me; for when the LORD delivered me into your hand, you did not kill me.
19 "For if a man finds his enemy, will he let him get away safely? Therefore may the LORD reward you with good for what you have done to me this day.
20 "And now I know indeed that you shall surely be king, and that the kingdom of Israel shall be established in your hand.
21 "Therefore swear now to me by the LORD that you will not cut off my descendants after me, and that you will not destroy my name from my father's house."
22 So David swore to Saul. And Saul went home, but David and his men went up to the stronghold.

Death of Samuel

25 Then Samuel died; and the Israelites gathered together and lamented for him, and buried him at his home in Ramah. And David arose and went down to the Wilderness of Paran.[a]

David and the Wife of Nabal

2 Now *there was* a man in Maon whose business *was* in Carmel, and the man *was* very rich. He had three thousand sheep and a thousand goats. And he was shearing his sheep in Carmel.
3 The name of the man *was* Nabal, and the name of his wife Abigail. And *she was* a woman of good understanding and beautiful appearance; but the man *was* harsh and evil in *his* doings. He *was of the house of* Caleb.
4 When David heard in the wilderness that Nabal was shearing his sheep,
5 David sent ten young men; and David said

25:1 [a]Following Masoretic Text, Syriac, Targum, and Vulgate; Septuagint reads *Maon*.

LIFE LESSONS

➤ 24:6 — *And he said to his men, "The LORD forbid that I should do this thing to my master, the LORD's anointed, to stretch out my hand against him, seeing he is the anointed of the LORD."*

David knew that God's blessing had left Saul. He knew that he would become king. Yet because God had anointed Saul, David refused to lay a hand on him. David honored the Lord by sparing Saul's life.

➤ 24:12 — *"Let the LORD judge between you and me, and let the LORD avenge me on you. But my hand shall not be against you."*

David would not usurp God's place. If Saul needed to be removed as king to make way for David, then God would have to do it. Even if urged by his friends, David would not strike the Lord's anointed.

to the young men, "Go up to Carmel, go to Nabal, and greet him in my name.

6 "And thus you shall say to him who lives *in prosperity:* 'Peace *be* to you, peace to your house, and peace to all that you have!

7 'Now I have heard that you have shearers. Your shepherds were with us, and we did not hurt them, nor was there anything missing from them all the while they were in Carmel.

8 'Ask your young men, and they will tell you. Therefore let *my* young men find favor in your eyes, for we come on a feast day. Please give whatever comes to your hand to your servants and to your son David.' "

9 So when David's young men came, they spoke to Nabal according to all these words in the name of David, and waited.

10 Then Nabal answered David's servants, and said, "Who *is* David, and who *is* the son of Jesse? There are many servants nowadays who break away each one from his master.

11 "Shall I then take my bread and my water and my meat that I have killed for my shearers, and give *it* to men when I do not know where they *are* from?"

12 So David's young men turned on their heels and went back; and they came and told him all these words.

13 Then David said to his men, "Every man gird on his sword." So every man girded on his sword, and David also girded on his sword. And about four hundred men went with David, and two hundred stayed with the supplies.

14 Now one of the young men told Abigail, Nabal's wife, saying, "Look, David sent messengers from the wilderness to greet our master; and he reviled them.

15 "But the men *were* very good to us, and we were not hurt, nor did we miss anything as long as we accompanied them, when we were in the fields.

16 "They were a wall to us both by night and day, all the time we were with them keeping the sheep.

17 "Now therefore, know and consider what you will do, for harm is determined against our master and against all his household. For he *is such* a scoundrel[a] that *one* cannot speak to him."

18 Then Abigail made haste and took two hundred *loaves* of bread, two skins of wine, five sheep already dressed, five seahs of roasted *grain,* one hundred clusters of raisins, and two hundred cakes of figs, and loaded *them* on donkeys.

19 And she said to her servants, "Go on before me; see, I am coming after you." But she did not tell her husband Nabal.

20 So it was, *as* she rode on the donkey, that she went down under cover of the hill; and there were David and his men, coming down toward her, and she met them.

21 Now David had said, "Surely in vain I have protected all that this *fellow* has in the wilderness, so that nothing was missed of all that *belongs* to him. And he has repaid me evil for good.

22 "May God do so, and more also, to the enemies of David, if I leave one male of all who *belong* to him by morning light."

23 Now when Abigail saw David, she dismounted quickly from the donkey, fell on her face before David, and bowed down to the ground.

24 So she fell at his feet and said: "On me, my lord, *on* me *let* this iniquity *be!* And please let your maidservant speak in your ears, and hear the words of your maidservant.

25 "Please, let not my lord regard this scoundrel Nabal. For as his name *is,* so *is* he: Nabal[a] *is* his name, and folly *is* with him! But I, your maidservant, did not see the young men of my lord whom you sent.

26 "Now therefore, my lord, *as* the LORD lives and *as* your soul lives, since the LORD has held you back from coming to bloodshed and from avenging yourself with your own hand, now then, let your enemies and those who seek harm for my lord be as Nabal.

27 "And now this present which your maidservant has brought to my lord, let it be given to the young men who follow my lord.

28 "Please forgive the trespass of your maidservant. For the LORD will certainly make for my lord an enduring house, because my lord fights the battles of the LORD, and evil is not found in you throughout your days.

29 "Yet a man has risen to pursue you and seek your life, but the life of my lord shall be bound in the bundle of the living with the LORD your God; and the lives of your enemies He shall sling out, *as from* the pocket of a sling.

30 "And it shall come to pass, when the LORD has done for my lord according to all the good that He has spoken concerning you, and has appointed you ruler over Israel,

31 "that this will be no grief to you, nor

25:17 [a]Literally *son of Belial* **25:25** [a]Literally *Fool*

LIFE LESSONS

➤ **25:21 — *Now David had said, "Surely in vain I have protected all that this fellow has in the wilderness, so that nothing was missed of all that belongs to him. And he has repaid me evil for good."***

Sometimes we doubt whether it benefits us at all to do good. But the Word tells us, "let us not grow weary while doing good, for in due season we shall reap if we do not lose heart" (Gal. 6:9).

offense of heart to my lord, either that you
have shed blood without cause, or that my
lord has avenged himself. But when the LORD
has dealt well with my lord, then remember
your maidservant."
32 Then David said to Abigail: "Blessed *is* the
LORD God of Israel, who sent you this day to
meet me!
33 "And blessed *is* your advice and blessed
are you, because you have kept me this day
from coming to bloodshed and from avenging
myself with my own hand.
➤ 34 "For indeed, *as* the LORD God of Israel
lives, who has kept me back from hurting
you, unless you had hurried and come to meet
me, surely by morning light no males would
have been left to Nabal!"
35 So David received from her hand what she
had brought him, and said to her, "Go up in
peace to your house. See, I have heeded your
voice and respected your person."
36 Now Abigail went to Nabal, and there he
was, holding a feast in his house, like the feast
of a king. And Nabal's heart *was* merry within
him, for he *was* very drunk; therefore she told
him nothing, little or much, until morning
light.
37 So it was, in the morning, when the wine
had gone from Nabal, and his wife had told
him these things, that his heart died within
him, and he became *like* a stone.
38 Then it happened, *after* about ten days,
that the LORD struck Nabal, and he died.
39 So when David heard that Nabal was
dead, he said, "Blessed *be* the LORD, who has
pleaded the cause of my reproach from the
hand of Nabal, and has kept His servant from
evil! For the LORD has returned the wickedness of Nabal on his own head." And David
sent and proposed to Abigail, to take her as
his wife.
40 When the servants of David had come to
Abigail at Carmel, they spoke to her saying,
"David sent us to you, to ask you to become
his wife."
41 Then she arose, bowed her face to the
earth, and said, "Here is your maidservant, a
servant to wash the feet of the servants of my
lord."
42 So Abigail rose in haste and rode on a
donkey, attended by five of her maidens; and
she followed the messengers of David, and
became his wife.
43 David also took Ahinoam of Jezreel, and
so both of them were his wives.
44 But Saul had given Michal his daughter,
David's wife, to Palti[a] the son of Laish, who
was from Gallim.

David Spares Saul a Second Time

26 Now the Ziphites came to Saul at
Gibeah, saying, "Is David not hiding in
the hill of Hachilah, opposite Jeshimon?"
2 Then Saul arose and went down to the
Wilderness of Ziph, having three thousand
chosen men of Israel with him, to seek David
in the Wilderness of Ziph.
3 And Saul encamped in the hill of Hachilah, which *is* opposite Jeshimon, by the road.
But David stayed in the wilderness, and he
saw that Saul came after him into the wilderness.
4 David therefore sent out spies, and understood that Saul had indeed come.
5 So David arose and came to the place
where Saul had encamped. And David saw the
place where Saul lay, and Abner the son of
Ner, the commander of his army. Now Saul lay
within the camp, with the people encamped all
around him.
6 Then David answered, and said to Ahimelech the Hittite and to Abishai the son of
Zeruiah, brother of Joab, saying, "Who will
go down with me to Saul in the camp?" And
Abishai said, "I will go down with you."
7 So David and Abishai came to the people
by night; and there Saul lay sleeping within
the camp, with his spear stuck in the ground
by his head. And Abner and the people lay all
around him.
8 Then Abishai said to David, "God has delivered your enemy into your hand this day.
Now therefore, please, let me strike him at
once with the spear, right to the earth; and I
will not *have to strike* him a second time!"
9 But David said to Abishai, "Do not destroy
him; for who can stretch out his hand against
the LORD's anointed, and be guiltless?"
10 David said furthermore, "*As* the LORD ➤
lives, the LORD shall strike him, or his day

25:44 [a]Spelled *Paltiel* in 2 Samuel 3:15

LIFE LESSONS

➤ 25:34 — *"For indeed, as the LORD God of Israel lives, who has kept me back from hurting you, unless you had hurried and come to meet me, surely by morning light no males would have been left to Nabal!"*

It was Abigail's quick thinking and wise actions that kept David from annihilating all the males in Nabal's family, but David rightly saw it as the Lord keeping him from bloodshed. Our sovereign Lord works in many ways!

➤ 26:10 — *David said furthermore, "As the LORD lives, the LORD shall strike him, or his day shall come to die, or he shall go out to battle and perish."*

Once more David refused to kill Saul when he had the chance. David's aide saw the opportunity as a divine blessing, but David saw it is a test. He would wait for God to act in His own time.

shall come to die, or he shall go out to battle
and perish.
11 "The LORD forbid that I should stretch out
my hand against the LORD's anointed. But
please, take now the spear and the jug of
water that *are* by his head, and let us go."
12 So David took the spear and the jug of
water *by* Saul's head, and they got away; and
no man saw or knew *it* or awoke. For they
were all asleep, because a deep sleep from the
LORD had fallen on them.
13 Now David went over to the other side,
and stood on the top of a hill afar off, a great
distance *being* between them.
14 And David called out to the people and to
Abner the son of Ner, saying, "Do you not
answer, Abner?" Then Abner answered
and said, "Who *are* you, calling out to the
king?"
15 So David said to Abner, "*Are* you not a
man? And who *is* like you in Israel? Why then
have you not guarded your lord the king? For
one of the people came in to destroy your lord
the king.
16 "This thing that you have done *is* not good.
As the LORD lives, you deserve to die, because
you have not guarded your master, the LORD's
anointed. And now see where the king's spear
is, and the jug of water that *was* by his head."
17 Then Saul knew David's voice, and said,
"*Is* that your voice, my son David?" David
said, "*It is* my voice, my lord, O king."
18 And he said, "Why does my lord thus pursue his servant? For what have I done, or what
evil *is* in my hand?
19 "Now therefore, please, let my lord the
king hear the words of his servant: If the
LORD has stirred you up against me, let Him
accept an offering. But if *it is* the children of
men, *may* they *be* cursed before the LORD, for
they have driven me out this day from sharing
in the inheritance of the LORD, saying, 'Go,
serve other gods.'
20 "So now, do not let my blood fall to the
earth before the face of the LORD. For the king
of Israel has come out to seek a flea, as when
one hunts a partridge in the mountains."
➤ **21** Then Saul said, "I have sinned. Return, my
son David. For I will harm you no more, because my life was precious in your eyes this
day. Indeed I have played the fool and erred
exceedingly."
22 And David answered and said, "Here is
the king's spear. Let one of the young men
come over and get it.
23 "May the LORD repay every man *for* his
righteousness and his faithfulness; for the
LORD delivered you into *my* hand today, but I
would not stretch out my hand against the
LORD's anointed.
24 "And indeed, as your life was valued much
this day in my eyes, so let my life be valued
much in the eyes of the LORD, and let Him deliver me out of all tribulation."
25 Then Saul said to David, "*May* you *be*
blessed, my son David! You shall both do
great things and also still prevail." So David
went on his way, and Saul returned to his
place.

David Allied with the Philistines

27 And David said in his heart, "Now I
shall perish someday by the hand of
Saul. *There is* nothing better for me than that
I should speedily escape to the land of the
Philistines; and Saul will despair of me, to
seek me anymore in any part of Israel. So I
shall escape out of his hand."
2 Then David arose and went over with the
six hundred men who *were* with him to
Achish the son of Maoch, king of Gath.
3 So David dwelt with Achish at Gath, he
and his men, each man with his household,
and David with his two wives, Ahinoam the
Jezreelitess, and Abigail the Carmelitess,
Nabal's widow.
4 And it was told Saul that David had fled to
Gath; so he sought him no more.
5 Then David said to Achish, "If I have now
found favor in your eyes, let them give me a
place in some town in the country, that I may
dwell there. For why should your servant
dwell in the royal city with you?"
6 So Achish gave him Ziklag that day.
Therefore Ziklag has belonged to the kings of
Judah to this day.
7 Now the time that David dwelt in the
country of the Philistines was one full year
and four months.
8 And David and his men went up and
raided the Geshurites, the Girzites,[a] and the
Amalekites. For those *nations* were the inhabitants of the land from of old, as you go to
Shur, even as far as the land of Egypt.
9 Whenever David attacked the land, he left
neither man nor woman alive, but took away
the sheep, the oxen, the donkeys, the camels,
and the apparel, and returned and came to
Achish.
10 Then Achish would say, "Where have you

27:8 [a]Or *Gezrites*

LIFE LESSONS

➤ **26:21 — *Then Saul said, "I have sinned. Return, my son David. For I will harm you no more, because my life was precious in your eyes this day. Indeed I have played the fool and erred exceedingly."***

It is one thing to know that you have acted foolishly and made a grave mistake; it is another to repent of the foolishness and the error. Saul did the first, but not the latter. God calls us to do both.

made a raid today?" And David would say, "Against the southern *area* of Judah, or against the southern *area* of the Jerahmeelites, or against the southern *area* of the Kenites."
11 David would save neither man nor woman alive, to bring *news* to Gath, saying, "Lest they should inform on us, saying, 'Thus David did.'" And thus *was* his behavior all the time he dwelt in the country of the Philistines.
12 So Achish believed David, saying, "He has made his people Israel utterly abhor him; therefore he will be my servant forever."

28 Now it happened in those days that the Philistines gathered their armies together for war, to fight with Israel. And Achish said to David, "You assuredly know that you will go out with me to battle, you and your men."
2 So David said to Achish, "Surely you know what your servant can do." And Achish said to David, "Therefore I will make you one of my chief guardians forever."

Saul Consults a Medium

3 Now Samuel had died, and all Israel had lamented for him and buried him in Ramah, in his own city. And Saul had put the mediums and the spiritists out of the land.
4 Then the Philistines gathered together, and came and encamped at Shunem. So Saul gathered all Israel together, and they encamped at Gilboa.
➤ 5 When Saul saw the army of the Philistines, he was afraid, and his heart trembled greatly.
6 And when Saul inquired of the LORD, the LORD did not answer him, either by dreams or by Urim or by the prophets.
7 Then Saul said to his servants, "Find me a woman who is a medium, that I may go to her and inquire of her." And his servants said to him, "In fact, *there is* a woman who is a medium at En Dor."
8 So Saul disguised himself and put on other clothes, and he went, and two men with him; and they came to the woman by night. And he said, "Please conduct a séance for me, and bring up for me the one I shall name to you."
9 Then the woman said to him, "Look, you know what Saul has done, how he has cut off the mediums and the spiritists from the land. Why then do you lay a snare for my life, to cause me to die?"
10 And Saul swore to her by the LORD, saying, "*As* the LORD lives, no punishment shall come upon you for this thing." ➤
11 Then the woman said, "Whom shall I bring up for you?" And he said, "Bring up Samuel for me."
12 When the woman saw Samuel, she cried out with a loud voice. And the woman spoke to Saul, saying, "Why have you deceived me? For you *are* Saul!"
13 And the king said to her, "Do not be afraid. What did you see?" And the woman said to Saul, "I saw a spirit[a] ascending out of the earth."
14 So he said to her, "What *is* his form?" And she said, "An old man is coming up, and he *is* covered with a mantle." And Saul perceived that it *was* Samuel, and he stooped with *his* face to the ground and bowed down.
15 Now Samuel said to Saul, "Why have you disturbed me by bringing me up?" And Saul answered, "I am deeply distressed; for the Philistines make war against me, and God has departed from me and does not answer me anymore, neither by prophets nor by dreams. Therefore I have called you, that you may reveal to me what I should do."
16 Then Samuel said: "So why do you ask me, seeing the LORD has departed from you and has become your enemy?
17 "And the LORD has done for Himself[a] as He spoke by me. For the LORD has torn the kingdom out of your hand and given it to your neighbor, David.
18 "Because you did not obey the voice of the LORD nor execute His fierce wrath upon Amalek, therefore the LORD has done this thing to you this day.
19 "Moreover the LORD will also deliver Israel with you into the hand of the Philistines. And tomorrow you and your sons *will be* with ➤

28:13 [a]Hebrew *elohim* **28:17** [a]Or *him,* that is, David

LIFE LESSONS

➤ **28:5, 7 — *When Saul saw the army of the Philistines, he was afraid . . . . Then Saul said to his servants, "Find me a woman who is a medium . . . ."***

Once more Saul allows his fear to spur him on to a foolish and wicked choice. If we do not deal with our fear by bringing it to the Lord, it will eventually crush us.

➤ **28:10 — *And Saul swore to her by the LORD, saying, "As the LORD lives, no punishment shall come upon you for this thing."***

By this point in the story, Saul is an absolute mess spiritually. He even swears by the Lord not to do what the Lord has commanded (Lev. 20:27)! Outward professions of faith will never substitute for genuine, obedient faith.

➤ **28:19 — *"Moreover the LORD will also deliver Israel with you into the hand of the Philistines. And tomorrow you and your sons will be with me . . . ."***

Samuel had not mellowed, even in death. He still proclaimed the same uncompromising message that he delivered while alive—and God still fulfilled his words. His Word is a rock on which we can build our entire lives.

me. The LORD will also deliver the army of Israel into the hand of the Philistines."
20 Immediately Saul fell full length on the ground, and was dreadfully afraid because of the words of Samuel. And there was no strength in him, for he had eaten no food all day or all night.
21 And the woman came to Saul and saw that he was severely troubled, and said to him, "Look, your maidservant has obeyed your voice, and I have put my life in my hands and heeded the words which you spoke to me.
22 "Now therefore, please, heed also the voice of your maidservant, and let me set a piece of bread before you; and eat, that you may have strength when you go on *your* way."
23 But he refused and said, "I will not eat." So his servants, together with the woman, urged him; and he heeded their voice. Then he arose from the ground and sat on the bed.
24 Now the woman had a fatted calf in the house, and she hastened to kill it. And she took flour and kneaded *it,* and baked unleavened bread from it.
25 So she brought *it* before Saul and his servants, and they ate. Then they rose and went away that night.

The Philistines Reject David

29 Then the Philistines gathered together all their armies at Aphek, and the Israelites encamped by a fountain which *is* in Jezreel.
2 And the lords of the Philistines passed in review by hundreds and by thousands, but David and his men passed in review at the rear with Achish.
3 Then the princes of the Philistines said, "What *are* these Hebrews *doing here?*" And Achish said to the princes of the Philistines, "*Is* this not David, the servant of Saul king of Israel, who has been with me these days, or these years? And to this day I have found no fault in him since he defected *to me.*"
4 But the princes of the Philistines were angry with him; so the princes of the Philistines said to him, "Make this fellow return, that he may go back to the place which you have appointed for him, and do not let him go down with us to battle, lest in the battle he become our adversary. For with what could he reconcile himself to his master, if not with the heads of these men?
5 "*Is* this not David, of whom they sang to one another in dances, saying:
'Saul has slain his thousands,
And David his ten thousands'?"[a]
6 Then Achish called David and said to him, "Surely, *as* the LORD lives, you have been upright, and your going out and your coming in with me in the army *is* good in my sight. For to this day I have not found evil in you since the day of your coming to me. Nevertheless the lords do not favor you.
7 "Therefore return now, and go in peace, that you may not displease the lords of the Philistines."
8 So David said to Achish, "But what have I done? And to this day what have you found in your servant as long as I have been with you, that I may not go and fight against the enemies of my lord the king?"
9 Then Achish answered and said to David, "I know that you *are* as good in my sight as an angel of God; nevertheless the princes of the Philistines have said, 'He shall not go up with us to the battle.'
10 "Now therefore, rise early in the morning with your master's servants who have come with you.[a] And as soon as you are up early in the morning and have light, depart."
11 So David and his men rose early to depart in the morning, to return to the land of the Philistines. And the Philistines went up to Jezreel.

David's Conflict with the Amalekites

30 Now it happened, when David and his men came to Ziklag, on the third day, that the Amalekites had invaded the South and Ziklag, attacked Ziklag and burned it with fire,
2 and had taken captive the women and those who *were* there, from small to great; they did not kill anyone, but carried *them* away and went their way.
3 So David and his men came to the city, and there it was, burned with fire; and their wives, their sons, and their daughters had been taken captive.
4 Then David and the people who *were* with him lifted up their voices and wept, until they had no more power to weep.
5 And David's two wives, Ahinoam the

29:5 [a]Compare 1 Samuel 18:7 **29:10** [a]Following Masoretic Text, Targum, and Vulgate; Septuagint adds *and go to the place which I have selected for you there; and set no bothersome word in your heart, for you are good before me. And rise on your way.*

LIFE LESSONS

➤ 30:1, 2 — . . . *the Amalekites had invaded the South and Ziklag, attacked Ziklag and burned it with fire, and had taken captive the women and those who were there, from small to great . . . .*

The blessing and anointing of the Lord does not exempt a person from hardship and tragedy. Yet the Lord is at work even through tragedy, and He asks us to trust Him even in the hard times.

LIFE PRINCIPLE 7

THE DARK MOMENTS OF OUR LIFE WILL LAST ONLY SO LONG AS IS NECESSARY FOR GOD TO ACCOMPLISH HIS PURPOSE IN US.

1 SAM. 30:1–6

If you want God's best for your life and desire to be used by Him, at some point you will have to travel the road of adversity. This means that God's purpose for adversity cannot be bad—and yet, sadly, many people allow adversity to become a major point of setback and defeat. You don't have to be among them!

God has designed adversity, regardless of its source, to become a turning point from which you take your greatest leaps forward in spiritual growth. He allows adversity to remain in your life only until it has enabled Him to accomplish His purpose in you. He will not keep it in your life one second longer than is necessary.

Some people are almost wiped out by trials, while others learn to stand in the confidence of God's faithfulness. The latter have an overwhelming sense of stability and immovable strength. They weather the storm, head held high, confident, bold, not repressing anything. They feel absolutely certain that their God is going to see them through the heartache and bring them out whole and joyful and more mature on the other side.

Adversity also shows us where we stand in our faith. Do we doubt God? Do we thank Him for His faithfulness in the stormy, heart-wrenching times? Can we trust Him when He says He will never leave or forsake us? Adversity is God's most accurate barometer for faith. It also reveals our endurance level. None of us knows how much physical or emotional pain we can withstand.

Right now, right where you are, remember this: *God has put a limit on all adversity.* Because you are a child of God, the Holy Spirit is living inside of you. He knows how much you can bear. You can endure the suffering and hardship to the limit God has given, as the psalmist said: "Many are the afflictions of the righteous; but the LORD delivers him out of them all" (Ps. 34:19). And, "As a father pities his children, so the LORD pities those who fear Him. For He knows our frame; He remembers that we are dust" (Ps. 103:13, 14).

Adversity shows us where we stand in our faith.

When we learn and mature in the midst of tremendous adversity, God is pleased because He sees His purpose being fulfilled in us. We are growing spiritually, becoming stronger in areas of weakness, and increasingly being conformed to the likeness of Christ. God is thrilled when we respond correctly to adversity!

I believe God weaves three principle threads into all adversity:

1. Adversity is God's choice tool for building godly, spiritual character into our lives. Until we experience heartache, disappointment, and pain, we are not properly equipped for service. He uses adversity to mold and shape us; He does not bring it into our lives without purpose.

2. Adversity usually comes in the areas where we feel the most confident. God wants to break us of the idea that we are sufficient on our own. He made us for a loving, dependant relationship with Himself, and He uses adversity to remind us of the fact.

God allows adversity to mold and shape you.

3. God's ultimate design is to conform you to the likeness of Jesus. He has something definite in mind. God allows adversity to mold and shape you, but He uses it only so long as it is needed. Once it has performed its function, He takes it away.

What do you think God has in mind when He allows adversity to invade your life? I believe God wants to accomplish several goals in your life and mine by allowing suffering and heartache into our experience. Adversity . . .

- *gets our attention*
- *delivers us from pride*
- *reveals our weaknesses and strengths*
- *increases our hatred of sin*
- *demonstrates the faithfulness of God*
- *strengthens our faith*
- *removes pride and self-centeredness*
- *prepares us for future service*
- *enables us to comfort others facing adversity*

Through adversity, He is molding you into a mature child of God. Whenever God sees you, He sees a saint—sometimes struggling, sometimes falling, but justified, redeemed, forgiven, and reconciled to Him. He sees a saint full of His unconditional love, indwelt by His presence, sealed by the Holy Spirit of promise, whose name is written in the Lamb's Book of Life. He sees you on your way to heaven, with purpose and direction in your life. He sees someone in whom adversity can never take up permanent residence.

See the Life Principles Index for further study.

Jezreelitess, and Abigail the widow of Nabal
the Carmelite, had been taken captive.
6 Now David was greatly distressed, for the
people spoke of stoning him, because the soul
of all the people was grieved, every man for
his sons and his daughters. But David
strengthened himself in the LORD his God.
7 Then David said to Abiathar the priest,
Ahimelech's son, "Please bring the ephod
here to me." And Abiathar brought the ephod
to David.
8 So David inquired of the LORD, saying,
"Shall I pursue this troop? Shall I overtake
them?" And He answered him, "Pursue, for
you shall surely overtake *them* and without
fail recover *all*."
9 So David went, he and the six hundred
men who *were* with him, and came to the
Brook Besor, where those stayed who were
left behind.
10 But David pursued, he and four hundred
men; for two hundred stayed *behind*, who
were so weary that they could not cross the
Brook Besor.
11 Then they found an Egyptian in the field,
and brought him to David; and they gave him
bread and he ate, and they let him drink
water.
12 And they gave him a piece of a cake of figs
and two clusters of raisins. So when he had
eaten, his strength came back to him; for he
had eaten no bread nor drunk water for three
days and three nights.
13 Then David said to him, "To whom do you
belong, and where *are* you from?" And he
said, "I *am* a young man from Egypt, servant
of an Amalekite; and my master left me behind, because three days ago I fell sick.
14 "We made an invasion of the southern
area of the Cherethites, in the *territory* which
belongs to Judah, and of the southern *area* of
Caleb; and we burned Ziklag with fire."
15 And David said to him, "Can you take me
down to this troop?" So he said, "Swear to me
by God that you will neither kill me nor deliver me into the hands of my master, and I
will take you down to this troop."
16 And when he had brought him down, there
they were, spread out over all the land, eating
and drinking and dancing, because of all the
great spoil which they had taken from the land
of the Philistines and from the land of Judah.
17 Then David attacked them from twilight
until the evening of the next day. Not a man of
them escaped, except four hundred young
men who rode on camels and fled.
18 So David recovered all that the Amalekites had carried away, and David rescued his
two wives.
19 And nothing of theirs was lacking, either
small or great, sons or daughters, spoil or
anything which they had taken from them;
David recovered all.
20 Then David took all the flocks and herds
they had driven before those *other* livestock,
and said, "This *is* David's spoil."
21 Now David came to the two hundred men
who had been so weary that they could not
follow David, whom they also had made to
stay at the Brook Besor. So they went out to
meet David and to meet the people who *were*
with him. And when David came near the
people, he greeted them.
22 Then all the wicked and worthless men[a] of
those who went with David answered and
said, "Because they did not go with us, we will
not give them *any* of the spoil that we have
recovered, except for every man's wife and
children, that they may lead *them* away and
depart."
23 But David said, "My brethren, you shall
not do so with what the LORD has given us,
who has preserved us and delivered into our
hand the troop that came against us.
24 "For who will heed you in this matter? But
as his part *is* who goes down to the battle, so
shall his part *be* who stays by the supplies;
they shall share alike."
25 So it was, from that day forward; he made
it a statute and an ordinance for Israel to this
day.

30:22 [a]Literally *men of Belial*

LIFE LESSONS

➤ 30:6 — . . . *But David strengthened himself in the LORD his God.*

In a previous hard time, Jonathan, David's friend, had encouraged him in his faith (1 Sam. 23:16). But in his friend's absence, David chose to strengthen himself in God. We must encourage each other so that we can strengthen ourselves.

➤ 30:20 — *Then David took all the flocks and herds they had driven before those other livestock, and said, "This is David's spoil."*

As He had done with Joseph centuries before, God took a personal tragedy for David and turned it into a personal blessing. Obedience always brings blessing, even in dark and puzzling times.

➤ 30:22 — *Then all the wicked and worthless men of those who went with David answered and said, "Because they did not go with us, we will not give them any of the spoil that we have recovered . . . ."*

Even after times of victory, "the wicked and the worthless" can raise their complaints. God allows the wheat and the tares to grow together (Matt. 13:24–30), and we must be ready for this—and make sure we're the wheat.

26 Now when David came to Ziklag, he sent
some of the spoil to the elders of Judah, to his
friends, saying, "Here is a present for you
from the spoil of the enemies of the LORD"—
27 to *those* who *were* in Bethel, *those* who
were in Ramoth of the South, *those* who *were*
in Jattir,
28 *those* who *were* in Aroer, *those* who *were*
in Siphmoth, *those* who *were* in Eshtemoa,
29 *those* who *were* in Rachal, *those* who
were in the cities of the Jerahmeelites, *those*
who *were* in the cities of the Kenites,
30 *those* who *were* in Hormah, *those* who
were in Chorashan,[a] *those* who *were* in
Athach,
31 *those* who *were* in Hebron, and to all the
places where David himself and his men were
accustomed to rove.

The Tragic End of Saul and His Sons

31 Now the Philistines fought against
Israel; and the men of Israel fled from
before the Philistines, and fell slain on Mount
Gilboa.
➤ 2 Then the Philistines followed hard after
Saul and his sons. And the Philistines killed
Jonathan, Abinadab, and Malchishua, Saul's
sons.
3 The battle became fierce against Saul. The
archers hit him, and he was severely wounded
by the archers.
4 Then Saul said to his armorbearer, "Draw
your sword, and thrust me through with it,
lest these uncircumcised men come and
thrust me through and abuse me." But his armorbearer would not, for he was greatly
afraid. Therefore Saul took a sword and fell
on it.
5 And when his armorbearer saw that Saul
was dead, he also fell on his sword, and died
with him.
6 So Saul, his three sons, his armorbearer,
and all his men died together that same day.
7 And when the men of Israel who were on
the other side of the valley, and *those* who
were on the other side of the Jordan, saw that
the men of Israel had fled and that Saul and
his sons were dead, they forsook the cities
and fled; and the Philistines came and dwe
in them.
8 So it happened the next day, when the Phi
listines came to strip the slain, that they found
Saul and his three sons fallen on Moun
Gilboa.
9 And they cut off his head and stripped off
his armor, and sent *word* throughout the lan
of the Philistines, to proclaim *it in* the templ
of their idols and among the people.
10 Then they put his armor in the temple
the Ashtoreths, and they fastened his body
the wall of Beth Shan.[a]
11 Now when the inhabitants of Jabe
Gilead heard what the Philistines had done
Saul,
12 all the valiant men arose and traveled
night, and took the body of Saul and the bo
ies of his sons from the wall of Beth Sha
and they came to Jabesh and burned the
there.
13 Then they took their bones and buri
them under the tamarisk tree at Jabesh, an
fasted seven days.

30:30 [a]Or *Borashan* **31:10** [a]Spelled *Beth Shean* in Joshua 17:1
and elsewhere

LIFE LESSONS

➤ 31:2 — *Then the Philistines followed hard after Saul and his sons. And the Philistines killed Jonathan, Abinadab, and Malchishua, Saul's sons.*

Jonathan loved God and delighted in his close friend, David—and yet the Lord allowed the Philistines to kill him. Why? We could speculate, but God does not tell us why. Even in tragedy, our job is to trust.

➤ 31:9 — *And they cut off his head and stripped off his armor, and sent word throughout the land of the Philistines, to proclaim it in the temple of their idols and among the people.*

God sometimes allows His enemies to triumph and even to celebrate and believe that they have overcome Him . . . but only for a while. God takes the long view of history, and always triumphs in the end.

THE SECOND BOOK OF

SAMUEL

After many long years of preparation, David finally assumed the throne as Israel's king. God had taken David through many battles. Now it was time for David to take his rightful place as God's chosen leader of God's chosen people.

The Book of 2 Samuel records the highlights of King David's reign, first over the territory of Judah, and finally over the entire nation of Israel. It traces the ascension of David to the throne, his ugly sins of adultery and murder, and the shattering consequences of those sins upon his family and the nation.

Second Samuel paints a picture of a man who loved God deeply, a leader of God's own choosing who became Israel's greatest king, a warrior who fought and won many battles on behalf of his God and his people. David truly was a hero of the faith—but he was far from perfect. Second Samuel also tells the story of David's fall into sin, his repentance, and his restoration. David, the warrior king, could often be drawn aside by his passions.

Still, David never lost his desire to know and please God. He became mighty in spirit because he never wavered in his love for God. David grew close to the Lord because of his heart's desire to spend time alone with the Lord. This is where spiritual greatness is born—in the presence of God.

Second Samuel teaches us that God isn't looking for perfect people to serve Him, but rather for those who have a heart of love and commitment for Him and who will willingly present themselves and all their flaws and imperfections to Him for service.

Themes: God will sovereignly act to bring about His own perfect will. Despite much opposition and several brushes with death, David ascended to the throne in God's way and in God's timing. Second Samuel also shows us that we never get away with sin and that it always has consequences. At the same time, we see that God loves to forgive and restore us.

Author: Unknown

Time: David became King of Judah around 1010 B.C. and over all of Israel around 1004 B.C. His reign lasted 40 years.

Structure: Second Samuel can be divided into four parts: David's ascension to the throne and his early reign (chapters 1–9); his great military conquests (chapter 10); his falling into sin and the resulting consequences (chapters 11–19); and the last years of his reign (chapters 20–24).

As you read 2 Samuel, watch for several life principles that play an important role in this book:

10. If necessary, God will move heaven and earth to show us His will. *See 2 Samuel 2:1; page 356.*

23. You can never outgive God. *See 2 Samuel 7:1–17; page 361.*

6. You reap what you sow, more than you sow, and later than you sow. *See 2 Samuel 12:7–12; page 369.*

16. Whatever you acquire outside of God's will eventually turns to ashes. *See 2 Samuel 15:13, 14; page 373.*

8. Fight all your battles on your knees and you win every time. *See 2 Samuel 15:31; page 374.*

The Report of Saul's Death

1 Now it came to pass after the death of
Saul, when David had returned from the
slaughter of the Amalekites, and David had
stayed two days in Ziklag,
2 on the third day, behold, it happened that
a man came from Saul's camp with his
clothes torn and dust on his head. So it was,
when he came to David, that he fell to the
ground and prostrated himself.
3 And David said to him, "Where have you
come from?" So he said to him, "I have escaped from the camp of Israel."
4 Then David said to him, "How did the matter go? Please tell me." And he answered,
"The people have fled from the battle, many
of the people are fallen and dead, and Saul
and Jonathan his son are dead also."
5 So David said to the young man who told
him, "How do you know that Saul and Jonathan his son are dead?"
6 Then the young man who told him said,
"As I happened by chance *to be* on Mount
Gilboa, there was Saul, leaning on his spear;
and indeed the chariots and horsemen followed hard after him.
7 "Now when he looked behind him, he saw
me and called to me. And I answered, 'Here I
am.'
8 "And he said to me, 'Who *are* you?' So I
answered him, 'I *am* an Amalekite.'
9 "He said to me again, 'Please stand over
me and kill me, for anguish has come upon
me, but my life still *remains* in me.'
10 "So I stood over him and killed him,
because I was sure that he could not live after
he had fallen. And I took the crown that
was on his head and the bracelet that *was* on
his arm, and have brought them here to my
lord."
11 Therefore David took hold of his own
clothes and tore them, and *so did* all the men
who *were* with him.
12 And they mourned and wept and fasted
until evening for Saul and for Jonathan his
son, for the people of the LORD and for the
house of Israel, because they had fallen by the
sword.
13 Then David said to the young man who
told him, "Where *are* you from?" And he answered, "I *am* the son of an alien, an Amalekite."
14 So David said to him, "How was it you
were not afraid to put forth your hand to destroy the LORD's anointed?"
15 Then David called one of the young men
and said, "Go near, *and* execute him!" And he
struck him so that he died.
16 So David said to him, "Your blood is on ➤
your own head, for your own mouth has testified against you, saying, 'I have killed the
LORD's anointed.'"

The Song of the Bow

17 Then David lamented with this lamenta
tion over Saul and over Jonathan his son,
18 and he told *them* to teach the children of
Judah *the Song of* the Bow; indeed *it is* written in the Book of Jasher:

19 "The beauty of Israel is slain on your high
places!
How the mighty have fallen!
20 Tell *it* not in Gath,
Proclaim *it* not in the streets of
Ashkelon—
Lest the daughters of the Philistines
rejoice,
Lest the daughters of the uncircumcised
triumph.

21 "O mountains of Gilboa,
Let there be no dew nor rain upon you,
Nor fields of offerings.
For the shield of the mighty is cast away
there!
The shield of Saul, not anointed with oil
22 From the blood of the slain,
From the fat of the mighty,
The bow of Jonathan did not turn back,
And the sword of Saul did not return
empty.

23 "Saul and Jonathan *were* beloved and
pleasant in their lives,
And in their death they were not divided
They were swifter than eagles,
They were stronger than lions.

24 "O daughters of Israel, weep over Saul,
Who clothed you in scarlet, with luxury;
Who put ornaments of gold on your ap-
parel.

25 "How the mighty have fallen in the midst
of the battle!
Jonathan *was* slain in your high places.

LIFE LESSONS

➤ **1:16 — *So David said to him, "Your blood is on your own head, for your own mouth has testified against you, saying, 'I have killed the LORD's anointed.'"***

Hoping for a reward (2 Sam. 4:10), the Amalekite lied about his role in Saul's death; but he had just stripped the dead king of some personal effects. David rewarded him with death, since no man had the right to kill the Lord's anointed.

➤ 26 I am distressed for you, my brother
Jonathan;
You have been very pleasant to me;
Your love to me was wonderful,
Surpassing the love of women.

27 "How the mighty have fallen,
And the weapons of war perished!"

David Anointed King of Judah

2 It happened after this that David inquired
of the LORD, saying, "Shall I go up to any
of the cities of Judah?" And the LORD said to
him, "Go up." David said, "Where shall I go
up?" And He said, "To Hebron."
2 So David went up there, and his two wives
also, Ahinoam the Jezreelitess, and Abigail
the widow of Nabal the Carmelite.
3 And David brought up the men who *were*
with him, every man with his household. So
they dwelt in the cities of Hebron.
4 Then the men of Judah came, and there
they anointed David king over the house of
Judah. And they told David, saying, "The men
of Jabesh Gilead *were the ones* who buried
Saul."
5 So David sent messengers to the men of
Jabesh Gilead, and said to them, "You *are*
blessed of the LORD, for you have shown this
kindness to your lord, to Saul, and have
buried him.
6 "And now may the LORD show kindness
and truth to you. I also will repay you this
kindness, because you have done this thing.
7 "Now therefore, let your hands be
strengthened, and be valiant; for your master
Saul is dead, and also the house of Judah has
anointed me king over them."

Ishbosheth Made King of Israel

8 But Abner the son of Ner, commander of
Saul's army, took Ishbosheth[a] the son of Saul
and brought him over to Mahanaim;
9 and he made him king over Gilead, over
the Ashurites, over Jezreel, over Ephraim,
over Benjamin, and over all Israel.
10 Ishbosheth, Saul's son, *was* forty years old ➤
when he began to reign over Israel, and he
reigned two years. Only the house of Judah
followed David.
11 And the time that David was king in Hebron
over the house of Judah was seven years
and six months.

Israel and Judah at War

12 Now Abner the son of Ner, and the servants
of Ishbosheth the son of Saul, went out
from Mahanaim to Gibeon.
13 And Joab the son of Zeruiah, and the servants
of David, went out and met them by the
pool of Gibeon. So they sat down, one on one
side of the pool and the other on the other
side of the pool.
14 Then Abner said to Joab, "Let the young
men now arise and compete before us." And
Joab said, "Let them arise."
15 So they arose and went over by number,
twelve from Benjamin, *followers* of Ishbosheth
the son of Saul, and twelve from the servants
of David.
16 And each one grasped his opponent by the
head and *thrust* his sword in his opponent's
side; so they fell down together. Therefore
that place was called the Field of Sharp
Swords,[a] which *is* in Gibeon.
17 So there was a very fierce battle that day,
and Abner and the men of Israel were beaten
before the servants of David.
18 Now the three sons of Zeruiah were there:
Joab and Abishai and Asahel. And Asahel
was as fleet of foot as a wild gazelle.
19 So Asahel pursued Abner, and in going he
did not turn to the right hand or to the left
from following Abner.
20 Then Abner looked behind him and said,
"*Are* you Asahel?" He answered, "I *am*."
21 And Abner said to him, "Turn aside to
your right hand or to your left, and lay hold
on one of the young men and take his armor

2:8 [a]Called *Esh-Baal* in 1 Chronicles 8:33 and 9:39
2:16 [a]Hebrew *Helkath Hazzurim*

LIFE LESSONS

➤ 1:26 — *"I am distressed for you, my brother Jonathan; you have been very pleasant to me; your love to me was wonderful, surpassing the love of women."*

David honored Saul in his lament, but he celebrated Jonathan, his dear friend. David became what he was at least in part because of Jonathan. Friends play an important role in shaping our spiritual destinies.

➤ 2:1 — *. . . David inquired of the LORD, saying, "Shall I go up to any of the cities of Judah?" And the LORD said to him, "Go up." David said, "Where shall I go up?" And He said, "To Hebron."*

David asked God for His leading even in the matter of where he should live. Listening to God is essential to walking with God.

➤ 2:10 — *Ishbosheth, Saul's son, was forty years old when he began to reign over Israel, and he reigned two years. Only the house of Judah followed David.*

Abner, not God, made Saul's son king over Israel. The arrangement lasted for two years, but in the end, it brought the nation nothing but heartache. Whatever we acquire outside of God's will eventually turns to ashes.

for yourself." But Asahel would not turn aside from following him.

22 So Abner said again to Asahel, "Turn aside from following me. Why should I strike you to the ground? How then could I face your brother Joab?"

23 However, he refused to turn aside. Therefore Abner struck him in the stomach with the blunt end of the spear, so that the spear came out of his back; and he fell down there and died on the spot. So it was *that* as many as came to the place where Asahel fell down and died, stood still.

24 Joab and Abishai also pursued Abner. And the sun was going down when they came to the hill of Ammah, which *is* before Giah by the road to the Wilderness of Gibeon.

25 Now the children of Benjamin gathered together behind Abner and became a unit, and took their stand on top of a hill.

26 Then Abner called to Joab and said, "Shall the sword devour forever? Do you not know that it will be bitter in the latter end? How long will it be then until you tell the people to return from pursuing their brethren?"

27 And Joab said, "*As* God lives, unless you had spoken, surely then by morning all the people would have given up pursuing their brethren."

28 So Joab blew a trumpet; and all the people stood still and did not pursue Israel anymore, nor did they fight anymore.

29 Then Abner and his men went on all that night through the plain, crossed over the Jordan, and went through all Bithron; and they came to Mahanaim.

30 So Joab returned from pursuing Abner. And when he had gathered all the people together, there were missing of David's servants nineteen men and Asahel.

31 But the servants of David had struck down, of Benjamin and Abner's men, three hundred and sixty men who died.

32 Then they took up Asahel and buried him in his father's tomb, which *was in* Bethlehem. And Joab and his men went all night, and they came to Hebron at daybreak.

➤ **3** Now there was a long war between the house of Saul and the house of David. But David grew stronger and stronger, and the house of Saul grew weaker and weaker.

Sons of David

2 Sons were born to David in Hebron: His firstborn was Amnon by Ahinoam the Jezreelitess;

3 his second, Chileab, by Abigail the widow of Nabal the Carmelite; the third, Absalom the son of Maacah, the daughter of Talmai, king of Geshur;

4 the fourth, Adonijah the son of Haggith; the fifth, Shephatiah the son of Abital;

5 and the sixth, Ithream, by David's wife Eglah. These were born to David in Hebron.

Abner Joins Forces with David

6 Now it was so, while there was war between the house of Saul and the house of David, that Abner was strengthening *his hold* on the house of Saul.

7 And Saul had a concubine, whose name *was* Rizpah, the daughter of Aiah. So *Ishbosheth* said to Abner, "Why have you gone in to my father's concubine?"

8 Then Abner became very angry at the words of Ishbosheth, and said, "*Am* I a dog's head that belongs to Judah? Today I show loyalty to the house of Saul your father, to his brothers, and to his friends, and have not delivered you into the hand of David; and you charge me today with a fault concerning this woman?

9 "May God do so to Abner, and more also, if I do not do for David as the LORD has sworn to him—

10 "to transfer the kingdom from the house of Saul, and set up the throne of David over Israel and over Judah, from Dan to Beersheba."

11 And he could not answer Abner another word, because he feared him.

12 Then Abner sent messengers on his behalf to David, saying, "Whose *is* the land?" saying *also*, "Make your covenant with me, and indeed my hand *shall be* with you to bring all Israel to you."

13 And *David* said, "Good, I will make a covenant with you. But one thing I require of you: you shall not see my face unless you first bring Michal, Saul's daughter, when you come to see my face."

14 So David sent messengers to Ishbosheth, Saul's son, saying, "Give *me* my wife Michal, whom I betrothed to myself for a hundred foreskins of the Philistines."

LIFE LESSONS

➤ 3:1 — *Now there was a long war between the house of Saul and the house of David. But David grew stronger and stronger, and the house of Saul grew weaker and weaker.*

God had given the kingdom to David, but it took a long time for him to finally bring the nation together under his rule. Yet what God promises, He delivers—even if it takes longer than we had expected.

➤ 3:9 — *"May God do so to Abner, and more also, if I do not do for David as the LORD has sworn to him . . . ."*

Abner knew of the promise God had made to David, yet until this point he had acted against that promise. Why? Apparently, to give himself a better position. But anything you hold too tightly, you will lose.

15 And Ishbosheth sent and took her from her husband, from Paltiel[a] the son of Laish.

16 Then her husband went along with her to Bahurim, weeping behind her. So Abner said to him, "Go, return!" And he returned.

17 Now Abner had communicated with the elders of Israel, saying, "In time past you were seeking for David *to be* king over you.

18 "Now then, do *it!* For the LORD has spoken of David, saying, 'By the hand of My servant David, I[a] will save My people Israel from the hand of the Philistines and the hand of all their enemies.'"

19 And Abner also spoke in the hearing of Benjamin. Then Abner also went to speak in the hearing of David in Hebron all that seemed good to Israel and the whole house of Benjamin.

20 So Abner and twenty men with him came to David at Hebron. And David made a feast for Abner and the men who *were* with him.

21 Then Abner said to David, "I will arise and go, and gather all Israel to my lord the king, that they may make a covenant with you, and that you may reign over all that your heart desires." So David sent Abner away, and he went in peace.

Joab Murders Abner

22 At that moment the servants of David and Joab came from a raid and brought much spoil with them. But Abner *was* not with David in Hebron, for he had sent him away, and he had gone in peace.

23 When Joab and all the troops that *were* with him had come, they told Joab, saying, "Abner the son of Ner came to the king, and he sent him away, and he has gone in peace."

24 Then Joab came to the king and said, "What have you done? Look, Abner came to you; why *is* it *that* you sent him away, and he has already gone?

25 "Surely you realize that Abner the son of Ner came to deceive you, to know your going out and your coming in, and to know all that you are doing."

26 And when Joab had gone from David's presence, he sent messengers after Abner, who brought him back from the well of Sirah. But David did not know *it.*

27 Now when Abner had returned to Hebron, Joab took him aside in the gate to speak with him privately, and there stabbed him in the stomach, so that he died for the blood of Asahel his brother.

28 Afterward, when David heard *it,* he said, "My kingdom and I *are* guiltless before the LORD forever of the blood of Abner the son of Ner.

29 "Let it rest on the head of Joab and on all his father's house; and let there never fail to be in the house of Joab one who has a discharge or is a leper, who leans on a staff or falls by the sword, or who lacks bread."

30 So Joab and Abishai his brother killed Abner, because he had killed their brother Asahel at Gibeon in the battle.

David's Mourning for Abner

31 Then David said to Joab and to all the people who were with him, "Tear your clothes, gird yourselves with sackcloth, and mourn for Abner." And King David followed the coffin.

32 So they buried Abner in Hebron; and the king lifted up his voice and wept at the grave of Abner, and all the people wept.

33 And the king sang *a lament* over Abner and said:

"Should Abner die as a fool dies?
34 Your hands were not bound
Nor your feet put into fetters;
As a man falls before wicked men, *so* you
fell."

Then all the people wept over him again.

35 And when all the people came to persuade David to eat food while it was still day, David took an oath, saying, "God do so to me, and more also, if I taste bread or anything else till the sun goes down!"

36 Now all the people took note *of it,* and it pleased them, since whatever the king did pleased all the people.

37 For all the people and all Israel understood that day that it had not been the king's *intent* to kill Abner the son of Ner.

38 Then the king said to his servants, "Do you not know that a prince and a great man has fallen this day in Israel?

39 "And I *am* weak today, though anointed king; and these men, the sons of Zeruiah, *are* too harsh for me. The LORD shall repay the evildoer according to his wickedness."

Ishbosheth Is Murdered

4 When Saul's son[a] heard that Abner had died in Hebron, he lost heart, and all Israel was troubled.

3:15 [a]Spelled *Palti* in 1 Samuel 25:44 **3:18** [a]Following many Hebrew manuscripts, Septuagint, Syriac, and Targum; Masoretic Text reads *he.* **4:1** [a]That is, Ishbosheth

LIFE LESSONS

➤ 3:37 — *For all the people and all Israel understood that day that it had not been the king's intent to kill Abner the son of Ner.*

David not only declared his innocence in the death of Abner, he acted wisely to back up his words. When our words and our actions match, everyone benefits.

2 Now Saul's son *had* two men *who were* captains of troops. The name of one *was* Baanah and the name of the other Rechab, the sons of Rimmon the Beerothite, of the children of Benjamin. (For Beeroth also was *part* of Benjamin,

3 because the Beerothites fled to Gittaim and have been sojourners there until this day.)

4 Jonathan, Saul's son, had a son *who was* lame in *his* feet. He was five years old when the news about Saul and Jonathan came from Jezreel; and his nurse took him up and fled. And it happened, as she made haste to flee, that he fell and became lame. His name *was* Mephibosheth.[a]

5 Then the sons of Rimmon the Beerothite, Rechab and Baanah, set out and came at about the heat of the day to the house of Ishbosheth, who was lying on his bed at noon.

6 And they came there, all the way into the house, *as though* to get wheat, and they stabbed him in the stomach. Then Rechab and Baanah his brother escaped.

7 For when they came into the house, he was lying on his bed in his bedroom; then they struck him and killed him, beheaded him and took his head, and were all night escaping through the plain.

➤ 8 And they brought the head of Ishbosheth to David at Hebron, and said to the king, "Here is the head of Ishbosheth, the son of Saul your enemy, who sought your life; and the LORD has avenged my lord the king this day of Saul and his descendants."

➤ **9** But David answered Rechab and Baanah his brother, the sons of Rimmon the Beerothite, and said to them, "As the LORD lives, who has redeemed my life from all adversity,

10 "when someone told me, saying, 'Look, Saul is dead,' thinking to have brought good news, I arrested him and had him executed in Ziklag—the one who *thought* I would give him a reward for *his* news.

11 "How much more, when wicked men have killed a righteous person in his own house on his bed? Therefore, shall I not now require his blood at your hand and remove you from the earth?"

12 So David commanded his young men, and they executed them, cut off their hands and feet, and hanged *them* by the pool in Hebron. But they took the head of Ishbosheth and buried *it* in the tomb of Abner in Hebron.

David Reigns over All Israel

5 Then all the tribes of Israel came to David at Hebron and spoke, saying, "Indeed we *are* your bone and your flesh.

2 "Also, in time past, when Saul was king over us, you were the one who led Israel out and brought them in; and the LORD said to you, 'You shall shepherd My people Israel, and be ruler over Israel.'"

3 Therefore all the elders of Israel came to the king at Hebron, and King David made a covenant with them at Hebron before the LORD. And they anointed David king over Israel.

4 David *was* thirty years old when he began to reign, *and* he reigned forty years.

5 In Hebron he reigned over Judah seven years and six months, and in Jerusalem he reigned thirty-three years over all Israel and Judah.

The Conquest of Jerusalem

6 And the king and his men went to Jerusalem against the Jebusites, the inhabitants of the land, who spoke to David, saying, "You shall not come in here; but the blind and the lame will repel you," thinking, "David cannot come in here."

7 Nevertheless David took the stronghold of Zion (that *is,* the City of David).

8 Now David said on that day, "Whoever climbs up by way of the water shaft and defeats the Jebusites (the lame and the blind, *who are* hated by David's soul), *he shall be chief and captain.*"[a] Therefore they say, "The blind and the lame shall not come into the house."

9 Then David dwelt in the stronghold, and called it the City of David. And David built all around from the Millo[a] and inward.

10 So David went on and became great, and the LORD God of hosts *was* with him. ➤

11 Then Hiram king of Tyre sent messengers to David, and cedar trees, and carpenters and masons. And they built David a house.

4:4 [a]Called *Merib-Baal* in 1 Chronicles 8:34 and 9:40
5:8 [a]Compare 1 Chronicles 11:6 **5:9** [a]Literally *The Landfill*

LIFE LESSONS

➤ ***4:8 — And they brought the head of Ishbosheth to David at Hebron . . . .***

David was not impressed by spiritual words when he saw evil deeds. As a man after God's own heart, he could not delight in wickedness, even if it appeared to benefit him.

➤ ***4:9 — "As the LORD lives, who has redeemed my life from all adversity . . . ."***

The Lord loves to "redeem our lives from all adversity." David realized that adversity is a setback from which we take our greatest leaps forward.

➤ ***5:10 — So David went on and became great, and the LORD God of hosts was with him.***

When we follow the Lord wholeheartedly as David did, we too will enjoy the presence of the Lord. And just as He did with David, He can cause us to advance and even to become great.

12 So David knew that the LORD had established him as king over Israel, and that He
had exalted His kingdom for the sake of His
people Israel.
13 And David took more concubines and
wives from Jerusalem, after he had come
from Hebron. Also more sons and daughters
were born to David.
14 Now these *are* the names of those who
were born to him in Jerusalem: Shammua,[a]
Shobab, Nathan, Solomon,
15 Ibhar, Elishua,[a] Nepheg, Japhia,
16 Elishama, Eliada, and Eliphelet.

The Philistines Defeated

17 Now when the Philistines heard that they
had anointed David king over Israel, all the
Philistines went up to search for David. And
David heard *of it* and went down to the stronghold.
18 The Philistines also went and deployed
themselves in the Valley of Rephaim.
➤ 19 So David inquired of the LORD, saying,
"Shall I go up against the Philistines? Will You
deliver them into my hand?" And the LORD
said to David, "Go up, for I will doubtless deliver the Philistines into your hand."
20 So David went to Baal Perazim, and David
defeated them there; and he said, "The LORD
has broken through my enemies before me,
like a breakthrough of water." Therefore he
called the name of that place Baal Perazim.[a]
21 And they left their images there, and David and his men carried them away.
22 Then the Philistines went up once again
and deployed themselves in the Valley of
Rephaim.
➤ 23 Therefore David inquired of the LORD, and
He said, "You shall not go up; circle around
behind them, and come upon them in front of
the mulberry trees.
24 "And it shall be, when you hear the sound
of marching in the tops of the mulberry trees,
then you shall advance quickly. For then the
LORD will go out before you to strike the camp
of the Philistines."
25 And David did so, as the LORD commanded him; and he drove back the Philistines from Geba[a] as far as Gezer.

The Ark Brought to Jerusalem

6 Again David gathered all *the* choice *men*
of Israel, thirty thousand.
2 And David arose and went with all the
people who *were* with him from Baale Judah
to bring up from there the ark of God, whose
name is called by the Name,[a] the LORD of
Hosts, who dwells *between* the cherubim.
3 So they set the ark of God on a new cart, ➤
and brought it out of the house of Abinadab,
which *was* on the hill; and Uzzah and Ahio,
the sons of Abinadab, drove the new cart.[a]
4 And they brought it out of the house of
Abinadab, which *was* on the hill, accompanying the ark of God; and Ahio went before
the ark.
5 Then David and all the house of Israel
played *music* before the LORD on all kinds of
instruments of fir wood, on harps, on stringed
instruments, on tambourines, on sistrums,
and on cymbals.
6 And when they came to Nachon's threshing floor, Uzzah put out *his hand* to the ark of
God and took hold of it, for the oxen stumbled.
7 Then the anger of the LORD was aroused
against Uzzah, and God struck him there for
his error; and he died there by the ark of God.
8 And David became angry because of the
LORD's outbreak against Uzzah; and he called
the name of the place Perez Uzzah[a] to this
day.
9 David was afraid of the LORD that day; and ➤
he said, "How can the ark of the LORD come to
me?"

5:14 [a]Spelled *Shimea* in 1 Chronicles 3:6 **5:15** [a]Spelled *Elishama* in 1 Chronicles 3:6 **5:20** [a]Literally *Master of Breakthroughs* **5:25** [a]Following Masoretic Text, Targum, and Vulgate; Septuagint reads *Gibeon*. **6:2** [a]Septuagint, Targum, and Vulgate omit *by the Name;* many Hebrew manuscripts and Syriac read *there*. **6:3** [a]Septuagint adds *with the ark*. **6:8** [a]Literally *Outburst Against Uzzah*

LIFE LESSONS

➤ 5:19 — *So David inquired of the LORD, saying, "Shall I go up against the Philistines? Will You deliver them into my hand?" And the LORD said to David, "Go up, for I will doubtless deliver the Philistines into your hand."*

As long as David asked for the Lord's guidance, he enjoyed success. When he stopped listening for the Lord's voice, he landed in trouble. The same is true for us.

➤ 5:23 — *Therefore David inquired of the LORD, and He said, "You shall not go up; circle around behind them, and come upon them in front of the mulberry trees."*

The Lord gives His people different strategies for success at different times. We dare not push forward out of habit, or rely on our own wisdom. Listening to God is essential to walking with God.

➤ 6:3 — *So they set the ark of God on a new cart, and brought it out of the house of Abinadab, which was on the hill; and Uzzah and Ahio, the sons of Abinadab, drove the new cart.*

David failed to consult the Word of God before he moved the ark; if he had, he would have learned the specific way God instructed His people to transport it (Ex. 25:12–14). God never blesses disobedience.

➤ 6:9 — *David was afraid of the LORD that day . . . .*

David, the man after God's own heart, learned a hard lesson about the infinite holiness of God and the necessity of obeying His words completely. God is our Friend, but He never ceases to be Lord.

10 So David would not move the ark of the LORD with him into the City of David; but David took it aside into the house of Obed-Edom the Gittite.
11 The ark of the LORD remained in the house of Obed-Edom the Gittite three months. And the LORD blessed Obed-Edom and all his household.
12 Now it was told King David, saying, "The LORD has blessed the house of Obed-Edom and all that *belongs* to him, because of the ark of God." So David went and brought up the ark of God from the house of Obed-Edom to the City of David with gladness.
➤ 13 And so it was, when those bearing the ark of the LORD had gone six paces, that he sacrificed oxen and fatted sheep.
14 Then David danced before the LORD with all *his* might; and David *was* wearing a linen ephod.
15 So David and all the house of Israel brought up the ark of the LORD with shouting and with the sound of the trumpet.
16 Now as the ark of the LORD came into the City of David, Michal, Saul's daughter, looked through a window and saw King David leaping and whirling before the LORD; and she despised him in her heart.
17 So they brought the ark of the LORD, and set it in its place in the midst of the tabernacle that David had erected for it. Then David offered burnt offerings and peace offerings before the LORD.
18 And when David had finished offering burnt offerings and peace offerings, he blessed the people in the name of the LORD of hosts.
19 Then he distributed among all the people, among the whole multitude of Israel, both the women and the men, to everyone a loaf of bread, a piece *of meat,* and a cake of raisins. So all the people departed, everyone to his house.
20 Then David returned to bless his household. And Michal the daughter of Saul came out to meet David, and said, "How glorious was the king of Israel today, uncovering himself today in the eyes of the maids of his servants, as one of the base fellows shamelessly uncovers himself!"
21 So David said to Michal, "*It was* before the LORD, who chose me instead of your father and all his house, to appoint me ruler over the people of the LORD, over Israel. Therefore I will play *music* before the LORD.
22 "And I will be even more undignified than this, and will be humble in my own sight. But as for the maidservants of whom you have spoken, by them I will be held in honor."
23 Therefore Michal the daughter of Saul had no children to the day of her death.

God's Covenant with David

7 Now it came to pass when the king was dwelling in his house, and the LORD had given him rest from all his enemies all around,
2 that the king said to Nathan the prophet, "See now, I dwell in a house of cedar, but the ark of God dwells inside tent curtains."
3 Then Nathan said to the king, "Go, do all that *is* in your heart, for the LORD *is* with you."
4 But it happened that night that the word of the LORD came to Nathan, saying,
5 "Go and tell My servant David, 'Thus says the LORD: "Would you build a house for Me to dwell in?
6 "For I have not dwelt in a house since the time that I brought the children of Israel up from Egypt, even to this day, but have moved about in a tent and in a tabernacle.
7 "Wherever I have moved about with all the children of Israel, have I ever spoken a word to anyone from the tribes of Israel, whom I commanded to shepherd My people Israel, saying, 'Why have you not built Me a house of cedar?'"'
8 "Now therefore, thus shall you say to My servant David, 'Thus says the LORD of hosts: "I took you from the sheepfold, from following the sheep, to be ruler over My people, over Israel.
9 "And I have been with you wherever you have gone, and have cut off all your enemies from before you, and have made you a great name, like the name of the great men who *are* on the earth.
10 "Moreover I will appoint a place for My people Israel, and will plant them, that they may dwell in a place of their own and move no more; nor shall the sons of wickedness oppress them anymore, as previously,

LIFE LESSONS

➤ 6:13 — *And so it was, when those bearing the ark of the LORD had gone six paces, that he sacrificed oxen and fatted sheep.*

David learned from his costly error and this time moved the ark in the prescribed way. Gladness resulted, for obedience always brings blessing.

➤ 6:22 — *"And I will be even more undignified than this, and will be humble in my own sight . . . ."*

David did not care if anyone thought him undignified because of the unbridled way he demonstrated his love for God. David accomplished as much as he did because he gave himself unreservedly to God.

➤ 7:8 — *"I took you from the sheepfold, from following the sheep, to be ruler over My people, over Israel."*

When we begin to enjoy some success, we would do well to remind ourselves of where we came from and how we arrived at our place of blessing. It is all God's doing.

ANSWERS TO LIFE'S QUESTIONS

What does it mean to "sit before the Lord"?

2 SAM. 7:18

Perhaps the greatest key to spiritual growth is spending time alone with the Lord. This means taking the time to speak with God about whatever is on your heart—and, even more importantly, allowing Him to speak to you.

King David has been called a "man after God's own heart." To win that kind of reputation, David first needed to know the mind and heart of God so that he might be and do what the Lord desired of him. David sought to know God. He frequently "inquired" of the Lord. He spent time in the Lord's presence, singing to the Lord from the depths of his heart. In 2 Samuel 7:18 we read, "Then King David went in and sat before the LORD; and said, 'Who am I, O Lord GOD? And what is my house, that You have brought me this far?'"

What did it mean for David to "sit" before the Lord? It means that he spent time alone in the presence of the Lord, communicating with the Lord from the depths of his heart, asking questions of God, and listening quietly before the Lord for the Lord's answers.

Jesus frequently sought time apart with His heavenly Father. Time with the Father provided Him with a source of comfort and strength. Jesus also sought time alone with His disciples so that He might teach them and they might find spiritual refreshment (see Luke 9:10).

We are wise if we choose to spend time alone with God, in a place without distractions or interruptions, for a period sufficient for us to relax completely and focus our attention fully upon the Lord and His Word. We must be willing to wait in the Lord's presence until we receive God's directives or His words of comfort.

Why don't many of us desire to spend time alone with God? The foremost reason is that we don't feel sure of our relationship with God and, therefore, we feel afraid of God.

But those who are born again spiritually have a Father-child relationship with the Lord. Our heavenly Father loves us unconditionally and deals with us tenderly and patiently. The more we learn what He's really like—the more we see Him as Jesus saw Him—the more we will long to spend time alone with Him . . . and the more we will know the fullness of His grace.

See the Life Principles Index for further study:

1. *Our intimacy with God—His highest priority for our lives—determines the impact of our lives.*

27. *Prayer is life's greatest time saver.*

11 "since the time that I commanded judges *to be* over My people Israel, and have caused you
to rest from all your enemies. Also the LORD
tells you that He will make you a house.[a]
12 "When your days are fulfilled and you rest
with your fathers, I will set up your seed after
you, who will come from your body, and I will
establish his kingdom.
13 "He shall build a house for My name, and
I will establish the throne of his kingdom forever.
14 "I will be his Father, and he shall be My
son. If he commits iniquity, I will chasten him
with the rod of men and with the blows of the
sons of men.
15 "But My mercy shall not depart from him,
as I took *it* from Saul, whom I removed from
before you.
16 "And your house and your kingdom shall
be established forever before you.[a] Your
throne shall be established forever."'"
17 According to all these words and according
to all this vision, so Nathan spoke to David.

David's Thanksgiving to God

18 Then King David went in and sat before
the LORD; and he said: "Who *am* I, O Lord

7:11 [a]That is, a royal dynasty **7:16** [a]Septuagint reads *Me*.

LIFE LESSONS

➤ 7:11 — *"Also the LORD tells you that He will make you a house."*

David wanted to build a house of cedar for the Lord; the Lord replied that He would build a living house for David. You can never out give God.

➤ 7:16 — *"And your house and your kingdom shall be established forever before you. Your throne shall be established forever."*

The Lord ultimately fulfilled this promise in the "Son of David," Jesus Christ, who rules forever.

GOD? And what is my house, that You have
brought me this far?
19 "And yet this was a small thing in Your
sight, O Lord GOD; and You have also spoken
of Your servant's house for a great while to
come. *Is* this the manner of man, O Lord GOD?
20 "Now what more can David say to You?
For You, Lord GOD, know Your servant.
➤ 21 "For Your word's sake, and according to
Your own heart, You have done all these great
things, to make Your servant know *them.*
22 "Therefore You are great, O Lord GOD.[a] For
there is none like You, nor *is there any* God
besides You, according to all that we have
heard with our ears.
23 "And who *is* like Your people, like Israel,
the one nation on the earth whom God went
to redeem for Himself as a people, to make
for Himself a name—and to do for Yourself
great and awesome deeds for Your land—before Your people whom You redeemed for
Yourself from Egypt, the nations, and their
gods?
24 "For You have made Your people Israel
Your very own people forever; and You, LORD,
have become their God.
25 "Now, O LORD God, the word which You
have spoken concerning Your servant and
concerning his house, establish *it* forever and
do as You have said.
26 "So let Your name be magnified forever,
saying, 'The LORD of hosts *is* the God over Israel.' And let the house of Your servant David
be established before You.
27 "For You, O LORD of hosts, God of Israel,
have revealed *this* to Your servant, saying, 'I
will build you a house.' Therefore Your servant has found it in his heart to pray this
prayer to You.
✳ 28 "And now, O Lord GOD, You are God, and
Your words are true, and You have promised
this goodness to Your servant.
➤ 29 "Now therefore, let it please You to bless
the house of Your servant, that it may continue before You forever; for You, O Lord GOD,
have spoken *it,* and with Your blessing let the
house of Your servant be blessed forever."

David's Further Conquests

8 After this it came to pass that David
attacked the Philistines and subdued
them. And David took Metheg Ammah from
the hand of the Philistines.
2 Then he defeated Moab. Forcing them
down to the ground, he measured them off
with a line. With two lines he measured off
those to be put to death, and with one full line
those to be kept alive. So the Moabites became David's servants, *and* brought tribute.
3 David also defeated Hadadezer the son of
Rehob, king of Zobah, as he went to recover
his territory at the River Euphrates.
4 David took from him one thousand *chariots,* seven hundred[a] horsemen, and twenty
thousand foot soldiers. Also David hamstrung
all the chariot *horses,* except that he spared
enough of them for one hundred chariots.
5 When the Syrians of Damascus came to
help Hadadezer king of Zobah, David killed
twenty-two thousand of the Syrians.
6 Then David put garrisons in Syria of Da- ➤
mascus; and the Syrians became David's servants, *and* brought tribute. So the LORD
preserved David wherever he went.
7 And David took the shields of gold that
had belonged to the servants of Hadadezer,
and brought them to Jerusalem.
8 Also from Betah[a] and from Berothai, cities
of Hadadezer, King David took a large
amount of bronze.
9 When Toi[a] king of Hamath heard that David had defeated all the army of Hadadezer,
10 then Toi sent Joram[a] his son to King David, to greet him and bless him, because he
had fought against Hadadezer and defeated
him (for Hadadezer had been at war with
Toi); and *Joram* brought with him articles of
silver, articles of gold, and articles of bronze.
11 King David also dedicated these to the
LORD, along with the silver and gold that he

7:22 [a]Targum and Syriac read *O LORD God.* **8:4** [a]Or *seven thousand* (compare 1 Chronicles 18:4) **8:8** [a]Spelled *Tibhath* in 1 Chronicles 18:8 **8:9** [a]Spelled *Tou* in 1 Chronicles 18:9 **8:10** [a]Spelled *Hadoram* in 1 Chronicles 18:10

LIFE LESSONS

➤ 7:21 — *"For Your word's sake, and according to Your own heart, You have done all these great things, to make Your servant know them."*

God blesses us in line with His own loving character and to honor and keep His Word. We do not deserve His blessings, but we can set ourselves up for them by our willing obedience to the Lord.

➤ 7:29 — *"Now therefore, let it please You to bless the house of Your servant, that it may continue forever before You; for You, O Lord GOD, have spoken it, and with Your blessing let the house of Your servant be blessed forever."*

David responded to God's gracious promise by praying that God would fulfill the promise He spoke. David understood that by praying according to God's promise, he aligned himself with God's will. We can do the same thing.

➤ 8:6 — *. . . The LORD preserved David wherever he went.*

As the Lord preserved David wherever he went, so He can preserve us wherever we go. If we make the Lord our delight, as David did, then we can enjoy the same kind of blessing that David did.

WHAT THE BIBLE SAYS ABOUT THE IMMENSE VALUE OF MEDITATION

2 Sam. 7:29

The mere mention of the word "meditation" tends to conjure up images foreign to the Western mind. Perhaps that's why so many contemporary believers have removed the word from their vocabulary. But we do this at our great peril, because scriptural meditation greatly helps us to listen accurately to God.

Perhaps no man pursued this godly endeavor more fervently and fruitfully than King David. Many psalms resulted from his quiet waiting and reflecting upon God. As a "man after God's own heart," David first had to know the mind and heart of God. To a large extent, David accomplished this through the persistent practice of godly mediation.

In our over-scheduled lives, we often find it difficult to see a purpose in what we do. With so many things and people clamoring for our time, we must return to one of life's most important activities—meditation.

Godly meditation means lifting your heart heavenward and listening to God.

Godly meditation means lifting your heart heavenward and listening to God.

It is focusing your attention on Christ and shutting out everything else. Without practicing daily meditation on the Lord, it is impossible to experience:

- *Holiness of heart*: Meditation allows you to concentrate on who God is and to grow into oneness with Him.
- *Contentment*: With meditation on God comes great contentment of soul.
- *Being a help to someone else*: If we don't draw our strength from God, we soon run out of strength.

In order to continue the habit of meditating on the Lord, we must guard against meditating simply out of habit. We must have a pure purpose for meditation: to get to know God more intimately. We must also have a plan for when we come to Him, including a portion of time when we meditate on His Word, and a prayer journal in which to offer up prayers and write what God tells us through the Holy Spirit and the Scriptures.

Meditate on the Lord's goodness, His faithfulness, His plan for your life, His will for you, His glory, and His promises. Meditate on who He is—and you will come to know His character and His desires in a deep, fresh way.

See the Life Principles Index for further study:
3. God's Word is an immovable anchor in times of storm.

had dedicated from all the nations which he
had subdued—
12 from Syria,[a] from Moab, from the people
of Ammon, from the Philistines, from Amalek, and from the spoil of Hadadezer the son
of Rehob, king of Zobah.
13 And David made *himself* a name when he
returned from killing eighteen thousand Syrians[a] in the Valley of Salt.
14 He also put garrisons in Edom; throughout all Edom he put garrisons, and all the
Edomites became David's servants. And the
LORD preserved David wherever he went.

David's Administration

15 So David reigned over all Israel; and David administered judgment and justice to all
his people.
16 Joab the son of Zeruiah *was* over the
army; Jehoshaphat the son of Ahilud *was*
recorder;
17 Zadok the son of Ahitub and Ahimelech
the son of Abiathar *were* the priests; Seraiah[a]
was the scribe;
18 Benaiah the son of Jehoiada *was over*
both the Cherethites and the Pelethites; and
David's sons were chief ministers.

David's Kindness to Mephibosheth

9 Now David said, "Is there still anyone who
is left of the house of Saul, that I may
show him kindness for Jonathan's sake?"
2 And *there was* a servant of the house of
Saul whose name *was* Ziba. So when they
had called him to David, the king said to him,
"*Are* you Ziba?" He said, "At your service!"
3 Then the king said, "*Is* there not still
someone of the house of Saul, to whom I may
show the kindness of God?" And Ziba said to
the king, "There is still a son of Jonathan *who*
is lame in *his* feet."
4 So the king said to him, "Where *is* he?"
And Ziba said to the king, "Indeed he *is* in the
house of Machir the son of Ammiel, in Lo
Debar."
5 Then King David sent and brought him
out of the house of Machir the son of Ammiel,
from Lo Debar.
6 Now when Mephibosheth the son of Jonathan, the son of Saul, had come to David, he
fell on his face and prostrated himself. Then
David said, "Mephibosheth?" And he answered, "Here is your servant!"
➤7 So David said to him, "Do not fear, for I
will surely show you kindness for Jonathan
your father's sake, and will restore to you all
the land of Saul your grandfather; and you
shall eat bread at my table continually."
8 Then he bowed himself, and said, "What *is*
your servant, that you should look upon such
a dead dog as I?"
9 And the king called to Ziba, Saul's servant, and said to him, "I have given to your
master's son all that belonged to Saul and to
all his house.
10 "You therefore, and your sons and your
servants, shall work the land for him, and you
shall bring in *the harvest,* that your master's
son may have food to eat. But Mephibosheth
your master's son shall eat bread at my table
always." Now Ziba had fifteen sons and
twenty servants.
11 Then Ziba said to the king, "According to
all that my lord the king has commanded his
servant, so will your servant do." "As for
Mephibosheth," *said the king,* "he shall eat at
my table[a] like one of the king's sons."
12 Mephibosheth had a young son whose
name *was* Micha. And all who dwelt in the
house of Ziba *were* servants of Mephibosheth.
13 So Mephibosheth dwelt in Jerusalem, for
he ate continually at the king's table. And he
was lame in both his feet.

The Ammonites and Syrians Defeated

10 It happened after this that the king of
the people of Ammon died, and Hanun
his son reigned in his place.
2 Then David said, "I will show kindness to
Hanun the son of Nahash, as his father
showed kindness to me." So David sent by the
hand of his servants to comfort him concerning his father. And David's servants came into
the land of the people of Ammon.
3 And the princes of the people of Ammon
said to Hanun their lord, "Do you think
that David really honors your father because
he has sent comforters to you? Has David not
rather sent his servants to you to search the
city, to spy it out, and to overthrow it?"
4 Therefore Hanun took David's servants,
shaved off half of their beards, cut off their

8:12 [a]Septuagint, Syriac, and some Hebrew manuscripts read *Edom.* **8:13** [a]Septuagint, Syriac, and some Hebrew manuscripts read *Edomites* (compare 1 Chronicles 18:12). **8:17** [a]Spelled *Shavsha* in 1 Chronicles 18:16 **9:11** [a]Septuagint reads *David's table.*

LIFE LESSONS

➤ 9:7 — *So David said to him, "Do not fear, for I will surely show you kindness for Jonathan your father's sake . . . ."*

David remembered the promise he had made to Jonathan (1 Sam. 20:14–17) and worked hard to honor it. David remembered with gratitude his friend's help and responded with generosity.

garments in the middle, at their buttocks, and
sent them away.
5 When they told David, he sent to meet
them, because the men were greatly ashamed.
And the king said, "Wait at Jericho until your
beards have grown, and *then* return."
6 When the people of Ammon saw that they
had made themselves repulsive to David, the
people of Ammon sent and hired the Syrians
of Beth Rehob and the Syrians of Zoba,
twenty thousand foot soldiers; and from the
king of Maacah one thousand men, and from
Ish-Tob twelve thousand men.
7 Now when David heard *of it*, he sent Joab
and all the army of the mighty men.
8 Then the people of Ammon came out and
put themselves in battle array at the entrance
of the gate. And the Syrians of Zoba, Beth
Rehob, Ish-Tob, and Maacah *were* by themselves in the field.
9 When Joab saw that the battle line was
against him before and behind, he chose
some of Israel's best and put *them* in battle
array against the Syrians.
10 And the rest of the people he put under
the command of Abishai his brother, that he
might set *them* in battle array against the
people of Ammon.
11 Then he said, "If the Syrians are too
strong for me, then you shall help me; but if
the people of Ammon are too strong for you,
then I will come and help you.
➤ 12 "Be of good courage, and let us be strong
for our people and for the cities of our God.
And may the LORD do *what is* good in His
sight."
13 So Joab and the people who *were* with
him drew near for the battle against the Syrians, and they fled before him.
14 When the people of Ammon saw that the
Syrians were fleeing, they also fled before
Abishai, and entered the city. So Joab returned from the people of Ammon and went
to Jerusalem.
15 When the Syrians saw that they had been
defeated by Israel, they gathered together.
16 Then Hadadezer[a] sent and brought out the
Syrians who *were* beyond the River,[b] and they
came to Helam. And Shobach the commander
of Hadadezer's army *went* before them.
17 When it was told David, he gathered all Israel, crossed over the Jordan, and came to
Helam. And the Syrians set themselves in battle array against David and fought with him.
18 Then the Syrians fled before Israel; and
David killed seven hundred charioteers and
forty thousand horsemen of the Syrians,
and struck Shobach the commander of their
army, who died there.
19 And when all the kings *who were* servants
to Hadadezer[a] saw that they were defeated by
Israel, they made peace with Israel and
served them. So the Syrians were afraid to
help the people of Ammon anymore.

David, Bathsheba, and Uriah

11 It happened in the spring of the year, at
the time when kings go out *to battle*,
that David sent Joab and his servants with
him, and all Israel; and they destroyed the
people of Ammon and besieged Rabbah. But
David remained at Jerusalem.
2 Then it happened one evening that David
arose from his bed and walked on the roof of ➤
the king's house. And from the roof he saw a
woman bathing, and the woman *was* very
beautiful to behold.
3 So David sent and inquired about the
woman. And *someone* said, "*Is* this not Bathsheba, the daughter of Eliam, the wife of
Uriah the Hittite?"
4 Then David sent messengers, and took
her; and she came to him, and he lay with her,
for she was cleansed from her impurity; and
she returned to her house.
5 And the woman conceived; so she sent
and told David, and said, "I *am* with child."
6 Then David sent to Joab, *saying*, "Send me
Uriah the Hittite." And Joab sent Uriah to David.
7 When Uriah had come to him, David
asked how Joab was doing, and how the people were doing, and how the war prospered.
8 And David said to Uriah, "Go down to
your house and wash your feet." So Uriah departed from the king's house, and a gift of
food from the king followed him.
9 But Uriah slept at the door of the king's

10:16 [a]Hebrew *Hadarezer* [b]That is, the Euphrates
10:19 [a]Hebrew *Hadarezer*

LIFE LESSONS

➤ 10:12 — *"Be of good courage, and let us be strong for our people and for the cities of our God. And may the LORD do what is good in His sight."*

When we face some major challenge, we can do no better than to find courage in God and to ask the Lord to "do what is good in His sight." The Lord loves to honor those who honor Him (1 Sam. 2:30).

➤ 11:2 — *. . . And from the roof he saw a woman bathing, and the woman was very beautiful to behold.*

David did not sin by catching a glimpse of a bathing beauty. He sinned when he failed to take his eyes off of her. Soon he discovered that lust gives birth to sin, and full-grown sin brings forth death (James 1:15).

ANSWERS TO LIFE'S QUESTIONS

How can we effectively guard against temptation?

2 SAM. 11:2–4

The mind is subject to the will. We each control what we choose to think about. Paul wrote to the Corinthians that they should bring "every thought into captivity to the obedience of Christ" (2 Cor. 10:5). We have the ability to screen, select, admit, and cultivate what goes into our minds. We can keep our minds from wandering into evil thoughts by choosing to focus instead upon what is good (Phil. 4:8).

We also have the ability to choose *how* we will think about what we perceive with our senses. While we have no control over some things that come into our field of vision or within our range of hearing, we *do* control how we will think about what we perceive or sense, and how we will act on that information.

For example, David *saw* Bathsheba. He wasn't looking for her. One night he was out walking on his balcony, and while surveying the city below, he saw a beautiful woman bathing. That could have been the end of the story. David could have turned and walked back into his palace and thought nothing more about what he had seen.

Instead, David began to *think* about what he saw. He turned over in his mind the beautiful feminine form he had just glimpsed. Soon he "sent and inquired about the woman" (2 Sam. 11:3). He did some research and began to dwell on what it would be like to get a closer look at her and what it might be like to be with her physically. Eventually he sent for her, sinned with her, and suffered serious consequences for that sin.

When things come into our range of sensation or perception, we must immediately evaluate them through the "filter" of God's Word. If we find ourselves dwelling on a thought, we must ask ourselves, "Why am I thinking this? What is at the root of my thought? What will happen if I continue to think this way? Is that really the direction I want my life to go?"

We do not need to act out of ungodly impulses, desires, and lusts. We can govern what we *choose* to think and then what we *choose* to do. And in so doing, we can "do all to the glory of God" (1 Cor. 10:31).

See the Life Principles Index for further study:
2. Obey God and leave all the consequences to Him.

house with all the servants of his lord, and did
not go down to his house.
10 So when they told David, saying, "Uriah
did not go down to his house," David said to
Uriah, "Did you not come from a journey?
Why did you not go down to your house?"
11 And Uriah said to David, "The ark and Israel and Judah are dwelling in tents, and my
lord Joab and the servants of my lord are encamped in the open fields. Shall I then go to
my house to eat and drink, and to lie with my
wife? *As* you live, and *as* your soul lives, I will
not do this thing."
12 Then David said to Uriah, "Wait here
today also, and tomorrow I will let you depart." So Uriah remained in Jerusalem that
day and the next.
13 Now when David called him, he ate and
drank before him; and he made him drunk.
And at evening he went out to lie on his bed
with the servants of his lord, but he did not go
down to his house.
14 In the morning it happened that David
wrote a letter to Joab and sent *it* by the hand
of Uriah.
15 And he wrote in the letter, saying, "Set
Uriah in the forefront of the hottest battle,
and retreat from him, that he may be struck
down and die."
16 So it was, while Joab besieged the city,
that he assigned Uriah to a place where he
knew there *were* valiant men.
17 Then the men of the city came out and
fought with Joab. And *some* of the people of
the servants of David fell; and Uriah the Hittite died also.

LIFE LESSONS

➢ 11:11 — *". . . my lord Joab and the servants of my lord are encamped in the open fields. Shall I then go to my house to eat and drink, and to lie with my wife? . . . I will not do this thing."*

Uriah had a pagan background, and yet he showed far more concern for the Lord and for His people than David did. We cannot afford to forget Jesus' words: "Watch and pray, lest you enter into temptation . . ." (Matt. 26:41).

Life Examples:

NATHAN

The Value of Godly Counsel

2 SAM. 12:1-14

God often uses other believers to strengthen, encourage, and enrich our lives. Despite countless negative influences around us, we can still find wisdom through the counsel of godly men and women.

A wonderful example of this is the prophet Nathan in his confrontation with King David (2 Sam. 12:1-14). God used Nathan to bring His servant, David, to repentance. Although the intense conviction greatly pained David, it was absolutely necessary in order for him to regain a right relationship with God.

The Book of Proverbs teaches us repeatedly to seek out godly counsel (Prov. 12:15; 13:10; 15:31; 19:20). We must be careful that the person giving us counsel is in step with the Lord. While we are all fellow travelers on the path toward godly wisdom, we would be wise to lean on each other for support along the way.

See the Life Principles Index for further study:
28. No Christian has ever been called to "go it alone" in his or her walk of faith.

18 Then Joab sent and told David all the
things concerning the war,
19 and charged the messenger, saying,
"When you have finished telling the matters
of the war to the king,
20 "if it happens that the king's wrath rises,
and he says to you: 'Why did you approach so
near to the city when you fought? Did you not
know that they would shoot from the wall?
21 'Who struck Abimelech the son of
Jerubbesheth?[a] Was it not a woman who cast
a piece of a millstone on him from the wall, so
that he died in Thebez? Why did you go near
the wall?'—then you shall say, 'Your servant
Uriah the Hittite is dead also.'"
22 So the messenger went, and came and told
David all that Joab had sent by him.
23 And the messenger said to David, "Surely
the men prevailed against us and came out to
us in the field; then we drove them back as far
as the entrance of the gate.
24 "The archers shot from the wall at your
servants; and *some* of the king's servants are
dead, and your servant Uriah the Hittite is
dead also."
25 Then David said to the messenger, "Thus
you shall say to Joab: 'Do not let this thing
displease you, for the sword devours one as
well as another. Strengthen your attack
against the city, and overthrow it.' So encourage him."
26 When the wife of Uriah heard that Uriah
her husband was dead, she mourned for her
husband.
27 And when her mourning was over, David
sent and brought her to his house, and she became his wife and bore him a son. But the
thing that David had done displeased the
LORD.

Nathan's Parable and David's Confession

12 Then the LORD sent Nathan to David.
And he came to him, and said to him:
"There were two men in one city, one rich and
the other poor.
2 "The rich *man* had exceedingly many
flocks and herds.
3 "But the poor *man* had nothing, except
one little ewe lamb which he had bought and
nourished; and it grew up together with him
and with his children. It ate of his own food
and drank from his own cup and lay in his
bosom; and it was like a daughter to him.
4 "And a traveler came to the rich man, who
refused to take from his own flock and from
his own herd to prepare one for the wayfaring
man who had come to him; but he took the
poor man's lamb and prepared it for the man
who had come to him."
5 So David's anger was greatly aroused
against the man, and he said to Nathan, "As

11:21 [a]Same as *Jerubbaal* (Gideon), Judges 6:32ff

LIFE LESSONS

➤ 11:25 — *Then David said to the messenger, "Thus you shall say to Joab: 'Do not let this thing displease you, for the sword devours one as well as another.'"*

Unconfessed sin has a way of making us callous toward the value of human life. It deadens the spirit and distances us from God. Without confession and repentance, we descend ever further into the prison of sin.

➤ 12:4 — *". . . but he took the poor man's lamb and prepared it for the man who had come to him."*

Nathan used a story that reminded David of his youth to break through the king's resistance and bring him to a place of repentance. A prayer-bathed, creative approach can usually accomplish far more than an iron hammer.

the LORD lives, the man who has done this
shall surely die!
6 "And he shall restore fourfold for the
lamb, because he did this thing and because
he had no pity."
7 Then Nathan said to David, "You *are* the
man! Thus says the LORD God of Israel: 'I
anointed you king over Israel, and I delivered
you from the hand of Saul.
8 'I gave you your master's house and your
master's wives into your keeping, and gave
you the house of Israel and Judah. And if *that
had been* too little, I also would have given
you much more!
9 'Why have you despised the commandment
of the LORD, to do evil in His sight? You have
killed Uriah the Hittite with the sword; you have
taken his wife *to be* your wife, and have killed
him with the sword of the people of Ammon.
10 'Now therefore, the sword shall never depart from your house, because you have despised Me, and have taken the wife of Uriah
the Hittite to be your wife.'
11 "Thus says the LORD: 'Behold, I will raise
up adversity against you from your own house;
and I will take your wives before your eyes and
give *them* to your neighbor, and he shall lie
with your wives in the sight of this sun.
12 'For you did *it* secretly, but I will do this
thing before all Israel, before the sun.'"
13 So David said to Nathan, "I have sinned
against the LORD." And Nathan said to David,
"The LORD also has put away your sin; you
shall not die.
➤ 14 "However, because by this deed you have
given great occasion to the enemies of the
LORD to blaspheme, the child also *who is* born
to you shall surely die."
15 Then Nathan departed to his house.

The Death of David's Son

And the LORD struck the child that Uriah's
wife bore to David, and it became ill.
16 David therefore pleaded with God for the
child, and David fasted and went in and lay
all night on the ground.
17 So the elders of his house arose *and went*
to him, to raise him up from the ground. But
he would not, nor did he eat food with them.
18 Then on the seventh day it came to pass
that the child died. And the servants of David
were afraid to tell him that the child was
dead. For they said, "Indeed, while the child
was alive, we spoke to him, and he would not
heed our voice. How can we tell him that the
child is dead? He may do some harm!"

Life Examples:

DAVID

A Case Study in Repentance

2 SAM. 12:13

What happens when we sin and delay our repentance? Are there consequences?

When David committed adultery with Bathsheba, he didn't repent immediately. Only some time later did David admit to his sin. And even then, he didn't do it on his own accord; God had to send a prophet to confront him (2 Sam. 12:1–14). Only after Nathan's visit did David confess his sin and then repent of it. God's discipline followed, in a severe form—perhaps so severe because of David's failure to repent sooner.

If you and I deal with our sin genuinely, openly, and immediately, God can lessen the severity of our discipline. This makes sense in the light of the nature of discipline. Discipline is designed to get us to change, to obey. If God sees that we want to cooperate and that we have purposed in our hearts to obey the next time, then stern discipline is not usually needed.

See the Life Principles Index for further study:
15. Brokenness is God's requirement for maximum usefulness.

19 When David saw that his servants were
whispering, David perceived that the child
was dead. Therefore David said to his servants, "Is the child dead?" And they said, "He
is dead."
20 So David arose from the ground, washed
and anointed himself, and changed his clothes;
and he went into the house of the LORD and
worshiped. Then he went to his own house; and
when he requested, they set food before him,
and he ate.
21 Then his servants said to him, "What *is*
this that you have done? You fasted and wept

LIFE LESSONS

➤ 12:14 — *"However, because by this deed you have given great occasion to the enemies of the LORD to blaspheme, the child also who is born to you shall surely die."*

God takes intense interest in how we behave as children of God, since His reputation is bound up in our conduct.

for the child *while he was* alive, but when the
child died, you arose and ate food."
➤ 22 And he said, "While the child was alive, I
fasted and wept; for I said, 'Who can tell
whether the LORD[a] will be gracious to me, that
the child may live?'
23 "But now he is dead; why should I fast?
Can I bring him back again? I shall go to him,
but he shall not return to me."

Solomon Is Born

➤ **24** Then David comforted Bathsheba his
wife, and went in to her and lay with her. So
she bore a son, and he[a] called his name Solomon. Now the LORD loved him,
25 and He sent *word* by the hand of Nathan
the prophet: So he[a] called his name Jedidiah,[b]
because of the LORD.

Rabbah Is Captured

26 Now Joab fought against Rabbah of the
people of Ammon, and took the royal city.
27 And Joab sent messengers to David, and
said, "I have fought against Rabbah, and I
have taken the city's water *supply.*
28 "Now therefore, gather the rest of the people together and encamp against the city and
take it, lest I take the city and it be called after
my name."
29 So David gathered all the people together
and went to Rabbah, fought against it, and
took it.
30 Then he took their king's crown from his
head. Its weight *was* a talent of gold, with precious stones. And it was *set* on David's head.
Also he brought out the spoil of the city in
great abundance.
31 And he brought out the people who *were*
in it, and put *them to work* with saws and
iron picks and iron axes, and made them
cross over to the brick works. So he did to all
the cities of the people of Ammon. Then David and all the people returned to Jerusalem.

Amnon and Tamar

13 After this Absalom the son of David
had a lovely sister, whose name *was*
Tamar; and Amnon the son of David loved her.
2 Amnon was so distressed over his sister
Tamar that he became sick; for she *was* a virgin. And it was improper for Amnon to do
anything to her.
3 But Amnon had a friend whose name *was*
Jonadab the son of Shimeah, David's brother.
Now Jonadab *was* a very crafty man.
4 And he said to him, "Why *are* you, the
king's son, becoming thinner day after day?
Will you not tell me?"Amnon said to him, "I
love Tamar, my brother Absalom's sister."
5 So Jonadab said to him, "Lie down on
your bed and pretend to be ill. And when your
father comes to see you, say to him, 'Please let
my sister Tamar come and give me food, and
prepare the food in my sight, that I may see *it*
and eat it from her hand.'"
6 Then Amnon lay down and pretended to
be ill; and when the king came to see him,
Amnon said to the king, "Please let Tamar my
sister come and make a couple of cakes for
me in my sight, that I may eat from her hand."
7 And David sent home to Tamar, saying,
"Now go to your brother Amnon's house, and
prepare food for him."
8 So Tamar went to her brother Amnon's
house; and he was lying down. Then she took
flour and kneaded *it,* made cakes in his sight,
and baked the cakes.
9 And she took the pan and placed *them* out
before him, but he refused to eat. Then
Amnon said, "Have everyone go out from
me." And they all went out from him.
10 Then Amnon said to Tamar, "Bring the
food into the bedroom, that I may eat from
your hand." And Tamar took the cakes which
she had made, and brought *them* to Amnon
her brother in the bedroom.
11 Now when she had brought *them* to him ➤
to eat, he took hold of her and said to her,
"Come, lie with me, my sister."
12 But she answered him, "No, my brother, do
not force me, for no such thing should be

12:22 [a]A few Hebrew manuscripts and Syriac read *God.*
12:24 [a]Following Kethib, Septuagint, and Vulgate; Qere, a few Hebrew manuscripts, Syriac, and Targum read *she.* **12:25** [a]Qere, some Hebrew manuscripts, Syriac, and Targum read *she.* [b]Literally *Beloved of the LORD*

LIFE LESSONS

➤ **12:22 — *And he said, "While the child was alive, I fasted and wept; for I said, 'Who can tell whether the LORD will be gracious to me, that the child may live?'"***

God does not owe us His grace. David knew he had sinned, yet He pleaded for God's mercy on his child. Because the king understood the nature of grace, he did not blame God when the child died.

➤ **12:24 — *So she bore a son, and he called his name Solomon. Now the LORD loved him . . . .***

Why did the Lord love Solomon? Look no further than His grace. David did not earn it; the newborn Solomon certainly did not earn it. We find the reason for God's love always in His own character, not in ours.

➤ **13:11 — *Now when she had brought them to him to eat, he took hold of her and said to her, "Come, lie with me, my sister."***

With his many wives and concubines and his illicit affair with Bathsheba, David had not modeled for his sons a godly love life. Children learn better by example than by words.

done in Israel. Do not do this disgraceful
thing!
13 "And I, where could I take my shame? And
as for you, you would be like one of the fools
in Israel. Now therefore, please speak to the
king; for he will not withhold me from you."
14 However, he would not heed her voice;
and being stronger than she, he forced her
and lay with her.
➤ **15** Then Amnon hated her exceedingly, so
that the hatred with which he hated her *was*
greater than the love with which he had loved
her. And Amnon said to her, "Arise, be gone!"
16 So she said to him, "No, indeed! This evil
of sending me away *is* worse than the other
that you did to me." But he would not listen to
her.
17 Then he called his servant who attended
him, and said, "Here! Put this *woman* out,
away from me, and bolt the door behind her."
18 Now she had on a robe of many colors, for
the king's virgin daughters wore such apparel. And his servant put her out and bolted
the door behind her.
19 Then Tamar put ashes on her head, and
tore her robe of many colors that *was* on her,
and laid her hand on her head and went away
crying bitterly.
20 And Absalom her brother said to her, "Has
Amnon your brother been with you? But now
hold your peace, my sister. He *is* your brother;
do not take this thing to heart." So Tamar remained desolate in her brother Absalom's
house.
21 But when King David heard of all these
things, he was very angry.
➤ 22 And Absalom spoke to his brother Amnon
neither good nor bad. For Absalom hated
Amnon, because he had forced his sister Tamar.

Absalom Murders Amnon

23 And it came to pass, after two full years,
that Absalom had sheepshearers in Baal
Hazor, which *is* near Ephraim; so Absalom invited all the king's sons.
24 Then Absalom came to the king and said,
"Kindly note, your servant has sheepshearers; please, let the king and his servants go
with your servant."
25 But the king said to Absalom, "No, my son,
let us not all go now, lest we be a burden to
you." Then he urged him, but he would not go;
and he blessed him.
26 Then Absalom said, "If not, please let my
brother Amnon go with us." And the king said
to him, "Why should he go with you?"
27 But Absalom urged him; so he let Amnon
and all the king's sons go with him.
28 Now Absalom had commanded his servants, saying, "Watch now, when Amnon's
heart is merry with wine, and when I say to
you, 'Strike Amnon!' then kill him. Do not be
afraid. Have I not commanded you? Be courageous and valiant."
29 So the servants of Absalom did to Amnon
as Absalom had commanded. Then all the
king's sons arose, and each one got on his
mule and fled.
30 And it came to pass, while they were on
the way, that news came to David, saying,
"Absalom has killed all the king's sons, and
not one of them is left!"
31 So the king arose and tore his garments
and lay on the ground, and all his servants
stood by with their clothes torn.
32 Then Jonadab the son of Shimeah, David's brother, answered and said, "Let not my
lord suppose they have killed all the young
men, the king's sons, for only Amnon is dead.
For by the command of Absalom this has
been determined from the day that he forced
his sister Tamar.
33 "Now therefore, let not my lord the king
take the thing to his heart, to think that all the
king's sons are dead. For only Amnon is
dead."

Absalom Flees to Geshur

34 Then Absalom fled. And the young
man who was keeping watch lifted his eyes
and looked, and there, many people were
coming from the road on the hillside behind
him.[a]
35 And Jonadab said to the king, "Look, the

13:34 [a]Septuagint adds *And the watchman went and told the king, and said, "I see men from the way of Horonaim, from the regions of the mountains."*

LIFE LESSONS

➤ 13:15 — *Then Amnon hated her exceedingly, so that the hatred with which he hated her was greater than the love with which he had loved her . . . .*

Lust relieved frequently gives way to hatred expressed. Lust often masquerades as love, but the two result in profoundly different outcomes.

➤ 13:22 — *And Absalom spoke to his brother Amnon neither good nor bad. For Absalom hated Amnon, because he had forced his sister Tamar.*

Anger must be resolved, or it festers and turns into violent hatred. For this reason the Bible tells us, "do not let the sun go down on your wrath" (Eph. 4:26).

➤ 13:28 — *Now Absalom had commanded his servants . . . "'Strike Amnon!' then kill him. Do not be afraid. Have I not commanded you? Be courageous and valiant."*

The wicked can also be urged to courage and valiance. But courage in the service of evil is never valiant.

➤ 13:32 — *Then Jonadab . . . answered and said, "Let not my lord suppose they have killed all the young men, the king's sons, for only Amnon is dead . . . ."*

The same man who advised Amnon how to rape his half-sister Tamar told David that not all of his sons had been killed. Since we never know the heart of another, we must always listen carefully for God's counsel.

king's sons are coming; as your servant said, so it is."

36 So it was, as soon as he had finished speaking, that the king's sons indeed came, and they lifted up their voice and wept. Also the king and all his servants wept very bitterly.

37 But Absalom fled and went to Talmai the son of Ammihud, king of Geshur. And *David* mourned for his son every day.

38 So Absalom fled and went to Geshur, and was there three years.

39 And King David[a] longed to go to[b] Absalom. For he had been comforted concerning Amnon, because he was dead.

Absalom Returns to Jerusalem

14 So Joab the son of Zeruiah perceived that the king's heart *was* concerned about Absalom.

2 And Joab sent to Tekoa and brought from there a wise woman, and said to her, "Please pretend to be a mourner, and put on mourning apparel; do not anoint yourself with oil, but act like a woman who has been mourning a long time for the dead.

3 "Go to the king and speak to him in this manner." So Joab put the words in her mouth.

4 And when the woman of Tekoa spoke[a] to the king, she fell on her face to the ground and prostrated herself, and said, "Help, O king!"

5 Then the king said to her, "What troubles you?" And she answered, "Indeed I *am* a widow, my husband is dead.

6 "Now your maidservant had two sons; and the two fought with each other in the field, and *there was* no one to part them, but the one struck the other and killed him.

7 "And now the whole family has risen up against your maidservant, and they said, 'Deliver him who struck his brother, that we may execute him for the life of his brother whom he killed; and we will destroy the heir also.' So they would extinguish my ember that is left, and leave to my husband *neither* name nor remnant on the earth."

8 Then the king said to the woman, "Go to your house, and I will give orders concerning you."

9 And the woman of Tekoa said to the king, "My lord, O king, *let* the iniquity *be* on me and on my father's house, and the king and his throne *be* guiltless."

10 So the king said, "Whoever says *anything* to you, bring him to me, and he shall not touch you anymore."

11 Then she said, "Please let the king remember the LORD your God, and do not permit the avenger of blood to destroy anymore, lest they destroy my son." And he said, "*As* the LORD lives, not one hair of your son shall fall to the ground."

12 Therefore the woman said, "Please, let your maidservant speak *another* word to my lord the king." And he said, "Say on."

13 So the woman said: "Why then have you schemed such a thing against the people of God? For the king speaks this thing as one who is guilty, *in that* the king does not bring his banished one home again.

14 "For we will surely die and *become* like water spilled on the ground, which cannot be gathered up again. Yet God does not take away a life; but He devises means, so that His banished ones are not expelled from Him.

15 "Now therefore, I have come to speak of this thing to my lord the king because the people have made me afraid. And your maidservant said, 'I will now speak to the king; it may be that the king will perform the request of his maidservant.

16 'For the king will hear and deliver his maidservant from the hand of the man *who would* destroy me and my son together from the inheritance of God.'

17 "Your maidservant said, 'The word of my lord the king will now be comforting; for as the angel of God, so *is* my lord the king in discerning good and evil. And may the LORD your God be with you.'"

18 Then the king answered and said to the woman, "Please do not hide from me anything that I ask you." And the woman said, "Please, let my lord the king speak."

19 So the king said, "*Is* the hand of Joab with you in all this?" And the woman answered and said, "*As* you live, my lord the king, no one can turn to the right hand or to the left from anything that my lord the king has spoken. For your servant Joab commanded me, and he put all these words in the mouth of your maidservant.

20 "To bring about this change of affairs your servant Joab has done this thing; but my lord *is* wise, according to the wisdom of the angel of God, to know everything that *is* in the earth."

21 And the king said to Joab, "All right, I have granted this thing. Go therefore, bring back the young man Absalom."

22 Then Joab fell to the ground on his face and bowed himself, and thanked the king. And Joab said, "Today your servant knows that I have found favor in your sight, my lord, O king, in that the king has fulfilled the request of his servant."

23 So Joab arose and went to Geshur, and brought Absalom to Jerusalem.

13:39 [a]Following Masoretic Text, Syriac, and Vulgate; Septuagint reads *the spirit of the king;* Targum reads *the soul of King David.* [b]Following Masoretic Text and Targum; Septuagint and Vulgate read *ceased to pursue after.* **14:4** [a]Many Hebrew manuscripts, Septuagint, Syriac, and Vulgate read *came.*

24 And the king said, "Let him return to his
own house, but do not let him see my face." So
Absalom returned to his own house, but did
not see the king's face.

David Forgives Absalom

25 Now in all Israel there was no one who
was praised as much as Absalom for his good
looks. From the sole of his foot to the crown
of his head there was no blemish in him.
26 And when he cut the hair of his head—at
the end of every year he cut *it* because it was
heavy on him—when he cut it, he weighed the
hair of his head at two hundred shekels according to the king's standard.
27 To Absalom were born three sons, and one
daughter whose name *was* Tamar. She was a
woman of beautiful appearance.
28 And Absalom dwelt two full years in Jerusalem, but did not see the king's face.
29 Therefore Absalom sent for Joab, to send
him to the king, but he would not come to
him. And when he sent again the second time,
he would not come.
30 So he said to his servants, "See, Joab's
field is near mine, and he has barley there; go
and set it on fire." And Absalom's servants set
the field on fire.
31 Then Joab arose and came to Absalom's
house, and said to him, "Why have your servants set my field on fire?"
32 And Absalom answered Joab, "Look, I
sent to you, saying, 'Come here, so that I may
send you to the king, to say, "Why have I come
from Geshur? *It would be* better for me *to be*
there still."' Now therefore, let me see the
king's face; but if there is iniquity in me, let
him execute me."
33 So Joab went to the king and told him.
And when he had called for Absalom, he
came to the king and bowed himself on his
face to the ground before the king. Then the
king kissed Absalom.

Absalom's Treason

15 After this it happened that Absalom
provided himself with chariots and
horses, and fifty men to run before him.
2 Now Absalom would rise early and stand
beside the way to the gate. *So* it was, whenever anyone who had a lawsuit came to the
king for a decision, that Absalom would call
to him and say, "What city *are* you from?"
And he would say, "Your servant *is* from such
and such a tribe of Israel."
3 Then Absalom would say to him, "Look,
your case *is* good and right; but *there is* no
deputy of the king to hear you."
4 Moreover Absalom would say, "Oh, that I
were made judge in the land, and everyone
who has any suit or cause would come to me;
then I would give him justice."
5 And *so* it was, whenever anyone came
near to bow down to him, that he would put
out his hand and take him and kiss him.
6 In this manner Absalom acted toward all
Israel who came to the king for judgment. So
Absalom stole the hearts of the men of Israel.
7 Now it came to pass after forty[a] years that
Absalom said to the king, "Please, let me go to
Hebron and pay the vow which I made to the
LORD.
8 "For your servant took a vow while I dwelt
at Geshur in Syria, saying, 'If the LORD indeed
brings me back to Jerusalem, then I will serve
the LORD.'"
9 And the king said to him, "Go in peace."
So he arose and went to Hebron.
10 Then Absalom sent spies throughout all
the tribes of Israel, saying, "As soon as you
hear the sound of the trumpet, then you shall
say, 'Absalom reigns in Hebron!'"
11 And with Absalom went two hundred men
invited from Jerusalem, and they went along
innocently and did not know anything.
12 Then Absalom sent for Ahithophel the
Gilonite, David's counselor, from his city—
from Giloh—while he offered sacrifices. And
the conspiracy grew strong, for the people
with Absalom continually increased in number.

David Escapes from Jerusalem

13 Now a messenger came to David, saying,
"The hearts of the men of Israel are with Absalom."
14 So David said to all his servants who *were*

15:7 [a]Septuagint manuscripts, Syriac, and Josephus read *four.*

LIFE LESSONS

➤ 14:32 — *"Now therefore, let me see the king's face; but if there is iniquity in me, let him execute me."*

Absalom never repented of his sin; he wanted acceptance, not forgiveness. But such shortcuts never work and cause more trouble in the end.

➤ 15:6 — *So Absalom stole the hearts of the men of Israel.*

It has always been possible to steal the hearts of the people through empty promises and a feigned concern for justice (2 Pet. 2:19). Mature Christians must always stay on the alert.

➤ 15:8 — *"For your servant took a vow while I dwelt at Geshur in Syria, saying, 'If the LORD indeed brings me back to Jerusalem, then I will serve the LORD.'"*

Absalom became a very good spiritual impostor, even deceiving his own father. We must remember that even the devil can quote Scripture (Matt. 4:6).

with him at Jerusalem, "Arise, and let us flee,
or we shall not escape from Absalom. Make
haste to depart, lest he overtake us suddenly
and bring disaster upon us, and strike the city
with the edge of the sword."
15 And the king's servants said to the king,
"We *are* your servants, *ready to do* whatever
my lord the king commands."
16 Then the king went out with all his household after him. But the king left ten women,
concubines, to keep the house.
17 And the king went out with all the people
after him, and stopped at the outskirts.
18 Then all his servants passed before him;
and all the Cherethites, all the Pelethites, and
all the Gittites, six hundred men who had
followed him from Gath, passed before the
king.
19 Then the king said to Ittai the Gittite,
"Why are you also going with us? Return and
remain with the king. For you *are* a foreigner
and also an exile from your own place.
20 "In fact, you came *only* yesterday. Should I
make you wander up and down with us today,
since I go I know not where? Return, and take
your brethren back. Mercy and truth *be* with
you."
➤ 21 But Ittai answered the king and said, "*As*
the LORD lives, and *as* my lord the king lives,
surely in whatever place my lord the king
shall be, whether in death or life, even there
also your servant will be."
22 So David said to Ittai, "Go, and cross over."
Then Ittai the Gittite and all his men and all
the little ones who *were* with him crossed
over.
23 And all the country wept with a loud
voice, and all the people crossed over. The
king himself also crossed over the Brook
Kidron, and all the people crossed over toward the way of the wilderness.
24 There was Zadok also, and all the Levites
with him, bearing the ark of the covenant of
God. And they set down the ark of God, and
Abiathar went up until all the people had finished crossing over from the city.
➤ 25 Then the king said to Zadok, "Carry the
ark of God back into the city. If I find favor in
the eyes of the LORD, He will bring me back
and show me *both* it and His dwelling place.
26 "But if He says thus: 'I have no delight in
you,' here I am, let Him do to me as seems
good to Him."
27 The king also said to Zadok the priest,
"*Are* you *not* a seer? Return to the city in
peace, and your two sons with you, Ahimaaz
your son, and Jonathan the son of Abiathar.
28 "See, I will wait in the plains of the wilderness until word comes from you to inform
me."
29 Therefore Zadok and Abiathar carried the
ark of God back to Jerusalem. And they remained there.
30 So David went up by the Ascent of the
Mount of Olives, and wept as he went up; and
he had his head covered and went barefoot.
And all the people who *were* with him covered their heads and went up, weeping as
they went up.
31 Then *someone* told David, saying, "Ahith- ➤
ophel *is* among the conspirators with Absalom." And David said, "O LORD, I pray, turn
the counsel of Ahithophel into foolishness!"
32 Now it happened when David had come to
the top *of the mountain,* where he worshiped
God—there was Hushai the Archite coming to
meet him with his robe torn and dust on his
head.
33 David said to him, "If you go on with me,
then you will become a burden to me.
34 "But if you return to the city, and say to
Absalom, 'I will be your servant, O king; *as* I
was your father's servant previously, so I *will*
now also *be* your servant,' then you may defeat the counsel of Ahithophel for me.
35 "And *do* you not *have* Zadok and Abiathar
the priests with you there? Therefore it will be
that whatever you hear from the king's
house, you shall tell to Zadok and Abiathar
the priests.
36 "Indeed *they have* there with them their
two sons, Ahimaaz, Zadok's *son,* and Jonathan, Abiathar's *son;* and by them you shall
send me everything you hear."
37 So Hushai, David's friend, went into the
city. And Absalom came into Jerusalem.

LIFE LESSONS

➤ 15:21 — *". . . surely in whatever place my lord the king shall be, whether in death or life, even there also your servant will be."*

Ittai the Gittite answered the king much as Ruth had answered her mother-in-law many years before (Ruth 1:17). By God's grace, faith can find a home in the unlikeliest of hearts.

➤ 15:25 — *Then the king said to Zadok, "Carry the ark of God back into the city. If I find favor in the eyes of the LORD, He will bring me back and show me both it and His dwelling place."*

David had learned to trust in the grace and mercy of the Lord, even though he did not know what lay ahead for him. God assumes full responsibility for our needs when we obey him.

➤ 15:31 — *"Ahithophel is among the conspirators with Absalom."*

By comparing 2 Samuel 11:3 with 2 Samuel 23:34, we learn that Ahithophel was Bathsheba's grandfather. Apparently he had nursed a grudge against David ever since the murder of his granddaughter's husband.

Mephibosheth's Servant

16 When David was a little past the top *of
the mountain,* there was Ziba the servant of Mephibosheth, who met him with a
couple of saddled donkeys, and on them two
hundred *loaves* of bread, one hundred clusters of raisins, one hundred summer fruits,
and a skin of wine.
2 And the king said to Ziba, "What do you
mean to do with these?" So Ziba said, "The
donkeys *are* for the king's household to ride
on, the bread and summer fruit for the young
men to eat, and the wine for those who are
faint in the wilderness to drink."
➤ 3 Then the king said, "And where *is* your
master's son?" And Ziba said to the king, "Indeed he is staying in Jerusalem, for he said,
'Today the house of Israel will restore the
kingdom of my father to me.'"
4 So the king said to Ziba, "Here, all that
belongs to Mephibosheth *is* yours." And
Ziba said, "I humbly bow before you, *that*
I may find favor in your sight, my lord,
O king!"

Shimei Curses David

5 Now when King David came to Bahurim,
there was a man from the family of the house
of Saul, whose name *was* Shimei the son of
Gera, coming from there. He came out, cursing continuously as he came.
6 And he threw stones at David and at all
the servants of King David. And all the people
and all the mighty men *were* on his right
hand and on his left.
7 Also Shimei said thus when he cursed:
"Come out! Come out! You bloodthirsty man,
you rogue!
8 "The LORD has brought upon you all the
blood of the house of Saul, in whose place you
have reigned; and the LORD has delivered the
kingdom into the hand of Absalom your son.
So now you *are caught* in your own evil, because you are a bloodthirsty man!"
9 Then Abishai the son of Zeruiah said to
the king, "Why should this dead dog curse my
lord the king? Please, let me go over and take
off his head!"
➤ 10 But the king said, "What have I to do with
you, you sons of Zeruiah? So let him curse,
because the LORD has said to him, 'Curse David.' Who then shall say, 'Why have you done
so?'"
11 And David said to Abishai and all his servants, "See how my son who came from my
own body seeks my life. How much more now
may this Benjamite? Let him alone, and let
him curse; for so the LORD has ordered him.
12 "It may be that the LORD will look on my ✳
affliction,[a] and that the LORD will repay me
with good for his cursing this day."
13 And as David and his men went along the
road, Shimei went along the hillside opposite
him and cursed as he went, threw stones at
him and kicked up dust.
14 Now the king and all the people who *were*
with him became weary; so they refreshed
themselves there.

The Advice of Ahithophel

15 Meanwhile Absalom and all the people,
the men of Israel, came to Jerusalem; and
Ahithophel *was* with him.
16 And so it was, when Hushai the Archite,
David's friend, came to Absalom, that Hushai
said to Absalom, "*Long* live the king! *Long*
live the king!"
17 So Absalom said to Hushai, "*Is* this your
loyalty to your friend? Why did you not go
with your friend?"
18 And Hushai said to Absalom, "No, but
whom the LORD and this people and all the
men of Israel choose, his I will be, and with
him I will remain.
19 "Furthermore, whom should I serve?
Should I not *serve* in the presence of his son?
As I have served in your father's presence, so
will I be in your presence."
20 Then Absalom said to Ahithophel, "Give
advice as to what we should do."
21 And Ahithophel said to Absalom, "Go in to ➤
your father's concubines, whom he has left to
keep the house; and all Israel will hear that
you are abhorred by your father. Then the
hands of all who are with you will be strong."

16:12 [a]Following Kethib, Septuagint, Syriac, and Vulgate; Qere reads *my eyes;* Targum reads *tears of my eyes.*

LIFE LESSONS

➤ 16:3 — *Ziba said to the king, "Indeed he is staying in Jerusalem, for he said, 'Today the house of Israel will restore the kingdom of my father to me.'"*

Ziba lied about Mephibosheth (see 2 Sam. 19:24–30) and used bribery to gain the king's favor—and so gained a financial boon. But he would find out that whatever you acquire outside of God's will turns to ashes.

➤ 16:10 — *But the king said, ". . . So let him curse, because the LORD has said to him, 'Curse David.' Who then shall say, 'Why have you done so?'"*

A lesser man would have given the order to silence Shimei's tongue, but David left such judgments in God's hands. Perhaps he remembered the Lord's words: "Vengeance is Mine, and recompense . . ." (Deut. 32:35).

➤ 16:21 — *And Ahithophel said to Absalom, "Go in to your father's concubines, whom he has left to keep the house . . . ."*

As David violated Bathsheba, the granddaughter of Ahithophel and the wife of Uriah, so Ahithophel advised Absalom to violate David's concubines. The evil we do often comes back to us in even greater quantity.

LIFE PRINCIPLE 8

FIGHT ALL YOUR BATTLES ON YOUR KNEES AND YOU WIN EVERY TIME.

2 SAM. 15:31

The term *resistance movement* describes situations in which oppressed people rise up against their oppressors. Resistance fighters take the stance, "I'm not going to stand idly by and allow this evil to continue. I choose to resist the wrongs. Whether I live or die in resisting my oppressor, I will no longer live as I have been."

Resistance in prayer is the biblical approach to confronting and overcoming the devil. Peter wrote, "Resist him, steadfast in the faith" (1 Pet. 5:9). James echoed this teaching: "Submit to God. Resist the devil and he will flee from you. Draw near to God and He will draw near to you" (James 4:7, 8). Both Peter and James make clear that we are to actively resist evil through our persevering prayers.

On the surface, resistance may appear to be passive. In practice, it is anything but passive. It is an active stance, both intentional and powerful.

What would you do if a weight began to press against you, attempting to push you off a position rightfully yours? How would you resist? You would lean into the weight and press back. The pressure you exert would equal or exceed the pressure exerted against you. That's a posture of resistance.

Resistance is first and foremost a firm decision to join the struggle against evil in prayer, rather than turning away, backing off, or retreating. Such resistance takes strength and courage. It also takes patience and perseverance. That's why Luke includes a parable designed to teach us "that men always ought to pray and not lose heart" (Luke 18:1).

Peter and James point to two key words at the heart of our ability to resist the devil through our prayers: submission to God and faith.

Submission to God is saying, "I can't, but You can." In our battlefield prayers we might say, "Lord, I can't defeat the devil on my own. But with You, I can." This is the position the apostle Paul took when he said, "I can do all things through Christ who strengthens me" (Phil. 4:13).

James taught that submission occurs when we seek to develop a closer relationship to God. As we spend time with God, we get to know Him better and discover *how* He wants us to overcome evil and experience blessing.

We draw near to God through prayer and by spending time in His Word. We draw near to God when we set aside time solely to listen to God and to wait upon Him for direction and guidance. We draw near to God when we periodically

Resistance is a decision to join the struggle against evil in prayer.

shut ourselves away, closing off all other influences that might distract us from knowing Him better. The better we know Him, the more we see His awesome power, experience His vast love, learn from His wisdom, and grow in our faith. We come to an even greater realization: "Yes, God *can* defeat the devil on my behalf. Yes, God *will* win in any conflict with the devil. Yes, God *does* want me to be able to overcome my adversary and to live in victory in Christ Jesus."

Faith is saying to God, "I believe You will." In our battle to overcome the enemy, we might pray this way: "I believe You will defeat the enemy and cause him to flee from me as I resist him and put my trust in You." Again and again, David made this declaration of faith to the Lord: "O my God, I trust in You" (See Ps. 25:2; also 31:6; 55:23; 56:3; 143:8).

We grow in faith by exercising it, by trusting God in situation after situation, circumstance after circumstance, relationship after relationship. We develop a personal history in which we obey God and He remains faithful in His loving care of us.

It is impossible for you to resist the devil for very long if you do not believe that Christ Jesus through you can and *will* defeat the devil. Furthermore, you can remain firm in your faith only when you completely submit to God—in all areas of your life. When you do not submit an area to God, you are saying to Him, "I can handle this. I don't need Your help." That's precisely the place the devil will attack you!

The good news is that God has given each of us a measure of faith to develop. He gives us the ability to submit. Therefore, we are capable of resisting the devil through our prayers. Afterwards he must flee.

See the Life Principles Index for further study.

We grow in faith by exercising it.

22 So they pitched a tent for Absalom on the
top of the house, and Absalom went in to his
father's concubines in the sight of all Israel.
23 Now the advice of Ahithophel, which he
gave in those days, *was* as if one had inquired
at the oracle of God. So *was* all the advice of
Ahithophel both with David and with Absalom.

17 Moreover Ahithophel said to Absalom,
"Now let me choose twelve thousand
men, and I will arise and pursue David tonight.
2 "I will come upon him while he *is* weary
and weak, and make him afraid. And all the
people who *are* with him will flee, and I will
strike only the king.
3 "Then I will bring back all the people to
you. When all return except the man whom
you seek, all the people will be at peace."
4 And the saying pleased Absalom and all
the elders of Israel.

The Advice of Hushai

5 Then Absalom said, "Now call Hushai the
Archite also, and let us hear what he says
too."
6 And when Hushai came to Absalom, Absalom spoke to him, saying, "Ahithophel has
spoken in this manner. Shall we do as he
says? If not, speak up."
7 So Hushai said to Absalom: "The advice
that Ahithophel has given *is* not good at this
time.
8 "For," said Hushai, "you know your father
and his men, that they *are* mighty men, and
they *are* enraged in their minds, like a bear
robbed of her cubs in the field; and your father *is* a man of war, and will not camp with
the people.
9 "Surely by now he is hidden in some pit,
or in some *other* place. And it will be, when
some of them are overthrown at the first, that
whoever hears *it* will say, 'There is a slaughter among the people who follow Absalom.'
10 "And even he *who is* valiant, whose heart
is like the heart of a lion, will melt completely.
For all Israel knows that your father *is* a
mighty man, and *those* who *are* with him *are*
valiant men.
11 "Therefore I advise that all Israel be fully
gathered to you, from Dan to Beersheba, like
the sand that *is* by the sea for multitude, and
that you go to battle in person.
12 "So we will come upon him in some place
where he may be found, and we will fall on
him as the dew falls on the ground. And of
him and all the men who *are* with him there
shall not be left so much as one.
13 "Moreover, if he has withdrawn into a city,
then all Israel shall bring ropes to that city;
and we will pull it into the river, until there is
not one small stone found there."
14 So Absalom and all the men of Israel said,
"The advice of Hushai the Archite *is* better
than the advice of Ahithophel." For the LORD
had purposed to defeat the good advice of
Ahithophel, to the intent that the LORD might
bring disaster on Absalom.

Hushai Warns David to Escape

15 Then Hushai said to Zadok and Abiathar
the priests, "Thus and so Ahithophel advised
Absalom and the elders of Israel, and thus
and so I have advised.
16 Now therefore, send quickly and tell David, saying, 'Do not spend this night in the
plains of the wilderness, but speedily cross
over, lest the king and all the people who *are*
with him be swallowed up.'"
17 Now Jonathan and Ahimaaz stayed at En
Rogel, for they dared not be seen coming into
the city; so a female servant would come and
tell them, and they would go and tell King David.
18 Nevertheless a lad saw them, and told Absalom. But both of them went away quickly
and came to a man's house in Bahurim, who
had a well in his court; and they went down
into it.
19 Then the woman took and spread a covering over the well's mouth, and spread ground
grain on it; and the thing was not known.
20 And when Absalom's servants came to the
woman at the house, they said, "Where *are*
Ahimaaz and Jonathan?" So the woman said
to them, "They have gone over the water
brook." And when they had searched and
could not find *them*, they returned to Jerusalem.
21 Now it came to pass, after they had departed, that they came up out of the well and
went and told King David, and said to David,
"Arise and cross over the water quickly. For
thus has Ahithophel advised against you."
22 So David and all the people who *were*
with him arose and crossed over the Jordan.
By morning light not one of them was left
who had not gone over the Jordan.
23 Now when Ahithophel saw that his advice
was not followed, he saddled a donkey, and
arose and went home to his house, to his city.
Then he put his household in order, and
hanged himself, and died; and he was buried
in his father's tomb.
24 Then David went to Mahanaim. And Absalom crossed over the Jordan, he and all the
men of Israel with him.
25 And Absalom made Amasa captain of
the army instead of Joab. This Amasa *was* the
son of a man whose name *was* Jithra,[a] an Israelite,[b] who had gone in to Abigail the
daughter of Nahash, sister of Zeruiah, Joab's
mother.

17:25 [a]Spelled *Jether* in 1 Chronicles 2:17 and elsewhere
[b]Following Masoretic Text, some manuscripts of the Septuagint,
and Targum; some manuscripts of the Septuagint read *Ishmaelite*
(compare 1 Chronicles 2:17); Vulgate reads *of Jezrael*.

26 So Israel and Absalom encamped in the
land of Gilead.
27 Now it happened, when David had come
to Mahanaim, that Shobi the son of Nahash
from Rabbah of the people of Ammon, Machir
the son of Ammiel from Lo Debar, and Barzillai the Gileadite from Rogelim,
28 brought beds and basins, earthen vessels
and wheat, barley and flour, parched *grain*
and beans, lentils and parched *seeds,*
29 honey and curds, sheep and cheese of the
herd, for David and the people who *were* with
him to eat. For they said, "The people are
hungry and weary and thirsty in the wilderness."

Absalom's Defeat and Death

18 And David numbered the people who
were with him, and set captains of thousands and captains of hundreds over them.
2 Then David sent out one third of the people under the hand of Joab, one third under
the hand of Abishai the son of Zeruiah, Joab's
brother, and one third under the hand of Ittai
the Gittite. And the king said to the people, "I
also will surely go out with you myself."
3 But the people answered, "You shall not
go out! For if we flee away, they will not care
about us; nor if half of us die, will they care
about us. But *you are* worth ten thousand of
us now. For you are now more help to us in
the city."
4 Then the king said to them, "Whatever
seems best to you I will do." So the king stood
beside the gate, and all the people went out by
hundreds and by thousands.
5 Now the king had commanded Joab,
Abishai, and Ittai, saying, "*Deal* gently for my
sake with the young man Absalom." And all
the people heard when the king gave all the
captains orders concerning Absalom.
6 So the people went out into the field of
battle against Israel. And the battle was in the
woods of Ephraim.
7 The people of Israel were overthrown
there before the servants of David, and a
great slaughter of twenty thousand took place
there that day.
8 For the battle there was scattered over the
face of the whole countryside, and the woods
devoured more people that day than the
sword devoured.
9 Then Absalom met the servants of David.
Absalom rode on a mule. The mule went
under the thick boughs of a great terebinth
tree, and his head caught in the terebinth; so
he was left hanging between heaven and
earth. And the mule which *was* under him
went on.
10 Now a certain man saw *it* and told Joab,
and said, "I just saw Absalom hanging in a
terebinth tree!"
11 So Joab said to the man who told him,
"You just saw *him!* And why did you not
strike him there to the ground? I would have
given you ten *shekels* of silver and a belt."
12 But the man said to Joab, "Though I were
to receive a thousand *shekels* of silver in my
hand, I would not raise my hand against the
king's son. For in our hearing the king commanded you and Abishai and Ittai, saying,
'Beware lest anyone *touch* the young man
Absalom!'[a]
13 "Otherwise I would have dealt falsely
against my own life. For there is nothing hidden from the king, and you yourself would
have set yourself against *me.*"
14 Then Joab said, "I cannot linger with you."
And he took three spears in his hand and
thrust them through Absalom's heart, while
he was *still* alive in the midst of the terebinth
tree.
15 And ten young men who bore Joab's
armor surrounded Absalom, and struck and
killed him.
16 So Joab blew the trumpet, and the people
returned from pursuing Israel. For Joab held
back the people.
17 And they took Absalom and cast him into
a large pit in the woods, and laid a very large
heap of stones over him. Then all Israel fled,
everyone to his tent.
18 Now Absalom in his lifetime had taken
and set up a pillar for himself, which *is* in the
King's Valley. For he said, "I have no son to
keep my name in remembrance." He called
the pillar after his own name. And to this day
it is called Absalom's Monument.

David Hears of Absalom's Death

19 Then Ahimaaz the son of Zadok said, "Let
me run now and take the news to the king,
how the LORD has avenged him of his enemies."
20 And Joab said to him, "You shall not take
the news this day, for you shall take the news
another day. But today you shall take no
news, because the king's son is dead."
21 Then Joab said to the Cushite, "Go, tell the

18:12 [a]The ancient versions read *'Protect the young man Absalom for me!'*

LIFE LESSONS

➤ **18:18 — *Now Absalom in his lifetime had taken and set up a pillar for himself, which is in the King's Valley . . . .***

Absalom left behind a stone monument in his name, but nothing else. Whatever we acquire outside of God's will turns to ashes.

king what you have seen." So the Cushite
bowed himself to Joab and ran.
22 And Ahimaaz the son of Zadok said again
to Joab, "But whatever happens, please let me
also run after the Cushite." So Joab said,
"Why will you run, my son, since you have no
news ready?"
23 "But whatever happens," *he said,* "let me
run." So he said to him, "Run." Then Ahimaaz
ran by way of the plain, and outran the
Cushite.
24 Now David was sitting between the two
gates. And the watchman went up to the roof
over the gate, to the wall, lifted his eyes and
looked, and there was a man, running alone.
25 Then the watchman cried out and told the
king. And the king said, "If he *is* alone, *there
is* news in his mouth." And he came rapidly
and drew near.
26 Then the watchman saw *another* man running, and the watchman called to the gate-
keeper and said, "There is *another* man,
running alone!" And the king said, "He also
brings news."
27 So the watchman said, "I think the running of the first is like the running of Ahimaaz the son of Zadok." And the king said,
"He *is* a good man, and comes with good
news."
28 So Ahimaaz called out and said to the
king, "All is well!" Then he bowed down with
his face to the earth before the king, and said,
"Blessed *be* the LORD your God, who has delivered up the men who raised their hand
against my lord the king!"
29 The king said, "Is the young man Absalom
safe?"Ahimaaz answered, "When Joab sent
the king's servant and *me* your servant, I saw
a great tumult, but I did not know what *it was
about.*"
30 And the king said, "Turn aside *and* stand
here." So he turned aside and stood still.
31 Just then the Cushite came, and the
Cushite said, "There is good news, my lord
the king! For the LORD has avenged you this
day of all those who rose against you."
32 And the king said to the Cushite, "Is the
young man Absalom safe?" So the Cushite
answered, "May the enemies of my lord the
king, and all who rise against you to do harm,
be like *that* young man!"

David's Mourning for Absalom

33 Then the king was deeply moved, and
went up to the chamber over the gate, and
wept. And as he went, he said thus: "O my son
Absalom—my son, my son Absalom—if only I
had died in your place! O Absalom my son,
my son!"

19 And Joab was told, "Behold, the king is
weeping and mourning for Absalom."
2 So the victory that day was *turned* into
mourning for all the people. For the people
heard it said that day, "The king is grieved for
his son."
3 And the people stole back into the city
that day, as people who are ashamed steal
away when they flee in battle.
4 But the king covered his face, and the king
cried out with a loud voice, "O my son Absalom! O Absalom, my son, my son!"
5 Then Joab came into the house to the
king, and said, "Today you have disgraced all
your servants who today have saved your life,
the lives of your sons and daughters, the lives
of your wives and the lives of your concubines,
6 "in that you love your enemies and hate
your friends. For you have declared today that
you regard neither princes nor servants; for
today I perceive that if Absalom had lived and
all of us had died today, then it would have
pleased you well.
7 "Now therefore, arise, go out and speak
comfort to your servants. For I swear by the
LORD, if you do not go out, not one will stay
with you this night. And that will be worse for
you than all the evil that has befallen you
from your youth until now."
8 Then the king arose and sat in the gate.
And they told all the people, saying, "There is
the king, sitting in the gate." So all the people
came before the king. For everyone of Israel
had fled to his tent.

David Returns to Jerusalem

9 Now all the people were in a dispute
throughout all the tribes of Israel, saying,
"The king saved us from the hand of our enemies, he delivered us from the hand of the
Philistines, and now he has fled from the land
because of Absalom.
10 "But Absalom, whom we anointed over
us, has died in battle. Now therefore, why do
you say nothing about bringing back the
king?"
11 So King David sent to Zadok and Abiathar
the priests, saying, "Speak to the elders of Judah, saying, 'Why are you the last to bring the
king back to his house, since the words of all
Israel have come to the king, to his *very* house?
12 'You *are* my brethren, you *are* my bone

LIFE LESSONS

➤ 19:4 — *"O my son Absalom! O Absalom, my son, my son!"*

The sword continued to devour David's house, as Nathan had predicted. God's promises always come true, whether for blessing or for judgment.

and my flesh. Why then are you the last to
bring back the king?'
13 "And say to Amasa, '*Are* you not my bone
and my flesh? God do so to me, and more
also, if you are not commander of the army
before me continually in place of Joab.'"
14 So he swayed the hearts of all the men of
Judah, just as *the heart of* one man, so that
they sent *this word* to the king: "Return, you
and all your servants!"
15 Then the king returned and came to the
Jordan. And Judah came to Gilgal, to go to
meet the king, to escort the king across the
Jordan.
16 And Shimei the son of Gera, a Benjamite,
who *was* from Bahurim, hurried and came
down with the men of Judah to meet King David.
17 *There were* a thousand men of Benjamin
with him, and Ziba the servant of the house of
Saul, and his fifteen sons and his twenty servants with him; and they went over the Jordan before the king.
18 Then a ferryboat went across to carry over
the king's household, and to do what he
thought good.

David's Mercy to Shimei

Now Shimei the son of Gera fell down before the king when he had crossed the Jordan.
19 Then he said to the king, "Do not let my
lord impute iniquity to me, or remember what
wrong your servant did on the day that my
lord the king left Jerusalem, that the king
should take *it* to heart.
20 "For I, your servant, know that I have
sinned. Therefore here I am, the first to come
today of all the house of Joseph to go down to
meet my lord the king."
21 But Abishai the son of Zeruiah answered
and said, "Shall not Shimei be put to death for
this, because he cursed the LORD's anointed?"
22 And David said, "What have I to do with
you, you sons of Zeruiah, that you should be
adversaries to me today? Shall any man be
put to death today in Israel? For do I not know
that today I *am* king over Israel?"
23 Therefore the king said to Shimei, "You
shall not die." And the king swore to him.

David and Mephibosheth Meet

24 Now Mephibosheth the son of Saul came
down to meet the king. And he had not cared
for his feet, nor trimmed his mustache, nor
washed his clothes, from the day the king departed until the day he returned in peace.
25 So it was, when he had come to Jerusalem
to meet the king, that the king said to him,
"Why did you not go with me, Mephibosheth?"
26 And he answered, "My lord, O king, my
servant deceived me. For your servant said, 'I
will saddle a donkey for myself, that I may
ride on it and go to the king,' because your
servant *is* lame.
27 "And he has slandered your servant to my
lord the king, but my lord the king *is* like the
angel of God. Therefore do *what is* good in
your eyes.
28 "For all my father's house were but dead
men before my lord the king. Yet you set your
servant among those who eat at your own
table. Therefore what right have I still to cry
out anymore to the king?"
29 So the king said to him, "Why do you
speak anymore of your matters? I have said,
'You and Ziba divide the land.'"
30 Then Mephibosheth said to the king,
"Rather, let him take it all, inasmuch as my
lord the king has come back in peace to his
own house."

David's Kindness to Barzillai

31 And Barzillai the Gileadite came down
from Rogelim and went across the Jordan
with the king, to escort him across the Jordan.
32 Now Barzillai was a very aged man,
eighty years old. And he had provided the
king with supplies while he stayed at Mahanaim, for he *was* a very rich man.
33 And the king said to Barzillai, "Come
across with me, and I will provide for you
while you are with me in Jerusalem."
34 But Barzillai said to the king, "How long
have I to live, that I should go up with the king
to Jerusalem?
35 "I *am* today eighty years old. Can I discern
between the good and bad? Can your servant
taste what I eat or what I drink? Can I hear
any longer the voice of singing men and
singing women? Why then should your servant be a further burden to my lord the king?
36 "Your servant will go a little way across
the Jordan with the king. And why should the
king repay me *with* such a reward?
37 "Please let your servant turn back again,
that I may die in my own city, near the grave
of my father and mother. But here is your servant Chimham; let him cross over with my
lord the king, and do for him what seems
good to you."
38 And the king answered, "Chimham shall
cross over with me, and I will do for him what
seems good to you. Now whatever you request of me, I will do for you."
39 Then all the people went over the Jordan.
And when the king had crossed over, the king
kissed Barzillai and blessed him, and he returned to his own place.

The Quarrel About the King

40 Now the king went on to Gilgal, and
Chimham[a] went on with him. And all the peo-

19:40 [a]Masoretic Text reads *Chimhan.*

ple of Judah escorted the king, and also half
the people of Israel.
41 Just then all the men of Israel came to the
king, and said to the king, "Why have our
brethren, the men of Judah, stolen you away
and brought the king, his household, and all
David's men with him across the Jordan?"
42 So all the men of Judah answered the men
of Israel, "Because the king *is* a close relative
of ours. Why then are you angry over this
matter? Have we ever eaten at the king's *expense*? Or has he given us any gift?"
43 And the men of Israel answered the men
of Judah, and said, "We have ten shares in the
king; therefore we also have more *right* to
David than you. Why then do you despise
us—were we not the first to advise bringing
back our king?" Yet the words of the men of
Judah were fiercer than the words of the men
of Israel.

The Rebellion of Sheba

20 And there happened to be there a
rebel,[a] whose name *was* Sheba the son
of Bichri, a Benjamite. And he blew a trumpet, and said:

"We have no share in David,
Nor do we have inheritance in the son of
Jesse;
Every man to his tents, O Israel!"

2 So every man of Israel deserted David,
and followed Sheba the son of Bichri. But the
men of Judah, from the Jordan as far as Jerusalem, remained loyal to their king.
3 Now David came to his house at Jerusalem. And the king took the ten women, his
concubines whom he had left to keep the
house, and put them in seclusion and supported them, but did not go in to them. So
they were shut up to the day of their death,
living in widowhood.
4 And the king said to Amasa, "Assemble
the men of Judah for me within three days,
and be present here yourself."
5 So Amasa went to assemble *the men of*
Judah. But he delayed longer than the set
time which David had appointed him.
6 And David said to Abishai, "Now Sheba
the son of Bichri will do us more harm than
Absalom. Take your lord's servants and pursue him, lest he find for himself fortified
cities, and escape us."
7 So Joab's men, with the Cherethites, the
Pelethites, and all the mighty men, went out
after him. And they went out of Jerusalem to
pursue Sheba the son of Bichri.
8 When they *were* at the large stone which
is in Gibeon, Amasa came before them.
Now Joab was dressed in battle armor; on it
was a belt *with* a sword fastened in its sheath
at his hips; and as he was going forward, it
fell out.
9 Then Joab said to Amasa, "*Are* you in
health, my brother?" And Joab took Amasa
by the beard with his right hand to kiss him.
10 But Amasa did not notice the sword
that *was* in Joab's hand. And he struck
him with it in the stomach, and his entrails
poured out on the ground; and he did not
strike him again. Thus he died. Then Joab and
Abishai his brother pursued Sheba the son of
Bichri.
11 Meanwhile one of Joab's men stood near
Amasa, and said, "Whoever favors Joab and
whoever *is* for David—follow Joab!"
12 But Amasa wallowed in *his* blood in the
middle of the highway. And when the man
saw that all the people stood still, he moved
Amasa from the highway to the field and
threw a garment over him, when he saw that
everyone who came upon him halted.
13 When he was removed from the highway,
all the people went on after Joab to pursue
Sheba the son of Bichri.
14 And he went through all the tribes of Israel to Abel and Beth Maachah and all the
Berites. So they were gathered together and
also went after *Sheba*.[a]
15 Then they came and besieged him in Abel
of Beth Maachah; and they cast up a siege
mound against the city, and it stood by the
rampart. And all the people who *were* with
Joab battered the wall to throw it down.
16 Then a wise woman cried out from the
city, "Hear, hear! Please say to Joab, 'Come
nearby, that I may speak with you.'"
17 When he had come near to her, the
woman said, "*Are* you Joab?" He answered, "I
am." Then she said to him, "Hear the words of
your maidservant." And he answered, "I am
listening."
18 So she spoke, saying, "They used to talk in
former times, saying, 'They shall surely seek
guidance at Abel,' and so they would end *disputes*.
19 "I *am among the* peaceable *and* faithful in
Israel. You seek to destroy a city and a mother
in Israel. Why would you swallow up the inheritance of the LORD?"
20 And Joab answered and said, "Far be it,
far be it from me, that I should swallow up or
destroy!
21 "That *is* not so. But a man from the mountains of Ephraim, Sheba the son of Bichri by
name, has raised his hand against the king,
against David. Deliver him only, and I will depart from the city." So the woman said to
Joab, "Watch, his head will be thrown to you
over the wall."
22 Then the woman in her wisdom went to all
the people. And they cut off the head of Sheba
the son of Bichri, and threw *it* out to Joab.
Then he blew a trumpet, and they withdrew

20:1 [a]Literally *man of Belial* **20:14** [a]Literally *him*

from the city, every man to his tent. So Joab
returned to the king at Jerusalem.

David's Government Officers

23 And Joab *was* over all the army of Israel;
Benaiah the son of Jehoiada *was* over the
Cherethites and the Pelethites;
24 Adoram *was* in charge of revenue; Jehoshaphat the son of Ahilud *was* recorder;
25 Sheva *was* scribe; Zadok and Abiathar
were the priests;
26 and Ira the Jairite was a chief minister
under David.

David Avenges the Gibeonites

➤21 Now there was a famine in the days of
David for three years, year after year;
and David inquired of the LORD. And the
LORD answered, "*It is* because of Saul and *his*
bloodthirsty house, because he killed the Gibeonites."
2 So the king called the Gibeonites and
spoke to them. Now the Gibeonites *were* not
of the children of Israel, but of the remnant of
the Amorites; the children of Israel had sworn
protection to them, but Saul had sought to kill
them in his zeal for the children of Israel and
Judah.
3 Therefore David said to the Gibeonites,
"What shall I do for you? And with what shall
I make atonement, that you may bless the inheritance of the LORD?"
4 And the Gibeonites said to him, "We will
have no silver or gold from Saul or from his
house, nor shall you kill any man in Israel for
us." So he said, "Whatever you say, I will do
for you."
5 Then they answered the king, "As for the
man who consumed us and plotted against
us, *that* we should be destroyed from remaining in any of the territories of Israel,
6 "let seven men of his descendants be
delivered to us, and we will hang them before
the LORD in Gibeah of Saul, *whom* the
LORD chose." And the king said, "I will give
them."
7 But the king spared Mephibosheth the son
of Jonathan, the son of Saul, because of the
LORD's oath that *was* between them, between
David and Jonathan the son of Saul.
8 So the king took Armoni and Mephibosheth, the two sons of Rizpah the daughter
of Aiah, whom she bore to Saul, and the five
sons of Michal[a] the daughter of Saul, whom
she brought up for Adriel the son of Barzillai
the Meholathite;
9 and he delivered them into the hands of
the Gibeonites, and they hanged them on the
hill before the LORD. So they fell, *all* seven together, and were put to death in the days of
harvest, in the first *days*, in the beginning of
barley harvest.
10 Now Rizpah the daughter of Aiah took
sackcloth and spread it for herself on the
rock, from the beginning of harvest until the
late rains poured on them from heaven. And
she did not allow the birds of the air to rest on
them by day nor the beasts of the field by
night.
11 And David was told what Rizpah the
daughter of Aiah, the concubine of Saul, had
done.
12 Then David went and took the bones of
Saul, and the bones of Jonathan his son, from
the men of Jabesh Gilead who had stolen
them from the street of Beth Shan,[a] where the
Philistines had hung them up, after the Philistines had struck down Saul in Gilboa.
13 So he brought up the bones of Saul and
the bones of Jonathan his son from there; and
they gathered the bones of those who had
been hanged.
14 They buried the bones of Saul and Jonathan his son in the country of Benjamin in
Zelah, in the tomb of Kish his father. So they
performed all that the king commanded. And
after that God heeded the prayer for the land.

Philistine Giants Destroyed

15 When the Philistines were at war again
with Israel, David and his servants with him
went down and fought against the Philistines;
and David grew faint.
16 Then Ishbi-Benob, who *was* one of the
sons of the giant, the weight of whose bronze
spear *was* three hundred *shekels*, who was
bearing a new *sword*, thought he could kill
David.
17 But Abishai the son of Zeruiah came to his
aid, and struck the Philistine and killed him.
Then the men of David swore to him, saying,
"You shall go out no more with us to battle,
lest you quench the lamp of Israel."
18 Now it happened afterward that there was
again a battle with the Philistines at Gob.

21:8 [a]Or *Merab* (compare 1 Samuel 18:19 and 25:44; 2 Samuel 3:14 and 6:23) **21:12** [a]Spelled *Beth Shean* in Joshua 17:11 and elsewhere

LIFE LESSONS

➤ 21:1 — *Now there was a famine . . . and David inquired of the LORD. And the LORD answered, "It is because of Saul and his bloodthirsty house, because he killed the Gibeonites."*

Saul in his mistaken zeal had violated a covenant made in God's name (Josh. 9:16–21), and Israel paid for it. We reap what we sow, more than we sow, and later than we sow.

Then Sibbechai the Hushathite killed Saph,[a]
who *was* one of the sons of the giant.
19 Again there was war at Gob with the Philistines, where Elhanan the son of Jaare-
Oregim[a] the Bethlehemite killed *the brother
of* Goliath the Gittite, the shaft of whose spear
was like a weaver's beam.
20 Yet again there was war at Gath, where
there was a man of *great* stature, who had six
fingers on each hand and six toes on each
foot, twenty-four in number; and he also was
born to the giant.
21 So when he defied Israel, Jonathan the
son of Shimea,[a] David's brother, killed him.
22 These four were born to the giant in Gath,
and fell by the hand of David and by the hand
of his servants.

Praise for God's Deliverance

22 Then David spoke to the LORD the words of this song, on the day when the LORD had delivered him from the hand of all his enemies, and from the hand of Saul.
2 And he said:[a]

"The LORD *is* my rock and my fortress and
my deliverer;
3 The God of my strength, in whom I will
trust;
My shield and the horn of my salvation,
My stronghold and my refuge;
My Savior, You save me from violence.
4 I will call upon the LORD, *who is worthy*
to be praised;
So shall I be saved from my enemies.

5 "When the waves of death surrounded me,
The floods of ungodliness made me
afraid.
6 The sorrows of Sheol surrounded me;
The snares of death confronted me.
7 In my distress I called upon the LORD,
And cried out to my God;
He heard my voice from His temple,
And my cry *entered* His ears.

8 "Then the earth shook and trembled;
The foundations of heaven[a] quaked and
were shaken,
Because He was angry.
9 Smoke went up from His nostrils,
And devouring fire from His mouth;
Coals were kindled by it.
10 He bowed the heavens also, and came
down
With darkness under His feet.
11 He rode upon a cherub, and flew;
And He was seen[a] upon the wings of the
wind.
12 He made darkness canopies around
Him,
Dark waters *and* thick clouds of the
skies.
13 From the brightness before Him
Coals of fire were kindled.

14 "The LORD thundered from heaven,
And the Most High uttered His voice.
15 He sent out arrows and scattered them;
Lightning bolts, and He vanquished
them.
16 Then the channels of the sea were seen,
The foundations of the world were
uncovered,
At the rebuke of the LORD,
At the blast of the breath of His nostrils.

17 "He sent from above, He took me,
He drew me out of many waters.
18 He delivered me from my strong
enemy,
From those who hated me;
For they were too strong for me.
19 They confronted me in the day of my
calamity,
But the LORD was my support.
20 He also brought me out into a broad
place;
He delivered me because He delighted in
me.

21 "The LORD rewarded me according to my
righteousness;
According to the cleanness of my
hands
He has recompensed me.
22 For I have kept the ways of the LORD,
And have not wickedly departed from my
God.
23 For all His judgments *were* before me;
And *as for* His statutes, I did not depart
from them.
24 I was also blameless before Him,
And I kept myself from my iniquity.

21:18 [a]Spelled *Sippai* in 1 Chronicles 20:4 **21:19** [a]Spelled *Jair* in 1 Chronicles 20:5 **21:21** [a]Spelled *Shammah* in 1 Samuel 16:9 and elsewhere **22:2** [a]Compare Psalm 18 **22:8** [a]Following Masoretic Text, Septuagint, and Targum; Syriac and Vulgate read *hills* (compare Psalm 18:7). **22:11** [a]Following Masoretic Text and Septuagint; many Hebrew manuscripts, Syriac, and Vulgate read *He flew* (compare Psalm 18:10); Targum reads *He spoke with power.*

LIFE LESSONS

➤ **22:18 — *He delivered me from my strong enemy, from those who hated me; for they were too strong for me.***

Our enemies are often too strong for us, but they are never too strong for the Lord.

25 Therefore the LORD has recompensed me
according to my righteousness,
According to my cleanness in His eyes.[a]

✻ 26"With the merciful You will show Yourself
merciful;
With a blameless man You will show
Yourself blameless;
27 With the pure You will show Yourself
pure;
And with the devious You will show
Yourself shrewd.
➤ 28 You will save the humble people;
But Your eyes *are* on the haughty, *that*
You may bring *them* down.

29"For You *are* my lamp, O LORD;
The LORD shall enlighten my darkness.
30 For by You I can run against a troop;
By my God I can leap over a wall.
31 *As for* God, His way *is* perfect;
The word of the LORD *is* proven;
He *is* a shield to all who trust in Him.

32"For who *is* God, except the LORD?
And who *is* a rock, except our God?
33 God *is* my strength *and* power,[a]
And He makes my[b] way perfect.
34 He makes my[a] feet like the *feet* of deer,
And sets me on my high places.
35 He teaches my hands to make war,
So that my arms can bend a bow of
bronze.

36"You have also given me the shield of
Your salvation;
Your gentleness has made me great.
37 You enlarged my path under me;
So my feet did not slip.

38"I have pursued my enemies and
destroyed them;
Neither did I turn back again till they
were destroyed.
39 And I have destroyed them and wounded
them,
So that they could not rise;
They have fallen under my feet.
40 For You have armed me with strength for
the battle;
You have subdued under me those who
rose against me.
41 You have also given me the necks of my
enemies,
So that I destroyed those who hated me.
42 They looked, but *there was* none to save;
Even to the LORD, but He did not answer
them.
43 Then I beat them as fine as the dust of
the earth;
I trod them like dirt in the streets,
And I spread them out.

44"You have also delivered me from the
strivings of my people;
You have kept me as the head of the
nations.
A people I have not known shall serve
me.
45 The foreigners submit to me;
As soon as they hear, they obey me.
46 The foreigners fade away,
And come frightened[a] from their hideouts.

47"The LORD lives!
Blessed *be* my Rock!
Let God be exalted,
The Rock of my salvation!
48 *It is* God who avenges me,
And subdues the peoples under me;
49 He delivers me from my enemies.
You also lift me up above those who rise
against me;
You have delivered me from the violent
man.
50 Therefore I will give thanks to You,
O LORD, among the Gentiles,
And sing praises to Your name.

51"*He* is the tower of salvation to His king,
And shows mercy to His anointed,
To David and his descendants
forevermore."

David's Last Words

23 Now these *are* the last words of David.
Thus says David the son of Jesse;
Thus says the man raised up on high,
The anointed of the God of Jacob,
And the sweet psalmist of Israel:

22:25 [a]Septuagint, Syriac, and Vulgate read *the cleanness of my hands in His sight* (compare Psalm 18:24); Targum reads *my cleanness before His word.* **22:33** [a]Dead Sea Scrolls, Septuagint, Syriac, and Vulgate read *It is God who arms me with strength* (compare Psalm 18:32); Targum reads *It is God who sustains me with strength.* [b]Following Qere, Septuagint, Syriac, Targum, and Vulgate (compare Psalm 18:32); Kethib reads *His.* **22:34** [a]Following Qere, Septuagint, Syriac, Targum, and Vulgate (compare Psalm 18:33); Kethib reads *His.* **22:46** [a]Following Septuagint, Targum, and Vulgate (compare Psalm 18:45); Masoretic Text reads *gird themselves.*

LIFE LESSONS

➤ ***22:28 — You will save the humble people; but Your eyes are on the haughty, that You may bring them down.***

All throughout Scripture, God tells us that He will save the humble but oppose the proud (Prov. 3:34; James 4:6; 1 Pet. 5:5). The proud try to put themselves in God's place, and that He will never allow.

2 "The Spirit of the LORD spoke by me,
And His word *was* on my tongue.
3 The God of Israel said,
The Rock of Israel spoke to me:
'He who rules over men *must be* just,
Ruling in the fear of God.
4 And *he shall be* like the light of the morning *when* the sun rises,
A morning without clouds,
Like the tender grass *springing* out of the earth,
By clear shining after rain.'

5 "Although my house *is* not so with God,
Yet He has made with me an everlasting covenant,
Ordered in all *things* and secure.
For *this is* all my salvation and all *my* desire;
Will He not make *it* increase?
6 But *the sons* of rebellion *shall* all *be* as thorns thrust away,
Because they cannot be taken with hands.
7 But the man *who* touches them
Must be armed with iron and the shaft of a spear,
And they shall be utterly burned with fire in *their* place."

David's Mighty Men

8 These *are* the names of the mighty men whom David had: Josheb-Basshebeth[a] the Tachmonite, chief among the captains.[b] He was called Adino the Eznite, because he had killed eight hundred men at one time.
9 And after him *was* Eleazar the son of Dodo,[a] the Ahohite, *one* of the three mighty men with David when they defied the Philistines *who* were gathered there for battle, and the men of Israel had retreated.
10 He arose and attacked the Philistines until his hand was weary, and his hand stuck to the sword. The LORD brought about a great victory that day; and the people returned after him only to plunder.
11 And after him *was* Shammah the son of Agee the Hararite. The Philistines had gathered together into a troop where there was a piece of ground full of lentils. So the people fled from the Philistines.
12 But he stationed himself in the middle of the field, defended it, and killed the Philistines. So the LORD brought about a great victory.
13 Then three of the thirty chief men went down at harvest time and came to David at the cave of Adullam. And the troop of Philistines encamped in the Valley of Rephaim.
14 David *was* then in the stronghold, and the garrison of the Philistines *was* then *in* Bethlehem.
15 And David said with longing, "Oh, that someone would give me a drink of the water from the well of Bethlehem, which *is* by the gate!"
16 So the three mighty men broke through the camp of the Philistines, drew water from the well of Bethlehem that *was* by the gate, and took it and brought *it* to David. Nevertheless he would not drink it, but poured it out to the LORD.
17 And he said, "Far be it from me, O LORD, that I should do this! Is *this not* the blood of the men who went in *jeopardy* of their lives?" Therefore he would not drink it. These things were done by the three mighty men.
18 Now Abishai the brother of Joab, the son of Zeruiah, was chief of *another* three.[a] He lifted his spear against three hundred *men*, killed *them*, and won a name among *these* three.
19 Was he not the most honored of three? Therefore he became their captain. However, he did not attain to the *first* three.
20 Benaiah *was* the son of Jehoiada, the son of a valiant man from Kabzeel, who had done many deeds. He had killed two lion-like heroes of Moab. He also had gone down and killed a lion in the midst of a pit on a snowy day.
21 And he killed an Egyptian, a spectacular man. The Egyptian *had* a spear in his hand; so he went down to him with a staff, wrested the spear out of the Egyptian's hand, and killed him with his own spear.
22 These *things* Benaiah the son of Jehoiada did, and won a name among three mighty men.
23 He was more honored than the thirty, but he did not attain to the *first* three. And David appointed him over his guard.
24 Asahel the brother of Joab *was* one of the thirty; Elhanan the son of Dodo of Bethlehem,
25 Shammah the Harodite, Elika the Harodite,
26 Helez the Paltite, Ira the son of Ikkesh the Tekoite,
27 Abiezer the Anathothite, Mebunnai the Hushathite,
28 Zalmon the Ahohite, Maharai the Netophathite,
29 Heleb the son of Baanah (the Netophathite), Ittai the son of Ribai from Gibeah of the children of Benjamin,
30 Benaiah a Pirathonite, Hiddai from the brooks of Gaash,
31 Abi-Albon the Arbathite, Azmaveth the Barhumite,

23:8 [a]Literally *One Who Sits in the Seat* (compare 1 Chronicles 11:11) [b]Following Masoretic Text and Targum; Septuagint and Vulgate read *the three.* **23:9** [a]Spelled *Dodai* in 1 Chronicles 27:4 **23:18** [a]Following Masoretic Text, Septuagint, and Vulgate; some Hebrew manuscripts and Syriac read *thirty;* Targum reads *the mighty men.*

32 Eliahba the Shaalbonite (of the sons of Jashen), Jonathan,
33 Shammah the Hararite, Ahiam the son of Sharar the Hararite,
34 Eliphelet the son of Ahasbai, the son of the Maachathite, Eliam the son of Ahithophel the Gilonite,
35 Hezrai[a] the Carmelite, Paarai the Arbite,
36 Igal the son of Nathan of Zobah, Bani the Gadite,
37 Zelek the Ammonite, Naharai the Beerothite (armorbearer of Joab the son of Zeruiah),
38 Ira the Ithrite, Gareb the Ithrite,
39 *and* Uriah the Hittite: thirty-seven in all.

David's Census of Israel and Judah

24 Again the anger of the LORD was aroused against Israel, and He moved David against them to say, "Go, number Israel and Judah."
2 So the king said to Joab the commander of the army who *was* with him, "Now go throughout all the tribes of Israel, from Dan to Beersheba, and count the people, that I may know the number of the people."
3 And Joab said to the king, "Now may the LORD your God add to the people a hundred times more than there are, and may the eyes of my lord the king see *it*. But why does my lord the king desire this thing?"
4 Nevertheless the king's word prevailed against Joab and against the captains of the army. Therefore Joab and the captains of the army went out from the presence of the king to count the people of Israel.
5 And they crossed over the Jordan and camped in Aroer, on the right side of the town which *is* in the midst of the ravine of Gad, and toward Jazer.
6 Then they came to Gilead and to the land of Tahtim Hodshi; they came to Dan Jaan and around to Sidon;
7 and they came to the stronghold of Tyre and to all the cities of the Hivites and the Canaanites. Then they went out to South Judah *as far as* Beersheba.
8 So when they had gone through all the land, they came to Jerusalem at the end of nine months and twenty days.
9 Then Joab gave the sum of the number of the people to the king. And there were in Israel eight hundred thousand valiant men who drew the sword, and the men of Judah were five hundred thousand men.

The Judgment on David's Sin

10 And David's heart condemned him after he had numbered the people. So David said to the LORD, "I have sinned greatly in what I have done; but now, I pray, O LORD, take away the iniquity of Your servant, for I have done very foolishly."
11 Now when David arose in the morning, the word of the LORD came to the prophet Gad, David's seer, saying,
12 "Go and tell David, 'Thus says the LORD: "I offer you three *things;* choose one of them for yourself, that I may do *it* to you." ' "
13 So Gad came to David and told him; and he said to him, "Shall seven[a] years of famine come to you in your land? Or shall you flee three months before your enemies, while they pursue you? Or shall there be three days' plague in your land? Now consider and see what answer I should take back to Him who sent me."
14 And David said to Gad, "I am in great distress. Please let us fall into the hand of the LORD, for His mercies *are* great; but do not let me fall into the hand of man."
15 So the LORD sent a plague upon Israel from the morning till the appointed time. From Dan to Beersheba seventy thousand men of the people died.
16 And when the angel[a] stretched out His hand over Jerusalem to destroy it, the LORD relented from the destruction, and said to the angel who was destroying the people, "It is enough; now restrain your hand." And the angel of the LORD was by the threshing floor of Araunah[b] the Jebusite.
17 Then David spoke to the LORD when he saw the angel who was striking the people, and said, "Surely I have sinned, and I have done wickedly; but these sheep, what have they done? Let Your hand, I pray, be against me and against my father's house."

The Altar on the Threshing Floor

18 And Gad came that day to David and said to him, "Go up, erect an altar to the LORD on the threshing floor of Araunah the Jebusite."
19 So David, according to the word of Gad, went up as the LORD commanded.

23:35 [a]Spelled *Hezro* in 1 Chronicles 11:37 **24:13** [a]Following Masoretic Text, Syriac, Targum, and Vulgate; Septuagint reads *three* (compare 1 Chronicles 21:12). **24:16** [a]Or *Angel* [b]Spelled *Ornan* in 1 Chronicles 21:15

LIFE LESSONS

➤ **24:14 — *And David said to Gad, "I am in great distress. Please let us fall into the hand of the LORD, for His mercies are great . . . ."***

David counted on the mercy of God, not to remove from him all consequences for his sin, but to spare his life and the life of his nation. Even in judgment, God shows mercy.

20 Now Araunah looked, and saw the king
and his servants coming toward him. So
Araunah went out and bowed before the king
with his face to the ground.
21 Then Araunah said, "Why has my lord the
king come to his servant?" And David said,
"To buy the threshing floor from you, to build
an altar to the LORD, that the plague may be
withdrawn from the people."
22 Now Araunah said to David, "Let my lord
the king take and offer up whatever *seems*
good to him. Look, *here are* oxen for burnt
sacrifice, and threshing implements and the
yokes of the oxen for wood.
23 "All these, O king, Araunah has given to
the king." And Araunah said to the king, "May
the LORD your God accept you."
24 Then the king said to Araunah, "No, but I
will surely buy *it* from you for a price; nor
will I offer burnt offerings to the LORD my
God with that which costs me nothing." So
David bought the threshing floor and the
oxen for fifty shekels of silver.
25 And David built there an altar to the
LORD, and offered burnt offerings and peace
offerings. So the LORD heeded the prayers for
the land, and the plague was withdrawn from
Israel.

LIFE LESSONS

➤ ***24:24 — Then the king said to Araunah, "No, but I will surely buy it from you for a price; nor will I offer burnt offerings to the LORD my God with that which costs me nothing."***

David felt that he could not honor God by offering a gift that cost him nothing. God wants our best, not because He needs it, but because by giving we demonstrate that our goods are not our God.

THE FIRST BOOK OF KINGS

Like the two books of Samuel, the two books of Kings originally were one in the Hebrew Bible. The original Hebrew title of Kings was *Melechim*, which means "Kings." The Septuagint artificially divided the book in the middle of the story of Ahaziah; it called the books of Samuel "First and Second Kingdoms" and the books of Kings, "Third and Fourth Kingdoms." It may have divided these books in this way because the text in Greek required a greater amount of scroll space than did the Hebrew.

The first half of 1 Kings traces the life of Solomon. Under his leadership, Israel rises to the peak of her size, power and glory. Solomon's great accomplishments, including the construction of the holy temple in Jerusalem, bring him worldwide fame and respect. This truly was Israel's golden age!

Sadly, Solomon's zeal for God diminishes in his later years, as pagan wives turn his heart away from worshiping the Lord in His holy temple. As a result, the king with the divided heart leaves behind a divided kingdom. The Book of 1 Kings records what happens over the next century: two sets of kings and two nations of disobedient people who grow increasingly indifferent to God's prophets and precepts.

Theme: Faithfulness to God must remain an individual's and a kingdom's first priority. While King Solomon and the people of Israel remained faithful to their God, He blessed them and caused their kingdom to grow in power, wealth, and respect. But when Solomon and the people turned from God, their once-great kingdom tore itself apart and later fell to vicious conquerors, leaving Jerusalem in ruins and its people languishing in brutal captivity in a foreign land.

Author: Unknown

Time: The book begins at the close of the magnificent reign of King David and the ascension of his son Solomon to the throne (around 970 B.C.). It records Solomon's compromises and falling away from God, followed by the civil war that divided the nation into the Northern Kingdom (Israel) and Southern Kingdom (Judah) around 930 B.C. First Kings closes with the ministry of the prophet Elijah. Altogether, the two books of Kings cover almost four centuries of Israel's history.

Structure: The historical narrative records Solomon's reign (1–11), starting with his ascension to the throne following David's death and ending with his own death, then moving on to record the decline and fall of the once-great kingdom (12–22).

As you read 1 Kings, watch for several life principles that play an important role in this book.

12. Peace with God is the fruit of oneness with Him. *See 1 Kings 4:24, 25; page 396.*

17. We stand tallest and strongest on our knees. *See 1 Kings 8:30–48; page 402.*

20. Disappointments are inevitable; discouragement is a choice. *See 1 Kings 8:17, 18; page 401.*

15. Brokenness is God's requirement for maximum usefulness. *See 1 Kings 11:9–14; page 407.*

Adonijah Presumes to Be King

1 Now King David was old, advanced in
years; and they put covers on him, but he
could not get warm.
2 Therefore his servants said to him, "Let a
young woman, a virgin, be sought for our lord
the king, and let her stand before the king,
and let her care for him; and let her lie in your
bosom, that our lord the king may be warm."
3 So they sought for a lovely young woman
throughout all the territory of Israel, and
found Abishag the Shunammite, and brought
her to the king.
4 The young woman *was* very lovely; and
she cared for the king, and served him; but
the king did not know her.
➤ **5** Then Adonijah the son of Haggith exalted
himself, saying, "I will be king"; and he prepared for himself chariots and horsemen, and
fifty men to run before him.
➤ 6 (And his father had not rebuked him at
any time by saying, "Why have you done so?"
He *was* also very good-looking. *His mother*
had borne him after Absalom.)
7 Then he conferred with Joab the son of
Zeruiah and with Abiathar the priest, and
they followed and helped Adonijah.
8 But Zadok the priest, Benaiah the son of
Jehoiada, Nathan the prophet, Shimei, Rei,
and the mighty men who *belonged* to David
were not with Adonijah.
9 And Adonijah sacrificed sheep and oxen
and fattened cattle by the stone of Zoheleth,
which *is* by En Rogel; he also invited all his
brothers, the king's sons, and all the men of
Judah, the king's servants.
10 But he did not invite Nathan the prophet,
Benaiah, the mighty men, or Solomon his
brother.
11 So Nathan spoke to Bathsheba the mother
of Solomon, saying, "Have you not heard that
Adonijah the son of Haggith has become
king, and David our lord does not know *it*?
12 "Come, please, let me now give you advice, that you may save your own life and the
life of your son Solomon.
13 "Go immediately to King David and say to
him, 'Did you not, my lord, O king, swear to
your maidservant, saying, "Assuredly your
son Solomon shall reign after me, and he
shall sit on my throne"? Why then has Adonijah become king?'
14 "Then, while you are still talking there
with the king, I also will come in after you
and confirm your words."
15 So Bathsheba went into the chamber to
the king. (Now the king was very old, and
Abishag the Shunammite was serving the
king.)
16 And Bathsheba bowed and did homage to
the king. Then the king said, "What is your
wish?"
17 Then she said to him, "My lord, you swore
by the LORD your God to your maidservant,
saying, 'Assuredly Solomon your son shall
reign after me, and he shall sit on my throne.'
18 "So now, look! Adonijah has become king;
and now, my lord the king, you do not know
about *it*.
19 "He has sacrificed oxen and fattened cattle and sheep in abundance, and has invited
all the sons of the king, Abiathar the priest,
and Joab the commander of the army; but
Solomon your servant he has not invited.
20 "And as for you, my lord, O king, the eyes
of all Israel *are* on you, that you should tell
them who will sit on the throne of my lord the
king after him.
21 "Otherwise it will happen, when my lord
the king rests with his fathers, that I and my
son Solomon will be counted as offenders."
22 And just then, while she was still talking
with the king, Nathan the prophet also came in.
23 So they told the king, saying, "Here is Nathan the prophet." And when he came in before the king, he bowed down before the king
with his face to the ground.
24 And Nathan said, "My lord, O king, have
you said, 'Adonijah shall reign after me, and
he shall sit on my throne'?
25 "For he has gone down today, and has sacrificed oxen and fattened cattle and sheep in
abundance, and has invited all the king's
sons, and the commanders of the army, and
Abiathar the priest; and look! They are eating
and drinking before him; and they say, '*Long*
live King Adonijah!'
26 "But he has not invited me—me your servant—nor Zadok the priest, nor Benaiah the
son of Jehoiada, nor your servant Solomon.
27 "Has this thing been done by my lord the
king, and you have not told your servant who
should sit on the throne of my lord the king
after him?"

LIFE LESSONS

➤ 1:5 — *Then Adonijah the son of Haggith exalted himself, saying, "I will be king"; and he prepared for himself chariots and horsemen, and fifty men to run before him.*

By exalting ourselves we can, for a time, obtain the fame or position or notoriety we seek. But whatever we acquire outside of God's will turns to ashes.

➤ 1:6 — *And his father had not rebuked him at any time by saying, "Why have you done so?"*

What do Eli the priest, Samuel the prophet, and David the king all have in common? In their personal lives they served and honored God, but as fathers they failed to raise their children in the fear of God.

David Proclaims Solomon King
28 Then King David answered and said, "Call
Bathsheba to me." So she came into the king's
presence and stood before the king.
29 And the king took an oath and said, "*As*
the LORD lives, who has redeemed my life
from every distress,
30 "just as I swore to you by the LORD God of Israel, saying, 'Assuredly Solomon your son shall
be king after me, and he shall sit on my throne
in my place,' so I certainly will do this day."
31 Then Bathsheba bowed with *her* face to
the earth, and paid homage to the king, and
said, "Let my lord King David live forever!"
32 And King David said, "Call to me Zadok
the priest, Nathan the prophet, and Benaiah
the son of Jehoiada." So they came before the
king.
33 The king also said to them, "Take with you
the servants of your lord, and have Solomon
my son ride on my own mule, and take him
down to Gihon.
34 "There let Zadok the priest and Nathan the
prophet anoint him king over Israel; and blow
the horn, and say, '*Long* live King Solomon!'
35 "Then you shall come up after him, and he
shall come and sit on my throne, and he shall
be king in my place. For I have appointed him
to be ruler over Israel and Judah."
36 Benaiah the son of Jehoiada answered the
king and said, "Amen! May the LORD God of
my lord the king say so *too*.
37 "As the LORD has been with my lord the
king, even so may He be with Solomon, and
make his throne greater than the throne of
my lord King David."
38 So Zadok the priest, Nathan the prophet,
Benaiah the son of Jehoiada, the Cherethites,
and the Pelethites went down and had Solomon ride on King David's mule, and took
him to Gihon.
39 Then Zadok the priest took a horn of oil
from the tabernacle and anointed Solomon.
And they blew the horn, and all the people
said, "*Long* live King Solomon!"
40 And all the people went up after him; and
the people played the flutes and rejoiced with
great joy, so that the earth *seemed to* split
with their sound.
41 Now Adonijah and all the guests who *were*
with him heard *it* as they finished eating. And
when Joab heard the sound of the horn, he
said, "Why *is* the city in such a noisy uproar?"
42 While he was still speaking, there came
Jonathan, the son of Abiathar the priest. And
Adonijah said to him, "Come in, for you *are* a
prominent man, and bring good news."
43 Then Jonathan answered and said to Adonijah, "No! Our lord King David has made
Solomon king.
44 "The king has sent with him Zadok the
priest, Nathan the prophet, Benaiah the son
of Jehoiada, the Cherethites, and the Pelethites; and they have made him ride on the
king's mule.
45 "So Zadok the priest and Nathan the
prophet have anointed him king at Gihon;
and they have gone up from there rejoicing,
so that the city is in an uproar. This *is* the
noise that you have heard.
46 "Also Solomon sits on the throne of the
kingdom.
47 "And moreover the king's servants have
gone to bless our lord King David, saying,
'May God make the name of Solomon better
than your name, and may He make his throne
greater than your throne.' Then the king
bowed himself on the bed.
48 "Also the king said thus, 'Blessed *be* the
LORD God of Israel, who has given *one* to sit
on my throne this day, while my eyes see *it!*'"
49 So all the guests who were with Adonijah
were afraid, and arose, and each one went his
way.
50 Now Adonijah was afraid of Solomon; so
he arose, and went and took hold of the horns
of the altar.
51 And it was told Solomon, saying, "Indeed
Adonijah is afraid of King Solomon; for look,
he has taken hold of the horns of the altar,
saying, 'Let King Solomon swear to me today
that he will not put his servant to death with
the sword.'"
52 Then Solomon said, "If he proves himself
a worthy man, not one hair of him shall fall to
the earth; but if wickedness is found in him,
he shall die."
53 So King Solomon sent them to bring him
down from the altar. And he came and fell
down before King Solomon; and Solomon
said to him, "Go to your house."

David's Instructions to Solomon
2 Now the days of David drew near that he
should die, and he charged Solomon his
son, saying:
2 "I go the way of all the earth; be strong,
therefore, and prove yourself a man.
3 "And keep the charge of the LORD your
God: to walk in His ways, to keep His statutes,

LIFE LESSONS

➤ **1:51 — *"Indeed Adonijah is afraid of King Solomon; for look, he has taken hold of the horns of the altar . . . ."***

There is a big difference between regretting the consequences of sin and repenting of it. Adonijah feared the possible consequences of his actions, but never repented of them. And eventually that would cost him everything.

His commandments, His judgments, and His
testimonies, as it is written in the Law of Moses, that you may prosper in all that you do
and wherever you turn;
4 "that the LORD may fulfill His word which
He spoke concerning me, saying, 'If your sons
take heed to their way, to walk before Me in
truth with all their heart and with all their
soul,' He said, 'you shall not lack a man on the
throne of Israel.'
5 "Moreover you know also what Joab the
son of Zeruiah did to me, *and* what he did to
the two commanders of the armies of Israel,
to Abner the son of Ner and Amasa the son of
Jether, whom he killed. And he shed the blood
of war in peacetime, and put the blood of war
on his belt that *was* around his waist, and on
his sandals that *were* on his feet.
➤ 6 "Therefore do according to your wisdom,
and do not let his gray hair go down to the
grave in peace.
7 "But show kindness to the sons of Barzillai the Gileadite, and let them be among those
who eat at your table, for so they came to me
when I fled from Absalom your brother.
8 "And see, *you have* with you Shimei the
son of Gera, a Benjamite from Bahurim, who
cursed me with a malicious curse in the day
when I went to Mahanaim. But he came down
to meet me at the Jordan, and I swore to him
by the LORD, saying, 'I will not put you to
death with the sword.'
➤ 9 "Now therefore, do not hold him guiltless,
for you *are* a wise man and know what you
ought to do to him; but bring his gray hair
down to the grave with blood."

Death of David

10 So David rested with his fathers, and was
buried in the City of David.
11 The period that David reigned over Israel
was forty years; seven years he reigned in Hebron, and in Jerusalem he reigned thirty-
three years.
12 Then Solomon sat on the throne of his father David; and his kingdom was firmly established.

Solomon Executes Adonijah

13 Now Adonijah the son of Haggith came to
Bathsheba the mother of Solomon. So she
said, "Do you come peaceably?" And he said,
"Peaceably."
14 Moreover he said, "I have something *to
say* to you." And she said, "Say it."
15 Then he said, "You know that the kingdom
was mine, and all Israel had set their expectations on me, that I should reign. However,
the kingdom has been turned over, and has
become my brother's; for it was his from the
LORD.
16 "Now I ask one petition of you; do not
deny me." And she said to him, "Say it."
17 Then he said, "Please speak to King
Solomon, for he will not refuse you, that he
may give me Abishag the Shunammite as
wife."
18 So Bathsheba said, "Very well, I will speak
for you to the king."
19 Bathsheba therefore went to King Solomon, to speak to him for Adonijah. And the
king rose up to meet her and bowed down to
her, and sat down on his throne and had a
throne set for the king's mother; so she sat at
his right hand.
20 Then she said, "I desire one small petition
of you; do not refuse me." And the king said
to her, "Ask it, my mother, for I will not refuse
you."
21 So she said, "Let Abishag the Shunammite be given to Adonijah your brother as
wife."
22 And King Solomon answered and said to
his mother, "Now why do you ask Abishag the
Shunammite for Adonijah? Ask for him the
kingdom also—for he *is* my older brother—
for him, and for Abiathar the priest, and for
Joab the son of Zeruiah."
23 Then King Solomon swore by the LORD,
saying, "May God do so to me, and more also,
if Adonijah has not spoken this word against
his own life!
24 "Now therefore, *as* the LORD lives, who
has confirmed me and set me on the throne of
David my father, and who has established a
house[a] for me, as He promised, Adonijah shall
be put to death today!"

2:24 [a]That is, a royal dynasty

LIFE LESSONS

➤ 2:3 — *"And keep the charge of the LORD your God: to walk in His ways, to keep His statutes . . . ."*

We are to daily encourage one another in the faith, "lest any of you be hardened through the deceitfulness of sin" (Heb. 3:13).

➤ 2:6, 9 — *"Therefore do according to your wisdom . . . you are a wise man and know what you ought to do . . . ."*

Even at the beginning of his reign, Solomon was considered a wise man. Yet God is able to multiply even what we have, so that we can better serve Him and bless His people.

➤ 2:15 — *"You know that the kingdom was mine, and all Israel had set their expectations on me . . . ."*

Adonijah revealed a heart still bent on evil when he connected his failed attempt to become king with his request to marry King David's concubine. God can never bless unrepentant sin.

25 So King Solomon sent by the hand of Benaiah the son of Jehoiada; and he struck him down, and he died.

Abiathar Exiled, Joab Executed

26 And to Abiathar the priest the king said, "Go to Anathoth, to your own fields, for you *are* deserving of death; but I will not put you to death at this time, because you carried the ark of the Lord GOD before my father David, and because you were afflicted every time my father was afflicted."

➤ 27 So Solomon removed Abiathar from being priest to the LORD, that he might fulfill the word of the LORD which He spoke concerning the house of Eli at Shiloh.

28 Then news came to Joab, for Joab had defected to Adonijah, though he had not defected to Absalom. So Joab fled to the tabernacle of the LORD, and took hold of the horns of the altar.

29 And King Solomon was told, "Joab has fled to the tabernacle of the LORD; there *he is,* by the altar." Then Solomon sent Benaiah the son of Jehoiada, saying, "Go, strike him down."

30 So Benaiah went to the tabernacle of the LORD, and said to him, "Thus says the king, 'Come out!'" And he said, "No, but I will die here." And Benaiah brought back word to the king, saying, "Thus said Joab, and thus he answered me."

31 Then the king said to him, "Do as he has said, and strike him down and bury him, that you may take away from me and from the house of my father the innocent blood which Joab shed.

➤ 32 "So the LORD will return his blood on his head, because he struck down two men more righteous and better than he, and killed them with the sword—Abner the son of Ner, the commander of the army of Israel, and Amasa the son of Jether, the commander of the army of Judah—though my father David did not know *it.*

33 "Their blood shall therefore return upon the head of Joab and upon the head of his descendants forever. But upon David and his descendants, upon his house and his throne, there shall be peace forever from the LORD."

34 So Benaiah the son of Jehoiada went up and struck and killed him; and he was buried in his own house in the wilderness.

35 The king put Benaiah the son of Jehoiada in his place over the army, and the king put Zadok the priest in the place of Abiathar.

Shimei Executed

36 Then the king sent and called for Shimei, and said to him, "Build yourself a house in Jerusalem and dwell there, and do not go out from there anywhere.

37 "For it shall be, on the day you go out and cross the Brook Kidron, know for certain you shall surely die; your blood shall be on your own head."

38 And Shimei said to the king, "The saying *is* good. As my lord the king has said, so your servant will do." So Shimei dwelt in Jerusalem many days.

39 Now it happened at the end of three years, that two slaves of Shimei ran away to Achish the son of Maachah, king of Gath. And they told Shimei, saying, "Look, your slaves *are* in Gath!"

40 So Shimei arose, saddled his donkey, and went to Achish at Gath to seek his slaves. And Shimei went and brought his slaves from Gath.

41 And Solomon was told that Shimei had gone from Jerusalem to Gath and had come back.

42 Then the king sent and called for Shimei, and said to him, "Did I not make you swear by the LORD, and warn you, saying, 'Know for certain that on the day you go out and travel anywhere, you shall surely die'? And you said to me, 'The word I have heard *is* good.'

43 "Why then have you not kept the oath of the LORD and the commandment that I gave you?"

44 The king said moreover to Shimei, "You know, as your heart acknowledges, all the wickedness that you did to my father David; therefore the LORD will return your wickedness on your own head.

45 "But King Solomon *shall be* blessed, and the throne of David shall be established before the LORD forever."

46 So the king commanded Benaiah the son of Jehoiada; and he went out and struck him down, and he died. Thus the kingdom was established in the hand of Solomon.

LIFE LESSONS

➤ **2:27 — *So Solomon removed Abiathar from being priest to the LORD, that he might fulfill the word of the LORD which He spoke concerning the house of Eli at Shiloh.***

We can always place our full confidence in God's Word, for He has the unlimited power and wisdom to fulfill His promises to the letter.

➤ **2:32 — *"So the LORD will return his blood on his head, because he struck down two men more righteous and better than he, and killed them with the sword . . . ."***

No one ultimately "gets away with" any sinful act. As Paul writes, "Some men's sins are clearly evident, preceding them to judgment, but those of some men follow later" (1 Tim. 5:24).

Solomon Requests Wisdom
3 Now Solomon made a treaty with Pharaoh
king of Egypt, and married Pharaoh's
daughter; then he brought her to the City of
David until he had finished building his own
house, and the house of the LORD, and the wall
all around Jerusalem.
2 Meanwhile the people sacrificed at the
high places, because there was no house built
for the name of the LORD until those days.
➤ 3 And Solomon loved the LORD, walking in
the statutes of his father David, except that he
sacrificed and burned incense at the high
places.
4 Now the king went to Gibeon to sacrifice
there, for that *was* the great high place: Solomon offered a thousand burnt offerings on
that altar.
5 At Gibeon the LORD appeared to Solomon
in a dream by night; and God said, "Ask! What
shall I give you?"
6 And Solomon said: "You have shown great
mercy to Your servant David my father, because he walked before You in truth, in righteousness, and in uprightness of heart with
You; You have continued this great kindness
for him, and You have given him a son to sit
on his throne, as *it is* this day.
7 "Now, O LORD my God, You have made
Your servant king instead of my father David,
but I *am* a little child; I do not know *how* to go
out or come in.
8 "And Your servant *is* in the midst of Your
people whom You have chosen, a great people, too numerous to be numbered or counted.
➤ 9 "Therefore give to Your servant an understanding heart to judge Your people, that I
may discern between good and evil. For who
is able to judge this great people of Yours?"
10 The speech pleased the Lord, that Solomon had asked this thing.
11 Then God said to him: "Because you have
asked this thing, and have not asked long life
for yourself, nor have asked riches for yourself, nor have asked the life of your enemies,
but have asked for yourself understanding to
discern justice,
12 "behold, I have done according to your
words; see, I have given you a wise and understanding heart, so that there has not been
anyone like you before you, nor shall any like
you arise after you.
13 "And I have also given you what you have
not asked: both riches and honor, so that
there shall not be anyone like you among the
kings all your days.
14 "So if you walk in My ways, to keep My
statutes and My commandments, as your father David walked, then I will lengthen your
days."
15 Then Solomon awoke; and indeed it had
been a dream. And he came to Jerusalem and
stood before the ark of the covenant of the
LORD, offered up burnt offerings, offered
peace offerings, and made a feast for all his
servants.

Solomon's Wise Judgment
16 Now two women *who were* harlots came
to the king, and stood before him.
17 And one woman said, "O my lord, this
woman and I dwell in the same house; and I
gave birth while she *was* in the house.
18 "Then it happened, the third day after I had
given birth, that this woman also gave birth.
And we *were* together; no one *was* with us in
the house, except the two of us in the house.
19 "And this woman's son died in the night,
because she lay on him.
20 "So she arose in the middle of the night and
took my son from my side, while your maidservant slept, and laid him in her bosom, and
laid her dead child in my bosom.
21 "And when I rose in the morning to nurse
my son, there he was, dead. But when I had
examined him in the morning, indeed, he was
not my son whom I had borne."
22 Then the other woman said, "No! But the
living one *is* my son, and the dead one *is* your
son." And the first woman said, "No! But the
dead one *is* your son, and the living one *is* my
son." Thus they spoke before the king.
23 And the king said, "The one says, 'This *is*
my son, who lives, and your son *is* the dead
one'; and the other says, 'No! But your son *is*
the dead one, and my son *is* the living one.'"
24 Then the king said, "Bring me a sword." So
they brought a sword before the king.
25 And the king said, "Divide the living child
in two, and give half to one, and half to the
other."
26 Then the woman whose son *was* living
spoke to the king, for she yearned with compassion for her son; and she said, "O my lord,

LIFE LESSONS

➤ 3:3 — *And Solomon loved the LORD, walking in the statutes of his father David, except that he sacrificed and burned incense at the high places.*

At the beginning, Solomon loved the Lord and obeyed His commandments. But note the one word that led to his downfall: "except." The Lord wants wholehearted commitment to Him, not partial devotion.

➤ 3:9 — *"Therefore give to Your servant an understanding heart to judge Your people, that I may discern between good and evil. For who is able to judge this great people of Yours?"*

Solomon wanted the ability to wisely lead his people. This was a good and honorable request—but note that he left out any mention of God. "The fear of the LORD is the beginning of wisdom" (Prov. 9:10).

WHAT THE BIBLE SAYS ABOUT ASKING GOD FOR SPECIFIC THINGS

1 Kin. 3:5

Many Bible passages challenge believers to ask God for very specific things. Read the following familiar verses to remind yourself how important it is to ask God for the things you need. God expects you to *ask*!

- At Gibeon the LORD appeared to Solomon in a dream by night; and God said, "Ask! What shall I give you?" (1 Kin. 3:5)
- [Jesus said,] "Whatever things you ask in prayer, believing, you will receive." (Matt. 21:22)
- [Jesus said,] "Until now you have asked nothing in My name. Ask, and you will receive, that your joy may be full." (John 16:24)
- If any of you lacks wisdom, let him ask of God, who gives to all liberally and without reproach, and it will be given to him. But let him ask in faith, with no doubting, for he who doubts is like a wave of the sea driven and tossed by the wind. (James 1:5, 6)

God expects you to *ask*!

If we were to summarize these verses, we would find some very clear and concise principles related to our asking:

- God wants us to ask Him to meet all of our needs.
- God delights in revealing to us His desires and His ways of doing things.
- We can ask God for all things, including those that relate to the natural world.
- We are wise to ask in agreement with others.
- We must always ask in faith and in the name of Jesus.
- God will respond to our need not in a way that opposes His commandments, but in a way that pleases Him and brings Him glory.
- We can be assured that whenever we ask God for something, He hears and responds to us, giving us precisely what we need—which may not be what we think we need, but which always benefits us most.

The Bible tells us, "You do not have because you do not ask" (James 4:2). For what things in your life have you failed to ask God?

See the Life Principles Index for further study:
8. Fight all your battles on your knees and you win every time.
27. Prayer is life's greatest time saver.

give her the living child, and by no means kill
him!" But the other said, "Let him be neither
mine nor yours, *but* divide *him.*"
27 So the king answered and said, "Give the
first woman the living child, and by no means
kill him; she *is* his mother."
28 And all Israel heard of the judgment
which the king had rendered; and they feared
the king, for they saw that the wisdom of God
was in him to administer justice.

Solomon's Administration

4 So King Solomon was king over all Israel.
2 And these *were* his officials: Azariah the
son of Zadok, the priest;
3 Elihoreph and Ahijah, the sons of Shisha,
scribes; Jehoshaphat the son of Ahilud, the
recorder;
4 Benaiah the son of Jehoiada, over the
army; Zadok and Abiathar, the priests;
5 Azariah the son of Nathan, over the officers; Zabud the son of Nathan, a priest *and*
the king's friend;
6 Ahishar, over the household; and Adoniram the son of Abda, over the labor force.
7 And Solomon had twelve governors over
all Israel, who provided food for the king and
his household; each one made provision for
one month of the year.
8 These *are* their names: Ben-Hur,[a] in the
mountains of Ephraim;
9 Ben-Deker,[a] in Makaz, Shaalbim, Beth
Shemesh, and Elon Beth Hanan;
10 Ben-Hesed,[a] in Arubboth; to him *belonged*
Sochoh and all the land of Hepher;
11 Ben-Abinadab,[a] *in* all the regions of Dor;
he had Taphath the daughter of Solomon as
wife;
12 Baana the son of Ahilud, *in* Taanach,
Megiddo, and all Beth Shean, which *is* beside
Zaretan below Jezreel, from Beth Shean to
Abel Meholah, as far as the other side of
Jokneam;
13 Ben-Geber,[a] in Ramoth Gilead; to him *belonged* the towns of Jair the son of Manasseh,
in Gilead; to him *also belonged* the region of
Argob in Bashan—sixty large cities with
walls and bronze gate-bars;
14 Ahinadab the son of Iddo, *in* Mahanaim;
15 Ahimaaz, in Naphtali; he also took Basemath the daughter of Solomon as wife;
16 Baanah the son of Hushai, in Asher and
Aloth;
17 Jehoshaphat the son of Paruah, in Issachar;
18 Shimei the son of Elah, in Benjamin;
19 Geber the son of Uri, in the land of Gilead,
in the country of Sihon king of the Amorites,
and of Og king of Bashan. *He was* the only
governor who *was* in the land.

Prosperity and Wisdom of Solomon's Reign

20 Judah and Israel *were* as numerous as the ➤
sand by the sea in multitude, eating and
drinking and rejoicing.
21 So Solomon reigned over all kingdoms
from the River[a] *to* the land of the Philistines,
as far as the border of Egypt. *They* brought
tribute and served Solomon all the days of his
life.
22 Now Solomon's provision for one day was
thirty kors of fine flour, sixty kors of meal,
23 ten fatted oxen, twenty oxen from the pastures, and one hundred sheep, besides deer,
gazelles, roebucks, and fatted fowl.
24 For he had dominion over all *the region* on
this side of the River[a] from Tiphsah even to
Gaza, namely over all the kings on this side of
the River; and he had peace on every side all
around him.
25 And Judah and Israel dwelt safely, each
man under his vine and his fig tree, from
Dan as far as Beersheba, all the days of Solomon.
26 Solomon had forty[a] thousand stalls of
horses for his chariots, and twelve thousand
horsemen.
27 And these governors, each man in his
month, provided food for King Solomon and
for all who came to King Solomon's table.
There was no lack in their supply.
28 They also brought barley and straw to the
proper place, for the horses and steeds, each
man according to his charge.
29 And God gave Solomon wisdom and exceedingly great understanding, and largeness
of heart like the sand on the seashore.
30 Thus Solomon's wisdom excelled the wisdom of all the men of the East and all the wisdom of Egypt.
31 For he was wiser than all men—than
Ethan the Ezrahite, and Heman, Chalcol, and
Darda, the sons of Mahol; and his fame was in
all the surrounding nations.
32 He spoke three thousand proverbs, and
his songs were one thousand and five.

4:8 [a]Literally *Son of Hur* **4:9** [a]Literally *Son of Deker* **4:10** [a]Literally *Son of Hesed* **4:11** [a]Literally *Son of Abinadab* **4:13** [a]Literally *Son of Geber* **4:21** [a]That is, the Euphrates **4:24** [a]That is, the Euphrates **4:26** [a]Following Masoretic Text and most other authorities; some manuscripts of the Septuagint read *four* (compare 2 Chronicles 9:25).

LIFE LESSONS

➤ ***4:20 — Judah and Israel were as numerous as the sand by the sea in multitude, eating and drinking and rejoicing.***

When we enjoy times of "eating and drinking and rejoicing," we are to remember that all these blessings come from the Lord, and He is the one who enables us to enjoy them (Eccl. 5:19).

33 Also he spoke of trees, from the cedar tree
of Lebanon even to the hyssop that springs
out of the wall; he spoke also of animals, of
birds, of creeping things, and of fish.
34 And men of all nations, from all the kings
of the earth who had heard of his wisdom,
came to hear the wisdom of Solomon.

Solomon Prepares to Build the Temple

5 Now Hiram king of Tyre sent his servants
to Solomon, because he heard that they
had anointed him king in place of his father,
for Hiram had always loved David.
2 Then Solomon sent to Hiram, saying:

3 You know how my father David could not build a house for the name of the LORD his God because of the wars which were fought against him on every side, until the LORD put *his foes*[a] under the soles of his feet.
4 But now the LORD my God has given me rest on every side; *there is* neither adversary nor evil occurrence.
5 And behold, I propose to build a house for the name of the LORD my God, as the LORD spoke to my father David, saying, "Your son, whom I will set on your throne in your place, he shall build the house for My name."
6 Now therefore, command that they cut down cedars for me from Lebanon; and my servants will be with your servants, and I will pay you wages for your servants according to whatever you say. For you know *there is* none among us who has skill to cut timber like the Sidonians.

7 So it was, when Hiram heard the words of
Solomon, that he rejoiced greatly and said,

Blessed *be* the LORD this day, for He has given David a wise son over this great people!

8 Then Hiram sent to Solomon, saying:

I have considered *the message* which you sent me, *and* I will do all you desire concerning the cedar and cypress logs.
9 My servants shall bring *them* down from Lebanon to the sea; I will float them in rafts by sea to the place you indicate to me, and will have them broken apart there; then you can take *them* away. And you shall fulfill my desire by giving food for my household.

10 Then Hiram gave Solomon cedar and cypress logs *according to* all his desire.
11 And Solomon gave Hiram twenty thousand kors of wheat *as* food for his household,
and twenty[a] kors of pressed oil. Thus Solomon gave to Hiram year by year.
12 So the LORD gave Solomon wisdom, as He ➤
had promised him; and there was peace between Hiram and Solomon, and the two of
them made a treaty together.
13 Then King Solomon raised up a labor
force out of all Israel; and the labor force was
thirty thousand men.
14 And he sent them to Lebanon, ten thousand a month in shifts: they were one month
in Lebanon *and* two months at home; Adoniram *was* in charge of the labor force.
15 Solomon had seventy thousand who carried burdens, and eighty thousand who quarried *stone* in the mountains,
16 besides three thousand three hundred[a]
from the chiefs of Solomon's deputies, who
supervised the people who labored in the
work.
17 And the king commanded them to quarry
large stones, costly stones, *and* hewn stones,
to lay the foundation of the temple.[a]
18 So Solomon's builders, Hiram's builders,
and the Gebalites quarried *them;* and they
prepared timber and stones to build the temple.

Solomon Builds the Temple

6 And it came to pass in the four hundred
and eightieth[a] year after the children of Israel had come out of the land of Egypt, in the
fourth year of Solomon's reign over Israel, in
the month of Ziv, which *is* the second month,
that he began to build the house of the LORD.
2 Now the house which King Solomon built
for the LORD, its length *was* sixty cubits, its
width twenty, and its height thirty cubits.
3 The vestibule in front of the sanctuary[a] of
the house *was* twenty cubits long across the
width of the house, *and* the width of *the
vestibule*[b] *extended* ten cubits from the front
of the house.

5:3 [a]Literally *them* **5:11** [a]Following Masoretic Text, Targum, and Vulgate; Septuagint and Syriac read *twenty thousand*. **5:16** [a]Following Masoretic Text, Targum, and Vulgate; Septuagint reads *three thousand six hundred*. **5:17** [a]Literally *house,* and so frequently throughout this book **6:1** [a]Following Masoretic Text, Targum, and Vulgate; Septuagint reads *fortieth*. **6:3** [a]Hebrew *heykal;* here the main room of the temple, elsewhere called the holy place (compare Exodus 26:33 and Ezekiel 41:1) [b]Literally *it*

LIFE LESSONS

➤ **5:12 — *So the LORD gave Solomon wisdom, as He had promised him . . . .***

The Lord always follows through on His promises. We may not see how He could fulfill a promise, but trusting God means looking beyond what we can see to what God can see.

4 And he made for the house windows with
beveled frames.
5 Against the wall of the temple he built
chambers all around, *against* the walls of the
temple, all around the sanctuary and the inner sanctuary.[a] Thus he made side chambers
all around it.
6 The lowest chamber *was* five cubits wide,
the middle *was* six cubits wide, and the third
was seven cubits wide; for he made narrow
ledges around the outside of the temple, so
that *the support beams* would not be fastened
into the walls of the temple.
7 And the temple, when it was being built,
was built with stone finished at the quarry, so
that no hammer or chisel *or* any iron tool was
heard in the temple while it was being built.
8 The doorway for the middle story[a] *was* on
the right side of the temple. They went up by
stairs to the middle *story,* and from the middle to the third.
9 So he built the temple and finished it, and
he paneled the temple with beams and boards
of cedar.
10 And he built side chambers against the
entire temple, each five cubits high; they were
attached to the temple with cedar beams.
11 Then the word of the LORD came to Solomon, saying:
➤ 12 "*Concerning* this temple which you are
building, if you walk in My statutes, execute
My judgments, keep all My commandments,
and walk in them, then I will perform My
word with you, which I spoke to your father
David.
13 "And I will dwell among the children of Israel, and will not forsake My people Israel."
14 So Solomon built the temple and finished it.
15 And he built the inside walls of the temple
with cedar boards; from the floor of the temple to the ceiling he paneled the inside with
wood; and he covered the floor of the temple
with planks of cypress.
16 Then he built the twenty-cubit room at the
rear of the temple, from floor to ceiling, with
cedar boards; he built *it* inside as the inner
sanctuary, as the Most Holy *Place.*
17 And in front of it the temple sanctuary
was forty cubits *long.*
18 The inside of the temple was cedar, carved
with ornamental buds and open flowers. All
was cedar; there was no stone *to be* seen.
19 And he prepared the inner sanctuary inside the temple, to set the ark of the covenant
of the LORD there.
20 The inner sanctuary *was* twenty cubits
long, twenty cubits wide, and twenty cubits
high. He overlaid it with pure gold, and overlaid the altar of cedar.
21 So Solomon overlaid the inside of the temple with pure gold. He stretched gold chains
across the front of the inner sanctuary, and
overlaid it with gold.
22 The whole temple he overlaid with gold,
until he had finished all the temple; also he
overlaid with gold the entire altar that *was* by
the inner sanctuary.
23 Inside the inner sanctuary he made two
cherubim *of* olive wood, *each* ten cubits high.
24 One wing of the cherub *was* five cubits,
and the other wing of the cherub five cubits:
ten cubits from the tip of one wing to the tip
of the other.
25 And the other cherub *was* ten cubits; both
cherubim *were* of the same size and shape.
26 The height of one cherub *was* ten cubits,
and so *was* the other cherub.
27 Then he set the cherubim inside the inner
room;[a] and they stretched out the wings of the
cherubim so that the wing of the one touched
one wall, and the wing of the other cherub
touched the other wall. And their wings
touched each other in the middle of the room.
28 Also he overlaid the cherubim with gold.
29 Then he carved all the walls of the temple
all around, both the inner and outer *sanctuaries,* with carved figures of cherubim, palm
trees, and open flowers.
30 And the floor of the temple he overlaid
with gold, both the inner and outer *sanctuaries.*
31 For the entrance of the inner sanctuary he
made doors *of* olive wood; the lintel *and* doorposts *were* one-fifth *of the wall.*
32 The two doors *were of* olive wood; and he
carved on them figures of cherubim, palm
trees, and open flowers, and overlaid *them*
with gold; and he spread gold on the cherubim and on the palm trees.
33 So for the door of the sanctuary he also
made doorposts *of* olive wood, one-fourth *of
the wall.*

6:5 [a]Hebrew *debir;* here the inner room of the temple, elsewhere called the Most Holy Place (compare verse 16) **6:8** [a]Following Masoretic Text and Vulgate; Septuagint reads *upper story;* Targum reads *ground story.* **6:27** [a]Literally *house*

LIFE LESSONS

➤ ***6:12 — ". . . if you walk in My statutes, execute My judgments, keep all My commandments, and walk in them, then I will perform My word with you . . . ."***

Many of God's promises to us are conditional in nature: *if* we will do this, *then* God will do that. He is under no obligation to fulfill a conditional promise if we neglect our part of the deal.

34 And the two doors *were of* cypress wood; two panels *comprised* one folding door, and two panels *comprised* the other folding door.

35 Then he carved cherubim, palm trees, and open flowers *on them,* and overlaid *them* with gold applied evenly on the carved work.

36 And he built the inner court with three rows of hewn stone and a row of cedar beams.

37 In the fourth year the foundation of the house of the LORD was laid, in the month of Ziv.

38 And in the eleventh year, in the month of Bul, which is the eighth month, the house was finished in all its details and according to all its plans. So he was seven years in building it.

Solomon's Other Buildings

➤ **7** But Solomon took thirteen years to build his own house; so he finished all his house.

2 He also built the House of the Forest of Lebanon; its length *was* one hundred cubits, its width fifty cubits, and its height thirty cubits, with four rows of cedar pillars, and cedar beams on the pillars.

3 And *it was* paneled with cedar above the beams that *were* on forty-five pillars, fifteen *to* a row.

4 *There were* windows *with beveled frames in* three rows, and window *was* opposite window *in* three tiers.

5 And all the doorways and doorposts *had* rectangular frames; and window *was* opposite window *in* three tiers.

6 He also made the Hall of Pillars: its length *was* fifty cubits, and its width thirty cubits; and in front of them *was* a portico with pillars, and a canopy *was* in front of them.

7 Then he made a hall for the throne, the Hall of Judgment, where he might judge; and *it was* paneled with cedar from floor to ceiling.[a]

8 And the house where he dwelt *had* another court inside the hall, of like workmanship. Solomon also made a house like this hall for Pharaoh's daughter, whom he had taken *as wife.*

9 All these *were of* costly stones cut to size, trimmed with saws, inside and out, from the foundation to the eaves, and also on the outside to the great court.

10 The foundation *was of* costly stones, large stones, some ten cubits and some eight cubits.

11 And above *were* costly stones, hewn to size, and cedar wood.

12 The great court *was* enclosed with three rows of hewn stones and a row of cedar beams. So were the inner court of the house of the LORD and the vestibule of the temple.

Hiram the Craftsman

13 Now King Solomon sent and brought Huram[a] from Tyre.

14 He *was* the son of a widow from the tribe of Naphtali, and his father *was* a man of Tyre, a bronze worker; he was filled with wisdom and understanding and skill in working with all kinds of bronze work. So he came to King Solomon and did all his work.

The Bronze Pillars for the Temple

15 And he cast two pillars of bronze, each one eighteen cubits high, and a line of twelve cubits measured the circumference of each.

16 Then he made two capitals *of* cast bronze, to set on the tops of the pillars. The height of one capital *was* five cubits, and the height of the other capital *was* five cubits.

17 *He made* a lattice network, with wreaths of chainwork, for the capitals which *were* on top of the pillars: seven chains for one capital and seven for the other capital.

18 So he made the pillars, and two rows of pomegranates above the network all around to cover the capitals that *were* on top; and thus he did for the other capital.

19 The capitals which *were* on top of the pillars in the hall *were* in the shape of lilies, four cubits.

20 The capitals on the two pillars also *had pomegranates* above, by the convex surface which *was* next to the network; and there *were* two hundred such pomegranates in rows on each of the capitals all around.

21 Then he set up the pillars by the vestibule of the temple; he set up the pillar on the right and called its name Jachin, and he set up the pillar on the left and called its name Boaz.

22 The tops of the pillars were in the shape of lilies. So the work of the pillars was finished.

The Sea and the Oxen

23 And he made the Sea of cast bronze, ten cubits from one brim to the other; *it was* completely round. Its height *was* five cubits, and a line of thirty cubits measured its circumference.

24 Below its brim *were* ornamental buds encircling it all around, ten to a cubit, all the

7:7 [a]Literally *floor,* that is, of the upper level **7:13** [a]Hebrew *Hiram* (compare 2 Chronicles 2:13, 14)

LIFE LESSONS

➤ **7:1 — *But Solomon took thirteen years to build his own house; so he finished all his house.***

Although Solomon took seven years to build the temple, he took almost twice as long to build his own palace. Could this have revealed a mistaken priority?

way around the Sea. The ornamental buds
were cast in two rows when it was cast.
25 It stood on twelve oxen: three looking toward the north, three looking toward the
west, three looking toward the south, and
three looking toward the east; the Sea *was set*
upon them, and all their back parts *pointed*
inward.
26 It *was* a handbreadth thick; and its brim
was shaped like the brim of a cup, *like* a lily
blossom. It contained two thousand[a] baths.

The Carts and the Lavers

27 He also made ten carts of bronze; four cubits *was* the length of each cart, four cubits its
width, and three cubits its height.
28 And this *was* the design of the carts: They
had panels, and the panels *were* between
frames;
29 on the panels that *were* between the
frames *were* lions, oxen, and cherubim. And
on the frames *was* a pedestal on top. Below
the lions and oxen *were* wreaths of plaited
work.
30 Every cart had four bronze wheels and
axles of bronze, and its four feet had supports. Under the laver *were* supports of cast
bronze beside each wreath.
31 Its opening inside the crown at the top
was one cubit in diameter; and the opening
was round, shaped *like* a pedestal, one and a
half cubits in outside diameter; and also on
the opening *were* engravings, but the panels
were square, not round.
32 Under the panels *were* the four wheels,
and the axles of the wheels *were joined* to the
cart. The height of a wheel *was* one and a half
cubits.
33 The workmanship of the wheels *was* like
the workmanship of a chariot wheel; their
axle pins, their rims, their spokes, and their
hubs *were* all of cast *bronze*.
34 And *there were* four supports at the four
corners of each cart; its supports *were* part of
the cart itself.
35 On the top of the cart, at the height of half
a cubit, *it was* perfectly round. And on the top
of the cart, its flanges and its panels *were* of
the same casting.
36 On the plates of its flanges and on its panels he engraved cherubim, lions, and palm
trees, wherever there was a clear space on
each, with wreaths all around.
37 Thus he made the ten carts. All of them
were of the same mold, one measure, *and* one
shape.
38 Then he made ten lavers of bronze; each
laver contained forty baths, *and* each laver
was four cubits. On each of the ten carts *was*
a laver.
39 And he put five carts on the right side of
the house, and five on the left side of the
house. He set the Sea on the right side of the
house, toward the southeast.

Furnishings of the Temple

40 Huram[a] made the lavers and the shovels
and the bowls. So Huram finished doing all
the work that he was to do for King Solomon
for the house of the LORD:
41 the two pillars, the *two* bowl-shaped capitals that *were* on top of the two pillars;
the two networks covering the two bowl-
shaped capitals which *were* on top of the pillars;
42 four hundred pomegranates for the two
networks (two rows of pomegranates for each
network, to cover the two bowl-shaped capitals that *were* on top of the pillars);
43 the ten carts, and ten lavers on the carts;
44 one Sea, and twelve oxen under the Sea;
45 the pots, the shovels, and the bowls. All
these articles which Huram[a] made for King
Solomon *for* the house of the LORD *were of*
burnished bronze.
46 In the plain of Jordan the king had them
cast in clay molds, between Succoth and
Zaretan.
47 And Solomon did not weigh all the articles, because *there were* so many; the weight
of the bronze was not determined.
48 Thus Solomon had all the furnishings
made for the house of the LORD: the altar of
gold, and the table of gold on which *was* the
showbread;
49 the lampstands of pure gold, five on
the right *side* and five on the left in front of
the inner sanctuary, with the flowers and the
lamps and the wick-trimmers of gold;
50 the basins, the trimmers, the bowls, the ladles, and the censers of pure gold; and the
hinges of gold, *both* for the doors of the inner
room (the Most Holy *Place*) *and* for the doors
of the main hall of the temple.
51 So all the work that King Solomon had
done for the house of the LORD was finished;
and Solomon brought in the things which his
father David had dedicated: the silver and the
gold and the furnishings. He put them in the
treasuries of the house of the LORD.

The Ark Brought into the Temple

8 Now Solomon assembled the elders of Israel and all the heads of the tribes, the
chief fathers of the children of Israel, to King
Solomon in Jerusalem, that they might bring
up the ark of the covenant of the LORD from
the City of David, which *is* Zion.
2 Therefore all the men of Israel assembled
with King Solomon at the feast in the month
of Ethanim, which *is* the seventh month.
3 So all the elders of Israel came, and the
priests took up the ark.
4 Then they brought up the ark of the LORD,
the tabernacle of meeting, and all the holy

7:26 [a]Or *three thousand* (compare 2 Chronicles 4:5)
7:40 [a]Hebrew *Hiram* (compare 2 Chronicles 2:13, 14)
7:45 [a]Hebrew *Hiram* (compare 2 Chronicles 2:13, 14)

furnishings that *were* in the tabernacle. The
priests and the Levites brought them up.
5 Also King Solomon, and all the congregation of Israel who were assembled with him,
were with him before the ark, sacrificing
sheep and oxen that could not be counted or
numbered for multitude.
6 Then the priests brought in the ark of the
covenant of the LORD to its place, into the
inner sanctuary of the temple, to the Most
Holy *Place*, under the wings of the cherubim.
7 For the cherubim spread *their* two wings
over the place of the ark, and the cherubim
overshadowed the ark and its poles.
8 The poles extended so that the ends of the
poles could be seen from the holy *place*, in
front of the inner sanctuary; but they could
not be seen from outside. And they are there
to this day.
9 Nothing *was* in the ark except the two
tablets of stone which Moses put there at
Horeb, when the LORD made *a covenant* with
the children of Israel, when they came out of
the land of Egypt.
➤ 10 And it came to pass, when the priests
came out of the holy *place*, that the cloud
filled the house of the LORD,
11 so that the priests could not continue ministering because of the cloud; for the glory of
the LORD filled the house of the LORD.
12 Then Solomon spoke:

"The LORD said He would dwell in the
dark cloud.
13 I have surely built You an exalted house,
And a place for You to dwell in forever."

Solomon's Speech at Completion of the Work

14 Then the king turned around and blessed
the whole assembly of Israel, while all the assembly of Israel was standing.
15 And he said: "Blessed *be* the LORD God of
Israel, who spoke with His mouth to my father David, and with His hand has fulfilled *it*,
saying,
16 'Since the day that I brought My people Israel out of Egypt, I have chosen no city from
any tribe of Israel *in which* to build a house,
that My name might be there; but I chose David to be over My people Israel.'
17 "Now it was in the heart of my father David to build a temple[a] for the name of the
LORD God of Israel.
18 "But the LORD said to my father David,
'Whereas it was in your heart to build a temple for My name, you did well that it was in
your heart.
19 'Nevertheless you shall not build the temple, but your son who will come from your
body, he shall build the temple for My name.'
20 "So the LORD has fulfilled His word which
He spoke; and I have filled the position of my
father David, and sit on the throne of Israel,
as the LORD promised; and I have built a temple for the name of the LORD God of Israel.
21 "And there I have made a place for the ark,
in which *is* the covenant of the LORD which
He made with our fathers, when He brought
them out of the land of Egypt."

Solomon's Prayer of Dedication

22 Then Solomon stood before the altar of
the LORD in the presence of all the assembly
of Israel, and spread out his hands toward
heaven;
23 and he said: "LORD God of Israel, *there is*
no God in heaven above or on earth below
like You, who keep *Your* covenant and mercy
with Your servants who walk before You with
all their hearts.
24 "You have kept what You promised Your
servant David my father; You have both spoken with Your mouth and fulfilled *it* with Your
hand, as *it is* this day.
25 "Therefore, LORD God of Israel, now keep
what You promised Your servant David my father, saying, 'You shall not fail to have a man
sit before Me on the throne of Israel, only if
your sons take heed to their way, that they
walk before Me as you have walked before
Me.'
26 "And now I pray, O God of Israel, let Your
word come true, which You have spoken to
Your servant David my father.

8:17 [a]Literally *house*, and so in verses 18–20

LIFE LESSONS

➤ **8:10 — *And it came to pass, when the priests came out of the holy place, that the cloud filled the house of the LORD . . . .***

Sometimes the presence of the Lord becomes so obvious and mighty that we must cease our ministering and simply worship. In those moments of intimacy we fulfill our highest purpose.

➤ **8:18, 19 — *"Whereas it was in your heart to build a temple for My name, you did well that it was in your heart. Nevertheless you shall not build the temple . . . ."***

God may put a good thing in our heart, and yet not allow us to accomplish it. Yet He will use even that to fulfill His own purposes. Our job is to trust and obey.

➤ **8:24 — *"You have kept what You promised Your servant David my father; You have both spoken with Your mouth and fulfilled it with Your hand, as it is this day."***

It honors God and blesses us when we publicly acknowledge that our God keeps all of His promises. He is absolutely trustworthy, and we can build our lives on His Word.

➤ 27 "But will God indeed dwell on the earth?
Behold, heaven and the heaven of heavens
cannot contain You. How much less this temple which I have built!
28 "Yet regard the prayer of Your servant and
his supplication, O LORD my God, and listen
to the cry and the prayer which Your servant
is praying before You today:
29 "that Your eyes may be open toward this
temple night and day, toward the place of
which You said, 'My name shall be there,' that
You may hear the prayer which Your servant
makes toward this place.
30 "And may You hear the supplication of Your
servant and of Your people Israel, when they
pray toward this place. Hear in heaven Your
dwelling place; and when You hear, forgive.
31 "When anyone sins against his neighbor,
and is forced to take an oath, and comes *and*
takes an oath before Your altar in this temple,
32 "then hear in heaven, and act, and judge
Your servants, condemning the wicked,
bringing his way on his head, and justifying
the righteous by giving him according to his
righteousness.
33 "When Your people Israel are defeated before an enemy because they have sinned
against You, and when they turn back to You
and confess Your name, and pray and make
supplication to You in this temple,
34 "then hear in heaven, and forgive the sin
of Your people Israel, and bring them back to
the land which You gave to their fathers.
35 "When the heavens are shut up and there
is no rain because they have sinned against
You, when they pray toward this place and
confess Your name, and turn from their sin because You afflict them,
36 "then hear in heaven, and forgive the sin
of Your servants, Your people Israel, that You
may teach them the good way in which they
should walk; and send rain on Your land
which You have given to Your people as an inheritance.
37 "When there is famine in the land, pestilence *or* blight *or* mildew, locusts *or* grasshoppers; when their enemy besieges them in the
land of their cities; whatever plague or whatever sickness *there is;*
38 "whatever prayer, whatever supplication ➤
is made by anyone, *or* by all Your people Israel, when each one knows the plague of his
own heart, and spreads out his hands toward
this temple:
39 "then hear in heaven Your dwelling place,
and forgive, and act, and give to everyone according to all his ways, whose heart You know
(for You alone know the hearts of all the sons
of men),
40 "that they may fear You all the days that
they live in the land which You gave to our fathers.
41 "Moreover, concerning a foreigner, who *is*
not of Your people Israel, but has come from a
far country for Your name's sake
42 "(for they will hear of Your great name
and Your strong hand and Your outstretched
arm), when he comes and prays toward this
temple,
43 "hear in heaven Your dwelling place, and do ➤
according to all for which the foreigner calls to
You, that all peoples of the earth may know
Your name and fear You, as *do* Your people Israel, and that they may know that this temple
which I have built is called by Your name.
44 "When Your people go out to battle against
their enemy, wherever You send them, and
when they pray to the LORD toward the city
which You have chosen and the temple which
I have built for Your name,
45 "then hear in heaven their prayer and
their supplication, and maintain their cause.
46 "When they sin against You (for *there is* no
one who does not sin), and You become angry
with them and deliver them to the enemy, and
they take them captive to the land of the
enemy, far or near;
47 "*yet* when they come to themselves in the
land where they were carried captive, and repent, and make supplication to You in the land
of those who took them captive, saying, 'We
have sinned and done wrong, we have committed wickedness';
48 "and *when* they return to You with all their
heart and with all their soul in the land of
their enemies who led them away captive, and
pray to You toward their land which You gave
to their fathers, the city which You have cho-

LIFE LESSONS

➤ 8:27 — *"But will God indeed dwell on the earth? Behold, heaven and the heaven of heavens cannot contain You. How much less this temple which I have built!"*

Our God fills the universe, yet He chose to dwell in a special way in the Jerusalem temple. Today, He lives not in a manmade temple, but in the hearts of all those who believe in Christ (1 Cor. 6:19).

➤ 8:38 — *". . . when each one knows the plague of his own heart . . . ."*

It is important that each of us knows "the plague of his own heart." We are not to dwell morbidly over our own sinfulness, but we need to know our personal tendencies toward certain kinds of sin.

➤ 8:43 — *". . . do according to all for which the foreigner calls to You, that all peoples of the earth may know Your name and fear You . . . ."*

From the very beginning, God desired that the whole world come to know, love, worship and serve Him. Intimacy with God is His highest priority everywhere on earth.

sen and the temple which I have built for Your
name:
49 "then hear in heaven Your dwelling place
their prayer and their supplication, and maintain their cause,
50 "and forgive Your people who have sinned
against You, and all their transgressions
which they have transgressed against You;
and grant them compassion before those who
took them captive, that they may have compassion on them
51 "(for they *are* Your people and Your inheritance, whom You brought out of Egypt, out of
the iron furnace),
52 "that Your eyes may be open to the supplication of Your servant and the supplication of
Your people Israel, to listen to them whenever
they call to You.
53 "For You separated them from among all
the peoples of the earth *to be* Your inheritance, as You spoke by Your servant Moses,
when You brought our fathers out of Egypt,
O Lord GOD."

Solomon Blesses the Assembly

54 And so it was, when Solomon had finished
praying all this prayer and supplication to the
LORD, that he arose from before the altar of
the LORD, from kneeling on his knees with his
hands spread up to heaven.
55 Then he stood and blessed all the assembly of Israel with a loud voice, saying:
✳ 56 "Blessed *be* the LORD, who has given rest to
His people Israel, according to all that He
promised. There has not failed one word of all
His good promise, which He promised through
His servant Moses.
57 "May the LORD our God be with us, as He
was with our fathers. May He not leave us nor
forsake us,
➤ 58 "that He may incline our hearts to Himself,
to walk in all His ways, and to keep His commandments and His statutes and His judgments, which He commanded our fathers.
59 "And may these words of mine, with which
I have made supplication before the LORD, be
near the LORD our God day and night, that He
may maintain the cause of His servant and
the cause of His people Israel, as each day
may require,
60 "that all the peoples of the earth may
know that the LORD *is* God; *there is* no other.
61 "Let your heart therefore be loyal to the
LORD our God, to walk in His statutes and
keep His commandments, as at this day."

Solomon Dedicates the Temple

62 Then the king and all Israel with him offered sacrifices before the LORD.
63 And Solomon offered a sacrifice of peace
offerings, which he offered to the LORD,
twenty-two thousand bulls and one hundred
and twenty thousand sheep. So the king and
all the children of Israel dedicated the house
of the LORD.
64 On the same day the king consecrated the
middle of the court that *was* in front of the
house of the LORD; for there he offered burnt
offerings, grain offerings, and the fat of the
peace offerings, because the bronze altar that
was before the LORD *was* too small to receive
the burnt offerings, the grain offerings, and
the fat of the peace offerings.
65 At that time Solomon held a feast, and all
Israel with him, a great assembly from the entrance of Hamath to the Brook of Egypt, before the LORD our God, seven days and seven
more days—fourteen days.
66 On the eighth day he sent the people ➤
away; and they blessed the king, and went to
their tents joyful and glad of heart for all the
good that the LORD had done for His servant
David, and for Israel His people.

God's Second Appearance to Solomon

9 And it came to pass, when Solomon had
finished building the house of the LORD
and the king's house, and all Solomon's desire which he wanted to do,
2 that the LORD appeared to Solomon the
second time, as He had appeared to him at
Gibeon.
3 And the LORD said to him: "I have heard ➤
your prayer and your supplication that you
have made before Me; I have consecrated this
house which you have built to put My name
there forever, and My eyes and My heart will
be there perpetually.
4 "Now if you walk before Me as your father
David walked, in integrity of heart and in

LIFE LESSONS

➤ 8:58 — *"that He may incline our hearts to Himself, to walk in all His ways, and to keep His commandments . . . ."*

Since we are all prone to wandering (1 Kin. 8:46), it is wise to pray regularly that God would give us a great love for Him and grant us the desire to walk in His ways and joyfully obey His Word.

➤ 8:66 — *. . . they blessed the king, and went to their tents joyful and glad of heart for all the good that the LORD had done . . . .*

It is important to periodically gather as the people of God to celebrate with joyful and glad hearts all the good that the Lord does for us. This not only honors Him; it encourages us to stay true to Him.

➤ 9:3 — *And the LORD said to him: "I have heard your prayer and your supplication that you have made before Me . . . ."*

When we bring our requests to God, He hears. It may not always seem as though He hears. Sometimes it may feel as though we speak into the air. But He hears, and He acts for those who wait for Him.

uprightness, to do according to all that I have
commanded you, *and* if you keep My statutes
and My judgments,
5 "then I will establish the throne of your
kingdom over Israel forever, as I promised
David your father, saying, 'You shall not fail
to have a man on the throne of Israel.'
6 "*But* if you or your sons at all turn from
following Me, and do not keep My commandments *and* My statutes which I have set before you, but go and serve other gods and
worship them,
7 "then I will cut off Israel from the land
which I have given them; and this house
which I have consecrated for My name I will
cast out of My sight. Israel will be a proverb
and a byword among all peoples.
8 "And *as for* this house, *which* is exalted,
everyone who passes by it will be astonished
and will hiss, and say, 'Why has the LORD
done thus to this land and to this house?'
9 "Then they will answer, 'Because they forsook the LORD their God, who brought their
fathers out of the land of Egypt, and have embraced other gods, and worshiped them and
served them; therefore the LORD has brought
all this calamity on them.'"

Solomon and Hiram Exchange Gifts

10 Now it happened at the end of twenty
years, when Solomon had built the two
houses, the house of the LORD and the king's
house
11 (Hiram the king of Tyre had supplied Solomon with cedar and cypress and gold, as
much as he desired), *that* King Solomon then
gave Hiram twenty cities in the land of Galilee.
12 Then Hiram went from Tyre to see the
cities which Solomon had given him, but they
did not please him.
13 So he said, "What *kind of* cities *are* these
which you have given me, my brother?" And
he called them the land of Cabul,[a] as they are
to this day.
14 Then Hiram sent the king one hundred
and twenty talents of gold.

Solomon's Additional Achievements

15 And this *is* the reason for the labor force
which King Solomon raised: to build the
house of the LORD, his own house, the Millo,[a]
the wall of Jerusalem, Hazor, Megiddo, and
Gezer.
16 (Pharaoh king of Egypt had gone up and
taken Gezer and burned it with fire, had
killed the Canaanites who dwelt in the city,
and had given it *as* a dowry to his daughter,
Solomon's wife.)
17 And Solomon built Gezer, Lower Beth
Horon,
18 Baalath, and Tadmor in the wilderness, in
the land *of Judah*,
19 all the storage cities that Solomon had,
cities for his chariots and cities for his cavalry, and whatever Solomon desired to build
in Jerusalem, in Lebanon, and in all the land
of his dominion.
20 All the people *who were* left of the Amorites, Hittites, Perizzites, Hivites, and Jebusites,
who *were* not of the children of Israel—
21 that is, their descendants who were left in
the land after them, whom the children of Israel had not been able to destroy completely—from these Solomon raised forced
labor, as it is to this day.
22 But of the children of Israel Solomon
made no forced laborers, because they *were*
men of war and his servants: his officers, his
captains, commanders of his chariots, and his
cavalry.
23 Others *were* chiefs of the officials who
were over Solomon's work: five hundred and
fifty, who ruled over the people who did the
work.
24 But Pharaoh's daughter came up from the
City of David to her house which *Solomon*[a]
had built for her. Then he built the Millo.
25 Now three times a year Solomon offered
burnt offerings and peace offerings on the
altar which he had built for the LORD, and he
burned incense with them *on the altar* that
was before the LORD. So he finished the temple.
26 King Solomon also built a fleet of ships at
Ezion Geber, which *is* near Elath[a] on the
shore of the Red Sea, in the land of Edom.
27 Then Hiram sent his servants with the
fleet, seamen who knew the sea, to work with
the servants of Solomon.
28 And they went to Ophir, and acquired four
hundred and twenty talents of gold from
there, and brought *it* to King Solomon.

The Queen of Sheba's Praise of Solomon

10 Now when the queen of Sheba heard of
the fame of Solomon concerning the
name of the LORD, she came to test him with
hard questions.
2 She came to Jerusalem with a very great
retinue, with camels that bore spices, very
much gold, and precious stones; and when
she came to Solomon, she spoke with him
about all that was in her heart.
3 So Solomon answered all her questions;
there was nothing so difficult for the king that
he could not explain *it* to her.
4 And when the queen of Sheba had seen all
the wisdom of Solomon, the house that he
had built,
5 the food on his table, the seating of his servants, the service of his waiters and their apparel, his cupbearers, and his entryway by

9:13 [a]Literally *Good for Nothing* **9:15** [a]Literally *The Landfill*
9:24 [a]Literally *he* (compare 2 Chronicles 8:11) **9:26** [a]Hebrew
Eloth (compare 2 Kings 14:22)

which he went up to the house of the LORD,
there was no more spirit in her.
6 Then she said to the king: "It was a true report which I heard in my own land about your
words and your wisdom.
7 "However I did not believe the words until
I came and saw with my own eyes; and indeed
the half was not told me. Your wisdom and
prosperity exceed the fame of which I heard.
8 "Happy *are* your men and happy *are* these
your servants, who stand continually before
you *and* hear your wisdom!
9 "Blessed be the LORD your God, who delighted in you, setting you on the throne of Israel! Because the LORD has loved Israel
forever, therefore He made you king, to do
justice and righteousness."
10 Then she gave the king one hundred and
twenty talents of gold, spices in great quantity, and precious stones. There never again
came such abundance of spices as the queen
of Sheba gave to King Solomon.
11 Also, the ships of Hiram, which brought
gold from Ophir, brought great quantities
of almug[a] wood and precious stones from
Ophir.
12 And the king made steps of the almug
wood for the house of the LORD and for the
king's house, also harps and stringed instruments for singers. There never again came
such almug wood, nor has the like been seen
to this day.
13 Now King Solomon gave the queen of
Sheba all she desired, whatever she asked,
besides what Solomon had given her according to the royal generosity. So she turned and
went to her own country, she and her servants.

Solomon's Great Wealth

14 The weight of gold that came to Solomon
yearly was six hundred and sixty-six talents
of gold,
15 besides *that* from the traveling merchants, from the income of traders, from all
the kings of Arabia, and from the governors
of the country.
16 And King Solomon made two hundred
large shields *of* hammered gold; six hundred
shekels of gold went into each shield.
17 He also *made* three hundred shields *of*
hammered gold; three minas of gold went
into each shield. The king put them in the
House of the Forest of Lebanon.
18 Moreover the king made a great throne of
ivory, and overlaid it with pure gold.
19 The throne had six steps, and the top of
the throne *was* round at the back; *there were*
armrests on either side of the place of the
seat, and two lions stood beside the armrests.
20 Twelve lions stood there, one on each side
of the six steps; nothing like *this* had been
made for any *other* kingdom.
21 All King Solomon's drinking vessels *were*
gold, and all the vessels of the House of the
Forest of Lebanon *were* pure gold. Not *one*
was silver, for this was accounted as nothing
in the days of Solomon.
22 For the king had merchant ships[a] at sea
with the fleet of Hiram. Once every three
years the merchant ships came bringing gold,
silver, ivory, apes, and monkeys.[b]
23 So King Solomon surpassed all the kings
of the earth in riches and wisdom.
24 Now all the earth sought the presence of
Solomon to hear his wisdom, which God had
put in his heart.
25 Each man brought his present: articles of
silver and gold, garments, armor, spices,
horses, and mules, at a set rate year by year.
26 And Solomon gathered chariots and
horsemen; he had one thousand four hundred
chariots and twelve thousand horsemen,
whom he stationed[a] in the chariot cities and
with the king at Jerusalem.
27 The king made silver *as common* in Jerusalem as stones, and he made cedar trees as
abundant as the sycamores which *are* in the
lowland.
28 Also Solomon had horses imported from
Egypt and Keveh; the king's merchants
bought them in Keveh at the *current* price.
29 Now a chariot that was imported from
Egypt cost six hundred *shekels* of silver, and
a horse one hundred and fifty; and thus,
through their agents,[a] they exported *them* to
all the kings of the Hittites and the kings of
Syria.

Solomon's Heart Turns from the LORD

11 But King Solomon loved many foreign
women, as well as the daughter of

10:11 [a]Or *algum* (compare 2 Chronicles 9:10, 11)
10:22 [a]Literally *ships of Tarshish,* deep-sea vessels [b]Or *peacocks*
10:26 [a]Following Septuagint, Syriac, Targum, and Vulgate (compare 2 Chronicles 9:25); Masoretic Text reads *led.*
10:29 [a]Literally *by their hands*

LIFE LESSONS

➤ 10:23 — *So King Solomon surpassed all the kings of the earth in riches and wisdom.*

The Lord had promised to make Solomon the wisest man in history and the richest king of his age, and He fulfilled that promise within twenty years of giving it.

➤ 10:28 — *11:1—Also Solomon had horses imported from Egypt and Keveh . . . King Solomon loved many foreign women . . . .*

Everything that the Lord had forbidden kings to do in Deuteronomy 17:16–17, Solomon did. He accumulated Egyptian horses, silver and gold, and foreign wives—and so lost the blessing of God.

ANSWERS TO LIFE'S QUESTIONS

Where do we draw the line between healthy and unhealthy compromise?

1 KIN. 11:4

Compromise can be defined as making a concession in order to gain something. At times, compromise can be a good thing. If you've ever had to compromise on what restaurant to choose or how much to pay for a new car, you don't need an explanation of how compromise works.

We engage in *healthy* compromise when we can give in to another without compromising our core values and beliefs. Every healthy human relationship experiences an element of give and take. *Unhealthy* compromise, on the other hand, involves abandoning sound and godly ideas and standards, leaving us morally and spiritually bankrupt.

The story of Solomon illustrates how unhealthy compromise ends in tragedy. Solomon surpassed every ruler of his time in wisdom and riches. People from all over the world sought out Solomon for his wisdom. Yet Solomon deliberately disobeyed God's warning against intermarriage with other religions (see Deut. 7:3). The result? Solomon's heart turned away from absolute devotion to His God and began to cling to the gods of his wives. No man ever soared so high but fell so low.

We live in a world full of temptations that urges us to compromise our godly values. But when we choose to compromise, we pay a price, even though it may not seem immediately apparent to others (or even to ourselves). Satan wants us to believe the lie that no one gets hurt when we compromise our core values. But that lie has cost men their jobs and ministries, children their innocence, and at times, it has cost individuals their very lives.

God's righteousness is forever. He doesn't wink at compromise. Consider Solomon. After his compromise came collapse. God didn't waste any words. He said he would rip the kingdom out of Solomon's hands because of his compromise. That is exactly what happened (1 Kin. 11:11).

Unhealthy compromise is costly. It corrupts. It brings collapse.

Has God put His finger on something in your life? Perhaps you've crossed the line and are no longer flirting with compromise but have jumped headlong into it. Satan is both cunning and powerful, and if he can get you to give up what is important to you, he can send you down a dark road that could cost you dearly. Don't fall for it. Don't give in. Don't compromise what you shouldn't. Trust God and leave all the consequences to Him.

See the Life Principles Index for further study:
2. Obey God and leave all the consequences to Him.

Pharaoh: women of the Moabites, Ammonites, Edomites, Sidonians, *and* Hittites—
2 from the nations of whom the LORD had
said to the children of Israel, "You shall not
intermarry with them, nor they with you.
Surely they will turn away your hearts after
their gods." Solomon clung to these in love.
3 And he had seven hundred wives, princesses, and three hundred concubines; and
his wives turned away his heart.
4 For it was so, when Solomon was old, that
his wives turned his heart after other gods;
and his heart was not loyal to the LORD his
God, as *was* the heart of his father David.
5 For Solomon went after Ashtoreth the
goddess of the Sidonians, and after Milcom
the abomination of the Ammonites.
6 Solomon did evil in the sight of the LORD,
and did not fully follow the LORD, as *did* his
father David.
7 Then Solomon built a high place for
Chemosh the abomination of Moab, on the
hill that *is* east of Jerusalem, and for Molech
the abomination of the people of Ammon.

LIFE LESSONS

➤ 11:4 — *For it was so, when Solomon was old, that his wives turned his heart after other gods . . . .*

Healthy compromise occurs when we can "give in" without sacrificing our values and beliefs. But a different kind of compromise leads us to abandon sound ideas or standards, leaving us morally and spiritually bankrupt.

8 And he did likewise for all his foreign wives, who burned incense and sacrificed to their gods.

9 So the LORD became angry with Solomon, because his heart had turned from the LORD God of Israel, who had appeared to him twice,

10 and had commanded him concerning this thing, that he should not go after other gods; but he did not keep what the LORD had commanded.

11 Therefore the LORD said to Solomon, "Because you have done this, and have not kept My covenant and My statutes, which I have commanded you, I will surely tear the kingdom away from you and give it to your servant.

12 "Nevertheless I will not do it in your days, for the sake of your father David; I will tear it out of the hand of your son.

13 "However I will not tear away the whole kingdom; I will give one tribe to your son for the sake of My servant David, and for the sake of Jerusalem which I have chosen."

Adversaries of Solomon

➤ **14** Now the LORD raised up an adversary against Solomon, Hadad the Edomite; he *was* a descendant of the king in Edom.

15 For it happened, when David was in Edom, and Joab the commander of the army had gone up to bury the slain, after he had killed every male in Edom

16 (because for six months Joab remained there with all Israel, until he had cut down every male in Edom),

17 that Hadad fled to go to Egypt, he and certain Edomites of his father's servants with him. Hadad *was* still a little child.

18 Then they arose from Midian and came to Paran; and they took men with them from Paran and came to Egypt, to Pharaoh king of Egypt, who gave him a house, apportioned food for him, and gave him land.

19 And Hadad found great favor in the sight of Pharaoh, so that he gave him as wife the sister of his own wife, that is, the sister of Queen Tahpenes.

20 Then the sister of Tahpenes bore him Genubath his son, whom Tahpenes weaned in Pharaoh's house. And Genubath was in Pharaoh's household among the sons of Pharaoh.

21 So when Hadad heard in Egypt that David rested with his fathers, and that Joab the commander of the army was dead, Hadad said to Pharaoh, "Let me depart, that I may go to my own country."

22 Then Pharaoh said to him, "But what have you lacked with me, that suddenly you seek to go to your own country?" So he answered, "Nothing, but do let me go anyway."

23 And God raised up *another* adversary against him, Rezon the son of Eliadah, who had fled from his lord, Hadadezer king of Zobah.

24 So he gathered men to him and became captain over a band *of raiders*, when David killed those *of Zobah*. And they went to Damascus and dwelt there, and reigned in Damascus.

25 He was an adversary of Israel all the days of Solomon (besides the trouble that Hadad *caused*); and he abhorred Israel, and reigned over Syria.

Jeroboam's Rebellion

26 Then Solomon's servant, Jeroboam the son of Nebat, an Ephraimite from Zereda, whose mother's name *was* Zeruah, a widow, also rebelled against the king.

27 And this *is* what caused him to rebel against the king: Solomon had built the Millo *and* repaired the damages to the City of David his father.

28 The man Jeroboam *was* a mighty man of valor; and Solomon, seeing that the young man was industrious, made him the officer over all the labor force of the house of Joseph.

29 Now it happened at that time, when Jeroboam went out of Jerusalem, that the prophet Ahijah the Shilonite met him on the way; and he had clothed himself with a new garment, and the two *were* alone in the field.

30 Then Ahijah took hold of the new garment that *was* on him, and tore it *into* twelve pieces.

31 And he said to Jeroboam, "Take for yourself ten pieces, for thus says the LORD, the God of Israel: 'Behold, I will tear the kingdom out of the hand of Solomon and will give ten tribes to you

32 '(but he shall have one tribe for the sake of My servant David, and for the sake of Jerusalem, the city which I have chosen out of all the tribes of Israel),

33 'because they have[a] forsaken Me, and

11:33 [a]Following Masoretic Text and Targum; Septuagint, Syriac, and Vulgate read *he has*.

LIFE LESSONS

➤ 11:14 — *Now the LORD raised up an adversary against Solomon, Hadad the Edomite . . . .*

When the Lord raises up an adversary against us, He does so not only to discipline us, but to bring us back to wholehearted devotion to Him. Even in judgment, He shows mercy.

worshiped Ashtoreth the goddess of the Sidonians, Chemosh the god of the Moabites, and
Milcom the god of the people of Ammon, and
have not walked in My ways to do *what is*
right in My eyes and *keep* My statutes and My
judgments, as *did* his father David.
34 'However I will not take the whole kingdom out of his hand, because I have made
him ruler all the days of his life for the sake of
My servant David, whom I chose because he
kept My commandments and My statutes.
35 'But I will take the kingdom out of his
son's hand and give it to you—ten tribes.
36 'And to his son I will give one tribe, that
My servant David may always have a lamp
before Me in Jerusalem, the city which I have
chosen for Myself, to put My name there.
37 'So I will take you, and you shall reign
over all your heart desires, and you shall be
king over Israel.
38 'Then it shall be, if you heed all that I command you, walk in My ways, and do *what is*
right in My sight, to keep My statutes and My
commandments, as My servant David did,
then I will be with you and build for you an
enduring house, as I built for David, and will
give Israel to you.
39 'And I will afflict the descendants of David
because of this, but not forever.' "
➤ 40 Solomon therefore sought to kill Jeroboam. But Jeroboam arose and fled to
Egypt, to Shishak king of Egypt, and was in
Egypt until the death of Solomon.

Death of Solomon

41 Now the rest of the acts of Solomon, all
that he did, and his wisdom, *are* they not written in the book of the acts of Solomon?
42 And the period that Solomon reigned in
Jerusalem over all Israel *was* forty years.
43 Then Solomon rested with his fathers, and
was buried in the City of David his father.
And Rehoboam his son reigned in his place.

The Revolt Against Rehoboam

12 And Rehoboam went to Shechem, for
all Israel had gone to Shechem to make
him king.
2 So it happened, when Jeroboam the son of
Nebat heard *it* (he was still in Egypt, for he
had fled from the presence of King Solomon
and had been dwelling in Egypt),
3 that they sent and called him. Then Jeroboam and the whole assembly of Israel
came and spoke to Rehoboam, saying,
4 "Your father made our yoke heavy; now
therefore, lighten the burdensome service of
your father, and his heavy yoke which he put
on us, and we will serve you."
5 So he said to them, "Depart *for* three days,
then come back to me." And the people departed.
6 Then King Rehoboam consulted the elders who stood before his father Solomon
while he still lived, and he said, "How do you
advise *me* to answer these people?"
7 And they spoke to him, saying, "If you will
be a servant to these people today, and serve
them, and answer them, and speak good
words to them, then they will be your servants forever."
8 But he rejected the advice which the elders had given him, and consulted the young
men who had grown up with him, who stood
before him.
9 And he said to them, "What advice do you
give? How should we answer this people who
have spoken to me, saying, 'Lighten the yoke
which your father put on us'?"
10 Then the young men who had grown up
with him spoke to him, saying, "Thus you
should speak to this people who have spoken
to you, saying, 'Your father made our yoke
heavy, but you make *it* lighter on us'—thus
you shall say to them: 'My little *finger* shall be
thicker than my father's waist!
11 'And now, whereas my father put a heavy
yoke on you, I will add to your yoke; my father chastised you with whips, but I will chastise you with scourges!' "[a]
12 So Jeroboam and all the people came to Rehoboam the third day, as the king had directed,
saying, "Come back to me the third day."
13 Then the king answered the people
roughly, and rejected the advice which the
elders had given him;
14 and he spoke to them according to the advice of the young men, saying, "My father
made your yoke heavy, but I will add to your
yoke; my father chastised you with whips, but
I will chastise you with scourges!"[a]
15 So the king did not listen to the people; for ➤
the turn *of events* was from the LORD, that He

12:11 [a]Literally *scorpions* **12:14** [a]Literally *scorpions*

LIFE LESSONS

➤ 11:40 — *Solomon therefore sought to kill Jeroboam . . . .*

Apparently Solomon heard of this prophecy against him, and instead of repenting, sought to frustrate it. But "there is no wisdom or understanding or counsel against the LORD" (Prov. 21:30).

➤ 12:15 — *So the king did not listen to the people; for the turn of events was from the LORD, that He might fulfill His word . . . .*

Whatever the Lord must do to fulfill His Word, He does. That is why God's word is an immovable anchor in times of storm.

might fulfill His word, which the LORD had spoken by Ahijah the Shilonite to Jeroboam the son of Nebat.
16 Now when all Israel saw that the king did not listen to them, the people answered the king, saying:

"What share have we in David?
We have no inheritance in the son of Jesse.
To your tents, O Israel!
Now, see to your own house, O David!"

So Israel departed to their tents.
17 But Rehoboam reigned over the children of Israel who dwelt in the cities of Judah.
18 Then King Rehoboam sent Adoram, who *was* in charge of the revenue; but all Israel stoned him with stones, and he died. Therefore King Rehoboam mounted his chariot in haste to flee to Jerusalem.
19 So Israel has been in rebellion against the house of David to this day.
20 Now it came to pass when all Israel heard that Jeroboam had come back, they sent for him and called him to the congregation, and made him king over all Israel. There was none who followed the house of David, but the tribe of Judah only.
21 And when Rehoboam came to Jerusalem, he assembled all the house of Judah with the tribe of Benjamin, one hundred and eighty thousand chosen *men* who were warriors, to fight against the house of Israel, that he might restore the kingdom to Rehoboam the son of Solomon.
22 But the word of God came to Shemaiah the man of God, saying,
23 "Speak to Rehoboam the son of Solomon, king of Judah, to all the house of Judah and Benjamin, and to the rest of the people, saying,
24 'Thus says the LORD: "You shall not go up nor fight against your brethren the children of Israel. Let every man return to his house, for this thing is from Me."'" Therefore they obeyed the word of the LORD, and turned back, according to the word of the LORD.

Jeroboam's Gold Calves

25 Then Jeroboam built Shechem in the mountains of Ephraim, and dwelt there. Also he went out from there and built Penuel.
26 And Jeroboam said in his heart, "Now the kingdom may return to the house of David:
27 If these people go up to offer sacrifices in the house of the LORD at Jerusalem, then the heart of this people will turn back to their lord, Rehoboam king of Judah, and they will kill me and go back to Rehoboam king of Judah."
28 Therefore the king asked advice, made two calves of gold, and said to the people, "It is too much for you to go up to Jerusalem. Here are your gods, O Israel, which brought you up from the land of Egypt!"
29 And he set up one in Bethel, and the other he put in Dan.
30 Now this thing became a sin, for the people went *to worship* before the one as far as Dan.
31 He made shrines[a] on the high places, and made priests from every class of people, who were not of the sons of Levi.
32 Jeroboam ordained a feast on the fifteenth day of the eighth month, like the feast that *was* in Judah, and offered sacrifices on the altar. So he did at Bethel, sacrificing to the calves that he had made. And at Bethel he installed the priests of the high places which he had made.
33 So he made offerings on the altar which he had made at Bethel on the fifteenth day of the eighth month, in the month which he had devised in his own heart. And he ordained a feast for the children of Israel, and offered sacrifices on the altar and burned incense.

The Message of the Man of God

13 And behold, a man of God went from Judah to Bethel by the word of the LORD, and Jeroboam stood by the altar to burn incense.

12:31 [a]Literally *a house*

LIFE LESSONS

➤ 12:28 — *Therefore the king asked advice, made two calves of gold, and said to the people, "It is too much for you to go up to Jerusalem. Here are your gods, O Israel . . . ."*

Centuries before, the Israelites had constructed a golden idol and proclaimed, "This is your god, O Israel, that brought you out of the land of Egypt!" (Ex. 32:4). Satan seldom changes his tactics; unfortunately, he doesn't need to.

➤ 12:33 — *So he made offerings on the altar which he had made at Bethel on the fifteenth day of the eighth month, in the month which he had devised in his own heart . . . .*

Religion really can be made to serve political purposes. But the existence of a counterfeit does not invalidate the genuine article. God still wants an intimate relationship with us.

➤ 13:1 — *And behold, a man of God went from Judah to Bethel by the word of the LORD, and Jeroboam stood by the altar to burn incense.*

A number of unnamed "men of God" populate the Bible. They are like most of us, who serve God in anonymity—but God remembers both our works and our names, and will reward all faithful service to Him.

➤ 2 Then he cried out against the altar by the
word of the LORD, and said, "O altar, altar!
Thus says the LORD: 'Behold, a child, Josiah
by name, shall be born to the house of David;
and on you he shall sacrifice the priests of the
high places who burn incense on you, and
men's bones shall be burned on you.'"
3 And he gave a sign the same day, saying,
"This *is* the sign which the LORD has spoken:
Surely the altar shall split apart, and the
ashes on it shall be poured out."
4 So it came to pass when King Jeroboam
heard the saying of the man of God, who cried
out against the altar in Bethel, that he
stretched out his hand from the altar, saying,
"Arrest him!" Then his hand, which he
stretched out toward him, withered, so that he
could not pull it back to himself.
5 The altar also was split apart, and the
ashes poured out from the altar, according to
the sign which the man of God had given by
the word of the LORD.
6 Then the king answered and said to the
man of God, "Please entreat the favor of
the LORD your God, and pray for me, that
my hand may be restored to me." So the man
of God entreated the LORD, and the king's
hand was restored to him, and became as before.
7 Then the king said to the man of God,
"Come home with me and refresh yourself,
and I will give you a reward."
8 But the man of God said to the king, "If
you were to give me half your house, I would
not go in with you; nor would I eat bread nor
drink water in this place.
9 "For so it was commanded me by the word
of the LORD, saying, 'You shall not eat bread,
nor drink water, nor return by the same way
you came.'"
10 So he went another way and did not return by the way he came to Bethel.

Death of the Man of God

11 Now an old prophet dwelt in Bethel, and
his sons came and told him all the works that
the man of God had done that day in Bethel;
they also told their father the words which he
had spoken to the king.
12 And their father said to them, "Which
way did he go?" For his sons had seen[a] which
way the man of God went who came from Judah.
13 Then he said to his sons, "Saddle the donkey for me." So they saddled the donkey for
him; and he rode on it,
14 and went after the man of God, and found
him sitting under an oak. Then he said to him,
"*Are* you the man of God who came from Judah?" And he said, "I *am*."
15 Then he said to him, "Come home with me
and eat bread."
16 And he said, "I cannot return with you nor
go in with you; neither can I eat bread nor
drink water with you in this place.
17 "For I have been told by the word of the
LORD, 'You shall not eat bread nor drink water
there, nor return by going the way you
came.'"
18 He said to him, "I too *am* a prophet as you
are, and an angel spoke to me by the word of
the LORD, saying, 'Bring him back with you to
your house, that he may eat bread and drink
water.'" (He was lying to him.)
19 So he went back with him, and ate bread
in his house, and drank water.
20 Now it happened, as they sat at the table,
that the word of the LORD came to the prophet
who had brought him back;
21 and he cried out to the man of God who
came from Judah, saying, "Thus says the
LORD: 'Because you have disobeyed the word
of the LORD, and have not kept the commandment which the LORD your God commanded
you,
22 'but you came back, ate bread, and drank
water in the place of which *the LORD* said to
you, "Eat no bread and drink no water," your
corpse shall not come to the tomb of your fathers.'"
23 So it was, after he had eaten bread and
after he had drunk, that he saddled the donkey for him, the prophet whom he had
brought back.
24 When he was gone, a lion met him on the
road and killed him. And his corpse was
thrown on the road, and the donkey stood by
it. The lion also stood by the corpse.
25 And there, men passed by and saw the
corpse thrown on the road, and the lion
standing by the corpse. Then they went and
told *it* in the city where the old prophet dwelt.
26 Now when the prophet who had brought ➤
him back from the way heard *it*, he said, "It *is*

13:12 [a]Septuagint, Syriac, Targum, and Vulgate read *showed him.*

LIFE LESSONS

➤ 13:2 — *"Thus says the LORD: 'Behold, a child, Josiah by name, shall be born to the house of David . . . .'"*

Only rarely in the Bible does God reveal the name of a person in the future who will act in some crucial way. Here he identifies Josiah by name, who lived centuries later (2 Kin. 23:15–20).

➤ 13:26 — *". . . Therefore the LORD has delivered him to the lion, which has torn him and killed him, according to the word of the LORD which He spoke to him."*

When we know we have heard from the Lord, we cannot let anyone convince us that He has changed His mind—regardless of the source of the supposed new revelation (see Gal. 1:8).

the man of God who was disobedient to the
word of the LORD. Therefore the LORD has delivered him to the lion, which has torn him
and killed him, according to the word of the
LORD which He spoke to him."
27 And he spoke to his sons, saying, "Saddle
the donkey for me." So they saddled *it*.
28 Then he went and found his corpse
thrown on the road, and the donkey and the
lion standing by the corpse. The lion had not
eaten the corpse nor torn the donkey.
29 And the prophet took up the corpse of the
man of God, laid it on the donkey, and
brought it back. So the old prophet came to
the city to mourn, and to bury him.
30 Then he laid the corpse in his own tomb;
and they mourned over him, *saying*, "Alas, my
brother!"
31 So it was, after he had buried him, that
he spoke to his sons, saying, "When I am
dead, then bury me in the tomb where the
man of God *is* buried; lay my bones beside his
bones.
32 "For the saying which he cried out by the
word of the LORD against the altar in Bethel,
and against all the shrines[a] on the high places
which *are* in the cities of Samaria, will surely
come to pass."
➤ **33** After this event Jeroboam did not turn
from his evil way, but again he made priests
from every class of people for the high places;
whoever wished, he consecrated him, and
he became *one* of the priests of the high
places.
34 And this thing was the sin of the house of
Jeroboam, so as to exterminate and destroy *it*
from the face of the earth.

Judgment on the House of Jeroboam

14 At that time Abijah the son of Jeroboam became sick.
➤ 2 And Jeroboam said to his wife, "Please
arise, and disguise yourself, that they may not
recognize you as the wife of Jeroboam, and
go to Shiloh. Indeed, Ahijah the prophet *is*
there, who told me that *I would be* king over
this people.
3 "Also take with you ten loaves, *some* cakes,
and a jar of honey, and go to him; he will tell
you what will become of the child."
4 And Jeroboam's wife did so; she arose and
went to Shiloh, and came to the house of Ahijah. But Ahijah could not see, for his eyes
were glazed by reason of his age.
5 Now the LORD had said to Ahijah, "Here is
the wife of Jeroboam, coming to ask you
something about her son, for he *is* sick. Thus
and thus you shall say to her; for it will be,
when she comes in, that she will pretend *to be*
another *woman*."
6 And so it was, when Ahijah heard the
sound of her footsteps as she came through
the door, he said, "Come in, wife of Jeroboam.
Why do you pretend *to be* another *person*?
For I *have been* sent to you *with* bad *news*.
7 "Go, tell Jeroboam, 'Thus says the LORD
God of Israel: "Because I exalted you from
among the people, and made you ruler over
My people Israel,
8 "and tore the kingdom away from the
house of David, and gave it to you; and *yet*
you have not been as My servant David, who
kept My commandments and who followed
Me with all his heart, to do only *what was*
right in My eyes;
9 "but you have done more evil than all who
were before you, for you have gone and made
for yourself other gods and molded images to
provoke Me to anger, and have cast Me behind your back—
10 "therefore behold! I will bring disaster on
the house of Jeroboam, and will cut off from
Jeroboam every male in Israel, bond and free;
I will take away the remnant of the house of
Jeroboam, as one takes away refuse until it is
all gone.
11 "The dogs shall eat whoever belongs to
Jeroboam and dies in the city, and the birds of
the air shall eat whoever dies in the field; for
the LORD has spoken!"'
12 "Arise therefore, go to your own house.
When your feet enter the city, the child shall
die.

13:32 [a]Literally *houses* 14:15 [a]That is, the Euphrates [b]Hebrew *Asherim*, Canaanite deities

LIFE LESSONS

➤ 13:33 — *After this event Jeroboam did not turn from his evil way, but again he made priests from every class of people for the high places . . . .*

Regret for the unpleasant consequences of sin does not equal repentance of the sin. "He who is often rebuked, and hardens his neck, will suddenly be destroyed" (Prov. 29:1).

➤ 14:2 — *"Please arise, and disguise yourself, that they may not recognize you as the wife of Jeroboam, and go to Shiloh. Indeed, Ahijah the prophet is there . . . ."*

Jeroboam recognized his own prophets as frauds and acknowledged Ahijah as the genuine article, and yet refused to follow his counsel. He provides a clear illustration of Hosea 8:2, 3.

➤ 14:5 — *Now the LORD had said to Ahijah, "Here is the wife of Jeroboam . . . for it will be, when she comes in, that she will pretend to be another woman."*

No one can outmaneuver the Lord or deceive Him. What human eyes cannot see, God sees with unmatched clarity. This is why we can trust in Him even when our way seems dark and uncertain.

➤ 13 "And all Israel shall mourn for him and bury him, for he is the only one of Jeroboam who shall come to the grave, because in him there is found something good toward the LORD God of Israel in the house of Jeroboam.
14 "Moreover the LORD will raise up for Himself a king over Israel who shall cut off the house of Jeroboam; this is the day. What? Even now!
15 "For the LORD will strike Israel, as a reed is shaken in the water. He will uproot Israel from this good land which He gave to their fathers, and will scatter them beyond the River,[a] because they have made their wooden images,[b] provoking the LORD to anger.
16 "And He will give Israel up because of the sins of Jeroboam, who sinned and who made Israel sin."
17 Then Jeroboam's wife arose and departed, and came to Tirzah. When she came to the threshold of the house, the child died.
18 And they buried him; and all Israel mourned for him, according to the word of the LORD which He spoke through His servant Ahijah the prophet.

Death of Jeroboam

19 Now the rest of the acts of Jeroboam, how he made war and how he reigned, indeed they *are* written in the book of the chronicles of the kings of Israel.
20 The period that Jeroboam reigned *was* twenty-two years. So he rested with his fathers. Then Nadab his son reigned in his place.

Rehoboam Reigns in Judah

21 And Rehoboam the son of Solomon reigned in Judah. Rehoboam *was* forty-one years old when he became king. He reigned seventeen years in Jerusalem, the city which the LORD had chosen out of all the tribes of Israel, to put His name there. His mother's name *was* Naamah, an Ammonitess.
22 Now Judah did evil in the sight of the LORD, and they provoked Him to jealousy with their sins which they committed, more than all that their fathers had done.
23 For they also built for themselves high places, *sacred* pillars, and wooden images on every high hill and under every green tree.
24 And there were also perverted persons[a] in the land. They did according to all the abominations of the nations which the LORD had cast out before the children of Israel.
25 It happened in the fifth year of King Rehoboam *that* Shishak king of Egypt came up against Jerusalem.
26 And he took away the treasures of the house of the LORD and the treasures of the king's house; he took away everything. He also took away all the gold shields which Solomon had made.
27 Then King Rehoboam made bronze shields in their place, and committed *them* to the hands of the captains of the guard, who guarded the doorway of the king's house.
28 And whenever the king entered the house of the LORD, the guards carried them, then brought them back into the guardroom.
29 Now the rest of the acts of Rehoboam, and all that he did, *are* they not written in the book of the chronicles of the kings of Judah?
30 And there was war between Rehoboam and Jeroboam all *their* days.
31 So Rehoboam rested with his fathers, and was buried with his fathers in the City of David. His mother's name *was* Naamah, an Ammonitess. Then Abijam[a] his son reigned in his place.

Abijam Reigns in Judah

15 In the eighteenth year of King Jeroboam the son of Nebat, Abijam became king over Judah.
2 He reigned three years in Jerusalem. His mother's name *was* Maachah the granddaughter of Abishalom.
3 And he walked in all the sins of his father, which he had done before him; his heart was not loyal to the LORD his God, as was the heart of his father David.
4 Nevertheless for David's sake the LORD ◄ his God gave him a lamp in Jerusalem, by setting up his son after him and by establishing Jerusalem;
5 because David did *what was* right in the eyes of the LORD, and had not turned aside from anything that He commanded him all the days of his life, except in the matter of Uriah the Hittite.

14:24 [a]Hebrew *qadesh,* that is, one practicing sodomy and prostitution in religious rituals **14:31** [a]Spelled *Abijah* in 2 Chronicles 12:16ff

LIFE LESSONS

➤ 14:13 — *". . . he is the only one of Jeroboam who shall come to the grave, because in him there is found something good toward the LORD God of Israel . . . ."*

The Lord said He would take the life of the only one in Jeroboam's family who had any good in him. Why? Sometimes God takes the life of the righteous to spare them from evil (Is. 57:1).

➤ 15:4 — *Nevertheless for David's sake the LORD his God gave him a lamp in Jerusalem, by setting up his son after him and by establishing Jerusalem.*

We can be glad that while God always blesses obedience, He also shows mercy when none is deserved. "If You, LORD, should mark iniquities, O Lord, who could stand?" (Ps. 130:3).

6 And there was war between Rehoboam[a] and Jeroboam all the days of his life.

7 Now the rest of the acts of Abijam, and all that he did, *are* they not written in the book of the chronicles of the kings of Judah? And there was war between Abijam and Jeroboam.

8 So Abijam rested with his fathers, and they buried him in the City of David. Then Asa his son reigned in his place.

Asa Reigns in Judah

9 In the twentieth year of Jeroboam king of Israel, Asa became king over Judah.

10 And he reigned forty-one years in Jerusalem. His grandmother's name *was* Maachah the granddaughter of Abishalom.

11 Asa did *what was* right in the eyes of the LORD, as *did* his father David.

12 And he banished the perverted persons[a] from the land, and removed all the idols that his fathers had made.

13 Also he removed Maachah his grandmother from *being* queen mother, because she had made an obscene image of Asherah.[a] And Asa cut down her obscene image and burned *it* by the Brook Kidron.

14 But the high places were not removed. Nevertheless Asa's heart was loyal to the LORD all his days.

15 He also brought into the house of the LORD the things which his father had dedicated, and the things which he himself had dedicated: silver and gold and utensils.

16 Now there was war between Asa and Baasha king of Israel all their days.

17 And Baasha king of Israel came up against Judah, and built Ramah, that he might let none go out or come in to Asa king of Judah.

➤ 18 Then Asa took all the silver and gold *that was* left in the treasuries of the house of the LORD and the treasuries of the king's house, and delivered them into the hand of his servants. And King Asa sent them to Ben-Hadad the son of Tabrimmon, the son of Hezion, king of Syria, who dwelt in Damascus, saying,

19 "*Let there be* a treaty between you and me, as there was between my father and your father. See, I have sent you a present of silver and gold. Come and break your treaty with Baasha king of Israel, so that he will withdraw from me."

20 So Ben-Hadad heeded King Asa, and sent the captains of his armies against the cities of Israel. He attacked Ijon, Dan, Abel Beth Maachah, and all Chinneroth, with all the land of Naphtali.

21 Now it happened, when Baasha heard *it*, that he stopped building Ramah, and remained in Tirzah.

22 Then King Asa made a proclamation throughout all Judah; none *was* exempted. And they took away the stones and timber of Ramah, which Baasha had used for building; and with them King Asa built Geba of Benjamin, and Mizpah.

23 The rest of all the acts of Asa, all his might, all that he did, and the cities which he built, *are* they not written in the book of the chronicles of the kings of Judah? But in the time of his old age he was diseased in his feet.

24 So Asa rested with his fathers, and was buried with his fathers in the City of David his father. Then Jehoshaphat his son reigned in his place.

Nadab Reigns in Israel

25 Now Nadab the son of Jeroboam became king over Israel in the second year of Asa king of Judah, and he reigned over Israel two years.

26 And he did evil in the sight of the LORD, and walked in the way of his father, and in his sin by which he had made Israel sin.

27 Then Baasha the son of Ahijah, of the house of Issachar, conspired against him. And Baasha killed him at Gibbethon, which *belonged* to the Philistines, while Nadab and all Israel laid siege to Gibbethon.

28 Baasha killed him in the third year of Asa king of Judah, and reigned in his place. ➤

29 And it was so, when he became king, *that* he killed all the house of Jeroboam. He did not leave to Jeroboam anyone that breathed, until he had destroyed him, according to the

15:6 [a]Following Masoretic Text, Septuagint, Targum, and Vulgate; some Hebrew manuscripts and Syriac read *Abijam*.
15:12 [a]Hebrew *qedeshim*, that is, those practicing sodomy and prostitution in religious rituals **15:13** [a]A Canaanite goddess

LIFE LESSONS

➤ 15:18 — *Then Asa took all the silver and gold that was left in the treasuries of the house of the LORD and the treasuries of the king's house, and . . . sent them to Ben-Hadad . . . .*

We must beware the temptation to rely on pragmatism rather than on trusting the Lord. In 2 Chronicles 16:7–9 Asa is rebuked for depending on political alliances rather than on the Lord.

➤ 15:28 — *Baasha killed him in the third year of Asa king of Judah, and reigned in his place.*

Jeroboam could have established an enduring royal line, if he had chosen to obey the Lord (1 Kin. 11:38). Instead, he chose to rebel and so brought on his family a deadly curse. God wants us to choose life.

word of the LORD which He had spoken by
His servant Ahijah the Shilonite,
30 because of the sins of Jeroboam, which he
had sinned and by which he had made Israel
sin, because of his provocation with which
he had provoked the LORD God of Israel to
anger.
31 Now the rest of the acts of Nadab, and all
that he did, *are* they not written in the book of
the chronicles of the kings of Israel?
32 And there was war between Asa and
Baasha king of Israel all their days.

Baasha Reigns in Israel

33 In the third year of Asa king of Judah,
Baasha the son of Ahijah became king over
all Israel in Tirzah, and *reigned* twenty-four
years.
34 He did evil in the sight of the LORD, and
walked in the way of Jeroboam, and in his sin
by which he had made Israel sin.

16 Then the word of the LORD came to
Jehu the son of Hanani, against Baasha,
saying:
➤ 2 "Inasmuch as I lifted you out of the dust
and made you ruler over My people Israel,
and you have walked in the way of Jeroboam,
and have made My people Israel sin, to provoke Me to anger with their sins,
3 "surely I will take away the posterity of
Baasha and the posterity of his house, and I
will make your house like the house of Jeroboam the son of Nebat.
4 "The dogs shall eat whoever belongs to
Baasha and dies in the city, and the birds
of the air shall eat whoever dies in the
fields."
5 Now the rest of the acts of Baasha, what
he did, and his might, *are* they not written in
the book of the chronicles of the kings of Israel?
6 So Baasha rested with his fathers and was
buried in Tirzah. Then Elah his son reigned in
his place.
7 And also the word of the LORD came by
the prophet Jehu the son of Hanani against
Baasha and his house, because of all the evil
that he did in the sight of the LORD in provoking Him to anger with the work of his hands,
in being like the house of Jeroboam, and because he killed them.

Elah Reigns in Israel

8 In the twenty-sixth year of Asa king of Judah, Elah the son of Baasha became king over
Israel, *and reigned* two years in Tirzah.
9 Now his servant Zimri, commander of half
his chariots, conspired against him as he was
in Tirzah drinking himself drunk in the house
of Arza, steward of *his* house in Tirzah.
10 And Zimri went in and struck him and
killed him in the twenty-seventh year of Asa
king of Judah, and reigned in his place.
11 Then it came to pass, when he began to
reign, as soon as he was seated on his throne,
that he killed all the household of Baasha; he
did not leave him one male, neither of his relatives nor of his friends.
12 Thus Zimri destroyed all the household of
Baasha, according to the word of the LORD,
which He spoke against Baasha by Jehu the
prophet,
13 for all the sins of Baasha and the sins of
Elah his son, by which they had sinned and
by which they had made Israel sin, in provoking the LORD God of Israel to anger with their
idols.
14 Now the rest of the acts of Elah, and all
that he did, *are* they not written in the book of
the chronicles of the kings of Israel?

Zimri Reigns in Israel

15 In the twenty-seventh year of Asa king of
Judah, Zimri had reigned in Tirzah seven
days. And the people *were* encamped against
Gibbethon, which *belonged* to the Philistines.
16 Now the people *who were* encamped
heard it said, "Zimri has conspired and also
has killed the king." So all Israel made Omri,
the commander of the army, king over Israel
that day in the camp.
17 Then Omri and all Israel with him went up
from Gibbethon, and they besieged Tirzah.
18 And it happened, when Zimri saw that the ◄
city was taken, that he went into the citadel of
the king's house and burned the king's house
down upon himself with fire, and died,
19 because of the sins which he had committed in doing evil in the sight of the LORD, in
walking in the way of Jeroboam, and in his
sin which he had committed to make Israel
sin.
20 Now the rest of the acts of Zimri, and the

LIFE LESSONS

➤ **16:2 — *"Inasmuch as I lifted you out of the dust and made you ruler over My people Israel, and you have walked in the way of Jeroboam, and have made My people Israel sin . . . ."***

God allowed the wicked king Baasha to reign in Israel for twenty-four years—plenty of time to repent (see Rev. 2:21)—but he refused. So God did to his line what He promised (1 Kin. 16:12). He always keeps His word.

➤ **16:18 — *And it happened, when Zimri saw that the city was taken, that he went into the citadel of the king's house and burned the king's house down upon himself with fire, and died . . . .***

Sometimes God allows wicked men to flourish for years; sometimes he judges them very quickly. The evil King Zimri lasted just seven days. God is sovereign, and "removes kings and raises up kings" (Dan. 2:21).

treason he committed, *are* they not written in
the book of the chronicles of the kings of Israel?

Omri Reigns in Israel

21 Then the people of Israel were divided
into two parts: half of the people followed
Tibni the son of Ginath, to make him king,
and half followed Omri.
22 But the people who followed Omri prevailed over the people who followed Tibni the
son of Ginath. So Tibni died and Omri reigned.
23 In the thirty-first year of Asa king of Judah, Omri became king over Israel, *and
reigned* twelve years. Six years he reigned in
Tirzah.
24 And he bought the hill of Samaria from
Shemer for two talents of silver; then he built
on the hill, and called the name of the city
which he built, Samaria, after the name of
Shemer, owner of the hill.
25 Omri did evil in the eyes of the LORD, and
did worse than all who *were* before him.
26 For he walked in all the ways of Jeroboam
the son of Nebat, and in his sin by which he
had made Israel sin, provoking the LORD God
of Israel to anger with their idols.
27 Now the rest of the acts of Omri which he
did, and the might that he showed, *are* they
not written in the book of the chronicles of
the kings of Israel?
28 So Omri rested with his fathers and was
buried in Samaria. Then Ahab his son reigned
in his place.

Ahab Reigns in Israel

29 In the thirty-eighth year of Asa king of Judah, Ahab the son of Omri became king over
Israel; and Ahab the son of Omri reigned over
Israel in Samaria twenty-two years.
➤ 30 Now Ahab the son of Omri did evil in the
sight of the LORD, more than all who *were* before him.
31 And it came to pass, as though it had been
a trivial thing for him to walk in the sins of
Jeroboam the son of Nebat, that he took as
wife Jezebel the daughter of Ethbaal, king of
the Sidonians; and he went and served Baal
and worshiped him.
32 Then he set up an altar for Baal in the
temple of Baal, which he had built in Samaria.
33 And Ahab made a wooden image.[a] Ahab
did more to provoke the LORD God of Israel to
anger than all the kings of Israel who were
before him.
34 In his days Hiel of Bethel built Jericho. He
laid its foundation with Abiram his firstborn,
and with his youngest *son* Segub he set up its
gates, according to the word of the LORD,
which He had spoken through Joshua the son
of Nun.[a]

Elijah Proclaims a Drought

17 And Elijah the Tishbite, of the inhabitants of Gilead, said to Ahab, "*As* the
LORD God of Israel lives, before whom I stand,
there shall not be dew nor rain these years,
except at my word."
2 Then the word of the LORD came to him,
saying,
3 "Get away from here and turn eastward,
and hide by the Brook Cherith, which flows
into the Jordan.
4 "And it will be *that* you shall drink from
the brook, and I have commanded the ravens
to feed you there."
5 So he went and did according to the
word of the LORD, for he went and stayed by
the Brook Cherith, which flows into the Jordan.
6 The ravens brought him bread and meat in ◄
the morning, and bread and meat in the
evening; and he drank from the brook.
7 And it happened after a while that the
brook dried up, because there had been no
rain in the land.

Elijah and the Widow

8 Then the word of the LORD came to him,
saying,
9 "Arise, go to Zarephath, which *belongs* to ◄
Sidon, and dwell there. See, I have commanded a widow there to provide for you."

16:33 [a]Hebrew *Asherah,* a Canaanite goddess **16:34** [a]Compare Joshua 6:26

LIFE LESSONS

➤ 16:30 — *Now Ahab the son of Omri did evil in the sight of the LORD, more than all who were before him.*

Although King Ahab did more evil than all his predecessors, the Lord allowed him to reign for twenty-two years. But we should never mistake God's patience for either indulgence or indifference (Jer. 5:12; Zeph. 1:12).

➤ 17:6 — *The ravens brought him bread and meat in the morning, and bread and meat in the evening; and he drank from the brook.*

Although miracles accompanied Elijah from the beginning of his recorded ministry, most of the people refused to believe in God. Miracles are great, but they do not produce faith (Luke 16:31).

➤ 17:9 — *"Arise, go to Zarephath, which belongs to Sidon, and dwell there. See, I have commanded a widow there to provide for you."*

God "commanded" a widow to provide for Elijah, and yet she knew nothing about it. She learned God's will as she walked in faith, just as we do.

10 So he arose and went to Zarephath. And
when he came to the gate of the city, indeed a
widow *was* there gathering sticks. And he
called to her and said, "Please bring me a little water in a cup, that I may drink."
11 And as she was going to get *it*, he called to
her and said, "Please bring me a morsel of
bread in your hand."
12 So she said, "As the LORD your God lives, I
do not have bread, only a handful of flour in
a bin, and a little oil in a jar; and see, I *am*
gathering a couple of sticks that I may go in
and prepare it for myself and my son, that we
may eat it, and die."
13 And Elijah said to her, "Do not fear; go
and do as you have said, but make me a small
cake from it first, and bring *it* to me; and afterward make *some* for yourself and your
son.
14 "For thus says the LORD God of Israel: 'The
bin of flour shall not be used up, nor shall the
jar of oil run dry, until the day the LORD sends
rain on the earth.'"
15 So she went away and did according to the
word of Elijah; and she and he and her household ate for *many* days.
16 The bin of flour was not used up, nor did
the jar of oil run dry, according to the word of
the LORD which He spoke by Elijah.

Elijah Revives the Widow's Son

➤ **17** Now it happened after these things *that*
the son of the woman who owned the house
became sick. And his sickness was so serious
that there was no breath left in him.
18 So she said to Elijah, "What have I to do
with you, O man of God? Have you come to
me to bring my sin to remembrance, and to
kill my son?"
19 And he said to her, "Give me your son." So
he took him out of her arms and carried him
to the upper room where he was staying, and
laid him on his own bed.
20 Then he cried out to the LORD and said,
"O LORD my God, have You also brought
tragedy on the widow with whom I lodge, by
killing her son?"
21 And he stretched himself out on the child
three times, and cried out to the LORD and
said, "O LORD my God, I pray, let this child's
soul come back to him."
22 Then the LORD heard the voice of Elijah;
and the soul of the child came back to him,
and he revived.
23 And Elijah took the child and brought him
down from the upper room into the house,
and gave him to his mother. And Elijah said,
"See, your son lives!"
24 Then the woman said to Elijah, "Now by
this I know that you *are* a man of God, *and*
that the word of the LORD in your mouth *is* the
truth."

Elijah's Message to Ahab

18 And it came to pass *after* many days
that the word of the LORD came to Elijah, in the third year, saying, "Go, present
yourself to Ahab, and I will send rain on the
earth."
2 So Elijah went to present himself to Ahab;
and *there was* a severe famine in Samaria.
3 And Ahab had called Obadiah, who *was* ◄
in charge of *his* house. (Now Obadiah feared
the LORD greatly.
4 For so it was, while Jezebel massacred the
prophets of the LORD, that Obadiah had taken
one hundred prophets and hidden them, fifty
to a cave, and had fed them with bread and
water.)
5 And Ahab had said to Obadiah, "Go into
the land to all the springs of water and to all
the brooks; perhaps we may find grass to
keep the horses and mules alive, so that we
will not have to kill any livestock."
6 So they divided the land between them to
explore it; Ahab went one way by himself,
and Obadiah went another way by himself.
7 Now as Obadiah was on his way, suddenly
Elijah met him; and he recognized him, and
fell on his face, and said, "*Is* that you, my lord
Elijah?"
8 And he answered him, "*It is* I. Go, tell your
master, 'Elijah *is here*.'"
9 So he said, "How have I sinned, that you
are delivering your servant into the hand of
Ahab, to kill me?
10 "*As* the LORD your God lives, there is no
nation or kingdom where my master has not
sent someone to hunt for you; and when they
said, '*He is* not *here*,' he took an oath from the
kingdom or nation that they could not find
you.
11 "And now you say, 'Go, tell your master,
"Elijah *is here*"'!

LIFE LESSONS

➤ 17:17 — ***. . . the son of the woman who owned the house became sick. And his sickness was so serious that there was no breath left in him.***

Tragedy comes into the life of the faithful, just as it does to the lives of the ungodly. But in the lives of obedient believers, God loves to take even tragedy and use it for His glory.

➤ 18:3 — ***And Ahab had called Obadiah, who was in charge of his house. (Now Obadiah feared the LORD greatly . . . .)***

A sovereign God often puts a godly man in the service of a wicked man, not to frustrate or aggravate him, but to provide a unique platform from which to rescue and bless His people.

➤ 12 "And it shall come to pass, *as soon as* I am
gone from you, that the Spirit of the LORD will
carry you to a place I do not know; so when I
go and tell Ahab, and he cannot find you, he
will kill me. But I your servant have feared
the LORD from my youth.
13 "Was it not reported to my lord what I did
when Jezebel killed the prophets of the LORD,
how I hid one hundred men of the LORD's
prophets, fifty to a cave, and fed them with
bread and water?
14 "And now you say, 'Go, tell your master,
"Elijah *is here*."' He will kill me!"
15 Then Elijah said, "*As* the LORD of hosts
lives, before whom I stand, I will surely present myself to him today."
16 So Obadiah went to meet Ahab, and told
him; and Ahab went to meet Elijah.
17 Then it happened, when Ahab saw Elijah,
that Ahab said to him, "*Is that* you, O troubler
of Israel?"
18 And he answered, "I have not troubled Israel, but you and your father's house *have*, in
that you have forsaken the commandments of
the LORD and have followed the Baals.
19 "Now therefore, send *and* gather all Israel
to me on Mount Carmel, the four hundred
and fifty prophets of Baal, and the four hundred prophets of Asherah,[a] who eat at Jezebel's table."

Elijah's Mount Carmel Victory

20 So Ahab sent for all the children of Israel,
and gathered the prophets together on Mount
Carmel.
➤ 21 And Elijah came to all the people, and
said, "How long will you falter between two
opinions? If the LORD *is* God, follow Him; but
if Baal, follow him." But the people answered
him not a word.
22 Then Elijah said to the people, "I alone am
left a prophet of the LORD; but Baal's prophets
are four hundred and fifty men.
23 "Therefore let them give us two bulls; and
let them choose one bull for themselves, cut it
in pieces, and lay *it* on the wood, but put no
fire *under it;* and I will prepare the other bull,
and lay *it* on the wood, but put no fire *under it.*
24 "Then you call on the name of your gods,
and I will call on the name of the LORD; and
the God who answers by fire, He is God." So
all the people answered and said, "It is well
spoken."
25 Now Elijah said to the prophets of Baal,
"Choose one bull for yourselves and prepare *it* first, for you *are* many; and call on
the name of your god, but put no fire *under
it*."
26 So they took the bull which was given
them, and they prepared *it*, and called on the
name of Baal from morning even till noon,
saying, "O Baal, hear us!" But *there was* no
voice; no one answered. Then they leaped
about the altar which they had made.
27 And so it was, at noon, that Elijah mocked
them and said, "Cry aloud, for he *is* a god; either he is meditating, or he is busy, or he is on
a journey, *or* perhaps he is sleeping and must
be awakened."
28 So they cried aloud, and cut themselves,
as was their custom, with knives and lances,
until the blood gushed out on them.
29 And when midday was past, they prophesied until the *time* of the offering of the *evening* sacrifice. But *there was* no voice; no one
answered, no one paid attention.
30 Then Elijah said to all the people, "Come
near to me." So all the people came near to
him. And he repaired the altar of the LORD
that was broken down.
31 And Elijah took twelve stones, according
to the number of the tribes of the sons of Jacob, to whom the word of the LORD had come,
saying, "Israel shall be your name."[a]
32 Then with the stones he built an altar in
the name of the LORD; and he made a trench
around the altar large enough to hold two
seahs of seed.
33 And he put the wood in order, cut the bull
in pieces, and laid *it* on the wood, and said,
"Fill four waterpots with water, and pour *it* on
the burnt sacrifice and on the wood."
34 Then he said, "Do *it* a second time," and
they did *it* a second time; and he said, "Do *it*
a third time," and they did *it* a third time.
35 So the water ran all around the altar; and
he also filled the trench with water.
36 And it came to pass, at *the time of* the offering of the *evening* sacrifice, that Elijah the
prophet came near and said, "LORD God of
Abraham, Isaac, and Israel, let it be known
this day that You *are* God in Israel and I *am*
Your servant, and *that* I have done all these
things at Your word.

18:19 [a]A Canaanite goddess **18:31** [a]Genesis 32:28

LIFE LESSONS

➤ 18:12 — *". . . I your servant have feared the LORD from my youth."*

Obadiah had learned to fear God from a young age, no doubt through the influence of his parents, even though they lived in a wicked land. Parents have a great opportunity to train their children to love the Lord.

➤ 18:21 — *"How long will you falter between two opinions? If the LORD is God, follow Him; but if Baal, follow him."*

At some point, we have to make up our minds: Will we serve God or not? Is He who He claims to be, or not? We have to take a stand and move on from there. No one can "keep their options open" forever.

WHAT THE BIBLE SAYS ABOUT
HOW TO PRAY WITH AUTHORITY

1 Kin. 18:20–40

The prophet Elijah is an amazing example of what can happen when believers pray with authority, when they come confidently to God asking Him to do something that glorifies Him. With the people of Israel and the prophets of Baal gathered at Mt. Carmel for a "showdown" between the Lord and Baal, Elijah confidently prayed:

> LORD God of Abraham, Isaac, and Israel, let it be known this day that You are God in Israel and I am Your servant, and that I have done all these things at Your word. Hear me, O LORD, hear me, that this people may know that You are the LORD God, and that You have turned their hearts back to You again (1 Kin. 18:36, 37).

When Elijah had finished his prayer, the fire of the Lord fell and consumed the sacrifice, as well as the wood, the stones, the dust, and all the water in the trench. When the people saw what had happened, they fell on their faces and said, "The LORD, He is God! The LORD, He is God!"

God tells us to come boldly into His presence.

Elijah didn't pray in secret, off in some corner where nobody could see or hear him. He prayed openly and publicly. There was nothing tricky or shady about what he did; there was no doubt about what he said.

God tells us to come boldly into His presence. He grants us the privilege to come before Him with authority because of our position in Christ Jesus. We are to be bold in our faith that God will do what He desires to do and what He says He will do.

The New Testament tells us, "For we do not have a High Priest who cannot sympathize with our weaknesses, but was in all points tempted as we are, yet without sin. Let us therefore come boldly to the throne of grace, that we may obtain mercy and find grace to help in time of need" (Heb. 4:15, 16), and, "let us draw near with a true heart in full assurance of faith" (Heb. 10:19). We have God's invitation; will we accept?

See the Life Principles Index for further study:
17. We stand tallest and strongest on our knees.

➤ 37 "Hear me, O LORD, hear me, that this people may know that You *are* the LORD God, and
that You have turned their hearts back *to You*
again."
38 Then the fire of the LORD fell and consumed the burnt sacrifice, and the wood and
the stones and the dust, and it licked up the
water that *was* in the trench.
39 Now when all the people saw *it*, they fell
on their faces; and they said, "The LORD, He *is*
God! The LORD, He *is* God!"
40 And Elijah said to them, "Seize the prophets of Baal! Do not let one of them escape!" So
they seized them; and Elijah brought them
down to the Brook Kishon and executed them
there.

The Drought Ends

41 Then Elijah said to Ahab, "Go up, eat and
drink; for *there is* the sound of abundance of
rain."
42 So Ahab went up to eat and drink. And
Elijah went up to the top of Carmel; then he
bowed down on the ground, and put his face
between his knees,
➤ 43 and said to his servant, "Go up now, look
toward the sea." So he went up and looked,
and said, "*There is* nothing." And seven times
he said, "Go again."
44 Then it came to pass the seventh *time*, that
he said, "There is a cloud, as small as a man's
hand, rising out of the sea!" So he said, "Go
up, say to Ahab, 'Prepare *your chariot*, and go
down before the rain stops you.'"
45 Now it happened in the meantime that the
sky became black with clouds and wind, and
there was a heavy rain. So Ahab rode away
and went to Jezreel.
46 Then the hand of the LORD came upon Elijah; and he girded up his loins and ran ahead
of Ahab to the entrance of Jezreel.

Elijah Escapes from Jezebel

19 And Ahab told Jezebel all that Elijah
had done, also how he had executed all
the prophets with the sword.
➤ 2 Then Jezebel sent a messenger to Elijah,
saying, "So let the gods do *to me*, and more

Life Examples:

ELIJAH

Responding to Stress

1 KIN. 19:3

Stressful situations can drive us to inappropriate responses. The prophet Elijah illustrates the importance of viewing circumstances from God's perspective.

God sent the prophet to rescue Israel from its moral and spiritual decline. Elijah confronted and defeated the prophets of Baal, but the wicked Queen Jezebel immediately threatened to kill him for executing her false prophets.

Instead of holding fast to God's faithfulness, Elijah panicked, ran, and hid (1 Kin. 19:3). Only when he recalled God's past faithfulness did he realize it was sufficient for his present circumstances. If God could protect and provide for seven thousand others in Israel, He could sustain Elijah. So after a rest, the prophet returned to his mission for God.

Like Elijah, we need to rest in God, recall His faithfulness, and trust Him for the future. God remains active in our lives even when it feels as though He has fallen silent.

See the Life Principles Index for further study:
4. The awareness of God's presence energizes us for our work.

also, if I do not make your life as the life of
one of them by tomorrow about this time."
3 And when he saw *that*, he arose and ran
for his life, and went to Beersheba, which *belongs* to Judah, and left his servant there.
4 But he himself went a day's journey into ➤

LIFE LESSONS

➤ 18:37 — *"Hear me, O LORD, hear me, that this people may know that You are the LORD God, and that You have turned their hearts back to You again."*

It is God who turns our hearts back to Him. By His grace He reaches out to us and invites us to come home.

➤ 18:43 — *So he went up and looked, and said, "There is nothing." And seven times he said, "Go again."*

We must not grow impatient in prayer. Jesus taught that we "always ought to pray and not lose heart" (Luke 18:1). God acts on behalf of those who wait for Him.

➤ 19:2 — *"So let the gods do to me, and more also, if I do not make your life as the life of one of them by tomorrow about this time."*

Great challenges often follow great victories. Elijah had just seen God do a great miracle, but Jezebel's threat unnerved him. None of us stand strong in faith all the time—and God uses us anyway.

➤ 19:4 — *"It is enough! Now, LORD, take my life, for I am no better than my fathers!"*

How many of God's faithful servants have prayed that they might die when confronted with stubborn unbelief or fierce opposition? Time alone with God can provide a remedy.

ANSWERS TO LIFE'S QUESTIONS

How can I develop and maintain an attitude of active listening before the Lord?

1 KIN. 19:11–13

Many people seem uncomfortable with silence, especially if they are alone. In silence, however, we are able to hear the "still, small voice" of the Lord. Certainly the prophet Elijah knew this. After receiving a death threat from Queen Jezebel, Elijah escaped to an isolated desert area. There in a cave, he heard the Lord say to him,

> "Go out, and stand on the mountain before the LORD." And behold, the LORD passed by, and a great and strong wind tore into the mountains and broke the rocks in pieces before the LORD, but the LORD was not in the wind; and after the wind an earthquake, but the LORD was not in the earthquake; and after the earthquake a fire, but the LORD was not in the fire; and after the fire a still small voice. So it was, when Elijah heard it, that he wrapped his face in his mantle and went out and stood in the entrance of the cave. Suddenly a voice came to him, and said, "What are you doing here, Elijah?" (1 Kin. 19:11–13).

Quietness is essential to listening. If we are too busy to sit in silence in His presence; if we are preoccupied with thoughts or concerns about the day; if we have filled our minds for hour upon hour with carnal interference and aimless chatter—then we are going to have difficulty truly listening to that still, small voice of God.

Set aside times to "wait upon the Lord" in silence. You may find that late night or early morning is a good time of solitude and quiet for you. A noonday walk in the park may be a time when you can quiet your soul before the Lord. Ask the Lord to reveal to you a time and a place where you might turn off the cares and worries of the world for a few moments and listen to Him.

So often we spend our prayer time by talking to the Lord, without spending any time just waiting in silence to see what the Lord might have to say to us. Take time to intentionally sit or kneel in silence before the Lord. Empty your mind of all other thoughts. Concentrate on His Word and His presence with you. Ask Him to speak to you.

See the Life Principles Index for further study:
13. Listening to God is essential to walking with God.
1. Our intimacy with God—His highest priority for our lives—determines the impact of our lives.

the wilderness, and came and sat down under
a broom tree. And he prayed that he might
die, and said, "It is enough! Now, LORD, take
my life, for I *am* no better than my fathers!"
5 Then as he lay and slept under a broom
tree, suddenly an angel[a] touched him, and
said to him, "Arise *and* eat."
6 Then he looked, and there by his head *was*
a cake baked on coals, and a jar of water. So
he ate and drank, and lay down again.
7 And the angel[a] of the LORD came back the
second time, and touched him, and said,
"Arise *and* eat, because the journey *is* too
great for you."
8 So he arose, and ate and drank; and he
went in the strength of that food forty days
and forty nights as far as Horeb, the mountain of God.
9 And there he went into a cave, and spent
the night in that place; and behold, the word
of the LORD *came* to him, and He said to him,
"What are you doing here, Elijah?"
10 So he said, "I have been very zealous for
the LORD God of hosts; for the children of Israel have forsaken Your covenant, torn down
Your altars, and killed Your prophets with the
sword. I alone am left; and they seek to take
my life."

God's Revelation to Elijah

11 Then He said, "Go out, and stand on the
mountain before the LORD." And behold, the
LORD passed by, and a great and strong wind
tore into the mountains and broke the rocks
in pieces before the LORD, *but* the LORD *was*
not in the wind; and after the wind an earthquake, *but* the LORD *was* not in the earthquake;
12 and after the earthquake a fire, *but* the
LORD *was* not in the fire; and after the fire a
still small voice.
13 So it was, when Elijah heard *it*, that he
wrapped his face in his mantle and went out
and stood in the entrance of the cave. Suddenly a voice *came* to him, and said, "What
are you doing here, Elijah?"

19:5 [a]Or *Angel* 19:7 [a]Or *Angel*

14 And he said, "I have been very zealous for
the LORD God of hosts; because the children
of Israel have forsaken Your covenant, torn
down Your altars, and killed Your prophets
with the sword. I alone am left; and they seek
to take my life."
15 Then the LORD said to him: "Go, return on
your way to the Wilderness of Damascus; and
when you arrive, anoint Hazael *as* king over
Syria.
16 "Also you shall anoint Jehu the son of
Nimshi *as* king over Israel. And Elisha the
son of Shaphat of Abel Meholah you shall
anoint *as* prophet in your place.
17 "It shall be *that* whoever escapes the
sword of Hazael, Jehu will kill; and whoever
escapes the sword of Jehu, Elisha will kill.
➤ 18 "Yet I have reserved seven thousand in Israel, all whose knees have not bowed to Baal,
and every mouth that has not kissed him."

Elisha Follows Elijah

19 So he departed from there, and found Elisha the son of Shaphat, who *was* plowing
with twelve yoke *of oxen* before him, and he
was with the twelfth. Then Elijah passed by
him and threw his mantle on him.
20 And he left the oxen and ran after Elijah,
and said, "Please let me kiss my father and
my mother, and *then* I will follow you." And
he said to him, "Go back again, for what have
I done to you?"
21 So *Elisha* turned back from him, and took
a yoke of oxen and slaughtered them and
boiled their flesh, using the oxen's equipment, and gave it to the people, and they ate.
Then he arose and followed Elijah, and became his servant.

Ahab Defeats the Syrians

20 Now Ben-Hadad the king of Syria
gathered all his forces together; thirty-
two kings *were* with him, with horses and
chariots. And he went up and besieged Samaria, and made war against it.
2 Then he sent messengers into the city to
Ahab king of Israel, and said to him, "Thus
says Ben-Hadad:
3 'Your silver and your gold *are* mine; your
loveliest wives and children are mine.'"
4 And the king of Israel answered and said,
"My lord, O king, just as you say, I and all that
I have *are* yours."
5 Then the messengers came back and said,
"Thus speaks Ben-Hadad, saying, 'Indeed I
have sent to you, saying, "You shall deliver to
me your silver and your gold, your wives and
your children";
6 'but I will send my servants to you tomorrow about this time, and they shall search
your house and the houses of your servants.
And it shall be, *that* whatever is pleasant in
your eyes, they will put *it* in their hands and
take *it*.'"
7 So the king of Israel called all the elders of
the land, and said, "Notice, please, and see
how this *man* seeks trouble, for he sent to me
for my wives, my children, my silver, and my
gold; and I did not deny him."
8 And all the elders and all the people said
to him, "Do not listen or consent."
9 Therefore he said to the messengers of
Ben-Hadad, "Tell my lord the king, 'All that
you sent for to your servant the first time I
will do, but this thing I cannot do.'" And the
messengers departed and brought back word
to him.
10 Then Ben-Hadad sent to him and said,
"The gods do so to me, and more also, if
enough dust is left of Samaria for a handful
for each of the people who follow me."
11 So the king of Israel answered and said,
"Tell *him*, 'Let not the one who puts on *his
armor* boast like the one who takes *it off*.'"
12 And it happened when *Ben-Hadad* heard
this message, as he and the kings *were* drinking at the command post, that he said to his
servants, "Get ready." And they got ready to
attack the city.
13 Suddenly a prophet approached Ahab
king of Israel, saying, "Thus says the LORD:
'Have you seen all this great multitude? Behold, I will deliver it into your hand today, and
you shall know that I *am* the LORD.'"
14 So Ahab said, "By whom?" And he said,
"Thus says the LORD: 'By the young leaders of
the provinces.'" Then he said, "Who will set
the battle in order?" And he answered, "You."
15 Then he mustered the young leaders of the
provinces, and there were two hundred and
thirty-two; and after them he mustered all the
people, all the children of Israel—seven thousand.
16 So they went out at noon. Meanwhile
Ben-Hadad and the thirty-two kings helping
him were getting drunk at the command
post.
17 The young leaders of the provinces went

LIFE LESSONS

➤ 19:18 — *"Yet I have reserved seven thousand in Israel, all whose knees have not bowed to Baal, and every mouth that has not kissed him."*

Even in the worst of times, God will not leave Himself without a remnant and a witness. When we feel isolated and all alone, we aren't; God is at work in hearts that we never see.

out first. And Ben-Hadad sent out *a patrol,*
and they told him, saying, "Men are coming
out of Samaria!"
18 So he said, "If they have come out for
peace, take them alive; and if they have come
out for war, take them alive."
19 Then these young leaders of the provinces
went out of the city with the army which followed them.
20 And each one killed his man; so the Syrians fled, and Israel pursued them; and Ben-
Hadad the king of Syria escaped on a horse
with the cavalry.
21 Then the king of Israel went out and attacked the horses and chariots, and killed the
Syrians with a great slaughter.
22 And the prophet came to the king of Israel
and said to him, "Go, strengthen yourself;
take note, and see what you should do, for in
the spring of the year the king of Syria will
come up against you."

The Syrians Again Defeated

23 Then the servants of the king of Syria said
to him, "Their gods *are* gods of the hills.
Therefore they were stronger than we; but if
we fight against them in the plain, surely we
will be stronger than they.
24 "So do this thing: Dismiss the kings, each
from his position, and put captains in their
places;
25 "and you shall muster an army like the
army that you have lost, horse for horse and
chariot for chariot. Then we will fight against
them in the plain; surely we will be stronger
than they." And he listened to their voice and
did so.
26 So it was, in the spring of the year, that
Ben-Hadad mustered the Syrians and went
up to Aphek to fight against Israel.
27 And the children of Israel were mustered
and given provisions, and they went against
them. Now the children of Israel encamped
before them like two little flocks of goats,
while the Syrians filled the countryside.
➤ **28** Then a man of God came and spoke to the
king of Israel, and said, "Thus says the LORD:
'Because the Syrians have said, "The LORD *is*
God of the hills, but He *is* not God of the valleys," therefore I will deliver all this great
multitude into your hand, and you shall know
that I *am* the LORD.'"
29 And they encamped opposite each other
for seven days. So it was that on the seventh
day the battle was joined; and the children of
Israel killed one hundred thousand foot soldiers *of* the Syrians in one day.
30 But the rest fled to Aphek, into the city;
then a wall fell on twenty-seven thousand
of the men *who were* left. And Ben-Hadad
fled and went into the city, into an inner
chamber.

Ahab's Treaty with Ben-Hadad

31 Then his servants said to him, "Look now,
we have heard that the kings of the house of
Israel *are* merciful kings. Please, let us put
sackcloth around our waists and ropes
around our heads, and go out to the king of Israel; perhaps he will spare your life."
32 So they wore sackcloth around their
waists and *put* ropes around their heads,
and came to the king of Israel and said,
"Your servant Ben-Hadad says, 'Please let me
live.'" And he said, "*Is* he still alive? He *is* my
brother."
33 Now the men were watching closely to see
whether *any sign of mercy would come* from
him; and they quickly grasped *at this word*
and said, "Your brother Ben-Hadad." So he
said, "Go, bring him." Then Ben-Hadad came
out to him; and he had him come up into the
chariot.
34 So *Ben-Hadad* said to him, "The cities
which my father took from your father I will
restore; and you may set up marketplaces for
yourself in Damascus, as my father did in Samaria." Then *Ahab said,* "I will send you away
with this treaty." So he made a treaty with
him and sent him away.

Ahab Condemned

35 Now a certain man of the sons of the
prophets said to his neighbor by the word of
the LORD, "Strike me, please." And the man
refused to strike him.
36 Then he said to him, "Because you have
not obeyed the voice of the LORD, surely, as
soon as you depart from me, a lion shall kill
you." And as soon as he left him, a lion found
him and killed him.
37 And he found another man, and said,
"Strike me, please." So the man struck him,
inflicting a wound.
38 Then the prophet departed and waited for
the king by the road, and disguised himself
with a bandage over his eyes.
39 Now as the king passed by, he cried out to
the king and said, "Your servant went out into

LIFE LESSONS

➤ **20:28 — *"Because the Syrians have said, 'The LORD is God of the hills, but He is not God of the valleys,' therefore I will deliver all this great multitude into your hand, and you shall know that I am the LORD."***

God delivered the massive enemy army into the hands of wicked Ahab, not because of Ahab, but because of God. He wanted to show the world that the Lord God reigns over all the earth.

the midst of the battle; and there, a man came
over and brought a man to me, and said,
'Guard this man; if by any means he is missing, your life shall be for his life, or else you
shall pay a talent of silver.'
40 "While your servant was busy here and
there, he was gone." Then the king of Israel
said to him, "So *shall* your judgment *be;* you
yourself have decided *it.*"
41 And he hastened to take the bandage
away from his eyes; and the king of Israel recognized him as one of the prophets.
42 Then he said to him, "Thus says the LORD:
'Because you have let slip out of *your* hand a
man whom I appointed to utter destruction,
therefore your life shall go for his life, and
your people for his people.'"
43 So the king of Israel went to his house
sullen and displeased, and came to Samaria.

Naboth Is Murdered for His Vineyard

21 And it came to pass after these things
that Naboth the Jezreelite had a vineyard which *was* in Jezreel, next to the palace
of Ahab king of Samaria.
2 So Ahab spoke to Naboth, saying, "Give
me your vineyard, that I may have it for a
vegetable garden, because it *is* near, next to
my house; and for it I will give you a vineyard
better than it. *Or,* if it seems good to you, I will
give you its worth in money."
3 But Naboth said to Ahab, "The LORD forbid that I should give the inheritance of my
fathers to you!"
4 So Ahab went into his house sullen and
displeased because of the word which Naboth
the Jezreelite had spoken to him; for he had
said, "I will not give you the inheritance of my
fathers." And he lay down on his bed, and
turned away his face, and would eat no food.
5 But Jezebel his wife came to him, and said
to him, "Why is your spirit so sullen that you
eat no food?"
6 He said to her, "Because I spoke to Naboth
the Jezreelite, and said to him, 'Give me your
vineyard for money; or else, if it pleases you,
I will give you *another* vineyard for it.' And he
answered, 'I will not give you my vineyard.'"
7 Then Jezebel his wife said to him, "You
now exercise authority over Israel! Arise, eat
food, and let your heart be cheerful; I will give
you the vineyard of Naboth the Jezreelite."
8 And she wrote letters in Ahab's name,
sealed *them* with his seal, and sent the letters
to the elders and the nobles who *were*
dwelling in the city with Naboth.
9 She wrote in the letters, saying,

> Proclaim a fast, and seat Naboth with
> high honor among the people;
> 10 and seat two men, scoundrels, before him
> to bear witness against him, saying, "You
> have blasphemed God and the king."
> *Then* take him out, and stone him, that he
> may die.

11 So the men of his city, the elders and nobles who were inhabitants of his city, did as
Jezebel had sent to them, as it *was* written in
the letters which she had sent to them.
12 They proclaimed a fast, and seated Naboth
with high honor among the people.
13 And two men, scoundrels, came in and sat
before him; and the scoundrels witnessed
against him, against Naboth, in the presence
of the people, saying, "Naboth has blasphemed God and the king!" Then they took
him outside the city and stoned him with
stones, so that he died.
14 Then they sent to Jezebel, saying, "Naboth
has been stoned and is dead."
15 And it came to pass, when Jezebel heard
that Naboth had been stoned and was dead,
that Jezebel said to Ahab, "Arise, take possession of the vineyard of Naboth the Jezreelite,
which he refused to give you for money; for
Naboth is not alive, but dead."
16 So it was, when Ahab heard that Naboth
was dead, that Ahab got up and went down to
take possession of the vineyard of Naboth the
Jezreelite.

The LORD Condemns Ahab

17 Then the word of the LORD came to Elijah
the Tishbite, saying,
18 "Arise, go down to meet Ahab king of Israel, who *lives* in Samaria. There *he is,* in the
vineyard of Naboth, where he has gone down
to take possession of it.
19 "You shall speak to him, saying, 'Thus
says the LORD: "Have you murdered and also
taken possession?"' And you shall speak to
him, saying, 'Thus says the LORD: "In the
place where dogs licked the blood of Naboth,
dogs shall lick your blood, even yours."'"
20 So Ahab said to Elijah, "Have you found
me, O my enemy?" And he answered, "I have
found *you,* because you have sold yourself to
do evil in the sight of the LORD:
21 'Behold, I will bring calamity on you. I will

LIFE LESSONS

➤ 21:14 — *Then they sent to Jezebel, saying, "Naboth has been stoned and is dead."*

Naboth lost his life for obeying God, while Jezebel got her way by disobeying Him (see Ex. 23:7). Yet this life is not all there is, and God promises to set all accounts right (Rom. 2:6–8).

take away your posterity, and will cut off from
Ahab every male in Israel, both bond and
free.
22 'I will make your house like the house of
Jeroboam the son of Nebat, and like the
house of Baasha the son of Ahijah, because of
the provocation with which you have provoked *Me* to anger, and made Israel sin.'
23 "And concerning Jezebel the LORD also
spoke, saying, 'The dogs shall eat Jezebel by
the wall[a] of Jezreel.'
24 "The dogs shall eat whoever belongs to
Ahab and dies in the city, and the birds of the
air shall eat whoever dies in the field."
➤ **25** But there was no one like Ahab who sold
himself to do wickedness in the sight of
the LORD, because Jezebel his wife stirred
him up.
26 And he behaved very abominably in following idols, according to all *that* the Amorites had done, whom the LORD had cast out
before the children of Israel.
27 So it was, when Ahab heard those words,
that he tore his clothes and put sackcloth on
his body, and fasted and lay in sackcloth, and
went about mourning.
28 And the word of the LORD came to Elijah
the Tishbite, saying,
➤ 29 "See how Ahab has humbled himself before Me? Because he has humbled himself before Me, I will not bring the calamity in his
days. In the days of his son I will bring the
calamity on his house."

Micaiah Warns Ahab

22 Now three years passed without war
between Syria and Israel.
2 Then it came to pass, in the third year, that
Jehoshaphat the king of Judah went down to
visit the king of Israel.
3 And the king of Israel said to his servants,
"Do you know that Ramoth in Gilead *is* ours,
but we hesitate to take it out of the hand of
the king of Syria?"
4 So he said to Jehoshaphat, "Will you go
with me to fight at Ramoth Gilead?" Jehoshaphat said to the king of Israel, "I *am* as you
are, my people as your people, my horses as
your horses."
5 Also Jehoshaphat said to the king of Is- ➤
rael, "Please inquire for the word of the LORD
today."
6 Then the king of Israel gathered the
prophets together, about four hundred men,
and said to them, "Shall I go against Ramoth
Gilead to fight, or shall I refrain?" So they
said, "Go up, for the Lord will deliver *it* into
the hand of the king."
7 And Jehoshaphat said, "*Is there* not still a
prophet of the LORD here, that we may inquire
of Him?"[a]
8 So the king of Israel said to Jehoshaphat,
"*There is* still one man, Micaiah the son of
Imlah, by whom we may inquire of the
LORD; but I hate him, because he does not
prophesy good concerning me, but evil." And
Jehoshaphat said, "Let not the king say such
things!"
9 Then the king of Israel called an officer
and said, "Bring Micaiah the son of Imlah
quickly!"
10 The king of Israel and Jehoshaphat the
king of Judah, having put on *their* robes, sat
each on his throne, at a threshing floor at the
entrance of the gate of Samaria; and all the
prophets prophesied before them.
11 Now Zedekiah the son of Chenaanah had
made horns of iron for himself; and he said,
"Thus says the LORD: 'With these you shall
gore the Syrians until they are destroyed.'"
12 And all the prophets prophesied so, saying, "Go up to Ramoth Gilead and prosper, for
the LORD will deliver *it* into the king's hand."
13 Then the messenger who had gone to call ➤
Micaiah spoke to him, saying, "Now listen,
the words of the prophets with one accord encourage the king. Please, let your word be like
the word of one of them, and speak encouragement."
14 And Micaiah said, "*As* the LORD lives, what-

21:23 [a]Following Masoretic Text and Septuagint; some Hebrew manuscripts, Syriac, Targum, and Vulgate read *plot of ground* (compare 2 Kings 9:36). **22:7** [a]Or *him*

LIFE LESSONS

➤ **21:25 — *But there was no one like Ahab who sold himself to do wickedness in the sight of the LORD, because Jezebel his wife stirred him up.***

Time after time in the Bible we see how a poor choice of mate leads to physical and moral ruin. What kind of king might Ahab have become had he married a godly woman? We'll never know.

➤ **21:29 — *"See how Ahab has humbled himself before Me? . . . I will not bring the calamity in his days."***

Even in judgment, God shows mercy. He does not desire the death of the wicked, but rather that they should repent and live (see Ezek. 18:32).

➤ **22:5 — *Also Jehoshaphat said to the king of Israel, "Please inquire for the word of the LORD today."***

The godly King Jehoshaphat of Judah did a foolish thing by allying himself with the wicked King Ahab, but at least he insisted on hearing a genuine word from the Lord. Perhaps that word saved him.

➤ **22:13 — *"Please, let your word be like the word of one of them, and speak encouragement."***

We live in an age that desires only encouraging words. Sometimes, however, we need correction or even rebuke rather than encouragement. God loves us enough to give us what we truly need.

ever the LORD says to me, that I will speak."
15 Then he came to the king; and the king
said to him, "Micaiah, shall we go to war
against Ramoth Gilead, or shall we refrain?"
And he answered him, "Go and prosper, for
the LORD will deliver *it* into the hand of the
king!"
16 So the king said to him, "How many times
shall I make you swear that you tell me nothing but the truth in the name of the LORD?"
17 Then he said, "I saw all Israel scattered on
the mountains, as sheep that have no shepherd. And the LORD said, 'These have no master. Let each return to his house in peace.'"
18 And the king of Israel said to Jehoshaphat, "Did I not tell you he would not prophesy good concerning me, but evil?"
19 Then *Micaiah* said, "Therefore hear the
word of the LORD: I saw the LORD sitting on
His throne, and all the host of heaven standing by, on His right hand and on His left.
20 "And the LORD said, 'Who will persuade
Ahab to go up, that he may fall at Ramoth
Gilead?' So one spoke in this manner, and another spoke in that manner.
21 "Then a spirit came forward and stood
before the LORD, and said, 'I will persuade
him.'
22 "The LORD said to him, 'In what way?' So
he said, 'I will go out and be a lying spirit in
the mouth of all his prophets.' And the LORD
said, 'You shall persuade *him*, and also prevail. Go out and do so.'
23 "Therefore look! The LORD has put a lying
spirit in the mouth of all these prophets of
yours, and the LORD has declared disaster
against you."
24 Now Zedekiah the son of Chenaanah
went near and struck Micaiah on the cheek,
and said, "Which way did the spirit from the
LORD go from me to speak to you?"
25 And Micaiah said, "Indeed, you shall see
on that day when you go into an inner chamber to hide!"
26 So the king of Israel said, "Take Micaiah,
and return him to Amon the governor of the
city and to Joash the king's son;
27 "and say, 'Thus says the king: "Put this *fellow* in prison, and feed him with bread of affliction and water of affliction, until I come in
peace."'"
➤ 28 But Micaiah said, "If you ever return in
peace, the LORD has not spoken by me." And
he said, "Take heed, all you people!"

Ahab Dies in Battle

29 So the king of Israel and Jehoshaphat the
king of Judah went up to Ramoth Gilead.
30 And the king of Israel said to Jehoshaphat, "I will disguise myself and go into battle; but you put on your robes." So the king of
Israel disguised himself and went into battle.
31 Now the king of Syria had commanded
the thirty-two captains of his chariots, saying,
"Fight with no one small or great, but only
with the king of Israel."
32 So it was, when the captains of the chariots saw Jehoshaphat, that they said, "Surely it
is the king of Israel!" Therefore they turned
aside to fight against him, and Jehoshaphat
cried out.
33 And it happened, when the captains of the
chariots saw that it *was* not the king of Israel,
that they turned back from pursuing him.
34 Now a *certain* man drew a bow at ran- ➤
dom, and struck the king of Israel between
the joints of his armor. So he said to the driver
of his chariot, "Turn around and take me out
of the battle, for I am wounded."
35 The battle increased that day; and the
king was propped up in his chariot, facing the
Syrians, and died at evening. The blood ran
out from the wound onto the floor of the chariot.
36 Then, as the sun was going down, a shout
went throughout the army, saying, "Every
man to his city, and every man to his own
country!"
37 So the king died, and was brought to Samaria. And they buried the king in Samaria.
38 Then *someone* washed the chariot at a
pool in Samaria, and the dogs licked up his
blood while the harlots bathed,[a] according to
the word of the LORD which He had spoken.
39 Now the rest of the acts of Ahab, and all
that he did, the ivory house which he built
and all the cities that he built, *are* they not
written in the book of the chronicles of the
kings of Israel?
40 So Ahab rested with his fathers. Then
Ahaziah his son reigned in his place.

Jehoshaphat Reigns in Judah

41 Jehoshaphat the son of Asa had become
king over Judah in the fourth year of Ahab
king of Israel.

22:38 [a]Syriac and Targum read *they washed his armor.*

LIFE LESSONS

➤ 22:28 — *But Micaiah said, "If you ever return in peace, the LORD has not spoken by me."*

The events of any prophecy supposedly from the Lord must take place as declared, or that prophecy proves itself to be from another source. Micaiah staked his life on it.

➤ 22:34 — *Now a certain man drew a bow at random, and struck the king of Israel between the joints of his armor.*

God takes "random" acts and uses them to fulfill His will and His Word. Only a sovereign Lord can do that!

42 Jehoshaphat *was* thirty-five years old
when he became king, and he reigned twenty-
five years in Jerusalem. His mother's name
was Azubah the daughter of Shilhi.
43 And he walked in all the ways of his father
Asa. He did not turn aside from them, doing
what was right in the eyes of the LORD. Nevertheless the high places were not taken
away, *for* the people offered sacrifices and
burned incense on the high places.
44 Also Jehoshaphat made peace with the
king of Israel.
45 Now the rest of the acts of Jehoshaphat,
the might that he showed, and how he made
war, *are* they not written in the book of the
chronicles of the kings of Judah?
46 And the rest of the perverted persons,[a]
who remained in the days of his father Asa,
he banished from the land.
47 *There was* then no king in Edom, only a
deputy of the king.
48 Jehoshaphat made merchant ships[a] to go
to Ophir for gold; but they never sailed, for
the ships were wrecked at Ezion Geber.
49 Then Ahaziah the son of Ahab said to Jehoshaphat, "Let my servants go with your servants in the ships." But Jehoshaphat would
not.
50 And Jehoshaphat rested with his fathers,
and was buried with his fathers in the City of
David his father. Then Jehoram his son
reigned in his place.

Ahaziah Reigns in Israel

51 Ahaziah the son of Ahab became king
over Israel in Samaria in the seventeenth year
of Jehoshaphat king of Judah, and reigned
two years over Israel.
52 He did evil in the sight of the LORD, and
walked in the way of his father and in the way
of his mother and in the way of Jeroboam the
son of Nebat, who had made Israel sin;
53 for he served Baal and worshiped him,
and provoked the LORD God of Israel to anger,
according to all that his father had done.

22:46 [a]Hebrew *qadesh,* that is, one practicing sodomy and prostitution in religious rituals **22:48** [a]Or *ships of Tarshish*

THE SECOND BOOK OF

KINGS

Second Kings continues the drama begun in 1 Kings—the tragic history of two erring nations on a collision course with captivity. The author systematically traces the reigning monarchs of Israel and Judah, first by carrying forward one nation's history, then retracing the same period for the other nation.

Nineteen consecutive evil kings rule in Israel, leading to the Assyrian captivity. The picture shines a little brighter in Judah, where godly kings occasionally emerge to reform the evils of their predecessors. In the end, however, sin outweighs righteousness and Judah gets marched off to Babylon.

As much as anything, however, 2 Kings records the ministry of the prophet Elisha, the successor to Elijah, both of whom ministered in very dark times. While Elijah used mostly words in his prophetic ministry, Elisha underscored his message with frequent miracles. Elisha began his ministry by asking God for a double portion of grace (2:9), then went on to part the waters of the Jordan River (2:14), raise a child from the dead (4:18–37), purify deadly food (4:38–41), feed a multitude of people (4:42–44), heal a leper (5:5–15), pronounce leprosy on another man (5:20–27), and pronounce blindness on the Syrians, whose king had planned to kill him (6:1–20)—among other miracles. In addition to the miracles, Elisha authorized the anointing of Jehu as king of Israel (9:1–6).

Themes: A people will eventually reap what they sow. After centuries of apostasy and rebellion, the people who once comprised the nation of Israel were taken into captivity and removed from the Promised Land. On the positive side, 2 Kings demonstrates what one man can accomplish if he is willing to ask God for a double portion of His grace.

Author: Unknown

Time: Second Kings covers a time span from late in the reigns of King Ahaziah in Israel and King Jehoram in Judah (both began around 853 B.C.) to the Babylonian destruction of Jerusalem and the subsequent captivity of the people of Judah (around 587 B.C.).

Structure: Second Kings picks up the historical narrative where 1 Kings leaves off. It begins with the closing years of Elijah's ministry (1:1—2:11), records the ministry of the prophet Elisha (2:12—13:25), and ends with the captivity of the people of Judah.

As you read 2 Kings, watch for several life principles that play an important role in this book:

9. Trusting God means looking beyond what we can see to what God sees. *See 2 Kings 6:17; page 435.*

14. God acts on behalf of those who wait for Him. *See 2 Kings 6:32—7:19; page 438.*

6. You reap what you sow, more than you sow, and later than you sow. *See 2 Kings 18:9–12; page 453.*

26. Adversity is a bridge to a deeper relationship with God. *See 2 Kings 19:14–37; page 455.*

God Judges Ahaziah

1 Moab rebelled against Israel after the death
of Ahab.
2 Now Ahaziah fell through the lattice of his
upper room in Samaria, and was injured; so
he sent messengers and said to them, "Go, inquire of Baal-Zebub, the god of Ekron,
whether I shall recover from this injury."
3 But the angel[a] of the LORD said to Elijah
the Tishbite, "Arise, go up to meet the messengers of the king of Samaria, and say to
them, '*Is it* because *there is* no God in Israel
that you are going to inquire of Baal-Zebub,
the god of Ekron?'
4 "Now therefore, thus says the LORD: 'You
shall not come down from the bed to which
you have gone up, but you shall surely die.'"
So Elijah departed.
5 And when the messengers returned to
him, he said to them, "Why have you come
back?"
6 So they said to him, "A man came up to
meet us, and said to us, 'Go, return to the
king who sent you, and say to him, "Thus
says the LORD: '*Is it* because *there is* no God
in Israel *that* you are sending to inquire
of Baal-Zebub, the god of Ekron? Therefore
you shall not come down from the bed to
which you have gone up, but you shall surely
die.'"'"
7 Then he said to them, "What kind of man
was it who came up to meet you and told you
these words?"
8 So they answered him, "A hairy man
wearing a leather belt around his waist." And
he said, "It *is* Elijah the Tishbite."
9 Then the king sent to him a captain of fifty
with his fifty men. So he went up to him; and
there he was, sitting on the top of a hill. And
he spoke to him: "Man of God, the king has
said, 'Come down!'"
➤ 10 So Elijah answered and said to the captain
of fifty, "If I *am* a man of God, then let fire
come down from heaven and consume you
and your fifty men." And fire came down from
heaven and consumed him and his fifty.
11 Then he sent to him another captain of
fifty with his fifty men. And he answered and
said to him: "Man of God, thus has the king
said, 'Come down quickly!'"
12 So Elijah answered and said to them, "If I
am a man of God, let fire come down from
heaven and consume you and your fifty men."
And the fire of God came down from heaven
and consumed him and his fifty.
13 Again, he sent a third captain of fifty with
his fifty men. And the third captain of fifty
went up, and came and fell on his knees before Elijah, and pleaded with him, and said to
him: "Man of God, please let my life and the
life of these fifty servants of yours be precious
in your sight.
14 "Look, fire has come down from heaven
and burned up the first two captains of fifties
with their fifties. But let my life now be precious in your sight."
15 And the angel[a] of the LORD said to Elijah,
"Go down with him; do not be afraid of him."
So he arose and went down with him to the
king.
16 Then he said to him, "Thus says the LORD:
'Because you have sent messengers to inquire
of Baal-Zebub, the god of Ekron, *is it* because
there is no God in Israel to inquire of His
word? Therefore you shall not come down
from the bed to which you have gone up, but
you shall surely die.'"
17 So *Ahaziah* died according to the word of
the LORD which Elijah had spoken. Because
he had no son, Jehoram[a] became king in his
place, in the second year of Jehoram the son
of Jehoshaphat, king of Judah.
18 Now the rest of the acts of Ahaziah which
he did, *are* they not written in the book of the
chronicles of the kings of Israel?

Elijah Ascends to Heaven

2 And it came to pass, when the LORD was
about to take up Elijah into heaven by a
whirlwind, that Elijah went with Elisha from
Gilgal.
2 Then Elijah said to Elisha, "Stay here,
please, for the LORD has sent me on to Bethel."
But Elisha said, "*As* the LORD lives, and *as*
your soul lives, I will not leave you!" So they
went down to Bethel.
3 Now the sons of the prophets who *were* at
Bethel came out to Elisha, and said to him,
"Do you know that the LORD will take away
your master from over you today?" And he
said, "Yes, I know; keep silent!"
4 Then Elijah said to him, "Elisha, stay here,
please, for the LORD has sent me on to Jericho." But he said, "*As* the LORD lives, and *as*
your soul lives, I will not leave you!" So they
came to Jericho.

1:3 [a]Or *Angel* **1:15** [a]Or *Angel* **1:17** [a]The son of Ahab king of Israel (compare 3:1)

LIFE LESSONS

➤ ***1:10 — So Elijah answered and said to the captain of fifty, "If I am a man of God, then let fire come down from heaven and consume you and your fifty men."***

This hardly seems like the same prophet who ran away at the death threats of Jezebel. What happened? Time alone with God had convinced Elijah of God's presence, and His presence energizes us for our work.

5 Now the sons of the prophets who *were* at
Jericho came to Elisha and said to him, "Do
you know that the LORD will take away your
master from over you today?" So he answered, "Yes, I know; keep silent!"
➤ 6 Then Elijah said to him, "Stay here, please,
for the LORD has sent me on to the Jordan." But
he said, "*As* the LORD lives, and *as* your soul
lives, I will not leave you!" So the two of them
went on.
7 And fifty men of the sons of the prophets went and stood facing *them* at a distance, while the two of them stood by the
Jordan.
8 Now Elijah took his mantle, rolled *it* up,
and struck the water; and it was divided this
way and that, so that the two of them crossed
over on dry ground.
➤ **9** And so it was, when they had crossed
over, that Elijah said to Elisha, "Ask! What
may I do for you, before I am taken away
from you?" Elisha said, "Please let a double
portion of your spirit be upon me."
10 So he said, "You have asked a hard thing.
Nevertheless, if you see me *when I am* taken
from you, it shall be so for you; but if not, it
shall not be *so.*"
11 Then it happened, as they continued on
and talked, that suddenly a chariot of fire *appeared* with horses of fire, and separated the
two of them; and Elijah went up by a whirlwind into heaven.
12 And Elisha saw *it,* and he cried out, "My
father, my father, the chariot of Israel and its
horsemen!" So he saw him no more. And he
took hold of his own clothes and tore them
into two pieces.
13 He also took up the mantle of Elijah that
had fallen from him, and went back and stood
by the bank of the Jordan.
14 Then he took the mantle of Elijah that had
fallen from him, and struck the water, and said,
"Where *is* the LORD God of Elijah?" And when
he also had struck the water, it was divided this
way and that; and Elisha crossed over.
15 Now when the sons of the prophets who
were from Jericho saw him, they said, "The
spirit of Elijah rests on Elisha." And they
came to meet him, and bowed to the ground
before him.
16 Then they said to him, "Look now, there ◄
are fifty strong men with your servants.
Please let them go and search for your master, lest perhaps the Spirit of the LORD has
taken him up and cast him upon some mountain or into some valley." And he said, "You
shall not send anyone."
17 But when they urged him till he was
ashamed, he said, "Send *them!*" Therefore
they sent fifty men, and they searched for
three days but did not find him.
18 And when they came back to him, for he
had stayed in Jericho, he said to them, "Did I
not say to you, 'Do not go'?"

Elisha Performs Miracles

19 Then the men of the city said to Elisha,
"Please notice, the situation of this city *is*
pleasant, as my lord sees; but the water *is*
bad, and the ground barren."
20 And he said, "Bring me a new bowl, and
put salt in it." So they brought *it* to him.
21 Then he went out to the source of the ◄
water, and cast in the salt there, and said,
"Thus says the LORD: 'I have healed this
water; from it there shall be no more death or
barrenness.'"
22 So the water remains healed to this day,
according to the word of Elisha which he
spoke.
23 Then he went up from there to Bethel; and
as he was going up the road, some youths
came from the city and mocked him, and said
to him, "Go up, you baldhead! Go up, you
baldhead!"
24 So he turned around and looked at them,
and pronounced a curse on them in the name
of the LORD. And two female bears came out
of the woods and mauled forty-two of the
youths.

LIFE LESSONS

➤ 2:6 — *Then Elijah said to him, "Stay here, please, for the LORD has sent me on to the Jordan."*

The Lord sent Elijah on a quick cycle of trips to Bethel, Jericho, and to the Jordan. Why? We aren't told. But because Elijah listened to the Lord in the little things, He entrusted the prophet with big things.

➤ 2:9 — *Elijah said to Elisha, "Ask! What may I do for you, before I am taken away from you?" Elisha said, "Please let a double portion of your spirit be upon me."*

Elisha made a big request because he had come to know a big God. What "big things" might God be pleased to do in your life if only you would ask Him?

➤ 2:16 — *"Please let them go and search for your master . . . ." And he said, "You shall not send anyone."*

Our God does not promise to do one thing and then do another. He promised to take Elijah into heaven, and that is what He did. We can place our full confidence in everything God says.

➤ 2:21 — *Then he went out to the source of the water, and cast in the salt there, and said, "Thus says the LORD: 'I have healed this water . . . .'"*

The salt did not heal the water, nor did Elisha's words; the Lord healed the water. Yet the Lord usually chooses to work through both people and things to accomplish His work.

25 Then he went from there to Mount Carmel, and from there he returned to Samaria.

Moab Rebels Against Israel

3 Now Jehoram the son of Ahab became king over Israel at Samaria in the eighteenth year of Jehoshaphat king of Judah, and reigned twelve years.

2 And he did evil in the sight of the LORD, but not like his father and mother; for he put away the *sacred* pillar of Baal that his father had made.

3 Nevertheless he persisted in the sins of Jeroboam the son of Nebat, who had made Israel sin; he did not depart from them.

4 Now Mesha king of Moab was a sheepbreeder, and he regularly paid the king of Israel one hundred thousand lambs and the wool of one hundred thousand rams.

5 But it happened, when Ahab died, that the king of Moab rebelled against the king of Israel.

6 So King Jehoram went out of Samaria at that time and mustered all Israel.

➤ 7 Then he went and sent to Jehoshaphat king of Judah, saying, "The king of Moab has rebelled against me. Will you go with me to fight against Moab?" And he said, "I will go up; I *am* as you *are*, my people as your people, my horses as your horses."

8 Then he said, "Which way shall we go up?" And he answered, "By way of the Wilderness of Edom."

9 So the king of Israel went with the king of Judah and the king of Edom, and they marched on that roundabout route seven days; and there was no water for the army, nor for the animals that followed them.

10 And the king of Israel said, "Alas! For the LORD has called these three kings together to deliver them into the hand of Moab."

11 But Jehoshaphat said, "*Is there* no prophet of the LORD here, that we may inquire of the LORD by him?" So one of the servants of the king of Israel answered and said, "Elisha the son of Shaphat *is* here, who poured water on the hands of Elijah."

12 And Jehoshaphat said, "The word of the LORD is with him." So the king of Israel and Jehoshaphat and the king of Edom went down to him.

13 Then Elisha said to the king of Israel, "What have I to do with you? Go to the prophets of your father and the prophets of your mother." But the king of Israel said to him, "No, for the LORD has called these three kings *together* to deliver them into the hand of Moab."

14 And Elisha said, "*As* the LORD of hosts lives, before whom I stand, surely were it not that I regard the presence of Jehoshaphat king of Judah, I would not look at you, nor see you.

15 "But now bring me a musician." Then it happened, when the musician played, that the hand of the LORD came upon him.

16 And he said, "Thus says the LORD: 'Make this valley full of ditches.'

17 "For thus says the LORD: 'You shall not see wind, nor shall you see rain; yet that valley shall be filled with water, so that you, your cattle, and your animals may drink.'

18 "And this is a simple matter in the sight of the LORD; He will also deliver the Moabites into your hand. ➤

19 "Also you shall attack every fortified city and every choice city, and shall cut down every good tree, and stop up every spring of water, and ruin every good piece of land with stones."

20 Now it happened in the morning, when the grain offering was offered, that suddenly water came by way of Edom, and the land was filled with water.

21 And when all the Moabites heard that the kings had come up to fight against them, all who were able to bear arms and older were gathered; and they stood at the border.

22 Then they rose up early in the morning, and the sun was shining on the water; and the Moabites saw the water on the other side *as* red as blood.

23 And they said, "This is blood; the kings have surely struck swords and have killed one another; now therefore, Moab, to the spoil!"

24 So when they came to the camp of Israel, Israel rose up and attacked the Moabites, so that they fled before them; and they entered *their* land, killing the Moabites.

25 Then they destroyed the cities, and each man threw a stone on every good piece of land and filled it; and they stopped up all the springs of water and cut down all the good

LIFE LESSONS

➤ 3:7 — *"I will go up; I am as you are, my people as your people, my horses as your horses."*

Why did the righteous King Jehoshaphat keep allying himself with wicked kings? Perhaps it made sense to him politically. But God does not require us to understand His will, just obey it, even if it seems unreasonable.

➤ 3:18 — *"And this is a simple matter in the sight of the LORD; He will also deliver the Moabites into your hand."*

Even our most difficult problems are nothing but "a simple matter" for God.

trees. But they left the stones of Kir Haraseth
intact. However the slingers surrounded and
attacked it.
26 And when the king of Moab saw that the
battle was too fierce for him, he took with him
seven hundred men who drew swords, to
break through to the king of Edom, but they
could not.
27 Then he took his eldest son who would
have reigned in his place, and offered him *as*
a burnt offering upon the wall; and there was
great indignation against Israel. So they departed from him and returned to *their own*
land.

Elisha and the Widow's Oil

4 A certain woman of the wives of the sons
of the prophets cried out to Elisha, saying,
"Your servant my husband is dead, and you
know that your servant feared the LORD. And
the creditor is coming to take my two sons to
be his slaves."
➤ 2 So Elisha said to her, "What shall I do for
you? Tell me, what do you have in the house?"
And she said, "Your maidservant has nothing
in the house but a jar of oil."
3 Then he said, "Go, borrow vessels from
everywhere, from all your neighbors—empty
vessels; do not gather just a few.
4 "And when you have come in, you shall
shut the door behind you and your sons; then
pour it into all those vessels, and set aside the
full ones."
5 So she went from him and shut the door
behind her and her sons, who brought *the
vessels* to her; and she poured *it* out.
6 Now it came to pass, when the vessels
were full, that she said to her son, "Bring me
another vessel." And he said to her, "*There is*
not another vessel." So the oil ceased.
7 Then she came and told the man of
God. And he said, "Go, sell the oil and pay
your debt; and you *and* your sons live on the
rest."

Elisha Raises the Shunammite's Son

8 Now it happened one day that Elisha went
to Shunem, where there *was* a notable
woman, and she persuaded him to eat some
food. So it was, as often as he passed by, he
would turn in there to eat some food.
9 And she said to her husband, "Look now, I
know that this *is* a holy man of God, who
passes by us regularly.
10 "Please, let us make a small upper room
on the wall; and let us put a bed for him there,
and a table and a chair and a lampstand; so it
will be, whenever he comes to us, he can turn
in there."
11 And it happened one day that he came
there, and he turned in to the upper room and
lay down there.
12 Then he said to Gehazi his servant, "Call
this Shunammite woman." When he had
called her, she stood before him.
13 And he said to him, "Say now to her,
'Look, you have been concerned for us
with all this care. What *can I* do for you?
Do you want me to speak on your behalf to
the king or to the commander of the army?'"
She answered, "I dwell among my own people."
14 So he said, "What then *is* to be done for
her?" And Gehazi answered, "Actually, she
has no son, and her husband is old."
15 So he said, "Call her." When he had called
her, she stood in the doorway.
16 Then he said, "About this time next year
you shall embrace a son." And she said, "No,
my lord. Man of God, do not lie to your
maidservant!"
17 But the woman conceived, and bore a son ◄
when the appointed time had come, of which
Elisha had told her.
18 And the child grew. Now it happened one
day that he went out to his father, to the
reapers.
19 And he said to his father, "My head, my
head!" So he said to a servant, "Carry him to
his mother."
20 When he had taken him and brought him ◄
to his mother, he sat on her knees till noon,
and *then* died.
21 And she went up and laid him on the bed
of the man of God, shut *the door* upon him,
and went out.
22 Then she called to her husband, and said,

LIFE LESSONS

➤ 4:2 — *"What shall I do for you? Tell me, what do you have in the house?"*

God loves to take our "nothing" and make it into something that takes away our breath. Elisha's command may have seemed silly to the woman, but she obeyed—and God blessed her obedience.

➤ 4:17 — *But the woman conceived, and bore a son when the appointed time had come, of which Elisha had told her.*

God loves to bless His obedient people with gifts far beyond anything they could ever hope for or imagine (see Eph. 3:20).

➤ 4:20 — *When he had taken him and brought him to his mother, he sat on her knees till noon, and then died.*

Life is never an unbroken string of joyful blessings and extraordinary miracles. We live on a fallen planet where bad things happen. Yet God calls us to trust Him with the end of the story as well as its beginning.

WHAT THE BIBLE SAYS ABOUT GAGGING ON FINANCIAL INDEBTEDNESS

2 Kin. 4:1

The Bible leaves no doubt about God's opinion regarding debt. The following two verses speak clearly on this subject, a painful one for millions:

> Owe no one anything except to love one another, for he who loves another has fulfilled the law (Rom. 13:8).
>
> The rich rules over the poor,
> And the borrower is servant to the lender (Prov. 22:7).

As a nation, the United States has ignored these truths. One in five families in this country sits on the brink of bankruptcy. Millions of people are no more than sixty days away from becoming homeless or in dire financial need. We have bought into a buy-now and pay-later philosophy that has been sold to us for decades by advertisers who tempt us to believe we must have their product in order to feel good about ourselves and to project an image of worth.

We have swallowed a lie, and we are gagging on it.

We have swallowed a lie, and we are gagging on it.

A debt like a mortgage on a house to live in makes sense, but God does not want His people to be in unnecessary financial debt. The only thing we are to owe others is our love, which we are to give freely and in tangible forms. The price for indebtedness can be high indeed.

Listen to the heart's cry of a widow who said to the prophet Elisha, "Your servant my husband is dead, and you know that your servant feared the LORD. And the creditor is coming to take my two sons to be his slaves" (2 Kin. 4:1).

The deceased husband of this woman, a prophet associated with Elisha, apparently had left his family in debt. The woman appeared to have only one way to repay what her husband owed: sell her children into slavery.

We may protest, "How horrible! How could a parent sell her children to work off a debt?" And yet that is exactly what we in the United States are doing in strapping our children with a huge national debt. In just a few decades we have gone from being the world's largest creditor nation to debtor status—and our children will be forced to pay for our foolishness.

We are to be givers, not borrowers.

See the Life Principles Index for further study:
11. God assumes full responsibility for our needs when we obey Him.
16. Whatever you acquire outside of God's will eventually turns to ashes.

"Please send me one of the young men and
one of the donkeys, that I may run to the man
of God and come back."
23 So he said, "Why are you going to him
today? *It is* neither the New Moon nor the
Sabbath." And she said, "*It is* well."
24 Then she saddled a donkey, and said to
her servant, "Drive, and go forward; do not
slacken the pace for me unless I tell you."
25 And so she departed, and went to the man
of God at Mount Carmel. So it was, when the
man of God saw her afar off, that he said to
his servant Gehazi, "Look, the Shunammite
woman!
26 "Please run now to meet her, and say to
her, '*Is it* well with you? *Is it* well with your
husband? *Is it* well with the child?'" And she
answered, "*It is* well."
➤ 27 Now when she came to the man of God at
the hill, she caught him by the feet, but Gehazi came near to push her away. But the man
of God said, "Let her alone; for her soul *is* in
deep distress, and the LORD has hidden *it*
from me, and has not told me."
28 So she said, "Did I ask a son of my lord?
Did I not say, 'Do not deceive me'?"
29 Then he said to Gehazi, "Get yourself
ready, and take my staff in your hand, and
be on your way. If you meet anyone, do not
greet him; and if anyone greets you, do not
answer him; but lay my staff on the face of the
child."
30 And the mother of the child said, "*As* the
LORD lives, and *as* your soul lives, I will not
leave you." So he arose and followed her.
31 Now Gehazi went on ahead of them, and
laid the staff on the face of the child; but *there
was* neither voice nor hearing. Therefore he
went back to meet him, and told him, saying,
"The child has not awakened."
32 When Elisha came into the house, there
was the child, lying dead on his bed.
33 He went in therefore, shut the door behind
the two of them, and prayed to the LORD.
➤ 34 And he went up and lay on the child, and
put his mouth on his mouth, his eyes on his
eyes, and his hands on his hands; and he
stretched himself out on the child, and the
flesh of the child became warm.
35 He returned and walked back and forth in
the house, and again went up and stretched
himself out on him; then the child sneezed
seven times, and the child opened his eyes.
36 And he called Gehazi and said, "Call this
Shunammite woman." So he called her. And
when she came in to him, he said, "Pick up
your son."
37 So she went in, fell at his feet, and bowed
to the ground; then she picked up her son and
went out.

Elisha Purifies the Pot of Stew

38 And Elisha returned to Gilgal, and *there
was* a famine in the land. Now the sons of the
prophets *were* sitting before him; and he said
to his servant, "Put on the large pot, and boil
stew for the sons of the prophets."
39 So one went out into the field to gather
herbs, and found a wild vine, and gathered
from it a lapful of wild gourds, and came and
sliced *them* into the pot of stew, though they
did not know *what they were*.
40 Then they served it to the men to eat. Now
it happened, as they were eating the stew,
that they cried out and said, "Man of God,
there is death in the pot!" And they could not
eat *it*.
41 So he said, "Then bring some flour." And
he put *it* into the pot, and said, "Serve *it* to the
people, that they may eat." And there was
nothing harmful in the pot.

Elisha Feeds One Hundred Men

42 Then a man came from Baal Shalisha, and
brought the man of God bread of the firstfruits, twenty loaves of barley bread, and
newly ripened grain in his knapsack. And he
said, "Give *it* to the people, that they may
eat."
43 But his servant said, "What? Shall I set
this before one hundred men?" He said again,
"Give it to the people, that they may eat; for
thus says the LORD: 'They shall eat and have
some left over.'"
44 So he set *it* before them; and they ate and ➤
had *some* left over, according to the word of
the LORD.

LIFE LESSONS

➤ 4:27 — "Let her alone; for her soul is in deep distress, and the LORD has hidden it from me, and has not told me."

Why did the Lord hide this tragedy from Elisha? We are not told. But we do know that God works in the lives of all His people to build their faith and trust in Him. That's true both for Elijah and for us.

➤ 4:34 — And he went up and lay on the child, and put his mouth on his mouth, his eyes on his eyes, and his hands on his hands . . . .

The way God performed this miracle looked nothing like how He performed another one through Elijah (1 Kin. 17:17–22). We cannot pin God down on how He "must" do things. He is sovereign and works in His own way.

➤ 4:44 — So he set it before them; and they ate and had some left over, according to the word of the LORD.

Elisha fed one hundred men with twenty loaves of barley bread; Jesus fed five thousand men with five loaves and two fish, and four thousand men with seven loaves and a few fish. Can anyone doubt who was the greater?

Naaman's Leprosy Healed

5 Now Naaman, commander of the army of
the king of Syria, was a great and honorable man in the eyes of his master, because by
him the LORD had given victory to Syria. He
was also a mighty man of valor, *but* a leper.
2 And the Syrians had gone out on raids,
and had brought back captive a young girl
from the land of Israel. She waited on Naaman's wife.
3 Then she said to her mistress, "If only my
master *were* with the prophet who *is* in Samaria! For he would heal him of his leprosy."
4 And *Naaman* went in and told his master,
saying, "Thus and thus said the girl who *is*
from the land of Israel."
5 Then the king of Syria said, "Go now, and
I will send a letter to the king of Israel." So he
departed and took with him ten talents of silver, six thousand *shekels* of gold, and ten
changes of clothing.
6 Then he brought the letter to the king of
Israel, which said,

> Now be advised, when this letter comes to you, that I have sent Naaman my servant to you, that you may heal him of his leprosy.

7 And it happened, when the king of Israel
read the letter, that he tore his clothes and
said, "*Am* I God, to kill and make alive, that
this man sends a man to me to heal him of his
leprosy? Therefore please consider, and see
how he seeks a quarrel with me."
8 So it was, when Elisha the man of God
heard that the king of Israel had torn his
clothes, that he sent to the king, saying, "Why
have you torn your clothes? Please let him
come to me, and he shall know that there is a
prophet in Israel."
9 Then Naaman went with his horses and
chariot, and he stood at the door of Elisha's
house.
10 And Elisha sent a messenger to him, saying, "Go and wash in the Jordan seven times,
and your flesh shall be restored to you, and
you shall be clean."
➤ 11 But Naaman became furious, and went
away and said, "Indeed, I said to myself, 'He
will surely come out *to me,* and stand and call
on the name of the LORD his God, and wave
his hand over the place, and heal the leprosy.'
12 "*Are* not the Abanah[a] and the Pharpar, the
rivers of Damascus, better than all the waters
of Israel? Could I not wash in them and be
clean?" So he turned and went away in a rage.
13 And his servants came near and spoke to
him, and said, "My father, *if* the prophet had
told you *to do* something great, would you not
have done *it?* How much more then, when he
says to you, 'Wash, and be clean'?"
14 So he went down and dipped seven times ➤
in the Jordan, according to the saying of the
man of God; and his flesh was restored like
the flesh of a little child, and he was clean.
15 And he returned to the man of God, he
and all his aides, and came and stood before
him; and he said, "Indeed, now I know that
there is no God in all the earth, except in Israel; now therefore, please take a gift from
your servant."
16 But he said, "*As* the LORD lives, before
whom I stand, I will receive nothing." And he
urged him to take *it,* but he refused.
17 So Naaman said, "Then, if not, please let
your servant be given two mule-loads of
earth; for your servant will no longer offer either burnt offering or sacrifice to other gods,
but to the LORD.
18 "Yet in this thing may the LORD pardon
your servant: when my master goes into the
temple of Rimmon to worship there, and he
leans on my hand, and I bow down in the temple of Rimmon—when I bow down in the
temple of Rimmon, may the LORD please pardon your servant in this thing."
19 Then he said to him, "Go in peace." So he
departed from him a short distance.

Gehazi's Greed

20 But Gehazi, the servant of Elisha the man
of God, said, "Look, my master has spared
Naaman this Syrian, while not receiving from
his hands what he brought; but *as* the LORD
lives, I will run after him and take something
from him."
21 So Gehazi pursued Naaman. When Naaman saw *him* running after him, he got down
from the chariot to meet him, and said, "*Is* all
well?"
22 And he said, "All *is* well. My master has

5:12 [a]Following Kethib, Septuagint, and Vulgate; Qere, Syriac, and Targum read *Amanah.*

LIFE LESSONS

➤ **5:11 — *But Naaman . . . said, "Indeed, I said to myself, 'He will surely come out to me, and stand and call on the name of the LORD his God, and wave his hand over the place, and heal the leprosy.'"***

We sometimes want God to make a great show of His work; He usually prefers to do His work quietly and without a lot of fanfare. Yet it is His work nonetheless.

➤ **5:14 — *So he went down and dipped seven times in the Jordan, according to the saying of the man of God; and his flesh was restored like the flesh of a little child, and he was clean.***

God does not require us to understand His will, just obey it, even if it seems unreasonable. And obedience always brings blessing.

sent me, saying, 'Indeed, just now two young men of the sons of the prophets have come to me from the mountains of Ephraim. Please give them a talent of silver and two changes of garments.'"

23 So Naaman said, "Please, take two talents." And he urged him, and bound two talents of silver in two bags, with two changes of garments, and handed *them* to two of his servants; and they carried *them* on ahead of him.

24 When he came to the citadel, he took *them* from their hand, and stored *them* away in the house; then he let the men go, and they departed.

25 Now he went in and stood before his master. Elisha said to him, "Where *did you go,* Gehazi?" And he said, "Your servant did not go anywhere."

26 Then he said to him, "Did not my heart go *with you* when the man turned back from his chariot to meet you? *Is it* time to receive money and to receive clothing, olive groves and vineyards, sheep and oxen, male and female servants?

27 "Therefore the leprosy of Naaman shall cling to you and your descendants forever." And he went out from his presence leprous, *as white* as snow.

The Floating Ax Head

6 And the sons of the prophets said to Elisha, "See now, the place where we dwell with you is too small for us.

2 "Please, let us go to the Jordan, and let every man take a beam from there, and let us make there a place where we may dwell." So he answered, "Go."

3 Then one said, "Please consent to go with your servants." And he answered, "I will go."

4 So he went with them. And when they came to the Jordan, they cut down trees.

5 But as one was cutting down a tree, the iron *ax head* fell into the water; and he cried out and said, "Alas, master! For it was borrowed."

6 So the man of God said, "Where did it fall?" And he showed him the place. So he cut off a stick, and threw *it* in there; and he made the iron float.

7 Therefore he said, "Pick *it* up for yourself." So he reached out his hand and took it.

The Blinded Syrians Captured

8 Now the king of Syria was making war against Israel; and he consulted with his servants, saying, "My camp *will be* in such and such a place."

9 And the man of God sent to the king of Israel, saying, "Beware that you do not pass this place, for the Syrians are coming down there."

10 Then the king of Israel sent *someone* to the place of which the man of God had told him. Thus he warned him, and he was watchful there, not just once or twice.

11 Therefore the heart of the king of Syria was greatly troubled by this thing; and he called his servants and said to them, "Will you not show me which of us *is* for the king of Israel?"

12 And one of his servants said, "None, my lord, O king; but Elisha, the prophet who *is* in Israel, tells the king of Israel the words that you speak in your bedroom."

13 So he said, "Go and see where he *is,* that I may send and get him." And it was told him, saying, "Surely *he is* in Dothan."

14 Therefore he sent horses and chariots and a great army there, and they came by night and surrounded the city.

15 And when the servant of the man of God arose early and went out, there was an army, surrounding the city with horses and chariots. And his servant said to him, "Alas, my master! What shall we do?"

16 So he answered, "Do not fear, for those who *are* with us *are* more than those who *are* with them."

17 And Elisha prayed, and said, "LORD, I pray, open his eyes that he may see." Then the LORD opened the eyes of the young man, and he saw. And behold, the mountain *was* full of horses and chariots of fire all around Elisha.

18 So when *the Syrians* came down to him, Elisha prayed to the LORD, and said, "Strike

LIFE LESSONS

➤ **6:12 — *"Elisha, the prophet who is in Israel, tells the king of Israel the words that you speak in your bedroom."***

Nothing is hidden from God, not a word or a thought. Jesus tells us, "there is nothing covered that will not be revealed, and hidden that will not be known." And so He tells us, "do not fear" (Matt. 10:26).

➤ **6:15 — *. . . there was an army, surrounding the city with horses and chariots. And his servant said to him, "Alas, my master! What shall we do?"***

When we focus on the challenges and troubles we face, we become alarmed. But when we focus on the unseen God of heaven, the picture changes radically. And our hearts find peace.

➤ **6:17 — *Then the LORD opened the eyes of the young man, and he saw. And behold, the mountain was full of horses and chariots of fire all around Elisha.***

Elisha did not pray that his servant would stop seeing the enemy; he prayed that he would start seeing the goodness of the Lord. Trusting God means looking beyond what we can see to what God sees.

LIFE PRINCIPLE 9

TRUSTING GOD MEANS LOOKING BEYOND WHAT WE CAN SEE TO WHAT GOD SEES.

2 KIN. 6:17

Staring across the Elah Valley into the eyes of Goliath, David recalled the times God had delivered him from the brink of disaster. God had always given him the ability he needed to triumph. Now he faced one of the greatest challenges of his life—a trained and well-armed warrior named Goliath.

At some point, each of us will face what will look like mammoth trials and difficulties. That is why we must know how to respond to every threat by laying hold of the kind of victorious faith that looks beyond what we can see to what God sees.

The secret of David's success was his ability to trust and obey God. Had he looked merely at the giant challenge facing him, he would have turned around and run away, as did the rest of the Israelites. But through faith, David saw what his countrymen did not.

In times of extreme pressure, God stretches our faith and deepens our dependence on Him. Without a strong, abiding faith, we can quickly yield to temptation and fear, especially when the trial or difficulty is intense or prolonged. God developed David's trust until it became unshakeable.

Whatever Goliath you face, you need to bury one truth deep within your heart: God loves you, and when you place your trust in Him, He will not allow you to suffer defeat. You may go through times of failure. Life may not always turn out the way you planned—but ultimately, God will be glorified, and you will be blessed.

Every challenge presents an opportunity for God to display His faithfulness and love. Instead of yielding to thoughts of fear and failure, make a commitment to trust God, even when you do not know what the next day will bring. Train yourself to look beyond what you can see to what God sees.

David founded his faith in the sovereignty of God; that's why he knew he would not fail in his quest to defeat the Philistine giant.

How can you gain that kind of faith?

- *Recall past victories.* David recalled how God had delivered him from the paw of the lion and the grasp of the bear (1 Sam. 17:32–37). You first win spiritual victories in

Through faith, David saw what his countrymen did not.

your mind. If you cave into feelings of fear and doubt, you will lose. When you focus on the truth of God's Word, you win every time.

- *Reject discouraging words.* No one in the Israelite camp encouraged David in his quest to defeat Goliath. The soldiers laughed at him. His brothers felt embarrassed by his presence and urged him to go home. Even King Saul doubted David. If he had listened to their disparaging comments, he would have given up—but he turned his heart toward God and there found the encouragement he needed.
- *Recognize the true nature of the battle.* David entered the battle shouting to his arrogant opponent the memorable words, "the battle is the Lord's, and He will give you into our hands" (1 Sam. 17:47). What a victorious way to say, "God wins!"

Triumph comes because of God's ability.

- *Respond to the challenge with a positive confession.* David asked the fearful Israelites, "Who is this uncircumcised Philistine, that he should defy the armies of the living God?" (1 Sam. 17:26). To Saul he said, "The Lord will deliver me from the hand of the Philistine." To Goliath he said, "I come to you in the name of the Lord of hosts, the God of the armies of Israel" (17:37, 45). David firmly declared his belief that he could not lose because God was with him.
- *Rely on the power of God.* David did not need a spear or a javelin to defeat Goliath. He needed only his faith and a homemade slingshot. "Then all this assembly shall know that the LORD does not save with sword and spear" (1 Sam. 17:47). God provided the victory, and God received the glory.
- *Reckon the victory.* Even before he stepped onto the battlefield, David knew he would not lose. He knew it wasn't his reputation on the line, but God's. He knew it wasn't his strength or cunning that would win the battle, but God's strength and wisdom.

You can face any circumstance with confidence and hope, because it is not your strength, wisdom, energy, or power that brings victory. Triumph comes because of God's ability, and when you place your trust in Him, you tap into an irresistible force that no one and nothing can successfully oppose.

See the Life Principles Index for further study.

Life Examples:

ELISHA

Enjoying a Hedge of Angels

2 KIN. 6:18

Who knows what God may accomplish through prayer?

The prophet Elisha experienced the miraculous protection of God as the result of prayer. The king of Syria sought to kill Elisha, who kept telling the Israelite army his every move. When the Syrian king discovered Elisha in Dothan, he sent a huge army to surround the city.

Early the next morning, Elisha saw the army ready to attack. When his frightened servant asked Elisha what they should do, Elisha asked God to open the eyes of the young man. Immediately the servant could see the hillside around Elisha filled with horses and chariots of fire—a hedge of angels.

As the Syrian army approached, Elisha prayed, "Strike this people, I pray, with blindness" (2 Kin. 6:18). Elisha then led the blind army all the way to Samaria before God opened their eyes, again through the prayers of Elisha!

What miracles might God want to do through your prayers?

See the Life Principles Index for further study:
8. Fight all your battles on your knees and you win every time.

this people, I pray, with blindness." And He
struck them with blindness according to the
word of Elisha.
19 Now Elisha said to them, "This *is* not the
way, nor *is* this the city. Follow me, and I will
bring you to the man whom you seek." But he
led them to Samaria.
20 So it was, when they had come to Samaria, that Elisha said, "LORD, open the eyes
of these *men,* that they may see." And the
LORD opened their eyes, and they saw; and
there *they were,* inside Samaria!
21 Now when the king of Israel saw them, he
said to Elisha, "My father, shall I kill *them?*
Shall I kill *them?*"
22 But he answered, "You shall not kill *them.*
Would you kill those whom you have taken
captive with your sword and your bow? Set
food and water before them, that they may eat
and drink and go to their master."
23 Then he prepared a great feast for them;
and after they ate and drank, he sent them
away and they went to their master. So the
bands of Syrian *raiders* came no more into
the land of Israel.

Syria Besieges Samaria in Famine

24 And it happened after this that Ben-Hadad
king of Syria gathered all his army, and went
up and besieged Samaria.
25 And there was a great famine in Samaria;
and indeed they besieged it until a donkey's
head was *sold* for eighty *shekels* of silver, and
one-fourth of a kab of dove droppings for five
shekels of silver.
26 Then, as the king of Israel was passing by
on the wall, a woman cried out to him, saying,
"Help, my lord, O king!"
27 And he said, "If the LORD does not help
you, where can I find help for you? From the
threshing floor or from the winepress?"
28 Then the king said to her, "What is troubling you?" And she answered, "This woman
said to me, 'Give your son, that we may
eat him today, and we will eat my son tomorrow.'
29 "So we boiled my son, and ate him. And I
said to her on the next day, 'Give your son, that
we may eat him'; but she has hidden her son."
30 Now it happened, when the king heard the
words of the woman, that he tore his clothes;
and as he passed by on the wall, the people
looked, and there underneath *he had* sackcloth on his body.
31 Then he said, "God do so to me and more ➤
also, if the head of Elisha the son of Shaphat
remains on him today!"
32 But Elisha was sitting in his house, and
the elders were sitting with him. And *the king*
sent a man ahead of him, but before the messenger came to him, he said to the elders, "Do
you see how this son of a murderer has sent
someone to take away my head? Look, when
the messenger comes, shut the door, and hold
him fast at the door. *Is* not the sound of his
master's feet behind him?"

LIFE LESSONS

➤ **6:31 — *Then he said, "God do so to me and more also, if the head of Elisha the son of Shaphat remains on him today."***

The king blamed Elisha for the disaster, rather than his own sin. So long as we blame others for the trouble our sin causes, we remain "stuck." God wants us to confess and repent so that He can bless us again.

ANSWERS TO LIFE'S QUESTIONS

What steps can I take when I *really* need to hear from God?

2 KIN. 7:1

Throughout the Bible, we read of prophets and other men and women of God who implored their people to hear the word of the Lord. Obviously, God earnestly wanted His people to hear His voice.

He still does.

So how do we hear God when He speaks to us today? What steps can we take to make ourselves ready to hear what He has to say?

We tend to complicate the process. When we want to ask God what He desires in our lives, we often act as though we would like to receive a phone call from heaven in which the Lord gives us a detailed plan for the next five years. In fact, we already have everything we need in order to discover what He wants for us.

Developing daily spiritual disciplines helps us to hear the Lord's voice clearly and seek His direction continually. Ponder the following basic steps you can take to enable you to hear the Lord when He speaks to you:

- *Read God's Word*. By diving every day into God's Word, we begin to see His established order for our lives. We learn about God's truth, mercy, love, and forgiveness.
- *Seek Him in prayer*: Many times, bowing our heads is the best way to see God's face and hear His voice. In opening ourselves up before the Lord, we can honestly discuss our circumstances with Him, listening for His direction as we remain still. Prayer is more than just a wish list for God—it's a conversation in which we interact with Him.
- *Meditation*: Dwelling on what God speaks to our hearts is a great way to let His truths take root in our souls. Not only will what we read and hear from Him impact our lives, but by meditating on it, God has the building materials to lay an unshakeable foundation in our hearts. The psalmist said to the Lord, "I have more understanding than all my teachers, for Your testimonies are my meditation" (Ps. 119:99).
- *Listen*: You hear with your ears. If you have normal hearing, you can't help hearing sounds within a certain audio range. Listening, however, goes further, involving the mind. Genuine listening is active, meaning that it puts the mind in gear and hears everything said, looking intently for the meaning. That's how God wants us to listen to Him—actively!

See the Life Principles Index for further study:
3. God's Word is an immovable anchor in times of storm.
27. Prayer is life's greatest time saver.
13. Listening to God is essential to walking with God.

33 And while he was still talking with them,
there was the messenger, coming down to
him; and then *the king* said, "Surely this
calamity *is* from the LORD; why should I wait
for the LORD any longer?"
7 Then Elisha said, "Hear the word of the
LORD. Thus says the LORD: 'Tomorrow
about this time a seah of fine flour *shall be
sold* for a shekel, and two seahs of barley for
a shekel, at the gate of Samaria.'"
2 So an officer on whose hand the king
leaned answered the man of God and said,
"Look, *if* the LORD would make windows in
heaven, could this thing be?" And he said, "In
fact, you shall see *it* with your eyes, but you
shall not eat of it."

The Syrians Flee
3 Now there were four leprous men at
the entrance of the gate; and they said to one

LIFE LESSONS

➤ 6:33 — *. . . and then the king said, "Surely this calamity is from the LORD; why should I wait for the LORD any longer?"*

The king correctly saw the calamity as from the Lord. But he was dead wrong about not waiting for God. The Lord acts on behalf of those who wait for Him, even when His timing seems off.

➤ 7:2 — *So an officer . . . said, "Look, if the LORD would make windows in heaven, could this thing be?" And he said, "In fact, you shall see it with your eyes, but you shall not eat of it."*

It is always foolish to question the promises of God. They will continue to be fulfilled—but the doubter may not experience any of their benefits.

another, "Why are we sitting here until we
die?
4 "If we say, 'We will enter the city,' the
famine *is* in the city, and we shall die there.
And if we sit here, we die also. Now therefore,
come, let us surrender to the army of the Syrians. If they keep us alive, we shall live; and if
they kill us, we shall only die."
5 And they rose at twilight to go to the camp
of the Syrians; and when they had come to
the outskirts of the Syrian camp, to their surprise no one *was* there.
➤ 6 For the Lord had caused the army of the
Syrians to hear the noise of chariots and the
noise of horses—the noise of a great army; so
they said to one another, "Look, the king of
Israel has hired against us the kings of the
Hittites and the kings of the Egyptians to attack us!"
7 Therefore they arose and fled at twilight,
and left the camp intact—their tents, their
horses, and their donkeys—and they fled for
their lives.
8 And when these lepers came to the outskirts of the camp, they went into one tent
and ate and drank, and carried from it silver
and gold and clothing, and went and hid
them; then they came back and entered another tent, and carried *some* from there *also*,
and went and hid *it*.
➤ **9** Then they said to one another, "We are not
doing right. This day *is* a day of good news,
and we remain silent. If we wait until morning
light, some punishment will come upon us.
Now therefore, come, let us go and tell the
king's household."
10 So they went and called to the gatekeepers of the city, and told them, saying, "We
went to the Syrian camp, and surprisingly no
one *was* there, not a human sound—only
horses and donkeys tied, and the tents intact."
11 And the gatekeepers called out, and they
told *it* to the king's household inside.
12 So the king arose in the night and said to
his servants, "Let me now tell you what the
Syrians have done to us. They know that we
are hungry; therefore they have gone out of
the camp to hide themselves in the field, saying, 'When they come out of the city, we shall
catch them alive, and get into the city.'"
13 And one of his servants answered and
said, "Please, let several *men* take five of the
remaining horses which are left in the city.
Look, they *may either become* like all the
multitude of Israel that are left in it; or indeed,
I say, they *may become* like all the multitude
of Israel left from those who are consumed;
so let us send them and see."
14 Therefore they took two chariots with
horses; and the king sent them in the direction of the Syrian army, saying, "Go and see."
15 And they went after them to the Jordan;
and indeed all the road *was* full of garments
and weapons which the Syrians had thrown
away in their haste. So the messengers returned and told the king.
16 Then the people went out and plundered
the tents of the Syrians. So a seah of fine flour
was *sold* for a shekel, and two seahs of barley
for a shekel, according to the word of the
LORD.
17 Now the king had appointed the officer
on whose hand he leaned to have charge of
the gate. But the people trampled him in the
gate, and he died, just as the man of God had
said, who spoke when the king came down to
him.
18 So it happened just as the man of God had
spoken to the king, saying, "Two seahs of barley for a shekel, and a seah of fine flour for a
shekel, shall be *sold* tomorrow about this time
in the gate of Samaria."
19 Then that officer had answered the man
of God, and said, "Now look, *if* the LORD
would make windows in heaven, could such
a thing be?" And he had said, "In fact, you
shall see *it* with your eyes, but you shall not
eat of it."
20 And so it happened to him, for the people
trampled him in the gate, and he died.

The King Restores the Shunammite's Land

8 Then Elisha spoke to the woman whose
son he had restored to life, saying, "Arise
and go, you and your household, and stay
wherever you can; for the LORD has called for
a famine, and furthermore, it will come upon
the land for seven years."
2 So the woman arose and did according to
the saying of the man of God, and she went
with her household and dwelt in the land of
the Philistines seven years.
3 It came to pass, at the end of seven years,
that the woman returned from the land of the

LIFE LESSONS

➤ **7:6 — *For the LORD had caused the army of the Syrians to hear the noise of chariots and the noise of horses—the noise of a great army . . . .***

To win a battle or a war, the Lord does not need state-of-the-art weapons or massive armies. In His hands, even noise—nothing but sound—can bring victory. Will we trust Him?

➤ **7:9 — *"We are not doing right. This day is a day of good news, and we remain silent. If we wait until morning light, some punishment will come upon us. Now therefore, come, let us go and tell the king's household."***

God calls us to share the good news we know. We are not to hide it or keep silent about it, but to bless others by speaking it clearly and joyfully.

Philistines; and she went to make an appeal
to the king for her house and for her land.
4 Then the king talked with Gehazi, the servant of the man of God, saying, "Tell me,
please, all the great things Elisha has done."
➤ 5 Now it happened, as he was telling the
king how he had restored the dead to life, that
there was the woman whose son he had restored to life, appealing to the king for her
house and for her land. And Gehazi said, "My
lord, O king, this *is* the woman, and this *is* her
son whom Elisha restored to life."
6 And when the king asked the woman, she
told him. So the king appointed a certain officer for her, saying, "Restore all that *was* hers,
and all the proceeds of the field from the day
that she left the land until now."

Death of Ben-Hadad

7 Then Elisha went to Damascus, and
Ben-Hadad king of Syria was sick; and it was
told him, saying, "The man of God has come
here."
8 And the king said to Hazael, "Take a present in your hand, and go to meet the man of
God, and inquire of the LORD by him, saying,
'Shall I recover from this disease?'"
9 So Hazael went to meet him and took a
present with him, of every good thing of Damascus, forty camel-loads; and he came and
stood before him, and said, "Your son Ben-
Hadad king of Syria has sent me to you, saying, 'Shall I recover from this disease?'"
10 And Elisha said to him, "Go, say to
him, 'You shall certainly recover.' However
the LORD has shown me that he will really
die."
11 Then he set his countenance in a stare
until he was ashamed; and the man of God
wept.
12 And Hazael said, "Why is my lord weeping?" He answered, "Because I know the evil
that you will do to the children of Israel: Their
strongholds you will set on fire, and their
young men you will kill with the sword; and
you will dash their children, and rip open
their women with child."
13 So Hazael said, "But what *is* your servant—
a dog, that he should do this gross thing?" And
Elisha answered, "The LORD has shown me
that you *will become* king over Syria."
14 Then he departed from Elisha, and came
to his master, who said to him, "What did Elisha say to you?" And he answered, "He told
me you would surely recover."
15 But it happened on the next day that he
took a thick cloth and dipped *it* in water, and
spread *it* over his face so that he died; and
Hazael reigned in his place.

Jehoram Reigns in Judah

16 Now in the fifth year of Joram the son of
Ahab, king of Israel, Jehoshaphat *having*
been king of Judah, Jehoram the son of Jehoshaphat began to reign as king of Judah.
17 He was thirty-two years old when he became king, and he reigned eight years in Jerusalem.
18 And he walked in the way of the kings of ◄
Israel, just as the house of Ahab had done, for
the daughter of Ahab was his wife; and he did
evil in the sight of the LORD.
19 Yet the LORD would not destroy Judah, for
the sake of His servant David, as He promised
him to give a lamp to him *and* his sons forever.
20 In his days Edom revolted against Judah's
authority, and made a king over themselves.
21 So Joram[a] went to Zair, and all his chariots with him. Then he rose by night and attacked the Edomites who had surrounded
him and the captains of the chariots; and the
troops fled to their tents.
22 Thus Edom has been in revolt against Judah's authority to this day. And Libnah revolted at that time.
23 Now the rest of the acts of Joram, and all
that he did, *are* they not written in the book of
the chronicles of the kings of Judah?
24 So Joram rested with his fathers, and was
buried with his fathers in the City of David.
Then Ahaziah his son reigned in his place.

Ahaziah Reigns in Judah

25 In the twelfth year of Joram the son of
Ahab, king of Israel, Ahaziah the son of Jehoram, king of Judah, began to reign.
26 Ahaziah *was* twenty-two years old when
he became king, and he reigned one year in
Jerusalem. His mother's name *was* Athaliah
the granddaughter of Omri, king of Israel.

8:21 [a]Spelled *Jehoram* in verse 16

LIFE LESSONS

➤ **8:5 —** ***Now it happened, as he was telling the king how he had restored the dead to life, that there was the woman whose son he had restored to life, appealing to the king for her house and for her land.***

How many "coincidences" are there in our lives that actually occur by the hand of God, and we do not know it?

➤ **8:18 —** ***And he walked in the way of the kings of Israel, just as the house of Ahab had done, for the daughter of Ahab was his wife . . . .***

Jehoshaphat, the righteous king of Judah, foolishly allowed the crown prince to marry the daughter of one of the most wicked kings in Israel's history. And so all the good he had accomplished quickly came unraveled.

27 And he walked in the way of the house of
Ahab, and did evil in the sight of the LORD,
like the house of Ahab, for he *was* the son-in-
law of the house of Ahab.
28 Now he went with Joram the son of Ahab
to war against Hazael king of Syria at Ramoth
Gilead; and the Syrians wounded Joram.
29 Then King Joram went back to Jezreel to
recover from the wounds which the Syrians
had inflicted on him at Ramah, when he
fought against Hazael king of Syria. And
Ahaziah the son of Jehoram, king of Judah,
went down to see Joram the son of Ahab in
Jezreel, because he was sick.

Jehu Anointed King of Israel

9 And Elisha the prophet called one of the
sons of the prophets, and said to him, "Get
yourself ready, take this flask of oil in your
hand, and go to Ramoth Gilead.
2 "Now when you arrive at that place, look
there for Jehu the son of Jehoshaphat, the son
of Nimshi, and go in and make him rise up
from among his associates, and take him to
an inner room.
3 "Then take the flask of oil, and pour *it* on
his head, and say, 'Thus says the LORD: "I have
anointed you king over Israel."' Then open
the door and flee, and do not delay."
4 So the young man, the servant of the
prophet, went to Ramoth Gilead.
5 And when he arrived, there *were* the captains of the army sitting; and he said, "I have
a message for you, Commander." Jehu said,
"For which *one* of us?" And he said, "For you,
Commander."
6 Then he arose and went into the house.
And he poured the oil on his head, and said to
him, "Thus says the LORD God of Israel: 'I
have anointed you king over the people of the
LORD, over Israel.
7 'You shall strike down the house of Ahab
your master, that I may avenge the blood of
My servants the prophets, and the blood of all
the servants of the LORD, at the hand of
Jezebel.
8 'For the whole house of Ahab shall perish;
and I will cut off from Ahab all the males in
Israel, both bond and free.
9 'So I will make the house of Ahab like the
house of Jeroboam the son of Nebat, and like
the house of Baasha the son of Ahijah.
10 'The dogs shall eat Jezebel on the plot *of
ground* at Jezreel, and *there shall be* none to
bury *her*.'" And he opened the door and fled.
11 Then Jehu came out to the servants of
his master, and *one* said to him, "*Is* all well?
Why did this madman come to you?" And he
said to them, "You know the man and his bab-
ble."
12 And they said, "A lie! Tell us now." So he
said, "Thus and thus he spoke to me, saying,
'Thus says the LORD: "I have anointed you
king over Israel."'"
13 Then each man hastened to take his garment and put *it* under him on the top of the
steps; and they blew trumpets, saying, "Jehu
is king!"

Joram of Israel Killed

14 So Jehu the son of Jehoshaphat, the son
of Nimshi, conspired against Joram. (Now
Joram had been defending Ramoth Gilead,
he and all Israel, against Hazael king of
Syria.
15 But King Joram had returned to Jezreel to
recover from the wounds which the Syrians
had inflicted on him when he fought with
Hazael king of Syria.) And Jehu said, "If you
are so minded, let no one leave *or* escape from
the city to go and tell *it* in Jezreel."
16 So Jehu rode in a chariot and went to
Jezreel, for Joram was laid up there; and
Ahaziah king of Judah had come down to see
Joram.
17 Now a watchman stood on the tower
in Jezreel, and he saw the company of Jehu
as he came, and said, "I see a company of
men." And Joram said, "Get a horseman and
send him to meet them, and let him say, '*Is it*
peace?'"
18 So the horseman went to meet him, and
said, "Thus says the king: '*Is it* peace?'" And
Jehu said, "What have you to do with peace?
Turn around and follow me." So the watchman reported, saying, "The messenger went
to them, but is not coming back."
19 Then he sent out a second horseman who
came to them, and said, "Thus says the king:
'*Is it* peace?'" And Jehu answered, "What have
you to do with peace? Turn around and follow
me."
20 So the watchman reported, saying, "He
went up to them and is not coming back; and
the driving *is* like the driving of Jehu the son
of Nimshi, for he drives furiously!"
21 Then Joram said, "Make ready." And his
chariot was made ready. Then Joram king of
Israel and Ahaziah king of Judah went out,
each in his chariot; and they went out to meet
Jehu, and met him on the property of Naboth
the Jezreelite.
22 Now it happened, when Joram saw Jehu,
that he said, "*Is it* peace, Jehu?" So he answered, "What peace, as long as the harlotries
of your mother Jezebel and her witchcraft *are*
so many?"
23 Then Joram turned around and fled, and
said to Ahaziah, "Treachery, Ahaziah!"
24 Now Jehu drew his bow with full strength
and shot Jehoram between his arms; and the
arrow came out at his heart, and he sank
down in his chariot.
25 Then *Jehu* said to Bidkar his captain,
"Pick *him* up, *and* throw him into the tract of
the field of Naboth the Jezreelite; for remember, when you and I were riding together be-

hind Ahab his father, that the LORD laid this burden upon him:
26 'Surely I saw yesterday the blood of Naboth and the blood of his sons,' says the LORD, 'and I will repay you in this plot,' says the LORD. Now therefore, take *and* throw him on the plot *of ground,* according to the word of the LORD."

Ahaziah of Judah Killed

27 But when Ahaziah king of Judah saw *this,* he fled by the road to Beth Haggan.[a] So Jehu pursued him, and said, "Shoot him also in the chariot." *And they shot him* at the Ascent of Gur, which is by Ibleam. Then he fled to Megiddo, and died there.
28 And his servants carried him in the chariot to Jerusalem, and buried him in his tomb with his fathers in the City of David.
29 In the eleventh year of Joram the son of Ahab, Ahaziah had become king over Judah.

Jezebel's Violent Death

30 Now when Jehu had come to Jezreel, Jezebel heard *of it;* and she put paint on her eyes and adorned her head, and looked through a window.
31 Then, as Jehu entered at the gate, she said, "*Is it* peace, Zimri, murderer of your master?"
32 And he looked up at the window, and said, "Who *is* on my side? Who?" So two *or* three eunuchs looked out at him.
33 Then he said, "Throw her down." So they threw her down, and *some* of her blood spattered on the wall and on the horses; and he trampled her underfoot.
34 And when he had gone in, he ate and drank. Then he said, "Go now, see to this accursed *woman,* and bury her, for she was a king's daughter."
35 So they went to bury her, but they found no more of her than the skull and the feet and the palms of *her* hands.
➤ 36 Therefore they came back and told him. And he said, "This *is* the word of the LORD, which He spoke by His servant Elijah the Tishbite, saying, 'On the plot *of ground* at Jezreel dogs shall eat the flesh of Jezebel;[a]
37 'and the corpse of Jezebel shall be as refuse on the surface of the field, in the plot at Jezreel, so that they shall not say, "Here *lies* Jezebel." ' "

Ahab's Seventy Sons Killed

10 Now Ahab had seventy sons in Samaria. And Jehu wrote and sent letters to Samaria, to the rulers of Jezreel,[a] to the elders, and to those who reared Ahab's *sons,* saying:

2 Now as soon as this letter comes to you, since your master's sons *are* with you, and you have chariots and horses, a fortified city also, and weapons,
3 choose the best qualified of your master's sons, set *him* on his father's throne, and fight for your master's house.

4 But they were exceedingly afraid, and said, "Look, two kings could not stand up to him; how then can we stand?"
5 And he who *was* in charge of the house, and he who *was* in charge of the city, the elders also, and those who reared *the sons,* sent to Jehu, saying, "We *are* your servants, we will do all you tell us; but we will not make anyone king. Do *what is* good in your sight."
6 Then he wrote a second letter to them, saying:

If you *are* for me and will obey my voice, take the heads of the men, your master's sons, and come to me at Jezreel by this time tomorrow.

Now the king's sons, seventy persons, *were* with the great men of the city, *who* were rearing them.
7 So it was, when the letter came to them, that they took the king's sons and slaughtered seventy persons, put their heads in baskets and sent *them* to him at Jezreel.
8 Then a messenger came and told him, saying, "They have brought the heads of the king's sons." And he said, "Lay them in two heaps at the entrance of the gate until morning."
9 So it was, in the morning, that he went out and stood, and said to all the people, "You *are* righteous. Indeed I conspired against my master and killed him; but who killed all these?
10 "Know now that nothing shall fall to the earth of the word of the LORD which the LORD spoke concerning the house of Ahab; for the

9:27 [a]Literally *The Garden House* **9:36** [a]1 Kings 21:23
10:1 [a]Following Masoretic Text, Syriac, and Targum; Septuagint reads *Samaria;* Vulgate reads *city.*

LIFE LESSONS

➤ 9:36 — *Therefore they came back and told him. And he said, "This is the word of the LORD, which He spoke by His servant Elijah the Tishbite, saying, 'On the plot of ground at Jezreel dogs shall eat the flesh of Jezebel . . . .'"*

The Word of the Lord always comes to pass, for blessing or for judgment.

LORD has done what He spoke by His servant Elijah."
11 So Jehu killed all who remained of the house of Ahab in Jezreel, and all his great men and his close acquaintances and his priests, until he left him none remaining.

Ahaziah's Forty-two Brothers Killed

12 And he arose and departed and went to Samaria. On the way, at Beth Eked[a] of the Shepherds,
13 Jehu met with the brothers of Ahaziah king of Judah, and said, "Who *are* you?" So they answered, "We *are* the brothers of Ahaziah; we have come down to greet the sons of the king and the sons of the queen mother."
14 And he said, "Take them alive!" So they took them alive, and killed them at the well of Beth Eked, forty-two men; and he left none of them.

The Rest of Ahab's Family Killed

15 Now when he departed from there, he met Jehonadab the son of Rechab, *coming* to meet him; and he greeted him and said to him, "Is your heart right, as my heart *is* toward your heart?" And Jehonadab answered, "It is." *Jehu said,* "If it is, give *me* your hand." So he gave *him* his hand, and he took him up to him into the chariot.
16 Then he said, "Come with me, and see my zeal for the LORD." So they had him ride in his chariot.
17 And when he came to Samaria, he killed all who remained to Ahab in Samaria, till he had destroyed them, according to the word of the LORD which He spoke to Elijah.

Worshipers of Baal Killed

18 Then Jehu gathered all the people together, and said to them, "Ahab served Baal a little, Jehu will serve him much.
19 "Now therefore, call to me all the prophets of Baal, all his servants, and all his priests. Let no one be missing, for I have a great sacrifice for Baal. Whoever is missing shall not live." But Jehu acted deceptively, with the intent of destroying the worshipers of Baal.
20 And Jehu said, "Proclaim a solemn assembly for Baal." So they proclaimed *it.*
21 Then Jehu sent throughout all Israel; and all the worshipers of Baal came, so that there was not a man left who did not come. So they came into the temple[a] of Baal, and the temple of Baal was full from one end to the other.
22 And he said to the one in charge of the wardrobe, "Bring out vestments for all the worshipers of Baal." So he brought out vestments for them.
23 Then Jehu and Jehonadab the son of Rechab went into the temple of Baal, and said to the worshipers of Baal, "Search and see that no servants of the LORD are here with you, but only the worshipers of Baal."
24 So they went in to offer sacrifices and burnt offerings. Now Jehu had appointed for himself eighty men on the outside, and had said, "*If* any of the men whom I have brought into your hands escapes, *whoever lets him escape, it shall be* his life for the life of the other."
25 Now it happened, as soon as he had made an end of offering the burnt offering, that Jehu said to the guard and to the captains, "Go in *and* kill them; let no one come out!" And they killed them with the edge of the sword; then the guards and the officers threw *them* out, and went into the inner room of the temple of Baal.
26 And they brought the *sacred* pillars out of the temple of Baal and burned them.
27 Then they broke down the *sacred* pillar of Baal, and tore down the temple of Baal and made it a refuse dump to this day.
28 Thus Jehu destroyed Baal from Israel.
29 However Jehu did not turn away from the sins of Jeroboam the son of Nebat, who had made Israel sin, *that is,* from the golden calves that *were* at Bethel and Dan.
30 And the LORD said to Jehu, "Because you have done well in doing *what is* right in My sight, *and* have done to the house of Ahab all that *was* in My heart, your sons shall sit on the throne of Israel to the fourth *generation.*"
31 But Jehu took no heed to walk in the law of the LORD God of Israel with all his heart; for he did not depart from the sins of Jeroboam, who had made Israel sin.

Death of Jehu

32 In those days the LORD began to cut off *parts* of Israel; and Hazael conquered them in all the territory of Israel
33 from the Jordan eastward: all the land of Gilead—Gad, Reuben, and Manasseh—from

10:12 [a]Or *The Shearing House* 10:21 [a]Literally *house,* and so elsewhere in this chapter

LIFE LESSONS

➤ 10:29 — *However Jehu did not turn away from the sins of Jeroboam the son of Nebat, who had made Israel sin, that is, from the golden calves that were at Bethel and Dan.*

Jehu zealously obeyed the Word of the Lord . . . so long as it advanced his his career. But to maintain control over his people, he followed the pattern set by the evil Jeroboam. Incomplete obedience is blatant rebellion.

Aroer, which *is* by the River Arnon, including Gilead and Bashan.

34 Now the rest of the acts of Jehu, all that he did, and all his might, *are* they not written in the book of the chronicles of the kings of Israel?

35 So Jehu rested with his fathers, and they buried him in Samaria. Then Jehoahaz his son reigned in his place.

36 And the period that Jehu reigned over Israel in Samaria *was* twenty-eight years.

Athaliah Reigns in Judah

11 When Athaliah the mother of Ahaziah saw that her son was dead, she arose and destroyed all the royal heirs.

➤ 2 But Jehosheba, the daughter of King Joram, sister of Ahaziah, took Joash the son of Ahaziah, and stole him away from among the king's sons *who were* being murdered; and they hid him and his nurse in the bedroom, from Athaliah, so that he was not killed.

3 So he was hidden with her in the house of the LORD for six years, while Athaliah reigned over the land.

Joash Crowned King of Judah

4 In the seventh year Jehoiada sent and brought the captains of hundreds—of the bodyguards and the escorts—and brought them into the house of the LORD to him. And he made a covenant with them and took an oath from them in the house of the LORD, and showed them the king's son.

5 Then he commanded them, saying, "This *is* what you shall do: One-third of you who come on duty on the Sabbath shall be keeping watch over the king's house,

6 "one-third *shall be* at the gate of Sur, and one-third at the gate behind the escorts. You shall keep the watch of the house, lest it be broken down.

7 "The two contingents of you who go off duty on the Sabbath shall keep the watch of the house of the LORD for the king.

8 "But you shall surround the king on all sides, every man with his weapons in his hand; and whoever comes within range, let him be put to death. You are to be with the king as he goes out and as he comes in."

9 So the captains of the hundreds did according to all that Jehoiada the priest commanded. Each of them took his men who were to be on duty on the Sabbath, with those who were going off duty on the Sabbath, and came to Jehoiada the priest.

10 And the priest gave the captains of hundreds the spears and shields which *had belonged* to King David, that were in the temple of the LORD.

11 Then the escorts stood, every man with his weapons in his hand, all around the king, from the right side of the temple to the left side of the temple, by the altar and the house.

12 And he brought out the king's son, put the crown on him, and *gave him* the Testimony;[a] they made him king and anointed him, and they clapped their hands and said, "Long live the king!"

Death of Athaliah

13 Now when Athaliah heard the noise of the escorts *and* the people, she came to the people *in* the temple of the LORD.

14 When she looked, there was the king standing by a pillar according to custom; and the leaders and the trumpeters were by the king. All the people of the land were rejoicing and blowing trumpets. So Athaliah tore her clothes and cried out, "Treason! Treason!"

15 And Jehoiada the priest commanded the captains of the hundreds, the officers of the army, and said to them, "Take her outside under guard, and slay with the sword whoever follows her." For the priest had said, "Do not let her be killed in the house of the LORD."

16 So they seized her; and she went by way of the horses' entrance *into* the king's house, and there she was killed.

17 Then Jehoiada made a covenant between the LORD, the king, and the people, that they should be the LORD's people, and *also* between the king and the people. ➤

18 And all the people of the land went to the temple of Baal, and tore it down. They thoroughly broke in pieces its altars and images, and killed Mattan the priest of Baal before the altars. And the priest appointed officers over the house of the LORD.

11:12 [a]That is, the Law (compare Exodus 25:16, 21 and Deuteronomy 31:9)

LIFE LESSONS

➤ **11:2** — ***But Jehosheba, the daughter of King Joram, sister of Ahaziah, took Joash the son of Ahaziah, and stole him away from among the king's sons who were being murdered; and they hid him . . . .***

Through Athaliah, Satan tried to wipe out the Davidic line and so frustrate the promise of God leading to the Messiah. But no one, not even the devil, can derail any of God's promises.

➤ **11:17** — ***Then Jehoiada made a covenant between the LORD, the king, and the people, that they should be the LORD's people, and also between the king and the people.***

Jehoiada is a bright light in a dark time. He demonstrates that we can remain faithful to God and His Word even when the culture around us decays and turns rotten.

19 Then he took the captains of hundreds,
the bodyguards, the escorts, and all the people of the land; and they brought the king
down from the house of the LORD, and went
by way of the gate of the escorts to the king's
house. Then he sat on the throne of the kings.
20 So all the people of the land rejoiced; and
the city was quiet, for they had slain Athaliah
with the sword *in* the king's house.
21 Jehoash *was* seven years old when he became king.

Jehoash Repairs the Temple

12 In the seventh year of Jehu, Jehoash[a]
became king, and he reigned forty years
in Jerusalem. His mother's name *was* Zibiah
of Beersheba.
➤ 2 Jehoash did *what was* right in the sight of
the LORD all the days in which Jehoiada the
priest instructed him.
3 But the high places were not taken away;
the people still sacrificed and burned incense
on the high places.
4 And Jehoash said to the priests, "All the
money of the dedicated gifts that are brought
into the house of the LORD—each man's census money, each man's assessment money[a]—
and all the money that a man purposes in his
heart to bring into the house of the LORD,
5 "let the priests take *it* themselves, each
from his constituency; and let them repair the
damages of the temple, wherever any dilapi-
dation is found."
6 Now it was so, by the twenty-third year of
King Jehoash, *that* the priests had not repaired the damages of the temple.
7 So King Jehoash called Jehoiada the
priest and the *other* priests, and said to them,
"Why have you not repaired the damages of
the temple? Now therefore, do not take *more*
money from your constituency, but deliver it
for repairing the damages of the temple."
8 And the priests agreed that they would
neither receive *more* money from the people,
nor repair the damages of the temple.
9 Then Jehoiada the priest took a chest,
bored a hole in its lid, and set it beside the
altar, on the right side as one comes into the
house of the LORD; and the priests who kept
the door put there all the money brought into
the house of the LORD.
10 So it was, whenever they saw that *there*
was much money in the chest, that the king's
scribe and the high priest came up and put it
in bags, and counted the money that was
found in the house of the LORD.
11 Then they gave the money, which had
been apportioned, into the hands of those
who did the work, who had the oversight of
the house of the LORD; and they paid it out
to the carpenters and builders who worked on
the house of the LORD,
12 and to masons and stonecutters, and for
buying timber and hewn stone, to repair the
damage of the house of the LORD, and for all
that was paid out to repair the temple.
13 However there were not made for the
house of the LORD basins of silver, trimmers,
sprinkling-bowls, trumpets, any articles of
gold or articles of silver, from the money
brought into the house of the LORD.
14 But they gave that to the workmen, and
they repaired the house of the LORD with it.
15 Moreover they did not require an account ➤
from the men into whose hand they delivered
the money to be paid to workmen, for they
dealt faithfully.
16 The money from the trespass offerings
and the money from the sin offerings was not
brought into the house of the LORD. It belonged to the priests.

Hazael Threatens Jerusalem

17 Hazael king of Syria went up and fought
against Gath, and took it; then Hazael set his
face to go up to Jerusalem.
18 And Jehoash king of Judah took all the sacred things that his fathers, Jehoshaphat and
Jehoram and Ahaziah, kings of Judah, had
dedicated, and his own sacred things, and all
the gold found in the treasuries of the house
of the LORD and in the king's house, and sent
them to Hazael king of Syria. Then he went
away from Jerusalem.

Death of Joash

19 Now the rest of the acts of Joash,[a] and all
that he did, *are* they not written in the book of
the chronicles of the kings of Judah?
20 And his servants arose and formed a conspiracy, and killed Joash in the house of the
Millo,[a] which goes down to Silla.

12:1 [a]Spelled *Joash* in 11:2ff **12:4** [a]Compare Leviticus 27:2ff **12:19** [a]Spelled *Jehoash* in 12:1ff **12:20** [a]Literally *The Landfill*

LIFE LESSONS

➤ 12:2 — *Jehoash did what was right in the sight of the LORD all the days in which Jehoiada the priest instructed him.*

Jehoash illustrates that we must make our faith our own. We must individually choose to make Jesus Christ the Lord over each of our hearts. We cannot long survive on the faith of others.

➤ 12:15 — *Moreover they did not require an account from the men into whose hand they delivered the money to be paid to workmen, for they dealt faithfully.*

God looks for faithful men and women to do His work. The Bible asks, "who can find a faithful man?" (Prov. 20:6). Are you such a faithful person?

21 For Jozachar[a] the son of Shimeath and Jehozabad the son of Shomer,[b] his servants,
struck him. So he died, and they buried him
with his fathers in the City of David. Then
Amaziah his son reigned in his place.

Jehoahaz Reigns in Israel

13 In the twenty-third year of Joash[a] the
son of Ahaziah, king of Judah, Jehoahaz the son of Jehu became king over Israel
in Samaria, *and reigned* seventeen years.
2 And he did evil in the sight of the LORD,
and followed the sins of Jeroboam the son of
Nebat, who had made Israel sin. He did not
depart from them.
3 Then the anger of the LORD was aroused
against Israel, and He delivered them into the
hand of Hazael king of Syria, and into the
hand of Ben-Hadad the son of Hazael, all
their days.
➤ 4 So Jehoahaz pleaded with the LORD, and
the LORD listened to him; for He saw the oppression of Israel, because the king of Syria
oppressed them.
5 Then the LORD gave Israel a deliverer, so
that they escaped from under the hand of the
Syrians; and the children of Israel dwelt in
their tents as before.
6 Nevertheless they did not depart from the
sins of the house of Jeroboam, who had made
Israel sin, *but* walked in them; and the
wooden image[a] also remained in Samaria.
7 For He left of the army of Jehoahaz only
fifty horsemen, ten chariots, and ten thousand foot soldiers; for the king of Syria had
destroyed them and made them like the dust
at threshing.
8 Now the rest of the acts of Jehoahaz, all
that he did, and his might, *are* they not written in the book of the chronicles of the kings
of Israel?
9 So Jehoahaz rested with his fathers, and
they buried him in Samaria. Then Joash his
son reigned in his place.

Jehoash Reigns in Israel

10 In the thirty-seventh year of Joash king of
Judah, Jehoash[a] the son of Jehoahaz became
king over Israel in Samaria, *and reigned* sixteen years.
11 And he did evil in the sight of the LORD. He
did not depart from all the sins of Jeroboam
the son of Nebat, who made Israel sin, *but*
walked in them.
12 Now the rest of the acts of Joash, all that
he did, and his might with which he fought
against Amaziah king of Judah, *are* they not
written in the book of the chronicles of the
kings of Israel?
13 So Joash rested with his fathers. Then Jeroboam sat on his throne. And Joash was
buried in Samaria with the kings of Israel.

Death of Elisha

14 Elisha had become sick with the illness of ➤
which he would die. Then Joash the king of
Israel came down to him, and wept over his
face, and said, "O my father, my father, the
chariots of Israel and their horsemen!"
15 And Elisha said to him, "Take a bow and
some arrows." So he took himself a bow and
some arrows.
16 Then he said to the king of Israel, "Put your
hand on the bow." So he put his hand *on it*, and
Elisha put his hands on the king's hands.
17 And he said, "Open the east window";
and he opened *it*. Then Elisha said, "Shoot";
and he shot. And he said, "The arrow of the
LORD's deliverance and the arrow of deliverance from Syria; for you must strike the Syrians at Aphek till you have destroyed *them*."
18 Then he said, "Take the arrows"; so he
took *them*. And he said to the king of Israel,
"Strike the ground"; so he struck three times,
and stopped.
19 And the man of God was angry with him,
and said, "You should have struck five or six
times; then you would have struck Syria till
you had destroyed *it!* But now you will strike
Syria *only* three times."
20 Then Elisha died, and they buried him.
And the *raiding* bands from Moab invaded
the land in the spring of the year.
21 So it was, as they were burying a man,
that suddenly they spied a band *of raiders;*
and they put the man in the tomb of Elisha;
and when the man was let down and touched
the bones of Elisha, he revived and stood on
his feet.

12:21 [a]Called *Zabad* in 2 Chronicles 24:26 [b]Called *Shimrith* in 2 Chronicles 24:26 **13:1** [a]Spelled *Jehoash* in 12:1ff **13:6** [a]Hebrew *Asherah,* a Canaanite goddess **13:10** [a]Spelled *Joash* in verse 9

LIFE LESSONS

➤ 13:4 — *So Jehoahaz pleaded with the LORD, and the LORD listened to him; for He saw the oppression of Israel, because the king of Syria oppressed them.*

It is the Lord's nature to show mercy and to respond with compassion to suffering. And yet He will not tolerate rebellion forever.

➤ 13:14 — *Elisha had become sick with the illness of which he would die . . . .*

Elisha performed twice as many miracles as Elijah and raised a boy from the dead, yet he himself died of an illness. Lack of faith? Hardly. God endorsed his ministry by performing one final miracle through him after his death (2 Kin. 13:21).

Israel Recaptures Cities from Syria
22 And Hazael king of Syria oppressed Israel
all the days of Jehoahaz.
➤ 23 But the LORD was gracious to them, had
compassion on them, and regarded them, because of His covenant with Abraham, Isaac,
and Jacob, and would not yet destroy them or
cast them from His presence.
24 Now Hazael king of Syria died. Then Ben-
Hadad his son reigned in his place.
25 And Jehoash[a] the son of Jehoahaz recaptured from the hand of Ben-Hadad, the son of
Hazael, the cities which he had taken out of
the hand of Jehoahaz his father by war. Three
times Joash defeated him and recaptured the
cities of Israel.

Amaziah Reigns in Judah
14 In the second year of Joash the son of
Jehoahaz, king of Israel, Amaziah the
son of Joash, king of Judah, became king.
2 He was twenty-five years old when he became king, and he reigned twenty-nine years
in Jerusalem. His mother's name was Jehoaddan of Jerusalem.
3 And he did *what was* right in the sight of
the LORD, yet not like his father David; he did
everything as his father Joash had done.
4 However the high places were not taken
away, and the people still sacrificed and
burned incense on the high places.
5 Now it happened, as soon as the kingdom
was established in his hand, that he executed
his servants who had murdered his father the
king.
6 But the children of the murderers he did
not execute, according to what is written in
the Book of the Law of Moses, in which the
LORD commanded, saying, "Fathers shall not
be put to death for their children, nor shall
children be put to death for their fathers; but
a person shall be put to death for his own
sin."[a]
7 He killed ten thousand Edomites in the
Valley of Salt, and took Sela by war, and
called its name Joktheel to this day.
8 Then Amaziah sent messengers to Jehoash[a] the son of Jehoahaz, the son of Jehu,
king of Israel, saying, "Come, let us face one
another *in battle*."
9 And Jehoash king of Israel sent to
Amaziah king of Judah, saying, "The thistle
that *was* in Lebanon sent to the cedar that
was in Lebanon, saying, 'Give your daughter
to my son as wife'; and a wild beast that *was*
in Lebanon passed by and trampled the thistle.
10 "You have indeed defeated Edom, and ➤
your heart has lifted you up. Glory *in that,*
and stay at home; for why should you meddle
with trouble so that you fall—you and Judah
with you?"
11 But Amaziah would not heed. Therefore
Jehoash king of Israel went out; so he and
Amaziah king of Judah faced one another at
Beth Shemesh, which *belongs* to Judah.
12 And Judah was defeated by Israel, and
every man fled to his tent.
13 Then Jehoash king of Israel captured
Amaziah king of Judah, the son of Jehoash,
the son of Ahaziah, at Beth Shemesh; and he
went to Jerusalem, and broke down the wall
of Jerusalem from the Gate of Ephraim to the
Corner Gate—four hundred cubits.
14 And he took all the gold and silver, all the
articles that were found in the house of the
LORD and in the treasuries of the king's house,
and hostages, and returned to Samaria.
15 Now the rest of the acts of Jehoash which
he did—his might, and how he fought with
Amaziah king of Judah—*are* they not written
in the book of the chronicles of the kings of
Israel?
16 So Jehoash rested with his fathers, and
was buried in Samaria with the kings of Israel. Then Jeroboam his son reigned in his
place.
17 Amaziah the son of Joash, king of Judah,
lived fifteen years after the death of Jehoash
the son of Jehoahaz, king of Israel.
18 Now the rest of the acts of Amaziah, *are*
they not written in the book of the chronicles
of the kings of Judah?
19 And they formed a conspiracy against him
in Jerusalem, and he fled to Lachish; but they
sent after him to Lachish and killed him
there.
20 Then they brought him on horses, and he
was buried at Jerusalem with his fathers in
the City of David.

13:25 [a]Spelled *Joash* in verses 12–14, 25 **14:6** [a]Deuteronomy 24:16 **14:8** [a]Spelled *Joash* in 13:12ff and 2 Chronicles 25:17ff

LIFE LESSONS

➤ **13:23 — *But the LORD was gracious to them, had compassion on them, and regarded them, because of His covenant with Abraham, Isaac, and Jacob . . . .***

We owe our very lives to the promises of God. He shows us compassion, grace, and favor not because we earn it, but because His loving nature does not change (see Mal. 3:6).

➤ **14:10 — *"You have indeed defeated Edom, and your heart has lifted you up. Glory in that, and stay at home; for why should you meddle with trouble so that you fall—you and Judah with you?"***

Pride can urge us to do foolish things. God tells us, "Pride goes before destruction, and a haughty spirit before a fall" (Prov. 16:18). God used a wicked king to admonish Amaziah, but he refused to listen.

21 And all the people of Judah took Azariah,[a]
who *was* sixteen years old, and made him
king instead of his father Amaziah.
22 He built Elath and restored it to Judah,
after the king rested with his fathers.

Jeroboam II Reigns in Israel

23 In the fifteenth year of Amaziah the son of
Joash, king of Judah, Jeroboam the son of
Joash, king of Israel, became king in Samaria, *and reigned* forty-one years.
24 And he did evil in the sight of the LORD; he
did not depart from all the sins of Jeroboam
the son of Nebat, who had made Israel sin.
25 He restored the territory of Israel from the
entrance of Hamath to the Sea of the Arabah,
according to the word of the LORD God of Israel, which He had spoken through His servant Jonah the son of Amittai, the prophet
who *was* from Gath Hepher.
26 For the LORD saw *that* the affliction of Israel *was* very bitter; and whether bond or
free, there was no helper for Israel.
➤ 27 And the LORD did not say that He would
blot out the name of Israel from under
heaven; but He saved them by the hand of Jeroboam the son of Joash.
28 Now the rest of the acts of Jeroboam, and
all that he did—his might, how he made war,
and how he recaptured for Israel, from Damascus and Hamath, *what had belonged* to
Judah—*are* they not written in the book of the
chronicles of the kings of Israel?
29 So Jeroboam rested with his fathers, the
kings of Israel. Then Zechariah his son reigned
in his place.

Azariah Reigns in Judah

15 In the twenty-seventh year of Jeroboam king of Israel, Azariah the son
of Amaziah, king of Judah, became king.
2 He was sixteen years old when he became
king, and he reigned fifty-two years in Jerusalem. His mother's name *was* Jecholiah of Jerusalem.
3 And he did *what was* right in the sight of
the LORD, according to all that his father
Amaziah had done,
4 except that the high places were not removed; the people still sacrificed and burned
incense on the high places.
5 Then the LORD struck the king, so that he ≺
was a leper until the day of his death; so he
dwelt in an isolated house. And Jotham the
king's son *was* over the *royal* house, judging
the people of the land.
6 Now the rest of the acts of Azariah, and all
that he did, *are* they not written in the book of
the chronicles of the kings of Judah?
7 So Azariah rested with his fathers, and
they buried him with his fathers in the City of
David. Then Jotham his son reigned in his
place.

Zechariah Reigns in Israel

8 In the thirty-eighth year of Azariah king
of Judah, Zechariah the son of Jeroboam
reigned over Israel in Samaria six months.
9 And he did evil in the sight of the LORD, as
his fathers had done; he did not depart from
the sins of Jeroboam the son of Nebat, who
had made Israel sin.
10 Then Shallum the son of Jabesh conspired
against him, and struck and killed him in
front of the people; and he reigned in his
place.
11 Now the rest of the acts of Zechariah, indeed they *are* written in the book of the
chronicles of the kings of Israel.
12 This *was* the word of the LORD which He ≺
spoke to Jehu, saying, "Your sons shall sit on
the throne of Israel to the fourth *generation*."[a]
And so it was.

Shallum Reigns in Israel

13 Shallum the son of Jabesh became king in
the thirty-ninth year of Uzziah[a] king of Judah; and he reigned a full month in Samaria.
14 For Menahem the son of Gadi went up
from Tirzah, came to Samaria, and struck
Shallum the son of Jabesh in Samaria and
killed him; and he reigned in his place.
15 Now the rest of the acts of Shallum, and
the conspiracy which he led, indeed they *are*

14:21 [a]Called *Uzziah* in 2 Chronicles 26:1ff, Isaiah 6:1, and elsewhere **15:12** [a]2 Kings 10:30 **15:13** [a]Called *Azariah* in 14:21ff and 15:1ff

LIFE LESSONS

➤ 14:27 — *And the LORD did not say that He would blot out the name of Israel from under heaven; but He saved them by the hand of Jeroboam the son of Joash.*

The sovereign Lord uses both good and evil men to fulfill His purposes. What He has said, He will do; but we must take care not to misrepresent or misconstrue His words.

➤ 15:5 — *Then the LORD struck the king, so that he was a leper until the day of his death; so he dwelt in an isolated house.*

Why did God strike Amaziah with leprosy? Second Chronicles 26:16–21 tells us that when the king became strong, he became proud and attempted to usurp the duties of a priest. God immediately made him a leper.

➤ 15:12 — *This was the word of the LORD which He spoke to Jehu, saying, "Your sons shall sit on the throne of Israel to the fourth generation." And so it was.*

Why does the Bible so often point out that the predictions made by God's prophets came true? So that we would have confidence that whatever God speaks is absolutely true.

written in the book of the chronicles of the
kings of Israel.
➤ 16 Then from Tirzah, Menahem attacked Tiph-
sah, all who *were* there, and its territory. Because they did not surrender, therefore he
attacked *it*. All the women there who were
with child he ripped open.

Menahem Reigns in Israel

17 In the thirty-ninth year of Azariah king of
Judah, Menahem the son of Gadi became
king over Israel, *and reigned* ten years in Samaria.
18 And he did evil in the sight of the LORD; he
did not depart all his days from the sins of
Jeroboam the son of Nebat, who had made Israel sin.
19 Pul[a] king of Assyria came against the
land; and Menahem gave Pul a thousand talents of silver, that his hand might be with him
to strengthen the kingdom under his control.
20 And Menahem exacted the money from
Israel, from all the very wealthy, from each
man fifty shekels of silver, to give to the king
of Assyria. So the king of Assyria turned
back, and did not stay there in the land.
21 Now the rest of the acts of Menahem, and
all that he did, *are* they not written in the
book of the chronicles of the kings of Israel?
22 So Menahem rested with his fathers. Then
Pekahiah his son reigned in his place.

Pekahiah Reigns in Israel

23 In the fiftieth year of Azariah king of Judah, Pekahiah the son of Menahem became
king over Israel in Samaria, *and reigned* two
years.
24 And he did evil in the sight of the LORD; he
did not depart from the sins of Jeroboam the
son of Nebat, who had made Israel sin.
25 Then Pekah the son of Remaliah, an officer of his, conspired against him and killed
him in Samaria, in the citadel of the king's
house, along with Argob and Arieh; and with
him were fifty men of Gilead. He killed him
and reigned in his place.
26 Now the rest of the acts of Pekahiah, and
all that he did, indeed they *are* written in the
book of the chronicles of the kings of Israel.

Pekah Reigns in Israel

27 In the fifty-second year of Azariah king of
Judah, Pekah the son of Remaliah became
king over Israel in Samaria, *and reigned*
twenty years.
28 And he did evil in the sight of the LORD; he
did not depart from the sins of Jeroboam the
son of Nebat, who had made Israel sin.
29 In the days of Pekah king of Israel,
Tiglath-Pileser king of Assyria came and took
Ijon, Abel Beth Maachah, Janoah, Kedesh,
Hazor, Gilead, and Galilee, all the land of
Naphtali; and he carried them captive to Assyria.
30 Then Hoshea the son of Elah led a conspiracy against Pekah the son of Remaliah,
and struck and killed him; so he reigned in
his place in the twentieth year of Jotham the
son of Uzziah.
31 Now the rest of the acts of Pekah, and all
that he did, indeed they *are* written in the
book of the chronicles of the kings of Israel.

Jotham Reigns in Judah

32 In the second year of Pekah the son of Remaliah, king of Israel, Jotham the son of
Uzziah, king of Judah, began to reign.
33 He was twenty-five years old when he became king, and he reigned sixteen years in Jerusalem. His mother's name *was* Jerusha[a] the
daughter of Zadok.
34 And he did *what was* right in the sight of
the LORD; he did according to all that his father Uzziah had done.
35 However the high places were not removed; the people still sacrificed and burned
incense on the high places. He built the Upper
Gate of the house of the LORD.
36 Now the rest of the acts of Jotham, and all
that he did, *are* they not written in the book of
the chronicles of the kings of Judah?
37 In those days the LORD began to send
Rezin king of Syria and Pekah the son of Remaliah against Judah.
38 So Jotham rested with his fathers, and
was buried with his fathers in the City of David his father. Then Ahaz his son reigned in
his place.

Ahaz Reigns in Judah

16 In the seventeenth year of Pekah the
son of Remaliah, Ahaz the son of
Jotham, king of Judah, began to reign.
2 Ahaz *was* twenty years old when he became king, and he reigned sixteen years in Jerusalem; and he did not do *what was* right in
the sight of the LORD his God, as his father
David *had done.*
3 But he walked in the way of the kings of

15:19 [a]That is, Tiglath-Pileser III (compare verse 29)
15:33 [a]Spelled *Jerushah* in 2 Chronicles 27:1

LIFE LESSONS

➤ 15:16 — *Then from Tirzah, Menahem attacked Tiph-sah, all who were there, and its territory. Because they did not surrender, therefore he attacked it.*

As God prepares to judge His rebellious people, He usually first gives them a taste of the judgment to come, giving them a further opportunity to repent. But Israel ignored His warnings.

Israel; indeed he made his son pass through
the fire, according to the abominations of the
nations whom the LORD had cast out from before the children of Israel.
4 And he sacrificed and burned incense on
the high places, on the hills, and under every
green tree.
5 Then Rezin king of Syria and Pekah the
son of Remaliah, king of Israel, came up to Jerusalem to *make* war; and they besieged
Ahaz but could not overcome *him*.
6 At that time Rezin king of Syria captured
Elath for Syria, and drove the men of Judah
from Elath. Then the Edomites[a] went to Elath,
and dwell there to this day.
7 So Ahaz sent messengers to Tiglath-
Pileser king of Assyria, saying, "I *am* your
servant and your son. Come up and save me
from the hand of the king of Syria and from
the hand of the king of Israel, who rise up
against me."
8 And Ahaz took the silver and gold that
was found in the house of the LORD, and in the
treasuries of the king's house, and sent *it as* a
present to the king of Assyria.
9 So the king of Assyria heeded him; for the
king of Assyria went up against Damascus
and took it, carried *its people* captive to Kir,
and killed Rezin.
10 Now King Ahaz went to Damascus to
meet Tiglath-Pileser king of Assyria, and saw
an altar that *was* at Damascus; and King
Ahaz sent to Urijah the priest the design of
the altar and its pattern, according to all its
workmanship.
11 Then Urijah the priest built an altar according to all that King Ahaz had sent from
Damascus. So Urijah the priest made *it* before King Ahaz came back from Damascus.
12 And when the king came back from Damascus, the king saw the altar; and the king
approached the altar and made offerings on
it.
13 So he burned his burnt offering and his
grain offering; and he poured his drink offering and sprinkled the blood of his peace offerings on the altar.
14 He also brought the bronze altar which
was before the LORD, from the front of the
temple—from between the *new* altar and the
house of the LORD—and put it on the north
side of the *new* altar.
15 Then King Ahaz commanded Urijah the
priest, saying, "On the great *new* altar burn
the morning burnt offering, the evening grain
offering, the king's burnt sacrifice, and his
grain offering, with the burnt offering of all
the people of the land, their grain offering,
and their drink offerings; and sprinkle on it
all the blood of the burnt offering and all the
blood of the sacrifice. And the bronze altar
shall be for me to inquire *by*."
16 Thus did Urijah the priest, according to all
that King Ahaz commanded.
17 And King Ahaz cut off the panels of the
carts, and removed the lavers from them; and
he took down the Sea from the bronze oxen
that *were* under it, and put it on a pavement of
stones.
18 Also he removed the Sabbath pavilion
which they had built in the temple, and he removed the king's outer entrance from the
house of the LORD, on account of the king of
Assyria.
19 Now the rest of the acts of Ahaz which he
did, *are* they not written in the book of the
chronicles of the kings of Judah?
20 So Ahaz rested with his fathers, and was
buried with his fathers in the City of David.
Then Hezekiah his son reigned in his place.

Hoshea Reigns in Israel

17 In the twelfth year of Ahaz king of
Judah, Hoshea the son of Elah became
king of Israel in Samaria, *and he reigned* nine
years.
2 And he did evil in the sight of the LORD,
but not as the kings of Israel who were before
him.
3 Shalmaneser king of Assyria came up
against him; and Hoshea became his vassal,
and paid him tribute money.
4 And the king of Assyria uncovered a conspiracy by Hoshea; for he had sent messengers to So, king of Egypt, and brought no
tribute to the king of Assyria, as *he had done*
year by year. Therefore the king of Assyria
shut him up, and bound him in prison.

Israel Carried Captive to Assyria

5 Now the king of Assyria went throughout
all the land, and went up to Samaria and besieged it for three years.
6 In the ninth year of Hoshea, the king of
Assyria took Samaria and carried Israel away
to Assyria, and placed them in Halah and by
the Habor, the River of Gozan, and in the
cities of the Medes.
7 For so it was that the children of Israel had
sinned against the LORD their God, who had
brought them up out of the land of Egypt,
from under the hand of Pharaoh king of
Egypt; and they had feared other gods,
8 and had walked in the statutes of the nations whom the LORD had cast out from before the children of Israel, and of the kings of
Israel, which they had made.
9 Also the children of Israel secretly did
against the LORD their God things that *were*
not right, and they built for themselves high
places in all their cities, from watchtower to
fortified city.
10 They set up for themselves *sacred* pillars
and wooden images[a] on every high hill and
under every green tree.

16:6 [a]Some ancient authorities read *Syrians.* **17:10** [a]Hebrew *Asherim,* Canaanite deities

11 There they burned incense on all the
high places, like the nations whom the
LORD had carried away before them; and they
did wicked things to provoke the LORD to anger,
12 for they served idols, of which the LORD
had said to them, "You shall not do this thing."
13 Yet the LORD testified against Israel and
against Judah, by all of His prophets, every
seer, saying, "Turn from your evil ways, and
keep My commandments *and* My statutes, according to all the law which I commanded
your fathers, and which I sent to you by My
servants the prophets."
➤ 14 Nevertheless they would not hear, but
stiffened their necks, like the necks of their
fathers, who did not believe in the LORD their
God.
15 And they rejected His statutes and His
covenant that He had made with their fathers,
and His testimonies which He had testified
against them; they followed idols, became
idolaters, and *went* after the nations who
were all around them, *concerning* whom the
LORD had charged them that they should not
do like them.
16 So they left all the commandments of the
LORD their God, made for themselves a
molded image *and* two calves, made a
wooden image and worshiped all the host of
heaven, and served Baal.
17 And they caused their sons and daughters
to pass through the fire, practiced witchcraft
and soothsaying, and sold themselves to do
evil in the sight of the LORD, to provoke Him
to anger.
➤ 18 Therefore the LORD was very angry with
Israel, and removed them from His sight;
there was none left but the tribe of Judah
alone.
19 Also Judah did not keep the commandments of the LORD their God, but walked in
the statutes of Israel which they made.
20 And the LORD rejected all the descendants
of Israel, afflicted them, and delivered them
into the hand of plunderers, until He had cast
them from His sight.
21 For He tore Israel from the house of David, and they made Jeroboam the son of
Nebat king. Then Jeroboam drove Israel from
following the LORD, and made them commit a
great sin.
22 For the children of Israel walked in all the
sins of Jeroboam which he did; they did not
depart from them,
23 until the LORD removed Israel out of His
sight, as He had said by all His servants
the prophets. So Israel was carried away
from their own land to Assyria, *as it is* to this
day.

Assyria Resettles Samaria

24 Then the king of Assyria brought *people*
from Babylon, Cuthah, Ava, Hamath, and
from Sepharvaim, and placed *them* in the
cities of Samaria instead of the children of Israel; and they took possession of Samaria
and dwelt in its cities.
25 And it was so, at the beginning of their
dwelling there, *that* they did not fear the
LORD; therefore the LORD sent lions among
them, which killed *some* of them.
26 So they spoke to the king of Assyria, saying, "The nations whom you have removed
and placed in the cities of Samaria do not
know the rituals of the God of the land;
therefore He has sent lions among them, and
indeed, they are killing them because they
do not know the rituals of the God of the
land."
27 Then the king of Assyria commanded,
saying, "Send there one of the priests whom
you brought from there; let him go and dwell
there, and let him teach them the rituals of
the God of the land."
28 Then one of the priests whom they had
carried away from Samaria came and dwelt
in Bethel, and taught them how they should
fear the LORD.
29 However every nation continued to make
gods of its own, and put *them* in the shrines
on the high places which the Samaritans had
made, *every* nation in the cities where they
dwelt.
30 The men of Babylon made Succoth
Benoth, the men of Cuth made Nergal, the
men of Hamath made Ashima,
31 and the Avites made Nibhaz and Tartak;
and the Sepharvites burned their children in
fire to Adrammelech and Anammelech, the
gods of Sepharvaim.
32 So they feared the LORD, and from every
class they appointed for themselves priests of
the high places, who sacrificed for them in
the shrines of the high places.

LIFE LESSONS

➤ 17:14 — *Nevertheless they would not hear, but stiffened their necks, like the necks of their fathers, who did not believe in the LORD their God.*

The real root of disobedience is unbelief. We disobey God when we do not believe either what He promises or what He instructs.

➤ 17:18 — *Therefore the LORD was very angry with Israel, and removed them from His sight; there was none left but the tribe of Judah alone.*

God is amazingly patient, but as David said, "He will not always strive with us, nor will He keep His anger forever" (Ps. 103:9). There is a point of no return.

33 They feared the LORD, yet served their
own gods—according to the rituals of the nations from among whom they were carried
away.
34 To this day they continue practicing the
former rituals; they do not fear the LORD, nor
do they follow their statutes or their ordinances, or the law and commandment which
the LORD had commanded the children of Jacob, whom He named Israel,
35 with whom the LORD had made a covenant
and charged them, saying: "You shall not fear
other gods, nor bow down to them nor serve
them nor sacrifice to them;
36 "but the LORD, who brought you up from
the land of Egypt with great power and an
outstretched arm, Him you shall fear, Him
you shall worship, and to Him you shall offer
sacrifice.
37 "And the statutes, the ordinances, the law,
and the commandment which He wrote for
you, you shall be careful to observe forever;
you shall not fear other gods.
38 "And the covenant that I have made with
you, you shall not forget, nor shall you fear
other gods.
39 "But the LORD your God you shall fear;
and He will deliver you from the hand of all
your enemies."
40 However they did not obey, but they followed their former rituals.
41 So these nations feared the LORD, yet
served their carved images; also their children and their children's children have continued doing as their fathers did, even to this
day.

Hezekiah Reigns in Judah

18 Now it came to pass in the third year of
Hoshea the son of Elah, king of Israel,
that Hezekiah the son of Ahaz, king of Judah,
began to reign.
2 He was twenty-five years old when he became king, and he reigned twenty-nine years
in Jerusalem. His mother's name *was* Abi[a] the
daughter of Zechariah.
3 And he did *what was* right in the sight of
the LORD, according to all that his father David had done.
4 He removed the high places and broke the
sacred pillars, cut down the wooden image[a]
and broke in pieces the bronze serpent that
Moses had made; for until those days the children of Israel burned incense to it, and called
it Nehushtan.[b]
5 He trusted in the LORD God of Israel, so
that after him was none like him among all
the kings of Judah, nor who were before him.
6 For he held fast to the LORD; he did not depart from following Him, but kept His commandments, which the LORD had commanded
Moses.
7 The LORD was with him; he prospered
wherever he went. And he rebelled against
the king of Assyria and did not serve him.
8 He subdued the Philistines, as far as Gaza
and its territory, from watchtower to fortified
city.
9 Now it came to pass in the fourth year of
King Hezekiah, which *was* the seventh year
of Hoshea the son of Elah, king of Israel, *that*
Shalmaneser king of Assyria came up against
Samaria and besieged it.
10 And at the end of three years they took it.
In the sixth year of Hezekiah, that *is*, the
ninth year of Hoshea king of Israel, Samaria
was taken.
11 Then the king of Assyria carried Israel
away captive to Assyria, and put them in
Halah and by the Habor, the River of Gozan,
and in the cities of the Medes,
12 because they did not obey the voice of the
LORD their God, but transgressed His covenant *and* all that Moses the servant of the
LORD had commanded; and they would neither hear nor do *them*.
13 And in the fourteenth year of King
Hezekiah, Sennacherib king of Assyria came
up against all the fortified cities of Judah and
took them.
14 Then Hezekiah king of Judah sent to the

18:2 [a]Called *Abijah* in 2 Chronicles 29:1ff **18:4** [a]Hebrew *Asherah*, a Canaanite goddess [b]Literally *Bronze Thing*

LIFE LESSONS

17:33 — *They feared the LORD, yet served their own gods—according to the rituals of the nations from among whom they were carried away.*

God demands and deserves our exclusive allegiance. He will not share our love with other gods. Jesus said, "You shall worship the Lord your God, and Him only you shall serve" (Matt. 4:10).

17:34 — *To this day they continue practicing the former rituals; they do not fear the LORD, nor do they follow their statutes or their ordinances. . . .*

To fear the Lord AND to serve other gods is not to fear the Lord at all.

18:4 — *He . . . broke in pieces the bronze serpent that Moses had made; for until those days the children of Israel burned incense to it, and called it Nehushtan.*

When we take something made to be good and turn it into something vile, it is time to get rid of it entirely, no matter how much good tradition lies behind it.

18:7 — *The LORD was with him; he prospered wherever he went.*

Because Hezekiah wholeheartedly followed the Lord, he obeyed Him. And because the king obeyed Him, "the LORD was with him" and "he prospered wherever he went."

king of Assyria at Lachish, saying, "I have
done wrong; turn away from me; whatever
you impose on me I will pay." And the king of
Assyria assessed Hezekiah king of Judah
three hundred talents of silver and thirty talents of gold.
15 So Hezekiah gave *him* all the silver that
was found in the house of the LORD and in the
treasuries of the king's house.
16 At that time Hezekiah stripped *the gold*
from the doors of the temple of the LORD, and
from the pillars which Hezekiah king of Judah had overlaid, and gave it to the king of
Assyria.

Sennacherib Boasts Against the LORD

17 Then the king of Assyria sent *the* Tartan,[a]
the Rabsaris,[b] *and the* Rabshakeh[c] from Lachish, with a great army against Jerusalem, to
King Hezekiah. And they went up and came
to Jerusalem. When they had come up, they
went and stood by the aqueduct from the
upper pool, which *was* on the highway to the
Fuller's Field.
18 And when they had called to the king, Eliakim the son of Hilkiah, who *was* over the
household, Shebna the scribe, and Joah the
son of Asaph, the recorder, came out to them.
19 Then *the* Rabshakeh said to them, "Say
now to Hezekiah, 'Thus says the great king,
the king of Assyria: "What confidence *is* this
in which you trust?
20 "You speak of *having* plans and power for
war; but *they are* mere words. And in whom
do you trust, that you rebel against me?
21 "Now look! You are trusting in the staff of
this broken reed, Egypt, on which if a man
leans, it will go into his hand and pierce it. So
is Pharaoh king of Egypt to all who trust in
him.
22 "But if you say to me, 'We trust in the LORD
our God,' *is* it not He whose high places and
whose altars Hezekiah has taken away, and
said to Judah and Jerusalem, 'You shall worship before this altar in Jerusalem'?"'
23 "Now therefore, I urge you, give a pledge
to my master the king of Assyria, and I will
give you two thousand horses—if you are able
on your part to put riders on them!
24 "How then will you repel one captain of
the least of my master's servants, and put your
trust in Egypt for chariots and horsemen?
25 "Have I now come up without the LORD
against this place to destroy it? The LORD said
to me, 'Go up against this land, and destroy it.'"
26 Then Eliakim the son of Hilkiah, Shebna,
and Joah said to *the* Rabshakeh, "Please speak
to your servants in Aramaic, for we understand *it;* and do not speak to us in Hebrew[a] in
the hearing of the people who *are* on the wall."
27 But *the* Rabshakeh said to them, "Has my
master sent me to your master and to you to
speak these words, and not to the men who sit
on the wall, who will eat and drink their own
waste with you?"
28 Then *the* Rabshakeh stood and called out
with a loud voice in Hebrew, and spoke, saying, "Hear the word of the great king, the king
of Assyria!
29 "Thus says the king: 'Do not let Hezekiah
deceive you, for he shall not be able to deliver
you from his hand;
30 'nor let Hezekiah make you trust in the
LORD, saying, "The LORD will surely deliver
us; this city shall not be given into the hand of
the king of Assyria."'
31 "Do not listen to Hezekiah; for thus says
the king of Assyria: 'Make *peace* with me by
a present and come out to me; and every one
of you eat from his own vine and every one
from his own fig tree, and every one of you
drink the waters of his own cistern;
32 'until I come and take you away to a land like
your own land, a land of grain and new wine, a
land of bread and vineyards, a land of olive
groves and honey, that you may live and not die.
But do not listen to Hezekiah, lest he persuade
you, saying, "The LORD will deliver us."
33 'Has any of the gods of the nations at all
delivered its land from the hand of the king of
Assyria?
34 'Where *are* the gods of Hamath and
Arpad? Where *are* the gods of Sepharvaim
and Hena and Ivah? Indeed, have they delivered Samaria from my hand?
35 'Who among all the gods of the lands have
delivered their countries from my hand, that
the LORD should deliver Jerusalem from my
hand?'"
36 But the people held their peace and an-

18:17 [a]A title, probably *Commander in Chief* [b]A title, probably *Chief Officer* [c]A title, probably *Chief of Staff* or *Governor*
18:26 [a]Literally *Judean*

LIFE LESSONS

➤ 18:25 — *"Have I now come up without the LORD against this place to destroy it? The LORD said to me, 'Go up against this land, and destroy it.'"*

The Assyrians had no command from the Lord to destroy Jerusalem, but they used religious language to dishearten God's people. We must always be discerning and not believe someone just because he uses the "right" words.

➤ 18:35 — *"Who among all the gods of the lands have delivered their countries from my hand, that the LORD should deliver Jerusalem from my hand?"*

Here we see the true heart of the invaders. They did not regard God, but exalted themselves above Him and thought Him no different from pagan gods. Those who set themselves against the Lord invite destruction (Ps. 2:2; Dan. 5:23).

swered him not a word; for the king's commandment was, "Do not answer him."
37 Then Eliakim the son of Hilkiah, who *was*
over the household, Shebna the scribe, and
Joah the son of Asaph, the recorder, came to
Hezekiah with *their* clothes torn, and told
him the words of *the* Rabshakeh.

Isaiah Assures Deliverance

19 And so it was, when King Hezekiah
heard *it,* that he tore his clothes, covered himself with sackcloth, and went into
the house of the LORD.
2 Then he sent Eliakim, who *was* over the
household, Shebna the scribe, and the elders
of the priests, covered with sackcloth, to Isaiah the prophet, the son of Amoz.
3 And they said to him, "Thus says Hezekiah: 'This day *is* a day of trouble, and rebuke,
and blasphemy; for the children have come to
birth, but *there is* no strength to bring them
forth.
➤ 4 'It may be that the LORD your God will hear
all the words of *the* Rabshakeh, whom his
master the king of Assyria has sent to reproach
the living God, and will rebuke the words
which the LORD your God has heard. Therefore
lift up *your* prayer for the remnant that is left.'"
5 So the servants of King Hezekiah came to
Isaiah.
6 And Isaiah said to them, "Thus you shall
say to your master, 'Thus says the LORD: "Do
not be afraid of the words which you have
heard, with which the servants of the king of
Assyria have blasphemed Me.
➤ 7 "Surely I will send a spirit upon him, and
he shall hear a rumor and return to his own
land; and I will cause him to fall by the sword
in his own land."'"

Sennacherib's Threat and Hezekiah's Prayer

8 Then *the* Rabshakeh returned and found
the king of Assyria warring against Libnah, for
he heard that he had departed from Lachish.
9 And the king heard concerning Tirhakah
king of Ethiopia, "Look, he has come out to
make war with you." So he again sent messengers to Hezekiah, saying,
10 "Thus you shall speak to Hezekiah king of
Judah, saying: 'Do not let your God in whom
you trust deceive you, saying, "Jerusalem
shall not be given into the hand of the king of
Assyria."
11 'Look! You have heard what the kings of
Assyria have done to all lands by utterly destroying them; and shall you be delivered?
12 'Have the gods of the nations delivered
those whom my fathers have destroyed,
Gozan and Haran and Rezeph, and the people
of Eden who *were* in Telassar?
13 'Where *is* the king of Hamath, the king of
Arpad, and the king of the city of Sepharvaim, Hena, and Ivah?'"
14 And Hezekiah received the letter from the
hand of the messengers, and read it; and
Hezekiah went up to the house of the LORD,
and spread it before the LORD.
15 Then Hezekiah prayed before the LORD,
and said: "O LORD God of Israel, *the One* who
dwells *between* the cherubim, You are God,
You alone, of all the kingdoms of the earth.
You have made heaven and earth.
16 "Incline Your ear, O LORD, and hear; open
Your eyes, O LORD, and see; and hear the
words of Sennacherib, which he has sent to
reproach the living God.
17 "Truly, LORD, the kings of Assyria have ➤
laid waste the nations and their lands,
18 "and have cast their gods into the fire; for
they *were* not gods, but the work of men's
hands—wood and stone. Therefore they destroyed them.
19 "Now therefore, O LORD our God, I pray,
save us from his hand, that all the kingdoms
of the earth may know that You *are* the LORD
God, You alone."

The Word of the LORD Concerning Sennacherib

20 Then Isaiah the son of Amoz sent to ➤
Hezekiah, saying, "Thus says the LORD God

LIFE LESSONS

➤ 19:4 — *"It may be that the LORD your God will hear all the words of the Rabshakeh, whom his master the king of Assyria has sent to reproach the living God . . . . Therefore lift up your prayer for the remnant that is left."*

The king asked Isaiah to pray for the nation not merely on the basis of a great need, but in order to exalt the name of the Lord, whom the invaders had insulted. Such a genuine prayer has great power.

➤ 19:7 — *"Surely I will send a spirit upon him, and he shall hear a rumor and return to his own land; and I will cause him to fall by the sword in his own land."*

God can use even a "rumor" to protect and save His people. What looks impossible to us, is easy for the Lord.

➤ 19:17 — *"Truly, LORD, the kings of Assyria have laid waste the nations and their lands . . . ."*

Hezekiah did not dispute the account of the Assyrians' war record; he did not close his eyes to historical truth. He refused, however, to class God with any other deity, and looked to God alone for deliverance.

➤ 19:20 — *Then Isaiah the son of Amoz sent to Hezekiah, saying, "Thus says the LORD God of Israel: 'Because you have prayed to Me against Sennacherib king of Assyria, I have heard.'"*

God acted in a mighty way against the king of Assyria because Hezekiah had prayed for Him to intervene. When we fight our battles on our knees, we win every time.

of Israel: 'Because you have prayed to Me against Sennacherib king of Assyria, I have heard.'
21 "This *is* the word which the LORD has spoken concerning him:

'The virgin, the daughter of Zion,
Has despised you, laughed you to scorn;
The daughter of Jerusalem
Has shaken *her* head behind your back!
22'Whom have you reproached and blasphemed?
Against whom have you raised *your* voice,
And lifted up your eyes on high?
Against the Holy *One* of Israel.
23 By your messengers you have reproached the Lord,
And said: "By the multitude of my chariots
I have come up to the height of the mountains,
To the limits of Lebanon;
I will cut down its tall cedars
And its choice cypress trees;
I will enter the extremity of its borders,
To its fruitful forest.
24 I have dug and drunk strange water,
And with the soles of my feet I have dried up
All the brooks of defense."

25'Did you not hear long ago
How I made it,
From ancient times that I formed it?
Now I have brought it to pass,
That you should be
For crushing fortified cities *into* heaps of ruins.
26 Therefore their inhabitants had little power;
They were dismayed and confounded;
They were *as* the grass of the field
And the green herb,
As the grass on the housetops
And *grain* blighted before it is grown.
27'But I know your dwelling place,
Your going out and your coming in,
And your rage against Me.
28 Because your rage against Me and your tumult
Have come up to My ears,
Therefore I will put My hook in your nose
And My bridle in your lips,
And I will turn you back
By the way which you came.

29'This *shall be* a sign to you:
You shall eat this year such as grows of itself,
And in the second year what springs from the same;
Also in the third year sow and reap,
Plant vineyards and eat the fruit of them.
30 And the remnant who have escaped of the house of Judah
Shall again take root downward,
And bear fruit upward.
31 For out of Jerusalem shall go a remnant,
And those who escape from Mount Zion.
The zeal of the LORD of hosts[a] will do this.'

32 "Therefore thus says the LORD concerning the king of Assyria:

'He shall not come into this city,
Nor shoot an arrow there,
Nor come before it with shield,
Nor build a siege mound against it.
33 By the way that he came,
By the same shall he return;
And he shall not come into this city,'
Says the LORD.

34'For I will defend this city, to save it
For My own sake and for My servant David's sake.'"

Sennacherib's Defeat and Death

35 And it came to pass on a certain night that
the angel[a] of the LORD went out, and killed in
the camp of the Assyrians one hundred and
eighty-five thousand; and when *people* arose
early in the morning, there were the corpses—
all dead.
36 So Sennacherib king of Assyria departed
and went away, returned *home*, and remained
at Nineveh.
37 Now it came to pass, as he was worshiping
in the temple of Nisroch his god, that his sons

19:31 [a]Following many Hebrew manuscripts and ancient versions (compare Isaiah 37:32); Masoretic Text omits *of hosts*. **19:35** [a]Or *Angel*

LIFE LESSONS

➤ 19:34 — *"For I will defend this city, to save it for My own sake and for My servant David's sake."*

God redeems and saves and rescues, not because we deserve His help, but because of His own loving nature and because of the promises He has made to His people. Therefore we have a living hope.

➤ 19:35 — *. . . the angel of the LORD went out, and killed in the camp of the Assyrians one hundred and eighty-five thousand . . . .*

A solitary angel killed 185,000 trained Assyrian troops—the best in the world at that time—in a single night. "The angel of the LORD encamps all around those who fear Him, and delivers them" (Ps. 34:7).

Adrammelech and Sharezer struck him down
with the sword; and they escaped into the land
of Ararat. Then Esarhaddon his son reigned in
his place.

Hezekiah's Life Extended

20 In those days Hezekiah was sick and
near death. And Isaiah the prophet, the
son of Amoz, went to him and said to him,
"Thus says the LORD: 'Set your house in order,
for you shall die, and not live.'"
2 Then he turned his face toward the wall,
and prayed to the LORD, saying,
3 "Remember now, O LORD, I pray, how I
have walked before You in truth and with a
loyal heart, and have done *what was* good in
Your sight." And Hezekiah wept bitterly.
4 And it happened, before Isaiah had gone
out into the middle court, that the word of the
LORD came to him, saying,
➤ 5 "Return and tell Hezekiah the leader of
My people, 'Thus says the LORD, the God of
David your father: "I have heard your prayer,
I have seen your tears; surely I will heal you.
On the third day you shall go up to the house
of the LORD.
6 "And I will add to your days fifteen years.
I will deliver you and this city from the hand
of the king of Assyria; and I will defend this
city for My own sake, and for the sake of My
servant David."'"
7 Then Isaiah said, "Take a lump of figs." So
they took and laid *it* on the boil, and he recovered.
8 And Hezekiah said to Isaiah, "What *is* the
sign that the LORD will heal me, and that I
shall go up to the house of the LORD the third
day?"
9 Then Isaiah said, "This is the sign to you
from the LORD, that the LORD will do the thing
which He has spoken: *shall* the shadow go
forward ten degrees or go backward ten degrees?"
10 And Hezekiah answered, "It is an easy
thing for the shadow to go down ten degrees;
no, but let the shadow go backward ten degrees."
➤ 11 So Isaiah the prophet cried out to the
LORD, and He brought the shadow ten degrees
backward, by which it had gone down on the
sundial of Ahaz.

The Babylonian Envoys

12 At that time Berodach-Baladan[a] the son of
Baladan, king of Babylon, sent letters and a
present to Hezekiah, for he heard that Hezekiah had been sick.
13 And Hezekiah was attentive to them, and
showed them all the house of his treasures—
the silver and gold, the spices and precious
ointment, and all[a] his armory—all that was
found among his treasures. There was nothing in his house or in all his dominion that
Hezekiah did not show them.
14 Then Isaiah the prophet went to King
Hezekiah, and said to him, "What did these
men say, and from where did they come to
you?" So Hezekiah said, "They came from a
far country, from Babylon."
15 And he said, "What have they seen in your
house?" So Hezekiah answered, "They have
seen all that *is* in my house; there is nothing
among my treasures that I have not shown
them."
16 Then Isaiah said to Hezekiah, "Hear the
word of the LORD:
17 'Behold, the days are coming when all ➤
that *is* in your house, and what your fathers
have accumulated until this day, shall be carried to Babylon; nothing shall be left,' says the
LORD.
18 'And they shall take away some of your
sons who will descend from you, whom you
will beget; and they shall be eunuchs in the
palace of the king of Babylon.'"
19 So Hezekiah said to Isaiah, "The word of
the LORD which you have spoken *is* good!" For
he said, "Will there not be peace and truth at
least in my days?"

Death of Hezekiah

20 Now the rest of the acts of Hezekiah—all
his might, and how he made a pool and a tunnel and brought water into the city—*are* they
not written in the book of the chronicles of
the kings of Judah?
21 So Hezekiah rested with his fathers. Then
Manasseh his son reigned in his place.

20:12 [a]Spelled *Merodach-Baladan* in Isaiah 39:1
20:13 [a]Following many Hebrew manuscripts, Syriac, and Targum; Masoretic Text omits *all*.

LIFE LESSONS

➤ **20:5 — *"I have heard your prayer, I have seen your tears; surely I will heal you."***

God healed Hezekiah in response to the king's heartfelt, urgent prayers. Prayer not only saves time, it can save lives.

➤ **20:11 — *So Isaiah the prophet cried out to the LORD, and He brought the shadow ten degrees backward, by which it had gone down on the sundial of Ahaz.***

How did the Lord accomplish this miracle? Who knows? But nothing is too hard for God (Jer. 32:17).

➤ **20:17 — *"Behold, the days are coming when all that is in your house, and what your fathers have accumulated until this day, shall be carried to Babylon . . . ."***

In God's name, Isaiah made this prophecy about the Babylonian exile more than a century before it happened, when Babylon was still a relatively weak nation. When God speaks, we must listen.

Manasseh Reigns in Judah

21 Manasseh *was* twelve years old when he became king, and he reigned fifty-five years in Jerusalem. His mother's name *was* Hephzibah.
2 And he did evil in the sight of the LORD, according to the abominations of the nations whom the LORD had cast out before the children of Israel.
3 For he rebuilt the high places which Hezekiah his father had destroyed; he raised up altars for Baal, and made a wooden image,[a] as Ahab king of Israel had done; and he worshiped all the host of heaven[b] and served them.
4 He also built altars in the house of the LORD, of which the LORD had said, "In Jerusalem I will put My name."
5 And he built altars for all the host of heaven in the two courts of the house of the LORD.
6 Also he made his son pass through the fire, practiced soothsaying, used witchcraft, and consulted spiritists and mediums. He did much evil in the sight of the LORD, to provoke *Him* to anger.
7 He even set a carved image of Asherah[a] that he had made, in the house of which the LORD had said to David and to Solomon his son, "In this house and in Jerusalem, which I have chosen out of all the tribes of Israel, I will put My name forever;
8 "and I will not make the feet of Israel wander anymore from the land which I gave their fathers—only if they are careful to do according to all that I have commanded them, and according to all the law that My servant Moses commanded them."
9 But they paid no attention, and Manasseh seduced them to do more evil than the nations whom the LORD had destroyed before the children of Israel.
10 And the LORD spoke by His servants the prophets, saying,
11 "Because Manasseh king of Judah has done these abominations (he has acted more wickedly than all the Amorites who *were* before him, and has also made Judah sin with his idols),
12 "therefore thus says the LORD God of Israel: 'Behold, *I* am bringing *such* calamity upon Jerusalem and Judah, that whoever hears of it, both his ears will tingle.
13 'And I will stretch over Jerusalem the measuring line of Samaria and the plummet of the house of Ahab; I will wipe Jerusalem as *one* wipes a dish, wiping *it* and turning *it* upside down.
14 'So I will forsake the remnant of My inheritance and deliver them into the hand of their enemies; and they shall become victims of plunder to all their enemies,
15 'because they have done evil in My sight, and have provoked Me to anger since the day their fathers came out of Egypt, even to this day.'"
16 Moreover Manasseh shed very much innocent blood, till he had filled Jerusalem from one end to another, besides his sin by which he made Judah sin, in doing evil in the sight of the LORD.
17 Now the rest of the acts of Manasseh—all that he did, and the sin that he committed—*are* they not written in the book of the chronicles of the kings of Judah?
18 So Manasseh rested with his fathers, and was buried in the garden of his own house, in the garden of Uzza. Then his son Amon reigned in his place.

Amon's Reign and Death

19 Amon *was* twenty-two years old when he became king, and he reigned two years in Jerusalem. His mother's name *was* Meshullemeth the daughter of Haruz of Jotbah.
20 And he did evil in the sight of the LORD, as his father Manasseh had done.
21 So he walked in all the ways that his father had walked; and he served the idols that his father had served, and worshiped them.
22 He forsook the LORD God of his fathers, and did not walk in the way of the LORD.
23 Then the servants of Amon conspired against him, and killed the king in his own house.

21:3 [a]Hebrew *Asherah,* a Canaanite goddess [b]The gods of the Assryians **21:7** [a]A Canaanite goddess

LIFE LESSONS

➤ 21:1 — *Manasseh was twelve years old when he became king, and he reigned fifty-five years in Jerusalem.*

No Israelite king ruled longer than Manasseh, and no king acted more wickedly. So why did God allow him such a long reign? God is patient with us, "not willing that any should perish but that all should come to repentance" (2 Pet. 3:9; compare 2 Chr. 33:12–19).

➤ 21:2 — *And he did evil in the sight of the LORD, according to the abominations of the nations whom the LORD had cast out before the children of Israel.*

Manasseh, the worst king in Judah's history, was the son of Hezekiah, one of the best kings in Judah's history. Faith does not transfer from generation to generation; each one of us must make it our own.

➤ 21:9 — . . . *Manasseh seduced them to do more evil than the nations whom the LORD had destroyed before the children of Israel.*

Other wicked kings had followed the corrupt practices of the pagan nations around them; Manasseh descended even further. Sin, left unchecked, always leads to perversion and eventually to destruction (2 Pet. 2:20, 21).

24 But the people of the land executed all those who had conspired against King Amon. Then the people of the land made his son Josiah king in his place.
25 Now the rest of the acts of Amon which he did, *are* they not written in the book of the chronicles of the kings of Judah?
26 And he was buried in his tomb in the garden of Uzza. Then Josiah his son reigned in his place.

Josiah Reigns in Judah

22 Josiah *was* eight years old when he became king, and he reigned thirty-one years in Jerusalem. His mother's name *was* Jedidah the daughter of Adaiah of Bozkath.
2 And he did *what was* right in the sight of the LORD, and walked in all the ways of his father David; he did not turn aside to the right hand or to the left.

Hilkiah Finds the Book of the Law

3 Now it came to pass, in the eighteenth year of King Josiah, *that* the king sent Shaphan the scribe, the son of Azaliah, the son of Meshullam, to the house of the LORD, saying:
4 "Go up to Hilkiah the high priest, that he may count the money which has been brought into the house of the LORD, which the doorkeepers have gathered from the people.
5 "And let them deliver it into the hand of those doing the work, who are the overseers in the house of the LORD; let them give it to those who *are* in the house of the LORD doing the work, to repair the damages of the house—
6 "to carpenters and builders and masons—and to buy timber and hewn stone to repair the house.
7 "However there need be no accounting made with them of the money delivered into their hand, because they deal faithfully."
8 Then Hilkiah the high priest said to Shaphan the scribe, "I have found the Book of the Law in the house of the LORD." And Hilkiah gave the book to Shaphan, and he read it.
9 So Shaphan the scribe went to the king, bringing the king word, saying, "Your servants have gathered the money that was found in the house, and have delivered it into the hand of those who do the work, who oversee the house of the LORD."
10 Then Shaphan the scribe showed the king, saying, "Hilkiah the priest has given me a book." And Shaphan read it before the king.
11 Now it happened, when the king heard the words of the Book of the Law, that he tore his clothes.
12 Then the king commanded Hilkiah the priest, Ahikam the son of Shaphan, Achbor[a] the son of Michaiah, Shaphan the scribe, and Asaiah a servant of the king, saying,
13 "Go, inquire of the LORD for me, for the people and for all Judah, concerning the words of this book that has been found; for great *is* the wrath of the LORD that is aroused against us, because our fathers have not obeyed the words of this book, to do according to all that is written concerning us."
14 So Hilkiah the priest, Ahikam, Achbor, Shaphan, and Asaiah went to Huldah the prophetess, the wife of Shallum the son of Tikvah, the son of Harhas, keeper of the wardrobe. (She dwelt in Jerusalem in the Second Quarter.) And they spoke with her.
15 Then she said to them, "Thus says the LORD God of Israel, 'Tell the man who sent you to Me,
16 "Thus says the LORD: 'Behold, I will bring calamity on this place and on its inhabitants—all the words of the book which the king of Judah has read—
17 'because they have forsaken Me and burned incense to other gods, that they might provoke Me to anger with all the works of their hands. Therefore My wrath shall be aroused against this place and shall not be quenched.'"'
18 "But as for the king of Judah, who sent you to inquire of the LORD, in this manner you shall speak to him, 'Thus says the LORD God of Israel: "*Concerning* the words which you have heard—
19 "because your heart was tender, and you humbled yourself before the LORD when you heard what I spoke against this place and against its inhabitants, that they would become a desolation and a curse, and you tore your clothes and wept before Me, I also have heard *you*," says the LORD.
20 "Surely, therefore, I will gather you to your fathers, and you shall be gathered to

22:12 [a]*Abdon the son of Micah* in 2 Chronicles 34:20

LIFE LESSONS

➤ 22:10 — *Then Shaphan the scribe showed the king, saying, "Hilkiah the priest has given me a book."*

The people of Judah had plummeted to such a spiritual low that the Bible had practically disappeared; when found, they called it simply, "a book." But God's Word remains strong and reliable, even if ignored.

➤ 22:19 — *". . . because your heart was tender, and you humbled yourself before the LORD . . . I also have heard you," says the LORD.*

God responds in powerful ways to those who humble themselves before Him and who make their hearts tender toward His Word.

your grave in peace; and your eyes shall not
see all the calamity which I will bring on this
place.'"' So they brought back word to the
king.

Josiah Restores True Worship

23 Now the king sent them to gather all
the elders of Judah and Jerusalem to
him.
2 The king went up to the house of the LORD
with all the men of Judah, and with him all
the inhabitants of Jerusalem—the priests and
the prophets and all the people, both small
and great. And he read in their hearing all the
words of the Book of the Covenant which had
been found in the house of the LORD.
3 Then the king stood by a pillar and made
a covenant before the LORD, to follow the
LORD and to keep His commandments and
His testimonies and His statutes, with all *his*
heart and all *his* soul, to perform the words of
this covenant that were written in this book.
And all the people took a stand for the covenant.
4 And the king commanded Hilkiah the
high priest, the priests of the second order,
and the doorkeepers, to bring out of the temple of the LORD all the articles that were made
for Baal, for Asherah,[a] and for all the host of
heaven;[b] and he burned them outside Jerusalem in the fields of Kidron, and carried their
ashes to Bethel.
5 Then he removed the idolatrous priests
whom the kings of Judah had ordained to
burn incense on the high places in the cities
of Judah and in the places all around Jerusalem, and those who burned incense to Baal, to
the sun, to the moon, to the constellations,
and to all the host of heaven.
6 And he brought out the wooden image[a]
from the house of the LORD, to the Brook
Kidron outside Jerusalem, burned it at the
Brook Kidron and ground *it* to ashes, and
threw its ashes on the graves of the common
people.
7 Then he tore down the *ritual* booths of the
perverted persons[a] that *were* in the house of
the LORD, where the women wove hangings
for the wooden image.
8 And he brought all the priests from the
cities of Judah, and defiled the high places
where the priests had burned incense, from
Geba to Beersheba; also he broke down the
high places at the gates which *were* at the entrance of the Gate of Joshua the governor of
the city, which *were* to the left of the city gate.
9 Nevertheless the priests of the high places
did not come up to the altar of the LORD in Jerusalem, but they ate unleavened bread
among their brethren.
10 And he defiled Topheth, which *is* in the
Valley of the Son[a] of Hinnom, that no man
might make his son or his daughter pass
through the fire to Molech.
11 Then he removed the horses that the kings
of Judah had dedicated to the sun, at the entrance to the house of the LORD, by the chamber of Nathan-Melech, the officer who *was* in
the court; and he burned the chariots of the
sun with fire.
12 The altars that *were* on the roof, the upper
chamber of Ahaz, which the kings of Judah
had made, and the altars which Manasseh
had made in the two courts of the house of the
LORD, the king broke down and pulverized
there, and threw their dust into the Brook
Kidron.
13 Then the king defiled the high places that
were east of Jerusalem, which *were* on the
south of the Mount of Corruption, which
Solomon king of Israel had built for Ashtoreth the abomination of the Sidonians, for
Chemosh the abomination of the Moabites,
and for Milcom the abomination of the people
of Ammon.
14 And he broke in pieces the *sacred* pillars
and cut down the wooden images, and filled
their places with the bones of men.
15 Moreover the altar that *was* at Bethel, *and*
the high place which Jeroboam the son of
Nebat, who made Israel sin, had made, both
that altar and the high place he broke down;
and he burned the high place *and* crushed *it*
to powder, and burned the wooden image.
16 As Josiah turned, he saw the tombs that
were there on the mountain. And he sent and
took the bones out of the tombs and burned
them on the altar, and defiled it according to
the word of the LORD which the man of God
proclaimed, who proclaimed these words.
17 Then he said, "What gravestone *is* this that
I see?" So the men of the city told him, "*It is*
the tomb of the man of God who came from
Judah and proclaimed these things which you
have done against the altar of Bethel."
18 And he said, "Let him alone; let no one
move his bones." So they let his bones alone,
with the bones of the prophet who came from
Samaria.
19 Now Josiah also took away all the shrines
of the high places that *were* in the cities of Samaria, which the kings of Israel had made to
provoke the LORD[a] to anger; and he did to
them according to all the deeds he had done
in Bethel.
20 He executed all the priests of the high
places who *were* there, on the altars, and
burned men's bones on them; and he returned
to Jerusalem.
21 Then the king commanded all the people,

23:4 [a]A Canaanite goddess [b]The gods of the Assyrians
23:6 [a]Hebrew *Asherah,* a Canaanite goddess **23:7** [a]Hebrew *qedeshim,* that is, those practicing sodomy and prostitution in religious rituals **23:10** [a]Kethib reads *Sons.* **23:19** [a]Following Septuagint, Syriac, and Vulgate; Masoretic Text and Targum omit *the LORD.*

saying, "Keep the Passover to the LORD your
God, as *it is* written in this Book of the Covenant."
22 Such a Passover surely had never been
held since the days of the judges who judged
Israel, nor in all the days of the kings of Israel
and the kings of Judah.
23 But in the eighteenth year of King Josiah
this Passover was held before the LORD in Jerusalem.
24 Moreover Josiah put away those who consulted mediums and spiritists, the household
gods and idols, all the abominations that were
seen in the land of Judah and in Jerusalem,
that he might perform the words of the law
which were written in the book that Hilkiah
the priest found in the house of the LORD.
➤ 25 Now before him there was no king like
him, who turned to the LORD with all his
heart, with all his soul, and with all his might,
according to all the Law of Moses; nor after
him did *any* arise like him.

Impending Judgment on Judah

26 Nevertheless the LORD did not turn from
the fierceness of His great wrath, with which
His anger was aroused against Judah, because of all the provocations with which Manasseh had provoked Him.
27 And the LORD said, "I will also remove Judah from My sight, as I have removed Israel,
and will cast off this city Jerusalem which I
have chosen, and the house of which I said,
'My name shall be there.'"[a]

Josiah Dies in Battle

28 Now the rest of the acts of Josiah, and all
that he did, *are* they not written in the book of
the chronicles of the kings of Judah?
➤ 29 In his days Pharaoh Necho king of Egypt
went to the aid of the king of Assyria, to the
River Euphrates; and King Josiah went
against him. And *Pharaoh Necho* killed him
at Megiddo when he confronted him.
30 Then his servants moved his body in a
chariot from Megiddo, brought him to Jerusalem, and buried him in his own tomb. And the
people of the land took Jehoahaz the son of
Josiah, anointed him, and made him king in
his father's place.

The Reign and Captivity of Jehoahaz

31 Jehoahaz *was* twenty-three years old
when he became king, and he reigned three
months in Jerusalem. His mother's name *was*
Hamutal the daughter of Jeremiah of Libnah.
32 And he did evil in the sight of the LORD,
according to all that his fathers had done.
33 Now Pharaoh Necho put him in prison at
Riblah in the land of Hamath, that he might
not reign in Jerusalem; and he imposed on
the land a tribute of one hundred talents of
silver and a talent of gold.

Life Examples:

JOSIAH

Committed to Following the Lord

2 KIN. 23:25

Josiah became king of Judah when he was just eight years old, after the murder of his idolatrous father, Amon. Having no living example and no parental instruction in the ways of God, he walked in the ways of his forefather, the great King David.

Josiah committed himself to follow the Lord, keeping all His mandates and decrees. When he renewed the covenant of his forefathers, all the people with him pledged themselves to the Lord as well. Josiah's extensive reforms throughout Judah and Samaria make him stand out as one of Judah's most faithful kings (2 Kin. 23:25).

When you make the Lord and His Word the focus of your life, He will help you just as He did Josiah. Make your heart tender, and humble yourself before the Lord. He will establish you, and by Him you will become mighty for God.

See the Life Principles Index for further study:
21. Obedience always brings blessing.

23:27 [a]1 Kings 8:29

LIFE LESSONS

➤ 23:25 — *Now before him there was no king like him, who turned to the LORD with all his heart, with all his soul, and with all his might . . . .*

Genuine devotion to God involves much more than intense feeling or heightened emotion. Those who follow God with all their heart, soul, and might, also eagerly obey His commands.

➤ 23:29 — *Pharaoh Necho king of Egypt went to the aid of the king of Assyria, to the River Euphrates; and King Josiah went against him. And Pharaoh Necho killed him at Megiddo . . . .*

Although Josiah was a godly king, excelling in devotion to God above all others before him, yet a pagan king killed him in battle. Sometimes, God takes the godly home in order to spare them coming disaster (see Is. 57:1).

34 Then Pharaoh Necho made Eliakim the
son of Josiah king in place of his father
Josiah, and changed his name to Jehoiakim.
And *Pharaoh* took Jehoahaz and went to
Egypt, and he[a] died there.

Jehoiakim Reigns in Judah

35 So Jehoiakim gave the silver and gold to
Pharaoh; but he taxed the land to give money
according to the command of Pharaoh; he exacted the silver and gold from the people of
the land, from every one according to his assessment, to give *it* to Pharaoh Necho.
36 Jehoiakim *was* twenty-five years old when
he became king, and he reigned eleven years
in Jerusalem. His mother's name *was* Zebudah
the daughter of Pedaiah of Rumah.
37 And he did evil in the sight of the LORD,
according to all that his fathers had done.

Judah Overrun by Enemies

24 In his days Nebuchadnezzar king of
Babylon came up, and Jehoiakim became his vassal *for* three years. Then he
turned and rebelled against him.
2 And the LORD sent against him *raiding*
bands of Chaldeans, bands of Syrians, bands of
Moabites, and bands of the people of Ammon;
He sent them against Judah to destroy it, according to the word of the LORD which He had
spoken by His servants the prophets.
3 Surely at the commandment of the LORD
this came upon Judah, to remove *them* from
His sight because of the sins of Manasseh, according to all that he had done,
4 and also because of the innocent blood
that he had shed; for he had filled Jerusalem
with innocent blood, which the LORD would
not pardon.
5 Now the rest of the acts of Jehoiakim, and
all that he did, *are* they not written in the
book of the chronicles of the kings of Judah?
6 So Jehoiakim rested with his fathers.
Then Jehoiachin his son reigned in his place.
7 And the king of Egypt did not come out of
his land anymore, for the king of Babylon had
taken all that belonged to the king of Egypt
from the Brook of Egypt to the River Euphrates.

The Reign and Captivity of Jehoiachin

8 Jehoiachin *was* eighteen years old when
he became king, and he reigned in Jerusalem
three months. His mother's name *was* Nehushta the daughter of Elnathan of Jerusalem.
9 And he did evil in the sight of the LORD,
according to all that his father had done.
10 At that time the servants of Nebuchadnezzar king of Babylon came up against Jerusalem, and the city was besieged.
11 And Nebuchadnezzar king of Babylon
came against the city, as his servants were be-
sieging it.
12 Then Jehoiachin king of Judah, his mother,
his servants, his princes, and his officers went
out to the king of Babylon; and the king of
Babylon, in the eighth year of his reign, took
him prisoner.

The Captivity of Jerusalem

13 And he carried out from there all the
treasures of the house of the LORD and the
treasures of the king's house, and he cut in
pieces all the articles of gold which Solomon
king of Israel had made in the temple of the
LORD, as the LORD had said.
14 Also he carried into captivity all Jerusalem: all the captains and all the mighty men
of valor, ten thousand captives, and all the
craftsmen and smiths. None remained except
the poorest people of the land.
15 And he carried Jehoiachin captive to
Babylon. The king's mother, the king's wives,
his officers, and the mighty of the land he carried into captivity from Jerusalem to Babylon.
16 All the valiant men, seven thousand, and
craftsmen and smiths, one thousand, all *who
were* strong *and* fit for war, these the king of
Babylon brought captive to Babylon.

Zedekiah Reigns in Judah

17 Then the king of Babylon made Mattaniah, *Jehoiachin's*[a] uncle, king in his place,
and changed his name to Zedekiah.
18 Zedekiah *was* twenty-one years old when
he became king, and he reigned eleven years
in Jerusalem. His mother's name *was* Hamutal the daughter of Jeremiah of Libnah.
19 He also did evil in the sight of the LORD,
according to all that Jehoiakim had done.
20 For because of the anger of the LORD *this*
happened in Jerusalem and Judah, that He finally cast them out from His presence. Then
Zedekiah rebelled against the king of Babylon.

The Fall and Captivity of Judah

25 Now it came to pass in the ninth year of
his reign, in the tenth month, on the
tenth *day* of the month, *that* Nebuchadnezzar
king of Babylon and all his army came against
Jerusalem and encamped against it; and they
built a siege wall against it all around.

23:34 [a]That is, Jehoahaz **24:17** [a]Literally *his*

LIFE LESSONS

➤ ***24:20 — For because of the anger of the LORD this happened in Jerusalem and Judah, that He finally cast them out from His presence.***

More than a hundred years after Isaiah made his prophecy about the fall of Jerusalem to the Babylonians, it happened. Though God seems to delay the fulfillment of His Word, "wait for it; because it will surely come" (Hab. 2:3).

2 So the city was besieged until the eleventh
year of King Zedekiah.
3 By the ninth *day* of the *fourth* month the
famine had become so severe in the city that
there was no food for the people of the land.
4 Then the city wall was broken through,
and all the men of war *fled* at night by way of
the gate between two walls, which was by the
king's garden, even though the Chaldeans
were still encamped all around against the
city. And *the king*[a] went by way of the plain.[b]
5 But the army of the Chaldeans pursued the
king, and they overtook him in the plains of
Jericho. All his army was scattered from him.
6 So they took the king and brought him up
to the king of Babylon at Riblah, and they
pronounced judgment on him.
7 Then they killed the sons of Zedekiah before his eyes, put out the eyes of Zedekiah,
bound him with bronze fetters, and took him
to Babylon.
8 And in the fifth month, on the seventh *day*
of the month (which *was* the nineteenth year of
King Nebuchadnezzar king of Babylon), Nebuzaradan the captain of the guard, a servant of
the king of Babylon, came to Jerusalem.
9 He burned the house of the LORD and the
king's house; all the houses of Jerusalem, that is,
all the houses of the great, he burned with fire.
10 And all the army of the Chaldeans who
were with the captain of the guard broke
down the walls of Jerusalem all around.
11 Then Nebuzaradan the captain of the
guard carried away captive the rest of the
people *who* remained in the city and the defectors who had deserted to the king of Babylon, with the rest of the multitude.
12 But the captain of the guard left *some* of
the poor of the land as vinedressers and farmers.
13 The bronze pillars that *were* in the house
of the LORD, and the carts and the bronze Sea
that *were* in the house of the LORD, the
Chaldeans broke in pieces, and carried their
bronze to Babylon.
14 They also took away the pots, the shovels,
the trimmers, the spoons, and all the bronze
utensils with which the priests ministered.
15 The firepans and the basins, the things of
solid gold and solid silver, the captain of the
guard took away.
16 The two pillars, one Sea, and the carts,
which Solomon had made for the house of the
LORD, the bronze of all these articles was beyond measure.
17 The height of one pillar *was* eighteen cubits, and the capital on it *was* of bronze. The
height of the capital was three cubits, and
the network and pomegranates all around the
capital were all of bronze. The second pillar
was the same, with a network.
18 And the captain of the guard took Seraiah
the chief priest, Zephaniah the second priest,
and the three doorkeepers.
19 He also took out of the city an officer who
had charge of the men of war, five men of the
king's close associates who were found in the
city, the chief recruiting officer of the army,
who mustered the people of the land, and
sixty men of the people of the land *who were*
found in the city.
20 So Nebuzaradan, captain of the guard,
took these and brought them to the king of
Babylon at Riblah.
21 Then the king of Babylon struck them and
put them to death at Riblah in the land of
Hamath. Thus Judah was carried away captive from its own land.

Gedaliah Made Governor of Judah

22 Then he made Gedaliah the son of Ahikam,
the son of Shaphan, governor over the people
who remained in the land of Judah, whom
Nebuchadnezzar king of Babylon had left.
23 Now when all the captains of the armies,
they and *their* men, heard that the king of
Babylon had made Gedaliah governor, they
came to Gedaliah at Mizpah—Ishmael the
son of Nethaniah, Johanan the son of Careah,
Seraiah the son of Tanhumeth the Netophathite, and Jaazaniah[a] the son of a Maachathite, they and their men.
24 And Gedaliah took an oath before them
and their men, and said to them, "Do not be
afraid of the servants of the Chaldeans. Dwell
in the land and serve the king of Babylon, and
it shall be well with you."
25 But it happened in the seventh month that
Ishmael the son of Nethaniah, the son of Elishama, of the royal family, came with ten
men and struck and killed Gedaliah, the Jews,
as well as the Chaldeans who were with him
at Mizpah.
26 And all the people, small and great, and
the captains of the armies, arose and went to
Egypt; for they were afraid of the Chaldeans.

Jehoiachin Released from Prison

27 Now it came to pass in the thirty-seventh
year of the captivity of Jehoiachin king of Judah, in the twelfth month, on the twenty-seventh *day* of the month, *that* Evil-Merodach[a]
king of Babylon, in the year that he began to
reign, released Jehoiachin king of Judah from
prison.
28 He spoke kindly to him, and gave him a
more prominent seat than those of the kings
who *were* with him in Babylon.
29 So Jehoiachin changed from his prison
garments, and he ate bread regularly before
the king all the days of his life.
30 And as for his provisions, *there was* a regular ration given him by the king, a portion
for each day, all the days of his life.

25:4 [a]Literally *he* [b]Or *Arabah,* that is, the Jordan Valley
25:23 [a]Spelled *Jezaniah* in Jeremiah 40:8 **25:27** [a]Literally *Man of Marduk*

THE FIRST BOOK OF

CHRONICLES

First and Second Chronicles were originally one continuous work in the Hebrew text. In the third-century B.C. the Septuagint divided Chronicles into two parts. At that time it was given the title, "Of Things Omitted," referring to the events left out of Samuel and Kings. The name "Chronicles" comes from Jerome in his Latin Vulgate Bible (A.D. 385–405). He meant his title in the sense of the "Chronicles of the Whole of Sacred History."

The books of 1 and 2 Chronicles cover the same period of Jewish history described in 2 Samuel through 2 Kings, but the perspective is different. These books do not merely repeat the same material, but rather provide a divine editorial on the history of God's people. While 2 Samuel and 1 and 2 Kings give a political history of Israel and Judah, 1 and 2 Chronicles present a religious history of the Davidic dynasty of Judah. Much more information is given here, for example, about the construction of the temple and Israel's worship. The former books are written from a prophetic and moral viewpoint; the latter from a priestly and spiritual perspective. The Book of 1 Chronicles begins with the royal line of David and then traces the spiritual significance of David's righteous reign.

Themes: The book highlights the proper worship of the true and living God of Israel, beautifully demonstrated in the life of David. First Chronicles also emphasizes the sovereignty of God.

Author: Uncertain, but thought to be compiled and edited by Ezra.

Time: Scholars think 1 and 2 Chronicles were written shortly after the Babylonian exile, which took place from 586 to 538 B.C. (The Jews rebuilt the temple in Jerusalem in 516 B.C., seventy years after the Babylonians had destroyed it and the city.) First Chronicles covers the life of David, Israel's greatest king, beginning with his ancestry, all the way back to Adam and Eve, and ending with his final words and deeds (1:1—9:44; 29:10–30). In between we read of David's early years as King of Israel, his kingdom and covenant with God, and his preparation for worship in the holy temple (10:1—29:9).

Structure: First Chronicles is straightforward narrative history, with a more spiritual focus than what we find in 2 Samuel or 1 and 2 Kings.

As you read 1 Chronicles, watch for several life principles that play an important role in this book:

6. You reap what you sow, more than you sow, and later than you sow. *See 1 Chronicles 10:13, 14; page 475.*

2. Obey God and leave all the consequences to Him. *See 1 Chronicles 21:1–19; page 485.*

12. Peace with God is the fruit of oneness with God. *See 1 Chronicles 22:9; page 486.*

23. You can never outgive God. *See 1 Chronicles 29:13–17; page 494.*

The Family of Adam—Seth to Abraham

➤ **1** Adam, Seth, Enosh,
2 Cainan,[a] Mahalalel, Jared,
3 Enoch, Methuselah, Lamech,
4 Noah,[a] Shem, Ham, and Japheth.
5 The sons of Japheth *were* Gomer, Magog, Madai, Javan, Tubal, Meshech, and Tiras.
6 The sons of Gomer *were* Ashkenaz, Diphath,[a] and Togarmah.
7 The sons of Javan *were* Elishah, Tarshishah,[a] Kittim, and Rodanim.[b]
8 The sons of Ham *were* Cush, Mizraim, Put, and Canaan.
9 The sons of Cush *were* Seba, Havilah, Sabta,[a] Raama,[b] and Sabtecha. The sons of Raama *were* Sheba and Dedan.
10 Cush begot Nimrod; he began to be a mighty one on the earth.
11 Mizraim begot Ludim, Anamim, Lehabim, Naphtuhim,
12 Pathrusim, Casluhim (from whom came the Philistines and the Caphtorim).
13 Canaan begot Sidon, his firstborn, and Heth;
14 the Jebusite, the Amorite, and the Girgashite;
15 the Hivite, the Arkite, and the Sinite;
16 the Arvadite, the Zemarite, and the Hamathite.
17 The sons of Shem *were* Elam, Asshur, Arphaxad, Lud, Aram, Uz, Hul, Gether, and Meshech.[a]
18 Arphaxad begot Shelah, and Shelah begot Eber.
19 To Eber were born two sons: the name of one *was* Peleg,[a] for in his days the earth was divided; and his brother's name *was* Joktan.
20 Joktan begot Almodad, Sheleph, Hazarmaveth, Jerah,
21 Hadoram, Uzal, Diklah,
22 Ebal,[a] Abimael, Sheba,
23 Ophir, Havilah, and Jobab. All these *were* the sons of Joktan.
24 Shem, Arphaxad, Shelah,
25 Eber, Peleg, Reu,
26 Serug, Nahor, Terah,
27 and Abram, who *is* Abraham.
28 The sons of Abraham *were* Isaac and Ishmael.

The Family of Ishmael

29 These *are* their genealogies: The firstborn of Ishmael *was* Nebajoth; then Kedar, Adbeel, Mibsam,
30 Mishma, Dumah, Massa, Hadad,[a] Tema,
31 Jetur, Naphish, and Kedemah. These *were* the sons of Ishmael.

The Family of Keturah

32 Now the sons born to Keturah, Abraham's concubine, *were* Zimran, Jokshan, Medan, Midian, Ishbak, and Shuah. The sons of Jokshan *were* Sheba and Dedan.
33 The sons of Midian *were* Ephah, Epher, Hanoch, Abida, and Eldaah. All these were the children of Keturah.

The Family of Isaac

34 And Abraham begot Isaac. The sons of Isaac *were* Esau and Israel.
35 The sons of Esau *were* Eliphaz, Reuel, Jeush, Jaalam, and Korah.
36 And the sons of Eliphaz *were* Teman, Omar, Zephi,[a] Gatam, *and* Kenaz; and *by* Timna,[b] Amalek.
37 The sons of Reuel *were* Nahath, Zerah, Shammah, and Mizzah.

The Family of Seir

38 The sons of Seir *were* Lotan, Shobal, Zibeon, Anah, Dishon, Ezer, and Dishan.
39 And the sons of Lotan *were* Hori and Homam; Lotan's sister *was* Timna.
40 The sons of Shobal *were* Alian,[a] Manahath, Ebal, Shephi,[b] and Onam. The sons of Zibeon *were* Ajah and Anah.
41 The son of Anah *was* Dishon. The sons of Dishon *were* Hamran,[a] Eshban, Ithran, and Cheran.
42 The sons of Ezer *were* Bilhan, Zaavan, *and* Jaakan.[a] The sons of Dishan *were* Uz and Aran.

The Kings of Edom

43 Now these *were* the kings who reigned in the land of Edom before a king reigned over the children of Israel: Bela the son of Beor, and the name of his city was Dinhabah.
44 And when Bela died, Jobab the son of Zerah of Bozrah reigned in his place.

1:2 [a]Hebrew *Qenan* **1:4** [a]Following Masoretic Text and Vulgate; Septuagint adds *the sons of Noah.* **1:6** [a]Spelled *Riphath* in Genesis 10:3 **1:7** [a]Spelled *Tarshish* in Genesis 10:4 [b]Spelled *Dodanim* in Genesis 10:4 **1:9** [a]Spelled *Sabtah* in Genesis 10:7 [b]Spelled *Raamah* in Genesis 10:7 **1:17** [a]Spelled *Mash* in Genesis 10:23 **1:19** [a]Literally *Division* **1:22** [a]Spelled *Obal* in Genesis 10:28 **1:30** [a]Spelled *Hadar* in Genesis 25:15 **1:36** [a]Spelled *Zepho* in Genesis 36:11 [b]Compare Genesis 36:12 **1:40** [a]Spelled *Alvan* in Genesis 36:23 [b]Spelled *Shepho* in Genesis 36:23 **1:41** [a]Spelled *Hemdan* in Genesis 36:26 **1:42** [a]Spelled *Akan* in Genesis 36:27

LIFE LESSONS

➤ **1:1 — *Adam, Seth, Enosh . . . .***

Why spend so much time and take up so much space with genealogies? For one thing, God wants us to remember that the Bible tells us of *real* people with *real* lives and *real* problems and *real* challenges. Just like us!

45 When Jobab died, Husham of the land of
the Temanites reigned in his place.
46 And when Husham died, Hadad the son of
Bedad, who attacked Midian in the field of
Moab, reigned in his place. The name of his
city *was* Avith.
47 When Hadad died, Samlah of Masrekah
reigned in his place.
48 And when Samlah died, Saul of Re-
hoboth-by-the-River reigned in his place.
49 When Saul died, Baal-Hanan the son of
Achbor reigned in his place.
50 And when Baal-Hanan died, Hadad[a]
reigned in his place; and the name of his city
was Pai.[b] His wife's name was Mehetabel the
daughter of Matred, the daughter of Mezahab.
51 Hadad died also. And the chiefs of Edom
were Chief Timnah, Chief Aliah,[a] Chief Jetheth,
52 Chief Aholibamah, Chief Elah, Chief
Pinon,
53 Chief Kenaz, Chief Teman, Chief Mibzar,
54 Chief Magdiel, and Chief Iram. These
were the chiefs of Edom.

The Family of Israel

2 These *were* the sons of Israel: Reuben,
Simeon, Levi, Judah, Issachar, Zebulun,
2 Dan, Joseph, Benjamin, Naphtali, Gad,
and Asher.

From Judah to David

3 The sons of Judah *were* Er, Onan, and
Shelah. *These* three were born to him by the
daughter of Shua, the Canaanitess. Er, the
firstborn of Judah, was wicked in the sight of
the LORD; so He killed him.
4 And Tamar, his daughter-in-law, bore him
Perez and Zerah. All the sons of Judah *were*
five.
5 The sons of Perez *were* Hezron and
Hamul.
6 The sons of Zerah *were* Zimri, Ethan,
Heman, Calcol, and Dara—five of them in all.
7 The son of Carmi *was* Achar,[a] the troubler
of Israel, who transgressed in the accursed
thing.
8 The son of Ethan *was* Azariah.
9 Also the sons of Hezron who were born to
him *were* Jerahmeel, Ram, and Chelubai.[a]
10 Ram begot Amminadab, and Amminadab
begot Nahshon, leader of the children of Judah;
11 Nahshon begot Salma,[a] and Salma begot
Boaz;
12 Boaz begot Obed, and Obed begot Jesse;
13 Jesse begot Eliab his firstborn, Abinadab
the second, Shimea[a] the third,
14 Nethanel the fourth, Raddai the fifth,
15 Ozem the sixth, *and* David the seventh.
16 Now their sisters *were* Zeruiah and Abigail. And the sons of Zeruiah *were* Abishai,
Joab, and Asahel—three.
17 Abigail bore Amasa; and the father of
Amasa *was* Jether the Ishmaelite.[a]

The Family of Hezron

18 Caleb the son of Hezron had children
by Azubah, *his* wife, and by Jerioth. Now
these were her sons: Jesher, Shobab, and
Ardon.
19 When Azubah died, Caleb took Ephrath[a]
as his wife, who bore him Hur.
20 And Hur begot Uri, and Uri begot Bezalel.
21 Now afterward Hezron went in to the
daughter of Machir the father of Gilead,
whom he married when he *was* sixty years
old; and she bore him Segub.
22 Segub begot Jair, who had twenty-three
cities in the land of Gilead.
23 (Geshur and Syria took from them the
towns of Jair, with Kenath and its towns—
sixty towns.) All these *belonged to* the sons of
Machir the father of Gilead.
24 After Hezron died in Caleb Ephrathah,
Hezron's wife Abijah bore him Ashhur the father of Tekoa.

The Family of Jerahmeel

25 The sons of Jerahmeel, the firstborn of
Hezron, *were* Ram, the firstborn, and Bunah,
Oren, Ozem, *and* Ahijah.
26 Jerahmeel had another wife, whose name
was Atarah; she was the mother of Onam.
27 The sons of Ram, the firstborn of Jerahmeel, were Maaz, Jamin, and Eker.
28 The sons of Onam were Shammai and
Jada. The sons of Shammai *were* Nadab and
Abishur.
29 And the name of the wife of Abishur
was Abihail, and she bore him Ahban and
Molid.
30 The sons of Nadab *were* Seled and Appaim; Seled died without children.
31 The son of Appaim *was* Ishi, the son of
Ishi *was* Sheshan, and Sheshan's son *was*
Ahlai.
32 The sons of Jada, the brother of Shammai,
were Jether and Jonathan; Jether died without children.
33 The sons of Jonathan *were* Peleth and
Zaza. These were the sons of Jerahmeel.
34 Now Sheshan had no sons, only daughters. And Sheshan had an Egyptian servant
whose name *was* Jarha.
35 Sheshan gave his daughter to Jarha his
servant as wife, and she bore him Attai.
36 Attai begot Nathan, and Nathan begot
Zabad;

1:50 [a]Spelled *Hadar* in Genesis 36:39 [b]Spelled *Pau* in Genesis 36:39 **1:51** [a]Spelled *Alvah* in Genesis 36:40 **2:7** [a]Spelled *Achan* in Joshua 7:1 and elsewhere **2:9** [a]Spelled *Caleb* in 2:18, 42 **2:11** [a]Spelled *Salmon* in Ruth 4:21 and Luke 3:32 **2:13** [a]Spelled *Shammah* in 1 Samuel 16:9 and elsewhere **2:17** [a]Compare 2 Samuel 17:25 **2:19** [a]Spelled *Ephrathah* elsewhere

37 Zabad begot Ephlal, and Ephlal begot Obed;
38 Obed begot Jehu, and Jehu begot Azariah;
39 Azariah begot Helez, and Helez begot Eleasah;
40 Eleasah begot Sismai, and Sismai begot Shallum;
41 Shallum begot Jekamiah, and Jekamiah begot Elishama.

The Family of Caleb

42 The descendants of Caleb the brother of Jerahmeel *were* Mesha, his firstborn, who was the father of Ziph, and the sons of Mareshah the father of Hebron.
43 The sons of Hebron *were* Korah, Tappuah, Rekem, and Shema.
44 Shema begot Raham the father of Jorkoam, and Rekem begot Shammai.
45 And the son of Shammai *was* Maon, and Maon *was* the father of Beth Zur.
46 Ephah, Caleb's concubine, bore Haran, Moza, and Gazez; and Haran begot Gazez.
47 And the sons of Jahdai *were* Regem, Jotham, Geshan, Pelet, Ephah, and Shaaph.
48 Maachah, Caleb's concubine, bore Sheber and Tirhanah.
49 She also bore Shaaph the father of Madmannah, Sheva the father of Machbenah and the father of Gibea. And the daughter of Caleb *was* Achsah.
50 These were the descendants of Caleb: The sons of Hur, the firstborn of Ephrathah, *were* Shobal the father of Kirjath Jearim,
51 Salma the father of Bethlehem, *and* Hareph the father of Beth Gader.
52 And Shobal the father of Kirjath Jearim had descendants: Haroeh, *and* half of the *families of* Manuhoth.[a]
53 The families of Kirjath Jearim *were* the Ithrites, the Puthites, the Shumathites, and the Mishraites. From these came the Zorathites and the Eshtaolites.
54 The sons of Salma *were* Bethlehem, the Netophathites, Atroth Beth Joab, half of the Manahethites, and the Zorites.
55 And the families of the scribes who dwelt at Jabez *were* the Tirathites, the Shimeathites, *and* the Suchathites. These *were* the Kenites who came from Hammath, the father of the house of Rechab.

The Family of David

3 Now these were the sons of David who were born to him in Hebron: The firstborn *was* Amnon, by Ahinoam the Jezreelitess; the second, Daniel,[a] by Abigail the Carmelitess;
2 the third, Absalom the son of Maacah, the daughter of Talmai, king of Geshur; the fourth, Adonijah the son of Haggith;
3 the fifth, Shephatiah, by Abital; the sixth, Ithream, by his wife Eglah.
4 *These* six were born to him in Hebron. There he reigned seven years and six months, and in Jerusalem he reigned thirty-three years.
5 And these were born to him in Jerusalem: Shimea,[a] Shobab, Nathan, and Solomon—four by Bathshua[b] the daughter of Ammiel.[c]
6 Also *there* were Ibhar, Elishama,[a] Eliphelet,[b]
7 Nogah, Nepheg, Japhia,
8 Elishama, Eliada,[a] and Eliphelet—nine *in all.*
9 *These were* all the sons of David, besides the sons of the concubines, and Tamar their sister.

The Family of Solomon

10 Solomon's son *was* Rehoboam; Abijah[a] *was* his son, Asa his son, Jehoshaphat his son,
11 Joram[a] his son, Ahaziah his son, Joash[b] his son,
12 Amaziah his son, Azariah[a] his son, Jotham his son,
13 Ahaz his son, Hezekiah his son, Manasseh his son,
14 Amon his son, *and* Josiah his son.
15 The sons of Josiah *were* Johanan the firstborn, the second Jehoiakim, the third Zedekiah, and the fourth Shallum.[a]
16 The sons of Jehoiakim *were* Jeconiah his son *and* Zedekiah[a] his son.

The Family of Jeconiah

17 And the sons of Jeconiah[a] *were* Assir,[b] Shealtiel his son,
18 *and* Malchiram, Pedaiah, Shenazzar, Jecamiah, Hoshama, and Nedabiah.
19 The sons of Pedaiah *were* Zerubbabel and Shimei. The sons of Zerubbabel *were* Meshullam, Hananiah, Shelomith their sister,
20 and Hashubah, Ohel, Berechiah, Hasadiah, and Jushab-Hesed—five *in all.*
21 The sons of Hananiah *were* Pelatiah and Jeshaiah, the sons of Rephaiah, the sons of Arnan, the sons of Obadiah, and the sons of Shechaniah.
22 The son of Shechaniah was Shemaiah. The sons of Shemaiah *were* Hattush, Igal, Bariah, Neariah, and Shaphat—six *in all.*
23 The sons of Neariah *were* Elioenai, Hezekiah, and Azrikam—three *in all.*

2:52 [a]Same as *the Manahethites,* verse 54 **3:1** [a]Called *Chileab* in 2 Samuel 3:3 **3:5** [a]Spelled *Shammua* in 14:4 and 2 Samuel 5:14 [b]Spelled *Bathsheba* in 2 Samuel 11:3 [c]Called *Eliam* in 2 Samuel 11:3 **3:6** [a]Spelled *Elishua* in 14:5 and 2 Samuel 5:15 [b]Spelled *Elpelet* in 14:5 **3:8** [a]Spelled *Beeliada* in 14:7 **3:10** [a]Spelled *Abijam* in 1 Kings 15:1 **3:11** [a]Spelled *Jehoram* in 2 Kings 1:17 and 8:16 [b]Spelled *Jehoash* in 2 Kings 12:1 **3:12** [a]Called *Uzziah* in Isaiah 6:1 **3:15** [a]Called *Jehoahaz* in 2 Kings 23:31 **3:16** [a]Compare 2 Kings 24:17 **3:17** [a]Also called *Coniah* in Jeremiah 22:24 and *Jehoiachin* in 2 Kings 24:8 [b]Or *Jeconiah the captive were*

24 The sons of Elioenai *were* Hodaviah,
Eliashib, Pelaiah, Akkub, Johanan, Delaiah,
and Anani—seven *in all.*

The Family of Judah

4 The sons of Judah *were* Perez, Hezron,
Carmi, Hur, and Shobal.
2 And Reaiah the son of Shobal begot
Jahath, and Jahath begot Ahumai and La-
had. These *were* the families of the Zorathites.
3 These *were the sons of* the father of Etam:
Jezreel, Ishma, and Idbash; and the name of
their sister *was* Hazelelponi;
4 and Penuel *was* the father of Gedor, and
Ezer *was the* father of Hushah. These *were*
the sons of Hur, the firstborn of Ephrathah
the father of Bethlehem.
5 And Ashhur the father of Tekoa had two
wives, Helah and Naarah.
6 Naarah bore him Ahuzzam, Hepher,
Temeni, and Haahashtari. These *were* the
sons of Naarah.
7 The sons of Helah *were* Zereth, Zohar, and
Ethnan;
8 and Koz begot Anub, Zobebah, and the
families of Aharhel the son of Harum.
9 Now Jabez was more honorable than his
brothers, and his mother called his name
Jabez,[a] saying, "Because I bore *him* in pain."
➤ 10 And Jabez called on the God of Israel saying, "Oh, that You would bless me indeed, and
enlarge my territory, that Your hand would be
with me, and that You would keep *me* from
evil, that I may not cause pain!" So God
granted him what he requested.
11 Chelub the brother of Shuhah begot
Mehir, who *was* the father of Eshton.
12 And Eshton begot Beth-Rapha, Paseah,
and Tehinnah the father of Ir-Nahash. These
were the men of Rechah.
13 The sons of Kenaz *were* Othniel and Seraiah. The sons of Othniel *were* Hathath,[a]
14 and Meonothai *who* begot Ophrah. Seraiah begot Joab the father of Ge Harashim,[a] for
they were craftsmen.
15 The sons of Caleb the son of Jephunneh
were Iru, Elah, and Naam. The son of Elah
was Kenaz.
16 The sons of Jehallelel *were* Ziph, Ziphah,
Tiria, and Asarel.
17 The sons of Ezrah *were* Jether, Mered,
Epher, and Jalon. And *Mered's wife*[a] bore Miriam, Shammai, and Ishbah the father of Eshtemoa.
18 (His wife Jehudijah[a] bore Jered the father
of Gedor, Heber the father of Sochoh, and
Jekuthiel the father of Zanoah.) And these
were the sons of Bithiah the daughter of
Pharaoh, whom Mered took.
19 The sons of Hodiah's wife, the sister of
Naham, *were* the fathers of Keilah the Gar-
mite and of Eshtemoa the Maachathite.
20 And the sons of Shimon *were* Amnon,
Rinnah, Ben-Hanan, and Tilon. And the sons
of Ishi *were* Zoheth and Ben-Zoheth.
21 The sons of Shelah the son of Judah *were*
Er the father of Lecah, Laadah the father of
Mareshah, and the families of the house of
the linen workers of the house of Ashbea;
22 also Jokim, the men of Chozeba, and
Joash; Saraph, who ruled in Moab, and
Jashubi-Lehem. Now the records are ancient.
23 These *were* the potters and those who
dwell at Netaim[a] and Gederah;[b] there they
dwelt with the king for his work.

The Family of Simeon

24 The sons of Simeon *were* Nemuel, Jamin,
Jarib,[a] Zerah,[b] *and* Shaul,
25 Shallum his son, Mibsam his son, and
Mishma his son.
26 And the sons of Mishma *were* Hamuel his
son, Zacchur his son, and Shimei his son.
27 Shimei had sixteen sons and six daughters; but his brothers did not have many children, nor did any of their families multiply as
much as the children of Judah.
28 They dwelt at Beersheba, Moladah, Hazar
Shual,
29 Bilhah, Ezem, Tolad,
30 Bethuel, Hormah, Ziklag,
31 Beth Marcaboth, Hazar Susim, Beth Biri,
and at Shaaraim. These *were* their cities until
the reign of David.
32 And their villages *were* Etam, Ain, Rimmon, Tochen, and Ashan—five cities—
33 and all the villages that *were* around these
cities as far as Baal.[a] These *were* their
dwelling places, and they maintained their
genealogy:
34 Meshobab, Jamlech, and Joshah the son
of Amaziah;

4:9 [a]Literally *He Will Cause Pain* **4:13** [a]Septuagint and Vulgate add *and Meonothai.* **4:14** [a]Literally *Valley of Craftsmen* **4:17** [a]Literally *she* **4:18** [a]Or *His Judean wife* **4:23** [a]Literally *Plants* [b]Literally *Hedges* **4:24** [a]Called *Jachin* in Genesis 46:10 [b]Called *Zohar* in Genesis 46:10 **4:33** [a]Or *Baalath Beer* (compare Joshua 19:8)

LIFE LESSONS

➤ 4:10 — *And Jabez called on the God of Israel . . . . God granted him what he requested.*

Jabez lived an "honorable" life (1 Chr. 4:9) and made specific prayer requests to God—and the Lord heard him and answered his prayers. Prayer is life's greatest time saver.

35 Joel, and Jehu the son of Joshibiah, the
son of Seraiah, the son of Asiel;
36 Elioenai, Jaakobah, Jeshohaiah, Asaiah,
Adiel, Jesimiel, and Benaiah;
37 Ziza the son of Shiphi, the son of Allon,
the son of Jedaiah, the son of Shimri, the son
of Shemaiah—
38 these mentioned by name *were* leaders in
their families, and their father's house increased greatly.
39 So they went to the entrance of Gedor, as
far as the east side of the valley, to seek pasture for their flocks.
40 And they found rich, good pasture, and
the land *was* broad, quiet, and peaceful; for
some Hamites formerly lived there.
41 These recorded by name came in the days
of Hezekiah king of Judah; and they attacked
their tents and the Meunites who were found
there, and utterly destroyed them, as it is to
this day. So they dwelt in their place, because
there was pasture for their flocks there.
42 Now *some* of them, five hundred men of
the sons of Simeon, went to Mount Seir, having as their captains Pelatiah, Neariah,
Rephaiah, and Uzziel, the sons of Ishi.
43 And they defeated the rest of the Amalekites who had escaped. They have dwelt there
to this day.

The Family of Reuben

5 Now the sons of Reuben the firstborn of
Israel—he *was* indeed the firstborn, but
because he defiled his father's bed, his
birthright was given to the sons of Joseph, the
son of Israel, so that the genealogy is not
listed according to the birthright;
2 yet Judah prevailed over his brothers, and
from him *came* a ruler, although the
birthright was Joseph's—
3 the sons of Reuben the firstborn of Israel
were Hanoch, Pallu, Hezron, and Carmi.
4 The sons of Joel *were* Shemaiah his son,
Gog his son, Shimei his son,
5 Micah his son, Reaiah his son, Baal his
son,
6 and Beerah his son, whom Tiglath-Pileser[a]
king of Assyria carried into captivity. He *was*
leader of the Reubenites.
7 And his brethren by their families, when
the genealogy of their generations was registered: the chief, Jeiel, and Zechariah,
8 and Bela the son of Azaz, the son of
Shema, the son of Joel, who dwelt in Aroer, as
far as Nebo and Baal Meon.
9 Eastward they settled as far as the entrance of the wilderness this side of the River
Euphrates, because their cattle had multiplied
in the land of Gilead.
10 Now in the days of Saul they made war
with the Hagrites, who fell by their hand; and
they dwelt in their tents throughout the entire
area east of Gilead.

The Family of Gad

11 And the children of Gad dwelt next to
them in the land of Bashan as far as Salcah:
12 Joel *was* the chief, Shapham the next, then
Jaanai and Shaphat in Bashan,
13 and their brethren of their father's house:
Michael, Meshullam, Sheba, Jorai, Jachan,
Zia, and Eber—seven *in all.*
14 These *were* the children of Abihail the son
of Huri, the son of Jaroah, the son of Gilead,
the son of Michael, the son of Jeshishai, the
son of Jahdo, the son of Buz;
15 Ahi the son of Abdiel, the son of Guni, *was*
chief of their father's house.
16 And *the Gadites* dwelt in Gilead, in
Bashan and in its villages, and in all the common-lands of Sharon within their borders.
17 All these were registered by genealogies
in the days of Jotham king of Judah, and in
the days of Jeroboam king of Israel.
18 The sons of Reuben, the Gadites, and half
the tribe of Manasseh *had* forty-four thousand seven hundred and sixty valiant men,
men able to bear shield and sword, to shoot
with the bow, and skillful in war, who went to
war.
19 They made war with the Hagrites, Jetur,
Naphish, and Nodab.
20 And they were helped against them, and ➤
the Hagrites were delivered into their hand,
and all who *were* with them, for they cried out
to God in the battle. He heeded their prayer,
because they put their trust in Him.
21 Then they took away their livestock—fifty
thousand of their camels, two hundred and
fifty thousand of their sheep, and two thousand of their donkeys—also one hundred
thousand of their men;
22 for many fell dead, because the war *was*
God's. And they dwelt in their place until the
captivity.

The Family of Manasseh (East)

23 So the children of the half-tribe of

5:6 [a]Hebrew *Tilgath-Pilneser*

LIFE LESSONS

➤ **5:20 — *He heeded their prayer, because they put their trust in Him.***

God loves to answer the prayers of those who put their trust in Him and cry out to Him for deliverance. When we fight all our battles on our knees, we win every time.

Manasseh dwelt in the land. Their *numbers*
increased from Bashan to Baal Hermon, that
is, to Senir, or Mount Hermon.
24 These *were* the heads of their fathers'
houses: Epher, Ishi, Eliel, Azriel, Jeremiah,
Hodaviah, and Jahdiel. They were mighty
men of valor, famous men, *and* heads of their
fathers' houses.
25 And they were unfaithful to the God of
their fathers, and played the harlot after the
gods of the peoples of the land, whom God
had destroyed before them.
➤ 26 So the God of Israel stirred up the spirit of
Pul king of Assyria, that is, Tiglath-Pileser[a]
king of Assyria. He carried the Reubenites,
the Gadites, and the half-tribe of Manasseh
into captivity. He took them to Halah, Habor,
Hara, and the river of Gozan to this day.

The Family of Levi

6 The sons of Levi *were* Gershon, Kohath,
and Merari.
2 The sons of Kohath *were* Amram, Izhar,
Hebron, and Uzziel.
3 The children of Amram *were* Aaron, Moses, and Miriam. And the sons of Aaron *were*
Nadab, Abihu, Eleazar, and Ithamar.
4 Eleazar begot Phinehas, *and* Phinehas
begot Abishua;
5 Abishua begot Bukki, and Bukki begot
Uzzi;
6 Uzzi begot Zerahiah, and Zerahiah begot
Meraioth;
7 Meraioth begot Amariah, and Amariah
begot Ahitub;
8 Ahitub begot Zadok, and Zadok begot
Ahimaaz;
9 Ahimaaz begot Azariah, and Azariah
begot Johanan;
10 Johanan begot Azariah (it was he who
ministered as priest in the temple that Solomon built in Jerusalem);
11 Azariah begot Amariah, and Amariah
begot Ahitub;
12 Ahitub begot Zadok, and Zadok begot
Shallum;
13 Shallum begot Hilkiah, and Hilkiah begot
Azariah;
14 Azariah begot Seraiah, and Seraiah begot
Jehozadak.
15 Jehozadak went *into captivity* when the
LORD carried Judah and Jerusalem into captivity by the hand of Nebuchadnezzar.
16 The sons of Levi *were* Gershon,[a] Kohath,
and Merari.
17 These are the names of the sons of Gershon: Libni and Shimei.
18 The sons of Kohath *were* Amram, Izhar,
Hebron, and Uzziel.
19 The sons of Merari *were* Mahli and Mushi.
Now these *are* the families of the Levites according to their fathers:
20 Of Gershon *were* Libni his son, Jahath his
son, Zimmah his son,
21 Joah his son, Iddo his son, Zerah his son,
and Jeatherai his son.
22 The sons of Kohath *were* Amminadab his
son, Korah his son, Assir his son,
23 Elkanah his son, Ebiasaph his son, Assir
his son,
24 Tahath his son, Uriel his son, Uzziah his
son, and Shaul his son.
25 The sons of Elkanah *were* Amasai and
Ahimoth.
26 *As for* Elkanah,[a] the sons of Elkanah *were*
Zophai[b] his son, Nahath[c] his son,
27 Eliab[a] his son, Jeroham his son, *and* Elkanah his son.
28 The sons of Samuel *were Joel*[a] the firstborn, and Abijah the second.[b]
29 The sons of Merari *were* Mahli, Libni his
son, Shimei his son, Uzzah his son,
30 Shimea his son, Haggiah his son, *and* Asaiah his son.

Musicians in the House of the LORD

31 Now these are the men whom David appointed over the service of song in the house
of the LORD, after the ark came to rest.
32 They were ministering with music before
the dwelling place of the tabernacle of meeting, until Solomon had built the house of the
LORD in Jerusalem, and they served in their
office according to their order.
33 And these *are* the ones who ministered
with their sons: Of the sons of the Kohathites
were Heman the singer, the son of Joel, the
son of Samuel,
34 the son of Elkanah, the son of Jeroham,
the son of Eliel,[a] the son of Toah,[b]
35 the son of Zuph, the son of Elkanah, the
son of Mahath, the son of Amasai,
36 the son of Elkanah, the son of Joel, the son
of Azariah, the son of Zephaniah,
37 the son of Tahath, the son of Assir, the son
of Ebiasaph, the son of Korah,

5:26 [a]Hebrew *Tilgath-Pilneser* **6:16** [a]Hebrew *Gershom* (alternate spelling of *Gershon,* as in verses 1, 17, 20, 43, 62, and 71) **6:26** [a]Compare verse 35 [b]Spelled *Zuph* in verse 35 and 1 Samuel 1:1 [c]Compare verse 34 **6:27** [a]Compare verse 34 **6:28** [a]Following Septuagint, Syriac, and Arabic (compare verse 33 and 1 Samuel 8:2) [b]Hebrew *Vasheni* **6:34** [a]Spelled *Elihu* in 1 Samuel 1:1 [b]Spelled *Tohu* in 1 Samuel 1:1

LIFE LESSONS

➤ **5:26 — *He carried the Reubenites, the Gadites, and the half-tribe of Manasseh into captivity.***

While eager obedience brings blessing, stubborn disobedience brings judgment.

38 the son of Izhar, the son of Kohath, the son
of Levi, the son of Israel.
39 And his brother Asaph, who stood at his
right hand, *was* Asaph the son of Berachiah,
the son of Shimea,
40 the son of Michael, the son of Baaseiah,
the son of Malchijah,
41 the son of Ethni, the son of Zerah, the son
of Adaiah,
42 the son of Ethan, the son of Zimmah, the
son of Shimei,
43 the son of Jahath, the son of Gershon, the
son of Levi.
44 Their brethren, the sons of Merari, on the
left hand, *were* Ethan the son of Kishi, the son
of Abdi, the son of Malluch,
45 the son of Hashabiah, the son of Amaziah,
the son of Hilkiah,
46 the son of Amzi, the son of Bani, the son of
Shamer,
47 the son of Mahli, the son of Mushi, the son
of Merari, the son of Levi.
48 And their brethren, the Levites, *were* appointed to every kind of service of the tabernacle of the house of God.

The Family of Aaron

49 But Aaron and his sons offered sacrifices
on the altar of burnt offering and on the altar
of incense, for all the work of the Most Holy
Place, and to make atonement for Israel, according to all that Moses the servant of God
had commanded.
50 Now these *are* the sons of Aaron: Eleazar
his son, Phinehas his son, Abishua his son,
51 Bukki his son, Uzzi his son, Zerahiah his
son,
52 Meraioth his son, Amariah his son, Ahitub
his son,
53 Zadok his son, *and* Ahimaaz his son.

Dwelling Places of the Levites

54 Now these *are* their dwelling places
throughout their settlements in their territory,
for they were *given* by lot to the sons of
Aaron, of the family of the Kohathites:
55 They gave them Hebron in the land of Judah, with its surrounding common-lands.
56 But the fields of the city and its villages
they gave to Caleb the son of Jephunneh.
57 And to the sons of Aaron they gave *one of*
the cities of refuge, Hebron; also Libnah with
its common-lands, Jattir, Eshtemoa with its
common-lands,
58 Hilen[a] with its common-lands, Debir with
its common-lands,
59 Ashan[a] with its common-lands, and Beth
Shemesh with its common-lands.
60 And from the tribe of Benjamin: Geba
with its common-lands, Alemeth[a] with its
common-lands, and Anathoth with its common-lands. All their cities among their families *were* thirteen.
61 To the rest of the family of the tribe of the
Kohathites *they gave* by lot ten cities from
half the tribe of Manasseh.
62 And to the sons of Gershon, throughout
their families, *they gave* thirteen cities from
the tribe of Issachar, from the tribe of Asher,
from the tribe of Naphtali, and from the tribe
of Manasseh in Bashan.
63 To the sons of Merari, throughout their
families, *they gave* twelve cities from the tribe
of Reuben, from the tribe of Gad, and from
the tribe of Zebulun.
64 So the children of Israel gave *these* cities
with their common-lands to the Levites.
65 And they gave by lot from the tribe of the
children of Judah, from the tribe of the children of Simeon, and from the tribe of the children of Benjamin these cities which are called
by *their* names.
66 Now some of the families of the sons of
Kohath *were given* cities as their territory
from the tribe of Ephraim.
67 And they gave them *one of* the cities of
refuge, Shechem with its common-lands, in
the mountains of Ephraim, also Gezer with its
common-lands,
68 Jokmeam with its common-lands, Beth
Horon with its common-lands,
69 Aijalon with its common-lands, and Gath
Rimmon with its common-lands.
70 And from the half-tribe of Manasseh:
Aner with its common-lands and Bileam with
its common-lands, for the rest of the family of
the sons of Kohath.
71 From the family of the half-tribe of Manasseh the sons of Gershon *were given* Golan in
Bashan with its common-lands and Ashtaroth
with its common-lands.
72 And from the tribe of Issachar: Kedesh
with its common-lands, Daberath with its
common-lands,
73 Ramoth with its common-lands, and
Anem with its common-lands.
74 And from the tribe of Asher: Mashal with
its common-lands, Abdon with its common-
lands,
75 Hukok with its common-lands, and Rehob
with its common-lands.
76 And from the tribe of Naphtali: Kedesh in
Galilee with its common-lands, Hammon with
its common-lands, and Kirjathaim with its
common-lands.
77 From the tribe of Zebulun the rest of the
children of Merari *were given* Rimmon[a] with
its common-lands and Tabor with its common-lands.
78 And on the other side of the Jordan,
across from Jericho, on the east side of the
Jordan, *they were given* from the tribe of Reuben: Bezer in the wilderness with its common-lands, Jahzah with its common-lands,

---

6:58 [a]Spelled *Holon* in Joshua 21:15 **6:59** [a]Spelled *Ain* in Joshua 21:16 **6:60** [a]Spelled *Almon* in Joshua 21:18
6:77 [a]Hebrew *Rimmono,* alternate spelling of *Rimmon;* see 4:32

79 Kedemoth with its common-lands, and
Mephaath with its common-lands.
80 And from the tribe of Gad: Ramoth in
Gilead with its common-lands, Mahanaim
with its common-lands,
81 Heshbon with its common-lands, and
Jazer with its common-lands.

The Family of Issachar

7 The sons of Issachar *were* Tola, Puah,[a]
Jashub, and Shimron—four *in all.*
2 The sons of Tola *were* Uzzi, Rephaiah,
Jeriel, Jahmai, Jibsam, and Shemuel, heads of
their father's house. *The sons* of Tola *were*
mighty men of valor in their generations;
their number in the days of David *was*
twenty-two thousand six hundred.
3 The son of Uzzi *was* Izrahiah, and the
sons of Izrahiah *were* Michael, Obadiah, Joel,
and Ishiah. All five of them *were* chief men.
4 And with them, by their generations, according to their fathers' houses, *were* thirty-
six thousand troops ready for war; for they
had many wives and sons.
5 Now their brethren among all the families
of Issachar *were* mighty men of valor, listed
by their genealogies, eighty-seven thousand
in all.

The Family of Benjamin

6 *The sons* of Benjamin *were* Bela, Becher,
and Jediael—three *in all.*
7 The sons of Bela were Ezbon, Uzzi, Uzziel,
Jerimoth, and Iri—five *in all.* They *were* heads
of *their* fathers' houses, and they were listed
by their genealogies, twenty-two thousand
and thirty-four mighty men of valor.
8 The sons of Becher *were* Zemirah, Joash,
Eliezer, Elioenai, Omri, Jerimoth, Abijah,
Anathoth, and Alemeth. All these *are* the sons
of Becher.
9 And they were recorded by genealogy according to their generations, heads of their fathers' houses, twenty thousand two hundred
mighty men of valor.
10 The son of Jediael *was* Bilhan, and the
sons of Bilhan *were* Jeush, Benjamin, Ehud,
Chenaanah, Zethan, Tharshish, and Ahisha-
har.
11 All these sons of Jediael *were* heads of
their fathers' houses; *there were* seventeen
thousand two hundred mighty men of valor
fit to go out for war *and* battle.
12 Shuppim and Huppim[a] *were* the sons of Ir,
and Hushim *was* the son of Aher.

The Family of Naphtali

13 The sons of Naphtali *were* Jahziel,[a] Guni,
Jezer, and Shallum,[b] the sons of Bilhah.

The Family of Manasseh (West)

14 The descendants of Manasseh: his Syrian
concubine bore him Machir the father of
Gilead, the father of Asriel.[a]
15 Machir took as his wife *the sister* of Huppim and Shuppim,[a] whose name *was* Maachah. The name of *Gilead's* grandson[b] *was*
Zelophehad,[c] but Zelophehad begot only
daughters.
16 (Maachah the wife of Machir bore a son,
and she called his name Peresh. The name of
his brother *was* Sheresh, and his sons *were*
Ulam and Rakem.
17 The son of Ulam *was* Bedan.) These *were*
the descendants of Gilead the son of Machir,
the son of Manasseh.
18 His sister Hammoleketh bore Ishhod,
Abiezer, and Mahlah.
19 And the sons of Shemida were Ahian,
Shechem, Likhi, and Aniam.

The Family of Ephraim

20 The sons of Ephraim *were* Shuthelah,
Bered his son, Tahath his son, Eladah his son,
Tahath his son,
21 Zabad his son, Shuthelah his son, and
Ezer and Elead. The men of Gath who were
born in *that* land killed *them* because they
came down to take away their cattle.
22 Then Ephraim their father mourned
many days, and his brethren came to comfort
him.
23 And when he went in to his wife, she conceived and bore a son; and he called his name
Beriah,[a] because tragedy had come upon his
house.
24 Now his daughter *was* Sheerah, who built
Lower and Upper Beth Horon and Uzzen
Sheerah;
25 and Rephah *was* his son, *as well* as
Resheph, and Telah his son, Tahan his son,
26 Laadan his son, Ammihud his son, Elishama his son,
27 Nun[a] his son, and Joshua his son.
28 Now their possessions and dwelling
places *were* Bethel and its towns: to the east
Naaran, to the west Gezer and its towns, and
Shechem and its towns, as far as Ayyah[a] and
its towns;
29 and by the borders of the children of Manasseh *were* Beth Shean and its towns,
Taanach and its towns, Megiddo and its
towns, Dor and its towns. In these dwelt the
children of Joseph, the son of Israel.

The Family of Asher

30 The sons of Asher *were* Imnah, Ishvah,
Ishvi, Beriah, and their sister Serah.

7:1 [a]Spelled *Puvah* in Genesis 46:13 **7:12** [a]Called *Hupham* in Numbers 26:39 **7:13** [a]Spelled *Jahzeel* in Genesis 46:24 [b]Spelled *Shillem* in Genesis 46:24 **7:14** [a]The son of Gilead (compare Numbers 26:30, 31) **7:15** [a]Compare verse 12 [b]Literally *the second* [c]Compare Numbers 26:30–33 **7:23** [a]Literally *In Tragedy* **7:27** [a]Hebrew *Non* **7:28** [a]Many Hebrew manuscripts, Bomberg, Septuagint, Targum, and Vulgate read *Gazza.*

31 The sons of Beriah *were* Heber and Malchiel, who was the father of Birzaith.[a]
32 And Heber begot Japhlet, Shomer,[a] Hotham,[b] and their sister Shua.
33 The sons of Japhlet *were* Pasach, Bimhal, and Ashvath. These *were* the children of Japhlet.
34 The sons of Shemer *were* Ahi, Rohgah, Jehubbah, and Aram.
35 And the sons of his brother Helem *were* Zophah, Imna, Shelesh, and Amal.
36 The sons of Zophah *were* Suah, Harnepher, Shual, Beri, Imrah,
37 Bezer, Hod, Shamma, Shilshah, Jithran,[a] and Beera.
38 The sons of Jether *were* Jephunneh, Pispah, and Ara.
39 The sons of Ulla *were* Arah, Haniel, and Rizia.
40 All these *were* the children of Asher, heads of *their* fathers' houses, choice men, mighty men of valor, chief leaders. And they were recorded by genealogies among the army fit for battle; their number *was* twenty-six thousand.

The Family Tree of King Saul of Benjamin

8 Now Benjamin begot Bela his firstborn, Ashbel the second, Aharah[a] the third,
2 Nohah the fourth, and Rapha the fifth.
3 The sons of Bela *were* Addar,[a] Gera, Abihud,
4 Abishua, Naaman, Ahoah,
5 Gera, Shephuphan, and Huram.
6 These *are* the sons of Ehud, who were the heads of the fathers' *houses* of the inhabitants of Geba, and who forced them to move to Manahath:
7 Naaman, Ahijah, and Gera who forced them to move. He begot Uzza and Ahihud.
8 Also Shaharaim had children in the country of Moab, after he had sent away Hushim and Baara his wives.
9 By Hodesh his wife he begot Jobab, Zibia, Mesha, Malcam,
10 Jeuz, Sachiah, and Mirmah. These *were* his sons, heads of their fathers' *houses.*
11 And by Hushim he begot Abitub and Elpaal.
12 The sons of Elpaal *were* Eber, Misham, and Shemed, who built Ono and Lod with its towns;
13 and Beriah and Shema, who *were* heads of their fathers' *houses* of the inhabitants of Aijalon, who drove out the inhabitants of Gath.
14 Ahio, Shashak, Jeremoth,
15 Zebadiah, Arad, Eder,
16 Michael, Ispah, and Joha *were* the sons of Beriah.
17 Zebadiah, Meshullam, Hizki, Heber,
18 Ishmerai, Jizliah, and Jobab *were* the sons of Elpaal.
19 Jakim, Zichri, Zabdi,
20 Elienai, Zillethai, Eliel,
21 Adaiah, Beraiah, and Shimrath *were* the sons of Shimei.
22 Ishpan, Eber, Eliel,
23 Abdon, Zichri, Hanan,
24 Hananiah, Elam, Antothijah,
25 Iphdeiah, and Penuel *were* the sons of Shashak.
26 Shamsherai, Shehariah, Athaliah,
27 Jaareshiah, Elijah, and Zichri *were* the sons of Jeroham.
28 These *were* heads of the fathers' *houses* by their generations, chief men. These dwelt in Jerusalem.
29 Now the father of Gibeon, whose wife's name *was* Maacah, dwelt at Gibeon.
30 And his firstborn son *was* Abdon, then Zur, Kish, Baal, Nadab,
31 Gedor, Ahio, Zecher,
32 and Mikloth, *who* begot Shimeah.[a] They also dwelt alongside their relatives in Jerusalem, with their brethren.
33 Ner[a] begot Kish, Kish begot Saul, and Saul begot Jonathan, Malchishua, Abinadab,[b] and Esh-Baal.[c]
34 The son of Jonathan *was* Merib-Baal,[a] and Merib-Baal begot Micah.
35 The sons of Micah *were* Pithon, Melech, Tarea, and Ahaz.
36 And Ahaz begot Jehoaddah;[a] Jehoaddah begot Alemeth, Azmaveth, and Zimri; and Zimri begot Moza.
37 Moza begot Binea, Raphah[a] his son, Eleasah his son, *and* Azel his son.
38 Azel had six sons whose names *were* these: Azrikam, Bocheru, Ishmael, Sheariah, Obadiah, and Hanan. All these *were* the sons of Azel.
39 And the sons of Eshek his brother *were* Ulam his firstborn, Jeush the second, and Eliphelet the third.
40 The sons of Ulam were mighty men of valor—archers. *They* had many sons and grandsons, one hundred and fifty *in all.* These *were* all sons of Benjamin.

9 So all Israel was recorded by genealogies, and indeed, they *were* inscribed in the book of the kings of Israel. But Judah was carried away captive to Babylon because of their unfaithfulness.
2 And the first inhabitants who *dwelt* in their possessions in their cities *were* Israelites, priests, Levites, and the Nethinim.

7:31 [a]Or *Birzavith* or *Birzoth* **7:32** [a]Spelled *Shemer* in verse 34 [b]Spelled *Helem* in verse 35 **7:37** [a]Spelled *Jether* in verse 38 **8:1** [a]Spelled *Ahiram* in Numbers 26:38 **8:3** [a]Called *Ard* in Numbers 26:40 **8:32** [a]Spelled *Shimeam* in 9:38 **8:33** [a]Also the son of Gibeon (compare 9:36, 39) [b]Called *Jishui* in 1 Samuel 14:49 [c]Called *Ishbosheth* in 2 Samuel 2:8 and elsewhere **8:34** [a]Called *Mephibosheth* in 2 Samuel 4:4 **8:36** [a]Spelled *Jarah* in 9:42 **8:37** [a]Spelled *Rephaiah* in 9:43

Dwellers in Jerusalem

3 Now in Jerusalem the children of Judah dwelt, and some of the children of Benjamin, and of the children of Ephraim and Manasseh:

4 Uthai the son of Ammihud, the son of Omri, the son of Imri, the son of Bani, of the descendants of Perez, the son of Judah.

5 Of the Shilonites: Asaiah the firstborn and his sons.

6 Of the sons of Zerah: Jeuel, and their brethren—six hundred and ninety.

7 Of the sons of Benjamin: Sallu the son of Meshullam, the son of Hodaviah, the son of Hassenuah;

8 Ibneiah the son of Jeroham; Elah the son of Uzzi, the son of Michri; Meshullam the son of Shephatiah, the son of Reuel, the son of Ibnijah;

9 and their brethren, according to their generations—nine hundred and fifty-six. All these men *were* heads of a father's *house* in their fathers' houses.

The Priests at Jerusalem

10 Of the priests: Jedaiah, Jehoiarib, and Jachin;

11 Azariah the son of Hilkiah, the son of Meshullam, the son of Zadok, the son of Meraioth, the son of Ahitub, the officer over the house of God;

12 Adaiah the son of Jeroham, the son of Pashur, the son of Malchijah; Maasai the son of Adiel, the son of Jahzerah, the son of Meshullam, the son of Meshillemith, the son of Immer;

13 and their brethren, heads of their fathers' houses—one thousand seven hundred and sixty. *They were* very able men for the work of the service of the house of God.

The Levites at Jerusalem

14 Of the Levites: Shemaiah the son of Hasshub, the son of Azrikam, the son of Hashabiah, of the sons of Merari;

15 Bakbakkar, Heresh, Galal, and Mattaniah the son of Micah, the son of Zichri, the son of Asaph;

16 Obadiah the son of Shemaiah, the son of Galal, the son of Jeduthun; and Berechiah the son of Asa, the son of Elkanah, who lived in the villages of the Netophathites.

The Levite Gatekeepers

17 And the gatekeepers *were* Shallum, Akkub, Talmon, Ahiman, and their brethren. Shallum *was* the chief.

18 Until then *they had been* gatekeepers for the camps of the children of Levi at the King's Gate on the east.

19 Shallum the son of Kore, the son of Ebiasaph, the son of Korah, and his brethren, from his father's house, the Korahites, *were* in charge of the work of the service, gatekeepers of the tabernacle. Their fathers had been keepers of the entrance to the camp of the LORD.

20 And Phinehas the son of Eleazar had been the officer over them in time past; the LORD *was* with him.

21 Zechariah the son of Meshelemiah *was* keeper of the door of the tabernacle of meeting.

22 All those chosen as gatekeepers *were* two hundred and twelve. They were recorded by their genealogy, in their villages. David and Samuel the seer had appointed them to their trusted office.

23 So they and their children *were* in charge of the gates of the house of the LORD, the house of the tabernacle, by assignment.

24 The gatekeepers were assigned to the four directions: the east, west, north, and south.

25 And their brethren in their villages *had* to come with them from time to time for seven days.

26 For in this trusted office *were* four chief gatekeepers; they were Levites. And they had charge over the chambers and treasuries of the house of God.

27 And they lodged *all* around the house of God because they *had* the responsibility, and they *were* in charge of opening *it* every morning.

Other Levite Responsibilities

28 Now *some* of them were in charge of the serving vessels, for they brought them in and took them out by count.

29 *Some* of them *were* appointed over the furnishings and over all the implements of the sanctuary, and over the fine flour and the wine and the oil and the incense and the spices.

30 And *some* of the sons of the priests made the ointment of the spices.

31 Mattithiah of the Levites, the firstborn of Shallum the Korahite, had the trusted office over the things that were baked in the pans.

32 And some of their brethren of the sons of

LIFE LESSONS

➤ **9:1 — *But Judah was carried away captive to Babylon because of their unfaithfulness.***

Judah did not get dragged to Babylon because it lacked political power, military strength, diplomatic connections, or financial resources. Unfaithfulness to God caused the exile. We reap what we sow, more than we sow, and later than we sow.

the Kohathites *were* in charge of preparing
the showbread for every Sabbath.
33 These are the singers, heads of the fathers'
houses of the Levites, *who lodged* in the
chambers, *and were* free *from other duties;*
for they were employed in *that* work day and
night.
34 These heads of the fathers' *houses* of the
Levites *were* heads throughout their generations. They dwelt at Jerusalem.

The Family of King Saul

35 Jeiel the father of Gibeon, whose wife's
name *was* Maacah, dwelt at Gibeon.
36 His firstborn son *was* Abdon, then Zur,
Kish, Baal, Ner, Nadab,
37 Gedor, Ahio, Zechariah,[a] and Mikloth.
38 And Mikloth begot Shimeam.[a] They also
dwelt alongside their relatives in Jerusalem,
with their brethren.
39 Ner begot Kish, Kish begot Saul, and Saul
begot Jonathan, Malchishua, Abinadab, and
Esh-Baal.
40 The son of Jonathan *was* Merib-Baal, and
Merib-Baal begot Micah.
41 The sons of Micah *were* Pithon, Melech,
Tahrea,[a] and Ahaz.[b]
42 And Ahaz begot Jarah;[a] Jarah begot
Alemeth, Azmaveth, and Zimri; and Zimri
begot Moza;
43 Moza begot Binea, Rephaiah[a] his son,
Eleasah his son, and Azel his son.
44 And Azel had six sons whose names *were*
these: Azrikam, Bocheru, Ishmael, Sheariah,
Obadiah, and Hanan; these *were* the sons of
Azel.

Tragic End of Saul and His Sons

10 Now the Philistines fought against Israel; and the men of Israel fled from before the Philistines, and fell slain on Mount
Gilboa.
2 Then the Philistines followed hard after
Saul and his sons. And the Philistines killed
Jonathan, Abinadab, and Malchishua, Saul's
sons.
3 The battle became fierce against Saul. The
archers hit him, and he was wounded by the
archers.
4 Then Saul said to his armorbearer, "Draw
your sword, and thrust me through with it,
lest these uncircumcised men come and
abuse me." But his armorbearer would not,
for he was greatly afraid. Therefore Saul took
a sword and fell on it.
5 And when his armorbearer saw that Saul
was dead, he also fell on his sword and died.
6 So Saul and his three sons died, and all his
house died together.
7 And when all the men of Israel who *were*
in the valley saw that they had fled and that
Saul and his sons were dead, they forsook
their cities and fled; then the Philistines came
and dwelt in them.
8 So it happened the next day, when the Philistines came to strip the slain, that they found
Saul and his sons fallen on Mount Gilboa.
9 And they stripped him and took his head
and his armor, and sent word throughout the
land of the Philistines to proclaim the news *in
the temple* of their idols and among the people.
10 Then they put his armor in the temple of
their gods, and fastened his head in the temple of Dagon.
11 And when all Jabesh Gilead heard all that
the Philistines had done to Saul,
12 all the valiant men arose and took the
body of Saul and the bodies of his sons; and
they brought them to Jabesh, and buried their
bones under the tamarisk tree at Jabesh, and
fasted seven days.
13 So Saul died for his unfaithfulness which
he had committed against the LORD, because
he did not keep the word of the LORD, and also
because he consulted a medium for guidance.
14 But *he* did not inquire of the LORD; therefore He killed him, and turned the kingdom
over to David the son of Jesse.

David Made King over All Israel

11 Then all Israel came together to David
at Hebron, saying, "Indeed we *are* your
bone and your flesh.
2 "Also, in time past, even when Saul was
king, you *were* the one who led Israel out and
brought them in; and the LORD your God said
to you, 'You shall shepherd My people Israel,
and be ruler over My people Israel.'"
3 Therefore all the elders of Israel came to the
king at Hebron, and David made a covenant

9:37 [a]Called *Zecher* in 8:31 **9:38** [a]Spelled *Shimeah* in 8:32 **9:41** [a]Spelled *Tarea* in 8:35 [b]Following Arabic, Syriac, Targum, and Vulgate (compare 8:35); Masoretic Text and Septuagint omit *and Ahaz.* **9:42** [a]Spelled *Jehoaddah* in 8:36 **9:43** [a]Spelled *Raphah* in 8:37

LIFE LESSONS

➤ 10:14 — *But he did not inquire of the LORD; therefore He killed him, and turned the kingdom over to David the son of Jesse.*

In all matters that require guidance, whether large or small, God wants us to come to Him first. If necessary, He will move heaven and earth to show us His will.

➤ 11:2 — *". . . and the LORD your God said to you, 'You shall shepherd My people Israel, and be ruler over My people Israel.'"*

David was to rule Israel much as he had shepherded his father's flocks: up close, tenderly, wisely, for their benefit and not merely for his own gain. He was to picture God's care of us as the great Shepherd (Heb. 13:20).

with them at Hebron before the LORD. And they
anointed David king over Israel, according to
the word of the LORD by Samuel.

The City of David

4 And David and all Israel went to Jerusalem, which is Jebus, where the Jebusites
were, the inhabitants of the land.
5 But the inhabitants of Jebus said to David,
"You shall not come in here!" Nevertheless
David took the stronghold of Zion (that is, the
City of David).
6 Now David said, "Whoever attacks the Jebusites first shall be chief and captain." And
Joab the son of Zeruiah went up first, and became chief.
7 Then David dwelt in the stronghold; therefore they called it the City of David.
8 And he built the city around it, from the
Millo[a] to the surrounding area. Joab repaired
the rest of the city.
➤ 9 So David went on and became great, and
the LORD of hosts *was* with him.

The Mighty Men of David

10 Now these *were* the heads of the mighty
men whom David had, who strengthened
themselves with him in his kingdom, with all
Israel, to make him king, according to the
word of the LORD concerning Israel.
11 And this *is* the number of the mighty men
whom David had: Jashobeam the son of a
Hachmonite, chief of the captains;[a] he had
lifted up his spear against three hundred,
killed *by him* at one time.
12 After him *was* Eleazar the son of Dodo,
the Ahohite, who *was one* of the three mighty
men.
13 He was with David at Pasdammim. Now
there the Philistines were gathered for battle,
and there was a piece of ground full of barley.
So the people fled from the Philistines.
14 But they stationed themselves in the middle of *that* field, defended it, and killed the
Philistines. So the LORD brought about a great
victory.
15 Now three of the thirty chief men went
down to the rock to David, into the cave of
Adullam; and the army of the Philistines encamped in the Valley of Rephaim.
16 David *was* then in the stronghold, and the
garrison of the Philistines *was* then in Bethlehem.
17 And David said with longing, "Oh, that
someone would give me a drink of water
from the well of Bethlehem, which is by the
gate!"
18 So the three broke through the camp of
the Philistines, drew water from the well of
Bethlehem that *was* by the gate, and took *it*
and brought *it* to David. Nevertheless David
would not drink it, but poured it out to the
LORD.
19 And he said, "Far be it from me, O my God,
that I should do this! Shall I drink the blood
of these men *who have put* their lives *in jeopardy*? For at the risk of their lives they
brought it." Therefore he would not drink it.
These things were done by the three mighty
men.
20 Abishai the brother of Joab was chief of
another three.[a] He had lifted up his spear
against three hundred *men*, killed *them*, and
won a name among *these* three.
21 Of the three he was more honored than
the other two men. Therefore he became their
captain. However he did not attain to the *first*
three.
22 Benaiah was the son of Jehoiada, the son
of a valiant man from Kabzeel, who had done
many deeds. He had killed two lion-like heroes of Moab. He also had gone down and
killed a lion in the midst of a pit on a snowy
day.
23 And he killed an Egyptian, a man of *great*
height, five cubits tall. In the Egyptian's hand
there was a spear like a weaver's beam; and
he went down to him with a staff, wrested the
spear out of the Egyptian's hand, and killed
him with his own spear.
24 These *things* Benaiah the son of Jehoiada
did, and won a name among three mighty
men.
25 Indeed he was more honored than the
thirty, but he did not attain to the *first* three.
And David appointed him over his guard.
26 Also the mighty warriors *were* Asahel the
brother of Joab, Elhanan the son of Dodo of
Bethlehem,
27 Shammoth the Harorite,[a] Helez the Pelonite,[b]
28 Ira the son of Ikkesh the Tekoite, Abiezer
the Anathothite,
29 Sibbechai the Hushathite, Ilai the Ahohite,
30 Maharai the Netophathite, Heled[a] the son
of Baanah the Netophathite,
31 Ithai[a] the son of Ribai of Gibeah, of the
sons of Benjamin, Benaiah the Pirathonite,

11:8 [a]Literally *The Landfill* **11:11** [a]Following Qere; Kethib, Septuagint, and Vulgate read *the thirty* (compare 2 Samuel 23:8). **11:20** [a]Following Masoretic Text, Septuagint, and Vulgate; Syriac reads *thirty*. **11:27** [a]Spelled *Harodite* in 2 Samuel 23:25 [b]Called *Paltite* in 2 Samuel 23:26 **11:30** [a]Spelled *Heleb* in 2 Samuel 23:29 and *Heldai* in 1 Chronicles 27:15 **11:31** [a]Spelled *Ittai* in 2 Samuel 23:29

LIFE LESSONS

➤ 11:9 — *So David went on and became great, and the LORD of hosts was with him.*

David became great because the Lord was with him. Only when David acted without the Lord did he become something much less than great.

32 Hurai[a] of the brooks of Gaash, Abiel[b] the Arbathite,
33 Azmaveth the Baharumite,[a] Eliahba the Shaalbonite,
34 the sons of Hashem the Gizonite, Jonathan the son of Shageh the Hararite,
35 Ahiam the son of Sacar the Hararite, Eliphal the son of Ur,
36 Hepher the Mecherathite, Ahijah the Pelonite,
37 Hezro the Carmelite, Naarai the son of Ezbai,
38 Joel the brother of Nathan, Mibhar the son of Hagri,
39 Zelek the Ammonite, Naharai the Berothite[a] (the armorbearer of Joab the son of Zeruiah),
40 Ira the Ithrite, Gareb the Ithrite,
41 Uriah the Hittite, Zabad the son of Ahlai,
42 Adina the son of Shiza the Reubenite (a chief of the Reubenites) and thirty with him,
43 Hanan the son of Maachah, Joshaphat the Mithnite,
44 Uzzia the Ashterathite, Shama and Jeiel the sons of Hotham the Aroerite,
45 Jediael the son of Shimri, and Joha his brother, the Tizite,
46 Eliel the Mahavite, Jeribai and Joshaviah the sons of Elnaam, Ithmah the Moabite,
47 Eliel, Obed, and Jaasiel the Mezobaite.

The Growth of David's Army

12 Now these *were* the men who came to David at Ziklag while he was still a fugitive from Saul the son of Kish; and they *were* among the mighty men, helpers in the war,
2 armed with bows, using both the right hand and the left in *hurling* stones and *shooting* arrows with the bow. *They were* of Benjamin, Saul's brethren.
3 The chief *was* Ahiezer, then Joash, the sons of Shemaah the Gibeathite; Jeziel and Pelet the sons of Azmaveth; Berachah, and Jehu the Anathothite;
4 Ishmaiah the Gibeonite, a mighty man among the thirty, and over the thirty; Jeremiah, Jahaziel, Johanan, and Jozabad the Gederathite;
5 Eluzai, Jerimoth, Bealiah, Shemariah, and Shephatiah the Haruphite;
6 Elkanah, Jisshiah, Azarel, Joezer, and Jashobeam, the Korahites;
7 and Joelah and Zebadiah the sons of Jeroham of Gedor.
8 *Some* Gadites joined David at the stronghold in the wilderness, mighty men of valor, men trained for battle, who could handle shield and spear, whose faces *were like* the faces of lions, and *were* as swift as gazelles on the mountains:
9 Ezer the first, Obadiah the second, Eliab the third,
10 Mishmannah the fourth, Jeremiah the fifth,
11 Attai the sixth, Eliel the seventh,
12 Johanan the eighth, Elzabad the ninth,
13 Jeremiah the tenth, and Machbanai the eleventh.
14 These *were* from the sons of Gad, captains of the army; the least was over a hundred, and the greatest was over a thousand.
15 These *are* the ones who crossed the Jordan in the first month, when it had overflowed all its banks; and they put to flight all *those* in the valleys, to the east and to the west.
16 Then some of the sons of Benjamin and Judah came to David at the stronghold.
17 And David went out to meet them, and answered and said to them, "If you have come peaceably to me to help me, my heart will be united with you; but if to betray me to my enemies, since *there is* no wrong in my hands, may the God of our fathers look and bring judgment."
18 Then the Spirit came upon Amasai, chief of the captains, *and he said:*

"*We are* yours, O David;
We *are* on your side, O son of Jesse!
Peace, peace to you,
And peace to your helpers!
For your God helps you."

So David received them, and made them captains of the troop.
19 And *some* from Manasseh defected to David when he was going with the Philistines to battle against Saul; but they did not help them, for the lords of the Philistines sent him away by agreement, saying, "He may defect to his master Saul *and endanger* our heads."

11:32 [a]Spelled *Hiddai* in 2 Samuel 23:30 [b]Spelled *Abi-Albon* in 2 Samuel 23:31 **11:33** [a]Spelled *Barhumite* in 2 Samuel 23:31 **11:39** [a]Spelled *Beerothite* in 2 Samuel 23:37

LIFE LESSONS

➤ **12:18 — *Then the Spirit came upon Amasai, chief of the captains, and he said: "We are yours, O David . . . . Peace, peace to you, and peace to your helpers! For your God helps you."***

When the Spirit leads us to join God's people in a developing work of God, we must listen and obey, regardless of how undeveloped the work appears. To walk in the Spirit is to obey the initial promptings of the Spirit.

20 When he went to Ziklag, those of Manasseh who defected to him were Adnah, Jozabad, Jediael, Michael, Jozabad, Elihu, and
Zillethai, captains of the thousands who *were*
from Manasseh.
21 And they helped David against the bands
of raiders, for they *were* all mighty men of
valor, and they were captains in the army.
22 For at *that* time they came to David day by
day to help him, until *it was* a great army, like
the army of God.

David's Army at Hebron

23 Now these *were* the numbers of the divisions *that were* equipped for war, *and* came
to David at Hebron to turn *over* the kingdom
of Saul to him, according to the word of the
LORD:
24 of the sons of Judah bearing shield and
spear, six thousand eight hundred armed for
war;
25 of the sons of Simeon, mighty men of
valor fit for war, seven thousand one hundred;
26 of the sons of Levi four thousand six hundred;
27 Jehoiada, the leader of the Aaronites, and
with him three thousand seven hundred;
28 Zadok, a young man, a valiant warrior,
and from his father's house twenty-two captains;
29 of the sons of Benjamin, relatives of Saul,
three thousand (until then the greatest part of
them had remained loyal to the house of
Saul);
30 of the sons of Ephraim twenty thousand
eight hundred, mighty men of valor, famous
men throughout their father's house;
31 of the half-tribe of Manasseh eighteen
thousand, who were designated by name to
come and make David king;
32 of the sons of Issachar who had understanding of the times, to know what Israel
ought to do, their chiefs were two hundred;
and all their brethren were at their command;
33 of Zebulun there were fifty thousand who
went out to battle, expert in war with all
weapons of war, stouthearted men who could
keep ranks;
34 of Naphtali one thousand captains, and
with them thirty-seven thousand with shield
and spear;
35 of the Danites who could keep battle formation, twenty-eight thousand six hundred;
36 of Asher, those who could go out to war,
able to keep battle formation, forty thousand;
37 of the Reubenites and the Gadites and the
half-tribe of Manasseh, from the other side of
the Jordan, one hundred and twenty thousand armed for battle with every *kind* of
weapon of war.
38 All these men of war, who could keep
ranks, came to Hebron with a loyal heart, to
make David king over all Israel; and all the
rest of Israel *were* of one mind to make David
king.
39 And they were there with David three
days, eating and drinking, for their brethren
had prepared for them.
40 Moreover those who were near to them,
from as far away as Issachar and Zebulun
and Naphtali, were bringing food on donkeys
and camels, on mules and oxen—provisions
of flour and cakes of figs and cakes of raisins,
wine and oil and oxen and sheep abundantly,
for *there was* joy in Israel.

The Ark Brought from Kirjath Jearim

13 Then David consulted with the captains of thousands and hundreds, *and*
with every leader.
2 And David said to all the assembly of Israel, "If *it seems* good to you, and if it is of the
LORD our God, let us send out to our brethren
everywhere *who are* left in all the land of Israel, and with them to the priests and Levites
who are in their cities *and* their common-
lands, that they may gather together to us;
3 "and let us bring the ark of our God back
to us, for we have not inquired at it since the
days of Saul."
4 Then all the assembly said that they
would do so, for the thing was right in the
eyes of all the people.
5 So David gathered all Israel together, from
Shihor in Egypt to as far as the entrance of
Hamath, to bring the ark of God from Kirjath
Jearim.
6 And David and all Israel went up to Baalah,[a] to Kirjath Jearim, which belonged to
Judah, to bring up from there the ark of God
the LORD, who dwells *between* the cherubim,
where *His* name is proclaimed.
7 So they carried the ark of God on a new
cart from the house of Abinadab, and Uzza
and Ahio drove the cart.

13:6 [a]Called *Baale Judah* in 2 Samuel 6:2

LIFE LESSONS

➤ ***13:3 — ". . . and let us bring the ark of our God back to us, for we have not inquired at it since the days of Saul."***

David saw the ark as a means to draw even closer to God than he had previously. We are made for an intimate relationship with God, and we should employ every godly means possible to draw close to Him.

8 Then David and all Israel played *music* before God with all *their* might, with singing, on
harps, on stringed instruments, on tambourines, on cymbals, and with trumpets.
9 And when they came to Chidon's[a] threshing floor, Uzza put out his hand to hold the
ark, for the oxen stumbled.
10 Then the anger of the LORD was aroused
against Uzza, and He struck him because he
put his hand to the ark; and he died there before God.
11 And David became angry because of the
LORD's outbreak against Uzza; therefore that
place is called Perez Uzza[a] to this day.
12 David was afraid of God that day, saying,
"How can I bring the ark of God to me?"
13 So David would not move the ark with
him into the City of David, but took it aside
into the house of Obed-Edom the Gittite.
➤ 14 The ark of God remained with the family
of Obed-Edom in his house three months.
And the LORD blessed the house of Obed-
Edom and all that he had.

David Established at Jerusalem

14 Now Hiram king of Tyre sent messengers to David, and cedar trees, with
masons and carpenters, to build him a house.
2 So David knew that the LORD had established him as king over Israel, for his kingdom was highly exalted for the sake of His
people Israel.
3 Then David took more wives in Jerusalem,
and David begot more sons and daughters.
4 And these are the names of his children
whom he had in Jerusalem: Shammua,[a]
Shobab, Nathan, Solomon,
5 Ibhar, Elishua,[a] Elpelet,[b]
6 Nogah, Nepheg, Japhia,
7 Elishama, Beeliada,[a] and Eliphelet.

The Philistines Defeated

8 Now when the Philistines heard that David had been anointed king over all Israel, all
the Philistines went up to search for David.
And David heard *of it* and went out against
them.
9 Then the Philistines went and made a raid
on the Valley of Rephaim.
10 And David inquired of God, saying, "Shall
I go up against the Philistines? Will You deliver them into my hand?" The LORD said to
him, "Go up, for I will deliver them into your
hand."
11 So they went up to Baal Perazim, and David defeated them there. Then David said,
"God has broken through my enemies by my
hand like a breakthrough of water." Therefore
they called the name of that place Baal Perazim.[a]
12 And when they left their gods there, David ➤
gave a commandment, and they were burned
with fire.
13 Then the Philistines once again made a
raid on the valley.
14 Therefore David inquired again of God,
and God said to him, "You shall not go up
after them; circle around them, and come
upon them in front of the mulberry trees.
15 "And it shall be, when you hear a sound of
marching in the tops of the mulberry trees,
then you shall go out to battle, for God has
gone out before you to strike the camp of the
Philistines."
16 So David did as God commanded him, and
they drove back the army of the Philistines
from Gibeon as far as Gezer.
17 Then the fame of David went out into all
lands, and the LORD brought the fear of him
upon all nations.

The Ark Brought to Jerusalem

15 *David* built houses for himself in the
City of David; and he prepared a place
for the ark of God, and pitched a tent for it.
2 Then David said, "No one may carry the
ark of God but the Levites, for the LORD has
chosen them to carry the ark of God and to
minister before Him forever."
3 And David gathered all Israel together at
Jerusalem, to bring up the ark of the LORD to
its place, which he had prepared for it.
4 Then David assembled the children of
Aaron and the Levites:
5 of the sons of Kohath, Uriel the chief, and
one hundred and twenty of his brethren;
6 of the sons of Merari, Asaiah the chief,
and two hundred and twenty of his brethren;

13:9 [a]Called *Nachon* in 2 Samuel 6:6 **13:11** [a]Literally *Outburst Against Uzza* **14:4** [a]Spelled *Shimea* in 3:5 **14:5** [a]Spelled *Elishama* in 3:6 [b]Spelled *Eliphelet* in 3:6 **14:7** [a]Spelled *Eliada* in 3:8 **14:11** [a]Literally *Master of Breakthroughs*

LIFE LESSONS

➤ 13:14 — *The ark of God remained with the family of Obed-Edom in his house three months. And the LORD blessed the house of Obed-Edom and all that he had.*

God used His blessing on Obed-Edom's house to show David that although He would always judge sin, He desires to draw close to His people and bless them.

➤ 14:12 — *And when they left their gods there, David gave a commandment, and they were burned with fire.*

Unlike some of his predecessors and many of his successors, David did not collect the idols of his defeated enemies, but burned them, as God commanded (Deut. 7:5). Obedience always brings blessing.

7 of the sons of Gershom, Joel the chief, and one hundred and thirty of his brethren;

8 of the sons of Elizaphan, Shemaiah the chief, and two hundred of his brethren;

9 of the sons of Hebron, Eliel the chief, and eighty of his brethren;

10 of the sons of Uzziel, Amminadab the chief, and one hundred and twelve of his brethren.

11 And David called for Zadok and Abiathar the priests, and for the Levites: for Uriel, Asaiah, Joel, Shemaiah, Eliel, and Amminadab.

12 He said to them, "You *are* the heads of the fathers' *houses* of the Levites; sanctify yourselves, you and your brethren, that you may bring up the ark of the LORD God of Israel to *the place* I have prepared for it.

➤ 13 "For because you *did* not *do it* the first *time,* the LORD our God broke out against us, because we did not consult Him about the proper order."

14 So the priests and the Levites sanctified themselves to bring up the ark of the LORD God of Israel.

15 And the children of the Levites bore the ark of God on their shoulders, by its poles, as Moses had commanded according to the word of the LORD.

16 Then David spoke to the leaders of the Levites to appoint their brethren *to be* the singers accompanied by instruments of music, stringed instruments, harps, and cymbals, by raising the voice with resounding joy.

17 So the Levites appointed Heman the son of Joel; and of his brethren, Asaph the son of Berechiah; and of their brethren, the sons of Merari, Ethan the son of Kushaiah;

18 and with them their brethren of the second *rank:* Zechariah, Ben,[a] Jaaziel, Shemiramoth, Jehiel, Unni, Eliab, Benaiah, Maaseiah, Mattithiah, Elipheleh, Mikneiah, Obed-Edom, and Jeiel, the gatekeepers;

19 the singers, Heman, Asaph, and Ethan, *were* to sound the cymbals of bronze;

20 Zechariah, Aziel, Shemiramoth, Jehiel, Unni, Eliab, Maaseiah, and Benaiah, with strings according to Alamoth;

21 Mattithiah, Elipheleh, Mikneiah, Obed-Edom, Jeiel, and Azaziah, to direct with harps on the Sheminith;

22 Chenaniah, leader of the Levites, was instructor *in charge of* the music, because he *was* skillful;

23 Berechiah and Elkanah *were* doorkeepers for the ark;

24 Shebaniah, Joshaphat, Nethanel, Amasai, Zechariah, Benaiah, and Eliezer, the priests, were to blow the trumpets before the ark of God; and Obed-Edom and Jehiah, doorkeepers for the ark.

25 So David, the elders of Israel, and the captains over thousands went to bring up the ark of the covenant of the LORD from the house of Obed-Edom with joy.

26 And so it was, when God helped the Levites who bore the ark of the covenant of the LORD, that they offered seven bulls and seven rams. ≺

27 David was clothed with a robe of fine linen, as were all the Levites who bore the ark, the singers, and Chenaniah the music master *with* the singers. David also wore a linen ephod.

28 Thus all Israel brought up the ark of the covenant of the LORD with shouting and with the sound of the horn, with trumpets and with cymbals, making music with stringed instruments and harps.

29 And it happened, *as* the ark of the covenant of the LORD came to the City of David, that Michal, Saul's daughter, looked through a window and saw King David whirling and playing music; and she despised him in her heart. ≺

The Ark Placed in the Tabernacle

16 So they brought the ark of God, and set it in the midst of the tabernacle that David had erected for it. Then they offered burnt offerings and peace offerings before God.

15:18 [a]Following Masoretic Text and Vulgate; Septuagint omits *Ben.*

LIFE LESSONS

➤ **15:13 — *"For because you did not do it the first time, the LORD our God broke out against us, because we did not consult Him about the proper order."***

David did not make the same mistake twice regarding the transportation of the ark. This time he carefully followed God's instructions (Deut. 10:8), and received great blessing for it.

➤ **15:26 — *And so it was, when God helped the Levites who bore the ark of the covenant of the LORD, that they offered seven bulls and seven rams.***

God helps us in the work He commissions us to do. He does not merely give us a task and leave us alone to do it; He gives us His strength and His presence to make our work successful.

➤ **15:29 — *. . . Michal, Saul's daughter, looked through a window and saw King David whirling and playing music; and she despised him in her heart.***

David's wife despised him when she saw him celebrating the return of the ark in a manner she thought undignified for a king. But God is after the heart, and David delighted to give his whole heart to the Lord, regardless of appearances.

2 And when David had finished offering the
burnt offerings and the peace offerings, he
blessed the people in the name of the LORD.
3 Then he distributed to everyone of Israel,
both man and woman, to everyone a loaf of
bread, a piece *of meat*, and a cake of raisins.
4 And he appointed some of the Levites to
minister before the ark of the LORD, to commemorate, to thank, and to praise the LORD
God of Israel:
5 Asaph the chief, and next to him
Zechariah, *then* Jeiel, Shemiramoth, Jehiel,
Mattithiah, Eliab, Benaiah, and Obed-Edom:
Jeiel with stringed instruments and harps, but
Asaph made music with cymbals;
6 Benaiah and Jahaziel the priests regularly
blew the trumpets before the ark of the covenant of God.

David's Song of Thanksgiving

➤ 7 On that day David first delivered *this*
psalm into the hand of Asaph and his
brethren, to thank the LORD:

8 Oh, give thanks to the LORD!
Call upon His name;
Make known His deeds among the peoples!
9 Sing to Him, sing psalms to Him;
Talk of all His wondrous works!
10 Glory in His holy name;
Let the hearts of those rejoice who seek
the LORD!
11 Seek the LORD and His strength;
Seek His face evermore!
12 Remember His marvelous works which
He has done,
His wonders, and the judgments of His
mouth,
13 O seed of Israel His servant,
You children of Jacob, His chosen ones!
14 He *is* the LORD our God;
His judgments *are* in all the earth.
15 Remember His covenant forever,
The word which He commanded, for a
thousand generations,
16 *The covenant which* He made with
Abraham,
And His oath to Isaac,
17 And confirmed it to Jacob for a statute,
To Israel *for* an everlasting covenant,
18 Saying, "To you I will give the land of
Canaan
As the allotment of your inheritance,"
19 When you were few in number,
Indeed very few, and strangers in it.
20 When they went from one nation to
another,
And from *one* kingdom to another
people,
21 He permitted no man to do them wrong;
Yes, He rebuked kings for their sakes,
22 *Saying*, "Do not touch My anointed ones,
And do My prophets no harm."[a]

23 Sing to the LORD, all the earth;
Proclaim the good news of His salvation
from day to day.
24 Declare His glory among the nations, ➤
His wonders among all peoples.

25 For the LORD *is* great and greatly to be
praised;
He *is* also to be feared above all gods.
26 For all the gods of the peoples *are* idols,
But the LORD made the heavens.
27 Honor and majesty *are* before Him;
Strength and gladness are in His place.
28 Give to the LORD, O families of the
peoples,
Give to the LORD glory and strength.
29 Give to the LORD the glory *due* His
name;
Bring an offering, and come before Him.
Oh, worship the LORD in the beauty of[a]
holiness!
30 Tremble before Him, all the earth.
The world also is firmly established,
It shall not be moved.

31 Let the heavens rejoice, and let the earth
be glad;
And let them say among the nations,
"The LORD reigns."
32 Let the sea roar, and all its fullness;
Let the field rejoice, and all that *is* in it.
33 Then the trees of the woods shall rejoice
before the LORD,
For He is coming to judge the earth.[a]
34 Oh, give thanks to the LORD, for *He is*
good!
For His mercy *endures* forever.[a]

16:22 [a]Compare verses 8–22 with Psalm 105:1–15
16:33 [a]Compare verses 23–33 with Psalm 96:1–13
16:34 [a]Compare verse 34 with Psalm 106:1

LIFE LESSONS

➤ 16:7 — *On that day David first delivered this psalm into the hand of Asaph and his brethren, to thank the* LORD.

David, the great warrior-king, took great pleasure in crafting worship songs for praising the Lord. If we want to grow close to God, we must also make time for our own times of personal worship.

➤ 16:24 — *Declare His glory among the nations, His wonders among all peoples.*

God's plan has always called for the entire world to acknowledge Him, honor Him, and enjoy the blessings He loves to shower on those who gladly obey Him.

35 And say, "Save us, O God of our
salvation;
Gather us together, and deliver us from
the Gentiles,
To give thanks to Your holy name,
To triumph in Your praise."

36 Blessed *be* the LORD God of Israel
From everlasting to everlasting![a]

And all the people said, "Amen!" and praised the LORD.

Regular Worship Maintained

37 So he left Asaph and his brothers there before the ark of the covenant of the LORD to minister before the ark regularly, as every day's work required;
38 and Obed-Edom with his sixty-eight brethren, including Obed-Edom the son of Jeduthun, and Hosah, *to be* gatekeepers;
39 and Zadok the priest and his brethren the priests, before the tabernacle of the LORD at the high place that *was* at Gibeon,
40 to offer burnt offerings to the LORD on the altar of burnt offering regularly morning and evening, and *to do* according to all that is written in the Law of the LORD which He commanded Israel;
41 and with them Heman and Jeduthun and the rest who were chosen, who were designated by name, to give thanks to the LORD, because His mercy *endures* forever;
42 and with them Heman and Jeduthun, to sound aloud with trumpets and cymbals and the musical instruments of God. Now the sons of Jeduthun *were* gatekeepers.
43 Then all the people departed, every man to his house; and David returned to bless his house.

God's Covenant with David

➤ 17 Now it came to pass, when David was dwelling in his house, that David said to Nathan the prophet, "See now, I dwell in a house of cedar, but the ark of the covenant of the LORD *is* under tent curtains."
2 Then Nathan said to David, "Do all that *is* in your heart, for God *is* with you."
3 But it happened that night that the word of God came to Nathan, saying,
4 "Go and tell My servant David, 'Thus says the LORD: "You shall not build Me a house to dwell in.
5 "For I have not dwelt in a house since the time that I brought up Israel, even to this day, but have gone from tent to tent, and from *one* tabernacle *to another.*
6 "Wherever I have moved about with all Israel, have I ever spoken a word to any of the judges of Israel, whom I commanded to shepherd My people, saying, 'Why have you not built Me a house of cedar?'"'
7 "Now therefore, thus shall you say to My servant David, 'Thus says the LORD of hosts: "I took you from the sheepfold, from following the sheep, to be ruler over My people Israel.
8 "And I have been with you wherever you have gone, and have cut off all your enemies from before you, and have made you a name like the name of the great men who *are* on the earth. ➤
9 "Moreover I will appoint a place for My people Israel, and will plant them, that they may dwell in a place of their own and move no more; nor shall the sons of wickedness oppress them anymore, as previously,
10 "since the time that I commanded judges *to be* over My people Israel. Also I will subdue all your enemies. Furthermore I tell you that the LORD will build you a house.[a]
11 "And it shall be, when your days are fulfilled, when you must go *to be* with your fathers, that I will set up your seed after you, who will be of your sons; and I will establish his kingdom.
12 "He shall build Me a house, and I will establish his throne forever. ➤
13 "I will be his Father, and he shall be My son; and I will not take My mercy away from him, as I took *it* from *him* who was before you.
14 "And I will establish him in My house and in My kingdom forever; and his throne shall be established forever."'"
15 According to all these words and accord-

16:36 [a]Compare verses 35, 36 with Psalm 106:47, 48
17:10 [a]That is, a royal dynasty

LIFE LESSONS

➤ 17:1 — *. . . David said to Nathan the prophet, "See now, I dwell in a house of cedar, but the ark of the covenant of the LORD is under tent curtains."*

It bothered David that he lived in a better "house" than the one provided for the ark. He wanted to give the Lord his best—and he would soon find out that no one out gives the Lord.

➤ 17:8 — *"And I have been with you wherever you have gone, and have cut off all your enemies from before you, and have made you a name . . . ."*

Everything good and wonderful that had happened to David occurred because God was with him, giving him grace after grace. It is the same with us (see James 1:17).

➤ 17:12 — *"He shall build Me a house, and I will establish his throne forever."*

Jesus Christ is the "Son of David" who will rule on David's throne forever (see Acts 2:29–33).

ing to all this vision, so Nathan spoke to David.
16 Then King David went in and sat before
the LORD; and he said: "Who am I, O LORD
God? And what is my house, that You have
brought me this far?
17 "And yet this was a small thing in Your
sight, O God; and You have also spoken of
Your servant's house for a great while to
come, and have regarded me according to
the rank of a man of high degree, O LORD
God.
18 "What more can David say to You for the
honor of Your servant? For You know Your servant.
19 "O LORD, for Your servant's sake, and according to Your own heart, You have done all
this greatness, in making known all these
great things.
20 "O LORD, there is none like You, nor is
there any God besides You, according to all
that we have heard with our ears.
21 "And who is like Your people Israel, the
one nation on the earth whom God went to redeem for Himself as a people—to make for
Yourself a name by great and awesome deeds,
by driving out nations from before Your people whom You redeemed from Egypt?
22 "For You have made Your people Israel
Your very own people forever; and You, LORD,
have become their God.
23 "And now, O LORD, the word which You
have spoken concerning Your servant and
concerning his house, *let it* be established
forever, and do as You have said.
24 "So let it be established, that Your name
may be magnified forever, saying, 'The LORD
of hosts, the God of Israel, *is* Israel's God.'
And let the house of Your servant David be
established before You.
25 "For You, O my God, have revealed to Your
servant that You will build him a house.
Therefore Your servant has found it *in his
heart* to pray before You.
26 "And now, LORD, You are God, and have
promised this goodness to Your servant.
27 "Now You have been pleased to bless
the house of Your servant, that it may continue before You forever; for You have blessed
it, O LORD, and *it shall be* blessed forever."

David's Further Conquests

18 After this it came to pass that David attacked the Philistines, subdued them,
and took Gath and its towns from the hand of
the Philistines.
2 Then he defeated Moab, and the Moabites
became David's servants, *and* brought tribute.
3 And David defeated Hadadezer[a] king of
Zobah *as far as* Hamath, as he went to establish his power by the River Euphrates.
4 David took from him one thousand chariots, seven thousand[a] horsemen, and twenty
thousand foot soldiers. Also David hamstrung
all the chariot *horses*, except that he spared
enough of them for one hundred chariots.
5 When the Syrians of Damascus came to
help Hadadezer king of Zobah, David killed
twenty-two thousand of the Syrians.
6 Then David put *garrisons* in Syria of Damascus; and the Syrians became David's servants, *and* brought tribute. So the LORD
preserved David wherever he went.
7 And David took the shields of gold that
were on the servants of Hadadezer, and
brought them to Jerusalem.
8 Also from Tibhath[a] and from Chun, cities of
Hadadezer, David brought a large amount of
bronze, with which Solomon made the bronze
Sea, the pillars, and the articles of bronze.
9 Now when Tou[a] king of Hamath heard
that David had defeated all the army of
Hadadezer king of Zobah,
10 he sent Hadoram[a] his son to King David,
to greet him and bless him, because he had
fought against Hadadezer and defeated him
(for Hadadezer had been at war with Tou);
and *Hadoram brought with him* all kinds of
articles of gold, silver, and bronze.
11 King David also dedicated these to the
LORD, along with the silver and gold that he
had brought from all *these* nations—from
Edom, from Moab, from the people of
Ammon, from the Philistines, and from Amalek.

18:3 [a]Hebrew *Hadarezer,* and so throughout chapters 18 and 19 **18:4** [a]Or *seven hundred* (compare 2 Samuel 8:4) **18:8** [a]Spelled *Betah* in 2 Samuel 8:8 **18:9** [a]Spelled *Toi* in 2 Samuel 8:9, 10 **18:10** [a]Spelled *Joram* in 2 Samuel 8:10

LIFE LESSONS

➤ 17:16 — *"Who am I, O LORD God? And what is my house, that You have brought me this far?"*

God values genuine humility more than we can possibly imagine. As king, David had a strong sense of self, but he gladly bowed down to the real King, the Lord of hosts.

➤ 17:19 — *"O LORD, for Your servant's sake, and according to Your own heart, You have done all this greatness, in making known all these great things."*

God acts for our benefit, not because we have earned His favor or deserve His grace, but because His loving heart desires to bless those who have given Him their heart.

➤ 18:8 — *. . . David brought a large amount of bronze, with which Solomon made the bronze Sea, the pillars, and the articles of bronze.*

God did not allow David to build the temple, but He did allow him to make preparations for it and to provide many of its supplies. Even when He says "no," God shows us His grace!

12 Moreover Abishai the son of Zeruiah killed eighteen thousand Edomites[a] in the Valley of Salt.
13 He also put garrisons in Edom, and all the Edomites became David's servants. And the LORD preserved David wherever he went.

David's Administration

14 So David reigned over all Israel, and administered judgment and justice to all his people.
15 Joab the son of Zeruiah *was* over the army; Jehoshaphat the son of Ahilud *was* recorder;
16 Zadok the son of Ahitub and Abimelech the son of Abiathar *were* the priests; Shavsha[a] *was* the scribe;
17 Benaiah the son of Jehoiada *was* over the Cherethites and the Pelethites; and David's sons *were* chief ministers at the king's side.

The Ammonites and Syrians Defeated

19 It happened after this that Nahash the king of the people of Ammon died, and his son reigned in his place.
2 Then David said, "I will show kindness to Hanun the son of Nahash, because his father showed kindness to me." So David sent messengers to comfort him concerning his father. And David's servants came to Hanun in the land of the people of Ammon to comfort him.
3 And the princes of the people of Ammon said to Hanun, "Do you think that David really honors your father because he has sent comforters to you? Did his servants not come to you to search and to overthrow and to spy out the land?"
4 Therefore Hanun took David's servants, shaved them, and cut off their garments in the middle, at their buttocks, and sent them away.
5 Then *some* went and told David about the men; and he sent to meet them, because the men were greatly ashamed. And the king said, "Wait at Jericho until your beards have grown, and *then* return."
6 When the people of Ammon saw that they had made themselves repulsive to David, Hanun and the people of Ammon sent a thousand talents of silver to hire for themselves chariots and horsemen from Mesopotamia,[a] from Syrian Maacah, and from Zobah.[b]
7 So they hired for themselves thirty-two thousand chariots, with the king of Maacah and his people, who came and encamped before Medeba. Also the people of Ammon gathered together from their cities, and came to battle.
8 Now when David heard *of it*, he sent Joab and all the army of the mighty men.
9 Then the people of Ammon came out and put themselves in battle array before the gate of the city, and the kings who had come *were* by themselves in the field.
10 When Joab saw that the battle line was
against him be[...] and behind, he chose
some of Israel's b[...] and put them in battle
array against the S[...]
11 And the rest of [...] he put under
the command of Abis[...] other, and they
set *themselves* in battle [...] inst the people of Ammon.
12 Then he said, "If [...] are too
strong for me, then you [...]
the people of Ammon are [...] but if
then I will help you.
13 "Be of good courage, an[...]
for our people and for the c[...]
And may the LORD do *what*[...]ou,
sight."
14 So Joab and the people w[...]
him drew near for the battle aga[...]
ians, and they fled before him.
15 When the people of Ammon sa[...]
Syrians were fleeing, they also fl[...]
Abishai his brother, and entered the[...]
Joab went to Jerusalem.
16 Now when the Syrians saw that th[...]
been defeated by Israel, they sent messe[...]
and brought the Syrians who were bey[...]
the River,[a] and Shophach[b] the commande[...]
Hadadezer's army *went* before them.
17 When it was told David, he gathered all Israel, crossed over the Jordan and came upon them, and set up in *battle* array against them. So when David had set up in battle array against the Syrians, they fought with him.
18 Then the Syrians fled before Israel; and David killed seven thousand[a] charioteers and forty thousand foot soldiers[b] of the Syrians, and killed Shophach the commander of the army.
19 And when the servants of Hadadezer saw that they were defeated by Israel, they made peace with David and became his servants. So the Syrians were not willing to help the people of Ammon anymore.

Rabbah Is Conquered

20 It happened in the spring of the year, at the time kings go out *to battle*, that Joab led out the armed forces and ravaged the country of the people of Ammon, and came and besieged Rabbah. But David stayed at Jerusalem. And Joab defeated Rabbah and overthrew it.
2 Then David took their king's crown from his head, and found it to weigh a talent of gold, and *there were* precious stones in it. And it was set on David's head. Also he brought out the spoil of the city in great abundance.

18:12 [a]Or *Syrians* (compare 2 Samuel 8:13) **18:16** [a]Spelled *Seraiah* in 2 Samuel 8:17 **19:6** [a]Hebrew *Aram Naharaim* [b]Spelled *Zoba* in 2 Samuel 10:6 **19:16** [a]That is, the Euphrates [b]Spelled *Shobach* in 2 Samuel 10:16 **19:18** [a]Or *seven hundred* (compare 2 Samuel 10:18) [b]Or *horsemen* (compare 2 Samuel 10:18)

3 And he brought out the people who *were*
in it, and put *them* to work[a] with saws, with
iron picks, and with axes. So David did to all
the cities of the people of Ammon. Then David and all the people returned *to* Jerusalem.

Philistine Giants Destroyed

4 Now it happened afterward that war
broke out at Gezer with the Philistines, at
which time Sibbechai the Hushathite killed
Sippai,[a] *who was one* of the sons of the giant.
And they were subdued.
5 Again there was war with the Philistines,
and Elhanan the son of Jair[a] killed Lahmi the
brother of Goliath the Gittite, the shaft of
whose spear *was* like a weaver's beam.
6 Yet again there was war at Gath, where
there was a man of *great* stature, with
twenty-four fingers and toes, six *on each
hand* and six *on each foot;* and he also was
born to the giant.
7 So when he defied Israel, Jonathan the
son of Shimea,[a] David's brother, killed him.
8 These were born to the giant in Gath, and
they fell by the hand of David and by the
hand of his servants.

The Census of Israel and Judah

➤ 21 Now Satan stood up against Israel, and
moved David to number Israel.
2 So David said to Joab and to the leaders of
the people, "Go, number Israel from Beersheba to Dan, and bring the number of them
to me that I may know *it.*"
3 And Joab answered, "May the LORD make
His people a hundred times more than they
are. But, my lord the king, *are* they not all my
lord's servants? Why then does my lord require this thing? Why should he be a cause of
guilt in Israel?"
4 Nevertheless the king's word prevailed
against Joab. Therefore Joab departed and
went throughout all Israel and came to Jerusalem.
5 Then Joab gave the sum of the number of
the people to David. All Israel *had* one million
one hundred thousand men who drew the
sword, and Judah *had* four hundred and seventy thousand men who drew the sword.
6 But he did not count Levi and Benjamin
among them, for the king's word was abominable to Joab.
7 And God was displeased with this thing;
therefore He struck Israel.
8 So David said to God, "I have sinned
greatly, because I have done this thing; but
now, I pray, take away the iniquity of Your servant, for I have done very foolishly."
9 Then the LORD spoke to Gad, David's seer,
saying,
10 "Go and tell David, saying, 'Thus says
the LORD: "I offer you three *things;* choose
one of them for yourself, that I may do *it* to
you."'"
11 So Gad came to David and said to him,
"Thus says the LORD: 'Choose for yourself,
12 'either three[a] years of famine, or three
months to be defeated by your foes with the
sword of your enemies overtaking *you,* or else
for three days the sword of the LORD—the
plague in the land, with the angel[b] of the LORD
destroying throughout all the territory of Israel.' Now consider what answer I should
take back to Him who sent me."
13 And David said to Gad, "I am in great distress. Please let me fall into the hand of the
LORD, for His mercies *are* very great; but do
not let me fall into the hand of man."
14 So the LORD sent a plague upon Israel, and ➤
seventy thousand men of Israel fell.
15 And God sent an angel to Jerusalem to destroy it. As he[a] was destroying, the LORD
looked and relented of the disaster, and said
to the angel who was destroying, "It is
enough; now restrain your[b] hand." And the
angel of the LORD stood by the threshing floor
of Ornan[c] the Jebusite.
16 Then David lifted his eyes and saw the ➤
angel of the LORD standing between earth and
heaven, having in his hand a drawn sword
stretched out over Jerusalem. So David and

20:3 [a]Septuagint reads *cut them.* **20:4** [a]Spelled *Saph* in 2 Samuel 21:18 **20:5** [a]Spelled *Jaare-Oregim* in 2 Samuel 21:19 **20:7** [a]Spelled *Shimeah* in 2 Samuel 21:21 and *Shammah* in 1 Samuel 16:9 **21:12** [a]Or *seven* (compare 2 Samuel 24:13) [b]Or *Angel,* and so elsewhere in this chapter **21:15** [a]Or *He* [b]Or *Your* [c]Spelled *Araunah* in 2 Samuel 24:16

LIFE LESSONS

➤ 21:1 — *Now Satan stood up against Israel, and moved David to number Israel.*

David took this census to gauge his own military strength, apart from any divine commandment. He slipped in his devotion, and it cost him greatly. Until the day we die, we must guard our hearts (Prov. 4:23).

➤ 21:14 — *So the LORD sent a plague upon Israel, and seventy thousand men of Israel fell.*

The sin of one man, David, caused the deaths of seventy thousand Israelites. God's people can never justify their sin by saying it affects only themselves; sin has a way of injuring everyone it touches.

➤ 21:16 — *Then David lifted his eyes and saw the angel of the LORD standing between earth and heaven, having in his hand a drawn sword stretched out over Jerusalem.*

At select times and places, God lifts the curtain that obscures our vision of spiritual realities and we see clearly what He is up to—but He remains active even when we do not see.

the elders, clothed in sackcloth, fell on their
faces.
17 And David said to God, "Was it not I who
commanded the people to be numbered? I am
the one who has sinned and done evil indeed;
but these sheep, what have they done? Let
Your hand, I pray, O LORD my God, be against
me and my father's house, but not against
Your people that they should be plagued."
18 Therefore, the angel of the LORD commanded Gad to say to David that David
should go and erect an altar to the LORD on
the threshing floor of Ornan the Jebusite.
19 So David went up at the word of Gad,
which he had spoken in the name of the LORD.
20 Now Ornan turned and saw the angel; and
his four sons *who were* with him hid themselves, but Ornan continued threshing wheat.
21 So David came to Ornan, and Ornan
looked and saw David. And he went out from
the threshing floor, and bowed before David
with *his* face to the ground.
22 Then David said to Ornan, "Grant me the
place of *this* threshing floor, that I may build
an altar on it to the LORD. You shall grant it to
me at the full price, that the plague may be
withdrawn from the people."
23 But Ornan said to David, "Take *it* to yourself, and let my lord the king do *what is* good
in his eyes. Look, I *also* give *you* the oxen for
burnt offerings, the threshing implements for
wood, and the wheat for the grain offering; I
give *it* all."
24 Then King David said to Ornan, "No, but I
will surely buy *it* for the full price, for I will
not take what is yours for the LORD, nor offer
burnt offerings with *that which* costs *me*
nothing."
25 So David gave Ornan six hundred shekels
of gold by weight for the place.
26 And David built there an altar to the LORD,
and offered burnt offerings and peace offerings, and called on the LORD; and He answered him from heaven by fire on the altar
of burnt offering.
27 So the LORD commanded the angel, and he
returned his sword to its sheath.
28 At that time, when David saw that the
LORD had answered him on the threshing
floor of Ornan the Jebusite, he sacrificed
there.
29 For the tabernacle of the LORD and the
altar of the burnt offering, which Moses had
made in the wilderness, *were* at that time at
the high place in Gibeon.
30 But David could not go before it to inquire
of God, for he was afraid of the sword of the
angel of the LORD.

David Prepares to Build the Temple

22 Then David said, "This *is* the house of
the LORD God, and this *is* the altar of
burnt offering for Israel."
2 So David commanded to gather the aliens
who *were* in the land of Israel; and he appointed masons to cut hewn stones to build
the house of God.
3 And David prepared iron in abundance
for the nails of the doors of the gates and for
the joints, and bronze in abundance beyond
measure,
4 and cedar trees in abundance; for the
Sidonians and those from Tyre brought much
cedar wood to David.
5 Now David said, "Solomon my son *is*
young and inexperienced, and the house to be
built for the LORD *must be* exceedingly magnificent, famous and glorious throughout all
countries. I will now make preparation for it."
So David made abundant preparations before
his death.
6 Then he called for his son Solomon, and
charged him to build a house for the LORD
God of Israel.
7 And David said to Solomon: "My son, as
for me, it was in my mind to build a house to
the name of the LORD my God;
8 "but the word of the LORD came to me, saying, 'You have shed much blood and have
made great wars; you shall not build a house
for My name, because you have shed much
blood on the earth in My sight.
9 'Behold, a son shall be born to you, who
shall be a man of rest; and I will give him rest
from all his enemies all around. His name
shall be Solomon,[a] for I will give peace and
quietness to Israel in his days.
10 'He shall build a house for My name, and
he shall be My son, and I *will be* his Father;
and I will establish the throne of his kingdom
over Israel forever.'
11 "Now, my son, may the LORD be with you;
and may you prosper, and build the house of
the LORD your God, as He has said to you.
12 "Only may the LORD give you wisdom and
understanding, and give you charge concerning Israel, that you may keep the law of the
LORD your God.

22:9 [a]Literally *Peaceful*

LIFE LESSONS

➤ ***22:9 — "Behold, a son shall be born to you . . . I will give him rest from all his enemies all around. His name shall be Solomon, for I will give peace and quietness to Israel in his days."***

God is the one who gives us rest and peace and quietness. While there is no peace for the wicked (Is. 57:21), God provides His obedient people with abundant peace (Jer. 33:6).

ANSWERS TO LIFE'S QUESTIONS

What should I do during times of adversity?

1 CHR. 22:13

Part of life is facing adversity, even the kind of adversity that challenges our faith. King David provides us some great advice when it comes to facing times of adversity.

As part of his final blessing to his son Solomon, David said to him, "You will prosper, if you take care to fulfill the statutes and judgments with which the LORD charged Moses concerning Israel. Be strong and of good courage; do not fear or be dismayed" (1 Chr. 22:13).

That's good advice for us today too. It's still true that obedience always brings blessing.

Time and again in the Law of Moses, we find the word *keep.* The children of Israel were commanded to keep the feasts, to keep the law and commandments, to keep the Sabbath day holy, to keep their oaths to God, to keep themselves from evil. Moses said to the children of Israel as he led them into a covenant relationship with God, "Therefore keep the words of this covenant, and do them, that you may prosper in all that you do" (Deut. 29:9).

To keep means to hold fast and to cherish at the same time. When adversity strikes, that should be our mind-set: above all else, we need to hold fast to the Lord and to cherish our relationship with Him. Rather than blame God or turn from God, we need to turn to God and rely on His help. Keeping God's laws in the face of adversity actually leads us toward prosperity—a better state of being.

When adversity hits, those around you may criticize you for clinging to faith or reaffirming your belief that God is a good and benevolent heavenly Father. They may mock you or scorn you. Don't feel dismayed if that happens. Continue to keep God's Word and remain faithful in your relationship with the Lord. Remember what David said: "I hear the slander of many; fear is on every side; while they take counsel together against me, they scheme to take away my life. But as for me, I trust in You, O LORD; I say, 'You are my God.' My times are in Your hand; deliver me from the hand of my enemies" (Ps. 31:13–15).

Ask the Lord to give you courage to withstand the hurtful comments of others and to be able to give a bold witness about God's power and presence even in your time of trouble.

See the Life Principles Index for further study:
21. Obedience always brings blessing.

✻ 13 "Then you will prosper, if you take care to
➤ fulfill the statutes and judgments with which
the LORD charged Moses concerning Israel.
Be strong and of good courage; do not fear
nor be dismayed.
14 "Indeed I have taken much trouble to prepare for the house of the LORD one hundred
thousand talents of gold and one million talents of silver, and bronze and iron beyond
measure, for it is so abundant. I have prepared timber and stone also, and you may add
to them.
15 "Moreover *there are* workmen with you in
abundance: woodsmen and stonecutters, and
all types of skillful men for every kind of work.
16 "Of gold and silver and bronze and iron
there is no limit. Arise and begin working,
and the LORD be with you."
17 David also commanded all the leaders of
Israel to help Solomon his son, *saying,*
18 "*Is* not the LORD your God with you? And
has He *not* given you rest on every side? For
He has given the inhabitants of the land into
my hand, and the land is subdued before the
LORD and before His people.
19 "Now set your heart and your soul to seek ➤

LIFE LESSONS

➤ 22:13 — *"Then you will prosper, if you take care to fulfill the statutes and judgments with which the LORD charged Moses concerning Israel. Be strong and of good courage; do not fear nor be dismayed."*

When we take care to obey the Lord, and act with courage and strength, He takes care to prosper us. God assumes full responsibility for our needs when we obey Him.

➤ 22:19 — *"Now set your heart and your soul to seek the LORD your God."*

We are to encourage one another to seek the Lord with all our heart and soul; Hebrews 3:13 instructs us to do this daily. We need each other, for no Christian has ever been called to a solitary faith.

the LORD your God. Therefore arise and build
the sanctuary of the LORD God, to bring the
ark of the covenant of the LORD and the holy
articles of God into the house that is to be
built for the name of the LORD."

The Divisions of the Levites

23 So when David was old and full of
days, he made his son Solomon king
over Israel.
2 And he gathered together all the leaders
of Israel, with the priests and the Levites.
3 Now the Levites were numbered from the
age of thirty years and above; and the number
of individual males was thirty-eight thousand.
4 Of these, twenty-four thousand *were* to
look after the work of the house of the LORD,
six thousand *were* officers and judges,
5 four thousand *were* gatekeepers, and four
thousand praised the LORD with *musical* instruments, "which I made," *said David,* "for
giving praise."
6 Also David separated them into divisions
among the sons of Levi: Gershon, Kohath,
and Merari.
7 Of the Gershonites: Laadan[a] and Shimei.
8 The sons of Laadan: the first Jehiel, then
Zetham and Joel—three *in all.*
9 The sons of Shimei: Shelomith, Haziel,
and Haran—three *in all.* These were the
heads of the fathers' *houses* of Laadan.
10 And the sons of Shimei: Jahath, Zina,[a]
Jeush, and Beriah. These *were* the four sons
of Shimei.
11 Jahath was the first and Zizah the second.
But Jeush and Beriah did not have many sons;
therefore they were assigned as one father's
house.
12 The sons of Kohath: Amram, Izhar, Hebron, and Uzziel—four *in all.*
13 The sons of Amram: Aaron and Moses;
and Aaron was set apart, he and his sons forever, that he should sanctify the most holy
things, to burn incense before the LORD, to
minister to Him, and to give the blessing in
His name forever.
14 Now the sons of Moses the man of God
were reckoned to the tribe of Levi.
15 The sons of Moses *were* Gershon[a] and
Eliezer.
16 Of the sons of Gershon, Shebuel[a] *was* the
first.
17 Of the descendants of Eliezer, Rehabiah
was the first. And Eliezer had no other sons,
but the sons of Rehabiah were very many.
18 Of the sons of Izhar, Shelomith *was* the
first.
19 Of the sons of Hebron, Jeriah *was* the
first, Amariah the second, Jahaziel the third,
and Jekameam the fourth.
20 Of the sons of Uzziel, Michah *was* the first
and Jesshiah the second.
21 The sons of Merari *were* Mahli and Mushi.
The sons of Mahli *were* Eleazar and Kish.
22 And Eleazar died, and had no sons, but
only daughters; and their brethren, the sons
of Kish, took them *as wives.*
23 The sons of Mushi *were* Mahli, Eder, and
Jeremoth—three *in all.*
24 These *were* the sons of Levi by their fathers' houses—the heads of the fathers'
houses as they were counted individually by
the number of their names, who did the work
for the service of the house of the LORD, from
the age of twenty years and above.
25 For David said, "The LORD God of Israel
has given rest to His people, that they may
dwell in Jerusalem forever";
26 and also to the Levites, "They shall no
longer carry the tabernacle, or any of the articles for its service."
27 For by the last words of David the Levites
were numbered from twenty years old and
above;
28 because their duty *was* to help the sons of
Aaron in the service of the house of the LORD,
in the courts and in the chambers, in the purifying of all holy things and the work of the
service of the house of God,
29 both with the showbread and the fine
flour for the grain offering, with the unleavened cakes and *what is baked in* the pan, with
what is mixed and with all kinds of measures
and sizes;
30 to stand every morning to thank and
praise the LORD, and likewise at evening;
31 and at every presentation of a burnt offering to the LORD on the Sabbaths and on the
New Moons and on the set feasts, by number
according to the ordinance governing them,
regularly before the LORD;
32 and that they should attend to the needs of
the tabernacle of meeting, the needs of the
holy *place,* and the needs of the sons of Aaron
their brethren in the work of the house of the
LORD.

The Divisions of the Priests

24 Now *these are* the divisions of the sons
of Aaron. The sons of Aaron *were*
Nadab, Abihu, Eleazar, and Ithamar.
2 And Nadab and Abihu died before their
father, and had no children; therefore Eleazar
and Ithamar ministered as priests.
3 Then David with Zadok of the sons of
Eleazar, and Ahimelech of the sons of
Ithamar, divided them according to the
schedule of their service.
4 There were more leaders found of the
sons of Eleazar than of the sons of Ithamar,
and *thus* they were divided. Among the sons
of Eleazar *were* sixteen heads of *their* fathers'
houses, and eight heads of their fathers'
houses among the sons of Ithamar.

23:7 [a]Spelled *Libni* in Exodus 6:17 **23:10** [a]Septuagint and Vulgate read *Zizah* (compare verse 11). **23:15** [a]Hebrew *Gershom* (compare 6:16) **23:16** [a]Spelled *Shubael* in 24:20

5 Thus they were divided by lot, one group
as another, for there were officials of the
sanctuary and officials *of the house* of God,
from the sons of Eleazar and from the sons of
Ithamar.
6 And the scribe, Shemaiah the son of
Nethanel, *one of* the Levites, wrote them
down before the king, the leaders, Zadok the
priest, Ahimelech the son of Abiathar, and the
heads of the fathers' *houses* of the priests and
Levites, one father's house taken for Eleazar
and *one* for Ithamar.
7 Now the first lot fell to Jehoiarib, the second to Jedaiah,
8 the third to Harim, the fourth to Seorim,
9 the fifth to Malchijah, the sixth to Mijamin,
10 the seventh to Hakkoz, the eighth to Abijah,
11 the ninth to Jeshua, the tenth to Shecaniah,
12 the eleventh to Eliashib, the twelfth to
Jakim,
13 the thirteenth to Huppah, the fourteenth
to Jeshebeab,
14 the fifteenth to Bilgah, the sixteenth to
Immer,
15 the seventeenth to Hezir, the eighteenth to
Happizzez,[a]
16 the nineteenth to Pethahiah, the twentieth
to Jehezekel,[a]
17 the twenty-first to Jachin, the twenty-second to Gamul,
18 the twenty-third to Delaiah, the twenty-
fourth to Maaziah.
19 This *was* the schedule of their service for
coming into the house of the LORD according
to their ordinance by the hand of Aaron their
father, as the LORD God of Israel had commanded him.

Other Levites

20 And the rest of the sons of Levi: of the
sons of Amram, Shubael;[a] of the sons of
Shubael, Jehdeiah.
21 Concerning Rehabiah, of the sons of Rehabiah, the first *was* Isshiah.
22 Of the Izharites, Shelomoth;[a] of the sons
of Shelomoth, Jahath.
23 Of the sons *of Hebron,*[a] Jeriah *was the
first,*[b] Amariah the second, Jahaziel the third,
and Jekameam the fourth.
24 *Of* the sons of Uzziel, Michah; of the sons
of Michah, Shamir.
25 The brother of Michah, Isshiah; of the
sons of Isshiah, Zechariah.
26 The sons of Merari *were* Mahli and Mushi;
the son of Jaaziah, Beno.
27 The sons of Merari by Jaaziah *were* Beno,
Shoham, Zaccur, and Ibri.
28 Of Mahli: Eleazar, who had no sons.
29 Of Kish: the son of Kish, Jerahmeel.
30 Also the sons of Mushi *were* Mahli,
Eder, and Jerimoth. These *were* the sons of
the Levites according to their fathers'
houses.
31 These also cast lots just as their brothers
the sons of Aaron did, in the presence of King
David, Zadok, Ahimelech, and the heads of
the fathers' *houses* of the priests and Levites.
The chief fathers *did* just as their younger
brethren.

The Musicians

25 Moreover David and the captains of the
army separated for the service *some* of
the sons of Asaph, of Heman, and of Jeduthun, who *should* prophesy with harps,
stringed instruments, and cymbals. And the
number of the skilled men performing their
service was:
2 Of the sons of Asaph: Zaccur, Joseph,
Nethaniah, and Asharelah;[a] the sons of Asaph
were under the direction of Asaph, who
prophesied according to the order of the king.
3 Of Jeduthun, the sons of Jeduthun:
Gedaliah, Zeri,[a] Jeshaiah, *Shimei*, Hashabiah,
and Mattithiah, six,[b] under the direction of
their father Jeduthun, who prophesied with a
harp to give thanks and to praise the LORD.
4 Of Heman, the sons of Heman: Bukkiah,
Mattaniah, Uzziel,[a] Shebuel,[b] Jerimoth,[c]
Hananiah, Hanani, Eliathah, Giddalti, Romamti-Ezer, Joshbekashah, Mallothi, Hothir,
and Mahazioth.
5 All these *were* the sons of Heman the
king's seer in the words of God, to exalt his
horn.[a] For God gave Heman fourteen sons
and three daughters.
6 All these *were* under the direction of their
father for the music *in* the house of the LORD,
with cymbals, stringed instruments, and
harps, for the service of the house of God.
Asaph, Jeduthun, and Heman *were* under the
authority of the king.
7 So the number of them, with their
brethren who were instructed in the songs of
the LORD, all who were skillful, *was* two hundred and eighty-eight.
8 And they cast lots for their duty, the small
as well as the great, the teacher with the student.
9 Now the first lot for Asaph came out for
Joseph; the second for Gedaliah, him with his
brethren and sons, twelve;

24:15 [a]Septuagint and Vulgate read *Aphses.* **24:16** [a]Masoretic Text reads *Jehezkel.* **24:20** [a]Spelled *Shebuel* in 23:16
24:22 [a]Spelled *Shelomith* in 23:18 **24:23** [a]Supplied from 23:19 (following some Hebrew manuscripts and Septuagint manuscripts) [b]Supplied from 23:19 (following some Hebrew manuscripts and Septuagint manuscripts) **25:2** [a]Spelled *Jesharelah* in verse 14 **25:3** [a]Spelled *Jizri* in verse 11 [b]*Shimei,* appearing in one Hebrew and several Septuagint manuscripts, completes the total of six sons (compare verse 17).
25:4 [a]Spelled *Azarel* in verse 18 [b]Spelled *Shubael* in verse 20 [c]Spelled *Jeremoth* in verse 22 **25:5** [a]That is, to increase his power or influence

10 the third for Zaccur, his sons and his
brethren, twelve;
11 the fourth for Jizri,[a] his sons and his
brethren, twelve;
12 the fifth for Nethaniah, his sons and his
brethren, twelve;
13 the sixth for Bukkiah, his sons and his
brethren, twelve;
14 the seventh for Jesharelah,[a] his sons and
his brethren, twelve;
15 the eighth for Jeshaiah, his sons and his
brethren, twelve;
16 the ninth for Mattaniah, his sons and his
brethren, twelve;
17 the tenth for Shimei, his sons and his
brethren, twelve;
18 the eleventh for Azarel,[a] his sons and his
brethren, twelve;
19 the twelfth for Hashabiah, his sons and his
brethren, twelve;
20 the thirteenth for Shubael,[a] his sons and
his brethren, twelve;
21 the fourteenth for Mattithiah, his sons and
his brethren, twelve;
22 the fifteenth for Jeremoth,[a] his sons and
his brethren, twelve;
23 the sixteenth for Hananiah, his sons and
his brethren, twelve;
24 the seventeenth for Joshbekashah, his
sons and his brethren, twelve;
25 the eighteenth for Hanani, his sons and
his brethren, twelve;
26 the nineteenth for Mallothi, his sons and
his brethren, twelve;
27 the twentieth for Eliathah, his sons and
his brethren, twelve;
28 the twenty-first for Hothir, his sons and
his brethren, twelve;
29 the twenty-second for Giddalti, his sons
and his brethren, twelve;
30 the twenty-third for Mahazioth, his sons
and his brethren, twelve;
31 the twenty-fourth for Romamti-Ezer, his
sons and his brethren, twelve.

The Gatekeepers

26 Concerning the divisions of the gatekeepers: of the Korahites, Meshelemiah
the son of Kore, of the sons of Asaph.
2 And the sons of Meshelemiah *were*
Zechariah the firstborn, Jediael the second,
Zebadiah the third, Jathniel the fourth,
3 Elam the fifth, Jehohanan the sixth,
Eliehoenai the seventh.
4 Moreover the sons of Obed-Edom *were*
Shemaiah the firstborn, Jehozabad the second, Joah the third, Sacar the fourth,
Nethanel the fifth,
5 Ammiel the sixth, Issachar the seventh,
Peulthai the eighth; for God blessed him.
6 Also to Shemaiah his son were sons born
who governed their fathers' houses, because
they *were* men of great ability.
7 The sons of Shemaiah *were* Othni,
Rephael, Obed, and Elzabad, whose brothers
Elihu and Semachiah *were* able men.
8 All these *were* of the sons of Obed-Edom,
they and their sons and their brethren, able
men with strength for the work: sixty-two of
Obed-Edom.
9 And Meshelemiah had sons and brethren,
eighteen able men.
10 Also Hosah, of the children of Merari, had
sons: Shimri the first (for *though* he was not
the firstborn, his father made him the first),
11 Hilkiah the second, Tebaliah the third,
Zechariah the fourth; all the sons and
brethren of Hosah *were* thirteen.
12 Among these *were* the divisions of the
gatekeepers, among the chief men, *having* duties just like their brethren, to serve in the
house of the LORD.
13 And they cast lots for each gate, the small
as well as the great, according to their father's
house.
14 The lot for the East *Gate* fell to
Shelemiah. Then they cast lots *for* his son
Zechariah, a wise counselor, and his lot came
out for the North Gate;
15 to Obed-Edom the South Gate, and to his
sons the storehouse.[a]
16 To Shuppim and Hosah *the lot came out*
for the West Gate, with the Shallecheth Gate
on the ascending highway—watchman opposite watchman.
17 On the east *were* six Levites, on the north
four each day, on the south four each day, and
for the storehouse[a] two by two.
18 As for the Parbar[a] on the west, *there were*
four on the highway *and* two at the Parbar.
19 These were the divisions of the gatekeepers among the sons of Korah and among the
sons of Merari.

The Treasuries and Other Duties

20 Of the Levites, Ahijah *was* over the treasuries of the house of God and over the treasuries of the dedicated things.
21 The sons of Laadan, the descendants of
the Gershonites of Laadan, heads of their fathers' *houses,* of Laadan the Gershonite: Jehieli.
22 The sons of Jehieli, Zetham and Joel his
brother, *were* over the treasuries of the house
of the LORD.
23 Of the Amramites, the Izharites, the Hebronites, and the Uzzielites:
24 Shebuel the son of Gershom, the son of
Moses, *was* overseer of the treasuries.
25 And his brethren by Eliezer *were* Rehabiah his son, Jeshaiah his son, Joram his
son, Zichri his son, and Shelomith his son.

25:11 [a]Spelled *Zeri* in verse 3 **25:14** [a]Spelled *Asharelah* in verse 2 **25:18** [a]Spelled *Uzziel* in verse 4 **25:20** [a]Spelled *Shebuel* in verse 4 **25:22** [a]Spelled *Jerimoth* in verse 4 **26:15** [a]Hebrew *asuppim* **26:17** [a]Hebrew *asuppim* **26:18** [a]Probably a court or colonnade extending west of the temple

26 This Shelomith and his brethren *were* over
all the treasuries of the dedicated things which
King David and the heads of fathers' *houses,*
the captains over thousands and hundreds,
and the captains of the army, had dedicated.
27 Some of the spoils won in battles they
dedicated to maintain the house of the LORD.
28 And all that Samuel the seer, Saul the son
of Kish, Abner the son of Ner, and Joab the
son of Zeruiah had dedicated, every dedicated *thing,* was under the hand of Shelomith
and his brethren.
29 Of the Izharites, Chenaniah and his sons
performed duties as officials and judges over
Israel outside Jerusalem.
30 Of the Hebronites, Hashabiah and his
brethren, one thousand seven hundred able
men, had the oversight of Israel on the west
side of the Jordan for all the business of the
LORD, and in the service of the king.
31 Among the Hebronites, Jerijah *was* head
of the Hebronites according to his genealogy
of the fathers. In the fortieth year of the reign
of David they were sought, and there were
found among them capable men at Jazer of
Gilead.
32 And his brethren *were* two thousand
seven hundred able men, heads of fathers'
houses, whom King David made officials over
the Reubenites, the Gadites, and the half-tribe
of Manasseh, for every matter pertaining to
God and the affairs of the king.

The Military Divisions

27 And the children of Israel, according to
their number, the heads of fathers'
houses, the captains of thousands and hundreds and their officers, served the king in
every matter of the *military* divisions. *These*
divisions came in and went out month by
month throughout all the months of the year,
each division *having* twenty-four thousand.
2 Over the first division for the first month
was Jashobeam the son of Zabdiel, and in his
division *were* twenty-four thousand;
3 *he was* of the children of Perez, and the
chief of all the captains of the army for the
first month.
4 Over the division of the second month *was*
Dodai[a] an Ahohite, and of his division Mikloth also *was* the leader; in his division *were*
twenty-four thousand.
5 The third captain of the army for the third
month *was* Benaiah, the son of Jehoiada the
priest, who was chief; in his division *were*
twenty-four thousand.
6 This was the Benaiah *who was* mighty
among the thirty, and was over the thirty; in
his division *was* Ammizabad his son.
7 The fourth *captain* for the fourth month
was Asahel the brother of Joab, and Zebadiah
his son after him; in his division *were* twenty-
four thousand.
8 The fifth captain for the fifth month *was*
Shamhuth[a] the Izrahite; in his division were
twenty-four thousand.
9 The sixth *captain* for the sixth month *was*
Ira the son of Ikkesh the Tekoite; in his division *were* twenty-four thousand.
10 The seventh *captain* for the seventh
month *was* Helez the Pelonite, of the children
of Ephraim; in his division *were* twenty-four
thousand.
11 The eighth *captain* for the eighth month
was Sibbechai the Hushathite, of the
Zarhites; in his division *were* twenty-four
thousand.
12 The ninth *captain* for the ninth month *was*
Abiezer the Anathothite, of the Benjamites; in
his division *were* twenty-four thousand.
13 The tenth *captain* for the tenth month *was*
Maharai the Netophathite, of the Zarhites; in
his division *were* twenty-four thousand.
14 The eleventh *captain* for the eleventh
month *was* Benaiah the Pirathonite, of the
children of Ephraim; in his division *were*
twenty-four thousand.
15 The twelfth *captain* for the twelfth month
was Heldai[a] the Netophathite, of Othniel; in
his division *were* twenty-four thousand.

Leaders of Tribes

16 Furthermore, over the tribes of Israel: the
officer over the Reubenites *was* Eliezer the
son of Zichri; over the Simeonites, Shephatiah the son of Maachah;
17 *over* the Levites, Hashabiah the son of Kemuel; over the Aaronites, Zadok;
18 *over* Judah, Elihu, *one* of David's brothers;
over Issachar, Omri the son of Michael;
19 *over* Zebulun, Ishmaiah the son of Obadiah; *over* Naphtali, Jerimoth the son of Azriel;
20 *over* the children of Ephraim, Hoshea the
son of Azaziah; *over* the half-tribe of Manasseh, Joel the son of Pedaiah;
21 *over* the half-*tribe* of Manasseh in Gilead,
Iddo the son of Zechariah; *over* Benjamin,
Jaasiel the son of Abner;
22 *over* Dan, Azarel the son of Jeroham.
These *were* the leaders of the tribes of Israel.
23 But David did not take the number of
those twenty years old and under, because the
LORD had said He would multiply Israel like
the stars of the heavens.
24 Joab the son of Zeruiah began a census,
but he did not finish, for wrath came upon Israel because of this census; nor was the number recorded in the account of the chronicles
of King David.

Other State Officials

25 And Azmaveth the son of Adiel *was* over
the king's treasuries; and Jehonathan the son

27:4 [a]Hebrew *Dodai,* usually spelled *Dodo* (compare 2 Samuel 23:9) **27:8** [a]Spelled *Shammoth* in 11:27 and *Shammah* in 2 Samuel 23:11 **27:15** [a]Spelled *Heled* in 11:30 and *Heleb* in 2 Samuel 23:29

of Uzziah was over the storehouses in the
field, in the cities, in the villages, and in the
fortresses.
26 Ezri the son of Chelub was over those who
did the work of the field for tilling the ground.
27 And Shimei the Ramathite *was* over the
vineyards, and Zabdi the Shiphmite was over
the produce of the vineyards for the supply of
wine.
28 Baal-Hanan the Gederite was over the
olive trees and the sycamore trees that *were*
in the lowlands, and Joash *was* over the store
of oil.
29 And Shitrai the Sharonite *was* over the
herds that fed in Sharon, and Shaphat the son
of Adlai was over the herds *that were* in the
valleys.
30 Obil the Ishmaelite *was* over the camels,
Jehdeiah the Meronothite *was* over the donkeys,
31 and Jaziz the Hagrite *was* over the flocks.
All these *were* the officials over King David's
property.
32 Also Jehonathan, David's uncle, *was* a
counselor, a wise man, and a scribe; and Jehiel the son of Hachmoni *was* with the king's
sons.
33 Ahithophel *was* the king's counselor, and
Hushai the Archite *was* the king's companion.
34 After Ahithophel *was* Jehoiada the son of
Benaiah, then Abiathar. And the general of
the king's army *was* Joab.

Solomon Instructed to Build the Temple

28 Now David assembled at Jerusalem all
the leaders of Israel: the officers of the
tribes and the captains of the divisions who
served the king, the captains over thousands
and captains over hundreds, and the stewards
over all the substance and possessions of the
king and of his sons, with the officials, the
valiant men, and all the mighty men of valor.
2 Then King David rose to his feet and said,
"Hear me, my brethren and my people: I *had*
it in my heart to build a house of rest for the
ark of the covenant of the LORD, and for the
footstool of our God, and had made preparations to build it.
3 "But God said to me, 'You shall not build a
house for My name, because you *have been* a
man of war and have shed blood.'
4 "However the LORD God of Israel chose
me above all the house of my father to be king
over Israel forever, for He has chosen Judah
to be the ruler. And of the house of Judah, the
house of my father, and among the sons of my
father, He was pleased with me to make *me*
king over all Israel.
5 "And of all my sons (for the LORD has
given me many sons) He has chosen my son
Solomon to sit on the throne of the kingdom
of the LORD over Israel.
6 "Now He said to me, 'It is your son Solomon *who* shall build My house and My
courts; for I have chosen him *to be* My son,
and I will be his Father.
7 'Moreover I will establish his kingdom
forever, if he is steadfast to observe My commandments and My judgments, as it is this
day.'
8 "Now therefore, in the sight of all Israel,
the assembly of the LORD, and in the hearing
of our God, be careful to seek out all the commandments of the LORD your God, that you
may possess this good land, and leave *it* as an
inheritance for your children after you forever.
9 "As for you, my son Solomon, know the
God of your father, and serve Him with a loyal
heart and with a willing mind; for the LORD
searches all hearts and understands all the intent of the thoughts. If you seek Him, He will
be found by you; but if you forsake Him, He
will cast you off forever.
10 "Consider now, for the LORD has chosen
you to build a house for the sanctuary; be
strong, and do it."
11 Then David gave his son Solomon the
plans for the vestibule, its houses, its treasuries, its upper chambers, its inner chambers,
and the place of the mercy seat;
12 and the plans for all that he had by the
Spirit, of the courts of the house of the LORD,
of all the chambers all around, of the treasuries of the house of God, and of the treasuries
for the dedicated things;
13 also for the division of the priests and the
Levites, for all the work of the service of the
house of the LORD, and for all the articles of
service in the house of the LORD.
14 *He gave* gold by weight for *things* of
gold, for all articles used in every kind of
service; also *silver* for all articles of silver by

LIFE LESSONS

➤ 28:5 — *"And of all my sons (for the LORD has given me many sons) He has chosen my son Solomon to sit on the throne of the kingdom of the LORD over Israel."*

Solomon, like his father David before him, ascended to the throne of Israel by the word of the Lord. God chose him to rule. As in all things, we are to ask the Lord who He has chosen to lead us.

➤ 28:9 — *" . . . know the God of your father, and serve Him with a loyal heart and with a willing mind; for the LORD searches all hearts and understands all the intent of the thoughts. If you seek Him, He will be found by you . . . ."*

God promises that we will find Him when we seek Him with all of our hearts (see Jer. 29:13). James says it like this: "Draw near to God and He will draw near to you" (James 4:8).

ANSWERS TO LIFE'S QUESTIONS

How do I deal with the temptation toward pride?

1 CHR. 28:9

Before his death, David told his son and successor Solomon, "As for you, my son Solomon, know the God of your father, and serve Him with a loyal heart and with a willing mind; for the LORD searches all hearts and understands all the intent of the thoughts. If you seek Him, He will be found by you" (1 Chr. 28:9).

Our ability to know and seek God and serve Him with our whole hearts begins with one word: Humility. As the apostle James wrote, "God resists the proud, but gives grace to the humble" (James 4:6).

Sadly, Solomon did not cling to his father's words of advice. Instead, he abandoned their instruction and married women who worshiped other gods. But sin has consequences, and while God did not forsake His promise, he did remove His blessing from Solomon's life.

If you desire God's wisdom, be sure you are willing to humble yourself and follow wisdom's pathway. God told Solomon he could ask for anything and it would be his. Instead of asking for great wealth or power, Solomon chose to ask for wisdom, which God provided abundantly. As Solomon grew older, however, he relied on his wisdom alone instead of leaning on God to inform that wisdom. In his early years, he had trusted God and wanted to do the Lord's will; but eventually Solomon stopped relying on the Lord and began to rely entirely on his own ability. That was his downfall.

When we fail to humbly listen to God—

- We begin to listen to the wrong voices: our own, the devil's, and those who don't have God's very best for us in mind.
- We get easily deceived—and decisions outside the will of God quickly turn disastrous.
- We become prideful and in various haughty ways express our independence from God.
- We begin to make decisions that appeal to our own desires and not the Lord's.
- We hurt those around us.
- We miss out on God's very best.

How can you avoid these perils? Ask God to open your heart to His truth. Be willing to obey His Word, even if it means giving up something you hold as precious. Obedience is always better than the richest sacrifice. Our God is a God of restoration, and He will never refuse your sincere desire to obey and please Him.

See the Life Principles Index for further study:

2. Obey God and leave all the consequences to Him.

19. Anything you hold too tightly you will lose.

weight, for all articles used in every kind of service;
15 the weight for the lampstands of gold, and their lamps of gold, by weight for each lampstand and its lamps; for the lampstands of silver by weight, for the lampstand and its lamps, according to the use of each lampstand.
16 And by weight *he gave* gold for the tables of the showbread, for each table, and silver for the tables of silver;
17 also pure gold for the forks, the basins, the pitchers of pure gold, and the golden bowls—*he gave gold* by weight for every bowl; and for the silver bowls, *silver* by weight for every bowl;
18 and refined gold by weight for the altar of incense, and for the construction of the chariot, that is, the gold cherubim that spread *their wings* and overshadowed the ark of the covenant of the LORD.
19 "All *this,*" *said David,* "the LORD made me ➤

LIFE LESSONS

➤ 28:19 — *"All this," said David, "the LORD made me understand in writing, by His hand upon me, all the works of these plans."*

Inspired by the Spirit of God, David drew up plans for the temple. If we will allow the Spirit to work unhindered in our lives, we can draw upon His guidance and wisdom in all areas of life.

understand in writing, by *His* hand upon me, all the works of these plans."

20 And David said to his son Solomon, "Be strong and of good courage, and do *it;* do not fear nor be dismayed, for the LORD God—my God—*will be* with you. He will not leave you nor forsake you, until you have finished all the work for the service of the house of the LORD.

21 "*Here are* the divisions of the priests and the Levites for all the service of the house of God; and every willing craftsman *will be* with you for all manner of workmanship, for every kind of service; also the leaders and all the people *will be* completely at your command."

Offerings for Building the Temple

29 Furthermore King David said to all the assembly: "My son Solomon, whom alone God has chosen, *is* young and inexperienced; and the work *is* great, because the temple[a] *is* not for man but for the LORD God.

2 "Now for the house of my God I have prepared with all my might: gold for *things to be made of* gold, silver for *things of* silver, bronze for *things of* bronze, iron for *things of* iron, wood for *things of* wood, onyx stones, *stones* to be set, glistening stones of various colors, all kinds of precious stones, and marble slabs in abundance.

3 "Moreover, because I have set my affection on the house of my God, I have given to the house of my God, over and above all that I have prepared for the holy house, my own special treasure of gold and silver:

4 "three thousand talents of gold, of the gold of Ophir, and seven thousand talents of refined silver, to overlay the walls of the houses;

5 "the gold for *things of* gold and the silver for *things of* silver, and for all kinds of work *to be done* by the hands of craftsmen. Who *then* is willing to consecrate himself this day to the LORD?"

6 Then the leaders of the fathers' *houses,* leaders of the tribes of Israel, the captains of thousands and of hundreds, with the officers over the king's work, offered willingly.

7 They gave for the work of the house of God five thousand talents and ten thousand darics of gold, ten thousand talents of silver, eighteen thousand talents of bronze, and one hundred thousand talents of iron.

8 And whoever had *precious* stones gave *them* to the treasury of the house of the LORD, into the hand of Jehiel[a] the Gershonite.

9 Then the people rejoiced, for they had offered willingly, because with a loyal heart they had offered willingly to the LORD; and King David also rejoiced greatly.

David's Praise to God

10 Therefore David blessed the LORD before all the assembly; and David said:

"Blessed are You, LORD God of Israel, our
 Father, forever and ever.
11 Yours, O LORD, *is* the greatness,
The power and the glory,
The victory and the majesty;
For all *that is* in heaven and in earth *is*
 Yours;
Yours *is* the kingdom, O LORD,
And You are exalted as head over all.
12 Both riches and honor *come* from You,
And You reign over all.
In Your hand *is* power and might;
In Your hand *it is* to make great
And to give strength to all.

13 "Now therefore, our God,
We thank You
And praise Your glorious name.
14 But who *am* I, and who *are* my people,
That we should be able to offer so
 willingly as this?
For all things *come* from You,
And of Your own we have given You.
15 For we *are* aliens and pilgrims before
 You,
As *were* all our fathers;
Our days on earth *are* as a shadow,
And without hope.

29:1 [a]Literally *palace* **29:8** [a]Possibly the same as *Jehieli* (compare 26:21, 22)

LIFE LESSONS

➤ 29:3 — *". . . because I have set my affection on the house of my God, I have given to the house of my God, over and above all that I have prepared for the holy house, my own special treasure of gold and silver . . . ."*

When the Lord fills our heart, we delight to honor Him with our wallet.

➤ 29:9 — *Then the people rejoiced, for they had offered willingly, because with a loyal heart they had offered willingly to the LORD . . . .*

Willing offerings to the Lord's work result in great joy for the givers. We can never out give God!

➤ 29:12 — *"Both riches and honor come from You, and You reign over all. In Your hand is power and might; in Your hand it is to make great and to give strength to all."*

Riches come from God. Honor comes from God. In His sovereignty and boundless power, God gives strength to all and makes some great. Who would not worship such a God?

➤ 29:14 — *"But who am I, and who are my people, that we should be able to offer so willingly as this? For all things come from You, and of Your own we have given You."*

We give nothing to God that He has not first given to us.

WHAT THE BIBLE SAYS ABOUT HOW GOD DEFINES WEALTH

1 Chr. 29:12

Each year various publications list the one hundred wealthiest persons in America. The magazines categorize the individuals by total income, usually in the millions and billions. Such is the predominant viewpoint regarding the meaning of wealth.

But is that the way God defines wealth? Hardly. From God's standpoint, wealth includes much more than currency. The bank accounts of rich men and women may overflow, but misery often enshrouds their souls.

Biblical wealth, by contrast, may be defined as the ability to experience and enjoy God's blessings. The poor individual who knows God as Savior has indescribable wealth compared to the rich one who rejects Him.

The Bible insists that God is the source of all gain: "Both riches and honor come from You, and You reign over all. In Your hand is power and might; in Your hand it is to make great and to give strength to all" (1 Chr. 29:12).

God gives it all and God owns it all.

Apart from the benevolence of God, we cannot amass wealth. While our labor, diligence, planning, and wisdom are vital, God remains the sole source of blessing. He is the fountainhead of life, health, food, sun, and all other elements necessary for prosperity. As Creator, all of life is His gift. He is the Prime Giver. "Every good gift and every perfect gift is from above, and comes down from the Father of lights" (James 1:17).

As God prepared to take the Israelites into fertile and fruitful Canaan, He warned them not to forget the source of their new-found affluence: " . . . then you say in your heart, 'My power and the might of my hand have gained me this wealth.' And you shall remember the LORD your God, for it is He who gives you power to get wealth" (Deut. 8:17).

Since all wealth flows from the provision of God, our role is to act as sensible, faithful stewards. God gives it all and God owns it all. He designates us as caretakers of His assets. Our spending and investments then become extensions of His will. By following the careful guidelines of Scripture, we can wisely manage God's riches.

See the Life Principles Index for further study:

23. You can never outgive God.

25. God blesses us so that we might bless others.

16 "O LORD our God, all this abundance that
we have prepared to build You a house for
Your holy name is from Your hand, and *is* all
Your own.
17 "I know also, my God, that You test the
heart and have pleasure in uprightness. As
for me, in the uprightness of my heart I have
willingly offered all these *things;* and now
with joy I have seen Your people, who are
present here to offer willingly to You.
18 "O LORD God of Abraham, Isaac, and Israel, our fathers, keep this forever in the intent of the thoughts of the heart of Your
people, and fix their heart toward You.
19 "And give my son Solomon a loyal heart to
keep Your commandments and Your testimonies and Your statutes, to do all *these
things*, and to build the temple[a] for which I
have made provision."
20 Then David said to all the assembly, "Now
bless the LORD your God." So all the assembly
blessed the LORD God of their fathers, and
bowed their heads and prostrated themselves
before the LORD and the king.

Solomon Anointed King

21 And they made sacrifices to the LORD
and offered burnt offerings to the LORD on
the next day: a thousand bulls, a thousand
rams, a thousand lambs, with their drink offerings, and sacrifices in abundance for all Israel.
22 So they ate and drank before the LORD
with great gladness on that day. And they
made Solomon the son of David king the second time, and anointed *him* before the LORD
to be the leader, and Zadok *to be* priest.
23 Then Solomon sat on the throne of the
LORD as king instead of David his father, and
prospered; and all Israel obeyed him.
24 All the leaders and the mighty men, and
also all the sons of King David, submitted
themselves to King Solomon.
25 So the LORD exalted Solomon exceedingly
in the sight of all Israel, and bestowed on him
such royal majesty as had not been on any
king before him in Israel.

The Close of David's Reign

26 Thus David the son of Jesse reigned over
all Israel.
27 And the period that he reigned over Israel
was forty years; seven years he reigned in Hebron, and thirty-three *years* he reigned in Jerusalem.
28 So he died in a good old age, full of days
and riches and honor; and Solomon his son
reigned in his place.
29 Now the acts of King David, first and last,
indeed they *are* written in the book of Samuel
the seer, in the book of Nathan the prophet,
and in the book of Gad the seer,
30 with all his reign and his might, and the
events that happened to him, to Israel, and to
all the kingdoms of the lands.

29:19 [a]Literally *palace*

THE SECOND BOOK OF

CHRONICLES

Second Chronicles, a sequel to 1 Chronicles, parallels 1 and 2 Kings but virtually ignores the northern kingdom of Israel because of its false worship and refusal to acknowledge the temple in Jerusalem. While the book tells the story of a nation that fell further and further away from its God—and the dreadful consequences of that apostasy—it focuses particular attention on the kings who patterned their lives and reigns after the life and reign of the godly King David, taking special note of the efforts of five godly kings who attempted to cleanse the nation of idol worship. It gives extended treatment to such zealous reformers as Asa (chapter 15), Jehoshaphat (chapter 17), Joash (chapter 23), Hezekiah (chapters 29–31), and Josiah (chapters 34–35).

The temple and its worship, central throughout the book, befit a nation whose worship of God makes possible its very survival. The book begins with the construction of Solomon's glorious temple and concludes with Cyrus's edict to allow the Jews to return home and rebuild their ruined temple, more than four hundred years later.

Themes: The temple and the worship surrounding it are strong themes in the Book of 2 Chronicles, even though it records the sad story of a people who strayed further and further from God. Apostasy and revival also provide strong themes throughout the book. Second Chronicles demonstrates that God will continue to accomplish His purposes for all of humankind, even when His own people turn away from Him in rebellion.

Authors: Uncertain, but thought to be compiled and edited by Ezra.

Time: Second Chronicles starts with Solomon's construction of the temple in Jerusalem (around 966 B.C.) and ends with the Persian king Cyrus's edict to allow the Jews to return to their homeland following the Babylonian exile (around 538 B.C.).

Structure: Mostly historic with a more sustained spiritual emphasis than in 1 Chronicles. This book can be divided into several parts, each covering the reign of various kings following Solomon. Second Chronicles gives special attention both to Solomon and his construction of the temple. Upon the death of Solomon, Rehoboam his son takes the throne—but his rule leads to disaster, resulting in the division of the kingdom. The book highlights the rule of five kings who struggled valiantly to bring the nation of Judah back to its God centuries after Solomon's death.

As you read 2 Chronicles, watch for several life principles that play an important role in this book:

11. **God assumes full responsibility for our needs when we obey Him.** *See 2 Chronicles 14:4; 34:31; pages 509; 535.*

8. **Fight all your battles on your knees and you win every time.** *See 2 Chronicles 20:1–30; page 514.*

10. **If necessary, God will move heaven and earth to show us His will.** *See 2 Chronicles 20:12; page 516.*

7. **The dark moments of our life will last only so long as is necessary for God to accomplish His purpose in us.** *See 2 Chronicles 32:24–29; page 533.*

15. **Brokenness is God's requirement for maximum usefulness.** *See 2 Chronicles 33; page 533.*

Solomon Requests Wisdom

➤ 1 Now Solomon the son of David was strengthened in his kingdom, and the LORD his God *was* with him and exalted him exceedingly.

2 And Solomon spoke to all Israel, to the captains of thousands and of hundreds, to the judges, and to every leader in all Israel, the heads of the fathers' *houses.*

3 Then Solomon, and all the assembly with him, went to the high place that *was* at Gibeon; for the tabernacle of meeting with God was there, which Moses the servant of the LORD had made in the wilderness.

4 But David had brought up the ark of God from Kirjath Jearim to *the place* David had prepared for it, for he had pitched a tent for it at Jerusalem.

5 Now the bronze altar that Bezalel the son of Uri, the son of Hur, had made, he put[a] before the tabernacle of the LORD; Solomon and the assembly sought Him *there.*

6 And Solomon went up there to the bronze altar before the LORD, which *was* at the tabernacle of meeting, and offered a thousand burnt offerings on it.

7 On that night God appeared to Solomon, and said to him, "Ask! What shall I give you?"

8 And Solomon said to God: "You have shown great mercy to David my father, and have made me king in his place.

9 "Now, O LORD God, let Your promise to David my father be established, for You have made me king over a people like the dust of the earth in multitude.

10 "Now give me wisdom and knowledge, that I may go out and come in before this people; for who can judge this great people of Yours?"

11 Then God said to Solomon: "Because this was in your heart, and you have not asked riches or wealth or honor or the life of your enemies, nor have you asked long life—but have asked wisdom and knowledge for yourself, that you may judge My people over whom I have made you king—

12 "wisdom and knowledge *are* granted to you; and I will give you riches and wealth and honor, such as none of the kings have had who *were* before you, nor shall any after you have the like."

Solomon's Military and Economic Power

13 So Solomon came to Jerusalem from the high place that *was* at Gibeon, from before the tabernacle of meeting, and reigned over Israel.

14 And Solomon gathered chariots and horsemen; he had one thousand four hundred chariots and twelve thousand horsemen, whom he stationed in the chariot cities and with the king in Jerusalem.

15 Also the king made silver and gold as common in Jerusalem as stones, and he made cedars as abundant as the sycamores which *are* in the lowland.

16 And Solomon had horses imported from Egypt and Keveh; the king's merchants bought them in Keveh at the *current* price.

17 They also acquired and imported from Egypt a chariot for six hundred *shekels* of silver, and a horse for one hundred and fifty; thus, through their agents,[a] they exported them to all the kings of the Hittites and the kings of Syria.

Solomon Prepares to Build the Temple

2 Then Solomon determined to build a temple for the name of the LORD, and a royal house for himself.

2 Solomon selected seventy thousand men to bear burdens, eighty thousand to quarry *stone* in the mountains, and three thousand six hundred to oversee them.

3 Then Solomon sent to Hiram[a] king of Tyre, saying:

> As you have dealt with David my father, and sent him cedars to build himself a house to dwell in, *so deal with me.*
>
> 4 Behold, I am building a temple for the name of the LORD my God, to dedicate *it* to Him, to burn before Him sweet incense, for the continual showbread, for the burnt offerings morning and evening, on the Sabbaths, on the New Moons, and on the set feasts of the LORD our God. This *is an ordinance* forever to Israel.
>
> 5 And the temple which I build *will be* great, for our God is greater than all gods. ➤

1:5 [a]Some authorities read *it was there.* **1:17** [a]Literally *by their hands* **2:3** [a]Hebrew *Huram* (compare 1 Kings 5:1)

LIFE LESSONS

➤ 1:1 — *Now Solomon the son of David was strengthened in his kingdom, and the LORD his God was with him and exalted him exceedingly.*

We choose life when we follow the Lord, death when we don't. So long as Solomon obeyed God, God prospered him; but when he rebelled, he doomed his kingdom to destruction.

➤ 2:5 — *"And the temple which I build will be great, for our God is greater than all gods."*

A great God deserved a great temple. But even more He deserves our wholehearted devotion and joyful obedience.

6 But who is able to build Him a temple, since heaven and the heaven of heavens cannot contain Him? Who *am* I then, that I should build Him a temple, except to burn sacrifice before Him?
7 Therefore send me at once a man skillful to work in gold and silver, in bronze and iron, in purple and crimson and blue, who has skill to engrave with the skillful men who are with me in Judah and Jerusalem, whom David my father provided.
8 Also send me cedar and cypress and algum logs from Lebanon, for I know that your servants have skill to cut timber in Lebanon; and indeed my servants *will be* with your servants,
9 to prepare timber for me in abundance, for the temple which I am about to build *shall be* great and wonderful.
10 And indeed I will give to your servants, the woodsmen who cut timber, twenty thousand kors of ground wheat, twenty thousand kors of barley, twenty thousand baths of wine, and twenty thousand baths of oil.

11 Then Hiram king of Tyre answered in writing, which he sent to Solomon:

Because the LORD loves His people, He has made you king over them.

12 Hiram[a] also said:

Blessed *be* the LORD God of Israel, who made heaven and earth, for He has given King David a wise son, endowed with prudence and understanding, who will build a temple for the LORD and a royal house for himself!
13 And now I have sent a skillful man, endowed with understanding, Huram[a] my master[b] *craftsman*
14 (the son of a woman of the daughters of Dan, and his father was a man of Tyre), skilled to work in gold and silver, bronze and iron, stone and wood, purple and blue, fine linen and crimson, and to make any engraving and to accomplish any plan which may be given to him, with your skillful men and with the skillful men of my lord David your father.
15 Now therefore, the wheat, the barley, the oil, and the wine which my lord has spoken of, let him send to his servants.
16 And we will cut wood from Lebanon, as much as you need; we will bring it to you in rafts by sea to Joppa, and you will carry it up to Jerusalem.

17 Then Solomon numbered all the aliens who *were* in the land of Israel, after the census in which David his father had numbered them; and there were found to be one hundred and fifty-three thousand six hundred.
18 And he made seventy thousand of them bearers of burdens, eighty thousand stonecutters in the mountain, and three thousand six hundred overseers to make the people work.

Solomon Builds the Temple

3 Now Solomon began to build the house of the LORD at Jerusalem on Mount Moriah, where *the LORD*[a] had appeared to his father David, at the place that David had prepared on the threshing floor of Ornan[b] the Jebusite.
2 And he began to build on the second *day* of the second month in the fourth year of his reign.
3 This is the foundation which Solomon laid for building the house of God: The length *was* sixty cubits (by cubits according to the former measure) and the width twenty cubits.
4 And the vestibule that *was* in front *of the sanctuary*[a] was twenty cubits long across the width of the house, and the height *was* one hundred and[b] twenty. He overlaid the inside with pure gold.
5 The larger room[a] he paneled with cypress which he overlaid with fine gold, and he carved palm trees and chainwork on it.
6 And he decorated the house with precious stones for beauty, and the gold *was* gold from Parvaim.
7 He also overlaid the house—the beams and doorposts, its walls and doors—with gold; and he carved cherubim on the walls.
8 And he made the Most Holy Place. Its length was according to the width of the house, twenty cubits, and its width twenty cubits. He overlaid it with six hundred talents of fine gold.
9 The weight of the nails *was* fifty shekels of gold; and he overlaid the upper area with gold.
10 In the Most Holy Place he made two cherubim, fashioned by carving, and overlaid them with gold.
11 The wings of the cherubim *were* twenty cubits in *overall* length: one wing *of the one cherub was* five cubits, touching the wall of the room, and the other wing *was* five cubits, touching the wing of the other cherub;
12 *one* wing of the other cherub *was* five cubits, touching the wall of the room, and the other wing *also was* five cubits, touching the wing of the other cherub.
13 The wings of these cherubim spanned twenty cubits overall. They stood on their feet, and they faced inward.

2:12 [a]Hebrew *Huram* (compare 1 Kings 5:1) **2:13** [a]Spelled *Hiram* in 1 Kings 7:13 [b]Literally *father* (compare 1 Kings 7:13, 14) **3:1** [a]Literally *He*, following Masoretic Text and Vulgate; Septuagint reads *the LORD;* Targum reads *the Angel of the LORD.* [b]Spelled *Araunah* in 2 Samuel 24:16ff **3:4** [a]The main room of the temple; elsewhere called the holy place (compare 1 Kings 6:3) [b]Following Masoretic Text, Septuagint, and Vulgate; Arabic, some manuscripts of the Septuagint, and Syriac omit *one hundred and.* **3:5** [a]Literally *house*

14 And he made the veil of blue, purple, crimson, and fine linen, and wove cherubim into it.

15 Also he made in front of the temple[a] two pillars thirty-five[b] cubits high, and the capital that *was* on the top of each of *them* was five cubits.

16 He made wreaths of chainwork, as in the inner sanctuary, and put *them* on top of the pillars; and he made one hundred pomegranates, and put *them* on the wreaths of chainwork.

17 Then he set up the pillars before the temple, one on the right hand and the other on the left; he called the name of the one on the right hand Jachin, and the name of the one on the left Boaz.

Furnishings of the Temple

4 Moreover he made a bronze altar: twenty cubits was its length, twenty cubits its width, and ten cubits its height.

2 Then he made the Sea of cast *bronze,* ten cubits from one brim to the other; *it was* completely round. Its height *was* five cubits, and a line of thirty cubits measured its circumference.

3 And under it *was* the likeness of oxen encircling it all around, ten to a cubit, all the way around the Sea. The oxen *were* cast in two rows, when it was cast.

4 It stood on twelve oxen: three looking toward the north, three looking toward the west, three looking toward the south, and three looking toward the east; the Sea *was set* upon them, and all their back parts *pointed* inward.

5 It *was* a handbreadth thick; and its brim was shaped like the brim of a cup, *like* a lily blossom. It contained three thousand[a] baths.

6 He also made ten lavers, and put five on the right side and five on the left, to wash in them; such things as they offered for the burnt offering they would wash in them, but the Sea *was* for the priests to wash in.

7 And he made ten lampstands of gold according to their design, and set *them* in the temple, five on the right side and five on the left.

8 He also made ten tables, and placed *them* in the temple, five on the right side and five on the left. And he made one hundred bowls of gold.

9 Furthermore he made the court of the priests, and the great court and doors for the court; and he overlaid these doors with bronze.

10 He set the Sea on the right side, toward the southeast.

11 Then Huram made the pots and the shovels and the bowls. So Huram finished doing the work that he was to do for King Solomon for the house of God:

12 the two pillars and the bowl-shaped capitals *that were* on top of the two pillars; the two networks covering the two bowl-shaped capitals which *were* on top of the pillars;

13 four hundred pomegranates for the two networks (two rows of pomegranates for each network, to cover the two bowl-shaped capitals that *were* on the pillars);

14 he also made carts and the lavers on the carts;

15 one Sea and twelve oxen under it;

16 also the pots, the shovels, the forks—and all their articles Huram his master[a] *craftsman* made of burnished bronze for King Solomon for the house of the LORD.

17 In the plain of Jordan the king had them cast in clay molds, between Succoth and Zeredah.[a]

18 And Solomon had all these articles made in such great abundance that the weight of the bronze was not determined.

19 Thus Solomon had all the furnishings made for the house of God: the altar of gold and the tables on which *was* the showbread;

20 the lampstands with their lamps of pure gold, to burn in the prescribed manner in front of the inner sanctuary,

21 with the flowers and the lamps and the wick-trimmers of gold, of purest gold;

22 the trimmers, the bowls, the ladles, and the censers of pure gold. As for the entry of the sanctuary, its inner doors to the Most Holy *Place,* and the doors of the main hall of the temple, *were* gold.

5 So all the work that Solomon had done for the house of the LORD was finished; and Solomon brought in the things which his father David had dedicated: the silver and the gold and all the furnishings. And he put *them* in the treasuries of the house of God.

The Ark Brought into the Temple

2 Now Solomon assembled the elders of Israel and all the heads of the tribes, the chief fathers of the children of Israel, in Jerusalem, that they might bring the ark of the covenant of the LORD up from the City of David, which *is* Zion.

3 Therefore all the men of Israel assembled with the king at the feast, which *was* in the seventh month.

4 So all the elders of Israel came, and the Levites took up the ark.

5 Then they brought up the ark, the tabernacle of meeting, and all the holy furnishings that *were* in the tabernacle. The priests and the Levites brought them up.

6 Also King Solomon, and all the congregation of Israel who were assembled with him before the ark, were sacrificing sheep and

---

3:15 [a]Literally *house* [b]Or *eighteen* (compare 1 Kings 7:15; 2 Kings 25:17; and Jeremiah 52:21) **4:5** [a]Or *two thousand* (compare 1 Kings 7:26) **4:16** [a]Literally *father* **4:17** [a]Spelled *Zaretan* in 1 Kings 7:46

oxen that could not be counted or numbered for multitude.

7 Then the priests brought in the ark of the covenant of the LORD to its place, into the inner sanctuary of the temple,[a] to the Most Holy *Place*, under the wings of the cherubim.

8 For the cherubim spread *their* wings over the place of the ark, and the cherubim overshadowed the ark and its poles.

9 The poles extended so that the ends of the poles of the ark could be seen from *the holy place*, in front of the inner sanctuary; but they could not be seen from outside. And they are there to this day.

10 Nothing was in the ark except the two tablets which Moses put *there* at Horeb, when the LORD made *a covenant* with the children of Israel, when they had come out of Egypt.

11 And it came to pass when the priests came out of the *Most* Holy *Place* (for all the priests who *were* present had sanctified themselves, without keeping to their divisions),

12 and the Levites *who were* the singers, all those of Asaph and Heman and Jeduthun, with their sons and their brethren, stood at the east end of the altar, clothed in white linen, having cymbals, stringed instruments and harps, and with them one hundred and twenty priests sounding with trumpets—

13 indeed it came to pass, when the trumpeters and singers *were* as one, to make one sound to be heard in praising and thanking the LORD, and when they lifted up their voice with the trumpets and cymbals and instruments of music, and praised the LORD, *saying*:

"*For He is* good,
For His mercy *endures* forever,"[a]

That the house, the house of the LORD, was filled with a cloud,

14 so that the priests could not continue ministering because of the cloud; for the glory of the LORD filled the house of God.

6 Then Solomon spoke:

"The LORD said He would dwell in the
dark cloud.
2 I have surely built You an exalted house,
And a place for You to dwell in forever."

Solomon's Speech upon Completion of the Work

3 Then the king turned around and blessed the whole assembly of Israel, while all the assembly of Israel was standing.

4 And he said: "Blessed *be* the LORD God of Israel, who has fulfilled with His hands *what* He spoke with His mouth to my father David, saying,

5 'Since the day that I brought My people out of the land of Egypt, I have chosen no city from any tribe of Israel *in which* to build a house, that My name might be there, nor did I choose any man to be a ruler over My people Israel.

6 'Yet I have chosen Jerusalem, that My name may be there, and I have chosen David to be over My people Israel.'

7 "Now it was in the heart of my father David to build a temple[a] for the name of the LORD God of Israel.

8 "But the LORD said to my father David, 'Whereas it was in your heart to build a temple for My name, you did well in that it was in your heart.

9 'Nevertheless you shall not build the temple, but your son who will come from your body, he shall build the temple for My name.'

10 "So the LORD has fulfilled His word which He spoke, and I have filled the position of my father David, and sit on the throne of Israel, as the LORD promised; and I have built the temple for the name of the LORD God of Israel.

11 "And there I have put the ark, in which *is* the covenant of the LORD which He made with the children of Israel."

Solomon's Prayer of Dedication

12 Then *Solomon*[a] stood before the altar of the LORD in the presence of all the assembly of Israel, and spread out his hands

13 (for Solomon had made a bronze platform five cubits long, five cubits wide, and three cubits high, and had set it in the midst of the court; and he stood on it, knelt down on his knees before all the assembly of Israel, and spread out his hands toward heaven);

14 and he said: "LORD God of Israel, *there is* no God in heaven or on earth like You, who keep *Your* covenant and mercy with Your servants who walk before You with all their hearts.

15 "You have kept what You promised Your servant David my father; You have both spoken with Your mouth and fulfilled *it* with Your hand, as *it is* this day.

5:7 [a]Literally *house* **5:13** [a]Compare Psalm 106:1 **6:7** [a]Literally *house*, and so in verses 8–10 **6:12** [a]Literally *he* (compare 1 Kings 8:22)

LIFE LESSONS

➤ ***6:15 — "You have kept what You promised Your servant David my father; You have both spoken with Your mouth and fulfilled it with Your hand, as it is this day."***

What God speaks with His mouth, He fulfills with His hand. God's Word is an immovable anchor in times of storm.

16 "Therefore, LORD God of Israel, now keep
what You promised Your servant David my father, saying, 'You shall not fail to have a man
sit before Me on the throne of Israel, only if
your sons take heed to their way, that they
walk in My law as you have walked before Me.'
17 "And now, O LORD God of Israel, let Your
word come true, which You have spoken to
Your servant David.
18 "But will God indeed dwell with men on
the earth? Behold, heaven and the heaven of
heavens cannot contain You. How much less
this temple[a] which I have built!
19 "Yet regard the prayer of Your servant and
his supplication, O LORD my God, and listen
to the cry and the prayer which Your servant
is praying before You:
20 "that Your eyes may be open toward this
temple day and night, toward the place where
You said *You would* put Your name, that You
may hear the prayer which Your servant
makes toward this place.
21 "And may You hear the supplications of
Your servant and of Your people Israel, when
they pray toward this place. Hear from
heaven Your dwelling place, and when You
hear, forgive.
22 "If anyone sins against his neighbor, and
is forced to take an oath, and comes *and* takes
an oath before Your altar in this temple,
23 "then hear from heaven, and act, and
judge Your servants, bringing retribution on
the wicked by bringing his way on his own
head, and justifying the righteous by giving
him according to his righteousness.
24 "Or if Your people Israel are defeated before an enemy because they have sinned
against You, and return and confess Your
name, and pray and make supplication before
You in this temple,
25 "then hear from heaven and forgive the
sin of Your people Israel, and bring them
back to the land which You gave to them and
their fathers.
26 "When the heavens are shut up and there
is no rain because they have sinned against
You, when they pray toward this place and
confess Your name, and turn from their sin because You afflict them,
27 "then hear *in* heaven, and forgive the sin
of Your servants, Your people Israel, that You
may teach them the good way in which they
should walk; and send rain on Your land
which You have given to Your people as an inheritance.
28 "When there is famine in the land, pestilence or blight or mildew, locusts or grasshoppers; when their enemies besiege them in
the land of their cities; whatever plague or
whatever sickness *there is;*
29 "whatever prayer, whatever supplication ➤
is *made* by anyone, or by all Your people Israel, when each one knows his own burden
and his own grief, and spreads out his hands
to this temple:
30 "then hear from heaven Your dwelling ➤
place, and forgive, and give to everyone according to all his ways, whose heart You know
(for You alone know the hearts of the sons of
men),
31 "that they may fear You, to walk in Your
ways as long as they live in the land which
You gave to our fathers.
32 "Moreover, concerning a foreigner, who is
not of Your people Israel, but has come from a
far country for the sake of Your great name
and Your mighty hand and Your outstretched
arm, when they come and pray in this temple;
33 "then hear from heaven Your dwelling
place, and do according to all for which the
foreigner calls to You, that all peoples of the
earth may know Your name and fear You, as
do Your people Israel, and that they may know
that this temple which I have built is called by
Your name.
34 "When Your people go out to battle against
their enemies, wherever You send them, and
when they pray to You toward this city which
You have chosen and the temple which I have
built for Your name,
35 "then hear from heaven their prayer and
their supplication, and maintain their cause.
36 "When they sin against You (for *there is* no
one who does not sin), and You become angry
with them and deliver them to the enemy, and
they take them captive to a land far or near;
37 "*yet* when they come to themselves in the
land where they were carried captive, and repent, and make supplication to You in the land
of their captivity, saying, 'We have sinned, we
have done wrong, and have committed
wickedness';
38 "and *when* they return to You with all their
heart and with all their soul in the land of
their captivity, where they have been carried
captive, and pray toward their land which You
gave to their fathers, the city which You have

6:18 [a]Literally *house*

LIFE LESSONS

➤ ***6:29, 30 — ". . . whatever prayer, whatever supplication is made by anyone . . . then hear from heaven Your dwelling place, and forgive, and give to everyone according to all his ways . . . ."***

We might consider this verse the Old Testament equivalent of Philippians 4:6: "In everything by prayer and supplication, with thanksgiving, let your requests be made known to God." God invites our prayers!

chosen, and toward the temple which I have
built for Your name:
39 "then hear from heaven Your dwelling
place their prayer and their supplications,
and maintain their cause, and forgive Your
people who have sinned against You.
40 "Now, my God, I pray, let Your eyes be
open and *let* Your ears *be* attentive to the
prayer *made* in this place.

41 "Now therefore,
Arise, O LORD God, to Your resting place,
You and the ark of Your strength.
Let Your priests, O LORD God, be clothed
with salvation,
And let Your saints rejoice in goodness.
42 "O LORD God, do not turn away the face of
Your Anointed;
Remember the mercies of Your servant
David."[a]

Solomon Dedicates the Temple

7 When Solomon had finished praying, fire
came down from heaven and consumed
the burnt offering and the sacrifices; and the
glory of the LORD filled the temple.[a]
2 And the priests could not enter the house
of the LORD, because the glory of the LORD
had filled the LORD's house.
3 When all the children of Israel saw how
the fire came down, and the glory of the LORD
on the temple, they bowed their faces to the
ground on the pavement, and worshiped and
praised the LORD, *saying:*

"For *He is* good,
For His mercy *endures* forever."[a]

4 Then the king and all the people offered
sacrifices before the LORD.
5 King Solomon offered a sacrifice of
twenty-two thousand bulls and one hundred
and twenty thousand sheep. So the king and
all the people dedicated the house of God.
6 And the priests attended to their services;
the Levites also with instruments of the music
of the LORD, which King David had made to
praise the LORD, saying, "For His mercy *endures* forever,"[a] whenever David offered
praise by their ministry. The priests sounded
trumpets opposite them, while all Israel
stood.
7 Furthermore Solomon consecrated the
middle of the court that *was* in front of the
house of the LORD; for there he offered burnt
offerings and the fat of the peace offerings,
because the bronze altar which Solomon had
made was not able to receive the burnt offerings, the grain offerings, and the fat.
8 At that time Solomon kept the feast seven
days, and all Israel with him, a very great assembly from the entrance of Hamath to the
Brook of Egypt.[a]
9 And on the eighth day they held a sacred
assembly, for they observed the dedication
of the altar seven days, and the feast seven
days.
10 On the twenty-third day of the seventh
month he sent the people away to their tents,
joyful and glad of heart for the good that the
LORD had done for David, for Solomon, and
for His people Israel.
11 Thus Solomon finished the house of the
LORD and the king's house; and Solomon successfully accomplished all that came into his
heart to make in the house of the LORD and in
his own house.

God's Second Appearance to Solomon

12 Then the LORD appeared to Solomon by
night, and said to him: "I have heard your
prayer, and have chosen this place for Myself
as a house of sacrifice.
13 "When I shut up heaven and there is no
rain, or command the locusts to devour
the land, or send pestilence among My people,
14 "if My people who are called by My name
will humble themselves, and pray and seek
My face, and turn from their wicked ways,
then I will hear from heaven, and will forgive
their sin and heal their land.
15 "Now My eyes will be open and My ears
attentive to prayer *made* in this place.
16 "For now I have chosen and sanctified this
house, that My name may be there forever;
and My eyes and My heart will be there perpetually.
17 "As for you, if you walk before Me as your
father David walked, and do according to all
that I have commanded you, and if you keep
My statutes and My judgments,
18 "then I will establish the throne of your
kingdom, as I covenanted with David your father, saying, 'You shall not fail *to have* a man
as ruler in Israel.'
19 "But if you turn away and forsake My
statutes and My commandments which I have
set before you, and go and serve other gods,
and worship them,
20 "then I will uproot them from My land
which I have given them; and this house
which I have sanctified for My name I will
cast out of My sight, and will make it a
proverb and a byword among all peoples.
21 "And *as for* this house, which is exalted,
everyone who passes by it will be astonished
and say, 'Why has the LORD done thus to this
land and this house?'
22 "Then they will answer, 'Because they forsook the LORD God of their fathers, who
brought them out of the land of Egypt, and
embraced other gods, and worshiped them

6:42 [a]Compare Psalm 132:8–10 **7:1** [a]Literally *house*
7:3 [a]Compare Psalm 106:1 **7:6** [a]Compare Psalm 106:1
7:8 [a]That is, the Shihor (compare 1 Chronicles 13:5)

ANSWERS TO LIFE'S QUESTIONS

What can I do to help change the spiritual and moral climate of my nation?

2 CHR. 7:14

Because the problems we face in our country seem overwhelming, getting a grip on any of them is a big challenge. One aspect of the national landscape in particular shows a steep decline after our government took a stand against the Word of God, under the guise of separation of church and state.

Forty years ago, while Bible and prayer still had an important place in the public school system, teachers reported the following as the major school problems: (1) talking in class; (2) chewing gum; (3) making noise; (4) running in the halls; (5) getting out of line; (6) wearing improper clothing; and (7) missing the wastebasket.

Today, they report a very different set of main problems: (1) drug abuse; (2) suicide; (3) alcohol abuse; (4) pregnancy; (5) rape; (6) murder; and (7) assault. Sounds like the description of a penitentiary instead of a public school!

Talking in class versus drug abuse just don't compare with one another, do they? And chewing gum versus suicide screams to the world, "SOMETHING WENT WRONG!"

Indeed it has! But God's Word gives us reason for hope regarding both a nation and a culture in serious moral decline. According to 2 Chronicles 7:14, righting our national ship begins with prayer. God has placed the solution to our country's woes in the laps of those who acknowledge Him. God's strategy for change goes something like the following.

First, we must humble ourselves. We agree with God that we are not worthy to be fixed. Although America is the greatest nation on earth, we're not really that great. We must take personal responsibility for the decline: "Father, my country is in the shape it is because I have not done my part to change it."

Second, we must pray. We must plead for this land. We must pray for every Supreme Court justice by name. We must pray for our president, for those who counsel him, for the members of the Senate and the House. Get the names of state and local authorities and pray specifically for them also.

Third, we must seek His face. We must seek and desperately want what God wants: "Lord, what can I do? Where do I fit in? Where can I have the most impact for righteousness?" And when God gives us direction, we must follow through on what He is telling us. We must not be merely hearers of His word, but doers (James 1:22).

See the Life Principles Index for further study:

8. Fight all your battles on your knees and you win every time.

15. Brokenness is God's requirement for maximum usefulness.

and served them; therefore He has brought all
this calamity on them.'"

Solomon's Additional Achievements

8 It came to pass at the end of twenty years,
when Solomon had built the house of the
LORD and his own house,
2 that the cities which Hiram[a] had given to
Solomon, Solomon built them; and he settled
the children of Israel there.
3 And Solomon went to Hamath Zobah and
seized it.
4 He also built Tadmor in the wilderness,
and all the storage cities which he built in
Hamath.
5 He built Upper Beth Horon and Lower
Beth Horon, fortified cities *with* walls, gates,
and bars,
6 also Baalath and all the storage cities that
Solomon had, and all the chariot cities and
the cities of the cavalry, and all that Solomon
desired to build in Jerusalem, in Lebanon,
and in all the land of his dominion.
7 All the people *who were* left of the Hittites,
Amorites, Perizzites, Hivites, and Jebusites,
who *were* not of Israel—
8 that is, their descendants who were left in
the land after them, whom the children of Israel
did not destroy—from these Solomon
raised forced labor, as it is to this day.
9 But Solomon did not make the children of
Israel servants for his work. Some *were* men
of war, captains of his officers, captains of his
chariots, and his cavalry.
10 And others *were* chiefs of the officials of
King Solomon: two hundred and fifty, who
ruled over the people.

8:2 [a]Hebrew *Huram* (compare 2 Chronicles 2:3)

➤ 11 Now Solomon brought the daughter of Pharaoh up from the City of David to the house he had built for her, for he said, "My wife shall not dwell in the house of David king of Israel, because *the places* to which the ark of the LORD has come are holy."

12 Then Solomon offered burnt offerings to the LORD on the altar of the LORD which he had built before the vestibule,

13 according to the daily rate, offering according to the commandment of Moses, for the Sabbaths, the New Moons, and the three appointed yearly feasts—the Feast of Unleavened Bread, the Feast of Weeks, and the Feast of Tabernacles.

14 And, according to the order of David his father, he appointed the divisions of the priests for their service, the Levites for their duties (to praise and serve before the priests) as the duty of each day required, and the gatekeepers by their divisions at each gate; for so David the man of God had commanded.

15 They did not depart from the command of the king to the priests and Levites concerning any matter or concerning the treasuries.

16 Now all the work of Solomon was well-ordered from[a] the day of the foundation of the house of the LORD until it was finished. So the house of the LORD was completed.

17 Then Solomon went to Ezion Geber and Elath[a] on the seacoast, in the land of Edom.

18 And Hiram sent him ships by the hand of his servants, and servants who knew the sea. They went with the servants of Solomon to Ophir, and acquired four hundred and fifty talents of gold from there, and brought it to King Solomon.

The Queen of Sheba's Praise of Solomon

9 Now when the queen of Sheba heard of the fame of Solomon, she came to Jerusalem to test Solomon with hard questions, *having* a very great retinue, camels that bore spices, gold in abundance, and precious stones; and when she came to Solomon, she spoke with him about all that was in her heart.

2 So Solomon answered all her questions; there was nothing so difficult for Solomon that he could not explain it to her.

3 And when the queen of Sheba had seen the wisdom of Solomon, the house that he had built,

4 the food on his table, the seating of his servants, the service of his waiters and their apparel, his cupbearers and their apparel, and his entryway by which he went up to the house of the LORD, there was no more spirit in her.

5 Then she said to the king: "*It was* a true report which I heard in my own land about your words and your wisdom.

6 "However I did not believe their words until I came and saw with my own eyes; and indeed the half of the greatness of your wisdom was not told me. You exceed the fame of which I heard.

7 "Happy *are* your men and happy *are* these your servants, who stand continually before you and hear your wisdom! ➤

8 "Blessed be the LORD your God, who delighted in you, setting you on His throne *to be* king for the LORD your God! Because your God has loved Israel, to establish them forever, therefore He made you king over them, to do justice and righteousness."

9 And she gave the king one hundred and twenty talents of gold, spices in great abundance, and precious stones; there never were any spices such as those the queen of Sheba gave to King Solomon.

10 Also, the servants of Hiram and the servants of Solomon, who brought gold from Ophir, brought algum[a] wood and precious stones.

11 And the king made walkways *of* the algum[a] wood for the house of the LORD and for the king's house, also harps and stringed instruments for singers; and there were none such *as these* seen before in the land of Judah.

12 Now King Solomon gave to the queen of Sheba all she desired, whatever she asked, *much more* than she had brought to the king. So she turned and went to her own country, she and her servants.

8:16 [a]Following Septuagint, Syriac, and Vulgate; Masoretic Text reads *as far as*. **8:17** [a]Hebrew *Eloth* (compare 2 Kings 14:22) **9:10** [a]Or *almug* (compare 1 Kings 10:11, 12) **9:11** [a]Or *almug* (compare 1 Kings 10:11, 12)

LIFE LESSONS

➤ 8:11 — *Now Solomon brought the daughter of Pharaoh up from the City of David . . . for he said, "My wife shall not dwell in the house of David king of Israel, because the places to which the ark of the LORD has come are holy."*

Solomon knew that he had married a woman who had no place in the worship of Israel and no connection to his nation's God. He knowingly sinned; but he did not know how his sin would ruin him.

➤ 9:7 — *"Happy are your men and happy are these your servants, who stand continually before you and hear your wisdom!"*

Perhaps Solomon listened too eagerly to glowing declarations of his great wisdom. He knew he had received this gift from God, yet we have no record that he reminded the queen of the fact.

Solomon's Great Wealth

13 The weight of gold that came to Solomon
yearly was six hundred and sixty-six talents
of gold,
14 besides *what* the traveling merchants and
traders brought. And all the kings of Arabia
and governors of the country brought gold
and silver to Solomon.
15 And King Solomon made two hundred
large shields of hammered gold; six hundred
shekels of hammered gold went into each
shield.
16 *He* also *made* three hundred shields of
hammered gold; three hundred *shekels*[a] of
gold went into each shield. The king put them
in the House of the Forest of Lebanon.
17 Moreover the king made a great throne of
ivory, and overlaid it with pure gold.
18 The throne *had* six steps, with a footstool
of gold, *which were* fastened to the throne;
there were armrests on either side of the
place of the seat, and two lions stood beside
the armrests.
19 Twelve lions stood there, one on each side
of the six steps; nothing like *this* had been
made for any *other* kingdom.
20 All King Solomon's drinking vessels *were*
gold, and all the vessels of the House of the
Forest of Lebanon *were* pure gold. Not *one*
was silver, for this was accounted as nothing
in the days of Solomon.
21 For the king's ships went to Tarshish with
the servants of Hiram.[a] Once every three
years the merchant ships[b] came, bringing
gold, silver, ivory, apes, and monkeys.[c]
22 So King Solomon surpassed all the kings
of the earth in riches and wisdom.
23 And all the kings of the earth sought the
presence of Solomon to hear his wisdom,
which God had put in his heart.
24 Each man brought his present: articles of
silver and gold, garments, armor, spices,
horses, and mules, at a set rate year by year.
25 Solomon had four thousand stalls for
horses and chariots, and twelve thousand
horsemen whom he stationed in the chariot
cities and with the king at Jerusalem.
26 So he reigned over all the kings from the
River[a] to the land of the Philistines, as far as
the border of Egypt.
27 The king made silver *as common* in Jerusalem as stones, and he made cedar trees as
abundant as the sycamores which *are* in the
lowland.
28 And they brought horses to Solomon from
Egypt and from all lands.

Death of Solomon

29 Now the rest of the acts of Solomon, first
and last, *are* they not written in the book of
Nathan the prophet, in the prophecy of Ahijah the Shilonite, and in the visions of Iddo
the seer concerning Jeroboam the son of
Nebat?
30 Solomon reigned in Jerusalem over all Israel forty years.
31 Then Solomon rested with his fathers,
and was buried in the City of David his
father. And Rehoboam his son reigned in his
place.

The Revolt Against Rehoboam

10 And Rehoboam went to Shechem, for
all Israel had gone to Shechem to make
him king.
2 So it happened, when Jeroboam the son of
Nebat heard *it* (he was in Egypt, where he
had fled from the presence of King Solomon),
that Jeroboam returned from Egypt.
3 Then they sent for him and called him.
And Jeroboam and all Israel came and spoke
to Rehoboam, saying,
4 "Your father made our yoke heavy; now
therefore, lighten the burdensome service of
your father and his heavy yoke which he put
on us, and we will serve you."
5 So he said to them, "Come back to me
after three days." And the people departed.
6 Then King Rehoboam consulted the elders who stood before his father Solomon
while he still lived, saying, "How do you advise *me* to answer these people?"
7 And they spoke to him, saying, "If you are
kind to these people, and please them, and
speak good words to them, they will be your
servants forever."
8 But he rejected the advice which the elders had given him, and consulted the young
men who had grown up with him, who stood
before him.
9 And he said to them, "What advice do you
give? How should we answer this people who
have spoken to me, saying, 'Lighten the yoke
which your father put on us'?"
10 Then the young men who had grown up
with him spoke to him, saying, "Thus you
should speak to the people who have spoken
to you, saying, 'Your father made our yoke
heavy, but you make *it* lighter on us'—thus
you shall say to them: 'My little *finger* shall be
thicker than my father's waist!
11 'And now, whereas my father put a heavy
yoke on you, I will add to your yoke; my father chastised you with whips, but I *will chas-*
tise you with scourges!'"[a]
12 So Jeroboam and all the people came to
Rehoboam on the third day, as the king had
directed, saying, "Come back to me the third
day."
13 Then the king answered them roughly.
King Rehoboam rejected the advice of the
elders,

9:16 [a]Or *three minas* (compare 1 Kings 10:17) **9:21** [a]Hebrew *Huram* (compare 1 Kings 10:22) [b]Literally *ships of Tarshish,* deep-sea vessels [c]Or *peacocks* **9:26** [a]That is, the Euphrates **10:11** [a]Literally *scorpions*

14 and he spoke to them according to the advice of the young men, saying, "My father[a]
made your yoke heavy, but I will add to it; my
father chastised you with whips, but I *will*
chastise you with scourges!"[b]
15 So the king did not listen to the people; for
the turn *of events* was from God, that the
LORD might fulfill His word, which He had
spoken by the hand of Ahijah the Shilonite to
Jeroboam the son of Nebat.
16 Now when all Israel *saw* that the king did
not listen to them, the people answered the
king, saying:

"What share have we in David?
We have no inheritance in the son of
Jesse.
Every man to your tents, O Israel!
Now see to your own house, O David!"

So all Israel departed to their tents.
17 But Rehoboam reigned over the children
of Israel who dwelt in the cities of Judah.
18 Then King Rehoboam sent Hadoram, who
was in charge of revenue; but the children of
Israel stoned him with stones, and he died.
Therefore King Rehoboam mounted *his* chariot in haste to flee to Jerusalem.
19 So Israel has been in rebellion against the
house of David to this day.

11 Now when Rehoboam came to Jerusalem, he assembled from the house of
Judah and Benjamin one hundred and eighty
thousand chosen *men* who were warriors, to
fight against Israel, that he might restore the
kingdom to Rehoboam.
2 But the word of the LORD came to Shemaiah the man of God, saying,
3 "Speak to Rehoboam the son of Solomon,
king of Judah, and to all Israel in Judah and
Benjamin, saying,
4 'Thus says the LORD: "You shall not go up
or fight against your brethren! Let every man
return to his house, for this thing is from
Me."'" Therefore they obeyed the words of
the LORD, and turned back from attacking
Jeroboam.

Rehoboam Fortifies the Cities

5 So Rehoboam dwelt in Jerusalem, and
built cities for defense in Judah.
6 And he built Bethlehem, Etam, Tekoa,
7 Beth Zur, Sochoh, Adullam,
8 Gath, Mareshah, Ziph,
9 Adoraim, Lachish, Azekah,
10 Zorah, Aijalon, and Hebron, which are in
Judah and Benjamin, fortified cities.
11 And he fortified the strongholds, and put
captains in them, and stores of food, oil, and
wine.
12 Also in every city *he put* shields and
spears, and made them very strong, having
Judah and Benjamin on his side.

Priests and Levites Move to Judah

13 And from all their territories the priests
and the Levites who *were* in all Israel took
their stand with him.
14 For the Levites left their common-lands
and their possessions and came to Judah and
Jerusalem, for Jeroboam and his sons had rejected them from serving as priests to the
LORD.
15 Then he appointed for himself priests for
the high places, for the demons, and the calf
idols which he had made.
16 And after *the Levites left*,[a] those from all
the tribes of Israel, such as set their heart to
seek the LORD God of Israel, came to Jerusalem to sacrifice to the LORD God of their fathers.
17 So they strengthened the kingdom of Judah, and made Rehoboam the son of Solomon
strong for three years, because they walked in
the way of David and Solomon for three
years.

The Family of Rehoboam

18 Then Rehoboam took for himself as wife
Mahalath the daughter of Jerimoth the son of
David, *and of* Abihail the daughter of Eliah
the son of Jesse.
19 And she bore him children: Jeush,
Shamariah, and Zaham.
20 After her he took Maachah the granddaughter[a] of Absalom; and she bore him Abijah, Attai, Ziza, and Shelomith.
21 Now Rehoboam loved Maachah the
granddaughter of Absalom more than all his
wives and his concubines; for he took eighteen wives and sixty concubines, and begot
twenty-eight sons and sixty daughters.
22 And Rehoboam appointed Abijah the son
of Maachah as chief, *to be* leader among his
brothers; for he *intended* to make him king.
23 He dealt wisely, and dispersed some of his
sons throughout all the territories of Judah

10:14 [a]Following many Hebrew manuscripts, Septuagint, Syriac, and Vulgate (compare verse 10 and 1 Kings 12:14); Masoretic Text reads *I*. [b]Literally *scorpions* **11:16** [a]Literally *after them* **11:20** [a]Literally *daughter,* but in the broader sense of granddaughter (compare 2 Chronicles 13:2)

LIFE LESSONS

➢ 11:15 — *Then he appointed for himself priests for the high places, for the demons, and the calf idols which he had made.*

This is one of the few places in the Bible where we learn that pagan worship actually honors demons (see also Deut. 32:17; Ps. 106:37; 1 Cor. 10:20). We are to worship God alone.

and Benjamin, to every fortified city; and he
gave them provisions in abundance. He also
sought many wives *for them.*

Egypt Attacks Judah

➤ 12 Now it came to pass, when Rehoboam
had established the kingdom and had
strengthened himself, that he forsook the law
of the LORD, and all Israel along with him.
2 And it happened in the fifth year of King
Rehoboam *that* Shishak king of Egypt came
up against Jerusalem, because they had
transgressed against the LORD,
3 with twelve hundred chariots, sixty thousand horsemen, and people without number
who came with him out of Egypt—the Lubim
and the Sukkiim and the Ethiopians.
4 And he took the fortified cities of Judah
and came to Jerusalem.
5 Then Shemaiah the prophet came to Rehoboam and the leaders of Judah, who were
gathered together in Jerusalem because of
Shishak, and said to them, "Thus says
the LORD: 'You have forsaken Me, and
therefore I also have left you in the hand of
Shishak.'"
6 So the leaders of Israel and the king humbled themselves; and they said, "The LORD *is*
righteous."
➤ 7 Now when the LORD saw that they humbled themselves, the word of the LORD came
to Shemaiah, saying, "They have humbled
themselves; *therefore* I will not destroy them,
but I will grant them some deliverance. My
wrath shall not be poured out on Jerusalem
by the hand of Shishak.
➤ 8 "Nevertheless they will be his servants,
that they may distinguish My service from the
service of the kingdoms of the nations."
9 So Shishak king of Egypt came up against
Jerusalem, and took away the treasures of the
house of the LORD and the treasures of the
king's house; he took everything. He also carried away the gold shields which Solomon
had made.
10 Then King Rehoboam made bronze
shields in their place, and committed *them* to
the hands of the captains of the guard, who
guarded the doorway of the king's house.
11 And whenever the king entered the house
of the LORD, the guard would go and bring
them out; then they would take them back
into the guardroom.
12 When he humbled himself, the wrath of
the LORD turned from him, so as not to destroy *him* completely; and things also went
well in Judah.

The End of Rehoboam's Reign

13 Thus King Rehoboam strengthened himself in Jerusalem and reigned. Now Rehoboam *was* forty-one years old when he
became king; and he reigned seventeen years
in Jerusalem, the city which the LORD had
chosen out of all the tribes of Israel, to put His
name there. His mother's name *was* Naamah,
an Ammonitess.
14 And he did evil, because he did not prepare his heart to seek the LORD.
15 The acts of Rehoboam, first and last, *are*
they not written in the book of Shemaiah the
prophet, and of Iddo the seer concerning genealogies? And *there were* wars between Rehoboam and Jeroboam all their days.
16 So Rehoboam rested with his fathers, and
was buried in the City of David. Then Abijah[a]
his son reigned in his place.

Abijah Reigns in Judah

13 In the eighteenth year of King Jeroboam, Abijah became king over Judah.
2 He reigned three years in Jerusalem. His
mother's name *was* Michaiah[a] the daughter
of Uriel of Gibeah. And there was war between Abijah and Jeroboam.
3 Abijah set the battle in order with an army
of valiant warriors, four hundred thousand
choice men. Jeroboam also drew up in battle

12:16 [a]Spelled *Abijam* in 1 Kings 14:31 **13:2** [a]Spelled *Maachah* in 11:20, 21 and 1 Kings 15:2

LIFE LESSONS

➤ 12:1 — *Now it came to pass, when Rehoboam had established the kingdom and had strengthened himself, that he forsook the law of the LORD, and all Israel along with him.*

If we should grow strong and prosperous, we must beware the temptation to attribute our prosperity to our own ingenuity (see Deut. 8:17, 18). God alone prospers us; we never outgrow our need for Him.

➤ 12:7 — *. . . the word of the LORD came to Shemaiah, saying, "They have humbled themselves; therefore I will not destroy them, but I will grant them some deliverance."*

In His grace, the Lord granted some deliverance to the disobedient leaders of Israel who humbled themselves—but he still let them taste the serious consequences of their rebellion.

➤ 12:8 — *"Nevertheless they will be his servants, that they may distinguish My service from the service of the kingdoms of the nations."*

We can choose: will we serve the Lord, or will we serve someone else? Whoever we choose, we will find that the wages they pay differ significantly.

formation against him with eight hundred thousand choice men, mighty men of valor.

4 Then Abijah stood on Mount Zemaraim, which *is* in the mountains of Ephraim, and said, "Hear me, Jeroboam and all Israel:

5 "Should you not know that the LORD God of Israel gave the dominion over Israel to David forever, to him and his sons, by a covenant of salt?

6 "Yet Jeroboam the son of Nebat, the servant of Solomon the son of David, rose up and rebelled against his lord.

7 "Then worthless rogues gathered to him, and strengthened themselves against Rehoboam the son of Solomon, when Rehoboam was young and inexperienced and could not withstand them.

8 "And now you think to withstand the kingdom of the LORD, which is in the hand of the sons of David; and you *are* a great multitude, and with you are the gold calves which Jeroboam made for you as gods.

9 "Have you not cast out the priests of the LORD, the sons of Aaron, and the Levites, and made for yourselves priests, like the peoples of *other* lands, so that whoever comes to consecrate himself with a young bull and seven rams may be a priest of *things that are* not gods?

10 "But as for us, the LORD *is* our God, and we have not forsaken Him; and the priests who minister to the LORD *are* the sons of Aaron, and the Levites *attend* to *their* duties.

11 "And they burn to the LORD every morning and every evening burnt sacrifices and sweet incense; *they* also *set* the showbread *in order on* the pure *gold* table, and the lampstand of gold with its lamps to burn every evening; for we keep the command of the LORD our God, but you have forsaken Him.

➤ 12 "Now look, God Himself is with us as *our* head, and His priests with sounding trumpets to sound the alarm against you. O children of Israel, do not fight against the LORD God of your fathers, for you shall not prosper!"

13 But Jeroboam caused an ambush to go around behind them; so they were in front of Judah, and the ambush *was* behind them.

14 And when Judah looked around, to their surprise the battle line *was* at both front and rear; and they cried out to the LORD, and the priests sounded the trumpets.

15 Then the men of Judah gave a shout; and as the men of Judah shouted, it happened that God struck Jeroboam and all Israel before Abijah and Judah.

16 And the children of Israel fled before Judah, and God delivered them into their hand.

17 Then Abijah and his people struck them with a great slaughter; so five hundred thousand choice men of Israel fell slain.

18 Thus the children of Israel were subdued at that time; and the children of Judah prevailed, because they relied on the LORD God of their fathers. ◄

19 And Abijah pursued Jeroboam and took cities from him: Bethel with its villages, Jeshanah with its villages, and Ephrain[a] with its villages.

20 So Jeroboam did not recover strength again in the days of Abijah; and the LORD struck him, and he died.

21 But Abijah grew mighty, married fourteen wives, and begot twenty-two sons and sixteen daughters.

22 Now the rest of the acts of Abijah, his ways, and his sayings *are* written in the annals of the prophet Iddo.

14 So Abijah rested with his fathers, and they buried him in the City of David. Then Asa his son reigned in his place. In his days the land was quiet for ten years.

Asa Reigns in Judah

2 Asa did *what was* good and right in the eyes of the LORD his God,

3 for he removed the altars of the foreign *gods* and the high places, and broke down the *sacred* pillars and cut down the wooden images.

4 He commanded Judah to seek the LORD God of their fathers, and to observe the law and the commandment. ◄

5 He also removed the high places and the incense altars from all the cities of Judah, and the kingdom was quiet under him.

6 And he built fortified cities in Judah, for

13:19 [a]Or *Ephron*

LIFE LESSONS

➤ 13:12 — *"O children of Israel, do not fight against the LORD God of your fathers, for you shall not prosper!"*

No one who opposes the Lord and His kingdom will ultimately prevail. God rules over all, and He knows how to deliver His people.

➤ 13:18 — *Thus the children of Israel were subdued at that time; and the children of Judah prevailed, because they relied on the LORD God of their fathers.*

The people of Judah prevailed despite clever military tactics by the enemy. Why? Only one reason: they relied on the Lord. As children of a sovereign God, we are never victims of our circumstances.

➤ 14:4 — *He commanded Judah to seek the LORD God of their fathers, and to observe the law and the commandment.*

It is impossible to obey God without first seeking Him. We must seek Him first, appropriate His strength, and then obey His commands by the power of His Spirit.

the land had rest; he had no war in those
years, because the LORD had given him rest.
7 Therefore he said to Judah, "Let us build
these cities and make walls around *them,* and
towers, gates, and bars, *while* the land *is* yet
before us, because we have sought the LORD
our God; we have sought *Him,* and He has
given us rest on every side." So they built and
prospered.
8 And Asa had an army of three hundred
thousand from Judah who carried shields
and spears, and from Benjamin two hundred and eighty thousand men who carried
shields and drew bows; all these *were* mighty
men of valor.
9 Then Zerah the Ethiopian came out
against them with an army of a million men
and three hundred chariots, and he came to
Mareshah.
10 So Asa went out against him, and they set
the troops in battle array in the Valley of
Zephathah at Mareshah.
➤ 11 And Asa cried out to the LORD his God,
and said, "LORD, *it is* nothing for You to help,
whether with many or with those who have
no power; help us, O LORD our God, for we
rest on You, and in Your name we go against
this multitude. O LORD, You *are* our God; do
not let man prevail against You!"
12 So the LORD struck the Ethiopians before
Asa and Judah, and the Ethiopians fled.
13 And Asa and the people who *were* with
him pursued them to Gerar. So the Ethiopians
were overthrown, and they could not recover,
for they were broken before the LORD and His
army. And they carried away very much spoil.
14 Then they defeated all the cities around
Gerar, for the fear of the LORD came upon
them; and they plundered all the cities, for
there was exceedingly much spoil in them.
15 They also attacked the livestock enclo-
sures, and carried off sheep and camels in
abundance, and returned to Jerusalem.

The Reforms of Asa

15 Now the Spirit of God came upon
Azariah the son of Oded.
2 And he went out to meet Asa, and said to
him: "Hear me, Asa, and all Judah and Benjamin. The LORD *is* with you while you are with
Him. If you seek Him, He will be found by
you; but if you forsake Him, He will forsake
you.
3 "For a long time Israel *has been* without
the true God, without a teaching priest, and
without law;
4 "but when in their trouble they turned to ◄
the LORD God of Israel, and sought Him, He
was found by them.
5 "And in those times *there was* no peace to
the one who went out, nor to the one who
came in, but great turmoil *was* on all the inhabitants of the lands.
6 "So nation was destroyed by nation, and
city by city, for God troubled them with every
adversity.
7 "But you, be strong and do not let your ◄
hands be weak, for your work shall be rewarded!"
8 And when Asa heard these words and the
prophecy of Oded[a] the prophet, he took
courage, and removed the abominable idols
from all the land of Judah and Benjamin and
from the cities which he had taken in the
mountains of Ephraim; and he restored the
altar of the LORD that *was* before the vestibule
of the LORD.
9 Then he gathered all Judah and Benjamin,
and those who dwelt with them from
Ephraim, Manasseh, and Simeon, for they
came over to him in great numbers from Israel when they saw that the LORD his God was
with him.
10 So they gathered together at Jerusalem in
the third month, in the fifteenth year of the
reign of Asa.
11 And they offered to the LORD at that time
seven hundred bulls and seven thousand
sheep from the spoil they had brought.
12 Then they entered into a covenant to seek
the LORD God of their fathers with all their
heart and with all their soul;
13 and whoever would not seek the LORD
God of Israel was to be put to death, whether
small or great, whether man or woman.

15:8 [a]Following Masoretic Text and Septuagint; Syriac and Vulgate read *Azariah the son of Oded* (compare verse 1).

LIFE LESSONS

➤ 14:11 — *And Asa cried out to the LORD his God, and said, "LORD, it is nothing for You to help, whether with many or with those who have no power; help us, O LORD our God, for we rest on You . . . ."*

What looks daunting and even impossible to us, is precisely "nothing" to the Lord. When we fight our battles on our knees, we win every time.

➤ 15:4 — *". . . when in their trouble they turned to the LORD God of Israel, and sought Him, He was found by them."*

No matter our backgrounds, regardless of our personal histories, despite the terrible things we may have done, God invites us and urges us to repent and turn to Him. When we seek Him, we will find Him.

➤ 15:7 — *"But you, be strong and do not let your hands be weak, for your work shall be rewarded!"*

God loves to reward those who serve Him wholeheartedly and with great joy. Obedience always brings blessing.

14 Then they took an oath before the LORD with a loud voice, with shouting and trumpets and rams' horns.

15 And all Judah rejoiced at the oath, for they had sworn with all their heart and sought Him with all their soul; and He was found by them, and the LORD gave them rest all around.

16 Also he removed Maachah, the mother of Asa the king, from *being* queen mother, because she had made an obscene image of Asherah;[a] and Asa cut down her obscene image, then crushed and burned *it* by the Brook Kidron.

17 But the high places were not removed from Israel. Nevertheless the heart of Asa was loyal all his days.

18 He also brought into the house of God the things that his father had dedicated and that he himself had dedicated: silver and gold and utensils.

19 And there was no war until the thirty-fifth year of the reign of Asa.

Asa's Treaty with Syria

16 In the thirty-sixth year of the reign of Asa, Baasha king of Israel came up against Judah and built Ramah, that he might let none go out or come in to Asa king of Judah.

2 Then Asa brought silver and gold from the treasuries of the house of the LORD and of the king's house, and sent to Ben-Hadad king of Syria, who dwelt in Damascus, saying,

3 "*Let there be* a treaty between you and me, as there was between my father and your father. See, I have sent you silver and gold; come, break your treaty with Baasha king of Israel, so that he will withdraw from me."

4 So Ben-Hadad heeded King Asa, and sent the captains of his armies against the cities of Israel. They attacked Ijon, Dan, Abel Maim, and all the storage cities of Naphtali.

5 Now it happened, when Baasha heard *it,* that he stopped building Ramah and ceased his work.

6 Then King Asa took all Judah, and they carried away the stones and timber of Ramah, which Baasha had used for building; and with them he built Geba and Mizpah.

Hanani's Message to Asa

7 And at that time Hanani the seer came to Asa king of Judah, and said to him: "Because you have relied on the king of Syria, and have not relied on the LORD your God, therefore the army of the king of Syria has escaped from your hand.

8 "Were the Ethiopians and the Lubim not a huge army with very many chariots and horsemen? Yet, because you relied on the LORD, He delivered them into your hand.

9 "For the eyes of the LORD run to and fro throughout the whole earth, to show Himself strong on behalf of *those* whose heart *is* loyal to Him. In this you have done foolishly; therefore from now on you shall have wars."

10 Then Asa was angry with the seer, and put him in prison, for *he was* enraged at him because of this. And Asa oppressed *some* of the people at that time.

Illness and Death of Asa

11 Note that the acts of Asa, first and last, are indeed written in the book of the kings of Judah and Israel.

12 And in the thirty-ninth year of his reign, Asa became diseased in his feet, and his malady was severe; yet in his disease he did not seek the LORD, but the physicians.

13 So Asa rested with his fathers; he died in the forty-first year of his reign.

14 They buried him in his own tomb, which he had made for himself in the City of David; and they laid him in the bed which was filled with spices and various ingredients prepared in a mixture of ointments. They made a very great burning for him.

Jehoshaphat Reigns in Judah

17 Then Jehoshaphat his son reigned in his place, and strengthened himself against Israel.

2 And he placed troops in all the fortified cities of Judah, and set garrisons in the land of Judah and in the cities of Ephraim which Asa his father had taken.

15:16 [a]A Canaanite deity

LIFE LESSONS

➤ **15:17 — *But the high places were not removed from Israel. Nevertheless the heart of Asa was loyal all his days.***

Some sinful practices are harder to eliminate than others, whether because of family ties, public pressure, or similar obstacles. What "high places" in your own heart still need to be removed?

➤ **16:7 — *"Because you have relied on the king of Syria, and have not relied on the LORD your God, therefore the army of the king of Syria has escaped from your hand."***

Asa's political solution "worked" in the short term to remove a threat, but it backfired in the long run. Trusting God is a day-by-day, moment-by-moment pursuit. We must trust the Lord today, every day.

➤ **16:12 — *And in the thirty-ninth year of his reign, Asa became diseased in his feet, and his malady was severe; yet in his disease he did not seek the LORD, but the physicians.***

Although we stand tallest and strongest on our knees, Asa chose to remain weak and low to the ground by refusing to humble himself before the Lord in prayer. And so he stayed there.

3 Now the LORD was with Jehoshaphat, because he walked in the former ways of his father David; he did not seek the Baals,
4 but sought the God[a] of his father, and
walked in His commandments and not according to the acts of Israel.
5 Therefore the LORD established the kingdom in his hand; and all Judah gave presents
to Jehoshaphat, and he had riches and honor
in abundance.
➤6 And his heart took delight in the ways of
the LORD; moreover he removed the high
places and wooden images from Judah.
7 Also in the third year of his reign he sent
his leaders, Ben-Hail, Obadiah, Zechariah,
Nethanel, and Michaiah, to teach in the cities
of Judah.
8 And with them *he sent* Levites: Shemaiah,
Nethaniah, Zebadiah, Asahel, Shemiramoth,
Jehonathan, Adonijah, Tobijah, and To-
badonijah—the Levites; and with them Elishama and Jehoram, the priests.
9 So they taught in Judah, and *had* the Book
of the Law of the LORD with them; they went
throughout all the cities of Judah and taught
the people.
➤**10** And the fear of the LORD fell on all the
kingdoms of the lands that *were* around Judah, so that they did not make war against Jehoshaphat.
11 Also *some* of the Philistines brought Jehoshaphat presents and silver as tribute; and
the Arabians brought him flocks, seven thousand seven hundred rams and seven thousand seven hundred male goats.
12 So Jehoshaphat became increasingly
powerful, and he built fortresses and storage
cities in Judah.
13 He had much property in the cities of Judah; and the men of war, mighty men of valor,
were in Jerusalem.
14 These *are* their numbers, according to their
fathers' houses. Of Judah, the captains of thousands: Adnah the captain, and with him three
hundred thousand mighty men of valor;
15 and next to him *was* Jehohanan the captain, and with him two hundred and eighty
thousand;
16 and next to him *was* Amasiah the son of
Zichri, who willingly offered himself to the
LORD, and with him two hundred thousand
mighty men of valor.
17 Of Benjamin: Eliada a mighty man of
valor, and with him two hundred thousand
men armed with bow and shield;
18 and next to him *was* Jehozabad, and with
him one hundred and eighty thousand prepared for war.
19 These served the king, besides those the
king put in the fortified cities throughout all
Judah.

Micaiah Warns Ahab

18 Jehoshaphat had riches and honor in
abundance; and by marriage he allied
himself with Ahab.
2 After some years he went down to *visit*
Ahab in Samaria; and Ahab killed sheep and
oxen in abundance for him and the people
who were with him, and persuaded him to go
up *with him* to Ramoth Gilead.
3 So Ahab king of Israel said to Jehoshaphat king of Judah, "Will you go with me
against Ramoth Gilead?" And he answered
him, "I *am* as you *are,* and my people as your
people; *we will be* with you in the war."
4 Also Jehoshaphat said to the king of Israel, "Please inquire for the word of the LORD
today."
5 Then the king of Israel gathered the prophets together, four hundred men, and said to
them, "Shall we go to war against Ramoth
Gilead, or shall I refrain?" So they said, "Go up,
for God will deliver it into the king's hand."
6 But Jehoshaphat said, "*Is there* not still a
prophet of the LORD here, that we may inquire
of Him?"[a]
7 So the king of Israel said to Jehoshaphat,
"*There is* still one man by whom we may inquire of the LORD; but I hate him, because he
never prophesies good concerning me, but always evil. He *is* Micaiah the son of Imla." And
Jehoshaphat said, "Let not the king say such
things!"
8 Then the king of Israel called one *of his* officers and said, "Bring Micaiah the son of
Imla quickly!"
9 The king of Israel and Jehoshaphat king
of Judah, clothed in *their* robes, sat each on
his throne; and they sat at a threshing floor at
the entrance of the gate of Samaria; and all
the prophets prophesied before them.

17:4 [a]Septuagint reads *LORD* God. **18:6** [a]Or *him*

LIFE LESSONS

➤ 17:6 — *And his heart took delight in the ways of the LORD; moreover he removed the high places and wooden images from Judah.*

God is not after brute, grudging obedience, but joyful and even delighted submission. But the only way we can delight in God's commands is to delight in Him.

➤ 17:10 — *And the fear of the LORD fell on all the kingdoms of the lands that were around Judah, so that they did not make war against Jehoshaphat.*

The Lord has untold weapons in His heavenly arsenal to protect His obedient people. Here he used a general sense of fear to keep Israel's enemies at bay. Who knows how the Lord is protecting you right now?

10 Now Zedekiah the son of Chenaanah had made horns of iron for himself; and he said, "Thus says the LORD: 'With these you shall gore the Syrians until they are destroyed.'"
11 And all the prophets prophesied so, saying, "Go up to Ramoth Gilead and prosper, for the LORD will deliver *it* into the king's hand."
12 Then the messenger who had gone to call Micaiah spoke to him, saying, "Now listen, the words of the prophets with one accord encourage the king. Therefore please let your word be like *the word of* one of them, and speak encouragement."
13 And Micaiah said, "*As* the LORD lives, whatever my God says, that I will speak."
14 Then he came to the king; and the king said to him, "Micaiah, shall we go to war against Ramoth Gilead, or shall I refrain?" And he said, "Go and prosper, and they shall be delivered into your hand!"
15 So the king said to him, "How many times shall I make you swear that you tell me nothing but the truth in the name of the LORD?"
➤ 16 Then he said, "I saw all Israel scattered on the mountains, as sheep that have no shepherd. And the LORD said, 'These have no master. Let each return to his house in peace.'"
17 And the king of Israel said to Jehoshaphat, "Did I not tell you he would not prophesy good concerning me, but evil?"
18 Then *Micaiah* said, "Therefore hear the word of the LORD: I saw the LORD sitting on His throne, and all the host of heaven standing on His right hand and His left.
19 "And the LORD said, 'Who will persuade Ahab king of Israel to go up, that he may fall at Ramoth Gilead?' So one spoke in this manner, and another spoke in that manner.
20 "Then a spirit came forward and stood before the LORD, and said, 'I will persuade him.' The LORD said to him, 'In what way?'
21 "So he said, 'I will go out and be a lying spirit in the mouth of all his prophets.' And *the LORD* said, 'You shall persuade *him* and also prevail; go out and do so.'
22 "Therefore look! The LORD has put a lying spirit in the mouth of these prophets of yours, and the LORD has declared disaster against you."
23 Then Zedekiah the son of Chenaanah went near and struck Micaiah on the cheek, and said, "Which way did the spirit from the LORD go from me to speak to you?"

Life Examples:

MICAIAH

Bold Servant of God

2 CHR. 18:13

The prophet Micaiah never shied away from speaking God's words, no matter how difficult they might be to hear. On one occasion, royal advisers urged Micaiah to speak encouragingly to a wicked king. But Micaiah had no interest in sugarcoating his message. "As the LORD lives," he declared, "whatever my God says, that I will speak" (2 Chr. 18:13).

Regardless of what others may want us to proclaim about or from the Lord, we must remain faithful to speak whatever He prompts us to say. We must listen closely to the One who gives us the message and then convey it accurately and faithfully.

And how can we gain the strength to do this? When we truly experience God's love, we have no fear to proclaim His word. As John wrote, "There is no fear in love; but perfect love casts out fear, because fear involves torment" (1 John 4:18).

See the Life Principles Index for further study:
4. The awareness of God's presence energizes us for our work.

24 And Micaiah said, "Indeed you shall see on that day when you go into an inner chamber to hide!"
25 Then the king of Israel said, "Take Micaiah, and return him to Amon the governor of the city and to Joash the king's son;
26 "and say, 'Thus says the king: "Put this *fellow* in prison, and feed him with bread of affliction and water of affliction, until I return in peace."'"
27 But Micaiah said, "If you ever return in peace, the LORD has not spoken by me." And he said, "Take heed, all you people!"

LIFE LESSONS

➤ 18:16 — *"I saw all Israel scattered on the mountains, as sheep that have no shepherd. And the LORD said, 'These have no master. Let each return to his house in peace.'"*

Why did godly King Jehoshaphat accompany Ahab to battle after hearing the prophecy of doom uttered by Micaiah? Who knows? God in His grace spared him, but things could easily have turned out much worse.

Ahab Dies in Battle

28 So the king of Israel and Jehoshaphat the
king of Judah went up to Ramoth Gilead.
29 And the king of Israel said to Jehoshaphat, "I will disguise myself and go into battle; but you put on your robes." So the king of
Israel disguised himself, and they went into
battle.
30 Now the king of Syria had commanded
the captains of the chariots who *were* with
him, saying, "Fight with no one small or great,
but only with the king of Israel."
➤ 31 So it was, when the captains of the chariots saw Jehoshaphat, that they said, "It *is* the
king of Israel!" Therefore they surrounded
him to attack; but Jehoshaphat cried out, and
the LORD helped him, and God diverted them
from him.
32 For so it was, when the captains of the
chariots saw that it was not the king of Israel,
that they turned back from pursuing him.
33 Now a certain man drew a bow at random,
and struck the king of Israel between the
joints of his armor. So he said to the driver of
his chariot, "Turn around and take me out of
the battle, for I am wounded."
34 The battle increased that day, and the king
of Israel propped *himself* up in *his* chariot facing the Syrians until evening; and about the
time of sunset he died.

19 Then Jehoshaphat the king of Judah
returned safely to his house in Jerusalem.
➤ 2 And Jehu the son of Hanani the seer went
out to meet him, and said to King Jehoshaphat, "Should you help the wicked and love
those who hate the LORD? Therefore the
wrath of the LORD *is* upon you.
3 "Nevertheless good things are found in
you, in that you have removed the wooden images from the land, and have prepared your
heart to seek God."

The Reforms of Jehoshaphat

➤ 4 So Jehoshaphat dwelt at Jerusalem; and
he went out again among the people from
Beersheba to the mountains of Ephraim, and
brought them back to the LORD God of their
fathers.
5 Then he set judges in the land throughout
all the fortified cities of Judah, city by city,
6 and said to the judges, "Take heed to what
you are doing, for you do not judge for man but
for the LORD, who *is* with you in the judgment.
7 "Now therefore, let the fear of the LORD be
upon you; take care and do *it,* for *there is* no
iniquity with the LORD our God, no partiality,
nor taking of bribes."
8 Moreover in Jerusalem, for the judgment
of the LORD and for controversies, Jehoshaphat appointed some of the Levites and
priests, and some of the chief fathers of Israel,
when they returned to Jerusalem.[a]
9 And he commanded them, saying, "Thus
you shall act in the fear of the LORD, faithfully
and with a loyal heart:
10 "Whatever case comes to you from your
brethren who dwell in their cities, whether of
bloodshed or offenses against law or commandment, against statutes or ordinances,
you shall warn them, lest they trespass
against the LORD and wrath come upon you
and your brethren. Do this, and you will not
be guilty.
11 "And take notice: Amariah the chief priest
is over you in all matters of the LORD; and Zebadiah the son of Ishmael, the ruler of the
house of Judah, for all the king's matters; also
the Levites *will be* officials before you. Behave courageously, and the LORD will be with
the good."

Ammon, Moab, and Mount Seir Defeated

20 It happened after this *that* the people
of Moab with the people of Ammon,
and *others* with them besides the Ammonites,[a] came to battle against Jehoshaphat.
2 Then some came and told Jehoshaphat,
saying, "A great multitude is coming against
you from beyond the sea, from Syria;[a] and
they are in Hazazon Tamar" (which *is* En
Gedi).

19:8 [a]Septuagint and Vulgate read *for the inhabitants of Jerusalem.* **20:1** [a]Following Masoretic Text and Vulgate; Septuagint reads *Meunites* (compare 26:7). **20:2** [a]Following Masoretic Text, Septuagint, and Vulgate; some Hebrew manuscripts and Old Latin read *Edom.*

LIFE LESSONS

➤ 18:31 — *So it was, when the captains of the chariots saw Jehoshaphat, that they said, "It is the king of Israel!" Therefore they surrounded him to attack; but Jehoshaphat cried out, and the LORD helped him . . . .*

The Lord helped Jehoshaphat out of a tight spot that he never should have been in. God's grace covers a multitude of our sins—but we should never presume upon it.

➤ 19:2 — *"Should you help the wicked and love those who hate the LORD? Therefore the wrath of the LORD is upon you."*

The Bible tells us, "Do not be deceived: 'Evil company corrupts good habits'" (1 Cor. 15:33). Through his unholy alliance with the wicked Ahab, Jehoshaphat ended up ruining his own family.

➤ 19:4 — *So Jehoshaphat . . . brought them back to the LORD God of their fathers.*

In the matter of evangelism and discipleship, at least, we may consider Jehoshaphat wise. The Bible tells us, "he who wins souls is wise" (Prov. 11:30).

ANSWERS TO LIFE'S QUESTIONS

What is our authority in prayer?

2 CHR. 20:3

One day King Jehoshaphat and the people of Judah saw that a great multitude had risen up against them. Three groups of aggressors—the Moabites, the Ammonites, and the people of Mount Seir—launched a major assault against Jerusalem.

Jehoshaphat felt deeply afraid, but rather than cower in fear, he "set himself to seek the LORD" (2 Chr. 20:3). He proclaimed a fast throughout all Judah and called the people together to join him in seeking the Lord. He stood before the people in the house of the Lord and prayed, "O LORD God of our fathers, are You not God in heaven, and do You not rule over all the kingdoms of the nations, and in Your hand is there not power and might, so that no one is able to withstand You?" (20:6).

Jehoshaphat did not express doubt in the power of God, but rather publicly proclaimed his trust in an almighty God. He declared that he was putting all of his hope in the Lord of unlimited power. In addition, Jehoshaphat stated very plainly that he, even as king of Judah, stood in total humility and weakness before the Lord. He claimed no authority in or for himself. He said to God:

- You are the One who gave us this land.
- You are the One who has allowed Your people to dwell in it and build a sanctuary in it.
- You are the One who said that we should cry out to You in our affliction and You would hear and save us.
- You are the One who told us to spare these enemy people when we first came to occupy this land.
- You are the only One capable of judging these enemies who are rising against us—we have no power and no plan.

He concluded his prayer by admitting, "our eyes are upon You." In effect, Jehoshaphat was saying, "If You don't exercise Your authority in this matter, we are doomed. We are putting our entire trust and confidence in You and You alone."

We see no trace of egotism in Jehoshaphat. He made no demand that God do something that God did not desire to do. Jehoshaphat claimed no authority in himself, and also no power for himself. But he wisely recognized that all power and all authority rest in God alone, and from that understanding he petitioned the God of heaven.

See the Life Principles Index for further study:
17. We stand tallest and strongest on our knees.

3 And Jehoshaphat feared, and set himself ≺
to seek the LORD, and proclaimed a fast
throughout all Judah.
4 So Judah gathered together to ask *help* ≺
from the LORD; and from all the cities of Judah they came to seek the LORD.
5 Then Jehoshaphat stood in the assembly
of Judah and Jerusalem, in the house of the
LORD, before the new court,
6 and said: "O LORD God of our fathers, *are*
You not God in heaven, and do You *not* rule
over all the kingdoms of the nations, and in
Your hand *is there not* power and might, so
that no one is able to withstand You?
7 "*Are* You not our God, *who* drove out the
inhabitants of this land before Your people Israel, and gave it to the descendants of Abraham Your friend forever?
8 "And they dwell in it, and have built You a
sanctuary in it for Your name, saying,
9 'If disaster comes upon us—sword, judgment, pestilence, or famine—we will stand before this temple and in Your presence (for Your
name *is* in this temple), and cry out to You in
our affliction, and You will hear and save.'
10 "And now, here are the people of Ammon,
Moab, and Mount Seir—whom You would not
let Israel invade when they came out of the
land of Egypt, but they turned from them and
did not destroy them—
11 "here they are, rewarding us by coming to

LIFE LESSONS

➤ **20:3, 4 — *And Jehoshaphat feared, and set himself to seek the LORD, and proclaimed a fast throughout all Judah. So Judah gathered together to ask help from the LORD . . . .***

When great fear engulfed the king, he did what all of us should do in frightening times: he sought the Lord with his whole heart and drafted as many people to pray as possible.

throw us out of Your possession which You
have given us to inherit.
12 "O our God, will You not judge them? For
we have no power against this great multitude that is coming against us; nor do we
know what to do, but our eyes *are* upon You."
13 Now all Judah, with their little ones, their
wives, and their children, stood before the
LORD.
14 Then the Spirit of the LORD came upon Jahaziel the son of Zechariah, the son of Benaiah, the son of Jeiel, the son of Mattaniah, a
Levite of the sons of Asaph, in the midst of
the assembly.
➤ 15 And he said, "Listen, all you of Judah and
you inhabitants of Jerusalem, and you, King
Jehoshaphat! Thus says the LORD to you: 'Do
not be afraid nor dismayed because of this
great multitude, for the battle *is* not yours, but
God's.
16 'Tomorrow go down against them. They
will surely come up by the Ascent of Ziz, and
you will find them at the end of the brook before the Wilderness of Jeruel.
17 'You will not *need* to fight in this *battle.*
Position yourselves, stand still and see the
salvation of the LORD, who is with you, O Judah and Jerusalem!' Do not fear or be dismayed; tomorrow go out against them, for the
LORD *is* with you."
18 And Jehoshaphat bowed his head with *his*
face to the ground, and all Judah and the inhabitants of Jerusalem bowed before the
LORD, worshiping the LORD.
19 Then the Levites of the children of the Kohathites and of the children of the Korahites
stood up to praise the LORD God of Israel with
voices loud and high.
➤ **20** So they rose early in the morning and
went out into the Wilderness of Tekoa; and as
they went out, Jehoshaphat stood and said,
"Hear me, O Judah and you inhabitants of Jerusalem: Believe in the LORD your God, and
you shall be established; believe His prophets, and you shall prosper."
21 And when he had consulted with the people, he appointed those who should sing to
the LORD, and who should praise the beauty
of holiness, as they went out before the army
and were saying:

"Praise the LORD,
For His mercy *endures* forever."[a]

22 Now when they began to sing and to
praise, the LORD set ambushes against the
people of Ammon, Moab, and Mount Seir,
who had come against Judah; and they were
defeated.
23 For the people of Ammon and Moab stood
up against the inhabitants of Mount Seir to
utterly kill and destroy *them.* And when they
had made an end of the inhabitants of Seir,
they helped to destroy one another.
24 So when Judah came to a place overlook-
ing the wilderness, they looked toward the
multitude; and there *were* their dead bodies,
fallen on the earth. No one had escaped.
25 When Jehoshaphat and his people came ➤
to take away their spoil, they found among
them an abundance of valuables on the dead
bodies,[a] and precious jewelry, which they
stripped off for themselves, more than they
could carry away; and they were three days
gathering the spoil because there was so
much.
26 And on the fourth day they assembled in
the Valley of Berachah, for there they blessed
the LORD; therefore the name of that place
was called The Valley of Berachah[a] until this
day.
27 Then they returned, every man of Judah
and Jerusalem, with Jehoshaphat in front of
them, to go back to Jerusalem with joy, for the
LORD had made them rejoice over their enemies.
28 So they came to Jerusalem, with stringed
instruments and harps and trumpets, to the
house of the LORD.
29 And the fear of God was on all the kingdoms of *those* countries when they heard that
the LORD had fought against the enemies of
Israel.

20:21 [a]Compare Psalm 106:1 **20:25** [a]A few Hebrew manuscripts, Old Latin, and Vulgate read *garments;* Septuagint reads *armor.* **20:26** [a]Literally *Blessing*

LIFE LESSONS

➤ 20:15 — *"Thus says the LORD to you: 'Do not be afraid nor dismayed because of this great multitude, for the battle is not yours, but God's.'"*

When we align ourselves with God and His will, the Lord takes the battle out of our hands and places it in His. Big enemies become small potatoes when God leads the charge.

➤ 20:20 — *"Hear me, O Judah and you inhabitants of Jerusalem: Believe in the LORD your God, and you shall be established; believe His prophets, and you shall prosper."*

If you want to prosper in life, you can do no better than to trust in God and believe in His Word. Stake your life on it!

➤ 20:25 — *When Jehoshaphat and his people came to take away their spoil, they found among them an abundance of valuables on the dead bodies . . . and they were three days gathering the spoil because there was so much.*

The very thing that Satan had intended to use to ruin God's people, the Lord used to bless and enrich them. God loves to answer the prayers of His obedient people in surprising ways!

WHAT THE BIBLE SAYS ABOUT **GOD'S LIMITATIONS ON ADVERSITY**

2 Chr. 20:29

The Lord uses adversity in the life of the believer for many purposes, all of them ultimately good. He limits adversity in the life of the believer and provides a way of escape.

But none of these statements can be made on behalf of the unbeliever.

The unbeliever stands before God in a position of estrangement and alienation. While God loves unbelievers and wants them to come to repentance, they also are subject to harsh treatment if they injure God's children or attempt to interfere with God's plans. "And the fear of God was on all the kingdoms of those countries when they heard that the LORD had fought against the enemies of Israel" (2 Chr. 20:29).

Time and again in the Scriptures we read that God showed no mercy to His enemies. He defeated them soundly and decisively, and often He commanded the Israelites "to utterly destroy" their enemies.

Enemies of God sit in a very precarious position. Not only are unsaved persons spiritually lost, but they remain in danger physically, emotionally, and mentally. Satan has total access to an unbeliever, limited only by the prayers of God's faithful people.

He limits adversity in the life of the believer and provides a way of escape.

God responds to the unsaved person according to the person's willful sin and acts of transgression. The Lord does not sit on His throne, survey the world, and take potshots at people. God is not a bully; rather, the Lord moves decisively against sin. God is just and righteous. He *must* judge and oppose sin. That is the message of the Book of Lamentations when Jeremiah concludes that the Lord does not willingly afflict the children of men (Lam. 3:33).

The Lord does not desire adversity for His people; rather, He responds appropriately to their actions. When we sin, He responds to our sin even as He loves us beyond measure. Fortunately, the dark moments of our lives will last only so long as is necessary for God to accomplish His purpose in us.

See the Life Principles Index for further study:

7. The dark moments of our life will last only so long as is necessary for God to accomplish His purpose in us.

26. Adversity is a bridge to a deeper relationship with God.

30 Then the realm of Jehoshaphat was quiet, for his God gave him rest all around.

The End of Jehoshaphat's Reign

31 So Jehoshaphat was king over Judah. *He was* thirty-five years old when he became king, and he reigned twenty-five years in Jerusalem. His mother's name *was* Azubah the daughter of Shilhi.

32 And he walked in the way of his father Asa, and did not turn aside from it, doing *what was* right in the sight of the LORD.

33 Nevertheless the high places were not taken away, for as yet the people had not directed their hearts to the God of their fathers.

34 Now the rest of the acts of Jehoshaphat, first and last, indeed they *are* written in the book of Jehu the son of Hanani, which *is* mentioned in the book of the kings of Israel.

35 After this Jehoshaphat king of Judah allied himself with Ahaziah king of Israel, who acted very wickedly.

36 And he allied himself with him to make ships to go to Tarshish, and they made the ships in Ezion Geber.

➤ 37 But Eliezer the son of Dodavah of Mareshah prophesied against Jehoshaphat, saying, "Because you have allied yourself with Ahaziah, the LORD has destroyed your works." Then the ships were wrecked, so that they were not able to go to Tarshish.

Jehoram Reigns in Judah

21 And Jehoshaphat rested with his fathers, and was buried with his fathers in the City of David. Then Jehoram his son reigned in his place.

2 He had brothers, the sons of Jehoshaphat: Azariah, Jehiel, Zechariah, Azaryahu, Michael, and Shephatiah; all these *were* the sons of Jehoshaphat king of Israel.

3 Their father gave them great gifts of silver and gold and precious things, with fortified cities in Judah; but he gave the kingdom to Jehoram, because he *was* the firstborn.

4 Now when Jehoram was established over the kingdom of his father, he strengthened himself and killed all his brothers with the sword, and also *others* of the princes of Israel.

5 Jehoram *was* thirty-two years old when he became king, and he reigned eight years in Jerusalem.

6 And he walked in the way of the kings of Israel, just as the house of Ahab had done, for he had the daughter of Ahab as a wife; and he did evil in the sight of the LORD.

7 Yet the LORD would not destroy the house of David, because of the covenant that He had made with David, and since He had promised to give a lamp to him and to his sons forever.

8 In his days Edom revolted against Judah's authority, and made a king over themselves.

9 So Jehoram went out with his officers, and all his chariots with him. And he rose by night and attacked the Edomites who had surrounded him and the captains of the chariots.

10 Thus Edom has been in revolt against Judah's authority to this day. At that time Libnah revolted against his rule, because he had forsaken the LORD God of his fathers.

11 Moreover he made high places in the mountains of Judah, and caused the inhabitants of Jerusalem to commit harlotry, and led Judah astray.

12 And a letter came to him from Elijah the prophet, saying,

Thus says the LORD God of your father
David:
Because you have not walked in the
ways of Jehoshaphat your father, or in
the ways of Asa king of Judah,
13 but have walked in the way of the kings
of Israel, and have made Judah and the
inhabitants of Jerusalem to play the harlot
like the harlotry of the house of
Ahab, and also have killed your brothers,
those of your father's household,
who were better than yourself,
14 behold, the LORD will strike your people
with a serious affliction—your children,
your wives, and all your possessions;
15 and you *will become* very sick with a
disease of your intestines, until your intestines
come out by reason of the sickness,
day by day.

16 Moreover the LORD stirred up against Jehoram the spirit of the Philistines and the Arabians who *were* near the Ethiopians.

17 And they came up into Judah and invaded it, and carried away all the possessions that were found in the king's house, and also his sons and his wives, so that there was not a son left to him except Jehoahaz,[a] the youngest of his sons.

21:17 [a]Elsewhere called *Ahaziah* (compare 2 Chronicles 22:1)

LIFE LESSONS

➤ ***20:37 — "Because you have allied yourself with Ahaziah, the LORD has destroyed your works." Then the ships were wrecked, so that they were not able to go to Tarshish.***

Most of us have at least one "blind spot" that gives us trouble. Jehoshaphat's was his tendency to make foolish alliances outside of God's will. He discovered that whatever we acquire outside of the will of God turns to ashes.

18 After all this the LORD struck him in his intestines with an incurable disease.

➤ 19 Then it happened in the course of time, after the end of two years, that his intestines came out because of his sickness; so he died in severe pain. And his people made no burning for him, like the burning for his fathers.

20 He was thirty-two years old when he became king. He reigned in Jerusalem eight years and, to no one's sorrow, departed. However they buried him in the City of David, but not in the tombs of the kings.

Ahaziah Reigns in Judah

22 Then the inhabitants of Jerusalem made Ahaziah his youngest son king in his place, for the raiders who came with the Arabians into the camp had killed all the older *sons*. So Ahaziah the son of Jehoram, king of Judah, reigned.

2 Ahaziah *was* forty-two[a] years old when he became king, and he reigned one year in Jerusalem. His mother's name *was* Athaliah the granddaughter of Omri.

3 He also walked in the ways of the house of Ahab, for his mother advised him to do wickedly.

➤ 4 Therefore he did evil in the sight of the LORD, like the house of Ahab; for they were his counselors after the death of his father, to his destruction.

5 He also followed their advice, and went with Jehoram[a] the son of Ahab king of Israel to war against Hazael king of Syria at Ramoth Gilead; and the Syrians wounded Joram.

6 Then he returned to Jezreel to recover from the wounds which he had received at Ramah, when he fought against Hazael king of Syria. And Azariah[a] the son of Jehoram, king of Judah, went down to see Jehoram the son of Ahab in Jezreel, because he was sick.

7 His going to Joram was God's occasion for Ahaziah's downfall; for when he arrived, he went out with Jehoram against Jehu the son of Nimshi, whom the LORD had anointed to cut off the house of Ahab.

8 And it happened, when Jehu was executing judgment on the house of Ahab, and found the princes of Judah and the sons of Ahaziah's brothers who served Ahaziah, that he killed them.

9 Then he searched for Ahaziah; and they caught him (he was hiding in Samaria), and brought him to Jehu. When they had killed him, they buried him, "because," they said, "he is the son of Jehoshaphat, who sought the LORD with all his heart." So the house of Ahaziah had no one to assume power over the kingdom.

Athaliah Reigns in Judah

10 Now when Athaliah the mother of Ahaziah saw that her son was dead, she arose and destroyed all the royal heirs of the house of Judah.

11 But Jehoshabeath,[a] the daughter of the king, took Joash the son of Ahaziah, and stole him away from among the king's sons who were being murdered, and put him and his nurse in a bedroom. So Jehoshabeath, the daughter of King Jehoram, the wife of Jehoiada the priest (for she was the sister of Ahaziah), hid him from Athaliah so that she did not kill him.

12 And he was hidden with them in the house of God for six years, while Athaliah reigned over the land.

Joash Crowned King of Judah

23 In the seventh year Jehoiada strengthened himself, *and made a* covenant with the captains of hundreds: Azariah the son of Jeroham, Ishmael the son of Jehohanan, Azariah the son of Obed, Maaseiah the son of Adaiah, and Elishaphat the son of Zichri.

2 And they went throughout Judah and gathered the Levites from all the cities of Judah, and the chief fathers of Israel, and they came to Jerusalem.

3 Then all the assembly made a covenant with the king in the house of God. And he said to them, "Behold, the king's son shall reign, as the LORD has said of the sons of David.

4 "This *is* what you shall do: One-third of ➤
you entering on the Sabbath, of the priests

22:2 [a]Or *twenty-two* (compare 2 Kings 8:26) **22:5** [a]Also spelled *Joram* (compare verses 5 and 7; 2 Kings 8:28; and elsewhere) **22:6** [a]Some Hebrew manuscripts, Septuagint, Syriac, Vulgate, and 2 Kings 8:29 read *Ahaziah*. **22:11** [a]Spelled *Jehosheba* in 2 Kings 11:2

LIFE LESSONS

➤ 21:19 — *. . . after the end of two years . . . his intestines came out because of his sickness; so he died in severe pain.*

The wages of sin are never very pleasant, but they can be bountiful.

➤ 22:4 — *Therefore he did evil in the sight of the LORD, like the house of Ahab; for they were his counselors after the death of his father, to his destruction.*

To follow any advice that opposes the Word of God is to invite destruction.

➤ 23:4 — *"This is what you shall do: One-third of you entering on the Sabbath, of the priests and the Levites, shall be keeping watch over the doors . . . ."*

Trusting God and depending on Him for strength and protection never means that we should fail to make wise plans. "Commit your works to the LORD, and your thoughts will be established" (Prov. 16:3).

LIFE PRINCIPLE 10

IF NECESSARY, GOD WILL MOVE HEAVEN AND EARTH TO SHOW US HIS WILL.

2 CHR. 20:12

God always wants the best for us, and He is committed to showing us how to follow the specific plan He has designed for each of our lives. He wants us to listen for His voice, to hear what He wants us to do and how He wants us to do it (see Is. 30:19, 21).

When we begin to wander from the course God has set for us, He will take all kinds of measures to capture our attention and protect us from harm. He has a wide variety of ways to help us to take notice, among them:

1. A restless spirit

Sometimes God gets our attention by making us restless (see Esther 6). If you experience a restlessness deep within—something you cannot quite identify—then stop and pray, "Lord, are You trying to say something to me?" Each time God was about to move me from one pastorate to another, I became very restless.

2. A spoken word

God also gets our attention by using the words of others. God gave a message both to a young Samuel and to the old priest Eli through this method (1 Sam. 3:4–18). If several people in a short span of time begin telling you the same thing, then ask the Lord if He is trying to speak to you through them.

3. An unusual blessing

God may bless us in an unusual way to gain our attention. Of course, if you are an overly self-sufficient person, the Lord may more likely use some other method to get your focus on Him. But remember that no matter which method He uses, it expresses His love.

4. Unanswered prayer

Sometimes God will answer a prayer with "No." Despite David's prayers for God to save his infant son's life—the child born through the king's adultery—the boy died (2 Sam. 12:15–18). The Lord may close the doors of heaven and refuse to answer our prayers as a way of forcing us to examine ourselves.

5. Disappointment

When the nation of Israel refused God's instruction to take possession of the Promised Land, God judged the people for their unbelief. They quickly changed their mind and said they now desired to enter the land; but the Lord said no, it was too late (Num. 14). God got their attention through a tremendous

God has a wide variety of ways to help us to take notice.

sense of disappointment. In a similar way, God may allow setbacks to keep us from charting our own course.

6. Extraordinary circumstances

Sometimes God will use unusual circumstances to get us to stop and listen. Moses saw a flaming bush that didn't burn up. As he approached to investigate, the Lord spoke to Him from the fire (Ex. 3). You and I must learn to look for the presence of God in every circumstance of life. He leaves His footprints and handiwork all around us.

7. Defeat

God may use defeat to show us the truth. Following the Lord's stunning victory over Jericho, the Israelites approached a small town with overconfidence and neglected to fight in God's strength or with His guidance (Josh. 7). God got Joshua's attention by letting him fail miserably. But even a terrible defeat may prove to be the greatest stepping-stone to success when we ask, "Lord, what are You saying?"

God knows precisely what it will take to get your attention.

8. Financial troubles

In the time of the Judges, when "everyone did what was right in his own eyes" (Judg. 17:6) the nation fell into idolatry and disobedience. God brought judgment through the Midianites, who devastated the land. Only when He took away every material belonging did they cry out to Him (Judg. 6:6). God knew exactly what it would take to get their attention. When they did return to Him, He delivered them from their oppressors and blessed them.

9. Tragedy, sickness, and affliction

We should regard our tragedies and afflictions as reasons to inquire of the Lord, "What are You trying to say?" When King Hezekiah became prideful, God used illness to alert him to the problem (2 Chr. 32:24). Similarly, when Saul of Tarsus persecuted Christians, God struck him with blindness—a tactic that certainly got his attention!

God always knows exactly where you are in your journey of faith and precisely what it will take to get your attention. So stay alert; notice if any of these divine methods are occurring—or recurring—in your life. If they are, ask Him what He wants to tell you, and then listen, not simply to hear, but to obey.

See the Life Principles Index for further study.

and the Levites, *shall be* keeping watch over
the doors;
5 "one-third *shall be* at the king's house; and
one-third at the Gate of the Foundation. All
the people *shall be* in the courts of the house
of the LORD.
6 "But let no one come into the house of the
LORD except the priests and those of the
Levites who serve. They may go in, for they
are holy; but all the people shall keep the
watch of the LORD.
7 "And the Levites shall surround the king
on all sides, every man with his weapons in
his hand; and whoever comes into the house,
let him be put to death. You are to be with the
king when he comes in and when he goes
out."
8 So the Levites and all Judah did according
to all that Jehoiada the priest commanded.
And each man took his men who were to be
on duty on the Sabbath, with those who were
going *off duty* on the Sabbath; for Jehoiada
the priest had not dismissed the divisions.
9 And Jehoiada the priest gave to the captains of hundreds the spears and the large
and small shields which *had belonged* to King
David, that *were* in the temple of God.
10 Then he set all the people, every man with
his weapon in his hand, from the right side of
the temple to the left side of the temple, along
by the altar and by the temple, all around the
king.
11 And they brought out the king's son, put
the crown on him, *gave him* the Testimony,[a]
and made him king. Then Jehoiada and his
sons anointed him, and said, "*Long* live the
king!"

Death of Athaliah

12 Now when Athaliah heard the noise of the
people running and praising the king, she
came to the people *in* the temple of the LORD.
13 *When* she looked, there was the king
standing by his pillar at the entrance; and the
leaders and the trumpeters *were* by the king.
All the people of the land were rejoicing and
blowing trumpets, also the singers with musical instruments, and those who led in praise.
So Athaliah tore her clothes and said, "Treason! Treason!"
14 And Jehoiada the priest brought out the
captains of hundreds who were set over the
army, and said to them, "Take her outside
under guard, and slay with the sword whoever follows her." For the priest had said, "Do
not kill her in the house of the LORD."
15 So they seized her; and she went by way
of the entrance of the Horse Gate *into* the
king's house, and they killed her there.
16 Then Jehoiada made a covenant between
himself, the people, and the king, that they
should be the LORD's people.
17 And all the people went to the temple[a] of
Baal, and tore it down. They broke in pieces
its altars and images, and killed Mattan the
priest of Baal before the altars.
18 Also Jehoiada appointed the oversight of
the house of the LORD to the hand of the
priests, the Levites, whom David had assigned in the house of the LORD, to offer the
burnt offerings of the LORD, as *it is* written in
the Law of Moses, with rejoicing and with
singing, *as it was established* by David.
19 And he set the gatekeepers at the gates of
the house of the LORD, so that no one *who was*
in any way unclean should enter.
20 Then he took the captains of hundreds,
the nobles, the governors of the people, and
all the people of the land, and brought the
king down from the house of the LORD; and
they went through the Upper Gate to the
king's house, and set the king on the throne of
the kingdom.
21 So all the people of the land rejoiced; and
the city was quiet, for they had slain Athaliah
with the sword.

Joash Repairs the Temple

24 Joash *was* seven years old when he be
came king, and he reigned forty years
in Jerusalem. His mother's name *was* Zibiah
of Beersheba.
2 Joash did *what was* right in the sight of
the LORD all the days of Jehoiada the priest.
3 And Jehoiada took two wives for him, and
he had sons and daughters.
4 Now it happened after this *that* Joash set
his heart on repairing the house of the LORD.
5 Then he gathered the priests and the
Levites, and said to them, "Go out to the cities
of Judah, and gather from all Israel money to
repair the house of your God from year to
year, and see that you do it quickly." However
the Levites did not do it quickly.
6 So the king called Jehoiada the chief
priest, and said to him, "Why have you not
required the Levites to bring in from Judah
and from Jerusalem the collection, *according
to the commandment* of Moses the servant of
the LORD and of the assembly of Israel, for the
tabernacle of witness?"
7 For the sons of Athaliah, that wicked
woman, had broken into the house of God,
and had also presented all the dedicated
things of the house of the LORD to the Baals.
8 Then at the king's command they made a
chest, and set it outside at the gate of the
house of the LORD.
9 And they made a proclamation throughout Judah and Jerusalem to bring to the LORD
the collection *that* Moses the servant of God
had imposed on Israel in the wilderness.
10 Then all the leaders and all the people rejoiced, brought their contributions, and put
them into the chest until all had given.

23:11 [a]That is, the Law (compare Exodus 25:16, 21; 31:18)
23:17 [a]Literally *house*

11 So it was, at that time, when the chest was
brought to the king's official by the hand of
the Levites, and when they saw that *there
was* much money, that the king's scribe and
the high priest's officer came and emptied the
chest, and took it and returned it to its place.
Thus they did day by day, and gathered
money in abundance.
12 The king and Jehoiada gave it to those
who did the work of the service of the house
of the LORD; and they hired masons and
carpenters to repair the house of the LORD,
and also those who worked in iron and
bronze to restore the house of the LORD.
13 So the workmen labored, and the work
was completed by them; they restored the
house of God to its original condition and re-
inforced it.
14 When they had finished, they brought the
rest of the money before the king and Jehoiada; they made from it articles for the
house of the LORD, articles for serving and offering, spoons and vessels of gold and silver.
And they offered burnt offerings in the house
of the LORD continually all the days of Jehoiada.

Apostasy of Joash

15 But Jehoiada grew old and was full of
days, and he died; *he was* one hundred and
thirty years old when he died.
16 And they buried him in the City of David
among the kings, because he had done good
in Israel, both toward God and His house.
17 Now after the death of Jehoiada the leaders of Judah came and bowed down to the
king. And the king listened to them.
18 Therefore they left the house of the LORD
God of their fathers, and served wooden images and idols; and wrath came upon Judah
and Jerusalem because of their trespass.
19 Yet He sent prophets to them, to bring
them back to the LORD; and they testified
against them, but they would not listen.
20 Then the Spirit of God came upon
Zechariah the son of Jehoiada the priest, who
stood above the people, and said to them,
"Thus says God: 'Why do you transgress the
commandments of the LORD, so that you cannot prosper? Because you have forsaken the
LORD, He also has forsaken you.'"
21 So they conspired against him, and at the
command of the king they stoned him with
stones in the court of the house of the LORD.
22 Thus Joash the king did not remember the
kindness which Jehoiada his father had done
to him, but killed his son; and as he died, he
said, "The LORD look on *it*, and repay!"

Death of Joash

23 So it happened in the spring of the year
that the army of Syria came up against him;
and they came to Judah and Jerusalem, and
destroyed all the leaders of the people from
among the people, and sent all their spoil to
the king of Damascus.
24 For the army of the Syrians came with a
small company of men; but the LORD delivered a very great army into their hand, because they had forsaken the LORD God of
their fathers. So they executed judgment
against Joash.
25 And when they had withdrawn from him
(for they left him severely wounded), his own
servants conspired against him because of
the blood of the sons[a] of Jehoiada the priest,
and killed him on his bed. So he died. And
they buried him in the City of David, but they
did not bury him in the tombs of the kings.
26 These are the ones who conspired against
him: Zabad[a] the son of Shimeath the Ammonitess, and Jehozabad the son of Shimrith[b]
the Moabitess.
27 Now *concerning* his sons, and the many
oracles about him, and the repairing of the
house of God, indeed they *are* written in the
annals of the book of the kings. Then
Amaziah his son reigned in his place.

Amaziah Reigns in Judah

25 Amaziah *was* twenty-five years old
when he became king, and he reigned

24:25 [a]Septuagint and Vulgate read *son* (compare verses 20–22).
24:26 [a]Or *Jozachar* (compare 2 Kings 12:21) [b]Or *Shomer* (compare 2 Kings 12:21)

LIFE LESSONS

➤ 24:17 — *Now after the death of Jehoiada the leaders of Judah came and bowed down to the king. And the king listened to them.*

As soon as these leaders suggested that Judah worship other gods, Joash should have executed them (Deut. 13:6–10). But since the king had never made the faith of Abraham his own, he adopted the faith of whoever advised him.

➤ 24:21 — *So they conspired against him, and at the command of the king they stoned him with stones in the court of the house of the LORD.*

For his faithfulness to God, Zechariah was stoned to death. Where is the reward in that? Jesus answers, "Be faithful until death, and I will give you the crown of life" (Rev. 2:10).

➤ 24:24 — *For the army of the Syrians came with a small company of men; but the LORD delivered a very great army into their hand, because they had forsaken the LORD God of their fathers.*

Just as God handed over huge enemy armies to the small but faithful forces of Israel, so He handed a huge but unfaithful Israelite army over to a small pagan force. The presence of God, not the size of the army, is what really matters.

twenty-nine years in Jerusalem. His mother's
name *was* Jehoaddan of Jerusalem.
2 And he did *what was* right in the sight of
the LORD, but not with a loyal heart.
3 Now it happened, as soon as the kingdom
was established for him, that he executed his
servants who had murdered his father the
king.
4 However he did not execute their children,
but *did* as *it is* written in the Law in the Book
of Moses, where the LORD commanded, saying, "The fathers shall not be put to death for
their children, nor shall the children be put to
death for their fathers; but a person shall die
for his own sin."[a]

The War Against Edom

5 Moreover Amaziah gathered Judah together and set over them captains of thousands and captains of hundreds, according to
their fathers' houses, throughout all Judah
and Benjamin; and he numbered them from
twenty years old and above, and found them
to be three hundred thousand choice *men,*
able to go to war, who could handle spear and
shield.
6 He also hired one hundred thousand
mighty men of valor from Israel for one hundred talents of silver.
7 But a man of God came to him, saying,
"O king, do not let the army of Israel go with
you, for the LORD *is* not with Israel—*not with*
any of the children of Ephraim.
➤ 8 "But if you go, be gone! Be strong in battle! *Even so,* God shall make you fall before
the enemy; for God has power to help and to
overthrow."
➤ 9 Then Amaziah said to the man of God,
"But what *shall we* do about the hundred talents which I have given to the troops of Israel?" And the man of God answered, "The
LORD is able to give you much more than
this."
10 So Amaziah discharged the troops that
had come to him from Ephraim, to go back
home. Therefore their anger was greatly
aroused against Judah, and they returned
home in great anger.
11 Then Amaziah strengthened himself, and
leading his people, he went to the Valley of
Salt and killed ten thousand of the people of
Seir.
12 Also the children of Judah took captive
ten thousand alive, brought them to the top of
the rock, and cast them down from the top
of the rock, so that they all were dashed in
pieces.
13 But as for the soldiers of the army which
Amaziah had discharged, so that they would
not go with him to battle, they raided the
cities of Judah from Samaria to Beth Horon,
killed three thousand in them, and took much
spoil.
14 Now it was so, after Amaziah came from
the slaughter of the Edomites, that he brought
the gods of the people of Seir, set them up *to*
be his gods, and bowed down before them
and burned incense to them.
15 Therefore the anger of the LORD was
aroused against Amaziah, and He sent him a
prophet who said to him, "Why have you
sought the gods of the people, which could
not rescue their own people from your hand?"
16 So it was, as he talked with him, that *the*
king said to him, "Have we made you the
king's counselor? Cease! Why should you be
killed?" Then the prophet ceased, and said, "I
know that God has determined to destroy
you, because you have done this and have not
heeded my advice."

Israel Defeats Judah

17 Now Amaziah king of Judah asked advice
and sent to Joash[a] the son of Jehoahaz, the
son of Jehu, king of Israel, saying, "Come, let
us face one another *in battle.*"
18 And Joash king of Israel sent to Amaziah
king of Judah, saying, "The thistle that *was* in
Lebanon sent to the cedar that was in Lebanon, saying, 'Give your daughter to my son as
wife'; and a wild beast that *was* in Lebanon
passed by and trampled the thistle.
19 "Indeed you say that you have defeated
the Edomites, and your heart is lifted up to

25:4 [a]Deuteronomy 24:16 **25:17** [a]Spelled *Jehoash* in 2 Kings 14:8ff

LIFE LESSONS

➤ 25:8 — *". . . God has power to help and to overthrow."*

God has the power to assist and rescue and He has the power to judge and destroy. Which we will receive depends on our attitude toward Him and toward His Word.

➤ 25:9 — *Then Amaziah said to the man of God, "But what shall we do about the hundred talents which I have given to the troops of Israel?" And the man of God answered, "The LORD is able to give you much more than this."*

Never shrink back from following the Lord out of fear of financial loss. God can bless you far more through your faithfulness than you can ever acquire through faithlessness.

➤ 25:14 — *. . . after Amaziah came from the slaughter of the Edomites . . . he brought the gods of the people of Seir, set them up to be his gods . . . .*

It makes no sense: after Amaziah won a great victory by depending on the Lord, he turned around and started worshiping the impotent gods of the people he had just defeated. We must continually guard our hearts!

boast. Stay at home now; why should you
meddle with trouble, that you should fall—
you and Judah with you?"
20 But Amaziah would not heed, for it *came*
from God, that He might give them into the
hand *of their enemies*, because they sought
the gods of Edom.
21 So Joash king of Israel went out; and he
and Amaziah king of Judah faced one another at Beth Shemesh, which *belongs* to Judah.
22 And Judah was defeated by Israel, and
every man fled to his tent.
23 Then Joash the king of Israel captured
Amaziah king of Judah, the son of Joash, the
son of Jehoahaz, at Beth Shemesh; and he
brought him to Jerusalem, and broke down
the wall of Jerusalem from the Gate of
Ephraim to the Corner Gate—four hundred
cubits.
24 And *he took* all the gold and silver, all the
articles that were found in the house of God
with Obed-Edom, the treasures of the king's
house, and hostages, and returned to Samaria.

Death of Amaziah

25 Amaziah the son of Joash, king of Judah,
lived fifteen years after the death of Joash the
son of Jehoahaz, king of Israel.
26 Now the rest of the acts of Amaziah, from
first to last, indeed *are* they not written in the
book of the kings of Judah and Israel?
27 After the time that Amaziah turned away
from following the LORD, they made a conspiracy against him in Jerusalem, and he fled
to Lachish; but they sent after him to Lachish
and killed him there.
28 Then they brought him on horses and
buried him with his fathers in the City of Judah.

Uzziah Reigns in Judah

26 Now all the people of Judah took
Uzziah,[a] who *was* sixteen years old,
and made him king instead of his father
Amaziah.
2 He built Elath[a] and restored it to Judah,
after the king rested with his fathers.
3 Uzziah *was* sixteen years old when he became king, and he reigned fifty-two years in
Jerusalem. His mother's name was Jecholiah
of Jerusalem.
4 And he did *what was* right in the sight of
the LORD, according to all that his father
Amaziah had done.
5 He sought God in the days of Zechariah,
who had understanding in the visions[a] of
God; and as long as he sought the LORD, God
made him prosper.
6 Now he went out and made war against
the Philistines, and broke down the wall of
Gath, the wall of Jabneh, and the wall of Ashdod; and he built cities *around* Ashdod and
among the Philistines.
7 God helped him against the Philistines,
against the Arabians who lived in Gur Baal,
and against the Meunites.
8 Also the Ammonites brought tribute to
Uzziah. His fame spread as far as the entrance of Egypt, for he became exceedingly
strong.
9 And Uzziah built towers in Jerusalem at
the Corner Gate, at the Valley Gate, and at the
corner buttress of the wall; then he fortified
them.
10 Also he built towers in the desert. He dug
many wells, for he had much livestock, both
in the lowlands and in the plains; *he also had*
farmers and vinedressers in the mountains
and in Carmel, for he loved the soil.
11 Moreover Uzziah had an army of fighting
men who went out to war by companies, according to the number on their roll as prepared by Jeiel the scribe and Maaseiah the
officer, under the hand of Hananiah, *one* of
the king's captains.
12 The total number of chief officers[a] of the
mighty men of valor *was* two thousand six
hundred.
13 And under their authority *was* an army of
three hundred and seven thousand five hundred, that made war with mighty power, to
help the king against the enemy.
14 Then Uzziah prepared for them, for the
entire army, shields, spears, helmets, body
armor, bows, and slings *to cast* stones.
15 And he made devices in Jerusalem, invented by skillful men, to be on the towers and
the corners, to shoot arrows and large stones.
So his fame spread far and wide, for he was
marvelously helped till he became strong.

The Penalty for Uzziah's Pride

16 But when he was strong his heart was lifted
up, to *his* destruction, for he transgressed

26:1 [a]Called *Azariah* in 2 Kings 14:21ff **26:2** [a]Hebrew *Eloth*
26:5 [a]Several Hebrew manuscripts, Septuagint, Syriac, Targum, and Arabic read *fear.* **26:12** [a]Literally *chief fathers*

LIFE LESSONS

➤ **26:5 — *. . . as long as he sought the LORD, God made him prosper.***

God prospers those who seek Him with their whole hearts.

➤ **26:16 — *But when he was strong his heart was lifted up, to his destruction . . . .***

Our greatest tests often come not during times of weakness or tragedy, but in times of prosperity and success. Pride brings down more men and women than any weapon of war ever invented.

Life Examples:

U Z Z I A H

The Downfall of Pride

2 CHR. 26:16–23

When we rely on our own strength to combat sin, our defeat draws very near. The "Big I" is no match for the Prince of Darkness; we're like an inflated balloon, just waiting to be popped.

Uzziah, a famous king and ferocious warrior, enjoyed great success "as long as he sought the LORD" (2 Chr. 26:5). He could have enjoyed a lifetime of victory . . . if he hadn't enthroned the "Big I."

Uzziah looked at all he had accomplished and gave in to pride—and predictably, corrupt behavior and unfaithfulness to the Lord followed. God consequently struck Uzziah with leprosy for usurping the work of the priests, and he died tragically (26:16–23).

Pride will take us places we have no business being, and before long it will destroy us. If we want to walk with God, we must listen to Him when He tells us to humble ourselves.

See the Life Principles Index for further study:
15. Brokenness is God's requirement for maximum usefulness.

against the LORD his God by entering the temple of the LORD to burn incense on the altar of
incense.
17 So Azariah the priest went in after him,
and with him were eighty priests of the
LORD—valiant men.
18 And they withstood King Uzziah, and said
to him, "*It is* not for you, Uzziah, to burn incense to the LORD, but for the priests, the sons
of Aaron, who are consecrated to burn incense. Get out of the sanctuary, for you have
trespassed! You *shall have* no honor from the
LORD God."
19 Then Uzziah became furious; and he *had*
a censer in his hand to burn incense. And
while he was angry with the priests, leprosy
broke out on his forehead, before the priests
in the house of the LORD, beside the incense
altar.
20 And Azariah the chief priest and all the
priests looked at him, and there, on his forehead, he *was* leprous; so they thrust him out
of that place. Indeed he also hurried to get
out, because the LORD had struck him.
21 King Uzziah was a leper until the day of
his death. He dwelt in an isolated house, because he was a leper; for he was cut off from
the house of the LORD. Then Jotham his son
was over the king's house, judging the people
of the land.
22 Now the rest of the acts of Uzziah, from
first to last, the prophet Isaiah the son of
Amoz wrote.
23 So Uzziah rested with his fathers, and
they buried him with his fathers in the field of
burial which *belonged* to the kings, for they
said, "He is a leper." Then Jotham his son
reigned in his place.

Jotham Reigns in Judah

27 Jotham *was* twenty-five years old
when he became king, and he reigned
sixteen years in Jerusalem. His mother's
name *was* Jerushah[a] the daughter of Zadok.
2 And he did *what was* right in the sight of
the LORD, according to all that his father
Uzziah had done (although he did not enter
the temple of the LORD). But still the people
acted corruptly.
3 He built the Upper Gate of the house of
the LORD, and he built extensively on the wall
of Ophel.
4 Moreover he built cities in the mountains
of Judah, and in the forests he built fortresses
and towers.
5 He also fought with the king of the Ammonites and defeated them. And the people of
Ammon gave him in that year one hundred
talents of silver, ten thousand kors of wheat,
and ten thousand of barley. The people of
Ammon paid this to him in the second and
third years also.
6 So Jotham became mighty, because he
prepared his ways before the LORD his God.
7 Now the rest of the acts of Jotham, and all
his wars and his ways, indeed they *are* written
in the book of the kings of Israel and Judah.
8 He was twenty-five years old when he became king, and he reigned sixteen years in Jerusalem.
9 So Jotham rested with his fathers, and
they buried him in the City of David. Then
Ahaz his son reigned in his place.

Ahaz Reigns in Judah

28 Ahaz *was* twenty years old when he
became king, and he reigned sixteen
years in Jerusalem; and he did not do *what*
was right in the sight of the LORD, as his father David *had done.*
2 For he walked in the ways of the kings of
Israel, and made molded images for the
Baals.

27:1 [a]Spelled *Jerusha* in 2 Kings 15:33

3 He burned incense in the Valley of the Son of Hinnom, and burned his children in the fire, according to the abominations of the nations whom the LORD had cast out before the children of Israel.
4 And he sacrificed and burned incense on the high places, on the hills, and under every green tree.

Syria and Israel Defeat Judah

5 Therefore the LORD his God delivered him into the hand of the king of Syria. They defeated him, and carried away a great multitude of them as captives, and brought *them* to Damascus. Then he was also delivered into the hand of the king of Israel, who defeated him with a great slaughter.
➤ 6 For Pekah the son of Remaliah killed one hundred and twenty thousand in Judah in one day, all valiant men, because they had forsaken the LORD God of their fathers.
7 Zichri, a mighty man of Ephraim, killed Maaseiah the king's son, Azrikam the officer over the house, and Elkanah *who was* second to the king.
8 And the children of Israel carried away captive of their brethren two hundred thousand women, sons, and daughters; and they also took away much spoil from them, and brought the spoil to Samaria.

Israel Returns the Captives

9 But a prophet of the LORD was there, whose name *was* Oded; and he went out before the army that came to Samaria, and said to them: "Look, because the LORD God of your fathers was angry with Judah, He has delivered them into your hand; but you have killed them in a rage *that* reaches up to heaven.
10 "And now you propose to force the children of Judah and Jerusalem to be your male and female slaves; *but are* you not also guilty before the LORD your God?
11 "Now hear me, therefore, and return the captives, whom you have taken captive from your brethren, for the fierce wrath of the LORD *is* upon you."
12 Then some of the heads of the children of Ephraim, Azariah the son of Johanan, Berechiah the son of Meshillemoth, Jehizkiah the son of Shallum, and Amasa the son of Hadlai, stood up against those who came from the war,
13 and said to them, "You shall not bring the captives here, for we *already* have offended the LORD. You intend to add to our sins and to our guilt; for our guilt is great, and *there is* fierce wrath against Israel."
14 So the armed men left the captives and the spoil before the leaders and all the assembly.
15 Then the men who were designated by name rose up and took the captives, and from the spoil they clothed all who were naked among them, dressed them and gave them sandals, gave them food and drink, and anointed them; and they let all the feeble ones ride on donkeys. So they brought them to their brethren at Jericho, the city of palm trees. Then they returned to Samaria.

Assyria Refuses to Help Judah

16 At the same time King Ahaz sent to the kings[a] of Assyria to help him.
17 For again the Edomites had come, attacked Judah, and carried away captives.
18 The Philistines also had invaded the cities of the lowland and of the South of Judah, and had taken Beth Shemesh, Aijalon, Gederoth, Sochoh with its villages, Timnah with its villages, and Gimzo with its villages; and they dwelt there.
19 For the LORD brought Judah low because of Ahaz king of Israel, for he had encouraged moral decline in Judah and had been continually unfaithful to the LORD.
20 Also Tiglath-Pileser[a] king of Assyria came to him and distressed him, and did not assist him.
21 For Ahaz took part *of the treasures* from the house of the LORD, from the house of the king, and from the leaders, and he gave *it* to the king of Assyria; but he did not help him.

Apostasy and Death of Ahaz

22 Now in the time of his distress King Ahaz became increasingly unfaithful to the LORD. This *is that* King Ahaz. ➤
23 For he sacrificed to the gods of Damascus which had defeated him, saying, "Because the

28:16 [a]Septuagint, Syriac, and Vulgate read *king* (compare verse 20). **28:20** [a]Hebrew *Tilgath-Pilneser*

LIFE LESSONS

➤ **28:6 — *For Pekah the son of Remaliah killed one hundred and twenty thousand in Judah in one day, all valiant men, because they had forsaken the LORD God of their fathers.***

Even multitudes of valiant men cannot prosper when they forsake the living God. The Lord promised that if His people abandoned Him, "I will hide My face from them, and they shall be devoured" (Deut. 31:17).

➤ **28:22 — *Now in the time of his distress King Ahaz became increasingly unfaithful to the LORD.***

God wants to use our times of distress to bring us closer to Him, not to drive us further away. We usually learn more in our valley experiences than on our mountaintops.

gods of the kings of Syria help them, I will
sacrifice to them that they may help me." But
they were the ruin of him and of all Israel.
24 So Ahaz gathered the articles of the house
of God, cut in pieces the articles of the house
of God, shut up the doors of the house of the
LORD, and made for himself altars in every
corner of Jerusalem.
25 And in every single city of Judah he made
high places to burn incense to other gods, and
provoked to anger the LORD God of his fathers.
26 Now the rest of his acts and all his ways,
from first to last, indeed they *are* written in
the book of the kings of Judah and Israel.
27 So Ahaz rested with his fathers, and they
buried him in the city, in Jerusalem; but they
did not bring him into the tombs of the kings
of Israel. Then Hezekiah his son reigned in
his place.

Hezekiah Reigns in Judah

29 Hezekiah became king *when he was*
twenty-five years old, and he reigned
twenty-nine years in Jerusalem. His mother's
name *was* Abijah[a] the daughter of Zechariah.
2 And he did *what was* right in the sight of
the LORD, according to all that his father David had done.

Hezekiah Cleanses the Temple

3 In the first year of his reign, in the first
month, he opened the doors of the house of
the LORD and repaired them.
4 Then he brought in the priests and the
Levites, and gathered them in the East
Square,
5 and said to them: "Hear me, Levites! Now
sanctify yourselves, sanctify the house of the
LORD God of your fathers, and carry out the
rubbish from the holy *place*.
6 "For our fathers have trespassed and done
evil in the eyes of the LORD our God; they
have forsaken Him, have turned their faces
away from the dwelling place of the LORD,
and turned *their* backs *on Him*.
7 "They have also shut up the doors of the
vestibule, put out the lamps, and have not
burned incense or offered burnt offerings in
the holy *place* to the God of Israel.
8 "Therefore the wrath of the LORD fell upon
Judah and Jerusalem, and He has given them
up to trouble, to desolation, and to jeering, as
you see with your eyes.
9 "For indeed, because of this our fathers
have fallen by the sword; and our sons, our
daughters, and our wives *are* in captivity.
10 "Now *it is* in my heart to make a covenant
with the LORD God of Israel, that His fierce
wrath may turn away from us.
11 "My sons, do not be negligent now, for the
LORD has chosen you to stand before Him, to
serve Him, and that you should minister to
Him and burn incense."
12 Then these Levites arose: Mahath the son
of Amasai and Joel the son of Azariah, of the
sons of the Kohathites; of the sons of Merari,
Kish the son of Abdi and Azariah the son of
Jehallelel; of the Gershonites, Joah the son of
Zimmah and Eden the son of Joah;
13 of the sons of Elizaphan, Shimri and Jeiel;
of the sons of Asaph, Zechariah and Mattaniah;
14 of the sons of Heman, Jehiel and Shimei;
and of the sons of Jeduthun, Shemaiah and
Uzziel.
15 And they gathered their brethren, sanctified themselves, and went according to the
commandment of the king, at the words of the
LORD, to cleanse the house of the LORD.
16 Then the priests went into the inner part
of the house of the LORD to cleanse *it*, and
brought out all the debris that they found in
the temple of the LORD to the court of the
house of the LORD. And the Levites took *it* out
and carried *it* to the Brook Kidron.
17 Now they began to sanctify on the first
day of the first month, and on the eighth day
of the month they came to the vestibule of the
LORD. So they sanctified the house of the
LORD in eight days, and on the sixteenth day
of the first month they finished.
18 Then they went in to King Hezekiah and
said, "We have cleansed all the house of the
LORD, the altar of burnt offerings with all its
articles, and the table of the showbread with
all its articles.
19 "Moreover all the articles which King
Ahaz in his reign had cast aside in his transgression we have prepared and sanctified; and
there they *are*, before the altar of the LORD."

Hezekiah Restores Temple Worship

20 Then King Hezekiah rose early, gathered
the rulers of the city, and went up to the house
of the LORD.
21 And they brought seven bulls, seven rams,
seven lambs, and seven male goats for a sin
offering for the kingdom, for the sanctuary,
and for Judah. Then he commanded the
priests, the sons of Aaron, to offer *them* on
the altar of the LORD.
22 So they killed the bulls, and the priests received the blood and sprinkled *it* on the altar.
Likewise they killed the rams and sprinkled
the blood on the altar. They also killed the
lambs and sprinkled the blood on the altar.
23 Then they brought out the male goats *for*
the sin offering before the king and the assembly, and they laid their hands on them.
24 And the priests killed them; and they presented their blood on the altar as a sin offering to make an atonement for all Israel, for
the king commanded *that* the burnt offering
and the sin offering *be made* for all Israel.

29:1 [a]Spelled *Abi* in 2 Kings 18:2

25 And he stationed the Levites in the house of the LORD with cymbals, with stringed instruments, and with harps, according to the commandment of David, of Gad the king's seer, and of Nathan the prophet; for thus *was* the commandment of the LORD by His prophets.
26 The Levites stood with the instruments of David, and the priests with the trumpets.
27 Then Hezekiah commanded *them* to offer the burnt offering on the altar. And when the burnt offering began, the song of the LORD *also* began, with the trumpets and with the instruments of David king of Israel.
28 So all the assembly worshiped, the singers sang, and the trumpeters sounded; all *this continued* until the burnt offering was finished.
29 And when they had finished offering, the king and all who were present with him bowed and worshiped.
30 Moreover King Hezekiah and the leaders commanded the Levites to sing praise to the LORD with the words of David and of Asaph the seer. So they sang praises with gladness, and they bowed their heads and worshiped.
31 Then Hezekiah answered and said, "Now *that* you have consecrated yourselves to the LORD, come near, and bring sacrifices and thank offerings into the house of the LORD." So the assembly brought in sacrifices and thank offerings, and as many as were of a willing heart *brought* burnt offerings.
32 And the number of the burnt offerings which the assembly brought was seventy bulls, one hundred rams, *and* two hundred lambs; all these *were* for a burnt offering to the LORD.
33 The consecrated things *were* six hundred bulls and three thousand sheep.
34 But the priests were too few, so that they could not skin all the burnt offerings; therefore their brethren the Levites helped them until the work was ended and until the *other* priests had sanctified themselves, for the Levites were more diligent in sanctifying themselves than the priests.
35 Also the burnt offerings *were* in abundance, with the fat of the peace offerings and *with* the drink offerings for *every* burnt offering. So the service of the house of the LORD was set in order.
36 Then Hezekiah and all the people rejoiced that God had prepared the people, since the events took place so suddenly.

Hezekiah Keeps the Passover

30 And Hezekiah sent to all Israel and Judah, and also wrote letters to Ephraim and Manasseh, that they should come to the house of the LORD at Jerusalem, to keep the Passover to the LORD God of Israel.
2 For the king and his leaders and all the assembly in Jerusalem had agreed to keep the Passover in the second month.
3 For they could not keep it at the regular time,[a] because a sufficient number of priests had not consecrated themselves, nor had the people gathered together at Jerusalem.
4 And the matter pleased the king and all the assembly.
5 So they resolved to make a proclamation throughout all Israel, from Beersheba to Dan, that they should come to keep the Passover to the LORD God of Israel at Jerusalem, since they had not done *it* for a long *time* in the *prescribed* manner.
6 Then the runners went throughout all Israel and Judah with the letters from the king and his leaders, and spoke according to the command of the king: "Children of Israel, return to the LORD God of Abraham, Isaac, and Israel; then He will return to the remnant of you who have escaped from the hand of the kings of Assyria.
7 "And do not be like your fathers and your brethren, who trespassed against the LORD God of their fathers, so that He gave them up to desolation, as you see.
8 "Now do not be stiff-necked, as your fathers *were, but* yield yourselves to the LORD; and enter His sanctuary, which He has sanctified forever, and serve the LORD your God, that the fierceness of His wrath may turn away from you.
9 "For if you return to the LORD, your brethren and your children *will be treated* with compassion by those who lead them captive, so that they may come back to this land; for the LORD your God *is* gracious and merciful, and will not turn *His* face from you if you return to Him."

30:3 [a]That is, the first month (compare Leviticus 23:5); literally *at that time*

LIFE LESSONS

➤ 29:36 — *Then Hezekiah and all the people rejoiced that God had prepared the people, since the events took place so suddenly.*

Good things can happen suddenly when God goes ahead of us to prepare hearts. We can rejoice that He makes it a habit to go ahead of His obedient people (Ex. 23:20; Deut. 31:3; Matt. 26:32).

➤ 30:9 — *". . . for the LORD your God is gracious and merciful, and will not turn His face from you if you return to Him."*

Some people worry that they have committed "the unpardonable sin," but God will never turn away anyone who genuinely repents of His sin and places his faith in Christ.

➤ **10** So the runners passed from city to city
through the country of Ephraim and Manasseh, as far as Zebulun; but they laughed at
them and mocked them.
➤ 11 Nevertheless some from Asher, Manasseh,
and Zebulun humbled themselves and came
to Jerusalem.
12 Also the hand of God was on Judah to give
them singleness of heart to obey the command of the king and the leaders, at the word
of the LORD.
13 Now many people, a very great assembly,
gathered at Jerusalem to keep the Feast of
Unleavened Bread in the second month.
14 They arose and took away the altars that
were in Jerusalem, and they took away all the
incense altars and cast *them* into the Brook
Kidron.
15 Then they slaughtered the Passover *lambs*
on the fourteenth *day* of the second month.
The priests and the Levites were ashamed,
and sanctified themselves, and brought the
burnt offerings to the house of the LORD.
16 They stood in their place according to
their custom, according to the Law of Moses
the man of God; the priests sprinkled the
blood *received* from the hand of the Levites.
17 For *there were* many in the assembly who
had not sanctified themselves; therefore the
Levites had charge of the slaughter of the
Passover *lambs* for everyone *who was* not
clean, to sanctify *them* to the LORD.
➤ 18 For a multitude of the people, many from
Ephraim, Manasseh, Issachar, and Zebulun,
had not cleansed themselves, yet they ate the
Passover contrary to what was written. But
Hezekiah prayed for them, saying, "May the
good LORD provide atonement for everyone
➤ 19 "*who* prepares his heart to seek God, the
LORD God of his fathers, though *he is* not
cleansed according to the purification of the
sanctuary."
20 And the LORD listened to Hezekiah and
healed the people.
21 So the children of Israel who were present
at Jerusalem kept the Feast of Unleavened
Bread seven days with great gladness; and
the Levites and the priests praised the LORD
day by day, *singing* to the LORD, accompanied
by loud instruments.
22 And Hezekiah gave encouragement to all
the Levites who taught the good knowledge of
the LORD; and they ate throughout the feast
seven days, offering peace offerings and making confession to the LORD God of their fathers.
23 Then the whole assembly agreed to keep
the feast another seven days, and they kept it
another seven days with gladness.
24 For Hezekiah king of Judah gave to the assembly a thousand bulls and seven thousand
sheep, and the leaders gave to the assembly a
thousand bulls and ten thousand sheep; and a
great number of priests sanctified themselves.
25 The whole assembly of Judah rejoiced,
also the priests and Levites, all the assembly
that came from Israel, the sojourners who
came from the land of Israel, and those who
dwelt in Judah.
26 So there was great joy in Jerusalem, for
since the time of Solomon the son of David,
king of Israel, *there had* been nothing like
this in Jerusalem.
27 Then the priests, the Levites, arose and
blessed the people, and their voice was heard;
and their prayer came *up* to His holy dwelling
place, to heaven.

The Reforms of Hezekiah

31 Now when all this was finished, all Is- ➤
rael who were present went out to the
cities of Judah and broke the *sacred* pillars in
pieces, cut down the wooden images, and
threw down the high places and the altars—
from all Judah, Benjamin, Ephraim, and Manasseh—until they had utterly destroyed them
all. Then all the children of Israel returned to
their own cities, every man to his possession.
2 And Hezekiah appointed the divisions of
the priests and the Levites according to their
divisions, each man according to his service,
the priests and Levites for burnt offerings and
peace offerings, to serve, to give thanks, and to
praise in the gates of the camp[a] of the LORD.

31:2 [a]That is, the temple

LIFE LESSONS

➤ 30:10, 11 — *So the runners passed from city to city through the country of Ephraim and Manasseh, as far as Zebulun; but they laughed at them and mocked them. Nevertheless some from Asher, Manasseh, and Zebulun humbled themselves . . . .*

Many will mock and laugh at hearing an offer of new life in Christ, but some will humbly respond. We must continue to speak the Good News for the benefit of the few, regardless of the scorn of the many.

➤ 30:18, 19 — *"May the good LORD provide atonement for everyone who prepares his heart to seek God, the LORD God of his fathers, though he is not cleansed according to the purification of the sanctuary."*

God is not a legalist; when the heart is right, He accepts the whole man. Jesus said, "But if you had known what this means, 'I desire mercy and not sacrifice,' you would not have condemned the guiltless" (Matt. 12:7).

➤ 31:1 — *. . . all Israel who were present went out to the cities of Judah and broke the sacred pillars in pieces, cut down the wooden images, and threw down the high places and the altars . . . until they had utterly destroyed them all.*

True devotion to God changes a person from the inside out, so that obedience to the Lord brings more pleasure than does sin. When the heart changes, behavior changes.

3 The king also *appointed* a portion of his
possessions for the burnt offerings: for the
morning and evening burnt offerings, the
burnt offerings for the Sabbaths and the New
Moons and the set feasts, as *it is* written in the
Law of the LORD.
4 Moreover he commanded the people
who dwelt in Jerusalem to contribute support
for the priests and the Levites, that they
might devote themselves to the Law of the
LORD.
5 As soon as the commandment was circulated, the children of Israel brought in abundance the firstfruits of grain and wine, oil and
honey, and of all the produce of the field; and
they brought in abundantly the tithe of everything.
6 And the children of Israel and Judah, who
dwelt in the cities of Judah, brought the tithe
of oxen and sheep; also the tithe of holy
things which were consecrated to the LORD
their God they laid in heaps.
7 In the third month they began laying them
in heaps, and they finished in the seventh
month.
8 And when Hezekiah and the leaders came
and saw the heaps, they blessed the LORD and
His people Israel.
9 Then Hezekiah questioned the priests and
the Levites concerning the heaps.
10 And Azariah the chief priest, from the
house of Zadok, answered him and said,
"Since *the people* began to bring the offerings
into the house of the LORD, we have had
enough to eat and have plenty left, for the
LORD has blessed His people; and what is left
is this great abundance."
11 Now Hezekiah commanded *them* to prepare rooms in the house of the LORD, and they
prepared them.
12 Then they faithfully brought in the offerings, the tithes, and the dedicated things;
Cononiah the Levite had charge of them, and
Shimei his brother *was* the next.
13 Jehiel, Azaziah, Nahath, Asahel, Jerimoth,
Jozabad, Eliel, Ismachiah, Mahath, and Benaiah *were* overseers under the hand of Cononiah and Shimei his brother, at the
commandment of Hezekiah the king and
Azariah the ruler of the house of God.
14 Kore the son of Imnah the Levite, the
keeper of the East Gate, *was* over the freewill
offerings to God, to distribute the offerings of
the LORD and the most holy things.
15 And under him *were* Eden, Miniamin,
Jeshua, Shemaiah, Amariah, and Shecaniah,
his faithful assistants in the cities of the
priests, to distribute allotments to their
brethren by divisions, to the great as well as
the small.
16 Besides those males from three years old
and up who were written in the genealogy,
they distributed to everyone who entered the
house of the LORD his daily portion for the
work of his service, by his division,
17 and to the priests who were written in
the genealogy according to their father's
house, and to the Levites from twenty years
old and up according to their work, by their
divisions,
18 and to all who were written in the genealogy—their little ones and their wives, their
sons and daughters, the whole company of
them—for in their faithfulness they sanctified
themselves in holiness.
19 Also for the sons of Aaron the priests, *who
were* in the fields of the common-lands of
their cities, in every single city, *there were*
men who were designated by name to distribute portions to all the males among the
priests and to all who were listed by genealogies among the Levites.
20 Thus Hezekiah did throughout all Judah,
and he did what *was* good and right and true
before the LORD his God.
21 And in every work that he began in the
service of the house of God, in the law and in
the commandment, to seek his God, he did *it*
with all his heart. So he prospered.

Sennacherib Boasts Against the LORD

32 After these deeds of faithfulness, Sennacherib king of Assyria came and entered Judah; he encamped against the fortified cities, thinking to win them over to
himself.
2 And when Hezekiah saw that Sennacherib had come, and that his purpose was
to make war against Jerusalem,
3 he consulted with his leaders and commanders[a] to stop the water from the springs

32:3 [a]Literally *mighty men*

LIFE LESSONS

➤ **31:21 —** ***And in every work that he began in the service of the house of God, in the law and in the commandment, to seek his God, he did it with all his heart. So he prospered.***

When we seek the Lord with all our heart, the natural result is joyful and earnest obedience. And obedience always brings blessing.

➤ **32:1 —** ***After these deeds of faithfulness, Sennacherib king of Assyria came and entered Judah; he encamped against the fortified cities, thinking to win them over to himself.***

On this fallen planet, stiff challenges to our faith often follow faithful obedience. We can ask, "Is this how You repay me, Lord?" Or we can say, "You have helped me before. Now I ask you to help me again."

which *were* outside the city; and they helped
him.
4 Thus many people gathered together who
stopped all the springs and the brook that ran
through the land, saying, "Why should the
kings[a] of Assyria come and find much
water?"
5 And he strengthened himself, built up
all the wall that was broken, raised *it* up to
the towers, and *built* another wall outside;
also he repaired the Millo[a] *in* the City of David, and made weapons and shields in abundance.
6 Then he set military captains over the people, gathered them together to him in the
open square of the city gate, and gave them
encouragement, saying,
7 "Be strong and courageous; do not be
afraid nor dismayed before the king of Assyria, nor before all the multitude that *is* with
him; for *there are* more with us than with
him.
8 "With him *is* an arm of flesh; but with us *is*
the LORD our God, to help us and to fight our
battles." And the people were strengthened by
the words of Hezekiah king of Judah.
9 After this Sennacherib king of Assyria
sent his servants to Jerusalem (but he and all
the forces with him *laid siege* against Lachish), to Hezekiah king of Judah, and to all
Judah who *were* in Jerusalem, saying,
10 "Thus says Sennacherib king of Assyria:
'In what do you trust, that you remain under
siege in Jerusalem?
11 'Does not Hezekiah persuade you to give
yourselves over to die by famine and by thirst,
saying, "The LORD our God will deliver us
from the hand of the king of Assyria"?
12 'Has not the same Hezekiah taken away
His high places and His altars, and commanded Judah and Jerusalem, saying, "You
shall worship before one altar and burn incense on it"?
13 'Do you not know what I and my fathers
have done to all the peoples of *other* lands?
Were the gods of the nations of those lands in
any way able to deliver their lands out of my
hand?
14 'Who *was there* among all the gods of
those nations that my fathers utterly destroyed that could deliver his people from my
hand, that your God should be able to deliver
you from my hand?
15 'Now therefore, do not let Hezekiah deceive you or persuade you like this, and do
not believe him; for no god of any nation or
kingdom was able to deliver his people from
my hand or the hand of my fathers. How
much less will your God deliver you from my
hand?'"
16 Furthermore, his servants spoke against
the LORD God and against His servant
Hezekiah.
17 He also wrote letters to revile the LORD ➤
God of Israel, and to speak against Him, saying, "As the gods of the nations of *other* lands
have not delivered their people from my
hand, so the God of Hezekiah will not deliver
His people from my hand."
18 Then they called out with a loud voice in
Hebrew[a] to the people of Jerusalem who *were*
on the wall, to frighten them and trouble
them, that they might take the city.
19 And they spoke against the God of Jerusalem, as against the gods of the people of the
earth—the work of men's hands.

Sennacherib's Defeat and Death

20 Now because of this King Hezekiah and
the prophet Isaiah, the son of Amoz, prayed
and cried out to heaven.
21 Then the LORD sent an angel who cut
down every mighty man of valor, leader, and
captain in the camp of the king of Assyria. So
he returned shamefaced to his own land. And
when he had gone into the temple of his god,
some of his own offspring struck him down
with the sword there.
22 Thus the LORD saved Hezekiah and the inhabitants of Jerusalem from the hand of Sennacherib the king of Assyria, and from the
hand of all *others,* and guided them[a] on every
side.
23 And many brought gifts to the LORD at Jerusalem, and presents to Hezekiah king of Judah, so that he was exalted in the sight of all
nations thereafter.

32:4 [a]Following Masoretic Text and Vulgate; Arabic, Septuagint, and Syriac read *king.* **32:5** [a]Literally *The Landfill* **32:18** [a]Literally *Judean* **32:22** [a]Septuagint reads *gave them rest;* Vulgate reads *gave them treasures.*

LIFE LESSONS

➤ 32:3 — . . . he consulted with his leaders and commanders to stop the water from the springs which were outside the city; and they helped him.

Hezekiah not only prayed to God for deliverance when the Assyrians advanced against him; he also took wise action. Faithful, believing prayer does not encourage passivity or inaction.

➤ 32:17 — He also wrote letters to revile the LORD God of Israel . . . "As the gods of the nations of other lands have not delivered their people from my hand, so the God of Hezekiah will not deliver His people from my hand."

The God of Israel differs from the gods of the nations. Therefore, all roads do not lead to the one, true God. A single such road exists, the one God built Himself using the blood of His Son (John 14:6; Acts 4:12).

Hezekiah Humbles Himself

24 In those days Hezekiah was sick and near death, and he prayed to the LORD; and He spoke to him and gave him a sign.

➤ 25 But Hezekiah did not repay according to the favor *shown* him, for his heart was lifted up; therefore wrath was looming over him and over Judah and Jerusalem.

26 Then Hezekiah humbled himself for the pride of his heart, he and the inhabitants of Jerusalem, so that the wrath of the LORD did not come upon them in the days of Hezekiah.

Hezekiah's Wealth and Honor

27 Hezekiah had very great riches and honor. And he made himself treasuries for silver, for gold, for precious stones, for spices, for shields, and for all kinds of desirable items;

28 storehouses for the harvest of grain, wine, and oil; and stalls for all kinds of livestock, and folds for flocks.[a]

29 Moreover he provided cities for himself, and possessions of flocks and herds in abundance; for God had given him very much property.

30 This same Hezekiah also stopped the water outlet of Upper Gihon, and brought the water by tunnel[a] to the west side of the City of David. Hezekiah prospered in all his works.

➤ **31** However, *regarding* the ambassadors of the princes of Babylon, whom they sent to him to inquire about the wonder that was *done* in the land, God withdrew from him, in order to test him, that He might know all *that was* in his heart.

Death of Hezekiah

32 Now the rest of the acts of Hezekiah, and his goodness, indeed they *are* written in the vision of Isaiah the prophet, the son of Amoz, *and* in the book of the kings of Judah and Israel.

33 So Hezekiah rested with his fathers, and they buried him in the upper tombs of the sons of David; and all Judah and the inhabitants of Jerusalem honored him at his death. Then Manasseh his son reigned in his place.

Manasseh Reigns in Judah

33 Manasseh *was* twelve years old when he became king, and he reigned fifty-five years in Jerusalem.

2 But he did evil in the sight of the LORD, according to the abominations of the nations whom the LORD had cast out before the children of Israel.

3 For he rebuilt the high places which Hezekiah his father had broken down; he raised up altars for the Baals, and made wooden images; and he worshiped all the host of heaven[a] and served them.

4 He also built altars in the house of the LORD, of which the LORD had said, "In Jerusalem shall My name be forever."

5 And he built altars for all the host of heaven in the two courts of the house of the LORD.

6 Also he caused his sons to pass through the fire in the Valley of the Son of Hinnom; he practiced soothsaying, used witchcraft and sorcery, and consulted mediums and spiritists. He did much evil in the sight of the LORD, to provoke Him to anger.

7 He even set a carved image, the idol which he had made, in the house of God, of which God had said to David and to Solomon his son, "In this house and in Jerusalem, which I have chosen out of all the tribes of Israel, I will put My name forever;

8 "and I will not again remove the foot of Israel from the land which I have appointed for your fathers—only if they are careful to do all that I have commanded them, according to the whole law and the statutes and the ordinances by the hand of Moses."

9 So Manasseh seduced Judah and the inhabitants of Jerusalem to do more evil than the nations whom the LORD had destroyed before the children of Israel.

Manasseh Restored After Repentance

10 And the LORD spoke to Manasseh and his people, but they would not listen. ➤

11 Therefore the LORD brought upon them the captains of the army of the king of Assyria, who took Manasseh with hooks,[a]

32:28 [a]Following Septuagint and Vulgate; Arabic and Syriac omit *folds for flocks;* Masoretic Text reads *flocks for sheepfolds.*
32:30 [a]Literally *brought it straight* (compare 2 Kings 20:20)
33:3 [a]The gods of the Assyrians **33:11** [a]That is, nose hooks (compare 2 Kings 19:28)

LIFE LESSONS

➤ **32:25 — *But Hezekiah did not repay according to the favor shown him, for his heart was lifted up; therefore wrath was looming over him and over Judah and Jerusalem.***

Pride can take root in the most faithful of hearts. The only antidote is humility. "A man's pride will bring him low, but the humble in spirit will retain honor" (Prov. 29:23).

➤ **32:31 — *However, regarding the ambassadors of the princes of Babylon, whom they sent to him to inquire about the wonder that was done in the land, God withdrew from him, in order to test him, that He might know all that was in his heart.***

The Babylonian ambassadors came to hear about the miracle God had done in Judah; Hezekiah instead showed them his riches. What might have happened had the king boasted to them about God and not about himself?

➤ **33:10 — *And the LORD spoke to Manasseh and his people, but they would not listen.***

The Lord speaks to us continually. Are we listening for His voice?

bound him with bronze *fetters,* and carried
him off to Babylon.
➤ 12 Now when he was in affliction, he implored the LORD his God, and humbled himself greatly before the God of his fathers,
➤ 13 and prayed to Him; and He received his
entreaty, heard his supplication, and brought
him back to Jerusalem into his kingdom.
Then Manasseh knew that the LORD *was* God.
14 After this he built a wall outside the City
of David on the west side of Gihon, in the valley, as far as the entrance of the Fish Gate;
and *it* enclosed Ophel, and he raised it to a
very great height. Then he put military captains in all the fortified cities of Judah.
15 He took away the foreign gods and the
idol from the house of the LORD, and all the altars that he had built in the mount of the
house of the LORD and in Jerusalem; and he
cast *them* out of the city.
16 He also repaired the altar of the LORD, sacrificed peace offerings and thank offerings on
it, and commanded Judah to serve the LORD
God of Israel.
17 Nevertheless the people still sacrificed on
the high places, *but* only to the LORD their
God.

Death of Manasseh

18 Now the rest of the acts of Manasseh, his
prayer to his God, and the words of the seers
who spoke to him in the name of the LORD
God of Israel, indeed they *are written* in the
book[a] of the kings of Israel.
19 Also his prayer and *how God* received his
entreaty, and all his sin and trespass, and the
sites where he built high places and set up
wooden images and carved images, before he
was humbled, indeed they *are* written among
the sayings of Hozai.[a]
20 So Manasseh rested with his fathers, and
they buried him in his own house. Then his
son Amon reigned in his place.

Amon's Reign and Death

21 Amon *was* twenty-two years old when he
became king, and he reigned two years in Jerusalem.
22 But he did evil in the sight of the LORD, as
his father Manasseh had done; for Amon sacrificed to all the carved images which his father Manasseh had made, and served them.
23 And he did not humble himself before the
LORD, as his father Manasseh had humbled
himself; but Amon trespassed more and
more.
24 Then his servants conspired against him,
and killed him in his own house.
25 But the people of the land executed all
those who had conspired against King Amon.
Then the people of the land made his son
Josiah king in his place.

Josiah Reigns in Judah

34 Josiah *was* eight years old when he became king, and he reigned thirty-one
years in Jerusalem.
2 And he did *what was* right in the sight of
the LORD, and walked in the ways of his father
David; *he* did *not* turn aside to the right hand
or to the left.
3 For in the eighth year of his reign, while ◄
he was still young, he began to seek the God
of his father David; and in the twelfth year he
began to purge Judah and Jerusalem of the
high places, the wooden images, the carved
images, and the molded images.
4 They broke down the altars of the Baals in
his presence, and the incense altars which
were above them he cut down; and the
wooden images, the carved images, and the
molded images he broke in pieces, and made
dust of them and scattered *it* on the graves of
those who had sacrificed to them.
5 He also burned the bones of the priests on
their altars, and cleansed Judah and Jerusalem.
6 And *so he did* in the cities of Manasseh,
Ephraim, and Simeon, as far as Naphtali and
all around, with axes.[a]
7 When he had broken down the altars and
the wooden images, had beaten the carved
images into powder, and cut down all the incense altars throughout all the land of Israel,
he returned to Jerusalem.

Hilkiah Finds the Book of the Law

8 In the eighteenth year of his reign, when
he had purged the land and the temple,[a] he
sent Shaphan the son of Azaliah, Maaseiah
the governor of the city, and Joah the son of

33:18 [a]Literally *words* **33:19** [a]Septuagint reads *the seers.*
34:6 [a]Literally *swords* **34:8** [a]Literally *house*

LIFE LESSONS

➤ **33:12, 13 — *Now when he was in affliction, he implored the LORD his God, and humbled himself greatly before the God of his fathers, and prayed to Him; and He received his entreaty . . . .***

If the Lord will hear and answer the humble, repentant prayer of a desperately wicked man like Manasseh, then truly no one is outside the reach of His saving grace.

➤ **34:3 — *For in the eighth year of his reign, while he was still young, he began to seek the God of his father David . . . .***

It is never too early to urge our children to seek the Lord. God can work in young hearts as well as in older ones—many times, more effectively.

Joahaz the recorder, to repair the house of the LORD his God.

9 When they came to Hilkiah the high priest, they delivered the money that was brought into the house of God, which the Levites who kept the doors had gathered from the hand of Manasseh and Ephraim, from all the remnant of Israel, from all Judah and Benjamin, and *which* they had brought back to Jerusalem.

10 Then they put *it* in the hand of the foremen who had the oversight of the house of the LORD; and they gave it to the workmen who worked in the house of the LORD, to repair and restore the house.

11 They gave *it* to the craftsmen and builders to buy hewn stone and timber for beams, and to floor the houses which the kings of Judah had destroyed.

12 And the men did the work faithfully. Their overseers *were* Jahath and Obadiah the Levites, of the sons of Merari, and Zechariah and Meshullam, of the sons of the Kohathites, to supervise. *Others of* the Levites, all of whom were skillful with instruments of music,

13 *were* over the burden bearers and *were* overseers of all who did work in any kind of service. And *some* of the Levites *were* scribes, officers, and gatekeepers.

14 Now when they brought out the money that was brought into the house of the LORD, Hilkiah the priest found the Book of the Law of the LORD *given* by Moses.

15 Then Hilkiah answered and said to Shaphan the scribe, "I have found the Book of the Law in the house of the LORD." And Hilkiah gave the book to Shaphan.

16 So Shaphan carried the book to the king, bringing the king word, saying, "All that was committed to your servants they are doing.

17 "And they have gathered the money that was found in the house of the LORD, and have delivered it into the hand of the overseers and the workmen."

18 Then Shaphan the scribe told the king, saying, "Hilkiah the priest has given me a book." And Shaphan read it before the king.

19 Thus it happened, when the king heard the words of the Law, that he tore his clothes.

20 Then the king commanded Hilkiah, Ahikam the son of Shaphan, Abdon[a] the son of Micah, Shaphan the scribe, and Asaiah a servant of the king, saying,

21 "Go, inquire of the LORD for me, and for those who are left in Israel and Judah, concerning the words of the book that is found; for great *is* the wrath of the LORD that is poured out on us, because our fathers have not kept the word of the LORD, to do according to all that is written in this book."

22 So Hilkiah and those the king *had appointed* went to Huldah the prophetess, the wife of Shallum the son of Tokhath,[a] the son of Hasrah,[b] keeper of the wardrobe. (She dwelt in Jerusalem in the Second Quarter.) And they spoke to her to that *effect*.

23 Then she answered them, "Thus says the LORD God of Israel, 'Tell the man who sent you to Me,

24 "Thus says the LORD: 'Behold, I will bring calamity on this place and on its inhabitants, all the curses that are written in the book which they have read before the king of Judah,

25 'because they have forsaken Me and burned incense to other gods, that they might provoke Me to anger with all the works of their hands. Therefore My wrath will be poured out on this place, and not be quenched.'"'

26 "But as for the king of Judah, who sent you to inquire of the LORD, in this manner you shall speak to him, 'Thus says the LORD God of Israel: "*Concerning* the words which you have heard—

27 "because your heart was tender, and you humbled yourself before God when you heard His words against this place and against its inhabitants, and you humbled yourself before Me, and you tore your clothes and wept before Me, I also have heard *you*," says the LORD.

28 "Surely I will gather you to your fathers, and you shall be gathered to your grave in peace; and your eyes shall not see all the calamity which I will bring on this place and its inhabitants."'" So they brought back word to the king.

Josiah Restores True Worship

29 Then the king sent and gathered all the elders of Judah and Jerusalem.

30 The king went up to the house of the LORD, with all the men of Judah and the inhabitants of Jerusalem—the priests and the Levites, and all the people, great and small. And he read in their hearing all the words of the Book of the Covenant which had been found in the house of the LORD.

31 Then the king stood in his place and made a covenant before the LORD, to follow the LORD, and to keep His commandments and His testimonies and His statutes with all his heart and all his soul, to perform the words of the covenant that were written in this book.

32 And he made all who were present in Jerusalem and Benjamin take a stand. So the inhabitants of Jerusalem did according to the covenant of God, the God of their fathers.

33 Thus Josiah removed all the abominations from all the country that *belonged* to the children of Israel, and made all who were present in Israel diligently serve the LORD their God. All his days they did not depart from following the LORD God of their fathers.

34:20 [a]*Achbor the son of Michaiah* in 2 Kings 22:12

34:22 [a]Spelled *Tikvah* in 2 Kings 22:14 [b]Spelled *Harhas* in 2 Kings 22:14

Josiah Keeps the Passover

35 Now Josiah kept a Passover to the LORD in Jerusalem, and they slaughtered the Passover *lambs* on the fourteenth *day* of the first month.
2 And he set the priests in their duties and encouraged them for the service of the house of the LORD.
➤ 3 Then he said to the Levites who taught all Israel, who were holy to the LORD: "Put the holy ark in the house which Solomon the son of David, king of Israel, built. *It shall* no longer *be* a burden on *your* shoulders. Now serve the LORD your God and His people Israel.
4 "Prepare *yourselves* according to your fathers' houses, according to your divisions, following the written instruction of David king of Israel and the written instruction of Solomon his son.
5 "And stand in the holy *place* according to the divisions of the fathers' houses of your brethren the *lay* people, and *according to* the division of the father's house of the Levites.
6 "So slaughter the Passover *offerings,* consecrate yourselves, and prepare *them* for your brethren, that *they* may do according to the word of the LORD by the hand of Moses."
7 Then Josiah gave the *lay* people lambs and young goats from the flock, all for Passover *offerings* for all who were present, to the number of thirty thousand, as well as three thousand cattle; these *were* from the king's possessions.
8 And his leaders gave willingly to the people, to the priests, and to the Levites. Hilkiah, Zechariah, and Jehiel, rulers of the house of God, gave to the priests for the Passover *offerings* two thousand six hundred *from the flock,* and three hundred cattle.
9 Also Conaniah, his brothers Shemaiah and Nethanel, and Hashabiah and Jeiel and Jozabad, chief of the Levites, gave to the Levites for Passover *offerings* five thousand *from the flock* and five hundred cattle.
10 So the service was prepared, and the priests stood in their places, and the Levites in their divisions, according to the king's command.
11 And they slaughtered the Passover *offerings;* and the priests sprinkled *the blood* with their hands, while the Levites skinned *the animals.*
12 Then they removed the burnt offerings that *they* might give them to the divisions of the fathers' houses of the *lay* people, to offer to the LORD, as *it is* written in the Book of Moses. And so *they did* with the cattle.
13 Also they roasted the Passover *offerings* with fire according to the ordinance; but the *other* holy *offerings* they boiled in pots, in caldrons, and in pans, and divided *them* quickly among all the *lay* people.
14 Then afterward they prepared portions for themselves and for the priests, because the priests, the sons of Aaron, *were busy* in offering burnt offerings and fat until night; therefore the Levites prepared portions for themselves and for the priests, the sons of Aaron.
15 And the singers, the sons of Asaph, *were* in their places, according to the command of David, Asaph, Heman, and Jeduthun the king's seer. Also the gatekeepers were at each gate; they did not have to leave their position, because their brethren the Levites prepared portions for them.
16 So all the service of the LORD was prepared the same day, to keep the Passover and to offer burnt offerings on the altar of the LORD, according to the command of King Josiah.
17 And the children of Israel who were present kept the Passover at that time, and the Feast of Unleavened Bread for seven days.
18 There had been no Passover kept in Israel like that since the days of Samuel the prophet; and none of the kings of Israel had kept such a Passover as Josiah kept, with the priests and the Levites, all Judah and Israel who were present, and the inhabitants of Jerusalem.
19 In the eighteenth year of the reign of Josiah this Passover was kept.

Josiah Dies in Battle

20 After all this, when Josiah had prepared the temple, Necho king of Egypt came up to fight against Carchemish by the Euphrates; and Josiah went out against him.
21 But he sent messengers to him, saying, "What have I to do with you, king of Judah? *I have* not *come* against you this day, but against the house with which I have war; for God commanded me to make haste. Refrain *from meddling with* God, who *is* with me, lest He destroy you."
22 Nevertheless Josiah would not turn his ➤

LIFE LESSONS

➤ 35:3 — *"Put the holy ark in the house which Solomon the son of David, king of Israel, built. It shall no longer be a burden on your shoulders."*

In the dark days of Manasseh's reign, Levites faithful to the Lord apparently took the ark from the temple and carried it elsewhere for safekeeping. We need those who will risk their lives for the name of Christ (Acts 15:26).

➤ 35:22 — *Nevertheless Josiah would not turn his face from him, but disguised himself so that he might fight with him, and did not heed the words of Necho from the mouth of God.*

God can speak to us in many ways and from many sources, some quite surprising. Our job is to listen for His voice and to discern whether it really is God speaking.

face from him, but disguised himself so that
he might fight with him, and did not heed the
words of Necho from the mouth of God. So he
came to fight in the Valley of Megiddo.
23 And the archers shot King Josiah; and the
king said to his servants, "Take me away, for I
am severely wounded."
24 His servants therefore took him out of that
chariot and put him in the second chariot that
he had, and they brought him to Jerusalem.
So he died, and was buried in *one of* the
tombs of his fathers. And all Judah and Jerusalem mourned for Josiah.
25 Jeremiah also lamented for Josiah. And to
this day all the singing men and the singing
women speak of Josiah in their lamentations.
They made it a custom in Israel; and indeed
they *are* written in the Laments.
26 Now the rest of the acts of Josiah and his
goodness, according to *what was* written in
the Law of the LORD,
27 and his deeds from first to last, indeed
they *are* written in the book of the kings of Israel and Judah.

The Reign and Captivity of Jehoahaz

36 Then the people of the land took Jehoahaz the son of Josiah, and made
him king in his father's place in Jerusalem.
2 Jehoahaz[a] *was* twenty-three years old
when he became king, and he reigned three
months in Jerusalem.
3 Now the king of Egypt deposed him at Jerusalem; and he imposed on the land a tribute
of one hundred talents of silver and a talent of
gold.
4 Then the king of Egypt made *Jehoahaz's*[a]
brother Eliakim king over Judah and Jerusalem, and changed his name to Jehoiakim. And
Necho took Jehoahaz[b] his brother and carried him off to Egypt.

The Reign and Captivity of Jehoiakim

5 Jehoiakim *was* twenty-five years old
when he became king, and he reigned eleven
years in Jerusalem. And he did evil in the
sight of the LORD his God.
6 Nebuchadnezzar king of Babylon came up
against him, and bound him in bronze *fetters*
to carry him off to Babylon.
7 Nebuchadnezzar also carried off *some* of
the articles from the house of the LORD to
Babylon, and put them in his temple at Babylon.
8 Now the rest of the acts of Jehoiakim, the
abominations which he did, and what was
found against him, indeed they *are* written in
the book of the kings of Israel and Judah.
Then Jehoiachin his son reigned in his place.

The Reign and Captivity of Jehoiachin

9 Jehoiachin *was* eight[a] years old when he
became king, and he reigned in Jerusalem
three months and ten days. And he did evil in
the sight of the LORD.
10 At the turn of the year King Nebuchadnezzar summoned *him* and took him to Babylon, with the costly articles from the house of
the LORD, and made Zedekiah, *Jehoiakim's*[a]
brother, king over Judah and Jerusalem.

Zedekiah Reigns in Judah

11 Zedekiah *was* twenty-one years old when
he became king, and he reigned eleven years
in Jerusalem.
12 He did evil in the sight of the LORD his
God, *and* did not humble himself before Jeremiah the prophet, *who spoke* from the mouth
of the LORD.
13 And he also rebelled against King Nebuchadnezzar, who had made him swear *an
oath* by God; but he stiffened his neck and
hardened his heart against turning to the
LORD God of Israel.
14 Moreover all the leaders of the priests and
the people transgressed more and more, *according* to all the abominations of the nations,
and defiled the house of the LORD which He
had consecrated in Jerusalem.

The Fall of Jerusalem

15 And the LORD God of their fathers sent
warnings to them by His messengers, rising
up early and sending *them*, because He had
compassion on His people and on His
dwelling place.
16 But they mocked the messengers of God,

36:2 [a]Masoretic Text reads *Joahaz.* **36:4** [a]Literally *his*
[b]Masoretic Text reads *Joahaz.* **36:9** [a]Some Hebrew manuscripts, Septuagint, Syriac, and 2 Kings 24:8 read *eighteen.*
36:10 [a]Literally *his* (compare 2 Kings 24:17)

LIFE LESSONS

➤ **36:15 — *And the LORD God of their fathers sent warnings to them by His messengers, rising up early and sending them, because He had compassion on His people and on His dwelling place.***

God issues severe warnings against disobedience, not out of anger, but out of compassion. He does not willingly "afflict" us—but He will do so when we leave Him no other options (Lam. 3:32, 33).

➤ **36:16 — *But they mocked the messengers of God, despised His words, and scoffed at His prophets, until the wrath of the LORD arose against His people, till there was no remedy.***

When a culture or a person comes to despise God's Word and habitually mocks and scoffs at His messengers, judgment cannot be far away. Death is imminent for terminally ill patients who reject the only doctor who can help.

despised His words, and scoffed at His prophets, until the wrath of the LORD arose against
His people, till *there was* no remedy.
17 Therefore He brought against them the
king of the Chaldeans, who killed their young
men with the sword in the house of their
sanctuary, and had no compassion on young
man or virgin, on the aged or the weak; He
gave *them* all into his hand.
18 And all the articles from the house of God,
great and small, the treasures of the house of
the LORD, and the treasures of the king and of
his leaders, all *these* he took to Babylon.
19 Then they burned the house of God, broke
down the wall of Jerusalem, burned all its
palaces with fire, and destroyed all its precious possessions.
20 And those who escaped from the sword he
carried away to Babylon, where they became
servants to him and his sons until the rule of
the kingdom of Persia,
21 to fulfill the word of the LORD by the
mouth of Jeremiah, until the land had enjoyed
her Sabbaths. As long as she lay desolate she
kept Sabbath, to fulfill seventy years.

The Proclamation of Cyrus

22 Now in the first year of Cyrus king of Persia, that the word of the LORD by the mouth of
Jeremiah might be fulfilled, the LORD stirred
up the spirit of Cyrus king of Persia, so that
he made a proclamation throughout all his
kingdom, and also *put it* in writing, saying,

23 Thus says Cyrus king of Persia: All the
kingdoms of the earth the LORD God of
heaven has given me. And He has commanded me to build Him a house at Jerusalem which is in Judah. Who *is*
among you of all His people? May the
LORD his God *be* with him, and let him
go up!

LIFE LESSONS

➤ ***36:23 — "Thus says Cyrus king of Persia: All the kingdoms of the earth the LORD God of heaven has given me. And He has commanded me to build Him a house at Jerusalem which is in Judah."***

A pagan king carried Israel into exile, and a pagan king sent them back. Our sovereign God allows the dark moments of our lives to last only so long as it takes for Him to accomplish His purposes in us.

THE BOOK OF EZRA

The Book of Ezra begins where 2 Chronicles ended, by showing how God fulfills His promise to return His people to the Land of Promise after seventy years of exile. Israel's "second exodus," this one from Babylon, is far less impressive than the return from Egypt because only a remnant chose to leave Babylon.

The Book of Ezra relates the story of two returns from Babylon—the first led by Zerubbabel to rebuild the temple (1–6), and the second under the leadership of Ezra to rebuild the spiritual condition of the people (7–10). Between these two accounts stretches a gap of nearly six decades, during which Esther lives and rules as queen of Persia.

Ezra tells a wonderful story of redemption and deliverance. But it also shows us that we can count on the Word of God in all circumstances, no matter how dire they may seem. God, speaking 150 years earlier through the prophet Isaiah (44:28—45:7), had foretold the arrival of one who would free the Jews from captivity. That man was King Cyrus of Persia, who, shortly after defeating the Babylonians, decreed that the Jews would be allowed to return to their homeland.

More than 2,500 years ago, God's people saw firsthand that they could count on their Lord to keep His promises. We can count on Him to do the same. If God said it, we can count on it!

Theme: Ezra highlights the power and reliability of the Word of God. In the very first verse of the book, the author tells us that the events then occurring happened in fulfillment of God's promise: "In the first year of Cyrus king of Persia, *in order to fulfill the word of the Lord* spoken by Jeremiah . . . ."

Author: Unknown. It is generally accepted that while Ezra did not author the entire book, he may have had a hand in writing and compiling parts of it.

Time: Ezra begins with the proclamation of King Cyrus of Persia that sets in motion the homeward journey of the first wave of Jewish captives (around 538–537 B.C.). Fifty-eight years later, after the reconstruction of the temple, a second wave of Jewish captives, under the leadership of Ezra, leaves Babylon and heads for home.

Structure: The Book of Ezra is divided into three main parts: Cyrus's edict and the return of the first wave of Jews to their homeland (1–2); the long-delayed endeavor to rebuild the holy temple (3–6); the exodus of the second wave of Jews from Babylon and the spiritual reforms that took place under the leadership of Ezra (7–10).

As you read Ezra, watch for several life principles that play an important role in this book.

3. God's Word is an immovable anchor in times of storm. *See Ezra 1:1; page 540.*

20. Disappointments are inevitable; discouragement is a choice. *See Ezra 4:1–5; page 543.*

17. We stand tallest and strongest on our knees. *See Ezra 8:21–23; 9:6–15; pages 549; 550.*

15. Brokenness is God's requirement for maximum usefulness. *See Ezra 10:1–4; page 551.*

Life Examples:

CYRUS

An Instrument of God

EZRA 1:1

Mighty men and ruthless conquerors may come and go, imposing their will on those in their path—but the Bible reminds us that the will of only one Ruler ultimately matters.

While the decree of the Persian king Cyrus sent Ezra back to Jerusalem, Scripture makes it clear that he did only what God prompted him to do. The Bible says, "the LORD stirred up the spirit of Cyrus king of Persia Cyrus" to issue his proclamation, "that the word of the LORD by the mouth of Jeremiah might be fulfilled" (2 Chr. 36:22; Ezra 1:1).

Exactly this had been prophesied more than a century before by the prophet Isaiah, who called Cyrus God's "anointed" and "shepherd" and said the king would do everything the Lord had called him to do—even though God had said of Cyrus, "you have not known Me" (Is. 44:24–28; 45:1–5). God rules! And He uses whomever He chooses.

See the Life Principles Index for further study: 18. As children of a sovereign God, we are never victims of our circumstances.

End of the Babylonian Captivity

➤ 1 Now in the first year of Cyrus king of Persia, that the word of the LORD by the
mouth of Jeremiah might be fulfilled, the
LORD stirred up the spirit of Cyrus king of
Persia, so that he made a proclamation
throughout all his kingdom, and also *put it* in
writing, saying,

2 Thus says Cyrus king of Persia: All the kingdoms of the earth the LORD God of heaven has given me. And He has commanded me to build Him a house at Jerusalem which *is* in Judah.
3 Who *is* among you of all His people? May his God be with him, and let him go up to Jerusalem which *is* in Judah, and build the house of the LORD God of Israel (He *is* God), which *is* in Jerusalem.
4 And whoever is left in any place where he dwells, let the men of his place help him with silver and gold, with goods and livestock, besides the freewill offerings for the house of God which *is* in Jerusalem.

5 Then the heads of the fathers' *houses* of ➤
Judah and Benjamin, and the priests and the
Levites, with all whose spirits God had
moved, arose to go up and build the house of
the LORD which *is* in Jerusalem.
6 And all those who *were* around them en- ➤
couraged them with articles of silver and
gold, with goods and livestock, and with precious things, besides all *that* was willingly offered.
7 King Cyrus also brought out the articles of
the house of the LORD, which Nebuchadnezzar had taken from Jerusalem and put in the
temple of his gods;
8 and Cyrus king of Persia brought them out
by the hand of Mithredath the treasurer, and
counted them out to Sheshbazzar the prince
of Judah.
9 This *is* the number of them: thirty gold
platters, one thousand silver platters, twenty-
nine knives,
10 thirty gold basins, four hundred and ten
silver basins of a similar *kind, and* one thousand other articles.
11 All the articles of gold and silver *were* five
thousand four hundred. All *these* Sheshbazzar took with the captives who were brought
from Babylon to Jerusalem.

LIFE LESSONS

➤ **1:1 — *. . . the LORD stirred up the spirit of Cyrus king of Persia . . . .***

Just as the Lord stirred up the spirit of Cyrus to act on behalf of His people, so can He act in the hearts of those in authority over you for your benefit. He is sovereign, and He acts in response to prayer.

➤ **1:5 — *Then the heads of the fathers' houses of Judah and Benjamin, and the priests and the Levites, with all whose spirits God had moved, arose to go up and build the house of the LORD . . . .***

God not only moves the spirits of unbelievers such as Cyrus to act in certain ways, but he also moves the spirits of His people to particular actions. To walk in the Spirit is to obey the initial promptings of the Spirit.

➤ **1:6 — *And all those who were around them encouraged them with articles of silver and gold, with goods and livestock, and with precious things, besides all that was willingly offered.***

God loves to bless what we willingly offer to Him. So the Bible counsels us to give "not grudgingly or of necessity; for God loves a cheerful giver" (2 Cor. 9:7).

The Captives Who Returned to Jerusalem

2 Now[a] these *are* the people of the province
who came back from the captivity, of
those who had been carried away, whom
Nebuchadnezzar the king of Babylon had
carried away to Babylon, and who returned to
Jerusalem and Judah, everyone to his *own*
city.
2 *Those* who came with Zerubbabel *were*
Jeshua, Nehemiah, Seraiah, Reelaiah, Mordecai, Bilshan, Mispar,[a] Bigvai, Rehum,[b] *and*
Baanah. The number of the men of the people
of Israel:
3 the people of Parosh, two thousand one
hundred and seventy-two;
4 the people of Shephatiah, three hundred
and seventy-two;
5 the people of Arah, seven hundred and
seventy-five;
6 the people of Pahath-Moab, of the people
of Jeshua *and* Joab, two thousand eight hundred and twelve;
7 the people of Elam, one thousand two
hundred and fifty-four;
8 the people of Zattu, nine hundred and
forty-five;
9 the people of Zaccai, seven hundred and
sixty;
10 the people of Bani,[a] six hundred and forty-
two;
11 the people of Bebai, six hundred and
twenty-three;
12 the people of Azgad, one thousand two
hundred and twenty-two;
13 the people of Adonikam, six hundred and
sixty-six;
14 the people of Bigvai, two thousand and
fifty-six;
15 the people of Adin, four hundred and fifty-
four;
16 the people of Ater of Hezekiah, ninety-
eight;
17 the people of Bezai, three hundred and
twenty-three;
18 the people of Jorah,[a] one hundred and
twelve;
19 the people of Hashum, two hundred and
twenty-three;
20 the people of Gibbar,[a] ninety-five;
21 the people of Bethlehem, one hundred and
twenty-three;
22 the men of Netophah, fifty-six;
23 the men of Anathoth, one hundred and
twenty-eight;
24 the people of Azmaveth,[a] forty-two;
25 the people of Kirjath Arim,[a] Chephirah,
and Beeroth, seven hundred and forty-three;
26 the people of Ramah and Geba, six hundred and twenty-one;
27 the men of Michmas, one hundred and
twenty-two;
28 the men of Bethel and Ai, two hundred
and twenty-three;
29 the people of Nebo, fifty-two;
30 the people of Magbish, one hundred and
fifty-six;
31 the people of the other Elam, one thousand two hundred and fifty-four;
32 the people of Harim, three hundred and
twenty;
33 the people of Lod, Hadid, and Ono, seven
hundred and twenty-five;
34 the people of Jericho, three hundred and
forty-five;
35 the people of Senaah, three thousand six
hundred and thirty.
36 The priests: the sons of Jedaiah, of the
house of Jeshua, nine hundred and seventy-
three;
37 the sons of Immer, one thousand and fifty-
two;
38 the sons of Pashhur, one thousand two
hundred and forty-seven;
39 the sons of Harim, one thousand and seventeen.
40 The Levites: the sons of Jeshua and Kadmiel, of the sons of Hodaviah,[a] seventy-four.
41 The singers: the sons of Asaph, one hundred and twenty-eight.
42 The sons of the gatekeepers: the sons of
Shallum, the sons of Ater, the sons of Talmon,
the sons of Akkub, the sons of Hatita, and the
sons of Shobai, one hundred and thirty-nine
in all.
43 The Nethinim: the sons of Ziha, the sons
of Hasupha, the sons of Tabbaoth,
44 the sons of Keros, the sons of Siaha,[a] the
sons of Padon,
45 the sons of Lebanah, the sons of Hagabah,
the sons of Akkub,
46 the sons of Hagab, the sons of Shalmai,
the sons of Hanan,
47 the sons of Giddel, the sons of Gahar, the
sons of Reaiah,
48 the sons of Rezin, the sons of Nekoda, the
sons of Gazzam,
49 the sons of Uzza, the sons of Paseah, the
sons of Besai,
50 the sons of Asnah, the sons of Meunim,
the sons of Nephusim,[a]
51 the sons of Bakbuk, the sons of Hakupha,
the sons of Harhur,
52 the sons of Bazluth,[a] the sons of Mehida,
the sons of Harsha,
53 the sons of Barkos, the sons of Sisera, the
sons of Tamah,
54 the sons of Neziah, and the sons of
Hatipha.

2:1 [a]Compare this chapter with Nehemiah 7:6–73. **2:2** [a]Spelled *Mispereth* in Nehemiah 7:7 [b]Spelled *Nehum* in Nehemiah 7:7 **2:10** [a]Spelled *Binnui* in Nehemiah 7:15 **2:18** [a]Called *Hariph* in Nehemiah 7:24 **2:20** [a]Called *Gibeon* in Nehemiah 7:25 **2:24** [a]Called *Beth Azmaveth* in Nehemiah 7:28 **2:25** [a]Called *Kirjath Jearim* in Nehemiah 7:29 **2:40** [a]Spelled *Hodevah* in Nehemiah 7:43 **2:44** [a]Spelled *Sia* in Nehemiah 7:47 **2:50** [a]Spelled *Nephishesim* in Nehemiah 7:52 **2:52** [a]Spelled *Bazlith* in Nehemiah 7:54

55 The sons of Solomon's servants: the sons of Sotai, the sons of Sophereth, the sons of Peruda,[a]
56 the sons of Jaala, the sons of Darkon, the sons of Giddel,
57 the sons of Shephatiah, the sons of Hattil, the sons of Pochereth of Zebaim, and the sons of Ami.[a]
58 All the Nethinim and the children of Solomon's servants were three hundred and ninety-two.
59 And these *were* the ones who came up from Tel Melah, Tel Harsha, Cherub, Addan,[a] and Immer; but they could not identify their father's house or their genealogy,[b] whether they *were* of Israel:
60 the sons of Delaiah, the sons of Tobiah, and the sons of Nekoda, six hundred and fifty-two;
61 and of the sons of the priests: the sons of Habaiah, the sons of Koz,[a] and the sons of Barzillai, who took a wife of the daughters of Barzillai the Gileadite, and was called by their name.
62 These sought their listing *among* those who were registered by genealogy, but they were not found; therefore they *were excluded* from the priesthood as defiled.
63 And the governor[a] said to them that they should not eat of the most holy things till a priest could consult with the Urim and Thummim.
64 The whole assembly together *was* forty-two thousand three hundred *and* sixty,
65 besides their male and female servants, of whom *there were* seven thousand three hundred and thirty-seven; and they had two hundred men and women singers.
66 Their horses *were* seven hundred and thirty-six, their mules two hundred and forty-five,
67 their camels four hundred and thirty-five, and *their* donkeys six thousand seven hundred and twenty.
68 *Some* of the heads of the fathers' *houses*, when they came to the house of the LORD which *is* in Jerusalem, offered freely for the house of God, to erect it in its place:
➤ 69 According to their ability, they gave to the treasury for the work sixty-one thousand gold drachmas, five thousand minas of silver, and one hundred priestly garments.
70 So the priests and the Levites, *some* of the people, the singers, the gatekeepers, and the Nethinim, dwelt in their cities, and all Israel in their cities.

Worship Restored at Jerusalem

3 And when the seventh month had come, and the children of Israel *were* in the cities, the people gathered together as one man to Jerusalem.
2 Then Jeshua the son of Jozadak[a] and his brethren the priests, and Zerubbabel the son of Shealtiel and his brethren, arose and built the altar of the God of Israel, to offer burnt offerings on it, as *it is* written in the Law of Moses the man of God.
3 Though fear *had come* upon them because ➤
of the people of those countries, they set the altar on its bases; and they offered burnt offerings on it to the LORD, *both* the morning and evening burnt offerings.
4 They also kept the Feast of Tabernacles, as *it is* written, and *offered* the daily burnt offerings in the number required by ordinance for each day.
5 Afterwards *they offered* the regular burnt offering, and *those* for New Moons and for all the appointed feasts of the LORD that were consecrated, and *those* of everyone who willingly offered a freewill offering to the LORD.
6 From the first day of the seventh month they began to offer burnt offerings to the LORD, although the foundation of the temple of the LORD had not been laid.
7 They also gave money to the masons and the carpenters, and food, drink, and oil to the people of Sidon and Tyre to bring cedar logs from Lebanon to the sea, to Joppa, according to the permission which they had from Cyrus king of Persia.

Restoration of the Temple Begins

8 Now in the second month of the second year of their coming to the house of God at Jerusalem, Zerubbabel the son of Shealtiel, Jeshua the son of Jozadak,[a] and the rest of their brethren the priests and the Levites, and all those who had come out of the captivity to

2:55 [a]Spelled *Perida* in Nehemiah 7:57 **2:57** [a]Spelled *Amon* in Nehemiah 7:59 **2:59** [a]Spelled *Addon* in Nehemiah 7:61 [b]Literally *seed* **2:61** [a]Or *Hakkoz* **2:63** [a]Hebrew *Tirshatha* **3:2** [a]Spelled *Jehozadak* in 1 Chronicles 6:14 **3:8** [a]Spelled *Jehozadak* in 1 Chronicles 6:14

LIFE LESSONS

➤ ***2:69 — According to their ability, they gave to the treasury for the work . . . .***

God asks us to give according to our ability, not according to what we do not have (Acts 11:29; 2 Cor. 8:12). But God will never be a debtor to anyone. You can never out give God!

➤ ***3:3 — Though fear had come upon them because of the people of those countries, they set the altar on its bases; and they offered burnt offerings on it to the LORD . . . .***

To do what God asks us to do, despite our fear, is to walk in faith. Disappointments are inevitable; discouragement—and shrinking back in fear—is a choice.

Jerusalem, began *work* and appointed the Levites from twenty years old and above to oversee the work of the house of the LORD.
9 Then Jeshua *with* his sons and brothers, Kadmiel *with* his sons, and the sons of Judah,[a] arose as one to oversee those working on the house of God: the sons of Henadad *with* their sons and their brethren the Levites.
10 When the builders laid the foundation of the temple of the LORD, the priests stood[a] in their apparel with trumpets, and the Levites, the sons of Asaph, with cymbals, to praise the LORD, according to the ordinance of David king of Israel.
✳ 11 And they sang responsively, praising and
➤ giving thanks to the LORD:

"For *He is* good,
For His mercy *endures* forever toward
Israel."[a]

Then all the people shouted with a great shout, when they praised the LORD, because the foundation of the house of the LORD was laid.
12 But many of the priests and Levites and heads of the fathers' *houses*, old men who had seen the first temple, wept with a loud voice when the foundation of this temple was laid before their eyes. Yet many shouted aloud for joy,
13 so that the people could not discern the noise of the shout of joy from the noise of the weeping of the people, for the people shouted with a loud shout, and the sound was heard afar off.

Resistance to Rebuilding the Temple

4 Now when the adversaries of Judah and Benjamin heard that the descendants of the captivity were building the temple of the LORD God of Israel,
➤ 2 they came to Zerubbabel and the heads of the fathers' *houses*, and said to them, "Let us build with you, for we seek your God as you *do;* and we have sacrificed to Him since the days of Esarhaddon king of Assyria, who brought us here."
3 But Zerubbabel and Jeshua and the rest of the heads of the fathers' *houses* of Israel said to them, "You may do nothing with us to build a house for our God; but we alone will build to the LORD God of Israel, as King Cyrus the king of Persia has commanded us."
4 Then the people of the land tried to discourage the people of Judah. They troubled them in building,
5 and hired counselors against them to frustrate their purpose all the days of Cyrus king of Persia, even until the reign of Darius king of Persia.

Rebuilding of Jerusalem Opposed

6 In the reign of Ahasuerus, in the beginning of his reign, they wrote an accusation against the inhabitants of Judah and Jerusalem.
7 In the days of Artaxerxes also, Bishlam, Mithredath, Tabel, and the rest of their companions wrote to Artaxerxes king of Persia; and the letter *was* written in Aramaic script, and translated into the Aramaic language.
8 Rehum[a] the commander and Shimshai the scribe wrote a letter against Jerusalem to King Artaxerxes in this fashion:

9 From[a] Rehum the commander, Shimshai the scribe, and the rest of their companions—*representatives* of the Dinaites, the Apharsathchites, the Tarpelites, the people of Persia and Erech and Babylon and Shushan,[b] the Dehavites, the Elamites,
10 and the rest of the nations whom the great and noble Osnapper took captive and settled in the cities of Samaria and the remainder beyond the River[a]—and so forth.[b]

11 (This *is* a copy of the letter that they sent him)

To King Artaxerxes from your servants, the men *of the region* beyond the River, and so forth:[a]

12 Let it be known to the king that the Jews who came up from you have come to us at Jerusalem, and are building the rebellious and evil city, and are finishing *its* walls and repairing the foundations.
13 Let it now be known to the king that, if

3:9 [a]Or *Hodaviah* (compare 2:40) 3:10 [a]Following Septuagint, Syriac, and Vulgate; Masoretic Text reads *they stationed the priests.* 3:11 [a]Compare Psalm 136:1 4:8 [a]The original language of Ezra 4:8 through 6:18 is Aramaic. 4:9 [a]Literally *Then* [b]Or *Susa* 4:10 [a]That is, the Euphrates [b]Literally *and now* 4:11 [a]Literally *and now*

LIFE LESSONS

➤ 3:11 — *And they sang responsively, praising and giving thanks to the LORD.*

Throughout the Bible, singing plays a large role in the worship of God and a walk of faith. Joyful singing connects our hearts to God, and our hearts are what He's really after.

➤ 4:2 — *. . . they came to Zerubbabel and the heads of the fathers' houses, and said to them, "Let us build with you, for we seek your God as you do . . . ."*

The adversaries of God and of His people do not always attack with a frontal assault; sometimes they try to seem friendly and sympathetic. A life of faith requires us to remain alert at all times (1 Pet. 5:8).

ANSWERS TO LIFE'S QUESTIONS

How can I find the strength to endure when I face spiritual opposition?

EZRA 4:1–24

In the Book of Ezra we read of a beleaguered people who faced opposition in doing what God had commissioned them to do. They sought to rebuild the holy temple that was destroyed by Nebuchadnezzar decades earlier, and they faced stiff opposition from the locals, deceitful offers of "help," and open attacks from the outside.

Still, God's people successfully completed the temple restoration. How? By developing a spiritual quality we all need in the Christian life: endurance.

God knows the Christian life is not easy. And it never will get easy, no matter how long we live. In this world, we will face opposition, both from the world and from the enemy of our souls, the devil. Jesus told us, "In the world you will have tribulation" (John 16:33).

Surrounded by such opposition, if we're going to live in a way that pleases God, then we must develop endurance. The Bible is full of examples of people who endured opposition to their work and who received their reward as a result. Hebrews 11, often called the "Faith Hall of Fame," lists some of those heroes.

But what exactly is involved in endurance? At least four things play a big role:

❶ ***Encouragement from others.***
The writer of Hebrews encourages us to ponder the lives of those he lists in chapter 11. He refers to them as "a cloud of witnesses" (Heb. 12:1). We cannot see this cloud of witnesses, but we can read about them and glean from their inspiring stories of endurance.

❷ ***Getting rid of hindrances.***
Hebrews tells us, "Let us lay aside every weight, and the sin which so easily ensnares us" (12:1). This means we need to identify those things that could slow us down, including the sin God has brought to our attention.

❸ ***Running the race.***
Hebrews 12:1 ends by telling us, "and let us run with endurance the race that is set before us." When the going gets rough, we don't run away. We can't be quitters. The longer we push the limits, the stronger our faith becomes.

❹ ***Fixing our eyes on Christ.***
Hebrews 12:2 advises us to keep "looking unto Jesus, the author and finisher of our faith." Nothing helps us endure like seeing the final prize before us—and that prize is Christ Himself. Do you want the prize? Then you must endure. And Jesus promises to help you.

See the Life Principles Index for further study:
28. No Christian has ever been called to "go it alone" in his or her walk of faith.
18. As children of a sovereign God, we are never victims of our circumstances.

this city is built and the walls completed, they will not pay tax, tribute, or custom, and the king's treasury will be diminished.
14 Now because we receive support from the palace, it was not proper for us to see the king's dishonor; therefore we have sent and informed the king,
15 that search may be made in the book of the records of your fathers. And you will find in the book of the records and know that this city *is* a rebellious city, harmful to kings and provinces, and that they have incited sedition within the city in former times, for which cause this city was destroyed.
16 We inform the king that if this city is rebuilt and its walls are completed, the result will be that you will have no dominion beyond the River.

17 The king sent an answer:

To Rehum the commander, *to* Shimshai the scribe, *to* the rest of their companions who dwell in Samaria, and *to* the remainder beyond the River:

Peace, and so forth.[a]

18 The letter which you sent to us has been clearly read before me.
19 And I gave the command, and a search has been made, and it was found that

4:17 [a]Literally *and now*

this city in former times has revolted against kings, and rebellion and sedition have been fostered in it.
20 There have also been mighty kings over Jerusalem, who have ruled over all *the region* beyond the River; and tax, tribute, and custom were paid to them.
21 Now give the command to make these men cease, that this city may not be built until the command is given by me.
22 Take heed now that you do not fail to do this. Why should damage increase to the hurt of the kings?

➤ **23** Now when the copy of King Artaxerxes' letter *was* read before Rehum, Shimshai the scribe, and their companions, they went up in haste to Jerusalem against the Jews, and by force of arms made them cease.
24 Thus the work of the house of God which *is* at Jerusalem ceased, and it was discontinued until the second year of the reign of Darius king of Persia.

Restoration of the Temple Resumed

➤ **5** Then the prophet Haggai and Zechariah the son of Iddo, prophets, prophesied to the Jews who *were* in Judah and Jerusalem, in the name of the God of Israel, *who was* over them.
➤ 2 So Zerubbabel the son of Shealtiel and Jeshua the son of Jozadak[a] rose up and began to build the house of God which *is* in Jerusalem; and the prophets of God *were* with them, helping them.
3 At the same time Tattenai the governor of *the region* beyond the River[a] and Shethar-Boznai and their companions came to them and spoke thus to them: "Who has commanded you to build this temple and finish this wall?"
4 Then, accordingly, we told them the names of the men who were constructing this building.
5 But the eye of their God was upon the elders of the Jews, so that they could not make them cease till a report could go to Darius. Then a written answer was returned concerning this *matter.*
6 This is a copy of the letter that Tattenai sent:

The governor of *the region* beyond the River, and Shethar-Boznai, and his companions, the Persians who *were in the region* beyond the River, to Darius the king.

7 (They sent a letter to him, in which was written thus)

To Darius the king:

All peace.

8 Let it be known to the king that we went into the province of Judea, to the temple of the great God, which is being built with heavy stones, and timber is being laid in the walls; and this work goes on diligently and prospers in their hands.
9 Then we asked those elders, *and* spoke thus to them: "Who commanded you to build this temple and to finish these walls?"
10 We also asked them their names to inform you, that we might write the names of the men who *were* chief among them.
11 And thus they returned us an answer, saying: "We are the servants of the God of heaven and earth, and we are rebuilding the temple that was built many years ago, which a great king of Israel built and completed.
12 "But because our fathers provoked the God of heaven to wrath, He gave them into the hand of Nebuchadnezzar king of Babylon, the Chaldean, *who* destroyed this temple and carried the people away to Babylon.
13 "However, in the first year of Cyrus king of Babylon, King Cyrus issued a decree to build this house of God.
14 "Also, the gold and silver articles of the house of God, which Nebuchadnezzar had taken from the temple that *was* in Jerusalem and carried into the temple of Babylon—those King Cyrus took from the temple of Babylon, and they were given to one named Sheshbazzar, whom he had made governor.

5:2 [a]Spelled *Jehozadak* in 1 Chronicles 6:14 **5:3** [a]That is, the Euphrates

LIFE LESSONS

➤ **4:23 —** ***Now when the copy of King Artaxerxes' letter was read before Rehum, Shimshai the scribe, and their companions, they went up in haste to Jerusalem against the Jews, and by force of arms made them cease.***

Sometimes God allows opposition to His will to succeed for a time. We may not know why, and unexpected developments may dishearten us. But adversity is merely a setback from which we take our greatest leaps forward.

➤ **5:1, 2 —** ***Haggai and Zechariah . . . prophesied to the Jews who were in Judah and Jerusalem . . . . So Zerubbabel the son of Shealtiel and Jeshua the son of Jozadak rose up and began to build the house of God . . . .***

God gave His people strength to continue the work through the words of His faithful prophets. It is always so. God's Word is an immovable anchor in times of storm.

15 “And he said to him, ‘Take these articles;
go, carry them to the temple *site* that *is*
in Jerusalem, and let the house of God
be rebuilt on its former site.’
16 “Then the same Sheshbazzar came *and*
laid the foundation of the house of God
which *is* in Jerusalem; but from that
time even until now it has been under
construction, and it is not finished.”

17 Now therefore, if *it seems* good to the
king, let a search be made in the king’s
treasure house, which *is* there in
Babylon, whether it is *so* that a decree
was issued by King Cyrus to build this
house of God at Jerusalem, and let the
king send us his pleasure concerning
this *matter.*

The Decree of Darius

6 Then King Darius issued a decree, and a
search was made in the archives,[a] where
the treasures were stored in Babylon.
2 And at Achmetha,[a] in the palace that *is* in
the province of Media, a scroll was found, and
in it a record *was* written thus:

3 In the first year of King Cyrus, King
Cyrus issued a decree *concerning* the
house of God at Jerusalem: “Let the
house be rebuilt, the place where they
offered sacrifices; and let the
foundations of it be firmly laid, its
height sixty cubits *and* its width sixty
cubits,
4 *with* three rows of heavy stones and one
row of new timber. Let the expenses be
paid from the king’s treasury.
5 Also let the gold and silver articles of
the house of God, which Nebuchadnezzar took from the temple which *is* in Jerusalem and brought to Babylon, be
restored and taken back to the temple
which *is* in Jerusalem, *each* to its place;
and deposit *them* in the house of God”—
6 Now *therefore,* Tattenai, governor of *the
region* beyond the River, and Shethar-
Boznai, and your companions the Persians who *are* beyond the River, keep
yourselves far from there.
7 Let the work of this house of God alone;
let the governor of the Jews and the elders of the Jews build this house of God
on its site.
8 Moreover I issue a decree *as to* what
you shall do for the elders of these Jews,
for the building of this house of God:
Let the cost be paid at the king’s
expense from taxes *on the region*
beyond the River; this is to be given
immediately to these men, so that they
are not hindered.
9 And whatever they need—young bulls,
rams, and lambs for the burnt offerings
of the God of heaven, wheat, salt, wine,
and oil, according to the request of the
priests who *are* in Jerusalem—let it be
given them day by day without fail,
10 that they may offer sacrifices of sweet
aroma to the God of heaven, and pray
for the life of the king and his sons.
11 Also I issue a decree that whoever alters
this edict, let a timber be pulled from his
house and erected, and let him be
hanged on it; and let his house be made
a refuse heap because of this.
12 And may the God who causes His name
to dwell there destroy any king or people who put their hand to alter it, or to
destroy this house of God which is in Jerusalem. I Darius issue a decree; let it be
done diligently.

The Temple Completed and Dedicated

13 Then Tattenai, governor of *the region* beyond the River, Shethar-Boznai, and their
companions diligently did according to what
King Darius had sent.
14 So the elders of the Jews built, and they
prospered through the prophesying of Haggai
the prophet and Zechariah the son of Iddo.
And they built and finished *it,* according to
the commandment of the God of Israel, and
according to the command of Cyrus, Darius,
and Artaxerxes king of Persia.
15 Now the temple was finished on the third
day of the month of Adar, which was in the
sixth year of the reign of King Darius.
16 Then the children of Israel, the priests and
the Levites and the rest of the descendants of

6:1 [a]Literally *house of the scrolls* **6:2** [a]Probably *Ecbatana,* the ancient capital of Media

LIFE LESSONS

➤ **6:12 — *“And may the God who causes His name to dwell there destroy any king or people who put their hand to alter it, or to destroy this house of God which is in Jerusalem. I Darius issue a decree . . . .”***

When men once more tried to stop the work that God had decreed (5:3), the Lord used their opposition to further his cause. As children of a sovereign God, we are never victims of our circumstances.

➤ **6:16 — *Then the children of Israel, the priests and the Levites and the rest of the descendants of the captivity, celebrated the dedication of this house of God with joy.***

No life of faith is complete without regular celebrations of joy. Jesus spoke His word to us, “that My joy may remain in you, and that your joy may be full” (John 15:11).

the captivity, celebrated the dedication of this
house of God with joy.
17 And they offered sacrifices at the dedication of this house of God, one hundred bulls,
two hundred rams, four hundred lambs, and
as a sin offering for all Israel twelve male
goats, according to the number of the tribes of
Israel.
18 They assigned the priests to their divisions and the Levites to their divisions, over
the service of God in Jerusalem, as it is written in the Book of Moses.

The Passover Celebrated

19 And the descendants of the captivity kept
the Passover on the fourteenth *day* of the first
month.
20 For the priests and the Levites had purified themselves; all of them *were ritually*
clean. And they slaughtered the Passover
lambs for all the descendants of the captivity,
for their brethren the priests, and for themselves.
➤ 21 Then the children of Israel who had returned from the captivity ate together with all
who had separated themselves from the filth
of the nations of the land in order to seek the
LORD God of Israel.
22 And they kept the Feast of Unleavened
Bread seven days with joy; for the LORD made
them joyful, and turned the heart of the king
of Assyria toward them, to strengthen their
hands in the work of the house of God, the
God of Israel.

The Arrival of Ezra

7 Now after these things, in the reign of Artaxerxes king of Persia, Ezra the son of
Seraiah, the son of Azariah, the son of
Hilkiah,
2 the son of Shallum, the son of Zadok, the
son of Ahitub,
3 the son of Amariah, the son of Azariah,
the son of Meraioth,
4 the son of Zerahiah, the son of Uzzi, the
son of Bukki,
5 the son of Abishua, the son of Phinehas,
the son of Eleazar, the son of Aaron the chief
priest—
6 this Ezra came up from Babylon; and he ➤
was a skilled scribe in the Law of Moses,
which the LORD God of Israel had given. The
king granted him all his request, according to
the hand of the LORD his God upon him.
7 *Some* of the children of Israel, the priests,
the Levites, the singers, the gatekeepers, and
the Nethinim came up to Jerusalem in the
seventh year of King Artaxerxes.
8 And Ezra came to Jerusalem in the fifth
month, which *was* in the seventh year of the
king.
9 On the first *day* of the first month he
began *his* journey from Babylon, and on the
first *day* of the fifth month he came to Jerusalem, according to the good hand of his God
upon him.
10 For Ezra had prepared his heart to seek ➤
the Law of the LORD, and to do *it*, and to teach
statutes and ordinances in Israel.

The Letter of Artaxerxes to Ezra

11 This *is* a copy of the letter that King Artaxerxes gave Ezra the priest, the scribe, expert in the words of the commandments of the
LORD, and of His statutes to Israel:

12 Artaxerxes,[a] king of kings,

To Ezra the priest, a scribe of the Law of
the God of heaven:
Perfect *peace*, and so forth.[b]

13 I issue a decree that all those of the
people of Israel and the priests and
Levites in my realm, who volunteer to
go up to Jerusalem, may go with you.
14 And whereas you are being sent by the
king and his seven counselors to inquire
concerning Judah and Jerusalem, with
regard to the Law of your God which *is*
in your hand;
15 and *whereas you are* to carry the silver
and gold which the king and his counselors have freely offered to the God of
Israel, whose dwelling *is* in Jerusalem;
16 and *whereas* all the silver and gold that

7:12 [a]The original language of Ezra 7:12–26 is Aramaic.
[b]Literally *and now*

LIFE LESSONS

➤ 6:21 — *Then the children of Israel who had returned from the captivity ate together with all who had separated themselves from the filth of the nations of the land in order to seek the LORD God of Israel.*

If we truly want to seek the Lord, we have to separate ourselves from the evil practices of an unbelieving world. James reminds us that, "friendship with the world is enmity with God" (James 4:4).

➤ 7:6 — . . . *The king granted him all his request, according to the hand of the LORD his God upon him.*

When the hand of God is upon us, even kings support our causes.

➤ 7:10 — *For Ezra had prepared his heart to seek the Law of the LORD, and to do it, and to teach statutes and ordinances in Israel.*

Spiritual maturity requires spiritual preparation. It does not happen by chance or simply through the passage of time. If we wish to grow in God, we must prepare our hearts to do so.

Life Examples:

EZRA

Applying God's Word

EZRA 7:10

Ezra is a great example of what commitment to applying God's Word can do for both an individual and a nation.

The Persian king Artaxerxes gave Ezra permission to travel from Babylon to his ancestral homeland in Jerusalem. As a godly priest, Ezra felt compelled to improve the spiritual condition of the remnant of his people, and so he worked diligently to bring about several religious and cultural reforms among his discouraged countrymen.

Ezra's life demonstrates the importance not merely of learning and knowing the Word of God, but also of practicing how to regularly apply it in daily life. Because God had put him in a position of spiritual authority, Ezra also did everything he could think of to pass on to others what he had learned in his Bible study. Ezra wasn't just a hearer of God's Word; he was also an effective and deeply committed doer of it (see James 1:22).

See the Life Principles Index for further study:
3. God's Word is an immovable anchor in times of storm.

you may find in all the province of
Babylon, along with the freewill offering
of the people and the priests, *are to be*
freely offered for the house of their God
in Jerusalem—
17 now therefore, be careful to buy with
this money bulls, rams, and lambs, with
their grain offerings and their drink offerings, and offer them on the altar of
the house of your God in Jerusalem.
18 And whatever seems good to you and
your brethren to do with the rest of the
silver and the gold, do it according to
the will of your God.
19 Also the articles that are given to you
for the service of the house of your God,
deliver in full before the God of Jerusalem.
20 And whatever more may be needed for
the house of your God, which you may
have occasion to provide, pay *for it* from
the king's treasury.
21 And I, *even* I, Artaxerxes the king, issue
a decree to all the treasurers who *are in
the region* beyond the River, that
whatever Ezra the priest, the scribe of
the Law of the God of heaven, may
require of you, let it be done diligently,
22 up to one hundred talents of silver, one
hundred kors of wheat, one hundred
baths of wine, one hundred baths of oil,
and salt without prescribed limit.
23 Whatever is commanded by the God of
heaven, let it diligently be done for the
house of the God of heaven. For why
should there be wrath against the realm
of the king and his sons?
24 Also we inform you that it shall not be
lawful to impose tax, tribute, or custom
on any of the priests, Levites, singers,
gatekeepers, Nethinim, or servants of
this house of God.
25 And you, Ezra, according to your God-
given wisdom, set magistrates and
judges who may judge all the people
who *are in the region* beyond the River,
all such as know the laws of your God;
and teach those who do not know *them.*
26 Whoever will not observe the law of
your God and the law of the king, let
judgment be executed speedily on him,
whether *it be* death, or banishment, or
confiscation of goods, or imprisonment.

27 Blessed *be* the LORD God of our fathers,
who has put *such a thing* as this in the king's
heart, to beautify the house of the LORD which
is in Jerusalem,
28 and has extended mercy to me before the
king and his counselors, and before all the
king's mighty princes.
So I was encouraged, as the hand of the
LORD my God *was* upon me; and I gathered
leading men of Israel to go up with me.

Heads of Families Who Returned with Ezra

8 These *are* the heads of their fathers'
houses, and *this is* the genealogy of those
who went up with me from Babylon, in the
reign of King Artaxerxes:

LIFE LESSONS

➤ **7:25 — *And you, Ezra, according to your God-given wisdom, set magistrates and judges who may judge all the people . . . .***

The king did not grant all his requests simply because something odd came over him. He had been watching Ezra and recognized him as a man with "God-given wisdom." Our behavior *matters.*

2 of the sons of Phinehas, Gershom; of the
sons of Ithamar, Daniel; of the sons of David,
Hattush;
3 of the sons of Shecaniah, of the sons of
Parosh, Zechariah; and registered with him
were one hundred and fifty males;
4 of the sons of Pahath-Moab, Eliehoenai
the son of Zerahiah, and with him two hundred males;
5 of the sons of Shechaniah,[a] Ben-Jahaziel,
and with him three hundred males;
6 of the sons of Adin, Ebed the son of Jonathan, and with him fifty males;
7 of the sons of Elam, Jeshaiah the son of
Athaliah, and with him seventy males;
8 of the sons of Shephatiah, Zebadiah the
son of Michael, and with him eighty males;
9 of the sons of Joab, Obadiah the son of Jehiel, and with him two hundred and eighteen
males;
10 of the sons of Shelomith,[a] Ben-Josiphiah,
and with him one hundred and sixty males;
11 of the sons of Bebai, Zechariah the son of
Bebai, and with him twenty-eight males;
12 of the sons of Azgad, Johanan the son of
Hakkatan, and with him one hundred and ten
males;
13 of the last sons of Adonikam, whose
names *are* these—Eliphelet, Jeiel, and Shemaiah—and with them sixty males;
14 also of the sons of Bigvai, Uthai and Zab-
bud, and with them seventy males.

Servants for the Temple

15 Now I gathered them by the river that
flows to Ahava, and we camped there three
days. And I looked among the people and the
priests, and found none of the sons of Levi
there.
16 Then I sent for Eliezer, Ariel, Shemaiah, Elnathan, Jarib, Elnathan, Nathan, Zechariah,
and Meshullam, leaders; also for Joiarib and
Elnathan, men of understanding.
17 And I gave them a command for Iddo the
chief man at the place Casiphia, and I told
them what they should say to Iddo *and* his
brethren[a] the Nethinim at the place
Casiphia—that they should bring us servants
for the house of our God.
18 Then, by the good hand of our God upon
us, they brought us a man of understanding,
of the sons of Mahli the son of Levi, the son of
Israel, namely Sherebiah, with his sons and
brothers, eighteen men;
19 and Hashabiah, and with him Jeshaiah of
the sons of Merari, his brothers and their
sons, twenty men;
20 also of the Nethinim, whom David and the
leaders had appointed for the service of the
Levites, two hundred and twenty Nethinim.
All of them were designated by name.

Fasting and Prayer for Protection

21 Then I proclaimed a fast there at the river
of Ahava, that we might humble ourselves before our God, to seek from Him the right way
for us and our little ones and all our possessions.
22 For I was ashamed to request of the king
an escort of soldiers and horsemen to help us
against the enemy on the road, because we
had spoken to the king, saying, "The hand of
our God *is* upon all those for good who seek
Him, but His power and His wrath *are* against
all those who forsake Him."
23 So we fasted and entreated our God for
this, and He answered our prayer.

Gifts for the Temple

24 And I separated twelve of the leaders of
the priests—Sherebiah, Hashabiah, and ten of
their brethren with them—
25 and weighed out to them the silver, the
gold, and the articles, the offering for the
house of our God which the king and his
counselors and his princes, and all Israel *who
were* present, had offered.
26 I weighed into their hand six hundred and
fifty talents of silver, silver articles *weighing*
one hundred talents, one hundred talents of
gold,
27 twenty gold basins *worth* a thousand
drachmas, and two vessels of fine polished
bronze, precious as gold.
28 And I said to them, "You *are* holy to the
LORD; the articles *are* holy also; and the silver
and the gold *are* a freewill offering to the
LORD God of your fathers.
29 "Watch and keep *them* until you weigh
them before the leaders of the priests and the
Levites and heads of the fathers' *houses* of Israel in Jerusalem, *in* the chambers of the
house of the LORD."
30 So the priests and the Levites received the

8:5 [a]Following Masoretic Text and Vulgate; Septuagint reads *the sons of Zatho, Shechaniah.* **8:10** [a]Following Masoretic Text and Vulgate; Septuagint reads *the sons of Banni, Shelomith.* **8:17** [a]Following Vulgate; Masoretic Text reads *to Iddo his brother;* Septuagint reads *to their brethren.*

LIFE LESSONS

➤ 8:21 — *Then I proclaimed a fast there at the river of Ahava, that we might humble ourselves before our God, to seek from Him the right way for us and our little ones and all our possessions.*

Ezra prayed not only for what we call "traveling mercies," but also that God might lead them on the way along exactly the right route. Prayer is life's greatest time saver.

silver and the gold and the articles by weight,
to bring *them* to Jerusalem to the house of
our God.

The Return to Jerusalem

➤ **31** Then we departed from the river of Ahava
on the twelfth *day* of the first month, to go to
Jerusalem. And the hand of our God was
upon us, and He delivered us from the hand of
the enemy and from ambush along the road.
32 So we came to Jerusalem, and stayed
there three days.
33 Now on the fourth day the silver and the
gold and the articles were weighed in the
house of our God by the hand of Meremoth
the son of Uriah the priest, and with him *was*
Eleazar the son of Phinehas; with them *were*
the Levites, Jozabad the son of Jeshua and
Noadiah the son of Binnui,
34 with the number *and* weight of everything. All the weight was written down at that
time.
35 The children of those who had been carried away captive, who had come from the
captivity, offered burnt offerings to the God of
Israel: twelve bulls for all Israel, ninety-six
rams, seventy-seven lambs, and twelve male
goats *as* a sin offering. All *this was* a burnt offering to the LORD.
36 And they delivered the king's orders to the
king's satraps and the governors *in the region*
beyond the River. So they gave support to the
people and the house of God.

Intermarriage with Pagans

9 When these things were done, the leaders
came to me, saying, "The people of Israel
and the priests and the Levites have not separated themselves from the peoples of the
lands, with respect to the abominations of the
Canaanites, the Hittites, the Perizzites, the Jebusites, the Ammonites, the Moabites, the
Egyptians, and the Amorites.
2 "For they have taken some of their daughters *as wives* for themselves and their sons, so
that the holy seed is mixed with the peoples
of *those* lands. Indeed, the hand of the leaders
and rulers has been foremost in this trespass."
3 So when I heard this thing, I tore my garment and my robe, and plucked out some of
the hair of my head and beard, and sat down
astonished.
4 Then everyone who trembled at the words
of the God of Israel assembled to me, because
of the transgression of those who had been
carried away captive, and I sat astonished
until the evening sacrifice.
5 At the evening sacrifice I arose from my
fasting; and having torn my garment and
my robe, I fell on my knees and spread out my
hands to the LORD my God.
6 And I said: "O my God, I am too ashamed
and humiliated to lift up my face to You, my
God; for our iniquities have risen higher than
our heads, and our guilt has grown up to the
heavens.
7 "Since the days of our fathers to this day
we *have been* very guilty, and for our iniquities we, our kings, *and* our priests have been
delivered into the hand of the kings of the
lands, to the sword, to captivity, to plunder,
and to humiliation, as *it is* this day.
8 "And now for a little while grace has been
shown from the LORD our God, to leave us a
remnant to escape, and to give us a peg in His
holy place, that our God may enlighten our
eyes and give us a measure of revival in our
bondage.
9 "For we *were* slaves. Yet our God did not
forsake us in our bondage; but He extended
mercy to us in the sight of the kings of Persia,
to revive us, to repair the house of our God, to
rebuild its ruins, and to give us a wall in Judah and Jerusalem.
10 "And now, O our God, what shall we say
after this? For we have forsaken Your commandments,
11 "which You commanded by Your servants
the prophets, saying, 'The land which you are
entering to possess is an unclean land, with
the uncleanness of the peoples of the lands,
with their abominations which have filled it
from one end to another with their impurity.

LIFE LESSONS

➤ ***8:31 — Then we departed from the river of Ahava . . . . And the hand of our God was upon us, and He delivered us from the hand of the enemy and from ambush along the road.***

Would Ezra have arrived safely at Jerusalem without prayer? Would bandits have ambushed him or enemies attacked him had he not prayed? Because he did not want to find out, he fought and won those battles ahead of time through prayer.

➤ ***9:3 — So when I heard this thing, I tore my garment and my robe, and plucked out some of the hair of my head and beard, and sat down astonished.***

That we should sin blatantly in the presence of God's Word and in full view of His response to past sin should astonish all of us. And our astonishment should lead to quick confession and repentance.

➤ ***9:9 — "For we were slaves. Yet our God did not forsake us in our bondage; but He extended mercy to us in the sight of the kings of Persia . . . ."***

Even in judgment, God loves to show mercy. We must be careful not to presume upon His grace, but rather must thank Him for it and seek to obey His word through that same grace.

12 'Now therefore, do not give your daughters as wives for their sons, nor take their daughters to your sons; and never seek their peace or prosperity, that you may be strong and eat the good of the land, and leave *it* as an inheritance to your children forever.'
13 "And after all that has come upon us for our evil deeds and for our great guilt, since You our God have punished us less than our iniquities *deserve,* and have given us *such* deliverance as this,
14 "should we again break Your commandments, and join in marriage with the people *committing* these abominations? Would You not be angry with us until You had consumed *us,* so that *there would be* no remnant or survivor?
15 "O LORD God of Israel, You *are* righteous, for we are left as a remnant, as *it is* this day. Here we *are* before You, in our guilt, though no one can stand before You because of this!"

Confession of Improper Marriages

10 Now while Ezra was praying, and while he was confessing, weeping, and bowing down before the house of God, a very large assembly of men, women, and children gathered to him from Israel; for the people wept very bitterly.
➤ 2 And Shechaniah the son of Jehiel, *one* of the sons of Elam, spoke up and said to Ezra, "We have trespassed against our God, and have taken pagan wives from the peoples of the land; yet now there is hope in Israel in spite of this.
➤ 3 "Now therefore, let us make a covenant with our God to put away all these wives and those who have been born to them, according to the advice of my master and of those who tremble at the commandment of our God; and let it be done according to the law.
4 "Arise, for *this* matter *is* your *responsibility.* We also *are* with you. Be of good courage, and do *it.*"
5 Then Ezra arose, and made the leaders of the priests, the Levites, and all Israel swear an oath that they would do according to this word. So they swore an oath.
6 Then Ezra rose up from before the house of God, and went into the chamber of Jehohanan the son of Eliashib; and *when* he came there, he ate no bread and drank no water, for he mourned because of the guilt of those from the captivity.
7 And they issued a proclamation throughout Judah and Jerusalem to all the descendants of the captivity, that they must gather at Jerusalem,
8 and that whoever would not come within three days, according to the instructions of the leaders and elders, all his property would be confiscated, and he himself would be separated from the assembly of those from the captivity.
9 So all the men of Judah and Benjamin gathered at Jerusalem within three days. It *was* the ninth month, on the twentieth of the month; and all the people sat in the open square of the house of God, trembling because of *this* matter and because of heavy rain.
10 Then Ezra the priest stood up and said to them, "You have transgressed and have taken pagan wives, adding to the guilt of Israel.
11 "Now therefore, make confession to the LORD God of your fathers, and do His will; separate yourselves from the peoples of the land, and from the pagan wives."
12 Then all the assembly answered and said with a loud voice, "Yes! As you have said, so we must do.
13 "But *there are* many people; *it is* the season for heavy rain, and we are not able to stand outside. Nor *is this* the work of one or two days, for *there are* many of us who have transgressed in this matter.
14 "Please, let the leaders of our entire assembly stand; and let all those in our cities who have taken pagan wives come at appointed times, together with the elders and judges of their cities, until the fierce wrath of our God is turned away from us in this matter."
15 Only Jonathan the son of Asahel and Jahaziah the son of Tikvah opposed this, and Meshullam and Shabbethai the Levite gave them support.
16 Then the descendants of the captivity did so. And Ezra the priest, *with* certain heads of the fathers' *households,* were set apart by the fathers' households, each of them by name;

LIFE LESSONS

➤ 10:2 — "We have trespassed against our God, and have taken pagan wives from the peoples of the land; yet now there is hope in Israel in spite of this."

Who can fathom the great grace of God? Despite our rebellion and sin, yet there is hope. While we must never take this for granted, we should continually give God praise and thanks for it.

➤ 10:3 — ". . . let us make a covenant with our God to put away all these wives and those who have been born to them, according to the advice of my master and of those who tremble at the commandment of our God . . . ."

Why should we "tremble at the commandment of our God"? Because He always means what He says, in regard to both blessing and judgment. We need more trembling at His Word!

and they sat down on the first day of the tenth
month to examine the matter.
17 By the first day of the first month they finished *questioning* all the men who had taken pagan wives.

Pagan Wives Put Away

18 And among the sons of the priests who had taken pagan wives *the following* were found of the sons of Jeshua the son of Jozadak,[a] and his brothers: Maaseiah, Eliezer, Jarib, and Gedaliah.
19 And they gave their promise that they would put away their wives; and *being* guilty, *they presented* a ram of the flock as their trespass offering.
20 Also of the sons of Immer: Hanani and Zebadiah;
21 of the sons of Harim: Maaseiah, Elijah, Shemaiah, Jehiel, and Uzziah;
22 of the sons of Pashhur: Elioenai, Maaseiah, Ishmael, Nethanel, Jozabad, and Elasah.
23 Also of the Levites: Jozabad, Shimei, Kelaiah (the same *is* Kelita), Pethahiah, Judah, and Eliezer.
24 Also of the singers: Eliashib; and of the gatekeepers: Shallum, Telem, and Uri.
25 And others of Israel: of the sons of Parosh: Ramiah, Jeziah, Malchiah, Mijamin, Eleazar, Malchijah, and Benaiah;
26 of the sons of Elam: Mattaniah, Zechariah, Jehiel, Abdi, Jeremoth, and Eliah;
27 of the sons of Zattu: Elioenai, Eliashib, Mattaniah, Jeremoth, Zabad, and Aziza;
28 of the sons of Bebai: Jehohanan, Hananiah, Zabbai, *and* Athlai;
29 of the sons of Bani: Meshullam, Malluch, Adaiah, Jashub, Sheal, *and* Ramoth;[a]
30 of the sons of Pahath-Moab: Adna, Chelal, Benaiah, Maaseiah, Mattaniah, Bezalel, Binnui, and Manasseh;
31 *of* the sons of Harim: Eliezer, Ishijah, Malchijah, Shemaiah, Shimeon,
32 Benjamin, Malluch, *and* Shemariah;
33 of the sons of Hashum: Mattenai, Mattattah, Zabad, Eliphelet, Jeremai, Manasseh, *and* Shimei;
34 of the sons of Bani: Maadai, Amram, Uel,
35 Benaiah, Bedeiah, Cheluh,[a]
36 Vaniah, Meremoth, Eliashib,
37 Mattaniah, Mattenai, Jaasai,[a]
38 Bani, Binnui, Shimei,
39 Shelemiah, Nathan, Adaiah,
40 Machnadebai, Shashai, Sharai,
41 Azarel, Shelemiah, Shemariah,
42 Shallum, Amariah, *and* Joseph;
43 of the sons of Nebo: Jeiel, Mattithiah, Zabad, Zebina, Jaddai,[a] Joel, *and* Benaiah.
44 All these had taken pagan wives, and *some* of them had wives *by whom* they had children.

10:18 [a]Spelled *Jehozadak* in 1 Chronicles 6:14 **10:29** [a]Or *Jeremoth* **10:35** [a]Or *Cheluhi,* or *Cheluhu* **10:37** [a]Or *Jaasu* **10:43** [a]Or *Jaddu*

THE BOOK OF

NEHEMIAH

The Hebrew name for the Book of Nehemiah is *Nehemyah*, meaning, "Comfort of Yahweh." The book is named after its chief character, whose name appears in the opening verse.

Perhaps nowhere is the expression of good leadership better exemplified than in the remarkable life of Nehemiah. As cupbearer to King Artaxerxes of Persia, Nehemiah held a prominent position in the royal court. As cupbearer, Nehemiah was far more than a mere servant. His duties included advising the king and acting as his bodyguard and food-taster (to make sure no one had poisoned the king's food). All of these were high-level positions requiring loyalty and trustworthiness.

Nehemiah, a contemporary of Ezra, leads the third and last return to Jerusalem after the Babylonian exile. His concern for the welfare of Jerusalem and its inhabitants prompts him to take bold action. It all started when Jews who had survived the Babylonian captivity entered the Persian capital and encountered Nehemiah, who inquired of the people's welfare in Jerusalem. They responded that the walls surrounding the city lay in ruins, the people felt disillusioned and weary, and the situation had become very depressing. Their discouraging words launched Nehemiah into action.

Granted permission to return to his homeland by the king, Nehemiah challenged his countrymen to arise and rebuild the shattered wall of Jerusalem. Despite opposition from without and abuse from within, they completed the task in only fifty-two days—a feat even the enemies of Israel had to attribute to God's enabling. By contrast, the task of reviving and reforming the people of God within the rebuilt wall demanded years of Nehemiah's godly life and leadership.

Theme: The Book of Nehemiah emphasizes restoration, both physical and spiritual. As soon as Nehemiah heard of the nation's great need, he went to God in prayer (Neh. 1:5–11), then inspected the walls around Jerusalem, then addressed the spiritual condition of the people who lived there—and through his efforts, God restored both the city and its people.

Author: Unknown, but a large portion of this book is thought to be Nehemiah's autobiography.

Time: The events in the Book of Nehemiah took place around 445 to 420 B.C., a span of about twenty-five years.

Structure: Chapters 1 through 7 record the rebuilding of the walls around Jerusalem; chapters 8 through 13 deal with the restoration of the people's spiritual lives.

As you read Nehemiah, watch for several life principles that play an important role in this book:

14. God acts on behalf of those who wait for Him.. *See Nehemiah 1:4—2:6; page 554.*

8. Fight all your battles on your knees and you win every time. *See Nehemiah 1:4; 2:4; 4:9; 6:9; pages 554; 556; 559; 562.*

13. Listening to God is essential to walking with God. *See Nehemiah 9:30; page 567.*

ANSWERS TO LIFE'S QUESTIONS

What good does fasting do us?

NEH. 1:4

Upon hearing the sad news of Jerusalem's pitiful state, Nehemiah agonized over the city's plight. His response can teach us all something useful: "When I heard these words, I sat down and wept and mourned for days, and I was fasting and praying before the God of heaven" (Neh. 1:4).

When we reach points of despondency, despair, confusion or desperation, going before the Lord in payer and fasting can bring peace, clarity, and direction to our situations. Jerusalem's devastation led Nehemiah to his knees in prayer and fasting.

Fasting in the biblical context means to abstain from food for a given period of time. Fasting doesn't just mean "going hungry" for a few days. It means abstaining for the purpose of focusing your attention on God and what He might have to say to you.

Consider many excellent reasons for fasting:

To receive divine intervention when we are helpless. Nehemiah needed God's guidance, so he fasted and prayed. And he received what he needed.

To know God's will for our lives. When Daniel felt unsure about God's next step for his life, he sought him through fasting (Dan. 9:3). Fasting clears the mind and allows us to hear more clearly what God is saying to us.

To respond to times of crisis. During times of crisis, we need more than ever to focus on what God wants us to do. When King Jehoshaphat and Judah landed in trouble, fasting was the recommended course of action (2 Chr. 20:3).

To prepare for ministry. We need to clearly hear the Lord's voice before we embark on His work. As we prepare for what God calls us to, fasting puts us in a proper attitude before God to conform us to that purpose and to His image.

For personal cleansing. Fasting is often practiced as a means of personal cleansing for the physical body, as a way to remove impurities. But it works the same way in our spiritual lives. When we realize that we are steeped in sin, fasting helps bring healing and cleansing (Joel 2:12).

For victory over temptation, habits, and bondage. Fasting equips us for the battle we wage against Satan and against our own flesh. When we fail repeatedly to defeat some sin, we should seek the Lord's help—and fasting is one of the spiritual disciplines that can help us secure victory (Is. 58:6).

See the Life Principles Index for further study:
27. Prayer is life's greatest time saver.
10. If necessary, God will move heaven and earth to show us His will.

Nehemiah Prays for His People

1 The words of Nehemiah the son of Hachaliah.
It came to pass in the month of Chislev, *in* the twentieth year, as I was in Shushan[a] the citadel,
2 that Hanani one of my brethren came with men from Judah; and I asked them concerning the Jews who had escaped, who had survived the captivity, and concerning Jerusalem.
3 And they said to me, "The survivors who are left from the captivity in the province *are* there in great distress and reproach. The wall of Jerusalem *is* also broken down, and its gates are burned with fire."
4 So it was, when I heard these words, that I sat down and wept, and mourned *for many* days; I was fasting and praying before the God of heaven.

1:1 [a]Or *Susa*

LIFE LESSONS

➤ ***1:4 — So it was, when I heard these words, that I sat down and wept, and mourned for many days; I was fasting and praying before the God of heaven.***

Have you ever noticed how many of the great things God does for His people get started with fasting and prayer? Fasting helps to focus our prayers, and through our prayers we tap into the limitless power of God.

WHAT THE BIBLE SAYS ABOUT **EFFECTIVELY TACKLING A PRAYER BURDEN**

Neh. 1:4–6

When Nehemiah heard that his people lived in great distress and reproach, that the walls of Jerusalem lay in ruins, and that the gates of the city remained burned and broken, he responded with prayer:

"I sat down and wept, and mourned for many days . . . . And I said: 'I pray, LORD God of heaven, O great and awesome God, You who keep Your covenant and mercy with those who love You and observe Your commandments, please let Your ear be attentive and Your eyes open, that You may hear the prayer of Your servant which I pray before You now, day and night.'" (Neh. 1:4–6)

Nehemiah was experiencing a prayer burden.

A prayer burden can be defined as a strong motivation to pray for others and to carry the needs of others before God in prayer until God responds.

The Bible has a great deal to say about burdens. We are to bear one another's burdens (Gal. 6:2). We are to go the second mile in helping another person (Matt. 5:41). Much of our ability to bear natural burdens is derived from developing our ability to carry spiritual burdens in prayer.

A sense of spiritual weight usually accompanies a prayer burden.

A sense of spiritual weight usually accompanies a prayer burden—a heaviness of heart, a drag on one's emotions, a spirit of mourning, or a feeling of restlessness that we can't seem to shift ourselves away from a problem or need that has come to our attention.

God does not act in many situations because we do not pray. God waits for either the co-instigator of the negative situation to cry out to Him for forgiveness, or for the victim of the negative situation to cry out to Him for mercy. Then He will act.

If you feel burdened to pray for another person, God desires to act on that person's behalf. He places the burden to pray on your heart, and He moves through the opening. As you pray, you can get in on the blessing that God has for that person through an answered prayer.

See the Life Principles Index for further study:
8. Fight all your battles on your knees and you win every time.
17. We stand tallest and strongest on our knees.

➤ 5 And I said: "I pray, LORD God of heaven, O great and awesome God, *You* who keep *Your* covenant and mercy with those who love You[a] and observe Your[b] commandments,
6 "please let Your ear be attentive and Your eyes open, that You may hear the prayer of Your servant which I pray before You now, day and night, for the children of Israel Your servants, and confess the sins of the children of Israel which we have sinned against You. Both my father's house and I have sinned.
7 "We have acted very corruptly against You, and have not kept the commandments, the statutes, nor the ordinances which You commanded Your servant Moses.
➤ 8 "Remember, I pray, the word that You commanded Your servant Moses, saying, '*If* you are unfaithful, I will scatter you among the nations;[a]
9 'but *if* you return to Me, and keep My commandments and do them, though some of you were cast out to the farthest part of the heavens, *yet* I will gather them from there, and bring them to the place which I have chosen as a dwelling for My name.'[a]
10 "Now these *are* Your servants and Your people, whom You have redeemed by Your great power, and by Your strong hand.
11 "O Lord, I pray, please let Your ear be attentive to the prayer of Your servant, and to the prayer of Your servants who desire to fear Your name; and let Your servant prosper this day, I pray, and grant him mercy in the sight of this man." For I was the king's cupbearer.

Nehemiah Sent to Judah

2 And it came to pass in the month of Nisan, in the twentieth year of King Artaxerxes, *when* wine *was* before him, that I took the wine and gave it to the king. Now I had never been sad in his presence before.
2 Therefore the king said to me, "Why *is* your face sad, since you *are* not sick? This *is* nothing but sorrow of heart." So I became dreadfully afraid,
3 and said to the king, "May the king live forever! Why should my face not be sad, when the city, the place of my fathers' tombs, *lies* waste, and its gates are burned with fire?"
4 Then the king said to me, "What do you request?" So I prayed to the God of heaven. ◄
5 And I said to the king, "If it pleases the king, and if your servant has found favor in your sight, I ask that you send me to Judah, to the city of my fathers' tombs, that I may rebuild it."
6 Then the king said to me (the queen also sitting beside him), "How long will your journey be? And when will you return?" So it pleased the king to send me; and I set him a time.
7 Furthermore I said to the king, "If it pleases the king, let letters be given to me for the governors *of the region* beyond the River,[a] that they must permit me to pass through till I come to Judah,
8 "and a letter to Asaph the keeper of the king's forest, that he must give me timber to make beams for the gates of the citadel which *pertains* to the temple,[a] for the city wall, and for the house that I will occupy." And the king granted *them* to me according to the good hand of my God upon me. ◄
9 Then I went to the governors *in the region* beyond the River, and gave them the king's letters. Now the king had sent captains of the army and horsemen with me.
10 When Sanballat the Horonite and Tobiah the Ammonite official[a] heard *of it,* they were deeply disturbed that a man had come to seek the well-being of the children of Israel.

Nehemiah Views the Wall of Jerusalem

11 So I came to Jerusalem and was there three days.

1:5 [a]Literally *Him* [b]Literally *His* **1:8** [a]Leviticus 26:33 **1:9** [a]Deuteronomy 30:2–5 **2:7** [a]That is, the Euphrates, and so elsewhere in this book **2:8** [a]Literally *house* **2:10** [a]Literally *servant,* and so elsewhere in this book

LIFE LESSONS

➤ 1:5 — *". . . O great and awesome God, You who keep Your covenant and mercy with those who love You and observe Your commandments . . . ."*

Love for God is what enables us to keep His commandments; that's why it must always come first. Jesus said, "If you love Me, keep My commandments" (John 14:15).

➤ 1:8 — *"Remember, I pray, the word that You commanded Your servant Moses . . . ."*

We pray powerfully when we pray according to the promises of God. When we pray based on who He is and what He has done rather than on who we are and what we have done, we attract God's blessing.

➤ 2:4 — *Then the king said to me, "What do you request?" So I prayed to the God of heaven.*

Potent prayers can be of many types. This must be one of the shortest on record, uttered wordlessly in the seconds after the king's question. But when God is in our prayers, mighty things happen.

➤ 2:8 — *And the king granted them to me according to the good hand of my God upon me.*

Nehemiah found out the truth of Proverbs 21:1: "The king's heart is in the hand of the LORD, like the rivers of water; He turns it wherever He wishes."

ANSWERS TO LIFE'S QUESTIONS

What should I do when I feel the need to act in haste?

NEH. 2:3

Nowhere in Scripture does God tell anyone to rush into a decision. He just doesn't operate that way.

Anyone in the financial world knows that success rarely follows a snap decision. Though at times we may need to hear from God quickly, God will never tell us to rush in blindly. We may have to move swiftly, but we can move swiftly in the will of God and still not hurry into a situation.

Satan always encourages us to act immediately, because he knows if we back off and think long enough, we may reconsider. How many people have made decisions they regretted for the rest of their lives? Psalm 27:14 exhorts us, "Wait on the LORD; Be of good courage, and He shall strengthen your heart; wait, I say, on the LORD!" Psalm 62:5 explains, "My soul, wait silently for God alone, for my expectation is from Him."

If we feel an overwhelming urge to act spontaneously, we had better pull in the reins. God wants us to get all the details in their proper places.

King Saul lost his throne because he acted hastily. The prophet Samuel told him to wait for him seven days at Gilgal, "till I come to you and show you what you should do" (1 Sam. 10:8). By the seventh day, Samuel still hadn't arrived. With a hostile Philistine army pressing in on him, Saul decided to take matters in his own hands and he prepared burnt offerings to invoke the Lord's favor. As soon as he completed the offering, Samuel appeared. Saul offered some lame excuses, but his rashness disqualified him for a long and peaceful reign. Getting ahead of God is a terrible mistake, with distasteful consequences.

On the other hand, Nehemiah, cupbearer to King Artaxerxes, patiently waited for God's timing . . . with glorious results. He fasted and prayed "for many days" (1:4), then waited for the right time to bring his concern before the king. Rather than dash into action, Nehemiah waited before God. In fact, he beseeched the Lord for a period of four months, until one day the king himself asked Nehemiah why he seemed so downcast. Nehemiah explained the situation, and within days, the king sent him off to Jerusalem with all the necessary authority and building materials (2:1–11). Nehemiah waited until God put all the particulars in place, and then he moved.

We should do the same.

See the Life Principles Index for further study:
14. God acts on behalf of those who wait for Him.

➤ 12 Then I arose in the night, I and a few men
with me; I told no one what my God had put
in my heart to do at Jerusalem; nor was there
any animal with me, except the one on which
I rode.
13 And I went out by night through the Valley
Gate to the Serpent Well and the Refuse Gate,
and viewed the walls of Jerusalem which
were broken down and its gates which were
burned with fire.
14 Then I went on to the Fountain Gate and to
the King's Pool, but *there was* no room for the
animal under me to pass.
15 So I went up in the night by the valley,
and viewed the wall; then I turned back
and entered by the Valley Gate, and so returned.
16 And the officials did not know where I
had gone or what I had done; I had not yet
told the Jews, the priests, the nobles, the officials, or the others who did the work.
17 Then I said to them, "You see the distress
that we *are* in, how Jerusalem *lies* waste, and
its gates are burned with fire. Come and let us

LIFE LESSONS

➤ 2:12 — *Then I arose in the night, I and a few men with me; I told no one what my God had put in my heart to do at Jerusalem . . . .*

Nehemiah showed himself to be a man of God when he obeyed the initial promptings of God's Spirit.

➤ 2:18 — *And I told them of the hand of my God which had been good upon me, and also of the king's words that he had spoken to me. So they said, "Let us rise up and build."*

Nehemiah could not have accomplished what God put on his heart unless he had encouraged God's people

build the wall of Jerusalem, that we may no
longer be a reproach."
➤ 18 And I told them of the hand of my God
which had been good upon me, and also of
the king's words that he had spoken to me. So
they said, "Let us rise up and build." Then
they set their hands to *this* good *work*.
19 But when Sanballat the Horonite, Tobiah
the Ammonite official, and Geshem the Arab
heard *of it*, they laughed at us and despised
us, and said, "What *is* this thing that you are
doing? Will you rebel against the king?"
✳ 20 So I answered them, and said to them,
➤ "The God of heaven Himself will prosper us;
therefore we His servants will arise and build,
but you have no heritage or right or memorial
in Jerusalem."

Rebuilding the Wall

3 Then Eliashib the high priest rose up with
his brethren the priests and built the
Sheep Gate; they consecrated it and hung its
doors. They built as far as the Tower of the
Hundred,[a] *and* consecrated it, then as far as
the Tower of Hananel.
2 Next to *Eliashib*[a] the men of Jericho built.
And next to them Zaccur the son of Imri built.
3 Also the sons of Hassenaah built the Fish
Gate; they laid its beams and hung its doors
with its bolts and bars.
4 And next to them Meremoth the son
of Urijah, the son of Koz,[a] made repairs. Next
to them Meshullam the son of Berechiah,
the son of Meshezabel, made repairs. Next
to them Zadok the son of Baana made repairs.
➤ 5 Next to them the Tekoites made repairs;
but their nobles did not put their shoulders[a] to
the work of their Lord.
6 Moreover Jehoiada the son of Paseah and
Meshullam the son of Besodeiah repaired the
Old Gate; they laid its beams and hung its
doors, with its bolts and bars.
7 And next to them Melatiah the Gibeonite,
Jadon the Meronothite, the men of Gibeon
and Mizpah, repaired the residence[a] of the
governor *of the region* beyond the River.
8 Next to him Uzziel the son of Harhaiah,
one of the goldsmiths, made repairs. Also
next to him Hananiah, one[a] of the perfumers,
made repairs; and they fortified Jerusalem as
far as the Broad Wall.
9 And next to them Rephaiah the son of
Hur, leader of half the district of Jerusalem,
made repairs.
10 Next to them Jedaiah the son of
Harumaph made repairs in front of his house.
And next to him Hattush the son of Hashabniah made repairs.
11 Malchijah the son of Harim and Hashub
the son of Pahath-Moab repaired another section, as well as the Tower of the Ovens.
12 And next to him was Shallum the son of
Hallohesh, leader of half the district of Jerusalem; he and his daughters made repairs.
13 Hanun and the inhabitants of Zanoah repaired the Valley Gate. They built it, hung its
doors with its bolts and bars, and *repaired* a
thousand cubits of the wall as far as the
Refuse Gate.
14 Malchijah the son of Rechab, leader of the
district of Beth Haccerem, repaired the
Refuse Gate; he built it and hung its doors
with its bolts and bars.
15 Shallun the son of Col-Hozeh, leader of
the district of Mizpah, repaired the Fountain
Gate; he built it, covered it, hung its doors
with its bolts and bars, and repaired the wall
of the Pool of Shelah by the King's Garden, as
far as the stairs that go down from the City of
David.
16 After him Nehemiah the son of Azbuk,
leader of half the district of Beth Zur, made
repairs as far as *the place* in front of the
tombs[a] of David, to the man-made pool, and
as far as the House of the Mighty.
17 After him the Levites, *under* Rehum the
son of Bani, made repairs. Next to him
Hashabiah, leader of half the district of
Keilah, made repairs for his district.
18 After him their brethren, *under* Bavai[a] the
son of Henadad, leader of the *other* half of the
district of Keilah, made repairs.
19 And next to him Ezer the son of Jeshua,
the leader of Mizpah, repaired another section in front of the Ascent to the Armory at
the buttress.

3:1 [a]Hebrew *Hammeah*, also at 12:39 **3:2** [a]Literally *On his hand* **3:4** [a]Or *Hakkoz* **3:5** [a]Literally *necks* **3:7** [a]Literally *throne* **3:8** [a]Literally *the son* **3:16** [a]Septuagint, Syriac, and Vulgate read *tomb*. **3:18** [a]Following Masoretic Text and Vulgate; some Hebrew manuscripts, Septuagint, and Syriac read *Binnui* (compare verse 24).

LIFE LESSONS

in the task. None of us are in this adventure alone; God wants us to walk it together.

➤ **2:20 — *"The God of heaven Himself will prosper us; therefore we His servants will arise and build, but you have no heritage or right or memorial in Jerusalem."***

Nehemiah understood his task to be not primarily political or civic, but spiritual, even though it concerned the building of a physical wall. When God puts something on our heart, the core issue is always spiritual.

➤ **3:5 — *Next to them the Tekoites made repairs; but their nobles did not put their shoulders to the work of their Lord.***

Even if our leaders or the prominent men and women among us do not put their shoulders to the task, we are to move ahead in faith anyway. Obedience always brings blessing.

20 After him Baruch the son of Zabbai[a] carefully repaired the other section, from the buttress to the door of the house of Eliashib the high priest.
21 After him Meremoth the son of Urijah, the son of Koz,[a] repaired another section, from the door of the house of Eliashib to the end of the house of Eliashib.
22 And after him the priests, the men of the plain, made repairs.
23 After him Benjamin and Hasshub made repairs opposite their house. After them Azariah the son of Maaseiah, the son of Ananiah, made repairs by his house.
24 After him Binnui the son of Henadad repaired another section, from the house of Azariah to the buttress, even as far as the corner.
25 Palal the son of Uzai *made repairs* opposite the buttress, and on the tower which projects from the king's upper house that *was* by the court of the prison. After him Pedaiah the son of Parosh *made repairs.*
26 Moreover the Nethinim who dwelt in Ophel *made repairs* as far as *the place* in front of the Water Gate toward the east, and on the projecting tower.
27 After them the Tekoites repaired another section, next to the great projecting tower, and as far as the wall of Ophel.
28 Beyond the Horse Gate the priests made repairs, each in front of his *own* house.
29 After them Zadok the son of Immer made repairs in front of his *own* house. After him Shemaiah the son of Shechaniah, the keeper of the East Gate, made repairs.
30 After him Hananiah the son of Shelemiah, and Hanun, the sixth son of Zalaph, repaired another section. After him Meshullam the son of Berechiah made repairs in front of his dwelling.
31 After him Malchijah, one of the goldsmiths, made repairs as far as the house of the Nethinim and of the merchants, in front of the Miphkad[a] Gate, and as far as the upper room at the corner.
32 And between the upper room at the corner, as far as the Sheep Gate, the goldsmiths and the merchants made repairs.

The Wall Defended Against Enemies

4 But it so happened, when Sanballat heard
that we were rebuilding the wall, that he was furious and very indignant, and mocked the Jews.
2 And he spoke before his brethren and the army of Samaria, and said, "What are these feeble Jews doing? Will they fortify themselves? Will they offer sacrifices? Will they complete it in a day? Will they revive the stones from the heaps of rubbish—*stones* that are burned?"
3 Now Tobiah the Ammonite *was* beside him, and he said, "Whatever they build, if even a fox goes up *on it,* he will break down their stone wall."
4 Hear, O our God, for we are despised; turn their reproach on their own heads, and give them as plunder to a land of captivity!
5 Do not cover their iniquity, and do not let their sin be blotted out from before You; for they have provoked *You* to anger before the builders.
6 So we built the wall, and the entire wall was joined together up to half its *height,* for the people had a mind to work.
7 Now it happened, when Sanballat, Tobiah, the Arabs, the Ammonites, and the Ashdodites heard that the walls of Jerusalem were being restored and the gaps were beginning to be closed, that they became very angry,
8 and all of them conspired together to come *and* attack Jerusalem and create confusion.
9 Nevertheless we made our prayer to our God, and because of them we set a watch against them day and night.
10 Then Judah said, "The strength of the laborers is failing, and *there is* so much rubbish that we are not able to build the wall."
11 And our adversaries said, "They will neither know nor see anything, till we come into their midst and kill them and cause the work to cease."
12 So it was, when the Jews who dwelt near

3:20 [a]A few Hebrew manuscripts, Syriac, and Vulgate read *Zaccai.* **3:21** [a]Or *Hakkoz* **3:31** [a]Literally *Inspection* or *Recruiting*

LIFE LESSONS

➤ **4:1 — *But it so happened, when Sanballat heard that we were rebuilding the wall, that he was furious and very indignant, and mocked the Jews.***

Dogs bark, mockers mock. Let them mock; our task is to obey God and leave all the consequences to Him.

➤ **4:4 — *Hear, O our God, for we are despised; turn their reproach on their own heads, and give them as plunder to a land of captivity!***

Nehemiah responded to his enemies' scorn not with sharp barbs of his own, but with prayer. He knew that we stand tallest and strongest on our knees.

➤ **4:9 — *Nevertheless we made our prayer to our God, and because of them we set a watch against them day and night.***

When we pray for God's protection, He often inspires us to take sensible precautions against the danger we see. We ask God to do only what only He can do, and we do what He gives us the strength and wisdom to do.

Life Examples: NEHEMIAH

Daring to Believe

NEH. 4:14

Despite moments of doubt and unease, Nehemiah demonstrated great faith in God. Driven by a vision that he believed came from God, he dared to trust in a sovereign Lord who always keeps His promises.

Nehemiah told the people, "The God of heaven Himself will prosper us; therefore we His servants will arise and build" (Neh. 2:20). Nehemiah understood that if He didn't depend on God to get the job done, it would never get done. But he also understood that genuine belief requires practical action, so he told his colleagues, "Remember the Lord, great and awesome, and fight for your brethren" (4:14)—an ancient version of "praise the Lord and pass the ammunition."

Because Nehemiah trusted God and moved forward, he successfully completed the vision God had given him. Whatever challenge confronts you, God has promised to grant you success when you put your trust in Him.

See the Life Principles Index for further study:
9. Trusting God means looking beyond what we can see to what God sees.

them came, that they told us ten times, "From
whatever place you turn, *they will be* upon
us."
13 Therefore I positioned *men* behind the
lower parts of the wall, at the openings; and I
set the people according to their families,
with their swords, their spears, and their
bows.
➤ 14 And I looked, and arose and said to the
nobles, to the leaders, and to the rest of the
people, "Do not be afraid of them. Remember
the Lord, great and awesome, and fight for
your brethren, your sons, your daughters,
your wives, and your houses."
15 And it happened, when our enemies heard
that it was known to us, and *that* God had
brought their plot to nothing, that all of us returned to the wall, everyone to his work.
16 So it was, from that time on, *that* half of
my servants worked at construction, while
the other half held the spears, the shields, the
bows, and *wore* armor; and the leaders *were*
behind all the house of Judah.
17 Those who built on the wall, and those
who carried burdens, loaded themselves so
that with one hand they worked at construction, and with the other held a weapon.
18 Every one of the builders had his sword
girded at his side as he built. And the one who
sounded the trumpet *was* beside me.
19 Then I said to the nobles, the rulers, and
the rest of the people, "The work *is* great and
extensive, and we are separated far from one
another on the wall.
20 "Wherever you hear the sound of the
trumpet, rally to us there. Our God will fight
for us."
21 So we labored in the work, and half of *the*
men[a] held the spears from daybreak until the
stars appeared.
22 At the same time I also said to the people,
"Let each man and his servant stay at night in
Jerusalem, that they may be our guard by
night and a working party by day."
23 So neither I, my brethren, my servants,
nor the men of the guard who followed me
took off our clothes, *except* that everyone
took them off for washing.

Nehemiah Deals with Oppression

5 And there was a great outcry of the people
and their wives against their Jewish
brethren.
2 For there were those who said, "We, our
sons, and our daughters *are* many; therefore
let us get grain, that we may eat and live."
3 There were also *some* who said, "We have
mortgaged our lands and vineyards and
houses, that we might buy grain because of
the famine."
4 There were also those who said, "We have
borrowed money for the king's tax *on* our
lands and vineyards.
5 "Yet now our flesh *is* as the flesh of our
brethren, our children as their children; and
indeed we are forcing our sons and our

4:21 [a]Literally *them*

LIFE LESSONS

➤ **4:14 — *"Do not be afraid of them. Remember the Lord, great and awesome, and fight for your brethren, your sons, your daughters, your wives, and your houses."***

The best way to fight fear is to "remember the Lord, great and awesome." When we fear Him most of all, other fears diminish and eventually disappear.

daughters to be slaves, and *some* of our daughters have been brought into slavery. *It is* not in our power *to redeem them*, for other men have our lands and vineyards."

6 And I became very angry when I heard their outcry and these words.

➤ 7 After serious thought, I rebuked the nobles and rulers, and said to them, "Each of you is exacting usury from his brother." So I called a great assembly against them.

8 And I said to them, "According to our ability we have redeemed our Jewish brethren who were sold to the nations. Now indeed, will you even sell your brethren? Or should they be sold to us?" Then they were silenced and found nothing *to say*.

➤ 9 Then I said, "What you are doing *is* not good. Should you not walk in the fear of our God because of the reproach of the nations, our enemies?

10 "I also, *with* my brethren and my servants, am lending them money and grain. Please, let us stop this usury!

11 "Restore now to them, even this day, their lands, their vineyards, their olive groves, and their houses, also a hundredth of the money and the grain, the new wine and the oil, that you have charged them."

12 So they said, "We will restore *it*, and will require nothing from them; we will do as you say." Then I called the priests, and required an oath from them that they would do according to this promise.

13 Then I shook out the fold of my garment[a] and said, "So may God shake out each man from his house, and from his property, who does not perform this promise. Even thus may he be shaken out and emptied." And all the assembly said, "Amen!" and praised the LORD. Then the people did according to this promise.

The Generosity of Nehemiah

14 Moreover, from the time that I was appointed to be their governor in the land of Judah, from the twentieth year until the thirty-second year of King Artaxerxes, twelve years, neither I nor my brothers ate the governor's provisions.

15 But the former governors who *were* before me laid burdens on the people, and took from them bread and wine, besides forty shekels of silver. Yes, even their servants bore rule over the people, but I did not do so, because of the fear of God.

16 Indeed, I also continued the work on this wall, and we[a] did not buy any land. All my servants *were* gathered there for the work.

17 And at my table *were* one hundred and fifty Jews and rulers, besides those who came to us from the nations around us.

18 Now *that* which was prepared daily *was* one ox *and* six choice sheep. Also fowl were prepared for me, and once every ten days an abundance of all kinds of wine. Yet in spite of this I did not demand the governor's provisions, because the bondage was heavy on this people.

19 Remember me, my God, for good, *according to* all that I have done for this people. ➤

Conspiracy Against Nehemiah

6 Now it happened when Sanballat, Tobiah, Geshem the Arab, and the rest of our enemies heard that I had rebuilt the wall, and *that* there were no breaks left in it (though at that time I had not hung the doors in the gates),

2 that Sanballat and Geshem sent to me, saying, "Come, let us meet together among the villages in the plain of Ono." But they thought to do me harm. ➤

3 So I sent messengers to them, saying, "I *am* doing a great work, so that I cannot come down. Why should the work cease while I leave it and go down to you?"

4 But they sent me this message four times, and I answered them in the same manner.

5 Then Sanballat sent his servant to me as before, the fifth time, with an open letter in his hand.

5:13 [a]Literally *my lap* **5:16** [a]Following Masoretic Text; Septuagint, Syriac, and Vulgate read *I*.

LIFE LESSONS

➤ 5:7 — *After serious thought, I rebuked the nobles and rulers . . . .*

A solid prayer life and a close relationship to God do not minimize the need for clear and extensive thinking. Rather, these things empower and sharpen our thoughts.

➤ 5:9 — *Then I said, "What you are doing is not good. Should you not walk in the fear of our God because of the reproach of the nations, our enemies?"*

Part of walking in the fear of God means that we watch carefully how we behave in front of those who do not yet know God. As Paul wrote, "Walk in wisdom toward those who are outside" (Col. 4:5).

➤ 5:19 — *Remember me, my God, for good, according to all that I have done for this people.*

Praying for your own blessing is not selfish, but biblical, especially when you labor on behalf of others, as Nehemiah did.

➤ 6:2 — *Sanballat and Geshem sent to me, saying, "Come, let us meet together among the villages in the plain of Ono." But they thought to do me harm.*

What the devil cannot accomplish by scorn and intimidation, he will try to accomplish by deception and hateful schemes. Only by immersing ourselves in the Word of God and through prayer will we avoid his traps.

6 In it *was* written:

It is reported among the nations, and
Geshem[a] says, *that* you and the Jews
plan to rebel; therefore, according to
these rumors, you are rebuilding the wall,
that you may be their king.
7 And you have also appointed prophets to
proclaim concerning you at Jerusalem,
saying, "*There is* a king in Judah!" Now
these matters will be reported to the king.
So come, therefore, and let us consult together.

8 Then I sent to him, saying, "No such things
as you say are being done, but you invent
them in your own heart."
9 For they all *were trying to* make us afraid,
saying, "Their hands will be weakened in the
work, and it will not be done."

Now therefore, *O God,* strengthen my
hands.
10 Afterward I came to the house of Shemaiah
the son of Delaiah, the son of Mehetabel,
who *was* a secret informer; and he said, "Let
us meet together in the house of God, within
the temple, and let us close the doors of the
temple, for they are coming to kill you; indeed,
at night they will come to kill you."
11 And I said, "Should such a man as I flee?
And who *is there* such as I who would go into
the temple to save his life? I will not go in!"
12 Then I perceived that God had not sent
him at all, but that he pronounced *this*
prophecy against me because Tobiah and
Sanballat had hired him.
➤ 13 For this reason he *was* hired, that I should
be afraid and act that way and sin, so *that*
they might have *cause* for an evil report, that
they might reproach me.
14 My God, remember Tobiah and Sanballat,
according to these their works, and the
prophetess Noadiah and the rest of the
prophets who would have made me afraid.

The Wall Completed

15 So the wall was finished on the twenty-fifth
day of Elul, in fifty-two days.
16 And it happened, when all our enemies
heard *of it,* and all the nations around us saw
these things, that they were very disheartened
in their own eyes; for they perceived
that this work was done by our God.
17 Also in those days the nobles of Judah
sent many letters to Tobiah, and *the letters of*
Tobiah came to them.
18 For many in Judah were pledged to him,
because he was the son-in-law of Shechaniah
the son of Arah, and his son Jehohanan had
married the daughter of Meshullam the son of
Berechiah.
19 Also they reported his good deeds before
me, and reported my words to him. Tobiah
sent letters to frighten me.

7 Then it was, when the wall was built and I
had hung the doors, when the gatekeepers,
the singers, and the Levites had been appointed,
2 that I gave the charge of Jerusalem to my ➤
brother Hanani, and Hananiah the leader of
the citadel, for he *was* a faithful man and
feared God more than many.
3 And I said to them, "Do not let the gates of
Jerusalem be opened until the sun is hot; and
while they stand *guard,* let them shut and bar
the doors; and appoint guards from among
the inhabitants of Jerusalem, one at his watch
station and another in front of his own
house."

The Captives Who Returned to Jerusalem

4 Now the city *was* large and spacious, but
the people in it *were* few, and the houses *were*
not rebuilt.
5 Then my God put it into my heart to ➤
gather the nobles, the rulers, and the people,
that they might be registered by genealogy.
And I found a register of the genealogy of
those who had come up in the first *return,*
and found written in it:

6 These[a] *are* the people of the province who
came back from the captivity, of those

6:6 [a]Hebrew *Gashmu* **7:6** [a]Compare verses 6–72 with Ezra 2:1–70

LIFE LESSONS

➤ 6:13 — *For this reason he was hired, that I should be afraid and act that way and sin, so that they might have cause for an evil report, that they might reproach me.*

We hurt our own cause when we give in to fear and intimidation and act as though the Lord God almighty does not reign on high. Prudence never means cowardice.

➤ 7:2 — *. . . I gave the charge of Jerusalem to my brother Hanani, and Hananiah the leader of the citadel, for he was a faithful man and feared God more than many.*

Do others consider you a faithful person? Do you fear God more than many? These are essential qualities in anyone who aspires to spiritual leadership.

➤ 7:5 — *Then my God put it into my heart to gather the nobles, the rulers, and the people, that they might be registered by genealogy.*

How does God put things into our hearts? He may use our own observation and experience, the counsel of others, or perhaps work more directly. However He does it, we walk in the Spirit when we obey His initial promptings.

who had been carried away, whom Nebuchadnezzar the king of Babylon had carried away, and who returned to Jerusalem and Judah, everyone to his city.

7 Those who came with Zerubbabel *were* Jeshua, Nehemiah, Azariah, Raamiah, Nahamani, Mordecai, Bilshan, Mispereth,[a] Bigvai, Nehum, and Baanah.

The number of the men of the people of Israel:

8 the sons of Parosh, two thousand one hundred and seventy-two;
9 the sons of Shephatiah, three hundred and seventy-two;
10 the sons of Arah, six hundred and fifty-two;
11 the sons of Pahath-Moab, of the sons of Jeshua and Joab, two thousand eight hundred and eighteen;
12 the sons of Elam, one thousand two hundred and fifty-four;
13 the sons of Zattu, eight hundred and forty-five;
14 the sons of Zaccai, seven hundred and sixty;
15 the sons of Binnui,[a] six hundred and forty-eight;
16 the sons of Bebai, six hundred and twenty-eight;
17 the sons of Azgad, two thousand three hundred and twenty-two;
18 the sons of Adonikam, six hundred and sixty-seven;
19 the sons of Bigvai, two thousand and sixty-seven;
20 the sons of Adin, six hundred and fifty-five;
21 the sons of Ater of Hezekiah, ninety-eight;
22 the sons of Hashum, three hundred and twenty-eight;
23 the sons of Bezai, three hundred and twenty-four;
24 the sons of Hariph,[a] one hundred and twelve;
25 the sons of Gibeon,[a] ninety-five;
26 the men of Bethlehem and Netophah, one hundred and eighty-eight;
27 the men of Anathoth, one hundred and twenty-eight;
28 the men of Beth Azmaveth,[a] forty-two;
29 the men of Kirjath Jearim, Chephirah, and Beeroth, seven hundred and forty-three;
30 the men of Ramah and Geba, six hundred and twenty-one;
31 the men of Michmas, one hundred and twenty-two;
32 the men of Bethel and Ai, one hundred and twenty-three;
33 the men of the other Nebo, fifty-two;
34 the sons of the other Elam, one thousand two hundred and fifty-four;
35 the sons of Harim, three hundred and twenty;
36 the sons of Jericho, three hundred and forty-five;
37 the sons of Lod, Hadid, and Ono, seven hundred and twenty-one;
38 the sons of Senaah, three thousand nine hundred and thirty.

39 The priests: the sons of Jedaiah, of the house of Jeshua, nine hundred and seventy-three;
40 the sons of Immer, one thousand and fifty-two;
41 the sons of Pashhur, one thousand two hundred and forty-seven;
42 the sons of Harim, one thousand and seventeen.

43 The Levites: the sons of Jeshua, of Kadmiel, *and* of the sons of Hodevah,[a] seventy-four.
44 The singers: the sons of Asaph, one hundred and forty-eight.
45 The gatekeepers: the sons of Shallum, the sons of Ater, the sons of Talmon, the sons of Akkub, the sons of Hatita, the sons of Shobai, one hundred and thirty-eight.

46 The Nethinim: the sons of Ziha, the sons of Hasupha, the sons of Tabbaoth,
47 the sons of Keros, the sons of Sia,[a] the sons of Padon,
48 the sons of Lebana,[a] the sons of Hagaba,[b] the sons of Salmai,[c]
49 the sons of Hanan, the sons of Giddel, the sons of Gahar,
50 the sons of Reaiah, the sons of Rezin, the sons of Nekoda,
51 the sons of Gazzam, the sons of Uzza, the sons of Paseah,
52 the sons of Besai, the sons of Meunim, the sons of Nephishesim,[a]
53 the sons of Bakbuk, the sons of Hakupha, the sons of Harhur,
54 the sons of Bazlith,[a] the sons of Mehida, the sons of Harsha,
55 the sons of Barkos, the sons of Sisera, the sons of Tamah,
56 the sons of Neziah, and the sons of Hatipha.

57 The sons of Solomon's servants: the sons of Sotai, the sons of Sophereth, the sons of Perida,[a]
58 the sons of Jaala, the sons of Darkon, the sons of Giddel,
59 the sons of Shephatiah, the sons of Hattil, the sons of Pochereth of Zebaim, and the sons of Amon.[a]

7:7 [a]Spelled *Mispar* in Ezra 2:2 **7:15** [a]Spelled *Bani* in Ezra 2:10 **7:24** [a]Called *Jorah* in Ezra 2:18 **7:25** [a]Called *Gibbar* in Ezra 2:20 **7:28** [a]Called *Azmaveth* in Ezra 2:24 **7:43** [a]Spelled *Hodaviah* in Ezra 2:40 **7:47** [a]Spelled *Siaha* in Ezra 2:44 **7:48** [a]Masoretic Text reads *Lebanah.* [b]Masoretic Text reads *Hogabah.* [c]Or *Shalmai,* or *Shamlai* **7:52** [a]Spelled *Nephusim* in Ezra 2:50 **7:54** [a]Spelled *Bazluth* in Ezra 2:52 **7:57** [a]Spelled *Peruda* in Ezra 2:55 **7:59** [a]Spelled *Ami* in Ezra 2:57

60 All the Nethinim, and the sons of Solomon's servants, *were* three hundred and ninety-two.

61 And these *were* the ones who came up from Tel Melah, Tel Harsha, Cherub, Addon,[a] and Immer, but they could not identify their father's house nor their lineage, whether they *were* of Israel:

62 the sons of Delaiah, the sons of Tobiah, the sons of Nekoda, six hundred and forty-two;

63 and of the priests: the sons of Habaiah, the sons of Koz,[a] the sons of Barzillai, who took a wife of the daughters of Barzillai the Gileadite, and was called by their name.

64 These sought their listing *among* those who were registered by genealogy, but it was not found; therefore they were excluded from the priesthood as defiled.

65 And the governor[a] said to them that they should not eat of the most holy things till a priest could consult with the Urim and Thummim.

66 Altogether the whole assembly *was* forty-two thousand three hundred and sixty,

67 besides their male and female servants, of whom *there were* seven thousand three hundred and thirty-seven; and they had two hundred and forty-five men and women singers.

68 Their horses were seven hundred and thirty-six, their mules two hundred and forty-five,

69 *their* camels four hundred and thirty-five, *and* donkeys six thousand seven hundred and twenty.

70 And some of the heads of the fathers' *houses* gave to the work. The governor[a] gave to the treasury one thousand gold drachmas, fifty basins, and five hundred and thirty priestly garments.

71 Some of the heads of the fathers' *houses* gave to the treasury of the work twenty thousand gold drachmas, and two thousand two hundred silver minas.

72 And that which the rest of the people gave *was* twenty thousand gold drachmas, two thousand silver minas, and sixty-seven priestly garments.

73 So the priests, the Levites, the gatekeepers, the singers, *some* of the people, the Nethinim, and all Israel dwelt in their cities.

Ezra Reads the Law

When the seventh month came, the children of Israel *were* in their cities.

8 Now all the people gathered together as one man in the open square that *was* in front of the Water Gate; and they told Ezra the scribe to bring the Book of the Law of Moses, which the LORD had commanded Israel.

2 So Ezra the priest brought the Law before the assembly of men and women and all who *could* hear with understanding on the first day of the seventh month.

3 Then he read from it in the open square that *was* in front of the Water Gate from morning until midday, before the men and women and those who could understand; and the ears of all the people *were attentive* to the Book of the Law.

4 So Ezra the scribe stood on a platform of wood which they had made for the purpose; and beside him, at his right hand, stood Mattithiah, Shema, Anaiah, Urijah, Hilkiah, and Maaseiah; and at his left hand Pedaiah, Mishael, Malchijah, Hashum, Hashbadana, Zechariah, *and* Meshullam.

5 And Ezra opened the book in the sight of all the people, for he was *standing* above all the people; and when he opened it, all the people stood up.

6 And Ezra blessed the LORD, the great God. Then all the people answered, "Amen, Amen!" while lifting up their hands. And they bowed their heads and worshiped the LORD with *their* faces to the ground.

7 Also Jeshua, Bani, Sherebiah, Jamin, Akkub, Shabbethai, Hodijah, Maaseiah, Kelita, Azariah, Jozabad, Hanan, Pelaiah, and the Levites, helped the people to understand the Law; and the people *stood* in their place.

8 So they read distinctly from the book, in the Law of God; and they gave the sense, and helped *them* to understand the reading.

9 And Nehemiah, who *was* the governor,[a] Ezra the priest *and* scribe, and the Levites who taught the people said to all the people, "This day *is* holy to the LORD your God; do not mourn nor weep." For all the people wept, when they heard the words of the Law.

10 Then he said to them, "Go your way, eat

7:61 [a]Spelled *Addan* in Ezra 2:59 **7:63** [a]Or *Hakkoz* **7:65** [a]Hebrew *Tirshatha* **7:70** [a]Hebrew *Tirshatha* **8:9** [a]Hebrew *Tirshatha*

LIFE LESSONS

➤ **8:6 — *And they bowed their heads and worshiped the LORD with their faces to the ground.***

Seldom do we worship anymore with our faces to the ground—but perhaps we should. Such a posture would remind us that God is the King and we are His subjects. He is sovereign; we are not.

➤ **8:8 — *So they read distinctly from the book, in the Law of God; and they gave the sense, and helped them to understand the reading.***

While all of us need to immerse ourselves in the Word of God on our own, there is no substitute for regularly gathering as the people of God to hear the Bible clearly explained and applied.

the fat, drink the sweet, and send portions to
those for whom nothing is prepared; for *this*
day *is* holy to our Lord. Do not sorrow, for the
joy of the LORD is your strength."
11 So the Levites quieted all the people, saying, "Be still, for the day *is* holy; do not be
grieved."
12 And all the people went their way to eat
and drink, to send portions and rejoice
greatly, because they understood the words
that were declared to them.

The Feast of Tabernacles

13 Now on the second day the heads of the
fathers' *houses* of all the people, with the
priests and Levites, were gathered to Ezra the
scribe, in order to understand the words of
the Law.
14 And they found written in the Law, which
the LORD had commanded by Moses, that the
children of Israel should dwell in booths during the feast of the seventh month,
15 and that they should announce and proclaim in all their cities and in Jerusalem, saying, "Go out to the mountain, and bring olive
branches, branches of oil trees, myrtle
branches, palm branches, and branches of
leafy trees, to make booths, as *it is* written."
16 Then the people went out and brought
them and made themselves booths, each one
on the roof of his house, or in their courtyards
or the courts of the house of God, and in the
open square of the Water Gate and in the
open square of the Gate of Ephraim.
➤ 17 So the whole assembly of those who had
returned from the captivity made booths and
sat under the booths; for since the days of
Joshua the son of Nun until that day the children of Israel had not done so. And there was
very great gladness.
18 Also day by day, from the first day until
the last day, he read from the Book of the Law
of God. And they kept the feast seven days;
and on the eighth day *there was* a sacred assembly, according to the *prescribed* manner.

The People Confess Their Sins

9 Now on the twenty-fourth day of this
month the children of Israel were assembled with fasting, in sackcloth, and with dust
on their heads.[a]
➤ 2 Then those of Israelite lineage separated
themselves from all foreigners; and they
stood and confessed their sins and the iniquities of their fathers.
3 And they stood up in their place and read
from the Book of the Law of the LORD their
God *for one*-fourth of the day; and *for another*
fourth they confessed and worshiped the
LORD their God.
4 Then Jeshua, Bani, Kadmiel, Shebaniah,
Bunni, Sherebiah, Bani, *and* Chenani stood
on the stairs of the Levites and cried out with
a loud voice to the LORD their God.
5 And the Levites, Jeshua, Kadmiel, Bani,
Hashabniah, Sherebiah, Hodijah, Shebaniah,
and Pethahiah, said:

"Stand up *and* bless the LORD your God
Forever and ever!

"Blessed be Your glorious name,
Which is exalted above all blessing and
praise!
6 You alone *are* the LORD;
You have made heaven,
The heaven of heavens, with all their
host,
The earth and everything on it,
The seas and all that is in them,
And You preserve them all.
The host of heaven worships You.

7 "You *are* the LORD God,
Who chose Abram,
And brought him out of Ur of the
Chaldeans,
And gave him the name Abraham;
8 You found his heart faithful before You,
And made a covenant with him
To give the land of the Canaanites,
The Hittites, the Amorites,
The Perizzites, the Jebusites,
And the Girgashites—
To give *it* to his descendants.
You have performed Your words,
For You *are* righteous.

9 "You saw the affliction of our fathers in
Egypt,
And heard their cry by the Red Sea.
10 You showed signs and wonders against
Pharaoh,

9:1 [a]Literally *earth on them*

LIFE LESSONS

➤ **8:17 — *So the whole assembly . . . made booths and sat under the booths; for since the days of Joshua the son of Nun until that day the children of Israel had not done so. And there was very great gladness.***

There is great joy in obeying the Word of God when we do so eagerly and by His Spirit. Joyful obedience pleases God and blesses us.

➤ **9:2 — *Then those of Israelite lineage . . . stood and confessed their sins and the iniquities of their fathers.***

Why confess our sins? First, because God tells us to (James 5:16). Second, because confessing a sin breaks its power over us, since the power of sin grows more readily in the dark.

Against all his servants,
And against all the people of his land.
For You knew that they acted proudly
against them.
So You made a name for Yourself, as *it is*
this day.
11 And You divided the sea before them,
So that they went through the midst of
the sea on the dry land;
And their persecutors You threw into the
deep,
As a stone into the mighty waters.
12 Moreover You led them by day with a
cloudy pillar,
And by night with a pillar of fire,
To give them light on the road
Which they should travel.

13 "You came down also on Mount Sinai,
And spoke with them from heaven,
And gave them just ordinances and true
laws,
Good statutes and commandments.
14 You made known to them Your holy
Sabbath,
And commanded them precepts, statutes
and laws,
By the hand of Moses Your servant.
15 You gave them bread from heaven for
their hunger,
And brought them water out of the rock
for their thirst,
And told them to go in to possess the
land
Which You had sworn to give them.

16 "But they and our fathers acted proudly,
Hardened their necks,
And did not heed Your commandments.
✳ 17 They refused to obey,
And they were not mindful of Your
wonders
That You did among them.
But they hardened their necks,
And in their rebellion[a]
They appointed a leader
To return to their bondage.
But You *are* God,
Ready to pardon,
Gracious and merciful,
Slow to anger,
Abundant in kindness,
And did not forsake them.

18 "Even when they made a molded calf for
themselves,
And said, 'This *is* your god
That brought you up out of Egypt,'
And worked great provocations,
19 Yet in Your manifold mercies
You did not forsake them in the
wilderness.
The pillar of the cloud did not depart
from them by day,
To lead them on the road;
Nor the pillar of fire by night,
To show them light,
And the way they should go.
20 You also gave Your good Spirit to instruct
them,
And did not withhold Your manna from
their mouth,
And gave them water for their thirst.
21 Forty years You sustained them in the
wilderness;
They lacked nothing;
Their clothes did not wear out[a]
And their feet did not swell.

22 "Moreover You gave them kingdoms and
nations,
And divided them into districts.[a]
So they took possession of the land of
Sihon,
The land of[b] the king of Heshbon,
And the land of Og king of Bashan.
23 You also multiplied their children as the
stars of heaven,
And brought them into the land
Which You had told their fathers
To go in and possess.
24 So the people went in
And possessed the land;
You subdued before them the inhabitants
of the land,
The Canaanites,
And gave them into their hands,
With their kings
And the people of the land,
That they might do with them as they
wished.
25 And they took strong cities and a rich
land,
And possessed houses full of all goods,
Cisterns *already* dug, vineyards, olive
groves,
And fruit trees in abundance.
So they ate and were filled and grew fat,
And delighted themselves in Your great
goodness.

26 "Nevertheless they were disobedient
And rebelled against You,
Cast Your law behind their backs
And killed Your prophets, who testified
against them
To turn them to Yourself;
And they worked great provocations.
27 Therefore You delivered them into the
hand of their enemies,
Who oppressed them;
And in the time of their trouble,
When they cried to You,
You heard from heaven;
And according to Your abundant mercies

9:17 [a]Following Masoretic Text and Vulgate; Septuagint reads *in Egypt*. **9:21** [a]Compare Deuteronomy 29:5 **9:22** [a]Literally *corners* [b]Following Masoretic Text and Vulgate; Septuagint omits *The land of*.

You gave them deliverers who saved them
From the hand of their enemies.

28 "But after they had rest,
They again did evil before You.
Therefore You left them in the hand of
their enemies,
So that they had dominion over them;
Yet when they returned and cried out to
You,
You heard from heaven;
And many times You delivered them
according to Your mercies,
29 And testified against them,
That You might bring them back to Your
law.
Yet they acted proudly,
And did not heed Your commandments,
But sinned against Your judgments,
'Which if a man does, he shall live by
them.'[a]
And they shrugged their shoulders,
Stiffened their necks,
And would not hear.
30 Yet for many years You had patience with
them,
And testified against them by Your Spirit
in Your prophets.
Yet they would not listen;
Therefore You gave them into the hand of
the peoples of the lands.
31 Nevertheless in Your great mercy
You did not utterly consume them nor
forsake them;
For You *are* God, gracious and merciful.

32 "Now therefore, our God,
The great, the mighty, and awesome God,
Who keeps covenant and mercy:
Do not let all the trouble seem small
before You
That has come upon us,
Our kings and our princes,
Our priests and our prophets,
Our fathers and on all Your people,
From the days of the kings of Assyria
until this day.
33 However You *are* just in all that has
befallen us;
For You have dealt faithfully,
But we have done wickedly.
34 Neither our kings nor our princes,
Our priests nor our fathers,
Have kept Your law,
Nor heeded Your commandments and
Your testimonies,
With which You testified against them.
35 For they have not served You in their
kingdom,
Or in the many good *things* that You gave
them,
Or in the large and rich land which You
set before them;
Nor did they turn from their wicked
works.

36 "Here we *are*, servants today!
And the land that You gave to our fathers,
To eat its fruit and its bounty,
Here we *are*, servants in it!
37 And it yields much increase to the kings
You have set over us,
Because of our sins;
Also they have dominion over our bodies
and our cattle
At their pleasure;
And we *are* in great distress.

38 "And because of all this,
We make a sure *covenant* and write *it;*
Our leaders, our Levites, *and* our priests
seal *it*."

The People Who Sealed the Covenant

10 Now those who placed *their* seal on *the document were:*
Nehemiah the governor, the son of Ha-
caliah, and Zedekiah,
2 Seraiah, Azariah, Jeremiah,
3 Pashhur, Amariah, Malchijah,
4 Hattush, Shebaniah, Malluch,
5 Harim, Meremoth, Obadiah,
6 Daniel, Ginnethon, Baruch,
7 Meshullam, Abijah, Mijamin,
8 Maaziah, Bilgai, *and* Shemaiah. These
were the priests.
9 The Levites: Jeshua the son of Azaniah,
Binnui of the sons of Henadad, *and* Kadmiel.
10 Their brethren: Shebaniah, Hodijah, Kelita, Pelaiah, Hanan,
11 Micha, Rehob, Hashabiah,
12 Zaccur, Sherebiah, Shebaniah,
13 Hodijah, Bani, *and* Beninu.
14 The leaders of the people: Parosh, Pahath-
Moab, Elam, Zattu, Bani,
15 Bunni, Azgad, Bebai,
16 Adonijah, Bigvai, Adin,
17 Ater, Hezekiah, Azzur,
18 Hodijah, Hashum, Bezai,
19 Hariph, Anathoth, Nebai,
20 Magpiash, Meshullam, Hezir,
21 Meshezabel, Zadok, Jaddua,
22 Pelatiah, Hanan, Anaiah,
23 Hoshea, Hananiah, Hasshub,
24 Hallohesh, Pilha, Shobek,
25 Rehum, Hashabnah, Maaseiah,
26 Ahijah, Hanan, Anan,
27 Malluch, Harim, *and* Baanah.

The Covenant That Was Sealed

28 Now the rest of the people—the priests,
the Levites, the gatekeepers, the singers, the
Nethinim, and all those who had separated
themselves from the peoples of the lands to
the Law of God, their wives, their sons, and
their daughters, everyone who had knowledge and understanding—
29 these joined with their brethren, their no-

9:29 [a]Leviticus 18:5

bles, and entered into a curse and an oath to
walk in God's Law, which was given by Moses
the servant of God, and to observe and do all
the commandments of the LORD our Lord, and
His ordinances and His statutes:
30 We would not give our daughters as wives
to the peoples of the land, nor take their
daughters for our sons;
31 *if* the peoples of the land brought wares or
any grain to sell on the Sabbath day, we
would not buy it from them on the Sabbath,
or on a holy day; and we would forego the
seventh year's *produce* and the exacting of
every debt.
32 Also we made ordinances for ourselves, to
exact from ourselves yearly one-third of a
shekel for the service of the house of our God:
33 for the showbread, for the regular grain
offering, for the regular burnt offering of the
Sabbaths, the New Moons, and the set feasts;
for the holy things, for the sin offerings to
make atonement for Israel, and all the work
of the house of our God.
34 We cast lots among the priests, the
Levites, and the people, for bringing the wood
offering into the house of our God, according
to our fathers' houses, at the appointed times
year by year, to burn on the altar of the LORD
our God as *it is* written in the Law.
35 And *we made ordinances* to bring the
firstfruits of our ground and the firstfruits of
all fruit of all trees, year by year, to the house
of the LORD;
36 to bring the firstborn of our sons and our
cattle, as *it is* written in the Law, and the firstborn of our herds and our flocks, to the house
of our God, to the priests who minister in the
house of our God;
37 to bring the firstfruits of our dough, our
offerings, the fruit from all kinds of trees, *the*
new wine and oil, to the priests, to the storerooms of the house of our God; and to bring
the tithes of our land to the Levites, for the
Levites should receive the tithes in all our
farming communities.
➤ 38 And the priest, the descendant of Aaron,
shall be with the Levites when the Levites receive tithes; and the Levites shall bring up a
tenth of the tithes to the house of our God, to
the rooms of the storehouse.
39 For the children of Israel and the children
of Levi shall bring the offering of the grain, of
the new wine and the oil, to the storerooms
where the articles of the sanctuary *are, where*
the priests who minister and the gatekeepers
and the singers *are;* and we will not neglect
the house of our God.

The People Dwelling in Jerusalem

11 Now the leaders of the people dwelt at
Jerusalem; the rest of the people cast
lots to bring one out of ten to dwell in Jerusalem, the holy city, and nine-tenths *were to*
dwell in *other* cities.
2 And the people blessed all the men who ➤
willingly offered themselves to dwell at Jerusalem.
3 These *are* the heads of the province who
dwelt in Jerusalem. (But in the cities of Judah
everyone dwelt in his own possession in their
cities—Israelites, priests, Levites, Nethinim,
and descendants of Solomon's servants.)
4 Also in Jerusalem dwelt *some* of the children of Judah and of the children of Benjamin.
The children of Judah: Athaiah the son of
Uzziah, the son of Zechariah, the son of Amariah, the son of Shephatiah, the son of Mahalalel, of the children of Perez;
5 and Maaseiah the son of Baruch, the son
of Col-Hozeh, the son of Hazaiah, the son of
Adaiah, the son of Joiarib, the son of
Zechariah, the son of Shiloni.
6 All the sons of Perez who dwelt at Jerusalem *were* four hundred and sixty-eight valiant
men.
7 And these are the sons of Benjamin: Sallu
the son of Meshullam, the son of Joed, the son
of Pedaiah, the son of Kolaiah, the son of Maaseiah, the son of Ithiel, the son of Jeshaiah;
8 and after him Gabbai *and* Sallai, nine hundred and twenty-eight.
9 Joel the son of Zichri *was* their overseer,
and Judah the son of Senuah[a] *was* second
over the city.
10 Of the priests: Jedaiah the son of Joiarib,
and Jachin;
11 Seraiah the son of Hilkiah, the son of
Meshullam, the son of Zadok, the son of
Meraioth, the son of Ahitub, *was* the leader
of the house of God.

11:9 [a]Or *Hassenuah*

LIFE LESSONS

➤ **10:38 — *And the priest, the descendant of Aaron, shall be with the Levites when the Levites receive tithes; and the Levites shall bring up a tenth of the tithes to the house of our God . . . .***

Giving back to God has always been an important part of a walk of faith. By giving, we show that our goods are not our gods. And no one ever out gives God!

➤ **11:2 — *And the people blessed all the men who willingly offered themselves to dwell at Jerusalem.***

It could not have been easy to leave a comfortable home in order to live in the ruined city, but many did this for the good of God's people. How often do we sacrifice for the benefit of other believers?

12 Their brethren who did the work of
the house *were* eight hundred and twenty-
two; and Adaiah the son of Jeroham, the son
of Pelaliah, the son of Amzi, the son of
Zechariah, the son of Pashhur, the son of
Malchijah,
13 and his brethren, heads of the fathers'
houses, were two hundred and forty-two; and
Amashai the son of Azarel, the son of Ahzai,
the son of Meshillemoth, the son of Immer,
14 and their brethren, mighty men of valor,
were one hundred and twenty-eight. Their
overseer *was* Zabdiel the son of *one of* the
great men.[a]
15 Also of the Levites: Shemaiah the son
of Hasshub, the son of Azrikam, the son of
Hashabiah, the son of Bunni;
16 Shabbethai and Jozabad, of the heads of
the Levites, *had* the oversight of the business
outside of the house of God;
17 Mattaniah the son of Micha,[a] the son of
Zabdi, the son of Asaph, the leader *who*
began the thanksgiving with prayer; Bakbukiah, the second among his brethren; and
Abda the son of Shammua, the son of Galal,
the son of Jeduthun.
18 All the Levites in the holy city *were* two
hundred and eighty-four.
19 Moreover the gatekeepers, Akkub, Talmon, and their brethren who kept the gates,
were one hundred and seventy-two.
20 And the rest of Israel, of the priests *and*
Levites, *were* in all the cities of Judah, everyone in his inheritance.
21 But the Nethinim dwelt in Ophel. And
Ziha and Gishpa *were* over the Nethinim.
22 Also the overseer of the Levites at Jerusalem *was* Uzzi the son of Bani, the son of
Hashabiah, the son of Mattaniah, the son of
Micha, of the sons of Asaph, the singers in
charge of the service of the house of God.
23 For *it was* the king's command concerning them that a certain portion should be for
the singers, a quota day by day.
24 Pethahiah the son of Meshezabel, of the
children of Zerah the son of Judah, *was*
the king's deputy[a] in all matters concerning
the people.

The People Dwelling Outside Jerusalem

25 And as for the villages with their fields,
some of the children of Judah dwelt in Kirjath
Arba and its villages, Dibon and its villages,
Jekabzeel and its villages;
26 in Jeshua, Moladah, Beth Pelet,
27 Hazar Shual, and Beersheba and its villages;
28 in Ziklag and Meconah and its villages;
29 in En Rimmon, Zorah, Jarmuth,
30 Zanoah, Adullam, and their villages; in
Lachish and its fields; in Azekah and its villages. They dwelt from Beersheba to the Valley of Hinnom.
31 Also the children of Benjamin from Geba
dwelt in Michmash, Aija, and Bethel, and
their villages;
32 in Anathoth, Nob, Ananiah;
33 in Hazor, Ramah, Gittaim;
34 in Hadid, Zeboim, Neballat;
35 in Lod, Ono, *and* the Valley of Craftsmen.
36 Some of the Judean divisions of Levites
were in Benjamin.

The Priests and Levites

12 Now these *are* the priests and the
Levites who came up with Zerubbabel
the son of Shealtiel, and Jeshua: Seraiah, Jeremiah, Ezra,
2 Amariah, Malluch, Hattush,
3 Shechaniah, Rehum, Meremoth,
4 Iddo, Ginnethoi,[a] Abijah,
5 Mijamin, Maadiah, Bilgah,
6 Shemaiah, Joiarib, Jedaiah,
7 Sallu, Amok, Hilkiah, *and* Jedaiah.
These *were* the heads of the priests and
their brethren in the days of Jeshua.
8 Moreover the Levites *were* Jeshua, Binnui,
Kadmiel, Sherebiah, Judah, *and* Mattaniah
who led the thanksgiving *psalms,* he and his
brethren.
9 Also Bakbukiah and Unni, their brethren,
stood across from them in *their* duties.
10 Jeshua begot Joiakim, Joiakim begot
Eliashib, Eliashib begot Joiada,
11 Joiada begot Jonathan, and Jonathan
begot Jaddua.
12 Now in the days of Joiakim, the priests,
the heads of the fathers' *houses were:* of Seraiah, Meraiah; of Jeremiah, Hananiah;
13 of Ezra, Meshullam; of Amariah, Jehohanan;
14 of Melichu,[a] Jonathan; of Shebaniah,[b] Joseph;
15 of Harim,[a] Adna; of Meraioth,[b] Helkai;
16 of Iddo, Zechariah; of Ginnethon, Meshullam;
17 of Abijah, Zichri; *the son* of Minjamin;[a] of
Moadiah,[b] Piltai;
18 of Bilgah, Shammua; of Shemaiah, Jehonathan;
19 of Joiarib, Mattenai; of Jedaiah, Uzzi;
20 of Sallai,[a] Kallai; of Amok, Eber;
21 of Hilkiah, Hashabiah; *and* of Jedaiah,
Nethanel.
22 During the reign of Darius the Persian, a
record *was also kept* of the Levites and
priests *who had been* heads of their fathers'
houses in the days of Eliashib, Joiada, Johanan, and Jaddua.
23 The sons of Levi, the heads of the fathers'

11:14 [a]Or *the son of Haggedolim* **11:17** [a]Or *Michah* **11:24** [a]Literally *at the king's hand* **12:4** [a]Or *Ginnethon* (compare verse 16) **12:14** [a]Or *Malluch* (compare verse 2) [b]Or *Shechaniah* (compare verse 3) **12:15** [a]Or *Rehum* (compare verse 3) [b]Or *Meremoth* (compare verse 3) **12:17** [a]Or *Mijamin* (compare verse 5) [b]Or *Maadiah* (compare verse 5) **12:20** [a]Or *Sallu* (compare verse 7)

houses until the days of Johanan the son of Eliashib, *were* written in the book of the chronicles.
24 And the heads of the Levites *were* Hashabiah, Sherebiah, and Jeshua the son of Kadmiel, with their brothers across from them, to praise *and* give thanks, group alternating with group, according to the command of David the man of God.
25 Mattaniah, Bakbukiah, Obadiah, Meshullam, Talmon, and Akkub *were* gatekeepers keeping the watch at the storerooms of the gates.
26 These *lived* in the days of Joiakim the son of Jeshua, the son of Jozadak,[a] and in the days of Nehemiah the governor, and of Ezra the priest, the scribe.

Nehemiah Dedicates the Wall

➤ **27** Now at the dedication of the wall of Jerusalem they sought out the Levites in all their places, to bring them to Jerusalem to celebrate the dedication with gladness, both with thanksgivings and singing, *with* cymbals and stringed instruments and harps.
28 And the sons of the singers gathered together from the countryside around Jerusalem, from the villages of the Netophathites,
29 from the house of Gilgal, and from the fields of Geba and Azmaveth; for the singers had built themselves villages all around Jerusalem.
30 Then the priests and Levites purified themselves, and purified the people, the gates, and the wall.
31 So I brought the leaders of Judah up on the wall, and appointed two large thanksgiving choirs. *One* went to the right hand on the wall toward the Refuse Gate.
32 After them went Hoshaiah and half of the leaders of Judah,
33 and Azariah, Ezra, Meshullam,
34 Judah, Benjamin, Shemaiah, Jeremiah,
35 and some of the priests' sons with trumpets—Zechariah the son of Jonathan, the son of Shemaiah, the son of Mattaniah, the son of Michaiah, the son of Zaccur, the son of Asaph,
36 and his brethren, Shemaiah, Azarel, Milalai, Gilalai, Maai, Nethanel, Judah, *and* Hanani, with the musical instruments of David the man of God. Ezra the scribe *went* before them.
37 By the Fountain Gate, in front of them, they went up the stairs of the City of David, on the stairway of the wall, beyond the house of David, as far as the Water Gate eastward.
38 The other thanksgiving choir went the opposite *way,* and I *was* behind them with half of the people on the wall, going past the Tower of the Ovens as far as the Broad Wall,
39 and above the Gate of Ephraim, above the Old Gate, above the Fish Gate, the Tower of Hananel, the Tower of the Hundred, as far as the Sheep Gate; and they stopped by the Gate of the Prison.
40 So the two thanksgiving choirs stood in the house of God, likewise I and the half of the rulers with me;
41 and the priests, Eliakim, Maaseiah, Minjamin,[a] Michaiah, Elioenai, Zechariah, *and* Hananiah, with trumpets;
42 also Maaseiah, Shemaiah, Eleazar, Uzzi, Jehohanan, Malchijah, Elam, and Ezer. The singers sang loudly with Jezrahiah the director.
43 Also that day they offered great sacrifices, ➤
and rejoiced, for God had made them rejoice with great joy; the women and the children also rejoiced, so that the joy of Jerusalem was heard afar off.

Temple Responsibilities

44 And at the same time some were appointed over the rooms of the storehouse for the offerings, the firstfruits, and the tithes, to gather into them from the fields of the cities the portions specified by the Law for the priests and Levites; for Judah rejoiced over the priests and Levites who ministered.
45 Both the singers and the gatekeepers kept the charge of their God and the charge of the purification, according to the command of David *and* Solomon his son.
46 For in the days of David and Asaph of old *there were* chiefs of the singers, and songs of praise and thanksgiving to God.

12:26 [a]Spelled *Jehozadak* in 1 Chronicles 6:14 **12:41** [a]Or *Mijamin* (compare verse 5)

LIFE LESSONS

➤ **12:27 — *Now at the dedication of the wall of Jerusalem they sought out the Levites . . . to celebrate the dedication with gladness, both with thanksgivings and singing, with cymbals and stringed instruments and harps.***

It is good to celebrate what God has accomplished through His willing servants. This not only honors and praises the God who made it possible, but encourages us to acknowledge His gracious work among us.

➤ **12:43 — *Also that day they offered great sacrifices, and rejoiced, for God had made them rejoice with great joy; the women and the children also rejoiced, so that the joy of Jerusalem was heard afar off.***

Great joy is a sign of the redeemed heart and powerfully attracts the attention of those who would like to experience it.

47 In the days of Zerubbabel and in the days
of Nehemiah all Israel gave the portions for
the singers and the gatekeepers, a portion for
each day. They also consecrated *holy things*
for the Levites, and the Levites consecrated
them for the children of Aaron.

Principles of Separation

13 On that day they read from the Book of
Moses in the hearing of the people, and
in it was found written that no Ammonite or
Moabite should ever come into the assembly
of God,
➤ 2 because they had not met the children of
Israel with bread and water, but hired Balaam
against them to curse them. However, our
God turned the curse into a blessing.
3 So it was, when they had heard the Law,
that they separated all the mixed multitude
from Israel.

The Reforms of Nehemiah

4 Now before this, Eliashib the priest, having authority over the storerooms of the
house of our God, *was* allied with Tobiah.
5 And he had prepared for him a large
room, where previously they had stored the
grain offerings, the frankincense, the articles,
the tithes of grain, the new wine and oil,
which were commanded *to be given* to the
Levites and singers and gatekeepers, and the
offerings for the priests.
6 But during all this I was not in Jerusalem,
for in the thirty-second year of Artaxerxes
king of Babylon I had returned to the king.
Then after certain days I obtained leave from
the king,
7 and I came to Jerusalem and discovered
the evil that Eliashib had done for Tobiah, in
preparing a room for him in the courts of the
house of God.
8 And it grieved me bitterly; therefore I
threw all the household goods of Tobiah out
of the room.
9 Then I commanded them to cleanse the
rooms; and I brought back into them the articles of the house of God, with the grain offering and the frankincense.
10 I also realized that the portions for the
Levites had not been given *them;* for each of
the Levites and the singers who did the work
had gone back to his field.
11 So I contended with the rulers, and said,
"Why is the house of God forsaken?" And I
gathered them together and set them in their
place.
12 Then all Judah brought the tithe of the
grain and the new wine and the oil to the
storehouse.
13 And I appointed as treasurers over the
storehouse Shelemiah the priest and Zadok
the scribe, and of the Levites, Pedaiah; and
next to them *was* Hanan the son of Zaccur,
the son of Mattaniah; for they were considered faithful, and their task *was* to distribute
to their brethren.
14 Remember me, O my God, concerning
this, and do not wipe out my good deeds that
I have done for the house of my God, and for
its services!
15 In those days I saw *people* in Judah treading winepresses on the Sabbath, and bringing
in sheaves, and loading donkeys with wine,
grapes, figs, and all *kinds of* burdens, which
they brought into Jerusalem on the Sabbath
day. And I warned *them* about the day on
which they were selling provisions.
16 Men of Tyre dwelt there also, who brought
in fish and all kinds of goods, and sold *them*
on the Sabbath to the children of Judah, and
in Jerusalem.
17 Then I contended with the nobles of Judah, and said to them, "What evil thing *is* this
that you do, by which you profane the Sabbath day?
18 "Did not your fathers do thus, and did not
our God bring all this disaster on us and on
this city? Yet you bring added wrath on Israel
by profaning the Sabbath."
19 So it was, at the gates of Jerusalem, as it
began to be dark before the Sabbath, that I
commanded the gates to be shut, and charged
that they must not be opened till after the
Sabbath. Then I posted *some* of my servants
at the gates, *so that* no burdens would be
brought in on the Sabbath day.
20 Now the merchants and sellers of all kinds
of wares lodged outside Jerusalem once or
twice.
21 Then I warned them, and said to them, ➤
"Why do you spend the night around the
wall? If you do *so* again, I will lay hands on
you!" From that time on they came no *more*
on the Sabbath.
22 And I commanded the Levites that they
should cleanse themselves, and that they

LIFE LESSONS

➤ **13:2 — *However, our God turned the curse into a blessing.***

God is an expert at turning curses into blessing. When did He last do this for you?

➤ **13:21 — *Then I warned them, and said to them, "Why do you spend the night around the wall? If you do so again, I will lay hands on you!"***

Too many of us confuse the words "nice" and "godly." They are not the same thing. A godly man may at times have to speak forcefully and with great zeal; a nice man never would.

should go and guard the gates, to sanctify the
Sabbath day.

Remember me, O my God, *concerning* this
also, and spare me according to the greatness
of Your mercy!
23 In those days I also saw Jews *who* had
married women of Ashdod, Ammon, *and*
Moab.
24 And half of their children spoke the language of Ashdod, and could not speak the
language of Judah, but spoke according to the
language of one or the other people.
25 So I contended with them and cursed
them, struck some of them and pulled out
their hair, and made them swear by God, *saying*, "You shall not give your daughters as
wives to their sons, nor take their daughters
for your sons or yourselves.
➤26 "Did not Solomon king of Israel sin by
these things? Yet among many nations there
was no king like him, who was beloved of his
God; and God made him king over all Israel.
Nevertheless pagan women caused even him
to sin.
27 "Should we then hear of your doing all
this great evil, transgressing against our God
by marrying pagan women?"
28 And *one* of the sons of Joiada, the son of
Eliashib the high priest, *was* a son-in-law of
Sanballat the Horonite; therefore I drove him
from me.
29 Remember them, O my God, because they
have defiled the priesthood and the covenant
of the priesthood and the Levites.
30 Thus I cleansed them of everything pagan.
I also assigned duties to the priests and the
Levites, each to his service,
31 and *to bringing* the wood offering and the
firstfruits at appointed times.

Remember me, O my God, for good!

LIFE LESSONS

➤ 13:26 — "Did not Solomon king of Israel sin by these things? Yet among many nations there was no king like him, who was beloved of his God; and God made him king over all Israel. Nevertheless pagan women caused even him to sin."

Because intimacy with God is His highest priority for our life, the Lord forbids mixed marriages between believers and unbelievers. Why would we ever want to do anything that threatens to damage a close relationship with Him?

THE BOOK OF
ESTHER

Esther's Hebrew name was *Hadassah*, meaning "Myrtle" (2:7), but her Persian name, *Ester*, came from the Persian word meaning "Star" (*stara*). The Greek title for this book is *Esther*.

Despite her heritage as a Hebrew exile, Esther became Queen of Persia through unusual circumstances. This Jewish orphan, raised by her cousin Mordecai, seemed a most unlikely candidate for the king's harem. Her remarkable beauty won her a spot among the many women who longed to catch the king's eye, however, and while her looks drew the king's favor, her deeper spiritual qualities undoubtedly sealed his affections.

The Book of Esther is a great story of intrigue and heroism, but a story whose inclusion in the Scriptures has been debated for centuries since God fails to get even a single mention in the book. In fact, the only reference of any kind to spiritual discipline comes in a few short references to prayer and fasting. Nevertheless, God's hand of providence and protection stands out throughout the book, especially when God's people appear in grave danger of annihilation.

As with many great stories, both heroes and villains populate the Book of Esther. The heroes include Esther herself and Mordecai. The chief villain is the king's right-hand man, Haman, who hatches a dastardly plot to kill Mordecai and exterminate the Jews. After Esther learned of the scheme against the Jews, she made a decision to try to save her people, even if it meant her own death. With a little encouragement from Mordecai, she willingly seized the opportunity God had placed before her. Esther did not turn away in fear but stepped forward in faith. So the courage of beautiful Esther and the counsel of the wise Mordecai foil Haman's plot, resulting in a great deliverance for God's people. And the Feast of Purim became an annual reminder of God's faithfulness to His people.

Through these circumstances God demonstrated His eternal love and ability to protect those who are His. God took a plan to exterminate His people and turned it into an occasion for their blessing.

Theme: God's invisible hand of providence cares for, protects, and delivers those who are His. Sometimes He uses godly people willing to stand up to opposition, even in the face of grave danger to themselves.

Author: Unknown.

Time: The story of Esther is set in the fifth century B.C. Esther was a contemporary of Zerubbabel, Ezra, and Nehemiah.

Structure: The Book of Esther is written as a historical narrative. The book is filled with interesting plot twists and heroism in the face of grave personal danger.

As you read Esther, watch for several life principles that play an important role in this book.

2. Obey God and leave all the consequences to Him. *See Esther 4:13–16; page 578.*

18. As children of a sovereign God, we are never victims of our circumstances. *See Esther 6:10, 11; page 580.*

26. Adversity is a bridge to a deeper relationship with God. *See Esther 9:1–17; page 582.*

The King Dethrones Queen Vashti

1 Now it came to pass in the days of Ahasuerus[a] (this *was* the Ahasuerus who reigned over one hundred and twenty-seven provinces, from India to Ethiopia),

2 in those days when King Ahasuerus sat on the throne of his kingdom, which *was* in Shushan[a] the citadel,

3 *that* in the third year of his reign he made a feast for all his officials and servants—the powers of Persia and Media, the nobles, and the princes of the provinces *being* before him—

4 when he showed the riches of his glorious kingdom and the splendor of his excellent majesty for many days, one hundred and eighty days *in all.*

5 And when these days were completed, the king made a feast lasting seven days for all the people who were present in Shushan the citadel, from great to small, in the court of the garden of the king's palace.

6 *There were* white and blue linen *curtains* fastened with cords of fine linen and purple on silver rods and marble pillars; *and the* couches *were* of gold and silver on a *mosaic* pavement of alabaster, turquoise, and white and black marble.

7 And they served drinks in golden vessels, each vessel being different from the other, with royal wine in abundance, according to the generosity of the king.

8 In accordance with the law, the drinking was not compulsory; for so the king had ordered all the officers of his household, that they should do according to each man's pleasure.

9 Queen Vashti also made a feast for the women *in* the royal palace which *belonged* to King Ahasuerus.

10 On the seventh day, when the heart of the king was merry with wine, he commanded Mehuman, Biztha, Harbona, Bigtha, Abagtha, Zethar, and Carcas, seven eunuchs who served in the presence of King Ahasuerus,

11 to bring Queen Vashti before the king, *wearing* her royal crown, in order to show her beauty to the people and the officials, for she *was* beautiful to behold.

12 But Queen Vashti refused to come at the king's command *brought* by *his* eunuchs; therefore the king was furious, and his anger burned within him.

13 Then the king said to the wise men who understood the times (for this *was* the king's manner toward all who knew law and justice,

14 those closest to him *being* Carshena, Shethar, Admatha, Tarshish, Meres, Marsena, and Memucan, the seven princes of Persia and Media, who had access to the king's presence, *and* who ranked highest in the kingdom):

15 "What *shall we* do to Queen Vashti, according to law, because she did not obey the command of King Ahasuerus *brought to her* by the eunuchs?"

16 And Memucan answered before the king and the princes: "Queen Vashti has not only wronged the king, but also all the princes, and all the people who *are* in all the provinces of King Ahasuerus.

17 "For the queen's behavior will become known to all women, so that they will despise their husbands in their eyes, when they report, 'King Ahasuerus commanded Queen Vashti to be brought in before him, but she did not come.'

18 "This very day the *noble* ladies of Persia and Media will say to all the king's officials that they have heard of the behavior of the queen. Thus *there will be* excessive contempt and wrath.

19 "If it pleases the king, let a royal decree go out from him, and let it be recorded in the laws of the Persians and the Medes, so that it will not be altered, that Vashti shall come no more before King Ahasuerus; and let the king give her royal position to another who is better than she.

20 "When the king's decree which he will make is proclaimed throughout all his empire (for it is great), all wives will honor their husbands, both great and small."

21 And the reply pleased the king and the princes, and the king did according to the word of Memucan.

22 Then he sent letters to all the king's provinces, to each province in its own script, and to every people in their own language, that each man should be master in his own house, and speak in the language of his own people.

1:1 [a]Generally identified with Xerxes I (485–464 B.C.) **1:2** [a]Or *Susa,* and so throughout this book

LIFE LESSONS

➤ 1:13 — *Then the king said to the wise men who understood the times . . . .*

We are wise to make the effort to "understand the times," to gain an accurate picture of how people of our era tend to think, behave, and communicate. Then we can have a maximum impact on our culture for Christ.

➤ 1:18 — *"This very day the noble ladies of Persia and Media will say to all the king's officials that they have heard of the behavior of the queen. Thus there will be excessive contempt and wrath."*

Those in authority—officials, teachers, parents, etc.—can have a huge impact on the people around them just by the way they act, whether for good or ill (see 1 Cor. 15:33; 1 Tim. 4:12).

Esther Becomes Queen

2 After these things, when the wrath of King Ahasuerus subsided, he remembered Vashti, what she had done, and what had been decreed against her.
2 Then the king's servants who attended him said: "Let beautiful young virgins be sought for the king;
3 "and let the king appoint officers in all the provinces of his kingdom, that they may gather all the beautiful young virgins to Shushan the citadel, into the women's quarters, under the custody of Hegai[a] the king's eunuch, custodian of the women. And let beauty preparations be given *them.*
4 "Then let the young woman who pleases the king be queen instead of Vashti." This thing pleased the king, and he did so.
5 In Shushan the citadel there was a certain Jew whose name *was* Mordecai the son of Jair, the son of Shimei, the son of Kish, a Benjamite.
6 *Kish*[a] had been carried away from Jerusalem with the captives who had been captured with Jeconiah[b] king of Judah, whom Nebuchadnezzar the king of Babylon had carried away.
7 And *Mordecai* had brought up Hadassah, that *is,* Esther, his uncle's daughter, for she had neither father nor mother. The young woman *was* lovely and beautiful. When her father and mother died, Mordecai took her as his own daughter.
8 So it was, when the king's command and decree were heard, and when many young women were gathered at Shushan the citadel, *under* the custody of Hegai, that Esther also was taken to the king's palace, into the care of Hegai the custodian of the women.
➤9 Now the young woman pleased him, and she obtained his favor; so he readily gave beauty preparations to her, besides her allowance. Then seven choice maidservants were provided for her from the king's palace, and he moved her and her maidservants to the best *place* in the house of the women.
10 Esther had not revealed her people or family, for Mordecai had charged her not to reveal *it.* ➤
11 And every day Mordecai paced in front of the court of the women's quarters, to learn of Esther's welfare and what was happening to her.
12 Each young woman's turn came to go in to King Ahasuerus after she had completed twelve months' preparation, according to the regulations for the women, for thus were the days of their preparation apportioned: six months with oil of myrrh, and six months with perfumes and preparations for beautifying women.
13 Thus *prepared, each* young woman went to the king, and she was given whatever she desired to take with her from the women's quarters to the king's palace.
14 In the evening she went, and in the morning she returned to the second house of the women, to the custody of Shaashgaz, the king's eunuch who kept the concubines. She would not go in to the king again unless the king delighted in her and called for her by name.
15 Now when the turn came for Esther the daughter of Abihail the uncle of Mordecai, who had taken her as his daughter, to go in to the king, she requested nothing but what Hegai the king's eunuch, the custodian of the women, advised. And Esther obtained favor in the sight of all who saw her. ➤
16 So Esther was taken to King Ahasuerus, into his royal palace, in the tenth month, which *is* the month of Tebeth, in the seventh year of his reign.
17 The king loved Esther more than all the *other* women, and she obtained grace and favor in his sight more than all the virgins; so he set the royal crown upon her head and made her queen instead of Vashti. ➤
18 Then the king made a great feast, the Feast of Esther, for all his officials and ser-

2:3 [a]Hebrew *Hege* **2:6** [a]Literally *Who* [b]Same as *Jehoiachin,* 2 Kings 24:6 and elsewhere

LIFE LESSONS

➤ **2:9 — *Now the young woman pleased him, and she obtained his favor . . . .***

God often demonstrates His grace to His godly children by giving them the unexpected favor of powerful or influential individuals. Whenever this happens, it is no accident; it is the work of our sovereign God.

➤ **2:10 — *Esther had not revealed her people or family, for Mordecai had charged her not to reveal it.***

Esther's obedience in a small thing led eventually to a great blessing in a difficult time. *Every* act of godly obedience brings the smile of God!

➤ **2:15 — *Now when the turn came for Esther . . . to go in to the king, she requested nothing but what Hegai the king's eunuch, the custodian of the women, advised.***

Esther not only had an obedient spirit, but she also possessed a humble heart. She realized that she did not know best in this unfamiliar situation, and so wisely acted on the advice of a more experienced person.

➤ **2:17 — *The king loved Esther more than all the other women, and she obtained grace and favor in his sight more than all the virgins; so he set the royal crown upon her head . . . .***

Esther did not know at the time the king showed her "grace and favor" that the Lord actually was behind these events. But God remains intimately involved in our lives even when we don't realize it.

Life Examples:

MORDECAI

Bowing Before No Man

ESTH. 3:2

If anyone ever had reason to fudge on what he knew was right, it was Mordecai. Mordecai had a choice: either bow before a powerful Persian official, or lose his life. Mordecai stood strong, however, and refused to disobey God's commandment against bowing in worship to anyone but Him (Ex. 20:3).

Day after day, the lackeys of this vain official tried to "reason" with Mordecai. But Mordecai refused to bow. Perhaps he remembered God's words: "Who are you that you should be afraid of a man who will die, and of the son of a man who will be made like grass? And you forget the LORD your Maker . . ." (Is. 51:12, 13).

In the end, God not only spared Mordecai's life, but He made him a powerful and honored public official (Esth. 10:3). God means it when He says, "those who honor Me I will honor" (1 Sam. 2:30)!

See the Life Principles Index for further study: 21. Obedience always brings blessing.

vants; and he proclaimed a holiday in the
provinces and gave gifts according to the generosity of a king.

Mordecai Discovers a Plot

19 When virgins were gathered together a
second time, Mordecai sat within the king's
gate.
20 *Now* Esther had not revealed her family
and her people, just as Mordecai had charged
her, for Esther obeyed the command of
Mordecai as when she was brought up by
him.
21 In those days, while Mordecai sat within
the king's gate, two of the king's eunuchs,
Bigthan and Teresh, doorkeepers, became furious and sought to lay hands on King Ahasuerus.
22 So the matter became known to Mordecai,
who told Queen Esther, and Esther informed
the king in Mordecai's name.
23 And when an inquiry was made into the
matter, it was confirmed, and both were
hanged on a gallows; and it was written in the
book of the chronicles in the presence of the
king.

Haman's Conspiracy Against the Jews

3 After these things King Ahasuerus promoted Haman, the son of Hammedatha
the Agagite, and advanced him and set
his seat above all the princes who *were* with
him.
2 And all the king's servants who *were*
within the king's gate bowed and paid homage to Haman, for so the king had commanded concerning him. But Mordecai would
not bow or pay homage.
3 Then the king's servants who *were* within
the king's gate said to Mordecai, "Why do you
transgress the king's command?"
4 Now it happened, when they spoke to him
daily and he would not listen to them, that
they told *it* to Haman, to see whether Mordecai's words would stand; for *Mordecai* had
told them that he *was* a Jew.
5 When Haman saw that Mordecai did not
bow or pay him homage, Haman was filled
with wrath.
6 But he disdained to lay hands on Mordecai alone, for they had told him of the people
of Mordecai. Instead, Haman sought to destroy all the Jews who *were* throughout the
whole kingdom of Ahasuerus—the people of
Mordecai.

LIFE LESSONS

➤ **2:23 — *And when an inquiry was made into the matter, it was confirmed, and both were hanged on a gallows; and it was written in the book of the chronicles in the presence of the king.***

God can use even secular records to accomplish His will and bless His people. No one knew at the time how important this incident would become—no one, of course, except God (see Esther 6).

➤ **3:2 — *And all the king's servants who were within the king's gate bowed and paid homage to Haman, for so the king had commanded concerning him. But Mordecai would not bow or pay homage.***

Mordecai owed his allegiance to God alone, and refused to bow in worship to any man, regardless of how powerful he might be. If we fear God, we will not be afraid of any man.

➤ **3:4 — *Now it happened, when they spoke to him daily and he would not listen to them, that they told it to Haman, to see whether Mordecai's words would stand . . . .***

People who do not know the Lord will often try to convince us and urge us and even coerce us into violating our convictions, but if we wish to honor God, we will obey His voice above all others.

7 In the first month, which is the month of Nisan, in the twelfth year of King Ahasuerus, they cast Pur (that *is,* the lot), before Haman to determine the day and the month,[a] until *it fell on the* twelfth *month,*[b] which *is* the month of Adar.

8 Then Haman said to King Ahasuerus, "There is a certain people scattered and dispersed among the people in all the provinces of your kingdom; their laws *are* different from all *other* people's, and they do not keep the king's laws. Therefore it *is* not fitting for the king to let them remain.

9 "If it pleases the king, let *a decree* be written that they be destroyed, and I will pay ten thousand talents of silver into the hands of those who do the work, to bring *it* into the king's treasuries."

➤ 10 So the king took his signet ring from his hand and gave it to Haman, the son of Hammedatha the Agagite, the enemy of the Jews.

11 And the king said to Haman, "The money and the people *are* given to you, to do with them as seems good to you."

12 Then the king's scribes were called on the thirteenth day of the first month, and *a decree* was written according to all that Haman commanded—to the king's satraps, to the governors who *were* over each province, to the officials of all people, to every province according to its script, and to every people in their language. In the name of King Ahasuerus it was written, and sealed with the king's signet ring.

13 And the letters were sent by couriers into all the king's provinces, to destroy, to kill, and to annihilate all the Jews, both young and old, little children and women, in one day, on the thirteenth *day* of the twelfth month, which *is* the month of Adar, and to plunder their possessions.[a]

14 A copy of the document was to be issued as law in every province, being published for all people, that they should be ready for that day.

15 The couriers went out, hastened by the king's command; and the decree was proclaimed in Shushan the citadel. So the king and Haman sat down to drink, but the city of Shushan was perplexed.

Esther Agrees to Help the Jews

4 When Mordecai learned all that had happened, he tore his clothes and put on sackcloth and ashes, and went out into the midst of the city. He cried out with a loud and bitter cry.

2 He went as far as the front of the king's gate, for no one *might* enter the king's gate clothed with sackcloth.

3 And in every province where the king's command and decree arrived, *there was* great mourning among the Jews, with fasting, weeping, and wailing; and many lay in sackcloth and ashes. ➤

4 So Esther's maids and eunuchs came and told her, and the queen was deeply distressed. Then she sent garments to clothe Mordecai and take his sackcloth away from him, but he would not accept *them.*

5 Then Esther called Hathach, *one* of the king's eunuchs whom he had appointed to attend her, and she gave him a command concerning Mordecai, to learn what and why this *was.*

6 So Hathach went out to Mordecai in the city square that *was* in front of the king's gate.

7 And Mordecai told him all that had happened to him, and the sum of money that Haman had promised to pay into the king's treasuries to destroy the Jews.

8 He also gave him a copy of the written decree for their destruction, which was given at Shushan, that he might show it to Esther and explain it to her, and that he might command her to go in to the king to make supplication to him and plead before him for her people.

9 So Hathach returned and told Esther the words of Mordecai.

10 Then Esther spoke to Hathach, and gave him a command for Mordecai:

11 "All the king's servants and the people of the king's provinces know that any man or ➤

3:7 [a]Septuagint adds *to destroy the people of Mordecai in one day;* Vulgate adds *the nation of the Jews should be destroyed.* [b]Following Masoretic Text and Vulgate; Septuagint reads *and the lot fell on the fourteenth of the month.* **3:13** [a]Septuagint adds the text of the letter here.

LIFE LESSONS

➤ ***3:10 — So the king took his signet ring from his hand and gave it to Haman, the son of Hammedatha the Agagite, the enemy of the Jews.***

Those who plot against the people of God become not only the enemies of God's people, but the enemies of God Himself. God says to His obedient people, "I will be an enemy to your enemies" (Ex. 23:22).

➤ ***4:3 — And in every province where the king's command and decree arrived, there was great mourning among the Jews, with fasting, weeping, and wailing; and many lay in sackcloth and ashes.***

Although prayer is not explicitly mentioned here, the references to fasting strongly suggest it. When catastrophe looms, prayer and fasting will do more for us than any other response.

➤ ***4:11 — ". . . any man or woman who goes into the inner court to the king, who has not been called, he has but one law: put all to death, except the one to whom the king holds out the golden scepter . . . ."***

When something threatens our lives, we naturally feel great fear. There is no sin in this. It's how we respond to that fear—with a courageous trust in God or a spineless desire for self-preservation—that makes the difference.

woman who goes into the inner court to the
king, who has not been called, *he has* but one
law: put *all* to death, except the one to whom
the king holds out the golden scepter, that he
may live. Yet I myself have not been called to
go in to the king these thirty days."
12 So they told Mordecai Esther's words.
13 And Mordecai told *them* to answer Esther:
"Do not think in your heart that you will escape
in the king's palace any more than all
the other Jews.
✳ 14 "For if you remain completely silent at this
time, relief and deliverance will arise for the
Jews from another place, but you and your father's
house will perish. Yet who knows
whether you have come to the kingdom for
such a time as this?"
15 Then Esther told *them* to reply to Mordecai:
16 "Go, gather all the Jews who are present
in Shushan, and fast for me; neither eat nor
drink for three days, night or day. My maids
and I will fast likewise. And so I will go to the
king, which *is* against the law; and if I perish,
I perish!"
➤ 17 So Mordecai went his way and did according
to all that Esther commanded him.[a]

Esther's Banquet

5 Now it happened on the third day that Esther
put on *her* royal *robes* and stood in
the inner court of the king's palace, across
from the king's house, while the king sat on
his royal throne in the royal house, facing the
entrance of the house.[a]
2 So it was, when the king saw Queen Esther
standing in the court, *that* she found
favor in his sight, and the king held out to Esther
the golden scepter that *was* in his hand.
Then Esther went near and touched the top of
the scepter.
3 And the king said to her, "What do you
wish, Queen Esther? What *is* your request? It
shall be given to you—up to half the kingdom!"
➤ 4 So Esther answered, "If it pleases the king,
let the king and Haman come today to the
banquet that I have prepared for him."
5 Then the king said, "Bring Haman quickly,
that he may do as Esther has said." So the
king and Haman went to the banquet that Esther
had prepared.
6 At the banquet of wine the king said to Esther,
"What *is* your petition? It shall be
granted you. What *is* your request, up to half
the kingdom? It shall be done!"
7 Then Esther answered and said, "My petition
and request *is this:*
8 "If I have found favor in the sight of the
king, and if it pleases the king to grant my petition
and fulfill my request, then let the king
and Haman come to the banquet which I will
prepare for them, and tomorrow I will do as
the king has said."

Haman's Plot Against Mordecai

9 So Haman went out that day joyful and
with a glad heart; but when Haman saw
Mordecai in the king's gate, and that he did
not stand or tremble before him, he was filled
with indignation against Mordecai.
10 Nevertheless Haman restrained himself
and went home, and he sent and called for his
friends and his wife Zeresh.
11 Then Haman told them of his great riches,
the multitude of his children, everything in
which the king had promoted him, and how
he had advanced him above the officials and
servants of the king.
12 Moreover Haman said, "Besides, Queen
Esther invited no one but me to come in with
the king to the banquet that she prepared;
and tomorrow I am again invited by her,
along with the king.
13 "Yet all this avails me nothing, so long as I
see Mordecai the Jew sitting at the king's
gate."
14 Then his wife Zeresh and all his friends
said to him, "Let a gallows be made, fifty cubits
high, and in the morning suggest to the
king that Mordecai be hanged on it; then go
merrily with the king to the banquet." And the
thing pleased Haman; so he had the gallows
made.

4:17 [a]Septuagint adds a prayer of Mordecai here.
5:1 [a]Septuagint adds many extra details in verses 1 and 2.

LIFE LESSONS

➤ 4:14 — *"For if you remain completely silent at this time, relief and deliverance will arise for the Jews from another place . . . ."*

God is never bound by our faithlessness or cowardice. He desires to use us to bless His people, but if we fail to trust Him, He will use someone else. But He will always accomplish His will.

➤ 4:17 — *So Mordecai went his way and did according to all that Esther commanded him.*

To this point in the story, Esther has always obeyed the words of Mordecai. Now the tables turn, and Mordecai obeys the words of Queen Esther. Thus this pair pictures a godly mutual submission (see Eph. 5:21).

➤ 5:4 — *"If it pleases the king, let the king and Haman come today to the banquet that I have prepared for him."*

Esther demonstrates as well as anyone in Scripture the wisdom of God's Word when it tells us to honor those who deserve honor, such as the king (Rom. 13:1–7; 1 Pet. 2:17). God honors us when we honor His Word!

WHAT THE BIBLE SAYS ABOUT THE BENEFITS OF PRAYER AND FASTING

Esth. 4:16

When God calls us to prayer and fasting, He always does so for our benefit. The Scriptures point out at least seven benefits to prayer and fasting.

1. *Our attitudes, feelings, and thoughts get sifted, pruned and purified so that God might entrust us with a greater ministry.* By fasting and praying, we become more disciplined toward the things of the Father. We give Him opportunity to cut away from us those things that will slow us down, do us in, or keep us from His plans and purposes.

2. *We are able to discern more clearly the will of God for our lives.* Fasting clears our spiritual eyes and ears so we can accurately discern what God desires to reveal to us.

3. *We are confronted with our sins and shortcomings so we might confess them to God, receive forgiveness for them, and walk in greater righteousness.* Many times we break stubborn, sinful habits when we fast and pray. Fasting and prayer cleanse us and purify us from the errors that have kept us entangled in sin and folly.

4. *We experience a release of supernatural power.* Genuine fasting and prayer result in spiritual growth, including a renewed outpouring of supernatural power. Certain problems and situations cannot be resolved apart from fasting and prayer.

5. *We can influence national issues and concerns through our prayers.* As we fast and pray for our nation, God will move. He will pour out His Spirit, in His ways and in His timing. We can count on it.

6. *We can help build up God's people.* Prayer is the generator of the church. It gives power to its ministers. It propels outreach to the lost. It creates a climate in which evangelistic efforts succeed.

7. *Our minds are sharpened.* When we fast and pray, we begin to understand the Scriptures as never before. We become sensitive to God's timing and direction, with an increased awareness and ability to discern. We become keenly aware of what God desires to do and accomplish not only in our lives, but also in the lives of those around us.

Genuine fasting and prayer result in spiritual growth.

See the Life Principles Index for further study:
15. Brokenness is God's requirement for maximum usefulness.
25. God blesses us so that we might bless others.

Life Examples:

KING AHASUERUS

A Restless Spirit

ESTH. 6:1

God often uses a restless spirit to get a person's attention.

After Haman tricked King Ahasuerus into signing an edict for the annihilation of the Jews, the king could not sleep. Because of his restless spirit, he "commanded to bring the book of the records of the chronicles; and they were read before the king" (Esth. 6:1). That night Ahasuerus discovered that Mordecai had earlier saved the king's life. And in the end, Mordecai was honored and Haman died on the gallows.

God frequently uses a persistent restlessness to direct us. This type of restlessness originates in the deepest aspect of a person's being and persists over time.

When you have that feeling, stop and ask the Lord what He is trying to say. Spend extended time in the Word and in prayer. Set aside a block of time to quiet yourself before the Lord so you can hear from Him clearly.

See the Life Principles Index for further study:
22. To walk in the Spirit is to obey the initial promptings of the Spirit.

The King Honors Mordecai

6 That night the king could not sleep. So one
was commanded to bring the book of the
records of the chronicles; and they were read
before the king.
2 And it was found written that Mordecai
had told of Bigthana and Teresh, two of the
king's eunuchs, the doorkeepers who had
sought to lay hands on King Ahasuerus.
3 Then the king said, "What honor or dignity
has been bestowed on Mordecai for this?" And
the king's servants who attended him said,
"Nothing has been done for him."
4 So the king said, "Who *is* in the court?"
Now Haman had *just* entered the outer court
of the king's palace to suggest that the king
hang Mordecai on the gallows that he had
prepared for him.
5 The king's servants said to him, "Haman
is there, standing in the court." And the king
said, "Let him come in."
6 So Haman came in, and the king asked
him, "What shall be done for the man whom
the king delights to honor?" Now Haman
thought in his heart, "Whom would the king
delight to honor more than me?"
7 And Haman answered the king, "*For* the
man whom the king delights to honor,
8 "let a royal robe be brought which the
king has worn, and a horse on which the king
has ridden, which has a royal crest placed on
its head.
9 "Then let this robe and horse be delivered
to the hand of one of the king's most noble
princes, that he may array the man whom
the king delights to honor. Then parade him
on horseback through the city square, and
proclaim before him: 'Thus shall it be done
to the man whom the king delights to
honor!'"
10 Then the king said to Haman, "Hurry, take ➤
the robe and the horse, as you have suggested, and do so for Mordecai the Jew who
sits within the king's gate! Leave nothing undone of all that you have spoken."
11 So Haman took the robe and the horse, arrayed Mordecai and led him on horseback
through the city square, and proclaimed before him, "Thus shall it be done to the man
whom the king delights to honor!"
12 Afterward Mordecai went back to the
king's gate. But Haman hurried to his house,
mourning and with his head covered.
13 When Haman told his wife Zeresh and all
his friends everything that had happened to
him, his wise men and his wife Zeresh said to
him, "If Mordecai, before whom you have
begun to fall, is of Jewish descent, you will
not prevail against him but will surely fall before him."
14 While they *were* still talking with him, the
king's eunuchs came, and hastened to bring
Haman to the banquet which Esther had prepared.

Haman Hanged Instead of Mordecai

7 So the king and Haman went to dine with
Queen Esther.
2 And on the second day, at the banquet

LIFE LESSONS

➤ **6:10 — *Then the king said to Haman, "Hurry, take the robe and the horse, as you have suggested, and do so for Mordecai the Jew . . . ."***

God loves to use for good what men intend for evil. In doing so, He shows that He alone is sovereign.

of wine, the king again said to Esther,
"What *is* your petition, Queen Esther? It
shall be granted you. And what *is* your request, up to half the kingdom? It shall be
done!"
➤ 3 Then Queen Esther answered and said,
"If I have found favor in your sight, O king,
and if it pleases the king, let my life be given
me at my petition, and my people at my request.
4 "For we have been sold, my people and I,
to be destroyed, to be killed, and to be annihilated. Had we been sold as male and female
slaves, I would have held my tongue, although
the enemy could never compensate for the
king's loss."
5 So King Ahasuerus answered and said to
Queen Esther, "Who is he, and where is he,
who would dare presume in his heart to do
such a thing?"
6 And Esther said, "The adversary and enemy *is* this wicked Haman!" So Haman was
terrified before the king and queen.
7 Then the king arose in his wrath from the
banquet of wine *and went* into the palace garden; but Haman stood before Queen Esther,
pleading for his life, for he saw that evil was
determined against him by the king.
8 When the king returned from the palace
garden to the place of the banquet of wine,
Haman had fallen across the couch where Esther *was*. Then the king said, "Will he also assault the queen while I *am* in the house?" As
the word left the king's mouth, they covered
Haman's face.
➤ 9 Now Harbonah, one of the eunuchs, said
to the king, "Look! The gallows, fifty cubits
high, which Haman made for Mordecai, who
spoke good on the king's behalf, is standing
at the house of Haman." Then the king said,
"Hang him on it!"
10 So they hanged Haman on the gallows
that he had prepared for Mordecai. Then the
king's wrath subsided.

Esther Saves the Jews

8 On that day King Ahasuerus gave Queen
Esther the house of Haman, the enemy of
the Jews. And Mordecai came before the
king, for Esther had told how he *was related*
to her.
2 So the king took off his signet ring, which ≺
he had taken from Haman, and gave it to
Mordecai; and Esther appointed Mordecai
over the house of Haman.
3 Now Esther spoke again to the king, fell
down at his feet, and implored him with tears
to counteract the evil of Haman the Agagite,
and the scheme which he had devised against
the Jews.
4 And the king held out the golden scepter
toward Esther. So Esther arose and stood before the king,
5 and said, "If it pleases the king, and if I
have found favor in his sight and the thing
seems right to the king and I am pleasing in
his eyes, let it be written to revoke the letters
devised by Haman, the son of Hammedatha
the Agagite, which he wrote to annihilate the
Jews who *are* in all the king's provinces.
6 "For how can I endure to see the evil that
will come to my people? Or how can I endure
to see the destruction of my countrymen?"
7 Then King Ahasuerus said to Queen Esther and Mordecai the Jew, "Indeed, I have
given Esther the house of Haman, and they
have hanged him on the gallows because he
tried to lay his hand on the Jews.
8 "You yourselves write *a decree* concerning ≺
the Jews, as you please, in the king's name,
and seal *it* with the king's signet ring; for
whatever is written in the king's name and
sealed with the king's signet ring no one can
revoke."
9 So the king's scribes were called at that
time, in the third month, which *is* the month
of Sivan, on the twenty-third *day;* and it was
written, according to all that Mordecai commanded, to the Jews, the satraps, the gover-

LIFE LESSONS

➤ 7:3 — *"If I have found favor in your sight, O king, and if it pleases the king, let my life be given me at my petition, and my people at my request."*

Even in her urgent request, Esther demonstrates a humble spirit and a restrained attitude—thus endearing her even more to the king. Her godly self-control wins her far more than a violent outburst ever could.

➤ 7:9 — *"The gallows, fifty cubits high, which Haman made for Mordecai, who spoke good on the king's behalf, is standing at the house of Haman." Then the king said, "Hang him on it!"*

The reversals of fortune just keep happening. Even when the skies grow darkest, we can stand on God's Word and pray that He will intervene for our good and His glory (see Ps. 9:15; 57:6).

➤ 8:2 — *So the king took off his signet ring, which he had taken from Haman, and gave it to Mordecai; and Esther appointed Mordecai over the house of Haman.*

The story of Mordecai and Haman well illustrates Proverbs 13:22: "A good man leaves an inheritance to his children's children, but the wealth of the sinner is stored up for the righteous."

➤ 8:8 — *". . . write a decree . . . in the king's name, and seal it with the king's signet ring; for whatever is written in the king's name and sealed with the king's signet ring no one can revoke."*

Not even the king could revoke his own order, but he could issue another order that would supersede his first one. God does whatever He needs to in order to bless His obedient people!

nors, and the princes of the provinces from
India to Ethiopia, one hundred and twenty-
seven provinces *in all,* to every province in its
own script, to every people in their own language, and to the Jews in their own script and
language.
10 And he wrote in the name of King Ahasuerus, sealed *it* with the king's signet ring,
and sent letters by couriers on horseback, riding on royal horses bred from swift steeds.[a]
11 By these letters the king permitted the
Jews who *were* in every city to gather together and protect their lives—to destroy, kill,
and annihilate all the forces of any people or
province that would assault them, *both* little
children and women, and to plunder their
possessions,
➤ 12 on one day in all the provinces of King
Ahasuerus, on the thirteenth *day* of the
twelfth month, which *is* the month of Adar.[a]
13 A copy of the document was to be issued
as a decree in every province and published
for all people, so that the Jews would be ready
on that day to avenge themselves on their enemies.
14 The couriers who rode on royal horses
went out, hastened and pressed on by the
king's command. And the decree was issued
in Shushan the citadel.
15 So Mordecai went out from the presence
of the king in royal apparel of blue and white,
with a great crown of gold and a garment of
fine linen and purple; and the city of Shushan
rejoiced and was glad.
16 The Jews had light and gladness, joy and
honor.
17 And in every province and city, wherever
the king's command and decree came, the
Jews had joy and gladness, a feast and a holiday. Then many of the people of the land became Jews, because fear of the Jews fell upon
them.

The Jews Destroy Their Tormentors

✳➤ 9 Now in the twelfth month, that *is,* the
month of Adar, on the thirteenth day, *the*
time came for the king's command and his decree to be executed. On the day that the enemies of the Jews had hoped to overpower them,
the opposite occurred, in that the Jews themselves overpowered those who hated them.
2 The Jews gathered together in their cities
throughout all the provinces of King Ahasuerus to lay hands on those who sought their
harm. And no one could withstand them, because fear of them fell upon all people.
3 And all the officials of the provinces, the
satraps, the governors, and all those doing the
king's work, helped the Jews, because the
fear of Mordecai fell upon them.
4 For Mordecai *was* great in the king's
palace, and his fame spread throughout all
the provinces; for this man Mordecai became
increasingly prominent.
5 Thus the Jews defeated all their enemies
with the stroke of the sword, with slaughter
and destruction, and did what they pleased
with those who hated them.
6 And in Shushan the citadel the Jews killed
and destroyed five hundred men.
7 Also Parshandatha, Dalphon, Aspatha,
8 Poratha, Adalia, Aridatha,
9 Parmashta, Arisai, Aridai, and Vajezatha—
10 the ten sons of Haman the son of Hammedatha, the enemy of the Jews—they killed; but
they did not lay a hand on the plunder.
11 On that day the number of those who were
killed in Shushan the citadel was brought to
the king.
12 And the king said to Queen Esther, "The
Jews have killed and destroyed five hundred
men in Shushan the citadel, and the ten sons
of Haman. What have they done in the rest of
the king's provinces? Now what *is* your petition? It shall be granted to you. Or what *is*
your further request? It shall be done."
13 Then Esther said, "If it pleases the king, let
it be granted to the Jews who *are* in Shushan
to do again tomorrow according to today's
decree, and let Haman's ten sons be hanged
on the gallows."
14 So the king commanded this to be done;
the decree was issued in Shushan, and they
hanged Haman's ten sons.
15 And the Jews who *were* in Shushan gathered together again on the fourteenth day of
the month of Adar and killed three hundred
men at Shushan; but they did not lay a hand
on the plunder.
16 The remainder of the Jews in the king's
provinces gathered together and protected

8:10 [a]Literally *sons of the swift horses* **8:12** [a]Septuagint adds the text of the letter here.

LIFE LESSONS

➤ **8:12 — *. . . on one day in all the provinces of King Ahasuerus, on the thirteenth day of the twelfth month, which is the month of Adar.***

This decree was to take effect just before Haman's genocidal order could be carried out. God often waits until the last moment to rescue His people. Will we trust Him even then?

➤ **9:1 — *On the day that the enemies of the Jews had hoped to overpower them, the opposite occurred, in that the Jews themselves overpowered those who hated them.***

Haman never lived to see the total reversal of his diabolical plan. God loves to act on behalf of those who wait for Him!

their lives, had rest from their enemies, and
killed seventy-five thousand of their enemies;
but they did not lay a hand on the plunder.
17 *This was* on the thirteenth day of the
month of Adar. And on the fourteenth of *the
month*[a] they rested and made it a day of feasting and gladness.

The Feast of Purim

18 But the Jews who *were* at Shushan assembled together on the thirteenth *day,* as well as
on the fourteenth; and on the fifteenth of *the
month*[a] they rested, and made it a day of
feasting and gladness.
19 Therefore the Jews of the villages who
dwelt in the unwalled towns celebrated the
fourteenth day of the month of Adar *with*
gladness and feasting, as a holiday, and for
sending presents to one another.
20 And Mordecai wrote these things and sent
letters to all the Jews, near and far, who *were*
in all the provinces of King Ahasuerus,
21 to establish among them that they should
celebrate yearly the fourteenth and fifteenth
days of the month of Adar,
22 as the days on which the Jews had rest
from their enemies, as the month which was
turned from sorrow to joy for them, and from
mourning to a holiday; that they should make
them days of feasting and joy, of sending
presents to one another and gifts to the poor.
23 So the Jews accepted the custom which
they had begun, as Mordecai had written to
them,
24 because Haman, the son of Hammedatha
the Agagite, the enemy of all the Jews, had
plotted against the Jews to annihilate them,
and had cast Pur (that *is,* the lot), to consume
them and destroy them;
25 but when *Esther*[a] came before the king, he
commanded by letter that this[b] wicked plot
which *Haman* had devised against the Jews
should return on his own head, and that he
and his sons should be hanged on the gallows.
26 So they called these days Purim, after
the name Pur. Therefore, because of all the
words of this letter, what they had seen concerning this matter, and what had happened
to them,
27 the Jews established and imposed it upon
themselves and their descendants and all
who would join them, that without fail they
should celebrate these two days every year,
according to the written *instructions* and according to the *prescribed* time,
28 *that* these days *should be* remembered
and kept throughout every generation, every
family, every province, and every city, that
these days of Purim should not fail *to be observed* among the Jews, and *that* the memory
of them should not perish among their descendants.
29 Then Queen Esther, the daughter of Abihail, with Mordecai the Jew, wrote with full
authority to confirm this second letter about
Purim.
30 And *Mordecai* sent letters to all the Jews,
to the one hundred and twenty-seven
provinces of the kingdom of Ahasuerus, *with*
words of peace and truth,
31 to confirm these days of Purim at their *appointed* time, as Mordecai the Jew and Queen
Esther had prescribed for them, and as they
had decreed for themselves and their descendants concerning matters of their fasting and
lamenting.
32 So the decree of Esther confirmed these
matters of Purim, and it was written in the
book.

Mordecai's Advancement

10 And King Ahasuerus imposed tribute
on the land and *on* the islands of the
sea.
2 Now all the acts of his power and his
might, and the account of the greatness of
Mordecai, to which the king advanced him,
are they not written in the book of the chronicles of the kings of Media and Persia?
3 For Mordecai the Jew *was* second to King
Ahasuerus, and was great among the Jews
and well received by the multitude of his
brethren, seeking the good of his people and
speaking peace to all his countrymen.[a]

9:17 [a]Literally *it* **9:18** [a]Literally *it* **9:25** [a]Literally *she* or *it* [b]Literally *his* **10:3** [a]Literally *seed.* Septuagint and Vulgate add a dream of Mordecai here; Vulgate adds six more chapters.

LIFE LESSONS

➤ 9:22 — *. . . the month . . . was turned from sorrow to joy for them, and from mourning to a holiday . . . days of feasting and joy, of sending presents to one another and gifts to the poor.*

What Satan intended to be a day of slaughter and mourning for the Jews, God turned into a day of rejoicing and sending presents. The sky never grows so dark that God can't make a brilliant rainbow out of it.

➤ 10:3 — *For Mordecai the Jew was second to King Ahasuerus, and was great among the Jews and well received by the multitude of his brethren, seeking the good of his people . . . .*

Mordecai took his place, along with Joseph and Daniel before him, as a godly man living in exile whom God raised to a position of authority second only to the king. God is sovereign, and God is good!

THE BOOK OF

JOB

Job is perhaps the oldest book of the Bible. Set in the period of the patriarchs (Abraham, Isaac, Jacob, and Joseph), it tells the story of a man who loses everything—his wealth, his family, his reputation, his health—and wrestles with the question, "Why?"

The book begins with a heavenly debate between God and Satan, moves through three cycles of earthly debates between Job and his friends, and concludes with a dramatic "divine diagnosis" of Job's problem. In the end, Job acknowledges the sovereignty of God in his life and receives back more than he had accumulated before his trials.

Job's name is also the Hebrew title for this book. The name is thought to mean "persecuted."

Themes: God is sovereign, even in the face of life's very worst trials. He will not allow us to be tested beyond our ability to withstand whatever adversity confronts us.

Author: Unknown. (Job, Moses, and Solomon have been suggested.)

Time: When was the Book of Job written? Scholars have debated this question for generations. Many scholars regard it as the oldest book in the Bible, while others believe it was written as late as the time of the Babylonian exile.

Structure: The first part of the book (1:1—2:10) describes the identity of Job, what happened to him, and who caused it. The second part (2:11—31:40) covers the arrival of Job's three friends and the conversations that took place between them and Job. Part three (chapters 32–37) describes Job's instruction from a younger man named Elihu. Part four (chapters 38, 39) gives God's reply to Job's questions about his suffering. Part five (40:1—42:9) covers Job's two confessions, as well as God's rebuke of Eliphaz, Bildad, and Zophar, and His demand that they make sacrifices for their sinful words. The final scene (42:10–17) describes Job's prayers for his friends and the restoration of his wealth and position.

As you read Job, watch for several life principles that play an important role in this book:

9. Trusting God means looking beyond what we can see to what God sees. *See Job 1:20–22; page 585.*

26. Adversity is a bridge to a deeper relationship with God. *See Job 42:1–6; page 618.*

11. God assumes full responsibility for our needs when we obey Him. *See Job 42:7–17; page 619.*

7. The dark moments of our life will last only so long as is necessary for God to accomplish His purposes in us. *See Job 42:10; page 619.*

14. God acts on behalf of those who wait for Him. *See Job 42:12–17; page 619.*

Job and His Family in Uz

1 There was a man in the land of Uz, whose
name *was* Job; and that man was blameless and upright, and one who feared God and
shunned evil.
2 And seven sons and three daughters were
born to him.
3 Also, his possessions were seven thousand sheep, three thousand camels, five hundred yoke of oxen, five hundred female
donkeys, and a very large household, so that
this man was the greatest of all the people of
the East.
4 And his sons would go and feast *in their*
houses, each on his *appointed* day, and would
send and invite their three sisters to eat and
drink with them.
5 So it was, when the days of feasting had
run their course, that Job would send and
sanctify them, and he would rise early in the
morning and offer burnt offerings *according
to* the number of them all. For Job said, "It
may be that my sons have sinned and
cursed[a] God in their hearts." Thus Job did
regularly.

Satan Attacks Job's Character

6 Now there was a day when the sons of
God came to present themselves before the
LORD, and Satan[a] also came among them.
7 And the LORD said to Satan, "From where
do you come?" So Satan answered the LORD
and said, "From going to and fro on the earth,
and from walking back and forth on it."
8 Then the LORD said to Satan, "Have
you considered My servant Job, that *there is*
none like him on the earth, a blameless and
upright man, one who fears God and shuns
evil?"
9 So Satan answered the LORD and said,
"Does Job fear God for nothing?
10 "Have You not made a hedge around him,
around his household, and around all that he
has on every side? You have blessed the work
of his hands, and his possessions have increased in the land.
11 "But now, stretch out Your hand and touch
all that he has, and he will surely curse You to
Your face!"
12 And the LORD said to Satan, "Behold, all
that he has *is* in your power; only do not lay a
hand on his *person*." So Satan went out from
the presence of the LORD.

Job Loses His Property and Children

13 Now there was a day when his sons and
daughters *were* eating and drinking wine in
their oldest brother's house;
14 and a messenger came to Job and said,
"The oxen were plowing and the donkeys
feeding beside them,
15 "when the Sabeans[a] raided *them* and took
them away—indeed they have killed the servants with the edge of the sword; and I alone
have escaped to tell you!"
16 While he *was* still speaking, another also
came and said, "The fire of God fell from
heaven and burned up the sheep and the servants, and consumed them; and I alone have
escaped to tell you!"
17 While he *was* still speaking, another also
came and said, "The Chaldeans formed three
bands, raided the camels and took them away,
yes, and killed the servants with the edge of
the sword; and I alone have escaped to tell
you!"
18 While he *was* still speaking, another also
came and said, "Your sons and daughters
were eating and drinking wine in their oldest
brother's house,
19 "and suddenly a great wind came from
across[a] the wilderness and struck the four
corners of the house, and it fell on the young
people, and they are dead; and I alone have
escaped to tell you!"
20 Then Job arose, tore his robe, and shaved
his head; and he fell to the ground and worshiped.
21 And he said:

"Naked I came from my mother's womb,
And naked shall I return there.
The LORD gave, and the LORD has taken
away;
Blessed be the name of the LORD."

1:5 [a]Literally *blessed,* but used here in the evil sense, and so in verse 11 and 2:5, 9 **1:6** [a]Literally *the Adversary,* and so throughout this book **1:15** [a]Literally *Sheba* (compare 6:19) **1:19** [a]Septuagint omits *across.*

LIFE LESSONS

1:1 — . . . *Job . . . was blameless and upright, and one who feared God and shunned evil.*

Our behavior *matters*. Those who are in Christ must learn to invite Jesus to live His life in and through them, so that they can increasingly please God and turn away from evil.

1:10 — *"Have You not made a hedge around him, around his household, and around all that he has on every side?"*

Job had no idea of the extent of God's protection that surrounded him and his family. When we joyfully obey God by His Spirit, as Job did, the Lord does the same thing for us that He did for him.

1:20 — *Then Job arose, tore his robe, and shaved his head; and he fell to the ground and worshiped.*

When tragedy strikes, believers hurt just as much as anyone else. They grieve, but not "as others who have no hope" (1 Thess. 4:13). We can worship, even in tragedy, because nothing can separate us from God and His love.

WHAT THE BIBLE SAYS ABOUT HOW GOD LIMITS OUR ADVERSITY

Job 1:12—2:6

Although God may allow Satan to persecute and accuse us, the Lord also puts a limit on the amount of adversity He allows Satan to send our way. In the case of Job, the Lord stopped Satan the first time by commanding him, "Do not lay a hand on his person" (Job 1:12), and the second time with the limiting command, "Spare his life" (2:6). Satan had to comply both times—just as he has to comply today with God's limitations on the amount of adversity you and I suffer as God's children.

There is a limit to adversity. It will come to an end.

One woman quoted to me a favorite Bible phrase of hers: "and it came to pass." She said, "Just think—*it came to pass*. It didn't come to stay!"

Remember that today's troubles are just that: *today's* troubles. A season of trouble is just that: *a season* of trouble. Crises pass. Circumstances change. Situations evolve. God works in and through adversity to bring it to an end, according to His timetable.

It came to pass. It didn't come to stay!

Daniel noted this when he prophesied that the "beast" would be allowed to persecute the saints "for a time and times and half a time" (Dan. 7:23–25). The Aramaic word for "persecute" in verse 24 literally means "wear out." The enemy of our souls attempts to grind us down, to wear us out, to wring us dry. But God says, "Not completely!" Satan can do nothing to us or in us beyond a certain point, if we will continue to trust God and resist the devil.

Furthermore, the Lord does not allow us to be tempted or persecuted beyond our ability to endure: "No temptation has overtaken you except such as is common to man; but God is faithful, who will not allow you to be tempted beyond what you are able, but with the temptation will also make the way of escape, that you may be able to bear it" (1 Cor. 10:13).

What good news this is! God will limit our trials and tribulations, and eventually provide a way of escape from them.

See the Life Principles Index for further study:

7. The dark moments of our life will last only so long as is necessary for God to accomplish His purpose in us.

ANSWERS TO LIFE'S QUESTIONS

What role does Satan play in our adversity?

JOB 2:4–7

In one sense, Satan is ultimately behind all adversity. He is directly responsible for leading Adam and Eve astray and for the catastrophe that followed. But his involvement in adversity extends far beyond his activity in the Garden of Eden.

Several biblical accounts illustrate Satan's role in adversity. We find the clearest example in the story of Job. Those who attribute all adversity to sin of some kind or to a lack of faith have a difficult time with this narrative. They attribute Job's problems to his pride or the sin of his children. But the Bible puts those theories to rest in the first verse of the book, where it describes Job as "blameless, upright, one who fears God and shuns evil." Later in the same chapter, God himself says of Job, "For there is no one like him on earth, a blameless and upright man, fearing God and turning away from evil" (Job 1:8).

Job was a righteous man whose adversity did *not* come as a result of sin. In fact, an ensuing discussion between God and Satan spells out why Job suffered the way he did. Satan accused Job of following God only because the Lord had blessed him and protected him. Take away that protection, Satan challenged, and Job would curse God to His face.

So Satan sets out to destroy all Job has. Yet Job continues to serve God and walk in His ways, so Satan makes another request of God, asking Him permission to afflict Job's body (2:4–7).

Clearly, Job's adversity came from Satan, who dared God to send adversity into Job's life. God, in turn, permits Satan to do the dirty work. The permission came from God; the adversity came from the devil.

Peter tells us that Satan roams around like a lion, seeking whom he can destroy (1 Pet. 5:8). Oftentimes we take Peter's words as referring to Satan's involvement in our temptations, but the real context is that of suffering. Satan roams the earth, looking for ways to bring adversity into our lives. He wants us to suffer, for suffering has the power to damage or even destroy one's faith in God. Peter instructs believers to be on the alert so that in the midst of their suffering they will not lose sight of who is causing it, as well as how God is going to use it (1 Pet. 5:9, 10).

See the Life Principles Index for further study:
26. Adversity is a bridge to a deeper relationship with God.

22 In all this Job did not sin nor charge God
with wrong.

Satan Attacks Job's Health

2 Again there was a day when the sons of
God came to present themselves before
the LORD, and Satan came also among them
to present himself before the LORD.
2 And the LORD said to Satan, "From where
do you come?" Satan answered the LORD and
said, "From going to and fro on the earth, and
from walking back and forth on it."
3 Then the LORD said to Satan, "Have you
considered My servant Job, that *there is* none
like him on the earth, a blameless and upright
man, one who fears God and shuns evil? And
still he holds fast to his integrity, although
you incited Me against him, to destroy him
without cause."
4 So Satan answered the LORD and said,
"Skin for skin! Yes, all that a man has he will
give for his life.
5 "But stretch out Your hand now, and touch
his bone and his flesh, and he will surely
curse You to Your face!"
6 And the LORD said to Satan, "Behold, he *is*
in your hand, but spare his life."
7 So Satan went out from the presence of
the LORD, and struck Job with painful boils
from the sole of his foot to the crown of his
head.
8 And he took for himself a potsherd with
which to scrape himself while he sat in the
midst of the ashes.
9 Then his wife said to him, "Do you still
hold fast to your integrity? Curse God and
die!"
10 But he said to her, "You speak as one of

LIFE LESSONS

➤ **2:10 — *"Shall we indeed accept good from God, and shall we not accept adversity?"***

If God is sovereign, and if He loves us, then we must believe that nothing reaches us without first passing through His omnipotent hands.

ANSWERS TO LIFE'S QUESTIONS

How can I handle criticism during times of adversity?

JOB 2:10

In times of adversity, life can sometimes seem so bleak and dark that we feel on the verge of giving up hope. Others around us may foretell doom and encourage us to face what they see as inevitable. Job's wife was one such person. After painful boils covered Job from the soles of his feet to the crown of his head, she said to him, "Do you still hold fast to your integrity? Curse God and die!" (Job 2:9).

Job wisely responded to her, "You speak as one of the foolish women speaks. Shall we indeed accept good from God, and shall we not accept adversity?" The Scriptures add this important line: "In all this Job did not sin with his lips" (2:10).

When you face difficult circumstances and then have to endure negative opinions and comments from others, you need the courage to stay positive—to continue to believe that the Lord is with you. Hope and faith are not automatic responses in times of hardship and trial; they require an exercise of the will, bolstered with courage. So the psalmist said, "Why are you cast down, O my soul? And why are you disquieted within me? Hope in God, for I shall yet praise Him for the help of His countenance" (Ps. 42:5).

At times, you must say aloud to yourself, "I know that God has a purpose in this. I know that God will bring me through this. I know that God is a good and loving Father and that He is doing a good and eternal work in my life." If no one else speaks hope to you, then you need to speak it to yourself.

You may also need courage to withstand the enemies moving against your life—in other words, those who are causing your adversity. Moses realized that Joshua and the Israelites would face such trials, so he said to God's people, "Be strong and of good courage, do not fear nor be afraid of them; for the LORD your God, He is the One who goes with you. He will not leave you nor forsake you" (Deut. 31:6).

Ask the Lord to give you the courage to continue to believe in Him and in His presence with you as you go through adversity. Ask Him to renew your hope and faith. And know that He loves to honor such faithful requests.

See the Life Principles Index for further study:
29. We learn more in our valley experiences than on our mountaintops.

the foolish women speaks. Shall we indeed accept good from God, and shall we not accept adversity?" In all this Job did not sin with his lips.

Job's Three Friends

11 Now when Job's three friends heard of all this adversity that had come upon him, each one came from his own place—Eliphaz the Temanite, Bildad the Shuhite, and Zophar the Naamathite. For they had made an appointment together to come and mourn with him, and to comfort him. ➤

12 And when they raised their eyes from afar, and did not recognize him, they lifted their voices and wept; and each one tore his robe and sprinkled dust on his head toward heaven.

13 So they sat down with him on the ground seven days and seven nights, and no one spoke a word to him, for they saw that *his* grief was very great.

Job Deplores His Birth

3 After this Job opened his mouth and cursed the day of his *birth.*

2 And Job spoke, and said:

3 "May the day perish on which I was born,
And the night *in which* it was said,
'A male child is conceived.'
4 May that day be darkness;
May God above not seek it,
Nor the light shine upon it.
5 May darkness and the shadow of death
claim it;

LIFE LESSONS

➤ **2:11 — *For they had made an appointment together to come and mourn with him, and to comfort him.***

We need each other, especially in the dark times of life. While compassion should flow from us naturally, it doesn't hurt to make a plan about how best to show that compassion.

May a cloud settle on it;
May the blackness of the day terrify it.
6 *As for* that night, may darkness seize it;
May it not rejoice[a] among the days of the year,
May it not come into the number of the months.
7 Oh, may that night be barren!
May no joyful shout come into it!
8 May those curse it who curse the day,
Those who are ready to arouse Leviathan.
9 May the stars of its morning be dark;
May it look for light, but *have* none,
And not see the dawning of the day;
10 Because it did not shut up the doors of my *mother's* womb,
Nor hide sorrow from my eyes.

➤ 11 "Why did I not die at birth?
Why did I *not* perish when I came from the womb?
12 Why did the knees receive me?
Or why the breasts, that I should nurse?
13 For now I would have lain still and been quiet,
I would have been asleep;
Then I would have been at rest
14 With kings and counselors of the earth,
Who built ruins for themselves,
15 Or with princes who had gold,
Who filled their houses *with* silver;
16 Or *why* was I not hidden like a stillborn child,
Like infants who never saw light?
17 There the wicked cease *from* troubling,
And there the weary are at rest.
18 *There* the prisoners rest together;
They do not hear the voice of the oppressor.
19 The small and great are there,
And the servant *is* free from his master.

20 "Why is light given to him who is in misery,
And life to the bitter of soul,
21 Who long for death, but it does not *come*,
And search for it more than hidden treasures;
22 Who rejoice exceedingly,
And are glad when they can find the grave?
23 *Why is light given* to a man whose way is hidden,
And whom God has hedged in?
24 For my sighing comes before I eat,[a]
And my groanings pour out like water.
25 For the thing I greatly feared has come upon me, ➤
And what I dreaded has happened to me.
26 I am not at ease, nor am I quiet;
I have no rest, for trouble comes."

Eliphaz: Job Has Sinned

4 Then Eliphaz the Temanite answered and said:
2 "If one attempts a word with you, will you become weary?
But who can withhold himself from speaking?
3 Surely you have instructed many,
And you have strengthened weak hands.
4 Your words have upheld him who was stumbling, ➤
And you have strengthened the feeble knees;
5 But now it comes upon you, and you are weary;
It touches you, and you are troubled.
6 *Is* not your reverence your confidence?
And the integrity of your ways your hope?

7 "Remember now, who *ever* perished being innocent? ➤
Or where were the upright *ever* cut off?
8 Even as I have seen,
Those who plow iniquity
And sow trouble reap the same.
9 By the blast of God they perish,
And by the breath of His anger they are consumed.

3:6 [a]Septuagint, Syriac, Targum, and Vulgate read *be joined*.
3:24 [a]Literally *my bread*

LIFE LESSONS

➤ 3:11 — *"Why did I not die at birth? Why did I not perish when I came from the womb?"*

Intense suffering often prompts us to say things we don't really mean. Fortunately, we serve a God who "remembers that we are dust" (Ps. 103:14) and who promises not to break the bruised reed of our souls (Is. 42:3).

➤ 3:25 — *"For the thing I greatly feared has come upon me, and what I dreaded has happened to me."*

We all have secret fears and underground worries, things that make us say, "If *this* happened, I don't know what I'd do." God wants us to take even these fears to Him and say, " . . . but I put my trust in You."

➤ 4:4, 5 — *" . . . you have strengthened the feeble knees; but now it comes upon you, and you are weary . . . ."*

It's one thing to say, "I trust God" when you feel good and your body's healthy. It's quite another to say, "I trust God," when you feel lousy and your body's falling apart. Only genuine faith can bridge the gap.

➤ 4:7 — *"Remember now, who ever perished being innocent?"*

It's tempting to think that good boys always get the apple and bad boys always get the stick. It's tempting, but not true. No one was ever more innocent than Jesus, yet he perished for *our* sins.

10 The roaring of the lion,
The voice of the fierce lion,
And the teeth of the young lions are broken.
11 The old lion perishes for lack of prey,
And the cubs of the lioness are scattered.

12 "Now a word was secretly brought to me,
And my ear received a whisper of it.
13 In disquieting thoughts from the visions of the night,
When deep sleep falls on men,
14 Fear came upon me, and trembling,
Which made all my bones shake.
15 Then a spirit passed before my face;
The hair on my body stood up.
16 It stood still,
But I could not discern its appearance.
A form *was* before my eyes;
There was silence;
Then I heard a voice *saying:*
➤ 17 'Can a mortal be more righteous than God?
Can a man be more pure than his Maker?
18 If He puts no trust in His servants,
If He charges His angels with error,
19 How much more those who dwell in houses of clay,
Whose foundation is in the dust,
Who are crushed before a moth?
20 They are broken in pieces from morning till evening;
They perish forever, with no one regarding.
21 Does not their own excellence go away?
They die, even without wisdom.'

Eliphaz: Job Is Chastened by God

5 "Call out now;
Is there anyone who will answer you?
And to which of the holy ones will you turn?
2 For wrath kills a foolish man,
And envy slays a simple one.
3 I have seen the foolish taking root,
But suddenly I cursed his dwelling place.
4 His sons are far from safety,
They are crushed in the gate,
And *there is* no deliverer.
5 Because the hungry eat up his harvest,
Taking it even from the thorns,[a]
And a snare snatches their substance.[b]
6 For affliction does not come from the dust,
Nor does trouble spring from the ground;
7 Yet man is born to trouble, ➤
As the sparks fly upward.

8 "But as for me, I would seek God, ➤
And to God I would commit my cause—
9 Who does great things, and unsearchable,
Marvelous things without number.
10 He gives rain on the earth,
And sends waters on the fields.
11 He sets on high those who are lowly,
And those who mourn are lifted to safety.
12 He frustrates the devices of the crafty,
So that their hands cannot carry out their plans.
13 He catches the wise in their own craftiness,
And the counsel of the cunning comes quickly upon them.
14 They meet with darkness in the daytime,
And grope at noontime as in the night.
15 But He saves the needy from the sword, ✳
From the mouth of the mighty,
And from their hand.
16 So the poor have hope,
And injustice shuts her mouth.

17 "Behold, happy *is* the man whom God corrects;
Therefore do not despise the chastening of the Almighty.
18 For He bruises, but He binds up;
He wounds, but His hands make whole.
19 He shall deliver you in six troubles,
Yes, in seven no evil shall touch you.
20 In famine He shall redeem you from death,
And in war from the power of the sword.

5:5 [a]Septuagint reads *They shall not be taken from evil men;* Vulgate reads *And the armed man shall take him by violence.* [b]Septuagint reads *The might shall draw them off;* Vulgate reads *And the thirsty shall drink up their riches.*

LIFE LESSONS

➤ 4:17 — *"Can a mortal be more righteous than God? Can a man be more pure than his Maker?"*

Whenever we fault God's handling of the universe or angrily blame Him for a personal hardship, in fact we're calling ourselves more gracious and righteous than He is—and that's always a dangerous and foolish place to be.

➤ 5:7 — *"Yet man is born to trouble, as the sparks fly upward."*

Job's friends said many foolish and hurtful things, but at least here Eliphaz got it right. Jesus declared, "In the world you will have tribulation"—but then added, happily, "be of good cheer, I have overcome the world" (John 16:33).

➤ 5:8, 9 — *"God . . . does great things, and unsearchable, marvelous things without number."*

Even foolish people can occasionally say wise things; just as the devil can mix in truth with his lies. We must constantly discern between wheat and chaff, truth and error, God's reliable Word and Satan's half-truths.

21 You shall be hidden from the scourge of
the tongue,
And you shall not be afraid of
destruction when it comes.
22 You shall laugh at destruction and
famine,
And you shall not be afraid of the beasts
of the earth.
23 For you shall have a covenant with the
stones of the field,
And the beasts of the field shall be at
peace with you.
24 You shall know that your tent *is* in
peace;
You shall visit your dwelling and find
nothing amiss.
25 You shall also know that your
descendants *shall be* many,
And your offspring like the grass of the
earth.
26 You shall come to the grave at a full age,
As a sheaf of grain ripens in its season.
27 Behold, this we have searched out;
It *is* true.
Hear it, and know for yourself."

Job: My Complaint Is Just

6 Then Job answered and said:
2 "Oh, that my grief were fully weighed,
And my calamity laid with it on the
scales!
3 For then it would be heavier than the
sand of the sea—
Therefore my words have been rash.
4 For the arrows of the Almighty *are* within
me;
My spirit drinks in their poison;
The terrors of God are arrayed against
me.
5 Does the wild donkey bray when it has
grass,
Or does the ox low over its fodder?
6 Can flavorless food be eaten without salt?
Or is there *any* taste in the white of an
egg?
7 My soul refuses to touch them;
They *are* as loathsome food to me.

8 "Oh, that I might have my request,
That God would grant *me* the thing that I
long for!
9 That it would please God to crush me,
That He would loose His hand and cut
me off!
10 Then I would still have comfort;
Though in anguish I would exult,
He will not spare;
For I have not concealed the words of the
Holy One.

11 "What strength do I have, that I should
hope?
And what *is* my end, that I should
prolong my life?
12 *Is* my strength the strength of stones?
Or is my flesh bronze?
13 *Is* my help not within me?
And is success driven from me?

14 "To him who is afflicted, kindness *should
be shown* by his friend,
Even though he forsakes the fear of the
Almighty.
15 My brothers have dealt deceitfully like a
brook,
Like the streams of the brooks that pass
away,
16 Which are dark because of the ice,
And into which the snow vanishes.
17 When it is warm, they cease to flow;
When it is hot, they vanish from their
place.
18 The paths of their way turn aside,
They go nowhere and perish.
19 The caravans of Tema look,
The travelers of Sheba hope for them.
20 They are disappointed because they were
confident;
They come there and are confused.
21 For now you are nothing,
You see terror and are afraid.
22 Did I ever say, 'Bring *something* to me'?
Or, 'Offer a bribe for me from your
wealth'?
23 Or, 'Deliver me from the enemy's hand'?
Or, 'Redeem me from the hand of
oppressors'?

24 "Teach me, and I will hold my tongue;
Cause me to understand wherein I have
erred.
25 How forceful are right words!
But what does your arguing prove?
26 Do you intend to rebuke *my* words,
And the speeches of a desperate one,
which are as wind?

LIFE LESSONS

➤ 6:14 — *"To him who is afflicted, kindness should be shown by his friend, even though he forsakes the fear of the Almighty."*

Because people in great pain often say things they don't really mean, we must not judge too harshly their words, even when they offend us. Peter says, "love will cover a multitude of sins" (1 Pet. 4:8).

➤ 6:26 — *"Do you intend to rebuke my words, and the speeches of a desperate one, which are as wind?"*

Godly people in pain usually know when they speak rashly and unwisely, but they just can't seem to help themselves; their desperation drives them to it. In these times, we must remain "swift to hear, slow to speak" (James 1:19).

27 Yes, you overwhelm the fatherless,
And you undermine your friend.
28 Now therefore, be pleased to look at me;
For I would never lie to your face.
29 Yield now, let there be no injustice!
Yes, concede, my righteousness still stands!
30 Is there injustice on my tongue?
Cannot my taste discern the unsavory?

Job: My Suffering Is Comfortless

7 "*Is there* not a time of hard service for man on earth?
Are not his days also like the days of a hired man?
2 Like a servant who earnestly desires the shade,
And like a hired man who eagerly looks for his wages,
3 So I have been allotted months of futility,
And wearisome nights have been appointed to me.
4 When I lie down, I say, 'When shall I arise,
And the night be ended?'
For I have had my fill of tossing till dawn.
5 My flesh is caked with worms and dust,
My skin is cracked and breaks out afresh.

6 "My days are swifter than a weaver's shuttle,
And are spent without hope.
7 Oh, remember that my life *is* a breath!
My eye will never again see good.
8 The eye of him who sees me will see me no *more;*
While your eyes *are* upon me, I shall no longer *be.*
9 *As* the cloud disappears and vanishes away,
So he who goes down to the grave does not come up.
10 He shall never return to his house,
Nor shall his place know him anymore.

➤ 11 "Therefore I will not restrain my mouth;
I will speak in the anguish of my spirit;
I will complain in the bitterness of my soul.
12 *Am* I a sea, or a sea serpent,
That You set a guard over me?
13 When I say, 'My bed will comfort me,
My couch will ease my complaint,'
14 Then You scare me with dreams
And terrify me with visions,
15 So that my soul chooses strangling
And death rather than my body.[a]
16 I loathe *my life;*
I would not live forever.
Let me alone,
For my days *are but* a breath.

17 "What *is* man, that You should exalt him, ➤
That You should set Your heart on him,
18 That You should visit him every morning,
And test him every moment?
19 How long?
Will You not look away from me,
And let me alone till I swallow my saliva?
20 Have I sinned?
What have I done to You, O watcher of men?
Why have You set me as Your target,
So that I am a burden to myself?[a]
21 Why then do You not pardon my transgression,
And take away my iniquity?
For now I will lie down in the dust,
And You will seek me diligently,
But I *will* no longer *be.*"

Bildad: Job Should Repent

8 Then Bildad the Shuhite answered and said:
2 "How long will you speak these *things,*
And the words of your mouth *be like* a strong wind?
3 Does God subvert judgment?
Or does the Almighty pervert justice?
4 If your sons have sinned against Him, ➤
He has cast them away for their transgression.
5 If you would earnestly seek God
And make your supplication to the Almighty,

7:15 [a]Literally *my bones* **7:20** [a]Following Masoretic Text, Targum, and Vulgate; Septuagint and Jewish tradition read *to You.*

LIFE LESSONS

➤ 7:11 — *"Therefore I will not restrain my mouth; I will speak in the anguish of my spirit; I will complain in the bitterness of my soul."*

God instructs us to come to Him with all our concerns, all our fears, all our hurts. He can take whatever we have to say, for He knows more about our suffering than we do.

➤ 7:17, 18 — *"What is man, that You should . . . visit him every morning, and test him every moment?"*

God does not really test us "every moment," even though when we suffer it may feel like it. When He tests us, He does so for our own good—and His tests end once they have run their course.

➤ 8:4 — *"If your sons have sinned against Him, He has cast them away for their transgression."*

Job lost his sons tragically, and now his friend worsens his pain by suggesting that they had it coming. The truth is, we don't usually know the reason behind someone's misfortune—and to speculate like this is a sin.

6 If you *were* pure and upright,
Surely now He would awake for you,
And prosper your rightful dwelling place.
7 Though your beginning was small,
Yet your latter end would increase abundantly.

8 "For inquire, please, of the former age,
And consider the things discovered by their fathers;
9 For we *were born* yesterday, and know nothing,
Because our days on earth *are* a shadow.
10 Will they not teach you and tell you,
And utter words from their heart?

11 "Can the papyrus grow up without a marsh?
Can the reeds flourish without water?
12 While it *is* yet green *and* not cut down,
It withers before any *other* plant.
13 So *are* the paths of all who forget God;
And the hope of the hypocrite shall perish,
14 Whose confidence shall be cut off,
And whose trust *is* a spider's web.
15 He leans on his house, but it does not stand.
He holds it fast, but it does not endure.
16 He grows green in the sun,
And his branches spread out in his garden.
17 His roots wrap around the rock heap,
And look for a place in the stones.
18 If he is destroyed from his place,
Then *it* will deny him, *saying,* 'I have not seen you.'

19 "Behold, this is the joy of His way,
And out of the earth others will grow.
➤ 20 Behold, God will not cast away the blameless,
Nor will He uphold the evildoers.
21 He will yet fill your mouth with laughing,
And your lips with rejoicing.
22 Those who hate you will be clothed with shame,
And the dwelling place of the wicked will come to nothing."[a]

Job: There Is No Mediator

9 Then Job answered and said:

➤ 2 "Truly I know *it is* so,
But how can a man be righteous before God?
3 If one wished to contend with Him,
He could not answer Him one time out of a thousand.
4 God is wise in heart and mighty in strength.
Who has hardened *himself* against Him and prospered?
5 He removes the mountains, and they do not know
When He overturns them in His anger;
6 He shakes the earth out of its place,
And its pillars tremble;
7 He commands the sun, and it does not rise;
He seals off the stars;
8 He alone spreads out the heavens,
And treads on the waves of the sea;
9 He made the Bear, Orion, and the Pleiades,
And the chambers of the south;
10 He does great things past finding out,
Yes, wonders without number.
11 If He goes by me, I do not see *Him;*
If He moves past, I do not perceive Him;
12 If He takes away, who can hinder Him?
Who can say to Him, 'What are You doing?'
13 God will not withdraw His anger,
The allies of the proud[a] lie prostrate beneath Him.

14 "How then can I answer Him,
And choose my words *to reason* with Him?
15 For though I were righteous, I could not answer Him;
I would beg mercy of my Judge.
16 If I called and He answered me,
I would not believe that He was listening to my voice.
17 For He crushes me with a tempest,
And multiplies my wounds without cause.
18 He will not allow me to catch my breath,
But fills me with bitterness.
19 If *it is a matter* of strength, indeed *He is* strong;
And if of justice, who will appoint my day *in court?*
20 Though I were righteous, my own mouth would condemn me;
Though I *were* blameless, it would prove me perverse.

21 "I am blameless, yet I do not know myself;
I despise my life.

8:22 [a]Literally *will not be* **9:13** [a]Hebrew *rahab*

LIFE LESSONS

➤ 8:20 — *"Behold, God will not cast away the blameless, nor will He uphold the evildoers."*

Bildad was right, but not how he meant. He implied wrongly that Job suffered because he had sinned. God really will not reject His people or bless the wicked—even though, for a while, it may seem like He does.

➤ 9:2 — *"But how can a man be righteous before God?"*

Job recognized that while he had earned a reputation as a blameless man, yet as a sinner he lacked all righteousness before his holy God. We stand as righteous only when, by faith, we stand in the righteousness of Christ.

22 It *is* all one *thing;*
Therefore I say, 'He destroys the blameless and the wicked.'
23 If the scourge slays suddenly,
He laughs at the plight of the innocent.
24 The earth is given into the hand of the wicked.
He covers the faces of its judges.
If it is not *He,* who else could it be?

25 "Now my days are swifter than a runner;
They flee away, they see no good.
26 They pass by like swift ships,
Like an eagle swooping on its prey.
27 If I say, 'I will forget my complaint,
I will put off my sad face and wear a smile,'
28 I am afraid of all my sufferings;
I know that You will not hold me innocent.
29 *If* I am condemned,
Why then do I labor in vain?
30 If I wash myself with snow water,
And cleanse my hands with soap,
31 Yet You will plunge me into the pit,
And my own clothes will abhor me.

32 "For *He is* not a man, as I *am,*
That I may answer Him,
And that we should go to court together.
➤ 33 Nor is there any mediator between us,
Who may lay his hand on us both.
34 Let Him take His rod away from me,
And do not let dread of Him terrify me.
35 *Then* I would speak and not fear Him,
But it is not so with me.

Job: I Would Plead with God

10 "My soul loathes my life;
I will give free course to my complaint,
I will speak in the bitterness of my soul.
2 I will say to God, 'Do not condemn me;
Show me why You contend with me.
3 *Does it* seem good to You that You should oppress,
That You should despise the work of Your hands,
And smile on the counsel of the wicked?
4 Do You have eyes of flesh?
Or do You see as man sees?
5 *Are* Your days like the days of a mortal man?
Are Your years like the days of a mighty man,
6 That You should seek for my iniquity
And search out my sin,
7 Although You know that I am not wicked,
And *there is* no one who can deliver from Your hand?

8 'Your hands have made me and fashioned me,
An intricate unity;
Yet You would destroy me.
9 Remember, I pray, that You have made me like clay.
And will You turn me into dust again?
10 Did You not pour me out like milk,
And curdle me like cheese,
11 Clothe me with skin and flesh,
And knit me together with bones and sinews?
12 You have granted me life and favor, ✳
And Your care has preserved my spirit. ➤
13 'And these *things* You have hidden in Your heart;
I know that this *was* with You:
14 If I sin, then You mark me,
And will not acquit me of my iniquity.
15 If I am wicked, woe to me;
Even *if* I am righteous, I cannot lift up my head.
I am full of disgrace;
See my misery!
16 If *my head* is exalted,
You hunt me like a fierce lion,
And again You show Yourself awesome against me.
17 You renew Your witnesses against me,
And increase Your indignation toward me;
Changes and war are *ever* with me.

18 'Why then have You brought me out of the womb?
Oh, that I had perished and no eye had seen me!
19 I would have been as though I had not been.
I would have been carried from the womb to the grave.
20 Are not my days few? ➤
Cease! Leave me alone, that I may take a little comfort,

LIFE LESSONS

➤ 9:33 — *"Nor is there any mediator between us, who may lay his hand on us both."*

Job needed what we have: a sympathetic mediator between a holy God and a sinful people. Here's the good news: "For there is one God and one Mediator between God and men, the Man Christ Jesus" (1 Tim. 2:5).

➤ 10:12 — *"You have granted me life and favor, and Your care has preserved my spirit."*

Even in the middle of their bitter complaints, those with a genuine heart for God continue to hope in His grace and remember His many blessings. God sustains them, even when it feels as though He attacks them.

➤ 10:20 — *"Cease! Leave me alone, that I may take a little comfort . . . ."*

When we feel most discouraged and worn out, we may wish that God would just "leave us alone"—but thank God, He never does. He promises us, "I will never leave you nor forsake you" (Heb. 13:5).

21 Before I go *to the place from which* I
shall not return,
To the land of darkness and the shadow
of death,
22 A land as dark as darkness *itself,*
As the shadow of death, without any
order,
Where even the light *is* like darkness.'"

Zophar Urges Job to Repent

11 Then Zophar the Naamathite answered
and said:
2 "Should not the multitude of words be
answered?
And should a man full of talk be
vindicated?
3 Should your empty talk make men hold
their peace?
And when you mock, should no one
rebuke you?
4 For you have said,
'My doctrine *is* pure,
And I am clean in your eyes.'
5 But oh, that God would speak,
And open His lips against you,
6 That He would show you the secrets of
wisdom!
For *they would* double *your* prudence.
Know therefore that God exacts from you
Less than your iniquity *deserves.*
➤ 7 "Can you search out the deep things of
God?
Can you find out the limits of the
Almighty?
8 *They are* higher than heaven— what can
you do?
Deeper than Sheol— what can you
know?
9 Their measure *is* longer than the earth
And broader than the sea.
10 "If He passes by, imprisons, and gathers *to*
judgment,
Then who can hinder Him?
11 For He knows deceitful men;
He sees wickedness also.
Will He not then consider *it?*
➤ 12 For an empty-headed man will be wise,
When a wild donkey's colt is born a man.
13 "If you would prepare your heart,
And stretch out your hands toward Him;
14 If iniquity *were* in your hand, *and you* put
it far away,
And would not let wickedness dwell in
your tents;
15 Then surely you could lift up your face
without spot;
Yes, you could be steadfast, and not fear;
16 Because you would forget *your* misery,
And remember *it* as waters *that have*
passed away,
17 And *your* life would be brighter than
noonday.
Though you were dark, you would be like
the morning.
18 And you would be secure, because there
is hope;
Yes, you would dig *around you, and* take
your rest in safety.
19 You would also lie down, and no one
would make *you* afraid;
Yes, many would court your favor.
20 But the eyes of the wicked will fail,
And they shall not escape,
And their hope—loss of life!"

Job Answers His Critics

12 Then Job answered and said:
2 "No doubt you *are* the people,
And wisdom will die with you!
3 But I have understanding as well as you;
I *am* not inferior to you.
Indeed, who does not *know* such things
as these?
4 "I am one mocked by his friends,
Who called on God, and He answered him,
The just and blameless *who is* ridiculed.
5 A lamp[a] is despised in the thought of one
who is at ease;
It is made ready for those whose feet slip.
6 The tents of robbers prosper,
And those who provoke God are secure—
In what God provides by His hand.
7 "But now ask the beasts, and they will
teach you;

12:5 [a]Or *disaster*

LIFE LESSONS

➤ 11:7 — *"Can you search out the deep things of God? Can you find out the limits of the Almighty?"*

Zophar asked good questions, but he should have directed them at himself, not merely at Job. "God is in heaven," the Bible tells us, "and you on earth; therefore let your words be few" (Eccl. 5:2).

➤ 11:12 — *"For an empty-headed man will be wise, when a wild donkey's colt is born a man"*

Zophar meant these words as an insult. He essentially said, "You are a fool and a sinner, Job; why won't you admit the obvious truth?" But the insults of men will never accomplish the righteousness of God.

➤ 12:4 — *"I am one mocked by his friends . . . the just and blameless who is ridiculed."*

God had called Job a "blameless and upright man, one who fears God and shuns evil" (Job 1:8)—and yet Job's friends mocked and ridiculed him in his distress. When will we learn the truth of Matthew 12:7, that God desires mercy?

And the birds of the air, and they will tell
you;
8 Or speak to the earth, and it will teach you;
And the fish of the sea will explain to you.
9 Who among all these does not know
That the hand of the LORD has done this,
10 In whose hand *is* the life of every living
thing,
And the breath of all mankind?
11 Does not the ear test words
And the mouth taste its food?
12 Wisdom *is* with aged men,
And with length of days, understanding.

➤ 13 "With Him *are* wisdom and strength,
He has counsel and understanding.
14 If He breaks *a thing* down, it cannot be
rebuilt;
If He imprisons a man, there can be no
release.
15 If He withholds the waters, they dry up;
If He sends them out, they overwhelm the
earth.
16 With Him *are* strength and prudence.
The deceived and the deceiver *are* His.
17 He leads counselors away plundered,
And makes fools of the judges.
18 He loosens the bonds of kings,
And binds their waist with a belt.
19 He leads princes[a] away plundered,
And overthrows the mighty.
20 He deprives the trusted ones of speech,
And takes away the discernment of the
elders.
21 He pours contempt on princes,
And disarms the mighty.
22 He uncovers deep things out of darkness,
And brings the shadow of death to light.
23 He makes nations great, and destroys them;
He enlarges nations, and guides them.
24 He takes away the understanding[a] of the
chiefs of the people of the earth,
And makes them wander in a pathless
wilderness.
25 They grope in the dark without light,
And He makes them stagger like a
drunken *man*.

13 "Behold, my eye has seen all *this*,
My ear has heard and understood it.
2 What you know, I also know;
I *am* not inferior to you.
3 But I would speak to the Almighty,
And I desire to reason with God.
4 But you forgers of lies,
You *are* all worthless physicians.
5 Oh, that you would be silent, ➤
And it would be your wisdom!
6 Now hear my reasoning,
And heed the pleadings of my lips.
7 Will you speak wickedly for God,
And talk deceitfully for Him?
8 Will you show partiality for Him?
Will you contend for God?
9 Will it be well when He searches you out?
Or can you mock Him as one mocks a
man?
10 He will surely rebuke you
If you secretly show partiality.
11 Will not His excellence make you afraid,
And the dread of Him fall upon you?
12 Your platitudes *are* proverbs of ashes,
Your defenses are defenses of clay.

13 "Hold your peace with me, and let me
speak,
Then let come on me what *may!*
14 Why do I take my flesh in my teeth,
And put my life in my hands?
15 Though He slay me, yet will I trust Him. ➤
Even so, I will defend my own ways
before Him.
16 He also *shall* be my salvation,
For a hypocrite could not come before
Him.
17 Listen carefully to my speech,
And to my declaration with your ears.
18 See now, I have prepared *my* case,
I know that I shall be vindicated.
19 Who *is* he *who* will contend with me?
If now I hold my tongue, I perish.

Job's Despondent Prayer

20 "Only two *things* do not do to me,
Then I will not hide myself from You:
21 Withdraw Your hand far from me,
And let not the dread of You make me
afraid.
22 Then call, and I will answer;
Or let me speak, then You respond to me.
23 How many *are* my iniquities and sins?

12:19 [a]Literally *priests,* but not in a technical sense
12:24 [a]Literally *heart*

LIFE LESSONS

➤ **12:13 — *"With Him are wisdom and strength, He has counsel and understanding."***

Especially when we find ourselves in painful and distressing circumstances, we must turn to the Lord for His wisdom and strength and guidance and knowledge. Where else can we go to find the help we need?

➤ **13:5 — *"Oh, that you would be silent, and it would be your wisdom!"***

Very often—more frequently than we know—our best counsel and most helpful advice is to say precisely nothing. "Even a fool is counted wise when he holds his peace; when he shuts his lips, he is considered perceptive" (Prov. 17:28).

➤ **13:15 — *"Though He slay me, yet will I trust Him."***

God is either worth trusting all the way to the end, or He's not worth trusting at all. "Lord, to whom shall we go? You have the words of eternal life" (John 6:68).

Make me know my transgression and my sin.
24 Why do You hide Your face,
And regard me as Your enemy?
25 Will You frighten a leaf driven to and fro?
And will You pursue dry stubble?
26 For You write bitter things against me,
And make me inherit the iniquities of my youth.
27 You put my feet in the stocks,
And watch closely all my paths.
You set a limit[a] for the soles of my feet.

28 "*Man*[a] decays like a rotten thing,
Like a garment that is moth-eaten.

14 "Man *who is* born of woman
Is of few days and full of trouble.
2 He comes forth like a flower and fades away;
He flees like a shadow and does not continue.
3 And do You open Your eyes on such a one,
And bring me[a] to judgment with Yourself?
4 Who can bring a clean *thing* out of an unclean?
No one!
5 Since his days *are* determined,
The number of his months *is* with You;
You have appointed his limits, so that he cannot pass.
6 Look away from him that he may rest,
Till like a hired man he finishes his day.

7 "For there is hope for a tree,
If it is cut down, that it will sprout again,
And that its tender shoots will not cease.
8 Though its root may grow old in the earth,
And its stump may die in the ground,
9 *Yet* at the scent of water it will bud
And bring forth branches like a plant.
10 But man dies and is laid away;
Indeed he breathes his last
And where *is* he?
11 *As* water disappears from the sea,
And a river becomes parched and dries up,
12 So man lies down and does not rise.
Till the heavens *are* no more,
They will not awake
Nor be roused from their sleep.

13 "Oh, that You would hide me in the grave,
That You would conceal me until Your wrath is past,
That You would appoint me a set time, and remember me!
14 If a man dies, shall he live *again?*
All the days of my hard service I will wait,
Till my change comes.
15 You shall call, and I will answer You;
You shall desire the work of Your hands.
16 For now You number my steps,
But do not watch over my sin.
17 My transgression *is* sealed up in a bag,
And You cover[a] my iniquity.

18 "But *as* a mountain falls *and* crumbles away,
And *as* a rock is moved from its place;
19 *As* water wears away stones,
And as torrents wash away the soil of the earth;
So You destroy the hope of man.
20 You prevail forever against him, and he passes on;
You change his countenance and send him away.
21 His sons come to honor, and he does not know *it;*
They are brought low, and he does not perceive *it.*
22 But his flesh will be in pain over it,
And his soul will mourn over it."

Eliphaz Accuses Job of Folly

15 Then Eliphaz the Temanite answered and said:
2 "Should a wise man answer with empty knowledge,
And fill himself with the east wind?
3 Should he reason with unprofitable talk,
Or by speeches with which he can do no good?
4 Yes, you cast off fear,
And restrain prayer before God.
5 For your iniquity teaches your mouth,
And you choose the tongue of the crafty.
6 Your own mouth condemns you, and not I;
Yes, your own lips testify against you.

13:27 [a]Literally *inscribe a print* **13:28** [a]Literally *He*
14:3 [a]Septuagint, Syriac, and Vulgate read *him.* **14:17** [a]Literally *plaster over*

LIFE LESSONS

➤ 14:4 — *"Who can bring a clean thing out of an unclean? No one!"*

We have no more power to turn our sins into righteousness than a leopard can change its spots (Jer. 13:23). Yet Christ has the power to remove our sins and replace them with His spotlessness—if we will trust Him.

➤ 14:14 — *"If a man dies, shall he live again?"*

A dead man will live again, but only the saved will live in God's presence. "He who believes in the Son has everlasting life; and he who does not believe the Son shall not see life, but the wrath of God abides on him" (John 3:36).

7 "*Are* you the first man *who* was born?
Or were you made before the hills?
8 Have you heard the counsel of God?
Do you limit wisdom to yourself?
➤ 9 What do you know that we do not know?
What do you understand that *is* not in us?
10 Both the gray-haired and the aged *are* among us,
Much older than your father.
11 *Are* the consolations of God too small for you,
And the word *spoken* gently[a] with you?
12 Why does your heart carry you away,
And what do your eyes wink at,
13 That you turn your spirit against God,
And let *such* words go out of your mouth?

14 "What *is* man, that he could be pure?
And *he who is* born of a woman, that he could be righteous?
➤ 15 If *God* puts no trust in His saints,
And the heavens are not pure in His sight,
16 How much less man, *who is* abominable and filthy,
Who drinks iniquity like water!

17 "I will tell you, hear me;
What I have seen I will declare,
18 What wise men have told,
Not hiding *anything received* from their fathers,
19 To whom alone the land was given,
And no alien passed among them:
20 The wicked man writhes with pain all *his* days,
And the number of years is hidden from the oppressor.
21 Dreadful sounds *are* in his ears;
In prosperity the destroyer comes upon him.
22 He does not believe that he will return from darkness,
For a sword is waiting for him.
23 He wanders about for bread, *saying*, 'Where *is it?*'
He knows that a day of darkness is ready at his hand.
24 Trouble and anguish make him afraid;
They overpower him, like a king ready for battle.
25 For he stretches out his hand against God,
And acts defiantly against the Almighty,
26 Running stubbornly against Him
With his strong, embossed shield.

27 "Though he has covered his face with his fatness,
And made *his* waist heavy with fat,
28 He dwells in desolate cities,
In houses which no one inhabits,
Which are destined to become ruins.
29 He will not be rich,
Nor will his wealth continue,
Nor will his possessions overspread the earth.
30 He will not depart from darkness;
The flame will dry out his branches,
And by the breath of His mouth he will go away.
31 Let him not trust in futile *things*, deceiving himself,
For futility will be his reward.
32 It will be accomplished before his time,
And his branch will not be green.
33 He will shake off his unripe grape like a vine,
And cast off his blossom like an olive tree.
34 For the company of hypocrites *will be* barren,
And fire will consume the tents of bribery.
35 They conceive trouble and bring forth futility;
Their womb prepares deceit."

Job Reproaches His Pitiless Friends

16 Then Job answered and said:
2 "I have heard many such things;
Miserable comforters *are* you all!
3 Shall words of wind have an end?
Or what provokes you that you answer?
4 I also could speak as you *do*,
If your soul were in my soul's place.
I could heap up words against you,
And shake my head at you;
5 *But* I would strengthen you with my mouth, ➤
And the comfort of my lips would relieve *your grief*.

15:11 [a]Septuagint reads *a secret thing*.

LIFE LESSONS

➤ 15:9 — *"What do you know, that we do not know? What do you understand that is not in us?"*

When people start "measuring themselves by themselves, and comparing themselves among themselves," they "are not wise" (2 Cor. 10:12). Why? We are all ignorant in ways unknown to us—especially when compared to God.

➤ 15:15 — *"If God puts no trust in His saints . . . ."*

On the contrary, God has entrusted us with many wonderful things: His Word (Rom. 3:2); the gospel of Christ (1 Thess. 2:4); the Holy Spirit (2 Tim. 1:14); God's work (Titus 1:7); God's people (1 Pet. 5:3); the faith itself (Jude 1:3).

➤ 16:5 — *"But I would strengthen you with my mouth, and the comfort of my lips would relieve your grief."*

Our words have the power to tear down and bring grief, or the power to give strength and comfort. Every day we choose what kind of power we will wield—and God is watching (Matt. 12:36).

ANSWERS TO LIFE'S QUESTIONS

Does Satan cause all of our adversity?

JOB 16:11

The quick answer is, "No."

While the Book of Job makes it obvious that the devil can and does afflict us, some of our adversity comes simply because we live in a fallen world. All people—believers and nonbelievers alike—suffer adversity not "caused" by anything we or others have done. In Luke 13:1–5, Jesus declared that victims of two separate local tragedies died not because they had sinned worse than anyone else in Jerusalem, but simply because they were at the wrong place at the wrong time. In a fallen world, any of us could die at any time—and that is why we must always be ready to stand before God.

Adversity can also come into our lives as a result of personal sin. Each sin we commit carries some consequence, a natural outflow of adversity tailored to the nature of our disobedience. In cases like this, we can't blame God, the devil, or others. We must follow David's example and say, "I acknowledge my transgressions, and my sin is always before me. Against You, You only, have I sinned, and done this evil in Your sight" (Ps. 51:3, 4).

Let's say that I hear a juicy rumor and choose to gossip about it. Then imagine that the "news" turns out to be completely untrue. The result? No one trusts me anymore. I am rightly seen as a malicious gossip. I have destroyed my public witness. I can't blame anyone else for what happened; it was my own fault!

Finally, some adversity comes straight from almighty God. We don't like to think about this one, but let's be clear: *God is ultimately concerned with our spiritual growth*, not with our happiness or momentary pleasures. He always has the big picture in mind whenever He allows or sends adversity into our lives. So David wrote, "I know, O LORD, that Your judgments are right, and that in faithfulness You have afflicted me" (Ps. 119:75).

Unfortunately, adversity is often the only thing that will get our attention. I once heard a fine teacher explain it this way: God whispers to us in our pleasures, speaks to us in our conscience, but shouts to us in adversity. If God doesn't get our attention through His blessings or by stinging our conscience, then He will certainly put us flat on our backs in adversity so that we *can* get the message!

See the Life Principles Index for further study: 29. We learn more in our valley experiences than on our mountaintops.

6 "Though I speak, my grief is not relieved;
And *if* I remain silent, how am I eased?
7 But now He has worn me out;
You have made desolate all my company.
8 You have shriveled me up,
And it is a witness *against me;*
My leanness rises up against me
And bears witness to my face.
9 He tears *me* in His wrath, and hates me;
He gnashes at me with His teeth;
My adversary sharpens His gaze on me.
10 They gape at me with their mouth,
They strike me reproachfully on the cheek,
They gather together against me.
11 God has delivered me to the ungodly,
And turned me over to the hands of the wicked.
12 I was at ease, but He has shattered me;
He also has taken *me* by my neck, and shaken me to pieces;
He has set me up for His target,
13 His archers surround me.
He pierces my heart[a] and does not pity;
He pours out my gall on the ground.
14 He breaks me with wound upon wound;
He runs at me like a warrior.[a]
15 "I have sewn sackcloth over my skin,
And laid my head[a] in the dust.

16:13 [a]Literally *kidneys* **16:14** [a]Vulgate reads *giant.*
16:15 [a]Literally *horn*

LIFE LESSONS

➤ **16:9 — *"He tears me in His wrath, and hates me; He gnashes at me with His teeth."***

When we pray in our anguish and nothing seems to change, and we cry out in our pain and it only increases, we wonder if God has become our enemy. Never! He loves us, and always will (Rom. 8:39).

16 My face is flushed from weeping,
And on my eyelids *is* the shadow of death;
17 Although no violence *is* in my hands,
And my prayer *is* pure.

18 "O earth, do not cover my blood,
And let my cry have no *resting* place!
19 Surely even now my witness *is* in heaven,
And my evidence *is* on high.
20 My friends scorn me;
My eyes pour out *tears* to God.
21 Oh, that one might plead for a man with God,
As a man *pleads* for his neighbor!
22 For when a few years are finished,
I shall go the way of no return.

Job Prays for Relief

17 "My spirit is broken,
My days are extinguished,
The grave *is ready* for me.
2 *Are* not mockers with me?
And does not my eye dwell on their provocation?

3 "Now put down a pledge for me with Yourself.
Who *is* he *who* will shake hands with me?
4 For You have hidden their heart from understanding;
Therefore You will not exalt *them*.
5 He who speaks flattery to *his* friends,
Even the eyes of his children will fail.

6 "But He has made me a byword of the people,
And I have become one in whose face men spit.
7 My eye has also grown dim because of sorrow,
And all my members *are* like shadows.
8 Upright *men* are astonished at this,
And the innocent stirs himself up against the hypocrite.
9 Yet the righteous will hold to his way,
And he who has clean hands will be stronger and stronger.

10 "But please, come back again, all of you,[a]
For I shall not find *one* wise *man* among you.
11 My days are past,
My purposes are broken off,
Even the thoughts of my heart.
12 They change the night into day;
'The light *is* near,' *they say*, in the face of darkness.
13 If I wait *for* the grave *as* my house,
If I make my bed in the darkness,
14 If I say to corruption, 'You *are* my father,'
And to the worm, 'You *are* my mother and my sister,'
15 Where then *is* my hope?
As for my hope, who can see it?
16 *Will* they go down to the gates of Sheol?
Shall *we have* rest together in the dust?"

Bildad: The Wicked Are Punished

18 Then Bildad the Shuhite answered and said:
2 "How long *till* you put an end to words?
Gain understanding, and afterward we will speak.
3 Why are we counted as beasts,
And regarded as stupid in your sight?
4 You who tear yourself in anger,
Shall the earth be forsaken for you?
Or shall the rock be removed from its place?

5 "The light of the wicked indeed goes out,
And the flame of his fire does not shine.
6 The light is dark in his tent,
And his lamp beside him is put out.
7 The steps of his strength are shortened,
And his own counsel casts him down.
8 For he is cast into a net by his own feet,
And he walks into a snare.
9 The net takes *him* by the heel,
And a snare lays hold of him.
10 A noose *is* hidden for him on the ground,
And a trap for him in the road.
11 Terrors frighten him on every side,
And drive him to his feet.
12 His strength is starved,
And destruction *is* ready at his side.
13 It devours patches of his skin;
The firstborn of death devours his limbs.
14 He is uprooted from the shelter of his tent,
And they parade him before the king of terrors.
15 They dwell in his tent *who are* none of his;
Brimstone is scattered on his dwelling.
16 His roots are dried out below,
And his branch withers above.
17 The memory of him perishes from the earth,
And he has no name among the renowned.[a]

17:10 [a]Following some Hebrew manuscripts, Septuagint, Syriac, and Vulgate; Masoretic Text and Targum read *all of them*.
18:17 [a]Literally *before the outside*, meaning distinguished, famous

LIFE LESSONS

➤ 17:15 — *"Where then is my hope? As for my hope, who can see it?"*

In Christ, we have all the hope we will ever need. Regardless of our circumstances, God has "begotten us again to a living hope through the resurrection of Jesus Christ from the dead" (1 Pet. 1:3).

18 He is driven from light into darkness,
And chased out of the world.
19 He has neither son nor posterity among his people,
Nor any remaining in his dwellings.
20 Those in the west are astonished at his day,
As those in the east are frightened.
21 Surely such *are* the dwellings of the wicked,
And this *is* the place *of him who* does not know God."

Job Trusts in His Redeemer

19 Then Job answered and said:
2 "How long will you torment my soul,
And break me in pieces with words?
3 These ten times you have reproached me;
You are not ashamed *that* you have wronged me.[a]
4 And if indeed I have erred,
My error remains with me.
5 If indeed you exalt *yourselves* against me,
And plead my disgrace against me,
6 Know then that God has wronged me,
And has surrounded me with His net.

7 "If I cry out concerning wrong, I am not heard.
If I cry aloud, *there is* no justice.
8 He has fenced up my way, so that I cannot pass;
And He has set darkness in my paths.
9 He has stripped me of my glory,
And taken the crown *from* my head.
10 He breaks me down on every side,
And I am gone;
My hope He has uprooted like a tree.
11 He has also kindled His wrath against me,
And He counts me as *one of* His enemies.
12 His troops come together
And build up their road against me;
They encamp all around my tent.

13 "He has removed my brothers far from me,
And my acquaintances are completely estranged from me.
14 My relatives have failed,
And my close friends have forgotten me.
15 Those who dwell in my house, and my maidservants,
Count me as a stranger;
I am an alien in their sight.
16 I call my servant, but he gives no answer;
I beg him with my mouth.
17 My breath is offensive to my wife,
And I am repulsive to the children of my own body.
18 Even young children despise me;
I arise, and they speak against me.
19 All my close friends abhor me,
And those whom I love have turned against me.
20 My bone clings to my skin and to my flesh,
And I have escaped by the skin of my teeth.

21 "Have pity on me, have pity on me, O you my friends,
For the hand of God has struck me!
22 Why do you persecute me as God *does*,
And are not satisfied with my flesh?

23 "Oh, that my words were written! ➤
Oh, that they were inscribed in a book!
24 That they were engraved on a rock
With an iron pen and lead, forever!
25 For I know *that* my Redeemer lives, ✳
And He shall stand at last on the earth;
26 And after my skin is destroyed, this *I know*, ➤
That in my flesh I shall see God,
27 Whom I shall see for myself,
And my eyes shall behold, and not another.
How my heart yearns within me!
28 If you should say, 'How shall we persecute him?'—
Since the root of the matter is found in me,
29 Be afraid of the sword for yourselves;
For wrath *brings* the punishment of the sword,
That you may know *there is* a judgment."

Zophar's Sermon on the Wicked Man

20 Then Zophar the Naamathite answered and said:
2 "Therefore my anxious thoughts make me answer,
Because of the turmoil within me.

19:3 [a]A Jewish tradition reads *make yourselves strange to me.*

LIFE LESSONS

➤ 19:23 — *"Oh, that my words were written! Oh, that they were inscribed in a book!"*

Even as Job spoke these words, God was getting ready to put them in the Book of books, for all time and for the benefit of His hurting people. He is at work even when we do not know it.

➤ 19:26, 27 — *". . . in my flesh I shall see God, whom I shall see for myself, and my eyes shall behold, and not another."*

Everyone who has placed his or her faith in Jesus Christ will one day "see the King in His beauty" (Is. 33:17). And when we do, "we shall be like Him, for we shall see Him as He is" (1 John 3:2).

Life Examples:

JOB

Choosing to Trust

JOB 19:25, 26

Job was a good and righteous man who walked in the ways of the Lord. In fact, his righteousness prompted God Himself to say of him, "there is none like him on the earth" (Job 1:8). God blessed Job for his righteousness and so Job earned the title, "the greatest of all the people of the East" (Job 1:3).

Yet Job endured unspeakable suffering. Though he had done nothing wrong, he lost everything—his family, his wealth, his reputation, even his health. If that weren't enough, his wife and his friends offered him no real comfort. Job's friends told him that he had suffered because of some hidden sin in his life.

Job is a stark biblical example of a fact we need to understand: Even those who are right before God suffer adversity. Will we allow the suffering to tear down our faith or build it up? These are our only choices. Job chose to trust God, his Redeemer (Job 19:25, 26).

See the Life Principles Index for further study:
20. Disappointments are inevitable; discouragement is a choice.

3 I have heard the rebuke that reproaches
me,
And the spirit of my understanding
causes me to answer.

➤ 4 "Do you *not* know this of old,
Since man was placed on earth,
5 That the triumphing of the wicked is short,
And the joy of the hypocrite is *but* for a
moment?
6 Though his haughtiness mounts up to the
heavens,
And his head reaches to the clouds,
7 *Yet* he will perish forever like his own
refuse;
Those who have seen him will say,
'Where is he?'
8 He will fly away like a dream, and not be
found;
Yes, he will be chased away like a vision
of the night.
9 The eye *that* saw him will *see him* no
more,
Nor will his place behold him anymore.
10 His children will seek the favor of the
poor,
And his hands will restore his wealth.
11 His bones are full of his youthful vigor,
But it will lie down with him in the dust.

12 "Though evil is sweet in his mouth,
And he hides it under his tongue,
13 *Though* he spares it and does not forsake
it,
But still keeps it in his mouth,
14 *Yet* his food in his stomach turns sour;
It becomes cobra venom within him.
15 He swallows down riches
And vomits them up again;
God casts them out of his belly.
16 He will suck the poison of cobras;
The viper's tongue will slay him.
17 He will not see the streams,
The rivers flowing with honey and
cream.
18 He will restore that for which he labored,
And will not swallow *it* down;
From the proceeds of business
He will get no enjoyment.
19 For he has oppressed *and* forsaken the
poor,
He has violently seized a house which he
did not build.

20 "Because he knows no quietness in his
heart,[a]
He will not save anything he desires.
21 Nothing is left for him to eat;
Therefore his well-being will not last.
22 In his self-sufficiency he will be in
distress;
Every hand of misery will come against
him.
23 *When* he is about to fill his stomach,
God will cast on him the fury of His
wrath,
And will rain *it* on him while he is eating.
24 He will flee from the iron weapon;
A bronze bow will pierce him through.
25 It is drawn, and comes out of the body;

20:20 [a]Literally *belly*

LIFE LESSONS

➤ **20:4, 5 — *"Do you not know . . . that the triumphing of the wicked is short, and the joy of the hypocrite is but for a moment?"***

This is only half of the story. The other half is that the suffering of the righteous is short, and the agony of the godly is but for a moment (Rom. 8:18). Present pain does not necessarily reveal divine judgment.

Yes, the glittering *point comes* out of his
gall.
Terrors *come* upon him;
26 Total darkness *is* reserved for his treasures.
An unfanned fire will consume him;
It shall go ill with him who is left in his
tent.
27 The heavens will reveal his iniquity,
And the earth will rise up against him.
28 The increase of his house will depart,
And his goods will flow away in the day
of His wrath.
29 This *is* the portion from God for a wicked
man,
The heritage appointed to him by God."

Job's Discourse on the Wicked

21 Then Job answered and said:
2 "Listen carefully to my speech,
And let this be your consolation.
3 Bear with me that I may speak,
And after I have spoken, keep mocking.

4 "As for me, *is* my complaint against man?
And if *it were,* why should I not be
impatient?
5 Look at me and be astonished;
Put *your* hand over *your* mouth.
6 Even when I remember I am terrified,
And trembling takes hold of my flesh.
➤ 7 Why do the wicked live *and* become old,
Yes, become mighty in power?
8 Their descendants are established with
them in their sight,
And their offspring before their eyes.
9 Their houses *are* safe from fear,
Neither *is* the rod of God upon them.
10 Their bull breeds without failure;
Their cow calves without miscarriage.
11 They send forth their little ones like a
flock,
And their children dance.
12 They sing to the tambourine and harp,
And rejoice to the sound of the flute.
13 They spend their days in wealth,
And in a moment go down to the grave.[a]
14 Yet they say to God, 'Depart from us,
For we do not desire the knowledge of
Your ways.
15 Who *is* the Almighty, that we should
serve Him?
And what profit do we have if we pray to
Him?'
16 Indeed their prosperity *is* not in their
hand;
The counsel of the wicked is far from me.

17 "How often is the lamp of the wicked put
out?
How often does their destruction come
upon them,
The sorrows *God* distributes in His
anger?
18 They are like straw before the wind,
And like chaff that a storm carries away.
19 *They say,* 'God lays up one's[a] iniquity for
his children';
Let Him recompense him, that he may
know *it.*
20 Let his eyes see his destruction,
And let him drink of the wrath of the
Almighty.
21 For what does he care about his
household after him,
When the number of his months is cut in
half?

22 "Can *anyone* teach God knowledge, ➤
Since He judges those on high?
23 One dies in his full strength,
Being wholly at ease and secure;
24 His pails[a] are full of milk,
And the marrow of his bones is moist.
25 Another man dies in the bitterness of his
soul,
Never having eaten with pleasure.
26 They lie down alike in the dust,
And worms cover them.

27 "Look, I know your thoughts,
And the schemes *with which* you would
wrong me.
28 For you say,
'Where *is* the house of the prince?
And where *is* the tent,[a]
The dwelling place of the wicked?'
29 Have you not asked those who travel the
road?
And do you not know their signs?
30 For the wicked are reserved for the day
of doom;
They shall be brought out on the day of
wrath.
31 Who condemns his way to his face?

21:13 [a]Or *Sheol* **21:19** [a]Literally *his* **21:24** [a]Septuagint and Vulgate read *bowels;* Syriac reads *sides;* Targum reads *breasts.* **21:28** [a]Vulgate omits *the tent.*

LIFE LESSONS

➤ 21:7 — *"Why do the wicked live and become old, yes, become mighty in power?"*

God makes His sun shine on the evil and the good, and sends His rain on the just and the unjust (Matt. 5:45). Both the wicked and the righteous grow together—but Judgment Day *is* coming (Matt. 13:24–30).

➤ 21:22 — *"Can anyone teach God knowledge, since He judges those on high?"*

It may sometimes appear to us that God has gotten our life "wrong," that somehow He has crossed a few heavenly wires—but He hasn't. As Abraham knew, "the Judge of all the earth" will *always* do right (Gen. 18:25).

And who repays him *for what* he has
done?
32 Yet he shall be brought to the grave,
And a vigil kept over the tomb.
33 The clods of the valley shall be sweet to
him;
Everyone shall follow him,
As countless *have gone* before him.
34 How then can you comfort me with
empty words,
Since falsehood remains in your
answers?"

Eliphaz Accuses Job of Wickedness

22 Then Eliphaz the Temanite answered
and said:
2 "Can a man be profitable to God,
Though he who is wise may be profitable
to himself?
➤ 3 *Is it* any pleasure to the Almighty that
you are righteous?
Or *is it* gain *to Him* that you make your
ways blameless?
4 "Is it because of your fear of Him that He
corrects you,
And enters into judgment with you?
5 *Is* not your wickedness great,
And your iniquity without end?
6 For you have taken pledges from your
brother for no reason,
And stripped the naked of their clothing.
7 You have not given the weary water to
drink,
And you have withheld bread from the
hungry.
8 But the mighty man possessed the land,
And the honorable man dwelt in it.
9 You have sent widows away empty,
And the strength of the fatherless was
crushed.
10 Therefore snares *are* all around you,
And sudden fear troubles you,
11 Or darkness *so that* you cannot see;
And an abundance of water covers you.
12"Is not God in the height of heaven?
And see the highest stars, how lofty they
are!
13 And you say, 'What does God know?
Can He judge through the deep
darkness?
14 Thick clouds cover Him, so that He
cannot see,
And He walks above the circle of heaven.'
15 Will you keep to the old way
Which wicked men have trod,
16 Who were cut down before their time,
Whose foundations were swept away by
a flood?
17 They said to God, 'Depart from us!
What can the Almighty do to them?'[a]
18 Yet He filled their houses with good *things;*
But the counsel of the wicked is far from
me.
19"The righteous see *it* and are glad,
And the innocent laugh at them:
20'Surely our adversaries[a] are cut down,
And the fire consumes their remnant.'
21"Now acquaint yourself with Him, and be
at peace;
Thereby good will come to you.
22 Receive, please, instruction from His
mouth,
And lay up His words in your heart.
23 If you return to the Almighty, you will be
built up;
You will remove iniquity far from your
tents.
24 Then you will lay your gold in the dust,
And the *gold* of Ophir among the stones
of the brooks.
25 Yes, the Almighty will be your gold[a]
And your precious silver;
26 For then you will have your delight in the
Almighty,
And lift up your face to God.
27 You will make your prayer to Him,
He will hear you,
And you will pay your vows.
28 You will also declare a thing,
And it will be established for you;
So light will shine on your ways.
29 When they cast *you* down, and you say,
'Exaltation *will come!*'
Then He will save the humble *person.*
30 He will *even* deliver one who is not
innocent;
Yes, he will be delivered by the purity of
your hands."

Job Proclaims God's Righteous Judgments

23 Then Job answered and said:
2 "Even today my complaint is bitter;
My[a] hand is listless because of my
groaning.

22:17 [a]Septuagint and Syriac read *us.* **22:20** [a]Septuagint reads *substance.* **22:25** [a]The ancient versions suggest *defense;* Hebrew reads *gold* as in verse 24. **23:2** [a]Following Masoretic Text, Targum, and Vulgate; Septuagint and Syriac read *His.*

LIFE LESSONS

➤ **22:3 — *"Is it any pleasure to the Almighty that you are righteous? Or is it gain to Him that you make your ways blameless?"***

Actually, the answers are "yes" and "yes." In fact, God "delights" in the obedience of His people (1 Sam. 15:22) and "takes pleasure in those who fear Him, in those who hope in His mercy" (Ps. 147:11).

3 Oh, that I knew where I might find Him,
That I might come to His seat!
4 I would present *my* case before Him,
And fill my mouth with arguments.
5 I would know the words *which* He would
answer me,
And understand what He would say to me.
6 Would He contend with me in His great
power?
No! But He would take *note* of me.
7 There the upright could reason with Him,
And I would be delivered forever from
my Judge.

8 "Look, I go forward, but He is not *there,*
And backward, but I cannot perceive Him;
9 When He works on the left hand, I
cannot behold *Him;*
When He turns to the right hand, I
cannot see *Him.*
➢ 10 But He knows the way that I take;
When He has tested me, I shall come
forth as gold.
11 My foot has held fast to His steps;
I have kept His way and not turned aside.
➢ 12 I have not departed from the
commandment of His lips;
I have treasured the words of His mouth
More than my necessary *food.*

➢ 13 "But He *is* unique, and who can make Him
change?
And *whatever* His soul desires, *that* He
does.
14 For He performs *what is* appointed for
me,
And many such *things are* with Him.
15 Therefore I am terrified at His presence;
When I consider *this,* I am afraid of Him.
16 For God made my heart weak,
And the Almighty terrifies me;
17 Because I was not cut off from the
presence of darkness,
And He did *not* hide deep darkness from
my face.

Job Complains of Violence on the Earth

24 "*Since* times are not hidden from the
Almighty,
Why do those who know Him see not His
days?

2 "*Some* remove landmarks;
They seize flocks violently and feed *on*
them;
3 They drive away the donkey of the
fatherless;
They take the widow's ox as a pledge.
4 They push the needy off the road;
All the poor of the land are forced to hide.
5 Indeed, *like* wild donkeys in the desert,
They go out to their work, searching for
food.
The wilderness *yields* food for them *and*
for *their* children.
6 They gather their fodder in the field
And glean in the vineyard of the wicked.
7 They spend the night naked, without
clothing,
And have no covering in the cold.
8 They are wet with the showers of the
mountains,
And huddle around the rock for want of
shelter.

9 "*Some* snatch the fatherless from the
breast,
And take a pledge from the poor.
10 They cause *the poor* to go naked, without
clothing;
And they take away the sheaves from the
hungry.
11 They press out oil within their walls,
And tread winepresses, yet suffer thirst.
12 The dying groan in the city,
And the souls of the wounded cry out;
Yet God does not charge *them* with wrong.

13 "There are those who rebel against the
light;
They do not know its ways
Nor abide in its paths.
14 The murderer rises with the light;
He kills the poor and needy;
And in the night he is like a thief.
15 The eye of the adulterer waits for the
twilight,
Saying, 'No eye will see me';
And he disguises *his* face.
16 In the dark they break into houses
Which they marked for themselves in the
daytime;
They do not know the light.

LIFE LESSONS

➢ 23:10 — *"But He knows the way that I take; when He has tested me, I shall come forth as gold."*

Despite his calamities, Job still believed that God had a hand in his life for good. The dark moments of our lives will last only so long as is necessary for God to accomplish His purpose in us.

➢ 23:12 — *"I have treasured the words of His mouth more than my necessary food."*

If we turn away from the Lord when hard times hit, where will we find hope, or peace, or truth? God's Word is an immovable anchor in times of storm, and living bread for dying men and women.

➢ 23:13 — *"And whatever His soul desires, that He does."*

God is sovereign and "He does according to His will in the army of heaven and among the inhabitants of the earth. No one can restrain His hand or say to Him, 'What have you done?'" (Dan. 4:35).

17 For the morning is the same to them as
the shadow of death;
If *someone* recognizes *them,*
They are in the terrors of the shadow of
death.

18 "They *should be* swift on the face of the
waters,
Their portion *should be* cursed in the earth,
So that no *one would* turn into the way
of their vineyards.
19 As drought and heat consume the snow
waters,
So the grave[a] *consumes those who* have
sinned.
20 The womb *should* forget him,
The worm *should* feed sweetly on him;
He *should* be remembered no more,
And wickedness *should* be broken like a
tree.
21 For he preys on the barren *who* do not bear,
And does no good for the widow.

22 "But *God* draws the mighty away with His
power;
He rises up, but no *man* is sure of life.
23 He gives them security, and they rely *on it;*
Yet His eyes *are* on their ways.
➤ 24 They are exalted for a little while,
Then they are gone.
They are brought low;
They are taken out of the way like all
others;
They dry out like the heads of grain.

25 "Now if *it is* not *so,* who will prove me a
liar,
And make my speech worth nothing?"

Bildad: How Can Man Be Righteous?

25 Then Bildad the Shuhite answered and
said:

2 "Dominion and fear *belong* to Him;
He makes peace in His high places.
3 Is there any number to His armies?
Upon whom does His light not rise?
➤ 4 How then can man be righteous before
God?
Or how can he be pure *who is* born of a
woman?
5 If even the moon does not shine,
And the stars are not pure in His sight,
6 How much less man, *who is* a maggot,
And a son of man, *who is* a worm?"

Job: Man's Frailty and God's Majesty

26 But Job answered and said:

2 "How have you helped *him who is* without
power?
How have you saved the arm *that has* no
strength?
3 How have you counseled *one who has* no
wisdom?
And *how* have you declared sound advice
to many?
4 To whom have you uttered words?
And whose spirit came from you?

5 "The dead tremble,
Those under the waters and those
inhabiting them.
6 Sheol *is* naked before Him,
And Destruction has no covering.
7 He stretches out the north over empty ◄
space;
He hangs the earth on nothing.
8 He binds up the water in His thick clouds,
Yet the clouds are not broken under it.
9 He covers the face of *His* throne,
And spreads His cloud over it.
10 He drew a circular horizon on the face of
the waters,
At the boundary of light and darkness.
11 The pillars of heaven tremble,
And are astonished at His rebuke.
12 He stirs up the sea with His power,
And by His understanding He breaks up
the storm.
13 By His Spirit He adorned the heavens;
His hand pierced the fleeing serpent.
14 Indeed these *are* the mere edges of His ◄
ways,

24:19 [a]Or *Sheol*

LIFE LESSONS

➤ 24:24 — *"They are exalted for a little while, then they are gone."*

None of us lives forever. Even the strongest and most powerful eventually succumbs to injury or disease or old age. We are "a vapor that appears for a little time and then vanishes away" (James 4:4)—and yet He loves us.

➤ 25:4 — *". . . how can he be pure who is born of a woman?"*

Peace with God is the fruit of oneness with God—and purity blossoms from the same healthy stock: "Be an example to the believers in word, in conduct, in love, in spirit, in faith, in purity" (1 Tim. 4:12).

➤ 26:7 — *"He hangs the earth on nothing."*

Who but God could take nothing and hang the world on it? Who but God could take the "nothing" of a destitute widow and pay her bills with it (2 Kin. 4:1–7)? What could He do with *your* "nothing"?

➤ 26:14 — *"Indeed these are the mere edges of His ways, and how small a whisper we hear of Him! But the thunder of His power who can understand?"*

The greatest forces in nature give nothing but the tiniest hint of God's immeasurable power. And yet He makes all that power available to us through prayer!

And how small a whisper we hear of Him!
But the thunder of His power who can understand?"

Job Maintains His Integrity

27 Moreover Job continued his discourse, and said:

2 "*As* God lives, *who* has taken away my justice,
And the Almighty, *who* has made my soul bitter,
➤ 3 As long as my breath *is* in me,
And the breath of God in my nostrils,
4 My lips will not speak wickedness,
Nor my tongue utter deceit.
5 Far be it from me
That I should say you are right;
Till I die I will not put away my integrity from me.
6 My righteousness I hold fast, and will not let it go;
My heart shall not reproach *me* as long as I live.

7 "May my enemy be like the wicked,
And he who rises up against me like the unrighteous.
8 For what is the hope of the hypocrite,
Though he may gain *much,*
If God takes away his life?
9 Will God hear his cry
When trouble comes upon him?
10 Will he delight himself in the Almighty?
Will he always call on God?

11 "I will teach you about the hand of God;
What *is* with the Almighty I will not conceal.
12 Surely all of you have seen *it;*
Why then do you behave with complete nonsense?

13 "This is the portion of a wicked man with God,
And the heritage of oppressors, received from the Almighty:
14 If his children are multiplied, *it is* for the sword;
And his offspring shall not be satisfied with bread.
15 Those who survive him shall be buried in death,
And their[a] widows shall not weep,
16 Though he heaps up silver like dust,
And piles up clothing like clay—
17 He may pile *it* up, but the just will wear *it,*
And the innocent will divide the silver.
18 He builds his house like a moth,[a]
Like a booth *which* a watchman makes.
19 The rich man will lie down,
But not be gathered *up;*[a]
He opens his eyes,
And he *is* no more.
20 Terrors overtake him like a flood;
A tempest steals him away in the night.
21 The east wind carries him away, and he is gone;
It sweeps him out of his place.
22 It hurls against him and does not spare;
He flees desperately from its power.
23 *Men* shall clap their hands at him,
And shall hiss him out of his place.

Job's Discourse on Wisdom

28 "Surely there is a mine for silver,
And a place *where* gold is refined.
2 Iron is taken from the earth,
And copper *is* smelted *from* ore.
3 *Man* puts an end to darkness,
And searches every recess
For ore in the darkness and the shadow of death.
4 He breaks open a shaft away from people;
In places forgotten by feet
They hang far away from men;
They swing to and fro.
5 *As for* the earth, from it comes bread,
But underneath it is turned up as by fire;
6 Its stones *are* the source of sapphires,
And it contains gold dust.
7 *That* path no bird knows,
Nor has the falcon's eye seen it.
8 The proud lions[a] have not trodden it,
Nor has the fierce lion passed over it.
9 He puts his hand on the flint;
He overturns the mountains at the roots.
10 He cuts out channels in the rocks,
And his eye sees every precious thing.
11 He dams up the streams from trickling;
What is hidden he brings forth to light.

12 "But where can wisdom be found?
And where *is* the place of understanding?
13 Man does not know its value,
Nor is it found in the land of the living.

27:15 [a]Literally *his* **27:18** [a]Following Masoretic Text and Vulgate; Septuagint and Syriac read *spider* (compare 8:14); Targum reads *decay.* **27:19** [a]Following Masoretic Text and Targum; Septuagint and Syriac read *But shall not add* (that is, do it again); Vulgate reads *But take away nothing.* **28:8** [a]Literally *sons of pride,* figurative of the great lions

LIFE LESSONS

➤ 27:3, 4 — *"As long as my breath is in me, and the breath of God in my nostrils, My lips will not speak wickedness, nor my tongue utter deceit."*

Every breath we take is really the breath of God. It belongs to Him, and He can take it back at any time. So let us use our breath to glorify and praise Him, so long as we have it.

14 The deep says, *'It is* not in me';
And the sea says, *'It is* not with me.'
15 It cannot be purchased for gold,
Nor can silver be weighed *for* its price.
16 It cannot be valued in the gold of Ophir,
In precious onyx or sapphire.
17 Neither gold nor crystal can equal it,
Nor can it be exchanged for jewelry of fine gold.
18 No mention shall be made of coral or quartz,
For the price of wisdom *is* above rubies.
19 The topaz of Ethiopia cannot equal it,
Nor can it be valued in pure gold.

20 "From where then does wisdom come?
And where *is* the place of understanding?
21 It is hidden from the eyes of all living,
And concealed from the birds of the air.
22 Destruction and Death say,
'We have heard a report about it with our ears.'
23 God understands its way,
And He knows its place.
24 For He looks to the ends of the earth,
And sees under the whole heavens,
25 To establish a weight for the wind,
And apportion the waters by measure.
26 When He made a law for the rain,
And a path for the thunderbolt,
27 Then He saw *wisdom*[a] and declared it;
He prepared it, indeed, He searched it out.
➤ 28 And to man He said,
'Behold, the fear of the Lord, that *is* wisdom,
And to depart from evil *is* understanding.'"

Job's Summary Defense

29 Job further continued his discourse, and said:

➤ 2 "Oh, that I were as *in* months past,
As *in* the days *when* God watched over me;
3 When His lamp shone upon my head,
And when by His light I walked *through* darkness;
4 Just as I was in the days of my prime,
When the friendly counsel of God *was* over my tent;
5 When the Almighty *was* yet with me,
When my children *were* around me;
6 When my steps were bathed with cream,[a]
And the rock poured out rivers of oil for me!

7 "When I went out to the gate by the city,
When I took my seat in the open square,
8 The young men saw me and hid,
And the aged arose *and* stood;
9 The princes refrained from talking,
And put *their* hand on their mouth;
10 The voice of nobles was hushed,
And their tongue stuck to the roof of their mouth.
11 When the ear heard, then it blessed me,
And when the eye saw, then it approved me;
12 Because I delivered the poor who cried out,
The fatherless and *the one who* had no helper.
13 The blessing of a perishing *man* came upon me,
And I caused the widow's heart to sing for joy.
14 I put on righteousness, and it clothed me;
My justice *was* like a robe and a turban.
15 I *was* eyes to the blind,
And I *was* feet to the lame.
16 I *was* a father to the poor,
And I searched out the case *that* I did not know.
17 I broke the fangs of the wicked,
And plucked the victim from his teeth.

18 "Then I said, 'I shall die in my nest,
And multiply *my* days as the sand.
19 My root *is* spread out to the waters,
And the dew lies all night on my branch.
20 My glory *is* fresh within me,
And my bow is renewed in my hand.'

21 "*Men* listened to me and waited,
And kept silence for my counsel.
22 After my words they did not speak again,
And my speech settled on them *as dew.*
23 They waited for me *as* for the rain,
And they opened their mouth wide *as* for the spring rain.
24 *If* I mocked at them, they did not believe *it*,

28:27 [a]Literally *it* **29:6** [a]Masoretic Text reads *wrath;* ancient versions and some Hebrew manuscripts read *cream* (compare 20:17).

LIFE LESSONS

➤ 28:28 — *"Behold, the fear of the Lord, that is wisdom, and to depart from evil is understanding."*

Why is it wise to fear the Lord? How do we show insight when we obey Him? One day we will stand before Him, "that each one may receive the things done in the body . . . whether good or bad" (2 Cor. 5:10).

➤ 29:2 — *"Oh, that I were as in months past, as in the days when God watched over me . . . ."*

Job did not realize that, even as he uttered this wish, God was *still* closely and lovingly watching over him. His hardships did not mean that God had abandoned him. The same is true for you.

And the light of my countenance they did
not cast down.
25 I chose the way for them, and sat as
chief;
So I dwelt as a king in the army,
As one *who* comforts mourners.

30 "But now they mock at me, *men*
younger than I,
Whose fathers I disdained to put with the
dogs of my flock.
2 Indeed, what *profit* is the strength of
their hands to me?
Their vigor has perished.
3 *They are* gaunt from want and famine,
Fleeing late to the wilderness, desolate
and waste,
4 Who pluck mallow by the bushes,
And broom tree roots *for* their food.
5 They were driven out from among *men*,
They shouted at them as *at* a thief.
6 *They had* to live in the clefts of the
valleys,
In caves of the earth and the rocks.
7 Among the bushes they brayed,
Under the nettles they nestled.
8 *They were* sons of fools,
Yes, sons of vile men;
They were scourged from the land.

9 "And now I am their taunting song;
Yes, I am their byword.
10 They abhor me, they keep far from me;
They do not hesitate to spit in my face.
11 Because He has loosed my[a] bowstring
and afflicted me,
They have cast off restraint before me.
12 At *my* right *hand* the rabble arises;
They push away my feet,
And they raise against me their ways of
destruction.
13 They break up my path,
They promote my calamity;
They have no helper.
14 They come as broad breakers;
Under the ruinous storm they roll along.
15 Terrors are turned upon me;
They pursue my honor as the wind,
And my prosperity has passed like a
cloud.

16 "And now my soul is poured out because
of my *plight;*
The days of affliction take hold of me.
17 My bones are pierced in me at night,
And my gnawing pains take no rest.
18 By great force my garment is disfigured;
It binds me about as the collar of my coat.
19 He has cast me into the mire,
And I have become like dust and ashes.

20 "I cry out to You, but You do not answer
me;
I stand up, and You regard me.
21 *But* You have become cruel to me;
With the strength of Your hand You
oppose me.
22 You lift me up to the wind and cause me
to ride *on it;*
You spoil my success.
23 For I know *that* You will bring me *to*
death,
And *to* the house appointed for all living.

24 "Surely He would not stretch out *His* hand
against a heap of ruins,
If they cry out when He destroys *it*.
25 Have I not wept for him who was in
trouble?
Has *not* my soul grieved for the poor?
26 But when I looked for good, evil came *to
me;*
And when I waited for light, then came
darkness.
27 My heart is in turmoil and cannot rest;
Days of affliction confront me.
28 I go about mourning, but not in the sun;
I stand up in the assembly *and* cry out for
help.
29 I am a brother of jackals,
And a companion of ostriches.
30 My skin grows black and falls from me;
My bones burn with fever.
31 My harp is *turned* to mourning,
And my flute to the voice of those who
weep.

31 "I have made a covenant with my
eyes;
Why then should I look upon a young
woman?
2 For what *is* the allotment of God from
above,
And the inheritance of the Almighty from
on high?

30:11 [a]Following Masoretic Text, Syriac, and Targum; Septuagint and Vulgate read *His*.

LIFE LESSONS

➤ 30:20 — *"I cry out to You, but You do not answer me . . . ."*

Just because God waits to answer our prayers does not mean that He has forgotten us or that He has failed to hear our requests. He works on our behalf even as we complain that He's ignoring us.

➤ 31:1 — *"I have made a covenant with my eyes; why then should I look upon a young woman?"*

When hard times come, it can help to recall how God already has worked in our hearts to shape us into the likeness of Christ. God finishes what He starts, and what He began in us He will certainly complete.

3 *Is* it not destruction for the wicked,
And disaster for the workers of iniquity?
➤ 4 Does He not see my ways,
And count all my steps?

5 "If I have walked with falsehood,
Or if my foot has hastened to deceit,
6 Let me be weighed on honest scales,
That God may know my integrity.
7 If my step has turned from the way,
Or my heart walked after my eyes,
Or if any spot adheres to my hands,
8 *Then* let me sow, and another eat;
Yes, let my harvest be rooted out.

9 "If my heart has been enticed by a woman,
Or *if* I have lurked at my neighbor's door,
10 *Then* let my wife grind for another,
And let others bow down over her.
11 For that *would be* wickedness;
Yes, it *would be* iniquity *deserving of* judgment.
12 For that *would be* a fire *that* consumes to destruction,
And would root out all my increase.

13 "If I have despised the cause of my male or female servant
When they complained against me,
14 What then shall I do when God rises up?
When He punishes, how shall I answer Him?
15 Did not He who made me in the womb make them?
Did not the same One fashion us in the womb?

16 "If I have kept the poor from *their* desire,
Or caused the eyes of the widow to fail,
17 Or eaten my morsel by myself,
So that the fatherless could not eat of it
18 (But from my youth I reared him as a father,
And from my mother's womb I guided *the widow*[a]);
19 If I have seen anyone perish for lack of clothing,
Or any poor *man* without covering;
20 If his heart[a] has not blessed me,
And *if* he was *not* warmed with the fleece of my sheep;
21 If I have raised my hand against the fatherless,
When I saw I had help in the gate;
22 *Then* let my arm fall from my shoulder,
Let my arm be torn from the socket.
23 For destruction *from* God *is* a terror to me,
And because of His magnificence I cannot endure.

24 "If I have made gold my hope,
Or said to fine gold, '*You are* my confidence';
25 If I have rejoiced because my wealth *was* great,
And because my hand had gained much;
26 If I have observed the sun[a] when it shines,
Or the moon moving *in* brightness,
27 So that my heart has been secretly enticed,
And my mouth has kissed my hand;
28 This also *would be* an iniquity *deserving of* judgment,
For I would have denied God *who is* above.

29 "If I have rejoiced at the destruction of him who hated me,
Or lifted myself up when evil found him
30 (Indeed I have not allowed my mouth to sin
By asking for a curse on his soul);
31 If the men of my tent have not said,
'Who is there that has not been satisfied with his meat?'
32 (*But* no sojourner had to lodge in the street,
For I have opened my doors to the traveler[a]);
33 If I have covered my transgressions as Adam,
By hiding my iniquity in my bosom,
34 Because I feared the great multitude,
And dreaded the contempt of families,
So that I kept silence
And did not go out of the door—
35 Oh, that I had one to hear me!
Here is my mark.
Oh, that the Almighty would answer me,
That my Prosecutor had written a book!
36 Surely I would carry it on my shoulder,
And bind it on me *like* a crown;
37 I would declare to Him the number of my steps;
Like a prince I would approach Him.

31:18 [a]Literally *her* (compare verse 16) **31:20** [a]Literally *loins*
31:26 [a]Literally *light* **31:32** [a]Following Septuagint, Syriac, Targum, and Vulgate; Masoretic Text reads *road.*

LIFE LESSONS

➤ 31:4 — *"Does He not see my ways, and count all my steps?"*

God does indeed see everything we do, hear everything we say, and record everywhere we go. He desires an intimate relationship with us, and His intimate knowledge of us makes that possible.

38 "If my land cries out against me,
And its furrows weep together;
39 If I have eaten its fruit[a] without money,
Or caused its owners to lose their lives;
40 *Then* let thistles grow instead of wheat,
And weeds instead of barley."

The words of Job are ended.

Elihu Contradicts Job's Friends

32 So these three men ceased answering
Job, because he *was* righteous in his
own eyes.
2 Then the wrath of Elihu, the son of
Barachel the Buzite, of the family of Ram,
was aroused against Job; his wrath was
aroused because he justified himself rather
than God.
3 Also against his three friends his wrath
was aroused, because they had found no answer, and *yet* had condemned Job.
4 Now because they *were* years older than
he, Elihu had waited to speak to Job.[a]
5 When Elihu saw that *there was* no answer
in the mouth of these three men, his wrath
was aroused.
6 So Elihu, the son of Barachel the Buzite,
answered and said:

"I *am* young in years, and you *are* very old;
Therefore I was afraid,
And dared not declare my opinion to you.
7 I said, 'Age[a] should speak,
And multitude of years should teach wisdom.'
8 But *there is* a spirit in man,
And the breath of the Almighty gives him understanding.
9 Great men[a] are not *always* wise,
Nor do the aged *always* understand justice.

10 "Therefore I say, 'Listen to me,
I also will declare my opinion.'
11 Indeed I waited for your words,
I listened to your reasonings, while you searched out what to say.
12 I paid close attention to you;
And surely not one of you convinced Job,
Or answered his words—
13 Lest you say,
'We have found wisdom';
God will vanquish him, not man.
14 Now he has not directed *his* words against me;
So I will not answer him with your words.

15 "They are dismayed and answer no more;
Words escape them.
16 And I have waited, because they did not speak,
Because they stood still *and* answered no more.
17 I also will answer my part,
I too will declare my opinion.
18 For I am full of words;
The spirit within me compels me.
19 Indeed my belly *is* like wine *that* has no vent;
It is ready to burst like new wineskins.
20 I will speak, that I may find relief;
I must open my lips and answer.
21 Let me not, I pray, show partiality to anyone;
Nor let me flatter any man.
22 For I do not know how to flatter,
Else my Maker would soon take me away.

Elihu Contradicts Job

33 "But please, Job, hear my speech,
And listen to all my words.
2 Now, I open my mouth;
My tongue speaks in my mouth.
3 My words *come* from my upright heart;
My lips utter pure knowledge.
4 The Spirit of God has made me,
And the breath of the Almighty gives me life.
5 If you can answer me,
Set *your words* in order before me;
Take your stand.
6 Truly I *am* as your spokesman[a] before God;
I also have been formed out of clay.
7 Surely no fear of me will terrify you,
Nor will my hand be heavy on you.

8 "Surely you have spoken in my hearing,
And I have heard the sound of *your* words, *saying,*
9 'I *am* pure, without transgression;
I *am* innocent, and *there is* no iniquity in me.
10 Yet He finds occasions against me,
He counts me as His enemy;

31:39 [a]Literally *its strength* **32:4** [a]Vulgate reads *till Job had spoken.* **32:7** [a]Literally *Days,* that is, years **32:9** [a]Or *Men of many years* **33:6** [a]Literally *as your mouth*

LIFE LESSONS

➤ **32:18 — *"For I am full of words; the spirit within me compels me."***

Elihu had a difficult time holding his tongue. He thought he had much to add, but in fact he merely restated the foolish things already said. "In the multitude of words sin is not lacking" (Prov. 10:19).

11 He puts my feet in the stocks,
He watches all my paths.'

12"Look, *in* this you are not righteous.
I will answer you,
For God is greater than man.
13 Why do you contend with Him?
For He does not give an accounting of
any of His words.
➤ 14 For God may speak in one way, or in
another,
Yet man does not perceive it.
15 In a dream, in a vision of the night,
When deep sleep falls upon men,
While slumbering on their beds,
16 Then He opens the ears of men,
And seals their instruction.
17 In order to turn man *from his* deed,
And conceal pride from man,
18 He keeps back his soul from the Pit,
And his life from perishing by the sword.

19"*Man* is also chastened with pain on his
bed,
And with strong *pain* in many of his bones,
20 So that his life abhors bread,
And his soul succulent food.
21 His flesh wastes away from sight,
And his bones stick out *which once* were
not seen.
22 Yes, his soul draws near the Pit,
And his life to the executioners.

23"If there is a messenger for him,
A mediator, one among a thousand,
To show man His uprightness,
24 Then He is gracious to him, and says,
'Deliver him from going down to the Pit;
I have found a ransom';
25 His flesh shall be young like a child's,
He shall return to the days of his youth.
26 He shall pray to God, and He will delight
in him,
He shall see His face with joy,
For He restores to man His righteousness.
27 Then he looks at men and says,
'I have sinned, and perverted *what was*
right,
And it did not profit me.'
28 He will redeem his[a] soul from going
down to the Pit,
And his[b] life shall see the light.

29"Behold, God works all these *things*,
Twice, *in fact*, three *times* with a man,
30 To bring back his soul from the Pit,
That he may be enlightened with the
light of life.
31"Give ear, Job, listen to me;
Hold your peace, and I will speak.
32 If you have anything to say, answer me;
Speak, for I desire to justify you.
33 If not, listen to me;
Hold your peace, and I will teach you
wisdom."

Elihu Proclaims God's Justice

34 Elihu further answered and said:
2 "Hear my words, you wise *men;*
Give ear to me, you who have knowledge.
3 For the ear tests words
As the palate tastes food.
4 Let us choose justice for ourselves;
Let us know among ourselves what *is*
good.

5 "For Job has said, 'I am righteous,
But God has taken away my justice;
6 Should I lie concerning my right?
My wound *is* incurable, *though I am*
without transgression.'
7 What man *is* like Job,
Who drinks scorn like water,
8 Who goes in company with the workers
of iniquity,
And walks with wicked men?
9 For he has said, 'It profits a man nothing
That he should delight in God.'

10"Therefore listen to me, you men of
understanding:
Far be it from God *to do* wickedness,
And *from* the Almighty to *commit*
iniquity.
11 For He repays man *according to* his work,
And makes man to find a reward
according to *his* way.
12 Surely God will never do wickedly, ➤
Nor will the Almighty pervert justice.
13 Who gave Him charge over the earth?
Or who appointed *Him over* the whole
world?
14 If He should set His heart on it,
If He should gather to Himself His Spirit
and His breath,

33:28 [a]Or *my* (Kethib) [b]Or *my* (Kethib)

LIFE LESSONS

➤ 33:14 — *"For God may speak in one way, or in another, yet man does not perceive it."*

Because God may want to speak to us in any number of ways—some of them quite surprising—we must always keep our ears open and our spirits ready to listen for His voice.

➤ 34:12 — *"Surely God will never do wickedly, nor will the Almighty pervert justice."*

We may not understand why God allows some very bad things to happen to very godly people, but we never have to wonder about His character. He will *always* do what is right. That truth will never change.

15 All flesh would perish together,
And man would return to dust.

16 "If *you have* understanding, hear this;
Listen to the sound of my words:
17 Should one who hates justice govern?
Will you condemn *Him who is* most just?
18 *Is it fitting* to say to a king, '*You are* worthless,'
And to nobles, '*You are* wicked'?
19 Yet He is not partial to princes,
Nor does He regard the rich more than the poor;
For they *are* all the work of His hands.
20 In a moment they die, in the middle of the night;
The people are shaken and pass away;
The mighty are taken away without a hand.

21 "For His eyes *are* on the ways of man,
And He sees all his steps.
22 There is no darkness nor shadow of death
Where the workers of iniquity may hide themselves.
23 For He need not further consider a man,
That he should go before God in judgment.
24 He breaks in pieces mighty men without inquiry,
And sets others in their place.
25 Therefore He knows their works;
He overthrows *them* in the night,
And they are crushed.
26 He strikes them as wicked *men*
In the open sight of others,
27 Because they turned back from Him,
And would not consider any of His ways,
28 So that they caused the cry of the poor to come to Him;
For He hears the cry of the afflicted.
29 When He gives quietness, who then can make trouble?
And when He hides *His* face, who then can see Him,
Whether *it is* against a nation or a man alone?—
30 That the hypocrite should not reign,
Lest the people be ensnared.

31 "For has *anyone* said to God,
'I have borne *chastening;*
I will offend no more;
32 Teach me *what* I do not see;
If I have done iniquity, I will do no more'?
33 Should He repay *it* according to your *terms,*
Just because you disavow it?
You must choose, and not I;
Therefore speak what you know.

34 "Men of understanding say to me,
Wise men who listen to me:
35 'Job speaks without knowledge,
His words *are* without wisdom.'
36 Oh, that Job were tried to the utmost,
Because *his* answers *are like* those of wicked men!
37 For he adds rebellion to his sin;
He claps *his hands* among us,
And multiplies his words against God."

Elihu Condemns Self-Righteousness

35 Moreover Elihu answered and said:

2 "Do you think this is right?
Do you say,
'My righteousness is more than God's'?
3 For you say,
'What advantage will it be to You?
What profit shall I have, more than *if* I had sinned?'

4 "I will answer you,
And your companions with you.
5 Look to the heavens and see;
And behold the clouds—
They are higher than you.
6 If you sin, what do you accomplish against Him?
Or, *if* your transgressions are multiplied, what do you do to Him?
7 If you are righteous, what do you give Him?
Or what does He receive from your hand?
8 Your wickedness affects a man such as you,
And your righteousness a son of man.

9 "Because of the multitude of oppressions they cry out;
They cry out for help because of the arm of the mighty.
10 But no one says, 'Where *is* God my Maker,
Who gives songs in the night,
11 Who teaches us more than the beasts of the earth,
And makes us wiser than the birds of heaven?'
12 There they cry out, but He does not answer,
Because of the pride of evil men.
13 Surely God will not listen to empty *talk,*
Nor will the Almighty regard it.
14 Although you say you do not see Him,
Yet justice *is* before Him, and you must wait for Him.
15 And now, because He has not punished in His anger,
Nor taken much notice of folly,
16 Therefore Job opens his mouth in vain;
He multiplies words without knowledge."

Elihu Proclaims God's Goodness

36 Elihu also proceeded and said:

2 "Bear with me a little, and I will show you
That *there are* yet words to speak on God's behalf.

3 I will fetch my knowledge from afar;
I will ascribe righteousness to my Maker.
4 For truly my words *are* not false;
One who is perfect in knowledge *is* with you.

5 "Behold, God *is* mighty, but despises *no one;*
He is mighty in strength of understanding.
6 He does not preserve the life of the wicked,
But gives justice to the oppressed.
7 He does not withdraw His eyes from the righteous;
But *they are* on the throne with kings,
For He has seated them forever,
And they are exalted.
8 And if *they are* bound in fetters,
Held in the cords of affliction,
9 Then He tells them their work and their transgressions—
That they have acted defiantly.
10 He also opens their ear to instruction,
And commands that they turn from iniquity.
➤ 11 If they obey and serve *Him,*
They shall spend their days in prosperity,
And their years in pleasures.
12 But if they do not obey,
They shall perish by the sword,
And they shall die without knowledge.[a]

13 "But the hypocrites in heart store up wrath;
They do not cry for help when He binds them.
14 They die in youth,
And their life *ends* among the perverted persons.[a]
➤ 15 He delivers the poor in their affliction,
And opens their ears in oppression.

16 "Indeed He would have brought you out of dire distress,
Into a broad place where *there is* no restraint;
And what is set on your table *would be* full of richness.
17 But you are filled with the judgment due the wicked;
Judgment and justice take hold *of you.*
18 Because *there is* wrath, *beware* lest He take you away with *one* blow;
For a large ransom would not help you avoid *it.*
19 Will your riches,
Or all the mighty forces,
Keep you from distress?
20 Do not desire the night,
When people are cut off in their place.
21 Take heed, do not turn to iniquity,
For you have chosen this rather than affliction.

22 "Behold, God is exalted by His power;
Who teaches like Him?
23 Who has assigned Him His way,
Or who has said, 'You have done wrong'?

Elihu Proclaims God's Majesty

24 "Remember to magnify His work,
Of which men have sung.
25 Everyone has seen it;
Man looks on *it* from afar.

26 "Behold, God *is* great, and we do not know *Him;*
Nor can the number of His years *be* discovered.
27 For He draws up drops of water,
Which distill as rain from the mist,
28 Which the clouds drop down
And pour abundantly on man.
29 Indeed, can *anyone* understand the spreading of clouds,
The thunder from His canopy?
30 Look, He scatters His light upon it,
And covers the depths of the sea.
31 For by these He judges the peoples;
He gives food in abundance.
32 He covers *His* hands with lightning,
And commands it to strike.
33 His thunder declares it,
The cattle also, concerning the rising *storm.*

37 "At this also my heart trembles,
And leaps from its place.
2 Hear attentively the thunder of His voice,
And the rumbling *that* comes from His mouth.
3 He sends it forth under the whole heaven,
His lightning to the ends of the earth.

36:12 [a]Masoretic Text reads *as one without knowledge.*
36:14 [a]Hebrew *qedeshim,* that is, those practicing sodomy and prostitution in religious rituals

LIFE LESSONS

➤ 36:11 — *"If they obey and serve Him, they shall spend their days in prosperity, and their years in pleasures."*

While it is true that obedience always brings blessing, it is *not* true that obedience always brings prosperity and pleasure in *this* life. Yet we can be sure that our deeds will follow us, even after death (Rev. 14:13).

➤ 36:15 — *"He delivers the poor in their affliction, and opens their ears in oppression."*

God wants to use our afflictions, and the way He delivers us from them, to lead us into a deeper and richer relationship with Him. We should treat adversity as a bridge to a closer walk with God.

4 After it a voice roars;
He thunders with His majestic voice,
And He does not restrain them when His
voice is heard.
5 God thunders marvelously with His
voice;
He does great things which we cannot
comprehend.
6 For He says to the snow, 'Fall *on* the
earth';
Likewise to the gentle rain and the heavy
rain of His strength.
7 He seals the hand of every man,
That all men may know His work.
8 The beasts go into dens,
And remain in their lairs.
9 From the chamber *of the south* comes the
whirlwind,
And cold from the scattering winds *of the
north.*
10 By the breath of God ice is given,
And the broad waters are frozen.
11 Also with moisture He saturates the thick
clouds;
He scatters His bright clouds.
12 And they swirl about, being turned by
His guidance,
That they may do whatever He
commands them
On the face of the whole earth.[a]
13 He causes it to come,
Whether for correction,
Or for His land,
Or for mercy.

14 "Listen to this, O Job;
Stand still and consider the wondrous
works of God.
15 Do you know when God dispatches them,
And causes the light of His cloud to
shine?
16 Do you know how the clouds are
balanced,
Those wondrous works of Him who is
perfect in knowledge?
17 Why *are* your garments hot,
When He quiets the earth by the south
wind?
18 With Him, have you spread out the skies,
Strong as a cast metal mirror?

19 "Teach us what we should say to Him,
For we can prepare nothing because of
the darkness.
20 Should He be told that I *wish to* speak?
If a man were to speak, surely he would
be swallowed up.
21 Even now *men* cannot look at the light
when it is bright in the skies,
When the wind has passed and cleared
them.
22 He comes from the north *as* golden
splendor;
With God *is* awesome majesty.
23 *As for* the Almighty, we cannot find Him;
He is excellent in power,
In judgment and abundant justice;
He does not oppress.
24 Therefore men fear Him;
He shows no partiality to any *who are*
wise of heart."

The LORD Reveals His Omnipotence to Job

38 Then the LORD answered Job out of the
whirlwind, and said:

2 "Who *is* this who darkens counsel
By words without knowledge?
3 Now prepare yourself like a man;
I will question you, and you shall answer
Me.

4 "Where were you when I laid the
foundations of the earth?
Tell *Me,* if you have understanding.
5 Who determined its measurements?
Surely you know!
Or who stretched the line upon it?
6 To what were its foundations fastened?
Or who laid its cornerstone,
7 When the morning stars sang together,
And all the sons of God shouted for joy?

8 "Or *who* shut in the sea with doors,
When it burst forth *and* issued from the
womb;
9 When I made the clouds its garment,
And thick darkness its swaddling band;
10 When I fixed My limit for it,
And set bars and doors;
11 When I said,
'This far you may come, but no farther,
And here your proud waves must stop!'

12 "Have you commanded the morning since
your days *began,*
And caused the dawn to know its place,

37:12 [a]Literally *the world of the earth*

LIFE LESSONS

➤ 38:1 — *Then the LORD answered Job out of the whirlwind . . . .*

God speaks to His people through His Word, through other believers, in circumstances, in dreams, in visions, by angels, out of whirlwinds, and even through donkeys. Are we listening?

➤ 38:4 — *"Where were you when I laid the foundations of the earth? Tell Me, if you have understanding."*

It is good to remind ourselves that the Lord is God and we are not. He is the Creator; we are the created. He is the Original; we are the image. He is our Friend, but absolutely not our peer.

13 That it might take hold of the ends of the
earth,
And the wicked be shaken out of it?
14 It takes on form like clay *under* a seal,
And stands out like a garment.
15 From the wicked their light is withheld,
And the upraised arm is broken.

16 "Have you entered the springs of the sea?
Or have you walked in search of the
depths?
17 Have the gates of death been revealed to
you?
Or have you seen the doors of the
shadow of death?
18 Have you comprehended the breadth of
the earth?
Tell *Me,* if you know all this.

19 "Where *is* the way *to* the dwelling of light?
And darkness, where *is* its place,
20 That you may take it to its territory,
That you may know the paths *to* its
home?
21 Do you know *it,* because you were born
then,
Or *because* the number of your days *is*
great?

22 "Have you entered the treasury of snow,
Or have you seen the treasury of hail,
23 Which I have reserved for the time of
trouble,
For the day of battle and war?
24 By what way is light diffused,
Or the east wind scattered over the earth?

25 "Who has divided a channel for the
overflowing *water,*
Or a path for the thunderbolt,
26 To cause it to rain on a land *where there
is* no one,
A wilderness in which *there is* no man;
27 To satisfy the desolate waste,
And cause to spring forth the growth of
tender grass?
28 Has the rain a father?
Or who has begotten the drops of dew?
29 From whose womb comes the ice?
And the frost of heaven, who gives it
birth?
30 The waters harden like stone,
And the surface of the deep is frozen.

31 "Can you bind the cluster of the Pleiades,
Or loose the belt of Orion?
32 Can you bring out Mazzaroth[a] in its
season?
Or can you guide the Great Bear with its
cubs?
33 Do you know the ordinances of the
heavens?
Can you set their dominion over the earth?

34 "Can you lift up your voice to the clouds,
That an abundance of water may cover
you?
35 Can you send out lightnings, that they
may go,
And say to you, 'Here we *are!*'?
36 Who has put wisdom in the mind?[a]
Or who has given understanding to the
heart?
37 Who can number the clouds by wisdom?
Or who can pour out the bottles of
heaven,
38 When the dust hardens in clumps,
And the clods cling together?

39 "Can you hunt the prey for the lion,
Or satisfy the appetite of the young lions,
40 When they crouch in *their* dens,
Or lurk in their lairs to lie in wait?
41 Who provides food for the raven,
When its young ones cry to God,
And wander about for lack of food?

39

"Do you know the time when the wild
mountain goats bear young?
Or can you mark when the deer gives
birth?
2 Can you number the months *that* they
fulfill?
Or do you know the time when they bear
young?
3 They bow down,
They bring forth their young,
They deliver their offspring.[a]
4 Their young ones are healthy,
They grow strong with grain;
They depart and do not return to them.

5 "Who set the wild donkey free?
Who loosed the bonds of the onager,
6 Whose home I have made the wilderness,
And the barren land his dwelling?
7 He scorns the tumult of the city;
He does not heed the shouts of the driver.
8 The range of the mountains *is* his pasture,
And he searches after every green thing.

9 "Will the wild ox be willing to serve you?
Will he bed by your manger?
10 Can you bind the wild ox in the furrow
with ropes?
Or will he plow the valleys behind you?
11 Will you trust him because his strength *is*
great?
Or will you leave your labor to him?
12 Will you trust him to bring home your
grain,
And gather it to your threshing floor?

13 "The wings of the ostrich wave proudly,
But are her wings and pinions *like the*
kindly stork's?
14 For she leaves her eggs on the ground,
And warms them in the dust;
15 She forgets that a foot may crush them,
Or that a wild beast may break them.

38:32 [a]Literally *Constellations* **38:36** [a]Literally *inward parts*
39:3 [a]Literally *pangs,* figurative of offspring

16 She treats her young harshly, as though
they were not hers;
Her labor is in vain, without concern,
17 Because God deprived her of wisdom,
And did not endow her with
understanding.
18 When she lifts herself on high,
She scorns the horse and its rider.

19 "Have you given the horse strength?
Have you clothed his neck with thunder?[a]
20 Can you frighten him like a locust?
His majestic snorting strikes terror.
21 He paws in the valley, and rejoices in *his*
strength;
He gallops into the clash of arms.
22 He mocks at fear, and is not frightened;
Nor does he turn back from the sword.
23 The quiver rattles against him,
The glittering spear and javelin.
24 He devours the distance with fierceness
and rage;
Nor does he come to a halt because the
trumpet *has* sounded.
25 At *the blast of* the trumpet he says, 'Aha!'
He smells the battle from afar,
The thunder of captains and shouting.

26 "Does the hawk fly by your wisdom,
And spread its wings toward the south?
27 Does the eagle mount up at your command,
And make its nest on high?
28 On the rock it dwells and resides,
On the crag of the rock and the stronghold.
29 From there it spies out the prey;
Its eyes observe from afar.
30 Its young ones suck up blood;
And where the slain *are,* there it *is.*"

➤ **40** Moreover the LORD answered Job, and
said:
2 "Shall the one who contends with the
Almighty correct *Him?*
He who rebukes God, let him answer it."

Job's Response to God

3 Then Job answered the LORD and said:

➤ 4 "Behold, I am vile;
What shall I answer You?
I lay my hand over my mouth.
5 Once I have spoken, but I will not answer;
Yes, twice, but I will proceed no further."

God's Challenge to Job

6 Then the LORD answered Job out of the
whirlwind, and said:

7 "Now prepare yourself like a man;
I will question you, and you shall answer
Me:

8 "Would you indeed annul My judgment? ➤
Would you condemn Me that you may be
justified?
9 Have you an arm like God?
Or can you thunder with a voice like His?
10 Then adorn yourself *with* majesty and
splendor,
And array yourself with glory and beauty.
11 Disperse the rage of your wrath;
Look on everyone *who is* proud, and
humble him.
12 Look on everyone *who is* proud, *and*
bring him low;
Tread down the wicked in their place.
13 Hide them in the dust together,
Bind their faces in hidden *darkness.*
14 Then I will also confess to you
That your own right hand can save you.

15 "Look now at the behemoth,[a] which I
made *along* with you;
He eats grass like an ox.
16 See now, his strength *is* in his hips,
And his power *is* in his stomach muscles.
17 He moves his tail like a cedar;
The sinews of his thighs are tightly knit.
18 His bones *are like* beams of bronze,
His ribs like bars of iron.
19 He *is* the first of the ways of God;
Only He who made him can bring near
His sword.
20 Surely the mountains yield food for him,
And all the beasts of the field play there.
21 He lies under the lotus trees,
In a covert of reeds and marsh.
22 The lotus trees cover him *with* their shade;
The willows by the brook surround him.

39:19 [a]Or *a mane* **40:15** [a]A large animal, exact identity unknown

LIFE LESSONS

➤ 40:1, 2 — *Moreover the LORD answered Job, and said: "Shall the one who contends with the Almighty correct Him?"*

Frequently these days, people increasingly say foolish things like, "I'm going to tell God to His face that He has made a mistake." No, He hasn't; and no, they're not: "The LORD alone shall be exalted in that day" (Is. 2:11).

➤ 40:4 — *"Behold, I am vile; what shall I answer You? I lay my hand over my mouth."*

Even a "blameless" and "upright" man sees himself as "vile" when confronted by the majestic holiness of almighty God. Yet we can come boldly into God's presence when we come in faith, wrapped in Christ's righteousness.

➤ 40:8 — *"Would you indeed annul My judgment? Would you condemn Me that you may be justified?"*

We may not always understand God's ways, but we must never presume to judge God's ways. He is "a God of truth and without injustice; righteous and upright is He" (Deut. 32:4).

23 Indeed the river may rage,
Yet he is not disturbed;
He is confident, though the Jordan
gushes into his mouth,
24 *Though* he takes it in his eyes,
Or one pierces *his* nose with a snare.

41 "Can you draw out Leviathan[a] with a
hook,
Or *snare* his tongue with a line *which* you
lower?
2 Can you put a reed through his nose,
Or pierce his jaw with a hook?
3 Will he make many supplications to you?
Will he speak softly to you?
4 Will he make a covenant with you?
Will you take him as a servant forever?
5 Will you play with him as *with* a bird,
Or will you leash him for your maidens?
6 Will *your* companions make a banquet[a]
of him?
Will they apportion him among the
merchants?
7 Can you fill his skin with harpoons,
Or his head with fishing spears?
8 Lay your hand on him;
Remember the battle—
Never do it again!
9 Indeed, *any* hope of *overcoming* him is
false;
Shall *one not* be overwhelmed at the
sight of him?
10 No one *is so* fierce that he would dare stir
him up.
Who then is able to stand against Me?
11 Who has preceded Me, that I should pay
him?
Everything under heaven is Mine.
12 "I will not conceal[a] his limbs,
His mighty power, or his graceful
proportions.
13 Who can remove his outer coat?
Who can approach *him* with a double
bridle?
14 Who can open the doors of his face,
With his terrible teeth all around?
15 *His* rows of scales are *his* pride,
Shut up tightly *as with* a seal;
16 One is so near another
That no air can come between them;
17 They are joined one to another,
They stick together and cannot be parted.
18 His sneezings flash forth light,
And his eyes *are* like the eyelids of the
morning.
19 Out of his mouth go burning lights;
Sparks of fire shoot out.
20 Smoke goes out of his nostrils,
As *from* a boiling pot and burning rushes.
21 His breath kindles coals,
And a flame goes out of his mouth.
22 Strength dwells in his neck,
And sorrow dances before him.
23 The folds of his flesh are joined together;
They are firm on him and cannot be moved.
24 His heart is as hard as stone,
Even as hard as the lower *millstone.*
25 When he raises himself up, the mighty
are afraid;
Because of his crashings they are beside[a]
themselves.
26 *Though* the sword reaches him, it cannot
avail;
Nor does spear, dart, or javelin.
27 He regards iron as straw,
And bronze as rotten wood.
28 The arrow cannot make him flee;
Slingstones become like stubble to him.
29 Darts are regarded as straw;
He laughs at the threat of javelins.
30 His undersides *are* like sharp potsherds;
He spreads pointed *marks* in the mire.
31 He makes the deep boil like a pot;
He makes the sea like a pot of ointment.
32 He leaves a shining wake behind him;
One would think the deep had white hair.
33 On earth there is nothing like him,
Which is made without fear.
34 He beholds every high *thing;*
He *is* king over all the children of pride."

Job's Repentance and Restoration

42 Then Job answered the LORD and said:
2 "I know that You can do everything,
And that no purpose *of Yours* can be
withheld from You.
3 *You asked,* 'Who *is* this who hides
counsel without knowledge?'
Therefore I have uttered what I did not
understand,
Things too wonderful for me, which I did
not know.
4 Listen, please, and let me speak;
You said, 'I will question you, and you
shall answer Me.'
5 "I have heard of You by the hearing of the ear,
But now my eye sees You.
6 Therefore I abhor *myself,*
And repent in dust and ashes."

41:1 [a]A large sea creature, exact identity unknown **41:6** [a]Or *bargain over him* **41:12** [a]Literally *keep silent about* **41:25** [a]Or *purify themselves*

LIFE LESSONS

42:5, 6 — *"I have heard of You by the hearing of the ear, but now my eye sees You. Therefore I abhor myself, and repent in dust and ashes."*

It is one thing to learn facts about God from a safe distance. It is quite another to know Him personally, intimately, up close and face-to-face. "Who would not fear You, O King of the nations?" (Jer. 10:7).

7 And so it was, after the LORD had spoken these words to Job, that the LORD said to Eliphaz the Temanite, "My wrath is aroused against you and your two friends, for you have not spoken of Me *what is* right, as My servant Job *has*.

➤ 8 Now therefore, take for yourselves seven bulls and seven rams, go to My servant Job, and offer up for yourselves a burnt offering; and My servant Job shall pray for you. For I will accept him, lest I deal with you *according to your* folly; because you have not spoken of Me *what is* right, as My servant Job *has*."

9 So Eliphaz the Temanite and Bildad the Shuhite *and* Zophar the Naamathite went and did as the LORD commanded them; for the LORD had accepted Job.

➤ 10 And the LORD restored Job's losses[a] when he prayed for his friends. Indeed the LORD gave Job twice as much as he had before.

11 Then all his brothers, all his sisters, and all those who had been his acquaintances before, came to him and ate food with him in his house; and they consoled him and comforted him for all the adversity that the LORD had brought upon him. Each one gave him a piece of silver and each a ring of gold.

➤ 12 Now the LORD blessed the latter *days* of Job more than his beginning; for he had fourteen thousand sheep, six thousand camels, one thousand yoke of oxen, and one thousand female donkeys.

13 He also had seven sons and three daughters.

14 And he called the name of the first Jemimah, the name of the second Keziah, and the name of the third Keren-Happuch.

15 In all the land were found no women *so* beautiful as the daughters of Job; and their father gave them an inheritance among their brothers.

16 After this Job lived one hundred and forty years, and saw his children and grandchildren *for* four generations.

➤ 17 So Job died, old and full of days.

Life Examples:

JOB'S FRIENDS

Adamant, but Wrong

JOB 42:7–9

Eliphaz, Bildad, and Zophar heard of Job's plight and felt deeply burdened to comfort their old friend. But what they saw staggered them. They gasped, cried out, and tore their clothes, a demonstration of deep grief. Finally, they sat with Job and remained silent. They stayed that way for seven days.

Once they opened their mouths, however, Job's visitors didn't offer much help. They judged his pitiful situation to be the consequence of sin, and kept insisting that adversity comes only to the wicked, not to the righteous. Therefore, Job had to be suffering God's punishment for some secret wrongdoing.

Job rejected their diagnosis.

In the end, the Lord had the final word, and He rebuked Eliphaz, Bildad, and Zophar (Job 42:7–9). When God restored Job twofold, He proved Himself—and His promises—ever faithful. And He showed that blessings for obedience do not guarantee a life free of adversity.

See the Life Principles Index for further study: 18. As children of a sovereign God, we are never victims of our circumstances.

42:10 [a]Literally *Job's captivity,* that is, what was captured from Job

LIFE LESSONS

➤ 42:8 — *". . . My servant Job shall pray for you. For I will accept him . . . ."*

In his time of trouble, Job wondered whether God even heard his pain-filled prayers—but not only had God heard him, He accepted both him and his prayers. God acts on behalf of those who wait for Him!

➤ 42:10 — *And the LORD restored Job's losses when he prayed for his friends. Indeed the LORD gave Job twice as much as he had before.*

Notice that God restored *Job's* losses when Job prayed for *his friends*, as God had instructed him. God assumes full responsibility for our needs when we obey Him!

➤ 42:12 — *Now the LORD blessed the latter days of Job more than his beginning . . .*

Life is seldom a sustained march in a single direction. Job found that it has its highs and lows, its delights and its tragedies. But through it all, God is there—and so is His blessing for faithful obedience.

➤ 42:17 — *So Job died, old and full of days.*

In the anguish of his darkest days, Job wished that he had never been born. Do you think he felt the same way by the end of his life? Like it or not, brokenness is God's requirement for maximum usefulness.

LIFE PRINCIPLE 11

GOD ASSUMES FULL RESPONSIBILITY FOR OUR NEEDS WHEN WE OBEY HIM.

JOB 42:7–17

Do you really believe that God is able and eager to meet all of your needs?

Some people ask, "If God is all-powerful and all-knowing, and if He loves me unconditionally—and therefore, He not only is capable of meeting all my needs but also desires to meet my needs—then why doesn't He just meet all my needs right now? Why do I still have unmet needs?"

Others say, "I know God is capable of meeting my needs, but since I still have them, God must not want to meet them."

Still others question sincerely, "Why didn't God meet all my needs the moment I accepted Jesus Christ as my savior?"

These are excellent questions worthy of close examination.

At the outset, let me assure you that God is committed to meeting all of your needs. Jesus told us in Matthew 6 that we are not to worry about getting our needs met, for God has promised to take care of them. "But seek first the kingdom of God and His righteousness," He said, "and all these things shall be added to you" (Matt. 6:33). He had in mind "things" like food and drink and clothes. This is a promise, a commitment, a pledge of action. The value of any commitment is based upon two things:

1. The ability of the promise maker to fulfill the promise.

2. The integrity of the promise maker, whether he has the character to follow through on the promise.

God certainly qualifies on both accounts. He has all the wisdom, power, and ability necessary to fulfill His promises to us. He also has proven integrity—He has always done what He has said He would do. God is utterly faithful to His Word. He is holy and immutable; He is unchanging. His commandments, statutes, and promises have not changed; they reflect our unchanging God. He is "the same yesterday, today, and forever" (Heb. 13:8).

When you have an unmet need, the first place to look for a reason why is not at God or at His Son, Christ Jesus, but at yourself. You err greatly when you ask, "Why hasn't God lived up to His promise?" You are wise to ask instead, "What

God is committed to meeting all of your needs.

could I be doing that is keeping God from fulfilling this promise?"

You may respond, "Well, I'm not doing anything to keep this promise from being fulfilled. If you knew my circumstances or my situation——."

Let me assure you that no circumstance or situation can keep God from acting on your behalf. Nothing is too great or too powerful to stand in the way if God chooses to act. The real question remains, What are you doing in the midst of your circumstance or situation? Look again at Jesus' promise. He pledged that God would meet all your needs *when* you "seek first the kingdom of God and His righteousness." That means that He promises to meet all your needs as you faithfully obey, by the power of His Spirit, the commands He has given you. God assumes full responsibility for your needs when you obey Him.

Trust in His wisdom is one such command. Do you have a preconceived idea about how God must act to meet your needs, or whom God may use to meet your needs? Many people have said to me, "Well, if this man would just do such and such or she would agree to do so and so, then my need would be met." Or they have said, "Well, I did such and such and therefore God must do this and that."

Those who make such statements are not trusting a wise God to be their Need Meeter. Rather, they are demanding that God exert His power on behalf of their wishes and commands. God calls us to trust Him, and Him alone, to meet our needs and to be our total source of supply. Furthermore, God requires that we obey Him as part of our trusting Him. We have the situation completely backward anytime we start expecting God to trust *us* to know what is right and to obey *our* commands so that He might prove His love for us.

Do you want your needs met? Then tell God today, "I trust You completely to meet my needs, in Your timing and according to Your methods. And I will continue to obey You, by the power of Your Spirit, believing that as I do, You will take care of me."

See the Life Principles Index for further study.

God requires that we obey Him as part of our trusting Him.

THE BOOK OF

PSALMS

The Book of Psalms is perhaps the most widely used book in the Bible. It explores the full range of human experience in a very personal and practical way. Its 150 songs run in theme from the creation through the patriarchal, theocratic, monarchical, exilic, and postexilic periods.

The tremendous breadth of subject matter in the Psalms includes diverse topics such as jubilation, war, peace, worship, judgment, messianic prophecy, praise, and lament. In ancient Israel the psalms were set to the accompaniment of stringed instruments and served as the temple hymnal and devotional guide for the Jewish people, especially after the construction of the second temple following the Babylonian exile.

Individual psalms were collected over time and eventually became the Book of Psalms. In the beginning, the book had no name, perhaps due to its great variety of material.

In Hebrew the book came to be known as *Sepher Tehillim*—Book of Praises—because almost every psalm contains some note of praise to God. The Septuagint uses the Greek word *Psalmoi* as its title for this book, meaning "Poems Sung to the Accompaniment of Musical Instruments." It also calls it the *Psalterium* ("A Collection of Songs"), and this word is the basis for the English term *Psalter*.

Outside of Isaiah, the Psalms are the most-quoted Old Testament writings in the New Testament. Many of the most important and famous prophecies regarding the coming Messiah are found in the Psalms (for example, Ps. 2:7–9; 8:4–6; 9:8; 16:10; 22:1, 22; 40:6–8; 45:6–7; 68:18; 110:1, 4; 118:22; 130:8).

Themes: The Book of Psalms features a wide variety of themes, but the predominant ones emphasize prayer, praise, and worship.

Authors: The authorship of many of the Psalms is in doubt or unknown. Seventy-three Psalms are attributed to David. Other named writers include the sons of Korah (11 Psalms), Asaph (12), Heman (1), Ethan (1), Solomon (2), Moses (1), Haggai (1), Zechariah (1), and Ezra (1).

Time: The Psalms were written over a long period in Israelite history, ranging from the time of Moses through the end of the Babylonian captivity.

Structure: Each of the psalms is a "stand-alone" work emphasizing a particular topic. The psalms do not appear to be arranged in any discernible order or according to any particular "timeline."

As you read Psalms, watch for several life principles that play an important role in this book:

12. Peace with God is the fruit of oneness with God. *See Psalm 4:8; 29:11; pages 624; 642.*

26. Adversity is a bridge to a deeper relationship with God. *See Psalm 13; page 631.*

1. Our intimacy with God—His highest priority for our lives—determines the impact of our lives. *See Psalm 18:29; 36:10; pages 634; 647.*

4. The awareness of God's presence energizes us for our work. *See Psalm 46:4–11; page 655.*

13. Listening to God is essential to walking with God. *See Psalm 81:8; page 679.*

Book One: Psalms 1—41

PSALM 1

The Way of the Righteous and the End of the Ungodly

1 Blessed *is* the man
Who walks not in the counsel of the ungodly,
Nor stands in the path of sinners,
Nor sits in the seat of the scornful;
2 But his delight *is* in the law of the LORD,
And in His law he meditates day and night.
➤ 3 He shall be like a tree
Planted by the rivers of water,
That brings forth its fruit in its season,
Whose leaf also shall not wither;
And whatever he does shall prosper.
4 The ungodly *are* not so,
But *are* like the chaff which the wind drives away.
➤ 5 Therefore the ungodly shall not stand in the judgment,
Nor sinners in the congregation of the righteous.
6 For the LORD knows the way of the righteous,
But the way of the ungodly shall perish.

PSALM 2

The Messiah's Triumph and Kingdom

1 Why do the nations rage,
And the people plot a vain thing?
2 The kings of the earth set themselves,
And the rulers take counsel together,
Against the LORD and against His Anointed, *saying*,
3 "Let us break Their bonds in pieces
And cast away Their cords from us."
4 He who sits in the heavens shall laugh;
The Lord shall hold them in derision.
5 Then He shall speak to them in His wrath,
And distress them in His deep displeasure:
6 "Yet I have set My King
On My holy hill of Zion."
7 "I will declare the decree: ➤
The LORD has said to Me,
'You *are* My Son,
Today I have begotten You.
8 Ask of Me, and I will give *You*
The nations *for* Your inheritance,
And the ends of the earth *for* Your possession.
9 You shall break[a] them with a rod of iron;
You shall dash them to pieces like a potter's vessel.'"
10 Now therefore, be wise, O kings;
Be instructed, you judges of the earth.
11 Serve the LORD with fear, ➤
And rejoice with trembling.
12 Kiss the Son,[a] lest He[b] be angry,
And you perish *in* the way,
When His wrath is kindled but a little.
Blessed *are* all those who put their trust in Him.

PSALM 3

The LORD Helps His Troubled People

A Psalm of David when he fled from Absalom his son.

1 LORD, how they have increased who trouble me!
Many *are* they who rise up against me.
2 Many *are* they who say of me, ➤
"*There is* no help for him in God." Selah

2:9 [a]Following Masoretic Text and Targum; Septuagint, Syriac, and Vulgate read *rule* (compare Revelation 2:27).
2:12 [a]Septuagint and Vulgate read *Embrace discipline;* Targum reads *Receive instruction*. [b]Septuagint reads *the LORD*.

LIFE LESSONS

➤ 1:3 — *He shall be like a tree planted by the rivers of water, that brings forth its fruit in its season, whose leaf also shall not wither; and whatever he does shall prosper.*

God loves to bless His obedient children. He moves out ahead of them, preparing the way, bringing them into a good and pleasant place. He doesn't promise lack of trials, but He does promise eventual victory.

➤ 1:5 — *Therefore the ungodly shall not stand in the judgment, nor sinners in the congregation of the righteous.*

Sometimes when we look around us, it seems as though God makes no distinction between the righteous and the ungodly. We have to take the long view; don't judge the whole story by the page you're on now.

➤ 2:7 — *"I will declare the decree: the LORD has said to Me, 'You are My Son, today I have begotten You.'"*

The writer of Hebrews quotes this verse to show how far superior Jesus is to angels (Heb. 1:5). We have a savior who is fully one of us, even as He is fully God. And that is why we can trust Him fully.

➤ 2:11 — *Serve the LORD with fear, and rejoice with trembling.*

When we remember that, out of love, a holy God calls us into His service, we serve Him with fear. And when remember that, in His power, a majestic God calls us to praise Him, we rejoice with trembling.

➤ 3:2 — *Many are they who say of me, "There is no help for him in God."*

To make it in the Christian life, we have to surround ourselves with other believers who love the Lord and who love us. Doubters and skeptics we can find anywhere; in the church we should find encouragement.

3 But You, O LORD, *are* a shield for me,
My glory and the One who lifts up my head.
4 I cried to the LORD with my voice,
And He heard me from His holy hill. Selah

➤ 5 I lay down and slept;
I awoke, for the LORD sustained me.
6 I will not be afraid of ten thousands of people
Who have set *themselves* against me all around.
7 Arise, O LORD;
Save me, O my God!
For You have struck all my enemies on the cheekbone;
You have broken the teeth of the ungodly.
8 Salvation *belongs* to the LORD.
Your blessing *is* upon Your people. Selah

PSALM 4

The Safety of the Faithful

To the Chief Musician. With stringed instruments. A Psalm of David.

1 Hear me when I call, O God of my righteousness!
You have relieved me in *my* distress;
Have mercy on me, and hear my prayer.
2 How long, O you sons of men,
Will you turn my glory to shame?
How long will you love worthlessness
And seek falsehood? Selah
* 3 But know that the LORD has set apart[a]
for Himself him who is godly;
The LORD will hear when I call to Him.

4 Be angry, and do not sin.
Meditate within your heart on your bed, and be still. Selah
5 Offer the sacrifices of righteousness,
And put your trust in the LORD.

6 *There are* many who say,
"Who will show us *any* good?"
LORD, lift up the light of Your countenance upon us.
7 You have put gladness in my heart, ➤
More than in the season that their grain and wine increased.
8 I will both lie down in peace, and sleep; ➤
For You alone, O LORD, make me dwell in safety.

PSALM 5

A Prayer for Guidance

To the Chief Musician. With flutes.[a] A Psalm of David.

1 Give ear to my words, O LORD,
Consider my meditation.
2 Give heed to the voice of my cry,
My King and my God,
For to You I will pray.
3 My voice You shall hear in the morning, O LORD;
In the morning I will direct *it* to You,
And I will look up.

4 For You *are* not a God who takes pleasure in wickedness, ➤
Nor shall evil dwell with You.
5 The boastful shall not stand in Your sight;
You hate all workers of iniquity.
6 You shall destroy those who speak falsehood;
The LORD abhors the bloodthirsty and deceitful man.

7 But as for me, I will come into Your house in the multitude of Your mercy;
In fear of You I will worship toward Your holy temple.
8 Lead me, O LORD, in Your righteousness because of my enemies;
Make Your way straight before my face.

9 For *there is* no faithfulness in their mouth;
Their inward part *is* destruction;

4:3 [a]Many Hebrew manuscripts, Septuagint, Targum, and Vulgate read *made wonderful*. **5:title** [a]Hebrew *nehiloth*

LIFE LESSONS

➤ 3:5 — *I lay down and slept; I awoke, for the LORD sustained me.*

Every time you lay down and fall asleep, you are enjoying a good gift of God. Every time you wake up, you are enjoying another good gift of God. He sustains us, both waking and sleeping.

➤ 4:7 — *You have put gladness in my heart, more than in the season that their grain and wine increased.*

The joy of the Lord is a supernatural thing, deeper and stronger and tougher and more resilient than any joy derived from mere circumstances. Those without it cannot understand it; we need to help them experience it for themselves.

➤ 4:8 — *I will both lie down in peace, and sleep; for You alone, O LORD, make me dwell in safety.*

Jesus once slept soundly on a boat that pitched and rolled wildly in a stormy sea. Why? Out of exhaustion? No, because He knew the Lord would keep Him safe. God wants Jesus' kind of confidence to take root in us.

➤ 5:4 — *For You are not a God who takes pleasure in wickedness, nor shall evil dwell with You.*

Many believers today think grace means they can sin without consequence, that God loves them and forgives them, so they can do what they want. But grace never changes the way God feels about sin. He hates it.

Their throat *is* an open tomb;
They flatter with their tongue.
10 Pronounce them guilty, O God!
Let them fall by their own counsels;
Cast them out in the multitude of their transgressions,
For they have rebelled against You.

➤ 11 But let all those rejoice who put their trust in You;
Let them ever shout for joy, because You defend them;
Let those also who love Your name
Be joyful in You.

✳ 12 For You, O LORD, will bless the righteous;
With favor You will surround him as *with* a shield.

PSALM 6

A Prayer of Faith in Time of Distress

To the Chief Musician. With stringed instruments. On an eight-stringed harp.[a] A Psalm of David.

1 O LORD, do not rebuke me in Your anger,
Nor chasten me in Your hot displeasure.
2 Have mercy on me, O LORD, for I *am* weak;
O LORD, heal me, for my bones are troubled.
3 My soul also is greatly troubled;
But You, O LORD—how long?

➤ 4 Return, O LORD, deliver me!
Oh, save me for Your mercies' sake!
5 For in death *there is* no remembrance of You;
In the grave who will give You thanks?
6 I am weary with my groaning;
All night I make my bed swim;
I drench my couch with my tears.
7 My eye wastes away because of grief;
It grows old because of all my enemies.

8 Depart from me, all you workers of iniquity;
For the LORD has heard the voice of my weeping.

9 The LORD has heard my supplication; ➤
The LORD will receive my prayer.
10 Let all my enemies be ashamed and greatly troubled;
Let them turn back *and* be ashamed suddenly.

PSALM 7

Prayer and Praise for Deliverance from Enemies

A Meditation[a] of David, which he sang to the LORD concerning the words of Cush, a Benjamite.

1 O LORD my God, in You I put my trust;
Save me from all those who persecute me;
And deliver me,
2 Lest they tear me like a lion,
Rending *me* in pieces, while *there is* none to deliver.

3 O LORD my God, if I have done this:
If there is iniquity in my hands,
4 If I have repaid evil to him who was at peace with me,
Or have plundered my enemy without cause,
5 Let the enemy pursue me and overtake *me;*
Yes, let him trample my life to the earth,
And lay my honor in the dust. Selah

6 Arise, O LORD, in Your anger;
Lift Yourself up because of the rage of my enemies;
Rise up for me[a] *to* the judgment You have commanded!
7 So the congregation of the peoples shall surround You;
For their sakes, therefore, return on high.
8 The LORD shall judge the peoples;
Judge me, O LORD, according to my righteousness,
And according to my integrity within me.

6:title [a]Hebrew *sheminith* **7:title** [a]Hebrew *Shiggaion*
7:6 [a]Following Masoretic Text, Targum, and Vulgate; Septuagint reads *O LORD my God.*

LIFE LESSONS

➤ **5:11 — *But let all those rejoice who put their trust in You; let them ever shout for joy, because You defend them.***

A heart that puts its trust in God cannot be anything but a rejoicing heart. When attacked, it knows that God will defend it. And so it shouts with gladness. It can't help it.

➤ **6:4 — *Return, O LORD, deliver me! Oh, save me for Your mercies' sake!***

We do not ask God to rescue and deliver us because we deserve His help; we ask Him to come to our aid because He loves to show mercy to His humble, obedient children.

➤ **6:9 — *The LORD has heard my supplication; the LORD will receive my prayer.***

How did the psalmist know that God had heard his prayer? How could he express such confidence that the Lord would answer his request? Through faith. He prayed in faith and he expected an answer by faith—just like us.

LIFE PRINCIPLE 12

PEACE WITH GOD IS THE FRUIT OF ONENESS WITH GOD.

PS. 4:8

Every now and then we do well to take stock of our situation, so I'd like to ask you to look around. What's happening in your life and in the life of your family?

You may not be experiencing a difficult time. From your perspective, everything may seem sunny and clear. Storms come, however. At times, they roll over our lives with bounding blows. How do we maintain a sense of peace and spiritual balance when trials strike?

The answer is found in a close, abiding relationship with Jesus Christ. The words of Helen Lemmel's classic hymn, "Turn Your Eyes Upon Jesus," contain a vital and exciting truth: an unshakable peace is available to all who turn the eyes of their hearts to Jesus.

Chances are that when adversity strikes, one of the first things you do is to wonder why. Then you may question what kind of impact it will have on your life. While reactions such as these are normal, we also need another response, and that is to turn to the One who holds all comfort and security firmly within His grasp.

No one, outside of God, is equipped to handle our problems. He never meant for us to be strong on our own. He wants us to find courage and hope and strength in Him and His Word.

Many wonder what they can do to change the feelings of anxiety they feel when they come under pressure. One of the first steps is to recognize anxiety for what it is, the opposite of peace. It is the fan that flames the fires of doubt and confusion and has the ability to leave us helplessly bundled up in worry and fear. When we cave in to thoughts of anxiety, we lose our spiritual focus and mindset. The key to overcoming anxiety is found only in the presence of God.

Paul admonishes us: "Be anxious for nothing, but in everything by prayer and supplication, with thanksgiving, let your requests be made known to God; and the peace of God, which surpasses all understanding, will guard your hearts and your minds through Christ Jesus" (Phil. 4:6, 7).

Accepting God's timetable and the limitations He places on a given situation helps to dispel rising anxiety. Therefore, let Him provide for you in His timing. When you accept life as a gift from the hand of God, then you will do what Helen Lemmel's song says—you will turn your eyes toward Jesus. You will look full into His glorious face and there

The answer is found in a close, abiding relationship with Jesus Christ.

find mercy and grace, forgiveness and hope, peace and everlasting security.

What would you give to experience the peace of God? Are you willing to lay down the anger that haunts your soul because someone has done something to wound you? God knows the hurt you have experienced. Will you trust Him in quietness, knowing that He has not forgotten you but stands ready to heal you?

God's peace is unshakable because there has never been a time or an event when God has felt disturbed. His peace and presence are sure. They are immovable. You will accomplish many things—great and mighty—when you keep your focus on God.

At one of the most difficult points in his life, David wrote Psalm 91, which begins: "He who dwells in the shelter of the Most High will abide in the shadow of the Almighty. I will say to the LORD, 'My refuge and my fortress, my God, in whom I trust!'"

Hear His word to you: "Peace be with you."

How could David write such words, especially with King Saul trying to kill him? David had a divine, unshakable peace within his heart. He knew this was God's responsibility and David allowed Him to protect his life.

The safest place for you when trials come is in the everlasting arms of Jesus. After His resurrection, Jesus appeared to His disciples and said to them, "Peace be with you" (John 20:19). This was not a trite greeting; the Lord had a specific point in mind. He spoke of God's peace, immovable and eternal—the peace you need today.

Does something trouble you? Has a conflict, a sorrow, a situation escalated beyond your control? Hear His word to you: "Peace be with you."

Let His peace invade your heart. Tell Him all you are feeling. He understands and knows that life can be difficult—but He has a solution. Our peace resides in our Savior, who loves us unconditionally. He has promised to keep us and deliver us into the Father's loving arms.

See the Life Principles Index for further study.

9 Oh, let the wickedness of the wicked
come to an end,
But establish the just;
For the righteous God tests the hearts
and minds.
10 My defense *is* of God,
Who saves the upright in heart.
➤ 11 God *is* a just judge,
And God is angry *with the wicked*
every day.
12 If he does not turn back,
He will sharpen His sword;
He bends His bow and makes it ready.
13 He also prepares for Himself
instruments of death;
He makes His arrows into fiery shafts.
14 Behold, *the wicked* brings forth
iniquity;
Yes, he conceives trouble and brings
forth falsehood.
15 He made a pit and dug it out,
And has fallen into the ditch *which* he
made.
16 His trouble shall return upon his own
head,
And his violent dealing shall come
down on his own crown.
➤ 17 I will praise the LORD according to His
righteousness,
And will sing praise to the name of the
LORD Most High.

PSALM 8

The Glory of the LORD in Creation

To the Chief Musician. On the instrument of Gath.[a] A Psalm of David.

1 O LORD, our Lord,
How excellent *is* Your name in all the
earth,
Who have set Your glory above the
heavens!
2 Out of the mouth of babes and nursing
infants
You have ordained strength,
Because of Your enemies,
That You may silence the enemy and the
avenger.
3 When I consider Your heavens, the work
of Your fingers,
The moon and the stars, which You have
ordained,
4 What is man that You are mindful of
him, ➤
And the son of man that You visit him?
5 For You have made him a little lower
than the angels,[a]
And You have crowned him with glory
and honor.
6 You have made him to have dominion
over the works of Your hands;
You have put all *things* under his feet,
7 All sheep and oxen—
Even the beasts of the field,
8 The birds of the air,
And the fish of the sea
That pass through the paths of the seas.
9 O LORD, our Lord, ➤
How excellent *is* Your name in all the
earth!

PSALM 9

Prayer and Thanksgiving for the LORD's Righteous Judgments

To the Chief Musician. To *the tune of* "Death of the Son."[a] A Psalm of David.

1 I will praise *You,* O LORD, with my
whole heart;
I will tell of all Your marvelous works.
2 I will be glad and rejoice in You;
I will sing praise to Your name, O Most
High.
3 When my enemies turn back,
They shall fall and perish at Your
presence.

8:title [a]Hebrew *Al Gittith* **8:5** [a]Hebrew *Elohim, God;* Septuagint, Syriac, Targum, and Jewish tradition translate as *angels.* **9:title** [a]Hebrew *Muth Labben*

LIFE LESSONS

➤ 7:11 — *God is a just judge, and God is angry with the wicked every day.*

God loves the world and sent His Son to die for undeserving sinners (John 3:16), yet He remains a holy God and will certainly judge all those who reject His Son (John 3:36).

➤ 7:17 — *I will praise the LORD according to His righteousness, and will sing praise to the name of the LORD Most High.*

Everything God does, He does right. There will never come a time when someone can say, "Lord, I'm afraid You messed up here." Even when we don't understand what He does, we can be sure that He acts in righteousness.

➤ 8:4 — *What is man that You are mindful of him, and the son of man that You visit him?*

The more we learn about the vastness of the universe, the more powerful this question becomes. Although we are but a speck drifting in the immensity of the cosmos, God places His love and unwavering attention on us.

➤ 8:9 — *O LORD, our Lord, how excellent is Your name in all the earth!*

When we say that God's name is excellent, we mean that everything about Him—His character, His actions, His thoughts, His desires, His plans, His words—is excellent and praiseworthy and perfect.

4 For You have maintained my right and
my cause;
You sat on the throne judging in
righteousness.
5 You have rebuked the nations,
You have destroyed the wicked;
You have blotted out their name forever
and ever.

6 O enemy, destructions are finished
forever!
And you have destroyed cities;
Even their memory has perished.
➤ 7 But the LORD shall endure forever;
He has prepared His throne for
judgment.
8 He shall judge the world in
righteousness,
And He shall administer judgment for
the peoples in uprightness.

✳ 9 The LORD also will be a refuge for the
oppressed,
A refuge in times of trouble.
➤ 10 And those who know Your name will
put their trust in You;
For You, LORD, have not forsaken those
who seek You.

11 Sing praises to the LORD, who dwells in
Zion!
Declare His deeds among the people.
12 When He avenges blood, He remembers
them;
He does not forget the cry of the
humble.

13 Have mercy on me, O LORD!
Consider my trouble from those who
hate me,
You who lift me up from the gates of
death,
14 That I may tell of all Your praise
In the gates of the daughter of Zion.
I will rejoice in Your salvation.

15 The nations have sunk down in the pit
which they made;
In the net which they hid, their own foot
is caught.
16 The LORD is known *by* the judgment He
executes;
The wicked is snared in the work of his
own hands.
Meditation.[a] Selah

17 The wicked shall be turned into hell,
And all the nations that forget God.
18 For the needy shall not always be
forgotten;
The expectation of the poor shall *not*
perish forever.

19 Arise, O LORD,
Do not let man prevail;
Let the nations be judged in Your sight.
20 Put them in fear, O LORD,
That the nations may know themselves
to be but men. Selah

PSALM 10

A Song of Confidence in God's Triumph over Evil

1 Why do You stand afar off, O LORD? ➤
Why do You hide in times of trouble?
2 The wicked in *his* pride persecutes the
poor;
Let them be caught in the plots which
they have devised.

3 For the wicked boasts of his heart's
desire;
He blesses the greedy *and* renounces
the LORD.
4 The wicked in his proud countenance
does not seek *God;*
God *is* in none of his thoughts.

5 His ways are always prospering;
Your judgments *are* far above, out of his
sight;
As for all his enemies, he sneers at
them.
6 He has said in his heart, "I shall not be
moved;
I shall never be in adversity."
7 His mouth is full of cursing and deceit
and oppression;
Under his tongue *is* trouble and
iniquity.

9:16 [a]Hebrew *Higgaion*

LIFE LESSONS

➤ 9:7 — *But the LORD shall endure forever; He has prepared His throne for judgment.*

God never had a beginning, and He will never have an end. That makes Him the perfect judge, for He knows all the causes leading up to an event and all the consequences leading from it. He judges perfectly.

➤ 9:10 — *And those who know Your name will put their trust in You; for You, LORD, have not forsaken those who seek You.*

God never forsakes any man or woman who places his or her trust in Him. He may allow them to wade through some very deep and cold waters, but He will never abandon them. When everyone else flees, He remains.

➤ 10:1 — *Why do You stand afar off, O LORD? Why do You hide in times of trouble?*

During hard times in the desert, the Israelites thought God had abandoned them. But Moses told them, ". . . in the wilderness the LORD your God carried you, as a man carries his son . . ." (Deut. 1:31).

8 He sits in the lurking places of the villages;
In the secret places he murders the innocent;
His eyes are secretly fixed on the helpless.
9 He lies in wait secretly, as a lion in his den;
He lies in wait to catch the poor;
He catches the poor when he draws him into his net.
10 So he crouches, he lies low,
That the helpless may fall by his strength.
11 He has said in his heart,
"God has forgotten;
He hides His face;
He will never see."

12 Arise, O LORD!
O God, lift up Your hand!
Do not forget the humble.
13 Why do the wicked renounce God?
He has said in his heart,
"You will not require *an account.*"
➤ 14 But You have seen, for You observe trouble and grief,
To repay *it* by Your hand.
The helpless commits himself to You;
You are the helper of the fatherless.
15 Break the arm of the wicked and the evil *man;*
Seek out his wickedness *until* You find none.
16 The LORD *is* King forever and ever;
The nations have perished out of His land.
✳ 17 LORD, You have heard the desire of the humble;
You will prepare their heart;
You will cause Your ear to hear,
18 To do justice to the fatherless and the oppressed,
That the man of the earth may oppress no more.

PSALM 11

Faith in the LORD's Righteousness

To the Chief Musician. *A Psalm* of David.

➤ 1 In the LORD I put my trust;
How can you say to my soul,
"Flee *as* a bird to your mountain"?
2 For look! The wicked bend *their* bow,
They make ready their arrow on the string,
That they may shoot secretly at the upright in heart.
3 If the foundations are destroyed,
What can the righteous do?

4 The LORD *is* in His holy temple,
The LORD's throne *is* in heaven;
His eyes behold,
His eyelids test the sons of men.
5 The LORD tests the righteous,
But the wicked and the one who loves violence His soul hates.
6 Upon the wicked He will rain coals;
Fire and brimstone and a burning wind
Shall be the portion of their cup.
7 For the LORD *is* righteous,
He loves righteousness;
His countenance beholds the upright.[a]

PSALM 12

Man's Treachery and God's Constancy

To the Chief Musician. On an eight-stringed harp.[a] A Psalm of David.

1 Help, LORD, for the godly man ceases!
For the faithful disappear from among the sons of men.
2 They speak idly everyone with his neighbor;
With flattering lips *and* a double heart they speak.

3 May the LORD cut off all flattering lips,
And the tongue that speaks proud things,
4 Who have said,
"With our tongue we will prevail;
Our lips *are* our own;
Who *is* lord over us?"

11:7 [a]Or *The upright beholds His countenance* **12:title** [a]Hebrew *sheminith*

LIFE LESSONS

➤ **10:14 — *The helpless commits himself to You; You are the helper of the fatherless.***

No Christian is ever truly without a helper. If everyone else abandons you, God has pledged to remain with you and give you the help you need. That is why He deserves the name "Faithful and True" (Rev. 3:14).

➤ **11:1 — *In the LORD I put my trust; how can you say to my soul, "Flee as a bird to your mountain"?***

When foes urged Nehemiah to run from trouble, he replied, "Should such a man as I flee?" He realized that his enemies wanted to make him "afraid" and so "sin" by fleeing instead of trusting God (Neh. 6:11, 13).

➤ **11:7 — *For the LORD is righteous, He loves righteousness; His countenance beholds the upright.***

God made us in His image to reflect who He is, and so to bring Him glory. Since the Lord is righteous, He wants us to act in righteous ways. And through His Spirit He gives us the power we need.

➤ 5 "For the oppression of the poor, for the sighing of the needy,
Now I will arise," says the LORD;
"I will set *him* in the safety for which he yearns."
➤ 6 The words of the LORD *are* pure words,
Like silver tried in a furnace of earth,
Purified seven times.
7 You shall keep them, O LORD,
You shall preserve them from this generation forever.
8 The wicked prowl on every side,
When vileness is exalted among the sons of men.

PSALM 13

Trust in the Salvation of the LORD

To the Chief Musician. A Psalm of David.

➤ 1 How long, O LORD? Will You forget me forever?
How long will You hide Your face from me?
2 How long shall I take counsel in my soul,
Having sorrow in my heart daily?
How long will my enemy be exalted over me?
3 Consider *and* hear me, O LORD my God;
Enlighten my eyes,
Lest I sleep the *sleep of* death;
4 Lest my enemy say,
"I have prevailed against him";
Lest those who trouble me rejoice when I am moved.
➤ 5 But I have trusted in Your mercy;
My heart shall rejoice in Your salvation.
6 I will sing to the LORD,
Because He has dealt bountifully with me.

PSALM 14

Folly of the Godless, and God's Final Triumph

To the Chief Musician. A Psalm of David.

➤ 1 The fool has said in his heart,
"*There is* no God."
They are corrupt,
They have done abominable works,
There is none who does good.
2 The LORD looks down from heaven upon the children of men,
To see if there are any who understand, who seek God.
3 They have all turned aside,
They have together become corrupt;
There is none who does good,
No, not one.
4 Have all the workers of iniquity no knowledge,
Who eat up my people *as* they eat bread,
And do not call on the LORD?
5 There they are in great fear,
For God *is* with the generation of the righteous.
6 You shame the counsel of the poor,
But the LORD *is* his refuge.
7 Oh, that the salvation of Israel *would come* out of Zion!
When the LORD brings back the captivity of His people,
Let Jacob rejoice *and* Israel be glad.

PSALM 15

The Character of Those Who May Dwell with the LORD

A Psalm of David.

1 LORD, who may abide in Your tabernacle?
Who may dwell in Your holy hill?
2 He who walks uprightly,
And works righteousness,
And speaks the truth in his heart;
3 He *who* does not backbite with his tongue,
Nor does evil to his neighbor,
Nor does he take up a reproach against his friend;

LIFE LESSONS

➤ 12:5 — *"For the oppression of the poor, for the sighing of the needy, now I will arise," says the LORD; "I will set him in the safety for which he yearns."*

We all yearn for safety, to feel secure in our surroundings. Whenever events occur that make us feel unsafe and insecure, God urges us to ask Him to intervene. He alone is both our safety and our security.

➤ 12:6 — *The words of the LORD are pure words, like silver tried in a furnace of earth, purified seven times.*

God's Word is not like any other book on earth. It expresses the heart and mind of the Lord, and can be trusted beyond any shadow of doubt. It is an immovable anchor in times of storm.

➤ 13:1 — *How long, O LORD? Will You forget me forever? How long will You hide Your face from me?*

At times we might feel as though God has slammed the door to heaven in our face. Yet these times do not last. Often He is testing us to see if we will continue to follow Him, regardless.

➤ 13:5 — *But I have trusted in Your mercy; my heart shall rejoice in Your salvation.*

The Christian life thrives on both memory and hope. We remember how God has shown us mercy in the past, and so we look forward to how He will save us in the future.

➤ 14:1 — *The fool has said in his heart, "There is no God."*

Our society has a lot more "practical atheists" than it does self-proclaimed atheists. A practical atheist acts as though God does not exist, whatever he or she may proclaim to believe. Both views of God are foolish and self-destructive.

4 In whose eyes a vile person is despised,
But he honors those who fear the LORD;
He *who* swears to his own hurt and does not change;
5 He *who* does not put out his money at usury,
Nor does he take a bribe against the innocent.

He who does these *things* shall never be moved.

PSALM 16

The Hope of the Faithful, and the Messiah's Victory

A Michtam of David.

1 Preserve me, O God, for in You I put my trust.
2 *O my soul,* you have said to the LORD,
"You *are* my Lord,
My goodness is nothing apart from You."
3 As for the saints who *are* on the earth,
"They are the excellent ones, in whom is all my delight."
4 Their sorrows shall be multiplied who hasten *after* another *god;*
Their drink offerings of blood I will not offer,
Nor take up their names on my lips.
5 O LORD, *You are* the portion of my inheritance and my cup;
You maintain my lot.
6 The lines have fallen to me in pleasant *places;*
Yes, I have a good inheritance.
7 I will bless the LORD who has given me counsel;
My heart also instructs me in the night seasons.
8 I have set the LORD always before me;
Because *He is* at my right hand I shall not be moved.
9 Therefore my heart is glad, and my glory rejoices;
My flesh also will rest in hope.
10 For You will not leave my soul in Sheol,
Nor will You allow Your Holy One to see corruption.
11 You will show me the path of life;
In Your presence *is* fullness of joy;
At Your right hand *are* pleasures forevermore.

PSALM 17

Prayer with Confidence in Final Salvation

A Prayer of David.

1 Hear a just cause, O LORD,
Attend to my cry;
Give ear to my prayer *which is* not from deceitful lips.
2 Let my vindication come from Your presence;
Let Your eyes look on the things that are upright.
3 You have tested my heart;
You have visited *me* in the night;
You have tried me and have found nothing;
I have purposed that my mouth shall not transgress.
4 Concerning the works of men,
By the word of Your lips,
I have kept away from the paths of the destroyer.
5 Uphold my steps in Your paths,
That my footsteps may not slip.
6 I have called upon You, for You will hear me, O God;
Incline Your ear to me, *and* hear my speech.
7 Show Your marvelous lovingkindness by Your right hand,
O You who save those who trust *in You*
From those who rise up *against them.*
8 Keep me as the apple of Your eye;
Hide me under the shadow of Your wings,
9 From the wicked who oppress me,
From my deadly enemies who surround me.

LIFE LESSONS

➤ 15:4 — *He . . . swears to his own hurt and does not change . . . .*

A young woman said she had "peace" about her decision to go back on a contract she had signed to teach at a small school. "That's great," said the jilted principal, "she has the peace and we have the pieces."

➤ 16:7 — *I will bless the LORD who has given me counsel; my heart also instructs me in the night seasons.*

God often gives us His counsel when we grow quiet enough to listen to Him while in bed or getting ready for sleep. We must be ready to listen at all times, because He may be ready to speak at any time.

➤ 16:10 — *For You will not leave my soul in Sheol, nor will You allow Your Holy One to see corruption.*

This verse is an important prophecy about the resurrection of Jesus Christ, quoted by Peter in Acts 2:27. Peter argued that since David had died and his body decayed, the verse had to apply to the Messiah, Jesus.

➤ 17:8 — *Keep me as the apple of Your eye; hide me under the shadow of Your wings . . . .*

God delights in all those who place their trust in Him. He considers each one the apple of His eye, the object of His special devotion. They find both protection and shelter in His loving presence.

10 They have closed up their fat *hearts;*
With their mouths they speak proudly.
11 They have now surrounded us in our steps;
They have set their eyes, crouching down to the earth,
12 As a lion is eager to tear his prey,
And like a young lion lurking in secret places.
13 Arise, O LORD,
Confront him, cast him down;
Deliver my life from the wicked with Your sword,
14 With Your hand from men, O LORD,
From men of the world *who have* their portion in *this* life,
And whose belly You fill with Your hidden treasure.
They are satisfied with children,
And leave the rest of their *possession* for their babes.
➤ 15 As for me, I will see Your face in righteousness;
I shall be satisfied when I awake in Your likeness.

PSALM 18

God the Sovereign Savior

To the Chief Musician. A Psalm of David the servant of the LORD, who spoke to the LORD the words of this song on the day that the LORD delivered him from the hand of all his enemies and from the hand of Saul. And he said:

1 I will love You, O LORD, my strength.
➤ 2 The LORD is my rock and my fortress and my deliverer;
My God, my strength, in whom I will trust;
My shield and the horn of my salvation, my stronghold.
3 I will call upon the LORD, *who is worthy* to be praised;
So shall I be saved from my enemies.

4 The pangs of death surrounded me,
And the floods of ungodliness made me afraid.
5 The sorrows of Sheol surrounded me;
The snares of death confronted me.
6 In my distress I called upon the LORD,
And cried out to my God;
He heard my voice from His temple,
And my cry came before Him, *even* to His ears.
7 Then the earth shook and trembled;
The foundations of the hills also quaked and were shaken,
Because He was angry.
8 Smoke went up from His nostrils,
And devouring fire from His mouth;
Coals were kindled by it.
9 He bowed the heavens also, and came down
With darkness under His feet.
10 And He rode upon a cherub, and flew;
He flew upon the wings of the wind.
11 He made darkness His secret place;
His canopy around Him *was* dark waters
And thick clouds of the skies.
12 From the brightness before Him,
His thick clouds passed with hailstones and coals of fire.

13 The LORD thundered from heaven,
And the Most High uttered His voice,
Hailstones and coals of fire.[a]
14 He sent out His arrows and scattered the foe,
Lightnings in abundance, and He vanquished them.
15 Then the channels of the sea were seen,
The foundations of the world were uncovered
At Your rebuke, O LORD,
At the blast of the breath of Your nostrils.

16 He sent from above, He took me;
He drew me out of many waters.
17 He delivered me from my strong enemy,
From those who hated me,
For they were too strong for me.
18 They confronted me in the day of my calamity, ➤
But the LORD was my support.

18:13 [a]Following Masoretic Text, Targum, and Vulgate; a few Hebrew manuscripts and Septuagint omit *Hailstones and coals of fire.*

LIFE LESSONS

➤ 17:15 — *As for me, I will see Your face in righteousness; I shall be satisfied when I awake in Your likeness.*

We look forward to that great day when we will see Jesus as He is, when we will be transformed into His glorious image (1 John 3:2). It will be like waking from a deep sleep into a stunningly beautiful new day.

➤ 18:2 — *The LORD is my rock and my fortress and my deliverer; my God, my strength, in whom I will trust; my shield and the horn of my salvation, my stronghold.*

We are wise if we fill our minds with many graphic images of who God is for us: our Rock, our Fortress, our Shield, our Stronghold. How do you best like to think of Him? What is He to you?

➤ 18:18 — *They confronted me in the day of my calamity, but the LORD was my support.*

In this life, confrontation is inevitable. When things go bad, the finger-pointing often begins. Even in those dark days, we can count upon the Lord for His support. He has bound Himself to us forever.

19 He also brought me out into a broad place;
He delivered me because He delighted in me.
20 The LORD rewarded me according to my righteousness;
According to the cleanness of my hands
He has recompensed me.
21 For I have kept the ways of the LORD,
And have not wickedly departed from my God.
22 For all His judgments *were* before me,
And I did not put away His statutes from me.
23 I was also blameless before Him,
And I kept myself from my iniquity.
24 Therefore the LORD has recompensed me according to my righteousness,
According to the cleanness of my hands in His sight.
25 With the merciful You will show Yourself merciful;
With a blameless man You will show Yourself blameless;
26 With the pure You will show Yourself pure;
And with the devious You will show Yourself shrewd.
27 For You will save the humble people,
But will bring down haughty looks.
✳ 28 For You will light my lamp;
The LORD my God will enlighten my darkness.
29 For by You I can run against a troop,
By my God I can leap over a wall.
30 *As for* God, His way *is* perfect;
The word of the LORD is proven;
He *is* a shield to all who trust in Him.
31 For who *is* God, except the LORD?
And who *is* a rock, except our God?
32 *It is* God who arms me with strength,
And makes my way perfect.
33 He makes my feet like the *feet of* deer,
And sets me on my high places.
34 He teaches my hands to make war,
So that my arms can bend a bow of bronze.
35 You have also given me the shield of Your salvation;
Your right hand has held me up,
Your gentleness has made me great.
36 You enlarged my path under me,
So my feet did not slip.
37 I have pursued my enemies and overtaken them;
Neither did I turn back again till they were destroyed.
38 I have wounded them,
So that they could not rise;
They have fallen under my feet.
39 For You have armed me with strength for the battle;
You have subdued under me those who rose up against me.
40 You have also given me the necks of my enemies,
So that I destroyed those who hated me.
41 They cried out, but *there was* none to save;
Even to the LORD, but He did not answer them.
42 Then I beat them as fine as the dust before the wind;
I cast them out like dirt in the streets.
43 You have delivered me from the strivings of the people;
You have made me the head of the nations;
A people I have not known shall serve me.
44 As soon as they hear of me they obey me;
The foreigners submit to me.
45 The foreigners fade away,
And come frightened from their hideouts.

46 The LORD lives!
Blessed *be* my Rock!
Let the God of my salvation be exalted.
47 *It is* God who avenges me,
And subdues the peoples under me;
48 He delivers me from my enemies.
You also lift me up above those who rise against me;
You have delivered me from the violent man.
49 Therefore I will give thanks to You,
O LORD, among the Gentiles,
And sing praises to Your name.
50 Great deliverance He gives to His king,
And shows mercy to His anointed,
To David and his descendants forevermore.

PSALM 19

The Perfect Revelation of the LORD

To the Chief Musician. A Psalm of David.

1 The heavens declare the glory of God;
And the firmament shows His handiwork.
2 Day unto day utters speech,
And night unto night reveals knowledge.

LIFE LESSONS

➤ 19:1 — *The heavens declare the glory of God; and the firmament shows His handiwork.*

Go outside on some clear night and just stare up into the sky for several minutes. Soak in the grandeur and majesty and vastness of the starry host—and then think: *my God made all this.*

3 *There is* no speech nor language
Where their voice is not heard.
4 Their line[a] has gone out through all the earth,
And their words to the end of the world.

In them He has set a tabernacle for the sun,
5 Which *is* like a bridegroom coming out of his chamber,
And rejoices like a strong man to run its race.
6 Its rising *is* from one end of heaven,
And its circuit to the other end;
And there is nothing hidden from its heat.

7 The law of the LORD *is* perfect, converting the soul;
The testimony of the LORD *is* sure, making wise the simple;
8 The statutes of the LORD *are* right, rejoicing the heart;
The commandment of the LORD *is* pure, enlightening the eyes;
9 The fear of the LORD *is* clean, enduring forever;
The judgments of the LORD *are* true *and* righteous altogether.
10 More to be desired *are they* than gold,
Yea, than much fine gold;
Sweeter also than honey and the honeycomb.
11 Moreover by them Your servant is warned,
And in keeping them *there is* great reward.

12 Who can understand *his* errors?
Cleanse me from secret *faults.*
13 Keep back Your servant also from presumptuous *sins;*
Let them not have dominion over me.
Then I shall be blameless,
And I shall be innocent of great transgression.

➤ 14 Let the words of my mouth and the meditation of my heart
Be acceptable in Your sight,
O LORD, my strength and my Redeemer.

PSALM 20

The Assurance of God's Saving Work

To the Chief Musician. A Psalm of David.

1 May the LORD answer you in the day of trouble;
May the name of the God of Jacob defend you;
2 May He send you help from the sanctuary,
And strengthen you out of Zion;
3 May He remember all your offerings,
And accept your burnt sacrifice. Selah
4 May He grant you according to your heart's *desire,*
And fulfill all your purpose.
5 We will rejoice in your salvation,
And in the name of our God we will set up *our* banners!
May the LORD fulfill all your petitions.

6 Now I know that the LORD saves His anointed; ✳
He will answer him from His holy heaven
With the saving strength of His right hand.

7 Some *trust* in chariots, and some in horses; ➤
But we will remember the name of the LORD our God.
8 They have bowed down and fallen;
But we have risen and stand upright.

9 Save, LORD!
May the King answer us when we call.

PSALM 21

Joy in the Salvation of the LORD

To the Chief Musician. A Psalm of David.

1 The king shall have joy in Your strength, O LORD;
And in Your salvation how greatly shall he rejoice!
2 You have given him his heart's desire,
And have not withheld the request of his lips. Selah
3 For You meet him with the blessings of goodness;
You set a crown of pure gold upon his head.
4 He asked life from You, *and* You gave *it* to him—
Length of days forever and ever.
5 His glory *is* great in Your salvation;

19:4 [a]Septuagint, Syriac, and Vulgate read *sound;* Targum reads *business.*

LIFE LESSONS

➤ **19:14 — *Let the words of my mouth and the meditation of my heart be acceptable in Your sight, O LORD, my strength and my Redeemer.***

The God who made the universe by His almighty power offers to exercise that same power on our behalf to help us speak and think in a way that honors Him. He wants to be involved in every aspect of our lives.

➤ **20:7 — *Some trust in chariots, and some in horses; but we will remember the name of the LORD our God.***

We could change this verse to say, "Some trust in tanks, and some in missiles; but we will put our hope in the God and Father of our Lord Jesus Christ." The details of history change, but God stays the same.

Honor and majesty You have placed upon him.
➤ 6 For You have made him most blessed forever;
You have made him exceedingly glad with Your presence.
7 For the king trusts in the LORD,
And through the mercy of the Most High he shall not be moved.
➤ 8 Your hand will find all Your enemies;
Your right hand will find those who hate You.
9 You shall make them as a fiery oven in the time of Your anger;
The LORD shall swallow them up in His wrath,
And the fire shall devour them.
10 Their offspring You shall destroy from the earth,
And their descendants from among the sons of men.
11 For they intended evil against You;
They devised a plot *which* they are not able *to perform.*
12 Therefore You will make them turn their back;
You will make ready *Your arrows* on Your string toward their faces.
13 Be exalted, O LORD, in Your own strength!
We will sing and praise Your power.

PSALM 22

The Suffering, Praise, and Posterity of the Messiah

To the Chief Musician. Set to "The Deer of the Dawn."[a] A Psalm of David.

➤ 1 My God, My God, why have You forsaken Me?
Why are You so far from helping Me,
And from the words of My groaning?
2 O My God, I cry in the daytime, but You do not hear;
And in the night season, and am not silent.
3 But You *are* holy,
Enthroned in the praises of Israel.
4 Our fathers trusted in You;
They trusted, and You delivered them.
5 They cried to You, and were delivered;
They trusted in You, and were not ashamed.
6 But I *am* a worm, and no man;
A reproach of men, and despised by the people.
7 All those who see Me ridicule Me;
They shoot out the lip, they shake the head, *saying,*
8 "He trusted[a] in the LORD, let Him rescue Him;
Let Him deliver Him, since He delights in Him!"
9 But You *are* He who took Me out of the womb;
You made Me trust *while* on My mother's breasts.
10 I was cast upon You from birth.
From My mother's womb
You *have been* My God.
11 Be not far from Me,
For trouble *is* near;
For *there is* none to help.
12 Many bulls have surrounded Me;
Strong *bulls* of Bashan have encircled Me.
13 They gape at Me *with* their mouths,
Like a raging and roaring lion.
14 I am poured out like water,
And all My bones are out of joint;
My heart is like wax;
It has melted within Me.
15 My strength is dried up like a potsherd,
And My tongue clings to My jaws;
You have brought Me to the dust of death.
16 For dogs have surrounded Me;
The congregation of the wicked has enclosed Me.
They pierced[a] My hands and My feet;

22:title [a]Hebrew *Aijeleth Hashahar* **22:8** [a]Septuagint, Syriac, and Vulgate read *hoped;* Targum reads *praised.*
22:16 [a]Following some Hebrew manuscripts, Septuagint, Syriac, Vulgate; Masoretic Text reads *Like a lion.*

LIFE LESSONS

➤ 21:6 — *For You have made him most blessed forever; You have made him exceedingly glad with Your presence.*

God invites us to ask Him for things, but even the things He gives us will never make us happy; only His presence can do that. The deepest delights are found only in Him, not in any of His gifts.

➤ 21:8 — *Your hand will find all Your enemies; Your right hand will find those who hate You.*

A classic sermon of many years ago was titled, "Payday Someday." We can come to God in faith and receive His pardon and grace, or we can reject His offer of life and become His enemy. Those are the options.

➤ 22:1 — *My God, My God, why have You forsaken Me? Why are You so far from helping Me, and from the words of My groaning?*

Jesus Christ knew more about feeling abandoned by God than we ever will—but in His case, it was more than a feeling. For a moment, God turned His back on His Son when He became sin for us (Matt. 27:46).

17 I can count all My bones.
They look *and* stare at Me.
18 They divide My garments among them,
And for My clothing they cast lots.

19 But You, O LORD, do not be far from Me;
O My Strength, hasten to help Me!
20 Deliver Me from the sword,
My precious *life* from the power of the dog.
21 Save Me from the lion's mouth
And from the horns of the wild oxen!

You have answered Me.

22 I will declare Your name to My brethren;
In the midst of the assembly I will praise You.
23 You who fear the LORD, praise Him!
All you descendants of Jacob, glorify Him,
And fear Him, all you offspring of Israel!
➤ 24 For He has not despised nor abhorred the affliction of the afflicted;
Nor has He hidden His face from Him;
But when He cried to Him, He heard.

25 My praise *shall be* of You in the great assembly;
I will pay My vows before those who fear Him.
26 The poor shall eat and be satisfied;
Those who seek Him will praise the LORD.
Let your heart live forever!

27 All the ends of the world
Shall remember and turn to the LORD,
And all the families of the nations
Shall worship before You.[a]
28 For the kingdom *is* the LORD's,
And He rules over the nations.

29 All the prosperous of the earth
Shall eat and worship;
All those who go down to the dust
Shall bow before Him,
Even he who cannot keep himself alive.

30 A posterity shall serve Him.
It will be recounted of the Lord to the *next* generation,
31 They will come and declare His righteousness to a people who will be born,
That He has done *this*.

PSALM 23

The LORD the Shepherd of His People

A Psalm of David.

1 The LORD *is* my shepherd;
I shall not want.
2 He makes me to lie down in green pastures;
He leads me beside the still waters.
3 He restores my soul;
He leads me in the paths of righteousness
For His name's sake.
4 Yea, though I walk through the valley of the shadow of death,
I will fear no evil;
For You *are* with me;
Your rod and Your staff, they comfort me.
5 You prepare a table before me in the presence of my enemies;
You anoint my head with oil;
My cup runs over.
6 Surely goodness and mercy shall follow me
All the days of my life;
And I will dwell[a] in the house of the LORD
Forever.

PSALM 24

The King of Glory and His Kingdom

A Psalm of David.

1 The earth *is* the LORD's, and all its fullness,
The world and those who dwell therein.
2 For He has founded it upon the seas,
And established it upon the waters.

22:27 [a]Following Masoretic Text, Septuagint, and Targum; Arabic, Syriac, and Vulgate read *Him*. **23:6** [a]Following Septuagint, Syriac, Targum, and Vulgate; Masoretic Text reads *return*.

LIFE LESSONS

➤ 22:24 — *For He has not despised nor abhorred the affliction of the afflicted; nor has He hidden His face from Him; but when He cried to Him, He heard.*

Jesus clearly had this psalm on His mind as He hung from the cross, so He must also have taken great comfort from this part of the psalm. He knew that God heard His cries, and would cause Him to triumph.

➤ 23:1 — *The LORD is my shepherd; I shall not want.*

If you have the Lord, you have everything; if you don't have the Lord, you have nothing. Is the Lord *your* shepherd? Is Jesus *your* savior? Are *you* a part of God's flock?

➤ 23:6 — *Surely goodness and mercy shall follow me all the days of my life; and I will dwell in the house of the LORD forever.*

We cannot always see goodness and mercy ahead of us, but when we look behind us, we see them. That helps us to look ahead and see more clearly, where we glimpse our place at God's side forever.

➤ 24:1 — *The earth is the LORD's, and all its fullness, the world and those who dwell therein.*

Occasionally you may hear a teaching that claims this world is the legal property of Satan, obtained in the Fall. Don't believe it. This world always has been and always will be God's. He hands His sovereignty to nobody.

ANSWERS TO LIFE'S QUESTIONS

How can I find renewal and restoration?

PS. 23:2–4

"He leads me beside quiet waters, He restores my soul" (Ps. 23:2, 3). Most likely you have heard this passage quoted more times than you can count. No matter how often this much-loved psalm gets recited, however, we still seem to miss the full impact of the message: *God restores our souls.*

How does He do this? He restores our souls though fellowship with Himself. Even though at times we stray far from Him, He remains the Good Shepherd. Though we wander, He receives us back gladly and willingly pardons His wayward sheep.

Why would we ever leave such a loving Guide? Most likely you have never made a conscious decision to forsake the Father; instead you may have slipped away slowly and subtly as a result of wandering desires and selfish attempts to meet your own needs. But when you strive to attain comfort and safety apart from God, you stray farther and farther away from Him.

Luke 15 presents a wonderful picture of the warm reception awaiting a lost "sheep." Did the shepherd scold or punish the wayward lamb? No. Instead, all of heaven celebrated because the lost had been found. Likewise, heaven rejoices when a wandering child of God returns "to the fold." Jesus tells us "there will be more joy in heaven over one sinner who repents than over ninety-nine just persons who need no repentance" (Luke 15:7).

In restoring our souls, God is more than a *pardoning* Shepherd. He is also a *providing* Shepherd. He knows what we need before we even ask, and He delights in meeting our needs (Matt. 7:9–11). That means He knows what you need physically, emotionally, and spiritually, right now. In fact, He is already at work, accomplishing and providing the things you need, even though you may not even have thought of them yet.

Finally, God is our *protecting* Shepherd. What comforts the psalmist in Psalm 23:4? It is the Lord's rod and staff. Ancient shepherds used these tools to defend their sheep from vicious animals seeking a quick meal. In the same way, God moves before us, clearing the way of the enemy's snares.

Have you experienced God's provision, only to fall into subsequent doubt and fear because of loss or hardship? God has not left you. He remains your Good Shepherd, leading you through the darkness and into the light. It is there in His presence that He will pardon, provide for, and protect you. Always.

See the Life Principles Index for further study:

1. *Our intimacy with God—His highest priority for our lives—determines the impact of our lives.*
12. *Peace with God is the fruit of oneness with God.*

3 Who may ascend into the hill of the LORD?
Or who may stand in His holy place?
4 He who has clean hands and a pure heart,
Who has not lifted up his soul to an idol,
Nor sworn deceitfully.
5 He shall receive blessing from the LORD,
And righteousness from the God of his salvation.
6 This *is* Jacob, the generation of those who seek Him,
Who seek Your face. Selah

7 Lift up your heads, O you gates!
And be lifted up, you everlasting doors!
And the King of glory shall come in.
8 Who *is* this King of glory?
The LORD strong and mighty,
The LORD mighty in battle.
9 Lift up your heads, O you gates!
Lift up, you everlasting doors!
And the King of glory shall come in.

LIFE LESSONS

➤ 24:8 — *Who is this King of glory? The LORD strong and mighty, the LORD mighty in battle.*

The Lord is not only glorious; He is *the King* of glory. He is the greatest in glory, the pinnacle of excellence, the mountaintop of majesty, the summit of splendor. He is "over all, the eternally blessed God" (Rom. 9:5).

10 Who is this King of glory?
The LORD of hosts,
He *is* the King of glory. Selah

PSALM 25

A Plea for Deliverance and Forgiveness

A Psalm of David.

1 To You, O LORD, I lift up my soul.
2 O my God, I trust in You;
Let me not be ashamed;
Let not my enemies triumph over me.
3 Indeed, let no one who waits on You be ashamed;
Let those be ashamed who deal treacherously without cause.

➤ 4 Show me Your ways, O LORD;
Teach me Your paths.
➤ 5 Lead me in Your truth and teach me,
For You *are* the God of my salvation;
On You I wait all the day.

6 Remember, O LORD, Your tender mercies and Your lovingkindnesses,
For they *are* from of old.
7 Do not remember the sins of my youth, nor my transgressions;
According to Your mercy remember me,
For Your goodness' sake, O LORD.

8 Good and upright *is* the LORD;
Therefore He teaches sinners in the way.
9 The humble He guides in justice,
And the humble He teaches His way.
10 All the paths of the LORD *are* mercy and truth,
To such as keep His covenant and His testimonies.

➤ 11 For Your name's sake, O LORD,
Pardon my iniquity, for it *is* great.

12 Who *is* the man that fears the LORD?
Him shall He[a] teach in the way He[b] chooses.
13 He himself shall dwell in prosperity,
And his descendants shall inherit the earth.
14 The secret of the LORD *is* with those who fear Him,
And He will show them His covenant.
15 My eyes *are* ever toward the LORD,
For He shall pluck my feet out of the net.

16 Turn Yourself to me, and have mercy on me,
For I *am* desolate and afflicted.
17 The troubles of my heart have enlarged;
Bring me out of my distresses!
18 Look on my affliction and my pain,
And forgive all my sins.
19 Consider my enemies, for they are many;
And they hate me with cruel hatred.
20 Keep my soul, and deliver me;
Let me not be ashamed, for I put my trust in You.
21 Let integrity and uprightness preserve me,
For I wait for You.

22 Redeem Israel, O God,
Out of all their troubles!

PSALM 26

A Prayer for Divine Scrutiny and Redemption

A Psalm of David.

1 Vindicate me, O LORD,
For I have walked in my integrity.
I have also trusted in the LORD;
I shall not slip.
2 Examine me, O LORD, and prove me;
Try my mind and my heart.
3 For Your lovingkindness *is* before my eyes,
And I have walked in Your truth.
4 I have not sat with idolatrous mortals,
Nor will I go in with hypocrites.
5 I have hated the assembly of evildoers,
And will not sit with the wicked.
6 I will wash my hands in innocence;
So I will go about Your altar, O LORD,
7 That I may proclaim with the voice of thanksgiving,
And tell of all Your wondrous works.
8 LORD, I have loved the habitation of Your house,
And the place where Your glory dwells.

9 Do not gather my soul with sinners,
Nor my life with bloodthirsty men,
10 In whose hands *is* a sinister scheme,
And whose right hand is full of bribes.

25:12 [a]Or *he* [b]Or *he*

LIFE LESSONS

➤ 25:4, 5 — *Show me Your ways, O LORD; teach me Your paths. Lead me in Your truth and teach me, for You are the God of my salvation; on You I wait all the day.*

We learn God's ways and His truth over time; we do not become experts in the things of God overnight. He spends years to mold His servants into the likeness of His Son, so we must beware of growing impatient.

➤ 25:11 — *For Your name's sake, O LORD, pardon my iniquity, for it is great.*

God saves us, not because He thinks we're smart or worthy of His Son's work on our behalf, but because of His own nature and goodness. He saves us for His name's sake and for His glory.

11 But as for me, I will walk in my
integrity;
Redeem me and be merciful to me.
➤ 12 My foot stands in an even place;
In the congregations I will bless the LORD.

PSALM 27

An Exuberant Declaration of Faith

A Psalm of David.

➤ 1 The LORD *is* my light and my salvation;
Whom shall I fear?
The LORD *is* the strength of my life;
Of whom shall I be afraid?
2 When the wicked came against me
To eat up my flesh,
My enemies and foes,
They stumbled and fell.
3 Though an army may encamp against
me,
My heart shall not fear;
Though war may rise against me,
In this I *will be* confident.

4 One *thing* I have desired of the LORD,
That will I seek:
That I may dwell in the house of the
LORD
All the days of my life,
To behold the beauty of the LORD,
And to inquire in His temple.
5 For in the time of trouble
He shall hide me in His pavilion;
In the secret place of His tabernacle
He shall hide me;
He shall set me high upon a rock.
6 And now my head shall be lifted up
above my enemies all around me;
Therefore I will offer sacrifices of joy in
His tabernacle;
I will sing, yes, I will sing praises to the
LORD.
7 Hear, O LORD, *when* I cry with my voice!
Have mercy also upon me, and answer
me.
8 *When You said,* "Seek My face,"
My heart said to You, "Your face, LORD, I
will seek."
9 Do not hide Your face from me;
Do not turn Your servant away in anger;
You have been my help;
Do not leave me nor forsake me,
O God of my salvation.
10 When my father and my mother forsake
me,
Then the LORD will take care of me.

11 Teach me Your way, O LORD,
And lead me in a smooth path, because
of my enemies.
12 Do not deliver me to the will of my
adversaries;
For false witnesses have risen against
me,
And such as breathe out violence.
13 *I would have lost heart,* unless I had ➤
believed
That I would see the goodness of the
LORD
In the land of the living.
14 Wait on the LORD;
Be of good courage,
And He shall strengthen your heart;
Wait, I say, on the LORD!

PSALM 28

Rejoicing in Answered Prayer

A Psalm of David.

1 To You I will cry, O LORD my Rock:
Do not be silent to me,
Lest, if You *are* silent to me,
I become like those who go down to the
pit.
2 Hear the voice of my supplications
When I cry to You,
When I lift up my hands toward Your
holy sanctuary.

3 Do not take me away with the wicked
And with the workers of iniquity,
Who speak peace to their neighbors,
But evil *is* in their hearts.
4 Give them according to their deeds,
And according to the wickedness of
their endeavors;
Give them according to the work of
their hands;
Render to them what they deserve.
5 Because they do not regard the works
of the LORD,

LIFE LESSONS

➤ 26:12 — *. . . in the congregations I will bless the LORD.*

Some believers say, "I don't need to go to church; Jesus and I get along just fine on our own." But the Bible never endorses such a spirit. It always pictures believers coming together for worship and mutual encouragement.

➤ 27:1 — *The LORD is my light and my salvation; whom shall I fear? The LORD is the strength of my life; of whom shall I be afraid?*

We don't need to be afraid of the dark when the Lord gives us His light. We don't need to fear the power of enemies when we walk in the power of God's Spirit. John says, "perfect love casts out fear" (1 John 4:18).

➤ 27:13 — *I would have lost heart, unless I had believed that I would see the goodness of the LORD in the land of the living.*

Christians do not merely hope for "pie in the sky in the great by-and-by." We can expect and trust to receive God's help and salvation right now, in the heat of the battle.

WHAT THE BIBLE SAYS ABOUT SEEKING GOD'S GUIDANCE

Ps. 27:14

Life is full of choices, and if we want to make the right choices—those that glorify God and benefit us and others—we need God's guidance. All of us will eventually come to places and times when we will desperately need God's guidance. How can believers find that guidance? Seven words may help.

1. *Cleansing.* We need to ask, "Is anything in my life hindering me from hearing what You are saying? If so, what is it?" Cleansing comes by confession (1 John 1:9).

2. *Surrendering.* Submitting to the will of God is both a humbling and an uplifting experience (1 Pet. 5:6).

3. *Asking.* God promises that when we ask according to his will, He hears us. And when we know that He hears us, we know He has answered (1 John 5:14, 15)—even though the answer may come over a long period of time.

4. *Meditating.* God promises that His Word will be a light to our paths (Ps. 119:105), so the more we think about His Word, the clearer our path will become.

God promises that His Word will be a light to our paths.

5. *Believing.* In Mark's Gospel, we learn that when we ask, we must believe He is going to give us what we have requested (Mark 11:22–24).

6. *Waiting.* God promises that He acts on our behalf when we wait for Him (Is. 64:4). If we want to, we can run ahead of Him, dash in and try to fix things on our own, or manipulate circumstances. If we wait on the Lord, then our sovereign, divine, omnipotent God will act on our behalf. It's our choice.

7. *Receiving.* When we obediently seek the will of God, we can be sure that He'll hear us and give us the wisdom we need to make the right life choices (Matt. 7:7, 8; James 1:5).

You will find great peace and confidence in knowing that you are making choices based on God's guidance. Perhaps no one else will understand or agree with your decision—but you will have heard from the One who matters the most.

See the Life Principles Index for further study:
10. If necessary, God will move heaven and earth to show us His will.
27. Prayer is life's greatest time saver.

Nor the operation of His hands,
He shall destroy them
And not build them up.
6 Blessed *be* the LORD,
Because He has heard the voice of my supplications!
7 The LORD *is* my strength and my shield;
My heart trusted in Him, and I am helped;
Therefore my heart greatly rejoices,
And with my song I will praise Him.
8 The LORD *is* their strength,[a]
And He *is* the saving refuge of His anointed.
➤ 9 Save Your people,
And bless Your inheritance;
Shepherd them also,
And bear them up forever.

PSALM 29

Praise to God in His Holiness and Majesty

A Psalm of David.

1 Give unto the LORD, O you mighty ones,
Give unto the LORD glory and strength.
2 Give unto the LORD the glory due to His name;
Worship the LORD in the beauty of holiness.
3 The voice of the LORD *is* over the waters;
The God of glory thunders;
The LORD *is* over many waters.
4 The voice of the LORD *is* powerful;
The voice of the LORD *is* full of majesty.
5 The voice of the LORD breaks the cedars,
Yes, the LORD splinters the cedars of Lebanon.
6 He makes them also skip like a calf,
Lebanon and Sirion like a young wild ox.
7 The voice of the LORD divides the flames of fire.
8 The voice of the LORD shakes the wilderness;
The LORD shakes the Wilderness of Kadesh.
9 The voice of the LORD makes the deer give birth,
And strips the forests bare;
And in His temple everyone says, "Glory!"
10 The LORD sat *enthroned* at the Flood,
And the LORD sits as King forever.
11 The LORD will give strength to His people;
The LORD will bless His people with peace. ✳

PSALM 30

The Blessedness of Answered Prayer

A Psalm. A Song at the dedication of the house of David.

1 I will extol You, O LORD, for You have lifted me up,
And have not let my foes rejoice over me.
2 O LORD my God, I cried out to You,
And You healed me.
3 O LORD, You brought my soul up from the grave;
You have kept me alive, that I should not go down to the pit.[a]
4 Sing praise to the LORD, you saints of His,
And give thanks at the remembrance of His holy name.[a]
5 For His anger *is but for* a moment, ➤
His favor *is for* life;
Weeping may endure for a night,
But joy *comes* in the morning.
6 Now in my prosperity I said,
"I shall never be moved."
7 LORD, by Your favor You have made my mountain stand strong;
You hid Your face, *and* I was troubled.
8 I cried out to You, O LORD;
And to the LORD I made supplication:
9 "What profit *is there* in my blood,
When I go down to the pit?
Will the dust praise You?
Will it declare Your truth?
10 Hear, O LORD, and have mercy on me;
LORD, be my helper!"

28:8 [a]Following Masoretic Text and Targum; Septuagint, Syriac, and Vulgate read *the strength of His people.* **30:3** [a]Following Qere and Targum; Kethib, Septuagint, Syriac, and Vulgate read *from those who descend to the pit.* **30:4** [a]Or *His holiness*

LIFE LESSONS

➤ 28:9 — *Save Your people, and bless Your inheritance; shepherd them also, and bear them up forever.*

God gives us His hand of salvation right now, not just in heaven. He blesses us right now, not just in eternity. He leads us and sustains us every day, on earth. Heaven merely completes our relationship with Him.

➤ 30:5 — *For His anger is but for a moment, His favor is for life; weeping may endure for a night, but joy comes in the morning.*

A holy God must judge sin, but a loving God takes great pleasure in showing mercy and bestowing grace. Hard times may be a fact of life here, but one day He will wipe away all our tears (Rev. 7:17).

➤ 11 You have turned for me my mourning
into dancing;
You have put off my sackcloth and
clothed me with gladness,
12 To the end that *my* glory may sing
praise to You and not be silent.
O LORD my God, I will give thanks to
You forever.

PSALM 31

The LORD a Fortress in Adversity

To the Chief Musician. A Psalm of David.

1 In You, O LORD, I put my trust;
Let me never be ashamed;
Deliver me in Your righteousness.
2 Bow down Your ear to me,
Deliver me speedily;
Be my rock of refuge,
A fortress of defense to save me.
➤ 3 For You *are* my rock and my fortress;
Therefore, for Your name's sake,
Lead me and guide me.
4 Pull me out of the net which they have
secretly laid for me,
For You *are* my strength.
5 Into Your hand I commit my spirit;
You have redeemed me, O LORD God of
truth.
6 I have hated those who regard useless
idols;
But I trust in the LORD.
7 I will be glad and rejoice in Your mercy,
For You have considered my trouble;
You have known my soul in adversities,
8 And have not shut me up into the hand
of the enemy;
You have set my feet in a wide place.
9 Have mercy on me, O LORD, for I am in
trouble;
My eye wastes away with grief,
Yes, my soul and my body!
10 For my life is spent with grief,
And my years with sighing;
My strength fails because of my iniquity,
And my bones waste away.
11 I am a reproach among all my enemies,
But especially among my neighbors,
And *am* repulsive to my acquaintances;
Those who see me outside flee from me.
12 I am forgotten like a dead man, out of
mind;
I am like a broken vessel.
13 For I hear the slander of many;
Fear *is* on every side;
While they take counsel together
against me,
They scheme to take away my life.
14 But as for me, I trust in You, O LORD;
I say, "You *are* my God."
15 My times *are* in Your hand; ➤
Deliver me from the hand of my enemies,
And from those who persecute me.
16 Make Your face shine upon Your servant;
Save me for Your mercies' sake.
17 Do not let me be ashamed, O LORD, for I
have called upon You;
Let the wicked be ashamed;
Let them be silent in the grave.
18 Let the lying lips be put to silence,
Which speak insolent things proudly
and contemptuously against the
righteous.
19 Oh, how great *is* Your goodness,
Which You have laid up for those who
fear You,
Which You have prepared for those who
trust in You
In the presence of the sons of men!
20 You shall hide them in the secret place
of Your presence
From the plots of man;
You shall keep them secretly in a
pavilion
From the strife of tongues.
21 Blessed *be* the LORD,
For He has shown me His marvelous
kindness in a strong city!
22 For I said in my haste,
"I am cut off from before Your eyes";
Nevertheless You heard the voice of my
supplications
When I cried out to You.
23 Oh, love the LORD, all you His saints!
For the LORD preserves the faithful,
And fully repays the proud person.
24 Be of good courage, *
And He shall strengthen your heart,
All you who hope in the LORD.

LIFE LESSONS

➤ 30:11 — *You have turned for me my mourning into dancing; You have put off my sackcloth and clothed me with gladness.*

God never meant for life to be one long dirge. He never meant for His people to trudge through life with a perpetual cloud over their heads. To know God is to know joy, and even in sorrow we can rejoice in Him.

➤ 31:3 — *For You are my rock and my fortress; therefore, for Your name's sake, lead me and guide me.*

When we place our trust in God through Christ, He becomes our stronghold and identifies us with Him forever. Our destiny is bound up with His future. That is why we can confidently ask for His guidance.

➤ 31:15 — *My times are in Your hand; deliver me from the hand of my enemies, and from those who persecute me.*

The hand of men can oppose us and harass us, but as children of a sovereign God, we are never victims of our circumstances. The hands that really matter belong to God.

Life Examples:

DAVID

The Joy of Forgiveness

PS. 32:1–11

Psalm 32 is David's confession of his sin with Bathsheba. He wrote it after his encounter with the prophet Nathan, and probably after he had spent time alone with God in prayer and repentance.

If we were to give this psalm a title, a good one would be *The Joy of Forgiveness.* David writes; "How blessed is he whose transgression is forgiven, whose sin is covered." "How blessed" can be translated, "How happy!"

Sin blocks our fellowship with the Lord. It also keeps us from experiencing God's goodness. David could not enjoy the sweetness of God's presence so long as he had not repented of his sin.

When you find yourself discouraged because you have repeated a certain sin, turn to God in prayer. Ask Him to apply His forgiveness to your life and receive His mercy. He loves you and wants to enjoy your fellowship once again.

See the Life Principles Index for further study:
8. Fight all your battles on your knees and you win every time.
15. Brokenness is God's requirement for maximum usefulness.

PSALM 32

The Joy of Forgiveness

A Psalm of David. A Contemplation.[a]

1 Blessed *is he whose* transgression *is* forgiven,
Whose sin *is* covered.
2 Blessed *is* the man to whom the LORD does not impute iniquity,
And in whose spirit *there is* no deceit.

3 When I kept silent, my bones grew old
Through my groaning all the day long.
4 For day and night Your hand was heavy upon me;
My vitality was turned into the drought of summer. Selah
5 I acknowledged my sin to You,
And my iniquity I have not hidden.
I said, "I will confess my transgressions to the LORD,"
And You forgave the iniquity of my sin. Selah

6 For this cause everyone who is godly shall pray to You
In a time when You may be found;
Surely in a flood of great waters
They shall not come near him.
7 You *are* my hiding place;
You shall preserve me from trouble;
You shall surround me with songs of deliverance. Selah

8 I will instruct you and teach you in the way you should go;
I will guide you with My eye.
9 Do not be like the horse *or* like the mule,
Which have no understanding,
Which must be harnessed with bit and bridle,
Else they will not come near you.
10 Many sorrows *shall be* to the wicked;
But he who trusts in the LORD, mercy shall surround him.
11 Be glad in the LORD and rejoice, you righteous;
And shout for joy, all *you* upright in heart!

PSALM 33

The Sovereignty of the LORD in Creation and History

1 Rejoice in the LORD, O you righteous!
For praise from the upright is beautiful.

32:title [a]Hebrew *Maschil*

LIFE LESSONS

➤ 32:5 — *I acknowledged my sin to You, and my iniquity I have not hidden. I said, "I will confess my transgressions to the LORD," and You forgave the iniquity of my sin.*

Confession clears our hearts spiritually and makes it possible for us once more to experience deep fellowship with God. Unconfessed sin makes us weak, discouraged, and ultimately miserable.

➤ 32:9 — *Do not be like the horse or like the mule, which have no understanding, which must be harnessed with bit and bridle, else they will not come near you.*

We expect animals to do animal-like things, because God has not given them the ability to think His thoughts. It should not take pain to move us toward God, because we should delight to draw near to Him.

2 Praise the LORD with the harp;
Make melody to Him with an instrument of ten strings.
3 Sing to Him a new song;
Play skillfully with a shout of joy.
4 For the word of the LORD *is* right,
And all His work *is done* in truth.
5 He loves righteousness and justice;
The earth is full of the goodness of the LORD.
➤ 6 By the word of the LORD the heavens were made,
And all the host of them by the breath of His mouth.
7 He gathers the waters of the sea together as a heap;[a]
He lays up the deep in storehouses.
8 Let all the earth fear the LORD;
Let all the inhabitants of the world stand in awe of Him.
9 For He spoke, and it was *done;*
He commanded, and it stood fast.
10 The LORD brings the counsel of the nations to nothing;
He makes the plans of the peoples of no effect.
11 The counsel of the LORD stands forever,
The plans of His heart to all generations.
12 Blessed *is* the nation whose God *is* the LORD,
The people He has chosen as His own inheritance.
13 The LORD looks from heaven;
He sees all the sons of men.
14 From the place of His dwelling He looks
On all the inhabitants of the earth;
15 He fashions their hearts individually;
He considers all their works.
16 No king *is* saved by the multitude of an army;
A mighty man is not delivered by great strength.
➤ 17 A horse *is* a vain hope for safety;
Neither shall it deliver *any* by its great strength.
18 Behold, the eye of the LORD *is* on those who fear Him,
On those who hope in His mercy,
19 To deliver their soul from death,
And to keep them alive in famine.
20 Our soul waits for the LORD;
He *is* our help and our shield.
21 For our heart shall rejoice in Him,
Because we have trusted in His holy name.
22 Let Your mercy, O LORD, be upon us,
Just as we hope in You.

PSALM 34

The Happiness of Those Who Trust in God

A Psalm of David when he pretended madness before Abimelech, who drove him away, and he departed.

1 I will bless the LORD at all times; ➤
His praise *shall* continually *be* in my mouth.
2 My soul shall make its boast in the LORD;
The humble shall hear *of it* and be glad.
3 Oh, magnify the LORD with me,
And let us exalt His name together.
4 I sought the LORD, and He heard me,
And delivered me from all my fears.
5 They looked to Him and were radiant,
And their faces were not ashamed.
6 This poor man cried out, and the LORD heard *him,*
And saved him out of all his troubles.
7 The angel[a] of the LORD encamps all around those who fear Him, ➤
And delivers them.
8 Oh, taste and see that the LORD *is* good;
Blessed *is* the man *who* trusts in Him!
9 Oh, fear the LORD, you His saints!
There is no want to those who fear Him.

33:7 [a]Septuagint, Targum, and Vulgate read *in a vessel.*
34:7 [a]Or *Angel*

LIFE LESSONS

➤ **33:6 — *By the word of the LORD the heavens were made, and all the host of them by the breath of His mouth.***

The Gospel of John calls Jesus "the Word" and says, "All things were made through Him, and without Him nothing was made that was made" (John 1:3). Paul adds that everything was made for Him (Col. 1:16).

➤ **33:17 — *A horse is a vain hope for safety; neither shall it deliver any by its great strength.***

A horse is much stronger and faster than a man, but no wise person puts his hope in the animal for deliverance. There is no real safety outside of a close walk with God.

➤ **34:1 — *I will bless the LORD at all times; His praise shall continually be in my mouth.***

Even if it's not your practice, pick a day this week and praise God throughout the day. Praise Him when you wake up, praise Him when you eat, praise Him when you leave the house and when you return.

➤ **34:7 — *The angel of the LORD encamps all around those who fear Him, and delivers them.***

Who knows how often we have been protected or delivered or saved from harm by an angel assigned to guard us? Who knows how that angel is protecting you right now?

10 The young lions lack and suffer hunger;
But those who seek the LORD shall not lack any good *thing*.
11 Come, you children, listen to me;
I will teach you the fear of the LORD.
12 Who *is* the man *who* desires life,
And loves *many* days, that he may see good?
13 Keep your tongue from evil,
And your lips from speaking deceit.
14 Depart from evil and do good;
Seek peace and pursue it.

15 The eyes of the LORD *are* on the righteous,
And His ears *are open* to their cry.
16 The face of the LORD *is* against those who do evil,
To cut off the remembrance of them from the earth.

17 *The righteous* cry out, and the LORD hears,
And delivers them out of all their troubles.
18 The LORD *is* near to those who have a broken heart,
And saves such as have a contrite spirit.

* 19 Many *are* the afflictions of the righteous,
But the LORD delivers him out of them all.
20 He guards all his bones;
Not one of them is broken.
21 Evil shall slay the wicked,
And those who hate the righteous shall be condemned.
22 The LORD redeems the soul of His servants,
And none of those who trust in Him shall be condemned.

PSALM 35

The LORD the Avenger of His People

A Psalm of David.

1 Plead *my cause,* O LORD, with those who strive with me;
Fight against those who fight against me.
2 Take hold of shield and buckler,
And stand up for my help.
3 Also draw out the spear,
And stop those who pursue me.
Say to my soul,
"I *am* your salvation."

4 Let those be put to shame and brought to dishonor
Who seek after my life;
Let those be turned back and brought to confusion
Who plot my hurt.
5 Let them be like chaff before the wind,
And let the angel[a] of the LORD chase *them.*
6 Let their way be dark and slippery,
And let the angel of the LORD pursue them.
7 For without cause they have hidden their net for me *in* a pit,
Which they have dug without cause for my life.
8 Let destruction come upon him unexpectedly,
And let his net that he has hidden catch himself;
Into that very destruction let him fall.

9 And my soul shall be joyful in the LORD;
It shall rejoice in His salvation.
10 All my bones shall say,
"LORD, who *is* like You,
Delivering the poor from him who is too strong for him,
Yes, the poor and the needy from him who plunders him?"

11 Fierce witnesses rise up;
They ask me *things* that I do not know.
12 They reward me evil for good,
To the sorrow of my soul.
13 But as for me, when they were sick,
My clothing *was* sackcloth;
I humbled myself with fasting;
And my prayer would return to my own heart.
14 I paced about as though *he were* my friend *or* brother;
I bowed down heavily, as one who mourns *for his* mother.

15 But in my adversity they rejoiced
And gathered together;
Attackers gathered against me,
And I did not know *it;*
They tore *at me* and did not cease;
16 With ungodly mockers at feasts
They gnashed at me with their teeth.

17 Lord, how long will You look on?
Rescue me from their destructions,
My precious *life* from the lions.
18 I will give You thanks in the great assembly;
I will praise You among many people.

19 Let them not rejoice over me who are wrongfully my enemies;
Nor let them wink with the eye who hate me without a cause.
20 For they do not speak peace,
But they devise deceitful matters
Against *the* quiet ones in the land.
21 They also opened their mouth wide against me,
And said, "Aha, aha!
Our eyes have seen *it.*"

35:5 [a]Or *Angel*

22 *This* You have seen, O LORD;
Do not keep silence.
O Lord, do not be far from me.
23 Stir up Yourself, and awake to my vindication,
To my cause, my God and my Lord.
➤ 24 Vindicate me, O LORD my God, according to Your righteousness;
And let them not rejoice over me.
25 Let them not say in their hearts, "Ah, so we would have it!"
Let them not say, "We have swallowed him up."

26 Let them be ashamed and brought to mutual confusion
Who rejoice at my hurt;
Let them be clothed with shame and dishonor
Who exalt themselves against me.

➤ 27 Let them shout for joy and be glad,
Who favor my righteous cause;
And let them say continually,
"Let the LORD be magnified,
Who has pleasure in the prosperity of His servant."
28 And my tongue shall speak of Your righteousness
And of Your praise all the day long.

PSALM 36

Man's Wickedness and God's Perfections

To the Chief Musician. A Psalm of David the servant of the LORD.

1 An oracle within my heart concerning the transgression of the wicked:
There is no fear of God before his eyes.
2 For he flatters himself in his own eyes,
When he finds out his iniquity *and* when he hates.
3 The words of his mouth *are* wickedness and deceit;
He has ceased to be wise *and* to do good.
4 He devises wickedness on his bed;
He sets himself in a way *that is* not good;
He does not abhor evil.

5 Your mercy, O LORD, *is* in the heavens; ➤
Your faithfulness *reaches* to the clouds.
6 Your righteousness *is* like the great mountains;
Your judgments *are* a great deep;
O LORD, You preserve man and beast.

7 How precious *is* Your lovingkindness, O God!
Therefore the children of men put their trust under the shadow of Your wings.
8 They are abundantly satisfied with the fullness of Your house,
And You give them drink from the river of Your pleasures.
9 For with You *is* the fountain of life; ➤
In Your light we see light.

10 Oh, continue Your lovingkindness to those who know You,
And Your righteousness to the upright in heart.
11 Let not the foot of pride come against me,
And let not the hand of the wicked drive me away.
12 There the workers of iniquity have fallen;
They have been cast down and are not able to rise.

PSALM 37

The Heritage of the Righteous and the Calamity of the Wicked

A Psalm of David.

1 Do not fret because of evildoers,
Nor be envious of the workers of iniquity.
2 For they shall soon be cut down like the grass,
And wither as the green herb.

LIFE LESSONS

➤ **35:24 — *Vindicate me, O LORD my God, according to Your righteousness; and let them not rejoice over me.***

We pray powerfully when we pray in line with the righteousness of God—that is, when we pray for what is right, good, glorifying to Him and beneficial for His people. The Lord delights in such prayers.

➤ **35:27 — *And let them say continually, "Let the LORD be magnified, who has pleasure in the prosperity of His servant."***

When things don't go well, we may think the Lord disdains us. But the truth is that He takes great pleasure in our prosperity and rejoices in our welfare. He loves us, even in the hard times.

➤ **36:5 — *Your mercy, O LORD, is in the heavens; Your faithfulness reaches to the clouds.***

God loves to show mercy and remains eternally trustworthy to do exactly what He has promised. If He seems to delay in working on your behalf, wait for Him. He will *never* be unfaithful to you.

➤ **36:9 — *For with You is the fountain of life; in Your light we see light.***

God offers the only real life there is. When we give ourselves to Him and walk in the light He provides us, in His Word and by His Spirit, we begin to see more and more how we can enjoy life to the fullest.

ANSWERS TO LIFE'S QUESTIONS

How can I deal effectively with jealousy?

PS. 37:4

Have you ever felt jealous of someone else's success? Maybe your neighbor has a brand new car, or perhaps someone at work got the promotion you desired. When situations like these stir up unexpected reactions within us, we just might have a problem.

Jealousy is the emotion of extreme displeasure upon seeing someone else's good fortune—and it can poison good relationships, ruin our witness, and keep us from experiencing God's blessings. The Bible calls jealousy a work of the flesh (Gal. 5:19, 20).

Is it possible to take control of a jealous attitude? Yes! Since God wants His children to take charge over these volatile emotions, let's examine some specific things you can do to gain victory.

❶ ***Confess your jealousy.*** This emotion will always—*always*—take your eyes off the Lord and fix them on some other person or object. That, at its heart, is idolatry. Whenever you place a higher value on some "thing" than you place on God, you put yourself under divine judgment. Repent of that sin immediately!

❷ ***Realize that you disagree with God.*** If the Lord chooses to bring some specific blessing into another person's life, then that is His prerogative. Your jealousy merely declares that you think you deserve the blessing more than the other person. Bring this disagreement honestly before the Lord and ask Him to restore a godly perspective to you.

❸ ***Thank God for what He's doing in that person's life.*** You may not like this point! But when you praise God—even if you do not feel like it—you put yourself in a position to receive His blessings by showing that you fully trust His judgment.

❹ ***Ask God to place love in your heart for the other person.*** So often in Scripture the word *anger* follows the word *jealous.* Do not allow jealousy to stir up malice and hate. Instead, learn how to rejoice when others receive blessings, even when you believe you should have received those blessings instead.

❺ ***Keep your focus on God alone.*** Delight in Him, knowing that He's promised to give you the desires of your heart. Focus first and foremost on what He's done for you and on the promises He's made to you through His Word. Always remember that God is God, and that it is His prerogative to bless each one of us in exactly the way He sees fit.

See the Life Principles Index for further study:
24. To live the Christian Life is to allow Jesus to live his life in and through us.
9. Trusting God means looking beyond what we can see to what God sees.

3 Trust in the LORD, and do good;
Dwell in the land, and feed on His faithfulness.
4 Delight yourself also in the LORD,
And He shall give you the desires of your heart.
5 Commit your way to the LORD,
Trust also in Him,
And He shall bring *it* to pass.
6 He shall bring forth your righteousness as the light,
And your justice as the noonday.
7 Rest in the LORD, and wait patiently for Him;
Do not fret because of him who prospers in his way,
Because of the man who brings wicked schemes to pass.
8 Cease from anger, and forsake wrath;
Do not fret—*it* only *causes* harm.
9 For evildoers shall be cut off;
But those who wait on the LORD,
They shall inherit the earth.
10 For yet a little while and the wicked *shall be* no *more;*

LIFE LESSONS

➤ ***37:3 — Trust in the LORD, and do good; dwell in the land, and feed on His faithfulness.***

God calls us to do good to others so that they might see His goodness in us. But unless we "feed on His faithfulness"—unless we stay in close fellowship with Him—we won't have much good to offer anyone.

Indeed, you will look carefully for his
place,
But it *shall be* no *more.*
11 But the meek shall inherit the earth,
And shall delight themselves in the
abundance of peace.
12 The wicked plots against the just,
And gnashes at him with his teeth.
13 The Lord laughs at him,
For He sees that his day is coming.
14 The wicked have drawn the sword
And have bent their bow,
To cast down the poor and needy,
To slay those who are of upright
conduct.
15 Their sword shall enter their own heart,
And their bows shall be broken.
16 A little that a righteous man has
Is better than the riches of many
wicked.
17 For the arms of the wicked shall be
broken,
But the LORD upholds the righteous.
18 The LORD knows the days of the
upright,
And their inheritance shall be forever.
19 They shall not be ashamed in the evil
time,
And in the days of famine they shall be
satisfied.
20 But the wicked shall perish;
And the enemies of the LORD,
Like the splendor of the meadows, shall
vanish.
Into smoke they shall vanish away.
21 The wicked borrows and does not
repay,
But the righteous shows mercy and
gives.
22 For *those* blessed by Him shall inherit
the earth,
But *those* cursed by Him shall be cut
off.
23 The steps of a *good* man are ordered by
the LORD,
And He delights in his way.
24 Though he fall, he shall not be utterly
cast down;
For the LORD upholds *him with* His
hand.
25 I have been young, and *now* am old;
Yet I have not seen the righteous
forsaken,
Nor his descendants begging bread.
26 *He is* ever merciful, and lends;
And his descendants *are* blessed.
27 Depart from evil, and do good;
And dwell forevermore.
28 For the LORD loves justice,
And does not forsake His saints;
They are preserved forever,
But the descendants of the wicked shall
be cut off.
29 The righteous shall inherit the land,
And dwell in it forever.
30 The mouth of the righteous speaks
wisdom,
And his tongue talks of justice.
31 The law of his God *is* in his heart;
None of his steps shall slide.
32 The wicked watches the righteous,
And seeks to slay him.
33 The LORD will not leave him in his
hand,
Nor condemn him when he is judged.
34 Wait on the LORD,
And keep His way,
And He shall exalt you to inherit the
land;
When the wicked are cut off, you shall
see *it.*
35 I have seen the wicked in great power,
And spreading himself like a native
green tree.
36 Yet he passed away,[a] and behold, he
was no *more;*
Indeed I sought him, but he could not
be found.
37 Mark the blameless *man,* and observe
the upright;
For the future of *that* man *is* peace.
38 But the transgressors shall be destroyed
together;
The future of the wicked shall be cut
off.
39 But the salvation of the righteous *is*
from the LORD;
He is their strength in the time of
trouble.
40 And the LORD shall help them and
deliver them;
He shall deliver them from the wicked,
And save them,
Because they trust in Him.

37:36 [a]Following Masoretic Text, Septuagint, and Targum; Syriac and Vulgate read *I passed by.*

LIFE LESSONS

➤ **37:39 —** ***But the salvation of the righteous is from the LORD; He is their strength in the time of trouble.***

When hard times come, we often feel listless, powerless, weak, and worried. Even when we don't have these feelings, we still really *are* weak. We must find our strength in God, for His might never wavers.

PSALM 38

Prayer in Time of Chastening

A Psalm of David. To bring to remembrance.

1 O LORD, do not rebuke me in Your wrath,
Nor chasten me in Your hot displeasure!
2 For Your arrows pierce me deeply,
And Your hand presses me down.
3 *There is* no soundness in my flesh
Because of Your anger,
Nor *any* health in my bones
Because of my sin.
➤ 4 For my iniquities have gone over my head;
Like a heavy burden they are too heavy for me.
5 My wounds are foul *and* festering
Because of my foolishness.
6 I am troubled, I am bowed down greatly;
I go mourning all the day long.
7 For my loins are full of inflammation,
And *there is* no soundness in my flesh.
8 I am feeble and severely broken;
I groan because of the turmoil of my heart.
9 Lord, all my desire *is* before You;
And my sighing is not hidden from You.
10 My heart pants, my strength fails me;
As for the light of my eyes, it also has gone from me.
11 My loved ones and my friends stand aloof from my plague,
And my relatives stand afar off.
12 Those also who seek my life lay snares *for me;*
Those who seek my hurt speak of destruction,
And plan deception all the day long.
13 But I, like a deaf *man,* do not hear;
And *I am* like a mute *who* does not open his mouth.
14 Thus I am like a man who does not hear,
And in whose mouth *is* no response.
15 For in You, O LORD, I hope;
You will hear, O Lord my God.
16 For I said, "*Hear me,* lest they rejoice over me,
Lest, when my foot slips, they exalt *themselves* against me."
17 For I *am* ready to fall,
And my sorrow *is* continually before me.
18 For I will declare my iniquity;
I will be in anguish over my sin.
19 But my enemies *are* vigorous, *and* they are strong;
And those who hate me wrongfully have multiplied.
20 Those also who render evil for good,
They are my adversaries, because I follow *what is* good.
21 Do not forsake me, O LORD;
O my God, be not far from me!
22 Make haste to help me,
O Lord, my salvation!

PSALM 39

Prayer for Wisdom and Forgiveness

To the Chief Musician. To Jeduthun. A Psalm of David.

1 I said, "I will guard my ways, ➤
Lest I sin with my tongue;
I will restrain my mouth with a muzzle,
While the wicked are before me."
2 I was mute with silence,
I held my peace *even* from good;
And my sorrow was stirred up.
3 My heart was hot within me;
While I was musing, the fire burned.
Then I spoke with my tongue:
4 "LORD, make me to know my end,
And what *is* the measure of my days,
That I may know how frail I *am.*
5 Indeed, You have made my days *as* handbreadths,
And my age *is* as nothing before You;
Certainly every man at his best state *is* but vapor. Selah
6 Surely every man walks about like a shadow;
Surely they busy themselves in vain;
He heaps up *riches,*
And does not know who will gather them.
7 "And now, Lord, what do I wait for?
My hope *is* in You.
8 Deliver me from all my transgressions;
Do not make me the reproach of the foolish.
9 I was mute, I did not open my mouth,
Because it was You who did *it.*

LIFE LESSONS

➤ 38:4 — *For my iniquities have gone over my head; like a heavy burden they are too heavy for me.*

God knows that our sins weigh us down and keep us from God's best. When we confess them, we take them off our shoulders and place them on His. Only then can we walk with heads upright once more.

➤ 39:1 — *I said, "I will guard my ways, lest I sin with my tongue; I will restrain my mouth with a muzzle, while the wicked are before me."*

We should always watch carefully how we speak, but we must take special caution when in the presence of unbelievers. Let us never give them any reason to reject God because of ungodly things we say.

10 Remove Your plague from me;
I am consumed by the blow of Your hand.
➤ 11 When with rebukes You correct man for iniquity,
You make his beauty melt away like a moth;
Surely every man *is* vapor. Selah

12 "Hear my prayer, O LORD,
And give ear to my cry;
Do not be silent at my tears;
For I *am* a stranger with You,
A sojourner, as all my fathers *were*.
13 Remove Your gaze from me, that I may regain strength,
Before I go away and am no more."

PSALM 40

Faith Persevering in Trial

To the Chief Musician. A Psalm of David.

➤ 1 I waited patiently for the LORD;
And He inclined to me,
And heard my cry.
2 He also brought me up out of a horrible pit,
Out of the miry clay,
And set my feet upon a rock,
And established my steps.
3 He has put a new song in my mouth—
Praise to our God;
Many will see *it* and fear,
And will trust in the LORD.

4 Blessed *is* that man who makes the LORD his trust,
And does not respect the proud, nor such as turn aside to lies.
5 Many, O LORD my God, *are* Your wonderful works
Which You have done;
And Your thoughts toward us
Cannot be recounted to You in order;
If I would declare and speak *of them*,
They are more than can be numbered.

6 Sacrifice and offering You did not desire;
My ears You have opened.
Burnt offering and sin offering You did not require.
7 Then I said, "Behold, I come;
In the scroll of the book *it is* written of me.
8 I delight to do Your will, O my God, ➤
And Your law *is* within my heart."

9 I have proclaimed the good news of righteousness
In the great assembly;
Indeed, I do not restrain my lips,
O LORD, You Yourself know.
10 I have not hidden Your righteousness within my heart;
I have declared Your faithfulness and Your salvation;
I have not concealed Your lovingkindness and Your truth
From the great assembly.

11 Do not withhold Your tender mercies from me, O LORD;
Let Your lovingkindness and Your truth continually preserve me.
12 For innumerable evils have surrounded me;
My iniquities have overtaken me, so that I am not able to look up;
They are more than the hairs of my head;
Therefore my heart fails me.
13 Be pleased, O LORD, to deliver me;
O LORD, make haste to help me!
14 Let them be ashamed and brought to mutual confusion
Who seek to destroy my life;
Let them be driven backward and brought to dishonor
Who wish me evil.
15 Let them be confounded because of their shame,
Who say to me, "Aha, aha!"

16 Let all those who seek You rejoice and be glad in You;
Let such as love Your salvation say continually,
"The LORD be magnified!"
17 But I *am* poor and needy;
Yet the LORD thinks upon me.
You *are* my help and my deliverer;
Do not delay, O my God.

LIFE LESSONS

➤ **39:11 — *. . . surely every man is vapor.***

Life passes with lightning speed. We are on this earth for only a short time, so we must be diligent to live wisely and well. We may appear before God tomorrow—so let us live for Him today.

➤ **40:1 — *I waited patiently for the LORD; and He inclined to me, and heard my cry.***

Waiting is just a fact of life when it comes to our prayer lives. Sometimes God answers prayer immediately, but other times He makes us wait to see the answer. When we wait for Him, we show that we trust Him.

➤ **40:8 — *I delight to do Your will, O my God, and Your law is within my heart.***

God isn't seeking men and women who will obey Him grudgingly and reluctantly and resentfully. He desires children who will delight to obey Him, who find pleasure in living out the commands that reflect His heart.

PSALM 41

The Blessing and Suffering of the Godly

To the Chief Musician. A Psalm of David.

1 Blessed *is* he who considers the poor;
The LORD will deliver him in time of trouble.
2 The LORD will preserve him and keep him alive,
And he will be blessed on the earth;
You will not deliver him to the will of his enemies.
3 The LORD will strengthen him on his bed of illness;
You will sustain him on his sickbed.

4 I said, "LORD, be merciful to me;
Heal my soul, for I have sinned against You."
5 My enemies speak evil of me:
"When will he die, and his name perish?"
6 And if he comes to see *me,* he speaks lies;
His heart gathers iniquity to itself;
When he goes out, he tells *it.*
7 All who hate me whisper together against me;
Against me they devise my hurt.
8 "An evil disease," *they say,* "clings to him.
And *now* that he lies down, he will rise up no more."
9 Even my own familiar friend in whom I trusted,
Who ate my bread,
Has lifted up *his* heel against me.
10 But You, O LORD, be merciful to me, and raise me up,
That I may repay them.
11 By this I know that You are well pleased with me,
Because my enemy does not triumph over me.
12 As for me, You uphold me in my integrity,
And set me before Your face forever.

13 Blessed *be* the LORD God of Israel
From everlasting to everlasting!
Amen and Amen.

Book Two: Psalms 42—72

PSALM 42

Yearning for God in the Midst of Distresses

To the Chief Musician. A Contemplation[a] of the sons of Korah.

1 As the deer pants for the water brooks,
So pants my soul for You, O God.
2 My soul thirsts for God, for the living God.
When shall I come and appear before God?[a]
3 My tears have been my food day and night,
While they continually say to me,
"Where *is* your God?"

4 When I remember these *things,*
I pour out my soul within me.
For I used to go with the multitude;
I went with them to the house of God,
With the voice of joy and praise,
With a multitude that kept a pilgrim feast.

5 Why are you cast down, O my soul?
And *why* are you disquieted within me?
Hope in God, for I shall yet praise Him
For the help of His countenance.[a]

6 O my God,[a] my soul is cast down within me;
Therefore I will remember You from the land of the Jordan,
And from the heights of Hermon,
From the Hill Mizar.
7 Deep calls unto deep at the noise of Your waterfalls;
All Your waves and billows have gone over me.
8 The LORD will command His lovingkindness in the daytime,
And in the night His song *shall be* with me—
A prayer to the God of my life.

42:title [a]Hebrew *Maschil* **42:2** [a]Following Masoretic Text and Vulgate; some Hebrew manuscripts, Septuagint, Syriac, and Targum read *I see the face of God.* **42:5** [a]Following Masoretic Text and Targum; a few Hebrew manuscripts, Septuagint, Syriac, and Vulgate read *The help of my countenance, my God.* **42:6** [a]Following Masoretic Text and Targum; a few Hebrew manuscripts, Septuagint, Syriac, and Vulgate put *my God* at the end of verse 5.

LIFE LESSONS

➤ 41:3 — *The LORD will strengthen him on his bed of illness; You will sustain him on his sickbed.*

In this fallen world, we all get sick at some point. Some struggle with it often, some not much at all. But whenever we fall ill, God invites us to trust Him for strength and to pray for recovery.

➤ 41:9 — *Even my own familiar friend in whom I trusted, who ate my bread, has lifted up his heel against me.*

Jesus applied this verse to Judas Iscariot as a fulfillment of biblical prophecy (John 13:18). Just because someone says, "Lord, Lord," that does not mean they have a genuine relationship with God (Matt. 7:21).

➤ 42:1 — *As the deer pants for the water brooks, so pants my soul for You, O God.*

God's highest priority for our lives is to develop an intimate and growing relationship with Him. He made us to thirst for Him as we thirst for water and to seek Him as we seek relief from a parched throat.

9 I will say to God my Rock,
"Why have You forgotten me?
Why do I go mourning because of the oppression of the enemy?"
10 *As* with a breaking of my bones,
My enemies reproach me,
While they say to me all day long,
"Where *is* your God?"
➤ 11 Why are you cast down, O my soul?
And why are you disquieted within me?
Hope in God;
For I shall yet praise Him,
The help of my countenance and my God.

PSALM 43

Prayer to God in Time of Trouble

1 Vindicate me, O God,
And plead my cause against an ungodly nation;
Oh, deliver me from the deceitful and unjust man!
2 For You *are* the God of my strength;
Why do You cast me off?
Why do I go mourning because of the oppression of the enemy?
➤ 3 Oh, send out Your light and Your truth!
Let them lead me;
Let them bring me to Your holy hill
And to Your tabernacle.
4 Then I will go to the altar of God,
To God my exceeding joy;
And on the harp I will praise You,
O God, my God.
5 Why are you cast down, O my soul?
And why are you disquieted within me?
Hope in God;
For I shall yet praise Him,
The help of my countenance and my God.

PSALM 44

Redemption Remembered in Present Dishonor

To the Chief Musician. A Contemplation[a] of the sons of Korah.

1 We have heard with our ears, O God,
Our fathers have told us,
The deeds You did in their days,
In days of old:
2 You drove out the nations with Your hand,
But them You planted;
You afflicted the peoples, and cast them out.
3 For they did not gain possession of the land by their own sword,
Nor did their own arm save them;
But it was Your right hand, Your arm, and the light of Your countenance,
Because You favored them.
4 You are my King, O God;[a]
Command[b] victories for Jacob.
5 Through You we will push down our enemies;
Through Your name we will trample those who rise up against us.
6 For I will not trust in my bow, ➤
Nor shall my sword save me.
7 But You have saved us from our enemies, ➤
And have put to shame those who hated us.
8 In God we boast all day long,
And praise Your name forever. Selah
9 But You have cast *us* off and put us to shame,
And You do not go out with our armies.
10 You make us turn back from the enemy,
And those who hate us have taken spoil for themselves.
11 You have given us up like sheep *intended* for food,
And have scattered us among the nations.
12 You sell Your people for *next to* nothing,
And are not enriched by selling them.
13 You make us a reproach to our neighbors,
A scorn and a derision to those all around us.
14 You make us a byword among the nations,
A shaking of the head among the peoples.

44:title [a]Hebrew *Maschil* **44:4** [a]Following Masoretic Text and Targum; Septuagint and Vulgate read *and my God.* [b]Following Masoretic Text and Targum; Septuagint, Syriac, and Vulgate read *Who commands.*

LIFE LESSONS

➤ 42:11 — *Why are you cast down, O my soul? And why are you disquieted within me? Hope in God; for I shall yet praise Him . . . .*

Sometimes we do not even know why we feel discouraged or down or sad. It is good at those times to consciously put our hope in God, to draw on His strength, and to anticipate the grace He will show us.

➤ 43:3 — *Oh, send out Your light and Your truth! Let them lead me; let them bring me to Your holy hill and to Your tabernacle.*

One of the ways God draws us to Himself is by leading us to worship Him with His people. His Word consistently encourages us to gather with other believers to hear His truth and to praise Him together.

➤ 44:6, 7 — *For I will not trust in my bow, nor shall my sword save me. But You have saved us from our enemies, and have put to shame those who hated us.*

Regardless of the resources God gives us, we must not trust in them for success, but we must put our hope in Him alone. We should ask Him how to use those resources, but never count on them for deliverance.

15 My dishonor *is* continually before me,
And the shame of my face has covered me,
16 Because of the voice of him who reproaches and reviles,
Because of the enemy and the avenger.

17 All this has come upon us;
But we have not forgotten You,
Nor have we dealt falsely with Your covenant.
18 Our heart has not turned back,
Nor have our steps departed from Your way;
19 But You have severely broken us in the place of jackals,
And covered us with the shadow of death.

20 If we had forgotten the name of our God,
Or stretched out our hands to a foreign god,
21 Would not God search this out?
For He knows the secrets of the heart.
➤ 22 Yet for Your sake we are killed all day long;
We are accounted as sheep for the slaughter.

23 Awake! Why do You sleep, O Lord?
Arise! Do not cast *us* off forever.
24 Why do You hide Your face,
And forget our affliction and our oppression?
25 For our soul is bowed down to the dust;
Our body clings to the ground.
26 Arise for our help,
And redeem us for Your mercies' sake.

PSALM 45

The Glories of the Messiah and His Bride

To the Chief Musician. Set to "The Lilies."[a] A Contemplation[b] of the sons of Korah. A Song of Love.

1 My heart is overflowing with a good theme;
I recite my composition concerning the King;
My tongue *is* the pen of a ready writer.

2 You are fairer than the sons of men;
Grace is poured upon Your lips;
Therefore God has blessed You forever.

3 Gird Your sword upon *Your* thigh, O Mighty One,
With Your glory and Your majesty.
4 And in Your majesty ride prosperously because of truth, humility, *and* righteousness;
And Your right hand shall teach You awesome things.
5 Your arrows *are* sharp in the heart of the King's enemies;
The peoples fall under You.

6 Your throne, O God, *is* forever and ever;
A scepter of righteousness *is* the scepter of Your kingdom.
7 You love righteousness and hate wickedness;
Therefore God, Your God, has anointed You
With the oil of gladness more than Your companions.
8 All Your garments *are scented* with myrrh and aloes and cassia,
Out of the ivory palaces, by which they have made You glad.
9 Kings' daughters *are* among Your honorable women;
At Your right hand stands the queen in gold from Ophir.

10 Listen, O daughter,
Consider and incline your ear;
Forget your own people also, and your father's house;
11 So the King will greatly desire your beauty;
Because He *is* your Lord, worship Him.
12 And the daughter of Tyre *will come* with a gift;
The rich among the people will seek your favor.

13 The royal daughter *is* all glorious within *the palace;*
Her clothing *is* woven with gold.
14 She shall be brought to the King in robes of many colors;
The virgins, her companions who follow her, shall be brought to You.
15 With gladness and rejoicing they shall be brought;
They shall enter the King's palace.

45:title [a]Hebrew *Shoshannim* [b]Hebrew *Maschil*

LIFE LESSONS

➤ 44:22 — *Yet for Your sake we are killed all day long; we are accounted as sheep for the slaughter.*

Paul quotes this unsettling verse in the middle of a passage extolling God's love (Rom. 8:36). Why? Because he wanted us to know that even in the worst of circumstances, God's love for us remains unchanged.

➤ 45:7 — *You love righteousness and hate wickedness; therefore God, Your God, has anointed You with the oil of gladness more than Your companions.*

It really is *not* more fun to do evil than to do good. When we willingly obey God, He rewards our obedience with "the oil of gladness," a satisfaction and joy that penetrates all the way to the heart.

16 Instead of Your fathers shall be Your sons,
Whom You shall make princes in all the earth.
17 I will make Your name to be remembered in all generations;
Therefore the people shall praise You forever and ever.

PSALM 46

God the Refuge of His People and Conqueror of the Nations

To the Chief Musician. *A Psalm* of the sons of Korah. A Song for Alamoth.

➤ 1 God *is* our refuge and strength,
A very present help in trouble.
➤ 2 Therefore we will not fear,
Even though the earth be removed,
And though the mountains be carried into the midst of the sea;
3 *Though* its waters roar *and* be troubled,
Though the mountains shake with its swelling. Selah

4 *There is* a river whose streams shall make glad the city of God,
The holy *place* of the tabernacle of the Most High.
5 God *is* in the midst of her, she shall not be moved;
God shall help her, just at the break of dawn.
6 The nations raged, the kingdoms were moved;
He uttered His voice, the earth melted.
7 The LORD of hosts *is* with us;
The God of Jacob *is* our refuge. Selah
8 Come, behold the works of the LORD,
Who has made desolations in the earth.
9 He makes wars cease to the end of the earth;
He breaks the bow and cuts the spear in two;
He burns the chariot in the fire.
➤ 10 Be still, and know that I *am* God;
I will be exalted among the nations,
I will be exalted in the earth!

11 The LORD of hosts *is* with us;
The God of Jacob *is* our refuge. Selah

PSALM 47

Praise to God, the Ruler of the Earth

To the Chief Musician. A Psalm of the sons of Korah.

1 Oh, clap your hands, all you peoples!
Shout to God with the voice of triumph!
2 For the LORD Most High *is* awesome;
He is a great King over all the earth.
3 He will subdue the peoples under us,
And the nations under our feet.
4 He will choose our inheritance for us,
The excellence of Jacob whom He loves. Selah

5 God has gone up with a shout,
The LORD with the sound of a trumpet.
6 Sing praises to God, sing praises!
Sing praises to our King, sing praises!
7 For God *is* the King of all the earth; ➤
Sing praises with understanding.

8 God reigns over the nations;
God sits on His holy throne.
9 The princes of the people have gathered together,
The people of the God of Abraham.
For the shields of the earth *belong* to God;
He is greatly exalted.

PSALM 48

The Glory of God in Zion

A Song. A Psalm of the sons of Korah.

1 Great *is* the LORD, and greatly to be praised
In the city of our God,
In His holy mountain.
2 Beautiful in elevation,
The joy of the whole earth,
Is Mount Zion *on* the sides of the north,
The city of the great King.
3 God *is* in her palaces;
He is known as her refuge.

4 For behold, the kings assembled,
They passed by together.
5 They saw *it, and* so they marveled;
They were troubled, they hastened away.
6 Fear took hold of them there,
And pain, as of a woman in birth pangs,

LIFE LESSONS

➤ 46:1, 2 — *God is our refuge and strength, a very present help in trouble. Therefore we will not fear, even though the earth be removed, and though the mountains be carried into the midst of the sea . . . .*

On some days, the earth *is* removed; some days, the mountains *are* carried into the midst of the sea. But if we put our hope in God, we have no need to fear, because we have a refuge that can never be moved.

➤ 46:10 — *Be still, and know that I am God . . . .*

Only in the rarest of circumstances, and then usually in judgment, does God display His glory in blinding flashes impossible to ignore. Most of the time, we meet Him in the quietness of our hearts.

➤ 47:7 — *For God is the King of all the earth; sing praises with understanding.*

Are hymns better than praise songs? Are choruses superior to cantatas? We weary ourselves with foolish questions, when we should be asking, "Am I growing in my understanding of God through my worship?"

WHAT THE BIBLE SAYS ABOUT CONFIDENCE IN TIMES OF DISTRESS

Ps. 46:1–11

"I'm out of here!" Most of us feel this way at some point in our lives. When stress in daily living becomes unbearable, we want to escape. We may want out of jobs, relationships, a church, a neighborhood, or some other difficult situation. We think we can't handle things the way they are because they cause us too much stress, so we decide to walk away. Move on. Head for anywhere but where we are.

What does the Bible have to tell us about how to handle stress? How are we to respond when our fallen human natures cry out for us to stop and run?

God has a powerful truth for us to hear. We do not handle stressful situations by fighting against them; instead, God calls us to be at rest in Him. To the psalmist, this meant being still and knowing God (Ps. 46:10). To the apostle Peter, it meant refusing to carry burdens not meant for him: "casting all your care upon Him, for He cares for you" (1 Pet. 5:7). Jesus described it as a peacefulness that we both find and receive as we spend time learning from Him (Matt. 11:28–30). Our human instinct clamors for us to escape—but God calls us to draw near and absorb the truths of Scripture.

God calls us to be at rest in Him.

Most of all, the Lord wants us to know Him. As we believe in His sovereignty (1 Chr. 29:11) and accept both the absolute goodness of His plans (Jer. 29:11) and His deep, abiding love for us (Eph. 3:17–19), we will grow in trust. Then we will find it easier to "be still" and not to respond like the world, which says "I'm out of here!"

Our stress need not become *dis*tress. When we feel stress, we do not have to feel defeated and give in to the temptation to give up and run. With an accurate understanding of our heavenly Father and a firm belief in His care, we will be able to walk through the worst of circumstances with inner quietness (Gal. 5:22) and genuine confidence (Heb. 13:6).

That is our privilege as God's children.

See the Life Principles Index for further study:
12. Peace with God is the fruit of oneness with God.

7 *As when* You break the ships of Tarshish
With an east wind.
8 As we have heard,
So we have seen
In the city of the LORD of hosts,
In the city of our God:
God will establish it forever. Selah
9 We have thought, O God, on Your lovingkindness,
In the midst of Your temple.
➤ 10 According to Your name, O God,
So *is* Your praise to the ends of the earth;
Your right hand is full of righteousness.
11 Let Mount Zion rejoice,
Let the daughters of Judah be glad,
Because of Your judgments.
12 Walk about Zion,
And go all around her.
Count her towers;
13 Mark well her bulwarks;
Consider her palaces;
That you may tell *it* to the generation following.
✳ 14 For this *is* God,
Our God forever and ever;
He will be our guide
Even to death.[a]

PSALM 49

The Confidence of the Foolish

To the Chief Musician. A Psalm of the sons of Korah.

1 Hear this, all peoples;
Give ear, all inhabitants of the world,
2 Both low and high,
Rich and poor together.
3 My mouth shall speak wisdom,
And the meditation of my heart *shall give* understanding.
4 I will incline my ear to a proverb;
I will disclose my dark saying on the harp.
5 Why should I fear in the days of evil,
When the iniquity at my heels surrounds me?
6 Those who trust in their wealth
And boast in the multitude of their riches,
7 None *of them* can by any means redeem *his* brother,
Nor give to God a ransom for him—
8 For the redemption of their souls *is* costly,
And it shall cease forever—
9 That he should continue to live eternally,
And not see the Pit.
10 For he sees wise men die;
Likewise the fool and the senseless person perish,
And leave their wealth to others.
11 Their inner thought *is that* their houses *will last* forever,[a]
Their dwelling places to all generations;
They call *their* lands after their own names.
12 Nevertheless man, *though* in honor, does not remain;[a]
He is like the beasts *that* perish.
13 This is the way of those who *are* foolish,
And of their posterity who approve their sayings. Selah
14 Like sheep they are laid in the grave;
Death shall feed on them;
The upright shall have dominion over them in the morning;
And their beauty shall be consumed in the grave, far from their dwelling.
15 But God will redeem my soul from the power of the grave, ➤
For He shall receive me. Selah
16 Do not be afraid when one becomes rich,
When the glory of his house is increased;
17 For when he dies he shall carry nothing away;
His glory shall not descend after him.
18 Though while he lives he blesses himself
(For *men* will praise you when you do well for yourself),

48:14 [a]Following Masoretic Text and Syriac; Septuagint and Vulgate read *Forever.* **49:11** [a]Septuagint, Syriac, Targum, and Vulgate read *Their graves shall be their houses forever.*
49:12 [a]Following Masoretic Text and Targum; Septuagint, Syriac, and Vulgate read *understand* (compare verse 20).

LIFE LESSONS

➤ 48:10 — *According to Your name, O God, so is Your praise to the ends of the earth . . . .*

God deserves our very best praise and worship, for He has the very best name in all of the universe. The style never matters so much as the heart: Regardless of what we sing, do we bring to Him our best?

➤ 49:15 — *But God will redeem my soul from the power of the grave, for He shall receive me.*

Death will overtake all of us, unless we are still alive when Jesus comes back. But one day, God will break the power of death over us and bring us into fullness of life, for He will receive us in Jesus' name.

19 He shall go to the generation of his
fathers;
They shall never see light.
➤ 20 A man *who is* in honor, yet does not
understand,
Is like the beasts *that* perish.

PSALM 50

God the Righteous Judge

A Psalm of Asaph.

1 The Mighty One, God the LORD,
Has spoken and called the earth
From the rising of the sun to its going
down.
2 Out of Zion, the perfection of beauty,
God will shine forth.
➤ 3 Our God shall come, and shall not keep
silent;
A fire shall devour before Him,
And it shall be very tempestuous all
around Him.

4 He shall call to the heavens from above,
And to the earth, that He may judge His
people:
5 "Gather My saints together to Me,
Those who have made a covenant with
Me by sacrifice."
6 Let the heavens declare His
righteousness,
For God Himself *is* Judge. Selah

7 "Hear, O My people, and I will speak,
O Israel, and I will testify against you;
I *am* God, your God!
8 I will not rebuke you for your sacrifices
Or your burnt offerings,
Which are continually before Me.
9 I will not take a bull from your house,
Nor goats out of your folds.
10 For every beast of the forest *is* Mine,
And the cattle on a thousand hills.
11 I know all the birds of the mountains,
And the wild beasts of the field *are*
Mine.

➤ 12 "If I were hungry, I would not tell you;
For the world *is* Mine, and all its
fullness.
13 Will I eat the flesh of bulls,
Or drink the blood of goats?
14 Offer to God thanksgiving,
And pay your vows to the Most High.
15 Call upon Me in the day of trouble;
I will deliver you, and you shall glorify
Me." ✳

16 But to the wicked God says:
"What *right* have you to declare My
statutes,
Or take My covenant in your mouth,
17 Seeing you hate instruction
And cast My words behind you?
18 When you saw a thief, you consented[a]
with him,
And have been a partaker with
adulterers.
19 You give your mouth to evil,
And your tongue frames deceit.
20 You sit *and* speak against your brother;
You slander your own mother's son.
21 These *things* you have done, and I kept
silent;
You thought that I was altogether like
you;
But I will rebuke you,
And set *them* in order before your
eyes.

22 "Now consider this, you who forget God,
Lest I tear *you* in pieces,
And *there be* none to deliver:
23 Whoever offers praise glorifies Me;
And to him who orders *his* conduct
aright
I will show the salvation of God."

PSALM 51

A Prayer of Repentance

To the Chief Musician. A Psalm of David when Nathan the prophet went to him, after he had gone in to Bathsheba.

1 Have mercy upon me, O God,
According to Your lovingkindness;
According to the multitude of Your
tender mercies,
Blot out my transgressions.
2 Wash me thoroughly from my iniquity,
And cleanse me from my sin.

50:18 [a]Septuagint, Syriac, Targum, and Vulgate read *ran.*

LIFE LESSONS

➤ **49:20 —** ***A man who is in honor, yet does not understand, is like the beasts that perish.***

Amassing a fortune or winning the admiration of millions counts for exactly nothing on the eternal scale if the person in question does not know the Lord.

➤ **50:3 —** ***Our God shall come, and shall not keep silent; a fire shall devour before Him, and it shall be very tempestuous all around Him.***

When Jesus comes again, He will arrive "with His mighty angels, in flaming fire taking vengeance on those who do not know God, and on those who do not obey the gospel of our Lord Jesus Christ" (1 Thess. 1:7, 8).

➤ **50:12 —** ***"If I were hungry, I would not tell you; for the world is Mine, and all its fullness."***

If anyone said this but God, we would consider Him arrogant. God has no needs, and we do not make up for any divine deficiencies through our service. But because He loves us, He invites us to serve Him.

3 For I acknowledge my transgressions,
And my sin *is* always before me.
➤ 4 Against You, You only, have I sinned,
And done *this* evil in Your sight—
That You may be found just when You speak,[a]
And blameless when You judge.

5 Behold, I was brought forth in iniquity,
And in sin my mother conceived me.
6 Behold, You desire truth in the inward parts,
And in the hidden *part* You will make me to know wisdom.

7 Purge me with hyssop, and I shall be clean;
Wash me, and I shall be whiter than snow.
8 Make me hear joy and gladness,
That the bones You have broken may rejoice.
9 Hide Your face from my sins,
And blot out all my iniquities.

10 Create in me a clean heart, O God,
And renew a steadfast spirit within me.
11 Do not cast me away from Your presence,
And do not take Your Holy Spirit from me.

➤ 12 Restore to me the joy of Your salvation,
And uphold me *by Your* generous Spirit.
13 *Then* I will teach transgressors Your ways,
And sinners shall be converted to You.

14 Deliver me from the guilt of bloodshed, O God,
The God of my salvation,
And my tongue shall sing aloud of Your righteousness.
15 O Lord, open my lips,
And my mouth shall show forth Your praise.
16 For You do not desire sacrifice, or else I would give *it;*
You do not delight in burnt offering.
17 The sacrifices of God *are* a broken spirit,
A broken and a contrite heart—
These, O God, You will not despise.

18 Do good in Your good pleasure to Zion;
Build the walls of Jerusalem.
19 Then You shall be pleased with the sacrifices of righteousness,
With burnt offering and whole burnt offering;
Then they shall offer bulls on Your altar.

PSALM 52

The End of the Wicked and the Peace of the Godly

To the Chief Musician. A Contemplation[a] of David when Doeg the Edomite went and told Saul, and said to him, "David has gone to the house of Ahimelech."

1 Why do you boast in evil, O mighty man?
The goodness of God *endures* continually.
2 Your tongue devises destruction,
Like a sharp razor, working deceitfully.
3 You love evil more than good,
Lying rather than speaking righteousness. Selah
4 You love all devouring words,
You deceitful tongue.

5 God shall likewise destroy you forever;
He shall take you away, and pluck you out of *your* dwelling place,
And uproot you from the land of the living. Selah
6 The righteous also shall see and fear,
And shall laugh at him, *saying,*
7 "Here is the man *who* did not make God his strength, ➤
But trusted in the abundance of his riches,
And strengthened himself in his wickedness."

51:4 [a]Septuagint, Targum, and Vulgate read *in Your words.*
52:title [a]Hebrew *Maschil*

LIFE LESSONS

➤ **51:4 — *Against You, You only, have I sinned, and done this evil in Your sight—that You may be found just when You speak, and blameless when You judge.***

David had sinned against Uriah by committing adultery with his wife and plotting his murder. He had sinned against Bathsheba. He had sinned against his people. Yet *all* sin is ultimately against God and requires His forgiveness.

➤ **51:12 — *Restore to me the joy of Your salvation, and uphold me by Your generous Spirit.***

Although we can never lose our salvation once we genuinely come to Christ by faith, we can lose the *joy* of our salvation through our sin. Only through confession and reliance on His Spirit can we return to joy.

➤ **52:7 — *"Here is the man who did not make God his strength, but trusted in the abundance of his riches, and strengthened himself in his wickedness."***

Is God your strength? When threats appear, do you run to your resources or to the Lord? Has your success made you humble or arrogant? How would your associates answer that question?

➤ 8 But I *am* like a green olive tree in the house of God;
I trust in the mercy of God forever and ever.
9 I will praise You forever,
Because You have done *it;*
And in the presence of Your saints
I will wait on Your name, for *it is* good.

PSALM 53

Folly of the Godless, and the Restoration of Israel

To the Chief Musician. Set to "Mahalath." A Contemplation[a] of David.

1 The fool has said in his heart,
"*There is* no God."
They are corrupt, and have done abominable iniquity;
There is none who does good.
2 God looks down from heaven upon the children of men,
To see if there are *any* who understand, who seek God.
3 Every one of them has turned aside;
They have together become corrupt;
There is none who does good,
No, not one.
4 Have the workers of iniquity no knowledge,
Who eat up my people *as* they eat bread,
And do not call upon God?
5 There they are in great fear
Where no fear was,
For God has scattered the bones of him who encamps against you;
You have put *them* to shame,
Because God has despised them.
6 Oh, that the salvation of Israel would come out of Zion!
When God brings back the captivity of His people,
Let Jacob rejoice *and* Israel be glad.

PSALM 54

Answered Prayer for Deliverance from Adversaries

To the Chief Musician. With stringed instruments.[a] A Contemplation[b] of David when the Ziphites went and said to Saul, "Is David not hiding with us?"

1 Save me, O God, by Your name,
And vindicate me by Your strength.
2 Hear my prayer, O God;
Give ear to the words of my mouth.
3 For strangers have risen up against me,
And oppressors have sought after my life;
They have not set God before them. Selah
4 Behold, God *is* my helper;
The Lord *is* with those who uphold my life.
5 He will repay my enemies for their evil.
Cut them off in Your truth.
6 I will freely sacrifice to You; ➤
I will praise Your name, O LORD, for *it is* good.
7 For He has delivered me out of all trouble;
And my eye has seen *its desire* upon my enemies.

PSALM 55

Trust in God Concerning the Treachery of Friends

To the Chief Musician. With stringed instruments.[a] A Contemplation[b] of David.

1 Give ear to my prayer, O God,
And do not hide Yourself from my supplication.
2 Attend to me, and hear me;
I am restless in my complaint, and moan noisily,
3 Because of the voice of the enemy,
Because of the oppression of the wicked;
For they bring down trouble upon me,
And in wrath they hate me.
4 My heart is severely pained within me,
And the terrors of death have fallen upon me.
5 Fearfulness and trembling have come upon me,
And horror has overwhelmed me.
6 So I said, "Oh, that I had wings like a dove! ➤
I would fly away and be at rest.

53:title [a]Hebrew *Maschil* **54:title** [a]Hebrew *neginoth* [b]Hebrew *Maschil* **55:title** [a]Hebrew *neginoth* [b]Hebrew *Maschil*

LIFE LESSONS

➤ 52:8 — *I trust in the mercy of God forever and ever.*

God will never run out of mercy or love or grace. There will never come a day when He will say, "You know what? I'm tired. Come back in a month." Because He never changes, we can have an unchanging hope.

➤ 54:6 — *I will freely sacrifice to You; I will praise Your name, O LORD, for it is good.*

What does it mean to "freely sacrifice" to God? It means that we willingly and gladly put something precious of ours on the line for God, knowing that we can never out give God. No "sacrifice" is ultimately a sacrifice.

7 Indeed, I would wander far off,
And remain in the wilderness. Selah
8 I would hasten my escape
From the windy storm *and* tempest."

9 Destroy, O Lord, *and* divide their tongues,
For I have seen violence and strife in the city.
10 Day and night they go around it on its walls;
Iniquity and trouble *are* also in the midst of it.
11 Destruction *is* in its midst;
Oppression and deceit do not depart from its streets.
12 For *it is* not an enemy *who* reproaches me;
Then I could bear *it*.
Nor *is it* one *who* hates me who has exalted *himself* against me;
Then I could hide from him.
13 But *it was* you, a man my equal,
My companion and my acquaintance.
14 We took sweet counsel together,
And walked to the house of God in the throng.

15 Let death seize them;
Let them go down alive into hell,
For wickedness *is* in their dwellings *and* among them.

16 As for me, I will call upon God,
And the LORD shall save me.
17 Evening and morning and at noon
I will pray, and cry aloud,
And He shall hear my voice.
18 He has redeemed my soul in peace from the battle *that was* against me,
For there were many against me.
19 God will hear, and afflict them,
Even He who abides from of old. Selah
Because they do not change,
Therefore they do not fear God.

20 He has put forth his hands against those who were at peace with him;
He has broken his covenant.
21 *The words* of his mouth were smoother than butter,
But war *was* in his heart;
His words were softer than oil,
Yet they *were* drawn swords.

22 Cast your burden on the LORD,
And He shall sustain you;
He shall never permit the righteous to be moved.

23 But You, O God, shall bring them down to the pit of destruction;
Bloodthirsty and deceitful men shall not live out half their days;
But I will trust in You.

PSALM 56

Prayer for Relief from Tormentors

To the Chief Musician. Set to "The Silent Dove in Distant Lands."[a] A Michtam of David when the Philistines captured him in Gath.

1 Be merciful to me, O God, for man would swallow me up;
Fighting all day he oppresses me.
2 My enemies would hound *me* all day,
For *there are* many who fight against me, O Most High.

3 Whenever I am afraid,
I will trust in You.
4 In God (I will praise His word),
In God I have put my trust;
I will not fear.
What can flesh do to me?
5 All day they twist my words;
All their thoughts *are* against me for evil.
6 They gather together,
They hide, they mark my steps,
When they lie in wait for my life.
7 Shall they escape by iniquity?
In anger cast down the peoples, O God!
8 You number my wanderings;
Put my tears into Your bottle;
Are they not in Your book?
9 When I cry out *to You*,
Then my enemies will turn back;
This I know, because God *is* for me.
10 In God (I will praise *His* word),
In the LORD (I will praise *His* word),
11 In God I have put my trust;

56:title [a]Hebrew *Jonath Elem Rechokim*

LIFE LESSONS

➤ 55:6 — *So I said, "Oh, that I had wings like a dove! I would fly away and be at rest."*

When the walls close in and the floor gives way, we often wish we could be anywhere but where God has put us. Trusting God, however, means looking beyond what we can see to what God sees.

➤ 56:3 — *Whenever I am afraid, I will trust in You.*

The psalmist does not say, "*if* something ever scares me," he says, "*whenever* I am afraid." Fear is a natural human reaction to danger. God does not tell us to ignore our fears, but to bring them to Him.

➤ 56:11 — *In God I have put my trust; I will not be afraid. What can man do to me?*

Men can do all types of terrible things to believers—but only if our sovereign God so permits. Jesus told Pilate, "You could have no power at all against Me unless it had been given you from above" (John 19:11).

I will not be afraid.
What can man do to me?

12 Vows *made* to You *are binding* upon me, O God;
I will render praises to You,

13 For You have delivered my soul from death.
Have You not *kept* my feet from falling,
That I may walk before God
In the light of the living?

PSALM 57

Prayer for Safety from Enemies

To the Chief Musician. Set to "Do Not Destroy."[a] A Michtam of David when he fled from Saul into the cave.

➤ 1 Be merciful to me, O God, be merciful to me!
For my soul trusts in You;
And in the shadow of Your wings I will make my refuge,
Until *these* calamities have passed by.

2 I will cry out to God Most High,
To God who performs *all things* for me.

3 He shall send from heaven and save me;
He reproaches the one who would swallow me up. Selah
God shall send forth His mercy and His truth.

4 My soul *is* among lions;
I lie *among* the sons of men
Who are set on fire,
Whose teeth *are* spears and arrows,
And their tongue a sharp sword.

5 Be exalted, O God, above the heavens;
Let Your glory *be* above all the earth.

6 They have prepared a net for my steps;
My soul is bowed down;
They have dug a pit before me;
Into the midst of it they *themselves* have fallen. Selah

➤ 7 My heart is steadfast, O God, my heart is steadfast;
I will sing and give praise.

8 Awake, my glory!
Awake, lute and harp!
I will awaken the dawn.

9 I will praise You, O Lord, among the peoples;
I will sing to You among the nations.

10 For Your mercy reaches unto the heavens,
And Your truth unto the clouds.

11 Be exalted, O God, above the heavens;
Let Your glory *be* above all the earth.

PSALM 58

The Just Judgment of the Wicked

To the Chief Musician. Set to "Do Not Destroy."[a] A Michtam of David.

1 Do you indeed speak righteousness, you silent ones?
Do you judge uprightly, you sons of men?

2 No, in heart you work wickedness;
You weigh out the violence of your hands in the earth.

3 The wicked are estranged from the womb;
They go astray as soon as they are born, speaking lies.

4 Their poison *is* like the poison of a serpent;
They are like the deaf cobra *that* stops its ear,

5 Which will not heed the voice of charmers,
Charming ever so skillfully.

6 Break their teeth in their mouth, O God!
Break out the fangs of the young lions, O LORD!

7 Let them flow away as waters *which* run continually;
When he bends *his bow,*
Let his arrows be as if cut in pieces.

8 *Let them be* like a snail which melts away as it goes,
Like a stillborn child of a woman, that they may not see the sun.

9 Before your pots can feel *the burning* thorns,
He shall take them away as with a whirlwind,
As in His living and burning wrath.

57:title [a]Hebrew *Al Tashcheth* **58:title** [a]Hebrew *Al Tashcheth*

LIFE LESSONS

➤ ***57:1 — . . . my soul trusts in You; and in the shadow of Your wings I will make my refuge, until these calamities have passed by.***

Even when God doesn't keep us from calamity, He invites us to make Him our refuge while we pass through the calamity. Adversity is a bridge to a deeper relationship with God.

➤ ***57:7 — My heart is steadfast, O God, my heart is steadfast; I will sing and give praise.***

Our emotions skitter here and there, and our feelings rise and fall. But when through an act of our will we decide to praise our God, the world seems to stop shaking a little.

10 The righteous shall rejoice when he
sees the vengeance;
He shall wash his feet in the blood of
the wicked,
➤ 11 So that men will say,
"Surely *there is* a reward for the
righteous;
Surely He is God who judges in the earth."

PSALM 59

The Assured Judgment of the Wicked

To the Chief Musician. Set to "Do Not Destroy."[a] A Michtam of David when Saul sent men, and they watched the house in order to kill him.

1 Deliver me from my enemies, O my God;
Defend me from those who rise up
against me.
2 Deliver me from the workers of iniquity,
And save me from bloodthirsty men.
3 For look, they lie in wait for my life;
The mighty gather against me,
Not *for* my transgression nor *for* my sin,
O LORD.
4 They run and prepare themselves
through no fault *of mine.*
Awake to help me, and behold!
5 You therefore, O LORD God of hosts, the
God of Israel,
Awake to punish all the nations;
Do not be merciful to any wicked
transgressors. Selah

6 At evening they return,
They growl like a dog,
And go all around the city.
7 Indeed, they belch with their mouth;
Swords *are* in their lips;
For *they say,* "Who hears?"

8 But You, O LORD, shall laugh at them;
You shall have all the nations in derision.
9 I will wait for You, O You his Strength;[a]
For God *is* my defense.
10 My God of mercy[a] shall come to meet me;
God shall let me see *my desire* on my
enemies.

11 Do not slay them, lest my people forget;
Scatter them by Your power,
And bring them down,
O Lord our shield.
12 *For* the sin of their mouth *and* the
words of their lips,
Let them even be taken in their pride,
And for the cursing and lying *which*
they speak.
13 Consume *them* in wrath, consume
them,
That they *may* not *be;*
And let them know that God rules in
Jacob
To the ends of the earth. Selah

14 And at evening they return,
They growl like a dog,
And go all around the city.
15 They wander up and down for food,
And howl[a] if they are not satisfied.
16 But I will sing of Your power;
Yes, I will sing aloud of Your mercy in
the morning;
For You have been my defense
And refuge in the day of my trouble.
17 To You, O my Strength, I will sing
praises;
For God *is* my defense,
My God of mercy.

PSALM 60

Urgent Prayer for the Restored Favor of God

To the Chief Musician. Set to "Lily of the Testimony."[a] A Michtam of David. For teaching. When he fought against Mesopotamia and Syria of Zobah, and Joab returned and killed twelve thousand Edomites in the Valley of Salt.

1 O God, You have cast us off;
You have broken us down;
You have been displeased;
Oh, restore us again!
2 You have made the earth tremble;
You have broken it;
Heal its breaches, for it is shaking.

59:title [a]Hebrew *Al Tashcheth* **59:9** [a]Following Masoretic Text and Syriac; some Hebrew manuscripts, Septuagint, Targum, and Vulgate read *my Strength.* **59:10** [a]Following Qere; some Hebrew manuscripts, Septuagint, and Vulgate read *My God, His mercy;* Kethib, some Hebrew manuscripts and Targum read *O God, my mercy;* Syriac reads *O God, Your mercy.* **59:15** [a]Following Septuagint and Vulgate; Masoretic Text, Syriac, and Targum read *spend the night.* **60:title** [a]Hebrew *Shushan Eduth*

LIFE LESSONS

➤ 58:11 — *"Surely there is a reward for the righteous; surely He is God who judges in the earth."*

Throughout the Bible God promises His obedient people that He will reward their faithfulness, far beyond what their deeds deserve. "My reward is with Me," Jesus says, "to give to every one according to his work" (Rev. 22:12).

➤ 59:16 — *But I will sing of Your power; yes, I will sing aloud of Your mercy in the morning; for You have been my defense and refuge in the day of my trouble.*

Many of us don't have good singing voices, so why should singing play such a prominent role in spiritual growth? The act of singing tends to unite emotions and intellect—and God wants to commune with every part of us.

3 You have shown Your people hard things;
You have made us drink the wine of confusion.

4 You have given a banner to those who fear You,
That it may be displayed because of the truth. Selah
5 That Your beloved may be delivered,
Save *with* Your right hand, and hear me.

6 God has spoken in His holiness:
"I will rejoice;
I will divide Shechem
And measure out the Valley of Succoth.
7 Gilead *is* Mine, and Manasseh *is* Mine;
Ephraim also *is* the helmet for My head;
Judah *is* My lawgiver.
8 Moab *is* My washpot;
Over Edom I will cast My shoe;
Philistia, shout in triumph because of Me."

9 Who will bring me *to* the strong city?
Who will lead me to Edom?
10 *Is it* not You, O God, *who* cast us off?
And You, O God, *who* did not go out with our armies?
11 Give us help from trouble,
For the help of man *is* useless.
➤ 12 Through God we will do valiantly,
For *it is* He *who* shall tread down our enemies.[a]

PSALM 61

Assurance of God's Eternal Protection

To the Chief Musician. On a stringed instrument.[a] *A Psalm* of David.

1 Hear my cry, O God;
Attend to my prayer.
➤ 2 From the end of the earth I will cry to You,
When my heart is overwhelmed;
Lead me to the rock that is higher than I.
3 For You have been a shelter for me,
A strong tower from the enemy.
4 I will abide in Your tabernacle forever;
I will trust in the shelter of Your wings. Selah

5 For You, O God, have heard my vows;
You have given *me* the heritage of those who fear Your name.
6 You will prolong the king's life,
His years as many generations.
7 He shall abide before God forever.
Oh, prepare mercy and truth, *which* may preserve him!

8 So I will sing praise to Your name forever,
That I may daily perform my vows.

PSALM 62

A Calm Resolve to Wait for the Salvation of God

To the Chief Musician. To Jeduthun. A Psalm of David.

1 Truly my soul silently *waits* for God;
From Him *comes* my salvation.
2 He only *is* my rock and my salvation;
He is my defense;
I shall not be greatly moved.

3 How long will you attack a man?
You shall be slain, all of you,
Like a leaning wall and a tottering fence.
4 They only consult to cast *him* down from his high position;
They delight in lies;
They bless with their mouth,
But they curse inwardly. Selah

5 My soul, wait silently for God alone,
For my expectation *is* from Him.
6 He only *is* my rock and my salvation;
He is my defense;
I shall not be moved.
7 In God *is* my salvation and my glory;
The rock of my strength,
And my refuge, *is* in God.

8 Trust in Him at all times, you people;
Pour out your heart before Him;
God *is* a refuge for us. Selah

9 Surely men of low degree *are* a vapor,
Men of high degree *are* a lie;

60:12 [a]Compare verses 5–12 with 108:6–13 **61:title** [a]Hebrew *neginah*

LIFE LESSONS

➤ 60:12 — *Through God we will do valiantly, for it is He who shall tread down our enemies.*

While on our own we can do nothing, through faith in God we can "do valiantly." So Paul said, "I will not dare to speak of any of those things which Christ has not accomplished through me . . ." (Rom. 15:18).

➤ 61:2 — *From the end of the earth I will cry to You, when my heart is overwhelmed; lead me to the rock that is higher than I.*

No matter where in the world we travel, no matter what challenges face us, the Rock of God goes before us, inviting us to hand our troubled emotions to Him. If we will just look up, He will be there.

➤ 62:5 — *My soul, wait silently for God alone, for my expectation is from Him.*

Why does God instruct us to wait "silently" for Him? Why not tell everyone we meet, "I'm waiting on God for something "? Like prayer, waiting on God is not for show; it's deeply personal and intimate (Matt. 6:6).

If they are weighed on the scales,
They *are* altogether *lighter* than vapor.
10 Do not trust in oppression,
Nor vainly hope in robbery;
If riches increase,
Do not set *your* heart *on them.*
11 God has spoken once,
Twice I have heard this:
That power *belongs* to God.
➤ 12 Also to You, O Lord, *belongs* mercy;
For You render to each one according to his work.

PSALM 63

Joy in the Fellowship of God

A Psalm of David when he was in the wilderness of Judah.

➤ 1 O God, You *are* my God;
Early will I seek You;
My soul thirsts for You;
My flesh longs for You
In a dry and thirsty land
Where there is no water.
2 So I have looked for You in the sanctuary,
To see Your power and Your glory.
3 Because Your lovingkindness *is* better than life,
My lips shall praise You.
4 Thus I will bless You while I live;
I will lift up my hands in Your name.
5 My soul shall be satisfied as with marrow and fatness,
And my mouth shall praise *You* with joyful lips.

➤ 6 When I remember You on my bed,
I meditate on You in the *night* watches.
7 Because You have been my help,
Therefore in the shadow of Your wings I will rejoice.
8 My soul follows close behind You;
Your right hand upholds me.

9 But those *who* seek my life, to destroy *it*,
Shall go into the lower parts of the earth.
10 They shall fall by the sword;
They shall be a portion for jackals.

11 But the king shall rejoice in God;
Everyone who swears by Him shall glory;
But the mouth of those who speak lies shall be stopped.

PSALM 64

Oppressed by the Wicked but Rejoicing in the L*ORD*

To the Chief Musician. A Psalm of David.

1 Hear my voice, O God, in my meditation;
Preserve my life from fear of the enemy.
2 Hide me from the secret plots of the wicked, ➤
From the rebellion of the workers of iniquity,
3 Who sharpen their tongue like a sword,
And bend *their bows to shoot* their arrows—bitter words,
4 That they may shoot in secret at the blameless;
Suddenly they shoot at him and do not fear.

5 They encourage themselves *in* an evil matter;
They talk of laying snares secretly;
They say, "Who will see them?"
6 They devise iniquities:
"We have perfected a shrewd scheme."
Both the inward thought and the heart of man are deep.

7 But God shall shoot at them *with* an arrow;
Suddenly they shall be wounded.
8 So He will make them stumble over their own tongue;
All who see them shall flee away.
9 All men shall fear,
And shall declare the work of God;
For they shall wisely consider His doing.

LIFE LESSONS

➤ 62:12 — . . . *You render to each one according to his work.*

Salvation is a gift; rewards are earned. While every true Christian will make it to heaven, not all will receive rewards for faithful service. Some will "suffer loss," yet "will be saved, yet so as through fire" (1 Cor. 3:15).

➤ 63:1 — *O God, You are my God; early will I seek You; my soul thirsts for You; my flesh longs for You in a dry and thirsty land where there is no water.*

Do you long for God as the psalmist did? Do you seek Him "early" and pursue Him throughout your day? Or do you feel satisfied with an hour or two on Sunday? Your answer will determine the impact of your life.

➤ 63:6 — *When I remember You on my bed, I meditate on You in the night watches.*

When God brings a matter to your attention at bedtime, don't ignore it. Pursue it. Ask Him what He wants. To walk in the Spirit is to obey the initial promptings of the Spirit.

➤ 64:2 — *Hide me from the secret plots of the wicked, from the rebellion of the workers of iniquity.*

Believers become targets. Unseen enemies seek to injure us and cause us trouble. God doesn't want us to worry about these things, but to bring them to Him. He knows all about them and knows just how to respond.

10 The righteous shall be glad in the LORD,
and trust in Him.
And all the upright in heart shall glory.

PSALM 65

Praise to God for His Salvation and Providence

To the Chief Musician. A Psalm of David. A Song.

1 Praise is awaiting You, O God, in Zion;
And to You the vow shall be performed.
2 O You who hear prayer,
To You all flesh will come.
✳ 3 Iniquities prevail against me;
As for our transgressions,
You will provide atonement for them.
4 Blessed *is the man* You choose,
And cause to approach *You,*
That he may dwell in Your courts.
We shall be satisfied with the goodness
of Your house,
Of Your holy temple.

➤ 5 *By* awesome deeds in righteousness You
will answer us,
O God of our salvation,
You who are the confidence of all the
ends of the earth,
And of the far-off seas;
6 Who established the mountains by His
strength,
Being clothed with power;
➤ 7 You who still the noise of the seas,
The noise of their waves,
And the tumult of the peoples.
8 They also who dwell in the farthest
parts are afraid of Your signs;
You make the outgoings of the morning
and evening rejoice.
9 You visit the earth and water it,
You greatly enrich it;
The river of God is full of water;
You provide their grain,
For so You have prepared it.
10 You water its ridges abundantly,
You settle its furrows;
You make it soft with showers,
You bless its growth.
11 You crown the year with Your goodness,
And Your paths drip *with* abundance.
12 They drop *on* the pastures of the
wilderness,
And the little hills rejoice on every side.
13 The pastures are clothed with flocks;
The valleys also are covered with grain;
They shout for joy, they also sing.

PSALM 66

Praise to God for His Awesome Works

To the Chief Musician. A Song. A Psalm.

1 Make a joyful shout to God, all the
earth!
2 Sing out the honor of His name;
Make His praise glorious.
3 Say to God,
"How awesome are Your works!
Through the greatness of Your power
Your enemies shall submit themselves
to You.
4 All the earth shall worship You
And sing praises to You;
They shall sing praises *to* Your
name." Selah

5 Come and see the works of God;
He is awesome *in His* doing toward the
sons of men.
6 He turned the sea into dry *land;*
They went through the river on foot.
There we will rejoice in Him.
7 He rules by His power forever;
His eyes observe the nations;
Do not let the rebellious exalt
themselves. Selah

8 Oh, bless our God, you peoples!
And make the voice of His praise to be
heard,
9 Who keeps our soul among the living,
And does not allow our feet to be
moved.
10 For You, O God, have tested us; ➤
You have refined us as silver is refined.
11 You brought us into the net;
You laid affliction on our backs.
12 You have caused men to ride over our
heads;

LIFE LESSONS

➤ 65:5 — *By awesome deeds in righteousness You will answer us; O God of our salvation.*

Some answers to prayer can be described with no better word than "awesome." How has God "awesomely" answered some of your prayers? What "awesome" answer to prayer do you need right now?

➤ 65:7 — *You who still the noise of the seas, the noise of their waves, and the tumult of the peoples.*

During His earthly ministry, Jesus both stilled the raging sea and stilled the angry mob (Mark 4:39; Luke 4:29, 30). And so without saying a word, He demonstrated His divine status as Lord of all.

➤ 66:10 — *For You, O God, have tested us; You have refined us as silver is refined.*

God tests every believer, both to reveal the character of his or her heart and to lead him or her into a deeper relationship with Himself. We tend to learn more in the valley than on the mountaintop.

We went through fire and through water;
But You brought us out to rich *fulfillment*.

13 I will go into Your house with burnt offerings;
I will pay You my vows,
14 Which my lips have uttered
And my mouth has spoken when I was in trouble.
15 I will offer You burnt sacrifices of fat animals,
With the sweet aroma of rams;
I will offer bulls with goats. Selah

16 Come *and* hear, all you who fear God,
And I will declare what He has done for my soul.
17 I cried to Him with my mouth,
And He was extolled with my tongue.
➤ 18 If I regard iniquity in my heart,
The Lord will not hear.
19 *But* certainly God has heard *me;*
He has attended to the voice of my prayer.

20 Blessed *be* God,
Who has not turned away my prayer,
Nor His mercy from me!

PSALM 67

An Invocation and a Doxology

To the Chief Musician. On stringed instruments.[a] A Psalm. A Song.

➤ 1 God be merciful to us and bless us,
And cause His face to shine upon us, Selah
2 That Your way may be known on earth,
Your salvation among all nations.
3 Let the peoples praise You, O God;
Let all the peoples praise You.
4 Oh, let the nations be glad and sing for joy!
For You shall judge the people righteously,
And govern the nations on earth. Selah
5 Let the peoples praise You, O God;
Let all the peoples praise You.
6 *Then* the earth shall yield her increase;
God, our own God, shall bless us.
7 God shall bless us,
And all the ends of the earth shall fear Him.

PSALM 68

The Glory of God in His Goodness to Israel

To the Chief Musician. A Psalm of David. A Song.

1 Let God arise,
Let His enemies be scattered;
Let those also who hate Him flee before Him.
2 As smoke is driven away,
So drive *them* away;
As wax melts before the fire,
So let the wicked perish at the presence of God.
3 But let the righteous be glad;
Let them rejoice before God;
Yes, let them rejoice exceedingly.

4 Sing to God, sing praises to His name;
Extol Him who rides on the clouds,[a]
By His name YAH,
And rejoice before Him.
5 A father of the fatherless, a defender of widows,
Is God in His holy habitation.
6 God sets the solitary in families;
He brings out those who are bound into prosperity;
But the rebellious dwell in a dry *land.*
7 O God, when You went out before Your people,
When You marched through the wilderness, Selah
8 The earth shook;
The heavens also dropped *rain* at the presence of God;
Sinai itself *was moved* at the presence of God, the God of Israel.
9 You, O God, sent a plentiful rain,
Whereby You confirmed Your inheritance,
When it was weary.

67:title [a]Hebrew *neginoth* **68:4** [a]Masoretic Text reads *deserts;* Targum reads *heavens* (compare verse 34 and Isaiah 19:1).

LIFE LESSONS

➤ 66:18 — *If I regard iniquity in my heart, the Lord will not hear.*

If we refuse to admit to some sin, despite the conviction of the Holy Spirit on our heart, we can have no confidence in prayer and no right to expect a divine "yes." God blesses obedience, not stubbornness.

➤ 67:1 — *God be merciful to us and bless us, and cause His face to shine upon us.*

As sinners saved by grace, we all need God's mercy. We all need His blessing. And life goes much better when His face shines upon us. So why not ask Him for all three, as the psalmist did?

➤ 68:6 — *God sets the solitary in families; He brings out those who are bound into prosperity . . . .*

God designed the church to be our greater family. Jesus said, "everyone who has left houses or brothers or sisters or father or mother or wife or children or lands, for My name's sake, shall receive a hundredfold . . . ." (Matt. 19:29).

10 Your congregation dwelt in it;
You, O God, provided from Your goodness for the poor.

11 The Lord gave the word;
Great *was* the company of those who proclaimed *it:*
12 "Kings of armies flee, they flee,
And she who remains at home divides the spoil.
13 Though you lie down among the sheepfolds,
You will be like the wings of a dove covered with silver,
And her feathers with yellow gold."
14 When the Almighty scattered kings in it,
It was *white* as snow in Zalmon.
15 A mountain of God *is* the mountain of Bashan;
A mountain *of many* peaks *is* the mountain of Bashan.
16 Why do you fume with envy, you mountains of *many* peaks?
This is the mountain *which* God desires to dwell in;
Yes, the LORD will dwell *in it* forever.
17 The chariots of God *are* twenty thousand,
Even thousands of thousands;
The Lord is among them *as in* Sinai, in the Holy *Place.*
18 You have ascended on high,
You have led captivity captive;
You have received gifts among men,
Even *from* the rebellious,
That the LORD God might dwell *there.*

➤ 19 Blessed *be* the Lord,
Who daily loads us *with benefits,*
The God of our salvation! Selah
20 Our God *is* the God of salvation;
And to GOD the Lord *belong* escapes from death.
21 But God will wound the head of His enemies,
The hairy scalp of the one who still goes on in his trespasses.
22 The Lord said, "I will bring back from Bashan,
I will bring *them* back from the depths of the sea,
23 That your foot may crush *them*[a] in blood,
And the tongues of your dogs *may have* their portion from *your* enemies."

24 They have seen Your procession, O God,
The procession of my God, my King, into the sanctuary.
25 The singers went before, the players on instruments *followed* after;
Among *them were* the maidens playing timbrels.
26 Bless God in the congregations,
The Lord, from the fountain of Israel.
27 There *is* little Benjamin, their leader,
The princes of Judah *and* their company,
The princes of Zebulun *and* the princes of Naphtali.

28 Your God has commanded[a] your strength;
Strengthen, O God, what You have done for us.
29 Because of Your temple at Jerusalem,
Kings will bring presents to You.
30 Rebuke the beasts of the reeds,
The herd of bulls with the calves of the peoples,
Till everyone submits himself with pieces of silver.
Scatter the peoples *who* delight in war.
31 Envoys will come out of Egypt;
Ethiopia will quickly stretch out her hands to God.

32 Sing to God, you kingdoms of the earth;
Oh, sing praises to the Lord, Selah
33 To Him who rides on the heaven of heavens, *which were* of old!
Indeed, He sends out His voice, a mighty voice.
34 Ascribe strength to God;
His excellence *is* over Israel,
And His strength *is* in the clouds.
35 O God, *You are* more awesome than Your holy places.
The God of Israel *is* He who gives strength and power to *His* people.

Blessed *be* God!

PSALM 69

An Urgent Plea for Help in Trouble

To the Chief Musician. Set to "The Lilies."[a] *A Psalm* of David.

1 Save me, O God!
For the waters have come up to *my* neck.

68:23 [a]Septuagint, Syriac, Targum, and Vulgate read *you may dip your foot.* **68:28** [a]Septuagint, Syriac, Targum, and Vulgate read *Command, O God.* **69:title** [a]Hebrew *Shoshannim*

LIFE LESSONS

➤ ***68:19 — Blessed be the Lord, who daily loads us with benefits, the God of our salvation!***

We will never know how the Lord "loads us with benefits" every day of our lives. We take for granted many of His blessings: life, food, shelter, friends, family, clothes. But we should always praise Him for who He is!

2 I sink in deep mire,
Where *there is* no standing;
I have come into deep waters,
Where the floods overflow me.
3 I am weary with my crying;
My throat is dry;
My eyes fail while I wait for my God.
4 Those who hate me without a cause
Are more than the hairs of my head;
They are mighty who would destroy me,
Being my enemies wrongfully;
Though I have stolen nothing,
I *still* must restore *it.*
5 O God, You know my foolishness;
And my sins are not hidden from You.
➤ 6 Let not those who wait for You, O Lord GOD of hosts, be ashamed because of me;
Let not those who seek You be confounded because of me, O God of Israel.
7 Because for Your sake I have borne reproach;
Shame has covered my face.
8 I have become a stranger to my brothers,
And an alien to my mother's children;
9 Because zeal for Your house has eaten me up,
And the reproaches of those who reproach You have fallen on me.
10 When I wept *and chastened* my soul with fasting,
That became my reproach.
11 I also made sackcloth my garment;
I became a byword to them.
12 Those who sit in the gate speak against me,
And I *am* the song of the drunkards.
13 But as for me, my prayer *is* to You,
O LORD, *in* the acceptable time;
O God, in the multitude of Your mercy,
Hear me in the truth of Your salvation.
14 Deliver me out of the mire,
And let me not sink;
Let me be delivered from those who hate me,
And out of the deep waters.
15 Let not the floodwater overflow me,
Nor let the deep swallow me up;
And let not the pit shut its mouth on me.
16 Hear me, O LORD, for Your lovingkindness *is* good;
Turn to me according to the multitude of Your tender mercies.
17 And do not hide Your face from Your servant,
For I am in trouble;
Hear me speedily.
18 Draw near to my soul, *and* redeem it;
Deliver me because of my enemies.
19 You know my reproach, my shame, and my dishonor;
My adversaries *are* all before You.
20 Reproach has broken my heart,
And I am full of heaviness;
I looked *for someone* to take pity, but *there was* none;
And for comforters, but I found none.
21 They also gave me gall for my food, ➤
And for my thirst they gave me vinegar to drink.
22 Let their table become a snare before them,
And their well-being a trap.
23 Let their eyes be darkened, so that they do not see;
And make their loins shake continually.
24 Pour out Your indignation upon them,
And let Your wrathful anger take hold of them.
25 Let their dwelling place be desolate;
Let no one live in their tents.
26 For they persecute the *ones* You have struck,
And talk of the grief of those You have wounded.
27 Add iniquity to their iniquity,
And let them not come into Your righteousness.
28 Let them be blotted out of the book of the living,
And not be written with the righteous.
29 But I *am* poor and sorrowful;
Let Your salvation, O God, set me up on high.
30 I will praise the name of God with a song,

LIFE LESSONS

➤ 69:6 — *Let not those who wait for You, O Lord GOD of hosts, be ashamed because of me; let not those who seek You be confounded because of me, O God of Israel.*

What we do and how we live has a profound effect on those around us. They're watching us, even when we don't know it. So we should pray that God would enable us to represent Him well, at all times.

➤ 69:21 — *They also gave me gall for my food, and for my thirst they gave me vinegar to drink.*

The Roman soldiers crucifying Jesus entertained themselves by giving him wine mixed with gall, to make it bitter. Later, others gave him wine vinegar to drink (Matt. 27:34, 48). So God, in His grace, showed Jesus what lay ahead.

And will magnify Him with
thanksgiving.
31 *This* also shall please the LORD better
than an ox *or* bull,
Which has horns and hooves.
32 The humble shall see *this and* be glad;
And you who seek God, your hearts
shall live.
33 For the LORD hears the poor,
And does not despise His prisoners.

34 Let heaven and earth praise Him,
The seas and everything that moves in
them.
35 For God will save Zion
And build the cities of Judah,
That they may dwell there and possess it.
36 Also, the descendants of His servants
shall inherit it,
And those who love His name shall
dwell in it.

PSALM 70

Prayer for Relief from Adversaries

To the Chief Musician. *A Psalm* of David.
To bring to remembrance.

1 *Make haste,* O God, to deliver me!
Make haste to help me, O LORD!

2 Let them be ashamed and confounded
Who seek my life;
Let them be turned back[a] and confused
Who desire my hurt.
3 Let them be turned back because of
their shame,
Who say, "Aha, aha!"

➤ 4 Let all those who seek You rejoice and
be glad in You;
And let those who love Your salvation
say continually,
"Let God be magnified!"

5 But I *am* poor and needy;
Make haste to me, O God!
You *are* my help and my deliverer;
O LORD, do not delay.

PSALM 71

God the Rock of Salvation

1 In You, O LORD, I put my trust;
Let me never be put to shame.
2 Deliver me in Your righteousness, and
cause me to escape;
Incline Your ear to me, and save me.
3 Be my strong refuge,
To which I may resort continually;
You have given the commandment to
save me,
For You *are* my rock and my fortress.

4 Deliver me, O my God, out of the hand
of the wicked,
Out of the hand of the unrighteous and
cruel man.
5 For You are my hope, O Lord GOD; ➤
You are my trust from my youth.
6 By You I have been upheld from birth;
You are He who took me out of my
mother's womb.
My praise *shall be* continually of You.

7 I have become as a wonder to many,
But You *are* my strong refuge.
8 Let my mouth be filled *with* Your praise
And with Your glory all the day.

9 Do not cast me off in the time of old age;
Do not forsake me when my strength
fails.
10 For my enemies speak against me;
And those who lie in wait for my life
take counsel together,
11 Saying, "God has forsaken him;
Pursue and take him, for *there is* none
to deliver *him.*"

12 O God, do not be far from me;
O my God, make haste to help me!
13 Let them be confounded *and* consumed
Who are adversaries of my life;
Let them be covered *with* reproach and
dishonor
Who seek my hurt.

14 But I will hope continually,
And will praise You yet more and more.
15 My mouth shall tell of Your
righteousness
And Your salvation all the day,
For I do not know *their* limits.
16 I will go in the strength of the Lord
GOD;
I will make mention of Your
righteousness, of Yours only.

70:2 [a]Following Masoretic Text, Septuagint, Targum, and Vulgate; some Hebrew manuscripts and Syriac read *be appalled* (compare 40:15).

LIFE LESSONS

➤ 70:4 — *Let all those who seek You rejoice and be glad in You; and let those who love Your salvation say continually, "Let God be magnified!"*

God invites us to express our joy in Him by testifying about it to others. We are not to keep the Good News to ourselves, but are to share it with others.

➤ 71:5 — *For You are my hope, O Lord GOD; You are my trust from my youth.*

Some caution against leading children to Christ, but this is an unbiblical mistake. If you don't lead your children to faith in Jesus, others will try to lead them to trust in something else.

17 O God, You have taught me from my youth;
And to this *day* I declare Your wondrous works.
18 Now also when *I am* old and grayheaded,
O God, do not forsake me,
Until I declare Your strength to *this* generation,
Your power to everyone *who* is to come.
19 Also Your righteousness, O God, *is* very high,
You who have done great things;
O God, who *is* like You?
20 *You*, who have shown me great and severe troubles,
Shall revive me again,
And bring me up again from the depths of the earth.
21 You shall increase my greatness,
And comfort me on every side.

22 Also with the lute I will praise You—
And Your faithfulness, O my God!
To You I will sing with the harp,
O Holy One of Israel.
23 My lips shall greatly rejoice when I sing to You,
And my soul, which You have redeemed.
➤ 24 My tongue also shall talk of Your righteousness all the day long;
For they are confounded,
For they are brought to shame
Who seek my hurt.

PSALM 72

Glory and Universality of the Messiah's Reign

A Psalm of Solomon.

1 Give the king Your judgments, O God,
And Your righteousness to the king's Son.
2 He will judge Your people with righteousness,
And Your poor with justice.
3 The mountains will bring peace to the people,
And the little hills, by righteousness.
✳ 4 He will bring justice to the poor of the people;
He will save the children of the needy,
And will break in pieces the oppressor.

5 They shall fear You[a]
As long as the sun and moon endure,
Throughout all generations.
6 He shall come down like rain upon the grass before mowing,
Like showers *that* water the earth.
7 In His days the righteous shall flourish,
And abundance of peace,
Until the moon is no more.

8 He shall have dominion also from sea to sea,
And from the River to the ends of the earth.
9 Those who dwell in the wilderness will bow before Him,
And His enemies will lick the dust.
10 The kings of Tarshish and of the isles
Will bring presents;
The kings of Sheba and Seba
Will offer gifts.
11 Yes, all kings shall fall down before Him; ➤
All nations shall serve Him.

12 For He will deliver the needy when he cries,
The poor also, and *him* who has no helper.
13 He will spare the poor and needy,
And will save the souls of the needy.
14 He will redeem their life from oppression and violence;
And precious shall be their blood in His sight.

15 And He shall live;
And the gold of Sheba will be given to Him;
Prayer also will be made for Him continually,
And daily He shall be praised.

16 There will be an abundance of grain in the earth,
On the top of the mountains;
Its fruit shall wave like Lebanon;
And *those* of the city shall flourish like grass of the earth.

17 His name shall endure forever; ➤
His name shall continue as long as the sun.
And *men* shall be blessed in Him;
All nations shall call Him blessed.

72:5 [a]Following Masoretic Text and Targum; Septuagint and Vulgate read *They shall continue*.

LIFE LESSONS

➤ **71:24 — *My tongue also shall talk of Your righteousness all the day long . . . .***

While faith is a deeply personal affair, God never meant for it to be a solitary affair. We usually love speaking about what gives us joy. If God is our joy, then He should also be on our tongues.

➤ **72:11 — *Yes, all kings shall fall down before Him; all nations shall serve Him.***

One day, perhaps soon, "every knee" will bow and "every tongue" will confess that, "Jesus Christ is Lord, to the glory of God the Father" (Phil. 2:10, 11).

➤ **72:17 — *His name shall endure forever; His name shall continue as long as the sun. And men shall be blessed in Him; all nations shall call Him blessed.***

Jesus will receive a kingdom that will never end, and He will rule over all the nations in righteousness and truth. And even then, obedience will bring blessing.

18 Blessed *be* the LORD God, the God of
Israel,
Who only does wondrous things!
19 And blessed *be* His glorious name forever!
And let the whole earth be filled *with*
His glory.
Amen and Amen.
20 The prayers of David the son of Jesse
are ended.

Book Three: Psalms 73—89

PSALM 73

The Tragedy of the Wicked, and the Blessedness of Trust in God

A Psalm of Asaph.

1 Truly God *is* good to Israel,
To such as are pure in heart.
2 But as for me, my feet had almost
stumbled;
My steps had nearly slipped.
3 For I *was* envious of the boastful,
When I saw the prosperity of the wicked.
4 For *there are* no pangs in their death,
But their strength *is* firm.
5 They *are* not in trouble *as other* men,
Nor are they plagued like *other* men.
6 Therefore pride serves as their necklace;
Violence covers them *like* a garment.
7 Their eyes bulge[a] with abundance;
They have more than heart could wish.
8 They scoff and speak wickedly
concerning oppression;
They speak loftily.
9 They set their mouth against the heavens,
And their tongue walks through the earth.
10 Therefore his people return here,
And waters of a full *cup* are drained by
them.
11 And they say, "How does God know?
And is there knowledge in the Most
High?"
12 Behold, these *are* the ungodly,
Who are always at ease;
They increase *in* riches.
13 Surely I have cleansed my heart *in* vain,
And washed my hands in innocence.
14 For all day long I have been plagued,
And chastened every morning.
15 If I had said, "I will speak thus,"
Behold, I would have been untrue to the
generation of Your children.
16 When I thought *how* to understand this,
It *was* too painful for me—
17 Until I went into the sanctuary of God;
Then I understood their end.
18 Surely You set them in slippery places;
You cast them down to destruction.
19 Oh, how they are *brought* to desolation,
as in a moment!
They are utterly consumed with terrors.
20 As a dream when *one* awakes,
So, Lord, when You awake,
You shall despise their image.
21 Thus my heart was grieved,
And I was vexed in my mind.
22 I *was* so foolish and ignorant;
I was *like* a beast before You.
23 Nevertheless I *am* continually with You;
You hold *me* by my right hand.
24 You will guide me with Your counsel,
And afterward receive me *to* glory.
25 Whom have I in heaven *but You?*
And *there is* none upon earth *that* I
desire besides You.
26 My flesh and my heart fail;
But God *is* the strength of my heart and
my portion forever.
27 For indeed, those who are far from You
shall perish;
You have destroyed all those who desert
You for harlotry.
28 But *it is* good for me to draw near to God;
I have put my trust in the Lord GOD,
That I may declare all Your works.

PSALM 74

A Plea for Relief from Oppressors

A Contemplation[a] of Asaph.

1 O God, why have You cast *us* off
forever?

73:7 [a]Targum reads *face bulges;* Septuagint, Syriac, and Vulgate read *iniquity bulges.* **74:title** [a]Hebrew *Maschil*

LIFE LESSONS

➤ 73:22 — *I was so foolish and ignorant; I was like a beast before You.*

When we leave the path God lays out for us and walk our own way, we may think (for a while) that we are pursuing a better or more enjoyable course of action; but sin is always the wrong choice. Always.

➤ 73:26 — *My flesh and my heart fail; but God is the strength of my heart and my portion forever.*

Some people think that only the weak need God, but the fact is that *all* of us are weak. Our flesh fails; our heart fails. But when we find our strength in God, our weakness turns to strength (see 2 Cor. 12:10).

➤ 74:1 — *O God, why have You cast us off forever? Why does Your anger smoke against the sheep of Your pasture?*

The psalmist knew of no unresolved sin in his life, and yet his circumstances continued to look bleak. We may not know why God seems to ignore our prayers, but even in such dark times, He calls us to trust Him.

Why does Your anger smoke against the sheep of Your pasture?
2 Remember Your congregation, *which* You have purchased of old,
The tribe of Your inheritance, *which* You have redeemed—
This Mount Zion where You have dwelt.
3 Lift up Your feet to the perpetual desolations.
The enemy has damaged everything in the sanctuary.
4 Your enemies roar in the midst of Your meeting place;
They set up their banners *for* signs.
5 They seem like men who lift up
Axes among the thick trees.
6 And now they break down its carved work, all at once,
With axes and hammers.
7 They have set fire to Your sanctuary;
They have defiled the dwelling place of Your name to the ground.
8 They said in their hearts,
"Let us destroy them altogether."
They have burned up all the meeting places of God in the land.

9 We do not see our signs;
There is no longer any prophet;
Nor *is there* any among us who knows how long.
10 O God, how long will the adversary reproach?
Will the enemy blaspheme Your name forever?
11 Why do You withdraw Your hand, even Your right hand?
Take it out of Your bosom and destroy *them.*
12 For God *is* my King from of old,
Working salvation in the midst of the earth.
13 You divided the sea by Your strength;
You broke the heads of the sea serpents in the waters.
14 You broke the heads of Leviathan in pieces,
And gave him *as* food to the people inhabiting the wilderness.
15 You broke open the fountain and the flood;
You dried up mighty rivers.
16 The day *is* Yours, the night also *is* Yours;
You have prepared the light and the sun.
17 You have set all the borders of the earth;
You have made summer and winter.

18 Remember this, *that* the enemy has reproached, O LORD,
And *that* a foolish people has blasphemed Your name.
19 Oh, do not deliver the life of Your turtledove to the wild beast!
Do not forget the life of Your poor forever.
20 Have respect to the covenant;
For the dark places of the earth are full of the haunts of cruelty.
21 Oh, do not let the oppressed return ashamed!
Let the poor and needy praise Your name.

22 Arise, O God, plead Your own cause;
Remember how the foolish man reproaches You daily.
23 Do not forget the voice of Your enemies;
The tumult of those who rise up against You increases continually.

PSALM 75

Thanksgiving for God's Righteous Judgment

To the Chief Musician. Set to "Do Not Destroy."[a] A Psalm of Asaph. A Song.

1 We give thanks to You, O God, we give thanks!
For Your wondrous works declare *that* Your name is near.

2 "When I choose the proper time,
I will judge uprightly.
3 The earth and all its inhabitants are dissolved;
I set up its pillars firmly. Selah

4 "I said to the boastful, 'Do not deal boastfully,'
And to the wicked, 'Do not lift up the horn.
5 Do not lift up your horn on high;
Do *not* speak with a stiff neck.'"
6 For exaltation *comes* neither from the east
Nor from the west nor from the south.
7 But God *is* the Judge:
He puts down one,
And exalts another.

75:title [a]Hebrew *Al Tashcheth*

LIFE LESSONS

➢ 74:22 — *Arise, O God, plead Your own cause; remember how the foolish man reproaches You daily.*

Many Bible prayers are based on genuine concern for God's reputation and glory. When we plead for God to act in order to defend His name, we pray on very high ground.

➢ 75:6 — *For exaltation comes neither from the east nor from the south.*

God's people are not to curry favor with powerful figures in an attempt to selfishly advance their own careers or positions. They are to work "as to the Lord" (Col. 3:23) and leave advancement in His hands.

8 For in the hand of the LORD *there is* a cup,
And the wine is red;
It is fully mixed, and He pours it out;
Surely its dregs shall all the wicked of the earth
Drain *and* drink down.

9 But I will declare forever,
I will sing praises to the God of Jacob.

10 "All the horns of the wicked I will also cut off,
But the horns of the righteous shall be exalted."

PSALM 76

The Majesty of God in Judgment

To the Chief Musician. On stringed instruments.[a] A Psalm of Asaph. A Song.

1 In Judah God *is* known;
His name *is* great in Israel.
2 In Salem[a] also is His tabernacle,
And His dwelling place in Zion.
3 There He broke the arrows of the bow,
The shield and sword of battle. Selah

4 You *are* more glorious and excellent
Than the mountains of prey.
5 The stouthearted were plundered;
They have sunk into their sleep;
And none of the mighty men have found the use of their hands.
6 At Your rebuke, O God of Jacob,
Both the chariot and horse were cast into a dead sleep.

➤ 7 You, Yourself, *are* to be feared;
And who may stand in Your presence
When once You are angry?
8 You caused judgment to be heard from heaven;
The earth feared and was still,
9 When God arose to judgment,
To deliver all the oppressed of the earth. Selah

10 Surely the wrath of man shall praise You;
With the remainder of wrath You shall gird Yourself.

11 Make vows to the LORD your God, and pay *them;*
Let all who are around Him bring presents to Him who ought to be feared.
12 He shall cut off the spirit of princes;
He is awesome to the kings of the earth.

PSALM 77

The Consoling Memory of God's Redemptive Works

To the Chief Musician. To Jeduthun. A Psalm of Asaph.

1 I cried out to God with my voice—
To God with my voice;
And He gave ear to me.
2 In the day of my trouble I sought the Lord;
My hand was stretched out in the night without ceasing;
My soul refused to be comforted.
3 I remembered God, and was troubled;
I complained, and my spirit was overwhelmed. Selah

4 You hold my eyelids *open;*
I am so troubled that I cannot speak.
5 I have considered the days of old,
The years of ancient times.
6 I call to remembrance my song in the night;
I meditate within my heart,
And my spirit makes diligent search.

7 Will the Lord cast off forever?
And will He be favorable no more? ➤
8 Has His mercy ceased forever?
Has *His* promise failed forevermore?
9 Has God forgotten to be gracious?
Has He in anger shut up His tender mercies? Selah ➤

10 And I said, "This *is* my anguish;
But I will remember the years of the right hand of the Most High."
11 I will remember the works of the LORD;
Surely I will remember Your wonders of old.
12 I will also meditate on all Your work,
And talk of Your deeds.
13 Your way, O God, *is* in the sanctuary;
Who *is* so great a God as *our* God?

76:title [a]Hebrew *neginoth* **76:2** [a]That is, Jerusalem

LIFE LESSONS

➤ 76:7 — *You, Yourself, are to be feared; and who may stand in Your presence when once You are angry?*

The contemporary American church has lost most of its fear of God, and that is one big reason why it is so weak. Jesus says, "Fear Him who, after He has killed, has power to cast into hell" (Luke 12:5).

➤ 77:8 — *Has His mercy ceased forever? Has His promise failed forevermore?*

When we're in the middle of some adversity, the answers to these questions often seem to be "yes" and "yes." In fact, however, they are "no" and "no." God loves mercy, and He keeps His promises. Always.

➤ 77:10 — *And I said, "This is my anguish; but I will remember the years of the right hand of the Most High."*

When hardship stalks us and we feel at our lowest point, it can bring great comfort to dwell on the fact that God never changes and that He will always act on behalf of those who wait for Him.

14 You *are* the God who does wonders;
You have declared Your strength among
the peoples.
15 You have with *Your* arm redeemed Your
people,
The sons of Jacob and Joseph. Selah
16 The waters saw You, O God;
The waters saw You, they were afraid;
The depths also trembled.
17 The clouds poured out water;
The skies sent out a sound;
Your arrows also flashed about.
18 The voice of Your thunder *was* in the
whirlwind;
The lightnings lit up the world;
The earth trembled and shook.
19 Your way *was* in the sea,
Your path in the great waters,
And Your footsteps were not known.
20 You led Your people like a flock
By the hand of Moses and Aaron.

PSALM 78

God's Kindness to Rebellious Israel

A Contemplation[a] of Asaph.

1 Give ear, O my people, *to* my law;
Incline your ears to the words of my
mouth.
2 I will open my mouth in a parable;
I will utter dark sayings of old,
3 Which we have heard and known,
And our fathers have told us.
➤4 We will not hide *them* from their
children,
Telling to the generation to come the
praises of the LORD,
And His strength and His wonderful
works that He has done.
5 For He established a testimony in
Jacob,
And appointed a law in Israel,
Which He commanded our fathers,
That they should make them known to
their children;
6 That the generation to come might
know *them*,
The children *who* would be born,
That they may arise and declare *them*
to their children,
7 That they may set their hope in God,
And not forget the works of God,
But keep His commandments;
8 And may not be like their fathers,
A stubborn and rebellious generation,
A generation *that* did not set its heart
aright,
And whose spirit was not faithful to
God.
9 The children of Ephraim, *being* armed
and carrying bows,
Turned back in the day of battle.
10 They did not keep the covenant of God;
They refused to walk in His law,
11 And forgot His works
And His wonders that He had shown
them.
12 Marvelous things He did in the sight of
their fathers,
In the land of Egypt, *in* the field of
Zoan.
13 He divided the sea and caused them to
pass through;
And He made the waters stand up like a
heap.
14 In the daytime also He led them with
the cloud,
And all the night with a light of fire.
15 He split the rocks in the wilderness,
And gave *them* drink in abundance like
the depths.
16 He also brought streams out of the rock,
And caused waters to run down like
rivers.
17 But they sinned even more against Him
By rebelling against the Most High in
the wilderness.
18 And they tested God in their heart
By asking for the food of their fancy.
19 Yes, they spoke against God:
They said, "Can God prepare a table in
the wilderness?
20 Behold, He struck the rock,
So that the waters gushed out,
And the streams overflowed.
Can He give bread also?
Can He provide meat for His people?"
21 Therefore the LORD heard *this* and was
furious;
So a fire was kindled against Jacob,
And anger also came up against Israel,
22 Because they did not believe in God,
And did not trust in His salvation.
23 Yet He had commanded the clouds
above,
And opened the doors of heaven,

78:title [a]Hebrew *Maschil*

LIFE LESSONS

➤ 78:4 — *We will not hide them from their children, telling to the generation to come the praises of the LORD, and His strength and His wonderful works that He has done.*

It is our job to tell our children not only the great things God did in Bible times, but also the wonderful works He has performed in our own lives. They need to see God at work in us.

24 Had rained down manna on them to eat,
And given them of the bread of heaven.
25 Men ate angels' food;
He sent them food to the full.
26 He caused an east wind to blow in the heavens;
And by His power He brought in the south wind.
27 He also rained meat on them like the dust,
Feathered fowl like the sand of the seas;
28 And He let *them* fall in the midst of their camp,
All around their dwellings.
29 So they ate and were well filled,
For He gave them their own desire.
30 They were not deprived of their craving;
But while their food *was* still in their mouths,
31 The wrath of God came against them,
And slew the stoutest of them,
And struck down the choice *men* of Israel.
32 In spite of this they still sinned,
And did not believe in His wondrous works.
33 Therefore their days He consumed in futility,
And their years in fear.
34 When He slew them, then they sought Him;
And they returned and sought earnestly for God.
35 Then they remembered that God *was* their rock,
And the Most High God their Redeemer.
36 Nevertheless they flattered Him with their mouth,
And they lied to Him with their tongue;
37 For their heart was not steadfast with Him,
Nor were they faithful in His covenant.
➤ 38 But He, *being* full of compassion, forgave *their* iniquity,
And did not destroy *them*.
Yes, many a time He turned His anger away,
And did not stir up all His wrath;
39 For He remembered that they *were but* flesh,
A breath that passes away and does not come again.
40 How often they provoked Him in the wilderness,
And grieved Him in the desert!
41 Yes, again and again they tempted God,
And limited the Holy One of Israel.
42 They did not remember His power:
The day when He redeemed them from the enemy,
43 When He worked His signs in Egypt,
And His wonders in the field of Zoan;
44 Turned their rivers into blood,
And their streams, that they could not drink.
45 He sent swarms of flies among them, which devoured them,
And frogs, which destroyed them.
46 He also gave their crops to the caterpillar,
And their labor to the locust.
47 He destroyed their vines with hail,
And their sycamore trees with frost.
48 He also gave up their cattle to the hail,
And their flocks to fiery lightning.
49 He cast on them the fierceness of His anger,
Wrath, indignation, and trouble,
By sending angels of destruction *among them*.
50 He made a path for His anger;
He did not spare their soul from death,
But gave their life over to the plague,
51 And destroyed all the firstborn in Egypt,
The first of *their* strength in the tents of Ham.
52 But He made His own people go forth like sheep,
And guided them in the wilderness like a flock;
53 And He led them on safely, so that they did not fear;
But the sea overwhelmed their enemies.
54 And He brought them to His holy border,
This mountain *which* His right hand had acquired.
55 He also drove out the nations before them,
Allotted them an inheritance by survey,
And made the tribes of Israel dwell in their tents.
56 Yet they tested and provoked the Most High God,
And did not keep His testimonies,
57 But turned back and acted unfaithfully like their fathers;

LIFE LESSONS

➤ 78:38 — *But He, being full of compassion, forgave their iniquity, and did not destroy them. Yes, many a time He turned His anger away, and did not stir up all His wrath . . . .*

It is a blessed truth that God "has not dealt with us according to our sins" (Ps. 103:10). For the sake of His name and of His Son, He restrains His anger and pours out mercy rather than wrath.

They were turned aside like a deceitful bow.
58 For they provoked Him to anger with their high places,
And moved Him to jealousy with their carved images.
59 When God heard *this,* He was furious,
And greatly abhorred Israel,
60 So that He forsook the tabernacle of Shiloh,
The tent He had placed among men,
61 And delivered His strength into captivity,
And His glory into the enemy's hand.
62 He also gave His people over to the sword,
And was furious with His inheritance.
63 The fire consumed their young men,
And their maidens were not given in marriage.
64 Their priests fell by the sword,
And their widows made no lamentation.

65 Then the Lord awoke as *from* sleep,
Like a mighty man who shouts because of wine.
66 And He beat back His enemies;
He put them to a perpetual reproach.

67 Moreover He rejected the tent of Joseph,
And did not choose the tribe of Ephraim,
68 But chose the tribe of Judah,
Mount Zion which He loved.
69 And He built His sanctuary like the heights,
Like the earth which He has established forever.
70 He also chose David His servant,
And took him from the sheepfolds;
71 From following the ewes that had young He brought him,
To shepherd Jacob His people,
And Israel His inheritance.
72 So he shepherded them according to the integrity of his heart,
And guided them by the skillfulness of his hands.

PSALM 79

A Dirge and a Prayer for Israel, Destroyed by Enemies

A Psalm of Asaph.

1 O God, the nations have come into Your inheritance;
Your holy temple they have defiled;
They have laid Jerusalem in heaps.
2 The dead bodies of Your servants
They have given *as* food for the birds of the heavens,
The flesh of Your saints to the beasts of the earth.
3 Their blood they have shed like water all around Jerusalem,
And *there was* no one to bury *them.*
4 We have become a reproach to our neighbors,
A scorn and derision to those who are around us.

5 How long, LORD?
Will You be angry forever?
Will Your jealousy burn like fire?
6 Pour out Your wrath on the nations that do not know You,
And on the kingdoms that do not call on Your name.
7 For they have devoured Jacob,
And laid waste his dwelling place.

8 Oh, do not remember former iniquities against us!
Let Your tender mercies come speedily to meet us,
For we have been brought very low.
9 Help us, O God of our salvation,
For the glory of Your name;
And deliver us, and provide atonement for our sins,
For Your name's sake!
10 Why should the nations say,
"Where *is* their God?"
Let there be known among the nations in our sight
The avenging of the blood of Your servants *which has been* shed.

11 Let the groaning of the prisoner come before You;
According to the greatness of Your power
Preserve those who are appointed to die;
12 And return to our neighbors sevenfold into their bosom
Their reproach with which they have reproached You, O Lord.

13 So we, Your people and sheep of Your pasture,
Will give You thanks forever;
We will show forth Your praise to all generations.

LIFE LESSONS

79:9 — *Help us, O God of our salvation, for the glory of Your name; and deliver us, and provide atonement for our sins, for Your name's sake!*

When we pray about something for the sake of God's name, we urge Him to act in order to defend His reputation, to make His glory known, to honor Him and to let others see His majesty and greatness.

ANSWERS TO LIFE'S QUESTIONS

How does my relationship with the Lord affect what and how I hear from Him?

PS. 79:13

Our relationship with God—the most important aspect of our lives—affects greatly what we hear when we pray and listen. The only message an unbeliever will ever hear from God is that he is a sinner who needs Jesus as his Savior. Until that person knows Christ as his personal Messiah, he will not hear God speak on any subject other than salvation.

In the life of a believer, that speaker/hearer relationship has two main features.

First, we are saved. When by faith we receive Jesus Christ as our personal Savior, the Bible says we are born again. God takes us from the kingdom of darkness and places us into the kingdom of light. We become children of God. Our salvation experience begins our relationship with Him.

Second, we are identified with Him. Our salvation takes care of our eternal security, while our identification takes care of our daily walk of victory. By identification, I mean that Christ's life is now mine and mine is His. "It is no longer I who live, but Christ lives in me" (Gal. 2:20). What happened to Christ at Calvary, also happened to me. Christ was crucified; I was crucified. Christ was buried; I was buried. Christ was raised; I was raised.

One who is safe and secure in the love of God and sustained by His grace no longer hears from a distant God. He now listens to Someone who loves him enough to bring him into a close, personal relationship—and that makes all the difference. We no longer come to Him, groping and pleading, wondering whether He accepts us.

Through my identification with Him, I come gladly and boldly, knowing that I am accepted, not by my behavior, but because of my belief in Him and in what He has already accomplished. Thus I can approach Him with confidence and great assurance.

Jesus is now my personal, faithful, and merciful High Priest. He is my Father with whom I enjoy intimate communication. I no longer have to stand on the perimeter, squinting into the distance for a glimpse of His presence. Jesus has paid the price of relationship with God through His shed blood, so that now I am a full member of His own family, sitting daily before Him, totally secure in my sonship.

Why do I hear His voice? I hear it because I am one of the "sheep of His pasture."

See the Life Principles Index for further study:

4. The awareness of God's presence energizes us for our work.

1. Our intimacy with God—His highest priority for our lives—determines the impact of our lives.

17. We stand tallest and strongest on our knees.

PSALM 80

Prayer for Israel's Restoration

To the Chief Musician. Set to "The Lilies."[a] A Testimony[b] of Asaph. A Psalm.

1 Give ear, O Shepherd of Israel,
You who lead Joseph like a flock;
You who dwell *between* the cherubim, shine forth!
2 Before Ephraim, Benjamin, and Manasseh,
Stir up Your strength,
And come *and* save us!
3 Restore us, O God;
Cause Your face to shine,
And we shall be saved!

4 O LORD God of hosts,
How long will You be angry
Against the prayer of Your people?
5 You have fed them with the bread of tears,

80:title [a]Hebrew *Shoshannim* [b]Hebrew *Eduth*

LIFE LESSONS

➤ 80:3 — *Restore us, O God; cause Your face to shine, and we shall be saved!*

It would be great if we all marched from spiritual childhood to spiritual maturity without a hitch, but the truth is we all need to be restored from time to time. Prayer is a necessary step to restoration.

And given them tears to drink in great
measure.
6 You have made us a strife to our
neighbors,
And our enemies laugh among
themselves.

7 Restore us, O God of hosts;
Cause Your face to shine,
And we shall be saved!

8 You have brought a vine out of Egypt;
You have cast out the nations, and
planted it.
9 You prepared *room* for it,
And caused it to take deep root,
And it filled the land.
10 The hills were covered with its shadow,
And the mighty cedars with its boughs.
11 She sent out her boughs to the Sea,[a]
And her branches to the River.[b]

12 Why have You broken down her hedges,
So that all who pass by the way pluck
her *fruit?*
13 The boar out of the woods uproots it,
And the wild beast of the field devours it.

14 Return, we beseech You, O God of hosts;
Look down from heaven and see,
And visit this vine
15 And the vineyard which Your right hand
has planted,
And the branch *that* You made strong
for Yourself.
16 *It is* burned with fire, *it is* cut down;
They perish at the rebuke of Your
countenance.
17 Let Your hand be upon the man of Your
right hand,
Upon the son of man *whom* You made
strong for Yourself.
18 Then we will not turn back from You;
Revive us, and we will call upon Your
name.

19 Restore us, O LORD God of hosts;
Cause Your face to shine,
And we shall be saved!

PSALM 81

An Appeal for Israel's Repentance

To the Chief Musician. On an instrument of Gath.[a] *A Psalm* of Asaph.

1 Sing aloud to God our strength;
Make a joyful shout to the God of Jacob.
2 Raise a song and strike the timbrel,
The pleasant harp with the lute.

3 Blow the trumpet at the time of the New
Moon,
At the full moon, on our solemn feast day.
4 For this *is* a statute for Israel,
A law of the God of Jacob.
5 This He established in Joseph *as* a
testimony,
When He went throughout the land of
Egypt,
Where I heard a language I did not
understand.

6 "I removed his shoulder from the burden;
His hands were freed from the baskets.
7 You called in trouble, and I delivered you;
I answered you in the secret place of
thunder;
I tested you at the waters of
Meribah. Selah

8 "Hear, O My people, and I will admonish
you!
O Israel, if you will listen to Me!
9 There shall be no foreign god among
you;
Nor shall you worship any foreign god.
10 I *am* the LORD your God,
Who brought you out of the land of
Egypt;
Open your mouth wide, and I will fill it.

11 "But My people would not heed My voice,
And Israel would *have* none of Me.
12 So I gave them over to their own
stubborn heart,
To walk in their own counsels.

13 "Oh, that My people would listen to Me,
That Israel would walk in My ways!
14 I would soon subdue their enemies,
And turn My hand against their
adversaries.
15 The haters of the LORD would pretend
submission to Him,
But their fate would endure forever.
16 He would have fed them also with the
finest of wheat;
And with honey from the rock I would
have satisfied you."

80:11 [a]That is, the Mediterranean [b]That is, the Euphrates
81:title [a]Hebrew *Al Gittith*

LIFE LESSONS

➤ ***81:10 — "I am the LORD Your God, who brought you out of the land of Egypt; open your mouth wide, and I will fill it."***

Here we see the heart of God: to bless His people beyond their imagination. But we also see our part in the process: to willingly receive what He has to offer. We get filled only when we obey His instructions.

➤ ***81:13, 16 — "Oh, that My people would listen to Me, that Israel would walk in My ways! . . . He would have fed them also with the finest of wheat; and with honey from the rock I would have satisfied you."***

God loves to bless His people when they obey His commands. He wants us to understand that "the good life" comes to us only through Him, and not through any other means.

LIFE PRINCIPLE 13

LISTENING TO GOD IS ESSENTIAL TO WALKING WITH GOD.

PS. 81:8

One of the most important lessons we can ever learn is how to listen to God. In our complex and hectic lives, nothing is more urgent, nothing more necessary, and nothing more rewarding than hearing what God has to say to us.

A true conversation, of course, involves both talking and listening. Most of us do better with the talking part.

I used to be so occupied doing the Lord's work that I had no time to pay close attention to God's voice. I preached six times a week, taped two television programs, traveled across the nation, wrote books, pastored the church, and administrated a large church staff and broadcast ministry (among other daily duties). I spent time talking to God, very often about the needs of my personal life and ministry—but not much time listening to God.

I ended up in the hospital for a week and out of circulation for three months.

If we don't learn how to listen to God, we can make unwise and very costly mistakes.

You may ask, "Does God really speak to us today?" The Bible assures us that He does. The book of Hebrews opens this way: "God, who at various times and in various ways spoke in time past to the fathers by the prophets, has in these last days spoken to us by His Son . . . ." (Heb. 1:1, 2).

Our God is not silent. Our Heavenly Father is alive and active. He speaks to us individually. Furthermore, He doesn't speak in veiled terms, riddles, or mysteries. He speaks plainly. The goal of any communicator is to be understood, not merely to speak well. God speaks in a way that we can hear Him, receive His message clearly, and understand precisely what He wants us to do.

God speaks not only in general and absolute terms, but also to each one of us personally. God is an infinite God, fully capable of communicating with each of us, right where we are—in the midst of our circumstances—in very personal, direct, and explicit terms.

This may be the most important concept you will ever grasp in learning how to listen to God. When God speaks, He is speaking to *you*. Everything in the Bible applies to your life in some way. Every message or communication based on the Word of God carries truth meant for you. There is no such thing as a chapter in the Bible, a sermon based on God's Word, or a book that explains God's Word, that is not for you. Each of us must take God's Word personally!

A true conversation involves both talking and listening.

This is not to say that God has an exclusive word for select individuals. God doesn't deal in secrets. He won't reveal truth to one person and deny it to another. Be on guard if you hear somebody say, "God told me something, but I can't tell anybody else," or "God had a word that's just for me and not for you."

God doesn't play favorites. He doesn't speak to one child and ignore His other children. His word of correction to you may be so personal that you don't want to share it with others, but ultimately, God's word of correction applies to everyone. The same goes for God's promises, provisions, and insights.

God doesn't speak frivolously. He doesn't joke around. God means what He says and will do what He says. God is serious about His relationship with you. He expects you to respond to His voice, heed His Word, and act on it.

God means what He says and will do what He says.

Can you remember last Sunday's sermon? Can you recall what you read in God's Word yesterday? You'll be able to remember if you were listening for what God had to say to you and if you seriously believe that God intends for you to act upon what you heard.

God always speaks for your benefit. He wants you to listen to Him and then respond in obedience. Sometimes He will challenge you to change your thinking or to release certain unhealthy feelings and opinions. Sometimes He will command you to change aspects of your behavior. He desires to encourage you so that you might live with greater joy and strength. Always, however, God's Word is for your transformation. He means for it to change you in some way.

Listening to God is not a casual pastime or a let's-try-it-and-see-if-you-like-it activity. Listening to God is the most important thing you can do, for the sake of your eternal soul.

See the Life Principles Index for further study.

PSALM 82

A Plea for Justice

A Psalm of Asaph.

1 God stands in the congregation of the mighty;
He judges among the gods.[a]
2 How long will you judge unjustly,
And show partiality to the wicked? Selah
3 Defend the poor and fatherless;
Do justice to the afflicted and needy.
4 Deliver the poor and needy;
Free *them* from the hand of the wicked.
5 They do not know, nor do they understand;
They walk about in darkness;
All the foundations of the earth are unstable.

➤ 6 I said, "You *are* gods,[a]
And all of you *are* children of the Most High.
7 But you shall die like men,
And fall like one of the princes."

8 Arise, O God, judge the earth;
For You shall inherit all nations.

PSALM 83

Prayer to Frustrate Conspiracy Against Israel

A Song. A Psalm of Asaph.

➤ 1 Do not keep silent, O God!
Do not hold Your peace,
And do not be still, O God!
2 For behold, Your enemies make a tumult;
And those who hate You have lifted up their head.
3 They have taken crafty counsel against Your people,
And consulted together against Your sheltered ones.
4 They have said, "Come, and let us cut them off from *being* a nation,
That the name of Israel may be remembered no more."

5 For they have consulted together with one consent;
They form a confederacy against You:
6 The tents of Edom and the Ishmaelites;
Moab and the Hagrites;
7 Gebal, Ammon, and Amalek;
Philistia with the inhabitants of Tyre;
8 Assyria also has joined with them;
They have helped the children of Lot. Selah

9 Deal with them as *with* Midian,
As *with* Sisera,
As *with* Jabin at the Brook Kishon,
10 Who perished at En Dor,
Who became *as* refuse on the earth.
11 Make their nobles like Oreb and like Zeeb,
Yes, all their princes like Zebah and Zalmunna,
12 Who said, "Let us take for ourselves
The pastures of God for a possession."

13 O my God, make them like the whirling dust,
Like the chaff before the wind!
14 As the fire burns the woods,
And as the flame sets the mountains on fire,
15 So pursue them with Your tempest,
And frighten them with Your storm.
16 Fill their faces with shame,
That they may seek Your name, O LORD.
17 Let them be confounded and dismayed forever;
Yes, let them be put to shame and perish,
18 That they may know that You, whose name alone *is* the LORD,
Are the Most High over all the earth.

PSALM 84

The Blessedness of Dwelling in the House of God

To the Chief Musician. On an instrument of Gath.[a] A Psalm of the sons of Korah.

1 How lovely *is* Your tabernacle,
O LORD of hosts!
2 My soul longs, yes, even faints
For the courts of the LORD;
My heart and my flesh cry out for the living God.

3 Even the sparrow has found a home,
And the swallow a nest for herself,

82:1 [a]Hebrew *elohim, mighty ones;* that is, the judges
82:6 [a]Hebrew *elohim, mighty ones;* that is, the judges
84:title [a]Hebrew *Al Gittith*

LIFE LESSONS

➤ 82:6 — *I said, "You are gods, and all of you are children of the Most High."*

Jesus quoted this verse and highlighted the staggering privilege of receiving the Word of God (John 10:34). Let us treat the Bible as the great gift it is, and daily feed upon it to honor the One who gave it to us.

➤ 83:1 — *Do not keep silent, O God! Do not hold Your peace, and do not be still, O God!*

The Book of Psalms is full of pleas for God to act in power, to rescue His beleaguered people. Often God does not act until we feel an urgency for Him to do so; that way, He gets all the glory.

Where she may lay her young—
Even Your altars, O LORD of hosts,
My King and my God.
4 Blessed *are* those who dwell in Your house;
They will still be praising You. Selah
5 Blessed *is* the man whose strength *is* in You,
Whose heart *is* set on pilgrimage.
6 *As they* pass through the Valley of Baca,
They make it a spring;
The rain also covers it with pools.
7 They go from strength to strength;
Each one appears before God in Zion.[a]
8 O LORD God of hosts, hear my prayer;
Give ear, O God of Jacob! Selah
9 O God, behold our shield,
And look upon the face of Your anointed.
➤ 10 For a day in Your courts *is* better than a thousand.
I would rather be a doorkeeper in the house of my God
Than dwell in the tents of wickedness.
✳ 11 For the LORD God *is* a sun and shield;
The LORD will give grace and glory;
No good *thing* will He withhold
From those who walk uprightly.
12 O LORD of hosts,
Blessed *is* the man who trusts in You!

PSALM 85

Prayer that the LORD Will Restore Favor to the Land

To the Chief Musician. A Psalm of the sons of Korah.

1 LORD, You have been favorable to Your land;
You have brought back the captivity of Jacob.
2 You have forgiven the iniquity of Your people;
You have covered all their sin. Selah
3 You have taken away all Your wrath;
You have turned from the fierceness of Your anger.
4 Restore us, O God of our salvation,
And cause Your anger toward us to cease.
5 Will You be angry with us forever?
Will You prolong Your anger to all generations?
➤ 6 Will You not revive us again,
That Your people may rejoice in You?
7 Show us Your mercy, LORD,
And grant us Your salvation.
➤ 8 I will hear what God the LORD will speak,
For He will speak peace
To His people and to His saints;
But let them not turn back to folly.
9 Surely His salvation *is* near to those who fear Him,
That glory may dwell in our land.
10 Mercy and truth have met together;
Righteousness and peace have kissed.
11 Truth shall spring out of the earth,
And righteousness shall look down from heaven.
12 Yes, the LORD will give *what is* good;
And our land will yield its increase.
13 Righteousness will go before Him,
And shall make His footsteps *our* pathway.

PSALM 86

Prayer for Mercy, with Meditation on the Excellencies of the LORD

A Prayer of David.

1 Bow down Your ear, O LORD, hear me;
For I *am* poor and needy.
2 Preserve my life, for I *am* holy;
You are my God;
Save Your servant who trusts in You!
3 Be merciful to me, O Lord,
For I cry to You all day long.
4 Rejoice the soul of Your servant,
For to You, O Lord, I lift up my soul.
5 For You, Lord, *are* good, and ready to forgive,
And abundant in mercy to all those who call upon You.
6 Give ear, O LORD, to my prayer;
And attend to the voice of my supplications.

84:7 [a]Septuagint, Syriac, and Vulgate read *The God of gods shall be seen.*

LIFE LESSONS

➤ **84:10 — *For a day in Your courts is better than a thousand. I would rather be a doorkeeper in the house of my God than dwell in the tents of wickedness.***

Since we were made for an intimate relationship with God, anywhere with Him is better than anywhere else without Him. We find deep and ultimate satisfaction only in Him.

➤ **85:6 — *Will You not revive us again, that Your people may rejoice in You?***

Spiritual revival is not only about getting right with God; even more it is about returning to a place where we can delight in God, where we can joyfully celebrate His goodness and love and mercy.

➤ **85:8 — *. . . He will speak peace to His people and to His saints; but let them not turn back to folly.***

Salvation not only rescues us from the penalty of our sins, it delivers us from the impulse to practice our sins. Paul says, "to the degree we have already attained, let us walk by the same rule" (Phil. 3:16).

7 In the day of my trouble I will call upon You,
For You will answer me.

8 Among the gods *there is* none like You, O Lord;
Nor *are there any works* like Your works.
9 All nations whom You have made
Shall come and worship before You, O Lord,
And shall glorify Your name.
10 For You *are* great, and do wondrous things;
You alone *are* God.

➤ 11 Teach me Your way, O LORD;
I will walk in Your truth;
Unite my heart to fear Your name.
12 I will praise You, O Lord my God, with all my heart,
And I will glorify Your name forevermore.
13 For great *is* Your mercy toward me,
And You have delivered my soul from the depths of Sheol.

14 O God, the proud have risen against me,
And a mob of violent *men* have sought my life,
And have not set You before them.
15 But You, O Lord, *are* a God full of compassion, and gracious,
Longsuffering and abundant in mercy and truth.
16 Oh, turn to me, and have mercy on me!
Give Your strength to Your servant,
And save the son of Your maidservant.
17 Show me a sign for good,
That those who hate me may see *it* and be ashamed,
Because You, LORD, have helped me and comforted me.

PSALM 87

The Glories of the City of God

A Psalm of the sons of Korah. A Song.

1 His foundation *is* in the holy mountains.
2 The LORD loves the gates of Zion
More than all the dwellings of Jacob.
3 Glorious things are spoken of you,
O city of God! Selah

4 "I will make mention of Rahab and Babylon to those who know Me;
Behold, O Philistia and Tyre, with Ethiopia:
'This *one* was born there.'"
5 And of Zion it will be said,
"This *one* and that *one* were born in her;
And the Most High Himself shall establish her."
6 The LORD will record,
When He registers the peoples:
"This *one* was born there." Selah

7 Both the singers and the players on instruments *say,*
"All my springs *are* in you."

PSALM 88

A Prayer for Help in Despondency

A Song. A Psalm of the sons of Korah. To the Chief Musician. Set to "Mahalath Leannoth." A Contemplation[a] of Heman the Ezrahite.

1 O LORD, God of my salvation,
I have cried out day and night before You.
2 Let my prayer come before You;
Incline Your ear to my cry.

3 For my soul is full of troubles, ➤
And my life draws near to the grave.
4 I am counted with those who go down to the pit;
I am like a man *who has* no strength,
5 Adrift among the dead,
Like the slain who lie in the grave,
Whom You remember no more,
And who are cut off from Your hand.

6 You have laid me in the lowest pit,
In darkness, in the depths.
7 Your wrath lies heavy upon me,
And You have afflicted *me* with all Your waves. Selah
8 You have put away my acquaintances far from me;
You have made me an abomination to them;
I am shut up, and I cannot get out;
9 My eye wastes away because of affliction.

LORD, I have called daily upon You;
I have stretched out my hands to You.
10 Will You work wonders for the dead?
Shall the dead arise *and* praise You? Selah

88:title [a]Hebrew *Maschil*

LIFE LESSONS

➤ 86:11 — *. . . unite my heart to fear Your name.*

Our hearts can be a jumble of conflicting emotions and competing interests. At the same time we can feel torn in several warring directions. So God instructs us to pray for a united heart, at one in Him.

➤ 88:3 — *For my soul is full of troubles, and my life draws near to the grave.*

An obedient life leads to a blessed life, but that doesn't mean a trouble-free life. Paul and Barnabas said, "We must through many tribulations enter the kingdom of God" (Acts 14:22).

11 Shall Your lovingkindness be declared in the grave?
Or Your faithfulness in the place of destruction?
12 Shall Your wonders be known in the dark?
And Your righteousness in the land of forgetfulness?

13 But to You I have cried out, O LORD,
And in the morning my prayer comes before You.
14 LORD, why do You cast off my soul?
Why do You hide Your face from me?
15 I *have been* afflicted and ready to die from *my* youth;
I suffer Your terrors;
I am distraught.
16 Your fierce wrath has gone over me;
Your terrors have cut me off.
17 They came around me all day long like water;
They engulfed me altogether.
18 Loved one and friend You have put far from me,
And my acquaintances into darkness.

PSALM 89

Remembering the Covenant with David, and Sorrow for Lost Blessings

A Contemplation[a] of Ethan the Ezrahite.

1 I will sing of the mercies of the LORD forever;
With my mouth will I make known Your faithfulness to all generations.
2 For I have said, "Mercy shall be built up forever;
Your faithfulness You shall establish in the very heavens."

3 "I have made a covenant with My chosen,
I have sworn to My servant David:
4 'Your seed I will establish forever,
And build up your throne to all generations.'" Selah

5 And the heavens will praise Your wonders, O LORD;
Your faithfulness also in the assembly of the saints.
6 For who in the heavens can be compared to the LORD?
Who among the sons of the mighty can be likened to the LORD?
7 God is greatly to be feared in the assembly of the saints,
And to be held in reverence by all *those* around Him.
8 O LORD God of hosts,
Who *is* mighty like You, O LORD?
Your faithfulness also surrounds You.
9 You rule the raging of the sea;
When its waves rise, You still them.
10 You have broken Rahab in pieces, as one who is slain;
You have scattered Your enemies with Your mighty arm.

11 The heavens *are* Yours, the earth also *is* Yours;
The world and all its fullness, You have founded them.
12 The north and the south, You have created them;
Tabor and Hermon rejoice in Your name.
13 You have a mighty arm;
Strong is Your hand, *and* high is Your right hand.
14 Righteousness and justice *are* the foundation of Your throne;
Mercy and truth go before Your face.
15 Blessed *are* the people who know the joyful sound!
They walk, O LORD, in the light of Your countenance.
16 In Your name they rejoice all day long,
And in Your righteousness they are exalted.
17 For You *are* the glory of their strength,
And in Your favor our horn is exalted.
18 For our shield *belongs* to the LORD,
And our king to the Holy One of Israel.

19 Then You spoke in a vision to Your holy one,[a]
And said: "I have given help to *one who is* mighty;
I have exalted one chosen from the people.
20 I have found My servant David;
With My holy oil I have anointed him,
21 With whom My hand shall be established;
Also My arm shall strengthen him.
22 The enemy shall not outwit him,
Nor the son of wickedness afflict him.
23 I will beat down his foes before his face,
And plague those who hate him.

24 "But My faithfulness and My mercy *shall be* with him,
And in My name his horn shall be exalted.
25 Also I will set his hand over the sea,
And his right hand over the rivers.
26 He shall cry to Me, 'You *are* my Father,
My God, and the rock of my salvation.'
27 Also I will make him *My* firstborn,
The highest of the kings of the earth.
28 My mercy I will keep for him forever,
And My covenant shall stand firm with him.
29 His seed also I will make *to endure* forever,
And his throne as the days of heaven.

89:title [a]Hebrew *Maschil* **89:19** [a]Following many Hebrew manuscripts; Masoretic Text, Septuagint, Targum, and Vulgate read *holy ones*.

30 "If his sons forsake My law
And do not walk in My judgments,
31 If they break My statutes
And do not keep My commandments,
32 Then I will punish their transgression with the rod,
And their iniquity with stripes.
➤ 33 Nevertheless My lovingkindness I will not utterly take from him,
Nor allow My faithfulness to fail.
34 My covenant I will not break,
Nor alter the word that has gone out of My lips.
➤ 35 Once I have sworn by My holiness;
I will not lie to David:
➤ 36 His seed shall endure forever,
And his throne as the sun before Me;
37 It shall be established forever like the moon,
Even *like* the faithful witness in the sky." Selah

38 But You have cast off and abhorred,
You have been furious with Your anointed.
39 You have renounced the covenant of Your servant;
You have profaned his crown *by casting it* to the ground.
40 You have broken down all his hedges;
You have brought his strongholds to ruin.
41 All who pass by the way plunder him;
He is a reproach to his neighbors.
42 You have exalted the right hand of his adversaries;
You have made all his enemies rejoice.
43 You have also turned back the edge of his sword,
And have not sustained him in the battle.
44 You have made his glory cease,
And cast his throne down to the ground.
45 The days of his youth You have shortened;
You have covered him with shame. Selah

46 How long, LORD?
Will You hide Yourself forever?
Will Your wrath burn like fire?
47 Remember how short my time is;
For what futility have You created all the children of men?
48 What man can live and not see death?
Can he deliver his life from the power of the grave? Selah

49 Lord, where *are* Your former lovingkindnesses,
Which You swore to David in Your truth?
50 Remember, Lord, the reproach of Your servants—
How I bear in my bosom *the reproach of* all the many peoples,
51 With which Your enemies have reproached, O LORD,
With which they have reproached the footsteps of Your anointed.

52 Blessed *be* the LORD forevermore!
Amen and Amen.

Book Four: Psalms 90—106

PSALM 90

The Eternity of God, and Man's Frailty

A Prayer of Moses the man of God.

1 Lord, You have been our dwelling place[a] in all generations.
2 Before the mountains were brought forth,
Or ever You had formed the earth and the world,
Even from everlasting to everlasting, You *are* God.

3 You turn man to destruction,
And say, "Return, O children of men."
4 For a thousand years in Your sight ➤
Are like yesterday when it is past,
And *like* a watch in the night.
5 You carry them away *like* a flood;
They are like a sleep.
In the morning they are like grass *which* grows up:
6 In the morning it flourishes and grows up;
In the evening it is cut down and withers.

90:1 [a]Septuagint, Targum, and Vulgate read *refuge*.

LIFE LESSONS

➤ 89:33 — *Nevertheless My lovingkindness I will not utterly take from him, nor allow My faithfulness to fail.*

God chastens and corrects His erring children, but we should never mistake His discipline for rejection. He will never allow His faithfulness to fail us, and even in judgment He shows mercy.

➤ 89:35, 36 — *Once I have sworn by My holiness; I will not lie to David; his seed shall endure forever, and his throne as the sun before Me.*

If Jesus Christ were not God's Messiah, then this promise would be broken, since David's house is no more. But since Jesus is the Messiah, His eternal rule fulfills this promise to the letter.

➤ 90:4 — *For a thousand years in Your sight are like yesterday when it is past, and like a watch in the night.*

Because God is infinite and "inhabits eternity" (Is. 57:15), He is not bound by the same constraints of time that limit and frustrate us. What seems like a delay to us is right on time to Him.

7 For we have been consumed by Your
anger,
And by Your wrath we are terrified.
8 You have set our iniquities before You,
Our secret *sins* in the light of Your
countenance.
9 For all our days have passed away in
Your wrath;
We finish our years like a sigh.
10 The days of our lives *are* seventy years;
And if by reason of strength *they are*
eighty years,
Yet their boast *is* only labor and sorrow;
For it is soon cut off, and we fly away.
11 Who knows the power of Your anger?
For as the fear of You, *so is* Your wrath.
12 So teach *us* to number our days,
That we may gain a heart of wisdom.

13 Return, O LORD!
How long?
And have compassion on Your servants.
➤ 14 Oh, satisfy us early with Your mercy,
That we may rejoice and be glad all our
days!
15 Make us glad according to the days *in
which* You have afflicted us,
The years *in which* we have seen evil.
16 Let Your work appear to Your servants,
And Your glory to their children.
17 And let the beauty of the LORD our God
be upon us,
And establish the work of our hands for
us;
Yes, establish the work of our hands.

PSALM 91

Safety of Abiding in the Presence of God

1 He who dwells in the secret place of the
Most High
Shall abide under the shadow of the
Almighty.
2 I will say of the LORD, "*He is* my refuge
and my fortress;
My God, in Him I will trust."
3 Surely He shall deliver you from the
snare of the fowler[a]
And from the perilous pestilence.
4 He shall cover you with His feathers,
And under His wings you shall take
refuge;
His truth *shall be your* shield and
buckler.
5 You shall not be afraid of the terror by
night, ➤
Nor of the arrow *that* flies by day,
6 *Nor* of the pestilence *that* walks in
darkness,
Nor of the destruction *that* lays waste
at noonday.

7 A thousand may fall at your side,
And ten thousand at your right hand;
But it shall not come near you.
8 Only with your eyes shall you look,
And see the reward of the wicked.

9 Because you have made the LORD, *who
is* my refuge,
Even the Most High, your dwelling
place,
10 No evil shall befall you,
Nor shall any plague come near your
dwelling;
11 For He shall give His angels charge
over you,
To keep you in all your ways.
12 In *their* hands they shall bear you up,
Lest you dash your foot against a
stone.
13 You shall tread upon the lion and the
cobra,
The young lion and the serpent you
shall trample underfoot.

14 "Because he has set his love upon Me,
therefore I will deliver him; ✳
I will set him on high, because he has
known My name.
15 He shall call upon Me, and I will answer
him; ➤
I *will be* with him in trouble;
I will deliver him and honor him.
16 With long life I will satisfy him,
And show him My salvation."

91:3 [a]That is, one who catches birds in a trap or snare

LIFE LESSONS

➤ 90:14 — *Oh, satisfy us early with Your mercy, that we may rejoice and be glad all our days!*

God wants our relationship with Him to fill us with joy and gladness, as an advertisement to the world of His goodness and mercy. "In Your presence is fullness of joy . . ." (Ps. 16:11).

➤ 91:5 — *You shall not be afraid of the terror by night, nor of the arrow that flies by day . . . .*

Some nights *are* filled with terror, and some arrows *do* fly by day. Yet when we find our security in the Lord, they do not have to terrify or intimidate us; He is our safety, and in Him we find rest.

➤ 91:15 — *He shall call upon Me, and I will answer him; I will be with him in trouble; I will deliver him and honor him.*

In prayer, we connect our need to God's supply. We bring our emptiness to God's fullness and ask Him to satisfy us. Our deficits are no match for His abundance, and our cries find a home in His ears.

PSALM 92

Praise to the LORD *for His Love and Faithfulness*

A Psalm. A Song for the Sabbath day.

1 *It is* good to give thanks to the LORD,
And to sing praises to Your name,
O Most High;
➤ 2 To declare Your lovingkindness in the morning,
And Your faithfulness every night,
3 On an instrument of ten strings,
On the lute,
And on the harp,
With harmonious sound.
4 For You, LORD, have made me glad through Your work;
I will triumph in the works of Your hands.
5 O LORD, how great are Your works!
Your thoughts are very deep.
6 A senseless man does not know,
Nor does a fool understand this.
7 When the wicked spring up like grass,
And when all the workers of iniquity flourish,
It is that they may be destroyed forever.
8 But You, LORD, *are* on high forevermore.
9 For behold, Your enemies, O LORD,
For behold, Your enemies shall perish;
All the workers of iniquity shall be scattered.
10 But my horn You have exalted like a wild ox;
I have been anointed with fresh oil.
11 My eye also has seen *my desire* on my enemies;
My ears hear *my desire* on the wicked
Who rise up against me.
12 The righteous shall flourish like a palm tree,
He shall grow like a cedar in Lebanon.
13 Those who are planted in the house of the LORD
Shall flourish in the courts of our God.
➤ 14 They shall still bear fruit in old age;
They shall be fresh and flourishing,
15 To declare that the LORD is upright;
He is my rock, and *there is* no unrighteousness in Him.

PSALM 93

The Eternal Reign of the LORD

1 The LORD reigns, He is clothed with majesty; ➤
The LORD is clothed,
He has girded Himself with strength.
Surely the world is established, so that it cannot be moved.
2 Your throne *is* established from of old;
You *are* from everlasting.
3 The floods have lifted up, O LORD,
The floods have lifted up their voice;
The floods lift up their waves.
4 The LORD on high *is* mightier
Than the noise of many waters,
Than the mighty waves of the sea.
5 Your testimonies are very sure;
Holiness adorns Your house,
O LORD, forever.

PSALM 94

God the Refuge of the Righteous

1 O LORD God, to whom vengeance belongs—
O God, to whom vengeance belongs, shine forth!
2 Rise up, O Judge of the earth;
Render punishment to the proud.
3 LORD, how long will the wicked,
How long will the wicked triumph?
4 They utter speech, *and* speak insolent things;
All the workers of iniquity boast in themselves.
5 They break in pieces Your people, O LORD,
And afflict Your heritage.
6 They slay the widow and the stranger,
And murder the fatherless.
7 Yet they say, "The LORD does not see,
Nor does the God of Jacob understand."

LIFE LESSONS

➤ 92:2 — *To declare Your lovingkindness in the morning, and Your faithfulness every night.*

This verse points to the moment-by-moment relationship that God wants with us. He has little interest in a law—"do this in the morning and this in the evening"—but rather wants to enjoy our company all day long.

➤ 92:14 — *They shall still bear fruit in old age; they shall be fresh and flourishing . . . .*

Bodies grow old and frail, but God wants us to bear fruit so long as we live on this earth. The kind of fruit may vary depending on our season of life, but He calls us to fruitfulness in all seasons.

➤ 93:1 — *The LORD reigns, He is clothed with majesty; the LORD is clothed, He has girded Himself with strength.*

We are children of a sovereign God who has the power and the wisdom to make happen everything He desires to do. Nothing can frustrate His plans and no one can derail His promises. That's why we can trust Him!

8 Understand, you senseless among the people;
And *you* fools, when will you be wise?
9 He who planted the ear, shall He not hear?
He who formed the eye, shall He not see?
10 He who instructs the nations, shall He not correct,
He who teaches man knowledge?
11 The LORD knows the thoughts of man,
That they *are* futile.

➤ 12 Blessed *is* the man whom You instruct, O LORD,
And teach out of Your law,
➤ 13 That You may give him rest from the days of adversity,
Until the pit is dug for the wicked.
14 For the LORD will not cast off His people,
Nor will He forsake His inheritance.
15 But judgment will return to righteousness,
And all the upright in heart will follow it.

16 Who will rise up for me against the evildoers?
Who will stand up for me against the workers of iniquity?
17 Unless the LORD *had been* my help,
My soul would soon have settled in silence.
18 If I say, "My foot slips,"
Your mercy, O LORD, will hold me up.
➤ 19 In the multitude of my anxieties within me,
Your comforts delight my soul.

20 Shall the throne of iniquity, which devises evil by law,
Have fellowship with You?
21 They gather together against the life of the righteous,
And condemn innocent blood.
22 But the LORD has been my defense,
And my God the rock of my refuge.
23 He has brought on them their own iniquity,
And shall cut them off in their own wickedness;
The LORD our God shall cut them off.

PSALM 95

A Call to Worship and Obedience

1 Oh come, let us sing to the LORD!
Let us shout joyfully to the Rock of our salvation.
2 Let us come before His presence with thanksgiving;
Let us shout joyfully to Him with psalms.
3 For the LORD *is* the great God,
And the great King above all gods.
4 In His hand *are* the deep places of the earth;
The heights of the hills *are* His also.
5 The sea *is* His, for He made it;
And His hands formed the dry *land.*

6 Oh come, let us worship and bow down; ➤
Let us kneel before the LORD our Maker.
7 For He *is* our God, ➤
And we *are* the people of His pasture,
And the sheep of His hand.

Today, if you will hear His voice:
8 "Do not harden your hearts, as in the rebellion,[a] ➤
As *in* the day of trial[b] in the wilderness,
9 When your fathers tested Me;
They tried Me, though they saw My work.
10 For forty years I was grieved with *that* generation,
And said, 'It *is* a people who go astray in their hearts,
And they do not know My ways.'
11 So I swore in My wrath,
'They shall not enter My rest.'"

95:8 [a]Or *Meribah* [b]Or *Massah*

LIFE LESSONS

➤ 94:12, 13 — *Blessed is the man whom You instruct, O LORD, and teach out of Your law, that You may give him rest from the days of adversity . . . .*

In this verse God gives us yet another reason to study His Word: when we do, He may shorten the seasons of adversity that trouble us, perhaps by showing us how we may have contributed to the trouble.

➤ 94:19 — *In the multitude of my anxieties within me, Your comforts delight my soul.*

God is an ever-present comfort, even when our emotions bounce off the wall and our hearts zigzag in a thousand directions. God wants to calm our anxieties, but even before that happens, He comforts us in our distress.

➤ 95:6 — *Oh come, let us worship and bow down; let us kneel before the LORD our Maker.*

In most churches the accommodations discourage us from physically bowing down before God in worship; but why not kneel before Him in private worship at home? A humble posture can help to remind us of God's majesty.

➤ 95:7, 8 — *Today, if you will hear His voice: "Do not harden your hearts, as in the rebellion, as in the day of trial in the wilderness . . . ."*

The writer of Hebrews quotes this verse three times in one short section of his letter (Heb. 3:7, 8, 15; 4:7) to encourage his readers to listen carefully to God and to demonstrate their faith by obeying Him.

PSALM 96

A Song of Praise to God Coming in Judgment

➤ 1 Oh, sing to the LORD a new song!
Sing to the LORD, all the earth.
2 Sing to the LORD, bless His name;
Proclaim the good news of His salvation from day to day.
3 Declare His glory among the nations,
His wonders among all peoples.

4 For the LORD *is* great and greatly to be praised;
He *is* to be feared above all gods.
5 For all the gods of the peoples *are* idols,
But the LORD made the heavens.
6 Honor and majesty *are* before Him;
Strength and beauty *are* in His sanctuary.

7 Give to the LORD, O families of the peoples,
Give to the LORD glory and strength.
8 Give to the LORD the glory *due* His name;
Bring an offering, and come into His courts.
➤ 9 Oh, worship the LORD in the beauty of holiness!
Tremble before Him, all the earth.

✳ 10 Say among the nations, "The LORD reigns;
The world also is firmly established,
It shall not be moved;
He shall judge the peoples righteously."

11 Let the heavens rejoice, and let the earth be glad;
Let the sea roar, and all its fullness;
12 Let the field be joyful, and all that *is* in it.
Then all the trees of the woods will rejoice
13 before the LORD.

For He is coming, for He is coming to judge the earth.
He shall judge the world with righteousness,
And the peoples with His truth.

PSALM 97

A Song of Praise to the Sovereign LORD

1 The LORD reigns;
Let the earth rejoice;
Let the multitude of isles be glad!

2 Clouds and darkness surround Him;
Righteousness and justice *are* the foundation of His throne.
3 A fire goes before Him,
And burns up His enemies round about.
4 His lightnings light the world;
The earth sees and trembles.
5 The mountains melt like wax at the presence of the LORD,
At the presence of the Lord of the whole earth.
6 The heavens declare His righteousness,
And all the peoples see His glory.

7 Let all be put to shame who serve carved images,
Who boast of idols.
Worship Him, all *you* gods.
8 Zion hears and is glad,
And the daughters of Judah rejoice
Because of Your judgments, O LORD.
9 For You, LORD, *are* most high above all the earth;
You are exalted far above all gods.

10 You who love the LORD, hate evil! ➤
He preserves the souls of His saints;
He delivers them out of the hand of the wicked.
11 Light is sown for the righteous,
And gladness for the upright in heart.
12 Rejoice in the LORD, you righteous,
And give thanks at the remembrance of His holy name.[a]

PSALM 98

A Song of Praise to the LORD for His Salvation and Judgment

A Psalm.

1 Oh, sing to the LORD a new song!
For He has done marvelous things;

97:12 [a]Or *His holiness*

LIFE LESSONS

➤ **96:1 — *Oh, sing to the LORD a new song!***

Why does Scripture encourage us to sing a "new" song to the Lord? Old songs are good too, but new songs help us to see God in a fresh light and to appreciate Him in a new way.

➤ **96:9 — *Oh, worship the LORD in the beauty of holiness!***

We are to worship the Lord for His beautiful holiness—His purity, His righteousness, His spotlessness—as we worship Him beautifully through pure, blameless, and upright lives.

➤ **97:10 — *You who love the LORD, hate evil!***

As our taste for the Lord and His loving, holy nature grows, our distaste for anything that dishonors and displeases Him should also grow. Our love for God should prompt us to help others love Him, too.

His right hand and His holy arm have
gained Him the victory.
2 The LORD has made known His
salvation;
His righteousness He has revealed in
the sight of the nations.
3 He has remembered His mercy and His
faithfulness to the house of Israel;
All the ends of the earth have seen the
salvation of our God.

4 Shout joyfully to the LORD, all the earth;
Break forth in song, rejoice, and sing
praises.
5 Sing to the LORD with the harp,
With the harp and the sound of a psalm,
6 With trumpets and the sound of a horn;
Shout joyfully before the LORD, the
King.

7 Let the sea roar, and all its fullness,
The world and those who dwell in it;
8 Let the rivers clap *their* hands;
Let the hills be joyful together
➤ 9 before the LORD,
for He is coming to judge the earth.
With righteousness He shall judge the
world,
And the peoples with equity.

PSALM 99

Praise to the LORD for His Holiness

➤ 1 The LORD reigns;
Let the peoples tremble!
He dwells *between* the cherubim;
Let the earth be moved!
2 The LORD *is* great in Zion,
And He *is* high above all the peoples.
3 Let them praise Your great and
awesome name—
He *is* holy.

4 The King's strength also loves justice;
You have established equity;
You have executed justice and
righteousness in Jacob.
5 Exalt the LORD our God,
And worship at His footstool—
He *is* holy.

6 Moses and Aaron were among His
priests,
And Samuel was among those who
called upon His name;
They called upon the LORD, and He
answered them.
7 He spoke to them in the cloudy pillar;
They kept His testimonies and the
ordinance He gave them.

8 You answered them, O LORD our God; ➤
You were to them God-Who-Forgives,
Though You took vengeance on their
deeds.
9 Exalt the LORD our God,
And worship at His holy hill;
For the LORD our God *is* holy.

PSALM 100

A Song of Praise for the Faithfulness to His People

A Psalm of Thanksgiving.

1 Make a joyful shout to the LORD, all you
lands!
2 Serve the LORD with gladness; ➤
Come before His presence with singing.
3 Know that the LORD, He *is* God; ➤
It is He *who* has made us, and not we
ourselves;[a]
We are His people and the sheep of His
pasture.

4 Enter into His gates with thanksgiving,
And into His courts with praise.

100:3 [a]Following Kethib, Septuagint, and Vulgate; Qere, many Hebrew manuscripts, and Targum read *we are His*.

LIFE LESSONS

➤ **98:9 — *For He is coming to judge the earth. With righteousness He shall judge the world, and the peoples with equity.***

Jesus told His disciples that, "the Father judges no one, but has committed all judgment to the Son" (John 5:22). When He returns, Jesus will fulfill this verse and bring God's justice to our troubled planet.

➤ **99:1 — *The LORD reigns; let the peoples tremble! He dwells between the cherubim; let the earth be moved!***

Why should we "tremble" when we ponder God's sovereignty? Why should our hearts "be moved" when we consider His presence? Because He is "the King of kings and Lord of lords, who alone has immortality . . ." (1 Tim. 6:15, 16).

➤ **99:8 — *You were to them God-Who-Forgives, though You took vengeance on their deeds.***

God's forgiveness is not incompatible with or opposed to His discipline. When we place our faith in Christ, He forgives our sins—past, present, and future—but He still promises to discipline us when necessary (Heb. 12:4–11).

➤ **100:2 — *Serve the LORD with gladness; come before His presence with singing.***

If the Lord's presence makes us joyful, then so should serving Him make us happy. Only when one takes no pleasure in God does serving Him seem like a chore and a burden.

➤ **100:3 — *Know that the LORD, He is God; it is He who has made us, and not we ourselves; we are His people and the sheep of His pasture.***

God is the Shepherd; we are His flock. God is the Creator; we are His creations. God is the Father; we are His children. When we remember these basic truths, life goes a lot smoother for everyone.

Be thankful to Him, *and* bless His name.
✳5 For the LORD *is* good;
His mercy *is* everlasting,
And His truth *endures* to all
generations.

PSALM 101

Promised Faithfulness to the LORD

A Psalm of David.

1 I will sing of mercy and justice;
To You, O LORD, I will sing praises.
➤2 I will behave wisely in a perfect way.
Oh, when will You come to me?
I will walk within my house with a
perfect heart.
➤3 I will set nothing wicked before my eyes;
I hate the work of those who fall away;
It shall not cling to me.
4 A perverse heart shall depart from me;
I will not know wickedness.
5 Whoever secretly slanders his neighbor,
Him I will destroy;
The one who has a haughty look and a
proud heart,
Him I will not endure.
6 My eyes *shall be* on the faithful of the
land,
That they may dwell with me;
He who walks in a perfect way,
He shall serve me.
7 He who works deceit shall not dwell
within my house;
He who tells lies shall not continue in
my presence.
8 Early I will destroy all the wicked of the
land,
That I may cut off all the evildoers from
the city of the LORD.

PSALM 102

The LORD's Eternal Love

A Prayer of the afflicted, when he is overwhelmed and pours out his complaint before the LORD.

1 Hear my prayer, O LORD,
And let my cry come to You.
2 Do not hide Your face from me in the
day of my trouble;
Incline Your ear to me;
In the day that I call, answer me speedily.
3 For my days are consumed like smoke,
And my bones are burned like a hearth.
4 My heart is stricken and withered like
grass,
So that I forget to eat my bread.
5 Because of the sound of my groaning
My bones cling to my skin.
6 I am like a pelican of the wilderness;
I am like an owl of the desert.
7 I lie awake,
And am like a sparrow alone on the
housetop.
8 My enemies reproach me all day long;
Those who deride me swear an oath
against me.
9 For I have eaten ashes like bread,
And mingled my drink with weeping,
10 Because of Your indignation and Your
wrath;
For You have lifted me up and cast me
away.
11 My days *are* like a shadow that lengthens,
And I wither away like grass.
12 But You, O LORD, shall endure forever,
And the remembrance of Your name to
all generations.
13 You will arise *and* have mercy on Zion;
For the time to favor her,
Yes, the set time, has come.
14 For Your servants take pleasure in her
stones,
And show favor to her dust.
15 So the nations shall fear the name of
the LORD,
And all the kings of the earth Your glory.
16 For the LORD shall build up Zion;
He shall appear in His glory.
17 He shall regard the prayer of the
destitute,
And shall not despise their prayer.
18 This will be written for the generation ◄
to come,
That a people yet to be created may
praise the LORD.

LIFE LESSONS

➤ 101:2 — *I will walk within my house with a perfect heart.*

It's one thing to behave in a godly way in public, when you know many eyes are watching. It's another to reflect His goodness and righteousness at home, where only family members see. God calls us to both.

➤ 101:3 — *I will set nothing wicked before my eyes . . . .*

How many affairs begin with just a "harmless glance"? How many thefts start with an envious gaze? How many addictive habits get rolling with prolonged exposure to the wrong thing?

➤ 102:18 — *This will be written for the generation to come, that a people yet to be created may praise the LORD.*

Most of us reading this are the "people yet to be created" spoken of in this verse. *You* are a fulfillment of prophecy! But to fulfill it completely, you must be in the habit of praising the Lord. Are you?

19 For He looked down from the height of His sanctuary;
From heaven the LORD viewed the earth,
20 To hear the groaning of the prisoner,
To release those appointed to death,
21 To declare the name of the LORD in Zion,
And His praise in Jerusalem,
22 When the peoples are gathered together,
And the kingdoms, to serve the LORD.
23 He weakened my strength in the way;
He shortened my days.
24 I said, "O my God,
Do not take me away in the midst of my days;
Your years *are* throughout all generations.
25 Of old You laid the foundation of the earth,
And the heavens *are* the work of Your hands.
➤ 26 They will perish, but You will endure;
Yes, they will all grow old like a garment;
Like a cloak You will change them,
And they will be changed.
➤ 27 But You *are* the same,
And Your years will have no end.
28 The children of Your servants will continue,
And their descendants will be established before You."

PSALM 103

Praise for the LORD's Mercies

A Psalm of David.

➤ 1 Bless the LORD, O my soul;
And all that is within me, *bless* His holy name!
2 Bless the LORD, O my soul,
And forget not all His benefits:
3 Who forgives all your iniquities,
Who heals all your diseases,
4 Who redeems your life from destruction,
Who crowns you with lovingkindness and tender mercies,
5 Who satisfies your mouth with good *things*,
So that your youth is renewed like the eagle's.

6 The LORD executes righteousness
And justice for all who are oppressed.
7 He made known His ways to Moses,
His acts to the children of Israel.
8 The LORD *is* merciful and gracious,
Slow to anger, and abounding in mercy.
9 He will not always strive *with us*,
Nor will He keep *His anger* forever.
10 He has not dealt with us according to our sins,
Nor punished us according to our iniquities.

11 For as the heavens are high above the earth,
So great is His mercy toward those who fear Him;
12 As far as the east is from the west,
So far has He removed our transgressions from us.

13 As a father pities *his* children, ➤
So the LORD pities those who fear Him.
14 For He knows our frame;
He remembers that we *are* dust.

15 *As for* man, his days *are* like grass;
As a flower of the field, so he flourishes.
16 For the wind passes over it, and it is gone,
And its place remembers it no more.[a]
17 But the mercy of the LORD *is* from everlasting to everlasting
On those who fear Him,
And His righteousness to children's children,
18 To such as keep His covenant,
And to those who remember His commandments to do them.

19 The LORD has established His throne in heaven,
And His kingdom rules over all.

103:16 [a]Compare Job 7:10

LIFE LESSONS

➤ 102:26, 27 — *They will perish, but You will endure; yes, they will all grow old like a garment; like a cloak You will change them, and they will be changed. But You are the same, and Your years will have no end.*

As people with comparatively short life spans, we view the stars as if they were everlasting. Our eternal God sees them more like threadbare clothes ready for the rag bin. And yet for all His majesty, He sets His love on *us*!

➤ 103:1 — *Bless the LORD, O my soul; and all that is within me, bless His holy name!*

God wants every part of us—body, soul and spirit—to grow close to Him and to enter into a joyful relationship with Him. He seeks worshipers who will gladly give everything they are to Him.

➤ 103:13 — *As a father pities his children, so the LORD pities those who fear Him.*

How does a father "pity" His children? He considers their weakness, immaturity, and ignorance, and so does not require of them more than they can handle. Our Father does the same with us (1 Cor. 10:13).

20 Bless the LORD, you His angels,
Who excel in strength, who do His word,
Heeding the voice of His word.
21 Bless the LORD, all *you* His hosts,
You ministers of His, who do His pleasure.
22 Bless the LORD, all His works,
In all places of His dominion.

Bless the LORD, O my soul!

PSALM 104

Praise to the Sovereign LORD for His Creation and Providence

1 Bless the LORD, O my soul!

O LORD my God, You are very great:
You are clothed with honor and majesty,
2 Who cover *Yourself* with light as *with* a garment,
Who stretch out the heavens like a curtain.

3 He lays the beams of His upper chambers in the waters,
Who makes the clouds His chariot,
Who walks on the wings of the wind,
➤ 4 Who makes His angels spirits,
His ministers a flame of fire.

5 *You who* laid the foundations of the earth,
So *that* it should not be moved forever,
6 You covered it with the deep as *with* a garment;
The waters stood above the mountains.
7 At Your rebuke they fled;
At the voice of Your thunder they hastened away.
8 They went up over the mountains;
They went down into the valleys,
To the place which You founded for them.
9 You have set a boundary that they may not pass over,
That they may not return to cover the earth.

10 He sends the springs into the valleys;
They flow among the hills.
11 They give drink to every beast of the field;
The wild donkeys quench their thirst.
12 By them the birds of the heavens have their home;
They sing among the branches.
13 He waters the hills from His upper chambers;
The earth is satisfied with the fruit of Your works.

14 He causes the grass to grow for the cattle,
And vegetation for the service of man,
That he may bring forth food from the earth,
15 And wine *that* makes glad the heart of man,
Oil to make *his* face shine,
And bread *which* strengthens man's heart.
16 The trees of the LORD are full *of sap*,
The cedars of Lebanon which He planted,
17 Where the birds make their nests;
The stork has her home in the fir trees.
18 The high hills *are* for the wild goats;
The cliffs are a refuge for the rock badgers.[a]

19 He appointed the moon for seasons;
The sun knows its going down.
20 You make darkness, and it is night,
In which all the beasts of the forest creep about.
21 The young lions roar after their prey,
And seek their food from God.
22 *When* the sun rises, they gather together
And lie down in their dens.
23 Man goes out to his work
And to his labor until the evening.

24 O LORD, how manifold are Your works! ➤
In wisdom You have made them all.
The earth is full of Your possessions—
25 This great and wide sea,
In which *are* innumerable teeming things,
Living things both small and great.
26 There the ships sail about;
There is that Leviathan
Which You have made to play there.

27 These all wait for You,

104:18 [a]Or *rock hyrax* (compare Leviticus 11:5)

LIFE LESSONS

➤ 104:4 — *Who makes His angels spirits, His ministers a flame of fire.*

The angels of God are not the cute, harmless little cherubs often pictured in popular culture. They are spirits of enormous power, sent to do God's will. Often God in His mercy sends them to help us.

➤ 104:24 — *O LORD, how manifold are Your works! In wisdom You have made them all.*

The creation reveals a God with a vast intellect that we cannot begin to comprehend. Our best scientists must regularly revise their theories to try to explain what He created—and He puts all His wisdom at our service.

That You may give *them* their food in
due season.
28 *What* You give them they gather in;
You open Your hand, they are filled with
good.
29 You hide Your face, they are troubled;
You take away their breath, they die
and return to their dust.
30 You send forth Your Spirit, they are
created;
And You renew the face of the earth.

31 May the glory of the LORD endure
forever;
May the LORD rejoice in His works.
32 He looks on the earth, and it trembles;
He touches the hills, and they smoke.

33 I will sing to the LORD as long as I live;
I will sing praise to my God while I
have my being.
34 May my meditation be sweet to Him;
I will be glad in the LORD.
35 May sinners be consumed from the
earth,
And the wicked be no more.

Bless the LORD, O my soul!
Praise the LORD!

PSALM 105

The Eternal Faithfulness of the LORD

1 Oh, give thanks to the LORD!
Call upon His name;
Make known His deeds among the
peoples!
2 Sing to Him, sing psalms to Him;
Talk of all His wondrous works!
3 Glory in His holy name;
Let the hearts of those rejoice who seek
the LORD!
➤4 Seek the LORD and His strength;
Seek His face evermore!
5 Remember His marvelous works which
He has done,
His wonders, and the judgments of His
mouth,
6 O seed of Abraham His servant,
You children of Jacob, His chosen ones!

7 He *is* the LORD our God;
His judgments *are* in all the earth.
8 He remembers His covenant forever,
The word *which* He commanded, for a
thousand generations,
9 *The covenant* which He made with
Abraham,
And His oath to Isaac,
10 And confirmed it to Jacob for a statute,
To Israel *as* an everlasting covenant,
11 Saying, "To you I will give the land of
Canaan
As the allotment of your inheritance,"
12 When they were few in number,
Indeed very few, and strangers in it.

13 When they went from one nation to
another,
From *one* kingdom to another people,
14 He permitted no one to do them wrong;
Yes, He rebuked kings for their sakes,
15 *Saying*, "Do not touch My anointed
ones,
And do My prophets no harm."

16 Moreover He called for a famine in the
land;
He destroyed all the provision of bread.
17 He sent a man before them—
Joseph—*who* was sold as a slave.
18 They hurt his feet with fetters,
He was laid in irons.
19 Until the time that his word came to ➤
pass,
The word of the LORD tested him.
20 The king sent and released him,
The ruler of the people let him go free.
21 He made him lord of his house,
And ruler of all his possessions,
22 To bind his princes at his pleasure,
And teach his elders wisdom.

23 Israel also came into Egypt,
And Jacob dwelt in the land of Ham.
24 He increased His people greatly,
And made them stronger than their
enemies.
25 He turned their heart to hate His
people,
To deal craftily with His servants.

26 He sent Moses His servant,
And Aaron whom He had chosen.
27 They performed His signs among them,
And wonders in the land of Ham.
28 He sent darkness, and made *it* dark;
And they did not rebel against His
word.
29 He turned their waters into blood,
And killed their fish.

LIFE LESSONS

➤ **105:4 — *Seek the Lord and His strength; seek His face evermore!***

Since God is infinite, we will never run out of new and surprising territory to explore regarding His character and nature. The great adventure of seeking God and His ways will continue our whole lives.

➤ **105:19 — *Until the time that his word came to pass, the word of the LORD tested him.***

Whomever God uses greatly, He first tests thoroughly. As a teenager, Joseph prophesied through the Spirit that his brothers and father would one day bow down to him. But before that happened, he had to endure much hardship.

30 Their land abounded with frogs,
Even in the chambers of their kings.
31 He spoke, and there came swarms of flies,
And lice in all their territory.
32 He gave them hail for rain,
And flaming fire in their land.
33 He struck their vines also, and their fig trees,
And splintered the trees of their territory.
34 He spoke, and locusts came,
Young locusts without number,
35 And ate up all the vegetation in their land,
And devoured the fruit of their ground.
36 He also destroyed all the firstborn in their land,
The first of all their strength.

37 He also brought them out with silver and gold,
And *there was* none feeble among His tribes.
38 Egypt was glad when they departed,
For the fear of them had fallen upon them.
39 He spread a cloud for a covering,
And fire to give light in the night.
40 *The people* asked, and He brought quail,
And satisfied them with the bread of heaven.
41 He opened the rock, and water gushed out;
It ran in the dry places *like* a river.

42 For He remembered His holy promise,
And Abraham His servant.
43 He brought out His people with joy,
His chosen ones with gladness.
44 He gave them the lands of the Gentiles,
And they inherited the labor of the nations,
45 That they might observe His statutes
And keep His laws.

Praise the LORD!

PSALM 106

Joy in Forgiveness of Israel's Sins

1 Praise the LORD!

Oh, give thanks to the LORD, for *He is* good!
For His mercy *endures* forever.
2 Who can utter the mighty acts of the LORD?
Who can declare all His praise?
3 Blessed *are* those who keep justice,
And he who does[a] righteousness at all times!

4 Remember me, O LORD, with the favor
You have toward Your people.
Oh, visit me with Your salvation,
5 That I may see the benefit of Your chosen ones,
That I may rejoice in the gladness of Your nation,
That I may glory with Your inheritance.

6 We have sinned with our fathers,
We have committed iniquity,
We have done wickedly.
7 Our fathers in Egypt did not understand Your wonders;
They did not remember the multitude of Your mercies,
But rebelled by the sea—the Red Sea.

8 Nevertheless He saved them for His name's sake,
That He might make His mighty power known.
9 He rebuked the Red Sea also, and it dried up;
So He led them through the depths,
As through the wilderness.
10 He saved them from the hand of him who hated *them*,
And redeemed them from the hand of the enemy.
11 The waters covered their enemies;
There was not one of them left.
12 Then they believed His words;
They sang His praise.

13 They soon forgot His works;
They did not wait for His counsel,
14 But lusted exceedingly in the wilderness,
And tested God in the desert.
15 And He gave them their request,
But sent leanness into their soul.

16 When they envied Moses in the camp,
And Aaron the saint of the LORD,
17 The earth opened up and swallowed Dathan,
And covered the faction of Abiram.

106:3 [a]Septuagint, Syriac, Targum, and Vulgate read *those who do.*

LIFE LESSONS

➤ 106:3 — *Blessed are those who keep justice, and he who does righteousness at all times!*

God often pairs "justice" with "righteousness." He insists that the good things He is doing with us on the inside must work their way outside of us to bless others (Phil. 2:12).

➤ 106:15 — *He gave them their request, but sent leanness into their soul.*

We should thank God regularly that He *doesn't* answer many of our prayers. When the Israelites demanded meat in the desert, God gave them what they asked for—but the request ended up killing thousands of them.

18 A fire was kindled in their company;
The flame burned up the wicked.

19 They made a calf in Horeb,
And worshiped the molded image.
20 Thus they changed their glory
Into the image of an ox that eats grass.
21 They forgot God their Savior,
Who had done great things in Egypt,
22 Wondrous works in the land of Ham,
Awesome things by the Red Sea.
23 Therefore He said that He would destroy them,
Had not Moses His chosen one stood before Him in the breach,
To turn away His wrath, lest He destroy *them.*

24 Then they despised the pleasant land;
They did not believe His word,
25 But complained in their tents,
And did not heed the voice of the LORD.
26 Therefore He raised His hand *in an oath* against them,
To overthrow them in the wilderness,
27 To overthrow their descendants among the nations,
And to scatter them in the lands.

28 They joined themselves also to Baal of Peor,
And ate sacrifices made to the dead.
29 Thus they provoked *Him* to anger with their deeds,
And the plague broke out among them.
30 Then Phinehas stood up and intervened,
And the plague was stopped.
31 And that was accounted to him for righteousness
To all generations forevermore.

32 They angered *Him* also at the waters of strife,[a]
So that it went ill with Moses on account of them;
33 Because they rebelled against His Spirit,
So that he spoke rashly with his lips.

34 They did not destroy the peoples,
Concerning whom the LORD had commanded them,
35 But they mingled with the Gentiles
And learned their works;
36 They served their idols,
Which became a snare to them.
37 They even sacrificed their sons
And their daughters to demons,
38 And shed innocent blood,
The blood of their sons and daughters,
Whom they sacrificed to the idols of Canaan;
And the land was polluted with blood.
39 Thus they were defiled by their own works,
And played the harlot by their own deeds.

40 Therefore the wrath of the LORD was kindled against His people,
So that He abhorred His own inheritance.
41 And He gave them into the hand of the Gentiles,
And those who hated them ruled over them.
42 Their enemies also oppressed them,
And they were brought into subjection under their hand.
43 Many times He delivered them;
But they rebelled in their counsel,
And were brought low for their iniquity.
44 Nevertheless He regarded their affliction,
When He heard their cry;
45 And for their sake He remembered His covenant,
And relented according to the multitude of His mercies.
46 He also made them to be pitied
By all those who carried them away captive.

47 Save us, O LORD our God,
And gather us from among the Gentiles,
To give thanks to Your holy name,
To triumph in Your praise.

48 Blessed *be* the LORD God of Israel
From everlasting to everlasting!
And let all the people say, "Amen!"

Praise the LORD!

Book Five: Psalms 107—150

PSALM 107

Thanksgiving to the LORD for His Great Works of Deliverance

1 Oh, give thanks to the LORD, for *He is* good!
For His mercy *endures* forever.
2 Let the redeemed of the LORD say *so,*
Whom He has redeemed from the hand of the enemy,
3 And gathered out of the lands,
From the east and from the west,
From the north and from the south.

4 They wandered in the wilderness in a desolate way;
They found no city to dwell in.
5 Hungry and thirsty,
Their soul fainted in them.
6 Then they cried out to the LORD in their trouble,
And He delivered them out of their distresses.
7 And He led them forth by the right way,
That they might go to a city for a dwelling place.

106:32 [a]Or *Meribah*

8 Oh, that *men* would give thanks to the
LORD *for* His goodness,
And *for* His wonderful works to the
children of men!
➤ 9 For He satisfies the longing soul,
And fills the hungry soul with
goodness.
10 Those who sat in darkness and in the
shadow of death,
Bound in affliction and irons—
11 Because they rebelled against the words
of God,
And despised the counsel of the Most
High,
12 Therefore He brought down their heart
with labor;
They fell down, and *there was* none to
help.
13 Then they cried out to the LORD in their
trouble,
And He saved them out of their
distresses.
14 He brought them out of darkness and
the shadow of death,
And broke their chains in pieces.
15 Oh, that *men* would give thanks to the
LORD *for* His goodness,
And *for* His wonderful works to the
children of men!
16 For He has broken the gates of bronze,
And cut the bars of iron in two.

17 Fools, because of their transgression,
And because of their iniquities, were
afflicted.
18 Their soul abhorred all manner of food,
And they drew near to the gates of
death.
➤ 19 Then they cried out to the LORD in their
trouble,
And He saved them out of their
distresses.
20 He sent His word and healed them,
And delivered *them* from their
destructions.
21 Oh, that *men* would give thanks to the
LORD *for* His goodness,
And *for* His wonderful works to the
children of men!
22 Let them sacrifice the sacrifices of
thanksgiving,
And declare His works with rejoicing.

23 Those who go down to the sea in ships,
Who do business on great waters,
24 They see the works of the LORD,
And His wonders in the deep.
25 For He commands and raises the
stormy wind,
Which lifts up the waves of the sea.
26 They mount up to the heavens,
They go down again to the depths;
Their soul melts because of trouble.
27 They reel to and fro, and stagger like a
drunken man,
And are at their wits' end.
28 Then they cry out to the LORD in their
trouble,
And He brings them out of their
distresses.
29 He calms the storm,
So that its waves are still.
30 Then they are glad because they are
quiet;
So He guides them to their desired
haven.
31 Oh, that *men* would give thanks to the
LORD *for* His goodness,
And *for* His wonderful works to the
children of men!
32 Let them exalt Him also in the
assembly of the people,
And praise Him in the company of the
elders.

33 He turns rivers into a wilderness,
And the watersprings into dry ground;
34 A fruitful land into barrenness,
For the wickedness of those who dwell
in it.
35 He turns a wilderness into pools of
water,
And dry land into watersprings.
36 There He makes the hungry dwell,
That they may establish a city for a
dwelling place,
37 And sow fields and plant vineyards,
That they may yield a fruitful harvest.
38 He also blesses them, and they multiply
greatly;
And He does not let their cattle
decrease.

39 When they are diminished and brought
low
Through oppression, affliction, and
sorrow,
40 He pours contempt on princes,
And causes them to wander in the
wilderness *where there is* no way;

LIFE LESSONS

➤ 107:9 — *He satisfies the longing soul, and fills the hungry with goodness.*

God wants the undefined longing we feel in our souls to drive us to Him. He wants to satisfy our spiritual hunger with heaping helpings of Himself. He is truly the soul's end.

➤ 107:19 — *Then they cried out to the LORD in their trouble, and He saved them out of their distresses.*

Sometimes, the trouble that comes upon us is really a blessing in disguise, for it prompts us to seek God as never before. Are you in some trouble today? Then call upon God, for He delights in rescuing you.

41 Yet He sets the poor on high, far from
affliction,
And makes *their* families like a flock.
42 The righteous see *it* and rejoice,
And all iniquity stops its mouth.
43 Whoever *is* wise will observe these
things,
And they will understand the
lovingkindness of the LORD.

PSALM 108

Assurance of God's Victory over Enemies

A Song. A Psalm of David.

1 O God, my heart is steadfast;
I will sing and give praise, even with my
glory.
2 Awake, lute and harp!
I will awaken the dawn.
3 I will praise You, O LORD, among the
peoples,
And I will sing praises to You among the
nations.
4 For Your mercy *is* great above the
heavens,
And Your truth *reaches* to the clouds.
5 Be exalted, O God, above the heavens,
And Your glory above all the earth;
6 That Your beloved may be delivered,
Save *with* Your right hand, and hear me.
7 God has spoken in His holiness:
"I will rejoice;
I will divide Shechem
And measure out the Valley of Succoth.
8 Gilead *is* Mine; Manasseh *is* Mine;
Ephraim also *is* the helmet for My
head;
Judah *is* My lawgiver.
9 Moab *is* My washpot;
Over Edom I will cast My shoe;
Over Philistia I will triumph."
10 Who will bring me *into* the strong city?
Who will lead me to Edom?
11 *Is it* not *You*, O God, *who* cast us off?
And *You*, O God, *who* did not go out
with our armies?
➤ 12 Give us help from trouble,
For the help of man is useless.
13 Through God we will do valiantly,
For *it is* He *who* shall tread down our
enemies.[a]

PSALM 109

Plea for Judgment of False Accusers

To the Chief Musician. A Psalm of David.

1 Do not keep silent,
O God of my praise!
2 For the mouth of the wicked and the
mouth of the deceitful
Have opened against me;
They have spoken against me with a
lying tongue.
3 They have also surrounded me with
words of hatred,
And fought against me without a cause.
4 In return for my love they are my ➤
accusers,
But I *give myself to* prayer.
5 Thus they have rewarded me evil for
good,
And hatred for my love.
6 Set a wicked man over him,
And let an accuser[a] stand at his right
hand.
7 When he is judged, let him be found
guilty,
And let his prayer become sin.
8 Let his days be few,
And let another take his office.
9 Let his children be fatherless,
And his wife a widow.
10 Let his children continually be
vagabonds, and beg;
Let them seek *their bread*[a] also from
their desolate places.
11 Let the creditor seize all that he has,
And let strangers plunder his labor.
12 Let there be none to extend mercy to him,
Nor let there be any to favor his
fatherless children.
13 Let his posterity be cut off,
And in the generation following let their
name be blotted out.
14 Let the iniquity of his fathers be
remembered before the LORD,
And let not the sin of his mother be
blotted out.
15 Let them be continually before the
LORD,

108:13 [a]Compare verses 6–13 with 60:5–12 **109:6** [a]Hebrew *satan* **109:10** [a]Following Masoretic Text and Targum; Septuagint and Vulgate read *be cast out.*

LIFE LESSONS

➤ ***108:12 — Give us help from trouble, for the help of man is useless.***

The real question is, where do we go *first* when trouble hits? Do we rush to secure the aid of a friend or relative? Or do we take our problems directly to the Lord, and ask Him to send us to the help we need?

➤ ***109:4 — In return for my love they are my accusers, but I give myself to prayer.***

When someone betrays us or turns against us, God instructs us not to seek revenge, but to seek His face in prayer. He knows how to best deal with the situation, and we need to hear from Him.

That He may cut off the memory of
them from the earth;
16 Because he did not remember to show
mercy,
But persecuted the poor and needy man,
That he might even slay the broken in
heart.
17 As he loved cursing, so let it come to him;
As he did not delight in blessing, so let
it be far from him.
18 As he clothed himself with cursing as
with his garment,
So let it enter his body like water,
And like oil into his bones.
19 Let it be to him like the garment which
covers him,
And for a belt with which he girds
himself continually.
20 *Let* this *be* the LORD's reward to my
accusers,
And to those who speak evil against my
person.
21 But You, O GOD the Lord,
Deal with me for Your name's sake;
Because Your mercy *is* good, deliver me.
22 For I *am* poor and needy,
And my heart is wounded within me.
23 I am gone like a shadow when it
lengthens;
I am shaken off like a locust.
24 My knees are weak through fasting,
And my flesh is feeble from lack of
fatness.
25 I also have become a reproach to them;
When they look at me, they shake their
heads.
26 Help me, O LORD my God!
Oh, save me according to Your mercy,
➤ 27 That they may know that this *is* Your
hand—
That You, LORD, have done it!
28 Let them curse, but You bless;
When they arise, let them be ashamed,
But let Your servant rejoice.
29 Let my accusers be clothed with shame,
And let them cover themselves with
their own disgrace as with a
mantle.
30 I will greatly praise the LORD with my
mouth;
Yes, I will praise Him among the
multitude.
31 For He shall stand at the right hand of
the poor,
To save *him* from those who condemn
him.

PSALM 110

Announcement of the Messiah's Reign

A Psalm of David.

1 The LORD said to my Lord, ➤
"Sit at My right hand,
Till I make Your enemies Your footstool."
2 The LORD shall send the rod of Your
strength out of Zion.
Rule in the midst of Your enemies!
3 Your people *shall be* volunteers
In the day of Your power;
In the beauties of holiness, from the
womb of the morning,
You have the dew of Your youth.
4 The LORD has sworn ➤
And will not relent,
"You *are* a priest forever
According to the order of Melchizedek."
5 The Lord *is* at Your right hand;
He shall execute kings in the day of His
wrath.
6 He shall judge among the nations,
He shall fill *the places* with dead bodies,
He shall execute the heads of many
countries.
7 He shall drink of the brook by the
wayside;
Therefore He shall lift up the head.

PSALM 111

Praise to God for His Faithfulness and Justice

1 Praise the LORD!
I will praise the LORD with *my* whole
heart,
In the assembly of the upright and *in*
the congregation.

LIFE LESSONS

➤ 109:27 — *That they may know that this is Your hand—that You, LORD, have done it!*

When we pray for someone's deliverance or for God to intervene in some situation, it is entirely appropriate to ask God to make it plain that what happens is no coincidence, but a direct answer to prayer.

➤ 110:1 — *The LORD said to my Lord, "Sit at My right hand, till I make Your enemies Your footstool."*

The New Testament quotes this psalm, written by David, more than any other. Jesus used this verse to prove that He, the Messiah, was both David's "son" and David's Lord (Matt. 22:41–46).

➤ 110:4 — *The LORD has sworn and will not relent, "You are a priest forever according to the order of Melchizedek."*

Melchizedek was a mysterious Old Testament figure who served as a priest of God long before Aaron came along (Gen. 14:18–20). The Book of Hebrews tells us that Jesus is our eternal priest (Heb. 5:6).

➤ 2 The works of the LORD *are* great,
Studied by all who have pleasure in them.
3 His work *is* honorable and glorious,
And His righteousness endures forever.
4 He has made His wonderful works to be remembered;
The LORD *is* gracious and full of compassion.
5 He has given food to those who fear Him;
He will ever be mindful of His covenant.
6 He has declared to His people the power of His works,
In giving them the heritage of the nations.
7 The works of His hands *are* verity and justice;
All His precepts *are* sure.
8 They stand fast forever and ever,
And are done in truth and uprightness.
9 He has sent redemption to His people;
He has commanded His covenant forever:
Holy and awesome *is* His name.

➤ 10 The fear of the LORD *is* the beginning of wisdom;
A good understanding have all those who do *His commandments.*
His praise endures forever.

PSALM 112

The Blessed State of the Righteous

1 Praise the LORD!

Blessed *is* the man *who* fears the LORD,
Who delights greatly in His commandments.

➤ 2 His descendants will be mighty on earth;
The generation of the upright will be blessed.
3 Wealth and riches *will be* in his house,
And his righteousness endures forever.
4 Unto the upright there arises light in the darkness;
He is gracious, and full of compassion, and righteous.
5 A good man deals graciously and lends;
He will guide his affairs with discretion.
6 Surely he will never be shaken;
The righteous will be in everlasting remembrance.
7 He will not be afraid of evil tidings;
His heart is steadfast, trusting in the LORD.
8 His heart *is* established;
He will not be afraid,
Until he sees *his desire* upon his enemies.

9 He has dispersed abroad,
He has given to the poor;
His righteousness endures forever;
His horn will be exalted with honor.
10 The wicked will see *it* and be grieved;
He will gnash his teeth and melt away;
The desire of the wicked shall perish.

PSALM 113

The Majesty and Condescension of God

1 Praise the LORD!

Praise, O servants of the LORD,
Praise the name of the LORD!
2 Blessed be the name of the LORD
From this time forth and forevermore!
3 From the rising of the sun to its going down
The LORD's name *is* to be praised.

4 The LORD *is* high above all nations,
His glory above the heavens.
5 Who *is* like the LORD our God,
Who dwells on high,
6 Who humbles Himself to behold
The things that are in the heavens and in the earth?

7 He raises the poor out of the dust, ➤
And lifts the needy out of the ash heap,
8 That He may seat *him* with princes— ➤
With the princes of His people.
9 He grants the barren woman a home,
Like a joyful mother of children.

Praise the LORD!

LIFE LESSONS

➤ 111:2 — *The works of the LORD are great, studied by all who have pleasure in them.*

We always take a keen interest in the activities and projects of those we deeply love. So it is natural that we should love to study the works of God, beginning with the Bible.

➤ 111:10 — *. . . a good understanding have all those who do His commandments.*

The more we strive by God's Spirit to obey God's commandments, the more understanding He gives us of His Word. Jesus said, "If anyone wills to do His will, he shall know concerning the doctrine . . ." (John 7:17).

➤ 112:2 — *. . . the generation of the upright will be blessed.*

God loves to bless the obedient. He delights to show "mercy to thousands, to those who love Me and keep My commandments" (Ex. 20:6).

➤ 113:7, 8 — *He raises the poor out of the dust, and lifts the needy out of the ash heap, that He may seat him with princes . . . .*

Throughout the Bible, we see God exalting the humble and humbling the proud. Jesus said it like this: "So the last will be first, and the first last" (Matt. 20:16).

PSALM 114

The Power of God in His Deliverance of Israel

1 When Israel went out of Egypt,
The house of Jacob from a people of strange language,
2 Judah became His sanctuary,
And Israel His dominion.

3 The sea saw *it* and fled;
Jordan turned back.
4 The mountains skipped like rams,
The little hills like lambs.
5 What ails you, O sea, that you fled?
O Jordan, *that* you turned back?
6 O mountains, *that* you skipped like rams?
O little hills, like lambs?

➤ 7 Tremble, O earth, at the presence of the Lord,
At the presence of the God of Jacob,
8 Who turned the rock *into* a pool of water,
The flint into a fountain of waters.

PSALM 115

The Futility of Idols and the Trustworthiness of God

➤ 1 Not unto us, O LORD, not unto us,
But to Your name give glory,
Because of Your mercy,
Because of Your truth.
2 Why should the Gentiles say,
"So where *is* their God?"

➤ 3 But our God *is* in heaven;
He does whatever He pleases.
4 Their idols *are* silver and gold,
The work of men's hands.
5 They have mouths, but they do not speak;
Eyes they have, but they do not see;
6 They have ears, but they do not hear;
Noses they have, but they do not smell;
7 They have hands, but they do not handle;
Feet they have, but they do not walk;
Nor do they mutter through their throat.
8 Those who make them are like them;
So is everyone who trusts in them.

9 O Israel, trust in the LORD;
He *is* their help and their shield.
10 O house of Aaron, trust in the LORD;
He *is* their help and their shield.
11 You who fear the LORD, trust in the LORD;
He *is* their help and their shield.

12 The LORD has been mindful of *us;*
He will bless us;
He will bless the house of Israel;
He will bless the house of Aaron.
13 He will bless those who fear the LORD, ➤
Both small and great.

14 May the LORD give you increase more and more,
You and your children.
15 *May* you *be* blessed by the LORD,
Who made heaven and earth.

16 The heaven, *even* the heavens, *are* the LORD'S;
But the earth He has given to the children of men.
17 The dead do not praise the LORD,
Nor any who go down into silence.
18 But we will bless the LORD
From this time forth and forevermore.

Praise the LORD!

PSALM 116

Thanksgiving for Deliverance from Death

1 I love the LORD, because He has heard
My voice *and* my supplications.
2 Because He has inclined His ear to me,
Therefore I will call *upon Him* as long as I live.

3 The pains of death surrounded me,
And the pangs of Sheol laid hold of me;
I found trouble and sorrow.

LIFE LESSONS

➤ 114:7 — *Tremble, O earth, at the presence of the LORD, at the presence of the God of Jacob.*

There are at least two kinds of "trembling" in Scripture. Both describe genuine fear in the presence of overwhelming power, but one takes quaking pleasure in that power, while the other sees in it only destruction.

➤ 115:1 — *Not unto us, O LORD, not unto us, but to Your name give glory, because of Your mercy, because of Your truth.*

God's mercy and truth make up a large part of His glory, and when we pray that He might gain glory for Himself by answering our requests, we pray with the kind of power that can move mountains.

➤ 115:3 — *But our God is in heaven; He does whatever He pleases.*

To say that God is sovereign is to say that He has the power and the wisdom to accomplish everything and anything He desires. He is the absolute Monarch of the universe, and His will rules all.

➤ 115:13 — *He will bless those who fear the LORD, both small and great.*

God does not play favorites when it comes to handing out His blessings. He does not favor pastors more than policemen, or missionaries more than moms. If you fear the Lord, He will bless you.

4 Then I called upon the name of the LORD:
"O LORD, I implore You, deliver my soul!"

5 Gracious *is* the LORD, and righteous;
Yes, our God *is* merciful.
6 The LORD preserves the simple;
I was brought low, and He saved me.
7 Return to your rest, O my soul,
For the LORD has dealt bountifully with you.

8 For You have delivered my soul from death,
My eyes from tears,
And my feet from falling.
9 I will walk before the LORD
In the land of the living.
➤ 10 I believed, therefore I spoke,
"I am greatly afflicted."
11 I said in my haste,
"All men *are* liars."

12 What shall I render to the LORD
For all His benefits toward me?
13 I will take up the cup of salvation,
And call upon the name of the LORD.
14 I will pay my vows to the LORD
Now in the presence of all His people.

➤ 15 Precious in the sight of the LORD
Is the death of His saints.

16 O LORD, truly I *am* Your servant;
I *am* Your servant, the son of Your maidservant;
You have loosed my bonds.
17 I will offer to You the sacrifice of thanksgiving,
And will call upon the name of the LORD.
18 I will pay my vows to the LORD
Now in the presence of all His people,
19 In the courts of the LORD's house,
In the midst of you, O Jerusalem.

Praise the LORD!

PSALM 117

Let All Peoples Praise the LORD

1 Praise the LORD, all you Gentiles!
Laud Him, all you peoples!
2 For His merciful kindness is great toward us,
And the truth of the LORD *endures* forever.

Praise the LORD!

PSALM 118

Praise to God for His Everlasting Mercy

1 Oh, give thanks to the LORD, for *He is* good!
For His mercy *endures* forever.

2 Let Israel now say,
"His mercy *endures* forever."
3 Let the house of Aaron now say,
"His mercy *endures* forever."
4 Let those who fear the LORD now say,
"His mercy *endures* forever."

5 I called on the LORD in distress;
The LORD answered me *and set me* in a broad place.
6 The LORD *is* on my side;
I will not fear.
What can man do to me?
7 The LORD is for me among those who help me;
Therefore I shall see *my desire* on those who hate me.
8 *It is* better to trust in the LORD
Than to put confidence in man.
9 *It is* better to trust in the LORD
Than to put confidence in princes.

10 All nations surrounded me,
But in the name of the LORD I will destroy them.
11 They surrounded me,
Yes, they surrounded me;
But in the name of the LORD I will destroy them.
12 They surrounded me like bees;
They were quenched like a fire of thorns;
For in the name of the LORD I will destroy them.
13 You pushed me violently, that I might fall,
But the LORD helped me.

LIFE LESSONS

➤ 116:10 — *I believed, therefore I spoke.*

Paul uses this little verse to show that those who really believe in the death and resurrection of Christ ought to speak of their conviction to others (2 Cor. 4:13–15). We act on what we think is true.

➤ 116:15 — *Precious in the sight of the LORD is the death of His saints.*

We rightly grieve when a loved one dies, but God has a very different reaction: He rejoices that another one of His children has entered His eternal presence. Death is not the end, but a new beginning.

➤ 117:2 — *. . . the truth of the LORD endures forever.*

God's truth does not change from year to year or decade to decade or century to century. It does not vary depending on current style or alter based on popular opinion. In a world of change, His truth remains constant.

➤ 118:8, 9 — *It is better to trust in the LORD than to put confidence in man. It is better to trust in the LORD than to put confidence in princes.*

Even the best of friends can say one thing and do another. Even the most trusted public officials can break their promises. But God always does what He says and keeps every promise He makes. So trust Him!

14 The LORD *is* my strength and song,
And He has become my salvation.[a]
15 The voice of rejoicing and salvation
Is in the tents of the righteous;
The right hand of the LORD does valiantly.
16 The right hand of the LORD is exalted;
The right hand of the LORD does valiantly.
17 I shall not die, but live,
And declare the works of the LORD.
18 The LORD has chastened me severely,
But He has not given me over to death.
19 Open to me the gates of righteousness;
I will go through them,
And I will praise the LORD.
20 This is the gate of the LORD,
Through which the righteous shall enter.
21 I will praise You,
For You have answered me,
And have become my salvation.
➤ 22 The stone *which* the builders rejected
Has become the chief cornerstone.
➤ 23 This was the LORD's doing;
It *is* marvelous in our eyes.
24 This *is* the day the LORD has made;
We will rejoice and be glad in it.
25 Save now, I pray, O LORD;
O LORD, I pray, send now prosperity.
26 Blessed *is* he who comes in the name of the LORD!
We have blessed you from the house of the LORD.
27 God *is* the LORD,
And He has given us light;
Bind the sacrifice with cords to the horns of the altar.
28 You *are* my God, and I will praise You;
You are my God, I will exalt You.
29 Oh, give thanks to the LORD, for *He is* good!
For His mercy *endures* forever.

PSALM 119

Meditations on the Excellencies of the Word of God

א ALEPH

1 Blessed *are* the undefiled in the way,
Who walk in the law of the LORD!
2 Blessed *are* those who keep His testimonies,
Who seek Him with the whole heart!
3 They also do no iniquity;
They walk in His ways.
4 You have commanded *us*
To keep Your precepts diligently.
5 Oh, that my ways were directed
To keep Your statutes!
6 Then I would not be ashamed,
When I look into all Your commandments.
7 I will praise You with uprightness of heart,
When I learn Your righteous judgments.
8 I will keep Your statutes;
Oh, do not forsake me utterly!

ב BETH

9 How can a young man cleanse his way? ◄
By taking heed according to Your word.
10 With my whole heart I have sought You;
Oh, let me not wander from Your commandments!
11 Your word I have hidden in my heart, ◄
That I might not sin against You.
12 Blessed *are* You, O LORD!
Teach me Your statutes.
13 With my lips I have declared
All the judgments of Your mouth.
14 I have rejoiced in the way of Your testimonies,
As *much as* in all riches.
15 I will meditate on Your precepts,
And contemplate Your ways.
16 I will delight myself in Your statutes;
I will not forget Your word.

118:14 [a]Compare Exodus 15:2

LIFE LESSONS

➤ 118: 22, 23 — *The stone which the builders rejected has become the chief cornerstone.*

The religious leaders of Jesus' day rejected Him as the Messiah (Matt. 21:42), but as Peter declared, "God has made this Jesus, whom you crucified, both Lord and Christ" (Acts 2:36).

➤ 119:9 — *How can a young man cleanse his way? By taking heed according to Your word.*

If we want to please God and honor Him with our lives, we must get to know His Word. The Bible warns us of dangers ahead, steers us toward the heart of God, and gives us wisdom to flourish in a dark age.

➤ 119:11 — *Your word I have hidden in my heart, that I might not sin against You.*

Many Christians today have never experienced the power and encouragement available to them through memorizing Scripture. When we lock portions of God's Word in our mind, they remain available always to help and strengthen us in tough times.

ג GIMEL

17 Deal bountifully with Your servant,
That I may live and keep Your word.
18 Open my eyes, that I may see
Wondrous things from Your law.
19 I *am* a stranger in the earth;
Do not hide Your commandments from me.
20 My soul breaks with longing
For Your judgments at all times.
21 You rebuke the proud—the cursed,
Who stray from Your commandments.
22 Remove from me reproach and contempt,
For I have kept Your testimonies.
23 Princes also sit *and* speak against me,
But Your servant meditates on Your statutes.
24 Your testimonies also *are* my delight
And my counselors.

ד DALETH

25 My soul clings to the dust;
Revive me according to Your word.
26 I have declared my ways, and You answered me;
Teach me Your statutes.
27 Make me understand the way of Your precepts;
So shall I meditate on Your wonderful works.
➤ 28 My soul melts from heaviness;
Strengthen me according to Your word.
29 Remove from me the way of lying,
And grant me Your law graciously.
30 I have chosen the way of truth;
Your judgments I have laid *before me.*
31 I cling to Your testimonies;
O LORD, do not put me to shame!
32 I will run the course of Your commandments,
For You shall enlarge my heart.

ה HE

33 Teach me, O LORD, the way of Your statutes,
And I shall keep it *to* the end.
34 Give me understanding, and I shall keep Your law;
Indeed, I shall observe it with *my* whole heart.
35 Make me walk in the path of Your commandments,
For I delight in it.
36 Incline my heart to Your testimonies,
And not to covetousness.
37 Turn away my eyes from looking at worthless things,
And revive me in Your way.[a]
38 Establish Your word to Your servant,
Who *is devoted* to fearing You.
39 Turn away my reproach which I dread,
For Your judgments *are* good.
40 Behold, I long for Your precepts;
Revive me in Your righteousness.

ו WAW

41 Let Your mercies come also to me, O LORD—
Your salvation according to Your word.
42 So shall I have an answer for him who reproaches me,
For I trust in Your word.
43 And take not the word of truth utterly out of my mouth,
For I have hoped in Your ordinances.
44 So shall I keep Your law continually,
Forever and ever.
45 And I will walk at liberty,
For I seek Your precepts.
46 I will speak of Your testimonies also before kings,
And will not be ashamed.
47 And I will delight myself in Your commandments,
Which I love.
48 My hands also I will lift up to Your commandments,
Which I love,
And I will meditate on Your statutes.

ז ZAYIN

49 Remember the word to Your servant,
Upon which You have caused me to hope.
50 This *is* my comfort in my affliction,
For Your word has given me life.
51 The proud have me in great derision,
Yet I do not turn aside from Your law.
52 I remembered Your judgments of old, O LORD,
And have comforted myself.
53 Indignation has taken hold of me
Because of the wicked, who forsake Your law.

119:37 [a]Following Masoretic Text, Septuagint, and Vulgate; Targum reads *Your words.*

LIFE LESSONS

➤ **119:28 — *My soul melts from heaviness; strengthen me according to Your word.***

When we feel discouraged, down, and low in spirit, reading just the right portion of God's Word can give us renewed hope and fresh strength. His words have a power all their own that defies description.

54 Your statutes have been my songs
In the house of my pilgrimage.
55 I remember Your name in the night,
O LORD,
And I keep Your law.
56 This has become mine,
Because I kept Your precepts.

ח HETH

57 *You are* my portion, O LORD;
I have said that I would keep Your
words.
58 I entreated Your favor with *my* whole
heart;
Be merciful to me according to Your
word.
59 I thought about my ways,
And turned my feet to Your testimonies.
60 I made haste, and did not delay
To keep Your commandments.
61 The cords of the wicked have bound me,
But I have not forgotten Your law.
62 At midnight I will rise to give thanks to
You,
Because of Your righteous judgments.
63 I *am* a companion of all who fear You,
And of those who keep Your precepts.
64 The earth, O LORD, is full of Your mercy;
Teach me Your statutes.

ט TETH

65 You have dealt well with Your servant,
O LORD, according to Your word.
66 Teach me good judgment and knowledge,
For I believe Your commandments.
➤ 67 Before I was afflicted I went astray,
But now I keep Your word.
68 You *are* good, and do good;
Teach me Your statutes.
69 The proud have forged a lie against me,
But I will keep Your precepts with *my*
whole heart.
70 Their heart is as fat as grease,
But I delight in Your law.
71 *It is* good for me that I have been
afflicted,
That I may learn Your statutes.
72 The law of Your mouth *is* better to me
Than thousands of *coins of* gold and
silver.

י YOD

73 Your hands have made me and
fashioned me;
Give me understanding, that I may
learn Your commandments.
74 Those who fear You will be glad when
they see me,
Because I have hoped in Your word.
75 I know, O LORD, that Your judgments *are*
right,
And *that* in faithfulness You have
afflicted me.
76 Let, I pray, Your merciful kindness be
for my comfort,
According to Your word to Your servant.
77 Let Your tender mercies come to me,
that I may live;
For Your law *is* my delight.
78 Let the proud be ashamed,
For they treated me wrongfully with
falsehood;
But I will meditate on Your precepts.
79 Let those who fear You turn to me,
Those who know Your testimonies.
80 Let my heart be blameless regarding
Your statutes,
That I may not be ashamed.

כ KAPH

81 My soul faints for Your salvation,
But I hope in Your word.
82 My eyes fail *from searching* Your word,
Saying, "When will You comfort me?"
83 For I have become like a wineskin in
smoke,
Yet I do not forget Your statutes.
84 How many *are* the days of Your servant?
When will You execute judgment on
those who persecute me?
85 The proud have dug pits for me,
Which *is* not according to Your law.
86 All Your commandments *are* faithful;
They persecute me wrongfully;
Help me!
87 They almost made an end of me on
earth,
But I did not forsake Your precepts.
88 Revive me according to Your
lovingkindness,
So that I may keep the testimony of
Your mouth.

ל LAMED

89 Forever, O LORD,
Your word is settled in heaven.
90 Your faithfulness *endures* to all
generations;
You established the earth, and it abides.
91 They continue this day according to
Your ordinances,
For all *are* Your servants.

LIFE LESSONS

➤ 119:67 — *Before I was afflicted I went astray, but now I keep Your word.*

God uses affliction, not as a whip to force us in line, but as a messenger to urge us back into a safe place. Affliction is a bridge to a deeper relationship with God.

92 Unless Your law *had been* my delight,
I would then have perished in my affliction.
93 I will never forget Your precepts,
For by them You have given me life.
94 I *am* Yours, save me;
For I have sought Your precepts.
95 The wicked wait for me to destroy me,
But I will consider Your testimonies.
96 I have seen the consummation of all perfection,
But Your commandment *is* exceedingly broad.

מ MEM

97 Oh, how I love Your law!
It *is* my meditation all the day.
98 You, through Your commandments, make me wiser than my enemies;
For they *are* ever with me.
99 I have more understanding than all my teachers,
For Your testimonies *are* my meditation.
100 I understand more than the ancients,
Because I keep Your precepts.
101 I have restrained my feet from every evil way,
That I may keep Your word.
102 I have not departed from Your judgments,
For You Yourself have taught me.
103 How sweet are Your words to my taste,
Sweeter than honey to my mouth!
104 Through Your precepts I get understanding;
Therefore I hate every false way.

נ NUN

➤ 105 Your word *is* a lamp to my feet
And a light to my path.
106 I have sworn and confirmed
That I will keep Your righteous judgments.
107 I am afflicted very much;
Revive me, O LORD, according to Your word.
108 Accept, I pray, the freewill offerings of my mouth, O LORD,
And teach me Your judgments.
109 My life *is* continually in my hand,
Yet I do not forget Your law.
110 The wicked have laid a snare for me,
Yet I have not strayed from Your precepts.
111 Your testimonies I have taken as a heritage forever,
For they *are* the rejoicing of my heart.
112 I have inclined my heart to perform Your statutes
Forever, to the very end.

ס SAMEK

113 I hate the double-minded,
But I love Your law.
114 You *are* my hiding place and my shield;
I hope in Your word.
115 Depart from me, you evildoers,
For I will keep the commandments of my God!
116 Uphold me according to Your word, that I may live;
And do not let me be ashamed of my hope.
117 Hold me up, and I shall be safe,
And I shall observe Your statutes continually.
118 You reject all those who stray from Your statutes,
For their deceit *is* falsehood.
119 You put away all the wicked of the earth *like* dross;
Therefore I love Your testimonies.
120 My flesh trembles for fear of You,
And I am afraid of Your judgments.

ע AYIN

121 I have done justice and righteousness;
Do not leave me to my oppressors.
122 Be surety for Your servant for good;
Do not let the proud oppress me.
123 My eyes fail *from seeking* Your salvation
And Your righteous word.
124 Deal with Your servant according to Your mercy,
And teach me Your statutes.
125 I *am* Your servant; ➤
Give me understanding,
That I may know Your testimonies.
126 *It is* time for *You* to act, O LORD,
For they have regarded Your law as void.

LIFE LESSONS

➤ 119:105 — *Your word is a lamp to my feet and a light to my path.*

Left to ourselves, we often don't know which way leads to life and which way ends in death; we remain in the dark. But God's Word provides us with a searchlight to cut through the darkness and lead us to safety.

➤ 119:125 — *I am Your servant; give me understanding, that I may know Your testimonies.*

God doesn't want ignorant servants, but well-informed ones. Jesus tells us, "I have called you friends, for all things that I heard from My Father I have made known to you" (John 15:15). God's Word tells us how to succeed.

127 Therefore I love Your commandments
More than gold, yes, than fine gold!
128 Therefore all *Your* precepts *concerning* all *things*
I consider *to be* right;
I hate every false way.

פ PE

129 Your testimonies are wonderful;
Therefore my soul keeps them.
130 The entrance of Your words gives light;
It gives understanding to the simple.
131 I opened my mouth and panted,
For I longed for Your commandments.
132 Look upon me and be merciful to me,
As Your custom *is* toward those who love Your name.
133 Direct my steps by Your word,
And let no iniquity have dominion over me.
134 Redeem me from the oppression of man,
That I may keep Your precepts.
135 Make Your face shine upon Your servant,
And teach me Your statutes.
136 Rivers of water run down from my eyes,
Because *men* do not keep Your law.

צ TSADDE

137 Righteous *are* You, O LORD,
And upright *are* Your judgments.
138 Your testimonies, *which* You have commanded,
Are righteous and very faithful.
139 My zeal has consumed me,
Because my enemies have forgotten Your words.
140 Your word *is* very pure;
Therefore Your servant loves it.
141 I *am* small and despised,
Yet I do not forget Your precepts.
142 Your righteousness *is* an everlasting righteousness,
And Your law *is* truth.
143 Trouble and anguish have overtaken me,
Yet Your commandments *are* my delights.
144 The righteousness of Your testimonies *is* everlasting;
Give me understanding, and I shall live.

ק QOPH

145 I cry out with *my* whole heart;
Hear me, O LORD!
I will keep Your statutes.
146 I cry out to You;
Save me, and I will keep Your testimonies.
147 I rise before the dawning of the morning,
And cry for help;
I hope in Your word.
148 My eyes are awake through the *night* watches,
That I may meditate on Your word.
149 Hear my voice according to Your lovingkindness;
O LORD, revive me according to Your justice.
150 They draw near who follow after wickedness;
They are far from Your law.
151 You *are* near, O LORD,
And all Your commandments *are* truth.
152 Concerning Your testimonies,
I have known of old that You have founded them forever.

ר RESH

153 Consider my affliction and deliver me,
For I do not forget Your law.
154 Plead my cause and redeem me;
Revive me according to Your word.
155 Salvation *is* far from the wicked,
For they do not seek Your statutes.
156 Great *are* Your tender mercies, O LORD;
Revive me according to Your judgments.
157 Many *are* my persecutors and my enemies,
Yet I do not turn from Your testimonies.
158 I see the treacherous, and am disgusted,
Because they do not keep Your word.
159 Consider how I love Your precepts;
Revive me, O LORD, according to Your lovingkindness.
160 The entirety of Your word *is* truth,
And every one of Your righteous judgments *endures* forever.

ש SHIN

161 Princes persecute me without a cause,
But my heart stands in awe of Your word.
162 I rejoice at Your word
As one who finds great treasure.

LIFE LESSONS

➤ ***119:162 — I rejoice at Your word as one who finds great treasure.***

If we think of the Bible as a mysterious book that's hard to understand, we won't value it much and will read it even less. But if we see it as priceless treasure, we'll dive into it often and reap its amazing benefits.

163 I hate and abhor lying,
But I love Your law.
164 Seven times a day I praise You,
Because of Your righteous judgments.
165 Great peace have those who love Your law,
And nothing causes them to stumble.
166 LORD, I hope for Your salvation,
And I do Your commandments.
167 My soul keeps Your testimonies,
And I love them exceedingly.
168 I keep Your precepts and Your testimonies,
For all my ways *are* before You.

ת TAU

169 Let my cry come before You, O LORD;
Give me understanding according to Your word.
170 Let my supplication come before You;
Deliver me according to Your word.
171 My lips shall utter praise,
For You teach me Your statutes.
172 My tongue shall speak of Your word,
For all Your commandments *are* righteousness.
173 Let Your hand become my help,
For I have chosen Your precepts.
174 I long for Your salvation, O LORD,
And Your law *is* my delight.
175 Let my soul live, and it shall praise You;
And let Your judgments help me.
176 I have gone astray like a lost sheep;
Seek Your servant,
For I do not forget Your commandments.

PSALM 120

Plea for Relief from Bitter Foes

A Song of Ascents.

1 In my distress I cried to the LORD,
And He heard me.
2 Deliver my soul, O LORD, from lying lips
And from a deceitful tongue.

3 What shall be given to you,
Or what shall be done to you,
You false tongue?
4 Sharp arrows of the warrior,
With coals of the broom tree!
5 Woe is me, that I dwell in Meshech,
That I dwell among the tents of Kedar!
6 My soul has dwelt too long
With one who hates peace.
7 I *am for* peace;
But when I speak, they *are* for war.

PSALM 121

God the Help of Those Who Seek Him

A Song of Ascents.

1 I will lift up my eyes to the hills—
From whence comes my help?
2 My help *comes* from the LORD,
Who made heaven and earth.

3 He will not allow your foot to be moved;
He who keeps you will not slumber.
4 Behold, He who keeps Israel
Shall neither slumber nor sleep.

5 The LORD *is* your keeper;
The LORD *is* your shade at your right hand.
6 The sun shall not strike you by day,
Nor the moon by night.

7 The LORD shall preserve you from all evil;
He shall preserve your soul.
8 The LORD shall preserve your going out and your coming in
From this time forth, and even forevermore.

PSALM 122

The Joy of Going to the House of the LORD

A Song of Ascents. Of David.

1 I was glad when they said to me,
"Let us go into the house of the LORD."
2 Our feet have been standing
Within your gates, O Jerusalem!

3 Jerusalem is built
As a city that is compact together,
4 Where the tribes go up,
The tribes of the LORD,
To the Testimony of Israel,
To give thanks to the name of the LORD.
5 For thrones are set there for judgment,
The thrones of the house of David.

6 Pray for the peace of Jerusalem:
"May they prosper who love you.
7 Peace be within your walls,
Prosperity within your palaces."
8 For the sake of my brethren and companions,
I will now say, "Peace *be* within you."

LIFE LESSONS

➤ 121:3 — *He who keeps you will not slumber.*

When Jesus asked three trusted disciples to pray with Him in His darkest hour, they all fell asleep—not once, but three times (Matt. 26:36–45). God will never do that to us. Even when we sleep, He stays wide awake.

➤ 122:1 — *I was glad when they said to me, "Let us go into the house of the LORD."*

What made the psalmist glad? First, he saw it as an opportunity to meet with God. Second, he considered it a chance to worship with friends. Third, it fulfilled the purpose for which God had created him.

9 Because of the house of the LORD our God
I will seek your good.

PSALM 123

Prayer for Relief from Contempt

A Song of Ascents.

1 Unto You I lift up my eyes,
O You who dwell in the heavens.
➤2 Behold, as the eyes of servants *look* to the hand of their masters,
As the eyes of a maid to the hand of her mistress,
So our eyes *look* to the LORD our God,
Until He has mercy on us.
3 Have mercy on us, O LORD, have mercy on us!
For we are exceedingly filled with contempt.
4 Our soul is exceedingly filled
With the scorn of those who are at ease,
With the contempt of the proud.

PSALM 124

The LORD the Defense of His People

A Song of Ascents. Of David.

➤1 "If it had not been the LORD who was on our side,"
Let Israel now say—
2 "If it had not been the LORD who was on our side,
When men rose up against us,
➤3 Then they would have swallowed us alive,
When their wrath was kindled against us;
4 Then the waters would have overwhelmed us,
The stream would have gone over our soul;
5 Then the swollen waters
Would have gone over our soul."
6 Blessed *be* the LORD,
Who has not given us *as* prey to their teeth.
7 Our soul has escaped as a bird from the snare of the fowlers;[a]
The snare is broken, and we have escaped.
8 Our help *is* in the name of the LORD,
Who made heaven and earth.

PSALM 125

The LORD the Strength of His People

A Song of Ascents.

1 Those who trust in the LORD
Are like Mount Zion,
Which cannot be moved, *but* abides forever.
2 As the mountains surround Jerusalem, ➤
So the LORD surrounds His people
From this time forth and forever.
3 For the scepter of wickedness shall not rest
On the land allotted to the righteous,
Lest the righteous reach out their hands to iniquity.
4 Do good, O LORD, to *those who are* good,
And to *those who are* upright in their hearts.
5 As for such as turn aside to their crooked ways,
The LORD shall lead them away
With the workers of iniquity.
Peace *be* upon Israel!

PSALM 126

A Joyful Return to Zion

A Song of Ascents.

1 When the LORD brought back the captivity of Zion,
We were like those who dream.
2 Then our mouth was filled with laughter,
And our tongue with singing.
Then they said among the nations,
"The LORD has done great things for them."
3 The LORD has done great things for us,
And we are glad.

124:7 [a]That is, persons who catch birds in a trap or snare

LIFE LESSONS

➤ **123:2 — *Behold, as the eyes of servants look to the hand of their masters, as the eyes of a maid to the hand of her mistress, so our eyes look to the LORD our God, until He has mercy on us.***

There may be many reasons why God does not immediately answer our prayers for help and mercy, but one thing is sure: He instructs us to keep on asking until He grants our request (see Luke 18:1–8).

➤ **124:1, 3 — *"If it had not been the LORD who was on our side," let Israel now say . . . then they would have swallowed us alive, when their wrath was kindled against us.***

God instructs us in His Word to encourage each other by verbally reminding one another of how He has acted on our behalf in the past. None of us are called to "go it alone" in our walk of faith.

➤ **125:2 — *As the mountains surround Jerusalem, so the LORD surrounds His people from this time forth and forever.***

God "surrounds" His people like a thick wall surrounded ancient cities. He covers us on every side so that nothing can reach us without first passing through His loving hands—the best security system ever devised.

4 Bring back our captivity, O LORD,
As the streams in the South.

*5 Those who sow in tears
➤ Shall reap in joy.
6 He who continually goes forth weeping,
Bearing seed for sowing,
Shall doubtless come again with rejoicing,
Bringing his sheaves *with him.*

PSALM 127

Laboring and Prospering with the LORD

A Song of Ascents. Of Solomon.

➤1 Unless the LORD builds the house,
They labor in vain who build it;
Unless the LORD guards the city,
The watchman stays awake in vain.
2 *It is* vain for you to rise up early,
To sit up late,
To eat the bread of sorrows;
For so He gives His beloved sleep.
3 Behold, children *are* a heritage from the LORD,
The fruit of the womb *is* a reward.
4 Like arrows in the hand of a warrior,
So *are* the children of one's youth.
5 Happy *is* the man who has his quiver full of them;
They shall not be ashamed,
But shall speak with their enemies in the gate.

PSALM 128

Blessings of Those Who Fear the LORD

A Song of Ascents.

1 Blessed *is* every one who fears the LORD,
Who walks in His ways.

2 When you eat the labor of your hands,
You *shall be* happy, and *it shall be* well with you.
3 Your wife *shall be* like a fruitful vine
In the very heart of your house,
Your children like olive plants
All around your table.
4 Behold, thus shall the man be blessed
Who fears the LORD.

5 The LORD bless you out of Zion,
And may you see the good of Jerusalem
All the days of your life.
6 Yes, may you see your children's children.

Peace *be* upon Israel!

PSALM 129

Song of Victory over Zion's Enemies

A Song of Ascents.

1 "Many a time they have afflicted me from my youth,"
Let Israel now say—
2 "Many a time they have afflicted me from my youth;
Yet they have not prevailed against me.
3 The plowers plowed on my back;
They made their furrows long."
4 The LORD *is* righteous;
He has cut in pieces the cords of the wicked.

5 Let all those who hate Zion
Be put to shame and turned back.
6 Let them be as the grass *on* the housetops,
Which withers before it grows up,
7 With which the reaper does not fill his hand,
Nor he who binds sheaves, his arms.
8 Neither let those who pass by them say,
"The blessing of the LORD *be* upon you;
We bless you in the name of the LORD!"

PSALM 130

Waiting for the Redemption of the LORD

A Song of Ascents.

1 Out of the depths I have cried to You, O LORD;
2 Lord, hear my voice!
Let Your ears be attentive
To the voice of my supplications.

3 If You, LORD, should mark iniquities,
O Lord, who could stand?
4 But *there is* forgiveness with You,
That You may be feared.

5 I wait for the LORD, my soul waits, ➤
And in His word I do hope.

LIFE LESSONS

➤ 126:5 — *Those who sow in tears shall reap in joy.*

God never pretends that this life will be free of hardship or pain, but He insists that, for those who know and love Him, our tears are nothing but seeds that will bloom one day into enormous trees of joy.

➤ 127:1 — *Unless the LORD builds the house, they labor in vain who build it; unless the LORD guards the city, the watchman stays awake in vain.*

All our efforts are useless and futile if we do not partner with God in what He wants, where He wants, and how He wants it. The blessing of the Lord spells the difference between success and failure, satisfaction and regret.

➤ 130:5 — *I wait for the LORD, my soul waits, and in His word I do hope.*

God does not spring into action on our timetable. In fact, He often waits to the very last moment to intervene. Why? Waiting is God's training ground for building strong faith. As we wait, we learn to trust.

6 My soul *waits* for the Lord
More than those who watch for the morning—
Yes, more than those who watch for the morning.
7 O Israel, hope in the LORD;
For with the LORD *there is* mercy,
And with Him *is* abundant redemption.
8 And He shall redeem Israel
From all his iniquities.

PSALM 131

Simple Trust in the LORD

A Song of Ascents. Of David.

➤ 1 LORD, my heart is not haughty,
Nor my eyes lofty.
Neither do I concern myself with great matters,
Nor with things too profound for me.
2 Surely I have calmed and quieted my soul,
Like a weaned child with his mother;
Like a weaned child *is* my soul within me.
3 O Israel, hope in the LORD
From this time forth and forever.

PSALM 132

The Eternal Dwelling of God in Zion

A Song of Ascents.

1 LORD, remember David
And all his afflictions;
2 How he swore to the LORD,
And vowed to the Mighty One of Jacob:
3 "Surely I will not go into the chamber of my house,
Or go up to the comfort of my bed;
4 I will not give sleep to my eyes
Or slumber to my eyelids,
5 Until I find a place for the LORD,
A dwelling place for the Mighty One of Jacob."
6 Behold, we heard of it in Ephrathah;
We found it in the fields of the woods.[a]
7 Let us go into His tabernacle;
Let us worship at His footstool.
8 Arise, O LORD, to Your resting place,
You and the ark of Your strength.
9 Let Your priests be clothed with righteousness,
And let Your saints shout for joy.
10 For Your servant David's sake,
Do not turn away the face of Your Anointed.
11 The LORD has sworn *in* truth to David;
He will not turn from it:
"I will set upon your throne the fruit of your body.
12 If your sons will keep My covenant
And My testimony which I shall teach them,
Their sons also shall sit upon your throne forevermore."
13 For the LORD has chosen Zion;
He has desired *it* for His dwelling place:
14 "This *is* My resting place forever;
Here I will dwell, for I have desired it.
15 I will abundantly bless her provision;
I will satisfy her poor with bread.
16 I will also clothe her priests with salvation,
And her saints shall shout aloud for joy.
17 There I will make the horn of David grow;
I will prepare a lamp for My Anointed.
18 His enemies I will clothe with shame,
But upon Himself His crown shall flourish."

PSALM 133

Blessed Unity of the People of God

A Song of Ascents. Of David.

1 Behold, how good and how pleasant *it is* ➤
For brethren to dwell together in unity!
2 *It is* like the precious oil upon the head,
Running down on the beard,
The beard of Aaron,
Running down on the edge of his garments.
3 *It is* like the dew of Hermon,
Descending upon the mountains of Zion;
For there the LORD commanded the blessing—
Life forevermore.

132:6 [a]Hebrew *Jaar*

LIFE LESSONS

➤ ***131:1 — LORD, my heart is not haughty, nor my eyes lofty. Neither do I concern myself with great matters, nor with things too profound for me.***

It takes humility to admit that some things are bigger than us or just plain beyond us. If the great David could call himself a "flea" and a "dead dog" (1 Sam. 24:14), maybe we have more to learn about humility.

➤ ***133:1 — Behold, how good and how pleasant it is for brethren to dwell together in unity!***

If we all serve the same God, who is love, then why shouldn't His love express itself in us through unity? It really should: "be of one mind, live in peace" (2 Cor. 13:11).

PSALM 134

Praising the LORD in His House at Night

A Song of Ascents.

1 Behold, bless the LORD,
All *you* servants of the LORD,
Who by night stand in the house of the LORD!
2 Lift up your hands *in* the sanctuary,
And bless the LORD.

3 The LORD who made heaven and earth
Bless you from Zion!

PSALM 135

Praise to God in Creation and Redemption

1 Praise the LORD!

Praise the name of the LORD;
Praise *Him,* O you servants of the LORD!
2 You who stand in the house of the LORD,
In the courts of the house of our God,
3 Praise the LORD, for the LORD *is* good;
Sing praises to His name, for *it is* pleasant.
4 For the LORD has chosen Jacob for Himself,
Israel for His special treasure.

5 For I know that the LORD *is* great,
And our Lord *is* above all gods.
➤ 6 Whatever the LORD pleases He does,
In heaven and in earth,
In the seas and in all deep places.
7 He causes the vapors to ascend from the ends of the earth;
He makes lightning for the rain;
He brings the wind out of His treasuries.
8 He destroyed the firstborn of Egypt,
Both of man and beast.
9 He sent signs and wonders into the midst of you, O Egypt,
Upon Pharaoh and all his servants.
10 He defeated many nations
And slew mighty kings—
11 Sihon king of the Amorites,
Og king of Bashan,
And all the kingdoms of Canaan—
12 And gave their land *as* a heritage,
A heritage to Israel His people.

13 Your name, O LORD, *endures* forever,
Your fame, O LORD, throughout all generations.
14 For the LORD will judge His people,
And He will have compassion on His servants.

15 The idols of the nations *are* silver and gold,
The work of men's hands.
16 They have mouths, but they do not speak;
Eyes they have, but they do not see;
17 They have ears, but they do not hear;
Nor is there *any* breath in their mouths.
18 Those who make them are like them;
So is everyone who trusts in them.

19 Bless the LORD, O house of Israel!
Bless the LORD, O house of Aaron!
20 Bless the LORD, O house of Levi!
You who fear the LORD, bless the LORD!
21 Blessed be the LORD out of Zion,
Who dwells in Jerusalem!

Praise the LORD!

PSALM 136

Thanksgiving to God for His Enduring Mercy

1 Oh, give thanks to the LORD, for *He is* good!
For His mercy *endures* forever.
2 Oh, give thanks to the God of gods!
For His mercy *endures* forever.
3 Oh, give thanks to the Lord of lords!
For His mercy *endures* forever:

4 To Him who alone does great wonders,
For His mercy *endures* forever;
5 To Him who by wisdom made the heavens,
For His mercy *endures* forever;
6 To Him who laid out the earth above the waters,
For His mercy *endures* forever;
7 To Him who made great lights,
For His mercy *endures* forever—
8 The sun to rule by day,
For His mercy *endures* forever;
9 The moon and stars to rule by night,
For His mercy *endures* forever.

10 To Him who struck Egypt in their firstborn,
For His mercy *endures* forever;
11 And brought out Israel from among them,
For His mercy *endures* forever;
12 With a strong hand, and with an outstretched arm,
For His mercy *endures* forever;

LIFE LESSONS

➤ 135:6 — *Whatever the LORD pleases He does, in heaven and in earth, in the seas and in all deep places.*

It may be simplistic to say that God does whatever He wants to, but it really isn't. The key is, what does He *want* to do? It pleases the Lord to do good, to show mercy, to bestow grace. And nothing can stop Him!

13 To Him who divided the Red Sea in two,
For His mercy *endures* forever;
14 And made Israel pass through the midst of it,
For His mercy *endures* forever;
15 But overthrew Pharaoh and his army in the Red Sea,
For His mercy *endures* forever;
16 To Him who led His people through the wilderness,
For His mercy *endures* forever;
17 To Him who struck down great kings,
For His mercy *endures* forever;
18 And slew famous kings,
For His mercy *endures* forever—
19 Sihon king of the Amorites,
For His mercy *endures* forever;
20 And Og king of Bashan,
For His mercy *endures* forever—
21 And gave their land as a heritage,
For His mercy *endures* forever;
22 A heritage to Israel His servant,
For His mercy *endures* forever.

23 Who remembered us in our lowly state,
For His mercy *endures* forever;
24 And rescued us from our enemies,
For His mercy *endures* forever;
25 Who gives food to all flesh,
For His mercy *endures* forever.

➤ 26 Oh, give thanks to the God of heaven!
For His mercy *endures* forever.

PSALM 137

Longing for Zion in a Foreign Land

1 By the rivers of Babylon,
There we sat down, yea, we wept
When we remembered Zion.
2 We hung our harps
Upon the willows in the midst of it.
3 For there those who carried us away captive asked of us a song,
And those who plundered us *requested* mirth,
Saying, "Sing us *one* of the songs of Zion!"

➤ 4 How shall we sing the LORD's song
In a foreign land?
5 If I forget you, O Jerusalem,
Let my right hand forget *its skill!*
6 If I do not remember you,
Let my tongue cling to the roof of my mouth—
If I do not exalt Jerusalem
Above my chief joy.

7 Remember, O LORD, against the sons of Edom
The day of Jerusalem,
Who said, "Raze *it*, raze *it*,
To its very foundation!"

8 O daughter of Babylon, who are to be destroyed,
Happy the one who repays you as you have served us!
9 Happy the one who takes and dashes
Your little ones against the rock!

PSALM 138

The LORD's Goodness to the Faithful

A Psalm of David.

1 I will praise You with my whole heart;
Before the gods I will sing praises to You.
2 I will worship toward Your holy temple, ➤
And praise Your name
For Your lovingkindness and Your truth;
For You have magnified Your word above all Your name.
3 In the day when I cried out, You answered me,
And made me bold *with* strength in my soul.

4 All the kings of the earth shall praise You, O LORD,
When they hear the words of Your mouth.
5 Yes, they shall sing of the ways of the LORD,
For great *is* the glory of the LORD.
6 Though the LORD *is* on high,
Yet He regards the lowly;
But the proud He knows from afar.

7 Though I walk in the midst of trouble, ✳
You will revive me;

LIFE LESSONS

➤ **136:26 — *Oh, give thanks to the God of heaven! For His mercy endures forever.***

Whenever you see an "Oh" at the beginning of a verse, it means that great emotion motivates the writer. Giving thanks to God is not a perfunctory thing, but a deeply felt expression of wholehearted gratitude.

➤ **137:4 — *How shall we sing the LORD's song in a foreign land?***

While our surroundings and circumstances can greatly influence our natural ability to worship God, true worship has less to do with outward conditions than with a decision of the will to draw on the inward resources of the Spirit.

➤ **138:2 — *. . . You have magnified Your word above all Your name.***

The Bible is not merely one holy book among several; God has identified His name with His book. And as God is above all other gods, so is His book above all other books. There is nothing else like it.

You will stretch out Your hand
Against the wrath of my enemies,
And Your right hand will save me.
8 The LORD will perfect *that which* concerns me;
Your mercy, O LORD, *endures* forever;
Do not forsake the works of Your hands.

PSALM 139

God's Perfect Knowledge of Man

For the Chief Musician. A Psalm of David.

1 O LORD, You have searched me and known *me.*
2 You know my sitting down and my rising up;
You understand my thought afar off.
3 You comprehend my path and my lying down,
And are acquainted with all my ways.
4 For *there is* not a word on my tongue,
But behold, O LORD, You know it altogether.
5 You have hedged me behind and before,
And laid Your hand upon me.
6 *Such* knowledge *is* too wonderful for me;
It is high, I cannot *attain* it.

➤ 7 Where can I go from Your Spirit?
Or where can I flee from Your presence?
8 If I ascend into heaven, You *are* there;
If I make my bed in hell, behold, You *are there.*
9 *If* I take the wings of the morning,
And dwell in the uttermost parts of the sea,
10 Even there Your hand shall lead me,
And Your right hand shall hold me.
11 If I say, "Surely the darkness shall fall[a] on me,"
Even the night shall be light about me;
12 Indeed, the darkness shall not hide from You,
But the night shines as the day;
The darkness and the light *are* both alike *to You.*
13 For You formed my inward parts;
You covered me in my mother's womb.
14 I will praise You, for I am fearfully *and* wonderfully made;[a]
Marvelous are Your works,
And *that* my soul knows very well.
15 My frame was not hidden from You,
When I was made in secret,
And skillfully wrought in the lowest parts of the earth.
16 Your eyes saw my substance, being yet unformed.
And in Your book they all were written,
The days fashioned for me,
When *as yet there were* none of them.

17 How precious also are Your thoughts to me, O God!
How great is the sum of them!
18 *If* I should count them, they would be more in number than the sand;
When I awake, I am still with You.

19 Oh, that You would slay the wicked, O God!
Depart from me, therefore, you bloodthirsty men.
20 For they speak against You wickedly;
Your enemies take *Your name* in vain.[a]
21 Do I not hate them, O LORD, who hate You?
And do I not loathe those who rise up against You?
22 I hate them with perfect hatred;
I count them my enemies.

23 Search me, O God, and know my heart; ➤
Try me, and know my anxieties;
24 And see if *there is any* wicked way in me,
And lead me in the way everlasting.

PSALM 140

Prayer for Deliverance from Evil Men

To the Chief Musician. A Psalm of David.

1 Deliver me, O LORD, from evil men;
Preserve me from violent men,
2 Who plan evil things in *their* hearts;
They continually gather together *for* war.
3 They sharpen their tongues like a serpent;
The poison of asps *is* under their lips. Selah

139:11 [a]Vulgate and Symmachus read *cover.* **139:14** [a]Following Masoretic Text and Targum; Septuagint, Syriac, and Vulgate read *You are fearfully wonderful.* **139:20** [a]Septuagint and Vulgate read *They take your cities in vain.*

LIFE LESSONS

➤ 139:7 — *Where can I go from Your Spirit? Or where can I flee from Your presence?*

God answered the psalmist's question in Jeremiah 23:24: "'Can anyone hide himself in secret places, so I shall not see him?' says the LORD; 'Do I not fill heaven and earth?"'

➤ 139:23 — *Search me, O God, and know my heart; try me, and know my anxieties . . . .*

When we cannot understand ourselves or comprehend our feelings, God invites us to take our internal struggles to Him and ask Him for insight. He understands what we do not, and knows what to do when we don't.

WHAT THE BIBLE SAYS ABOUT GOD'S DESIRE TO COMMUNICATE WITH US

Ps. 139:1–24

How many times have we heard someone say, "Why would God want to speak to *me*? I am not a preacher or in full-time Christian service. Why in the world would he want to communicate with me?"

The truth is, we are all saved by grace (Eph. 2:8); we are all washed and sanctified (1 Cor. 6:11); we are all saints (1 Cor. 1:2); and we are all children of the living God (John 1:12). Fathers just naturally want to speak to their children.

Unfortunately, we often see ourselves in an unworthy light—and when we do, we wonder why a great, magnificent God would ever want to speak to us. In that case, God could scream into our ears, but we would not hear Him.

We *must* see ourselves as God sees us: that is, as children who need Him to speak, who need to listen, who need guidance every day of their lives. If we have a pauper-like image of ourselves, wondering why the God who created the heavens and the earth would engage in meaningful conversation with insignificant us, then communication shuts down to minimal levels at best. *It all depends on relationship*. We are children of God, and our Father eagerly seeks to speak to us!

Fathers just naturally want to speak to their children.

Psalm 139 provides us with marvelous insight into the Father's perfect knowledge of us and His abundant love for us, just the way we are. He knows how we are made. He knows our weaknesses. He knows our sinful desires, and our transgressions are not hidden from Him. He knows our innermost hurts, fears, and frustrations—and yet He longs to gain intimacy with us.

Jesus has chosen to put His unmatched presence into these scarred, earthen vessels. He is at home in these tattered earthly tents. We need not be ill at ease, but instead we can relax and enjoy His fellowship, knowing that He died for us while were yet hopeless sinners (Rom. 5:6–8). He has permanently accepted us into His family, with *all* our undesirable baggage. We are His—lock, stock, and barrel!

See the Life Principles Index for further study:

13. Listening to God is essential to walking with God.

18. As children of a sovereign God, we are never victims of our circumstances.

4 Keep me, O LORD, from the hands of the wicked;
Preserve me from violent men,
Who have purposed to make my steps stumble.
5 The proud have hidden a snare for me, and cords;
They have spread a net by the wayside;
They have set traps for me. Selah

6 I said to the LORD: "You *are* my God;
Hear the voice of my supplications, O LORD.
➤ 7 O GOD the Lord, the strength of my salvation,
You have covered my head in the day of battle.
8 Do not grant, O LORD, the desires of the wicked;
Do not further his *wicked* scheme,
Lest they be exalted. Selah

9 "*As for* the head of those who surround me,
Let the evil of their lips cover them;
10 Let burning coals fall upon them;
Let them be cast into the fire,
Into deep pits, that they rise not up again.
11 Let not a slanderer be established in the earth;
Let evil hunt the violent man to overthrow *him*."

✳ 12 I know that the LORD will maintain
The cause of the afflicted,
And justice for the poor.
13 Surely the righteous shall give thanks to Your name;
The upright shall dwell in Your presence.

PSALM 141

Prayer for Safekeeping from Wickedness

A Psalm of David.

1 LORD, I cry out to You;
Make haste to me!
Give ear to my voice when I cry out to You.
2 Let my prayer be set before You *as* incense,
The lifting up of my hands *as* the evening sacrifice.

3 Set a guard, O LORD, over my mouth;
Keep watch over the door of my lips.
4 Do not incline my heart to any evil thing,
To practice wicked works
With men who work iniquity;
And do not let me eat of their delicacies.

5 Let the righteous strike me;
It shall be a kindness.
And let him rebuke me;
It shall be as excellent oil;
Let my head not refuse it.

For still my prayer *is* against the deeds of the wicked.
6 Their judges are overthrown by the sides of the cliff,
And they hear my words, for they are sweet.
7 Our bones are scattered at the mouth of the grave,
As when one plows and breaks up the earth.

8 But my eyes *are* upon You, O GOD the Lord;
In You I take refuge;
Do not leave my soul destitute.
9 Keep me from the snares they have laid for me,
And from the traps of the workers of iniquity.
10 Let the wicked fall into their own nets,
While I escape safely.

PSALM 142

A Plea for Relief from Persecutors

A Contemplation[a] of David. A Prayer when he was in the cave.

1 I cry out to the LORD with my voice;
With my voice to the LORD I make my supplication.
2 I pour out my complaint before Him;
I declare before Him my trouble.

3 When my spirit was overwhelmed within me,
Then You knew my path.

142:title [a]Hebrew *Maschil*

LIFE LESSONS

➤ ***140:7 — O GOD the Lord, the strength of my salvation, You have covered my head in the day of battle.***

It's usually wise to heed the counsel, "Keep your head down!" But what if you can't? What if your neck is so far out there that it invites chopping? Then God steps in. He protects us in our most vulnerable times.

➤ ***141:5 — Let the righteous strike me; it shall be a kindness. And let him rebuke me; it shall be as excellent oil; let my head not refuse it.***

When the righteous "strike" us through a stern rebuke or painful correction, they do so for our own good. Only a fool would call for ice cream when he really needs penicillin.

In the way in which I walk
They have secretly set a snare for me.
4 Look on *my* right hand and see,
For *there is* no one who acknowledges me;
Refuge has failed me;
No one cares for my soul.

5 I cried out to You, O LORD:
I said, "You *are* my refuge,
My portion in the land of the living.
6 Attend to my cry,
For I am brought very low;
Deliver me from my persecutors,
For they are stronger than I.
➤ 7 Bring my soul out of prison,
That I may praise Your name;
The righteous shall surround me,
For You shall deal bountifully with me."

PSALM 143

An Earnest Appeal for Guidance and Deliverance

A Psalm of David.

1 Hear my prayer, O LORD,
Give ear to my supplications!
In Your faithfulness answer me,
And in Your righteousness.
2 Do not enter into judgment with Your servant,
For in Your sight no one living is righteous.

3 For the enemy has persecuted my soul;
He has crushed my life to the ground;
He has made me dwell in darkness,
Like those who have long been dead.
4 Therefore my spirit is overwhelmed within me;
My heart within me is distressed.
5 I remember the days of old;
I meditate on all Your works;
I muse on the work of Your hands.
6 I spread out my hands to You;
My soul *longs* for You like a thirsty land. Selah

7 Answer me speedily, O LORD;
My spirit fails!
Do not hide Your face from me,
Lest I be like those who go down into the pit.
➤ 8 Cause me to hear Your lovingkindness in the morning,
For in You do I trust;
Cause me to know the way in which I should walk,
For I lift up my soul to You.

9 Deliver me, O LORD, from my enemies;
In You I take shelter.[a]
➤ 10 Teach me to do Your will,
For You *are* my God;
Your Spirit *is* good.
Lead me in the land of uprightness.

11 Revive me, O LORD, for Your name's sake!
For Your righteousness' sake bring my soul out of trouble.
12 In Your mercy cut off my enemies,
And destroy all those who afflict my soul;
For I *am* Your servant.

PSALM 144

A Song to the LORD Who Preserves and Prospers His People

A Psalm of David.

1 Blessed *be* the LORD my Rock,
Who trains my hands for war,
And my fingers for battle—
2 My lovingkindness and my fortress,
My high tower and my deliverer,
My shield and *the One* in whom I take refuge,
Who subdues my people[a] under me.

3 LORD, what *is* man, that You take knowledge of him?
Or the son of man, that You are mindful of him?
4 Man is like a breath;
His days *are* like a passing shadow.

5 Bow down Your heavens, O LORD, and come down;

143:9 [a]Septuagint and Vulgate read *To You I flee.*
144:2 [a]Following Masoretic Text, Septuagint, and Vulgate; Syriac and Targum read *the peoples* (compare 18:47).

LIFE LESSONS

➤ 142:7 — *Bring my soul out of prison, that I may praise Your name . . . .*

Our souls get in prison in many ways. Sometimes we put ourselves there through sin. Sometimes enemies put us there. Sometimes we're just at the wrong place at the wrong time. But our God is a specialist at prison escapes!

➤ 143:8 — *. . . cause me to know the way in which I should walk, for I lift up my soul to You.*

If we want God's guidance—and we all need it every day—then He instructs us to ask for it. We must ask in faith and then listen carefully for His voice. He always guides those who really want to follow.

➤ 143:10 — *Teach me to do Your will, for You are my God . . . .*

Every day we obey someone. Paul says that we can obey sin, which leads to death; or we can obey God, which leads to righteousness (Rom. 6:16). If God is our Master, shouldn't we learn to obey Him?

Touch the mountains, and they shall
smoke.
6 Flash forth lightning and scatter them;
Shoot out Your arrows and destroy
them.
7 Stretch out Your hand from above;
Rescue me and deliver me out of great
waters,
From the hand of foreigners,
8 Whose mouth speaks lying words,
And whose right hand *is* a right hand of
falsehood.

➤ 9 I will sing a new song to You, O God;
On a harp of ten strings I will sing
praises to You,
10 *The One* who gives salvation to kings,
Who delivers David His servant
From the deadly sword.

11 Rescue me and deliver me from the
hand of foreigners,
Whose mouth speaks lying words,
And whose right hand *is* a right hand of
falsehood—
12 That our sons *may be* as plants grown
up in their youth;
That our daughters *may be* as pillars,
Sculptured in palace style;
13 *That* our barns *may be* full,
Supplying all kinds of produce;
That our sheep may bring forth
thousands
And ten thousands in our fields;
14 *That* our oxen *may be* well laden;
That there be no breaking in or going
out;
That there be no outcry in our streets.
15 Happy *are* the people who are in such a
state;
Happy *are* the people whose God *is* the
LORD!

PSALM 145

A Song of God's Majesty and Love

A Praise of David.

1 I will extol You, my God, O King;
And I will bless Your name forever and
ever.
2 Every day I will bless You,
And I will praise Your name forever and
ever.
3 Great *is* the LORD, and greatly to be
praised;
And His greatness *is* unsearchable.
4 One generation shall praise Your works
to another,
And shall declare Your mighty acts.
5 I[a] will meditate on the glorious splendor ➤
of Your majesty,
And on Your wondrous works.[b]
6 *Men* shall speak of the might of Your
awesome acts,
And I will declare Your greatness.
7 They shall utter the memory of Your
great goodness,
And shall sing of Your righteousness.

8 The LORD *is* gracious and full of
compassion,
Slow to anger and great in mercy.
9 The LORD *is* good to all,
And His tender mercies *are* over all His
works.

10 All Your works shall praise You, O LORD,
And Your saints shall bless You.
11 They shall speak of the glory of Your
kingdom,
And talk of Your power,
12 To make known to the sons of men His
mighty acts,
And the glorious majesty of His
kingdom.
13 Your kingdom *is* an everlasting
kingdom,
And Your dominion *endures* throughout
all generations.[a]

14 The LORD upholds all who fall,
And raises up all *who are* bowed down.
15 The eyes of all look expectantly to You, ➤
And You give them their food in due
season.

145:5 [a]Following Masoretic Text and Targum; Dead Sea Scrolls, Septuagint, Syriac, and Vulgate read *They.* [b]Literally *on the words of Your wondrous works* **145:13** [a]Following Masoretic Text and Targum; Dead Sea Scrolls, Septuagint, Syriac, and Vulgate add *The LORD is faithful in all His words, And holy in all His works.*

LIFE LESSONS

➤ 144:9 — *I will sing a new song to You, O God; on a harp of ten strings I will sing praises to You.*

If we have instrumental abilities, the Lord invites us to use them to praise Him. If we have only a mediocre voice, He invites us to use that to praise Him. The point is to praise Him with all we have.

➤ 145:5 — *I will meditate on the glorious splendor of Your majesty, and on Your wondrous works.*

How can we meditate on God's majestic splendor? We can recall the personal victories He has given us. We can ponder His attributes. We can glory in a mountain peak. And most of all, we can focus on His Son.

➤ 145:15 — *The eyes of all look expectantly to You, and You give them their food in due season.*

God is the great Provider. As Paul said, "He gives to all life, breath, and all things" (Acts 17:25). We do not look to God presumptuously for what we need, but expectantly, for we put our hope in His great love.

16 You open Your hand
And satisfy the desire of every living
thing.
17 The LORD *is* righteous in all His ways,
Gracious in all His works.
✳18 The LORD *is* near to all who call upon
Him,
To all who call upon Him in truth.
19 He will fulfill the desire of those who
fear Him;
He also will hear their cry and save
them.
20 The LORD preserves all who love Him,
But all the wicked He will destroy.
21 My mouth shall speak the praise of the
LORD,
And all flesh shall bless His holy name
Forever and ever.

PSALM 146

The Happiness of Those Whose Help Is the LORD

1 Praise the LORD!

Praise the LORD, O my soul!
2 While I live I will praise the LORD;
I will sing praises to my God while I
have my being.

3 Do not put your trust in princes,
Nor in a son of man, in whom *there is*
no help.
4 His spirit departs, he returns to his
earth;
In that very day his plans perish.

5 Happy *is he* who *has* the God of Jacob
for his help,
Whose hope *is* in the LORD his God,
6 Who made heaven and earth,
The sea, and all that *is* in them;
Who keeps truth forever,
7 Who executes justice for the oppressed,
Who gives food to the hungry.
The LORD gives freedom to the
prisoners.

➤8 The LORD opens *the eyes of* the blind;
The LORD raises those who are bowed
down;
The LORD loves the righteous.
9 The LORD watches over the strangers;
He relieves the fatherless and widow;
But the way of the wicked He turns
upside down.

10 The LORD shall reign forever—
Your God, O Zion, to all generations.

Praise the LORD!

PSALM 147

Praise to God for His Word and Providence

1 Praise the LORD!
For *it is* good to sing praises to our God;
For *it is* pleasant, *and* praise is
beautiful.

2 The LORD builds up Jerusalem;
He gathers together the outcasts of
Israel.
3 He heals the brokenhearted ➤
And binds up their wounds.
4 He counts the number of the stars;
He calls them all by name.
5 Great *is* our Lord, and mighty in power;
His understanding *is* infinite.
6 The LORD lifts up the humble;
He casts the wicked down to the
ground.

7 Sing to the LORD with thanksgiving;
Sing praises on the harp to our God,
8 Who covers the heavens with clouds,
Who prepares rain for the earth,
Who makes grass to grow on the
mountains.
9 He gives to the beast its food,
And to the young ravens that cry.
10 He does not delight in the strength of
the horse;
He takes no pleasure in the legs of a
man.
11 The LORD takes pleasure in those who ➤
fear Him,
In those who hope in His mercy.

12 Praise the LORD, O Jerusalem!
Praise your God, O Zion!
13 For He has strengthened the bars of
your gates;
He has blessed your children within
you.

LIFE LESSONS

➤ 146:8 — *The LORD opens the eyes of the blind . . . .*

The Old Testament prophets performed many mighty miracles, but not one of them ever caused a blind man to see. Jesus, however, made healing the blind something of a specialty (Matt. 9:30; 11:5; 12:22; John 9:32).

➤ 147:3 — *He heals the brokenhearted and binds up their wounds.*

When Jesus began His public ministry, He quoted from Isaiah 61:1, telling the crowd that God had sent Him to fulfill it: " . . . the Spirit of the LORD has anointed Me . . . to heal the brokenhearted. . ." (Luke 4:18).

➤ 147:11 — *The LORD takes pleasure in those who fear Him, in those who hope in His mercy.*

It may seem odd to "fear" and "hope" in the same person, but they work together to produce a profound and deep kind of faith that has the staying power to bring us safely through all hardship and calamity.

14 He makes peace *in* your borders,
And fills you with the finest wheat.
15 He sends out His command *to the* earth;
His word runs very swiftly.
16 He gives snow like wool;
He scatters the frost like ashes;
17 He casts out His hail like morsels;
Who can stand before His cold?
18 He sends out His word and melts them;
He causes His wind to blow, *and* the waters flow.

19 He declares His word to Jacob,
His statutes and His judgments to Israel.
20 He has not dealt thus with any nation;
And *as for His* judgments, they have not known them.

Praise the LORD!

PSALM 148

Praise to the LORD from Creation

1 Praise the LORD!

Praise the LORD from the heavens;
Praise Him in the heights!
2 Praise Him, all His angels;
Praise Him, all His hosts!
3 Praise Him, sun and moon;
Praise Him, all you stars of light!
4 Praise Him, you heavens of heavens,
And you waters above the heavens!

5 Let them praise the name of the LORD,
For He commanded and they were created.
6 He also established them forever and ever;
He made a decree which shall not pass away.

7 Praise the LORD from the earth,
You great sea creatures and all the depths;
➤ 8 Fire and hail, snow and clouds;
Stormy wind, fulfilling His word;
9 Mountains and all hills;
Fruitful trees and all cedars;
10 Beasts and all cattle;
Creeping things and flying fowl;
11 Kings of the earth and all peoples;
Princes and all judges of the earth;
12 Both young men and maidens;
Old men and children.

13 Let them praise the name of the LORD,
For His name alone is exalted;
His glory *is* above the earth and heaven.
14 And He has exalted the horn of His people,
The praise of all His saints—
Of the children of Israel,
A people near to Him.

Praise the LORD!

PSALM 149

Praise to God for His Salvation and Judgment

1 Praise the LORD!

Sing to the LORD a new song,
And His praise in the assembly of saints.

2 Let Israel rejoice in their Maker;
Let the children of Zion be joyful in their King.
3 Let them praise His name with the dance;
Let them sing praises to Him with the timbrel and harp.
4 For the LORD takes pleasure in His people; ➤
He will beautify the humble with salvation.

5 Let the saints be joyful in glory;
Let them sing aloud on their beds.
6 *Let* the high praises of God *be* in their mouth,
And a two-edged sword in their hand,
7 To execute vengeance on the nations,
And punishments on the peoples;
8 To bind their kings with chains,
And their nobles with fetters of iron;
9 To execute on them the written judgment—
This honor have all His saints.

Praise the LORD!

PSALM 150

Let All Things Praise the LORD

1 Praise the LORD!

Praise God in His sanctuary;
Praise Him in His mighty firmament!

LIFE LESSONS

➤ 148:8 — *Fire and hail, snow and clouds; stormy wind, fulfilling His word . . . .*

God has used fire (Ex. 3:2), hail (Ex. 9:19), snow (Ps. 147:16), clouds (Deut. 4:1), storm (Ex. 9:24), and wind (Gen. 8:1) to accomplish His will. They all obey every whisper of His command. Do we?

➤ 149:4 — *For the LORD takes pleasure in His people; He will beautify the humble with salvation.*

Do you know that God takes pleasure in *you?* He delights in your growth and rejoices over your desire to obey Him. One day He will give you the ultimate beauty treatment: He will make you like His Son (1 John 3:2).

ANSWERS TO LIFE'S QUESTIONS

What happens when we praise God?

PS. 150:1–6

Perhaps no book exemplifies the spirit of praise and worship more than the book of Psalms. It records more verses of praise than any other book of the Bible. Obviously, God wants the praises of His people.

God tells us to give Him thanks in everything (1 Thess. 5:18), even when things press against our souls. We may not understand what is happening; we may never understand. But God's will in each circumstance is that we praise and thank Him.

But why? It's because praise is the clearest and most direct means by which you declare your dependence on God. It repeats your trust in Him in the midst of darkness. It confesses your allegiance and devotion to the One who was crucified for you and to whom you are eternally joined.

Consider a few of the specific benefits we derive from praising the Lord:

Praise magnifies God: Praise puts our focus on God, not on our problems. God's power, presence, and ability transform our thinking.

Praise humbles us: When we worship God, we gain a right view of ourselves. Praise deflates excess pride and ego. We gain a healthy self-image, based on God's view of us. By removing pride, praise strengthens us against temptation.

Praise reveals our devotion to God: If I love Christ, I will praise Him. If He has first place in my life, I will honor Him with worship and thanksgiving.

Praise motivates us to holy living: Praise opens our hearts to want to live the way God desires—holy and separated unto Him, to do His will above our own, to want to be like Him more than like anyone else. The more we worship Him, the more like Him we will become.

Praise increases our joy: Joy is the constant companion of praise. If we feel depressed or discouraged, praising God will soon bring us joy.

Praise establishes our faith: The greater we see our God, the smaller we see our problems.

Praise elevates our emotions: Worry, fear, and doubt cannot survive for long in an atmosphere of praise.

If you want to see a difference in your relationship with Christ and in your walk with Him, start to praise Him today. Continue even when you feel prone to give up. Commit yourself to a life of praise and fellowship with Jesus—and experience the fullness of what God means by "joy."

See the Life Principles Index for further study:

1. Our intimacy with God—His highest priority for our lives—determines the impact of our lives.

2 **Praise Him for His mighty acts;**
Praise Him according to His excellent greatness!

3 **Praise Him with the sound of the trumpet;**
Praise Him with the lute and harp!

4 **Praise Him with the timbrel and dance;**
Praise Him with stringed instruments and flutes!

5 **Praise Him with loud cymbals;**
Praise Him with clashing cymbals!

6 **Let everything that has breath praise the LORD.**

Praise the LORD!

LIFE LESSONS

➤ **150:6 — *Let everything that has breath praise the LORD. Praise the LORD!***

Do you have breath? Then praise the Lord! Praise Him before you turn the page. Praise Him in your car. Praise Him at home. Praise Him while you work. As long as you draw breath, praise Him!

THE BOOK OF

PROVERBS

The key word in the Book of Proverbs is "wisdom," the ability to live life skillfully. Living a godly life in an ungodly world, however, is no simple assignment. Proverbs provides a divine commentary on how to deal successfully with the practical affairs of everyday life: how to relate to God, parents, children, neighbors, government, and others. Proverbs tackles topics as wide-ranging as pride, greed, procrastination, slothfulness, sexual sin, anger, friendship, and speech—among many others.

Solomon, the principal author, uses a combination of poetry, parables, leading questions, short stories, and wise sayings—all wrapped in striking and memorable nuggets—to enable God's people to gain the divine perspective necessary to handle life's issues. He does not issue divine promises or guarantees, but instead says to us, in essence, "If you live wisely according to the guidelines set down in God's Word, then blessing is the usual result. If you live foolishly, however, and follow your own stubborn path, then you should expect regret and pain and destruction."

Because Solomon, who represents the pinnacle of Israel's wisdom tradition, wrote the majority of the book, its Hebrew title is *Mishle Shelomoh*, "Proverbs of Solomon" (1:1). The Latin title, *Liber Proverbiorum*, "Book of Proverbs," combines the words *Pro* ("for") and *Verba* ("words") to describe how the proverbs concentrate the meaning of many words into a very few.

Themes: Proverbs presents time-tested wisdom for achieving a successful everyday life. The book takes the principles of the Law of Moses and expresses them in a practical, easy-to-understand form that anyone can understand and apply. The phrase "the fear of the LORD" appears more than a dozen times in Proverbs and provides the underlying theological concept for the entire book.

Authors: Solomon is the generally accepted author of Proverbs 1–29. Agur and Lemuel are credited with writing chapters 30 and 31.

Date: Solomon ruled Israel in the tenth century B.C. Apparently King Hezekiah's men compiled and edited many of his proverbs during the revival of their day (about 715–686 B.C.), a fact briefly noted in Proverbs 25:1.

Structure: Chapters 1–7 of Proverbs take the form of "fatherly advice" concerning the acquisition of wisdom. Chapters 8 and 9 issue Solomon's call to wisdom. Chapters 10–20 contrast wisdom and foolishness, godliness and ungodliness, good and evil. Chapters 21–24 offer wisdom in the form of maxims and counsel, and chapters 25–29 present more of Solomon's proverbs, compiled and edited during King Hezekiah's time. Chapter 30 gives us the words of "Agur," while 31:1–9 are from "King Lemuel." Proverbs 31:10–31 describes an ideal wife.

As you read Proverbs, watch for several life principles that play an important role in this book:

13. **Listening is essential to walking with God.** *See Proverbs 1:5; 8:32, 33; 16:20; pages 724; 731; 740.*

6. **You reap what you sow, more than you sow, and later than you sow.** *See Proverbs 11:18; 22:8; pages 733; 746.*

23. **You can never outgive God.** *See Proverbs 19:17; 22:9; 28:20; pages 744; 746; 752.*

The Beginning of Knowledge

1 The proverbs of Solomon the son of David, king of Israel:

2 To know wisdom and instruction,
To perceive the words of understanding,
3 To receive the instruction of wisdom,
Justice, judgment, and equity;
4 To give prudence to the simple,
To the young man knowledge and discretion—
5 A wise *man* will hear and increase learning,
And a man of understanding will attain wise counsel,
6 To understand a proverb and an enigma,
The words of the wise and their riddles.

➤ 7 The fear of the LORD *is* the beginning of knowledge,
But fools despise wisdom and instruction.

Shun Evil Counsel

8 My son, hear the instruction of your father,
And do not forsake the law of your mother;
9 For they *will be* a graceful ornament on your head,
And chains about your neck.

➤ 10 My son, if sinners entice you,
Do not consent.
11 If they say, "Come with us,
Let us lie in wait to *shed* blood;
Let us lurk secretly for the innocent without cause;
12 Let us swallow them alive like Sheol,[a]
And whole, like those who go down to the Pit;
13 We shall find all *kinds* of precious possessions,
We shall fill our houses with spoil;
14 Cast in your lot among us,
Let us all have one purse"—
15 My son, do not walk in the way with them,
Keep your foot from their path;
16 For their feet run to evil,
And they make haste to shed blood.
17 Surely, in vain the net is spread
In the sight of any bird;
18 But they lie in wait for their *own* blood,
They lurk secretly for their *own* lives.
19 So *are* the ways of everyone who is greedy for gain;
It takes away the life of its owners.

The Call of Wisdom

20 Wisdom calls aloud outside;
She raises her voice in the open squares.
21 She cries out in the chief concourses,[a]
At the openings of the gates in the city
She speaks her words:
22 "How long, you simple ones, will you love simplicity?
For scorners delight in their scorning,
And fools hate knowledge.
23 Turn at my rebuke;
Surely I will pour out my spirit on you;
I will make my words known to you.
24 Because I have called and you refused,
I have stretched out my hand and no one regarded,
25 Because you disdained all my counsel,
And would have none of my rebuke,
26 I also will laugh at your calamity;
I will mock when your terror comes,
27 When your terror comes like a storm,
And your destruction comes like a whirlwind,
When distress and anguish come upon you.

28 "Then they will call on me, but I will not answer;
They will seek me diligently, but they will not find me.
29 Because they hated knowledge
And did not choose the fear of the LORD,
30 They would have none of my counsel
And despised my every rebuke.
31 Therefore they shall eat the fruit of their own way,
And be filled to the full with their own fancies.
32 For the turning away of the simple will slay them,
And the complacency of fools will destroy them;
33 But whoever listens to me will dwell safely,
And will be secure, without fear of evil."

1:12 [a]Or *the grave* **1:21** [a]Septuagint, Syriac, and Targum read *top of the walls;* Vulgate reads *the head of multitudes.*

LIFE LESSONS

➤ 1:7 — *The fear of the LORD is the beginning of knowledge . . . .*

When we start with the truth of God—His holiness, power, love, wisdom, goodness—we build on an unchanging reality that provides us with a firm foundation for life.

➤ 1:10 — *My son, if sinners entice you, do not consent.*

The devil doesn't "make" anyone sin; neither does anyone else. We consent to it. When we remember that God's wages pay a lot better than Satan's, we'll find it easier to obey.

ANSWERS TO LIFE'S QUESTIONS

How can I gain wisdom from God?

PROV. 2:1–7

A growing number of people in our world fail to seek God for His wisdom. Instead, they strive to satisfy their passions and desires without regard to their future or to the consequences of their decisions.

For a believer, this is a spiritually dangerous way to live. When we try to live apart from the counsel of God's wisdom, we suffer disillusionment, fear, doubt, worry, and frustration. Our lives fall apart when we do not involve the Savior in our decisions.

The wisest approach to life's challenges is to seek God for His plan, direction, and spiritual insight. But how can we do that? The next time you face a challenge or an important decision, seek God's wisdom by doing the following:

- *Seek Him*—If you want to know God's heart on a given issue or when you have to make a difficult decision, ask Him. Take time to pray—but in your times of prayer, don't do all the talking. Listen for God's still, small voice.
- *Meditate on God's Word*—You will gain insight into God's mind and heart by studying Scripture and meditating on its truth. Difficult decisions become easier to make when God is the One guiding you.
- *Obey the principles of Scripture*—When you set your heart on obeying God, He will teach you how to apply His truth in your life. Then you will know the way of wisdom.
- *Observe the faithfulness of God*—The Lord has never failed to keep a single promise He has made. The Bible is full of testimonies that celebrate His goodness and love. Learn to claim His promises as you read His Word.
- *Heed godly counsel*—God can use a pastor or trusted Christian friend to help you see beyond your weaknesses. Don't hesitate to share your needs and fears with those who love the Lord and you.
- *Associate with wise people*—Choose your friends wisely. Include God in every relationship, and you will establish a strong, godly base from which you can make wise decisions.

Because God loves us, we have no need to worry about the future. He has a plan, not only for our lives, but also for every problem we face. Oswald Chambers said, "All our fret and worry is caused by calculating without God." Take time today to renew your trust in God and His ability to provide the wisdom you need.

See the Life Principles Index for further study:
3. God's Word is an immovable anchor in times of storm.

The Value of Wisdom

2 My son, if you receive my words,
And treasure my commands within you,
2 So that you incline your ear to wisdom,
And apply your heart to understanding;
3 Yes, if you cry out for discernment,
And lift up your voice for understanding,
4 If you seek her as silver,
And search for her as *for* hidden treasures;
5 Then you will understand the fear of the LORD,
And find the knowledge of God.
6 For the LORD gives wisdom;
From His mouth *come* knowledge and understanding;
7 He stores up sound wisdom for the upright;
He is a shield to those who walk uprightly;
8 He guards the paths of justice,
And preserves the way of His saints.
9 Then you will understand righteousness and justice,
Equity *and* every good path.
10 When wisdom enters your heart,
And knowledge is pleasant to your soul,

LIFE LESSONS

2:6 — *For the LORD gives wisdom; from His mouth come knowledge and understanding.*

And how do we appropriate His wisdom? We ask for it: "If any of you lacks wisdom, let him ask of God, who gives to all liberally and without reproach, and it will be given to him" (James 1:5).

Life Examples:

KING SOLOMON

We All Need God's Wisdom

PROV. 3:5, 6

When God invited Solomon to ask for whatever he wanted, the king requested wisdom (1 Kin. 3:9). That God-given wisdom taught Solomon that only a fool tries to solve life's problems without God's help.

Any time we spend wondering about how to get out of a touchy situation is time wasted. God's guidance is more than sufficient for all the tests or trials we might have to face—but in order to benefit from it, we have to seek it out, just as Solomon did so long ago.

In this life, tests come in all shapes and sizes. Some we anticipate; others blindside us in the middle of a rainy afternoon. Some tests require us to endure; others ask us to make the right decision immediately. Regardless of the package in which the test comes wrapped, God instructs us to come to Him for the wisdom we so desperately need.

See the Life Principles Index for further study:
13. Listening to God is essential to walking with God.

11 Discretion will preserve you;
Understanding will keep you,
12 To deliver you from the way of evil,
From the man who speaks perverse things,
13 From those who leave the paths of uprightness
To walk in the ways of darkness;
14 Who rejoice in doing evil,
And delight in the perversity of the wicked;
15 Whose ways *are* crooked,
And *who are* devious in their paths;
16 To deliver you from the immoral woman,
From the seductress *who* flatters with her words,
17 Who forsakes the companion of her youth,
And forgets the covenant of her God.
18 For her house leads down to death,
And her paths to the dead;
19 None who go to her return,
Nor do they regain the paths of life—
20 So you may walk in the way of goodness,
And keep *to* the paths of righteousness.
21 For the upright will dwell in the land,
And the blameless will remain in it;
22 But the wicked will be cut off from the earth,
And the unfaithful will be uprooted from it.

Guidance for the Young

3 My son, do not forget my law,
But let your heart keep my commands;
2 For length of days and long life
And peace they will add to you.

3 Let not mercy and truth forsake you;
Bind them around your neck,
Write them on the tablet of your heart,
4 *And* so find favor and high esteem
In the sight of God and man.

5 Trust in the LORD with all your heart,
And lean not on your own understanding;
6 In all your ways acknowledge Him,
And He shall direct[a] your paths.

7 Do not be wise in your own eyes;
Fear the LORD and depart from evil.
8 It will be health to your flesh,[a]
And strength[b] to your bones.

9 Honor the LORD with your possessions,
And with the firstfruits of all your increase;
10 So your barns will be filled with plenty,
And your vats will overflow with new wine.

11 My son, do not despise the chastening of the LORD,
Nor detest His correction;
12 For whom the LORD loves He corrects,
Just as a father the son *in whom* he delights.

3:6 [a]Or *make smooth* or *straight* **3:8** [a]Literally *navel,* figurative of the body [b]Literally *drink* or *refreshment*

LIFE LESSONS

➤ ***3:3, 4 — Let not mercy and truth forsake you; bind them around your neck, write them on the tablet of your heart, and so find favor and high esteem in the sight of God and man.***

Mercy without truth can lead to ungodly compromise; truth without mercy can lead to unfeeling legalism. When we pursue both equally and simultaneously, we reflect the heart of God and bring Him great pleasure.

13 Happy *is* the man *who* finds wisdom,
And the man *who* gains understanding;
14 For her proceeds *are* better than the profits of silver,
And her gain than fine gold.
15 She *is* more precious than rubies,
And all the things you may desire cannot compare with her.
16 Length of days *is* in her right hand,
In her left hand riches and honor.
17 Her ways *are* ways of pleasantness,
And all her paths *are* peace.
18 She *is* a tree of life to those who take hold of her,
And happy *are all* who retain her.

19 The LORD by wisdom founded the earth;
By understanding He established the heavens;
20 By His knowledge the depths were broken up,
And clouds drop down the dew.

21 My son, let them not depart from your eyes—
Keep sound wisdom and discretion;
22 So they will be life to your soul
And grace to your neck.
23 Then you will walk safely in your way,
And your foot will not stumble.
24 When you lie down, you will not be afraid;
Yes, you will lie down and your sleep will be sweet.
25 Do not be afraid of sudden terror,
Nor of trouble from the wicked when it comes;
26 For the LORD will be your confidence,
And will keep your foot from being caught.

➤ 27 Do not withhold good from those to whom it is due,
When it is in the power of your hand to do *so*.
28 Do not say to your neighbor,
"Go, and come back,
And tomorrow I will give *it*,"
When you have it with you.
29 Do not devise evil against your neighbor,
For he dwells by you for safety's sake.
30 Do not strive with a man without cause,
If he has done you no harm.

31 Do not envy the oppressor,
And choose none of his ways;
32 For the perverse *person is* an abomination to the LORD,
But His secret counsel *is* with the upright.
33 The curse of the LORD *is* on the house of the wicked, ✳
But He blesses the home of the just.
34 Surely He scorns the scornful,
But gives grace to the humble.
35 The wise shall inherit glory,
But shame shall be the legacy of fools.

Security in Wisdom

4 Hear, *my* children, the instruction of a father,
And give attention to know understanding;
2 For I give you good doctrine:
Do not forsake my law.
3 When I was my father's son,
Tender and the only one in the sight of my mother,
4 He also taught me, and said to me:
"Let your heart retain my words;
Keep my commands, and live.
5 Get wisdom! Get understanding!
Do not forget, nor turn away from the words of my mouth.
6 Do not forsake her, and she will preserve you;
Love her, and she will keep you.
7 Wisdom *is* the principal thing;
Therefore get wisdom.
And in all your getting, get understanding.
8 Exalt her, and she will promote you;
She will bring you honor, when you embrace her.
9 She will place on your head an ornament of grace;
A crown of glory she will deliver to you."

10 Hear, my son, and receive my sayings,
And the years of your life will be many.
11 I have taught you in the way of wisdom;
I have led you in right paths.
12 When you walk, your steps will not be hindered,
And when you run, you will not stumble.
13 Take firm hold of instruction, do not let go;
Keep her, for she *is* your life.

14 Do not enter the path of the wicked,
And do not walk in the way of evil.
15 Avoid it, do not travel on it;
Turn away from it and pass on.
16 For they do not sleep unless they have done evil;

LIFE LESSONS

➤ ***3:27 — Do not withhold good from those to whom it is due, when it is in the power of your hand to do so.***

"But he doesn't deserve it!" Neither do you, but God lavishes good things on you every day. We should look for ways to bless others, and so demonstrate to the world the boundless love of God.

And their sleep is taken away unless they
make *someone* fall.
17 For they eat the bread of wickedness,
And drink the wine of violence.

18 But the path of the just *is* like the shining
sun,[a]
That shines ever brighter unto the perfect
day.
19 The way of the wicked *is* like darkness;
They do not know what makes them
stumble.

20 My son, give attention to my words;
Incline your ear to my sayings.
21 Do not let them depart from your eyes;
Keep them in the midst of your heart;
22 For they *are* life to those who find them,
And health to all their flesh.
23 Keep your heart with all diligence,
For out of it *spring* the issues of life.
24 Put away from you a deceitful mouth,
And put perverse lips far from you.
25 Let your eyes look straight ahead,
And your eyelids look right before you.
➤ 26 Ponder the path of your feet,
And let all your ways be established.
27 Do not turn to the right or the left;
Remove your foot from evil.

The Peril of Adultery

5 My son, pay attention to my wisdom;
Lend your ear to my understanding,
2 That you may preserve discretion,
And your lips may keep knowledge.
3 For the lips of an immoral woman drip
honey,
And her mouth *is* smoother than oil;
4 But in the end she is bitter as wormwood,
Sharp as a two-edged sword.
5 Her feet go down to death,
Her steps lay hold of hell.[a]
6 Lest you ponder *her* path of life—
Her ways are unstable;
You do not know *them*.

7 Therefore hear me now, *my* children,
And do not depart from the words of my
mouth.
➤ 8 Remove your way far from her,
And do not go near the door of her house,
9 Lest you give your honor to others,
And your years to the cruel *one;*
10 Lest aliens be filled with your wealth,
And your labors *go* to the house of a
foreigner;
11 And you mourn at last,
When your flesh and your body are
consumed,
12 And say:
"How I have hated instruction,
And my heart despised correction!
13 I have not obeyed the voice of my
teachers,
Nor inclined my ear to those who
instructed me!
14 I was on the verge of total ruin,
In the midst of the assembly and
congregation."

15 Drink water from your own cistern,
And running water from your own
well.
16 Should your fountains be dispersed
abroad,
Streams of water in the streets?
17 Let them be only your own,
And not for strangers with you.
18 Let your fountain be blessed,
And rejoice with the wife of your youth.
19 *As a* loving deer and a graceful doe,
Let her breasts satisfy you at all times;
And always be enraptured with her
love.
20 For why should you, my son, be
enraptured by an immoral woman,
And be embraced in the arms of a
seductress?

21 For the ways of man *are* before the eyes
of the LORD, ◄
And He ponders all his paths.
22 His own iniquities entrap the wicked
man,
And he is caught in the cords of his sin.
23 He shall die for lack of instruction,
And in the greatness of his folly he shall
go astray.

4:18 [a]Literally *light* **5:5** [a]Or *Sheol*

LIFE LESSONS

➤ 4:26 — *Ponder the path of your feet . . . .*

Sometimes we fall into sin, not because we plan to, but because we aren't looking where we are going. God calls us to stay spiritually alert at all times, and that includes taking regular inventory of our life's direction.

➤ 5:8 — *Remove your way far from her, and do not go near the door of her house . . . .*

God's Word tells us to "flee sexual immorality" (1 Cor. 6:18), not to test our spiritual maturity by seeing how close we can get to it without falling into it. If you know something tempts you, stay away from it.

➤ 5:21 — *For the ways of man are before the eyes of the LORD, and He ponders all his paths.*

God is constantly watching over us, noting our decisions, pondering our plans, observing our behavior—not primarily for judgment, but for blessing. He knows exactly what we need, and so He invites us to ask Him for His counsel.

Dangerous Promises

6 My son, if you become surety for your friend,
If you have shaken hands in pledge for a stranger,
2 You are snared by the words of your mouth;
You are taken by the words of your mouth.
3 So do this, my son, and deliver yourself;
For you have come into the hand of your friend:
Go and humble yourself;
Plead with your friend.
4 Give no sleep to your eyes,
Nor slumber to your eyelids.
5 Deliver yourself like a gazelle from the hand *of the hunter,*
And like a bird from the hand of the fowler.[a]

The Folly of Indolence

➤ 6 Go to the ant, you sluggard!
Consider her ways and be wise,
7 Which, having no captain,
Overseer or ruler,
8 Provides her supplies in the summer,
And gathers her food in the harvest.
9 How long will you slumber, O sluggard?
When will you rise from your sleep?
10 A little sleep, a little slumber,
A little folding of the hands to sleep—
11 So shall your poverty come on you like a prowler,
And your need like an armed man.

The Wicked Man

12 A worthless person, a wicked man,
Walks with a perverse mouth;
13 He winks with his eyes,
He shuffles his feet,
He points with his fingers;
14 Perversity *is* in his heart,
He devises evil continually,
He sows discord.
15 Therefore his calamity shall come suddenly;
Suddenly he shall be broken without remedy.

16 These six *things* the LORD hates,
Yes, seven *are* an abomination to Him:
17 A proud look,
A lying tongue,
Hands that shed innocent blood,
18 A heart that devises wicked plans,
Feet that are swift in running to evil,
19 A false witness *who* speaks lies,
And one who sows discord among brethren.

Beware of Adultery

20 My son, keep your father's command,
And do not forsake the law of your mother.
21 Bind them continually upon your heart;
Tie them around your neck.
22 When you roam, they[a] will lead you;
When you sleep, they will keep you;
And *when* you awake, they will speak with you.
23 For the commandment *is* a lamp, ➤
And the law a light;
Reproofs of instruction *are* the way of life,
24 To keep you from the evil woman,
From the flattering tongue of a seductress.
25 Do not lust after her beauty in your heart,
Nor let her allure you with her eyelids.
26 For by means of a harlot
A man is reduced to a crust of bread;
And an adulteress[a] will prey upon his precious life.
27 Can a man take fire to his bosom,
And his clothes not be burned?
28 Can one walk on hot coals,
And his feet not be seared?
29 So *is* he who goes in to his neighbor's wife;
Whoever touches her shall not be innocent.

30 *People* do not despise a thief
If he steals to satisfy himself when he is starving.
31 Yet *when* he is found, he must restore sevenfold;
He may have to give up all the substance of his house.
32 Whoever commits adultery with a woman lacks understanding;
He *who* does so destroys his own soul.
33 Wounds and dishonor he will get,
And his reproach will not be wiped away.

6:5 [a]That is, one who catches birds in a trap or snare
6:22 [a]Literally *it* **6:26** [a]Literally *a man's wife,* that is, of another

LIFE LESSONS

➤ 6:6 — *Go to the ant, you sluggard! Consider her ways and be wise . . . .*

God loves to use nature as a ready source of spiritual object lessons. While observing nature is no substitute for spending time in His Word, it can open our eyes to spiritual truth in a way nothing else does.

➤ 6:23 — *For the commandment is a lamp, and the law a light . . . .*

We live in a dark world, and without getting familiar with God's Word and learning how to effectively shine its light on our problems, we will certainly stumble in the blackness.

34 For jealousy *is* a husband's fury;
Therefore he will not spare in the day of vengeance.
35 He will accept no recompense,
Nor will he be appeased though you give many gifts.

7 My son, keep my words,
And treasure my commands within you.
➤ 2 Keep my commands and live,
And my law as the apple of your eye.
3 Bind them on your fingers;
Write them on the tablet of your heart.
4 Say to wisdom, "You *are* my sister,"
And call understanding *your* nearest kin,
5 That they may keep you from the immoral woman,
From the seductress *who* flatters with her words.

The Crafty Harlot

6 For at the window of my house
I looked through my lattice,
7 And saw among the simple,
I perceived among the youths,
A young man devoid of understanding,
8 Passing along the street near her corner;
And he took the path to her house
9 In the twilight, in the evening,
In the black and dark night.

10 And there a woman met him,
With the attire of a harlot, and a crafty heart.
11 She *was* loud and rebellious,
Her feet would not stay at home.
12 At times *she was* outside, at times in the open square,
Lurking at every corner.
➤ 13 So she caught him and kissed him;
With an impudent face she said to him:
14 "*I have* peace offerings with me;
Today I have paid my vows.
15 So I came out to meet you,
Diligently to seek your face,
And I have found you.
16 I have spread my bed with tapestry,
Colored coverings of Egyptian linen.
17 I have perfumed my bed
With myrrh, aloes, and cinnamon.
18 Come, let us take our fill of love until morning;
Let us delight ourselves with love.
19 For my husband *is* not at home;
He has gone on a long journey;
20 He has taken a bag of money with him,
And will come home on the appointed day."

21 With her enticing speech she caused him to yield,
With her flattering lips she seduced him.
22 Immediately he went after her, as an ox goes to the slaughter,
Or as a fool to the correction of the stocks,[a]
23 Till an arrow struck his liver.
As a bird hastens to the snare,
He did not know it *would cost* his life.

24 Now therefore, listen to me, *my* children;
Pay attention to the words of my mouth:
25 Do not let your heart turn aside to her ways,
Do not stray into her paths;
26 For she has cast down many wounded,
And all who were slain by her were strong *men.*
27 Her house *is* the way to hell,[a]
Descending to the chambers of death.

The Excellence of Wisdom

8 Does not wisdom cry out,
And understanding lift up her voice?
2 She takes her stand on the top of the high hill,
Beside the way, where the paths meet.
3 She cries out by the gates, at the entry of the city,
At the entrance of the doors:
4 "To you, O men, I call,
And my voice *is* to the sons of men.
5 O you simple ones, understand prudence,
And you fools, be of an understanding heart.
6 Listen, for I will speak of excellent things,
And from the opening of my lips *will come* right things;
7 For my mouth will speak truth;
Wickedness *is* an abomination to my lips.
8 All the words of my mouth *are* with righteousness;
Nothing crooked or perverse *is* in them.

7:22 [a]Septuagint, Syriac, and Targum read *as a dog to bonds;* Vulgate reads *as a lamb . . . to bonds.* **7:27** [a]Or *Sheol*

LIFE LESSONS

➤ 7:2 — *Keep my commands and live, and my law as the apple of your eye.*

How do we approach our time in Scripture? As a grinding duty to be completed as quickly as possible, or as a delightful opportunity to get to know God? David exclaimed, "Oh, how I love Your law!" (Ps. 119:97).

➤ 7:13, 14 — *With an impudent face she said to him: "I have peace offerings with me; today I have paid my vows."*

People have long used religious language to entice naïve believers into sin. Others confuse religious practices with genuine godliness. But we should never confuse sentiment with true spirituality.

9 They *are* all plain to him who
understands,
And right to those who find knowledge.
10 Receive my instruction, and not silver,
And knowledge rather than choice gold;
11 For wisdom *is* better than rubies,
And all the things one may desire cannot
be compared with her.

12"I, wisdom, dwell with prudence,
And find out knowledge *and* discretion.
➤ 13 The fear of the LORD *is* to hate evil;
Pride and arrogance and the evil way
And the perverse mouth I hate.
14 Counsel *is* mine, and sound wisdom;
I *am* understanding, I have strength.
15 By me kings reign,
And rulers decree justice.
16 By me princes rule, and nobles,
All the judges of the earth.[a]
17 I love those who love me,
And those who seek me diligently will
find me.
18 Riches and honor *are* with me,
Enduring riches and righteousness.
19 My fruit *is* better than gold, yes, than fine
gold,
And my revenue than choice silver.
20 I traverse the way of righteousness,
In the midst of the paths of justice,
21 That I may cause those who love me to
inherit wealth,
That I may fill their treasuries.

22"The LORD possessed me at the beginning
of His way,
Before His works of old.
23 I have been established from everlasting,
From the beginning, before there was
ever an earth.
24 When *there were* no depths I was
brought forth,
When *there were* no fountains abounding
with water.
25 Before the mountains were settled,
Before the hills, I was brought forth;
26 While as yet He had not made the earth
or the fields,
Or the primal dust of the world.
27 When He prepared the heavens, I *was*
there,
When He drew a circle on the face of the
deep,
28 When He established the clouds above,
When He strengthened the fountains of
the deep,
29 When He assigned to the sea its limit,
So that the waters would not transgress
His command,
When He marked out the foundations of
the earth,
30 Then I was beside Him *as* a master
craftsman;[a]
And I was daily *His* delight,
Rejoicing always before Him,
31 Rejoicing in His inhabited world,
And my delight *was* with the sons of
men.

32"Now therefore, listen to me, *my* children,
For blessed *are those who* keep my ways.
33 Hear instruction and be wise,
And do not disdain *it*.
34 Blessed is the man who listens to me,
Watching daily at my gates,
Waiting at the posts of my doors.
35 For whoever finds me finds life,
And obtains favor from the LORD;
36 But he who sins against me wrongs his
own soul;
All those who hate me love death."

The Way of Wisdom

9 Wisdom has built her house,
She has hewn out her seven pillars;
2 She has slaughtered her meat,
She has mixed her wine,
She has also furnished her table.
3 She has sent out her maidens,
She cries out from the highest places of
the city,
4 "Whoever *is* simple, let him turn in here!"
As for him who lacks understanding, she
says to him,
5 "Come, eat of my bread
And drink of the wine I have mixed.
6 Forsake foolishness and live,
And go in the way of understanding.

7 "He who corrects a scoffer gets shame for
himself,
And he who rebukes a wicked *man only*
harms himself.
8 Do not correct a scoffer, lest he hate you;
Rebuke a wise *man*, and he will love you.
9 Give *instruction* to a wise *man*, and he
will be still wiser;
Teach a just *man*, and he will increase in
learning.

8:16 [a]Masoretic Text, Syriac, Targum, and Vulgate read *righteousness;* Septuagint, Bomberg, and some manuscripts and editions read *earth.* **8:30** [a]A Jewish tradition reads *one brought up.*

LIFE LESSONS

➤ **8:13 — *The fear of the LORD is to hate evil . . . .***

As we grow spiritually, we gradually change from trying to stop doing the evil thing that we really want to do, to actually hating the evil thing so that we no longer want to do it.

10 "The fear of the LORD *is* the beginning of wisdom,
And the knowledge of the Holy One *is* understanding.
11 For by me your days will be multiplied,
And years of life will be added to you.
12 If you are wise, you are wise for yourself,
And *if* you scoff, you will bear *it* alone."

The Way of Folly

13 A foolish woman is clamorous;
She is simple, and knows nothing.
14 For she sits at the door of her house,
On a seat *by* the highest places of the city,
15 To call to those who pass by,
Who go straight on their way:
16 "Whoever *is* simple, let him turn in here";
And *as for* him who lacks understanding, she says to him,
➤ 17 "Stolen water is sweet,
And bread *eaten* in secret is pleasant."
18 But he does not know that the dead *are* there,
That her guests *are* in the depths of hell.[a]

Wise Sayings of Solomon

10 The proverbs of Solomon:

A wise son makes a glad father,
But a foolish son *is* the grief of his mother.
➤ 2 Treasures of wickedness profit nothing,
But righteousness delivers from death.
3 The LORD will not allow the righteous soul to famish,
But He casts away the desire of the wicked.

4 He who has a slack hand becomes poor,
But the hand of the diligent makes rich.
5 He who gathers in summer *is* a wise son;
He who sleeps in harvest *is* a son who causes shame.

6 Blessings *are* on the head of the righteous,
But violence covers the mouth of the wicked.
7 The memory of the righteous *is* blessed,
But the name of the wicked will rot.

8 The wise in heart will receive commands,
But a prating fool will fall.
9 He who walks with integrity walks securely,
But he who perverts his ways will become known.

10 He who winks with the eye causes trouble,
But a prating fool will fall.

11 The mouth of the righteous *is* a well of life,
But violence covers the mouth of the wicked.

12 Hatred stirs up strife, ➤
But love covers all sins.

13 Wisdom is found on the lips of him who has understanding,
But a rod *is* for the back of him who is devoid of understanding.

14 Wise *people* store up knowledge,
But the mouth of the foolish *is* near destruction.

15 The rich man's wealth *is* his strong city;
The destruction of the poor *is* their poverty.

16 The labor of the righteous *leads* to life,
The wages of the wicked to sin.

17 He who keeps instruction *is in* the way of life,
But he who refuses correction goes astray.

18 Whoever hides hatred *has* lying lips,
And whoever spreads slander *is* a fool.

19 In the multitude of words sin is not lacking,
But he who restrains his lips *is* wise.
20 The tongue of the righteous *is* choice silver;
The heart of the wicked *is worth* little.
21 The lips of the righteous feed many,
But fools die for lack of wisdom.[a]

22 The blessing of the LORD makes *one* rich, ✳
And He adds no sorrow with it.

9:18 [a]Or *Sheol* **10:21** [a]Literally *heart*

LIFE LESSONS

➤ 9:17, 18 — *"Stolen water is sweet, and bread eaten in secret is pleasant." But he does not know that the dead are there . . . .*

There is a certain thrill in doing forbidden things that no one sees you do. An adrenaline rush often accompanies this kind of "living on the edge"—but it ends when you fall off the cliff.

➤ 10:2 — *Treasures of wickedness profit nothing . . . .*

The Bible never tries to hide the fact that the wicked can indeed amass "treasures" through their wicked deeds. But it also insists that those ill-gotten treasures will benefit them not at all in the end.

➤ 10:12 — *Hatred stirs up strife, but love covers all sins.*

We all make mistakes in our relationships, and the natural reaction to an offense is anger. But if we want our relationships to work, we have to learn to apply love, not bitterness, to the wounds we suffer.

23 To do evil *is* like sport to a fool,
But a man of understanding has wisdom.
24 The fear of the wicked will come upon him,
And the desire of the righteous will be granted.
25 When the whirlwind passes by, the wicked *is* no *more,*
But the righteous *has* an everlasting foundation.

26 As vinegar to the teeth and smoke to the eyes,
So *is* the lazy *man* to those who send him.

27 The fear of the LORD prolongs days,
But the years of the wicked will be shortened.
28 The hope of the righteous *will be* gladness,
But the expectation of the wicked will perish.
29 The way of the LORD *is* strength for the upright,
But destruction *will come* to the workers of iniquity.

30 The righteous will never be removed,
But the wicked will not inhabit the earth.
31 The mouth of the righteous brings forth wisdom,
But the perverse tongue will be cut out.
32 The lips of the righteous know what is acceptable,
But the mouth of the wicked *what is* perverse.

➤ **11** Dishonest scales *are* an abomination to the LORD,
But a just weight *is* His delight.
2 When pride comes, then comes shame;
But with the humble *is* wisdom.
3 The integrity of the upright will guide them,
But the perversity of the unfaithful will destroy them.
4 Riches do not profit in the day of wrath,
But righteousness delivers from death.
5 The righteousness of the blameless will direct[a] his way aright,
But the wicked will fall by his own wickedness.
6 The righteousness of the upright will deliver them,
But the unfaithful will be caught by *their* lust.

7 When a wicked man dies, *his* expectation will perish,
And the hope of the unjust perishes.
8 The righteous is delivered from trouble,
And it comes to the wicked instead.
9 The hypocrite with *his* mouth destroys his neighbor,
But through knowledge the righteous will be delivered.
10 When it goes well with the righteous, the city rejoices;
And when the wicked perish, *there is* jubilation.
11 By the blessing of the upright the city is exalted,
But it is overthrown by the mouth of the wicked.

12 He who is devoid of wisdom despises his neighbor,
But a man of understanding holds his peace.

13 A talebearer reveals secrets,
But he who is of a faithful spirit conceals a matter.

14 Where *there is* no counsel, the people fall;
But in the multitude of counselors *there is* safety.

15 He who is surety for a stranger will suffer,
But one who hates being surety is secure.

16 A gracious woman retains honor,
But ruthless *men* retain riches.
17 The merciful man does good for his own soul, ➤
But *he who is* cruel troubles his own flesh.
18 The wicked *man* does deceptive work,
But he who sows righteousness *will have* a sure reward.
19 As righteousness *leads* to life,
So he who pursues evil *pursues it* to his own death.

11:5 [a]Or *make smooth* or *straight*

LIFE LESSONS

➤ 11:1 — *Dishonest scales are an abomination to the LORD, but a just weight is His delight.*

The writer refers to "abomination to the LORD." God is as concerned that His people conduct fair and honest business practices as He is that their sexual lives honor Him (Lev. 18:22). He delights in a "just weight" because it reflects His righteousness.

➤ 11:17 — *The merciful man does good for his own soul, but he who is cruel troubles his own flesh.*

The Lord calls us to do what is good and right, not only because godly living reflects His own holy character, but also because it benefits and blesses us. Living by God's Word is the healthy way to live.

20 Those who are of a perverse heart *are* an
abomination to the LORD,
But *the* blameless in their ways *are* His
delight.
21 *Though they* join forces,[a] the wicked will
not go unpunished;
But the posterity of the righteous will be
delivered.
22 *As* a ring of gold in a swine's snout,
So is a lovely woman who lacks discretion.
23 The desire of the righteous *is* only good,
But the expectation of the wicked *is*
wrath.
24 There is *one* who scatters, yet increases
more;
And there is *one* who withholds more
than is right,
But it *leads* to poverty.
25 The generous soul will be made rich,
And he who waters will also be watered
himself.
26 The people will curse him who withholds
grain,
But blessing *will be* on the head of him
who sells *it*.
27 He who earnestly seeks good finds favor,
But trouble will come to him who seeks
evil.
28 He who trusts in his riches will fall,
But the righteous will flourish like foliage.
29 He who troubles his own house will
inherit the wind,
And the fool *will be* servant to the wise of
heart.
30 The fruit of the righteous *is a* tree of life,
And he who wins souls *is* wise.
31 If the righteous will be recompensed on
the earth,
How much more the ungodly and the
sinner.

12 Whoever loves instruction loves
knowledge,
But he who hates correction *is* stupid.
2 A good *man* obtains favor from the LORD,
But a man of wicked intentions He will
condemn.
3 A man is not established by wickedness,
But the root of the righteous cannot be
moved.
4 An excellent[a] wife *is* the crown of her
husband,
But she who causes shame *is* like
rottenness in his bones.
5 The thoughts of the righteous *are* right,
But the counsels of the wicked *are*
deceitful.
6 The words of the wicked *are,* "Lie in wait
for blood,"
But the mouth of the upright will deliver
them.
7 The wicked are overthrown and *are* no
more,
But the house of the righteous will stand.
8 A man will be commended according to
his wisdom,
But he who is of a perverse heart will be
despised.
9 Better *is the one* who is slighted but has
a servant,
Than he who honors himself but lacks
bread.
10 A righteous *man* regards the life of his
animal,
But the tender mercies of the wicked *are*
cruel.
11 He who tills his land will be satisfied
with bread,
But he who follows frivolity *is* devoid of
understanding.[a]
12 The wicked covet the catch of evil *men,*
But the root of the righteous yields *fruit.*
13 The wicked is ensnared by the
transgression of *his* lips,
But the righteous will come through
trouble.
14 A man will be satisfied with good by the
fruit of *his* mouth,
And the recompense of a man's hands
will be rendered to him.
15 The way of a fool *is* right in his own eyes, ➤
But he who heeds counsel *is* wise.
16 A fool's wrath is known at once,
But a prudent *man* covers shame.
17 He *who* speaks truth declares
righteousness,
But a false witness, deceit.

11:21 [a]Literally *hand to hand* **12:4** [a]Literally *A wife of valor*
12:11 [a]Literally *heart*

LIFE LESSONS

➤ ***12:15 — The way of a fool is right in his own eyes, but he who heeds counsel is wise.***

We all naturally assume our own opinions are right; no one thinks, *I'll believe this, because I know it's untrue.* Wise people, however, listen to contrary opinions to see if they might have made a mistake; fools don't.

18 There is one who speaks like the
piercings of a sword,
But the tongue of the wise *promotes*
health.
19 The truthful lip shall be established
forever,
But a lying tongue *is* but for a moment.
20 Deceit is in the heart of those who devise
evil,
But counselors of peace have joy.
21 No grave trouble will overtake the
righteous,
But the wicked shall be filled with evil.
➤ 22 Lying lips *are* an abomination to the LORD,
But those who deal truthfully *are* His
delight.

23 A prudent man conceals knowledge,
But the heart of fools proclaims
foolishness.

24 The hand of the diligent will rule,
But the lazy *man* will be put to forced
labor.

➤ 25 Anxiety in the heart of man causes
depression,
But a good word makes it glad.

26 The righteous should choose his friends
carefully,
For the way of the wicked leads them
astray.

27 The lazy *man* does not roast what he
took in hunting,
But diligence *is* man's precious
possession.

28 In the way of righteousness *is* life,
And in *its* pathway *there is* no death.

13 A wise son *heeds* his father's
instruction,
But a scoffer does not listen to rebuke.

2 A man shall eat well by the fruit of *his*
mouth,
But the soul of the unfaithful feeds on
violence.

➤ 3 He who guards his mouth preserves his
life,
But he who opens wide his lips shall
have destruction.

4 The soul of a lazy *man* desires, and *has*
nothing;
But the soul of the diligent shall be made
rich.

5 A righteous *man* hates lying,
But a wicked *man* is loathsome and
comes to shame.
6 Righteousness guards *him whose* way is
blameless,
But wickedness overthrows the sinner.

7 There is one who makes himself rich, yet
has nothing;
And one who makes himself poor, yet *has*
great riches.
8 The ransom of a man's life *is* his riches,
But the poor does not hear rebuke.

9 The light of the righteous rejoices,
But the lamp of the wicked will be put
out.
10 By pride comes nothing but strife,
But with the well-advised *is* wisdom.

11 Wealth *gained by* dishonesty will be
diminished,
But he who gathers by labor will
increase.

12 Hope deferred makes the heart sick,
But *when* the desire comes, *it is* a tree of
life.

13 He who despises the word will be
destroyed,
But he who fears the commandment will
be rewarded.
14 The law of the wise *is* a fountain of life,
To turn *one* away from the snares of
death.

15 Good understanding gains favor,
But the way of the unfaithful *is* hard.
16 Every prudent *man* acts with knowledge,
But a fool lays open *his* folly.

17 A wicked messenger falls into trouble,
But a faithful ambassador *brings* health.

LIFE LESSONS

➤ 12:22 — *Lying lips are an abomination to the LORD, but those who deal truthfully are His delight.*

When we say that God always keeps His promises, it's another way of saying that He always speaks the truth. He delights in the truth, and so we please Him when we tell the truth.

➤ 12:25 — *Anxiety in the heart of man causes depression, but a good word makes it glad.*

We ought to become experts at giving encouragement. The world has more than enough of naysayers, critics, scoffers, ridiculers and detractors. A "good word" is hard to find; why not give it a home in *your* mouth?

➤ 13:3 — *He who guards his mouth preserves his life, but he who opens wide his lips shall have destruction.*

"Loose lips sink ships," was a popular World War II motto. It reminded people to guard their words so that nothing they said would endanger American troops. Preventing casualties in a spiritual war takes the same kind of caution.

ANSWERS TO LIFE'S QUESTIONS

Where can I look for good advice?

PROV. 13:10

God often leads us to seek advice from others. When He does so, He wants us to check out the lifestyle of the person from whom we hope to receive counsel. If "the fear of the LORD is the beginning of wisdom," (Prov. 9:10), then we had better know where the person stands with the Lord.

Why should a believer go to a non-believer to get advice that will affect the rest of his life? Some may question such an approach, but I challenge you to consider the spiritual and moral track record of anyone from whom you obtain important advice or counsel, especially if the decision you make affects your entire family and future.

Certainly, unsaved people may have sound wisdom and good advice to offer; but a wise believer can add the crucial dimension of spiritual insight. Some counselors dispense unscriptural advice that leads to ruin and destruction. "There is a way that seems right to a man," the Bible warns us, "but its end is the way of death" (Prov. 14:12).

Proverbs has a lot to say about the value of wise counsel. Proverbs 13:10 declares, "By pride comes nothing but strife, but with the well-advised is wisdom." Proverbs 15:22 proclaims, "Without counsel, plans go awry, but in the multitude of counselors they are established." And Proverbs 20:5 instructs us, "Counsel in the heart of man is like deep water, but a man of understanding will draw it out."

I remember when my grandfather, a minister, told me one day, "Charles, whatever you do in life, always obey God fully. If He tells you to run your head through a brick wall, go forward, expecting Him to make a hole." I have never forgotten that advice, and it has remained a main girder of truth supporting my personal ministry over the last many decades—and it reminds me that the most important counsel we can ever get comes from the Lord Himself.

Regardless of the situation or circumstance, we should always go first to God for *His* counsel. We should tell our own souls what King Jehoshaphat told the king of Israel: "Please inquire for the word of the LORD today" (1 Kin. 22:5). When we do so, we go to the wellspring of all wisdom, for we go to "the LORD of hosts, who is wonderful in counsel and excellent in guidance" (Is. 28:29).

See the Life Principles Index for further study:
3. God's Word is an immovable anchor in times of storm.

18 Poverty and shame *will come* to him who disdains correction,
But he who regards a rebuke will be honored. ➤

19 A desire accomplished is sweet to the soul,
But *it is* an abomination to fools to depart from evil.

20 He who walks with wise *men* will be wise,
But the companion of fools will be destroyed.

21 Evil pursues sinners,
But to the righteous, good shall be repaid.

22 A good *man* leaves an inheritance to his children's children,
But the wealth of the sinner is stored up for the righteous.

23 Much food *is in* the fallow *ground* of the poor,
And for lack of justice there is waste.[a]

24 He who spares his rod hates his son,
But he who loves him disciplines him promptly.

25 The righteous eats to the satisfying of his soul,
But the stomach of the wicked shall be in want.

13:23 [a]Literally *what is swept away*

LIFE LESSONS

➤ **13:18 — *Poverty and shame will come to him who disdains correction, but he who regards a rebuke will be honored.***

We all need correction at many points along life's journey, but not all of us graciously and willingly accept the correction we need. We need correction to keep us off the wrong path that leads to the wrong destination.

ANSWERS TO LIFE'S QUESTIONS

How can I deal with the anger or bitterness of another?

PROV. 14:10

The unfortunate fact is, sooner or later, all of us will run into someone who feels angry or bitter toward us. What should you do when you find yourself the object of another's bitterness? How should you respond to someone's red-hot anger aimed straight at you? Responding to bitterness with more bitterness leads only to a combative and even explosive situation. So what should you do?

First, tell yourself the truth about the situation. What happened? How did the situation unfold? Are you really at fault? It may be that you can't entirely reconstruct the event in question, but try your best to honestly recall what led to the outburst.

Second, listen carefully to what the bitter person is saying. Bitterness and anger are usually the offshoots of deep hurt. Say something like, "It seems that you are really upset. Can we talk about it?" Even such a simple question may help to defuse the situation. And even if it doesn't—you may not be able to turn the bitterness around in someone else's life—you can stop it from taking root in your own heart by asking God to help you understand why this person feels the way he or she does.

Third, any time you come under personal attack, it is very important to recall God's personal love for you. You may have made mistakes, but that does not change the Lord's feelings about you. Ask Him to encourage you through His Word.

Fourth, ask God to help you respond with His love and grace, and to protect you from angry attacks. In Psalm 64, we read how one man prayed for God's deliverance from the attacks of an embittered enemy. Bitterness is a much deeper and more complex reaction than a simple expression of quick anger. It is a satanic stronghold and needs to be faced in an honest manner. God tells us to beware "lest any root of bitterness springing up cause trouble, and by this many become defiled" (Heb. 12:15).

When you find yourself the target of a bitter accusation or a hateful personal attack, pray for God's protection. Ask Him to give you wisdom in dealing with the other person, as well as a healthy perspective on the entire matter. Your reaction to the assault is the most important issue with God. Therefore, be firm but loving in what you do and say.

See the Life Principles Index for further study:
8. Fight all your battles on your knees and you win every time.
27. Prayer is life's greatest time saver.

14 The wise woman builds her house,
But the foolish pulls it down with her hands.
2 He who walks in his uprightness fears the LORD,
But *he who is* perverse in his ways despises Him.
3 In the mouth of a fool *is* a rod of pride,
But the lips of the wise will preserve them.
4 Where no oxen *are,* the trough *is* clean;
But much increase *comes* by the strength of an ox.
5 A faithful witness does not lie,
But a false witness will utter lies.
6 A scoffer seeks wisdom and does not *find it,*
But knowledge *is* easy to him who understands.
7 Go from the presence of a foolish man,
When you do not perceive *in him* the lips of knowledge.
8 The wisdom of the prudent *is* to understand his way,
But the folly of fools *is* deceit.
9 Fools mock at sin,
But among the upright *there is* favor.
10 The heart knows its own bitterness,
And a stranger does not share its joy.
11 The house of the wicked will be overthrown,
But the tent of the upright will flourish.
12 There is a way *that seems* right to a man,
But its end *is* the way of death.
13 Even in laughter the heart may sorrow,
And the end of mirth *may be* grief.
14 The backslider in heart will be filled with his own ways,
But a good man *will be satisfied* from above.[a]

14:14 [a]Literally *from above himself*

15 The simple believes every word,
But the prudent considers well his steps.
16 A wise *man* fears and departs from evil,
But a fool rages and is self-confident.
17 A quick-tempered *man* acts foolishly,
And a man of wicked intentions is hated.
18 The simple inherit folly,
But the prudent are crowned with knowledge.
19 The evil will bow before the good,
And the wicked at the gates of the righteous.

20 The poor *man* is hated even by his own neighbor,
But the rich *has* many friends.
21 He who despises his neighbor sins;
But he who has mercy on the poor, happy *is* he.

22 Do they not go astray who devise evil?
But mercy and truth *belong* to those who devise good.

23 In all labor there is profit,
But idle chatter[a] *leads* only to poverty.

24 The crown of the wise is their riches,
But the foolishness of fools *is* folly.

25 A true witness delivers souls,
But a deceitful *witness* speaks lies.

26 In the fear of the LORD *there is* strong confidence,
And His children will have a place of refuge.
27 The fear of the LORD *is* a fountain of life,
To turn *one* away from the snares of death.
28 In a multitude of people *is* a king's honor,
But in the lack of people *is* the downfall of a prince.

➤ 29 *He who is* slow to wrath has great understanding,
But *he who is* impulsive[a] exalts folly.

30 A sound heart *is* life to the body,
But envy *is* rottenness to the bones.

31 He who oppresses the poor reproaches his Maker,
But he who honors Him has mercy on the needy.

32 The wicked is banished in his wickedness,
But the righteous has a refuge in his death.

33 Wisdom rests in the heart of him who has understanding,
But *what is* in the heart of fools is made known.

34 Righteousness exalts a nation,
But sin *is* a reproach to *any* people.

35 The king's favor *is* toward a wise servant,
But his wrath *is against* him who causes shame.

15 A soft answer turns away wrath,
But a harsh word stirs up anger.
2 The tongue of the wise uses knowledge rightly,
But the mouth of fools pours forth foolishness.

3 The eyes of the LORD *are* in every place, ➤
Keeping watch on the evil and the good.

4 A wholesome tongue *is* a tree of life,
But perverseness in it breaks the spirit.

5 A fool despises his father's instruction,
But he who receives correction is prudent.

6 *In* the house of the righteous *there is* much treasure,
But in the revenue of the wicked is trouble.

7 The lips of the wise disperse knowledge,
But the heart of the fool *does* not *do* so.

8 The sacrifice of the wicked *is* an abomination to the LORD,
But the prayer of the upright *is* His delight.
9 The way of the wicked *is* an abomination to the LORD,
But He loves him who follows righteousness.

10 Harsh discipline *is* for him who forsakes the way,
And he who hates correction will die.

11 Hell[a] and Destruction[b] *are* before the LORD;
So how much more the hearts of the sons of men.

14:23 [a]Literally *talk of the lips* **14:29** [a]Literally *short of spirit*
15:11 [a]Or *Sheol* [b]Hebrew *Abaddon*

LIFE LESSONS

➤ 14:29 — *He who is slow to wrath has great understanding, but he who is impulsive exalts folly.*

It may feel good (for a short while) to vent our anger at someone, but "the wrath of man does not produce the righteousness of God" (James 1:20). Failure to control a quick temper leads only to heartache.

➤ 15:3 — *The eyes of the LORD are in every place, keeping watch on the evil and the good.*

Nothing ever escapes the notice of God, so nothing ever surprises Him. Since nothing ever surprises Him, He always has exactly the right plans in place to accomplish precisely what He desires—for reward or for judgment.

12 A scoffer does not love one who corrects him,
Nor will he go to the wise.

13 A merry heart makes a cheerful countenance,
But by sorrow of the heart the spirit is broken.

14 The heart of him who has understanding seeks knowledge,
But the mouth of fools feeds on foolishness.

15 All the days of the afflicted *are* evil,
But he who is of a merry heart *has* a continual feast.

16 Better *is* a little with the fear of the LORD,
Than great treasure with trouble.

17 Better *is* a dinner of herbs[a] where love is,
Than a fatted calf with hatred.

18 A wrathful man stirs up strife,
But *he who is* slow to anger allays contention.

19 The way of the lazy *man is* like a hedge of thorns,
But the way of the upright *is* a highway.

20 A wise son makes a father glad,
But a foolish man despises his mother.

21 Folly *is* joy *to him who is* destitute of discernment,
But a man of understanding walks uprightly.

➤ 22 Without counsel, plans go awry,
But in the multitude of counselors they are established.

23 A man has joy by the answer of his mouth,
And a word *spoken* in due season, how good *it is!*

24 The way of life *winds* upward for the wise,
That he may turn away from hell[a] below.

25 The LORD will destroy the house of the proud,
But He will establish the boundary of the widow.

26 The thoughts of the wicked *are* an abomination to the LORD,
But the words of the pure *are* pleasant.

27 He who is greedy for gain troubles his own house,
But he who hates bribes will live.

28 The heart of the righteous studies how to answer,
But the mouth of the wicked pours forth evil.

29 The LORD *is* far from the wicked,
But He hears the prayer of the righteous.

30 The light of the eyes rejoices the heart,
And a good report makes the bones healthy.[a]

31 The ear that hears the rebukes of life
Will abide among the wise.

32 He who disdains instruction despises his own soul,
But he who heeds rebuke gets understanding.

33 The fear of the LORD *is* the instruction of wisdom,
And before honor *is* humility.

16 The preparations of the heart *belong* to man,
But the answer of the tongue *is* from the LORD.

2 All the ways of a man *are* pure in his own eyes,
But the LORD weighs the spirits.

3 Commit your works to the LORD,
And your thoughts will be established. ➤

4 The LORD has made all for Himself,
Yes, even the wicked for the day of doom.

5 Everyone proud in heart *is* an abomination to the LORD;
Though they join forces,[a] none will go unpunished.

6 In mercy and truth
Atonement is provided for iniquity;
And by the fear of the LORD *one* departs from evil.

7 When a man's ways please the LORD,
He makes even his enemies to be at peace with him.

8 Better *is* a little with righteousness,
Than vast revenues without justice.

15:17 [a]Or *vegetables* **15:24** [a]Or *Sheol* **15:30** [a]Literally *fat*
16:5 [a]Literally *hand to hand*

LIFE LESSONS

➤ 15:22 — *Without counsel, plans go awry, but in the multitude of counselors they are established.*

Since none of us has an unlimited perspective, we need to invite multiple viewpoints outside of our own to inform our most important decisions and plans. God often uses the perspective of others to show us His will.

➤ 16:3 — *Commit your works to the LORD, and your thoughts will be established.*

How do we commit our works to the Lord? Not merely by asking Him to bless what we've already done, but by committing ourselves and our plans to Him before, during, and after we have done our work.

✳ 9 A man's heart plans his way,
But the LORD directs his steps.

10 Divination *is* on the lips of the king;
His mouth must not transgress in judgment.
11 Honest weights and scales *are* the LORD's;
All the weights in the bag *are* His work.
12 *It is* an abomination for kings to commit wickedness,
For a throne is established by righteousness.
13 Righteous lips *are* the delight of kings,
And they love him who speaks *what is* right.
14 As messengers of death *is* the king's wrath,
But a wise man will appease it.
15 In the light of the king's face *is* life,
And his favor *is* like a cloud of the latter rain.

16 How much better to get wisdom than gold!
And to get understanding is to be chosen rather than silver.

17 The highway of the upright *is* to depart from evil;
He who keeps his way preserves his soul.

18 Pride *goes* before destruction,
And a haughty spirit before a fall.
19 Better *to be* of a humble spirit with the lowly,
Than to divide the spoil with the proud.

➤ 20 He who heeds the word wisely will find good,
And whoever trusts in the LORD, happy *is* he.
21 The wise in heart will be called prudent,
And sweetness of the lips increases learning.
22 Understanding *is* a wellspring of life to him who has it.
But the correction of fools *is* folly.
23 The heart of the wise teaches his mouth,
And adds learning to his lips.
24 Pleasant words *are like* a honeycomb,
Sweetness to the soul and health to the bones.

25 There is a way *that seems* right to a man,
But its end *is* the way of death.
26 The person who labors, labors for himself,
For his *hungry* mouth drives him *on.*

27 An ungodly man digs up evil,
And *it is* on his lips like a burning fire.
28 A perverse man sows strife,
And a whisperer separates the best of friends.
29 A violent man entices his neighbor,
And leads him in a way *that is* not good.
30 He winks his eye to devise perverse things;
He purses his lips *and* brings about evil.

31 The silver-haired head *is* a crown of glory,
If it is found in the way of righteousness.

32 *He who is* slow to anger *is* better than the mighty,
And he who rules his spirit than he who takes a city.

33 The lot is cast into the lap,
But its every decision *is* from the LORD.

17 Better *is* a dry morsel with quietness,
Than a house full of feasting[a] *with* strife.

2 A wise servant will rule over a son who causes shame,
And will share an inheritance among the brothers.

3 The refining pot *is* for silver and the furnace for gold,
But the LORD tests the hearts.

4 An evildoer gives heed to false lips;
A liar listens eagerly to a spiteful tongue.

5 He who mocks the poor reproaches his Maker; ◄
He who is glad at calamity will not go unpunished.

6 Children's children *are* the crown of old men,
And the glory of children *is* their father.

7 Excellent speech is not becoming to a fool,
Much less lying lips to a prince.

8 A present *is* a precious stone in the eyes of its possessor;
Wherever he turns, he prospers.

17:1 [a]Or *sacrificial meals*

LIFE LESSONS

➤ 16:20 — . . . *whoever trusts in the LORD, happy is he.*

No one will ever find true happiness by disobeying a clear command of God, for happiness is found in trusting God—and those who disobey show that they do not trust Him to make them happy.

➤ 17:5 — *He who mocks the poor reproaches his Maker . . . .*

God made us all in His image, and to mock anyone for something like poverty is to mock God. God said the poor would always exist (Deut. 15:11; Matt. 26:11); we are to help them, not mock them.

WHAT THE BIBLE SAYS ABOUT GOD'S HATRED OF HUMAN PRIDE

Prov. 16:18

The Bible makes it very clear that God hates human pride. James 4:6 states very clearly, "God resists the proud, but gives grace to the humble." The same message gets stated in the Scripture no less than three times (see also Prov. 3:34 and 1 Pet. 5:5).

Elsewhere, the Bible lists pride among four things that the Lord hates: pride gets lumped together with arrogance, the evil way, and the perverse mouth (Prov. 8:13). In yet another passage, pride finds a place among seven things that are an abomination to God: "A proud look, a lying tongue, hands that shed innocent blood, a heart that devises wicked plans, feet that are swift in running to evil, a false witness who speaks lies, and one who sows discord among brethren" (Prov. 6:17–19).

God puts pride in the same category with murder!

Why does God hate human pride so much? Because it is the one sin that keeps us from allowing God to use us for His purposes. When we commit ourselves to doing things our way, we are in no position to do things God's way. Pride renders us useless in the kingdom of God. We fall prey to pride when we forget that God does not exist for us, but we exist for Him.

The Lord refuses to share His glory with anyone.

The Lord refuses to share His glory with anyone. When we seek to take His glory for ourselves—saying, in effect, "Look at what I have accomplished! Look at me! Look at who I am!"—we deny that everything we accomplish comes about because God enables and empowers us to accomplish it. Any good in us is by His design and redemption. Anything noteworthy that we become, we become because He wills it. We have no goodness part from God's goodness imparted to us.

Most people know some version of Proverbs 16:18: "Pride goes before destruction, and a haughty spirit before a fall." While not all destructions are caused by pride, pride *always* ends in destruction—and usually, we lose the very thing we feel most proud about having achieved, earned, owned, or accomplished.

See the Life Principles Index for further study:
15. Brokenness is God's requirement for maximum usefulness.

9 He who covers a transgression seeks love,
But he who repeats a matter separates friends.

10 Rebuke is more effective for a wise *man*
Than a hundred blows on a fool.

11 An evil *man* seeks only rebellion;
Therefore a cruel messenger will be sent against him.

12 Let a man meet a bear robbed of her cubs,
Rather than a fool in his folly.

13 Whoever rewards evil for good,
Evil will not depart from his house.

14 The beginning of strife *is like* releasing water;
Therefore stop contention before a quarrel starts.

15 He who justifies the wicked, and he who condemns the just,
Both of them alike *are* an abomination to the LORD.

16 Why *is there* in the hand of a fool the purchase price of wisdom,
Since *he has* no heart *for it?*

17 A friend loves at all times,
And a brother is born for adversity.

18 A man devoid of understanding shakes hands in a pledge,
And becomes surety for his friend.

19 He who loves transgression loves strife,
And he who exalts his gate seeks destruction.

20 He who has a deceitful heart finds no good,
And he who has a perverse tongue falls into evil.

21 He who begets a scoffer *does so* to his sorrow,
And the father of a fool has no joy.

22 A merry heart does good, *like* medicine,[a]
But a broken spirit dries the bones.

23 A wicked *man* accepts a bribe behind the back[a]
To pervert the ways of justice.

24 Wisdom *is* in the sight of him who has understanding,
But the eyes of a fool *are* on the ends of the earth.

25 A foolish son *is* a grief to his father,
And bitterness to her who bore him.

26 Also, to punish the righteous *is* not good,
Nor to strike princes for *their* uprightness.

27 He who has knowledge spares his words,
And a man of understanding is of a calm spirit.

28 Even a fool is counted wise when he holds his peace;
When he shuts his lips, *he is considered* perceptive.

18 A man who isolates himself seeks his own desire;
He rages against all wise judgment.

2 A fool has no delight in understanding,
But in expressing his own heart.

3 When the wicked comes, contempt comes also;
And with dishonor *comes* reproach.

4 The words of a man's mouth *are* deep waters;
The wellspring of wisdom *is* a flowing brook.

5 *It is* not good to show partiality to the wicked,
Or to overthrow the righteous in judgment.

6 A fool's lips enter into contention,
And his mouth calls for blows.

7 A fool's mouth *is* his destruction,
And his lips *are* the snare of his soul.

8 The words of a talebearer *are* like tasty trifles,[a]
And they go down into the inmost body.

9 He who is slothful in his work
Is a brother to him who is a great destroyer.

10 The name of the LORD *is* a strong tower;
The righteous run to it and are safe.

17:22 [a]Or *makes medicine even better* **17:23** [a]Literally *from the bosom* **18:8** [a]A Jewish tradition reads *wounds.*

LIFE LESSONS

➤ **17:28 — *Even a fool is counted wise when he holds his peace; when he shuts his lips, he is considered perceptive.***

There are times when we must speak up (Esth. 4:14; Acts 18:9), but there are vastly more times when we ought to keep silent. "Meditate within your heart . . . and be still" (Ps. 4:4).

➤ **18:10 — *The name of the LORD is a strong tower; the righteous run to it and are safe.***

Where do you run when trouble comes? How do you react at the first sign of hardship? Do you run directly to the tower of God, or do you jump into pits of despair or flee to earthbound huts?

11 The rich man's wealth *is* his strong city,
And like a high wall in his own esteem.

12 Before destruction the heart of a man is haughty,
And before honor *is* humility.

13 He who answers a matter before he hears *it*,
It *is* folly and shame to him.

14 The spirit of a man will sustain him in sickness,
But who can bear a broken spirit?

15 The heart of the prudent acquires knowledge,
And the ear of the wise seeks knowledge.

16 A man's gift makes room for him,
And brings him before great men.

➤ 17 The first *one* to plead his cause *seems* right,
Until his neighbor comes and examines him.

18 Casting lots causes contentions to cease,
And keeps the mighty apart.

19 A brother offended *is harder to win* than a strong city,
And contentions *are* like the bars of a castle.

20 A man's stomach shall be satisfied from the fruit of his mouth;
From the produce of his lips he shall be filled.

21 Death and life *are* in the power of the tongue,
And those who love it will eat its fruit.

22 *He who* finds a wife finds a good *thing*,
And obtains favor from the LORD.

23 The poor *man* uses entreaties,
But the rich answers roughly.

24 A man *who has* friends must himself be friendly,[a]
But there is a friend *who* sticks closer than a brother.

19

Better *is* the poor who walks in his integrity
Than *one who is* perverse in his lips, and is a fool.

2 Also it is not good *for* a soul *to be* without knowledge,
And he sins who hastens with *his* feet.

3 The foolishness of a man twists his way,
And his heart frets against the LORD.

4 Wealth makes many friends,
But the poor is separated from his friend.

5 A false witness will not go unpunished,
And *he who* speaks lies will not escape.

6 Many entreat the favor of the nobility,
And every man *is* a friend to one who gives gifts.

7 All the brothers of the poor hate him;
How much more do his friends go far from him!
He may pursue *them with* words, *yet* they abandon *him*.

8 He who gets wisdom loves his own soul;
He who keeps understanding will find good.

9 A false witness will not go unpunished,
And *he who* speaks lies shall perish.

10 Luxury is not fitting for a fool,
Much less for a servant to rule over princes.

11 The discretion of a man makes him slow to anger, ◄
And his glory *is* to overlook a transgression.

12 The king's wrath *is* like the roaring of a lion,
But his favor *is* like dew on the grass.

13 A foolish son *is* the ruin of his father,
And the contentions of a wife *are* a continual dripping.

14 Houses and riches *are* an inheritance from fathers,
But a prudent wife *is* from the LORD.

15 Laziness casts *one* into a deep sleep,
And an idle person will suffer hunger.

16 He who keeps the commandment keeps his soul,
But he who is careless[a] of his ways will die.

18:24 [a]Following Greek manuscripts, Syriac, Targum, and Vulgate; Masoretic Text reads *may come to ruin*. **19:16** [a]Literally *despises*, figurative of recklessness or carelessness

LIFE LESSONS

➤ 18:17 — *The first one to plead his cause seems right, until his neighbor comes and examines him.*

We must guard against making snap judgments. Scripture insists that we listen to the testimony of two or three witnesses (Deut. 19:15; Matt. 18:16; 2 Cor. 13:1; 1 Tim. 5:19), precisely so we don't make hasty judgments.

➤ 19:11 — *The discretion of a man makes him slow to anger, and his glory is to overlook a transgression.*

Many of us get into real trouble in our relationships because we insist on being "right." We demand that everyone see things our way; and because we refuse to overlook a transgression, we end up alienating our friends and family.

17 He who has pity on the poor lends to the LORD,
And He will pay back what he has given.

18 Chasten your son while there is hope,
And do not set your heart on his destruction.[a]

19 *A man of* great wrath will suffer punishment;
For if you rescue *him,* you will have to do it again.

20 Listen to counsel and receive instruction,
That you may be wise in your latter days.

21 There are many plans in a man's heart,
Nevertheless the LORD's counsel—that will stand.

22 What is desired in a man is kindness,
And a poor man is better than a liar.

✳ 23 The fear of the LORD *leads* to life,
And *he who has it* will abide in satisfaction;
He will not be visited with evil.

24 A lazy *man* buries his hand in the bowl,[a]
And will not so much as bring it to his mouth again.

25 Strike a scoffer, and the simple will become wary;
Rebuke one who has understanding, *and* he will discern knowledge.

26 He who mistreats *his* father *and* chases away *his* mother
Is a son who causes shame and brings reproach.

➤ 27 Cease listening to instruction, my son,
And you will stray from the words of knowledge.

28 A disreputable witness scorns justice,
And the mouth of the wicked devours iniquity.

29 Judgments are prepared for scoffers,
And beatings for the backs of fools.

20

Wine *is* a mocker,
Strong drink *is* a brawler,
And whoever is led astray by it is not wise.

2 The wrath[a] of a king *is* like the roaring of a lion;
Whoever provokes him to anger sins *against* his own life.

3 *It is* honorable for a man to stop striving,
Since any fool can start a quarrel.

4 The lazy *man* will not plow because of winter;
He will beg during harvest and *have* nothing.

5 Counsel in the heart of man *is like* deep water,
But a man of understanding will draw it out.

6 Most men will proclaim each his own goodness,
But who can find a faithful man?

7 The righteous *man* walks in his integrity; ➤
His children *are* blessed after him.

8 A king who sits on the throne of judgment
Scatters all evil with his eyes.

9 Who can say, "I have made my heart clean,
I am pure from my sin"?

10 Diverse weights *and* diverse measures,
They *are* both alike, an abomination to the LORD.

11 Even a child is known by his deeds,
Whether what he does *is* pure and right.

12 The hearing ear and the seeing eye,
The LORD has made them both.

13 Do not love sleep, lest you come to poverty;
Open your eyes, *and* you will be satisfied with bread.

14 "*It is* good for nothing,"[a] cries the buyer;
But when he has gone his way, then he boasts.

15 There is gold and a multitude of rubies,
But the lips of knowledge *are* a precious jewel.

16 Take the garment of one who is surety *for* a stranger,

19:18 [a]Literally *to put him to death;* a Jewish tradition reads *on his crying.* **19:24** [a]Septuagint and Syriac read *bosom;* Targum and Vulgate read *armpit.* **20:2** [a]Literally *fear* or *terror* which is produced by the king's wrath **20:14** [a]Literally *evil, evil*

LIFE LESSONS

➤ 19:27 — *Cease listening to instruction, my son, and you will stray from the words of knowledge.*

We must never stop learning. Not only do we forget lessons once learned, new lessons always lie ahead of us. Peter said, "I will not be negligent to remind you always of these things, though you know" them (2 Pet. 1:12).

➤ 20:7 — *The righteous man walks in his integrity; his children are blessed after him.*

It would be hard to think of a greater legacy to leave behind than a personal record of godly integrity. Those who develop sound moral character bless their children with a gift that lasts for generations.

And hold it as a pledge *when it* is for a
seductress.

17 Bread gained by deceit *is* sweet to a man,
But afterward his mouth will be filled
with gravel.

18 Plans are established by counsel;
By wise counsel wage war.

➤ 19 He who goes about *as* a talebearer
reveals secrets;
Therefore do not associate with one who
flatters with his lips.

20 Whoever curses his father or his mother,
His lamp will be put out in deep darkness.

21 An inheritance gained hastily at the
beginning
Will not be blessed at the end.

22 Do not say, "I will recompense evil";
Wait for the LORD, and He will save you.

23 Diverse weights *are* an abomination to
the LORD,
And dishonest scales *are* not good.

24 A man's steps *are* of the LORD;
How then can a man understand his own
way?

25 *It is* a snare for a man to devote rashly
something as holy,
And afterward to reconsider *his* vows.

26 A wise king sifts out the wicked,
And brings the threshing wheel over
them.

27 The spirit of a man *is* the lamp of the
LORD,
Searching all the inner depths of his
heart.[a]

28 Mercy and truth preserve the king,
And by lovingkindness he upholds his
throne.

29 The glory of young men *is* their strength,
And the splendor of old men *is* their gray
head.

30 Blows that hurt cleanse away evil,
As *do* stripes the inner depths of the
heart.[a]

21

1 The king's heart *is* in the hand of the
LORD,
Like the rivers of water; He turns it
wherever He wishes.

2 Every way of a man *is* right in his own
eyes,
But the LORD weighs the hearts.

3 To do righteousness and justice ➤
Is more acceptable to the LORD than
sacrifice.

4 A haughty look, a proud heart,
And the plowing[a] of the wicked *are* sin.

5 The plans of the diligent *lead* surely to ➤
plenty,
But *those of* everyone *who is* hasty,
surely to poverty.

6 Getting treasures by a lying tongue
Is the fleeting fantasy of those who seek
death.[a]

7 The violence of the wicked will destroy
them,[a]
Because they refuse to do justice.

8 The way of a guilty man *is* perverse;[a]
But *as for* the pure, his work *is* right.

9 Better to dwell in a corner of a housetop,
Than in a house shared with a
contentious woman.

10 The soul of the wicked desires evil;
His neighbor finds no favor in his eyes.

11 When the scoffer is punished, the simple
is made wise;
But when the wise is instructed, he
receives knowledge.

12 The righteous *God* wisely considers the
house of the wicked,
Overthrowing the wicked for *their*
wickedness.

20:27 [a]Literally *the rooms of the belly* **20:30** [a]Literally *the rooms of the belly* **21:4** [a]Or *lamp* **21:6** [a]Septuagint reads *Pursue vanity on the snares of death;* Vulgate reads *Is vain and foolish, and shall stumble on the snares of death;* Targum reads *They shall be destroyed, and they shall fall who seek death.*
21:7 [a]Literally *drag them away* **21:8** [a]Or *The way of a man is perverse and strange*

LIFE LESSONS

➤ **20:19 — *He who goes about as a talebearer reveals secrets; therefore do not associate with one who flatters with his lips.***

Flattery is often nothing but a ruse to get someone to reveal information that would better be left unsaid—information that inevitably makes its way into the public square.

➤ **21:3 — *To do righteousness and justice is more acceptable to the LORD than sacrifice.***

God wants the heart. He is not interested in outward compliance without an inward desire to willingly and joyfully obey. In fact, He hates religious pretense, because it mocks His heart's desire for us (Amos 5:21).

➤ **21:5 — *The plans of the diligent lead surely to plenty, but those of everyone who is hasty, surely to poverty.***

"Get rich quick" schemes have been around for millennia, and they've never worked. For every man who gets rich quick, ten thousand get poor even quicker.

13 Whoever shuts his ears to the cry of the poor
Will also cry himself and not be heard.

14 A gift in secret pacifies anger,
And a bribe behind the back,[a] strong wrath.

15 *It is* a joy for the just to do justice,
But destruction *will come* to the workers of iniquity.

16 A man who wanders from the way of understanding
Will rest in the assembly of the dead.

17 He who loves pleasure *will be* a poor man;
He who loves wine and oil will not be rich.

18 The wicked *shall be* a ransom for the righteous,
And the unfaithful for the upright.

19 Better to dwell in the wilderness,
Than with a contentious and angry woman.

20 *There is* desirable treasure,
And oil in the dwelling of the wise,
But a foolish man squanders it.

21 He who follows righteousness and mercy
Finds life, righteousness, and honor.

22 A wise *man* scales the city of the mighty,
And brings down the trusted stronghold.

23 Whoever guards his mouth and tongue
Keeps his soul from troubles.

24 A proud *and* haughty *man*—"Scoffer" *is* his name;
He acts with arrogant pride.

25 The desire of the lazy *man* kills him,
For his hands refuse to labor.
26 He covets greedily all day long,
But the righteous gives and does not spare.

27 The sacrifice of the wicked *is* an abomination;
How much more *when* he brings it with wicked intent!

28 A false witness shall perish,
But the man who hears *him* will speak endlessly.

29 A wicked man hardens his face,
But *as for* the upright, he establishes[a] his way.

30 *There is* no wisdom or understanding
Or counsel against the LORD.

31 The horse *is* prepared for the day of battle,
But deliverance *is* of the LORD.

22 A *good* name is to be chosen rather than great riches,
Loving favor rather than silver and gold.

2 The rich and the poor have this in common,
The LORD *is* the maker of them all.

3 A prudent *man* foresees evil and hides himself,
But the simple pass on and are punished.

4 By humility *and* the fear of the LORD
Are riches and honor and life.

5 Thorns *and* snares *are* in the way of the perverse;
He who guards his soul will be far from them.

6 Train up a child in the way he should go,
And when he is old he will not depart from it.

7 The rich rules over the poor,
And the borrower *is* servant to the lender.

8 He who sows iniquity will reap sorrow,
And the rod of his anger will fail.

9 He who has a generous eye will be blessed,
For he gives of his bread to the poor.

10 Cast out the scoffer, and contention will leave;
Yes, strife and reproach will cease.

11 He who loves purity of heart
And has grace on his lips,
The king *will be* his friend.

12 The eyes of the LORD preserve knowledge,
But He overthrows the words of the faithless.

13 The lazy *man* says, "*There is* a lion outside!
I shall be slain in the streets!"

21:14 [a]Literally *in the bosom* **21:29** [a]Qere and Septuagint read *understands.*

LIFE LESSONS

➤ 22:4 — *By humility and the fear of the LORD are riches and honor and life.*

The truly humble recognize two things: that they are not God; and that God is. When we serve our almighty Creator with humility and gratitude, He blesses us in ways that stagger the imagination.

14 The mouth of an immoral woman *is* a
deep pit;
He who is abhorred by the LORD will fall
there.

15 Foolishness *is* bound up in the heart of a
child;
The rod of correction will drive it far
from him.

16 He who oppresses the poor to increase
his *riches*,
And he who gives to the rich, *will* surely
come to poverty.

Sayings of the Wise

17 Incline your ear and hear the words of
the wise,
And apply your heart to my knowledge;
18 For *it is* a pleasant thing if you keep them
within you;
Let them all be fixed upon your lips,
19 So that your trust may be in the LORD;
I have instructed you today, even you.
20 Have I not written to you excellent things
Of counsels and knowledge,
21 That I may make you know the certainty
of the words of truth,
That you may answer words of truth
To those who send to you?
22 Do not rob the poor because he *is* poor,
Nor oppress the afflicted at the gate;
23 For the LORD will plead their cause,
And plunder the soul of those who
plunder them.
24 Make no friendship with an angry man,
And with a furious man do not go,
25 Lest you learn his ways
And set a snare for your soul.

26 Do not be one of those who shakes hands
in a pledge,
One of those who is surety for debts;
27 If you have nothing *with which* to pay,
Why should he take away your bed from
under you?

28 Do not remove the ancient landmark
Which your fathers have set.

29 Do you see a man *who* excels in his work?
He will stand before kings;
He will not stand before unknown *men*.

23 When you sit down to eat with a ruler,
Consider carefully what *is* before you;
2 And put a knife to your throat
If you *are* a man given to appetite.
3 Do not desire his delicacies,
For they *are* deceptive food.

4 Do not overwork to be rich;
Because of your own understanding, cease!
5 Will you set your eyes on that which is
not?
For *riches* certainly make themselves
wings;
They fly away like an eagle *toward*
heaven.

6 Do not eat the bread of a miser,[a]
Nor desire his delicacies;
7 For as he thinks in his heart, so *is* he.
"Eat and drink!" he says to you,
But his heart is not with you.
8 The morsel you have eaten, you will
vomit up,
And waste your pleasant words.

9 Do not speak in the hearing of a fool,
For he will despise the wisdom of your
words.

10 Do not remove the ancient landmark,
Nor enter the fields of the fatherless;
11 For their Redeemer *is* mighty;
He will plead their cause against you.

12 Apply your heart to instruction,
And your ears to words of knowledge.

13 Do not withhold correction from a child,
For *if* you beat him with a rod, he will not
die.
14 You shall beat him with a rod,
And deliver his soul from hell.[a]

15 My son, if your heart is wise,
My heart will rejoice—indeed, I myself;
16 Yes, my inmost being will rejoice
When your lips speak right things.

17 Do not let your heart envy sinners,
But *be zealous* for the fear of the LORD all
the day;
18 For surely there is a hereafter,
And your hope will not be cut off.

19 Hear, my son, and be wise;
And guide your heart in the way.
20 Do not mix with winebibbers,
Or with gluttonous eaters of meat;
21 For the drunkard and the glutton will
come to poverty,
And drowsiness will clothe *a man* with
rags.

23:6 [a]Literally *one who has an evil eye* **23:14** [a]Or *Sheol*

LIFE LESSONS

➤ ***23:4, 5 — Do not overwork to be rich; because of your own understanding, cease! . . . For riches certainly make themselves wings . . . .***

When we focus our energies on gaining wealth, we cannot focus our attention on gaining an intimate relationship with God. That's why Jesus said, "You cannot serve God and mammon [money]" (Luke 16:13).

22 Listen to your father who begot you,
And do not despise your mother when
she is old.

23 Buy the truth, and do not sell *it*,
Also wisdom and instruction and
understanding.

24 The father of the righteous will greatly
rejoice,
And he who begets a wise *child* will
delight in him.

25 Let your father and your mother be glad,
And let her who bore you rejoice.

26 My son, give me your heart,
And let your eyes observe my ways.
27 For a harlot *is* a deep pit,
And a seductress *is* a narrow well.
28 She also lies in wait as *for* a victim,
And increases the unfaithful among men.

29 Who has woe?
Who has sorrow?
Who has contentions?
Who has complaints?
Who has wounds without cause?
Who has redness of eyes?
30 Those who linger long at the wine,
Those who go in search of mixed wine.
31 Do not look on the wine when it is red,
When it sparkles in the cup,
When it swirls around smoothly;
32 At the last it bites like a serpent,
And stings like a viper.
33 Your eyes will see strange things,
And your heart will utter perverse things.
34 Yes, you will be like one who lies down in
the midst of the sea,
Or like one who lies at the top of the
mast, *saying*:
35 "They have struck me, *but* I was not hurt;
They have beaten me, but I did not feel *it*.
When shall I awake, that I may seek
another *drink*?"

➤ **24** Do not be envious of evil men,
Nor desire to be with them;
2 For their heart devises violence,
And their lips talk of troublemaking.

3 Through wisdom a house is built,
And by understanding it is established;
4 By knowledge the rooms are filled
With all precious and pleasant riches.

5 A wise man *is* strong,
Yes, a man of knowledge increases
strength;
6 For by wise counsel you will wage your
own war,
And in a multitude of counselors *there is*
safety.

7 Wisdom *is* too lofty for a fool;
He does not open his mouth in the gate.

8 He who plots to do evil
Will be called a schemer.
9 The devising of foolishness *is* sin,
And the scoffer *is* an abomination to men.

10 *If* you faint in the day of adversity,
Your strength *is* small.

11 Deliver *those who* are drawn toward
death,
And hold back *those* stumbling to the
slaughter.
12 If you say, "Surely we did not know this,"
Does not He who weighs the hearts
consider *it*?
He who keeps your soul, does He *not*
know *it*?
And will He *not* render to *each* man
according to his deeds?

13 My son, eat honey because *it is* good,
And the honeycomb *which is* sweet to
your taste;
14 So *shall* the knowledge of wisdom *be* to
your soul;
If you have found *it*, there is a prospect,
And your hope will not be cut off.

15 Do not lie in wait, O wicked *man*, against
the dwelling of the righteous;
Do not plunder his resting place;
16 For a righteous *man* may fall seven times
And rise again,
But the wicked shall fall by calamity.

17 Do not rejoice when your enemy falls,
And do not let your heart be glad when
he stumbles;
18 Lest the LORD see *it*, and it displease Him,
And He turn away His wrath from him.

19 Do not fret because of evildoers,
Nor be envious of the wicked;
20 For there will be no prospect for the evil
man;
The lamp of the wicked will be put out.

21 My son, fear the LORD and the king;
Do not associate with those given to
change;
22 For their calamity will rise suddenly,
And who knows the ruin those two can
bring?

LIFE LESSONS

➤ **24:1, 2 — *Do not be envious of evil men, nor desire to be with them; for their heart devises violence, and their lips talk of troublemaking.***

It may seem like the wicked have better lives than we do, but it's a big mistake to envy them. In the end, they have nothing; "but God is the strength of my heart and my portion forever" (Ps. 73:26).

Further Sayings of the Wise

23 These *things* also *belong* to the wise:

It is not good to show partiality in
judgment.
24 He who says to the wicked, "You *are*
righteous,"
Him the people will curse;
Nations will abhor him.
25 But those who rebuke *the wicked* will
have delight,
And a good blessing will come upon
them.

26 He who gives a right answer kisses the
lips.

27 Prepare your outside work,
Make it fit for yourself in the field;
And afterward build your house.

28 Do not be a witness against your
neighbor without cause,
For would you deceive[a] with your lips?
➤ 29 Do not say, "I will do to him just as he
has done to me;
I will render to the man according to his
work."

30 I went by the field of the lazy *man,*
And by the vineyard of the man devoid of
understanding;
31 And there it was, all overgrown with
thorns;
Its surface was covered with nettles;
Its stone wall was broken down.
32 When I saw *it,* I considered *it* well;
I looked on *it and* received instruction:
33 A little sleep, a little slumber,
A little folding of the hands to rest;
34 So shall your poverty come *like* a
prowler,
And your need like an armed man.

Further Wise Sayings of Solomon

25 These also *are* proverbs of Solomon
which the men of Hezekiah king of Judah copied:

➤ 2 *It is* the glory of God to conceal a matter,
But the glory of kings *is* to search out a
matter.

3 *As* the heavens for height and the earth
for depth,
So the heart of kings *is* unsearchable.
4 Take away the dross from silver,
And it will go to the silversmith *for*
jewelry.
5 Take away the wicked from before the
king,
And his throne will be established in
righteousness.

6 Do not exalt yourself in the presence of
the king,
And do not stand in the place of the great;
7 For *it is* better that he say to you,
"Come up here,"
Than that you should be put lower in the
presence of the prince,
Whom your eyes have seen.

8 Do not go hastily to court;
For what will you do in the end,
When your neighbor has put you to
shame?
9 Debate your case with your neighbor,
And do not disclose the secret to another;
10 Lest he who hears *it* expose your shame,
And your reputation be ruined.

11 A word fitly spoken *is like* apples of gold
In settings of silver.
12 *Like* an earring of gold and an ornament
of fine gold
Is a wise rebuker to an obedient ear.

13 Like the cold of snow in time of harvest
Is a faithful messenger to those who send
him,
For he refreshes the soul of his masters.

14 Whoever falsely boasts of giving
Is like clouds and wind without rain.

15 By long forbearance a ruler is persuaded,
And a gentle tongue breaks a bone.

16 Have you found honey?
Eat only as much as you need,
Lest you be filled with it and vomit.

17 Seldom set foot in your neighbor's house,
Lest he become weary of you and hate
you.

18 A man who bears false witness against
his neighbor
Is like a club, a sword, and a sharp arrow.

24:28 [a]Septuagint and Vulgate read *Do not deceive.*

LIFE LESSONS

➤ 24:29 — *Do not say, "I will do to him just as he has done to me; I will render to the man according to his work."*

It is not up to us to settle accounts and to avenge personal scores. We do not have all the facts, and we may well get it wrong. Since God knows everything, He says, "Vengeance is Mine, I will repay" (Rom. 12:19).

➤ Proverbs 25:2 — *It is the glory of God to conceal a matter . . . .*

God not only reveals things we didn't know; He also hides things so that we *can't* know them. Elisha found this out (2 Kin. 4:27), as did Moses (Deut. 29:29). And Isaiah says, "You are God, who hide Yourself. . ." (Is. 45:15).

19 Confidence in an unfaithful *man* in time
of trouble
Is like a bad tooth and a foot out of joint.
20 *Like* one who takes away a garment in
cold weather,
And like vinegar on soda,
Is one who sings songs to a heavy heart.
21 If your enemy is hungry, give him bread
to eat;
And if he is thirsty, give him water to
drink;
22 For *so* you will heap coals of fire on his
head,
And the LORD will reward you.
23 The north wind brings forth rain,
And a backbiting tongue an angry
countenance.
24 *It is* better to dwell in a corner of a
housetop,
Than in a house shared with a
contentious woman.
25 *As* cold water to a weary soul,
So *is* good news from a far country.
26 A righteous *man* who falters before the
wicked
Is like a murky spring and a polluted well.
27 *It is* not good to eat much honey;
So to seek one's own glory *is not* glory.
28 Whoever *has* no rule over his own spirit
Is like a city broken down, without walls.

26 As snow in summer and rain in
harvest,
So honor is not fitting for a fool.
2 Like a flitting sparrow, like a flying swallow,
So a curse without cause shall not alight.
3 A whip for the horse,
A bridle for the donkey,
And a rod for the fool's back.
➤ 4 Do not answer a fool according to his folly,
Lest you also be like him.
5 Answer a fool according to his folly,
Lest he be wise in his own eyes.
6 He who sends a message by the hand of
a fool
Cuts off *his own* feet *and* drinks violence.
7 *Like* the legs of the lame that hang limp
Is a proverb in the mouth of fools.
8 Like one who binds a stone in a sling
Is he who gives honor to a fool.
9 *Like* a thorn *that* goes into the hand of a
drunkard
Is a proverb in the mouth of fools.
10 The great *God* who formed everything
Gives the fool *his* hire and the
transgressor *his* wages.[a]
11 As a dog returns to his own vomit,
So a fool repeats his folly.
12 Do you see a man wise in his own eyes?
There is more hope for a fool than for him.

13 The lazy *man* says, "*There is* a lion in the
road!
A fierce lion *is* in the streets!"
14 *As* a door turns on its hinges,
So *does* the lazy *man* on his bed.
15 The lazy *man* buries his hand in the bowl;[a]
It wearies him to bring it back to his
mouth.
16 The lazy *man is* wiser in his own eyes
Than seven men who can answer
sensibly.

17 He who passes by *and* meddles in a
quarrel not his own
Is like one who takes a dog by the ears.
18 Like a madman who throws firebrands,
arrows, and death,
19 *Is* the man *who* deceives his neighbor,
And says, "I was only joking!"
20 Where *there is* no wood, the fire goes
out;
And where *there is* no talebearer, strife
ceases.
21 *As* charcoal *is* to burning coals, and
wood to fire,
So *is* a contentious man to kindle strife.
22 The words of a talebearer *are* like tasty
trifles,
And they go down into the inmost body.
23 Fervent lips with a wicked heart
Are like earthenware covered with silver
dross.
24 He who hates, disguises *it* with his lips,
And lays up deceit within himself;
25 When he speaks kindly, do not believe
him,
For *there are* seven abominations in his
heart;
26 *Though his* hatred is covered by deceit,
His wickedness will be revealed before
the assembly.

26:10 [a]The Hebrew is difficult; ancient and modern translators differ greatly. **26:15** [a]Compare 19:24

LIFE LESSONS

➤ **26:4, 5 —** ***Do not answer a fool according to his folly, lest you also be like him. Answer a fool according to his folly, lest he be wise in his own eyes.***

Some may say, "There you have it: a direct contradiction in the Bible!" Well, not quite. Both statements can be true, although in different situations and at different times. It takes a wise person to know which one applies.

27 Whoever digs a pit will fall into it,
And he who rolls a stone will have it roll back on him.

28 A lying tongue hates *those who are* crushed by it,
And a flattering mouth works ruin.

27 Do not boast about tomorrow,
For you do not know what a day may bring forth.

➤ 2 Let another man praise you, and not your own mouth;
A stranger, and not your own lips.

3 A stone *is* heavy and sand *is* weighty,
But a fool's wrath *is* heavier than both of them.

4 Wrath *is* cruel and anger a torrent,
But who *is* able to stand before jealousy?

5 Open rebuke *is* better
Than love carefully concealed.

6 Faithful *are* the wounds of a friend,
But the kisses of an enemy *are* deceitful.

7 A satisfied soul loathes the honeycomb,
But to a hungry soul every bitter thing *is* sweet.

8 Like a bird that wanders from its nest
Is a man who wanders from his place.

9 Ointment and perfume delight the heart,
And the sweetness of a man's friend *gives delight* by hearty counsel.

10 Do not forsake your own friend or your father's friend,
Nor go to your brother's house in the day of your calamity;
Better *is* a neighbor nearby than a brother far away.

11 My son, be wise, and make my heart glad,
That I may answer him who reproaches me.

➤ 12 A prudent *man* foresees evil *and* hides himself;
The simple pass on *and* are punished.

13 Take the garment of him who is surety for a stranger,
And hold it in pledge *when* he is surety for a seductress.

14 He who blesses his friend with a loud voice, rising early in the morning,
It will be counted a curse to him.

15 A continual dripping on a very rainy day
And a contentious woman are alike;
16 Whoever restrains her restrains the wind,
And grasps oil with his right hand.

17 *As* iron sharpens iron,
So a man sharpens the countenance of his friend.

18 Whoever keeps the fig tree will eat its fruit;
So he who waits on his master will be honored.

19 As in water face *reflects* face,
So a man's heart *reveals* the man.

20 Hell[a] and Destruction[b] are never full;
So the eyes of man are never satisfied.

21 The refining pot *is* for silver and the furnace for gold,
And a man *is valued* by what others say of him.

22 Though you grind a fool in a mortar with a pestle along with crushed grain,
Yet his foolishness will not depart from him.

23 Be diligent to know the state of your flocks,
And attend to your herds;
24 For riches *are* not forever,
Nor does a crown *endure* to all generations.
25 *When* the hay is removed, and the tender grass shows itself,
And the herbs of the mountains are gathered in,
26 The lambs *will provide* your clothing,
And the goats the price of a field;
27 *You shall have* enough goats' milk for your food,
For the food of your household,
And the nourishment of your maidservants.

28 The wicked flee when no one pursues,
But the righteous are bold as a lion.

2 Because of the transgression of a land,
many *are* its princes;

27:20 [a]Or *Sheol* [b]Hebrew *Abaddon*

LIFE LESSONS

➤ 27:2 — *Let another man praise you, and not your own mouth; a stranger, and not your own lips.*

Our God loathes human self-promotion. Our society seems to take it for granted, especially in athletics and entertainment, but "God is the Judge; He puts down one, and exalts another" (Ps. 75:7).

➤ 27:12 — *A prudent man foresees evil and hides himself; the simple pass on and are punished.*

Trust in God does not mean that we turn off our brains or skip through life without any thought about our surroundings or the challenges we face. Fools remain oblivious; the wise stay alert and take appropriate action.

But by a man of understanding *and* knowledge
Right will be prolonged.

3 A poor man who oppresses the poor
Is like a driving rain which leaves no food.

4 Those who forsake the law praise the wicked,
But such as keep the law contend with them.

5 Evil men do not understand justice,
But those who seek the LORD understand all.

➤ 6 Better *is* the poor who walks in his integrity
Than one perverse *in his* ways, though he *be* rich.

7 Whoever keeps the law *is* a discerning son,
But a companion of gluttons shames his father.

8 One who increases his possessions by usury and extortion
Gathers it for him who will pity the poor.

9 One who turns away his ear from hearing the law,
Even his prayer *is* an abomination.

10 Whoever causes the upright to go astray in an evil way,
He himself will fall into his own pit;
But the blameless will inherit good.

11 The rich man *is* wise in his own eyes,
But the poor who has understanding searches him out.

12 When the righteous rejoice, *there is* great glory;
But when the wicked arise, men hide themselves.

➤ 13 He who covers his sins will not prosper,
But whoever confesses and forsakes *them* will have mercy.

14 Happy *is* the man who is always reverent,
But he who hardens his heart will fall into calamity.

15 *Like* a roaring lion and a charging bear
Is a wicked ruler over poor people.

16 A ruler who lacks understanding *is* a great oppressor,
But he who hates covetousness will prolong *his* days.

17 A man burdened with bloodshed will flee into a pit;
Let no one help him.

18 Whoever walks blamelessly will be saved,
But *he who is* perverse *in his* ways will suddenly fall.

19 He who tills his land will have plenty of bread,
But he who follows frivolity will have poverty enough!

20 A faithful man will abound with blessings,
But he who hastens to be rich will not go unpunished.

21 To show partiality *is* not good,
Because for a piece of bread a man will transgress.

22 A man with an evil eye hastens after riches,
And does not consider that poverty will come upon him.

23 He who rebukes a man will find more favor afterward
Than he who flatters with the tongue.

24 Whoever robs his father or his mother,
And says, "*It is* no transgression,"
The same *is* companion to a destroyer.

25 He who is of a proud heart stirs up strife,
But he who trusts in the LORD will be prospered.

26 He who trusts in his own heart is a fool,
But whoever walks wisely will be delivered.

27 He who gives to the poor will not lack,
But he who hides his eyes will have many curses.

28 When the wicked arise, men hide themselves;
But when they perish, the righteous increase.

LIFE LESSONS

➤ 28:6 — *Better is the poor who walks in his integrity than one perverse in his ways, though he be rich.*

No amount of money can make a vile person honorable, and no level of poverty can make a person of integrity anything but honored. As it is said, "We name our dogs Nero, but our sons Paul."

➤ 28:13 — *He who covers his sins will not prosper, but whoever confesses and forsakes them will have mercy.*

Sins left covered and in the dark retain their awful power over us, while sins exposed to the light of truth through confession lose their ability to keep us bound. Confession is not self-mutilation, but freedom.

29 He who is often rebuked, *and* hardens
his neck,
Will suddenly be destroyed, and that
without remedy.

2 When the righteous are in authority, the
people rejoice;
But when a wicked *man* rules, the people
groan.

3 Whoever loves wisdom makes his father
rejoice,
But a companion of harlots wastes *his*
wealth.

4 The king establishes the land by justice,
But he who receives bribes overthrows it.

5 A man who flatters his neighbor
Spreads a net for his feet.

6 By transgression an evil man is snared,
But the righteous sings and rejoices.

7 The righteous considers the cause of the
poor,
But the wicked does not understand *such*
knowledge.

8 Scoffers set a city aflame,
But wise *men* turn away wrath.

9 *If* a wise man contends with a foolish man,
Whether *the fool* rages or laughs, *there is*
no peace.

10 The bloodthirsty hate the blameless,
But the upright seek his well-being.[a]

11 A fool vents all his feelings,[a]
But a wise *man* holds them back.

12 If a ruler pays attention to lies,
All his servants *become* wicked.

13 The poor *man* and the oppressor have
this in common:
The LORD gives light to the eyes of both.

14 The king who judges the poor with truth,
His throne will be established forever.

15 The rod and rebuke give wisdom,
But a child left *to himself* brings shame
to his mother.

16 When the wicked are multiplied,
transgression increases;
But the righteous will see their fall.

17 Correct your son, and he will give you
rest;
Yes, he will give delight to your soul.

18 Where *there is* no revelation,[a] the people
cast off restraint;
But happy *is* he who keeps the law.

19 A servant will not be corrected by mere
words;
For though he understands, he will not
respond.

20 Do you see a man hasty in his words?
There is more hope for a fool than for him.

21 He who pampers his servant from
childhood
Will have him as a son in the end.

22 An angry man stirs up strife,
And a furious man abounds in
transgression.

23 A man's pride will bring him low,
But the humble in spirit will retain honor.

24 Whoever is a partner with a thief hates
his own life;
He swears to tell the truth,[a] but reveals
nothing.

25 The fear of man brings a snare,
But whoever trusts in the LORD shall be
safe.

26 Many seek the ruler's favor,
But justice for man *comes* from the LORD.

27 An unjust man *is* an abomination to the
righteous,
And *he who is* upright in the way *is* an
abomination to the wicked.

The Wisdom of Agur

30 The words of Agur the son of Jakeh, *his*
utterance. This man declared to Ithiel—
to Ithiel and Ucal:

2 Surely I *am* more stupid than *any* man,
And do not have the understanding of a
man.

3 I neither learned wisdom
Nor have knowledge of the Holy One.

4 Who has ascended into heaven, or
descended?
Who has gathered the wind in His fists?
Who has bound the waters in a garment?
Who has established all the ends of the
earth?

29:10 [a]Literally *soul* **29:11** [a]Literally *spirit* **29:18** [a]Or *prophetic vision* **29:24** [a]Literally *hears the adjuration*

LIFE LESSONS

➤ ***29:18 — Where there is no revelation, the people cast off restraint . . . .***

What happens when a society rejects God's revelation and everyone does as he sees fit? You get a culture that looks a lot like the perverted one described in the Book of Judges (17:6; 21:25). And it never works.

What *is* His name, and what *is* His Son's
name,
If you know?

5 Every word of God *is* pure;
He *is* a shield to those who put their trust
in Him.
6 Do not add to His words,
Lest He rebuke you, and you be found a
liar.

7 Two *things* I request of You
(Deprive me not before I die):
8 Remove falsehood and lies far from me;
Give me neither poverty nor riches—
Feed me with the food allotted to me;
9 Lest I be full and deny *You*,
And say, "Who *is* the LORD?"
Or lest I be poor and steal,
And profane the name of my God.

10 Do not malign a servant to his master,
Lest he curse you, and you be found
guilty.

11 *There is* a generation *that* curses its
father,
And does not bless its mother.
12 *There is* a generation *that is* pure in its
own eyes,
Yet is not washed from its filthiness.
13 *There is* a generation—oh, how lofty are
their eyes!
And their eyelids are lifted up.
14 *There is* a generation whose teeth *are like*
swords,
And whose fangs *are like* knives,
To devour the poor from off the earth,
And the needy from *among* men.

15 The leech has two daughters—
Give *and* Give!

There are three *things that* are never
satisfied,
Four never say, "Enough!":
16 The grave,[a]
The barren womb,
The earth *that* is not satisfied with water—
And the fire never says, "Enough!"

17 The eye *that* mocks *his* father,
And scorns obedience to *his* mother,
The ravens of the valley will pick it out,
And the young eagles will eat it.

18 There are three *things which* are too
wonderful for me,
Yes, four *which* I do not understand:
19 The way of an eagle in the air,
The way of a serpent on a rock,
The way of a ship in the midst of the sea,
And the way of a man with a virgin.

20 This *is* the way of an adulterous woman:
She eats and wipes her mouth,
And says, "I have done no wickedness."

21 For three *things* the earth is perturbed,
Yes, for four it cannot bear up:
22 For a servant when he reigns,
A fool when he is filled with food,
23 A hateful *woman* when she is married,
And a maidservant who succeeds her
mistress.

24 There are four *things which* are little on
the earth,
But they *are* exceedingly wise:
25 The ants *are* a people not strong,
Yet they prepare their food in the summer;
26 The rock badgers[a] are a feeble folk,
Yet they make their homes in the crags;
27 The locusts have no king,
Yet they all advance in ranks;
28 The spider[a] skillfully grasps with its hands,
And it is in kings' palaces.

29 There are three *things which* are majestic
in pace,
Yes, four *which* are stately in walk:
30 A lion, *which is* mighty among beasts
And does not turn away from any;
31 A greyhound,[a]
A male goat also,
And a king *whose* troops *are* with him.[b]

32 If you have been foolish in exalting
yourself,
Or if you have devised evil, *put your*
hand on *your* mouth.

30:16 [a]Or *Sheol* **30:26** [a]Or *hyraxes* **30:28** [a]Or *lizard*
30:31 [a]Exact identity unknown [b]A Jewish tradition reads *a king against whom there is no uprising.*

LIFE LESSONS

➤ 30:6 — *Do not add to His words, lest He rebuke you, and you be found a liar.*

We must be careful to distinguish between our own opinions and interpretations of Scripture, and what God actually says in His Word. Paul says we are "not to think beyond what is written" (1 Cor. 4:6).

➤ 30:20 — *This is the way of an adulterous woman: she eats and wipes her mouth, and says, "I have done no wickedness."*

It's become a mantra in our society: "But I'm really a good person!" Unbelievers and believers alike often make this claim after they do what God's Word calls sin. But sin requires repentance, not self-justification or denial.

➤ 30:32 — *If you have been foolish in exalting yourself, or if you have devised evil, put your hand on your mouth.*

Job literally put his hand over his mouth when God appeared to him in a whirlwind to admonish him for his rash demands (Job 40:4). We must control our tongues by the Spirit, or they will control us (James 3:8).

33 For *as* the churning of milk produces
butter,
And wringing the nose produces blood,
So the forcing of wrath produces strife.

The Words of King Lemuel's Mother

31 The words of King Lemuel, the utterance which his mother taught him:

2 What, my son?
And what, son of my womb?
And what, son of my vows?
3 Do not give your strength to women,
Nor your ways to that which destroys
kings.

4 *It is* not for kings, O Lemuel,
It is not for kings to drink wine,
Nor for princes intoxicating drink;
5 Lest they drink and forget the law,
And pervert the justice of all the afflicted.
6 Give strong drink to him who is
perishing,
And wine to those who are bitter of
heart.
7 Let him drink and forget his poverty,
And remember his misery no more.
8 Open your mouth for the speechless,
In the cause of all *who are* appointed to
die.[a]
9 Open your mouth, judge righteously,
And plead the cause of the poor and
needy.

The Virtuous Wife

10 Who[a] can find a virtuous[b] wife?
For her worth *is* far above rubies.
11 The heart of her husband safely trusts
her;
So he will have no lack of gain.
12 She does him good and not evil
All the days of her life.
13 She seeks wool and flax,
And willingly works with her hands.
14 She is like the merchant ships,
She brings her food from afar.
15 She also rises while it is yet night,
And provides food for her household,
And a portion for her maidservants.
16 She considers a field and buys it;
From her profits she plants a vineyard.
17 She girds herself with strength,
And strengthens her arms.
18 She perceives that her merchandise *is*
good,
And her lamp does not go out by night.
19 She stretches out her hands to the distaff,
And her hand holds the spindle.
20 She extends her hand to the poor,
Yes, she reaches out her hands to the
needy.
21 She is not afraid of snow for her
household,
For all her household *is* clothed with
scarlet.
22 She makes tapestry for herself;
Her clothing *is* fine linen and purple.
23 Her husband is known in the gates,
When he sits among the elders of the
land.
24 She makes linen garments and sells *them,*
And supplies sashes for the merchants.
25 Strength and honor *are* her clothing;
She shall rejoice in time to come.
26 She opens her mouth with wisdom,
And on her tongue *is* the law of kindness.
27 She watches over the ways of her
household,
And does not eat the bread of idleness.
28 Her children rise up and call her blessed;
Her husband *also,* and he praises her:
29 "Many daughters have done well,
But you excel them all."
30 Charm *is* deceitful and beauty *is* passing, ≺
But a woman *who* fears the LORD, she
shall be praised.
31 Give her of the fruit of her hands,
And let her own works praise her in the
gates.

31:8 [a]Literally *sons of passing away* **31:10** [a]Verses 10 through 31 are an alphabetic acrostic in Hebrew (compare Psalm 119). [b]Literally *a wife of valor,* in the sense of all forms of excellence

LIFE LESSONS

➤ ***31:30 — Charm is deceitful and beauty is passing, but a woman who fears the LORD, she shall be praised.***

The Book of Proverbs ends where it began, with a focus on the fear of the Lord (see Prov. 1:7). Those who know and worship God for who He really is find both success in life and praise after it.

THE BOOK OF

ECCLESIASTES

The key word in Ecclesiastes is "vanity," the emptiness of trying to be happy apart from God. The Preacher (traditionally identified as Solomon, the wisest, richest king in Israel's history; Eccl. 1:1, 12), looks at life "under the sun" (1:9), and from a purely human perspective he declares it all to be empty. Power, popularity, prestige, pleasure—nothing can fill the God-shaped vacuum in man's life but God Himself.

Once seen from God's perspective, however, life takes on great meaning and purpose, causing Solomon to exclaim, "eat . . . drink . . . rejoice . . . do good . . . live joyfully . . . fear God . . . and keep His commandments!" Skepticism and despair melt away when we view life as a daily gift from God.

The Hebrew title, *Qoheleth*, is a rare term in the Bible, found only in Ecclesiastes (1:1, 2, 12; 7:27; 12:8–10). It comes from the word *qahal*, "to convoke an assembly, to assemble." Thus, it means, "one who addresses an assembly; a preacher." The Septuagint uses the word *Ekklesiastes* as its title for this book, a name derived from the Greek term *ekklesia*, "assembly," "congregation," "church."

Because of the largely negative and pessimistic tone of the book, ancient Hebrews debated whether it even belonged in the Bible. In God's sovereignty, however, Ecclesiastes took its place among the other thirty-eight books of the Old Testament, and so it continues to speak its powerful truths to our own increasingly secular culture. Life without God just does not "work," even if one can manage to accumulate wealth, fame, popularity and power. So the conclusion of the ancient Preacher stands: "Fear God, and keep His commandments, for this is man's all" (12:13).

Themes: Outside of a real and dynamic relationship with God, even a "successful" life will be full of futility and vanity.

Author: Uncertain, but thought to be King Solomon.

Time: Solomon ruled Israel in the tenth century B.C.

Structure: The introduction to Ecclesiastes declares the futility of human effort apart from a living relationship with God (1:1–11). Still, life is to be enjoyed as a gift from God's own hand (1:12—11:6); and because death is coming sooner than we think, in our enjoyment of life we should remember that God's judgment also is coming (11:7—12:8). The book concludes with a charge to fear God and obey His commandments (12:9–14).

As you read Ecclesiastes, watch for several life principles that play an important role in this book:

16. Whatever you acquire outside of God's will eventually turn to ashes. *See Ecclesiastes 2:4–11, 18–23; 5:13–15; pages 757-758; 762.*

4. The awareness of God's presence energizes us for our work. *See Ecclesiastes 3:9–13; 5:18–20; pages 760; 762.*

28. No Christian has ever been called to "go it alone" in his or her walk of faith. *See Ecclesiastes 4:7–12; page 761.*

The Vanity of Life

1 The words of the Preacher, the son of David, king in Jerusalem.

2 "Vanity[a] of vanities," says the Preacher;
"Vanity of vanities, all *is* vanity."

3 What profit has a man from all his labor
In which he toils under the sun?
4 *One* generation passes away, and *another*
generation comes;
But the earth abides forever.
5 The sun also rises, and the sun goes down,
And hastens to the place where it arose.
6 The wind goes toward the south,
And turns around to the north;
The wind whirls about continually,
And comes again on its circuit.
7 All the rivers run into the sea,
Yet the sea *is* not full;
To the place from which the rivers come,
There they return again.
8 All things *are* full of labor;
Man cannot express *it*.
The eye is not satisfied with seeing,
Nor the ear filled with hearing.

9 That which has been *is* what will be,
That which *is* done is what will be done,
And *there is* nothing new under the sun.
10 Is there anything of which it may be said,
"See, this *is* new"?
It has already been in ancient times
before us.
11 *There is* no remembrance of former *things*,
Nor will there be any remembrance of
things that are to come
By *those* who will come after.

The Grief of Wisdom

12 I, the Preacher, was king over Israel in Jerusalem.
13 And I set my heart to seek and search out by wisdom concerning all that is done under heaven; this burdensome task God has given to the sons of man, by which they may be exercised.
14 I have seen all the works that are done under the sun; and indeed, all *is* vanity and grasping for the wind.

15 *What is* crooked cannot be made straight,
And what is lacking cannot be numbered.

16 I communed with my heart, saying, "Look, I have attained greatness, and have gained more wisdom than all who were before me in Jerusalem. My heart has understood great wisdom and knowledge."
17 And I set my heart to know wisdom and to know madness and folly. I perceived that this also is grasping for the wind.

18 For in much wisdom *is* much grief,
And he who increases knowledge
increases sorrow.

The Vanity of Pleasure

2 I said in my heart, "Come now, I will test you with mirth; therefore enjoy pleasure"; but surely, this also *was* vanity.
2 I said of laughter—"Madness!"; and of mirth, "What does it accomplish?"
3 I searched in my heart *how* to gratify my flesh with wine, while guiding my heart with wisdom, and how to lay hold on folly, till I might see what *was* good for the sons of men to do under heaven all the days of their lives.
4 I made my works great, I built myself houses, and planted myself vineyards.
5 I made myself gardens and orchards, and I planted all *kinds* of fruit trees in them.
6 I made myself water pools from which to water the growing trees of the grove.
7 I acquired male and female servants, and had servants born in my house. Yes, I had greater possessions of herds and flocks than all who were in Jerusalem before me.
8 I also gathered for myself silver and gold and the special treasures of kings and of the provinces. I acquired male and female singers, the delights of the sons of men, *and* musical instruments[a] of all kinds.
9 So I became great and excelled more than all who were before me in Jerusalem. Also my wisdom remained with me.

10 Whatever my eyes desired I did not keep
from them.
I did not withhold my heart from any
pleasure,
For my heart rejoiced in all my labor;
And this was my reward from all my
labor.
11 Then I looked on all the works that my
hands had done
And on the labor in which I had toiled;

1:2 [a]Or *Absurdity, Frustration, Futility, Nonsense;* and so throughout this book **2:8** [a]Exact meaning unknown

LIFE LESSONS

➢ 1:18 — *For in much wisdom is much grief, and he who increases knowledge increases sorrow.*

Solomon's big mistake is that he depended on his great wisdom alone, apart from a vibrant walk with God. We were made for an intimate relationship with God, and pursuing *anything* apart from Him will lead to discouragement.

➢ 2:11 — *Then I looked on all the works that my hands had done . . . and indeed all was vanity and grasping for the wind.*

Long before the phrase was invented, Solomon climbed the world's ladder of success, only to find it leaning against the wrong wall. Only when we walk through life with God do we find ultimate meaning.

Life Examples:

THE PREACHER

Rich Doesn't Mean Expensive

ECCL. 2:4

The Preacher is a great example of how "the good life" lacks the power to make anyone truly happy. He wrote that he built houses, planted vineyards, made gardens and orchards, possessed flocks and herds, and collected silver and gold and the treasures of kings. He did not refuse himself any desire. And what was the result? "All was vanity and grasping for wind . . ." (Eccl. 2:4–11).

The richest moments in life are not the most expensive. Often they are the cheapest—the laughter of a child, a hug from a grandparent, a cup of coffee with a friend, a fishing trip with Dad, an "I love you" from Mom. The next time you find yourself wishing you had more, ask God to show you how rich you really are in Him.

See the Life Principles Index for further study:

11. God assumes full responsibility for our needs when we obey Him.

9. Trusting God means looking beyond what we can see to what God sees.

And indeed all *was* vanity and grasping for the wind.
There was no profit under the sun.

The End of the Wise and the Fool

12 Then I turned myself to consider wisdom and madness and folly;
For what *can* the man *do* who succeeds the king?—
Only what he has already done.
13 Then I saw that wisdom excels folly
As light excels darkness.
14 The wise man's eyes *are* in his head,
But the fool walks in darkness.
Yet I myself perceived
That the same event happens to them all.

15 So I said in my heart,
"As it happens to the fool,
It also happens to me,
And why was I then more wise?"
Then I said in my heart,
"This also *is* vanity."
16 For *there is* no more remembrance of the wise than of the fool forever,
Since all that now *is* will be forgotten in the days to come.
And how does a wise *man* die?
As the fool!

17 Therefore I hated life because the work that was done under the sun *was* distressing to me, for all *is* vanity and grasping for the wind.
18 Then I hated all my labor in which I had toiled under the sun, because I must leave it to the man who will come after me.
19 And who knows whether he will be wise or a fool? Yet he will rule over all my labor in which I toiled and in which I have shown myself wise under the sun. This also *is* vanity.
20 Therefore I turned my heart and despaired of all the labor in which I had toiled under the sun.
21 For there is a man whose labor *is* with wisdom, knowledge, and skill; yet he must leave his heritage to a man who has not labored for it. This also *is* vanity and a great evil.
22 For what has man for all his labor, and for the striving of his heart with which he has toiled under the sun?
23 For all his days *are* sorrowful, and his work burdensome; even in the night his heart takes no rest. This also is vanity.
24 Nothing *is* better for a man *than* that he should eat and drink, and *that* his soul should enjoy good in his labor. This also, I saw, was from the hand of God.
25 For who can eat, or who can have enjoyment, more than I?[a]
26 For *God* gives wisdom and knowledge and joy to a man who *is* good in His sight; but to the sinner He gives the work of gathering and collecting, that he may give to *him who is* good before God. This also *is* vanity and grasping for the wind.

2:25 [a]Following Masoretic Text, Targum, and Vulgate; some Hebrew manuscripts, Septuagint, and Syriac read *without Him.*

LIFE LESSONS

➤ 2:17 — *Therefore I hated life because the work that was done under the sun was distressing to me, for all is vanity and grasping for the wind.*

How many throughout history have conquered vast territories, built great works, written brilliant prose, earned immense riches, won worldwide fame . . . only to end up hating life? Without God, life can't help but disappoint.

WHAT THE BIBLE SAYS ABOUT ENJOYING GOD'S PRESENCE

Eccl. 2:26

Over and over again in Scripture, God declares that He wants us to enjoy His presence. As Ecclesiastes tells us, "For God gives wisdom and knowledge and joy to a man who is good in His sight" (Eccl. 2:26). Why, then, do so many people fail to enjoy God's presence?

First, they don't really know Him. Often they see God as an untouchable, invisible force that cares very little about His creation. But nothing is further from the truth! God desires a close, abiding relationship with you. When you fail to realize the depth of His love, you miss a great blessing. He says to you today, as He did to His ancient people, "Yes, I have loved you with an everlasting love; therefore with lovingkindness I have drawn you" (Jer. 31:3).

Second, they have a wrong view of God's attitude. God is no legalist. He isn't scrutinizing your actions or investigating your motives, in order to condemn you. Instead, Jesus says He came to set you free (see John 8:32). Remember this: "God did not send His Son into the world to condemn the world, but that the world through Him might be saved" (John 3:17).

Third, they are afraid of Him. God calls you to reverence His holiness, but never to be afraid of Him. This is why He so often tells His people, "do not be afraid!" (see Gen. 15:1; Josh. 8:1; Luke 1:30).

Fourth, sin breaks the fellowship God wants us to enjoy with Him. Sin not only blocks God's best for us, it eliminates joy. Forsaking sin puts us in a prime position for God's blessing. Not only does God extend forgiveness, He also promises restoration.

Fifth, they refuse God's acceptance. God loves you the way you are! There is nothing you can do to become more acceptable to Him. His love for you is unconditional and never ending.

How can you begin to enjoy God? Realize He enjoys being with you, and then learn to spend time with Him and begin to trust Him to meet all your needs.

He enjoys being with you.

See the Life Principles Index for further study:

1. *Our intimacy with God—His highest priority for our lives—determines the impact of our lives.*
4. *The awareness of God's presence energizes us for our work.*

Everything Has Its Time

➤ 3 To everything *there is* a season,
A time for every purpose under heaven:

2 A time to be born,
And a time to die;
A time to plant,
And a time to pluck *what is* planted;
3 A time to kill,
And a time to heal;
A time to break down,
And a time to build up;
4 A time to weep,
And a time to laugh;
A time to mourn,
And a time to dance;
5 A time to cast away stones,
And a time to gather stones;
A time to embrace,
And a time to refrain from embracing;
6 A time to gain,
And a time to lose;
A time to keep,
And a time to throw away;
7 A time to tear,
And a time to sew;
A time to keep silence,
And a time to speak;
8 A time to love,
And a time to hate;
A time of war,
And a time of peace.

The God-Given Task

9 What profit has the worker from that in
which he labors?
10 I have seen the God-given task with which
the sons of men are to be occupied.
11 He has made everything beautiful in its
time. Also He has put eternity in their hearts,
except that no one can find out the work that
God does from beginning to end.
➤ 12 I know that nothing *is* better for them than
to rejoice, and to do good in their lives,
13 and also that every man should eat and
drink and enjoy the good of all his labor—it *is*
the gift of God.

14 I know that whatever God does,
It shall be forever.
Nothing can be added to it,
And nothing taken from it.
God does *it,* that men should fear before
Him.
15 That which is has already been,
And what is to be has already been;
And God requires an account of what is
past.

Injustice Seems to Prevail

16 Moreover I saw under the sun:

In the place of judgment,
Wickedness *was* there;
And *in* the place of righteousness,
Iniquity *was* there.

17 I said in my heart,

"God shall judge the righteous and the
wicked,
For *there is* a time there for every
purpose and for every work."

18 I said in my heart, "Concerning the condition of the sons of men, God tests them, that
they may see that they themselves are *like* animals."
19 For what happens to the sons of men also
happens to animals; one thing befalls them:
as one dies, so dies the other. Surely, they all
have one breath; man has no advantage over
animals, for all *is* vanity.
20 All go to one place: all are from the dust,
and all return to dust.
21 Who knows the spirit of the sons of men,
which goes upward, and the spirit of the animal, which goes down to the earth?[a]
22 So I perceived that nothing *is* better than
that a man should rejoice in his own works,
for that *is* his heritage. For who can bring him
to see what will happen after him?
4 Then I returned and considered all the oppression that is done under the sun:

And look! The tears of the oppressed,
But they have no comforter—
On the side of their oppressors *there is*
power,
But they have no comforter.

3:21 [a]Septuagint, Syriac, Targum, and Vulgate read *Who knows whether the spirit . . . goes upward, and whether . . . goes downward to the earth?*

LIFE LESSONS

➤ **3:1, 2 —** ***To everything there is a season, a time for every purpose under heaven: A time to be born, and a time to die; a time to plant, and a time to pluck what is planted . . . .***

In His wisdom and sovereignty, God sets an appropriate time for everything. At the right time, Christ was born (Gal. 4:4); at the right time, He lifts us up (1 Pet. 5:6). Don't run ahead of God's timing!

➤ **3:12, 13 —** ***I know that nothing is better for them than to rejoice, and to do good in their lives, and also that every man should eat and drink and enjoy the good of all his labor—it is the gift of God.***

God "gives us richly all things to enjoy," but He warns us not "to trust in uncertain riches but in the living God" and urges us to "be rich in good works, ready to give" (1 Tim. 6:17, 18).

2 Therefore I praised the dead who were
already dead,
More than the living who are still alive.
3 Yet, better than both *is he* who has never
existed,
Who has not seen the evil work that is
done under the sun.

The Vanity of Selfish Toil

4 Again, I saw that for all toil and every
skillful work a man is envied by his neighbor.
This also *is* vanity and grasping for the wind.

5 The fool folds his hands
And consumes his own flesh.
➤ 6 Better a handful *with* quietness
Than both hands full, *together with* toil
and grasping for the wind.

7 Then I returned, and I saw vanity under
the sun:

8 There is one alone, without companion:
He has neither son nor brother.
Yet *there is* no end to all his labors,
Nor is his eye satisfied with riches.
But he never asks,
"For whom do I toil and deprive myself of
good?"
This also *is* vanity and a grave
misfortune.

The Value of a Friend

➤ **9** Two *are* better than one,
Because they have a good reward for
their labor.
10 For if they fall, one will lift up his
companion.
But woe to him *who is* alone when he
falls,
For *he has* no one to help him up.
11 Again, if two lie down together, they will
keep warm;
But how can one be warm *alone?*
12 Though one may be overpowered by
another, two can withstand him.
And a threefold cord is not quickly
broken.

Popularity Passes Away

13 Better a poor and wise youth
Than an old and foolish king who will be
admonished no more.
14 For he comes out of prison to be king,
Although he was born poor in his
kingdom.
15 I saw all the living who walk under the
sun;
They were with the second youth who
stands in his place.
16 *There was* no end of all the people over
whom he was made king;
Yet those who come afterward will not
rejoice in him.
Surely this also *is* vanity and grasping
for the wind.

Fear God, Keep Your Vows

5 Walk prudently when you go to the house
of God; and draw near to hear rather than
to give the sacrifice of fools, for they do not
know that they do evil.

2 Do not be rash with your mouth,
And let not your heart utter anything
hastily before God.
For God *is* in heaven, and you on earth;
Therefore let your words be few.
3 For a dream comes through much activity,
And a fool's voice *is known* by *his* many
words.

4 When you make a vow to God, do not
delay to pay it;
For *He has* no pleasure in fools.
Pay what you have vowed—
5 Better not to vow than to vow and not
pay.

6 Do not let your mouth cause your flesh to
sin, nor say before the messenger *of God* that
it *was* an error. Why should God be angry at
your excuse[a] and destroy the work of your
hands?
7 For in the multitude of dreams and many
words *there is* also vanity. But fear God.

The Vanity of Gain and Honor

8 If you see the oppression of the poor, and
the violent perversion of justice and righteousness in a province, do not marvel at the
matter; for high official watches over high official, and higher officials are over them.
9 Moreover the profit of the land is for all;
even the king is served from the field.

5:6 [a]Literally *voice*

LIFE LESSONS

➤ **4:6 — *Better a handful with quietness than both hands full, together with toil and grasping for the wind.***

Paul tells us that "godliness with contentment is great gain" (1 Tim. 6:6) and that those who walk closely with God can learn "both to be full and to be hungry, both to abound and to suffer need" (Phil. 4:12).

➤ **4:9, 10 — *Two are better than one, because they have a good reward for their labor. For if they fall, one will lift up his companion. But woe to him who is alone when he falls, for he has no one to help him up.***

God never calls on any of His children to "go it alone" in their walk with Him. We need each other, not only to receive help and encouragement, but to give it as well.

10 He who loves silver will not be satisfied
with silver;
Nor he who loves abundance, with
increase.
This also *is* vanity.

11 When goods increase,
They increase who eat them;
So what profit have the owners
Except to see *them* with their eyes?

12 The sleep of a laboring man *is* sweet,
Whether he eats little or much;
But the abundance of the rich will not
permit him to sleep.

13 There is a severe evil *which* I have seen
under the sun:
Riches kept for their owner to his hurt.
14 But those riches perish through
misfortune;
When he begets a son, *there is* nothing in
his hand.
➤ 15 As he came from his mother's womb,
naked shall he return,
To go as he came;
And he shall take nothing from his labor
Which he may carry away in his hand.

16 And this also *is* a severe evil—
Just exactly as he came, so shall he go.
And what profit has he who has labored
for the wind?
17 All his days he also eats in darkness,
And *he has* much sorrow and sickness
and anger.

18 Here is what I have seen: *It is* good and fitting *for one* to eat and drink, and to enjoy the
good of all his labor in which he toils under
the sun all the days of his life which God
gives him; for it *is* his heritage.
➤ 19 As for every man to whom God has given
riches and wealth, and given him power to eat
of it, to receive his heritage and rejoice in his
labor—this *is* the gift of God.
20 For he will not dwell unduly on the days of
his life, because God keeps *him* busy with the
joy of his heart.

6 There is an evil which I have seen under
the sun, and it *is* common among men:
2 A man to whom God has given riches and
wealth and honor, so that he lacks nothing for
himself of all he desires; yet God does not
give him power to eat of it, but a foreigner
consumes it. This *is* vanity, and it *is* an evil affliction.
3 If a man begets a hundred *children* and
lives many years, so that the days of his years
are many, but his soul is not satisfied with
goodness, or indeed he has no burial, I say
that a stillborn child *is* better than he—
4 for it comes in vanity and departs in darkness, and its name is covered with darkness.
5 Though it has not seen the sun or known
anything, this has more rest than that man,
6 even if he lives a thousand years twice—
but has not seen goodness. Do not all go to
one place?

7 All the labor of man *is* for his mouth,
And yet the soul is not satisfied.
8 For what more has the wise *man* than the
fool?
What does the poor man have,
Who knows *how* to walk before the living?
9 Better *is* the sight of the eyes than the
wandering of desire.
This also *is* vanity and grasping for the
wind.

10 Whatever one is, he has been named
already,
For it is known that he *is* man;
And he cannot contend with Him who is
mightier than he.
11 Since there are many things that increase
vanity,
How *is* man the better?

12 For who knows what *is* good for man in
life, all the days of his vain life which he
passes like a shadow? Who can tell a man
what will happen after him under the sun?

The Value of Practical Wisdom

7 A good name *is* better than precious
ointment,
And the day of death than the day of
one's birth;
2 Better to go to the house of mourning
Than to go to the house of feasting,
For that *is* the end of all men;
And the living will take *it* to heart.
3 Sorrow *is* better than laughter,
For by a sad countenance the heart is
made better.

LIFE LESSONS

➤ 5:15 — *As he came from his mother's womb, naked shall he return, to go as he came; and he shall take nothing from his labor which he may carry away in his hand.*

Would we spend less of our time in trivial and useless pursuits if we regularly called to mind this truth? Paul said, "For we brought nothing into this world, and it is certain we can carry nothing out" (1 Tim. 6:7).

➤ 5:19 — *As for every man to whom God has given riches and wealth, and given him power to eat of it, to receive his heritage and rejoice in his labor—this is the gift of God.*

God allows certain amounts of wealth and possessions to come into our hands so that we might use them to bless others. We are to be a funnel for God's blessings, not a container in which to hoard them.

4 The heart of the wise *is* in the house of mourning,
But the heart of fools *is* in the house of mirth.
➤ 5 *It is* better to hear the rebuke of the wise
Than for a man to hear the song of fools.
6 For like the crackling of thorns under a pot,
So *is* the laughter of the fool.
This also is vanity.
7 Surely oppression destroys a wise *man's* reason,
And a bribe debases the heart.
8 The end of a thing *is* better than its beginning;
The patient in spirit *is* better than the proud in spirit.
9 Do not hasten in your spirit to be angry,
For anger rests in the bosom of fools.
10 Do not say,
"Why were the former days better than these?"
For you do not inquire wisely concerning this.

11 Wisdom *is* good with an inheritance,
And profitable to those who see the sun.
12 For wisdom *is* a defense *as* money *is* a defense,
But the excellence of knowledge *is that* wisdom gives life to those who have it.

13 Consider the work of God;
For who can make straight what He has made crooked?
➤ 14 In the day of prosperity be joyful,
But in the day of adversity consider:
Surely God has appointed the one as well as the other,
So that man can find out nothing *that will come* after him.

15 I have seen everything in my days of vanity:

There is a just *man* who perishes in his righteousness,
And there is a wicked *man* who prolongs *life* in his wickedness.

16 Do not be overly righteous,
Nor be overly wise:
Why should you destroy yourself?
17 Do not be overly wicked,
Nor be foolish:
Why should you die before your time?
18 *It is* good that you grasp this,
And also not remove your hand from the other;
For he who fears God will escape them all.

19 Wisdom strengthens the wise
More than ten rulers of the city.
20 For *there is* not a just man on earth who does good
And does not sin.

21 Also do not take to heart everything people say,
Lest you hear your servant cursing you.
22 For many times, also, your own heart has known
That even you have cursed others.

23 All this I have proved by wisdom.
I said, "I will be wise";
But it *was* far from me.
24 As for that which is far off and exceedingly deep,
Who can find it out?
25 I applied my heart to know,
To search and seek out wisdom and the reason *of things*,
To know the wickedness of folly,
Even of foolishness *and* madness.
26 And I find more bitter than death
The woman whose heart *is* snares and nets,
Whose hands *are* fetters.
He who pleases God shall escape from her,
But the sinner shall be trapped by her.

27 "Here is what I have found," says the Preacher,
"*Adding* one thing to the other to find out the reason,
28 Which my soul still seeks but I cannot find:
One man among a thousand I have found,
But a woman among all these I have not found.
29 Truly, this only I have found:
That God made man upright,
But they have sought out many schemes."

LIFE LESSONS

➤ **7:5 — *It is better to hear the rebuke of the wise than for a man to hear the song of fools.***

We live in an entertainment age, in which people increasingly value mindless diversions over substantive pursuits that might require some thinking. Fun is great, but never as the main goal of life.

➤ **7:14 — *In the day of prosperity be joyful, but in the day of adversity consider: Surely God has appointed the one as well as the other . . .***

We tend to see good times as the blessing of God and bad times as the work of the devil, but such a view is shortsighted. Nothing reaches us without first passing through the hands of our sovereign God.

8 Who *is* like a wise *man?*
And who knows the interpretation of a thing?
A man's wisdom makes his face shine,
And the sternness of his face is changed.

Obey Authorities for God's Sake

2 I *say,* "Keep the king's commandment for
the sake of your oath to God.
3 Do not be hasty to go from his presence.
Do not take your stand for an evil thing, for
he does whatever pleases him."

4 Where the word of a king *is, there is* power;
And who may say to him, "What are you doing?"
➤ 5 He who keeps his command will experience nothing harmful;
And a wise man's heart discerns both time and judgment,
6 Because for every matter there is a time and judgment,
Though the misery of man increases greatly.
7 For he does not know what will happen;
So who can tell him when it will occur?
8 No one has power over the spirit to retain the spirit,
And no one has power in the day of death.
There is no release from that war,
And wickedness will not deliver those who are given to it.

9 All this I have seen, and applied my heart
to every work that is done under the sun:
There is a time in which one man rules over
another to his own hurt.

Death Comes to All

10 Then I saw the wicked buried, who had
come and gone from the place of holiness,
and they were forgotten[a] in the city where
they had so done. This also *is* vanity.
11 Because the sentence against an evil work
is not executed speedily, therefore the heart
of the sons of men is fully set in them to do
evil.
➤ 12 Though a sinner does evil a hundred
times, and his *days* are prolonged, yet I surely
know that it will be well with those who fear
God, who fear before Him.
13 But it will not be well with the wicked; nor
will he prolong *his* days, *which are* as a
shadow, because he does not fear before God.
14 There is a vanity which occurs on earth,
that there are just *men* to whom it happens
according to the work of the wicked; again,
there are wicked *men* to whom it happens according to the work of the righteous. I said
that this also *is* vanity.
15 So I commended enjoyment, because a
man has nothing better under the sun than to
eat, drink, and be merry; for this will remain
with him in his labor *all* the days of his life
which God gives him under the sun.
16 When I applied my heart to know wisdom
and to see the business that is done on earth,
even though one sees no sleep day or night,
17 then I saw all the work of God, that a man
cannot find out the work that is done under
the sun. For though a man labors to discover
it, yet he will not find *it;* moreover, though a
wise *man* attempts to know *it,* he will not be
able to find *it.*

9 For I considered all this in my heart, so
that I could declare it all: that the righteous and the wise and their works *are* in the
hand of God. People know neither love nor
hatred *by* anything *they see* before them.
2 All things *come* alike to all: ➤

One event *happens* to the righteous and the wicked;
To the good,[a] the clean, and the unclean;
To him who sacrifices and him who does not sacrifice.
As is the good, so *is* the sinner;
He who takes an oath as *he* who fears an oath.

3 This *is* an evil in all that is done under the
sun: that one thing *happens* to all. Truly the
hearts of the sons of men are full of evil; mad-

8:10 [a]Some Hebrew manuscripts, Septuagint, and Vulgate read *praised.* **9:2** [a]Septuagint, Syriac, and Vulgate read *good and bad.*

LIFE LESSONS

➤ 8:5 — *. . . a wise man's heart discerns both time and judgment . . . .*

The wisest men and women seek God's will, and often that will has much to say about timing and method, about the when and the how. God moves heaven and earth to show us His will when we seek Him wholeheartedly.

➤ 8:12 — *Though a sinner does evil a hundred times, and his days are prolonged, yet I surely know that it will be well with those who fear God, who fear before Him.*

To really understand the promises of God, we have to take the long view. Sometimes the wicked prosper . . . for a while. And sometimes the righteous suffer . . . for a while. But all accounts get balanced in eternity.

➤ 9:2 — *All things come alike to all: One event happens to the righteous and the wicked; to the good, the clean, and the unclean . . . .*

Good things can happen to bad people, and bad things can happen to good people. That's the world we live in. But this world is coming to an end, and the next one will feature a very different story.

ANSWERS TO LIFE'S QUESTIONS

How can I find fulfillment in my work?

ECCL. 9:10

We all enjoy weekends. Recreation with our families and friends is important for a well-balanced life. But if we live for the weekends only, we thwart God's desire to bless us in the task that occupies most of our adult life—work.

Work is not the result of the curse placed on our planet when Adam and Eve sinned. God had instructed them to till the soil and reap its fruit *before* the fall. Work is a gift from God—given for our enjoyment and blessing. That is why the Preacher can say, "I know that nothing is better for them than to rejoice, and to do good in their lives, and also that every man should eat and drink and enjoy the good of all his labor—it is the gift of God" (Eccl. 3:12, 13).

"Wait a minute," you might be saying. "If you knew who my boss is, you would understand! How can I possibly enjoy my work with such an unpleasant supervisor?"

True enough, some work may not fit our ideal job description—but consider the alternative. Have you ever known anyone to feel happy and satisfied while standing in an unemployment line? If you have a job, thank God for it. Not everyone is so blessed.

Wherever you find yourself working today—on the factory line, under a sink, at a desk, in a truck or on the phone—thank God for your work. It may be less than perfect, but that is where God has placed you, at least for now.

We must come to see every detail of our jobs as an opportunity to serve God. The apostle Paul tells us, "whether you eat or drink, or whatever you do, do all to the glory of God" (1 Cor. 10:31). And he reminds us, "whatever you do, do it heartily, as to the Lord and not to men, knowing that from the Lord you will receive the reward of the inheritance; for you serve the Lord Christ" (Col. 3:23, 24). Such an attitude can transform the workplace from a mere workstation to a practical pulpit that says more about your relationship with Christ than words ever could.

See work as God's gift! Give Him thanks for the opportunity and the privilege of working, not just for a living, but for Him. Then you can start anticipating the weekday as much as the weekend.

See the Life Principles Index for further study:
4. The awareness of God's presence energizes us for our work.

ness *is* in their hearts while they live, and
after that *they go* to the dead.
4 But for him who is joined to all the living
there is hope, for a living dog is better than a
dead lion.

5 For the living know that they will die;
But the dead know nothing,
And they have no more reward,
For the memory of them is forgotten.
6 Also their love, their hatred, and their
envy have now perished;
Nevermore will they have a share
In anything done under the sun.

7 Go, eat your bread with joy,
And drink your wine with a merry heart;
For God has already accepted your
works.
8 Let your garments always be white,
And let your head lack no oil.

9 Live joyfully with the wife whom you love
all the days of your vain life which He has
given you under the sun, all your days of vanity; for that *is* your portion in life, and in the
labor which you perform under the sun.
10 Whatever your hand finds to do, do *it* with ➤
your might; for *there is* no work or device or
knowledge or wisdom in the grave where you
are going.
11 I returned and saw under the sun that—

The race *is* not to the swift,
Nor the battle to the strong,

LIFE LESSONS

➤ 9:10 — *Whatever your hand finds to do, do it with your might . . . .*

God doesn't appreciate halfhearted anything. He denounces halfhearted devotion to Him (Rev. 3:15, 16) and He urges us to work at our day jobs with all our hearts (Col. 3:23). Enthusiasm for Him should translate into enthusiasm for life.

Nor bread to the wise,
Nor riches to men of understanding,
Nor favor to men of skill;
But time and chance happen to them all.
12 For man also does not know his time:
Like fish taken in a cruel net,
Like birds caught in a snare,
So the sons of men *are* snared in an evil time,
When it falls suddenly upon them.

Wisdom Superior to Folly

13 This wisdom I have also seen under the
sun, and it *seemed* great to me:
14 *There was* a little city with few men in it;
and a great king came against it, besieged it,
and built great snares[a] around it.
15 Now there was found in it a poor wise
man, and he by his wisdom delivered the city.
Yet no one remembered that same poor man.
16 Then I said:

"Wisdom *is* better than strength.
Nevertheless the poor man's wisdom *is* despised,
And his words are not heard.
17 Words of the wise, *spoken* quietly, *should be* heard
Rather than the shout of a ruler of fools.
18 Wisdom *is* better than weapons of war;
But one sinner destroys much good."

10 Dead flies putrefy[a] the perfumer's ointment,
And cause it to give off a foul odor;
So does a little folly to one respected for wisdom *and* honor.
2 A wise man's heart *is* at his right hand,
But a fool's heart at his left.
3 Even when a fool walks along the way,
He lacks wisdom,
And he shows everyone *that* he *is* a fool.
4 If the spirit of the ruler rises against you,
Do not leave your post;
For conciliation pacifies great offenses.

5 There is an evil I have seen under the sun,
As an error proceeding from the ruler:
6 Folly is set in great dignity,
While the rich sit in a lowly place.
7 I have seen servants on horses,
While princes walk on the ground like servants.

8 He who digs a pit will fall into it,
And whoever breaks through a wall will be bitten by a serpent.
9 He who quarries stones may be hurt by them,
And he who splits wood may be endangered by it.
10 If the ax is dull,
And one does not sharpen the edge,
Then he must use more strength;
But wisdom brings success.

11 A serpent may bite when *it is* not charmed;
The babbler is no different.
12 The words of a wise man's mouth *are* gracious,
But the lips of a fool shall swallow him up;
13 The words of his mouth begin with foolishness,
And the end of his talk *is* raving madness.
14 A fool also multiplies words.
No man knows what is to be;
Who can tell him what will be after him?
15 The labor of fools wearies them,
For they do not even know how to go to the city!

16 Woe to you, O land, when your king *is* a child,
And your princes feast in the morning!
17 Blessed *are* you, O land, when your king *is* the son of nobles,
And your princes feast at the proper time—
For strength and not for drunkenness!
18 Because of laziness the building decays,
And through idleness of hands the house leaks.
19 A feast is made for laughter,
And wine makes merry;
But money answers everything.

20 Do not curse the king, even in your thought;
Do not curse the rich, even in your bedroom;
For a bird of the air may carry your voice,
And a bird in flight may tell the matter.

9:14 [a]Septuagint, Syriac, and Vulgate read *bulwarks.*
10:1 [a]Targum and Vulgate omit *putrefy.*

LIFE LESSONS

➤ 10:18 — *Because of laziness the building decays, and through idleness of hands the house leaks.*

The Bible contrasts laziness with working diligently. The pursuit of godly goals takes energy. The building of godly relationships takes diligence and effort. The pursuit of godly success takes an expenditure of time and creativity.

The Value of Diligence

11 Cast your bread upon the waters,
For you will find it after many days.
2 Give a serving to seven, and also to
eight,
For you do not know what evil will be on
the earth.

3 If the clouds are full of rain,
They empty *themselves* upon the earth;
And if a tree falls to the south or the
north,
In the place where the tree falls, there it
shall lie.
4 He who observes the wind will not sow,
And he who regards the clouds will not
reap.

5 As you do not know what *is* the way of
the wind,[a]
Or how the bones *grow* in the womb of
her who is with child,
So you do not know the works of God
who makes everything.
6 In the morning sow your seed,
And in the evening do not withhold your
hand;
For you do not know which will prosper,
Either this or that,
Or whether both alike *will be* good.

7 Truly the light is sweet,
And *it is* pleasant for the eyes to behold
the sun;
8 But if a man lives many years
And rejoices in them all,
Yet let him remember the days of
darkness,
For they will be many.
All that is coming *is* vanity.

Seek God in Early Life

9 Rejoice, O young man, in your youth,
And let your heart cheer you in the days
of your youth;
Walk in the ways of your heart,
And in the sight of your eyes;
But know that for all these
God will bring you into judgment.
10 Therefore remove sorrow from your
heart,
And put away evil from your flesh,
For childhood and youth *are* vanity.

12 Remember now your Creator in the
days of your youth,
Before the difficult days come,
And the years draw near when you say,
"I have no pleasure in them":
2 While the sun and the light,
The moon and the stars,
Are not darkened,
And the clouds do not return after the
rain;
3 In the day when the keepers of the house
tremble,
And the strong men bow down;
When the grinders cease because they
are few,
And those that look through the windows
grow dim;
4 When the doors are shut in the streets,
And the sound of grinding is low;
When one rises up at the sound of a
bird,
And all the daughters of music are
brought low.
5 Also they are afraid of height,
And of terrors in the way;
When the almond tree blossoms,
The grasshopper is a burden,
And desire fails.
For man goes to his eternal home,
And the mourners go about the streets.

6 *Remember your Creator* before the silver
cord is loosed,[a]
Or the golden bowl is broken,
Or the pitcher shattered at the fountain,
Or the wheel broken at the well.
7 Then the dust will return to the earth as
it was,
And the spirit will return to God who
gave it.

11:5 [a]Or *spirit* **12:6** [a]Following Qere and Targum; Kethib reads *removed;* Septuagint and Vulgate read *broken.*

LIFE LESSONS

➤ 11:4 — *He who observes the wind will not sow, and he who regards the clouds will not reap.*

The procrastinator can easily miss out on God's best for his life. Let your motto be: "I'll do it now, as the Lord directs and enables me." It will save a lot of heartache later.

➤ 11:5 — *As you do not know what is the way of the wind, or how the bones grow in the womb of her who is with child, so you do not know the works of God who makes everything.*

God's ways are higher than ours, and His thoughts far loftier and greater (Is. 55: 8, 9). And yet what He has revealed, He has given so that we might follow Him joyfully (Deut. 29:29). Let us treasure God's Word!

➤ 12:1 — *Remember now your Creator in the days of your youth, before the difficult days come, and the years draw near when you say, "I have no pleasure in them."*

Toward the end of his life, Solomon did not walk with God, and so he dreaded growing old. Let us strive to be more like Moses, who at the end still had bright eyes and a zest for life (Deut. 34:7).

WHAT THE BIBLE SAYS ABOUT **THE VALUE OF DILIGENCE**

Eccl. 11:6

"The early bird gets the worm." "Sharp as a tack."

You've probably heard these time-worn clichés many times. But have you ever realized that both overflow with biblical significance regarding a character trait vital to any successful venture?

That character trait is diligence, frequently contrasted in the Bible with laziness and procrastination. The Hebrew language uses two word pictures to illustrate diligence: "dawn" and "knife," thus portraying an individual who is fully awake and alert (the early bird) and whose skills are sharpened and honed (sharp as a tack).

"He who observes the wind will not sow, and he who regards the clouds will not reap," the Preacher tells us (Eccl. 11:4). We can't spend our time daydreaming, nor can we wait to get started until all conditions look absolutely optimal. "In the morning sow your seed, and in the evening do not withhold your hand, for you do not know which will prosper, either this or that, or whether both alike will be good" (11:6).

A diligent man is a satisfied man.

A diligent man is a satisfied man. The lazy man is always dreaming and wanting but never willing to pay the price of perseverance. Thus he comes to frustration and emptiness.

Before the apostle Peter listed his character building blocks, such as faith, virtue, knowledge, and self-control, he exhorted his readers to apply "all diligence" (2 Pet. 1:5). Such qualities are not found in a superficial Christian. They take root in one's character only through steadfast application and pursuit.

The overriding motivation for the cultivation and attainment of diligence is not material gain, but the urgency of our Christian witness. "I must work the work of Him who sent Me while it is day," Jesus said. "The night is coming when no one can work" (John 9:4).

Our pilgrimage on earth is brief. A diligent lifestyle alert to every opportunity to share Christ and make Him known will have the greatest influence on the kingdom of God. Time is precious. We redeem it for His purposes as we remain diligent in our work, our study, our witness, and our prayers.

See the Life Principles Index for further study:
4. The awareness of God's presence energizes us for our work.

8 "Vanity of vanities," says the Preacher,
"All *is* vanity."

The Whole Duty of Man

9 And moreover, because the Preacher was
wise, he still taught the people knowledge;
yes, he pondered and sought out *and* set in
order many proverbs.
10 The Preacher sought to find acceptable
words; and *what was* written *was* upright—
words of truth.
11 The words of the wise are like goads, and
the words of scholars[a] are like well-driven
nails, given by one Shepherd.
12 And further, my son, be admonished by
these. Of making many books *there is* no end,
and much study *is* wearisome to the flesh.
13 Let us hear the conclusion of the whole
matter:

Fear God and keep His commandments,
For this is man's all.

14 For God will bring every work into
judgment,
Including every secret thing,
Whether good or evil.

12:11 [a]Literally *masters of the assemblies*

LIFE LESSONS

➤ 12:13 — *Fear God and keep His commandments, for this is man's all.*

From Genesis to Revelation, God instructs and urges His people to obey His commands and to fear His great Name. Yet we are to do so with joy in our souls and love in our hearts (see 1 Cor. 16:22).

THE SONG OF

SOLOMON

Does God have anything to say to us about love, sex, and intimacy? For many people, the words "romance" and "Bible" conjure up a long list of religious "thou shalt nots." But God never intended for us to view love in a negative way. He created us in love and for love, and for that reason, the Bible has a great deal to say about romantic love. In fact, it often uses pictures of human love to help us understand God's love for us.

As one key example, consider the Song of Solomon.

The Song of Solomon is a beautiful love poem written by Solomon that abounds in colorful metaphors and eastern imagery. When considered literally, it depicts the wooing and wedding of a shepherdess by King Solomon, and the joys and thrills and heartaches and surprises of wedded love.

Throughout the ages, scholars have also looked at the book through an allegorical lens. When considered in this way, it pictures Israel as God's betrothed bride (Hos. 2:19, 20), and the church as the bride of Christ. As human life finds its highest fulfillment in the love of man and woman, so spiritual life finds its highest fulfillment in the love of God for His people and Christ for His church.

The Hebrew title, *Shir Hashirim*, comes from 1:1, "the song of songs." The superlative form declares it to be Solomon's most exquisite song. The Latin title, *Canticum Canticorum*, also means "Song of Songs" or "The Best Song." The alternative name for the book, *Canticles*, is derived from the Latin title. Because Solomon is mentioned in 1:1, the book is also known as the Song of Solomon.

Themes: God demonstrates His grace to us through the joys of romantic love that He enables husbands and wives to share. That human love can also serve as a picture of His divine love for us.

Authors: Solomon.

Time: Solomon ruled over Israel in the tenth century B.C.

Structure: The book is arranged like scenes in a drama with three main speakers: the bride (Shulamite), the groom (Solomon), and a chorus (daughters of Jerusalem).

As you read the Song of Solomon, watch for two life principles that play an important role in this book:

1. Our intimacy with God—His highest priority for our lives—determines the impact of our lives. *See Song of Solomon 2:1; page 771.*

12. Peace with God is the fruit of oneness with God. *See Song of Solomon 7:10; page 778.*

1 The song of songs, which *is* Solomon's.

The Banquet

THE SHULAMITE[a]

2 Let him kiss me with the kisses of his mouth—
For your[b] love *is* better than wine.
3 Because of the fragrance of your good ointments,
Your name *is* ointment poured forth;
Therefore the virgins love you.
4 Draw me away!

THE DAUGHTERS OF JERUSALEM

We will run after you.[a]

THE SHULAMITE

The king has brought me into his chambers.

THE DAUGHTERS OF JERUSALEM

We will be glad and rejoice in you.[b]
We will remember your[c] love more than wine.

THE SHULAMITE

Rightly do they love you.[d]
5 I *am* dark, but lovely,
O daughters of Jerusalem,
Like the tents of Kedar,
Like the curtains of Solomon.
6 Do not look upon me, because I *am* dark,
Because the sun has tanned me.
My mother's sons were angry with me;
They made me the keeper of the vineyards,
But my own vineyard I have not kept.

(TO HER BELOVED)

7 Tell me, O you whom I love,
Where you feed *your flock,*
Where you make *it* rest at noon.
For why should I be as one who veils herself[a]
By the flocks of your companions?

THE BELOVED

8 If you do not know, O fairest among women,
Follow in the footsteps of the flock,
And feed your little goats
Beside the shepherds' tents.
9 I have compared you, my love,
To my filly among Pharaoh's chariots.
10 Your cheeks are lovely with ornaments,
Your neck with chains *of gold.*

THE DAUGHTERS OF JERUSALEM

11 We will make you[a] ornaments of gold
With studs of silver.

THE SHULAMITE

12 While the king *is* at his table,
My spikenard sends forth its fragrance.
13 A bundle of myrrh *is* my beloved to me,
That lies all night between my breasts.
14 My beloved *is* to me a cluster of henna *blooms*
In the vineyards of En Gedi.

THE BELOVED

15 Behold, you *are* fair, my love!
Behold, you *are* fair!
You *have* dove's eyes.

THE SHULAMITE

16 Behold, you *are* handsome, my beloved!
Yes, pleasant!
Also our bed *is* green.
17 The beams of our houses *are* cedar,
And our rafters of fir.

2 I *am* the rose of Sharon,
And the lily of the valleys.

THE BELOVED

2 Like a lily among thorns,
So is my love among the daughters.

1:2 [a]A Palestinian young woman (compare 6:13). The speaker and audience are identified according to the number, gender, and person of the Hebrew words. Occasionally the identity is not certain. [b]Masculine singular, that is, the Beloved
1:4 [a]Masculine singular, that is, the Beloved [b]Feminine singular, that is, the Shulamite [c]Masculine singular, that is, the Beloved [d]Masculine singular, that is, the Beloved **1:7** [a]Septuagint, Syriac, and Vulgate read *wanders.* **1:11** [a]Feminine singular, that is, the Shulamite

LIFE LESSONS

➤ 1:4 — *We will be glad and rejoice in you. We will remember your love more than wine.*

To make both our marriages and our churches work as God wants them to, we must get involved with others of like mind who delight in us and our successes. No one grows in perpetual solitude.

➤ 1:15 — *Behold, you are fair, my love! Behold, you are fair! You have dove's eyes.*

Human love grows best in a bright atmosphere of frequent and heartfelt praise. Lovers do not tire of hearing their beloved exult over them. And by the way, neither does God.

THE SHULAMITE

➤ 3 Like an apple tree among the trees of the woods,
So *is* my beloved among the sons.
I sat down in his shade with great delight,
And his fruit *was* sweet to my taste.

THE SHULAMITE TO THE DAUGHTERS OF JERUSALEM

4 He brought me to the banqueting house,
And his banner over me *was* love.
5 Sustain me with cakes of raisins,
Refresh me with apples,
For I *am* lovesick.

6 His left hand *is* under my head,
And his right hand embraces me.
7 I charge you, O daughters of Jerusalem,
By the gazelles or by the does of the field,
Do not stir up nor awaken love
Until it pleases.

The Beloved's Request

THE SHULAMITE

8 The voice of my beloved!
Behold, he comes
Leaping upon the mountains,
Skipping upon the hills.
9 My beloved is like a gazelle or a young stag.
Behold, he stands behind our wall;
He is looking through the windows,
Gazing through the lattice.

10 My beloved spoke, and said to me:
"Rise up, my love, my fair one,
And come away.
11 For lo, the winter is past,
The rain is over *and* gone.
12 The flowers appear on the earth;
The time of singing has come,
And the voice of the turtledove
Is heard in our land.
➤ 13 The fig tree puts forth her green figs,
And the vines *with* the tender grapes
Give a *good* smell.
Rise up, my love, my fair one,
And come away!

14 "O my dove, in the clefts of the rock,
In the secret *places* of the cliff,
Let me see your face,
Let me hear your voice;
For your voice *is* sweet,
And your face *is* lovely."

HER BROTHERS

15 Catch us the foxes,
The little foxes that spoil the vines,
For our vines *have* tender grapes.

THE SHULAMITE

16 My beloved *is* mine, and I *am* his.
He feeds *his flock* among the lilies.

(TO HER BELOVED)

17 Until the day breaks
And the shadows flee away,
Turn, my beloved,
And be like a gazelle
Or a young stag
Upon the mountains of Bether.[a]

A Troubled Night

THE SHULAMITE

3 By night on my bed I sought the one I love;
I sought him, but I did not find him.
2 "I will rise now," *I said,*
"And go about the city;
In the streets and in the squares
I will seek the one I love."
I sought him, but I did not find him.
3 The watchmen who go about the city found me;
I said,
"Have you seen the one I love?"

4 Scarcely had I passed by them,
When I found the one I love.
I held him and would not let him go,
Until I had brought him to the house of my mother,
And into the chamber of her who conceived me.

5 I charge you, O daughters of Jerusalem,
By the gazelles or by the does of the field,
Do not stir up nor awaken love
Until it pleases.

2:17 [a]Literally *Separation*

LIFE LESSONS

➤ 2:3 — *Like an apple tree among the trees of the woods, so is my beloved among the sons.*

Men and women in love almost can't help but brag about their loved one to others. This kind of expression endears the lovers to one another. In a similar way, the best evangelism also flows naturally out of love for God.

➤ 2:13 — *Rise up, my love, my fair one, and come away!*

Marital love will not flourish without some "alone time" between the lovers. In a similar way, our relationship with God will not blossom without spending some private time with Him.

WHAT THE BIBLE SAYS ABOUT GOD AS OUR LOVER

Song 2:4

Love—as in, "his banner over me was love" (Song 2:4). It is the greatest gift God offers us, and yet it is the one we have the most difficulty receiving. Why?

First, we do not think we deserve His love—which is true. "God demonstrates His own love toward us," the apostle Paul writes, "in that while we were still sinners, Christ died for us" (Rom. 5:8).

Second, we do not understand it, for the quality of His love differs tremendously from our own. We somehow want to believe that He loves us the way we love others. Such a viewpoint, however, leaves us doubtful that He will always love us as the Bible promises He will.

Love is a commitment to the satisfaction, peace, security, joy, and development of another person. God's love is not based on emotion, but flows out of His changeless character. The Bible tells us that God *is* love (see 1 John 4:8). Since it is impossible for Him to do anything contrary to His nature, His love will forever remain certain and dependable.

His love will forever remain certain and dependable.

In addition, His *gift* is love. James 1:17 implies that God's love does not change, and it exists independently of our feelings about "deserving" it. We cannot earn it or give anything in return for it—God offers His love to us freely, as a gift.

Furthermore, the love of our heavenly Father is perfect. Every one of God's attributes represents the peak of perfection and cannot be improved to any degree. Since His love is perfect, we know it will bless us forever. He will always treat each of us in accordance with His love.

Every day, you and I walk under the canopy of God's amazing love, which remains perfect and changeless, even if we wander from His will or fall into disobedience. Never allow yourself to think, *the canopy must be down.* It never is! We did not erect the canopy, and neither can we dismantle it.

God has always loved you and always will. Release any misconceptions therefore, and rejoice under His canopy of love.

See the Life Principles Index for further study:
1. Our intimacy with God—His highest priority for our lives—determines the impact of our lives.

The Coming of Solomon

THE SHULAMITE

6 Who *is* this coming out of the wilderness
Like pillars of smoke,
Perfumed with myrrh and frankincense,
With all the merchant's fragrant
powders?
7 Behold, it *is* Solomon's couch,
With sixty valiant men around it,
Of the valiant of Israel.
8 They all hold swords,
Being expert in war.
Every man *has* his sword on his thigh
Because of fear in the night.

9 Of the wood of Lebanon
Solomon the King
Made himself a palanquin:[a]
10 He made its pillars *of* silver,
Its support *of* gold,
Its seat *of* purple,
Its interior paved *with* love
By the daughters of Jerusalem.
11 Go forth, O daughters of Zion,
And see King Solomon with the crown
With which his mother crowned him
On the day of his wedding,
The day of the gladness of his heart.

THE BELOVED

4 Behold, you *are* fair, my love!
Behold, you *are* fair!
You *have* dove's eyes behind your veil.
Your hair *is* like a flock of goats,
Going down from Mount Gilead.
2 Your teeth *are* like a flock of shorn
sheep
Which have come up from the
washing,
Every one of which bears twins,
And none *is* barren among them.
3 Your lips *are* like a strand of scarlet,
And your mouth is lovely.
Your temples behind your veil
Are like a piece of pomegranate.
4 Your neck *is* like the tower of David,
Built for an armory,
On which hang a thousand bucklers,
All shields of mighty men.
5 Your two breasts *are* like two fawns,
Twins of a gazelle,
Which feed among the lilies.

6 Until the day breaks
And the shadows flee away,
I will go my way to the mountain of
myrrh
And to the hill of frankincense.

7 You *are* all fair, my love,
And *there is* no spot in you.
8 Come with me from Lebanon, *my* spouse,
With me from Lebanon.
Look from the top of Amana,
From the top of Senir and Hermon,
From the lions' dens,
From the mountains of the leopards.

9 You have ravished my heart,
My sister, *my* spouse;
You have ravished my heart
With one *look* of your eyes,
With one link of your necklace.
10 How fair is your love,
My sister, *my* spouse!
How much better than wine is your love,
And the scent of your perfumes
Than all spices!
11 Your lips, O *my* spouse,
Drip as the honeycomb;
Honey and milk *are* under your tongue;
And the fragrance of your garments
Is like the fragrance of Lebanon.

12 A garden enclosed
Is my sister, *my* spouse,
A spring shut up,
A fountain sealed.
13 Your plants *are* an orchard of
pomegranates
With pleasant fruits,
Fragrant henna with spikenard,
14 Spikenard and saffron,
Calamus and cinnamon,
With all trees of frankincense,
Myrrh and aloes,
With all the chief spices—
15 A fountain of gardens,
A well of living waters,
And streams from Lebanon.

THE SHULAMITE

16 Awake, O north *wind*,
And come, O south!
Blow upon my garden,

3:9 [a]A portable enclosed chair

LIFE LESSONS

➤ **4:9** — ***You have ravished my heart, my sister, my spouse; you have ravished my heart with one look of your eyes . . . .***

Not only do husbands and wives need to praise each other's good qualities, but in the best marriages, they also love to describe the wonderful way they make each other feel.

➤ **4:16** — ***Let my beloved come to his garden and eat its pleasant fruits.***

While sex is not the all-important prize our culture claims, it is a delightful and important part of any growing marriage. So Paul instructs, "Do not deprive one another except with consent for a time . . ." (1 Cor. 7:5).

That its spices may flow out.
Let my beloved come to his garden
And eat its pleasant fruits.

THE BELOVED

5 I have come to my garden, my sister, *my* spouse;
I have gathered my myrrh with my spice;
I have eaten my honeycomb with my honey;
I have drunk my wine with my milk.

(TO HIS FRIENDS)

Eat, O friends!
Drink, yes, drink deeply,
O beloved ones!

The Shulamite's Troubled Evening

THE SHULAMITE

2 I sleep, but my heart is awake;
It is the voice of my beloved!
He knocks, *saying,*
"Open for me, my sister, my love,
My dove, my perfect one;
For my head is covered with dew,
My locks with the drops of the night."

3 I have taken off my robe;
How can I put it on *again?*
I have washed my feet;
How can I defile them?
4 My beloved put his hand
By the latch *of the door,*
And my heart yearned for him.
5 I arose to open for my beloved,
And my hands dripped *with* myrrh,
My fingers with liquid myrrh,
On the handles of the lock.
6 I opened for my beloved,
But my beloved had turned away *and* was gone.
My heart leaped up when he spoke.
I sought him, but I could not find him;
I called him, but he gave me no answer.
7 The watchmen who went about the city found me.
They struck me, they wounded me;
The keepers of the walls
Took my veil away from me.
8 I charge you, O daughters of Jerusalem,
If you find my beloved,
That you tell him I *am* lovesick!

THE DAUGHTERS OF JERUSALEM

9 What *is* your beloved
More than *another* beloved,
O fairest among women?
What *is* your beloved
More than *another* beloved,
That you so charge us?

THE SHULAMITE

10 My beloved *is* white and ruddy,
Chief among ten thousand.
11 His head *is like* the finest gold;
His locks *are* wavy,
And black as a raven.
12 His eyes *are* like doves
By the rivers of waters,
Washed with milk,
And fitly set.
13 His cheeks *are* like a bed of spices,
Banks of scented herbs.
His lips *are* lilies,
Dripping liquid myrrh.

14 His hands *are* rods of gold
Set with beryl.
His body *is* carved ivory
Inlaid *with* sapphires.
15 His legs *are* pillars of marble
Set on bases of fine gold.
His countenance *is* like Lebanon,
Excellent as the cedars.
16 His mouth *is* most sweet,
Yes, he *is* altogether lovely.
This *is* my beloved,
And this *is* my friend,
O daughters of Jerusalem!

THE DAUGHTERS OF JERUSALEM

6 Where has your beloved gone,
O fairest among women?
Where has your beloved turned aside,
That we may seek him with you?

THE SHULAMITE

2 My beloved has gone to his garden,
To the beds of spices,
To feed *his flock* in the gardens,
And to gather lilies.
3 I *am* my beloved's,
And my beloved *is* mine.
He feeds *his flock* among the lilies.

LIFE LESSONS

➤ 5:16 — *This is my beloved, and this is my friend, O daughters of Jerusalem!*

How many marriages fall apart because the spouses forget to nurture their friendship along with their romance? All important relationships are first good friendships—and that includes the one we have with God.

➤ 6:3 — *I am my beloved's, and my beloved is mine.*

Husbands and wives do not "own" each other, but they do belong to each other in an exclusive way that no one else can share. "Adulterer" is an ugly word in any language, in heaven as on earth.

WHAT THE BIBLE SAYS ABOUT **THE BEST FRIEND YOU WILL EVER HAVE**

Song 5:16

Many of us know the familiar hymn, "What a Friend We Have in Jesus." We all consider our Savior a great friend—but none of us have an exhaustive knowledge of the heights, depths, and breadth of His amazing friendship. Consider just a few of the elements of Jesus' loving relationship with you.

1. He has committed Himself to you as a friend for life. In fact, this commitment lasts more than an earthly lifetime; it's eternal. He will never leave you, no matter what you do. You may suffer some dashed expectations in your lifetime, but the Lord Himself will never disappoint you.

2. He remains open and transparent to you at all times. Jesus will show you as much about Himself as you desire to learn and are able to appreciate. He will never keep from you anything about Himself that you need to know.

3. He renews His loving overtures to you every day. He knows how to meet your deepest longings, and He remains sensitive to your wants as well as your needs.

What a friend we have in Jesus.

Jesus is an inspiring, comforting listener who will never thoughtlessly interrupt or be quick to criticize you. He attends wholeheartedly to your requests. He has so lovingly fixed His eyes on you that His heart hears exactly what you say.

What kind of friend is Jesus? John 15:13 answers that question: "Greater love has no one than this, than to lay down one's life for his friends." Jesus is the kind of friend who willingly laid down His life as payment for your sins—past, present, and future. Without complaint, He bore all your sorrows and suffering, while pledging never to leave you or forsake you (see John 14:18). Jesus is the friend who sticks closer than a brother (see Prov. 18:24), the friend who walks by your side through everything.

And because Jesus gave Himself once for many people, we His followers can give ourselves for a few. "He became poor, that you through His poverty might become rich" (2 Cor. 8:9). Who in your circle of influence needs the sacrifice of your time or caring?

See the Life Principles Index for further study:

1. *Our intimacy with God—His highest priority for our lives—determines the impact of our lives.*

25. *God blesses us so that we might bless others.*

ANSWERS TO LIFE'S QUESTIONS

What does God's love look like?

SONG 6:4

The notion of "true love" dominates much of popular culture. We purchase cards, shop for gifts, and plan romantic outings with our cherished one in mind.

God Himself places a high value on love (1 Cor. 13:13) and delights in expressing His wonderful love to us. Much of the time, however, we don't *feel* loved, do we? Sin has spoiled our capacity to understand God's love, to receive His love, and to love Him in return.

Thank God that our Savior, Jesus Christ, has remedied this problem! By liberating us from the power of sin and providing us with a new nature, we can now understand—at least, a little—our heavenly Father's wonderful love for us.

Divine love is *unconditional*—He showers us with it, regardless of who we are, where we have been, or what mistakes we have made. What matters to the Lord is that we belong to Him.

His love for us is also *absolute*—it never wavers or varies and knows no limitations. It always seeks our best, helping us to grow into the likeness of Jesus. Even when God disciplines us, He does so as a loving Father.

Understanding how much we are loved, and accepting God's love for us, frees us to live and love God's way. By loving Him with all our heart, soul, mind, and strength, we find the wisdom and power to love our neighbors in return.

What does loving God look like? Loving God means spending time deepening our relationship with Jesus and submitting to Him. We love Him when we give ourselves wholeheartedly to knowing Him and learning what pleases Him. We express our love when we obey Him.

The Word of God also tells us that when we love others, we are loving Jesus (Matt. 25:40). Loving others God's way means we will pursue God's best for them. We will ask God to show us what we can say and do on behalf of others. We will seek to answer the question, "How can I build them up and help them grow into Christ's likeness?" When we love people in obedience to God, we will find ourselves looking for ways to express God's love to them. Love demonstrates that we belong to Jesus (John 13:35).

We are created to be lovers of God and others. Dear child of God, won't you receive God's outpouring of love today?

See the Life Principles Index for further study:

1. Our intimacy with God—His highest priority for our lives—determines the impact of our lives.

12. Peace with God is the fruit of oneness with God.

25. God blesses us so that we might bless others.

Praise of the Shulamite's Beauty

THE BELOVED

4 O my love, you *are as* beautiful as Tirzah,
Lovely as Jerusalem,
Awesome as *an army* with banners!
5 Turn your eyes away from me,
For they have overcome me.
Your hair *is* like a flock of goats
Going down from Gilead.
6 Your teeth *are* like a flock of sheep
Which have come up from the washing;
Every one bears twins,
And none *is* barren among them.
7 Like a piece of pomegranate
Are your temples behind your veil.
8 There are sixty queens
And eighty concubines,
And virgins without number.
9 My dove, my perfect one,
Is the only one,
The only one of her mother,
The favorite of the one who bore her.
The daughters saw her
And called her blessed,
The queens and the concubines,
And they praised her.

10 Who is she who looks forth as the morning,
Fair as the moon,
Clear as the sun,
Awesome as *an army* with banners?

THE SHULAMITE

11 I went down to the garden of nuts
To see the verdure of the valley,

To see whether the vine had budded
And the pomegranates had bloomed.
12 Before I was even aware,
My soul had made me
As the chariots of my noble people.[a]

THE BELOVED AND HIS FRIENDS

13 Return, return, O Shulamite;
Return, return, that we may look upon
you!

THE SHULAMITE

What would you see in the Shulamite—
As it were, the dance of the two camps?[a]

Expressions of Praise

THE BELOVED

7 How beautiful are your feet in sandals,
O prince's daughter!
The curves of your thighs *are* like jewels,
The work of the hands of a skillful
workman.
2 Your navel *is* a rounded goblet;
It lacks no blended beverage.
Your waist *is* a heap of wheat
Set about with lilies.
3 Your two breasts *are* like two fawns,
Twins of a gazelle.
4 Your neck *is* like an ivory tower,
Your eyes *like* the pools in Heshbon
By the gate of Bath Rabbim.
Your nose *is* like the tower of Lebanon
Which looks toward Damascus.
5 Your head *crowns* you like *Mount* Carmel,
And the hair of your head *is* like purple;
A king *is* held captive by *your* tresses.

6 How fair and how pleasant you are,
O love, with your delights!
7 This stature of yours is like a palm tree,
And your breasts *like* its clusters.
8 I said, "I will go up to the palm tree,
I will take hold of its branches."
Let now your breasts be like clusters of
the vine,
The fragrance of your breath like apples,
9 And the roof of your mouth like the best
wine.

THE SHULAMITE

The wine goes *down* smoothly for my
beloved,
Moving gently the lips of sleepers.[a]

10 I *am* my beloved's,
And his desire *is* toward me.

11 Come, my beloved,
Let us go forth to the field;
Let us lodge in the villages.
12 Let us get up early to the vineyards;
Let us see if the vine has budded,
Whether the grape blossoms are open,
And the pomegranates are in bloom.
There I will give you my love.
13 The mandrakes give off a fragrance,
And at our gates *are* pleasant *fruits*,
All manner, new and old,
Which I have laid up for you, my
beloved.

8 Oh, that you were like my brother,
Who nursed at my mother's breasts!
If I should find you outside,
I would kiss you;
I would not be despised.
2 I would lead you *and* bring you
Into the house of my mother,
She *who* used to instruct me.
I would cause you to drink of spiced
wine,
Of the juice of my pomegranate.

(TO THE DAUGHTERS OF JERUSALEM)

3 His left hand *is* under my head,
And his right hand embraces me.
4 I charge you, O daughters of Jerusalem,
Do not stir up nor awaken love
Until it pleases.

Love Renewed in Lebanon

A RELATIVE

5 Who *is* this coming up from the
wilderness,
Leaning upon her beloved?

I awakened you under the apple tree.
There your mother brought you forth;
There she *who* bore you brought *you*
forth.

THE SHULAMITE TO HER BELOVED

6 Set me as a seal upon your heart,
As a seal upon your arm;
For love *is as* strong as death,

6:12 [a]Hebrew *Ammi Nadib* **6:13** [a]Hebrew *Mahanaim*
7:9 [a]Septuagint, Syriac, and Vulgate read *lips and teeth.*

LIFE LESSONS

➤ ***8:6 — Set me as a seal upon your heart, as a seal upon your arm . . . .***

True devotion begins in the heart and works its way out in loving expressions involving the rest of the body. Spouses want and need all of each other—and God wants the same thing.

Jealousy *as* cruel as the grave;[a]
Its flames *are* flames of fire,
A most vehement flame.[b]

✳ 7 Many waters cannot quench love,
Nor can the floods drown it.
If a man would give for love
All the wealth of his house,
It would be utterly despised.

THE SHULAMITE'S BROTHERS

8 We have a little sister,
And she has no breasts.
What shall we do for our sister
In the day when she is spoken for?
9 If she *is* a wall,
We will build upon her
A battlement of silver;
And if she *is* a door,
We will enclose her
With boards of cedar.

THE SHULAMITE

10 I *am* a wall,
And my breasts like towers;
Then I became in his eyes
As one who found peace.

11 Solomon had a vineyard at Baal Hamon;
He leased the vineyard to keepers;
Everyone was to bring for its fruit
A thousand silver *coins*.

(TO SOLOMON)

12 My own vineyard *is* before me.
You, O Solomon, *may have* a thousand,
And those who tend its fruit two hundred.

THE BELOVED

13 You who dwell in the gardens,
The companions listen for your voice—
Let me hear it!

THE SHULAMITE

14 Make haste, my beloved,
And be like a gazelle
Or a young stag
On the mountains of spices.

8:6 [a]Or *Sheol* [b]Literally *A flame of* YAH (a poetic form of *YHWH*, *the* LORD)

THE BOOK OF ISAIAH

Isaiah is something like a miniature Bible. The Bible's chapter divisions and even some of the book divisions have been developed over time by men, but it's interesting nevertheless: The first thirty-nine chapters of Isaiah (like the thirty-nine books of the Old Testament) predict judgment after judgment upon immoral and idolatrous people. Judah has sinned; the surrounding nations have sinned; the whole earth has sinned. Judgment must come, for God cannot allow such blatant sin to go unpunished forever. The final twenty-seven chapters (like the twenty-seven books of the New Testament), focus more on a message of hope. The Messiah is coming as a Savior and a Sovereign to bear a cross and to wear a crown, and the Lord will restore the fortunes of His people and give them a heart to follow Him completely.

The English name "Isaiah" comes from the Hebrew *Yesha'yahu* and its shortened form, *Yeshaiah*, which means "Yahweh is salvation." This name provides an excellent summary of the contents of the book. God saves! And He does so, not because His people deserve it, but because of His great name and amazing love (43:25; 48:11).

Isaiah's prophetic ministry spanned the reigns of four kings of Judah (Uzziah, Jotham, Ahaz, and Hezekiah) and covered at least forty years, and perhaps as many as sixty. Tradition says he was sawn in half during the reign of the evil king Manasseh (compare Heb. 11:37).

Isaiah is the most-quoted Old Testament book in the New Testament, and the prophet Isaiah is generally regarded as the greatest of the Old Testament "writing prophets" (those who wrote books eventually included in the Bible) because so many of his prophecies focus on the coming Messiah and on an age of remarkable divine blessing, when "the earth shall be full of the knowledge of the LORD as the waters cover the sea" (11:9).

Themes: The "Holy One of Israel" (see 1:4; 5:19; 10:20; etc.) calls His people to a life of righteousness and justice, but when they turn their backs on Him and His ways, the inevitable result is judgment. Yet God will always preserve a remnant for Himself and will save and rescue them in amazing ways that will ultimately bless the whole world.

Author: Isaiah, the son of Amoz.

Time: Isaiah prophesied from the time of Uzziah (c. 740 B.C.) to the time of Hezekiah (c. 681 B.C.).

Structure: Chapters 1—39 of Isaiah cover events and prophecies in Israel's history leading up to the Babylonian captivity. Chapters 40—66 contain warnings, predictions, and prophecies concerning Judah from the time of the Babylonian captivity through the arrival of the Messiah, Jesus Christ, and on into the distant future.

As you read Isaiah, watch for several life principles that play an important role in this book:

13. Listening to God is essential to walking with God. *See Isaiah 1:2, 10; 28:12, 23; pages 781; 807; 808.*

21. Obedience always brings blessing. *See Isaiah 1:18, 19; page 781.*

14. God acts on behalf of those who wait for Him. *See Isaiah 8:17; 26:8; 30:18; 64:4; pages 789; 804; 810; 847.*

1 The vision of Isaiah the son of Amoz, which he saw concerning Judah and Jerusalem in the days of Uzziah, Jotham, Ahaz, *and* Hezekiah, kings of Judah.

The Wickedness of Judah

2 Hear, O heavens, and give ear, O earth!
For the LORD has spoken:
"I have nourished and brought up children,
And they have rebelled against Me;
3 The ox knows its owner
And the donkey its master's crib;
But Israel does not know,
My people do not consider."

4 Alas, sinful nation,
A people laden with iniquity,
A brood of evildoers,
Children who are corrupters!
They have forsaken the LORD,
They have provoked to anger
The Holy One of Israel,
They have turned away backward.

➤ 5 Why should you be stricken again?
You will revolt more and more.
The whole head is sick,
And the whole heart faints.
6 From the sole of the foot even to the head,
There is no soundness in it,
But wounds and bruises and putrefying sores;
They have not been closed or bound up,
Or soothed with ointment.

7 Your country *is* desolate,
Your cities *are* burned with fire;
Strangers devour your land in your presence;
And *it is* desolate, as overthrown by strangers.
8 So the daughter of Zion is left as a booth in a vineyard,
As a hut in a garden of cucumbers,
As a besieged city.
9 Unless the LORD of hosts
Had left to us a very small remnant,
We would have become like Sodom,
We would have been made like Gomorrah.

10 Hear the word of the LORD,
You rulers of Sodom;
Give ear to the law of our God,
You people of Gomorrah:
11 "To what purpose *is* the multitude of your sacrifices to Me?"
Says the LORD.
"I have had enough of burnt offerings of rams
And the fat of fed cattle.
I do not delight in the blood of bulls,
Or of lambs or goats.

12 "When you come to appear before Me,
Who has required this from your hand,
To trample My courts?
13 Bring no more futile sacrifices;
Incense is an abomination to Me.
The New Moons, the Sabbaths, and the calling of assemblies—
I cannot endure iniquity and the sacred meeting.
14 Your New Moons and your appointed feasts
My soul hates;
They are a trouble to Me,
I am weary of bearing *them*.
15 When you spread out your hands,
I will hide My eyes from you;
Even though you make many prayers,
I will not hear.
Your hands are full of blood.

16 "Wash yourselves, make yourselves clean;
Put away the evil of your doings from before My eyes.
Cease to do evil,
17 Learn to do good;
Seek justice,
Rebuke the oppressor;[a]
Defend the fatherless,
Plead for the widow.

18 "Come now, and let us reason together," ➤
Says the LORD,
"Though your sins are like scarlet,
They shall be as white as snow;
Though they are red like crimson,
They shall be as wool.
19 If you are willing and obedient, ✳
You shall eat the good of the land;
20 But if you refuse and rebel,
You shall be devoured by the sword";
For the mouth of the LORD has spoken.

The Degenerate City

21 How the faithful city has become a harlot!

1:17 [a]Some ancient versions read *the oppressed.*

LIFE LESSONS

➤ 1:5 — *Why should you be stricken again?*

The Lord wants to bless us for our obedience, not discipline us for our disobedience. So He urges us to turn from our sin and follow Him, so that He can do good to us.

➤ 1:18 — *"Come now, and let us reason together."*

Dialogue builds relationships. Genuine prayer has all of the qualities and characteristics of a deeply meaningful conversation between two people. This image of God and man sitting down together for a good talk is our best image of prayer.

It was full of justice;
Righteousness lodged in it,
But now murderers.
22 Your silver has become dross,
Your wine mixed with water.
23 Your princes *are* rebellious,
And companions of thieves;
Everyone loves bribes,
And follows after rewards.
They do not defend the fatherless,
Nor does the cause of the widow come before them.

24 Therefore the Lord says,
The LORD of hosts, the Mighty One of Israel,
"Ah, I will rid Myself of My adversaries,
And take vengeance on My enemies.
25 I will turn My hand against you,
And thoroughly purge away your dross,
And take away all your alloy.
26 I will restore your judges as at the first,
And your counselors as at the beginning.
Afterward you shall be called the city of righteousness, the faithful city."

27 Zion shall be redeemed with justice,
And her penitents with righteousness.
28 The destruction of transgressors and of sinners *shall be* together,
And those who forsake the LORD shall be consumed.
29 For they[a] shall be ashamed of the terebinth trees
Which you have desired;
And you shall be embarrassed because of the gardens
Which you have chosen.
30 For you shall be as a terebinth whose leaf fades,
And as a garden that has no water.
31 The strong shall be as tinder,
And the work of it as a spark;
Both will burn together,
And no one shall quench *them*.

The Future House of God

2 The word that Isaiah the son of Amoz saw concerning Judah and Jerusalem.

2 Now it shall come to pass in the latter days
That the mountain of the LORD's house
Shall be established on the top of the mountains,
And shall be exalted above the hills;
And all nations shall flow to it.
3 Many people shall come and say,
"Come, and let us go up to the mountain of the LORD,
To the house of the God of Jacob;
He will teach us His ways,
And we shall walk in His paths."
For out of Zion shall go forth the law,
And the word of the LORD from Jerusalem.
4 He shall judge between the nations,
And rebuke many people;
They shall beat their swords into plowshares,
And their spears into pruning hooks;
Nation shall not lift up sword against nation,
Neither shall they learn war anymore.

The Day of the LORD

5 O house of Jacob, come and let us walk
In the light of the LORD.

6 For You have forsaken Your people, the house of Jacob,
Because they are filled with eastern ways;
They *are* soothsayers like the Philistines,
And they are pleased with the children of foreigners.
7 Their land is also full of silver and gold,
And there is no end to their treasures;
Their land is also full of horses,
And there is no end to their chariots.
8 Their land is also full of idols;
They worship the work of their own hands,
That which their own fingers have made.
9 People bow down,
And each man humbles himself;
Therefore do not forgive them.

10 Enter into the rock, and hide in the dust,
From the terror of the LORD
And the glory of His majesty.
11 The lofty looks of man shall be humbled,
The haughtiness of men shall be bowed down,
And the LORD alone shall be exalted in that day.

12 For the day of the LORD of hosts
Shall come upon everything proud and lofty,

1:29 [a]Following Masoretic Text, Septuagint, and Vulgate; some Hebrew manuscripts and Targum read *you*.

LIFE LESSONS

➤ 2:3 — *" . . . He will teach us His ways, and we shall walk in His paths . . . ."*

God designed a life of faith to be a community affair. He teaches *us* His ways, so that *we* can walk in His paths. If you're trying to go it alone in your faith, you'll never grow as God wants you to.

Upon everything lifted up—
And it shall be brought low—
13 Upon all the cedars of Lebanon *that are* high and lifted up,
And upon all the oaks of Bashan;
14 Upon all the high mountains,
And upon all the hills *that are* lifted up;
15 Upon every high tower,
And upon every fortified wall;
16 Upon all the ships of Tarshish,
And upon all the beautiful sloops.
➤ 17 The loftiness of man shall be bowed down,
And the haughtiness of men shall be brought low;
The LORD alone will be exalted in that day,
18 But the idols He shall utterly abolish.

19 They shall go into the holes of the rocks,
And into the caves of the earth,
From the terror of the LORD
And the glory of His majesty,
When He arises to shake the earth mightily.

20 In that day a man will cast away his idols of silver
And his idols of gold,
Which they made, *each* for himself to worship,
To the moles and bats,
21 To go into the clefts of the rocks,
And into the crags of the rugged rocks,
From the terror of the LORD
And the glory of His majesty,
When He arises to shake the earth mightily.

22 Sever yourselves from such a man,
Whose breath *is* in his nostrils;
For of what account is he?

Judgment on Judah and Jerusalem

3 For behold, the Lord, the LORD of hosts,
Takes away from Jerusalem and from Judah
The stock and the store,
The whole supply of bread and the whole supply of water;
2 The mighty man and the man of war,
The judge and the prophet,
And the diviner and the elder;
3 The captain of fifty and the honorable man,
The counselor and the skillful artisan,
And the expert enchanter.

4 "I will give children *to be* their princes,
And babes shall rule over them.
5 The people will be oppressed,
Every one by another and every one by his neighbor;
The child will be insolent toward the elder,
And the base toward the honorable."

6 When a man takes hold of his brother
In the house of his father, *saying,*
"You have clothing;
You be our ruler,
And *let* these ruins *be* under your power,"[a]
7 In that day he will protest, saying,
"I cannot cure *your* ills,
For in my house *is* neither food nor clothing;
Do not make me a ruler of the people."

8 For Jerusalem stumbled,
And Judah is fallen,
Because their tongue and their doings
Are against the LORD,
To provoke the eyes of His glory.
9 The look on their countenance witnesses against them,
And they declare their sin as Sodom;
They do not hide *it.*
Woe to their soul!
For they have brought evil upon themselves.

10 "Say to the righteous that *it shall be* well *with them,*

3:6 [a]Literally *hand*

LIFE LESSONS

➤ 2:17 — *The loftiness of man shall be bowed down, and the haughtiness of men shall be brought low; the LORD alone will be exalted in that day . . . .*

A day is coming when human pride and arrogance will be smashed forever, and the entire world will acknowledge that God alone rules. As followers of Christ, we can anticipate that day by willingly humbling ourselves.

➤ 3:8 — *. . . Judah is fallen, because their tongue and their doings are against the LORD, to provoke the eyes of His glory.*

Sin is an affront to the glory of God, an insult to His goodness and righteousness. It is especially serious when a believer sins, for God has connected His holy name with that believer, whose conduct reflects on God's character.

➤ 3:10 — *"Say to the righteous that it shall be well with them, for they shall eat the fruit of their doings."*

God always rewards faithful and obedient behavior. Although God would judge Judah for her sin, He wanted to encourage the few righteous believers who remained to continue living for Him, for He would remember their good deeds.

For they shall eat the fruit of their
doings.
11 Woe to the wicked! *It shall be* ill *with
him,*
For the reward of his hands shall be
given him.
12 *As for* My people, children *are* their
oppressors,
And women rule over them.
O My people! Those who lead you cause
you to err,
And destroy the way of your paths."

Oppression and Luxury Condemned

13 The LORD stands up to plead,
And stands to judge the people.
14 The LORD will enter into judgment
With the elders of His people
And His princes:
"For you have eaten up the vineyard;
The plunder of the poor *is* in your
houses.
15 What do you mean by crushing My
people
And grinding the faces of the poor?"
Says the Lord GOD of hosts.

16 Moreover the LORD says:

"Because the daughters of Zion are
haughty,
And walk with outstretched necks
And wanton eyes,
Walking and mincing *as* they go,
Making a jingling with their feet,
17 Therefore the Lord will strike with a scab
The crown of the head of the daughters
of Zion,
And the LORD will uncover their secret
parts."

18 In that day the Lord will take away the
finery:
The jingling anklets, the scarves, and the
crescents;
19 The pendants, the bracelets, and the veils;
20 The headdresses, the leg ornaments, and
the headbands;
The perfume boxes, the charms,
21 and the rings;
The nose jewels,
22 the festal apparel, and the mantles;
The outer garments, the purses,
23 and the mirrors;
The fine linen, the turbans, and the robes.

24 And so it shall be:

Instead of a sweet smell there will be a
stench;
Instead of a sash, a rope;
Instead of well-set hair, baldness;
Instead of a rich robe, a girding of
sackcloth;
And branding instead of beauty.
25 Your men shall fall by the sword,
And your mighty in the war.

26 Her gates shall lament and mourn,
And she *being* desolate shall sit on the
ground.

4 And in that day seven women shall take
hold of one man, saying,
"We will eat our own food and wear our
own apparel;
Only let us be called by your name,
To take away our reproach."

The Renewal of Zion

2 In that day the Branch of the LORD shall
be beautiful and glorious;
And the fruit of the earth *shall be*
excellent and appealing
For those of Israel who have escaped.

3 And it shall come to pass that *he who is*
left in Zion and remains in Jerusalem will be
called holy—everyone who is recorded
among the living in Jerusalem.
4 When the Lord has washed away the filth
of the daughters of Zion, and purged the
blood of Jerusalem from her midst, by the
spirit of judgment and by the spirit of burning,
5 then the LORD will create above every
dwelling place of Mount Zion, and above her
assemblies, a cloud and smoke by day and the
shining of a flaming fire by night. For over all
the glory there *will be* a covering.
6 And there will be a tabernacle for shade in
the daytime from the heat, for a place of
refuge, and for a shelter from storm and rain.

God's Disappointing Vineyard

5 Now let me sing to my Well-beloved
A song of my Beloved regarding His
vineyard:

My Well-beloved has a vineyard
On a very fruitful hill.
2 He dug it up and cleared out its stones,
And planted it with the choicest vine.
He built a tower in its midst,
And also made a winepress in it;

LIFE LESSONS

➤ ***4:2 — In that day the Branch of the Lord shall be beautiful and glorious . . . .***

Isaiah is the first prophet to call the coming Messiah by the name "Branch." He sees a time when Jesus will reign in glory and bring prosperity and joy to the whole world (Is. 11:1; Jer. 23:5; 33:15).

So He expected *it* to bring forth *good* grapes,
But it brought forth wild grapes.

3 "And now, O inhabitants of Jerusalem and men of Judah,
Judge, please, between Me and My vineyard.
4 What more could have been done to My vineyard
That I have not done in it?
Why then, when I expected *it* to bring forth *good* grapes,
Did it bring forth wild grapes?
5 And now, please let Me tell you what I will do to My vineyard:
I will take away its hedge, and it shall be burned;
And break down its wall, and it shall be trampled down.
6 I will lay it waste;
It shall not be pruned or dug,
But there shall come up briers and thorns.
I will also command the clouds
That they rain no rain on it."
7 For the vineyard of the LORD of hosts *is* the house of Israel,
And the men of Judah are His pleasant plant.
He looked for justice, but behold, oppression;
For righteousness, but behold, a cry *for help*.

Impending Judgment on Excesses

8 Woe to those who join house to house;
They add field to field,
Till *there is* no place
Where they may dwell alone in the midst of the land!
9 In my hearing the LORD of hosts *said,*
"Truly, many houses shall be desolate,
Great and beautiful ones, without inhabitant.
10 For ten acres of vineyard shall yield one bath,
And a homer of seed shall yield one ephah."

11 Woe to those who rise early in the morning,
That they may follow intoxicating drink;
Who continue until night, *till* wine inflames them!
12 The harp and the strings,
The tambourine and flute,
And wine are in their feasts;
But they do not regard the work of the LORD,
Nor consider the operation of His hands.

13 Therefore my people have gone into captivity,
Because *they have* no knowledge;
Their honorable men *are* famished,
And their multitude dried up with thirst.
14 Therefore Sheol has enlarged itself
And opened its mouth beyond measure;
Their glory and their multitude and their pomp,
And he who is jubilant, shall descend into it.
15 People shall be brought down,
Each man shall be humbled,
And the eyes of the lofty shall be humbled.
16 But the LORD of hosts shall be exalted in judgment,
And God who is holy shall be hallowed in righteousness.
17 Then the lambs shall feed in their pasture,
And in the waste places of the fat ones strangers shall eat.

18 Woe to those who draw iniquity with cords of vanity,
And sin as if with a cart rope;
19 That say, "Let Him make speed *and* hasten His work,
That we may see *it;*
And let the counsel of the Holy One of Israel draw near and come,
That we may know *it.*"

20 Woe to those who call evil good, and good evil;
Who put darkness for light, and light for darkness;
Who put bitter for sweet, and sweet for bitter!

21 Woe to *those who are* wise in their own eyes,
And prudent in their own sight!

LIFE LESSONS

➢ **5:12 — *The harp and the strings, the tambourine and flute, and wine are in their feasts; but they do not regard the work of the LORD, nor consider the operation of His hands.***

God gives us music and food and celebrations to enjoy, but never to enjoy apart from Him or instead of Him or in neglect of Him. He is to be at the center of all we do, all the time.

➢ **5:20 — *Woe to those who call evil good, and good evil; who put darkness for light, and light for darkness; who put bitter for sweet, and sweet for bitter!***

When God in His Word calls something evil, it is evil. When He labels a thing bitter, no multitude of religious authorities can make it sweet through their solemn declarations. God is our absolute authority.

Life Examples:

ISAIAH

A Life-Changing Encounter

IS. 6:1–7

Isaiah's whole life changed when he saw the majestic Lord seated on His heavenly throne. His awesome vision of God pierced him to the very core and prompted him to cry out, "I am a man of unclean lips . . . . For my eyes have seen the King, the LORD of hosts" (6:5).

You will never deal effectively with your sin without first realizing who God is. When you study His Word and begin to grasp His holiness, a deep reverence for Him grows in your heart. You, like Isaiah, are humbled before Him and realize that you fall far short of His holiness. Yet before discouragement can creep in, you also realize that God loves you deeply.

Through Jesus' death on the cross, God takes away your sins and shows you His amazing love. The crucifixion and resurrection are the beautiful visions God gives *you* of His awesome holiness and majesty.

See the Life Principles Index for further study:

4. The awareness of God's presence energizes us for our work.

15. Brokenness is God's requirement for maximum usefulness.

22 Woe to men mighty at drinking wine,
Woe to men valiant for mixing intoxicating drink,
23 Who justify the wicked for a bribe,
And take away justice from the righteous man!

24 Therefore, as the fire devours the stubble,
And the flame consumes the chaff,
So their root will be as rottenness,
And their blossom will ascend like dust;
Because they have rejected the law of the LORD of hosts,
And despised the word of the Holy One of Israel.
25 Therefore the anger of the LORD is aroused against His people;
He has stretched out His hand against them
And stricken them,
And the hills trembled.
Their carcasses *were* as refuse in the midst of the streets.

For all this His anger is not turned away,
But His hand *is* stretched out still.

26 He will lift up a banner to the nations from afar,
And will whistle to them from the end of the earth;
Surely they shall come with speed, swiftly.
27 No one will be weary or stumble among them,
No one will slumber or sleep;
Nor will the belt on their loins be loosed,
Nor the strap of their sandals be broken;
28 Whose arrows *are* sharp,
And all their bows bent;
Their horses' hooves will seem like flint,
And their wheels like a whirlwind.
29 Their roaring *will be* like a lion,
They will roar like young lions;
Yes, they will roar
And lay hold of the prey;
They will carry *it* away safely,
And no one will deliver.
30 In that day they will roar against them
Like the roaring of the sea.
And if *one* looks to the land,
Behold, darkness *and* sorrow;
And the light is darkened by the clouds.

Isaiah Called to Be a Prophet

6 In the year that King Uzziah died, I saw
the Lord sitting on a throne, high and
lifted up, and the train of His *robe* filled the
temple.
2 Above it stood seraphim; each one had six
wings: with two he covered his face, with two
he covered his feet, and with two he flew.
3 And one cried to another and said: ➤

"Holy, holy, holy *is* the LORD of hosts;
The whole earth *is* full of His glory!"

LIFE LESSONS

➤ **6:3 — *"Holy, holy, holy is the LORD of hosts; the whole earth is full of His glory!"***

When the angels cry out that God is "holy," they mean that He is absolutely pure, completely separated from sin, righteous and just and spotless. So He tells us, "Be holy, for I am holy" (1 Pet. 1:16).

4 And the posts of the door were shaken by
the voice of him who cried out, and the house
was filled with smoke.
5 So I said:

"Woe *is* me, for I am undone!
Because I *am* a man of unclean lips,
And I dwell in the midst of a people of
unclean lips;
For my eyes have seen the King,
The LORD of hosts."

6 Then one of the seraphim flew to me, having in his hand a live coal *which* he had taken
with the tongs from the altar.
7 And he touched my mouth *with it*, and
said:

"Behold, this has touched your lips;
Your iniquity is taken away,
And your sin purged."

➤ **8** Also I heard the voice of the Lord, saying:

"Whom shall I send,
And who will go for Us?"

Then I said, "Here *am* I! Send me."
9 And He said, "Go, and tell this people:

'Keep on hearing, but do not understand;
Keep on seeing, but do not perceive.'

10 "Make the heart of this people dull,
And their ears heavy,
And shut their eyes;
Lest they see with their eyes,
And hear with their ears,
And understand with their heart,
And return and be healed."

11 Then I said, "Lord, how long?" And He answered:

"Until the cities are laid waste and without
inhabitant,
The houses are without a man,
The land is utterly desolate,
12 The LORD has removed men far away,
And the forsaken places *are* many in the
midst of the land.
13 But yet a tenth *will be* in it,
And will return and be for consuming,
As a terebinth tree or as an oak,
Whose stump *remains* when it is cut
down.
So the holy seed *shall be* its stump."

Isaiah Sent to King Ahaz

7 Now it came to pass in the days of Ahaz
the son of Jotham, the son of Uzziah, king
of Judah, *that* Rezin king of Syria and Pekah
the son of Remaliah, king of Israel, went up to
Jerusalem to *make* war against it, but could
not prevail against it.
2 And it was told to the house of David, saying, "Syria's forces are deployed in Ephraim."
So his heart and the heart of his people were
moved as the trees of the woods are moved
with the wind.
3 Then the LORD said to Isaiah, "Go out now
to meet Ahaz, you and Shear-Jashub[a] your
son, at the end of the aqueduct from the upper
pool, on the highway to the Fuller's Field,
4 "and say to him: 'Take heed, and be quiet;
do not fear or be fainthearted for these two
stubs of smoking firebrands, for the fierce
anger of Rezin and Syria, and the son of Remaliah.
5 'Because Syria, Ephraim, and the son of
Remaliah have plotted evil against you, saying,
6 "Let us go up against Judah and trouble it,
and let us make a gap in its wall for ourselves,
and set a king over them, the son of Tabel"—
7 'thus says the Lord GOD:

"It shall not stand,
Nor shall it come to pass.
8 For the head of Syria *is* Damascus,
And the head of Damascus *is* Rezin.
Within sixty-five years Ephraim will be
broken,
So that it will not *be* a people.
9 The head of Ephraim *is* Samaria, ➤
And the head of Samaria *is* Remaliah's
son.
If you will not believe,
Surely you shall not be established."'"

The Immanuel Prophecy

10 Moreover the LORD spoke again to Ahaz,
saying,
11 "Ask a sign for yourself from the LORD
your God; ask it either in the depth or in the
height above."
12 But Ahaz said, "I will not ask, nor will I
test the LORD!"

7:3 [a]Literally *A Remnant Shall Return*

LIFE LESSONS

➤ **6:8 — *Also I heard the voice of the Lord, saying: "Whom shall I send, and who will go for Us?" Then I said, "Here am I! Send me."***

God first prepared Isaiah for service, then Isaiah offered himself to serve. God will never call us to do something for which He hasn't equipped us, nor will He force us to serve Him. He wants equipped, willing servants.

➤ **7:9 — *". . . If you will not believe, surely you shall not be established."***

We will never go wrong by putting our trust in God and living by His promises, but we will have no end of trouble if we refuse to believe that He will do exactly as He has said.

13 Then he said, "Hear now, O house of David! *Is it* a small thing for you to weary men, but will you weary my God also?
➤ 14 "Therefore the Lord Himself will give you a sign: Behold, the virgin shall conceive and bear a Son, and shall call His name Immanuel.[a]
15 "Curds and honey He shall eat, that He may know to refuse the evil and choose the good.
16 "For before the Child shall know to refuse the evil and choose the good, the land that you dread will be forsaken by both her kings.
17 "The LORD will bring the king of Assyria upon you and your people and your father's house—days that have not come since the day that Ephraim departed from Judah."

18 And it shall come to pass in that day
That the LORD will whistle for the fly
That *is* in the farthest part of the rivers of
Egypt,
And for the bee that *is* in the land of
Assyria.
19 They will come, and all of them will rest
In the desolate valleys and in the clefts of
the rocks,
And on all thorns and in all pastures.

20 In the same day the Lord will shave with
a hired razor,
With those from beyond the River,[a] with
the king of Assyria,
The head and the hair of the legs,
And will also remove the beard.

21 It shall be in that day
That a man will keep alive a young cow
and two sheep;
22 So it shall be, from the abundance of
milk they give,
That he will eat curds;
For curds and honey everyone will eat
who is left in the land.

23 It shall happen in that day,
That wherever there could be a thousand
vines
Worth a thousand *shekels* of silver,
It will be for briers and thorns.
24 With arrows and bows *men* will come
there,
Because all the land will become briers
and thorns.

25 And to any hill which could be dug with
the hoe,
You will not go there for fear of briers
and thorns;
But it will become a range for oxen
And a place for sheep to roam.

Assyria Will Invade the Land

8 Moreover the LORD said to me, "Take a large scroll, and write on it with a man's pen concerning Maher-Shalal-Hash-Baz.[a]
2 "And I will take for Myself faithful witnesses to record, Uriah the priest and Zechariah the son of Jeberechiah."
3 Then I went to the prophetess, and she conceived and bore a son. Then the LORD said to me, "Call his name Maher-Shalal-Hash-Baz;
4 "for before the child shall have knowledge to cry 'My father' and 'My mother,' the riches of Damascus and the spoil of Samaria will be taken away before the king of Assyria."
5 The LORD also spoke to me again, saying:

6 "Inasmuch as these people refused
The waters of Shiloah that flow softly,
And rejoice in Rezin and in Remaliah's
son;
7 Now therefore, behold, the Lord brings
up over them
The waters of the River,[a] strong and
mighty—
The king of Assyria and all his glory;
He will go up over all his channels
And go over all his banks.
8 He will pass through Judah,
He will overflow and pass over,
He will reach up to the neck;
And the stretching out of his wings
Will fill the breadth of Your land,
O Immanuel.[a]

9 "Be shattered, O you peoples, and be
broken in pieces!
Give ear, all you from far countries.
Gird yourselves, but be broken in
pieces;
Gird yourselves, but be broken in
pieces.
10 Take counsel together, but it will come to
nothing;
Speak the word, but it will not stand,
For God *is* with us."[a]

7:14 [a]Literally *God-With-Us* **7:20** [a]That is, the Euphrates **8:1** [a]Literally *Speed the Spoil, Hasten the Booty* **8:7** [a]That is, the Euphrates **8:8** [a]Literally *God-With-Us* **8:10** [a]Hebrew *Immanuel*

LIFE LESSONS

➤ **7:14 — . . . *Behold, the virgin shall conceive and bear a Son, and shall call His name Immanuel.***

"Immanuel" means "God with us" and functions more as a title than a proper name. The angel told Mary to call her Son "Jesus," which means "God saves." So Jesus is the God among us who saves (Matt. 1:21, 23).

Fear God, Heed His Word

11 For the LORD spoke thus to me with a strong hand, and instructed me that I should not walk in the way of this people, saying:

12 "Do not say, 'A conspiracy,'
Concerning all that this people call a conspiracy,
Nor be afraid of their threats, nor be troubled.
➤ 13 The LORD of hosts, Him you shall hallow;
Let Him *be* your fear,
And *let* Him *be* your dread.
14 He will be as a sanctuary,
But a stone of stumbling and a rock of offense
To both the houses of Israel,
As a trap and a snare to the inhabitants of Jerusalem.
15 And many among them shall stumble;
They shall fall and be broken,
Be snared and taken."

16 Bind up the testimony,
Seal the law among my disciples.
17 And I will wait on the LORD,
Who hides His face from the house of Jacob;
And I will hope in Him.
18 Here am I and the children whom the LORD has given me!
We are for signs and wonders in Israel
From the LORD of hosts,
Who dwells in Mount Zion.

19 And when they say to you, "Seek those who are mediums and wizards, who whisper and mutter," should not a people seek their God? *Should they seek* the dead on behalf of the living?
➤ 20 To the law and to the testimony! If they do not speak according to this word, *it is* because *there is* no light in them.
21 They will pass through it hard-pressed and hungry; and it shall happen, when they are hungry, that they will be enraged and curse their king and their God, and look upward.
22 Then they will look to the earth, and see trouble and darkness, gloom of anguish; and *they will be* driven into darkness.

The Government of the Promised Son

9 Nevertheless the gloom *will* not *be* upon her who *is* distressed,
As when at first He lightly esteemed
The land of Zebulun and the land of Naphtali,
And afterward more heavily oppressed *her*,
By the way of the sea, beyond the Jordan,
In Galilee of the Gentiles.
2 The people who walked in darkness ➤
Have seen a great light;
Those who dwelt in the land of the shadow of death,
Upon them a light has shined.

3 You have multiplied the nation
And increased its joy;[a]
They rejoice before You
According to the joy of harvest,
As *men* rejoice when they divide the spoil.
4 For You have broken the yoke of his burden
And the staff of his shoulder,
The rod of his oppressor,
As in the day of Midian.
5 For every warrior's sandal from the noisy battle,
And garments rolled in blood,
Will be used for burning *and* fuel of fire.

6 For unto us a Child is born,
Unto us a Son is given;
And the government will be upon His shoulder.
And His name will be called
Wonderful, Counselor, Mighty God,
Everlasting Father, Prince of Peace.
7 Of the increase of *His* government and peace
There will be no end,
Upon the throne of David and over His kingdom,
To order it and establish it with judgment and justice

9:3 [a]Following Qere and Targum; Kethib and Vulgate read *not increased joy;* Septuagint reads *Most of the people You brought down in Your joy.*

LIFE LESSONS

➤ 8:13 — *"The LORD of hosts, Him you shall hallow; let Him be your fear, and let Him be your dread."*

We do not have to fear the threats of men if we fear God above all else. When human threats seem more real to us than the promises of God, remember: God's Word will stand when men turn to dust.

➤ 8:20 — *To the law and to the testimony! If they do not speak according to this word, it is because there is no light in them.*

We live in a time when men demean the Bible and value their wisdom and insight above all else. But never bet against the Word of God! Regardless of current opinion, it proclaims the truth and will be completely vindicated.

➤ 9:2 — *The people who walked in darkness have seen a great light . . . .*

Jesus grew up in Nazareth of Galilee, the area in view here. His parents learned that He would be "a light to bring revelation to the Gentiles" (Luke 2:32), and He called Himself "the light of the world" (John 8:12).

From that time forward, even forever.
The zeal of the Lord of hosts will perform this.

The Punishment of Samaria

8 The Lord sent a word against Jacob,
And it has fallen on Israel.
9 All the people will know—
Ephraim and the inhabitant of Samaria—
Who say in pride and arrogance of heart:
10 "The bricks have fallen down,
But we will rebuild with hewn stones;
The sycamores are cut down,
But we will replace *them* with cedars."
11 Therefore the LORD shall set up
The adversaries of Rezin against him,
And spur his enemies on,
12 The Syrians before and the Philistines behind;
And they shall devour Israel with an open mouth.

For all this His anger is not turned away,
But His hand *is* stretched out still.

➤ **13** For the people do not turn to Him who strikes them,
Nor do they seek the LORD of hosts.
14 Therefore the LORD will cut off head and tail from Israel,
Palm branch and bulrush in one day.
15 The elder and honorable, he *is* the head;
The prophet who teaches lies, he *is* the tail.
16 For the leaders of this people cause *them* to err,
And *those who are* led by them are destroyed.
17 Therefore the Lord will have no joy in their young men,
Nor have mercy on their fatherless and widows;
For everyone *is* a hypocrite and an evildoer,
And every mouth speaks folly.

For all this His anger is not turned away,
But His hand *is* stretched out still.

18 For wickedness burns as the fire;
It shall devour the briers and thorns,
And kindle in the thickets of the forest;
They shall mount up *like* rising smoke.
19 Through the wrath of the LORD of hosts
The land is burned up,
And the people shall be as fuel for the fire;
No man shall spare his brother.
20 And he shall snatch on the right hand
And be hungry;
He shall devour on the left hand
And not be satisfied;
Every man shall eat the flesh of his own arm.
21 Manasseh *shall devour* Ephraim, and Ephraim Manasseh;
Together they *shall be* against Judah.

For all this His anger is not turned away,
But His hand *is* stretched out still.

10 "Woe to those who decree unrighteous decrees,
Who write misfortune,
Which they have prescribed
2 To rob the needy of justice,
And to take what is right from the poor of My people,
That widows may be their prey,
And *that* they may rob the fatherless.
3 What will you do in the day of punishment,
And in the desolation *which* will come from afar?
To whom will you flee for help?
And where will you leave your glory?
4 Without Me they shall bow down among the prisoners,
And they shall fall among the slain."

For all this His anger is not turned away,
But His hand *is* stretched out still.

Arrogant Assyria Also Judged

5 "Woe to Assyria, the rod of My anger
And the staff in whose hand is My indignation.
6 I will send him against an ungodly nation,
And against the people of My wrath
I will give him charge,
To seize the spoil, to take the prey,
And to tread them down like the mire of the streets.
7 Yet he does not mean so,
Nor does his heart think so;
But *it is* in his heart to destroy,
And cut off not a few nations.
8 For he says,
'*Are* not my princes altogether kings?
9 *Is* not Calno like Carchemish?
Is not Hamath like Arpad?
Is not Samaria like Damascus?

LIFE LESSONS

➤ **9:13 — *For the people do not turn to Him who strikes them, nor do they seek the LORD of hosts.***

God spent many years warning Israel to turn from its wicked ways before He finally sent the Assyrians to destroy the nation and carry her people into captivity. He uses adversity to turn us to Him, not to destroy us.

10 As my hand has found the kingdoms of
the idols,
Whose carved images excelled those of
Jerusalem and Samaria,
11 As I have done to Samaria and her idols,
Shall I not do also to Jerusalem and her
idols?'"

12 Therefore it shall come to pass, when the
Lord has performed all His work on Mount
Zion and on Jerusalem, *that He will say,* "I
will punish the fruit of the arrogant heart of
the king of Assyria, and the glory of his
haughty looks."
13 For he says:

"By the strength of my hand I have done
it,
And by my wisdom, for I am prudent;
Also I have removed the boundaries of
the people,
And have robbed their treasuries;
So I have put down the inhabitants like a
valiant *man.*
14 My hand has found like a nest the riches
of the people,
And as one gathers eggs *that are* left,
I have gathered all the earth;
And there was no one who moved *his*
wing,
Nor opened *his* mouth with even a peep."

➤ **15** Shall the ax boast itself against him who
chops with it?
Or shall the saw exalt itself against him
who saws with it?
As if a rod could wield *itself* against
those who lift it up,
Or as if a staff could lift up, *as if it were*
not wood!
16 Therefore the Lord, the Lord[a] of hosts,
Will send leanness among his fat ones;
And under his glory
He will kindle a burning
Like the burning of a fire.
17 So the Light of Israel will be for a fire,
And his Holy One for a flame;
It will burn and devour
His thorns and his briers in one day.
18 And it will consume the glory of his
forest and of his fruitful field,
Both soul and body;
And they will be as when a sick man
wastes away.
19 Then the rest of the trees of his forest
Will be so few in number
That a child may write them.

The Returning Remnant of Israel

20 And it shall come to pass in that day
That the remnant of Israel,
And such as have escaped of the house of
Jacob,
Will never again depend on him who
defeated them,
But will depend on the LORD, the Holy
One of Israel, in truth.
21 The remnant will return, the remnant of
Jacob,
To the Mighty God.
22 For though your people, O Israel, be as
the sand of the sea,
A remnant of them will return;
The destruction decreed shall overflow
with righteousness.
23 For the Lord GOD of hosts
Will make a determined end
In the midst of all the land.

24 Therefore thus says the Lord GOD of hosts:
"O My people, who dwell in Zion, do not be
afraid of the Assyrian. He shall strike you
with a rod and lift up his staff against you, in
the manner of Egypt.
25 For yet a very little while and the indigna- ➤
tion will cease, as will My anger in their destruction."
26 And the LORD of hosts will stir up a
scourge for him like the slaughter of Midian
at the rock of Oreb; *as* His rod was on the sea,
so will He lift it up in the manner of Egypt.

27 It shall come to pass in that day
That his burden will be taken away from
your shoulder,
And his yoke from your neck,
And the yoke will be destroyed because
of the anointing oil.

28 He has come to Aiath,
He has passed Migron;
At Michmash he has attended to his
equipment.
29 They have gone along the ridge,
They have taken up lodging at Geba.

10:16 [a]Following Bomberg; Masoretic Text and Dead Sea Scrolls read *YHWH* (*the LORD*).

LIFE LESSONS

➤ 10:15 — *Shall the ax boast itself against him who chops with it? Or shall the saw exalt itself against him who saws with it?*

Any success we achieve, any accomplishments we make, we owe to the will and favor of God. As Paul asks, "For who makes you differ from another? And what do you have that you did not receive?" (1 Cor. 4:7).

➤ 10:25 — *"For yet a very little while and the indignation will cease, as will My anger in their destruction."*

The dark moments of our lives will last only so long as is necessary for God to accomplish His purpose in us. "His anger is but for a moment, His favor is for life" (Ps. 30:5).

Ramah is afraid,
Gibeah of Saul has fled.
30 Lift up your voice,
O daughter of Gallim!
Cause it to be heard as far as Laish—
O poor Anathoth![a]
31 Madmenah has fled,
The inhabitants of Gebim seek refuge.
32 As yet he will remain at Nob that day;
He will shake his fist at the mount of the daughter of Zion,
The hill of Jerusalem.

33 Behold, the Lord,
The LORD of hosts,
Will lop off the bough with terror;
Those of high stature *will be* hewn down,
And the haughty will be humbled.
34 He will cut down the thickets of the forest with iron,
And Lebanon will fall by the Mighty One.

The Reign of Jesse's Offspring

11 There shall come forth a Rod from the stem of Jesse,
And a Branch shall grow out of his roots.
2 The Spirit of the LORD shall rest upon Him,
The Spirit of wisdom and understanding,
The Spirit of counsel and might,
The Spirit of knowledge and of the fear of the LORD.

➤ 3 His delight *is* in the fear of the LORD,
And He shall not judge by the sight of His eyes,
Nor decide by the hearing of His ears;
4 But with righteousness He shall judge the poor,
And decide with equity for the meek of the earth;
He shall strike the earth with the rod of His mouth,
And with the breath of His lips He shall slay the wicked.
5 Righteousness shall be the belt of His loins,
And faithfulness the belt of His waist.

✳ **6** "The wolf also shall dwell with the lamb,
The leopard shall lie down with the young goat,
The calf and the young lion and the fatling together;
And a little child shall lead them.
7 The cow and the bear shall graze;
Their young ones shall lie down together;
And the lion shall eat straw like the ox.
8 The nursing child shall play by the cobra's hole,
And the weaned child shall put his hand in the viper's den.
9 They shall not hurt nor destroy in all My holy mountain, ➤
For the earth shall be full of the knowledge of the LORD
As the waters cover the sea.

10 "And in that day there shall be a Root of Jesse, ✳
Who shall stand as a banner to the people;
For the Gentiles shall seek Him,
And His resting place shall be glorious."

11 It shall come to pass in that day
That the Lord shall set His hand again the second time
To recover the remnant of His people who are left,
From Assyria and Egypt,
From Pathros and Cush,
From Elam and Shinar,
From Hamath and the islands of the sea.
12 He will set up a banner for the nations,
And will assemble the outcasts of Israel,
And gather together the dispersed of Judah
From the four corners of the earth.
13 Also the envy of Ephraim shall depart,
And the adversaries of Judah shall be cut off;
Ephraim shall not envy Judah,
And Judah shall not harass Ephraim.
14 But they shall fly down upon the shoulder of the Philistines toward the west;
Together they shall plunder the people of the East;
They shall lay their hand on Edom and Moab;
And the people of Ammon shall obey them.
15 The LORD will utterly destroy[a] the tongue of the Sea of Egypt;
With His mighty wind He will shake His fist over the River,[b]

10:30 [a]Following Masoretic Text, Targum, and Vulgate; Septuagint and Syriac read *Listen to her, O Anathoth.*
11:15 [a]Following Masoretic Text and Vulgate; Septuagint, Syriac, and Targum read *dry up.* [b]That is, the Euphrates

LIFE LESSONS

➤ 11:3 — *His delight is in the fear of the LORD . . . .*

Isaiah foresaw that Jesus would "delight" in the fear of God. He didn't mean that Jesus would delight in the emotion so much as in the awesome, majestic, all-powerful God who inspires godly fear.

➤ 11:9 — *For the earth shall be full of the knowledge of the LORD as the waters cover the sea.*

We look forward to the day when God will rule on earth as He does in heaven, a day when righteousness will reign and evil will not be allowed to oppress anyone.

And strike it in the seven streams,
And make *men* cross over dry-shod.
16 There will be a highway for the remnant of His people
Who will be left from Assyria,
As it was for Israel
In the day that he came up from the land of Egypt.

A Hymn of Praise

12 And in that day you will say:

"O LORD, I will praise You;
Though You were angry with me,
Your anger is turned away, and You comfort me.
➤ 2 Behold, God *is* my salvation,
I will trust and not be afraid;
'For YAH, the LORD, *is* my strength and song;
He also has become my salvation.'"[a]
➤ 3 Therefore with joy you will draw water
From the wells of salvation.

4 And in that day you will say:

"Praise the LORD, call upon His name;
Declare His deeds among the peoples,
Make mention that His name is exalted.
5 Sing to the LORD,
For He has done excellent things;
This *is* known in all the earth.
6 Cry out and shout, O inhabitant of Zion,
For great *is* the Holy One of Israel in your midst!"

Proclamation Against Babylon

13 The burden against Babylon which Isaiah the son of Amoz saw.

2 "Lift up a banner on the high mountain,
Raise your voice to them;
Wave your hand, that they may enter the gates of the nobles.
3 I have commanded My sanctified ones;
I have also called My mighty ones for My anger—
Those who rejoice in My exaltation."

4 The noise of a multitude in the mountains,
Like that of many people!
A tumultuous noise of the kingdoms of nations gathered together!
The LORD of hosts musters
The army for battle.
5 They come from a far country,
From the end of heaven—
The LORD and His weapons of indignation,
To destroy the whole land.

6 Wail, for the day of the LORD *is* at hand!
It will come as destruction from the Almighty.
7 Therefore all hands will be limp,
Every man's heart will melt,
8 And they will be afraid.
Pangs and sorrows will take hold of *them;*
They will be in pain as a woman in childbirth;
They will be amazed at one another;
Their faces *will be like* flames.

9 Behold, the day of the LORD comes,
Cruel, with both wrath and fierce anger,
To lay the land desolate;
And He will destroy its sinners from it.
10 For the stars of heaven and their constellations
Will not give their light;
The sun will be darkened in its going forth,
And the moon will not cause its light to shine.

11 "I will punish the world for *its* evil, ➤
And the wicked for their iniquity;
I will halt the arrogance of the proud,
And will lay low the haughtiness of the terrible.
12 I will make a mortal more rare than fine gold,
A man more than the golden wedge of Ophir.
13 Therefore I will shake the heavens,
And the earth will move out of her place,
In the wrath of the LORD of hosts
And in the day of His fierce anger.

12:2 [a]Exodus 15:2

LIFE LESSONS

➤ 12:2 — *Behold, God is my salvation, I will trust and not be afraid . . . .*

When hard times come around, we always have the choice of whether to trust Him or to fear. "I lost my job"—trust or fear? "We can't pay the mortgage"—trust or fear? "I don't feel well"—trust or fear?

➤ 12:3 — *Therefore with joy you will draw water from the wells of salvation.*

Our salvation should give us joy every day, not merely in the period immediately following our conversion. God's salvation is not about eternal life only, but about an abundant life right now.

➤ 13:11 — *"I will punish the world for its evil, and the wicked for their iniquity . . . ."*

Hollywood may glamorize it, pundits may mock it, leaders may ignore it and most may misunderstand it, but Judgment Day really is coming. Now is the time to get right with God, before it comes.

14 It shall be as the hunted gazelle,
And as a sheep that no man takes up;
Every man will turn to his own people,
And everyone will flee to his own land.
15 Everyone who is found will be thrust through,
And everyone who is captured will fall by the sword.
16 Their children also will be dashed to pieces before their eyes;
Their houses will be plundered
And their wives ravished.
➤ 17 "Behold, I will stir up the Medes against them,
Who will not regard silver;
And *as for* gold, they will not delight in it.
18 Also *their* bows will dash the young men to pieces,
And they will have no pity on the fruit of the womb;
Their eye will not spare children.
19 And Babylon, the glory of kingdoms,
The beauty of the Chaldeans' pride,
Will be as when God overthrew Sodom and Gomorrah.
20 It will never be inhabited,
Nor will it be settled from generation to generation;
Nor will the Arabian pitch tents there,
Nor will the shepherds make their sheepfolds there.
21 But wild beasts of the desert will lie there,
And their houses will be full of owls;
Ostriches will dwell there,
And wild goats will caper there.
22 The hyenas will howl in their citadels,
And jackals in their pleasant palaces.
Her time *is* near to come,
And her days will not be prolonged."

Mercy on Jacob

14 For the LORD will have mercy on Jacob,
and will still choose Israel, and settle
them in their own land. The strangers will be
joined with them, and they will cling to the
house of Jacob.
2 Then people will take them and bring
them to their place, and the house of Israel
will possess them for servants and maids in
the land of the LORD; they will take them captive whose captives they were, and rule over
their oppressors.

Fall of the King of Babylon

3 It shall come to pass in the day the LORD
gives you rest from your sorrow, and from
your fear and the hard bondage in which you
were made to serve,
4 that you will take up this proverb against
the king of Babylon, and say:

"How the oppressor has ceased,
The golden[a] city ceased!
5 The LORD has broken the staff of the wicked,
The scepter of the rulers;
6 He who struck the people in wrath with a continual stroke,
He who ruled the nations in anger,
Is persecuted *and* no one hinders.
7 The whole earth is at rest *and* quiet;
They break forth into singing.
8 Indeed the cypress trees rejoice over you,
And the cedars of Lebanon,
Saying, 'Since you were cut down,
No woodsman has come up against us.'

9 "Hell from beneath is excited about you,
To meet *you* at your coming;
It stirs up the dead for you,
All the chief ones of the earth;
It has raised up from their thrones
All the kings of the nations.
10 They all shall speak and say to you:
'Have you also become as weak as we?
Have you become like us?
11 Your pomp is brought down to Sheol,
And the sound of your stringed instruments;
The maggot is spread under you,
And worms cover you.'

The Fall of Lucifer

12 "How you are fallen from heaven,
O Lucifer,[a] son of the morning!
How you are cut down to the ground,
You who weakened the nations!
13 For you have said in your heart: ◄
'I will ascend into heaven,
I will exalt my throne above the stars of God;
I will also sit on the mount of the congregation
On the farthest sides of the north;

14:4 [a]Or *insolent* **14:12** [a]Literally *Day Star*

LIFE LESSONS

➤ 13:17 — *"Behold, I will stir up the Medes against them . . . ."*

When Isaiah made this prophecy, the Babylonians were far from the world's mightiest superpower and more than 150 years away from conquering Judah. Yet it was the Medes who eventually toppled them, just as God declared.

➤ 14:13 — *For you have said in your heart: "I will ascend into heaven, I will exalt my throne above the stars of God . . . ."*

Isaiah uses the arrogant king of Babylon to picture the insolent pride of Satan. The devil fell from his lofty position because he wanted to usurp God's place. He even tried to get Jesus to worship him (Matt. 4:9).

14 I will ascend above the heights of the
clouds,
I will be like the Most High.'
15 Yet you shall be brought down to Sheol,
To the lowest depths of the Pit.

16 "Those who see you will gaze at you,
And consider you, *saying*:
'*Is* this the man who made the earth
tremble,
Who shook kingdoms,
17 Who made the world as a wilderness
And destroyed its cities,
Who did not open the house of his
prisoners?'

18 "All the kings of the nations,
All of them, sleep in glory,
Everyone in his own house;
19 But you are cast out of your grave
Like an abominable branch,
Like the garment of those who are slain,
Thrust through with a sword,
Who go down to the stones of the pit,
Like a corpse trodden underfoot.
20 You will not be joined with them in burial,
Because you have destroyed your land
And slain your people.
The brood of evildoers shall never be
named.
21 Prepare slaughter for his children
Because of the iniquity of their fathers,
Lest they rise up and possess the land,
And fill the face of the world with cities."

Babylon Destroyed
22 "For I will rise up against them," says the
LORD of hosts,
"And cut off from Babylon the name and
remnant,
And offspring and posterity," says the
LORD.
23 "I will also make it a possession for the
porcupine,
And marshes of muddy water;
I will sweep it with the broom of
destruction," says the LORD of hosts.

Assyria Destroyed
➤ **24** The LORD of hosts has sworn, saying,
"Surely, as I have thought, so it shall come
to pass,
And as I have purposed, *so* it shall stand:
25 That I will break the Assyrian in My
land,
And on My mountains tread him
underfoot.
Then his yoke shall be removed from
them,
And his burden removed from their
shoulders.
26 This *is* the purpose that is purposed
against the whole earth,
And this *is* the hand that is stretched out
over all the nations.
27 For the LORD of hosts has purposed,
And who will annul *it*?
His hand *is* stretched out,
And who will turn it back?"

Philistia Destroyed
28 This is the burden which came in the year
that King Ahaz died.

29 "Do not rejoice, all you of Philistia,
Because the rod that struck you is
broken;
For out of the serpent's roots will come
forth a viper,
And its offspring *will be* a fiery flying
serpent.
30 The firstborn of the poor will feed,
And the needy will lie down in safety;
I will kill your roots with famine,
And it will slay your remnant.
31 Wail, O gate! Cry, O city!
All you of Philistia *are* dissolved;
For smoke will come from the north,
And no one *will be* alone in his appointed
times."

32 What will they answer the messengers of
the nation?
That the LORD has founded Zion,
And the poor of His people shall take
refuge in it.

Proclamation Against Moab
15 The burden against Moab.

Because in the night Ar of Moab is laid
waste
And destroyed,
Because in the night Kir of Moab is laid
waste
And destroyed,
2 He has gone up to the temple[a] and Dibon,
To the high places to weep.

15:2 [a]Hebrew *bayith*, literally *house*

LIFE LESSONS

➤ **14:24 — *The Lord of hosts has sworn, saying, "Surely, as I have thought, so it shall come to pass, and as I have purposed, so it shall stand . . . ."***

Disobedience never makes sense, because God will always—*always*—follow through on both His promises and His warnings. If He tells us, "you reap what you sow," then we'd be fools not to believe Him.

Moab will wail over Nebo and over
Medeba;
On all their heads *will be* baldness,
And every beard cut off.
3 In their streets they will clothe
themselves with sackcloth;
On the tops of their houses
And in their streets
Everyone will wail, weeping bitterly.
4 Heshbon and Elealeh will cry out,
Their voice shall be heard as far as
Jahaz;
Therefore the armed soldiers[a] of Moab
will cry out;
His life will be burdensome to him.

5 "My heart will cry out for Moab;
His fugitives *shall flee* to Zoar,
Like a three-year-old heifer.[a]
For by the Ascent of Luhith
They will go up with weeping;
For in the way of Horonaim
They will raise up a cry of destruction,
6 For the waters of Nimrim will be
desolate,
For the green grass has withered away;
The grass fails, there is nothing green.
7 Therefore the abundance they have
gained,
And what they have laid up,
They will carry away to the Brook of the
Willows.
8 For the cry has gone all around the
borders of Moab,
Its wailing to Eglaim
And its wailing to Beer Elim.
9 For the waters of Dimon[a] will be full of
blood;
Because I will bring more upon Dimon,[b]
Lions upon him who escapes from Moab,
And on the remnant of the land."

Moab Destroyed

16 Send the lamb to the ruler of the land,
From Sela to the wilderness,
To the mount of the daughter of Zion.
2 For it shall be as a wandering bird
thrown out of the nest;
So shall be the daughters of Moab at the
fords of the Arnon.

3 "Take counsel, execute judgment;
Make your shadow like the night in the
middle of the day;
Hide the outcasts,
Do not betray him who escapes.
4 Let My outcasts dwell with you, O Moab;
Be a shelter to them from the face of the
spoiler.
For the extortioner is at an end,
Devastation ceases,
The oppressors are consumed out of the
land.
* 5 In mercy the throne will be established;
And One will sit on it in truth, in the
tabernacle of David,
Judging and seeking justice and
hastening righteousness."

6 We have heard of the pride of Moab—
He is very proud—
Of his haughtiness and his pride and his
wrath;
But his lies *shall* not *be* so.
7 Therefore Moab shall wail for Moab;
Everyone shall wail.
For the foundations of Kir Hareseth you
shall mourn;
Surely *they are* stricken.

8 For the fields of Heshbon languish,
And the vine of Sibmah;
The lords of the nations have broken
down its choice plants,
Which have reached to Jazer
And wandered through the wilderness.
Her branches are stretched out,
They are gone over the sea.
9 Therefore I will bewail the vine of
Sibmah,
With the weeping of Jazer;
I will drench you with my tears,
O Heshbon and Elealeh;
For battle cries have fallen
Over your summer fruits and your
harvest.

10 Gladness is taken away,
And joy from the plentiful field;
In the vineyards there will be no
singing,
Nor will there be shouting;
No treaders will tread out wine in the
presses;
I have made their shouting cease.
11 Therefore my heart shall resound like a
harp for Moab,
And my inner being for Kir Heres.

12 And it shall come to pass,
When it is seen that Moab is weary on
the high place,
That he will come to his sanctuary to
pray;
But he will not prevail.

13 This *is* the word which the LORD has spoken concerning Moab since that time.
14 But now the LORD has spoken, saying,
"Within three years, as the years of a hired
man, the glory of Moab will be despised with
all that great multitude, and the remnant *will
be* very small *and* feeble."

15:4 [a]Following Masoretic Text, Targum, and Vulgate; Septuagint and Syriac read *loins*. 15:5 [a]Or *The Third Eglath*, an unknown city (compare Jeremiah 48:34) 15:9 [a]Following Masoretic Text and Targum; Dead Sea Scrolls and Vulgate read *Dibon;* Septuagint reads *Rimon*. [b]Following Masoretic Text and Targum; Dead Sea Scrolls and Vulgate read *Dibon;* Septuagint reads *Rimon*.

Proclamation Against Syria and Israel

17 The burden against Damascus.

"Behold, Damascus will cease from *being* a city,
And it will be a ruinous heap.
2 The cities of Aroer *are* forsaken;[a]
They will be for flocks
Which lie down, and no one will make *them* afraid.
3 The fortress also will cease from Ephraim,
The kingdom from Damascus,
And the remnant of Syria;
They will be as the glory of the children of Israel,"
Says the LORD of hosts.

4 "In that day it shall come to pass
That the glory of Jacob will wane,
And the fatness of his flesh grow lean.
5 It shall be as when the harvester gathers the grain,
And reaps the heads with his arm;
It shall be as he who gathers heads of grain
In the Valley of Rephaim.
6 Yet gleaning grapes will be left in it,
Like the shaking of an olive tree,
Two *or* three olives at the top of the uppermost bough,
Four *or* five in its most fruitful branches,"
Says the LORD God of Israel.

➤ 7 In that day a man will look to his Maker,
And his eyes will have respect for the Holy One of Israel.
8 He will not look to the altars,
The work of his hands;
He will not respect what his fingers have made,
Nor the wooden images[a] nor the incense altars.

9 In that day his strong cities will be as a forsaken bough[a]
And an uppermost branch,[b]
Which they left because of the children of Israel;
And there will be desolation.

10 Because you have forgotten the God of your salvation,
And have not been mindful of the Rock of your stronghold,
Therefore you will plant pleasant plants
And set out foreign seedlings;
11 In the day you will make your plant to grow,
And in the morning you will make your seed to flourish;
But the harvest *will be* a heap of ruins
In the day of grief and desperate sorrow.

12 Woe to the multitude of many people
Who make a noise like the roar of the seas,
And to the rushing of nations
That make a rushing like the rushing of mighty waters!
13 The nations will rush like the rushing of many waters;
But *God* will rebuke them and they will flee far away,
And be chased like the chaff of the mountains before the wind,
Like a rolling thing before the whirlwind.
14 Then behold, at eventide, trouble!
And before the morning, he *is* no more.
This *is* the portion of those who plunder us,
And the lot of those who rob us.

Proclamation Against Ethiopia

18 Woe to the land shadowed with buzzing wings,
Which *is* beyond the rivers of Ethiopia,
2 Which sends ambassadors by sea,
Even in vessels of reed on the waters, *saying,*
"Go, swift messengers, to a nation tall and smooth *of skin,*
To a people terrible from their beginning onward,
A nation powerful and treading down,
Whose land the rivers divide."

3 All inhabitants of the world and dwellers on the earth:
When he lifts up a banner on the mountains, you see *it;*
And when he blows a trumpet, you hear *it.*
4 For so the LORD said to me,
"I will take My rest,

17:2 [a]Following Masoretic Text and Vulgate; Septuagint reads *It shall be forsaken forever;* Targum reads *Its cities shall be forsaken and desolate.* **17:8** [a]Hebrew *Asherim,* Canaanite deities
17:9 [a]Septuagint reads *Hivites;* Targum reads *laid waste;* Vulgate reads *as the plows.* [b]Septuagint reads *Amorites;* Targum reads *in ruins;* Vulgate reads *corn.*

LIFE LESSONS

➤ 17:7 — *In that day a man will look to his Maker, and his eyes will have respect for the Holy One of Israel.*

Isaiah pictures a future time, but we can look to our Maker and have respect for the Holy One of Israel right now. At this very moment we can enjoy the blessings of intimate connection to our God.

And I will look from My dwelling place
Like clear heat in sunshine,
Like a cloud of dew in the heat of harvest."
5 For before the harvest, when the bud is perfect
And the sour grape is ripening in the flower,
He will both cut off the sprigs with pruning hooks
And take away *and* cut down the branches.
6 They will be left together for the mountain birds of prey
And for the beasts of the earth;
The birds of prey will summer on them,
And all the beasts of the earth will winter on them.

7 In that time a present will be brought to the LORD of hosts
From[a] a people tall and smooth *of skin*,
And from a people terrible from their beginning onward,
A nation powerful and treading down,
Whose land the rivers divide—
To the place of the name of the LORD of hosts,
To Mount Zion.

Proclamation Against Egypt

19 The burden against Egypt.

Behold, the LORD rides on a swift cloud,
And will come into Egypt;
The idols of Egypt will totter at His presence,
And the heart of Egypt will melt in its midst.

2 "I will set Egyptians against Egyptians;
Everyone will fight against his brother,
And everyone against his neighbor,
City against city, kingdom against kingdom.
3 The spirit of Egypt will fail in its midst;
I will destroy their counsel,
And they will consult the idols and the charmers,
The mediums and the sorcerers.
4 And the Egyptians I will give
Into the hand of a cruel master,
And a fierce king will rule over them,"
Says the Lord, the LORD of hosts.

5 The waters will fail from the sea,
And the river will be wasted and dried up.
6 The rivers will turn foul;
The brooks of defense will be emptied and dried up;
The reeds and rushes will wither.
7 The papyrus reeds by the River,[a] by the mouth of the River,
And everything sown by the River,
Will wither, be driven away, and be no more.
8 The fishermen also will mourn;
All those will lament who cast hooks into the River,
And they will languish who spread nets on the waters.
9 Moreover those who work in fine flax
And those who weave fine fabric will be ashamed;
10 And its foundations will be broken.
All who make wages *will be* troubled of soul.

11 Surely the princes of Zoan *are* fools;
Pharaoh's wise counselors give foolish counsel.
How do you say to Pharaoh, "I *am* the son of the wise,
The son of ancient kings?"
12 Where *are* they?
Where are your wise men?
Let them tell you now,
And let them know what the LORD of hosts has purposed against Egypt.
13 The princes of Zoan have become fools;
The princes of Noph[a] are deceived;
They have also deluded Egypt,
Those who are the mainstay of its tribes.
14 The LORD has mingled a perverse spirit in her midst;
And they have caused Egypt to err in all her work,
As a drunken man staggers in his vomit.
15 Neither will there be *any* work for Egypt,
Which the head or tail,
Palm branch or bulrush, may do.[a]

16 In that day Egypt will be like women, and
will be afraid and fear because of the waving
of the hand of the LORD of hosts, which He
waves over it.
17 And the land of Judah will be a terror to
Egypt; everyone who makes mention of it will
be afraid in himself, because of the counsel of
the LORD of hosts which He has determined
against it.

Egypt, Assyria, and Israel Blessed

18 In that day five cities in the land of Egypt
will speak the language of Canaan and swear
by the LORD of hosts; one will be called the
City of Destruction.[a]
19 In that day there will be an altar to the
LORD in the midst of the land of Egypt, and a
pillar to the LORD at its border.
20 And it will be for a sign and for a witness
to the LORD of hosts in the land of Egypt; for

18:7 [a]Following Dead Sea Scrolls, Septuagint, and Vulgate; Masoretic Text omits *From;* Targum reads *To.* **19:7** [a]That is, the Nile **19:13** [a]That is, ancient Memphis **19:15** [a]Compare Isaiah 9:14–16 **19:18** [a]Some Hebrew manuscripts, Arabic, Dead Sea Scrolls, Targum, and Vulgate read *Sun;* Septuagint reads *Asedek* (literally *Righteousness*).

they will cry to the LORD because of the oppressors, and He will send them a Savior and a Mighty One, and He will deliver them.
21 Then the LORD will be known to Egypt, and the Egyptians will know the LORD in that day, and will make sacrifice and offering; yes, they will make a vow to the LORD and perform *it*.
22 And the LORD will strike Egypt, He will strike and heal *it;* they will return to the LORD, and He will be entreated by them and heal them.
23 In that day there will be a highway from Egypt to Assyria, and the Assyrian will come into Egypt and the Egyptian into Assyria, and the Egyptians will serve with the Assyrians.
24 In that day Israel will be one of three with Egypt and Assyria—a blessing in the midst of the land,
➤ 25 whom the LORD of hosts shall bless, saying, "Blessed *is* Egypt My people, and Assyria the work of My hands, and Israel My inheritance."

The Sign Against Egypt and Ethiopia

20 In the year that Tartan[a] came to Ashdod, when Sargon the king of Assyria sent him, and he fought against Ashdod and took it,
➤ 2 at the same time the LORD spoke by Isaiah the son of Amoz, saying, "Go, and remove the sackcloth from your body, and take your sandals off your feet." And he did so, walking naked and barefoot.
3 Then the LORD said, "Just as My servant Isaiah has walked naked and barefoot three years *for* a sign and a wonder against Egypt and Ethiopia,
4 "so shall the king of Assyria lead away the Egyptians as prisoners and the Ethiopians as captives, young and old, naked and barefoot, with their buttocks uncovered, to the shame of Egypt.
5 "Then they shall be afraid and ashamed of Ethiopia their expectation and Egypt their glory.
6 "And the inhabitant of this territory will say in that day, 'Surely such *is* our expectation, wherever we flee for help to be delivered from the king of Assyria; and how shall we escape?'"

The Fall of Babylon Proclaimed

21 The burden against the Wilderness of the Sea.

As whirlwinds in the South pass through,
So it comes from the desert, from a terrible land.
2 A distressing vision is declared to me;
The treacherous dealer deals treacherously,
And the plunderer plunders.
Go up, O Elam!
Besiege, O Media!
All its sighing I have made to cease.

3 Therefore my loins are filled with pain;
Pangs have taken hold of me, like the pangs of a woman in labor.
I was distressed when *I* heard *it;*
I was dismayed when *I* saw *it*.
4 My heart wavered, fearfulness frightened me;
The night for which I longed He turned into fear for me.
5 Prepare the table,
Set a watchman in the tower,
Eat and drink.
Arise, you princes,
Anoint the shield!

6 For thus has the Lord said to me:
"Go, set a watchman,
Let him declare what he sees."
7 And he saw a chariot *with* a pair of horsemen,
A chariot of donkeys, *and* a chariot of camels,
And he listened earnestly with great care.
8 Then he cried, "A lion,[a] my Lord!
I stand continually on the watchtower in the daytime;
I have sat at my post every night.
9 And look, here comes a chariot of men *with* a pair of horsemen!"

20:1 [a]Or *the Commander in Chief* **21:8** [a]Dead Sea Scrolls read *Then the observer cried.*

LIFE LESSONS

➤ 19:20 — . . . *they will cry to the LORD because of the oppressors, and He will send them a Savior and a Mighty One, and He will deliver them.*

We expect the Bible to tell us of a Savior coming to deliver Israel—but this text speaks of a Savior coming to rescue Egypt, Israel's longtime nemesis! Our God is a global God, and He wants to bless all peoples.

➤ 19:25 — . . . *the LORD of hosts shall bless, saying, "Blessed is Egypt My people, and Assyria the work of My hands, and Israel My inheritance."*

In the Exodus, God severely judged Egypt; He destroyed Assyria after the deportation of the northern kingdom; and many times He judged rebellious Israel. Yet God loves to show mercy, not exercise judgment!

➤ 20:2 — . . . *the LORD spoke by Isaiah the son of Amoz, saying, "Go, and remove the sackcloth from your body, and take your sandals off your feet." And he did so, walking naked and barefoot.*

God will take extraordinary measures to get our attention when we have walked away from Him and stand in danger of severe discipline. Is He trying to get your attention right now?

Then he answered and said,
"Babylon is fallen, is fallen!
And all the carved images of her gods
He has broken to the ground."
10 Oh, my threshing and the grain of my floor!
That which I have heard from the LORD of hosts,
The God of Israel,
I have declared to you.

Proclamation Against Edom

11 The burden against Dumah.

He calls to me out of Seir,
"Watchman, what of the night?
Watchman, what of the night?"
12 The watchman said,
"The morning comes, and also the night.
If you will inquire, inquire;
Return! Come back!"

Proclamation Against Arabia

13 The burden against Arabia.

In the forest in Arabia you will lodge,
O you traveling companies of Dedanites.
14 O inhabitants of the land of Tema,
Bring water to him who is thirsty;
With their bread they met him who fled.
15 For they fled from the swords, from the drawn sword,
From the bent bow, and from the distress of war.

16 For thus the LORD has said to me: "Within
a year, according to the year of a hired man,
all the glory of Kedar will fail;
17 and the remainder of the number of
archers, the mighty men of the people of
Kedar, will be diminished; for the LORD God
of Israel has spoken *it*."

Proclamation Against Jerusalem

22 The burden against the Valley of Vision.

What ails you now, that you have all gone up to the housetops,
2 You who are full of noise,
A tumultuous city, a joyous city?
Your slain *men are* not slain with the sword,
Nor dead in battle.
3 All your rulers have fled together;
They are captured by the archers.
All who are found in you are bound together;
They have fled from afar.
4 Therefore I said, "Look away from me,
I will weep bitterly;
Do not labor to comfort me
Because of the plundering of the daughter of my people."
5 For *it is* a day of trouble and treading down and perplexity
By the Lord GOD of hosts
In the Valley of Vision—
Breaking down the walls
And of crying to the mountain.
6 Elam bore the quiver
With chariots of men *and* horsemen,
And Kir uncovered the shield.
7 It shall come to pass *that* your choicest valleys
Shall be full of chariots,
And the horsemen shall set themselves in array at the gate.

8 He removed the protection of Judah.
You looked in that day to the armor of the House of the Forest;
9 You also saw the damage to the city of David,
That it was great;
And you gathered together the waters of the lower pool.
10 You numbered the houses of Jerusalem,
And the houses you broke down
To fortify the wall.
11 You also made a reservoir between the two walls
For the water of the old pool.
But you did not look to its Maker,
Nor did you have respect for Him who fashioned it long ago.

12 And in that day the Lord GOD of hosts
Called for weeping and for mourning,
For baldness and for girding with sackcloth.
13 But instead, joy and gladness,
Slaying oxen and killing sheep,
Eating meat and drinking wine:
"Let us eat and drink, for tomorrow we die!"

14 Then it was revealed in my hearing by the LORD of hosts,
"Surely for this iniquity there will be no atonement for you,
Even to your death," says the Lord GOD of hosts.

The Judgment on Shebna

15 Thus says the Lord GOD of hosts:

"Go, proceed to this steward,
To Shebna, who *is* over the house, *and say:*
16 'What have you here, and whom have you here,
That you have hewn a sepulcher here,
As he who hews himself a sepulcher on high,
Who carves a tomb for himself in a rock?
17 Indeed, the LORD will throw you away violently,
O mighty man,
And will surely seize you.

18 He will surely turn violently and toss you
like a ball
Into a large country;
There you shall die, and there your
glorious chariots
Shall be the shame of your master's
house.
19 So I will drive you out of your office,
And from your position he will pull you
down.[a]

20 'Then it shall be in that day,
That I will call My servant Eliakim the
son of Hilkiah;
21 I will clothe him with your robe
And strengthen him with your belt;
I will commit your responsibility into his
hand.
He shall be a father to the inhabitants of
Jerusalem
And to the house of Judah.
➤ 22 The key of the house of David
I will lay on his shoulder;
So he shall open, and no one shall shut;
And he shall shut, and no one shall open.
23 I will fasten him *as* a peg in a secure
place,
And he will become a glorious throne to
his father's house.

24 'They will hang on him all the glory of his
father's house, the offspring and the posterity,
all vessels of small quantity, from the cups to
all the pitchers.
25 In that day,' says the LORD of hosts, 'the
peg that is fastened in the secure place will be
removed and be cut down and fall, and the
burden that *was* on it will be cut off; for the
LORD has spoken.'"

Proclamation Against Tyre

23 The burden against Tyre.

Wail, you ships of Tarshish!
For it is laid waste,
So that there is no house, no harbor;
From the land of Cyprus[a] it is revealed to
them.

2 Be still, you inhabitants of the coastland,
You merchants of Sidon,
Whom those who cross the sea have
filled.[a]
3 And on great waters the grain of Shihor,
The harvest of the River,[a] *is* her revenue;
And she is a marketplace for the nations.
4 Be ashamed, O Sidon;
For the sea has spoken,
The strength of the sea, saying,
"I do not labor, nor bring forth children;
Neither do I rear young men,
Nor bring up virgins."
5 When the report *reaches* Egypt,
They also will be in agony at the report
of Tyre.

6 Cross over to Tarshish;
Wail, you inhabitants of the coastland!
7 *Is* this your joyous *city*,
Whose antiquity *is* from ancient days,
Whose feet carried her far off to dwell?
8 Who has taken this counsel against Tyre,
the crowning *city*,
Whose merchants *are* princes,
Whose traders *are* the honorable of the
earth?
9 The LORD of hosts has purposed it,
To bring to dishonor the pride of all
glory,
To bring into contempt all the honorable
of the earth.

10 Overflow through your land like the
River,[a]
O daughter of Tarshish;
There is no more strength.
11 He stretched out His hand over the sea,
He shook the kingdoms;
The LORD has given a commandment
against Canaan
To destroy its strongholds.
12 And He said, "You will rejoice no
more,
O you oppressed virgin daughter of
Sidon.
Arise, cross over to Cyprus;
There also you will have no rest."

13 Behold, the land of the Chaldeans,
This people *which* was not;
Assyria founded it for wild beasts of the
desert.
They set up its towers,
They raised up its palaces,
And brought it to ruin.

22:19 [a]Septuagint omits *he will pull you down;* Syriac, Targum, and Vulgate read *I will pull you down.* **23:1** [a]Hebrew *Kittim,* western lands, especially Cyprus **23:2** [a]Following Masoretic Text and Vulgate; Septuagint and Targum read *Passing over the water;* Dead Sea Scrolls read *Your messengers passing over the sea.* **23:3** [a]That is, the Nile **23:10** [a]That is, the Nile

LIFE LESSONS

➤ ***22:22 — ". . . So he shall open, and no one shall shut; and he shall shut, and no one shall open."***

Revelation 3:7 applies this verse to Jesus. When He gives us an open door of ministry and beckons us to walk through it, we are to do so without fear that it will slam shut behind us. He is sovereign!

14 Wail, you ships of Tarshish!
For your strength is laid waste.

15 Now it shall come to pass in that day that
Tyre will be forgotten seventy years, according to the days of one king. At the end of seventy years it will happen to Tyre as *in* the
song of the harlot:

16 "Take a harp, go about the city,
You forgotten harlot;
Make sweet melody, sing many songs,
That you may be remembered."

17 And it shall be, at the end of seventy years,
that the LORD will deal with Tyre. She will return to her hire, and commit fornication with
all the kingdoms of the world on the face of
the earth.
18 Her gain and her pay will be set apart for
the LORD; it will not be treasured nor laid up,
for her gain will be for those who dwell before the LORD, to eat sufficiently, and for fine
clothing.

Impending Judgment on the Earth

24 Behold, the LORD makes the earth
empty and makes it waste,
Distorts its surface
And scatters abroad its inhabitants.
2 And it shall be:
As with the people, so with the priest;
As with the servant, so with his master;
As with the maid, so with her mistress;
As with the buyer, so with the seller;
As with the lender, so with the borrower;
As with the creditor, so with the debtor.
3 The land shall be entirely emptied and
utterly plundered,
For the LORD has spoken this word.

4 The earth mourns *and* fades away,
The world languishes *and* fades away;
The haughty people of the earth
languish.
➤ 5 The earth is also defiled under its
inhabitants,
Because they have transgressed the laws,
Changed the ordinance,
Broken the everlasting covenant.
6 Therefore the curse has devoured the
earth,
And those who dwell in it are desolate.
Therefore the inhabitants of the earth are
burned,
And few men *are* left.

7 The new wine fails, the vine languishes,
All the merry-hearted sigh.
8 The mirth of the tambourine ceases,
The noise of the jubilant ends,
The joy of the harp ceases.
9 They shall not drink wine with a song;
Strong drink is bitter to those who drink it.
10 The city of confusion is broken down;
Every house is shut up, so that none may
go in.
11 *There is* a cry for wine in the streets,
All joy is darkened,
The mirth of the land is gone.
12 In the city desolation is left,
And the gate is stricken with destruction.
13 When it shall be thus in the midst of the
land among the people,
It shall be like the shaking of an olive
tree,
Like the gleaning of grapes when the
vintage is done.

14 They shall lift up their voice, they shall
sing;
For the majesty of the LORD
They shall cry aloud from the sea.
15 Therefore glorify the LORD in the
dawning light,
The name of the LORD God of Israel in
the coastlands of the sea.
16 From the ends of the earth we have heard
songs:
"Glory to the righteous!"
But I said, "I am ruined, ruined!
Woe to me!
The treacherous dealers have dealt
treacherously,
Indeed, the treacherous dealers have
dealt very treacherously."

17 Fear and the pit and the snare
Are upon you, O inhabitant of the earth.
18 And it shall be
That he who flees from the noise of the
fear
Shall fall into the pit,
And he who comes up from the midst of
the pit
Shall be caught in the snare;
For the windows from on high are open,
And the foundations of the earth are
shaken.

19 The earth is violently broken,
The earth is split open,
The earth is shaken exceedingly.

LIFE LESSONS

➤ 24:5, 6 — *The earth is also defiled under its inhabitants, because they have transgressed the laws, changed the ordinance, broken the everlasting covenant. Therefore the curse has devoured the earth, and those who dwell in it are desolate.*

Sin not only destroys us spiritually, it also plays havoc with the earth. Paul says "the whole creation groans and labors with birth pangs" (Rom. 8:22) and looks forward to its day of redemption.

ANSWERS TO LIFE'S QUESTIONS

When is the appropriate time to praise the Lord?

IS. 25:1

Praise the Lord often, regardless of your circumstances. Many people praise the Lord only when something good happens to them or when they receive an unexpected blessing—but the Lord is worthy of our praise at all times, in all circumstances.

We do not praise the Lord on the basis of our circumstances; we praise the Lord on the basis of who He is in the midst of our circumstances.

We do not praise the Lord because of the way we feel; we praise the Lord because of who He is and the way He feels about us.

Don't limit your praise to the songs you sing at the Sunday church service. Praise the Lord often, in both words and songs that you create spontaneously. All around you, at all times, you can find countless things for which to praise the Lord. Look for those things, and throughout the day voice your heartfelt praise and thanksgiving to God.

When you ride alone in your car, get into an empty elevator, sit alone in your office or work space, or find yourself alone in your home, take every opportunity to voice praise to the Lord for who He is. Praise Him for what He has done through the ages, for what He has done in your life and in the lives of your loved ones, and for what you know without doubt the Lord is doing for you and will do for you both now and throughout all eternity.

You can never run out of things for which to praise the Lord!

When you voice your praise to the Lord, you open yourself up to experiencing the presence of God with you. The Bible tells us that the Lord is "enthroned" in the praises of His people (Ps. 22:3).

The greater your praise, the smaller your problems will appear.

The more frequent your praise, the less you will find yourself with time to worry or feel anxious.

The more you praise the Lord, the more you are going to "see" things worthy of His praise.

As you praise Him, your entire attitude will shift from an unhealthy "I focus" and "problem focus," to a healthy and joyful "God focus" and "answer focus." So take a cue from the prophet Isaiah and proclaim: "O LORD, You are my God, I will exalt You, I will praise Your name, for you have done wonderful things; Your counsels of old are faithfulness and truth" (Is. 25:1).

See the Life Principles Index for further study:

2. Obey God and leave all the consequences to Him.

1. Our intimacy with God—His highest priority for our lives—determines the impact of our lives.

➤ 20 The earth shall reel to and fro like a drunkard,
And shall totter like a hut;
Its transgression shall be heavy upon it,
And it will fall, and not rise again.

21 It shall come to pass in that day
That the LORD will punish on high the host of exalted ones,
And on the earth the kings of the earth.
22 They will be gathered together,
As prisoners are gathered in the pit,
And will be shut up in the prison;
After many days they will be punished.
23 Then the moon will be disgraced
And the sun ashamed;
For the LORD of hosts will reign
On Mount Zion and in Jerusalem
And before His elders, gloriously.

Praise to God

25 O LORD, You *are* my God.
I will exalt You,
I will praise Your name,

LIFE LESSONS

➤ 24:20 — *The earth shall reel to and fro like a drunkard, and shall totter like a hut; its transgression shall be heavy upon it . . . .*

The prophets speak often about "the Day of the LORD," describing it as a time of horrific destruction, planet-wide judgments, and fierce divine wrath. Jesus said, "unless those days were shortened, no flesh would be saved" (Matt. 24:22).

For You have done wonderful *things;*
Your counsels of old *are* faithfulness *and* truth.
2 For You have made a city a ruin,
A fortified city a ruin,
A palace of foreigners to be a city no more;
It will never be rebuilt.
3 Therefore the strong people will glorify You;
The city of the terrible nations will fear You.
➤ 4 For You have been a strength to the poor,
A strength to the needy in his distress,
A refuge from the storm,
A shade from the heat;
For the blast of the terrible ones *is* as a storm *against* the wall.
5 You will reduce the noise of aliens,
As heat in a dry place;
As heat in the shadow of a cloud,
The song of the terrible ones will be diminished.
6 And in this mountain
The LORD of hosts will make for all people
A feast of choice pieces,
A feast of wines on the lees,
Of fat things full of marrow,
Of well-refined wines on the lees.
7 And He will destroy on this mountain
The surface of the covering cast over all people,
And the veil that is spread over all nations.
✳ 8 He will swallow up death forever,
And the Lord GOD will wipe away tears from all faces;
The rebuke of His people
He will take away from all the earth;
For the LORD has spoken.
➤ **9** And it will be said in that day:
"Behold, this *is* our God;
We have waited for Him, and He will save us.
This *is* the LORD;
We have waited for Him;
We will be glad and rejoice in His salvation."
10 For on this mountain the hand of the LORD will rest,
And Moab shall be trampled down under Him,
As straw is trampled down for the refuse heap.
11 And He will spread out His hands in their midst
As a swimmer reaches out to swim,
And He will bring down their pride
Together with the trickery of their hands.
12 The fortress of the high fort of your walls
He will bring down, lay low,
And bring to the ground, down to the dust.

A Song of Salvation

26 In that day this song will be sung in the land of Judah:
"We have a strong city;
God will appoint salvation *for* walls and bulwarks.
2 Open the gates,
That the righteous nation which keeps the truth may enter in.
3 You will keep *him* in perfect peace,
Whose mind *is* stayed *on You,*
Because he trusts in You. ✳
4 Trust in the LORD forever,
For in YAH, the LORD, *is* everlasting strength.[a]
5 For He brings down those who dwell on high,
The lofty city;
He lays it low,
He lays it low to the ground,
He brings it down to the dust.
6 The foot shall tread it down—
The feet of the poor
And the steps of the needy."
7 The way of the just *is* uprightness;
O Most Upright,
You weigh the path of the just.
8 Yes, in the way of Your judgments,
O LORD, we have waited for You; ➤
The desire of *our* soul *is* for Your name
And for the remembrance of You.

26:4 [a]Or *Rock of Ages*

LIFE LESSONS

➤ **25:4 — *For You have been a strength to the poor, a strength to the needy in his distress, a refuge from the storm, a shade from the heat . . . .***

Whatever we need God to be for us, He is. He gives strength to the weak, shelter to the homeless, shade to those fainting in the scorching sun. Our Redeemer is all this to us, and more.

➤ **25:9 — *"Behold, this is our God; we have waited for Him, and He will save us."***

Throughout the Bible, God promises to act on behalf of those who wait for Him. In the act of waiting, we demonstrate that we believe the promises of God and that we trust Him to fulfill them all.

➤ **26:8 — *The desire of our soul is for Your name and for the remembrance of You.***

God designed us to enjoy a heart-to-heart closeness with Him, and we find our life's highest calling and priority in coming to know Him intimately and love Him deeply.

ANSWERS TO LIFE'S QUESTIONS

How can I have God's peace?

IS. 26:3

The key element in true, lasting peace is the presence of God. Isaiah says to God, "You will keep him in perfect peace, whose mind is stayed on You, because he trusts in You" (26:3). Christ is our peace—His presence is the presence of peace within us (Eph. 2:14). And so Jesus declares, "in Me you may have peace" (John 16:33).

What is this peace? It is an inner sense of contentment and quietness, regardless of life's circumstances. It is steadfast confidence in our ever-faithful, immutable heavenly Father. It is the presence of joy in the midst of unhappiness.

True peace does not merely paint our pain with a pretty color. A person who has genuine, godly peace can endure an avalanche of hardship and difficulty and still enjoy an inner peace that surpasses all human understanding. Why? Because it does not come from pleasant circumstances, nice events, or good things others may do to us. Instead, it is based on the fact that the Spirit of a holy, omnipotent, and never-changing God lives within us.

Does enjoying God's perfect peace mean that you'll never feel the effects of the storms raging around you? Hardly. But His peace is complete, adequate, and sufficient for anything you face. Keep in mind three keys to experiencing sustained peace.

1. ***Focus on God.*** Perfect peace comes when you fix your mind on God. You must discipline yourself to meditate on God's presence and work. When you spend time concentrating on a problem, does it not seem to grow bigger? In the same way, you will have a greater sense of God's presence and provision as you fix your mind on Him.
2. ***Trust Him.*** You never have to worry about God acting too late or providing insufficient help. His timing and purposes are perfect; in fact, He uses your tribulations to reveal more of Himself to you. His Word is full of rock-solid promises, many of which involve granting you peace. Know that He will always honor them!
3. ***Meditate on His Word.*** Psalm 119:165 emphasizes that those who love God's Word have great peace and nothing causes them to stumble. Your most precious material possession is your Bible. Every believer should love God's Word and feast on it daily. If you love it, you're gong to believe what it says—and then it will guide and anchor your life.

See the Life Principles Index for further study:
12. Peace with God is the fruit of oneness with God.

9 With my soul I have desired You in the night,
Yes, by my spirit within me I will seek You early;
For when Your judgments *are* in the earth,
The inhabitants of the world will learn righteousness.
10 Let grace be shown to the wicked,
Yet he will not learn righteousness;
In the land of uprightness he will deal unjustly,
And will not behold the majesty of the LORD.
11 LORD, *when* Your hand is lifted up, they will not see.
But they will see and be ashamed
For *their* envy of people;
Yes, the fire of Your enemies shall devour them.
12 LORD, You will establish peace for us,
For You have also done all our works in us.
13 O LORD our God, masters besides You
Have had dominion over us;

LIFE LESSONS

➤ ***26:12 — LORD, You will establish peace for us, for You have also done all our works in us.***

To live the Christian life is to allow Jesus to live His life in us and through us. That means that all we accomplish, we accomplish through His Spirit. And that kind of wonderful partnership results in peace.

But by You only we make mention of Your
name.
14 *They are* dead, they will not live;
They are deceased, they will not rise.
Therefore You have punished and
destroyed them,
And made all their memory to perish.
15 You have increased the nation, O LORD,
You have increased the nation;
You are glorified;
You have expanded all the borders of the
land.

16 LORD, in trouble they have visited You,
They poured out a prayer *when* Your
chastening *was* upon them.
17 As a woman with child
Is in pain and cries out in her pangs,
When she draws near the time of her
delivery,
So have we been in Your sight, O LORD.
18 We have been with child, we have been in
pain;
We have, as it were, brought forth wind;
We have not accomplished any
deliverance in the earth,
Nor have the inhabitants of the world
fallen.

✳ 19 Your dead shall live;
Together with my dead body[a] they shall
arise.
Awake and sing, you who dwell in dust;
For your dew *is like* the dew of herbs,
And the earth shall cast out the dead.

Take Refuge from the Coming Judgment
20 Come, my people, enter your chambers,
And shut your doors behind you;
Hide yourself, as it were, for a little
moment,
Until the indignation is past.
21 For behold, the LORD comes out of His
place
To punish the inhabitants of the earth for
their iniquity;
The earth will also disclose her blood,
And will no more cover her slain.

27 In that day the LORD with His severe
sword, great and strong,
Will punish Leviathan the fleeing
serpent,
Leviathan that twisted serpent;
And He will slay the reptile that *is* in the
sea.

The Restoration of Israel
2 In that day sing to her,
"A vineyard of red wine![a]
3 I, the LORD, keep it,
I water it every moment;
Lest any hurt it,
I keep it night and day.
4 Fury *is* not in Me.
Who would set briers *and* thorns
Against Me in battle?
I would go through them,
I would burn them together.
5 Or let him take hold of My strength,
That he may make peace with Me;
And he shall make peace with Me."

6 Those who come He shall cause to take
root in Jacob;
Israel shall blossom and bud,
And fill the face of the world with fruit.

7 Has He struck Israel as He struck those
who struck him?
Or has He been slain according to the
slaughter of those who were slain by
Him?
8 In measure, by sending it away,
You contended with it.
He removes *it* by His rough wind
In the day of the east wind.
9 Therefore by this the iniquity of Jacob
will be covered;
And this *is* all the fruit of taking away his
sin:
When he makes all the stones of the altar
Like chalkstones that are beaten to dust,
Wooden images[a] and incense altars shall
not stand.
10 Yet the fortified city *will be* desolate,
The habitation forsaken and left like a
wilderness;
There the calf will feed, and there it will
lie down
And consume its branches.
11 When its boughs are withered, they will
be broken off;
The women come *and* set them on fire.
For it *is* a people of no understanding;
Therefore He who made them will not
have mercy on them,
And He who formed them will show
them no favor.

12 And it shall come to pass in that day
That the LORD will thresh,
From the channel of the River[a] to the
Brook of Egypt;
And you will be gathered one by one,
O you children of Israel.

13 So it shall be in that day:
The great trumpet will be blown;
They will come, who are about to perish
in the land of Assyria,
And they who are outcasts in the land of
Egypt,

26:19 [a]Following Masoretic Text and Vulgate; Syriac and Targum read *their dead bodies;* Septuagint reads *those in the tombs.*
27:2 [a]Following Masoretic Text (Kittel's *Biblia Hebraica*), Bomberg, and Vulgate; Masoretic Text (*Biblia Hebraica Stuttgartensia*), some Hebrew manuscripts, and Septuagint read *delight;* Targum reads *choice vineyard.* **27:9** [a]Hebrew *Asherim,* Canaanite deities
27:12 [a]That is, the Euphrates

And shall worship the LORD in the holy
mount at Jerusalem.

Woe to Ephraim and Jerusalem

28 Woe to the crown of pride, to the
drunkards of Ephraim,
Whose glorious beauty *is* a fading flower
Which *is* at the head of the verdant
valleys,
To those who are overcome with wine!
2 Behold, the Lord has a mighty and strong
one,
Like a tempest of hail and a destroying
storm,
Like a flood of mighty waters
overflowing,
Who will bring *them* down to the earth
with *His* hand.
3 The crown of pride, the drunkards of
Ephraim,
Will be trampled underfoot;
4 And the glorious beauty is a fading
flower
Which *is* at the head of the verdant
valley,
Like the first fruit before the summer,
Which an observer sees;
He eats it up while it is still in his hand.

➤ 5 In that day the LORD of hosts will be
For a crown of glory and a diadem of
beauty
To the remnant of His people,
6 For a spirit of justice to him who sits in
judgment,
And for strength to those who turn back
the battle at the gate.

7 But they also have erred through wine,
And through intoxicating drink are out of
the way;
The priest and the prophet have erred
through intoxicating drink,
They are swallowed up by wine,
They are out of the way through
intoxicating drink;
They err in vision, they stumble *in*
judgment.
8 For all tables are full of vomit *and* filth;
No place *is clean.*

9 "Whom will he teach knowledge?
And whom will he make to understand
the message?
Those *just* weaned from milk?
Those *just* drawn from the breasts?
10 For precept *must be* upon precept,
precept upon precept,
Line upon line, line upon line,
Here a little, there a little."

11 For with stammering lips and another
tongue
He will speak to this people,
12 To whom He said, "This *is* the rest *with
which*
You may cause the weary to rest,"
And, "This *is* the refreshing";
Yet they would not hear.
13 But the word of the LORD was to
them,
"Precept upon precept, precept upon
precept,
Line upon line, line upon line,
Here a little, there a little,"
That they might go and fall backward,
and be broken
And snared and caught.

14 Therefore hear the word of the LORD, you
scornful men,
Who rule this people who *are* in
Jerusalem,
15 Because you have said, "We have made a
covenant with death,
And with Sheol we are in agreement.
When the overflowing scourge passes
through,
It will not come to us,
For we have made lies our refuge,
And under falsehood we have hidden
ourselves."

A Cornerstone in Zion

16 Therefore thus says the Lord GOD:

"Behold, I lay in Zion a stone for a
foundation,
A tried stone, a precious cornerstone, a
sure foundation;
Whoever believes will not act hastily.
17 Also I will make justice the measuring
line,
And righteousness the plummet;
The hail will sweep away the refuge of
lies,
And the waters will overflow the hiding
place.
18 Your covenant with death will be
annulled,
And your agreement with Sheol will not
stand;

LIFE LESSONS

➤ **28:5 — *In that day the LORD of hosts will be for a crown of glory and a diadem of beauty to the remnant of His people . . . .***

Do you consider the Lord your greatest treasure, your most precious possession, the deepest joy of your heart? He longs to be closer to us than parents, mates, or children. We are His treasure, and He wants to be ours.

When the overflowing scourge passes through,
Then you will be trampled down by it.
19 As often as it goes out it will take you;
For morning by morning it will pass over,
And by day and by night;
It will be a terror just to understand the report."
20 For the bed is too short to stretch out *on,*
And the covering so narrow that one cannot wrap himself *in it.*
21 For the LORD will rise up as *at* Mount Perazim,
He will be angry as in the Valley of Gibeon—
That He may do His work, His awesome work,
And bring to pass His act, His unusual act.
22 Now therefore, do not be mockers,
Lest your bonds be made strong;
For I have heard from the Lord GOD of hosts,
A destruction determined even upon the whole earth.

Listen to the Teaching of God

23 Give ear and hear my voice,
Listen and hear my speech.
24 Does the plowman keep plowing all day to sow?
Does he keep turning his soil and breaking the clods?
25 When he has leveled its surface,
Does he not sow the black cummin
And scatter the cummin,
Plant the wheat in rows,
The barley in the appointed place,
And the spelt in its place?
26 For He instructs him in right judgment,
His God teaches him.

27 For the black cummin is not threshed with a threshing sledge,
Nor is a cartwheel rolled over the cummin;
But the black cummin is beaten out with a stick,
And the cummin with a rod.
28 Bread *flour* must be ground;
Therefore he does not thresh it forever,
Break *it with* his cartwheel,
Or crush it *with* his horsemen.
➤ 29 This also comes from the LORD of hosts,
Who is wonderful in counsel *and* excellent in guidance.

Woe to Jerusalem

29 "Woe to Ariel,[a] to Ariel, the city *where* David dwelt!
Add year to year;
Let feasts come around.
2 Yet I will distress Ariel;
There shall be heaviness and sorrow,
And it shall be to Me as Ariel.
3 I will encamp against you all around,
I will lay siege against you with a mound,
And I will raise siegeworks against you.
4 You shall be brought down,
You shall speak out of the ground;
Your speech shall be low, out of the dust;
Your voice shall be like a medium's, out of the ground;
And your speech shall whisper out of the dust.

5 "Moreover the multitude of your foes
Shall be like fine dust,
And the multitude of the terrible ones
Like chaff that passes away;
Yes, it shall be in an instant, suddenly.
6 You will be punished by the LORD of hosts
With thunder and earthquake and great noise,
With storm and tempest
And the flame of devouring fire.
7 The multitude of all the nations who fight against Ariel,
Even all who fight against her and her fortress,
And distress her,
Shall be as a dream of a night vision.
8 It shall even be as when a hungry man dreams,
And look—he eats;
But he awakes, and his soul is still empty;
Or as when a thirsty man dreams,
And look—he drinks;
But he awakes, and indeed *he is* faint,
And his soul still craves:
So the multitude of all the nations shall be,
Who fight against Mount Zion."

29:1 [a]That is, Jerusalem

LIFE LESSONS

➤ **28:29 — *This also comes from the LORD of hosts, who is wonderful in counsel and excellent in guidance.***

Have you experienced the wonderful counsel of God? Have you invited Him to guide you to excellent places? He wants to lead you into a great future—but you must listen to His voice and obey His directions.

The Blindness of Disobedience

9 Pause and wonder!
Blind yourselves and be blind!
They are drunk, but not with wine;
They stagger, but not with intoxicating drink.
10 For the LORD has poured out on you
The spirit of deep sleep,
And has closed your eyes, namely, the prophets;
And He has covered your heads, *namely,* the seers.

11 The whole vision has become to you like
the words of a book that is sealed, which *men*
deliver to one who is literate, saying, "Read
this, please." And he says, "I cannot, for it *is*
sealed."
12 Then the book is delivered to one who is
illiterate, saying, "Read this, please." And he
says, "I am not literate."
➤ **13** Therefore the Lord said:

"Inasmuch as these people draw near with their mouths
And honor Me with their lips,
But have removed their hearts far from Me,
And their fear toward Me is taught by the commandment of men,
14 Therefore, behold, I will again do a marvelous work
Among this people,
A marvelous work and a wonder;
For the wisdom of their wise *men* shall perish,
And the understanding of their prudent *men* shall be hidden."

15 Woe to those who seek deep to hide their counsel far from the LORD,
And their works are in the dark;
They say, "Who sees us?" and, "Who knows us?"
16 Surely you have things turned around!
Shall the potter be esteemed as the clay;
For shall the thing made say of him who made it,
"He did not make me"?
Or shall the thing formed say of him who formed it,
"He has no understanding"?

Future Recovery of Wisdom

17 *Is* it not yet a very little while
Till Lebanon shall be turned into a fruitful field,
And the fruitful field be esteemed as a forest?
18 In that day the deaf shall hear the words of the book,
And the eyes of the blind shall see out of obscurity and out of darkness.
19 The humble also shall increase *their* joy in the LORD,
And the poor among men shall rejoice
In the Holy One of Israel.
20 For the terrible one is brought to nothing,
The scornful one is consumed,
And all who watch for iniquity are cut off—
21 Who make a man an offender by a word,
And lay a snare for him who reproves in the gate,
And turn aside the just by empty words.

22 Therefore thus says the LORD, who redeemed Abraham, concerning the house of
Jacob:

"Jacob shall not now be ashamed,
Nor shall his face now grow pale;
23 But when he sees his children,
The work of My hands, in his midst,
They will hallow My name,
And hallow the Holy One of Jacob,
And fear the God of Israel.
24 These also who erred in spirit will come to understanding, ➤
And those who complained will learn doctrine."

Future Confidence in Egypt

30 "Woe to the rebellious children," says the LORD, ➤
"Who take counsel, but not of Me,
And who devise plans, but not of My Spirit,
That they may add sin to sin;

LIFE LESSONS

➤ 29:13 — *". . . these people draw near with their mouths and honor Me with their lips, but have removed their hearts far from Me . . . ."*

God not only isn't impressed with passionless prayers and dead devotion, He detests them. He has no interest in outward compliance devoid of inward desire to please Him. He wants *us*, not our words, deeds, or possessions.

➤ 29:24 — *"These also who erred in spirit will come to understanding, and those who complained will learn doctrine."*

God disciplines us only to bring us to a better state than we had before. He uses adversity to teach us, because we tend to learn more in our valley experiences than on our mountaintops.

➤ 30:1 — *"Woe to the rebellious children," says the LORD, "who take counsel, but not of Me, and who devise plans, but not of My Spirit . . . ."*

We find it terribly easy to jump ahead of the Lord, to get our plans in order and our projects in motion before we ask Him for His counsel. But He wants to be the engine, not the caboose.

2 Who walk to go down to Egypt,
And have not asked My advice,
To strengthen themselves in the strength of Pharaoh,
And to trust in the shadow of Egypt!
3 Therefore the strength of Pharaoh
Shall be your shame,
And trust in the shadow of Egypt
Shall be *your* humiliation.
4 For his princes were at Zoan,
And his ambassadors came to Hanes.
5 They were all ashamed of a people *who* could not benefit them,
Or be help or benefit,
But a shame and also a reproach."

6 The burden against the beasts of the South.

Through a land of trouble and anguish,
From which *came* the lioness and lion,
The viper and fiery flying serpent,
They will carry their riches on the backs of young donkeys,
And their treasures on the humps of camels,
To a people *who* shall not profit;
7 For the Egyptians shall help in vain and to no purpose.
Therefore I have called her
Rahab-Hem-Shebeth.[a]

A Rebellious People

8 Now go, write it before them on a tablet,
And note it on a scroll,
That it may be for time to come,
Forever and ever:
9 That this *is* a rebellious people,
Lying children,
Children *who* will not hear the law of the LORD;
10 Who say to the seers, "Do not see,"
And to the prophets, "Do not prophesy to us right things;
Speak to us smooth things, prophesy deceits.
11 Get out of the way,
Turn aside from the path,
Cause the Holy One of Israel
To cease from before us."

12 Therefore thus says the Holy One of Israel:

"Because you despise this word,
And trust in oppression and perversity,
And rely on them,
13 Therefore this iniquity shall be to you
Like a breach ready to fall,
A bulge in a high wall,
Whose breaking comes suddenly, in an instant.
14 And He shall break it like the breaking of the potter's vessel,
Which is broken in pieces;
He shall not spare.
So there shall not be found among its fragments
A shard to take fire from the hearth,
Or to take water from the cistern."

15 For thus says the Lord GOD, the Holy One of Israel:

"In returning and rest you shall be saved;
In quietness and confidence shall be your strength."
But you would not,
16 And you said, "No, for we will flee on horses"—
Therefore you shall flee!
And, "We will ride on swift *horses*"—
Therefore those who pursue you shall be swift!
17 One thousand *shall flee* at the threat of one,
At the threat of five you shall flee,
Till you are left as a pole on top of a mountain
And as a banner on a hill.

God Will Be Gracious

18 Therefore the LORD will wait, that He may be gracious to you;
And therefore He will be exalted, that He may have mercy on you.
For the LORD *is* a God of justice;
Blessed *are* all those who wait for Him.

19 For the people shall dwell in Zion at Jerusalem;
You shall weep no more.
He will be very gracious to you at the sound of your cry;
When He hears it, He will answer you.
20 And *though* the Lord gives you
The bread of adversity and the water of affliction,
Yet your teachers will not be moved into a corner anymore,
But your eyes shall see your teachers.

30:7 [a]Literally *Rahab Sits Idle*

LIFE LESSONS

30:15 — *"In returning and rest you shall be saved; in quietness and confidence shall be your strength."*

God asks us to work hard for His kingdom (1 Thess. 5:12), but He never instructs us to strive for anything apart from the empowering of His Spirit. Dependence upon Him leads to a quiet, confident spirit.

➤ 21 Your ears shall hear a word behind you, saying,
"This *is* the way, walk in it,"
Whenever you turn to the right hand
Or whenever you turn to the left.
22 You will also defile the covering of your images of silver,
And the ornament of your molded images of gold.
You will throw them away as an unclean thing;
You will say to them, "Get away!"

23 Then He will give the rain for your seed
With which you sow the ground,
And bread of the increase of the earth;
It will be fat and plentiful.
In that day your cattle will feed
In large pastures.
24 Likewise the oxen and the young donkeys that work the ground
Will eat cured fodder,
Which has been winnowed with the shovel and fan.
25 There will be on every high mountain
And on every high hill
Rivers *and* streams of waters,
In the day of the great slaughter,
When the towers fall.
26 Moreover the light of the moon will be as the light of the sun,
And the light of the sun will be sevenfold,
As the light of seven days,
In the day that the LORD binds up the bruise of His people
And heals the stroke of their wound.

Judgment on Assyria

27 Behold, the name of the LORD comes from afar,
Burning *with* His anger,
And *His* burden *is* heavy;
His lips are full of indignation,
And His tongue like a devouring fire.
28 His breath is like an overflowing stream,
Which reaches up to the neck,
To sift the nations with the sieve of futility;
And *there shall be* a bridle in the jaws of the people,
Causing *them* to err.
29 You shall have a song
As in the night *when* a holy festival is kept,
And gladness of heart as when one goes with a flute,
To come into the mountain of the LORD,
To the Mighty One of Israel.
30 The LORD will cause His glorious voice to be heard,
And show the descent of His arm,
With the indignation of *His* anger
And the flame of a devouring fire,
With scattering, tempest, and hailstones.
31 For through the voice of the LORD
Assyria will be beaten down,
As He strikes with the rod.
32 And *in* every place where the staff of punishment passes,
Which the LORD lays on him,
It will be with tambourines and harps;
And in battles of brandishing He will fight with it.
33 For Tophet *was* established of old,
Yes, for the king it is prepared.
He has made *it* deep and large;
Its pyre *is* fire with much wood;
The breath of the LORD, like a stream of brimstone,
Kindles it.

The Folly of Not Trusting God

31 Woe to those who go down to Egypt for help, ➤
And rely on horses,
Who trust in chariots because *they are* many,
And in horsemen because they are very strong,
But who do not look to the Holy One of Israel,
Nor seek the LORD!
2 Yet He also *is* wise and will bring disaster,
And will not call back His words,
But will arise against the house of evildoers,
And against the help of those who work iniquity.
3 Now the Egyptians *are* men, and not God;
And their horses are flesh, and not spirit.

LIFE LESSONS

➤ 30:21 — *Your ears shall hear a word behind you, saying, "This is the way, walk in it," whenever you turn to the right hand or whenever you turn to the left.*

The Lord promises to lead and to guide His people. He doesn't play "hide and seek," trying to make it difficult for us to find Him and His will. If we really want to do His will, He promises to make it clear to us.

➤ 31:1 — *Woe to those who go down to Egypt for help, and rely on horses . . . but who do not look to the Holy One of Israel, nor seek the LORD!*

What is your "Egypt"? What are your "horses"? To what do you instinctively turn for help, other than your God? Those other things may seem more "practical" to eyes of flesh, but only God provides aid that will last.

WHAT THE BIBLE SAYS ABOUT THE THRILLING ADVENTURE OF OBEDIENCE

Is. 30:21

Christians sometimes approach obedience as a way of avoiding the negative consequences of disobedience. They see obedience as a burden, not as a wide road to blessing.

But God intended our walk of faith to be a thrilling adventure, motivated by our love for Jesus Christ. Obedience is about discovering God, not about avoiding unpleasant consequences. That is why John can say, "For this is the love of God, that we keep His commandments. And His commandments are not burdensome" (1 John 5:3).

When we place our trust in the omnipotence of the Lord and act on His prompting, life becomes exciting. We need not be afraid of the future because God already knows the outcome of our obedience—and we can trust in His promise that he does everything for our good (Rom. 8:28).

Walking in faith is so thrilling because each step leads to a fantastic blessing from Almighty God. The Lord continuously moves us through a variety of circumstances toward His overriding purpose for our lives. If we back off from obedience because of a mistaken desire for safety, we deprive God of the opportunity to demonstrate His awesome power in us. Small choices may seem insignificant, but they lead toward a lifetime of walking with God.

As God's children, we should ask Him what He wants us to do every day. "What would You have me say here, Lord?" or "What is the best decision now?" We must learn to listen to our heavenly Father and remain sensitive to the quiet voice that prompts us throughout the day. Isaiah says, "Your ears shall hear a word behind you, saying, 'This is the way, walk in it,' whenever you turn to the right hand or whenever you turn to the left" (Is. 30:21).

When we keep our minds attuned to Him, we will begin to understand the significance of some decisions we might otherwise barely notice. Ultimately this awareness will lead to a lifestyle of walking with the Lord and receiving his best for us.

As you look at the day ahead of you—what is *your* next step of obedience?

God intended our walk of faith to be a thrilling adventure.

See the Life Principles Index for further study:

2. Obey God and leave all the consequences to Him.

11. God assumes full responsibility for our needs when we obey Him.

21. Obedience always brings blessing.

When the LORD stretches out His hand,
Both he who helps will fall,
And he who is helped will fall down;
They all will perish together.

God Will Deliver Jerusalem

4 For thus the LORD has spoken to me:

"As a lion roars,
And a young lion over his prey
(When a multitude of shepherds is summoned against him,
He will not be afraid of their voice
Nor be disturbed by their noise),
So the LORD of hosts will come down
To fight for Mount Zion and for its hill.
5 Like birds flying about,
So will the LORD of hosts defend Jerusalem.
Defending, He will also deliver *it;*
Passing over, He will preserve *it.*"

6 Return *to Him* against whom the children
of Israel have deeply revolted.
7 For in that day every man shall throw
away his idols of silver and his idols of gold—
sin, which your own hands have made for
yourselves.

8 "Then Assyria shall fall by a sword not of man,
And a sword not of mankind shall devour him.
But he shall flee from the sword,
And his young men shall become forced labor.
9 He shall cross over to his stronghold for fear,
And his princes shall be afraid of the banner,"
Says the LORD,
Whose fire *is* in Zion
And whose furnace *is* in Jerusalem.

A Reign of Righteousness

32 Behold, a king will reign in righteousness,
And princes will rule with justice.
2 A man will be as a hiding place from the wind,
And a cover from the tempest,
As rivers of water in a dry place,
As the shadow of a great rock in a weary land.
3 The eyes of those who see will not be dim,
And the ears of those who hear will listen.
4 Also the heart of the rash will understand knowledge,
And the tongue of the stammerers will be ready to speak plainly.
5 The foolish person will no longer be called generous,
Nor the miser said *to be* bountiful;
6 For the foolish person will speak foolishness,
And his heart will work iniquity:
To practice ungodliness,
To utter error against the LORD,
To keep the hungry unsatisfied,
And he will cause the drink of the thirsty to fail.
7 Also the schemes of the schemer *are* evil;
He devises wicked plans
To destroy the poor with lying words,
Even when the needy speaks justice.
8 But a generous man devises generous things,
And by generosity he shall stand.

Consequences of Complacency

9 Rise up, you women who are at ease,
Hear my voice;
You complacent daughters,
Give ear to my speech.
10 In a year and *some* days
You will be troubled, you complacent women;
For the vintage will fail,
The gathering will not come.
11 Tremble, you *women* who are at ease;
Be troubled, you complacent ones;
Strip yourselves, make yourselves bare,
And gird *sackcloth* on *your* waists.
12 People shall mourn upon their breasts
For the pleasant fields, for the fruitful vine.
13 On the land of my people will come up thorns *and* briers,
Yes, on all the happy homes *in* the joyous city;
14 Because the palaces will be forsaken,
The bustling city will be deserted.
The forts and towers will become lairs forever,
A joy of wild donkeys, a pasture of flocks—
15 Until the Spirit is poured upon us from on high,
And the wilderness becomes a fruitful field,
And the fruitful field is counted as a forest.

The Peace of God's Reign

16 Then justice will dwell in the wilderness,
And righteousness remain in the fruitful field.
17 The work of righteousness will be peace, *
And the effect of righteousness, quietness and assurance forever.
18 My people will dwell in a peaceful habitation,
In secure dwellings, and in quiet resting places,
19 Though hail comes down on the forest,
And the city is brought low in humiliation.

20 Blessed *are* you who sow beside all
waters,
Who send out freely the feet of the ox
and the donkey.

A Prayer in Deep Distress

33 Woe to you who plunder, though you
have not *been* plundered;
And you who deal treacherously, though
they have not dealt treacherously
with you!
When you cease plundering,
You will be plundered;
When you make an end of dealing
treacherously,
They will deal treacherously with you.

➤ 2 O LORD, be gracious to us;
We have waited for You.
Be their[a] arm every morning,
Our salvation also in the time of trouble.
3 At the noise of the tumult the people
shall flee;
When You lift Yourself up, the nations
shall be scattered;
4 And Your plunder shall be gathered
Like the gathering of the caterpillar;
As the running to and fro of locusts,
He shall run upon them.

5 The LORD is exalted, for He dwells on
high;
He has filled Zion with justice and
righteousness.
6 Wisdom and knowledge will be the
stability of your times,
And the strength of salvation;
The fear of the LORD *is* His treasure.

7 Surely their valiant ones shall cry
outside,
The ambassadors of peace shall weep
bitterly.
8 The highways lie waste,
The traveling man ceases.
He has broken the covenant,
He has despised the cities,[a]
He regards no man.
9 The earth mourns *and* languishes,
Lebanon is shamed *and* shriveled;
Sharon is like a wilderness,
And Bashan and Carmel shake off *their*
fruits.

Impending Judgment on Zion

10 "Now I will rise," says the LORD;
"Now I will be exalted,
Now I will lift Myself up.
11 You shall conceive chaff,
You shall bring forth stubble;
Your breath, *as* fire, shall devour you.
12 And the people shall be *like* the burnings
of lime;
Like thorns cut up they shall be burned
in the fire.
13 Hear, you *who are* afar off, what I have
done;
And you *who are* near, acknowledge My
might."

14 The sinners in Zion are afraid;
Fearfulness has seized the hypocrites:
"Who among us shall dwell with the
devouring fire?
Who among us shall dwell with
everlasting burnings?"
15 He who walks righteously and speaks
uprightly,
He who despises the gain of oppressions,
Who gestures with his hands, refusing
bribes,
Who stops his ears from hearing of
bloodshed,
And shuts his eyes from seeing evil:
16 He will dwell on high;
His place of defense *will be* the fortress
of rocks;
Bread will be given him,
His water *will be* sure.

The Land of the Majestic King

17 Your eyes will see the King in His
beauty;
They will see the land that is very far off. ✳
18 Your heart will meditate on terror:
"Where *is* the scribe?
Where *is* he who weighs?
Where *is* he who counts the towers?"
19 You will not see a fierce people,
A people of obscure speech, beyond
perception,
Of a stammering tongue *that you* cannot
understand.

20 Look upon Zion, the city of our
appointed feasts;
Your eyes will see Jerusalem, a quiet
home,
A tabernacle *that* will not be taken
down;

33:2 [a]Septuagint omits *their;* Syriac, Targum, and Vulgate read *our.* **33:8** [a]Following Masoretic Text and Vulgate; Dead Sea Scrolls read *witnesses;* Septuagint omits *cities;* Targum reads *They have been removed from their cities.*

LIFE LESSONS

➤ **33:2 — *. . . Be their arm every morning . . . .***

When you first get out of bed in the morning, where do your thoughts run? Not everyone does devotions in the morning, but every one of us can and should begin our day with a grateful acknowledgment of God's presence.

Not one of its stakes will ever be
removed,
Nor will any of its cords be broken.
21 But there the majestic LORD *will be* for us
A place of broad rivers *and* streams,
In which no galley with oars will sail,
Nor majestic ships pass by
➤ 22 (For the LORD *is* our Judge,
The LORD *is* our Lawgiver,
The LORD *is* our King;
He will save us);
23 Your tackle is loosed,
They could not strengthen their mast,
They could not spread the sail.

Then the prey of great plunder is divided;
The lame take the prey.
24 And the inhabitant will not say, "I am
sick";
The people who dwell in it *will be*
forgiven *their* iniquity.

Judgment on the Nations

34 Come near, you nations, to hear;
And heed, you people!
Let the earth hear, and all that is in it,
The world and all things that come forth
from it.
2 For the indignation of the LORD *is* against
all nations,
And *His* fury against all their armies;
He has utterly destroyed them,
He has given them over to the slaughter.
3 Also their slain shall be thrown out;
Their stench shall rise from their corpses,
And the mountains shall be melted with
their blood.
➤ 4 All the host of heaven shall be dissolved,
And the heavens shall be rolled up like a
scroll;
All their host shall fall down
As the leaf falls from the vine,
And as *fruit* falling from a fig tree.

5 "For My sword shall be bathed in heaven;
Indeed it shall come down on Edom,
And on the people of My curse, for
judgment.
6 The sword of the LORD is filled with
blood,
It is made overflowing with fatness,
With the blood of lambs and goats,
With the fat of the kidneys of rams.
For the LORD has a sacrifice in Bozrah,
And a great slaughter in the land of
Edom.
7 The wild oxen shall come down with
them,
And the young bulls with the mighty
bulls;
Their land shall be soaked with blood,
And their dust saturated with fatness."

8 For *it is* the day of the LORD's vengeance,
The year of recompense for the cause of
Zion.
9 Its streams shall be turned into pitch,
And its dust into brimstone;
Its land shall become burning pitch.
10 It shall not be quenched night or day;
Its smoke shall ascend forever.
From generation to generation it shall lie
waste;
No one shall pass through it forever and
ever.
11 But the pelican and the porcupine shall
possess it,
Also the owl and the raven shall dwell in
it.
And He shall stretch out over it
The line of confusion and the stones of
emptiness.
12 They shall call its nobles to the kingdom,
But none *shall be* there, and all its
princes shall be nothing.

13 And thorns shall come up in its palaces,
Nettles and brambles in its fortresses;
It shall be a habitation of jackals,
A courtyard for ostriches.
14 The wild beasts of the desert shall also
meet with the jackals,
And the wild goat shall bleat to its
companion;
Also the night creature shall rest there,
And find for herself a place of rest.
15 There the arrow snake shall make her
nest and lay *eggs*
And hatch, and gather *them* under her
shadow;
There also shall the hawks be gathered,
Every one with her mate.

16 "Search from the book of the LORD, and
read:
Not one of these shall fail;
Not one shall lack her mate.
For My mouth has commanded it, and
His Spirit has gathered them.

LIFE LESSONS

➤ 33:22 — *(For the LORD is our Judge, the LORD is our Lawgiver, the LORD is our King; He will save us.)*

God is our Judge—He will give us what we deserve (2 Cor. 5:10). He is our Lawgiver—He instructs us how to live. And He is our King—He rules over all. How amazing that He is also our Savior!

➤ 34:4 — *All the host of heaven shall be dissolved, and the heavens shall be rolled up like a scroll . . . .*

Peter saw this same staggering event, and asked, "since all these things will be dissolved, what manner of persons ought you to be in holy conduct and godliness . . .?" (2 Pet. 3:10, 11).

17 He has cast the lot for them,
And His hand has divided it among them with a measuring line.
They shall possess it forever;
From generation to generation they shall dwell in it."

The Future Glory of Zion

35 The wilderness and the wasteland shall be glad for them,
And the desert shall rejoice and blossom as the rose;
➤ 2 It shall blossom abundantly and rejoice,
Even with joy and singing.
The glory of Lebanon shall be given to it,
The excellence of Carmel and Sharon.
They shall see the glory of the LORD,
The excellency of our God.

3 Strengthen the weak hands,
And make firm the feeble knees.
✳ 4 Say to those *who are* fearful-hearted,
"Be strong, do not fear!
Behold, your God will come *with* vengeance,
With the recompense of God;
He will come and save you."

5 Then the eyes of the blind shall be opened,
And the ears of the deaf shall be unstopped.
6 Then the lame shall leap like a deer,
And the tongue of the dumb sing.
For waters shall burst forth in the wilderness,
And streams in the desert.
7 The parched ground shall become a pool,
And the thirsty land springs of water;
In the habitation of jackals, where each lay,
There shall be grass with reeds and rushes.

8 A highway shall be there, and a road,
And it shall be called the Highway of Holiness.
The unclean shall not pass over it,
But it *shall be* for others.
Whoever walks the road, although a fool,
Shall not go astray.
9 No lion shall be there,
Nor shall *any* ravenous beast go up on it;
It shall not be found there.
But the redeemed shall walk *there*,
10 And the ransomed of the LORD shall return, ➤
And come to Zion with singing,
With everlasting joy on their heads.
They shall obtain joy and gladness,
And sorrow and sighing shall flee away.

Sennacherib Boasts Against the LORD

36 Now it came to pass in the fourteenth
year of King Hezekiah *that* Sennacherib king of Assyria came up against all
the fortified cities of Judah and took them.
2 Then the king of Assyria sent *the* Rabshakeh[a] with a great army from Lachish to
King Hezekiah at Jerusalem. And he stood by
the aqueduct from the upper pool, on the
highway to the Fuller's Field.
3 And Eliakim the son of Hilkiah, who was
over the household, Shebna the scribe, and
Joah the son of Asaph, the recorder, came out
to him.
4 Then *the* Rabshakeh said to them, "Say
now to Hezekiah, 'Thus says the great king,
the king of Assyria: "What confidence is this
in which you trust?
5 "I say you speak of having plans and
power for war; but *they are* mere words. Now
in whom do you trust, that you rebel against
me?
6 "Look! You are trusting in the staff of this
broken reed, Egypt, on which if a man leans,
it will go into his hand and pierce it. So *is*
Pharaoh king of Egypt to all who trust in him. ➤
7 "But if you say to me, 'We trust in the LORD
our God,' *is it* not He whose high places and
whose altars Hezekiah has taken away, and
said to Judah and Jerusalem, 'You shall worship before this altar'?"'

36:2 [a]A title, probably *Chief of Staff* or *Governor*

LIFE LESSONS

➤ 35:2 — *. . . They shall see the glory of the LORD, the excellency of our God.*

Although we can experience some of the glory and excellency of God right now, "we see in a mirror, dimly" (1 Cor. 13:12). One day, however, we will not only see His glory; we will share in it (Rom. 8:17).

➤ 35:10 — *And the ransomed of the LORD shall return, and come to Zion with singing, with everlasting joy on their heads . . . and sorrow and sighing shall flee away.*

We look forward to a time when God's goodness and righteousness will bless every believer in an unmeasured way and will banish all evil, pain, and grief. Our sorrows now cannot compare to our joy then.

➤ 36:7 — *"But if you say to me, 'We trust in the LORD our God,' is it not He whose high places and whose altars Hezekiah has taken away? . . ."*

Those who do not know the Lord simply cannot understand what a real life of faith is all about. Hezekiah removed those altars, of course, because God told him to. Religious expression does not necessarily mean spiritual reality.

8 "Now therefore, I urge you, give a pledge
to my master the king of Assyria, and I will
give you two thousand horses—if you are able
on your part to put riders on them!
9 "How then will you repel one captain of
the least of my master's servants, and put your
trust in Egypt for chariots and horsemen?
10 "Have I now come up without the LORD
against this land to destroy it? The LORD said
to me, 'Go up against this land, and destroy
it.'"
11 Then Eliakim, Shebna, and Joah said to
the Rabshakeh, "Please speak to your servants in Aramaic, for we understand *it;* and
do not speak to us in Hebrew[a] in the hearing
of the people who *are* on the wall."
12 But *the* Rabshakeh said, "Has my master
sent me to your master and to you to speak
these words, and not to the men who sit on
the wall, who will eat and drink their own
waste with you?"
13 Then *the* Rabshakeh stood and called out
with a loud voice in Hebrew, and said, "Hear
the words of the great king, the king of Assyria!
14 "Thus says the king: 'Do not let Hezekiah
deceive you, for he will not be able to deliver
you;
➤ 15 'nor let Hezekiah make you trust in the
LORD, saying, "The LORD will surely deliver
us; this city will not be given into the hand of
the king of Assyria."'
16 "Do not listen to Hezekiah; for thus says
the king of Assyria: 'Make *peace* with me *by
a* present and come out to me; and every one
of you eat from his own vine and every one
from his own fig tree, and every one of you
drink the waters of his own cistern;
17 'until I come and take you away to a land
like your own land, a land of grain and new
wine, a land of bread and vineyards.
18 '*Beware* lest Hezekiah persuade you, saying, "The LORD will deliver us." Has any one
of the gods of the nations delivered its land
from the hand of the king of Assyria?
19 'Where *are* the gods of Hamath and
Arpad? Where *are* the gods of Sepharvaim?
Indeed, have they delivered Samaria from my
hand?
20 'Who among all the gods of these lands
have delivered their countries from my hand,
that the LORD should deliver Jerusalem from
my hand?'"
21 But they held their peace and answered
him not a word; for the king's commandment
was, "Do not answer him."
22 Then Eliakim the son of Hilkiah, who *was*
over the household, Shebna the scribe, and
Joah the son of Asaph, the recorder, came to
Hezekiah with *their* clothes torn, and told
him the words of *the* Rabshakeh.

Isaiah Assures Deliverance

37 And so it was, when King Hezekiah
heard *it,* that he tore his clothes, covered himself with sackcloth, and went into
the house of the LORD.
2 Then he sent Eliakim, who *was* over the
household, Shebna the scribe, and the elders
of the priests, covered with sackcloth, to Isaiah the prophet, the son of Amoz.
3 And they said to him, "Thus says
Hezekiah: 'This day *is* a day of trouble and rebuke and blasphemy; for the children have
come to birth, but *there is* no strength to
bring them forth.
4 'It may be that the LORD your God will hear ➤
the words of *the* Rabshakeh, whom his master
the king of Assyria has sent to reproach the
living God, and will rebuke the words which
the LORD your God has heard. Therefore lift up
your prayer for the remnant that is left.'"
5 So the servants of King Hezekiah came to
Isaiah.
6 And Isaiah said to them, "Thus you shall
say to your master, 'Thus says the LORD: "Do
not be afraid of the words which you have
heard, with which the servants of the king of
Assyria have blasphemed Me.
7 "Surely I will send a spirit upon him, and
he shall hear a rumor and return to his own
land; and I will cause him to fall by the sword
in his own land."'"

Sennacherib's Threat and Hezekiah's Prayer

8 Then *the* Rabshakeh returned, and found
the king of Assyria warring against Libnah,
for he heard that he had departed from Lachish.
9 And the king heard concerning Tirhakah
king of Ethiopia, "He has come out to make
war with you." So when he heard *it,* he sent
messengers to Hezekiah, saying,

36:11 [a]Literally *Judean*

LIFE LESSONS

➤ 36:15 — *". . . nor let Hezekiah make you trust in the LORD, saying, 'The LORD will surely deliver us . . . .'"*

People try to make us doubt the existence, power, and love of God all the time. They will encourage us to "get with the program" and "be smart" and abandon what they see as religious nonsense—but God still rules.

➤ 37:4 — *". . . Therefore lift up your prayer for the remnant that is left."*

Individual prayer is crucial, but corporate prayer is also important. Throughout the Bible we see godly leaders organizing their people to pray as a group. But how can we pray corporately if we never gather with God's people?

➤ 10 "Thus you shall speak to Hezekiah king of
Judah, saying: 'Do not let your God in whom
you trust deceive you, saying, "Jerusalem
shall not be given into the hand of the king of
Assyria."
11 'Look! You have heard what the kings of
Assyria have done to all lands by utterly destroying them; and shall you be delivered?
12 'Have the gods of the nations delivered
those whom my fathers have destroyed,
Gozan and Haran and Rezeph, and the people
of Eden who *were* in Telassar?
13 'Where *is* the king of Hamath, the king of
Arpad, and the king of the city of Sepharvaim, Hena, and Ivah?'"
14 And Hezekiah received the letter from the
hand of the messengers, and read it; and
Hezekiah went up to the house of the LORD,
and spread it before the LORD.
15 Then Hezekiah prayed to the LORD, saying:
16 "O LORD of hosts, God of Israel, *the One*
who dwells *between* the cherubim, You *are*
God, You alone, of all the kingdoms of the
earth. You have made heaven and earth.
17 "Incline Your ear, O LORD, and hear; open
Your eyes, O LORD, and see; and hear all the
words of Sennacherib, which he has sent to
reproach the living God.
18 "Truly, LORD, the kings of Assyria have
laid waste all the nations and their lands,
19 "and have cast their gods into the fire; for
they *were* not gods, but the work of men's
hands—wood and stone. Therefore they destroyed them.
➤ 20 "Now therefore, O LORD our God, save us
from his hand, that all the kingdoms of the
earth may know that You *are* the LORD, You
alone."

The Word of the LORD Concerning Sennacherib

21 Then Isaiah the son of Amoz sent to
Hezekiah, saying, "Thus says the LORD God of
Israel, 'Because you have prayed to Me
against Sennacherib king of Assyria,
22 'this *is* the word which the LORD has spoken concerning him:

"The virgin, the daughter of Zion,
Has despised you, laughed you to scorn;
The daughter of Jerusalem
Has shaken *her* head behind your back!

23 "Whom have you reproached and blasphemed?
Against whom have you raised *your* voice,
And lifted up your eyes on high?
Against the Holy One of Israel.
24 By your servants you have reproached the Lord,
And said, 'By the multitude of my chariots
I have come up to the height of the mountains,
To the limits of Lebanon;
I will cut down its tall cedars
And its choice cypress trees;
I will enter its farthest height,
To its fruitful forest.
25 I have dug and drunk water,
And with the soles of my feet I have dried up
All the brooks of defense.'

26 "Did you not hear long ago
How I made it,
From ancient times that I formed it?
Now I have brought it to pass,
That you should be
For crushing fortified cities *into* heaps of ruins.
27 Therefore their inhabitants *had* little power;
They were dismayed and confounded;
They were *as* the grass of the field
And the green herb,
As the grass on the housetops
And *grain* blighted before it is grown.

28 "But I know your dwelling place,
Your going out and your coming in,
And your rage against Me.
29 Because your rage against Me and your tumult
Have come up to My ears,
Therefore I will put My hook in your nose
And My bridle in your lips,
And I will turn you back
By the way which you came."'

30 "This *shall be* a sign to you:

You shall eat this year such as grows of itself,
And the second year what springs from the same;

LIFE LESSONS

➤ 37:10 — *"Thus you shall speak to Hezekiah king of Judah, saying, 'Do not let your God in whom you trust deceive you . . . .'"*

God will never deceive anyone, but His enemies will often try to convince His people that He is not worth trusting. This was Satan's tack in the Garden of Eden, and he still uses the same tactic today.

➤ 37:20 — *"Now therefore, O LORD our God, save us from his hand, that all the kingdoms of the earth may know that You are the LORD, You alone."*

Hezekiah prayed that God might act on Judah's behalf so that the world might know that He is Lord. "He is, and He is a rewarder of those who diligently seek Him" (Heb. 11:6).

Also in the third year sow and reap,
Plant vineyards and eat the fruit of them.
31 And the remnant who have escaped of the house of Judah
Shall again take root downward,
And bear fruit upward.
32 For out of Jerusalem shall go a remnant,
And those who escape from Mount Zion.
The zeal of the LORD of hosts will do this.

33 "Therefore thus says the LORD concerning
the king of Assyria:

'He shall not come into this city,
Nor shoot an arrow there,
Nor come before it with shield,
Nor build a siege mound against it.
34 By the way that he came,
By the same shall he return;
And he shall not come into this city,'
Says the LORD.
35 'For I will defend this city, to save it
For My own sake and for My servant David's sake.'"

Sennacherib's Defeat and Death

36 Then the angel[a] of the LORD went out, and
killed in the camp of the Assyrians one hundred and eighty-five thousand; and when *people* arose early in the morning, there were the
corpses—all dead.
37 So Sennacherib king of Assyria departed
and went away, returned *home,* and remained
at Nineveh.
38 Now it came to pass, as he was worshiping
in the house of Nisroch his god, that his sons
Adrammelech and Sharezer struck him down
with the sword; and they escaped into the
land of Ararat. Then Esarhaddon his son
reigned in his place.

Hezekiah's Life Extended

38 In those days Hezekiah was sick and
near death. And Isaiah the prophet, the
son of Amoz, went to him and said to him,
"Thus says the LORD: 'Set your house in order,
for you shall die and not live.'"
2 Then Hezekiah turned his face toward the
wall, and prayed to the LORD,
3 and said, "Remember now, O LORD, I pray,
how I have walked before You in truth and
with a loyal heart, and have done *what is*
good in Your sight." And Hezekiah wept bitterly.
4 And the word of the LORD came to Isaiah,
saying,
5 "Go and tell Hezekiah, 'Thus says the
LORD, the God of David your father: "I have
heard your prayer, I have seen your tears;
surely I will add to your days fifteen years.
6 "I will deliver you and this city from the
hand of the king of Assyria, and I will defend
this city."'
7 "And this *is* the sign to you from the LORD,
that the LORD will do this thing which He has
spoken:
8 "Behold, I will bring the shadow on the
sundial, which has gone down with the sun
on the sundial of Ahaz, ten degrees backward." So the sun returned ten degrees on the
dial by which it had gone down.
9 This is the writing of Hezekiah king of Judah, when he had been sick and had recovered from his sickness:

10 I said,
"In the prime of my life
I shall go to the gates of Sheol;
I am deprived of the remainder of my years."
11 I said,
"I shall not see YAH,
The LORD[a] in the land of the living;
I shall observe man no more among the inhabitants of the world.[b]
12 My life span is gone,
Taken from me like a shepherd's tent;
I have cut off my life like a weaver.
He cuts me off from the loom;
From day until night You make an end of me.
13 I have considered until morning—
Like a lion,
So He breaks all my bones;
From day until night You make an end of me.
14 Like a crane *or* a swallow, so I chattered;
I mourned like a dove;
My eyes fail *from looking* upward.
O LORD,[a] I am oppressed;
Undertake for me!
15 "What shall I say?
He has both spoken to me,[a]

37:36 [a]Or *Angel* **38:11** [a]Hebrew *YAH, YAH* [b]Following some Hebrew manuscripts; Masoretic Text and Vulgate read *rest;* Septuagint omits *among the inhabitants of the world;* Targum reads *land.* **38:14** [a]Following Bomberg; Masoretic Text and Dead Sea Scrolls read *Lord.* **38:15** [a]Following Masoretic Text and Vulgate; Dead Sea Scrolls and Targum read *And shall I say to Him;* Septuagint omits first half of this verse.

LIFE LESSONS

➤ 38:14 — *My eyes fail from looking upward. O LORD, I am oppressed; undertake for me!*

We should not feel surprised if God seems to delay in delivering us from some trouble. Sometimes He makes us wait longer than we think we can hold on. But genuine trust perseveres no matter what.

And He Himself has done *it*.
I shall walk carefully all my years
In the bitterness of my soul.
16 O Lord, by these *things men* live;
And in all these *things is* the life of my spirit;
So You will restore me and make me live.
➤ 17 Indeed *it was* for *my own* peace
That I had great bitterness;
But You have lovingly *delivered* my soul from the pit of corruption,
For You have cast all my sins behind Your back.
18 For Sheol cannot thank You,
Death cannot praise You;
Those who go down to the pit cannot hope for Your truth.
19 The living, the living man, he shall praise You,
As I *do* this day;
The father shall make known Your truth to the children.

20 "The LORD *was ready* to save me;
Therefore we will sing my songs with stringed instruments
All the days of our life, in the house of the LORD."

21 Now Isaiah had said, "Let them take a
lump of figs, and apply *it* as a poultice on the
boil, and he shall recover."
22 And Hezekiah had said, "What *is* the sign
that I shall go up to the house of the LORD?"

The Babylonian Envoys

39 At that time Merodach-Baladan[a] the
son of Baladan, king of Babylon, sent
letters and a present to Hezekiah, for he
heard that he had been sick and had recovered.
2 And Hezekiah was pleased with them, and
showed them the house of his treasures—the
silver and gold, the spices and precious ointment, and all his armory—all that was found
among his treasures. There was nothing in his
house or in all his dominion that Hezekiah
did not show them.
3 Then Isaiah the prophet went to King
Hezekiah, and said to him, "What did these
men say, and from where did they come to
you?" So Hezekiah said, "They came to me
from a far country, from Babylon."
4 And he said, "What have they seen in your
house?" So Hezekiah answered, "They have
seen all that *is* in my house; there is nothing
among my treasures that I have not shown
them."
5 Then Isaiah said to Hezekiah, "Hear the
word of the LORD of hosts:
6 'Behold, the days are coming when all that
is in your house, and what your fathers have
accumulated until this day, shall be carried to
Babylon; nothing shall be left,' says the LORD.
7 'And they shall take away *some* of your
sons who will descend from you, whom you
will beget; and they shall be eunuchs in the
palace of the king of Babylon.'"
8 So Hezekiah said to Isaiah, "The word of
the LORD which you have spoken *is* good!" For
he said, "At least there will be peace and truth
in my days."

God's People Are Comforted

40 "Comfort, yes, comfort My people!"
Says your God.
2 "Speak comfort to Jerusalem, and cry out to her,
That her warfare is ended,
That her iniquity is pardoned;
For she has received from the LORD's hand
Double for all her sins."

3 The voice of one crying in the wilderness:
"Prepare the way of the LORD;
Make straight in the desert[a]
A highway for our God.
4 Every valley shall be exalted
And every mountain and hill brought low;
The crooked places shall be made straight
And the rough places smooth;
5 The glory of the LORD shall be revealed,
And all flesh shall see *it* together;
For the mouth of the LORD has spoken."

39:1 [a]Spelled *Berodach-Baladan* in 2 Kings 20:12
40:3 [a]Following Masoretic Text, Targum, and Vulgate; Septuagint omits *in the desert.*

LIFE LESSONS

➤ 38:17 — *Indeed it was for my own peace that I had great bitterness . . . .*

Adversity is a bridge to a deeper relationship with God. He brings bitterness into our lives only so that we can experience peace.

➤ 39:6 — *"Behold, the days are coming when all that is in your house, and what your fathers have accumulated until this day, shall be carried to Babylon . . . ."*

About a century and a half after Isaiah spoke this prophecy, it came true in 586 B.C., when the Babylonian forces of Nebuchadnezzar destroyed Jerusalem. What God speaks always comes true.

➤ 40:1 — *"Comfort, yes, comfort My people," says your God.*

Through a prophet's eyes, Isaiah saw both the destruction of his people and their eventual regathering and redemption. But even before the judgment fell, he prophesied of grace to come. That is God's way.

6 The voice said, "Cry out!"
And he[a] said, "What shall I cry?"

"All flesh *is* grass,
And all its loveliness *is* like the flower of the field.
7 The grass withers, the flower fades,
Because the breath of the LORD blows upon it;
Surely the people *are* grass.
➤ 8 The grass withers, the flower fades,
But the word of our God stands forever."

9 O Zion,
You who bring good tidings,
Get up into the high mountain;
O Jerusalem,
You who bring good tidings,
Lift up your voice with strength,
Lift *it* up, be not afraid;
Say to the cities of Judah, "Behold your God!"

10 Behold, the Lord GOD shall come with a strong *hand*,
And His arm shall rule for Him;
Behold, His reward *is* with Him,
And His work before Him.
➤ 11 He will feed His flock like a shepherd;
He will gather the lambs with His arm,
And carry *them* in His bosom,
And gently lead those who are with young.

12 Who has measured the waters[a] in the hollow of His hand,
Measured heaven with a span
And calculated the dust of the earth in a measure?
Weighed the mountains in scales
And the hills in a balance?
13 Who has directed the Spirit of the LORD,
Or *as* His counselor has taught Him?
14 With whom did He take counsel, and *who* instructed Him,
And taught Him in the path of justice?
Who taught Him knowledge,
And showed Him the way of understanding?

15 Behold, the nations *are* as a drop in a bucket,
And are counted as the small dust on the scales;
Look, He lifts up the isles as a very little thing.
16 And Lebanon *is* not sufficient to burn,
Nor its beasts sufficient for a burnt offering.
17 All nations before Him *are* as nothing,
And they are counted by Him less than nothing and worthless.

18 To whom then will you liken God?
Or what likeness will you compare to Him?
19 The workman molds an image,
The goldsmith overspreads it with gold,
And the silversmith casts silver chains.
20 Whoever *is* too impoverished for *such* a contribution
Chooses a tree *that* will not rot;
He seeks for himself a skillful workman
To prepare a carved image *that* will not totter.

21 Have you not known?
Have you not heard?
Has it not been told you from the beginning?
Have you not understood from the foundations of the earth?
22 *It is* He who sits above the circle of the earth,
And its inhabitants *are* like grasshoppers,
Who stretches out the heavens like a curtain,
And spreads them out like a tent to dwell in.
23 He brings the princes to nothing;
He makes the judges of the earth useless.

24 Scarcely shall they be planted,
Scarcely shall they be sown,
Scarcely shall their stock take root in the earth,
When He will also blow on them,
And they will wither,
And the whirlwind will take them away like stubble.

25 "To whom then will you liken Me,
Or *to whom* shall I be equal?" says the Holy One. ◄

40:6 [a]Following Masoretic Text and Targum; Dead Sea Scrolls, Septuagint, and Vulgate read *I.* **40:12** [a]Following Masoretic Text, Septuagint, and Vulgate; Dead Sea Scrolls read *waters of the sea;* Targum reads *waters of the world.*

LIFE LESSONS

➤ **40:8 — *"The grass withers, the flower fades, but the word of our God stands forever."***

Critics have attacked the Bible for centuries, but it still stands. They die; it remains. Their works are forgotten; it still generates front page news. We can bank our lives on the trustworthy Word of God.

➤ **40:11 — *He will feed His flock like a Shepherd; He will gather the lambs with His arm, and carry them in His bosom, and gently lead those who are with young.***

Jesus loved to refer to Himself as the Shepherd of God's people (John 10:11–16). The New Testament writers also considered Jesus their Shepherd (Heb. 13:20; 1 Pet. 5:4). He is both God's Lamb and our Shepherd (Rev. 7:17).

➤ **40:25 — *"To whom then will you liken Me, or to whom shall I be equal," says the Holy One.***

God has no rivals, no peers, and no equals. Satan is merely a fallen angel. God therefore deserves all our trust, and promises to reward that trust in ways beyond our comprehension.

ANSWERS TO LIFE'S QUESTIONS

How do I deal with burnout?

IS. 40:28–31

Burnout. The very expression seems to make us sigh, doesn't it? In this fast-paced, overworked world, most of us have felt the tiring numbness of burnout. How should a believer in Christ respond to these feelings?

❶ *Surrender.* You may think this means to throw up your hands and cry, "I give up!" but that is not what we must do. Rather, we should surrender everything we have to the Lord. His hands are large enough to hold anything we need Him to handle. Remember what God says: "I have made the earth, and created man on it. I—My hands—stretched out the heavens, and all their host I have commanded" (Is. 45:12). When we try to keep everything in our puny hands, we will eventually start dropping it all.

❷ *Depend on Him.* Have you ever relinquished a concern to the Lord, only to find yourself trying to pull it back out of His hand? We tend to want to fix things ourselves. The truth is, however, that only God has both the power and perspective to bring all matters to their proper conclusion (Rom. 11:33–36). When we try to take things back from Him, we only interfere with the solution He wants to bring about.

❸ *Trust Him.* Do not overlook this vital point: God loves you! Because of His great love, God wants to take care of you—and that means He wants to handle all of your worries (Matt. 6:25–34).

God does not want you to run yourself into exhaustion, even by doing "good deeds" or "church work." Instead, He desires that you rejoice in His rest (Matt. 11:29, 30). You may have reached the end of your rope, but God never will: "Have you not known? Have you not heard? The everlasting God, the LORD, the Creator of the ends of the earth, neither faints nor is weary. His understanding is unsearchable. He gives power to the weak, and to those who have no might He increases strength. Even the youths shall faint and be weary, and the young men shall utterly fall, but those who wait on the LORD shall renew their strength; they shall mount up with wings like eagles, they shall run and not be weary, they shall walk and not faint" (Is. 40:28–31).

Are you burning out? If so, return to the Flame and be rekindled today.

See the Life Principles Index for further study:
4. The awareness of God's presence energizes us for our work.

26 Lift up your eyes on high,
And see who has created these *things,*
Who brings out their host by number;
He calls them all by name,
By the greatness of His might
And the strength of *His* power;
Not one is missing.

27 Why do you say, O Jacob,
And speak, O Israel:
"My way is hidden from the LORD,
And my just claim is passed over by my God"?
28 Have you not known?
Have you not heard?
The everlasting God, the LORD,
The Creator of the ends of the earth,
Neither faints nor is weary.
His understanding is unsearchable.
29 He gives power to the weak,
And to *those who have* no might He increases strength.
30 Even the youths shall faint and be weary,
And the young men shall utterly fall,
31 But those who wait on the LORD
Shall renew *their* strength;
They shall mount up with wings like eagles,
They shall run and not be weary,
They shall walk and not faint.

LIFE LESSONS

➤ 40:29 — *He gives power to the weak, and to those who have no might He increases strength.*

Paul said, "when I am weak, then I am strong" (2 Cor. 12:10). He meant that, "the weakness of God is stronger than men" (1 Cor. 1:25)—that is, we become truly strong only when we depend on His strength.

Israel Assured of God's Help

41 "Keep silence before Me, O coastlands,
And let the people renew *their* strength!
Let them come near, then let them speak;
Let us come near together for judgment.
2 "Who raised up one from the east?
Who in righteousness called him to His feet?
Who gave the nations before him,
And made *him* rule over kings?
Who gave *them* as the dust *to* his sword,
As driven stubble to his bow?
3 Who pursued them, *and* passed safely
By the way *that* he had not gone with his feet?
➤ 4 Who has performed and done *it*,
Calling the generations from the beginning?
'I, the LORD, am the first;
And with the last I *am* He.'"
5 The coastlands saw *it* and feared,
The ends of the earth were afraid;
They drew near and came.
6 Everyone helped his neighbor,
And said to his brother,
"Be of good courage!"
7 So the craftsman encouraged the goldsmith;
He who smooths *with* the hammer
inspired him who strikes the anvil,
Saying, "It *is* ready for the soldering";
Then he fastened it with pegs,
That it might not totter.
8 "But you, Israel, *are* My servant,
Jacob whom I have chosen,
The descendants of Abraham My friend.
9 *You* whom I have taken from the ends of the earth,
And called from its farthest regions,
And said to you,
'You *are* My servant,
I have chosen you and have not cast you away:
✳ 10 Fear not, for I *am* with you;
➤ Be not dismayed, for I *am* your God.
I will strengthen you,
Yes, I will help you,
I will uphold you with My righteous right hand.'
11 "Behold, all those who were incensed against you
Shall be ashamed and disgraced;
They shall be as nothing,
And those who strive with you shall perish.
12 You shall seek them and not find them—
Those who contended with you.
Those who war against you
Shall be as nothing,
As a nonexistent thing.
13 For I, the LORD your God, will hold your right hand,
Saying to you, 'Fear not, I will help you.'
14 "Fear not, you worm Jacob,
You men of Israel!
I will help you," says the LORD
And your Redeemer, the Holy One of Israel.
15 "Behold, I will make you into a new threshing sledge with sharp teeth;
You shall thresh the mountains and beat *them* small,
And make the hills like chaff.
16 You shall winnow them, the wind shall carry them away,
And the whirlwind shall scatter them;
You shall rejoice in the LORD,
And glory in the Holy One of Israel.
17 "The poor and needy seek water, but *there is* none, ➤
Their tongues fail for thirst.
I, the LORD, will hear them;
I, the God of Israel, will not forsake them.
18 I will open rivers in desolate heights,
And fountains in the midst of the valleys;
I will make the wilderness a pool of water,
And the dry land springs of water.
19 I will plant in the wilderness the cedar and the acacia tree,
The myrtle and the oil tree;
I will set in the desert the cypress tree *and* the pine
And the box tree together,
20 That they may see and know,
And consider and understand together,
That the hand of the LORD has done this,
And the Holy One of Israel has created it.

LIFE LESSONS

➤ 41:4 — *". . . I, the LORD, am the first; and with the last I am He."*

Three times the book of Revelation appropriates this title—the First and the Last—for Jesus (Rev. 1:17; 2:8; 22:13). He who was from the beginning and always shall be knows how to rescue us from all our troubles.

➤ 41:10 — *"Fear not, for I am with you; be not dismayed, for I am your God. I will strengthen you, yes, I will help you, I will uphold you with My righteous right hand."*

Each of us will face fear at some point; it is what we do with it that matters most. We must claim our position as God's children. We have the power to overcome fear when we apply His Word to our lives.

➤ 41:17 — *"The poor and needy seek water, but there is none, their tongues fail for thirst. I, the LORD, will hear them; I, the God of Israel, will not forsake them."*

Hard times come when we run out of what we need to live. We hunger, we thirst, and so we cry out to God. God does not promise to spare us these times, but rather to sustain us in them.

The Futility of Idols

21 "Present your case," says the LORD.
"Bring forth your strong *reasons*," says the King of Jacob.
22 "Let them bring forth and show us what will happen;
Let them show the former things, what they *were*,
That we may consider them,
And know the latter end of them;
Or declare to us things to come.
23 Show the things that are to come hereafter,
That we may know that you *are* gods;
Yes, do good or do evil,
That we may be dismayed and see *it* together.
24 Indeed you *are* nothing,
And your work *is* nothing;
He who chooses you *is* an abomination.

25 "I have raised up one from the north,
And he shall come;
From the rising of the sun he shall call on My name;
And he shall come against princes as *though* mortar,
As the potter treads clay.
26 Who has declared from the beginning, that we may know?
And former times, that we may say, *'He is* righteous'?
Surely *there is* no one who shows,
Surely *there is* no one who declares,
Surely *there is* no one who hears your words.
27 The first time *I said* to Zion,
'Look, there they are!'
And I will give to Jerusalem one who brings good tidings.
28 For I looked, and *there was* no man;
I looked among them, but *there was* no counselor,
Who, when I asked of them, could answer a word.
29 Indeed they *are* all worthless;[a]
Their works *are* nothing;
Their molded images *are* wind and confusion.

The Servant of the LORD

42 "Behold! My Servant whom I uphold,
My Elect One *in whom* My soul delights!
I have put My Spirit upon Him;
He will bring forth justice to the Gentiles.
2 He will not cry out, nor raise *His voice,*
Nor cause His voice to be heard in the street.
3 A bruised reed He will not break,
And smoking flax He will not quench;
He will bring forth justice for truth.
4 He will not fail nor be discouraged,
Till He has established justice in the earth;
And the coastlands shall wait for His law."

5 Thus says God the LORD,
Who created the heavens and stretched them out,
Who spread forth the earth and that which comes from it,
Who gives breath to the people on it,
And spirit to those who walk on it:
6 "I, the LORD, have called You in righteousness,
And will hold Your hand;
I will keep You and give You as a covenant to the people,
As a light to the Gentiles,
7 To open blind eyes,
To bring out prisoners from the prison,
Those who sit in darkness from the prison house.
8 I *am* the LORD, that *is* My name;
And My glory I will not give to another,
Nor My praise to carved images.
9 Behold, the former things have come to pass,
And new things I declare;
Before they spring forth I tell you of them."

Praise to the LORD

10 Sing to the LORD a new song,
And His praise from the ends of the earth,
You who go down to the sea, and all that is in it,
You coastlands and you inhabitants of them!
11 Let the wilderness and its cities lift up *their voice,*
The villages *that* Kedar inhabits.
Let the inhabitants of Sela sing,
Let them shout from the top of the mountains.

41:29 [a]Following Masoretic Text and Vulgate; Dead Sea Scrolls, Syriac, and Targum read *nothing;* Septuagint omits the first line.

LIFE LESSONS

➤ 42:3 — *A bruised reed He will not break, and smoking flax He will not quench . . . .*

We never need to worry that when we humbly come to Christ for forgiveness or restoration or strength or wisdom, that He will despise our weakness and refuse our request. He treats the bruised and the scorched with tenderness.

12 Let them give glory to the LORD,
And declare His praise in the coastlands.
13 The LORD shall go forth like a mighty man;
He shall stir up *His* zeal like a man of war.
He shall cry out, yes, shout aloud;
He shall prevail against His enemies.

Promise of the LORD's Help

➤ **14**"I have held My peace a long time,
I have been still and restrained Myself.
Now I will cry like a woman in labor,
I will pant and gasp at once.
15 I will lay waste the mountains and hills,
And dry up all their vegetation;
I will make the rivers coastlands,
And I will dry up the pools.
16 I will bring the blind by a way they did not know;
I will lead them in paths they have not known.
I will make darkness light before them,
And crooked places straight.
These things I will do for them,
And not forsake them.
17 They shall be turned back,
They shall be greatly ashamed,
Who trust in carved images,
Who say to the molded images,
'You *are* our gods.'

18"Hear, you deaf;
And look, you blind, that you may see.
19 Who *is* blind but My servant,
Or deaf as My messenger *whom* I send?
Who *is* blind as *he who is* perfect,
And blind as the LORD's servant?
20 Seeing many things, but you do not observe;
Opening the ears, but he does not hear."

Israel's Obstinate Disobedience

21 The LORD is well pleased for His righteousness' sake;
He will exalt the law and make *it* honorable.
22 But this *is* a people robbed and plundered;
All of them are snared in holes,
And they are hidden in prison houses;
They are for prey, and no one delivers;
For plunder, and no one says, "Restore!"

23 Who among you will give ear to this?
Who will listen and hear for the time to come?
24 Who gave Jacob for plunder, and Israel to the robbers?
Was it not the LORD,
He against whom we have sinned?
For they would not walk in His ways,
Nor were they obedient to His law.
25 Therefore He has poured on him the fury of His anger
And the strength of battle;
It has set him on fire all around,
Yet he did not know;
And it burned him,
Yet he did not take *it* to heart.

The Redeemer of Israel

43 But now, thus says the LORD, who created you, O Jacob, ✳
And He who formed you, O Israel:
"Fear not, for I have redeemed you;
I have called *you* by your name;
You *are* Mine.
2 When you pass through the waters, I *will be* with you; ✳
And through the rivers, they shall not overflow you.
When you walk through the fire, you shall not be burned,
Nor shall the flame scorch you.
3 For I *am* the LORD your God,
The Holy One of Israel, your Savior;
I gave Egypt for your ransom,
Ethiopia and Seba in your place.
4 Since you were precious in My sight,
You have been honored,
And I have loved you;
Therefore I will give men for you,
And people for your life.
5 Fear not, for I *am* with you;
I will bring your descendants from the east,
And gather you from the west;
6 I will say to the north, 'Give them up!'
And to the south, 'Do not keep them back!'
Bring My sons from afar,
And My daughters from the ends of the earth—
7 Everyone who is called by My name, ➤
Whom I have created for My glory;
I have formed him, yes, I have made him."

LIFE LESSONS

➤ **42:14 — *"I have held My peace a long time, I have been still and restrained Myself. Now I will cry like a woman in labor, I will pant and gasp at once."***

We often wonder why God seems to restrain His hand when we need Him to act, or why He remains silent when we need Him to speak. When He acts in power, He often does so suddenly and explosively.

➤ **43:7 — *"Everyone who is called by My name, whom I have created for My glory . . . ."***

Do you realize that the God of heaven has created *you* for His glory? He wants the world to see some of His majesty and goodness through you, and He wants to crown you with His own splendor.

8 Bring out the blind people who have eyes,
And the deaf who have ears.
9 Let all the nations be gathered together,
And let the people be assembled.
Who among them can declare this,
And show us former things?
Let them bring out their witnesses, that
they may be justified;
Or let them hear and say, "*It is* truth."
10 "You *are* My witnesses," says the LORD,
"And My servant whom I have chosen,
That you may know and believe Me,
And understand that I *am* He.
Before Me there was no God formed,
Nor shall there be after Me.
11 I, *even* I, *am* the LORD,
And besides Me *there is* no savior.
12 I have declared and saved,
I have proclaimed,
And *there was* no foreign *god* among you;
Therefore you *are* My witnesses,"
Says the LORD, "that I *am* God.
13 Indeed before the day *was,* I *am* He;
And *there is* no one who can deliver out
of My hand;
I work, and who will reverse it?"

14 Thus says the LORD, your Redeemer,
The Holy One of Israel:
"For your sake I will send to Babylon,
And bring them all down as fugitives—
The Chaldeans, who rejoice in their ships.
15 I *am* the LORD, your Holy One,
The Creator of Israel, your King."

16 Thus says the LORD, who makes a way in
the sea
And a path through the mighty waters,
17 Who brings forth the chariot and horse,
The army and the power
(They shall lie down together, they shall
not rise;
They are extinguished, they are
quenched like a wick):
18 "Do not remember the former things,
Nor consider the things of old.
➤ 19 Behold, I will do a new thing,
Now it shall spring forth;
Shall you not know it?
I will even make a road in the wilderness
And rivers in the desert.
➤ 20 The beast of the field will honor Me,
The jackals and the ostriches,
Because I give waters in the wilderness
And rivers in the desert,
To give drink to My people, My chosen.
21 This people I have formed for Myself;
They shall declare My praise.

Pleading with Unfaithful Israel

22 "But you have not called upon Me,
O Jacob;
And you have been weary of Me,
O Israel.
23 You have not brought Me the sheep for
your burnt offerings,
Nor have you honored Me with your
sacrifices.
I have not caused you to serve with grain
offerings,
Nor wearied you with incense.
24 You have bought Me no sweet cane with
money,
Nor have you satisfied Me with the fat of
your sacrifices;
But you have burdened Me with your sins,
You have wearied Me with your
iniquities.

25 "I, *even* I, *am* He who blots out your ✳
transgressions for My own sake;
And I will not remember your sins.
26 Put Me in remembrance;
Let us contend together;
State your *case,* that you may be
acquitted.
27 Your first father sinned,
And your mediators have transgressed
against Me.
28 Therefore I will profane the princes of
the sanctuary;
I will give Jacob to the curse,
And Israel to reproaches.

God's Blessing on Israel

44 "Yet hear me now, O Jacob My
servant,
And Israel whom I have chosen.
2 Thus says the LORD who made you
And formed you from the womb, *who*
will help you:
'Fear not, O Jacob My servant;
And you, Jeshurun, whom I have chosen.
3 For I will pour water on him who is
thirsty,
And floods on the dry ground;
I will pour My Spirit on your descendants,
And My blessing on your offspring;

LIFE LESSONS

➤ 43:19 — *"Behold, I will do a new thing, now it shall spring forth; shall you not know it?"*

God loves *new* things: new songs, new hearts, new heavens, new earth, new names. We should not always look for Him to do in our lives what He has done before, but should learn to expect the unexpected.

➤ 43:20 — *". . . I give waters in the wilderness and rivers in the desert, to give drink to My people, My chosen."*

God does not promise to keep us out of the wilderness or away from the desert. But if we belong to Him, He does promise to sustain us there and renew our lives even in the tough times.

4 They will spring up among the grass
Like willows by the watercourses.'
5 One will say, 'I *am* the LORD's';
Another will call *himself* by the name of Jacob;
Another will write *with* his hand, 'The LORD's,'
And name *himself* by the name of Israel.

There Is No Other God

6 "Thus says the LORD, the King of Israel,
And his Redeemer, the LORD of hosts:
'I *am* the First and I *am* the Last;
Besides Me *there is* no God.
7 And who can proclaim as I do?
Then let him declare it and set it in order for Me,
Since I appointed the ancient people.
And the things that are coming and shall come,
Let them show these to them.
➤ 8 Do not fear, nor be afraid;
Have I not told you from that time, and declared *it?*
You *are* My witnesses.
Is there a God besides Me?
Indeed *there is* no other Rock;
I know not *one.*'"

Idolatry Is Foolishness

9 Those who make an image, all of them *are* useless,
And their precious things shall not profit;
They *are* their own witnesses;
They neither see nor know, that they may be ashamed.
10 Who would form a god or mold an image
That profits him nothing?
11 Surely all his companions would be ashamed;
And the workmen, they *are* mere men.
Let them all be gathered together,
Let them stand up;
Yet they shall fear,
They shall be ashamed together.

12 The blacksmith with the tongs works one in the coals,
Fashions it with hammers,
And works it with the strength of his arms.
Even so, he is hungry, and his strength fails;
He drinks no water and is faint.

13 The craftsman stretches out *his* rule,
He marks one out with chalk;
He fashions it with a plane,
He marks it out with the compass,
And makes it like the figure of a man,
According to the beauty of a man, that it may remain in the house.
14 He cuts down cedars for himself,
And takes the cypress and the oak;
He secures *it* for himself among the trees of the forest.
He plants a pine, and the rain nourishes *it.*

15 Then it shall be for a man to burn,
For he will take some of it and warm himself;
Yes, he kindles *it* and bakes bread;
Indeed he makes a god and worships *it;*
He makes it a carved image, and falls down to it.
16 He burns half of it in the fire;
With this half he eats meat;
He roasts a roast, and is satisfied.
He even warms *himself* and says,
"Ah! I am warm,
I have seen the fire."
17 And the rest of it he makes into a god,
His carved image.
He falls down before it and worships *it,*
Prays to it and says,
"Deliver me, for you *are* my god!"

18 They do not know nor understand;
For He has shut their eyes, so that they cannot see,
And their hearts, so that they cannot understand.
19 And no one considers in his heart,
Nor *is there* knowledge nor understanding to say,
"I have burned half of it in the fire,
Yes, I have also baked bread on its coals;
I have roasted meat and eaten *it;*
And shall I make the rest of it an abomination?
Shall I fall down before a block of wood?"
20 He feeds on ashes;
A deceived heart has turned him aside;
And he cannot deliver his soul,
Nor say, "*Is there* not a lie in my right hand?"

Israel Is Not Forgotten

21 "Remember these, O Jacob,
And Israel, for you *are* My servant;
I have formed you, you *are* My servant;
O Israel, you will not be forgotten by Me!

LIFE LESSONS

➤ 44:8 — *". . . Is there a God besides Me? Indeed there is no other Rock; I know not one."*

Scripture consistently teaches that only one true God exists. All other "so-called gods" (1 Cor. 8:5) are actually nothing but demons trying to usurp the worship that belongs to God alone (1 Cor. 10:20).

WHAT THE BIBLE SAYS ABOUT **HOW TO HANDLE FEELINGS OF GUILT**

Is. 44:9–11

Many teachers find true-or-false tests a useful tool to determine what their students know. Some people seem able to discern right away what is true. Others ponder the question at length and realize they can't with confidence identify the truth.

How would *you* answer the following questions?

True or False? *It is the responsibility of the Holy Spirit to convict us of sin.*

The answer is TRUE (John 16:8). When we have sinned, the Holy Spirit will cause us to feel guilty. Why? So we will ask God's forgiveness and allow Him to restore us to a proper fellowship with Him.

It is possible, of course, to engage in sin for so long that feelings of shame and guilt evaporate. Isaiah marveled that his countrymen could create lifeless idols to worship and yet feel no shame (Is. 44:9–11). And the apostle Paul said that people can wallow in sin for so long that their consciences become seared as with a hot iron (1 Tim. 4:2). Nevertheless, it is the Holy Spirit's job—*not* ours—to convict people of their sin.

Accept the truth that God loves you.

True or False? *All guilty feelings come because of sin.*

The answer is FALSE. Guilty feelings can come for reasons other than our sin. A wrong view of God may cause us to feel guilty. We feel guilty when we imagine God is gleefully noticing our mistakes, pointing His finger at us, and eagerly pronouncing judgment. At other times we feel guilty and do not know why. The New Testament proclaims that "there is therefore now no condemnation to those who are in Christ Jesus" (Rom. 8:1). Jesus came to take away our guilt (Is. 53:10)—and the Spirit-filled life is designed to overflow with joy and peace.

Spend this week learning to know God as the Bible reveals Him. Look especially at the love and compassion Jesus had for the crowds who followed Him (Matt. 14:14), the widow (Luke 7:13), the leper (Mark 1:40–42), and the tax collector (Matt. 9:9–12). Accept the truth that God loves you, and allow any "false" guilt feelings to melt away.

See the Life Principles Index for further study:
15. Brokenness is God's requirement for maximum usefulness.

And compare Me, that we should be alike?
6 They lavish gold out of the bag,
And weigh silver on the scales;
They hire a goldsmith, and he makes it a god;
They prostrate themselves, yes, they worship.
7 They bear it on the shoulder, they carry it
And set it in its place, and it stands;
From its place it shall not move.
Though *one* cries out to it, yet it cannot answer
Nor save him out of his trouble.

8 "Remember this, and show yourselves men;
Recall to mind, O you transgressors.
➢ 9 Remember the former things of old,
For I *am* God, and *there is* no other;
I am God, and *there is* none like Me,
10 Declaring the end from the beginning,
And from ancient times *things* that are not *yet* done,
Saying, 'My counsel shall stand,
And I will do all My pleasure,'
11 Calling a bird of prey from the east,
The man who executes My counsel, from a far country.
Indeed I have spoken *it;*
I will also bring it to pass.
I have purposed *it;*
I will also do it.

12 "Listen to Me, you stubborn-hearted,
Who *are* far from righteousness:
13 I bring My righteousness near, it shall not be far off;
My salvation shall not linger.
And I will place salvation in Zion,
For Israel My glory.

The Humiliation of Babylon

47 "Come down and sit in the dust,
O virgin daughter of Babylon;
Sit on the ground without a throne,
O daughter of the Chaldeans!
For you shall no more be called
Tender and delicate.
2 Take the millstones and grind meal.
Remove your veil,
Take off the skirt,
Uncover the thigh,
Pass through the rivers.
3 Your nakedness shall be uncovered,
Yes, your shame will be seen;
I will take vengeance,
And I will not arbitrate with a man."
4 *As for* our Redeemer, the LORD of hosts *is* His name,
The Holy One of Israel.

5 "Sit in silence, and go into darkness,
O daughter of the Chaldeans;
For you shall no longer be called
The Lady of Kingdoms.
6 I was angry with My people;
I have profaned My inheritance,
And given them into your hand.
You showed them no mercy;
On the elderly you laid your yoke very heavily.
7 And you said, 'I shall be a lady forever,'
So that you did not take these *things* to heart,
Nor remember the latter end of them.

8 "Therefore hear this now, *you who are* given to pleasures,
Who dwell securely,
Who say in your heart, 'I *am*, and *there is* no one else besides me;
I shall not sit *as* a widow,
Nor shall I know the loss of children';
9 But these two *things* shall come to you
In a moment, in one day:
The loss of children, and widowhood.
They shall come upon you in their fullness
Because of the multitude of your sorceries,
For the great abundance of your enchantments.

10 "For you have trusted in your wickedness;
You have said, 'No one sees me';
Your wisdom and your knowledge have warped you;
And you have said in your heart,
'I *am*, and *there is* no one else besides me.'
11 Therefore evil shall come upon you;
You shall not know from where it arises.
And trouble shall fall upon you;
You will not be able to put it off.
And desolation shall come upon you suddenly,
Which you shall not know.

12 "Stand now with your enchantments
And the multitude of your sorceries,
In which you have labored from your youth—
Perhaps you will be able to profit,
Perhaps you will prevail.
13 You are wearied in the multitude of your counsels;

LIFE LESSONS

➢ **46:9, 10 — "*. . . I am God, and there is none like Me, declaring the end from the beginning, and from ancient times things that are not yet done . . . .*"**

According to some estimates, almost thirty percent of the Bible concerned future events at the time it was written. God declares to us "the end from the beginning" so that we might trust both Him and His Word.

Let now the astrologers, the stargazers,
And the monthly prognosticators
Stand up and save you
From what shall come upon you.
14 Behold, they shall be as stubble,
The fire shall burn them;
They shall not deliver themselves
From the power of the flame;
It shall not *be* a coal to be warmed by,
Nor a fire to sit before!
15 Thus shall they be to you
With whom you have labored,
Your merchants from your youth;
They shall wander each one to his quarter.
No one shall save you.

Israel Refined for God's Glory

48 "Hear this, O house of Jacob,
Who are called by the name of Israel,
And have come forth from the wellsprings of Judah;
Who swear by the name of the LORD,
And make mention of the God of Israel,
But not in truth or in righteousness;
2 For they call themselves after the holy city,
And lean on the God of Israel;
The LORD of hosts *is* His name:

3 "I have declared the former things from the beginning;
They went forth from My mouth, and I caused them to hear it.
Suddenly I did *them*, and they came to pass.
4 Because I knew that you *were* obstinate,
And your neck *was* an iron sinew,
And your brow bronze,
5 Even from the beginning I have declared *it* to you;
Before it came to pass I proclaimed *it* to you,
Lest you should say, 'My idol has done them,
And my carved image and my molded image
Have commanded them.'

6 "You have heard;
See all this.
And will you not declare *it*?
I have made you hear new things from this time,
Even hidden things, and you did not know them.
7 They are created now and not from the beginning;
And before this day you have not heard them,
Lest you should say, 'Of course I knew them.'
8 Surely you did not hear,
Surely you did not know;
Surely from long ago your ear was not opened.
For I knew that you would deal very treacherously,
And were called a transgressor from the womb.

9 "For My name's sake I will defer My anger,
And *for* My praise I will restrain it from you,
So that I do not cut you off.
10 Behold, I have refined you, but not as silver;
I have tested you in the furnace of affliction.
11 For My own sake, for My own sake, I will do *it;*
For how should *My name* be profaned?
And I will not give My glory to another.

God's Ancient Plan to Redeem Israel

12 "Listen to Me, O Jacob,
And Israel, My called:
I *am* He, I *am* the First,
I *am* also the Last.
13 Indeed My hand has laid the foundation of the earth,
And My right hand has stretched out the heavens;
When I call to them,
They stand up together.

14 "All of you, assemble yourselves, and hear!
Who among them has declared these *things?*
The LORD loves him;
He shall do His pleasure on Babylon,
And His arm *shall be against* the Chaldeans.
15 I, *even* I, have spoken;
Yes, I have called him,
I have brought him, and his way will prosper.

16 "Come near to Me, hear this:
I have not spoken in secret from the beginning;
From the time that it was, I *was* there.
And now the Lord GOD and His Spirit
Have[a] sent Me."

48:16 [a]The Hebrew verb is singular.

LIFE LESSONS

➤ 48:9 — *"For My name's sake I will defer My anger, and for My praise I will restrain it from you, so that I do not cut you off."*

We owe our salvation to the love and grace of God, and not to anything else. God saved us for His name's sake, not because we deserved it or were somehow worth more than the Son who died for us.

➤ 17 Thus says the LORD, your Redeemer,
The Holy One of Israel:
"I *am* the LORD your God,
Who teaches you to profit,
Who leads you by the way you should go.
18 Oh, that you had heeded My commandments!
Then your peace would have been like a river,
And your righteousness like the waves of the sea.
19 Your descendants also would have been like the sand,
And the offspring of your body like the grains of sand;
His name would not have been cut off
Nor destroyed from before Me."

20 Go forth from Babylon!
Flee from the Chaldeans!
With a voice of singing,
Declare, proclaim this,
Utter it to the end of the earth;
Say, "The LORD has redeemed
His servant Jacob!"
21 And they did not thirst
When He led them through the deserts;
He caused the waters to flow from the rock for them;
He also split the rock, and the waters gushed out.

22 "*There is* no peace," says the LORD, "for the wicked."

The Servant, the Light to the Gentiles

49 "Listen, O coastlands, to Me,
And take heed, you peoples from afar!
The LORD has called Me from the womb;
From the matrix of My mother He has made mention of My name.
2 And He has made My mouth like a sharp sword;
In the shadow of His hand He has hidden Me,
And made Me a polished shaft;
In His quiver He has hidden Me."

3 "And He said to me,
'You *are* My servant, O Israel,
In whom I will be glorified.'
4 Then I said, 'I have labored in vain,
I have spent my strength for nothing and in vain;
Yet surely my just reward *is* with the LORD,
And my work with my God.'"

5 "And now the LORD says,
Who formed Me from the womb *to be* His Servant,
To bring Jacob back to Him,
So that Israel is gathered to Him[a]
(For I shall be glorious in the eyes of the LORD,
And My God shall be My strength),
6 Indeed He says,
'It is too small a thing that You should be My Servant
To raise up the tribes of Jacob,
And to restore the preserved ones of Israel;
I will also give You as a light to the Gentiles,
That You should be My salvation to the ends of the earth.'"

7 Thus says the LORD,
The Redeemer of Israel, their Holy One,
To Him whom man despises,
To Him whom the nation abhors,
To the Servant of rulers:
"Kings shall see and arise,
Princes also shall worship,
Because of the LORD who is faithful,
The Holy One of Israel;
And He has chosen You."
8 Thus says the LORD:

"In an acceptable time I have heard You,
And in the day of salvation I have helped You;
I will preserve You and give You
As a covenant to the people,
To restore the earth,
To cause them to inherit the desolate heritages;
9 That You may say to the prisoners, 'Go forth,'
To those who *are* in darkness, 'Show yourselves.'

"They shall feed along the roads,
And their pastures *shall be* on all desolate heights.
10 They shall neither hunger nor thirst,
Neither heat nor sun shall strike them;
For He who has mercy on them will lead them,
Even by the springs of water He will guide them.

49:5 [a]Qere, Dead Sea Scrolls, and Septuagint read *is gathered to Him;* Kethib reads *is not gathered.*

LIFE LESSONS

➤ **48:17 — *"I am the LORD your God, who teaches you to profit, who leads you by the way you should go."***

God may sometimes lead you into tight spots and difficult circumstances (see Mark 6:45; Luke 10:1), but wherever He guides you, He does it "to do you good in the end" (Deut. 8:16).

11 I will make each of My mountains a road,
And My highways shall be elevated.
12 Surely these shall come from afar;
Look! Those from the north and the west,
And these from the land of Sinim."

✳ 13 Sing, O heavens!
Be joyful, O earth!
And break out in singing, O mountains!
For the LORD has comforted His people,
And will have mercy on His afflicted.

God Will Remember Zion

14 But Zion said, "The LORD has forsaken me,
And my Lord has forgotten me."

➤ 15 "Can a woman forget her nursing child,
And not have compassion on the son of her womb?
Surely they may forget,
Yet I will not forget you.
16 See, I have inscribed you on the palms *of My hands;*
Your walls *are* continually before Me.
17 Your sons[a] shall make haste;
Your destroyers and those who laid you waste
Shall go away from you.
18 Lift up your eyes, look around and see;
All these gather together *and* come to you.
As I live," says the LORD,
"You shall surely clothe yourselves with them all as an ornament,
And bind them *on you* as a bride *does.*

19 "For your waste and desolate places,
And the land of your destruction,
Will even now be too small for the inhabitants;
And those who swallowed you up will be far away.
20 The children you will have,
After you have lost the others,
Will say again in your ears,
'The place *is* too small for me;
Give me a place where I may dwell.'
21 Then you will say in your heart,
'Who has begotten these for me,
Since I have lost my children and am desolate,
A captive, and wandering to and fro?
And who has brought these up?
There I was, left alone;
But these, where *were* they?'"

22 Thus says the Lord GOD:

"Behold, I will lift My hand in an oath to the nations,
And set up My standard for the peoples;
They shall bring your sons in *their* arms,
And your daughters shall be carried on *their* shoulders;
23 Kings shall be your foster fathers,
And their queens your nursing mothers;
They shall bow down to you with *their* faces to the earth,
And lick up the dust of your feet.
Then you will know that I *am* the LORD,
For they shall not be ashamed who wait for Me."

24 Shall the prey be taken from the mighty,
Or the captives of the righteous[a] be delivered?

25 But thus says the LORD:

"Even the captives of the mighty shall be taken away,
And the prey of the terrible be delivered;
For I will contend with him who contends with you,
And I will save your children.
26 I will feed those who oppress you with their own flesh,
And they shall be drunk with their own blood as with sweet wine.
All flesh shall know
That I, the LORD, *am* your Savior,
And your Redeemer, the Mighty One of Jacob."

The Servant, Israel's Hope

50 Thus says the LORD:

"Where *is* the certificate of your mother's divorce,
Whom I have put away?
Or which of My creditors *is it* to whom I have sold you?
For your iniquities you have sold yourselves,
And for your transgressions your mother has been put away.
2 Why, when I came, *was there* no man?
Why, when I called, *was there* none to answer?
Is My hand shortened at all that it cannot redeem?
Or have I no power to deliver?
Indeed with My rebuke I dry up the sea,

49:17 [a]Dead Sea Scrolls, Septuagint, Targum, and Vulgate read *builders.* **49:24** [a]Following Masoretic Text and Targum; Dead Sea Scrolls, Syriac, and Vulgate read *the mighty;* Septuagint reads *unjustly.*

LIFE LESSONS

➤ **49:15 — *"Can a woman forget her nursing child, and not have compassion on the son of her womb? Surely they may forget, yet I will not forget you."***

God loves you more than any mother has ever loved her own son or daughter. Everything He does in your life, He does out of love and for love's sake. He allows even the hard times for your benefit.

I make the rivers a wilderness;
Their fish stink because *there is* no water,
And die of thirst.
3 I clothe the heavens with blackness,
And I make sackcloth their covering."

4 "The Lord God has given Me
The tongue of the learned,
That I should know how to speak
A word in season to *him who is* weary.
He awakens Me morning by morning,
He awakens My ear
To hear as the learned.
5 The Lord God has opened My ear;
And I was not rebellious,
Nor did I turn away.
6 I gave My back to those who struck *Me,*
And My cheeks to those who plucked out the beard;
I did not hide My face from shame and spitting.

➤ 7 "For the Lord God will help Me;
Therefore I will not be disgraced;
Therefore I have set My face like a flint,
And I know that I will not be ashamed.
8 *He is* near who justifies Me;
Who will contend with Me?
Let us stand together.
Who *is* My adversary?
Let him come near Me.
9 Surely the Lord God will help Me;
Who *is* he *who* will condemn Me?
Indeed they will all grow old like a garment;
The moth will eat them up.

➤ 10 "Who among you fears the LORD?
Who obeys the voice of His Servant?
Who walks in darkness
And has no light?
Let him trust in the name of the LORD
And rely upon his God.
11 Look, all you who kindle a fire,
Who encircle *yourselves* with sparks:
Walk in the light of your fire and in the sparks you have kindled—
This you shall have from My hand:
You shall lie down in torment.

The LORD Comforts Zion

51 "Listen to Me, you who follow after righteousness,
You who seek the LORD:
Look to the rock *from which* you were hewn,
And to the hole of the pit *from which* you were dug.
2 Look to Abraham your father,
And to Sarah *who* bore you;
For I called him alone,
And blessed him and increased him."
3 For the LORD will comfort Zion,
He will comfort all her waste places;
He will make her wilderness like Eden,
And her desert like the garden of the LORD;
Joy and gladness will be found in it,
Thanksgiving and the voice of melody.

4 "Listen to Me, My people;
And give ear to Me, O My nation:
For law will proceed from Me,
And I will make My justice rest
As a light of the peoples.
5 My righteousness *is* near,
My salvation has gone forth,
And My arms will judge the peoples;
The coastlands will wait upon Me,
And on My arm they will trust.
6 Lift up your eyes to the heavens,
And look on the earth beneath.
For the heavens will vanish away like smoke,
The earth will grow old like a garment,
And those who dwell in it will die in like manner;
But My salvation will be forever,
And My righteousness will not be abolished.

7 "Listen to Me, you who know righteousness, ✳
You people in whose heart *is* My law:
Do not fear the reproach of men,
Nor be afraid of their insults.
8 For the moth will eat them up like a garment,
And the worm will eat them like wool;
But My righteousness will be forever,
And My salvation from generation to generation."

9 Awake, awake, put on strength,
O arm of the LORD!
Awake as in the ancient days,
In the generations of old.
Are You not *the arm* that cut Rahab apart,
And wounded the serpent?

LIFE LESSONS

➤ 50:7 — *"For the Lord GOD will help Me; therefore I will not be disgraced; therefore I have set My face like a flint, and I know that I will not be ashamed."*

If you know and feel certain that God is for you, then you too can set your face like a flint, and "be steadfast, immovable, always abounding in the work of the Lord, knowing that your labor is not in vain" (1 Cor. 15:58).

➤ 50:10 — *". . . Who walks in darkness and has no light? Let him trust in the name of the LORD and rely upon his God."*

Dark times come upon all of us; that's part of life in a fallen world. But we do not have to grope blindly, as those without hope. We trust God in the dark, take His hand, and go where He leads.

10 *Are* You not *the One* who dried up the
sea,
The waters of the great deep;
That made the depths of the sea a road
For the redeemed to cross over?
11 So the ransomed of the LORD shall
return,
And come to Zion with singing,
With everlasting joy on their heads.
They shall obtain joy and gladness;
Sorrow and sighing shall flee away.

➤ 12 "I, *even* I, *am* He who comforts you.
Who *are* you that you should be afraid
Of a man *who* will die,
And of the son of a man *who* will be
made like grass?
13 And you forget the LORD your Maker,
Who stretched out the heavens
And laid the foundations of the earth;
You have feared continually every day
Because of the fury of the oppressor,
When *he has* prepared to destroy.
And where *is* the fury of the oppressor?
14 The captive exile hastens, that he may be
loosed,
That he should not die in the pit,
And that his bread should not fail.
15 But I *am* the LORD your God,
Who divided the sea whose waves
roared—
The LORD of hosts *is* His name.
16 And I have put My words in your mouth;
I have covered you with the shadow of
My hand,
That I may plant the heavens,
Lay the foundations of the earth,
And say to Zion, 'You *are* My people.'"

God's Fury Removed

17 Awake, awake!
Stand up, O Jerusalem,
You who have drunk at the hand of the
LORD
The cup of His fury;
You have drunk the dregs of the cup of
trembling,
And drained *it* out.
18 *There is* no one to guide her
Among all the sons she has brought
forth;
Nor *is there any* who takes her by the
hand
Among all the sons she has brought up.
19 These two *things* have come to you;
Who will be sorry for you?—
Desolation and destruction, famine and
sword—
By whom will I comfort you?
20 Your sons have fainted,
They lie at the head of all the streets,
Like an antelope in a net;
They are full of the fury of the LORD,
The rebuke of your God.

21 Therefore please hear this, you afflicted,
And drunk but not with wine.
22 Thus says your Lord,
The LORD and your God,
Who pleads the cause of His people:
"See, I have taken out of your hand
The cup of trembling,
The dregs of the cup of My fury;
You shall no longer drink it.
23 But I will put it into the hand of those
who afflict you,
Who have said to you,[a]
'Lie down, that we may walk over you.'
And you have laid your body like the
ground,
And as the street, for those who walk
over."

God Redeems Jerusalem

52 Awake, awake!
Put on your strength, O Zion;
Put on your beautiful garments,
O Jerusalem, the holy city!
For the uncircumcised and the unclean
Shall no longer come to you.
2 Shake yourself from the dust, arise;
Sit down, O Jerusalem!
Loose yourself from the bonds of your
neck,
O captive daughter of Zion!

3 For thus says the LORD:

"You have sold yourselves for nothing,
And you shall be redeemed without
money."

4 For thus says the Lord GOD:

"My people went down at first
Into Egypt to dwell there;
Then the Assyrian oppressed them
without cause.

51:23 [a]Literally *your soul*

LIFE LESSONS

➤ 51:12 — *"I, even I, am He who comforts you . . . ."*

God does not leave us comfortless. He always comes with words of hope and mercy. His goal in allowing hurt is not to break us, but to teach us to draw close to Him in times of heartache and extreme pressure.

➤ 52:3 — *For thus says the LORD: "You have sold yourselves for nothing, and you shall be redeemed without money."*

Why do we sin? We sin because we think that it gives us a better deal than whatever God is offering. But we always get burned. We sell ourselves for nothing—and then God buys us back with Himself.

5 Now therefore, what have I here," says
the LORD,
"That My people are taken away for
nothing?
Those who rule over them
Make them wail,"[a] says the LORD,
"And My name *is* blasphemed continually
every day.
6 Therefore My people shall know My
name;
Therefore *they shall know* in that day
That I *am* He who speaks:
'Behold, *it is* I.'"

7 How beautiful upon the mountains
Are the feet of him who brings good news,
Who proclaims peace,
Who brings glad tidings of good *things*,
Who proclaims salvation,
Who says to Zion,
"Your God reigns!"
8 Your watchmen shall lift up *their* voices,
With their voices they shall sing together;
For they shall see eye to eye
When the LORD brings back Zion.
9 Break forth into joy, sing together,
You waste places of Jerusalem!
For the LORD has comforted His people,
He has redeemed Jerusalem.
10 The LORD has made bare His holy arm
In the eyes of all the nations;
And all the ends of the earth shall see
The salvation of our God.

11 Depart! Depart! Go out from there,
Touch no unclean *thing*;
Go out from the midst of her,
Be clean,
You who bear the vessels of the LORD.
12 For you shall not go out with haste,
Nor go by flight;
For the LORD will go before you,
And the God of Israel *will* be your rear
guard.

The Sin-Bearing Servant

13 Behold, My Servant shall deal prudently;
He shall be exalted and extolled and be
very high.
➤ 14 Just as many were astonished at you,
So His visage was marred more than any
man,
And His form more than the sons of men;
15 So shall He sprinkle[a] many nations.
Kings shall shut their mouths at Him;
For what had not been told them they
shall see,
And what they had not heard they shall
consider.

53 Who has believed our report?
And to whom has the arm of the LORD
been revealed?
2 For He shall grow up before Him as a
tender plant,
And as a root out of dry ground.
He has no form or comeliness;
And when we see Him,
There is no beauty that we should desire
Him.
3 He is despised and rejected by men,
A Man of sorrows and acquainted with
grief.
And we hid, as it were, *our* faces from
Him;
He was despised, and we did not esteem
Him.

4 Surely He has borne our griefs
And carried our sorrows;
Yet we esteemed Him stricken,
Smitten by God, and afflicted.
5 But He *was* wounded for our ◄
transgressions,
He was bruised for our iniquities;
The chastisement for our peace *was* upon
Him,
And by His stripes we are healed.
6 All we like sheep have gone astray;
We have turned, every one, to his own
way;
And the LORD has laid on Him the
iniquity of us all.

7 He was oppressed and He was afflicted,
Yet He opened not His mouth;
He was led as a lamb to the slaughter,
And as a sheep before its shearers is
silent,
So He opened not His mouth.
8 He was taken from prison and from
judgment,

52:5 [a]Dead Sea Scrolls read *Mock;* Septuagint reads *Marvel and wail;* Targum reads *Boast themselves;* Vulgate reads *Treat them unjustly.* **52:15** [a]Or *startle*

LIFE LESSONS

➤ 52:14 — ***His visage was marred more than any man, and His form more than the sons of men . . . .***

Jesus went through agony for our sakes. He suffered, not through any personal fault, but because of our sins. He willingly died for us, that we might live. "If you love Me," He says, "keep my commandments" (John 14:15).

➤ 53:5 — ***But He was wounded for our transgressions, He was bruised for our iniquities; the chastisement for our peace was upon Him, and by His stripes we are healed.***

On the cross, Jesus willingly became our substitute. God made Jesus "who knew no sin to be sin for us, that we might become the righteousness of God in Him" (2 Cor. 5:21).

And who will declare His generation?
For He was cut off from the land of the living;
For the transgressions of My people He was stricken.
9 And they[a] made His grave with the wicked—
But with the rich at His death,
Because He had done no violence,
Nor *was any* deceit in His mouth.

10 Yet it pleased the LORD to bruise Him;
He has put *Him* to grief.
When You make His soul an offering for sin,
He shall see *His* seed, He shall prolong *His* days,
And the pleasure of the LORD shall prosper in His hand.
➤ 11 He shall see the labor of His soul,[a] *and* be satisfied.
By His knowledge My righteous Servant shall justify many,
For He shall bear their iniquities.
12 Therefore I will divide Him a portion with the great,
And He shall divide the spoil with the strong,
Because He poured out His soul unto death,
And He was numbered with the transgressors,
And He bore the sin of many,
And made intercession for the transgressors.

A Perpetual Covenant of Peace

54 "Sing, O barren,
You *who* have not borne!
Break forth into singing, and cry aloud,
You *who* have not labored with child!
For more *are* the children of the desolate
Than the children of the married woman," says the LORD.
2 "Enlarge the place of your tent,
And let them stretch out the curtains of your dwellings;
Do not spare;
Lengthen your cords,
And strengthen your stakes.
3 For you shall expand to the right and to the left,
And your descendants will inherit the nations,
And make the desolate cities inhabited.
4 "Do not fear, for you will not be ashamed;
Neither be disgraced, for you will not be put to shame;
For you will forget the shame of your youth,
And will not remember the reproach of your widowhood anymore.
5 For your Maker *is* your husband,
The LORD of hosts *is* His name;
And your Redeemer *is* the Holy One of Israel;
He is called the God of the whole earth.
6 For the LORD has called you
Like a woman forsaken and grieved in spirit,
Like a youthful wife when you were refused,"
Says your God.
7 "For a mere moment I have forsaken you,
But with great mercies I will gather you.
8 With a little wrath I hid My face from you ➤
for a moment;
But with everlasting kindness I will have mercy on you,"
Says the LORD, your Redeemer.

9 "For this *is* like the waters of Noah to Me;
For as I have sworn
That the waters of Noah would no longer cover the earth,
So have I sworn
That I would not be angry with you, nor rebuke you.
10 For the mountains shall depart
And the hills be removed,
But My kindness shall not depart from you,
Nor shall My covenant of peace be removed,"
Says the LORD, who has mercy on you.

11 "O you afflicted one,
Tossed with tempest, *and* not comforted,
Behold, I will lay your stones with colorful gems,
And lay your foundations with sapphires.
12 I will make your pinnacles of rubies,
Your gates of crystal,
And all your walls of precious stones.
13 All your children *shall be* taught by the LORD,

53:9 [a]Literally *he* or *He* **53:11** [a]Following Masoretic Text, Targum, and Vulgate; Dead Sea Scrolls and Septuagint read *From the labor of His soul He shall see light.*

LIFE LESSONS

➤ **53:11 — *By His knowledge My righteous Servant shall justify many, for He shall bear their iniquities.***

Jesus nailed your sins to the cross and made you "alive together with Him, having forgiven you all trespasses, having wiped out the handwriting of requirements that was against us" (Col. 2:13, 14).

➤ **54:8 — *"With a little wrath I hid My face from you for a moment, but with everlasting kindness I will have mercy on you," says the LORD, your Redeemer.***

God calls you to obey Him so "that the LORD may turn from the fierceness of His anger and show you mercy, have compassion on you and multiply you" (Deut. 13:17). He wants to do us good, not harm.

And great *shall be* the peace of your
children.
14 In righteousness you shall be established;
You shall be far from oppression, for you
shall not fear;
And from terror, for it shall not come
near you.
15 Indeed they shall surely assemble, *but*
not because of Me.
Whoever assembles against you shall fall
for your sake.
16 "Behold, I have created the blacksmith
Who blows the coals in the fire,
Who brings forth an instrument for his
work;
And I have created the spoiler to destroy.
17 No weapon formed against you shall
prosper,
And every tongue *which* rises against you
in judgment
You shall condemn.
This *is* the heritage of the servants of the
LORD,
And their righteousness *is* from Me,"
Says the LORD.

An Invitation to Abundant Life

55 "Ho! Everyone who thirsts,
Come to the waters;
And you who have no money,
Come, buy and eat.
Yes, come, buy wine and milk
Without money and without price.
➤ 2 Why do you spend money for *what is* not
bread,
And your wages for *what* does not satisfy?
Listen carefully to Me, and eat *what is*
good,
And let your soul delight itself in
abundance.
3 Incline your ear, and come to Me.
Hear, and your soul shall live;
And I will make an everlasting covenant
with you—
The sure mercies of David.
4 Indeed I have given him *as* a witness to
the people,
A leader and commander for the people.
5 Surely you shall call a nation you do not
know,
And nations *who* do not know you shall
run to you,
Because of the LORD your God,
And the Holy One of Israel;
For He has glorified you."

6 Seek the LORD while He may be found, ➤
Call upon Him while He is near.
7 Let the wicked forsake his way, ✳
And the unrighteous man his thoughts;
Let him return to the LORD,
And He will have mercy on him;
And to our God,
For He will abundantly pardon.
8 "For My thoughts *are* not your thoughts,
Nor *are* your ways My ways," says the LORD.
9 "For *as* the heavens are higher than the ➤
earth,
So are My ways higher than your ways,
And My thoughts than your thoughts.
10 "For as the rain comes down, and the
snow from heaven,
And do not return there,
But water the earth,
And make it bring forth and bud,
That it may give seed to the sower
And bread to the eater,
11 So shall My word be that goes forth from ➤
My mouth;
It shall not return to Me void,
But it shall accomplish what I please,
And it shall prosper *in the thing* for
which I sent it.
12 "For you shall go out with joy,
And be led out with peace;
The mountains and the hills
Shall break forth into singing before you,
And all the trees of the field shall clap
their hands.

LIFE LESSONS

➤ 55:2 — *". . . Listen carefully to Me, and eat what is good, and let your soul delight itself in abundance."*

To obey God is to bless yourself; to disobey Him is to curse yourself. "I have come," Jesus said, "that they may have life, and that they may have it more abundantly" (John 10:10).

➤ 55:6 — *Seek the LORD while He may be found, call upon Him while He is near.*

The Lord invites us to come "boldly" into His presence, any time of day or night, to receive His counsel, confess our sins, make requests, and just enjoy His company (Heb. 4:16).

➤ 55:9 — *"For as the heavens are higher than the earth, so are My ways higher than your ways, and My thoughts than your thoughts."*

Even when we do not understand what God is up to in our lives—which may happen frequently—He asks us to trust Him. He knows what He is doing, even if we cannot comprehend His methods or timing.

➤ 55:11 — *". . . My word . . . shall not return to Me void, but it shall accomplish what I please, and it shall prosper in the thing for which I sent it."*

God promises to bless His Word, not ours, so we are wise if we honor that Word and represent it as accurately and effectively as we can whenever we get the opportunity to speak on God's behalf.

13 Instead of the thorn shall come up the
cypress tree,
And instead of the brier shall come up
the myrtle tree;
And it shall be to the LORD for a name,
For an everlasting sign *that* shall not be
cut off."

Salvation for the Gentiles

56 Thus says the LORD:
"Keep justice, and do righteousness,
For My salvation *is* about to come,
And My righteousness to be revealed.
2 Blessed *is* the man *who* does this,
And the son of man *who* lays hold on it;
Who keeps from defiling the Sabbath,
And keeps his hand from doing any evil."

3 Do not let the son of the foreigner
Who has joined himself to the LORD
Speak, saying,
"The LORD has utterly separated me from
His people";
Nor let the eunuch say,
"Here I am, a dry tree."
4 For thus says the LORD:
"To the eunuchs who keep My Sabbaths,
And choose what pleases Me,
And hold fast My covenant,
5 Even to them I will give in My house
And within My walls a place and a name
Better than that of sons and daughters;
I will give them[a] an everlasting name
That shall not be cut off.

6 "Also the sons of the foreigner
Who join themselves to the LORD, to
serve Him,
And to love the name of the LORD, to be
His servants—
Everyone who keeps from defiling the
Sabbath,
And holds fast My covenant—
➤ 7 Even them I will bring to My holy
mountain,
And make them joyful in My house of
prayer.
Their burnt offerings and their sacrifices
Will be accepted on My altar;
For My house shall be called a house of
prayer for all nations."
8 The Lord GOD, who gathers the outcasts
of Israel, says,
"Yet I will gather to him
Others besides those who are gathered to
him."

Israel's Irresponsible Leaders

9 All you beasts of the field, come to
devour,
All you beasts in the forest.
10 His watchmen *are* blind,
They are all ignorant;
They *are* all dumb dogs,
They cannot bark;
Sleeping, lying down, loving to slumber.
11 Yes, *they are* greedy dogs
Which never have enough.
And they *are* shepherds
Who cannot understand;
They all look to their own way,
Every one for his own gain,
From his *own* territory.
12 "Come," *one says,* "I will bring wine,
And we will fill ourselves with
intoxicating drink;
Tomorrow will be as today,
And much more abundant."

Israel's Futile Idolatry

57 The righteous perishes, ➤
And no man takes *it* to heart;
Merciful men *are* taken away,
While no one considers
That the righteous is taken away from
evil.
2 He shall enter into peace;
They shall rest in their beds,
Each one walking *in* his uprightness.

3 "But come here,
You sons of the sorceress,
You offspring of the adulterer and the
harlot!
4 Whom do you ridicule?
Against whom do you make a wide
mouth
And stick out the tongue?
Are you not children of transgression,
Offspring of falsehood,
5 Inflaming yourselves with gods under
every green tree,
Slaying the children in the valleys,
Under the clefts of the rocks?

56:5 [a]Literally *him*

LIFE LESSONS

➤ 56:7 — *". . . For My house shall be called a house of prayer for all nations."*

God is serious about prayer and about His people, from throughout the world, gathering to pray together. Jesus quoted this verse when He drove the merchants and money changers out of the temple (Mark 11:15–17).

➤ 57:1 — *The righteous perishes, and no man takes it to heart; merciful men are taken away, while no one considers that the righteous is taken away from evil.*

We will never know until heaven how many godly men and women have died early in life as a result of God's grace. He takes some home so that evil things might not touch them.

6 Among the smooth *stones* of the stream
Is your portion;
They, they, *are* your lot!
Even to them you have poured a drink
offering,
You have offered a grain offering.
Should I receive comfort in these?

7 "On a lofty and high mountain
You have set your bed;
Even there you went up
To offer sacrifice.
8 Also behind the doors and their posts
You have set up your remembrance;
For you have uncovered yourself *to those
other* than Me,
And have gone up to them;
You have enlarged your bed
And made *a covenant* with them;
You have loved their bed,
Where you saw *their* nudity.[a]
9 You went to the king with ointment,
And increased your perfumes;
You sent your messengers far off,
And *even* descended to Sheol.
10 You are wearied in the length of your way;
Yet you did not say, 'There is no hope.'
You have found the life of your hand;
Therefore you were not grieved.

➤ 11 "And of whom have you been afraid, or
feared,
That you have lied
And not remembered Me,
Nor taken *it* to your heart?
Is it not because I have held My peace
from of old
That you do not fear Me?
12 I will declare your righteousness
And your works,
For they will not profit you.
13 When you cry out,
Let your collection *of idols* deliver you.
But the wind will carry them all away,
A breath will take *them*.
But he who puts his trust in Me shall
possess the land,
And shall inherit My holy mountain."

Healing for the Backslider

14 And one shall say,
"Heap it up! Heap it up!
Prepare the way,
Take the stumbling block out of the way
of My people."

15 For thus says the High and Lofty One ➤
Who inhabits eternity, whose name *is*
Holy:
"I dwell in the high and holy *place*,
With him *who* has a contrite and humble
spirit,
To revive the spirit of the humble,
And to revive the heart of the contrite ones.
16 For I will not contend forever,
Nor will I always be angry;
For the spirit would fail before Me,
And the souls *which* I have made.
17 For the iniquity of his covetousness
I was angry and struck him;
I hid and was angry,
And he went on backsliding in the way of
his heart.
18 I have seen his ways, and will heal him;
I will also lead him,
And restore comforts to him
And to his mourners.

19 "I create the fruit of the lips: ✳
Peace, peace to *him who is* far off and to
him who is near,"
Says the LORD,
"And I will heal him."
20 But the wicked *are* like the troubled sea,
When it cannot rest,
Whose waters cast up mire and dirt.

21 "*There is* no peace," ➤
Says my God, "for the wicked."

Fasting that Pleases God

58 "Cry aloud, spare not;
Lift up your voice like a trumpet;
Tell My people their transgression,
And the house of Jacob their sins.
2 Yet they seek Me daily,
And delight to know My ways,
As a nation that did righteousness,
And did not forsake the ordinance of
their God.
They ask of Me the ordinances of justice;
They take delight in approaching God.

57:8 [a]Literally *hand,* a euphemism

LIFE LESSONS

➤ 57:11 — *". . . Is it not because I have held My peace from of old that you do not fear Me?"*

The silence of God leads many to believe either that He doesn't exist or that He doesn't care enough to make Himself obvious. Both are mistakes. The Lord can "roar," but He prefers to speak in a Shepherd's voice (Jer. 25:30; John 10:16).

➤ 57:15 — *"I dwell in the high and holy place, with him who has a contrite and humble spirit . . . ."*

The Lord longs for an intimate relationship with us. Time spent in communication with Him is the best way to grow close to Him, as we recognize His majesty and our own need.

➤ 57:21 — *"There is no peace," says my God, "for the wicked."*

In the absence of peace *with* God through faith in Christ (Rom. 5:1), there can be no peace *of* God (Phil. 4:7) flooding the heart with quiet confidence and putting it at rest.

3 'Why have we fasted,' *they say,* 'and You
have not seen?
Why have we afflicted our souls, and You
take no notice?'
"In fact, in the day of your fast you find
pleasure,
And exploit all your laborers.
4 Indeed you fast for strife and debate,
And to strike with the fist of wickedness.
You will not fast as *you do* this day,
To make your voice heard on high.
5 Is it a fast that I have chosen,
A day for a man to afflict his soul?
Is it to bow down his head like a bulrush,
And to spread out sackcloth and ashes?
Would you call this a fast,
And an acceptable day to the LORD?

➤ 6 "*Is* this not the fast that I have chosen:
To loose the bonds of wickedness,
To undo the heavy burdens,
To let the oppressed go free,
And that you break every yoke?
7 *Is it* not to share your bread with the
hungry,
And that you bring to your house the
poor who are cast out;
When you see the naked, that you cover
him,
And not hide yourself from your own
flesh?
8 Then your light shall break forth like the
morning,
Your healing shall spring forth speedily,
And your righteousness shall go before
you;
The glory of the LORD shall be your rear
guard.
9 Then you shall call, and the LORD will
answer;
You shall cry, and He will say, 'Here I *am.*'
"If you take away the yoke from your
midst,
The pointing of the finger, and speaking
wickedness,
10 *If* you extend your soul to the hungry
And satisfy the afflicted soul,
Then your light shall dawn in the
darkness,
And your darkness shall *be* as the
noonday.
11 The LORD will guide you continually,
And satisfy your soul in drought,
And strengthen your bones;
You shall be like a watered garden,
And like a spring of water, whose waters
do not fail.
12 Those from among you
Shall build the old waste places;
You shall raise up the foundations of
many generations;
And you shall be called the Repairer of
the Breach,
The Restorer of Streets to Dwell In.

13 "If you turn away your foot from the
Sabbath,
From doing your pleasure on My holy day,
And call the Sabbath a delight,
The holy *day* of the LORD honorable,
And shall honor Him, not doing your
own ways,
Nor finding your own pleasure,
Nor speaking *your own* words,
14 Then you shall delight yourself in the
LORD;
And I will cause you to ride on the high
hills of the earth,
And feed you with the heritage of Jacob
your father.
The mouth of the LORD has spoken."

Separated from God

59 Behold, the LORD's hand is not
shortened,
That it cannot save;
Nor His ear heavy,
That it cannot hear.
2 But your iniquities have separated you ➤
from your God;
And your sins have hidden *His* face from
you,
So that He will not hear.
3 For your hands are defiled with blood,
And your fingers with iniquity;
Your lips have spoken lies,
Your tongue has muttered perversity.

4 No one calls for justice,
Nor does *any* plead for truth.
They trust in empty words and speak lies;
They conceive evil and bring forth
iniquity.

LIFE LESSONS

➤ 58:6 — *"Is this not the fast that I have chosen: to loose the bonds of wickedness, to undo the heavy burdens, to let the oppressed go free, and that you break every yoke?"*

God expects that the righteousness He puts in our hearts through faith in Christ will work its way out into acts of justice and mercy for the oppressed and disadvantaged around us. Because we have received, we give.

➤ 59:2 — *But your iniquities have separated you from your God; and your sins have hidden His face from you, so that He will not hear.*

God may refuse to hear our prayers when we stubbornly refuse to abandon some sin or evil course of action. Peter says, for example, that husbands may hinder their prayers by treating a spouse with disrespect (1 Pet. 3:7)

5 They hatch vipers' eggs and weave the
spider's web;
He who eats of their eggs dies,
And *from* that which is crushed a viper
breaks out.
6 Their webs will not become garments,
Nor will they cover themselves with their
works;
Their works *are* works of iniquity,
And the act of violence *is* in their hands.
7 Their feet run to evil,
And they make haste to shed innocent
blood;
Their thoughts *are* thoughts of iniquity;
Wasting and destruction *are* in their paths.
8 The way of peace they have not known,
And *there is* no justice in their ways;
They have made themselves crooked
paths;
Whoever takes that way shall not know
peace.

Sin Confessed

9 Therefore justice is far from us,
Nor does righteousness overtake us;
We look for light, but there is darkness!
For brightness, *but* we walk in blackness!
10 We grope for the wall like the blind,
And we grope as if *we had* no eyes;
We stumble at noonday as at twilight;
We are as dead *men* in desolate places.
11 We all growl like bears,
And moan sadly like doves;
We look for justice, but *there is* none;
For salvation, *but* it is far from us.
12 For our transgressions are multiplied
before You,
And our sins testify against us;
For our transgressions *are* with us,
And *as for* our iniquities, we know them:
13 In transgressing and lying against the
LORD,
And departing from our God,
Speaking oppression and revolt,
Conceiving and uttering from the heart
words of falsehood.
14 Justice is turned back,
And righteousness stands afar off;
For truth is fallen in the street,
And equity cannot enter.
15 So truth fails,
And he *who* departs from evil makes
himself a prey.

The Redeemer of Zion

Then the LORD saw *it*, and it displeased
Him
That *there was* no justice.
16 He saw that *there was* no man,
And wondered that *there was* no
intercessor;
Therefore His own arm brought salvation
for Him;
And His own righteousness, it sustained
Him.
17 For He put on righteousness as a
breastplate,
And a helmet of salvation on His head;
He put on the garments of vengeance for
clothing,
And was clad with zeal as a cloak.
18 According to *their* deeds, accordingly He
will repay,
Fury to His adversaries,
Recompense to His enemies;
The coastlands He will fully repay.
19 So shall they fear
The name of the LORD from the west,
And His glory from the rising of the sun;
When the enemy comes in like a flood,
The Spirit of the LORD will lift up a
standard against him.

20"The Redeemer will come to Zion,
And to those who turn from
transgression in Jacob,"
Says the LORD.

21 "As for Me," says the LORD, "this *is* My covenant with them: My Spirit who *is* upon you,
and My words which I have put in your
mouth, shall not depart from your mouth, nor
from the mouth of your descendants, nor
from the mouth of your descendants' descendants," says the LORD, "from this time and
forevermore."

The Gentiles Bless Zion

60 Arise, shine;
For your light has come!
And the glory of the LORD is risen upon
you.
2 For behold, the darkness shall cover the
earth,
And deep darkness the people;
But the LORD will arise over you,
And His glory will be seen upon you.
3 The Gentiles shall come to your light,
And kings to the brightness of your
rising.

4 "Lift up your eyes all around, and see:
They all gather together, they come to
you;
Your sons shall come from afar,
And your daughters shall be nursed at
your side.
5 Then you shall see and become radiant,
And your heart shall swell with joy;
Because the abundance of the sea shall
be turned to you,
The wealth of the Gentiles shall come to
you.
6 The multitude of camels shall cover your
land,
The dromedaries of Midian and Ephah;
All those from Sheba shall come;
They shall bring gold and incense,

And they shall proclaim the praises of
the LORD.
7 All the flocks of Kedar shall be gathered
together to you,
The rams of Nebaioth shall minister to
you;
They shall ascend with acceptance on My
altar,
And I will glorify the house of My glory.

8 "Who *are* these *who* fly like a cloud,
And like doves to their roosts?
9 Surely the coastlands shall wait for Me;
And the ships of Tarshish *will come* first,
To bring your sons from afar,
Their silver and their gold with them,
To the name of the LORD your God,
And to the Holy One of Israel,
Because He has glorified you.

10 "The sons of foreigners shall build up your
walls,
And their kings shall minister to you;
For in My wrath I struck you,
But in My favor I have had mercy on you.
11 Therefore your gates shall be open
continually;
They shall not be shut day or night,
That *men* may bring to you the wealth of
the Gentiles,
And their kings in procession.
12 For the nation and kingdom which will
not serve you shall perish,
And *those* nations shall be utterly ruined.

13 "The glory of Lebanon shall come to you,
The cypress, the pine, and the box tree
together,
To beautify the place of My sanctuary;
And I will make the place of My feet
glorious.
14 Also the sons of those who afflicted you
Shall come bowing to you,
And all those who despised you shall fall
prostrate at the soles of your feet;
And they shall call you The City of the
LORD,
Zion of the Holy One of Israel.

15 "Whereas you have been forsaken and
hated,
So that no one went through *you*,
I will make you an eternal excellence,
A joy of many generations.
16 You shall drink the milk of the Gentiles,
And milk the breast of kings;
You shall know that I, the LORD, *am* your
Savior
And your Redeemer, the Mighty One of
Jacob.

17 "Instead of bronze I will bring gold,
Instead of iron I will bring silver,
Instead of wood, bronze,
And instead of stones, iron.
I will also make your officers peace,
And your magistrates righteousness.
18 Violence shall no longer be heard in your
land,
Neither wasting nor destruction within
your borders;
But you shall call your walls Salvation,
And your gates Praise.

God the Glory of His People

19 "The sun shall no longer be your light by
day,
Nor for brightness shall the moon give
light to you;
But the LORD will be to you an
everlasting light,
And your God your glory.
20 Your sun shall no longer go down,
Nor shall your moon withdraw itself;
For the LORD will be your everlasting
light,
And the days of your mourning shall be
ended.
21 Also your people *shall* all *be* righteous;
They shall inherit the land forever,
The branch of My planting,
The work of My hands,
That I may be glorified.
22 A little one shall become a thousand,
And a small one a strong nation.
I, the LORD, will hasten it in its time."

The Good News of Salvation

61 "The Spirit of the Lord GOD *is*
upon Me,
Because the LORD has anointed Me
To preach good tidings to the poor;
He has sent Me to heal the brokenhearted,
To proclaim liberty to the captives,
And the opening of the prison to *those*
who are bound;

LIFE LESSONS

➢ 60:19 — *"The sun shall no longer be your light by day, nor for brightness shall the moon give light to you; but the LORD will be to you an everlasting light, and your God your glory."*

John tells us that in the future New Jerusalem there will be "no need of the sun or of the moon to shine in it" (Rev. 21:23). The glory of God will illuminate it, he says, and "the Lamb is its light."

➢ 61:1 — *"The Spirit of the Lord GOD is upon Me, because the Lord has anointed Me to preach good tidings to the poor . . . ."*

Jesus began His public ministry by returning to his boyhood synagogue in Nazareth and delivering a short sermon based on this passage (Luke 4:16–21). He told the astonished crowd that He fulfilled this Scripture.

2 To proclaim the acceptable year of the LORD,
And the day of vengeance of our God;
To comfort all who mourn,
3 To console those who mourn in Zion,
To give them beauty for ashes,
The oil of joy for mourning,
The garment of praise for the spirit of heaviness;
That they may be called trees of righteousness,
The planting of the LORD, that He may be glorified."

4 And they shall rebuild the old ruins,
They shall raise up the former desolations,
And they shall repair the ruined cities,
The desolations of many generations.
5 Strangers shall stand and feed your flocks,
And the sons of the foreigner
Shall be your plowmen and your vinedressers.
6 But you shall be named the priests of the LORD,
They shall call you the servants of our God.
You shall eat the riches of the Gentiles,
And in their glory you shall boast.
7 Instead of your shame *you shall have* double *honor,*
And *instead of* confusion they shall rejoice in their portion.
Therefore in their land they shall possess double;
Everlasting joy shall be theirs.

8 "For I, the LORD, love justice;
I hate robbery for burnt offering;
I will direct their work in truth,
And will make with them an everlasting covenant.
9 Their descendants shall be known among the Gentiles,
And their offspring among the people.
All who see them shall acknowledge them,
That they *are* the posterity *whom* the LORD has blessed."

10 I will greatly rejoice in the LORD,
My soul shall be joyful in my God;
For He has clothed me with the garments of salvation,
He has covered me with the robe of righteousness,
As a bridegroom decks *himself* with ornaments,
And as a bride adorns *herself* with her jewels.
✳ 11 For as the earth brings forth its bud,
As the garden causes the things that are sown in it to spring forth,
So the Lord GOD will cause righteousness and praise to spring forth before all the nations.

Assurance of Zion's Salvation

62 For Zion's sake I will not hold My peace,
And for Jerusalem's sake I will not rest,
Until her righteousness goes forth as brightness,
And her salvation as a lamp *that* burns.
2 The Gentiles shall see your righteousness,
And all kings your glory.
You shall be called by a new name,
Which the mouth of the LORD will name.
3 You shall also be a crown of glory
In the hand of the LORD,
And a royal diadem
In the hand of your God.
4 You shall no longer be termed Forsaken,
Nor shall your land any more be termed Desolate;
But you shall be called Hephzibah,[a] and your land Beulah;[b]
For the LORD delights in you,
And your land shall be married.
5 For *as* a young man marries a virgin,
So shall your sons marry you;
And *as* the bridegroom rejoices over the bride,
So shall your God rejoice over you.

6 I have set watchmen on your walls, O Jerusalem;
They shall never hold their peace day or night.
You who make mention of the LORD, do not keep silent,
7 And give Him no rest till He establishes
And till He makes Jerusalem a praise in the earth.

8 The LORD has sworn by His right hand
And by the arm of His strength:
"Surely I will no longer give your grain
As food for your enemies;
And the sons of the foreigner shall not drink your new wine,
For which you have labored.
9 But those who have gathered it shall eat it,
And praise the LORD;
Those who have brought it together shall drink it in My holy courts."

10 Go through,
Go through the gates!
Prepare the way for the people;
Build up,
Build up the highway!
Take out the stones,
Lift up a banner for the peoples!

62:4 [a]Literally *My Delight Is in Her* [b]Literally *Married*

➤ 11 Indeed the LORD has proclaimed
To the end of the world:
"Say to the daughter of Zion,
'Surely your salvation is coming;
Behold, His reward *is* with Him,
And His work before Him.'"
12 And they shall call them The Holy People,
The Redeemed of the LORD;
And you shall be called Sought Out,
A City Not Forsaken.

The LORD in Judgment and Salvation

63 Who *is* this who comes from Edom,
With dyed garments from Bozrah,
This *One who is* glorious in His apparel,
Traveling in the greatness of His strength?—

"I who speak in righteousness, mighty to save."

2 Why *is* Your apparel red,
And Your garments like one who treads in the winepress?

3 "I have trodden the winepress alone,
And from the peoples no one *was* with Me.
For I have trodden them in My anger,
And trampled them in My fury;
Their blood is sprinkled upon My garments,
And I have stained all My robes.
4 For the day of vengeance *is* in My heart,
And the year of My redeemed has come.
5 I looked, but *there was* no one to help,
And I wondered
That *there was* no one to uphold;
Therefore My own arm brought salvation for Me;
And My own fury, it sustained Me.
6 I have trodden down the peoples in My anger,
Made them drunk in My fury,
And brought down their strength to the earth."

God's Mercy Remembered

7 I will mention the lovingkindnesses of the LORD
And the praises of the LORD,
According to all that the LORD has bestowed on us,
And the great goodness toward the house of Israel,
Which He has bestowed on them according to His mercies,
According to the multitude of His lovingkindnesses.
8 For He said, "Surely they *are* My people,
Children *who* will not lie."
So He became their Savior.
9 In all their affliction He was afflicted, ➤
And the Angel of His Presence saved them;
In His love and in His pity He redeemed them;
And He bore them and carried them
All the days of old.
10 But they rebelled and grieved His Holy Spirit;
So He turned Himself against them as an enemy,
And He fought against them.

11 Then he remembered the days of old,
Moses *and* his people, *saying:*
"Where *is* He who brought them up out of the sea
With the shepherd of His flock?
Where *is* He who put His Holy Spirit within them,
12 Who led *them* by the right hand of Moses,
With His glorious arm,
Dividing the water before them
To make for Himself an everlasting name,
13 Who led them through the deep,
As a horse in the wilderness,
That they might not stumble?"

14 As a beast goes down into the valley, ➤
And the Spirit of the LORD causes him to rest,
So You lead Your people,
To make Yourself a glorious name.

A Prayer of Penitence

15 Look down from heaven,
And see from Your habitation, holy and glorious.
Where *are* Your zeal and Your strength,
The yearning of Your heart and Your mercies toward me?
Are they restrained?
16 Doubtless You *are* our Father,
Though Abraham was ignorant of us,

LIFE LESSONS

➤ 62:11 — *"Surely your salvation is coming; behold, His reward is with Him . . . ."*

Jesus is our salvation, and He is coming again to judge His followers. "And behold," He says, "I am coming quickly, and My reward is with Me, to give to every one according to his work" (Rev. 22:12).

➤ 63:9 — *In all their affliction He was afflicted, and the Angel of His Presence saved them . . . .*

God understands what we are going through. He feels what we feel and none of our anguish escapes His attention. He does not merely feel, however; He also acts to save us and rescue us.

➤ 63:14 — *As a beast goes down into the valley, and the Spirit of the LORD causes him to rest, so You lead Your people, to make Yourself a glorious name.*

The prophet seems to ask, "If God cares enough to lead wild animals to a safe place of rest, then don't you think He will care enough to lead you to a place of prosperity and safety?"

ANSWERS TO LIFE'S QUESTIONS

Where is God when I'm in pain?

IS. 63:9

Children periodically need painful immunizations. Often they do not understand that while inoculations hurt, they also protect from serious diseases. From their point of view, the doctor is assaulting them—and someone who loves them is allowing it!

Such an experience gives us a little insight into God's dealings with His own children. It helps to answer one of the questions we often ask when painful things happen to us: *Where is God?*

The Bible tells us that when the ancient Israelites suffered many kinds of hardships, God was right there with them. "In all their affliction He was afflicted," says the prophet (Is. 63:9).

Do you remember your earthly father restraining you so that the doctor could administer the painful injection? Perhaps you recall him commenting that the experience hurt him more than it did you. That is exactly what God is describing in this passage. To a childish mind, such an action seems utterly incomprehensible; but when we have children of our own, we grasp it clearly. Then we begin to understand what kind of Father we really have. He Himself enters into all our agony, and He has tasted the last drop in our own cup of suffering.

Where is God when we suffer? He is where the pain is. "He was bruised for our iniquities, the chastisement for peace was on Him" (Is. 53:5). God does not pick up and leave us when the hard times come; instead, He is right there with us, ever mindful of the pain we endure.

But not only does God "feel" for us; He also acts on our behalf, even when we don't know it. So Isaiah says, "the Angel of His Presence saved them; in His love and in His pity He redeemed them; and He bore them and carried them all the days of old" (Is. 63:9). Did ancient Israel realize that God was carrying them through all their trials? No. But He did, nonetheless.

As you face adversity, look into the Savior's tear-strained face—you won't see anything but love. If we would follow Jesus, we must bear the fellowship of His suffering. As Paul reminds us, "For to you it has been granted on behalf of Christ, not only to believe in Him, but also to suffer for His sake" (Phil. 1:29). We must go where He is—and the cross is one of the sweetest places to find Him.

See the Life Principles Index for further study:
26. Adversity is a bridge to a deeper relationship with God.
29. We learn more in our valley experiences than on our mountaintops.

And Israel does not acknowledge us.
You, O LORD, *are* our Father;
Our Redeemer from Everlasting *is* Your name.
17 O LORD, why have You made us stray from Your ways,
And hardened our heart from Your fear?
Return for Your servants' sake,
The tribes of Your inheritance.
18 Your holy people have possessed *it* but a little while;
Our adversaries have trodden down Your sanctuary.
19 We have become *like* those of old, over whom You never ruled,
Those who were never called by Your name.

64 Oh, that You would rend the heavens!
That You would come down!
That the mountains might shake at Your presence—
2 As fire burns brushwood,
As fire causes water to boil—
To make Your name known to Your adversaries,
That the nations may tremble at Your presence!
3 When You did awesome things *for which* we did not look,
You came down,
The mountains shook at Your presence.
4 For since the beginning of the world
Men have not heard nor perceived by the ear,

LIFE LESSONS

➤ 64:4 — *For since the beginning of the world men have not heard nor perceived by the ear, nor has the eye seen any God besides You, who acts for the one who waits for Him.*

We cannot imagine how God will move on our behalf—He does "exceedingly abundantly above all that we ask or think" (Eph. 3:20)—but we confidently expect that He *will* act when we wait for Him in faith.

LIFE PRINCIPLE 14

GOD ACTS ON BEHALF OF THOSE WHO WAIT FOR HIM.

IS. 64:4

In this hurry-up world, waiting for anything can cause us to lose our temper, our good sense, and our tongues—more frequently than we care to admit! No one enjoys waiting in line. We don't like waiting at stoplights. We don't like waiting for dinner. We don't even like waiting for good things, like for fish to bite. We want what we want *right now*.

Yet the Word of God insists that we learn some of life's greatest lessons while we wait. Waiting rooms can be hard classrooms, but God promises vast rewards to those who wait for Him. God plans to use the long pauses in our lives for our blessing . . . if we let him.

Why does God so often ask us to wait? Let's consider five major rewards of waiting.

1. We discover God's will and purpose in the things that most concern us.

"The LORD is good to those who wait for Him, to the soul who seeks Him" (Lam. 3:25). God does not string us out to tantalize us. He does not dangle carrots in front of our noses to lead us along. He does not say, as do many earthly parents, "We'll see." No. Right now, even as we wait, He is working all things together for our good and His glory (Rom. 8:28).

2. We receive supernatural physical energy and strength.

God invites us to claim His promise in Isaiah 40:29–31: "He gives power to the weak, and to those who have no might He increases strength. Even the youths shall faint and be weary, and the young men shall utterly fall, but those who wait on the LORD shall renew their strength; they shall mount up with wings like eagles, they shall run and not be weary, they shall walk and not faint."

God promises that as we wait on Him, He will supply us with supernatural, physical energy. While our impatience makes us weary and worn, actively waiting on Him energizes us. Five or ten minutes of waiting on God can be like a two-hour nap. Waiting on Him is never wasted time!

3. We win battles.

"Wait for the LORD, and He will save you" (Prov. 20:22). How wonderful to see the Lord rescue us and bless us with His favor! When we do things our way, in our own hurried time, we end up defeated. But waiting on God will ensure our victory and keep us from foolish and precipitous acts.

4. We see the fulfillment of our faith.

Actively waiting on God energizes us.

"They shall not be ashamed who wait for Me" (Isaiah 49:23). In the end, we'll never feel embarrassed for waiting on God; it's always the smart thing to do. When others encourage us to forge ahead instead of waiting on the Lord, we need to remember that we will never ultimately be put to shame. "But Lord," we may say during a long wait, "suppose it doesn't work out?" His answer? He'll never let us down!

5. We see God working on our behalf.

Isaiah spoke of the God "who acts for the one who waits for Him" (Is. 64:4). What a wonderful promise! While *we* actively wait, *He* actively works. Think of this: every single day, we have the greatest Mediator working on our behalf, when things go wrong or when they go right.

Although waiting can be one of the more difficult things in the Christian life, it is *not* wasted time. God gives us instructions through periods of actively waiting. He may change our circumstances while we wait. He keeps us in step with Himself and prepares us for His answers. He uses the time to sift our motives and strengthen our faith. And when we choose to wait, God rewards us with blessings both large and unexpected.

Think of waiting on God as something like planting a garden. You put a seed under the soil and water it. And then you wait.

And wait.

And wait.

After the sun and rain pelt the earth, the seeds begin to grow; and one day, finally, you begin to see evidence of what you planted. Now, suppose you had grown impatient and dug up your seeds because nothing seemed to be happening? You would have ruined your garden.

Remember, some fruit takes a long time to mature—and the One who wants to bring it forth in our lives knows exactly how long we need to wait. Waiting makes possible the most luscious fruit of all.

See the Life Principles Index for further study.

Some fruit takes a long time to mature.

Nor has the eye seen any God besides
You,
Who acts for the one who waits for Him.
5 You meet him who rejoices and does
righteousness,
Who remembers You in Your ways.
You are indeed angry, for we have
sinned—
In these ways we continue;
And we need to be saved.

6 But we are all like an unclean *thing*,
And all our righteousnesses *are* like
filthy rags;
We all fade as a leaf,
And our iniquities, like the wind,
Have taken us away.
7 And *there is* no one who calls on Your
name,
Who stirs himself up to take hold of You;
For You have hidden Your face from us,
And have consumed us because of our
iniquities.

➤ 8 But now, O LORD,
You *are* our Father;
We *are* the clay, and You our potter;
And all we *are* the work of Your hand.
9 Do not be furious, O LORD,
Nor remember iniquity forever;
Indeed, please look—we all *are* Your
people!
10 Your holy cities are a wilderness,
Zion is a wilderness,
Jerusalem a desolation.
11 Our holy and beautiful temple,
Where our fathers praised You,
Is burned up with fire;
And all our pleasant things are laid
waste.
12 Will You restrain Yourself because of
these *things*, O LORD?
Will You hold Your peace, and afflict us
very severely?

The Righteousness of God's Judgment

65 "I was sought by *those who* did not
ask *for Me;*
I was found by *those who* did not seek
Me.
I said, 'Here I am, here I am,'
To a nation *that* was not called by My
name.
2 I have stretched out My hands all day
long to a rebellious people,
Who walk in a way *that is* not good,
According to their own thoughts;
3 A people who provoke Me to anger
continually to My face;
Who sacrifice in gardens,
And burn incense on altars of brick;
4 Who sit among the graves,
And spend the night in the tombs;
Who eat swine's flesh,
And the broth of abominable things is *in*
their vessels;
5 Who say, 'Keep to yourself,
Do not come near me,
For I am holier than you!'
These *are* smoke in My nostrils,
A fire that burns all the day.

6 "Behold, *it is* written before Me:
I will not keep silence, but will repay—
Even repay into their bosom—
7 Your iniquities and the iniquities of your
fathers together,"
Says the LORD,
"Who have burned incense on the
mountains
And blasphemed Me on the hills;
Therefore I will measure their former
work into their bosom."

8 Thus says the LORD:
"As the new wine is found in the cluster,
And *one* says, 'Do not destroy it,
For a blessing *is* in it,'
So will I do for My servants' sake,
That I may not destroy them all.
9 I will bring forth descendants from Jacob,
And from Judah an heir of My
mountains;
My elect shall inherit it,
And My servants shall dwell there.
10 Sharon shall be a fold of flocks,
And the Valley of Achor a place for herds
to lie down,
For My people who have sought Me.

11 "But you *are* those who forsake the LORD,
Who forget My holy mountain,
Who prepare a table for Gad,[a]
And who furnish a drink offering for
Meni.[b]
12 Therefore I will number you for the
sword,
And you shall all bow down to the
slaughter;
Because, when I called, you did not
answer;

65:11 [a]Literally *Troop* or *Fortune,* a pagan deity [b]Literally *Number* or *Destiny,* a pagan deity

LIFE LESSONS

➤ **64:8 — *But now, O LORD, You are our Father; we are the clay, and You our potter; and all we are the work of Your hand.***

As our Father, God acts for our benefit in ways that childlike minds cannot always understand. As our potter, He molds us and shapes us in ways that sometimes hurt. But always He deals with us in love.

WHAT THE BIBLE SAYS ABOUT **HOW TO CONTROL OUR ANGER**

Is. 64:9

In Isaiah 64:9, the prophet implores God with these words: "Do not be furious, O LORD, nor remember iniquity forever." This passage implies that God measures His anger in a way appropriate to each occasion. We, too, can learn how to measure our anger and focus it so that we do no harm. How do we go about that?

In Ephesians 4:26, God exhorts us to control our anger so that we don't sin. While anger itself is not sinful, it can quickly lead to sin. A line exists that we must not cross. How do we know when we have crossed it? Clearly we must avoid verbal abuse and physical violence, but anger can lead to other sins just as deadly. Whenever you see the following in your life, you know you have crossed the line:

1. *Strife*—Proverbs 29:22 tells us that "an angry man stirs up strife." Strife can take many forms, but it always pits one person against another, even if things don't become loud or violent. Isaiah warned against employers who took unfair advantage of their workers, yet tried to cover their tracks with religious observance: "Indeed you fast for strife and debate, and to strike with the fist of wickedness." But it wouldn't work: "You will not fast as you do this day, to make your voice heard on high" (Is. 58:4).

2. *Bitterness*—Psalm 30:5 says that God's "anger is but for a moment," and Ephesians 4:26 warns us against staying angry overnight. Extended anger usually leads to bitterness. So God instructs us, "Let all bitterness, wrath, anger, clamor, and evil speaking be put away from you, with all malice" (Eph. 4:31).

3. *Isolation*—nursing our anger leads to people becoming separated from each other. Proverbs 16:28 warns us against this by pointing out that "a whisperer separates the best of friends."

4. *Retaliation*—Romans 12:19 addresses this directly: "Do not avenge yourselves, but rather give place to wrath; for it is written, 'Vengeance is Mine, I will repay,' says the Lord."

Remember, "the wrath of man does not produce the righteousness of God" (James 1:20).

A line exists that we must not cross.

See the Life Principles Index for further study:
5. *God does not require us to understand His will, just obey it, even if it seems unreasonable.*
24. *To live the Christian life is to allow Jesus to live His life in and through us.*

When I spoke, you did not hear,
But did evil before My eyes,
And chose *that* in which I do not delight."

13 Therefore thus says the Lord GOD:

"Behold, My servants shall eat,
But you shall be hungry;
Behold, My servants shall drink,
But you shall be thirsty;
Behold, My servants shall rejoice,
But you shall be ashamed;
14 Behold, My servants shall sing for joy of heart,
But you shall cry for sorrow of heart,
And wail for grief of spirit.
15 You shall leave your name as a curse to My chosen;
For the Lord GOD will slay you,
And call His servants by another name;
16 So that he who blesses himself in the earth
Shall bless himself in the God of truth;
And he who swears in the earth
Shall swear by the God of truth;
Because the former troubles are forgotten,
And because they are hidden from My eyes.

The Glorious New Creation

17 "For behold, I create new heavens and a new earth;
And the former shall not be remembered or come to mind.
18 But be glad and rejoice forever in what I create;
For behold, I create Jerusalem *as* a rejoicing,
And her people a joy.
19 I will rejoice in Jerusalem,
And joy in My people;
The voice of weeping shall no longer be heard in her,
Nor the voice of crying.

20 "No more shall an infant from there *live but a few* days,
Nor an old man who has not fulfilled his days;
For the child shall die one hundred years old,
But the sinner *being* one hundred years old shall be accursed.
21 They shall build houses and inhabit *them;*
They shall plant vineyards and eat their fruit.
22 They shall not build and another inhabit;
They shall not plant and another eat;
For as the days of a tree, *so shall be* the days of My people,
And My elect shall long enjoy the work of their hands.
23 They shall not labor in vain,
Nor bring forth children for trouble;
For they *shall be* the descendants of the blessed of the LORD,
And their offspring with them.

24 "It shall come to pass
That before they call, I will answer;
And while they are still speaking, I will hear.
25 The wolf and the lamb shall feed together,
The lion shall eat straw like the ox,
And dust *shall be* the serpent's food.
They shall not hurt nor destroy in all My holy mountain,"
Says the LORD.

True Worship and False

66 Thus says the LORD:

"Heaven *is* My throne,
And earth *is* My footstool.
Where *is* the house that you will build Me?
And where *is* the place of My rest?
2 For all those *things* My hand has made,
And all those *things* exist,"
Says the LORD.
"But on this *one* will I look:
On *him who is* poor and of a contrite spirit,
And who trembles at My word.

3 "He who kills a bull *is as if* he slays a man;
He who sacrifices a lamb, *as if* he breaks a dog's neck;
He who offers a grain offering, *as if he offers* swine's blood;
He who burns incense, *as if* he blesses an idol.
Just as they have chosen their own ways,
And their soul delights in their abominations,
4 So will I choose their delusions,
And bring their fears on them;
Because, when I called, no one answered,
When I spoke they did not hear;
But they did evil before My eyes,
And chose *that* in which I do not delight."

LIFE LESSONS

➤ **65:18 — *"But be glad and rejoice forever in what I create; for behold, I create Jerusalem as a rejoicing, and her people a joy."***

Our God is surrounded by joy, and He plans to bring all of us into His happiness forever. It's just as Peter quotes David from Psalm 16: "You will make me full of joy in Your presence" (Acts 2:28).

The LORD Vindicates Zion

5 Hear the word of the LORD,
You who tremble at His word:
"Your brethren who hated you,
Who cast you out for My name's sake, said,
'Let the LORD be glorified,
That we may see your joy.'
But they shall be ashamed."

6 The sound of noise from the city!
A voice from the temple!
The voice of the LORD,
Who fully repays His enemies!

7 "Before she was in labor, she gave birth;
Before her pain came,
She delivered a male child.
8 Who has heard such a thing?
Who has seen such things?
Shall the earth be made to give birth in one day?
Or shall a nation be born at once?
For as soon as Zion was in labor,
She gave birth to her children.
9 Shall I bring to the time of birth, and not cause delivery?" says the LORD.
"Shall I who cause delivery shut up *the* womb?" says your God.
10 "Rejoice with Jerusalem,
And be glad with her, all you who love her;
Rejoice for joy with her, all you who mourn for her;
11 That you may feed and be satisfied
With the consolation of her bosom,
That you may drink deeply and be delighted
With the abundance of her glory."

12 For thus says the LORD:

"Behold, I will extend peace to her like a river,
And the glory of the Gentiles like a flowing stream.
Then you shall feed;
On *her* sides shall you be carried,
And be dandled on *her* knees.
13 As one whom his mother comforts,
So I will comfort you;
And you shall be comforted in Jerusalem."

The Reign and Indignation of God

14 When you see *this,* your heart shall rejoice,
And your bones shall flourish like grass;
The hand of the LORD shall be known to His servants,
And *His* indignation to His enemies.
15 For behold, the LORD will come with fire
And with His chariots, like a whirlwind,
To render His anger with fury,
And His rebuke with flames of fire.
16 For by fire and by His sword
The LORD will judge all flesh;
And the slain of the LORD shall be many.

17 "Those who sanctify themselves and purify themselves,
To go to the gardens
After an *idol* in the midst,
Eating swine's flesh and the abomination and the mouse,
Shall be consumed together," says the LORD.

18 "For I *know* their works and their
thoughts. It shall be that I will gather all nations and tongues; and they shall come and
see My glory.
19 "I will set a sign among them; and those
among them who escape I will send to the nations: *to* Tarshish and Pul[a] and Lud, who
draw the bow, and Tubal and Javan, *to* the
coastlands afar off who have not heard My
fame nor seen My glory. And they shall declare My glory among the Gentiles.
20 "Then they shall bring all your brethren
for an offering to the LORD out of all nations,
on horses and in chariots and in litters, on
mules and on camels, to My holy mountain
Jerusalem," says the LORD, "as the children of
Israel bring an offering in a clean vessel into
the house of the LORD.
21 "And I will also take some of them for
priests *and* Levites," says the LORD.

22 "For as the new heavens and the new earth
Which I will make shall remain before Me," says the LORD,
"So shall your descendants and your name remain.
23 And it shall come to pass
That from one New Moon to another,
And from one Sabbath to another,
All flesh shall come to worship before Me," says the LORD.

24 "And they shall go forth and look
Upon the corpses of the men
Who have transgressed against Me.
For their worm does not die,
And their fire is not quenched.
They shall be an abhorrence to all flesh."

66:19 [a]Following Masoretic Text and Targum; Septuagint reads *Put* (compare Jeremiah 46:9).

LIFE LESSONS

66:22 — *"For as the new heavens and the new earth which I will make shall remain before Me," says the LORD, "so shall your descendants and your name remain."*

God loves us so much that He wants our relationship with Him to continue to grow for all eternity. He will never grow weary of us or toss us away, and there will always be more of Him for us to explore.

THE BOOK OF

JEREMIAH

The Book of Jeremiah records the frequently dark prophecies of a man from the priestly city of Anathoth, whom God called to a difficult ministry while the prophet was still in his youth.

Yirmeyahu or *Yirmeyah* literally means "Yahweh throws," perhaps in the sense of laying a foundation. It may effectively mean, "Yahweh establishes, appoints, or sends." The Latin form of the name is *Jeremias.*

Jeremiah, who has been called "the weeping prophet," labors for more than forty years proclaiming a message of doom to the stiff-necked and unrepentant people of Judah. In his long ministry he wrote a long book; Jeremiah contains more words than any other book in the Bible. And as the people of Judah and their king rejected his message, it became even longer (see Jer. 36:32). For all these reasons, Jeremiah is a heartbroken prophet with a heartbreaking message. Despised and persecuted by his countrymen, Jeremiah bathes his harsh prophecies in tears of compassion.

Jeremiah often rebukes his people that they have "forgotten God" and have refused to listen for His voice. The persistent prophet accuses both religious and civil leaders of abandoning God's agenda and substituting a morally bankrupt system that they have artificially contrived. Through his uncompromising sermons and memorable object lessons, he faithfully declares that surrender to God's will is the only way to escape calamity—and the only route to certain blessing.

Themes: Jeremiah decries the apostasy of God's chosen people, predicts their bondage at the hands of the Babylonians, and looks forward to their eventual restoration through the mercy and grace of God.

Author: Jeremiah, the son of Hilkiah.

Time: The Book of Jeremiah covers a dark period in the history of Judah, beginning with the thirteenth year of the reign of Josiah (c. 627 B.C.), Judah's last good and godly king (for whom Jeremiah issued a deeply emotional lament in 2 Chr. 35:25), until several years after the Babylonian captivity (c. 586 B.C.).

Structure: Jeremiah's broken heart causes him to write a broken book, which is difficult to arrange either chronologically or topically. In its current form, the book begins with a description of the prophet's divine call (chapter 1); then records several warnings and exhortations to the rebellious nation (chapters 2–35); describes the hardships of the persecuted prophet (chapters 36–38); chronicles the destruction of Jerusalem and the nation's subsequent ruin (chapters 39–45); declares judgment against many surrounding nations (chapters 46–51); and ends with a historical postscript (chapters 52).

As you read Jeremiah, watch for several life principles that play an important role in this book:

26. Adversity is a bridge to a deeper relationship with God. *See Jeremiah 1:7–19; 12:1–13; pages 855; 872.*

13. Listening to God is essential to walking with God. *See Jeremiah 6:10, 17; 7:13, 24–27; pages 863; 864; 865.*

15. Brokenness is God's requirement for maximum usefulness. *See Jeremiah 15:19; page 876.*

1 The words of Jeremiah the son of Hilkiah,
of the priests who *were* in Anathoth in the
land of Benjamin,
2 to whom the word of the LORD came in the
days of Josiah the son of Amon, king of Judah, in the thirteenth year of his reign.
3 It came also in the days of Jehoiakim the
son of Josiah, king of Judah, until the end of
the eleventh year of Zedekiah the son of
Josiah, king of Judah, until the carrying away
of Jerusalem captive in the fifth month.

The Prophet Is Called

4 Then the word of the LORD came to me,
saying:

➤ 5 "Before I formed you in the womb I knew
you;
Before you were born I sanctified you;
I ordained you a prophet to the nations."

6 Then said I:

"Ah, Lord GOD!
Behold, I cannot speak, for I *am* a youth."

7 But the LORD said to me:

"Do not say, 'I *am* a youth,'
For you shall go to all to whom I send you,
And whatever I command you, you shall
speak.
✳ 8 Do not be afraid of their faces,
For I *am* with you to deliver you," says
the LORD.

9 Then the LORD put forth His hand and
touched my mouth, and the LORD said
to me:

"Behold, I have put My words in your
mouth.
10 See, I have this day set you over the
nations and over the kingdoms,
To root out and to pull down,
To destroy and to throw down,
To build and to plant."

11 Moreover the word of the LORD came to
me, saying, "Jeremiah, what do you see?" And
I said, "I see a branch of an almond tree."
12 Then the LORD said to me, "You have seen
well, for I am ready to perform My word."
13 And the word of the LORD came to me the
second time, saying, "What do you see?" And
I said, "I see a boiling pot, and it is facing
away from the north."

14 Then the LORD said to me:

"Out of the north calamity shall break
forth
On all the inhabitants of the land.
15 For behold, I am calling
All the families of the kingdoms of the
north," says the LORD;
"They shall come and each one set his
throne
At the entrance of the gates of Jerusalem,
Against all its walls all around,
And against all the cities of Judah.
16 I will utter My judgments
Against them concerning all their
wickedness,
Because they have forsaken Me,
Burned incense to other gods,
And worshiped the works of their own
hands.

17 "Therefore prepare yourself and arise, ➤
And speak to them all that I command
you.
Do not be dismayed before their faces,
Lest I dismay you before them.
18 For behold, I have made you this day
A fortified city and an iron pillar,
And bronze walls against the whole land—
Against the kings of Judah,
Against its princes,
Against its priests,
And against the people of the land.
19 They will fight against you,
But they shall not prevail against you.
For I *am* with you," says the LORD, "to
deliver you."

God's Case Against Israel

2 Moreover the word of the LORD came to
me, saying,
2 "Go and cry in the hearing of Jerusalem,
saying, 'Thus says the LORD:

"I remember you,
The kindness of your youth,
The love of your betrothal,
When you went after Me in the wilderness,
In a land not sown.
3 Israel *was* holiness to the LORD,
The firstfruits of His increase.
All that devour him will offend;
Disaster will come upon them," says the
LORD.'"

LIFE LESSONS

➤ 1:5 — *"Before I formed you in the womb I knew you; before you were born I sanctified you . . . ."*

God has a plan for our lives. We are not accidents, nor do we exist by chance. Before we take our first breath, God knows how long we'll live (Ps. 139:16). Long before we're born, He even knows our name (Is. 44:28).

➤ 1:17 — *"Therefore prepare yourself and arise, and speak to them all that I command you . . . ."*

As servants of the living God, we are to speak His words, not merely what we think best. Paul told the Ephesian elders, "I have not shunned to declare to you the whole counsel of God" (Acts 20:27).

WHAT THE BIBLE SAYS ABOUT GOD'S EMPOWERING PRESENCE

Jer. 1:6–10

When did you last feel the presence of God in your life? I don't mean a merely intellectual recognition that God is with you, for He is everywhere; but rather, when did you last recognize in your heart that God is personally, intimately abiding in you?

If you are like many believers, it may have been a while since you really felt His presence. Too many people go about their lives without a genuine sense of God's closeness. What a tragedy!

Repeatedly in Scripture, we see that whenever God calls someone into His service, He first reminds the person of His enduring presence. We see this in the stories of Moses (Ex. 3:11, 12), Joshua (Josh. 1:1–9), Gideon (Judg. 6:12), and Jeremiah (Jer. 1:6–8), to name just a few. These men discovered, as we can, that the awareness of God's presence energizes us for our work.

Why does God repeatedly assure His followers of His presence? He does so because we need to be reminded of the reasons for our confidence. Each time God calls a servant into action, He essentially says, "You can be strong and courageous because I am with you. Victory isn't about *your* abilities, *your* strength, *your* skill, *your* armor, *your* gifts, or *your* dedication; it has to do with *My* presence. You can be strong because I will be strong in you."

God knows how difficult life can be.

When Jeremiah trembled at the thought of the difficult ministry ahead of him, the Lord strengthened him with these words: "'They will fight against you, but they shall not prevail against you. For I am with you,' says the LORD, 'to deliver you'" (Jer. 1:19).

God knows how difficult life can be and He knows every detail of each struggle you will ever face. As a believer in Christ Jesus, you can trust that your heavenly Father will keep His Word. He is with you right now, and He always will be, as He promises in His Word: "'I will never leave you nor forsake you.' So we may boldly say, 'The LORD is my helper; I will not fear. What can man do to me?'" (Heb. 13:5, 6).

See the Life Principles Index for further study:
4. The awareness of God's presence energizes us for our work.

4 Hear the word of the LORD, O house of Jacob and all the families of the house of Israel.
5 Thus says the LORD:

"What injustice have your fathers found in Me,
That they have gone far from Me,
Have followed idols,
And have become idolaters?
6 Neither did they say, 'Where *is* the LORD,
Who brought us up out of the land of Egypt,
Who led us through the wilderness,
Through a land of deserts and pits,
Through a land of drought and the shadow of death,
Through a land that no one crossed
And where no one dwelt?'
7 I brought you into a bountiful country,
To eat its fruit and its goodness.
But when you entered, you defiled My land
And made My heritage an abomination.
8 The priests did not say, 'Where *is* the LORD?'
And those who handle the law did not know Me;
The rulers also transgressed against Me;
The prophets prophesied by Baal,
And walked after *things that* do not profit.

9 "Therefore I will yet bring charges against you," says the LORD,
"And against your children's children I will bring charges.
10 For pass beyond the coasts of Cyprus[a] and see,
Send to Kedar[b] and consider diligently,
And see if there has been such *a thing*.
11 Has a nation changed *its* gods,
Which *are* not gods?
But My people have changed their Glory
For *what* does not profit.
12 Be astonished, O heavens, at this,
And be horribly afraid;
Be very desolate," says the LORD.
13 "For My people have committed two evils:
They have forsaken Me, the fountain of living waters,
And hewn themselves cisterns—broken cisterns that can hold no water.

14 "*Is* Israel a servant?
Is he a homeborn *slave*?
Why is he plundered?
15 The young lions roared at him, *and* growled;
They made his land waste;
His cities are burned, without inhabitant.
16 Also the people of Noph[a] and Tahpanhes
Have broken the crown of your head.
17 Have you not brought this on yourself,
In that you have forsaken the LORD your God
When He led you in the way?
18 And now why take the road to Egypt,
To drink the waters of Sihor?
Or why take the road to Assyria,
To drink the waters of the River?[a]
19 Your own wickedness will correct you,
And your backslidings will rebuke you.
Know therefore and see that *it is* an evil and bitter *thing*
That you have forsaken the LORD your God,
And the fear of Me *is* not in you,"
Says the Lord GOD of hosts.

20 "For of old I have broken your yoke *and* burst your bonds;
And you said, 'I will not transgress,'
When on every high hill and under every green tree
You lay down, playing the harlot.
21 Yet I had planted you a noble vine, a seed of highest quality.
How then have you turned before Me
Into the degenerate plant of an alien vine?
22 For though you wash yourself with lye, and use much soap,
Yet your iniquity is marked before Me," says the Lord GOD.
23 "How can you say, 'I am not polluted,
I have not gone after the Baals'?
See your way in the valley;
Know what you have done:
You are a swift dromedary breaking loose in her ways,

2:10 [a]Hebrew *Kittim,* western lands, especially Cyprus [b]In the northern Arabian desert, representative of the eastern cultures **2:16** [a]That is, Memphis in ancient Egypt **2:18** [a]That is, the Euphrates

LIFE LESSONS

2:5 — "What injustice have your fathers found in Me, that they have gone far from Me . . . ?"

No one will ever be able to blame God for their sin or for their wandering habits. James says that "each one is tempted when he is drawn away by his own desires and enticed" (James 1:14).

2:11 — " . . . My people have changed their Glory for what does not profit."

We never make a good deal when we exchange God for anything else. Money, fame, power, sex, pleasure, influence—if we choose any of them instead of God, we end up with nothing in the end but death.

2:19 — "Your own wickedness will correct you, and your backslidings will rebuke you . . . ."

In many cases, the consequences for choosing sin are bound up in the sin itself. God doesn't have to add punishment to many sins, because they include punishment in their results (see Rom. 1:27).

ANSWERS TO LIFE'S QUESTIONS

How does God define sin?

JER. 2:13

Some people define sin as "missing the mark"—just as an arrow misses a bull's-eye on a target. God's commandments are the target, and we miss God's best when we sin.

Others define sin as "falling short" of God's perfect will. God desires that we live in wholeness and follow all His commandments; when we fail to do so, that is sin.

Still others define sin as "trespassing." God designates certain areas of behavior as off-limits and when we trespass into those territories, we become subject to penalty.

My personal favorite definition of sin comes from Jeremiah 2:13: "For My people have committed two evils: They have forsaken Me, the fountain of living waters, and hewn themselves cisterns—broken cisterns that can hold no water."

Cisterns are reservoirs dug into the earth, usually out of solid rock, designed to hold water. A fountain, on the other hand, is an artesian spring, bubbling up from the earth with an unending supply of fresh, pure water. But instead of choosing God's living water, too often we choose to build our own cisterns. To build is an act of the will. When we choose our way over God's, we reject the artesian spring for a well of our own creation. And the Lord notes with sadness but with certainty, "It doesn't work. It can't. It's broken."

Jesus once told a Samaritan woman by the well of Sychar, "If you knew the gift of God, and who it is who says to you, 'Give Me a drink,' you would have asked Him, and He would have given you living water" (John 4:10). In this way He used the same word picture developed in Jeremiah to describe Himself. Jesus has life to give, eternal and freely offered. His forgiveness—and the eternal life associated with it—is a fountain from which we can freely draw forever, whenever we like.

We have a choice to make. We can dig and dig, make cistern after cistern, and strive and struggle all we want—but it will never bring us fulfillment or forgiveness. Or we can choose God's way.

Only God's forgiveness, granted God's way, brings the results we need. Any time we attempt to meet our own needs or accomplish anything without God, we sin and set ourselves up for failure. We build broken cisterns that cannot hold water. So why not rather go to the fountain and drink our fill?

See the Life Principles Index for further study:

1. *Our intimacy with God—His highest priority for our lives—determines the impact of our lives.*
16. *Whatever you acquire outside of God's will eventually turns to ashes.*

24 A wild donkey used to the wilderness,
That sniffs at the wind in her desire;
In her time of mating, who can turn her away?
All those who seek her will not weary themselves;
In her month they will find her.
25 Withhold your foot from being unshod,
and your throat from thirst.
But you said, 'There is no hope.
No! For I have loved aliens, and after them I will go.'

26"As the thief is ashamed when he is found out,
So is the house of Israel ashamed;
They and their kings and their princes,
and their priests and their prophets,
27 Saying to a tree, 'You *are* my father,'
And to a stone, 'You gave birth to me.'
For they have turned *their* back to Me,
and not *their* face.
But in the time of their trouble
They will say, 'Arise and save us.'
28 But where *are* your gods that you have made for yourselves?
Let them arise,
If they can save you in the time of your trouble;
For *according to* the number of your cities
Are your gods, O Judah.

29"Why will you plead with Me?
You all have transgressed against Me,"
says the LORD.
30"In vain I have chastened your children;
They received no correction.
Your sword has devoured your prophets
Like a destroying lion.
31"O generation, see the word of the LORD!
Have I been a wilderness to Israel,
Or a land of darkness?
Why do My people say, 'We are lords;
We will come no more to You'?

➤ 32 Can a virgin forget her ornaments,
Or a bride her attire?
Yet My people have forgotten Me days
without number.

33 "Why do you beautify your way to seek
love?
Therefore you have also taught
The wicked women your ways.
34 Also on your skirts is found
The blood of the lives of the poor
innocents.
I have not found it by secret search,
But plainly on all these things.
35 Yet you say, 'Because I am innocent,
Surely His anger shall turn from me.'
Behold, I will plead My case against you,
Because you say, 'I have not sinned.'
36 Why do you gad about so much to
change your way?
Also you shall be ashamed of Egypt as
you were ashamed of Assyria.
37 Indeed you will go forth from him
With your hands on your head;
For the LORD has rejected your trusted
allies,
And you will not prosper by them.

Israel Is Shameless

➤ 3 "They say, 'If a man divorces his wife,
And she goes from him
And becomes another man's,
May he return to her again?'
Would not that land be greatly polluted?
But you have played the harlot with
many lovers;
Yet return to Me," says the LORD.

2 "Lift up your eyes to the desolate heights
and see:
Where have you not lain *with men*?
By the road you have sat for them
Like an Arabian in the wilderness;
And you have polluted the land
With your harlotries and your
wickedness.
3 Therefore the showers have been
withheld,
And there has been no latter rain.
You have had a harlot's forehead;
You refuse to be ashamed.
4 Will you not from this time cry to Me,
'My Father, You *are* the guide of my youth?
5 Will He remain angry forever?
Will He keep it to the end?'
Behold, you have spoken and done evil
things,
As you were able."

A Call to Repentance

6 The LORD said also to me in the days of
Josiah the king: "Have you seen what backsliding Israel has done? She has gone up on
every high mountain and under every green
tree, and there played the harlot.
7 "And I said, after she had done all these
things, 'Return to Me.' But she did not return.
And her treacherous sister Judah saw it.
8 "Then I saw that for all the causes for
which backsliding Israel had committed adultery, I had put her away and given her a certificate of divorce; yet her treacherous sister
Judah did not fear, but went and played the
harlot also.
9 "So it came to pass, through her casual
harlotry, that she defiled the land and committed adultery with stones and trees.
10 "And yet for all this her treacherous sister
Judah has not turned to Me with her whole
heart, but in pretense," says the LORD.
11 Then the LORD said to me, "Backsliding Israel has shown herself more righteous than
treacherous Judah.
12 "Go and proclaim these words toward the ➤
north, and say:

'Return, backsliding Israel,' says the LORD;
'I will not cause My anger to fall on you.
For I *am* merciful,' says the LORD;
'I will not remain angry forever.
13 Only acknowledge your iniquity,
That you have transgressed against the
LORD your God,
And have scattered your charms
To alien deities under every green tree,
And you have not obeyed My voice,' says
the LORD.

14 "Return, O backsliding children," says the
LORD; "for I am married to you. I will take
you, one from a city and two from a family,
and I will bring you to Zion.

LIFE LESSONS

➤ 2:32 — *"Can a virgin forget her ornaments, or a bride her attire? Yet My people have forgotten Me days without number."*

We do not tend to forget what we really love. What captures our hearts also tends to capture our time and our energy. God wants an intimate relationship with us, not merely a place on our schedules.

➤ 3:1 — *". . . you have played the harlot with many lovers; yet return to Me," says the LORD.*

Despite our sin, despite our rebellion, despite our tendency to wander, God still wants to build a strong and loving relationship with us. Wherever you have been, He calls to you: "Come home!"

➤ 3:12 — *"Return, backsliding Israel," says the LORD; "I will not cause My anger to fall on you. For I am merciful," says the LORD.*

God does not want to inflict His wrath upon us, but instead wants to show us mercy. He makes it possible for us to return to Him and to get to know Him as Friend and Savior, not as Judge.

15 "And I will give you shepherds according
to My heart, who will feed you with knowledge and understanding.
16 "Then it shall come to pass, when you are
multiplied and increased in the land in those
days," says the LORD, "that they will say no
more, 'The ark of the covenant of the LORD.' It
shall not come to mind, nor shall they remember it, nor shall they visit *it*, nor shall it
be made anymore.
17 "At that time Jerusalem shall be called The
Throne of the LORD, and all the nations shall
be gathered to it, to the name of the LORD, to
Jerusalem. No more shall they follow the dictates of their evil hearts.
18 "In those days the house of Judah shall
walk with the house of Israel, and they shall
come together out of the land of the north to
the land that I have given as an inheritance to
your fathers.
19 "But I said:

'How can I put you among the children
And give you a pleasant land,
A beautiful heritage of the hosts of nations?'

"And I said:

'You shall call Me, "My Father,"
And not turn away from Me.'
20 Surely, *as* a wife treacherously departs
from her husband,
So have you dealt treacherously with Me,
O house of Israel," says the LORD.

21 A voice was heard on the desolate heights,
Weeping *and* supplications of the
children of Israel.
For they have perverted their way;
They have forgotten the LORD their God.

✳ 22 "Return, you backsliding children,
And I will heal your backslidings."

"Indeed we do come to You,
For You are the LORD our God.
23 Truly, in vain *is salvation hoped for* from
the hills,
And from the multitude of mountains;
Truly, in the LORD our God
Is the salvation of Israel.
24 For shame has devoured
The labor of our fathers from our youth—
Their flocks and their herds,
Their sons and their daughters.
25 We lie down in our shame,
And our reproach covers us.
For we have sinned against the LORD our
God,
We and our fathers,
From our youth even to this day,
And have not obeyed the voice of the
LORD our God."

4 "If you will return, O Israel," says the
LORD,
"Return to Me;
And if you will put away your
abominations out of My sight,
Then you shall not be moved.
2 And you shall swear, 'The LORD lives,'
In truth, in judgment, and in
righteousness;
The nations shall bless themselves in Him,
And in Him they shall glory."

3 For thus says the LORD to the men of Judah and Jerusalem:

"Break up your fallow ground,
And do not sow among thorns.
4 Circumcise yourselves to the LORD,
And take away the foreskins of your
hearts,
You men of Judah and inhabitants of
Jerusalem,
Lest My fury come forth like fire,
And burn so that no one can quench *it*,
Because of the evil of your doings."

An Imminent Invasion

5 Declare in Judah and proclaim in Jerusalem, and say:

"Blow the trumpet in the land;
Cry, 'Gather together,'
And say, 'Assemble yourselves,
And let us go into the fortified cities.'
6 Set up the standard toward Zion.
Take refuge! Do not delay!
For I will bring disaster from the north,
And great destruction."

7 The lion has come up from his thicket,
And the destroyer of nations is on his
way.
He has gone forth from his place
To make your land desolate.
Your cities will be laid waste,
Without inhabitant.
8 For this, clothe yourself with sackcloth,
Lament and wail.
For the fierce anger of the LORD
Has not turned back from us.
9 "And it shall come to pass in that day,"
says the LORD,
"*That* the heart of the king shall perish,
And the heart of the princes;
The priests shall be astonished,
And the prophets shall wonder."

10 Then I said, "Ah, Lord GOD!
Surely You have greatly deceived this
people and Jerusalem,
Saying, 'You shall have peace,'
Whereas the sword reaches to the heart."

11 At that time it will be said
To this people and to Jerusalem,
"A dry wind of the desolate heights *blows*
in the wilderness
Toward the daughter of My people—
Not to fan or to cleanse—

12 A wind too strong for these will come for
Me;
Now I will also speak judgment against
them."

13 "Behold, he shall come up like clouds,
And his chariots like a whirlwind.
His horses are swifter than eagles.
Woe to us, for we are plundered!"

➤ 14 O Jerusalem, wash your heart from
wickedness,
That you may be saved.
How long shall your evil thoughts lodge
within you?
15 For a voice declares from Dan
And proclaims affliction from Mount
Ephraim:
16 "Make mention to the nations,
Yes, proclaim against Jerusalem,
That watchers come from a far country
And raise their voice against the cities of
Judah.
17 Like keepers of a field they are against
her all around,
Because she has been rebellious against
Me," says the LORD.
18 "Your ways and your doings
Have procured these *things* for you.
This *is* your wickedness,
Because it is bitter,
Because it reaches to your heart."

Sorrow for the Doomed Nation

19 O my soul, my soul!
I am pained in my very heart!
My heart makes a noise in me;
I cannot hold my peace,
Because you have heard, O my soul,
The sound of the trumpet,
The alarm of war.
20 Destruction upon destruction is cried,
For the whole land is plundered.
Suddenly my tents are plundered,
And my curtains in a moment.
21 How long will I see the standard,
And hear the sound of the trumpet?

➤ 22 "For My people *are* foolish,
They have not known Me.
They *are* silly children,
And they have no understanding.
They *are* wise to do evil,
But to do good they have no knowledge."

23 I beheld the earth, and indeed *it was*
without form, and void;
And the heavens, they *had* no light.
24 I beheld the mountains, and indeed they
trembled,
And all the hills moved back and forth.
25 I beheld, and indeed *there was* no man,
And all the birds of the heavens had fled.
26 I beheld, and indeed the fruitful land *was*
a wilderness,
And all its cities were broken down
At the presence of the LORD,
By His fierce anger.

27 For thus says the LORD:

"The whole land shall be desolate;
Yet I will not make a full end.
28 For this shall the earth mourn,
And the heavens above be black,
Because I have spoken.
I have purposed and will not relent,
Nor will I turn back from it.
29 The whole city shall flee from the noise
of the horsemen and bowmen.
They shall go into thickets and climb up
on the rocks.
Every city *shall be* forsaken,
And not a man shall dwell in it.

30 "And *when* you *are* plundered,
What will you do?
Though you clothe yourself with crimson,
Though you adorn *yourself* with
ornaments of gold,
Though you enlarge your eyes with paint,
In vain you will make yourself fair;
Your lovers will despise you;
They will seek your life.

31 "For I have heard a voice as of a woman in
labor,
The anguish as of her who brings forth
her first child,
The voice of the daughter of Zion
bewailing herself;
She spreads her hands, *saying*,
'Woe *is* me now, for my soul is weary
Because of murderers!'

The Justice of God's Judgment

5 "Run to and fro through the streets of
Jerusalem;
See now and know;

LIFE LESSONS

➤ 4:14 — *". . . wash your heart from wickedness, that you may be saved. How long shall your evil thoughts lodge within you?"*

God saves us not merely to enable us to escape the punishment our sins deserve, but to free us from the power of sin. "Let everyone who names the name of Christ depart from iniquity" (2 Tim. 2:19).

➤ 4:22 — *"My people are foolish, they have not known Me. They are silly children, and they have no understanding. They are wise to do evil, but to do good they have no knowledge."*

To know God is to know righteousness. To love God is to love righteousness. To serve God is to serve righteously. "They profess to know God, but in works they deny Him . . ." (Titus 1:16).

And seek in her open places
If you can find a man,
If there is *anyone* who executes judgment,
Who seeks the truth,
And I will pardon her.
2 Though they say, 'As the LORD lives,'
Surely they swear falsely."

3 O LORD, *are* not Your eyes on the truth?
You have stricken them,
But they have not grieved;
You have consumed them,
But they have refused to receive correction.
They have made their faces harder than rock;
They have refused to return.

4 Therefore I said, "Surely these *are* poor.
They are foolish;
For they do not know the way of the LORD,
The judgment of their God.
5 I will go to the great men and speak to them,
For they have known the way of the LORD,
The judgment of their God."

But these have altogether broken the yoke
And burst the bonds.
6 Therefore a lion from the forest shall slay them,
A wolf of the deserts shall destroy them;
A leopard will watch over their cities.
Everyone who goes out from there shall be torn in pieces,
Because their transgressions are many;
Their backslidings have increased.

7 "How shall I pardon you for this?
Your children have forsaken Me
And sworn by *those that are* not gods.
When I had fed them to the full,
Then they committed adultery
And assembled themselves by troops in the harlots' houses.
➤ 8 They were *like* well-fed lusty stallions;
Every one neighed after his neighbor's wife.
9 Shall I not punish *them* for these *things?"* says the LORD.
"And shall I not avenge Myself on such a nation as this?

10 "Go up on her walls and destroy,
But do not make a complete end.
Take away her branches,
For they *are* not the LORD's.
11 For the house of Israel and the house of Judah
Have dealt very treacherously with Me,"
says the LORD.

12 They have lied about the LORD, ◀
And said, "*It is* not He.
Neither will evil come upon us,
Nor shall we see sword or famine.
13 And the prophets become wind,
For the word *is* not in them.
Thus shall it be done to them."

14 Therefore thus says the LORD God of hosts:

"Because you speak this word,
Behold, I will make My words in your mouth fire,
And this people wood,
And it shall devour them.
15 Behold, I will bring a nation against you from afar,
O house of Israel," says the LORD.
"It *is* a mighty nation,
It *is* an ancient nation,
A nation whose language you do not know,
Nor can you understand what they say.
16 Their quiver *is* like an open tomb;
They *are* all mighty men.
17 And they shall eat up your harvest and your bread,
Which your sons and daughters should eat.
They shall eat up your flocks and your herds;
They shall eat up your vines and your fig trees;
They shall destroy your fortified cities,
In which you trust, with the sword.

18 "Nevertheless in those days," says the
LORD, "I will not make a complete end of you.
19 "And it will be when you say, 'Why does
the LORD our God do all these *things* to us?'
then you shall answer them, 'Just as you have
forsaken Me and served foreign gods in your
land, so you shall serve aliens in a land *that*
is not yours.'

20 "Declare this in the house of Jacob
And proclaim it in Judah, saying,

LIFE LESSONS

➤ 5:8 — *"They were like well-fed lusty stallions; every one neighed after his neighbor's wife."*

In a culture where rampant immorality exists, it becomes harder and harder to maintain a God-honoring lifestyle. But it also becomes increasingly important to shine a light into the growing night (Matt. 5:15, 16).

➤ 5:12 — *They have lied about the LORD, and said, "It is not He. Neither will evil come upon us, nor shall we see sword or famine."*

We lie about the Lord when we say that He takes pleasure in what the Bible calls evil, or when we say that He will bless what He has sworn to judge. God *always* judges sin and blesses obedience.

21 'Hear this now, O foolish people,
Without understanding,
Who have eyes and see not,
And who have ears and hear not:
22 Do you not fear Me?' says the LORD.
'Will you not tremble at My presence,
Who have placed the sand as the bound of the sea,
By a perpetual decree, that it cannot pass beyond it?
And though its waves toss to and fro,
Yet they cannot prevail;
Though they roar, yet they cannot pass over it.
23 But this people has a defiant and rebellious heart;
They have revolted and departed.
24 They do not say in their heart,
"Let us now fear the LORD our God,
Who gives rain, both the former and the latter, in its season.
He reserves for us the appointed weeks of the harvest."
25 Your iniquities have turned these *things* away,
And your sins have withheld good from you.
26 'For among My people are found wicked *men;*
They lie in wait as one who sets snares;
They set a trap;
They catch men.
27 As a cage is full of birds,
So their houses *are* full of deceit.
Therefore they have become great and grown rich.
28 They have grown fat, they are sleek;
Yes, they surpass the deeds of the wicked;
They do not plead the cause,
The cause of the fatherless;
Yet they prosper,
And the right of the needy they do not defend.
29 Shall I not punish *them* for these *things?*' says the LORD.
'Shall I not avenge Myself on such a nation as this?'

➤ **30** "An astonishing and horrible thing
Has been committed in the land:
31 The prophets prophesy falsely,
And the priests rule by their *own* power;
And My people love *to have it* so.
But what will you do in the end?

Impending Destruction from the North

6 "O you children of Benjamin,
Gather yourselves to flee from the midst of Jerusalem!
Blow the trumpet in Tekoa,
And set up a signal-fire in Beth Haccerem;
For disaster appears out of the north,
And great destruction.
2 I have likened the daughter of Zion
To a lovely and delicate woman.
3 The shepherds with their flocks shall come to her.
They shall pitch *their* tents against her all around.
Each one shall pasture in his own place."
4 "Prepare war against her;
Arise, and let us go up at noon.
Woe to us, for the day goes away,
For the shadows of the evening are lengthening.
5 Arise, and let us go by night,
And let us destroy her palaces."

6 For thus has the LORD of hosts said:

"Cut down trees,
And build a mound against Jerusalem.
This *is* the city to be punished.
She *is* full of oppression in her midst.
7 As a fountain wells up with water,
So she wells up with her wickedness.
Violence and plundering are heard in her.
Before Me continually *are* grief and wounds.
8 Be instructed, O Jerusalem,
Lest My soul depart from you;
Lest I make you desolate,
A land not inhabited."

9 Thus says the LORD of hosts:

"They shall thoroughly glean as a vine the remnant of Israel;
As a grape-gatherer, put your hand back into the branches."
10 To whom shall I speak and give warning,
That they may hear?
Indeed their ear *is* uncircumcised,
And they cannot give heed.
Behold, the word of the LORD is a reproach to them;
They have no delight in it.
11 Therefore I am full of the fury of the LORD.

LIFE LESSONS

➤ **5:30, 31 — *"An astonishing and horrible thing has been committed in the land: the prophets prophesy falsely, and the priests rule by their own power; and My people love to have it so. But what will you do in the end?"***

We live in an era when many religious authorities try to bless what God has condemned and arrogantly replace divine authority with public opinion. God allows them to continue their activities for a time—but not forever.

I am weary of holding *it* in.
"I will pour it out on the children outside,
And on the assembly of young men together;
For even the husband shall be taken with the wife,
The aged with *him who is* full of days.
12 And their houses shall be turned over to others,
Fields and wives together;
For I will stretch out My hand
Against the inhabitants of the land," says the LORD.
13 "Because from the least of them even to the greatest of them,
Everyone *is* given to covetousness;
And from the prophet even to the priest,
Everyone deals falsely.
➤ 14 They have also healed the hurt of My people slightly,
Saying, 'Peace, peace!'
When *there is* no peace.
➤ 15 Were they ashamed when they had committed abomination?
No! They were not at all ashamed;
Nor did they know how to blush.
Therefore they shall fall among those who fall;
At the time I punish them,
They shall be cast down," says the LORD.

✳ **16** Thus says the LORD:
"Stand in the ways and see,
And ask for the old paths, where the good way *is,*
And walk in it;
Then you will find rest for your souls.
But they said, 'We will not walk *in it.*'
17 Also, I set watchmen over you, *saying,*
'Listen to the sound of the trumpet!'
But they said, 'We will not listen.'
18 Therefore hear, you nations,
And know, O congregation, what *is* among them.
19 Hear, O earth!
Behold, I will certainly bring calamity on this people—
The fruit of their thoughts,
Because they have not heeded My words
Nor My law, but rejected it.
20 For what purpose to Me
Comes frankincense from Sheba,
And sweet cane from a far country?
Your burnt offerings *are* not acceptable,
Nor your sacrifices sweet to Me."

21 Therefore thus says the LORD:
"Behold, I will lay stumbling blocks before this people,
And the fathers and the sons together shall fall on them.
The neighbor and his friend shall perish."

22 Thus says the LORD:
"Behold, a people comes from the north country,
And a great nation will be raised from the farthest parts of the earth.
23 They will lay hold on bow and spear;
They *are* cruel and have no mercy;
Their voice roars like the sea;
And they ride on horses,
As men of war set in array against you, O daughter of Zion."

24 We have heard the report of it;
Our hands grow feeble.
Anguish has taken hold of us,
Pain as of a woman in labor.
25 Do not go out into the field,
Nor walk by the way.
Because of the sword of the enemy,
Fear *is* on every side.
26 O daughter of my people,
Dress in sackcloth
And roll about in ashes!
Make mourning *as for* an only son, most bitter lamentation;
For the plunderer will suddenly come upon us.

27 "I have set you *as* an assayer *and* a fortress among My people,
That you may know and test their way.
28 They *are* all stubborn rebels, walking as slanderers.
They are bronze and iron,
They *are* all corrupters;
29 The bellows blow fiercely,
The lead is consumed by the fire;
The smelter refines in vain,
For the wicked are not drawn off.
30 *People* will call them rejected silver,
Because the LORD has rejected them."

LIFE LESSONS

➤ 6:14 — *"They have also healed the hurt of My people slightly, saying, 'Peace, peace!' when there is no peace."*

It was because of the love of God that Jeremiah warned his erring people to repent and turn back to God. There is no genuine peace or safety in open rebellion, and he wanted them safe in God's arms.

➤ 6:15 — *Were they ashamed when they had committed abomination? No! They were not at all ashamed; nor did they know how to blush.*

Shame is not a bad thing when it alerts us to our error and helps to turn us back to God in repentance and confession. But when we start identifying good as evil and evil as good, divine judgment draws near.

Trusting in Lying Words

7 The word that came to Jeremiah from the
LORD, saying,
2 "Stand in the gate of the LORD's house,
and proclaim there this word, and say, 'Hear
the word of the LORD, all *you of* Judah who
enter in at these gates to worship the LORD!'"
3 Thus says the LORD of hosts, the God of Israel: "Amend your ways and your doings, and
I will cause you to dwell in this place.
4 "Do not trust in these lying words, saying,
'The temple of the LORD, the temple of the
LORD, the temple of the LORD *are* these.'
5 "For if you thoroughly amend your ways
and your doings, if you thoroughly execute
judgment between a man and his neighbor,
6 "*if* you do not oppress the stranger, the fatherless, and the widow, and do not shed innocent blood in this place, or walk after other
gods to your hurt,
7 "then I will cause you to dwell in this
place, in the land that I gave to your fathers
forever and ever.
8 "Behold, you trust in lying words that cannot profit.
9 "Will you steal, murder, commit adultery,
swear falsely, burn incense to Baal, and walk
after other gods whom you do not know,
10 "and *then* come and stand before Me in
this house which is called by My name, and
say, 'We are delivered to do all these
abominations'?
11 "Has this house, which is called by My
name, become a den of thieves in your eyes?
Behold, I, even I, have seen *it*," says the LORD.
➤ **12** "But go now to My place which *was* in
Shiloh, where I set My name at the first, and
see what I did to it because of the wickedness
of My people Israel.
13 "And now, because you have done all these
works," says the LORD, "and I spoke to you,
rising up early and speaking, but you did not
hear, and I called you, but you did not answer,
14 "therefore I will do to the house which is
called by My name, in which you trust, and to
this place which I gave to you and your fathers, as I have done to Shiloh.
15 "And I will cast you out of My sight, as I
have cast out all your brethren—the whole
posterity of Ephraim.
16 "Therefore do not pray for this people, nor
lift up a cry or prayer for them, nor make intercession to Me; for I will not hear you.
17 "Do you not see what they do in the cities
of Judah and in the streets of Jerusalem?
18 "The children gather wood, the fathers
kindle the fire, and the women knead dough,
to make cakes for the queen of heaven; and
they pour out drink offerings to other gods,
that they may provoke Me to anger.
19 "Do they provoke Me to anger?" says the
LORD. "*Do they* not *provoke* themselves, to
the shame of their own faces?"
20 Therefore thus says the Lord GOD: "Behold, My anger and My fury will be poured
out on this place—on man and on beast, on
the trees of the field and on the fruit of the
ground. And it will burn and not be
quenched."
21 Thus says the LORD of hosts, the God of Israel: "Add your burnt offerings to your sacrifices and eat meat.
22 "For I did not speak to your fathers, or
command them in the day that I brought them
out of the land of Egypt, concerning burnt offerings or sacrifices.
23 "But this is what I commanded them, say- ➤
ing, 'Obey My voice, and I will be your God,
and you shall be My people. And walk in all
the ways that I have commanded you, that it
may be well with you.'
24 "Yet they did not obey or incline their ear,
but followed the counsels *and* the dictates of
their evil hearts, and went backward and not
forward.
25 "Since the day that your fathers came out
of the land of Egypt until this day, I have even
sent to you all My servants the prophets, daily
rising up early and sending *them*.
26 "Yet they did not obey Me or incline their
ear, but stiffened their neck. They did worse
than their fathers.
27 "Therefore you shall speak all these words
to them, but they will not obey you. You shall
also call to them, but they will not answer
you.

Judgment on Obscene Religion

28 "So you shall say to them, 'This *is* a nation
that does not obey the voice of the LORD their
God nor receive correction. Truth has perished and has been cut off from their mouth.

LIFE LESSONS

➤ 7:12 — *"But go now to My place which was in Shiloh, where I set My name at the first, and see what I did to it because of the wickedness of My people Israel."*

God has no nostalgic ties to shrines or holy places or houses of worship. We are never "safe" merely because we live near or around a "sacred place." God wants clean hearts, not impressive grounds.

➤ 7:23 — *"Obey My voice, and I will be your God, and you shall be My people. And walk in all the ways that I have commanded you, that it may be well with you."*

God desires prosperity for you. He wants you to be a whole person, balanced and growing and fruitful and fulfilling His purpose for your life. So ask yourself: What do I desire? How am I acting on it?

29 'Cut off your hair and cast *it* away, and
take up a lamentation on the desolate heights;
for the LORD has rejected and forsaken the
generation of His wrath.'
30 "For the children of Judah have done evil
in My sight," says the LORD. "They have set
their abominations in the house which is
called by My name, to pollute it.
➤ 31 "And they have built the high places of
Tophet, which *is* in the Valley of the Son of
Hinnom, to burn their sons and their daughters in the fire, which I did not command, nor
did it come into My heart.
32 "Therefore behold, the days are coming,"
says the LORD, "when it will no more be called
Tophet, or the Valley of the Son of Hinnom,
but the Valley of Slaughter; for they will bury
in Tophet until there is no room.
33 "The corpses of this people will be food for
the birds of the heaven and for the beasts of
the earth. And no one will frighten *them away.*
34 "Then I will cause to cease from the cities
of Judah and from the streets of Jerusalem
the voice of mirth and the voice of gladness,
the voice of the bridegroom and the voice of
the bride. For the land shall be desolate.

8 "At that time," says the LORD, "they shall
bring out the bones of the kings of Judah,
and the bones of its princes, and the bones of
the priests, and the bones of the prophets, and
the bones of the inhabitants of Jerusalem, out
of their graves.
2 "They shall spread them before the sun
and the moon and all the host of heaven, which
they have loved and which they have served
and after which they have walked, which they
have sought and which they have worshiped.
They shall not be gathered nor buried; they
shall be like refuse on the face of the earth.
3 "Then death shall be chosen rather than
life by all the residue of those who remain of
this evil family, who remain in all the places
where I have driven them," says the LORD of
hosts.

The Peril of False Teaching

4 "Moreover you shall say to them, 'Thus
says the LORD:

"Will they fall and not rise?
Will one turn away and not return?
5 Why has this people slidden back,
Jerusalem, in a perpetual backsliding?
They hold fast to deceit,
They refuse to return.
6 I listened and heard,
But they do not speak aright.
No man repented of his wickedness,
Saying, 'What have I done?'
Everyone turned to his own course,
As the horse rushes into the battle.

7 "Even the stork in the heavens ➤
Knows her appointed times;
And the turtledove, the swift, and the
swallow
Observe the time of their coming.
But My people do not know the judgment
of the LORD.

8 "How can you say, 'We *are* wise,
And the law of the LORD *is* with us'?
Look, the false pen of the scribe certainly
works falsehood.
9 The wise men are ashamed, ➤
They are dismayed and taken.
Behold, they have rejected the word of
the LORD;
So what wisdom do they have?
10 Therefore I will give their wives to
others,
And their fields to those who will inherit
them;
Because from the least even to the
greatest
Everyone is given to covetousness;
From the prophet even to the priest
Everyone deals falsely.
11 For they have healed the hurt of the
daughter of My people slightly,
Saying, 'Peace, peace!'
When *there is* no peace.
12 Were they ashamed when they had
committed abomination?
No! They were not at all ashamed,
Nor did they know how to blush.
Therefore they shall fall among those
who fall;

LIFE LESSONS

➤ 7:31 — *"And they have built the high places of Tophet . . . to burn their sons and their daughters in the fire, which I did not command, nor did it come into My heart."*

Pagan deities might be believed to call for human sacrifice in worship, but God never does that. He wants to give life, not take it. He wants to bless us, not terrify us. He wants us to love Him, not cower before Him.

➤ 8:7 — *" . . . the turtledove, the swift, and the swallow observe the time of their coming. But My people do not know the judgment of the LORD."*

Instinct drives many animals to regular cycles of hibernation or migration. God asks us, "If they can be so wise about the way they live, then why don't you use the wisdom I gave you to draw near to Me?"

➤ 8:9 — *"Behold, they have rejected the word of the LORD; so what wisdom do they have?"*

Whenever we disobey the Word of God, we reject God's wisdom for what we consider to be more potent or effective wisdom. But it never turns out that way. "Wisdom" apart from God always leads to death.

In the time of their punishment
They shall be cast down," says the LORD.

13 "I will surely consume them," says the
LORD.
"No grapes *shall be* on the vine,
Nor figs on the fig tree,
And the leaf shall fade;
And *the things* I have given them shall
pass away from them." ' "

14 "Why do we sit still?
Assemble yourselves,
And let us enter the fortified cities,
And let us be silent there.
For the LORD our God has put us to
silence
And given us water of gall to drink,
Because we have sinned against the
LORD.

15 "*We* looked for peace, but no good *came;*
And for a time of health, and there was
trouble!
16 The snorting of His horses was heard
from Dan.
The whole land trembled at the sound of
the neighing of His strong ones;
For they have come and devoured the
land and all that is in it,
The city and those who dwell in it."

17 "For behold, I will send serpents among
you,
Vipers which cannot be charmed,
And they shall bite you," says the LORD.

The Prophet Mourns for the People
18 I would comfort myself in sorrow;
My heart *is* faint in me.
19 Listen! The voice,
The cry of the daughter of my people
From a far country:
"*Is* not the LORD in Zion?
Is not her King in her?"

"Why have they provoked Me to anger
With their carved images—
With foreign idols?"

20 "The harvest is past,
The summer is ended,
And we are not saved!"

21 For the hurt of the daughter of my people
I am hurt.
I am mourning;
Astonishment has taken hold of me.
➤ 22 *Is there* no balm in Gilead,
Is there no physician there?
Why then is there no recovery
For the health of the daughter of my
people?

9 Oh, that my head were waters,
And my eyes a fountain of tears,
That I might weep day and night
For the slain of the daughter of my
people!
2 Oh, that I had in the wilderness
A lodging place for travelers;
That I might leave my people,
And go from them!
For they *are* all adulterers,
An assembly of treacherous men.

3 "And *like* their bow they have bent their
tongues *for* lies.
They are not valiant for the truth on the
earth.
For they proceed from evil to evil,
And they do not know Me," says the LORD.
4 "Everyone take heed to his neighbor,
And do not trust any brother;
For every brother will utterly supplant,
And every neighbor will walk with
slanderers.
5 Everyone will deceive his neighbor,
And will not speak the truth;
They have taught their tongue to speak
lies;
They weary themselves to commit
iniquity.
6 Your dwelling place *is* in the midst of
deceit;
Through deceit they refuse to know Me,"
says the LORD.

7 Therefore thus says the LORD of hosts:

"Behold, I will refine them and try them;
For how shall I deal with the daughter of
My people?
8 Their tongue *is* an arrow shot out;
It speaks deceit;
One speaks peaceably to his neighbor
with his mouth,
But in his heart he lies in wait.
9 Shall I not punish them for these *things?*"
says the LORD.
"Shall I not avenge Myself on such a
nation as this?"

10 I will take up a weeping and wailing for
the mountains,
And for the dwelling places of the
wilderness a lamentation,
Because they are burned up,

LIFE LESSONS

➤ **8:22 — *Is there no balm in Gilead, is there no physician there? Why then is there no recovery for the health of the daughter of my people?***

Even in Jeremiah's day, God offered hope and healing to His spiritually diseased people—but they had to come to Him and accept His prescription to find life. We will never find life anywhere else.

WHAT THE BIBLE SAYS ABOUT GOD AS OUR COMFORTER

Jer. 8:18

The recognition of God's power to heal your hurts is a key component to experiencing His tender love. In the midst of great pain, Jeremiah acknowledged his sadness and the ability of God to comfort him. So he cried out, "I would comfort myself in sorrow; my heart is faint in me" (Jer. 8:18).

Centuries earlier, King David moaned, "Reproach has broken my heart, and I am full of heaviness; I looked for someone to take pity, but there was none; and for comforters, but I found none" (Ps. 69:20). In the people around him he could find no solace; but near the end of his song, his tune had changed: "And you who seek God, your hearts shall live. For the LORD hears the poor, and does not despise His prisoners" (Ps. 69:32, 33).

Where do *you* look for comfort? If you have relied on human remedies, you know how their effectiveness diminishes over time. Some try food, or alcohol, or drugs, or escape into fantasy—anything to attempt to outrun the pain. But when the artificial glow wears off and the dream ends, the ache remains.

There is no such thing as a life without pain and trial, and therefore no such thing as a person without need of comfort. Don't let anyone deceive you into thinking that the key to leading a joy-filled Christian life is avoiding pain; that simply is not possible in this sinful world, and neither is it profitable for us. God could choose to insulate you from hurt, but instead He allows you to experience the tough times that draw you closer to Him.

Out of your pain comes a need for God. As He ministers to you and you accept it with thanksgiving and a desire to learn, you become equipped to minister to those He places within your reach (see 2 Cor. 1:3, 4). Hurting individuals know there is no substitute for experience.

You can reach for God's comfort right now. Ask Him to give you solace—and find yourself wrapped in the love that will not let you go.

You can reach for God's comfort right now.

See the Life Principles Index for further study:

12. *Peace with God is the fruit of oneness with God.*
15. *Brokenness is God's requirement for maximum usefulness.*

So that no one can pass through;
Nor can *men* hear the voice of the cattle.
Both the birds of the heavens and the beasts have fled;
They are gone.
11 "I will make Jerusalem a heap of ruins, a den of jackals.
I will make the cities of Judah desolate, without an inhabitant."

12 Who *is* the wise man who may understand
this? And *who is he* to whom the mouth of the
LORD has spoken, that he may declare it? Why
does the land perish *and* burn up like a
wilderness, so that no one can pass through?
13 And the LORD said, "Because they have
forsaken My law which I set before them, and
have not obeyed My voice, nor walked according to it,
14 "but they have walked according to the
dictates of their own hearts and after the
Baals, which their fathers taught them,"
15 therefore thus says the LORD of hosts, the
God of Israel: "Behold, I will feed them, this
people, with wormwood, and give them water
of gall to drink.
16 "I will scatter them also among the Gentiles, whom neither they nor their fathers
have known. And I will send a sword after
them until I have consumed them."

The People Mourn in Judgment

17 Thus says the LORD of hosts:

"Consider and call for the mourning women,
That they may come;
And send for skillful *wailing* women,
That they may come.
18 Let them make haste
And take up a wailing for us,
That our eyes may run with tears,
And our eyelids gush with water.
19 For a voice of wailing is heard from Zion:
'How we are plundered!
We are greatly ashamed,
Because we have forsaken the land,
Because we have been cast out of our dwellings.'"
20 Yet hear the word of the LORD, O women,
And let your ear receive the word of His mouth;
Teach your daughters wailing,
And everyone her neighbor a lamentation.
21 For death has come through our windows,
Has entered our palaces,
To kill off the children—*no longer to be* outside!
And the young men—*no longer* on the streets!
22 Speak, "Thus says the LORD:
'Even the carcasses of men shall fall as refuse on the open field,
Like cuttings after the harvester,
And no one shall gather *them*.'"

23 Thus says the LORD:

"Let not the wise *man* glory in his wisdom,
Let not the mighty *man* glory in his might,
Nor let the rich *man* glory in his riches;
24 But let him who glories glory in this,
That he understands and knows Me,
That I *am* the LORD, exercising lovingkindness, judgment, and righteousness in the earth.
For in these I delight," says the LORD.

25 "Behold, the days are coming," says the
LORD, "that I will punish all *who are* circumcised with the uncircumcised—
26 "Egypt, Judah, Edom, the people of
Ammon, Moab, and all *who are* in the farthest
corners, who dwell in the wilderness. For all
these nations *are* uncircumcised, and all the
house of Israel *are* uncircumcised in the
heart."

Idols and the True God

10 Hear the word which the LORD speaks to you, O house of Israel.
2 Thus says the LORD:

"Do not learn the way of the Gentiles;
Do not be dismayed at the signs of heaven,
For the Gentiles are dismayed at them.
3 For the customs of the peoples *are* futile;
For *one* cuts a tree from the forest,
The work of the hands of the workman, with the ax.
4 They decorate it with silver and gold;
They fasten it with nails and hammers
So that it will not topple.
5 They *are* upright, like a palm tree,
And they cannot speak;
They must be carried,

LIFE LESSONS

➤ 9:23, 24 — *"Let not the wise man glory in his wisdom, let not the mighty man glory in his might, nor let the rich man glory in his riches; but let him who glories glory in this, that he understands and knows Me . . . ."*

Intelligence, power, and riches all give human beings the illusion of being in control—but the illusion always comes to an end. When we put our confidence in God alone, however, we find something worth our boasting.

Because they cannot go *by themselves.*
Do not be afraid of them,
For they cannot do evil,
Nor can they do any good."

6 Inasmuch as *there is* none like You, O LORD
(You *are* great, and Your name *is* great in might),
➤ 7 Who would not fear You, O King of the nations?
For this is Your rightful due.
For among all the wise *men* of the nations,
And in all their kingdoms,
There is none like You.
8 But they are altogether dull-hearted and foolish;
A wooden idol *is* a worthless doctrine.
9 Silver is beaten into plates;
It is brought from Tarshish,
And gold from Uphaz,
The work of the craftsman
And of the hands of the metalsmith;
Blue and purple *are* their clothing;
They *are* all the work of skillful *men.*
10 But the LORD *is* the true God;
He *is* the living God and the everlasting King.
At His wrath the earth will tremble,
And the nations will not be able to endure His indignation.

11 Thus you shall say to them: "The gods that
have not made the heavens and the earth
shall perish from the earth and from under
these heavens."

12 He has made the earth by His power,
He has established the world by His wisdom,
And has stretched out the heavens at His discretion.
13 When He utters His voice,
There is a multitude of waters in the heavens:
"And He causes the vapors to ascend from the ends of the earth.
He makes lightning for the rain,
He brings the wind out of His treasuries."[a]
14 Everyone is dull-hearted, without knowledge;
Every metalsmith is put to shame by an image;
For his molded image *is* falsehood,
And *there is* no breath in them.
15 They *are* futile, a work of errors;
In the time of their punishment they shall perish.
16 The Portion of Jacob *is* not like them,
For He *is* the Maker of all *things*,
And Israel *is* the tribe of His inheritance;
The LORD of hosts *is* His name.

The Coming Captivity of Judah

17 Gather up your wares from the land,
O inhabitant of the fortress!
18 For thus says the LORD:
"Behold, I will throw out at this time
The inhabitants of the land,
And will distress them,
That they may find *it so.*"
19 Woe is me for my hurt!
My wound is severe.
But I say, "Truly this *is* an infirmity,
And I must bear it."
20 My tent is plundered,
And all my cords are broken;
My children have gone from me,
And they *are* no more.
There is no one to pitch my tent anymore,
Or set up my curtains.
21 For the shepherds have become dull-hearted,
And have not sought the LORD;
Therefore they shall not prosper,
And all their flocks shall be scattered.
22 Behold, the noise of the report has come,
And a great commotion out of the north country,
To make the cities of Judah desolate, a den of jackals.
23 O LORD, I know the way of man *is* not in himself; ➤
It is not in man who walks to direct his own steps.
24 O LORD, correct me, but with justice;
Not in Your anger, lest You bring me to nothing.
25 Pour out Your fury on the Gentiles, who do not know You,
And on the families who do not call on Your name;
For they have eaten up Jacob,
Devoured him and consumed him,
And made his dwelling place desolate.

10:13 [a]Psalm 135:7

LIFE LESSONS

➤ 10:7 — *"Who would not fear You, O King of the nations? For this is Your rightful due . . . ."*

For reasons of His own, God chooses to veil His glory most of the time. If men and women fall prostrate whenever they see an unveiled angel (Rev. 19:10), imagine what they would feel if they saw God!

➤ 10:23 — *O LORD, I know the way of man is not in himself; it is not in man who walks to direct his own steps.*

God made us to depend on Him, to look for His guidance and direction and counsel. We commit our lives to Him, not merely for salvation, but for what we need and where we go every moment of our life.

The Broken Covenant

11 The word that came to Jeremiah from the LORD, saying,

2 "Hear the words of this covenant, and speak to the men of Judah and to the inhabitants of Jerusalem;

3 "and say to them, 'Thus says the LORD God of Israel: "Cursed *is* the man who does not obey the words of this covenant

4 "which I commanded your fathers in the day I brought them out of the land of Egypt, from the iron furnace, saying, 'Obey My voice, and do according to all that I command you; so shall you be My people, and I will be your God,'

5 "that I may establish the oath which I have sworn to your fathers, to give them 'a land flowing with milk and honey,'[a] as *it is* this day."'" And I answered and said, "So be it, LORD."

6 Then the LORD said to me, "Proclaim all these words in the cities of Judah and in the streets of Jerusalem, saying: 'Hear the words of this covenant and do them.

7 'For I earnestly exhorted your fathers in the day I brought them up out of the land of Egypt, until this day, rising early and exhorting, saying, "Obey My voice."

8 'Yet they did not obey or incline their ear, but everyone followed the dictates of his evil heart; therefore I will bring upon them all the words of this covenant, which I commanded *them* to do, but *which* they have not done.'"

9 And the LORD said to me, "A conspiracy has been found among the men of Judah and among the inhabitants of Jerusalem.

10 "They have turned back to the iniquities of their forefathers who refused to hear My words, and they have gone after other gods to serve them; the house of Israel and the house of Judah have broken My covenant which I made with their fathers."

11 Therefore thus says the LORD: "Behold, I will surely bring calamity on them which they will not be able to escape; and though they cry out to Me, I will not listen to them.

12 "Then the cities of Judah and the inhabitants of Jerusalem will go and cry out to the gods to whom they offer incense, but they will not save them at all in the time of their trouble.

13 "For *according to* the number of your cities were your gods, O Judah; and *according to* the number of the streets of Jerusalem you have set up altars to *that* shameful thing, altars to burn incense to Baal.

14 "So do not pray for this people, or lift up a cry or prayer for them; for I will not hear *them* in the time that they cry out to Me because of their trouble.

15 "What has My beloved to do in My house,
Having done lewd deeds with many?
And the holy flesh has passed from you.
When you do evil, then you rejoice.
16 The LORD called your name,
Green Olive Tree, Lovely *and* of Good Fruit.
With the noise of a great tumult
He has kindled fire on it,
And its branches are broken.

17 "For the LORD of hosts, who planted you, has pronounced doom against you for the evil of the house of Israel and of the house of Judah, which they have done against themselves to provoke Me to anger in offering incense to Baal."

Jeremiah's Life Threatened

18 Now the LORD gave me knowledge *of it*, and I know *it;* for You showed me their doings.

19 But I *was* like a docile lamb brought to the slaughter; and I did not know that they had devised schemes against me, *saying*, "Let us destroy the tree with its fruit, and let us cut him off from the land of the living, that his name may be remembered no more."

20 But, O LORD of hosts,
You who judge righteously,
Testing the mind and the heart,
Let me see Your vengeance on them,
For to You I have revealed my cause.

21 "Therefore thus says the LORD concerning the men of Anathoth who seek your life, saying, 'Do not prophesy in the name of the LORD, lest you die by our hand'—

22 "therefore thus says the LORD of hosts: 'Behold, I will punish them. The young men shall die by the sword, their sons and their daughters shall die by famine;

23 "and there shall be no remnant of them, for I will bring catastrophe on the men of Anathoth, *even* the year of their punishment.'"

11:5 [a]Exodus 3:8

LIFE LESSONS

➤ 11:14 — *"So do not pray for this people, or lift up a cry or prayer for them; for I will not hear them in the time that they cry out to Me because of their trouble."*

God banned Jeremiah from praying for the welfare of his rebellious people. They had gone so far down a road of destruction that it had become too late for them—a time known to God alone (see 1 John 5:16).

Jeremiah's Question

12 Righteous *are* You, O LORD, when I
plead with You;
Yet let me talk with You about *Your*
judgments.
Why does the way of the wicked prosper?
Why are those happy who deal so
treacherously?
2 You have planted them, yes, they have
taken root;
They grow, yes, they bear fruit.
You *are* near in their mouth
But far from their mind.

3 But You, O LORD, know me;
You have seen me,
And You have tested my heart toward You.
Pull them out like sheep for the slaughter,
And prepare them for the day of
slaughter.
4 How long will the land mourn,
And the herbs of every field wither?
The beasts and birds are consumed,
For the wickedness of those who dwell
there,
Because they said, "He will not see our
final end."

The LORD Answers Jeremiah

➤ **5** "If you have run with the footmen, and
they have wearied you,
Then how can you contend with horses?
And *if* in the land of peace,
In which you trusted, *they wearied you,*
Then how will you do in the floodplain[a]
of the Jordan?
6 For even your brothers, the house of your
father,
Even they have dealt treacherously with
you;
Yes, they have called a multitude after
you.
Do not believe them,
Even though they speak smooth words to
you.

7 "I have forsaken My house, I have left My
heritage;
I have given the dearly beloved of My
soul into the hand of her enemies.
8 My heritage is to Me like a lion in the
forest;
It cries out against Me;
Therefore I have hated it.
9 My heritage *is* to Me *like* a speckled
vulture;
The vultures all around *are* against her.
Come, assemble all the beasts of the
field,
Bring them to devour!

10 "Many rulers[a] have destroyed My
vineyard,
They have trodden My portion underfoot;
They have made My pleasant portion a
desolate wilderness.
11 They have made it desolate;
Desolate, it mourns to Me;
The whole land is made desolate,
Because no one takes *it* to heart.
12 The plunderers have come
On all the desolate heights in the
wilderness,
For the sword of the LORD shall devour
From *one* end of the land to the *other* end
of the land;
No flesh shall have peace.
13 They have sown wheat but reaped thorns;
They have put themselves to pain *but* do
not profit.
But be ashamed of your harvest
Because of the fierce anger of the LORD."

14 Thus says the LORD: "Against all My evil
neighbors who touch the inheritance which I
have caused My people Israel to inherit—behold, I will pluck them out of their land and
pluck out the house of Judah from among
them.
15 "Then it shall be, after I have plucked
them out, that I will return and have compassion on them and bring them back, everyone
to his heritage and everyone to his land.
16 "And it shall be, if they will learn carefully
the ways of My people, to swear by My name,
'As the LORD lives,' as they taught My people
to swear by Baal, then they shall be established in the midst of My people.
17 "But if they do not obey, I will utterly pluck
up and destroy that nation," says the LORD.

Symbol of the Linen Sash

13 Thus the LORD said to me: "Go and get ➤
yourself a linen sash, and put it around
your waist, but do not put it in water."

12:5 [a]Or *thicket* **12:10** [a]Literally *shepherds* or *pastors*

LIFE LESSONS

➤ **12:5 — *"If you have run with the footmen, and they have wearied you, then how can you contend with horses?"***

God encourages us, but He also challenges us. He speaks soft words to us when we need them, but He speaks harder words to us when we need them. He always gives us exactly what we need.

➤ **13:1 — *Thus the LORD said to me: "Go and get yourself a linen sash, and put it around your waist, but do not put it in water."***

God often had His prophets participate in graphic object lessons, but frequently He didn't tell them what He was up to until after they had obeyed. We are to obey even when God's instructions don't seem to make much sense.

2 So I got a sash according to the word of
the LORD, and put *it* around my waist.
3 And the word of the LORD came to me the
second time, saying,
4 "Take the sash that you acquired, which *is*
around your waist, and arise, go to the Euphrates,[a] and hide it there in a hole in the
rock."
5 So I went and hid it by the Euphrates, as
the LORD commanded me.
6 Now it came to pass after many days that
the LORD said to me, "Arise, go to the Euphrates, and take from there the sash which I
commanded you to hide there."
7 Then I went to the Euphrates and dug, and
I took the sash from the place where I had
hidden it; and there was the sash, ruined. It
was profitable for nothing.
8 Then the word of the LORD came to me,
saying,
9 "Thus says the LORD: 'In this manner I will
ruin the pride of Judah and the great pride of
Jerusalem.
10 "This evil people, who refuse to hear My
words, who follow the dictates of their hearts,
and walk after other gods to serve them and
worship them, shall be just like this sash
which is profitable for nothing.
➤ 11 'For as the sash clings to the waist of a
man, so I have caused the whole house of Israel and the whole house of Judah to cling to
Me,' says the LORD, 'that they may become My
people, for renown, for praise, and for glory;
but they would not hear.'

Symbol of the Wine Bottles

12 "Therefore you shall speak to them this
word: 'Thus says the LORD God of Israel:
"Every bottle shall be filled with wine."' And
they will say to you, 'Do we not certainly know
that every bottle will be filled with wine?'
13 "Then you shall say to them, 'Thus says
the LORD: "Behold, I will fill all the inhabitants of this land—even the kings who sit on
David's throne, the priests, the prophets, and
all the inhabitants of Jerusalem—with drunkenness!
14 "And I will dash them one against another,
even the fathers and the sons together," says
the LORD. "I will not pity nor spare nor have
mercy, but will destroy them."'"

Pride Precedes Captivity

15 Hear and give ear:
Do not be proud,
For the LORD has spoken.
16 Give glory to the LORD your God
Before He causes darkness,
And before your feet stumble
On the dark mountains,
And while you are looking for light,
He turns it into the shadow of death
And makes *it* dense darkness.
17 But if you will not hear it,
My soul will weep in secret for *your* pride;
My eyes will weep bitterly
And run down with tears,
Because the LORD's flock has been taken
captive.

18 Say to the king and to the queen mother,
"Humble yourselves;
Sit down,
For your rule shall collapse, the crown of
your glory."
19 The cities of the South shall be shut up,
And no one shall open *them;*
Judah shall be carried away captive, all
of it;
It shall be wholly carried away captive.

20 Lift up your eyes and see
Those who come from the north.
Where *is* the flock *that* was given to you,
Your beautiful sheep?
21 What will you say when He punishes you?
For you have taught them
To be chieftains, to be head over you.
Will not pangs seize you,
Like a woman in labor?
22 And if you say in your heart,
"Why have these things come upon me?"
For the greatness of your iniquity
Your skirts have been uncovered,
Your heels made bare.
23 Can the Ethiopian change his skin or the
leopard its spots?
Then may you also do good who are
accustomed to do evil.

24 "Therefore I will scatter them like stubble
That passes away by the wind of the
wilderness.
25 This is your lot,
The portion of your measures from Me,"
says the LORD,
"Because you have forgotten Me
And trusted in falsehood.
26 Therefore I will uncover your skirts over
your face,
That your shame may appear.

13:4 [a]Hebrew *Perath*

LIFE LESSONS

➤ ***13:11 — "I have caused the whole house of Israel and the whole house of Judah to cling to Me," says the LORD, "that they may become My people, for renown, for praise, and for glory . . . ."***

Here we see the heart of God: a passionate longing to become one with His people, to bless them, to identify them with Him in such a way that they receive honor and He receives glory.

Life Examples:

JEREMIAH

Sorrowful Compassion

JER. 14:17

Jeremiah is often called the "weeping prophet," for little in his writings evokes ease or comfort. He wept because the people of his time had turned from God and had begun to reap the dreadful consequences of their sin.

He also wept because, with the careful eye of a true prophet of God, Jeremiah saw the devastation to come. And even though he occasionally urged the Lord to give His wandering people the full measure of what they deserved (see Jer. 11:20), most of the time he pled for mercy and the divine grace needed to lead them back to repentance (Jer. 8:20–22).

Do we weep when we see people wandering away from God and heading straight toward judgment? Do we strive to show godly compassion to those in great spiritual danger? Or do we keep silent, hoping to see God's wrath poured out on our enemies?

See the Life Principles Index for further study:

24. To live the Christian life is to allow Jesus to live His life in and through us.

27 I have seen your adulteries
And your *lustful* neighings,
The lewdness of your harlotry,
Your abominations on the hills in the fields.
Woe to you, O Jerusalem!
Will you still not be made clean?"

Sword, Famine, and Pestilence

14 The word of the LORD that came to Jeremiah concerning the droughts.

2 "Judah mourns,
And her gates languish;
They mourn for the land,
And the cry of Jerusalem has gone up.
3 Their nobles have sent their lads for water;
They went to the cisterns *and* found no water.
They returned with their vessels empty;
They were ashamed and confounded
And covered their heads.
4 Because the ground is parched,
For there was no rain in the land,
The plowmen were ashamed;
They covered their heads.
5 Yes, the deer also gave birth in the field,
But left because there was no grass.
6 And the wild donkeys stood in the desolate heights;
They sniffed at the wind like jackals;
Their eyes failed because *there was* no grass."

7 O LORD, though our iniquities testify against us,
Do it for Your name's sake;
For our backslidings are many,
We have sinned against You.
8 O the Hope of Israel, his Savior in time of trouble,
Why should You be like a stranger in the land,
And like a traveler *who* turns aside to tarry for a night?
9 Why should You be like a man astonished,
Like a mighty one *who* cannot save?
Yet You, O LORD, *are* in our midst,
And we are called by Your name;
Do not leave us!

10 Thus says the LORD to this people:
"Thus they have loved to wander;
They have not restrained their feet.
Therefore the LORD does not accept them;
He will remember their iniquity now,
And punish their sins."

11 Then the LORD said to me, "Do not pray for
this people, for *their* good.
12 "When they fast, I will not hear their cry;
and when they offer burnt offering and grain
offering, I will not accept them. But I will consume them by the sword, by the famine, and
by the pestilence."
13 Then I said, "Ah, Lord GOD! Behold, the
prophets say to them, 'You shall not see the
sword, nor shall you have famine, but I will
give you assured peace in this place.'"
14 And the LORD said to me, "The prophets
prophesy lies in My name. I have not sent
them, commanded them, nor spoken to them;
they prophesy to you a false vision, divination,
a worthless thing, and the deceit of their heart.
15 "Therefore thus says the LORD concerning
the prophets who prophesy in My name,
whom I did not send, and who say, 'Sword and
famine shall not be in this land'—'By sword
and famine those prophets shall be consumed!
16 'And the people to whom they prophesy
shall be cast out in the streets of Jerusalem
because of the famine and the sword; they
will have no one to bury them—them nor
their wives, their sons nor their daughters—
for I will pour their wickedness on them.'
17 "Therefore you shall say this word to
them:

'Let my eyes flow with tears night and day,
And let them not cease;

For the virgin daughter of my people
Has been broken with a mighty stroke,
with a very severe blow.
18 If I go out to the field,
Then behold, those slain with the sword!
And if I enter the city,
Then behold, those sick from famine!
Yes, both prophet and priest go about in
a land they do not know.'"

The People Plead for Mercy

19 Have You utterly rejected Judah?
Has Your soul loathed Zion?
Why have You stricken us so that *there is*
no healing for us?
We looked for peace, but *there was* no
good;
And for the time of healing, and there
was trouble.
➤ 20 We acknowledge, O LORD, our wickedness
And the iniquity of our fathers,
For we have sinned against You.
21 Do not abhor *us*, for Your name's sake;
Do not disgrace the throne of Your glory.
Remember, do not break Your covenant
with us.
➤ 22 Are there any among the idols of the
nations that can cause rain?
Or can the heavens give showers?
Are You not He, O LORD our God?
Therefore we will wait for You,
Since You have made all these.

The LORD Will Not Relent

15 Then the LORD said to me, "*Even* if
Moses and Samuel stood before Me,
My mind *would* not *be* favorable toward this
people. Cast *them* out of My sight, and let
them go forth.
2 "And it shall be, if they say to you, 'Where
should we go?' then you shall tell them, 'Thus
says the LORD:

"Such as *are* for death, to death;
And such as *are* for the sword, to the
sword;
And such as *are* for the famine, to the
famine;
And such as *are* for the captivity, to the
captivity."'
3 "And I will appoint over them four forms *of*
destruction," says the LORD: "the sword to slay,
the dogs to drag, the birds of the heavens and
the beasts of the earth to devour and destroy.
4 "I will hand them over to trouble, to all
kingdoms of the earth, because of Manasseh
the son of Hezekiah, king of Judah, for what
he did in Jerusalem.

5 "For who will have pity on you,
O Jerusalem?
Or who will bemoan you?
Or who will turn aside to ask how you
are doing?
6 You have forsaken Me," says the LORD,
"You have gone backward.
Therefore I will stretch out My hand
against you and destroy you;
I am weary of relenting!
7 And I will winnow them with a winnowing
fan in the gates of the land;
I will bereave *them* of children;
I will destroy My people,
Since they do not return from their ways.
8 Their widows will be increased to Me
more than the sand of the seas;
I will bring against them,
Against the mother of the young men,
A plunderer at noonday;
I will cause anguish and terror to fall on
them suddenly.
9 "She languishes who has borne seven;
She has breathed her last;
Her sun has gone down
While *it was* yet day;
She has been ashamed and confounded.
And the remnant of them I will deliver to
the sword
Before their enemies," says the LORD.

Jeremiah's Dejection

10 Woe is me, my mother,
That you have borne me,
A man of strife and a man of contention
to the whole earth!
I have neither lent for interest,
Nor have men lent to me for interest.
Every one of them curses me.

11 The LORD said: ✳

"Surely it will be well with your remnant;
Surely I will cause the enemy to
intercede with you
In the time of adversity and in the time of
affliction.

LIFE LESSONS

➤ **14:20 — *"We acknowledge, O LORD, our wickedness and the iniquity of our fathers, for we have sinned against You."***

Confession of sin rips away the thick shroud of darkness that sin weaves around our heads, and allows the light of God to penetrate our souls and fill us with life and joy.

➤ **14:22 — *Are there any among the idols of the nations that can cause rain? Or can the heavens give showers? Are You not He, O LORD our God? Therefore we will wait for You, since You have made all these.***

We pray to God because He alone is the Creator. He created rain; He made the clouds to drench the land with life-giving water. Since He alone created the world, He alone has the power to answer our prayers.

12 Can anyone break iron,
The northern iron and the bronze?
13 Your wealth and your treasures
I will give as plunder without price,
Because of all your sins,
Throughout your territories.
14 And I will make *you* cross over with[a]
your enemies
Into a land *which* you do not know;
For a fire is kindled in My anger,
Which shall burn upon you."

15 O LORD, You know;
Remember me and visit me,
And take vengeance for me on my
persecutors.
In Your enduring patience, do not take me
away.
Know that for Your sake I have suffered
rebuke.
➤ 16 Your words were found, and I ate them,
And Your word was to me the joy and
rejoicing of my heart;
For I am called by Your name,
O LORD God of hosts.
17 I did not sit in the assembly of the
mockers,
Nor did I rejoice;
I sat alone because of Your hand,
For You have filled me with indignation.
18 Why is my pain perpetual
And my wound incurable,
Which refuses to be healed?
Will You surely be to me like an
unreliable stream,
As waters *that* fail?

The LORD Reassures Jeremiah

19 Therefore thus says the LORD:

"If you return,
Then I will bring you back;
You shall stand before Me;
If you take out the precious from the vile,
You shall be as My mouth.
Let them return to you,
But you must not return to them.
20 And I will make you to this people a
fortified bronze wall;
And they will fight against you,
But they shall not prevail against you;
For I *am* with you to save you
And deliver you," says the LORD.
21 "I will deliver you from the hand of the
wicked,
And I will redeem you from the grip of
the terrible."

Jeremiah's Lifestyle and Message

16 The word of the LORD also came to me,
saying,
2 "You shall not take a wife, nor shall you
have sons or daughters in this place."
3 For thus says the LORD concerning the sons
and daughters who are born in this place, and
concerning their mothers who bore them and
their fathers who begot them in this land:
4 "They shall die gruesome deaths; they
shall not be lamented nor shall they be buried, *but* they shall be like refuse on the face of
the earth. They shall be consumed by the
sword and by famine, and their corpses shall
be meat for the birds of heaven and for the
beasts of the earth."
5 For thus says the LORD: "Do not enter the
house of mourning, nor go to lament or bemoan them; for I have taken away My peace
from this people," says the LORD, "lovingkindness and mercies.
6 "Both the great and the small shall die in
this land. They shall not be buried; neither
shall men lament for them, cut themselves,
nor make themselves bald for them.
7 "Nor shall *men* break *bread* in mourning
for them, to comfort them for the dead; nor
shall *men* give them the cup of consolation to
drink for their father or their mother.
8 "Also you shall not go into the house of
feasting to sit with them, to eat and drink."
9 For thus says the LORD of hosts, the God of
Israel: "Behold, I will cause to cease from this
place, before your eyes and in your days, the
voice of mirth and the voice of gladness,
the voice of the bridegroom and the voice of
the bride.
10 "And it shall be, when you show this people all these words, and they say to you, 'Why
has the LORD pronounced all this great disaster against us? Or what *is* our iniquity? Or
what *is* our sin that we have committed
against the LORD our God?'
11 "then you shall say to them, 'Because your
fathers have forsaken Me,' says the LORD;
'they have walked after other gods and have
served them and worshiped them, and have
forsaken Me and not kept My law.
12 "And you have done worse than your fathers, for behold, each one follows the dictates of his own evil heart, so that no one
listens to Me.
13 'Therefore I will cast you out of this land

15:14 [a]Following Masoretic Text and Vulgate; Septuagint, Syriac, and Targum read *cause you to serve* (compare 17:4).

LIFE LESSONS

➤ **15:16 — *Your words were found, and I ate them, and Your word was to me the joy and rejoicing of my heart; for I am called by Your name, O LORD God of hosts.***

God invites us to spend daily time with Him in His Word, not just because it provides us with spiritual bread (Matt. 4:4), but because as a reflection of Him, it gives us joy. Does it give *you* joy?

into a land that you do not know, neither you nor your fathers; and there you shall serve other gods day and night, where I will not show you favor.'

God Will Restore Israel

14 "Therefore behold, the days are coming," says the LORD, "that it shall no more be said, 'The LORD lives who brought up the children of Israel from the land of Egypt,'
15 "but, 'The LORD lives who brought up the children of Israel from the land of the north and from all the lands where He had driven them.' For I will bring them back into their land which I gave to their fathers.
➤ **16** "Behold, I will send for many fishermen," says the LORD, "and they shall fish them; and afterward I will send for many hunters, and they shall hunt them from every mountain and every hill, and out of the holes of the rocks.
17 "For My eyes *are* on all their ways; they are not hidden from My face, nor is their iniquity hidden from My eyes.
18 "And first I will repay double for their iniquity and their sin, because they have defiled My land; they have filled My inheritance with the carcasses of their detestable and abominable idols."

19 O LORD, my strength and my fortress,
My refuge in the day of affliction,
The Gentiles shall come to You
From the ends of the earth and say,
"Surely our fathers have inherited lies,
Worthlessness and unprofitable *things*."
20 Will a man make gods for himself,
Which *are* not gods?

21 "Therefore behold, I will this once cause them to know,
I will cause them to know
My hand and My might;
And they shall know that My name *is* the LORD.

Judah's Sin and Punishment

17 "The sin of Judah *is* written with a pen of iron;
With the point of a diamond *it is* engraved
On the tablet of their heart,
And on the horns of your altars,
2 While their children remember
Their altars and their wooden images[a]
By the green trees on the high hills.
3 O My mountain in the field,
I will give as plunder your wealth, all your treasures,
And your high places of sin within all your borders.
4 And you, even yourself,
Shall let go of your heritage which I gave you;
And I will cause you to serve your enemies
In the land which you do not know;
For you have kindled a fire in My anger *which* shall burn forever."

5 Thus says the LORD:

"Cursed *is* the man who trusts in man
And makes flesh his strength,
Whose heart departs from the LORD.
6 For he shall be like a shrub in the desert,
And shall not see when good comes,
But shall inhabit the parched places in the wilderness,
In a salt land *which is* not inhabited.

7 "Blessed *is* the man who trusts in the LORD,
And whose hope is the LORD.
8 For he shall be like a tree planted by the waters,
Which spreads out its roots by the river,
And will not fear[a] when heat comes;
But its leaf will be green,
And will not be anxious in the year of drought,
Nor will cease from yielding fruit.

9 "The heart *is* deceitful above all *things*,
And desperately wicked;
Who can know it?
10 I, the LORD, search the heart,
I test the mind,

17:2 [a]Hebrew *Asherim*, Canaanite deities **17:8** [a]Qere and Targum read *see*.

LIFE LESSONS

➤ **16:16 — *"Behold, I will send for many fishermen," says the LORD, "and they shall fish them; and afterward I will send for many hunters, and they shall hunt them from every mountain and every hill, and out of the holes of the rocks."***

God will spare no effort to bless us, just as He promised. If we feel forgotten at the bottom of the sea or marooned on the far side of the moon, even from there He will retrieve us to bless us.

➤ **17:5 — *"Cursed is the man who trusts in man and makes flesh his strength, whose heart departs from the LORD."***

God made us for a dynamic and deep relationship with Himself, and trying to replace Him with *anything* else will always result in a curse. We are to find our strength in Him, not in ourselves.

➤ **17:9 — *"The heart is deceitful above all things, and desperately wicked; who can know it?"***

Only God knows the human heart. We cannot understand the twists and turns and deceptions and dead ends of our own hearts; so when our hearts condemn us, we turn to the Maker of our hearts (1 John 3:20).

LIFE PRINCIPLE 15

BROKENNESS IS GOD'S REQUIREMENT FOR MAXIMUM USEFULNESS.

JER. 15:19

Someone once said, "A soul is converted in a moment of time, but to become a saint takes a lifetime." Conversion happens instantly; maturity takes many years. To bring us to maturity, God has to break us over and over again.

So often I see Christians struggling to get to what they perceive as the top. They gather and accumulate and arrange and amass—all the while forging their long list of accomplishments, perhaps with the hope that they will one day be able to hand their resume to God and say, "See what I've done for You?"

God's work through brokenness calls us not to accumulate, but to discard. He calls us to get rid of this, toss that, purge ourselves of this trait and that habit, repent of that desire and that goal, and finally strip ourselves of all self until we can truly say, "All that I am and all that I have is God's. He is in me and I am in Him, and that's all that matters."

What is God stripping away from your life? What comes to mind when you think of being broken? What have you put between you and total surrender to God? What do you trust more than you trust God? What do you love more than you love God?

God will break you, change you, and cause you to grow until you reach spiritual maturity. No matter how long it takes or how difficult the process may be, God will continue to break you and bring you to a place of wholeness and spiritual maturity so that he might use you as his tool in bringing still others to wholeness and spiritual maturity.

We can't reach spiritual maturity without suffering and pain, and we can't engage in ministry without being willing to endure even more suffering and pain. The joy set before us, however, is the joy of knowing that God is with us, working in us and through us, and that God is pleased with us.

Friend, there's no greater joy than that.

Maybe you are facing a time of brokenness and it feels as though the emotional pain is more than you can bear. Or perhaps you are dealing with a series of disappointments. Instead of becoming fearful—a frequent ploy of Satan to pull you away from God—ask the Lord to reveal what He is up to in your life.

God did not remove the "thorn" from the apostle Paul's life, yet He did help him to understand why He allowed the trial to persist. The Holy Spirit revealed an element of pride in Paul's life; the "thorn" was given to humble him and cause him to rely only on Christ (see 2 Cor. 12:1–11).

What is God stripping away from your life?

In visiting God's altar of brokenness, you will find a spiritual depth not present before the trial began. Peter writes: "Beloved, do not think it strange concerning the fiery trial which is to try you, as though some strange thing happened to you; but rejoice to the extent that you partake of Christ's sufferings, that when His glory is revealed, you may also be glad with exceeding joy" (1 Pet. 4:12, 13).

Charles Spurgeon wrote: "God knows that soldiers are only to be made in battle; they are not to be grown in peaceful times . . . . Warriors are really educated by the smell of powder, in the midst of whizzing bullets and roaring cannonades . . . . Is He not developing in you the qualities of the soldier by throwing you into the heat of battle, and should you not use every application to come off conqueror?"

Brokenness is a sign of God's love and activity in your life. He breaks your self-reliance because He loves you. He knows that, left on your own, you would yield to pride and selfishness. Any discipline you experience in times of brokenness is God's way of preparing you for future service.

Keep in mind that God uses brokenness to deepen your understanding in at least three ways:

- *You gain a new perspective of His mercy and provision*
- *You develop a more complete comprehension of yourself*
- *Your compassion and understanding for others' suffering grows*

The Lord has one thing in mind for brokenness: spiritual victory. You will soon discover that only Jesus Christ can take your weakness and turn it into strength, hope, and honor. Will you trust Him to change your life?

See the Life Principles Index for further study.

Brokenness is a sign of God's love and activity in your life.

Even to give every man according to his
ways,
According to the fruit of his doings.
11 "*As* a partridge that broods but does not
hatch,
So is he who gets riches, but not by
right;
It will leave him in the midst of his
days,
And at his end he will be a fool."

12 A glorious high throne from the
beginning
Is the place of our sanctuary.
13 O LORD, the hope of Israel,
All who forsake You shall be ashamed.

"Those who depart from Me
Shall be written in the earth,
Because they have forsaken the LORD,
The fountain of living waters."

Jeremiah Prays for Deliverance

14 Heal me, O LORD, and I shall be healed;
Save me, and I shall be saved,
For You *are* my praise.
15 Indeed they say to me,
"Where *is* the word of the LORD?
Let it come now!"
16 As for me, I have not hurried away from
being a shepherd *who* follows You,
Nor have I desired the woeful day;
You know what came out of my lips;
It was right there before You.
17 Do not be a terror to me;
You *are* my hope in the day of doom.
18 Let them be ashamed who
persecute me,
But do not let me be put to shame;
Let them be dismayed,
But do not let me be dismayed.
Bring on them the day of doom,
And destroy them with double
destruction!

Hallow the Sabbath Day

19 Thus the LORD said to me: "Go and stand
in the gate of the children of the people, by
which the kings of Judah come in and by
which they go out, and in all the gates of Jerusalem;
20 "and say to them, 'Hear the word of the
LORD, you kings of Judah, and all Judah, and
all the inhabitants of Jerusalem, who enter by
these gates.
21 'Thus says the LORD: "Take heed to yourselves, and bear no burden on the Sabbath
day, nor bring *it* in by the gates of Jerusalem;
22 "nor carry a burden out of your houses on
the Sabbath day, nor do any work, but hallow
the Sabbath day, as I commanded your fathers.
23 "But they did not obey nor incline their
ear, but made their neck stiff, that they might
not hear nor receive instruction.
24 "And it shall be, if you heed Me carefully,"
says the LORD, "to bring no burden through
the gates of this city on the Sabbath day, but
hallow the Sabbath day, to do no work in it,
25 "then shall enter the gates of this city
kings and princes sitting on the throne of David, riding in chariots and on horses, they and
their princes, accompanied by the men of Judah and the inhabitants of Jerusalem; and
this city shall remain forever.
26 "And they shall come from the cities of Judah and from the places around Jerusalem,
from the land of Benjamin and from the lowland, from the mountains and from the South,
bringing burnt offerings and sacrifices, grain
offerings and incense, bringing sacrifices of
praise to the house of the LORD.
27 "But if you will not heed Me to hallow the
Sabbath day, such as not carrying a burden
when entering the gates of Jerusalem on the
Sabbath day, then I will kindle a fire in its
gates, and it shall devour the palaces of Jerusalem, and it shall not be quenched." ' "

The Potter and the Clay

18 The word which came to Jeremiah
from the LORD, saying:
2 "Arise and go down to the potter's house,
and there I will cause you to hear My words."
3 Then I went down to the potter's house,
and there he was, making something at the
wheel.
4 And the vessel that he made of clay was
marred in the hand of the potter; so he made
it again into another vessel, as it seemed good
to the potter to make.
5 Then the word of the LORD came to me,
saying:
6 "O house of Israel, can I not do with you as ➤
this potter?" says the LORD. "Look, as the clay
is in the potter's hand, so *are* you in My hand,
O house of Israel!
7 "The instant I speak concerning a nation
and concerning a kingdom, to pluck up, to
pull down, and to destroy *it*,

LIFE LESSONS

➤ **18:6 — *"Look, as the clay is in the potter's hand, so are you in My hand, house of Israel!"***

God wants to mold us and shape us into something of indescribable beauty. The process is not quick, nor does it always feel pleasant, but we can trust the hand of the Potter to finish what He has started.

WHAT THE BIBLE SAYS ABOUT THE PROCESS OF SPIRITUAL GROWTH

Jer. 18:1–6

Young Christians often complain that the Christian growth process feels slow and tedious. They become discouraged and stop growing because they want instant knowledge and maturity without going through the time and effort it takes to mature in their faith.

Seasoned Christians have some of the same difficulties, only in a different way. They perceive themselves as having all the knowledge necessary to live the Christian life, so they stop growing and risk becoming hardened to the intimate love of God.

The Lord has a solution for both of these spiritual problems. It is called being molded into the likeness of Christ, and it's much more than a one or two year process. Through it we grow abundantly as children of God and fall so much in love with Christ that there's no time for boredom or pride. As we allow the Lord to shape and mold us, we "shall also bear the image of the heavenly Man," that is, Jesus Christ (1 Cor. 15:49).

The Potter longs to mold and shape your life.

Being molded and shaped into Christ's image, however, can take many twists and turns we don't expect. It can take longer than we thought and involve events we never imagined. We might not be able to discern the shape of the vase or pot or pitcher the Lord wants to make out of us, and so we may resist His work, to our own detriment. Yet the Lord says to us, "Look, as the clay is in the potter's hand, so are you in My hand" (Jer. 18:6).

As Elizabeth Elliot said, holiness is God's loving purpose for us, and it is the equivalent of joy in God's kingdom. Holiness is a priority with God. When we seek to be like Christ, we seek holiness. But in order to become holy, we must submit ourselves to the shaping and molding of God's loving hands.

Clay cries out to be molded into something beautiful. The Potter longs to mold and shape your life. Allow Him to take whatever time He needs to create in you a joy and devotion of immeasurable worth.

See the Life Principles Index for further study:

7. *The dark moments of our life will last only so long as is necessary for God to accomplish His purpose in us.*
14. *God acts on behalf of those who wait for Him.*

➤ 8 "if that nation against whom I have spoken turns from its evil, I will relent of the disaster that I thought to bring upon it.
9 "And the instant I speak concerning a nation and concerning a kingdom, to build and
to plant *it*,
10 "if it does evil in My sight so that it does not
obey My voice, then I will relent concerning
the good with which I said I would benefit it.
11 "Now therefore, speak to the men of Judah and to the inhabitants of Jerusalem, saying, 'Thus says the LORD: "Behold, I am
fashioning a disaster and devising a plan
against you. Return now every one from his
evil way, and make your ways and your doings good."'"

God's Warning Rejected

12 And they said, "That is hopeless! So we
will walk according to our own plans, and we
will every one obey the dictates of his evil
heart."
13 Therefore thus says the LORD:

"Ask now among the Gentiles,
Who has heard such things?
The virgin of Israel has done a very
horrible thing.
14 Will *a man* leave the snow water of
Lebanon,
Which comes from the rock of the field?
Will the cold flowing waters be forsaken
for strange waters?

15 "Because My people have forgotten Me,
They have burned incense to worthless
idols.
And they have caused themselves to
stumble in their ways,
From the ancient paths,
To walk in pathways and not on a
highway,
16 To make their land desolate *and* a
perpetual hissing;
Everyone who passes by it will be
astonished
And shake his head.
17 I will scatter them as with an east wind
before the enemy;
I will show them[a] the back and not the
face
In the day of their calamity."

Jeremiah Persecuted

18 Then they said, "Come and let us devise
plans against Jeremiah; for the law shall not
perish from the priest, nor counsel from the
wise, nor the word from the prophet. Come
and let us attack him with the tongue, and let
us not give heed to any of his words."

19 Give heed to me, O LORD,
And listen to the voice of those who
contend with me!
20 Shall evil be repaid for good?
For they have dug a pit for my life.
Remember that I stood before You
To speak good for them,
To turn away Your wrath from them.
21 Therefore deliver up their children to the
famine,
And pour out their *blood*
By the force of the sword;
Let their wives *become* widows
And bereaved of their children.
Let their men be put to death,
Their young men *be* slain
By the sword in battle.
22 Let a cry be heard from their houses,
When You bring a troop suddenly upon
them;
For they have dug a pit to take me,
And hidden snares for my feet.
23 Yet, LORD, You know all their counsel
Which is against me, to slay *me*.
Provide no atonement for their iniquity,
Nor blot out their sin from Your sight;
But let them be overthrown before You.
Deal *thus* with them
In the time of Your anger.

The Sign of the Broken Flask

19 Thus says the LORD: "Go and get a potter's earthen flask, and *take* some of
the elders of the people and some of the elders of the priests.
2 "And go out to the Valley of the Son of Hinnom, which *is* by the entry of the Potsherd
Gate; and proclaim there the words that I will
tell you,
3 "and say, 'Hear the word of the LORD, O
kings of Judah and inhabitants of Jerusalem.
Thus says the LORD of hosts, the God of Israel:
"Behold, I will bring such a catastrophe on
this place, that whoever hears of it, his ears
will tingle.
4 "Because they have forsaken Me and
made this an alien place, because they have
burned incense in it to other gods whom neither they, their fathers, nor the kings of Judah

18:17 [a]Following Septuagint, Syriac, Targum, and Vulgate; Masoretic Text reads *look them in*.

LIFE LESSONS

➤ **18:8 — *". . . if that nation against whom I have spoken turns from its evil, I will relent of the disaster that I thought to bring upon it."***

In the days of Jonah the prophet, God spared the wicked city of Nineveh, even though He had sent Jonah there to proclaim, "Yet forty days, and Nineveh shall be overthrown!" (Jon. 3:4). God loves mercy above judgment.

have known, and have filled this place with
the blood of the innocents
5 "(they have also built the high places of
Baal, to burn their sons with fire *for* burnt offerings to Baal, which I did not command or
speak, nor did it come into My mind),
6 "therefore behold, the days are coming,"
says the LORD, "that this place shall no more
be called Tophet or the Valley of the Son of
Hinnom, but the Valley of Slaughter.
7 "And I will make void the counsel of Judah
and Jerusalem in this place, and I will cause
them to fall by the sword before their enemies
and by the hands of those who seek their
lives; their corpses I will give as meat for the
birds of the heaven and for the beasts of the
earth.
8 "I will make this city desolate and a hissing; everyone who passes by it will be astonished and hiss because of all its plagues.
9 "And I will cause them to eat the flesh of
their sons and the flesh of their daughters,
and everyone shall eat the flesh of his friend
in the siege and in the desperation with which
their enemies and those who seek their lives
shall drive them to despair."'
10 "Then you shall break the flask in the
sight of the men who go with you,
11 "and say to them, 'Thus says the LORD of
hosts: "Even so I will break this people and
this city, as *one* breaks a potter's vessel,
which cannot be made whole again; and they
shall bury *them* in Tophet till *there is* no place
to bury.
12 "Thus I will do to this place," says the
LORD, "and to its inhabitants, and make this
city like Tophet.
13 "And the houses of Jerusalem and the
houses of the kings of Judah shall be defiled
like the place of Tophet, because of all the
houses on whose roofs they have burned incense to all the host of heaven, and poured
out drink offerings to other gods."'"
14 Then Jeremiah came from Tophet, where
the LORD had sent him to prophesy; and he
stood in the court of the Lord's house and
said to all the people,
15 "Thus says the LORD of hosts, the God of
Israel: 'Behold, I will bring on this city and on
all her towns all the doom that I have pronounced against it, because they have stiffened their necks that they might not hear My
words.'"

The Word of God to Pashhur

20 Now Pashhur the son of Immer, the
priest who *was* also chief governor in
the house of the LORD, heard that Jeremiah
prophesied these things.
2 Then Pashhur struck Jeremiah the ➤
prophet, and put him in the stocks that *were*
in the high gate of Benjamin, which *was* by
the house of the LORD.
3 And it happened on the next day that
Pashhur brought Jeremiah out of the stocks.
Then Jeremiah said to him, "The LORD has not
called your name Pashhur, but Magor-Missabib.[a]
4 "For thus says the LORD: 'Behold, I will
make you a terror to yourself and to all your
friends; and they shall fall by the sword of
their enemies, and your eyes shall see *it*. I will
give all Judah into the hand of the king of
Babylon, and he shall carry them captive to
Babylon and slay them with the sword.
5 'Moreover I will deliver all the wealth of
this city, all its produce, and all its precious
things; all the treasures of the kings of Judah
I will give into the hand of their enemies, who
will plunder them, seize them, and carry them
to Babylon.
6 'And you, Pashhur, and all who dwell in
your house, shall go into captivity. You shall
go to Babylon, and there you shall die, and be
buried there, you and all your friends, to
whom you have prophesied lies.'"

Jeremiah's Unpopular Ministry

7 O LORD, You induced me, and I was
persuaded;
You are stronger than I, and have
prevailed.
I am in derision daily;
Everyone mocks me.
8 For when I spoke, I cried out;
I shouted, "Violence and plunder!"
Because the word of the LORD was made
to me
A reproach and a derision daily.
9 Then I said, "I will not make mention of ➤
Him,
Nor speak anymore in His name."
But *His word* was in my heart like a
burning fire

20:3 [a]Literally *Fear on Every Side*

LIFE LESSONS

➤ **20:2 — *Then Pashhur struck Jeremiah the prophet, and put him in the stocks that were in the high gate of Benjamin, which was by the house of the LORD.***

Jeremiah suffered greatly for faithfully proclaiming the word that God told him to speak. To an observer, it might not have looked as though God always rewards obedience. But a snapshot does not equal the whole movie.

➤ **20:9 — *". . . His word was in my heart like a burning fire shut up in my bones; I was weary of holding it back, and I could not."***

If your goals are truly from the Lord, you will have a feeling deep within that you *must* accomplish them in order to obey the Lord and to bring benefit to others. You won't be able to do otherwise.

Shut up in my bones;
I was weary of holding *it* back,
And I could not.
10 For I heard many mocking:
"Fear on every side!"
"Report," *they say,* "and we will report it!"
All my acquaintances watched for my stumbling, *saying,*
"Perhaps he can be induced;
Then we will prevail against him,
And we will take our revenge on him."

*11 But the LORD *is* with me as a mighty, awesome One.
Therefore my persecutors will stumble, and will not prevail.
They will be greatly ashamed, for they will not prosper.
Their everlasting confusion will never be forgotten.
12 But, O LORD of hosts,
You who test the righteous,
And see the mind and heart,
Let me see Your vengeance on them;
For I have pleaded my cause before You.

13 Sing to the LORD! Praise the LORD!
For He has delivered the life of the poor
From the hand of evildoers.

14 Cursed *be* the day in which I was born!
Let the day not be blessed in which my mother bore me!
15 Let the man *be* cursed
Who brought news to my father, saying,
"A male child has been born to you!"
Making him very glad.
16 And let that man be like the cities
Which the LORD overthrew, and did not relent;
Let him hear the cry in the morning
And the shouting at noon,
17 Because he did not kill me from the womb,
That my mother might have been my grave,
And her womb always enlarged *with me.*
18 Why did I come forth from the womb to see labor and sorrow,
That my days should be consumed with shame?

Jerusalem's Doom Is Sealed

21 The word which came to Jeremiah
from the LORD when King Zedekiah
sent to him Pashhur the son of Melchiah, and
Zephaniah the son of Maaseiah, the priest,
saying,
2 "Please inquire of the LORD for us, for
Nebuchadnezzar[a] king of Babylon makes war
against us. Perhaps the LORD will deal with us
according to all His wonderful works, that *the*
king may go away from us."
3 Then Jeremiah said to them, "Thus you
shall say to Zedekiah,
4 'Thus says the LORD God of Israel: "Behold, I will turn back the weapons of war that
are in your hands, with which you fight
against the king of Babylon and the
Chaldeans[a] who besiege you outside the
walls; and I will assemble them in the midst
of this city.
5 "I Myself will fight against you with an
outstretched hand and with a strong arm,
even in anger and fury and great wrath.
6 "I will strike the inhabitants of this city,
both man and beast; they shall die of a great
pestilence.
7 "And afterward," says the LORD, "I will deliver Zedekiah king of Judah, his servants
and the people, and such as are left in this city
from the pestilence and the sword and the
famine, into the hand of Nebuchadnezzar
king of Babylon, into the hand of their enemies, and into the hand of those who seek
their life; and he shall strike them with the
edge of the sword. He shall not spare them, or
have pity or mercy."'
8 "Now you shall say to this people, 'Thus
says the LORD: "Behold, I set before you the
way of life and the way of death.
9 "He who remains in this city shall die by
the sword, by famine, and by pestilence; but
he who goes out and defects to the Chaldeans
who besiege you, he shall live, and his life
shall be as a prize to him.
10 "For I have set My face against this city for
adversity and not for good," says the LORD. "It
shall be given into the hand of the king of
Babylon, and he shall burn it with fire."'

Message to the House of David

11 "And concerning the house of the king of
Judah, *say,* 'Hear the word of the LORD,
12 'O house of David! Thus says the LORD:

"Execute judgment in the morning;
And deliver *him who is* plundered
Out of the hand of the oppressor,
Lest My fury go forth like fire
And burn so that no one can quench *it,*
Because of the evil of your doings.

13 "Behold, I *am* against you, O inhabitant of the valley,
And rock of the plain," says the LORD,
"Who say, 'Who shall come down against us?
Or who shall enter our dwellings?'
14 But I will punish you according to the fruit of your doings," says the LORD;
"I will kindle a fire in its forest,
And it shall devour all things around it."'"

22 Thus says the LORD: "Go down to the
house of the king of Judah, and there
speak this word,

21:2 [a]Hebrew *Nebuchadrezzar,* and so elsewhere **21:4** [a]Or *Babylonians*

2 "and say, 'Hear the word of the LORD, O king of Judah, you who sit on the throne of David, you and your servants and your people who enter these gates!
3 'Thus says the LORD: "Execute judgment and righteousness, and deliver the plundered out of the hand of the oppressor. Do no wrong and do no violence to the stranger, the fatherless, or the widow, nor shed innocent blood in this place.
4 "For if you indeed do this thing, then shall enter the gates of this house, riding on horses and in chariots, accompanied by servants and people, kings who sit on the throne of David.
5 "But if you will not hear these words, I swear by Myself," says the LORD, "that this house shall become a desolation."'"
6 For thus says the LORD to the house of the king of Judah:

"You *are* Gilead to Me,
The head of Lebanon;
Yet I surely will make you a wilderness,
Cities *which* are not inhabited.
7 I will prepare destroyers against you,
Everyone with his weapons;
They shall cut down your choice cedars
And cast *them* into the fire.

8 "And many nations will pass by this city; and everyone will say to his neighbor, 'Why has the LORD done so to this great city?'
9 "Then they will answer, 'Because they have forsaken the covenant of the LORD their God, and worshiped other gods and served them.'"

10 Weep not for the dead, nor bemoan him;
Weep bitterly for him who goes away,
For he shall return no more,
Nor see his native country.

Message to the Sons of Josiah

11 For thus says the LORD concerning Shallum[a] the son of Josiah, king of Judah, who reigned instead of Josiah his father, who went from this place: "He shall not return here anymore,
12 "but he shall die in the place where they have led him captive, and shall see this land no more.

13 "Woe to him who builds his house by unrighteousness
And his chambers by injustice,
Who uses his neighbor's service without wages
And gives him nothing for his work,
14 Who says, 'I will build myself a wide house with spacious chambers,
And cut out windows for it,
Paneling *it* with cedar
And painting *it* with vermilion.'

15 "Shall you reign because you enclose *yourself* in cedar?
Did not your father eat and drink,
And do justice and righteousness?
Then *it was* well with him.
16 He judged the cause of the poor and needy;
Then *it was* well.
Was not this knowing Me?" says the LORD.
17 "Yet your eyes and your heart *are* for nothing but your covetousness,
For shedding innocent blood,
And practicing oppression and violence."

18 Therefore thus says the LORD concerning Jehoiakim the son of Josiah, king of Judah:

"They shall not lament for him,
Saying, 'Alas, my brother!' or 'Alas, my sister!'
They shall not lament for him,
Saying, 'Alas, master!' or 'Alas, his glory!'
19 He shall be buried with the burial of a donkey,
Dragged and cast out beyond the gates of Jerusalem.

20 "Go up to Lebanon, and cry out,
And lift up your voice in Bashan;
Cry from Abarim,
For all your lovers are destroyed.
21 I spoke to you in your prosperity,
But you said, 'I will not hear.'
This *has been* your manner from your youth,
That you did not obey My voice.
22 The wind shall eat up all your rulers,
And your lovers shall go into captivity;
Surely then you will be ashamed and humiliated
For all your wickedness.
23 O inhabitant of Lebanon,
Making your nest in the cedars,

22:11 [a]Also called *Jehoahaz*

LIFE LESSONS

➢ 22:16 — *"He judged the cause of the poor and needy; then it was well. Was not this knowing Me?" says the LORD.*

To know God is not merely to have a peaceful feeling in the heart; to know God is to act for the benefit of others, especially for those who cannot pay you back. Those who know God love to serve Him.

➢ 22:21 — *"I spoke to you in your prosperity, but you said, 'I will not hear.' This has been your manner from your youth, that you did not obey My voice."*

God speaks to us in both our prosperity and our hardship; our job in both cases is to listen carefully for His voice, and to hear and obey what He says. What has God been saying to you lately?

ANSWERS TO LIFE'S QUESTIONS

Why do I sometimes fail to hear God when He speaks?

JER. 22:21

Jeremiah repeatedly reminded his people that while God had been speaking to them, they did not hear. "I spoke to you in your prosperity," the Lord declared through the prophet, "but you said, 'I will not hear.' This has been your manner from your youth, that you did not obey My voice" (Jer. 22:21).

We often have the same problem; the Lord may be speaking to us, but we don't hear Him. Why do so many of us fail to hear what God is saying?

One significant obstacle is that we often consider the act of listening to be a passive experience—we assume we can simply sit and absorb what is being said. Good listening, however, is an active endeavor, involving both attitude and action.

We will have difficulty listening if we come to God with uncertainty, doubting that He is going to speak. Instead, we are to approach God confidently and expectantly, anticipating that He will communicate with us. Such an attitude expresses our faith and demonstrates that we believe His promises.

The Bible instructs us, "Be still, and know that I am God" (Ps. 46:10). To hear God we must come quietly to Him and allow Him to do the talking. While there is nothing wrong with keeping a prayer list, a devotional time ought to include more than just a litany of requests. We should take time to hear what God says to us.

We must approach the Lord with an attitude of patience (Ps. 40:1). While none of us enjoys waiting, God will not tell us everything at once. Sometimes He withholds information until we are prepared to listen.

We must also listen actively. Colossians 3:16 says, "Let the word of Christ dwell in you richly in all wisdom." In other words, the truth of God's Word is to deeply and abundantly overflow in us. That happens when we read and meditate on Scripture.

Remember also to listen humbly and submissively. We depend absolutely upon the Holy Spirit to reveal God's truth to us (John 14:26)! Apart from the work of the Spirit, we are helpless to hear from God—whether He speaks through Scripture, circumstances, prayer, or other people. Only the Spirit enables us to hear.

So when God speaks to you, listen attentively and prepare to submit to whatever He tells you. Obedience pleases Your heavenly Father and He desires to bless you for listening well.

See the Life Principles Index for further study:

11. God assumes full responsibility for our needs when we obey Him.

10. If necessary, God will move heaven and earth to show us His will.

How gracious will you be when pangs
come upon you,
Like the pain of a woman in labor?

Message to Coniah

24 "*As* I live," says the LORD, "though Coniah[a]
the son of Jehoiakim, king of Judah, were the
signet on My right hand, yet I would pluck
you off;
25 "and I will give you into the hand of those
who seek your life, and into the hand *of those*
whose face you fear—the hand of Nebuchadnezzar king of Babylon and the hand of the
Chaldeans.
26 "So I will cast you out, and your mother
who bore you, into another country where
you were not born; and there you shall die.
27 "But to the land to which they desire to return, there they shall not return.

28 "Is this man Coniah a despised, broken
idol—
A vessel in which *is* no pleasure?
Why are they cast out, he and his
descendants,
And cast into a land which they do not
know?
29 O earth, earth, earth,
Hear the word of the LORD!
30 Thus says the LORD:
'Write this man down as childless,
A man *who* shall not prosper in his
days;
For none of his descendants shall
prosper,
Sitting on the throne of David,
And ruling anymore in Judah.'"

22:24 [a]Also called *Jeconiah* and *Jehoiachin*

The Branch of Righteousness

23 "Woe to the shepherds who destroy and scatter the sheep of My pasture!" says the LORD.
2 Therefore thus says the LORD God of Israel against the shepherds who feed My people: "You have scattered My flock, driven them away, and not attended to them. Behold, I will attend to you for the evil of your doings," says the LORD.
➢ 3 "But I will gather the remnant of My flock out of all countries where I have driven them, and bring them back to their folds; and they shall be fruitful and increase.
4 "I will set up shepherds over them who will feed them; and they shall fear no more, nor be dismayed, nor shall they be lacking," says the LORD.

✳ 5 "Behold, *the* days are coming," says the LORD,
"That I will raise to David a Branch of righteousness;
A King shall reign and prosper,
And execute judgment and righteousness in the earth.
➢ 6 In His days Judah will be saved,
And Israel will dwell safely;
Now this *is* His name by which He will be called:

THE LORD OUR RIGHTEOUSNESS.[a]

7 "Therefore, behold, *the* days are coming," says the LORD, "that they shall no longer say, 'As the LORD lives who brought up the children of Israel from the land of Egypt,'
8 "but, 'As the LORD lives who brought up and led the descendants of the house of Israel from the north country and from all the countries where I had driven them.' And they shall dwell in their own land."

False Prophets and Empty Oracles

9 My heart within me is broken
Because of the prophets;
All my bones shake.
I am like a drunken man,
And like a man whom wine has overcome,
Because of the LORD,
And because of His holy words.
10 For the land is full of adulterers;
For because of a curse the land mourns.
The pleasant places of the wilderness are dried up.
Their course of life is evil,
And their might *is* not right.

11 "For both prophet and priest are profane;
Yes, in My house I have found their wickedness," says the LORD.
12 "Therefore[R] their way shall be to them
Like slippery *ways;*
In the darkness they shall be driven on
And fall in them;
For I will bring disaster on them,
The year of their punishment," says the LORD.
13 "And I have seen folly in the prophets of Samaria:
They prophesied by Baal
And caused My people Israel to err.
14 Also I have seen a horrible thing in the prophets of Jerusalem:
They commit adultery and walk in lies;
They also strengthen the hands of evildoers,
So that no one turns back from his wickedness.
All of them are like Sodom to Me,
And her inhabitants like Gomorrah.

15 "Therefore thus says the LORD of hosts concerning the prophets:

'Behold, I will feed them with wormwood,
And make them drink the water of gall;
For from the prophets of Jerusalem
Profaneness has gone out into all the land.'"

16 Thus says the LORD of hosts:

"Do not listen to the words of the prophets who prophesy to you.
They make you worthless;
They speak a vision of their own heart,
Not from the mouth of the LORD.
17 They continually say to those who despise Me, ➣
'The LORD has said, "You shall have peace"';

23:6 [a]Hebrew *YHWH Tsidkenu*

LIFE LESSONS

➢ **23:3 — *"But I will gather the remnant of My flock out of all countries where I have driven them, and bring them back to their folds; and they shall be fruitful and increase."***

God desires to bless His people and to make them fruitful and numerous. Just as He promises to one day gather Israel and bless her (Rom. 11), so He longs to bless you when you obey Him.

➢ **23:6 — *In His days Judah will be saved, and Israel will dwell safely; now this is His name by which He will be called: THE LORD OUR RIGHTEOUSNESS.***

When we come to Jesus Christ in faith, *He* becomes our righteousness. We stand before God, not on the basis of our efforts or record, but because of what He has done for us on the cross.

➢ **23:17 — *"They continually say to those who despise Me, 'The LORD has said, "You shall have peace"'; and to everyone who walks according to the dictates of his own heart, they say, 'No evil shall come upon you.'"***

If God calls a thing sin, and declares that He will judge it, don't listen to anyone who says He will bless it. Grace never turns sin into something lovely; rather, grace gives us the power to turn from sin.

And *to* everyone who walks according to
the dictates of his own heart, they
say,
'No evil shall come upon you.'"

18 For who has stood in the counsel of the
LORD,
And has perceived and heard His word?
Who has marked His word and heard *it?*
19 Behold, a whirlwind of the LORD has
gone forth in fury—
A violent whirlwind!
It will fall violently on the head of the
wicked.
20 The anger of the LORD will not turn back
Until He has executed and performed the
thoughts of His heart.
In the latter days you will understand it
perfectly.

21"I have not sent these prophets, yet they
ran.
I have not spoken to them, yet they
prophesied.
22 But if they had stood in My counsel,
And had caused My people to hear My
words,
Then they would have turned them from
their evil way
And from the evil of their doings.

23"*Am* I a God near at hand," says the LORD,
"And not a God afar off?
24 Can anyone hide himself in secret places,
So I shall not see him?" says the LORD;
"Do I not fill heaven and earth?" says the
LORD.

25 "I have heard what the prophets have said
who prophesy lies in My name, saying, 'I have
dreamed, I have dreamed!'
26 "How long will *this* be in the heart of the
prophets who prophesy lies? Indeed *they are*
prophets of the deceit of their own heart,
27 "who try to make My people forget My
name by their dreams which everyone tells
his neighbor, as their fathers forgot My name
for Baal.

28"The prophet who has a dream, let him
tell a dream;
And he who has My word, let him speak
My word faithfully.
What *is* the chaff to the wheat?" says the
LORD.
29"*Is* not My word like a fire?" says the
LORD,
"And like a hammer *that* breaks the rock
in pieces?

30 "Therefore behold, I *am* against the
prophets," says the LORD, "who steal My
words every one from his neighbor.
31 "Behold, I *am* against the prophets," says
the LORD, "who use their tongues and say, 'He
says.'
32 "Behold, I *am* against those who prophesy
false dreams," says the LORD, "and tell them,
and cause My people to err by their lies and
by their recklessness. Yet I did not send them
or command them; therefore they shall not
profit this people at all," says the LORD.
33 "So when these people or the prophet or
the priest ask you, saying, 'What is the oracle
of the LORD?' you shall then say to them,
'What oracle?'[a] I will even forsake you," says
the LORD.
34 "And *as for* the prophet and the priest and
the people who say, 'The oracle of the LORD!'
I will even punish that man and his house.
35 "Thus every one of you shall say to his
neighbor, and every one to his brother, 'What
has the LORD answered?' and, 'What has the
LORD spoken?'
36 "And the oracle of the LORD you shall
mention no more. For every man's word will
be his oracle, for you have perverted the
words of the living God, the LORD of hosts,
our God.
37 "Thus you shall say to the prophet, 'What
has the LORD answered you?' and, 'What has
the LORD spoken?'
38 "But since you say, 'The oracle of the
LORD!' therefore thus says the LORD: 'Because
you say this word, "The oracle of the LORD!"
and I have sent to you, saying, "Do not say,
'The oracle of the LORD!'"
39 'therefore behold, I, even I, will utterly forget you and forsake you, and the city that I
gave you and your fathers, and *will cast you*
out of My presence.
40 'And I will bring an everlasting reproach
upon you, and a perpetual shame, which shall
not be forgotten.'"

23:33 [a]Septuagint, Targum, and Vulgate read *'You are the burden.'*

LIFE LESSONS

23:24 — "Can anyone hide himself in secret places, so I shall not see him?" says the LORD; "Do I not fill heaven and earth?"

God is never so busy with a new star in Orion or an erupting volcano on Venus that He has no time for you. He fills the universe, so He can listen to your prayers even as He cares for everything else.

23:29 — "Is not My word like a fire?" says the LORD, "and like a hammer that breaks the rock in pieces?"

The words of great human authors may inspire us, but the words of God last forever and always accomplish the work God gives them to do. They can burn through the toughest soul and smash through the hardest heart.

The Sign of Two Baskets of Figs

24 The LORD showed me, and there were
two baskets of figs set before the temple of the LORD, after Nebuchadnezzar king
of Babylon had carried away captive Jeconiah the son of Jehoiakim, king of Judah, and
the princes of Judah with the craftsmen and
smiths, from Jerusalem, and had brought
them to Babylon.
2 One basket *had* very good figs, like the
figs *that are* first ripe; and the other basket
had very bad figs which could not be eaten,
they were so bad.
3 Then the LORD said to me, "What do you
see, Jeremiah?" And I said, "Figs, the good
figs, very good; and the bad, very bad, which
cannot be eaten, they are so bad."
4 Again the word of the LORD came to me,
saying,
5 "Thus says the LORD, the God of Israel:
'Like these good figs, so will I acknowledge
those who are carried away captive from Judah, whom I have sent out of this place for
their own good, into the land of the
Chaldeans.
6 'For I will set My eyes on them for good,
and I will bring them back to this land; I will
build them and not pull *them* down, and I will
plant them and not pluck *them* up.
➤ 7 'Then I will give them a heart to know Me,
that I *am* the LORD; and they shall be My people, and I will be their God, for they shall return to Me with their whole heart.
8 'And as the bad figs which cannot be
eaten, they are so bad'—surely thus says the
LORD—'so will I give up Zedekiah the king of
Judah, his princes, the residue of Jerusalem
who remain in this land, and those who dwell
in the land of Egypt.
9 'I will deliver them to trouble into all the
kingdoms of the earth, for *their* harm, *to be* a
reproach and a byword, a taunt and a curse,
in all places where I shall drive them.
10 'And I will send the sword, the famine, and
the pestilence among them, till they are consumed from the land that I gave to them and
their fathers.'"

Seventy Years of Desolation

25 The word that came to Jeremiah concerning all the people of Judah, in the
fourth year of Jehoiakim the son of Josiah,
king of Judah (which *was* the first year of
Nebuchadnezzar king of Babylon),
2 which Jeremiah the prophet spoke to all
the people of Judah and to all the inhabitants
of Jerusalem, saying:
3 "From the thirteenth year of Josiah the
son of Amon, king of Judah, even to this day,
this *is* the twenty-third year in which the
word of the LORD has come to me; and I have
spoken to you, rising early and speaking, but
you have not listened.
4 "And the LORD has sent to you all His servants the prophets, rising early and sending
them, but you have not listened nor inclined
your ear to hear.
5 "They said, 'Repent now everyone of his
evil way and his evil doings, and dwell in the
land that the LORD has given to you and your
fathers forever and ever.
6 'Do not go after other gods to serve them
and worship them, and do not provoke Me to
anger with the works of your hands; and I
will not harm you.'
7 "Yet you have not listened to Me," says the
LORD, "that you might provoke Me to anger
with the works of your hands to your own hurt.
8 "Therefore thus says the LORD of hosts:
'Because you have not heard My words,
9 'behold, I will send and take all the families of the north,' says the LORD, 'and Nebuchadnezzar the king of Babylon, My
servant, and will bring them against this land,
against its inhabitants, and against these nations all around, and will utterly destroy
them, and make them an astonishment, a
hissing, and perpetual desolations.
10 'Moreover I will take from them the voice
of mirth and the voice of gladness, the voice
of the bridegroom and the voice of the bride,
the sound of the millstones and the light of
the lamp.
11 'And this whole land shall be a desolation
and an astonishment, and these nations shall ◄
serve the king of Babylon seventy years.
12 'Then it will come to pass, when seventy
years are completed, *that* I will punish the
king of Babylon and that nation, the land of
the Chaldeans, for their iniquity,' says the
LORD; 'and I will make it a perpetual desolation.
13 'So I will bring on that land all My words
which I have pronounced against it, all that is

LIFE LESSONS

➤ 24:7 — *"Then I will give them a heart to know Me, that I am the LORD; and they shall be My people, and I will be their God, for they shall return to Me with their whole heart."*

God wants our whole hearts. He wants an intimate relationship with us that affects every part of our lives—our work, our families, our friendships, our money, everything. He wants *us*, not what we have.

➤ 25:11 — *"And this whole land shall be a desolation and an astonishment, and these nations shall serve the king of Babylon seventy years."*

Before enemy troops ever set foot in Jerusalem, Jeremiah predicted that the Babylonian captivity would last seventy years. And that is exactly how long it lasted, no less, no more. You can always trust God's Word!

written in this book, which Jeremiah has
prophesied concerning all the nations.
14 '(For many nations and great kings shall
be served by them also; and I will repay them
according to their deeds and according to the
works of their own hands.)'"

Judgment on the Nations

15 For thus says the LORD God of Israel to me:
"Take this wine cup of fury from My hand,
and cause all the nations, to whom I send you,
to drink it.
16 "And they will drink and stagger and go
mad because of the sword that I will send
among them."
17 Then I took the cup from the LORD's hand,
and made all the nations drink, to whom the
LORD had sent me:
18 Jerusalem and the cities of Judah, its
kings and its princes, to make them a desolation, an astonishment, a hissing, and a curse,
as *it is* this day;
19 Pharaoh king of Egypt, his servants, his
princes, and all his people;
20 all the mixed multitude, all the kings of
the land of Uz, all the kings of the land of the
Philistines (namely, Ashkelon, Gaza, Ekron,
and the remnant of Ashdod);
21 Edom, Moab, and the people of Ammon;
22 all the kings of Tyre, all the kings of Sidon,
and the kings of the coastlands which *are*
across the sea;
23 Dedan, Tema, Buz, and all *who are* in the
farthest corners;
24 all the kings of Arabia and all the kings of
the mixed multitude who dwell in the desert;
25 all the kings of Zimri, all the kings of
Elam, and all the kings of the Medes;
26 all the kings of the north, far and near, one
with another; and all the kingdoms of the
world which *are* on the face of the earth. Also
the king of Sheshach[a] shall drink after them.
27 "Therefore you shall say to them, 'Thus
says the LORD of hosts, the God of Israel:
"Drink, be drunk, and vomit! Fall and rise no
more, because of the sword which I will send
among you."'
28 "And it shall be, if they refuse to take the
cup from your hand to drink, then you shall
say to them, 'Thus says the LORD of hosts:
"You shall certainly drink!
29 "For behold, I begin to bring calamity on
the city which is called by My name, and
should you be utterly unpunished? You shall
not be unpunished, for I will call for a sword
on all the inhabitants of the earth," says the
LORD of hosts.'

30 "Therefore prophesy against them all
these words, and say to them:

'The LORD will roar from on high,
And utter His voice from His holy
habitation;
He will roar mightily against His fold.
He will give a shout, as those who tread
the grapes,
Against all the inhabitants of the earth.
31 A noise will come to the ends of the
earth—
For the LORD has a controversy with the
nations;
He will plead His case with all flesh.
He will give those *who are* wicked to the
sword,' says the LORD."

32 Thus says the LORD of hosts:

"Behold, disaster shall go forth
From nation to nation,
And a great whirlwind shall be raised up
From the farthest parts of the earth.

33 "And at that day the slain of the LORD shall
be from *one* end of the earth even to the *other*
end of the earth. They shall not be lamented,
or gathered, or buried; they shall become refuse on the ground.

34 "Wail, shepherds, and cry!
Roll about *in the ashes,*
You leaders of the flock!
For the days of your slaughter and your
dispersions are fulfilled;
You shall fall like a precious vessel.
35 And the shepherds will have no way to
flee,
Nor the leaders of the flock to escape.
36 A voice of the cry of the shepherds,
And a wailing of the leaders to the flock
will be heard.
For the LORD has plundered their pasture,
37 And the peaceful dwellings are cut down
Because of the fierce anger of the LORD.
38 He has left His lair like the lion;
For their land is desolate
Because of the fierceness of the Oppressor,
And because of His fierce anger."

Jeremiah Saved from Death

26 In the beginning of the reign of Jehoiakim the son of Josiah, king of Judah, this word came from the LORD, saying,
2 "Thus says the LORD: 'Stand in the court of
the LORD's house, and speak to all the cities of

25:26 [a]A code word for Babylon (compare 51:41)

LIFE LESSONS

➤ **26:2 — *"Thus says the LORD: 'Stand in the court of the LORD's house, and speak . . . all the words that I command you to speak to them. Do not diminish a word.'"***

Jeremiah knew that partial obedience is blatant rebellion. He may have feared to speak *every* word that God told him to proclaim, but he did it. Only through the Spirit can we obey like this.

Judah, which come to worship *in* the LORD's
house, all the words that I command you to
speak to them. Do not diminish a word.
3 'Perhaps everyone will listen and turn
from his evil way, that I may relent concerning the calamity which I purpose to bring on
them because of the evil of their doings.'
4 "And you shall say to them, 'Thus says the
LORD: "If you will not listen to Me, to walk in
My law which I have set before you,
5 "to heed the words of My servants the
prophets whom I sent to you, both rising up
early and sending *them* (but you have not
heeded),
6 "then I will make this house like Shiloh,
and will make this city a curse to all the nations of the earth." ' "
7 So the priests and the prophets and all the
people heard Jeremiah speaking these words
in the house of the LORD.
8 Now it happened, when Jeremiah had
made an end of speaking all that the LORD
had commanded *him* to speak to all the people, that the priests and the prophets and all
the people seized him, saying, "You will
surely die!
9 "Why have you prophesied in the name of
the LORD, saying, 'This house shall be like
Shiloh, and this city shall be desolate, without
an inhabitant'?" And all the people were gathered against Jeremiah in the house of the LORD.
10 When the princes of Judah heard these
things, they came up from the king's house to
the house of the LORD and sat down in the
entry of the New Gate of the LORD's *house.*
11 And the priests and the prophets spoke to
the princes and all the people, saying, "This
man deserves to die! For he has prophesied
against this city, as you have heard with your
ears."
12 Then Jeremiah spoke to all the princes
and all the people, saying: "The LORD sent me
to prophesy against this house and against
this city with all the words that you have
heard.
➤ 13 "Now therefore, amend your ways and
your doings, and obey the voice of the LORD
your God; then the LORD will relent concerning the doom that He has pronounced against
you.
14 "As for me, here I am, in your hand; do
with me as seems good and proper to you.
15 "But know for certain that if you put me to
death, you will surely bring innocent blood on
yourselves, on this city, and on its inhabitants;
for truly the LORD has sent me to you to speak
all these words in your hearing."
16 So the princes and all the people said to
the priests and the prophets, "This man does
not deserve to die. For he has spoken to us in
the name of the LORD our God."
17 Then certain of the elders of the land rose
up and spoke to all the assembly of the people, saying:
18 "Micah of Moresheth prophesied in the
days of Hezekiah king of Judah, and spoke to
all the people of Judah, saying, 'Thus says the
LORD of hosts:

"Zion shall be plowed *like* a field,
Jerusalem shall become heaps of ruins,
And the mountain of the temple[a]
Like the bare hills of the forest." '[b]

19 "Did Hezekiah king of Judah and all Judah ever put him to death? Did he not fear the
LORD and seek the LORD's favor? And the
LORD relented concerning the doom which
He had pronounced against them. But we are
doing great evil against ourselves."
20 Now there was also a man who prophesied in the name of the LORD, Urijah the son
of Shemaiah of Kirjath Jearim, who prophesied against this city and against this land according to all the words of Jeremiah.
21 And when Jehoiakim the king, with all his
mighty men and all the princes, heard his
words, the king sought to put him to death;
but when Urijah heard *it,* he was afraid and
fled, and went to Egypt.
22 Then Jehoiakim the king sent men to
Egypt: Elnathan the son of Achbor, and *other*
men *who went* with him to Egypt.
23 And they brought Urijah from Egypt
and brought him to Jehoiakim the king,
who killed him with the sword and cast his
dead body into the graves of the common
people.
24 Nevertheless the hand of Ahikam the son ◄
of Shaphan was with Jeremiah, so that they
should not give him into the hand of the people to put him to death.

26:18 [a]Literally *house* [b]Compare Micah 3:12

LIFE LESSONS

➤ **26:13 — *"Now therefore, amend your ways and your doings, and obey the voice of the LORD your God; then the LORD will relent concerning the doom that He has pronounced against you."***

God delights in showing mercy far more than in fulfilling His threats of judgment. He wants to bless us, not judge us; but what we experience from His hand is largely up to us.

➤ **26:24 — *Nevertheless the hand of Ahikam the son of Shaphan was with Jeremiah, so that they should not give him into the hand of the people to put him to death.***

At strategic points along his difficult ministry, God provided Jeremiah with both encouragement and friends to help him complete his mission. God does the same for us, to help us succeed in our own divinely-appointed tasks.

Symbol of the Bonds and Yokes

27 In the beginning of the reign of Jehoiakim[a] the son of Josiah, king of Judah, this word came to Jeremiah from the
LORD, saying,[b]
2 "Thus says the LORD to me: 'Make for
yourselves bonds and yokes, and put them on
your neck,
3 'and send them to the king of Edom, the
king of Moab, the king of the Ammonites,
the king of Tyre, and the king of Sidon, by the
hand of the messengers who come to Jerusalem to Zedekiah king of Judah.
4 'And command them to say to their masters, "Thus says the LORD of hosts, the God of
Israel—thus you shall say to your masters:
5 'I have made the earth, the man and the
beast that *are* on the ground, by My great
power and by My outstretched arm, and have
given it to whom it seemed proper to Me.
6 'And now I have given all these lands into
the hand of Nebuchadnezzar the king of
Babylon, My servant; and the beasts of the
field I have also given him to serve him.
7 'So all nations shall serve him and his son
and his son's son, until the time of his land
comes; and then many nations and great
kings shall make him serve them.
8 'And it shall be, *that* the nation and kingdom which will not serve Nebuchadnezzar
the king of Babylon, and which will not put its
neck under the yoke of the king of Babylon,
that nation I will punish,' says the LORD, 'with
the sword, the famine, and the pestilence,
until I have consumed them by his hand.
9 'Therefore do not listen to your prophets,
your diviners, your dreamers, your soothsayers, or your sorcerers, who speak to you, saying, "You shall not serve the king of Babylon."
10 'For they prophesy a lie to you, to remove
you far from your land; and I will drive you
out, and you will perish.
11 'But the nations that bring their necks
under the yoke of the king of Babylon and
serve him, I will let them remain in their own
land,' says the LORD, 'and they shall till it and
dwell in it.'"'"
12 I also spoke to Zedekiah king of Judah according to all these words, saying, "Bring your
necks under the yoke of the king of Babylon,
and serve him and his people, and live!
13 "Why will you die, you and your people,
by the sword, by the famine, and by the pestilence, as the LORD has spoken against the nation that will not serve the king of Babylon?
14 "Therefore do not listen to the words of
the prophets who speak to you, saying, 'You
shall not serve the king of Babylon,' for they
prophesy a lie to you;
15 "for I have not sent them," says the LORD,
"yet they prophesy a lie in My name, that I
may drive you out, and that you may perish,
you and the prophets who prophesy to you."
16 Also I spoke to the priests and to all this
people, saying, "Thus says the LORD: 'Do not
listen to the words of your prophets who
prophesy to you, saying, "Behold, the vessels
of the LORD's house will now shortly be
brought back from Babylon"; for they prophesy a lie to you.
17 'Do not listen to them; serve the king of
Babylon, and live! Why should this city be
laid waste?
18 'But if they *are* prophets, and if the word
of the LORD is with them, let them now make
intercession to the LORD of hosts, that the vessels which are left in the house of the LORD, *in*
the house of the king of Judah, and at Jerusalem, do not go to Babylon.'
19 "For thus says the LORD of hosts concerning the pillars, concerning the Sea, concerning the carts, and concerning the remainder
of the vessels that remain in this city,
20 "which Nebuchadnezzar king of Babylon
did not take, when he carried away captive
Jeconiah the son of Jehoiakim, king of Judah,
from Jerusalem to Babylon, and all the nobles
of Judah and Jerusalem—
21 "yes, thus says the LORD of hosts, the God
of Israel, concerning the vessels that remain
in the house of the LORD, and in the house of
the king of Judah and of Jerusalem:
22 'They shall be carried to Babylon, and ➤
there they shall be until the day that I visit
them,' says the LORD. 'Then I will bring them
up and restore them to this place.'"

Hananiah's Falsehood and Doom

28 And it happened in the same year, at
the beginning of the reign of Zedekiah
king of Judah, in the fourth year *and* in the
fifth month, *that* Hananiah the son of Azur
the prophet, who *was* from Gibeon, spoke to
me in the house of the LORD in the presence of
the priests and of all the people, saying,
2 "Thus speaks the LORD of hosts, the God
of Israel, saying: 'I have broken the yoke of
the king of Babylon.

27:1 [a]Following Masoretic Text, Targum, and Vulgate; some Hebrew manuscripts, Arabic, and Syriac read *Zedekiah* (compare 27:3, 12; 28:1). [b]Septuagint omits verse 1.

LIFE LESSONS

➤ ***27:22 — "They shall be carried to Babylon, and there they shall be until the day that I visit them," says the LORD.***

The Lord never abandoned His people, nor did He leave them alone; but for most of their years of captivity, life would seem pretty dreary—until God blessed them. We are to wait for God until He moves in power.

3 'Within two full years I will bring back to
this place all the vessels of the LORD's house,
that Nebuchadnezzar king of Babylon took
away from this place and carried to Babylon.
4 'And I will bring back to this place Jeconiah the son of Jehoiakim, king of Judah,
with all the captives of Judah who went to
Babylon,' says the LORD, 'for I will break the
yoke of the king of Babylon.'"
5 Then the prophet Jeremiah spoke to the
prophet Hananiah in the presence of the
priests and in the presence of all the people
who stood in the house of the LORD,
6 and the prophet Jeremiah said, "Amen!
The LORD do so; the LORD perform your words
which you have prophesied, to bring back the
vessels of the LORD's house and all who were
carried away captive, from Babylon to this
place.
7 "Nevertheless hear now this word that I
speak in your hearing and in the hearing of
all the people:
8 "The prophets who have been before me
and before you of old prophesied against
many countries and great kingdoms—of war
and disaster and pestilence.
9 "As for the prophet who prophesies of
peace, when the word of the prophet comes to
pass, the prophet will be known *as* one whom
the LORD has truly sent."
10 Then Hananiah the prophet took the yoke
off the prophet Jeremiah's neck and broke it.
11 And Hananiah spoke in the presence of all
the people, saying, "Thus says the LORD:
'Even so I will break the yoke of Nebuchadnezzar king of Babylon from the neck of all
nations within the space of two full years.'"
And the prophet Jeremiah went his way.
12 Now the word of the LORD came to Jeremiah, after Hananiah the prophet had broken
the yoke from the neck of the prophet Jeremiah, saying,
13 "Go and tell Hananiah, saying, 'Thus says
the LORD: "You have broken the yokes of
wood, but you have made in their place yokes
of iron."
14 'For thus says the LORD of hosts, the God
of Israel: "I have put a yoke of iron on the
neck of all these nations, that they may serve
Nebuchadnezzar king of Babylon; and they
shall serve him. I have given him the beasts of
the field also."'"
15 Then the prophet Jeremiah said to Hananiah the prophet, "Hear now, Hananiah, the
LORD has not sent you, but you make this people trust in a lie.
16 "Therefore thus says the LORD: 'Behold, I
will cast you from the face of the earth. This
year you shall die, because you have taught
rebellion against the LORD.'"
17 So Hananiah the prophet died the same
year in the seventh month.

Jeremiah's Letter to the Captives

29 Now these *are* the words of the letter
that Jeremiah the prophet sent from Jerusalem to the remainder of the elders who
were carried away captive—to the priests, the
prophets, and all the people whom Nebuchadnezzar had carried away captive from
Jerusalem to Babylon.
2 (This happened after Jeconiah the king,
the queen mother, the eunuchs, the princes of
Judah and Jerusalem, the craftsmen, and the
smiths had departed from Jerusalem.)
3 *The letter was sent* by the hand of Elasah
the son of Shaphan, and Gemariah the son of
Hilkiah, whom Zedekiah king of Judah sent
to Babylon, to Nebuchadnezzar king of Babylon, saying,

4 Thus says the LORD of hosts, the God of
Israel, to all who were carried away
captive, whom I have caused to be
carried away from Jerusalem to Babylon:
5 Build houses and dwell *in them;* plant
gardens and eat their fruit.
6 Take wives and beget sons and daughters;
and take wives for your sons and give
your daughters to husbands, so that they
may bear sons and daughters—that you
may be increased there, and not diminished.
7 And seek the peace of the city where I
have caused you to be carried away captive, and pray to the LORD for it; for in its
peace you will have peace.
8 For thus says the LORD of hosts, the God of
Israel: Do not let your prophets and your
diviners who are in your midst deceive

LIFE LESSONS

➤ 28:16, 17 — *"Therefore thus says the LORD: 'Behold, I will cast you from the face of the earth. This year you shall die, because you have taught rebellion against the LORD.'" So Hananiah the prophet died the same year in the seventh month.*

How did Hananiah teach rebellion against the Lord? He did it through a message of false peace! We never earn God's favor by convincing anyone that sin is anything other than sin.

➤ 29:7 — *"And seek the peace of the city where I have caused you to be carried away captive, and pray to the LORD for it; for in its peace you will have peace."*

God caused His rebellious people to be carried away by force to wicked Babylon, and yet He instructed them to pray for the peace of the pagan city. Even in Babylon, He wanted to bless His people!

ANSWERS TO LIFE'S QUESTIONS

How can I deal with discouragement?

JER. 29:11

Do you ever feel tempted to give up? Perhaps right now you feel overlooked, forgotten, mistreated, and you want to quit. Satan's goal is to get you to do just that—throw in the towel and call it quits. Discouragement is his favorite weapon.

But remember this: while disappointments are inevitable, discouragement is a choice.

Once we yield to the devil's debilitating whispers of doubt and fear, we quickly find ourselves trapped in a web of self-pity. Soon afterwards we try to justify our feelings of anger, envy, and jealousy. Encouragement rarely comes to those looking for ways to justify themselves.

During a very troubling time in Israel's history, God directed Jeremiah to speak words of hope and encouragement to the disheartened exiles in Babylon: "For I know the thoughts that I think toward you, says the LORD, thoughts of peace and not of evil, to give you a future and a hope." If we are ever going to reach our full potential, we must understand a very important truth: *God is for us.* He is not against us. In Babylon, Israel sorted out her faith and rediscovered her deep need for the Lord.

God often uses trials to position us for greater blessing. Even in times of great disappointment, He has our best in mind. He knows how He wants to use the disappointment or hardship for our benefit, and He desires that we see Him as our only source of salvation and blessing.

When you feel tempted to yield to discouragement, go to God in prayer. Tell Him all you are feeling—the unkind ways you have been treated that do not seem fair to you. God has an objective view of the situation. He sees the future and knows the direction your life will take. He also wants you to totally depend on Him and not rely on the compliments or resources of others. While disappointments will come—you live in a fallen world, after all—you can live above it by focusing your heart on Jesus Christ.

If you are in an emotionally or physically difficult spot right now, refuse to become discouraged. Ask the Lord to reveal His will and plan for your life. Commit yourself fully to Him and pray to obey no matter what it costs. If you take this approach, then God will provide for you in ways that far exceed human understanding.

See the Life Principles Index for further study:
20. Disappointments are inevitable; discouragement is a choice.
8. Fight all your battles on your knees and you win every time.

you, nor listen to your dreams which you
cause to be dreamed.
9 For they prophesy falsely to you in My
name; I have not sent them, says the LORD.
10 For thus says the LORD: After seventy
years are completed at Babylon, I will
visit you and perform My good word
toward you, and cause you to return to
this place.
11 For I know the thoughts that I think to- ✳
ward you, says the LORD, thoughts of
peace and not of evil, to give you a future
and a hope.
12 Then you will call upon Me and go and
pray to Me, and I will listen to you.
13 And you will seek Me and find *Me,* when ➤
you search for Me with all your heart.
14 I will be found by you, says the LORD, and
I will bring you back from your captivity;
I will gather you from all the nations and
from all the places where I have driven
you, says the LORD, and I will bring you to
the place from which I cause you to be
carried away captive.

15 Because you have said, "The LORD has
raised up prophets for us in Babylon"—
16 therefore thus says the LORD concerning

LIFE LESSONS

➤ **29:13 — *"And you will seek Me and find Me, when you search for Me with all your heart."***

Do you *really* want to know God's will for your life? Do you *really* want to learn His plans for you? God promises to reveal His will to everyone who will obey whatever He tells them to do.

the king who sits on the throne of David, concerning all the people who dwell in this city, and concerning your brethren who have not gone out with you into captivity—
17 thus says the LORD of hosts: Behold, I will send on them the sword, the famine, and the pestilence, and will make them like rotten figs that cannot be eaten, they are so bad.
18 And I will pursue them with the sword, with famine, and with pestilence; and I will deliver them to trouble among all the kingdoms of the earth—to be a curse, an astonishment, a hissing, and a reproach among all the nations where I have driven them,
19 because they have not heeded My words, says the LORD, which I sent to them by My servants the prophets, rising up early and sending *them;* neither would you heed, says the LORD.
20 Therefore hear the word of the LORD, all you of the captivity, whom I have sent from Jerusalem to Babylon.
21 Thus says the LORD of hosts, the God of Israel, concerning Ahab the son of Kolaiah, and Zedekiah the son of Maaseiah, who prophesy a lie to you in My name: Behold, I will deliver them into the hand of Nebuchadnezzar king of Babylon, and he shall slay them before your eyes.
22 And because of them a curse shall be taken up by all the captivity of Judah who *are* in Babylon, saying, "The LORD make you like Zedekiah and Ahab, whom the king of Babylon roasted in the fire";
23 because they have done disgraceful things in Israel, have committed adultery with their neighbors' wives, and have spoken lying words in My name, which I have not commanded them. Indeed I know, and *am* a witness, says the LORD.

24 You shall also speak to Shemaiah the Nehelamite, saying,
25 Thus speaks the LORD of hosts, the God of Israel, saying: You have sent letters in your name to all the people who *are* at Jerusalem, to Zephaniah the son of Maaseiah the priest, and to all the priests, saying,
26 "The LORD has made you priest instead of Jehoiada the priest, so that there should be officers *in* the house of the LORD over every man *who* is demented and considers himself a prophet, that you should put him in prison and in the stocks.
27 Now therefore, why have you not rebuked Jeremiah of Anathoth who makes himself a prophet to you?
28 For he has sent to us *in* Babylon, saying, 'This *captivity is* long; build houses and dwell *in them,* and plant gardens and eat their fruit.'"
29 Now Zephaniah the priest read this letter in the hearing of Jeremiah the prophet.
30 Then the word of the LORD came to Jeremiah, saying:
31 Send to all those in captivity, saying, Thus says the LORD concerning Shemaiah the Nehelamite: Because Shemaiah has prophesied to you, and I have not sent him, and he has caused you to trust in a lie—
32 therefore thus says the LORD: Behold, I will punish Shemaiah the Nehelamite and his family: he shall not have anyone to dwell among this people, nor shall he see the good that I will do for My people, says the LORD, because he has taught rebellion against the LORD.

Restoration of Israel and Judah

30 The word that came to Jeremiah from the LORD, saying,
2 "Thus speaks the LORD God of Israel, saying: 'Write in a book for yourself all the words that I have spoken to you.
3 'For behold, the days are coming,' says the LORD, 'that I will bring back from captivity My people Israel and Judah,' says the LORD. 'And I will cause them to return to the land that I gave to their fathers, and they shall possess it.'"
4 Now these *are* the words that the LORD spoke concerning Israel and Judah.
5 "For thus says the LORD:

'We have heard a voice of trembling,
Of fear, and not of peace.
6 Ask now, and see,
Whether a man is ever in labor with child?
So why do I see every man *with* his hands on his loins
Like a woman in labor,
And all faces turned pale?
7 Alas! For that day *is* great,
So that none *is* like it;
And it *is* the time of Jacob's trouble,
But he shall be saved out of it.

8 'For it shall come to pass in that day,'
Says the LORD of hosts,
'*That* I will break his yoke from your neck,
And will burst your bonds;
Foreigners shall no more enslave them.
9 But they shall serve the LORD their God,
And David their king,
Whom I will raise up for them.

10 'Therefore do not fear, O My servant Jacob,' says the LORD,
'Nor be dismayed, O Israel;
For behold, I will save you from afar,
And your seed from the land of their captivity.
Jacob shall return, have rest and be quiet,
And no one shall make *him* afraid.

➢ 11 For I *am* with you,' says the LORD, 'to
save you;
Though I make a full end of all nations
where I have scattered you,
Yet I will not make a complete end of
you.
But I will correct you in justice,
And will not let you go altogether
unpunished.'

12 "For thus says the LORD:

'Your affliction *is* incurable,
Your wound *is* severe.
13 *There is* no one to plead your cause,
That you may be bound up;
You have no healing medicines.
14 All your lovers have forgotten you;
They do not seek you;
For I have wounded you with the wound
of an enemy,
With the chastisement of a cruel one,
For the multitude of your iniquities,
Because your sins have increased.
15 Why do you cry about your affliction?
Your sorrow *is* incurable.
Because of the multitude of your
iniquities,
Because your sins have increased,
I have done these things to you.

16 'Therefore all those who devour you shall
be devoured;
And all your adversaries, every one of
them, shall go into captivity;
Those who plunder you shall become
plunder,
And all who prey upon you I will make a
prey.
17 For I will restore health to you
And heal you of your wounds,' says the
LORD,
'Because they called you an outcast
saying:
"This *is* Zion;
No one seeks her." '

18 "Thus says the LORD:

'Behold, I will bring back the captivity of
Jacob's tents,
And have mercy on his dwelling
places;
The city shall be built upon its own
mound,
And the palace shall remain according to
its own plan.
19 Then out of them shall proceed
thanksgiving
And the voice of those who make merry;
I will multiply them, and they shall not
diminish;
I will also glorify them, and they shall not
be small.
20 Their children also shall be as before,
And their congregation shall be
established before Me;
And I will punish all who oppress them.
21 Their nobles shall be from among them,
And their governor shall come from their
midst;
Then I will cause him to draw near,
And he shall approach Me;
For who *is* this who pledged his heart to
approach Me?' says the LORD.
22 'You shall be My people,
And I will be your God.' "

23 Behold, the whirlwind of the LORD
Goes forth with fury,
A continuing whirlwind;
It will fall violently on the head of the
wicked.
24 The fierce anger of the LORD will not
return until He has done it,
And until He has performed the intents
of His heart.
In the latter days you will consider it.

The Remnant of Israel Saved

31 "At the same time," says the LORD, "I
will be the God of all the families of Israel, and they shall be My people."
2 Thus says the LORD:

"The people who survived the sword
Found grace in the wilderness—
Israel, when I went to give him rest."

3 The LORD has appeared of old to me, ➤
saying:
"Yes, I have loved you with an everlasting
love;
Therefore with lovingkindness I have
drawn you.

LIFE LESSONS

➢ 30:11 — *"I am with you," says the LORD, "to save you; though I make a full end of all nations where I have scattered you, yet I will not make a complete end of you. But I will correct you in justice, and will not let you go altogether unpunished."*

Complete and total forgiveness of sin does not necessarily mean complete and total eradication of all consequences for sin. Jesus forgave the thief on the cross and gave him eternal life, but the thief still died (Luke 23:43).

➢ 31:3 — *The LORD has appeared of old to me, saying: "Yes, I have loved you with an everlasting love; therefore with lovingkindness I have drawn you."*

God has pledged His love to you. He walks with you through disappointment and never gets disillusioned by your wayward acts, for He has seen the finished portrait. He knows that, through Christ, you can and will succeed (Phil. 4:13).

4 Again I will build you, and you shall be rebuilt,
O virgin of Israel!
You shall again be adorned with your tambourines,
And shall go forth in the dances of those who rejoice.
5 You shall yet plant vines on the mountains of Samaria;
The planters shall plant and eat *them* as ordinary food.
6 For there shall be a day
When the watchmen will cry on Mount Ephraim,
'Arise, and let us go up *to* Zion,
To the LORD our God.'"
7 For thus says the LORD:

"Sing with gladness for Jacob,
And shout among the chief of the nations;
Proclaim, give praise, and say,
'O LORD, save Your people,
The remnant of Israel!'
8 Behold, I will bring them from the north country,
And gather them from the ends of the earth,
Among them the blind and the lame,
The woman with child
And the one who labors with child, together;
A great throng shall return there.
9 They shall come with weeping,
And with supplications I will lead them.
I will cause them to walk by the rivers of waters,
In a straight way in which they shall not stumble;
For I am a Father to Israel,
And Ephraim *is* My firstborn.
10"Hear the word of the LORD, O nations,
And declare *it* in the isles afar off, and say,
'He who scattered Israel will gather him,
And keep him as a shepherd *does* his flock.'
11 For the LORD has redeemed Jacob,
And ransomed him from the hand of one stronger than he.
12 Therefore they shall come and sing in the height of Zion,
Streaming to the goodness of the LORD—
For wheat and new wine and oil,
For the young of the flock and the herd;
Their souls shall be like a well-watered garden,
And they shall sorrow no more at all.
13"Then shall the virgin rejoice in the dance,
And the young men and the old, together;
For I will turn their mourning to joy,
Will comfort them,
And make them rejoice rather than sorrow.
14 I will satiate the soul of the priests with abundance,
And My people shall be satisfied with My goodness, says the LORD."

Mercy on Ephraim
15 Thus says the LORD:

"A voice was heard in Ramah,
Lamentation *and* bitter weeping,
Rachel weeping for her children,
Refusing to be comforted for her children,
Because they *are* no more."
16 Thus says the LORD:

"Refrain your voice from weeping,
And your eyes from tears;
For your work shall be rewarded, says the LORD,
And they shall come back from the land of the enemy.
17 There is hope in your future, says the LORD,
That *your* children shall come back to their own border.
18"I have surely heard Ephraim bemoaning himself:
'You have chastised me, and I was chastised,
Like an untrained bull;
Restore me, and I will return,
For You *are* the LORD my God.
19 Surely, after my turning, I repented;
And after I was instructed, I struck myself on the thigh;
I was ashamed, yes, even humiliated,
Because I bore the reproach of my youth.'
20 *Is* Ephraim My dear son?
Is he a pleasant child?

LIFE LESSONS

➤ 31:14 — *"I will satiate the soul of the priests with abundance, and My people shall be satisfied with My goodness, says the LORD."*

The Lord does not want to wait until heaven to satisfy our soul with abundance, or fill us with His goodness. He desires to bless us *right now* with all the good things of His Spirit.

➤ 31:20 — *"Is Ephraim My dear son? Is he a pleasant child? For though I spoke against him, I earnestly remember him still; therefore My heart yearns for him; I will surely have mercy on him, says the LORD."*

In these words you can hear the turmoil that we often cause our Lord. He loves us and wants to bless us, but He can never simply ignore our rebellion and sin. Yet He loves mercy above judgment.

For though I spoke against him,
I earnestly remember him still;
Therefore My heart yearns for him;
I will surely have mercy on him, says the LORD.

21 "Set up signposts,
Make landmarks;
Set your heart toward the highway,
The way in *which* you went.
Turn back, O virgin of Israel,
Turn back to these your cities.
22 How long will you gad about,
O you backsliding daughter?
For the LORD has created a new thing in the earth—
A woman shall encompass a man."

Future Prosperity of Judah

23 Thus says the LORD of hosts, the God of Israel: "They shall again use this speech in the land of Judah and in its cities, when I bring back their captivity: 'The LORD bless you, O home of justice, *and* mountain of holiness!'
24 "And there shall dwell in Judah itself, and in all its cities together, farmers and those going out with flocks.
25 "For I have satiated the weary soul, and I have replenished every sorrowful soul."
26 After this I awoke and looked around, and my sleep was sweet to me.
27 "Behold, the days are coming, says the LORD, that I will sow the house of Israel and the house of Judah with the seed of man and the seed of beast.
28 "And it shall come to pass, *that* as I have watched over them to pluck up, to break down, to throw down, to destroy, and to afflict, so I will watch over them to build and to plant, says the LORD.
29 In those days they shall say no more:

'The fathers have eaten sour grapes,
And the children's teeth are set on edge.'

30 But every one shall die for his own iniquity; every man who eats the sour grapes, his teeth shall be set on edge.

A New Covenant

➤ 31 "Behold, the days are coming, says the LORD, when I will make a new covenant with the house of Israel and with the house of Judah—
32 "not according to the covenant that I made with their fathers in the day *that* I took them by the hand to lead them out of the land of Egypt, My covenant which they broke, though I was a husband to them,[a] says the LORD.
33 "But this *is* the covenant that I will make with the house of Israel after those days, says the LORD: I will put My law in their minds, and write it on their hearts; and I will be their God, and they shall be My people.
34 "No more shall every man teach his neighbor, and every man his brother, saying, 'Know the LORD,' for they all shall know Me, from the least of them to the greatest of them, says the LORD. For I will forgive their iniquity, and their sin I will remember no more."

35 Thus says the LORD,
Who gives the sun for a light by day,
The ordinances of the moon and the stars for a light by night,
Who disturbs the sea,
And its waves roar
(The LORD of hosts *is* His name):

36 "If those ordinances depart
From before Me, says the LORD,
Then the seed of Israel shall also cease
From being a nation before Me forever."

37 Thus says the LORD:

"If heaven above can be measured,
And the foundations of the earth searched out beneath,
I will also cast off all the seed of Israel
For all that they have done, says the LORD.

38 "Behold, the days are coming, says the LORD, that the city shall be built for the LORD from the Tower of Hananel to the Corner Gate.
39 "The surveyor's line shall again extend straight forward over the hill Gareb; then it shall turn toward Goath.
40 "And the whole valley of the dead bodies and of the ashes, and all the fields as far as the Brook Kidron, to the corner of the Horse Gate toward the east, *shall be* holy to the LORD. It shall not be plucked up or thrown down anymore forever."

Jeremiah Buys a Field

32 The word that came to Jeremiah from the LORD in the tenth year of Zedekiah king of Judah, which was the eighteenth year of Nebuchadnezzar.

31:32 [a]Following Masoretic Text, Targum, and Vulgate; Septuagint and Syriac read *and I turned away from them.*

LIFE LESSONS

➤ 31:31 — *"Behold, the days are coming, says the LORD, when I will make a new covenant with the house of Israel and with the house of Judah . . . ."*

We are a "new covenant" people, a blessed group of men and women who can come boldly into God's presence by His Spirit and through faith in His Son, Jesus Christ (Heb. 8:7–13; 9:15; 12:24).

2 For then the king of Babylon's army besieged Jerusalem, and Jeremiah the prophet was shut up in the court of the prison, which *was in* the king of Judah's house.
3 For Zedekiah king of Judah had shut him up, saying, "Why do you prophesy and say, 'Thus says the LORD: "Behold, I will give this city into the hand of the king of Babylon, and he shall take it;
4 "and Zedekiah king of Judah shall not escape from the hand of the Chaldeans, but shall surely be delivered into the hand of the king of Babylon, and shall speak with him face to face,[a] and see him eye to eye;
5 "then he shall lead Zedekiah to Babylon, and there he shall be until I visit him," says the LORD; "though you fight with the Chaldeans, you shall not succeed"'?"
6 And Jeremiah said, "The word of the LORD came to me, saying,
7 'Behold, Hanamel the son of Shallum your uncle will come to you, saying, "Buy my field which *is* in Anathoth, for the right of redemption *is* yours to buy *it*."'
8 "Then Hanamel my uncle's son came to me in the court of the prison according to the word of the LORD, and said to me, 'Please buy my field that *is* in Anathoth, which *is* in the country of Benjamin; for the right of inheritance *is* yours, and the redemption yours; buy *it* for yourself.' Then I knew that this was the word of the LORD.
9 "So I bought the field from Hanamel, the son of my uncle who *was* in Anathoth, and weighed *out to* him the money—seventeen shekels of silver.
10 "And I signed the deed and sealed *it*, took witnesses, and weighed the money on the scales.
11 "So I took the purchase deed, *both* that which was sealed *according* to the law and custom, and that which was open;
12 "and I gave the purchase deed to Baruch the son of Neriah, son of Mahseiah, in the presence of Hanamel my uncle's *son*, and in the presence of the witnesses who signed the purchase deed, before all the Jews who sat in the court of the prison.
13 "Then I charged Baruch before them, saying,
14 'Thus says the LORD of hosts, the God of Israel: "Take these deeds, both this purchase deed which is sealed and this deed which is open, and put them in an earthen vessel, that they may last many days."
15 'For thus says the LORD of hosts, the God of Israel: "Houses and fields and vineyards shall be possessed again in this land."'

Jeremiah Prays for Understanding

16 "Now when I had delivered the purchase deed to Baruch the son of Neriah, I prayed to the LORD, saying:
17 'Ah, Lord GOD! Behold, You have made the heavens and the earth by Your great power and outstretched arm. There is nothing too hard for You.
18 '*You* show lovingkindness to thousands, and repay the iniquity of the fathers into the bosom of their children after them—the Great, the Mighty God, whose name *is* the LORD of hosts.
19 '*You are* great in counsel and mighty in work, for Your eyes *are* open to all the ways of the sons of men, to give everyone according to his ways and according to the fruit of his doings.
20 'You have set signs and wonders in the land of Egypt, to this day, and in Israel and among *other* men; and You have made Yourself a name, as it is this day.
21 'You have brought Your people Israel out of the land of Egypt with signs and wonders, with a strong hand and an outstretched arm, and with great terror;
22 'You have given them this land, of which You swore to their fathers to give them—"a land flowing with milk and honey."[a]
23 'And they came in and took possession of it, but they have not obeyed Your voice or walked in Your law. They have done nothing of all that You commanded them to do; therefore You have caused all this calamity to come upon them.
24 'Look, the siege mounds! They have come to the city to take it; and the city has been given into the hand of the Chaldeans who fight against it, because of the sword and famine and pestilence. What You have spoken has happened; there You see *it!*
25 'And You have said to me, O Lord GOD, "Buy the field for money, and take witnesses"!—yet the city has been given into the hand of the Chaldeans.'"

God's Assurance of the People's Return

26 Then the word of the LORD came to Jeremiah, saying,

32:4 [a]Literally *mouth to mouth* **32:22** [a]Exodus 3:8

LIFE LESSONS

32:17 — *"Ah, Lord GOD! Behold, You have made the heavens and the earth by Your great power and outstretched arm. There is nothing too hard for You."*

Jeremiah states rightly that God can do whatever He desires—and yet when it comes to his life, he wonders (Jer. 32:24). How like us! In theory, we agree; but in our own lives? Yet nothing is too hard for God.

➤ 27 "Behold, I *am* the LORD, the God of all flesh. Is there anything too hard for Me?

28 "Therefore thus says the LORD: 'Behold, I will give this city into the hand of the Chaldeans, into the hand of Nebuchadnezzar king of Babylon, and he shall take it.

29 'And the Chaldeans who fight against this city shall come and set fire to this city and burn it, with the houses on whose roofs they have offered incense to Baal and poured out drink offerings to other gods, to provoke Me to anger;

30 'because the children of Israel and the children of Judah have done only evil before Me from their youth. For the children of Israel have provoked Me only to anger with the work of their hands,' says the LORD.

31 'For this city has been to Me *a provocation of* My anger and My fury from the day that they built it, even to this day; so I will remove it from before My face

32 'because of all the evil of the children of Israel and the children of Judah, which they have done to provoke Me to anger—they, their kings, their princes, their priests, their prophets, the men of Judah, and the inhabitants of Jerusalem.

33 'And they have turned to Me the back, and not the face; though I taught them, rising up early and teaching *them*, yet they have not listened to receive instruction.

34 'But they set their abominations in the house which is called by My name, to defile it.

35 'And they built the high places of Baal which *are* in the Valley of the Son of Hinnom, to cause their sons and their daughters to pass through *the fire* to Molech, which I did not command them, nor did it come into My mind that they should do this abomination, to cause Judah to sin.'

36 "Now therefore, thus says the LORD, the God of Israel, concerning this city of which you say, 'It shall be delivered into the hand of the king of Babylon by the sword, by the famine, and by the pestilence':

37 'Behold, I will gather them out of all countries where I have driven them in My anger, in My fury, and in great wrath; I will bring them back to this place, and I will cause them to dwell safely.

38 'They shall be My people, and I will be their God;

39 'then I will give them one heart and one way, that they may fear Me forever, for the good of them and their children after them. ≺

40 'And I will make an everlasting covenant with them, that I will not turn away from doing them good; but I will put My fear in their hearts so that they will not depart from Me.

41 'Yes, I will rejoice over them to do them good, and I will assuredly plant them in this land, with all My heart and with all My soul.' ≺

42 "For thus says the LORD: 'Just as I have brought all this great calamity on this people, so I will bring on them all the good that I have promised them. ≺

43 'And fields will be bought in this land of which you say, "*It is* desolate, without man or beast; it has been given into the hand of the Chaldeans."

44 'Men will buy fields for money, sign deeds and seal *them*, and take witnesses, in the land of Benjamin, in the places around Jerusalem, in the cities of Judah, in the cities of the mountains, in the cities of the lowland, and in the cities of the South; for I will cause their captives to return,' says the LORD."

Excellence of the Restored Nation

33 Moreover the word of the LORD came to Jeremiah a second time, while he was still shut up in the court of the prison, saying,

2 "Thus says the LORD who made it, the LORD who formed it to establish it (the LORD *is* His name):

3 'Call to Me, and I will answer you, and show you great and mighty things, which you do not know.' ≺

4 "For thus says the LORD, the God of Israel, concerning the houses of this city and the

LIFE LESSONS

➤ 32:27 — *"Behold, I am the LORD, the God of all flesh. Is there anything too hard for Me?"*

Abraham had to learn this lesson (Gen. 18:14). Mary, the mother of Jesus, had to learn this lesson (Luke 1:37). Peter and the other disciples had to learn this lesson (Luke 18:27). And so do we.

➤ 32:39 — *". . . I will give them one heart and one way, that they may fear Me forever, for the good of them and their children after them."*

Everything God does for us, He does for our good. He gives us a heart to love Him, a will to obey Him, and a spirit to fear Him, for our good and the good of our children.

➤ 32:41 — *"Yes, I will rejoice over them to do them good, and I will assuredly plant them in this land, with all My heart and with all My soul."*

God wants to bless us with all His heart and with all His soul—that is, with everything within Him. Who can measure that kind of blessing? Who can comprehend it? But that is exactly what He has for us.

➤ 32:42 — *"For thus says the LORD: 'Just as I have brought all this great calamity on this people, so I will bring on them all the good that I have promised them.'"*

God keeps all of His promises, for both judgment and blessing—but He loves to bless His people, not judge them. He will not shrink from judging us (1 Pet. 4:17), but He would much prefer to bless us.

ANSWERS TO LIFE'S QUESTIONS

How can I make my prayer life fresh and new?

JER. 33:1–3

The prophet Jeremiah was not a popular man. When he declared the truth God had given him—that Judah would soon start seventy long years in captivity—the people threw him into prison.

Yet in such dire circumstances, Jeremiah learned something profound about prayer. Jeremiah 33:1–3 says: "The word of the LORD came to Jeremiah a second time, while he was still shut up in the court of the prison, saying, 'Thus says the LORD who made it, the Lord who formed it to establish it (the LORD is His name): "Call to Me, and I will answer you, and show you great and mighty things, which you do not know." ' "

Prayer is a very real part of a vital relationship with God. It is not for some special spiritual elite; it is for *you*. Three principles within these verses can transform your old notions about prayer into something fresh and new.

First, God says, "Call to Me." He wants to hear from you. His all-loving, omnipotent heart desires to hear your innermost thoughts and feelings. He wants to hear from you in the hard times and when life is going smoothly. In fact, your sweetest times of prayer happen when you come before Him simply to praise and worship and give thanks for what He has done.

Second, God says, "I will answer you." Do you believe that? Perhaps you once asked God for something He did not give you, and since then, you have harbored secret worries that He did not hear or did not care to answer. But God Himself says to you, "I will answer you." That answer may not take the form you anticipate or come when you desire, but He *will* respond. He might say "yes," "no," or "wait." You may not understand the reasons behind His answer—but you can trust that they are best for you (Rom. 8:28).

Third, God says, "I will show you great and mighty things, which you do not know." You have finite wisdom and understanding; God knows all. He knows the big picture; you see merely a tiny piece. When you ask Him to guide you, He works to direct you as a part of His higher vision and calling.

If you take that first step of calling out to Him, prayer can become an important part of a dynamic relationship with almighty God. Do it today—He waits to hear your voice.

See the Life Principles Index for further study:

8. Fight all your battles on your knees and you win every time.

17. We stand tallest and strongest on our knees.

houses of the kings of Judah, which have
been pulled down *to fortify*[a] against the siege
mounds and the sword:
5 'They come to fight with the Chaldeans,
but *only* to fill their places[a] with the dead bodies of men whom I will slay in My anger and
My fury, all for whose wickedness I have hidden My face from this city.
6 'Behold, I will bring it health and healing;
I will heal them and reveal to them the abundance of peace and truth.
7 'And I will cause the captives of Judah and
the captives of Israel to return, and will rebuild those places as at the first.
8 'I will cleanse them from all their iniquity
by which they have sinned against Me, and I
will pardon all their iniquities by which they
have sinned and by which they have transgressed against Me.

33:4 [a]Compare Isaiah 22:10 33:5 [a]Compare 2 Kings 23:14

LIFE LESSONS

➤ 33:3 — *"Call to Me, and I will answer you, and show you great and mighty things, which you do not know."*

Throughout the Bible, God promises to speak to His children—but we must listen for His voice. To listen actively, we must come before the Lord expectantly. We must eagerly anticipate Him speaking to us.

➤ 33:6 — *"Behold, I will bring it health and healing; I will heal them and reveal to them the abundance of peace and truth."*

For such a dark book, Jeremiah has some blindingly bright spots. God desires to bring us health and healing, not sickness and injury. He wants to shower us with peace and truth, not keep either from us.

➤ 9 'Then it shall be to Me a name of joy, a
praise, and an honor before all nations of the
earth, who shall hear all the good that I do to
them; they shall fear and tremble for all the
goodness and all the prosperity that I provide
for it.'
10 "Thus says the LORD: 'Again there shall be
heard in this place—of which you say, "It *is*
desolate, without man and without beast"—in
the cities of Judah, in the streets of Jerusalem
that are desolate, without man and without
inhabitant and without beast,
11 'the voice of joy and the voice of gladness, the voice of the bridegroom and the
voice of the bride, the voice of those who will
say:

"Praise the LORD of hosts,
For the LORD *is* good,
For His mercy *endures* forever"—

and of those *who will* bring the sacrifice of
praise into the house of the LORD. For I will
cause the captives of the land to return as at
the first,' says the LORD.
12 "Thus says the LORD of hosts: 'In this place
which is desolate, without man and without
beast, and in all its cities, there shall again be
a dwelling place of shepherds causing *their*
flocks to lie down.
13 'In the cities of the mountains, in the cities
of the lowland, in the cities of the South, in
the land of Benjamin, in the places around Jerusalem, and in the cities of Judah, the flocks
shall again pass under the hands of him who
counts *them*,' says the LORD.
14 'Behold, the days are coming,' says the
LORD, 'that I will perform that good thing
which I have promised to the house of Israel
and to the house of Judah:

15 'In those days and at that time
I will cause to grow up to David
A Branch of righteousness;
He shall execute judgment and
righteousness in the earth.
16 In those days Judah will be saved,
And Jerusalem will dwell safely.
And this *is the name* by which she will
be called:
THE LORD OUR RIGHTEOUSNESS.'[a]

17 "For thus says the LORD: 'David shall
never lack a man to sit on the throne of the
house of Israel;
18 nor shall the priests, the Levites, lack a
man to offer burnt offerings before Me, to
kindle grain offerings, and to sacrifice continually.'"

The Permanence of God's Covenant

19 And the word of the LORD came to Jeremiah, saying,
20 "Thus says the LORD: 'If you can break My
covenant with the day and My covenant with
the night, so that there will not be day and
night in their season,
21 'then My covenant may also be broken
with David My servant, so that he shall not
have a son to reign on his throne, and with
the Levites, the priests, My ministers.
22 'As the host of heaven cannot be numbered, nor the sand of the sea measured, so
will I multiply the descendants of David My
servant and the Levites who minister to Me.'"
23 Moreover the word of the LORD came to
Jeremiah, saying,
24 "Have you not considered what these people have spoken, saying, 'The two families
which the LORD has chosen, He has also cast
them off'? Thus they have despised My people, as if they should no more be a nation before them.
25 "Thus says the LORD: 'If My covenant *is*
not with day and night, *and if* I have not appointed the ordinances of heaven and earth,
26 'then I will cast away the descendants of
Jacob and David My servant, *so* that I will not
take *any* of his descendants *to be* rulers over
the descendants of Abraham, Isaac, and Jacob. For I will cause their captives to return,
and will have mercy on them.'"

Zedekiah Warned by God

34 The word which came to Jeremiah
from the LORD, when Nebuchadnezzar
king of Babylon and all his army, all the kingdoms of the earth under his dominion, and all
the people, fought against Jerusalem and all
its cities, saying,
2 "Thus says the LORD, the God of Israel: 'Go
and speak to Zedekiah king of Judah and tell
him, "Thus says the LORD: 'Behold, I will give
this city into the hand of the king of Babylon,
and he shall burn it with fire.
3 'And you shall not escape from his hand,
but shall surely be taken and delivered into
his hand; your eyes shall see the eyes of the
king of Babylon, he shall speak with you face
to face,[a] and you shall go to Babylon.'"'

33:16 [a]Compare 23:5, 6 **34:3** [a]Literally *mouth to mouth*

LIFE LESSONS

➤ 33:9 — *"Then it shall be to Me a name of joy, a praise, and an honor before all nations of the earth, who shall hear all the good that I do to them; they shall fear and tremble for all the goodness and all the prosperity that I provide for it."*

When will we learn that the heart of God yearns to lavish on His obedient people joy, praise, honor, goodness, and prosperity? He does not wait in heaven, just itching for us to fall, but rather longs to do good to us.

4 "Yet hear the word of the LORD, O Zedekiah king of Judah! Thus says the LORD concerning you: 'You shall not die by the sword.
5 'You shall die in peace; as in the ceremonies of your fathers, the former kings who
were before you, so they shall burn *incense*
for you and lament for you, *saying*, "Alas,
lord!" For I have pronounced the word, says
the LORD.'"
6 Then Jeremiah the prophet spoke all these
words to Zedekiah king of Judah in Jerusalem,
7 when the king of Babylon's army fought
against Jerusalem and all the cities of Judah
that were left, against Lachish and Azekah;
for *only* these fortified cities remained of the
cities of Judah.

Treacherous Treatment of Slaves
8 *This is* the word that came to Jeremiah
from the LORD, after King Zedekiah had made
a covenant with all the people who *were* at Jerusalem to proclaim liberty to them:
9 that every man should set free his male
and female slave—a Hebrew man or
woman—that no one should keep a Jewish
brother in bondage.
10 Now when all the princes and all the people, who had entered into the covenant, heard
that everyone should set free his male and female slaves, that no one should keep them in
bondage anymore, they obeyed and let *them*
go.
11 But afterward they changed their minds
and made the male and female slaves return,
whom they had set free, and brought them
into subjection as male and female slaves.
12 Therefore the word of the LORD came to
Jeremiah from the LORD, saying,
13 "Thus says the LORD, the God of Israel: 'I
made a covenant with your fathers in the day
that I brought them out of the land of Egypt,
out of the house of bondage, saying,
14 "At the end of seven years let every man
set free his Hebrew brother, who has been
sold to him; and when he has served you six
years, you shall let him go free from you." But
your fathers did not obey Me nor incline their
ear.
15 'Then you recently turned and did what
was right in My sight—every man proclaiming liberty to his neighbor; and you made a
covenant before Me in the house which is
called by My name.
16 'Then you turned around and profaned
My name, and every one of you brought back
his male and female slaves, whom you had set
at liberty, at their pleasure, and brought them
back into subjection, to be your male and female slaves.'
17 "Therefore thus says the LORD: 'You have
not obeyed Me in proclaiming liberty, every
one to his brother and every one to his neighbor. Behold, I proclaim liberty to you,' says
the LORD—'to the sword, to pestilence, and to
famine! And I will deliver you to trouble
among all the kingdoms of the earth.
18 'And I will give the men who have transgressed My covenant, who have not performed the words of the covenant which they
made before Me, when they cut the calf in two
and passed between the parts of it—
19 'the princes of Judah, the princes of Jerusalem, the eunuchs, the priests, and all the
people of the land who passed between the
parts of the calf—
20 'I will give them into the hand of their enemies and into the hand of those who seek
their life. Their dead bodies shall be for meat
for the birds of the heaven and the beasts of
the earth.
21 'And I will give Zedekiah king of Judah
and his princes into the hand of their enemies, into the hand of those who seek their
life, and into the hand of the king of Babylon's army which has gone back from you.
22 'Behold, I will command,' says the LORD,
'and cause them to return to this city. They
will fight against it and take it and burn it
with fire; and I will make the cities of Judah a
desolation without inhabitant.'"

The Obedient Rechabites
35 The word which came to Jeremiah
from the LORD in the days of Jehoiakim
the son of Josiah, king of Judah, saying,
2 "Go to the house of the Rechabites, speak
to them, and bring them into the house of the
LORD, into one of the chambers, and give
them wine to drink."
3 Then I took Jaazaniah the son of Jeremiah, the son of Habazziniah, his brothers
and all his sons, and the whole house of the
Rechabites,
4 and I brought them into the house of the
LORD, into the chamber of the sons of Hanan
the son of Igdaliah, a man of God, which *was*
by the chamber of the princes, above the
chamber of Maaseiah the son of Shallum, the
keeper of the door.
5 Then I set before the sons of the house of
the Rechabites bowls full of wine, and cups;
and I said to them, "Drink wine."
6 But they said, "We will drink no wine, for
Jonadab the son of Rechab, our father, commanded us, saying, 'You shall drink no wine,
you nor your sons, forever.
7 'You shall not build a house, sow seed,
plant a vineyard, nor have *any of these;* but
all your days you shall dwell in tents, that you
may live many days in the land where you are
sojourners.'
8 "Thus we have obeyed the voice of Jonadab the son of Rechab, our father, in all that
he charged us, to drink no wine all our days,
we, our wives, our sons, or our daughters,
9 "nor to build ourselves houses to dwell in;
nor do we have vineyard, field, or seed.

10 "But we have dwelt in tents, and have obeyed and done according to all that Jonadab our father commanded us.

11 "But it came to pass, when Nebuchadnezzar king of Babylon came up into the land, that we said, 'Come, let us go to Jerusalem for fear of the army of the Chaldeans and for fear of the army of the Syrians.' So we dwell at Jerusalem."

12 Then came the word of the LORD to Jeremiah, saying,

13 "Thus says the LORD of hosts, the God of Israel: 'Go and tell the men of Judah and the inhabitants of Jerusalem, "Will you not receive instruction to obey My words?" says the LORD.

14 "The words of Jonadab the son of Rechab, which he commanded his sons, not to drink wine, are performed; for to this day they drink none, and obey their father's commandment. But although I have spoken to you, rising early and speaking, you did not obey Me.

15 "I have also sent to you all My servants the prophets, rising up early and sending *them*, saying, 'Turn now everyone from his evil way, amend your doings, and do not go after other gods to serve them; then you will dwell in the land which I have given you and your fathers.' But you have not inclined your ear, nor obeyed Me.

16 "Surely the sons of Jonadab the son of Rechab have performed the commandment of their father, which he commanded them, but this people has not obeyed Me."'

17 "Therefore thus says the LORD God of hosts, the God of Israel: 'Behold, I will bring on Judah and on all the inhabitants of Jerusalem all the doom that I have pronounced against them; because I have spoken to them but they have not heard, and I have called to them but they have not answered.'"

18 And Jeremiah said to the house of the Rechabites, "Thus says the LORD of hosts, the God of Israel: 'Because you have obeyed the commandment of Jonadab your father, and kept all his precepts and done according to all that he commanded you,

19 'therefore thus says the LORD of hosts, the God of Israel: "Jonadab the son of Rechab shall not lack a man to stand before Me forever."'"

The Scroll Read in the Temple

36 Now it came to pass in the fourth year of Jehoiakim the son of Josiah, king of Judah, *that* this word came to Jeremiah from the LORD, saying:

2 "Take a scroll of a book and write on it all the words that I have spoken to you against Israel, against Judah, and against all the nations, from the day I spoke to you, from the days of Josiah even to this day.

3 "It may be that the house of Judah will hear all the adversities which I purpose to bring upon them, that everyone may turn from his evil way, that I may forgive their iniquity and their sin."

4 Then Jeremiah called Baruch the son of Neriah; and Baruch wrote on a scroll of a book, at the instruction of Jeremiah,[a] all the words of the LORD which He had spoken to him.

5 And Jeremiah commanded Baruch, saying, "I *am* confined, I cannot go into the house of the LORD.

6 "You go, therefore, and read from the scroll which you have written at my instruction,[a] the words of the LORD, in the hearing of the people in the LORD's house on the day of fasting. And you shall also read them in the hearing of all Judah who come from their cities.

7 "It may be that they will present their supplication before the LORD, and everyone will turn from his evil way. For great *is* the anger and the fury that the LORD has pronounced against this people."

8 And Baruch the son of Neriah did according to all that Jeremiah the prophet commanded him, reading from the book the words of the LORD in the LORD's house.

9 Now it came to pass in the fifth year of Jehoiakim the son of Josiah, king of Judah, in the ninth month, *that* they proclaimed a fast before the LORD to all the people in Jerusalem, and to all the people who came from the cities of Judah to Jerusalem.

10 Then Baruch read from the book the words of Jeremiah in the house of the LORD, in the chamber of Gemariah the son of Shaphan the scribe, in the upper court at the entry of the New Gate of the LORD's house, in the hearing of all the people.

The Scroll Read in the Palace

11 When Michaiah the son of Gemariah, the son of Shaphan, heard all the words of the LORD from the book,

12 he then went down to the king's house,

36:4 [a]Literally *from Jeremiah's mouth* **36:6** [a]Literally *from my mouth*

LIFE LESSONS

➤ 36:7 — *"It may be that they will present their supplication before the LORD, and everyone will turn from his evil way."*

Since we never know when someone has "crossed the point of no return," we should always urge men and women to repent and return to the Lord so that He might heal them.

into the scribe's chamber; and there all the princes were sitting—Elishama the scribe, Delaiah the son of Shemaiah, Elnathan the son of Achbor, Gemariah the son of Shaphan, Zedekiah the son of Hananiah, and all the princes.
13 Then Michaiah declared to them all the words that he had heard when Baruch read the book in the hearing of the people.
14 Therefore all the princes sent Jehudi the son of Nethaniah, the son of Shelemiah, the son of Cushi, to Baruch, saying, "Take in your hand the scroll from which you have read in the hearing of the people, and come." So Baruch the son of Neriah took the scroll in his hand and came to them.
15 And they said to him, "Sit down now, and read it in our hearing." So Baruch read *it* in their hearing.
16 Now it happened, when they had heard all the words, that they looked in fear from one to another, and said to Baruch, "We will surely tell the king of all these words."
17 And they asked Baruch, saying, "Tell us now, how did you write all these words—at his instruction?"[a]
18 So Baruch answered them, "He proclaimed with his mouth all these words to me, and I wrote *them* with ink in the book."
19 Then the princes said to Baruch, "Go and hide, you and Jeremiah; and let no one know where you are."

The King Destroys Jeremiah's Scroll

20 And they went to the king, into the court; but they stored the scroll in the chamber of Elishama the scribe, and told all the words in the hearing of the king.
21 So the king sent Jehudi to bring the scroll, and he took it from Elishama the scribe's chamber. And Jehudi read it in the hearing of the king and in the hearing of all the princes who stood beside the king.
22 Now the king was sitting in the winter house in the ninth month, with *a fire* burning on the hearth before him.
23 And it happened, when Jehudi had read three or four columns, *that the king* cut it with the scribe's knife and cast *it* into the fire that *was* on the hearth, until all the scroll was consumed in the fire that *was* on the hearth.
➤ 24 Yet they were not afraid, nor did they tear their garments, the king nor any of his servants who heard all these words.
25 Nevertheless Elnathan, Delaiah, and Gemariah implored the king not to burn the scroll; but he would not listen to them.
26 And the king commanded Jerahmeel the king's[a] son, Seraiah the son of Azriel, and Shelemiah the son of Abdeel, to seize Baruch the scribe and Jeremiah the prophet, but the LORD hid them.

Jeremiah Rewrites the Scroll

27 Now after the king had burned the scroll with the words which Baruch had written at the instruction of Jeremiah,[a] the word of the LORD came to Jeremiah, saying:
28 "Take yet another scroll, and write on it all the former words that were in the first scroll which Jehoiakim the king of Judah has burned.
29 "And you shall say to Jehoiakim king of Judah, 'Thus says the LORD: "You have burned this scroll, saying, 'Why have you written in it that the king of Babylon will certainly come and destroy this land, and cause man and beast to cease from here?'"
30 'Therefore thus says the LORD concerning Jehoiakim king of Judah: "He shall have no one to sit on the throne of David, and his dead body shall be cast out to the heat of the day and the frost of the night.
31 "I will punish him, his family, and his servants for their iniquity; and I will bring on them, on the inhabitants of Jerusalem, and on the men of Judah all the doom that I have pronounced against them; but they did not heed."'"
32 Then Jeremiah took another scroll and gave it to Baruch the scribe, the son of Neriah, who wrote on it at the instruction of Jeremiah[a] all the words of the book which Jehoiakim king of Judah had burned in the fire. And besides, there were added to them many similar words.

Zedekiah's Vain Hope

37 Now King Zedekiah the son of Josiah reigned instead of Coniah the son of Jehoiakim, whom Nebuchadnezzar king of Babylon made king in the land of Judah.
2 But neither he nor his servants nor the people of the land gave heed to the words of

36:17 [a]Literally *with his mouth* **36:26** [a]Hebrew *Hammelech*
36:27 [a]Literally *from Jeremiah's mouth* **36:32** [a]Literally *from Jeremiah's mouth*

LIFE LESSONS

➤ **36:24 — *Yet they were not afraid, nor did they tear their garments, the king nor any of his servants who heard all these words.***

Until God actually comes in judgment, it is possible to mock His Word and ridicule His servants, right up until the floodwaters arrive. It is possible to doubt His existence . . . until one's own comes into question.

Life Examples:

KING JEHOIAKIM

God's Word Stands

JER. 36:30, 31

The evil king Jehoiakim of Judah proves that while someone may physically destroy the pages of the Bible, no one may prevent the fulfillment of even a single word spoken by the mouth of God. His Word stands, regardless of what men may do.

When Jehoiakim heard words of divine judgment pronounced on him and his wicked kingdom, the king took the offending scroll and "cut it with the scribe's knife and cast it into the fire that was on the hearth, until all the scroll was consumed" (Jer. 36:23). He did so probably to show his contempt for the messenger and to demonstrate his lack of fear regarding the message.

God let the king's insolence stand for seven years. But when he refused to repent, the Lord fulfilled every threat that He had made regarding the king (36:30, 31). God always keeps His promises, whether for blessing or judgment.

See the Life Principles Index for further study:

3. God's Word is an immovable anchor in times of storm.

the LORD which He spoke by the prophet Jeremiah.
3 And Zedekiah the king sent Jehucal the
son of Shelemiah, and Zephaniah the son of
Maaseiah, the priest, to the prophet Jeremiah,
saying, "Pray now to the LORD our God for us."
4 Now Jeremiah was coming and going
among the people, for they had not *yet* put
him in prison.
5 Then Pharaoh's army came up from
Egypt; and when the Chaldeans who were be-
sieging Jerusalem heard news of them, they
departed from Jerusalem.
6 Then the word of the LORD came to the
prophet Jeremiah, saying,
7 "Thus says the LORD, the God of Israel,
'Thus you shall say to the king of Judah, who
sent you to Me to inquire of Me: "Behold,
Pharaoh's army which has come up to help
you will return to Egypt, to their own land.
8 "And the Chaldeans shall come back and
fight against this city, and take it and burn it
with fire."'
9 "Thus says the LORD: 'Do not deceive yourselves, saying, "The Chaldeans will surely depart from us," for they will not depart.
10 'For though you had defeated the whole
army of the Chaldeans who fight against you,
and there remained *only* wounded men
among them, they would rise up, every man in
his tent, and burn the city with fire.'"

Jeremiah Imprisoned

11 And it happened, when the army of the
Chaldeans left *the siege* of Jerusalem for fear
of Pharaoh's army,
12 that Jeremiah went out of Jerusalem to go
into the land of Benjamin to claim his property there among the people.
13 And when he was in the Gate of Benjamin,
a captain of the guard *was* there whose name
was Irijah the son of Shelemiah, the son of
Hananiah; and he seized Jeremiah the
prophet, saying, "You are defecting to the
Chaldeans!"
14 Then Jeremiah said, "False! I am not defecting to the Chaldeans." But he did not listen to him. So Irijah seized Jeremiah and
brought him to the princes.
15 Therefore the princes were angry with Jeremiah, and they struck him and put him in
prison in the house of Jonathan the scribe.
For they had made that the prison.
16 When Jeremiah entered the dungeon and
the cells, and Jeremiah had remained there
many days,
17 then Zedekiah the king sent and took him
out. The king asked him secretly in his house,
and said, "Is there *any* word from the LORD?"
And Jeremiah said, "There is." Then he said,
"You shall be delivered into the hand of the
king of Babylon!"
18 Moreover Jeremiah said to King Zedekiah, "What offense have I committed against
you, against your servants, or against this
people, that you have put me in prison?

LIFE LESSONS

➤ 37:16 — *Jeremiah entered the dungeon and the cells, and Jeremiah . . . remained there many days . . . .*

God never left Jeremiah, yet the prophet spent many lonely and discouraging days in His service. Jeremiah's obedience did not translate to instant and obvious blessing. It took faith to believe that God would remain faithful to the end.

19 "Where now *are* your prophets who prophesied to you, saying, 'The king of Babylon will
not come against you or against this land'?
20 "Therefore please hear now, O my lord
the king. Please, let my petition be accepted
before you, and do not make me return to
the house of Jonathan the scribe, lest I die
there."
21 Then Zedekiah the king commanded that
they should commit Jeremiah to the court of
the prison, and that they should give him
daily a piece of bread from the bakers' street,
until all the bread in the city was gone. Thus
Jeremiah remained in the court of the prison.

Jeremiah in the Dungeon

38 Now Shephatiah the son of Mattan,
Gedaliah the son of Pashhur, Jucal[a] the
son of Shelemiah, and Pashhur the son of
Malchiah heard the words that Jeremiah had
spoken to all the people, saying,
2 "Thus says the LORD: 'He who remains in
this city shall die by the sword, by famine, and
by pestilence; but he who goes over to the
Chaldeans shall live; his life shall be as a
prize to him, and he shall live.'[a]
3 "Thus says the LORD: 'This city shall
surely be given into the hand of the king of
Babylon's army, which shall take it.'"
4 Therefore the princes said to the king,
"Please, let this man be put to death, for thus
he weakens the hands of the men of war who
remain in this city, and the hands of all the
people, by speaking such words to them. For
this man does not seek the welfare of this
people, but their harm."
5 Then Zedekiah the king said, "Look, he *is*
in your hand. For the king can *do* nothing
against you."
➤ 6 So they took Jeremiah and cast him into
the dungeon of Malchiah the king's[a] son,
which *was* in the court of the prison, and they
let Jeremiah down with ropes. And in the dungeon *there was* no water, but mire. So Jeremiah sank in the mire.
➤ 7 Now Ebed-Melech the Ethiopian, one of
the eunuchs, who was in the king's house,
heard that they had put Jeremiah in the dungeon. When the king was sitting at the Gate of
Benjamin,
8 Ebed-Melech went out of the king's house
and spoke to the king, saying:
9 "My lord the king, these men have done
evil in all that they have done to Jeremiah the
prophet, whom they have cast into the dungeon, and he is likely to die from hunger in
the place where he is. For *there is* no more
bread in the city."
10 Then the king commanded Ebed-Melech
the Ethiopian, saying, "Take from here thirty
men with you, and lift Jeremiah the prophet
out of the dungeon before he dies."
11 So Ebed-Melech took the men with him
and went into the house of the king under the
treasury, and took from there old clothes and
old rags, and let them down by ropes into the
dungeon to Jeremiah.
12 Then Ebed-Melech the Ethiopian said to
Jeremiah, "Please put these old clothes and
rags under your armpits, under the ropes."
And Jeremiah did so.
13 So they pulled Jeremiah up with ropes
and lifted him out of the dungeon. And Jeremiah remained in the court of the prison.

Zedekiah's Fears and Jeremiah's Advice

14 Then Zedekiah the king sent and had Jeremiah the prophet brought to him at the third
entrance of the house of the LORD. And the
king said to Jeremiah, "I will ask you something. Hide nothing from me."
15 Jeremiah said to Zedekiah, "If I declare *it*
to you, will you not surely put me to death?
And if I give you advice, you will not listen to
me."
16 So Zedekiah the king swore secretly to
Jeremiah, saying, "*As* the LORD lives, who
made our very souls, I will not put you to
death, nor will I give you into the hand of
these men who seek your life."
17 Then Jeremiah said to Zedekiah, "Thus
says the LORD, the God of hosts, the God of Israel: 'If you surely surrender to the king of
Babylon's princes, then your soul shall live;
this city shall not be burned with fire, and you
and your house shall live.
18 'But if you do not surrender to the king of
Babylon's princes, then this city shall be
given into the hand of the Chaldeans; they
shall burn it with fire, and you shall not escape from their hand.'"
19 And Zedekiah the king said to Jeremiah,
"I am afraid of the Jews who have defected to

38:1 [a]Same as *Jehucal* (compare 37:3) **38:2** [a]Compare 21:9
38:6 [a]Hebrew *Hammelech*

LIFE LESSONS

➤ **38:6 — *So they took Jeremiah and cast him into the dungeon . . . and they let Jeremiah down with ropes . . . . So Jeremiah sank in the mire.***

Jeremiah went from a bad situation to an even worse situation. But like Joseph long before him (Gen. 37:24), even in the well, God was with the prophet to deliver him.

➤ **38:7–9 — *"My lord the king, these men have done evil in all that they have done to Jeremiah the prophet . . . ."***

With all Jeremiah's fellow Israelites around him, it took a foreigner, Ebed-Melech the Ethiopian, to give him the help he needed. God loves to provide help from unexpected sources, so that He gets the glory and not us.

the Chaldeans, lest they deliver me into their hand, and they abuse me."
20 But Jeremiah said, "They shall not deliver *you.* Please, obey the voice of the LORD which I speak to you. So it shall be well with you, and your soul shall live.
21 "But if you refuse to surrender, this *is* the word that the LORD has shown me:
22 'Now behold, all the women who are left in the king of Judah's house *shall be* surrendered to the king of Babylon's princes, and those *women* shall say:

"Your close friends have set upon you
And prevailed against you;
Your feet have sunk in the mire,
And they have turned away again."

23 'So they shall surrender all your wives and children to the Chaldeans. You shall not escape from their hand, but shall be taken by the hand of the king of Babylon. And you shall cause this city to be burned with fire.'"
24 Then Zedekiah said to Jeremiah, "Let no one know of these words, and you shall not die.
25 "But if the princes hear that I have talked with you, and they come to you and say to you, 'Declare to us now what you have said to the king, and also what the king said to you; do not hide *it* from us, and we will not put you to death,'
26 "then you shall say to them, 'I presented my request before the king, that he would not make me return to Jonathan's house to die there.'"
27 Then all the princes came to Jeremiah and asked him. And he told them according to all these words that the king had commanded. So they stopped speaking with him, for the conversation had not been heard.
28 Now Jeremiah remained in the court of the prison until the day that Jerusalem was taken. And he was *there* when Jerusalem was taken.

The Fall of Jerusalem

39 In the ninth year of Zedekiah king of Judah, in the tenth month, Nebuchadnezzar king of Babylon and all his army came against Jerusalem, and besieged it.
2 In the eleventh year of Zedekiah, in the fourth month, on the ninth *day* of the month, the city was penetrated.
3 Then all the princes of the king of Babylon came in and sat in the Middle Gate: Nergal-Sharezer, Samgar-Nebo, Sarsechim, Rab-saris,[a] Nergal-Sarezer, Rabmag,[b] with the rest of the princes of the king of Babylon.
4 So it was, when Zedekiah the king of Judah and all the men of war saw them, that they fled and went out of the city by night, by way of the king's garden, by the gate between the two walls. And he went out by way of the plain.[a]
5 But the Chaldean army pursued them and overtook Zedekiah in the plains of Jericho. And when they had captured him, they brought him up to Nebuchadnezzar king of Babylon, to Riblah in the land of Hamath, where he pronounced judgment on him.
6 Then the king of Babylon killed the sons of Zedekiah before his eyes in Riblah; the king of Babylon also killed all the nobles of Judah.
7 Moreover he put out Zedekiah's eyes, and bound him with bronze fetters to carry him off to Babylon.
8 And the Chaldeans burned the king's house and the houses of the people with fire, and broke down the walls of Jerusalem.
9 Then Nebuzaradan the captain of the guard carried away captive to Babylon the remnant of the people who remained in the city and those who defected to him, with the rest of the people who remained.
10 But Nebuzaradan the captain of the guard left in the land of Judah the poor people, who had nothing, and gave them vineyards and fields at the same time.

Jeremiah Goes Free

11 Now Nebuchadnezzar king of Babylon gave charge concerning Jeremiah to Nebuzaradan the captain of the guard, saying,
12 "Take him and look after him, and do him no harm; but do to him just as he says to you."
13 So Nebuzaradan the captain of the guard sent Nebushasban, Rabsaris, Nergal-Sharezer, Rabmag, and all the king of Babylon's chief officers;
14 then they sent *someone* to take Jeremiah from the court of the prison, and committed him to Gedaliah the son of Ahikam, the son of Shaphan, that he should take him home. So he dwelt among the people.

39:3 [a]A title, probably *Chief Officer;* also verse 13 [b]A title, probably *Troop Commander;* also verse 13 **39:4** [a]Or *the Arabah,* that is, the Jordan Valley

LIFE LESSONS

➤ 38:20 — *" . . . Please, obey the voice of the LORD which I speak to you. So it shall be well with you, and your soul shall live."*

Obedience is always the smart choice, the wise choice, the choice of blessing. Obedience always brings blessing, and we bless others when we remind them of this simple fact.

15 Meanwhile the word of the LORD had
come to Jeremiah while he was shut up in the
court of the prison, saying,
16 "Go and speak to Ebed-Melech the Ethiopian, saying, 'Thus says the LORD of hosts, the
God of Israel: "Behold, I will bring My words
upon this city for adversity and not for good,
and they shall be *performed* in that day before you.
17 "But I will deliver you in that day," says the
LORD, "and you shall not be given into the
hand of the men of whom you *are* afraid.
➤ 18 "For I will surely deliver you, and you
shall not fall by the sword; but your life shall
be as a prize to you, because you have put
your trust in Me," says the LORD.'"

Jeremiah with Gedaliah the Governor

40 The word that came to Jeremiah from
the LORD after Nebuzaradan the captain of the guard had let him go from Ramah,
when he had taken him bound in chains
among all who were carried away captive
from Jerusalem and Judah, who were carried
away captive to Babylon.
2 And the captain of the guard took Jeremiah and said to him: "The LORD your God
has pronounced this doom on this place.
3 "Now the LORD has brought *it,* and has
done just as He said. Because you *people* have
sinned against the LORD, and not obeyed His
voice, therefore this thing has come upon you.
4 "And now look, I free you this day from
the chains that *were* on your hand. If it seems
good to you to come with me to Babylon,
come, and I will look after you. But if it seems
wrong for you to come with me to Babylon,
remain here. See, all the land *is* before you;
wherever it seems good and convenient for
you to go, go there."
5 Now while Jeremiah had not yet gone
back, *Nebuzaradan said,* "Go back to
Gedaliah the son of Ahikam, the son of
Shaphan, whom the king of Babylon has
made governor over the cities of Judah, and
dwell with him among the people. Or go
wherever it seems convenient for you to go."
So the captain of the guard gave him rations
and a gift and let him go.
6 Then Jeremiah went to Gedaliah the son
of Ahikam, to Mizpah, and dwelt with him
among the people who were left in the land.
7 And when all the captains of the armies
who *were* in the fields, they and their men,
heard that the king of Babylon had made
Gedaliah the son of Ahikam governor in the
land, and had committed to him men, women,
children, and the poorest of the land who had
not been carried away captive to Babylon,
8 then they came to Gedaliah at Mizpah—
Ishmael the son of Nethaniah, Johanan and
Jonathan the sons of Kareah, Seraiah the son
of Tanhumeth, the sons of Ephai the Netophathite, and Jezaniah[a] the son of a Maachathite, they and their men.
9 And Gedaliah the son of Ahikam, the son
of Shaphan, took an oath before them and
their men, saying, "Do not be afraid to serve
the Chaldeans. Dwell in the land and serve
the king of Babylon, and it shall be well with
you.
10 "As for me, I will indeed dwell at Mizpah
and serve the Chaldeans who come to us. But
you, gather wine and summer fruit and oil,
put *them* in your vessels, and dwell in your
cities that you have taken."
11 Likewise, when all the Jews who *were* in
Moab, among the Ammonites, in Edom, and
who *were* in all the countries, heard that the
king of Babylon had left a remnant of Judah,
and that he had set over them Gedaliah the
son of Ahikam, the son of Shaphan,
12 then all the Jews returned out of all places
where they had been driven, and came to the
land of Judah, to Gedaliah at Mizpah, and
gathered wine and summer fruit in abundance.
13 Moreover Johanan the son of Kareah and
all the captains of the forces that *were* in the
fields came to Gedaliah at Mizpah,
14 and said to him, "Do you certainly know
that Baalis the king of the Ammonites has
sent Ishmael the son of Nethaniah to murder
you?" But Gedaliah the son of Ahikam did not
believe them.
15 Then Johanan the son of Kareah spoke secretly to Gedaliah in Mizpah, saying, "Let me
go, please, and I will kill Ishmael the son of
Nethaniah, and no one will know *it.* Why
should he murder you, so that all the Jews
who are gathered to you would be scattered,
and the remnant in Judah perish?"
16 But Gedaliah the son of Ahikam said to
Johanan the son of Kareah, "You shall not do
this thing, for you speak falsely concerning
Ishmael."

40:8 [a]Spelled *Jaazaniah* in 2 Kings 25:23

LIFE LESSONS

➤ 39:18 — *"For I will surely deliver you, and you shall not fall by the sword; but your life shall be as a prize to you, because you have put your trust in Me," says the LORD.*

Ebed-Melech the Ethiopian had no way of knowing that when he helped Jeremiah he was actually helping himself. He displayed his genuine faith by risking his life for the prophet, and God gave him his life as a reward.

Insurrection Against Gedaliah

41 Now it came to pass in the seventh
month *that* Ishmael the son of Nethaniah, the son of Elishama, of the royal family
and of the officers of the king, came with ten
men to Gedaliah the son of Ahikam, at Mizpah. And there they ate bread together in
Mizpah.
2 Then Ishmael the son of Nethaniah, and
the ten men who were with him, arose and
struck Gedaliah the son of Ahikam, the son of
Shaphan, with the sword, and killed him
whom the king of Babylon had made governor over the land.
3 Ishmael also struck down all the Jews
who were with him, *that is,* with Gedaliah at
Mizpah, and the Chaldeans who were found
there, the men of war.
4 And it happened, on the second day after
he had killed Gedaliah, when as yet no one
knew *it,*
5 that certain men came from Shechem,
from Shiloh, and from Samaria, eighty men
with their beards shaved and their clothes
torn, having cut themselves, with offerings
and incense in their hand, to bring *them* to
the house of the LORD.
6 Now Ishmael the son of Nethaniah went
out from Mizpah to meet them, weeping as he
went along; and it happened as he met them
that he said to them, "Come to Gedaliah the
son of Ahikam!"
7 So it was, when they came into the midst
of the city, that Ishmael the son of Nethaniah
killed them *and cast them* into the midst of a
pit, he and the men who were with him.
8 But ten men were found among them who
said to Ishmael, "Do not kill us, for we have
treasures of wheat, barley, oil, and honey in
the field." So he desisted and did not kill them
among their brethren.
9 Now the pit into which Ishmael had cast
all the dead bodies of the men whom he had
slain, because of Gedaliah, *was* the same one
Asa the king had made for fear of Baasha
king of Israel. Ishmael the son of Nethaniah
filled it with *the* slain.
10 Then Ishmael carried away captive all the
rest of the people who *were* in Mizpah, the
king's daughters and all the people who remained in Mizpah, whom Nebuzaradan the
captain of the guard had committed to
Gedaliah the son of Ahikam. And Ishmael the
son of Nethaniah carried them away captive
and departed to go over to the Ammonites.
11 But when Johanan the son of Kareah and
all the captains of the forces that *were* with
him heard of all the evil that Ishmael the son
of Nethaniah had done,
12 they took all the men and went to fight
with Ishmael the son of Nethaniah; and they
found him by the great pool that *is* in Gibeon.
13 So it was, when all the people who *were*
with Ishmael saw Johanan the son of Kareah,
and all the captains of the forces who *were*
with him, that they were glad.
14 Then all the people whom Ishmael had
carried away captive from Mizpah turned
around and came back, and went to Johanan
the son of Kareah.
15 But Ishmael the son of Nethaniah escaped
from Johanan with eight men and went to the
Ammonites.
16 Then Johanan the son of Kareah, and all
the captains of the forces that were with him,
took from Mizpah all the rest of the people
whom he had recovered from Ishmael the son
of Nethaniah after he had murdered Gedaliah
the son of Ahikam—the mighty men of war
and the women and the children and the eunuchs, whom he had brought back from Gibeon.
17 And they departed and dwelt in the habitation of Chimham, which is near Bethlehem,
as they went on their way to Egypt,
18 because of the Chaldeans; for they were
afraid of them, because Ishmael the son of
Nethaniah had murdered Gedaliah the son of
Ahikam, whom the king of Babylon had made
governor in the land.

The Flight to Egypt Forbidden

42 Now all the captains of the forces, Johanan the son of Kareah, Jezaniah the
son of Hoshaiah, and all the people, from the
least to the greatest, came near
2 and said to Jeremiah the prophet, "Please,
let our petition be acceptable to you, and pray
for us to the LORD your God, for all this remnant (since we are left *but* a few of many, as
you can see),
3 "that the LORD your God may show us the
way in which we should walk and the thing
we should do."

LIFE LESSONS

➤ 41:15 — *But Ishmael the son of Nethaniah escaped from Johanan with eight men and went to the Ammonites.*

In Hollywood, the bad guy usually "gets it" in the end. But the Bible is realistic; it admits that life doesn't always happen that way . . . at least, on this side of heaven. But no one escapes the final judgment.

➤ 42:2, 3 — *"Please . . . pray for us to the LORD your God . . . that the LORD your God may show us the way in which we should walk and the thing we should do."*

The men who said these things mouthed all the right words, but they had no intention of obeying God. They already had a plan; they merely wanted Jeremiah to bless it. Such prayers and plans God will never honor.

ANSWERS TO LIFE'S QUESTIONS

What role does obedience play in a mature Christian's life?

JER. 42:1–6

Those who know the greatness and goodness of God—and those who seek to identify fully with Christ's life—have a great passion to obey God.

Obedience is active, not passive. It is a joyful "living out" of what we know to be true, right, and good. It is to follow the Lord daily, saying and doing what Jesus would do if He were living in our place. Obedience is total submission to what God desires.

Our heavenly Father places a high value on obedience. He prefers it even to sacrifice, or the outward expression of worship (1 Sam. 15:22). In fact, our obedience is the ultimate expression of worship and service (Prov. 21:3).

A mature Christian expresses a passion to obey God in three general ways:

❶ ***A hunger to know the Bible.*** To know what God requires of us, we must know what He has commanded. God's commandments have not changed through the ages, nor have they been altered according to culture, custom, or technological advances. God's Word is absolute and enduring (see Josh. 24:24; Ps. 119:15, 16, 105, 106; 143:10).

❷ ***A passion to live in righteousness.*** Very simply, living in righteousness is doing what is "right" before the Lord. It is gladly keeping His commandments and statutes. It is turning way from sin and toward what is holy and acceptable to God (see Rom. 2:7–10; Ps. 97:10–12; Heb. 12:1, 2; Prov. 11:30; 12: 12, 13).

❸ ***A passion to receive daily direction from the Lord.*** To have a heart for obedience is to have a deep desire to receive daily direction from the Holy Spirit. To obey is to "walk in His ways," step by step—trusting that God is leading you and that He will correct you should you make an error. We must observe what God is doing around us and daily ask Him, "What is my role?" (see Ps. 25:4, 5; 141:3, 4, 8–10; Jer. 42:1–6).

Ultimately, these three desires work together. The more we explore God's Word, the greater our understanding of righteousness and how the Holy Spirit works in us. The more we trust the Holy Spirit, the more He reminds us of God's Word and leads us into righteousness. The more we desire to be "right" before the Father, the more we will want to read His Word and listen for His voice.

See the Life Principles Index for further study:
2. Obey God and leave all the consequences to Him.
11. God assumes full responsibility for our needs when we obey Him.
21. Obedience always brings blessing.

4 Then Jeremiah the prophet said to them,
"I have heard. Indeed, I will pray to the LORD
your God according to your words, and it
shall be, *that* whatever the LORD answers
you, I will declare *it* to you. I will keep nothing back from you."
5 So they said to Jeremiah, "Let the LORD be
a true and faithful witness between us, if we
do not do according to everything which the
LORD your God sends us by you.
6 "Whether *it is* pleasing or displeasing, we ➤
will obey the voice of the LORD our God to
whom we send you, that it may be well with
us when we obey the voice of the LORD our
God."
7 And it happened after ten days that the
word of the LORD came to Jeremiah.
8 Then he called Johanan the son of
Kareah, all the captains of the forces which
were with him, and all the people from the
least even to the greatest,
9 and said to them, "Thus says the LORD, the
God of Israel, to whom you sent me to present
your petition before Him:

LIFE LESSONS

➤ 42:6 — *"Whether it is pleasing or displeasing, we will obey the voice of the LORD our God to whom we send you, that it may be well with us when we obey the voice of the LORD our God."*

These men spoke truth, but harbored lies. It is not hard to play the part of regular churchgoer and hymn-singer, but God is after genuine faith, not well-rehearsed lines spoken convincingly.

10 'If you will still remain in this land, then I
will build you and not pull *you* down, and I
will plant you and not pluck *you* up. For I relent concerning the disaster that I have
brought upon you.
11 'Do not be afraid of the king of Babylon, of
whom you are afraid; do not be afraid of him,'
says the LORD, 'for I *am* with you, to save you
and deliver you from his hand.
12 'And I will show you mercy, that he may
have mercy on you and cause you to return to
your own land.'
13 "But if you say, 'We will not dwell in this
land,' disobeying the voice of the LORD your
God,
14 "saying, 'No, but we will go to the land of
Egypt where we shall see no war, nor hear the
sound of the trumpet, nor be hungry for
bread, and there we will dwell'—
15 "Then hear now the word of the LORD,
O remnant of Judah! Thus says the LORD of
hosts, the God of Israel: 'If you wholly set
your faces to enter Egypt, and go to dwell
there,
16 'then it shall be *that* the sword which you
feared shall overtake you there in the land of
Egypt; the famine of which you were afraid
shall follow close after you there *in* Egypt;
and there you shall die.
17 'So shall it be with all the men who set
their faces to go to Egypt to dwell there. They
shall die by the sword, by famine, and by
pestilence. And none of them shall remain or
escape from the disaster that I will bring upon
them.'
18 "For thus says the LORD of hosts, the God
of Israel: 'As My anger and My fury have been
poured out on the inhabitants of Jerusalem,
so will My fury be poured out on you when
you enter Egypt. And you shall be an oath, an
astonishment, a curse, and a reproach; and
you shall see this place no more.'
19 "The LORD has said concerning you, O
remnant of Judah, 'Do not go to Egypt!' Know
certainly that I have admonished you this
day.
➤ 20 "For you were hypocrites in your hearts
when you sent me to the LORD your God, saying, 'Pray for us to the LORD our God, and according to all that the LORD your God says, so
declare to us and we will do *it*.'
21 "And I have this day declared *it* to you, but
you have not obeyed the voice of the LORD
your God, or anything which He has sent you
by me.
22 "Now therefore, know certainly that you
shall die by the sword, by famine, and by
pestilence in the place where you desire to go
to dwell."

Jeremiah Taken to Egypt

43 Now it happened, when Jeremiah had
stopped speaking to all the people all
the words of the LORD their God, for which
the LORD their God had sent him to them, all
these words,
2 that Azariah the son of Hoshaiah, Johanan the son of Kareah, and all the proud
men spoke, saying to Jeremiah, "You speak
falsely! The LORD our God has not sent you to
say, 'Do not go to Egypt to dwell there.'
3 "But Baruch the son of Neriah has set you
against us, to deliver us into the hand of the
Chaldeans, that they may put us to death or
carry us away captive to Babylon."
4 So Johanan the son of Kareah, all the captains of the forces, and all the people would
not obey the voice of the LORD, to remain in
the land of Judah.
5 But Johanan the son of Kareah and all the ➤
captains of the forces took all the remnant of
Judah who had returned to dwell in the land
of Judah, from all nations where they had
been driven—
6 men, women, children, the king's daugh- ➤
ters, and every person whom Nebuzaradan
the captain of the guard had left with
Gedaliah the son of Ahikam, the son of
Shaphan, and Jeremiah the prophet and
Baruch the son of Neriah.
7 So they went to the land of Egypt, for they
did not obey the voice of the LORD. And they
went as far as Tahpanhes.
8 Then the word of the LORD came to Jeremiah in Tahpanhes, saying,
9 "Take large stones in your hand, and hide
them in the sight of the men of Judah, in the
clay in the brick courtyard which *is* at the entrance to Pharaoh's house in Tahpanhes;
10 "and say to them, 'Thus says the LORD of
hosts, the God of Israel: "Behold, I will send
and bring Nebuchadnezzar the king of Baby-

LIFE LESSONS

➤ **42:20 — *"For you were hypocrites in your hearts when you sent me to the LORD your God, saying, 'Pray for us to the LORD our God, and according to all that the LORD your God says, so declare to us and we will do it.'"***

Before these men ever acted on their deception, Jeremiah openly revealed their hearts. We may fool others, but we do not fool God. We can never manipulate Him into giving us what we want.

➤ **43:5, 6 — *But Johanan the son of Kareah and all the captains of the forces took all the remnant of Judah . . . and Jeremiah the prophet and Baruch the son of Neriah.***

Jeremiah told the remnant not to move to Egypt, but they disobeyed and moved there anyway—and took him along for the ride. He suffered for their disobedience. By faith—he had nothing else—Jeremiah expected God to vindicate him.

lon, My servant, and will set his throne above these stones that I have hidden. And he will spread his royal pavilion over them.

11 "When he comes, he shall strike the land of Egypt *and deliver* to death *those appointed* for death, and to captivity *those appointed* for captivity, and to the sword *those appointed* for the sword.

12 "I[a] will kindle a fire in the houses of the gods of Egypt, and he shall burn them and carry them away captive. And he shall array himself with the land of Egypt, as a shepherd puts on his garment, and he shall go out from there in peace.

13 "He shall also break the *sacred* pillars of Beth Shemesh[a] that *are* in the land of Egypt; and the houses of the gods of the Egyptians he shall burn with fire."'"

Israelites Will Be Punished in Egypt

44 The word that came to Jeremiah concerning all the Jews who dwell in the land of Egypt, who dwell at Migdol, at Tahpanhes, at Noph,[a] and in the country of Pathros, saying,

2 "Thus says the LORD of hosts, the God of Israel: 'You have seen all the calamity that I have brought on Jerusalem and on all the cities of Judah; and behold, this day they *are* a desolation, and no one dwells in them,

3 'because of their wickedness which they have committed to provoke Me to anger, in that they went to burn incense *and* to serve other gods whom they did not know, they nor you nor your fathers.

➤ 4 'However I have sent to you all My servants the prophets, rising early and sending *them,* saying, "Oh, do not do this abominable thing that I hate!"

5 'But they did not listen or incline their ear to turn from their wickedness, to burn no incense to other gods.

6 'So My fury and My anger were poured out and kindled in the cities of Judah and in the streets of Jerusalem; and they are wasted *and* desolate, as it is this day.'

7 "Now therefore, thus says the LORD, the God of hosts, the God of Israel: 'Why do you commit *this* great evil against yourselves, to cut off from you man and woman, child and infant, out of Judah, leaving none to remain,

8 'in that you provoke Me to wrath with the works of your hands, burning incense to other gods in the land of Egypt where you have gone to dwell, that you may cut yourselves off and be a curse and a reproach among all the nations of the earth?

9 'Have you forgotten the wickedness of your fathers, the wickedness of the kings of Judah, the wickedness of their wives, your own wickedness, and the wickedness of your wives, which they committed in the land of Judah and in the streets of Jerusalem?

10 'They have not been humbled, to this day, nor have they feared; they have not walked in My law or in My statutes that I set before you and your fathers.'

11 "Therefore thus says the LORD of hosts, the God of Israel: 'Behold, I will set My face against you for catastrophe and for cutting off all Judah.

12 'And I will take the remnant of Judah who have set their faces to go into the land of Egypt to dwell there, and they shall all be consumed *and* fall in the land of Egypt. They shall be consumed by the sword *and* by famine. They shall die, from the least to the greatest, by the sword and by famine; and they shall be an oath, an astonishment, a curse and a reproach!

13 'For I will punish those who dwell in the land of Egypt, as I have punished Jerusalem, by the sword, by famine, and by pestilence,

14 'so that none of the remnant of Judah who have gone into the land of Egypt to dwell there shall escape or survive, lest they return to the land of Judah, to which they desire to return and dwell. For none shall return except those who escape.'"

15 Then all the men who knew that their wives had burned incense to other gods, with all the women who stood by, a great multitude, and all the people who dwelt in the land of Egypt, in Pathros, answered Jeremiah, saying:

16 "*As for* the word that you have spoken to us in the name of the LORD, we will not listen to you!

17 "But we will certainly do whatever has gone out of our own mouth, to burn incense to the queen of heaven and pour out drink offerings to her, as we have done, we and our fathers, our kings and our princes, in the cities of Judah and in the streets of Jerusalem. For *then* we had plenty of food, were well-off, and saw no trouble.

43:12 [a]Following Masoretic Text and Targum; Septuagint, Syriac, and Vulgate read *He.* **43:13** [a]Literally *House of the Sun,* ancient On; later called Heliopolis **44:1** [a]That is, ancient Memphis

LIFE LESSONS

➤ 44:4 — *" . . . I have sent to you all My servants the prophets, rising early and sending them, saying, 'Oh, do not do this abominable thing that I hate!'"*

We never have to wonder whether something we're considering might offend or anger God. He goes out of His way to make His will clear to us. Will we listen carefully for what He says?

➤ 18 "But since we stopped burning incense to
the queen of heaven and pouring out drink offerings to her, we have lacked everything and
have been consumed by the sword and by
famine."
19 *The women also said,* "And when we
burned incense to the queen of heaven and
poured out drink offerings to her, did we
make cakes for her, to worship her, and pour
out drink offerings to her without our husbands' *permission?*"
20 Then Jeremiah spoke to all the people—
the men, the women, and all the people who
had given him *that* answer—saying:
21 "The incense that you burned in the cities
of Judah and in the streets of Jerusalem, you
and your fathers, your kings and your
princes, and the people of the land, did not
the LORD remember them, and did it *not* come
into His mind?
22 "So the LORD could no longer bear *it,* because of the evil of your doings *and* because
of the abominations which you committed.
Therefore your land is a desolation, an astonishment, a curse, and without an inhabitant,
as *it is* this day.
23 "Because you have burned incense and
because you have sinned against the LORD,
and have not obeyed the voice of the LORD or
walked in His law, in His statutes or in His
testimonies, therefore this calamity has happened to you, as *at* this day."
24 Moreover Jeremiah said to all the people
and to all the women, "Hear the word of the
LORD, all Judah who *are* in the land of Egypt!
25 "Thus says the LORD of hosts, the God of
Israel, saying: 'You and your wives have spoken with your mouths and fulfilled with your
hands, saying, "We will surely keep our vows
that we have made, to burn incense to the
queen of heaven and pour out drink offerings
to her." You will surely keep your vows and
perform your vows!'
26 "Therefore hear the word of the LORD, all
Judah who dwell in the land of Egypt: 'Behold, I have sworn by My great name,' says
the LORD, 'that My name shall no more be
named in the mouth of any man of Judah in
all the land of Egypt, saying, "The Lord GOD
lives."
27 'Behold, I will watch over them for adversity and not for good. And all the men of Judah who *are* in the land of Egypt shall be
consumed by the sword and by famine, until
there is an end to them.
28 'Yet a small number who escape the sword ◄
shall return from the land of Egypt to the land
of Judah; and all the remnant of Judah, who
have gone to the land of Egypt to dwell there,
shall know whose words will stand, Mine or
theirs.
29 'And this *shall be* a sign to you,' says the
LORD, 'that I will punish you in this place, that
you may know that My words will surely
stand against you for adversity.'
30 "Thus says the LORD: 'Behold, I will give
Pharaoh Hophra king of Egypt into the hand
of his enemies and into the hand of those who
seek his life, as I gave Zedekiah king of Judah
into the hand of Nebuchadnezzar king of
Babylon, his enemy who sought his life.'"

Assurance to Baruch

45 The word that Jeremiah the prophet
spoke to Baruch the son of Neriah,
when he had written these words in a book at
the instruction of Jeremiah,[a] in the fourth
year of Jehoiakim the son of Josiah, king of
Judah, saying,
2 "Thus says the LORD, the God of Israel, to
you, O Baruch:
3 'You said, "Woe is me now! For the LORD
has added grief to my sorrow. I fainted in my
sighing, and I find no rest."'
4 "Thus you shall say to him, 'Thus says the
LORD: "Behold, what I have built I will break
down, and what I have planted I will pluck up,
that is, this whole land.
5 "And do you seek great things for yourself? ◄

45:1 [a]Literally *from Jeremiah's mouth*

LIFE LESSONS

➤ **44:18 — *"But since we stopped burning incense to the queen of heaven and pouring out drink offerings to her, we have lacked everything and have been consumed by the sword and by famine."***

The rebels of Jeremiah's day saw profit in rebellion and poverty in righteousness. So they chose rebellion—and suffered ultimate poverty. Only living by the long view gives us the perspective we need to help us thrive.

➤ **44:28 — *"Yet a small number who escape the sword shall . . . know whose words will stand, Mine or theirs."***

It's as if God says to us, "Do you think you know better than Me? OK, then go ahead. Do the thing I forbid. But we'll see whose words end up proving true, Mine or yours." *Never* bet against the Word of God.

➤ **45:5 — *"'And do you seek great things for yourself? Do not seek them; for behold, I will bring adversity on all flesh,' says the LORD. 'But I will give your life to you as a prize in all places, wherever you go.'"***

As He did with Ebed-Melech, God promised to spare the life of Jeremiah's servant, Baruch—but Baruch wanted more. We must remember that God has a distinct plan for each of us, and our best is always God's best for us.

Life Examples:

BARUCH

Given His Life as a Prize

JER. 45:1–5

Baruch served Jeremiah well through much of the prophet's difficult ministry. When Jeremiah instructed him to record his frightful words and read them to the people, Baruch did so (Jer. 36:4–19). When the king destroyed the scroll and threatened to harm Baruch, the scribe obeyed Jeremiah and replaced the ruined scroll (36:23–26, 32). And when the people mistakenly blamed Baruch for inspiring the awful threats of Jeremiah's prophecies, he bore their anger and accepted the same fate as the prophet (43:3–7).

God saw Baruch's loyalty and faithfulness and would not allow his obedience to go unrewarded. Yet He did not promise the scribe an easy life. "And do you seek great things for yourself?" the Lord asked Baruch. "Do not seek them . . . . But I will give your life to you as a prize in all places, wherever you go" (45:5).

See the Life Principles Index for further study:

21. Obedience always brings blessing.

2. Obey God and leave all the consequences to Him.

Do not seek *them;* for behold, I will bring adversity on all flesh," says the LORD. "But I will give your life to you as a prize in all places, wherever you go."'"

Judgment on Egypt

46 The word of the LORD which came to Jeremiah the prophet against the nations.

2 Against Egypt.

Concerning the army of Pharaoh Necho, king of Egypt, which was by the River Euphrates in Carchemish, and which Nebuchadnezzar king of Babylon defeated in the fourth year of Jehoiakim the son of Josiah, king of Judah:

3 "Order the buckler and shield,
And draw near to battle!
4 Harness the horses,
And mount up, you horsemen!
Stand forth with *your* helmets,
Polish the spears,
Put on the armor!
5 Why have I seen them dismayed *and* turned back?
Their mighty ones are beaten down;
They have speedily fled,
And did not look back,
For fear *was* all around," says the LORD.
6 "Do not let the swift flee away,
Nor the mighty man escape;
They will stumble and fall
Toward the north, by the River Euphrates.

7 "Who *is* this coming up like a flood,
Whose waters move like the rivers?
8 Egypt rises up like a flood,
And *its* waters move like the rivers;
And he says, 'I will go up *and* cover the earth,
I will destroy the city and its inhabitants.'
9 Come up, O horses, and rage, O chariots!
And let the mighty men come forth:
The Ethiopians and the Libyans who handle the shield,
And the Lydians who handle *and* bend the bow.
10 For this *is* the day of the Lord GOD of hosts,
A day of vengeance,
That He may avenge Himself on His adversaries.
The sword shall devour;
It shall be satiated and made drunk with their blood;
For the Lord GOD of hosts has a sacrifice
In the north country by the River Euphrates.

11 "Go up to Gilead and take balm,
O virgin, the daughter of Egypt;
In vain you will use many medicines;
You shall not be cured.
12 The nations have heard of your shame,
And your cry has filled the land;
For the mighty man has stumbled against the mighty;
They both have fallen together."

Babylonia Will Strike Egypt

13 The word that the LORD spoke to Jeremiah the prophet, how Nebuchadnezzar king of Babylon would come *and* strike the land of Egypt.

14 "Declare in Egypt, and proclaim in Migdol;
Proclaim in Noph[a] and in Tahpanhes;
Say, 'Stand fast and prepare yourselves,
For the sword devours all around you.'
15 Why are your valiant *men* swept away?
They did not stand
Because the LORD drove them away.

46:14 [a]That is, ancient Memphis

16 He made many fall;
Yes, one fell upon another.
And they said, 'Arise!
Let us go back to our own people
And to the land of our nativity
From the oppressing sword.'
17 They cried there,
'Pharaoh, king of Egypt, *is but* a noise.
He has passed by the appointed time!'

18 "*As* I live," says the King,
Whose name *is* the LORD of hosts,
"Surely as Tabor *is* among the mountains
And as Carmel by the sea, *so* he shall come.
19 O you daughter dwelling in Egypt,
Prepare yourself to go into captivity!
For Noph[a] shall be waste and desolate,
without inhabitant.

20 "Egypt *is* a very pretty heifer,
But destruction comes, it comes from the north.
21 Also her mercenaries are in her midst
like fat bulls,
For they also are turned back,
They have fled away together.
They did not stand,
For the day of their calamity had come
upon them,
The time of their punishment.
22 Her noise shall go like a serpent,
For they shall march with an army
And come against her with axes,
Like those who chop wood.

23 "They shall cut down her forest," says the LORD,
"Though it cannot be searched,
Because they *are* innumerable,
And more numerous than grasshoppers.
24 The daughter of Egypt shall be ashamed;
She shall be delivered into the hand
Of the people of the north."

25 The LORD of hosts, the God of Israel, says:
"Behold, I will bring punishment on Amon[a] of
No,[b] and Pharaoh and Egypt, with their gods
and their kings—Pharaoh and those who
trust in him.
26 "And I will deliver them into the hand of
those who seek their lives, into the hand of
Nebuchadnezzar king of Babylon and the
hand of his servants. Afterward it shall be inhabited as in the days of old," says the LORD.

God Will Preserve Israel

27 "But do not fear, O My servant Jacob,
And do not be dismayed, O Israel!
For behold, I will save you from afar,
And your offspring from the land of their
captivity;
Jacob shall return, have rest and be at
ease;
No one shall make *him* afraid.
28 Do not fear, O Jacob My servant," says
the LORD,
"For I *am* with you;
For I will make a complete end of all the
nations
To which I have driven you,
But I will not make a complete end of
you.
I will rightly correct you,
For I will not leave you wholly
unpunished."

Judgment on Philistia

47 The word of the LORD that came to Jeremiah the prophet against the Philistines, before Pharaoh attacked Gaza.
2 Thus says the LORD:

"Behold, waters rise out of the north,
And shall be an overflowing flood;
They shall overflow the land and all that
is in it,
The city and those who dwell within;
Then the men shall cry,
And all the inhabitants of the land shall
wail.
3 At the noise of the stamping hooves of
his strong horses,
At the rushing of his chariots,
At the rumbling of his wheels,
The fathers will not look back for *their*
children,
Lacking courage,
4 Because of the day that comes to plunder
all the Philistines,
To cut off from Tyre and Sidon every
helper who remains;
For the LORD shall plunder the
Philistines,
The remnant of the country of Caphtor.
5 Baldness has come upon Gaza,
Ashkelon is cut off
With the remnant of their valley.
How long will you cut yourself?

6 "O you sword of the LORD,
How long until you are quiet?

46:19 [a]That is, ancient Memphis **46:25** [a]A sun god [b]That is, ancient Thebes

LIFE LESSONS

➤ 46:28 — *"Do not fear, O Jacob My servant," says the LORD, "For I am with you . . . ."*

If God fills our heart, then fear has no place to make a home there. The storms of life may whistle and howl around us, but when God is with us, we have no reason to fear their threats.

Put yourself up into your scabbard,
Rest and be still!
7 How can it be quiet,
Seeing the LORD has given it a charge
Against Ashkelon and against the seashore?
There He has appointed it."

Judgment on Moab

48 Against Moab.
Thus says the LORD of hosts, the God of Israel:
"Woe to Nebo!
For it is plundered,
Kirjathaim is shamed *and* taken;
The high stronghold[a] is shamed and dismayed—
2 No more praise of Moab.
In Heshbon they have devised evil against her:
'Come, and let us cut her off as a nation.'
You also shall be cut down, O Madmen![a]
The sword shall pursue you;
3 A voice of crying *shall be* from Horonaim:
'Plundering and great destruction!'
4 "Moab is destroyed;
Her little ones have caused a cry to be heard;[a]
5 For in the Ascent of Luhith they ascend with continual weeping;
For in the descent of Horonaim the enemies have heard a cry of destruction.

6 "Flee, save your lives!
And be like the juniper[a] in the wilderness.
7 For because you have trusted in your works and your treasures,
You also shall be taken.
And Chemosh shall go forth into captivity,
His priests and his princes together.
8 And the plunderer shall come against every city;
No one shall escape.
The valley also shall perish,
And the plain shall be destroyed,
As the LORD has spoken.

9 "Give wings to Moab,
That she may flee and get away;
For her cities shall be desolate,
Without any to dwell in them.
10 Cursed *is* he who does the work of the LORD deceitfully,
And cursed *is* he who keeps back his sword from blood.

11 "Moab has been at ease from his[a] youth;
He has settled on his dregs,
And has not been emptied from vessel to vessel,
Nor has he gone into captivity.
Therefore his taste remained in him,
And his scent has not changed.

12 "Therefore behold, the days are coming," says the LORD,
"That I shall send him wine-workers
Who will tip him over
And empty his vessels
And break the bottles.
13 Moab shall be ashamed of Chemosh,
As the house of Israel was ashamed of Bethel, their confidence.

14 "How can you say, 'We *are* mighty
And strong men for the war'?
15 Moab is plundered and gone up *from* her cities;
Her chosen young men have gone down to the slaughter," says the King,
Whose name *is* the LORD of hosts.

16 "The calamity of Moab *is* near at hand,
And his affliction comes quickly.
17 Bemoan him, all you who are around him;
And all you who know his name,
Say, 'How the strong staff is broken,
The beautiful rod!'

18 "O daughter inhabiting Dibon,
Come down from *your* glory,
And sit in thirst;
For the plunderer of Moab has come against you,
He has destroyed your strongholds.
19 O inhabitant of Aroer,
Stand by the way and watch;
Ask him who flees
And her who escapes;
Say, 'What has happened?'
20 Moab is shamed, for he is broken down.
Wail and cry!
Tell it in Arnon, that Moab is plundered.

21 "And judgment has come on the plain country:
On Holon and Jahzah and Mephaath,
22 On Dibon and Nebo and Beth Diblathaim,
23 On Kirjathaim and Beth Gamul and Beth Meon,
24 On Kerioth and Bozrah,
On all the cities of the land of Moab,
Far or near.
25 The horn of Moab is cut off,
And his arm is broken," says the LORD.

26 "Make him drunk,
Because he exalted *himself* against the LORD.

48:1 [a]Hebrew *Misgab* **48:2** [a]A city of Moab **48:4** [a]Following Masoretic Text, Targum, and Vulgate; Septuagint reads *Proclaim it in Zoar*. **48:6** [a]Or *Aroer,* a city of Moab **48:11** [a]The Hebrew uses masculine and feminine pronouns interchangeably in this chapter.

Moab shall wallow in his vomit,
And he shall also be in derision.
27 For was not Israel a derision to you?
Was he found among thieves?
For whenever you speak of him,
You shake *your head in scorn.*
28 You who dwell in Moab,
Leave the cities and dwell in the rock,
And be like the dove *which* makes her nest
In the sides of the cave's mouth.

29"We have heard the pride of Moab
(He *is* exceedingly proud),
Of his loftiness and arrogance and pride,
And of the haughtiness of his heart."

30"I know his wrath," says the LORD,
"But it *is* not right;
His lies have made nothing right.
31 Therefore I will wail for Moab,
And I will cry out for all Moab;
I[a] will mourn for the men of Kir Heres.
32 O vine of Sibmah! I will weep for you
with the weeping of Jazer.
Your plants have gone over the sea,
They reach to the sea of Jazer.
The plunderer has fallen on your summer
fruit and your vintage.
33 Joy and gladness are taken
From the plentiful field
And from the land of Moab;
I have caused wine to fail from the
winepresses;
No one will tread with joyous shouting—
Not joyous shouting!

34"From the cry of Heshbon to Elealeh and
to Jahaz
They have uttered their voice,
From Zoar to Horonaim,
Like a three-year-old heifer;[a]
For the waters of Nimrim also shall be
desolate.

35"Moreover," says the LORD,
"I will cause to cease in Moab
The one who offers *sacrifices* in the high
places
And burns incense to his gods.
36 Therefore My heart shall wail like flutes
for Moab,
And like flutes My heart shall wail
For the men of Kir Heres.
Therefore the riches they have acquired
have perished.

37"For every head *shall be* bald, and every
beard clipped;
On all the hands *shall be* cuts, and on the
loins sackcloth—
38 A general lamentation
On all the housetops of Moab,
And in its streets;
For I have broken Moab like a vessel in
which *is* no pleasure," says the LORD.
39"They shall wail:
'How she is broken down!
How Moab has turned her back with
shame!'
So Moab shall be a derision
And a dismay to all those about her."

40 For thus says the LORD:

"Behold, one shall fly like an eagle,
And spread his wings over Moab.
41 Kerioth is taken,
And the strongholds are surprised;
The mighty men's hearts in Moab on that
day shall be
Like the heart of a woman in birth pangs.
42 And Moab shall be destroyed as a people, ≺
Because he exalted *himself* against the
LORD.
43 Fear and the pit and the snare *shall be*
upon you,
O inhabitant of Moab," says the LORD.
44"He who flees from the fear shall fall into
the pit,
And he who gets out of the pit shall be
caught in the snare.
For upon Moab, upon it I will bring
The year of their punishment," says the
LORD.

45"Those who fled stood under the shadow
of Heshbon
Because of exhaustion.
But a fire shall come out of Heshbon,
A flame from the midst of Sihon,
And shall devour the brow of Moab,
The crown of the head of the sons of tumult.
46 Woe to you, O Moab!
The people of Chemosh perish;
For your sons have been taken captive,
And your daughters captive.

47"Yet I will bring back the captives of Moab
In the latter days," says the LORD.

Thus far *is* the judgment of Moab.

48:31 [a]Following Dead Sea Scrolls, Septuagint, and Vulgate; Masoretic Text reads *He.* **48:34** [a]Or *The Third Eglath,* an unknown city (compare Isaiah 15:5)

LIFE LESSONS

➤ 48:42 — *"And Moab shall be destroyed as a people, because he exalted himself against the LORD."*

God *always* judges pride. Always. Whether He finds the arrogance and pride in the heart of an angel (Satan), a man (Nebuchadnezzar), or a nation (Moab), He will always judge it. He has no rivals.

Judgment on Ammon

49 Against the Ammonites.
Thus says the LORD:
"Has Israel no sons?
Has he no heir?
Why *then* does Milcom[a] inherit Gad,
And his people dwell in its cities?
2 Therefore behold, the days are coming,"
says the LORD,
"That I will cause to be heard an alarm of war
In Rabbah of the Ammonites;
It shall be a desolate mound,
And her villages shall be burned with fire.
Then Israel shall take possession of his inheritance," says the LORD.
3 "Wail, O Heshbon, for Ai is plundered!
Cry, you daughters of Rabbah,
Gird yourselves with sackcloth!
Lament and run to and fro by the walls;
For Milcom shall go into captivity
With his priests and his princes together.
4 Why do you boast in the valleys,
Your flowing valley, O backsliding daughter?
Who trusted in her treasures, *saying,*
'Who will come against me?'
5 Behold, I will bring fear upon you,"
Says the Lord GOD of hosts,
"From all those who are around you;
You shall be driven out, everyone headlong,
And no one will gather those who wander off.
6 But afterward I will bring back
The captives of the people of Ammon,"
says the LORD.

Judgment on Edom

7 Against Edom.
Thus says the LORD of hosts:
"*Is* wisdom no more in Teman?
Has counsel perished from the prudent?
Has their wisdom vanished?
8 Flee, turn back, dwell in the depths, O inhabitants of Dedan!
For I will bring the calamity of Esau upon him,
The time *that* I will punish him.
9 If grape-gatherers came to you,
Would they not leave *some* gleaning grapes?
If thieves by night,
Would they not destroy until they have enough?
10 But I have made Esau bare;
I have uncovered his secret places,[a]
And he shall not be able to hide himself.
His descendants are plundered,
His brethren and his neighbors,
And he *is* no more.
11 Leave your fatherless children,
I will preserve *them* alive;
And let your widows trust in Me."

12 For thus says the LORD: "Behold, those
whose judgment *was* not to drink of the cup
have assuredly drunk. And *are* you the one
who will altogether go unpunished? You shall
not go unpunished, but you shall surely drink
of it.
13 "For I have sworn by Myself," says the
LORD, "that Bozrah shall become a desolation,
a reproach, a waste, and a curse. And all its
cities shall be perpetual wastes."

14 I have heard a message from the LORD,
And an ambassador has been sent to the nations:
"Gather together, come against her,
And rise up to battle!

15 "For indeed, I will make you small among nations,
Despised among men.
16 Your fierceness has deceived you,
The pride of your heart,
O you who dwell in the clefts of the rock,
Who hold the height of the hill!
Though you make your nest as high as the eagle,
I will bring you down from there," says the LORD.[a]
17 "Edom also shall be an astonishment;
Everyone who goes by it will be astonished
And will hiss at all its plagues.
18 As in the overthrow of Sodom and Gomorrah
And their neighbors," says the LORD,
"No one shall remain there,
Nor shall a son of man dwell in it.

19 "Behold, he shall come up like a lion from the floodplain[a] of the Jordan

49:1 [a]Hebrew *Malcam,* literally *their king,* a god of the Ammonites; also called *Molech* (compare verse 3)
49:10 [a]Compare Obadiah 5, 6 **49:16** [a]Compare Obadiah 3, 4
49:19 [a]Or *thicket*

LIFE LESSONS

➢ 49:19 — *"For who is like Me? Who will arraign Me? And who is that shepherd who will withstand Me?"*

No one and nothing is like God. He has no peers, no equals, no judges and no accusers. No one will prevent Him from accomplishing exactly what He plans to accomplish, when He wants to accomplish it.

Against the dwelling place of the strong;
But I will suddenly make him run away from her.
And who *is* a chosen *man that* I may appoint over her?
For who *is* like Me?
Who will arraign Me?
And who *is* that shepherd
Who will withstand Me?"

20 Therefore hear the counsel of the LORD that He has taken against Edom,
And His purposes that He has proposed against the inhabitants of Teman:
Surely the least of the flock shall draw them out;
Surely He shall make their dwelling places desolate with them.
21 The earth shakes at the noise of their fall;
At the cry its noise is heard at the Red Sea.
22 Behold, He shall come up and fly like the eagle,
And spread His wings over Bozrah;
The heart of the mighty men of Edom in that day shall be
Like the heart of a woman in birth pangs.

Judgment on Damascus

23 Against Damascus.

"Hamath and Arpad are shamed,
For they have heard bad news.
They are fainthearted;
There is trouble on the sea;
It cannot be quiet.
24 Damascus has grown feeble;
She turns to flee,
And fear has seized *her.*
Anguish and sorrows have taken her like a woman in labor.
25 Why is the city of praise not deserted, the city of My joy?
26 Therefore her young men shall fall in her streets,
And all the men of war shall be cut off in that day," says the LORD of hosts.
27 "I will kindle a fire in the wall of Damascus,
And it shall consume the palaces of Ben-Hadad."[a]

Judgment on Kedar and Hazor

28 Against Kedar and against the kingdoms of Hazor, which Nebuchadnezzar king of Babylon shall strike.
Thus says the LORD:

"Arise, go up to Kedar,
And devastate the men of the East!
29 Their tents and their flocks they shall take away.
They shall take for themselves their curtains,
All their vessels and their camels;
And they shall cry out to them,
'Fear *is* on every side!'
30 "Flee, get far away! Dwell in the depths,
O inhabitants of Hazor!" says the LORD.
"For Nebuchadnezzar king of Babylon has taken counsel against you,
And has conceived a plan against you.
31 "Arise, go up to the wealthy nation that dwells securely," says the LORD,
"Which has neither gates nor bars,
Dwelling alone.
32 Their camels shall be for booty,
And the multitude of their cattle for plunder.
I will scatter to all winds those in the farthest corners,
And I will bring their calamity from all its sides," says the LORD.
33 "Hazor shall be a dwelling for jackals, a desolation forever;
No one shall reside there,
Nor son of man dwell in it."

Judgment on Elam

34 The word of the LORD that came to Jeremiah the prophet against Elam, in the beginning of the reign of Zedekiah king of Judah,
saying,
35 "Thus says the LORD of hosts:

'Behold, I will break the bow of Elam,
The foremost of their might.
36 Against Elam I will bring the four winds
From the four quarters of heaven,
And scatter them toward all those winds;
There shall be no nations where the outcasts of Elam will not go.
37 For I will cause Elam to be dismayed before their enemies
And before those who seek their life.
I will bring disaster upon them,
My fierce anger,' says the LORD;
'And I will send the sword after them
Until I have consumed them.
38 I will set My throne in Elam,
And will destroy from there the king and the princes,' says the LORD.

39 'But it shall come to pass in the latter days:
I will bring back the captives of Elam,'
says the LORD."

Judgment on Babylon and Babylonia

50 The word that the LORD spoke against Babylon *and* against the land of the Chaldeans by Jeremiah the prophet.

2 "Declare among the nations,
Proclaim, and set up a standard;
Proclaim—do not conceal *it*—
Say, 'Babylon is taken, Bel is shamed.

49:27 [a]Compare Amos 1:4

Merodach[a] is broken in pieces;
Her idols are humiliated,
Her images are broken in pieces.'
3 For out of the north a nation comes up against her,
Which shall make her land desolate,
And no one shall dwell therein.
They shall move, they shall depart,
Both man and beast.

4 "In those days and in that time," says the LORD,
"The children of Israel shall come,
They and the children of Judah together;
With continual weeping they shall come,
And seek the LORD their God.
5 They shall ask the way to Zion,
With their faces toward it, *saying*,
'Come and let us join ourselves to the LORD
In a perpetual covenant
That will not be forgotten.'

6 "My people have been lost sheep.
Their shepherds have led them astray;
They have turned them away *on* the mountains.
They have gone from mountain to hill;
They have forgotten their resting place.
7 All who found them have devoured them;
And their adversaries said, 'We have not offended,
Because they have sinned against the LORD, the habitation of justice,
The LORD, the hope of their fathers.'
8 "Move from the midst of Babylon,
Go out of the land of the Chaldeans;
And be like the rams before the flocks.
9 For behold, I will raise and cause to come up against Babylon
An assembly of great nations from the north country,
And they shall array themselves against her;
From there she shall be captured.
Their arrows *shall be* like *those* of an expert warrior;[a]
None shall return in vain.
10 And Chaldea shall become plunder;
All who plunder her shall be satisfied," says the LORD.

11 "Because you were glad, because you rejoiced,
You destroyers of My heritage,
Because you have grown fat like a heifer threshing grain,
And you bellow like bulls,
12 Your mother shall be deeply ashamed;
She who bore you shall be ashamed.
Behold, the least of the nations *shall be* a wilderness,
A dry land and a desert.
13 Because of the wrath of the LORD
She shall not be inhabited,
But she shall be wholly desolate.
Everyone who goes by Babylon shall be horrified
And hiss at all her plagues.

14 "Put yourselves in array against Babylon all around,
All you who bend the bow;
Shoot at her, spare no arrows,
For she has sinned against the LORD.
15 Shout against her all around;
She has given her hand,
Her foundations have fallen,
Her walls are thrown down;
For it *is* the vengeance of the LORD.
Take vengeance on her.
As she has done, so do to her.
16 Cut off the sower from Babylon,
And him who handles the sickle at harvest time.
For fear of the oppressing sword
Everyone shall turn to his own people,
And everyone shall flee to his own land.

17 "Israel *is* like scattered sheep;
The lions have driven *him* away.
First the king of Assyria devoured him;
Now at last this Nebuchadnezzar king of Babylon has broken his bones."

18 Therefore thus says the LORD of hosts, the God of Israel:

"Behold, I will punish the king of Babylon and his land,
As I have punished the king of Assyria.
19 But I will bring back Israel to his home,
And he shall feed on Carmel and Bashan;
His soul shall be satisfied on Mount Ephraim and Gilead.
20 In those days and in that time," says the LORD,
"The iniquity of Israel shall be sought, but *there shall be* none;
And the sins of Judah, but they shall not be found;
For I will pardon those whom I preserve.

21 "Go up against the land of Merathaim, against it,
And against the inhabitants of Pekod.
Waste and utterly destroy them," says the LORD,
"And do according to all that I have commanded you.
22 A sound of battle *is* in the land,
And of great destruction.
23 How the hammer of the whole earth has been cut apart and broken!
How Babylon has become a desolation among the nations!

50:2 [a]A Babylonian god; sometimes spelled *Marduk*
50:9 [a]Following some Hebrew manuscripts, Septuagint, and Syriac; Masoretic Text, Targum, and Vulgate read *a warrior who makes childless.*

24 I have laid a snare for you;
You have indeed been trapped,
O Babylon,
And you were not aware;
You have been found and also caught,
Because you have contended against the LORD.
25 The LORD has opened His armory,
And has brought out the weapons of His indignation;
For this *is* the work of the Lord GOD of hosts
In the land of the Chaldeans.
26 Come against her from the farthest border;
Open her storehouses;
Cast her up as heaps of ruins,
And destroy her utterly;
Let nothing of her be left.
27 Slay all her bulls,
Let them go down to the slaughter.
Woe to them!
For their day has come, the time of their punishment.
28 The voice of those who flee and escape from the land of Babylon
Declares in Zion the vengeance of the LORD our God,
The vengeance of His temple.

29"Call together the archers against Babylon.
All you who bend the bow, encamp against it all around;
Let none of them escape.[a]
Repay her according to her work;
According to all she has done, do to her;
For she has been proud against the LORD,
Against the Holy One of Israel.
30 Therefore her young men shall fall in the streets,
And all her men of war shall be cut off in that day," says the LORD.
31"Behold, I *am* against you,
O most haughty one!" says the Lord GOD of hosts;
"For your day has come,
The time *that* I will punish you.[a]
32 The most proud shall stumble and fall,
And no one will raise him up;
I will kindle a fire in his cities,
And it will devour all around him."

33 Thus says the LORD of hosts:

"The children of Israel *were* oppressed,
Along with the children of Judah;
All who took them captive have held them fast;
They have refused to let them go.
34 Their Redeemer *is* strong;
The LORD of hosts *is* His name.
He will thoroughly plead their case,
That He may give rest to the land,
And disquiet the inhabitants of Babylon.

35"A sword *is* against the Chaldeans," says the LORD,
"Against the inhabitants of Babylon,
And against her princes and her wise men.
36 A sword *is* against the soothsayers, and they will be fools.
A sword *is* against her mighty men, and they will be dismayed.
37 A sword *is* against their horses,
Against their chariots,
And against all the mixed peoples who *are* in her midst;
And they will become like women.
A sword *is* against her treasures, and they will be robbed.
38 A drought[a] *is* against her waters, and they will be dried up.
For it *is* the land of carved images,
And they are insane with *their* idols.

39"Therefore the wild desert beasts shall dwell *there* with the jackals,
And the ostriches shall dwell in it.
It shall be inhabited no more forever,
Nor shall it be dwelt in from generation to generation.
40 As God overthrew Sodom and Gomorrah
And their neighbors," says the LORD,
"*So* no one shall reside there,
Nor son of man dwell in it.

41"Behold, a people shall come from the north,
And a great nation and many kings
Shall be raised up from the ends of the earth.
42 They shall hold the bow and the lance;
They *are* cruel and shall not show mercy.
Their voice shall roar like the sea;
They shall ride on horses,
Set in array, like a man for the battle,
Against you, O daughter of Babylon.

43"The king of Babylon has heard the report about them,
And his hands grow feeble;
Anguish has taken hold of him,
Pangs as of a woman in childbirth.

44"Behold, he shall come up like a lion from the floodplain[a] of the Jordan
Against the dwelling place of the strong;
But I will make them suddenly run away from her.
And who *is* a chosen *man that* I may appoint over her?
For who *is* like Me?
Who will arraign Me?
And who *is* that shepherd
Who will withstand Me?"

50:29 [a]Qere, some Hebrew manuscripts, Septuagint, and Targum add *to her*. **50:31** [a]Following Masoretic Text and Targum; Septuagint and Vulgate read *The time of your punishment*. **50:38** [a]Following Masoretic Text, Targum, and Vulgate; Syriac reads *sword;* Septuagint omits *A drought is*. **50:44** [a]Or *thicket*

45 Therefore hear the counsel of the LORD
that He has taken against Babylon,
And His purposes that He has proposed
against the land of the Chaldeans:
Surely the least of the flock shall draw
them out;
Surely He will make their dwelling place
desolate with them.
46 At the noise of the taking of Babylon
The earth trembles,
And the cry is heard among the nations.

The Utter Destruction of Babylon

51 Thus says the LORD:

Behold, I will raise up against Babylon,
Against those who dwell in Leb Kamai,[a]
A destroying wind.
2 And I will send winnowers to Babylon,
Who shall winnow her and empty her
land.
For in the day of doom
They shall be against her all around.
3 Against *her* let the archer bend his bow,
And lift himself up against *her* in his armor.
Do not spare her young men;
Utterly destroy all her army.
4 Thus the slain shall fall in the land of the
Chaldeans,
And *those* thrust through in her streets.
➤ 5 For Israel is not forsaken, nor Judah,
By his God, the LORD of hosts,
Though their land was filled with sin
against the Holy One of Israel."

6 Flee from the midst of Babylon,
And every one save his life!
Do not be cut off in her iniquity,
For this *is* the time of the LORD's
vengeance;
He shall recompense her.
7 Babylon *was* a golden cup in the LORD's
hand,
That made all the earth drunk.
The nations drank her wine;
Therefore the nations are deranged.
8 Babylon has suddenly fallen and been
destroyed.
Wail for her!
Take balm for her pain;
Perhaps she may be healed.

9 We would have healed Babylon,
But she is not healed.
Forsake her, and let us go everyone to his
own country;
For her judgment reaches to heaven and
is lifted up to the skies.
10 The LORD has revealed our righteousness.
Come and let us declare in Zion the work
of the LORD our God.

11 Make the arrows bright!
Gather the shields!
The LORD has raised up the spirit of the
kings of the Medes.
For His plan *is* against Babylon to
destroy it,
Because it *is* the vengeance of the LORD,
The vengeance for His temple.
12 Set up the standard on the walls of
Babylon;
Make the guard strong,
Set up the watchmen,
Prepare the ambushes.
For the LORD has both devised and done
What He spoke against the inhabitants of
Babylon.
13 O you who dwell by many waters,
Abundant in treasures,
Your end has come,
The measure of your covetousness.
14 The LORD of hosts has sworn by Himself:
"Surely I will fill you with men, as with
locusts,
And they shall lift up a shout against
you."

15 He has made the earth by His power;
He has established the world by His
wisdom,
And stretched out the heaven by His
understanding.
16 When He utters *His* voice—
There is a multitude of waters in the
heavens:
"He causes the vapors to ascend from the
ends of the earth;
He makes lightnings for the rain;
He brings the wind out of His
treasuries."[a]

17 Everyone is dull-hearted, without
knowledge;
Every metalsmith is put to shame by the
carved image;
For his molded image *is* falsehood,
And *there is* no breath in them.

51:1 [a]A code word for Chaldea (Babylonia); may be translated *The Midst of Those Who Rise Up Against Me* **51:16** [a]Psalm 135:7

LIFE LESSONS

➤ 51:5 — *"For Israel is not forsaken, nor Judah, by his God, the LORD of hosts, though their land was filled with sin against the Holy One of Israel."*

Jeremiah knew that while God would certainly judge His people for their sin, He would never completely abandon them. He had promised Abraham that He would be with them forever, and He always keeps His promises.

18 They *are* futile, a work of errors;
In the time of their punishment they shall perish.
19 The Portion of Jacob *is* not like them,
For He *is* the Maker of all things;
And *Israel is* the tribe of His inheritance.
The LORD of hosts *is* His name.

20 "You *are* My battle-ax *and* weapons of war:
For with you I will break the nation in pieces;
With you I will destroy kingdoms;
21 With you I will break in pieces the horse and its rider;
With you I will break in pieces the chariot and its rider;
22 With you also I will break in pieces man and woman;
With you I will break in pieces old and young;
With you I will break in pieces the young man and the maiden;
23 With you also I will break in pieces the shepherd and his flock;
With you I will break in pieces the farmer and his yoke of oxen;
And with you I will break in pieces governors and rulers.

24 "And I will repay Babylon
And all the inhabitants of Chaldea
For all the evil they have done
In Zion in your sight," says the LORD.

25 "Behold, I *am* against you, O destroying mountain,
Who destroys all the earth," says the LORD.
"And I will stretch out My hand against you,
Roll you down from the rocks,
And make you a burnt mountain.
26 They shall not take from you a stone for a corner
Nor a stone for a foundation,
But you shall be desolate forever," says the LORD.

27 Set up a banner in the land,
Blow the trumpet among the nations!
Prepare the nations against her,
Call the kingdoms together against her:
Ararat, Minni, and Ashkenaz.
Appoint a general against her;
Cause the horses to come up like the bristling locusts.
28 Prepare against her the nations,
With the kings of the Medes,
Its governors and all its rulers,
All the land of his dominion.
29 And the land will tremble and sorrow;
For every purpose of the LORD shall be performed against Babylon,
To make the land of Babylon a desolation without inhabitant.
30 The mighty men of Babylon have ceased fighting,
They have remained in their strongholds;
Their might has failed,
They became *like* women;
They have burned her dwelling places,
The bars of her *gate* are broken.
31 One runner will run to meet another,
And one messenger to meet another,
To show the king of Babylon that his city is taken on *all* sides;
32 The passages are blocked,
The reeds they have burned with fire,
And the men of war are terrified.

33 For thus says the LORD of hosts, the God of Israel:

"The daughter of Babylon *is* like a threshing floor
When it is time to thresh her;
Yet a little while
And the time of her harvest will come."

34 "Nebuchadnezzar the king of Babylon
Has devoured me, he has crushed me;
He has made me an empty vessel,
He has swallowed me up like a monster;
He has filled his stomach with my delicacies,
He has spit me out.
35 Let the violence *done* to me and my flesh *be* upon Babylon,"
The inhabitant of Zion will say;
"And my blood be upon the inhabitants of Chaldea!"
Jerusalem will say.

36 Therefore thus says the LORD:

"Behold, I will plead your case and take vengeance for you.
I will dry up her sea and make her springs dry.
37 Babylon shall become a heap,
A dwelling place for jackals,
An astonishment and a hissing,
Without an inhabitant.
38 They shall roar together like lions,
They shall growl like lions' whelps.
39 In their excitement I will prepare their feasts;
I will make them drunk,
That they may rejoice,
And sleep a perpetual sleep
And not awake," says the LORD.
40 "I will bring them down
Like lambs to the slaughter,
Like rams with male goats.

41 "Oh, how Sheshach[a] is taken!
Oh, how the praise of the whole earth is seized!
How Babylon has become desolate among the nations!

51:41 [a]A code word for Babylon (compare Jeremiah 25:26)

42 The sea has come up over Babylon;
She is covered with the multitude of its waves.
43 Her cities are a desolation,
A dry land and a wilderness,
A land where no one dwells,
Through which no son of man passes.
44 I will punish Bel in Babylon,
And I will bring out of his mouth what he has swallowed;
And the nations shall not stream to him anymore.
Yes, the wall of Babylon shall fall.

45 "My people, go out of the midst of her!
And let everyone deliver himself from the fierce anger of the LORD.
46 And lest your heart faint,
And you fear for the rumor that *will be* heard in the land
(A rumor will come *one* year,
And after that, in *another* year
A rumor *will come*,
And violence in the land,
Ruler against ruler),
47 Therefore behold, the days are coming
That I will bring judgment on the carved images of Babylon;
Her whole land shall be ashamed,
And all her slain shall fall in her midst.
48 Then the heavens and the earth and all that *is* in them
Shall sing joyously over Babylon;
For the plunderers shall come to her from the north," says the LORD.

49 As Babylon *has caused* the slain of Israel to fall,
So at Babylon the slain of all the earth shall fall.
50 You who have escaped the sword,
Get away! Do not stand still!
Remember the LORD afar off,
And let Jerusalem come to your mind.

51 We are ashamed because we have heard reproach.
Shame has covered our faces,
For strangers have come into the sanctuaries of the LORD's house.

52 "Therefore behold, the days are coming," says the LORD,
"That I will bring judgment on her carved images,
And throughout all her land the wounded shall groan.
53 Though Babylon were to mount up to heaven,
And though she were to fortify the height of her strength,
Yet from Me plunderers would come to her," says the LORD.

54 The sound of a cry *comes* from Babylon,
And great destruction from the land of the Chaldeans,
55 Because the LORD is plundering Babylon
And silencing her loud voice,
Though her waves roar like great waters,
And the noise of their voice is uttered,
56 Because the plunderer comes against her, against Babylon,
And her mighty men are taken.
Every one of their bows is broken;
For the LORD *is* the God of recompense,
He will surely repay.

57 "And I will make drunk
Her princes and wise men,
Her governors, her deputies, and her mighty men.
And they shall sleep a perpetual sleep
And not awake," says the King,
Whose name *is* the LORD of hosts.

58 Thus says the LORD of hosts:

"The broad walls of Babylon shall be utterly broken,
And her high gates shall be burned with fire;
The people will labor in vain,
And the nations, because of the fire;
And they shall be weary."

Jeremiah's Command to Seraiah

59 The word which Jeremiah the prophet
commanded Seraiah the son of Neriah, the
son of Mahseiah, when he went with Zedekiah the king of Judah to Babylon in the
fourth year of his reign. And Seraiah *was* the
quartermaster.
60 So Jeremiah wrote in a book all the evil
that would come upon Babylon, all these
words that are written against Babylon.
61 And Jeremiah said to Seraiah, "When you
arrive in Babylon and see it, and read all
these words,
62 "then you shall say, 'O LORD, You have
spoken against this place to cut it off, so that
none shall remain in it, neither man nor
beast, but it shall be desolate forever.'
63 "Now it shall be, when you have finished
reading this book, *that* you shall tie a stone to
it and throw it out into the Euphrates.
64 "Then you shall say, 'Thus Babylon shall
sink and not rise from the catastrophe that I
will bring upon her. And they shall be
weary.'" Thus far *are* the words of Jeremiah.

The Fall of Jerusalem Reviewed

52 Zedekiah *was* twenty-one years old
when he became king, and he reigned
eleven years in Jerusalem. His mother's name
was Hamutal the daughter of Jeremiah of
Libnah.
2 He also did evil in the sight of the LORD,
according to all that Jehoiakim had done.
3 For because of the anger of the LORD *this*
happened in Jerusalem and Judah, till He fi-

nally cast them out from His presence. Then
Zedekiah rebelled against the king of Babylon.
4 Now it came to pass in the ninth year of
his reign, in the tenth month, on the tenth *day*
of the month, *that* Nebuchadnezzar king of
Babylon and all his army came against Jerusalem and encamped against it; and *they* built
a siege wall against it all around.
5 So the city was besieged until the eleventh
year of King Zedekiah.
6 By the fourth month, on the ninth day of
the month, the famine had become so severe
in the city that there was no food for the people of the land.
7 Then the city *wall* was broken through,
and all the men of war fled and went out of
the city at night by way of the gate between
the two walls, which *was* by the king's garden, even though the Chaldeans *were* near
the city all around. And they went by way of
the plain.[a]
8 But the army of the Chaldeans pursued
the king, and they overtook Zedekiah in the
plains of Jericho. All his army was scattered
from him.
9 So they took the king and brought him up
to the king of Babylon at Riblah in the land of
Hamath, and he pronounced judgment on
him.
10 Then the king of Babylon killed the sons
of Zedekiah before his eyes. And he killed all
the princes of Judah in Riblah.
11 He also put out the eyes of Zedekiah; and
the king of Babylon bound him in bronze fetters, took him to Babylon, and put him in
prison till the day of his death.

The Temple and City Plundered and Burned
12 Now in the fifth month, on the tenth *day* of
the month (which *was* the nineteenth year of
King Nebuchadnezzar king of Babylon), Nebuzaradan, the captain of the guard, *who*
served the king of Babylon, came to Jerusalem.
13 He burned the house of the LORD and the
king's house; all the houses of Jerusalem, that
is, all the houses of the great, he burned with
fire.
14 And all the army of the Chaldeans
who *were* with the captain of the guard
broke down all the walls of Jerusalem all
around.
15 Then Nebuzaradan the captain of the
guard carried away captive *some* of the poor
people, the rest of the people who remained
in the city, the defectors who had deserted to
the king of Babylon, and the rest of the craftsmen.
16 But Nebuzaradan the captain of the guard
left *some* of the poor of the land as vinedressers and farmers.
17 The bronze pillars that *were* in the house
of the LORD, and the carts and the bronze Sea
that *were* in the house of the LORD, the
Chaldeans broke in pieces, and carried all
their bronze to Babylon.
18 They also took away the pots, the shovels,
the trimmers, the bowls, the spoons, and all
the bronze utensils with which the *priests*
ministered.
19 The basins, the firepans, the bowls, the
pots, the lampstands, the spoons, and the
cups, whatever *was* solid gold and whatever
was solid silver, the captain of the guard took
away.
20 The two pillars, one Sea, the twelve
bronze bulls which *were* under *it, and* the
carts, which King Solomon had made for the
house of the LORD—the bronze of all these articles was beyond measure.
21 Now *concerning* the pillars: the height of
one pillar *was* eighteen cubits, a measuring
line of twelve cubits could measure its circumference, and its thickness *was* four fingers; *it was* hollow.
22 A capital of bronze *was* on it; and the
height of one capital *was* five cubits, with a
network and pomegranates all around the
capital, all of bronze. The second pillar, with
pomegranates was the same.
23 There were ninety-six pomegranates on
the sides; all the pomegranates, all around on
the network, *were* one hundred.

The People Taken Captive to Babylonia
24 The captain of the guard took Seraiah the
chief priest, Zephaniah the second priest, and
the three doorkeepers.
25 He also took out of the city an officer who
had charge of the men of war, seven men of
the king's close associates who were found in
the city, the principal scribe of the army who
mustered the people of the land, and sixty
men of the people of the land who were found
in the midst of the city.
26 And Nebuzaradan the captain of the
guard took these and brought them to the
king of Babylon at Riblah.
27 Then the king of Babylon struck them and
put them to death at Riblah in the land of
Hamath. Thus Judah was carried away captive from its own land.
28 These *are* the people whom Nebuchadnezzar carried away captive: in the seventh year,
three thousand and twenty-three Jews;
29 in the eighteenth year of Nebuchadnezzar
he carried away captive from Jerusalem eight
hundred and thirty-two persons;
30 in the twenty-third year of Nebuchadnezzar, Nebuzaradan the captain of the guard
carried away captive of the Jews seven hundred and forty-five persons. All the persons
were four thousand six hundred.

52:7 [a]Or *the Arabah,* that is, the Jordan Valley

Jehoiachin Released from Prison
31 Now it came to pass in the thirty-seventh
year of the captivity of Jehoiachin king of Judah, in the twelfth month, on the twenty-fifth
day of the month, *that* Evil-Merodach[a] king
of Babylon, in the *first* year of his reign, lifted
up the head of Jehoiachin king of Judah and
brought him out of prison.
32 And he spoke kindly to him and gave him
a more prominent seat than those of the kings
who *were* with him in Babylon.
33 So Jehoiachin changed from his prison
garments, and he ate bread regularly before
the *king* all the days of his life.
34 And as for his provisions, there was a regular ration given him by the king of Babylon,
a portion for each day until the day of his
death, all the days of his life.

52:31 [a]Or *Awil-Marduk*

LIFE LESSONS

➤ ***52:34 — And as for his provisions, there was a regular ration given him by the king of Babylon, a portion for each day until the day of his death, all the days of his life.***

While Jeremiah had predicted that King Jehoiachin would die in Babylon (Jer. 22:26), the false prophet Hananiah predicted that the king would return in triumph to Jerusalem (Jer. 28:4). Guess who was right.

THE BOOK OF

LAMENTATIONS

Lamentations describes the funeral of a city. Think of it as the tearstained portrait of a once-proud Jerusalem, now reduced to rubble by invaders bent on destruction.

In a five-poem dirge, Jeremiah lays bare his ragged emotions. A death has occurred; Jerusalem lies barren and desolate. Lamentations records the horrible aftermath of the overthrow of Jerusalem and the exile of the Jews at the hands of the Babylonians. It laments what has happened to the city, to its inhabitants, and Jeremiah's own persecutions.

But even in the midst of this holocaust, Jeremiah triumphantly cries out, "Great is Your faithfulness" (3:23). In the face of death and destruction, with life seemingly coming apart, the prophet turns tragedy into a triumph of faith. God has never failed him in the past, and God has promised to remain faithful in the future. In the light of the God he knows and loves, Jeremiah finds hope and comfort.

The Hebrew title of this book comes from the first word of chapters 1, 2, and 4: *Ekah*, "Ah, how!" Another Hebrew word, *qinot* ("Elegies" or "Lamentations"), has also been used as the title because it better represents the contents of the book. The subtitle in Jerome's Latin Vulgate reads, "*Id est lamentationes Jeremiae prophetae*," and this became the basis for the English title, "The Lamentations of Jeremiah."

Themes: When we refuse to repent of our sin, affliction is the inevitable consequence.

Author: Jeremiah the prophet.

Time: Lamentations is set at the time of the Babylonian exile (586 B.C.), which left the city of Jerusalem in ruins and its inhabitants dead or in exile.

Structure: Jeremiah writes his lament in acrostic or alphabetical fashion. Beginning each section with the first Hebrew letter, Aleph, he progresses through the entire Hebrew alphabet four times in the first four chapters (in the initial letter verse by verse in chapters 1, 2, and 4, and every three verses in chapter 3), weeping literally from A to Z.

As you read Lamentations, watch for these life principles that play an important role in this book:

26. Adversity is a bridge to a deeper relationship with God. *See Lamentations 3:22–24; page 932.*

15. Brokenness is God's requirement for maximum usefulness. *See Lamentations 3:31–33; page 932.*

Jerusalem in Affliction

1 How lonely sits the city
That was full of people!
How like a widow is she,
Who *was* great among the nations!
The princess among the provinces
Has become a slave!

2 She weeps bitterly in the night,
Her tears *are* on her cheeks;
Among all her lovers
She has none to comfort *her.*
All her friends have dealt treacherously with her;
They have become her enemies.

3 Judah has gone into captivity,
Under affliction and hard servitude;
She dwells among the nations,
She finds no rest;
All her persecutors overtake her in dire straits.

4 The roads to Zion mourn
Because no one comes to the set feasts.
All her gates are desolate;
Her priests sigh,
Her virgins are afflicted,
And she *is* in bitterness.

5 Her adversaries have become the master,
Her enemies prosper;
For the LORD has afflicted her
Because of the multitude of her transgressions.
Her children have gone into captivity before the enemy.

6 And from the daughter of Zion
All her splendor has departed.
Her princes have become like deer
That find no pasture,
That flee without strength
Before the pursuer.

7 In the days of her affliction and roaming,
Jerusalem remembers all her pleasant things
That she had in the days of old.
When her people fell into the hand of the enemy,
With no one to help her,
The adversaries saw her
And mocked at her downfall.[a]

➤ 8 Jerusalem has sinned gravely,
Therefore she has become vile.[a]
All who honored her despise her
Because they have seen her nakedness;
Yes, she sighs and turns away.

9 Her uncleanness *is* in her skirts;
She did not consider her destiny;
Therefore her collapse was awesome;
She had no comforter.
"O LORD, behold my affliction,
For *the* enemy is exalted!"

10 The adversary has spread his hand
Over all her pleasant things;
For she has seen the nations enter her sanctuary,
Those whom You commanded
Not to enter Your assembly.

11 All her people sigh,
They seek bread;
They have given their valuables for food to restore life.
"See, O LORD, and consider,
For I am scorned."

12 "*Is it* nothing to you, all you who pass by?
Behold and see
If there is any sorrow like my sorrow,
Which has been brought on me,
Which the LORD has inflicted
In the day of His fierce anger.

13 "From above He has sent fire into my bones,
And it overpowered them;
He has spread a net for my feet
And turned me back;
He has made me desolate
And faint all the day.

14 "The yoke of my transgressions was bound;[a]
They were woven together by His hands,
And thrust upon my neck.
He made my strength fail;
The Lord delivered me into the hands of *those whom* I am not able to withstand.

15 "The Lord has trampled underfoot all my mighty *men* in my midst;
He has called an assembly against me
To crush my young men;
The Lord trampled *as* in a winepress
The virgin daughter of Judah.

1:7 [a]Vulgate reads *her Sabbaths.* **1:8** [a]Septuagint and Vulgate read *moved* or *removed.* **1:14** [a]Following Masoretic Text and Targum; Septuagint, Syriac, and Vulgate read *watched over.*

LIFE LESSONS

➤ 1:8 — *Jerusalem has sinned gravely, therefore she has become vile.*

Sin does not make us cool, hip, fashionable, or trendy. It does not make us sophisticated, mature or attractive. It only makes us vile.

➤ 1:9 — *She did not consider her destiny; therefore her collapse was awesome . . . .*

Every one of us is rushing along one path or another. How often do we take stock of whether that direction leads to God's destiny for us?

16 "For these *things* I weep;
My eye, my eye overflows with water;
Because the comforter, who should
restore my life,
Is far from me.
My children are desolate
Because the enemy prevailed."

17 Zion spreads out her hands,
But no one comforts her;
The LORD has commanded concerning
Jacob
That those around him *become* his
adversaries;
Jerusalem has become an unclean thing
among them.

18 "The LORD is righteous,
For I rebelled against His commandment.
Hear now, all peoples,
And behold my sorrow;
My virgins and my young men
Have gone into captivity.

19 "I called for my lovers,
But they deceived me;
My priests and my elders
Breathed their last in the city,
While they sought food
To restore their life.

20 "See, O LORD, that I *am* in distress;
My soul is troubled;
My heart is overturned within me,
For I have been very rebellious.
Outside the sword bereaves,
At home *it is* like death.

21 "They have heard that I sigh,
But no one comforts me.
All my enemies have heard of my trouble;
They are glad that You have done *it*.
Bring on the day You have announced,
That they may become like me.

22 "Let all their wickedness come before You,
And do to them as You have done to me
For all my transgressions;
For my sighs *are* many,
And my heart *is* faint."

God's Anger with Jerusalem

2 How the Lord has covered the daughter
of Zion
With a cloud in His anger!
He cast down from heaven to the earth
The beauty of Israel,
And did not remember His footstool
In the day of His anger.

2 The Lord has swallowed up and has not
pitied
All the dwelling places of Jacob.
He has thrown down in His wrath
The strongholds of the daughter of Judah;
He has brought *them* down to the
ground;
He has profaned the kingdom and its
princes.

3 He has cut off in fierce anger
Every horn of Israel;
He has drawn back His right hand
From before the enemy.
He has blazed against Jacob like a
flaming fire
Devouring all around.

4 Standing like an enemy, He has bent His
bow;
With His right hand, like an adversary,
He has slain all *who were* pleasing to His
eye;
On the tent of the daughter of Zion,
He has poured out His fury like fire.

5 The Lord was like an enemy.
He has swallowed up Israel,
He has swallowed up all her palaces;
He has destroyed her strongholds,
And has increased mourning and
lamentation
In the daughter of Judah.

6 He has done violence to His tabernacle,
As if it were a garden;
He has destroyed His place of assembly;
The LORD has caused
The appointed feasts and Sabbaths to be
forgotten in Zion.
In His burning indignation He has
spurned the king and the priest.

7 The Lord has spurned His altar,
He has abandoned His sanctuary;
He has given up the walls of her
palaces
Into the hand of the enemy.
They have made a noise in the house of
the LORD
As on the day of a set feast.

8 The LORD has purposed to destroy
The wall of the daughter of Zion.
He has stretched out a line;
He has not withdrawn His hand from
destroying;
Therefore He has caused the rampart and
wall to lament;
They languished together.

9 Her gates have sunk into the ground;
He has destroyed and broken her bars.
Her king and her princes *are* among the
nations;
The Law *is* no *more*,
And her prophets find no vision from the
LORD.

10 The elders of the daughter of Zion
Sit on the ground *and* keep silence;
They throw dust on their heads
And gird themselves with sackcloth.
The virgins of Jerusalem
Bow their heads to the ground.

11 My eyes fail with tears,
My heart is troubled;
My bile is poured on the ground
Because of the destruction of the daughter of my people,
Because the children and the infants
Faint in the streets of the city.

12 They say to their mothers,
"Where *is* grain and wine?"
As they swoon like the wounded
In the streets of the city,
As their life is poured out
In their mothers' bosom.

13 How shall I console you?
To what shall I liken you,
O daughter of Jerusalem?
What shall I compare with you, that I may comfort you,
O virgin daughter of Zion?
For your ruin *is* spread wide as the sea;
Who can heal you?

➤ 14 Your prophets have seen for you
False and deceptive visions;
They have not uncovered your iniquity,
To bring back your captives,
But have envisioned for you false prophecies and delusions.

15 All who pass by clap *their* hands at you;
They hiss and shake their heads
At the daughter of Jerusalem:
"*Is* this the city that is called
'The perfection of beauty,
The joy of the whole earth'?"

16 All your enemies have opened their mouth against you;
They hiss and gnash *their* teeth.
They say, "We have swallowed *her* up!
Surely this *is* the day we have waited for;
We have found *it*, we have seen *it*!"

➤ 17 The LORD has done what He purposed;
He has fulfilled His word
Which He commanded in days of old.
He has thrown down and has not pitied,
And He has caused an enemy to rejoice over you;
He has exalted the horn of your adversaries.

18 Their heart cried out to the Lord,
"O wall of the daughter of Zion,
Let tears run down like a river day and night;
Give yourself no relief;
Give your eyes no rest.

19 "Arise, cry out in the night,
At the beginning of the watches;
Pour out your heart like water before the face of the Lord.
Lift your hands toward Him
For the life of your young children,
Who faint from hunger at the head of every street."

20 "See, O LORD, and consider!
To whom have You done this?
Should the women eat their offspring,
The children they have cuddled?[a]
Should the priest and prophet be slain
In the sanctuary of the Lord?

21 "Young and old lie
On the ground in the streets;
My virgins and my young men
Have fallen by the sword;
You have slain *them* in the day of Your anger,
You have slaughtered *and* not pitied.

22 "You have invited as to a feast day
The terrors that surround me.
In the day of the LORD's anger
There was no refugee or survivor.
Those whom I have borne and brought up
My enemies have destroyed."

The Prophet's Anguish and Hope

3 I *am* the man *who* has seen affliction by the rod of His wrath.
2 He has led me and made *me* walk
In darkness and not *in* light.
3 Surely He has turned His hand against me
Time and time again throughout the day.

4 He has aged my flesh and my skin,
And broken my bones.
5 He has besieged me
And surrounded *me* with bitterness and woe.
6 He has set me in dark places
Like the dead of long ago.

2:20 [a]Vulgate reads *a span long.*

LIFE LESSONS

➤ 2:14 — ***Your prophets have seen for you false and deceptive visions; they have not uncovered your iniquity . . . .***

We can trust God's Word, not only because it speaks to us of pleasant things like heaven and grace and love, but also because it uncovers and lays bare our sins, so that we may turn from it and live.

➤ 2:17 — ***The LORD has done what He purposed; He has fulfilled His word which He commanded in days of old.***

We never have to wonder whether the Lord will keep His promises. We never have to question whether He will really fulfill His word in your case or mine. Whatever He says, He will do (Matt. 5:18).

7 He has hedged me in so that I cannot get
out;
He has made my chain heavy.
8 Even when I cry and shout,
He shuts out my prayer.
9 He has blocked my ways with hewn
stone;
He has made my paths crooked.

10 He *has been* to me a bear lying in wait,
Like a lion in ambush.
11 He has turned aside my ways and torn
me in pieces;
He has made me desolate.
12 He has bent His bow
And set me up as a target for the arrow.
13 He has caused the arrows of His quiver
To pierce my loins.[a]
14 I have become the ridicule of all my
people—
Their taunting song all the day.
15 He has filled me with bitterness,
He has made me drink wormwood.

16 He has also broken my teeth with gravel,
And covered me with ashes.
17 You have moved my soul far from
peace;
I have forgotten prosperity.
18 And I said, "My strength and my hope
Have perished from the LORD."

19 Remember my affliction and roaming,
The wormwood and the gall.
20 My soul still remembers
And sinks within me.
21 This I recall to my mind,
Therefore I have hope.

22 *Through* the LORD's mercies we are not
consumed,
Because His compassions fail not.
23 *They are* new every morning;
Great *is* Your faithfulness.
24 "The LORD *is* my portion," says my soul,
"Therefore I hope in Him!"

25 The LORD *is* good to those who wait for
Him,
To the soul *who* seeks Him.
26 *It is* good that *one* should hope and wait
quietly
For the salvation of the LORD.
27 *It is* good for a man to bear
The yoke in his youth.

28 Let him sit alone and keep silent,
Because *God* has laid *it* on him;
29 Let him put his mouth in the dust—
There may yet be hope.
30 Let him give *his* cheek to the one who
strikes him,
And be full of reproach.

31 For the Lord will not cast off forever.
32 Though He causes grief,
Yet He will show compassion
According to the multitude of His mercies.
33 For He does not afflict willingly,
Nor grieve the children of men.

34 To crush under one's feet
All the prisoners of the earth,
35 To turn aside the justice *due* a man
Before the face of the Most High,
36 Or subvert a man in his cause—
The Lord does not approve.

37 Who *is* he *who* speaks and it comes to
pass,
When the Lord has not commanded *it*?
38 *Is it* not from the mouth of the Most High
That woe and well-being proceed?
39 Why should a living man complain,
A man for the punishment of his sins?

40 Let us search out and examine our ways,
And turn back to the LORD;
41 Let us lift our hearts and hands
To God in heaven.
42 We have transgressed and rebelled;
You have not pardoned.

43 You have covered *Yourself* with anger
And pursued us;
You have slain *and* not pitied.
44 You have covered Yourself with a cloud,
That prayer should not pass through.

3:13 [a]Literally *kidneys*

LIFE LESSONS

3:22 — *Through the LORD's mercies we are not consumed, because His compassions fail not.*

Do you know the Lord as trustworthy, reliable, and consistent? Or do you question whether God will be there for you in your hour of need? From cover to cover, the Bible proclaims, "God is there, and He cares!" He never abandons us.

3:25 — *The LORD is good to those who wait for Him, to the soul who seeks Him.*

Waiting upon God isn't passive. We don't sit with folded hands and smiling faces. Instead we inquire, we take preliminary steps, we pray, we obtain counsel. We ask, seek, and knock in a prudent fashion.

3:31, 32 — *For the Lord will not cast off forever. Though He causes grief, Yet He will show compassion according to the multitude of His mercies.*

The Lord sometimes brings affliction into our lives, not to make us squirm, but to shape and mold us increasingly into the image of His Son. Adversity is a bridge to a deeper relationship with God.

WHAT THE BIBLE SAYS ABOUT FINDING CONFIDENCE IN GOD

Lam. 3:23, 24

God's people have only one way to face life: confidently. After all, He loves us, has saved us from eternal death, and is committed to guiding us through every moment of life. God wants us to live confidently—but too often we allow feelings of personal inadequacy and unworthiness to derail our confidence.

The apostle Paul lived through horrendous circumstances—rejected by his Jewish peers, stoned, abandoned for dead, ridiculed, ignored, and often beaten and imprisoned for his devotion to Christ. But Paul continued to maintain a confident hope, right up to the very end. How did he manage this?

When the apostle did not think he could face another day, he recalled one simple truth: "I can do all things through Christ who strengthens me" (Phil. 4:13). He focused on his Lord, just as Jeremiah had: "Great is Your faithfulness. 'The Lord is my portion,' says my soul, 'therefore I hope in Him!'" (Lam. 3:23, 24).

Roll the burden of your heart onto Him.

The classic hymn *Great Is Thy Faithfulness* expands on this important idea. Next time you sing it, don't miss the wonder of it: God is faithful and does not change (Heb. 13:8). In this one truth we find our reason for hope and unwavering confidence. God's unchanging nature teaches us that even when we feel unlovely, we remain beautiful to Him. We can do nothing to change His love for us—it is unconditional and flows freely from His throne of grace.

If God decided to change who He is, then every promise He has made would be in jeopardy. He would become untrustworthy. But the legacy of God is this: He loved us unconditionally yesterday, and He loves us with the same love today and tomorrow.

Do you trust Him? Have you experienced a strong assurance that comes from placing your faith in His unfailing love? Roll the burden of your heart onto Him and you will discover that you too can sing, "great is thy faithfulness."

See the Life Principles Index for further study:
11. God assumes full responsibility for our needs when we obey Him.

ANSWERS TO LIFE'S QUESTIONS

How can I praise God when life doesn't go well?

LAM. 3:40

When life's twists and turns take you down unexpected and difficult roads, it can sometimes feel strange to praise the Lord. Yet He seeks our praise in *all* things—whether they appear good to us or not.

So how can you praise God when adversity finds its way into your life?

First, remember that our God is good and *always* gives us ample reason to praise Him. When you find yourself not wanting to praise Him (or not knowing how), try some of the following ideas:

- Make a list of blessings God has bestowed on you—from giving you friends and family to salvation in His Son.
- Tell someone about your salvation experience. Re-telling the moment when God lovingly adopted you into His family helps you recall the beauty of His matchless grace.
- Read a psalm each day. David praised God through hardship and great trial; we can learn from his example.
- Try to imagine how God could use negative circumstances to glorify Himself. Could He use the death of a loved one to get a lost person thinking about the meaning of life? Could He use the loss of a job to help you focus on Him and find out how you can experience His best? Could He use an illness to give you the opportunity to minister to the sick souls of your doctors and nurses as they minister to your sick body?

Second, remember that God's overriding purpose in your life is to glorify Him and that He will use any means necessary to accomplish that. Ask Him to change your perspective so that you will see your life circumstances as He does. For example, God has a decidedly different viewpoint on the death of believers than we often do: "Precious in the sight of the LORD is the death of His saints" (Ps. 116:15). When we begin to see things as He does, we begin to see the truth—and praise once more can find a home on our lips.

Third, by exercising your will, make a conscious choice to praise Him. David did this: "While I live I will praise the LORD; I will sing praises to my God while I have my being" (Ps. 146:2).

Despite how you may feel, praise really can flow from you like a fountain—beginning right now.

See the Life Principles Index for further study:
9. Trusting God means looking beyond what we can see to what God sees.
20. Disappointments are inevitable; discouragement is a choice.

45 You have made us an offscouring and refuse
In the midst of the peoples.

46 All our enemies
Have opened their mouths against us.
47 Fear and a snare have come upon us,
Desolation and destruction.
48 My eyes overflow with rivers of water
For the destruction of the daughter of my people.

49 My eyes flow and do not cease,
Without interruption,
50 Till the LORD from heaven
Looks down and sees.
51 My eyes bring suffering to my soul
Because of all the daughters of my city.

52 My enemies without cause
Hunted me down like a bird.
53 They silenced[a] my life in the pit
And threw stones at me.
54 The waters flowed over my head;
I said, "I am cut off!"

55 I called on Your name, O LORD,
From the lowest pit.
56 You have heard my voice:
"Do not hide Your ear
From my sighing, from my cry for help."
57 You drew near on the day I called on You,
And said, "Do not fear!"

58 O Lord, You have pleaded the case for my soul;
You have redeemed my life.
59 O LORD, You have seen *how* I am wronged;
Judge my case.

3:53 [a]Septuagint reads *put to death.*

60 You have seen all their vengeance,
All their schemes against me.

61 You have heard their reproach, O LORD,
All their schemes against me,
62 The lips of my enemies
And their whispering against me all the day.
63 Look at their sitting down and their rising up;
I *am* their taunting song.

64 Repay them, O LORD,
According to the work of their hands.
65 Give them a veiled[a] heart;
Your curse *be* upon them!
66 In Your anger,
Pursue and destroy them
From under the heavens of the LORD.

The Degradation of Zion

4 How the gold has become dim!
How changed the fine gold!
The stones of the sanctuary are scattered
At the head of every street.

2 The precious sons of Zion,
Valuable as fine gold,
How they are regarded as clay pots,
The work of the hands of the potter!

3 Even the jackals present their breasts
To nurse their young;
But the daughter of my people *is* cruel,
Like ostriches in the wilderness.

4 The tongue of the infant clings
To the roof of its mouth for thirst;
The young children ask for bread,
But no one breaks *it* for them.

5 Those who ate delicacies
Are desolate in the streets;
Those who were brought up in scarlet
Embrace ash heaps.

6 The punishment of the iniquity of the daughter of my people
Is greater than the punishment of the sin of Sodom,
Which was overthrown in a moment,
With no hand to help her!

7 Her Nazirites[a] were brighter than snow
And whiter than milk;
They were more ruddy in body than rubies,
Like sapphire in their appearance.

8 *Now* their appearance is blacker than soot;
They go unrecognized in the streets;
Their skin clings to their bones,
It has become as dry as wood.

9 *Those* slain by the sword are better off
Than *those* who die of hunger;
For these pine away,
Stricken *for lack* of the fruits of the field.

10 The hands of the compassionate women
Have cooked their own children;
They became food for them
In the destruction of the daughter of my people.

11 The LORD has fulfilled His fury,
He has poured out His fierce anger.
He kindled a fire in Zion,
And it has devoured its foundations.

12 The kings of the earth,
And all inhabitants of the world,
Would not have believed
That the adversary and the enemy
Could enter the gates of Jerusalem—

13 Because of the sins of her prophets
And the iniquities of her priests,
Who shed in her midst
The blood of the just.

14 They wandered blind in the streets;
They have defiled themselves with blood,
So that no one would touch their garments.

15 They cried out to them,
"Go away, unclean!
Go away, go away,
Do not touch us!"
When they fled and wandered,
Those among the nations said,
"They shall no longer dwell *here*."

16 The face[a] of the LORD scattered them;
He no longer regards them.
The people do not respect the priests
Nor show favor to the elders.

17 Still our eyes failed us,
Watching vainly for our help;
In our watching we watched
For a nation *that* could not save *us*.

18 They tracked our steps
So that we could not walk in our streets.
Our end was near;
Our days were over,
For our end had come.

3:65 [a]A Jewish tradition reads *sorrow of.* **4:7** [a]Or *nobles*
4:16 [a]Targum reads *anger.*

LIFE LESSONS

➤ 4:17 — . . . *In our watching we watched for a nation that could not save us.*

When trouble storms into your life, where do you *first* look for help? The doctor? The police? Your congressman? Your parents? Your rich uncle? God may use any of them; but only He saves.

19 Our pursuers were swifter
Than the eagles of the heavens.
They pursued us on the mountains
And lay in wait for us in the wilderness.

20 The breath of our nostrils, the anointed of the LORD,
Was caught in their pits,
Of whom we said, "Under his shadow
We shall live among the nations."

21 Rejoice and be glad, O daughter of Edom,
You who dwell in the land of Uz!
The cup shall also pass over to you
And you shall become drunk and make yourself naked.

22 *The punishment of* your iniquity is accomplished,
O daughter of Zion;
He will no longer send you into captivity.
He will punish your iniquity,
O daughter of Edom;
He will uncover your sins!

A Prayer for Restoration

5 Remember, O LORD, what has come upon us;
Look, and behold our reproach!
2 Our inheritance has been turned over to aliens,
And our houses to foreigners.
3 We have become orphans and waifs,
Our mothers *are* like widows.

4 We pay for the water we drink,
And our wood comes at a price.
5 *They* pursue at our heels;[a]
We labor *and* have no rest.
6 We have given our hand *to* the Egyptians
And the Assyrians, to be satisfied with bread.

➤ 7 Our fathers sinned *and are* no more,
But we bear their iniquities.

8 Servants rule over us;
There is none to deliver *us* from their hand.
9 We get our bread *at the risk* of our lives,
Because of the sword in the wilderness.

10 Our skin is hot as an oven,
Because of the fever of famine.
11 They ravished the women in Zion,
The maidens in the cities of Judah.
12 Princes were hung up by their hands,
And elders were not respected.
13 Young men ground at the millstones;
Boys staggered under *loads of* wood.
14 The elders have ceased *gathering at* the gate,
And the young men from their music.

15 The joy of our heart has ceased;
Our dance has turned into mourning.
16 The crown has fallen *from* our head.
Woe to us, for we have sinned!
17 Because of this our heart is faint;
Because of these *things* our eyes grow dim;
18 Because of Mount Zion which is desolate,
With foxes walking about on it.

19 You, O LORD, remain forever;
Your throne from generation to generation.
20 Why do You forget us forever,
And forsake us for so long a time?
21 Turn us back to You, O LORD, and we will be restored;
Renew our days as of old,
22 Unless You have utterly rejected us,
And are very angry with us!

5:5 [a]Literally *necks*

LIFE LESSONS

➤ 5:7 — *Our fathers sinned and are no more, but we bear their iniquities.*

God does not punish the son for the sins of his father (see Deut. 24:16), and yet the father may, through his sin, inflict a great deal of suffering on his innocent son. Sin has a way of multiplying consequences.

➤ 5:19 — *You, O LORD, remain forever; Your throne from generation to generation.*

We live in a time of enormous and rapid change—and yet God remains exactly the same today as He was in the days of Jeremiah. The changes do not surprise Him, nor do they impress Him. Praise Him today!

THE BOOK OF

EZEKIEL

Ezekiel, a priest and a prophet, ministered during the darkest days of Judah's history: the seventy years of Babylonian captivity. Carried to Babylon before the final assault on Jerusalem, Ezekiel uses prophecies, parables, object lessons, and symbols to dramatize God's message to His exiled people. Though they are like dry bones baking in the sun, God will reassemble them and breathe life into the nation once again (37:1–14). Present judgment will be followed by future glory, so that "you shall know that I am the LORD" (6:7).

The Hebrew name for Ezekiel, *Yehezke'l*, means "God Strengthens" or "Strengthened by God." Ezekiel is indeed strengthened by God for the prophetic ministry to which God calls him (3:8, 9). The name occurs twice in this book and nowhere else in the Old Testament.

Ezekiel's prophecies for God's people can be seen as the companion piece to those of Jeremiah. While Jeremiah delivered a frightening message primarily of judgment and destruction, Ezekiel's message focuses more on restoration and reconstruction.

A large portion of Ezekiel's book (40–48) focuses on a temple in Jerusalem that has yet to be built. Its dimensions and features are distinctly different from any Jewish temple ever constructed, leading many scholars to assume this temple has a yet future role to play in Israel's history. In Ezekiel's vision the Lord says of this temple, "this is the place of My throne and the place of the soles of My feet, where I will dwell in the midst of the children of Israel forever" (43:7). Even the city where the temple sits will have a new name: "and the name of the city from that day shall be: THE LORD IS THERE" (48:35).

Themes: God promises to restore His people when they repent of their sin and return to Him with their whole hearts.

Author: Ezekiel the prophet.

Time: Ezekiel's prophecies are set during the latter part of Judah's decline and during the Babylonian exile (approximately 592–570 B.C.)

Structure: The first part of the book (1–24) details God's judgment against His wayward people. The second part (25–32) speaks of God's judgment against the nations. The third part (33–48) predicts God's renewed blessing on His repentant people.

As you read Ezekiel, watch for several life principles that play an important role in this book:

4. The awareness of God's presence energizes us for our work. *See Ezekiel 2:3–8; page 939.*

22. To walk in the Spirit is to obey the initial promptings of the Spirit. *See Ezekiel 3:24; page 940.*

16. Whatever you acquire outside of God's will eventually turns to ashes. *See Ezekiel 25:6, 7; page 964.*

7. The dark moments of our life will last only so long as is necessary for God to accomplish His purpose in us. *See Ezekiel 43:6–9; page 988.*

Ezekiel's Vision of God

➤ 1 Now it came to pass in the thirtieth year, in the fourth *month,* on the fifth *day* of the month, as I *was* among the captives by the River Chebar, *that* the heavens were opened and I saw visions[a] of God.

2 On the fifth *day* of the month, which *was* in the fifth year of King Jehoiachin's captivity,

3 the word of the LORD came expressly to Ezekiel the priest, the son of Buzi, in the land of the Chaldeans[a] by the River Chebar; and the hand of the LORD was upon him there.

4 Then I looked, and behold, a whirlwind was coming out of the north, a great cloud with raging fire engulfing itself; and brightness *was* all around it and radiating out of its midst like the color of amber, out of the midst of the fire.

5 Also from within it *came* the likeness of four living creatures. And this *was* their appearance: they had the likeness of a man.

6 Each one had four faces, and each one had four wings.

7 Their legs *were* straight, and the soles of their feet *were* like the soles of calves' feet. They sparkled like the color of burnished bronze.

8 The hands of a man *were* under their wings on their four sides; and each of the four had faces and wings.

9 Their wings touched one another. *The creatures* did not turn when they went, but each one went straight forward.

10 As for the likeness of their faces, *each* had the face of a man; each of the four had the face of a lion on the right side, each of the four had the face of an ox on the left side, and each of the four had the face of an eagle.

11 Thus *were* their faces. Their wings stretched upward; two *wings* of each one touched one another, and two covered their bodies.

12 And each one went straight forward; they went wherever the spirit wanted to go, and they did not turn when they went.

13 As for the likeness of the living creatures, their appearance *was* like burning coals of fire, like the appearance of torches going back and forth among the living creatures. The fire was bright, and out of the fire went lightning.

14 And the living creatures ran back and forth, in appearance like a flash of lightning.

15 Now as I looked at the living creatures, behold, a wheel *was* on the earth beside each living creature with its four faces.

16 The appearance of the wheels and their workings *was* like the color of beryl, and all four had the same likeness. The appearance of their workings *was,* as it were, a wheel in the middle of a wheel.

17 When they moved, they went toward any one of four directions; they did not turn aside when they went.

18 As for their rims, they were so high they were awesome; and their rims *were* full of eyes, all around the four of them.

19 When the living creatures went, the wheels went beside them; and when the living creatures were lifted up from the earth, the wheels were lifted up.

20 Wherever the spirit wanted to go, they went, *because* there the spirit went; and the wheels were lifted together with them, for the spirit of the living creatures[a] *was* in the wheels.

21 When those went, *these* went; when those stood, *these* stood; and when those were lifted up from the earth, the wheels were lifted up together with them, for the spirit of the living creatures[a] *was* in the wheels.

22 The likeness of the firmament above the heads of the living creatures[a] *was* like the color of an awesome crystal, stretched out over their heads.

23 And under the firmament their wings *spread out* straight, one toward another. Each one had two which covered one side, and each one had two which covered the other side of the body.

24 When they went, I heard the noise of their wings, like the noise of many waters, like the voice of the Almighty, a tumult like the noise of an army; and when they stood still, they let down their wings.

25 A voice came from above the firmament that *was* over their heads; whenever they stood, they let down their wings.

26 And above the firmament over their heads *was* the likeness of a throne, in appearance like a sapphire stone; on the likeness of the

---

1:1 [a]Following Masoretic Text, Septuagint, and Vulgate; Syriac and Targum read *a vision.* **1:3** [a]Or *Babylonians,* and so elsewhere in this book **1:20** [a]Literally *living creature;* Septuagint and Vulgate read *spirit of life;* Targum reads *creatures.* **1:21** [a]Literally *living creature;* Septuagint and Vulgate read *spirit of life;* Targum reads *creatures.* **1:22** [a]Following Septuagint, Targum, and Vulgate; Masoretic Text reads *living creature.*

LIFE LESSONS

➤ **1:1 — . . . *the heavens were opened and I saw visions of God.***

Ezekiel did not choose to see "visions of God"; God took the initiative: " . . . prophecy never came by the will of man, but holy men of God spoke as they were moved by the Holy Spirit" (2 Pet. 1:21).

throne *was* a likeness with the appearance of
a man high above it.
27 Also from the appearance of His waist and
upward I saw, as it were, the color of amber
with the appearance of fire all around within
it; and from the appearance of His waist and
downward I saw, as it were, the appearance of
fire with brightness all around.
➤ 28 Like the appearance of a rainbow in a
cloud on a rainy day, so *was* the appearance
of the brightness all around it. This *was* the
appearance of the likeness of the glory of the
LORD.

Ezekiel Sent to Rebellious Israel

So when I saw *it*, I fell on my face, and I
heard a voice of One speaking.
➤ 2 And He said to me, "Son of man, stand on
your feet, and I will speak to you."
2 Then the Spirit entered me when He
spoke to me, and set me on my feet; and I
heard Him who spoke to me.
3 And He said to me: "Son of man, I am
sending you to the children of Israel, to a rebellious nation that has rebelled against Me;
they and their fathers have transgressed
against Me to this very day.
4 "For *they are* impudent and stubborn children. I am sending you to them, and you shall
say to them, 'Thus says the Lord GOD.'
5 "As for them, whether they hear or
whether they refuse—for they *are* a rebellious
house—yet they will know that a prophet has
been among them.
➤ **6** "And you, son of man, do not be afraid of
them nor be afraid of their words, though
briers and thorns *are* with you and you dwell
among scorpions; do not be afraid of their
words or dismayed by their looks, though
they *are* a rebellious house.
7 "You shall speak My words to them,
whether they hear or whether they refuse, for
they *are* rebellious.
8 "But you, son of man, hear what I say to you.
Do not be rebellious like that rebellious house;
open your mouth and eat what I give you."
9 Now when I looked, there was a hand
stretched out to me; and behold, a scroll of a
book *was* in it.
10 Then He spread it before me; and *there*
was writing on the inside and on the outside,
and written on it *were* lamentations and
mourning and woe.
3 Moreover He said to me, "Son of man, eat
what you find; eat this scroll, and go,
speak to the house of Israel."
2 So I opened my mouth, and He caused me
to eat that scroll.
3 And He said to me, "Son of man, feed your
belly, and fill your stomach with this scroll
that I give you." So I ate, and it was in my
mouth like honey in sweetness.
4 Then He said to me: "Son of man, go to the
house of Israel and speak with My words to
them.
5 "For you *are* not sent to a people of unfamiliar speech and of hard language, *but* to
the house of Israel,
6 "not to many people of unfamiliar speech
and of hard language, whose words you cannot understand. Surely, had I sent you to
them, they would have listened to you.
7 "But the house of Israel will not listen to
you, because they will not listen to Me; for all
the house of Israel *are* impudent and hardhearted.
8 "Behold, I have made your face strong
against their faces, and your forehead strong
against their foreheads.
9 "Like adamant stone, harder than flint, I
have made your forehead; do not be afraid of
them, nor be dismayed at their looks, though
they *are* a rebellious house."
10 Moreover He said to me: "Son of man, re- ➤
ceive into your heart all My words that I
speak to you, and hear with your ears.
11 "And go, get to the captives, to the children
of your people, and speak to them and tell
them, 'Thus says the Lord GOD,' whether they
hear, or whether they refuse."
12 Then the Spirit lifted me up, and I
heard behind me a great thunderous voice:

LIFE LESSONS

➤ **1:28 — . . . *This was the appearance of the likeness of the glory of the LORD.***

It is impossible to fully describe the splendor that is God. The best Ezekiel can do is to say, "it looked something like an expression of something else." God's glory is radically different from everything in the universe.

➤ **2:1, 2 — *And He said to me, "Son of man, stand on your feet, and I will speak to you." Then the Spirit entered me when He spoke to me, and set me on my feet . . . .***

God never gives us a command that He doesn't also give us the ability to fulfill. He never calls us to a task without also enabling us to complete it. God makes possible what He commands.

➤ **2:6 — *"And you, son of man, do not be afraid of them nor be afraid of their words, though briers and thorns are with you and you dwell among scorpions . . . ."***

God sent Ezekiel to speak to a nation He called "rebellious" and "impudent" and "stubborn" and "hardhearted"—not an easy task! But since God would be with Ezekiel, the prophet did not have to fear.

➤ **3:10 — *"Son of man, receive into your heart all My words that I speak to you, and hear with your ears."***

Listening to God is essential to walking with God. Listening requires not only straining to hear His voice, but taking His words so seriously that they set up shop in the deepest place of our hearts.

“Blessed *is* the glory of the LORD from His
place!”
13 *I* also *heard* the noise of the wings of the
living creatures that touched one another, and
the noise of the wheels beside them, and a
great thunderous noise.
14 So the Spirit lifted me up and took me
away, and I went in bitterness, in the heat of
my spirit; but the hand of the LORD was strong
upon me.
15 Then I came to the captives at Tel Abib,
who dwelt by the River Chebar; and I sat
where they sat, and remained there astonished among them seven days.

Ezekiel Is a Watchman

16 Now it came to pass at the end of seven
days that the word of the LORD came to me,
saying,
17 “Son of man, I have made you a watchman
for the house of Israel; therefore hear a word
from My mouth, and give them warning from
Me:
18 “When I say to the wicked, ‘You shall
surely die,’ and you give him no warning, nor
speak to warn the wicked from his wicked
way, to save his life, that same wicked *man*
shall die in his iniquity; but his blood I will require at your hand.
19 “Yet, if you warn the wicked, and he does
not turn from his wickedness, nor from his
wicked way, he shall die in his iniquity; but
you have delivered your soul.
20 “Again, when a righteous *man* turns from
his righteousness and commits iniquity, and I
lay a stumbling block before him, he shall die;
because you did not give him warning, he
shall die in his sin, and his righteousness
which he has done shall not be remembered;
but his blood I will require at your hand.
21 “Nevertheless if you warn the righteous
man that the righteous should not sin, and he
does not sin, he shall surely live because he
took warning; also you will have delivered
your soul.”
22 Then the hand of the LORD was upon me
there, and He said to me, “Arise, go out into
the plain, and there I shall talk with you.”
23 So I arose and went out into the plain, and
behold, the glory of the LORD stood there, like
the glory which I saw by the River Chebar;
and I fell on my face.
24 Then the Spirit entered me and set me on
my feet, and spoke with me and said to me:
“Go, shut yourself inside your house.
25 “And you, O son of man, surely they will
put ropes on you and bind you with them, so
that you cannot go out among them.
26 “I will make your tongue cling to the roof
of your mouth, so that you shall be mute and
not be one to rebuke them, for they *are* a rebellious house.
27 “But when I speak with you, I will open
your mouth, and you shall say to them, ‘Thus
says the Lord GOD.’ He who hears, let him
hear; and he who refuses, let him refuse; for
they *are* a rebellious house.

The Siege of Jerusalem Portrayed

4 “You also, son of man, take a clay tablet
and lay it before you, and portray on it a
city, Jerusalem.
2 “Lay siege against it, build a siege wall
against it, and heap up a mound against it; set
camps against it also, and place battering
rams against it all around.
3 “Moreover take for yourself an iron plate,
and set it *as* an iron wall between you and the
city. Set your face against it, and it shall be
besieged, and you shall lay siege against it.
This *will be* a sign to the house of Israel.
4 “Lie also on your left side, and lay the iniquity of the house of Israel upon it. *According* to the number of the days that you lie on
it, you shall bear their iniquity.
5 “For I have laid on you the years of their
iniquity, according to the number of the days,
three hundred and ninety days; so you shall
bear the iniquity of the house of Israel.
6 “And when you have completed them, lie
again on your right side; then you shall bear
the iniquity of the house of Judah forty days.
I have laid on you a day for each year.
7 “Therefore you shall set your face toward
the siege of Jerusalem; your arm *shall be*
uncovered, and you shall prophesy against it.
8 “And surely I will restrain you so that you
cannot turn from one side to another till you
have ended the days of your siege.
9 “Also take for yourself wheat, barley,
beans, lentils, millet, and spelt; put them into
one vessel, and make bread of them for yourself. *During* the number of days that you lie
on your side, three hundred and ninety days,
you shall eat it.
10 “And your food which you eat *shall be* by

LIFE LESSONS

➤ 3:27 — *“. . . He who hears, let him hear; and he who refuses, let him refuse . . . .”*

God lets us choose whether we will open our ears to listen or whether we will refuse to hear. Jesus often said, “He who has ears to hear, let him hear!” (Mark 4:9). We get what we choose (Rev. 22:11).

➤ 4:1 — *“You also, son of man, take a clay tablet and lay it before you, and portray on it a city, Jerusalem.”*

Ezekiel was to publicly “lay siege” to his model city to dramatize the coming siege against the real Jerusalem. God uses a wild variety of ways to try to help us understand His Word.

weight, twenty shekels a day; from time to
time you shall eat it.
11 "You shall also drink water by measure,
one-sixth of a hin; from time to time you shall
drink.
12 "And you shall eat it *as* barley cakes; and
bake it using fuel of human waste in their
sight."
13 Then the LORD said, "So shall the children
of Israel eat their defiled bread among the
Gentiles, where I will drive them."
14 So I said, "Ah, Lord GOD! Indeed I have
never defiled myself from my youth till now; I
have never eaten what died of itself or was
torn by beasts, nor has abominable flesh ever
come into my mouth."
➤ 15 Then He said to me, "See, I am giving you
cow dung instead of human waste, and you
shall prepare your bread over it."
16 Moreover He said to me, "Son of man,
surely I will cut off the supply of bread in Jerusalem;
they shall eat bread by weight and
with anxiety, and shall drink water by measure
and with dread,
17 "that they may lack bread and water, and
be dismayed with one another, and waste
away because of their iniquity.

A Sword Against Jerusalem

5 "And you, son of man, take a sharp sword,
take it as a barber's razor, and pass *it* over
your head and your beard; then take scales to
weigh and divide the *hair.*
2 "You shall burn with fire one-third in the
midst of the city, when the days of the siege
are finished; then you shall take one-third
and strike around *it* with the sword, and one-third
you shall scatter in the wind: I will draw
out a sword after them.
3 "You shall also take a small number of
them and bind them in the edge of your *garment.*
4 "Then take some of them again and throw
them into the midst of the fire, and burn them
in the fire. From there a fire will go out into all
the house of Israel.
5 "Thus says the Lord GOD: 'This *is* Jerusalem;
I have set her in the midst of the nations
and the countries all around her.
6 'She has rebelled against My judgments
by doing wickedness more than the nations,
and against My statutes more than the countries
that *are* all around her; for they have refused
My judgments, and they have not
walked in My statutes.'
7 "Therefore thus says the Lord GOD: 'Because
you have multiplied *disobedience* more
than the nations that *are* all around you, have
not walked in My statutes nor kept My judgments,
nor even done[a] according to the judgments
of the nations that *are* all around you'—
8 "therefore thus says the Lord GOD: 'Indeed
I, even I, *am* against you and will execute judgments
in your midst in the sight of the nations.
9 'And I will do among you what I have
never done, and the like of which I will never
do again, because of all your abominations.
10 'Therefore fathers shall eat *their* sons in
your midst, and sons shall eat their fathers;
and I will execute judgments among you, and
all of you who remain I will scatter to all the
winds.
11 'Therefore, *as* I live,' says the Lord GOD,
'surely, because you have defiled My sanctuary
with all your detestable things and with
all your abominations, therefore I will also diminish
you; My eye will not spare, nor will I
have any pity.
12 'One-third of you shall die of the pestilence,
and be consumed with famine in your
midst; and one-third shall fall by the sword all
around you; and I will scatter another third to
all the winds, and I will draw out a sword
after them.
13 'Thus shall My anger be spent, and I will
cause My fury to rest upon them, and I will be
avenged; and they shall know that I, the LORD,
have spoken *it* in My zeal, when I have spent
My fury upon them.
14 'Moreover I will make you a waste and a
reproach among the nations that *are* all
around you, in the sight of all who pass by.
15 'So it[a] shall be a reproach, a taunt, a lesson, ➤
and an astonishment to the nations that
are all around you, when I execute judgments
among you in anger and in fury and in furious
rebukes. I, the LORD, have spoken.
16 'When I send against them the terrible arrows
of famine which shall be for destruction,

5:7 [a]Following Masoretic Text, Septuagint, Targum, and Vulgate; many Hebrew manuscripts and Syriac read *but have done* (compare 11:12). 5:15 [a]Septuagint, Syriac, Targum, and Vulgate read *you.*

LIFE LESSONS

➤ 4:15 — *Then He said to me, "See, I am giving you cow dung instead of human waste, and you shall prepare your bread over it."*

God graciously works within our human limitations to accomplish His purpose. When Ezekiel recoiled from an object lesson involving ceremonial uncleanness, God accommodated him.

➤ 5:15 — *"So it shall be a reproach, a taunt, a lesson, and an astonishment to the nations that are all around you, when I execute judgments among you in anger and in fury and in furious rebukes."*

All along, God intended for Israel to serve as an advertisement to the world's nations regarding the goodness and holiness of God. If she refused to play the role in blessing, she would play it in judgment.

which I will send to destroy you, I will increase the famine upon you and cut off your
supply of bread.
17 'So I will send against you famine and
wild beasts, and they will bereave you. Pestilence and blood shall pass through you, and I
will bring the sword against you. I, the LORD,
have spoken.' "

Judgment on Idolatrous Israel

6 Now the word of the LORD came to me,
saying:
2 "Son of man, set your face toward the
mountains of Israel, and prophesy against
them,
3 "and say, 'O mountains of Israel, hear the
word of the Lord GOD! Thus says the Lord
GOD to the mountains, to the hills, to the
ravines, and to the valleys: "Indeed I, *even* I,
will bring a sword against you, and I will destroy your high places.
4 "Then your altars shall be desolate, your
incense altars shall be broken, and I will cast
down your slain *men* before your idols.
5 "And I will lay the corpses of the children
of Israel before their idols, and I will scatter
your bones all around your altars.
6 "In all your dwelling places the cities shall
be laid waste, and the high places shall be desolate, so that your altars may be laid waste and
made desolate, your idols may be broken and
made to cease, your incense altars may be cut
down, and your works may be abolished.
7 "The slain shall fall in your midst, and you
shall know that I *am* the LORD.
8 "Yet I will leave a remnant, so that you
may have *some* who escape the sword among
the nations, when you are scattered through
the countries.
➤9 "Then those of you who escape will remember Me among the nations where they
are carried captive, because I was crushed by
their adulterous heart which has departed
from Me, and by their eyes which play the
harlot after their idols; they will loathe themselves for the evils which they committed in
all their abominations.
10 "And they shall know that I *am* the LORD;
I have not said in vain that I would bring this
calamity upon them."
11 'Thus says the Lord GOD: "Pound your
fists and stamp your feet, and say, 'Alas, for
all the evil abominations of the house of Israel! For they shall fall by the sword, by
famine, and by pestilence.
12 'He who is far off shall die by the pestilence,
he who is near shall fall by the sword, and he
who remains and is besieged shall die by the
famine. Thus will I spend My fury upon them.
13 'Then you shall know that I *am* the LORD,
when their slain are among their idols all
around their altars, on every high hill, on all
the mountaintops, under every green tree,
and under every thick oak, wherever they offered sweet incense to all their idols.
14 'So I will stretch out My hand against ◄
them and make the land desolate, yes, more
desolate than the wilderness toward Diblah,
in all their dwelling places. Then they shall
know that I *am* the LORD.' " ' "

Judgment on Israel Is Near

7 Moreover the word of the LORD came to
me, saying,
2 "And you, son of man, thus says the Lord
GOD to the land of Israel:

'An end! The end has come upon the four
corners of the land.
3 Now the end *has come* upon you,
And I will send My anger against you;
I will judge you according to your ways,
And I will repay you for all your
abominations.
4 My eye will not spare you,
Nor will I have pity;
But I will repay your ways,
And your abominations will be in your
midst;
Then you shall know that I *am* the LORD!'

5 "Thus says the Lord GOD:

'A disaster, a singular disaster;
Behold, it has come!
6 An end has come,
The end has come;
It has dawned for you;
Behold, it has come!
7 Doom has come to you, you who dwell in
the land;
The time has come,
A day of trouble *is* near,
And not of rejoicing in the mountains.
8 Now upon you I will soon pour out My
fury,
And spend My anger upon you;

LIFE LESSONS

➤ **6:9 — *" . . . I was crushed by their adulterous heart which has departed from Me, and by their eyes which play the harlot after their idols . . . ."***

The Lord has a staggering emotional investment in His relationship with us. He created us to connect with Him on a heart-to-heart level, and when we give our hearts to something else, it deeply grieves Him.

➤ **6:14 — *" . . . Then they shall know that I am the LORD."***

This phrase recurs throughout the Book of Ezekiel. Over and over again God says that He will execute mighty judgments and secure redemption so that the whole world will know that He alone is God.

I will judge you according to your ways,
And I will repay you for all your
abominations.

9 'My eye will not spare,
Nor will I have pity;
I will repay you according to your ways,
And your abominations will be in your
midst.
Then you shall know that I *am* the LORD
who strikes.

10 'Behold, the day!
Behold, it has come!
Doom has gone out;
The rod has blossomed,
Pride has budded.
11 Violence has risen up into a rod of
wickedness;
None of them *shall remain,*
None of their multitude,
None of them;
Nor *shall there be* wailing for them.
12 The time has come,
The day draws near.
'Let not the buyer rejoice,
Nor the seller mourn,
For wrath *is* on their whole multitude.
13 For the seller shall not return to what has
been sold,
Though he may still be alive;
For the vision concerns the whole
multitude,
And it shall not turn back;
No one will strengthen himself
Who lives in iniquity.

14 'They have blown the trumpet and made
everyone ready,
But no one goes to battle;
For My wrath *is* on all their multitude.
15 The sword *is* outside,
And the pestilence and famine within.
Whoever *is* in the field
Will die by the sword;
And whoever *is* in the city,
Famine and pestilence will devour him.

16 'Those who survive will escape and be on
the mountains
Like doves of the valleys,
All of them mourning,
Each for his iniquity.
17 Every hand will be feeble,
And every knee will be *as* weak *as* water.
18 They will also be girded with sackcloth;
Horror will cover them;
Shame *will be* on every face,
Baldness on all their heads.

19 'They will throw their silver into the streets, ➤
And their gold will be like refuse;
Their silver and their gold will not be
able to deliver them
In the day of the wrath of the LORD;
They will not satisfy their souls,
Nor fill their stomachs,
Because it became their stumbling block
of iniquity.

20 'As for the beauty of his ornaments,
He set it in majesty;
But they made from it
The images of their abominations—
Their detestable things;
Therefore I have made it
Like refuse to them.
21 I will give it as plunder
Into the hands of strangers,
And to the wicked of the earth as spoil;
And they shall defile it.
22 I will turn My face from them,
And they will defile My secret place;
For robbers shall enter it and defile it.

23 'Make a chain,
For the land is filled with crimes of blood,
And the city is full of violence.
24 Therefore I will bring the worst of the
Gentiles,
And they will possess their houses;
I will cause the pomp of the strong to
cease,
And their holy places shall be defiled.
25 Destruction comes;
They will seek peace, but *there shall be*
none.
26 Disaster will come upon disaster,
And rumor will be upon rumor.
Then they will seek a vision from a prophet;
But the law will perish from the priest,
And counsel from the elders.

27 'The king will mourn, ➤
The prince will be clothed with desolation,
And the hands of the common people
will tremble.
I will do to them according to their way,
And according to what they deserve I will
judge them;
Then they shall know that I *am* the LORD!'"

LIFE LESSONS

➤ 7:19 — *"Their silver and their gold will not be able to deliver them in the day of the wrath of the LORD . . . ."*

When the time of God's judgment arrives, no amount of planning or scheming will be able to rescue a person intended for judgment. Nothing can stand in the way of God accomplishing His purposes.

➤ 7:27 — *"I will do to them according to their way, and according to what they deserve I will judge them . . . ."*

The Bible tells us that God keeps careful records of what we say and do and even think, to make sure that everyone gets exactly his due at the final judgment (Dan. 7:10; Rev. 20:12).

Abominations in the Temple

8 And it came to pass in the sixth year, in the sixth *month,* on the fifth *day* of the month, as I sat in my house with the elders of Judah sitting before me, that the hand of the Lord GOD fell upon me there.

2 Then I looked, and there was a likeness, like the appearance of fire—from the appearance of His waist and downward, fire; and from His waist and upward, like the appearance of brightness, like the color of amber.

➤ 3 He stretched out the form of a hand, and took me by a lock of my hair; and the Spirit lifted me up between earth and heaven, and brought me in visions of God to Jerusalem, to the door of the north gate of the inner *court,* where the seat of the image of jealousy *was,* which provokes to jealousy.

4 And behold, the glory of the God of Israel *was* there, like the vision that I saw in the plain.

5 Then He said to me, "Son of man, lift your eyes now toward the north." So I lifted my eyes toward the north, and there, north of the altar gate, was this image of jealousy in the entrance.

6 Furthermore He said to me, "Son of man, do you see what they are doing, the great abominations that the house of Israel commits here, to make Me go far away from My sanctuary? Now turn again, you will see greater abominations."

7 So He brought me to the door of the court; and when I looked, there was a hole in the wall.

8 Then He said to me, "Son of man, dig into the wall"; and when I dug into the wall, there was a door.

9 And He said to me, "Go in, and see the wicked abominations which they are doing there."

10 So I went in and saw, and there—every sort of creeping thing, abominable beasts, and all the idols of the house of Israel, portrayed all around on the walls.

11 And there stood before them seventy men of the elders of the house of Israel, and in their midst stood Jaazaniah the son of Shaphan. Each man had a censer in his hand, and a thick cloud of incense went up.

12 Then He said to me, "Son of man, have you seen what the elders of the house of Israel do in the dark, every man in the room of his idols? For they say, 'The LORD does not see us, the LORD has forsaken the land.'"

13 And He said to me, "Turn again, *and* you will see greater abominations that they are doing."

14 So He brought me to the door of the north gate of the LORD's house; and to my dismay, women were sitting there weeping for Tammuz.

15 Then He said to me, "Have you seen *this,* O son of man? Turn again, you will see greater abominations than these."

16 So He brought me into the inner court of the LORD's house; and there, at the door of the temple of the LORD, between the porch and the altar, *were* about twenty-five men with their backs toward the temple of the LORD and their faces toward the east, and they were worshiping the sun toward the east.

17 And He said to me, "Have you seen *this,* O son of man? Is it a trivial thing to the house of Judah to commit the abominations which they commit here? For they have filled the land with violence; then they have returned to provoke Me to anger. Indeed they put the branch to their nose. ➤

18 Therefore I also will act in fury. My eye will not spare nor will I have pity; and though they cry in My ears with a loud voice, I will not hear them."

The Wicked Are Slain

9 Then He called out in my hearing with a loud voice, saying, "Let those who have charge over the city draw near, each *with* a deadly weapon in his hand."

2 And suddenly six men came from the direction of the upper gate, which faces north, each with his battle-ax in his hand. One man among them *was* clothed with linen and had a writer's inkhorn at his side. They went in and stood beside the bronze altar.

3 Now the glory of the God of Israel had gone up from the cherub, where it had been, to the threshold of the temple.[a] And He called to the man clothed with linen, who *had* the writer's inkhorn at his side;

9:3 [a]Literally *house*

LIFE LESSONS

➤ **8:3 — *. . . the Spirit lifted me up between earth and heaven, and brought me in visions of God to Jerusalem . . . .***

Ezekiel gives us more vivid descriptions of the prophetic process than almost any other Old Testament prophet. God speaks to us in uncounted ways. Are we watching and listening?

➤ **8:17 — *"Is it a trivial thing to the house of Judah to commit the abominations which they commit here?"***

Sin is never a "trivial thing." We may get so used to some offense that it seems harmless and even inconsequential, but God's holy nature never changes. Sin never becomes acceptable to Him.

➤ 4 and the LORD said to him, "Go through the midst of the city, through the midst of Jerusalem, and put a mark on the foreheads of the men who sigh and cry over all the abominations that are done within it."

5 To the others He said in my hearing, "Go after him through the city and kill; do not let your eye spare, nor have any pity.

6 "Utterly slay old *and* young men, maidens and little children and women; but do not come near anyone on whom *is* the mark; and begin at My sanctuary." So they began with the elders who *were* before the temple.

7 Then He said to them, "Defile the temple, and fill the courts with the slain. Go out!" And they went out and killed in the city.

8 So it was, that while they were killing them, I was left *alone;* and I fell on my face and cried out, and said, "Ah, Lord GOD! Will You destroy all the remnant of Israel in pouring out Your fury on Jerusalem?"

➤ 9 Then He said to me, "The iniquity of the house of Israel and Judah *is* exceedingly great, and the land is full of bloodshed, and the city full of perversity; for they say, 'The LORD has forsaken the land, and the LORD does not see!'

10 "And as for Me also, My eye will neither spare, nor will I have pity, *but* I will recompense their deeds on their own head."

11 Just then, the man clothed with linen, who *had* the inkhorn at his side, reported back and said, "I have done as You commanded me."

The Glory Departs from the Temple

10 And I looked, and there in the firmament that was above the head of the cherubim, there appeared something like a sapphire stone, having the appearance of the likeness of a throne.

2 Then He spoke to the man clothed with linen, and said, "Go in among the wheels, under the cherub, fill your hands with coals of fire from among the cherubim, and scatter *them* over the city." And he went in as I watched.

3 Now the cherubim were standing on the south side of the temple[a] when the man went in, and the cloud filled the inner court.

4 Then the glory of the LORD went up from the cherub, *and paused* over the threshold of the temple; and the house was filled with the cloud, and the court was full of the brightness of the LORD's glory.

5 And the sound of the wings of the cherubim was heard *even* in the outer court, like the voice of Almighty God when He speaks.

6 Then it happened, when He commanded the man clothed in linen, saying, "Take fire from among the wheels, from among the cherubim," that he went in and stood beside the wheels.

7 And the cherub stretched out his hand from among the cherubim to the fire that *was* among the cherubim, and took *some of it* and put *it* into the hands of the *man* clothed with linen, who took *it* and went out.

8 The cherubim appeared to have the form of a man's hand under their wings.

9 And when I looked, there were four wheels by the cherubim, one wheel by one cherub and another wheel by each other cherub; the wheels appeared *to have* the color of a beryl stone.

10 *As for* their appearance, all four looked alike—as it were, a wheel in the middle of a wheel.

11 When they went, they went toward *any of* their four directions; they did not turn aside when they went, but followed in the direction the head was facing. They did not turn aside when they went.

12 And their whole body, with their back, their hands, their wings, and the wheels that the four had, *were* full of eyes all around.

13 As for the wheels, they were called in my hearing, "Wheel."

14 Each one had four faces: the first face *was* the face of a cherub, the second face the face of a man, the third the face of a lion, and the fourth the face of an eagle.

15 And the cherubim were lifted up. This *was* the living creature I saw by the River Chebar.

16 When the cherubim went, the wheels went beside them; and when the cherubim lifted their wings to mount up from the earth, the same wheels also did not turn from beside them.

17 When *the cherubim*[a] stood still, *the wheels* stood still, and when *one*[b] was lifted up, *the other*[c] lifted itself up, for the spirit of the living creature *was* in them.

10:3 [a]Literally *house,* also in verses 4 and 18 **10:17** [a]Literally *they* [b]Literally *they* [c]Literally *they*

LIFE LESSONS

➤ 9:4 — *"Go through the midst of the city . . . and put a mark on the foreheads of the men who sigh and cry over all the abominations that are done within it."*

God ordered His angels to distinguish between those who honored Him and those who did not. When it came time for judgment, He would spare His faithful people: "Do not come near anyone on whom is the mark" (9:6).

➤ 9:9 — *"The iniquity of the house of Israel and Judah is exceedingly great . . . for they say, 'The LORD has forsaken the land, and the LORD does not see!'"*

Most Israelites completely misunderstood what happened during the Babylonian invasions. They did not see them for what they were—a prophesied divine judgment—but rather as proof that God had lost interest. God considered this perspective deeply evil.

➤ 18 Then the glory of the LORD departed from
the threshold of the temple and stood over the
cherubim.
19 And the cherubim lifted their wings and
mounted up from the earth in my sight. When
they went out, the wheels *were* beside them;
and they stood at the door of the east gate of
the LORD's house, and the glory of the God of
Israel *was* above them.
20 This *is* the living creature I saw under the
God of Israel by the River Chebar, and I knew
they *were* cherubim.
21 Each one had four faces and each one four
wings, and the likeness of the hands of a man
was under their wings.
22 And the likeness of their faces *was* the
same *as* the faces which I had seen by the
River Chebar, their appearance and their persons. They each went straight forward.

Judgment on Wicked Counselors

11 Then the Spirit lifted me up and
brought me to the East Gate of the
LORD's house, which faces eastward; and
there at the door of the gate were twenty-five
men, among whom I saw Jaazaniah the son of
Azzur, and Pelatiah the son of Benaiah,
princes of the people.
2 And He said to me: "Son of man, these *are*
the men who devise iniquity and give wicked
counsel in this city,
3 "who say, '*The time is* not near to build
houses; this *city is* the caldron, and we *are* the
meat.'
4 "Therefore prophesy against them, prophesy, O son of man!"
➤ **5** Then the Spirit of the LORD fell upon me,
and said to me, "Speak! 'Thus says the LORD:
"Thus you have said, O house of Israel; for I
know the things that come into your mind.
6 "You have multiplied your slain in this city,
and you have filled its streets with the slain."
7 'Therefore thus says the Lord GOD: "Your
slain whom you have laid in its midst, they
are the meat, and this *city is* the caldron; but
I shall bring you out of the midst of it.
8 "You have feared the sword; and I will
bring a sword upon you," says the Lord GOD.
9 "And I will bring you out of its midst, and
deliver you into the hands of strangers, and
execute judgments on you.
10 "You shall fall by the sword. I will judge
you at the border of Israel. Then you shall
know that I *am* the LORD.
11 "This *city* shall not be your caldron, nor
shall you be the meat in its midst. I will judge
you at the border of Israel.
12 "And you shall know that I *am* the LORD;
for you have not walked in My statutes nor
executed My judgments, but have done according to the customs of the Gentiles which
are all around you."'"
13 Now it happened, while I was prophesying, that Pelatiah the son of Benaiah died.
Then I fell on my face and cried with a loud
voice, and said, "Ah, Lord GOD! Will You make
a complete end of the remnant of Israel?"

God Will Restore Israel

14 Again the word of the LORD came to me,
saying,
15 "Son of man, your brethren, your relatives, your countrymen, and all the house of
Israel in its entirety, *are* those about whom
the inhabitants of Jerusalem have said, 'Get
far away from the LORD; this land has been
given to us as a possession.'
16 "Therefore say, 'Thus says the Lord GOD: ➤
"Although I have cast them far off among the
Gentiles, and although I have scattered them
among the countries, yet I shall be a little
sanctuary for them in the countries where
they have gone."'
17 "Therefore say, 'Thus says the Lord GOD:
"I will gather you from the peoples, assemble
you from the countries where you have been
scattered, and I will give you the land of Israel."'
18 "And they will go there, and they will take
away all its detestable things and all its
abominations from there.
19 "Then I will give them one heart, and I will ✳
put a new spirit within them,[a] and take the
stony heart out of their flesh, and give them a
heart of flesh,

11:19 [a]Literally *you*

LIFE LESSONS

➤ **10:18 — *Then the glory of the LORD departed from the threshold of the temple and stood over the cherubim.***

Many in Israel thought Jerusalem could never be destroyed because the temple, God's "home," stood there. They never imagined that He would abandon the temple, even though He had warned of precisely that (1 Kin. 9:6, 7).

➤ **11:5 — *". . . for I know the things that come into your mind."***

The Lord knows us completely—our thoughts, our plans, our hopes, our feelings. We can hide nothing from Him, and we can never surprise Him. He knows us better than we know ourselves; that is why we can trust Him.

➤ **11:16 — *"Although I have cast them far off . . . yet I shall be a little sanctuary for them . . . ."***

Wherever we go, God is a sanctuary for us. Even when He judged Israel and sent her into captivity, even there in the land of the nation's exile, the Lord became "a little sanctuary" for her.

✳ 20 that they may walk in My statutes and
keep My judgments and do them; and they
shall be My people, and I will be their God.
21 "But *as for those* whose hearts follow the
desire for their detestable things and their
abominations, I will recompense their deeds
on their own heads," says the Lord GOD.
22 So the cherubim lifted up their wings, with
the wheels beside them, and the glory of the
God of Israel *was* high above them.
23 And the glory of the LORD went up from
the midst of the city and stood on the mountain, which *is* on the east side of the city.
24 Then the Spirit took me up and brought
me in a vision by the Spirit of God into
Chaldea,[a] to those in captivity. And the vision
that I had seen went up from me.
25 So I spoke to those in captivity of all the
things the LORD had shown me.

Judah's Captivity Portrayed

12 Now the word of the LORD came to me,
saying:
2 "Son of man, you dwell in the midst of a
rebellious house, which has eyes to see but
does not see, and ears to hear but does not
hear; for they *are* a rebellious house.
➤ 3 "Therefore, son of man, prepare your belongings for captivity, and go into captivity by
day in their sight. You shall go from your
place into captivity to another place in their
sight. It may be that they will consider,
though they *are* a rebellious house.
4 "By day you shall bring out your belongings in their sight, as though going into captivity; and at evening you shall go in their
sight, like those who go into captivity.
5 "Dig through the wall in their sight, and
carry *your belongings* out through it.
6 "In their sight you shall bear *them* on *your*
shoulders *and* carry *them* out at twilight; you
shall cover your face, so that you cannot see
the ground, for I have made you a sign to the
house of Israel."
7 So I did as I was commanded. I brought
out my belongings by day, as though going
into captivity, and at evening I dug through
the wall with my hand. I brought *them* out at
twilight, *and* I bore *them* on *my* shoulder in
their sight.
8 And in the morning the word of the LORD
came to me, saying,
9 "Son of man, has not the house of Israel,
the rebellious house, said to you, 'What are
you doing?'
10 "Say to them, 'Thus says the Lord GOD:
"This burden *concerns* the prince in Jerusalem and all the house of Israel who are among
them."'
11 Say, 'I *am* a sign to you. As I have done, so
shall it be done to them; they shall be carried
away into captivity.'
12 "And the prince who *is* among them shall
bear *his belongings* on *his* shoulder at twilight
and go out. They shall dig through the wall to
carry *them* out through it. He shall cover his
face, so that he cannot see the ground with *his*
eyes.
13 "I will also spread My net over him, and he
shall be caught in My snare. I will bring him
to Babylon, *to* the land of the Chaldeans; yet
he shall not see it, though he shall die there.
14 "I will scatter to every wind all who *are*
around him to help him, and all his troops;
and I will draw out the sword after them.
15 "Then they shall know that I *am* the LORD,
when I scatter them among the nations and
disperse them throughout the countries.
16 "But I will spare a few of their men from
the sword, from famine, and from pestilence,
that they may declare all their abominations
among the Gentiles wherever they go. Then
they shall know that I *am* the LORD."

Judgment Not Postponed

17 Moreover the word of the LORD came to
me, saying,
18 "Son of man, eat your bread with quaking,
and drink your water with trembling and anxiety.
19 "And say to the people of the land, 'Thus
says the Lord GOD to the inhabitants of Jerusalem *and* to the land of Israel: "They shall
eat their bread with anxiety, and drink their
water with dread, so that her land may be
emptied of all who are in it, because of the violence of all those who dwell in it.
20 "Then the cities that are inhabited shall be
laid waste, and the land shall become desolate; and you shall know that I *am* the
LORD."'"
21 And the word of the LORD came to me,
saying,
22 "Son of man, what *is* this proverb *that* you
people have about the land of Israel, which
says, 'The days are prolonged, and every vision fails'?

11:24 [a]Or *Babylon,* and so elsewhere in this book

LIFE LESSONS

➤ **12:3 — *"Therefore, son of man, prepare your belongings for captivity, and go into captivity by day in their sight . . . . It may be that they will consider, though they are a rebellious house."***

God instructed Ezekiel to perform many unusual actions in a last-ditch effort to prod the rebellious Israelites to return to the Lord with all their heart and soul. God will do all He can to hold off judgment.

23 "Tell them therefore, 'Thus says the Lord
GOD: "I will lay this proverb to rest, and they
shall no more use it as a proverb in Israel."
But say to them, "The days are at hand, and
the fulfillment of every vision.
24 "For no more shall there be any false vision or flattering divination within the house
of Israel.
➤ 25 "For I *am* the LORD. I speak, and the word
which I speak will come to pass; it will no
more be postponed; for in your days, O rebellious house, I will say the word and perform
it," says the Lord GOD.'"
26 Again the word of the LORD came to me,
saying,
27 "Son of man, look, the house of Israel is
saying, 'The vision that he sees *is* for many
days *from now,* and he prophesies of times far
off.'
28 "Therefore say to them, 'Thus says the
Lord GOD: "None of My words will be postponed any more, but the word which I speak
will be done," says the Lord GOD.'"

Woe to Foolish Prophets

13 And the word of the LORD came to me,
saying,
2 "Son of man, prophesy against the prophets of Israel who prophesy, and say to those
who prophesy out of their own heart, 'Hear
the word of the LORD!'"
3 Thus says the Lord GOD: "Woe to the foolish prophets, who follow their own spirit and
have seen nothing!
4 "O Israel, your prophets are like foxes in
the deserts.
5 "You have not gone up into the gaps to
build a wall for the house of Israel to stand in
battle on the day of the LORD.
6 "They have envisioned futility and false
divination, saying, 'Thus says the LORD!' But
the LORD has not sent them; yet they hope
that the word may be confirmed.
7 "Have you not seen a futile vision, and
have you not spoken false divination? You say,
'The LORD says,' but I have not spoken."
8 Therefore thus says the Lord GOD: "Because you have spoken nonsense and envisioned lies, therefore I *am* indeed against
you," says the Lord GOD.
9 "My hand will be against the prophets
who envision futility and who divine lies; they
shall not be in the assembly of My people, nor
be written in the record of the house of Israel,
nor shall they enter into the land of Israel.
Then you shall know that I *am* the Lord GOD.
10 "Because, indeed, because they have seduced My people, saying, 'Peace!' when *there
is* no peace—and one builds a wall, and they
plaster it with untempered *mortar*—
11 "say to those who plaster *it* with untempered *mortar,* that it will fall. There will be
flooding rain, and you, O great hailstones,
shall fall; and a stormy wind shall tear *it* down.
12 "Surely, when the wall has fallen, will it
not be said to you, 'Where *is* the mortar with
which you plastered *it?*'"
13 Therefore thus says the Lord GOD: "I will
cause a stormy wind to break forth in My fury;
and there shall be a flooding rain in My anger,
and great hailstones in fury to consume *it.*
14 "So I will break down the wall you have
plastered with untempered *mortar,* and bring
it down to the ground, so that its foundation
will be uncovered; it will fall, and you shall be
consumed in the midst of it. Then you shall
know that I *am* the LORD.
15 "Thus will I accomplish My wrath on the
wall and on those who have plastered it with
untempered *mortar;* and I will say to you, 'The
wall *is* no *more,* nor those who plastered it,
16 '*that is,* the prophets of Israel who prophesy concerning Jerusalem, and who see visions of peace for her when *there is* no peace,'"
says the Lord GOD.
17 "Likewise, son of man, set your face
against the daughters of your people, who
prophesy out of their own heart; prophesy
against them,
18 "and say, 'Thus says the Lord GOD: "Woe
to the *women* who sew *magic* charms on their
sleeves[a] and make veils for the heads of people of every height to hunt souls! Will you
hunt the souls of My people, and keep yourselves alive?
19 "And will you profane Me among My peo- ➤
ple for handfuls of barley and for pieces of
bread, killing people who should not die, and
keeping people alive who should not live, by
your lying to My people who listen to lies?"

13:18 [a]Literally *over all the joints of My hands;* Vulgate reads *under every elbow;* Septuagint and Targum read *on all elbows of the hands.*

LIFE LESSONS

➤ 12:25 — *"'For I am the LORD. I speak, and the word which I speak will come to pass . . . .'"*

You can rely completely on the truth and accuracy of the Word of God. When Jesus disputed with Satan in the wilderness, He responded repeatedly with an authoritative, "It is written . . ." (Matt. 4:4, 7, 10).

➤ 13:19 — *"And will you profane Me among My people for handfuls of barley and for pieces of bread, killing people who should not die, and keeping people alive who should not live, by your lying to My people who listen to lies?"*

When we stray from the God's truth, we quickly wind up in a cesspool of ugly transgressions: blasphemy, murder, bribery, perjury. One sin tends to grease the skids for many more sins.

20 'Therefore thus says the Lord GOD: "Behold, I *am* against your *magic* charms by which you hunt souls there like birds. I will tear them from your arms, and let the souls go, the souls you hunt like birds.
21 "I will also tear off your veils and deliver My people out of your hand, and they shall no longer be as prey in your hand. Then you shall know that I *am* the LORD.
➤ 22 "Because with lies you have made the heart of the righteous sad, whom I have not made sad; and you have strengthened the hands of the wicked, so that he does not turn from his wicked way to save his life.
23 "Therefore you shall no longer envision futility nor practice divination; for I will deliver My people out of your hand, and you shall know that I *am* the LORD."'"

Idolatry Will Be Punished

14 Now some of the elders of Israel came to me and sat before me.
2 And the word of the LORD came to me, saying,
➤ 3 "Son of man, these men have set up their idols in their hearts, and put before them that which causes them to stumble into iniquity. Should I let Myself be inquired of at all by them?
4 "Therefore speak to them, and say to them, 'Thus says the Lord GOD: "Everyone of the house of Israel who sets up his idols in his heart, and puts before him what causes him to stumble into iniquity, and then comes to the prophet, I the LORD will answer him who comes, according to the multitude of his idols,
5 "that I may seize the house of Israel by their heart, because they are all estranged from Me by their idols."'
6 "Therefore say to the house of Israel, 'Thus says the Lord GOD: "Repent, turn away from your idols, and turn your faces away from all your abominations.
7 "For anyone of the house of Israel, or of the strangers who dwell in Israel, who separates himself from Me and sets up his idols in his heart and puts before him what causes him to stumble into iniquity, then comes to a prophet to inquire of him concerning Me, I the LORD will answer him by Myself.
8 "I will set My face against that man and make him a sign and a proverb, and I will cut him off from the midst of My people. Then you shall know that I *am* the LORD.
9 "And if the prophet is induced to speak anything, I the LORD have induced that prophet, and I will stretch out My hand against him and destroy him from among My people Israel.
10 "And they shall bear their iniquity; the punishment of the prophet shall be the same as the punishment of the one who inquired,
11 "that the house of Israel may no longer stray from Me, nor be profaned anymore with all their transgressions, but that they may be My people and I may be their God," says the Lord GOD.'"

Judgment on Persistent Unfaithfulness

12 The word of the LORD came again to me, saying:
13 "Son of man, when a land sins against Me by persistent unfaithfulness, I will stretch out My hand against it; I will cut off its supply of bread, send famine on it, and cut off man and beast from it.
14 "Even *if* these three men, Noah, Daniel, and Job, were in it, they would deliver *only* themselves by their righteousness," says the Lord GOD.
15 "If I cause wild beasts to pass through the land, and they empty it, and make it so desolate that no man may pass through because of the beasts,
16 "*even though* these three men *were* in it, *as* I live," says the Lord GOD, "they would deliver neither sons nor daughters; only they would be delivered, and the land would be desolate.
17 "Or *if* I bring a sword on that land, and say, 'Sword, go through the land,' and I cut off man and beast from it,
18 "even *though* these three men *were* in it, *as* I live," says the Lord GOD, "they would deliver neither sons nor daughters, but only they themselves would be delivered.
19 "Or *if* I send a pestilence into that land and pour out My fury on it in blood, and cut off from it man and beast,
20 "even *though* Noah, Daniel, and Job *were* in it, *as* I live," says the Lord GOD, "they would deliver neither son nor daughter; they would deliver *only* themselves by their righteousness."
21 For thus says the Lord GOD: "How much

LIFE LESSONS

➤ 13:22 — *". . . you have made the heart of the righteous sad, whom I have not made sad; and you have strengthened the hands of the wicked, so that he does not turn from his wicked way to save his life."*

We must be very careful how we represent God's message, neither adding to it nor taking away from it. Any true word from the Lord will encourage His people and urge the wicked to turn from evil.

➤ 14:3 — *"Son of man, these men have set up their idols in their hearts . . . ."*

We don't have to set up idols of wood and stone at a physical shrine in order to engage in idolatry. If there is anything that we honor above God, we have already made it an idol in our hearts.

more it shall be when I send My four severe
judgments on Jerusalem—the sword and
famine and wild beasts and pestilence—to cut
off man and beast from it?
22 "Yet behold, there shall be left in it a remnant who will be brought out, *both* sons and
daughters; surely they will come out to you,
and you will see their ways and their doings.
Then you will be comforted concerning the
disaster that I have brought upon Jerusalem,
all that I have brought upon it.
23 "And they will comfort you, when you see
their ways and their doings; and you shall
know that I have done nothing without cause
that I have done in it," says the Lord GOD.

The Outcast Vine

15 Then the word of the LORD came to me,
saying:
2 "Son of man, how is the wood of the vine
better than any other wood, the vine branch
which is among the trees of the forest?
3 "Is wood taken from it to make any object? Or can *men* make a peg from it to hang
any vessel on?
4 "Instead, it is thrown into the fire for fuel;
the fire devours both ends of it, and its middle
is burned. Is it useful for *any* work?
5 "Indeed, when it was whole, no object
could be made from it. How much less will it
be useful for *any* work when the fire has devoured it, and it is burned?
6 "Therefore thus says the Lord GOD: 'Like
the wood of the vine among the trees of the
forest, which I have given to the fire for fuel,
so I will give up the inhabitants of Jerusalem;
7 "and I will set My face against them. They
will go out from *one* fire, but *another* fire shall
devour them. Then you shall know that I *am*
the LORD, when I set My face against them.
➤ 8 "Thus I will make the land desolate, because they have persisted in unfaithfulness,'
says the Lord GOD."

God's Love for Jerusalem

16 Again the word of the LORD came to
me, saying,
2 "Son of man, cause Jerusalem to know her
abominations,
3 "and say, 'Thus says the Lord GOD to Jerusalem: "Your birth and your nativity *are* from
the land of Canaan; your father *was* an Amorite and your mother a Hittite.
4 "*As for* your nativity, on the day you were
born your navel cord was not cut, nor were
you washed in water to cleanse *you;* you
were not rubbed with salt nor wrapped in
swaddling cloths.
5 "No eye pitied you, to do any of these
things for you, to have compassion on you;
but you were thrown out into the open field,
when you yourself were loathed on the day
you were born.
6 "And when I passed by you and saw you ➤
struggling in your own blood, I said to you in
your blood, 'Live!' Yes, I said to you in your
blood, 'Live!'
7 "I made you thrive like a plant in the field;
and you grew, matured, and became very
beautiful. *Your* breasts were formed, your
hair grew, but you *were* naked and bare.
8 "When I passed by you again and looked
upon you, indeed your time *was* the time of
love; so I spread My wing over you and covered your nakedness. Yes, I swore an oath to
you and entered into a covenant with you,
and you became Mine," says the Lord GOD.
9 "Then I washed you in water; yes, I thoroughly washed off your blood, and I anointed
you with oil.
10 "I clothed you in embroidered cloth and
gave you sandals of badger skin; I clothed
you with fine linen and covered you with silk.
11 "I adorned you with ornaments, put bracelets on your wrists, and a chain on your neck.
12 "And I put a jewel in your nose, earrings in
your ears, and a beautiful crown on your head.
13 "Thus you were adorned with gold and silver, and your clothing *was of* fine linen, silk,
and embroidered cloth. You ate *pastry of* fine
flour, honey, and oil. You were exceedingly
beautiful, and succeeded to royalty.
14 "Your fame went out among the nations ➤
because of your beauty, for it *was* perfect

LIFE LESSONS

➤ 15:8 — *"Thus I will make the land desolate, because they have persisted in unfaithfulness," says the Lord GOD.*

To persist in unfaithfulness is to invite God's judgment. Paul says, "if we would judge ourselves, we would not be judged. But when we are judged, we are chastened by the Lord . . ." (1 Cor. 11:31, 32).

➤ 16:6 — *"And when I passed by you and saw you struggling in your own blood, I said to you in your blood, 'Live!'"*

We owe our very lives to God. Without Him, we are a mess. Without Him, we wallow in our own blood, unable to grow and thrive. He sees us in our moral ugliness and yet says to us, "Live!"

➤ 16:14 — *"Your fame went out among the nations because of your beauty, for it was perfect through My splendor which I had bestowed on you," says the Lord GOD.*

Israel forgot that any good thing it had, it had received from God. We should never make the same mistake. Any success, talent, ability, insight or strength we have comes from Him. We should use it for His glory.

ANSWERS TO LIFE'S QUESTIONS

How can I confront a believer who has fallen spiritually?

EZEK. 16:2

God gave Ezekiel a tremendous and ominous calling to confront His people about their sin. "Son of man," He told the prophet, "cause Jerusalem to know her abominations" (Ezek. 16:2; 20:4; 22:2; 23:36). A tough calling! Even so, at times He will call us to do the same thing. So how can we manage it effectively?

First, we must watch the spirit in which we confront the fallen one. We must be firm but gentle. We are to confront them "in a spirit of gentleness" (Gal. 6:1). Hurting people can be as fragile as glass; they don't need our condemnation. We don't go to them in anger or to vent our hurt. We go gently, remaining sensitive to their agony. We should not automatically interpret their inability to express grief as a lack of remorse or repentance. They may suffer so greatly that they can't get close to the physical tears for which their souls weep. We must remain firm in our efforts to bring the sin into the open, but we need to do so with gentleness and respect.

Second, we are to confront someone in the spirit of humility: "For if anyone thinks himself to be something, when he is nothing, he deceives himself" (Gal. 6:3). We can't go with a haughty attitude, as if we could never fall into such sin. That kind of attitude deeply offends God. We have to remember that we are *all* vulnerable to sin. If we go to hurting people with the attitude that we are way above them, they certainly won't respond to our efforts. In fact, we only build a wall that will obstruct the restoration process, which is the object of our confrontation. "Considering yourself lest you also be tempted" (Gal. 6:1) means to examine ourselves with a sharp eye.

Third, we are to go in love. Galatians 6:2 uses a word that means "heavy burdens." We need to get under the heavy burden and help the offenders carry it. We need to vicariously feel what they are feeling. We must go with the right spirit, or we may as well not go at all.

Those who walk with the Father are to gently, humbly, and lovingly confront the straying person, and then get under the load with the saint who has sinned. Confrontation is never easy, but it is often a prerequisite to restoration, the real goal.

See the Life Principles Index for further study:
2. *Obey God and leave all the consequences to Him.*
24. *To live the Christian Life is to allow Jesus to live His life in and through us.*

through My splendor which I had bestowed
on you," says the Lord GOD.

Jerusalem's Harlotry

15 "But you trusted in your own beauty,
played the harlot because of your fame, and
poured out your harlotry on everyone passing
by who *would have* it.
16 "You took some of your garments and
adorned multicolored high places for yourself,
and played the harlot on them. *Such*
things should not happen, nor be.
17 "You have also taken your beautiful jewelry
from My gold and My silver, which I had
given you, and made for yourself male images
and played the harlot with them.
18 "You took your embroidered garments
and covered them, and you set My oil and My
incense before them.
19 "Also My food which I gave you—the pastry
of fine flour, oil, and honey *which* I fed
you—you set it before them as sweet incense;
and *so* it was," says the Lord GOD.
20 "Moreover you took your sons and your
daughters, whom you bore to Me, and these
you sacrificed to them to be devoured. *Were*
your *acts* of harlotry a small matter,
21 "that you have slain My children and offered
them up to them by causing them to
pass through *the fire*?
22 "And in all your abominations and acts of
harlotry you did not remember the days of
your youth, when you were naked and bare,
struggling in your blood.
23 "Then it was so, after all your wickedness—'Woe,
woe to you!' says the Lord GOD—
24 "*that* you also built for yourself a shrine,
and made a high place for yourself in every
street.
25 "You built your high places at the head of
every road, and made your beauty to be abhorred.
You offered yourself to everyone who
passed by, and multiplied your acts of harlotry.
26 "You also committed harlotry with the
Egyptians, your very fleshly neighbors, and
increased your acts of harlotry to provoke Me
to anger.
27 "Behold, therefore, I stretched out My

hand against you, diminished your allotment, and gave you up to the will of those who hate you, the daughters of the Philistines, who were ashamed of your lewd behavior.
28 You also played the harlot with the Assyrians, because you were insatiable; indeed you played the harlot with them and still were not satisfied.
29 Moreover you multiplied your acts of harlotry as far as the land of the trader, Chaldea; and even then you were not satisfied.
30 "How degenerate is your heart!" says the Lord GOD, "seeing you do all these *things,* the deeds of a brazen harlot.

Jerusalem's Adultery

31 "You erected your shrine at the head of every road, and built your high place in every street. Yet you were not like a harlot, because you scorned payment.
32 *You are* an adulterous wife, *who* takes strangers instead of her husband.
33 Men make payment to all harlots, but you made your payments to all your lovers, and hired them to come to you from all around for your harlotry.
34 You are the opposite of *other* women in your harlotry, because no one solicited you to be a harlot. In that you gave payment but no payment was given you, therefore you are the opposite."

Jerusalem's Lovers Will Abuse Her

35 'Now then, O harlot, hear the word of the LORD!
36 'Thus says the Lord GOD: "Because your filthiness was poured out and your nakedness uncovered in your harlotry with your lovers, and with all your abominable idols, and because of the blood of your children which you gave to them,
37 "surely, therefore, I will gather all your lovers with whom you took pleasure, all those you loved, *and* all those you hated; I will gather them from all around against you and will uncover your nakedness to them, that they may see all your nakedness.
38 "And I will judge you as women who break wedlock or shed blood are judged; I will bring blood upon you in fury and jealousy.
39 "I will also give you into their hand, and they shall throw down your shrines and break down your high places. They shall also strip you of your clothes, take your beautiful jewelry, and leave you naked and bare.
40 "They shall also bring up an assembly against you, and they shall stone you with stones and thrust you through with their swords.
41 "They shall burn your houses with fire, and execute judgments on you in the sight of many women; and I will make you cease playing the harlot, and you shall no longer hire lovers.
42 "So I will lay to rest My fury toward you, and My jealousy shall depart from you. I will be quiet, and be angry no more.
43 "Because you did not remember the days of your youth, but agitated Me[a] with all these *things,* surely I will also recompense your deeds on *your own* head," says the Lord GOD. "And you shall not commit lewdness in addition to all your abominations.

More Wicked than Samaria and Sodom

44 "Indeed everyone who quotes proverbs will use *this* proverb against you: 'Like mother, like daughter!'
45 "You *are* your mother's daughter, loathing husband and children; and you *are* the sister of your sisters, who loathed their husbands and children; your mother *was* a Hittite and your father an Amorite.
46 "Your elder sister *is* Samaria, who dwells with her daughters to the north of you; and your younger sister, who dwells to the south of you, *is* Sodom and her daughters.
47 "You did not walk in their ways nor act according to their abominations; but, as *if that were* too little, you became more corrupt than they in all your ways.
48 "*As* I live," says the Lord GOD, "neither your sister Sodom nor her daughters have done as you and your daughters have done.
49 "Look, this was the iniquity of your sister Sodom: She and her daughter had pride, fullness of food, and abundance of idleness; neither did she strengthen the hand of the poor and needy.
50 "And they were haughty and committed abomination before Me; therefore I took them away as I saw *fit.*[a]
51 "Samaria did not commit half of your sins; but you have multiplied your abominations more than they, and have justified your sisters by all the abominations which you have done.
52 "You who judged your sisters, bear your own shame also, because the sins which you committed were more abominable than theirs; they are more righteous than you. Yes, be disgraced also, and bear your own shame, because you justified your sisters.
53 "When I bring back their captives, the captives of Sodom and her daughters, and the captives of Samaria and her daughters, then *I will also bring back* the captives of your captivity among them,
54 "that you may bear your own shame and be disgraced by all that you did when you comforted them.
55 "When your sisters, Sodom and her daughters, return to their former state, and Samaria and her daughters return to their former

---

16:43 [a]Following Septuagint, Syriac, Targum, and Vulgate; Masoretic Text reads *were agitated with Me.* **16:50** [a]Vulgate reads *you saw;* Septuagint reads *he saw;* Targum reads *as was revealed to Me.*

state, then you and your daughters will return
to your former state.
56 "For your sister Sodom was not a byword
in your mouth in the days of your pride,
57 "before your wickedness was uncovered.
It was like the time of the reproach of the
daughters of Syria[a] and all *those* around her,
and of the daughters of the Philistines, who
despise you everywhere.
58 "You have paid for your lewdness and
your abominations," says the LORD.
59 'For thus says the Lord GOD: "I will deal
with you as you have done, who despised the
oath by breaking the covenant.

An Everlasting Covenant

60 "Nevertheless I will remember My covenant with you in the days of your youth, and
I will establish an everlasting covenant with
you.
61 "Then you will remember your ways and
be ashamed, when you receive your older and
your younger sisters; for I will give them to
you for daughters, but not because of My covenant with you.
62 "And I will establish My covenant with
you. Then you shall know that I *am* the LORD,
63 "that you may remember and be ashamed,
and never open your mouth anymore because
of your shame, when I provide you an atonement for all you have done," says the Lord
GOD.'"

The Eagles and the Vine

17 And the word of the LORD came to me, saying,
2 "Son of man, pose a riddle, and speak a
parable to the house of Israel,
3 "and say, 'Thus says the Lord GOD:

"A great eagle with large wings and long
pinions,
Full of feathers of various colors,
Came to Lebanon
And took from the cedar the highest
branch.
4 He cropped off its topmost young twig
And carried it to a land of trade;
He set it in a city of merchants.
5 Then he took some of the seed of the
land
And planted it in a fertile field;
He placed *it* by abundant waters
And set it like a willow tree.
6 And it grew and became a spreading vine
of low stature;
Its branches turned toward him,
But its roots were under it.
So it became a vine,
Brought forth branches,
And put forth shoots.

7 "But there was another[a] great eagle with
large wings and many feathers;
And behold, this vine bent its roots
toward him,
And stretched its branches toward him,
From the garden terrace where it had
been planted,
That he might water it.
8 It was planted in good soil by many
waters,
To bring forth branches, bear fruit,
And become a majestic vine."'

9 "Say, 'Thus says the Lord GOD:

"Will it thrive?
Will he not pull up its roots,
Cut off its fruit,
And leave it to wither?
All of its spring leaves will wither,
And no great power or many people
Will be needed to pluck it up by its roots.
10 Behold, *it is* planted,
Will it thrive?
Will it not utterly wither when the east
wind touches it?
It will wither in the garden terrace where
it grew."'"

11 Moreover the word of the LORD came to
me, saying,
12 "Say now to the rebellious house: 'Do you
not know what these *things mean?*' Tell *them,*
'Indeed the king of Babylon went to Jerusalem and took its king and princes, and led
them with him to Babylon.
13 'And he took the king's offspring, made a
covenant with him, and put him under oath.
He also took away the mighty of the land,
14 'that the kingdom might be brought low
and not lift itself up, *but* that by keeping his
covenant it might stand.
15 'But he rebelled against him by sending
his ambassadors to Egypt, that they might
give him horses and many people. Will he
prosper? Will he who does such *things* escape? Can he break a covenant and still be
delivered?
16 '*As* I live,' says the Lord GOD, 'surely in the
place *where* the king *dwells* who made him
king, whose oath he despised and whose covenant he broke—with him in the midst of
Babylon he shall die.
17 'Nor will Pharaoh with *his* mighty army
and great company do anything in the war,
when they heap up a siege mound and build a
wall to cut off many persons.
18 'Since he despised the oath by breaking
the covenant, and in fact gave his hand and
still did all these *things,* he shall not escape.'"
19 Therefore thus says the Lord GOD: "*As* I
live, surely My oath which he despised, and

16:57 [a]Following Masoretic Text, Septuagint, Targum, and Vulgate; many Hebrew manuscripts and Syriac read *Edom.*
17:7 [a]Following Septuagint, Syriac, and Vulgate; Masoretic Text and Targum read *one.*

My covenant which he broke, I will recompense on his own head.
20 "I will spread My net over him, and he shall be taken in My snare. I will bring him to Babylon and try him there for the treason which he committed against Me.
21 "All his fugitives[a] with all his troops shall fall by the sword, and those who remain shall be scattered to every wind; and you shall know that I, the LORD, have spoken."

Israel Exalted at Last

22 Thus says the Lord GOD: "I will take also *one* of the highest branches of the high cedar and set *it* out. I will crop off from the topmost of its young twigs a tender one, and will plant *it* on a high and prominent mountain.
23 "On the mountain height of Israel I will plant it; and it will bring forth boughs, and bear fruit, and be a majestic cedar. Under it will dwell birds of every sort; in the shadow of its branches they will dwell.
➤ 24 "And all the trees of the field shall know that I, the LORD, have brought down the high tree and exalted the low tree, dried up the green tree and made the dry tree flourish; I, the LORD, have spoken and have done *it*."

A False Proverb Refuted

18 The word of the LORD came to me again, saying,
2 "What do you mean when you use this proverb concerning the land of Israel, saying:

'The fathers have eaten sour grapes,
And the children's teeth are set on edge'?

3 "*As* I live," says the Lord GOD, "you shall no longer use this proverb in Israel.

➤ 4 "Behold, all souls are Mine;
The soul of the father
As well as the soul of the son is Mine;
The soul who sins shall die.
5 But if a man is just
And does what is lawful and right;
6 If he has not eaten on the mountains,
Nor lifted up his eyes to the idols of the house of Israel,
Nor defiled his neighbor's wife,
Nor approached a woman during her impurity;
7 If he has not oppressed anyone,
But has restored to the debtor his pledge;
Has robbed no one by violence,
But has given his bread to the hungry
And covered the naked with clothing;
8 If he has not exacted usury
Nor taken any increase,
But has withdrawn his hand from iniquity
And executed true judgment between man and man;
9 *If* he has walked in My statutes
And kept My judgments faithfully—
He *is* just;
He shall surely live!"
Says the Lord GOD.

10 "If he begets a son *who is* a robber
Or a shedder of blood,
Who does any of these *things*
11 And does none of those *duties*,
But has eaten on the mountains
Or defiled his neighbor's wife;
12 If he has oppressed the poor and needy,
Robbed by violence,
Not restored the pledge,
Lifted his eyes to the idols,
Or committed abomination;
13 If he has exacted usury
Or taken increase—
Shall he then live?
He shall not live!
If he has done any of these abominations,
He shall surely die;
His blood shall be upon him.

14 "*If*, however, he begets a son
Who sees all the sins which his father has done,
And considers but does not do likewise;
15 *Who* has not eaten on the mountains,
Nor lifted his eyes to the idols of the house of Israel,
Nor defiled his neighbor's wife;
16 Has not oppressed anyone,
Nor withheld a pledge,
Nor robbed by violence,

17:21 [a]Following Masoretic Text and Vulgate; many Hebrew manuscripts and Syriac read *choice men;* Targum reads *mighty men;* Septuagint omits *All his fugitives*.

LIFE LESSONS

➤ 17:24 — *"And all the trees of the field shall know that I, the LORD, have brought down the high tree and exalted the low tree, dried up the green tree and made the dry tree flourish; I, the LORD, have spoken and have done it."*

The Lord wants us to remember that He is absolutely sovereign. If a nation rides high, it does so because He planned it. If a nation falls, it does so because He made it happen. God rules among the nations.

➤ 18:4 — *"Behold, all souls are Mine; the soul of the father as well as the soul of the son is Mine . . . ."*

As the Creator, every human being belongs to God, so all of us on the planet are His "offspring" (Acts 17:28). Yet only those who place their faith in Christ belong to God as members of His heavenly family (Gal. 6:10).

But has given his bread to the hungry
And covered the naked with clothing;
17 *Who* has withdrawn his hand from the poor[a]
And not received usury or increase,
But has executed My judgments
And walked in My statutes—
He shall not die for the iniquity of his father;
He shall surely live!

18 "*As for* his father,
Because he cruelly oppressed,
Robbed his brother by violence,
And did what *is* not good among his people,
Behold, he shall die for his iniquity.

Turn and Live

19 "Yet you say, 'Why should the son not bear
the guilt of the father?' Because the son has
done what is lawful and right, and has kept all
My statutes and observed them, he shall
surely live.
20 "The soul who sins shall die. The son shall
not bear the guilt of the father, nor the father
bear the guilt of the son. The righteousness of
the righteous shall be upon himself, and the
wickedness of the wicked shall be upon himself.
21 "But if a wicked man turns from all his
sins which he has committed, keeps all My
statutes, and does what is lawful and right, he
shall surely live; he shall not die.
22 "None of the transgressions which he has
committed shall be remembered against him;
because of the righteousness which he has
done, he shall live.
23 "Do I have any pleasure at all that the
wicked should die?" says the Lord GOD, "*and*
not that he should turn from his ways and
live?
24 "But when a righteous man turns away
from his righteousness and commits iniquity,
and does according to all the abominations
that the wicked *man* does, shall he live? All
the righteousness which he has done shall not
be remembered; because of the unfaithfulness of which he is guilty and the sin which he
has committed, because of them he shall die.
25 "Yet you say, 'The way of the Lord is not
fair.' Hear now, O house of Israel, is it not My
way which is fair, and your ways which are
not fair?
26 "When a righteous *man* turns away from
his righteousness, commits iniquity, and dies
in it, it is because of the iniquity which he has
done that he dies.
27 "Again, when a wicked *man* turns away
from the wickedness which he committed,
and does what is lawful and right, he preserves himself alive.
28 "Because he considers and turns away
from all the transgressions which he committed, he shall surely live; he shall not die.
29 "Yet the house of Israel says, 'The way of
the Lord is not fair.' O house of Israel, is it not
My ways which are fair, and your ways which
are not fair?
30 "Therefore I will judge you, O house of Israel, every one according to his ways," says
the Lord GOD. "Repent, and turn from all your
transgressions, so that iniquity will not be
your ruin.
31 "Cast away from you all the transgressions which you have committed, and get
yourselves a new heart and a new spirit. For
why should you die, O house of Israel?
32 "For I have no pleasure in the death of one
who dies," says the Lord GOD. "Therefore turn
and live!"

Israel Degraded

19 "Moreover take up a lamentation for
the princes of Israel,
2 "and say:

'What *is* your mother? A lioness:
She lay down among the lions;
Among the young lions she nourished her cubs.
3 She brought up one of her cubs,
And he became a young lion;
He learned to catch prey,
And he devoured men.
4 The nations also heard of him;
He was trapped in their pit,
And they brought him with chains to the land of Egypt.
5 'When she saw that she waited, *that* her hope was lost,
She took another of her cubs *and* made him a young lion.
6 He roved among the lions,
And became a young lion;
He learned to catch prey;
He devoured men.
7 He knew their desolate places,[a]
And laid waste their cities;
The land with its fullness was desolated
By the noise of his roaring.

18:17 [a]Following Masoretic Text, Targum, and Vulgate; Septuagint reads *iniquity* (compare verse 8). **19:7** [a]Septuagint reads *He stood in insolence;* Targum reads *He destroyed its palaces;* Vulgate reads *He learned to make widows.*

LIFE LESSONS

➤ 18:32 — *"For I have no pleasure in the death of one who dies," says the Lord GOD. "Therefore turn and live!"*

Death is the wages of sin, but God would rather we not pay it. He has already covered the cost of our sin in the death of His Son; we must simply accept His gift and come to Him on His terms.

8 Then the nations set against him from the provinces on every side,
And spread their net over him;
He was trapped in their pit.
9 They put him in a cage with chains,
And brought him to the king of Babylon;
They brought him in nets,
That his voice should no longer be heard on the mountains of Israel.

10 'Your mother *was* like a vine in your bloodline,[a]
Planted by the waters,
Fruitful and full of branches
Because of many waters.
11 She had strong branches for scepters of rulers.
She towered in stature above the thick branches,
And was seen in her height amid the dense foliage.
12 But she was plucked up in fury,
She was cast down to the ground,
And the east wind dried her fruit.
Her strong branches were broken and withered;
The fire consumed them.
13 And now she *is* planted in the wilderness,
In a dry and thirsty land.
14 Fire has come out from a rod of her branches
And devoured her fruit,
So that she has no strong branch— a scepter for ruling.' "

This *is* a lamentation, and has become a lamentation.

The Rebellions of Israel

20 It came to pass in the seventh year, in
the fifth *month,* on the tenth *day* of the
month, *that* certain of the elders of Israel
came to inquire of the LORD, and sat before
me.
2 Then the word of the LORD came to me,
saying,
3 "Son of man, speak to the elders of Israel,
and say to them, 'Thus says the Lord GOD:
"Have you come to inquire of Me? *As* I live,"
says the Lord GOD, "I will not be inquired of
by you." '
4 "Will you judge them, son of man, will you
judge *them?* Then make known to them the
abominations of their fathers.
5 "Say to them, 'Thus says the Lord GOD:
"On the day when I chose Israel and raised
My hand in an oath to the descendants of the
house of Jacob, and made Myself known to
them in the land of Egypt, I raised My hand in
an oath to them, saying, 'I *am* the LORD your
God.'
6 "On that day I raised My hand in an oath
to them, to bring them out of the land of
Egypt into a land that I had searched out for
them, 'flowing with milk and honey,'[a] the
glory of all lands.
7 "Then I said to them, 'Each of you, throw
away the abominations which are before his
eyes, and do not defile yourselves with the
idols of Egypt. I *am* the LORD your God.'
8 "But they rebelled against Me and would
not obey Me. They did not all cast away the
abominations which were before their eyes,
nor did they forsake the idols of Egypt. Then
I said, 'I will pour out My fury on them and
fulfill My anger against them in the midst of
the land of Egypt.'
9 "But I acted for My name's sake, that it
should not be profaned before the Gentiles
among whom they *were,* in whose sight I had
made Myself known to them, to bring them
out of the land of Egypt.
10 "Therefore I made them go out of the land
of Egypt and brought them into the wilderness.
11 "And I gave them My statutes and showed
them My judgments, 'which, *if* a man does, he
shall live by them.'[a]
12 "Moreover I also gave them My Sabbaths,
to be a sign between them and Me, that they
might know that I *am* the LORD who sanctifies
them.
13 "Yet the house of Israel rebelled against
Me in the wilderness; they did not walk in My
statutes; they despised My judgments, 'which,
if a man does, he shall live by them';[a] and they
greatly defiled My Sabbaths. Then I said I
would pour out My fury on them in the wilderness, to consume them.
14 "But I acted for My name's sake, that it ➤
should not be profaned before the Gentiles, in
whose sight I had brought them out.
15 "So I also raised My hand in an oath to
them in the wilderness, that I would not bring
them into the land which I had given *them,*
'flowing with milk and honey,'[a] the glory of all
lands,
16 "because they despised My judgments and

19:10 [a]Literally *blood,* following Masoretic Text, Syriac, and Vulgate; Septuagint reads *like a flower on a pomegranate tree;* Targum reads *in your likeness.* **20:6** [a]Exodus 3:8 **20:11** [a]Leviticus 18:5 **20:13** [a]Leviticus 18:5 **20:15** [a]Exodus 3:8

LIFE LESSONS

➤ **20:14 — *"But I acted for My name's sake, that it should not be profaned before the Gentiles, in whose sight I had brought them out."***

God rescued the stiff-necked Israelites out of Egyptian slavery, not because they deserved it, but as a demonstration of His grace and mercy. He wants the world to both see and enjoy His love and goodness.

did not walk in My statutes, but profaned My Sabbaths; for their heart went after their idols.
17 "Nevertheless My eye spared them from destruction. I did not make an end of them in the wilderness.
18 "But I said to their children in the wilderness, 'Do not walk in the statutes of your fathers, nor observe their judgments, nor defile yourselves with their idols.
19 'I *am* the LORD your God: Walk in My statutes, keep My judgments, and do them;
20 'hallow My Sabbaths, and they will be a sign between Me and you, that you may know that I *am* the LORD your God.'
21 "Notwithstanding, the children rebelled against Me; they did not walk in My statutes, and were not careful to observe My judgments, 'which, *if* a man does, he shall live by them';[a] but they profaned My Sabbaths. Then I said I would pour out My fury on them and fulfill My anger against them in the wilderness.
22 "Nevertheless I withdrew My hand and acted for My name's sake, that it should not be profaned in the sight of the Gentiles, in whose sight I had brought them out.
23 "Also I raised My hand in an oath to those in the wilderness, that I would scatter them among the Gentiles and disperse them throughout the countries,
24 "because they had not executed My judgments, but had despised My statutes, profaned My Sabbaths, and their eyes were fixed on their fathers' idols.
➤ 25 "Therefore I also gave them up to statutes *that were* not good, and judgments by which they could not live;
26 "and I pronounced them unclean because of their ritual gifts, in that they caused all their firstborn to pass through *the fire,* that I might make them desolate and that they might know that I am the LORD."'
27 "Therefore, son of man, speak to the house of Israel, and say to them, 'Thus says the Lord GOD: "In this too your fathers have blasphemed Me, by being unfaithful to Me.
28 "When I brought them into the land *concerning* which I had raised My hand in an oath to give them, and they saw all the high hills and all the thick trees, there they offered their sacrifices and provoked Me with their offerings. There they also sent up their sweet aroma and poured out their drink offerings.
29 "Then I said to them, 'What *is* this high place to which you go?' So its name is called Bamah[a] to this day."'
30 "Therefore say to the house of Israel, 'Thus says the Lord GOD: "Are you defiling yourselves in the manner of your fathers, and committing harlotry according to their abominations?
31 "For when you offer your gifts and make your sons pass through the fire, you defile yourselves with all your idols, even to this day. So shall I be inquired of by you, O house of Israel? *As* I live," says the Lord GOD, "I will not be inquired of by you.
32 "What you have in your mind shall never be, when you say, 'We will be like the Gentiles, like the families in other countries, serving wood and stone.'

God Will Restore Israel

33 "*As* I live," says the Lord GOD, "surely with a mighty hand, with an outstretched arm, and with fury poured out, I will rule over you.
34 "I will bring you out from the peoples and gather you out of the countries where you are scattered, with a mighty hand, with an outstretched arm, and with fury poured out.
35 "And I will bring you into the wilderness of the peoples, and there I will plead My case with you face to face.
36 "Just as I pleaded My case with your fathers in the wilderness of the land of Egypt, so I will plead My case with you," says the Lord GOD.
37 "I will make you pass under the rod, and I will bring you into the bond of the covenant;
38 "I will purge the rebels from among you, and those who transgress against Me; I will bring them out of the country where they dwell, but they shall not enter the land of Israel. Then you will know that I *am* the LORD.
39 "As for you, O house of Israel," thus says the Lord GOD: "Go, serve every one of you his idols—and hereafter—if you will not obey Me; but profane My holy name no more with your gifts and your idols.
40 "For on My holy mountain, on the mountain height of Israel," says the Lord GOD, "there all the house of Israel, all of them in the land, shall serve Me; there I will accept them, and there I will require your offerings and the firstfruits of your sacrifices, together with all your holy things.
41 "I will accept you as a sweet aroma when I bring you out from the peoples and gather you out of the countries where you have been

20:21 [a]Leviticus 18:5 **20:29** [a]Literally *High Place*

LIFE LESSONS

➤ ***20:25 — "Therefore I also gave them up to statutes that were not good, and judgments by which they could not live . . . ."***

If we refuse to live by God's wisdom, we will have to live by our own; and that's like choosing a square-wheeled, stone bicycle. Human wisdom always fails in ways that no one sees coming.

scattered; and I will be hallowed in you before
the Gentiles.
42 "Then you shall know that I *am* the LORD,
when I bring you into the land of Israel, into
the country *for* which I raised My hand in an
oath to give to your fathers.
43 "And there you shall remember your ways
and all your doings with which you were defiled; and you shall loathe yourselves in your
own sight because of all the evils that you
have committed.
➤ 44 "Then you shall know that I *am* the LORD,
when I have dealt with you for My name's
sake, not according to your wicked ways nor
according to your corrupt doings, O house of
Israel," says the Lord GOD.'"

Fire in the Forest

45 Furthermore the word of the LORD came to
me, saying,
46 "Son of man, set your face toward the
south; preach against the south and prophesy
against the forest land, the South,[a]
47 "and say to the forest of the South, 'Hear
the word of the LORD! Thus says the Lord
GOD: "Behold, I will kindle a fire in you, and it
shall devour every green tree and every dry
tree in you; the blazing flame shall not be
quenched, and all faces from the south to the
north shall be scorched by it.
48 "All flesh shall see that I, the LORD, have
kindled it; it shall not be quenched."'"
49 Then I said, "Ah, Lord GOD! They say of
me, 'Does he not speak parables?'"

Babylon, the Sword of God

21 And the word of the LORD came to me,
saying,
2 "Son of man, set your face toward Jerusalem, preach against the holy places, and
prophesy against the land of Israel;
3 "and say to the land of Israel, 'Thus says
the LORD: "Behold, I *am* against you, and I
will draw My sword out of its sheath and cut
off both righteous and wicked from you.
4 "Because I will cut off both righteous and
wicked from you, therefore My sword shall go
out of its sheath against all flesh from south
to north,
5 "that all flesh may know that I, the LORD,
have drawn My sword out of its sheath; it
shall not return anymore."'
6 "Sigh therefore, son of man, with a breaking heart, and sigh with bitterness before
their eyes.
7 "And it shall be when they say to you,
'Why are you sighing?' that you shall answer,
'Because of the news; when it comes, every
heart will melt, all hands will be feeble, every
spirit will faint, and all knees will be weak *as*
water. Behold, it is coming and shall be
brought to pass,' says the Lord GOD."
8 Again the word of the LORD came to me,
saying,
9 "Son of man, prophesy and say, 'Thus says
the LORD!' Say:

'A sword, a sword is sharpened
And also polished!
10 Sharpened to make a dreadful slaughter,
Polished to flash like lightning!
Should we then make mirth?
It despises the scepter of My son,
As it does all wood.
11 And He has given it to be polished,
That it may be handled;
This sword is sharpened, and it is
polished
To be given into the hand of the slayer.'

12 "Cry and wail, son of man;
For it will be against My people,
Against all the princes of Israel.
Terrors including the sword will be
against My people;
Therefore strike *your* thigh.

13 "Because *it is* a testing,
And what if *the sword* despises even the
scepter?
The scepter shall be no *more*,"

says the Lord GOD.

14 "You therefore, son of man, prophesy,
And strike *your* hands together.
The third time let the sword do double
damage.
It *is* the sword *that* slays,
The sword that slays the great *men*,
That enters their private chambers.
15 I have set the point of the sword against
all their gates,
That the heart may melt and many may
stumble.
Ah! *It is* made bright;
It is grasped for slaughter:
16 "Swords at the ready!
Thrust right!
Set your blade!
Thrust left—
Wherever your edge is ordered!

20:46 [a]Hebrew *Negev*

LIFE LESSONS

➤ 20:44 — *"Then you shall know that I am the LORD, when I have dealt with you for My name's sake, not according to your wicked ways nor according to your corrupt doings, O house of Israel," says the Lord GOD.*

If God did not deal with us on the basis of His mercy and grace, none of us would have any hope of a happy future. But because He acts according to His loving nature, we have the brightest future imaginable.

17"I also will beat My fists together,
And I will cause My fury to rest;
I, the LORD, have spoken."

18 The word of the LORD came to me again, saying:
19 "And son of man, appoint for yourself two
ways for the sword of the king of Babylon to
go; both of them shall go from the same land.
Make a sign; put *it* at the head of the road to
the city.
20 "Appoint a road for the sword to go to
Rabbah of the Ammonites, and to Judah, into
fortified Jerusalem.
21 "For the king of Babylon stands at the parting of the road, at the fork of the two roads, to
use divination: he shakes the arrows, he consults the images, he looks at the liver.
22 "In his right hand is the divination for Jerusalem: to set up battering rams, to call for a
slaughter, to lift the voice with shouting, to set
battering rams against the gates, to heap up a
siege mound, and to build a wall.
23 "And it will be to them like a false divination in the eyes of those who have sworn
oaths with them; but he will bring their iniquity to remembrance, that they may be taken.
24 "Therefore thus says the Lord GOD: 'Because you have made your iniquity to be remembered, in that your transgressions are
uncovered, so that in all your doings your sins
appear—because you have come to remembrance, you shall be taken in hand.
25 'Now to you, O profane, wicked prince of
Israel, whose day has come, whose iniquity
shall end,
26'thus says the Lord GOD:

"Remove the turban, and take off the crown;
Nothing *shall remain* the same.
Exalt the humble, and humble the exalted.
➤ 27 Overthrown, overthrown,
I will make it overthrown!
It shall be no *longer,*
Until He comes whose right it is,
And I will give it *to Him*."'

A Sword Against the Ammonites

28 "And you, son of man, prophesy and say,
'Thus says the Lord GOD concerning the Ammonites and concerning their reproach,' and
say:

'A sword, a sword *is* drawn,
Polished for slaughter,
For consuming, for flashing—
29 While they see false visions for you,
While they divine a lie to you,
To bring you on the necks of the wicked, the slain
Whose day has come,
Whose iniquity *shall* end.

30'Return *it* to its sheath.
I will judge you
In the place where you were created,
In the land of your nativity.
31 I will pour out My indignation on you;
I will blow against you with the fire of My wrath,
And deliver you into the hands of brutal men *who are* skillful to destroy.
32 You shall be fuel for the fire;
Your blood shall be in the midst of the land.
You shall not be remembered,
For I the LORD have spoken.'"

Sins of Jerusalem

22 Moreover the word of the LORD came to
me, saying,
2 "Now, son of man, will you judge, will you
judge the bloody city? Yes, show her all her
abominations!
3 "Then say, 'Thus says the Lord GOD: "The
city sheds blood in her own midst, that her
time may come; and she makes idols within
herself to defile herself.
4 "You have become guilty by the blood
which you have shed, and have defiled yourself with the idols which you have made. You
have caused your days to draw near, and have
come to *the end of* your years; therefore I
have made you a reproach to the nations, and
a mockery to all countries.
5 "*Those* near and *those* far from you will
mock you as infamous *and* full of tumult.
6 "Look, the princes of Israel: each one has
used his power to shed blood in you.
7 "In you they have made light of father and
mother; in your midst they have oppressed
the stranger; in you they have mistreated the
fatherless and the widow.
8 "You have despised My holy things and
profaned My Sabbaths.
9 "In you are men who slander to cause
bloodshed; in you are those who eat on the
mountains; in your midst they commit lewdness.
10 "In you men uncover their fathers' nakedness; in you they violate women who are set
apart during their impurity.

LIFE LESSONS

➤ **21:27 — *"It shall be no longer, until He comes whose right it is, and I will give it to Him."***

With the destruction of Jerusalem by the Babylonians, the line of David ceased to rule on Israel's throne. According to this prophecy, no other Davidic king will rule until Jesus Christ—and His rule will last forever.

11 "One commits abomination with his neighbor's wife; another lewdly defiles his daughter-in-law; and another in you violates his sister, his father's daughter.
12 "In you they take bribes to shed blood; you take usury and increase; you have made profit from your neighbors by extortion, and have forgotten Me," says the Lord GOD.
13 "Behold, therefore, I beat My fists at the dishonest profit which you have made, and at the bloodshed which has been in your midst.
➤ 14 "Can your heart endure, or can your hands remain strong, in the days when I shall deal with you? I, the LORD, have spoken, and will do *it*.
15 "I will scatter you among the nations, disperse you throughout the countries, and remove your filthiness completely from you.
16 "You shall defile yourself in the sight of the nations; then you shall know that I *am* the LORD."'"

Israel in the Furnace

17 The word of the LORD came to me, saying,
18 "Son of man, the house of Israel has become dross to Me; they *are* all bronze, tin, iron, and lead, in the midst of a furnace; they have become dross from silver.
19 "Therefore thus says the Lord GOD: 'Because you have all become dross, therefore behold, I will gather you into the midst of Jerusalem.
20 '*As men* gather silver, bronze, iron, lead, and tin into the midst of a furnace, to blow fire on it, to melt *it;* so I will gather *you* in My anger and in My fury, and I will leave *you there* and melt you.
21 'Yes, I will gather you and blow on you with the fire of My wrath, and you shall be melted in its midst.
22 'As silver is melted in the midst of a furnace, so shall you be melted in its midst; then you shall know that I, the LORD, have poured out My fury on you.'"

Israel's Wicked Leaders

23 And the word of the LORD came to me, saying,
24 "Son of man, say to her: 'You *are* a land that is not cleansed[a] or rained on in the day of indignation.'
25 "The conspiracy of her prophets[a] in her midst is like a roaring lion tearing the prey; they have devoured people; they have taken treasure and precious things; they have made many widows in her midst.
26 "Her priests have violated My law and profaned My holy things; they have not distinguished between the holy and unholy, nor have they made known *the difference* between the unclean and the clean; and they have hidden their eyes from My Sabbaths, so that I am profaned among them.
27 "Her princes in her midst *are* like wolves tearing the prey, to shed blood, to destroy people, and to get dishonest gain.
28 "Her prophets plastered them with untempered *mortar,* seeing false visions, and divining lies for them, saying, 'Thus says the Lord GOD,' when the LORD had not spoken.
29 "The people of the land have used oppressions, committed robbery, and mistreated the poor and needy; and they wrongfully oppress the stranger.
30 "So I sought for a man among them who ➤
would make a wall, and stand in the gap before Me on behalf of the land, that I should not destroy it; but I found no one.
31 "Therefore I have poured out My indignation on them; I have consumed them with the fire of My wrath; and I have recompensed their deeds on their own heads," says the Lord GOD.

Two Harlot Sisters

23 The word of the LORD came again to me, saying:

2 "Son of man, there were two women,
The daughters of one mother.
3 They committed harlotry in Egypt,
They committed harlotry in their youth;
Their breasts were there embraced,
Their virgin bosom was there pressed.
4 Their names: Oholah[a] the elder and
Oholibah[b] her sister;
They were Mine,
And they bore sons and daughters.
As for their names,
Samaria *is* Oholah, and Jerusalem *is*
Oholibah.

22:24 [a]Following Masoretic Text, Syriac, and Vulgate; Septuagint reads *showered upon*. **22:25** [a]Following Masoretic Text and Vulgate; Septuagint reads *princes;* Targum reads *scribes*.
23:4 [a]Literally *Her Own Tabernacle* [b]Literally *My Tabernacle Is in Her*

LIFE LESSONS

➤ 22:14 — *"Can your heart endure, or can your hands remain strong, in the days when I shall deal with you? I, the LORD, have spoken, and will do it."*

God knows how to turn up the heat slowly, until His wayward people admit their sin and turn from it. God *will* transform His people into the image of His Son, and He will do whatever it takes to accomplish it.

➤ 22:30 — *"So I sought for a man among them who would make a wall, and stand in the gap before Me on behalf of the land, that I should not destroy it; but I found no one."*

God calls us, His people, to "stand in the gap" and call those around us to repentance and new life in Christ. Who do you know that needs to hear the Good News? Whose heart needs the softening of your prayers?

ANSWERS TO LIFE'S QUESTIONS

How can I become a godly influence on others?

EZEK. 22:30

The United States Marine Corps is always on the lookout for what it calls "a few good men." The eyes of the Lord are likewise scanning the earth in order to find godly men and women who will step forward and use their influence to exalt righteousness (see 2 Chr. 16:9). We see this in Ezekiel, where God says, "So I sought for a man among them who would make a wall, and stand in the gap before Me on behalf of the land, that I should not destroy it" (Ezek. 22:30).

A "gap" is some place where error or falsehood has crept in, allowing satanic confusion and inviting the judgment of God. Sometimes these gaps are so serious that they imperil entire nations. Such a time faced Israel following the Exodus; but the Word of God records this remarkable statement: "Therefore He said that He would destroy them, had not Moses His chosen one stood before Him in the breach, to turn away His wrath" (Ps. 106:23).

Few of us will ever be called upon to save a nation. But we can build up walls of protection around our families and churches by insisting on speaking the whole counsel of God. We can resist the devil daily and refuse the sensuality and perversions of this age. In Moses' day, one man made all the difference. Why not be the one who makes a difference today?

A prostitute named Rahab made the right choice and became the ancestor of the Messiah. A widow named Ruth chose the God of Israel and became the great-grandmother of King David. An infertile wife named Hannah poured out her soul to God and became the mother of Samuel. A man called Abram responded to God, left his relatives behind, and became the father of all who believe. A woman named Mary poured expensive perfume on Jesus' head and gained for herself an eternal monument in the stream of history.

Who are the influential people of this earth? They are the ones who leave all to follow the Lord—men and women who prove themselves to be "blameless and harmless, children of God without fault in the midst of a crooked and perverse generation, among whom [they] shine as lights in the world" (Phil. 2:15). You may doubt that your light shines brightly by this world's standards—but since God calls you a luminary, keep on shining!

See the Life Principles Index for further study:

8. Fight all your battles on your knees and you win every time.

14. God acts on behalf of those who wait for Him.

The Older Sister, Samaria

5 "Oholah played the harlot even though
she was Mine;
And she lusted for her lovers, the
neighboring Assyrians,
6 *Who were* clothed in purple,
Captains and rulers,
All of them desirable young men,
Horsemen riding on horses.
7 Thus she committed her harlotry with
them,
All of them choice men of Assyria;
And with all for whom she lusted,
With all their idols, she defiled herself.
8 She has never given up her harlotry
brought from Egypt,
For in her youth they had lain with her,
Pressed her virgin bosom,
And poured out their immorality upon her.

9 "Therefore I have delivered her
Into the hand of her lovers,
Into the hand of the Assyrians,
For whom she lusted.
10 They uncovered her nakedness,
Took away her sons and daughters,
And slew her with the sword;
She became a byword among women,
For they had executed judgment on her.

The Younger Sister, Jerusalem

11 "Now although her sister Oholibah saw *this,* she became more corrupt in her lust than she, and in her harlotry more corrupt than her sister's harlotry.

12 "She lusted for the neighboring Assyrians,
Captains and rulers,
Clothed most gorgeously,
Horsemen riding on horses,
All of them desirable young men.
13 Then I saw that she was defiled;
Both *took* the same way.
14 But she increased her harlotry;
She looked at men portrayed on the wall,
Images of Chaldeans portrayed in
vermilion,

15 Girded with belts around their waists,
Flowing turbans on their heads,
All of them looking like captains,
In the manner of the Babylonians of
Chaldea,
The land of their nativity.
16 As soon as her eyes saw them,
She lusted for them
And sent messengers to them in Chaldea.

17 "Then the Babylonians came to her, into
the bed of love,
And they defiled her with their immorality;
So she was defiled by them, and
alienated herself from them.
18 She revealed her harlotry and uncovered
her nakedness.
Then I alienated Myself from her,
As I had alienated Myself from her sister.

19 "Yet she multiplied her harlotry
In calling to remembrance the days of
her youth,
When she had played the harlot in the
land of Egypt.
20 For she lusted for her paramours,
Whose flesh *is like* the flesh of donkeys,
And whose issue *is like* the issue of horses.
21 Thus you called to remembrance the
lewdness of your youth,
When the Egyptians pressed your bosom
Because of your youthful breasts.

Judgment on Jerusalem
22 "Therefore, Oholibah, thus says the Lord
GOD:

'Behold, I will stir up your lovers against
you,
From whom you have alienated yourself,
And I will bring them against you from
every side:
23 The Babylonians,
All the Chaldeans,
Pekod, Shoa, Koa,
All the Assyrians with them,
All of them desirable young men,
Governors and rulers,
Captains and men of renown,
All of them riding on horses.
24 And they shall come against you
With chariots, wagons, and war-horses,
With a horde of people.
They shall array against you
Buckler, shield, and helmet all around.

'I will delegate judgment to them,
And they shall judge you according to
their judgments.
25 I will set My jealousy against you,
And they shall deal furiously with you;
They shall remove your nose and your
ears,
And your remnant shall fall by the sword;
They shall take your sons and your
daughters,
And your remnant shall be devoured by
fire.
26 They shall also strip you of your clothes
And take away your beautiful jewelry.

27 'Thus I will make you cease your
lewdness and your harlotry
Brought from the land of Egypt,
So that you will not lift your eyes to them,
Nor remember Egypt anymore.'

28 "For thus says the Lord GOD: 'Surely I will
deliver you into the hand of those you hate,
into the hand *of those* from whom you alienated yourself.
29 'They will deal hatefully with you, take
away all you have worked for, and leave you
naked and bare. The nakedness of your harlotry shall be uncovered, both your lewdness
and your harlotry.
30 'I will do these *things* to you because you
have gone as a harlot after the Gentiles, because you have become defiled by their idols.
31 'You have walked in the way of your sister;
therefore I will put her cup in your hand.'
32 "Thus says the Lord GOD:

'You shall drink of your sister's cup,
The deep and wide one;
You shall be laughed to scorn
And held in derision;
It contains much.
33 You will be filled with drunkenness and
sorrow,
The cup of horror and desolation,
The cup of your sister Samaria.
34 You shall drink and drain it,
You shall break its shards,
And tear at your own breasts;
For I have spoken,'
Says the Lord GOD.

35 "Therefore thus says the Lord GOD:

'Because you have forgotten Me and cast
Me behind your back,
Therefore you shall bear the *penalty*
Of your lewdness and your harlotry.'"

Both Sisters Judged
36 The LORD also said to me: "Son of man,
will you judge Oholah and Oholibah? Then
declare to them their abominations.

LIFE LESSONS

➤ 23:35 — *"Because you have forgotten Me and cast Me behind your back, therefore you shall bear the penalty of your lewdness and your harlotry."*

God will never "go quietly into that good night." We may forget Him, but He will never forget us. We may try to put Him behind our back, but He will always insist on receiving the glory that belongs to Him alone.

37 "For they have committed adultery, and
blood *is* on their hands. They have committed
adultery with their idols, and even *sacrificed*
their sons whom they bore to Me, passing
them through *the fire,* to devour *them.*
38 "Moreover they have done this to Me:
They have defiled My sanctuary on the same
day and profaned My Sabbaths.
39 "For after they had slain their children for
their idols, on the same day they came into
My sanctuary to profane it; and indeed thus
they have done in the midst of My house.
40 "Furthermore you sent for men to come
from afar, to whom a messenger *was* sent;
and there they came. And you washed yourself for them, painted your eyes, and adorned
yourself with ornaments.
41 "You sat on a stately couch, with a table
prepared before it, on which you had set My
incense and My oil.
42 "The sound of a carefree multitude *was*
with her, and Sabeans *were* brought from the
wilderness with men of the common sort,
who put bracelets on their wrists and beautiful crowns on their heads.
43 "Then I said concerning *her who had
grown* old in adulteries, 'Will they commit
harlotry with her now, and she *with them*?'
44 "Yet they went in to her, as men go in to a
woman who plays the harlot; thus they went
in to Oholah and Oholibah, the lewd women.
45 "But righteous men will judge them after
the manner of adulteresses, and after the
manner of women who shed blood, because
they *are* adulteresses, and blood *is* on their
hands.
46 "For thus says the Lord GOD: 'Bring up an
assembly against them, give them up to trouble and plunder.
47 'The assembly shall stone them with
stones and execute them with their swords;
they shall slay their sons and their daughters,
and burn their houses with fire.
48 'Thus I will cause lewdness to cease from
the land, that all women may be taught not to
practice your lewdness.
49 'They shall repay you for your lewdness,
and you shall pay for your idolatrous sins.
Then you shall know that I *am* the Lord GOD.'"

Symbol of the Cooking Pot

24 Again, in the ninth year, in the tenth
month, on the tenth *day* of the month,
the word of the LORD came to me, saying,
2 "Son of man, write down the name of the
day, this very day—the king of Babylon
started his siege against Jerusalem this very
day.
3 "And utter a parable to the rebellious
house, and say to them, 'Thus says the Lord
GOD:

"Put on a pot, set *it* on,
And also pour water into it.
4 Gather pieces *of meat* in it,
Every good piece,
The thigh and the shoulder.
Fill *it* with choice cuts;
5 Take the choice of the flock.
Also pile *fuel* bones under it,
Make it boil well,
And let the cuts simmer in it."

6 'Therefore thus says the Lord GOD:

"Woe to the bloody city,
To the pot whose scum *is* in it,
And whose scum is not gone from it!
Bring it out piece by piece,
On which no lot has fallen.
7 For her blood is in her midst;
She set it on top of a rock;
She did not pour it on the ground,
To cover it with dust.
8 That it may raise up fury and take
vengeance,
I have set her blood on top of a rock,
That it may not be covered."

9 'Therefore thus says the Lord GOD:

"Woe to the bloody city!
I too will make the pyre great.
10 Heap on the wood,
Kindle the fire;
Cook the meat well,
Mix in the spices,
And let the cuts be burned up.

11 "Then set the pot empty on the coals,
That it may become hot and its bronze
may burn,
That its filthiness may be melted in it,
That its scum may be consumed.
12 She has grown weary with lies,
And her great scum has not gone from
her.
Let her scum *be* in the fire!
13 In your filthiness *is* lewdness.
Because I have cleansed you, and you
were not cleansed,
You will not be cleansed of your
filthiness anymore,
Till I have caused My fury to rest upon
you.
14 I, the LORD, have spoken *it;*
It shall come to pass, and I will do *it;*
I will not hold back,
Nor will I spare,
Nor will I relent;
According to your ways
And according to your deeds
They[a] will judge you,"
Says the Lord GOD.'"

The Prophet's Wife Dies

15 Also the word of the LORD came to me,
saying,

24:14 [a]Septuagint, Syriac, Targum, and Vulgate read *I*.

➤ 16 "Son of man, behold, I take away from you
the desire of your eyes with one stroke; yet
you shall neither mourn nor weep, nor shall
your tears run down.
17 "Sigh in silence, make no mourning for the
dead; bind your turban on your head, and put
your sandals on your feet; do not cover *your*
lips, and do not eat man's bread *of sorrow*."
18 So I spoke to the people in the morning,
and at evening my wife died; and the next
morning I did as I was commanded.
19 And the people said to me, "Will you not
tell us what these *things signify* to us, that you
behave so?"
20 Then I answered them, "The word of the
LORD came to me, saying,
21 'Speak to the house of Israel, "Thus says
the Lord GOD: 'Behold, I will profane My
sanctuary, your arrogant boast, the desire of
your eyes, the delight of your soul; and your
sons and daughters whom you left behind
shall fall by the sword.
22 'And you shall do as I have done; you shall
not cover *your* lips nor eat man's bread *of sorrow*.
23 'Your turbans shall be on your heads and
your sandals on your feet; you shall neither
mourn nor weep, but you shall pine away in
your iniquities and mourn with one another.
➤ 24 'Thus Ezekiel is a sign to you; according to
all that he has done you shall do; and when
this comes, you shall know that I *am* the Lord
GOD.'"
25 'And you, son of man—*will it* not *be* in the
day when I take from them their stronghold,
their joy and their glory, the desire of their
eyes, and that on which they set their minds,
their sons and their daughters:
26 '*that* on that day one who escapes will
come to you to let *you* hear *it* with *your* ears?
27 'On that day your mouth will be opened to
him who has escaped; you shall speak and no
longer be mute. Thus you will be a sign to
them, and they shall know that I *am* the LORD.'"

Proclamation Against Ammon

25 The word of the LORD came to me,
saying,
2 "Son of man, set your face against the Ammonites, and prophesy against them.
3 "Say to the Ammonites, 'Hear the word of
the Lord GOD! Thus says the Lord GOD: "Because you said, 'Aha!' against My sanctuary
when it was profaned, and against the land of
Israel when it was desolate, and against the
house of Judah when they went into captivity,
4 "indeed, therefore, I will deliver you as a
possession to the men of the East, and they
shall set their encampments among you and
make their dwellings among you; they shall
eat your fruit, and they shall drink your milk.
5 "And I will make Rabbah a stable for
camels and Ammon a resting place for flocks.
Then you shall know that I *am* the LORD."
6 'For thus says the Lord GOD: "Because you
clapped *your* hands, stamped your feet, and
rejoiced in heart with all your disdain for the
land of Israel,
7 "indeed, therefore, I will stretch out My
hand against you, and give you as plunder to
the nations; I will cut you off from the peoples, and I will cause you to perish from the
countries; I will destroy you, and you shall
know that I *am* the LORD."

Proclamation Against Moab

8 'Thus says the Lord GOD: "Because Moab
and Seir say, 'Look! The house of Judah *is* like
all the nations,'
9 "therefore, behold, I will clear the territory
of Moab of cities, of the cities on its frontier,
the glory of the country, Beth Jeshimoth, Baal
Meon, and Kirjathaim.
10 "To the men of the East I will give it as a
possession, together with the Ammonites,
that the Ammonites may not be remembered
among the nations.
11 "And I will execute judgments upon Moab,
and they shall know that I *am* the LORD."

Proclamation Against Edom

12 'Thus says the Lord GOD: "Because of
what Edom did against the house of Judah by
taking vengeance, and has greatly offended
by avenging itself on them,"
13 'therefore thus says the Lord GOD: "I will
also stretch out My hand against Edom, cut
off man and beast from it, and make it desolate from Teman; Dedan shall fall by the
sword.

LIFE LESSONS

➤ 24:16 — *"Son of man, behold, I take away from you the desire of your eyes with one stroke; yet you shall neither mourn nor weep, nor shall your tears run down."*

God required some hard things of His servants the prophets. Here he told Ezekiel not to weep when his beloved wife died. God will use the most extraordinary measures to try to wake up His sleeping people to their imminent danger.

➤ 24:24 — *"Thus Ezekiel is a sign to you; according to all that he has done you shall do; and when this comes, you shall know that I am the Lord GOD."*

God made Ezekiel's whole life into a "sign" or a living message to Israel. He will move heaven and earth, if necessary, to show us His will. Our job is to obey it through the power of the Spirit.

14 "I will lay My vengeance on Edom by the hand of My people Israel, that they may do in Edom according to My anger and according to My fury; and they shall know My vengeance," says the Lord GOD.

Proclamation Against Philistia

15 'Thus says the Lord GOD: "Because the Philistines dealt vengefully and took vengeance with a spiteful heart, to destroy because of the old hatred,"

16 'therefore thus says the Lord GOD: "I will stretch out My hand against the Philistines, and I will cut off the Cherethites and destroy the remnant of the seacoast.

17 "I will execute great vengeance on them with furious rebukes; and they shall know that I *am* the LORD, when I lay My vengeance upon them."'"

Proclamation Against Tyre

26 And it came to pass in the eleventh year, on the first *day* of the month, *that* the word of the LORD came to me, saying,

2 "Son of man, because Tyre has said against Jerusalem, 'Aha! She is broken who *was* the gateway of the peoples; now she is turned over to me; I shall be filled; she is laid waste.'

3 "Therefore thus says the Lord GOD: 'Behold, I *am* against you, O Tyre, and will cause many nations to come up against you, as the sea causes its waves to come up.

➤ 4 'And they shall destroy the walls of Tyre and break down her towers; I will also scrape her dust from her, and make her like the top of a rock.

5 'It shall be *a place for* spreading nets in the midst of the sea, for I have spoken,' says the Lord GOD; 'it shall become plunder for the nations.

6 'Also her daughter *villages* which *are* in the fields shall be slain by the sword. Then they shall know that I am the LORD.'

7 "For thus says the Lord GOD: 'Behold, I will bring against Tyre from the north Nebuchadnezzar[a] king of Babylon, king of kings, with horses, with chariots, and with horsemen, and an army with many people.

8 'He will slay with the sword your daughter *villages* in the fields; he will heap up a siege mound against you, build a wall against you, and raise a defense against you.

9 'He will direct his battering rams against your walls, and with his axes he will break down your towers.

10 'Because of the abundance of his horses, their dust will cover you; your walls will shake at the noise of the horsemen, the wagons, and the chariots, when he enters your gates, as men enter a city that has been breached.

11 'With the hooves of his horses he will trample all your streets; he will slay your people by the sword, and your strong pillars will fall to the ground.

12 'They will plunder your riches and pillage your merchandise; they will break down your walls and destroy your pleasant houses; they will lay your stones, your timber, and your soil in the midst of the water.

13 'I will put an end to the sound of your songs, and the sound of your harps shall be heard no more.

14 'I will make you like the top of a rock; you shall be *a place for* spreading nets, and you shall never be rebuilt, for I the LORD have spoken,' says the Lord GOD.

15 "Thus says the Lord GOD to Tyre: 'Will the coastlands not shake at the sound of your fall, when the wounded cry, when slaughter is made in the midst of you?

16 'Then all the princes of the sea will come down from their thrones, lay aside their robes, and take off their embroidered garments; they will clothe themselves with trembling; they will sit on the ground, tremble *every* moment, and be astonished at you.

17 'And they will take up a lamentation for you, and say to you:

"How you have perished,
O one inhabited by seafaring men,
O renowned city,
Who was strong at sea,
She and her inhabitants,
Who caused their terror *to be* on all her
inhabitants!
18 Now the coastlands tremble on the day of
your fall;
Yes, the coastlands by the sea are
troubled at your departure."'

19 "For thus says the Lord GOD: 'When I make you a desolate city, like cities that are not inhabited, when I bring the deep upon you, and great waters cover you,

20 'then I will bring you down with those who descend into the Pit, to the people of old, and I will make you dwell in the lowest part of the earth, in places desolate from antiquity,

26:7 [a]Hebrew *Nebuchadrezzar,* and so elsewhere in this book

LIFE LESSONS

➤ **26:4, 5 — *"And they shall destroy the walls of Tyre and break down her towers; I will also scrape her dust from her, and make her like the top of a rock. 'It shall be a place for spreading nets . . . ."***

Ezekiel's prophecy about the fate of Tyre is a remarkable example of fulfilled prophecy. While at the height of her power, Ezekiel predicted she would become a place to dry fishing nets—exactly what it is today.

LIFE PRINCIPLE 16

WHATEVER YOU ACQUIRE OUTSIDE OF GOD'S WILL EVENTUALLY TURNS TO ASHES.

EZEK. 25:6, 7

Some people think that God's refusal to give them some cherished need would be the worst thing that could ever happen to them. They think life would truly disappoint them if some urgent desire of theirs should go unmet.

So they pursue their desire, either in opposition to God's will or in disregard of it—and end up *truly* disappointed, even if they get what they think they wanted. They remind me of the Israelites in Moses' day who insisted on meat and got it: "He gave them their request, but sent leanness into their soul" (Ps. 106:15).

G. K. Chesterton said, "There are two ways to get enough: One is to accumulate more and more, the other is to desire less."

While you can always accumulate more things, more relationships, and more success, there will always be room for more. And when there's room for more, there's room for *wanting* more. The cycle never ends.

If you choose the second route of Chesterton's advice, "to desire less," the likelihood of living a fulfilling life increases. But how does one simply want less?

By going back to the one desire present in every human heart: to know God.

You may not understand this longing as a desire for God; you may simply feel dissatisfaction with your life. Maybe the relationship you wanted and attained isn't everything you thought it would be. Perhaps you have everything you'd ever wanted, yet still go through periods of longing, sadness, and loneliness.

The origin of dissatisfaction, unfulfilled expectations, and feelings of sadness or loneliness is the same: a raging hunger for what you cannot see and do not fully know: God. Centuries ago Augustine said to God, "You made us for Yourself, and our heart is restless until it rests in You."

There is always more to be uncovered about God. We will never "get to the bottom" of Him while we live on earth. But once we enter into a relationship with the Lord, He promises to reveal more of Himself to us as we fellowship with Him. Hosea 2:19, 20 says, "I will betroth you to Me forever; Yes, I will betroth you to Me in righteousness and justice. In lovingkindness and mercy I will betroth you to Me in

How does one simply want less?

faithfulness, and you shall know the LORD."

To "fellowship" with God—to talk to Him and listen to Him as you study the Bible—is to get to know Him better. He has "betrothed" (or engaged) His people to Himself for one reason: to let Himself be known.

When you discover something about God that you have never recognized, the proverbial light bulb illuminates your heart and mind, giving you a greater desire to know more—and leave your fleshly desires behind.

As we test the waters of worldly desire, only to find ourselves drowning in them, God's loyalty to us shines. As we find the things we acquire outside of His will turning to ashes, He rescues us and restores our desire for Him alone.

Glimpsing one of God's characteristics in His Word, and then seeing it come to life through our experiences, deepens:

There is always more to be uncovered about God.

- *Our humility.* As we see God's sovereignty unveiled, we more deeply understand our need for Him.
- *Our gratitude.* Knowing that God's lovingkindness motivates His forgiveness, deliverance, and guidance, gives us a thankful heart. Instead of coming to God with complaints about our unfulfilled, selfish desires, we come to Him with adoration and praise.
- *Our hunger.* When the Holy Spirit sheds new light on an old verse (one we've read many times), our quest for more gets stronger. Our appreciation of God's Word gives us a more profound delight in studying and applying its truth.
- *Our reverence.* Learning something new about our Creator reminds us that we don't know everything about Him. As we come to terms with the depths and heights of God, our awe of Him grows.
- *Our desire to please God.* When we have a right, holy, respectful fear of the Lord, our wants change from satisfying ourselves to satisfying our God. Pleasing Him is not a chore; rather it becomes a joy done out of humility and thankfulness.

Amazingly, as we pursue our desire for God, He fulfills the other desires He has given us (Ps. 37:4). And so we learn afresh that while acquiring *anything* outside of His will leaves dust in our mouths, He desires to fill us with "pleasures forevermore" (Ps. 16:11).

See the Life Principles Index for further study.

with those who go down to the Pit, so that you
may never be inhabited; and I shall establish
glory in the land of the living.
21 'I will make you a terror, and you *shall be*
no *more;* though you are sought for, you will
never be found again,' says the Lord GOD."

Lamentation for Tyre

27 The word of the LORD came again to
me, saying,
2 "Now, son of man, take up a lamentation
for Tyre,
3 "and say to Tyre, 'You who are situated at
the entrance of the sea, merchant of the peoples on many coastlands, thus says the Lord
GOD:

"O Tyre, you have said,
'I *am* perfect in beauty.'
4 Your borders *are* in the midst of the seas.
Your builders have perfected your beauty.
5 They made all *your* planks of fir trees
from Senir;
They took a cedar from Lebanon to make
you a mast.
6 *Of* oaks from Bashan they made your oars;
The company of Ashurites have inlaid
your planks
With ivory from the coasts of Cyprus.[a]
7 Fine embroidered linen from Egypt was
what you spread for your sail;
Blue and purple from the coasts of
Elishah was what covered you.

8 "Inhabitants of Sidon and Arvad were
your oarsmen;
Your wise men, O Tyre, were in you;
They became your pilots.
9 Elders of Gebal and its wise men
Were in you to caulk your seams;
All the ships of the sea
And their oarsmen were in you
To market your merchandise.

10 "Those from Persia, Lydia,[a] and Libya[b]
Were in your army as men of war;
They hung shield and helmet in you;
They gave splendor to you.
11 Men of Arvad with your army *were* on
your walls *all* around,
And the men of Gammad were in your
towers;
They hung their shields on your walls *all*
around;
They made your beauty perfect.

12 "Tarshish *was* your merchant because of
your many luxury goods. They gave you silver, iron, tin, and lead for your goods.
13 "Javan, Tubal, and Meshech *were* your
traders. They bartered human lives and vessels of bronze for your merchandise.
14 "Those from the house of Togarmah traded
for your wares with horses, steeds, and mules.
15 "The men of Dedan *were* your traders;
many isles *were* the market of your hand.
They brought you ivory tusks and ebony as
payment.
16 "Syria *was* your merchant because of the
abundance of goods you made. They gave you
for your wares emeralds, purple, embroidery,
fine linen, corals, and rubies.
17 "Judah and the land of Israel *were* your
traders. They traded for your merchandise
wheat of Minnith, millet, honey, oil, and balm.
18 "Damascus *was* your merchant because of
the abundance of goods you made, because of
your many luxury items, with the wine of Hel-
bon and with white wool.
19 "Dan and Javan paid for your wares, traversing back and forth. Wrought iron, cassia,
and cane were among your merchandise.
20 "Dedan *was* your merchant in saddle-
cloths for riding.
21 "Arabia and all the princes of Kedar *were*
your regular merchants. They traded with
you in lambs, rams, and goats.
22 "The merchants of Sheba and Raamah
were your merchants. They traded for your
wares the choicest spices, all kinds of precious stones, and gold.
23 "Haran, Canneh, Eden, the merchants of
Sheba, Assyria, *and* Chilmad *were* your merchants.
24 "These *were* your merchants in choice
items—in purple clothes, in embroidered garments, in chests of multicolored apparel, in
sturdy woven cords, which were in your marketplace.

25 "The ships of Tarshish were carriers of
your merchandise.
You were filled and very glorious in the
midst of the seas.
26 Your oarsmen brought you into many
waters,
But the east wind broke you in the midst
of the seas.

27 "Your riches, wares, and merchandise,
Your mariners and pilots,
Your caulkers and merchandisers,
All your men of war who *are* in you,
And the entire company which *is* in your
midst,
Will fall into the midst of the seas on the
day of your ruin.
28 The common-land will shake at the
sound of the cry of your pilots.

29 "All who handle the oar,
The mariners,
All the pilots of the sea
Will come down from their ships *and*
stand on the shore.
30 They will make their voice heard because
of you;

27:6 [a]Hebrew *Kittim,* western lands, especially Cyprus
27:10 [a]Hebrew *Lud* [b]Hebrew *Put*

They will cry bitterly and cast dust on
their heads;
They will roll about in ashes;
31 They will shave themselves completely
bald because of you,
Gird themselves with sackcloth,
And weep for you
With bitterness of heart *and* bitter wailing.
32 In their wailing for you
They will take up a lamentation,
And lament for you:
'What *city is* like Tyre,
Destroyed in the midst of the sea?

33 'When your wares went out by sea,
You satisfied many people;
You enriched the kings of the earth
With your many luxury goods and your
merchandise.
34 But you are broken by the seas in the
depths of the waters;
Your merchandise and the entire
company will fall in your midst.
35 All the inhabitants of the isles will be
astonished at you;
Their kings will be greatly afraid,
And *their* countenance will be troubled.
➤ 36 The merchants among the peoples will
hiss at you;
You will become a horror, and *be* no
more forever.'"'"

Proclamation Against the King of Tyre

28 The word of the LORD came to me
again, saying,
2 "Son of man, say to the prince of Tyre,
'Thus says the Lord GOD:

"Because your heart *is* lifted up,
And you say, 'I *am* a god,
I sit *in* the seat of gods,
In the midst of the seas,'
Yet you *are* a man, and not a god,
Though you set your heart as the heart of
a god
3 (Behold, you *are* wiser than Daniel!
There is no secret that can be hidden
from you!
4 With your wisdom and your
understanding
You have gained riches for yourself,
And gathered gold and silver into your
treasuries;
5 By your great wisdom in trade you have
increased your riches,
And your heart is lifted up because of
your riches),"
6 'Therefore thus says the Lord GOD:

"Because you have set your heart as the
heart of a god,
7 Behold, therefore, I will bring strangers
against you,
The most terrible of the nations;
And they shall draw their swords against
the beauty of your wisdom,
And defile your splendor.
8 They shall throw you down into the Pit,
And you shall die the death of the slain
In the midst of the seas.

9 "Will you still say before him who slays
you,
'I *am* a god'?
But you *shall be* a man, and not a god,
In the hand of him who slays you.
10 You shall die the death of the
uncircumcised
By the hand of aliens;
For I have spoken," says the Lord GOD.'"

Lamentation for the King of Tyre

11 Moreover the word of the LORD came to
me, saying,
12 "Son of man, take up a lamentation for the ➤
king of Tyre, and say to him, 'Thus says the
Lord GOD:

"You *were* the seal of perfection,
Full of wisdom and perfect in beauty.
13 You were in Eden, the garden of God;
Every precious stone *was* your covering:
The sardius, topaz, and diamond,
Beryl, onyx, and jasper,
Sapphire, turquoise, and emerald with
gold.
The workmanship of your timbrels and
pipes
Was prepared for you on the day you
were created.

14 "You *were* the anointed cherub who
covers;
I established you;
You were on the holy mountain of God;
You walked back and forth in the midst
of fiery stones.

LIFE LESSONS

➤ 27:36 — *"The merchants among the peoples will hiss at you; you will become a horror, and be no more forever."*

Despite a fabulous location and plenty of fresh water available, God foretold that Tyre would cease to be a city and remain a desolation forever. So He spoke, and so it has been even to this day.

➤ 28:12 — *"You were the seal of perfection, full of wisdom and perfect in beauty."*

Many scholars believe this passage speaks of Satan and how through his rebellion he lost his privileged place in heaven and became the devil. As a fallen angel, he possesses power, but not all power.

WHAT THE BIBLE SAYS ABOUT THE ORIGIN, WORK, AND DESTINY OF SATAN

Ezek. 28:12–19

Ezekiel 28:12–19 tells us that God created Satan as a beautiful and eminent angel, a being as real as any of us. The devil lusted after God's place and position and so rebelled against the Creator, who subsequently cast him and his co-conspirators to earth. Here he set up a counterfeit kingdom in order that he might reign as the god of this world (2 Cor. 4:4).

Satan uses deception and division to ensnare believers. He works tirelessly to tempt us, hoping that we will fall into sin, thereby damaging our relationship with God and ruining our witness for Christ. He also desires to keep unbelievers away from the saving grace of Jesus Christ, thereby destroying them. Jesus called him a murderer and the father of lies (John 8:44), and as such, he instigates pain, sorrow and death all over the world. When Satan speaks, he accuses and deceives. He condemns, antagonizes, and confuses us in an attempt to fill us with doubt and despair.

When Satan speaks, he accuses and deceives.

But Christians have no cause to fear Satan. This is true for two reasons.

First, "He who is in you is greater than he who is in the world" (1 John 4:4). We live under the protection of the Holy Spirit; nothing can happen to us that God does not allow, and we know that whatever He permits—no matter how bad it may seem—He can turn for our good (Rom. 8:28).

Second, all of us who have read Scripture have seen Satan's obituary. The Bible says he will be thrown into the lake of fire and eternally punished for his rebellion against almighty God (Rev. 20:10).

The apostle Peter refers to Satan as "a roaring lion, seeking whom he may devour" (1 Pet. 5:8). Yet even though the devil is a lion, he's a lion on a short leash. His eternal destination, like ours, is certain. While he may be able to harass us, tempt us, and prompt us to stumble, our ultimate victory over him and his work was secured for us when Jesus Christ defeated sin once and for all on the cross.

See the Life Principles Index for further study:

9. Trusting God means looking beyond what we can see to what God sees.

18. As children of a sovereign God, we are never victims of our circumstances.

15 You *were* perfect in your ways from the day you were created,
Till iniquity was found in you.

16 "By the abundance of your trading
You became filled with violence within,
And you sinned;
Therefore I cast you as a profane thing
Out of the mountain of God;
And I destroyed you, O covering cherub,
From the midst of the fiery stones.

➤ 17 "Your heart was lifted up because of your beauty;
You corrupted your wisdom for the sake of your splendor;
I cast you to the ground,
I laid you before kings,
That they might gaze at you.

18 "You defiled your sanctuaries
By the multitude of your iniquities,
By the iniquity of your trading;
Therefore I brought fire from your midst;
It devoured you,
And I turned you to ashes upon the earth
In the sight of all who saw you.
19 All who knew you among the peoples are astonished at you;
You have become a horror,
And *shall be* no more forever." ' "

Proclamation Against Sidon

20 Then the word of the LORD came to me,
saying,
21 "Son of man, set your face toward Sidon,
and prophesy against her,
22 "and say, 'Thus says the Lord GOD:

"Behold, I *am* against you, O Sidon;
I will be glorified in your midst;
And they shall know that I *am* the LORD,
When I execute judgments in her and am hallowed in her.
23 For I will send pestilence upon her,
And blood in her streets;
The wounded shall be judged in her midst
By the sword against her on every side;
Then they shall know that I *am* the LORD.

24 "And there shall no longer be a pricking
brier or a painful thorn for the house of Israel
from among all *who are* around them, who
despise them. Then they shall know that I *am*
the Lord GOD."

Israel's Future Blessing

25 'Thus says the Lord GOD: "When I have
gathered the house of Israel from the peoples
among whom they are scattered, and am hallowed in them in the sight of the Gentiles,
then they will dwell in their own land which I
gave to My servant Jacob.
26 "And they will dwell safely there, build
houses, and plant vineyards; yes, they will
dwell securely, when I execute judgments on
all those around them who despise them.
Then they shall know that I *am* the LORD their
God." ' "

Proclamation Against Egypt

29 In the tenth year, in the tenth *month*,
on the twelfth *day* of the month, the
word of the LORD came to me, saying,
2 "Son of man, set your face against
Pharaoh king of Egypt, and prophesy against
him, and against all Egypt.
3 "Speak, and say, 'Thus says the Lord GOD:

"Behold, I *am* against you,
O Pharaoh king of Egypt,
O great monster who lies in the midst of his rivers,
Who has said, 'My River[a] *is* my own;
I have made *it* for myself.'
4 But I will put hooks in your jaws,
And cause the fish of your rivers to stick to your scales;
I will bring you up out of the midst of your rivers,
And all the fish in your rivers will stick to your scales.
5 I will leave you in the wilderness,
You and all the fish of your rivers;
You shall fall on the open field;
You shall not be picked up or gathered.[a]
I have given you as food
To the beasts of the field
And to the birds of the heavens.

6 "Then all the inhabitants of Egypt
Shall know that I *am* the LORD,
Because they have been a staff of reed to the house of Israel.
7 When they took hold of you with the hand,
You broke and tore all their shoulders;[a]
When they leaned on you,
You broke and made all their backs quiver."

29:3 [a]That is, the Nile **29:5** [a]Following Masoretic Text, Septuagint, and Vulgate; some Hebrew manuscripts and Targum read *buried.* **29:7** [a]Following Masoretic Text and Vulgate; Septuagint and Syriac read *hand.*

LIFE LESSONS

➤ **28:17 — *"Your heart was lifted up because of your beauty; you corrupted your wisdom for the sake of your splendor . . . ."***

What made Lucifer into the devil? Pride. He forgot that any wisdom and beauty and splendor he had came as a gift from God, to reflect God's glory and not his own. We must beware the same deadly mistake.

8 'Therefore thus says the Lord GOD:
"Surely I will bring a sword upon you and cut
off from you man and beast.
9 "And the land of Egypt shall become desolate and waste; then they will know that I *am*
the LORD, because he said, 'The River *is* mine,
and I have made *it*.'
10 "Indeed, therefore, I *am* against you and
against your rivers, and I will make the land
of Egypt utterly waste and desolate, from
Migdol[a] *to* Syene, as far as the border of Ethiopia.
11 "Neither foot of man shall pass through it
nor foot of beast pass through it, and it shall
be uninhabited forty years.
12 "I will make the land of Egypt desolate in
the midst of the countries *that are* desolate;
and among the cities *that are* laid waste, her
cities shall be desolate forty years; and I will
scatter the Egyptians among the nations and
disperse them throughout the countries."
13 'Yet, thus says the Lord GOD: "At the end
of forty years I will gather the Egyptians from
the peoples among whom they were scattered.
14 "I will bring back the captives of Egypt
and cause them to return to the land of
Pathros, to the land of their origin, and there
they shall be a lowly kingdom.
➤ 15 "It shall be the lowliest of kingdoms; it
shall never again exalt itself above the nations, for I will diminish them so that they will
not rule over the nations anymore.
16 "No longer shall it be the confidence of the
house of Israel, but will remind them of *their*
iniquity when they turned to follow them.
Then they shall know that I *am* the Lord
GOD."'"

Babylonia Will Plunder Egypt

17 And it came to pass in the twenty-seventh
year, in the first *month,* on the first *day* of the
month, *that* the word of the LORD came to me,
saying,
18 "Son of man, Nebuchadnezzar king of
Babylon caused his army to labor strenuously
against Tyre; every head *was* made bald, and
every shoulder rubbed raw; yet neither he nor
his army received wages from Tyre, for the
labor which they expended on it.
19 "Therefore thus says the Lord GOD: 'Surely
I will give the land of Egypt to Nebuchadnezzar king of Babylon; he shall take away her
wealth, carry off her spoil, and remove her pillage; and that will be the wages for his army.
20 'I have given him the land of Egypt *for* his
labor, because they worked for Me,' says the
Lord GOD.
21 'In that day I will cause the horn of the
house of Israel to spring forth, and I will open
your mouth to speak in their midst. Then they
shall know that I *am* the LORD.'"

Egypt and Her Allies Will Fall

30 The word of the LORD came to me
again, saying,
2 "Son of man, prophesy and say, 'Thus says
the Lord GOD:

"Wail, 'Woe to the day!'
3 For the day *is* near,
Even the day of the LORD *is* near;
It will be a day of clouds, the time of the
Gentiles.
4 The sword shall come upon Egypt,
And great anguish shall be in Ethiopia,
When the slain fall in Egypt,
And they take away her wealth,
And her foundations are broken down.

5 "Ethiopia, Libya,[a] Lydia,[b] all the mingled
people, Chub, and the men of the lands who
are allied, shall fall with them by the sword."
6 'Thus says the LORD:

"Those who uphold Egypt shall fall,
And the pride of her power shall come
down.
From Migdol *to* Syene
Those within her shall fall by the sword,"
Says the Lord GOD.
7 "They shall be desolate in the midst of the
desolate countries,
And her cities shall be in the midst of the
cities *that are* laid waste.
8 Then they will know that I *am* the LORD,
When I have set a fire in Egypt
And all her helpers are destroyed.
9 On that day messengers shall go forth
from Me in ships
To make the careless Ethiopians afraid,
And great anguish shall come upon them,
As on the day of Egypt;
For indeed it is coming!"
10 'Thus says the Lord GOD:
"I will also make a multitude of Egypt to
cease
By the hand of Nebuchadnezzar king of
Babylon.

29:10 [a]Or *tower* 30:5 [a]Hebrew *Put* [b]Hebrew *Lud*

LIFE LESSONS

➤ 29:15 — *"It shall be the lowliest of kingdoms; it shall never again exalt itself above the nations, for I will diminish them so that they will not rule over the nations anymore."*

Who but God could have declared that Egypt, the ancient ruler of nations, would fall so completely from the heights and never again become a world superpower? No one at the time could have—except God.

11 He and his people with him, the most
terrible of the nations,
Shall be brought to destroy the land;
They shall draw their swords against
Egypt,
And fill the land with the slain.
12 I will make the rivers dry,
And sell the land into the hand of the
wicked;
I will make the land waste, and all that is
in it,
By the hand of aliens.
I, the LORD, have spoken."

13 'Thus says the Lord GOD:

"I will also destroy the idols,
And cause the images to cease from
Noph;[a]
There shall no longer be princes from the
land of Egypt;
I will put fear in the land of Egypt.
14 I will make Pathros desolate,
Set fire to Zoan,
And execute judgments in No.[a]
15 I will pour My fury on Sin,[a] the strength
of Egypt;
I will cut off the multitude of No,
16 And set a fire in Egypt;
Sin shall have great pain,
No shall be split open,
And Noph *shall be in* distress daily.
17 The young men of Aven[a] and Pi Beseth
shall fall by the sword,
And these *cities* shall go into captivity.
18 At Tehaphnehes[a] the day shall also be
darkened,[b]
When I break the yokes of Egypt there.
And her arrogant strength shall cease in
her;
As for her, a cloud shall cover her,
And her daughters shall go into captivity.
19 Thus I will execute judgments on Egypt,
Then they shall know that I *am* the
LORD."'"

Proclamation Against Pharaoh

20 And it came to pass in the eleventh year, in
the first *month*, on the seventh *day* of the
month, *that* the word of the LORD came to me,
saying,
21 "Son of man, I have broken the arm of
Pharaoh king of Egypt; and see, it has not
been bandaged for healing, nor a splint put
on to bind it, to make it strong enough to hold
a sword.
22 "Therefore thus says the Lord GOD:
'Surely I *am* against Pharaoh king of Egypt,
and will break his arms, both the strong one
and the one that was broken; and I will make
the sword fall out of his hand.
23 'I will scatter the Egyptians among the nations, and disperse them throughout the
countries.
24 'I will strengthen the arms of the king of
Babylon and put My sword in his hand; but I
will break Pharaoh's arms, and he will groan
before him with the groanings of a mortally
wounded *man*.
25 'Thus I will strengthen the arms of the
king of Babylon, but the arms of Pharaoh
shall fall down; they shall know that I *am* the
LORD, when I put My sword into the hand of
the king of Babylon and he stretches it out
against the land of Egypt.
26 'I will scatter the Egyptians among the nations and disperse them throughout the countries. Then they shall know that I *am* the
LORD.'"

Egypt Cut Down Like a Great Tree

31 Now it came to pass in the eleventh
year, in the third *month*, on the first
day of the month, *that* the word of the LORD
came to me, saying,
2 "Son of man, say to Pharaoh king of Egypt
and to his multitude:

'Whom are you like in your greatness?
3 Indeed Assyria *was* a cedar in Lebanon,
With fine branches that shaded the forest,
And of high stature;
And its top was among the thick boughs.
4 The waters made it grow;
Underground waters gave it height,
With their rivers running around the
place where it was planted,
And sent out rivulets to all the trees of
the field.

5 'Therefore its height was exalted above all
the trees of the field;
Its boughs were multiplied,
And its branches became long because of
the abundance of water,
As it sent them out.
6 All the birds of the heavens made their
nests in its boughs;
Under its branches all the beasts of the
field brought forth their young;
And in its shadow all great nations made
their home.
7 'Thus it was beautiful in greatness and in
the length of its branches,
Because its roots reached to abundant
waters.
8 The cedars in the garden of God could
not hide it;
The fir trees were not like its boughs,
And the chestnut[a] trees were not like its
branches;
No tree in the garden of God was like it
in beauty.

30:13 [a]That is, ancient Memphis **30:14** [a]That is, ancient Thebes **30:15** [a]That is, ancient Pelusium **30:17** [a]That is, ancient On (Heliopolis) **30:18** [a]Spelled *Tahpanhes* in Jeremiah 43:7 and elsewhere [b]Following many Hebrew manuscripts, Bomberg, Septuagint, Syriac, Targum, and Vulgate; Masoretic Text reads *refrained.* **31:8** [a]Hebrew *armon*

9 I made it beautiful with a multitude of
branches,
So that all the trees of Eden envied it,
That *were* in the garden of God.'

10 "Therefore thus says the Lord GOD: 'Because you have increased in height, and it set
its top among the thick boughs, and its heart
was lifted up in its height,
11 'therefore I will deliver it into the hand of
the mighty one of the nations, and he shall
surely deal with it; I have driven it out for its
wickedness.
12 'And aliens, the most terrible of the nations, have cut it down and left it; its branches
have fallen on the mountains and in all the
valleys; its boughs lie broken by all the rivers
of the land; and all the peoples of the earth
have gone from under its shadow and left it.

13 'On its ruin will remain all the birds of the
heavens,
And all the beasts of the field will come
to its branches—

14 'So that no trees by the waters may ever
again exalt themselves for their height, nor
set their tops among the thick boughs, that no
tree which drinks water may ever be high
enough to reach up to them.

'For they have all been delivered to death,
To the depths of the earth,
Among the children of men who go down
to the Pit.'

15 "Thus says the Lord GOD: 'In the day when
it went down to hell, I caused mourning. I covered the deep because of it. I restrained its
rivers, and the great waters were held back. I
caused Lebanon to mourn for it, and all the
trees of the field wilted because of it.
16 'I made the nations shake at the sound of
its fall, when I cast it down to hell together
with those who descend into the Pit; and all
the trees of Eden, the choice and best of Lebanon, all that drink water, were comforted in
the depths of the earth.
17 'They also went down to hell with it, with
those slain by the sword; and *those who were*
its *strong* arm dwelt in its shadows among the
nations.
18 'To which of the trees in Eden will you
then be likened in glory and greatness? Yet
you shall be brought down with the trees of
Eden to the depths of the earth; you shall lie
in the midst of the uncircumcised, with *those*
slain by the sword. This *is* Pharaoh and all his
multitude,' says the Lord GOD."

Lamentation for Pharaoh and Egypt

32 And it came to pass in the twelfth year,
in the twelfth *month,* on the first *day* of
the month, *that* the word of the LORD came to
me, saying,
2 "Son of man, take up a lamentation for
Pharaoh king of Egypt, and say to him:

'You are like a young lion among the
nations,
And you *are* like a monster in the seas,
Bursting forth in your rivers,
Troubling the waters with your feet,
And fouling their rivers.'

3 "Thus says the Lord GOD:

'I will therefore spread My net over you
with a company of many people,
And they will draw you up in My net.
4 Then I will leave you on the land;
I will cast you out on the open fields,
And cause to settle on you all the birds of
the heavens.
And with you I will fill the beasts of the
whole earth.
5 I will lay your flesh on the mountains,
And fill the valleys with your carcass.

6 'I will also water the land with the flow of
your blood,
Even to the mountains;
And the riverbeds will be full of you.
7 When *I* put out your light,
I will cover the heavens, and make its
stars dark;
I will cover the sun with a cloud,
And the moon shall not give her light.
8 All the bright lights of the heavens I will
make dark over you,
And bring darkness upon your land,'
Says the Lord GOD.

9 'I will also trouble the hearts of many peoples, when I bring your destruction among
the nations, into the countries which you have
not known.
10 'Yes, I will make many peoples astonished
at you, and their kings shall be horribly afraid
of you when I brandish My sword before them;
and they shall tremble *every* moment, every
man for his own life, in the day of your fall.'
11 "For thus says the Lord GOD: 'The sword of
the king of Babylon shall come upon you.
12 'By the swords of the mighty warriors, all
of them the most terrible of the nations, I will
cause your multitude to fall.

'They shall plunder the pomp of Egypt,
And all its multitude shall be destroyed.
13 Also I will destroy all its animals
From beside its great waters;
The foot of man shall muddy them no
more,
Nor shall the hooves of animals muddy
them.
14 Then I will make their waters clear,
And make their rivers run like oil,'
Says the Lord GOD.

15 'When I make the land of Egypt desolate,
And the country is destitute of all that
once filled it,
When I strike all who dwell in it,
Then they shall know that I *am* the LORD.

16 'This *is* the lamentation
With which they shall lament her;
The daughters of the nations shall lament her;
They shall lament for her, for Egypt,
And for all her multitude,'
Says the Lord GOD."

Egypt and Others Consigned to the Pit

17 It came to pass also in the twelfth year, on the fifteenth *day* of the month, *that* the word of the LORD came to me, saying:

18 "Son of man, wail over the multitude of Egypt,
And cast them down to the depths of the earth,
Her and the daughters of the famous nations,
With those who go down to the Pit:
19 'Whom do you surpass in beauty?
Go down, be placed with the uncircumcised.'

20 "They shall fall in the midst of *those* slain by the sword;
She is delivered to the sword,
Drawing her and all her multitudes.
21 The strong among the mighty
Shall speak to him out of the midst of hell
With those who help him:
'They have gone down,
They lie with the uncircumcised, slain by the sword.'

22 "Assyria *is* there, and all her company,
With their graves all around her,
All of them slain, fallen by the sword.
23 Her graves are set in the recesses of the Pit,
And her company is all around her grave,
All of them slain, fallen by the sword,
Who caused terror in the land of the living.

24 "There *is* Elam and all her multitude,
All around her grave,
All of them slain, fallen by the sword,
Who have gone down uncircumcised to the lower parts of the earth,
Who caused their terror in the land of the living;
Now they bear their shame with those who go down to the Pit.
25 They have set her bed in the midst of the slain,
With all her multitude,
With her graves all around it,
All of them uncircumcised, slain by the sword;
Though their terror was caused
In the land of the living,
Yet they bear their shame
With those who go down to the Pit;
It was put in the midst of the slain.

26 "There *are* Meshech and Tubal and all their multitudes,
With all their graves around it,
All of them uncircumcised, slain by the sword,
Though they caused their terror in the land of the living.
27 They do not lie with the mighty
Who are fallen of the uncircumcised,
Who have gone down to hell with their weapons of war;
They have laid their swords under their heads,
But their iniquities will be on their bones,
Because of the terror of the mighty in the land of the living.
28 Yes, you shall be broken in the midst of the uncircumcised,
And lie with *those* slain by the sword.

29 "There *is* Edom,
Her kings and all her princes,
Who despite their might
Are laid beside *those* slain by the sword;
They shall lie with the uncircumcised,
And with those who go down to the Pit.
30 There *are* the princes of the north,
All of them, and all the Sidonians,
Who have gone down with the slain
In shame at the terror which they caused by their might;
They lie uncircumcised with *those* slain by the sword,
And bear their shame with those who go down to the Pit.

31 "Pharaoh will see them
And be comforted over all his multitude,
Pharaoh and all his army,
Slain by the sword,"
Says the Lord GOD.

32 "For I have caused My terror in the land of the living;
And he shall be placed in the midst of the uncircumcised
With *those* slain by the sword,
Pharaoh and all his multitude,"
Says the Lord GOD.

The Watchman and His Message

33 Again the word of the LORD came to me, saying,
2 "Son of man, speak to the children of your people, and say to them: 'When I bring the sword upon a land, and the people of the land take a man from their territory and make him their watchman,
3 'when he sees the sword coming upon the land, if he blows the trumpet and warns the people,
4 'then whoever hears the sound of the trumpet and does not take warning, if the sword comes and takes him away, his blood shall be on his *own* head.

5 'He heard the sound of the trumpet, but did not take warning; his blood shall be upon himself. But he who takes warning will save his life.
6 'But if the watchman sees the sword coming and does not blow the trumpet, and the people are not warned, and the sword comes and takes *any* person from among them, he is taken away in his iniquity; but his blood I will require at the watchman's hand.'
7 "So you, son of man: I have made you a watchman for the house of Israel; therefore you shall hear a word from My mouth and warn them for Me.
8 "When I say to the wicked, 'O wicked *man,* you shall surely die!' and you do not speak to warn the wicked from his way, that wicked *man* shall die in his iniquity; but his blood I will require at your hand.
9 "Nevertheless if you warn the wicked to turn from his way, and he does not turn from his way, he shall die in his iniquity; but you have delivered your soul.
10 "Therefore you, O son of man, say to the house of Israel: 'Thus you say, "If our transgressions and our sins *lie* upon us, and we pine away in them, how can we then live?"'
➤ 11 "Say to them: '*As* I live,' says the Lord GOD, 'I have no pleasure in the death of the wicked, but that the wicked turn from his way and live. Turn, turn from your evil ways! For why should you die, O house of Israel?'

The Fairness of God's Judgment

12 "Therefore you, O son of man, say to the children of your people: 'The righteousness of the righteous man shall not deliver him in the day of his transgression; as for the wickedness of the wicked, he shall not fall because of it in the day that he turns from his wickedness; nor shall the righteous be able to live because of *his righteousness* in the day that he sins.'
13 "When I say to the righteous *that* he shall surely live, but he trusts in his own righteousness and commits iniquity, none of his righteous works shall be remembered; but because of the iniquity that he has committed, he shall die.
14 "Again, when I say to the wicked, 'You shall surely die,' if he turns from his sin and does what is lawful and right,
15 "*if* the wicked restores the pledge, gives back what he has stolen, and walks in the statutes of life without committing iniquity, he shall surely live; he shall not die.
16 "None of his sins which he has committed shall be remembered against him; he has done what is lawful and right; he shall surely live.
17 "Yet the children of your people say, 'The way of the Lord is not fair.' But it is their way which is not fair!
18 "When the righteous turns from his righteousness and commits iniquity, he shall die because of it.
19 "But when the wicked turns from his wickedness and does what is lawful and right, he shall live because of it.
20 "Yet you say, 'The way of the Lord is not fair.' O house of Israel, I will judge every one of you according to his own ways."

The Fall of Jerusalem

21 And it came to pass in the twelfth year of our captivity, in the tenth *month,* on the fifth *day* of the month, *that* one who had escaped from Jerusalem came to me and said, "The city has been captured!"
22 Now the hand of the LORD had been upon me the evening before the man came who had escaped. And He had opened my mouth; so when he came to me in the morning, my mouth was opened, and I was no longer mute.

The Cause of Judah's Ruin

23 Then the word of the LORD came to me, saying:
24 "Son of man, they who inhabit those ruins in the land of Israel are saying, 'Abraham was only one, and he inherited the land. But we *are* many; the land has been given to us as a possession.'
25 "Therefore say to them, 'Thus says the Lord GOD: "You eat *meat* with blood, you lift up your eyes toward your idols, and shed blood. Should you then possess the land?
26 "You rely on your sword, you commit abominations, and you defile one another's wives. Should you then possess the land?"'
27 "Say thus to them, 'Thus says the Lord GOD: "*As* I live, surely those who *are* in the ruins shall fall by the sword, and the one who *is* in the open field I will give to the beasts to be devoured, and those who *are* in the strongholds and caves shall die of the pestilence.
28 "For I will make the land most desolate, her arrogant strength shall cease, and the mountains of Israel shall be so desolate that no one will pass through.
29 "Then they shall know that I *am* the LORD, when I have made the land most desolate be-

LIFE LESSONS

➤ 33:11 — *"As I live," says the Lord GOD, "I have no pleasure in the death of the wicked, but that the wicked turn from his way and live."*

God does not want to judge anyone. He pleads with us to turn from our wicked ways and to return to Him with all our heart and all our soul. God will never reject anyone with a truly repentant heart.

cause of all their abominations which they
have committed." '

Hearing and Not Doing

30 "As for you, son of man, the children of
your people are talking about you beside the
walls and in the doors of the houses; and they
speak to one another, everyone saying to his
brother, 'Please come and hear what the word
is that comes from the LORD.'
31 "So they come to you as people do, they sit
before you *as* My people, and they hear your
words, but they do not do them; for with their
mouth they show much love, *but* their hearts
pursue their *own* gain.
32 "Indeed you *are* to them as a very lovely
song of one who has a pleasant voice and can
play well on an instrument; for they hear your
words, but they do not do them.
33 "And when this comes to pass—surely it
will come—then they will know that a
prophet has been among them."

Irresponsible Shepherds

34 And the word of the LORD came to me,
saying,
2 "Son of man, prophesy against the shepherds of Israel, prophesy and say to them,
'Thus says the Lord GOD to the shepherds:
"Woe to the shepherds of Israel who feed
themselves! Should not the shepherds feed
the flocks?
3 "You eat the fat and clothe yourselves with
the wool; you slaughter the fatlings, *but* you
do not feed the flock.
4 "The weak you have not strengthened, nor
have you healed those who were sick, nor
bound up the broken, nor brought back what
was driven away, nor sought what was lost;
but with force and cruelty you have ruled
them.
5 "So they were scattered because *there was*
no shepherd; and they became food for all the
beasts of the field when they were scattered.
6 "My sheep wandered through all the
mountains, and on every high hill; yes, My
flock was scattered over the whole face of the
earth, and no one was seeking or searching
for them."
7 'Therefore, you shepherds, hear the word
of the LORD:
8 "*As* I live," says the Lord GOD, "surely because My flock became a prey, and My flock
became food for every beast of the field, because *there was* no shepherd, nor did My
shepherds search for My flock, but the shepherds fed themselves and did not feed My
flock"—
9 'therefore, O shepherds, hear the word of
the LORD!
10 'Thus says the Lord GOD: "Behold, I *am*
against the shepherds, and I will require My
flock at their hand; I will cause them to cease
feeding the sheep, and the shepherds shall
feed themselves no more; for I will deliver My
flock from their mouths, that they may no
longer be food for them."

God, the True Shepherd

11 'For thus says the Lord GOD: "Indeed I Myself will search for My sheep and seek them
out.
12 "As a shepherd seeks out his flock on the
day he is among his scattered sheep, so will I
seek out My sheep and deliver them from all
the places where they were scattered on a
cloudy and dark day.
13 "And I will bring them out from the peoples and gather them from the countries, and
will bring them to their own land; I will feed
them on the mountains of Israel, in the valleys
and in all the inhabited places of the country.
14 "I will feed them in good pasture, and their
fold shall be on the high mountains of Israel.
There they shall lie down in a good fold and
feed in rich pasture on the mountains of Israel.
15 "I will feed My flock, and I will make them
lie down," says the Lord GOD.
16 "I will seek what was lost and bring back
what was driven away, bind up the broken
and strengthen what was sick; but I will destroy the fat and the strong, and feed them in
judgment."
17 'And *as for* you, O My flock, thus says the
Lord GOD: "Behold, I shall judge between
sheep and sheep, between rams and goats.
18 "*Is it* too little for you to have eaten up the
good pasture, that you must tread down with
your feet the residue of your pasture—and to
have drunk of the clear waters, that you must
foul the residue with your feet?
19 "And *as for* My flock, they eat what you

LIFE LESSONS

33:32 — *"Indeed you are to them as a very lovely song of one who has a pleasant voice and can play well on an instrument; for they hear your words, but they do not do them."*

The New Testament tells us that King Herod "feared" John the Baptist and "heard him gladly" (Mark 6:20)—until he killed him. Many people have their favorite preachers; the point, however, is not merely hearing, but doing (James 1:22).

34:15 — *"I will feed My flock, and I will make them lie down," says the Lord GOD.*

The Lord does what He does with us for our benefit. He feeds us what He knows will give us health. He makes us lie down when we would rather keep moving. He is the Good and Great Shepherd (John 10:11, 14).

have trampled with your feet, and they drink
what you have fouled with your feet."
20 'Therefore thus says the Lord GOD to
them: "Behold, I Myself will judge between
the fat and the lean sheep.
21 "Because you have pushed with side and
shoulder, butted all the weak ones with your
horns, and scattered them abroad,
22 "therefore I will save My flock, and they
shall no longer be a prey; and I will judge between sheep and sheep.
23 "I will establish one shepherd over them,
and he shall feed them—My servant David.
He shall feed them and be their shepherd.
24 "And I, the LORD, will be their God, and My
servant David a prince among them; I, the
LORD, have spoken.
25 "I will make a covenant of peace with
them, and cause wild beasts to cease from the
land; and they will dwell safely in the wilderness and sleep in the woods.
26 "I will make them and the places all
around My hill a blessing; and I will cause
showers to come down in their season; there
shall be showers of blessing.
27 "Then the trees of the field shall yield their
fruit, and the earth shall yield her increase.
They shall be safe in their land; and they shall
know that I *am* the LORD, when I have broken
the bands of their yoke and delivered them
from the hand of those who enslaved them.
28 "And they shall no longer be a prey for the
nations, nor shall beasts of the land devour
them; but they shall dwell safely, and no one
shall make *them* afraid.
29 "I will raise up for them a garden of
renown, and they shall no longer be consumed with hunger in the land, nor bear the
shame of the Gentiles anymore.
30 "Thus they shall know that I, the LORD
their God, *am* with them, and they, the house
of Israel, *are* My people," says the Lord GOD.'"
➤ 31 "You are My flock, the flock of My pasture; you *are* men, *and* I *am* your God," says
the Lord GOD.

Judgment on Mount Seir

35 Moreover the word of the LORD came to
me, saying,
2 "Son of man, set your face against Mount
Seir and prophesy against it,
3 "and say to it, 'Thus says the Lord GOD:

"Behold, O Mount Seir, I *am* against you;
I will stretch out My hand against you,
And make you most desolate;
4 I shall lay your cities waste,
And you shall be desolate.
Then you shall know that I *am* the LORD.

5 "Because you have had an ancient hatred,
and have shed *the blood of* the children of Israel by the power of the sword at the time of
their calamity, when their iniquity *came to an*
end,
6 "therefore, *as* I live," says the Lord GOD, "I
will prepare you for blood, and blood shall
pursue you; since you have not hated blood,
therefore blood shall pursue you.
7 "Thus I will make Mount Seir most desolate, and cut off from it the one who leaves
and the one who returns.
8 "And I will fill its mountains with the slain;
on your hills and in your valleys and in all
your ravines those who are slain by the sword
shall fall.
9 "I will make you perpetually desolate, and
your cities shall be uninhabited; then you
shall know that I *am* the LORD.
10 "Because you have said, 'These two nations and these two countries shall be mine,
and we will possess them,' although the LORD
was there,
11 "therefore, *as* I live," says the Lord GOD, "I
will do according to your anger and according to the envy which you showed in your hatred against them; and I will make Myself
known among them when I judge you.
12 "Then you shall know that I *am* the LORD.
I have heard all your blasphemies which you
have spoken against the mountains of Israel,
saying, 'They are desolate; they are given to
us to consume.'
13 "Thus with your mouth you have boasted
against Me and multiplied your words against
Me; I have heard *them*."
14 'Thus says the Lord GOD: "The whole
earth will rejoice when I make you desolate.
15 "As you rejoiced because the inheritance
of the house of Israel was desolate, so I will
do to you; you shall be desolate, O Mount
Seir, as well as all of Edom—all of it! Then
they shall know that I *am* the LORD."'

Blessing on Israel

36 "And you, son of man, prophesy to the
mountains of Israel, and say, 'O mountains of Israel, hear the word of the LORD!
2 'Thus says the Lord GOD: "Because the
enemy has said of you, 'Aha! The ancient
heights have become our possession,'"'
3 "therefore prophesy, and say, 'Thus says

LIFE LESSONS

➤ 34:31 — *"You are My flock, the flock of My pasture; you are men, and I am your God," says the Lord GOD.*

In both testaments, God calls His people His "flock." Why? For one thing, it's a term of endearment and a picture of close, personal connection. For another, it reveals our total dependence upon Him. Third, it honors Him as our Guide.

the Lord GOD: "Because they made *you* desolate and swallowed you up on every side, so
that you became the possession of the rest of
the nations, and you are taken up by the lips
of talkers and slandered by the people"—
4 'therefore, O mountains of Israel, hear the
word of the Lord GOD! Thus says the Lord
GOD to the mountains, the hills, the rivers, the
valleys, the desolate wastes, and the cities
that have been forsaken, which became plunder and mockery to the rest of the nations all
around—
5 'therefore thus says the Lord GOD: "Surely
I have spoken in My burning jealousy against
the rest of the nations and against all Edom,
who gave My land to themselves as a possession, with wholehearted joy *and* spiteful
minds, in order to plunder its open country." '
6 "Therefore prophesy concerning the land
of Israel, and say to the mountains, the hills,
the rivers, and the valleys, 'Thus says the
Lord GOD: "Behold, I have spoken in My jealousy and My fury, because you have borne
the shame of the nations."
7 'Therefore thus says the Lord GOD: "I have
raised My hand in an oath that surely the nations that *are* around you shall bear their own
shame.
8 "But you, O mountains of Israel, you shall
shoot forth your branches and yield your fruit
to My people Israel, for they are about to
come.
9 "For indeed I *am* for you, and I will turn to
you, and you shall be tilled and sown.
10 "I will multiply men upon you, all the
house of Israel, all of it; and the cities shall be
inhabited and the ruins rebuilt.
11 "I will multiply upon you man and beast;
and they shall increase and bear young; I will
make you inhabited as in former times, and
do better *for you* than at your beginnings.
Then you shall know that I *am* the LORD.
12 "Yes, I will cause men to walk on you, My
people Israel; they shall take possession of
you, and you shall be their inheritance; no
more shall you bereave them *of children.*"
13 'Thus says the Lord GOD: "Because they
say to you, 'You devour men and bereave your
nation *of children,*'
14 "therefore you shall devour men no more,
nor bereave your nation anymore," says the
Lord GOD.
15 "Nor will I let you hear the taunts of the nations anymore, nor bear the reproach of the
peoples anymore, nor shall you cause your nation to stumble anymore," says the Lord GOD.' "

The Renewal of Israel

16 Moreover the word of the LORD came to
me, saying:
17 "Son of man, when the house of Israel
dwelt in their own land, they defiled it by
their own ways and deeds; to Me their way
was like the uncleanness of a woman in her
customary impurity.
18 "Therefore I poured out My fury on them
for the blood they had shed on the land, and
for their idols *with which* they had defiled it.
19 "So I scattered them among the nations,
and they were dispersed throughout the
countries; I judged them according to their
ways and their deeds.
20 "When they came to the nations, wherever
they went, they profaned My holy name—
when they said of them, 'These *are* the people
of the LORD, *and* yet they have gone out of His
land.'
21 "But I had concern for My holy name,
which the house of Israel had profaned
among the nations wherever they went.
22 "Therefore say to the house of Israel,
'Thus says the Lord GOD: "I do not do *this* for
your sake, O house of Israel, but for My holy
name's sake, which you have profaned
among the nations wherever you went.
23 "And I will sanctify My great name, which
has been profaned among the nations, which
you have profaned in their midst; and the nations shall know that I *am* the LORD," says the
Lord GOD, "when I am hallowed in you before
their eyes.
24 "For I will take you from among the nations, gather you out of all countries, and
bring you into your own land.
25 "Then I will sprinkle clean water on you,
and you shall be clean; I will cleanse you from
all your filthiness and from all your idols.
26 "I will give you a new heart and put a new
spirit within you; I will take the heart of stone
out of your flesh and give you a heart of flesh.

LIFE LESSONS

➤ 36:21 — *"But I had concern for My holy name, which the house of Israel had profaned among the nations wherever they went."*

Our behavior not only reflects how much or little we love God (John 14:15; 1 John 5:3), but it also either attracts or repels those who do not yet know God. Our connection to God should draw others to God.

➤ 36:24 — *"For I will take you from among the nations, gather you out of all countries, and bring you into your own land."*

The Bible is full of predictions that God will bring His ancient people back to their Promised Land, and there give them a heart to joyfully follow Him. Paul saw this as tremendous news for Gentile Christians (Rom. 11:12).

➤ 36:26 — *"I will give you a new heart and put a new spirit within you; I will take the heart of stone out of your flesh and give you a heart of flesh."*

God does not want remodeled hearts, but brand new ones. He doesn't want a reform in character, but a new spirit that loves to do His will. He wants transformation, not mere accommodation.

ANSWERS TO LIFE'S QUESTIONS

How can I help to restore someone to fellowship with God?

EZEK. 36:16–38

The term "restore" is an interesting one. In ancient Greek, it means to set a broken bone back in place. In restoring someone we do not place bandages on small cuts, but instead we set broken spiritual bones. Therefore the work is often long and painful.

The steps to restoration are as follows:

❶ ***Lead the person to recognize his failure.*** Help him see the nature of the problem and to call it by its right name: sin. As long as a person can rationalize his behavior, he will never accept responsibility for it.

❷ ***Lead the person to acknowledge responsibility for his sin.*** Blaming others will do no good. Others may have been involved, but the person chose to sin—and claiming proper responsibility is essential to restoration.

❸ ***Lead the fallen saint to repent.*** Pray that the Holy Spirit will convict the person to feel remorse, regret, and grief. Repentance means a change of mind leading to a change of conduct. Paul taught that our thinking must change first; then our actions will follow (Rom. 12:2).

❹ ***Lead the person to receive the message God wants to teach him.*** Sometimes a person is stubborn and resistant and reluctant to learn. But failure is unprofitable only when we refuse to learn from the experience. If we learn and grow, we have not utterly failed—we have taken the opportunity to learn more about ourselves and about our God.

❺ ***Lead the sinful believer to respond to God's chastisement with gratitude.*** The one leading might point out two helpful verses: "Before I was afflicted I went astray, but now I keep Your word;" and, "It is good for me that I have been afflicted, that I may learn Your statutes" (Ps. 119:67, 71). Gently remind the person how wonderful it is that God loves us enough to chastise us and to mend us. God will *never* crush the one He loves so dearly.

The goal of all spiritual restoration is to help our sinning brothers and sisters "come to their senses and escape the snare of the devil, having been taken captive by him to do his will" (2 Tim. 2:26). What a joy is ours when we see God put a new heart and a new spirit in them, causing them to walk joyfully and willingly in His ways and to keep His commandments for their own good (Ezek. 36:26, 27)!

See the Life Principles Index for further study:
15. Brokenness is God's requirement for maximum usefulness.
29. We learn more in our valley experiences than on our mountaintops.

27 "I will put My Spirit within you and cause ✳
you to walk in My statutes, and you will keep
My judgments and do *them.*
28 "Then you shall dwell in the land that I
gave to your fathers; you shall be My people,
and I will be your God.
29 "I will deliver you from all your unclean-
nesses. I will call for the grain and multiply it,
and bring no famine upon you.
30 "And I will multiply the fruit of your trees
and the increase of your fields, so that you
need never again bear the reproach of famine
among the nations.
31 "Then you will remember your evil ways
and your deeds that *were* not good; and you
will loathe yourselves in your own sight, for
your iniquities and your abominations.
32 "Not for your sake do I do *this,*" says the
Lord GOD, "let it be known to you. Be
ashamed and confounded for your own ways,
O house of Israel!"
33 'Thus says the Lord GOD: "On the day that
I cleanse you from all your iniquities, I will
also enable *you* to dwell in the cities, and the
ruins shall be rebuilt.
34 "The desolate land shall be tilled instead of
lying desolate in the sight of all who pass by.
35 "So they will say, 'This land that was desolate has become like the garden of Eden; and
the wasted, desolate, and ruined cities *are*
now fortified *and* inhabited.'
36 "Then the nations which are left all
around you shall know that I, the LORD, have
rebuilt the ruined places *and* planted what
was desolate. I, the LORD, have spoken *it,* and
I will do *it.*"
37 'Thus says the Lord GOD: "I will also let
the house of Israel inquire of Me to do this for
them: I will increase their men like a flock.

38 "Like a flock *offered as* holy *sacrifices*,
like the flock at Jerusalem on its feast days,
so shall the ruined cities be filled with flocks
of men. Then they shall know that I *am* the
LORD."'"

The Dry Bones Live

37 The hand of the LORD came upon me
and brought me out in the Spirit of the
LORD, and set me down in the midst of the valley; and it *was* full of bones.
2 Then He caused me to pass by them all
around, and behold, *there were* very many in
the open valley; and indeed *they were* very
dry.
3 And He said to me, "Son of man, can these
bones live?" So I answered, "O Lord GOD, You
know."
4 Again He said to me, "Prophesy to these
bones, and say to them, 'O dry bones, hear the
word of the LORD!
5 'Thus says the Lord GOD to these bones:
"Surely I will cause breath to enter into you,
and you shall live.
➤ 6 "I will put sinews on you and bring flesh
upon you, cover you with skin and put breath
in you; and you shall live. Then you shall
know that I *am* the LORD."'"
7 So I prophesied as I was commanded; and
as I prophesied, there was a noise, and suddenly a rattling; and the bones came together,
bone to bone.
8 Indeed, as I looked, the sinews and the
flesh came upon them, and the skin covered
them over; but *there was* no breath in them.
9 Also He said to me, "Prophesy to the
breath, prophesy, son of man, and say to the
breath, 'Thus says the Lord GOD: "Come from
the four winds, O breath, and breathe on
these slain, that they may live."'"
10 So I prophesied as He commanded me,
and breath came into them, and they lived,
and stood upon their feet, an exceedingly
great army.
11 Then He said to me, "Son of man, these
bones are the whole house of Israel. They indeed say, 'Our bones are dry, our hope is lost,
and we ourselves are cut off!'
12 "Therefore prophesy and say to them,
'Thus says the Lord GOD: "Behold, O My people, I will open your graves and cause you to
come up from your graves, and bring you into
the land of Israel.
13 "Then you shall know that I *am* the LORD,
when I have opened your graves, O My people, and brought you up from your graves.

Life Examples:

EZEKIEL

Watching Dead Bones Come Alive

EZEK. 37:14

In his day, hope had become a rare commodity. Ezekiel must have felt as desolate and useless as the piles of bones that he had seen in a startling vision.

As the prophet sat in the middle of a valley, he knew that only a miracle could bring together his decimated and scattered people. Yet as Ezekiel watched, a miracle of life took place. Where before only dry bones had littered the landscape, the Lord added muscles, tendons, and tissue. And into those restored, silent bodies, God breathed new life.

Maybe you feel dry, defeated, emotionally scattered. Perhaps you sit alone, dejected, watching a panorama of death unfold before you. But do not despair! If the God of Ezekiel is your God, then know that even the dry bones before you can live again. In His grace they can live and stand upon their feet—an exceedingly great army.

See the Life Principles Index for further study:

20. Disappointments are inevitable; discouragement is a choice.

7. The dark moments of our life will last only so long as is necessary for God to accomplish His purpose in us.

14 "I will put My Spirit in you, and you shall
live, and I will place you in your own land.
Then you shall know that I, the LORD, have
spoken *it* and performed *it*," says the LORD.'"

One Kingdom, One King

15 Again the word of the LORD came to me,
saying,
16 "As for you, son of man, take a stick for

LIFE LESSONS

➤ 37:6 — *"I will put sinews on you and bring flesh upon you, cover you with skin and put breath in you; and you shall live. Then you shall know that I am the LORD."*

This passage looks forward to a day when God will gather the remnant of His ancient people to Israel again. He will breathe new life into them in such a way that the whole world will recognize the miraculous hand of God.

yourself and write on it: 'For Judah and for
the children of Israel, his companions.' Then
take another stick and write on it, 'For Joseph, the stick of Ephraim, and *for* all the
house of Israel, his companions.'
17 "Then join them one to another for yourself into one stick, and they will become one
in your hand.
18 "And when the children of your people
speak to you, saying, 'Will you not show us
what you *mean* by these?'—
19 "say to them, 'Thus says the Lord GOD:
"Surely I will take the stick of Joseph, which
is in the hand of Ephraim, and the tribes of Israel, his companions; and I will join them
with it, with the stick of Judah, and make
them one stick, and they will be one in My
hand." '
20 "And the sticks on which you write will be
in your hand before their eyes.
➤ 21 "Then say to them, 'Thus says the Lord
GOD: "Surely I will take the children of Israel
from among the nations, wherever they have
gone, and will gather them from every side
and bring them into their own land;
22 "and I will make them one nation in the
land, on the mountains of Israel; and one king
shall be king over them all; they shall no
longer be two nations, nor shall they ever be
divided into two kingdoms again.
23 "They shall not defile themselves anymore
with their idols, nor with their detestable
things, nor with any of their transgressions;
but I will deliver them from all their dwelling
places in which they have sinned, and will
cleanse them. Then they shall be My people,
and I will be their God.
24 "David My servant *shall be* king over
them, and they shall all have one shepherd;
they shall also walk in My judgments and observe My statutes, and do them.
25 "Then they shall dwell in the land that I
have given to Jacob My servant, where your
fathers dwelt; and they shall dwell there, they,
their children, and their children's children,
forever; and My servant David *shall be* their
prince forever.
✳ 26 "Moreover I will make a covenant of peace
with them, and it shall be an everlasting covenant with them; I will establish them and
multiply them, and I will set My sanctuary in
their midst forevermore.
27 "My tabernacle also shall be with them;
indeed I will be their God, and they shall be
My people.
28 "The nations also will know that I, the
LORD, sanctify Israel, when My sanctuary is in
their midst forevermore." '

Gog and Allies Attack Israel

38 Now the word of the LORD came to me,
saying,
2 "Son of man, set your face against Gog, of
the land of Magog, the prince of Rosh,[a]
Meshech, and Tubal, and prophesy against
him,
3 "and say, 'Thus says the Lord GOD: "Behold, I *am* against you, O Gog, the prince of
Rosh, Meshech, and Tubal.
4 "I will turn you around, put hooks into
your jaws, and lead you out, with all your
army, horses, and horsemen, all splendidly
clothed, a great company *with* bucklers and
shields, all of them handling swords.
5 "Persia, Ethiopia,[a] and Libya[b] are with
them, all of them *with* shield and helmet;
6 "Gomer and all its troops; the house of
Togarmah *from* the far north and all its
troops—many people *are* with you.
7 "Prepare yourself and be ready, you and
all your companies that are gathered about
you; and be a guard for them.
8 "After many days you will be visited. In
the latter years you will come into the land of
those brought back from the sword *and* gathered from many people on the mountains of
Israel, which had long been desolate; they
were brought out of the nations, and now all
of them dwell safely.
9 "You will ascend, coming like a storm,
covering the land like a cloud, you and all
your troops and many peoples with you."
10 'Thus says the Lord GOD: "On that day it
shall come to pass *that* thoughts will arise in
your mind, and you will make an evil plan:
11 "You will say, 'I will go up against a land
of unwalled villages; I will go to a peaceful
people, who dwell safely, all of them dwelling
without walls, and having neither bars nor
gates'—
12 "to take plunder and to take booty, to
stretch out your hand against the waste
places *that are again* inhabited, and against a
people gathered from the nations, who have
acquired livestock and goods, who dwell in
the midst of the land.
13 "Sheba, Dedan, the merchants of Tarshish,

38:2 [a]Targum, Vulgate, and Aquila read *chief prince of* (also verse 3). **38:5** [a]Hebrew *Cush* [b]Hebrew *Put*

LIFE LESSONS

➤ 37:21 — *"Surely I will take the children of Israel from among the nations, wherever they have gone, and will gather them from every side and bring them into their own land . . . ."*

No other nation in history has ever come back into existence after disappearing from the world stage for nineteen brutal centuries—but Israel did, in 1948. God will yet fulfill *all* His promises to His ancient people.

and all their young lions will say to you, 'Have
you come to take plunder? Have you gathered
your army to take booty, to carry away silver
and gold, to take away livestock and goods, to
take great plunder?'"'
14 "Therefore, son of man, prophesy and say
to Gog, 'Thus says the Lord GOD: "On that day
when My people Israel dwell safely, will you
not know *it*?
15 "Then you will come from your place out
of the far north, you and many peoples with
you, all of them riding on horses, a great company and a mighty army.
➤ 16 "You will come up against My people Israel
like a cloud, to cover the land. It will be in the
latter days that I will bring you against My
land, so that the nations may know Me, when I
am hallowed in you, O Gog, before their eyes."
17 'Thus says the Lord GOD: "Are *you* he of
whom I have spoken in former days by My
servants the prophets of Israel, who prophesied for years in those days that I would bring
you against them?

Judgment on Gog

18 "And it will come to pass at the same time,
when Gog comes against the land of Israel,"
says the Lord GOD, "*that* My fury will show in
My face.
19 "For in My jealousy *and* in the fire of My
wrath I have spoken: 'Surely in that day there
shall be a great earthquake in the land of Israel,
20 'so that the fish of the sea, the birds of the
heavens, the beasts of the field, all creeping
things that creep on the earth, and all men
who *are* on the face of the earth shall shake at
My presence. The mountains shall be thrown
down, the steep places shall fall, and every
wall shall fall to the ground.'
21 "I will call for a sword against Gog
throughout all My mountains," says the Lord
GOD. "Every man's sword will be against his
brother.
22 "And I will bring him to judgment with
pestilence and bloodshed; I will rain down on
him, on his troops, and on the many peoples
who *are* with him, flooding rain, great hailstones, fire, and brimstone.
➤ 23 Thus I will magnify Myself and sanctify
Myself, and I will be known in the eyes of
many nations. Then they shall know that I *am*
the LORD."'

Gog's Armies Destroyed

39 "And you, son of man, prophesy
against Gog, and say, 'Thus says the
Lord GOD: "Behold, I *am* against you, O Gog,
the prince of Rosh,[a] Meshech, and Tubal;
2 "and I will turn you around and lead you
on, bringing you up from the far north, and
bring you against the mountains of Israel.
3 "Then I will knock the bow out of your left
hand, and cause the arrows to fall out of your
right hand.
4 "You shall fall upon the mountains of Israel, you and all your troops and the peoples
who *are* with you; I will give you to birds of
prey of every sort and *to* the beasts of the
field to be devoured.
5 "You shall fall on the open field; for I have
spoken," says the Lord GOD.
6 "And I will send fire on Magog and on
those who live in security in the coastlands.
Then they shall know that I *am* the LORD.
7 "So I will make My holy name known in
the midst of My people Israel, and I will not
let them profane My holy name anymore.
Then the nations shall know that *I am* the
LORD, the Holy One in Israel.
8 "Surely it is coming, and it shall be done,"
says the Lord GOD. "This *is* the day of which I
have spoken.
9 "Then those who dwell in the cities of Israel will go out and set on fire and burn the
weapons, both the shields and bucklers, the
bows and arrows, the javelins and spears; and
they will make fires with them for seven
years.
10 "They will not take wood from the field
nor cut down *any* from the forests, because
they will make fires with the weapons; and
they will plunder those who plundered them,
and pillage those who pillaged them," says
the Lord GOD.

The Burial of Gog

11 "It will come to pass in that day *that* I will
give Gog a burial place there in Israel, the valley of those who pass by east of the sea; and
it will obstruct travelers, because there they
will bury Gog and all his multitude. Therefore
they will call *it* the Valley of Hamon Gog.[a]

39:1 [a]Targum, Vulgate and Aquila read *chief prince of.*
39:11 [a]Literally *The Multitude of Gog*

LIFE LESSONS

➤ 38:16 — *"It will be in the latter days that I will bring you against My land, so that the nations may know Me, when I am hallowed in you, O Gog, before their eyes."*

Just as God used stubborn Pharaoh to gain glory for Himself in the eyes of the watching nations (Josh. 2:10; 9:9), so will He use "Gog" one day to again gain glory for Himself on the world stage.

➤ 38:23 — *"Thus I will magnify Myself and sanctify Myself, and I will be known in the eyes of many nations. Then they shall know that I am the LORD."*

The entire world has always been in the crosshairs of God's divine sights. He wants to bless and favor the whole earth with His glory, and bring all nations into a joyful and obedient walk with Him.

12 "For seven months the house of Israel will
be burying them, in order to cleanse the land.
13 "Indeed all the people of the land will be
burying, and they will gain renown for it on
the day that I am glorified," says the Lord
GOD.
14 "They will set apart men regularly employed, with the help of a search party,[a] to
pass through the land and bury those bodies
remaining on the ground, in order to cleanse
it. At the end of seven months they will make
a search.
15 "The search party will pass through the
land; and *when anyone* sees a man's bone, he
shall set up a marker by it, till the buriers
have buried it in the Valley of Hamon Gog.
16 "*The* name of *the* city *will* also *be* Ha-
monah. Thus they shall cleanse the land."'

A Triumphant Festival

17 "And as for you, son of man, thus says the
Lord GOD, 'Speak to every sort of bird and to
every beast of the field:

"Assemble yourselves and come;
Gather together from all sides to My
sacrificial meal
Which I am sacrificing for you,
A great sacrificial meal on the mountains
of Israel,
That you may eat flesh and drink blood.
18 You shall eat the flesh of the mighty,
Drink the blood of the princes of the
earth,
Of rams and lambs,
Of goats and bulls,
All of them fatlings of Bashan.
19 You shall eat fat till you are full,
And drink blood till you are drunk,
At My sacrificial meal
Which I am sacrificing for you.
20 You shall be filled at My table
With horses and riders,
With mighty men
And with all the men of war," says the
Lord GOD.

Israel Restored to the Land

21 "I will set My glory among the nations; all
the nations shall see My judgment which I
have executed, and My hand which I have
laid on them.
➤ 22 "So the house of Israel shall know that I
am the LORD their God from that day forward.
23 "The Gentiles shall know that the house of
Israel went into captivity for their iniquity;
because they were unfaithful to Me, therefore
I hid My face from them. I gave them into the
hand of their enemies, and they all fell by the
sword.
24 "According to their uncleanness and according to their transgressions I have dealt
with them, and hidden My face from them."'
25 "Therefore thus says the Lord GOD: 'Now I
will bring back the captives of Jacob, and
have mercy on the whole house of Israel; and
I will be jealous for My holy name—
26 'after they have borne their shame, and all
their unfaithfulness in which they were
unfaithful to Me, when they dwelt safely in
their *own* land and no one made *them* afraid.
27 'When I have brought them back from the
peoples and gathered them out of their enemies' lands, and I am hallowed in them in the
sight of many nations,
28 'then they shall know that I *am* the LORD
their God, who sent them into captivity
among the nations, but also brought them
back to their land, and left none of them captive any longer.
29 'And I will not hide My face from them ✳
anymore; for I shall have poured out My Spirit
on the house of Israel,' says the Lord GOD."

A New City, a New Temple

40 In the twenty-fifth year of our captivity,
at the beginning of the year, on the
tenth *day* of the month, in the fourteenth year
after the city was captured, on the very same
day the hand of the LORD was upon me; and
He took me there.
2 In the visions of God He took me into the
land of Israel and set me on a very high
mountain; on it toward the south *was* something like the structure of a city.
3 He took me there, and behold, *there was* a
man whose appearance *was* like the appearance of bronze. He had a line of flax and a
measuring rod in his hand, and he stood in
the gateway.
4 And the man said to me, "Son of man, look
with your eyes and hear with your ears, and
fix your mind on everything I show you; for
you *were* brought here so that I might show
them to you. Declare to the house of Israel
everything you see."
5 Now there was a wall all around the outside of the temple.[a] In the man's hand was a

39:14 [a]Literally *those who pass through* **40:5** [a]Literally *house,* and so elsewhere in this book

LIFE LESSONS

➤ **39:22 — *"So the house of Israel shall know that I am the LORD their God from that day forward."***

We do not know why God waits to do some of the good things He has promised to do, but we can have total confidence that He will bring all of them about in His perfect time. He calls us to wait and to trust.

measuring rod six cubits *long, each being a* cubit and a handbreadth; and he measured the width of the wall structure, one rod; and the height, one rod.

The Eastern Gateway of the Temple

6 Then he went to the gateway which faced east; and he went up its stairs and measured the threshold of the gateway, *which was* one rod wide, and the other threshold *was* one rod wide.

7 Each gate chamber *was* one rod long and one rod wide; between the gate chambers *was a space of* five cubits; and the threshold of the gateway by the vestibule of the inside gate *was* one rod.

8 He also measured the vestibule of the inside gate, one rod.

9 Then he measured the vestibule of the gateway, eight cubits; and the gateposts, two cubits. The vestibule of the gate *was* on the inside.

10 In the eastern gateway *were* three gate chambers on one side and three on the other; the three *were* all the same size; also the gateposts were of the same size on this side and that side.

11 He measured the width of the entrance to the gateway, ten cubits; *and* the length of the gate, thirteen cubits.

12 *There was* a space in front of the gate chambers, one cubit *on this side* and one cubit on that side; the gate chambers *were* six cubits on this side and six cubits on that side.

13 Then he measured the gateway from the roof of *one* gate chamber to the roof of the other; the width *was* twenty-five cubits, as door faces door.

14 He measured the gateposts, sixty cubits high, and the court all around the gateway *extended* to the gatepost.

15 *From* the front of the entrance gate to the front of the vestibule of the inner gate *was* fifty cubits.

16 *There were* beveled window *frames* in the gate chambers and in their intervening archways on the inside of the gateway all around, and likewise in the vestibules. *There were* windows all around on the inside. And on each gatepost *were* palm trees.

The Outer Court

17 Then he brought me into the outer court; and *there were* chambers and a pavement made all around the court; thirty chambers faced the pavement.

18 The pavement was by the side of the gateways, corresponding to the length of the gateways; *this was* the lower pavement.

19 Then he measured the width from the front of the lower gateway to the front of the inner court exterior, one hundred cubits toward the east and the north.

The Northern Gateway

20 On the outer court was also a gateway facing north, and he measured its length and its width.

21 Its gate chambers, three on this side and three on that side, its gateposts and its archways, had the same measurements as the first gate; its length *was* fifty cubits and its width twenty-five cubits.

22 Its windows and those of its archways, and also its palm trees, *had* the same measurements as the gateway facing east; it was ascended by seven steps, and its archway *was* in front of it.

23 A gate of the inner court was opposite the northern gateway, just as the eastern *gateway;* and he measured from gateway to gateway, one hundred cubits.

The Southern Gateway

24 After that he brought me toward the south, and there a gateway was facing south; and he measured its gateposts and archways according to these same measurements.

25 *There were* windows in it and in its archways all around like those windows; its length *was* fifty cubits and its width twenty-five cubits.

26 Seven steps led up to it, and its archway *was* in front of them; and it had palm trees on its gateposts, one on this side and one on that side.

27 *There was* also a gateway on the inner court, facing south; and he measured from gateway to gateway toward the south, one hundred cubits.

Gateways of the Inner Court

28 Then he brought me to the inner court through the southern gateway; he measured the southern gateway according to these same measurements.

29 Also its gate chambers, its gateposts, and its archways *were* according to these same measurements; *there were* windows in it and in its archways all around; *it was* fifty cubits long and twenty-five cubits wide.

30 *There were* archways all around, twenty-five cubits long and five cubits wide.

31 Its archways faced the outer court, palm trees *were* on its gateposts, and going up to it *were* eight steps.

32 And he brought me into the inner court facing east; he measured the gateway according to these same measurements.

33 Also its gate chambers, its gateposts, and its archways *were* according to these same measurements; and *there were* windows in it and in its archways all around; *it was* fifty cubits long and twenty-five cubits wide.

34 Its archways faced the outer court, and palm trees *were* on its gateposts on this side and on that side; and going up to it *were* eight steps.

35 Then he brought me to the north gateway and measured *it* according to these same measurements—

36 also its gate chambers, its gateposts, and its archways. It had windows all around; its length *was* fifty cubits and its width twenty-five cubits.

37 Its gateposts faced the outer court, palm trees *were* on its gateposts on this side and on that side, and going up to it *were* eight steps.

Where Sacrifices Were Prepared

38 *There was* a chamber and its entrance by the gateposts of the gateway, where they washed the burnt offering.

39 In the vestibule of the gateway *were* two tables on this side and two tables on that side, on which to slay the burnt offering, the sin offering, and the trespass offering.

40 At the outer side of the *vestibule,* as one goes up to the entrance of the northern gateway, *were* two tables; and on the other side of the vestibule of the gateway *were* two tables.

41 Four tables *were* on this side and four tables on that side, by the side of the gateway, eight tables on which they slaughtered *the sacrifices.*

42 *There were* also four tables of hewn stone for the burnt offering, one cubit and a half long, one cubit and a half wide, and one cubit high; on these they laid the instruments with which they slaughtered the burnt offering and the sacrifice.

43 Inside *were* hooks, a handbreadth wide, fastened all around; and the flesh of the sacrifices *was* on the tables.

Chambers for Singers and Priests

44 Outside the inner gate *were* the chambers for the singers in the inner court, one facing south at the side of the northern gateway, and the other facing north at the side of the southern[a] gateway.

45 Then he said to me, "This chamber which faces south *is* for the priests who have charge of the temple.

46 "The chamber which faces north *is* for the priests who have charge of the altar; these *are* the sons of Zadok, from the sons of Levi, who come near the LORD to minister to Him."

Dimensions of the Inner Court and Vestibule

47 And he measured the court, one hundred cubits long and one hundred cubits wide, foursquare. The altar *was* in front of the temple.

48 Then he brought me to the vestibule of the temple and measured the doorposts of the vestibule, five cubits on this side and five cubits on that side; and the width of the gateway was three cubits on this side and three cubits on that side.

49 The length of the vestibule *was* twenty cubits, and the width eleven cubits; and by the steps which led up to it *there were* pillars by the doorposts, one on this side and another on that side.

Dimensions of the Sanctuary

41 Then he brought me into the sanctuary[a] and measured the doorposts, six cubits wide on one side and six cubits wide on the other side—the width of the tabernacle.

2 The width of the entryway *was* ten cubits, and the side walls of the entrance *were* five cubits on this side and five cubits on the other side; and he measured its length, forty cubits, and its width, twenty cubits.

3 Also he went inside and measured the doorposts, two cubits; and the entrance, six cubits *high;* and the width of the entrance, seven cubits.

4 He measured the length, twenty cubits; and the width, twenty cubits, beyond the sanctuary; and he said to me, "This *is* the Most Holy *Place.*"

The Side Chambers on the Wall

5 Next, he measured the wall of the temple, six cubits. The width of each side chamber all around the temple *was* four cubits on every side.

6 The side chambers *were* in three stories, one above the other, thirty chambers in each story; they rested on ledges which *were* for the side chambers all around, that they might be supported, but not fastened to the wall of the temple.

7 As one went up from story to story, the side chambers became wider all around, because their supporting ledges in the wall of the temple ascended like steps; therefore the width of the structure increased as one went up *from* the lowest *story* to the highest by way of the middle one.

8 I also saw an elevation all around the temple; it was the foundation of the side chambers, a full rod, *that is,* six cubits *high.*

9 The thickness of the outer wall of the side chambers *was* five cubits, and so also the remaining terrace by the place of the side chambers of the temple.

10 And between *it and* the *wall* chambers was a width of twenty cubits all around the temple on every side.

11 The doors of the side chambers opened on the terrace, one door toward the north and another toward the south; and the width of the terrace *was* five cubits all around.

The Building at the Western End

12 The building that faced the separating courtyard at its western end *was* seventy cubits wide; the wall of the building *was* five cu-

---

40:44 [a]Following Septuagint; Masoretic Text and Vulgate read *eastern.* **41:1** [a]Hebrew *heykal,* here the main room of the temple, sometimes called the *holy place* (compare Exodus 26:33)

bits thick all around, and its length ninety cubits.

Dimensions and Design of the Temple Area

13 So he measured the temple, one hundred
cubits long; and the separating courtyard
with the building and its walls *was* one hundred cubits long;
14 also the width of the eastern face of the
temple, including the separating courtyard,
was one hundred cubits.
15 He measured the length of the building
behind it, facing the separating courtyard,
with its galleries on the one side and on the
other side, one hundred cubits, as well as the
inner temple and the porches of the court,
16 their doorposts and the beveled window
frames. And the galleries all around their
three stories opposite the threshold were paneled with wood from the ground to the windows—the windows were covered—
17 from the space above the door, even to the
inner room,[a] as well as outside, and on every
wall all around, inside and outside, by measure.
18 And *it was* made with cherubim and palm
trees, a palm tree between cherub and
cherub. *Each* cherub had two faces,
19 so that the face of a man *was* toward a
palm tree on one side, and the face of a young
lion toward a palm tree on the other side; thus
it was made throughout the temple all
around.
20 From the floor to the space above the door,
and on the wall of the sanctuary, cherubim
and palm trees *were* carved.
21 The doorposts of the temple *were* square,
as was the front of the sanctuary; their appearance was similar.
22 The altar *was* of wood, three cubits high,
and its length two cubits. Its corners, its
length, and its sides *were* of wood; and he
said to me, "This *is* the table that *is* before the
LORD."
23 The temple and the sanctuary had two
doors.
24 The doors had two panels *apiece*, two
folding panels: two *panels* for one door and
two panels for the other *door*.
25 Cherubim and palm trees *were* carved on
the doors of the temple just as they *were*
carved on the walls. A wooden canopy *was* on
the front of the vestibule outside.
26 *There were* beveled window *frames* and
palm trees on one side and on the other, on
the sides of the vestibule—also on the side
chambers of the temple and on the canopies.

The Chambers for the Priests

42 Then he brought me out into the outer
court, by the way toward the north; and
he brought me into the chamber which *was*
opposite the separating courtyard, and which
was opposite the building toward the north.
2 Facing the length, *which was* one hundred
cubits (the width was fifty cubits), was the
north door.
3 Opposite the inner court of twenty *cubits*,
and opposite the pavement of the outer court,
was gallery against gallery in three *stories*.
4 In front of the chambers, toward the inside, *was* a walk ten cubits wide, at a distance
of one cubit; and their doors faced north.
5 Now the upper chambers *were* shorter, because the galleries took away *space* from
them more than from the lower and middle
stories of the building.
6 For they *were* in three *stories* and did not
have pillars like the pillars of the courts;
therefore *the upper level* was shortened more
than the lower and middle levels from the
ground up.
7 And a wall which *was* outside ran parallel
to the chambers, at the front of the chambers,
toward the outer court; its length *was* fifty
cubits.
8 The length of the chambers toward the
outer court *was* fifty cubits, whereas that facing the temple *was* one hundred cubits.
9 At the lower chambers *was* the entrance
on the east side, as one goes into them from
the outer court.
10 Also *there were* chambers in the thickness of the wall of the court toward the east,
opposite the separating courtyard and opposite the building.
11 *There was* a walk in front of them also,
and their appearance *was* like the chambers
which *were* toward the north; they *were* as
long and as wide as the others, and all their
exits and entrances *were* according to plan.
12 And corresponding to the doors of the
chambers that *were* facing south, as one enters them, *there was* a door in front of the
walk, the way directly in front of the wall toward the east.
13 Then he said to me, "The north chambers
and the south chambers, which *are* opposite
the separating courtyard, *are* the holy chambers where the priests who approach the
LORD shall eat the most holy offerings. There
they shall lay the most holy offerings—the
grain offering, the sin offering, and the trespass offering—for the place *is* holy.
14 When the priests enter them, they shall
not go out of the holy *chamber* into the outer
court; but there they shall leave their garments in which they minister, for they *are*
holy. They shall put on other garments; then
they may approach *that* which *is* for the people."

Outer Dimensions of the Temple

15 Now when he had finished measuring the
inner temple, he brought me out through the

41:17 [a]Literally *house*, here *the Most Holy Place*

gateway that faces toward the east, and measured it all around.
16 He measured the east side with the measuring rod,[a] five hundred rods by the measuring rod all around.
17 He measured the north side, five hundred rods by the measuring rod all around.
18 He measured the south side, five hundred rods by the measuring rod.
19 He came around to the west side *and* measured five hundred rods by the measuring rod.
20 He measured it on the four sides; it had a wall all around, five hundred *cubits* long and five hundred wide, to separate the holy areas from the common.

The Temple, the LORD's Dwelling Place

43 Afterward he brought me to the gate, the gate that faces toward the east.
➤ 2 And behold, the glory of the God of Israel came from the way of the east. His voice *was* like the sound of many waters; and the earth shone with His glory.
3 *It was* like the appearance of the vision which I saw—like the vision which I saw when I[a] came to destroy the city. The visions *were* like the vision which I saw by the River Chebar; and I fell on my face.
4 And the glory of the LORD came into the temple by way of the gate which faces toward the east.
5 The Spirit lifted me up and brought me into the inner court; and behold, the glory of the LORD filled the temple.
6 Then I heard *Him* speaking to me from the temple, while a man stood beside me.
✳ 7 And He said to me, "Son of man, *this is* the place of My throne and the place of the soles of My feet, where I will dwell in the midst of the children of Israel forever. No more shall the house of Israel defile My holy name, they nor their kings, by their harlotry or with the carcasses of their kings on their high places.
8 "When they set their threshold by My threshold, and their doorpost by My doorpost, with a wall between them and Me, they defiled My holy name by the abominations which they committed; therefore I have consumed them in My anger.
9 'Now let them put their harlotry and the carcasses of their kings far away from Me, and I will dwell in their midst forever.
10 "Son of man, describe the temple to the house of Israel, that they may be ashamed of their iniquities; and let them measure the pattern.
11 And if they are ashamed of all that they have done, make known to them the design of the temple and its arrangement, its exits and its entrances, its entire design and all its ordinances, all its forms and all its laws. Write *it* down in their sight, so that they may keep its whole design and all its ordinances, and perform them.
12 "This *is* the law of the temple: The whole area surrounding the mountaintop *is* most holy. Behold, this *is* the law of the temple.

Dimensions of the Altar

13 "These are the measurements of the altar in cubits (the cubit *is* one cubit and a handbreadth): the base one cubit high and one cubit wide, with a rim all around its edge of one span. This *is* the height of the altar:
14 "from the base on the ground to the lower ledge, two cubits; the width of the ledge, one cubit; from the smaller ledge to the larger ledge, four cubits; and the width of the ledge, *one* cubit.
15 "The altar hearth *is* four cubits high, with four horns extending upward from the hearth.
16 "The altar hearth *is* twelve *cubits* long, twelve wide, square at its four corners;
17 "the ledge, fourteen *cubits* long and fourteen wide on its four sides, with a rim of half a cubit around it; its base, one cubit all around; and its steps face toward the east."

Consecrating the Altar

18 And He said to me, "Son of man, thus says the Lord GOD: 'These *are* the ordinances for the altar on the day when it is made, for sacrificing burnt offerings on it, and for sprinkling blood on it.
19 'You shall give a young bull for a sin offering to the priests, the Levites, who are of the seed of Zadok, who approach Me to minister to Me,' says the Lord GOD.
20 'You shall take some of its blood and put *it* on the four horns of the altar, on the four corners of the ledge, and on the rim around it; thus you shall cleanse it and make atonement for it.
21 'Then you shall also take the bull of the sin offering, and burn it in the appointed place of the temple, outside the sanctuary.

42:16 [a]Compare 40:5 **43:3** [a]Some Hebrew manuscripts and Vulgate read *He.*

LIFE LESSONS

➤ **43:2 — *And behold, the glory of the God of Israel came from the way of the east. His voice was like the sound of many waters; and the earth shone with His glory.***

Even today the whole earth shines with the glory of God's creative genius, but one day it will shine with the glory of His redemptive and saving genius. When the Savior rules in fullness, complete joy will finally arrive.

22 'On the second day you shall offer a kid of
the goats without blemish for a sin offering;
and they shall cleanse the altar, as they
cleansed *it* with the bull.
23 'When you have finished cleansing *it,* you
shall offer a young bull without blemish, and
a ram from the flock without blemish.
24 'When you offer them before the LORD, the
priests shall throw salt on them, and they will
offer them up *as* a burnt offering to the LORD.
25 'Every day for seven days you shall prepare a goat *for* a sin offering; they shall also
prepare a young bull and a ram from the
flock, both without blemish.
26 'Seven days they shall make atonement for
the altar and purify it, and so consecrate *it.*
27 'When these days are over it shall be, on
the eighth day and thereafter, that the priests
shall offer your burnt offerings and your
peace offerings on the altar; and I will accept
you,' says the Lord GOD."

The East Gate and the Prince

44 Then He brought me back to the outer
gate of the sanctuary which faces toward the east, but it *was* shut.
2 And the LORD said to me, "This gate shall
be shut; it shall not be opened, and no man
shall enter by it, because the LORD God of Israel has entered by it; therefore it shall be
shut.
3 "*As for* the prince, *because* he *is* the
prince, he may sit in it to eat bread before the
LORD; he shall enter by way of the vestibule of
the gateway, and go out the same way."

Those Admitted to the Temple

4 Also He brought me by way of the north
gate to the front of the temple; so I looked,
and behold, the glory of the LORD filled the
house of the LORD; and I fell on my face.
5 And the LORD said to me, "Son of man,
mark well, see with your eyes and hear with
your ears, all that I say to you concerning all
the ordinances of the house of the LORD and
all its laws. Mark well who may enter the
house and all who go out from the sanctuary.
6 "Now say to the rebellious, to the house of
Israel, 'Thus says the Lord GOD: "O house of
Israel, let Us have no more of all your
abominations.
7 "When you brought in foreigners, uncircumcised in heart and uncircumcised in flesh,
to be in My sanctuary to defile it—My
house—and when you offered My food, the
fat and the blood, then they broke My covenant because of all your abominations.
8 "And you have not kept charge of My holy
things, but you have set *others* to keep charge
of My sanctuary for you."
9 'Thus says the Lord GOD: "No foreigner,
uncircumcised in heart or uncircumcised in
flesh, shall enter My sanctuary, including any
foreigner who *is* among the children of Israel.

Laws Governing Priests

10 "And the Levites who went far from Me,
when Israel went astray, who strayed away
from Me after their idols, they shall bear their
iniquity.
11 "Yet they shall be ministers in My sanctuary, *as* gatekeepers of the house and ministers of the house; they shall slay the burnt
offering and the sacrifice for the people, and
they shall stand before them to minister to
them.
12 "Because they ministered to them before
their idols and caused the house of Israel to
fall into iniquity, therefore I have raised My
hand in an oath against them," says the Lord
GOD, "that they shall bear their iniquity.
13 "And they shall not come near Me to minister to Me as priest, nor come near any of My
holy things, nor into the Most Holy *Place;* but
they shall bear their shame and their
abominations which they have committed.
14 "Nevertheless I will make them keep
charge of the temple, for all its work, and for
all that has to be done in it.
15 "But the priests, the Levites, the sons of
Zadok, who kept charge of My sanctuary
when the children of Israel went astray from
Me, they shall come near Me to minister to
Me; and they shall stand before Me to offer to
Me the fat and the blood," says the Lord GOD.
16 "They shall enter My sanctuary, and they
shall come near My table to minister to Me,
and they shall keep My charge.
17 "And it shall be, whenever they enter the
gates of the inner court, that they shall put on
linen garments; no wool shall come upon
them while they minister within the gates of
the inner court or within the house.
18 "They shall have linen turbans on their
heads and linen trousers on their bodies; they
shall not clothe themselves with *anything
that causes* sweat.
19 "When they go out to the outer court, to
the outer court to the people, they shall take
off their garments in which they have ministered, leave them in the holy chambers, and
put on other garments; and in their holy garments they shall not sanctify the people.
20 "They shall neither shave their heads, nor
let their hair grow long, but they shall keep
their hair well trimmed.
21 "No priest shall drink wine when he enters the inner court.
22 "They shall not take as wife a widow or a
divorced woman, but take virgins of the descendants of the house of Israel, or widows of
priests.
23 "And they shall teach My people *the difference* between the holy and the unholy, and
cause them to discern between the unclean
and the clean.
24 "In controversy they shall stand as judges,
and judge it according to My judgments. They
shall keep My laws and My statutes in all My

appointed meetings, and they shall hallow
My Sabbaths.
25 "They shall not defile *themselves* by coming near a dead person. Only for father or
mother, for son or daughter, for brother or unmarried sister may they defile themselves.
26 "After he is cleansed, they shall count
seven days for him.
27 "And on the day that he goes to the sanctuary to minister in the sanctuary, he must
offer his sin offering in the inner court," says
the Lord GOD.
28 "It shall be, in regard to their inheritance,
that I *am* their inheritance. You shall give
them no possession in Israel, for I *am* their
possession.
29 "They shall eat the grain offering, the sin
offering, and the trespass offering; every dedicated thing in Israel shall be theirs.
30 "The best of all firstfruits of any kind, and
every sacrifice of any kind from all your sacrifices, shall be the priest's; also you shall
give to the priest the first of your ground
meal, to cause a blessing to rest on your
house.
31 "The priests shall not eat anything, bird or
beast, that died naturally or was torn *by wild
beasts.*

The Holy District

45 "Moreover, when you divide the land
by lot into inheritance, you shall set
apart a district for the LORD, a holy section of
the land; its length *shall be* twenty-five thousand *cubits,* and the width ten thousand. It
shall be holy throughout its territory all
around.
2 "Of this there shall be a square plot for the
sanctuary, five hundred by five hundred *rods,*
with fifty cubits around it for an open space.
3 "So this is the district you shall measure:
twenty-five thousand *cubits* long and ten
thousand wide; in it shall be the sanctuary,
the Most Holy *Place.*
4 "It shall be a holy *section* of the land, belonging to the priests, the ministers of the
sanctuary, who come near to minister to the
LORD; it shall be a place for their houses and
a holy place for the sanctuary.
5 "*An area* twenty-five thousand *cubits* long
and ten thousand wide shall belong to the
Levites, the ministers of the temple; they shall
have twenty chambers as a possession.[a]

Properties of the City and the Prince

6 "You shall appoint as the property of the
city *an area* five thousand *cubits* wide and
twenty-five thousand long, adjacent to the
district of the holy *section;* it shall belong to
the whole house of Israel.
7 "The prince shall have *a section* on one
side and the other of the holy district and the
city's property; and bordering on the holy district and the city's property, extending westward on the west side and eastward on the
east side, the length *shall be* side by side with
one of the *tribal* portions, from the west border to the east border.
8 "The land shall be his possession in Israel;
and My princes shall no more oppress My
people, but they shall give *the rest of* the land
to the house of Israel, according to their tribes."

Laws Governing the Prince

9 'Thus says the Lord GOD: "Enough,
O princes of Israel! Remove violence and
plundering, execute justice and righteousness, and stop dispossessing My people," says
the Lord GOD.
10 "You shall have honest scales, an honest
ephah, and an honest bath.
11 "The ephah and the bath shall be of the
same measure, so that the bath contains one-
tenth of a homer, and the ephah one-tenth of
a homer; their measure shall be according to
the homer.
12 "The shekel *shall be* twenty gerahs;
twenty shekels, twenty-five shekels, *and* fifteen shekels shall be your mina.
13 "This *is* the offering which you shall offer:
you shall give one-sixth of an ephah from a
homer of wheat, and one-sixth of an ephah
from a homer of barley.
14 "The ordinance concerning oil, the bath of
oil, *is* one-tenth of a bath from a kor. *A kor is*
a homer or ten baths, for ten baths *are* a
homer.
15 "And one lamb shall be given from a flock
of two hundred, from the rich pastures of Israel. These shall be for grain offerings, burnt
offerings, and peace offerings, to make atonement for them," says the Lord GOD.
16 "All the people of the land shall give this
offering for the prince in Israel.
17 "Then it shall be the prince's part *to give*
burnt offerings, grain offerings, and drink offerings, at the feasts, the New Moons, the
Sabbaths, and at all the appointed seasons of
the house of Israel. He shall prepare the sin
offering, the grain offering, the burnt offering, and the peace offerings to make atonement for the house of Israel."

Keeping the Feasts

18 'Thus says the Lord GOD: "In the first
month, on the first *day* of the month, you
shall take a young bull without blemish and
cleanse the sanctuary.
19 "The priest shall take some of the blood of
the sin offering and put *it* on the doorposts of
the temple, on the four corners of the ledge
of the altar, and on the gateposts of the gate of
the inner court.
20 "And so you shall do on the seventh *day* of
the month for everyone who has sinned unin-

45:5 [a]Following Masoretic Text, Targum, and Vulgate; Septuagint reads *a possession, cities of dwelling.*

tentionally or in ignorance. Thus you shall
make atonement for the temple.
21 "In the first *month,* on the fourteenth day
of the month, you shall observe the Passover,
a feast of seven days; unleavened bread shall
be eaten.
22 "And on that day the prince shall prepare
for himself and for all the people of the land
a bull *for* a sin offering.
23 "On the seven days of the feast he shall
prepare a burnt offering to the LORD, seven
bulls and seven rams without blemish, daily
for seven days, and a kid of the goats daily *for*
a sin offering.
24 "And he shall prepare a grain offering of
one ephah for each bull and one ephah for
each ram, together with a hin of oil for each
ephah.
25 "In the seventh *month,* on the fifteenth
day of the month, at the feast, he shall do likewise for seven days, according to the sin offering, the burnt offering, the grain offering,
and the oil."

The Manner of Worship

46 'Thus says the Lord GOD: "The gateway
of the inner court that faces toward the
east shall be shut the six working days; but on
the Sabbath it shall be opened, and on the day
of the New Moon it shall be opened.
2 "The prince shall enter by way of the
vestibule of the gateway from the outside, and
stand by the gatepost. The priests shall prepare his burnt offering and his peace offerings. He shall worship at the threshold of the
gate. Then he shall go out, but the gate shall
not be shut until evening.
3 "Likewise the people of the land shall worship at the entrance to this gateway before the
LORD on the Sabbaths and the New Moons.
4 "The burnt offering that the prince offers
to the LORD on the Sabbath day *shall be* six
lambs without blemish, and a ram without
blemish;
5 "and the grain offering *shall be one* ephah
for a ram, and the grain offering for the
lambs, as much as he wants to give, as well as
a hin of oil with every ephah.
6 "On the day of the New Moon *it shall be* a
young bull without blemish, six lambs, and a
ram; they shall be without blemish.
7 "He shall prepare a grain offering of an
ephah for a bull, an ephah for a ram, as much
as he wants to give for the lambs, and a hin of
oil with every ephah.
8 "When the prince enters, he shall go in by
way of the vestibule of the gateway, and go
out the same way.
9 "But when the people of the land come before the LORD on the appointed feast days,
whoever enters by way of the north gate to
worship shall go out by way of the south gate;
and whoever enters by way of the south gate
shall go out by way of the north gate. He shall
not return by way of the gate through which
he came, but shall go out through the opposite gate.
10 "The prince shall then be in their midst.
When they go in, he shall go in; and when
they go out, he shall go out.
11 "At the festivals and the appointed feast
days the grain offering shall be an ephah for
a bull, an ephah for a ram, as much as he
wants to give for the lambs, and a hin of oil
with every ephah.
12 "Now when the prince makes a voluntary
burnt offering or voluntary peace offering to
the LORD, the gate that faces toward the east
shall then be opened for him; and he shall
prepare his burnt offering and his peace offerings as he did on the Sabbath day. Then he
shall go out, and after he goes out the gate
shall be shut.
13 "You shall daily make a burnt offering to
the LORD *of* a lamb of the first year without
blemish; you shall prepare it every morning.
14 "And you shall prepare a grain offering
with it every morning, a sixth of an ephah,
and a third of a hin of oil to moisten the fine
flour. This grain offering is a perpetual ordinance, to be made regularly to the LORD.
15 "Thus they shall prepare the lamb, the
grain offering, and the oil, *as* a regular burnt
offering every morning."

The Prince and Inheritance Laws

16 'Thus says the Lord GOD: "If the prince
gives a gift *of some* of his inheritance to any
of his sons, it shall belong to his sons; it is
their possession by inheritance.
17 "But if he gives a gift of some of his inheritance to one of his servants, it shall be his
until the year of liberty, after which it shall return to the prince. But his inheritance shall
belong to his sons; it shall become theirs.
18 "Moreover the prince shall not take any of
the people's inheritance by evicting them
from their property; he shall provide an inheritance for his sons from his own property,
so that none of My people may be scattered
from his property." ' "

How the Offerings Were Prepared

19 Now he brought me through the entrance,
which *was* at the side of the gate, into the holy
chambers of the priests which face toward the
north; and there a place *was* situated at their
extreme western end.
20 And he said to me, "This *is* the place
where the priests shall boil the trespass offering and the sin offering, *and* where they shall
bake the grain offering, so that they do not
bring *them* out into the outer court to sanctify
the people."
21 Then he brought me out into the outer
court and caused me to pass by the four corners of the court; and in fact, in every corner
of the court *there was another* court.

22 In the four corners of the court *were* enclosed courts, forty *cubits* long and thirty wide; all four corners *were* the same size.
23 *There was* a row *of building stones* all around in them, all around the four of them; and cooking hearths were made under the rows of stones all around.
24 And he said to me, "These *are* the kitchens where the ministers of the temple shall boil the sacrifices of the people."

The Healing Waters and Trees

47 Then he brought me back to the door of the temple; and there was water, flowing from under the threshold of the temple toward the east, for the front of the temple faced east; the water was flowing from under the right side of the temple, south of the altar.
2 He brought me out by way of the north gate, and led me around on the outside to the outer gateway that faces east; and there was water, running out on the right side.
3 And when the man went out to the east with the line in his hand, he measured one thousand cubits, and he brought me through the waters; the water *came up to my* ankles.
4 Again he measured one thousand and brought me through the waters; the water *came up to my* knees. Again he measured one thousand and brought me through; the water *came up to my* waist.
5 Again he measured one thousand, *and it was* a river that I could not cross; for the water was too deep, water in which one must swim, a river that could not be crossed.
6 He said to me, "Son of man, have you seen *this?*" Then he brought me and returned me to the bank of the river.
7 When I returned, there, along the bank of the river, *were* very many trees on one side and the other.
8 Then he said to me: "This water flows toward the eastern region, goes down into the valley, and enters the sea. *When it* reaches the sea, *its* waters are healed.
➤ 9 "And it shall be *that* every living thing that moves, wherever the rivers go, will live. There will be a very great multitude of fish, because these waters go there; for they will be healed, and everything will live wherever the river goes.
10 "It shall be *that* fishermen will stand by it from En Gedi to En Eglaim; they will be *places* for spreading their nets. Their fish will be of the same kinds as the fish of the Great Sea, exceedingly many.
11 "But its swamps and marshes will not be healed; they will be given over to salt.
12 "Along the bank of the river, on this side and that, will grow all *kinds of* trees used for food; their leaves will not wither, and their fruit will not fail. They will bear fruit every month, because their water flows from the sanctuary. Their fruit will be for food, and their leaves for medicine." ✳

Borders of the Land

13 Thus says the Lord GOD: "These *are* the borders by which you shall divide the land as an inheritance among the twelve tribes of Israel. Joseph *shall have two* portions.
14 "You shall inherit it equally with one another; for I raised My hand in an oath to give it to your fathers, and this land shall fall to you as your inheritance.
15 "This *shall be* the border of the land on the north: from the Great Sea, *by* the road to Hethlon, as one goes to Zedad,
16 "Hamath, Berothah, Sibraim (which *is* between the border of Damascus and the border of Hamath), to Hazar Hatticon (which *is* on the border of Hauran).
17 "Thus the boundary shall be from the Sea to Hazar Enan, the border of Damascus; and as for the north, northward, it is the border of Hamath. *This is* the north side.
18 "On the east side you shall mark out the border from between Hauran and Damascus, and between Gilead and the land of Israel, along the Jordan, and along the eastern side of the sea. *This is* the east side.
19 "The south side, toward the South,[a] *shall be* from Tamar to the waters of Meribah by Kadesh, along the brook to the Great Sea. *This is* the south side, toward the South.
20 "The west side *shall be* the Great Sea, from the *southern* boundary until one comes to a point opposite Hamath. This *is* the west side.
21 "Thus you shall divide this land among yourselves according to the tribes of Israel.
22 "It shall be that you will divide it by lot as an inheritance for yourselves, and for the strangers who dwell among you and who bear children among you. They shall be to you as native-born among the children of Is-

47:19 [a]Hebrew *Negev*

LIFE LESSONS

➤ 47:9 — *"There will be a very great multitude of fish, because these waters go there; for they will be healed, and everything will live wherever the river goes."*

A vibrant river pictures the abundant life that God offers all of those who come to Him in faith. John, like Ezekiel, envisions "a pure river of water of life, clear as crystal, proceeding from the throne of God and of the Lamb" (Rev. 22:1).

rael; they shall have an inheritance with you
among the tribes of Israel.
23 "And it shall be *that* in whatever tribe the
stranger dwells, there you shall give *him* his
inheritance," says the Lord GOD.

Division of the Land

48 "Now these *are* the names of the tribes:
From the northern border along the
road to Hethlon at the entrance of Hamath, to
Hazar Enan, the border of Damascus northward, in the direction of Hamath, *there shall
be* one *section for* Dan from its east to its west
side;
2 "by the border of Dan, from the east side
to the west, one *section for* Asher;
3 "by the border of Asher, from the east side
to the west, one *section for* Naphtali;
4 "by the border of Naphtali, from the east
side to the west, one *section for* Manasseh;
5 "by the border of Manasseh, from the east
side to the west, one *section for* Ephraim;
6 "by the border of Ephraim, from the east
side to the west, one *section for* Reuben;
7 "by the border of Reuben, from the east
side to the west, one *section for* Judah;
8 "by the border of Judah, from the east side
to the west, shall be the district which you
shall set apart, twenty-five thousand *cubits* in
width, and *in* length the same as one of the
other portions, from the east side to the west,
with the sanctuary in the center.
9 "The district that you shall set apart for
the LORD *shall be* twenty-five thousand *cubits*
in length and ten thousand in width.
10 "To these—to the priests—the holy district
shall belong: on the north twenty-five thousand *cubits in length,* on the west ten thousand in width, on the east ten thousand in
width, and on the south twenty-five thousand
in length. The sanctuary of the LORD shall be
in the center.
11 "*It shall be* for the priests of the sons of
Zadok, who are sanctified, who have kept My
charge, who did not go astray when the children of Israel went astray, as the Levites went
astray.
12 "And *this* district of land that is set apart
shall be to them a thing most holy by the border of the Levites.
13 "Opposite the border of the priests, the
Levites *shall have an area* twenty-five thousand *cubits* in length and ten thousand in
width; its entire length *shall be* twenty-five
thousand and its width ten thousand.
14 "And they shall not sell or exchange any
of it; they may not alienate this best *part* of
the land, for *it is* holy to the LORD.
15 "The five thousand *cubits* in width that remain, along the edge of the twenty-five thousand, shall be for general use by the city, for
dwellings and common-land; and the city
shall be in the center.
16 "These *shall be* its measurements: the
north side four thousand five hundred *cubits,*
the south side four thousand five hundred, the
east side four thousand five hundred, and the
west side four thousand five hundred.
17 "The common-land of the city shall be: to
the north two hundred and fifty *cubits,* to the
south two hundred and fifty, to the east two
hundred and fifty, and to the west two hundred and fifty.
18 "The rest of the length, alongside the district of the holy *section, shall be* ten thousand
cubits to the east and ten thousand to the
west. It shall be adjacent to the district of the
holy *section,* and its produce shall be food for
the workers of the city.
19 "The workers of the city, from all the
tribes of Israel, shall cultivate it.
20 "The entire district *shall be* twenty-five
thousand *cubits* by twenty-five thousand *cubits,* foursquare. You shall set apart the holy
district with the property of the city.
21 "The rest *shall belong* to the prince, on one
side and on the other of the holy district and
of the city's property, next to the twenty-five
thousand *cubits* of the *holy* district as far as
the eastern border, and westward next to the
twenty-five thousand as far as the western
border, adjacent to the *tribal* portions; *it shall
belong* to the prince. It shall be the holy district, and the sanctuary of the temple *shall be*
in the center.
22 "Moreover, apart from the possession of
the Levites and the possession of the city
which are in the midst of what *belongs* to the
prince, *the area* between the border of Judah
and the border of Benjamin shall belong to
the prince.
23 "As for the rest of the tribes, from the east
side to the west, Benjamin *shall have* one *section;*
24 "by the border of Benjamin, from the east
side to the west, Simeon *shall have* one *section;*
25 "by the border of Simeon, from the east
side to the west, Issachar *shall have* one *section;*
26 "by the border of Issachar, from the east
side to the west, Zebulun *shall have* one *section;*
27 "by the border of Zebulun, from the
east side to the west, Gad *shall have* one *section;*
28 "by the border of Gad, on the south side,
toward the South,[a] the border shall be from
Tamar *to* the waters of Meribah *by* Kadesh,
along the brook to the Great Sea.
29 "This *is* the land which you shall divide by
lot as an inheritance among the tribes of Israel, and these *are* their portions," says the
Lord GOD.

48:28 [a]Hebrew *Negev*

The Gates of the City and Its Name
30 "These *are* the exits of the city. On the
north side, measuring four thousand five hundred *cubits*
31 "(the gates of the city *shall be* named after
the tribes of Israel), the three gates northward: one gate for Reuben, one gate for Judah, and one gate for Levi;
32 "on the east side, four thousand five hundred *cubits*, three gates: one gate for Joseph,
one gate for Benjamin, and one gate for Dan;
33 "on the south side, measuring four thousand five hundred *cubits*, three gates: one
gate for Simeon, one gate for Issachar, and
one gate for Zebulun;
34 "on the west side, four thousand five hundred *cubits* with their three gates: one gate
for Gad, one gate for Asher, and one gate for
Naphtali.
35 "All the way around *shall be* eighteen
thousand *cubits;* and the name of the city
from *that* day *shall be:* THE LORD *IS*
THERE."[a]

48:35 [a]Hebrew *YHWH Shammah*

THE BOOK OF DANIEL

Daniel's life and ministry covered the entire seventy years of the Babylonian captivity. Deported to Babylon at approximately age sixteen and handpicked for government service, Daniel became God's prophetic mouthpiece to the Gentile and Jewish world, declaring God's present and eternal purpose. Daniel, a Hebrew, became prime minister of Babylon and worked for at least three kings: Nebuchadnezzar, Belshazzar, and Darius. His inspired work quotes both Nebuchadnezzar and Darius as declaring that Daniel's God is the living and true Lord of all.

The name *Daniye'l* or *Dani'el* means "God is my Judge." The Greek form *Daniel* in the Septuagint is the basis for the Latin and English titles.

The Book of Daniel details the life and prophecies of one of God's most trusted servants. It includes more fulfilled prophecy than any other book in the Bible and earns the endorsement of Christ Himself (Matt. 24:15). Several of the book's twelve chapters revolve around dreams, including God-given visions involving trees, animals, beasts, and images.

While many of the accounts in Daniel are retold in children's books, those accounts are too important and relevant to relegate exclusively to the pages of childhood literature. To be sure, Daniel in the lion's den—just like Daniel's description of the deliverance of Shadrach, Meshach, and Abednego in the fiery furnace, or the disembodied hand that spells doom for a Bablyonian despot—is a spectacular and colorful account. But what stands out is that a sovereign, omnipotent God consistently and swiftly reacts to the earnest prayers of his faithful servants.

Daniel prophesied the coming of many key historical figures, from Christ to Alexander the Great to Cleopatra. Daniel's famous "seventieth week" (9:27) describes the ancestry, rise, and fall of the antichrist, and the glorious Second Coming of Christ. The Book of Daniel is often seen as a companion to the New Testament Book of Revelation, largely because both contain a great deal of mysterious prophetic imagery and because Revelation draws upon much of Daniel's imagery.

Themes: God rules over the affairs of men, and no one can derail His plans or stop Him from acting. He is absolutely sovereign.

Author: Daniel.

Time: During and shortly after the seventy-year Babylonian captivity of Judah (c. 605–530 B.C.).

Structure: The first six chapters of Daniel cover the personal biographies of several key characters, plus some local history. The second six chapters cover visions and prophecies concerning God's controlling hand in the affairs of men.

As you read Daniel, watch for several life principles that play an important role in this book:

21. Obedience always brings blessing. *See Daniel 1:8–20; page 996.*

9. Trusting God means looking beyond what we can see to what God sees. *See Daniel 3:13–25; page 999.*

1. Our intimacy with God—His highest priority for our lives—determines the impact of our lives. *See Daniel 6:5–24; page 1005.*

17. We stand tallest and strongest on our knees. *See Daniel 6:10, 11; page 1005.*

18. As children of a sovereign God, we are never victims of our circumstances. *See Daniel 7:24–27; 11:32—12:3; pages 1010; 1016.*

ANSWERS TO LIFE'S QUESTIONS

How can I become a more obedient Christian?

DAN. 1:4–16

Obedience is the bottom line in the Christian life. So what is it? Obedience means compliance to the plan; conformity to the pattern; observance of the rules; adherence to the standard; and submission to another's will.

If we want to obey the Lord, we need to know what action God wants us to take. What attitude would most please Him? What required steps may be along the way? And how do we get ourselves to that point of obedience?

First, we have to know what God's commandments are. We cannot obey what we do not know or understand—and we get God's perspective by becoming familiar with His Word.

But simply knowing God's Word isn't enough. We must also tap into His power through the Holy Spirit, who helps us relate God's commands to our own situation and who assists us in determining the wisest course of action.

Once we decide to obey, we can expect a challenge to compromise. It takes commitment and courage to obey God in the face of these challenges: courage to give up what we like in order to do what he asks; courage to do things that may bring unwelcome results; courage to rearrange our schedule to match His plan; courage to love the unlovely, to forgive the seemingly unforgivable, and to give when we want to keep.

Since Satan doesn't want us to follow God, he will offer temptation after temptation to divert us to another place or to weaken us through small steps of disobedience. How can we counter his challenge to compromise? By renewing our resolve to obey, as Jesus did.

When Jesus neared the end of forty days of fasting and prayer following His baptism, Satan came at Him hard, tempting Him to compromise on His calling. But Jesus stood up to Satan with courage, answering temptation after temptation with the Word of God. Commitment like His involves loving God above all else, obedient action, a determined attitude, and a willingness to suffer any consequences that flow out of compliance.

Whenever you feel tempted to disobey God, remember that your faithfulness and devotion to Christ are at stake. Ask yourself: "Is my understanding of Scripture increasing? Am I able to hold to God's plan without compromise? How committed am I to obeying God? If I love Him, I'll obey Him—so how much do I really love Him?"

See the Life Principles Index for further study:
2. Obey God and leave all the consequences to Him.
21. Obedience always brings blessing.

Daniel and His Friends Obey God

1 In the third year of the reign of Jehoiakim king of Judah, Nebuchadnezzar
king of Babylon came to Jerusalem and besieged it.
2 And the Lord gave Jehoiakim king of Judah into his hand, with some of the articles of
the house of God, which he carried into the
land of Shinar to the house of his god; and he
brought the articles into the treasure house of
his god.
3 Then the king instructed Ashpenaz, the
master of his eunuchs, to bring some of the
children of Israel and some of the king's descendants and some of the nobles,
4 young men in whom *there was* no blemish, but good-looking, gifted in all wisdom, possessing knowledge and quick to
understand, who *had* ability to serve in the
king's palace, and whom they might teach
the language and literature of the Chaldeans.
5 And the king appointed for them a daily
provision of the king's delicacies and of the
wine which he drank, and three years of
training for them, so that at the end of *that
time* they might serve before the king.
6 Now from among those of the sons of Judah were Daniel, Hananiah, Mishael, and
Azariah.
7 To them the chief of the eunuchs gave
names: he gave Daniel *the name* Belteshazzar; to Hananiah, Shadrach; to Mishael, Meshach; and to Azariah, Abed-Nego.
8 But Daniel purposed in his heart that he ◄
would not defile himself with the portion of
the king's delicacies, nor with the wine which
he drank; therefore he requested of the chief
of the eunuchs that he might not defile himself.

9 Now God had brought Daniel into the
favor and goodwill of the chief of the eunuchs.
10 And the chief of the eunuchs said to Daniel, "I fear my lord the king, who has appointed your food and drink. For why should he see your faces looking worse than the young men who *are* your age? Then you would endanger my head before the king."
11 So Daniel said to the steward[a] whom the chief of the eunuchs had set over Daniel, Hananiah, Mishael, and Azariah,
12 "Please test your servants for ten days, and let them give us vegetables to eat and water to drink.
13 Then let our appearance be examined before you, and the appearance of the young men who eat the portion of the king's delicacies; and as you see fit, *so* deal with your servants."
14 So he consented with them in this matter, and tested them ten days.
15 And at the end of ten days their features appeared better and fatter in flesh than all the young men who ate the portion of the king's delicacies.
16 Thus the steward took away their portion of delicacies and the wine that they were to drink, and gave them vegetables.
➢ **17** As for these four young men, God gave them knowledge and skill in all literature and wisdom; and Daniel had understanding in all visions and dreams.
18 Now at the end of the days, when the king had said that they should be brought in, the chief of the eunuchs brought them in before Nebuchadnezzar.
19 Then the king interviewed[a] them, and among them all none was found like Daniel, Hananiah, Mishael, and Azariah; therefore they served before the king.
20 And in all matters of wisdom *and* understanding about which the king examined them, he found them ten times better than all the magicians *and* astrologers who *were* in all his realm.
21 Thus Daniel continued until the first year of King Cyrus.

Nebuchadnezzar's Dream

2 Now in the second year of Nebuchadnezzar's reign, Nebuchadnezzar had dreams; and his spirit was *so* troubled that his sleep left him.
2 Then the king gave the command to call the magicians, the astrologers, the sorcerers, and the Chaldeans to tell the king his dreams. So they came and stood before the king.
3 And the king said to them, "I have had a dream, and my spirit is anxious to know the dream."
4 Then the Chaldeans spoke to the king in Aramaic,[a] "O king, live forever! Tell your servants the dream, and we will give the interpretation."
5 The king answered and said to the Chaldeans, "My decision is firm: if you do not make known the dream to me, and its interpretation, you shall be cut in pieces, and your houses shall be made an ash heap.
6 "However, if you tell the dream and its interpretation, you shall receive from me gifts, rewards, and great honor. Therefore tell me the dream and its interpretation."
7 They answered again and said, "Let the king tell his servants the dream, and we will give its interpretation."
8 The king answered and said, "I know for certain that you would gain time, because you see that my decision is firm:
9 "if you do not make known the dream to me, *there is only* one decree for you! For you have agreed to speak lying and corrupt words before me till the time has changed. Therefore tell me the dream, and I shall know that you can give me its interpretation."
10 The Chaldeans answered the king, and said, "There is not a man on earth who can tell the king's matter; therefore no king, lord, or ruler has *ever* asked such things of any magician, astrologer, or Chaldean.
11 "*It is* a difficult thing that the king requests, and there is no other who can tell it to the king except the gods, whose dwelling is not with flesh."
12 For this reason the king was angry and very furious, and gave the command to destroy all the wise *men* of Babylon.
13 So the decree went out, and they began killing the wise *men;* and they sought Daniel and his companions, to kill *them.*

God Reveals Nebuchadnezzar's Dream

14 Then with counsel and wisdom Daniel

1:11 [a]Hebrew *Melzar,* also in verse 16 **1:19** [a]Literally *talked with them* **2:4** [a]The original language of Daniel 2:4b through 7:28 is Aramaic.

LIFE LESSONS

➢ **1:8 — *But Daniel purposed in his heart that he would not defile himself . . . .***

Godly obedience begins with an absolute commitment to honoring God above all else. When we "purpose in our heart" to put God first, then the particular temptation or challenge doesn't much matter.

➢ **1:17 — *. . . God gave them knowledge and skill in all literature and wisdom; and Daniel had understanding in all visions and dreams.***

God has the power and wisdom and resolve to equip you fully for whatever task or position He wants you to tackle. We will never fail in a God-given task because God failed to give us what we need.

answered Arioch, the captain of the king's guard, who had gone out to kill the wise *men* of Babylon;
15 he answered and said to Arioch the king's captain, "Why is the decree from the king so urgent?" Then Arioch made the decision known to Daniel.
➤ 16 So Daniel went in and asked the king to give him time, that he might tell the king the interpretation.
17 Then Daniel went to his house, and made the decision known to Hananiah, Mishael, and Azariah, his companions,
18 that they might seek mercies from the God of heaven concerning this secret, so that Daniel and his companions might not perish with the rest of the wise *men* of Babylon.
19 Then the secret was revealed to Daniel in a night vision. So Daniel blessed the God of heaven.
✳ 20 Daniel answered and said:

"Blessed be the name of God forever and ever,
For wisdom and might are His.
21 And He changes the times and the seasons;
He removes kings and raises up kings;
He gives wisdom to the wise
And knowledge to those who have understanding.
22 He reveals deep and secret things;
He knows what *is* in the darkness,
And light dwells with Him.

23 "I thank You and praise You,
O God of my fathers;
You have given me wisdom and might,
And have now made known to me what we asked of You,
For You have made known to us the king's demand."

Daniel Explains the Dream
24 Therefore Daniel went to Arioch, whom the king had appointed to destroy the wise *men* of Babylon. He went and said thus to him: "Do not destroy the wise *men* of Babylon; take me before the king, and I will tell the king the interpretation."
25 Then Arioch quickly brought Daniel before the king, and said thus to him, "I have found a man of the captives[a] of Judah, who will make known to the king the interpretation."
26 The king answered and said to Daniel, whose name *was* Belteshazzar, "Are you able to make known to me the dream which I have seen, and its interpretation?"
27 Daniel answered in the presence of the king, and said, "The secret which the king has demanded, the wise *men*, the astrologers, the magicians, and the soothsayers cannot declare to the king.
28 "But there is a God in heaven who reveals secrets, and He has made known to King Nebuchadnezzar what will be in the latter days. Your dream, and the visions of your head upon your bed, were these:
29 "As for you, O king, thoughts came *to* your *mind while* on your bed, *about* what would come to pass after this; and He who reveals secrets has made known to you what will be.
30 "But as for me, this secret has not been revealed to me because I have more wisdom than anyone living, but for *our* sakes who make known the interpretation to the king, and that you may know the thoughts of your heart.
31 "You, O king, were watching; and behold, a great image! This great image, whose splendor *was* excellent, stood before you; and its form *was* awesome.
32 "This image's head *was* of fine gold, its chest and arms of silver, its belly and thighs[a] of bronze,
33 "its legs of iron, its feet partly of iron and partly of clay.[a]
34 "You watched while a stone was cut out without hands, which struck the image on its feet of iron and clay, and broke them in pieces.
35 "Then the iron, the clay, the bronze, the silver, and the gold were crushed together, and became like chaff from the summer threshing floors; the wind carried them away so that no trace of them was found. And the stone that struck the image became a great mountain and filled the whole earth.
36 "This *is* the dream. Now we will tell the interpretation of it before the king.
37 "You, O king, *are* a king of kings. For the God of heaven has given you a kingdom, power, strength, and glory;
38 "and wherever the children of men dwell, or the beasts of the field and the birds of the heaven, He has given *them* into your hand, and has made you ruler over them all—you *are* this head of gold.
39 "But after you shall arise another king-

2:25 [a]Literally *of the sons of the captivity* **2:32** [a]Or *sides*
2:33 [a]Or *baked clay,* and so in verses 34, 35, and 42

LIFE LESSONS

➤ **2:16** — ***So Daniel went in and asked the king to give him time, that he might tell the king the interpretation.***

Before Daniel ever brought his urgent request to God, he demonstrated his trust in Him by telling the king that he would give him what he wanted. Trusting God means looking beyond what we can see to what God sees.

dom inferior to yours; then another, a third kingdom of bronze, which shall rule over all the earth.
40 "And the fourth kingdom shall be as strong as iron, inasmuch as iron breaks in pieces and shatters everything; and like iron that crushes, *that kingdom* will break in pieces and crush all the others.
41 "Whereas you saw the feet and toes, partly of potter's clay and partly of iron, the kingdom shall be divided; yet the strength of the iron shall be in it, just as you saw the iron mixed with ceramic clay.
42 "And *as* the toes of the feet *were* partly of iron and partly of clay, *so* the kingdom shall be partly strong and partly fragile.
43 "As you saw iron mixed with ceramic clay, they will mingle with the seed of men; but they will not adhere to one another, just as iron does not mix with clay.
➤ 44 "And in the days of these kings the God of heaven will set up a kingdom which shall never be destroyed; and the kingdom shall not be left to other people; it shall break in pieces and consume all these kingdoms, and it shall stand forever.
45 "Inasmuch as you saw that the stone was cut out of the mountain without hands, and that it broke in pieces the iron, the bronze, the clay, the silver, and the gold—the great God has made known to the king what will come to pass after this. The dream is certain, and its interpretation is sure."

Daniel and His Friends Promoted

46 Then King Nebuchadnezzar fell on his face, prostrate before Daniel, and commanded that they should present an offering and incense to him.
47 The king answered Daniel, and said, "Truly your God *is* the God of gods, the Lord of kings, and a revealer of secrets, since you could reveal this secret."
48 Then the king promoted Daniel and gave him many great gifts; and he made him ruler over the whole province of Babylon, and chief administrator over all the wise *men* of Babylon.
49 Also Daniel petitioned the king, and he set Shadrach, Meshach, and Abed-Nego over the affairs of the province of Babylon; but Daniel *sat* in the gate[a] of the king.

The Image of Gold

3 Nebuchadnezzar the king made an image of gold, whose height *was* sixty cubits *and* its width six cubits. He set it up in the plain of Dura, in the province of Babylon.
2 And King Nebuchadnezzar sent *word* to gather together the satraps, the administrators, the governors, the counselors, the treasurers, the judges, the magistrates, and all the officials of the provinces, to come to the dedication of the image which King Nebuchadnezzar had set up.
3 So the satraps, the administrators, the governors, the counselors, the treasurers, the judges, the magistrates, and all the officials of the provinces gathered together for the dedication of the image that King Nebuchadnezzar had set up; and they stood before the image that Nebuchadnezzar had set up.
4 Then a herald cried aloud: "To you it is commanded, O peoples, nations, and languages,
5 "*that* at the time you hear the sound of the horn, flute, harp, lyre, *and* psaltery, in symphony with all kinds of music, you shall fall down and worship the gold image that King Nebuchadnezzar has set up;
6 "and whoever does not fall down and worship shall be cast immediately into the midst of a burning fiery furnace."
7 So at that time, when all the people heard the sound of the horn, flute, harp, *and* lyre, in symphony with all kinds of music, all the people, nations, and languages fell down *and* worshiped the gold image which King Nebuchadnezzar had set up.

Daniel's Friends Disobey the King

8 Therefore at that time certain Chaldeans came forward and accused the Jews.
9 They spoke and said to King Nebuchadnezzar, "O king, live forever!
10 "You, O king, have made a decree that everyone who hears the sound of the horn, flute, harp, lyre, *and* psaltery, in symphony with all kinds of music, shall fall down and worship the gold image;
11 "and whoever does not fall down and worship shall be cast into the midst of a burning fiery furnace.
12 "There are certain Jews whom you have set over the affairs of the province of Babylon: Shadrach, Meshach, and Abed-Nego; these men, O king, have not paid due regard to you. They do not serve your gods or worship the gold image which you have set up."
13 Then Nebuchadnezzar, in rage and fury, gave the command to bring Shadrach, Meshach, and Abed-Nego. So they brought these men before the king.

2:49 [a]That is, the king's court

LIFE LESSONS

➤ ***2:44 — . . . The God of heaven will set up a kingdom which shall never be destroyed . . . .***

When we face various difficulties and challenges, it can give us great hope to remember that, whatever happens, we are intimately connected to the winning side.

Life Examples:

SHADRACH, MESHACH, AND ABEDNEGO

Facing the Fire

DAN. 3:19–29

As Nebuchadnezzar scanned the horizon, he saw people of many nationalities bowing down to the image he had made. He had declared that when the music began, everyone was to fall in worship before the immense gold statue he had set up. As far as he could see, people were obeying.

But then the king received word that three Hebrews—Shadrach, Meshach, and Abednego—refused to bow. Nebuchadnezzar flew into a rage and threatened to throw the three men into a raging furnace. They faced a decision: obey God and face the fire, or pay homage to Nebuchadnezzar and dishonor God.

They chose the former—and God delivered them.

God is just as able to deliver you from whatever fire you face. He can help you today, regardless of your struggle. Trust Him, for He is able and willing to deliver you.

See the Life Principles Index for further study:

2. Obey God and leave all the consequences to Him.

14 Nebuchadnezzar spoke, saying to them,
"*Is it* true, Shadrach, Meshach, and Abed-Nego, *that* you do not serve my gods or worship the gold image which I have set up?
➤ 15 "Now if you are ready at the time you hear
the sound of the horn, flute, harp, lyre, *and* psaltery, in symphony with all kinds of music, and you fall down and worship the image which I have made, *good!* But if you do not worship, you shall be cast immediately into the midst of a burning fiery furnace. And who *is* the god who will deliver you from my hands?"
16 Shadrach, Meshach, and Abed-Nego answered and said to the king, "O Nebuchadnezzar, we have no need to answer you in this matter.
17 "If that *is the case,* our God whom we serve is able to deliver us from the burning fiery furnace, and He will deliver *us* from your hand, O king.
18 "But if not, let it be known to you, O king, that we do not serve your gods, nor will we worship the gold image which you have set up."

Saved in Fiery Trial

19 Then Nebuchadnezzar was full of fury, and the expression on his face changed toward Shadrach, Meshach, and Abed-Nego. He spoke and commanded that they heat the furnace seven times more than it was usually heated.
20 And he commanded certain mighty men of valor who *were* in his army to bind Shadrach, Meshach, and Abed-Nego, *and* cast *them* into the burning fiery furnace.
21 Then these men were bound in their coats, their trousers, their turbans, and their *other* garments, and were cast into the midst of the burning fiery furnace.
22 Therefore, because the king's command was urgent, and the furnace exceedingly hot, the flame of the fire killed those men who took up Shadrach, Meshach, and Abed-Nego.
23 And these three men, Shadrach, Meshach, and Abed-Nego, fell down bound into the midst of the burning fiery furnace.
24 Then King Nebuchadnezzar was astonished; and he rose in haste *and* spoke, saying to his counselors, "Did we not cast three men bound into the midst of the fire?" They answered and said to the king, "True, O king."
25 "Look!" he answered, "I see four men loose, walking in the midst of the fire; and they are not hurt, and the form of the fourth is like the Son of God."[a]

Nebuchadnezzar Praises God

26 Then Nebuchadnezzar went near the mouth of the burning fiery furnace *and* spoke, saying, "Shadrach, Meshach, and Abed-Nego, servants of the Most High God, come out, and come *here.*" Then Shadrach,

3:25 [a]Or *a son of the gods*

LIFE LESSONS

➤ **3:15 — *". . . And who is the god who will deliver you from my hands?"***

Nebuchadnezzar could not conceive of a deity with the power to frustrate his wishes. Hadn't he already destroyed Jerusalem, where the temple of the Lord had been? God would not let his arrogant challenge stand.

Meshach, and Abed-Nego came from the
midst of the fire.
27 And the satraps, administrators, governors, and the king's counselors gathered together, and they saw these men on whose bodies the fire had no power; the hair of their head was not singed nor were their garments affected, and the smell of fire was not on them.
➤ 28 Nebuchadnezzar spoke, saying, "Blessed be the God of Shadrach, Meshach, and Abed-Nego, who sent His Angel[a] and delivered His servants who trusted in Him, and they have frustrated the king's word, and yielded their bodies, that they should not serve nor worship any god except their own God!
29 "Therefore I make a decree that any people, nation, or language which speaks anything amiss against the God of Shadrach, Meshach, and Abed-Nego shall be cut in pieces, and their houses shall be made an ash heap; because there is no other God who can deliver like this."
30 Then the king promoted Shadrach, Meshach, and Abed-Nego in the province of Babylon.

Nebuchadnezzar's Second Dream

4 Nebuchadnezzar the king,

To all peoples, nations, and languages that dwell in all the earth:

Peace be multiplied to you.

2 I thought it good to declare the signs and wonders that the Most High God has worked for me.

3 How great *are* His signs,
And how mighty His wonders!
His kingdom *is* an everlasting kingdom,
And His dominion *is* from generation to generation.

4 I, Nebuchadnezzar, was at rest in my house, and flourishing in my palace.
5 I saw a dream which made me afraid, and the thoughts on my bed and the visions of my head troubled me.
6 Therefore I issued a decree to bring in all the wise *men* of Babylon before me, that they might make known to me the interpretation of the dream.
7 Then the magicians, the astrologers, the Chaldeans, and the soothsayers came in, and I told them the dream; but they did not make known to me its interpretation.
8 But at last Daniel came before me (his name *is* Belteshazzar, according to the name of my god; in him *is* the Spirit of the Holy God), and I told the dream before him, *saying:*
9 "Belteshazzar, chief of the magicians, because I know that the Spirit of the Holy God *is* in you, and no secret troubles you, explain to me the visions of my dream that I have seen, and its interpretation.
10 "These *were* the visions of my head *while* on my bed:

"I was looking, and behold,
A tree in the midst of the earth,
And its height was great.
11 The tree grew and became strong;
Its height reached to the heavens,
And it could be seen to the ends of all the earth.
12 Its leaves *were* lovely,
Its fruit abundant,
And in it *was* food for all.
The beasts of the field found shade under it,
The birds of the heavens dwelt in its branches,
And all flesh was fed from it.

13 "I saw in the visions of my head *while* on my bed, and there was a watcher, a holy one, coming down from heaven.
14 He cried aloud and said thus:

'Chop down the tree and cut off its branches,
Strip off its leaves and scatter its fruit.
Let the beasts get out from under it,
And the birds from its branches.
15 Nevertheless leave the stump and roots in the earth,
Bound with a band of iron and bronze,
In the tender grass of the field.
Let it be wet with the dew of heaven,
And *let* him graze with the beasts
On the grass of the earth.
16 Let his heart be changed from *that of* a man,
Let him be given the heart of a beast,
And let seven times[a] pass over him.

3:28 [a]Or *angel* **4:16** [a]Possibly *seven years,* and so in verses 23, 25, and 32

LIFE LESSONS

➤ 3:28 — *". . . God . . . sent His Angel and delivered His servants who trusted in Him . . . ."*

Nebuchadnezzar noticed at least two things about the three Hebrew young men: they served God (they went to work for Him) and they trusted God (they placed their lives in His hands). God loves to rescue people like them.

17 'This decision *is* by the decree of the
watchers,
And the sentence by the word of the holy
ones,
In order that the living may know
That the Most High rules in the kingdom
of men,
Gives it to whomever He will,
And sets over it the lowest of men.'

18 "This dream I, King Nebuchadnezzar,
have seen. Now you, Belteshazzar, declare
its interpretation, since all the wise *men* of
my kingdom are not able to make known
to me the interpretation; but you *are* able,
for the Spirit of the Holy God *is* in you."

Daniel Explains the Second Dream

19 Then Daniel, whose name *was* Belteshazzar, was astonished for a time, and his
thoughts troubled him. *So* the king spoke,
and said, "Belteshazzar, do not let the
dream or its interpretation trouble you."
Belteshazzar answered and said, "My
lord, *may* the dream concern those who
hate you, and its interpretation concern
your enemies!
20 The tree that you saw, which grew and became strong, whose height reached to the
heavens and which *could be* seen by all
the earth,
21 whose leaves *were* lovely and its fruit
abundant, in which *was* food for all, under
which the beasts of the field dwelt, and in
whose branches the birds of the heaven
had their home—
22 it *is* you, O king, who have grown and become strong; for your greatness has
grown and reaches to the heavens, and
your dominion to the end of the earth.
23 And inasmuch as the king saw a watcher,
a holy one, coming down from heaven and
saying, 'Chop down the tree and destroy
it, but leave its stump and roots in the
earth, *bound* with a band of iron and
bronze in the tender grass of the field; let
it be wet with the dew of heaven, and let
him graze with the beasts of the field, till
seven times pass over him';
24 this is the interpretation, O king, and this
is the decree of the Most High, which has
come upon my lord the king:
25 They shall drive you from men, your
dwelling shall be with the beasts of the
field, and they shall make you eat grass
like oxen. They shall wet you with the dew
of heaven, and seven times shall pass over
you, till you know that the Most High rules
in the kingdom of men, and gives it to
whomever He chooses.
26 And inasmuch as they gave the command ➤
to leave the stump *and* roots of the tree,
your kingdom shall be assured to you,
after you come to know that Heaven rules.
27 Therefore, O king, let my advice be
acceptable to you; break off your sins
by *being* righteous, and your iniquities
by showing mercy to *the* poor. Perhaps
there may be a lengthening of your prosperity."

Nebuchadnezzar's Humiliation

28 All *this* came upon King Nebuchadnezzar.
29 At the end of the twelve months he was
walking about the royal palace of Babylon.
30 The king spoke, saying, "Is not this great
Babylon, that I have built for a royal
dwelling by my mighty power and for the
honor of my majesty?"
31 While the word *was still* in the king's
mouth, a voice fell from heaven: "King
Nebuchadnezzar, to you it is spoken: the
kingdom has departed from you!
32 And they shall drive you from men, and
your dwelling *shall be* with the beasts of
the field. They shall make you eat grass
like oxen; and seven times shall pass over
you, until you know that the Most High
rules in the kingdom of men, and gives it
to whomever He chooses."
33 That very hour the word was fulfilled concerning Nebuchadnezzar; he was driven
from men and ate grass like oxen; his
body was wet with the dew of heaven till
his hair had grown like eagles' *feathers*
and his nails like birds' *claws*.

Nebuchadnezzar Praises God

34 And at the end of the time[a] I, Nebuchadnezzar, lifted my eyes to heaven, and my
understanding returned to me; and I
blessed the Most High and praised and
honored Him who lives forever:

For His dominion *is* an everlasting
dominion,

4:34 [a]Literally *days*

LIFE LESSONS

➤ 4:26 — *". . . your kingdom shall be assured to you, after you come to know that Heaven rules."*

Heaven rules—that's the first lesson in politics that any leader ought to learn. God "rules in the kingdom of men, gives it to whomever He will, and sets over it the lowest of men" (Dan. 4:17).

And His kingdom *is* from generation to
generation.
35 All the inhabitants of the earth *are*
reputed as nothing;
He does according to His will in the army
of heaven
And *among* the inhabitants of the earth.
No one can restrain His hand
Or say to Him, "What have You done?"

36 At the same time my reason returned to me, and for the glory of my kingdom, my honor and splendor returned to me. My counselors and nobles resorted to me, I was restored to my kingdom, and excellent majesty was added to me.

➤ 37 Now I, Nebuchadnezzar, praise and extol and honor the King of heaven, all of whose works *are* truth, and His ways justice. And those who walk in pride He is able to put down.

Belshazzar's Feast

5 Belshazzar the king made a great feast for a thousand of his lords, and drank wine in the presence of the thousand.

2 While he tasted the wine, Belshazzar gave the command to bring the gold and silver vessels which his father Nebuchadnezzar had taken from the temple which *had been* in Jerusalem, that the king and his lords, his wives, and his concubines might drink from them.

3 Then they brought the gold vessels that had been taken from the temple of the house of God which *had been* in Jerusalem; and the king and his lords, his wives, and his concubines drank from them.

4 They drank wine, and praised the gods of gold and silver, bronze and iron, wood and stone.

5 In the same hour the fingers of a man's hand appeared and wrote opposite the lampstand on the plaster of the wall of the king's palace; and the king saw the part of the hand that wrote.

6 Then the king's countenance changed, and his thoughts troubled him, so that the joints of his hips were loosened and his knees knocked against each other.

7 The king cried aloud to bring in the astrologers, the Chaldeans, and the soothsayers. The king spoke, saying to the wise *men* of Babylon, "Whoever reads this writing, and tells me its interpretation, shall be clothed with purple and *have* a chain of gold around his neck; and he shall be the third ruler in the kingdom."

8 Now all the king's wise *men* came, but they could not read the writing, or make known to the king its interpretation.

9 Then King Belshazzar was greatly troubled, his countenance was changed, and his lords were astonished.

10 The queen, because of the words of the king and his lords, came to the banquet hall. The queen spoke, saying, "O king, live forever! Do not let your thoughts trouble you, nor let your countenance change.

Life Examples:

NEBUCHADNEZZAR

A Lesson in Humility

DAN. 4:30–37

Under Nebuchadnezzar's rule, Babylon expanded and grew in power and fame. The world looked to him as unto a god—and he unwisely started believing his own press.

"Is not this great Babylon, that I have built for a royal dwelling by my mighty power and for the honor of my majesty?" he congratulated himself (Dan. 4:30). In a flash, Nebuchadnezzar lost his kingdom and lived like a wild beast. Yet after a period of severe humbling, he came to his senses: "Now I, Nebuchadnezzar, praise and extol and honor the King of heaven . . . those who walk in pride He is able to put down" (Dan. 4:37).

God is love, but we must walk humbly before Him. When we begin to exalt ourselves, God will humble us. He deserves all our love and affection, and we must remember that He rules over all, we don't.

See the Life Principles Index for further study:

6. You reap what you sow, more than you sow, and later than you sow.

LIFE LESSONS

➤ 4:37 — *". . . And those who walk in pride He is able to put down."*

God opposes human pride wherever He finds it, and He always will. He declares, "I will halt the arrogance of the proud, and will lay low the haughtiness of the terrible" (Is. 13:11).

11 "There is a man in your kingdom in whom *is* the Spirit of the Holy God. And in the days of your father, light and understanding and wisdom, like the wisdom of the gods, were found in him; and King Nebuchadnezzar your father—your father the king—made him chief of the magicians, astrologers, Chaldeans, *and* soothsayers.
12 "Inasmuch as an excellent spirit, knowledge, understanding, interpreting dreams, solving riddles, and explaining enigmas[a] were found in this Daniel, whom the king named Belteshazzar, now let Daniel be called, and he will give the interpretation."

The Writing on the Wall Explained

13 Then Daniel was brought in before the king. The king spoke, and said to Daniel, "*Are* you that Daniel who is one of the captives[a] from Judah, whom my father the king brought from Judah?
14 "I have heard of you, that the Spirit of God *is* in you, and *that* light and understanding and excellent wisdom are found in you.
15 "Now the wise *men,* the astrologers, have been brought in before me, that they should read this writing and make known to me its interpretation, but they could not give the interpretation of the thing.
16 "And I have heard of you, that you can give interpretations and explain enigmas. Now if you can read the writing and make known to me its interpretation, you shall be clothed with purple and *have* a chain of gold around your neck, and shall be the third ruler in the kingdom."
➤ **17** Then Daniel answered, and said before the king, "Let your gifts be for yourself, and give your rewards to another; yet I will read the writing to the king, and make known to him the interpretation.
18 "O king, the Most High God gave Nebuchadnezzar your father a kingdom and majesty, glory and honor.
19 "And because of the majesty that He gave him, all peoples, nations, and languages trembled and feared before him. Whomever he wished, he executed; whomever he wished, he kept alive; whomever he wished, he set up; and whomever he wished, he put down.
20 "But when his heart was lifted up, and his spirit was hardened in pride, he was deposed from his kingly throne, and they took his glory from him.
21 "Then he was driven from the sons of men, his heart was made like the beasts, and his dwelling *was* with the wild donkeys. They fed him with grass like oxen, and his body was wet with the dew of heaven, till he knew that the Most High God rules in the kingdom of men, and appoints over it whomever He chooses.
22 "But you his son, Belshazzar, have not humbled your heart, although you knew all this.
23 "And you have lifted yourself up against the Lord of heaven. They have brought the vessels of His house before you, and you and your lords, your wives and your concubines, have drunk wine from them. And you have praised the gods of silver and gold, bronze and iron, wood and stone, which do not see or hear or know; and the God who *holds* your breath in His hand and owns all your ways, you have not glorified. ➤
24 "Then the fingers[a] of the hand were sent from Him, and this writing was written.
25 "And this is the inscription that was written:

MENE,[a] MENE, TEKEL,[b] UPHARSIN.[c]

26 "This *is* the interpretation of *each* word. MENE: God has numbered your kingdom, and finished it;
27 "TEKEL: You have been weighed in the balances, and found wanting;
28 "PERES: Your kingdom has been divided, and given to the Medes and Persians."[a]
29 Then Belshazzar gave the command, and they clothed Daniel with purple and *put* a chain of gold around his neck, and made a proclamation concerning him that he should be the third ruler in the kingdom.

Belshazzar's Fall

30 That very night Belshazzar, king of the Chaldeans, was slain.
31 And Darius the Mede received the kingdom, *being* about sixty-two years old.

5:12 [a]Literally *untying knots,* and so in verse 16 **5:13** [a]Literally *of the sons of the captivity* **5:24** [a]Literally *palm* **5:25** [a]Literally *a mina* (50 shekels) from the verb "to number" [b]Literally *a shekel* from the verb "to weigh" [c]Literally *and half-shekels* from the verb "to divide" **5:28** [a]Aramaic *Paras,* consonant with *Peres*

LIFE LESSONS

➤ 5:17 — *"Let your gifts be for yourself, and give your rewards to another . . . ."*

Like Abraham long before him, Daniel had no interest in being made rich by a wicked ruler (see Gen. 14:23). He also had no fear of the Babylonian king, for he feared the Lord above all (Is. 51:12, 13).

➤ 5:23 — *" . . . the God who holds your breath in His hand and owns all your ways . . . ."*

Whether men believe in God or not, He keeps them alive. Whether they serve Him or not, He gives them breath. Whether they revere Him or not, they remain alive at His good pleasure. God rules!

The Plot Against Daniel

6 It pleased Darius to set over the kingdom
one hundred and twenty satraps, to be
over the whole kingdom;
2 and over these, three governors, of whom
Daniel *was* one, that the satraps might give
account to them, so that the king would suffer
no loss.
3 Then this Daniel distinguished himself
above the governors and satraps, because an
excellent spirit *was* in him; and the king gave
thought to setting him over the whole realm.
4 So the governors and satraps sought to
find *some* charge against Daniel concerning
the kingdom; but they could find no charge or
fault, because he *was* faithful; nor was there
any error or fault found in him.
➤5 Then these men said, "We shall not find
any charge against this Daniel unless we find
it against him concerning the law of his God."
6 So these governors and satraps thronged
before the king, and said thus to him: "King
Darius, live forever!
7 "All the governors of the kingdom, the administrators and satraps, the counselors and
advisors, have consulted together to establish
a royal statute and to make a firm decree, that
whoever petitions any god or man for thirty
days, except you, O king, shall be cast into the
den of lions.
8 "Now, O king, establish the decree and
sign the writing, so that it cannot be changed,
according to the law of the Medes and Persians, which does not alter."
9 Therefore King Darius signed the written
decree.

Daniel in the Lions' Den

10 Now when Daniel knew that the writing was signed, he went home. And in his
upper room, with his windows open toward
Jerusalem, he knelt down on his knees three
times that day, and prayed and gave thanks
before his God, as was his custom since early
days.
11 Then these men assembled and found
Daniel praying and making supplication before his God.
12 And they went before the king, and spoke
concerning the king's decree: "Have you not
signed a decree that every man who petitions
any god or man within thirty days, except
you, O king, shall be cast into the den of
lions?" The king answered and said, "The
thing *is* true, according to the law of the
Medes and Persians, which does not alter."
13 So they answered and said before the
king, "That Daniel, who is one of the captives[a]
from Judah, does not show due regard for you,
O king, or for the decree that you have signed,
but makes his petition three times a day."

Life Examples:

DANIEL

A Man of Prayer

DAN. 6:10

The story of Daniel in the lion's den features such high drama that it is easy to overlook the reason why he ended up among hungry beasts.

Daniel got thrown to the lions because of his daily habit of prayer. Ordinarily, his faithfulness would have caused him no problem; but Daniel's enemies decided to use his godliness against him by secretly making it a crime to pray to anyone except Darius.

When Daniel learned of the offensive edict, he went home and prayed—right in front of his chamber windows, as always, where his enemies were certain to see him (Dan. 6:10). Daniel refused to alter his commitment to God in order to protect himself. He could have prayed in a windowless room. But Daniel knew that the eyes of more than his enemies were upon him—God watched, as did His frightened people.

May we choose faithfulness when faithlessness seems easier!

See the Life Principles Index for further study:

8. Fight all your battles on your knees and you win every time.

6:13 [a]Literally *of the sons of the captivity*

LIFE LESSONS

➤ 6:5 — *"We shall not find any charge against this Daniel unless we find it against him concerning the law of his God."*

As a powerful governmental official, Daniel no doubt had lots of closets—but his enemies could find no skeletons in any of them. So they tried to use his God against him—never a wise decision (see Dan. 6:24).

LIFE PRINCIPLE 17

WE STAND TALLEST AND STRONGEST ON OUR KNEES.

DAN. 6:10, 11

An older pastor got into the habit of challenging his congregation by quoting Jeremiah 33:3: "Call to Me, and I will answer you, and I will tell you great and mighty things, which you do not know." Leveling his eyes at those gathered before him, he would say, "Try it. It works!"

This is a very simple thought, but it carries a tremendous truth. God wants us to call to Him. Many times He allows disappointment to rake through our lives so that He might draw us closer to Himself. Prayer is the most powerful tool a believer has; nothing compares to it. In prayer we profess our need of Christ and His solution to our problems. In prayer we learn to worship Him and grow spiritually in His loving presence.

Don't worry about what to say; the Holy Spirit will show you. Tears are just as effective as words at times, and God is sensitive to every tear you cry. Just as He listens to the hurt you feel, so He knows how to deal with and guide you through any anger that has penetrated your life.

God is bigger than any problem you face. He knows the way before you, and only He can guide you through the difficulty. When a trial hits, always respond first by going to Him in prayer. As you pray, hope invades your life and fills you with the reassurance of His undergirding presence.

Several things are essential to establishing a powerful prayer life. One is to choose a definite time to spend in prayer. Setting a time, whether early in the morning or late in the evening, is not the issue. Consistency is the key here. Ask God to show you the perfect time when you can be alone with Him, even for fifteen minutes. God honors the prayers of His people! If you come to him, He will provide all you need for your prayer life.

If possible, select a place where you can be alone with Him. You may need to consider obligations with younger children. When it comes to prayer, you will find that God is very creative; He will provide the perfect place for you to seek Him. Making the commitment to pray is an essential step. This alone tells God that your heart is open to His heart and that you want to learn more about Him and the life He has planned for you.

As we spend time with Him, God lovingly teaches us how to pray and how to listen for His still, small voice as He replies to our humble requests. Prayer is the doorway to blessing and freedom from bondage. As we pray, God teaches us more about Himself and the spiritual warfare needed to combat the enemy. Every day God calls us to put on the

Tears are just as effective as words at times.

armor of God and to stand firm in our faith (Eph. 6:10–17). The only way to do this is through prayer and complete reliance on Jesus Christ, who is Lord over all.

I tell my congregation that the distance between success and failure and victory and defeat is about six to twelve inches, or whatever the distance is for you to drop to your knees and pray to your wondrous Lord and Savior. You never stand taller or stronger than while on your knees!

Over your lifetime, you will face many difficult situations. Some will feel very exciting and challenging. Whatever life sends your way, you can be sure that God cares. He enjoys seeing you excited over His blessings, and He mourns with you when tragedy strikes.

Over the years I have enjoyed keeping a journal that contains many prayers and God's insights for each request. You can do the same thing by writing out your need and the way God answers your prayers. Pray that He will provide specific verses that apply to your situation. Look for His promises in His Word. Claim them, write them down, and trust Him. You will never be disappointed!

My challenge to you is simple: Whatever you're facing, trust God with it. Ask Him to take away the anxiety, fear, and feelings of frustration. When you trust the Lord, you rest in His care.

You probably could name at least one place where you feel safe and accepted. But there is no place where you will feel more accepted or secure than in the presence of God. All of this and much more waits for you as you come to Him.

See the Life Principles Index for further study.

Whatever you're facing, trust God with it.

ANSWERS TO LIFE'S QUESTIONS

Why doesn't God keep us from tests and trials?

DAN. 6:16

Because we live in a fallen world, all of us will face times of suffering and heartache. Sometimes God keeps us from certain tests and trials, but at other times He allows them, knowing that the testing strengthens and perfects our faith in Him.

God wants us to have an unshakeable faith—and if trials, tests, and suffering are what it takes for us to have it, then He'll allow them. Even the strongest faith in God does not mean we will be spared life's trials.

Daniel's faith was severely tested, but he emerged victorious. Daniel refused to compromise his love for God by worshiping King Darius. He also understood that his obedience to God would jeopardize his life (Dan. 6:16)—but he chose the path of other faithful believers who "did not love their lives to the death" (Rev. 12:11).

Many of God's greatest saints—those in the Bible and others throughout Christian history—faced varying degrees of suffering. All of them, however, developed an unshakeable faith that provided the inner strength they needed to face every difficulty with hope and blessed assurance.

Do you have an unshakeable faith? Are you in an extreme place of testing?

If so, do not be afraid. God has planned this very moment, and He will teach you how to trust Him perfectly.

A person with an unshakeable faith never judges God's faithfulness by his or her feelings. Instead, he or she believes and trusts God through many seasons of life, knowing that in the end, God's plan will emerge as perfect.

At times in your walk with God, He may require you to do something that, from a human perspective, seems unreasonable. From His viewpoint, however, it will be in perfect alignment with His Word and will turn out for your ultimate benefit.

His goal is that you acquire a "perfect faith"—but He knows your weaknesses. Open your heart to His love and give Him the opportunity to prove His faithfulness. That is what Daniel did, and God made it possible for him to walk away from the lion's den with a song of victory on his lips.

What is your level of faith in God? Do you believe that He will do exactly what He has promised? Are you convinced that He has already moved heaven and earth for you, and all you have to do is move toward His blessing?

See the Life Principles Index for further study:
20. *Disappointments are inevitable; discouragement is a choice.*
26. *Adversity is a bridge to a deeper relationship with God.*

14 And the king, when he heard *these* words,
was greatly displeased with himself, and set
his heart on Daniel to deliver him; and he labored till the going down of the sun to deliver
him.
15 Then these men approached the king, and
said to the king, "Know, O king, that *it is* the
law of the Medes and Persians that no decree
or statute which the king establishes may be
changed."
* 16 So the king gave the command, and they
brought Daniel and cast *him* into the den of
lions. *But* the king spoke, saying to Daniel,
"Your God, whom you serve continually, He
will deliver you."
17 Then a stone was brought and laid on the
mouth of the den, and the king sealed it with
his own signet ring and with the signets of his
lords, that the purpose concerning Daniel
might not be changed.

Daniel Saved from the Lions
18 Now the king went to his palace and spent
the night fasting; and no musicians[a] were
brought before him. Also his sleep went from
him.
19 Then the king arose very early in the
morning and went in haste to the den of lions.
20 And when he came to the den, he cried out
with a lamenting voice to Daniel. The king
spoke, saying to Daniel, "Daniel, servant of
the living God, has your God, whom you serve
continually, been able to deliver you from the
lions?"
21 Then Daniel said to the king, "O king, live
forever!
22 "My God sent His angel and shut the lions'
mouths, so that they have not hurt me, because
I was found innocent before Him; and also,
O king, I have done no wrong before you."

6:18 [a]Exact meaning unknown

23 Now the king was exceedingly glad for him, and commanded that they should take Daniel up out of the den. So Daniel was taken up out of the den, and no injury whatever was found on him, because he believed in his God.

Darius Honors God

24 And the king gave the command, and they brought those men who had accused Daniel, and they cast *them* into the den of lions—them, their children, and their wives; and the lions overpowered them, and broke all their bones in pieces before they ever came to the bottom of the den.

25 Then King Darius wrote:

To all peoples, nations, and languages that dwell in all the earth:

Peace be multiplied to you.

✳ 26 I make a decree that in every dominion of my kingdom *men must* tremble and fear before the God of Daniel.

For He *is* the living God,
And steadfast forever;
His kingdom *is the one* which shall not be destroyed,
And His dominion *shall endure* to the end.
27 He delivers and rescues,
And He works signs and wonders
In heaven and on earth,
Who has delivered Daniel from the power of the lions.

➤ **28** So this Daniel prospered in the reign of Darius and in the reign of Cyrus the Persian.

Vision of the Four Beasts

7 In the first year of Belshazzar king of Babylon, Daniel had a dream and visions of his head *while* on his bed. Then he wrote down the dream, telling the main facts.[a]
2 Daniel spoke, saying, "I saw in my vision by night, and behold, the four winds of heaven were stirring up the Great Sea.
3 "And four great beasts came up from the sea, each different from the other.
4 "The first *was* like a lion, and had eagle's wings. I watched till its wings were plucked off; and it was lifted up from the earth and made to stand on two feet like a man, and a man's heart was given to it.
5 "And suddenly another beast, a second, like a bear. It was raised up on one side, and *had* three ribs in its mouth between its teeth. And they said thus to it: 'Arise, devour much flesh!'
6 "After this I looked, and there was another, like a leopard, which had on its back four wings of a bird. The beast also had four heads, and dominion was given to it.
7 "After this I saw in the night visions, and behold, a fourth beast, dreadful and terrible, exceedingly strong. It had huge iron teeth; it was devouring, breaking in pieces, and trampling the residue with its feet. It *was* different from all the beasts that *were* before it, and it had ten horns.
8 "I was considering the horns, and there was another horn, a little one, coming up among them, before whom three of the first horns were plucked out by the roots. And there, in this horn, *were* eyes like the eyes of a man, and a mouth speaking pompous words.

Vision of the Ancient of Days

9 "I watched till thrones were put in place,
And the Ancient of Days was seated;
His garment *was* white as snow,
And the hair of His head *was* like pure wool.
His throne *was* a fiery flame,
Its wheels a burning fire;
10 A fiery stream issued
And came forth from before Him.
A thousand thousands ministered to Him;
Ten thousand times ten thousand stood before Him.
The court[a] was seated,
And the books were opened.

11 "I watched then because of the sound of the pompous words which the horn was speaking; I watched till the beast was slain, and its body destroyed and given to the burning flame.
12 "As for the rest of the beasts, they had their dominion taken away, yet their lives were prolonged for a season and a time.

13 "I was watching in the night visions, ➤
And behold, *One* like the Son of Man,
Coming with the clouds of heaven!

7:1 [a]Literally *the head* (or *chief*) *of the words* **7:10** [a]Or *judgment*

LIFE LESSONS

➤ *6:28 — So this Daniel prospered in the reign of Darius and in the reign of Cyrus the Persian.*

God desires for you to live successfully regardless of your circumstances. Daniel lived well and lived successfully in the midst of his circumstances, and we are called to do the same.

➤ *7:13 — "I was watching in the night visions, and behold, One like the Son of Man, coming with the clouds of heaven!"*

Jesus claimed this verse for Himself in Matthew 26:64, causing an uproar in the Sanhedrin. They considered it blasphemy—but the only blasphemy that day was theirs, for not recognizing the Messiah in front of them.

He came to the Ancient of Days,
And they brought Him near before Him.
14 Then to Him was given dominion and glory and a kingdom,
That all peoples, nations, and languages should serve Him.
His dominion *is* an everlasting dominion,
Which shall not pass away,
And His kingdom *the one*
Which shall not be destroyed.

Daniel's Visions Interpreted

15 "I, Daniel, was grieved in my spirit within
my body, and the visions of my head troubled
me.
16 "I came near to one of those who stood by,
and asked him the truth of all this. So he told
me and made known to me the interpretation
of these things:
17 'Those great beasts, which are four, *are*
four kings[a] *which* arise out of the earth.
18 'But the saints of the Most High shall receive the kingdom, and possess the kingdom
forever, even forever and ever.'
19 "Then I wished to know the truth about
the fourth beast, which was different from all
the others, exceedingly dreadful, *with* its
teeth of iron and its nails of bronze, *which* devoured, broke in pieces, and trampled the
residue with its feet;
20 "and the ten horns that *were* on its head,
and the other *horn* which came up, before
which three fell, namely, that horn which had
eyes and a mouth which spoke pompous
words, whose appearance *was* greater than
his fellows.
21 "I was watching; and the same horn was
making war against the saints, and prevailing
against them,
22 "until the Ancient of Days came, and a
judgment was made *in favor* of the saints of
the Most High, and the time came for the
saints to possess the kingdom.
23 "Thus he said:

'The fourth beast shall be
A fourth kingdom on earth,
Which shall be different from all *other* kingdoms,
And shall devour the whole earth,
Trample it and break it in pieces.
24 The ten horns *are* ten kings
Who shall arise from this kingdom.
And another shall rise after them;
He shall be different from the first *ones*,
And shall subdue three kings.
25 He shall speak *pompous* words against the Most High,
Shall persecute[a] the saints of the Most High,
And shall intend to change times and law.
Then *the saints* shall be given into his hand
For a time and times and half a time.
26 'But the court shall be seated,
And they shall take away his dominion,
To consume and destroy *it* forever.
27 Then the kingdom and dominion,
And the greatness of the kingdoms under the whole heaven,
Shall be given to the people, the saints of the Most High.
His kingdom *is* an everlasting kingdom,
And all dominions shall serve and obey Him.'

28 "This *is* the end of the account.[a] As for me,
Daniel, my thoughts greatly troubled me, and
my countenance changed; but I kept the matter in my heart."

Vision of a Ram and a Goat

8 In the third year of the reign of King
Belshazzar a vision appeared *to* me—to
me, Daniel—after the one that appeared to
me the first time.
2 I saw in the vision, and it so happened
while I was looking, that I *was* in Shushan, the
citadel, which *is* in the province of Elam; and
I saw in the vision that I was by the River Ulai.
3 Then I lifted my eyes and saw, and there,
standing beside the river, was a ram which
had two horns, and the two horns *were* high;
but one *was* higher than the other, and the
higher *one* came up last.
4 I saw the ram pushing westward, northward, and southward, so that no animal could
withstand him; nor *was there any* that could
deliver from his hand, but he did according to
his will and became great.
5 And as I was considering, suddenly a male
goat came from the west, across the surface
of the whole earth, without touching the
ground; and the goat *had* a notable horn between his eyes.
6 Then he came to the ram that had two
horns, which I had seen standing beside the
river, and ran at him with furious power.

7:17 [a]Representing their kingdoms (compare verse 23)
7:25 [a]Literally *wear out* **7:28** [a]Literally *the word*

LIFE LESSONS

➤ 7:25 — *". . . Then the saints shall be given into his hand for a time and times and half a time."*

God's blessing for obedience is not always obvious or immediate. Many believers have died for their obedience, and many more will (Rev. 6:11). But the crown of life is well worth waiting for (Rev. 2:10).

7 And I saw him confronting the ram; he
was moved with rage against him, attacked
the ram, and broke his two horns. There was
no power in the ram to withstand him, but he
cast him down to the ground and trampled
him; and there was no one that could deliver
the ram from his hand.
8 Therefore the male goat grew very great;
but when he became strong, the large horn
was broken, and in place of it four notable
ones came up toward the four winds of
heaven.
9 And out of one of them came a little horn
which grew exceedingly great toward the
south, toward the east, and toward the Glorious *Land.*
10 And it grew up to the host of heaven; and
it cast down *some* of the host and *some* of the
stars to the ground, and trampled them.
11 He even exalted *himself* as high as the
Prince of the host; and by him the daily *sacrifices* were taken away, and the place of His
sanctuary was cast down.
12 Because of transgression, an army was
given over *to the horn* to oppose the daily
sacrifices; and he cast truth down to the
ground. He did *all this* and prospered.
13 Then I heard a holy one speaking; and *another* holy one said to that certain *one* who
was speaking, "How long *will* the vision *be,
concerning* the daily *sacrifices* and the transgression of desolation, the giving of both the
sanctuary and the host to be trampled underfoot?"
14 And he said to me, "For two thousand
three hundred days;[a] then the sanctuary shall
be cleansed."

Gabriel Interprets the Vision

15 Then it happened, when I, Daniel, had
seen the vision and was seeking the meaning,
that suddenly there stood before me one having the appearance of a man.
16 And I heard a man's voice between *the
banks of* the Ulai, who called, and said, "Gabriel, make this *man* understand the vision."
17 So he came near where I stood, and when
he came I was afraid and fell on my face; but
he said to me, "Understand, son of man, that
the vision *refers* to the time of the end."
18 Now, as he was speaking with me, I was in
a deep sleep with my face to the ground; but
he touched me, and stood me upright.
19 And he said, "Look, I am making known
to you what shall happen in the latter time of
the indignation; for at the appointed time the
end *shall be.*
20 "The ram which you saw, having the two
horns—*they are* the kings of Media and Persia.
21 "And the male goat *is* the kingdom[a] of
Greece. The large horn that *is* between its
eyes *is* the first king.
22 "As for the broken *horn* and the four that
stood up in its place, four kingdoms shall
arise out of that nation, but not with its power.

23 "And in the latter time of their kingdom,
When the transgressors have reached
their fullness,
A king shall arise,
Having fierce features,
Who understands sinister schemes.
24 His power shall be mighty, but not by his
own power;
He shall destroy fearfully,
And shall prosper and thrive;
He shall destroy the mighty, and *also* the
holy people.

25 "Through his cunning
He shall cause deceit to prosper under
his rule;[a]
And he shall exalt *himself* in his heart.
He shall destroy many in *their* prosperity.
He shall even rise against the Prince of
princes;
But he shall be broken without *human*
means.[b]

26 "And the vision of the evenings and
mornings
Which was told is true;
Therefore seal up the vision,
For *it refers* to many days *in the future.*"

27 And I, Daniel, fainted and was sick for
days; afterward I arose and went about the
king's business. I was astonished by the vision, but no one understood it.

Daniel's Prayer for the People

9 In the first year of Darius the son of
Ahasuerus, of the lineage of the Medes,
who was made king over the realm of the
Chaldeans—

8:14 [a]Literally *evening-mornings* **8:21** [a]Literally *king, representing his kingdom* (compare 7:17, 23) **8:25** [a]Literally *hand* [b]Literally *hand*

LIFE LESSONS

➤ 8:21 — *"And the male goat is the kingdom of Greece. The large horn that is between its eyes is the first king."*

This prophecy about Alexander the Great is so precise and clear that critics have tried to claim that it was written after the fact. God gives prophecies like this to build our trust in the truth and accuracy of His Word.

ANSWERS TO LIFE'S QUESTIONS

How can I learn to pray effectively?

DAN. 9:2

Daniel demonstrates how to pray with both power and confidence. When he discovered in the Book of Jeremiah that the Babylonian captivity would last seventy years (Dan. 9:2), he fell to his knees and began interceding for his people (Dan. 9:4–19).

In Daniel 9, we see a great example of what prayer should be. Its focus is on almighty God and His character. It includes sincere confession, unselfishness, and dependence on the Word of God.

Such prayer has great power. In Daniel's case, God sent the angel Gabriel with His answer even before the prophet had completed his supplication.

To find God during your own hardship, go to the portal Daniel knew best. Go to your knees. Model your prayer after Daniel's and model your life after Daniel 11:32: "The people who know their God shall be strong, and carry out great exploits."

The Bible tells us, "the effective, fervent prayer of a righteous man avails much" (James 5:16). *Effective*—that is exactly what we want our prayers to be, especially in a crisis. When we meet God's requirements, we can feel confident that He will act in the situation as a result of our earnest prayers. What are those requirements?

Requirement 1: Fervent prayer.

Fervent prayers are filled with passion and a strong sense of personal helplessness. They also have a narrow focus on some specific difficulty. Scripture calls this type of prayer "laboring fervently" (Col. 4:12).

Requirement 2: Righteousness.

At salvation, we become rightly related to God as His children. He permanently seals us with the Holy Spirit and declares us righteous forever because of our position in Jesus Christ. But the Bible also uses the word "righteous" to describe a believer's conduct. This means that to be called a "righteous person," we must be found in Christ (Phil. 3:9) *and* make it a habit to obey God (Eph. 4:1; Col. 1:10). If we willingly and knowingly engage in sin, then we do not live righteously and our prayers will lack power.

When the Lord hears the impassioned prayer of a righteous person whose life reflects God's ways, Scripture promises that the Holy Spirit will begin His divine work. God responds with great power to the prayers of even one righteous person. Friend, that person can be *you!*

See the Life Principles Index for further study:

8. Fight all your battles on your knees and you win every time.

17. We stand tallest and strongest on our knees.

2 in the first year of his reign I, Daniel, understood by the books the number of the
years *specified* by the word of the LORD
through Jeremiah the prophet, that He would
accomplish seventy years in the desolations
of Jerusalem.
3 Then I set my face toward the Lord God to
make request by prayer and supplications,
with fasting, sackcloth, and ashes.
4 And I prayed to the LORD my God, and
made confession, and said, "O Lord, great
and awesome God, who keeps His covenant
and mercy with those who love Him, and with
those who keep His commandments,
5 "we have sinned and committed iniquity,
we have done wickedly and rebelled, even by
departing from Your precepts and Your judgments.
6 "Neither have we heeded Your servants
the prophets, who spoke in Your name to our
kings and our princes, to our fathers and all
the people of the land.
7 "O Lord, righteousness *belongs* to You, but
to us shame of face, as *it is* this day—to the
men of Judah, to the inhabitants of Jerusalem
and all Israel, those near and those far off in
all the countries to which You have driven
them, because of the unfaithfulness which
they have committed against You.
8 "O Lord, to us *belongs* shame of face, to
our kings, our princes, and our fathers, because we have sinned against You.
9 "To the Lord our God *belong* mercy and
forgiveness, though we have rebelled against
Him.
10 "We have not obeyed the voice of the LORD
our God, to walk in His laws, which He set before us by His servants the prophets.
11 "Yes, all Israel has transgressed Your law,
and has departed so as not to obey Your voice;
therefore the curse and the oath written in the

Law of Moses the servant of God have been
poured out on us, because we have sinned
against Him.
12 "And He has confirmed His words, which
He spoke against us and against our judges
who judged us, by bringing upon us a great
disaster; for under the whole heaven such has
never been done as what has been done to Jerusalem.
13 "As *it is* written in the Law of Moses, all
this disaster has come upon us; yet we have
not made our prayer before the LORD our
God, that we might turn from our iniquities
and understand Your truth.
14 "Therefore the LORD has kept the disaster
in mind, and brought it upon us; for the LORD
our God *is* righteous in all the works which
He does, though we have not obeyed His
voice.
15 "And now, O Lord our God, who brought
Your people out of the land of Egypt with a
mighty hand, and made Yourself a name, as *it
is* this day—we have sinned, we have done
wickedly!
16 "O Lord, according to all Your righteousness, I pray, let Your anger and Your fury be
turned away from Your city Jerusalem, Your
holy mountain; because for our sins, and for
the iniquities of our fathers, Jerusalem and
Your people *are* a reproach to all *those*
around us.
17 "Now therefore, our God, hear the prayer
of Your servant, and his supplications, and for
the Lord's sake cause Your face to shine on
Your sanctuary, which is desolate.
➤ 18 "O my God, incline Your ear and hear;
open Your eyes and see our desolations, and
the city which is called by Your name; for we
do not present our supplications before You
because of our righteous deeds, but because
of Your great mercies.
19 "O Lord, hear! O Lord, forgive! O Lord, listen and act! Do not delay for Your own sake,
my God, for Your city and Your people are
called by Your name."

The Seventy-Weeks Prophecy

20 Now while I *was* speaking, praying, and
confessing my sin and the sin of my people Israel, and presenting my supplication before
the LORD my God for the holy mountain of my
God,
21 yes, while I *was* speaking in prayer, the
man Gabriel, whom I had seen in the vision at
the beginning, being caused to fly swiftly,
reached me about the time of the evening offering.
22 And he informed *me,* and talked with me,
and said, "O Daniel, I have now come forth to
give you skill to understand.
23 "At the beginning of your supplications
the command went out, and I have come to
tell *you,* for you *are* greatly beloved; therefore
consider the matter, and understand the vision:

24 "Seventy weeks[a] are determined
For your people and for your holy city,
To finish the transgression,
To make an end of[b] sins,
To make reconciliation for iniquity,
To bring in everlasting righteousness,
To seal up vision and prophecy,
And to anoint the Most Holy.

25 "Know therefore and understand,
That from the going forth of the command
To restore and build Jerusalem
Until Messiah the Prince,
There shall be seven weeks and sixty-two weeks;
The street[a] shall be built again, and the wall,[b]
Even in troublesome times.

26 "And after the sixty-two weeks ➤
Messiah shall be cut off, but not for Himself;
And the people of the prince who is to come
Shall destroy the city and the sanctuary.
The end of it *shall be* with a flood,
And till the end of the war desolations are determined.
27 Then he shall confirm a covenant with many for one week;
But in the middle of the week
He shall bring an end to sacrifice and offering.
And on the wing of abominations shall be one who makes desolate,

9:24 [a]Literally *sevens,* and so throughout the chapter [b]Following Qere, Septuagint, Syriac, and Vulgate; Kethib and Theodotion read *To seal up.* **9:25** [a]Or *open square* [b]Or *moat*

LIFE LESSONS

➤ 9:18 — *". . . we do not present our supplications before You because of our righteous deeds, but because of Your great mercies."*

We bring our prayers to God on the basis of who He is, not on the basis of who we are or what we have done. We stand tallest and strongest when we bow low in prayer.

➤ 9:26 — *"And after the sixty-two weeks Messiah shall be cut off, but not for Himself . . . ."*

Only one figure in history fits the time frame of this prophecy: Jesus of Nazareth. He died (was "cut off") for our sins, not for His own sins, since He never committed any. "He was wounded for our transgressions . . ." (Is. 53:5).

Even until the consummation, which is
determined,
Is poured out on the desolate."

Vision of the Glorious Man

10 In the third year of Cyrus king of
Persia a message was revealed to Daniel, whose name was called Belteshazzar. The
message *was* true, but the appointed time *was*
long;[a] and he understood the message, and
had understanding of the vision.
2 In those days I, Daniel, was mourning
three full weeks.
3 I ate no pleasant food, no meat or wine
came into my mouth, nor did I anoint myself
at all, till three whole weeks were fulfilled.
4 Now on the twenty-fourth day of the first
month, as I was by the side of the great river,
that *is*, the Tigris,[a]
5 I lifted my eyes and looked, and behold, a
certain man clothed in linen, whose waist *was*
girded with gold of Uphaz!
6 His body *was* like beryl, his face like the
appearance of lightning, his eyes like torches
of fire, his arms and feet like burnished
bronze in color, and the sound of his words
like the voice of a multitude.
➤ 7 And I, Daniel, alone saw the vision, for the
men who were with me did not see the vision;
but a great terror fell upon them, so that they
fled to hide themselves.
8 Therefore I was left alone when I saw this
great vision, and no strength remained in me;
for my vigor was turned to frailty in me, and
I retained no strength.
9 Yet I heard the sound of his words; and
while I heard the sound of his words I was in
a deep sleep on my face, with my face to the
ground.

Prophecies Concerning Persia and Greece

10 Suddenly, a hand touched me, which
made me tremble on my knees and *on* the
palms of my hands.
11 And he said to me, "O Daniel, man greatly
beloved, understand the words that I speak to
you, and stand upright, for I have now been
sent to you." While he was speaking this word
to me, I stood trembling.
12 Then he said to me, "Do not fear, Daniel,
for from the first day that you set your heart
to understand, and to humble yourself before
your God, your words were heard; and I have
come because of your words.
13 "But the prince of the kingdom of Persia ➤
withstood me twenty-one days; and behold,
Michael, one of the chief princes, came to
help me, for I had been left alone there with
the kings of Persia.
14 "Now I have come to make you understand what will happen to your people in the
latter days, for the vision *refers* to *many* days
yet *to come*."
15 When he had spoken such words to me, I
turned my face toward the ground and became speechless.
16 And suddenly, *one* having the likeness of
the sons[a] of men touched my lips; then I
opened my mouth and spoke, saying to him
who stood before me, "My lord, because of
the vision my sorrows have overwhelmed me,
and I have retained no strength.
17 "For how can this servant of my lord talk
with you, my lord? As for me, no strength remains in me now, nor is any breath left in
me."
18 Then again, *the one* having the likeness of
a man touched me and strengthened me.
19 And he said, "O man greatly beloved, fear
not! Peace *be* to you; be strong, yes, be
strong!" So when he spoke to me I was
strengthened, and said, "Let my lord speak,
for you have strengthened me."
20 Then he said, "Do you know why I have
come to you? And now I must return to fight
with the prince of Persia; and when I have
gone forth, indeed the prince of Greece will
come.
21 "But I will tell you what is noted in the
Scripture of Truth. (No one upholds me
against these, except Michael your prince.
11 "Also in the first year of Darius the
Mede, I, *even* I, stood up to confirm and
strengthen him.)
2 "And now I will tell you the truth: Behold,
three more kings will arise in Persia, and the
fourth shall be far richer than *them* all; by his
strength, through his riches, he shall stir up
all against the realm of Greece.
3 "Then a mighty king shall arise, who shall

10:1 [a]Or *and of great conflict* **10:4** [a]Hebrew *Hiddekel*
10:16 [a]Theodotion and Vulgate read *the son;* Septuagint reads *a hand.*

LIFE LESSONS

➤ 10:7 — *"And I, Daniel, alone saw the vision, for the men who were with me did not see the vision; but a great terror fell upon them . . . ."*

The Lord told Moses, "no man shall see Me, and live" (Ex. 33:20). Paul said God dwells "in unapproachable light, whom no man has seen or can see" (1 Tim. 6:16). And yet even God's invisible Presence makes men tremble.

➤ 10:13 — *"But the prince of the kingdom of Persia withstood me twenty-one days . . . ."*

We get a small glimpse here of the spiritual realities of unseen warfare that take place around the prayers of God's people. What if Daniel had ceased to pray when he did not immediately get an answer?

rule with great dominion, and do according to
his will.
4 "And when he has arisen, his kingdom
shall be broken up and divided toward the
four winds of heaven, but not among his posterity nor according to his dominion with
which he ruled; for his kingdom shall be uprooted, even for others besides these.

Warring Kings of North and South

5 "Also the king of the South shall become
strong, as well as *one* of his princes; and he
shall gain power over him and have dominion. His dominion *shall be* a great dominion.
6 "And at the end of *some* years they shall
join forces, for the daughter of the king of the
South shall go to the king of the North to
make an agreement; but she shall not retain
the power of her authority,[a] and neither he
nor his authority[b] shall stand; but she shall be
given up, with those who brought her, and
with him who begot her, and with him who
strengthened her in *those* times.
7 "But from a branch of her roots *one* shall
arise in his place, who shall come with an
army, enter the fortress of the king of the
North, and deal with them and prevail.
8 "And he shall also carry their gods captive
to Egypt, with their princes[a] *and* their precious articles of silver and gold; and he shall
continue *more* years than the king of the
North.
9 "Also *the king of the North* shall come to
the kingdom of the king of the South, but
shall return to his own land.
10 "However his sons shall stir up strife, and
assemble a multitude of great forces; and *one*
shall certainly come and overwhelm and pass
through; then he shall return to his fortress
and stir up strife.
11 "And the king of the South shall be moved
with rage, and go out and fight with him, with
the king of the North, who shall muster a
great multitude; but the multitude shall be
given into the hand of his *enemy.*
12 "When he has taken away the multitude,
his heart will be lifted up; and he will cast
down tens of thousands, but he will not prevail.
13 "For the king of the North will return and
muster a multitude greater than the former,
and shall certainly come at the end of some
years with a great army and much equipment.
14 "Now in those times many shall rise up
against the king of the South. Also, violent
men[a] of your people shall exalt themselves in
fulfillment of the vision, but they shall fall.
15 "So the king of the North shall come and
build a siege mound, and take a fortified city;
and the forces[a] of the South shall not withstand *him.* Even his choice troops *shall have*
no strength to resist.
16 "But he who comes against him shall do
according to his own will, and no one shall
stand against him. He shall stand in the Glorious Land with destruction in his power.[a]
17 "He shall also set his face to enter with the
strength of his whole kingdom, and upright
ones[a] with him; thus shall he do. And he shall
give him the daughter of women to destroy it;
but she shall not stand *with him,* or be for him.
18 "After this he shall turn his face to the
coastlands, and shall take many. But a ruler
shall bring the reproach against them to an
end; and with the reproach removed, he shall
turn back on him.
19 "Then he shall turn his face toward the
fortress of his own land; but he shall stumble
and fall, and not be found.
20 "There shall arise in his place one who imposes taxes *on* the glorious kingdom; but
within a few days he shall be destroyed, but
not in anger or in battle.
21 "And in his place shall arise a vile person,
to whom they will not give the honor of royalty; but he shall come in peaceably, and seize
the kingdom by intrigue.
22 "With the force[a] of a flood they shall be
swept away from before him and be broken,
and also the prince of the covenant.
23 "And after the league *is made* with him he
shall act deceitfully, for he shall come up and
become strong with a small *number of* people.
24 "He shall enter peaceably, even into the
richest places of the province; and he shall do
what his fathers have not done, nor his
forefathers: he shall disperse among them the
plunder, spoil, and riches; and he shall devise
his plans against the strongholds, but *only* for
a time.
25 "He shall stir up his power and his
courage against the king of the South with a
great army. And the king of the South shall be
stirred up to battle with a very great and
mighty army; but he shall not stand, for they
shall devise plans against him.
26 "Yes, those who eat of the portion of his
delicacies shall destroy him; his army shall be
swept away, and many shall fall down slain.
27 "Both these kings' hearts *shall be* bent on
evil, and they shall speak lies at the same
table; but it shall not prosper, for the end *will*
still *be* at the appointed time.
28 "While returning to his land with great
riches, his heart shall be *moved* against the
holy covenant; so he shall do *damage* and return to his own land.

The Northern King's Blasphemies

29 "At the appointed time he shall return and
go toward the south; but it shall not be like
the former or the latter.

11:6 [a]Literally *arm* [b]Literally *arm* **11:8** [a]Or *molded images* **11:14** [a]Or *robbers,* literally *sons of breakage* **11:15** [a]Literally *arms* **11:16** [a]Literally *hand* **11:17** [a]Or *bring equitable terms* **11:22** [a]Literally *arms*

30 "For ships from Cyprus[a] shall come
against him; therefore he shall be grieved, and
return in rage against the holy covenant, and
do *damage.* "So he shall return and show regard for those who forsake the holy covenant.
31 "And forces[a] shall be mustered by him,
and they shall defile the sanctuary fortress;
then they shall take away the daily *sacrifices,*
and place *there* the abomination of desolation.
➤ 32 "Those who do wickedly against the covenant he shall corrupt with flattery; but the
people who know their God shall be strong,
and carry out *great exploits.*
33 "And those of the people who understand
shall instruct many; yet *for many* days they
shall fall by sword and flame, by captivity and
plundering.
34 "Now when they fall, they shall be aided
with a little help; but many shall join with
them by intrigue.
✳ 35 "And *some* of those of understanding shall
fall, to refine them, purify *them,* and make
them white, *until* the time of the end; because
it is still for the appointed time.
36 "Then the king shall do according to his
own will: he shall exalt and magnify himself
above every god, shall speak blasphemies
against the God of gods, and shall prosper till
the wrath has been accomplished; for what
has been determined shall be done.
➤ 37 "He shall regard neither the God[a] of his fathers nor the desire of women, nor regard any
god; for he shall exalt himself above *them* all.
38 "But in their place he shall honor a god of
fortresses; and a god which his fathers did
not know he shall honor with gold and silver,
with precious stones and pleasant things.
39 "Thus he shall act against the strongest
fortresses with a foreign god, which he shall
acknowledge, *and* advance *its* glory; and he
shall cause them to rule over many, and divide the land for gain.

The Northern King's Conquests

40 "At the time of the end the king of the
South shall attack him; and the king of the
North shall come against him like a whirlwind, with chariots, horsemen, and with
many ships; and he shall enter the countries,
overwhelm *them,* and pass through.
41 "He shall also enter the Glorious Land,
and many *countries* shall be overthrown; but
these shall escape from his hand: Edom,
Moab, and the prominent people of Ammon.
42 "He shall stretch out his hand against the
countries, and the land of Egypt shall not escape.
43 "He shall have power over the treasures of
gold and silver, and over all the precious
things of Egypt; also the Libyans and Ethiopians *shall follow* at his heels.
44 "But news from the east and the north shall
trouble him; therefore he shall go out with
great fury to destroy and annihilate many.
45 "And he shall plant the tents of his palace
between the seas and the glorious holy mountain; yet he shall come to his end, and no one
will help him.

Prophecy of the End Time

12 "At that time Michael shall stand up,
The great prince who stands *watch*
over the sons of your people;
And there shall be a time of trouble,
Such as never was since there was a
nation,
Even to that time.
And at that time your people shall be
delivered,
Every one who is found written in the book.
2 And many of those who sleep in the dust ➤
of the earth shall awake,
Some to everlasting life,
Some to shame *and* everlasting contempt.
3 Those who are wise shall shine ✳
Like the brightness of the firmament,
And those who turn many to
righteousness
Like the stars forever and ever.
4 "But you, Daniel, shut up the words, and
seal the book until the time of the end; many
shall run to and fro, and knowledge shall increase."

11:30 [a]Hebrew *Kittim,* western lands, especially Cyprus
11:31 [a]Literally *arms* **11:37** [a]Or *gods*

LIFE LESSONS

➤ 11:32 — *". . . but the people who know their God shall be strong, and carry out great exploits."*

Our intimacy with God—his highest priority for our lives—determines the impact of our lives. The better we know and love God, the more "exploits" we will do—not in our own power, but in His.

➤ 11:37 — *". . . he shall exalt himself above them all."*

Most conservative scholars believe this verse describes the antichrist, who "opposes and exalts himself above all that is called God or that is worshiped, so that he sits as God in the temple of God, showing himself that he is God" (2 Thess. 2:4).

➤ 12:2 — *"And many of those who sleep in the dust of the earth shall awake, some to everlasting life, some to shame and everlasting contempt."*

Any hardships that God asks us to endure for His sake will one day seem like nothing in comparison to His reward (see Rom. 8:18)—and "nothing" *will* be the reward for choosing anything in His place (see Matt. 25:30).

5 Then I, Daniel, looked; and there stood two others, one on this riverbank and the other on that riverbank.
6 And *one* said to the man clothed in linen, who *was* above the waters of the river, "How long shall the fulfillment of these wonders *be?*"
7 Then I heard the man clothed in linen, who *was* above the waters of the river, when he held up his right hand and his left hand to heaven, and swore by Him who lives forever, that *it shall be* for a time, times, and half *a time;* and when the power of the holy people has been completely shattered, all these *things* shall be finished.
➤ 8 Although I heard, I did not understand. Then I said, "My lord, what *shall be* the end of these *things?*"
9 And he said, "Go *your way,* Daniel, for the words *are* closed up and sealed till the time of the end.
10 "Many shall be purified, made white, and refined, but the wicked shall do wickedly; and none of the wicked shall understand, but the wise shall understand.
11 "And from the time *that* the daily *sacrifice* is taken away, and the abomination of desolation is set up, *there shall be* one thousand two hundred and ninety days.
12 "Blessed *is* he who waits, and comes to the one thousand three hundred and thirty-five days.
13 "But you, go *your way* till the end; for you shall rest, and will arise to your inheritance at the end of the days."

LIFE LESSONS

➤ **12:8 — *"Although I heard, I did not understand . . . ."***

Are there some Bible passages that confuse you? Join the club. Even the great prophet Daniel couldn't understand some of the visions given to Him. Yet what we need to understand, God will help us to understand, in His time.

THE BOOK OF HOSEA

The prophet Hosea ministered to the northern kingdom of Israel before its destruction and deportation by the vicious Assyrians. During his time, the nation appeared to enjoy a season of prosperity and growth; but inwardly, moral corruption and spiritual adultery had thoroughly infected the people.

When God instructed Hosea to marry a promiscuous woman named Gomer, the prophet found his domestic life to be an accurate and tragic dramatization of the unfaithfulness of God's people. The Lord even had the prophet name two of his children Lo-Ruhamah ("no mercy") and Lo-Ammi ("not My people"), to try to shock the people of Israel into realizing how far they had fallen away from their God.

During his half century of prophetic ministry, Hosea repeatedly echoed a threefold message: God abhors the sins of His people; judgment is certain; but God's loyal love stands firm. Hosea insisted that while God would certainly punish His people for their persistent and blatant sins—prophecies which God fulfilled to the letter during the Assyrian invasion of 722 B.C.—yet He would never completely reject His people. A time would come when He would just as certainly draw them back to their land and give them a heart to obey Him joyfully, so He could bless them abundantly.

The names Hosea, Joshua, and Jesus all come from the same Hebrew root word. While the word *hoshea* means "salvation," the names of Joshua and Jesus include an additional idea: "Yahweh is Salvation." As God's messenger, Hosea offered salvation to the straying people if they would turn from idolatry back to God.

The Book of Hosea presents a compelling love story of God's unfailing, steadfast care for His people despite their unfaithfulness, ingratitude, and repeated rebellion. While God's people abandoned Him for pagan idols, His love would forever remain in place as He calls His people back to Himself.

Themes: Spiritual adultery will always bring God's judgment, but God will never abandon His steadfast love for His covenant people.

Author: Hosea.

Time: During the latter years of the northern kingdom of Israel and beyond, around 755–715 B.C.

Structure: The first section of Hosea (1–3) records the apostasy of the northern kingdom of Israel, symbolized in the prophet's marriage to the prostitute Gomer. The second section (4–13) chronicles Israel's sins and the prophetic consequences of those sins. The briefest section (14) outlines God's promised blessings for repentance.

As you read Hosea, watch for several life principles that play an important role in this book:

5. God does not require us to understand His will, just to obey it, even if it seems unreasonable. *See Hosea 1:2–9; page 1019.*

18. As children of a sovereign God, we are never victims of our circumstances. *See Hosea 3:4, 5; page 1021.*

6. You reap what you sow, more than you sow, and later than you sow. *See Hosea 4:7–10; page 1023.*

13. Listening to God is essential to walking with God. *See Hosea 5:1; page 1023.*

1 The word of the LORD that came to Hosea the son of Beeri, in the days of Uzziah, Jotham, Ahaz, *and* Hezekiah, kings of Judah, and in the days of Jeroboam the son of Joash, king of Israel.

The Family of Hosea

2 When the LORD began to speak by Hosea, the LORD said to Hosea:

"Go, take yourself a wife of harlotry
And children of harlotry,
For the land has committed great
harlotry
By departing from the LORD."

3 So he went and took Gomer the daughter of Diblaim, and she conceived and bore him a son.
4 Then the LORD said to him:

"Call his name Jezreel,
For in a little *while*
I will avenge the bloodshed of Jezreel on
the house of Jehu,
And bring an end to the kingdom of the
house of Israel.
5 It shall come to pass in that day
That I will break the bow of Israel in the
Valley of Jezreel."

➤ 6 And she conceived again and bore a daughter. Then *God* said to him:

"Call her name Lo-Ruhamah,[a]
For I will no longer have mercy on the
house of Israel,
But I will utterly take them away.[b]
7 Yet I will have mercy on the house of
Judah,
Will save them by the LORD their God,
And will not save them by bow,
Nor by sword or battle,
By horses or horsemen."

8 Now when she had weaned Lo-Ruhamah, she conceived and bore a son.
9 Then *God* said:

"Call his name Lo-Ammi,[a]
For you *are* not My people,
And I will not be your *God.*

The Restoration of Israel

➤ 10 "Yet the number of the children of Israel
Shall be as the sand of the sea,
Which cannot be measured or numbered.
And it shall come to pass
In the place where it was said to them,
'You *are* not My people,'[a]
There it shall be said to them,
'*You are* sons of the living God.'
11 Then the children of Judah and the
children of Israel
Shall be gathered together,
And appoint for themselves one head;
And they shall come up out of the land,
For great *will be* the day of Jezreel!

2 Say to your brethren, 'My people,'[a]
And to your sisters, 'Mercy[b] *is shown.*'

God's Unfaithful People

2 "Bring charges against your mother, bring
charges;
For she *is* not My wife, nor *am* I her
Husband!
Let her put away her harlotries from her
sight,
And her adulteries from between her
breasts;
3 Lest I strip her naked
And expose her, as in the day she was
born,
And make her like a wilderness,
And set her like a dry land,
And slay her with thirst.

4 "I will not have mercy on her children,
For they *are* the children of harlotry.
5 For their mother has played the harlot;
She who conceived them has behaved
shamefully.
For she said, 'I will go after my lovers,
Who give *me* my bread and my water,
My wool and my linen,
My oil and my drink.'

6 "Therefore, behold,
I will hedge up your way with thorns,
And wall her in,
So that she cannot find her paths.
7 She will chase her lovers,
But not overtake them;

1:6 [a]Literally *No-Mercy* [b]Or *That I may forgive them at all*
1:9 [a]Literally *Not-My-People* **1:10** [a]Hebrew *lo-ammi* (compare verse 9) **2:1** [a]Hebrew *Ammi* (compare 1:9, 10) [b]Hebrew *Ruhamah* (compare 1:6)

LIFE LESSONS

➤ 1:6, 7 — *". . . I will no longer have mercy on the house of Israel, but I will utterly take them away. Yet I will have mercy on the house of Judah . . . ."*

Mercy is not earned or deserved, any more than grace is earned or deserved. A compassionate God may show mercy, but mercy is no sinner's right: "I will have mercy on whomever I will have mercy" (Rom. 9:15).

➤ 1:10 — *". . . And it shall come to pass in the place where it was said to them, 'You are not my people,' there it shall be said to them, 'You are sons of the living God.'"*

Even in judgment, God shows mercy. Throughout the prophets, declarations of awful judgment get intertwined with promises of restoration and mercy. We owe everything to God's grace.

Life Examples:

GOMER

What Did She Want?

HOS. 2:14

It's difficult to understand a woman like Gomer. The prophet Hosea loved her faithfully, provided for her consistently, and invited her to enjoy a soul-to-soul relationship with him.

Instead, she opted for a series of "lovers" who sought nothing but their own pleasure and offered nothing but a few trinkets. What was her problem? What did she want?

Scripture never tells us—but we don't have to look far to find the likely answers, for the same wanderlust that corrupted her heart threatens ours as well. We commit the sin of Gomer every time we turn from the love of God in order to run after the "love" of something else:

- a bigger house
- a better job
- a prestigious neighborhood
- an exciting relationship

Yet God says to us, as He did to her, "behold, I will allure her, will bring her into the wilderness, and speak comfort to her" (Hos. 2:14).

See the Life Principles Index for further study:

15. Brokenness is God's requirement for maximum usefulness.

Yes, she will seek them, but not find
them.
Then she will say,
'I will go and return to my first husband,
For then *it was* better for me than now.'

8 For she did not know
That I gave her grain, new wine, and oil,
And multiplied her silver and gold—
Which they prepared for Baal.

9 "Therefore I will return and take away
My grain in its time
And My new wine in its season,
And will take back My wool and My linen,
Given to cover her nakedness.
10 Now I will uncover her lewdness in the sight of her lovers,
And no one shall deliver her from My hand.
11 I will also cause all her mirth to cease,
Her feast days,
Her New Moons,
Her Sabbaths—
All her appointed feasts.

12 "And I will destroy her vines and her fig trees,
Of which she has said,
'These *are* my wages that my lovers have given me.'
So I will make them a forest,
And the beasts of the field shall eat them.
13 I will punish her
For the days of the Baals to which she burned incense.
She decked herself with her earrings and jewelry,
And went after her lovers;
But Me she forgot," says the LORD.

God's Mercy on His People

14 "Therefore, behold, I will allure her,
Will bring her into the wilderness,
And speak comfort to her.
15 I will give her her vineyards from there,
And the Valley of Achor as a door of hope;
She shall sing there,
As in the days of her youth,
As in the day when she came up from the land of Egypt.

16 "And it shall be, in that day,"
Says the LORD,
"*That* you will call Me 'My Husband,'[a]
And no longer call Me 'My Master,'[b]

2:16 [a]Hebrew *Ishi* [b]Hebrew *Baali*

LIFE LESSONS

➢ 2:8 — *"For she did not know that I gave her grain, new wine, and oil, and multiplied her silver and gold—which they prepared for Baal."*

Every good thing we have and enjoy is nothing but a gift from the hand of God (James 1:17). We must beware of taking the good gifts of God and using them for evil purposes (James 3:9, 10).

➢ 2:16 — *"And it shall be, in that day," says the LORD, "that you will call Me 'My Husband,' and no longer call Me 'My Master.'"*

The Hebrew word *ishi* means "husband," while *baali* means "owner." The first word expresses the deepest desire of God's heart for us—that we would know Him intimately as a wife knows her mate.

17 For I will take from her mouth the names
of the Baals,
And they shall be remembered by their
name no more.
18 In that day I will make a covenant for
them
With the beasts of the field,
With the birds of the air,
And *with* the creeping things of the
ground.
Bow and sword of battle I will shatter
from the earth,
To make them lie down safely.

19 "I will betroth you to Me forever;
Yes, I will betroth you to Me
In righteousness and justice,
In lovingkindness and mercy;
20 I will betroth you to Me in faithfulness,
And you shall know the LORD.

21 "It shall come to pass in that day
That I will answer," says the LORD;
"I will answer the heavens,
And they shall answer the earth.
22 The earth shall answer
With grain,
With new wine,
And with oil;
They shall answer Jezreel.[a]
23 Then I will sow her for Myself in the
earth,
And I will have mercy on *her who had*
not obtained mercy;[a]
Then I will say to *those who were* not My
people,[b]
'You *are* My people!'
And they shall say, '*You are* my God!'"

Israel Will Return to God

3 Then the LORD said to me, "Go again, love
a woman *who is* loved by a lover[a] and is
committing adultery, just like the love of the
LORD for the children of Israel, who look to
other gods and love *the* raisin cakes *of the pagans*."
2 So I bought her for myself for fifteen
shekels of silver, and one and one-half
homers of barley.
3 And I said to her, "You shall stay with me
many days; you shall not play the harlot, nor
shall you have a man—so, too, *will* I *be* toward
you."
4 For the children of Israel shall abide many
days without king or prince, without sacrifice or *sacred* pillar, without ephod or teraphim.
5 Afterward the children of Israel shall return and seek the LORD their God and David
their king. They shall fear the LORD and His
goodness in the latter days.

God's Charge Against Israel

4 Hear the word of the LORD,
You children of Israel,
For the LORD *brings* a charge against the
inhabitants of the land:

"There is no truth or mercy
Or knowledge of God in the land.
2 *By* swearing and lying,
Killing and stealing and committing
adultery,
They break all restraint,
With bloodshed upon bloodshed.
3 Therefore the land will mourn;
And everyone who dwells there will
waste away
With the beasts of the field
And the birds of the air;
Even the fish of the sea will be taken
away.

4 "Now let no man contend, or rebuke
another;
For your people *are* like those who
contend with the priest.
5 Therefore you shall stumble in the day;
The prophet also shall stumble with you
in the night;
And I will destroy your mother.
6 My people are destroyed for lack of
knowledge.
Because you have rejected knowledge,
I also will reject you from being priest for
Me;
Because you have forgotten the law of
your God,
I also will forget your children.

2:22 [a]Literally *God Will Sow* 2:23 [a]Hebrew *lo-ruhamah*
[b]Hebrew *lo-ammi* 3:1 [a]Literally *friend* or *husband*

LIFE LESSONS

➢ 2:20 — *"I will betroth you to Me in faithfulness, and you shall know the LORD."*

God extends His lovingkindness to us, even when we stray from Him. As we test the waters of worldly desire, only to find ourselves drowning in them, God remains loyal to us, rescuing us and restoring our desire for Him alone.

➢ 3:5 — *. . . They shall fear the LORD and His goodness in the latter days.*

We may know what it means to "fear the Lord"—but what does it mean to fear "His goodness"? Hosea means that the goodness of God to us is so great and undeserved that it ought to make us tremble.

➢ 4:6 — *"My people are destroyed for lack of knowledge . . . ."*

If only in the Lord do we find life, then we had better make it a priority to learn as much about Him and His ways as possible—and that means spending prayerful and extended time in His Word.

WHAT THE BIBLE SAYS ABOUT KNOWING ALL OF GOD

Hos. 2:19, 20

Whether you made a commitment to God years ago or have yet to ask Him into your life, there always remains much more to learn about Him. We will never have a full understanding of His nature and ways while we live on earth.

Once we enter into a relationship with the Lord, however, He promises to reveal more of Himself to us. Hosea 2:19, 20 says, "I will betroth you to Me forever; yes, I will betroth you to Me in righteousness and justice, in lovingkindness and mercy; I will betroth you to Me in faithfulness, and you shall know the LORD." He has "betrothed" (or engaged) His people to Himself for one reason: to let Himself be known.

When you discover something new about God, the proverbial light bulb goes on, giving you a greater desire to know more. Grasping one of God's traits through His Word, and then seeing it come to life through our experience, deepens . . .

- *our humility.* As we see God's sovereignty unveiled, we better understand our need for Him. As we see how great He really is, we see how small we are by comparison.
- *our gratitude.* Instead of coming to God with complaints about our unfulfilled, selfish desires, we come to Him with adoration and praise. We love to shower Him with thanksgiving.
- *our hunger.* When the Holy Spirit sheds new light on a familiar verse (one we've read many times), we want more. We take great delight in His Word and want to mine it for its fabulous treasures.
- *our reverence.* As we come to terms with the depths and heights of God, our awe of Him intensifies.
- *our desire to please God.* When we have a right, holy, respectful fear of the Lord, our desire to satisfy self gets transformed into a desire to please God.

As we pursue God, He will fulfill the desires He has given us (Ps. 37:4).Yet even as He meets those desires, our longing for Him continues to grow. The goal remains the same: less of us and more of God.

As we pursue God, He will fulfill the desires He has given us.

See the Life Principles Index for further study:

1. Our intimacy with God—His highest priority for our lives—determines the impact of our lives.

7 "The more they increased,
The more they sinned against Me;
I will change[a] their glory[b] into shame.
8 They eat up the sin of My people;
They set their heart on their iniquity.
9 And it shall be: like people, like priest.
So I will punish them for their ways,
And reward them for their deeds.
➤ 10 For they shall eat, but not have enough;
They shall commit harlotry, but not increase;
Because they have ceased obeying the LORD.

The Idolatry of Israel

11 "Harlotry, wine, and new wine enslave the heart.
12 My people ask counsel from their wooden *idols*,
And their staff informs them.
For the spirit of harlotry has caused *them* to stray,
And they have played the harlot against their God.
13 They offer sacrifices on the mountaintops,
And burn incense on the hills,
Under oaks, poplars, and terebinths,
Because their shade *is* good.
Therefore your daughters commit harlotry,
And your brides commit adultery.

14 "I will not punish your daughters when they commit harlotry,
Nor your brides when they commit adultery;
For *the men* themselves go apart with harlots,
And offer sacrifices with a ritual harlot.[a]
Therefore people *who* do not understand will be trampled.

15 "Though you, Israel, play the harlot,
Let not Judah offend.
Do not come up to Gilgal,
Nor go up to Beth Aven,
Nor swear an oath, *saying*, 'As the LORD lives'—

16 "For Israel is stubborn
Like a stubborn calf;
Now the LORD will let them forage
Like a lamb in open country.

17 "Ephraim *is* joined to idols,
Let him alone.
18 Their drink is rebellion,
They commit harlotry continually.
Her rulers dearly[a] love dishonor.
19 The wind has wrapped her up in its wings,
And they shall be ashamed because of their sacrifices.

Impending Judgment on Israel and Judah

5 "Hear this, O priests!
Take heed, O house of Israel!
Give ear, O house of the king!
For yours *is* the judgment,
Because you have been a snare to Mizpah
And a net spread on Tabor.
2 The revolters are deeply involved in slaughter,
Though I rebuke them all.
3 I know Ephraim,
And Israel is not hidden from Me;
For now, O Ephraim, you commit harlotry;
Israel is defiled.

4 "They do not direct their deeds
Toward turning to their God,
For the spirit of harlotry is in their midst,
And they do not know the LORD.
5 The pride of Israel testifies to his face;
Therefore Israel and Ephraim stumble in their iniquity;
Judah also stumbles with them.

6 "With their flocks and herds
They shall go to seek the LORD,
But they will not find *Him;*
He has withdrawn Himself from them.
7 They have dealt treacherously with the LORD,
For they have begotten pagan children.
Now a New Moon shall devour them and their heritage.

8 "Blow the ram's horn in Gibeah,
The trumpet in Ramah!
Cry aloud *at* Beth Aven,
'*Look* behind you, O Benjamin!'
9 Ephraim shall be desolate in the day of rebuke;
Among the tribes of Israel I make known what is sure.

4:7 [a]Following Masoretic Text, Septuagint, and Vulgate; scribal tradition, Syriac, and Targum read *They will change.* [b]Following Masoretic Text, Septuagint, Syriac, Targum, and Vulgate; scribal tradition reads *My glory.* **4:14** [a]Compare Deuteronomy 23:18 **4:18** [a]Hebrew is difficult; a Jewish tradition reads *Her rulers shamefully love, 'Give!'*

LIFE LESSONS

➤ **4:10 — *"For they shall eat, but not have enough; they shall commit harlotry, but not increase; because they have ceased obeying the LORD."***

When we obey the Lord, He can take a little and make it stretch a long way (see 2 Kin. 4:2–7). But when we disobey, He can take a lot and make it seem like nothing (see Eccl. 6:3–6). The choice is ours.

LIFE PRINCIPLE 18

AS CHILDREN OF A SOVEREIGN GOD, WE ARE NEVER VICTIMS OF OUR CIRCUMSTANCES.

HOS. 3:4, 5

Life is not simple. We face many bumps and turns along the way. The race is real, the battle continuous, and the painful experiences piercing.

But our environment determines neither our circumstances nor our reaction to them.

Chapter 11 of Hebrews is populated with men and women who endured despite adverse circumstances. You may say, "Well, sure they endured. I mean, look how their story turned out!" Well, *they* didn't know how their story was going to turn out. And you don't know how yours is going to end either.

So how did they demonstrate such strong faith in God? They did so because they understood *God* knew how everything was going to turn out. It made perfect sense to them to entrust their futures to a sovereign Lord.

In the fifth grade a young man, now a pastor, had to memorize the entire chapter of Hebrews 11. His mother says that exercise probably became one of the most important parts of his education, although he went all the way through seminary. He committed to memory this repertoire of godly people who endured. When he went through a rough time in the ministry, the Lord reminded him of these great people of faith who endured.

When I look at the Bible's unseen cloud of witnesses, I think of Joseph, who endured though life was so unfair. I think of David, who endured though he was so lonely; and Moses, who took no shortcuts through the land with his grumbling people. I think of Peter, stumbling and falling, stumbling and falling, and getting up again and again.

We can say, "God, if they endured, so can I, because You are just as sovereign today as You were then. You love me just as much as You loved them."

Although I spent little time with my grandfather, he greatly encouraged me. Once he said to me, "Charles, obey God and leave the consequences to Him." That statement from an encourager has sustained me through many battles.

God knows the Christian life is not easy. It will never be easy, no matter how long you live. There is always a battle. You will deal with the world, the flesh, and the devil until you die. Satan is not going to say, "Well, he is sixty-two now and retired, so I guess I'll give him a

God knows the Christian life is not easy.

break." The enemy has an incredible record for perseverance.

Endurance requires something that doesn't come easily. We have to stand *for* something and *against* something, and we can do that only by trusting in a sovereign God.

When the going gets rough—and it will—we can't run away. We can't quit. The longer we push the limits, the stronger our faith becomes. We become ready for greater service and expanded ministry. We become strong, stalwart, and steadfast.

A woman noticed a friend hobbling along. When she asked about the problem, her friend sheepishly answered, "I am trying to lose weight through exercise, and my personal trainer is killing me."

We have a Personal Trainer who wants us fit for the race, but who will never "kill us" in the meantime. He knows our individual racetrack. He knows the pace we need to take. He knows what goal He has set for us. He knows what makes us weary. He is sovereign! We endure when we remember how He endured: "Looking unto Jesus, the author and finisher of our faith" (Heb. 12:2).

The One who endured the cross lives in you.

The One who endured the cross lives in you, so that you can endure yours. If you stumble, He is there to pick you up. If your trail gets real narrow or the bridge is out, don't turn around. Keep your eyes on Jesus. Don't quit. Endure.

When you received the Lord Jesus as your Savior and He set you on your course, He had it all mapped out as your sovereign Lord—bumps, quick turns, detours, up hills, down valleys. Everything. He didn't just fire the starting pistol and hope you could find your way. He sent the Holy Spirit to indwell you.

You aren't running alone. You don't have to clench your fists in order to endure. Just recognize that your sovereign Lord is with you in every situation, and call upon Him to infuse you with His power. You are *never* a victim of your circumstances, for your sovereign God has determined to use everything that happens to you for your blessing and His glory.

See the Life Principles Index for further study.

10 "The princes of Judah are like those who
remove a landmark;
I will pour out My wrath on them like
water.
➤ 11 Ephraim is oppressed *and* broken in
judgment,
Because he willingly walked by *human*
precept.
12 Therefore I *will be* to Ephraim like a
moth,
And to the house of Judah like rottenness.

13 "When Ephraim saw his sickness,
And Judah *saw* his wound,
Then Ephraim went to Assyria
And sent to King Jareb;
Yet he cannot cure you,
Nor heal you of your wound.
14 For I *will be* like a lion to Ephraim,
And like a young lion to the house of
Judah.
I, *even* I, will tear *them* and go away;
I will take *them* away, and no one shall
rescue.
➤ 15 I will return again to My place
Till they acknowledge their offense.
Then they will seek My face;
In their affliction they will earnestly
seek Me."

A Call to Repentance

✳ **6** Come, and let us return to the LORD;
For He has torn, but He will heal us;
He has stricken, but He will bind us up.
2 After two days He will revive us;
On the third day He will raise us up,
That we may live in His sight.
➤ 3 Let us know,
Let us pursue the knowledge of the LORD.
His going forth is established as the
morning;
He will come to us like the rain,
Like the latter *and* former rain to the
earth.

Impenitence of Israel and Judah

4 "O Ephraim, what shall I do to you?
O Judah, what shall I do to you?
For your faithfulness is like a morning
cloud,
And like the early dew it goes away.
5 Therefore I have hewn *them* by the
prophets,
I have slain them by the words of My
mouth;
And your judgments *are like* light *that*
goes forth.
6 For I desire mercy and not sacrifice, ➤
And the knowledge of God more than
burnt offerings.

7 "But like men[a] they transgressed the
covenant;
There they dealt treacherously with Me.
8 Gilead *is* a city of evildoers
And defiled with blood.
9 As bands of robbers lie in wait for a man,
So the company of priests murder on the
way to Shechem;
Surely they commit lewdness.
10 I have seen a horrible thing in the house
of Israel:
There *is* the harlotry of Ephraim;
Israel is defiled.
11 Also, O Judah, a harvest is appointed for
you,
When I return the captives of My
people.

7 "When I would have healed Israel,
Then the iniquity of Ephraim was
uncovered,
And the wickedness of Samaria.
For they have committed fraud;
A thief comes in;
A band of robbers takes spoil outside.
2 They do not consider in their hearts
That I remember all their wickedness;
Now their own deeds have surrounded
them;
They are before My face.
3 They make a king glad with their
wickedness,
And princes with their lies.

6:7 [a]Or *like Adam*

LIFE LESSONS

➤ **5:11 — *"Ephraim is oppressed and broken in judgment, because he willingly walked by human precept."***

God wants us to seek Him and come before Him with our requests and questions. He wants to be involved in the day-to-day business of our lives, and when we leave Him out, we open ourselves to unnecessary hardship.

➤ **5:15 — *". . . In their affliction they will earnestly seek Me."***

God does not use affliction because He enjoys it; He uses affliction because sometimes that is the only language we understand, the only warning we will heed.

➤ **6:3 — *"Let us know, let us pursue the knowledge of the LORD . . . ."***

Our highest pursuit in life is to get to know the Lord for who He really is. While we can do much of this on our own, God directs us to pursue Him *together*, with other believers who also love Him.

➤ **6:6 — *"For I desire mercy and not sacrifice, and the knowledge of God more than burnt offerings."***

Repeatedly in Scripture the Lord tells us that while He has no desire for half-hearted religious ritual, He greatly desires hearts on fire for Him—those who will joyfully love God and love others.

ANSWERS TO LIFE'S QUESTIONS

How can I get to *really* know God?

HOS. 6:6

Did you know that God wants to show you more of Himself every day? "For I desire mercy and not sacrifice, and the knowledge of God more than burnt offerings" (Hos. 6:6).

Are you seeking after God with all your strength? Does your time with the Lord revitalize you, or does it feel more like a ritualistic experience?

Contrast the experience of Gomer with that of an earlier Israelite, Hannah (see 1 Sam. 1–2). Gomer did not care to know God; Hannah desired to know God with all her heart. What made the difference? To better know God . . .

- *you must come to Him honestly.* Confessing your sins and inviting Jesus Christ into your heart requires you to be vulnerable—yet it is the best decision anyone can ever make.
- *you must understand your reliance upon Him.* Hannah saw God as her only source of comfort and power: "And she was in bitterness of soul, and prayed to the LORD and wept in anguish" (1 Sam. 1:10).
- *you must become interested in what interests Him.* Has your desire for spiritual insight and godly wisdom declined? If so, ask the Lord to restore your longing for Him and for the things that most concern Him.
- *you must know His Word.* By reading the Bible, you open your heart to Him. He has given you the Holy Spirit to help you interpret His Word, and He wants you to meditate on it so you can apply it to your life.
- *you must observe His characteristics and ways.* Read the promises that God makes in His Word. Ask Him to remind you of how He has already worked in your life.
- *you must accept His invitations and follow His commands.* God is constantly inviting you to walk with Him. Give the Lord total control of your decisions, your time, your talents, and your possessions.

Your knowledge of God grows as you increasingly recognize His love for you. God delights in your joyful praise and worship of Him. Psalm 46:10 says, "Be still, and know that I am God; I will be exalted among the nations, I will be exalted in the earth!"

As you get to know God on deeper levels, your ability to trust and obey Him will increase. You will find your life's fulfillment when you come to know and exalt the Lord of all creation.

See the Life Principles Index for further study:

1. *Our intimacy with God—His highest priority for our lives—determines the impact of our lives.*

12. *Peace with God is the fruit of oneness with God.*

4 "They *are* all adulterers.
Like an oven heated by a baker—
He ceases stirring *the fire* after kneading the dough,
Until it is leavened.
5 In the day of our king
Princes have made *him* sick, inflamed with wine;
He stretched out his hand with scoffers.
6 They prepare their heart like an oven,
While they lie in wait;
Their baker[a] sleeps all night;
In the morning it burns like a flaming fire.
7 They are all hot, like an oven,
And have devoured their judges;

7:6 [a]Following Masoretic Text and Vulgate; Syriac and Targum read *Their anger;* Septuagint reads *Ephraim.*

LIFE LESSONS

➤ 7:7 — *"None among them calls upon Me."*

The Lord invites us to come to Him in prayer at any time of the day, for any reason, with any problem or challenge or request. What keeps us from taking Him up on His open-ended offer?

All their kings have fallen.
None among them calls upon Me.
8 "Ephraim has mixed himself among the peoples;
Ephraim is a cake unturned.
9 Aliens have devoured his strength,
But he does not know *it;*
Yes, gray hairs are here and there on him,
Yet he does not know *it.*
10 And the pride of Israel testifies to his face,
But they do not return to the LORD their God,
Nor seek Him for all this.

Futile Reliance on the Nations

11 "Ephraim also is like a silly dove, without sense—
They call to Egypt,
They go to Assyria.
12 Wherever they go, I will spread My net on them;
I will bring them down like birds of the air;
I will chastise them
According to what their congregation has heard.

➤ 13 "Woe to them, for they have fled from Me!
Destruction to them,
Because they have transgressed against Me!
Though I redeemed them,
Yet they have spoken lies against Me.
➤ 14 They did not cry out to Me with their heart
When they wailed upon their beds.

"They assemble together for[a] grain and new wine,
They rebel against Me;[b]
15 Though I disciplined *and* strengthened their arms,
Yet they devise evil against Me;
16 They return, *but* not to the Most High;[a]
They are like a treacherous bow.
Their princes shall fall by the sword
For the cursings of their tongue.
This *shall be* their derision in the land of Egypt.

The Apostasy of Israel

8 "*Set* the trumpet[a] to your mouth!
He shall come like an eagle against the house of the LORD,
Because they have transgressed My covenant
And rebelled against My law.
2 Israel will cry to Me,
'My God, we know You!'
3 Israel has rejected the good;
The enemy will pursue him.

4 "They set up kings, but not by Me;
They made princes, but I did not acknowledge *them.*
From their silver and gold
They made idols for themselves—
That they might be cut off.
5 Your calf is rejected, O Samaria!
My anger is aroused against them—
How long until they attain to innocence?
6 For from Israel *is* even this:
A workman made it, and it *is* not God;
But the calf of Samaria shall be broken to pieces.

7 "They sow the wind,
And reap the whirlwind.
The stalk has no bud;
It shall never produce meal.
If it should produce,
Aliens would swallow it up.
8 Israel is swallowed up;
Now they are among the Gentiles
Like a vessel in which *is* no pleasure.
9 For they have gone up to Assyria,

7:14 [a]Following Masoretic Text and Targum; Vulgate reads *thought upon;* Septuagint reads *slashed themselves for* (compare 1 Kings 18:28). [b]Following Masoretic Text, Syriac, and Targum; Septuagint omits *They rebel against Me;* Vulgate reads *They departed from Me.* **7:16** [a]Or *upward* **8:1** [a]Hebrew *shophar,* ram's horn

LIFE LESSONS

➤ 7:13 — *". . . Though I redeemed them, yet they have spoken lies against Me."*

How do we speak lies against our Redeemer? We lie when we say that He has forgotten about us, that He doesn't keep His promises, that He plays favorites. Such lies bring us nothing but pain.

➤ 7:14 — *"They did not cry out to Me with their heart when they wailed upon their beds."*

Affliction does not necessarily bring us back to the Lord; it depends on what we do with it. Affliction is an invitation to repentance, not repentance itself. A cry of anguish is not the same as a cry for mercy.

➤ 8:4 — *"They set up kings, but not by Me . . . ."*

God wants to be intimately involved in all the details of our life, especially in the major decisions that shape our future. Israel chose her kings without the Lord's guidance—and never had a single good one.

➤ 8:7 — *"They sow the wind, and reap the whirlwind . . . ."*

Rarely do we immediately suffer the consequences of our foolish actions. But we do reap what we sow—much more than we sow, and later than we sow.

Like a wild donkey alone by itself;
Ephraim has hired lovers.
10 Yes, though they have hired among the nations,
Now I will gather them;
And they shall sorrow a little,[a]
Because of the burden[b] of the king of princes.

11 "Because Ephraim has made many altars for sin,
They have become for him altars for sinning.
12 I have written for him the great things of My law,
But they were considered a strange thing.
13 *For* the sacrifices of My offerings they sacrifice flesh and eat *it*,
But the LORD does not accept them.
Now He will remember their iniquity and punish their sins.
They shall return to Egypt.

14 "For Israel has forgotten his Maker,
And has built temples;[a]
Judah also has multiplied fortified cities;
But I will send fire upon his cities,
And it shall devour his palaces."

Judgment of Israel's Sin

9 Do not rejoice, O Israel, with joy like *other* peoples,
For you have played the harlot against your God.
You have made love *for* hire on every threshing floor.
2 The threshing floor and the winepress
Shall not feed them,
And the new wine shall fail in her.
3 They shall not dwell in the LORD's land,
But Ephraim shall return to Egypt,
And shall eat unclean *things* in Assyria.
4 They shall not offer wine *offerings* to the LORD,
Nor shall their sacrifices be pleasing to Him.
It shall be like bread of mourners to them;
All who eat it shall be defiled.
For their bread *shall be* for their *own* life;
It shall not come into the house of the LORD.
➤ 5 What will you do in the appointed day,
And in the day of the feast of the LORD?
6 For indeed they are gone because of destruction.
Egypt shall gather them up;
Memphis shall bury them.
Nettles shall possess their valuables of silver;
Thorns *shall be* in their tents.

7 The days of punishment have come;
The days of recompense have come.
Israel knows!
The prophet *is* a fool,
The spiritual man *is* insane,
Because of the greatness of your iniquity and great enmity.
8 The watchman of Ephraim *is* with my God;
But the prophet *is* a fowler's[a] snare in all his ways—
Enmity in the house of his God.
9 They are deeply corrupted,
As in the days of Gibeah.
He will remember their iniquity;
He will punish their sins.

10 "I found Israel
Like grapes in the wilderness;
I saw your fathers
As the firstfruits on the fig tree in its first season.
But they went to Baal Peor,
And separated themselves *to that* shame;
They became an abomination like the thing they loved.
11 *As for* Ephraim, their glory shall fly away like a bird—
No birth, no pregnancy, and no conception!
12 Though they bring up their children,
Yet I will bereave them to the last man.
Yes, woe to them when I depart from them!
13 Just as I saw Ephraim like Tyre, planted in a pleasant place,
So Ephraim will bring out his children to the murderer."

14 Give them, O LORD—
What will You give?
Give them a miscarrying womb
And dry breasts!

15 "All their wickedness *is* in Gilgal,
For there I hated them.

8:10 [a]Or *begin to diminish* [b]Or *oracle* **8:14** [a]Or *palaces*
9:8 [a]That is, one who catches birds in a trap or snare

LIFE LESSONS

➤ 9:5 — *What will you do in the appointed day, and in the day of the feast of the LORD?*

Never mistake the Lord's great patience for acceptance of evil. When we knowingly step out of His will, He gives us chance after chance to turn back to Him. But if we never turn back, that road will eventually end.

Because of the evil of their deeds
I will drive them from My house;
I will love them no more.
All their princes *are* rebellious.
16 Ephraim is stricken,
Their root is dried up;
They shall bear no fruit.
Yes, were they to bear children,
I would kill the darlings of their womb."
➤ 17 My God will cast them away,
Because they did not obey Him;
And they shall be wanderers among the nations.

Israel's Sin and Captivity

10 Israel empties *his* vine;
He brings forth fruit for himself.
According to the multitude of his fruit
He has increased the altars;
According to the bounty of his land
They have embellished *his sacred* pillars.
2 Their heart is divided;
Now they are held guilty.
He will break down their altars;
He will ruin their *sacred* pillars.

3 For now they say,
"We have no king,
Because we did not fear the LORD.
And as for a king, what would he do for us?"
4 They have spoken words,
Swearing falsely in making a covenant.
Thus judgment springs up like hemlock in the furrows of the field.

5 The inhabitants of Samaria fear
Because of the calf[a] of Beth Aven.
For its people mourn for it,
And its priests shriek for it—
Because its glory has departed from it.
6 *The idol* also shall be carried to Assyria
As a present for King Jareb.
Ephraim shall receive shame,
And Israel shall be ashamed of his own counsel.

7 *As for* Samaria, her king is cut off
Like a twig on the water.
➤ 8 Also the high places of Aven, the sin of Israel,
Shall be destroyed.
The thorn and thistle shall grow on their altars;
They shall say to the mountains, "Cover us!"
And to the hills, "Fall on us!"

9 "O Israel, you have sinned from the days of Gibeah;
There they stood.
The battle in Gibeah against the children of iniquity[a]
Did not overtake them.
10 When *it is* My desire, I will chasten them.
Peoples shall be gathered against them
When I bind them for their two transgressions.[a]
11 Ephraim *is* a trained heifer
That loves to thresh *grain;*
But I harnessed her fair neck,
I will make Ephraim pull *a plow.*
Judah shall plow;
Jacob shall break his clods."

12 Sow for yourselves righteousness;
Reap in mercy;
Break up your fallow ground,
For *it is* time to seek the LORD,
Till He comes and rains righteousness on you.

13 You have plowed wickedness;
You have reaped iniquity.
You have eaten the fruit of lies,
Because you trusted in your own way,
In the multitude of your mighty men.
14 Therefore tumult shall arise among your people,
And all your fortresses shall be plundered
As Shalman plundered Beth Arbel in the day of battle—
A mother dashed in pieces upon *her* children.
15 Thus it shall be done to you, O Bethel,
Because of your great wickedness.
At dawn the king of Israel
Shall be cut off utterly.

10:5 [a]Literally *calves* **10:9** [a]So read many Hebrew manuscripts, Septuagint, and Vulgate; Masoretic Text reads *unruliness.* **10:10** [a]Or *in their two habitations*

LIFE LESSONS

➤ 9:17 — *My God will cast them away, because they did not obey Him . . . .*

A chronic case of disobedience may reveal not just a rebellious heart, but an unbelieving one. The Hebrews who died in the wilderness wanderings refused to obey "because of unbelief" (Heb. 3:19).

➤ 10:8 — *They shall say to the mountains, "Cover us!" and to the hills, "Fall on us!"*

Jesus quoted this verse as the Romans led Him away to be crucified (Luke 23:30). And John alludes to it in a future scene of divine judgment (Rev. 6:16). How much better to call on God than on the tools of His judgment!

➤ 10:13 — *You have eaten the fruit of lies, because you trusted in your own way, in the multitude of your mighty men.*

God wants us to develop both our minds and our relationships, but He never wants us to put our hope for the future in either one. "A mighty man is not delivered by great strength" (Ps. 33:16).

God's Continuing Love for Israel

11 "When Israel *was* a child, I loved him,
And out of Egypt I called My son.
2 *As* they called them,[a]
So they went from them;[b]
They sacrificed to the Baals,
And burned incense to carved images.
➤ 3 "I taught Ephraim to walk,
Taking them by their arms;[a]
But they did not know that I healed
them.
➤ 4 I drew them with gentle cords,[a]
With bands of love,
And I was to them as those who take the
yoke from their neck.[b]
I stooped *and* fed them.
5 "He shall not return to the land of
Egypt;
But the Assyrian shall be his king,
Because they refused to repent.
6 And the sword shall slash in his cities,
Devour his districts,
And consume *them,*
Because of their own counsels.
7 My people are bent on backsliding
from Me.
Though they call to the Most High,[a]
None at all exalt *Him.*
8 "How can I give you up, Ephraim?
How can I hand you over, Israel?
How can I make you like Admah?
How can I set you like Zeboiim?
My heart churns within Me;
My sympathy is stirred.
✳ 9 I will not execute the fierceness of My
anger;
I will not again destroy Ephraim.
For I *am* God, and not man,
The Holy One in your midst;
And I will not come with terror.[a]
10 "They shall walk after the LORD.
He will roar like a lion.
When He roars,
Then *His* sons shall come trembling from
the west;
11 They shall come trembling like a bird
from Egypt,
Like a dove from the land of Assyria.
And I will let them dwell in their houses,"
Says the LORD.

Life Examples:

HOSEA

A Longing for Intimacy

HOS. 11:8, 9

Without questioning God, Hosea obeyed Him and took the prostitute Gomer to be his wife. Though she wandered and repeatedly slipped into unfaithfulness, Hosea obeyed the Lord and did not cast her way.

The moving poetry of Hosea reveals the longing of God for uninterrupted intimacy with His people. Can you feel the words of agony in the following words?

"How can I give you up, Ephraim? How can I hand you over, Israel? . . . My heart churns within Me; My sympathy is stirred. I will not execute the fierceness of My anger . . . " (Hosea 11:8, 9).

God longs for an intimate relationship with you. He will do anything to get your love—and He did. In the most dramatic display of love for all time, He provided His Son Jesus Christ as the means to make such fellowship possible. God is the passionate and faithful Lover of your soul.

See the Life Principles Index for further study:

1. *Our intimacy with God—His highest priority for our lives—determines the impact of our lives.*

11:2 [a]Following Masoretic Text and Vulgate; Septuagint reads *Just as I called them;* Targum interprets as *I sent prophets to a thousand of them.* [b]Following Masoretic Text, Targum, and Vulgate; Septuagint reads *from My face.* **11:3** [a]Some Hebrew manuscripts, Septuagint, Syriac, and Vulgate read *My arms.* **11:4** [a]Literally *cords of a man* [b]Literally *jaws* **11:7** [a]Or *upward* **11:9** [a]Or *I will not enter a city*

LIFE LESSONS

➤ 11:3 — *"I taught Ephraim to walk, taking them by their arms; but they did not know that I healed them."*

God "healed" Ephraim over and over again, even when His people disobeyed, even when they lacked the sense to recognize His loving hand. How has God healed you? Where do you recognize His hand in *your* life?

➤ 11:4 — *"I drew them with gentle cords, with bands of love, and I was to them as those who take the yoke from their neck."*

God prefers to deal with His people in love and grace, not in anger and judgment. Sometimes, however, it is that very tenderness that allows us to forget how seriously God takes our relationship with Him.

God's Charge Against Ephraim

12 "Ephraim has encircled Me with lies,
And the house of Israel with deceit;
But Judah still walks with God,
Even with the Holy One[a] *who is* faithful.

12 "Ephraim feeds on the wind,
And pursues the east wind;
He daily increases lies and desolation.
Also they make a covenant with the Assyrians,
And oil is carried to Egypt.

2 "The LORD also *brings* a charge against Judah,
And will punish Jacob according to his ways;
According to his deeds He will recompense him.
3 He took his brother by the heel in the womb,
And in his strength he struggled with God.[a]
4 Yes, he struggled with the Angel and prevailed;
He wept, and sought favor from Him.
He found Him *in* Bethel,
And there He spoke to us—
5 That is, the LORD God of hosts.
The LORD *is* His memorable name.
➤ 6 So you, by *the help of* your God, return;
Observe mercy and justice,
And wait on your God continually.

7 "A cunning Canaanite!
Deceitful scales *are* in his hand;
He loves to oppress.
8 And Ephraim said,
'Surely I have become rich,
I have found wealth for myself;
In all my labors
They shall find in me no iniquity that *is* sin.'

9 "But I *am* the LORD your God,
Ever since the land of Egypt;
I will again make you dwell in tents,
As in the days of the appointed feast.
10 I have also spoken by the prophets,
And have multiplied visions;
I have given symbols through the witness of the prophets."

11 Though Gilead *has* idols—
Surely they are vanity—
Though they sacrifice bulls in Gilgal,
Indeed their altars *shall be* heaps in the furrows of the field.

12 Jacob fled to the country of Syria;
Israel served for a spouse,
And for a wife he tended *sheep*.
13 By a prophet the LORD brought Israel out of Egypt,
And by a prophet he was preserved.
14 Ephraim provoked *Him* to anger most bitterly;
Therefore his Lord will leave the guilt of his bloodshed upon him,
And return his reproach upon him.

Relentless Judgment on Israel

13 When Ephraim spoke, trembling,
He exalted *himself* in Israel;
But when he offended through Baal *worship*, he died.
2 Now they sin more and more,
And have made for themselves molded images,
Idols of their silver, according to their skill;
All of it *is* the work of craftsmen.
They say of them,
"Let the men who sacrifice[a] kiss the calves!"
3 Therefore they shall be like the morning cloud
And like the early dew that passes away,
Like chaff blown off from a threshing floor
And like smoke from a chimney.

4 "Yet I *am* the LORD your God ➤
Ever since the land of Egypt,
And you shall know no God but Me;
For *there is* no savior besides Me.
5 I knew you in the wilderness,
In the land of great drought.
6 When they had pasture, they were filled; ➤
They were filled and their heart was exalted;
Therefore they forgot Me.
7 "So I will be to them like a lion;
Like a leopard by the road I will lurk;

11:12 [a]Or *holy ones* **12:3** [a]Compare Genesis 32:28 **13:2** [a]Or *those who offer human sacrifice*

LIFE LESSONS

➤ 12:6 — *"So you, by the help of your God, return; observe mercy and justice, and wait on your God continually."*

God wants to partner with us in *everything*, including those times when we need to repent. He actually helps us return to Him! Without His help, we could not show mercy or provide justice, or even wait for Him.

➤ 13:4 — *". . . and you shall know no God but Me; for there is no savior besides Me."*

Passages like these show us the truth of the Trinity. There is only one God, and He is our only Savior; yet Scripture plainly calls Jesus our Savior (Acts 13:23; Phil. 3:20; 2 Pet. 1:11). Therefore, Jesus and the Father are one (see John 10:30).

➤ 13:6 — *"When they had pasture, they were filled; they were filled and their heart was exalted; therefore they forgot Me."*

The history of Israel suggests that the nation turned from God most often, not in times of hardship, but in times of prosperity. We must beware of the same traps (Deut. 8:10–18).

8 I will meet them like a bear deprived *of her cubs;*
I will tear open their rib cage,
And there I will devour them like a lion.
The wild beast shall tear them.

9 "O Israel, you are destroyed,[a]
But your help[b] *is* from Me.
10 I will be your King;[a]
Where *is any other,*
That he may save you in all your cities?
And your judges to whom you said,
'Give me a king and princes'?
11 I gave you a king in My anger,
And took *him* away in My wrath.

12 "The iniquity of Ephraim *is* bound up;
His sin *is* stored up.
13 The sorrows of a woman in childbirth shall come upon him.
He *is* an unwise son,
For he should not stay long where children are born.

14 "I will ransom them from the power of the grave;[a]
I will redeem them from death.
O Death, I will be your plagues![b]
O Grave,[c] I will be your destruction![d]
Pity is hidden from My eyes."

15 Though he is fruitful among *his* brethren,
An east wind shall come;
The wind of the LORD shall come up from the wilderness.
Then his spring shall become dry,
And his fountain shall be dried up.
He shall plunder the treasury of every desirable prize.
16 Samaria is held guilty,[a]
For she has rebelled against her God.
They shall fall by the sword,
Their infants shall be dashed in pieces,
And their women with child ripped open.

Israel Restored at Last

14 O Israel, return to the LORD your God,
For you have stumbled because of your iniquity;
2 Take words with you,
And return to the LORD.
Say to Him,
"Take away all iniquity;
Receive *us* graciously,
For we will offer the sacrifices[a] of our lips.
3 Assyria shall not save us,
We will not ride on horses,
Nor will we say anymore to the work of our hands, '*You are* our gods.'
For in You the fatherless finds mercy."

4 "I will heal their backsliding,
I will love them freely,
For My anger has turned away from him.
5 I will be like the dew to Israel;
He shall grow like the lily,
And lengthen his roots like Lebanon.
6 His branches shall spread;
His beauty shall be like an olive tree,
And his fragrance like Lebanon.
7 Those who dwell under his shadow shall return;
They shall be revived *like* grain,
And grow like a vine.
Their scent[a] *shall be* like the wine of Lebanon.

8 "Ephraim *shall say,* 'What have I to do anymore with idols?'
I have heard and observed him.
I *am* like a green cypress tree;
Your fruit is found in Me."

9 Who *is* wise?
Let him understand these things.
Who is prudent?
Let him know them.
For the ways of the LORD *are* right;
The righteous walk in them,
But transgressors stumble in them.

13:9 [a]Literally *it* or *he destroyed you* [b]Literally *in your help* **13:10** [a]Septuagint, Syriac, Targum, and Vulgate read *Where is your king?* **13:14** [a]Or *Sheol* [b]Septuagint reads *where is your punishment?* [c]Or *Sheol* [d]Septuagint reads *where is your sting?* **13:16** [a]Septuagint reads *shall be disfigured* **14:2** [a]Literally *bull calves;* Septuagint reads *fruit.* **14:7** [a]Literally *remembrance*

LIFE LESSONS

➤ **14:2 — *Take words with you, and return to the LORD.***

Why does God insist that we confess our sins to Him (Ps. 32:5; 1 John 1:9)? Why should we "take words" with us when we return to the Lord? Confession breaks the power that sin wields over us in the dark.

➤ **14:9 — *For the ways of the LORD are right; the righteous walk in them . . . .***

Jesus died not only to save us from the penalty of sin, but also from its power. We are not free to sin because we live under grace (Rom. 6:15); rather, His grace enables us to walk in His righteous ways.

THE BOOK OF

JOEL

Disaster struck the southern kingdom of Judah without warning. An ominous black cloud descended upon the land—the dreaded locusts. In a matter of hours, every living green thing was stripped bare.

While it's not clear whether Joel wrote of a literal swarm of locusts or of a vision of things to come, he used the frightening image to proclaim God's message. Although the locust plague was a terrible judgment for sin, God's further judgments during "the day of the LORD" will make that plague pale by comparison. In that day, God will destroy His enemies but bring unparalleled blessing to those who faithfully obey Him.

The Hebrew name *Yo'el* means "Yahweh is God." The name is appropriate to the theme of the book, which emphasizes God's sovereign work in history. Both nature and nations are in His hand. Joel served as God's spokesman, and some scholars consider him one of the earliest of the writing prophets.

Peter quoted Joel as he stood to explain to the men of Jerusalem what they had seen on the day of Pentecost (Acts 2:16–21). Peter held that they had witnessed the outpouring of the Holy Spirit on all flesh, as prophesied in Joel 2:28–32.

Themes: Repentance must precede God's blessing.

Author: Joel the prophet.

Time: Perhaps during the reign of King Joash of Judah (835-796 B.C.), although some say later.

Structure: Chapter 1 of Joel focuses on what is either a literal or figurative plague of locusts on the land of Judah. Chapter 2 deals with "the day of the LORD," a time of severe judgment, a time of repentance and prayer, followed by a time of great blessing. Chapter 3 covers the judgment of the Gentile nations and God's blessings on Zion.

As you read Joel, watch for several life principles that play an important role in this book:

15. Brokenness is God's requirement for maximum usefulness. *See Joel 2:12–17; page 1037.*

7. The dark moments of our life will last only so long as is necessary for God to accomplish His purpose in us. *See Joel 2:18–27; page 1037, 1039.*

1 The word of the LORD that came to Joel the son of Pethuel.

The Land Laid Waste

2 Hear this, you elders,
And give ear, all you inhabitants of the land!
Has *anything like* this happened in your days,
Or even in the days of your fathers?
3 Tell your children about it,
Let your children *tell* their children,
And their children another generation.

4 What the chewing locust[a] left, the swarming locust has eaten;
What the swarming locust left, the crawling locust has eaten;
And what the crawling locust left, the consuming locust has eaten.

5 Awake, you drunkards, and weep;
And wail, all you drinkers of wine,
Because of the new wine,
For it has been cut off from your mouth.
6 For a nation has come up against My land,
Strong, and without number;
His teeth *are* the teeth of a lion,
And he has the fangs of a fierce lion.
7 He has laid waste My vine,
And ruined My fig tree;
He has stripped it bare and thrown *it* away;
Its branches are made white.

8 Lament like a virgin girded with sackcloth
For the husband of her youth.
9 The grain offering and the drink offering
Have been cut off from the house of the LORD;
The priests mourn, who minister to the LORD.
10 The field is wasted,
The land mourns;
For the grain is ruined,
The new wine is dried up,
The oil fails.

11 Be ashamed, you farmers,
Wail, you vinedressers,
For the wheat and the barley;
Because the harvest of the field has perished.
12 The vine has dried up,
And the fig tree has withered;
The pomegranate tree,
The palm tree also,
And the apple tree—
All the trees of the field are withered;
Surely joy has withered away from the sons of men.

Mourning for the Land

13 Gird yourselves and lament, you priests;
Wail, you who minister before the altar;
Come, lie all night in sackcloth,
You who minister to my God;
For the grain offering and the drink offering
Are withheld from the house of your God.
14 Consecrate a fast,
Call a sacred assembly;
Gather the elders
And all the inhabitants of the land
Into the house of the LORD your God,
And cry out to the LORD.

15 Alas for the day!
For the day of the LORD *is* at hand;
It shall come as destruction from the Almighty.
16 Is not the food cut off before our eyes,
Joy and gladness from the house of our God?
17 The seed shrivels under the clods,
Storehouses are in shambles;
Barns are broken down,
For the grain has withered.
18 How the animals groan!
The herds of cattle are restless,
Because they have no pasture;
Even the flocks of sheep suffer punishment.[a]
19 O LORD, to You I cry out;
For fire has devoured the open pastures,
And a flame has burned all the trees of the field.
20 The beasts of the field also cry out to You,
For the water brooks are dried up,
And fire has devoured the open pastures.

1:4 [a]Exact identity of these locusts is unknown.
1:18 [a]Septuagint and Vulgate read *are made desolate.*

LIFE LESSONS

➤ **1:18 — *How the animals groan! The herds of cattle are restless, because they have no pasture; even the flocks of sheep suffer punishment.***

How often have you heard it said, "Hey, what I do is no one's business, so long as I don't hurt anyone else"? The statement betrays a false assumption. Sin *always* hurts others—and even animals.

ANSWERS TO LIFE'S QUESTIONS

How can a good God allow suffering in a believer's life?

JOEL 1:19

Have you ever caught yourself wishing for "the good old days?" Most of us have. The truth is, however, if we had a chance to travel back to another time, we would find the same problems and trials that confront us now also existed back then. Trials come no matter who you are or what you do.

Suffering molds, prepares, and perfects us in a variety of ways. Pressure from without increases pressure within. We feel it as the darkness lingers, the pain increases, and the disappointment goes on and on.

In the spiritual realm, however, we do not have to yield to the mounting pressure. We can defuse it by placing it on the altar of God and allowing Him to handle our hurts.

Suffering beyond our control proves to us that we are not omnipotent. Suddenly we become acutely aware of an authority higher than ourselves, Someone whose insight and wisdom outranks our own. We need a Savior—Someone greater than our biggest fear, Someone able to meet all our needs. Only through His grace can we learn the truth concerning suffering: God uses it to help us experience His immense love.

Maybe you are facing a time of suffering, and you think the emotional pain is more than you can bear. Or perhaps you are dealing with a series of disappointments. Instead of becoming fearful—a frequent ploy of Satan to pull you away from the will of God—ask the Lord to show you what He is up to in your life.

The great preacher Charles Spurgeon wrote: "God knows that soldiers are to be made only in battle; they are not to be grown in peaceful times. We may grow the stuff of which soldiers are made; but warriors are really educated by the smell of powder, in the midst of whizzing bullets and roaring cannonades . . . . Is He not developing in you the qualities of the soldier by throwing you into the heat of battle, and should you not use every application to come off conqueror?"

See the Life Principles Index for further study:

7. The dark moments of our life will last only so long as is necessary for God to accomplish His purpose in us.

29. We learn more in our valley experiences than on our mountaintops.

The Day of the LORD

2 Blow the trumpet in Zion,
And sound an alarm in My holy
mountain!
Let all the inhabitants of the land tremble;
For the day of the LORD is coming,
For it is at hand:
2 A day of darkness and gloominess,
A day of clouds and thick darkness,
Like the morning *clouds* spread over the
mountains.
A people *come,* great and strong,
The like of whom has never been;
Nor will there ever be any *such* after
them,
Even for many successive generations.

3 A fire devours before them,
And behind them a flame burns;
The land *is* like the Garden of Eden
before them,
And behind them a desolate wilderness;
Surely nothing shall escape them.
4 Their appearance is like the appearance
of horses;
And like swift steeds, so they run.
5 With a noise like chariots
Over mountaintops they leap,
Like the noise of a flaming fire that
devours the stubble,
Like a strong people set in battle array.

6 Before them the people writhe in pain;
All faces are drained of color.[a]
7 They run like mighty men,
They climb the wall like men of war;
Every one marches in formation,
And they do not break ranks.
8 They do not push one another;
Every one marches in his own column.[a]
Though they lunge between the weapons,
They are not cut down.[b]
9 They run to and fro in the city,
They run on the wall;
They climb into the houses,
They enter at the windows like a thief.

10 The earth quakes before them,
The heavens tremble;

2:6 [a]Septuagint, Targum, and Vulgate read *gather blackness.*
2:8 [a]Literally *his own highway* [b]That is, they are not halted by losses

The sun and moon grow dark,
And the stars diminish their brightness.
➤ 11 The LORD gives voice before His army,
For His camp is very great;
For strong *is the One* who executes His word.
For the day of the LORD *is* great and very terrible;
Who can endure it?

A Call to Repentance

12 "Now, therefore," says the LORD,
"Turn to Me with all your heart,
With fasting, with weeping, and with mourning."
✳ 13 So rend your heart, and not your garments;
➤ Return to the LORD your God,
For He *is* gracious and merciful,
Slow to anger, and of great kindness;
And He relents from doing harm.
➤ 14 Who knows *if* He will turn and relent,
And leave a blessing behind Him—
A grain offering and a drink offering
For the LORD your God?

15 Blow the trumpet in Zion,
Consecrate a fast,
Call a sacred assembly;
16 Gather the people,
Sanctify the congregation,
Assemble the elders,
Gather the children and nursing babes;
Let the bridegroom go out from his chamber,
And the bride from her dressing room.
17 Let the priests, who minister to the LORD,
Weep between the porch and the altar;
Let them say, "Spare Your people, O LORD,
And do not give Your heritage to reproach,
That the nations should rule over them.
Why should they say among the peoples,
'Where *is* their God?'"

The Land Refreshed

18 Then the LORD will be zealous for His land,
And pity His people.
19 The LORD will answer and say to His people,
"Behold, I will send you grain and new wine and oil,
And you will be satisfied by them;
I will no longer make you a reproach among the nations.

20 "But I will remove far from you the northern *army*,
And will drive him away into a barren and desolate land,
With his face toward the eastern sea

Life Examples:

JOEL

Prophet of Revival

JOEL 2:13

Little is known about the prophet Joel, who ministered to the southern kingdom of Judah. His entire personal history is stated in a single verse: "The word of the LORD that came to Joel the son of Pethuel" (Joel 1:1).

Joel has been called "the prophet of religious revival." His unwavering message to the people of Judah: Repentance *must* precede revival. Therefore he told them, "So rend your heart, and not your garments; return to the LORD your God, for He is gracious and merciful, slow to anger, and of great kindness; and He relents from doing harm" (Joel 2:13).

God does not delight in sending hardship, nor does He glory in calamity. But to bring a rebellious people—or a disobedient believer—to repentance, He will use trials and even tragedies if He has to. He wants to bless His people, not judge them; and if that takes serious measures, so be it.

See the Life Principles Index for further study:
26. Adversity is a bridge to a deeper relationship with God.

LIFE LESSONS

➤ 2:11 — *For strong is the One who executes His word.*

Our omnipotent Lord will use all of His power to fulfill every one of His promises. Not one of them will or can fail. That is why we can build our lives on His every word.

➤ 2:13 — *So rend your heart, and not your garments . . . .*

God is always after the heart, not mere outward religious expression. He wants heartfelt prayer, not impressive oratory (Matt. 6:7). He wants genuine devotion, not smug declarations (Matt. 15:8). He wants your heart.

➤ 2:14 — *Who knows if He will turn and relent, and leave a blessing behind Him . . . ?*

God is under no obligation to show sinners His mercy, but since He delights in it (Mic. 7:18), we can hope not only for pardon when we repent, but even for a blessing.

WHAT THE BIBLE SAYS ABOUT **BROKENNESS, THE WAY TO BLESSING**

Joel 2:12–20

No one enjoys being broken emotionally, physically, or spiritually. It is difficult to understand how strength and blessing can result from brokenness, even though they do. Yet we seldom recognize the benefit of brokenness in the midst of our pain.

The apostle Paul faced discouragement and many intense trials, but he knew God was in control and so he placed his hope and faith in Jesus Christ: "We are hard-pressed on every side, yet not crushed; we are perplexed, but not in despair; persecuted, but not forsaken; struck down, but not destroyed—always carrying about in the body the dying of the Lord Jesus, that the life of Jesus also may be manifested in our body" (2 Cor. 4:8–10).

Paul believed that the trials in his life came with a purpose. He considered them tools in the hand of God, who reshaped, refined, and refocused his life so that it could better reflect the life of Christ, full of purpose and blessing.

Brokenness demands a sharp focus of the heart on Christ.

Just like us, Paul fought with emotional and physical difficulties. He laced his letter to the Corinthians with words of pain and difficulty, but even more he filled it with words of hope and divine intervention, designed to inspire and encourage all who face the agony of brokenness.

Clinging to what you want and think is right for your life can prolong the brokenness process. God's work in your life may not appear to make sense in the beginning, but He knows what lies ahead in your life. He disciplines, guides, and directs, not to hem you in, but to place you in a better position to live a free and blessed life.

For the Christian, brokenness demands a sharp focus of the heart on Christ. You may feel as though you are coming apart at the seams, but if you will transfer your fear and anxiety to Jesus, then something amazing will happen. Not only will you begin the process of transformation into the image of God's Son, but you will sense a greater strength growing within you.

See the Life Principles Index for further study:
15. Brokenness is God's requirement for maximum usefulness.

And his back toward the western sea;
His stench will come up,
And his foul odor will rise,
Because he has done monstrous things."

21 Fear not, O land;
Be glad and rejoice,
For the LORD has done marvelous things!
22 Do not be afraid, you beasts of the field;
For the open pastures are springing up,
And the tree bears its fruit;
The fig tree and the vine yield their strength.
23 Be glad then, you children of Zion,
And rejoice in the LORD your God;
For He has given you the former rain faithfully,[a]
And He will cause the rain to come down for you—
The former rain,
And the latter rain in the first *month*.
24 The threshing floors shall be full of wheat,
And the vats shall overflow with new wine and oil.

25 "So I will restore to you the years that the swarming locust has eaten,
The crawling locust,
The consuming locust,
And the chewing locust,[a]
My great army which I sent among you.
26 You shall eat in plenty and be satisfied,
And praise the name of the LORD your God,
Who has dealt wondrously with you;
And My people shall never be put to shame.
27 Then you shall know that I *am* in the midst of Israel:
I *am* the LORD your God
And there is no other.
My people shall never be put to shame.

God's Spirit Poured Out

28 "And it shall come to pass afterward
That I will pour out My Spirit on all flesh;
Your sons and your daughters shall prophesy,
Your old men shall dream dreams,
Your young men shall see visions.
29 And also on *My* menservants and on *My* maidservants
I will pour out My Spirit in those days.

30 "And I will show wonders in the heavens and in the earth:
Blood and fire and pillars of smoke.
31 The sun shall be turned into darkness,
And the moon into blood,
Before the coming of the great and awesome day of the LORD.
32 And it shall come to pass
That whoever calls on the name of the LORD
Shall be saved.
For in Mount Zion and in Jerusalem there shall be deliverance,
As the LORD has said,
Among the remnant whom the LORD calls.

God Judges the Nations

3 "For behold, in those days and at that time,
When I bring back the captives of Judah and Jerusalem,
2 I will also gather all nations,
And bring them down to the Valley of Jehoshaphat;
And I will enter into judgment with them there
On account of My people, My heritage Israel,
Whom they have scattered among the nations;
They have also divided up My land.
3 They have cast lots for My people,
Have given a boy *as payment* for a harlot,
And sold a girl for wine, that they may drink.

4 "Indeed, what have you to do with Me,
O Tyre and Sidon, and all the coasts of Philistia?
Will you retaliate against Me?
But if you retaliate against Me,
Swiftly and speedily I will return your retaliation upon your own head;
5 Because you have taken My silver and My gold,
And have carried into your temples My prized possessions.
6 Also the people of Judah and the people of Jerusalem
You have sold to the Greeks,
That you may remove them far from their borders.

2:23 [a]Or *the teacher of righteousness* **2:25** [a]Compare 1:4

LIFE LESSONS

2:29 — *"And also on My menservants and on My maidservants I will pour out My Spirit in those days."*

We live in the great day when God is pouring out His Spirit on all believers in Christ, filling them and empowering them to serve Him in holiness and great joy. Have you asked the Lord to fill you today?

7 "Behold, I will raise them
Out of the place to which you have sold them,
And will return your retaliation upon your own head.
8 I will sell your sons and your daughters
Into the hand of the people of Judah,
And they will sell them to the Sabeans,[a]
To a people far off;
For the LORD has spoken."

9 Proclaim this among the nations:
"Prepare for war!
Wake up the mighty men,
Let all the men of war draw near,
Let them come up.
10 Beat your plowshares into swords
And your pruning hooks into spears;
Let the weak say, 'I *am* strong.'"
11 Assemble and come, all you nations,
And gather together all around.
Cause Your mighty ones to go down there, O LORD.

12 "Let the nations be wakened, and come up to the Valley of Jehoshaphat;
For there I will sit to judge all the surrounding nations.
➤ 13 Put in the sickle, for the harvest is ripe.
Come, go down;
For the winepress is full,
The vats overflow—
For their wickedness *is* great."

14 Multitudes, multitudes in the valley of decision!
For the day of the LORD *is* near in the valley of decision.
15 The sun and moon will grow dark,
And the stars will diminish their brightness.
16 The LORD also will roar from Zion,
And utter His voice from Jerusalem;
The heavens and earth will shake;
But the LORD will be a shelter for His people,
And the strength of the children of Israel.

17 "So you shall know that I *am* the LORD your God,
Dwelling in Zion My holy mountain.
Then Jerusalem shall be holy,
And no aliens shall ever pass through her again."

God Blesses His People

18 And it will come to pass in that day
That the mountains shall drip with new wine,
The hills shall flow with milk,
And all the brooks of Judah shall be flooded with water;
A fountain shall flow from the house of the LORD
And water the Valley of Acacias.

19 "Egypt shall be a desolation,
And Edom a desolate wilderness,
Because of violence *against* the people of Judah,
For they have shed innocent blood in their land.
20 But Judah shall abide forever,
And Jerusalem from generation to generation.
21 For I will acquit them of the guilt of bloodshed, whom I had not acquitted;
For the LORD dwells in Zion."

3:8 [a]Literally *Shebaites* (compare Isaiah 60:6 and Ezekiel 27:22)

LIFE LESSONS

➤ 3:13 — *"Put in the sickle, for the harvest is ripe. Come, go down; for the winepress is full, the vats overflow—for their wickedness is great."*

Despite His grace, despite His mercy, despite His love, if we continue to disobey God and reject His Word, we may reach a point of no return where His judgment inevitably falls (see Gen. 15:16; Rev. 2:5).

THE BOOK OF

AMOS

Amos prophesied during a period of national optimism in Israel. Business was booming and boundaries were bulging—but below the surface, greed and injustice festered. Hypocritical religious motions had replaced true worship, creating a false sense of security and a growing callousness to God's disciplining hand. Famine, drought, plagues, death, destruction—it seemed that nothing could force the people to their knees.

Amos, the farmer-turned-prophet, lashed out at sin unflinchingly, trying to visualize the nearness of God's judgment and mobilize the nation to repentance. The complacent kingdom, like a basket of rotting fruit, stood ripe for judgment because of her hypocrisy and spiritual indifference.

Amos came from the southern kingdom of Judah but did his prophetic work in the northern kingdom of Israel, slightly earlier than the prophet Hosea. He was from Tekoa, a small town about eleven miles south of Jerusalem. He did not consider himself a prophet or the son of a prophet (7:14); his only qualification was the calling of God. Amos received his training as a prophet straight from the hand of God.

The name Amos is derived from the Hebrew root *amas*, "to lift a burden, to carry." Thus his name means "Burden" or "Burden-bearer." Amos lived up to the meaning of his name by his divinely given burden of declaring divine judgment to rebellious Israel. The Greek and Latin titles are both transliterated in English as *Amos.*

Themes: God will discipline those who become spiritually lax or indifferent.

Author: Amos

Time: Amos prophesied at the time when Uzziah sat on the throne of Judah (792–740 B.C.) and Jeroboam II was king of Israel (793–753 B.C.).

Structure: In the first two chapters, the prophet pronounces judgment against neighboring nations. The final seven chapters of Amos speak of judgment against the kingdom of Israel because of its oppression, social injustice, and hypocrisy. Five of Amos's visions (7–9) told the people that they still had time to turn back to God; but in the final two visions, judgment became inevitable. Only the closing verses of chapter 9 express hope beyond God's judgment.

As you read Amos, watch for several life principles that play an important role in this book:

6. You reap what you sow, more than you sow, and later than you sow. *See Amos 2:6–16; page 1043.*

13. Listening to God is essential to walking with God. *See Amos 5:4–7; page 1045.*

19. Anything you hold too tightly you will lose. *See Amos 6:6, 7; page 1047.*

1 The words of Amos, who was among the
sheepbreeders[a] of Tekoa, which he saw
concerning Israel in the days of Uzziah king
of Judah, and in the days of Jeroboam the son
of Joash, king of Israel, two years before the
earthquake.
2 And he said:

"The LORD roars from Zion,
And utters His voice from Jerusalem;
The pastures of the shepherds mourn,
And the top of Carmel withers."

Judgment on the Nations

3 Thus says the LORD:

"For three transgressions of Damascus, and for four,
I will not turn away its *punishment*,
Because they have threshed Gilead with implements of iron.
4 But I will send a fire into the house of Hazael,
Which shall devour the palaces of Ben-Hadad.
5 I will also break the *gate* bar of Damascus,
And cut off the inhabitant from the Valley of Aven,
And the one who holds the scepter from Beth Eden.
The people of Syria shall go captive to Kir,"
Says the LORD.

6 Thus says the LORD:

"For three transgressions of Gaza, and for four,
I will not turn away its *punishment*,
Because they took captive the whole captivity
To deliver *them* up to Edom.
7 But I will send a fire upon the wall of Gaza,
Which shall devour its palaces.
8 I will cut off the inhabitant from Ashdod,
And the one who holds the scepter from Ashkelon;
I will turn My hand against Ekron,
And the remnant of the Philistines shall perish,"
Says the Lord GOD.

9 Thus says the LORD:

"For three transgressions of Tyre, and for four,
I will not turn away its *punishment*,
Because they delivered up the whole captivity to Edom,
And did not remember the covenant of brotherhood.
10 But I will send a fire upon the wall of Tyre,
Which shall devour its palaces."

11 Thus says the LORD:

"For three transgressions of Edom, and for four,
I will not turn away its *punishment*,
Because he pursued his brother with the sword,
And cast off all pity;
His anger tore perpetually,
And he kept his wrath forever.
12 But I will send a fire upon Teman,
Which shall devour the palaces of Bozrah."

13 Thus says the LORD:

"For three transgressions of the people of Ammon, and for four,
I will not turn away its *punishment*,
Because they ripped open the women with child in Gilead,
That they might enlarge their territory.
14 But I will kindle a fire in the wall of Rabbah,
And it shall devour its palaces,
Amid shouting in the day of battle,
And a tempest in the day of the whirlwind.
15 Their king shall go into captivity,
He and his princes together,"
Says the LORD.

2 Thus says the LORD:

"For three transgressions of Moab, and for four,
I will not turn away its *punishment*,
Because he burned the bones of the king of Edom to lime.
2 But I will send a fire upon Moab,
And it shall devour the palaces of Kerioth;
Moab shall die with tumult,
With shouting *and* trumpet sound.
3 And I will cut off the judge from its midst,
And slay all its princes with him,"
Says the LORD.

Judgment on Judah

4 Thus says the LORD:

"For three transgressions of Judah, and for four,
I will not turn away its *punishment*,
Because they have despised the law of the LORD,
And have not kept His commandments.
Their lies lead them astray,
Lies which their fathers followed.

1:1 [a]Compare 2 Kings 3:4

LIFE LESSONS

➤ **2:4 — *"Their lies led them astray, lies which their fathers followed."***

If we do not immerse ourselves in the truth of God's Word, the lies that flourish all around us can easily take hold in our minds and lead us astray, to our own destruction.

5 But I will send a fire upon Judah,
And it shall devour the palaces of
Jerusalem."

Judgment on Israel

6 Thus says the LORD:

"For three transgressions of Israel, and for
four,
I will not turn away its *punishment*,
Because they sell the righteous for
silver,
And the poor for a pair of sandals.
7 They pant after[a] the dust of the earth
which is on the head of the poor,
And pervert the way of the humble.
A man and his father go in to the *same*
girl,
To defile My holy name.
8 They lie down by every altar on clothes
taken in pledge,
And drink the wine of the condemned *in*
the house of their god.

9 "Yet *it was* I *who* destroyed the Amorite
before them,
Whose height *was* like the height of the
cedars,
And he *was as* strong as the oaks;
Yet I destroyed his fruit above
And his roots beneath.
➤ 10 Also *it was* I *who* brought you up from
the land of Egypt,
And led you forty years through the
wilderness,
To possess the land of the Amorite.
11 I raised up some of your sons as
prophets,
And some of your young men as
Nazirites.
Is it not so, O you children of Israel?"
Says the LORD.
12 "But you gave the Nazirites wine to
drink,
And commanded the prophets saying,
'Do not prophesy!'

13 "Behold, I am weighed down by you,
As a cart full of sheaves is weighed
down.
14 Therefore flight shall perish from the
swift,
The strong shall not strengthen his
power,
Nor shall the mighty deliver
himself;

Life Examples:

AMOS

Obedient Without Compromise

AMOS 2:6

God called Amos from his flocks and groves to prophecy to the northern kingdom, and Amos obeyed. Without hesitation and without argument, this quiet man simply complied. He packed and traveled to a strange region so that he could prophesy God's word to unfamiliar tribes. He didn't object or complain. He simply went.

Amos knew he would fight an uphill battle. During this economic golden era, a haze of relaxed contentment had settled over the nation. The people did not welcome Amos' words of warning, yet he unceasingly fulfilled his divine task.

How many of us today have the mighty spirit of Amos? How many boldly face a hostile world and faithfully proclaim the truth of the Lord? How many obey, regardless of the repercussions? How many absorb blow after blow from the enemy, only to turn and take the next obedient step in their walk of faith?

See the Life Principles Index for further study:
2. Obey God and leave all the consequences to Him.

15 He shall not stand who handles the
bow,
The swift of foot shall not escape,
Nor shall he who rides a horse deliver
himself.
16 The most courageous men of might
Shall flee naked in that day,"
Says the LORD.

2:7 [a]Or *trample on*

LIFE LESSONS

➤ 2:10 — *"Also it was I who brought you up from the land of Egypt, and led you forty years through the wilderness, to possess the land of the Amorite."*

It is good to regularly remind ourselves how the Lord has helped and delivered us in the past, otherwise we tend to either forget His goodness to us or we begin to imagine that we have blessed ourselves.

Authority of the Prophet's Message

3 Hear this word that the LORD has spoken
against you, O children of Israel, against
the whole family which I brought up from the
land of Egypt, saying:

➤ 2 "You only have I known of all the families
of the earth;
Therefore I will punish you for all your
iniquities."

3 Can two walk together, unless they are
agreed?
4 Will a lion roar in the forest, when he has
no prey?
Will a young lion cry out of his den, if he
has caught nothing?
5 Will a bird fall into a snare on the earth,
where there is no trap for it?
Will a snare spring up from the earth, if it
has caught nothing at all?
6 If a trumpet is blown in a city, will not
the people be afraid?
If there is calamity in a city, will not the
LORD have done *it?*
✳ 7 Surely the Lord GOD does nothing,
Unless He reveals His secret to His
servants the prophets.
8 A lion has roared!
Who will not fear?
The Lord GOD has spoken!
Who can but prophesy?

Punishment of Israel's Sins

9 "Proclaim in the palaces at Ashdod,[a]
And in the palaces in the land of Egypt,
and say:
'Assemble on the mountains of Samaria;
See great tumults in her midst,
And the oppressed within her.
10 For they do not know to do right,'
Says the LORD,
'Who store up violence and robbery in
their palaces.'"

11 Therefore thus says the Lord GOD:

"An adversary *shall be* all around the
land;
He shall sap your strength from you,
And your palaces shall be plundered."

12 Thus says the LORD:

"As a shepherd takes from the mouth of a
lion
Two legs or a piece of an ear,
So shall the children of Israel be taken
out
Who dwell in Samaria—
In the corner of a bed and on the edge[a] of
a couch!
13 Hear and testify against the house of
Jacob,"
Says the Lord GOD, the God of hosts,
14 "That in the day I punish Israel for their
transgressions,
I will also visit *destruction* on the altars
of Bethel;
And the horns of the altar shall be cut off
And fall to the ground.
15 I will destroy the winter house along with ➤
the summer house;
The houses of ivory shall perish,
And the great houses shall have an end,"
Says the LORD.

4 Hear this word, you cows of Bashan, who
are on the mountain of Samaria,
Who oppress the poor,
Who crush the needy,
Who say to your husbands,[a] "Bring *wine,*
let us drink!"
2 The Lord GOD has sworn by His holiness: ➤
"Behold, the days shall come upon you
When He will take you away with
fishhooks,
And your posterity with fishhooks.
3 You will go out *through* broken *walls,*
Each one straight ahead of her,
And you will be cast into Harmon,"
Says the LORD.

4 "Come to Bethel and transgress,
At Gilgal multiply transgression;
Bring your sacrifices every morning,
Your tithes every three days.[a]
5 Offer a sacrifice of thanksgiving with
leaven,

3:9 [a]Following Masoretic Text; Septuagint reads *Assyria.*
3:12 [a]The Hebrew is uncertain. **4:1** [a]Literally *their lords* or *their masters* **4:4** [a]Or *years* (compare Deuteronomy 14:28)

LIFE LESSONS

➤ **3:2 — *"You only have I known of all the families of the earth; therefore I will punish you for all your iniquities."***

A relationship with God is not only a phenomenal privilege, it is also a great responsibility. "For the time has come for judgment to begin at the house of God" (1 Pet. 4:17).

➤ **3:15 — *"I will destroy the winter house along with the summer house; the houses of ivory shall perish, and the great houses shall have an end," says the LORD.***

The ancient Israelites had allowed their pursuit of material abundance to eclipse their commitment to God—and He will never allow for long anything or anyone to take the place that belongs to Him alone.

➤ **4:2 — *The Lord GOD has sworn by His holiness . . . .***

The Lord had called Israel to be "a kingdom of priests and a holy nation" (Ex. 19:6), but the people chose to spurn His holiness and go their own way instead. The only thing left was judgment.

Proclaim *and* announce the freewill
offerings;
For this you love,
You children of Israel!"
Says the Lord GOD.

Israel Did Not Accept Correction

6 "Also I gave you cleanness of teeth in all
your cities.
And lack of bread in all your places;
Yet you have not returned to Me,"
Says the LORD.

7 "I also withheld rain from you,
When *there were* still three months to the
harvest.
I made it rain on one city,
I withheld rain from another city.
One part was rained upon,
And where it did not rain the part
withered.
8 So two *or* three cities wandered to
another city to drink water,
But they were not satisfied;
Yet you have not returned to Me,"
Says the LORD.

9 "I blasted you with blight and mildew.
When your gardens increased,
Your vineyards,
Your fig trees,
And your olive trees,
The locust devoured *them;*
Yet you have not returned to Me,"
Says the LORD.

10 "I sent among you a plague after the
manner of Egypt;
Your young men I killed with a sword,
Along with your captive horses;
I made the stench of your camps come up
into your nostrils;
Yet you have not returned to Me,"
Says the LORD.

➤ 11 "I overthrew *some* of you,
As God overthrew Sodom and Gomorrah,
And you were like a firebrand plucked
from the burning;
Yet you have not returned to Me,"
Says the LORD.

12 "Therefore thus will I do to you, O Israel;
Because I will do this to you,
Prepare to meet your God, O Israel!"

13 For behold,
He who forms mountains,
And creates the wind,
Who declares to man what his[a] thought
is,
And makes the morning darkness,
Who treads the high places of the earth—
The LORD God of hosts *is* His name.

A Lament for Israel

5 Hear this word which I take up against
you, a lamentation, O house of Israel:

2 The virgin of Israel has fallen;
She will rise no more.
She lies forsaken on her land;
There is no one to raise her up.

3 For thus says the Lord GOD:

"The city that goes out by a thousand
Shall have a hundred left,
And that which goes out by a hundred
Shall have ten left to the house of Israel."

A Call to Repentance

4 For thus says the LORD to the house of Israel:

"Seek Me and live;
5 But do not seek Bethel,
Nor enter Gilgal,
Nor pass over to Beersheba;
For Gilgal shall surely go into captivity,
And Bethel shall come to nothing.
6 Seek the LORD and live,
Lest He break out like fire *in* the house of
Joseph,
And devour *it,*
With no one to quench *it* in Bethel—
7 You who turn justice to wormwood,
And lay righteousness to rest in the
earth!"

8 He made the Pleiades and Orion;
He turns the shadow of death into
morning
And makes the day dark as night;
He calls for the waters of the sea
And pours them out on the face of the
earth;
The LORD *is* His name.
9 He rains ruin upon the strong,
So that fury comes upon the fortress.

10 They hate the one who rebukes in the
gate,

4:13 [a]Or *His*

LIFE LESSONS

➤ **4:11 — *"I overthrew some of you, as God overthrew Sodom and Gomorrah, and you were like a firebrand plucked from the burning; yet you have not returned to Me," says the LORD.***

When we refuse to obey, God often gradually "turns up the heat" to prompt us to repent and turn back to Him. He does not want to send catastrophic judgment upon us, but uses affliction to get our attention.

And they abhor the one who speaks
uprightly.
11 Therefore, because you tread down the
poor
And take grain taxes from him,
Though you have built houses of hewn
stone,
Yet you shall not dwell in them;
You have planted pleasant vineyards,
But you shall not drink wine from them.
12 For I know your manifold transgressions
And your mighty sins:
Afflicting the just *and* taking bribes;
Diverting the poor *from justice* at the
gate.
13 Therefore the prudent keep silent at that
time,
For it *is* an evil time.
14 Seek good and not evil,
That you may live;
So the LORD God of hosts will be with you,
As you have spoken.
15 Hate evil, love good;
Establish justice in the gate.
It may be that the LORD God of hosts
Will be gracious to the remnant of Joseph.

The Day of the LORD

16 Therefore the LORD God of hosts, the
Lord, says this:

"*There shall be* wailing in all streets,
And they shall say in all the highways,
'Alas! Alas!'
They shall call the farmer to mourning,
And skillful lamenters to wailing.
17 In all vineyards *there shall be* wailing,
For I will pass through you,"
Says the LORD.

18 Woe to you who desire the day of the
LORD!
For what good *is* the day of the LORD to
you?
It *will be* darkness, and not light.
19 It *will be* as though a man fled from a lion,
And a bear met him!
Or *as though* he went into the house,
Leaned his hand on the wall,
And a serpent bit him!
20 *Is* not the day of the LORD darkness, and
not light?
Is it not very dark, with no brightness
in it?

21 "I hate, I despise your feast days,
And I do not savor your sacred
assemblies.
22 Though you offer Me burnt offerings and
your grain offerings,
I will not accept *them,*
Nor will I regard your fattened peace
offerings.
23 Take away from Me the noise of your
songs,
For I will not hear the melody of your
stringed instruments.
24 But let justice run down like water,
And righteousness like a mighty stream.

25 "Did you offer Me sacrifices and offerings
In the wilderness forty years, O house of
Israel?
26 You also carried Sikkuth[a] your king[b]
And Chiun,[c] your idols,
The star of your gods,
Which you made for yourselves.
27 Therefore I will send you into captivity
beyond Damascus,"
Says the LORD, whose name *is* the God of
hosts.

Warnings to Zion and Samaria

6 Woe to you *who are* at ease in Zion,
And trust in Mount Samaria,
Notable persons in the chief nation,
To whom the house of Israel comes!
2 Go over to Calneh and see;
And from there go to Hamath the great;
Then go down to Gath of the Philistines.
Are you better than these kingdoms?
Or is their territory greater than your
territory?

3 *Woe to* you who put far off the day of
doom,
Who cause the seat of violence to come
near;
4 Who lie on beds of ivory,
Stretch out on your couches,
Eat lambs from the flock
And calves from the midst of the stall;
5 Who sing idly to the sound of stringed
instruments,
And invent for yourselves musical
instruments like David;

5:26 [a]A pagan deity [b]Septuagint and Vulgate read *tabernacle of Moloch.* [c]A pagan deity

LIFE LESSONS

➤ 5:14 — *Seek good and not evil, that you may live; so the Lord God of hosts will be with you . . .*

We find life when we find the Lord, and we seek good when we seek God. Christ delivers from us our sins, not so we can wallow in them, but so we can joyfully live free of them.

➤ 5:24 — *"But let justice run down like water, and righteousness like a mighty stream."*

God intends for our personal righteousness to prompt us to actions of community justice. "If someone says, 'I love God,' and hates his brother, he is liar," John said (1 John 4:20).

6 Who drink wine from bowls,
And anoint yourselves with the best ointments,
But are not grieved for the affliction of Joseph.
7 Therefore they shall now go captive as the first of the captives,
And those who recline at banquets shall be removed.

8 The Lord GOD has sworn by Himself,
The LORD God of hosts says:
"I abhor the pride of Jacob,
And hate his palaces;
Therefore I will deliver up *the* city
And all that is in it."

9 Then it shall come to pass, that if ten men
remain in one house, they shall die.
10 And when a relative *of the dead,* with one
who will burn *the bodies,* picks up the bodies[a]
to take them out of the house, he will say to
one inside the house, "*Are there* any more
with you?" Then someone will say, "None."
And he will say, "Hold your tongue! For we
dare not mention the name of the LORD."

11 For behold, the LORD gives a command:
He will break the great house into bits,
And the little house into pieces.

12 Do horses run on rocks?
Does *one* plow *there* with oxen?
Yet you have turned justice into gall,
And the fruit of righteousness into wormwood,
13 You who rejoice over Lo Debar,[a]
Who say, "Have we not taken Karnaim[b] for ourselves
By our own strength?"

14 "But, behold, I will raise up a nation against you,
O house of Israel,"
Says the LORD God of hosts;
"And they will afflict you from the entrance of Hamath
To the Valley of the Arabah."

Vision of the Locusts

7 Thus the Lord GOD showed me: Behold,
He formed locust swarms at the beginning
of the late crop; indeed *it was* the late crop
after the king's mowings.
2 And so it was, when they had finished eating the grass of the land, that I said:

"O Lord GOD, forgive, I pray!
Oh, that Jacob may stand,
For he *is* small!"
3 *So* the LORD relented concerning this.
"It shall not be," said the LORD.

Vision of the Fire

4 Thus the Lord GOD showed me: Behold,
the Lord GOD called for conflict by fire, and it
consumed the great deep and devoured the
territory.
5 Then I said:

"O Lord GOD, cease, I pray!
Oh, that Jacob may stand,
For he *is* small!"
6 *So* the LORD relented concerning this.
"This also shall not be," said the Lord GOD.

Vision of the Plumb Line

7 Thus He showed me: Behold, the Lord
stood on a wall *made* with a plumb line, with
a plumb line in His hand.
8 And the LORD said to me, "Amos, what do
you see?" And I said, "A plumb line." Then the
Lord said:

"Behold, I am setting a plumb line
In the midst of My people Israel;
I will not pass by them anymore.
9 The high places of Isaac shall be desolate,
And the sanctuaries of Israel shall be laid waste.
I will rise with the sword against the house of Jeroboam."

Amaziah's Complaint

10 Then Amaziah the priest of Bethel sent to
Jeroboam king of Israel, saying, "Amos has
conspired against you in the midst of the
house of Israel. The land is not able to bear all
his words.
11 "For thus Amos has said:

'Jeroboam shall die by the sword,
And Israel shall surely be led away captive
From their own land.'"

12 Then Amaziah said to Amos:

"Go, you seer!
Flee to the land of Judah.
There eat bread,
And there prophesy.
13 But never again prophesy at Bethel,
For it *is* the king's sanctuary,
And it *is* the royal residence."

6:10 [a]Literally *bones* 6:13 [a]Literally *Nothing* [b]Literally *Horns,* symbol of strength

LIFE LESSONS

➤ 7:8 — *"Behold, I am setting a plumb line in the midst of My people Israel; I will not pass by them anymore."*

A plumb line pictures God's careful evaluation of the hearts and behavior of His people. Sometimes He delivers His defiant people up "to Satan for the destruction of the flesh, that his spirit may be saved" (1 Cor. 5:5).

LIFE PRINCIPLE 19

ANYTHING YOU HOLD TOO TIGHTLY YOU WILL LOSE.

AMOS 6:6, 7

In seventeenth century France, a humble church leader named Fénelon wrote a letter of encouragement to believers who sought spiritual perspective during some discouraging trials. He said,

> Do not worry about the future. It makes no sense to worry if God loves you and has taken care of you. However, when God blesses you, remember to keep your eyes on Him and not the blessing. Enjoy your blessings day by day, just as the Israelites enjoyed their manna; but do not try to store the blessings for the future . . . .
>
> Sometimes in this life of faith God will remove His blessings from you. But remember that He knows how and when to replace them, either through the ministry of others or by Himself. He can raise up children from the very stones.
>
> Eat then your daily bread without worrying about tomorrow. There is time enough tomorrow to think about the things tomorrow will bring. The same God who feeds you today is the very God who will feed you tomorrow. God will see to it that manna falls again from Heaven in the midst of the desert, before His children lack any good thing.

If we lived with faith of this kind, we would stop anxiety and worry and fretting in their tracks. Will we humbly depend on God to provide?

Admit it—in a tough situation, your first emotional "reflex" is to take control. We *all* want control. We want to live with the assurance that everything will be okay, and the things that aren't right can be fixed with concentrated effort. Secretly, we often think, "If I plan carefully and labor enough, I can dig myself out of any ditch." Or we say, "I can't give up this thing; it's my only hope."

The problem comes when the ground shakes harder than you expected, or the shovel you're using to dig yourself out breaks. God lets things like this happen for an important reason—He wants you to recognize that He's in control. Whatever you hold too tightly, you will lose; so why not willingly let go and receive a blessing for it?

A humorous bumper sticker reads, "If God is your Co-Pilot, switch seats." The Lord does not want merely to be the resource you call on when you're in trouble. God wants to be your all-sufficient Lord and Master, Savior

Keep your eyes on God and not the blessing.

and Friend. He knows you intimately; He formed your very cells and fibers (Ps. 139:13–16); He has a good plan for every day of your life (Eph. 2:10) and He knows how to get you there.

When you face circumstances that rapidly deplete your spiritual, emotional, and physical reserves, you want to cling to something strong. The urge is called fear. The question should not be how to get rid of or deny the fear, but what kind of fear it is and where it drives you—to the arms of God or to your own resources?

A woman trapped in a burning building stood on a ledge, several stories from the ground. Even when the fireman climbed a ladder to get her, she would not release her grip from the ledge; she remained frozen in fear. Finally, after the fireman talked to her firmly but gently, the woman understood he was there to help. Only when she let go and released herself into his care was she saved from the flames.

Are you hanging on to another support system besides the Lord?

Are you hanging on to another support system besides the Lord? He longs for you to release yourself into His control and eternal support. You do not have to worry about the consequences; He takes care of those, too, in the way that He knows is best, and sustains your spirit in the process (Phil. 4:6, 7).

When you feel ready to yield wholly to the Lord, Psalm 56 provides a wonderful model prayer: "Whenever I am afraid, I will trust in You. In God (I will praise His word), in God I have put my trust; I will not fear. What can flesh do to me?" (vv. 3, 4)

Maybe to this point in your relationship to the Lord you have not experienced a trial so extreme that it caused you to assess the true foundation of your trust. God has blessed you with a time of quiet strengthening.

But understand that He loves you too much to allow you any notions of self-sufficiency. He will test you in time, but always with the purpose of demonstrating His never-ending love.

See the Life Principles Index for further study.

➤ 14 Then Amos answered, and said to
Amaziah:

"I *was* no prophet,
Nor *was* I a son of a prophet,
But I *was* a sheepbreeder[a]
And a tender of sycamore fruit.
15 Then the LORD took me as I followed the flock,
And the LORD said to me,
'Go, prophesy to My people Israel.'
16 Now therefore, hear the word of the LORD:
You say, 'Do not prophesy against Israel,
And do not spout against the house of Isaac.'

17 "Therefore thus says the LORD:

'Your wife shall be a harlot in the city;
Your sons and daughters shall fall by the sword;
Your land shall be divided by *survey* line;
You shall die in a defiled land;
And Israel shall surely be led away captive
From his own land.'"

Vision of the Summer Fruit

8 Thus the Lord GOD showed me: Behold, a
basket of summer fruit.
2 And He said, "Amos, what do you see?" So
I said, "A basket of summer fruit." Then the
LORD said to me:

"The end has come upon My people Israel;
I will not pass by them anymore.
3 And the songs of the temple
Shall be wailing in that day,"
Says the Lord GOD—
"Many dead bodies everywhere,
They shall be thrown out in silence."

4 Hear this, you who swallow up[a] the needy,
And make the poor of the land fail,

➤ 5 Saying:

"When will the New Moon be past,
That we may sell grain?
And the Sabbath,
That we may trade wheat?
Making the ephah small and the shekel large,
Falsifying the scales by deceit,
6 That we may buy the poor for silver,
And the needy for a pair of sandals—
Even sell the bad wheat?"

7 The LORD has sworn by the pride of Jacob:
"Surely I will never forget any of their works.
8 Shall the land not tremble for this,
And everyone mourn who dwells in it?
All of it shall swell like the River,[a]
Heave and subside
Like the River of Egypt.

9 "And it shall come to pass in that day,"
says the Lord GOD,
"That I will make the sun go down at noon,
And I will darken the earth in broad daylight;
10 I will turn your feasts into mourning,
And all your songs into lamentation;
I will bring sackcloth on every waist,
And baldness on every head;
I will make it like mourning for an only *son*,
And its end like a bitter day.

11 "Behold, the days are coming," says the Lord GOD, ➤
"That I will send a famine on the land,
Not a famine of bread,
Nor a thirst for water,
But of hearing the words of the LORD.
12 They shall wander from sea to sea,
And from north to east;
They shall run to and fro, seeking the word of the LORD,
But shall not find *it*.

13 "In that day the fair virgins
And strong young men
Shall faint from thirst.
14 Those who swear by the sin[a] of Samaria,

7:14 [a]Compare 2 Kings 3:4 **8:4** [a]Or *trample on* (compare 2:7) **8:8** [a]That is, the Nile; some Hebrew manuscripts, Septuagint, Syriac, Targum, and Vulgate read *River;* Masoretic Text reads *the light.* **8:14** [a]Or *Ashima,* a Syrian goddess

LIFE LESSONS

➤ 7:14 — *"I was no prophet, nor was I a son of a prophet, but I was a sheepbreeder and a tender of sycamore fruit."*

Regardless of who you are or what you do for a living, God wants to use you to bring the Good News to those around you, and ultimately to the whole world. If you love Christ, *you* are God's ambassador (2 Cor. 5:20).

➤ 8:5 — *"When will the New Moon be past, that we may sell grain? And the Sabbath, that we may trade wheat?"*

Something has gone seriously wrong in our hearts when we see God's commandments and regular, corporate worship as a burden to get through rather than as a privilege to savor and enjoy.

➤ 8:11 — *"Behold, the days are coming," says the Lord GOD, "that I will send a famine on the land, not a famine of bread, nor a thirst for water, but of hearing the words of the LORD."*

From the time of the prophet Malachi to the time of John the Baptist—a period of almost 500 years—this drought withered the land. Let us daily feast on God's Word, and so avoid a similar drought in our souls.

Who say,
'As your god lives, O Dan!'
And, 'As the way of Beersheba lives!'
They shall fall and never rise again."

The Destruction of Israel

9 I saw the Lord standing by the altar, and He said:
"Strike the doorposts, that the thresholds may shake,
And break them on the heads of them all.
I will slay the last of them with the sword.
He who flees from them shall not get away,
And he who escapes from them shall not be delivered.

➤ 2 "Though they dig into hell,[a]
From there My hand shall take them;
Though they climb up to heaven,
From there I will bring them down;
3 And though they hide themselves on top of Carmel,
From there I will search and take them;
Though they hide from My sight at the bottom of the sea,
From there I will command the serpent, and it shall bite them;
4 Though they go into captivity before their enemies,
From there I will command the sword,
And it shall slay them.
I will set My eyes on them for harm and not for good."

5 The Lord GOD of hosts,
He who touches the earth and it melts,
And all who dwell there mourn;
All of it shall swell like the River,[a]
And subside like the River of Egypt.
6 He who builds His layers in the sky,
And has founded His strata in the earth;
Who calls for the waters of the sea,
And pours them out on the face of the earth—
The LORD *is* His name.

7 "*Are* you not like the people of Ethiopia to Me,
O children of Israel?" says the LORD.
"Did I not bring up Israel from the land of Egypt,
The Philistines from Caphtor,
And the Syrians from Kir?

8 "Behold, the eyes of the Lord GOD *are* on the sinful kingdom,
And I will destroy it from the face of the earth;
Yet I will not utterly destroy the house of Jacob,"
Says the LORD.
9 "For surely I will command,
And will sift the house of Israel among all nations,
As *grain* is sifted in a sieve;
Yet not the smallest grain shall fall to the ground.
10 All the sinners of My people shall die by the sword,
Who say, 'The calamity shall not overtake nor confront us.'

Israel Will Be Restored

11 "On that day I will raise up
The tabernacle[a] of David, which has fallen down,
And repair its damages;
I will raise up its ruins,
And rebuild it as in the days of old;
12 That they may possess the remnant of Edom,[a] ➤
And all the Gentiles who are called by My name,"
Says the LORD who does this thing.

13 "Behold, the days are coming," says the LORD, ✳
"When the plowman shall overtake the reaper,
And the treader of grapes him who sows seed;
The mountains shall drip with sweet wine,
And all the hills shall flow *with it.*
14 I will bring back the captives of My people Israel;
They shall build the waste cities and inhabit *them;*
They shall plant vineyards and drink wine from them;
They shall also make gardens and eat fruit from them.
15 I will plant them in their land,
And no longer shall they be pulled up
From the land I have given them,"
Says the LORD your God.

9:2 [a]Or *Sheol* **9:5** [a]That is, the Nile **9:11** [a]Literally *booth,* figure of a deposed dynasty **9:12** [a]Septuagint reads *mankind.*

LIFE LESSONS

➤ **9:2 — *"Though they dig into hell, from there My hand shall take them; though they climb up to heaven, from there I will bring them down."***

No one can prevent the Lord from doing all He has decided to do, whether for judgment or blessing. Since we serve a sovereign God, we should never think of ourselves as victims of our circumstances.

➤ **9:12 — *". . . and all the Gentiles who are called by My name."***

Our God is a global God, and He calls men and women, boys and girls into His family from every spot on earth and from every tribe and nation, so that we may "exalt His name together" (Ps. 34:3).

THE BOOK OF

OBADIAH

A struggle that began in the womb between twin brothers, Esau and Jacob, eventually erupted into a greater struggle between their respective descendants, the Edomites and the Israelites. The prophet Obadiah roundly condemned the Edomites for their stubborn refusal to aid Israel, first during the time of the wilderness wandering (Num. 20:14–21) and later during the time of the Babylonian invasion. This little-known prophet described their crimes, tried their case, and pronounced their judgment: total destruction. By contrast, God promised that his people would ultimately destroy their enemies and live in peace.

Obadiah is the shortest book of the Old Testament and in it, Obadiah addresses Edom's prideful and superior attitude after the enemies of Israel had crushed her. He knew that a similar end would come to Edom, and that God would eventually restore Israel to her land and place of prominence.

The Hebrew name *Obadyah* means "Worshiper of Yahweh" or "Servant of Yahweh." Nothing more is known of the prophet other than what he reveals in the brief twenty-one verses of his prophecy.

Themes: God provides and cares for His people and will execute judgment against those who oppose them.

Author: Obadiah.

Time: Approximately 840 B.C.

Structure: Verses 1–16 of Obadiah foretell the destruction of Edom, while verses 17–21 speak of the deliverance of Zion.

As you read Obadiah, watch for several life principles that play an important role in this book:

16. Whatever you acquire outside of God's will eventually turns to ashes. *See Obadiah 5–9; page 1053.*

6. You reap what you sow, more than you sow, and later than you sow. *See Obadiah 10–14; page 1053.*

The Coming Judgment on Edom

1 The vision of Obadiah.

Thus says the Lord GOD concerning
Edom
(We have heard a report from the LORD,
And a messenger has been sent among
the nations, *saying*,
"Arise, and let us rise up against her for
battle"):

2 "Behold, I will make you small among the
nations;
You shall be greatly despised.
➤ 3 The pride of your heart has deceived you,
You who dwell in the clefts of the rock,
Whose habitation is high;
You who say in your heart, 'Who will
bring me down to the ground?'
4 Though you ascend *as* high as the eagle,
And though you set your nest among the
stars,
From there I will bring you down," says
the LORD.

5 "If thieves had come to you,
If robbers by night—
Oh, how you will be cut off!—
Would they not have stolen till they had
enough?
If grape-gatherers had come to you,
Would they not have left *some* gleanings?

6 "Oh, how Esau shall be searched out!
How his hidden treasures shall be sought
after!
7 All the men in your confederacy
Shall force you to the border;
The men at peace with you
Shall deceive you *and* prevail against
you.
Those who eat your bread shall lay a
trap[a] for you.
No one is aware of it.

8 "Will I not in that day," says the LORD,
"Even destroy the wise *men* from Edom,
And understanding from the mountains
of Esau?
9 Then your mighty men, O Teman, shall
be dismayed,
To the end that everyone from the
mountains of Esau
May be cut off by slaughter.

Edom Mistreated His Brother

10"For violence against your brother Jacob,
Shame shall cover you,
And you shall be cut off forever.
11 In the day that you stood on the other
side—
In the day that strangers carried captive
his forces,
When foreigners entered his gates
And cast lots for Jerusalem—
Even you *were* as one of them.

12"But you should not have gazed on the
day of your brother
In the day of his captivity;[a]
Nor should you have rejoiced over the
children of Judah
In the day of their destruction;
Nor should you have spoken proudly
In the day of distress.
13 You should not have entered the gate of
My people
In the day of their calamity.
Indeed, you should not have gazed on
their affliction
In the day of their calamity,
Nor laid *hands* on their substance
In the day of their calamity.
14 You should not have stood at the
crossroads
To cut off those among them who
escaped;
Nor should you have delivered up those
among them who remained
In the day of distress.

15"For the day of the LORD upon all the
nations *is* near; ➤
As you have done, it shall be done to you;
Your reprisal shall return upon your own
head.
16 For as you drank on My holy mountain,
So shall all the nations drink continually;
Yes, they shall drink, and swallow,
And they shall be as though they had
never been.

Israel's Final Triumph

17"But on Mount Zion there shall be
deliverance, ✳
And there shall be holiness;
The house of Jacob shall possess their
possessions.
18 The house of Jacob shall be a fire,

7 [a]Or *wound,* or *plot* 12 [a]Literally *on the day he became a foreigner*

LIFE LESSONS

➤ 3 — *"The pride of your heart has deceived you . . . ."*

God hates pride, not only because it imagines itself a rival to God, but also because it blinds and deceives. Because it cannot see or accept the truth, it walks off of cliffs and runs into brick walls.

➤ 15 — *"As you have done, it shall be done to you; your reprisal shall return upon your own head."*

Repeatedly in Scripture God says that He will use a man's own sin against him in judgment. "He made a pit and dug it out," said David of the wicked, "and has fallen into the ditch which he made" (Ps. 7:15).

And the house of Joseph a flame;
But the house of Esau *shall be* stubble;
They shall kindle them and devour them,
And no survivor shall *remain* of the
house of Esau,"
For the LORD has spoken.

19 The South[a] shall possess the mountains
of Esau,
And the Lowland shall possess Philistia.
They shall possess the fields of Ephraim
And the fields of Samaria.
Benjamin *shall possess* Gilead.

20 And the captives of this host of the
children of Israel
Shall possess the land of the Canaanites
As far as Zarephath.
The captives of Jerusalem who are in
Sepharad
Shall possess the cities of the South.[a]

21 Then saviors[a] shall come to Mount Zion
To judge the mountains of Esau,
And the kingdom shall be the LORD's.

---

19 aHebrew *Negev* **20** aHebrew *Negev* **21** aOr *deliverers*

THE BOOK OF JONAH

Sometimes, geography is everything.

Nineveh lies northeast of Israel; Tarshish is west. But when God called Jonah to leave his home in Israel and travel to Nineveh to preach to the city's wicked residents, the prophet turned down the divine assignment and headed west rather than northeast. Why?

As a true prophet of the Lord (2 Kin. 14:25), Jonah knew God and recognized Him as a merciful, gracious God, "slow to anger and abundant in lovingkindness, One who relents from doing harm" (Jon. 4:2). Jonah despised the brutal Assyrian city of Nineveh, however, and did not want to give its citizens the opportunity to repent and so perhaps experience God's mercy. So he ran in the opposite direction.

Once God dampened the prophet's spirits, however—first by dumping him into the cold ocean currents and then into the fish's reeking stomach—Jonah realized just how serious God was about His command. Nineveh *must* hear the word of the Lord; therefore Jonah repented of his disobedience, traveled to Nineveh, and there preached the message God gave him.

Most preachers would feel delighted to speak to a receptive audience eager to respond positively to the featured message—but the Ninevites' humble reaction angered Jonah. Or rather, God's gracious response to the Ninevites' reaction embittered the prophet. He had to learn firsthand to glory in God's compassion for sinful men, regardless of who they might be.

Throughout modern times the story of Jonah often has been ridiculed as myth, but the Hebrew people accepted it as historical. Jesus Christ Himself also vouched for the truth of the book and the remarkable story it relates (Matt. 12:39–41).

Yonah is the Hebrew word for "dove." The Latin Vulgate used the title *Jonas*.

Theme: When we fail to obey God's calling, we go nowhere but "down."

Author: Jonah.

Time: Jonah lived during the reign of King Jeroboam II, around 760 B.C.

Structure: Chapter one of Jonah records the prophet's call and disobedience. Chapter two describes his distress in the belly of the fish. Chapter three recounts the prophet's declaration of judgment to the people of Nineveh. Chapter four records Jonah's displeasure at God's withholding of judgment after the Ninevites repent.

As you read Jonah, watch for several life principles that play an important role in this book:

13. Listening to God is essential to walking with God. *See Jonah 1:1–3; page 1056.*

26. Adversity is a bridge to a deeper relationship with God. *See Jonah 2:1–9; page 1057.*

2. Obey God and leave all the consequences to Him. *See Jonah 3:1–4; page 1057.*

21. Obedience always brings blessing. *See Jonah 3:5–10; page 1057.*

20. Disappointments are inevitable; discouragement is a choice. *See Jonah 4:1–11; page 1058, 1059.*

Life Examples:

JONAH

No Fleeing the God of Everywhere

JON. 1:3

The Bible tells us that Jonah bought a ticket to Tarshish in an effort to escape from the presence of the Lord and thereby avoid a God-given assignment—not because he thought he might fail, but because he feared he might succeed.

Apparently Jonah forgot what King David knew so well: "Where can I go from Your Spirit? Or where can I flee from Your presence?" (Ps. 139:7). The answer, of course, is "nowhere," as the prophet Jeremiah heard straight from the mouth of God: "'Am I a God near at hand . . . and not a God afar off? Can anyone hide himself in secret places, so I shall not see him? . . . Do I not fill heaven and earth?' says the LORD" (Jer. 23:23, 24).

We serve a God who fills heaven and earth. Everywhere we are, there He is—and He was there long before we arrived.

See the Life Principles Index for further study:
18. As children of a sovereign God, we are never victims of our circumstances.

Jonah's Disobedience

1 Now the word of the LORD came to Jonah the son of Amittai, saying,
2 "Arise, go to Nineveh, that great city, and cry out against it; for their wickedness has come up before Me."
3 But Jonah arose to flee to Tarshish from the presence of the LORD. He went down to Joppa, and found a ship going to Tarshish; so he paid the fare, and went down into it, to go with them to Tarshish from the presence of the LORD.

The Storm at Sea

4 But the LORD sent out a great wind on the sea, and there was a mighty tempest on the sea, so that the ship was about to be broken up.
5 Then the mariners were afraid; and every man cried out to his god, and threw the cargo that *was* in the ship into the sea, to lighten the load.[a] But Jonah had gone down into the lowest parts of the ship, had lain down, and was fast asleep.
6 So the captain came to him, and said to him, "What do you mean, sleeper? Arise, call on your God; perhaps your God will consider us, so that we may not perish."
7 And they said to one another, "Come, let us cast lots, that we may know for whose cause this trouble *has come* upon us." So they cast lots, and the lot fell on Jonah.
8 Then they said to him, "Please tell us! For whose cause *is* this trouble upon us? What is your occupation? And where do you come from? What is your country? And of what people are you?"
9 So he said to them, "I *am* a Hebrew; and I fear the LORD, the God of heaven, who made the sea and the dry *land*."

Jonah Thrown into the Sea

10 Then the men were exceedingly afraid, and said to him, "Why have you done this?" For the men knew that he fled from the presence of the LORD, because he had told them.
11 Then they said to him, "What shall we do to you that the sea may be calm for us?"—for the sea was growing more tempestuous.
12 And he said to them, "Pick me up and throw me into the sea; then the sea will become calm for you. For I know that this great tempest *is* because of me."
13 Nevertheless the men rowed hard to return to land, but they could not, for the sea continued to grow more tempestuous against them.
14 Therefore they cried out to the LORD and said, "We pray, O LORD, please do not let us perish for this man's life, and do not charge us with innocent blood; for You, O LORD, have done as it pleased You."
15 So they picked up Jonah and threw him into the sea, and the sea ceased from its raging.

1:5 [a]Literally *from upon them*

LIFE LESSONS

➤ 1:12 — *"Pick me up and throw me into the sea; then the sea will become calm for you. For I know that this great tempest is because of me."*

Jonah knew that his own disobedience had put the ship in peril, and yet he would rather die than return to land and obey God's command. But God does not give up so easily on us, and He had a fish ready to prove it.

16 Then the men feared the LORD exceedingly, and offered a sacrifice to the LORD and took vows.

Jonah's Prayer and Deliverance

17 Now the LORD had prepared a great fish to swallow Jonah. And Jonah was in the belly of the fish three days and three nights.

2 Then Jonah prayed to the LORD his God from the fish's belly.
2 And he said:

"I cried out to the LORD because of my affliction,
And He answered me.
"Out of the belly of Sheol I cried,
And You heard my voice.
3 For You cast me into the deep,
Into the heart of the seas,
And the floods surrounded me;
All Your billows and Your waves passed over me.
4 Then I said, 'I have been cast out of Your sight;
Yet I will look again toward Your holy temple.'
5 The waters surrounded me, *even* to my soul;
The deep closed around me;
Weeds were wrapped around my head.
6 I went down to the moorings of the mountains;
The earth with its bars *closed* behind me forever;
Yet You have brought up my life from the pit,
O LORD, my God.
7 "When my soul fainted within me,
I remembered the LORD;
And my prayer went *up* to You,
Into Your holy temple.

8 "Those who regard worthless idols
Forsake their own Mercy.
9 But I will sacrifice to You
With the voice of thanksgiving;
I will pay what I have vowed.
Salvation *is* of the LORD."

10 So the LORD spoke to the fish, and it vomited Jonah onto dry *land*.

Jonah Preaches at Nineveh

3 Now the word of the LORD came to Jonah the second time, saying,
2 "Arise, go to Nineveh, that great city, and preach to it the message that I tell you."
3 So Jonah arose and went to Nineveh, according to the word of the LORD. Now Nineveh was an exceedingly great city, a three-day journey[a] *in extent*.
4 And Jonah began to enter the city on the first day's walk. Then he cried out and said, "Yet forty days, and Nineveh shall be overthrown!"

The People of Nineveh Believe

5 So the people of Nineveh believed God, proclaimed a fast, and put on sackcloth, from the greatest to the least of them.
6 Then word came to the king of Nineveh; and he arose from his throne and laid aside his robe, covered *himself* with sackcloth and sat in ashes.
7 And he caused *it* to be proclaimed and published throughout Nineveh by the decree of the king and his nobles, saying,

Let neither man nor beast, herd nor flock, taste anything; do not let them eat, or drink water.
8 But let man and beast be covered with sackcloth, and cry mightily to God; yes, let every one turn from his evil way and from the violence that is in his hands.
9 Who can tell *if* God will turn and relent, and turn away from His fierce anger, so that we may not perish?

10 Then God saw their works, that they turned from their evil way; and God relented

3:3 [a]Exact meaning unknown

LIFE LESSONS

1:16 — *Then the men feared the LORD exceedingly, and offered a sacrifice to the LORD and took vows.*

God inspires prophecy not to satisfy our curiosity, but to prompt faith in His grace and glory. He tells us about the future so that we might live well in the present and get ready for what's to come.

2:2 — *"I cried out to the LORD because of my affliction, and He answered me."*

God will never turn away from a truly repentant heart, even if that heart beats in a man who tried to run away from Him. The Lord often uses affliction, not to punish us, but to bring us back to Him.

2:7 — *"When my soul fainted within me, I remembered the Lord . . . ."*

When we reach the end of our rope and the end of ourselves—when we hit rock bottom—only then are we sometimes ready to repent. But God is so loving and gracious, He will even accept that.

3:1 — *Now the word of the LORD came to Jonah the second time . . . .*

Did Jonah deserve a second chance to carry out God's assignment? No. Neither do we. But God, in His mercy, is not about keeping score, but about shaping us into the likeness of His Son.

ANSWERS TO LIFE'S QUESTIONS

How does God deal with our disobedience?

JON. 3:1

In the light of God's omniscience and omnipresence, it's easy to wonder why Christians still attempt to run from the Lord. Jonah certainly demonstrated that it could not be done, and yet many people still insist on trying. Why?

Sometimes they act out of pure selfishness. We have an unlimited capacity to believe we know what is best for us, regardless of what God says.

Sometimes we balk out of simple fear: We worry that we might not succeed, or that others will criticize our efforts, or that our obedience will cost us too much. What we fail to recognize, however, is the much higher price of fleeing from the Lord.

Jonah paid dearly for his rebellion. Not only did he suffer embarrassment, terror, and guilt, but he also jeopardized the lives of men whom God wanted to save. Jonah overlooked two essentials that we should all keep in mind.

First, he incorrectly assumed that fleeing from God would release him from having to obey God. He never imagined how persistent the Lord can be when He calls us to a duty station. Eventually Jonah found that God will pursue us in love, even to the depths of the sea, in order to conform us to His will and His plan for our lives. God simply will not be deterred by our slippery disobedience.

Second, Jonah forgot that by running from God, he went nowhere but down. In addition, when we run from God, we cannot help but inflict heavy punishment on those whom God wants to bless. How many parents walk away from their child and say, "I can do what I want. It's my own life"? No, it's not. If you are a Christian, God tells you, "you are not your own." In fact, "you were bought at a price," and both your body and your spirit belong to God (1 Cor. 6:19, 20). You cannot leave a child fatherless or motherless without reaping lifelong pain and suffering. Nor can you sin against the Lord without paying a terrible price yourself and hurting others in the process.

Despite these awful realities, it is also true that God is forgiving—He offers a second or third or fortieth or even millionth chance (Jon. 3:1). He kept after Jonah as long as it was necessary—and He will do the same with you.

See the Life Principles Index for further study:

7. The dark moments of our life will last only so long as is necessary for God to accomplish His purpose in us.

15. Brokenness is God's requirement for ultimate usefulness.

from the disaster that He had said He would
bring upon them, and He did not do it.

Jonah's Anger and God's Kindness

4 But it displeased Jonah exceedingly, and
he became angry.
∗ 2 So he prayed to the LORD, and said, "Ah,
LORD, was not this what I said when I was still
in my country? Therefore I fled previously to
Tarshish; for I know that You *are* a gracious
and merciful God, slow to anger and abundant in lovingkindness, One who relents from
doing harm.
3 "Therefore now, O LORD, please take my
life from me, for *it is* better for me to die than
to live!"
4 Then the LORD said, "*Is it* right for you to
be angry?"
5 So Jonah went out of the city and sat on
the east side of the city. There he made himself a shelter and sat under it in the shade, till
he might see what would become of the city.

LIFE LESSONS

➤ **3:10 — *Then God saw their works, that they turned from their evil way; and God relented from the disaster that He had said He would bring upon them . . . .***

Over and over again in Scripture, we see that God does not want to bring calamity or judgment upon anyone. So He pleads with us and urges us to repent. Only when no other option remains does judgment fall.

➤ 6 And the LORD God prepared a plant[a] and
made it come up over Jonah, that it might be
shade for his head to deliver him from his
misery. So Jonah was very grateful for the
plant.
7 But as morning dawned the next day God
prepared a worm, and it *so* damaged the plant
that it withered.
8 And it happened, when the sun arose, that
God prepared a vehement east wind; and the
sun beat on Jonah's head, so that he grew
faint. Then he wished death for himself, and
said, "*It is* better for me to die than to live."
9 Then God said to Jonah, "*Is it* right for you
to be angry about the plant?" And he said, "*It
is* right for me to be angry, even to death!"
10 But the LORD said, "You have had pity on
the plant for which you have not labored, nor
made it grow, which came up in a night and
perished in a night.
11 "And should I not pity Nineveh, that great ➤
city, in which are more than one hundred and
twenty thousand persons who cannot discern
between their right hand and their left—and
much livestock?"

4:6 [a]Hebrew *kikayon,* exact identity unknown

LIFE LESSONS

➤ 4:6–8 — *And the LORD God prepared a plant . . . the next day God prepared a worm . . . God prepared a vehement east wind . . . .*

God's providence watches over all the details of our lives. A plant, a worm, a wind—He prepares and uses them all to shape us into people who more closely resemble His Son.

➤ 4:11 — *"And should I not pity Nineveh . . . ?"*

Jonah didn't pity Nineveh. Perhaps as a prophet he had looked into the future and seen how it would one day bludgeon Israel. But God did pity it. He did spare it. Why? Because He loves mercy, not judgment.

THE BOOK OF

MICAH

Micah, called from a rustic home to be a prophet, left his familiar surroundings to deliver a stern message of judgment to the princes and people of Jerusalem. Angered by the abusive treatment of the poor by the rich and influential, the prophet turned his verbal rebukes upon any who would use their social or political power for personal gain.

Micah insisted that God's righteous demands upon His people remained clear at all times and in all ages: "to do justly, to love mercy, and to walk humbly with your God" (6:8).

Micah not only rebuked his people, however; he also issued several prophecies of the coming Messiah and described a future time of peace and prosperity when Israel would once more serve the Lord in holy gladness. The most famous of his Messianic prophecies is an annual favorite at Christmas time: "But you, Bethlehem Ephrathah, though you are little among the thousands of Judah, yet out of you shall come forth to Me the One to be Ruler in Israel, whose goings forth are from of old, from everlasting" (5:2).

The Hebrew name *Michayahu* ("Who is like Yahweh?") is shortened in the book to *Michaia.* In 7:18, Micah hints at his own name with the phrase "Who is a God like You?" He is fond of plays on words, as in 1:10, "Tell it not in Gath," where "Gath" sounds like the Hebrew word for "tell."

Themes: God insists that His people must reflect His holy character in the way they live; if they refuse, judgment is the inevitable result. Yet God will never abandon His covenant people and will send the Messiah to rescue them from their sins and to one day rule over them in righteousness and truth.

Author: Micah, a native of Moresheth in southern Judah.

Time: Micah prophesied during the reigns of Jotham, Ahaz, and Hezekiah (750–686 B.C.), and was a contemporary of the prophet Isaiah.

Structure: The first portion of Micah's book generally exposes the sins of his countrymen; then he focuses on the punishment God is about to send; and the final portion holds out the hope of restoration once that discipline has ended.

As you read Micah, watch for several life principles that play an important role in this book:

6. You reap what you sow, more than you sow, and later than you sow. *See Micah 1:2–7; page 1061.*

12. Peace with God is the fruit of oneness with God. *See Micah 5:2–5; page 1063, 1064.*

1 The word of the LORD that came to Micah of Moresheth in the days of Jotham, Ahaz, *and* Hezekiah, kings of Judah, which he saw concerning Samaria and Jerusalem.

The Coming Judgment on Israel

2 Hear, all you peoples!
Listen, O earth, and all that is in it!
Let the Lord GOD be a witness against you,
The Lord from His holy temple.

3 For behold, the LORD is coming out of His place;
He will come down
And tread on the high places of the earth.
4 The mountains will melt under Him,
And the valleys will split
Like wax before the fire,
Like waters poured down a steep place.
5 All this is for the transgression of Jacob
And for the sins of the house of Israel.
What *is* the transgression of Jacob?
Is it not Samaria?
And what *are* the high places of Judah?
Are they not Jerusalem?

6 "Therefore I will make Samaria a heap of ruins in the field,
Places for planting a vineyard;
I will pour down her stones into the valley,
And I will uncover her foundations.
7 All her carved images shall be beaten to pieces,
And all her pay as a harlot shall be burned with the fire;
All her idols I will lay desolate,
For she gathered *it* from the pay of a harlot,
And they shall return to the pay of a harlot."

Mourning for Israel and Judah

8 Therefore I will wail and howl,
I will go stripped and naked;
I will make a wailing like the jackals
And a mourning like the ostriches,
9 For her wounds *are* incurable.
For it has come to Judah;
It has come to the gate of My people—
To Jerusalem.

10 Tell *it* not in Gath,
Weep not at all;
In Beth Aphrah[a]
Roll yourself in the dust.
11 Pass by in naked shame, you inhabitant of Shaphir;
The inhabitant of Zaanan[a] does not go out.
Beth Ezel mourns;
Its place to stand is taken away from you.

12 For the inhabitant of Maroth pined[a] for good,
But disaster came down from the LORD
To the gate of Jerusalem.
13 O inhabitant of Lachish,
Harness the chariot to the swift steeds
(She *was* the beginning of sin to the daughter of Zion),
For the transgressions of Israel were found in you.

14 Therefore you shall give presents to Moresheth Gath;[a]
The houses of Achzib[b] *shall be* a lie to the kings of Israel.
15 I will yet bring an heir to you,
O inhabitant of Mareshah;[a]
The glory of Israel shall come to Adullam.
16 Make yourself bald and cut off your hair,
Because of your precious children;
Enlarge your baldness like an eagle,
For they shall go from you into captivity.

Woe to Evildoers

2 Woe to those who devise iniquity,
And work out evil on their beds!
At morning light they practice it,
Because it is in the power of their hand.
2 They covet fields and take *them* by violence,
Also houses, and seize *them*.
So they oppress a man and his house,
A man and his inheritance.

3 Therefore thus says the LORD:

"Behold, against this family I am devising disaster,
From which you cannot remove your necks;
Nor shall you walk haughtily,
For this *is* an evil time.
4 In that day *one* shall take up a proverb against you,
And lament with a bitter lamentation, saying:
'We are utterly destroyed!
He has changed the heritage of my people;
How He has removed *it* from me!
To a turncoat He has divided our fields.'"

5 Therefore you will have no one to determine boundaries[a] by lot
In the assembly of the LORD.

Lying Prophets

6 "Do not prattle," *you say to those* who prophesy.
So they shall not prophesy to you;[a]
They shall not return insult for insult.[b]

1:10 [a]Literally *House of Dust* **1:11** [a]Literally *Going Out* **1:12** [a]Literally *was sick* **1:14** [a]Literally *Possession of Gath* [b]Literally *Lie* **1:15** [a]Literally *Inheritance* **2:5** [a]Literally *one casting a surveyor's line* **2:6** [a]Literally *to these* [b]Vulgate reads *He shall not take shame.*

➤ 7 *You who are* named the house of Jacob:
"Is the Spirit of the LORD restricted?
Are these His doings?
Do not My words do good
To him who walks uprightly?

8 "Lately My people have risen up as an enemy—
You pull off the robe with the garment
From those who trust *you,* as they pass by,
Like men returned from war.
9 The women of My people you cast out
From their pleasant houses;
From their children
You have taken away My glory forever.

10 "Arise and depart,
For this *is* not *your* rest;
Because it is defiled, it shall destroy,
Yes, with utter destruction.
11 If a man should walk in a false spirit
And speak a lie, *saying,*
'I will prophesy to you of wine and drink,'
Even he would be the prattler of this people.

Israel Restored

12 "I will surely assemble all of you, O Jacob,
I will surely gather the remnant of Israel;
I will put them together like sheep of the fold,[a]
Like a flock in the midst of their pasture;
They shall make a loud noise because of *so many* people.
13 The one who breaks open will come up before them;
They will break out,
Pass through the gate,
And go out by it;
Their king will pass before them,
With the LORD at their head."

Wicked Rulers and Prophets

3 And I said:

"Hear now, O heads of Jacob,
And you rulers of the house of Israel:
Is it not for you to know justice?
2 You who hate good and love evil;
Who strip the skin from My people,[a]
And the flesh from their bones;
3 Who also eat the flesh of My people,
Flay their skin from them,
Break their bones,
And chop *them* in pieces
Like *meat* for the pot,
Like flesh in the caldron."

4 Then they will cry to the LORD,
But He will not hear them;
He will even hide His face from them at that time,
Because they have been evil in their deeds.

5 Thus says the LORD concerning the prophets
Who make my people stray;
Who chant "Peace"
While they chew with their teeth,
But who prepare war against him
Who puts nothing into their mouths:
6 "Therefore you shall have night without vision,
And you shall have darkness without divination;
The sun shall go down on the prophets,
And the day shall be dark for them.
7 So the seers shall be ashamed,
And the diviners abashed;
Indeed they shall all cover their lips;
For *there is* no answer from God."

8 But truly I am full of power by the Spirit of the LORD, ◄
And of justice and might,
To declare to Jacob his transgression
And to Israel his sin.
9 Now hear this,
You heads of the house of Jacob
And rulers of the house of Israel,
Who abhor justice
And pervert all equity,
10 Who build up Zion with bloodshed
And Jerusalem with iniquity:
11 Her heads judge for a bribe,
Her priests teach for pay,
And her prophets divine for money.
Yet they lean on the LORD, and say,
"Is not the LORD among us?
No harm can come upon us."
12 Therefore because of you
Zion shall be plowed *like* a field,
Jerusalem shall become heaps of ruins,
And the mountain of the temple[a]
Like the bare hills of the forest.

2:12 [a]Hebrew *Bozrah* **3:2** [a]Literally *them* **3:12** [a]Literally *house*

LIFE LESSONS

➤ 2:7 — *"Do not My words do good to him who walks uprightly?"*

God desires to bless us, not punish us, so even His words of rebuke and correction are good for us. "Let the righteous . . . rebuke me; it shall be as excellent oil; let my head not refuse it" (Ps. 141:5).

➤ 3:8 — *But truly I am full of power by the Spirit of the LORD . . . .*

God has given us, not a spirit of fear, but of power (2 Tim. 1:7), and that power comes from His Spirit: "But you shall receive power when the Holy Spirit has come upon you" (Acts 1:8; see also Eph. 3:16).

The LORD*'s Reign in Zion*

4 Now it shall come to pass in the latter
days
That the mountain of the LORD's house
Shall be established on the top of the
mountains,
And shall be exalted above the hills;
And peoples shall flow to it.
➤ 2 Many nations shall come and say,
"Come, and let us go up to the mountain
of the LORD,
To the house of the God of Jacob;
He will teach us His ways,
And we shall walk in His paths."
For out of Zion the law shall go forth,
And the word of the LORD from
Jerusalem.
✳ 3 He shall judge between many peoples,
And rebuke strong nations afar off;
They shall beat their swords into
plowshares,
And their spears into pruning hooks;
Nation shall not lift up sword against
nation,
Neither shall they learn war anymore.[a]
4 But everyone shall sit under his vine and
under his fig tree,
And no one shall make *them* afraid;
For the mouth of the LORD of hosts has
spoken.
5 For all people walk each in the name of
his god,
But we will walk in the name of the LORD
our God
Forever and ever.

Zion's Future Triumph

6 "In that day," says the LORD,
"I will assemble the lame,
I will gather the outcast
And those whom I have afflicted;
7 I will make the lame a remnant,
And the outcast a strong nation;
So the LORD will reign over them in
Mount Zion
From now on, even forever.
8 And you, O tower of the flock,
The stronghold of the daughter of Zion,
To you shall it come,
Even the former dominion shall come,
The kingdom of the daughter of
Jerusalem."
9 Now why do you cry aloud?
Is there no king in your midst?
Has your counselor perished?
For pangs have seized you like a woman
in labor.
10 Be in pain, and labor to bring forth,
O daughter of Zion,
Like a woman in birth pangs.
For now you shall go forth from the city,
You shall dwell in the field,
And to Babylon you shall go.
There you shall be delivered;
There the LORD will redeem you
From the hand of your enemies.
11 Now also many nations have gathered
against you,
Who say, "Let her be defiled,
And let our eye look upon Zion."
12 But they do not know the thoughts of the ➤
LORD,
Nor do they understand His counsel;
For He will gather them like sheaves to
the threshing floor.
13 "Arise and thresh, O daughter of Zion;
For I will make your horn iron,
And I will make your hooves bronze;
You shall beat in pieces many peoples;
I will consecrate their gain to the LORD,
And their substance to the Lord of the
whole earth."

5 Now gather yourself in troops,
O daughter of troops;
He has laid siege against us;
They will strike the judge of Israel with a
rod on the cheek.

The Coming Messiah

2 "But you, Bethlehem Ephrathah, ➤
Though you are little among the
thousands of Judah,
Yet out of you shall come forth to Me
The One to be Ruler in Israel,

4:3 [a]Compare Isaiah 2:2–4

LIFE LESSONS

➤ **4:2 — *"He will teach us His ways, and we shall walk in His paths."***

God does not leave us in the dark about His nature and will, and through His Spirit He enables us to reflect His nature and do His will. We walk in His paths when we allow Jesus to live through us.

➤ **4:12 — *But they do not know the thoughts of the* LORD*, nor do they understand His counsel . . . .***

Without loving the Lord, a person cannot understand and endorse His thoughts or counsel. Such a person cannot "receive the things of the Spirit of God nor can he know them, because they are spiritually discerned" (1 Cor. 2:14).

➤ **5:2 — *" . . . the One to be Ruler in Israel, whose goings forth are from of old, from everlasting."***

When Jesus told the Pharisees, "before Abraham was, I AM" (John 8:58), He was simply restating what Micah said here, that the Messiah would be the eternal God come to earth in the flesh.

Whose goings forth *are* from of old,
From everlasting."

3 Therefore He shall give them up,
Until the time *that* she who is in labor
has given birth;
Then the remnant of His brethren
Shall return to the children of Israel.

4 And He shall stand and feed *His flock*
In the strength of the LORD,
In the majesty of the name of the LORD
His God;
And they shall abide,
For now He shall be great
To the ends of the earth;

5 And this *One* shall be peace.

Judgment on Israel's Enemies

When the Assyrian comes into our land,
And when he treads in our palaces,
Then we will raise against him
Seven shepherds and eight princely men.

6 They shall waste with the sword the land
of Assyria,
And the land of Nimrod at its entrances;
Thus He shall deliver *us* from the
Assyrian,
When he comes into our land
And when he treads within our borders.

7 Then the remnant of Jacob
Shall be in the midst of many peoples,
Like dew from the LORD,
Like showers on the grass,
That tarry for no man
Nor wait for the sons of men.

8 And the remnant of Jacob
Shall be among the Gentiles,
In the midst of many peoples,
Like a lion among the beasts of the forest,
Like a young lion among flocks of sheep,
Who, if he passes through,
Both treads down and tears in pieces,
And none can deliver.

9 Your hand shall be lifted against your
adversaries,
And all your enemies shall be cut off.

10 "And it shall be in that day," says the
LORD,
"That I will cut off your horses from your
midst
And destroy your chariots.

11 I will cut off the cities of your land
And throw down all your strongholds.

12 I will cut off sorceries from your hand,
And you shall have no soothsayers.

13 Your carved images I will also cut off,
And your *sacred* pillars from your midst;
You shall no more worship the work of
your hands;

14 I will pluck your wooden images[a] from
your midst;
Thus I will destroy your cities.

15 And I will execute vengeance in anger
and fury
On the nations that have not heard."[a]

God Pleads with Israel

6 Hear now what the LORD says:

"Arise, plead your case before the
mountains,
And let the hills hear your voice.

2 Hear, O you mountains, the LORD's
complaint,
And you strong foundations of the earth;
For the LORD has a complaint against His
people,
And He will contend with Israel.

3 "O My people, what have I done to you?
And how have I wearied you?
Testify against Me.

4 For I brought you up from the land of
Egypt,
I redeemed you from the house of
bondage;
And I sent before you Moses, Aaron, and
Miriam.

5 O My people, remember now
What Balak king of Moab counseled,
And what Balaam the son of Beor
answered him,
From Acacia Grove[a] to Gilgal,
That you may know the righteousness of
the LORD."

6 With what shall I come before the LORD,
And bow myself before the High God?
Shall I come before Him with burnt
offerings,
With calves a year old?

7 Will the LORD be pleased with thousands
of rams,
Ten thousand rivers of oil?
Shall I give my firstborn *for* my
transgression,
The fruit of my body *for* the sin of my
soul?

5:14 [a]Hebrew *Asherim,* Canaanite deities **5:15** [a]Or *obeyed*
6:5 [a]Hebrew *Shittim* (compare Numbers 25:1; Joshua 2:1; 3:1)

LIFE LESSONS

➤ **5:4 — *And He shall stand and feed His flock . . . in the majesty of the name of the LORD His God . . . .***

During His earthly ministry, Jesus practically made this verse His motto when He said, "I am the good shepherd. The good shepherd gives His life for the sheep . . . I am the good shepherd" (John 10:11, 14).

WHAT THE BIBLE SAYS ABOUT TRUE RELIGION

Mic. 6:8

What a tragedy that we have lost our ability to function in society the way God originally intended! He left us here to be a light to our world. People should be able to look our way and see something wonderfully different about us. Not our clothes or our hairstyle—*US*! The good things God places on the inside of us should show up in practical ways on the outside.

The prophet Micah said it like this: "He has shown you, O man, what is good; and what does the LORD require of you but to do justly, to love mercy, and to walk humbly with your God?" (Mic. 6:8). And don't think Micah gave an exclusively Old Testament perspective! The New Testament tells us, "Pure and undefiled religion before God and the Father is this: to visit orphans and widows in their trouble, and to keep oneself unspotted from the world" (James 1:27).

This means there should be something different in the way we do business. There should be some clear differences in the way we raise our children. Our marriages should testify to the love of Christ. Those outside the church should feel powerfully attracted to the unity and love they see among believers.

Unfortunately, that rarely happens today. Consequently, our society has a warped view of the person and work of Christ. It is no wonder that so many non-Christians want nothing to do with Christ or His church. They know too many Christians!

We cannot expect anyone to embrace a Savior they know nothing about. We certainly cannot expect them to surrender to a Lord whose servants can't even get along with each other. As ambassadors for Christ, believers have the God-given responsibility to live in such a way that others see Christ in us. As the body of Christ, *we* are His hands and His feet. *We* are His mouthpiece.

Pardon the cliché, but we are the only Jesus most people will ever know.

See the Life Principles Index for further study:
24. To live the Christian life is to allow Jesus to live His life in and through us.

Our society has a warped view of the person and work of Christ.

8 He has shown you, O man, what *is* good;
And what does the LORD require of you
But to do justly,
To love mercy,
And to walk humbly with your God?

Punishment of Israel's Injustice

9 The LORD's voice cries to the city—
Wisdom shall see Your name:

"Hear the rod!
Who has appointed it?
10 Are there yet the treasures of wickedness
In the house of the wicked,
And the short measure *that is* an abomination?
11 Shall I count pure *those* with the wicked scales,
And with the bag of deceitful weights?
12 For her rich men are full of violence,
Her inhabitants have spoken lies,
And their tongue is deceitful in their mouth.
13 "Therefore I will also make *you* sick by striking you,
By making *you* desolate because of your sins.
14 You shall eat, but not be satisfied;
Hunger[a] *shall be* in your midst.
You may carry *some* away,[b] but shall not save *them;*
And what you do rescue I will give over to the sword.
15 "You shall sow, but not reap;
You shall tread the olives, but not anoint yourselves with oil;
And *make* sweet wine, but not drink wine.
16 For the statutes of Omri are kept;
All the works of Ahab's house *are done;*
And you walk in their counsels,
That I may make you a desolation,
And your inhabitants a hissing.
Therefore you shall bear the reproach of My people."[a]

Sorrow for Israel's Sins

7 Woe is me!
For I am like those who gather summer fruits,
Like those who glean vintage grapes;
There is no cluster to eat
Of the first-ripe fruit *which* my soul desires.
2 The faithful *man* has perished from the earth,
And *there is* no one upright among men.
They all lie in wait for blood;
Every man hunts his brother with a net.

3 That they may successfully do evil with both hands—
The prince asks *for gifts,*
The judge *seeks* a bribe,
And the great *man* utters his evil desire;
So they scheme together.
4 The best of them *is* like a brier;
The most upright *is sharper* than a thorn hedge;
The day of your watchman and your punishment comes;
Now shall be their perplexity.

5 Do not trust in a friend;
Do not put your confidence in a companion;
Guard the doors of your mouth
From her who lies in your bosom.
6 For son dishonors father,
Daughter rises against her mother,
Daughter-in-law against her mother-in-law;
A man's enemies *are* the men of his own household.
7 Therefore I will look to the LORD;
I will wait for the God of my salvation;
My God will hear me.

Israel's Confession and Comfort

8 Do not rejoice over me, my enemy;
When I fall, I will arise;
When I sit in darkness,
The LORD *will be* a light to me.
9 I will bear the indignation of the LORD,
Because I have sinned against Him,
Until He pleads my case
And executes justice for me.

6:14 [a]Or *Emptiness* or *Humiliation* [b]Targum and Vulgate read *You shall take hold.* **6:16** [a]Following Masoretic Text, Targum, and Vulgate; Septuagint reads *of nations.*

LIFE LESSONS

➤ 6:8 — *What does the LORD require of you but to do justly, to love mercy, and to walk humbly with your God?*

To be a "good Christian" requires more than personal devotions and a warm feeling inside. God wants us to show the outside world what He is doing inside of us—and that takes humble, merciful, just action.

➤ 7:7 — *I will look to the LORD; I will wait for the God of my salvation; My God will hear me.*

Whether we like it or not, waiting on God is a big part of our walk of faith. When we do all that we can, in faith, and then wait for God to do the rest, we demonstrate our trust and proclaim His faithfulness.

➤ 7:8 — *When I sit in darkness, the LORD will be a light to me.*

Micah says "when" I sit in darkness, not "if." All of us will go through difficult times. But the dark moments of our lives will last only so long as is necessary for God to accomplish His purpose in us.

He will bring me forth to the light;
I will see His righteousness.
10 Then *she who is* my enemy will see,
And shame will cover her who said to me,
"Where is the LORD your God?"
My eyes will see her;
Now she will be trampled down
Like mud in the streets.

11 *In* the day when your walls are to be built,
In that day the decree shall go far and wide.[a]
12 *In* that day they[a] shall come to you
From Assyria and the fortified cities,[b]
From the fortress[c] to the River,[d]
From sea to sea,
And mountain *to* mountain.
13 Yet the land shall be desolate
Because of those who dwell in it,
And for the fruit of their deeds.

God Will Forgive Israel
14 Shepherd Your people with Your staff,
The flock of Your heritage,
Who dwell solitarily *in* a woodland,
In the midst of Carmel;
Let them feed *in* Bashan and Gilead,
As in days of old.

15 "As in the days when you came out of the land of Egypt,
I will show them[a] wonders."

16 The nations shall see and be ashamed of all their might;
They shall put *their* hand over *their* mouth;
Their ears shall be deaf.
17 They shall lick the dust like a serpent;
They shall crawl from their holes like snakes of the earth.
They shall be afraid of the LORD our God,
And shall fear because of You.
18 Who *is* a God like You,
Pardoning iniquity
And passing over the transgression of the remnant of His heritage?

He does not retain His anger forever,
Because He delights *in* mercy.
19 He will again have compassion on us,
And will subdue our iniquities.

You will cast all our[a] sins
Into the depths of the sea.
20 You will give truth to Jacob
And mercy to Abraham,
Which You have sworn to our fathers
From days of old.

7:11 [a]Or *the boundary shall be extended* **7:12** [a]Literally *he,* collective of the captives [b]Hebrew *arey mazor,* possibly *cities of Egypt* [c]Hebrew *mazor,* possibly *Egypt* [d]That is, the Euphrates **7:15** [a]Literally *him,* collective for the captives **7:19** [a]Literally *their*

LIFE LESSONS

➤ 7:18 — *Who is a God like You, pardoning iniquity and passing over the transgression of the remnant of His heritage?*

God was never under any obligation to forgive our sins or pardon our iniquity. We do not deserve His mercy. But He loves us and so sent His Son to die for our sins. Who, indeed, is a God like that?

➤ 7:19 — *You will cast all our sins into the depths of the sea.*

When God forgives us in Christ, He does not merely turn His back on our sins or force Himself to overlook them. He deals with them radically and once-and-for-all, removing them from us forever.

THE BOOK OF

NAHUM

"For everyone to whom much is given, from him much will be required," Jesus declared (Luke 12:48). His words found graphic illustration in the fortunes of ancient Nineveh, the infamous capital of Assyria.

The great Gentile city had been given the privilege of knowing the one true God. Under Jonah's preaching, the people of the metropolis repented, and God had graciously withheld His promised judgment.

A hundred years later, however, Nahum proclaims the downfall of the same city. The Assyrians forgot their life-saving revival and returned to their habits of violence, idolatry, and arrogance. As a result, the Babylonians would so utterly destroy the city that no trace of it would remain—a prophecy fulfilled in painful detail. In fact, until modern times the exact location of Nineveh (near modern-day Mosul in Iraq) had been forgotten.

The Hebrew word *nahum* ("comfort," "consolation") is a shortened form of Nehemiah ("Comfort of Yahweh"). The destruction of the capital city of Assyria brings comfort and consolation to Judah and all who live in fear of the cruelty of the Assyrians.

Themes: God judges disobedience, but He gives the repentant a "second chance." Nahum is sometimes regarded as a sequel to the Book of Jonah.

Author: Nahum.

Time: Sometime before the fall of Nineveh (c. 660 B.C.).

Structure: The Book of Nahum can be divided simply into three parts. In chapter one, Nahum describes the Lord as Nineveh's judge. In chapter two, he proclaims Nineveh's judgment. In chapter three, he prophesies Nineveh's complete ruin.

As you read Nahum, watch for a couple of life principles that play an important role in this book:

6. You reap what you sow, more than you sow, and later than you sow. *See Nahum 1:14; page 1069.*

18. As children of a sovereign God, we are never victims of our circumstances. *See Nahum 2:2; page 1069.*

1

The burden[a] against Nineveh. The book of the vision of Nahum the Elkoshite.

God's Wrath on His Enemies

➤ **2** God *is* jealous, and the LORD avenges;
The LORD avenges and *is* furious.
The LORD will take vengeance on His adversaries,
And He reserves *wrath* for His enemies;
✳ 3 The LORD *is* slow to anger and great in power,
And will not at all acquit *the wicked.*

The LORD has His way
In the whirlwind and in the storm,
And the clouds *are* the dust of His feet.
4 He rebukes the sea and makes it dry,
And dries up all the rivers.
Bashan and Carmel wither,
And the flower of Lebanon wilts.
5 The mountains quake before Him,
The hills melt,
And the earth heaves[a] at His presence,
Yes, the world and all who dwell in it.

6 Who can stand before His indignation?
And who can endure the fierceness of His anger?
His fury is poured out like fire,
And the rocks are thrown down by Him.

✳ 7 The LORD *is* good,
A stronghold in the day of trouble;
And He knows those who trust in Him.
8 But with an overflowing flood
He will make an utter end of its place,
And darkness will pursue His enemies.

➤ **9** What do you conspire against the LORD?
He will make an utter end *of it.*
Affliction will not rise up a second time.
10 For while tangled *like* thorns,
And while drunken *like* drunkards,
They shall be devoured like stubble fully dried.
11 From you comes forth *one*
Who plots evil against the LORD,
A wicked counselor.

12 Thus says the LORD:

"Though *they are* safe, and likewise many,
Yet in this manner they will be cut down
When he passes through.
Though I have afflicted you,
I will afflict you no more;
13 For now I will break off his yoke from you,
And burst your bonds apart."

14 The LORD has given a command concerning you:
"Your name shall be perpetuated no longer.
Out of the house of your gods
I will cut off the carved image and the molded image.
I will dig your grave,
For you are vile."

15 Behold, on the mountains
The feet of him who brings good tidings,
Who proclaims peace!
O Judah, keep your appointed feasts,
Perform your vows.
For the wicked one shall no more pass through you;
He is utterly cut off.

The Destruction of Nineveh

2

He who scatters[a] has come up before your face. Man the fort!
Watch the road!
Strengthen *your* flanks!
Fortify *your* power mightily.

2 For the LORD will restore the excellence of Jacob
Like the excellence of Israel,
For the emptiers have emptied them out
And ruined their vine branches.

3 The shields of his mighty men *are* made red,
The valiant men *are* in scarlet.
The chariots *come* with flaming torches
In the day of his preparation,
And the spears are brandished.[a]
4 The chariots rage in the streets,
They jostle one another in the broad roads;
They seem like torches,
They run like lightning.

5 He remembers his nobles;
They stumble in their walk;

1:1 [a]Or *oracle* **1:5** [a]Targum reads *burns.* **2:1** [a]Vulgate reads *He who destroys.* **2:3** [a]Literally *the cypresses are shaken;* Septuagint and Syriac read *the horses rush about;* Vulgate reads *the drivers are stupefied.*

LIFE LESSONS

➤ **1:2 — *God is jealous, and the LORD avenges; the LORD avenges and is furious.***

God will not share our devotion with anyone else. In fact, He tells us His "name is Jealous" (Ex. 34:14). In warning us against dual allegiances, the New Testament asks, "do we provoke the Lord to jealousy?" (1 Cor. 10:22).

➤ **1:9 — *What do you conspire against the LORD? He will make an utter end of it.***

Disobedience and sin simply make no sense. No one ever gets away with anything, and everyone will one day stand before God to give an account of himself (Rom. 14:12). So why not choose obedience and blessing?

They make haste to her walls,
And the defense is prepared.
6 The gates of the rivers are opened,
And the palace is dissolved.
7 It is decreed:[a]
She shall be led away captive,
She shall be brought up;
And her maidservants shall lead *her* as
with the voice of doves,
Beating their breasts.

8 Though Nineveh of old *was* like a pool of
water,
Now they flee away.
"Halt! Halt!" *they cry;*
But no one turns back.
9 Take spoil of silver!
Take spoil of gold!
There is no end of treasure,
Or wealth of every desirable prize.
10 She is empty, desolate, and waste!
The heart melts, and the knees shake;
Much pain *is* in every side,
And all their faces are drained of color.[a]

11 Where *is* the dwelling of the lions,
And the feeding place of the young lions,
Where the lion walked, the lioness *and*
lion's cub,
And no one made *them* afraid?
12 The lion tore in pieces enough for his
cubs,
Killed for his lionesses,
Filled his caves with prey,
And his dens with flesh.

➤ 13 "Behold, I *am* against you," says the LORD
of hosts, "I will burn your[a] chariots in smoke,
and the sword shall devour your young lions;
I will cut off your prey from the earth, and the
voice of your messengers shall be heard no
more."

The Woe of Nineveh

3 Woe to the bloody city!
It *is* all full of lies *and* robbery.
Its victim never departs.
2 The noise of a whip
And the noise of rattling wheels,
Of galloping horses,
Of clattering chariots!
3 Horsemen charge with bright sword and
glittering spear.
There is a multitude of slain,
A great number of bodies,
Countless corpses—
They stumble over the corpses—
4 Because of the multitude of harlotries of
the seductive harlot,
The mistress of sorceries,
Who sells nations through her harlotries,
And families through her sorceries.

5 "Behold, I *am* against you," says the LORD
of hosts;
"I will lift your skirts over your face,
I will show the nations your nakedness,
And the kingdoms your shame.
6 I will cast abominable filth upon you,
Make you vile,
And make you a spectacle.
7 It shall come to pass *that* all who look
upon you
Will flee from you, and say,
'Nineveh is laid waste!
Who will bemoan her?'
Where shall I seek comforters for you?"

8 Are you better than No Amon[a]
That was situated by the River,[b]
That had the waters around her,
Whose rampart *was* the sea,
Whose wall *was* the sea?
9 Ethiopia and Egypt *were* her strength,
And *it was* boundless;
Put and Lubim were your[a] helpers.
10 Yet she *was* carried away,
She went into captivity;
Her young children also were dashed to
pieces
At the head of every street;
They cast lots for her honorable men,
And all her great men were bound in
chains.
11 You also will be drunk;
You will be hidden;
You also will seek refuge from the enemy.

12 All your strongholds *are* fig trees with
ripened figs:
If they are shaken,
They fall into the mouth of the eater.
13 Surely, your people in your midst *are*
women!
The gates of your land are wide open for
your enemies;
Fire shall devour the bars of your *gates*.

2:7 [a]Hebrew *Huzzab* **2:10** [a]Compare Joel 2:6 **2:13** [a]Literally *her* **3:8** [a]That is, ancient Thebes; Targum and Vulgate read *populous Alexandria.* [b]Literally *rivers,* that is, the Nile and the surrounding canals **3:9** [a]Septuagint reads *her.*

LIFE LESSONS

➤ 2:13 — *"Behold, I am against you," says the LORD of hosts . . . .*

You never want to hear God say to you, "I am against you." What God opposes ends in misery and destruction; what God supports ends in joy and blessing. Remember, obedience always brings blessing.

➤ 14 Draw your water for the siege!
Fortify your strongholds!
Go into the clay and tread the mortar!
Make strong the brick kiln!
15 There the fire will devour you,
The sword will cut you off;
It will eat you up like a locust.

Make yourself many—like the locust!
Make yourself many— like the *swarming* locusts!
16 You have multiplied your merchants more than the stars of heaven.
The locust plunders and flies away.
17 Your commanders *are* like *swarming* locusts,
And your generals like great grasshoppers,
Which camp in the hedges on a cold day;
When the sun rises they flee away,
And the place where they *are* is not known.

18 Your shepherds slumber, O king of Assyria;
Your nobles rest *in the dust.*
Your people are scattered on the mountains,
And no one gathers them.
19 Your injury *has* no healing, ➤
Your wound is severe.
All who hear news of you
Will clap *their* hands over you,
For upon whom has not your wickedness passed continually?

LIFE LESSONS

➤ 3:14 — *Draw your water for the siege! Fortify your strongholds! Go into the clay and tread the mortar! Make strong the brick kiln!*

God does not always plead with rebels to repent. The time comes when they reach a point of no return. Pharaoh did this (Ex. 9:12). Assyria did this. And some still do it (1 John 5:16). But you don't have to.

➤ 3:19 — *Your injury has no healing, your wound is severe.*

Those who refuse to come to God for their spiritual healing will never be healed. We were made for intimacy with God, and to seek a cure for spiritual wounds apart from God is to seek poison, not medicine.

THE BOOK OF

HABAKKUK

Habakkuk ministered during the final "death throes" of the nation of Judah. Although God had repeatedly called the nation to repentance, Judah stubbornly refused to change her sinful ways.

The prophet, knowing the hardheartedness of his countrymen, asked God how long such an intolerable condition could continue. God replied that He would use the brutal Babylonians as His chastening rod upon the wayward nation—an announcement that sent the prophet to his knees. How could God use a nation more wicked than Judah to punish Judah? God answered that, in His time, He would also punish the Babylonians.

Habakkuk did not entirely understand or celebrate God's plan, but He acknowledged that the just in any generation live by faith (Hab. 2:4). So he would leave the situation in God's holy hands. Habakkuk concluded his little book by praising God's wisdom, even though he did not fully grasp God's mysterious ways.

Habaqquq is an unusual Hebrew name, derived from the verb *habaq*, "embrace." Thus his name probably means "One Who Embraces (or Clings)." At the end of his book this name becomes especially appropriate because Habakkuk chose to cling firmly to God, regardless of what happened to him or to his nation (3:17–19).

Theme: God rules over the whole earth and uses whomever He chooses for His purposes. We are to trust God, despite the mysterious nature of His providence.

Author: Habakkuk.

Time: Uncertain. The prophet evidently lived during the Babylonian period. Many scholars fix the time of the prophecy during the reign of Jehoiakim (609-598 B.C.)

Structure: The first two chapters of Habakkuk feature a conversation between God and the prophet concerning evil and judgment. The third and final chapter reads like a psalm of prayer and praise for the sovereignty and providence of God.

As you read Habakkuk, watch for several life principles that play an important role in this book:

5. God does not require us to understand His will, just obey it, even if it seems unreasonable. *See Habakkuk 1:12—2:1; page 1073.*

9. Trusting God means looking beyond what we can see to what God sees. *See Habakkuk 2:4; page 1074.*

20. Disappointments are inevitable; discouragement is a choice. *See Habakkuk 3:17–19; page 1075, 1078.*

1 The burden[a] which the prophet Habakkuk saw.

The Prophet's Question

2 O LORD, how long shall I cry,
And You will not hear?
Even cry out to You, "Violence!"
And You will not save.
3 Why do You show me iniquity,
And cause *me* to see trouble?
For plundering and violence *are* before me;
There is strife, and contention arises.
4 Therefore the law is powerless,
And justice never goes forth.
For the wicked surround the righteous;
Therefore perverse judgment proceeds.

The LORD's Reply

5 "Look among the nations and watch—
Be utterly astounded!
For *I will* work a work in your days
Which you would not believe, though it were told *you.*
6 For indeed I am raising up the Chaldeans,
A bitter and hasty nation
Which marches through the breadth of the earth,
To possess dwelling places *that are* not theirs.
7 They are terrible and dreadful;
Their judgment and their dignity proceed from themselves.
8 Their horses also are swifter than leopards,
And more fierce than evening wolves.
Their chargers charge ahead;
Their cavalry comes from afar;
They fly as the eagle *that* hastens to eat.

9 "They all come for violence;
Their faces are set *like* the east wind.
They gather captives like sand.
10 They scoff at kings,
And princes are scorned by them.
They deride every stronghold,
For they heap up earthen *mounds* and seize it.
11 Then *his* mind[a] changes, and he transgresses;
He commits offense,
Ascribing this power to his god."

The Prophet's Second Question

12 Are You not from everlasting,
O LORD my God, my Holy One?
We shall not die.
O LORD, You have appointed them for judgment;
O Rock, You have marked them for correction.
13 *You are* of purer eyes than to behold evil,
And cannot look on wickedness.
Why do You look on those who deal treacherously,
And hold Your tongue when the wicked devours
A *person* more righteous than he?
14 *Why* do You make men like fish of the sea,
Like creeping things *that have* no ruler over them?

15 They take up all of them with a hook,
They catch them in their net,
And gather them in their dragnet.
Therefore they rejoice and are glad.
16 Therefore they sacrifice to their net,
And burn incense to their dragnet;
Because by them their share *is* sumptuous
And their food plentiful.
17 Shall they therefore empty their net,
And continue to slay nations without pity?

2 I will stand my watch
And set myself on the rampart,
And watch to see what He will say to me,
And what I will answer when I am corrected.

The Just Live by Faith

2 Then the LORD answered me and said:

"Write the vision
And make *it* plain on tablets,
That he may run who reads it.
3 For the vision *is* yet for an appointed time;

1:1 [a]Or *oracle* 1:11 [a]Literally *spirit* or *wind*

LIFE LESSONS

➢ 1:3 — *Why do You show me iniquity, and cause me to see trouble?*

When we focus on the sin and trouble around us, we quickly grow discouraged, anxious, and confused. God does not want us to look away, but to look toward Him and then do what we can to address the evil.

➢ 1:13 — *Why do you look on those who deal treacherously, and hold Your tongue when the wicked devours a person more righteous than he?*

We might prefer a world where God instantly judges every wrong, but that is not the world we have (nor would any of us long survive in it!). Yet in His time, He will certainly judge all evil and reward all good.

➢ 2:2 — *"Write the vision and make it plain on tablets, that he may run who reads it."*

God told Jeremiah, "Write in a book for yourself all the words that I have spoken to you" (Jer. 30:2). He also instructed Israel's kings to copy His Word (Deut. 17:18). Why? It's simple: we remember what we write.

But at the end it will speak, and it will
not lie.
Though it tarries, wait for it;
Because it will surely come,
It will not tarry.

4 "Behold the proud,
His soul is not upright in him;
But the just shall live by his faith.

Woe to the Wicked

5 "Indeed, because he transgresses by wine,
He is a proud man,
And he does not stay at home.
Because he enlarges his desire as hell,[a]
And he *is* like death, and cannot be
satisfied,
He gathers to himself all nations
And heaps up for himself all peoples.

6 "Will not all these take up a proverb
against him,
And a taunting riddle against him, and
say,
'Woe to him who increases
What is not his—how long?
And to him who loads himself with many
pledges'?[a]
7 Will not your creditors[a] rise up suddenly?
Will they not awaken who oppress you?
And you will become their booty.
8 Because you have plundered many
nations,
All the remnant of the people shall
plunder you,
Because of men's blood
And the violence of the land *and* the city,
And of all who dwell in it.

9 "Woe to him who covets evil gain for his
house,
That he may set his nest on high,
That he may be delivered from the power
of disaster!
10 You give shameful counsel to your house,
Cutting off many peoples,
And sin *against* your soul.
11 For the stone will cry out from the wall,
And the beam from the timbers will
answer it.

12 "Woe to him who builds a town with
bloodshed,
Who establishes a city by iniquity!
13 Behold, *is it* not of the LORD of hosts
That the peoples labor to feed the fire,[a]
And nations weary themselves in vain?
14 For the earth will be filled
With the knowledge of the glory of the
LORD,
As the waters cover the sea.

15 "Woe to him who gives drink to his
neighbor,
Pressing[a] *him to* your bottle,
Even to make *him* drunk,
That you may look on his nakedness!
16 You are filled with shame instead of
glory.
You also—drink!
And be exposed as uncircumcised![a]
The cup of the LORD's right hand *will be*
turned against you,
And utter shame will be on your glory.
17 For the violence *done to* Lebanon will
cover you,
And the plunder of beasts *which* made
them afraid,
Because of men's blood
And the violence of the land *and* the city,
And of all who dwell in it.

18 "What profit is the image, that its maker
should carve it,
The molded image, a teacher of lies,
That the maker of its mold should trust
in it,
To make mute idols?
19 Woe to him who says to wood, 'Awake!'
To silent stone, 'Arise! It shall teach!'
Behold, it is overlaid with gold and silver,
Yet in it there is no breath at all.

20 "But the LORD is in His holy temple.
Let all the earth keep silence before
Him."

The Prophet's Prayer

3 A prayer of Habakkuk the prophet, on
Shigionoth.[a]

2 O LORD, I have heard Your speech *and*
was afraid;

2:5 [a]Or *Sheol* **2:6** [a]Syriac and Vulgate read *thick clay.*
2:7 [a]Literally *those who bite you* **2:13** [a]Literally *for what satisfies fire,* that is, for what is of no lasting value **2:15** [a]Literally *Attaching* or *Joining* **2:16** [a]Dead Sea Scrolls and Septuagint read *And reel!;* Syriac and Vulgate read *And fall fast asleep!*
3:1 [a]Exact meaning unknown

LIFE LESSONS

➤ 2:4 — *"Behold the proud, his soul is not upright in him; but the just shall live by his faith."*

Why does God contrast pride with faith? Because, as C.S. Lewis noted, pride is the completely anti-God state of mind. Faith, on the other hand, looks to God for everything. God seeks worshipers, not rivals.

➤ 3:2 — *In wrath remember mercy.*

The psalmist asked, "If you, LORD, should mark iniquities, O Lord, who could stand?" (Ps. 130:3). The answer is, "nobody." Even when God must act to judge sin, He still shows mercy.

O LORD, revive Your work in the midst of
the years!
In the midst of the years make *it*
known;
In wrath remember mercy.

3 God came from Teman,
The Holy One from Mount Paran. Selah

His glory covered the heavens,
And the earth was full of His praise.
4 *His* brightness was like the light;
He had rays *flashing* from His hand,
And there His power *was* hidden.
5 Before Him went pestilence,
And fever followed at His feet.

6 He stood and measured the earth;
He looked and startled the nations.
And the everlasting mountains were
scattered,
The perpetual hills bowed.
His ways *are* everlasting.
7 I saw the tents of Cushan in affliction;
The curtains of the land of Midian
trembled.
8 O LORD, were *You* displeased with the
rivers,
Was Your anger against the rivers,
Was Your wrath against the sea,
That You rode on Your horses,
Your chariots of salvation?
9 Your bow was made quite ready;
Oaths were sworn over *Your*
arrows.[a] Selah

You divided the earth with rivers.
10 The mountains saw You *and* trembled;
The overflowing of the water passed by.
The deep uttered its voice,
And lifted its hands on high.
11 The sun and moon stood still in their
habitation;
At the light of Your arrows they went,
At the shining of Your glittering spear.

12 You marched through the land in
indignation;
You trampled the nations in anger.
13 You went forth for the salvation of Your
people,
For salvation with Your Anointed.
You struck the head from the house of
the wicked,
By laying bare from foundation to
neck. Selah

14 You thrust through with his own arrows
The head of his villages.
They came out like a whirlwind to
scatter me;
Their rejoicing was like feasting on the
poor in secret.
15 You walked through the sea with Your
horses,
Through the heap of great waters.

Life Examples:

HABAKKUK

Trusting God in the Dark

HAB. 3:17–19

We trust God to accomplish what He promises us in His Word. But the real battle of faith comes when He appears not to respond to our trust.

What should we do when God appears to have ignored our request? Will we continue to rely upon Him despite the disappointment? Or will we blaze our own path and turn away from the Lord in discouragement?

The prophet Habakkuk demonstrated the essence of true faith: to continue to trust in the Lord's wisdom and faithfulness, even when He seems inactive, or worse, uncaring.

In difficult times, faith becomes a matter of devoted allegiance to the Lord Jesus Christ. Do we have confidence in Him regardless of the circumstances? Do we cling to God and His Word despite the silence? Can we say, along with Habakkuk, that although all our resources and reserves vanish, "yet I will rejoice in the LORD" (Hab. 3:18)?

See the Life Principles Index for further study:
9. Trusting God means looking beyond what we can see to what God sees.
3. God's Word is an immovable anchor in times of storm.

16 When I heard, my body trembled;
My lips quivered at *the* voice;
Rottenness entered my bones;
And I trembled in myself,
That I might rest in the day of trouble.
When he comes up to the people,
He will invade them with his troops.

A Hymn of Faith
17 Though the fig tree may not blossom,
Nor fruit be on the vines;
Though the labor of the olive may
fail,
And the fields yield no food;

3:9 [a]Literally *rods* or *tribes* (compare verse 14)

LIFE PRINCIPLE 20

DISAPPOINTMENTS ARE INEVITABLE; DISCOURAGEMENT IS A CHOICE.

HAB. 3:17–19

"I'm so disappointed," he moaned. "I was just sure that deal would come through. We had a lock on it, but a competitor edged us out at the last minute."

She felt crushed; the whole weekend looked ruined. If only the basement hadn't flooded, she could have joined her friends for an unforgettable time of hiking and camping! Now she found herself stuck at home and alone, dealing with a faulty water pump and serious damage to her treasured possessions.

Everyone has known the ache of unfulfillment, the sadness that comes when life moves in an unanticipated direction. Disappointment may come as a result of a change in circumstances, such as a sudden reversal of plans; or it may be a more personal issue. If someone close to you behaves in a manner that lets you down, you may experience deep sensations of loss. If your disappointment comes as a result of a personal offense, it is tempting to lash out at the one who has damaged your plans. The vision or ideal you had cherished for so long now lies in ruins, and you don't know how to respond. Disappointment cuts so close to our sweetest dreams that we often find it difficult to sort through our swirling emotions.

Disappointment afflicted even the hearts of those who knew Jesus. Years before Jesus died, even before He was born, someone destined for a close relationship with Jesus faced unbelievable disappointment. This quiet carpenter lived a humble life and was betrothed to a young, godly woman named Mary. Like any Jewish man, he looked forward to the day when the one promised to him would become his wife.

Then the news came. Imagine the emotions in Joseph's heart when he heard of Mary's pregnancy! He knew he was not responsible, and the hard facts seemed to confirm that Mary must have been unfaithful.

What a devastating blow to Joseph's expectations! He knew the social consequences; people would surely talk. But it wasn't the threat of wagging tongues that bothered Joseph the most. It was the pain of having to let Mary go. His vision of the future had shattered, and no option looked good. Matthew 1:19 gives insight into the heart of this man who pondered his course of action: "Then Joseph her [betrothed] husband, being a

God has a unique plan for your life.

just man, and not wanting to make her a public example, was minded to put her away secretly."

If Joseph had been a hasty, rash, or self-centered individual, he could have loudly defended his own innocence at the expense of Mary's feelings. He could have let her reputation be ruined. In his love for her, however, he did not give personal disappointment the upper hand. Privately and quietly, he decided to break his engagement to Mary—but God soon changed his mind.

The Lord sent a special messenger to confirm Mary's extraordinary words to Joseph. It was true! Mary really was going to give birth to the Messiah; Joseph did not need to doubt that these confusing events were a part of God's plan. He obeyed immediately and brought Mary home to live with him, as a virgin, until the birth of Jesus (vv. 24, 25).

God holds your future in His hands.

God has a unique plan for your life, too, one that does not change according to unexpected circumstances. When you confront a situation that does not line up with your understanding of how God wants your life to proceed, you must stop and look to Him for direction. Sometimes God allows disappointments to occur so that you will learn to rely on Him more fully, to walk by faith and not by sight. But never forget this: while disappointments are inevitable, discouragement is a choice.

In the daily disappointments that threaten to consume your emotional resources and deflect your attention away from the Lord, you have real hope and a real choice for joy and abundant living in Christ. Circumstances do not control you; Jesus does. You never have to be the victim of your feelings. You can choose to look to God and listen, learn, and move ahead. As you do, the withered and dead-feeling places in your heart, the scars of old disappointments, will melt away in God's restoring love.

God does have blessings for you, more than you picture and in ways that you cannot imagine. Let go of disappointments and the fear of hoping and trusting again. God holds your future in His hands, and you will never lose by looking forward to what He has in store.

See the Life Principles Index for further study.

ANSWERS TO LIFE'S QUESTIONS

What can I do when my feelings go from discouraged to hopeless?

HAB. 3:17–19

If you feel hopeless, helpless, or powerless—unable to deal with people or problems and on the verge of exhaustion—take heart in the prophet Habakkuk's stirring conclusion to his short book.

Knowing that a savage army of Babylonians would soon plunder and pillage his homeland, Habakkuk recited a litany of probable destruction. Times would be hard. Food would be scarce. An agrarian culture's source of income would soon dry up and blow away (Hab. 3:17).

Yet despite this disheartening scenario, Habakkuk penned an amazing response: "Yet I will rejoice in the LORD, I will joy in the God of my salvation. The LORD God is my strength; He will make my feet like deer's feet, and he will make me walk on my high hills" (Hab. 3:18, 19).

Where did the prophet find such hope in the face of such terrible calamity? For one thing, clearly he had been spending time in God's Word. His expression of faith closely echoes the words of David, uttered centuries before: "The LORD is my rock and my fortress and my deliverer; my God, my strength, in whom I will trust; my shield and the horn of my salvation, my stronghold. I will call upon the LORD, who is worthy to be praised; so shall I be saved from my enemies" (Ps. 18:2, 3).

For another thing, Habakkuk had been spending a lot of time alone with God. His whole book is a record of his extended conversation with the Creator about the way the Lord does things. Habakkuk did not always understand (or particularly like) what he heard from God, but he recognized that the Lord knows what He's doing and so he chose to place his trust in Him.

When the outlook looks grim, Christ is your strength. When the circumstances seem volatile, Christ is your stability. When the future appears foreboding, Christ remains your hope. The strength of Christ is both inexhaustible and immeasurable—and it is yours to receive.

God delights in upholding the weary and reviving the fainthearted (Is. 40:29–31). Your reservoir of emotional and physical energy may feel nearly drained, but God's supply of spiritual stamina never runs out. Come to Him and His Word for the strength to carry on, and He will supply the power you need to traverse the rough terrain ahead. That's His promise, and God always keeps His promises.

See the Life Principles Index for further study:

2. *Obey God and leave all the consequences to Him.*
29. *We learn more in our valley experiences than on our mountaintops.*

Though the flock may be cut off from the fold,
And there be no herd in the stalls—
➤ 18 Yet I will rejoice in the LORD,
I will joy in the God of my salvation.

✳ 19 The LORD God[a] is my strength;
He will make my feet like deer's *feet*,
And He will make me walk on my high hills.

To the Chief Musician. With my stringed instruments.

3:19 [a]Hebrew *YHWH Adonai*

LIFE LESSONS

➤ **3:18 — *Yet I will rejoice in the LORD, I will joy in the God of my salvation.***

How should we respond when our situation seems dire, even hopeless? What should we do when God appears silent, even uninterested? Oftentimes, trusting God means looking beyond what we can see to what God sees.

THE BOOK OF

ZEPHANIAH

From time to time during Judah's chaotic political and religious history, reform swept the nation. Zephaniah's forceful prophecy may have been a factor in the reform that occurred during Josiah's reign—a "revival" that produced outward change but did not fully remove the heart of corruption that had come to characterize the nation.

Zephaniah repeatedly hammers home his message that "the day of the LORD"—Judgment Day—is coming like a flood, when God will deal decisively with the malignancy of sin. Israel and her Gentile neighbors will shortly experience the crushing hand of God's wrath. After the divine chastening process has run its course, however, blessing will come once more, this time in the person of the Messiah, a cause for great praise and singing.

Tsephan-yah means "Yahweh hides" or "Yahweh has hidden." Evidently Zephaniah was born during the latter part of the reign of the evil King Manasseh; his name may indicate that he was "hidden" from Manasseh's atrocities. He appears to have been a man of great social standing and may even have been related to the royal family. In any case, he demonstrates a great awareness of court life as well as knowledge of the political situation of the time.

Theme: Zephaniah memorably illustrates the "goodness and severity" of almighty God as described in Romans 11:22. The Lord will never wink at sin, but neither will He ever totally abandon His covenant people.

Author: The prophet Zephaniah, the son of Berekiah.

Time: This prophecy was given just two months after Haggai's prophecy and fifty years after the prophecy of Nahum. Zephaniah began his ministry as a prophet in the early days of the reign of King Josiah (640–609 B.C.).

Structure: The first two chapters of Zephaniah paint a grim picture of God's judgment—on the nations of the world and on Judah herself—but the final chapter focuses on the need for salvation and God's promises of restoration and salvation for His people.

As you read Zephaniah, watch for several life principles that play an important role in this book:

6. You reap what you sow, more than you sow, and later than you sow. *See Zephaniah 1:17; page 1080.*

15. Brokenness is God's requirement for maximum usefulness. *See Zephaniah 3:12; page 1082.*

1 The word of the LORD which came to
Zephaniah the son of Cushi, the son of
Gedaliah, the son of Amariah, the son of Hezekiah, in the days of Josiah the son of Amon,
king of Judah.

The Great Day of the LORD

2 "I will utterly consume everything
From the face of the land,"
Says the LORD;
3 "I will consume man and beast;
I will consume the birds of the heavens,
The fish of the sea,
And the stumbling blocks[a] along with the wicked.
I will cut off man from the face of the land,"
Says the LORD.

4 "I will stretch out My hand against Judah,
And against all the inhabitants of Jerusalem.
I will cut off every trace of Baal from this place,
The names of the idolatrous priests[a] with the *pagan* priests—
5 Those who worship the host of heaven on the housetops;
Those who worship and swear *oaths* by the LORD,
But who *also* swear by Milcom;[a]
6 Those who have turned back from *following* the LORD,
And have not sought the LORD, nor inquired of Him."

➤ 7 Be silent in the presence of the Lord GOD;
For the day of the LORD *is* at hand,
For the LORD has prepared a sacrifice;
He has invited[a] His guests.

8 "And it shall be,
In the day of the LORD's sacrifice,
That I will punish the princes and the king's children,
And all such as are clothed with foreign apparel.
9 In the same day I will punish
All those who leap over the threshold,[a]
Who fill their masters' houses with violence and deceit.

10 "And there shall be on that day," says the LORD,
"The sound of a mournful cry from the Fish Gate,
A wailing from the Second Quarter,
And a loud crashing from the hills.
11 Wail, you inhabitants of Maktesh![a]
For all the merchant people are cut down;
All those who handle money are cut off.

12 "And it shall come to pass at that time ➤
That I will search Jerusalem with lamps,
And punish the men
Who are settled in complacency,[a]
Who say in their heart,
'The LORD will not do good,
Nor will He do evil.'
13 Therefore their goods shall become booty,
And their houses a desolation;
They shall build houses, but not inhabit *them;*
They shall plant vineyards, but not drink their wine."

14 The great day of the LORD *is* near;
It is near and hastens quickly.
The noise of the day of the LORD is bitter;
There the mighty men shall cry out.
15 That day *is* a day of wrath,
A day of trouble and distress,
A day of devastation and desolation,
A day of darkness and gloominess,
A day of clouds and thick darkness,
16 A day of trumpet and alarm
Against the fortified cities
And against the high towers.

17 "I will bring distress upon men,
And they shall walk like blind men,
Because they have sinned against the LORD;
Their blood shall be poured out like dust,
And their flesh like refuse."
18 Neither their silver nor their gold
Shall be able to deliver them
In the day of the LORD's wrath;
But the whole land shall be devoured
By the fire of His jealousy,

1:3 [a]Figurative of idols **1:4** [a]Hebrew *chemarim* **1:5** [a]Or *Malcam,* an Ammonite god, also called *Molech* (compare Leviticus 18:21) **1:7** [a]Literally *set apart, consecrated* **1:9** [a]Compare 1 Samuel 5:5 **1:11** [a]Literally *Mortar,* a market district of Jerusalem **1:12** [a]Literally *on their lees,* that is, settled like the dregs of wine

LIFE LESSONS

➤ 1:7 — *Be silent in the presence of the Lord GOD . . . .*

God calls us to silence before Him for many reasons. His awesome power and glory surpass all words. To hear His voice, we need to remain quiet and carefully listen. And anticipating His mighty work stills our mouths.

➤ 1:12 — *"I will . . . punish the men who are settled in complacency, who say in their heart, 'The LORD will not do good, nor will He do evil.'"*

Complacency—a feeling of smug satisfaction—is always dangerous, especially in the spiritual realm. God may look inactive to us, but He never is. He observes, He plans, He waits—and then He acts.

For He will make speedy riddance
Of all those who dwell in the land.

A Call to Repentance

2 Gather yourselves together, yes, gather
together,
O undesirable[a] nation,
2 Before the decree is issued,
Or the day passes like chaff,
Before the LORD's fierce anger comes
upon you,
Before the day of the LORD's anger comes
upon you!
3 Seek the LORD, all you meek of the earth,
Who have upheld His justice.
Seek righteousness, seek humility.
It may be that you will be hidden
In the day of the LORD's anger.

Judgment on Nations

4 For Gaza shall be forsaken,
And Ashkelon desolate;
They shall drive out Ashdod at noonday,
And Ekron shall be uprooted.
5 Woe to the inhabitants of the seacoast,
The nation of the Cherethites!
The word of the LORD *is* against you,
O Canaan, land of the Philistines:
"I will destroy you;
So there shall be no inhabitant."

6 The seacoast shall be pastures,
With shelters[a] for shepherds and folds for
flocks.
7 The coast shall be for the remnant of the
house of Judah;
They shall feed *their* flocks there;
In the houses of Ashkelon they shall lie
down at evening.
For the LORD their God will intervene for
them,
And return their captives.

8 "I have heard the reproach of Moab,
And the insults of the people of Ammon,
With which they have reproached My
people,
And made arrogant threats against their
borders.
9 Therefore, as I live,"
Says the LORD of hosts, the God of Israel,
"Surely Moab shall be like Sodom,
And the people of Ammon like
Gomorrah—
Overrun with weeds and saltpits,
And a perpetual desolation.
The residue of My people shall plunder
them,
And the remnant of My people shall
possess them."
10 This they shall have for their pride,
Because they have reproached and made
arrogant threats
Against the people of the LORD of hosts.
11 The LORD *will be* awesome to them,
For He will reduce to nothing all the gods
of the earth;
People shall worship Him,
Each one from his place,
Indeed all the shores of the nations.

12 "You Ethiopians also,
You shall be slain by My sword."

13 And He will stretch out His hand against
the north,
Destroy Assyria,
And make Nineveh a desolation,
As dry as the wilderness.
14 The herds shall lie down in her midst,
Every beast of the nation.
Both the pelican and the bittern
Shall lodge on the capitals *of her pillars;*
Their voice shall sing in the windows;
Desolation *shall be* at the threshold;
For He will lay bare the cedar work.
15 This is the rejoicing city
That dwelt securely,
That said in her heart,
"I *am it,* and *there is* none besides me."
How has she become a desolation,
A place for beasts to lie down!
Everyone who passes by her
Shall hiss and shake his fist.

The Wickedness of Jerusalem

3 Woe to her who is rebellious and
polluted,
To the oppressing city!
2 She has not obeyed *His* voice,

2:1 [a]Or *shameless* 2:6 [a]Literally *excavations,* either underground huts or cisterns

LIFE LESSONS

➤ 2:3 — *Seek the LORD, all you meek of the earth, who have upheld His justice. Seek righteousness, seek humility.*

A genuine heart for God always results in a genuine love for people, especially for the poor and oppressed. Seeking the Lord means seeking community justice along with personal righteousness.

➤ 2:11 — *The LORD will be awesome to them, for He will reduce to nothing all the gods of the earth; people shall worship Him, each one from his place, indeed all the shores of the nations.*

The Lord wants the whole world to know Him and serve Him and worship Him and love Him. The gospel is for every kingdom, tribe, nation and tongue on earth, and God commissions us to be His ambassadors (2 Cor. 5:20).

She has not received correction;
She has not trusted in the LORD,
She has not drawn near to her God.
3 Her princes in her midst *are* roaring lions;
Her judges *are* evening wolves
That leave not a bone till morning.
4 Her prophets are insolent, treacherous people;
Her priests have polluted the sanctuary,
They have done violence to the law.
5 The LORD *is* righteous in her midst,
He will do no unrighteousness.
Every morning He brings His justice to light;
He never fails,
But the unjust knows no shame.

6 "I have cut off nations,
Their fortresses are devastated;
I have made their streets desolate,
With none passing by.
Their cities are destroyed;
There is no one, no inhabitant.
7 I said, 'Surely you will fear Me,
You will receive instruction'—
So that her dwelling would not be cut off,
Despite everything for which I punished her.
But they rose early and corrupted all their deeds.

A Faithful Remnant

8 "Therefore wait for Me," says the LORD,
"Until the day I rise up for plunder;[a]
My determination *is* to gather the nations
To My assembly of kingdoms,
To pour on them My indignation,
All My fierce anger;
All the earth shall be devoured
With the fire of My jealousy.

9 "For then I will restore to the peoples a pure language,
That they all may call on the name of the LORD,
To serve Him with one accord.
10 From beyond the rivers of Ethiopia
My worshipers,
The daughter of My dispersed ones,
Shall bring My offering.
11 In that day you shall not be shamed for any of your deeds
In which you transgress against Me;
For then I will take away from your midst
Those who rejoice in your pride,
And you shall no longer be haughty
In My holy mountain.
12 I will leave in your midst
A meek and humble people,
And they shall trust in the name of the LORD.
13 The remnant of Israel shall do no unrighteousness
And speak no lies,
Nor shall a deceitful tongue be found in their mouth;
For they shall feed *their* flocks and lie down,
And no one shall make *them* afraid."

Joy in God's Faithfulness

14 Sing, O daughter of Zion!
Shout, O Israel!
Be glad and rejoice with all *your* heart,
O daughter of Jerusalem!
15 The LORD has taken away your judgments,
He has cast out your enemy.
The King of Israel, the LORD, *is* in your midst;
You shall see[a] disaster no more.

16 In that day it shall be said to Jerusalem:
"Do not fear;
Zion, let not your hands be weak.
17 The LORD your God in your midst,
The Mighty One, will save;
He will rejoice over you with gladness,
He will quiet *you* with His love,
He will rejoice over you with singing."
18 "I will gather those who sorrow over the appointed assembly,
Who are among you,
To whom its reproach *is* a burden.
19 Behold, at that time
I will deal with all who afflict you;
I will save the lame,
And gather those who were driven out;

3:8 [a]Septuagint and Syriac read *for witness;* Targum reads *for the day of My revelation for judgment;* Vulgate reads *for the day of My resurrection that is to come.* **3:15** [a]Some Hebrew manuscripts, Septuagint, and Bomberg read *see;* Masoretic Text and Vulgate read *fear.*

LIFE LESSONS

3:9 — *"For then I will restore to the peoples a pure language, that they all may call on the name of the LORD, to serve Him with one accord."*

God multiplied human languages at Babel in order to frustrate human arrogance (Gen. 11:9), but one day He will use language to bring us together to serve Him in unity and humility. He longs for a close relationship with us!

ANSWERS TO LIFE'S QUESTIONS

How can I endure in my faith during hard times?

ZEPH. 3:17

You are God's masterpiece, and He has given you His Word as a testimony to the love and joy He has for you. Zephaniah 3:17 says: "The LORD your God in your midst, the Mighty One, will save; He will rejoice over you with gladness, He will quiet you with His love, He will rejoice over you with singing."

God rejoices over you, though He knows you are in the process of becoming all that He has planned for you to become. You are not yet what you will be when you step into the eternal presence of God (1 Cor. 13:12; 1 John 3:2). Until that time, God is patiently molding and shaping you into the image of His Son.

You never have a reason to give up (Gal. 6:9). You are not alone! Jesus is with you, cheering you on to victory. He is at your side to strengthen and encourage you. When you fix your eyes on Him and not on your circumstances, you will begin to see life differently. Instead of thinking negatively, the Holy Spirit will teach you to think about the things of God, pure thoughts that honor Jesus Christ.

God has pledged over and over to love you. He walks with you through disappointment and is never disillusioned by your wayward acts. He has seen the finished portrait! While on your own you can do nothing, He knows that through Christ you can and will succeed (Phil. 1:6; 4:13).

This does not mean that you won't suffer or feel pain. Jesus endured both, and yet He did not give up. He knew that in order to complete His mission He would have to endure until the end, and He wanted more than anything else to accomplish the Father's will.

How could He possibly bear the weight of all our sins and still remain victorious? God had given Him an eternal perspective. Long before it happened, Jesus saw the resurrection as a completed fact (Matt. 20:18, 19). And after three days, He rose again from the grave to walk in victory. God gives you such victory through the presence of the Holy Spirit.

You can walk in victory because Jesus is your example and His Spirit lives in you. Like colors on an artist's palette, God uses every frustration, fear, feeling of hopelessness, and even temptation to bring you closer to Himself.

See the Life Principles Index for further study:

12. *Peace of God is the fruit of oneness with God.*
18. *As children of a sovereign God, we are never victims of our circumstances.*

I will appoint them for praise and fame
In every land where they were put to shame.
20 At that time I will bring you back,
Even at the time I gather you;
For I will give you fame and praise
Among all the peoples of the earth,
When I return your captives before your eyes,"
Says the LORD.

THE BOOK OF
HAGGAI

With the Babylonian exile behind them, a newly returned group of Jews back in the holy land began rebuilding the temple. Sixteen years after the project got started, however, God's people had not finished it, for they had allowed their personal affairs to interfere with God's business. Because of their lapse, God withheld His natural blessings.

In response, the prophet Haggai preached a fiery series of sermonettes designed to stir up the nation to finish the temple. He called the builders to renewed courage in the Lord, renewed holiness of life, and renewed faith in the God who controls the future.

The meaning of the prophet's name, *Haggay*, is uncertain, but it may be derived from the Hebrew word *hag* ("festival"). It may also be an abbreviated form of *haggiah*, "festival of Yahweh." Thus Haggai's name probably means "festal" or "festive," perhaps because he was born on the day of a major feast, such as Tabernacles. In fact, Haggai's second message takes place during that feast (2:1).

Haggai has been called "the prophet of the temple" and possibly was born during the Babylonian captivity. He returned to Jerusalem with Zerubbabel, the governor of Jerusalem.

Haggai's stern call to duty proved to be just what the people of Judah needed to motivate them to finish what they had started. In response to the prophet's challenge, Joshua the high priest, Zerubbabel, and the rest of the people got busy and set about restoring the temple.

Theme: Haggai rebukes the people for failing to finish God's work and promises His blessings for completing it.

Author: Haggai.

Time: The events narrated in Haggai take place several years after the end of the Babylonian captivity (520–516 B.C.).

Structure: The book is built around four sermons. In the first message, Haggai called the people to rebuild the temple, and they responded (1:1–15). In the second, Haggai predicted that the rebuilt temple would be filled with God's glory (2:1–9). In the third, the prophet decried the people's sin and declared how God would bless obedience (2:10–19). In the fourth, Haggai encouraged Zerubbabel with prophesies of blessing for his obedience (2:20–23).

As you read Haggai, watch for several life principles that play an important role in this book:

11. God assumes full responsibility for our needs when we obey Him. *See Haggai 2:3–9; page 1085.*

21. Obedience always brings blessing. *See Haggai 2:15–19; page 1087.*

4. The awareness of God's presence energizes us for our work. *See Haggai 2:21–23; page 1088.*

The Command to Build God's House

1 In the second year of King Darius, in the
sixth month, on the first day of the month,
the word of the LORD came by Haggai the
prophet to Zerubbabel the son of Shealtiel,
governor of Judah, and to Joshua the son of
Jehozadak, the high priest, saying,
2 "Thus speaks the LORD of hosts, saying:
'This people says, "The time has not come, the
time that the LORD's house should be built."'"
3 Then the word of the LORD came by Haggai the prophet, saying,
4 "*Is it* time for you yourselves to dwell in
your paneled houses, and this temple[a] *to lie* in
ruins?"
5 Now therefore, thus says the LORD of hosts:
"Consider your ways!

6 "You have sown much, and bring in little;
You eat, but do not have enough;
You drink, but you are not filled with
drink;
You clothe yourselves, but no one is
warm;
And he who earns wages,
Earns wages *to put* into a bag with holes."

➤ 7 Thus says the LORD of hosts: "Consider
your ways!
8 "Go up to the mountains and bring wood
and build the temple, that I may take pleasure
in it and be glorified," says the LORD.
9 "*You* looked for much, but indeed *it came
to* little; and when you brought it home, I
blew it away. Why?" says the LORD of hosts.
"Because of My house that *is in* ruins, while
every one of you runs to his own house.
10 "Therefore the heavens above you withhold the dew, and the earth withholds its fruit.
11 "For I called for a drought on the land and
the mountains, on the grain and the new wine
and the oil, on whatever the ground brings
forth, on men and livestock, and on all the
labor of *your* hands."

The People's Obedience

12 Then Zerubbabel the son of Shealtiel, and
Joshua the son of Jehozadak, the high priest,
with all the remnant of the people, obeyed the
voice of the LORD their God, and the words of
Haggai the prophet, as the LORD their God
had sent him; and the people feared the presence of the LORD.
13 Then Haggai, the LORD's messenger,
spoke the LORD's message to the people, saying, "I *am* with you, says the LORD."
14 So the LORD stirred up the spirit of Zerubbabel the son of Shealtiel, governor of Judah,
and the spirit of Joshua the son of Jehozadak,
the high priest, and the spirit of all the remnant of the people; and they came and
worked on the house of the LORD of hosts,
their God,
15 on the twenty-fourth day of the sixth
month, in the second year of King Darius.

The Coming Glory of God's House

2 In the seventh *month,* on the twenty-first
of the month, the word of the LORD came
by Haggai the prophet, saying:
2 "Speak now to Zerubbabel the son of Shealtiel, governor of Judah, and to Joshua the
son of Jehozadak, the high priest, and to the
remnant of the people, saying:
3 'Who is left among you who saw this temple[a] in its former glory? And how do you see
it now? In comparison with it, *is this* not in
your eyes as nothing?
4 'Yet now be strong, Zerubbabel,' says the
LORD; 'and be strong, Joshua, son of Jehozadak, the high priest; and be strong, all
you people of the land,' says the LORD, 'and
work; for I *am* with you,' says the LORD of
hosts.
5 '*According to* the word that I covenanted
with you when you came out of Egypt, so My
Spirit remains among you; do not fear!'
6 "For thus says the LORD of hosts: 'Once
more (it *is* a little while) I will shake heaven
and earth, the sea and dry land;

1:4 [a]Literally *house,* and so in verse 8 **2:3** [a]Literally *house,* and so in verses 7 and 9

LIFE LESSONS

➤ 1:7 — *Thus says the Lord of hosts: "Consider your ways!"*

We ought to stop and periodically review our lives in light of God's Word. Very often this is all it would take to alert us to a dangerous trend or to confirm that we're heading in the right direction.

➤ 1:13 — *Then Haggai, the LORD's messenger, spoke the LORD's message to the people, saying, "I am with you, says the LORD."*

The Holy Spirit empowers us to carry out God's commands. He gives us the courage, strength, and ability we need. Do not hesitate to obey God in the midst of your trouble. He will equip you to carry out His command.

➤ 2:3 — *"Who is left among you who saw this temple in its former glory? And how do you see it now? In comparison with it, is this not in your eyes as nothing?"*

God knows we tend to compare our current circumstances with what went before, and to long for "the good old days." But He wants us to fix our eyes on Him and the still greater things He has planned for us.

➤ 2:4 — *". . . be strong, all you people of the land," says the LORD, "and work; for I am with you."*

We can work hard and effectively for the Lord when we remember that He has promised to be with us. The awareness of God's presence energizes us for our work.

WHAT THE BIBLE SAYS ABOUT SPIRITUAL SHORTSIGHTEDNESS IN GIVING

Hag. 1:2–11

It is no secret that over the past several years, a bear market has mauled many retirement accounts. Whether 401(k)s or IRAs, these savings accounts have been decimated by an unfortunate combination of market forces. Too many shortsighted people assumed that the expanding bull market of the 90s would last forever. Now these supposedly "safe havens" have turned out to be what the Bible calls "a bag with holes" (Hag. 1:6).

The market forces of Haggai's day differed considerably from those of today, but shortsightedness plagued God's people just as much then as it does now. Their experience illustrates the modern saying, "the faster I go, the behinder I get." The Lord put it this way: "You looked for much, but indeed it came to little; and when you brought it home, I blew it away. Why? . . . Because of My house that is in ruins, while every one of you runs to his own house" (Hag. 1:9).

> **"Every one of you runs to his own house."**

The problem came down to this: God's people assumed that they could put their own financial interests ahead of God's and still prosper financially. But the Lord had warned against this kind of flawed thinking long before: "Do not overwork to be rich; because of your own understanding, cease! Will you set your eyes on that which is not? For riches certainly make themselves wings; they fly away like an eagle toward heaven" (Prov. 23:4, 5).

A similar thing took place in Malachi's day. When the people failed to bring their tithes and offerings, God called it robbery and cursed their investments. He admonished them to "bring all the tithes into the storehouse" so he could open the windows of heaven and pour abundant prosperity upon them (Mal. 3:10).

We simply cannot afford shortsighted investment strategies that rob God of His due. So the apostle Paul reminds us, "He who sows sparingly will also reap sparingly, and he who sows bountifully will also reap bountifully. So let each one give as he purposes in his heart, not grudgingly or of necessity; for God loves a cheerful giver" (2 Cor. 9:6, 7).

See the Life Principles Index for further study:
23. You can never outgive God.

ANSWERS TO LIFE'S QUESTIONS

How can I feel secure in the Lord during troubled times?

HAG. 2:4

Of one thing you can be certain in any time of trouble, suffering, hardship, difficulty, pain, or tragedy: The Lord is with you! Time and again in His Word, the Lord assures you of His presence:

- "The LORD is with you while you are with Him. If you seek Him, He will be found by you" (2 Chr. 15:2).
- "Stand still and see the salvation of the LORD, who is with you . . . . Do not fear or be dismayed" (2 Chr. 20:17).
- "Do not be afraid of him," says the LORD, "for I am with you, to save you and deliver you from his hand" (Jer. 42:11).
- "Be strong, all you people of the land," says the LORD, "and work; for I am with you" (Hag. 2:4).

Jesus said the same thing to His disciples: "I am with you always" (Matt. 28:20).

The apostle Paul considered this truth and asked, "If God is for us, who can be against us?" (Rom. 8:31). Don't answer his question too quickly! For the truth is, many people can rise up against us. They can cheat us, harass us, persecute us, insult us, mock us, physically injure us, even kill us. But here's the point: *In the end, they can never win.* That is why Jesus could say, "You will be betrayed even by parents and brothers, relatives, and friends; and they will put some of you to death. And you will be hated by all for My name's sake. But not a hair of your head shall be lost" (Luke 21:16–18). If you belong to God, you are on the winning side. Period.

When rough times come, immerse yourself in God's Word. Read His promises to you, His beloved child. Read about His power, His strength, His wisdom, and His love. Read how He has helped countless men and women through the ages as they trusted in Him. Read about His saving, delivering, and restoring power.

The more you read and study God's Word, the stronger your faith will grow.

The more you trust God, the more you will grow in your understanding that He is trustworthy in all things, at all times.

The more you take courage in the Lord's presence with you, the more secure you will feel . . . even in the most troubling of times and the most trying of circumstances.

The Lord alone is your security, every moment of your life.

See the Life Principles Index for further study:
4. *The awareness of God's presence energizes us for our work.*

7 'and I will shake all nations, and they shall
come to the Desire of All Nations,[a] and I will
fill this temple with glory,' says the LORD of
hosts.
8 'The silver *is* Mine, and the gold *is* Mine,'
says the LORD of hosts.
9 'The glory of this latter temple shall be
greater than the former,' says the LORD of
hosts. 'And in this place I will give peace,'
says the LORD of hosts."

The People Are Defiled

10 On the twenty-fourth *day* of the ninth
month, in the second year of Darius, the word
of the LORD came by Haggai the prophet, saying,
11 "Thus says the LORD of hosts: 'Now, ask
the priests *concerning the* law, saying,
12 "If one carries holy meat in the fold of his
garment, and with the edge he touches bread
or stew, wine or oil, or any food, will it become holy?"'" Then the priests answered and
said, "No."
13 And Haggai said, "If *one who is* unclean
because of a dead body touches any of these,
will it be unclean?" So the priests answered
and said, "It shall be unclean."
14 Then Haggai answered and said, "'So is
this people, and so is this nation before Me,'
says the LORD, 'and so is every work of their
hands; and what they offer there is unclean.

Promised Blessing

15 'And now, carefully consider from this day
forward: from before stone was laid upon
stone in the temple of the LORD—
16 'since those *days,* when *one* came to a heap
of twenty ephahs, there were *but* ten; when
one came to the wine vat to draw out fifty
baths from the press, there were *but* twenty.

2:7 [a]Or *the desire of all nations*

17 'I struck you with blight and mildew and
hail in all the labors of your hands; yet you
did not *turn* to Me,' says the LORD.
18 'Consider now from this day forward,
from the twenty-fourth day of the ninth
month, from the day that the foundation of
the LORD's temple was laid—consider it:
➤ 19 'Is the seed still in the barn? As yet the
vine, the fig tree, the pomegranate, and the
olive tree have not yielded *fruit. But* from this
day I will bless *you.*'"

Zerubbabel Chosen as a Signet

20 And again the word of the LORD came to
Haggai on the twenty-fourth day of the
month, saying,
21 "Speak to Zerubbabel, governor of Judah,
saying:

'I will shake heaven and earth.
22 I will overthrow the throne of kingdoms;
I will destroy the strength of the Gentile
kingdoms.
I will overthrow the chariots
And those who ride in them;
The horses and their riders shall come
down,
Every one by the sword of his brother.

23 'In that day,' says the LORD of hosts, 'I will
take you, Zerubbabel My servant, the son of
Shealtiel,' says the LORD, 'and will make you
like a signet *ring;* for I have chosen you,' says
the LORD of hosts."

LIFE LESSONS

➤ **2:19 — *"Is the seed still in the barn? As yet the vine, the fig tree, the pomegranate, and the olive tree have not yielded fruit. But from this day I will bless you."***

God asks for our obedience today so that He may bless us tomorrow. God's blessings for obedience usually do not appear as soon as we obey; He's not a candy machine. But God works for those who wait for Him.

THE BOOK OF

ZECHARIAH

For a dozen years or more, the task of rebuilding the temple had remained only half completed. God commissioned Zechariah to encourage the people to complete their unfinished responsibility.

Zechariah sought to motivate his countrymen to the work by reminding them of the future importance of the temple. The temple must be built, for one day the Messiah's glory will inhabit it. Future blessing, however, depended upon present obedience. The people needed to remember that they were not merely building a facility; they were building the future. With that as their motivation, they could enter into the project with wholehearted zeal, for their Messiah is coming.

While Zechariah and his prophetic colleague, Haggai, prophesied regarding the same issue—the unfinished temple—they took very different approaches. Haggai tended to reprimand the people with strong words of rebuke, while Zechariah sought to encourage them. God inspired both approaches, working together, to urge and to coax His people into the kind of obedience that could attract His blessing. The "tag-team" of Haggai and Zechariah thus represents a common pairing found all the way through God's Word: cursing and blessing, threat and promise, warning and reward, the stick and the carrot. God uses both negative and positive means to motivate His people to willing obedience.

Zechariah contains a number of important Messianic prophecies, including: the Messiah's coming into Jerusalem on what we know as Palm Sunday (Zech. 9:9); the amount of money paid to the betrayer of the Messiah (11:12, 13); the death of Christ and the scattering of His disciples (13:7); the return of Christ (12:10–13); the rule of Christ (14:5–9).

The Hebrew name of the prophet, *Zekar-yah*, means "Yahweh remembers" or "Yahweh has remembered." This theme of divine remembrance dominates the whole Book of Zechariah: Israel will be blessed because Yahweh remembers the covenant He made with their fathers. The Greek and Latin version of the prophet's name is *Zacharias.*

Theme: God equips and strengthens us to do the work He calls us to do.

Author: Zechariah.

Time: Zechariah began his prophetic ministry about two months after Haggai (c. 520 B.C.), and may have continued into the reign of Artaxerxes I (465–424 B.C.).

Structure: The first eight chapters of Zechariah focus on the importance of finishing the uncompleted temple. The final six chapters focus on promises of blessing once work on the temple is finished.

As you read Zechariah, watch for several life principles that play an important role in this book:

4. The awareness of God's presence energizes us for our work. *See Zechariah 2:10–12; page 1091.*

9. Trusting God means looking beyond what we can see to what God sees. *See Zechariah 4:6–10; page 1093.*

21. Obedience always brings blessing. *See Zechariah 8:9–17; page 1095.*

A Call to Repentance

1 In the eighth month of the second year of
Darius, the word of the LORD came to
Zechariah the son of Berechiah, the son of
Iddo the prophet, saying,
2 "The LORD has been very angry with your
fathers.
➤3 "Therefore say to them, 'Thus says the
LORD of hosts: "Return to Me," says the LORD
of hosts, "and I will return to you," says the
LORD of hosts.
4 "Do not be like your fathers, to whom the
former prophets preached, saying, 'Thus says
the LORD of hosts: "Turn now from your evil
ways and your evil deeds."' But they did not
hear nor heed Me," says the LORD.

5 "Your fathers, where *are* they?
And the prophets, do they live forever?
6 Yet surely My words and My statutes,
Which I commanded My servants the prophets,
Did they not overtake your fathers?

"So they returned and said:

'Just as the LORD of hosts determined to do to us,
According to our ways and according to our deeds,
So He has dealt with us.'"'"

Vision of the Horses

7 On the twenty-fourth day of the eleventh
month, which is the month Shebat, in the second year of Darius, the word of the LORD
came to Zechariah the son of Berechiah, the
son of Iddo the prophet:
8 I saw by night, and behold, a man riding
on a red horse, and it stood among the myrtle
trees in the hollow; and behind him *were*
horses: red, sorrel, and white.
9 Then I said, "My lord, what *are* these?" So
the angel who talked with me said to me, "I
will show you what they *are*."
10 And the man who stood among the myrtle
trees answered and said, "These *are the ones*
whom the LORD has sent to walk to and fro
throughout the earth."
11 So they answered the Angel of the LORD,
who stood among the myrtle trees, and said,
"We have walked to and fro throughout the
earth, and behold, all the earth is resting quietly."

The LORD Will Comfort Zion

12 Then the Angel of the LORD answered and
said, "O LORD of hosts, how long will You not
have mercy on Jerusalem and on the cities of
Judah, against which You were angry these
seventy years?"
13 And the LORD answered the angel who
talked to me, *with* good *and* comforting
words.
14 So the angel who spoke with me said to
me, "Proclaim, saying, 'Thus says the LORD of
hosts:

"I am zealous for Jerusalem
And for Zion with great zeal.
15 I am exceedingly angry with the nations at ease;
For I was a little angry,
And they helped—*but* with evil *intent*."

16 'Therefore thus says the LORD:

"I am returning to Jerusalem with mercy;
My house shall be built in it," says the LORD of hosts,
"And a *surveyor's* line shall be stretched out over Jerusalem."'

17 "Again proclaim, saying, 'Thus says the ➤
LORD of hosts:

"My cities shall again spread out through prosperity;
The LORD will again comfort Zion,
And will again choose Jerusalem."'"

Vision of the Horns

18 Then I raised my eyes and looked, and
there *were* four horns.
19 And I said to the angel who talked with
me, "What *are* these?" So he answered me,
"These *are* the horns that have scattered Judah, Israel, and Jerusalem."
20 Then the LORD showed me four craftsmen.
21 And I said, "What are these coming to
do?" So he said, "These *are* the horns that
scattered Judah, so that no one could lift up
his head; but the craftsmen[a] are coming to
terrify them, to cast out the horns of the nations that lifted up *their* horn against the land
of Judah to scatter it."

1:21 [a]Literally *these*

LIFE LESSONS

➤ 1:3 — *"Return to Me," says the LORD of hosts, "and I will return to you . . . ."*

If we want peace with God, we must get on the same page with Him—and often that requires our repentance. The New Testament agrees: "Draw near to God and He will draw near to you" (James 4:8).

➤ 1:17 — *"The LORD will again comfort Zion, and will again choose Jerusalem."*

God judged Israel, not to vent His anger, but to bring the hearts of His people back to Him. Brokenness is God's requirement for maximum usefulness.

Vision of the Measuring Line

2 Then I raised my eyes and looked, and
behold, a man with a measuring line in his
hand.
2 So I said, "Where are you going?" And he
said to me, "To measure Jerusalem, to see
what *is* its width and what *is* its length."
3 And there *was* the angel who talked with
me, going out; and another angel was coming
out to meet him,
4 who said to him, "Run, speak to this young
man, saying: 'Jerusalem shall be inhabited *as*
towns without walls, because of the multitude
of men and livestock in it.
➤ 5 'For I,' says the LORD, 'will be a wall of fire
all around her, and I will be the glory in her
midst.'"

Future Joy of Zion and Many Nations

6 "Up, up! Flee from the land of the north,"
says the LORD; "for I have spread you abroad
like the four winds of heaven," says the LORD.
7 "Up, Zion! Escape, you who dwell with the
daughter of Babylon."
8 "For thus says the LORD of hosts: "He sent
Me after glory, to the nations which plunder
you; for he who touches you touches the apple of His eye.
9 "For surely I will shake My hand against
them, and they shall become spoil for their
servants. Then you will know that the LORD of
hosts has sent Me.
✳ **10** "Sing and rejoice, O daughter of Zion! For
➤ behold, I am coming and I will dwell in your
midst," says the LORD.
➤ 11 "Many nations shall be joined to the LORD
in that day, and they shall become My people.
And I will dwell in your midst. Then you will
know that the LORD of hosts has sent Me to
you.
12 "And the LORD will take possession of Judah as His inheritance in the Holy Land, and
will again choose Jerusalem.
13 "Be silent, all flesh, before the LORD, for
He is aroused from His holy habitation!"

Vision of the High Priest

3 Then he showed me Joshua the high priest ➤
standing before the Angel of the LORD,
and Satan standing at his right hand to oppose him.
2 And the LORD said to Satan, "The LORD rebuke you, Satan! The LORD who has chosen
Jerusalem rebuke you! *Is* this not a brand
plucked from the fire?"
3 Now Joshua was clothed with filthy garments, and was standing before the Angel.
4 Then He answered and spoke to those ➤
who stood before Him, saying, "Take away
the filthy garments from him." And to him He
said, "See, I have removed your iniquity from
you, and I will clothe you with rich robes."
5 And I said, "Let them put a clean turban
on his head." So they put a clean turban on
his head, and they put the clothes on him.
And the Angel of the LORD stood by.

The Coming Branch

6 Then the Angel of the LORD admonished
Joshua, saying,
7 "Thus says the LORD of hosts:

'If you will walk in My ways,
And if you will keep My command,
Then you shall also judge My house,
And likewise have charge of My courts;
I will give you places to walk
Among these who stand here.

8 'Hear, O Joshua, the high priest,
You and your companions who sit before
you,
For they are a wondrous sign;
For behold, I am bringing forth My
Servant the BRANCH.
9 For behold, the stone
That I have laid before Joshua:

LIFE LESSONS

➤ 2:5 — *"For I," says the LORD, "will be a wall of fire all around her, and I will be the glory in her midst."*

We can trust God's promises because He puts His heart and His soul and His infinite power into making sure they come to pass, just as He promised.

➤ 2:10 — *"Sing and rejoice, O daughter of Zion! For behold, I am coming and I will dwell in your midst," says the LORD.*

When we know that God is with us and that He desires to enjoy intimate fellowship with us, how can we not break out in song and rejoice with all our hearts?

➤ 2:11 — *"Many nations shall be joined to the LORD in that day, and they shall become My people."*

It has always been the Lord's plan to redeem people to God by the blood of Christ from "every tribe and tongue and people and nation" (Rev. 5:9). His love covers the world!

➤ 3:1 — *Then he showed me Joshua the high priest standing before the Angel of the LORD, and Satan standing at his right hand to oppose him.*

The Bible calls Satan "the accuser of our brethren," who opposes God's people "before God day and night" (Rev. 12:10). But thank God, we also "have an Advocate with the Father, Jesus Christ the righteous" (1 John 2:1).

➤ 3:4 — *"Take away the filthy garments from him." And to him He said, "See, I have removed your iniquity from you, and I will clothe you with rich robes."*

God says, "put off the old man with his deeds," and "put on the new man who is renewed in knowledge according to the image of Him who created him" (Col. 3:9, 10). We must wear Jesus like a garment.

ANSWERS TO LIFE'S QUESTIONS

How can I avoid burnout in doing God's work?

ZECH. 4:6, 7

God called Zerubbabel to do an important job, namely, finish rebuilding the Jerusalem temple. A group of Israelites had been released from captivity to return home to accomplish the monumental task. But when they ran into some opposition, they abandoned the project. For fifteen years the work came to a standstill.

Do you ever wonder how people serving the living God could become so discouraged or distracted that they would throw in the towel and walk away? In most cases, it seems to make little sense. Sure, there are pressures. But anybody with responsibility is going to face some pressure.

I believe there is a common denominator. Many of God's servants don't do God's work in God's way. Consequently, they are doomed to failure from the outset.

God knew that Zerubbabel and his team, like their predecessors, would face opposition. To prepare them for what lay ahead, He encouraged them through the prophet Zechariah: "This is the word of the LORD to Zerubbabel: 'Not by might nor by power, but by My Spirit,' says the LORD of hosts. 'What are you, O great mountain? Before Zerubbabel you will become a plain; and he will bring forth the top stone with shouts of "Grace, grace to it!"' (Zech. 4:6, 7).

This was God's way of saying to Zerubbabel, "The work *can* be completed. There are no immovable obstacles, when you do things My way and by My Spirit. And when it's finished, there will be a big celebration."

There are two ways to approach God's work. First, you can do it in the flesh. Doing God's work in the flesh boils down to depending on influence, personality, gifts, natural resources, education, and experience. Or second, you can carry it out under the direction of and in the power of the Holy Spirit. That's God's way.

When we do God's work in God's way, it will bear the unmistakable mark of the Holy Spirit. There will be something inexplicable about it. People will know that what has happened can never be repeated simply by bringing the right components together. The whole is divinely greater than the sum of the parts.

All of us who know the Lord—homemakers, bankers, mechanics, assembly line workers, construction workers—are involved in God's work. We are all a part of what He is doing. And we all need to do God's work in God's way.

See the Life Principles Index for further study:
24. To live the Christian life is to allow Jesus to live His life in and through us.

Upon the stone *are* seven eyes.
Behold, I will engrave its inscription,'
Says the LORD of hosts,
'And I will remove the iniquity of that
land in one day.
10 In that day,' says the LORD of hosts,
'Everyone will invite his neighbor
Under his vine and under his fig tree.'"

Vision of the Lampstand and Olive Trees

4 Now the angel who talked with me came
back and wakened me, as a man who is
wakened out of his sleep.
2 And he said to me, "What do you see?" So
I said, "I am looking, and there *is* a lampstand
of solid gold with a bowl on top of it, and on
the *stand* seven lamps with seven pipes to the
seven lamps.
3 "Two olive trees *are* by it, one at the right
of the bowl and the other at its left."
4 So I answered and spoke to the angel who
talked with me, saying, "What *are* these, my
lord?"
5 Then the angel who talked with me answered and said to me, "Do you not know
what these are?" And I said, "No, my lord."

LIFE LESSONS

➤ **4:5 — *Then the angel who talked with me answered and said to me, "Do you not know what these are?" And I said, "No, my lord."***

Never be afraid to admit your ignorance. When you come to a passage in the Bible that you don't understand, ask God to enlighten your mind. He loves to reveal His Word to those eager to hear and obey.

6 So he answered and said to me:
"This *is* the word of the LORD to
Zerubbabel:
'Not by might nor by power, but by My
Spirit,'
Says the LORD of hosts.
7 'Who *are* you, O great mountain?
Before Zerubbabel *you shall become* a
plain!
And he shall bring forth the capstone
With shouts of "Grace, grace to it!"'"

8 Moreover the word of the LORD came to me, saying:

9 "The hands of Zerubbabel
Have laid the foundation of this temple;[a]
His hands shall also finish *it*.
Then you will know
That the LORD of hosts has sent Me to you.
➤ 10 For who has despised the day of small
things?
For these seven rejoice to see
The plumb line in the hand of
Zerubbabel.
They are the eyes of the LORD,
Which scan to and fro throughout the
whole earth."

11 Then I answered and said to him, "What *are* these two olive trees—at the right of the lampstand and at its left?"
12 And I further answered and said to him, "What *are these* two olive branches that *drip* into the receptacles[a] of the two gold pipes from which the golden *oil* drains?"
13 Then he answered me and said, "Do you not know what these *are?*" And I said, "No, my lord."
14 So he said, "These *are* the two anointed ones, who stand beside the Lord of the whole earth."

Vision of the Flying Scroll

5 Then I turned and raised my eyes, and saw there a flying scroll.
2 And he said to me, "What do you see?" So I answered, "I see a flying scroll. Its length *is* twenty cubits and its width ten cubits."
3 Then he said to me, "This *is* the curse that goes out over the face of the whole earth: 'Every thief shall be expelled,' according *to* this side of *the scroll;* and, 'Every perjurer shall be expelled,' according *to* that side of it."

4 "I will send out *the curse,*" says the LORD
of hosts;
"It shall enter the house of the thief
And the house of the one who swears
falsely by My name.
It shall remain in the midst of his
house
And consume it, with its timber and
stones."

Vision of the Woman in a Basket

5 Then the angel who talked with me came out and said to me, "Lift your eyes now, and see what this *is* that goes forth."
6 So I asked, "What *is* it?" And he said, "It *is* a basket[a] that is going forth." He also said, "This *is* their resemblance throughout the earth:
7 "Here *is* a lead disc lifted up, and this *is* a woman sitting inside the basket";
8 then he said, "This *is* Wickedness!" And he thrust her down into the basket, and threw the lead cover[a] over its mouth.
9 Then I raised my eyes and looked, and there *were* two women, coming with the wind in their wings; for they had wings like the wings of a stork, and they lifted up the basket between earth and heaven.
10 So I said to the angel who talked with me, "Where are they carrying the basket?"
11 And he said to me, "To build a house for it in the land of Shinar;[a] when it is ready, *the basket* will be set there on its base."

Vision of the Four Chariots

6 Then I turned and raised my eyes and looked, and behold, four chariots *were* coming from between two mountains, and the mountains *were* mountains of bronze.
2 With the first chariot *were* red horses, with the second chariot black horses,
3 with the third chariot white horses, and with the fourth chariot dappled horses—strong *steeds.*
4 Then I answered and said to the angel who talked with me, "What *are* these, my lord?"
5 And the angel answered and said to me, "These *are* four spirits of heaven, who go out from *their* station before the Lord of all the earth.
6 "The one with the black horses is going to

4:9 [a]Literally *house* **4:12** [a]Literally *into the hands of*
5:6 [a]Hebrew *ephah,* a measuring container, and so elsewhere
5:8 [a]Literally *stone* **5:11** [a]That is, Babylon

LIFE LESSONS

➤ 4:10 — *"For who has despised the day of small things?"*

Never despise the "small" things God asks you to do, for a basic principle of spiritual growth is that God gives "bigger" and "greater" things and responsibilities to those who faithfully handle the "small things" (see Luke 16:10).

Life Examples:

JOSHUA

A Picture of the Messiah

ZECH. 6:9–13

The high priests of Israel had always worn turbans, not ornate crowns. But in the days of the prophet Zechariah, God commanded that a kingly crown of silver and gold be made for Joshua the high priest and that it be set upon his head.

Furthermore, the Lord said through the prophet, "He shall bear the glory, and shall sit and rule on His throne; so He shall be a priest on His throne, and the counsel of peace shall be between them both" (Zech. 6:13).

From earliest times, ancient Jews recognized this passage as a prophecy of the Messiah to come. In the Messiah, both the priestly and the royal lines would merge—something unprecedented and unique. So the high priest, Joshua (whose name means "God saves") provided a compelling picture of the greater Savior to come, Jesus (a different form of the same name).

See the Life Principles Index for further study:
3. God's Word is an immovable anchor in times of storm.

the north country, the white are going after them, and the dappled are going toward the south country."

7 Then the strong *steeds* went out, eager to go, that they might walk to and fro throughout the earth. And He said, "Go, walk to and fro throughout the earth." So they walked to and fro throughout the earth.

8 And He called to me, and spoke to me, saying, "See, those who go toward the north country have given rest to My Spirit in the north country."

The Command to Crown Joshua

9 Then the word of the LORD came to me, saying:

10 "Receive *the gift* from the captives—from Heldai, Tobijah, and Jedaiah, who have come from Babylon—and go the same day and enter the house of Josiah the son of Zephaniah.

11 "Take the silver and gold, make an elaborate crown, and set *it* on the head of Joshua the son of Jehozadak, the high priest.

12 "Then speak to him, saying, 'Thus says the LORD of hosts, saying:

"Behold, the Man whose name *is* the
BRANCH!
From His place He shall branch out,
And He shall build the temple of the
LORD;
13 Yes, He shall build the temple of the
LORD.
He shall bear the glory,
And shall sit and rule on His throne;
So He shall be a priest on His throne,
And the counsel of peace shall be
between them both."'

14 "Now the elaborate crown shall be for a memorial in the temple of the LORD for Helem,[a] Tobijah, Jedaiah, and Hen the son of Zephaniah.

15 "Even those from afar shall come and build the temple of the LORD. Then you shall know that the LORD of hosts has sent Me to you. And *this* shall come to pass if you diligently obey the voice of the LORD your God."

Obedience Better than Fasting

7 Now in the fourth year of King Darius it came to pass *that* the word of the LORD came to Zechariah, on the fourth *day* of the ninth month, Chislev,

2 when *the people*[a] sent Sherezer,[b] with Regem-Melech and his men, *to* the house of God,[c] to pray before the LORD,

3 *and* to ask the priests who *were* in the house of the LORD of hosts, and the prophets, saying, "Should I weep in the fifth month and fast as I have done for so many years?"

4 Then the word of the LORD of hosts came to me, saying,

6:14 [a]Following Masoretic Text, Targum, and Vulgate; Syriac reads *for Heldai* (compare verse 10); Septuagint reads *for the patient ones.* **7:2** [a]Literally *they* (compare verse 5) [b]Or *Sar-Ezer* [c]Hebrew *Bethel*

LIFE LESSONS

➤ 6:15 — *"And this shall come to pass if you diligently obey the voice of the LORD your God."*

Many of God's promises, in both Old and New Testaments, are conditional. When you see the word "if," understand that God is making His action contingent upon your obedience.

➤ 5 "Say to all the people of the land, and to
the priests: 'When you fasted and mourned in
the fifth and seventh *months* during those
seventy years, did you really fast for Me—for
Me?
6 'When you eat and when you drink, do
you not eat and drink *for yourselves?*
7 '*Should you* not *have obeyed* the words
which the LORD proclaimed through the former prophets when Jerusalem and the cities
around it were inhabited and prosperous, and
the South[a] and the Lowland were inhabited?'"

Disobedience Resulted in Captivity

8 Then the word of the LORD came to
Zechariah, saying,
➤ 9 "Thus says the LORD of hosts:

'Execute true justice,
Show mercy and compassion
Everyone to his brother.
10 Do not oppress the widow or the fatherless,
The alien or the poor.
Let none of you plan evil in his heart
Against his brother.'

11 "But they refused to heed, shrugged their
shoulders, and stopped their ears so that they
could not hear.
12 "Yes, they made their hearts like flint, refusing to hear the law and the words which
the LORD of hosts had sent by His Spirit
through the former prophets. Thus great
wrath came from the LORD of hosts.
13 "Therefore it happened, *that* just as He
proclaimed and they would not hear, so they
called out and I would not listen," says the
LORD of hosts.
14 "But I scattered them with a whirlwind
among all the nations which they had not
known. Thus the land became desolate after
them, so that no one passed through or returned; for they made the pleasant land desolate."

Jerusalem, Holy City of the Future

8 Again the word of the LORD of hosts came,
saying,
2 "Thus says the LORD of hosts:

'I am zealous for Zion with great zeal;
With great fervor I am zealous for her.'

3 "Thus says the LORD:

'I will return to Zion,
And dwell in the midst of Jerusalem.
Jerusalem shall be called the City of Truth,
The Mountain of the LORD of hosts,
The Holy Mountain.'

4 "Thus says the LORD of hosts:

'Old men and old women shall again sit
In the streets of Jerusalem,
Each one with his staff in his hand
Because of great age.
5 The streets of the city
Shall be full of boys and girls
Playing in its streets.'

6 "Thus says the LORD of hosts: ◄

'If it is marvelous in the eyes of the remnant of this people in these days,
Will it also be marvelous in My eyes?'
Says the LORD of hosts.

7 "Thus says the LORD of hosts:

'Behold, I will save My people from the land of the east
And from the land of the west;
8 I will bring them *back*,
And they shall dwell in the midst of Jerusalem.
They shall be My people
And I will be their God,
In truth and righteousness.'

9 "Thus says the LORD of hosts: ◄

7:7 [a]Hebrew *Negev*

LIFE LESSONS

➤ 7:5 — *"When you fasted and mourned in the fifth and seventh months during those seventy years, did you really fast for Me—for Me?"*

God is not interested in religious observance or sacred ritual apart from a genuine, heart-felt, intimate relationship with Him. Our intimacy with God determines the impact of our lives.

➤ 7:9 — *"Thus says the LORD of hosts: 'Execute true justice, show mercy and compassion everyone to his brother.'"*

A genuine and dynamic relationship with God leads naturally to genuine and dynamic relationships with others, in which you seek their best and treat them as you would like to be treated.

➤ 8:6 — *"Thus says the LORD of hosts: 'If it is marvelous in the eyes of the remnant of this people in these days, will it also be marvelous in My eyes?'"*

What we call miracles, God calls just another day at the office. What looks impossible to us is very easy for the Lord. That is why we can trust Him no matter how difficult our situation may seem.

➤ 8:9 — *"Let your hands be strong, you who have been hearing in these days these words by the mouth of the prophets . . . ."*

If you feel weak and need a shot of spiritual strength, determine right now to spend some extended time in the Scriptures. God delights to give us strength through His Word—but we have to be taking it in.

'Let your hands be strong,
You who have been hearing in these days
These words by the mouth of the prophets,
Who *spoke* in the day the foundation was laid
For the house of the LORD of hosts,
That the temple might be built.
10 For before these days
There were no wages for man nor any hire for beast;
There was no peace from the enemy for whoever went out or came in;
For I set all men, everyone, against his neighbor.

11 'But now I *will* not *treat* the remnant of
this people as in the former days,' says the
LORD of hosts.

12 'For the seed *shall be* prosperous,
The vine shall give its fruit,
The ground shall give her increase,
And the heavens shall give their dew—
I will cause the remnant of this people
To possess all these.
13 And it shall come to pass
That just as you were a curse among the nations,
O house of Judah and house of Israel,
So I will save you, and you shall be a blessing.
Do not fear,
Let your hands be strong.'

14 "For thus says the LORD of hosts:

'Just as I determined to punish you
When your fathers provoked Me to wrath,'
Says the LORD of hosts,
'And I would not relent,
15 So again in these days
I am determined to do good
To Jerusalem and to the house of Judah.
Do not fear.
16 These *are* the things you shall do:
Speak each man the truth to his neighbor;
Give judgment in your gates for truth, justice, and peace;
17 Let none of you think evil in your[a] heart against your neighbor;
And do not love a false oath.
For all these *are things* that I hate,'
Says the LORD."

18 Then the word of the LORD of hosts came
to me, saying,
19 "Thus says the LORD of hosts:

'The fast of the fourth *month,*
The fast of the fifth,
The fast of the seventh,
And the fast of the tenth,
Shall be joy and gladness and cheerful feasts
For the house of Judah.
Therefore love truth and peace.'

20 "Thus says the LORD of hosts:

'Peoples shall yet come,
Inhabitants of many cities;
21 The inhabitants of one *city* shall go to another, saying,
"Let us continue to go and pray before the LORD,
And seek the LORD of hosts.
I myself will go also."
22 Yes, many peoples and strong nations
Shall come to seek the LORD of hosts in Jerusalem,
And to pray before the LORD.'

23 "Thus says the LORD of hosts: 'In those
days ten men from every language of the nations shall grasp the sleeve of a Jewish man,
saying, "Let us go with you, for we have heard
that God *is* with you." ' "

Israel Defended Against Enemies

9 The burden[a] of the word of the LORD
Against the land of Hadrach,
And Damascus its resting place
(For the eyes of men
And all the tribes of Israel
Are on the LORD);
2 Also *against* Hamath, *which* borders on it,
And *against* Tyre and Sidon, though they are very wise.
3 For Tyre built herself a tower,
Heaped up silver like the dust,
And gold like the mire of the streets.
4 Behold, the Lord will cast her out;
He will destroy her power in the sea,
And she will be devoured by fire.

8:17 [a]Literally *his* **9:1** [a]Or *oracle*

LIFE LESSONS

➤ 8:13 — *". . . so I will save you, and you shall be a blessing."*

God blesses us so that we might be a blessing to others. He wants us to function as a conduit of blessing to those around us, not to become a stagnant pool of no use to anyone.

➤ 8:21 — *"Let us continue to go and pray before the LORD, and seek the LORD of hosts. I myself will go also."*

Prayer needs to be continual, God-centered, and personal. Occasional prayers will not cut it. Mere ritual will not cut it. Rote prayers will not cut it. We must daily seek the Lord through our heart-felt prayers.

5 Ashkelon shall see *it* and fear;
Gaza also shall be very sorrowful;
And Ekron, for He dried up her expectation.
The king shall perish from Gaza,
And Ashkelon shall not be inhabited.

6 "A mixed race shall settle in Ashdod,
And I will cut off the pride of the Philistines.
7 I will take away the blood from his mouth,
And the abominations from between his teeth.
But he who remains, even he *shall be* for our God,
And shall be like a leader in Judah,
And Ekron like a Jebusite.
8 I will camp around My house
Because of the army,
Because of him who passes by and him who returns.
No more shall an oppressor pass through them,
For now I have seen with My eyes.

The Coming King

➤ 9 "Rejoice greatly, O daughter of Zion!
Shout, O daughter of Jerusalem!
Behold, your King is coming to you;
He *is* just and having salvation,
Lowly and riding on a donkey,
A colt, the foal of a donkey.
10 I will cut off the chariot from Ephraim
And the horse from Jerusalem;
The battle bow shall be cut off.
He shall speak peace to the nations;
His dominion *shall be* 'from sea to sea,
And from the River to the ends of the earth.'[a]

God Will Save His People

11 "As for you also,
Because of the blood of your covenant,
I will set your prisoners free from the waterless pit.
12 Return to the stronghold,
You prisoners of hope.
Even today I declare
That I will restore double to you.
13 For I have bent Judah, My *bow*,
Fitted the bow with Ephraim,
And raised up your sons, O Zion,
Against your sons, O Greece,
And made you like the sword of a mighty man."

14 Then the LORD will be seen over them,
And His arrow will go forth like lightning.
The Lord GOD will blow the trumpet,
And go with whirlwinds from the south.
15 The LORD of hosts will defend them;
They shall devour and subdue with slingstones.
They shall drink *and* roar as if with wine;
They shall be filled *with blood* like basins,
Like the corners of the altar.
16 The LORD their God will save them in that day,
As the flock of His people.
For they *shall be like* the jewels of a crown,
Lifted like a banner over His land—
17 For how great is its[a] goodness
And how great its[b] beauty!
Grain shall make the young men thrive,
And new wine the young women.

Restoration of Judah and Israel

10 Ask the LORD for rain
In the time of the latter rain.[a]
The LORD will make flashing clouds;
He will give them showers of rain,
Grass in the field for everyone.

2 For the idols[a] speak delusion;
The diviners envision lies,
And tell false dreams;
They comfort in vain.
Therefore *the people* wend their way like sheep;
They are in trouble because *there is* no shepherd.

3 "My anger is kindled against the shepherds,
And I will punish the goatherds.
For the LORD of hosts will visit His flock,
The house of Judah,

9:10 [a]Psalm 72:8 **9:17** [a]Or *His* [b]Or *His* **10:1** [a]That is, spring rain **10:2** [a]Hebrew *teraphim*

LIFE LESSONS

➤ **9:9 — *"Rejoice greatly, O daughter of Zion! Shout, O daughter of Jerusalem! Behold, your King is coming to you; He is just and having salvation, lowly and riding on a donkey . . . ."***

We serve a just, humble Savior who doesn't wait for us to make our way to Him, but who willingly comes to us. How could we not praise and worship and gladly welcome such a glorious King?

➤ **9:16 — *The LORD their God will save them in that day, as the flock of His people.***

God loves to picture Himself as our loving Shepherd, ready and eager to rescue us from the vicious enemies and troubles that would otherwise overwhelm us. How can you trust your Shepherd today?

And will make them as His royal horse in
the battle.
4 From him comes the cornerstone,
From him the tent peg,
From him the battle bow,
From him every ruler[a] together.
5 They shall be like mighty men,
Who tread down *their enemies*
In the mire of the streets in the battle.
They shall fight because the LORD is with
them,
And the riders on horses shall be put to
shame.

6 "I will strengthen the house of Judah,
And I will save the house of Joseph.
I will bring them back,
Because I have mercy on them.
They shall be as though I had not cast
them aside;
For I *am* the LORD their God,
And I will hear them.
7 *Those of* Ephraim shall be like a mighty
man,
And their heart shall rejoice as if with
wine.
Yes, their children shall see *it* and be
glad;
Their heart shall rejoice in the LORD.
8 I will whistle for them and gather them,
For I will redeem them;
And they shall increase as they once
increased.

9 "I will sow them among the peoples,
And they shall remember Me in far
countries;
They shall live, together with their
children,
And they shall return.
10 I will also bring them back from the land
of Egypt,
And gather them from Assyria.
I will bring them into the land of Gilead
and Lebanon,
Until no *more room* is found for them.
11 He shall pass through the sea with
affliction,
And strike the waves of the sea:
All the depths of the River[a] shall dry up.
Then the pride of Assyria shall be
brought down,
And the scepter of Egypt shall depart.

12 "So I will strengthen them in the LORD,
And they shall walk up and down in His
name,"
Says the LORD.

Desolation of Israel

11 Open your doors, O Lebanon,
That fire may devour your cedars.
2 Wail, O cypress, for the cedar has fallen,
Because the mighty *trees* are ruined.
Wail, O oaks of Bashan,
For the thick forest has come down.
3 *There is* the sound of wailing shepherds!
For their glory is in ruins.
There is the sound of roaring lions!
For the pride[a] of the Jordan is in ruins.

Prophecy of the Shepherds

4 Thus says the LORD my God, "Feed the
flock for slaughter,
5 "whose owners slaughter them and feel no
guilt; those who sell them say, 'Blessed be the
LORD, for I am rich'; and their shepherds do
not pity them.
6 "For I will no longer pity the inhabitants of
the land," says the LORD. "But indeed I will
give everyone into his neighbor's hand and
into the hand of his king. They shall attack
the land, and I will not deliver *them* from
their hand."
7 So I fed the flock for slaughter, in particular the poor of the flock.[a] I took for myself two
staffs: the one I called Beauty,[b] and the other
I called Bonds;[c] and I fed the flock.
8 I dismissed the three shepherds in one
month. My soul loathed them, and their soul
also abhorred me.
9 Then I said, "I will not feed you. Let what
is dying die, and what is perishing perish. Let
those that are left eat each other's flesh."
10 And I took my staff, Beauty, and cut it in
two, that I might break the covenant which I
had made with all the peoples.
11 So it was broken on that day. Thus the
poor[a] of the flock, who were watching me,
knew that it *was* the word of the LORD.

10:4 [a]Or *despot* **10:11** [a]That is, the Nile **11:3** [a]Or *floodplain, thicket* **11:7** [a]Following Masoretic Text, Targum, and Vulgate; Septuagint reads *for the Canaanites.* [b]Or *Grace,* and so in verse 10 [c]Or *Unity,* and so in verse 14 **11:11** [a]Following Masoretic Text, Targum, and Vulgate; Septuagint reads *the Canaanites.*

LIFE LESSONS

10:6 — "I will save the house of Joseph. I will bring them back, because I have mercy on them. They shall be as though I had not cast them aside . . . ."

Even in judgment, God shows mercy. He does not desire to punish or cast aside anyone, but in love calls everyone to repentance and life (see Ezek. 33:11; 1 Tim. 2:4; 2 Pet. 3:9).

10:12 — "So I will strengthen them in the LORD, and they shall walk up and down in His name," says the LORD.

God wants us to become living advertisements for Him, walking billboards of His love and grace and mercy and holiness. But the only way for that to happen is to allow Jesus to live His life in and through us.

12 Then I said to them, "If it is agreeable to you, give *me* my wages; and if not, refrain." So they weighed out for my wages thirty *pieces* of silver.

➤ 13 And the LORD said to me, "Throw it to the potter"—that princely price they set on me. So I took the thirty *pieces* of silver and threw them into the house of the LORD for the potter.

14 Then I cut in two my other staff, Bonds, that I might break the brotherhood between Judah and Israel.

15 And the LORD said to me, "Next, take for yourself the implements of a foolish shepherd.

16 "For indeed I will raise up a shepherd in the land *who* will not care for those who are cut off, nor seek the young, nor heal those that are broken, nor feed those that still stand. But he will eat the flesh of the fat and tear their hooves in pieces.

17 "Woe to the worthless shepherd,
Who leaves the flock!
A sword *shall be* against his arm
And against his right eye;
His arm shall completely wither,
And his right eye shall be totally blinded."

The Coming Deliverance of Judah

➤ **12** The burden[a] of the word of the LORD against Israel. Thus says the LORD, who stretches out the heavens, lays the foundation of the earth, and forms the spirit of man within him:

2 "Behold, I will make Jerusalem a cup of drunkenness to all the surrounding peoples, when they lay siege against Judah and Jerusalem.

3 "And it shall happen in that day that I will make Jerusalem a very heavy stone for all peoples; all who would heave it away will surely be cut in pieces, though all nations of the earth are gathered against it.

4 "In that day," says the LORD, "I will strike every horse with confusion, and its rider with madness; I will open My eyes on the house of Judah, and will strike every horse of the peoples with blindness.

5 "And the governors of Judah shall say in their heart, 'The inhabitants of Jerusalem *are* my strength in the LORD of hosts, their God.'

6 "In that day I will make the governors of Judah like a firepan in the woodpile, and like a fiery torch in the sheaves; they shall devour all the surrounding peoples on the right hand and on the left, but Jerusalem shall be inhabited again in her own place—Jerusalem.

7 "The LORD will save the tents of Judah first, so that the glory of the house of David and the glory of the inhabitants of Jerusalem shall not become greater than that of Judah.

8 "In that day the LORD will defend the inhabitants of Jerusalem; the one who is feeble among them in that day shall be like David, and the house of David *shall be* like God, like the Angel of the LORD before them.

9 "It shall be in that day *that* I will seek to destroy all the nations that come against Jerusalem.

Mourning for the Pierced One

10 "And I will pour on the house of David and on the inhabitants of Jerusalem the Spirit of grace and supplication; then they will look on Me whom they pierced. Yes, they will mourn for Him as one mourns for *his* only *son,* and grieve for Him as one grieves for a firstborn. ✳ ➤

11 "In that day there shall be a great mourning in Jerusalem, like the mourning at Hadad Rimmon in the plain of Megiddo.[a]

12 "And the land shall mourn, every family by itself: the family of the house of David by itself, and their wives by themselves; the family of the house of Nathan by itself, and their wives by themselves;

13 "the family of the house of Levi by itself, and their wives by themselves; the family of Shimei by itself, and their wives by themselves;

14 "all the families that remain, every family by itself, and their wives by themselves.

12:1 [a]Or *oracle* **12:11** [a]Hebrew *Megiddon*

LIFE LESSONS

➤ 11:13 — *And the LORD said to me, "Throw it to the potter"—that princely price they set on me.*

Judas Iscariot fulfilled this prophecy when he betrayed the Lord Jesus for thirty pieces of silver (Matt. 27:3–10). How many of us have betrayed Him for less by choosing trinkets over Him?

➤ 12:1 — *Thus says the LORD, who stretches out the heavens, lays the foundation of the earth, and forms the spirit of man within him . . . .*

The same God who designed and created the vast universe around you, who devised and fashioned the earth you live on, also molded and shaped your very spirit. He knows you inside out—and wants you to know Him.

➤ 12:10 — *"And I will pour on the house of David and on the inhabitants of Jerusalem the Spirit of grace and supplication; then they will look on Me whom they pierced . . . ."*

The day will come when the resurrected Jesus will return to this earth to bring God's covenant people back into a close, warm, intimate relationship with Himself (Rom. 11:25–32). What a day that will be!

Idolatry Cut Off

➤ 13 "In that day a fountain shall be opened
for the house of David and for the inhabitants of Jerusalem, for sin and for uncleanness.
2 "It shall be in that day," says the LORD of
hosts, "*that* I will cut off the names of the
idols from the land, and they shall no longer
be remembered. I will also cause the prophets
and the unclean spirit to depart from the land.
3 "It shall come to pass *that* if anyone still
prophesies, then his father and mother who
begot him will say to him, 'You shall not live,
because you have spoken lies in the name of
the LORD.' And his father and mother who
begot him shall thrust him through when he
prophesies.
4 "And it shall be in that day *that* every
prophet will be ashamed of his vision when
he prophesies; they will not wear a robe of
coarse hair to deceive.
5 "But he will say, 'I *am* no prophet, I *am* a
farmer; for a man taught me to keep cattle
from my youth.'
6 "And *one* will say to him, 'What are these
wounds between your arms?'[a] Then he will
answer, '*Those* with which I was wounded in
the house of my friends.'

The Shepherd Savior

➤ 7 "Awake, O sword, against My Shepherd,
Against the Man who is My
Companion,"
Says the LORD of hosts.
"Strike the Shepherd,
And the sheep will be scattered;
Then I will turn My hand against the
little ones.
8 And it shall come to pass in all the land,"
Says the LORD,
"*That* two-thirds in it shall be cut off *and*
die,
But *one*-third shall be left in it:
9 I will bring the *one*-third through the
fire,
Will refine them as silver is refined,
And test them as gold is tested.
They will call on My name,
And I will answer them.
I will say, 'This *is* My people';
And each one will say, 'The LORD *is* my
God.'"

The Day of the LORD

14 Behold, the day of the LORD is coming,
And your spoil will be divided in your
midst.
2 For I will gather all the nations to battle
against Jerusalem;
The city shall be taken,
The houses rifled,
And the women ravished.
Half of the city shall go into captivity,
But the remnant of the people shall not
be cut off from the city.

3 Then the LORD will go forth
And fight against those nations,
As He fights in the day of battle.
4 And in that day His feet will stand on the
Mount of Olives,
Which faces Jerusalem on the east.
And the Mount of Olives shall be split in
two,
From east to west,
Making a very large valley;
Half of the mountain shall move toward
the north
And half of it toward the south.

5 Then you shall flee *through* My mountain ➤
valley,
For the mountain valley shall reach to
Azal.
Yes, you shall flee
As you fled from the earthquake
In the days of Uzziah king of Judah.

Thus the LORD my God will come,
And all the saints with You.[a]

6 It shall come to pass in that day
That there will be no light;
The lights will diminish.
7 It shall be one day
Which is known to the LORD—
Neither day nor night.
But at evening time it shall happen
That it will be light.

13:6 [a]Or *hands* **14:5** [a]Or *you;* Septuagint, Targum, and Vulgate read *Him.*

LIFE LESSONS

➤ 13:1 — *"In that day a fountain shall be opened for the house of David and for the inhabitants of Jerusalem, for sin and for uncleanness."*

God often uses a fountain to picture Himself as our source of salvation. As a fountain, He overflows with mercy and grace. As a fountain, He refreshes. And as a fountain, His love must be individually taken in.

➤ 13:7 — *"Awake, O sword, against My Shepherd, against the Man who is My Companion . . . ."*

Think of it: *the Lord* called for the sword against His Son, Jesus Christ. *He* planned the events of the cross; *He* willingly bruised His only Son (Is. 53:10; Acts 4:27, 28). And He did it *for you.*

➤ 14:5 — *Thus the LORD my God will come, and all the saints with You.*

Did you know that the Bible contains almost three times as many predictions of the Second Coming of Christ as it has for His first coming? He is coming again! And He wants us to be ready (Matt. 24:44).

➤ 8 And in that day it shall be
That living waters shall flow from
Jerusalem,
Half of them toward the eastern sea
And half of them toward the western sea;
In both summer and winter it shall occur.
✳ 9 And the LORD shall be King over all the
➤ earth.
In that day it shall be—
"The LORD *is* one,"[a]
And His name one.

10 All the land shall be turned into a plain
from Geba to Rimmon south of Jerusalem. *Je-*
rusalem[a] shall be raised up and inhabited in
her place from Benjamin's Gate to the place
of the First Gate and the Corner Gate, and
from the Tower of Hananel to the king's winepresses.

11 *The people* shall dwell in it;
And no longer shall there be utter
destruction,
But Jerusalem shall be safely inhabited.

12 And this shall be the plague with which
the LORD will strike all the people who fought
against Jerusalem:

Their flesh shall dissolve while they
stand on their feet,
Their eyes shall dissolve in their sockets,
And their tongues shall dissolve in their
mouths.

13 It shall come to pass in that day
That a great panic from the LORD will be
among them.
Everyone will seize the hand of his
neighbor,
And raise his hand against his neighbor's
hand;
14 Judah also will fight at Jerusalem.
And the wealth of all the surrounding
nations
Shall be gathered together:
Gold, silver, and apparel in great
abundance.

15 Such also shall be the plague
On the horse *and* the mule,
On the camel and the donkey,
And on all the cattle that will be in those
camps.
So *shall* this plague *be.*

The Nations Worship the King

16 And it shall come to pass *that* everyone
who is left of all the nations which came
against Jerusalem shall go up from year to
year to worship the King, the LORD of hosts,
and to keep the Feast of Tabernacles.
17 And it shall be *that* whichever of the families of the earth do not come up to Jerusalem
to worship the King, the LORD of hosts, on
them there will be no rain.
18 If the family of Egypt will not come up and
enter in, they *shall have* no *rain;* they shall receive the plague with which the LORD strikes
the nations who do not come up to keep the
Feast of Tabernacles.
19 This shall be the punishment of Egypt and
the punishment of all the nations that do not
come up to keep the Feast of Tabernacles.
20 In that day "HOLINESS TO THE LORD"
shall be *engraved* on the bells of the horses.
The pots in the LORD's house shall be like the
bowls before the altar.
21 Yes, every pot in Jerusalem and Judah
shall be holiness to the LORD of hosts.[a] Everyone who sacrifices shall come and take them
and cook in them. In that day there shall no
longer be a Canaanite in the house of the
LORD of hosts.

14:9 [a]Compare Deuteronomy 6:4 **14:10** [a]Literally *She*
14:21 [a]Or *on every pot . . . shall be (engraved) "HOLINESS TO THE LORD OF HOSTS"*

LIFE LESSONS

➤ 14:8 — *And in that day it shall be that living waters shall flow from Jerusalem . . . .*

Water brings life, and living water brings eternal life. God calls Himself our spring of living water (Jer. 2:13); the Spirit is a stream of living water in us (John 7:38, 39); and His living water is ours forever (Rev. 7:17).

➤ 14:9 — *In that day it shall be—"The LORD is one," and His name one.*

Today, many voices honor and serve many gods. But one day, the Lord says, "to Me every knee shall bow, every tongue shall take an oath" (Is. 45:23)—and they shall all say, "Jesus Christ is Lord" (Phil. 2:11).

THE BOOK OF

MALACHI

Years after God restored His people and returned them to the Promised Land, they again backslid and began falling into the same kinds of sin that led to God's judgment and the seven decade long Babylonian captivity. The priests were dishonoring God by leading the people astray, and Jewish men were marrying pagan women. The hearts of the people were growing hard.

Into this ugly scene God sent the prophet Malachi.

Malachi, a contemporary of Nehemiah, directed his message to a people plagued with corrupt priests, immoral lifestyles, and a false sense of security in their privileged relationship with God. Using a question-and-answer format, Malachi probed deeply into their habits of hypocrisy, infidelity, mixed marriages, divorce, false worship, and arrogance. Malachi may have prophesied in the period after Nehemiah left Jerusalem to serve the Persian king once more (433 B.C.), since the problems he tried to combat sound so similar to the ones Nehemiah later confronted upon his return to Jerusalem for a second tour of duty as governor (Neh. 13:7–31).

The name *Mal'aki* ("My messenger") is probably a shortened form of *Mal'akya*, "Messenger of Yahweh," an appropriate author for a book that speaks of the coming of the "messenger of the covenant" ("messenger" is mentioned three times: see Mal. 2:7; 3:1).

Theme: God's people need to reform their rebellious habits in order to prepare the way for the coming Messiah.

Author: Probably Malachi, although some believe the name Malachi actually functions more as a title ("My messenger").

Time: Written near the end of the prophetic period in Israel's history, around 430 B.C.

Structure: Malachi has three main parts: introductory remarks in which God reaffirms His promised love to Israel (1:1–5); stinging rebukes for various kinds of unfaithfulness (1:6—2:16); and prophecies of the coming of the Lord (2:17—4:6).

As you read Malachi, watch for several life principles that play an important role in this book:

23. You can never outgive God. *See Malachi 3:8–12; page 1105.*

2. Obey God and leave all the consequences to Him. *See Malachi 3:13–18; page 1105.*

1 The burden[a] of the word of the LORD to
Israel by Malachi.

Israel Beloved of God

2 "I have loved you," says the LORD.
"Yet you say, 'In what way have You loved
us?'
Was not Esau Jacob's brother?"
Says the LORD.
"Yet Jacob I have loved;
3 But Esau I have hated,
And laid waste his mountains and his
heritage
For the jackals of the wilderness."

4 Even though Edom has said,
"We have been impoverished,
But we will return and build the desolate
places,"
Thus says the LORD of hosts:

"They may build, but I will throw down;
They shall be called the Territory of
Wickedness,
And the people against whom the LORD
will have indignation forever.
5 Your eyes shall see,
And you shall say,
'The LORD is magnified beyond the border
of Israel.'

Polluted Offerings

6 "A son honors *his* father,
And a servant *his* master.
If then I am the Father,
Where *is* My honor?
And if I *am* a Master,
Where *is* My reverence?
Says the LORD of hosts
To you priests who despise My name.
Yet you say, 'In what way have we
despised Your name?'
7 "You offer defiled food on My altar,
But say,
'In what way have we defiled You?'
By saying,
'The table of the LORD is contemptible.'
8 And when you offer the blind as a
sacrifice,
Is it not evil?
And when you offer the lame and sick,
Is it not evil?
Offer it then to your governor!
Would he be pleased with you?
Would he accept you favorably?"
Says the LORD of hosts.

9 "But now entreat God's favor,
That He may be gracious to us.
While this is being *done* by your hands,
Will He accept you favorably?"
Says the LORD of hosts.
10 "Who *is there* even among you who would
shut the doors,
So that you would not kindle fire *on* My
altar in vain?
I have no pleasure in you,"
Says the LORD of hosts,
"Nor will I accept an offering from your
hands.
11 For from the rising of the sun, even to its
going down,
My name *shall be* great among the
Gentiles;
In every place incense *shall be* offered to
My name,
And a pure offering;
For My name shall be great among the
nations,"
Says the LORD of hosts.

12 "But you profane it,
In that you say,
'The table of the LORD[a] is defiled;
And its fruit, its food, *is* contemptible.'
13 You also say,
'Oh, what a weariness!'
And you sneer at it,"
Says the LORD of hosts.
"And you bring the stolen, the lame, and
the sick;
Thus you bring an offering!
Should I accept this from your hand?"
Says the LORD.
14 "But cursed *be* the deceiver
Who has in his flock a male,

1:1 [a]Or *oracle* **1:12** [a]Following Bomberg; Masoretic Text reads *Lord*.

LIFE LESSONS

➤ 1:2 — *"I have loved you," says the LORD.*

It's wrong to think of the Old Testament as a declaration of divine judgment while the New Testament declares God's love. Both testaments proclaim God's love for His people and portray Him as a compassionate Redeemer.

➤ 1:13 — *"And you bring the stolen, the lame, and the sick; thus you bring an offering! Should I accept this from your hand?" says the LORD.*

Don't bring God something left over that you do not want. Do not offer to God eight hours of labor in which you acted dishonestly or did as little as possible to get by. He deserves our best.

➤ 1:14 — *"For I am a great King," says the LORD of hosts, "and My name is to be feared among the nations."*

Kings are to be obeyed, and as a "great King," the Lord deserves our complete obedience. When we disobey, we profane His name among those who don't know Him, and they see no reason to fear Him.

And takes a vow,
But sacrifices to the Lord what is blemished—
For I *am* a great King,"
Says the LORD of hosts,
"And My name *is to be* feared among the nations.

Corrupt Priests

2 "And now, O priests, this commandment is for you.
2 If you will not hear,
And if you will not take *it* to heart,
To give glory to My name,"
Says the LORD of hosts,
"I will send a curse upon you,
And I will curse your blessings.
Yes, I have cursed them already,
Because you do not take *it* to heart.
3 "Behold, I will rebuke your descendants
And spread refuse on your faces,
The refuse of your solemn feasts;
And *one* will take you away with it.
4 Then you shall know that I have sent this commandment to you,
That My covenant with Levi may continue,"
Says the LORD of hosts.

➤ 5 "My covenant was with him, *one* of life and peace,
And I gave them to him *that he might* fear *Me;*
So he feared Me
And was reverent before My name.
6 The law of truth[a] was in his mouth,
And injustice was not found on his lips.
He walked with Me in peace and equity,
And turned many away from iniquity.
7 "For the lips of a priest should keep knowledge,
And *people* should seek the law from his mouth;
For he is the messenger of the LORD of hosts.
8 But you have departed from the way;
You have caused many to stumble at the law.
You have corrupted the covenant of Levi,"
Says the LORD of hosts.
9 "Therefore I also have made you contemptible and base
Before all the people,
Because you have not kept My ways
But have shown partiality in the law."

Treachery of Infidelity

10 Have we not all one Father?
Has not one God created us?
Why do we deal treacherously with one another
By profaning the covenant of the fathers?
11 Judah has dealt treacherously,
And an abomination has been committed in Israel and in Jerusalem,
For Judah has profaned
The LORD's holy *institution* which He loves:
He has married the daughter of a foreign god.
12 May the LORD cut off from the tents of Jacob
The man who does this, being awake and aware,[a]
Yet who brings an offering to the LORD of hosts!
13 And this is the second thing you do:
You cover the altar of the LORD with tears,
With weeping and crying;
So He does not regard the offering anymore,
Nor receive *it* with goodwill from your hands.
14 Yet you say, "For what reason?"
Because the LORD has been witness
Between you and the wife of your youth,
With whom you have dealt treacherously;
Yet she is your companion
And your wife by covenant.
15 But did He not make *them* one,
Having a remnant of the Spirit?
And why one?
He seeks godly offspring.
Therefore take heed to your spirit,
And let none deal treacherously with the wife of his youth.
16 "For the LORD God of Israel says ➤
That He hates divorce,

2:6 [a]Or *true instruction* **2:12** [a]Talmud and Vulgate read *teacher and student.*

LIFE LESSONS

➤ 2:5 — *"My covenant was with him, one of life and peace . . . ."*

God's commandments and promises and warnings are all for our benefit, to bless us with life and peace. When we turn away from His Word, we turn away from both life and peace.

➤ 2:16 — *"For the LORD God of Israel says that He hates divorce . . . ."*

God hates divorce because He meant for our marriages to mirror the love and grace and joy that the three Persons of the Godhead enjoy within the Trinity.

For it covers one's garment with
violence,"
Says the LORD of hosts.
"Therefore take heed to your spirit,
That you do not deal treacherously."

17 You have wearied the LORD with your
words;
Yet you say,
"In what way have we wearied *Him?*"
In that you say,
"Everyone who does evil
Is good in the sight of the LORD,
And He delights in them,"
Or, "Where *is* the God of justice?"

The Coming Messenger

3 "Behold, I send My messenger,
And he will prepare the way before Me.
And the Lord, whom you seek,
Will suddenly come to His temple,
Even the Messenger of the covenant,
In whom you delight.
Behold, He is coming,"
Says the LORD of hosts.

2 "But who can endure the day of His
coming?
And who can stand when He appears?
For He *is* like a refiner's fire
And like launderers' soap.
3 He will sit as a refiner and a purifier of
silver;
He will purify the sons of Levi,
And purge them as gold and silver,
That they may offer to the LORD
An offering in righteousness.

4 "Then the offering of Judah and
Jerusalem
Will be pleasant to the LORD,
As in the days of old,
As in former years.
5 And I will come near you for
judgment;
I will be a swift witness
Against sorcerers,
Against adulterers,
Against perjurers,
Against those who exploit wage earners
and widows and orphans,
And against those who turn away an
alien—
Because they do not fear Me,"
Says the LORD of hosts.

✳ 6 "For I *am* the LORD, I do not change;
➤ Therefore you are not consumed,
O sons of Jacob.
7 Yet from the days of your fathers
You have gone away from My
ordinances
And have not kept *them.*
Return to Me, and I will return to you,"
Says the LORD of hosts.
"But you said,
'In what way shall we return?'

Do Not Rob God

8 "Will a man rob God?
Yet you have robbed Me!
But you say,
'In what way have we robbed You?'
In tithes and offerings.
9 You are cursed with a curse,
For you have robbed Me,
Even this whole nation.
10 Bring all the tithes into the
storehouse, ✳
That there may be food in My house,
And try Me now in this,"
Says the LORD of hosts,
"If I will not open for you the windows
of heaven
And pour out for you *such* blessing
That *there will* not *be room* enough *to
receive it.*

11 "And I will rebuke the devourer for your
sakes,
So that he will not destroy the fruit of
your ground,
Nor shall the vine fail to bear fruit for
you in the field,"
Says the LORD of hosts;
12 "And all nations will call you blessed,
For you will be a delightful land,"
Says the LORD of hosts.

The People Complain Harshly

13 "Your words have been harsh
against Me,"
Says the LORD,
"Yet you say,
'What have we spoken against You?'
14 You have said,
'It is useless to serve God;
What profit *is it* that we have kept His
ordinance,
And that we have walked as mourners
Before the LORD of hosts?
15 So now we call the proud blessed,
For those who do wickedness are
raised up;
They even tempt God and go
free.'"

LIFE LESSONS

➤ 3:6 — *"For I am the LORD, I do not change; therefore you are not consumed, O sons of Jacob."*

Our God is immutable, meaning that He never changes. He operates on eternal, unchanging principles—and that is why we can build our lives on His promises.

ANSWERS TO LIFE'S QUESTIONS

Should I tithe when I am struggling financially?

MAL. 3:8–12

From the human perspective, the Bible is a book of paradoxes. It says, for example, that if we really want to have life, we must first lose it (Matt. 10:39). If we want to understand authority, we must first become a servant (Matt. 20:26, 27). If we want to get ahead in life, we must first humble ourselves (1 Pet. 5:6).

And giving to God is the first step toward financial freedom.

"Wow," you say. "How can I give God *anything* when I can't even pay my bills? Doesn't God expect me to take care of by debts first?"

At first glance, such a response sounds reasonable. The problem is, it's not God's response. He insists that if we don't give, then we are robbing Him—and we will end up in worse financial shape than ever.

We should always keep in mind that God gives us this tenth in the first place. It never is ours: "All things come from You, and of Your own we have given You" (1 Chron. 29:14).

The tithe is our way to renew God's blessing in our lives. It is always for our increase.

God's promises have been tried and proven. This includes the promises regarding tithing: "Bring all the tithes into the storehouse," the Lord tells us. And then He adds, ". . . and try Me now in this" (Mal. 3:10).

God invites us to try Him, to prove His wisdom, to test His truth. What a bold challenge! Will we take it up? If we do, He promises to open the "windows of heaven," and pour out blessing for you until it overflows (Mal. 3:10).

The challenge involves a tithe—a tenth of your income. That may frighten you; but remember, since God owns it all, He is asking only for a penny back out of every dime. He doesn't need the money; He simply wants us to discover the rewards of obedience.

Giving is God's supernatural means of priming the pump of divine supply. We initiate it by faith, not reason. Giving to God is the prerequisite for enjoying true financial freedom.

If you feel afraid to give a tenth of your income, then at least start somewhere. When you start to give and realize the wisdom of God's economic plan, it won't be long until you will be giving a tenth of your income . . . or even more.

See the Life Principles Index for further study:
21. Obedience always brings blessing.
23. You can never outgive God.

A Book of Remembrance

➤ 16 Then those who feared the LORD spoke to
one another,
And the LORD listened and heard *them;*
So a book of remembrance was written
before Him
For those who fear the LORD
And who meditate on His name.

17 "They shall be Mine," says the LORD of
hosts,
"On the day that I make them My jewels.[a]
And I will spare them
As a man spares his own son who serves
him."

18 Then you shall again discern
Between the righteous and the
wicked,
Between one who serves God
And one who does not serve Him.

The Great Day of God

4 "For behold, the day is coming,
Burning like an oven,
And all the proud, yes, all who do
wickedly will be stubble.
And the day which is coming shall burn
them up,"
Says the LORD of hosts,

3:17 [a]Literally *special treasure*

LIFE LESSONS

➤ **3:16 — *Then those who feared the LORD spoke to one another, and the LORD gave attention and heard them . . . .***

None of us are in this walk of faith on our own. We need to encourage one another to "stir up love and good works" (Heb. 10:24). Best of all, the Lord promises to reward such healthy obedience.

WHAT THE BIBLE SAYS ABOUT TITHING AND GIVING

Mal. 3:8–12

God has set forth very specific directives about what He expects us to give back to Him. Malachi 3:8–12 clearly teaches that we are to give Him a tithe, which is ten percent (the word *tithe* is based on the number ten in Hebrew).

Offerings were gifts, often of material goods, given above and beyond the tithe. People normally made offerings for specific reasons—to meet a special need, for example, or thanksgiving for a special blessing. The children of Israel gave such a generous offering at the time they built the tabernacle that Moses actually had to tell them to stop giving (see Ex. 35:4–36:7)!

The tithe is given to God *from* our increase and *for* our increase. It is the way we open the door of our finances to give and then to receive God's blessing. When we give the first tenth of our earnings back to God, we return to Him what was His in the first place, and what He asks us to give to Him so that He might give us even more.

The Lord is very specific in the way we are to give our tithes and offerings.

First, we are to bring them into His storehouse. Generally that meant His tabernacle or temple in the Old Testament, and the church in the New Testament. We are to give our tithes wherever we regularly worship the Lord—not to a mere charitable work, but to a work that bears the Lord's name.

Second, we are to make our gifts on a regular basis. Paul advised the Corinthians, "On the first day of the week let each one of you lay something aside, storing up as he may prosper, that there be no collections when I come" (1 Cor. 16:2).

Third, we are to make our gifts joyfully. People who give grudgingly, solely from a sense of duty, do not truly open up their lives to God's prosperity (2 Cor. 9:7–8). The joy in our hearts about giving is a direct expression of our trust in God to meet our needs.

See the Life Principles Index for further study:
23. You can never outgive God.

We return to Him what was His in the first place.

"That will leave them neither root nor
branch.
✳ 2 But to you who fear My name
The Sun of Righteousness shall arise
With healing in His wings;
And you shall go out
And grow fat like stall-fed calves.
3 You shall trample the wicked,
For they shall be ashes under the soles of
your feet
On the day that I do *this*,"
Says the LORD of hosts.

4 "Remember the Law of Moses, My
servant,
Which I commanded him in Horeb for all
Israel,
With the statutes and judgments.
5 Behold, I will send you Elijah the
prophet
Before the coming of the great and
dreadful day of the LORD.
6 And he will turn
The hearts of the fathers to the
children,
And the hearts of the children to their
fathers,
Lest I come and strike the earth with a
curse."

LIFE LESSONS

➤ 4:5 — *"Behold, I will send you Elijah the prophet before the coming of the great and dreadful day of the LORD."*

John the Baptist came in the "spirit and power of Elijah" (Luke 1:17), and Jesus said, "if you are willing to receive it, he [John] is Elijah who is to come" (Matt. 11:14; but see also Matt. 17:11–13).

➤ 4:6 — *"He will turn the hearts of the fathers to their children, and the hearts of the children to their fathers, lest I come and strike the land with a curse."*

The closest mission field we have is our own families. God says that He "seeks godly offspring" (Mal. 2:15), but children have to be trained to be godly—and that's the job of parents.

NEW TESTAMENT

THE GOSPEL ACCORDING TO

MATTHEW

Matthew presents Jesus as the King of the Jews, the long-awaited Messiah. Matthew wrote his Gospel primarily for a Jewish audience that had been waiting centuries for the Messiah's coming.

Through a carefully selected series of Old Testament quotations (more than sixty), Matthew documents Jesus Christ's claim to be that Messiah. Jesus' genealogy, baptism, message, and miracles all point to the same inescapable conclusion: Christ is King. Jesus turns even the seeming defeat of His death into victory through the Resurrection, and so the message again echoes forth: the King of the Jews *lives.*

At an early date, this Gospel received the title *Kata Matthaion*, "According to Matthew." As the name suggests, other Gospel accounts were known at the time. Matthew (which means "Gift of the Lord") was also named Levi (Mark 2:14; Luke 5:27).

Matthew is the first of the three "synoptic" Gospels, so called because they "see together" the life and teachings of Jesus. Matthew, Mark, and Luke each record basically the same events, but give them different emphases.

Themes: The word *fulfilled* appears repeatedly in the Gospel of Matthew, mostly referring to Jesus' fulfillment of Old Testament messianic prophecies.

Author: Matthew, a Jew who had collected taxes for the hated Romans.

Time: Most authorities believe that the Gospel of Mark predates Matthew and that Matthew follows Mark's account in many of its narratives; if this is so, Matthew could be dated in the A.D. 70s. Others believe Matthew was written earlier, in the A.D. 50s or 60s.

Structure: The Gospel of Matthew begins by tracing Jesus' family history, all the way back to Abraham, and recording a few incidents surrounding His birth (1–2). It then describes the preparation and beginnings of Jesus' earthly ministry, including the ministry of John the Baptist, Jesus' baptism, and His temptation (3–4). The Sermon on the Mount (5–7) is followed by various accounts of Jesus' healings and teachings (8–9) and His words on missions (10). The Gospel then reports Jesus' travels, in which He taught the masses, often using parables, and performed great miracles (11–23). A special section predicting the events leading up to and including the end times (24–25) is followed by a final portion that reports Jesus' arrest, sentencing, crucifixion, and resurrection (26–28).

As you read Matthew, watch for several life principles that play an important role in this book:

27. Prayer is life's greatest time saver. *See Matthew 6:5–9; page 1118.*

25. God blesses us so that we might bless others. *See Matthew 10:8; page 1126.*

21. Obedience always brings blessing. *See Matthew 14:17–21; 15:34–38; page 1132, 1134.*

30. An eager anticipation of the Lord's return keeps us living productively. *See Matthew 24:36–44; page 1147.*

The Genealogy of Jesus Christ

1 The book of the genealogy of Jesus Christ,
the Son of David, the Son of Abraham:
2 Abraham begot Isaac, Isaac begot Jacob,
and Jacob begot Judah and his brothers.
3 Judah begot Perez and Zerah by Tamar,
Perez begot Hezron, and Hezron begot Ram.
4 Ram begot Amminadab, Amminadab
begot Nahshon, and Nahshon begot Salmon.
➤ 5 Salmon begot Boaz by Rahab, Boaz begot
Obed by Ruth, Obed begot Jesse,
6 and Jesse begot David the king. David the
king begot Solomon by her *who had been the*
wife[a] of Uriah.
7 Solomon begot Rehoboam, Rehoboam
begot Abijah, and Abijah begot Asa.[a]
8 Asa begot Jehoshaphat, Jehoshaphat
begot Joram, and Joram begot Uzziah.
9 Uzziah begot Jotham, Jotham begot Ahaz,
and Ahaz begot Hezekiah.
10 Hezekiah begot Manasseh, Manasseh
begot Amon,[a] and Amon begot Josiah.
11 Josiah begot Jeconiah and his brothers
about the time they were carried away to
Babylon.
12 And after they were brought to Babylon,
Jeconiah begot Shealtiel, and Shealtiel begot
Zerubbabel.
13 Zerubbabel begot Abiud, Abiud begot Eliakim, and Eliakim begot Azor.
14 Azor begot Zadok, Zadok begot Achim,
and Achim begot Eliud.
15 Eliud begot Eleazar, Eleazar begot
Matthan, and Matthan begot Jacob.
16 And Jacob begot Joseph the husband of
Mary, of whom was born Jesus who is called
Christ.
17 So all the generations from Abraham to
David *are* fourteen generations, from David
until the captivity in Babylon *are* fourteen
generations, and from the captivity in Babylon until the Christ *are* fourteen generations.

Christ Born of Mary

➤ 18 Now the birth of Jesus Christ was as follows: After His mother Mary was betrothed to
Joseph, before they came together, she was
found with child of the Holy Spirit.
19 Then Joseph her husband, being a just
man, and not wanting to make her a public example, was minded to put her away secretly.
20 But while he thought about these things, ➤
behold, an angel of the Lord appeared to him in
a dream, saying, "Joseph, son of David, do not
be afraid to take to you Mary your wife, for that
which is conceived in her is of the Holy Spirit.
21 "And she will bring forth a Son, and you ✳
shall call His name JESUS, for He will save His
people from their sins."
22 So all this was done that it might be fulfilled which was spoken by the Lord through
the prophet, saying:
23 *"Behold, the virgin shall be with child, and*
bear a Son, and they shall call His name Im-
manuel,"[a] which is translated, "God with us."
24 Then Joseph, being aroused from sleep,
did as the angel of the Lord commanded him
and took to him his wife,
25 and did not know her till she had brought
forth her firstborn Son.[a] And he called His
name JESUS.

Wise Men from the East

2 Now after Jesus was born in Bethlehem of
Judea in the days of Herod the king, behold, wise men from the East came to Jerusalem,
2 saying, "Where is He who has been born
King of the Jews? For we have seen His star in
the East and have come to worship Him."
3 When Herod the king heard *this,* he was
troubled, and all Jerusalem with him.
4 And when he had gathered all the chief ➤
priests and scribes of the people together, he
inquired of them where the Christ was to be
born.

1:6 [a]Words in italic type have been added for clarity. They are not found in the original Greek. **1:7** [a]NU-Text reads *Asaph.*
1:10 [a]NU-Text reads *Amos.* **1:23** [a]Isaiah 7:14. Words in oblique type in the New Testament are quoted from the Old Testament.
1:25 [a]NU-Text reads *a Son.*

LIFE LESSONS

➤ 1:5 — *Salmon begot Boaz by Rahab, Boaz begot Obed by Ruth . . . .*

Four women are unexpectedly included in the genealogy of Jesus. At least three of them (Tamar, Ruth, and Rahab) were Gentiles; three (Tamar, Rahab, and Uriah's wife Bathsheba) were involved in blatant sexual sins. How appropriate for the Messiah who would save the world from sin!

➤ 1:18 — *Now the birth of Jesus Christ was as follows: After His mother Mary was betrothed to Joseph, before they came together, she was found with child of the Holy Spirit.*

Jesus Christ can be our sinless sin-bearer because He alone out of all the human family was born "without sin." Through the virgin birth, He could be both fully human *and* unstained by sin.

➤ 1:20 — *But while he thought about these things, behold, an angel of the Lord appeared to him in a dream . . . .*

Why didn't the angel Gabriel appear to Joseph when he appeared to Mary? We're not told. But God will always reveal His will to us, however He sees fit, when we really want to know (and do) it.

➤ 2:4 — *And when he had gathered all the chief priests and scribes of the people together, he inquired of them where the Christ was to be born.*

Herod believed enough in the Scriptures to inquire where they said the Messiah would be born, but not enough to shape his life according to its teachings. A little religion can be a dangerous thing.

ANSWERS TO LIFE'S QUESTIONS

What are the characteristics of a godly man?

MATT. 1:20, 21

Until he became engaged to Mary, Joseph's life probably resembled that of most other men in his hometown. No doubt he had business concerns and goals for the future—but nothing seriously interrupted his daily routine until Mary informed him she was pregnant. Then he revealed his godly traits.

While the news must have shocked him, he clearly felt troubled for her and her reputation. God saw the confusion building inside of Joseph and sent an angel to tell him, "Joseph, son of David, do not be afraid to take to you Mary your wife; for that which is conceived in her is of the Holy Spirit. And she will bring forth a Son, and you shall call His name JESUS, for He will save His people from their sins" (Matt. 1:20, 21).

From this point on, Joseph never doubted God's will in choosing him to watch over Mary and her son. He remained faithful not only to his wife, but also to God. He showed courage by ignoring the ugly rumors swirling around town about Mary's pregnancy; he valued God's plan above what others might think of him. He remained sensitive to the Holy Spirit, demonstrated by his acceptance of God's guidance. After the birth of Jesus, an angel appeared to him, warning him of impending danger. Joseph immediately took Mary and Jesus to Egypt, where they found safety until the threat passed (Matt. 2:13–15).

Joseph, a humble man, honored God by obeying His Word. He remained consistent and content, and could be counted on to follow God regardless of the personal costs.

How can you grow in your faith to become a godly individual? Start by committing yourself to a consistent, daily walk with Christ. Attend a church where the Word of God is proclaimed as the standard of life. Make an open commitment to God and to your loved ones that you will not abandon your devotion to Christ or to them.

You gain a sense of godly responsibility when you stand up for what is right. A godly person is not easily swayed, but is filled with conviction, faith, and prayer. When Joseph had no one else to guide and comfort him, he turned to God and found the strength and love he needed to get through the most difficult of circumstances.

Will you make Joseph's spiritual commitment your own today?

See the Life Principles Index for further study:

2. *Obey God and leave all the consequences to Him.*
22. *To walk in the Spirit is to obey the initial promptings of the Spirit.*
1. *Our intimacy with God—His highest priority for our lives—determines the impact of our lives.*

5 So they said to him, "In Bethlehem of
Judea, for thus it is written by the prophet:

6 '*But you, Bethlehem, in the land of Judah,*
Are not the least among the rulers of
Judah;
For out of you shall come a Ruler
Who will shepherd My people Israel.'"[a]

7 Then Herod, when he had secretly called
the wise men, determined from them what
time the star appeared.
8 And he sent them to Bethlehem and said,
"Go and search carefully for the young Child,
and when you have found *Him,* bring back
word to me, that I may come and worship
Him also."
9 When they heard the king, they departed;
and behold, the star which they had seen in
the East went before them, till it came and
stood over where the young Child was.

2:6 [a]Micah 5:2

LIFE LESSONS

➤ ***2:8 — And he sent them to Bethlehem and said, "Go and search carefully for the young Child, and when you have found Him, bring back word to me, that I may come and worship Him also."***

Herod was apparently a good actor and used his skill to convince the wise men of his sincerity. Anyone can pretend to love God—but the proof is in a person's character.

Life Examples:

THE WISE MEN

Giving Passionate Praise

MATT. 2:1–12

The wise men eagerly journeyed to Bethlehem to give a royal welcome to the great new ruler of the world. They packed gold, frankincense, and myrrh so they could join in the heavenly worship of the infant King.

The wise men formed an important part of the celebration that surrounded Jesus' birth. In fact, they represented *you* in God's great plan. They portrayed the countless stargazers who set out in search of a king and find the Son of the living God.

Through your own seeking and serving, you become part of the heavenly symphony that gives passionate praise to the Savior. Allow your heart to burst into song at the thought of Him. Permit the tune of your being to swell with the joy of who He is. Just like the wise men, you have joined the great multitude in never-ending worship. Seek Him and sing, for surely He is worthy.

See the Life Principles Index for further study:

1. *Our intimacy with God—His highest priority for our lives—determines the impact of our lives.*

12. *Peace with God is the fruit of oneness with God.*

10 When they saw the star, they rejoiced with
exceedingly great joy.
➢ 11 And when they had come into the house,
they saw the young Child with Mary His
mother, and fell down and worshiped Him.
And when they had opened their treasures,
they presented gifts to Him: gold, frankincense, and myrrh.
12 Then, being divinely warned in a dream
that they should not return to Herod, they departed for their own country another way.

The Flight into Egypt

13 Now when they had departed, behold, an
angel of the Lord appeared to Joseph in a
dream, saying, "Arise, take the young Child
and His mother, flee to Egypt, and stay there
until I bring you word; for Herod will seek the
young Child to destroy Him."
14 When he arose, he took the young Child
and His mother by night and departed for
Egypt,
15 and was there until the death of Herod,
that it might be fulfilled which was spoken by
the Lord through the prophet, saying, *"Out of
Egypt I called My Son."*[a]

Massacre of the Innocents

16 Then Herod, when he saw that he was deceived by the wise men, was exceedingly
angry; and he sent forth and put to death all
the male children who were in Bethlehem and
in all its districts, from two years old and
under, according to the time which he had determined from the wise men.
17 Then was fulfilled what was spoken by Jeremiah the prophet, saying:
18 *"A voice was heard in Ramah,*
Lamentation, weeping, and great mourning,
Rachel weeping for her children,
Refusing to be comforted,
Because they are no more."[a]

The Home in Nazareth

19 Now when Herod was dead, behold, an
angel of the Lord appeared in a dream to Joseph in Egypt,
20 saying, "Arise, take the young Child and
His mother, and go to the land of Israel, for
those who sought the young Child's life are
dead."
21 Then he arose, took the young Child and
His mother, and came into the land of Israel.
22 But when he heard that Archelaus was ➢
reigning over Judea instead of his father

2:15 [a]Hosea 11:1 2:18 [a]Jeremiah 31:15

LIFE LESSONS

➢ **2:11 — *And when they had come into the house, they saw the young Child with Mary His mother, and fell down and worshiped Him.***

The wise men probably visited Jesus when He was about two years old; they came to a "house" instead of a stable and saw a "young Child" rather than an infant. But regardless of His age, they worshiped Him.

➢ **2:22 — *And being warned by God in a dream, he turned aside into the region of Galilee.***

Four times in this short narrative, Joseph received divine instructions through dreams. On one occasion the wise men get warned through a dream. God uses many methods to communicate His will to us (see also Matt. 27:19).

Herod, he was afraid to go there. And being warned by God in a dream, he turned aside into the region of Galilee.

23 And he came and dwelt in a city called Nazareth, that it might be fulfilled which was spoken by the prophets, "He shall be called a Nazarene."

John the Baptist Prepares the Way

3 In those days John the Baptist came preaching in the wilderness of Judea,

2 and saying, "Repent, for the kingdom of heaven is at hand!"

3 For this is he who was spoken of by the prophet Isaiah, saying:

"The voice of one crying in the wilderness:
'Prepare the way of the LORD;
Make His paths straight.'"[a]

4 Now John himself was clothed in camel's hair, with a leather belt around his waist; and his food was locusts and wild honey.

5 Then Jerusalem, all Judea, and all the region around the Jordan went out to him

6 and were baptized by him in the Jordan, confessing their sins.

7 But when he saw many of the Pharisees and Sadducees coming to his baptism, he said to them, "Brood of vipers! Who warned you to flee from the wrath to come?

➤ 8 "Therefore bear fruits worthy of repentance,

9 "and do not think to say to yourselves, 'We have Abraham as *our* father.' For I say to you that God is able to raise up children to Abraham from these stones.

10 "And even now the ax is laid to the root of the trees. Therefore every tree which does not bear good fruit is cut down and thrown into the fire.

11 "I indeed baptize you with water unto repentance, but He who is coming after me is mightier than I, whose sandals I am not worthy to carry. He will baptize you with the Holy Spirit and fire.[a]

12 "His winnowing fan *is* in His hand, and He will thoroughly clean out His threshing floor, and gather His wheat into the barn; but He will burn up the chaff with unquenchable fire."

John Baptizes Jesus

13 Then Jesus came from Galilee to John at the Jordan to be baptized by him.

14 And John *tried to* prevent Him, saying, "I need to be baptized by You, and are You coming to me?"

15 But Jesus answered and said to him, "Permit *it to be so* now, for thus it is fitting for us to fulfill all righteousness." Then he allowed Him. ◀

16 When He had been baptized, Jesus came up immediately from the water; and behold, the heavens were opened to Him, and He[a] saw the Spirit of God descending like a dove and alighting upon Him.

17 And suddenly a voice *came* from heaven, saying, "This is My beloved Son, in whom I am well pleased." ◀

Satan Tempts Jesus

4 Then Jesus was led up by the Spirit into the wilderness to be tempted by the devil. ◀

2 And when He had fasted forty days and forty nights, afterward He was hungry.

3 Now when the tempter came to Him, he said, "If You are the Son of God, command that these stones become bread." ◀

4 But He answered and said, "It is written, *'Man shall not live by bread alone, but by every word that proceeds from the mouth of God.'"*[a] ◀

3:3 [a]Isaiah 40:3 **3:11** [a]M-Text omits *and fire.* **3:16** [a]Or *he*
4:4 [a]Deuteronomy 8:3

LIFE LESSONS

➤ 3:8 — *"Therefore bear fruits worthy of repentance . . . ."*

Genuine repentance leads not only to a change in attitude, but also to a change in behavior. Merely feeling sorry for some wrong action does not constitute repentance.

➤ 3:15 — *But Jesus answered and said to him, "Permit it to be so now, for thus it is fitting for us to fulfill all righteousness."*

While He walked this earth, Jesus submitted Himself to the Law and to doing the whole will of His Father. Because He completely fulfilled the Law, believers also have fulfilled the Law through Him.

➤ 3:17 — *And suddenly a voice came from heaven, saying, "This is My beloved Son, in whom I am well pleased."*

God the Father loved Jesus the Son and publicly stated His pleasure in Christ's righteous manner of living. Yet it also "pleased" God to send His Son to the cross on our behalf (see Is. 53:10).

➤ 4:1 — *Then Jesus was led up by the Spirit into the wilderness to be tempted by the devil.*

The Holy Spirit led Jesus to a barren place where the devil waited to tempt Him. We should never doubt God's leading just because we run into temptation. That is often God's way of testing us.

➤ 4:3 — *Now when the tempter came to Him, he said, "If You are the Son of God . . . ."*

Satan tries to get us to doubt the Word of God and test God's promises. He will urge us to think that God cannot quite be trusted, or that what He has said is not the whole truth.

➤ 4:4, 7, 10 — *"It is written . . . . It is written . . . . it is written . . . ."*

Jesus responded to each of Satan's three temptations by appealing to the unchanging Word of God: "It is written!" If we want to successfully overcome temptation, we *must* know what the Word says.

5 Then the devil took Him up into the holy
city, set Him on the pinnacle of the temple,
6 and said to Him, "If You are the Son of
God, throw Yourself down. For it is written:

'He shall give His angels charge over you,'

and,

'In their hands they shall bear you up,
Lest you dash your foot against a
stone.'"[a]

7 Jesus said to him, "It is written again, *'You
shall not tempt the LORD your God.'*"[a]
8 Again, the devil took Him up on an exceedingly high mountain, and showed Him all
the kingdoms of the world and their glory.
9 And he said to Him, "All these things I will
give You if You will fall down and worship
me."
10 Then Jesus said to him, "Away with you,[a]
Satan! For it is written, *'You shall worship the
LORD your God, and Him only you shall
serve.'*"[b]
11 Then the devil left Him, and behold, angels came and ministered to Him.

Jesus Begins His Galilean Ministry

12 Now when Jesus heard that John had
been put in prison, He departed to Galilee.
13 And leaving Nazareth, He came and dwelt
in Capernaum, which is by the sea, in the regions of Zebulun and Naphtali,
14 that it might be fulfilled which was spoken
by Isaiah the prophet, saying:

15 "*The land of Zebulun and the land of*
Naphtali,
By the way of the sea, beyond the
Jordan,
Galilee of the Gentiles:
16 *The people who sat in darkness have*
seen a great light,
And upon those who sat in the region
and shadow of death
Light has dawned."[a]

17 From that time Jesus began to preach and
to say, "Repent, for the kingdom of heaven is
at hand."

Four Fishermen Called as Disciples

18 And Jesus, walking by the Sea of Galilee,
saw two brothers, Simon called Peter, and Andrew his brother, casting a net into the sea;
for they were fishermen.
19 Then He said to them, "Follow Me, and I
will make you fishers of men."
20 They immediately left *their* nets and followed Him.
21 Going on from there, He saw two other
brothers, James *the son* of Zebedee, and John
his brother, in the boat with Zebedee their father, mending their nets. He called them,
22 and immediately they left the boat and
their father, and followed Him.

Jesus Heals a Great Multitude

23 And Jesus went about all Galilee, teaching ➤
in their synagogues, preaching the gospel of
the kingdom, and healing all kinds of sickness
and all kinds of disease among the people.
24 Then His fame went throughout all Syria;
and they brought to Him all sick people who
were afflicted with various diseases and torments, and those who were demon-possessed, epileptics, and paralytics; and He
healed them.
25 Great multitudes followed Him—from
Galilee, and *from* Decapolis, Jerusalem,
Judea, and beyond the Jordan.

The Beatitudes

5 And seeing the multitudes, He went up on
a mountain, and when He was seated His
disciples came to Him.
2 Then He opened His mouth and taught
them, saying:

3 "Blessed *are* the poor in spirit,
For theirs is the kingdom of heaven.
4 Blessed *are* those who mourn,
For they shall be comforted.
5 Blessed *are* the meek,
For they shall inherit the earth.
6 Blessed *are* those who hunger and thirst ➤
for righteousness,
For they shall be filled.
7 Blessed *are* the merciful,
For they shall obtain mercy.
8 Blessed *are* the pure in heart,
For they shall see God.
9 Blessed *are* the peacemakers,
For they shall be called sons of God.

4:6 [a]Psalm 91:11, 12 **4:7** [a]Deuteronomy 6:16 **4:10** [a]M-Text reads *Get behind Me.* [b]Deuteronomy 6:13 **4:16** [a]Isaiah 9:1, 2

LIFE LESSONS

➤ ***4:23 — And Jesus went about all Galilee, teaching in their synagogues, preaching the gospel of the kingdom, and healing all kinds of sickness and all kinds of disease among the people.***

The earthly ministry of Jesus focused on teaching, preaching, and healing. He instructed the people, exhorted the people, and cured the people. Why? So that they might enjoy a more intimate relationship with His Father.

➤ ***5:6 — "Blessed are those who hunger and thirst for righteousness, for they shall be filled."***

To hunger and thirst for righteousness ultimately means that one hungers and thirsts for God. And those who long for God—the real God, not a false deity of their own imagination—will find Him and be filled.

10 Blessed are those who are persecuted for
righteousness' sake,
For theirs is the kingdom of heaven.

11 "Blessed are you when they revile and
persecute you, and say all kinds of evil
against you falsely for My sake.
12 "Rejoice and be exceedingly glad, for great
is your reward in heaven, for so they persecuted the prophets who were before you.

Believers Are Salt and Light

➤ **13** "You are the salt of the earth; but if the salt
loses its flavor, how shall it be seasoned? It is
then good for nothing but to be thrown out
and trampled underfoot by men.
14 "You are the light of the world. A city that
is set on a hill cannot be hidden.
15 "Nor do they light a lamp and put it under
a basket, but on a lampstand, and it gives
light to all *who are* in the house.
➤ 16 "Let your light so shine before men, that
they may see your good works and glorify
your Father in heaven.

Christ Fulfills the Law

➤ **17** "Do not think that I came to destroy the
Law or the Prophets. I did not come to destroy
but to fulfill.
✳ 18 "For assuredly, I say to you, till heaven and
earth pass away, one jot or one tittle will by
no means pass from the law till all is fulfilled.
19 "Whoever therefore breaks one of the least
of these commandments, and teaches men so,
shall be called least in the kingdom of heaven;
but whoever does and teaches *them,* he shall
be called great in the kingdom of heaven.
20 "For I say to you, that unless your righteousness exceeds *the righteousness* of the
scribes and Pharisees, you will by no means
enter the kingdom of heaven.

Murder Begins in the Heart

21 "You have heard that it was said to those
of old, *'You shall not murder,'*[a] and whoever
murders will be in danger of the judgment.'
22 "But I say to you that whoever is angry
with his brother without a cause[a] shall be in
danger of the judgment. And whoever says to
his brother, 'Raca!' shall be in danger of the
council. But whoever says, 'You fool!' shall be
in danger of hell fire.
23 "Therefore if you bring your gift to the
altar, and there remember that your brother
has something against you,
24 "leave your gift there before the altar, and
go your way. First be reconciled to your
brother, and then come and offer your gift.
25 "Agree with your adversary quickly, while
you are on the way with him, lest your adversary deliver you to the judge, the judge hand
you over to the officer, and you be thrown into
prison.
26 "Assuredly, I say to you, you will by no
means get out of there till you have paid the
last penny.

Adultery in the Heart

27 "You have heard that it was said to those
of old,[a] *'You shall not commit adultery.'*[b]
28 "But I say to you that whoever looks at a ➤
woman to lust for her has already committed
adultery with her in his heart.
29 "If your right eye causes you to sin, pluck it
out and cast *it* from you; for it is more profitable for you that one of your members perish,
than for your whole body to be cast into hell.
30 "And if your right hand causes you to sin,
cut it off and cast *it* from you; for it is more
profitable for you that one of your members
perish, than for your whole body to be cast
into hell.

Marriage Is Sacred and Binding

31 "Furthermore it has been said, 'Whoever
divorces his wife, let him give her a certificate
of divorce.'

5:21 [a]Exodus 20:13; Deuteronomy 5:17 **5:22** [a]NU-Text omits *without a cause.* **5:27** [a]NU-Text and M-Text omit *to those of old.* [b]Exodus 20:14; Deuteronomy 5:18

LIFE LESSONS

➤ 5:13 — *"You are the salt of the earth; but if the salt loses its flavor, how shall it be seasoned? It is then good for nothing but to be thrown out and trampled underfoot by men."*

Jesus wants us to take seriously our role as "salt," a preservative. Our behavior is to be distinctly different from those who do not know God, and it must not reflect the same kinds of sin that corrupt a godless culture.

➤ 5:16 — *"Let your light so shine before men, that they may see your good works and glorify your Father in heaven."*

Does anyone know that you are a light burning with the fire of heaven? What "good works" do they see you doing that reflect well on your heavenly Father? How does your faith cause you to behave differently from anyone else?

➤ 5:17 — *"Do not think that I came to destroy the Law or the Prophets. I did not come to destroy but to fulfill."*

Some people mistakenly think that Jesus came to reveal a God totally different from the One revealed in the Old Testament, but this is false. Jesus came to do the will of His Father, not to replace it with His own.

➤ 5:28 — *"But I say to you that whoever looks at a woman to lust for her has already committed adultery with her in his heart."*

Jesus made it clear that God is not after outward compliance but inward change. He doesn't want religious fanatics, but transformed men and women. He wants people who love to do His will.

32 "But I say to you that whoever divorces his
wife for any reason except sexual immorality[a] causes her to commit adultery; and whoever marries a woman who is divorced commits adultery.

Jesus Forbids Oaths

33 "Again you have heard that it was said to
those of old, 'You shall not swear falsely, but shall perform your oaths to the Lord.'
34 "But I say to you, do not swear at all: nei-
ther by heaven, for it is God's throne;
35 "nor by the earth, for it is His footstool;
nor by Jerusalem, for it is the city of the great King.
36 "Nor shall you swear by your head, because
you cannot make one hair white or black.
➤ 37 "But let your 'Yes' be 'Yes,' and your 'No,'
'No.' For whatever is more than these is from the evil one.

Go the Second Mile

38 "You have heard that it was said, *'An eye*
for an eye and a tooth for a tooth.'[a]
39 "But I tell you not to resist an evil person.
But whoever slaps you on your right cheek, turn the other to him also.
40 "If anyone wants to sue you and take away
your tunic, let him have *your* cloak also.
41 "And whoever compels you to go one mile,
go with him two.
42 "Give to him who asks you, and from him
who wants to borrow from you do not turn away.

Love Your Enemies

43 "You have heard that it was said, *'You*
shall love your neighbor[a] and hate your enemy.'
44 "But I say to you, love your enemies, bless
those who curse you, do good to those who hate you, and pray for those who spitefully use you and persecute you,[a]
45 "that you may be sons of your Father in
heaven; for He makes His sun rise on the evil and on the good, and sends rain on the just and on the unjust.
46 "For if you love those who love you, what
reward have you? Do not even the tax collectors do the same?
47 "And if you greet your brethren[a] only,
what do you do more *than others?* Do not even the tax collectors[b] do so?
48 "Therefore you shall be perfect, just as ◄
your Father in heaven is perfect.

Do Good to Please God

6 "Take heed that you do not do your charitable deeds before men, to be seen by them. Otherwise you have no reward from your Father in heaven.
2 "Therefore, when you do a charitable deed,
do not sound a trumpet before you as the hypocrites do in the synagogues and in the streets, that they may have glory from men. Assuredly, I say to you, they have their reward.
3 "But when you do a charitable deed, do not
let your left hand know what your right hand is doing,
4 "that your charitable deed may be in se- ◄
cret; and your Father who sees in secret will Himself reward you openly.[a]

The Model Prayer

5 "And when you pray, you shall not be like
the hypocrites. For they love to pray standing in the synagogues and on the corners of the streets, that they may be seen by men. Assuredly, I say to you, they have their reward.
6 "But you, when you pray, go into your
room, and when you have shut your door, pray to your Father who *is* in the secret *place;* and your Father who sees in secret will reward you openly.[a]
7 "And when you pray, do not use vain repe- ◄
titions as the heathen *do.* For they think that they will be heard for their many words.

5:32 [a]Or *fornication* **5:38** [a]Exodus 21:24; Leviticus 24:20; Deuteronomy 19:21 **5:43** [a]Compare Leviticus 19:18
5:44 [a]NU-Text omits three clauses from this verse, leaving, *"But I say to you, love your enemies and pray for those who persecute you."* **5:47** [a]M-Text reads *friends.* [b]NU-Text reads *Gentiles.*
6:4 [a]NU-Text omits *openly.* **6:6** [a]NU-Text omits *openly.*

LIFE LESSONS

➤ 5:37 — *"But let your 'Yes' be 'Yes,' and your 'No,' 'No.' For whatever is more than these is from the evil one."*

Jesus frowned on oath-taking. We tend to break our oaths, and a broken oath reflects badly on God's holy character. Our word should be just as trustworthy as an oath.

➤ 5:48 — *"Therefore you shall be perfect, just as your Father in heaven is perfect."*

The only way to be "perfect" as the Father is "perfect" is to be clothed, through faith, with the righteousness of Christ. This is necessary, for without holiness "no one will see the Lord" (Heb. 12:14).

➤ 6:4 — *". . . and your Father who sees in secret will Himself reward you openly."*

We do not need to trumpet our Spirit-led good deeds or advertise the kind things we do out of fear that they might otherwise get overlooked. God gives the only rewards that matter, and He keeps careful tally.

➤ 6:7 — *"And when you pray, do not use vain repetitions as the heathen do. For they think that they will be heard for their many words."*

Effective prayer is not magic; it's not about speaking the right string of words or using the correct formula. Instead, it's about communicating on a heart-to-heart level with the God of the universe.

WHAT THE BIBLE SAYS ABOUT LOVING THE UNLOVABLE

Matt. 5:45

From the man who cuts you off in traffic to the former friend who has offended you, you often get hurt by the thoughtless or deliberate actions of others. How do you typically react?

Jesus tells us that our behavior must radically differ from that of the world: "But I say to you, love your enemies, bless those who curse you, do good to those who hate you, and pray for those who spitefully use you and persecute you" (Matt. 5:45).

So what should you do when someone offends you? Follow a few basic steps to help move you toward a Christ-centered response.

1. Forgive the offender.

Hurt, when not addressed properly, turns into bitterness and an unforgiving spirit. Through the grace of Jesus Christ, you have the spiritual resources to truly forgive others (Matt. 18:21–35; Eph. 4:32). When you release someone from the debt he or she owes you, you are free to see that person as Christ does—and anger and bitterness no longer have the power to rule your decisions.

2. Seek to understand before you seek to be understood.

Practice the skill of listening, and try to imagine the perspective of the offender. What might have motivated his actions? What is going on in her life? Many times, a person who hurts you is also a victim of hurt. Understanding the offender's private pains could be a key step toward reconciliation or preventing further conflicts.

3. Speak with noncombative yet truthful words.

Speaking truth in love does not mean that your words will lack a sharp point; sometimes truth can feel very unsettling. The individual who has wounded you may need to grapple with some tough issues.

Only the Lord can work with a person's heart, but He asks you to continue to extend patience and love. And who knows? Maybe someday your "worst enemy" could become your best friend in Christ. Whatever the result, you can be sure of God's blessing as you seek His way of dealing with those who hurt you.

How do you typically react?

See the Life Principles Index for further study:

24. To live the Christian life is to allow Jesus to live His life in and through us.

28. No Christian has ever been called to "go it alone" in his or her walk of faith.

8 "Therefore do not be like them. For your Father knows the things you have need of before you ask Him.
9 "In this manner, therefore, pray:

Our Father in heaven,
Hallowed be Your name.
10 Your kingdom come.
Your will be done
On earth as *it is* in heaven.
11 Give us this day our daily bread.
12 And forgive us our debts,
As we forgive our debtors.
13 And do not lead us into temptation,
But deliver us from the evil one.
For Yours is the kingdom and the power
and the glory forever. Amen.[a]

14 "For if you forgive men their trespasses, your heavenly Father will also forgive you.
15 "But if you do not forgive men their trespasses, neither will your Father forgive your trespasses.

Fasting to Be Seen Only by God

16 "Moreover, when you fast, do not be like the hypocrites, with a sad countenance. For they disfigure their faces that they may appear to men to be fasting. Assuredly, I say to you, they have their reward.
17 "But you, when you fast, anoint your head and wash your face,
18 "so that you do not appear to men to be fasting, but to your Father who *is* in the secret *place;* and your Father who sees in secret will reward you openly.[a]

Lay Up Treasures in Heaven

19 "Do not lay up for yourselves treasures on earth, where moth and rust destroy and where thieves break in and steal;
20 "but lay up for yourselves treasures in heaven, where neither moth nor rust destroys and where thieves do not break in and steal.
➤ 21 "For where your treasure is, there your heart will be also.

The Lamp of the Body

22 "The lamp of the body is the eye. If therefore your eye is good, your whole body will be full of light.
23 "But if your eye is bad, your whole body will be full of darkness. If therefore the light that is in you is darkness, how great *is* that darkness!

You Cannot Serve God and Riches

24 "No one can serve two masters; for either he will hate the one and love the other, or else he will be loyal to the one and despise the other. You cannot serve God and mammon.

Do Not Worry

25 "Therefore I say to you, do not worry about your life, what you will eat or what you will drink; nor about your body, what you will put on. Is not life more than food and the body more than clothing?
26 "Look at the birds of the air, for they neither sow nor reap nor gather into barns; yet your heavenly Father feeds them. Are you not of more value than they?
27 "Which of you by worrying can add one cubit to his stature?
28 "So why do you worry about clothing? Consider the lilies of the field, how they grow: they neither toil nor spin;
29 "and yet I say to you that even Solomon in all his glory was not arrayed like one of these.
30 "Now if God so clothes the grass of the field, which today is, and tomorrow is thrown into the oven, *will He* not much more *clothe* you, O you of little faith?
31 "Therefore do not worry, saying, 'What shall we eat?' or 'What shall we drink?' or 'What shall we wear?'
32 "For after all these things the Gentiles seek. For your heavenly Father knows that you need all these things.
33 "But seek first the kingdom of God and His righteousness, and all these things shall be added to you.
34 "Therefore do not worry about tomorrow, for tomorrow will worry about its own things. Sufficient for the day *is* its own trouble.

6:13 [a]NU-Text omits *For Yours* through *Amen.* 6:18 [a]NU-Text and M-Text omit *openly.*

LIFE LESSONS

➤ 6:21 — *"For where your treasure is, there your heart will be also."*

What do you think about most throughout the day? What gets your heart beating fastest and loudest? What do you think you couldn't live without? Whatever "it" is, it's your treasure—and nothing but God is worthy of it.

➤ 6:24 — *"No one can serve two masters; for either he will hate the one and love the other, or else he will be loyal to the one and despise the other."*

Too many of us try to serve two masters: God *and* work, or God *and* bank accounts, or God *and* family. But Jesus says this is impossible, for two masters inevitably give contradictory demands. Who will *you* serve?

➤ 6:32 — *". . . For your heavenly Father knows that you need all these things."*

God doesn't tell us to stop worrying over food and shelter and clothing because we don't really need them; He *knows* we need them. We can stop worrying because He has promised to take care of the essentials.

ANSWERS TO LIFE'S QUESTIONS

How can I overcome anxiety?

MATT. 6:25–34

God did not design you to be anxious or nervous. In His Sermon on the Mount, Jesus told the crowds, "Do not worry, saying, 'What shall we eat?' or 'What shall we drink?' or 'What shall we wear?' . . . Therefore do not worry about tomorrow . . . ." (Matt. 6:31, 34).

All of us have worried about the basics of life. When we reduce most of our anxieties to their lowest terms, we discover they involve fundamental things: where we live, what food we buy, what clothes to wear, what friends we have, what others think about us. In all these concerns, the issue for believers in Jesus Christ comes down to trust.

Do you believe that you are in charge of your life? Or do you acknowledge that God directs and provides? Your answer has everything to do with your anxiety level.

Have you ever watched a mouse running inside a wheel? The faster he runs, the faster the wheel moves—but he doesn't make the slightest progress. He does not even have the sense to get off the wheel.

That is what anxiety does to you. You run faster and faster, trying harder and harder to meet demands or prevent disaster—and still you do not have control over your circumstances. So when something does not go quite right, your frustration level continues to mount.

There is a way off the wheel, however. God created you. He knows your deepest needs (Ps. 68:19). He longs for you to end the anxiety cycle and let Him lead (Matt. 11:28). First Peter 5:6, 7 says, "Therefore humble yourselves under the mighty hand of God, that He may exalt you in due time, casting all your care upon Him, for He cares for you." The word "casting" is related to the Greek verb used in Luke 19:35, when on Palm Sunday the people of Jerusalem threw their garments onto a colt for Jesus to ride. The word describes the same motion: a deliberate action of setting something down and leaving it there.

Jesus wants you to throw your cares on Him *and leave them there.* You depend on Him for life itself, and you acknowledge this reliant relationship by saying, "Here, Jesus. Take my problems. You have the answers! I trust You to show me what to do and to take care of the consequences."

See the Life Principles Index for further study:

11. God assumes full responsibility for our needs when we obey Him.

9. Trusting God means looking beyond what we can see to what God sees.

Do Not Judge

7 "Judge not, that you be not judged.
2 "For with what judgment you judge, you
will be judged; and with the measure you use,
it will be measured back to you.
3 "And why do you look at the speck in your
brother's eye, but do not consider the plank in
your own eye?
4 "Or how can you say to your brother, 'Let
me remove the speck from your eye'; and
look, a plank *is* in your own eye?
5 "Hypocrite! First remove the plank from
your own eye, and then you will see clearly to
remove the speck from your brother's eye.
6 "Do not give what is holy to the dogs; nor
cast your pearls before swine, lest they trample them under their feet, and turn and tear
you in pieces.

Keep Asking, Seeking, Knocking

7 "Ask, and it will be given to you; seek, and
you will find; knock, and it will be opened to
you.
8 "For everyone who asks receives, and he

LIFE LESSONS

➤ 7:2 — *"For with what judgment you judge, you will be judged; and with the measure you use, it will be measured back to you."*

Living by this simple guideline would eliminate the vast majority of the squabbles and conflicts we endure. Would we want to be judged by the standards we judge others? Do we demand grace but never give mercy?

➤ 7:7 — *"Ask, and it will be given to you; seek, and you will find; knock, and it will be opened to you."*

We must get it out of our heads that God is stingy or miserly or tight-fisted with His grace and goodness. He delights in showering us with good things—but we have to present Him with our requests.

who seeks finds, and to him who knocks it
will be opened.
9 "Or what man is there among you who, if
his son asks for bread, will give him a stone?
10 "Or if he asks for a fish, will he give him a
serpent?
11 "If you then, being evil, know how to give
good gifts to your children, how much more
will your Father who is in heaven give good
things to those who ask Him!
12 "Therefore, whatever you want men to do
to you, do also to them, for this is the Law and
the Prophets.

The Narrow Way

13 "Enter by the narrow gate; for wide *is* the
gate and broad *is* the way that leads to destruction, and there are many who go in by it.
14 "Because[a] narrow *is* the gate and difficult
is the way which leads to life, and there are
few who find it.

You Will Know Them by Their Fruits

15 "Beware of false prophets, who come to
you in sheep's clothing, but inwardly they are
ravenous wolves.
16 "You will know them by their fruits. Do
men gather grapes from thornbushes or figs
from thistles?
17 "Even so, every good tree bears good fruit,
but a bad tree bears bad fruit.
18 "A good tree cannot bear bad fruit, nor
can a bad tree bear good fruit.
19 "Every tree that does not bear good fruit is
cut down and thrown into the fire.
20 "Therefore by their fruits you will know
them.

I Never Knew You

21 "Not everyone who says to Me, 'Lord,
Lord,' shall enter the kingdom of heaven, but
he who does the will of My Father in heaven.
22 "Many will say to Me in that day, 'Lord,
Lord, have we not prophesied in Your name,
cast out demons in Your name, and done
many wonders in Your name?'
23 "And then I will declare to them, 'I never
knew you; depart from Me, you who practice
lawlessness!'

Build on the Rock

24 "Therefore whoever hears these sayings
of Mine, and does them, I will liken him to a
wise man who built his house on the rock:
25 "and the rain descended, the floods came,
and the winds blew and beat on that house;
and it did not fall, for it was founded on the
rock.
26 "But everyone who hears these sayings of
Mine, and does not do them, will be like a
foolish man who built his house on the sand:
27 "and the rain descended, the floods came,
and the winds blew and beat on that house;
and it fell. And great was its fall."
28 And so it was, when Jesus had ended
these sayings, that the people were astonished at His teaching,
29 for He taught them as one having authority, and not as the scribes.

Jesus Cleanses a Leper

8 When He had come down from the mountain, great multitudes followed Him.
2 And behold, a leper came and worshiped
Him, saying, "Lord, if You are willing, You can
make me clean."
3 Then Jesus put out *His* hand and touched
him, saying, "I am willing; be cleansed." Immediately his leprosy was cleansed.
4 And Jesus said to him, "See that you tell
no one; but go your way, show yourself to the
priest, and offer the gift that Moses commanded, as a testimony to them."

Jesus Heals a Centurion's Servant

5 Now when Jesus had entered Capernaum,
a centurion came to Him, pleading with Him,
6 saying, "Lord, my servant is lying at home
paralyzed, dreadfully tormented."

7:14 [a]NU-Text and M-Text read *How . . . !*

LIFE LESSONS

➤ 7:12 — *"Therefore, whatever you want men to do to you, do also to them, for this is the Law and the Prophets."*

If we want to be treated kindly, we must treat others with kindness. If we want to be given the benefit of the doubt, we must give others the benefit of the doubt. If we want good things for us, we must want good things for others.

➤ 7:21 — *"Not everyone who says to Me, 'Lord, Lord,' shall enter the kingdom of heaven, but he who does the will of My Father in heaven."*

Willing and eager obedience is the hallmark of someone who has truly come to faith in Jesus Christ. They obey, not because they want to earn God's favor, but because they feel delighted already to have received it.

➤ 7:24 — *"Therefore whoever hears these sayings of Mine, and does them, I will liken him to a wise man who built his house on the rock . . . ."*

Joyful obedience to Christ creates a firm foundation for living. Those who obey out of love for Jesus build a solid life for themselves of strength and endurance. Terrible storms may hit them, but they can never destroy them.

➤ 7:29 — *. . . He taught them as one having authority, and not as the scribes.*

Some time, read straight through in your Bible from the prophets to the Gospels. You'll feel almost jolted by the huge difference between, "thus says the Lord" of the prophets, and "But I say to you," of Jesus.

7 And Jesus said to him, "I will come and heal him."
8 The centurion answered and said, "Lord, I am not worthy that You should come under my roof. But only speak a word, and my servant will be healed.
➤ 9 "For I also am a man under authority, having soldiers under me. And I say to this *one*, 'Go,' and he goes; and to another, 'Come,' and he comes; and to my servant, 'Do this,' and he does *it*."
10 When Jesus heard *it*, He marveled, and said to those who followed, "Assuredly, I say to you, I have not found such great faith, not even in Israel!
11 "And I say to you that many will come from east and west, and sit down with Abraham, Isaac, and Jacob in the kingdom of heaven.
12 "But the sons of the kingdom will be cast out into outer darkness. There will be weeping and gnashing of teeth."
➤ 13 Then Jesus said to the centurion, "Go your way; and as you have believed, so let it be done for you." And his servant was healed that same hour.

Peter's Mother-in-Law Healed

14 Now when Jesus had come into Peter's house, He saw his wife's mother lying sick with a fever.
15 So He touched her hand, and the fever left her. And she arose and served them.[a]

Many Healed in the Evening

16 When evening had come, they brought to Him many who were demon-possessed. And He cast out the spirits with a word, and healed all who were sick,
17 that it might be fulfilled which was spoken by Isaiah the prophet, saying:

"He Himself took our infirmities
And bore our sicknesses."[a]

The Cost of Discipleship

18 And when Jesus saw great multitudes about Him, He gave a command to depart to the other side.
19 Then a certain scribe came and said to Him, "Teacher, I will follow You wherever You go."
20 And Jesus said to him, "Foxes have holes and birds of the air *have* nests, but the Son of Man has nowhere to lay *His* head."
21 Then another of His disciples said to Him, "Lord, let me first go and bury my father."
22 But Jesus said to him, "Follow Me, and let the dead bury their own dead."

Wind and Wave Obey Jesus

23 Now when He got into a boat, His disciples followed Him.
24 And suddenly a great tempest arose on the sea, so that the boat was covered with the waves. But He was asleep.
25 Then His disciples came to *Him* and awoke Him, saying, "Lord, save us! We are perishing!"
26 But He said to them, "Why are you fearful, ➤
O you of little faith?" Then He arose and rebuked the winds and the sea, and there was a great calm.
27 So the men marveled, saying, "Who can this be, that even the winds and the sea obey Him?"

Two Demon-Possessed Men Healed

28 When He had come to the other side, to the country of the Gergesenes,[a] there met Him two demon-possessed *men*, coming out of the tombs, exceedingly fierce, so that no one could pass that way.
29 And suddenly they cried out, saying, "What have we to do with You, Jesus, You Son of God? Have You come here to torment us before the time?"
30 Now a good way off from them there was a herd of many swine feeding.
31 So the demons begged Him, saying, "If You cast us out, permit us to go away[a] into the herd of swine."
32 And He said to them, "Go." So when they had come out, they went into the herd of

8:15 [a]NU-Text and M-Text read *Him*. **8:17** [a]Isaiah 53:4
8:28 [a]NU-Text reads *Gadarenes*. **8:31** [a]NU-Text reads *send us*.

LIFE LESSONS

➤ 8:9 — *"For I also am a man under authority, having soldiers under me."*

The Roman centurion recognized in Jesus an authority far beyond what most observers detected. He trusted in the power and word of Jesus because He first saw and acknowledged His supernatural authority.

➤ 8:13 — *Then Jesus said to the centurion, "Go your way; and as you have believed, so let it be done for you." And his servant was healed that same hour.*

Why is faith such a powerful trigger for the miracles of God? God delights to do extraordinary things for those who bank their lives on His goodness and grace. When we exercise faith in God, we're telling Him, "I believe You."

➤ 8:26 — *But He said to them, "Why are you fearful, O you of little faith?" Then He arose and rebuked the winds and the sea, and there was a great calm.*

The storm terrified the disciples, but it didn't so much as raise an eyebrow on the Lord. Why the difference? Because Jesus trusted that God would get them to the other side.

Life Examples:

MATTHEW

Leaving It All Behind

MATT. 9:9–17

After years of counting out coins, writing out customs receipts, and collecting Roman taxes from his Jewish countrymen, Matthew finally heard an offer he could not refuse. "Follow me," Jesus said to him, and "he left all, rose up, and followed Him" (Luke 5:28).

Matthew left *everything.* The taxes. The extorted excess. The receipts. He left it all—except, praise God, his gift of accurate record-keeping!

Before his conversion, his name had been Levi, the son of Alphaeus (Mark 2:14). But after he came to Christ, he received a new name, Matthew ("Gift of the Lord"). When Luke and Mark refer to Matthew, they call him Levi. But in Matthew 10:3, he refers to himself as "Matthew the tax collector"—a pointed reminder of a past he had given up.

What "old life" did you leave behind in order to fully follow the Son of God?

See the Life Principles Index for further study:
23. You can never outgive God.
2. Obey God and leave all the consequences to Him.

swine. And suddenly the whole herd of swine ran violently down the steep place into the sea, and perished in the water.
33 Then those who kept *them* fled; and they went away into the city and told everything, including what *had happened* to the demon-possessed *men.*
34 And behold, the whole city came out to meet Jesus. And when they saw Him, they begged *Him* to depart from their region.

Jesus Forgives and Heals a Paralytic

9 So He got into a boat, crossed over, and came to His own city.
2 Then behold, they brought to Him a paralytic lying on a bed. When Jesus saw their faith, He said to the paralytic, "Son, be of good cheer; your sins are forgiven you."
3 And at once some of the scribes said within themselves, "This Man blasphemes!"
4 But Jesus, knowing their thoughts, said, "Why do you think evil in your hearts?
5 "For which is easier, to say, *'Your* sins are forgiven you,' or to say, 'Arise and walk'?
6 "But that you may know that the Son of Man has power on earth to forgive sins"—then He said to the paralytic, "Arise, take up your bed, and go to your house."
7 And he arose and departed to his house.
8 Now when the multitudes saw *it,* they marveled[a] and glorified God, who had given such power to men.

Matthew the Tax Collector

9 As Jesus passed on from there, He saw a man named Matthew sitting at the tax office. And He said to him, "Follow Me." So he arose and followed Him.
10 Now it happened, as Jesus sat at the table in the house, *that* behold, many tax collectors and sinners came and sat down with Him and His disciples.
11 And when the Pharisees saw *it,* they said to His disciples, "Why does your Teacher eat with tax collectors and sinners?"
12 When Jesus heard *that,* He said to them, "Those who are well have no need of a physician, but those who are sick.
13 "But go and learn what *this* means: *'I desire mercy and not sacrifice.'*[a] For I did not come to call the righteous, but sinners, to repentance."[b]

9:8 [a]NU-Text reads *were afraid.* **9:13** [a]Hosea 6:6 [b]NU-Text omits *to repentance.*

LIFE LESSONS

➤ 8:34 — *And behold, the whole city came out to meet Jesus. And when they saw Him, they begged Him to depart from their region.*

Not everyone is happy to see the wonder-working arm of God. Some would rather stick with their comfortable, familiar routines. A life of faith is not necessarily comfortable, but it is exciting.

➤ 9:2 — *When Jesus saw their faith . . . .*

It would be hard to "see" faith if it never worked its way out in meaningful action. If our faith does not affect the way we live or ever get noticed by others, then perhaps it is not genuine faith at all.

➤ 9:13 — *"But go and learn what this means: 'I desire mercy and not sacrifice.'"*

Throughout the Bible, God wants our hearts, not merely our lips. He wants genuine devotion to Him that results in beneficial action toward others. Dutiful religious activity means nothing without devotion to God and a real concern for others.

Jesus Is Questioned About Fasting

14 Then the disciples of John came to Him, saying, "Why do we and the Pharisees fast often,[a] but Your disciples do not fast?"

15 And Jesus said to them, "Can the friends of the bridegroom mourn as long as the bridegroom is with them? But the days will come when the bridegroom will be taken away from them, and then they will fast.

16 "No one puts a piece of unshrunk cloth on an old garment; for the patch pulls away from the garment, and the tear is made worse.

17 "Nor do they put new wine into old wineskins, or else the wineskins break, the wine is spilled, and the wineskins are ruined. But they put new wine into new wineskins, and both are preserved."

A Girl Restored to Life and a Woman Healed

18 While He spoke these things to them, behold, a ruler came and worshiped Him, saying, "My daughter has just died, but come and lay Your hand on her and she will live."

19 So Jesus arose and followed him, and so *did* His disciples.

20 And suddenly, a woman who had a flow of blood for twelve years came from behind and touched the hem of His garment.

21 For she said to herself, "If only I may touch His garment, I shall be made well."

22 But Jesus turned around, and when He saw her He said, "Be of good cheer, daughter; your faith has made you well." And the woman was made well from that hour.

23 When Jesus came into the ruler's house, and saw the flute players and the noisy crowd wailing,

➤ 24 He said to them, "Make room, for the girl is not dead, but sleeping." And they ridiculed Him.

25 But when the crowd was put outside, He went in and took her by the hand, and the girl arose.

26 And the report of this went out into all that land.

Two Blind Men Healed

27 When Jesus departed from there, two blind men followed Him, crying out and saying, "Son of David, have mercy on us!"

28 And when He had come into the house, the blind men came to Him. And Jesus said to them, "Do you believe that I am able to do this?" They said to Him, "Yes, Lord."

29 Then He touched their eyes, saying, "According to your faith let it be to you."

30 And their eyes were opened. And Jesus sternly warned them, saying, "See *that* no one knows *it*."

31 But when they had departed, they spread the news about Him in all that country.

A Mute Man Speaks

32 As they went out, behold, they brought to Him a man, mute and demon-possessed.

33 And when the demon was cast out, the mute spoke. And the multitudes marveled, saying, "It was never seen like this in Israel!"

34 But the Pharisees said, "He casts out demons by the ruler of the demons."

The Compassion of Jesus

35 Then Jesus went about all the cities and villages, teaching in their synagogues, preaching the gospel of the kingdom, and healing every sickness and every disease among the people.[a]

36 But when He saw the multitudes, He was moved with compassion for them, because they were weary[a] and scattered, like sheep having no shepherd. ➤

37 Then He said to His disciples, "The harvest truly *is* plentiful, but the laborers *are* few.

38 "Therefore pray the Lord of the harvest to send out laborers into His harvest."

The Twelve Apostles

10 And when He had called His twelve disciples to *Him*, He gave them power *over* unclean spirits, to cast them out, and to heal all kinds of sickness and all kinds of disease.

2 Now the names of the twelve apostles are these: first, Simon, who is called Peter, and Andrew his brother; James the *son* of Zebedee, and John his brother;

3 Philip and Bartholomew; Thomas and Matthew the tax collector; James the *son* of Alphaeus, and Lebbaeus, whose surname was[a] Thaddaeus;

9:14 [a]NU-Text brackets *often* as disputed. **9:35** [a]NU-Text omits *among the people.* **9:36** [a]NU-Text and M-Text read *harassed.* **10:3** [a]NU-Text omits *Lebbaeus, whose surname was.*

LIFE LESSONS

➤ ***9:24 — He said to them, "Make room, for the girl is not dead, but sleeping." And they ridiculed Him.***

Because Jesus looked beyond what people could see to what God sees, they ridiculed him. Faith often looks ridiculous to those who don't have it. But God does what no one else can.

➤ ***9:36 — But when He saw the multitudes, He was moved with compassion for them, because they were weary and scattered, like sheep having no shepherd.***

By this point in the story, Jesus and His men were tired and needed a rest. But when Jesus saw the haggard masses, He couldn't help but feel compassion for them, so He continued to minister to them. He is the Good Shepherd.

4 Simon the Cananite,[a] and Judas Iscariot, who also betrayed Him.

Sending Out the Twelve

5 These twelve Jesus sent out and commanded them, saying: "Do not go into the way of the Gentiles, and do not enter a city of the Samaritans.

6 "But go rather to the lost sheep of the house of Israel.

7 "And as you go, preach, saying, 'The kingdom of heaven is at hand.'

8 "Heal the sick, cleanse the lepers, raise the dead,[a] cast out demons. Freely you have received, freely give.

9 "Provide neither gold nor silver nor copper in your money belts,

10 "nor bag for *your* journey, nor two tunics, nor sandals, nor staffs; for a worker is worthy of his food.

11 "Now whatever city or town you enter, inquire who in it is worthy, and stay there till you go out.

12 "And when you go into a household, greet it.

13 "If the household is worthy, let your peace come upon it. But if it is not worthy, let your peace return to you.

14 "And whoever will not receive you nor hear your words, when you depart from that house or city, shake off the dust from your feet.

15 "Assuredly, I say to you, it will be more tolerable for the land of Sodom and Gomorrah in the day of judgment than for that city!

Persecutions Are Coming

16 "Behold, I send you out as sheep in the midst of wolves. Therefore be wise as serpents and harmless as doves.

17 "But beware of men, for they will deliver you up to councils and scourge you in their synagogues.

18 "You will be brought before governors and kings for My sake, as a testimony to them and to the Gentiles.

19 "But when they deliver you up, do not worry about how or what you should speak. For it will be given to you in that hour what you should speak;

20 "for it is not you who speak, but the Spirit of your Father who speaks in you.

21 "Now brother will deliver up brother to death, and a father *his* child; and children will rise up against parents and cause them to be put to death.

22 "And you will be hated by all for My name's sake. But he who endures to the end will be saved.

23 "When they persecute you in this city, flee to another. For assuredly, I say to you, you will not have gone through the cities of Israel before the Son of Man comes.

24 "A disciple is not above *his* teacher, nor a servant above his master.

25 "It is enough for a disciple that he be like his teacher, and a servant like his master. If they have called the master of the house Beelzebub,[a] how much more *will they call* those of his household!

26 "Therefore do not fear them. For there is nothing covered that will not be revealed, and hidden that will not be known.

Jesus Teaches the Fear of God

27 "Whatever I tell you in the dark, speak in the light; and what you hear in the ear, preach on the housetops.

28 "And do not fear those who kill the body but cannot kill the soul. But rather fear Him who is able to destroy both soul and body in hell.

29 "Are not two sparrows sold for a copper coin? And not one of them falls to the ground apart from your Father's will.

30 "But the very hairs of your head are all numbered.

31 "Do not fear therefore; you are of more value than many sparrows.

Confess Christ Before Men

32 "Therefore whoever confesses Me before men, him I will also confess before My Father who is in heaven.

33 "But whoever denies Me before men, him I will also deny before My Father who is in heaven.

10:4 [a]NU-Text reads *Cananaean.* **10:8** [a]NU-Text reads *raise the dead, cleanse the lepers;* M-Text omits *raise the dead.*
10:25 [a]NU-Text and M-Text read *Beelzebul.*

LIFE LESSONS

➤ 10:8 — *"Freely you have received, freely give."*

God blesses us so that we can bless others. He does not show us His goodness so that we can hoard it all to ourselves in heedless unconcern of the hurts of those around us.

➤ 10:16 — *"Behold, I send you out as sheep in the midst of wolves."*

Jesus was under no illusions as He sent His disciples out to minister. He knew what was waiting for them—and He knows what is waiting for us. Still He sends us, to represent Him under the protection of His Father.

➤ 10:28 — *"And do not fear those who kill the body but cannot kill the soul. But rather fear Him who is able to destroy both soul and body in hell."*

Just before His execution, Jesus told the Roman governor, Pilate, "You could have no power at all against Me unless it had been given you from above" (John 19:11). He didn't fear Pilate because God was in control.

Christ Brings Division

➤ **34** "Do not think that I came to bring peace on earth. I did not come to bring peace but a sword.
35 "For I have come to *'set a man against his father, a daughter against her mother, and a daughter-in-law against her mother-in-law';*
36 "and *'a man's enemies will be those of his own household.'*[a]
37 "He who loves father or mother more than Me is not worthy of Me. And he who loves son or daughter more than Me is not worthy of Me.
38 "And he who does not take his cross and follow after Me is not worthy of Me.
39 "He who finds his life will lose it, and he who loses his life for My sake will find it.

A Cup of Cold Water

40 "He who receives you receives Me, and he who receives Me receives Him who sent Me.
41 "He who receives a prophet in the name of a prophet shall receive a prophet's reward. And he who receives a righteous man in the name of a righteous man shall receive a righteous man's reward.
➤ 42 "And whoever gives one of these little ones only a cup of cold *water* in the name of a disciple, assuredly, I say to you, he shall by no means lose his reward."

John the Baptist Sends Messengers to Jesus

11 Now it came to pass, when Jesus finished commanding His twelve disciples, that He departed from there to teach and to preach in their cities.
2 And when John had heard in prison about the works of Christ, he sent two of[a] his disciples
3 and said to Him, "Are You the Coming One, or do we look for another?"
4 Jesus answered and said to them, "Go and tell John the things which you hear and see:
5 "*The* blind see and *the* lame walk; *the* lepers are cleansed and *the* deaf hear; *the* dead are raised up and *the* poor have the gospel preached to them.
6 "And blessed is he who is not offended because of Me."
7 As they departed, Jesus began to say to the multitudes concerning John: "What did you go out into the wilderness to see? A reed shaken by the wind?
8 "But what did you go out to see? A man clothed in soft garments? Indeed, those who wear soft *clothing* are in kings' houses.
9 "But what did you go out to see? A prophet? Yes, I say to you, and more than a prophet.
10 "For this is *he* of whom it is written:

'Behold, I send My messenger before
Your face,
Who will prepare Your way before You.'[a]

11 "Assuredly, I say to you, among those born of women there has not risen one greater than John the Baptist; but he who is least in the kingdom of heaven is greater than he. ➤
12 "And from the days of John the Baptist until now the kingdom of heaven suffers violence, and the violent take it by force.
13 "For all the prophets and the law prophesied until John.
14 "And if you are willing to receive *it*, he is Elijah who is to come.
15 "He who has ears to hear, let him hear!
16 "But to what shall I liken this generation? It is like children sitting in the marketplaces and calling to their companions,
17 "and saying:

'We played the flute for you,
And you did not dance;
We mourned to you,
And you did not lament.'

18 "For John came neither eating nor drinking, and they say, 'He has a demon.'
19 "The Son of Man came eating and drinking, and they say, 'Look, a glutton and a winebibber, a friend of tax collectors and sinners!' But wisdom is justified by her children."[a]

10:36 [a]Micah 7:6 **11:2** [a]NU-Text reads *by* for *two of.*
11:10 [a]Malachi 3:1 **11:19** [a]NU-Text reads *works.*

LIFE LESSONS

➤ 10:34 — *"Do not think that I came to bring peace on earth. I did not come to bring peace but a sword."*

Jesus always brings peace to the human heart, and one day He will bring peace to the whole planet. But these days, a person's faith in Him can often cause major rifts in families, friendships, and other relationships.

➤ 10:42 — *"And whoever gives one of these little ones only a cup of cold water in the name of a disciple, assuredly, I say to you, he shall by no means lose his reward."*

God doesn't reward only "big" jobs and "important" works. He loves to give and He loves to reward obedience, no matter how "small" or "insignificant" it may seem to us.

➤ 11:11 — *"Assuredly, I say to you, among those born of women there has not risen one greater than John the Baptist; but he who is least in the kingdom of heaven is greater than he."*

Today, believers have something unknown to believers in Old Testament times: the indwelling and permanent presence of the Holy Spirit. We are the temple of the Holy Spirit, and that makes us "great" in God's eyes.

Woe to the Impenitent Cities
20 Then He began to rebuke the cities in
which most of His mighty works had been
done, because they did not repent:
21 "Woe to you, Chorazin! Woe to you, Bethsaida! For if the mighty works which were
done in you had been done in Tyre and Sidon,
they would have repented long ago in sackcloth and ashes.
22 "But I say to you, it will be more tolerable
for Tyre and Sidon in the day of judgment
than for you.
23 "And you, Capernaum, who are exalted to
heaven, will be[a] brought down to Hades; for if
the mighty works which were done in you
had been done in Sodom, it would have remained until this day.
24 "But I say to you that it shall be more tolerable for the land of Sodom in the day of
judgment than for you."

Jesus Gives True Rest
25 At that time Jesus answered and said, "I
thank You, Father, Lord of heaven and earth,
that You have hidden these things from *the*
wise and prudent and have revealed them to
babes.
26 "Even so, Father, for so it seemed good in
Your sight.
27 "All things have been delivered to Me by
My Father, and no one knows the Son except
the Father. Nor does anyone know the Father
except the Son, and *the one* to whom the Son
wills to reveal *Him*.
✳ 28 "Come to Me, all *you* who labor and are
heavy laden, and I will give you rest.
➤ 29 "Take My yoke upon you and learn from
Me, for I am gentle and lowly in heart, and
you will find rest for your souls.
30 "For My yoke *is* easy and My burden is
light."

Jesus Is Lord of the Sabbath
12 At that time Jesus went through the
grainfields on the Sabbath. And His
disciples were hungry, and began to pluck
heads of grain and to eat.
2 And when the Pharisees saw *it*, they said
to Him, "Look, Your disciples are doing what
is not lawful to do on the Sabbath!"
3 But He said to them, "Have you not read
what David did when he was hungry, he and
those who were with him:
4 "how he entered the house of God and ate
the showbread which was not lawful for him
to eat, nor for those who were with him, but
only for the priests?
5 "Or have you not read in the law that on
the Sabbath the priests in the temple profane
the Sabbath, and are blameless?
6 "Yet I say to you that in this place there is
One greater than the temple.
7 "But if you had known what *this* means, *'I
desire mercy and not sacrifice,'*[a] you would
not have condemned the guiltless.
8 "For the Son of Man is Lord even[a] of the ◄
Sabbath."

Healing on the Sabbath
9 Now when He had departed from there,
He went into their synagogue.
10 And behold, there was a man who had a
withered hand. And they asked Him, saying,
"Is it lawful to heal on the Sabbath?"—that
they might accuse Him.
11 Then He said to them, "What man is there
among you who has one sheep, and if it falls
into a pit on the Sabbath, will not lay hold of
it and lift *it* out?
12 "Of how much more value then is a man
than a sheep? Therefore it is lawful to do
good on the Sabbath."
13 Then He said to the man, "Stretch out your
hand." And he stretched *it* out, and it was restored as whole as the other.
14 Then the Pharisees went out and plotted
against Him, how they might destroy Him.

Behold, My Servant
15 But when Jesus knew *it*, He withdrew
from there. And great multitudes[a] followed
Him, and He healed them all.
16 Yet He warned them not to make Him
known,
17 that it might be fulfilled which was spoken
by Isaiah the prophet, saying:
18 *"Behold! My Servant whom I have chosen,*
My Beloved in whom My soul is well
pleased!
I will put My Spirit upon Him,
And He will declare justice to the Gentiles.

11:23 [a]NU-Text reads *will you be exalted to heaven? No, you will be.* **12:7** [a]Hosea 6:6 **12:8** [a]NU-Text and M-Text omit *even.* **12:15** [a]NU-Text brackets *multitudes* as disputed.

LIFE LESSONS

➤ 11:29 — "Take My yoke upon you and learn from Me, for I am gentle and lowly in heart, and you will find rest for your souls."

All of us need rest, and Jesus promises to give it to us when we find our rest in Him. He will not scold us for being weak or scorn us for being foolish. He promises to gently and humbly refresh our weary souls.

➤ 12:8 — "For the Son of Man is Lord even of the Sabbath."

As the Creator of heaven and earth, Jesus was far greater than the Sabbath, a day instituted to remember His work of creation. Jesus is Lord of all, and the Sabbath was intended to honor Him.

19 *He will not quarrel nor cry out,*
Nor will anyone hear His voice in the streets.
20 *A bruised reed He will not break,*
And smoking flax He will not quench,
Till He sends forth justice to victory;
21 *And in His name Gentiles will trust."*[a]

A House Divided Cannot Stand

22 Then one was brought to Him who was
demon-possessed, blind and mute; and He
healed him, so that the blind and[a] mute man
both spoke and saw.
23 And all the multitudes were amazed and
said, "Could this be the Son of David?"
24 Now when the Pharisees heard *it* they said,
"This *fellow* does not cast out demons except
by Beelzebub,[a] the ruler of the demons."
➤ 25 But Jesus knew their thoughts, and said to
them: "Every kingdom divided against itself
is brought to desolation, and every city or
house divided against itself will not stand.
26 "If Satan casts out Satan, he is divided
against himself. How then will his kingdom
stand?
27 "And if I cast out demons by Beelzebub, by
whom do your sons cast *them* out? Therefore
they shall be your judges.
28 "But if I cast out demons by the Spirit of
God, surely the kingdom of God has come
upon you.
29 "Or how can one enter a strong man's
house and plunder his goods, unless he first
binds the strong man? And then he will plunder his house.
30 "He who is not with Me is against Me, and
he who does not gather with Me scatters
abroad.

The Unpardonable Sin

➤ **31** "Therefore I say to you, every sin and blasphemy will be forgiven men, but the blasphemy *against* the Spirit will not be forgiven
men.
32 "Anyone who speaks a word against the
Son of Man, it will be forgiven him; but whoever speaks against the Holy Spirit, it will not
be forgiven him, either in this age or in the
age to come.

A Tree Known by Its Fruit

33 "Either make the tree good and its fruit
good, or else make the tree bad and its fruit
bad; for a tree is known by *its* fruit.
34 "Brood of vipers! How can you, being evil,
speak good things? For out of the abundance
of the heart the mouth speaks.
35 "A good man out of the good treasure of
his heart[a] brings forth good things, and an
evil man out of the evil treasure brings forth
evil things.
36 "But I say to you that for every idle word
men may speak, they will give account of it in
the day of judgment.
37 "For by your words you will be justified,
and by your words you will be condemned."

The Scribes and Pharisees Ask for a Sign

38 Then some of the scribes and Pharisees
answered, saying, "Teacher, we want to see a
sign from You."
39 But He answered and said to them, "An
evil and adulterous generation seeks after a
sign, and no sign will be given to it except the
sign of the prophet Jonah.
40 "For as Jonah was three days and three
nights in the belly of the great fish, so will the
Son of Man be three days and three nights in
the heart of the earth.
41 "The men of Nineveh will rise up in the
judgment with this generation and condemn
it, because they repented at the preaching of
Jonah; and indeed a greater than Jonah *is*
here.
42 "The queen of the South will rise up in the
judgment with this generation and condemn
it, for she came from the ends of the earth to
hear the wisdom of Solomon; and indeed a
greater than Solomon *is* here.

An Unclean Spirit Returns

43 "When an unclean spirit goes out of a
man, he goes through dry places, seeking
rest, and finds none.
44 "Then he says, 'I will return to my house
from which I came.' And when he comes, he
finds *it* empty, swept, and put in order.
45 "Then he goes and takes with him seven
other spirits more wicked than himself, and
they enter and dwell there; and the last *state*
of that man is worse than the first. So shall it
also be with this wicked generation."

12:21 [a]Isaiah 42:1–4 **12:22** [a]NU-Text omits *blind and.* **12:24** [a]NU-Text and M-Text read *Beelzebul.* **12:35** [a]NU-Text and M-Text omit *of his heart.*

LIFE LESSONS

➤ **12:25 — *But Jesus knew their thoughts . . . .***

The Book of Hebrews says, "all things are naked and open to the eyes of Him to whom we must give account" (4:13). And Paul says the Lord will "reveal the counsels of the hearts" (1 Cor. 4:5).

➤ **12:31 — *"Therefore I say to you, every sin and blasphemy will be forgiven men, but the blasphemy against the Spirit will not be forgiven men."***

Blasphemy against the Spirit is unforgivable because it prevents repentance. Some worry that they have committed the unforgivable sin, but God will *never* reject anyone who is truly repentant.

Jesus' Mother and Brothers Send for Him

46 While He was still talking to the multitudes, behold, His mother and brothers stood outside, seeking to speak with Him.

47 Then one said to Him, "Look, Your mother and Your brothers are standing outside, seeking to speak with You."

48 But He answered and said to the one who told Him, "Who is My mother and who are My brothers?"

49 And He stretched out His hand toward His disciples and said, "Here are My mother and My brothers!

➤ 50 "For whoever does the will of My Father in heaven is My brother and sister and mother."

The Parable of the Sower

13 On the same day Jesus went out of the house and sat by the sea.

2 And great multitudes were gathered together to Him, so that He got into a boat and sat; and the whole multitude stood on the shore.

3 Then He spoke many things to them in parables, saying: "Behold, a sower went out to sow.

4 "And as he sowed, some *seed* fell by the wayside; and the birds came and devoured them.

5 "Some fell on stony places, where they did not have much earth; and they immediately sprang up because they had no depth of earth.

6 "But when the sun was up they were scorched, and because they had no root they withered away.

7 "And some fell among thorns, and the thorns sprang up and choked them.

8 "But others fell on good ground and yielded a crop: some a hundredfold, some sixty, some thirty.

9 "He who has ears to hear, let him hear!"

The Purpose of Parables

10 And the disciples came and said to Him, "Why do You speak to them in parables?"

11 He answered and said to them, "Because it has been given to you to know the mysteries of the kingdom of heaven, but to them it has not been given.

➤ 12 "For whoever has, to him more will be given, and he will have abundance; but whoever does not have, even what he has will be taken away from him.

13 "Therefore I speak to them in parables, because seeing they do not see, and hearing they do not hear, nor do they understand.

14 "And in them the prophecy of Isaiah is fulfilled, which says:

'Hearing you will hear and shall not
understand,
And seeing you will see and not
perceive;
15 *For the hearts of this people have grown*
dull.
Their ears are hard of hearing,
And their eyes they have closed,
Lest they should see with their eyes and
hear with their ears,
Lest they should understand with their
hearts and turn,
So that I should[a] *heal them.'*[b]

16 "But blessed *are* your eyes for they see, and your ears for they hear;

17 "for assuredly, I say to you that many prophets and righteous *men* desired to see what you see, and did not see *it,* and to hear what you hear, and did not hear *it.*

The Parable of the Sower Explained

18 "Therefore hear the parable of the sower:

19 "When anyone hears the word of the kingdom, and does not understand *it,* then the wicked *one* comes and snatches away what was sown in his heart. This is he who received seed by the wayside.

20 "But he who received the seed on stony places, this is he who hears the word and immediately receives it with joy;

21 "yet he has no root in himself, but endures only for a while. For when tribulation or persecution arises because of the word, immediately he stumbles.

22 "Now he who received seed among the thorns is he who hears the word, and the cares of this world and the deceitfulness of riches choke the word, and he becomes unfruitful.

23 "But he who received seed on the good ground is he who hears the word and under- ➤

13:15 [a]NU-Text and M-Text read *would.* [b]Isaiah 6:9, 10

LIFE LESSONS

➤ 12:50 — *"For whoever does the will of My Father in heaven is My brother and sister and mother."*

Jesus came to earth to do the will of His Father, and so anyone who has the same goal is one in spirit with Him. A genuine desire to please God creates a stronger bond than anything else in the universe.

➤ 13:12 — *"For whoever has, to him more will be given, and he will have abundance; but whoever does not have, even what he has will be taken away from him."*

This combination of promise and warning typifies a great deal of God's instruction in His Word. He motivates us to experience life through both offers of blessing and declarations of caution.

➤ 13:23 — *"But he who received seed on the good ground is he who hears the word and understands it, who indeed bears fruit and produces: some a hundredfold, some sixty, some thirty."*

God wants us to hear, understand, and put into practice His counsel and instruction. He doesn't see us as vaults into which He hides His Word, but rather as gardens in which His Word can sprout and grow.

stands *it,* who indeed bears fruit and produces: some a hundredfold, some sixty, some thirty."

The Parable of the Wheat and the Tares

24 Another parable He put forth to them, saying: "The kingdom of heaven is like a man who sowed good seed in his field;
25 "but while men slept, his enemy came and sowed tares among the wheat and went his way.
26 "But when the grain had sprouted and produced a crop, then the tares also appeared.
27 "So the servants of the owner came and said to him, 'Sir, did you not sow good seed in your field? How then does it have tares?'
28 "He said to them, 'An enemy has done this.' The servants said to him, 'Do you want us then to go and gather them up?'
29 "But he said, 'No, lest while you gather up the tares you also uproot the wheat with them.
30 'Let both grow together until the harvest, and at the time of harvest I will say to the reapers, "First gather together the tares and bind them in bundles to burn them, but gather the wheat into my barn." ' "

The Parable of the Mustard Seed

31 Another parable He put forth to them, saying: "The kingdom of heaven is like a mustard seed, which a man took and sowed in his field,
32 "which indeed is the least of all the seeds; but when it is grown it is greater than the herbs and becomes a tree, so that the birds of the air come and nest in its branches."

The Parable of the Leaven

33 Another parable He spoke to them: "The kingdom of heaven is like leaven, which a woman took and hid in three measures[a] of meal till it was all leavened."

Prophecy and the Parables

34 All these things Jesus spoke to the multitude in parables; and without a parable He did not speak to them,
35 that it might be fulfilled which was spoken by the prophet, saying:

"I will open My mouth in parables;
I will utter things kept secret from the foundation of the world."[a]

The Parable of the Tares Explained

36 Then Jesus sent the multitude away and went into the house. And His disciples came to Him, saying, "Explain to us the parable of the tares of the field."
37 He answered and said to them: "He who sows the good seed is the Son of Man.
38 "The field is the world, the good seeds are the sons of the kingdom, but the tares are the sons of the wicked *one.*
39 "The enemy who sowed them is the devil, the harvest is the end of the age, and the reapers are the angels.
40 "Therefore as the tares are gathered and burned in the fire, so it will be at the end of this age.
41 "The Son of Man will send out His angels, and they will gather out of His kingdom all things that offend, and those who practice lawlessness,
42 "and will cast them into the furnace of fire. There will be wailing and gnashing of teeth.
43 "Then the righteous will shine forth as the sun in the kingdom of their Father. He who has ears to hear, let him hear!

The Parable of the Hidden Treasure

44 "Again, the kingdom of heaven is like treasure hidden in a field, which a man found and hid; and for joy over it he goes and sells all that he has and buys that field.

The Parable of the Pearl of Great Price

45 "Again, the kingdom of heaven is like a merchant seeking beautiful pearls,
46 "who, when he had found one pearl of great price, went and sold all that he had and bought it.

The Parable of the Dragnet

47 "Again, the kingdom of heaven is like a dragnet that was cast into the sea and gathered some of every kind,
48 "which, when it was full, they drew to shore; and they sat down and gathered the good into vessels, but threw the bad away.
49 "So it will be at the end of the age. The angels will come forth, separate the wicked from among the just,
50 "and cast them into the furnace of fire. There will be wailing and gnashing of teeth."
51 Jesus said to them,[a] "Have you understood all these things?" They said to Him, "Yes, Lord."[b]
52 Then He said to them, "Therefore every scribe instructed concerning[a] the kingdom of

13:33 [a]Greek *sata,* approximately two pecks in all **13:35** [a]Psalm 78:2 **13:51** [a]NU-Text omits *Jesus said to them.* [b]NU-Text omits *Lord.* **13:52** [a]Or *for*

LIFE LESSONS

➤ **13:38 — *"The field is the world, the good seeds are the sons of the kingdom, but the tares are the sons of the wicked one."***

We may not like it, but God allows the righteous and the wicked to live alongside one another. The situation will change one day, but for now, we must remember that, "not all have faith" (1 Thess. 3:2).

heaven is like a householder who brings out of his treasure *things* new and old."

Jesus Rejected at Nazareth

53 Now it came to pass, when Jesus had finished these parables, that He departed from there.

54 When He had come to His own country, He taught them in their synagogue, so that they were astonished and said, "Where did this *Man* get this wisdom and *these* mighty works?

55 "Is this not the carpenter's son? Is not His mother called Mary? And His brothers James, Joses,[a] Simon, and Judas?

56 "And His sisters, are they not all with us? Where then did this *Man* get all these things?"

57 So they were offended at Him. But Jesus said to them, "A prophet is not without honor except in his own country and in his own house."

➤ 58 Now He did not do many mighty works there because of their unbelief.

John the Baptist Beheaded

14 At that time Herod the tetrarch heard the report about Jesus

2 and said to his servants, "This is John the Baptist; he is risen from the dead, and therefore these powers are at work in him."

3 For Herod had laid hold of John and bound him, and put *him* in prison for the sake of Herodias, his brother Philip's wife.

4 Because John had said to him, "It is not lawful for you to have her."

5 And although he wanted to put him to death, he feared the multitude, because they counted him as a prophet.

6 But when Herod's birthday was celebrated, the daughter of Herodias danced before them and pleased Herod.

7 Therefore he promised with an oath to give her whatever she might ask.

8 So she, having been prompted by her mother, said, "Give me John the Baptist's head here on a platter."

9 And the king was sorry; nevertheless, because of the oaths and because of those who sat with him, he commanded *it* to be given to *her.*

10 So he sent and had John beheaded in prison.

11 And his head was brought on a platter and given to the girl, and she brought *it* to her mother.

12 Then his disciples came and took away the body and buried it, and went and told Jesus.

Feeding the Five Thousand

13 When Jesus heard *it,* He departed from there by boat to a deserted place by Himself. But when the multitudes heard it, they followed Him on foot from the cities.

14 And when Jesus went out He saw a great multitude; and He was moved with compassion for them, and healed their sick. ➤

15 When it was evening, His disciples came to Him, saying, "This is a deserted place, and the hour is already late. Send the multitudes away, that they may go into the villages and buy themselves food."

16 But Jesus said to them, "They do not need to go away. You give them something to eat."

17 And they said to Him, "We have here only five loaves and two fish."

18 He said, "Bring them here to Me."

19 Then He commanded the multitudes to sit down on the grass. And He took the five loaves and the two fish, and looking up to heaven, He blessed and broke and gave the loaves to the disciples; and the disciples gave to the multitudes.

20 So they all ate and were filled, and they took up twelve baskets full of the fragments that remained.

21 Now those who had eaten were about five thousand men, besides women and children.

Jesus Walks on the Sea

22 Immediately Jesus made His disciples get into the boat and go before Him to the other side, while He sent the multitudes away.

23 And when He had sent the multitudes away, He went up on the mountain by Himself to pray. Now when evening came, He was alone there. ➤

13:55 [a]NU-Text reads *Joseph.*

LIFE LESSONS

➤ **13:58 — *Now He did not do many mighty works there because of their unbelief.***

Unbelief acts like a wet blanket on a smoldering fire, discouraging anything from really getting started. It does not prevent God from acting—as though we had the power to stop Him—but it does dampen the possibility.

➤ **14:14 — *And when Jesus went out He saw a great multitude; and He was moved with compassion for them, and healed their sick.***

Compassion is God's natural response to human suffering. Jesus had gone to a remote place to get alone, but when the crowds followed Him, He ministered to them and refused to send them away.

➤ **14:23 — *And when He had sent the multitudes away, He went up on the mountain by Himself to pray. Now when evening came, He was alone there.***

Jesus spent a good deal of His time alone with God in prayer. He made this a practice not only to make requests of His Father, but even more to stay in close fellowship with Him and enjoy His company.

24 But the boat was now in the middle of the
sea,[a] tossed by the waves, for the wind was
contrary.
25 Now in the fourth watch of the night Jesus
went to them, walking on the sea.
26 And when the disciples saw Him walking
on the sea, they were troubled, saying, "It is a
ghost!" And they cried out for fear.
➤ 27 But immediately Jesus spoke to them, saying, "Be of good cheer! It is I; do not be
afraid."
28 And Peter answered Him and said, "Lord,
if it is You, command me to come to You on the
water."
29 So He said, "Come." And when Peter had
come down out of the boat, he walked on the
water to go to Jesus.
30 But when he saw that the wind *was* boisterous,[a] he was afraid; and beginning to sink
he cried out, saying, "Lord, save me!"
31 And immediately Jesus stretched out *His*
hand and caught him, and said to him, "O you
of little faith, why did you doubt?"
32 And when they got into the boat, the wind
ceased.
33 Then those who were in the boat came
and[a] worshiped Him, saying, "Truly You are
the Son of God."

Many Touch Him and Are Made Well

34 When they had crossed over, they came to
the land of[a] Gennesaret.
35 And when the men of that place recognized Him, they sent out into all that surrounding region, brought to Him all who were
sick,
36 and begged Him that they might only
touch the hem of His garment. And as many
as touched *it* were made perfectly well.

Defilement Comes from Within

15 Then the scribes and Pharisees who
were from Jerusalem came to Jesus,
saying,
2 "Why do Your disciples transgress the tradition of the elders? For they do not wash
their hands when they eat bread."
➤ 3 He answered and said to them, "Why do
you also transgress the commandment of God
because of your tradition?
4 "For God commanded, saying, *'Honor your
father and your mother'*;[a] and, *'He who curses
father or mother, let him be put to death.'*[b]
5 "But you say, 'Whoever says to his father
or mother, "Whatever profit you might have
received from me *is* a gift *to God*"—
6 'then he need not honor his father or
mother.'[a] Thus you have made the commandment[b] of God of no effect by your tradition.
7 "Hypocrites! Well did Isaiah prophesy
about you, saying:
8 *'These people draw near to Me with their* ➤
mouth,
And[a] honor Me with their lips,
But their heart is far from Me.
9 *And in vain they worship Me,*
Teaching as doctrines the
commandments of men.'"[a]
10 When He had called the multitude to *Himself*, He said to them, "Hear and understand:
11 "Not what goes into the mouth defiles a
man; but what comes out of the mouth, this
defiles a man."
12 Then His disciples came and said to Him,
"Do You know that the Pharisees were offended when they heard this saying?"
13 But He answered and said, "Every plant
which My heavenly Father has not planted
will be uprooted.
14 "Let them alone. They are blind leaders of
the blind. And if the blind leads the blind,
both will fall into a ditch."
15 Then Peter answered and said to Him,
"Explain this parable to us."
16 So Jesus said, "Are you also still without
understanding?
17 "Do you not yet understand that whatever
enters the mouth goes into the stomach and is
eliminated?
18 "But those things which proceed out of the
mouth come from the heart, and they defile a
man.

14:24 [a]NU-Text reads *many furlongs away from the land.*
14:30 [a]NU-Text brackets *that* and *boisterous* as disputed.
14:33 [a]NU-Text omits *came and.* **14:34** [a]NU-Text reads *came to land at.* **15:4** [a]Exodus 20:12; Deuteronomy 5:16 [b]Exodus 21:17 **15:6** [a]NU-Text omits *or mother.* [b]NU-Text reads *word.* **15:8** [a]NU-Text omits *draw near to Me with their mouth, And.* **15:9** [a]Isaiah 29:13

LIFE LESSONS

➤ **14:27 — *But immediately Jesus spoke to them, saying, "Be of good cheer! It is I; do not be afraid."***

The unexpected way God often does things may startle us or even frighten us. We may not understand why He works in a certain way. So He continually tells us, "Do not be afraid. It is I!"

➤ **15:3 — *He answered and said to them, "Why do you also transgress the commandment of God because of your tradition?"***

We must beware of allowing religious customs and church rituals to take precedence over the clear Word of God. Just because something has been done in a certain way for a long time, that doesn't mean it pleases God.

➤ **15:8 — *"These people draw near to Me with their mouth, and honor Me with their lips, but their heart is far from Me."***

Human beings have a natural fondness for pomp and ceremony and ritual, and there's nothing wrong with that—unless it begins to replace a genuine connection to the living God. Our Lord wants our hearts.

19 "For out of the heart proceed evil thoughts,
murders, adulteries, fornications, thefts, false
witness, blasphemies.
20 "These are *the things* which defile a man,
but to eat with unwashed hands does not defile a man."

A Gentile Shows Her Faith

21 Then Jesus went out from there and departed to the region of Tyre and Sidon.
22 And behold, a woman of Canaan came
from that region and cried out to Him, saying,
"Have mercy on me, O Lord, Son of David!
My daughter is severely demon-possessed."
23 But He answered her not a word. And His
disciples came and urged Him, saying, "Send
her away, for she cries out after us."
24 But He answered and said, "I was not sent
except to the lost sheep of the house of Israel."
25 Then she came and worshiped Him, saying, "Lord, help me!"
26 But He answered and said, "It is not good
to take the children's bread and throw *it* to
the little dogs."
27 And she said, "Yes, Lord, yet even the little
dogs eat the crumbs which fall from their
masters' table."
➤ 28 Then Jesus answered and said to her, "O
woman, great *is* your faith! Let it be to you as
you desire." And her daughter was healed
from that very hour.

Jesus Heals Great Multitudes

29 Jesus departed from there, skirted the Sea
of Galilee, and went up on the mountain and
sat down there.
30 Then great multitudes came to Him, having with them *the* lame, blind, mute, maimed,
and many others; and they laid them down at
Jesus' feet, and He healed them.
31 So the multitude marveled when they saw
the mute speaking, *the* maimed made whole,
the lame walking, and *the* blind seeing; and
they glorified the God of Israel.

Feeding the Four Thousand

32 Now Jesus called His disciples to *Himself*
and said, "I have compassion on the multitude, because they have now continued with
Me three days and have nothing to eat. And I
do not want to send them away hungry, lest
they faint on the way."
33 Then His disciples said to Him, "Where
could we get enough bread in the wilderness
to fill such a great multitude?"
34 Jesus said to them, "How many loaves do
you have?" And they said, "Seven, and a few
little fish."
35 So He commanded the multitude to sit
down on the ground.
36 And He took the seven loaves and the fish
and gave thanks, broke *them* and gave *them*
to His disciples; and the disciples *gave* to the
multitude.
37 So they all ate and were filled, and they
took up seven large baskets full of the fragments that were left.
38 Now those who ate were four thousand
men, besides women and children.
39 And He sent away the multitude, got into
the boat, and came to the region of Magdala.[a]

The Pharisees and Sadducees Seek a Sign

16 Then the Pharisees and Sadducees
came, and testing Him asked that He
would show them a sign from heaven.
2 He answered and said to them, "When it is
evening you say, *'It will be* fair weather, for
the sky is red';
3 "and in the morning, *'It will be* foul
weather today, for the sky is red and threatening.' Hypocrites![a] You know how to discern
the face of the sky, but you cannot *discern* the
signs of the times.
4 "A wicked and adulterous generation ➤
seeks after a sign, and no sign shall be given
to it except the sign of the prophet[a] Jonah."
And He left them and departed.

The Leaven of the Pharisees and Sadducees

5 Now when His disciples had come to the
other side, they had forgotten to take bread.
6 Then Jesus said to them, "Take heed and
beware of the leaven of the Pharisees and the
Sadducees."
7 And they reasoned among themselves,
saying, "*It is* because we have taken no
bread."

15:39 [a]NU-Text reads *Magadan.* 16:3 [a]NU-Text omits *Hypocrites.*
16:4 [a]NU-Text omits *the prophet.*

LIFE LESSONS

➤ **15:28 — *Then Jesus answered and said to her, "O woman, great is your faith! Let it be to you as you desire." And her daughter was healed from that very hour.***

Only two people in the Gospels are said to have "great" faith, and both of them were Gentiles (the other was a Roman centurion, Matt. 8:10). Great faith does not depend on background or position, but on the heart.

➤ **16:4 — *"A wicked and adulterous generation seeks after a sign, and no sign shall be given to it except the sign of the prophet Jonah."***

Once before Jesus had spoken of the "sign of the prophet Jonah" (Matt. 12:39–41). As Jonah had spent three days in the belly of the great fish, so Jesus would spend three days "in the heart of the earth" before His resurrection.

8 But Jesus, being aware of *it*, said to them, "O you of little faith, why do you reason among yourselves because you have brought no bread?[a]

9 "Do you not yet understand, or remember the five loaves of the five thousand and how many baskets you took up?

10 "Nor the seven loaves of the four thousand and how many large baskets you took up?

11 "How is it you do not understand that I did not speak to you concerning bread?—*but* to beware of the leaven of the Pharisees and Sadducees."

12 Then they understood that He did not tell *them* to beware of the leaven of bread, but of the doctrine of the Pharisees and Sadducees.

Peter Confesses Jesus as the Christ

13 When Jesus came into the region of Caesarea Philippi, He asked His disciples, saying, "Who do men say that I, the Son of Man, am?"

14 So they said, "Some *say* John the Baptist, some Elijah, and others Jeremiah or one of the prophets."

➤ 15 He said to them, "But who do you say that I am?"

16 Simon Peter answered and said, "You are the Christ, the Son of the living God."

17 Jesus answered and said to him, "Blessed are you, Simon Bar-Jonah, for flesh and blood has not revealed *this* to you, but My Father who is in heaven.

✳ 18 "And I also say to you that you are Peter, and on this rock I will build My church, and the gates of Hades shall not prevail against it.

19 "And I will give you the keys of the kingdom of heaven, and whatever you bind on earth will be bound in heaven, and whatever you loose on earth will be loosed[a] in heaven."

20 Then He commanded His disciples that they should tell no one that He was Jesus the Christ.

Jesus Predicts His Death and Resurrection

➤ **21** From that time Jesus began to show to His disciples that He must go to Jerusalem, and suffer many things from the elders and chief priests and scribes, and be killed, and be raised the third day.

22 Then Peter took Him aside and began to rebuke Him, saying, "Far be it from You, Lord; this shall not happen to You!"

23 But He turned and said to Peter, "Get be- ➤

Life Examples:

PETER

Willing to Change

MATT. 16:18

What's in a name? The apostle Peter provides us with one of the best answers to Shakespeare's famous question.

The name Peter comes from the Greek *Petros*, meaning "Rock" or "Stone." Peter's original name was Simon Bar-Jona (or son of Jonah). Today, we might call him Simon Johnson or Simon Stone.

But whatever we call him, he was impetuous, impulsive, brash, outspoken, loud, self-confident, even arrogant. Why would Jesus pick such a man? For the same reason He picks us: He wants to take those same unlovely qualities and transform them for His use.

We can all learn from Peter. Perhaps his most compelling characteristic wasn't impulsiveness or outspokenness, but his willingness to change and, in Jesus' hands, become a person mightily used of God.

What's in a name? Today it isn't so important what we are called—just that we hear and obey when God calls us.

See the Life Principles Index for further study:
21. Obedience always brings blessing.

16:8 [a]NU-Text reads *you have no bread.* **16:19** [a]Or *will have been bound . . . will have been loosed*

LIFE LESSONS

➤ **16:15 — *He said to them, "But who do you say that I am?"***

Jesus has no interest in dispassionate, hypothetical views regarding His person and work. He wants to know what *you* think about Him. Who do *you* say that He is?

➤ **16:21 — *From that time Jesus began to show to His disciples that He must go to Jerusalem, and suffer many things from the elders and chief priests and scribes, and be killed, and be raised the third day.***

Jesus repeatedly told His disciples about the fate that awaited Him in Jerusalem, but they never really understood Him until after the Resurrection (Mark 9:32; Luke 24:8). Yet God's Word always bears fruit in its time.

➤ **16:23 — *But He turned and said to Peter, "Get behind Me, Satan! You are an offense to Me, for you are not mindful of the things of God, but the things of men."***

The "gentle Jesus" could be very stern when He had to be. He knows when to show us compassion, and He knows when we need correction or rebuke. He always gives us what we need, not necessarily what we want.

WHAT THE BIBLE SAYS ABOUT **BINDING SATAN**

Matt. 16:19

Because Jesus triumphed over Satan at the cross, the believer can claim victory over Satan in daily battles. A Christian is indwelt with the triumphant power of the Holy Spirit and has the privilege of exercising a divine authority more powerful than the authority of Satan (1 John 4:4). Through the power of the Holy Spirit, we can restore and release someone who has been bound, by exercising the higher authority of the Holy Spirit.

How can we bind Satan by the power of the Holy Spirit? There are three things we must have and use.

1. The name of Jesus

The Bible tells us to pray in Jesus' name (John 16:23). Throughout the New Testament, the apostles heal and do the works of the Lord in Jesus' name (Acts 3:6). You and I transact spiritual business, so to speak, by using the currency of the name of the Lord Jesus Christ. When we ask in Jesus' name, we are saying to the Father, "Jesus would have asked this if He were physically here now." Can you imagine what would happen to the church if believers took God at His Word and appropriated the power of the Holy Spirit?

The power to defeat Satan is available to every believer.

2. The blood of Jesus

We dare not come boldly into battle with Satan without the protection of the shed blood of Jesus Christ. Throughout the Scriptures, the shed blood is the symbol of protection and of our redemption. The blood of Christ's sacrifice paid the price of sin and eternally broke the power of Satan over us.

3. The Word of God

Jesus countered the temptation of Satan by quoting scripture: "It is written." He confronted Satan in spirit-to-spirit combat using the Word of God. We must rely on the guidance of God's Word.

The power to defeat Satan is available to every believer. Every one of us has the ability to deal with Satan by the almighty, supernatural power of God. We have the right to declare Satan bound, his work restricted, and the prisoner set free.

My friend, exercise courage to allow God to use you to the maximum every day.

See the Life Principles Index for further study:
8. Fight all our battles on your knees and you win every time.
3. God's Word is an immovable anchor in times of storm.

hind Me, Satan! You are an offense to Me, for
you are not mindful of the things of God, but
the things of men."

Take Up the Cross and Follow Him

➤ **24** Then Jesus said to His disciples, "If anyone desires to come after Me, let him deny
himself, and take up his cross, and follow Me.
✳ 25 "For whoever desires to save his life will
lose it, but whoever loses his life for My sake
will find it.
26 "For what profit is it to a man if he gains
the whole world, and loses his own soul?
Or what will a man give in exchange for his
soul?
➤ 27 "For the Son of Man will come in the glory
of His Father with His angels, and then He
will reward each according to his works.

Jesus Transfigured on the Mount

28 "Assuredly, I say to you, there are some
standing here who shall not taste death till
they see the Son of Man coming in His kingdom."

17 Now after six days Jesus took Peter,
James, and John his brother, led them
up on a high mountain by themselves;
2 and He was transfigured before them. His
face shone like the sun, and His clothes became as white as the light.
3 And behold, Moses and Elijah appeared to
them, talking with Him.
4 Then Peter answered and said to Jesus,
"Lord, it is good for us to be here; if You wish,
let us[a] make here three tabernacles: one for
You, one for Moses, and one for Elijah."
➤ 5 While he was still speaking, behold, a
bright cloud overshadowed them; and suddenly a voice came out of the cloud, saying,
"This is My beloved Son, in whom I am well
pleased. Hear Him!"
6 And when the disciples heard *it*, they fell
on their faces and were greatly afraid.
7 But Jesus came and touched them and
said, "Arise, and do not be afraid."
8 When they had lifted up their eyes, they
saw no one but Jesus only.
9 Now as they came down from the mountain, Jesus commanded them, saying, "Tell the
vision to no one until the Son of Man is risen
from the dead."
10 And His disciples asked Him, saying,
"Why then do the scribes say that Elijah must
come first?"
11 Jesus answered and said to them, "Indeed,
Elijah is coming first[a] and will restore all
things.
12 "But I say to you that Elijah has come already, and they did not know him but did to
him whatever they wished. Likewise the Son
of Man is also about to suffer at their hands."
13 Then the disciples understood that He
spoke to them of John the Baptist.

A Boy Is Healed

14 And when they had come to the multitude,
a man came to Him, kneeling down to Him
and saying,
15 "Lord, have mercy on my son, for he is an
epileptic[a] and suffers severely; for he often
falls into the fire and often into the water.
16 "So I brought him to Your disciples, but
they could not cure him."
17 Then Jesus answered and said, "O faith- ➤
less and perverse generation, how long shall I
be with you? How long shall I bear with you?
Bring him here to Me."
18 And Jesus rebuked the demon, and it
came out of him; and the child was cured
from that very hour.
19 Then the disciples came to Jesus privately
and said, "Why could we not cast it out?"
20 So Jesus said to them, "Because of your un- ✳
belief;[a] for assuredly, I say to you, if you have
faith as a mustard seed, you will say to this
mountain, 'Move from here to there,' and it will
move; and nothing will be impossible for you.

17:4 [a]NU-Text reads *I will.* **17:11** [a]NU-Text omits *first.*
17:15 [a]Literally *moonstruck* **17:20** [a]NU-Text reads *little faith.*

LIFE LESSONS

➤ 16:24 — *Then Jesus said to His disciples, "If anyone desires to come after Me, let him deny himself, and take up his cross, and follow Me."*

We take up the cross of Jesus anytime we suffer in some way for identifying with Him and His cause. "Cross bearing" is not suffering in general, but affliction that comes to us specifically because of our connection to Jesus.

➤ 16:27 — *"For the Son of Man will come in the glory of His Father with His angels, and then He will reward each according to his works."*

Jesus often motivated His disciples to "love and good works" by reminding them that He would return one day in great glory to reward all His faithful servants for whatever they had accomplished in His name.

➤ 17:5 — *"This is My beloved Son, in whom I am well pleased. Hear Him!"*

At both the baptism of Jesus and the Transfiguration, God the Father publicly declared His great pleasure in His only Son, Jesus. Jesus speaks for the Father, and we are to obey Him as we obey the Father.

➤ 17:17 — *Then Jesus answered and said, "O faithless and perverse generation, how long shall I be with you? How long shall I bear with you?"*

Jesus expects us to grow in our faith. Our trust in Him is to deepen as we depend upon Him to help us overcome difficulties and surmount challenges. He is not pleased with stagnant faith.

21 "However, this kind does not go out except
by prayer and fasting."[a]

Jesus Again Predicts His Death and Resurrection

22 Now while they were staying[a] in Galilee,
Jesus said to them, "The Son of Man is about
to be betrayed into the hands of men,
23 "and they will kill Him, and the third day
He will be raised up." And they were exceedingly sorrowful.

Peter and His Master Pay Their Taxes

24 When they had come to Capernaum,[a]
those who received the *temple* tax came to
Peter and said, "Does your Teacher not pay
the *temple* tax?"
25 He said, "Yes." And when he had come
into the house, Jesus anticipated him, saying,
"What do you think, Simon? From whom do
the kings of the earth take customs or taxes,
from their sons or from strangers?"
➤ 26 Peter said to Him, "From strangers." Jesus
said to him, "Then the sons are free.
27 "Nevertheless, lest we offend them, go to
the sea, cast in a hook, and take the fish that
comes up first. And when you have opened its
mouth, you will find a piece of money;[a] take
that and give it to them for Me and you."

Who Is the Greatest?

18 At that time the disciples came to
Jesus, saying, "Who then is greatest in
the kingdom of heaven?"
2 Then Jesus called a little child to Him, set
him in the midst of them,
➤ 3 and said, "Assuredly, I say to you, unless
you are converted and become as little children, you will by no means enter the kingdom
of heaven.
4 "Therefore whoever humbles himself as
this little child is the greatest in the kingdom
of heaven.
5 "Whoever receives one little child like this
in My name receives Me.

Jesus Warns of Offenses

6 "But whoever causes one of these little
ones who believe in Me to sin, it would be better for him if a millstone were hung around
his neck, and he were drowned in the depth of
the sea.
7 "Woe to the world because of offenses! For
offenses must come, but woe to that man by
whom the offense comes!
8 "If your hand or foot causes you to sin, cut
it off and cast *it* from you. It is better for you
to enter into life lame or maimed, rather than
having two hands or two feet, to be cast into
the everlasting fire.
9 "And if your eye causes you to sin, pluck it
out and cast *it* from you. It is better for you to
enter into life with one eye, rather than having two eyes, to be cast into hell fire.

The Parable of the Lost Sheep

10 "Take heed that you do not despise one of
these little ones, for I say to you that in
heaven their angels always see the face of My
Father who is in heaven.
11 "For the Son of Man has come to save that
which was lost.[a]
12 "What do you think? If a man has a hundred sheep, and one of them goes astray, does
he not leave the ninety-nine and go to the
mountains to seek the one that is straying?
13 "And if he should find it, assuredly, I say to
you, he rejoices more over that *sheep* than
over the ninety-nine that did not go astray.
14 "Even so it is not the will of your Father ➤
who is in heaven that one of these little ones
should perish.

Dealing with a Sinning Brother

15 "Moreover if your brother sins against
you, go and tell him his fault between you and
him alone. If he hears you, you have gained
your brother.
16 "But if he will not hear, take with you one
or two more, that *'by the mouth of two or
three witnesses every word may be established.'*[a]
17 "And if he refuses to hear them, tell *it* to
the church. But if he refuses even to hear the
church, let him be to you like a heathen and a
tax collector.
18 "Assuredly, I say to you, whatever you

17:21 [a]NU-Text omits this verse. **17:22** [a]NU-Text reads *gathering together.* **17:24** [a]NU-Text reads *Capharnaum* (here and elsewhere). **17:27** [a]Greek *stater,* the exact amount to pay the temple tax (didrachma) for two **18:11** [a]NU-Text omits this verse. **18:16** [a]Deuteronomy 19:15

LIFE LESSONS

➤ 17:26 — *Jesus said to him, "Then the sons are free."*

Freedom is one of the greatest gifts Jesus has bestowed on us. Paul says, "Stand fast therefore in the liberty by which Christ has made us free, and do not get entangled again with a yoke of bondage" (Gal. 5:1).

➤ 18:3 — *"Assuredly, I say to you, unless you are converted and become as little children, you will by no means enter the kingdom of heaven."*

Jesus has in mind the humility of little children and their unconcern for social status or public opinion. He encourages us to place childlike trust in Him, regardless of what others may think.

➤ 18:14 — *"Even so it is not the will of your Father who is in heaven that one of these little ones should perish."*

God wants "all men to be saved and to come to the knowledge of the truth" (1 Tim. 2:4). He is "not willing that any should perish but that all should come to repentance" (2 Pet. 3:9). That includes children.

bind on earth will be bound in heaven, and
whatever you loose on earth will be loosed in
heaven.
19 "Again I say[a] to you that if two of you
agree on earth concerning anything that they
ask, it will be done for them by My Father in
heaven.
20 "For where two or three are gathered together in My name, I am there in the midst of
them."

The Parable of the Unforgiving Servant

21 Then Peter came to Him and said, "Lord,
how often shall my brother sin against me,
and I forgive him? Up to seven times?"
22 Jesus said to him, "I do not say to you, up
to seven times, but up to seventy times seven.
23 "Therefore the kingdom of heaven is like a
certain king who wanted to settle accounts
with his servants.
24 "And when he had begun to settle accounts, one was brought to him who owed
him ten thousand talents.
25 "But as he was not able to pay, his master
commanded that he be sold, with his wife and
children and all that he had, and that payment be made.
26 "The servant therefore fell down before
him, saying, 'Master, have patience with me,
and I will pay you all.'
27 "Then the master of that servant was
moved with compassion, released him, and
forgave him the debt.
28 "But that servant went out and found one
of his fellow servants who owed him a hundred denarii; and he laid hands on him and
took *him* by the throat, saying, 'Pay me what
you owe!'
29 "So his fellow servant fell down at his feet[a]
and begged him, saying, 'Have patience with
me, and I will pay you all.'[b]
30 "And he would not, but went and threw
him into prison till he should pay the debt.
31 "So when his fellow servants saw what had
been done, they were very grieved, and came
and told their master all that had been done.
32 "Then his master, after he had called him,
said to him, 'You wicked servant! I forgave
you all that debt because you begged me.
33 'Should you not also have had compassion
on your fellow servant, just as I had pity on
you?'
34 "And his master was angry, and delivered
him to the torturers until he should pay all
that was due to him.
35 "So My heavenly Father also will do to you
if each of you, from his heart, does not forgive
his brother his trespasses."[a]

Marriage and Divorce

19 Now it came to pass, when Jesus had
finished these sayings, *that* He departed from Galilee and came to the region of
Judea beyond the Jordan.
2 And great multitudes followed Him, and
He healed them there.
3 The Pharisees also came to Him, testing
Him, and saying to Him, "Is it lawful for a
man to divorce his wife for *just* any reason?"
4 And He answered and said to them, "Have
you not read that He who made[a] *them* at the
beginning *'made them male and female,'*[b]
5 "and said, *'For this reason a man shall
leave his father and mother and be joined to
his wife, and the two shall become one
flesh'*?[a]
6 "So then, they are no longer two but one
flesh. Therefore what God has joined together, let not man separate."
7 They said to Him, "Why then did Moses
command to give a certificate of divorce, and
to put her away?"
8 He said to them, "Moses, because of the
hardness of your hearts, permitted you to divorce your wives, but from the beginning it
was not so.
9 "And I say to you, whoever divorces his
wife, except for sexual immorality,[a] and marries another, commits adultery; and whoever
marries her who is divorced commits adultery."
10 His disciples said to Him, "If such is the
case of the man with *his* wife, it is better not
to marry."

Jesus Teaches on Celibacy

11 But He said to them, "All cannot accept
this saying, but only *those* to whom it has
been given:
12 "For there are eunuchs who were born thus

18:19 [a]NU-Text and M-Text read *Again, assuredly, I say.*
18:29 [a]NU-Text omits *at his feet.* [b]NU-Text and M-Text omit *all.*
18:35 [a]NU-Text omits *his trespasses.* **19:4** [a]NU-Text reads *created.* [b]Genesis 1:27; 5:2 **19:5** [a]Genesis 2:24 **19:9** [a]Or *fornication*

LIFE LESSONS

18:20 — *"For where two or three are gathered together in My name, I am there in the midst of them."*

The Spirit of Jesus lives in each individual Christian, but He promises to be with them in a unique and special way when they gather "in His name" for worship, service, and mutual encouragement.

19:6 — *"So then, they are no longer two but one flesh. Therefore what God has joined together, let not man separate."*

Marriage is not merely a social convention, as many declare today. It is far more than a piece of paper. In marriage, *God* joins a man and a woman into a single family unit. This is what makes divorce such a tragedy.

from *their* mother's womb, and there are eunuchs who were made eunuchs by men, and there are eunuchs who have made themselves eunuchs for the kingdom of heaven's sake. He who is able to accept *it*, let him accept *it*."

Jesus Blesses Little Children

13 Then little children were brought to Him that He might put *His* hands on them and pray, but the disciples rebuked them.
14 But Jesus said, "Let the little children come to Me, and do not forbid them; for of such is the kingdom of heaven."
15 And He laid *His* hands on them and departed from there.

Jesus Counsels the Rich Young Ruler

16 Now behold, one came and said to Him, "Good[a] Teacher, what good thing shall I do that I may have eternal life?"
17 So He said to him, "Why do you call Me good?[a] No one *is* good but One, *that is*, God.[b] But if you want to enter into life, keep the commandments."
18 He said to Him, "Which ones?" Jesus said, "*'You shall not murder,' 'You shall not commit adultery,' 'You shall not steal,' 'You shall not bear false witness,'*
19 *'Honor your father and your mother,'*[a] and, *'You shall love your neighbor as yourself.'*"[b]
20 The young man said to Him, "All these things I have kept from my youth.[a] What do I still lack?"
21 Jesus said to him, "If you want to be perfect, go, sell what you have and give to the poor, and you will have treasure in heaven; and come, follow Me."
22 But when the young man heard that saying, he went away sorrowful, for he had great possessions.

With God All Things Are Possible

23 Then Jesus said to His disciples, "Assuredly, I say to you that it is hard for a rich man to enter the kingdom of heaven.
24 "And again I say to you, it is easier for a camel to go through the eye of a needle than for a rich man to enter the kingdom of God."
25 When His disciples heard *it*, they were greatly astonished, saying, "Who then can be saved?"
26 But Jesus looked at *them* and said to them, "With men this is impossible, but with God all things are possible."
27 Then Peter answered and said to Him, "See, we have left all and followed You. Therefore what shall we have?"
28 So Jesus said to them, "Assuredly I say to you, that in the regeneration, when the Son of Man sits on the throne of His glory, you who have followed Me will also sit on twelve thrones, judging the twelve tribes of Israel.
29 "And everyone who has left houses or brothers or sisters or father or mother or wife[a] or children or lands, for My name's sake, shall receive a hundredfold, and inherit eternal life.
30 "But many *who are* first will be last, and the last first.

The Parable of the Workers in the Vineyard

20 "For the kingdom of heaven is like a landowner who went out early in the morning to hire laborers for his vineyard.
2 "Now when he had agreed with the laborers for a denarius a day, he sent them into his vineyard.
3 "And he went out about the third hour and saw others standing idle in the marketplace,
4 "and said to them, 'You also go into the vineyard, and whatever is right I will give you.' So they went.
5 "Again he went out about the sixth and the ninth hour, and did likewise.
6 "And about the eleventh hour he went out and found others standing idle,[a] and said to them, 'Why have you been standing here idle all day?'
7 "They said to him, 'Because no one hired us.' He said to them, 'You also go into the vineyard, and whatever is right you will receive.'[a]
8 "So when evening had come, the owner of the vineyard said to his steward, 'Call the laborers and give them *their* wages, beginning with the last to the first.'

19:16 [a]NU-Text omits *Good.* **19:17** [a]NU-Text reads *Why do you ask Me about what is good?* [b]NU-Text reads *There is One who is good.* **19:19** [a]Exodus 20:12–16; Deuteronomy 5:16–20 [b]Leviticus 19:18 **19:20** [a]NU-Text omits *from my youth.* **19:29** [a]NU-Text omits *or wife.* **20:6** [a]NU-Text omits *idle.* **20:7** [a]NU-Text omits the last clause of this verse.

LIFE LESSONS

➤ 19:23 — *Then Jesus said to His disciples, "Assuredly, I say to you that it is hard for a rich man to enter the kingdom of heaven."*

Why is it hard for the rich to enter heaven? For the same reason it's hard for the strong, or the bright, or the politically connected. They tend to rely on their own resources; pride keeps them from trusting God's resources.

➤ 19:30 — *"But many who are first will be last, and the last first."*

God loves to exalt the humble and humble the proud. So Paul says, "not many wise according to the flesh, not many mighty, not many noble, are called" and "He who glories, let him glory in the Lord" (1 Cor. 1:26, 31).

9 "And when those came who *were hired*
about the eleventh hour, they each received a
denarius.
10 "But when the first came, they supposed
that they would receive more; and they likewise received each a denarius.
11 "And when they had received *it*, they complained against the landowner,
12 "saying, 'These last *men* have worked *only*
one hour, and you made them equal to us who
have borne the burden and the heat of the
day.'
13 "But he answered one of them and said,
'Friend, I am doing you no wrong. Did you not
agree with me for a denarius?
14 'Take *what is* yours and go your way. I
wish to give to this last man *the same* as to
you.
➤ 15 'Is it not lawful for me to do what I wish
with my own things? Or is your eye evil because I am good?'
16 "So the last will be first, and the first last.
For many are called, but few chosen."[a]

Jesus a Third Time Predicts His Death and Resurrection

17 Now Jesus, going up to Jerusalem, took
the twelve disciples aside on the road and
said to them,
18 "Behold, we are going up to Jerusalem,
and the Son of Man will be betrayed to the
chief priests and to the scribes; and they will
condemn Him to death,
19 "and deliver Him to the Gentiles to mock
and to scourge and to crucify. And the third
day He will rise again."

Greatness Is Serving

20 Then the mother of Zebedee's sons came
to Him with her sons, kneeling down and asking something from Him.
21 And He said to her, "What do you wish?"
She said to Him, "Grant that these two sons of
mine may sit, one on Your right hand and the
other on the left, in Your kingdom."
22 But Jesus answered and said, "You do not
know what you ask. Are you able to drink the
cup that I am about to drink, and be baptized
with the baptism that I am baptized with?"[a]
They said to Him, "We are able."
23 So He said to them, "You will indeed drink
My cup, and be baptized with the baptism
that I am baptized with;[a] but to sit on My right
hand and on My left is not Mine to give, but *it
is for those* for whom it is prepared by My Father."
24 And when the ten heard *it*, they were
greatly displeased with the two brothers.
25 But Jesus called them to *Himself* and said,
"You know that the rulers of the Gentiles lord
it over them, and those who are great exercise
authority over them.
26 "Yet it shall not be so among you; but who- ◄
ever desires to become great among you, let
him be your servant.
27 "And whoever desires to be first among
you, let him be your slave—
28 "just as the Son of Man did not come to be ◄
served, but to serve, and to give His life a ransom for many."

Two Blind Men Receive Their Sight

29 Now as they went out of Jericho, a great
multitude followed Him.
30 And behold, two blind men sitting by the
road, when they heard that Jesus was passing by, cried out, saying, "Have mercy on us,
O Lord, Son of David!"
31 Then the multitude warned them that they
should be quiet; but they cried out all the
more, saying, "Have mercy on us, O Lord, Son
of David!"
32 So Jesus stood still and called them, and
said, "What do you want Me to do for you?"
33 They said to Him, "Lord, that our eyes may
be opened."
34 So Jesus had compassion and touched
their eyes. And immediately their eyes received sight, and they followed Him.

The Triumphal Entry

21 Now when they drew near Jerusalem,
and came to Bethphage,[a] at the Mount
of Olives, then Jesus sent two disciples,

20:16 [a]NU-Text omits the last sentence of this verse.
20:22 [a]NU-Text omits *and be baptized with the baptism that I am baptized with.* **20:23** [a]NU-Text omits *and be baptized with the baptism that I am baptized with.* **21:1** [a]M-Text reads *Bethsphage.*

LIFE LESSONS

➤ **20:15 — *"Is it not lawful for me to do what I wish with my own things? Or is your eye evil because I am good?"***

The Lord can and does distribute His gifts and His goodness as He wills. By definition, grace cannot be earned or deserved, so God is completely free to parcel out His favor however He chooses.

➤ **20:26 — *". . . whoever desires to become great among you, let him be your servant."***

Christian leadership is never about exercising power over someone or putting someone in his or her place; whenever it comes to that, the "Christian" element has vanished. Christian leaders are always servants first.

➤ **20:28 — *". . . the Son of Man did not come to be served, but to serve, and to give His life a ransom for many."***

No one ever mistook Jesus for anything but a leader, and yet He came to serve, right up to the time He performed the ultimate service by giving His life so that we might not have to die.

2 saying to them, "Go into the village opposite you, and immediately you will find a donkey tied, and a colt with her. Loose *them* and
bring *them* to Me.
3 "And if anyone says anything to you, you
shall say, 'The Lord has need of them,' and
immediately he will send them."
➤ 4 All[a] this was done that it might be fulfilled
which was spoken by the prophet, saying:

5 *"Tell the daughter of Zion,*
'Behold, your King is coming to you,
Lowly, and sitting on a donkey,
A colt, the foal of a donkey.'"[a]

6 So the disciples went and did as Jesus
commanded them.
7 They brought the donkey and the colt, laid
their clothes on them, and set *Him*[a] on them.
8 And a very great multitude spread their
clothes on the road; others cut down
branches from the trees and spread *them* on
the road.
9 Then the multitudes who went before and
those who followed cried out, saying:

"Hosanna to the Son of David!
'Blessed is He who comes in the name of
the LORD*!'*[a]
Hosanna in the highest!"

10 And when He had come into Jerusalem,
all the city was moved, saying, "Who is this?"
11 So the multitudes said, "This is Jesus, the
prophet from Nazareth of Galilee."

Jesus Cleanses the Temple
➤ **12** Then Jesus went into the temple of God[a]
and drove out all those who bought and sold
in the temple, and overturned the tables of the
money changers and the seats of those who
sold doves.
13 And He said to them, "It is written, *'My*
house shall be called a house of prayer,'[a] but
you have made it a *'den of thieves.'*"[b]
14 Then *the* blind and *the* lame came to Him
in the temple, and He healed them.
15 But when the chief priests and scribes saw
the wonderful things that He did, and the
children crying out in the temple and saying,
"Hosanna to the Son of David!" they were indignant
16 and said to Him, "Do You hear what these
are saying?" And Jesus said to them, "Yes.
Have you never read,

'Out of the mouth of babes and nursing
infants
You have perfected praise'?"[a]

17 Then He left them and went out of the city
to Bethany, and He lodged there.

The Fig Tree Withered
18 Now in the morning, as He returned to the
city, He was hungry.
19 And seeing a fig tree by the road, He came
to it and found nothing on it but leaves, and
said to it, "Let no fruit grow on you ever again."
Immediately the fig tree withered away.

The Lesson of the Withered Fig Tree
20 And when the disciples saw *it,* they marveled, saying, "How did the fig tree wither
away so soon?"
21 So Jesus answered and said to them, "Assuredly, I say to you, if you have faith and do
not doubt, you will not only do what was done
to the fig tree, but also if you say to this mountain, 'Be removed and be cast into the sea,' it
will be done.
22 "And whatever things you ask in prayer,
believing, you will receive."

Jesus' Authority Questioned
23 Now when He came into the temple, the
chief priests and the elders of the people confronted Him as He was teaching, and said,
"By what authority are You doing these
things? And who gave You this authority?"
24 But Jesus answered and said to them, "I
also will ask you one thing, which if you tell
Me, I likewise will tell you by what authority
I do these things:
25 "The baptism of John—where was it from?
From heaven or from men?" And they reasoned among themselves, saying, "If we say,
'From heaven,' He will say to us, 'Why then
did you not believe him?'
26 "But if we say, 'From men,' we fear the
multitude, for all count John as a prophet."
27 So they answered Jesus and said, "We do
not know." And He said to them, "Neither
will I tell you by what authority I do these
things.

21:4 [a]NU-Text omits *All.* **21:5** [a]Zechariah 9:9 **21:7** [a]NU-Text reads *and He sat.* **21:9** [a]Psalm 118:26 **21:12** [a]NU-Text omits *of God.* **21:13** [a]Isaiah 56:7 [b]Jeremiah 7:11 **21:16** [a]Psalm 8:2

LIFE LESSONS

➤ 21:4 — *All this was done that it might be fulfilled which was spoken by the prophet . . . .*

God is serious about fulfilling His Word. If He makes sure that even "little" prophesied details take place (see Matt. 2:15; 13:35; John 19:24, 28), then we can expect that He will surely fulfill all the "big" ones.

➤ 21:12 — *Then Jesus went into the temple of God and drove out all those who bought and sold in the temple, and overturned the tables of the money changers . . . .*

God feels passionate that His name be honored and that His people be treated well. His silence may unnerve us at times, but He overlooks nothing and lets nothing "slide." The day of His justice is coming.

The Parable of the Two Sons
28 "But what do you think? A man had two
sons, and he came to the first and said, 'Son,
go, work today in my vineyard.'
29 "He answered and said, 'I will not,' but afterward he regretted it and went.
30 "Then he came to the second and said
likewise. And he answered and said, 'I go, sir,'
but he did not go.
31 "Which of the two did the will of *his* father?" They said to Him, "The first." Jesus said
to them, "Assuredly, I say to you that tax collectors and harlots enter the kingdom of God
before you.
32 "For John came to you in the way of righteousness, and you did not believe him; but tax
collectors and harlots believed him; and when
you saw *it,* you did not afterward relent and
believe him.

The Parable of the Wicked Vinedressers
33 "Hear another parable: There was a certain landowner who planted a vineyard and
set a hedge around it, dug a winepress in it
and built a tower. And he leased it to vinedressers and went into a far country.
34 "Now when vintage-time drew near, he
sent his servants to the vinedressers, that they
might receive its fruit.
35 "And the vinedressers took his servants,
beat one, killed one, and stoned another.
36 "Again he sent other servants, more than
the first, and they did likewise to them.
37 "Then last of all he sent his son to them,
saying, 'They will respect my son.'
38 "But when the vinedressers saw the son,
they said among themselves, 'This is the heir.
Come, let us kill him and seize his inheritance.'
39 "So they took him and cast *him* out of the
vineyard and killed *him.*
40 "Therefore, when the owner of the vineyard
comes, what will he do to those vinedressers?"
41 They said to Him, "He will destroy those
wicked men miserably, and lease *his* vineyard
to other vinedressers who will render to him
the fruits in their seasons."
42 Jesus said to them, "Have you never read
in the Scriptures:

> '*The stone which the builders rejected*
> *Has become the chief cornerstone.*
> *This was the* LORD*'s doing,*
> *And it is marvelous in our eyes*'?[a]

43 "Therefore I say to you, the kingdom of
God will be taken from you and given to a nation bearing the fruits of it.
44 "And whoever falls on this stone will be
broken; but on whomever it falls, it will grind
him to powder."
45 Now when the chief priests and Pharisees
heard His parables, they perceived that He
was speaking of them.
46 But when they sought to lay hands on
Him, they feared the multitudes, because they
took Him for a prophet.

The Parable of the Wedding Feast
22 And Jesus answered and spoke to them
again by parables and said:
2 "The kingdom of heaven is like a certain
king who arranged a marriage for his son,
3 "and sent out his servants to call those
who were invited to the wedding; and they
were not willing to come.
4 "Again, he sent out other servants, saying,
'Tell those who are invited, "See, I have prepared my dinner; my oxen and fatted cattle
are killed, and all things *are* ready. Come to
the wedding."'
5 "But they made light of it and went their
ways, one to his own farm, another to his
business.
6 "And the rest seized his servants, treated
them spitefully, and killed *them.*
7 "But when the king heard *about it,* he was
furious. And he sent out his armies, destroyed
those murderers, and burned up their city.
8 "Then he said to his servants, 'The wedding is ready, but those who were invited
were not worthy.
9 'Therefore go into the highways, and as
many as you find, invite to the wedding.'
10 "So those servants went out into the highways and gathered together all whom they
found, both bad and good. And the wedding
hall was filled with guests.
11 "But when the king came in to see the
guests, he saw a man there who did not have
on a wedding garment.
12 "So he said to him, 'Friend, how did you
come in here without a wedding garment?'
And he was speechless.
13 "Then the king said to the servants, 'Bind
him hand and foot, take him away, and[a] cast
him into outer darkness; there will be weeping and gnashing of teeth.'
14 "For many are called, but few *are* chosen."

21:42 [a]Psalm 118:22, 23 **22:13** [a]NU-Text omits *take him away, and.*

LIFE LESSONS

➤ **22:14 — *"For many are called, but few are chosen."***

God instructs us to share the gospel with anyone who will listen. Since we do not know who will respond and who will not—the most unlikely candidates often come to faith—we are to make our appeals to the "many."

The Pharisees: Is It Lawful to Pay Taxes to Caesar?

15 Then the Pharisees went and plotted how they might entangle Him in *His* talk.
16 And they sent to Him their disciples with the Herodians, saying, "Teacher, we know that You are true, and teach the way of God in truth; nor do You care about anyone, for You do not regard the person of men.
17 "Tell us, therefore, what do You think? Is it lawful to pay taxes to Caesar, or not?"
18 But Jesus perceived their wickedness, and said, "Why do you test Me, *you* hypocrites?
19 "Show Me the tax money." So they brought Him a denarius.
20 And He said to them, "Whose image and inscription *is* this?"
21 They said to Him, "Caesar's." And He said to them, "Render therefore to Caesar the things that are Caesar's, and to God the things that are God's."
22 When they had heard *these words,* they marveled, and left Him and went their way.

The Sadducees: What About the Resurrection?

23 The same day the Sadducees, who say there is no resurrection, came to Him and asked Him,
24 saying: "Teacher, Moses said that if a man dies, having no children, his brother shall marry his wife and raise up offspring for his brother.
25 "Now there were with us seven brothers. The first died after he had married, and having no offspring, left his wife to his brother.
26 "Likewise the second also, and the third, even to the seventh.
27 "Last of all the woman died also.
28 "Therefore, in the resurrection, whose wife of the seven will she be? For they all had her."
➤ 29 Jesus answered and said to them, "You are mistaken, not knowing the Scriptures nor the power of God.
30 "For in the resurrection they neither marry nor are given in marriage, but are like angels of God[a] in heaven.
31 "But concerning the resurrection of the dead, have you not read what was spoken to you by God, saying,
32 *'I am the God of Abraham, the God of Isaac, and the God of Jacob'*?[a] God is not the God of the dead, but of the living."
33 And when the multitudes heard *this,* they were astonished at His teaching.

The Scribes: Which Is the First Commandment of All?

34 But when the Pharisees heard that He had silenced the Sadducees, they gathered together.
35 Then one of them, a lawyer, asked *Him a question,* testing Him, and saying,
36 "Teacher, which *is* the great commandment in the law?"
37 Jesus said to him, "*'You shall love the* LORD *your God with all your heart, with all your soul, and with all your mind.'*[a]
38 "This is *the* first and great commandment.
39 "And *the* second *is* like it: *'You shall love your neighbor as yourself.'*[a]
40 "On these two commandments hang all the Law and the Prophets." ➤

Jesus: How Can David Call His Descendant Lord?

41 While the Pharisees were gathered together, Jesus asked them,
42 saying, "What do you think about the Christ? Whose Son is He?" They said to Him, "*The Son* of David."
43 He said to them, "How then does David in the Spirit call Him *'Lord,'* saying:

44 '*The* LORD *said to my Lord,*
"Sit at My right hand,
Till I make Your enemies Your
footstool"'?[a]

45 "If David then calls Him *'Lord,'* how is He his Son?"
46 And no one was able to answer Him a word, nor from that day on did anyone dare question Him anymore.

Woe to the Scribes and Pharisees

23 Then Jesus spoke to the multitudes and to His disciples,
2 saying: "The scribes and the Pharisees sit in Moses' seat.
3 "Therefore whatever they tell you to observe,[a] *that* observe and do, but do not do according to their works; for they say, and do not do.

22:30 [a]NU-Text omits *of God.* **22:32** [a]Exodus 3:6, 15
22:37 [a]Deuteronomy 6:5 **22:39** [a]Leviticus 19:18
22:44 [a]Psalm 110:1 **23:3** [a]NU-Text omits *to observe.*

LIFE LESSONS

➤ 22:29 — *Jesus answered and said to them, "You are mistaken, not knowing the Scriptures nor the power of God."*

We cannot base our faith on human logic or reasoning, but on the Word of God and the almighty power that brought it into being. If it seems foolish to some, so be it. The Word of God will stand when all else falls.

➤ 22:40 — *"On these two commandments hang all the Law and the Prophets."*

Love for God and love for all those made in His image form the backbone of everything God says to us in His Word. So Paul can say, "love is the fulfillment of the law" (Rom. 13:10).

4 "For they bind heavy burdens, hard to
bear, and lay *them* on men's shoulders; but
they *themselves* will not move them with one
of their fingers.
5 "But all their works they do to be seen by
men. They make their phylacteries broad and
enlarge the borders of their garments.
6 "They love the best places at feasts, the
best seats in the synagogues,
7 "greetings in the marketplaces, and to be
called by men, 'Rabbi, Rabbi.'
8 "But you, do not be called 'Rabbi'; for One
is your Teacher, the Christ,[a] and you are all
brethren.
9 "Do not call anyone on earth your father;
for One is your Father, He who is in heaven.
10 "And do not be called teachers; for One is
your Teacher, the Christ.
11 "But he who is greatest among you shall
be your servant.
12 "And whoever exalts himself will be humbled, and he who humbles himself will be exalted.
13 "But woe to you, scribes and Pharisees,
hypocrites! For you shut up the kingdom of
heaven against men; for you neither go in
yourselves, nor do you allow those who are
entering to go in.
14 "Woe to you, scribes and Pharisees, hypocrites! For you devour widows' houses, and
for a pretense make long prayers. Therefore
you will receive greater condemnation.[a]
15 "Woe to you, scribes and Pharisees, hypocrites! For you travel land and sea to win one
proselyte, and when he is won, you make him
twice as much a son of hell as yourselves.
16 "Woe to you, blind guides, who say, 'Whoever swears by the temple, it is nothing; but
whoever swears by the gold of the temple, he
is obliged *to perform it.*'
17 "Fools and blind! For which is greater, the
gold or the temple that sanctifies[a] the gold?
18 "And, 'Whoever swears by the altar, it is
nothing; but whoever swears by the gift that
is on it, he is obliged *to perform it.*'
19 "Fools and blind! For which is greater, the
gift or the altar that sanctifies the gift?
20 "Therefore he who swears by the altar,
swears by it and by all things on it.
21 "He who swears by the temple, swears by
it and by Him who dwells[a] in it.
22 "And he who swears by heaven, swears by
the throne of God and by Him who sits on it.
23 "Woe to you, scribes and Pharisees, hypocrites! For you pay tithe of mint and anise
and cummin, and have neglected the weightier *matters* of the law: justice and mercy and
faith. These you ought to have done, without
leaving the others undone.
24 "Blind guides, who strain out a gnat and
swallow a camel!
25 "Woe to you, scribes and Pharisees, hypocrites! For you cleanse the outside of the cup
and dish, but inside they are full of extortion
and self-indulgence.[a]
26 "Blind Pharisee, first cleanse the inside of
the cup and dish, that the outside of them may
be clean also.
27 "Woe to you, scribes and Pharisees, hypocrites! For you are like whitewashed tombs
which indeed appear beautiful outwardly, but
inside are full of dead *men's* bones and all
uncleanness.
28 "Even so you also outwardly appear righteous to men, but inside you are full of
hypocrisy and lawlessness.
29 "Woe to you, scribes and Pharisees, hypocrites! Because you build the tombs of the
prophets and adorn the monuments of the
righteous,
30 "and say, 'If we had lived in the days of our
fathers, we would not have been partakers
with them in the blood of the prophets.'
31 "Therefore you are witnesses against
yourselves that you are sons of those who
murdered the prophets.
32 "Fill up, then, the measure of your fathers'
guilt.
33 "Serpents, brood of vipers! How can you
escape the condemnation of hell?
34 "Therefore, indeed, I send you prophets,
wise men, and scribes: *some* of them you will
kill and crucify, and *some* of them you will
scourge in your synagogues and persecute
from city to city,
35 "that on you may come all the righteous
blood shed on the earth, from the blood of
righteous Abel to the blood of Zechariah, son
of Berechiah, whom you murdered between
the temple and the altar.
36 "Assuredly, I say to you, all these things
will come upon this generation.

23:8 [a]NU-Text omits *the Christ.* **23:14** [a]NU-Text omits this verse. **23:17** [a]NU-Text reads *sanctified.* **23:21** [a]M-Text reads *dwelt.* **23:25** [a]M-Text reads *unrighteousness.*

LIFE LESSONS

➤ 23:13 — *"But woe to you, scribes and Pharisees, hypocrites!"*

Eight times in Matthew 23, Jesus pronounces "woes" upon those He calls "hypocrites" and "fools" and "blind" and "serpents." When love speaks harshly, it does so because no other language has a chance of breaking through.

➤ 23:28 — *"Even so you also outwardly appear righteous to men, but inside you are full of hypocrisy and lawlessness."*

God despises disobedience of any kind, but He seems to have a special hatred for religious pretense. Why? Perhaps because those who only pretend to love God do a great job of keeping others away from God.

Jesus Laments over Jerusalem
➤ **37** "O Jerusalem, Jerusalem, the one who
kills the prophets and stones those who are
sent to her! How often I wanted to gather
your children together, as a hen gathers her
chicks under *her* wings, but you were not
willing!
38 "See! Your house is left to you desolate;
39 "for I say to you, you shall see Me no more
till you say, *'Blessed is He who comes in the
name of the LORD!'*"[a]

Jesus Predicts the Destruction of the Temple
24 Then Jesus went out and departed from
the temple, and His disciples came up
to show Him the buildings of the temple.
2 And Jesus said to them, "Do you not see
all these things? Assuredly, I say to you, not
one stone shall be left here upon another, that
shall not be thrown down."

The Signs of the Times and the End of the Age
3 Now as He sat on the Mount of Olives, the
disciples came to Him privately, saying, "Tell
us, when will these things be? And what *will
be* the sign of Your coming, and of the end of
the age?"
4 And Jesus answered and said to them:
"Take heed that no one deceives you.
➤ 5 "For many will come in My name, saying,
'I am the Christ,' and will deceive many.
6 "And you will hear of wars and rumors of
wars. See that you are not troubled; for all[a]
these things must come to pass, but the end is
not yet.
7 "For nation will rise against nation, and
kingdom against kingdom. And there will be
famines, pestilences,[a] and earthquakes in various places.
8 "All these *are* the beginning of sorrows.
9 "Then they will deliver you up to tribulation and kill you, and you will be hated by all
nations for My name's sake.
10 "And then many will be offended, will betray one another, and will hate one another.
11 "Then many false prophets will rise up
and deceive many.
12 "And because lawlessness will abound,
the love of many will grow cold.
13 "But he who endures to the end shall be
saved.
14 "And this gospel of the kingdom will be ➤
preached in all the world as a witness to all
the nations, and then the end will come.

The Great Tribulation
15 "Therefore when you see the *'abomination
of desolation,'*[a] spoken of by Daniel the
prophet, standing in the holy place" (whoever
reads, let him understand),
16 "then let those who are in Judea flee to the
mountains.
17 "Let him who is on the housetop not go
down to take anything out of his house.
18 "And let him who is in the field not go
back to get his clothes.
19 "But woe to those who are pregnant and to
those who are nursing babies in those days!
20 "And pray that your flight may not be in
winter or on the Sabbath.
21 "For then there will be great tribulation,
such as has not been since the beginning of
the world until this time, no, nor ever shall
be.
22 "And unless those days were shortened,
no flesh would be saved; but for the elect's
sake those days will be shortened.
23 "Then if anyone says to you, 'Look, here *is*
the Christ!' or 'There!' do not believe *it*.
24 "For false christs and false prophets will
rise and show great signs and wonders to deceive, if possible, even the elect.
25 "See, I have told you beforehand.
26 "Therefore if they say to you, 'Look, He is
in the desert!' do not go out; *or* 'Look, *He is* in
the inner rooms!' do not believe *it*.
27 "For as the lightning comes from the east
and flashes to the west, so also will the coming of the Son of Man be.
28 "For wherever the carcass is, there the eagles will be gathered together.

23:39 [a]Psalm 118:26 **24:6** [a]NU-Text omits *all*. **24:7** [a]NU-Text omits *pestilences*. **24:15** [a]Daniel 11:31; 12:11

LIFE LESSONS

➤ 23:37 — *"How often I wanted to gather your children together, as a hen gathers her chicks under her wings, but you were not willing!"*

God's greatest desire for us is always to develop and nurture a growing, satisfying relationship with Him. He created us for deep fellowship with Him, but we make the choice whether we will fulfill our purpose.

➤ 24:5 — *"For many will come in My name, saying, 'I am the Christ,' and will deceive many."*

There have always been deceivers in the church, leading people away from a relationship with Christ and into religious bondage. But Jesus says as the time nears for His return, such deception will markedly increase.

➤ 24:14 — *"And this gospel of the kingdom will be preached in all the world as a witness to all the nations, and then the end will come."*

God will not wind down human history until the whole world has had the opportunity to hear the Good News about Jesus Christ. His amazing patience leads to our rich salvation.

The Coming of the Son of Man
29 "Immediately after the tribulation of those
days the sun will be darkened, and the moon
will not give its light; the stars will fall from
heaven, and the powers of the heavens will be
shaken.
30 "Then the sign of the Son of Man will appear in heaven, and then all the tribes of the
earth will mourn, and they will see the Son of
Man coming on the clouds of heaven with
power and great glory.
31 "And He will send His angels with a great
sound of a trumpet, and they will gather together His elect from the four winds, from
one end of heaven to the other.

The Parable of the Fig Tree
32 "Now learn this parable from the fig tree:
When its branch has already become tender
and puts forth leaves, you know that summer
is near.
33 "So you also, when you see all these
things, know that it[a] is near—at the doors!
34 "Assuredly, I say to you, this generation
will by no means pass away till all these
things take place.
✳ 35 "Heaven and earth will pass away, but My
words will by no means pass away.

No One Knows the Day or Hour
36 "But of that day and hour no one knows,
not even the angels of heaven,[a] but My Father
only.
37 "But as the days of Noah *were,* so also will
the coming of the Son of Man be.
38 "For as in the days before the flood, they
were eating and drinking, marrying and giving in marriage, until the day that Noah entered the ark,
39 "and did not know until the flood came
and took them all away, so also will the coming of the Son of Man be.
40 "Then two *men* will be in the field: one will
be taken and the other left.
41 "Two *women will be* grinding at the mill:
one will be taken and the other left.
42 "Watch therefore, for you do not know
what hour[a] your Lord is coming.
43 "But know this, that if the master of the
house had known what hour the thief would
come, he would have watched and not allowed his house to be broken into.
➤ 44 "Therefore you also be ready, for the Son
of Man is coming at an hour you do not expect.

The Faithful Servant and the Evil Servant
45 "Who then is a faithful and wise servant,
whom his master made ruler over his household, to give them food in due season?
46 "Blessed *is* that servant whom his master,
when he comes, will find so doing.
47 "Assuredly, I say to you that he will make
him ruler over all his goods.
48 "But if that evil servant says in his heart,
'My master is delaying his coming,'[a]
49 "and begins to beat *his* fellow servants,
and to eat and drink with the drunkards,
50 "the master of that servant will come on a
day when he is not looking for *him* and at an
hour that he is not aware of,
51 "and will cut him in two and appoint *him*
his portion with the hypocrites. There shall be
weeping and gnashing of teeth.

The Parable of the Wise and Foolish Virgins
25 "Then the kingdom of heaven shall be
likened to ten virgins who took their
lamps and went out to meet the bridegroom.
2 "Now five of them were wise, and five
were foolish.
3 "Those who *were* foolish took their lamps
and took no oil with them,
4 "but the wise took oil in their vessels with
their lamps.
5 "But while the bridegroom was delayed,
they all slumbered and slept.
6 "And at midnight a cry was *heard:* 'Behold, the bridegroom is coming;[a] go out to
meet him!'
7 "Then all those virgins arose and trimmed
their lamps.
8 "And the foolish said to the wise, 'Give
us *some* of your oil, for our lamps are going
out.'
9 "But the wise answered, saying, '*No,* lest
there should not be enough for us and you;
but go rather to those who sell, and buy for
yourselves.'
10 "And while they went to buy, the bridegroom came, and those who were ready went
in with him to the wedding; and the door was
shut.
11 "Afterward the other virgins came also,
saying, 'Lord, Lord, open to us!'
12 "But he answered and said, 'Assuredly, I
say to you, I do not know you.'

24:33 [a]Or *He* **24:36** [a]NU-Text adds *nor the Son.*
24:42 [a]NU-Text reads *day.* **24:48** [a]NU-Text omits *his coming.*
25:6 [a]NU-Text omits *is coming.*

LIFE LESSONS

➤ **24:44 — *"Therefore you also be ready, for the Son of Man is coming at an hour you do not expect."***

Despite many attempts over the centuries to pinpoint the time of Jesus' return, God's Word stands: He will come "at an hour you do not expect." We are to remain in a perpetual state of readiness.

➤ 13 "Watch therefore, for you know neither
the day nor the hour[a] in which the Son of Man
is coming.

The Parable of the Talents

14 "For *the kingdom of heaven is* like a man
traveling to a far country, *who* called his own
servants and delivered his goods to them.
15 "And to one he gave five talents, to another two, and to another one, to each according to his own ability; and immediately
he went on a journey.
16 "Then he who had received the five talents
went and traded with them, and made another five talents.
17 "And likewise he who *had received* two
gained two more also.
18 "But he who had received one went and
dug in the ground, and hid his lord's money.
19 "After a long time the lord of those servants came and settled accounts with them.
20 "So he who had received five talents came
and brought five other talents, saying, 'Lord,
you delivered to me five talents; look, I have
gained five more talents besides them.'
21 "His lord said to him, 'Well *done*, good and
faithful servant; you were faithful over a few
things, I will make you ruler over many
things. Enter into the joy of your lord.'
22 "He also who had received two talents
came and said, 'Lord, you delivered to me two
talents; look, I have gained two more talents
besides them.'
23 "His lord said to him, 'Well *done*, good and
faithful servant; you have been faithful over a
few things, I will make you ruler over many
things. Enter into the joy of your lord.'
24 "Then he who had received the one talent
came and said, 'Lord, I knew you to be a hard
man, reaping where you have not sown, and
gathering where you have not scattered seed.
25 'And I was afraid, and went and hid your
talent in the ground. Look, *there* you have
what is yours.'
26 "But his lord answered and said to him,
'You wicked and lazy servant, you knew that
I reap where I have not sown, and gather
where I have not scattered seed.
27 'So you ought to have deposited my money
with the bankers, and at my coming I would
have received back my own with interest.
28 'Therefore take the talent from him, and
give *it* to him who has ten talents.
29 'For to everyone who has, more will be
given, and he will have abundance; but from
him who does not have, even what he has will
be taken away.
30 'And cast the unprofitable servant into the
outer darkness. There will be weeping and
gnashing of teeth.'

The Son of Man Will Judge the Nations

31 "When the Son of Man comes in His glory,
and all the holy[a] angels with Him, then He
will sit on the throne of His glory.
32 "All the nations will be gathered before
Him, and He will separate them one from another, as a shepherd divides *his* sheep from
the goats.
33 "And He will set the sheep on His right
hand, but the goats on the left.
34 "Then the King will say to those on His ➤
right hand, 'Come, you blessed of My Father,
inherit the kingdom prepared for you from
the foundation of the world:
35 'for I was hungry and you gave Me food; I
was thirsty and you gave Me drink; I was a
stranger and you took Me in;
36 'I *was* naked and you clothed Me; I was
sick and you visited Me; I was in prison and
you came to Me.'
37 "Then the righteous will answer Him, saying, 'Lord, when did we see You hungry and
feed *You*, or thirsty and give *You* drink?
38 'When did we see You a stranger and take
You in, or naked and clothe *You?*
39 'Or when did we see You sick, or in prison,
and come to You?'
40 "And the King will answer and say to
them, 'Assuredly, I say to you, inasmuch as
you did *it* to one of the least of these My
brethren, you did *it* to Me.'
41 "Then He will also say to those on the left
hand, 'Depart from Me, you cursed, into the
everlasting fire prepared for the devil and his
angels:
42 'for I was hungry and you gave Me no
food; I was thirsty and you gave Me no drink;
43 'I was a stranger and you did not take Me
in, naked and you did not clothe Me, sick and
in prison and you did not visit Me.'
44 "Then they also will answer Him,[a] saying,
'Lord, when did we see You hungry or thirsty

25:13 [a]NU-Text omits the rest of this verse. **25:31** [a]NU-Text omits *holy.* **25:44** [a]NU-Text and M-Text omit *Him.*

LIFE LESSONS

➤ 25:13 — *"Watch therefore, for you know neither the day nor the hour in which the Son of Man is coming."*

Some people have claimed to know the season of Christ's return, even though they cannot determine the day or hour, but all such speculation is useless. The point is to continually watch for His coming.

➤ 25:34 — *"Then the King will say to those on His right hand, 'Come, you blessed of My Father, inherit the kingdom prepared for you from the foundation of the world."*

Just as Jesus is "the Lamb slain from the foundation of the world" (Rev. 13:8), so has the coming kingdom been prepared for God's people "from the foundation of the world." His plan is as ancient as it is sure.

or a stranger or naked or sick or in prison,
and did not minister to You?'
45 "Then He will answer them, saying, 'Assuredly, I say to you, inasmuch as you did not
do *it* to one of the least of these, you did not
do *it* to Me.'
➤ 46 "And these will go away into everlasting
punishment, but the righteous into eternal life."

The Plot to Kill Jesus

26 Now it came to pass, when Jesus had
finished all these sayings, *that* He said
to His disciples,
2 "You know that after two days is the
Passover, and the Son of Man will be delivered up to be crucified."
3 Then the chief priests, the scribes,[a] and the
elders of the people assembled at the palace of
the high priest, who was called Caiaphas,
4 and plotted to take Jesus by trickery and
kill *Him.*
5 But they said, "Not during the feast, lest
there be an uproar among the people."

The Anointing at Bethany

6 And when Jesus was in Bethany at the
house of Simon the leper,
7 a woman came to Him having an alabaster
flask of very costly fragrant oil, and she
poured *it* on His head as He sat *at the table.*
8 But when His disciples saw *it,* they were
indignant, saying, "Why this waste?
9 "For this fragrant oil might have been sold
for much and given to *the* poor."
10 But when Jesus was aware of *it,* He said to
them, "Why do you trouble the woman? For
she has done a good work for Me.
11 "For you have the poor with you always,
but Me you do not have always.
12 "For in pouring this fragrant oil on My
body, she did *it* for My burial.
➤ 13 "Assuredly, I say to you, wherever this
gospel is preached in the whole world, what
this woman has done will also be told as a
memorial to her."

Judas Agrees to Betray Jesus

14 Then one of the twelve, called Judas Iscariot, went to the chief priests
15 and said, "What are you willing to give me
if I deliver Him to you?" And they counted out
to him thirty pieces of silver.
16 So from that time he sought opportunity
to betray Him.

Jesus Celebrates Passover with His Disciples

17 Now on the first *day of the Feast* of Unleavened Bread the disciples came to Jesus,
saying to Him, "Where do You want us to prepare for You to eat the Passover?"
18 And He said, "Go into the city to a certain
man, and say to him, 'The Teacher says, "My
time is at hand; I will keep the Passover at
your house with My disciples."'"
19 So the disciples did as Jesus had directed
them; and they prepared the Passover.
20 When evening had come, He sat down
with the twelve.
21 Now as they were eating, He said, "Assuredly, I say to you, one of you will betray
Me."
22 And they were exceedingly sorrowful, and
each of them began to say to Him, "Lord, is it
I?"
23 He answered and said, "He who dipped *his*
hand with Me in the dish will betray Me.
24 "The Son of Man indeed goes just as it is
written of Him, but woe to that man by whom
the Son of Man is betrayed! It would have
been good for that man if he had not been
born."
25 Then Judas, who was betraying Him, answered and said, "Rabbi, is it I?" He said to
him, "You have said it."

Jesus Institutes the Lord's Supper

26 And as they were eating, Jesus took bread,
blessed[a] and broke *it,* and gave *it* to the disciples and said, "Take, eat; this is My body."
27 Then He took the cup, and gave thanks,
and gave *it* to them, saying, "Drink from it, all
of you.
28 "For this is My blood of the new[a] covenant,
which is shed for many for the remission of
sins.
29 "But I say to you, I will not drink of this ◄
fruit of the vine from now on until that day

26:3 [a]NU-Text omits *the scribes.* **26:26** [a]M-Text reads *gave thanks for.* **26:28** [a]NU-Text omits *new.*

LIFE LESSONS

➤ 25:46 — *"And these will go away into everlasting punishment, but the righteous into eternal life."*

What we do with the Good News of Jesus has enormous consequences, because the punishment of those who reject Jesus is just as eternal as the reward of those who serve Him.

➤ 26:13 — *"Assuredly, I say to you, wherever this gospel is preached in the whole world, what this woman has done will also be told as a memorial to her."*

The woman could not have known that what she did that day would be memorialized in God's Word and distributed to the ends of the earth. God loves to reward faithful devotion to Him.

➤ 26:29 — *"But I say to you, I will not drink of this fruit of the vine from now on until that day when I drink it new with you in My Father's kingdom."*

The Lord's Supper not only looks back to the sacrifice of Christ's death, it also looks ahead to His glorious reign. It both memorializes and anticipates the work of Christ and invites us to remember and celebrate.

Life Examples:

JESUS

Example or Sacrifice?

MATT. 26:39

Some believe that Jesus came to show us how to live a good life—and to be sure, He *is* our example of righteousness. We are to become like Him. But that isn't the reason Jesus came. Jesus came to die, to become the sacrificial, substitutionary, all-sufficient atonement for our sins.

If Jesus didn't come to die, there is no purpose in the Cross or the Resurrection. The New Testament consistently confronts us with the message: *Christ died for us.* Jesus came so that you and I might transfer our guilt to Him and accept by faith that as the guiltless One, He has received our sin and taken it to Himself.

If you are looking for forgiveness on the basis of your pleas, promises, and performance, then you will remain in your sins. Only if you accept His sacrifice will you open yourself to receiving the fullness of God's life-giving Spirit.

See the Life Principles Index for further study:
24. To live the Christian life is to allow Jesus to live His life in and through us.
12. Peace with God is the fruit of oneness with God.

when I drink it new with you in My Father's kingdom."
30 And when they had sung a hymn, they went out to the Mount of Olives.

Jesus Predicts Peter's Denial
31 Then Jesus said to them, "All of you will be made to stumble because of Me this night, for it is written:

'I will strike the Shepherd,
And the sheep of the flock will be
scattered.'[a]

32 "But after I have been raised, I will go before you to Galilee."
33 Peter answered and said to Him, "Even if all are made to stumble because of You, I will never be made to stumble."
34 Jesus said to him, "Assuredly, I say to you that this night, before the rooster crows, you will deny Me three times."
35 Peter said to Him, "Even if I have to die with You, I will not deny You!" And so said all the disciples.

The Prayer in the Garden
36 Then Jesus came with them to a place called Gethsemane, and said to the disciples, "Sit here while I go and pray over there."
37 And He took with Him Peter and the two sons of Zebedee, and He began to be sorrowful and deeply distressed.
38 Then He said to them, "My soul is exceedingly sorrowful, even to death. Stay here and watch with Me."
39 He went a little farther and fell on His face, and prayed, saying, "O My Father, if it is possible, let this cup pass from Me; nevertheless, not as I will, but as You *will.*"
40 Then He came to the disciples and found them sleeping, and said to Peter, "What! Could you not watch with Me one hour?
41 "Watch and pray, lest you enter into temptation. The spirit indeed *is* willing, but the flesh *is* weak."
42 Again, a second time, He went away and prayed, saying, "O My Father, if this cup cannot pass away from Me unless[a] I drink it, Your will be done."
43 And He came and found them asleep again, for their eyes were heavy.
44 So He left them, went away again, and prayed the third time, saying the same words.
45 Then He came to His disciples and said to them, "Are *you* still sleeping and resting? Behold, the hour is at hand, and the Son of Man is being betrayed into the hands of sinners.
46 "Rise, let us be going. See, My betrayer is at hand."

26:31 [a]Zechariah 13:7 **26:42** [a]NU-Text reads *if this may not pass away unless.*

LIFE LESSONS

➤ 26:37 — *And He took with Him Peter and the two sons of Zebedee, and He began to be sorrowful and deeply distressed.*

Isaiah called the coming Messiah "a Man of sorrows and acquainted with grief" (Is. 53:3), and in the Garden of Gethsemane, Jesus faced sorrow like He had never known. Truly, "He was in all points tempted as we are" (Heb. 4:15).

Betrayal and Arrest in Gethsemane
47 And while He was still speaking, behold,
Judas, one of the twelve, with a great multitude with swords and clubs, came from the
chief priests and elders of the people.
48 Now His betrayer had given them a sign,
saying, "Whomever I kiss, He is the One; seize
Him."
49 Immediately he went up to Jesus and said,
"Greetings, Rabbi!" and kissed Him.
50 But Jesus said to him, "Friend, why have
you come?" Then they came and laid hands
on Jesus and took Him.
51 And suddenly, one of those *who were* with
Jesus stretched out *his* hand and drew his
sword, struck the servant of the high priest,
and cut off his ear.
52 But Jesus said to him, "Put your sword in
its place, for all who take the sword will perish[a] by the sword.
53 "Or do you think that I cannot now pray to
My Father, and He will provide Me with more
than twelve legions of angels?
54 "How then could the Scriptures be fulfilled, that it must happen thus?"
55 In that hour Jesus said to the multitudes,
"Have you come out, as against a robber, with
swords and clubs to take Me? I sat daily with
you, teaching in the temple, and you did not
seize Me.
56 "But all this was done that the Scriptures
of the prophets might be fulfilled." Then all
the disciples forsook Him and fled.

Jesus Faces the Sanhedrin
57 And those who had laid hold of Jesus led
Him away to Caiaphas the high priest, where
the scribes and the elders were assembled.
58 But Peter followed Him at a distance to the
high priest's courtyard. And he went in and
sat with the servants to see the end.
59 Now the chief priests, the elders,[a] and all
the council sought false testimony against Jesus to put Him to death,
60 but found none. Even though many false
witnesses came forward, they found none.[a]
But at last two false witnesses[b] came forward
61 and said, "This *fellow* said, 'I am able to
destroy the temple of God and to build it in
three days.'"
62 And the high priest arose and said to Him,
"Do You answer nothing? What *is it* these men
testify against You?"
63 But Jesus kept silent. And the high priest
answered and said to Him, "I put You under
oath by the living God: Tell us if You are the
Christ, the Son of God!"
✳ 64 Jesus said to him, "*It is as* you said. Nevertheless, I say to you, hereafter you will
see the Son of Man sitting at the right hand of
the Power, and coming on the clouds of
heaven."
65 Then the high priest tore his clothes, saying, "He has spoken blasphemy! What further
need do we have of witnesses? Look, now you
have heard His blasphemy!
66 "What do you think?" They answered and
said, "He is deserving of death."
67 Then they spat in His face and beat Him;
and others struck *Him* with the palms of their
hands,
68 saying, "Prophesy to us, Christ! Who is the
one who struck You?"

Peter Denies Jesus, and Weeps Bitterly
69 Now Peter sat outside in the courtyard.
And a servant girl came to him, saying, "You
also were with Jesus of Galilee."
70 But he denied it before *them* all, saying, "I
do not know what you are saying."
71 And when he had gone out to the gateway,
another *girl* saw him and said to those *who
were* there, "This *fellow* also was with Jesus
of Nazareth."
72 But again he denied with an oath, "I do not
know the Man!"
73 And a little later those who stood by came
up and said to Peter, "Surely you also are *one*
of them, for your speech betrays you."
74 Then he began to curse and swear, *saying*,
"I do not know the Man!" Immediately a rooster crowed.
75 And Peter remembered the word of Jesus
who had said to him, "Before the rooster
crows, you will deny Me three times." So he
went out and wept bitterly.

Jesus Handed Over to Pontius Pilate
27 When morning came, all the chief
priests and elders of the people plotted
against Jesus to put Him to death.
2 And when they had bound Him, they led
Him away and delivered Him to Pontius[a] Pilate the governor.

Judas Hangs Himself
3 Then Judas, His betrayer, seeing that He
had been condemned, was remorseful and
brought back the thirty pieces of silver to the
chief priests and elders,
4 saying, "I have sinned by betraying innocent blood." And they said, "What *is that* to
us? You see *to it!*"
5 Then he threw down the pieces of silver in
the temple and departed, and went and
hanged himself.
6 But the chief priests took the silver pieces
and said, "It is not lawful to put them into
the treasury, because they are the price of
blood."
7 And they consulted together and bought
with them the potter's field, to bury strangers
in.

26:52 [a]M-Text reads *die*. **26:59** [a]NU-Text omits *the elders*.
26:60 [a]NU-Text puts a comma after *but found none*, does not capitalize *Even*, and omits *they found none*. [b]NU-Text omits *false witnesses*. **27:2** [a]NU-Text omits *Pontius*.

8 Therefore that field has been called the
Field of Blood to this day.
9 Then was fulfilled what was spoken by Jeremiah the prophet, saying, *"And they took
the thirty pieces of silver, the value of Him
who was priced,* whom they of the children of
Israel priced,
10 *"and gave them for the potter's field, as
the LORD directed me."*[a]

Jesus Faces Pilate

11 Now Jesus stood before the governor. And
the governor asked Him, saying, "Are You the
King of the Jews?" Jesus said to him, *"It is as
you say."*
12 And while He was being accused by the
chief priests and elders, He answered nothing.
13 Then Pilate said to Him, "Do You not hear
how many things they testify against You?"
➤ 14 But He answered him not one word, so
that the governor marveled greatly.

Taking the Place of Barabbas

15 Now at the feast the governor was accustomed to releasing to the multitude one prisoner whom they wished.
16 And at that time they had a notorious prisoner called Barabbas.[a]
17 Therefore, when they had gathered together, Pilate said to them, "Whom do you
want me to release to you? Barabbas, or Jesus
who is called Christ?"
18 For he knew that they had handed Him
over because of envy.
➤ 19 While he was sitting on the judgment seat,
his wife sent to him, saying, "Have nothing to
do with that just Man, for I have suffered
many things today in a dream because of
Him."
20 But the chief priests and elders persuaded
the multitudes that they should ask for Barabbas and destroy Jesus.
21 The governor answered and said to them,
"Which of the two do you want me to release
to you?" They said, "Barabbas!"
22 Pilate said to them, "What then shall I do
with Jesus who is called Christ?" *They* all said
to him, "Let Him be crucified!"
23 Then the governor said, "Why, what evil
has He done?" But they cried out all the more,
saying, "Let Him be crucified!"
24 When Pilate saw that he could not prevail
at all, but rather *that* a tumult was rising, he
took water and washed *his* hands before the
multitude, saying, "I am innocent of the blood
of this just Person.[a] You see *to it.*"
25 And all the people answered and said,
"His blood *be* on us and on our children."
26 Then he released Barabbas to them; and
when he had scourged Jesus, he delivered
Him to be crucified.

The Soldiers Mock Jesus

27 Then the soldiers of the governor took Jesus into the Praetorium and gathered the
whole garrison around Him.
28 And they stripped Him and put a scarlet
robe on Him.
29 When they had twisted a crown of thorns,
they put *it* on His head, and a reed in His right
hand. And they bowed the knee before Him
and mocked Him, saying, "Hail, King of the
Jews!"
30 Then they spat on Him, and took the reed
and struck Him on the head.
31 And when they had mocked Him, they
took the robe off Him, put His *own* clothes on
Him, and led Him away to be crucified.

The King on a Cross

32 Now as they came out, they found a man
of Cyrene, Simon by name. Him they compelled to bear His cross.
33 And when they had come to a place called
Golgotha, that is to say, Place of a Skull,
34 they gave Him sour[a] wine mingled with
gall to drink. But when He had tasted *it,* He
would not drink.
35 Then they crucified Him, and divided His
garments, casting lots,[a] that it might be fulfilled which was spoken by the prophet:

"They divided My garments among them,
And for My clothing they cast lots."[b]

36 Sitting down, they kept watch over Him
there.
37 And they put up over His head the accusation written against Him:

27:10 [a]Jeremiah 32:6–9 **27:16** [a]NU-Text reads *Jesus Barabbas.*
27:24 [a]NU-Text omits *just.* **27:34** [a]NU-Text omits *sour.*
27:35 [a]NU-Text and M-Text omit the rest of this verse.
[b]Psalm 22:18

LIFE LESSONS

➤ ***27:14 — But He answered him not one word, so that the governor marveled greatly.***

Pilate was used to prisoners cowering in his presence; this one did not, and it unnerved him. Isaiah had predicted that the Messiah would keep silent before His accusers, and Jesus did exactly that (Is. 53:7).

➤ ***27:19 — While he was sitting on the judgment seat, his wife sent to him, saying, "Have nothing to do with that just Man, for I have suffered many things today in a dream because of Him."***

What did God tell Pilate's wife in this dream? What did He intend to accomplish through it? How should the dream have influenced events? We don't know—but we do know that God speaks to those with open ears.

THIS IS JESUS THE KING OF THE JEWS.
38 Then two robbers were crucified with Him, one on the right and another on the left.
39 And those who passed by blasphemed Him, wagging their heads
40 and saying, "You who destroy the temple and build *it* in three days, save Yourself! If You are the Son of God, come down from the cross."
41 Likewise the chief priests also, mocking with the scribes and elders,[a] said,
42 "He saved others; Himself He cannot save. If He is the King of Israel,[a] let Him now come down from the cross, and we will believe Him.[b]
43 "He trusted in God; let Him deliver Him now if He will have Him; for He said, 'I am the Son of God.'"
➤ 44 Even the robbers who were crucified with Him reviled Him with the same thing.

Jesus Dies on the Cross

45 Now from the sixth hour until the ninth hour there was darkness over all the land.
46 And about the ninth hour Jesus cried out with a loud voice, saying, "Eli, Eli, lama sabachthani?" that is, *"My God, My God, why have You forsaken Me?"*[a]
47 Some of those who stood there, when they heard *that,* said, "This Man is calling for Elijah!"
48 Immediately one of them ran and took a sponge, filled *it* with sour wine and put *it* on a reed, and offered it to Him to drink.
49 The rest said, "Let Him alone; let us see if Elijah will come to save Him."
50 And Jesus cried out again with a loud voice, and yielded up His spirit.
51 Then, behold, the veil of the temple was torn in two from top to bottom; and the earth quaked, and the rocks were split,
52 and the graves were opened; and many bodies of the saints who had fallen asleep were raised;
53 and coming out of the graves after His resurrection, they went into the holy city and appeared to many.
54 So when the centurion and those with him, who were guarding Jesus, saw the earthquake and the things that had happened, they feared greatly, saying, "Truly this was the Son of God!"
55 And many women who followed Jesus from Galilee, ministering to Him, were there looking on from afar,
56 among whom were Mary Magdalene, Mary the mother of James and Joses,[a] and the mother of Zebedee's sons.

Jesus Buried in Joseph's Tomb

57 Now when evening had come, there came a rich man from Arimathea, named Joseph, who himself had also become a disciple of Jesus.
58 This man went to Pilate and asked for the body of Jesus. Then Pilate commanded the body to be given to him.
59 When Joseph had taken the body, he wrapped it in a clean linen cloth,
60 and laid it in his new tomb which he had hewn out of the rock; and he rolled a large stone against the door of the tomb, and departed.
61 And Mary Magdalene was there, and the other Mary, sitting opposite the tomb.

Pilate Sets a Guard

62 On the next day, which followed the Day of Preparation, the chief priests and Pharisees gathered together to Pilate,
63 saying, "Sir, we remember, while He was still alive, how that deceiver said, 'After three days I will rise.' ➤
64 "Therefore command that the tomb be made secure until the third day, lest His disciples come by night[a] and steal Him *away,* and say to the people, 'He has risen from the dead.' So the last deception will be worse than the first."
65 Pilate said to them, "You have a guard; go your way, make *it* as secure as you know how."
66 So they went and made the tomb secure, sealing the stone and setting the guard.

He Is Risen

28 Now after the Sabbath, as the first *day* of the week began to dawn, Mary Magdalene and the other Mary came to see the tomb.

27:41 [a]M-Text reads *with the scribes, the Pharisees, and the elders.* **27:42** [a]NU-Text reads *He is the King of Israel!* [b]NU-Text and M-Text read *we will believe in Him.* **27:46** [a]Psalm 22:1 **27:56** [a]NU-Text reads *Joseph.* **27:64** [a]NU-Text omits *by night.*

LIFE LESSONS

➤ 27:44 — *Even the robbers who were crucified with Him reviled Him with the same thing.*

At the beginning of the crucifixion, both robbers jeered Jesus. But when one criminal saw how Jesus reacted to the angry mob with grace and forgiveness, he was struck to the heart and came to faith (Luke 23:40–43).

➤ 27:63 — *"Sir, we remember, while He was still alive, how that deceiver said, 'After three days I will rise.'"*

The enemies of Jesus often understood Him better than His friends and followers did. The disciples did not grasp until some time after the Resurrection that Jesus would actually rise from the dead (John 20:9).

ANSWERS TO LIFE'S QUESTIONS

Do I have a role to play in communicating God's truth to others?

MATT. 28:19, 20

God never gives us anything to keep for ourselves. Whether it is money, insight, or truth, He calls us to share it.

Jesus told us to make disciples of all the nations, "teaching them to observe all things that I have commanded you" (Matt. 28:19, 20). Just before He ascended to heaven, He told His disciples, "you shall be witnesses to Me in Jerusalem, and in all Judea and Samaria, and to the end of the earth" (Acts 1:8).

Jesus let His disciples know that they were not to keep the truth He had taught them in some personal reservoir of knowledge. They were to give away everything they had received.

Paul admonished his young pupil, Timothy, to communicate the truth he had learned to others who would, in turn, pass it along (2 Tim. 2:2). Elsewhere he noted that we are "ambassadors for Christ" (2 Cor. 5:20). The sole purpose of ambassadors is to relay the policies and decisions of their superiors to the people of the countries where they serve. We have an obligation to declare the divine plan and scriptural policies of our Master.

Each of us communicates something by what we say and don't say, by what we do and fail to do. A father who never reads the Bible states that he's smart enough to make his own decisions without input from God. The child who never sees her parents praying learns that trials and tribulations can be handled without any direction from the Lord. On the other hand, a father who tells his family, "We are going to trust the Lord to provide us with what we need," declares that God can be trusted in every facet of life.

Even when we remain silent, we subtly state something. Although the apostle Peter recognized the Gentiles as rightful recipients of God's grace, he developed the bad habit of withdrawing from them during meals. His fellow Jews soon picked up on his prideful practice, with the result "that even Barnabas was carried away with their hypocrisy" (Gal. 2:13). Without a word, Peter had effectively sent a message that the Gentiles were inferior.

We must honestly evaluate our responses to God's communications. Are we deliberately and daily applying what God has taught us over the years? When we comprehend the truth, are we conforming ourselves to the image of Christ? Are we then communicating this truth to others?

See the Life Principles Index for further study:
21. Obedience always brings blessing.
25. God blesses us so that we might bless others.

2 And behold, there was a great earthquake; for an angel of the Lord descended from heaven, and came and rolled back the stone from the door,[a] and sat on it.
3 His countenance was like lightning, and his clothing as white as snow.
4 And the guards shook for fear of him, and became like dead *men.*
5 But the angel answered and said to the women, "Do not be afraid, for I know that you seek Jesus who was crucified.
6 "He is not here; for He is risen, as He said. Come, see the place where the Lord lay.
7 "And go quickly and tell His disciples that He is risen from the dead, and indeed He is going before you into Galilee; there you will see Him. Behold, I have told you."
8 So they went out quickly from the tomb

28:2 [a]NU-Text omits *from the door.*

LIFE LESSONS

➤ 28:4, 5 — *And the guards shook for fear of him, and became like dead men. But the angel answered and said to the women . . . .*

The angel ignored the tough male guards—he even sat silently on the stone that covered the entrance to the tomb—but he did speak to the startled women. God speaks to those who want to listen.

➤ 28:6 — *"He is not here; for He is risen, as He said."*

Jesus did exactly what He had repeatedly said He would do. That is God's way, always. We can count on His promises and build our lives on them, for He always does just what He says.

with fear and great joy, and ran to bring His
disciples word.

The Women Worship the Risen Lord

9 And as they went to tell His disciples,[a] behold, Jesus met them, saying, "Rejoice!" So they came and held Him by the feet and worshiped Him.

10 Then Jesus said to them, "Do not be afraid. Go *and* tell My brethren to go to Galilee, and there they will see Me."

The Soldiers Are Bribed

11 Now while they were going, behold, some of the guard came into the city and reported to the chief priests all the things that had happened.

12 When they had assembled with the elders and consulted together, they gave a large sum of money to the soldiers,

13 saying, "Tell them, 'His disciples came at night and stole Him *away* while we slept.'

14 "And if this comes to the governor's ears, we will appease him and make you secure."

15 So they took the money and did as they were instructed; and this saying is commonly reported among the Jews until this day.

The Great Commission

16 Then the eleven disciples went away into Galilee, to the mountain which Jesus had appointed for them.

17 When they saw Him, they worshiped Him; but some doubted.

18 And Jesus came and spoke to them, saying, "All authority has been given to Me in heaven and on earth.

19 "Go therefore[a] and make disciples of all the nations, baptizing them in the name of the Father and of the Son and of the Holy Spirit,

20 "teaching them to observe all things that I have commanded you; and lo, I am with you always, *even* to the end of the age." Amen.[a]

28:9 [a]NU-Text omits the first clause of this verse. **28:19** [a]M-Text omits *therefore*. **28:20** [a]NU-Text omits *Amen*.

LIFE LESSONS

➤ 28:17 — *When they saw Him, they worshiped Him; but some doubted.*

God has set up this world so that an element of faith is always required to connect with Him. Why did some doubt? Had Jesus' appearance dramatically changed? The real question is, *will we trust Him?*

➤ 28:18, 19 — *"All authority has been given to Me in heaven and on earth. Go therefore and make disciples of all the nations . . . ."*

We can confidently bring the truth of Jesus to the world because we have Jesus' divine authority to back it up. Our job is to be His faithful messengers; His job is to prosper His Word.

THE GOSPEL ACCORDING TO

MARK

We see the essence of Mark's Gospel in a single verse: "For even the Son of man did not come to be served, but to serve, and to give His life a ransom for many" (10:45). Chapter after chapter, the book unfolds the dual focus of Christ's life: service and sacrifice.

Mark portrays Jesus as a Servant on the move, instantly responsive to the will of His Father. Preaching, teaching, and healing, Jesus is seen ministering to the needs of others even to the point of death. After the resurrection, we see Him commissioning His followers to continue His work in His power—servants following in the steps of the perfect Servant.

The ancient title for this Gospel was *Kata Markon*, "According to Mark." Acts 12:12, 25 refer to the author as "John whose surname was Mark."

Little is known about Mark. At one time he associated with the apostle Paul and his partner-in-missions, Barnabas, and accompanied them on a missionary journey to Antioch. While Mark was not one of Jesus' twelve apostles, tradition says he was very close to Peter, and that he based his Gospel account largely on Peter's teaching and recollections. Some ancient writers refer to Mark's Gospel as "The Gospel of Peter."

Because he never quotes the Jewish law, Mark appears to have written for first-century Greek and Roman Christians. Mark quotes the Old Testament only twice, the first time to announce the coming of John the Baptist as predicted in Isaiah 40:3. He often translates Aramaic words and phrases into Greek.

Mark is the shortest of the four Gospels. Unlike Matthew and Luke, Mark makes no reference to the genealogy of Jesus, nor to the virgin birth. He also leaves out the famous "Sermon on the Mount," which Matthew covers in three chapters. His book moves at a quick pace and he has a fondness for the word "immediately."

Theme: Jesus Christ, the dedicated servant of God and of humankind, is the Savior of the world.

Author: John Mark.

Time: Mark is generally considered the earliest of the Gospels, likely composed in the A.D. 50s or early 60s.

Structure: The first part of Mark describes the years leading up to Jesus' public ministry, focusing on John the Baptist (1:1–13). The book then focuses on Jesus' ministry in Galilee (1:14—6:29), followed by ministry outside of Galilee (6:30—9:32), and a final effort back inside Galilee (9:33–50). Mark next describes Jesus' work in Judea and Perea (10:1–52), the events leading up to His arrest, crucifixion, and burial (11:1—15:47), and His resurrection (16:1–20).

As you read Mark, watch for several life principles that play an important role in this book:

4. The awareness of God's presence energizes us for our work. *See Mark 3:13–15; page 1160.*

27. Prayer is life's greatest time saver. *See Mark 9:28, 29; page 1170.*

25. God blesses us so that we might bless others. *See Mark 10:35–45; page 1172.*

15. Brokenness is God's requirement for maximum usefulness. *See Mark 14:66–72; page 1179.*

John the Baptist Prepares the Way

1 The beginning of the gospel of Jesus Christ, the Son of God.
2 As it is written in the Prophets:[a]

"Behold, I send My messenger before
Your face,
Who will prepare Your way before
You."[b]
3 *"The voice of one crying in the*
wilderness:
'Prepare the way of the LORD;
Make His paths straight.'"[a]

4 John came baptizing in the wilderness
and preaching a baptism of repentance for
the remission of sins.
➤ 5 Then all the land of Judea, and those from
Jerusalem, went out to him and were all baptized by him in the Jordan River, confessing
their sins.
6 Now John was clothed with camel's hair
and with a leather belt around his waist, and
he ate locusts and wild honey.
7 And he preached, saying, "There comes
One after me who is mightier than I, whose
sandal strap I am not worthy to stoop down
and loose.
8 "I indeed baptized you with water, but He
will baptize you with the Holy Spirit."

John Baptizes Jesus

9 It came to pass in those days *that* Jesus
came from Nazareth of Galilee, and was baptized by John in the Jordan.
10 And immediately, coming up from[a] the
water, He saw the heavens parting and the
Spirit descending upon Him like a dove.
11 Then a voice came from heaven, "You are
My beloved Son, in whom I am well pleased."

Satan Tempts Jesus

12 Immediately the Spirit drove Him into the
wilderness.
13 And He was there in the wilderness forty
days, tempted by Satan, and was with the
wild beasts; and the angels ministered to
Him.

Jesus Begins His Galilean Ministry

14 Now after John was put in prison, Jesus
came to Galilee, preaching the gospel of the
kingdom[a] of God,
15 and saying, "The time is fulfilled, and the
kingdom of God is at hand. Repent, and believe in the gospel."

Four Fishermen Called as Disciples

16 And as He walked by the Sea of Galilee,
He saw Simon and Andrew his brother casting a net into the sea; for they were fishermen.
17 Then Jesus said to them, "Follow Me, and ✳
I will make you become fishers of men."
18 They immediately left their nets and followed Him.
19 When He had gone a little farther from
there, He saw James the *son* of Zebedee, and
John his brother, who also *were* in the boat
mending their nets.
20 And immediately He called them, and
they left their father Zebedee in the boat with
the hired servants, and went after Him.

Jesus Casts Out an Unclean Spirit

21 Then they went into Capernaum, and immediately on the Sabbath He entered the synagogue and taught.
22 And they were astonished at His teaching,
for He taught them as one having authority,
and not as the scribes.
23 Now there was a man in their synagogue
with an unclean spirit. And he cried out,
24 saying, "Let *us* alone! What have we to do
with You, Jesus of Nazareth? Did You come to
destroy us? I know who You are—the Holy
One of God!"
25 But Jesus rebuked him, saying, "Be quiet,
and come out of him!"
26 And when the unclean spirit had convulsed him and cried out with a loud voice, he
came out of him.
27 Then they were all amazed, so that they ➤
questioned among themselves, saying, "What
is this? What new doctrine *is* this? For with
authority[a] He commands even the unclean
spirits, and they obey Him."
28 And immediately His fame spread
throughout all the region around Galilee.

1:2 [a]NU-Text reads *Isaiah the prophet.* [b]Malachi 3:1
1:3 [a]Isaiah 40:3 **1:10** [a]NU-Text reads *out of.* **1:14** [a]NU-Text omits *of the kingdom.* **1:27** [a]NU-Text reads *What is this? A new doctrine with authority.*

LIFE LESSONS

➤ 1:5 — *Then all the land of Judea, and those from Jerusalem, went out to him and were all baptized by him in the Jordan River, confessing their sins.*

Confessing our sins reminds us of our guilt and inability to make ourselves right, even as it points us to the grace of God who alone can give us spiritual life.

➤ 1:27 — *Then they were all amazed, so that they questioned among themselves, saying, "What is this? What new doctrine is this? For with authority He commands even the unclean spirits, and they obey Him."*

Jesus closely connected His teaching with His miracles. The miracles were designed to point to the validity of both His teachings and His personal claims.

Peter's Mother-in-Law Healed
29 Now as soon as they had come out of the
synagogue, they entered the house of Simon
and Andrew, with James and John.
30 But Simon's wife's mother lay sick with a
fever, and they told Him about her at once.
31 So He came and took her by the hand and
lifted her up, and immediately the fever left
her. And she served them.

Many Healed After Sabbath Sunset
32 At evening, when the sun had set, they
brought to Him all who were sick and those
who were demon-possessed.
33 And the whole city was gathered together
at the door.
➤ 34 Then He healed many who were sick with
various diseases, and cast out many demons;
and He did not allow the demons to speak, because they knew Him.

Preaching in Galilee
➤ **35** Now in the morning, having risen a long
while before daylight, He went out and departed to a solitary place; and there He
prayed.
36 And Simon and those *who were* with Him
searched for Him.
37 When they found Him, they said to Him,
"Everyone is looking for You."
38 But He said to them, "Let us go into the
next towns, that I may preach there also, because for this purpose I have come forth."
39 And He was preaching in their synagogues throughout all Galilee, and casting out
demons.

Jesus Cleanses a Leper
40 Now a leper came to Him, imploring Him,
kneeling down to Him and saying to Him, "If
You are willing, You can make me clean."
41 Then Jesus, moved with compassion,
stretched out *His* hand and touched him, and
said to him, "I am willing; be cleansed."
42 As soon as He had spoken, immediately
the leprosy left him, and he was cleansed.
43 And He strictly warned him and sent him
away at once,
44 and said to him, "See that you say nothing
to anyone; but go your way, show yourself to
the priest, and offer for your cleansing those
things which Moses commanded, as a testimony to them."
45 However, he went out and began to proclaim *it* freely, and to spread the matter, so
that Jesus could no longer openly enter the
city, but was outside in deserted places; and
they came to Him from every direction.

Jesus Forgives and Heals a Paralytic
2 And again He entered Capernaum after
some days, and it was heard that He was
in the house.
2 Immediately[a] many gathered together, so
that there was no longer room to receive
them, not even near the door. And He
preached the word to them.
3 Then they came to Him, bringing a paralytic who was carried by four *men*.
4 And when they could not come near Him
because of the crowd, they uncovered the roof
where He was. So when they had broken
through, they let down the bed on which the
paralytic was lying.
5 When Jesus saw their faith, He said to the ➤
paralytic, "Son, your sins are forgiven you."
6 And some of the scribes were sitting there
and reasoning in their hearts,
7 "Why does this *Man* speak blasphemies
like this? Who can forgive sins but God
alone?"
8 But immediately, when Jesus perceived in
His spirit that they reasoned thus within
themselves, He said to them, "Why do you
reason about these things in your hearts?
9 "Which is easier, to say to the paralytic,
'*Your* sins are forgiven you,' or to say, 'Arise,
take up your bed and walk'?
10 "But that you may know that the Son of
Man has power on earth to forgive sins"—He
said to the paralytic,
11 "I say to you, arise, take up your bed, and
go to your house."
12 Immediately he arose, took up the bed,
and went out in the presence of them all, so
that all were amazed and glorified God, saying, "We never saw *anything* like this!"

2:2 [a]NU-Text omits *Immediately.*

LIFE LESSONS

➤ **1:34 — *. . . He did not allow the demons to speak, because they knew Him.***

Jesus does not need the testimony of evil spirits to corroborate His identity or to vouch for His holy character. We might be impressed with such supernatural witnesses, but Jesus dismissed them.

➤ **1:35 — *Now in the morning, having risen a long while before daylight, He went out and departed to a solitary place; and there He prayed.***

Jesus never got too busy to pray. If He had to get up a long time before sunrise in order to pray, that's what He did. He valued His time alone with His Father and pursued it His whole life.

➤ **2:5 — *When Jesus saw their faith, He said to the paralytic, "Son, your sins are forgiven you."***

In this instance, Jesus heals a man and forgives his sins, based not on the man's faith but on the faith of his friends. We are wise if we recruit godly friends to pray for us.

Matthew the Tax Collector

13 Then He went out again by the sea; and all the multitude came to Him, and He taught them.
14 As He passed by, He saw Levi the *son* of Alphaeus sitting at the tax office. And He said to him, "Follow Me." So he arose and followed Him.
15 Now it happened, as He was dining in *Levi's* house, that many tax collectors and sinners also sat together with Jesus and His disciples; for there were many, and they followed Him.
16 And when the scribes and[a] Pharisees saw Him eating with the tax collectors and sinners, they said to His disciples, "How *is it* that He eats and drinks with tax collectors and sinners?"
➤ 17 When Jesus heard *it*, He said to them, "Those who are well have no need of a physician, but those who are sick. I did not come to call *the* righteous, but sinners, to repentance."[a]

Jesus Is Questioned About Fasting

18 The disciples of John and of the Pharisees were fasting. Then they came and said to Him, "Why do the disciples of John and of the Pharisees fast, but Your disciples do not fast?"
19 And Jesus said to them, "Can the friends of the bridegroom fast while the bridegroom is with them? As long as they have the bridegroom with them they cannot fast.
20 "But the days will come when the bridegroom will be taken away from them, and then they will fast in those days.
21 "No one sews a piece of unshrunk cloth on an old garment; or else the new piece pulls away from the old, and the tear is made worse.
➤ 22 "And no one puts new wine into old wineskins; or else the new wine bursts the wineskins, the wine is spilled, and the wineskins are ruined. But new wine must be put into new wineskins."

Jesus Is Lord of the Sabbath

23 Now it happened that He went through the grainfields on the Sabbath; and as they went His disciples began to pluck the heads of grain.
24 And the Pharisees said to Him, "Look, why do they do what is not lawful on the Sabbath?"
25 But He said to them, "Have you never read what David did when he was in need and hungry, he and those with him:
26 "how he went into the house of God *in the days* of Abiathar the high priest, and ate the showbread, which is not lawful to eat except for the priests, and also gave some to those who were with him?"
27 And He said to them, "The Sabbath was made for man, and not man for the Sabbath. ➤
28 "Therefore the Son of Man is also Lord of the Sabbath."

Healing on the Sabbath

3 And He entered the synagogue again, and a man was there who had a withered hand.
2 So they watched Him closely, whether He would heal him on the Sabbath, so that they might accuse Him. ➤
3 And He said to the man who had the withered hand, "Step forward."
4 Then He said to them, "Is it lawful on the Sabbath to do good or to do evil, to save life or to kill?" But they kept silent.
5 And when He had looked around at them with anger, being grieved by the hardness of their hearts, He said to the man, "Stretch out your hand." And he stretched *it* out, and his hand was restored as whole as the other.[a] ➤

2:16 [a]NU-Text reads *of the.* **2:17** [a]NU-Text omits *to repentance.*
3:5 [a]NU-Text omits *as whole as the other.*

LIFE LESSONS

➤ 2:17 — *"Those who are well have no need of a physician, but those who are sick. I did not come to call the righteous, but sinners, to repentance."*

If you have troubles at home or with friends or at work, then you need a Savior. If you feel weary and discouraged and hopeless, then Jesus is the physician you need. He offers Himself to you right now.

➤ 2:22 — *"And no one puts new wine into old wineskins; or else the new wine bursts the wineskins, the wine is spilled, and the wineskins are ruined."*

All of us tend to resist change, but God's Spirit continually moves in new ways and in new directions. If we want to keep in step with the Spirit, we need to be willing to change the way we do things.

➤ 2:27 — *And He said to them, "The Sabbath was made for man, and not man for the Sabbath."*

God created the Sabbath to bless humankind, to give men and women a much-needed opportunity to rest and relax and regain strength. The Sabbath was not meant to be a burden but a blessing.

➤ 3:2 — *So they watched Him closely, whether He would heal him on the Sabbath, so that they might accuse Him.*

When we exchange the freedom of the Spirit for the straightjacket of legalism, the rules become far more important than the life that the rules were meant to guard. Legalism saps the life out of everyone it touches.

➤ 3:5 — *And when He had looked around at them with anger, being grieved by the hardness of their hearts . . . .*

Do you ever picture Jesus as angry, as grieved over hard hearts? As the perfect reflection of His heavenly Father, Jesus is both angered by sin and grieved by unrepentant hearts. He takes sin seriously.

6 Then the Pharisees went out and immediately plotted with the Herodians against Him, how they might destroy Him.

A Great Multitude Follows Jesus

7 But Jesus withdrew with His disciples to the sea. And a great multitude from Galilee followed Him, and from Judea
8 and Jerusalem and Idumea and beyond the Jordan; and those from Tyre and Sidon, a great multitude, when they heard how many things He was doing, came to Him.
9 So He told His disciples that a small boat should be kept ready for Him because of the multitude, lest they should crush Him.
10 For He healed many, so that as many as had afflictions pressed about Him to touch Him.
11 And the unclean spirits, whenever they saw Him, fell down before Him and cried out, saying, "You are the Son of God."
12 But He sternly warned them that they should not make Him known.

The Twelve Apostles

13 And He went up on the mountain and called to *Him* those He Himself wanted. And they came to Him.
➤ 14 Then He appointed twelve,[a] that they might be with Him and that He might send them out to preach,
15 and to have power to heal sicknesses and[a] to cast out demons:
16 Simon,[a] to whom He gave the name Peter;
17 James the *son* of Zebedee and John the brother of James, to whom He gave the name Boanerges, that is, "Sons of Thunder";
18 Andrew, Philip, Bartholomew, Matthew, Thomas, James the *son* of Alphaeus, Thaddaeus, Simon the Cananite;
19 and Judas Iscariot, who also betrayed Him. And they went into a house.

A House Divided Cannot Stand

20 Then the multitude came together again, so that they could not so much as eat bread.
➤ 21 But when His own people heard *about this,* they went out to lay hold of Him, for they said, "He is out of His mind."
22 And the scribes who came down from Jerusalem said, "He has Beelzebub," and, "By the ruler of the demons He casts out demons."
23 So He called them to *Himself* and said to them in parables: "How can Satan cast out Satan?
24 "If a kingdom is divided against itself, that kingdom cannot stand.
25 "And if a house is divided against itself, that house cannot stand.
26 "And if Satan has risen up against himself, and is divided, he cannot stand, but has an end.
27 "No one can enter a strong man's house and plunder his goods, unless he first binds the strong man. And then he will plunder his house.

The Unpardonable Sin

28 "Assuredly, I say to you, all sins will be forgiven the sons of men, and whatever blasphemies they may utter;
29 "but he who blasphemes against the Holy Spirit never has forgiveness, but is subject to eternal condemnation"—
30 because they said, "He has an unclean spirit."

Jesus' Mother and Brothers Send for Him

31 Then His brothers and His mother came, and standing outside they sent to Him, calling Him.
32 And a multitude was sitting around Him; and they said to Him, "Look, Your mother and Your brothers[a] are outside seeking You."
33 But He answered them, saying, "Who is My mother, or My brothers?"
34 And He looked around in a circle at those who sat about Him, and said, "Here are My mother and My brothers!
35 "For whoever does the will of God is My brother and My sister and mother."

The Parable of the Sower

4 And again He began to teach by the sea. And a great multitude was gathered to Him, so that He got into a boat and sat *in it* on the sea; and the whole multitude was on the land facing the sea.
2 Then He taught them many things by parables, and said to them in His teaching:
3 "Listen! Behold, a sower went out to sow.

3:14 [a]NU-Text adds *whom He also named apostles.* **3:15** [a]NU-Text omits *to heal sicknesses and.* **3:16** [a]NU-Text reads *and He appointed the twelve: Simon . . . .* **3:32** [a]NU-Text and M-Text add *and Your sisters.*

LIFE LESSONS

➤ 3:14 — *Then He appointed twelve, that they might be with Him. . . .*

Jesus trained His disciples primarily by being *with* them—walking with them, talking with them, eating with them, observing them, asking them questions. There is no substitute for investing time with others.

➤ 3:21 — *But when His own people heard about this, they went out to lay hold of Him, for they said, "He is out of His mind."*

When Jesus' family heard of the long hours He spent ministering to ever-growing crowds, they grew concerned for His well-being and sought to take Him home. Even some of them did not at first believe in Him.

4 "And it happened, as he sowed, *that* some
seed fell by the wayside; and the birds of the
air[a] came and devoured it.
5 "Some fell on stony ground, where it did
not have much earth; and immediately it
sprang up because it had no depth of earth.
6 "But when the sun was up it was scorched,
and because it had no root it withered away.
7 "And some *seed* fell among thorns; and
the thorns grew up and choked it, and it
yielded no crop.
8 "But other *seed* fell on good ground and
yielded a crop that sprang up, increased and
produced: some thirtyfold, some sixty, and
some a hundred."
➤ 9 And He said to them,[a] "He who has ears to
hear, let him hear!"

The Purpose of Parables

10 But when He was alone, those around
Him with the twelve asked Him about the
parable.
11 And He said to them, "To you it has been
given to know the mystery of the kingdom of
God; but to those who are outside, all things
come in parables,
12 "so that

'*Seeing they may see and not perceive,*
And hearing they may hear and not
understand;
Lest they should turn,
And their sins be forgiven them.'"[a]

The Parable of the Sower Explained

13 And He said to them, "Do you not understand this parable? How then will you understand all the parables?
14 "The sower sows the word.
15 "And these are the ones by the wayside
where the word is sown. When they hear, Satan comes immediately and takes away the
word that was sown in their hearts.
16 "These likewise are the ones sown on
stony ground who, when they hear the word,
immediately receive it with gladness;
➤ 17 "and they have no root in themselves, and
so endure only for a time. Afterward, when
tribulation or persecution arises for the
word's sake, immediately they stumble.
18 "Now these are the ones sown among
thorns; *they are* the ones who hear the word,
19 "and the cares of this world, the deceitfulness of riches, and the desires for other things
entering in choke the word, and it becomes
unfruitful.
20 "But these are the ones sown on good
ground, those who hear the word, accept *it*,
and bear fruit: some thirtyfold, some sixty,
and some a hundred."

Light Under a Basket

21 Also He said to them, "Is a lamp brought
to be put under a basket or under a bed? Is it
not to be set on a lampstand?
22 "For there is nothing hidden which will ✳
not be revealed, nor has anything been kept
secret but that it should come to light.
23 "If anyone has ears to hear, let him hear."
24 Then He said to them, "Take heed what
you hear. With the same measure you use, it
will be measured to you; and to you who hear,
more will be given.
25 "For whoever has, to him more will be
given; but whoever does not have, even what
he has will be taken away from him."

The Parable of the Growing Seed

26 And He said, "The kingdom of God is as if
a man should scatter seed on the ground,
27 "and should sleep by night and rise by day,
and the seed should sprout and grow, he himself does not know how.
28 "For the earth yields crops by itself: first
the blade, then the head, after that the full
grain in the head.
29 "But when the grain ripens, immediately
he puts in the sickle, because the harvest has
come."

The Parable of the Mustard Seed

30 Then He said, "To what shall we liken the
kingdom of God? Or with what parable shall
we picture it?
31 "*It is* like a mustard seed which, when it is
sown on the ground, is smaller than all the
seeds on earth;
32 "but when it is sown, it grows up and becomes greater than all herbs, and shoots out
large branches, so that the birds of the air
may nest under its shade."

4:4 [a]NU-Text and M-Text omit *of the air.* **4:9** [a]NU-Text and M-Text omit *to them.* **4:12** [a]Isaiah 6:9, 10

LIFE LESSONS

➤ 4:9 — *"He who has ears to hear, let him hear!"*

God does not force any of us to hear His words or listen to His counsel. He may employ a series of uncomfortable situations to try to get our attention, but whether we choose to hear is entirely up to us.

➤ 4:17 — *". . . they have no root in themselves, and so endure only for a time. Afterward, when tribulation or persecution arises for the word's sake, immediately they stumble."*

All of us need the help and encouragement of others to grow in our faith and send our roots deep into the soil of God's grace. We cannot endure on our own; we need each other to advance in our faith.

Jesus' Use of Parables

33 And with many such parables He spoke
the word to them as they were able to hear *it*.
34 But without a parable He did not speak to
them. And when they were alone, He explained all things to His disciples.

Wind and Wave Obey Jesus

35 On the same day, when evening had come,
He said to them, "Let us cross over to the
other side."
36 Now when they had left the multitude,
they took Him along in the boat as He was.
And other little boats were also with Him.
37 And a great windstorm arose, and the
waves beat into the boat, so that it was already filling.
➤ 38 But He was in the stern, asleep on a pillow.
And they awoke Him and said to Him,
"Teacher, do You not care that we are perishing?"
39 Then He arose and rebuked the wind, and
said to the sea, "Peace, be still!" And the wind
ceased and there was a great calm.
40 But He said to them, "Why are you so fearful? How *is it* that you have no faith?"[a]
41 And they feared exceedingly, and said to
one another, "Who can this be, that even the
wind and the sea obey Him!"

A Demon-Possessed Man Healed

5 Then they came to the other side of the
sea, to the country of the Gadarenes.[a]
2 And when He had come out of the boat,
immediately there met Him out of the tombs
a man with an unclean spirit,
3 who had *his* dwelling among the tombs;
and no one could bind him,[a] not even with
chains,
4 because he had often been bound with
shackles and chains. And the chains had been
pulled apart by him, and the shackles broken
in pieces; neither could anyone tame him.
5 And always, night and day, he was in the
mountains and in the tombs, crying out and
cutting himself with stones.
6 When he saw Jesus from afar, he ran and
worshiped Him.
7 And he cried out with a loud voice and
said, "What have I to do with You, Jesus, Son
of the Most High God? I implore You by God
that You do not torment me."
8 For He said to him, "Come out of the man,
unclean spirit!"
9 Then He asked him, "What *is* your name?"
And he answered, saying, "My name *is* Legion; for we are many."
10 Also he begged Him earnestly that He
would not send them out of the country.
11 Now a large herd of swine was feeding
there near the mountains.
12 So all the demons begged Him, saying,
"Send us to the swine, that we may enter
them."
13 And at once Jesus[a] gave them permission.
Then the unclean spirits went out and entered
the swine (there were about two thousand);
and the herd ran violently down the steep
place into the sea, and drowned in the sea.
14 So those who fed the swine fled, and they
told *it* in the city and in the country. And they
went out to see what it was that had happened.
15 Then they came to Jesus, and saw the one
who had been demon-possessed and had the
legion, sitting and clothed and in his right
mind. And they were afraid.
16 And those who saw it told them how it
happened to him *who had been* demon-possessed, and about the swine.
17 Then they began to plead with Him to depart from their region.
18 And when He got into the boat, he who
had been demon-possessed begged Him that
he might be with Him.
19 However, Jesus did not permit him, but ➤
said to him, "Go home to your friends, and tell
them what great things the Lord has done for
you, and how He has had compassion on
you."
20 And he departed and began to proclaim in
Decapolis all that Jesus had done for him;
and all marveled.

A Girl Restored to Life and a Woman Healed

21 Now when Jesus had crossed over again
by boat to the other side, a great multitude
gathered to Him; and He was by the sea.
22 And behold, one of the rulers of the synagogue came, Jairus by name. And when he
saw Him, he fell at His feet

4:40 [a]NU-Text reads *Have you still no faith?* **5:1** [a]NU-Text reads *Gerasenes.* **5:3** [a]NU-Text adds *anymore.* **5:13** [a]NU-Text reads *And He gave.*

LIFE LESSONS

➤ **4:38 — *And they awoke Him and said to Him, "Teacher, do You not care that we are perishing?"***

How often do we say things like this to our Lord? When we get into some trouble, we question His love, not His ability. And yet despite our lack of faith, He reaches out His hand and saves us.

➤ **5:19 — *Jesus did not permit him, but said to him, "Go home to your friends, and tell them what great things the Lord has done for you, and how He has had compassion on you."***

The former demoniac really wanted to go with Jesus; he probably did not think it very compassionate that Jesus refused to let him do so. But Jesus' compassion is much more than merely being nice.

WHAT THE BIBLE SAYS ABOUT HOW ADVERSITY REVEALS OUR LEVEL OF FAITH

Mark 4:35

When hardships come our way, do we respond, "God, I trust You to bring me through this"? Or do we tend to say, "I'm doomed, and there's nothing anybody can do"?

God once sent a storm on the Sea of Galilee to teach Jesus' disciples a lesson on faith. Jesus had said to His men, "Let us cross over to the other side" (Mark 4:35), and they should have taken His statement as a sure sign that He expected a safe trip. But when a terrible windstorm threatened the boat, they panicked. The terrified disciples asked Jesus, "Teacher, do You not care that we are perishing?"

How many times have we said the same thing? "Don't You care, Lord, that this is happening to me?" "Don't You love me enough, Lord, to do something about this hardship?"

Jesus rebuked the wind, and immediately a great calm settled on the lake. Then He turned to His disciples and said, "Why are you so fearful? How is it that you have no faith?" (Mark 4:40).

Faith says that God is in control.

God has given to each one of us a measure of faith (Rom. 12:3), and He expects us to use it to overcome our fear. Fear always accompanies adversity; in fact, a degree of fear is what makes something an adversity instead of just another experience. Fear causes us to project the very worst that can happen—that we will never recover, that all hope is lost, that we will never again enjoy some treasured thing.

Faith tells the opposite story. Faith says that God is in control and that all things work together for our good (Rom. 8:28). Faith says that we *will* recover and that our final state *will* be better than anything we have experienced thus far.

Allow adversity to call your faith to action rather than into question. Adversity reveals areas in which you need to act in faith and not fear. When hard times come, say to yourself, "Now is the time to use my faith in a new way." The more you use your faith, the greater it grows.

See the Life Principles Index for further study:

29. We learn more in our mountain experiences than on our mountaintops.

9. Trusting God means looking beyond what we can see to what God sees.

23 and begged Him earnestly, saying, "My little daughter lies at the point of death. Come
and lay Your hands on her, that she may be
healed, and she will live."
24 So *Jesus* went with him, and a great multitude followed Him and thronged Him.
25 Now a certain woman had a flow of blood
for twelve years,
26 and had suffered many things from many
physicians. She had spent all that she had and
was no better, but rather grew worse.
27 When she heard about Jesus, she came behind *Him* in the crowd and touched His garment.
28 For she said, "If only I may touch His
clothes, I shall be made well."
29 Immediately the fountain of her blood was
dried up, and she felt in *her* body that she was
healed of the affliction.
30 And Jesus, immediately knowing in Himself that power had gone out of Him, turned
around in the crowd and said, "Who touched
My clothes?"
31 But His disciples said to Him, "You see the
multitude thronging You, and You say, 'Who
touched Me?'"
32 And He looked around to see her who had
done this thing.
33 But the woman, fearing and trembling,
knowing what had happened to her, came
and fell down before Him and told Him the
whole truth.
34 And He said to her, "Daughter, your faith
has made you well. Go in peace, and be
healed of your affliction."
35 While He was still speaking, *some* came
from the ruler of the synagogue's *house* who
said, "Your daughter is dead. Why trouble the
Teacher any further?"
➤ 36 As soon as Jesus heard the word that was
spoken, He said to the ruler of the synagogue,
"Do not be afraid; only believe."
37 And He permitted no one to follow Him
except Peter, James, and John the brother of
James.
38 Then He came to the house of the ruler of
the synagogue, and saw a tumult and those
who wept and wailed loudly.
39 When He came in, He said to them, "Why
make this commotion and weep? The child is
not dead, but sleeping."
40 And they ridiculed Him. But when He had
put them all outside, He took the father and the
mother of the child, and those *who were* with
Him, and entered where the child was lying.
41 Then He took the child by the hand, and
said to her, "Talitha, cumi," which is translated, "Little girl, I say to you, arise."
42 Immediately the girl arose and walked, for
she was twelve years *of age.* And they were
overcome with great amazement.
43 But He commanded them strictly that no ➤
one should know it, and said that *something*
should be given her to eat.

Jesus Rejected at Nazareth

6 Then He went out from there and came to
His own country, and His disciples followed Him.
2 And when the Sabbath had come, He
began to teach in the synagogue. And many
hearing *Him* were astonished, saying, "Where
did this Man *get* these things? And what wisdom *is* this which is given to Him, that such
mighty works are performed by His hands!
3 "Is this not the carpenter, the Son of Mary,
and brother of James, Joses, Judas, and Simon? And are not His sisters here with us?"
So they were offended at Him.
4 But Jesus said to them, "A prophet is not
without honor except in his own country,
among his own relatives, and in his own
house."
5 Now He could do no mighty work there,
except that He laid His hands on a few sick
people and healed *them.*
6 And He marveled because of their unbe- ➤
lief. Then He went about the villages in a circuit, teaching.

Sending Out the Twelve

7 And He called the twelve to *Himself,* and
began to send them out two *by* two, and gave
them power over unclean spirits.
8 He commanded them to take nothing for
the journey except a staff—no bag, no bread,
no copper in *their* money belts—
9 but to wear sandals, and not to put on two
tunics.
10 Also He said to them, "In whatever place
you enter a house, stay there till you depart
from that place.

LIFE LESSONS

➤ 5:36 — *As soon as Jesus heard the word that was spoken, He said to the ruler of the synagogue, "Do not be afraid; only believe."*

Jesus did not comfort the man upon hearing the news of his daughter's death; he challenged him to faith instead. Regardless of our circumstances, God always urges us on to faith and away from fear.

➤ 5:43 — *But He . . . said that something should be given her to eat.*

If Jesus brought the little girl back to life, why didn't He also put something in her empty stomach? God does what only He can do; He instructs us to do what He equips us to do.

➤ 6:6 — *And He marveled because of their unbelief.*

Unbelief always causes Jesus to marvel, because He knows that the God who asks us to trust Him is almighty, all-wise, all-present, and all-loving. Why would someone *not* trust Him? The very idea is beyond understanding.

11 "And whoever[a] will not receive you nor hear you, when you depart from there, shake off the dust under your feet as a testimony against them.[b] Assuredly, I say to you, it will be more tolerable for Sodom and Gomorrah in the day of judgment than for that city!"
12 So they went out and preached that *people* should repent.
13 And they cast out many demons, and anointed with oil many who were sick, and healed *them*.

John the Baptist Beheaded
14 Now King Herod heard *of Him*, for His name had become well known. And he said, "John the Baptist is risen from the dead, and therefore these powers are at work in him."
15 Others said, "It is Elijah." And others said, "It is the Prophet, or[a] like one of the prophets."
16 But when Herod heard, he said, "This is John, whom I beheaded; he has been raised from the dead!"
17 For Herod himself had sent and laid hold of John, and bound him in prison for the sake of Herodias, his brother Philip's wife; for he had married her.
18 Because John had said to Herod, "It is not lawful for you to have your brother's wife."
19 Therefore Herodias held it against him and wanted to kill him, but she could not;
20 for Herod feared John, knowing that he *was* a just and holy man, and he protected him. And when he heard him, he did many things, and heard him gladly.
21 Then an opportune day came when Herod on his birthday gave a feast for his nobles, the high officers, and the chief *men* of Galilee.
22 And when Herodias' daughter herself came in and danced, and pleased Herod and those who sat with him, the king said to the girl, "Ask me whatever you want, and I will give *it* to you."
23 He also swore to her, "Whatever you ask me, I will give you, up to half my kingdom."
24 So she went out and said to her mother, "What shall I ask?" And she said, "The head of John the Baptist!"
25 Immediately she came in with haste to the king and asked, saying, "I want you to give me at once the head of John the Baptist on a platter."
26 And the king was exceedingly sorry; *yet*, because of the oaths and because of those who sat with him, he did not want to refuse her.
27 Immediately the king sent an executioner and commanded his head to be brought. And he went and beheaded him in prison,

Life Examples:
JOHN THE BAPTIST
A Man of Discernment

MARK 6:14–29

What would you think of a man who lived alone in the desert, wore camel skins, and ate wild honey and locusts? And how would you feel if this man said you needed to let God change your life?

You can see why many people who heard about John the Baptist went to see him out of sheer curiosity.

But John was no lunatic, and neither was his message his own. For almost thirty years, God prepared John to announce the coming of Jesus Christ, the Messiah. John was a man of great spiritual discernment who knew the difference between those who came with humble, repentant hearts, and those who came to mock or criticize.

When you ask God for discernment, He gives it to you freely. For those who truly seek His face and His direction for their lives, the Lord brings a wisdom that can come only from Him.

See the Life Principles Index for further study:
11. God assumes full responsibility for our needs when we obey Him.
10. If necessary, God will move heaven and earth to show us His will.

28 brought his head on a platter, and gave it to the girl; and the girl gave it to her mother.
29 When his disciples heard *of it*, they came and took away his corpse and laid it in a tomb.

Feeding the Five Thousand
30 Then the apostles gathered to Jesus and told Him all things, both what they had done and what they had taught.
31 And He said to them, "Come aside by ➤

6:11 [a]NU-Text reads *whatever place.* [b]NU-Text omits the rest of this verse. **6:15** [a]NU-Text and M-Text omit *or.*

LIFE LESSONS

➤ **6:31** — ***And He said to them, "Come aside by yourselves to a deserted place and rest a while."***

Jesus and His disciples worked hard, but they did not drive themselves to exhaustion. Jesus made sure that His men took care of themselves, not only spiritually, but physically as well.

yourselves to a deserted place and rest a while." For there were many coming and going, and they did not even have time to eat.
32 So they departed to a deserted place in the boat by themselves.
33 But the multitudes[a] saw them departing, and many knew Him and ran there on foot from all the cities. They arrived before them and came together to Him.
34 And Jesus, when He came out, saw a great multitude and was moved with compassion for them, because they were like sheep not having a shepherd. So He began to teach them many things.
35 When the day was now far spent, His disciples came to Him and said, "This is a deserted place, and already the hour *is* late.
36 "Send them away, that they may go into the surrounding country and villages and buy themselves bread;[a] for they have nothing to eat."
37 But He answered and said to them, "You give them something to eat." And they said to Him, "Shall we go and buy two hundred denarii worth of bread and give them *something* to eat?"
38 But He said to them, "How many loaves do you have? Go and see." And when they found out they said, "Five, and two fish."
39 Then He commanded them to make them all sit down in groups on the green grass.
40 So they sat down in ranks, in hundreds and in fifties.
41 And when He had taken the five loaves and the two fish, He looked up to heaven, blessed and broke the loaves, and gave *them* to His disciples to set before them; and the two fish He divided among *them* all.
42 So they all ate and were filled.
43 And they took up twelve baskets full of fragments and of the fish.
44 Now those who had eaten the loaves were about[a] five thousand men.

Jesus Walks on the Sea

45 Immediately He made His disciples get into the boat and go before Him to the other side, to Bethsaida, while He sent the multitude away.
➤ 46 And when He had sent them away, He departed to the mountain to pray.
47 Now when evening came, the boat was in the middle of the sea; and He *was* alone on the land.
48 Then He saw them straining at rowing, for the wind was against them. Now about the fourth watch of the night He came to them, walking on the sea, and would have passed them by.
49 And when they saw Him walking on the sea, they supposed it was a ghost, and cried out;
50 for they all saw Him and were troubled. But immediately He talked with them and said to them, "Be of good cheer! It is I; do not be afraid."
51 Then He went up into the boat to them, and the wind ceased. And they were greatly amazed in themselves beyond measure, and marveled.
52 For they had not understood about the loaves, because their heart was hardened. ◄

Many Touch Him and Are Made Well

53 When they had crossed over, they came to the land of Gennesaret and anchored there.
54 And when they came out of the boat, immediately the people recognized Him,
55 ran through that whole surrounding region, and began to carry about on beds those who were sick to wherever they heard He was.
56 Wherever He entered, into villages, cities, or the country, they laid the sick in the marketplaces, and begged Him that they might just touch the hem of His garment. And as many as touched Him were made well.

Defilement Comes from Within

7 Then the Pharisees and some of the scribes came together to Him, having come from Jerusalem.
2 Now when[a] they saw some of His disciples eat bread with defiled, that is, with unwashed hands, they found fault.
3 For the Pharisees and all the Jews do not eat unless they wash *their* hands in a special way, holding the tradition of the elders.
4 *When they come* from the marketplace, they do not eat unless they wash. And there are many other things which they have received and hold, *like* the washing of cups, pitchers, copper vessels, and couches.

6:33 [a]NU-Text and M-Text read *they.* **6:36** [a]NU-Text reads *something to eat* and omits the rest of this verse. **6:44** [a]NU-Text and M-Text omit *about.* **7:2** [a]NU-Text omits *when* and *they found fault.*

LIFE LESSONS

➤ 6:46 — *And when He had sent them away, He departed to the mountain to pray.*

Throughout the Gospels we find Jesus getting alone with God to pray. During these times of intimate fellowship He found renewed strength, direction, and a deep love for His Father.

➤ 6:52 — *For they had not understood about the loaves, because their heart was hardened.*

Had Jesus' disciples understood the meaning behind His first miracles—that they revealed Him as the Messiah, the Son of God—His other miracles would not have surprised them. They saw, but they did not understand.

5 Then the Pharisees and scribes asked
Him, "Why do Your disciples not walk according to the tradition of the elders, but eat bread
with unwashed hands?"
6 He answered and said to them, "Well did
Isaiah prophesy of you hypocrites, as it is
written:

'This people honors Me with their lips,
But their heart is far from Me.
7 *And in vain they worship Me,*
Teaching as doctrines the
commandments of men.'[a]

8 "For laying aside the commandment of
God, you hold the tradition of men[a]—the
washing of pitchers and cups, and many other
such things you do."
9 He said to them, "*All too* well you reject
the commandment of God, that you may keep
your tradition.
10 "For Moses said, *'Honor your father and
your mother'*;[a] and, *'He who curses father or
mother, let him be put to death.'*[b]
11 "But you say, 'If a man says to his father or
mother, "Whatever profit you might have received from me *is* Corban"—' (that is, a gift *to
God*),
12 "then you no longer let him do anything
for his father or his mother,
13 "making the word of God of no effect
through your tradition which you have
handed down. And many such things you do."
14 When He had called all the multitude to
Himself, He said to them, "Hear Me, everyone,
and understand:
➤ 15 "There is nothing that enters a man from
outside which can defile him; but the things
which come out of him, those are the things
that defile a man.
16 "If anyone has ears to hear, let him hear!"[a]
17 When He had entered a house away from
the crowd, His disciples asked Him concerning the parable.
18 So He said to them, "Are you thus without
understanding also? Do you not perceive that
whatever enters a man from outside cannot
defile him,
19 "because it does not enter his heart but his
stomach, and is eliminated, *thus* purifying all
foods?"[a]
20 And He said, "What comes out of a man,
that defiles a man.
21 "For from within, out of the heart of men,
proceed evil thoughts, adulteries, fornications, murders,
22 "thefts, covetousness, wickedness, deceit,
lewdness, an evil eye, blasphemy, pride, foolishness.
23 "All these evil things come from within
and defile a man."

A Gentile Shows Her Faith

24 From there He arose and went to the region of Tyre and Sidon.[a] And He entered a
house and wanted no one to know *it*, but He
could not be hidden.
25 For a woman whose young daughter had
an unclean spirit heard about Him, and she
came and fell at His feet.
26 The woman was a Greek, a Syro-Phoenician by birth, and she kept asking Him to cast
the demon out of her daughter.
27 But Jesus said to her, "Let the children be
filled first, for it is not good to take the children's bread and throw *it* to the little dogs."
28 And she answered and said to Him, "Yes,
Lord, yet even the little dogs under the table
eat from the children's crumbs."
29 Then He said to her, "For this saying go
your way; the demon has gone out of your
daughter."
30 And when she had come to her house, she
found the demon gone out, and her daughter
lying on the bed.

Jesus Heals a Deaf-Mute

31 Again, departing from the region of Tyre
and Sidon, He came through the midst of the
region of Decapolis to the Sea of Galilee.
32 Then they brought to Him one who was
deaf and had an impediment in his speech,
and they begged Him to put His hand on him.
33 And He took him aside from the multitude, and put His fingers in his ears, and He
spat and touched his tongue.
34 Then, looking up to heaven, He sighed,
and said to him, "Ephphatha," that is, "Be
opened."
35 Immediately his ears were opened, and
the impediment of his tongue was loosed, and
he spoke plainly.
36 Then He commanded them that they
should tell no one; but the more He com-

7:7 [a]Isaiah 29:13 **7:8** [a]NU-Text omits the rest of this verse.
7:10 [a]Exodus 20:12; Deuteronomy 5:16 [b]Exodus 21:17
7:16 [a]NU-Text omits this verse. **7:19** [a]NU-Text ends quotation with *eliminated,* setting off the final clause as Mark's comment that Jesus has declared all foods clean. **7:24** [a]NU-Text omits *and Sidon.*

LIFE LESSONS

➤ ***7:15 — "There is nothing that enters a man from outside which can defile him; but the things which come out of him, those are the things that defile a man."***

What a person eats and drinks cannot "defile" him, but what comes out of him—ungodly words and actions—certainly can. Jesus wanted His disciples to see that the core issue always comes down to the heart.

manded them, the more widely they proclaimed *it.*
➤ 37 And they were astonished beyond measure, saying, "He has done all things well. He makes both the deaf to hear and the mute to speak."

Feeding the Four Thousand

8 In those days, the multitude being very great and having nothing to eat, Jesus called His disciples *to Him* and said to them,
2 "I have compassion on the multitude, because they have now continued with Me three days and have nothing to eat.
3 "And if I send them away hungry to their own houses, they will faint on the way; for some of them have come from afar."
4 Then His disciples answered Him, "How can one satisfy these people with bread here in the wilderness?"
5 He asked them, "How many loaves do you have?" And they said, "Seven."
6 So He commanded the multitude to sit down on the ground. And He took the seven loaves and gave thanks, broke *them* and gave *them* to His disciples to set before *them;* and they set *them* before the multitude.
7 They also had a few small fish; and having blessed them, He said to set them also before *them.*
8 So they ate and were filled, and they took up seven large baskets of leftover fragments.
9 Now those who had eaten were about four thousand. And He sent them away,
10 immediately got into the boat with His disciples, and came to the region of Dalmanutha.

The Pharisees Seek a Sign

11 Then the Pharisees came out and began to dispute with Him, seeking from Him a sign from heaven, testing Him.
➤ 12 But He sighed deeply in His spirit, and said, "Why does this generation seek a sign? Assuredly, I say to you, no sign shall be given to this generation."

Beware of the Leaven of the Pharisees and Herod

13 And He left them, and getting into the boat again, departed to the other side.
14 Now the disciples[a] had forgotten to take bread, and they did not have more than one loaf with them in the boat.
15 Then He charged them, saying, "Take heed, beware of the leaven of the Pharisees and the leaven of Herod."
16 And they reasoned among themselves, saying, "*It is* because we have no bread."
17 But Jesus, being aware of *it,* said to them, "Why do you reason because you have no bread? Do you not yet perceive nor understand? Is your heart still[a] hardened?
18 "Having eyes, do you not see? And having ears, do you not hear? And do you not remember?
19 "When I broke the five loaves for the five thousand, how many baskets full of fragments did you take up?" They said to Him, "Twelve."
20 "Also, when I broke the seven for the four thousand, how many large baskets full of fragments did you take up?" And they said, "Seven."
21 So He said to them, "How *is it* you do not understand?" ➤

A Blind Man Healed at Bethsaida

22 Then He came to Bethsaida; and they brought a blind man to Him, and begged Him to touch him.
23 So He took the blind man by the hand and led him out of the town. And when He had spit on his eyes and put His hands on him, He asked him if he saw anything.
24 And he looked up and said, "I see men like trees, walking."
25 Then He put *His* hands on his eyes again and made him look up. And he was restored and saw everyone clearly.
26 Then He sent him away to his house, saying, "Neither go into the town, nor tell anyone in the town."[a]

Peter Confesses Jesus as the Christ

27 Now Jesus and His disciples went out to the towns of Caesarea Philippi; and on the road He asked His disciples, saying to them, "Who do men say that I am?"

8:14 [a]NU-Text and M-Text read *they.* **8:17** [a]NU-Text omits *still.* **8:26** [a]NU-Text reads *"Do not even go into the town."*

LIFE LESSONS

➤ **7:37 — *And they were astonished beyond measure, saying, "He has done all things well."***

Jesus does all things well, but He also usually does them in unexpected ways. He astonishes us, not only by the mighty works He performs, but also because He so often catches us off guard.

➤ **8:12 — *But He sighed deeply in His spirit . . . .***

Jesus sighed a lot during His earthly ministry. He never felt disillusioned by His disciples, since He had no illusions to begin with, but He often expressed His very human disappointment with their lack of spiritual progress.

➤ **8:21 — *So He said to them, "How is it you do not understand?"***

Sometimes we mistakenly think that grace excuses us from the hard work of growing in grace. It doesn't. The Bible says that "by reason of use" we have our "senses exercised to discern both good and evil" (Heb. 5:14).

28 So they answered, "John the Baptist; but some *say,* Elijah; and others, one of the prophets."
29 He said to them, "But who do you say that I am?" Peter answered and said to Him, "You are the Christ."
30 Then He strictly warned them that they should tell no one about Him.

Jesus Predicts His Death and Resurrection

31 And He began to teach them that the Son of Man must suffer many things, and be rejected by the elders and chief priests and scribes, and be killed, and after three days rise again.
32 He spoke this word openly. Then Peter took Him aside and began to rebuke Him.
33 But when He had turned around and looked at His disciples, He rebuked Peter, saying, "Get behind Me, Satan! For you are not mindful of the things of God, but the things of men."

Take Up the Cross and Follow Him

34 When He had called the people to *Himself,* with His disciples also, He said to them, "Whoever desires to come after Me, let him deny himself, and take up his cross, and follow Me.
35 "For whoever desires to save his life will lose it, but whoever loses his life for My sake and the gospel's will save it.
36 "For what will it profit a man if he gains the whole world, and loses his own soul?
37 "Or what will a man give in exchange for his soul?
38 "For whoever is ashamed of Me and My words in this adulterous and sinful generation, of him the Son of Man also will be ashamed when He comes in the glory of His Father with the holy angels."

Jesus Transfigured on the Mount

9 And He said to them, "Assuredly, I say to you that there are some standing here who will not taste death till they see the kingdom of God present with power."
2 Now after six days Jesus took Peter, James, and John, and led them up on a high mountain apart by themselves; and He was transfigured before them.
3 His clothes became shining, exceedingly white, like snow, such as no launderer on earth can whiten them.
4 And Elijah appeared to them with Moses, and they were talking with Jesus.
5 Then Peter answered and said to Jesus, "Rabbi, it is good for us to be here; and let us make three tabernacles: one for You, one for Moses, and one for Elijah"—
6 because he did not know what to say, for they were greatly afraid.
7 And a cloud came and overshadowed them; and a voice came out of the cloud, saying, "This is My beloved Son. Hear Him!"
8 Suddenly, when they had looked around, they saw no one anymore, but only Jesus with themselves.
9 Now as they came down from the mountain, He commanded them that they should tell no one the things they had seen, till the Son of Man had risen from the dead.
10 So they kept this word to themselves, questioning what the rising from the dead meant.
11 And they asked Him, saying, "Why do the scribes say that Elijah must come first?"
12 Then He answered and told them, "Indeed, Elijah is coming first and restores all things. And how is it written concerning the Son of Man, that He must suffer many things and be treated with contempt?
13 "But I say to you that Elijah has also come, and they did to him whatever they wished, as it is written of him."

A Boy Is Healed

14 And when He came to the disciples, He saw a great multitude around them, and scribes disputing with them.
15 Immediately, when they saw Him, all the people were greatly amazed, and running to *Him,* greeted Him.
16 And He asked the scribes, "What are you discussing with them?"
17 Then one of the crowd answered and said, "Teacher, I brought You my son, who has a mute spirit.
18 "And wherever it seizes him, it throws him down; he foams at the mouth, gnashes his teeth, and becomes rigid. So I spoke to Your

LIFE LESSONS

➤ 8:36 — *"For what will it profit a man if he gains the whole world, and loses his own soul?"*

The question is meant as rhetorical—nothing can make up for the loss of one's soul—and yet how many of us regularly exchange our lives for much less than "the whole world"?

➤ 9:4 — *And Elijah appeared to them with Moses, and they were talking with Jesus.*

How did Peter and the others instantly recognize Moses and Elijah, men they'd never met and who had died centuries before? In the Transfiguration we get a brief foretaste of heaven and its wonders.

➤ 9:10 — *So they kept this word to themselves, questioning what the rising from the dead meant.*

Jesus sometimes did speak figuratively (as in John 2:19–21), so perhaps we can sympathize with this failure to grasp the Lord's meaning (Mark 9:32). The words of God are not always easy to understand.

disciples, that they should cast it out, but they
could not."
19 He answered him and said, "O faithless
generation, how long shall I be with you?
How long shall I bear with you? Bring him to
Me."
20 Then they brought him to Him. And when
he saw Him, immediately the spirit convulsed
him, and he fell on the ground and wallowed,
foaming at the mouth.
21 So He asked his father, "How long has this
been happening to him?" And he said, "From
childhood.
22 "And often he has thrown him both into
the fire and into the water to destroy him. But
if You can do anything, have compassion on
us and help us."
✳ 23 Jesus said to him, "If you can believe,[a] all
things *are* possible to him who believes."
➤ 24 Immediately the father of the child cried
out and said with tears, "Lord, I believe; help
my unbelief!"
25 When Jesus saw that the people came running together, He rebuked the unclean spirit,
saying to it, "Deaf and dumb spirit, I command you, come out of him and enter him no
more!"
26 Then *the spirit* cried out, convulsed him
greatly, and came out of him. And he became
as one dead, so that many said, "He is dead."
27 But Jesus took him by the hand and lifted
him up, and he arose.
28 And when He had come into the house,
His disciples asked Him privately, "Why
could we not cast it out?"
29 So He said to them, "This kind can come
out by nothing but prayer and fasting."[a]

Jesus Again Predicts His Death and Resurrection

30 Then they departed from there and passed
through Galilee, and He did not want anyone
to know *it*.
31 For He taught His disciples and said to
them, "The Son of Man is being betrayed into
the hands of men, and they will kill Him. And
after He is killed, He will rise the third day."
32 But they did not understand this saying,
and were afraid to ask Him.

Who Is the Greatest?

33 Then He came to Capernaum. And when
He was in the house He asked them, "What
was it you disputed among yourselves on the
road?"
34 But they kept silent, for on the road they
had disputed among themselves who *would
be the* greatest.
35 And He sat down, called the twelve, and
said to them, "If anyone desires to be first, he
shall be last of all and servant of all."
36 Then He took a little child and set him in
the midst of them. And when He had taken
him in His arms, He said to them,
37 "Whoever receives one of these little children in My name receives Me; and whoever
receives Me, receives not Me but Him who
sent Me."

Jesus Forbids Sectarianism

38 Now John answered Him, saying,
"Teacher, we saw someone who does not follow us casting out demons in Your name, and
we forbade him because he does not follow
us."
39 But Jesus said, "Do not forbid him, for no
one who works a miracle in My name can
soon afterward speak evil of Me.
40 "For he who is not against us is on our[a]
side.
41 "For whoever gives you a cup of water to
drink in My name, because you belong to
Christ, assuredly, I say to you, he will by no
means lose his reward.

Jesus Warns of Offenses

42 "But whoever causes one of these little
ones who believe in Me to stumble, it would
be better for him if a millstone were hung
around his neck, and he were thrown into the
sea.
43 "If your hand causes you to sin, cut it off.
It is better for you to enter into life maimed,
rather than having two hands, to go to hell,
into the fire that shall never be quenched—
44 "where

> *'Their worm does not die*
> *And the fire is not quenched.'*[a]

45 "And if your foot causes you to sin, cut it
off. It is better for you to enter life lame, rather
than having two feet, to be cast into hell, into
the fire that shall never be quenched—
46 "where

> *'Their worm does not die*
> *And the fire is not quenched.'*[a]

9:23 [a]NU-Text reads *" 'If You can!' All things. . . ."* **9:29** [a]NU-Text omits *and fasting.* **9:40** [a]M-Text reads *against you is on your side.* **9:44** [a]NU-Text omits this verse. **9:46** [a]NU-Text omits the last clause of verse 45 and all of verse 46.

LIFE LESSONS

➤ ***9:24 — Immediately the father of the child cried out and said with tears, "Lord, I believe; help my unbelief!"***

The Lord does not demand that we have mountains of faith before He acts on our behalf; a little mustard seed of genuine faith is all He requires. And then He steps in and supplies what we lack.

47 "And if your eye causes you to sin, pluck it out. It is better for you to enter the kingdom of God with one eye, rather than having two eyes, to be cast into hell fire—
48 "where

'Their worm does not die
And the fire is not quenched.'[a]

Tasteless Salt Is Worthless

49 "For everyone will be seasoned with fire,[a] and every sacrifice will be seasoned with salt.
50 "Salt *is* good, but if the salt loses its flavor, how will you season it? Have salt in yourselves, and have peace with one another."

Marriage and Divorce

10 Then He arose from there and came to the region of Judea by the other side of the Jordan. And multitudes gathered to Him again, and as He was accustomed, He taught them again.
2 The Pharisees came and asked Him, "Is it lawful for a man to divorce *his* wife?" testing Him.
3 And He answered and said to them, "What did Moses command you?"
4 They said, "Moses permitted *a man* to write a certificate of divorce, and to dismiss *her.*"
➤5 And Jesus answered and said to them, "Because of the hardness of your heart he wrote you this precept.
6 "But from the beginning of the creation, God *'made them male and female.'*[a]
7 *'For this reason a man shall leave his father and mother and be joined to his wife,*
8 *'and the two shall become one flesh'*;[a] so then they are no longer two, but one flesh.
9 "Therefore what God has joined together, let not man separate."
10 In the house His disciples also asked Him again about the same *matter.*
11 So He said to them, "Whoever divorces his wife and marries another commits adultery against her.
12 "And if a woman divorces her husband and marries another, she commits adultery."

Jesus Blesses Little Children

13 Then they brought little children to Him, that He might touch them; but the disciples rebuked those who brought *them.*
14 But when Jesus saw *it,* He was greatly displeased and said to them, "Let the little children come to Me, and do not forbid them; for of such is the kingdom of God.
15 "Assuredly, I say to you, whoever does not receive the kingdom of God as a little child will by no means enter it." ✳
16 And He took them up in His arms, laid *His* hands on them, and blessed them.

Jesus Counsels the Rich Young Ruler

17 Now as He was going out on the road, one came running, knelt before Him, and asked Him, "Good Teacher, what shall I do that I may inherit eternal life?"
18 So Jesus said to him, "Why do you call Me good? No one *is* good but One, *that is,* God. ➤
19 "You know the commandments: *'Do not commit adultery,' 'Do not murder,' 'Do not steal,' 'Do not bear false witness,'* 'Do not defraud,' *'Honor your father and your mother.'*"[a]
20 And he answered and said to Him, "Teacher, all these things I have kept from my youth."
21 Then Jesus, looking at him, loved him, and said to him, "One thing you lack: Go your way, sell whatever you have and give to the poor, and you will have treasure in heaven; and come, take up the cross, and follow Me."
22 But he was sad at this word, and went away sorrowful, for he had great possessions.

With God All Things Are Possible

23 Then Jesus looked around and said to His disciples, "How hard it is for those who have riches to enter the kingdom of God!"
24 And the disciples were astonished at His words. But Jesus answered again and said to them, "Children, how hard it is for those who trust in riches[a] to enter the kingdom of God!
25 "It is easier for a camel to go through the eye of a needle than for a rich man to enter the kingdom of God."
26 And they were greatly astonished, saying among themselves, "Who then can be saved?"

9:48 [a]Isaiah 66:24 **9:49** [a]NU-Text omits the rest of this verse. **10:6** [a]Genesis 1:27; 5:2 **10:8** [a]Genesis 2:24 **10:19** [a]Exodus 20:12–16; Deuteronomy 5:16–20 **10:24** [a]NU-Text omits *for those who trust in riches.*

LIFE LESSONS

➤ 10:5 — *And Jesus answered and said to them, "Because of the hardness of your heart he wrote you this precept."*

God often acts in pragmatic ways toward us. He gives us a high standard to shoot for, but since "He remembers that we are dust" (Ps. 103:14), He also condescends to our weaknesses. And yet He calls us to grow.

➤ 10:18 — *So Jesus said to him, "Why do you call Me good? No one is good but One, that is, God."*

Jesus did not contradict the man's description of Him as "good." Jesus merely asked him why he used the term. As God in the flesh, Jesus was truly good—but He wanted the man to see it for himself.

✳ 27 But Jesus looked at them and said, "With
men *it is* impossible, but not with God; for
with God all things are possible."
28 Then Peter began to say to Him, "See, we
have left all and followed You."
29 So Jesus answered and said, "Assuredly, I
say to you, there is no one who has left house
or brothers or sisters or father or mother or
wife[a] or children or lands, for My sake and
the gospel's,
30 "who shall not receive a hundredfold now
in this time—houses and brothers and sisters
and mothers and children and lands, with
persecutions—and in the age to come, eternal
life.
31 "But many *who are* first will be last, and
the last first."

Jesus a Third Time Predicts His Death and Resurrection

➤ **32** Now they were on the road, going up to
Jerusalem, and Jesus was going before them;
and they were amazed. And as they followed
they were afraid. Then He took the twelve
aside again and began to tell them the things
that would happen to Him:
33 "Behold, we are going up to Jerusalem,
and the Son of Man will be betrayed to the
chief priests and to the scribes; and they will
condemn Him to death and deliver Him to the
Gentiles;
34 "and they will mock Him, and scourge
Him, and spit on Him, and kill Him. And the
third day He will rise again."

Greatness Is Serving

35 Then James and John, the sons of
Zebedee, came to Him, saying, "Teacher, we
want You to do for us whatever we ask."
36 And He said to them, "What do you want
Me to do for you?"
37 They said to Him, "Grant us that we may
sit, one on Your right hand and the other on
Your left, in Your glory."
38 But Jesus said to them, "You do not know
what you ask. Are you able to drink the cup
that I drink, and be baptized with the baptism
that I am baptized with?"
39 They said to Him, "We are able." So Jesus
said to them, "You will indeed drink the cup
that I drink, and with the baptism I am baptized with you will be baptized;
40 "but to sit on My right hand and on My left
is not Mine to give, but *it is for those* for
whom it is prepared."
41 And when the ten heard *it*, they began to
be greatly displeased with James and John.
42 But Jesus called them to *Himself* and said
to them, "You know that those who are considered rulers over the Gentiles lord it over
them, and their great ones exercise authority
over them.
43 "Yet it shall not be so among you; but whoever desires to become great among you shall
be your servant.
44 "And whoever of you desires to be first
shall be slave of all.
45 "For even the Son of Man did not come to
be served, but to serve, and to give His life a
ransom for many."

Jesus Heals Blind Bartimaeus

46 Now they came to Jericho. As He went out
of Jericho with His disciples and a great multitude, blind Bartimaeus, the son of Timaeus,
sat by the road begging.
47 And when he heard that it was Jesus of
Nazareth, he began to cry out and say, "Jesus,
Son of David, have mercy on me!"
48 Then many warned him to be quiet; but he
cried out all the more, "Son of David, have
mercy on me!"
49 So Jesus stood still and commanded him
to be called. Then they called the blind man,
saying to him, "Be of good cheer. Rise, He is
calling you."
50 And throwing aside his garment, he rose
and came to Jesus.
51 So Jesus answered and said to him, "What
do you want Me to do for you?" The blind
man said to Him, "Rabboni, that I may receive
my sight."
52 Then Jesus said to him, "Go your way;
your faith has made you well." And immediately he received his sight and followed Jesus
on the road.

The Triumphal Entry

11 Now when they drew near Jerusalem,
to Bethphage[a] and Bethany, at the
Mount of Olives, He sent two of His disciples;
2 and He said to them, "Go into the village
opposite you; and as soon as you have entered it you will find a colt tied, on which no
one has sat. Loose it and bring *it*.
3 "And if anyone says to you, 'Why are you
doing this?' say, 'The Lord has need of it,' and
immediately he will send it here."

10:29 [a]NU-Text omits *or wife*. **11:1** [a]M-Text reads *Bethsphage*.

LIFE LESSONS

➤ **10:32 — . . . *Jesus was going before them; and they were amazed. And as they followed they were afraid.***

Amazement and fear, astonishment and terror—certain emotions go together when we observe what happens in the presence of the Lord. His love staggers us and His power makes us tremble.

4 So they went their way, and found the[a] colt
tied by the door outside on the street, and
they loosed it.
5 But some of those who stood there said to
them, "What are you doing, loosing the colt?"
6 And they spoke to them just as Jesus had
commanded. So they let them go.
7 Then they brought the colt to Jesus and
threw their clothes on it, and He sat on it.
8 And many spread their clothes on the
road, and others cut down leafy branches
from the trees and spread *them* on the road.
9 Then those who went before and those
who followed cried out, saying:

"Hosanna!
'*Blessed is He who comes in the name of*
the L*ORD*!'[a]
➤ 10 Blessed *is* the kingdom of our father
David
That comes in the name of the Lord![a]
Hosanna in the highest!"

11 And Jesus went into Jerusalem and into
the temple. So when He had looked around at
all things, as the hour was already late, He
went out to Bethany with the twelve.

The Fig Tree Withered

12 Now the next day, when they had come
out from Bethany, He was hungry.
13 And seeing from afar a fig tree having
leaves, He went to see if perhaps He would
find something on it. When He came to it, He
found nothing but leaves, for it was not the
season for figs.
➤ 14 In response Jesus said to it, "Let no one
eat fruit from you ever again." And His disciples heard *it*.

Jesus Cleanses the Temple

15 So they came to Jerusalem. Then Jesus
went into the temple and began to drive out
those who bought and sold in the temple, and
overturned the tables of the money changers
and the seats of those who sold doves.
16 And He would not allow anyone to carry
wares through the temple.
17 Then He taught, saying to them, "Is it not
written, '*My house shall be called a house of*
prayer for all nations'?[a] But you have made it
a '*den of thieves*.'"[b]
18 And the scribes and chief priests heard it
and sought how they might destroy Him; for
they feared Him, because all the people were
astonished at His teaching.
19 When evening had come, He went out of
the city.

The Lesson of the Withered Fig Tree

20 Now in the morning, as they passed by,
they saw the fig tree dried up from the roots.
21 And Peter, remembering, said to Him,
"Rabbi, look! The fig tree which You cursed
has withered away."
22 So Jesus answered and said to them,
"Have faith in God.
23 "For assuredly, I say to you, whoever says
to this mountain, 'Be removed and be cast
into the sea,' and does not doubt in his heart,
but believes that those things he says will be
done, he will have whatever he says.
24 "Therefore I say to you, whatever things ✳
you ask when you pray, believe that you receive *them*, and you will have *them*.

Forgiveness and Prayer

25 "And whenever you stand praying, if you
have anything against anyone, forgive him,
that your Father in heaven may also forgive
you your trespasses.
26 "But if you do not forgive, neither will your
Father in heaven forgive your trespasses."[a]

Jesus' Authority Questioned

27 Then they came again to Jerusalem. And
as He was walking in the temple, the chief
priests, the scribes, and the elders came to
Him.
28 And they said to Him, "By what authority
are You doing these things? And who gave You
this authority to do these things?"
29 But Jesus answered and said to them, "I
also will ask you one question; then answer
Me, and I will tell you by what authority I do
these things:
30 "The baptism of John—was it from heaven
or from men? Answer Me."
31 And they reasoned among themselves,
saying, "If we say, 'From heaven,' He will say,
'Why then did you not believe him?'

11:4 [a]NU-Text and M-Text read *a*. **11:9** [a]Psalm 118:26 **11:10** [a]NU-Text omits *in the name of the Lord*. **11:17** [a]Isaiah 56:7 [b]Jeremiah 7:11 **11:26** [a]NU-Text omits this verse.

LIFE LESSONS

➤ 11:10 — *"Blessed is the kingdom of our father David that comes in the name of the Lord! Hosanna in the highest!"*

"Hosanna" means "save now!" Many in the crowd recognized Jesus as the Son of David who would come to reign, but they misunderstood the timing and the nature of His reign.

➤ 11:14 — *In response Jesus said to it, "Let no one eat fruit from you ever again."*

This is the only "destructive" miracle reported in the Gospels. Jesus meant it to picture God's displeasure with a people who appeared religious, but whose lives remained barren of the fruits of godliness.

32 "But if we say, 'From men'"—they feared
the people, for all counted John to have been
a prophet indeed.
33 So they answered and said to Jesus, "We
do not know." And Jesus answered and said
to them, "Neither will I tell you by what authority I do these things."

The Parable of the Wicked Vinedressers

12 Then He began to speak to them in
parables: "A man planted a vineyard
and set a hedge around *it*, dug *a place for* the
wine vat and built a tower. And he leased it to
vinedressers and went into a far country.
2 "Now at vintage-time he sent a servant to
the vinedressers, that he might receive some
of the fruit of the vineyard from the vinedressers.
3 "And they took *him* and beat him and sent
him away empty-handed.
4 "Again he sent them another servant, and
at him they threw stones,[a] wounded *him* in the
head, and sent *him* away shamefully treated.
5 "And again he sent another, and him they
killed; and many others, beating some and
killing some.
6 "Therefore still having one son, his
beloved, he also sent him to them last, saying,
'They will respect my son.'
7 "But those vinedressers said among themselves, 'This is the heir. Come, let us kill him,
and the inheritance will be ours.'
8 "So they took him and killed *him* and cast
him out of the vineyard.
9 "Therefore what will the owner of the
vineyard do? He will come and destroy the
vinedressers, and give the vineyard to others.
10 "Have you not even read this Scripture:

'*The stone which the builders rejected*
Has become the chief cornerstone.
11 *This was the* LORD*'s doing,*
And it is marvelous in our eyes'?"[a]

12 And they sought to lay hands on Him, but
feared the multitude, for they knew He had
spoken the parable against them. So they left
Him and went away.

The Pharisees: Is It Lawful to Pay Taxes to Caesar?

13 Then they sent to Him some of the Pharisees and the Herodians, to catch Him in *His*
words.
14 When they had come, they said to Him,
"Teacher, we know that You are true, and care
about no one; for You do not regard the person of men, but teach the way of God in truth.
Is it lawful to pay taxes to Caesar, or not?
15 "Shall we pay, or shall we not pay?" But
He, knowing their hypocrisy, said to them,
"Why do you test Me? Bring Me a denarius
that I may see *it*."
16 So they brought *it*. And He said to them,
"Whose image and inscription *is* this?" They
said to Him, "Caesar's."
17 And Jesus answered and said to them,
"Render to Caesar the things that are Caesar's, and to God the things that are God's."
And they marveled at Him.

The Sadducees: What About the Resurrection?

18 Then *some* Sadducees, who say there is no
resurrection, came to Him; and they asked
Him, saying:
19 "Teacher, Moses wrote to us that if a man's
brother dies, and leaves *his* wife behind, and
leaves no children, his brother should take his
wife and raise up offspring for his brother.
20 "Now there were seven brothers. The first
took a wife; and dying, he left no offspring.
21 "And the second took her, and he died; nor
did he leave any offspring. And the third likewise.
22 "So the seven had her and left no offspring. Last of all the woman died also.
23 "Therefore, in the resurrection, when they
rise, whose wife will she be? For all seven had
her as wife."
24 Jesus answered and said to them, "Are you
not therefore mistaken, because you do not
know the Scriptures nor the power of God?
25 "For when they rise from the dead, they
neither marry nor are given in marriage, but
are like angels in heaven.
26 "But concerning the dead, that they rise,
have you not read in the book of Moses, in the
burning bush *passage*, how God spoke to
him, saying, '*I am the God of Abraham, the
God of Isaac, and the God of Jacob*'?[a]
27 "He is not the God of the dead, but the God
of the living. You are therefore greatly mistaken."

12:4 [a]NU-Text omits *and at him they threw stones.*
12:11 [a]Psalm 118:22, 23 **12:26** [a]Exodus 3:6, 15

LIFE LESSONS

➤ **12:17 — *And Jesus answered and said to them, "Render to Caesar the things that are Caesar's, and to God the things that are God's."***

We have duties and responsibilities to civil authorities that our faith does not negate. Jesus never advocated rebellion against the occupying Romans, despite their brutality and godlessness.

➤ **12:27 — *"He is not the God of the dead, but the God of the living. You are therefore greatly mistaken."***

Luke 20:38 adds, "For He is not the God of the dead but of the living, *for all live to Him*." Abraham is dead to us, but not to God. The long-deceased patriarchs live in His glorious presence, as we will someday.

The Scribes: Which Is the First Commandment of All?

28 Then one of the scribes came, and having heard them reasoning together, perceiving[a] that He had answered them well, asked Him, "Which is the first commandment of all?"

29 Jesus answered him, "The first of all the commandments *is: 'Hear, O Israel, the* L*ORD our God, the* L*ORD is one.*

30 *'And you shall love the* L*ORD your God with all your heart, with all your soul, with all your mind, and with all your strength.'*[a] This *is* the first commandment.[b]

31 "And the second, like *it, is* this: *'You shall love your neighbor as yourself.'*[a] There is no other commandment greater than these."

32 So the scribe said to Him, "Well *said,* Teacher. You have spoken the truth, for there is one God, and there is no other but He.

33 "And to love Him with all the heart, with all the understanding, with all the soul,[a] and with all the strength, and to love one's neighbor as oneself, is more than all the whole burnt offerings and sacrifices."

➤ 34 Now when Jesus saw that he answered wisely, He said to him, "You are not far from the kingdom of God." But after that no one dared question Him.

Jesus: How Can David Call His Descendant Lord?

35 Then Jesus answered and said, while He taught in the temple, "How *is it* that the scribes say that the Christ is the Son of David?

36 "For David himself said by the Holy Spirit:

'The L*ORD said to my Lord,*
"Sit at My right hand,
Till I make Your enemies Your
footstool."'[a]

37 "Therefore David himself calls Him *'Lord'*; how is He *then* his Son?" And the common people heard Him gladly.

Beware of the Scribes

38 Then He said to them in His teaching, "Beware of the scribes, who desire to go around in long robes, *love* greetings in the marketplaces,

39 "the best seats in the synagogues, and the best places at feasts,

40 "who devour widows' houses, and for a pretense make long prayers. These will receive greater condemnation."

The Widow's Two Mites

41 Now Jesus sat opposite the treasury and saw how the people put money into the treasury. And many *who were* rich put in much.

42 Then one poor widow came and threw in two mites,[a] which make a quadrans.

43 So He called His disciples to *Himself* and said to them, "Assuredly, I say to you that this poor widow has put in more than all those who have given to the treasury;

44 "for they all put in out of their abundance, but she out of her poverty put in all that she had, her whole livelihood."

Jesus Predicts the Destruction of the Temple

13 Then as He went out of the temple, one of His disciples said to Him, "Teacher, see what manner of stones and what buildings *are here!*"

2 And Jesus answered and said to him, "Do you see these great buildings? Not *one* stone shall be left upon another, that shall not be thrown down."

The Signs of the Times and the End of the Age

3 Now as He sat on the Mount of Olives opposite the temple, Peter, James, John, and Andrew asked Him privately,

4 "Tell us, when will these things be? And what *will be* the sign when all these things will be fulfilled?"

5 And Jesus, answering them, began to say: "Take heed that no one deceives you.

6 "For many will come in My name, saying, 'I am *He,*' and will deceive many.

7 "But when you hear of wars and rumors of wars, do not be troubled; for *such things* must happen, but the end *is* not yet.

8 "For nation will rise against nation, and kingdom against kingdom. And there will be earthquakes in various places, and there will be famines and troubles.[a] These *are* the beginnings of sorrows.

9 "But watch out for yourselves, for they will deliver you up to councils, and you will be beaten in the synagogues. You will be brought[a] before rulers and kings for My sake, for a testimony to them.

12:28 [a]NU-Text reads *seeing.* **12:30** [a]Deuteronomy 6:4, 5 [b]NU-Text omits this sentence. **12:31** [a]Leviticus 19:18 **12:33** [a]NU-Text omits *with all the soul.* **12:36** [a]Psalm 110:1 **12:42** [a]Greek *lepta,* very small copper coins worth a fraction of a penny **13:8** [a]NU-Text omits *and troubles.* **13:9** [a]NU-Text and M-Text read *will stand.*

LIFE LESSONS

➤ **12:34 — *But after that no one dared question Him.***

Jesus' opponents never succeeded in getting Him to make a foolish statement. But when Jesus asked a question of His own—not a "trick" question, but a serious one—they fell silent. He really is Lord of all!

10 "And the gospel must first be preached to all the nations.

11 "But when they arrest *you* and deliver you up, do not worry beforehand, or premeditate[a] what you will speak. But whatever is given you in that hour, speak that; for it is not you who speak, but the Holy Spirit.

12 "Now brother will betray brother to death, and a father *his* child; and children will rise up against parents and cause them to be put to death.

➤ 13 "And you will be hated by all for My name's sake. But he who endures to the end shall be saved.

The Great Tribulation

14 "So when you see the '*abomination of desolation*,'[a] spoken of by Daniel the prophet,[b] standing where it ought not" (let the reader understand), "then let those who are in Judea flee to the mountains.

15 "Let him who is on the housetop not go down into the house, nor enter to take anything out of his house.

16 "And let him who is in the field not go back to get his clothes.

17 "But woe to those who are pregnant and to those who are nursing babies in those days!

18 "And pray that your flight may not be in winter.

19 "For *in* those days there will be tribulation, such as has not been since the beginning of the creation which God created until this time, nor ever shall be.

✳ 20 "And unless the Lord had shortened those days, no flesh would be saved; but for the elect's sake, whom He chose, He shortened the days.

21 "Then if anyone says to you, 'Look, here *is* the Christ!' or, 'Look, *He is* there!' do not believe it.

22 "For false christs and false prophets will rise and show signs and wonders to deceive, if possible, even the elect.

➤ 23 "But take heed; see, I have told you all things beforehand.

The Coming of the Son of Man

24 "But in those days, after that tribulation, the sun will be darkened, and the moon will not give its light;

25 "the stars of heaven will fall, and the powers in the heavens will be shaken.

26 "Then they will see the Son of Man coming in the clouds with great power and glory.

27 "And then He will send His angels, and gather together His elect from the four winds, from the farthest part of earth to the farthest part of heaven.

The Parable of the Fig Tree

28 "Now learn this parable from the fig tree: When its branch has already become tender, and puts forth leaves, you know that summer is near.

29 "So you also, when you see these things happening, know that it[a] is near—at the doors!

30 "Assuredly, I say to you, this generation will by no means pass away till all these things take place.

31 "Heaven and earth will pass away, but My words will by no means pass away.

No One Knows the Day or Hour

32 "But of that day and hour no one knows, not even the angels in heaven, nor the Son, but only the Father.

33 "Take heed, watch and pray; for you do not know when the time is.

34 "*It is* like a man going to a far country, who left his house and gave authority to his servants, and to each his work, and commanded the doorkeeper to watch. ➤

35 "Watch therefore, for you do not know when the master of the house is coming—in the evening, at midnight, at the crowing of the rooster, or in the morning—

36 "lest, coming suddenly, he find you sleeping.

37 "And what I say to you, I say to all: Watch!"

The Plot to Kill Jesus

14 After two days it was the Passover and *the Feast* of Unleavened Bread. And the chief priests and the scribes sought how

13:11 [a]NU-Text omits *or premeditate.* **13:14** [a]Daniel 11:31; 12:11 [b]NU-Text omits *spoken of by Daniel the prophet.*
13:29 [a]Or *He*

LIFE LESSONS

➤ 13:13 — *"And you will be hated by all for My name's sake."*

Millions of people have died throughout history for their faith in Jesus, and even in modern times the martyrs continue. We must be willing to suffer abuse for our connection to Christ.

➤ 13:23 — *"But take heed; see, I have told you all things beforehand."*

Why does Jesus tell us of frightful things like persecution and suffering? So that it will not surprise us when it comes. It would come regardless, and His prophecies of it simply demonstrate His great grace.

➤ 13:34 — *"It is like a man going to a far country, who left his house and gave authority to his servants, and to each his work, and commanded the doorkeeper to watch."*

God gives each of us our own work; He expects us to faithfully discharge whatever duties He may have given us in Jesus' absence. And always, we are to remain vigilant and watch for His return.

they might take Him by trickery and put *Him*
to death.
2 But they said, "Not during the feast, lest
there be an uproar of the people."

The Anointing at Bethany

3 And being in Bethany at the house of Simon the leper, as He sat at the table, a woman came having an alabaster flask of very costly oil of spikenard. Then she broke the flask and poured *it* on His head.
4 But there were some who were indignant
among themselves, and said, "Why was this
fragrant oil wasted?
5 "For it might have been sold for more than
three hundred denarii and given to the poor."
And they criticized her sharply.
6 But Jesus said, "Let her alone. Why do you
trouble her? She has done a good work for
Me.
7 "For you have the poor with you always,
and whenever you wish you may do them
good; but Me you do not have always.
8 "She has done what she could. She has
come beforehand to anoint My body for burial.
9 "Assuredly, I say to you, wherever this
gospel is preached in the whole world, what
this woman has done will also be told as a
memorial to her."

Judas Agrees to Betray Jesus

➤ **10** Then Judas Iscariot, one of the twelve,
went to the chief priests to betray Him to
them.
11 And when they heard *it*, they were glad,
and promised to give him money. So he
sought how he might conveniently betray
Him.

Jesus Celebrates the Passover with His Disciples

12 Now on the first day of Unleavened Bread,
when they killed the Passover *lamb*, His disciples said to Him, "Where do You want us to
go and prepare, that You may eat the
Passover?"
13 And He sent out two of His disciples and
said to them, "Go into the city, and a man will
meet you carrying a pitcher of water; follow
him.
14 "Wherever he goes in, say to the master of
the house, 'The Teacher says, "Where is the
guest room in which I may eat the Passover
with My disciples?"'
15 "Then he will show you a large upper
room, furnished *and* prepared; there make
ready for us."
16 So His disciples went out, and came into ➤
the city, and found it just as He had said to
them; and they prepared the Passover.
17 In the evening He came with the twelve.
18 Now as they sat and ate, Jesus said, "Assuredly, I say to you, one of you who eats with
Me will betray Me."
19 And they began to be sorrowful, and to
say to Him one by one, "*Is* it I?" And another
said, "*Is* it I?"[a]
20 He answered and said to them, "*It is* one
of the twelve, who dips with Me in the dish.
21 "The Son of Man indeed goes just as it is
written of Him, but woe to that man by whom
the Son of Man is betrayed! It would have
been good for that man if he had never been
born."

Jesus Institutes the Lord's Supper

22 And as they were eating, Jesus took bread,
blessed and broke *it*, and gave *it* to them and
said, "Take, eat;[a] this is My body."
23 Then He took the cup, and when He had
given thanks He gave *it* to them, and they all
drank from it.
24 And He said to them, "This is My blood of
the new[a] covenant, which is shed for many.
25 "Assuredly, I say to you, I will no longer
drink of the fruit of the vine until that day
when I drink it new in the kingdom of God."
26 And when they had sung a hymn, they
went out to the Mount of Olives.

Jesus Predicts Peter's Denial

27 Then Jesus said to them, "All of you will be
made to stumble because of Me this night,[a]
for it is written:

'I will strike the Shepherd,
And the sheep will be scattered.'[b]

28 "But after I have been raised, I will go before you to Galilee."
29 Peter said to Him, "Even if all are made to
stumble, yet I *will* not *be*."

14:19 [a]NU-Text omits this sentence. **14:22** [a]NU-Text omits *eat.* **14:24** [a]NU-Text omits *new.* **14:27** [a]NU-Text omits *because of Me this night.* [b]Zechariah 13:7

LIFE LESSONS

➤ ***14:10 — Then Judas Iscariot, one of the twelve, went to the chief priests to betray Him to them.***

Judas went to the religious authorities with his offer to betray Jesus immediately after Jesus rebuked him for criticizing a woman who had honored the Lord with an expensive gift (see John 12:6).

➤ ***14:16 — So His disciples went out, and came into the city, and found it just as He had said to them . . . .***

Just as the disciples found the Passover preparations just as Jesus had told them, so we will find life to be just as He tells us. We will always find our smoothest life path by carefully following Jesus' instructions.

30 Jesus said to him, "Assuredly, I say to you that today, *even* this night, before the rooster crows twice, you will deny Me three times."
31 But he spoke more vehemently, "If I have to die with You, I will not deny You!" And they all said likewise.

The Prayer in the Garden

32 Then they came to a place which was named Gethsemane; and He said to His disciples, "Sit here while I pray."
33 And He took Peter, James, and John with Him, and He began to be troubled and deeply distressed.
34 Then He said to them, "My soul is exceedingly sorrowful, *even* to death. Stay here and watch."
➤ 35 He went a little farther, and fell on the ground, and prayed that if it were possible, the hour might pass from Him.
36 And He said, "Abba, Father, all things *are* possible for You. Take this cup away from Me; nevertheless, not what I will, but what You *will.*"
37 Then He came and found them sleeping, and said to Peter, "Simon, are you sleeping? Could you not watch one hour?
38 "Watch and pray, lest you enter into temptation. The spirit indeed *is* willing, but the flesh *is* weak."
39 Again He went away and prayed, and spoke the same words.
40 And when He returned, He found them asleep again, for their eyes were heavy; and they did not know what to answer Him.
41 Then He came the third time and said to them, "Are you still sleeping and resting? It is enough! The hour has come; behold, the Son of Man is being betrayed into the hands of sinners.
42 "Rise, let us be going. See, My betrayer is at hand."

Betrayal and Arrest in Gethsemane

43 And immediately, while He was still speaking, Judas, one of the twelve, with a great multitude with swords and clubs, came from the chief priests and the scribes and the elders.
44 Now His betrayer had given them a signal, saying, "Whomever I kiss, He is the One; seize Him and lead *Him* away safely."
45 As soon as he had come, immediately he went up to Him and said to Him, "Rabbi, Rabbi!" and kissed Him.
46 Then they laid their hands on Him and took Him.
47 And one of those who stood by drew his sword and struck the servant of the high priest, and cut off his ear.
48 Then Jesus answered and said to them, "Have you come out, as against a robber, with swords and clubs to take Me?
49 "I was daily with you in the temple teaching, and you did not seize Me. But the Scriptures must be fulfilled."
50 Then they all forsook Him and fled.

A Young Man Flees Naked

51 Now a certain young man followed Him, having a linen cloth thrown around *his* naked *body.* And the young men laid hold of him,
52 and he left the linen cloth and fled from them naked.

Jesus Faces the Sanhedrin

53 And they led Jesus away to the high priest; and with him were assembled all the chief priests, the elders, and the scribes.
54 But Peter followed Him at a distance, right into the courtyard of the high priest. And he sat with the servants and warmed himself at the fire.
55 Now the chief priests and all the council sought testimony against Jesus to put Him to death, but found none.
56 For many bore false witness against Him, but their testimonies did not agree.
57 Then some rose up and bore false witness against Him, saying,
58 "We heard Him say, 'I will destroy this temple made with hands, and within three days I will build another made without hands.'"
59 But not even then did their testimony agree.
60 And the high priest stood up in the midst and asked Jesus, saying, "Do You answer nothing? What *is it* these men testify against You?"
61 But He kept silent and answered nothing. Again the high priest asked Him, saying to Him, "Are You the Christ, the Son of the Blessed?"
62 Jesus said, "I am. And you will see the Son of Man sitting at the right hand of the Power, and coming with the clouds of heaven."
63 Then the high priest tore his clothes and said, "What further need do we have of witnesses?
64 "You have heard the blasphemy! What do you think?" And they all condemned Him to be deserving of death.

LIFE LESSONS

➤ 14:35 — *He went a little farther, and fell on the ground, and prayed that if it were possible, the hour might pass from Him.*

In the Garden of Gethsemane, the will of Jesus regarding the will of His Father was tested—and yet Jesus did not sin. He willingly submitted Himself to His Father's will, even though He desired something else.

65 Then some began to spit on Him, and to
blindfold Him, and to beat Him, and to say to
Him, "Prophesy!" And the officers struck Him
with the palms of their hands.[a]

Peter Denies Jesus, and Weeps

66 Now as Peter was below in the courtyard,
one of the servant girls of the high priest
came.
67 And when she saw Peter warming himself,
she looked at him and said, "You also were
with Jesus of Nazareth."
68 But he denied it, saying, "I neither know
nor understand what you are saying." And
he went out on the porch, and a rooster
crowed.
69 And the servant girl saw him again, and
began to say to those who stood by, "This is
one of them."
70 But he denied it again. And a little later
those who stood by said to Peter again,
"Surely you are *one* of them; for you are a
Galilean, and your speech shows *it*."[a]
71 Then he began to curse and swear, "I do
not know this Man of whom you speak!"
72 A second time *the* rooster crowed. Then
Peter called to mind the word that Jesus had
said to him, "Before the rooster crows twice,
you will deny Me three times." And when he
thought about it, he wept.

Jesus Faces Pilate

15 Immediately, in the morning, the chief
priests held a consultation with the elders and scribes and the whole council; and
they bound Jesus, led *Him* away, and delivered *Him* to Pilate.
2 Then Pilate asked Him, "Are You the King
of the Jews?" He answered and said to him,
"*It is as* you say."
3 And the chief priests accused Him of
many things, but He answered nothing.
4 Then Pilate asked Him again, saying, "Do
You answer nothing? See how many things
they testify against You!"[a]
5 But Jesus still answered nothing, so that
Pilate marveled.

Taking the Place of Barabbas

6 Now at the feast he was accustomed to releasing one prisoner to them, whomever they
requested.
7 And there was one named Barabbas, *who
was* chained with his fellow rebels; they had
committed murder in the rebellion.
8 Then the multitude, crying aloud,[a] began
to ask *him to do* just as he had always done
for them.
9 But Pilate answered them, saying, "Do you
want me to release to you the King of the
Jews?"
10 For he knew that the chief priests had
handed Him over because of envy.
11 But the chief priests stirred up the crowd,
so that he should rather release Barabbas to
them.
12 Pilate answered and said to them again,
"What then do you want me to do *with Him*
whom you call the King of the Jews?"
13 So they cried out again, "Crucify Him!"
14 Then Pilate said to them, "Why, what evil
has He done?" But they cried out all the more,
"Crucify Him!"
15 So Pilate, wanting to gratify the crowd, released Barabbas to them; and he delivered Jesus, after he had scourged *Him*, to be
crucified.

The Soldiers Mock Jesus

16 Then the soldiers led Him away into the
hall called Praetorium, and they called together the whole garrison.
17 And they clothed Him with purple; and
they twisted a crown of thorns, put it on His
head,
18 and began to salute Him, "Hail, King of
the Jews!"
19 Then they struck Him on the head with a
reed and spat on Him; and bowing the knee,
they worshiped Him.
20 And when they had mocked Him, they
took the purple off Him, put His own clothes
on Him, and led Him out to crucify Him.

The King on a Cross

21 Then they compelled a certain man, Simon a Cyrenian, the father of Alexander and
Rufus, as he was coming out of the country
and passing by, to bear His cross.
22 And they brought Him to the place Golgotha, which is translated, Place of a Skull.
23 Then they gave Him wine mingled with
myrrh to drink, but He did not take *it*.
24 And when they crucified Him, they divided His garments, casting lots for them *to
determine* what every man should take.
25 Now it was the third hour, and they crucified Him.

14:65 [a]NU-Text reads *received Him with slaps.* **14:70** [a]NU-Text omits *and your speech shows it.* **15:4** [a]NU-Text reads *of which they accuse You.* **15:8** [a]NU-Text reads *going up.*

LIFE LESSONS

➤ ***15:19 — Then they struck Him on the head with a reed and spat on Him; and bowing the knee, they worshiped Him.***

How hard it would have been to take the brutality and cruel mocking, knowing that with a word Jesus could have summoned more than twelve legions of furious angels (Matt. 26:53)! Yet He bore it, for our sake.

Life Examples:

THE CENTURION

A Bold Confession

MARK 15:39

The breastplate that covered his heart bore the seal of his master, Caesar. He felt pride in commanding a hundred elite Roman soldiers.

The centurion looked at the crosses and stood vigil as death reduced them to a mass of lifeless flesh. Yet one victim seemed unlike any the veteran soldier had ever seen. This man didn't fight as the others had. Nor did He beg or curse, condemn or plead for mercy. In fact, He did something that tore at the centurion's heart.

He forgave.

In all his career, only Jesus had ever offered the centurion mercy. Even though he stood for everything that put Christ on that cross, Jesus forgave him.

In that moment, he could utter only one confession: "Surely this was the Son of God" (Mark 15:39).

Two thousand years later, people still look upon Jesus, the resurrected Son of God. What is your confession about Him?

See the Life Principles Index for further study:

9. Trusting God means looking beyond what we can see to what God sees.

1. Out intimacy with God—His highest priority for our lives—determines the impact of our lives.

26 And the inscription of His accusation was written above:

THE KING OF THE JEWS.

27 With Him they also crucified two robbers, one on His right and the other on His left.

28 So the Scripture was fulfilled[a] which says, *"And He was numbered with the transgressors."*[b]

29 And those who passed by blasphemed Him, wagging their heads and saying, "Aha! *You* who destroy the temple and build *it* in three days,

30 "save Yourself, and come down from the cross!"

31 Likewise the chief priests also, mocking among themselves with the scribes, said, "He saved others; Himself He cannot save.

32 "Let the Christ, the King of Israel, descend now from the cross, that we may see and believe."[a] Even those who were crucified with Him reviled Him.

Jesus Dies on the Cross

33 Now when the sixth hour had come, there was darkness over the whole land until the ninth hour.

34 And at the ninth hour Jesus cried out with a loud voice, saying, "Eloi, Eloi, lama sabachthani?" which is translated, *"My God, My God, why have You forsaken Me?"*[a]

35 Some of those who stood by, when they heard *that,* said, "Look, He is calling for Elijah!"

36 Then someone ran and filled a sponge full of sour wine, put *it* on a reed, and offered *it* to Him to drink, saying, "Let Him alone; let us see if Elijah will come to take Him down."

37 And Jesus cried out with a loud voice, and breathed His last.

38 Then the veil of the temple was torn in two from top to bottom.

39 So when the centurion, who stood opposite Him, saw that He cried out like this and breathed His last,[a] he said, "Truly this Man was the Son of God!"

40 There were also women looking on from afar, among whom were Mary Magdalene, Mary the mother of James the Less and of Joses, and Salome,

41 who also followed Him and ministered to Him when He was in Galilee, and many other women who came up with Him to Jerusalem.

15:28 [a]Isaiah 53:12 [b]NU-Text omits this verse. **15:32** [a]M-Text reads *believe Him.* **15:34** [a]Psalm 22:1 **15:39** [a]NU-Text reads *that He thus breathed His last.*

LIFE LESSONS

➤ **15:34 — *Jesus cried out with a loud voice, saying, "Eloi, Eloi, lama sabachthani?" which is translated, "My God, My God, why have You forsaken Me?"***

In His darkest hour, when the sins of the whole world were piled on His back, Jesus fixed His mind on the words of Scripture. Read Psalm 22 to see how God comforted Him even on the cross.

➤ **15:38 — *Then the veil of the temple was torn in two from top to bottom.***

By tearing the veil of the temple from top to bottom, God signified that He, through the death of His Son, had made free access to heaven possible for all those who trusted in His Son.

ANSWERS TO LIFE'S QUESTIONS

What tools has God provided to help me share my faith?

MARK 16:15

The only way to reach spiritually blind, captive, and dead people is through the divine work of almighty God, who is "not willing that any should perish but that all should come to repentance" (2 Pet. 3:9). We are His tools; He is the power.

The apostle Paul says, "For God has not given us a spirit of fear, but of power and of love and of a sound mind" (2 Tim. 1:7). We therefore have three supernatural change agents to help us share our faith.

Power. The gospel of God opens blind eyes, rescues the captive, and revives the dead. We share our faith by declaring that Christ died on the cross for our sins, was buried, and rose again from the dead. Bring the non-Christian to consider Jesus, the core of saving faith; any rejection you experience thus centers on Christ, not you. Do not attempt to share your faith without prayer, and make sure that you depend on the power of God through the Holy Spirit (Acts 1:8).

Love. The greatest force on earth is love. "By this all will know that you are My disciples, if you have love for one another" (John 13:35). We can showcase the love of God in uncounted practical ways (1 John 3:18). Perhaps you could keep a couple's children in order to give them a special night out, or invite them over for dinner, or take them food during sickness. Having loved through service, we can also love in word (Prov. 31:26). That means we encourage, praise, and point out the positive qualities of our lost friends.

A sound mind. The Christian faith is based on facts, not fiction. As the Christian apologist Josh McDowell says, "My heart cannot rejoice in what my mind rejects." Thus, sharing our faith doesn't mean we are unreasonable or irrational. Rather, we offer the trustworthy testimony of Scripture. Such evidence includes:

- The fact of the Resurrection (1 Cor. 15:6). The Resurrection is indeed a concrete, historical fact.
- The fact of fulfilled Scripture. Literally hundreds of Old Testament Scriptures were fulfilled in the New Testament, including many intricate details of Jesus' birth, life, death, and resurrection.
- The fact of manuscript and archaeological evidence. Thousands of ancient manuscripts attest to the reliability of the Bible. Archaeological evidence has consistently verified the historical data of the Bible.

See the Life Principles Index for further study:
8. Fight all your battles on your knees and you win every time.
25. God blesses us so that we might bless others.

Jesus Buried in Joseph's Tomb

42 Now when evening had come, because it
was the Preparation Day, that is, the day before the Sabbath,
43 Joseph of Arimathea, a prominent council
member, who was himself waiting for the kingdom of God, coming and taking courage, went
in to Pilate and asked for the body of Jesus.
44 Pilate marveled that He was already dead;
and summoning the centurion, he asked him
if He had been dead for some time.
45 So when he found out from the centurion,
he granted the body to Joseph.
46 Then he bought fine linen, took Him
down, and wrapped Him in the linen. And he
laid Him in a tomb which had been hewn out
of the rock, and rolled a stone against the
door of the tomb.
47 And Mary Magdalene and Mary *the
mother* of Joses observed where He was laid.

He Is Risen

16 Now when the Sabbath was past, Mary
Magdalene, Mary *the mother* of James,

LIFE LESSONS

➤ ***15:43 — Joseph of Arimathea . . . coming and taking courage, went in to Pilate and asked for the body of Jesus.***

To this point, Joseph had been a "secret" disciple for fear that he might jeopardize his position. But when all the Lord's disciples ran, he stepped forward and made public his allegiance to Christ.

and Salome bought spices, that they might come and anoint Him.

2 Very early in the morning, on the first *day* of the week, they came to the tomb when the sun had risen.

3 And they said among themselves, "Who will roll away the stone from the door of the tomb for us?"

4 But when they looked up, they saw that the stone had been rolled away—for it was very large.

5 And entering the tomb, they saw a young man clothed in a long white robe sitting on the right side; and they were alarmed.

6 But he said to them, "Do not be alarmed. You seek Jesus of Nazareth, who was crucified. He is risen! He is not here. See the place where they laid Him.

➤ 7 "But go, tell His disciples—and Peter—that He is going before you into Galilee; there you will see Him, as He said to you."

➤ 8 So they went out quickly[a] and fled from the tomb, for they trembled and were amazed. And they said nothing to anyone, for they were afraid.

Mary Magdalene Sees the Risen Lord

9 Now when *He* rose early on the first *day* of the week, He appeared first to Mary Magdalene, out of whom He had cast seven demons.

10 She went and told those who had been with Him, as they mourned and wept.

➤ 11 And when they heard that He was alive and had been seen by her, they did not believe.

Jesus Appears to Two Disciples

12 After that, He appeared in another form to two of them as they walked and went into the country.

13 And they went and told *it* to the rest, *but* they did not believe them either.

The Great Commission

14 Later He appeared to the eleven as they sat at the table; and He rebuked their unbelief and hardness of heart, because they did not believe those who had seen Him after He had risen.

15 And He said to them, "Go into all the world and preach the gospel to every creature.

16 "He who believes and is baptized will be saved; but he who does not believe will be condemned.

17 "And these signs will follow those who believe: In My name they will cast out demons; they will speak with new tongues;

18 "they[a] will take up serpents; and if they drink anything deadly, it will by no means hurt them; they will lay hands on the sick, and they will recover."

Christ Ascends to God's Right Hand

19 So then, after the Lord had spoken to them, He was received up into heaven, and sat down at the right hand of God.

20 And they went out and preached everywhere, the Lord working with *them* and confirming the word through the accompanying signs. Amen.[a]

16:8 [a]NU-Text and M-Text omit *quickly.* **16:18** [a]NU-Text reads *and in their hands they will.* **16:20** [a]Verses 9–20 are bracketed in NU-Text as not original. They are lacking in Codex Sinaiticus and Codex Vaticanus, although nearly all other manuscripts of Mark contain them.

LIFE LESSONS

➤ 16:7 — *"But go, tell His disciples—and Peter—that He is going before you into Galilee . . . ."*

Only Mark's Gospel tells us that the angel singled out Peter for the announcement that Christ had risen from the dead. Peter had denied the Lord three times—but Jesus would show him grace.

➤ 16:8 — *So they went out quickly and fled from the tomb, for they trembled and were amazed. And they said nothing to anyone, for they were afraid.*

Though He had told them repeatedly that He would rise from the dead, none of the Lord's disciples imagined that He really would. And fear reigned so long as they doubted.

➤ 16:11 — *And when they heard that He was alive and had been seen by her, they did not believe.*

The first hours after the Resurrection were anything but a triumphant display of faith and courage. Over and over, at first, we hear that the disciples "did not believe." Wishful thinking does *not* explain the Resurrection!

THE GOSPEL ACCORDING TO

LUKE

Luke, a physician, writes with the compassion and warmth of a family doctor as he carefully documents the perfect humanity of the Son of Man, Jesus Christ. He emphasizes Jesus' ancestry, birth, and early life before moving carefully and chronologically through His earthly ministry.

At the very beginning of his Gospel, Luke tells his audience that he wasn't an original apostle or even an eyewitness to Jesus' words and works. Many believe Luke came to faith in Christ through the ministry of the apostle Paul, whom he befriended and accompanied on some of his missionary journeys. Luke is the only non-Jewish writer of a New Testament book (he also penned the Acts of the Apostles). Luke has a fondness for parables; of the twenty-five he includes in his Gospel, seventeen appear nowhere else. He also describes seven of Jesus' miracles not mentioned in the other two synoptic Gospels.

Luke's Gospel includes many details of Jesus' life omitted from the other three Gospels. Only Luke records a detailed account of Jesus' birth and the events surrounding it, including the angelic announcement to Jesus' mother, Mary, that she would give birth to the Messiah. He also records the story of the conception and birth of John the Baptist. Only Luke includes anything about the boyhood of Jesus.

Luke presents Jesus as a man of great compassion and intense emotions. Luke alone, for example, records how Jesus looked out over the holy city of Jerusalem and wept over its coming destruction. Luke also shows us that Jesus had a very sympathetic attitude toward women, the poor, the sinners, the sick, and the dying—and His resurrection ensures that His purposes will be fulfilled: "to seek and to save that which was lost" (19:10).

Kata Loukon, "According to Luke," is the ancient title added to this Gospel at a very early date. The Greek name Luke appears only three times in the New Testament (Col. 4:14; 2 Tim. 4:11; Philem. 24).

Theme: Jesus is the Son of Man.

Authors: Luke

Time: Most scholars believe Luke wrote his Gospel a few years before he wrote the Acts of the Apostles, which he likely penned around A.D. 63 or 64.

Structure: Luke starts his Gospel by explaining that he had thoroughly investigated Jesus' story and had written his account based on his careful investigations. The first two chapters of this Gospel contain several incidents unique to Luke that are related to Jesus' birth and early life.

As you read Luke, watch for several life principles that play an important role in this book:

26. Adversity is a bridge to a deeper relationship with God. *See Luke 2:19, 35, 51; pages 1187, 1189.*

22. To walk in the Spirit is to obey the initial promptings of the Spirit. *See Luke 2:27; 4:1; pages 1187, 1190.*

9. Trusting God means looking beyond what we can see to what God sees. *See Luke 5:20; 7:9; pages 1192, 1195.*

21. Obedience always brings blessing. *See Luke 11:28; page 1203.*

30. An eager anticipation of the Lord's return keeps us living productively. *See Luke 17:20–37; page 1214.*

Dedication to Theophilus

1 Inasmuch as many have taken in hand to
set in order a narrative of those things
which have been fulfilled[a] among us,
2 just as those who from the beginning were
eyewitnesses and ministers of the word delivered them to us,
3 it seemed good to me also, having had perfect understanding of all things from the very
first, to write to you an orderly account, most
excellent Theophilus,
➤ 4 that you may know the certainty of those
things in which you were instructed.

John's Birth Announced to Zacharias

5 There was in the days of Herod, the king
of Judea, a certain priest named Zacharias, of
the division of Abijah. His wife *was* of the
daughters of Aaron, and her name *was* Elizabeth.
6 And they were both righteous before God,
walking in all the commandments and ordinances of the Lord blameless.
7 But they had no child, because Elizabeth
was barren, and they were both well advanced in years.
8 So it was, that while he was serving as
priest before God in the order of his division,
9 according to the custom of the priesthood,
his lot fell to burn incense when he went into
the temple of the Lord.
10 And the whole multitude of the people
was praying outside at the hour of incense.
11 Then an angel of the Lord appeared to
him, standing on the right side of the altar of
incense.
12 And when Zacharias saw *him*, he was
troubled, and fear fell upon him.
13 But the angel said to him, "Do not be
afraid, Zacharias, for your prayer is heard;
and your wife Elizabeth will bear you a son,
and you shall call his name John.
14 "And you will have joy and gladness, and
many will rejoice at his birth.
15 "For he will be great in the sight of the
Lord, and shall drink neither wine nor strong
drink. He will also be filled with the Holy
Spirit, even from his mother's womb.
16 "And he will turn many of the children of
Israel to the Lord their God.
➤ 17 "He will also go before Him in the spirit
and power of Elijah, *'to turn the hearts of the
fathers to the children,'*[a] and the disobedient
to the wisdom of the just, to make ready a
people prepared for the Lord."
18 And Zacharias said to the angel, "How
shall I know this? For I am an old man, and
my wife is well advanced in years."
19 And the angel answered and said to him,
"I am Gabriel, who stands in the presence of
God, and was sent to speak to you and bring
you these glad tidings.
20 "But behold, you will be mute and not able
to speak until the day these things take place,
because you did not believe my words which
will be fulfilled in their own time."
21 And the people waited for Zacharias, and
marveled that he lingered so long in the temple.
22 But when he came out, he could not speak
to them; and they perceived that he had seen
a vision in the temple, for he beckoned to
them and remained speechless.
23 So it was, as soon as the days of his service were completed, that he departed to his
own house.
24 Now after those days his wife Elizabeth
conceived; and she hid herself five months,
saying,
25 "Thus the Lord has dealt with me, in the
days when He looked on *me*, to take away my
reproach among people."

Christ's Birth Announced to Mary

26 Now in the sixth month the angel Gabriel
was sent by God to a city of Galilee named
Nazareth,
27 to a virgin betrothed to a man whose
name was Joseph, of the house of David. The
virgin's name *was* Mary.
28 And having come in, the angel said to her,
"Rejoice, highly favored *one*, the Lord *is* with
you; blessed *are* you among women!"[a]
29 But when she saw *him*,[a] she was troubled
at his saying, and considered what manner of
greeting this was.
30 Then the angel said to her, "Do not be ➤

1:1 [a]Or *are most surely believed* **1:17** [a]Malachi 4:5, 6
1:28 [a]NU-Text omits *blessed are you among women.*
1:29 [a]NU-Text omits *when she saw him.*

LIFE LESSONS

➤ 1:4 — *. . . that you may know the certainty of those things in which you were instructed.*

God wants us to know that the Bible teaches truth and can be trusted in all that it declares. The Gospels are not a collection of religious fairy tales. They are parts of the only written source of eternal truth, God's Word.

➤ 1:17 — *"He will also go before Him in the spirit and power of Elijah . . . to make ready a people prepared for the Lord."*

John the Baptist came "in the spirit and power of Elijah" to prepare the people for the coming of Jesus Christ. He was not Elijah (John 1:21), and Jesus declared that Elijah will yet come (Matt. 17:11).

➤ 1:30 — *Then the angel said to her, "Do not be afraid, Mary, for you have found favor with God."*

The favor of God is worth any discomfort it might entail. God chose Mary to bear the Savior of the world, but she also had to bear the public shame of being an unwed mother.

afraid, Mary, for you have found favor with
God.
* 31 "And behold, you will conceive in your
womb and bring forth a Son, and shall call
His name JESUS.
32 "He will be great, and will be called the
Son of the Highest; and the Lord God will
give Him the throne of His father David.
33 "And He will reign over the house of Jacob
forever, and of His kingdom there will be no
end."
34 Then Mary said to the angel, "How can
this be, since I do not know a man?"
35 And the angel answered and said to her,
"*The* Holy Spirit will come upon you, and the
power of the Highest will overshadow you;
therefore, also, that Holy One who is to be
born will be called the Son of God.
36 "Now indeed, Elizabeth your relative has
also conceived a son in her old age; and this
is now the sixth month for her who was called
barren.
➤ 37 "For with God nothing will be impossible."
38 Then Mary said, "Behold the maidservant
of the Lord! Let it be to me according to your
word." And the angel departed from her.

Mary Visits Elizabeth

39 Now Mary arose in those days and went
into the hill country with haste, to a city of Judah,
40 and entered the house of Zacharias and
greeted Elizabeth.
41 And it happened, when Elizabeth heard
the greeting of Mary, that the babe leaped in
her womb; and Elizabeth was filled with the
Holy Spirit.
42 Then she spoke out with a loud voice and
said, "Blessed *are* you among women, and
blessed *is* the fruit of your womb!
43 "But why *is* this *granted* to me, that the
mother of my Lord should come to me?
44 "For indeed, as soon as the voice of your
greeting sounded in my ears, the babe leaped
in my womb for joy.
➤ 45 "Blessed *is* she who believed, for there will
be a fulfillment of those things which were
told her from the Lord."

The Song of Mary

46 And Mary said:

"My soul magnifies the Lord,
47 And my spirit has rejoiced in God my
Savior.
48 For He has regarded the lowly state of
His maidservant;
For behold, henceforth all generations
will call me blessed.

Life Examples:

MARY

Woman of Faith

LUKE 1:31–38

The customary age for betrothal among Mary's people was thirteen or fourteen, so probably she was a young girl when her parents arranged her engagement to Joseph. The angel Gabriel visited her shortly afterwards and announced that she would bear the Savior of the world.

Jewish society treated unmarried pregnant women with shame and scorn, yet Mary remained strong in her faith. Expecting the worst from Joseph, her family, and her society, she gratefully accepted God's will for her life.

Mary was an ordinary girl with extraordinary godly character that gave her an uncommon faith. Completely trusting in her God, in every way Mary was a good and faithful servant.

Mary provides a model of inspiration for ordinary women who can fulfill their deepest vocation by placing themselves at the service of others. She lived her life in relative obscurity, yet the world has celebrated her obedience to God for nearly two thousand years.

See the Life Principles Index for further study:

2. *Obey God and leave all the consequences to Him.*
5. *God does not require us to understand His will, just obey it, even if it seems unreasonable.*

LIFE LESSONS

➤ 1:37 — *"For with God nothing will be impossible."*

We can trust God even in the most difficult of circumstances because no problem is too tough for Him to handle and no challenge is beyond His power to overcome. He has the ability to do what He says He will do.

➤ 1:45 — *"Blessed is she who believed, for there will be a fulfillment of those things which were told her from the Lord."*

What would have happened had Mary not believed Gabriel's words? Would she have disqualified herself to be the mother of Jesus? The fact is she did believe, and God did fulfill His word in her.

49 For He who is mighty has done great
things for me,
And holy *is* His name.
50 And His mercy *is* on those who fear Him
From generation to generation.
51 He has shown strength with His arm;
He has scattered *the* proud in the
imagination of their hearts.
52 He has put down the mighty from *their*
thrones,
And exalted *the* lowly.
53 He has filled *the* hungry with good things,
And *the* rich He has sent away empty.
54 He has helped His servant Israel,
In remembrance of *His* mercy,
55 As He spoke to our fathers,
To Abraham and to his seed forever."

56 And Mary remained with her about three
months, and returned to her house.

Birth of John the Baptist

57 Now Elizabeth's full time came for her to
be delivered, and she brought forth a son.
58 When her neighbors and relatives heard
how the Lord had shown great mercy to her,
they rejoiced with her.

Circumcision of John the Baptist

59 So it was, on the eighth day, that they
came to circumcise the child; and they would
have called him by the name of his father,
Zacharias.
60 His mother answered and said, "No; he
shall be called John."
61 But they said to her, "There is no one
among your relatives who is called by this
name."
62 So they made signs to his father—what he
would have him called.
63 And he asked for a writing tablet, and
wrote, saying, "His name is John." So they all
marveled.
64 Immediately his mouth was opened and
his tongue *loosed,* and he spoke, praising
God.
65 Then fear came on all who dwelt around
them; and all these sayings were discussed
throughout all the hill country of Judea.
66 And all those who heard *them* kept *them*
in their hearts, saying, "What kind of child
will this be?" And the hand of the Lord was
with him.

Zacharias' Prophecy

67 Now his father Zacharias was filled with
the Holy Spirit, and prophesied, saying:

68 "Blessed *is* the Lord God of Israel,
For He has visited and redeemed His
people,
69 And has raised up a horn of salvation
for us
In the house of His servant David,
70 As He spoke by the mouth of His holy
prophets,
Who *have been* since the world began,
71 That we should be saved from our
enemies
And from the hand of all who hate us,
72 To perform the mercy *promised* to our
fathers
And to remember His holy covenant,
73 The oath which He swore to our father
Abraham:
74 To grant us that we,
Being delivered from the hand of our
enemies,
Might serve Him without fear,
75 In holiness and righteousness before Him
all the days of our life.

76 "And you, child, will be called the prophet
of the Highest;
For you will go before the face of the
Lord to prepare His ways,
77 To give knowledge of salvation to His
people
By the remission of their sins,
78 Through the tender mercy of our God,
With which the Dayspring from on high
has visited[a] us;
79 To give light to those who sit in darkness
and the shadow of death,
To guide our feet into the way of
peace."

80 So the child grew and became strong in
spirit, and was in the deserts till the day of his
manifestation to Israel.

Christ Born of Mary

2 And it came to pass in those days *that* a
decree went out from Caesar Augustus
that all the world should be registered.
2 This census first took place while
Quirinius was governing Syria.
3 So all went to be registered, everyone to
his own city.
4 Joseph also went up from Galilee, out of
the city of Nazareth, into Judea, to the city of
David, which is called Bethlehem, because he
was of the house and lineage of David,

1:78 [a]NU-Text reads *shall visit.*

LIFE LESSONS

➤ 1:74, 75 — *". . . that we . . . might serve Him without fear, in holiness and righteousness before Him all the days of our life."*

Those who fear God do not have to fear anything else. When we commit ourselves wholeheartedly to serving God, we can enjoy the intense pleasures that come with holiness and righteousness.

5 to be registered with Mary, his betrothed
wife,[a] who was with child.
6 So it was, that while they were there, the
days were completed for her to be delivered.
7 And she brought forth her firstborn Son,
and wrapped Him in swaddling cloths, and
laid Him in a manger, because there was no
room for them in the inn.

Glory in the Highest

8 Now there were in the same country shepherds living out in the fields, keeping watch
over their flock by night.
9 And behold,[a] an angel of the Lord stood
before them, and the glory of the Lord shone
around them, and they were greatly afraid.
➤ 10 Then the angel said to them, "Do not be
afraid, for behold, I bring you good tidings of
great joy which will be to all people.
11 "For there is born to you this day in the
city of David a Savior, who is Christ the Lord.
12 "And this *will be* the sign to you: You will
find a Babe wrapped in swaddling cloths,
lying in a manger."
13 And suddenly there was with the angel a
multitude of the heavenly host praising God
and saying:

14 "Glory to God in the highest,
And on earth peace, goodwill toward
men!"[a]

15 So it was, when the angels had gone
away from them into heaven, that the shepherds said to one another, "Let us now go
to Bethlehem and see this thing that has
come to pass, which the Lord has made
known to us."
16 And they came with haste and found Mary
and Joseph, and the Babe lying in a manger.
17 Now when they had seen *Him*, they made
widely[a] known the saying which was told
them concerning this Child.
18 And all those who heard *it* marveled at
those things which were told them by the
shepherds.
19 But Mary kept all these things and pondered *them* in her heart.
20 Then the shepherds returned, glorifying
and praising God for all the things that they
had heard and seen, as it was told them.

Circumcision of Jesus

21 And when eight days were completed for
the circumcision of the Child,[a] His name was
called JESUS, the name given by the angel before He was conceived in the womb.

Jesus Presented in the Temple

22 Now when the days of her purification according to the law of Moses were completed,
they brought Him to Jerusalem to present
Him to the Lord
23 (as it is written in the law of the Lord,
*"Every male who opens the womb shall be
called holy to the LORD"*),[a]
24 and to offer a sacrifice according to what
is said in the law of the Lord, *"A pair of turtledoves or two young pigeons."*[a]

Simeon Sees God's Salvation

25 And behold, there was a man in Jerusalem
whose name *was* Simeon, and this man *was*
just and devout, waiting for the Consolation
of Israel, and the Holy Spirit was upon him.
26 And it had been revealed to him by the
Holy Spirit that he would not see death before
he had seen the Lord's Christ.
27 So he came by the Spirit into the temple.
And when the parents brought in the Child
Jesus, to do for Him according to the custom
of the law,
28 he took Him up in his arms and blessed
God and said:

29 "Lord, now You are letting Your servant
depart in peace,
According to Your word;
30 For my eyes have seen Your salvation
31 Which You have prepared before the face
of all peoples,
32 A light to *bring* revelation to the Gentiles,
And the glory of Your people Israel."

33 And Joseph and His mother[a] marveled at
those things which were spoken of Him.
34 Then Simeon blessed them, and said to
Mary His mother, "Behold, this *Child* is destined for the fall and rising of many in Israel,
and for a sign which will be spoken against
35 "(yes, a sword will pierce through your
own soul also), that the thoughts of many
hearts may be revealed."

Anna Bears Witness to the Redeemer

36 Now there was one, Anna, a prophetess,
the daughter of Phanuel, of the tribe of Asher.
She was of a great age, and had lived with a
husband seven years from her virginity;

2:5 [a]NU-Text omits *wife.* **2:9** [a]NU-Text omits *behold.* **2:14** [a]NU-Text reads *toward men of goodwill.* **2:17** [a]NU-Text omits *widely.* **2:21** [a]NU-Text reads *for His circumcision.* **2:23** [a]Exodus 13:2, 12, 15 **2:24** [a]Leviticus 12:8 **2:33** [a]NU-Text reads *And His father and mother.*

LIFE LESSONS

➤ ***2:10 — Then the angel said to them, "Do not be afraid, for behold, I bring you good tidings of great joy which will be to all people."***

The angel told the shepherds not to fear, but to open their eyes and look for the wonderfully good thing that God was doing for them and for the whole world—something that would bring great joy to everyone.

Life Examples:

SIMEON

Whole in the Arms of God

LUKE 2:25–35

The years are catching up to me, Simeon must have thought as he made his way to the temple. How many years had it been since he had received the special word of the Lord? Five? Ten? It didn't matter. Each day brought him closer to the fulfillment of God's promise: "You will not see death until you have seen the Lord's Christ" (see Luke 2:26).

At that moment, a young couple emerged onto the temple porch with a newborn son. *The child!* Simeon thought. He approached the young family, took the babe in his arms, and immediately knew *this* was the One for whom he had waited so long.

God had kept His promise. Posted at the crux of history, the old soldier foresaw that the greatest battle of all time would be faced, fought, and won by this tiny child. There he stood, breathing the breath of Christ, whole in the arms of God.

See the Life Principles Index for further study:

5. *God does not require us to understand His will, just obey it, even if it seems unreasonable.*
9. *Trusting God means looking beyond what we can see to what God sees.*
14. *God acts on behalf of those who wait for Him.*

37 and this woman *was* a widow of about
eighty-four years,[a] who did not depart from
the temple, but served *God* with fastings and
prayers night and day.
38 And coming in that instant she gave
thanks to the Lord,[a] and spoke of Him to all
those who looked for redemption in Jerusalem.

The Family Returns to Nazareth

39 So when they had performed all things according to the law of the Lord, they returned to Galilee, to their *own* city, Nazareth.
40 And the Child grew and became strong in
spirit,[a] filled with wisdom; and the grace of
God was upon Him.

The Boy Jesus Amazes the Scholars

41 His parents went to Jerusalem every year at the Feast of the Passover.
42 And when He was twelve years old, they
went up to Jerusalem according to the custom
of the feast.
43 When they had finished the days, as they
returned, the Boy Jesus lingered behind in Jerusalem. And Joseph and His mother[a] did not
know *it;*
44 but supposing Him to have been in the
company, they went a day's journey, and
sought Him among *their* relatives and acquaintances.
45 So when they did not find Him, they returned to Jerusalem, seeking Him.
46 Now so it was *that* after three days they
found Him in the temple, sitting in the midst
of the teachers, both listening to them and
asking them questions.
47 And all who heard Him were astonished
at His understanding and answers.
48 So when they saw Him, they were
amazed; and His mother said to Him, "Son,
why have You done this to us? Look, Your father and I have sought You anxiously."
49 And He said to them, "Why did you seek
Me? Did you not know that I must be about
My Father's business?"
50 But they did not understand the statement
which He spoke to them.

2:37 [a]NU-Text reads *a widow until she was eighty-four.*
2:38 [a]NU-Text reads *to God.* **2:40** [a]NU-Text omits *in spirit.*
2:43 [a]NU-Text reads *And His parents.*

LIFE LESSONS

➤ **2:40 — *And the Child grew and became strong in spirit, filled with wisdom; and the grace of God was upon Him.***

Jesus had to grow, just like every other human child. He became strong in spirit and filled with wisdom because He grew up in the grace of God. God's grace is what makes us both strong and wise.

➤ **2:47 — *And all who heard Him were astonished at His understanding and answers.***

From a very early age, Jesus spent a lot of time alone with His heavenly Father—a practice that made Him spiritually mature far beyond His years. You can always tell when someone has nurtured a close relationship with God.

➤ **2:50 — *But they did not understand the statement which He spoke to them.***

Even as a boy, Jesus spoke of spiritual issues in ways that His hearers often did not understand. Serious Christ followers, however, strive to gain understanding, as did Mary (Luke 2:51) and His disciples (8:9).

Jesus Advances in Wisdom and Favor
➤ **51** Then He went down with them and came
to Nazareth, and was subject to them, but His
mother kept all these things in her heart.
52 And Jesus increased in wisdom and
stature, and in favor with God and men.

John the Baptist Prepares the Way
3 Now in the fifteenth year of the reign of
Tiberius Caesar, Pontius Pilate being governor of Judea, Herod being tetrarch of Galilee, his brother Philip tetrarch of Iturea and
the region of Trachonitis, and Lysanias
tetrarch of Abilene,
2 while Annas and Caiaphas were high
priests,[a] the word of God came to John the
son of Zacharias in the wilderness.
3 And he went into all the region around the
Jordan, preaching a baptism of repentance
for the remission of sins,
4 as it is written in the book of the words of
Isaiah the prophet, saying:

"The voice of one crying in the
wilderness:
'Prepare the way of the L*ORD;*
Make His paths straight.
5 *Every valley shall be filled*
And every mountain and hill brought
low;
The crooked places shall be made
straight
And the rough ways smooth;
6 *And all flesh shall see the salvation of*
God.'"[a]

John Preaches to the People
7 Then he said to the multitudes that came
out to be baptized by him, "Brood of vipers!
Who warned you to flee from the wrath to
come?
8 "Therefore bear fruits worthy of repentance, and do not begin to say to yourselves,
'We have Abraham as *our* father.' For I say to
you that God is able to raise up children to
Abraham from these stones.
9 "And even now the ax is laid to the root of
the trees. Therefore every tree which does not
bear good fruit is cut down and thrown into
the fire."
10 So the people asked him, saying, "What
shall we do then?"
11 He answered and said to them, "He who
has two tunics, let him give to him who has
none; and he who has food, let him do likewise."
12 Then tax collectors also came to be baptized, and said to him, "Teacher, what shall
we do?"
13 And he said to them, "Collect no more
than what is appointed for you."
14 Likewise the soldiers asked him, saying,
"And what shall we do?" So he said to them,
"Do not intimidate anyone or accuse falsely,
and be content with your wages."
15 Now as the people were in expectation,
and all reasoned in their hearts about John,
whether he was the Christ *or* not,
16 John answered, saying to all, "I indeed
baptize you with water; but One mightier
than I is coming, whose sandal strap I am not
worthy to loose. He will baptize you with the
Holy Spirit and fire.
17 "His winnowing fan *is* in His hand, and
He will thoroughly clean out His threshing
floor, and gather the wheat into His barn; but
the chaff He will burn with unquenchable
fire."
18 And with many other exhortations he
preached to the people.
19 But Herod the tetrarch, being rebuked by
him concerning Herodias, his brother Philip's
wife,[a] and for all the evils which Herod had
done,
20 also added this, above all, that he shut
John up in prison.

John Baptizes Jesus
21 When all the people were baptized, it
came to pass that Jesus also was baptized;
and while He prayed, the heaven was opened.
22 And the Holy Spirit descended in bodily
form like a dove upon Him, and a voice came
from heaven which said, "You are My beloved
Son; in You I am well pleased."

3:2 [a]NU-Text and M-Text read *in the high priesthood of Annas and Caiaphas.* **3:6** [a]Isaiah 40:3–5 **3:19** [a]NU-Text reads *his brother's wife.*

LIFE LESSONS

➤ **2:51 — *Then He went down with them and came to Nazareth, and was subject to them . . . .***

Jesus was the only begotten Son of God. Yet God had placed Him in the care and under the authority of His parents; so He submitted to them, not as an inferior, but in obedience to God.

➤ **3:11 — *"He who has two tunics, let him give to him who has none; and he who has food, let him do likewise."***

An intimate relationship with God is about far more than enjoying warm feelings toward the Creator of the universe. Any genuine love of God moves a person to real acts of love toward others (1 John 3:17).

➤ **3:14 — *"Do not intimidate anyone or accuse falsely, and be content with your wages."***

John the Baptist did not advise soldiers to go into another profession. He did, however, instruct them to act justly and mercifully with those under their authority.

The Genealogy of Jesus Christ

➤ **23** Now Jesus Himself began *His ministry at* about thirty years of age, being (as was supposed) *the* son of Joseph, *the son* of Heli,
24 *the son* of Matthat,[a] *the son* of Levi, *the son* of Melchi, *the son* of Janna, *the son* of Joseph,
25 *the son* of Mattathiah, *the son* of Amos, *the son* of Nahum, *the son* of Esli, *the son* of Naggai,
26 *the son* of Maath, *the son* of Mattathiah, *the son* of Semei, *the son* of Joseph, *the son* of Judah,
27 *the son* of Joannas, *the son* of Rhesa, *the son* of Zerubbabel, *the son* of Shealtiel, *the son* of Neri,
28 *the son* of Melchi, *the son* of Addi, *the son* of Cosam, *the son* of Elmodam, *the son* of Er,
29 *the son* of Jose, *the son* of Eliezer, *the son* of Jorim, *the son* of Matthat, *the son* of Levi,
30 *the son* of Simeon, *the son* of Judah, *the son* of Joseph, *the son* of Jonan, *the son* of Eliakim,
31 *the son* of Melea, *the son* of Menan, *the son* of Mattathah, *the son* of Nathan, *the son* of David,
32 *the son* of Jesse, *the son* of Obed, *the son* of Boaz, *the son* of Salmon, *the son* of Nahshon,
33 *the son* of Amminadab, *the son* of Ram, *the son* of Hezron, *the son* of Perez, *the son* of Judah,
34 *the son* of Jacob, *the son* of Isaac, *the son* of Abraham, *the son* of Terah, *the son* of Nahor,
35 *the son* of Serug, *the son* of Reu, *the son* of Peleg, *the son* of Eber, *the son* of Shelah,
36 *the son* of Cainan, *the son* of Arphaxad, *the son* of Shem, *the son* of Noah, *the son* of Lamech,
37 *the son* of Methuselah, *the son* of Enoch, *the son* of Jared, *the son* of Mahalalel, *the son* of Cainan,
38 *the son* of Enosh, *the son* of Seth, *the son* of Adam, *the son* of God.

Satan Tempts Jesus

➤ **4** Then Jesus, being filled with the Holy Spirit, returned from the Jordan and was led by the Spirit into[a] the wilderness,
2 being tempted for forty days by the devil. And in those days He ate nothing, and afterward, when they had ended, He was hungry.
3 And the devil said to Him, "If You are the Son of God, command this stone to become bread."
4 But Jesus answered him, saying,[a] "It is written, *'Man shall not live by bread alone, but by every word of God.'*"[b]
5 Then the devil, taking Him up on a high mountain, showed Him[a] all the kingdoms of the world in a moment of time.
6 And the devil said to Him, "All this authority I will give You, and their glory; for *this* has been delivered to me, and I give it to whomever I wish.
7 "Therefore, if You will worship before me, all will be Yours."
8 And Jesus answered and said to him, "Get behind Me, Satan![a] For[b] it is written, *'You shall worship the* LORD *your God, and Him only you shall serve.'*"[c]
9 Then he brought Him to Jerusalem, set Him on the pinnacle of the temple, and said to Him, "If You are the Son of God, throw Yourself down from here.
10 "For it is written:

'He shall give His angels charge over you,
To keep you,'

11 "and,

'In their hands they shall bear you up,
Lest you dash your foot against a
stone.'"[a]

12 And Jesus answered and said to him, "It has been said, *'You shall not tempt the* LORD *your God.'*"[a]
13 Now when the devil had ended every ➤

3:24 [a]This and several other names in the genealogy are spelled somewhat differently in the NU-Text. Since the New King James Version uses the Old Testament spelling for persons mentioned in the New Testament, these variations, which come from the Greek, have not been footnoted. **4:1** [a]NU-Text reads *in.*
4:4 [a]Deuteronomy 8:3 [b]NU-Text omits *but by every word of God.* **4:5** [a]NU-Text reads *And taking Him up, he showed Him.*
4:8 [a]NU-Text omits *Get behind Me, Satan.* [b]NU-Text and M-Text omit *For.* [c]Deuteronomy 6:13 **4:11** [a]Psalm 91:11, 12
4:12 [a]Deuteronomy 6:16

LIFE LESSONS

➤ 3:23 — *Now Jesus Himself began His ministry at about thirty years of age . . . .*

God spent three decades preparing Jesus for His ministry, most of it in almost total obscurity. Anyone whom God uses greatly He first puts through a period of preparation outside of the bright lights.

➤ 4:1, 14 — *Then Jesus, being filled with the Holy Spirit . . . Then Jesus returned in the power of the Spirit to Galilee . . . .*

Luke shows that Jesus fulfilled His entire ministry by relying on the power and direction of the Holy Spirit. When we rely on the Spirit as Jesus did, we can follow in His ministry footsteps.

➤ 4:13 — *Now when the devil had ended every temptation, he departed from Him until an opportune time.*

Satan does not attack us in the same way at all times. He looks for "opportune" moments, when we feel weakest or most discouraged, to suggest that God cannot be trusted and we must take matters into our own hands.

temptation, he departed from Him until an
opportune time.

Jesus Begins His Galilean Ministry

➤ **14** Then Jesus returned in the power of the
Spirit to Galilee, and news of Him went out
through all the surrounding region.
15 And He taught in their synagogues, being
glorified by all.

Jesus Rejected at Nazareth

16 So He came to Nazareth, where He had
been brought up. And as His custom was, He
went into the synagogue on the Sabbath day,
and stood up to read.
17 And He was handed the book of the
prophet Isaiah. And when He had opened the
book, He found the place where it was written:

18 "*The Spirit of the LORD is upon Me,*
Because He has anointed Me
To preach the gospel to the poor;
He has sent Me to heal the
brokenhearted,[a]
To proclaim liberty to the captives
And recovery of sight to the blind,
To set at liberty those who are oppressed;
19 *To proclaim the acceptable year of the*
LORD."[a]

20 Then He closed the book, and gave *it* back
to the attendant and sat down. And the eyes
of all who were in the synagogue were fixed
on Him.
➤ 21 And He began to say to them, "Today this
Scripture is fulfilled in your hearing."
22 So all bore witness to Him, and marveled
at the gracious words which proceeded out of
His mouth. And they said, "Is this not Joseph's son?"
23 He said to them, "You will surely say this
proverb to Me, 'Physician, heal yourself!
Whatever we have heard done in Capernaum,[a] do also here in Your country.'"
24 Then He said, "Assuredly, I say to you, no
prophet is accepted in his own country.
25 "But I tell you truly, many widows were in
Israel in the days of Elijah, when the heaven
was shut up three years and six months, and
there was a great famine throughout all the
land;
26 "but to none of them was Elijah sent except to Zarephath,[a] *in the region* of Sidon, to
a woman *who was* a widow.
27 "And many lepers were in Israel in the
time of Elisha the prophet, and none of them
was cleansed except Naaman the Syrian."
28 So all those in the synagogue, when they
heard these things, were filled with wrath,
29 and rose up and thrust Him out of the city;
and they led Him to the brow of the hill on
which their city was built, that they might
throw Him down over the cliff.
30 Then passing through the midst of them,
He went His way.

Jesus Casts Out an Unclean Spirit

31 Then He went down to Capernaum, a city
of Galilee, and was teaching them on the
Sabbaths.
32 And they were astonished at His teaching,
for His word was with authority.
33 Now in the synagogue there was a man
who had a spirit of an unclean demon. And he
cried out with a loud voice,
34 saying, "Let *us* alone! What have we to do
with You, Jesus of Nazareth? Did You come to
destroy us? I know who You are—the Holy
One of God!"
35 But Jesus rebuked him, saying, "Be quiet,
and come out of him!" And when the demon
had thrown him in *their* midst, it came out of
him and did not hurt him.
36 Then they were all amazed and spoke
among themselves, saying, "What a word this
is! For with authority and power He commands the unclean spirits, and they come
out."
37 And the report about Him went out into
every place in the surrounding region.

Peter's Mother-in-Law Healed

38 Now He arose from the synagogue and entered Simon's house. But Simon's wife's
mother was sick with a high fever, and they
made request of Him concerning her.
39 So He stood over her and rebuked the
fever, and it left her. And immediately she
arose and served them.

Many Healed After Sabbath Sunset

40 When the sun was setting, all those who
had any that were sick with various diseases
brought them to Him; and He laid His hands
on every one of them and healed them.

4:18 [a]NU-Text omits *to heal the brokenhearted.*
4:19 [a]Isaiah 61:1, 2 **4:23** [a]Here and elsewhere the NU-Text spelling is *Capharnaum.* **4:26** [a]Greek *Sarepta*

LIFE LESSONS

➤ 4:21 — *And He began to say to them, "Today this Scripture is fulfilled in your hearing."*

Everyone knew that the text Jesus read (from Isaiah 61) referred to the ministry of the prophesied Messiah. Therefore, at the outset of His ministry Jesus was making a direct claim to be that Messiah.

41 And demons also came out of many, crying out and saying, "You are the Christ,[a] the
Son of God!" And He, rebuking *them,* did not
allow them to speak, for they knew that He
was the Christ.

Jesus Preaches in Galilee

42 Now when it was day, He departed and
went into a deserted place. And the crowd
sought Him and came to Him, and tried to
keep Him from leaving them;
43 but He said to them, "I must preach the
kingdom of God to the other cities also, because for this purpose I have been sent."
44 And He was preaching in the synagogues
of Galilee.[a]

Four Fishermen Called as Disciples

5 So it was, as the multitude pressed about
Him to hear the word of God, that He
stood by the Lake of Gennesaret,
2 and saw two boats standing by the lake;
but the fishermen had gone from them and
were washing *their* nets.
3 Then He got into one of the boats, which
was Simon's, and asked him to put out a little
from the land. And He sat down and taught
the multitudes from the boat.
4 When He had stopped speaking, He said
to Simon, "Launch out into the deep and let
down your nets for a catch."
5 But Simon answered and said to Him,
"Master, we have toiled all night and caught
nothing; nevertheless at Your word I will let
down the net."
6 And when they had done this, they caught
a great number of fish, and their net was
breaking.
7 So they signaled to *their* partners in the
other boat to come and help them. And they
came and filled both the boats, so that they
began to sink.
8 When Simon Peter saw *it,* he fell down at
Jesus' knees, saying, "Depart from me, for I
am a sinful man, O Lord!"
9 For he and all who were with him were astonished at the catch of fish which they had
taken;
10 and so also *were* James and John, the sons
of Zebedee, who were partners with Simon.
And Jesus said to Simon, "Do not be afraid.
From now on you will catch men."
11 So when they had brought their boats to
land, they forsook all and followed Him.

Jesus Cleanses a Leper

12 And it happened when He was in a certain
city, that behold, a man who was full of leprosy saw Jesus; and he fell on *his* face and implored Him, saying, "Lord, if You are willing,
You can make me clean."
13 Then He put out *His* hand and touched
him, saying, "I am willing; be cleansed." Immediately the leprosy left him.
14 And He charged him to tell no one, "But
go and show yourself to the priest, and make
an offering for your cleansing, as a testimony
to them, just as Moses commanded."
15 However, the report went around concerning Him all the more; and great multitudes
came together to hear, and to be healed by
Him of their infirmities.
16 So He Himself *often* withdrew into the
wilderness and prayed.

Jesus Forgives and Heals a Paralytic

17 Now it happened on a certain day, as He
was teaching, that there were Pharisees and
teachers of the law sitting by, who had come
out of every town of Galilee, Judea, and Jerusalem. And the power of the Lord was *present*
to heal them.[a]
18 Then behold, men brought on a bed a man
who was paralyzed, whom they sought to
bring in and lay before Him.
19 And when they could not find how they
might bring him in, because of the crowd,
they went up on the housetop and let him
down with *his* bed through the tiling into the
midst before Jesus.
20 When He saw their faith, He said to him,
"Man, your sins are forgiven you."
21 And the scribes and the Pharisees began
to reason, saying, "Who is this who speaks
blasphemies? Who can forgive sins but God
alone?"
22 But when Jesus perceived their thoughts,

4:41 [a]NU-Text omits *the Christ.* **4:44** [a]NU-Text reads *Judea.*
5:17 [a]NU-Text reads *present with Him to heal.*

LIFE LESSONS

➤ **5:11 — *So when they had brought their boats to land, they forsook all and followed Him.***

The particulars of what Jesus requires of His disciples varies tremendously, but of all followers He demands total allegiance. He must be Lord of all, not merely one significant voice among many others.

➤ **5:13 — *Then He put out His hand and touched him, saying, "I am willing; be cleansed." Immediately the leprosy left him.***

Jesus did not have to touch people to cure them (see Luke 7:1–10), but He made a point of touching the leper, a man no one dared to touch. Jesus always gives us exactly what we need.

➤ **5:16 — *So He Himself often withdrew into the wilderness and prayed.***

Jesus cherished his times alone with His heavenly Father. As our example, He shows us that none of us can afford to skimp on our devotional times with God. We were made for this!

He answered and said to them, "Why are you
reasoning in your hearts?
23 "Which is easier, to say, 'Your sins are forgiven you,' or to say, 'Rise up and walk'?
24 "But that you may know that the Son of
Man has power on earth to forgive sins"—He
said to the man who was paralyzed, "I say to
you, arise, take up your bed, and go to your
house."
25 Immediately he rose up before them, took
up what he had been lying on, and departed
to his own house, glorifying God.
26 And they were all amazed, and they glorified God and were filled with fear, saying,
"We have seen strange things today!"

Matthew the Tax Collector

27 After these things He went out and saw a
tax collector named Levi, sitting at the tax office. And He said to him, "Follow Me."
28 So he left all, rose up, and followed Him.
29 Then Levi gave Him a great feast in his
own house. And there were a great number of
tax collectors and others who sat down with
them.
30 And their scribes and the Pharisees[a] complained against His disciples, saying, "Why do
You eat and drink with tax collectors and sinners?"
31 Jesus answered and said to them, "Those
who are well have no need of a physician, but
those who are sick.
* 32 "I have not come to call *the* righteous, but
sinners, to repentance."

Jesus Is Questioned About Fasting

33 Then they said to Him, "Why do[a] the disciples of John fast often and make prayers, and
likewise those of the Pharisees, but Yours eat
and drink?"
34 And He said to them, "Can you make the
friends of the bridegroom fast while the
bridegroom is with them?
35 "But the days will come when the bridegroom will be taken away from them; then
they will fast in those days."
36 Then He spoke a parable to them: "No one
puts a piece from a new garment on an old
one;[a] otherwise the new makes a tear, and
also the piece that was *taken* out of the new
does not match the old.
37 "And no one puts new wine into old wineskins; or else the new wine will burst the
wineskins and be spilled, and the wineskins
will be ruined.
38 "But new wine must be put into new wineskins, and both are preserved.[a]
39 And no one, having drunk old *wine,* immediately[a] desires new; for he says, 'The old
is better.'"[b]

Jesus Is Lord of the Sabbath

6 Now it happened on the second Sabbath
after the first[a] that He went through the
grainfields. And His disciples plucked the
heads of grain and ate *them,* rubbing *them* in
their hands.
2 And some of the Pharisees said to them,
"Why are you doing what is not lawful to do
on the Sabbath?"
3 But Jesus answering them said, "Have you
not even read this, what David did when he
was hungry, he and those who were with him:
4 "how he went into the house of God, took
and ate the showbread, and also gave some to
those with him, which is not lawful for any
but the priests to eat?"
5 And He said to them, "The Son of Man is
also Lord of the Sabbath."

Healing on the Sabbath

6 Now it happened on another Sabbath,
also, that He entered the synagogue and
taught. And a man was there whose right
hand was withered.
7 So the scribes and Pharisees watched Him
closely, whether He would heal on the Sabbath, that they might find an accusation
against Him.
8 But He knew their thoughts, and said to
the man who had the withered hand, "Arise
and stand here." And he arose and stood.
9 Then Jesus said to them, "I will ask you
one thing: Is it lawful on the Sabbath to do
good or to do evil, to save life or to destroy?"[a]
10 And when He had looked around at them
all, He said to the man,[a] "Stretch out your
hand." And he did so, and his hand was restored as whole as the other.[b]
11 But they were filled with rage, and discussed with one another what they might do
to Jesus.

5:30 [a]NU-Text reads *But the Pharisees and their scribes.*
5:33 [a]NU-Text omits *Why do,* making the verse a statement.
5:36 [a]NU-Text reads *No one tears a piece from a new garment and puts it on an old one.* **5:38** [a]NU-Text omits *and both are preserved.* **5:39** [a]NU-Text omits *immediately.* [b]NU-Text reads *good.* **6:1** [a]NU-Text reads *on a Sabbath.* **6:9** [a]M-Text reads *to kill.* **6:10** [a]NU-Text and M-Text read *to him.* [b]NU-Text omits *as whole as the other.*

LIFE LESSONS

➤ 6:9 — *"Is it lawful on the Sabbath to do good or to do evil, to save life or to destroy?"*

Every law or commandment that God ever gave to His people, He gave for their own good (Deut. 10:13). God takes no pleasure in laws that destroy or injure, so the answer to Jesus' question should have been obvious.

The Twelve Apostles

➤ **12** Now it came to pass in those days that He went out to the mountain to pray, and continued all night in prayer to God.
13 And when it was day, He called His disciples to *Himself;* and from them He chose twelve whom He also named apostles:
14 Simon, whom He also named Peter, and Andrew his brother; James and John; Philip and Bartholomew;
15 Matthew and Thomas; James the *son* of Alphaeus, and Simon called the Zealot;
16 Judas *the son* of James, and Judas Iscariot who also became a traitor.

Jesus Heals a Great Multitude

17 And He came down with them and stood on a level place with a crowd of His disciples and a great multitude of people from all Judea and Jerusalem, and from the seacoast of Tyre and Sidon, who came to hear Him and be healed of their diseases,
18 as well as those who were tormented with unclean spirits. And they were healed.
19 And the whole multitude sought to touch Him, for power went out from Him and healed *them* all.

The Beatitudes

20 Then He lifted up His eyes toward His disciples, and said:

"Blessed *are you* poor,
For yours is the kingdom of God.
21 Blessed *are you* who hunger now,
For you shall be filled.
Blessed *are you* who weep now,
For you shall laugh.
22 Blessed are you when men hate you,
And when they exclude you,
And revile *you,* and cast out your name as evil,
For the Son of Man's sake.
23 Rejoice in that day and leap for joy!
For indeed your reward *is* great in heaven,
For in like manner their fathers did to the prophets.

Jesus Pronounces Woes

24 "But woe to you who are rich,
For you have received your consolation.
25 Woe to you who are full,
For you shall hunger.
Woe to you who laugh now,
For you shall mourn and weep.
26 Woe to you[a] when all[b] men speak well of you,
For so did their fathers to the false prophets.

Love Your Enemies

27 "But I say to you who hear: Love your enemies, do good to those who hate you,
28 "bless those who curse you, and pray for those who spitefully use you.
29 "To him who strikes you on the *one* cheek, offer the other also. And from him who takes away your cloak, do not withhold *your* tunic either.
30 "Give to everyone who asks of you. And from him who takes away your goods do not ask *them* back.
31 "And just as you want men to do to you, you also do to them likewise.
32 "But if you love those who love you, what credit is that to you? For even sinners love those who love them.
33 "And if you do good to those who do good to you, what credit is that to you? For even sinners do the same.
34 "And if you lend *to those* from whom you hope to receive back, what credit is that to you? For even sinners lend to sinners to receive as much back.
35 "But love your enemies, do good, and lend, hoping for nothing in return; and your reward will be great, and you will be sons of the Most High. For He is kind to the unthankful and evil. ✳ ➤
36 "Therefore be merciful, just as your Father also is merciful.

Do Not Judge

37 "Judge not, and you shall not be judged. Condemn not, and you shall not be condemned. Forgive, and you will be forgiven.
38 "Give, and it will be given to you: good measure, pressed down, shaken together, and running over will be put into your bosom. For with the same measure that you use, it will be measured back to you."

6:26 [a]NU-Text and M-Text omit *to you.* [b]M-Text omits *all.*

LIFE LESSONS

➤ **6:12 — *Now it came to pass in those days that He went out to the mountain to pray, and continued all night in prayer to God.***

Jesus spent all night in prayer immediately before He chose the twelve disciples who would accompany Him everywhere. Jesus wanted the counsel of His Father on all major decisions, and so should we.

➤ **6:35 — *"For He is kind to the unthankful and evil."***

If God were not kind to the unthankful and evil, where would any of us be? God will always judge sin, but He most desires that we turn from our sin and come to Him so that He can bless us, not judge us.

39 And He spoke a parable to them: "Can the blind lead the blind? Will they not both fall into the ditch?
40 "A disciple is not above his teacher, but everyone who is perfectly trained will be like his teacher.
41 "And why do you look at the speck in your brother's eye, but do not perceive the plank in your own eye?
42 "Or how can you say to your brother, 'Brother, let me remove the speck that *is* in your eye,' when you yourself do not see the plank that *is* in your own eye? Hypocrite! First remove the plank from your own eye, and then you will see clearly to remove the speck that is in your brother's eye.

A Tree Is Known by Its Fruit

43 "For a good tree does not bear bad fruit, nor does a bad tree bear good fruit.
➤ 44 "For every tree is known by its own fruit. For *men* do not gather figs from thorns, nor do they gather grapes from a bramble bush.
45 "A good man out of the good treasure of his heart brings forth good; and an evil man out of the evil treasure of his heart[a] brings forth evil. For out of the abundance of the heart his mouth speaks.

Build on the Rock

46 "But why do you call Me 'Lord, Lord,' and not do the things which I say?
47 "Whoever comes to Me, and hears My sayings and does them, I will show you whom he is like:
48 "He is like a man building a house, who dug deep and laid the foundation on the rock. And when the flood arose, the stream beat vehemently against that house, and could not shake it, for it was founded on the rock.[a]
49 "But he who heard and did nothing is like a man who built a house on the earth without a foundation, against which the stream beat vehemently; and immediately it fell.[a] And the ruin of that house was great."

Jesus Heals a Centurion's Servant

7 Now when He concluded all His sayings in the hearing of the people, He entered Capernaum.
2 And a certain centurion's servant, who was dear to him, was sick and ready to die.
3 So when he heard about Jesus, he sent elders of the Jews to Him, pleading with Him to come and heal his servant.
4 And when they came to Jesus, they begged Him earnestly, saying that the one for whom He should do this was deserving,
5 "for he loves our nation, and has built us a synagogue."
6 Then Jesus went with them. And when He was already not far from the house, the centurion sent friends to Him, saying to Him, "Lord, do not trouble Yourself, for I am not worthy that You should enter under my roof.
7 "Therefore I did not even think myself worthy to come to You. But say the word, and my servant will be healed.
8 "For I also am a man placed under authority, having soldiers under me. And I say to one, 'Go,' and he goes; and to another, 'Come,' and he comes; and to my servant, 'Do this,' and he does *it*."
9 When Jesus heard these things, He marveled at him, and turned around and said to the crowd that followed Him, "I say to you, I have not found such great faith, not even in Israel!"
10 And those who were sent, returning to the house, found the servant well who had been sick.[a]

Jesus Raises the Son of the Widow of Nain

11 Now it happened, the day after, *that* He went into a city called Nain; and many of His disciples went with Him, and a large crowd.
12 And when He came near the gate of the city, behold, a dead man was being carried out, the only son of his mother; and she was a widow. And a large crowd from the city was with her.
13 When the Lord saw her, He had compassion on her and said to her, "Do not weep."
14 Then He came and touched the open coffin, and those who carried *him* stood still. And He said, "Young man, I say to you, arise."
15 So he who was dead sat up and began to speak. And He presented him to his mother. ➤
16 Then fear came upon all, and they glorified God, saying, "A great prophet has risen up among us"; and, "God has visited His people."

6:45 [a]NU-Text omits *treasure of his heart.* **6:48** [a]NU-Text reads *for it was well built.* **6:49** [a]NU-Text reads *collapsed.* **7:10** [a]NU-Text omits *who had been sick.*

LIFE LESSONS

➤ 6:44 — *"For every tree is known by its own fruit."*

What kind of fruit do you bear? How would your coworkers describe you? Your next-door neighbor? Your family? If you feel dissatisfied either with the quality or the amount of your fruit, what can you do about it?

➤ 7:15 — *So he who was dead sat up and began to speak. And He presented him to his mother.*

This was not the only time Jesus raised a dead person back to life. He who is called the Word of life (1 John 1:1) is "Lord of both the dead and the living" (Rom. 14:9).

17 And this report about Him went throughout all Judea and all the surrounding region.

John the Baptist Sends Messengers to Jesus

18 Then the disciples of John reported to him concerning all these things.
19 And John, calling two of his disciples to *him,* sent *them* to Jesus,[a] saying, "Are You the Coming One, or do we look for another?"
20 When the men had come to Him, they said, "John the Baptist has sent us to You, saying, 'Are You the Coming One, or do we look for another?'"
➤ 21 And that very hour He cured many of infirmities, afflictions, and evil spirits; and to many blind He gave sight.
22 Jesus answered and said to them, "Go and tell John the things you have seen and heard: that *the* blind see, *the* lame walk, *the* lepers are cleansed, *the* deaf hear, *the* dead are raised, *the* poor have the gospel preached to them.
23 "And blessed is *he* who is not offended because of Me."
24 When the messengers of John had departed, He began to speak to the multitudes concerning John: "What did you go out into the wilderness to see? A reed shaken by the wind?
25 "But what did you go out to see? A man clothed in soft garments? Indeed those who are gorgeously appareled and live in luxury are in kings' courts.
26 "But what did you go out to see? A prophet? Yes, I say to you, and more than a prophet.
27 "This is *he* of whom it is written:

'Behold, I send My messenger before
Your face,
Who will prepare Your way before You.'[a]

28 "For I say to you, among those born of women there is not a greater prophet than John the Baptist;[a] but he who is least in the kingdom of God is greater than he."
29 And when all the people heard *Him,* even the tax collectors justified God, having been baptized with the baptism of John.
➤ 30 But the Pharisees and lawyers rejected the will of God for themselves, not having been baptized by him.
31 And the Lord said,[a] "To what then shall I liken the men of this generation, and what are they like?
32 "They are like children sitting in the marketplace and calling to one another, saying:

'We played the flute for you,
And you did not dance;
We mourned to you,
And you did not weep.'

33 "For John the Baptist came neither eating bread nor drinking wine, and you say, 'He has a demon.'
34 "The Son of Man has come eating and drinking, and you say, 'Look, a glutton and a winebibber, a friend of tax collectors and sinners!'
35 "But wisdom is justified by all her children."

A Sinful Woman Forgiven

36 Then one of the Pharisees asked Him to eat with him. And He went to the Pharisee's house, and sat down to eat.
37 And behold, a woman in the city who was a sinner, when she knew that *Jesus* sat at the table in the Pharisee's house, brought an alabaster flask of fragrant oil,
38 and stood at His feet behind *Him* weeping; and she began to wash His feet with her tears, and wiped *them* with the hair of her head; and she kissed His feet and anointed *them* with the fragrant oil.
39 Now when the Pharisee who had invited Him saw *this,* he spoke to himself, saying, "This Man, if He were a prophet, would know who and what manner of woman *this is* who is touching Him, for she is a sinner."
40 And Jesus answered and said to him, "Simon, I have something to say to you." So he said, "Teacher, say it."
41 "There was a certain creditor who had two debtors. One owed five hundred denarii, and the other fifty.
42 "And when they had nothing with which to repay, he freely forgave them both. Tell Me, therefore, which of them will love him more?"
43 Simon answered and said, "I suppose the

7:19 [a]NU-Text reads *the Lord.* **7:27** [a]Malachi 3:1 **7:28** [a]NU-Text reads *there is none greater than John.* **7:31** [a]NU-Text and M-Text omit *And the Lord said.*

LIFE LESSONS

➤ 7:21 — *And that very hour He cured many of infirmities, afflictions, and evil spirits; and to many blind He gave sight.*

In prison, John had begun to doubt whether Jesus was the promised Messiah. In His grace, the Lord showed the discouraged John the truth. In the number and variety of His miracles, Jesus was doing what no Old Testament prophet had ever done.

➤ 7:30 — *But the Pharisees and lawyers rejected the will of God for themselves . . . .*

It is possible to reject the will of God for your life. This will never happen accidentally, however, or take place despite your desires. If you want God's will for your life, you can have it. But you have to choose it.

one whom he forgave more." And He said to him, "You have rightly judged."
44 Then He turned to the woman and said to Simon, "Do you see this woman? I entered your house; you gave Me no water for My feet, but she has washed My feet with her tears and wiped *them* with the hair of her head.
45 "You gave Me no kiss, but this woman has not ceased to kiss My feet since the time I came in.
46 "You did not anoint My head with oil, but this woman has anointed My feet with fragrant oil.
➤ 47 "Therefore I say to you, her sins, which *are* many, are forgiven, for she loved much. But to whom little is forgiven, *the same* loves little."
48 Then He said to her, "Your sins are forgiven."
49 And those who sat at the table with Him began to say to themselves, "Who is this who even forgives sins?"
50 Then He said to the woman, "Your faith has saved you. Go in peace."

Many Women Minister to Jesus

8 Now it came to pass, afterward, that He went through every city and village, preaching and bringing the glad tidings of the kingdom of God. And the twelve *were* with Him,
➤ 2 and certain women who had been healed of evil spirits and infirmities—Mary called Magdalene, out of whom had come seven demons,
3 and Joanna the wife of Chuza, Herod's steward, and Susanna, and many others who provided for Him[a] from their substance.

The Parable of the Sower

4 And when a great multitude had gathered, and they had come to Him from every city, He spoke by a parable:
5 "A sower went out to sow his seed. And as he sowed, some fell by the wayside; and it was trampled down, and the birds of the air devoured it.
6 "Some fell on rock; and as soon as it sprang up, it withered away because it lacked moisture.
7 "And some fell among thorns, and the thorns sprang up with it and choked it.
8 "But others fell on good ground, sprang up, and yielded a crop a hundredfold." When He had said these things He cried, "He who has ears to hear, let him hear!"

The Purpose of Parables

9 Then His disciples asked Him, saying, "What does this parable mean?"
10 And He said, "To you it has been given to know the mysteries of the kingdom of God, but to the rest *it is given* in parables, that

'Seeing they may not see,
And hearing they may not understand.'[a]

The Parable of the Sower Explained

11 "Now the parable is this: The seed is the word of God.
12 "Those by the wayside are the ones who hear; then the devil comes and takes away the word out of their hearts, lest they should believe and be saved.
13 "But the ones on the rock *are those* who, when they hear, receive the word with joy; and these have no root, who believe for a while and in time of temptation fall away.
14 "Now the ones *that* fell among thorns are those who, when they have heard, go out and are choked with cares, riches, and pleasures of life, and bring no fruit to maturity.
15 "But the ones *that* fell on the good ground are those who, having heard the word with a noble and good heart, keep *it* and bear fruit with patience.

The Parable of the Revealed Light

16 "No one, when he has lit a lamp, covers it with a vessel or puts *it* under a bed, but sets *it* on a lampstand, that those who enter may see the light.
17 "For nothing is secret that will not be revealed, nor *anything* hidden that will not be known and come to light.
18 "Therefore take heed how you hear. For whoever has, to him *more* will be given; and whoever does not have, even what he seems to have will be taken from him."

Jesus' Mother and Brothers Come to Him

19 Then His mother and brothers came to Him, and could not approach Him because of the crowd.

8:3 [a]NU-Text and M-Text read *them.* **8:10** [a]Isaiah 6:9

LIFE LESSONS

➤ 7:47 — *"But to whom little is forgiven, the same loves little."*

If we do not see the magnitude of our sin, the Lord's sacrifice will not seem large; it might even seem like overkill. But when we know the true condition of our sinful hearts, His sacrifice will inspire deep love.

➤ 8:2, 3 — *. . . and certain women . . . provided for Him from their substance.*

Luke came from a culture that largely dismissed or at least downplayed the importance of women, yet he often highlights the contributions of women in the ministry of Jesus. He thus anticipates the message of Galatians 3:28.

20 And it was told Him *by some,* who said,
"Your mother and Your brothers are standing
outside, desiring to see You."
21 But He answered and said to them, "My
mother and My brothers are these who hear
the word of God and do it."

Wind and Wave Obey Jesus

22 Now it happened, on a certain day, that He
got into a boat with His disciples. And He said
to them, "Let us cross over to the other side of
the lake." And they launched out.
23 But as they sailed He fell asleep. And a
windstorm came down on the lake, and they
were filling *with water,* and were in jeopardy.
24 And they came to Him and awoke Him,
saying, "Master, Master, we are perishing!"
Then He arose and rebuked the wind and the
raging of the water. And they ceased, and
there was a calm.
25 But He said to them, "Where is your
faith?" And they were afraid, and marveled,
saying to one another, "Who can this be? For
He commands even the winds and water, and
they obey Him!"

A Demon-Possessed Man Healed

26 Then they sailed to the country of the
Gadarenes,[a] which is opposite Galilee.
27 And when He stepped out on the land,
there met Him a certain man from the city
who had demons for a long time. And he wore
no clothes,[a] nor did he live in a house but in
the tombs.
28 When he saw Jesus, he cried out, fell down
before Him, and with a loud voice said, "What
have I to do with You, Jesus, Son of the Most
High God? I beg You, do not torment me!"
29 For He had commanded the unclean spirit
to come out of the man. For it had often seized
him, and he was kept under guard, bound
with chains and shackles; and he broke the
bonds and was driven by the demon into the
wilderness.
30 Jesus asked him, saying, "What is your
name?" And he said, "Legion," because many
demons had entered him.
31 And they begged Him that He would not
command them to go out into the abyss.
32 Now a herd of many swine was feeding
there on the mountain. So they begged Him
that He would permit them to enter them. And
He permitted them.
33 Then the demons went out of the man and
entered the swine, and the herd ran violently
down the steep place into the lake and
drowned.
34 When those who fed *them* saw what had
happened, they fled and told *it* in the city and
in the country.
35 Then they went out to see what had happened, and came to Jesus, and found the man
from whom the demons had departed, sitting
at the feet of Jesus, clothed and in his right
mind. And they were afraid.
36 They also who had seen *it* told them by
what means he who had been demon-possessed was healed.
37 Then the whole multitude of the surrounding region of the Gadarenes[a] asked Him to
depart from them, for they were seized with
great fear. And He got into the boat and returned.
38 Now the man from whom the demons had
departed begged Him that he might be with
Him. But Jesus sent him away, saying,
39 "Return to your own house, and tell what
great things God has done for you." And he
went his way and proclaimed throughout the
whole city what great things Jesus had done
for him.

A Girl Restored to Life and a Woman Healed

40 So it was, when Jesus returned, that the
multitude welcomed Him, for they were all
waiting for Him.
41 And behold, there came a man named
Jairus, and he was a ruler of the synagogue.
And he fell down at Jesus' feet and begged
Him to come to his house,
42 for he had an only daughter about twelve
years of age, and she was dying. But as He
went, the multitudes thronged Him.
43 Now a woman, having a flow of blood for
twelve years, who had spent all her livelihood
on physicians and could not be healed by any,
44 came from behind and touched the border
of His garment. And immediately her flow of
blood stopped.
45 And Jesus said, "Who touched Me?" When
all denied it, Peter and those with him[a] said,
"Master, the multitudes throng and press You,
and You say, 'Who touched Me?'"[b]
46 But Jesus said, "Somebody touched Me,
for I perceived power going out from Me."
47 Now when the woman saw that she was
not hidden, she came trembling; and falling
down before Him, she declared to Him in the
presence of all the people the reason she had
touched Him and how she was healed immediately.
48 And He said to her, "Daughter, be of good
cheer;[a] your faith has made you well. Go in
peace."
49 While He was still speaking, someone
came from the ruler of the synagogue's
house, saying to him, "Your daughter is dead.
Do not trouble the Teacher."[a]
50 But when Jesus heard *it,* He answered
him, saying, "Do not be afraid; only believe,
and she will be made well."

8:26 [a]NU-Text reads *Gerasenes.* **8:27** [a]NU-Text reads *who had demons and for a long time wore no clothes.* **8:37** [a]NU-Text reads *Gerasenes.* **8:45** [a]NU-Text omits *and those with him.* [b]NU-Text omits *and You say, 'Who touched Me?'* **8:48** [a]NU-Text omits *be of good cheer.* **8:49** [a]NU-Text adds *anymore.*

51 When He came into the house, He permitted no one to go in[a] except Peter, James, and John,[b] and the father and mother of the girl.

52 Now all wept and mourned for her; but He said, "Do not weep; she is not dead, but sleeping."

➤ 53 And they ridiculed Him, knowing that she was dead.

54 But He put them all outside,[a] took her by the hand and called, saying, "Little girl, arise."

55 Then her spirit returned, and she arose immediately. And He commanded that she be given *something* to eat.

56 And her parents were astonished, but He charged them to tell no one what had happened.

Sending Out the Twelve

9 Then He called His twelve disciples together and gave them power and authority over all demons, and to cure diseases.

2 He sent them to preach the kingdom of God and to heal the sick.

3 And He said to them, "Take nothing for the journey, neither staffs nor bag nor bread nor money; and do not have two tunics apiece.

4 "Whatever house you enter, stay there, and from there depart.

5 "And whoever will not receive you, when you go out of that city, shake off the very dust from your feet as a testimony against them."

6 So they departed and went through the towns, preaching the gospel and healing everywhere.

Herod Seeks to See Jesus

7 Now Herod the tetrarch heard of all that was done by Him; and he was perplexed, because it was said by some that John had risen from the dead,

8 and by some that Elijah had appeared, and by others that one of the old prophets had risen again.

9 Herod said, "John I have beheaded, but who is this of whom I hear such things?" So he sought to see Him.

Feeding the Five Thousand

10 And the apostles, when they had returned, told Him all that they had done. Then He took them and went aside privately into a deserted place belonging to the city called Bethsaida.

11 But when the multitudes knew *it*, they followed Him; and He received them and spoke to them about the kingdom of God, and healed those who had need of healing.

12 When the day began to wear away, the twelve came and said to Him, "Send the multitude away, that they may go into the surrounding towns and country, and lodge and get provisions; for we are in a deserted place here."

13 But He said to them, "You give them something to eat." And they said, "We have no more than five loaves and two fish, unless we go and buy food for all these people." ➤

14 For there were about five thousand men. Then He said to His disciples, "Make them sit down in groups of fifty."

15 And they did so, and made them all sit down.

16 Then He took the five loaves and the two fish, and looking up to heaven, He blessed and broke them, and gave *them* to the disciples to set before the multitude.

17 So they all ate and were filled, and twelve baskets of the leftover fragments were taken up by them.

Peter Confesses Jesus as the Christ

18 And it happened, as He was alone praying, *that* His disciples joined Him, and He asked them, saying, "Who do the crowds say that I am?" ➤

19 So they answered and said, "John the Baptist, but some *say* Elijah; and others *say* that one of the old prophets has risen again."

20 He said to them, "But who do you say that I am?" Peter answered and said, "The Christ of God."

Jesus Predicts His Death and Resurrection

21 And He strictly warned and commanded them to tell this to no one,

22 saying, "The Son of Man must suffer many things, and be rejected by the elders and chief

8:51 [a]NU-Text adds *with Him.* [b]NU-Text and M-Text read *Peter, John, and James.* **8:54** [a]NU-Text omits *put them all outside.*

LIFE LESSONS

➤ 8:53 — *And they ridiculed Him, knowing that she was dead.*

As a physician, Luke wanted his audience to know that the child Jesus healed was really and truly dead. One day, Jesus will destroy death altogether (1 Cor. 15:21); but even before then, He showed His mastery over it.

➤ 9:13 — *But He said to them, "You give them something to eat."*

The Lord will never command us to do something without also providing whatever we need to obey His command. In this case, His command seemed impossible; but He provided what He told them to give.

➤ 9:18 — *And it happened, as He was alone praying, that His disciples joined Him . . . .*

The disciples often saw Jesus off by Himself, praying to His Father. Eventually, they asked Him to teach them to pray, as He did (Luke 11:1). Do our prayer lives inspire others to want to pray as we do?

priests and scribes, and be killed, and be raised the third day."

Take Up the Cross and Follow Him

23 Then He said to *them* all, "If anyone desires to come after Me, let him deny himself, and take up his cross daily,[a] and follow Me.
24 "For whoever desires to save his life will lose it, but whoever loses his life for My sake will save it.
25 "For what profit is it to a man if he gains the whole world, and is himself destroyed or lost?
26 "For whoever is ashamed of Me and My words, of him the Son of Man will be ashamed when He comes in His *own* glory, and *in His* Father's, and of the holy angels.
27 "But I tell you truly, there are some standing here who shall not taste death till they see the kingdom of God."

Jesus Transfigured on the Mount

28 Now it came to pass, about eight days after these sayings, that He took Peter, John, and James and went up on the mountain to pray.
29 As He prayed, the appearance of His face was altered, and His robe *became* white *and* glistening.
30 And behold, two men talked with Him, who were Moses and Elijah,
31 who appeared in glory and spoke of His decease which He was about to accomplish at Jerusalem.
32 But Peter and those with him were heavy with sleep; and when they were fully awake, they saw His glory and the two men who stood with Him.
33 Then it happened, as they were parting from Him, *that* Peter said to Jesus, "Master, it is good for us to be here; and let us make three tabernacles: one for You, one for Moses, and one for Elijah"—not knowing what he said.
34 While he was saying this, a cloud came and overshadowed them; and they were fearful as they entered the cloud.
35 And a voice came out of the cloud, saying, "This is My beloved Son.[a] Hear Him!"
36 When the voice had ceased, Jesus was found alone. But they kept quiet, and told no one in those days any of the things they had seen.

A Boy Is Healed

37 Now it happened on the next day, when they had come down from the mountain, that a great multitude met Him.
38 Suddenly a man from the multitude cried out, saying, "Teacher, I implore You, look on my son, for he is my only child.
39 "And behold, a spirit seizes him, and he suddenly cries out; it convulses him so that he foams *at the mouth;* and it departs from him with great difficulty, bruising him.
40 "So I implored Your disciples to cast it out, but they could not."
41 Then Jesus answered and said, "O faithless and perverse generation, how long shall I be with you and bear with you? Bring your son here."
42 And as he was still coming, the demon threw him down and convulsed *him.* Then Jesus rebuked the unclean spirit, healed the child, and gave him back to his father.

Jesus Again Predicts His Death

43 And they were all amazed at the majesty of God. But while everyone marveled at all the things which Jesus did, He said to His disciples,
44 "Let these words sink down into your ears, for the Son of Man is about to be betrayed into the hands of men."
45 But they did not understand this saying, and it was hidden from them so that they did not perceive it; and they were afraid to ask Him about this saying.

Who Is the Greatest?

46 Then a dispute arose among them as to which of them would be greatest.
47 And Jesus, perceiving the thought of their heart, took a little child and set him by Him,
48 and said to them, "Whoever receives this little child in My name receives Me; and whoever receives Me receives Him who sent Me. For he who is least among you all will be great."

Jesus Forbids Sectarianism

49 Now John answered and said, "Master, we saw someone casting out demons in Your name, and we forbade him because he does not follow with us."
50 But Jesus said to him, "Do not forbid *him,* for he who is not against us[a] is on our[b] side."

9:23 [a]M-Text omits *daily.* **9:35** [a]NU-Text reads *This is My Son, the Chosen One.* **9:50** [a]NU-Text reads *you.* [b]NU-Text reads *your.*

LIFE LESSONS

➤ ***9:43 — And they were all amazed at the majesty of God.***

The majesty of God takes many forms. In this case, it amounted to His irresistible power over an unclean spirit. What do you think of when you consider the majesty of God? What amazes you about His majesty?

A Samaritan Village Rejects the Savior
51 Now it came to pass, when the time had
come for Him to be received up, that He
steadfastly set His face to go to Jerusalem,
52 and sent messengers before His face. And
as they went, they entered a village of the Samaritans, to prepare for Him.
53 But they did not receive Him, because His
face was *set* for the journey to Jerusalem.
54 And when His disciples James and John
saw *this,* they said, "Lord, do You want us to
command fire to come down from heaven and
consume them, just as Elijah did?"[a]
➤ 55 But He turned and rebuked them,[a] and
said, "You do not know what manner of spirit
you are of.
✳ 56 "For the Son of Man did not come to destroy men's lives but to save *them.*"[a] And they
went to another village.

The Cost of Discipleship
57 Now it happened as they journeyed on the
road, *that* someone said to Him, "Lord, I will
follow You wherever You go."
58 And Jesus said to him, "Foxes have holes
and birds of the air *have* nests, but the Son of
Man has nowhere to lay *His* head."
59 Then He said to another, "Follow Me." But
he said, "Lord, let me first go and bury my father."
60 Jesus said to him, "Let the dead bury their
own dead, but you go and preach the kingdom of God."
61 And another also said, "Lord, I will follow
You, but let me first go *and* bid them farewell
who are at my house."
62 But Jesus said to him, "No one, having put
his hand to the plow, and looking back, is fit
for the kingdom of God."

The Seventy Sent Out
10 After these things the Lord appointed
seventy others also,[a] and sent them two
by two before His face into every city and
place where He Himself was about to go.
➤ 2 Then He said to them, "The harvest truly *is*
great, but the laborers *are* few; therefore pray
the Lord of the harvest to send out laborers
into His harvest.
3 "Go your way; behold, I send you out as
lambs among wolves.
4 "Carry neither money bag, knapsack, nor
sandals; and greet no one along the road.
5 "But whatever house you enter, first say,
'Peace to this house.'
6 "And if a son of peace is there, your peace
will rest on it; if not, it will return to you.
7 "And remain in the same house, eating
and drinking such things as they give, for the
laborer is worthy of his wages. Do not go
from house to house.
8 "Whatever city you enter, and they receive
you, eat such things as are set before you.
9 "And heal the sick there, and say to them,
'The kingdom of God has come near to you.'
10 "But whatever city you enter, and they do
not receive you, go out into its streets and
say,
11 'The very dust of your city which clings to
us[a] we wipe off against you. Nevertheless
know this, that the kingdom of God has come
near you.'
12 "But[a] I say to you that it will be more tolerable in that Day for Sodom than for that city.

Woe to the Impenitent Cities
13 "Woe to you, Chorazin! Woe to you, Bethsaida! For if the mighty works which were
done in you had been done in Tyre and Sidon,
they would have repented long ago, sitting in
sackcloth and ashes.
14 "But it will be more tolerable for Tyre and
Sidon at the judgment than for you.
15 "And you, Capernaum, who are exalted to
heaven, will be brought down to Hades.[a]
16 "He who hears you hears Me, he who rejects you rejects Me, and he who rejects Me
rejects Him who sent Me."

The Seventy Return with Joy
17 Then the seventy[a] returned with joy, saying, "Lord, even the demons are subject to us
in Your name."
18 And He said to them, "I saw Satan fall like
lightning from heaven.
19 "Behold, I give you the authority to trample on serpents and scorpions, and over all
the power of the enemy, and nothing shall by
any means hurt you.

9:54 [a]NU-Text omits *just as Elijah did.* **9:55** [a]NU-Text omits the rest of this verse. **9:56** [a]NU-Text omits the first sentence of this verse. **10:1** [a]NU-Text reads *seventy-two others.* **10:11** [a]NU-Text reads *our feet.* **10:12** [a]NU-Text and M-Text omit *But.* **10:15** [a]NU-Text reads *will you be exalted to heaven? You will be thrust down to Hades!* **10:17** [a]NU-Text reads *seventy-two.*

LIFE LESSONS

➤ **9:55 — *But He turned and rebuked them, and said, "You do not know what manner of spirit you are of."***

The disciples had no idea yet of who they really were in Christ. Sometimes we too do not act like the new men and women in Christ who we really are. Yet we are new creations all the same (2 Cor. 5:17).

➤ **10:2 — *"The harvest truly is great, but the laborers are few; therefore pray the Lord of the harvest to send out laborers into His harvest."***

The Lord invites us to partner with Him in expanding His kingdom! The curious fact is that, even when he uses an angel in an evangelistic role, He still leaves the proclamation of the message to us (see Acts 10).

20 "Nevertheless do not rejoice in this, that
the spirits are subject to you, but rather[a] rejoice because your names are written in
heaven."

Jesus Rejoices in the Spirit

21 In that hour Jesus rejoiced in the Spirit
and said, "I thank You, Father, Lord of heaven
and earth, that You have hidden these things
from *the* wise and prudent and revealed them
to babes. Even so, Father, for so it seemed
good in Your sight.
22 "All[a] things have been delivered to Me by
My Father, and no one knows who the Son is
except the Father, and who the Father is except the Son, and *the one* to whom the Son
wills to reveal *Him*."
23 Then He turned to *His* disciples and said
privately, "Blessed *are* the eyes which see the
things you see;
24 "for I tell you that many prophets and
kings have desired to see what you see, and
have not seen *it*, and to hear what you hear,
and have not heard *it*."

The Parable of the Good Samaritan

25 And behold, a certain lawyer stood up and
tested Him, saying, "Teacher, what shall I do
to inherit eternal life?"
26 He said to him, "What is written in the
law? What is your reading *of it*?"
27 So he answered and said, "'*You shall love
the* LORD *your God with all your heart, with
all your soul, with all your strength, and with
all your mind*,'[a] and '*your neighbor as yourself*.'"[b]
28 And He said to him, "You have answered
rightly; do this and you will live."
29 But he, wanting to justify himself, said to
Jesus, "And who is my neighbor?"
30 Then Jesus answered and said: "A certain
man went down from Jerusalem to Jericho,
and fell among thieves, who stripped him of
his clothing, wounded *him*, and departed,
leaving *him* half dead.
31 "Now by chance a certain priest came
down that road. And when he saw him, he
passed by on the other side.
32 "Likewise a Levite, when he arrived at the
place, came and looked, and passed by on the
other side.
33 "But a certain Samaritan, as he journeyed,
came where he was. And when he saw him,
he had compassion.
34 "So he went to *him* and bandaged his
wounds, pouring on oil and wine; and he set
him on his own animal, brought him to an
inn, and took care of him.
35 "On the next day, when he departed,[a] he
took out two denarii, gave *them* to the
innkeeper, and said to him, 'Take care of him;
and whatever more you spend, when I come
again, I will repay you.'
36 "So which of these three do you think was
neighbor to him who fell among the thieves?"
37 And he said, "He who showed mercy on
him." Then Jesus said to him, "Go and do likewise."

Mary and Martha Worship and Serve

38 Now it happened as they went that He entered a certain village; and a certain woman
named Martha welcomed Him into her house.
39 And she had a sister called Mary, who also
sat at Jesus'[a] feet and heard His word.
40 But Martha was distracted with much
serving, and she approached Him and said,
"Lord, do You not care that my sister has left
me to serve alone? Therefore tell her to help
me."
41 And Jesus[a] answered and said to her,
"Martha, Martha, you are worried and troubled about many things.
42 "But one thing is needed, and Mary has
chosen that good part, which will not be
taken away from her."

The Model Prayer

11 Now it came to pass, as He was praying
in a certain place, when He ceased,
that one of His disciples said to Him, "Lord,
teach us to pray, as John also taught his disciples."
2 So He said to them, "When you pray, say:

Our Father in heaven,[a]
Hallowed be Your name.
Your kingdom come.[b]

10:20 [a]NU-Text and M-Text omit *rather.* **10:22** [a]M-Text reads *And turning to the disciples He said, "All . . .* **10:27** [a]Deuteronomy 6:5 [b]Leviticus 19:18 **10:35** [a]NU-Text omits *when he departed.* **10:39** [a]NU-Text reads *the Lord's.* **10:41** [a]NU-Text reads *the Lord.* **11:2** [a]NU-Text omits *Our* and *in heaven.* [b]NU-Text omits the rest of this verse.

LIFE LESSONS

10:20 — *"Nevertheless do not rejoice in this, that the spirits are subject to you, but rather rejoice because your names are written in heaven."*

We tend to get excited about miracles like curing cancer and casting out demons, but the Lord insists that the greatest miracle is our salvation. Evangelism is therefore a "greater work" than we imagine (see John 14:12).

10:42 — *"But one thing is needed, and Mary has chosen that good part, which will not be taken away from her."*

God created us to enjoy a deep and intimate relationship with Himself, and while works of service are important, they must never eclipse the fellowship He wants to experience with each of us.

Your will be done
On earth as *it is* in heaven.
3 Give us day by day our daily bread.
4 And forgive us our sins,
For we also forgive everyone who is indebted to us.
And do not lead us into temptation,
But deliver us from the evil one." [a]

A Friend Comes at Midnight

5 And He said to them, "Which of you shall have a friend, and go to him at midnight and say to him, 'Friend, lend me three loaves;

6 'for a friend of mine has come to me on his journey, and I have nothing to set before him';

7 "and he will answer from within and say, 'Do not trouble me; the door is now shut, and my children are with me in bed; I cannot rise and give to you'?

8 "I say to you, though he will not rise and give to him because he is his friend, yet because of his persistence he will rise and give him as many as he needs.

Keep Asking, Seeking, Knocking

9 "So I say to you, ask, and it will be given to you; seek, and you will find; knock, and it will be opened to you.

10 "For everyone who asks receives, and he who seeks finds, and to him who knocks it will be opened.

11 "If a son asks for bread[a] from any father among you, will he give him a stone? Or if *he asks* for a fish, will he give him a serpent instead of a fish?

12 "Or if he asks for an egg, will he offer him a scorpion?

13 "If you then, being evil, know how to give good gifts to your children, how much more will *your* heavenly Father give the Holy Spirit to those who ask Him!"

A House Divided Cannot Stand

14 And He was casting out a demon, and it was mute. So it was, when the demon had gone out, that the mute spoke; and the multitudes marveled.

15 But some of them said, "He casts out demons by Beelzebub,[a] the ruler of the demons."

16 Others, testing *Him*, sought from Him a sign from heaven.

17 But He, knowing their thoughts, said to them: "Every kingdom divided against itself is brought to desolation, and a house *divided* against a house falls.

18 "If Satan also is divided against himself, how will his kingdom stand? Because you say I cast out demons by Beelzebub.

19 "And if I cast out demons by Beelzebub, by whom do your sons cast *them* out? Therefore they will be your judges.

20 "But if I cast out demons with the finger of God, surely the kingdom of God has come upon you.

21 "When a strong man, fully armed, guards his own palace, his goods are in peace.

22 "But when a stronger than he comes upon him and overcomes him, he takes from him all his armor in which he trusted, and divides his spoils.

23 "He who is not with Me is against Me, and he who does not gather with Me scatters.

An Unclean Spirit Returns

24 "When an unclean spirit goes out of a man, he goes through dry places, seeking rest; and finding none, he says, 'I will return to my house from which I came.'

25 "And when he comes, he finds *it* swept and put in order.

26 "Then he goes and takes with *him* seven other spirits more wicked than himself, and they enter and dwell there; and the last *state* of that man is worse than the first."

Keeping the Word

27 And it happened, as He spoke these things, that a certain woman from the crowd raised her voice and said to Him, "Blessed *is* the womb that bore You, and *the* breasts which nursed You!"

28 But He said, "More than that, blessed *are* those who hear the word of God and keep it!"

Seeking a Sign

29 And while the crowds were thickly gathered together, He began to say, "This is an evil generation. It seeks a sign, and no sign will be given to it except the sign of Jonah the prophet.[a]

30 "For as Jonah became a sign to the Ninevites, so also the Son of Man will be to this generation.

31 "The queen of the South will rise up in the judgment with the men of this generation and condemn them, for she came from the ends of the earth to hear the wisdom of Solomon; and indeed a greater than Solomon *is* here.

11:4 [a]NU-Text omits *But deliver us from the evil one.*
11:11 [a]NU-Text omits the words from *bread* through *for* in the next sentence. **11:15** [a]NU-Text and M-Text read *Beelzebul.*
11:29 [a]NU-Text omits *the prophet.*

LIFE LESSONS

➤ ***11:28 — "More than that, blessed are those who hear the word of God and keep it!"***

God always promises to bless joyful obedience. We delight God's heart when we choose to rely on the power of the Holy Spirit to do what He commands us to do.

LIFE PRINCIPLE 21

OBEDIENCE ALWAYS BRINGS BLESSING.

LUKE 11:28

The Lord's simple requests often serve as steppingstones to life's most wonderful blessings. Simon Peter illustrates what can happen when we say yes to God.

One day a large crowd pressed around Jesus while He preached (see Luke 5:1–11). The Lord wanted to use Peter's boat as a floating platform from which to address the multitude, so He asked the future apostle to push the vessel out a little way from shore (v. 3)—not in itself a particularly remarkable request. Peter's compliance paved the way for staggering blessings. From his example, we learn how essential it is to obey God in even the smallest matters.

The noisy crowd received the first blessing of Peter's obedience; the people could now clearly hear Jesus' words. At the conclusion of the lesson, the Lord said to Peter, "Launch out into the deep and let down your nets for a catch" (v. 4)—a second opportunity to say yes or no. But this time, Peter must have felt tempted to decline. After all, he had worked the entire night for a catch but had returned empty-handed. And now this young teacher—a carpenter, by the way, not a fisherman—was telling him to go fishing again?

But notice what happened as a result of Peter's second act of obedience: on a day that he and his partners must have counted as a total loss, they pulled in not one, but *two* overflowing boatloads of fish (v. 7). Saying yes to the Lord's request resulted in a miracle that transformed the fisherman's life.

Consider three reasons why obedience is critical to the successful Christian life:

1. Obeying God in small matters is an essential step to God's greatest blessings.

Suppose Peter had said, "Look, I'm busy cleaning my nets right now. I can't help you because I'm going fishing again tonight." Or he could have said, "Why don't you ask to use that other boat, over there?" or "I've already been fishing today; it would be a waste of time to go again." If Peter had said anything other than yes, he would have missed the greatest fishing experience of his life. But because of Peter's obedience, the Lord arranged a miracle that he would never forget.

Oftentimes, God's greatest blessings come as a result of our willingness to do something that appears very insignificant. So ask yourself, "Has God been challenging me to do something seemingly unimportant that I have not yet made an effort to accomplish? Is there anything I have rationalized by saying, 'It's too difficult,' 'I don't want to,' or 'I have to pray about it first'"?

Our obedience always benefits others.

2. Our obedience always benefits others.

Think of how many people got blessed by Peter's obedience. Not only could the crowd see the Lord and hear His lesson, but Jesus Himself also benefited: preaching from the boat enabled him to sit down in comfort while He spoke (v. 3). Then, of course, Peter's friends had a very profitable day—they took in two vessels so full of fish that both began to sink. More importantly, they had the opportunity to witness something supernatural.

God often rewards others—in particular, those closest to us—as a result of our obedience. For example, no father can obey God without a blessing pouring into the lives of his wife and children. Likewise, a child's obedience will bless his or her parents.

3. When we obey God, we will never be disappointed.

God's ways never end up disappointing us.

Peter no doubt assumed that Jesus' fishing instructions would amount to a waste of time. But when he complied with the Lord's simple request, the Lord brought about a miracle that gripped him with amazement. Jesus turned an empty boat into a full one.

We, like Peter, must recognize that obeying God is *always* the wisest course of action. He can also take our emptiness—whether related to finances, relationships, or career—and change it into something splendid.

Perhaps you hesitate to obey because you fear the consequences. Remember that the same sovereign, omnipotent God who keeps your heart beating and the planets orbiting is more than able to handle the results of your obedience. I don't mean that to obey will necessarily result in the outcome you desire; in fact, an intervening trial could well precede a blessing. But even when our expectations do not line up with God's purposes, His ways never end up disappointing us. On the contrary, however He chooses to bless our obedience always proves most satisfying in the end.

See the Life Principles Index for further study.

32 "The men of Nineveh will rise up in the
judgment with this generation and condemn
it, for they repented at the preaching of Jonah; and indeed a greater than Jonah *is* here.

The Lamp of the Body

33 "No one, when he has lit a lamp, puts *it* in
a secret place or under a basket, but on a
lampstand, that those who come in may see
the light.
34 "The lamp of the body is the eye. Therefore, when your eye is good, your whole body
also is full of light. But when *your eye* is bad,
your body also *is* full of darkness.
➤ 35 "Therefore take heed that the light which
is in you is not darkness.
36 "If then your whole body *is* full of light,
having no part dark, *the* whole *body* will be
full of light, as when the bright shining of a
lamp gives you light."

Woe to the Pharisees and Lawyers

37 And as He spoke, a certain Pharisee asked
Him to dine with him. So He went in and sat
down to eat.
38 When the Pharisee saw *it,* he marveled
that He had not first washed before dinner.
39 Then the Lord said to him, "Now you
Pharisees make the outside of the cup and
dish clean, but your inward part is full of
greed and wickedness.
40 "Foolish ones! Did not He who made the
outside make the inside also?
41 "But rather give alms of such things as you
have; then indeed all things are clean to you.
42 "But woe to you Pharisees! For you tithe
mint and rue and all manner of herbs, and
pass by justice and the love of God. These you
ought to have done, without leaving the others undone.
43 "Woe to you Pharisees! For you love the
best seats in the synagogues and greetings in
the marketplaces.
44 "Woe to you, scribes and Pharisees, hypocrites![a] For you are like graves which are not
seen, and the men who walk over *them* are
not aware *of them.*"
➤ 45 Then one of the lawyers answered and
said to Him, "Teacher, by saying these things
You reproach us also."
46 And He said, "Woe to you also, lawyers!
For you load men with burdens hard to bear,
and you yourselves do not touch the burdens
with one of your fingers.
47 "Woe to you! For you build the tombs of
the prophets, and your fathers killed them.
48 "In fact, you bear witness that you approve the deeds of your fathers; for they indeed killed them, and you build their tombs.
49 "Therefore the wisdom of God also said, 'I
will send them prophets and apostles, and
some of them they will kill and persecute,'
50 "that the blood of all the prophets which
was shed from the foundation of the world
may be required of this generation,
51 "from the blood of Abel to the blood of
Zechariah who perished between the altar
and the temple. Yes, I say to you, it shall be required of this generation.
52 "Woe to you lawyers! For you have taken
away the key of knowledge. You did not enter
in yourselves, and those who were entering in
you hindered."
53 And as He said these things to them,[a] the
scribes and the Pharisees began to assail *Him*
vehemently, and to cross-examine Him about
many things,
54 lying in wait for Him, and seeking to catch
Him in something He might say, that they
might accuse Him.[a]

Beware of Hypocrisy

12 In the meantime, when an innumerable
multitude of people had gathered together, so that they trampled one another, He
began to say to His disciples first *of all,* "Beware of the leaven of the Pharisees, which is
hypocrisy.
2 "For there is nothing covered that will not
be revealed, nor hidden that will not be
known.
3 "Therefore whatever you have spoken in
the dark will be heard in the light, and what
you have spoken in the ear in inner rooms
will be proclaimed on the housetops.

Jesus Teaches the Fear of God

4 "And I say to you, My friends, do not be
afraid of those who kill the body, and after
that have no more that they can do.
5 "But I will show you whom you should fear:
Fear Him who, after He has killed, has power
to cast into hell; yes, I say to you, fear Him!

11:44 [a]NU-Text omits *scribes and Pharisees, hypocrites.*
11:53 [a]NU-Text reads *And when He left there.* **11:54** [a]NU-Text omits *and seeking* and *that they might accuse Him.*

LIFE LESSONS

➤ 11:35 — *"Therefore take heed that the light which is in you is not darkness."*

How can the "light" within us actually be "darkness"? It happens when we mistake religious dogmatism and man-made tradition for genuine spirituality—"zeal for God, but not according to knowledge" (Rom. 10:2).

➤ 11:45 — *Then one of the lawyers answered and said to Him, "Teacher, by saying these things You reproach us also."*

Although Jesus knew how to answer tough questions and delight the masses, He did not neglect the truth to remain popular. He never shrank from rebuking those who needed it. He still doesn't.

6 "Are not five sparrows sold for two copper
coins?[a] And not one of them is forgotten before God.
7 "But the very hairs of your head are all
numbered. Do not fear therefore; you are of
more value than many sparrows.

Confess Christ Before Men

8 "Also I say to you, whoever confesses Me
before men, him the Son of Man also will confess before the angels of God.
9 "But he who denies Me before men will be
denied before the angels of God.
10 "And anyone who speaks a word against
the Son of Man, it will be forgiven him; but to
him who blasphemes against the Holy Spirit,
it will not be forgiven.
11 "Now when they bring you to the synagogues and magistrates and authorities, do
not worry about how or what you should answer, or what you should say.
12 "For the Holy Spirit will teach you in that
very hour what you ought to say."

The Parable of the Rich Fool

13 Then one from the crowd said to Him,
"Teacher, tell my brother to divide the inheritance with me."
14 But He said to him, "Man, who made Me a
judge or an arbitrator over you?"
15 And He said to them, "Take heed and beware of covetousness,[a] for one's life does not
consist in the abundance of the things he possesses."
16 Then He spoke a parable to them, saying:
"The ground of a certain rich man yielded
plentifully.
17 "And he thought within himself, saying,
'What shall I do, since I have no room to store
my crops?'
18 "So he said, 'I will do this: I will pull down
my barns and build greater, and there I will
store all my crops and my goods.
19 'And I will say to my soul, "Soul, you have
many goods laid up for many years; take your
ease; eat, drink, *and* be merry."'
20 "But God said to him, 'Fool! This night
your soul will be required of you; then whose
will those things be which you have provided?'
21 "So *is* he who lays up treasure for himself,
and is not rich toward God."

Do Not Worry

22 Then He said to His disciples, "Therefore I
say to you, do not worry about your life, what
you will eat; nor about the body, what you will
put on.
23 "Life is more than food, and the body *is*
more than clothing.
24 "Consider the ravens, for they neither sow
nor reap, which have neither storehouse nor
barn; and God feeds them. Of how much
more value are you than the birds?
25 "And which of you by worrying can add
one cubit to his stature?
26 "If you then are not able to do *the* least,
why are you anxious for the rest?
27 "Consider the lilies, how they grow: they
neither toil nor spin; and yet I say to you, even
Solomon in all his glory was not arrayed like
one of these.
28 "If then God so clothes the grass, which
today is in the field and tomorrow is thrown
into the oven, how much more *will He clothe*
you, O *you* of little faith?
29 "And do not seek what you should eat or
what you should drink, nor have an anxious
mind.
30 "For all these things the nations of the
world seek after, and your Father knows that
you need these things.
31 "But seek the kingdom of God, and all
these things[a] shall be added to you.
32 "Do not fear, little flock, for it is your Father's good pleasure to give you the kingdom.
33 "Sell what you have and give alms; provide yourselves money bags which do not
grow old, a treasure in the heavens that does
not fail, where no thief approaches nor moth
destroys.
34 "For where your treasure is, there your
heart will be also.

The Faithful Servant and the Evil Servant

35 "Let your waist be girded and *your* lamps
burning;
36 "and you yourselves be like men who wait
for their master, when he will return from the
wedding, that when he comes and knocks
they may open to him immediately.

12:6 [a]Greek *assarion,* a coin of very small value **12:15** [a]NU-Text reads *all covetousness.* **12:31** [a]NU-Text reads *His kingdom, and these things.*

LIFE LESSONS

12:6 — *"Are not five sparrows sold for two copper coins? And not one of them is forgotten before God."*

Jesus says that God remembers even the sparrows that end up for sale at a market. He knows their plight. Even so, He knows our situation. He never forgets us, even when our trials make it seem as though He has.

12:15 — *"Take heed and beware of covetousness, for one's life does not consist in the abundance of the things he possesses."*

True satisfaction in life flows out of fulfilling the purpose for which we were created, to enjoy an intimate relationship with God. As a substitute for God, acquiring material excess only makes the heart feel more hollow (see Eccl. 6:2).

➤ 37 "Blessed *are* those servants whom the master, when he comes, will find watching. Assuredly, I say to you that he will gird himself and have them sit down *to eat,* and will come and serve them.
38 "And if he should come in the second watch, or come in the third watch, and find *them* so, blessed are those servants.
39 "But know this, that if the master of the house had known what hour the thief would come, he would have watched and[a] not allowed his house to be broken into.
40 "Therefore you also be ready, for the Son of Man is coming at an hour you do not expect."
41 Then Peter said to Him, "Lord, do You speak this parable *only* to us, or to all *people?*"
42 And the Lord said, "Who then is that faithful and wise steward, whom *his* master will make ruler over his household, to give *them their* portion of food in due season?
43 "Blessed *is* that servant whom his master will find so doing when he comes.
44 "Truly, I say to you that he will make him ruler over all that he has.
45 "But if that servant says in his heart, 'My master is delaying his coming,' and begins to beat the male and female servants, and to eat and drink and be drunk,
46 "the master of that servant will come on a day when he is not looking for *him,* and at an hour when he is not aware, and will cut him in two and appoint *him* his portion with the unbelievers.
47 "And that servant who knew his master's will, and did not prepare *himself* or do according to his will, shall be beaten with many *stripes.*
➤ 48 "But he who did not know, yet committed things deserving of stripes, shall be beaten with few. For everyone to whom much is given, from him much will be required; and to whom much has been committed, of him they will ask the more.

Christ Brings Division

49 "I came to send fire on the earth, and how I wish it were already kindled!
50 "But I have a baptism to be baptized with, and how distressed I am till it is accomplished!
51 "Do *you* suppose that I came to give peace on earth? I tell you, not at all, but rather division.
52 "For from now on five in one house will be divided: three against two, and two against three.
53 "Father will be divided against son and son against father, mother against daughter and daughter against mother, mother-in-law against her daughter-in-law and daughter-in-law against her mother-in-law."

Discern the Time

54 Then He also said to the multitudes, "Whenever you see a cloud rising out of the west, immediately you say, 'A shower is coming'; and so it is.
55 "And when *you see* the south wind blow, you say, 'There will be hot weather'; and there is.
56 "Hypocrites! You can discern the face of the sky and of the earth, but how *is it* you do not discern this time?

Make Peace with Your Adversary

57 "Yes, and why, even of yourselves, do you not judge what is right?
58 "When you go with your adversary to the magistrate, make every effort along the way to settle with him, lest he drag you to the judge, the judge deliver you to the officer, and the officer throw you into prison.
59 "I tell you, you shall not depart from there till you have paid the very last mite."

Repent or Perish

13 There were present at that season some who told Him about the Galileans whose blood Pilate had mingled with their sacrifices.
2 And Jesus answered and said to them, "Do you suppose that these Galileans were worse sinners than all *other* Galileans, because they suffered such things?
3 "I tell you, no; but unless you repent you will all likewise perish. ➤

12:39 [a]NU-Text reads *he would not have allowed.*

LIFE LESSONS

➤ 12:37 — *"Blessed are those servants whom the master, when he comes, will find watching. Assuredly, I say to you that he will gird himself and have them sit down to eat, and will come and serve them."*

Servants serve and masters get served—at least, that's the way it works in this world. But Jesus says that *He,* the Master, will serve His faithful, prepared servants when He returns to settle accounts.

➤ 12:48 — *"For everyone to whom much is given, from him much will be required . . . ."*

Jesus does not give us gifts and talents and resources merely to spend them on ourselves. He gives them to us so that we might use them to expand His kingdom and to meet the needs of others, especially fellow believers.

➤ 13:3 — *"I tell you, no; but unless you repent you will all likewise perish."*

The victims of tragedies are not necessarily the recipients of divine judgment. Yet because we live in a dangerous world where tragedies occur without warning, we must always be ready to meet our God.

4 "Or those eighteen on whom the tower in Siloam fell and killed them, do you think that they were worse sinners than all *other* men who dwelt in Jerusalem?
5 "I tell you, no; but unless you repent you will all likewise perish."

The Parable of the Barren Fig Tree

6 He also spoke this parable: "A certain *man* had a fig tree planted in his vineyard, and he came seeking fruit on it and found none.
7 "Then he said to the keeper of his vineyard, 'Look, for three years I have come seeking fruit on this fig tree and find none. Cut it down; why does it use up the ground?'
8 "But he answered and said to him, 'Sir, let it alone this year also, until I dig around it and fertilize *it*.
9 'And if it bears fruit, *well*. But if not, after that[a] you can cut it down.'"

A Spirit of Infirmity

10 Now He was teaching in one of the synagogues on the Sabbath.
11 And behold, there was a woman who had a spirit of infirmity eighteen years, and was bent over and could in no way raise *herself* up.
12 But when Jesus saw her, He called *her* to *Him* and said to her, "Woman, you are loosed from your infirmity."
13 And He laid *His* hands on her, and immediately she was made straight, and glorified God.
14 But the ruler of the synagogue answered with indignation, because Jesus had healed on the Sabbath; and he said to the crowd, "There are six days on which men ought to work; therefore come and be healed on them, and not on the Sabbath day."
15 The Lord then answered him and said, "Hypocrite![a] Does not each one of you on the Sabbath loose his ox or donkey from the stall, and lead *it* away to water it?
➤ 16 "So ought not this woman, being a daughter of Abraham, whom Satan has bound—think of it—for eighteen years, be loosed from this bond on the Sabbath?"
17 And when He said these things, all His adversaries were put to shame; and all the multitude rejoiced for all the glorious things that were done by Him.

The Parable of the Mustard Seed

18 Then He said, "What is the kingdom of God like? And to what shall I compare it?
19 "It is like a mustard seed, which a man took and put in his garden; and it grew and became a large[a] tree, and the birds of the air nested in its branches."

The Parable of the Leaven

20 And again He said, "To what shall I liken the kingdom of God?
21 "It is like leaven, which a woman took and hid in three measures[a] of meal till it was all leavened."

The Narrow Way

22 And He went through the cities and villages, teaching, and journeying toward Jerusalem.
23 Then one said to Him, "Lord, are there few who are saved?" And He said to them,
24 "Strive to enter through the narrow gate, for many, I say to you, will seek to enter and will not be able. ➤
25 "When once the Master of the house has risen up and shut the door, and you begin to stand outside and knock at the door, saying, 'Lord, Lord, open for us,' and He will answer and say to you, 'I do not know you, where you are from,'
26 "then you will begin to say, 'We ate and drank in Your presence, and You taught in our streets.'
27 "But He will say, 'I tell you I do not know you, where you are from. Depart from Me, all you workers of iniquity.'
28 "There will be weeping and gnashing of teeth, when you see Abraham and Isaac and Jacob and all the prophets in the kingdom of God, and yourselves thrust out.
29 "They will come from the east and the west, from the north and the south, and sit down in the kingdom of God.
30 "And indeed there are last who will be first, and there are first who will be last."
31 On that very day[a] some Pharisees came,

13:9 [a]NU-Text reads *And if it bears fruit after that, well. But if not, you can cut it down.* **13:15** [a]NU-Text and M-Text read *Hypocrites.* **13:19** [a]NU-Text omits *large.* **13:21** [a]Greek *sata,* approximately two pecks in all **13:31** [a]NU-Text reads *In that very hour.*

LIFE LESSONS

➤ 13:16 — *"So ought not this woman, being a daughter of Abraham, whom Satan has bound—think of it—for eighteen years, be loosed from this bond on the Sabbath?"*

When we care more for keeping rules than we do for the welfare of people made in God's image, we miss the whole point of our existence. The Bible says, "love is the fulfillment of the law" (Rom. 13:10).

➤ 13:24 — *"Strive to enter through the narrow gate, for many, I say to you, will seek to enter and will not be able."*

Not all roads lead to God. Not all doors open to heaven. Jesus insisted He was the only doorway to Paradise, the only way to the Father (John 10:7; 14:6; see also Acts 4:12).

saying to Him, "Get out and depart from here,
for Herod wants to kill You."
32 And He said to them, "Go, tell that fox,
'Behold, I cast out demons and perform cures
today and tomorrow, and the third *day* I shall
be perfected.'
33 "Nevertheless I must journey today, tomorrow, and the *day* following; for it cannot
be that a prophet should perish outside of Jerusalem.

Jesus Laments over Jerusalem

34 "O Jerusalem, Jerusalem, the one who
kills the prophets and stones those who are
sent to her! How often I wanted to gather your
children together, as a hen *gathers* her brood
under *her* wings, but you were not willing!
35 "See! Your house is left to you desolate; and
assuredly,[a] I say to you, you shall not see Me
until *the time* comes when you say, *'Blessed
is He who comes in the name of the LORD!'*"[b]

A Man with Dropsy Healed on the Sabbath

14 Now it happened, as He went into the
house of one of the rulers of the Pharisees to eat bread on the Sabbath, that they
watched Him closely.
2 And behold, there was a certain man before Him who had dropsy.
3 And Jesus, answering, spoke to the
lawyers and Pharisees, saying, "Is it lawful to
heal on the Sabbath?"[a]
4 But they kept silent. And He took *him* and
healed him, and let him go.
5 Then He answered them, saying, "Which
of you, having a donkey[a] or an ox that has
fallen into a pit, will not immediately pull him
out on the Sabbath day?"
6 And they could not answer Him regarding
these things.

Take the Lowly Place

7 So He told a parable to those who were invited, when He noted how they chose the best
places, saying to them:
8 "When you are invited by anyone to a
wedding feast, do not sit down in the best
place, lest one more honorable than you be
invited by him;
9 "and he who invited you and him come
and say to you, 'Give place to this man,' and
then you begin with shame to take the lowest
place.
10 "But when you are invited, go and sit
down in the lowest place, so that when he
who invited you comes he may say to you,
'Friend, go up higher.' Then you will have
glory in the presence of those who sit at the
table with you.
11 "For whoever exalts himself will be humbled, and he who humbles himself will be exalted."
12 Then He also said to him who invited Him,
"When you give a dinner or a supper, do not
ask your friends, your brothers, your relatives, nor rich neighbors, lest they also invite
you back, and you be repaid.
13 "But when you give a feast, invite *the*
poor, *the* maimed, *the* lame, *the* blind.
14 "And you will be blessed, because they ➤
cannot repay you; for you shall be repaid at
the resurrection of the just."

The Parable of the Great Supper

15 Now when one of those who sat at the
table with Him heard these things, he said to
Him, "Blessed *is* he who shall eat bread[a] in
the kingdom of God!"
16 Then He said to him, "A certain man gave
a great supper and invited many,
17 "and sent his servant at supper time to say
to those who were invited, 'Come, for all
things are now ready.'
18 "But they all with one *accord* began to
make excuses. The first said to him, 'I have
bought a piece of ground, and I must go and
see it. I ask you to have me excused.'
19 "And another said, 'I have bought five
yoke of oxen, and I am going to test them. I
ask you to have me excused.'
20 "Still another said, 'I have married a wife,
and therefore I cannot come.'
21 "So that servant came and reported these
things to his master. Then the master of the
house, being angry, said to his servant, 'Go
out quickly into the streets and lanes of the
city, and bring in here *the* poor and *the*
maimed and *the* lame and *the* blind.'
22 "And the servant said, 'Master, it is done
as you commanded, and still there is room.'
23 "Then the master said to the servant, 'Go ➤
out into the highways and hedges, and com-

13:35 [a]NU-Text and M-Text omit *assuredly.* [b]Psalm 118:26
14:3 [a]NU-Text adds *or not.* **14:5** [a]NU-Text and M-Text read *son.*
14:15 [a]M-Text reads *dinner.*

LIFE LESSONS

➤ 14:14 — *"And you will be blessed, because they cannot repay you; for you shall be repaid at the resurrection of the just."*

No one ever outgives God. Any kind deed or blessing that we bestow upon someone else, in Jesus' name and for His sake, will be repaid, in abundance. God loves to reward His faithful people!

➤ 14:23 — *"Then the master said to the servant, 'Go out into the highways and hedges, and compel them to come in, that my house may be filled.'"*

Far from wanting to exclude people from heaven, God desires "all men to be saved and to come to the knowledge of the truth" (1 Tim. 2:4).

pel *them* to come in, that my house may be
filled.
24 'For I say to you that none of those men
who were invited shall taste my supper.'"

Leaving All to Follow Christ

25 Now great multitudes went with Him. And
He turned and said to them,
26 "If anyone comes to Me and does not hate
his father and mother, wife and children,
brothers and sisters, yes, and his own life
also, he cannot be My disciple.
27 "And whoever does not bear his cross and
come after Me cannot be My disciple.
28 "For which of you, intending to build a
tower, does not sit down first and count the
cost, whether he has *enough* to finish *it*—
29 "lest, after he has laid the foundation, and
is not able to finish, all who see *it* begin to
mock him,
30 "saying, 'This man began to build and was
not able to finish.'
31 "Or what king, going to make war against
another king, does not sit down first and consider whether he is able with ten thousand to
meet him who comes against him with twenty
thousand?
32 "Or else, while the other is still a great way
off, he sends a delegation and asks conditions
of peace.
33 "So likewise, whoever of you does not forsake all that he has cannot be My disciple.

Tasteless Salt Is Worthless

34 "Salt *is* good; but if the salt has lost its flavor, how shall it be seasoned?
35 "It is neither fit for the land nor for the
dunghill, *but* men throw it out. He who has
ears to hear, let him hear!"

The Parable of the Lost Sheep

15 Then all the tax collectors and the sinners drew near to Him to hear Him.
2 And the Pharisees and scribes complained, saying, "This Man receives sinners
and eats with them."
3 So He spoke this parable to them, saying:
4 "What man of you, having a hundred
sheep, if he loses one of them, does not leave
the ninety-nine in the wilderness, and go after
the one which is lost until he finds it?
5 "And when he has found *it*, he lays *it* on
his shoulders, rejoicing.
6 "And when he comes home, he calls together *his* friends and neighbors, saying to
them, 'Rejoice with me, for I have found my
sheep which was lost!'
7 "I say to you that likewise there will be
more joy in heaven over one sinner who repents than over ninety-nine just persons who
need no repentance.

The Parable of the Lost Coin

8 "Or what woman, having ten silver coins,[a]
if she loses one coin, does not light a lamp,
sweep the house, and search carefully until
she finds *it*?
9 "And when she has found *it*, she calls *her*
friends and neighbors together, saying, 'Rejoice with me, for I have found the piece
which I lost!'
10 "Likewise, I say to you, there is joy in the
presence of the angels of God over one sinner
who repents."

The Parable of the Lost Son

11 Then He said: "A certain man had two sons.
12 "And the younger of them said to *his* father,
'Father, give me the portion of goods that falls
to me.' So he divided to them *his* livelihood.
13 "And not many days after, the younger son
gathered all together, journeyed to a far country, and there wasted his possessions with
prodigal living.
14 "But when he had spent all, there arose a
severe famine in that land, and he began to be
in want.
15 "Then he went and joined himself to a citizen of that country, and he sent him into his
fields to feed swine.
16 "And he would gladly have filled his stomach with the pods that the swine ate, and no
one gave him *anything*.

15:8 [a]Greek *drachma*, a valuable coin often worn in a ten-piece garland by married women

LIFE LESSONS

➤ 14:26 — *"If anyone comes to Me and does not hate his father and mother, wife and children, brothers and sisters, yes, and his own life also, he cannot be My disciple."*

Jesus calls for an exclusive commitment to the Father through Him. In comparison to our love for Him, everything else—everything—should look like hatred. He alone must be enthroned in our hearts.

➤ 15:6 — *"And when he comes home, he calls together his friends and neighbors, saying to them, 'Rejoice with me, for I have found my sheep which was lost!'"*

The Lord is neither cold-hearted nor matter-of-fact about finding His lost sheep and bringing them home. He takes great joy and feels great excitement in re-establishing a close bond with His wandering creations.

➤ 15:10 — *"Likewise, I say to you, there is joy in the presence of the angels of God over one sinner who repents."*

Jesus cannot talk about heaven and about the redeemed who populate it without talking about joy and gladness. Heaven is a very happy place, because God is a very happy God.

17 "But when he came to himself, he said, 'How many of my father's hired servants have bread enough and to spare, and I perish with hunger!
18 'I will arise and go to my father, and will say to him, "Father, I have sinned against heaven and before you,
19 "and I am no longer worthy to be called your son. Make me like one of your hired servants."'
20 "And he arose and came to his father. But when he was still a great way off, his father saw him and had compassion, and ran and fell on his neck and kissed him.
21 "And the son said to him, 'Father, I have sinned against heaven and in your sight, and am no longer worthy to be called your son.'
22 "But the father said to his servants, 'Bring[a] out the best robe and put *it* on him, and put a ring on his hand and sandals on *his* feet.
23 'And bring the fatted calf here and kill *it*, and let us eat and be merry;
24 'for this my son was dead and is alive again; he was lost and is found.' And they began to be merry.
25 "Now his older son was in the field. And as he came and drew near to the house, he heard music and dancing.
26 "So he called one of the servants and asked what these things meant.
27 "And he said to him, 'Your brother has come, and because he has received him safe and sound, your father has killed the fatted calf.'
28 "But he was angry and would not go in. Therefore his father came out and pleaded with him.
29 "So he answered and said to *his* father, 'Lo, these many years I have been serving you; I never transgressed your commandment at any time; and yet you never gave me a young goat, that I might make merry with my friends.
30 'But as soon as this son of yours came, who has devoured your livelihood with harlots, you killed the fatted calf for him.'
31 "And he said to him, 'Son, you are always with me, and all that I have is yours.
➤ 32 'It was right that we should make merry and be glad, for your brother was dead and is alive again, and was lost and is found.'"

The Parable of the Unjust Steward

16 He also said to His disciples: "There was a certain rich man who had a steward, and an accusation was brought to him that this man was wasting his goods.
2 "So he called him and said to him, 'What is this I hear about you? Give an account of your stewardship, for you can no longer be steward.'
3 "Then the steward said within himself, 'What shall I do? For my master is taking the stewardship away from me. I cannot dig; I am ashamed to beg.
4 'I have resolved what to do, that when I am put out of the stewardship, they may receive me into their houses.'
5 "So he called every one of his master's debtors to *him*, and said to the first, 'How much do you owe my master?'
6 "And he said, 'A hundred measures[a] of oil.' So he said to him, 'Take your bill, and sit down quickly and write fifty.'
7 "Then he said to another, 'And how much do you owe?' So he said, 'A hundred measures[a] of wheat.' And he said to him, 'Take your bill, and write eighty.'
8 "So the master commended the unjust steward because he had dealt shrewdly. For the sons of this world are more shrewd in their generation than the sons of light.
9 "And I say to you, make friends for yourselves by unrighteous mammon, that when you fail,[a] they may receive you into an everlasting home.
10 "He who *is* faithful in *what is* least is faithful also in much; and he who is unjust in *what is* least is unjust also in much.
11 "Therefore if you have not been faithful in the unrighteous mammon, who will commit to your trust the true *riches*?
12 "And if you have not been faithful in what

15:22 [a]NU-Text reads *Quickly bring.* **16:6** [a]Greek *batos,* eight or nine gallons each (Old Testament *bath*) **16:7** [a]Greek *koros,* ten or twelve bushels each (Old Testament *kor*) **16:9** [a]NU-Text reads *it fails.*

LIFE LESSONS

➤ 15:32 — *"It was right that we should make merry and be glad, for your brother was dead and is alive again, and was lost and is found."*

Apart from a close relationship with God, we have nothing to look forward to but death. But connecting with Him on a deep level brings merriment and gladness and joy, both for us and for God.

➤ 16:8 — *For the sons of this world are more shrewd in their generation than the sons of light.*

Jesus calls us to be "wise as serpents and harmless as doves" (Matt. 10:16), but sometimes we're wise as doves and harmless as serpents. Jesus does not call us to turn off our brains, but to engage our hearts.

➤ 16:10 — *"He who is faithful in what is least is faithful also in much; and he who is unjust in what is least is unjust also in much."*

Faithfulness in the small things in the day of obscurity qualifies us for the opportunity to serve in greater and more influential ways. Be faithful where God plants you and watch what He does.

is another man's, who will give you what is
your own?
13 "No servant can serve two masters; for either he will hate the one and love the other, or
else he will be loyal to the one and despise the
other. You cannot serve God and mammon."

The Law, the Prophets, and the Kingdom

14 Now the Pharisees, who were lovers of
money, also heard all these things, and they
derided Him.
15 And He said to them, "You are those who
justify yourselves before men, but God knows
your hearts. For what is highly esteemed
among men is an abomination in the sight of
God.
16 "The law and the prophets *were* until John.
Since that time the kingdom of God has been
preached, and everyone is pressing into it.
17 "And it is easier for heaven and earth to
pass away than for one tittle of the law to fail.
18 "Whoever divorces his wife and marries
another commits adultery; and whoever marries her who is divorced from *her* husband
commits adultery.

The Rich Man and Lazarus

19 "There was a certain rich man who was
clothed in purple and fine linen and fared
sumptuously every day.
20 "But there was a certain beggar named
Lazarus, full of sores, who was laid at his gate,
21 "desiring to be fed with the crumbs which
fell[a] from the rich man's table. Moreover the
dogs came and licked his sores.
22 "So it was that the beggar died, and was
carried by the angels to Abraham's bosom.
The rich man also died and was buried.
23 "And being in torments in Hades, he lifted
up his eyes and saw Abraham afar off, and
Lazarus in his bosom.
24 "Then he cried and said, 'Father Abraham,
have mercy on me, and send Lazarus that he
may dip the tip of his finger in water and cool
my tongue; for I am tormented in this flame.'
25 "But Abraham said, 'Son, remember that
in your lifetime you received your good
things, and likewise Lazarus evil things; but
now he is comforted and you are tormented.
26 'And besides all this, between us and you
there is a great gulf fixed, so that those who
want to pass from here to you cannot, nor can
those from there pass to us.'
27 "Then he said, 'I beg you therefore, father,
that you would send him to my father's house,
28 'for I have five brothers, that he may testify to them, lest they also come to this place
of torment.'
29 "Abraham said to him, 'They have Moses
and the prophets; let them hear them.'
30 "And he said, 'No, father Abraham; but if
one goes to them from the dead, they will repent.'
31 "But he said to him, 'If they do not hear
Moses and the prophets, neither will they be
persuaded though one rise from the dead.'"

Jesus Warns of Offenses

17 Then He said to the disciples, "It is impossible that no offenses should come,
but woe *to him* through whom they do come!
2 "It would be better for him if a millstone
were hung around his neck, and he were
thrown into the sea, than that he should offend one of these little ones.
3 "Take heed to yourselves. If your brother
sins against you,[a] rebuke him; and if he repents, forgive him.
4 "And if he sins against you seven times in
a day, and seven times in a day returns to
you,[a] saying, 'I repent,' you shall forgive him."

Faith and Duty

5 And the apostles said to the Lord, "Increase our faith."
6 So the Lord said, "If you have faith as a
mustard seed, you can say to this mulberry
tree, 'Be pulled up by the roots and be planted
in the sea,' and it would obey you.
7 "And which of you, having a servant plowing or tending sheep, will say to him when he

16:21 [a]NU-Text reads *with what fell.* **17:3** [a]NU-Text omits *against you.* **17:4** [a]M-Text omits *to you.*

LIFE LESSONS

➤ 16:15 — *"For what is highly esteemed among men is an abomination in the sight of God."*

There is nothing wrong with desiring to be great; the problem arises in how we try to go about it. Human logic says the great must enforce their authority; God says the great must humbly serve.

➤ 16:31 — *"But he said to him, 'If they do not hear Moses and the prophets, neither will they be persuaded though one rise from the dead.'"*

Miracles never *make* anyone believe. Jesus performed all kinds of miracles—including raising a man named Lazarus from the dead (John 11)—and His enemies still crucified Him.

➤ 17:4 — *"And if he sins against you seven times in a day, and seven times in a day returns to you, saying, 'I repent,' you shall forgive him."*

Jesus is not encouraging irresponsible behavior on the part of the offender, but merciful and gracious behavior on the part of the offended. For "even as Christ forgave you, so you also must do" (Col. 3:13).

➤ 17:5 — *And the apostles said to the Lord, "Increase our faith."*

We do not need *more* faith to comply with the Lord's instructions, but *genuine* faith. It's not the amount that matters, but its nature. The almighty power of God can flow through any unobstructed channel.

has come in from the field, 'Come at once and
sit down to eat'?
8 "But will he not rather say to him, 'Prepare
something for my supper, and gird yourself
and serve me till I have eaten and drunk, and
afterward you will eat and drink'?
9 "Does he thank that servant because he
did the things that were commanded him? I
think not.[a]
➤ 10 "So likewise you, when you have done all
those things which you are commanded, say,
'We are unprofitable servants. We have done
what was our duty to do.'"

Ten Lepers Cleansed

11 Now it happened as He went to Jerusalem
that He passed through the midst of Samaria
and Galilee.
12 Then as He entered a certain village, there
met Him ten men who were lepers, who stood
afar off.
13 And they lifted up *their* voices and said,
"Jesus, Master, have mercy on us!"
14 So when He saw *them,* He said to them,
"Go, show yourselves to the priests." And so it
was that as they went, they were cleansed.
15 And one of them, when he saw that he was
healed, returned, and with a loud voice glorified God,
16 and fell down on *his* face at His feet, giving Him thanks. And he was a Samaritan.
17 So Jesus answered and said, "Were there
not ten cleansed? But where *are* the nine?
➤ 18 "Were there not any found who returned
to give glory to God except this foreigner?"
19 And He said to him, "Arise, go your way.
Your faith has made you well."

The Coming of the Kingdom

20 Now when He was asked by the Pharisees
when the kingdom of God would come, He
answered them and said, "The kingdom of
God does not come with observation;
21 "nor will they say, 'See here!' or 'See
there!'[a] For indeed, the kingdom of God is
within you."
22 Then He said to the disciples, "The days will
come when you will desire to see one of the
days of the Son of Man, and you will not see *it.*
23 "And they will say to you, 'Look here!' or
'Look there!'[a] Do not go after *them* or follow
them.
24 "For as the lightning that flashes out of
one *part* under heaven shines to the other
part under heaven, so also the Son of Man
will be in His day.
25 "But first He must suffer many things and
be rejected by this generation.
26 "And as it was in the days of Noah, so it
will be also in the days of the Son of Man:
27 "They ate, they drank, they married wives,
they were given in marriage, until the day
that Noah entered the ark, and the flood came
and destroyed them all.
28 "Likewise as it was also in the days of Lot:
They ate, they drank, they bought, they sold,
they planted, they built;
29 "but on the day that Lot went out of
Sodom it rained fire and brimstone from
heaven and destroyed *them* all.
30 "Even so will it be in the day when the Son
of Man is revealed.
31 "In that day, he who is on the housetop,
and his goods *are* in the house, let him not
come down to take them away. And likewise
the one who is in the field, let him not turn
back.
32 "Remember Lot's wife.
33 "Whoever seeks to save his life will lose it,
and whoever loses his life will preserve it.
34 "I tell you, in that night there will be two
men in one bed: the one will be taken and the
other will be left.
35 "Two *women* will be grinding together: the
one will be taken and the other left.
36 "Two *men* will be in the field: the one will
be taken and the other left."[a]
37 And they answered and said to Him,
"Where, Lord?" So He said to them, "Wherever the body is, there the eagles will be gathered together."

The Parable of the Persistent Widow

18 Then He spoke a parable to them, that ◄
men always ought to pray and not lose
heart,

17:9 [a]NU-Text ends verse with *commanded;* M-Text omits *him.*
17:21 [a]NU-Text reverses *here* and *there.* 17:23 [a]NU-Text reverses *here* and *there.* 17:36 [a]NU-Text and M-Text omit verse 36.

LIFE LESSONS

➤ 17:10 — *"So likewise you, when you have done all those things which you are commanded, say, 'We are unprofitable servants. We have done what was our duty to do.'"*

Jesus does not want us to grow proud over the things He enables us to accomplish by His Spirit. So Paul writes, "For if I preach the gospel, I have nothing to boast of, for necessity is laid upon me" (1 Cor. 9:16).

➤ 17:18 — *"Were there not any found who returned to give glory to God except this foreigner?"*

Oftentimes, the most unlikely people are the ones who obey God and give Him glory. God always accepts their praise and frequently uses them as the examples of a righteous heart.

➤ 18:1 — *Then He spoke a parable to them, that men always ought to pray and not lose heart . . . .*

There may be many reasons why God does not always answer our prayers quickly, but until He lets us know that we should stop praying about something, He calls us to persevere in our prayers.

WHAT THE BIBLE SAYS ABOUT GROWING IN OUR FAITH

Luke 18:1–8

While a "measure of faith" has been given to every person (Rom. 12:3), our faith is to grow. God desires that we develop great faith.

After Peter walked on the water, but then started to sink when he heard the howling wind and saw the wild waves, the Lord asked him, "O you of little faith, why did you doubt?" (Matt. 14:31). When the disciples awoke a sleeping Jesus to still the storm on the Sea of Galilee, He responded, "Why are you so fearful? How is it that you have no faith?" (Mark 4:40). In other words, Jesus was asking, "How is that you haven't used any of your faith in this situation?" Jesus clearly expected His followers to have faith, to use it, and to grow in their faith.

We grow in faith when we hear from God, obey what He says, and then acknowledge God's faithfulness to His word in our lives. If we aren't hearing from God, it's virtually impossible for us to grow in faith. The same is true if we aren't obeying Him and if we aren't looking for Him to fulfill His word in us.

God desires that we develop great faith.

A faith challenge requires consistency, endurance, perseverance, and watchfulness. We must continue to stand in faith until the thing for which God challenged us to believe comes to pass.

Jesus once told a parable about a widow who went repeatedly to a judge for justice until he responded to her. Jesus pointed out that God was not like the callous judge and said, "And shall God not avenge His own elect who cry out day and night to Him, though He bears long with them? I tell you that He will avenge them speedily." Then He added a comment about our tendency to give up too soon in matters that call for our faith to grow: "Nevertheless, when the Son of Man comes, will He really find faith on the earth?" (Luke 18:7, 8).

Persevere in your believing once you have heard God speak to you! Endure until you see the fulfillment of God's Word.

See the Life Principles Index for further study:
9. *Trusting God means looking beyond what we can see to what God sees.*
24. *To live the Christian life is to allow Jesus to live His life in and through us.*

2 saying: "There was in a certain city a judge who did not fear God nor regard man.
3 "Now there was a widow in that city; and she came to him, saying, 'Get justice for me from my adversary.'
4 "And he would not for a while; but afterward he said within himself, 'Though I do not fear God nor regard man,
5 'yet because this widow troubles me I will avenge her, lest by her continual coming she weary me.'"
6 Then the Lord said, "Hear what the unjust judge said.
7 "And shall God not avenge His own elect who cry out day and night to Him, though He bears long with them?
8 "I tell you that He will avenge them speedily. Nevertheless, when the Son of Man comes, will He really find faith on the earth?"

The Parable of the Pharisee and the Tax Collector

9 Also He spoke this parable to some who trusted in themselves that they were righteous, and despised others:
10 "Two men went up to the temple to pray, one a Pharisee and the other a tax collector.
11 "The Pharisee stood and prayed thus with himself, 'God, I thank You that I am not like other men—extortioners, unjust, adulterers, or even as this tax collector.
12 'I fast twice a week; I give tithes of all that I possess.'
13 "And the tax collector, standing afar off, would not so much as raise *his* eyes to heaven, but beat his breast, saying, 'God, be merciful to me a sinner!'
14 "I tell you, this man went down to his house justified *rather* than the other; for everyone who exalts himself will be humbled, and he who humbles himself will be exalted."

Jesus Blesses Little Children

15 Then they also brought infants to Him that He might touch them; but when the disciples saw *it,* they rebuked them.
16 But Jesus called them to *Him* and said, "Let the little children come to Me, and do not forbid them; for of such is the kingdom of God.
17 "Assuredly, I say to you, whoever does not receive the kingdom of God as a little child will by no means enter it."

Jesus Counsels the Rich Young Ruler

18 Now a certain ruler asked Him, saying, "Good Teacher, what shall I do to inherit eternal life?"
19 So Jesus said to him, "Why do you call Me good? No one *is* good but One, *that is,* God.
20 "You know the commandments: *'Do not commit adultery,' 'Do not murder,' 'Do not steal,' 'Do not bear false witness,' 'Honor your father and your mother.'*"[a]
21 And he said, "All these things I have kept from my youth."
22 So when Jesus heard these things, He said to him, "You still lack one thing. Sell all that you have and distribute to the poor, and you will have treasure in heaven; and come, follow Me."
23 But when he heard this, he became very sorrowful, for he was very rich.

With God All Things Are Possible

24 And when Jesus saw that he became very sorrowful, He said, "How hard it is for those who have riches to enter the kingdom of God!
25 "For it is easier for a camel to go through the eye of a needle than for a rich man to enter the kingdom of God."
26 And those who heard it said, "Who then can be saved?"
27 But He said, "The things which are impossible with men are possible with God."
28 Then Peter said, "See, we have left all[a] and followed You."
29 So He said to them, "Assuredly, I say to you, there is no one who has left house or parents or brothers or wife or children, for the sake of the kingdom of God,
30 "who shall not receive many times more in this present time, and in the age to come eternal life."

Jesus a Third Time Predicts His Death and Resurrection

31 Then He took the twelve aside and said to them, "Behold, we are going up to Jerusalem, and all things that are written by the prophets concerning the Son of Man will be accomplished.
32 "For He will be delivered to the Gentiles and will be mocked and insulted and spit upon.
33 "They will scourge *Him* and kill Him. And the third day He will rise again."
34 But they understood none of these things;

18:20 [a]Exodus 20:12–16; Deuteronomy 5:16–20
18:28 [a]NU-Text reads *our own.*

LIFE LESSONS

➤ **18:34 —** ***But they understood none of these things; this saying was hidden from them, and they did not know the things which were spoken.***

Why did the disciples so frequently misunderstand Jesus' words? Can we blame faulty expectations, disobedience, or some other cause? Luke says the truth was hidden from them. Those who really want to know will persevere to reach understanding.

this saying was hidden from them, and they did not know the things which were spoken.

A Blind Man Receives His Sight

35 Then it happened, as He was coming near Jericho, that a certain blind man sat by the road begging.
36 And hearing a multitude passing by, he asked what it meant.
37 So they told him that Jesus of Nazareth was passing by.
38 And he cried out, saying, "Jesus, Son of David, have mercy on me!"
39 Then those who went before warned him that he should be quiet; but he cried out all the more, "Son of David, have mercy on me!"
40 So Jesus stood still and commanded him to be brought to Him. And when he had come near, He asked him,
41 saying, "What do you want Me to do for you?" He said, "Lord, that I may receive my sight."
42 Then Jesus said to him, "Receive your sight; your faith has made you well."
43 And immediately he received his sight, and followed Him, glorifying God. And all the people, when they saw *it*, gave praise to God.

Jesus Comes to Zacchaeus' House

19 Then *Jesus* entered and passed through Jericho.
2 Now behold, *there was* a man named Zacchaeus who was a chief tax collector, and he was rich.
3 And he sought to see who Jesus was, but could not because of the crowd, for he was of short stature.
4 So he ran ahead and climbed up into a sycamore tree to see Him, for He was going to pass that *way*.
5 And when Jesus came to the place, He looked up and saw him,[a] and said to him, "Zacchaeus, make haste and come down, for today I must stay at your house."
6 So he made haste and came down, and received Him joyfully.
7 But when they saw *it*, they all complained, saying, "He has gone to be a guest with a man who is a sinner."
8 Then Zacchaeus stood and said to the Lord, "Look, Lord, I give half of my goods to the poor; and if I have taken anything from anyone by false accusation, I restore fourfold."
9 And Jesus said to him, "Today salvation has come to this house, because he also is a son of Abraham;

Life Examples:

ZACCHAEUS

A Life That Counts

LUKE 19:1–10

It wasn't easy being the most hated (and one of the shortest) men in the city, but Zacchaeus the tax collector had learned to handle it. In fact, he often overcame difficulties in unorthodox ways—which is how he ended up in a tree to get a look at the miracle worker he'd heard so much about.

Apparently, Jesus had also heard about him. "Zacchaeus," Jesus said, "make haste and come down, for today I must stay at your house" (Luke 19:5).

Within moments, Zacchaeus turned his life over to God. He stopped cheating the people and promised to restore four times all he had taken.

Zacchaeus eagerly surrendered everything he had to the Lord. For all his shortcomings, Zacchaeus realized that following the Savior was the only way to true meaning and purpose. He had spent many lonely nights counting his money; now he wanted his life to count.

See the Life Principles Index for further study:
4. The awareness of God's presence energizes us for our work.
23. You can never outgive God.

10 "for the Son of Man has come to seek and to save that which was lost."

The Parable of the Minas

11 Now as they heard these things, He spoke another parable, because He was near Jerusalem and because they thought the kingdom of God would appear immediately.

19:5 [a]NU-Text omits *and saw him.*

LIFE LESSONS

➤ 19:10 — *". . . the Son of Man has come to seek and to save that which was lost."*

Jesus came to earth, not merely to provide us with an example of godly living, but to make it possible for us to enjoy an intimate relationship with God. He did for us what we could never do on our own.

➤ 12 Therefore He said: "A certain nobleman went into a far country to receive for himself a kingdom and to return.
13 "So he called ten of his servants, delivered to them ten minas,[a] and said to them, 'Do business till I come.'
14 "But his citizens hated him, and sent a delegation after him, saying, 'We will not have this *man* to reign over us.'
15 "And so it was that when he returned, having received the kingdom, he then commanded these servants, to whom he had given the money, to be called to him, that he might know how much every man had gained by trading.
16 "Then came the first, saying, 'Master, your mina has earned ten minas.'
17 "And he said to him, 'Well *done*, good servant; because you were faithful in a very little, have authority over ten cities.'
18 "And the second came, saying, 'Master, your mina has earned five minas.'
19 "Likewise he said to him, 'You also be over five cities.'
20 "Then another came, saying, 'Master, here is your mina, which I have kept put away in a handkerchief.
21 'For I feared you, because you are an austere man. You collect what you did not deposit, and reap what you did not sow.'
22 "And he said to him, 'Out of your own mouth I will judge you, *you* wicked servant. You knew that I was an austere man, collecting what I did not deposit and reaping what I did not sow.
23 'Why then did you not put my money in the bank, that at my coming I might have collected it with interest?'
24 "And he said to those who stood by, 'Take the mina from him, and give *it* to him who has ten minas.'
25 ("But they said to him, 'Master, he has ten minas.')
26 'For I say to you, that to everyone who has will be given; and from him who does not have, even what he has will be taken away from him.
27 'But bring here those enemies of mine, who did not want me to reign over them, and slay *them* before me.'"

The Triumphal Entry

28 When He had said this, He went on ahead, going up to Jerusalem.
29 And it came to pass, when He drew near to Bethphage[a] and Bethany, at the mountain called Olivet, *that* He sent two of His disciples,
30 saying, "Go into the village opposite *you*, where as you enter you will find a colt tied, on which no one has ever sat. Loose it and bring *it here*.
31 "And if anyone asks you, 'Why are you loosing *it?*' thus you shall say to him, 'Because the Lord has need of it.'"
32 So those who were sent went their way and found *it* just as He had said to them.
33 But as they were loosing the colt, the owners of it said to them, "Why are you loosing the colt?"
34 And they said, "The Lord has need of him."
35 Then they brought him to Jesus. And they threw their own clothes on the colt, and they set Jesus on him.
36 And as He went, *many* spread their clothes on the road.
37 Then, as He was now drawing near the descent of the Mount of Olives, the whole multitude of the disciples began to rejoice and praise God with a loud voice for all the mighty works they had seen,
38 saying:

"'*Blessed is the King who comes in the*
name of the LORD!'[a]
Peace in heaven and glory in the
highest!"

39 And some of the Pharisees called to Him from the crowd, "Teacher, rebuke Your disciples."
40 But He answered and said to them, "I tell you that if these should keep silent, the stones would immediately cry out."

Jesus Weeps over Jerusalem

41 Now as He drew near, He saw the city and wept over it,
42 saying, "If you had known, even you, especially in this your day, the things *that make* for your peace! But now they are hidden from your eyes.
43 "For days will come upon you when your enemies will build an embankment around

19:13 [a]The *mina* (Greek *mna,* Hebrew *minah*) was worth about three months' salary. **19:29** [a]M-Text reads *Bethsphage.*
19:38 [a]Psalm 118:26

LIFE LESSONS

➤ 19:12 — *Therefore He said: "A certain nobleman went into a far country to receive for himself a kingdom and to return."*

Jesus gave a few clues like this one to indicate that He might not return to earth for a long time after His ascension. During His absence, we are to continue to faithfully do His work (compare John 9:4).

➤ 19:44 — *". . . you did not know the time of your visitation."*

How is it that the vast majority of people alive in Jesus' day did not realize that they were in the presence of God in the flesh? More to the point, do *we* realize it when God is doing something special in our midst?

you, surround you and close you in on every side,

44 “and level you, and your children within you, to the ground; and they will not leave in you one stone upon another, because you did not know the time of your visitation.”

Jesus Cleanses the Temple

45 Then He went into the temple and began to drive out those who bought and sold in it,[a]

46 saying to them, “It is written, *‘My house is*[a] *a house of prayer,’*[b] but you have made it a *‘den of thieves.’* ”[c]

47 And He was teaching daily in the temple. But the chief priests, the scribes, and the leaders of the people sought to destroy Him,

48 and were unable to do anything; for all the people were very attentive to hear Him.

Jesus’ Authority Questioned

20 Now it happened on one of those days, as He taught the people in the temple and preached the gospel, *that* the chief priests and the scribes, together with the elders, confronted *Him*

2 and spoke to Him, saying, “Tell us, by what authority are You doing these things? Or who is he who gave You this authority?”

3 But He answered and said to them, “I also will ask you one thing, and answer Me:

4 “The baptism of John—was it from heaven or from men?”

5 And they reasoned among themselves, saying, “If we say, ‘From heaven,’ He will say, ‘Why then[a] did you not believe him?’

6 “But if we say, ‘From men,’ all the people will stone us, for they are persuaded that John was a prophet.”

7 So they answered that they did not know where *it was* from.

8 And Jesus said to them, “Neither will I tell you by what authority I do these things.”

The Parable of the Wicked Vinedressers

9 Then He began to tell the people this parable: “A certain man planted a vineyard, leased it to vinedressers, and went into a far country for a long time.

10 “Now at vintage-time he sent a servant to the vinedressers, that they might give him some of the fruit of the vineyard. But the vinedressers beat him and sent *him* away empty-handed.

11 “Again he sent another servant; and they beat him also, treated *him* shamefully, and sent *him* away empty-handed.

12 “And again he sent a third; and they wounded him also and cast *him* out.

13 “Then the owner of the vineyard said, ‘What shall I do? I will send my beloved son. Probably they will respect *him* when they see him.’

14 “But when the vinedressers saw him, they reasoned among themselves, saying, ‘This is the heir. Come, let us kill him, that the inheritance may be ours.’

15 “So they cast him out of the vineyard and killed *him*. Therefore what will the owner of the vineyard do to them?

16 “He will come and destroy those vinedressers and give the vineyard to others.” And when they heard *it* they said, “Certainly not!”

17 Then He looked at them and said, “What then is this that is written:

> *‘The stone which the builders rejected*
> *Has become the chief cornerstone’*?[a]

18 “Whoever falls on that stone will be broken; but on whomever it falls, it will grind him to powder.”

19 And the chief priests and the scribes that very hour sought to lay hands on Him, but they feared the people[a]—for they knew He had spoken this parable against them.

The Pharisees: Is It Lawful to Pay Taxes to Caesar?

20 So they watched *Him*, and sent spies who pretended to be righteous, that they might seize on His words, in order to deliver Him to the power and the authority of the governor.

21 Then they asked Him, saying, “Teacher, we know that You say and teach rightly, and You do not show personal favoritism, but teach the way of God in truth:

22 “Is it lawful for us to pay taxes to Caesar or not?”

23 But He perceived their craftiness, and said to them, “Why do you test Me?[a]

24 “Show Me a denarius. Whose image and inscription does it have?” They answered and said, “Caesar’s.”

25 And He said to them, “Render therefore to Caesar the things that are Caesar’s, and to God the things that are God’s.”

19:45 [a]NU-Text reads *those who were selling.* **19:46** [a]NU-Text reads *shall be.* [b]Isaiah 56:7 [c]Jeremiah 7:11 **20:5** [a]NU-Text and M-Text omit *then.* **20:17** [a]Psalm 118:22 **20:19** [a]M-Text reads *but they were afraid.* **20:23** [a]NU-Text omits *Why do you test Me?*

LIFE LESSONS

➤ 20:20 — *So they watched Him, and sent spies who pretended to be righteous . . . .*

Every age has its religious phonies, ours included. Jesus told us to be on the alert for them—but even more to make sure that we do not become one of them ourselves. Each of us must guard our hearts (Prov. 4:23).

26 But they could not catch Him in His words
in the presence of the people. And they marveled at His answer and kept silent.

The Sadducees: What About the Resurrection?

27 Then some of the Sadducees, who deny
that there is a resurrection, came to *Him* and
asked Him,
28 saying: "Teacher, Moses wrote to us *that* if
a man's brother dies, having a wife, and he
dies without children, his brother should take
his wife and raise up offspring for his brother.
29 "Now there were seven brothers. And the
first took a wife, and died without children.
30 "And the second[a] took her as wife, and he
died childless.
31 "Then the third took her, and in like manner the seven also; and they left no children,[a]
and died.
32 "Last of all the woman died also.
33 "Therefore, in the resurrection, whose
wife does she become? For all seven had her
as wife."
34 Jesus answered and said to them, "The
sons of this age marry and are given in marriage.
35 "But those who are counted worthy to attain that age, and the resurrection from the
dead, neither marry nor are given in marriage;
36 "nor can they die anymore, for they are
equal to the angels and are sons of God, being
sons of the resurrection.
37 "But even Moses showed in the *burning*
bush *passage* that the dead are raised, when
he called the Lord *'the God of Abraham, the
God of Isaac, and the God of Jacob.'*[a]
38 "For He is not the God of the dead but of
the living, for all live to Him."
39 Then some of the scribes answered and
said, "Teacher, You have spoken well."
40 But after that they dared not question Him
anymore.

Jesus: How Can David Call His Descendant Lord?

41 And He said to them, "How can they say
that the Christ is the Son of David?
42 "Now David himself said in the Book of
Psalms:

' The LORD said to my Lord,
"Sit at My right hand,
43 *Till I make Your enemies Your*
footstool."'[a]

44 "Therefore David calls Him *'Lord'*; how is
He then his Son?"

Beware of the Scribes

45 Then, in the hearing of all the people, He
said to His disciples,
46 "Beware of the scribes, who desire to go
around in long robes, love greetings in the
marketplaces, the best seats in the synagogues, and the best places at feasts,
47 "who devour widows' houses, and for a
pretense make long prayers. These will receive greater condemnation."

The Widow's Two Mites

21 And He looked up and saw the rich
putting their gifts into the treasury,
2 and He saw also a certain poor widow putting in two mites.
3 So He said, "Truly I say to you that this
poor widow has put in more than all;
4 "for all these out of their abundance have
put in offerings for God,[a] but she out of her
poverty put in all the livelihood that she had."

Jesus Predicts the Destruction of the Temple

5 Then, as some spoke of the temple, how it
was adorned with beautiful stones and dona-
tions, He said,
6 "These things which you see—the days
will come in which not *one* stone shall be left
upon another that shall not be thrown down."

The Signs of the Times and the End of the Age

7 So they asked Him, saying, "Teacher, but
when will these things be? And what sign *will
there be* when these things are about to take
place?"
8 And He said: "Take heed that you not be
deceived. For many will come in My name,
saying, 'I am *He*,' and, 'The time has drawn
near.' Therefore[a] do not go after them.
9 "But when you hear of wars and commo-
tions, do not be terrified; for these things
must come to pass first, but the end *will* not
come immediately."
10 Then He said to them, "Nation will rise
against nation, and kingdom against kingdom.
11 "And there will be great earthquakes in

20:30 [a]NU-Text ends verse 30 here. **20:31** [a]NU-Text and M-Text read *the seven also left no children.* **20:37** [a]Exodus 3:6, 15 **20:43** [a]Psalm 110:1 **21:4** [a]NU-Text omits *for God.* **21:8** [a]NU-Text omits *Therefore.*

LIFE LESSONS

➤ 20:47 — *"These will receive greater condemnation."*

Just as faithful believers will receive greater rewards than those who disregard their divine assignments, so God's judgment will fall more severely on some than others. Each will receive what he has earned (Rom. 2:6).

various places, and famines and pestilences;
and there will be fearful sights and great
signs from heaven.
12 "But before all these things, they will lay
their hands on you and persecute *you*, delivering *you* up to the synagogues and prisons.
You will be brought before kings and rulers
for My name's sake.
➤ 13 "But it will turn out for you as an occasion
for testimony.
14 "Therefore settle *it* in your hearts not to
meditate beforehand on what you will answer;
✳ 15 "for I will give you a mouth and wisdom
which all your adversaries will not be able to
contradict or resist.
16 "You will be betrayed even by parents and
brothers, relatives and friends; and they will
put *some* of you to death.
17 "And you will be hated by all for My
name's sake.
➤ 18 "But not a hair of your head shall be lost.
19 "By your patience possess your souls.

The Destruction of Jerusalem

20 "But when you see Jerusalem surrounded
by armies, then know that its desolation is
near.
21 "Then let those who are in Judea flee to
the mountains, let those who are in the midst
of her depart, and let not those who are in the
country enter her.
22 "For these are the days of vengeance, that
all things which are written may be fulfilled.
23 "But woe to those who are pregnant and to
those who are nursing babies in those days!
For there will be great distress in the land and
wrath upon this people.
24 "And they will fall by the edge of the
sword, and be led away captive into all nations. And Jerusalem will be trampled by
Gentiles until the times of the Gentiles are fulfilled.

The Coming of the Son of Man

25 "And there will be signs in the sun, in the
moon, and in the stars; and on the earth distress of nations, with perplexity, the sea and
the waves roaring;
26 "men's hearts failing them from fear and
the expectation of those things which are
coming on the earth, for the powers of the
heavens will be shaken.
27 "Then they will see the Son of Man coming in a cloud with power and great glory.
28 "Now when these things begin to happen,
look up and lift up your heads, because your
redemption draws near."

The Parable of the Fig Tree

29 Then He spoke to them a parable: "Look
at the fig tree, and all the trees.
30 "When they are already budding, you see
and know for yourselves that summer is now
near.
31 "So you also, when you see these things
happening, know that the kingdom of God is
near.
32 "Assuredly, I say to you, this generation
will by no means pass away till all things take
place.
33 "Heaven and earth will pass away, but My
words will by no means pass away.

The Importance of Watching

34 "But take heed to yourselves, lest your ➤
hearts be weighed down with carousing,
drunkenness, and cares of this life, and that
Day come on you unexpectedly.
35 "For it will come as a snare on all those
who dwell on the face of the whole earth.
36 "Watch therefore, and pray always that ➤
you may be counted worthy[a] to escape all
these things that will come to pass, and to
stand before the Son of Man."
37 And in the daytime He was teaching in the
temple, but at night He went out and stayed
on the mountain called Olivet.
38 Then early in the morning all the people
came to Him in the temple to hear Him.

21:36 [a]NU-Text reads *may have strength*.

LIFE LESSONS

➤ 21:13 — *"But it will turn out for you as an occasion for testimony."*

Just as the imprisonments of the apostle Paul turned out to be divine opportunities to testify to the gospel of Christ (Acts 9:15; Phil. 1:12), so God will use persecutions to make His Word known.

➤ 21:18 — *"But not a hair of your head shall be lost."*

Jesus said that though His followers might lose their lives for His sake, yet not a hair of their head would perish. He meant that nothing was left up to chance or accident and that He would always remain in control.

➤ 21:34 — *"But take heed to yourselves, lest your hearts be weighed down with carousing, drunkenness, and cares of this life, and that Day come on you unexpectedly."*

A constant awareness that the Lord could return at any time keeps us spiritually alert and helps to make us productive for the kingdom of God. When we forget about the Second Coming, we become spiritually lazy.

➤ 21:36 — *"Watch therefore, and pray always that you may be counted worthy to escape all these things that will come to pass . . . ."*

God Himself instructs us to pray that we might escape certain kinds of trials and tribulations. We need faith to bear up under suffering, and we need faith to pray that God might spare us unnecessary suffering.

The Plot to Kill Jesus

22 Now the Feast of Unleavened Bread drew near, which is called Passover.
2 And the chief priests and the scribes sought how they might kill Him, for they feared the people.
➤ 3 Then Satan entered Judas, surnamed Iscariot, who was numbered among the twelve.
4 So he went his way and conferred with the chief priests and captains, how he might betray Him to them.
5 And they were glad, and agreed to give him money.
6 So he promised and sought opportunity to betray Him to them in the absence of the multitude.

Jesus and His Disciples Prepare the Passover

7 Then came the Day of Unleavened Bread, when the Passover must be killed.
8 And He sent Peter and John, saying, "Go and prepare the Passover for us, that we may eat."
9 So they said to Him, "Where do You want us to prepare?"
10 And He said to them, "Behold, when you have entered the city, a man will meet you carrying a pitcher of water; follow him into the house which he enters.
11 "Then you shall say to the master of the house, 'The Teacher says to you, "Where is the guest room where I may eat the Passover with My disciples?"'
12 "Then he will show you a large, furnished upper room; there make ready."
13 So they went and found it just as He had said to them, and they prepared the Passover.

Jesus Institutes the Lord's Supper

14 When the hour had come, He sat down, and the twelve[a] apostles with Him.
15 Then He said to them, "With *fervent* desire I have desired to eat this Passover with you before I suffer;
16 "for I say to you, I will no longer eat of it until it is fulfilled in the kingdom of God."
17 Then He took the cup, and gave thanks, and said, "Take this and divide *it* among yourselves;
18 "for I say to you,[a] I will not drink of the fruit of the vine until the kingdom of God comes."
19 And He took bread, gave thanks and broke *it,* and gave *it* to them, saying, "This is My body which is given for you; do this in remembrance of Me."
20 Likewise He also *took* the cup after supper, saying, "This cup *is* the new covenant in My blood, which is shed for you.
21 "But behold, the hand of My betrayer *is* with Me on the table.
22 "And truly the Son of Man goes as it has been determined, but woe to that man by whom He is betrayed!"
23 Then they began to question among themselves, which of them it was who would do this thing.

The Disciples Argue About Greatness

24 Now there was also a dispute among them, as to which of them should be considered the greatest.
25 And He said to them, "The kings of the Gentiles exercise lordship over them, and those who exercise authority over them are called 'benefactors.'
26 "But not so *among* you; on the contrary, he who is greatest among you, let him be as the younger, and he who governs as he who serves.
27 "For who *is* greater, he who sits at the table, or he who serves? *Is* it not he who sits at the table? Yet I am among you as the One who serves.
28 "But you are those who have continued with Me in My trials.
29 "And I bestow upon you a kingdom, just as My Father bestowed *one* upon Me,
30 "that you may eat and drink at My table in My kingdom, and sit on thrones judging the twelve tribes of Israel."

Jesus Predicts Peter's Denial

31 And the Lord said,[a] "Simon, Simon! Indeed, Satan has asked for you, that he may sift *you* as wheat. ◄
32 "But I have prayed for you, that your faith should not fail; and when you have returned to *Me,* strengthen your brethren."
33 But he said to Him, "Lord, I am ready to go with You, both to prison and to death."
34 Then He said, "I tell you, Peter, the rooster shall not crow this day before you will deny three times that you know Me."

22:14 [a]NU-Text omits *twelve.* **22:18** [a]NU-Text adds *from now on.* **22:31** [a]NU-Text omits *And the Lord said.*

LIFE LESSONS

➤ **22:3 — *Then Satan entered Judas, surnamed Iscariot, who was numbered among the twelve.***

Judas is the only person whom the Bible explicitly says was possessed by Satan. Many Bible scholars believe the Antichrist will be as well (Rev. 12, 13). Both men are called "the son of perdition" (John 17:12; 2 Thess. 2:3).

➤ **22:31 — *And the Lord said, "Simon, Simon! Indeed, Satan has asked for you, that he may sift you as wheat."***

When Peter denied Jesus three times, Satan was invisibly working behind the scenes to encourage his spiritual failure. We must always remain on the alert to detect the activity of our adversary (1 Pet. 5:8).

Supplies for the Road

35 And He said to them, "When I sent you without money bag, knapsack, and sandals, did you lack anything?" So they said, "Nothing."

36 Then He said to them, "But now, he who has a money bag, let him take *it,* and likewise a knapsack; and he who has no sword, let him sell his garment and buy one.

37 "For I say to you that this which is written must still be accomplished in Me: *'And He was numbered with the transgressors.'*[a] For the things concerning Me have an end."

38 So they said, "Lord, look, here *are* two swords." And He said to them, "It is enough."

The Prayer in the Garden

39 Coming out, He went to the Mount of Olives, as He was accustomed, and His disciples also followed Him.

40 When He came to the place, He said to them, "Pray that you may not enter into temptation."

41 And He was withdrawn from them about a stone's throw, and He knelt down and prayed,

42 saying, "Father, if it is Your will, take this cup away from Me; nevertheless not My will, but Yours, be done."

➤ 43 Then an angel appeared to Him from heaven, strengthening Him.

44 And being in agony, He prayed more earnestly. Then His sweat became like great drops of blood falling down to the ground.[a]

45 When He rose up from prayer, and had come to His disciples, He found them sleeping from sorrow.

46 Then He said to them, "Why do you sleep? Rise and pray, lest you enter into temptation."

Betrayal and Arrest in Gethsemane

47 And while He was still speaking, behold, a multitude; and he who was called Judas, one of the twelve, went before them and drew near to Jesus to kiss Him.

48 But Jesus said to him, "Judas, are you betraying the Son of Man with a kiss?"

49 When those around Him saw what was going to happen, they said to Him, "Lord, shall we strike with the sword?"

50 And one of them struck the servant of the high priest and cut off his right ear.

51 But Jesus answered and said, "Permit even this." And He touched his ear and healed him.

52 Then Jesus said to the chief priests, captains of the temple, and the elders who had come to Him, "Have you come out, as against a robber, with swords and clubs?

53 "When I was with you daily in the temple, you did not try to seize Me. But this is your hour, and the power of darkness."

Peter Denies Jesus, and Weeps Bitterly

54 Having arrested Him, they led *Him* and brought Him into the high priest's house. But Peter followed at a distance.

55 Now when they had kindled a fire in the midst of the courtyard and sat down together, Peter sat among them.

56 And a certain servant girl, seeing him as he sat by the fire, looked intently at him and said, "This man was also with Him."

57 But he denied Him,[a] saying, "Woman, I do not know Him."

58 And after a little while another saw him and said, "You also are of them." But Peter said, "Man, I am not!"

59 Then after about an hour had passed, another confidently affirmed, saying, "Surely this *fellow* also was with Him, for he is a Galilean."

60 But Peter said, "Man, I do not know what you are saying!" Immediately, while he was still speaking, the rooster[a] crowed.

61 And the Lord turned and looked at Peter. ➤ Then Peter remembered the word of the Lord, how He had said to him, "Before the rooster crows,[a] you will deny Me three times."

62 So Peter went out and wept bitterly.

Jesus Mocked and Beaten

63 Now the men who held Jesus mocked Him and beat Him.

64 And having blindfolded Him, they struck Him on the face and asked Him,[a] saying, "Prophesy! Who is the one who struck You?"

65 And many other things they blasphemously spoke against Him.

Jesus Faces the Sanhedrin

66 As soon as it was day, the elders of the people, both chief priests and scribes, came together and led Him into their council, saying,

---

22:37 [a]Isaiah 53:12 **22:44** [a]NU-Text brackets verses 43 and 44 as not in the original text. **22:57** [a]NU-Text reads *denied it.* **22:60** [a]NU-Text and M-Text read *a rooster.* **22:61** [a]NU-Text adds *today.* **22:64** [a]NU-Text reads *And having blindfolded Him, they asked Him.*

LIFE LESSONS

➤ 22:43 — *Then an angel appeared to Him from heaven, strengthening Him.*

During Jesus' most difficult hour, when He had to make the final decision to accept His Father's will and march to the cross, God sent Him angelic help to encourage Him. He will always give us just what we need.

➤ 22:61 — *And the Lord turned and looked at Peter.*

What kind of look was it? A look that said, "I told you so"? One that expressed compassion? Disappointment? Resignation? Sorrow? We don't know. We only know that Jesus used it to remind Peter of His prophetic word, and that look caused Peter to weep.

67 "If You are the Christ, tell us." But He said
to them, "If I tell you, you will by no means
believe.
68 "And if I also ask *you*, you will by no
means answer Me or let *Me* go.[a]
69 "Hereafter the Son of Man will sit on the
right hand of the power of God."
70 Then they all said, "Are You then the Son
of God?" So He said to them, "You *rightly* say
that I am."
71 And they said, "What further testimony do
we need? For we have heard it ourselves from
His own mouth."

Jesus Handed Over to Pontius Pilate

23 Then the whole multitude of them
arose and led Him to Pilate.
2 And they began to accuse Him, saying,
"We found this *fellow* perverting the[a] nation,
and forbidding to pay taxes to Caesar, saying
that He Himself is Christ, a King."
3 Then Pilate asked Him, saying, "Are You
the King of the Jews?" He answered him and
said, "*It is as* you say."
4 So Pilate said to the chief priests and the
crowd, "I find no fault in this Man."
5 But they were the more fierce, saying, "He
stirs up the people, teaching throughout all
Judea, beginning from Galilee to this place."

Jesus Faces Herod

6 When Pilate heard of Galilee,[a] he asked if
the Man were a Galilean.
7 And as soon as he knew that He belonged
to Herod's jurisdiction, he sent Him to Herod,
who was also in Jerusalem at that time.
➤ 8 Now when Herod saw Jesus, he was exceedingly glad; for he had desired for a long
time to see Him, because he had heard many
things about Him, and he hoped to see some
miracle done by Him.
9 Then he questioned Him with many
words, but He answered him nothing.
10 And the chief priests and scribes stood
and vehemently accused Him.
11 Then Herod, with his men of war, treated
Him with contempt and mocked *Him*, arrayed
Him in a gorgeous robe, and sent Him back to
Pilate.
12 That very day Pilate and Herod became
friends with each other, for previously they
had been at enmity with each other.

Taking the Place of Barabbas

13 Then Pilate, when he had called together
the chief priests, the rulers, and the people,
14 said to them, "You have brought this Man
to me, as one who misleads the people. And
indeed, having examined *Him* in your presence, I have found no fault in this Man concerning those things of which you accuse
Him;
15 "no, neither did Herod, for I sent you back
to him;[a] and indeed nothing deserving of
death has been done by Him.
16 "I will therefore chastise Him and release
Him"
17 (for it was necessary for him to release
one to them at the feast).[a]
18 And they all cried out at once, saying,
"Away with this *Man*, and release to us Barabbas"—
19 who had been thrown into prison for a
certain rebellion made in the city, and for
murder.
20 Pilate, therefore, wishing to release Jesus,
again called out to them.
21 But they shouted, saying, "Crucify *Him*,
crucify Him!"
22 Then he said to them the third time, "Why,
what evil has He done? I have found no reason for death in Him. I will therefore chastise
Him and let *Him* go."
23 But they were insistent, demanding with
loud voices that He be crucified. And the
voices of these men and of the chief priests
prevailed.[a]
24 So Pilate gave sentence that it should be
as they requested.
25 And he released to them[a] the one they requested, who for rebellion and murder had
been thrown into prison; but he delivered Jesus to their will.

The King on a Cross

26 Now as they led Him away, they laid hold
of a certain man, Simon a Cyrenian, who was
coming from the country, and on him they
laid the cross that he might bear *it* after Jesus.
27 And a great multitude of the people followed Him, and women who also mourned
and lamented Him.
28 But Jesus, turning to them, said, "Daughters of Jerusalem, do not weep for Me, but
weep for yourselves and for your children.

22:68 [a]NU-Text omits *also* and *Me or let Me go.* **23:2** [a]NU-Text reads *our.* **23:6** [a]NU-Text omits *of Galilee.* **23:15** [a]NU-Text reads *for he sent Him back to us.* **23:17** [a]NU-Text omits verse 17. **23:23** [a]NU-Text omits *and of the chief priests.* **23:25** [a]NU-Text and M-Text omit *to them.*

LIFE LESSONS

➤ **23:8 — *Now when Herod saw Jesus, he was exceedingly glad; for he had desired for a long time to see Him, because he . . . hoped to see some miracle done by Him.***

Herod had no interest in Jesus the Messiah or Jesus the Savior; he simply wanted to see a magic show. Jesus refused to speak a single word to the king. No one can ever manipulate Him into doing their bidding.

29 "For indeed the days are coming in which
they will say, 'Blessed *are* the barren, wombs
that never bore, and breasts which never
nursed!'
30 "Then they will begin *'to say to the mountains, "Fall on us!" and to the hills, "Cover
us!"'*[a]
31 "For if they do these things in the green
wood, what will be done in the dry?"
32 There were also two others, criminals, led
with Him to be put to death.
33 And when they had come to the place
called Calvary, there they crucified Him, and
the criminals, one on the right hand and the
other on the left.
34 Then Jesus said, "Father, forgive them, for
they do not know what they do."[a] And they divided His garments and cast lots.
35 And the people stood looking on. But even
the rulers with them sneered, saying, "He
saved others; let Him save Himself if He is the
Christ, the chosen of God."
36 The soldiers also mocked Him, coming
and offering Him sour wine,
37 and saying, "If You are the King of the
Jews, save Yourself."
38 And an inscription also was written over
Him in letters of Greek, Latin, and Hebrew:[a]

THIS IS THE KING OF THE JEWS.

39 Then one of the criminals who were
hanged blasphemed Him, saying, "If You are
the Christ,[a] save Yourself and us."
40 But the other, answering, rebuked him,
saying, "Do you not even fear God, seeing you
are under the same condemnation?
41 "And we indeed justly, for we receive the
due reward of our deeds; but this Man has
done nothing wrong."
42 Then he said to Jesus, "Lord,[a] remember
me when You come into Your kingdom."
➤ 43 And Jesus said to him, "Assuredly, I say to
you, today you will be with Me in Paradise."

Jesus Dies on the Cross

44 Now it was[a] about the sixth hour, and
there was darkness over all the earth until the
ninth hour.
45 Then the sun was darkened,[a] and the veil
of the temple was torn in two.
46 And when Jesus had cried out with a loud
voice, He said, "Father, *'into Your hands I
commit My spirit.'*"[a] Having said this, He
breathed His last.
47 So when the centurion saw what had happened, he glorified God, saying, "Certainly
this was a righteous Man!"
48 And the whole crowd who came together
to that sight, seeing what had been done, beat
their breasts and returned.
49 But all His acquaintances, and the women
who followed Him from Galilee, stood at a
distance, watching these things.

Jesus Buried in Joseph's Tomb

50 Now behold, *there was* a man named Joseph, a council member, a good and just man.
51 He had not consented to their decision
and deed. *He was* from Arimathea, a city of
the Jews, who himself was also waiting[a] for
the kingdom of God.
52 This man went to Pilate and asked for the
body of Jesus.
53 Then he took it down, wrapped it in linen,
and laid it in a tomb *that was* hewn out of the
rock, where no one had ever lain before.
54 That day was the Preparation, and the
Sabbath drew near.
55 And the women who had come with Him ➤
from Galilee followed after, and they observed the tomb and how His body was laid.
56 Then they returned and prepared spices
and fragrant oils. And they rested on the Sabbath according to the commandment.

He Is Risen

24 Now on the first *day* of the week, very
early in the morning, they, and certain
other women with them,[a] came to the tomb
bringing the spices which they had prepared.
2 But they found the stone rolled away from
the tomb.
3 Then they went in and did not find the
body of the Lord Jesus.
4 And it happened, as they were greatly[a]
perplexed about this, that behold, two men
stood by them in shining garments.
5 Then, as they were afraid and bowed *their*
faces to the earth, they said to them, "Why do
you seek the living among the dead?

23:30 [a]Hosea 10:8 **23:34** [a]NU-Text brackets the first sentence as a later addition. **23:38** [a]NU-Text omits *written* and *in letters of Greek, Latin, and Hebrew.* **23:39** [a]NU-Text reads *Are You not the Christ?* **23:42** [a]NU-Text reads *And he said, "Jesus, remember me.* **23:44** [a]NU-Text adds *already.* **23:45** [a]NU-Text reads *obscured.* **23:46** [a]Psalm 31:5 **23:51** [a]NU-Text reads *who was waiting.* **24:1** [a]NU-Text omits *and certain other women with them.* **24:4** [a]NU-Text omits *greatly.*

LIFE LESSONS

➤ 23:43 — *And Jesus said to him, "Assuredly, I say to you, today you will be with Me in Paradise."*

One thief had a change of heart while on the cross, and Jesus accepted his expression of faith as genuine. Did the thief deserve such mercy? No. None of us do. But the point is that God's grace saves us, not our merit.

➤ 23:55 — *And the women who had come with Him from Galilee followed after, and they observed the tomb and how His body was laid.*

Sometimes people who want to discredit the Resurrection claim that the disciples went to the wrong tomb. But this verse shows that the women carefully noted which tomb held Jesus' body.

6 "He is not here, but is risen! Remember how
He spoke to you when He was still in Galilee,
7 "saying, 'The Son of Man must be delivered into the hands of sinful men, and be crucified, and the third day rise again.'"
8 And they remembered His words.
9 Then they returned from the tomb and
told all these things to the eleven and to all
the rest.
10 It was Mary Magdalene, Joanna, Mary *the
mother* of James, and the other *women* with
them, who told these things to the apostles.
➤ 11 And their words seemed to them like idle
tales, and they did not believe them.
12 But Peter arose and ran to the tomb; and
stooping down, he saw the linen cloths lying[a]
by themselves; and he departed, marveling to
himself at what had happened.

The Road to Emmaus

13 Now behold, two of them were traveling
that same day to a village called Emmaus,
which was seven miles[a] from Jerusalem.
14 And they talked together of all these
things which had happened.
15 So it was, while they conversed and reasoned, that Jesus Himself drew near and went
with them.
➤ 16 But their eyes were restrained, so that
they did not know Him.
17 And He said to them, "What kind of conversation *is* this that you have with one another as you walk and are sad?"[a]
18 Then the one whose name was Cleopas
answered and said to Him, "Are You the only
stranger in Jerusalem, and have You not
known the things which happened there in
these days?"
19 And He said to them, "What things?" So
they said to Him, "The things concerning Jesus of Nazareth, who was a Prophet mighty in
deed and word before God and all the people,
20 "and how the chief priests and our rulers
delivered Him to be condemned to death, and
crucified Him.
21 "But we were hoping that it was He who
was going to redeem Israel. Indeed, besides
all this, today is the third day since these
things happened.
22 "Yes, and certain women of our company, who arrived at the tomb early, astonished us.
23 "When they did not find His body, they
came saying that they had also seen a vision
of angels who said He was alive.
24 "And certain of those *who were* with us
went to the tomb and found *it* just as the
women had said; but Him they did not see."
25 Then He said to them, "O foolish ones, and
slow of heart to believe in all that the prophets have spoken!
26 "Ought not the Christ to have suffered
these things and to enter into His glory?"
27 And beginning at Moses and all the
Prophets, He expounded to them in all the
Scriptures the things concerning Himself.

The Disciples' Eyes Opened

28 Then they drew near to the village where
they were going, and He indicated that He
would have gone farther.
29 But they constrained Him, saying, "Abide
with us, for it is toward evening, and the day
is far spent." And He went in to stay with
them.
30 Now it came to pass, as He sat at the table
with them, that He took bread, blessed and
broke *it*, and gave it to them.
31 Then their eyes were opened and they ➤
knew Him; and He vanished from their sight.
32 And they said to one another, "Did not our
heart burn within us while He talked with us
on the road, and while He opened the Scriptures to us?"
33 So they rose up that very hour and returned to Jerusalem, and found the eleven
and those *who were* with them gathered together,
34 saying, "The Lord is risen indeed, and has
appeared to Simon!"
35 And they told about the things *that had
happened* on the road, and how He was
known to them in the breaking of bread.

24:12 [a]NU-Text omits *lying.* 24:13 [a]Literally *sixty stadia*
24:17 [a]NU-Text reads *as you walk? And they stood still, looking sad.*

LIFE LESSONS

➤ 24:11 — *And their words seemed to them like idle tales, and they did not believe them.*

It took some real convincing to get the disciples to believe that Jesus really had risen from the dead. Only after they became convinced of its truth did they become powerhouse witnesses for Christ.

➤ 24:16 — *But their eyes were restrained, so that they did not know Him.*

In many accounts of the post-resurrection appearances of Jesus, the disciples did not at first recognize the Lord. Usually it took hearing His voice or seeing Him perform some recognizable action to open their eyes.

➤ 24:31 — *Then their eyes were opened and they knew Him; and He vanished from their sight.*

Why would Jesus vanish as soon as the disciples recognized Him? We might propose many theories, but they would be just that: theories. God often doesn't explain Himself. He simply calls us to trust Him.

ANSWERS TO LIFE'S QUESTIONS

How do I handle nagging doubt?

LUKE 24:38

Satan loves to use fear and doubt against believers. He knows if he can get you to question God, then maybe you will give up and abandon His will for your life. Feelings of fear often precede feelings of doubt and uncertainty. If left unattended, these runaway emotions can cause you to stop trusting God and His ability to provide for you.

A first step to defuse doubt is to determine its origin. Begin by asking yourself if your feelings of doubt have a legitimate basis. Many times we struggle with thoughts and feelings that have no validity.

Second, reading God's Word is a great way to combat fear and doubt. A daily reading program will show you many ways to handle doubt. The Book of Psalms highlights many personal battles over emotions such as fear, doubt, loneliness, and discouragement. David and others made a conscious decision to trust the Lord through tremendously difficult circumstances and found that God never once failed them.

Prayer is also essential in fighting fear and doubt. In essence, prayer is faith in action. When we pray, regardless of whether we feel like it, we make a statement of faith. We pray because we see God as the solution to what we face. If you are facing a difficult situation, don't be slow in asking God to show you the best way to handle it. If your level of trust seems low, don't worry. God is wise and kind. He wants to teach you more about Himself, not frighten you away. Your faith will increase as you get to know Him better.

Even if you don't have the emotional strength to trust God, you still can begin. God will be your strength. A. B. Simpson often told those who found themselves in a difficult spot, "When God tests you, it is a good time for you to test Him by putting His promises to the proof, and claiming from Him just as much as your trials have rendered necessary."

Always be honest with God; He knows it all anyway. Honesty breaks the pattern of doubt. The last thing Satan wants you to do is to go to God in prayer and tell Him you feel doubtful. He knows that God loves you with an eternal love and that if you come to Him for help, He will give you all the assistance you need.

See the Life Principles Index for further study:

9. Trusting God means looking beyond what we can see to what God sees.

8. Fight all your battles on your knees and you win every time.

Jesus Appears to His Disciples

36 Now as they said these things, Jesus Himself stood in the midst of them, and said to
them, "Peace to you."
37 But they were terrified and frightened,
and supposed they had seen a spirit.
38 And He said to them, "Why are you troubled? And why do doubts arise in your
hearts?
39 "Behold My hands and My feet, that it is I
Myself. Handle Me and see, for a spirit does
not have flesh and bones as you see I have."
40 When He had said this, He showed them
His hands and His feet.[a]
41 But while they still did not believe for joy,
and marveled, He said to them, "Have you any
food here?"
42 So they gave Him a piece of a broiled fish
and some honeycomb.[a]
43 And He took *it* and ate in their presence.

The Scriptures Opened

44 Then He said to them, "These *are* the
words which I spoke to you while I was still

24:40 [a]Some printed New Testaments omit this verse. It is found in nearly all Greek manuscripts. **24:42** [a]NU-Text omits *and some honeycomb.*

LIFE LESSONS

➤ **24:41 — *But while they still did not believe for joy, and marveled, He said to them, "Have you any food here?"***

Jesus had to prove to His unbelieving disciples that He was no ghost and no figment of their imagination before they would accept the truth of the Resurrection—another reason we can trust the Gospel accounts.

with you, that all things must be fulfilled
which were written in the Law of Moses and
the Prophets and *the* Psalms concerning Me."
➤ 45 And He opened their understanding, that
they might comprehend the Scriptures.
46 Then He said to them, "Thus it is written,
and thus it was necessary for the Christ to
suffer and to rise[a] from the dead the third day,
47 "and that repentance and remission of
sins should be preached in His name to all nations, beginning at Jerusalem.
48 "And you are witnesses of these things.
✳ 49 "Behold, I send the Promise of My Father
upon you; but tarry in the city of Jerusalem[a]
until you are endued with power from on high."

The Ascension
50 And He led them out as far as Bethany,
and He lifted up His hands and blessed them.
51 Now it came to pass, while He blessed
them, that He was parted from them and carried up into heaven.
52 And they worshiped Him, and returned to
Jerusalem with great joy,
53 and were continually in the temple praising and[a] blessing God. Amen.[b]

24:46 [a]NU-Text reads *written, that the Christ should suffer and rise.* **24:49** [a]NU-Text omits *of Jerusalem.* **24:53** [a]NU-Text omits *praising and.* [b]NU-Text omits *Amen.*

LIFE LESSONS

➤ 24:45 — *And He opened their understanding, that they might comprehend the Scriptures.*

It always takes God's influence to help us understand and accept the truth of His Word. Without spiritual discernment, the things of the Spirit of God are "foolishness" to the "natural man" (1 Cor. 2:14).

THE GOSPEL ACCORDING TO

JOHN

Just as every coin has two valid sides, so Jesus Christ has two natures, also both valid. While the Gospel of Luke presents Jesus in His humanity as the Son of Man, the Gospel of John showcases Christ in His divinity as the Son of God.

The writer of this final canonical Gospel was the apostle John, who, along with Peter and James, formed Jesus' inner circle of disciples. Interestingly, John never refers to himself by name, but always calls himself "the disciple whom Jesus loved" (13:23; 19:26; 20:2; 21:7, 20, 24).

John's account goes further back in time than any of the other Gospels, when the pre-incarnate Jesus as "the Word" created the universe (1:3). John thus highlights the glory of Christ as the Son of God, from His role in creation (1:14) to His miracles (2:11; 11:4), to His person (12:41), to His unique relationship with the Holy Spirit (16:14), to His return to a fully glorified state (17:5, 24).

John mentions "life" some thirty-six times, often connecting it with "light." He speaks a great deal about "believing" and always refers to Jesus' miracles as "signs," thus spotlighting their meaning for faith rather than the phenomenon itself. John uses the word "Father" 122 times and connects this term of affection with divine love, expressed both for Jesus and for His followers.

John includes an extended eyewitness description of the Upper Room meal and records several events leading up to the resurrection, the climactic proof that Jesus is who He claimed to be—the Son of God.

The Greek title of the fourth Gospel, *Kata Ioannen*, means "According to John." *Ioannes* is derived from the Hebrew name *Johanan*, "Yahweh Has Been Gracious."

Theme: John clearly states his theme and purpose: "that you may believe that Jesus is the Christ, the Son of God, and that believing you may have life in His name" (20:31).

Author: John, "the disciple Jesus loved."

Time: John was the last of the four canonical Gospels to be written. It was likely composed between A.D. 80 and 100. By then, the rest of the New Testament (other than John's writings), had been completed. It is widely believed that John wrote his Gospel in his old age while living in Ephesus in Asia Minor, where he served as the leader of the local church.

Structure: John's Gospel is not just chronological in structure, but it also has topical elements. Seven miracles ("signs") and seven "I am" statements by Christ provide thematic continuity.

As you read John, watch for several life principles that play an important role in this book:

9. Trusting God means looking beyond what we can see to what God sees. *See John 3:12; page 1233.*

21. Obedience always brings blessing. *See John 14:21–24; page 1252.*

24. To live the Christian life is to allow Jesus to live His life in and through us. *See John 15:1–8; 17:20–23; pages 1253, 1257.*

26. Adversity is a bridge to a deeper relationship with God. *See John 21:15–19; page 1262.*

The Eternal Word

1 In the beginning was the Word, and the
Word was with God, and the Word was
God.
2 He was in the beginning with God.
3 All things were made through Him, and
without Him nothing was made that was
made.
4 In Him was life, and the life was the light
of men.
5 And the light shines in the darkness, and
the darkness did not comprehend[a] it.

John's Witness: The True Light

6 There was a man sent from God, whose
name *was* John.
7 This man came for a witness, to bear witness of the Light, that all through him might
believe.
8 He was not that Light, but *was sent* to
bear witness of that Light.
9 That was the true Light which gives light
to every man coming into the world.[a]
10 He was in the world, and the world was
made through Him, and the world did not
know Him.
11 He came to His own,[a] and His own[b] did
not receive Him.
12 But as many as received Him, to them He
gave the right to become children of God, to
those who believe in His name:
13 who were born, not of blood, nor of the
will of the flesh, nor of the will of man, but of
God.

The Word Becomes Flesh

14 And the Word became flesh and dwelt
among us, and we beheld His glory, the glory
as of the only begotten of the Father, full of
grace and truth.
15 John bore witness of Him and cried out,
saying, "This was He of whom I said, 'He who
comes after me is preferred before me, for He
was before me.' "
16 And[a] of His fullness we have all received,
and grace for grace.
17 For the law was given through Moses, *but*
grace and truth came through Jesus Christ.
18 No one has seen God at any time. The only
begotten Son,[a] who is in the bosom of the Father, He has declared *Him*.

A Voice in the Wilderness

19 Now this is the testimony of John, when
the Jews sent priests and Levites from Jerusalem to ask him, "Who are you?"
20 He confessed, and did not deny, but confessed, "I am not the Christ."
21 And they asked him, "What then? Are you
Elijah?" He said, "I am not." "Are you the
Prophet?" And he answered, "No."
22 Then they said to him, "Who are you, that
we may give an answer to those who sent us?
What do you say about yourself?"
23 He said: "I *am*

'The voice of one crying in the
wilderness:
"Make straight the way of the LORD," '[a]

as the prophet Isaiah said."
24 Now those who were sent were from the
Pharisees.
25 And they asked him, saying, "Why then do
you baptize if you are not the Christ, nor Elijah, nor the Prophet?"
26 John answered them, saying, "I baptize
with water, but there stands One among you
whom you do not know.
27 "It is He who, coming after me, is preferred before me, whose sandal strap I am not
worthy to loose."
28 These things were done in Bethabara[a] beyond the Jordan, where John was baptizing.

The Lamb of God

29 The next day John saw Jesus coming toward him, and said, "Behold! The Lamb of
God who takes away the sin of the world!
30 "This is He of whom I said, 'After me
comes a Man who is preferred before me, for
He was before me.'

1:5 [a]Or *overcome* **1:9** [a]Or *That was the true Light which, coming into the world, gives light to every man.* **1:11** [a]That is, His own things or domain [b]That is, His own people **1:16** [a]NU-Text reads *For.* **1:18** [a]NU-Text reads *only begotten God.* **1:23** [a]Isaiah 40:3 **1:28** [a]NU-Text and M-Text read *Bethany.*

LIFE LESSONS

➤ 1:1 — *In the beginning was the Word, and the Word was with God, and the Word was God.*

Right at the beginning of his Gospel, John tells us that Jesus was far more than just a great teacher or a mighty prophet; in fact, He was God. Jesus is "the express image" of God's person (Heb. 1:3).

➤ 1:14 — *And the Word became flesh and dwelt among us, and we beheld His glory, the glory as of the only begotten of the Father, full of grace and truth.*

Whatever Jesus did, He did with grace. Whatever He said, He said in truth. He was not gracious some of the time and less gracious other times, any more than He varied in the amount of truth He spoke.

➤ 1:29 — *The next day John saw Jesus coming toward him, and said, "Behold! The Lamb of God who takes away the sin of the world!"*

Jesus is our Passover Lamb who willingly took the punishment we deserve (1 Cor. 5:7). God "made Him who knew no sin to be sin for us, that we might become the righteousness of God in Him" (2 Cor. 5:21).

31 "I did not know Him; but that He should
be revealed to Israel, therefore I came baptizing with water."
32 And John bore witness, saying, "I saw the
Spirit descending from heaven like a dove,
and He remained upon Him.
33 "I did not know Him, but He who sent me
to baptize with water said to me, 'Upon whom
you see the Spirit descending, and remaining
on Him, this is He who baptizes with the Holy
Spirit.'
34 "And I have seen and testified that this is
the Son of God."

The First Disciples

35 Again, the next day, John stood with two
of his disciples.
36 And looking at Jesus as He walked, he
said, "Behold the Lamb of God!"
37 The two disciples heard him speak, and
they followed Jesus.
38 Then Jesus turned, and seeing them following, said to them, "What do you seek?"
They said to Him, "Rabbi" (which is to say,
when translated, Teacher), "where are You
staying?"
39 He said to them, "Come and see." They
came and saw where He was staying, and remained with Him that day (now it was about
the tenth hour).
40 One of the two who heard John *speak,* and
followed Him, was Andrew, Simon Peter's
brother.
41 He first found his own brother Simon, and
said to him, "We have found the Messiah"
(which is translated, the Christ).
42 And he brought him to Jesus. Now when
Jesus looked at him, He said, "You are Simon
the son of Jonah.[a] You shall be called Cephas"
(which is translated, A Stone).

Philip and Nathanael

43 The following day Jesus wanted to go to
Galilee, and He found Philip and said to him,
"Follow Me."
44 Now Philip was from Bethsaida, the city of
Andrew and Peter.
45 Philip found Nathanael and said to him,
"We have found Him of whom Moses in the
law, and also the prophets, wrote—Jesus of
Nazareth, the son of Joseph."
46 And Nathanael said to him, "Can anything
good come out of Nazareth?" Philip said to
him, "Come and see."
47 Jesus saw Nathanael coming toward Him,
and said of him, "Behold, an Israelite indeed,
in whom is no deceit!"
48 Nathanael said to Him, "How do You know
me?" Jesus answered and said to him, "Before
Philip called you, when you were under the
fig tree, I saw you."
49 Nathanael answered and said to Him,
"Rabbi, You are the Son of God! You are the
King of Israel!"
50 Jesus answered and said to him, "Because
I said to you, 'I saw you under the fig tree,' do
you believe? You will see greater things than
these."
51 And He said to him, "Most assuredly, I say
to you, hereafter[a] you shall see heaven open,
and the angels of God ascending and descending upon the Son of Man."

Water Turned to Wine

2 On the third day there was a wedding in
Cana of Galilee, and the mother of Jesus
was there.
2 Now both Jesus and His disciples were invited to the wedding.
3 And when they ran out of wine, the
mother of Jesus said to Him, "They have no
wine."
4 Jesus said to her, "Woman, what does your
concern have to do with Me? My hour has not
yet come."
5 His mother said to the servants, "What- ➤
ever He says to you, do *it.*"
6 Now there were set there six waterpots of
stone, according to the manner of purification
of the Jews, containing twenty or thirty gallons apiece.
7 Jesus said to them, "Fill the waterpots with
water." And they filled them up to the brim.
8 And He said to them, "Draw *some* out
now, and take *it* to the master of the feast."
And they took *it.*
9 When the master of the feast had tasted
the water that was made wine, and did not
know where it came from (but the servants
who had drawn the water knew), the master
of the feast called the bridegroom.
10 And he said to him, "Every man at the beginning sets out the good wine, and when the
guests have well drunk, then the inferior. You
have kept the good wine until now!"
11 This beginning of signs Jesus did in Cana
of Galilee, and manifested His glory; and His
disciples believed in Him.
12 After this He went down to Capernaum,
He, His mother, His brothers, and His disciples; and they did not stay there many days.

1:42 [a]NU-Text reads *John.* **1:51** [a]NU-Text omits *hereafter.*

LIFE LESSONS

➤ ***2:5 — His mother said to the servants, "Whatever He says to you, do it."***

Jesus' mother did not understand everything her Son said or did, but she understood enough to know that it was always wise to do what He said. It still is.

Life Examples:

NICODEMUS

Unclean but Unblemished

JOHN 3:1–21

It all started at night, when Nicodemus, "the teacher of Israel," came to the Light.

Nicodemus makes three appearances in the Bible (John 3:1–21; 7:50–52; 19:39–42), and by the third time, we see that the seed Jesus planted by night blossoms in the light of a gloomy day. Nicodemus retrieved Jesus' body from the cross and prepared it for burial. According to his old way of life, Nicodemus became unclean; but in his new eternal life, he was unblemished.

Today, Nicodemus is still the teacher. We learn from him that Jesus is always there for us, night or day. We learn that in God's perfect timing, He will answer our most confounding questions. We learn that regardless of our status, nothing is more important than the life of Christ within us. And we learn that no matter how great our sacrifice, it can never compare to Christ's sacrifice.

See the Life Principles Index for further study:
12. Peace with God is the fruit of oneness with God.

Jesus Cleanses the Temple

13 Now the Passover of the Jews was at hand, and Jesus went up to Jerusalem.
14 And He found in the temple those who sold oxen and sheep and doves, and the money changers doing business.
15 When He had made a whip of cords, He drove them all out of the temple, with the sheep and the oxen, and poured out the changers' money and overturned the tables.
16 And He said to those who sold doves, "Take these things away! Do not make My Father's house a house of merchandise!"
17 Then His disciples remembered that it was written, *"Zeal for Your house has eaten*[a] *Me up."*[b]
18 So the Jews answered and said to Him, "What sign do You show to us, since You do these things?"
19 Jesus answered and said to them, "Destroy this temple, and in three days I will raise it up."
20 Then the Jews said, "It has taken forty-six years to build this temple, and will You raise it up in three days?"
21 But He was speaking of the temple of His body.
22 Therefore, when He had risen from the dead, His disciples remembered that He had said this to them;[a] and they believed the Scripture and the word which Jesus had said.

The Discerner of Hearts

23 Now when He was in Jerusalem at the Passover, during the feast, many believed in His name when they saw the signs which He did.
24 But Jesus did not commit Himself to them, because He knew all *men*,
25 and had no need that anyone should testify of man, for He knew what was in man.

The New Birth

3 There was a man of the Pharisees named Nicodemus, a ruler of the Jews.
2 This man came to Jesus by night and said to Him, "Rabbi, we know that You are a teacher come from God; for no one can do these signs that You do unless God is with him."
3 Jesus answered and said to him, "Most assuredly, I say to you, unless one is born again, he cannot see the kingdom of God."
4 Nicodemus said to Him, "How can a man be born when he is old? Can he enter a second time into his mother's womb and be born?"
5 Jesus answered, "Most assuredly, I say to you, unless one is born of water and the Spirit, he cannot enter the kingdom of God.

2:17 [a]NU-Text and M-Text read *will eat.* [b]Psalm 69:9
2:22 [a]NU-Text and M-Text omit *to them.*

LIFE LESSONS

➢ 2:17 — *Then His disciples remembered that it was written, "Zeal for Your house has eaten Me up."*

The disciples would not have been able to remember this text (Ps. 69:9) if they were not already familiar with it. For God to use His Word to encourage and instruct us, we have to spend time in it.

➢ 2:22 — *. . . when He had risen from the dead, His disciples remembered that He had said this to them; and they believed the Scripture and the word which Jesus had said.*

Sometimes we hesitate to spend time in God's Word because we don't feel as though we're getting anything out of it. But often a text does not "click" in our minds until some time later.

6 "That which is born of the flesh is flesh,
and that which is born of the Spirit is spirit.
7 "Do not marvel that I said to you, 'You
must be born again.'
8 "The wind blows where it wishes, and you
hear the sound of it, but cannot tell where it
comes from and where it goes. So is everyone
who is born of the Spirit."
9 Nicodemus answered and said to Him,
"How can these things be?"
10 Jesus answered and said to him, "Are you
the teacher of Israel, and do not know these
things?
11 "Most assuredly, I say to you, We speak
what We know and testify what We have seen,
and you do not receive Our witness.
12 "If I have told you earthly things and you
do not believe, how will you believe if I tell
you heavenly things?
13 "No one has ascended to heaven but He
who came down from heaven, *that is,* the Son
of Man who is in heaven.[a]
14 "And as Moses lifted up the serpent in the
wilderness, even so must the Son of Man be
lifted up,
15 "that whoever believes in Him should not
perish but[a] have eternal life.
16 "For God so loved the world that He gave
His only begotten Son, that whoever believes
in Him should not perish but have everlasting
life.
17 "For God did not send His Son into the
world to condemn the world, but that the
world through Him might be saved.
18 "He who believes in Him is not condemned; but he who does not believe is
condemned already, because he has not believed in the name of the only begotten Son of
God.
19 "And this is the condemnation, that the
light has come into the world, and men loved
darkness rather than light, because their
deeds were evil.
20 "For everyone practicing evil hates the
light and does not come to the light, lest his
deeds should be exposed.
21 "But he who does the truth comes to the
light, that his deeds may be clearly seen, that
they have been done in God."

John the Baptist Exalts Christ

22 After these things Jesus and His disciples
came into the land of Judea, and there He remained with them and baptized.
23 Now John also was baptizing in Aenon
near Salim, because there was much water
there. And they came and were baptized.
24 For John had not yet been thrown into
prison.
25 Then there arose a dispute between *some*
of John's disciples and the Jews about purification.
26 And they came to John and said to him,
"Rabbi, He who was with you beyond the Jordan, to whom you have testified—behold, He
is baptizing, and all are coming to Him!"
27 John answered and said, "A man can receive nothing unless it has been given to him
from heaven.
28 "You yourselves bear me witness, that I
said, 'I am not the Christ,' but, 'I have been
sent before Him.'
29 "He who has the bride is the bridegroom;
but the friend of the bridegroom, who stands
and hears him, rejoices greatly because of the
bridegroom's voice. Therefore this joy of
mine is fulfilled.
30 "He must increase, but I *must* decrease.
31 "He who comes from above is above all;
he who is of the earth is earthly and speaks of
the earth. He who comes from heaven is
above all.
32 "And what He has seen and heard, that He
testifies; and no one receives His testimony.
33 "He who has received His testimony has
certified that God is true.
34 "For He whom God has sent speaks the
words of God, for God does not give the Spirit
by measure.
35 "The Father loves the Son, and has given
all things into His hand.
36 "He who believes in the Son has everlasting life; and he who does not believe the Son
shall not see life, but the wrath of God abides
on him."

3:13 [a]NU-Text omits *who is in heaven.* **3:15** [a]NU-Text omits *not perish but.*

LIFE LESSONS

➤ 3:17 — *"For God did not send His Son into the world to condemn the world, but that the world through Him might be saved."*

While Jesus says that all judgment has been committed to Him (John 5:22), He insists that He did not come to earth to judge us but to save us. As James says, "Mercy triumphs over judgment" (James 2:13).

➤ 3:18 — *"He who believes in Him is not condemned; but he who does not believe is condemned already . . . ."*

Those who place their faith in Jesus will never be condemned, because Jesus has already taken their punishment upon Himself. But those who reject Jesus as Savior must bear the full penalty of their sins.

➤ 3:36 — *" . . . he who does not believe the Son shall not see life, but the wrath of God abides on him."*

God loves the world in the sense that He provided a sufficient sacrifice to atone for its sins in the person of His Son. But those who turn from God's love choose His wrath instead.

A Samaritan Woman Meets Her Messiah

4 Therefore, when the Lord knew that the Pharisees had heard that Jesus made and baptized more disciples than John
2 (though Jesus Himself did not baptize, but His disciples),
3 He left Judea and departed again to Galilee.
4 But He needed to go through Samaria.
5 So He came to a city of Samaria which is called Sychar, near the plot of ground that Jacob gave to his son Joseph.
6 Now Jacob's well was there. Jesus therefore, being wearied from *His* journey, sat thus by the well. It was about the sixth hour.
7 A woman of Samaria came to draw water. Jesus said to her, "Give Me a drink."
8 For His disciples had gone away into the city to buy food.
9 Then the woman of Samaria said to Him, "How is it that You, being a Jew, ask a drink from me, a Samaritan woman?" For Jews have no dealings with Samaritans.
10 Jesus answered and said to her, "If you knew the gift of God, and who it is who says to you, 'Give Me a drink,' you would have asked Him, and He would have given you living water."
11 The woman said to Him, "Sir, You have nothing to draw with, and the well is deep. Where then do You get that living water?
12 "Are You greater than our father Jacob, who gave us the well, and drank from it himself, as well as his sons and his livestock?"
13 Jesus answered and said to her, "Whoever drinks of this water will thirst again,
14 "but whoever drinks of the water that I shall give him will never thirst. But the water that I shall give him will become in him a fountain of water springing up into everlasting life."
15 The woman said to Him, "Sir, give me this water, that I may not thirst, nor come here to draw."
16 Jesus said to her, "Go, call your husband, and come here."
17 The woman answered and said, "I have no husband." Jesus said to her, "You have well said, 'I have no husband,'
18 "for you have had five husbands, and the one whom you now have is not your husband; in that you spoke truly."
19 The woman said to Him, "Sir, I perceive that You are a prophet.
20 "Our fathers worshiped on this mountain, and you *Jews* say that in Jerusalem is the place where one ought to worship."
21 Jesus said to her, "Woman, believe Me, the hour is coming when you will neither on this mountain, nor in Jerusalem, worship the Father.
22 "You worship what you do not know; we know what we worship, for salvation is of the Jews.
23 "But the hour is coming, and now is, when the true worshipers will worship the Father in spirit and truth; for the Father is seeking such to worship Him.
24 "God *is* Spirit, and those who worship Him must worship in spirit and truth."
25 The woman said to Him, "I know that Messiah is coming" (who is called Christ). "When He comes, He will tell us all things."
26 Jesus said to her, "I who speak to you am *He.*"

The Whitened Harvest

27 And at this *point* His disciples came, and they marveled that He talked with a woman; yet no one said, "What do You seek?" or, "Why are You talking with her?"
28 The woman then left her waterpot, went her way into the city, and said to the men,
29 "Come, see a Man who told me all things that I ever did. Could this be the Christ?"
30 Then they went out of the city and came to Him.
31 In the meantime His disciples urged Him, saying, "Rabbi, eat."
32 But He said to them, "I have food to eat of which you do not know."
33 Therefore the disciples said to one another, "Has anyone brought Him *anything* to eat?"
34 Jesus said to them, "My food is to do the will of Him who sent Me, and to finish His work.
35 "Do you not say, 'There are still four

LIFE LESSONS

➤ 4:10 — Jesus answered and said to her, "If you knew the gift of God, and who it is who says to you, 'Give Me a drink,' you would have asked Him, and He would have given you living water."

Even when God asks us to do certain things, it's really an invitation to receive greater things from Him. Jesus asked the woman for a drink of water so He could offer her a drink of living water.

➤ 4:23 — ". . . true worshipers will worship the Father in spirit and truth; for the Father is seeking such to worship Him."

God actively seeks men and women who will eagerly worship Him according to the truth of the Scripture and by the power of the Holy Spirit. In one sense, evangelism is nothing but seeking out authentic worshipers.

➤ 4:34 — Jesus said to them, "My food is to do the will of Him who sent Me, and to finish His work."

Jesus lived to the do the will of His Father. He wanted nothing more than to hear God's voice and please Him by depending on His Spirit to do exactly what He commanded.

ANSWERS TO LIFE'S QUESTIONS

How can I know if my worship pleases God?

JOHN 4:23, 24

Many ask, "How do I know if the way I worship pleases God?" Scripture gives few specific guidelines, other than Old Testament regulations for the Mosaic sacrificial system. But remember, *at all times* God looks at the heart of the worshiper.

Jesus tells us, "But the hour is coming, and now is, when the true worshipers will worship the Father in spirit and truth; for the Father is seeking such to worship Him. God is Spirit, and those who worship Him must worship in spirit and truth" (John 4:23, 24).

Jesus always emphasized the worshiper's heart. He felt disgusted by those who displayed their "devotion" in a pompous, attention-getting manner. He instructed us, "And when you pray, you shall not be like the hypocrites. For they love to pray standing in the synagogues and on the corners of the streets, that they may be seen by men. Assuredly, I say to you, they have their reward. But you, when you pray, go into your room, and when you have shut your door, pray to your Father who is in the secret place; and your Father who sees in secret will reward you openly" (Matt. 6:5, 6).

Nothing escapes the loving and sovereign eye of the Lord. One day, sitting in the temple, Jesus watched how people put coins in the offering box. The rich dumped in large amounts, making quite a scene. Then a poor widow put in what amounted to one cent. "So He called His disciples to Himself and said to them, 'Assuredly, I say to you that this poor widow has put in more than all those who have given to the treasury; for they all put in out of their abundance, but she out of her poverty put in all that she had, her whole livelihood'" (Mark 12:43, 44).

Are you noticing what is important to the Lord? That's right—always and ever the heart of the worshiper. Whether it is praising, giving thanks, singing, praying, or giving financially, the issue always comes down to motivation.

As you prepare to worship God in spirit and in truth, you begin to feel an excitement. Bringing glory to God is one of the primary sources of refreshment of your own spirit; that's the way God designed it. Fulfilling your purpose of worshiping Him satisfies your very being, and it helps you build intimacy in your relationship with Him.

See the Life Principles Index for further study:
1. Our intimacy with God—His highest priority for our lives—determines the impact of our lives.
12. Peace with God is the fruit of oneness with God.

months and *then* comes the harvest'? Behold,
I say to you, lift up your eyes and look at the
fields, for they are already white for harvest!
36 "And he who reaps receives wages, and
gathers fruit for eternal life, that both he who
sows and he who reaps may rejoice together.
37 "For in this the saying is true: 'One sows
and another reaps.'
38 "I sent you to reap that for which you have
not labored; others have labored, and you
have entered into their labors."

The Savior of the World

39 And many of the Samaritans of that city
believed in Him because of the word of the
woman who testified, "He told me all that I
ever did."
40 So when the Samaritans had come to
Him, they urged Him to stay with them; and
He stayed there two days.
41 And many more believed because of His
own word.
42 Then they said to the woman, "Now we believe, not because of what you said, for we
ourselves have heard *Him* and we know that
this is indeed [T]the Christ,[a] the Savior of the
world."

4:42 [a]NU-Text omits *the Christ.*

LIFE LESSONS

➤ 4:42 — *"Now we believe, not because of what you said, for we ourselves have heard Him and we know that this is indeed the Christ, the Savior of the world."*

Each of us has to make the faith our own. Our faith must become deeply personal, genuine, and an authentic expression of our heart. We must feel convinced in our own minds of the gospel's truth.

Welcome at Galilee

43 Now after the two days He departed from
there and went to Galilee.
44 For Jesus Himself testified that a prophet
has no honor in his own country.
45 So when He came to Galilee, the Galileans
received Him, having seen all the things He
did in Jerusalem at the feast; for they also had
gone to the feast.

A Nobleman's Son Healed

46 So Jesus came again to Cana of Galilee
where He had made the water wine. And
there was a certain nobleman whose son was
sick at Capernaum.
47 When he heard that Jesus had come out of
Judea into Galilee, he went to Him and implored Him to come down and heal his son,
for he was at the point of death.
48 Then Jesus said to him, "Unless you *people* see signs and wonders, you will by no
means believe."
49 The nobleman said to Him, "Sir, come
down before my child dies!"
50 Jesus said to him, "Go your way; your son
lives." So the man believed the word that Jesus spoke to him, and he went his way.
51 And as he was now going down, his servants met him and told *him,* saying, "Your son
lives!"
52 Then he inquired of them the hour when
he got better. And they said to him, "Yesterday at the seventh hour the fever left him."
53 So the father knew that *it was* at the same
hour in which Jesus said to him, "Your son
lives." And he himself believed, and his whole
household.
54 This again *is* the second sign Jesus did
when He had come out of Judea into Galilee.

A Man Healed at the Pool of Bethesda

5 After this there was a feast of the Jews,
and Jesus went up to Jerusalem.
2 Now there is in Jerusalem by the Sheep
Gate a pool, which is called in Hebrew,
Bethesda,[a] having five porches.
3 In these lay a great multitude of sick people, blind, lame, paralyzed, waiting for the
moving of the water.
4 For an angel went down at a certain time
into the pool and stirred up the water; then
whoever stepped in first, after the stirring of
the water, was made well of whatever disease
he had.[a]
5 Now a certain man was there who had an
infirmity thirty-eight years.
6 When Jesus saw him lying there, and
knew that he already had been *in that condition* a long time, He said to him, "Do you want
to be made well?"
7 The sick man answered Him, "Sir, I have
no man to put me into the pool when the
water is stirred up; but while I am coming, another steps down before me."
8 Jesus said to him, "Rise, take up your bed
and walk."
9 And immediately the man was made well,
took up his bed, and walked. And that day
was the Sabbath.
10 The Jews therefore said to him who was
cured, "It is the Sabbath; it is not lawful for
you to carry your bed."
11 He answered them, "He who made me
well said to me, 'Take up your bed and walk.'"
12 Then they asked him, "Who is the Man
who said to you, 'Take up your bed and
walk'?"
13 But the one who was healed did not know
who it was, for Jesus had withdrawn, a multitude being in *that* place.
14 Afterward Jesus found him in the temple,
and said to him, "See, you have been made
well. Sin no more, lest a worse thing come
upon you."
15 The man departed and told the Jews that
it was Jesus who had made him well.

Honor the Father and the Son

16 For this reason the Jews persecuted Jesus,
and sought to kill Him,[a] because He had done
these things on the Sabbath.
17 But Jesus answered them, "My Father has
been working until now, and I have been
working."
18 Therefore the Jews sought all the more to
kill Him, because He not only broke the Sabbath, but also said that God was His Father,
making Himself equal with God.

5:2 [a]NU-Text reads *Bethzatha.* **5:4** [a]NU-Text omits *waiting for the moving of the water* at the end of verse 3, and all of verse 4. **5:16** [a]NU-Text omits *and sought to kill Him.*

LIFE LESSONS

➤ 5:14 — *Afterward Jesus found him in the temple, and said to him, "See, you have been made well. Sin no more, lest a worse thing come upon you."*

Not all sickness is a result of sin (John 9:3), but some may be. Paul told the Corinthians that because of their sin, "many are weak and sick among you, and many sleep" (1 Cor. 11:30).

➤ 5:18 — *Therefore the Jews sought all the more to kill Him, because He not only broke the Sabbath, but also said that God was His Father, making Himself equal with God.*

Jesus' opponents understood very well that He made several claims to divinity, and He never objected that they had misunderstood. He often said He had come from heaven and would return there (John 3:13, 31; 6:33; 16:28).

19 Then Jesus answered and said to them,
"Most assuredly, I say to you, the Son can do
nothing of Himself, but what He sees the Father do; for whatever He does, the Son also
does in like manner.
20 "For the Father loves the Son, and shows
Him all things that He Himself does; and He
will show Him greater works than these, that
you may marvel.
21 "For as the Father raises the dead and
gives life to *them*, even so the Son gives life to
whom He will.
22 "For the Father judges no one, but has
committed all judgment to the Son,
23 "that all should honor the Son just as they
honor the Father. He who does not honor the
Son does not honor the Father who sent Him.

Life and Judgment Are Through the Son

✳ **24** "Most assuredly, I say to you, he who
hears My word and believes in Him who sent
Me has everlasting life, and shall not come
into judgment, but has passed from death into
life.
25 "Most assuredly, I say to you, the hour is
coming, and now is, when the dead will hear
the voice of the Son of God; and those who
hear will live.
26 "For as the Father has life in Himself, so He
has granted the Son to have life in Himself,
27 "and has given Him authority to execute
judgment also, because He is the Son of Man.
28 "Do not marvel at this; for the hour is coming in which all who are in the graves will
hear His voice
➤ 29 "and come forth—those who have done
good, to the resurrection of life, and those
who have done evil, to the resurrection of
condemnation.
➤ 30 "I can of Myself do nothing. As I hear, I
judge; and My judgment is righteous, because
I do not seek My own will but the will of the
Father who sent Me.

The Fourfold Witness

31 "If I bear witness of Myself, My witness is
not true.
32 "There is another who bears witness of
Me, and I know that the witness which He
witnesses of Me is true.
33 "You have sent to John, and he has borne
witness to the truth.
34 "Yet I do not receive testimony from man,
but I say these things that you may be saved.
35 "He was the burning and shining lamp,
and you were willing for a time to rejoice in
his light.
36 "But I have a greater witness than John's;
for the works which the Father has given
Me to finish—the very works that I do—
bear witness of Me, that the Father has
sent Me.
37 "And the Father Himself, who sent Me, has
testified of Me. You have neither heard His
voice at any time, nor seen His form.
38 "But you do not have His word abiding in
you, because whom He sent, Him you do not
believe.
39 "You search the Scriptures, for in them
you think you have eternal life; and these are
they which testify of Me.
40 "But you are not willing to come to Me
that you may have life.
41 "I do not receive honor from men.
42 "But I know you, that you do not have the
love of God in you.
43 "I have come in My Father's name, and
you do not receive Me; if another comes in his
own name, him you will receive.
44 "How can you believe, who receive honor
from one another, and do not seek the honor
that *comes* from the only God?
45 "Do not think that I shall accuse you to the
Father; there is *one* who accuses you—Moses,
in whom you trust.
46 "For if you believed Moses, you would believe Me; for he wrote about Me.
47 "But if you do not believe his writings,
how will you believe My words?"

Feeding the Five Thousand

6 After these things Jesus went over the Sea
of Galilee, which is *the Sea* of Tiberias.
2 Then a great multitude followed Him, because they saw His signs which He performed
on those who were diseased.
3 And Jesus went up on the mountain, and
there He sat with His disciples.
4 Now the Passover, a feast of the Jews, was
near.
5 Then Jesus lifted up *His* eyes, and seeing a
great multitude coming toward Him, He said
to Philip, "Where shall we buy bread, that
these may eat?"

LIFE LESSONS

➤ 5:29 — *". . . and come forth—those who have done good, to the resurrection of life, and those who have done evil, to the resurrection of condemnation."*

Every person who has ever lived will one day stand before God at the judgment, either to receive rewards for Spirit-empowered activity, or to receive condemnation for self-focused behavior.

➤ 5:30 — *"I can of Myself do nothing. As I hear, I judge; and My judgment is righteous, because I do not seek My own will but the will of the Father who sent Me."*

As the perfect reflection of His heavenly Father, Jesus spoke and acted just as God would speak or act if He were walking on earth. God the Father and God the Son always speak and act as one.

➤ 6 But this He said to test him, for He Himself
knew what He would do.
7 Philip answered Him, "Two hundred
denarii worth of bread is not sufficient for
them, that every one of them may have a little."
8 One of His disciples, Andrew, Simon Peter's brother, said to Him,
9 "There is a lad here who has five barley
loaves and two small fish, but what are they
among so many?"
10 Then Jesus said, "Make the people sit
down." Now there was much grass in the
place. So the men sat down, in number about
five thousand.
11 And Jesus took the loaves, and when He
had given thanks He distributed *them* to the
disciples, and the disciples[a] to those sitting
down; and likewise of the fish, as much as
they wanted.
12 So when they were filled, He said to His
disciples, "Gather up the fragments that remain, so that nothing is lost."
13 Therefore they gathered *them* up, and
filled twelve baskets with the fragments of
the five barley loaves which were left over by
those who had eaten.
14 Then those men, when they had seen the
sign that Jesus did, said, "This is truly the
Prophet who is to come into the world."

Jesus Walks on the Sea

15 Therefore when Jesus perceived that they
were about to come and take Him by force to
make Him king, He departed again to the
mountain by Himself alone.
16 Now when evening came, His disciples
went down to the sea,
17 got into the boat, and went over the sea toward Capernaum. And it was already dark,
and Jesus had not come to them.
18 Then the sea arose because a great wind
was blowing.
19 So when they had rowed about three or
four miles,[a] they saw Jesus walking on the sea
and drawing near the boat; and they were
afraid.
20 But He said to them, "It is I; do not be
afraid."
21 Then they willingly received Him into the
boat, and immediately the boat was at the
land where they were going.

The Bread from Heaven

22 On the following day, when the people
who were standing on the other side of the
sea saw that there was no other boat there,
except that one which His disciples had entered,[a] and that Jesus had not entered the
boat with His disciples, but His disciples had
gone away alone—
23 however, other boats came from Tiberias,
near the place where they ate bread after the
Lord had given thanks—
24 when the people therefore saw that Jesus
was not there, nor His disciples, they also got
into boats and came to Capernaum, seeking
Jesus.
25 And when they found Him on the other
side of the sea, they said to Him, "Rabbi,
when did You come here?"
26 Jesus answered them and said, "Most assuredly, I say to you, you seek Me, not because you saw the signs, but because you ate
of the loaves and were filled.
27 "Do not labor for the food which perishes,
but for the food which endures to everlasting
life, which the Son of Man will give you, because God the Father has set His seal on
Him."
28 Then they said to Him, "What shall we do,
that we may work the works of God?"
29 Jesus answered and said to them, "This is
the work of God, that you believe in Him
whom He sent."
30 Therefore they said to Him, "What sign
will You perform then, that we may see it and
believe You? What work will You do?
31 "Our fathers ate the manna in the desert;
as it is written, *'He gave them bread from
heaven to eat.'*"[a]
32 Then Jesus said to them, "Most assuredly,
I say to you, Moses did not give you the bread
from heaven, but My Father gives you the true
bread from heaven.
33 "For the bread of God is He who comes
down from heaven and gives life to the
world."
34 Then they said to Him, "Lord, give us this
bread always."
35 And Jesus said to them, "I am the bread of
life. He who comes to Me shall never hunger,
and he who believes in Me shall never thirst.
36 "But I said to you that you have seen Me
and yet do not believe.

6:11 [a]NU-Text omits *to the disciples, and the disciples.*
6:19 [a]Literally *twenty-five or thirty stadia* **6:22** [a]NU-Text omits *that* and *which His disciples had entered.* **6:31** [a]Exodus 16:4; Nehemiah 9:15; Psalm 78:24

LIFE LESSONS

➤ **6:6 — *But this He said to test him, for He Himself knew what He would do.***

Before Jesus ever sets before us an "impossible" task, He knows what He is going to do. But He watches us and tests us to see how we will react—either in fear, confusion, or faith.

✳ 37 "All that the Father gives Me will come to
Me, and the one who comes to Me I will by no
means cast out.
➤ 38 "For I have come down from heaven, not
to do My own will, but the will of Him who
sent Me.
39 "This is the will of the Father who sent Me,
that of all He has given Me I should lose nothing, but should raise it up at the last day.
40 "And this is the will of Him who sent Me,
that everyone who sees the Son and believes
in Him may have everlasting life; and I will
raise him up at the last day."

Rejected by His Own

41 The Jews then complained about Him, because He said, "I am the bread which came
down from heaven."
42 And they said, "Is not this Jesus, the son of
Joseph, whose father and mother we know?
How is it then that He says, 'I have come
down from heaven'?"
43 Jesus therefore answered and said to
them, "Do not murmur among yourselves.
44 "No one can come to Me unless the Father
who sent Me draws him; and I will raise him
up at the last day.
45 "It is written in the prophets, *'And they
shall all be taught by God.'*[a] Therefore everyone who has heard and learned[b] from the Father comes to Me.
46 "Not that anyone has seen the Father, except He who is from God; He has seen the Father.
47 "Most assuredly, I say to you, he who believes in Me[a] has everlasting life.
48 "I am the bread of life.
49 "Your fathers ate the manna in the wilderness, and are dead.
50 "This is the bread which comes down from
heaven, that one may eat of it and not die.
51 "I am the living bread which came down
from heaven. If anyone eats of this bread, he
will live forever; and the bread that I shall
give is My flesh, which I shall give for the life
of the world."
52 The Jews therefore quarreled among
themselves, saying, "How can this Man give
us *His* flesh to eat?"
53 Then Jesus said to them, "Most assuredly,
I say to you, unless you eat the flesh of the
Son of Man and drink His blood, you have no
life in you.
54 "Whoever eats My flesh and drinks My
blood has eternal life, and I will raise him up
at the last day.
55 "For My flesh is food indeed,[a] and My
blood is drink indeed.
56 "He who eats My flesh and drinks My
blood abides in Me, and I in him.
57 "As the living Father sent Me, and I live because of the Father, so he who feeds on Me
will live because of Me.
58 "This is the bread which came down from
heaven—not as your fathers ate the manna,
and are dead. He who eats this bread will live
forever."
59 These things He said in the synagogue as
He taught in Capernaum.

Many Disciples Turn Away

60 Therefore many of His disciples, when
they heard *this*, said, "This is a hard saying;
who can understand it?"
61 When Jesus knew in Himself that His disciples complained about this, He said to them,
"Does this offend you?
62 "*What* then if you should see the Son of
Man ascend where He was before?
63 "It is the Spirit who gives life; the flesh
profits nothing. The words that I speak to you
are spirit, and *they* are life.
64 "But there are some of you who do not believe." For Jesus knew from the beginning
who they were who did not believe, and who
would betray Him.
65 And He said, "Therefore I have said to you
that no one can come to Me unless it has been
granted to him by My Father."
66 From that *time* many of His disciples went ➤
back and walked with Him no more.
67 Then Jesus said to the twelve, "Do you
also want to go away?"
68 But Simon Peter answered Him, "Lord, to ➤

6:45 [a]Isaiah 54:13 [b]M-Text reads *hears and has learned.*
6:47 [a]NU-Text omits *in Me.* **6:55** [a]NU-Text reads *true food* and *true drink.*

LIFE LESSONS

➤ **6:38 — *"For I have come down from heaven, not to do My own will, but the will of Him who sent Me."***

We never grow out of our need to obey God; obedience always remains a part of our relationship with Him. Jesus was the Son of God, and yet He continually named obedience to His Father as His number one desire.

➤ **6:66 — *From that time many of His disciples went back and walked with Him no more.***

Jesus did not try to talk unwilling disciples into staying with Him, nor did He make things easier for them so that they would reconsider their relationship to Him. He wants eager followers, not fickle fans.

➤ **6:68 — *But Simon Peter answered Him, "Lord, to whom shall we go? You have the words of eternal life."***

Times come for all of us when a life of faith in Christ seems less attractive than we expected. Yet here's the question: Where can we find a better offer than the eternal life Jesus alone promises?

whom shall we go? You have the words of eternal life.
69 "Also we have come to believe and know that You are the Christ, the Son of the living God."[a]
70 Jesus answered them, "Did I not choose you, the twelve, and one of you is a devil?"
71 He spoke of Judas Iscariot, *the son* of Simon, for it was he who would betray Him, being one of the twelve.

Jesus' Brothers Disbelieve

7 After these things Jesus walked in Galilee; for He did not want to walk in Judea, because the Jews[a] sought to kill Him.
2 Now the Jews' Feast of Tabernacles was at hand.
3 His brothers therefore said to Him, "Depart from here and go into Judea, that Your disciples also may see the works that You are doing.
4 "For no one does anything in secret while he himself seeks to be known openly. If You do these things, show Yourself to the world."
5 For even His brothers did not believe in Him.
6 Then Jesus said to them, "My time has not yet come, but your time is always ready.
7 "The world cannot hate you, but it hates Me because I testify of it that its works are evil.
8 "You go up to this feast. I am not yet[a] going up to this feast, for My time has not yet fully come."
9 When He had said these things to them, He remained in Galilee.

The Heavenly Scholar

10 But when His brothers had gone up, then He also went up to the feast, not openly, but as it were in secret.
11 Then the Jews sought Him at the feast, and said, "Where is He?"
12 And there was much complaining among the people concerning Him. Some said, "He is good"; others said, "No, on the contrary, He deceives the people."
13 However, no one spoke openly of Him for fear of the Jews.
14 Now about the middle of the feast Jesus went up into the temple and taught.
15 And the Jews marveled, saying, "How does this Man know letters, having never studied?"
16 Jesus[a] answered them and said, "My doctrine is not Mine, but His who sent Me.
17 "If anyone wills to do His will, he shall know concerning the doctrine, whether it is from God or *whether* I speak on My own *authority.*
18 "He who speaks from himself seeks his own glory; but He who seeks the glory of the One who sent Him is true, and no unrighteousness is in Him.
19 "Did not Moses give you the law, yet none of you keeps the law? Why do you seek to kill Me?"
20 The people answered and said, "You have a demon. Who is seeking to kill You?"
21 Jesus answered and said to them, "I did one work, and you all marvel.
22 "Moses therefore gave you circumcision (not that it is from Moses, but from the fathers), and you circumcise a man on the Sabbath.
23 "If a man receives circumcision on the Sabbath, so that the law of Moses should not be broken, are you angry with Me because I made a man completely well on the Sabbath?
24 "Do not judge according to appearance, but judge with righteous judgment."

Could This Be the Christ?

25 Now some of them from Jerusalem said, "Is this not He whom they seek to kill?
26 "But look! He speaks boldly, and they say nothing to Him. Do the rulers know indeed that this is truly[a] the Christ?
27 "However, we know where this Man is from; but when the Christ comes, no one knows where He is from."
28 Then Jesus cried out, as He taught in the temple, saying, "You both know Me, and you know where I am from; and I have not come of Myself, but He who sent Me is true, whom you do not know.
29 "But[a] I know Him, for I am from Him, and He sent Me."

6:69 [a]NU-Text reads *You are the Holy One of God.* **7:1** [a]That is, the ruling authorities **7:8** [a]NU-Text omits *yet.* **7:16** [a]NU-Text and M-Text read *So Jesus.* **7:26** [a]NU-Text omits *truly.* **7:29** [a]NU-Text and M-Text omit *But.*

LIFE LESSONS

➤ 7:5 — *For even His brothers did not believe in Him.*

Jesus' younger brothers had grown up with Him in Nazareth, and while they might have heard about Jesus' extraordinary birth, they did not believe—until after the resurrection. Only then did they come to faith.

➤ 7:17 — *"If anyone wants to do His will, he shall know concerning the doctrine, whether it is from God or whether I speak on My own authority."*

The best way to understand the Word of God is to decide to obey it, whatever it says. We put ourselves in great spiritual danger by trying to understand the Bible without first committing to obey God (Luke 12:47, 48).

➤ 7:30 — *Therefore they sought to take Him; but no one laid a hand on Him, because His hour had not yet come.*

Several times Jesus' opponents wanted to take Him by force or eliminate Him, but God did not permit any of their plans to succeed until they fit His timing. His sovereign will controls all of history.

➤ 30 Therefore they sought to take Him; but no
one laid a hand on Him, because His hour had
not yet come.
31 And many of the people believed in Him,
and said, "When the Christ comes, will He do
more signs than these which this *Man* has
done?"

Jesus and the Religious Leaders

32 The Pharisees heard the crowd murmuring these things concerning Him, and the Pharisees and the chief priests sent officers to take Him.
33 Then Jesus said to them,[a] "I shall be with
you a little while longer, and *then* I go to Him
who sent Me.
34 "You will seek Me and not find *Me,* and
where I am you cannot come."
35 Then the Jews said among themselves,
"Where does He intend to go that we shall not
find Him? Does He intend to go to the Dispersion among the Greeks and teach the
Greeks?
36 "What is this thing that He said, 'You will
seek Me and not find Me, and where I am you
cannot come'?"

The Promise of the Holy Spirit

✳ **37** On the last day, that great *day* of the feast,
➤ Jesus stood and cried out, saying, "If anyone
thirsts, let him come to Me and drink.
38 "He who believes in Me, as the Scripture
has said, out of his heart will flow rivers of
living water."
39 But this He spoke concerning the Spirit,
whom those believing[a] in Him would receive;
for the Holy[b] Spirit was not yet *given,* because
Jesus was not yet glorified.

Who Is He?

40 Therefore many[a] from the crowd, when
they heard this saying, said, "Truly this is the
Prophet."
41 Others said, "This is the Christ." But some
said, "Will the Christ come out of Galilee?
42 "Has not the Scripture said that the Christ
comes from the seed of David and from the
town of Bethlehem, where David was?"
43 So there was a division among the people
because of Him.
44 Now some of them wanted to take Him,
but no one laid hands on Him.

Rejected by the Authorities

45 Then the officers came to the chief priests
and Pharisees, who said to them, "Why have
you not brought Him?"
46 The officers answered, "No man ever
spoke like this Man!"
47 Then the Pharisees answered them, "Are
you also deceived?
48 "Have any of the rulers or the Pharisees
believed in Him?
49 "But this crowd that does not know the
law is accursed."
50 Nicodemus (he who came to Jesus by
night,[a] being one of them) said to them,
51 "Does our law judge a man before it hears
him and knows what he is doing?"
52 They answered and said to him, "Are you
also from Galilee? Search and look, for no
prophet has arisen[a] out of Galilee."

An Adulteress Faces the Light of the World

53 And everyone went to his *own* house.[a]
8 But Jesus went to the Mount of Olives.
2 Now early[a] in the morning He came
again into the temple, and all the people came
to Him; and He sat down and taught them.
3 Then the scribes and Pharisees brought to
Him a woman caught in adultery. And when
they had set her in the midst,
4 they said to Him, "Teacher, this woman
was caught[a] in adultery, in the very act.
5 "Now Moses, in the law, commanded[a] us
that such should be stoned.[b] But what do You
say?"[c]
6 This they said, testing Him, that they
might have *something* of which to accuse
Him. But Jesus stooped down and wrote on
the ground with *His* finger, as though He did
not hear.[a]
7 So when they continued asking Him, He
raised Himself up[a] and said to them, "He who
is without sin among you, let him throw a
stone at her first."
8 And again He stooped down and wrote on
the ground.
9 Then those who heard *it,* being convicted
by *their* conscience,[a] went out one by one, beginning with the oldest *even* to the last. And

7:33 [a]NU-Text and M-Text omit *to them.* **7:39** [a]NU-Text reads *who believed.* [b]NU-Text omits *Holy.* **7:40** [a]NU-Text reads *some.* **7:50** [a]NU-Text reads *before.* **7:52** [a]NU-Text reads *is to rise.* **7:53** [a]The words *And everyone* through *sin no more* (8:11) are bracketed by NU-Text as not original. They are present in over 900 manuscripts. **8:2** [a]M-Text reads *very early.* **8:4** [a]M-Text reads *we found this woman.* **8:5** [a]M-Text reads *in our law Moses commanded.* [b]NU-Text and M-Text read *to stone such.* [c]M-Text adds *about her.* **8:6** [a]NU-Text and M-Text omit *as though He did not hear.* **8:7** [a]M-Text reads *He looked up.* **8:9** [a]NU-Text and M-Text omit *being convicted by their conscience.*

LIFE LESSONS

➤ **7:37 — *On the last day, that great day of the feast, Jesus stood and cried out, saying, "If anyone thirsts, let him come to Me and drink."***

Because God made us for an intimate relationship with Himself, we cannot get our deepest needs met anywhere else but in Him. Jesus offers the only satisfaction for spiritual thirst.

Jesus was left alone, and the woman standing
in the midst.
10 When Jesus had raised Himself up and
saw no one but the woman, He said to her,[a]
"Woman, where are those accusers of yours?[b]
Has no one condemned you?"
11 She said, "No one, Lord." And Jesus said
to her, "Neither do I condemn you; go and[a] sin
no more."
12 Then Jesus spoke to them again, saying, "I
am the light of the world. He who follows Me
shall not walk in darkness, but have the light
of life."

Jesus Defends His Self-Witness

13 The Pharisees therefore said to Him, "You
bear witness of Yourself; Your witness is not
true."
14 Jesus answered and said to them, "Even if
I bear witness of Myself, My witness is true,
for I know where I came from and where I am
going; but you do not know where I come
from and where I am going.
15 "You judge according to the flesh; I judge
no one.
16 "And yet if I do judge, My judgment is
true; for I am not alone, but I *am* with the Father who sent Me.
17 "It is also written in your law that the testimony of two men is true.
18 "I am One who bears witness of Myself,
and the Father who sent Me bears witness of
Me."
19 Then they said to Him, "Where is Your Father?" Jesus answered, "You know neither Me
nor My Father. If you had known Me, you
would have known My Father also."
20 These words Jesus spoke in the treasury,
as He taught in the temple; and no one laid
hands on Him, for His hour had not yet come.

Jesus Predicts His Departure

21 Then Jesus said to them again, "I am
going away, and you will seek Me, and will
die in your sin. Where I go you cannot come."
22 So the Jews said, "Will He kill Himself, because He says, 'Where I go you cannot
come'?"
23 And He said to them, "You are from beneath; I am from above. You are of this world;
I am not of this world.
24 "Therefore I said to you that you will die in
your sins; for if you do not believe that I am
He, you will die in your sins."
25 Then they said to Him, "Who are You?"
And Jesus said to them, "Just what I have
been saying to you from the beginning.
26 "I have many things to say and to judge
concerning you, but He who sent Me is true;
and I speak to the world those things which I
heard from Him."
27 They did not understand that He spoke to
them of the Father.
28 Then Jesus said to them, "When you lift up
the Son of Man, then you will know that I am
He, and *that* I do nothing of Myself; but as
My Father taught Me, I speak these things.
29 "And He who sent Me is with Me. The Father has not left Me alone, for I always do
those things that please Him."
30 As He spoke these words, many believed
in Him.

The Truth Shall Make You Free

31 Then Jesus said to those Jews who believed Him, "If you abide in My word, you are
My disciples indeed.
32 "And you shall know the truth, and the
truth shall make you free."
33 They answered Him, "We are Abraham's
descendants, and have never been in bondage
to anyone. How *can* You say, 'You will be
made free'?"
34 Jesus answered them, "Most assuredly, I
say to you, whoever commits sin is a slave of
sin.
35 "And a slave does not abide in the house
forever, *but* a son abides forever.
36 "Therefore if the Son makes you free, you
shall be free indeed.

Abraham's Seed and Satan's

37 "I know that you are Abraham's descendants, but you seek to kill Me, because My
word has no place in you.
38 "I speak what I have seen with My Father,
and you do what you have seen with[a] your father."
39 They answered and said to Him, "Abraham is our father." Jesus said to them, "If you
were Abraham's children, you would do the
works of Abraham.

8:10 [a]NU-Text omits *and saw no one but the woman;* M-Text reads *He saw her and said.* [b]NU-Text and M-Text omit *of yours.* **8:11** [a]NU-Text and M-Text add *from now on.* **8:38** [a]NU-Text reads *heard from.*

LIFE LESSONS

➤ 8:11 — *And Jesus said to her, "Neither do I condemn you; go and sin no more."*

Jesus is gracious and merciful, but He never ceases to be holy. He calls us to a life of holiness and obedience to His Father, and He gives us the spiritual resources we need to walk in righteousness.

➤ 8:32 — *"And you shall know the truth, and the truth shall make you free."*

Jesus offended His listeners when He made this statement, because they considered themselves in bondage to no one. But Jesus insisted that only faith in Him could free anyone from the power of sin.

ANSWERS TO LIFE'S QUESTIONS

What does it mean to be set free in Christ?

JOHN 8:31, 32

Jesus had quite an audience that day. The crowds had just witnessed an intense scene when the scribes and Pharisees brought to Jesus a woman who had been caught in the act of adultery (John 8:11). Then they saw Jesus' liberating love in action as He looked at her and said, "Neither do I condemn you; go and sin no more." This woman walked away forgiven, free, and saved from certain doom.

A little later, Jesus proclaimed: "If you abide in My word, you are My disciples indeed. And you shall know the truth, and the truth shall make you free" (John 8:31, 32).

Consider these verses the believer's emancipation proclamation. In verses 34–36, Jesus explains more of what He means: "Most assuredly, I say to you, whoever commits sin is a slave of sin. And a slave does not abide in the house forever, but a son abides forever. Therefore if the Son makes you free, you shall be free indeed."

On the surface, this sounds very simple; and in a foundational sense, it is. But it's one thing to believe that Jesus can set you free from patterns of sin. It's quite another to experience that freedom in your own life.

Most of us have difficulty in the action stage of belief, the vital link between knowing by intellect and knowing by experience (see James 2:14–26). You are saved by faith alone in Jesus Christ, but that does not mean that you leap immediately into a full understanding of your faith.

Your personal response to Jesus' commands determines whether you will be able to live in the joys of that salvation, with the freedom and exhilaration of learning to say no to daily sins. A man in prison can receive a signed pardon and the warden can unlock the jail door, but the man has to put one foot in front of the other and walk outside those prison walls.

What can you do to begin living in the freedom Christ purchased for you on the cross? There is no formula for discovering the richness of His truth. But by obeying Christ, you'll be on the road to the fresh, liberated life He designed for you. Always when you obey God, you can count on watching Him reveal exciting, new things. Remember, the key to crossing the bridge between belief and experience is obedience. You must take the step of faith and do what He says.

See the Life Principles Index for further study:
21. Obedience always brings blessings.
5. God does not require us to understand His will, just obey it, even if it seems unreasonable.

40 "But now you seek to kill Me, a Man who
has told you the truth which I heard from
God. Abraham did not do this.
41 "You do the deeds of your father." Then
they said to Him, "We were not born of fornication; we have one Father—God."
42 Jesus said to them, "If God were your Father, you would love Me, for I proceeded forth
and came from God; nor have I come of Myself, but He sent Me.
43 "Why do you not understand My speech?
Because you are not able to listen to My word.
44 "You are of *your* father the devil, and the
desires of your father you want to do. He was
a murderer from the beginning, and does not
stand in the truth, because there is no truth in
him. When he speaks a lie, he speaks from his
own *resources,* for he is a liar and the father
of it.
45 "But because I tell the truth, you do not believe Me.
46 "Which of you convicts Me of sin? And if I
tell the truth, why do you not believe Me?
47 "He who is of God hears God's words;
therefore you do not hear, because you are
not of God."

Before Abraham Was, I AM

48 Then the Jews answered and said to Him,
"Do we not say rightly that You are a Samaritan and have a demon?"
49 Jesus answered, "I do not have a demon;
but I honor My Father, and you dishonor Me.
50 "And I do not seek My *own* glory; there is
One who seeks and judges.
51 "Most assuredly, I say to you, if anyone
keeps My word he shall never see death."
52 Then the Jews said to Him, "Now we know
that You have a demon! Abraham is dead, and
the prophets; and You say, 'If anyone keeps
My word he shall never taste death.'
53 "Are You greater than our father Abraham,

who is dead? And the prophets are dead. Who
do You make Yourself out to be?"
54 Jesus answered, "If I honor Myself, My
honor is nothing. It is My Father who honors
Me, of whom you say that He is your[a] God.
55 "Yet you have not known Him, but I know
Him. And if I say, 'I do not know Him,' I shall
be a liar like you; but I do know Him and keep
His word.
56 "Your father Abraham rejoiced to see My
day, and he saw *it* and was glad."
57 Then the Jews said to Him, "You are not
yet fifty years old, and have You seen Abraham?"
➤ 58 Jesus said to them, "Most assuredly, I say
to you, before Abraham was, I AM."
59 Then they took up stones to throw at Him;
but Jesus hid Himself and went out of the
temple,[a] going through the midst of them, and
so passed by.

A Man Born Blind Receives Sight

9 Now as *Jesus* passed by, He saw a man
who was blind from birth.
2 And His disciples asked Him, saying,
"Rabbi, who sinned, this man or his parents,
that he was born blind?"
➤ 3 Jesus answered, "Neither this man nor his
parents sinned, but that the works of God
should be revealed in him.
4 "I[a] must work the works of Him who sent
Me while it is day; *the* night is coming when
no one can work.
5 "As long as I am in the world, I am the
light of the world."
6 When He had said these things, He spat
on the ground and made clay with the saliva;
and He anointed the eyes of the blind man
with the clay.
7 And He said to him, "Go, wash in the pool
of Siloam" (which is translated, Sent). So he
went and washed, and came back seeing.
8 Therefore the neighbors and those who
previously had seen that he was blind[a] said,
"Is not this he who sat and begged?"
9 Some said, "This is he." Others *said*, "He is
like him."[a] He said, "I am *he*."
10 Therefore they said to him, "How were
your eyes opened?"
11 He answered and said, "A Man called Jesus made clay and anointed my eyes and said
to me, 'Go to the pool of[a] Siloam and wash.'
So I went and washed, and I received sight."
12 Then they said to him, "Where is He?" He
said, "I do not know."

The Pharisees Excommunicate the Healed Man

13 They brought him who formerly was blind
to the Pharisees.
14 Now it was a Sabbath when Jesus made
the clay and opened his eyes.
15 Then the Pharisees also asked him again
how he had received his sight. He said to
them, "He put clay on my eyes, and I washed,
and I see."
16 Therefore some of the Pharisees said,
"This Man is not from God, because He does
not keep the Sabbath." Others said, "How can
a man who is a sinner do such signs?" And
there was a division among them.
17 They said to the blind man again, "What
do you say about Him because He opened
your eyes?" He said, "He is a prophet."
18 But the Jews did not believe concerning
him, that he had been blind and received his
sight, until they called the parents of him who
had received his sight.
19 And they asked them, saying, "Is this your
son, who you say was born blind? How then
does he now see?"
20 His parents answered them and said, "We
know that this is our son, and that he was
born blind;
21 "but by what means he now sees we do not
know, or who opened his eyes we do not
know. He is of age; ask him. He will speak for
himself."
22 His parents said these *things* because they
feared the Jews, for the Jews had agreed already that if anyone confessed *that* He *was*
Christ, he would be put out of the synagogue.
23 Therefore his parents said, "He is of age;
ask him."
24 So they again called the man who was ➤

8:54 [a]NU-Text and M-Text read *our*. **8:59** [a]NU-Text omits the rest of this verse. **9:4** [a]NU-Text reads *We*. **9:8** [a]NU-Text reads *a beggar*. **9:9** [a]NU-Text reads *"No, but he is like him."* **9:11** [a]NU-Text omits *the pool of*.

LIFE LESSONS

➤ 8:58 — *Jesus said to them, "Most assuredly, I say to you, before Abraham was, I AM."*

This may be the clearest claim Jesus ever made to be God in the flesh. He called Himself by the divine name, "I AM" (see Ex. 3:14; Is. 42:8), and said that He existed long before Abraham lived.

➤ 9:3 — *Jesus answered, "Neither this man nor his parents sinned, but that the works of God should be revealed in him."*

It is always dangerous to assume that some sin is to blame for a physical ailment. In this case, Jesus said that God designed the man's blindness to provide a platform for exalting His glory.

➤ 9:24 — *So they again called the man who was blind, and said to him, "Give God the glory! We know that this Man is a sinner."*

Religious speech often cloaks the darkest of hearts. These leaders wanted the man to speak a vicious lie about God's Son—something that, far from honoring God, would anger and offend Him.

blind, and said to him, "Give God the glory!
We know that this Man is a sinner."
25 He answered and said, "Whether He is a
sinner *or not* I do not know. One thing I know:
that though I was blind, now I see."
26 Then they said to him again, "What did He
do to you? How did He open your eyes?"
27 He answered them, "I told you already,
and you did not listen. Why do you want to
hear *it* again? Do you also want to become
His disciples?"
28 Then they reviled him and said, "You are
His disciple, but we are Moses' disciples.
29 "We know that God spoke to Moses; *as for*
this *fellow*, we do not know where He is
from."
30 The man answered and said to them,
"Why, this is a marvelous thing, that you do
not know where He is from; yet He has
opened my eyes!
31 "Now we know that God does not hear
sinners; but if anyone is a worshiper of God
and does His will, He hears him.
32 "Since the world began it has been un-
heard of that anyone opened the eyes of one
who was born blind.
33 "If this Man were not from God, He could
do nothing."
34 They answered and said to him, "You were
completely born in sins, and are you teaching
us?" And they cast him out.

True Vision and True Blindness

35 Jesus heard that they had cast him out;
and when He had found him, He said to him,
"Do you believe in the Son of God?"[a]
36 He answered and said, "Who is He, Lord,
that I may believe in Him?"
37 And Jesus said to him, "You have both
seen Him and it is He who is talking with
you."
38 Then he said, "Lord, I believe!" And he
worshiped Him.
39 And Jesus said, "For judgment I have
come into this world, that those who do not
see may see, and that those who see may be
made blind."
40 Then *some* of the Pharisees who were
with Him heard these words, and said to Him,
"Are we blind also?"
41 Jesus said to them, "If you were blind, you
would have no sin; but now you say, 'We see.'
Therefore your sin remains.

Jesus the True Shepherd

10 "Most assuredly, I say to you, he who
does not enter the sheepfold by the
door, but climbs up some other way, the same
is a thief and a robber.
2 "But he who enters by the door is the
shepherd of the sheep.
3 "To him the doorkeeper opens, and the
sheep hear his voice; and he calls his own
sheep by name and leads them out.
4 "And when he brings out his own sheep,
he goes before them; and the sheep follow
him, for they know his voice.
5 "Yet they will by no means follow a stranger, but will flee from him, for they do not
know the voice of strangers."
6 Jesus used this illustration, but they did
not understand the things which He spoke to
them.

Jesus the Good Shepherd

7 Then Jesus said to them again, "Most assuredly, I say to you, I am the door of the
sheep.
8 "All who *ever* came before Me[a] are thieves
and robbers, but the sheep did not hear them.
9 "I am the door. If anyone enters by Me, he
will be saved, and will go in and out and find
pasture.
10 "The thief does not come except to steal,
and to kill, and to destroy. I have come that
they may have life, and that they may have *it*
more abundantly.
11 "I am the good shepherd. The good shepherd gives His life for the sheep.
12 "But a hireling, *he who is* not the shepherd, one who does not own the sheep, sees
the wolf coming and leaves the sheep and
flees; and the wolf catches the sheep and scatters them.
13 "The hireling flees because he is a hireling
and does not care about the sheep.

9:35 [a]NU-Text reads *Son of Man.* **10:8** [a]M-Text omits *before Me.*

LIFE LESSONS

➤ 9:35 — *Jesus heard that they had cast him out; and when He had found him . . . .*

Jesus sought the man out after He heard what the religious leaders had done to him. He does the same thing with us. He seeks us out, offering us His help and encouragement to walk with God.

➤ 10:9 — *"I am the door. If anyone enters by Me, he will be saved, and will go in and out and find pasture."*

Jesus is not one of many doors to the Father, but the only door. He never claimed to be one route among several to an intimate relationship with God, but insisted He was the only way.

➤ 10:11 — *"I am the good shepherd. The good shepherd gives His life for the sheep."*

If Jesus willingly gave His life to save ours, how can we think He would ever keep back from us anything that would truly benefit us? He is the *good* shepherd, not the stingy shepherd or the tightfisted shepherd.

14 "I am the good shepherd; and I know My
sheep, and am known by My own.
15 "As the Father knows Me, even so I know
the Father; and I lay down My life for the sheep.
16 "And other sheep I have which are not of
this fold; them also I must bring, and they will
hear My voice; and there will be one flock
and one shepherd.
➤ 17 "Therefore My Father loves Me, because I
lay down My life that I may take it again.
18 "No one takes it from Me, but I lay it down
of Myself. I have power to lay it down, and I
have power to take it again. This command I
have received from My Father."
19 Therefore there was a division again
among the Jews because of these sayings.
20 And many of them said, "He has a demon
and is mad. Why do you listen to Him?"
21 Others said, "These are not the words of
one who has a demon. Can a demon open the
eyes of the blind?"

The Shepherd Knows His Sheep

22 Now it was the Feast of Dedication in Jerusalem, and it was winter.
23 And Jesus walked in the temple, in Solomon's porch.
24 Then the Jews surrounded Him and said
to Him, "How long do You keep us in doubt? If
You are the Christ, tell us plainly."
25 Jesus answered them, "I told you, and you
do not believe. The works that I do in My Father's name, they bear witness of Me.
26 "But you do not believe, because you are
not of My sheep, as I said to you.[a]
✳ 27 "My sheep hear My voice, and I know
them, and they follow Me.
28 "And I give them eternal life, and they
shall never perish; neither shall anyone
snatch them out of My hand.
29 "My Father, who has given *them* to Me, is
greater than all; and no one is able to snatch
them out of My Father's hand.
➤ 30 "I and *My* Father are one."

Renewed Efforts to Stone Jesus

31 Then the Jews took up stones again to
stone Him.
32 Jesus answered them, "Many good works
I have shown you from My Father. For which
of those works do you stone Me?"
33 The Jews answered Him, saying, "For a
good work we do not stone You, but for blasphemy, and because You, being a Man, make
Yourself God."
34 Jesus answered them, "Is it not written in
your law, *'I said, "You are gods"'*?[a]
35 "If He called them gods, to whom the word
of God came (and the Scripture cannot be
broken),
36 "do you say of Him whom the Father sanctified and sent into the world, 'You are blaspheming,' because I said, 'I am the Son of
God'?
37 "If I do not do the works of My Father, do
not believe Me;
38 "but if I do, though you do not believe Me, ➤
believe the works, that you may know and believe[a] that the Father *is* in Me, and I in Him."
39 Therefore they sought again to seize Him,
but He escaped out of their hand.

The Believers Beyond Jordan

40 And He went away again beyond the Jordan to the place where John was baptizing at
first, and there He stayed.
41 Then many came to Him and said, "John
performed no sign, but all the things that
John spoke about this Man were true."
42 And many believed in Him there.

The Death of Lazarus

11 Now a certain *man* was sick, Lazarus
of Bethany, the town of Mary and her
sister Martha.
2 It was *that* Mary who anointed the Lord
with fragrant oil and wiped His feet with her
hair, whose brother Lazarus was sick.
3 Therefore the sisters sent to Him, saying,
"Lord, behold, he whom You love is sick."
4 When Jesus heard *that,* He said, "This ➤
sickness is not unto death, but for the glory of

10:26 [a]NU-Text omits *as I said to you.* **10:34** [a]Psalm 82:6
10:38 [a]NU-Text reads *understand.*

LIFE LESSONS

➤ 10:17 — *"Therefore My Father loves Me, because I lay down My life that I may take it again."*

God gave Jesus the authority both to offer His life as a sacrifice for our sins and to rise from the dead in power and great glory. Jesus' death and resurrection were equally planned from eternity (Rev. 13:8).

➤ 10:30 — *"I and My Father are one."*

When Jesus used the words "I" and "My Father," He proclaimed a clear distinction in the two divine Persons. But in saying they are "one," He proclaimed their unity of nature and equality—and His hearers understood His claim.

➤ 10:38 — *". . . though you do not believe Me, believe the works, that you may know and believe . . . ."*

God often acts more like a pragmatist than an idealist. Jesus said it would be best if His audience would believe Him; but if they didn't, at least they could believe in the fact of His amazing actions.

➤ 11:4 — *"This sickness is not unto death, but for the glory of God, that the Son of God may be glorified through it."*

Jesus did not mean that Lazarus would not die—he did—but that the episode would not *end* in death. When Jesus is involved, death ends nothing; as the Lord of life, He triumphs over even death.

God, that the Son of God may be glorified
through it."
5 Now Jesus loved Martha and her sister
and Lazarus.
6 So, when He heard that he was sick, He
stayed two more days in the place where He
was.
7 Then after this He said to *the* disciples,
"Let us go to Judea again."
8 *The* disciples said to Him, "Rabbi, lately
the Jews sought to stone You, and are You
going there again?"
9 Jesus answered, "Are there not twelve
hours in the day? If anyone walks in the day,
he does not stumble, because he sees the light
of this world.
10 "But if one walks in the night, he stumbles,
because the light is not in him."
11 These things He said, and after that He
said to them, "Our friend Lazarus sleeps, but
I go that I may wake him up."
12 Then His disciples said, "Lord, if he sleeps
he will get well."
13 However, Jesus spoke of his death, but
they thought that He was speaking about taking rest in sleep.
➤ 14 Then Jesus said to them plainly, "Lazarus
is dead.
15 "And I am glad for your sakes that I was
not there, that you may believe. Nevertheless
let us go to him."
16 Then Thomas, who is called the Twin, said
to his fellow disciples, "Let us also go, that we
may die with Him."

I Am the Resurrection and the Life

17 So when Jesus came, He found that he had
already been in the tomb four days.
18 Now Bethany was near Jerusalem, about
two miles[a] away.
19 And many of the Jews had joined the
women around Martha and Mary, to comfort
them concerning their brother.
20 Now Martha, as soon as she heard that Jesus was coming, went and met Him, but Mary
was sitting in the house.
21 Now Martha said to Jesus, "Lord, if You
had been here, my brother would not have
died.
22 "But even now I know that whatever You
ask of God, God will give You."
23 Jesus said to her, "Your brother will rise
again."
24 Martha said to Him, "I know that he will
rise again in the resurrection at the last day."

Life Examples:

MARTHA

Worship as You Work

JOHN 11:19–44

After Jesus raised her brother from the dead, Martha finally understood the awesome power of Christ. She knew that nothing she could do would ever honor Him sufficiently—yet also that He would gladly receive anything done for Him out of a heart of genuine devotion (John 11:19–44).

God invites you to use your gifts to express praise to Him, especially if you use them with a grateful, joyful heart. If, however, they become your avenue for seeking acceptance and prestige—as with Martha at the beginning (Luke 10:38–42)—then they can become a source of bitterness and resentment. Your actions can either proclaim Christ or they can seek your own advancement. You can use your talents with an attitude of praise or an attitude of self-promotion.

As you express your gifts today, consider your testimony. Will you serve out of praise to Him? Will you choose work or worship?

See the Life Principles Index for further study:

4. The awareness of God's presence energizes us for our work.

15. Brokenness is God's requirement for maximum usefulness.

25 Jesus said to her, "I am the resurrection ✳
and the life. He who believes in Me, though he
may die, he shall live.
26 "And whoever lives and believes in Me
shall never die. Do you believe this?"
27 She said to Him, "Yes, Lord, I believe that

11:18 [a]Literally *fifteen stadia*

LIFE LESSONS

➤ **11:14, 15 — *Then Jesus said to them plainly, "Lazarus is dead. And I am glad for your sakes that I was not there, that you may believe."***

We have to understand that God is far more concerned with growing our faith than with making us comfortable. Jesus said He was "glad" about the death of Lazarus, because He valued his friends' faith over their tears.

You are the Christ, the Son of God, who is to
come into the world."

Jesus and Death, the Last Enemy

28 And when she had said these things, she
went her way and secretly called Mary her
sister, saying, "The Teacher has come and is
calling for you."
29 As soon as she heard *that,* she arose
quickly and came to Him.
30 Now Jesus had not yet come into the
town, but was[a] in the place where Martha met
Him.
31 Then the Jews who were with her in the
house, and comforting her, when they saw
that Mary rose up quickly and went out, followed her, saying, "She is going to the tomb to
weep there."[a]
32 Then, when Mary came where Jesus was,
and saw Him, she fell down at His feet, saying
to Him, "Lord, if You had been here, my
brother would not have died."
33 Therefore, when Jesus saw her weeping,
and the Jews who came with her weeping, He
groaned in the spirit and was troubled.
34 And He said, "Where have you laid him?"
They said to Him, "Lord, come and see."
35 Jesus wept.
36 Then the Jews said, "See how He loved
him!"
➤ 37 And some of them said, "Could not this
Man, who opened the eyes of the blind, also
have kept this man from dying?"

Lazarus Raised from the Dead

38 Then Jesus, again groaning in Himself,
came to the tomb. It was a cave, and a stone
lay against it.
39 Jesus said, "Take away the stone." Martha,
the sister of him who was dead, said to Him,
"Lord, by this time there is a stench, for he
has been *dead* four days."
40 Jesus said to her, "Did I not say to you that
if you would believe you would see the glory
of God?"
41 Then they took away the stone *from the
place* where the dead man was lying.[a] And Jesus lifted up *His* eyes and said, "Father, I
thank You that You have heard Me.
42 "And I know that You always hear Me, but
because of the people who are standing by I
said *this,* that they may believe that You sent
Me."
43 Now when He had said these things, He
cried with a loud voice, "Lazarus, come
forth!"
44 And he who had died came out bound
hand and foot with graveclothes, and his face
was wrapped with a cloth. Jesus said to them,
"Loose him, and let him go."

The Plot to Kill Jesus

45 Then many of the Jews who had come to
Mary, and had seen the things Jesus did, believed in Him.
46 But some of them went away to the Pharisees and told them the things Jesus did.
47 Then the chief priests and the Pharisees
gathered a council and said, "What shall we
do? For this Man works many signs.
48 "If we let Him alone like this, everyone will
believe in Him, and the Romans will come and
take away both our place and nation."
49 And one of them, Caiaphas, being high
priest that year, said to them, "You know
nothing at all,
50 "nor do you consider that it is expedient
for us[a] that one man should die for the people, and not that the whole nation should perish."
51 Now this he did not say on his own *authority;* but being high priest that year he
prophesied that Jesus would die for the nation,
52 and not for that nation only, but also that
He would gather together in one the children
of God who were scattered abroad.
53 Then, from that day on, they plotted to put
Him to death.
54 Therefore Jesus no longer walked openly
among the Jews, but went from there into the
country near the wilderness, to a city called
Ephraim, and there remained with His disciples.
55 And the Passover of the Jews was near,
and many went from the country up to Jerusalem before the Passover, to purify themselves.
56 Then they sought Jesus, and spoke among
themselves as they stood in the temple, "What
do you think—that He will not come to the
feast?"
57 Now both the chief priests and the Pharisees had given a command, that if anyone
knew where He was, he should report *it,* that
they might seize Him.

11:30 [a]NU-Text adds *still.* **11:31** [a]NU-Text reads *supposing that she was going to the tomb to weep there.* **11:41** [a]NU-Text omits *from the place where the dead man was lying.* **11:50** [a]NU-Text reads *you.*

LIFE LESSONS

➤ 11:37 — *And some of them said, "Could not this Man, who opened the eyes of the blind, also have kept this man from dying?"*

Yes, Jesus could have; but He chose to do something else. He did not spare His friends even great grief, because it benefited them more in the end to witness His power over death (see Rom. 8:18).

The Anointing at Bethany

12 Then, six days before the Passover, Jesus came to Bethany, where Lazarus
was who had been dead,[a] whom He had
raised from the dead.
2 There they made Him a supper; and Martha served, but Lazarus was one of those who
sat at the table with Him.
3 Then Mary took a pound of very costly oil
of spikenard, anointed the feet of Jesus, and
wiped His feet with her hair. And the house
was filled with the fragrance of the oil.
4 But one of His disciples, Judas Iscariot, Simon's *son,* who would betray Him, said,
5 "Why was this fragrant oil not sold for
three hundred denarii[a] and given to the
poor?"
6 This he said, not that he cared for the
poor, but because he was a thief, and had
the money box; and he used to take what was
put in it.
7 But Jesus said, "Let her alone; she has
kept[a] this for the day of My burial.
8 "For the poor you have with you always,
but Me you do not have always."

The Plot to Kill Lazarus

9 Now a great many of the Jews knew that
He was there; and they came, not for Jesus'
sake only, but that they might also see
Lazarus, whom He had raised from the dead.
10 But the chief priests plotted to put Lazarus
to death also,
11 because on account of him many of the
Jews went away and believed in Jesus.

The Triumphal Entry

12 The next day a great multitude that had
come to the feast, when they heard that Jesus
was coming to Jerusalem,
13 took branches of palm trees and went out
to meet Him, and cried out:

"Hosanna!
'*Blessed is He who comes in the name of*
the LORD!'[a]
The King of Israel!"

14 Then Jesus, when He had found a young
donkey, sat on it; as it is written:

15 "*Fear not, daughter of Zion;*
Behold, your King is coming,
Sitting on a donkey's colt."[a]

➤ 16 His disciples did not understand these
things at first; but when Jesus was glorified,
then they remembered that these things were
written about Him and *that* they had done
these things to Him.
17 Therefore the people, who were with Him
when He called Lazarus out of his tomb and
raised him from the dead, bore witness.
18 For this reason the people also met Him,

Life Examples:

MARY OF BETHANY

A Life Devoted to God

JOHN 12:1–8

Each time we look at the life of Mary of Bethany through the window afforded us in the Gospels, we find her at the feet of Jesus (John 11:32; 12:3). In Mary, Jesus discerned a heart of devotion and love for the things of God.

Mary accepted Jesus' words when He spoke of His death and resurrection, and she applied them to her life by humbling herself before God and desiring only to serve the Lord. Her attitude marked her as a woman mighty in spirit—and you too can have this trait when you commit yourself to Christ.

Ask Him to make you aware of anything that keeps you from sitting at His feet in heart devotion. Pray for the Holy Spirit to give you a deep love for God's Word. This is what Mary cherished—the Word of God spoken to her. And it is your greatest source of comfort and hope!

See the Life Principles Index for further study:

1. *Our intimacy with God—His highest priority for our lives—determines the impact of our lives.*
12. *Peace with God is the fruit of oneness with God.*

12:1 [a]NU-Text omits *who had been dead.* **12:5** [a]About one year's wages for a worker **12:7** [a]NU-Text reads *that she may keep.* **12:13** [a]Psalm 118:26 **12:15** [a]Zechariah 9:9

LIFE LESSONS

➤ ***12:16 — His disciples did not understand these things at first; but when Jesus was glorified, then they remembered that these things were written about Him . . . .***

Even though it took the disciples a long time to understand the meaning and significance of Scripture, when understanding finally came, it never left them, and it gave them the strength to continue despite great hardship.

because they heard that He had done this sign.
19 The Pharisees therefore said among themselves, "You see that you are accomplishing nothing. Look, the world has gone after Him!"

The Fruitful Grain of Wheat

20 Now there were certain Greeks among those who came up to worship at the feast.
21 Then they came to Philip, who was from Bethsaida of Galilee, and asked him, saying, "Sir, we wish to see Jesus."
22 Philip came and told Andrew, and in turn Andrew and Philip told Jesus.
23 But Jesus answered them, saying, "The hour has come that the Son of Man should be glorified.
24 "Most assuredly, I say to you, unless a grain of wheat falls into the ground and dies, it remains alone; but if it dies, it produces much grain.
25 "He who loves his life will lose it, and he who hates his life in this world will keep it for eternal life.
✳ 26 "If anyone serves Me, let him follow Me; and where I am, there My servant will be also. If anyone serves Me, him *My* Father will honor.

Jesus Predicts His Death on the Cross

27 "Now My soul is troubled, and what shall I say? 'Father, save Me from this hour'? But for this purpose I came to this hour.
28 "Father, glorify Your name." Then a voice came from heaven, *saying*, "I have both glorified *it* and will glorify *it* again."
29 Therefore the people who stood by and heard *it* said that it had thundered. Others said, "An angel has spoken to Him."
30 Jesus answered and said, "This voice did not come because of Me, but for your sake.
31 "Now is the judgment of this world; now the ruler of this world will be cast out.
➤ 32 "And I, if I am lifted up from the earth, will draw all *peoples* to Myself."
33 This He said, signifying by what death He would die.
34 The people answered Him, "We have heard from the law that the Christ remains forever; and how *can* You say, 'The Son of Man must be lifted up'? Who is this Son of Man?"
35 Then Jesus said to them, "A little while longer the light is with you. Walk while you have the light, lest darkness overtake you; he who walks in darkness does not know where he is going.
36 "While you have the light, believe in the light, that you may become sons of light." These things Jesus spoke, and departed, and was hidden from them.

Who Has Believed Our Report?

37 But although He had done so many signs before them, they did not believe in Him,
38 that the word of Isaiah the prophet might be fulfilled, which he spoke:

> *"Lord, who has believed our report?*
> *And to whom has the arm of the LORD*
> *been revealed?"*[a]

39 Therefore they could not believe, because Isaiah said again:

40 *"He has blinded their eyes and hardened*
> *their hearts,*
> *Lest they should see with their eyes,*
> *Lest they should understand with their*
> *hearts and turn,*
> *So that I should heal them."*[a]

41 These things Isaiah said when[a] he saw His glory and spoke of Him.

Walk in the Light

42 Nevertheless even among the rulers many believed in Him, but because of the Pharisees they did not confess *Him*, lest they should be put out of the synagogue;
43 for they loved the praise of men more than the praise of God.
44 Then Jesus cried out and said, "He who believes in Me, believes not in Me but in Him who sent Me.
45 "And he who sees Me sees Him who sent Me.
46 "I have come *as* a light into the world, that whoever believes in Me should not abide in darkness. ✳
47 "And if anyone hears My words and does not believe,[a] I do not judge him; for I did not come to judge the world but to save the world.
48 "He who rejects Me, and does not receive My words, has that which judges him—the word that I have spoken will judge him in the last day.
49 "For I have not spoken on My own *authority;* but the Father who sent Me gave Me a

12:38 [a]Isaiah 53:1 **12:40** [a]Isaiah 6:10 **12:41** [a]NU-Text reads *because.* **12:47** [a]NU-Text reads *keep them.*

LIFE LESSONS

➤ ***12:32 — "And I, if I am lifted up from the earth, will draw all peoples to Myself."***

Jesus says that it is His job to "draw" all peoples to Himself. We are to represent Him as well as we can, but we never convert anyone. It is Christ's job to cause faith to dawn in human hearts, not ours.

command, what I should say and what I
should speak.
50 "And I know that His command is everlasting life. Therefore, whatever I speak, just
as the Father has told Me, so I speak."

Jesus Washes the Disciples' Feet

13 Now before the Feast of the Passover,
when Jesus knew that His hour had
come that He should depart from this world
to the Father, having loved His own who were
in the world, He loved them to the end.
2 And supper being ended,[a] the devil having
already put it into the heart of Judas Iscariot,
Simon's *son,* to betray Him,
3 Jesus, knowing that the Father had given
all things into His hands, and that He had
come from God and was going to God,
4 rose from supper and laid aside His garments, took a towel and girded Himself.
5 After that, He poured water into a basin
and began to wash the disciples' feet, and to
wipe *them* with the towel with which He was
girded.
6 Then He came to Simon Peter. And *Peter*
said to Him, "Lord, are You washing my feet?"
7 Jesus answered and said to him, "What I
am doing you do not understand now, but you
will know after this."
8 Peter said to Him, "You shall never wash
my feet!" Jesus answered him, "If I do not
wash you, you have no part with Me."
9 Simon Peter said to Him, "Lord, not my
feet only, but also *my* hands and *my* head!"
10 Jesus said to him, "He who is bathed
needs only to wash *his* feet, but is completely
clean; and you are clean, but not all of you."
11 For He knew who would betray Him;
therefore He said, "You are not all clean."
12 So when He had washed their feet, taken
His garments, and sat down again, He said to
them, "Do you know what I have done to you?
13 "You call Me Teacher and Lord, and you
say well, for *so* I am.
14 "If I then, *your* Lord and Teacher, have
washed your feet, you also ought to wash one
another's feet.
15 "For I have given you an example, that you
should do as I have done to you.
16 "Most assuredly, I say to you, a servant is
not greater than his master; nor is he who is
sent greater than he who sent him.
17 "If you know these things, blessed are you
if you do them.

Jesus Identifies His Betrayer

18 "I do not speak concerning all of you. I
know whom I have chosen; but that the Scripture may be fulfilled, *'He who eats bread with
Me*[a] *has lifted up his heel against Me.'*[b]
19 "Now I tell you before it comes, that when
it does come to pass, you may believe that I
am *He.*
20 "Most assuredly, I say to you, he who receives whomever I send receives Me; and he
who receives Me receives Him who sent Me."
21 When Jesus had said these things, He was
troubled in spirit, and testified and said,
"Most assuredly, I say to you, one of you will
betray Me."
22 Then the disciples looked at one another,
perplexed about whom He spoke.
23 Now there was leaning on Jesus' bosom
one of His disciples, whom Jesus loved.
24 Simon Peter therefore motioned to him to
ask who it was of whom He spoke.
25 Then, leaning back[a] on Jesus' breast, he
said to Him, "Lord, who is it?"
26 Jesus answered, "It is he to whom I shall
give a piece of bread when I have dipped *it.*"
And having dipped the bread, He gave *it* to
Judas Iscariot, *the son* of Simon.
27 Now after the piece of bread, Satan entered him. Then Jesus said to him, "What you
do, do quickly."
28 But no one at the table knew for what reason He said this to him.
29 For some thought, because Judas had the
money box, that Jesus had said to him, "Buy
those things we need for the feast," or that he
should give something to the poor.
30 Having received the piece of bread, he
then went out immediately. And it was night.

The New Commandment

31 So, when he had gone out, Jesus said,
"Now the Son of Man is glorified, and God is
glorified in Him.
32 "If God is glorified in Him, God will also
glorify Him in Himself, and glorify Him immediately.
33 "Little children, I shall be with you a little
while longer. You will seek Me; and as I said
to the Jews, 'Where I am going, you cannot
come,' so now I say to you.

13:2 [a]NU-Text reads *And during supper.* **13:18** [a]NU-Text reads *My bread.* [b]Psalm 41:9 **13:25** [a]NU-Text and M-Text add *thus.*

LIFE LESSONS

13:1 — . . . *having loved His own who were in the world, He loved them to the end.*

Jesus always finishes what He starts. He never drops someone in mid-stream or gives up on a person halfway to the finish line. "He who has begun a good work in you will complete it . . . ." (Phil. 1:6).

13:17 — *"If you know these things, blessed are you if you do them."*

Knowing and doing are two separate things. Jesus reserves His blessing not merely for those who know His will, but for those who know it *and* do it. Genuine faith always leads to godly action.

34 "A new commandment I give to you, that
you love one another; as I have loved you, that
you also love one another.
➤ 35 "By this all will know that you are My disciples, if you have love for one another."

Jesus Predicts Peter's Denial

36 Simon Peter said to Him, "Lord, where are
You going?" Jesus answered him, "Where I am
going you cannot follow Me now, but you
shall follow Me afterward."
37 Peter said to Him, "Lord, why can I not follow You now? I will lay down my life for Your
sake."
38 Jesus answered him, "Will you lay down
your life for My sake? Most assuredly, I say to
you, the rooster shall not crow till you have
denied Me three times.

The Way, the Truth, and the Life

14 "Let not your heart be troubled; you
believe in God, believe also in Me.
✳ 2 "In My Father's house are many man-
sions;[a] if *it were* not *so,* I would have told you.
I go to prepare a place for you.[b]
3 "And if I go and prepare a place for you, I
will come again and receive you to Myself;
that where I am, *there* you may be also.
4 "And where I go you know, and the way
you know."
5 Thomas said to Him, "Lord, we do not
know where You are going, and how can we
know the way?"
➤ 6 Jesus said to him, "I am the way, the truth,
and the life. No one comes to the Father except through Me.

The Father Revealed

7 "If you had known Me, you would have
known My Father also; and from now on you
know Him and have seen Him."
8 Philip said to Him, "Lord, show us the Father, and it is sufficient for us."
➤ 9 Jesus said to him, "Have I been with you
so long, and yet you have not known Me,
Philip? He who has seen Me has seen the Father; so how can you say, 'Show us the Father'?
10 "Do you not believe that I am in the Father,
and the Father in Me? The words that I speak
to you I do not speak on My own *authority;*
but the Father who dwells in Me does the
works.
11 "Believe Me that I *am* in the Father and the
Father in Me, or else believe Me for the sake
of the works themselves.

The Answered Prayer

12 "Most assuredly, I say to you, he who be- ✳
lieves in Me, the works that I do he will do
also; and greater *works* than these he will do,
because I go to My Father.
13 "And whatever you ask in My name, that I
will do, that the Father may be glorified in the
Son.
14 "If you ask[a] anything in My name, I will do
it.

Jesus Promises Another Helper

15 "If you love Me, keep[a] My commandments.
16 "And I will pray the Father, and He will
give you another Helper, that He may abide
with you forever—
17 "the Spirit of truth, whom the world cannot receive, because it neither sees Him nor
knows Him; but you know Him, for He dwells
with you and will be in you.
18 "I will not leave you orphans; I will come
to you.

Indwelling of the Father and the Son

19 "A little while longer and the world will
see Me no more, but you will see Me. Because
I live, you will live also.
20 "At that day you will know that I *am* in My
Father, and you in Me, and I in you.
21 "He who has My commandments and
keeps them, it is he who loves Me. And he
who loves Me will be loved by My Father, and
I will love him and manifest Myself to him."
22 Judas (not Iscariot) said to Him, "Lord,
how is it that You will manifest Yourself to us,
and not to the world?"

14:2 [a]Literally *dwellings* [b]NU-Text adds a word which would cause the text to read either *if it were not so, would I have told you that I go to prepare a place for you?* or *if it were not so I would have told you; for I go to prepare a place for you.*
14:14 [a]NU-Text adds *Me.* **14:15** [a]NU-Text reads *you will keep.*

LIFE LESSONS

➤ 13:35 — *"By this all will know that you are My disciples, if you have love for one another."*

The method Jesus gave us to introduce ourselves to the world is love. The world does not know we are His disciples through correct doctrine or big buildings, but through our love for one another.

➤ 14:6 — *"I am the way, the truth, and the life. No one comes to the Father except through Me."*

The only way someone could come to the Father apart from Jesus is if that person had lived a completely sinless life, in thought, word, and deed—and no one but Jesus Himself fits that profile.

➤ 14:9 — *"He who has seen Me has seen the Father . . . ."*

Jesus was not a cardboard cutout or an abstract list of theological attributes. He exhibited a full range of potent emotions and showed His love in both gentle and tough ways. In other words, He mirrored God exactly.

23 Jesus answered and said to him, "If anyone loves Me, he will keep My word; and My
Father will love him, and We will come to him
and make Our home with him.
24 "He who does not love Me does not keep
My words; and the word which you hear is
not Mine but the Father's who sent Me.

The Gift of His Peace

25 "These things I have spoken to you while
being present with you.
26 "But the Helper, the Holy Spirit, whom the
Father will send in My name, He will teach
you all things, and bring to your remembrance all things that I said to you.
27 "Peace I leave with you, My peace I give to
you; not as the world gives do I give to you.
Let not your heart be troubled, neither let it
be afraid.
28 "You have heard Me say to you, 'I am
going away and coming *back* to you.' If you
loved Me, you would rejoice because I said,[a] 'I
am going to the Father,' for My Father is
greater than I.
29 "And now I have told you before it comes,
that when it does come to pass, you may believe.
30 "I will no longer talk much with you, for
the ruler of this world is coming, and he has
nothing in Me.
31 "But that the world may know that I love
the Father, and as the Father gave Me commandment, so I do. Arise, let us go from here.

The True Vine

15 "I am the true vine, and My Father is
the vinedresser.
2 "Every branch in Me that does not bear fruit
He takes away;[a] and every *branch* that bears
fruit He prunes, that it may bear more fruit.
3 "You are already clean because of the
word which I have spoken to you.
4 "Abide in Me, and I in you. As the branch
cannot bear fruit of itself, unless it abides in the
vine, neither can you, unless you abide in Me.
5 "I am the vine, you *are* the branches. He
who abides in Me, and I in him, bears much
fruit; for without Me you can do nothing.
6 "If anyone does not abide in Me, he is cast
out as a branch and is withered; and they
gather them and throw *them* into the fire, and
they are burned.
7 "If you abide in Me, and My words abide
in you, you will[a] ask what you desire, and it
shall be done for you.
8 "By this My Father is glorified, that you
bear much fruit; so you will be My disciples.

Love and Joy Perfected

9 "As the Father loved Me, I also have loved
you; abide in My love.
10 "If you keep My commandments, you will
abide in My love, just as I have kept My Father's commandments and abide in His love.
11 "These things I have spoken to you, that
My joy may remain in you, and *that* your joy
may be full.
12 "This is My commandment, that you love
one another as I have loved you.
13 "Greater love has no one than this, than to
lay down one's life for his friends.
14 "You are My friends if you do whatever I
command you.
15 "No longer do I call you servants, for a servant does not know what his master is doing;
but I have called you friends, for all things
that I heard from My Father I have made
known to you.
16 "You did not choose Me, but I chose you
and appointed you that you should go and
bear fruit, and *that* your fruit should remain,

14:28 [a]NU-Text omits *I said.* **15:2** [a]Or *lifts up* **15:7** [a]NU-Text omits *you will.*

LIFE LESSONS

➤ 14:23 — *"If anyone loves Me, he will keep My word; and My Father will love him, and We will come to him and make Our home with him."*

We obey Jesus not by gritting our teeth and doing what we hate, but by depending on His power to enable us to do what our love for Him compels us to do. Willing obedience leads to an intimate relationship.

➤ 14:27 — *"Peace I leave with you, My peace I give to you; not as the world gives do I give to you. Let not your heart be troubled, neither let it be afraid."*

The peace of Jesus "surpasses all understanding" (Phil. 4:7) because it has a supernatural source in the heart of Christ Himself. His peace keeps us from fear and worry because it brings us straight to Him.

➤ 15:4 — *"Abide in Me, and I in you. As the branch cannot bear fruit of itself, unless it abides in the vine, neither can you, unless you abide in Me."*

The only way we can play a significant role in the kingdom of God is to allow Jesus to live His life in and through us. While apart from Him we can do nothing, in Him we can do anything He calls us to do.

➤ 15:11 — *"These things I have spoken to you, that My joy may remain in you, and that your joy may be full."*

The Word of God, living and growing within us, produces lasting and increasing joy. A lack of joy in a Christian's life often can be traced to a lack of concentrated devotional time in God's Word.

➤ 15:16 — *"You did not choose Me, but I chose you and appointed you that you should go and bear fruit, and that your fruit should remain . . . ."*

Jesus does not want any of us to lead unproductive or unfocused lives. He chose us not only for salvation, but also to play a significant role in His kingdom. He wants each of us to fulfill a particular purpose.

that whatever you ask the Father in My name
He may give you.
17 "These things I command you, that you
love one another.

The World's Hatred

18 "If the world hates you, you know that it
hated Me before *it hated* you.
19 "If you were of the world, the world would
love its own. Yet because you are not of the
world, but I chose you out of the world, therefore the world hates you.
20 "Remember the word that I said to you, 'A
servant is not greater than his master.' If they
persecuted Me, they will also persecute you. If
they kept My word, they will keep yours also.
21 "But all these things they will do to you for
My name's sake, because they do not know
Him who sent Me.
22 "If I had not come and spoken to them,
they would have no sin, but now they have no
excuse for their sin.
23 "He who hates Me hates My Father also.
24 "If I had not done among them the works
which no one else did, they would have no
sin; but now they have seen and also hated
both Me and My Father.
25 "But *this happened* that the word might be
fulfilled which is written in their law, *'They
hated Me without a cause.'*[a]

The Coming Rejection

26 "But when the Helper comes, whom I shall
send to you from the Father, the Spirit of truth
who proceeds from the Father, He will testify
of Me.
27 "And you also will bear witness, because
you have been with Me from the beginning.

16 "These things I have spoken to you,
that you should not be made to stumble.
2 "They will put you out of the synagogues;
yes, the time is coming that whoever kills you
will think that he offers God service.
3 "And these things they will do to you[a] because they have not known the Father nor Me.
4 "But these things I have told you, that when
the[a] time comes, you may remember that I told
you of them. "And these things I did not say to
you at the beginning, because I was with you.

The Work of the Holy Spirit

5 "But now I go away to Him who sent Me,
and none of you asks Me, 'Where are You
going?'
6 "But because I have said these things to
you, sorrow has filled your heart.
7 "Nevertheless I tell you the truth. It is to
your advantage that I go away; for if I do not
go away, the Helper will not come to you; but
if I depart, I will send Him to you.
8 "And when He has come, He will convict
the world of sin, and of righteousness, and of
judgment:
9 "of sin, because they do not believe in Me;
10 "of righteousness, because I go to My Father and you see Me no more;
11 "of judgment, because the ruler of this
world is judged.
12 "I still have many things to say to you, but
you cannot bear *them* now.
13 "However, when He, the Spirit of truth, ✳
has come, He will guide you into all truth; for
He will not speak on His own *authority,* but
whatever He hears He will speak; and He will
tell you things to come.
14 "He will glorify Me, for He will take of
what is Mine and declare *it* to you.
15 "All things that the Father has are Mine.
Therefore I said that He will take of Mine and
declare *it* to you.[a]

Sorrow Will Turn to Joy

16 "A little while, and you will not see Me;
and again a little while, and you will see Me,
because I go to the Father."
17 Then *some* of His disciples said among
themselves, "What is this that He says to us,
'A little while, and you will not see Me; and
again a little while, and you will see Me'; and,
'because I go to the Father'?"
18 They said therefore, "What is this that He
says, 'A little while'? We do not know what He
is saying."
19 Now Jesus knew that they desired to ask
Him, and He said to them, "Are you inquiring
among yourselves about what I said, 'A little
while, and you will not see Me; and again a
little while, and you will see Me'?
20 "Most assuredly, I say to you that you will
weep and lament, but the world will rejoice;
and you will be sorrowful, but your sorrow
will be turned into joy.
21 "A woman, when she is in labor, has sorrow because her hour has come; but as soon
as she has given birth to the child, she no
longer remembers the anguish, for joy that a
human being has been born into the world.
22 "Therefore you now have sorrow; but I ➤

15:25 [a]Psalm 69:4 **16:3** [a]NU-Text and M-Text omit *to you.*
16:4 [a]NU-Text reads *their.* **16:15** [a]NU-Text and M-Text read *He takes of Mine and will declare it to you.*

LIFE LESSONS

➤ ***16:22 — " . . . you now have sorrow; but I will see you again and your heart will rejoice, and your joy no one will take from you."***

Sorrow and happiness are both a part of the human experience, and both depend largely on circumstances. When we unite ourselves to the risen Christ, however, He gives us a joy that no circumstances can dampen.

WHAT THE BIBLE SAYS ABOUT HOW THE HOLY SPIRIT GUIDES US

John 16:13

The Bible promises that the Holy Spirit will guide us, with an emphasis on the word "guide." Jesus doesn't promise that the Holy Spirit will control us. He doesn't promise that He will drive us. He doesn't say that the Holy Spirit will force us to do anything. He says He will guide us.

At times I wish the Holy Spirit *would* control me—when I feel tempted, or when it's a beautiful Saturday afternoon and I need to study, but everything in me wants to grab my camera and head for the mountains. Life would be much easier (and I would be a much more enjoyable person) if the Holy Spirit would just reach out and take control of me. But that is not the case.

He is our guide, not our controller. At no point do we lose our ability to choose to follow His leading. Consequently, we are always responsible for our words and actions.

The Holy Spirit guides believers into truth; that makes His guidance trustworthy. The Holy Spirit helps believers discern between what is true and what is not; what is wise and what is foolish; what is best and what is simply okay.

We are always responsible for our words and actions.

As the details of everyday living barrage you, the Holy Spirit will guide you. He will give you that extra, on-the-spot sense of discernment you need to make both big and small decisions. And as you develop greater sensitivity to His guidance, you will worry much less about the decisions you make.

The Holy Spirit never speaks on His own. Like Christ, this Person of the Trinity willingly submits to the authority of the Father. Everything He communicates to us is directly from the Father: "He will not speak on His own authority" (John 16:13). The Holy Spirit is God's mouthpiece to believers.

When you think about it, this makes perfect sense. After all, where does the Holy Spirit reside? In you and in me! Since He has direct access to our minds, emotions, and consciences, He is the perfect candidate for communicating God's will to us.

See the Life Principles Index for further study:

22. *To walk in the Spirit is to obey the initial promptings of the Spirit.*
10. *If necessary, God will move heaven and earth to show us His will.*

will see you again and your heart will rejoice,
and your joy no one will take from you.
23 "And in that day you will ask Me nothing.
Most assuredly, I say to you, whatever you
ask the Father in My name He will give you.
➤ 24 "Until now you have asked nothing in My
name. Ask, and you will receive, that your joy
may be full.

Jesus Christ Has Overcome the World

25 "These things I have spoken to you in figurative language; but the time is coming
when I will no longer speak to you in figurative language, but I will tell you plainly about
the Father.
26 "In that day you will ask in My name, and
I do not say to you that I shall pray the Father
for you;
27 "for the Father Himself loves you, because
you have loved Me, and have believed that I
came forth from God.
28 "I came forth from the Father and have
come into the world. Again, I leave the world
and go to the Father."
29 His disciples said to Him, "See, now You
are speaking plainly, and using no figure of
speech!
30 "Now we are sure that You know all
things, and have no need that anyone should
question You. By this we believe that You came
forth from God."
31 Jesus answered them, "Do you now believe?
32 "Indeed the hour is coming, yes, has now
come, that you will be scattered, each to his
own, and will leave Me alone. And yet I am
not alone, because the Father is with Me.
➤ 33 "These things I have spoken to you, that in
Me you may have peace. In the world you
will[a] have tribulation; but be of good cheer, I
have overcome the world."

Jesus Prays for Himself

17 Jesus spoke these words, lifted up His
eyes to heaven, and said: "Father, the
hour has come. Glorify Your Son, that Your
Son also may glorify You,
2 "as You have given Him authority over all
flesh, that He should[a] give eternal life to as
many as You have given Him.
3 "And this is eternal life, that they may ➤
know You, the only true God, and Jesus Christ
whom You have sent.
4 "I have glorified You on the earth. I have
finished the work which You have given Me to
do.
5 "And now, O Father, glorify Me together
with Yourself, with the glory which I had with
You before the world was.

Jesus Prays for His Disciples

6 "I have manifested Your name to the men
whom You have given Me out of the world.
They were Yours, You gave them to Me, and
they have kept Your word.
7 "Now they have known that all things
which You have given Me are from You.
8 "For I have given to them the words which
You have given Me; and they have received
them, and have known surely that I came
forth from You; and they have believed that
You sent Me.
9 "I pray for them. I do not pray for the
world but for those whom You have given Me,
for they are Yours.
10 "And all Mine are Yours, and Yours are
Mine, and I am glorified in them.
11 "Now I am no longer in the world, but
these are in the world, and I come to You. Holy
Father, keep through Your name those whom
You have given Me,[a] that they may be one as
We *are.*
12 "While I was with them in the world,[a] I
kept them in Your name. Those whom You
gave Me I have kept;[b] and none of them is lost
except the son of perdition, that the Scripture
might be fulfilled.
13 "But now I come to You, and these things I
speak in the world, that they may have My joy
fulfilled in themselves.

16:33 [a]NU-Text and M-Text omit *will.* **17:2** [a]M-Text reads *shall.* **17:11** [a]NU-Text and M-Text read *keep them through Your name which You have given Me.* **17:12** [a]NU-Text omits *in the world.* [b]NU-Text reads *in Your name which You gave Me. And I guarded them;* (or *it;*).

LIFE LESSONS

➤ 16:24 — *"Until now you have asked nothing in My name. Ask, and you will receive, that your joy may be full."*

To ask in Jesus' name means to connect your request with the will, plans, and purpose of Jesus Christ. It is not a magic add-on to hedge your bets, but it weds your request to the sovereignty of Jesus.

➤ 16:33 — *". . . be of good cheer, I have overcome the world."*

How could a man about to be crucified say that He had overcome the world? Jesus overcame the world by obeying His Father despite all challenges and opposition. In a similar way, we too can be overcomers (Rev. 3:21; 12:11).

➤ 17:3 — *"And this is eternal life, that they may know You, the only true God, and Jesus Christ whom You have sent."*

Eternal life comes by knowing and being connected to the Source of all life, God. Through faith in the risen Jesus, the life of Christ fills us and unites us forever with the Father (Rom. 8:11).

14 "I have given them Your word; and the world has hated them because they are not of the world, just as I am not of the world.
15 "I do not pray that You should take them out of the world, but that You should keep them from the evil one.
16 "They are not of the world, just as I am not of the world.
17 "Sanctify them by Your truth. Your word is truth.
18 "As You sent Me into the world, I also have sent them into the world.
19 "And for their sakes I sanctify Myself, that they also may be sanctified by the truth.

Jesus Prays for All Believers

➤ **20** "I do not pray for these alone, but also for those who will[a] believe in Me through their word;
21 "that they all may be one, as You, Father, *are* in Me, and I in You; that they also may be one in Us, that the world may believe that You sent Me.
22 "And the glory which You gave Me I have given them, that they may be one just as We are one:
23 "I in them, and You in Me; that they may be made perfect in one, and that the world may know that You have sent Me, and have loved them as You have loved Me.
➤ 24 "Father, I desire that they also whom You gave Me may be with Me where I am, that they may behold My glory which You have given Me; for You loved Me before the foundation of the world.
25 "O righteous Father! The world has not known You, but I have known You; and these have known that You sent Me.
26 "And I have declared to them Your name, and will declare *it*, that the love with which You loved Me may be in them, and I in them."

Betrayal and Arrest in Gethsemane

18 When Jesus had spoken these words, He went out with His disciples over the Brook Kidron, where there was a garden, which He and His disciples entered.
2 And Judas, who betrayed Him, also knew the place; for Jesus often met there with His disciples.
3 Then Judas, having received a detachment *of troops*, and officers from the chief priests and Pharisees, came there with lanterns, torches, and weapons.

Life Examples:

JUDAS

"Rabbi" Is Not Enough

JOHN 18:3

Possessor of the darkest of human hearts, Judas Iscariot could never be described as godly. But his betrayal (John 18:3) powerfully reminds us of the horrific possibilities within every human heart.

While Judas called Jesus "Rabbi" (Matt. 26:49), there is no record that he used the term "Lord." It has always been possible to claim allegiance to God without ever handing over the soul's title deed.

When Judas approached Jesus in Gethsemane, he received one final chance to win eternal asylum. But sin had so blinded Judas that he could not see the Way, the Truth, and the Life.

His story of the betrayal still resonates, not only because of Judas's evil kiss, but also because we realize the wickedness of our own flesh. How many attend church regularly and give Jesus intellectual assent, but not their hearts? How many call Him King, only to assume their own thrones?

What kind of kiss do *we* give the Lord?

See the Life Principles Index for further study:

24. To live the Christian life is to allow Jesus to live His life in and through us.

1. Our intimacy with God—His highest priority for our lives—determines the impact of our lives.

17:20 [a]NU-Text and M-Text omit *will.*

LIFE LESSONS

➤ 17:20 — *"I do not pray for these alone, but also for those who will believe in Me through their word . . . ."*

Jesus began His prayers for us way back in the garden of Gethsemane before His arrest. We have trusted in Jesus through the word of the apostles, and this prayer of His is therefore for us.

➤ 17:24 — *"Father, I desire that they also whom You gave Me may be with Me where I am, that they may behold My glory . . . ."*

Jesus wants us to be with Him where He is, and to see the majesty and splendor that belonged to Him even before He left heaven to fulfill His ministry on earth. Jesus wants to share His glory with us!

4 Jesus therefore, knowing all things that would come upon Him, went forward and said to them, "Whom are you seeking?"
5 They answered Him, "Jesus of Nazareth." Jesus said to them, "I am *He.*" And Judas, who betrayed Him, also stood with them.
6 Now when He said to them, "I am *He,*" they drew back and fell to the ground.
7 Then He asked them again, "Whom are you seeking?" And they said, "Jesus of Nazareth."
8 Jesus answered, "I have told you that I am *He.* Therefore, if you seek Me, let these go their way,"
9 that the saying might be fulfilled which He spoke, "Of those whom You gave Me I have lost none."
10 Then Simon Peter, having a sword, drew it and struck the high priest's servant, and cut off his right ear. The servant's name was Malchus.
➤ 11 So Jesus said to Peter, "Put your sword into the sheath. Shall I not drink the cup which My Father has given Me?"

Before the High Priest

12 Then the detachment *of troops* and the captain and the officers of the Jews arrested Jesus and bound Him.
13 And they led Him away to Annas first, for he was the father-in-law of Caiaphas who was high priest that year.
14 Now it was Caiaphas who advised the Jews that it was expedient that one man should die for the people.

Peter Denies Jesus

15 And Simon Peter followed Jesus, and so *did* another[a] disciple. Now that disciple was known to the high priest, and went with Jesus into the courtyard of the high priest.
16 But Peter stood at the door outside. Then the other disciple, who was known to the high priest, went out and spoke to her who kept the door, and brought Peter in.
17 Then the servant girl who kept the door said to Peter, "You are not also *one* of this Man's disciples, are you?" He said, "I am not."
18 Now the servants and officers who had made a fire of coals stood there, for it was cold, and they warmed themselves. And Peter stood with them and warmed himself.

Jesus Questioned by the High Priest

19 The high priest then asked Jesus about His disciples and His doctrine.
20 Jesus answered him, "I spoke openly to the world. I always taught in synagogues and in the temple, where the Jews always meet,[a] and in secret I have said nothing.
21 "Why do you ask Me? Ask those who have heard Me what I said to them. Indeed they know what I said."
22 And when He had said these things, one of the officers who stood by struck Jesus with the palm of his hand, saying, "Do You answer the high priest like that?"
23 Jesus answered him, "If I have spoken evil, bear witness of the evil; but if well, why do you strike Me?"
24 Then Annas sent Him bound to Caiaphas the high priest.

Peter Denies Twice More

25 Now Simon Peter stood and warmed himself. Therefore they said to him, "You are not also *one* of His disciples, are you?" He denied *it* and said, "I am not!"
26 One of the servants of the high priest, a relative *of him* whose ear Peter cut off, said, "Did I not see you in the garden with Him?"
27 Peter then denied again; and immediately a rooster crowed.

In Pilate's Court

28 Then they led Jesus from Caiaphas to the Praetorium, and it was early morning. But they themselves did not go into the Praetorium, lest they should be defiled, but that they might eat the Passover.
29 Pilate then went out to them and said, "What accusation do you bring against this Man?"
30 They answered and said to him, "If He were not an evildoer, we would not have delivered Him up to you."
31 Then Pilate said to them, "You take Him and judge Him according to your law." Therefore the Jews said to him, "It is not lawful for us to put anyone to death,"
32 that the saying of Jesus might be fulfilled which He spoke, signifying by what death He would die.
33 Then Pilate entered the Praetorium again, called Jesus, and said to Him, "Are You the King of the Jews?"
34 Jesus answered him, "Are you speaking for yourself about this, or did others tell you this concerning Me?"

18:15 [a]M-Text reads *the other.* **18:20** [a]NU-Text reads *where all the Jews meet.*

LIFE LESSONS

➤ 18:11 — *"Shall I not drink the cup which My Father has given Me?"*

Three times in the garden of Gethsemane Jesus had prayed that, if it were possible, God would remove the "cup" of the cross from Him (Matt. 26:36–46). He didn't, and so now Jesus would let nothing come between Him and that cup.

35 Pilate answered, "Am I a Jew? Your own
nation and the chief priests have delivered
You to me. What have You done?"
➤ 36 Jesus answered, "My kingdom is not of
this world. If My kingdom were of this world,
My servants would fight, so that I should not
be delivered to the Jews; but now My kingdom is not from here."
37 Pilate therefore said to Him, "Are You a
king then?" Jesus answered, "You say *rightly*
that I am a king. For this cause I was born,
and for this cause I have come into the world,
that I should bear witness to the truth. Everyone who is of the truth hears My voice."
38 Pilate said to Him, "What is truth?" And
when he had said this, he went out again to
the Jews, and said to them, "I find no fault in
Him at all.

Taking the Place of Barabbas

39 "But you have a custom that I should release someone to you at the Passover. Do you
therefore want me to release to you the King
of the Jews?"
40 Then they all cried again, saying, "Not this
Man, but Barabbas!" Now Barabbas was a
robber.

The Soldiers Mock Jesus

19 So then Pilate took Jesus and scourged
Him.
2 And the soldiers twisted a crown of thorns
and put *it* on His head, and they put on Him a
purple robe.
3 Then they said,[a] "Hail, King of the Jews!"
And they struck Him with their hands.
4 Pilate then went out again, and said to
them, "Behold, I am bringing Him out to you,
that you may know that I find no fault in Him."

Pilate's Decision

5 Then Jesus came out, wearing the crown
of thorns and the purple robe. And *Pilate* said
to them, "Behold the Man!"
6 Therefore, when the chief priests and officers saw Him, they cried out, saying, "Crucify
Him, crucify *Him!*" Pilate said to them, "You
take Him and crucify *Him,* for I find no fault
in Him."
7 The Jews answered him, "We have a law,
and according to our[a] law He ought to die, because He made Himself the Son of God."
8 Therefore, when Pilate heard that saying,
he was the more afraid,
9 and went again into the Praetorium, and
said to Jesus, "Where are You from?" But Jesus gave him no answer.
10 Then Pilate said to Him, "Are You not
speaking to me? Do You not know that I have
power to crucify You, and power to release
You?"
11 Jesus answered, "You could have no ➤
power at all against Me unless it had been
given you from above. Therefore the one who
delivered Me to you has the greater sin."
12 From then on Pilate sought to release Him,
but the Jews cried out, saying, "If you let this
Man go, you are not Caesar's friend. Whoever
makes himself a king speaks against Caesar."
13 When Pilate therefore heard that saying,
he brought Jesus out and sat down in the
judgment seat in a place that is called *The*
Pavement, but in Hebrew, Gabbatha.
14 Now it was the Preparation Day of the
Passover, and about the sixth hour. And he
said to the Jews, "Behold your King!"
15 But they cried out, "Away with *Him,* away ➤
with *Him!* Crucify Him!" Pilate said to them,
"Shall I crucify your King?" The chief priests
answered, "We have no king but Caesar!"
16 Then he delivered Him to them to be crucified. Then they took Jesus and led *Him*
away.[a]

The King on a Cross

17 And He, bearing His cross, went out to a
place called *the Place* of a Skull, which is
called in Hebrew, Golgotha,
18 where they crucified Him, and two others
with Him, one on either side, and Jesus in the
center.
19 Now Pilate wrote a title and put *it* on the
cross. And the writing was:

JESUS OF NAZARETH,
THE KING OF THE JEWS.

19:3 [a]NU-Text reads *And they came up to Him and said.*
19:7 [a]NU-Text reads *the law.* **19:16** [a]NU-Text omits *and led Him away.*

LIFE LESSONS

➤ 18:36 — *"My kingdom is not of this world."*

One day Jesus will return to earth "to rule all the nations with a rod of iron" (Rev. 12:5; see also Ps. 2:9; Rev. 2:27; 19:15). Until then, His kingdom focuses on redeeming the hearts of His followers.

➤ 19:11 — *"You could have no power at all against Me unless it had been given you from above."*

No one exercises any authority at all in this world unless God first gives it to him or her (Dan. 4:17; Rom. 13:1). As children of a sovereign God, we are *never* victims of our circumstances.

➤ 19:15 — *Pilate said to them, "Shall I crucify your King?" The chief priests answered, "We have no king but Caesar!"*

The opponents of Jesus wanted Him dead so badly that they confessed Caesar as their only king, thus rejecting God as their King. No one speaking by the Spirit of the Lord could ever give total allegiance to a human ruler.

20 Then many of the Jews read this title, for the place where Jesus was crucified was near the city; and it was written in Hebrew, Greek, *and* Latin.

21 Therefore the chief priests of the Jews said to Pilate, "Do not write, 'The King of the Jews,' but, 'He said, "I am the King of the Jews."'"

22 Pilate answered, "What I have written, I have written."

23 Then the soldiers, when they had crucified Jesus, took His garments and made four parts, to each soldier a part, and also the tunic. Now the tunic was without seam, woven from the top in one piece.

24 They said therefore among themselves, "Let us not tear it, but cast lots for it, whose it shall be," that the Scripture might be fulfilled which says:

> *"They divided My garments among them,*
> *And for My clothing they cast lots."*[a]

Therefore the soldiers did these things.

Behold Your Mother

25 Now there stood by the cross of Jesus His mother, and His mother's sister, Mary the *wife* of Clopas, and Mary Magdalene.

➤ 26 When Jesus therefore saw His mother, and the disciple whom He loved standing by, He said to His mother, "Woman, behold your son!"

27 Then He said to the disciple, "Behold your mother!" And from that hour that disciple took her to his own *home.*

It Is Finished

28 After this, Jesus, knowing[a] that all things were now accomplished, that the Scripture might be fulfilled, said, "I thirst!"

29 Now a vessel full of sour wine was sitting there; and they filled a sponge with sour wine, put *it* on hyssop, and put *it* to His mouth.

30 So when Jesus had received the sour wine, He said, "It is finished!" And bowing His head, He gave up His spirit.

Jesus' Side Is Pierced

31 Therefore, because it was the Preparation *Day,* that the bodies should not remain on the cross on the Sabbath (for that Sabbath was a high day), the Jews asked Pilate that their legs might be broken, and *that* they might be taken away.

32 Then the soldiers came and broke the legs of the first and of the other who was crucified with Him.

33 But when they came to Jesus and saw that He was already dead, they did not break His legs.

34 But one of the soldiers pierced His side with a spear, and immediately blood and water came out.

35 And he who has seen has testified, and his testimony is true; and he knows that he is telling the truth, so that you may believe.

36 For these things were done that the Scripture should be fulfilled, *"Not one of His bones shall be broken."*[a]

37 And again another Scripture says, *"They shall look on Him whom they pierced."*[a]

Jesus Buried in Joseph's Tomb

38 After this, Joseph of Arimathea, being a disciple of Jesus, but secretly, for fear of the Jews, asked Pilate that he might take away the body of Jesus; and Pilate gave *him* permission. So he came and took the body of Jesus.

39 And Nicodemus, who at first came to Jesus by night, also came, bringing a mixture of myrrh and aloes, about a hundred pounds.

40 Then they took the body of Jesus, and bound it in strips of linen with the spices, as the custom of the Jews is to bury.

41 Now in the place where He was crucified there was a garden, and in the garden a new tomb in which no one had yet been laid.

42 So there they laid Jesus, because of the Jews' Preparation *Day,* for the tomb was nearby.

The Empty Tomb

20 Now the first *day* of the week Mary Magdalene went to the tomb early, while it was still dark, and saw *that* the stone had been taken away from the tomb.

2 Then she ran and came to Simon Peter, and to the other disciple, whom Jesus loved, and said to them, "They have taken away the Lord out of the tomb, and we do not know where they have laid Him."

3 Peter therefore went out, and the other disciple, and were going to the tomb.

4 So they both ran together, and the other disciple outran Peter and came to the tomb first.

19:24 [a]Psalm 22:18 **19:28** [a]M-Text reads *seeing.*
19:36 [a]Exodus 12:46; Numbers 9:12; Psalm 34:20
19:37 [a]Zechariah 12:10

LIFE LESSONS

➤ 19:26 — When Jesus therefore saw His mother, and the disciple whom He loved standing by, He said to His mother, "Woman, behold your son!"

Even as He died, Jesus showed His deep and genuine concern for others. "The son of Man did not come to be served, but to serve, and to give His life a ransom for many" (Mark 10:45).

5 And he, stooping down and looking in, saw the linen cloths lying *there;* yet he did not go in.

6 Then Simon Peter came, following him, and went into the tomb; and he saw the linen cloths lying *there,*

7 and the handkerchief that had been around His head, not lying with the linen cloths, but folded together in a place by itself.

8 Then the other disciple, who came to the tomb first, went in also; and he saw and believed.

9 For as yet they did not know the Scripture, that He must rise again from the dead.

10 Then the disciples went away again to their own homes.

Mary Magdalene Sees the Risen Lord

11 But Mary stood outside by the tomb weeping, and as she wept she stooped down *and looked* into the tomb.

12 And she saw two angels in white sitting, one at the head and the other at the feet, where the body of Jesus had lain.

13 Then they said to her, "Woman, why are you weeping?" She said to them, "Because they have taken away my Lord, and I do not know where they have laid Him."

14 Now when she had said this, she turned around and saw Jesus standing *there,* and did not know that it was Jesus.

15 Jesus said to her, "Woman, why are you weeping? Whom are you seeking?" She, supposing Him to be the gardener, said to Him, "Sir, if You have carried Him away, tell me where You have laid Him, and I will take Him away."

16 Jesus said to her, "Mary!" She turned and said to Him,[a] "Rabboni!" (which is to say, Teacher).

17 Jesus said to her, "Do not cling to Me, for I have not yet ascended to My Father; but go to My brethren and say to them, 'I am ascending to My Father and your Father, and *to* My God and your God.'"

18 Mary Magdalene came and told the disciples that she had seen the Lord,[a] and *that* He had spoken these things to her.

The Apostles Commissioned

19 Then, the same day at evening, being the first *day* of the week, when the doors were shut where the disciples were assembled,[a] for fear of the Jews, Jesus came and stood in the midst, and said to them, "Peace *be* with you."

20 When He had said this, He showed them *His* hands and His side. Then the disciples were glad when they saw the Lord.

21 So Jesus said to them again, "Peace to you! As the Father has sent Me, I also send you."

22 And when He had said this, He breathed on *them,* and said to them, "Receive the Holy Spirit.

23 "If you forgive the sins of any, they are forgiven them; if you retain the *sins* of any, they are retained."

Seeing and Believing

24 Now Thomas, called the Twin, one of the twelve, was not with them when Jesus came.

25 The other disciples therefore said to him, "We have seen the Lord." So he said to them, "Unless I see in His hands the print of the nails, and put my finger into the print of the nails, and put my hand into His side, I will not believe."

26 And after eight days His disciples were again inside, and Thomas with them. Jesus came, the doors being shut, and stood in the midst, and said, "Peace to you!"

27 Then He said to Thomas, "Reach your finger here, and look at My hands; and reach your hand *here,* and put *it* into My side. Do not be unbelieving, but believing."

28 And Thomas answered and said to Him, "My Lord and my God!"

29 Jesus said to him, "Thomas,[a] because you have seen Me, you have believed. Blessed *are* those who have not seen and *yet* have believed."

That You May Believe

30 And truly Jesus did many other signs in the presence of His disciples, which are not written in this book;

31 but these are written that you may believe that Jesus is the Christ, the Son of God, and that believing you may have life in His name.

20:16 [a]NU-Text adds *in Hebrew.* **20:18** [a]NU-Text reads *disciples, "I have seen the Lord," . . .* **20:19** [a]NU-Text omits *assembled.* **20:29** [a]NU-Text and M-Text omit *Thomas.*

LIFE LESSONS

➢ ***20:21 — "As the Father has sent Me, I also send you."***

The Father sent His Son into the world to make it possible for sinful men and women to become holy, and the Son now sends His followers into the world to make it possible for others to hear about His work.

➢ ***20:31 — . . . these are written that you may believe that Jesus is the Christ, the Son of God, and that believing you may have life in His name.***

If the Word of God did not have God's stamp of approval, it would have fallen into obscurity long ago. But it still rings with the power of God to accomplish its purpose, to lead people to life in Christ.

Life Examples:

THOMAS

From Doubt to Faith

JOHN 20:24–29

The name Thomas is the Hebrew equivalent of the Greek name *Didymus*, which means "twin." Thomas reminds us of the similarities between doubt and faith—both originate from the same place: a confrontation with the unknown. Doubt concedes defeat, while faith claims the victory.

When Jesus appeared to Thomas, hope became reality. The resurrection renewed his confidence in God (John 20:24–29) and motivated him to spend the rest of his life proclaiming the certainty of the risen Christ. Tradition holds that Thomas spread the gospel to India and helped dispel others' disbelief about the resurrection.

If uncertainties have smothered your confidence in the Lord, remember His power so evident in the empty tomb. The crucifixion was not the end of the story—and neither is the trial you face. Choose the path of faith and declare that triumph lies just ahead. Allow His resurrection to strengthen your hope, renew your certainty, and be your greatest victory.

See the Life Principles Index for further study:
9. Trusting God means looking beyond what we can see to what God sees.

Breakfast by the Sea

21 After these things Jesus showed Himself again to the disciples at the Sea of
Tiberias, and in this way He showed *Himself:*
2 Simon Peter, Thomas called the Twin,
Nathanael of Cana in Galilee, the *sons* of
Zebedee, and two others of His disciples were
together.
3 Simon Peter said to them, "I am going
fishing." They said to him, "We are going with
you also." They went out and immediately[a]
got into the boat, and that night they caught
nothing.
4 But when the morning had now come, Jesus stood on the shore; yet the disciples did
not know that it was Jesus.
5 Then Jesus said to them, "Children, have
you any food?" They answered Him, "No."
6 And He said to them, "Cast the net on the
right side of the boat, and you will find *some.*"
So they cast, and now they were not able to
draw it in because of the multitude of fish.
7 Therefore that disciple whom Jesus loved
said to Peter, "It is the Lord!" Now when Simon Peter heard that it was the Lord, he put
on *his* outer garment (for he had removed it),
and plunged into the sea.
8 But the other disciples came in the little
boat (for they were not far from land, but
about two hundred cubits), dragging the net
with fish.
9 Then, as soon as they had come to land,
they saw a fire of coals there, and fish laid on
it, and bread.
10 Jesus said to them, "Bring some of the fish
which you have just caught."
11 Simon Peter went up and dragged the net
to land, full of large fish, one hundred and
fifty-three; and although there were so many,
the net was not broken.
12 Jesus said to them, "Come *and* eat breakfast." Yet none of the disciples dared ask Him,
"Who are You?"—knowing that it was the Lord.
13 Jesus then came and took the bread and
gave it to them, and likewise the fish.
14 This *is* now the third time Jesus showed
Himself to His disciples after He was raised
from the dead.

Jesus Restores Peter

15 So when they had eaten breakfast, Jesus
said to Simon Peter, "Simon, *son* of Jonah,[a] do
you love Me more than these?" He said to
Him, "Yes, Lord; You know that I love You." He
said to him, "Feed My lambs."
16 He said to him again a second time, "Simon, *son* of Jonah,[a] do you love Me?" He said
to Him, "Yes, Lord; You know that I love You."
He said to him, "Tend My sheep."
17 He said to him the third time, "Simon, *son*
of Jonah,[a] do you love Me?" Peter was grieved
because He said to him the third time, "Do

21:3 [a]NU-Text omits *immediately.* **21:15** [a]NU-Text reads *John.*
21:16 [a]NU-Text reads *John.* **21:17** [a]NU-Text reads *John.*

LIFE LESSONS

➤ **21:12 — *Jesus said to them, "Come and eat breakfast."***

If someone were making up the story, it would seem very odd to have a resurrected Savior making breakfast for His awestruck disciples. Yet God is interested in every detail of our lives, even the mundane ones.

you love Me?" And he said to Him, "Lord, You know all things; You know that I love You." Jesus said to him, "Feed My sheep.

18 "Most assuredly, I say to you, when you were younger, you girded yourself and walked where you wished; but when you are old, you will stretch out your hands, and another will gird you and carry *you* where you do not wish."

➤ 19 This He spoke, signifying by what death he would glorify God. And when He had spoken this, He said to him, "Follow Me."

The Beloved Disciple and His Book

20 Then Peter, turning around, saw the disciple whom Jesus loved following, who also had leaned on His breast at the supper, and said, "Lord, who is the one who betrays You?"

21 Peter, seeing him, said to Jesus, "But Lord, what *about* this man?"

22 Jesus said to him, "If I will that he remain till I come, what *is that* to you? You follow Me." ◄

23 Then this saying went out among the brethren that this disciple would not die. Yet Jesus did not say to him that he would not die, but, "If I will that he remain till I come, what *is that* to you?"

24 This is the disciple who testifies of these things, and wrote these things; and we know that his testimony is true.

25 And there are also many other things that Jesus did, which if they were written one by one, I suppose that even the world itself could not contain the books that would be written. Amen.

LIFE LESSONS

➤ **21:19 — *This He spoke, signifying by what death he would glorify God.***

From this moment on, Peter knew what kind of death—crucifixion—awaited him. And yet he loved the Savior who forgave him with such a passion that he never shrank from fulfilling his purpose, even to the very end.

➤ **21:22 — *Jesus said to him, "If I will that he remain till I come, what is that to you? You follow Me."***

We are to concern ourselves with what God wants to do in our lives, not to fret about what He might do in the life of another. What God does with His other servants is His business, not ours.

THE ACTS

OF THE APOSTLES

Jesus' last recorded words before His ascension—"you shall be witnesses to Me in Jerusalem, and in all Judea and Samaria, and to the end of the earth" (1:8)—prompted the great exploits recorded in the Book of Acts. Empowered by the Holy Spirit, godly men and women took seriously their Lord's final words and began to spread the news of the risen Savior to the most remote corners of the known world.

As the second volume in a two-part work by Luke, this book originally might have had no separate title. But all available Greek manuscripts designate it by the title *Praxeis*, "Acts," or by an expanded title such as, "The Acts of the Apostles." The term *Praxeis* was commonly used in Greek literature to summarize the accomplishments of outstanding men.

While the apostles are mentioned collectively at several points, this book emphasizes the acts of Peter (chapters 1–12) and of Paul (13–28). Peter took an immediate leadership role in the church at Jerusalem, while Paul took the lead in expanding the reach of the church to the Gentiles outside of Israel.

The Book of Acts covers about the first three decades of the church after the resurrection of Christ and spotlights important events that took place from Jerusalem to Rome. Scholars have noted and appreciated its careful attention to recording not only the successes of the early church, but also its challenges (see, for example, Acts 5:1–11; 11:1, 2; 15:1–5, 36–40).

Themes: The Book of Acts highlights the apostles' preaching regarding the resurrected Savior, Jesus Christ, and emphasizes how the Holy Spirit empowered, guided, protected and encouraged the members of the church to boldly serve as witnesses for Jesus.

Author: The physician Luke, who uses the pronoun "we" during some of the narrative.

Time: Some scholars believe the book was written about A.D. 63, while others prefer a date of A.D. 70 or later.

Structure: Each section of the book (chapters 1–7; 8–12; 13–28) focuses on a particular audience, a key personality, and a significant phase in the expansion of the gospel message. Acts begins with the ascension of Christ and moves through the coming of the Holy Spirit and the growth of the church in Jerusalem (1–7). The book next focuses on the expansion of the church to the surrounding area after an outbreak of persecution (8–12), and then it shifts focus to the three missionary journeys and the imprisonment journey of Paul that took the gospel message to Greece and other parts of Europe (13–28).

As you read Acts, watch for several life principles that play an important role in this book:

30. An eager anticipation of the Lord's return keeps us living productively. *See Acts 1:9–11; page 1265.*

22. To walk in the Spirit is to obey the initial promptings of the Spirit. *See Acts 1:24, 25; 6:1–5; 10:19; pages 1266, 1272, 1280.*

25. God blesses us so that we might bless others. *See Acts 2:44–47; 4:32–37; pages 1268, 1270.*

27. Prayer is life's greatest time saver. *See Acts 4:25–31; 12:5–17; pages 1270, 1284*

Prologue

1 The former account I made, O Theophilus,
of all that Jesus began both to do and teach,
2 until the day in which He was taken up,
after He through the Holy Spirit had given
commandments to the apostles whom He had
chosen,
3 to whom He also presented Himself alive
after His suffering by many infallible proofs,
being seen by them during forty days and
speaking of the things pertaining to the kingdom of God.

The Holy Spirit Promised

4 And being assembled together with *them,*
He commanded them not to depart from Jerusalem, but to wait for the Promise of the Father,
"which," *He said,* "you have heard from Me;
➤ 5 "for John truly baptized with water, but
you shall be baptized with the Holy Spirit not
many days from now."
6 Therefore, when they had come together,
they asked Him, saying, "Lord, will You at this
time restore the kingdom to Israel?"
7 And He said to them, "It is not for you to
know times or seasons which the Father has
put in His own authority.
➤ 8 "But you shall receive power when the Holy
Spirit has come upon you; and you shall be witnesses to Me[a] in Jerusalem, and in all Judea
and Samaria, and to the end of the earth."

Jesus Ascends to Heaven

9 Now when He had spoken these things,
while they watched, He was taken up, and a
cloud received Him out of their sight.
10 And while they looked steadfastly toward
heaven as He went up, behold, two men stood
by them in white apparel,
✳ 11 who also said, "Men of Galilee, why do
➤ you stand gazing up into heaven? This *same*
Jesus, who was taken up from you into
heaven, will so come in like manner as you
saw Him go into heaven."

The Upper Room Prayer Meeting

12 Then they returned to Jerusalem from the
mount called Olivet, which is near Jerusalem,
a Sabbath day's journey.
13 And when they had entered, they went up
into the upper room where they were staying:
Peter, James, John, and Andrew; Philip and
Thomas; Bartholomew and Matthew; James
the son of Alphaeus and Simon the Zealot;
and Judas *the son* of James.
14 These all continued with one accord in
prayer and supplication,[a] with the women
and Mary the mother of Jesus, and with His
brothers.

Matthias Chosen

15 And in those days Peter stood up in the
midst of the disciples[a] (altogether the number
of names was about a hundred and twenty),
and said,
16 "Men *and* brethren, this Scripture had to
be fulfilled, which the Holy Spirit spoke before by the mouth of David concerning Judas,
who became a guide to those who arrested
Jesus;
17 "for he was numbered with us and obtained a part in this ministry."
18 (Now this man purchased a field with the
wages of iniquity; and falling headlong, he
burst open in the middle and all his entrails
gushed out.
19 And it became known to all those dwelling
in Jerusalem; so that field is called in their
own language, Akel Dama, that is, Field of
Blood.)
20 "For it is written in the Book of Psalms:

> *'Let his dwelling place be desolate,*
> *And let no one live in it';*[a]

and,

> *'Let*[b] *another take his office.'*[c]

21 "Therefore, of these men who have accompanied us all the time that the Lord Jesus
went in and out among us,
22 "beginning from the baptism of John to
that day when He was taken up from us, one
of these must become a witness with us of His
resurrection."

1:8 [a]NU-Text reads *My witnesses.* **1:14** [a]NU-Text omits *and supplication.* **1:15** [a]NU-Text reads *brethren.* **1:20** [a]Psalm 69:25 [b]Psalm 109:8 [c]Greek *episkopen,* position of overseer

LIFE LESSONS

➤ 1:5 — *". . . for John truly baptized with water, but you shall be baptized with the Holy Spirit not many days from now."*

Every believer in Jesus is baptized by the Holy Spirit into the body of Christ at the moment of conversion (1 Cor. 12:13). From then on, the Spirit lives inside the believer, empowering him or her for service to Christ.

➤ 1:8 — *"But you shall receive power when the Holy Spirit has come upon you; and you shall be witnesses to Me in Jerusalem, and in all Judea and Samaria, and to the end of the earth."*

God calls us to be His ambassadors in this world, introducing people who don't yet know Jesus to the love and grace of God available to them in Christ. We become effective witnesses only through the power of the Spirit.

➤ 1:11 — *"Men of Galilee, why do you stand gazing up into heaven?"*

It is easy to get so mesmerized by the amazing power and miracles of God that we become mere observers rather than active participants in what He wants to do in this world. God calls us to Spirit-empowered action.

ANSWERS TO LIFE'S QUESTIONS

When and how am I filled with the Holy Spirit?

ACTS 2:4

What does the New Testament have to say about the believer's relationship with the Holy Spirit?

First, it is a curious fact that after the Book of Acts, the whole concept of being "filled with the Spirit" drops out of sight, except for one mention in Ephesians (5:18). In that passage, the grammar and word order indicate that Paul is talking about surrendering to the influence of the Spirit, not to the indwelling ministry of the Holy Spirit. While much confusion has stemmed from the refusal to deal with the implications of this simple biblical fact, there is no real cause for confusion.

The Holy Spirit arrived on the day of Pentecost, accompanied by extraordinary manifestations of His presence. These manifestations were sign oriented, not character oriented. In other words, the Bible doesn't say that after being filled with the Holy Spirit, those in the Upper Room went out with great patience, kindness, gentleness, and so on. Rather, it says they immediately began speaking in other tongues. That is how the unbelievers who heard them knew that something supernatural had taken place.

Initially, it appeared that the Spirit came to indwell only those gathered in the Upper Room (Acts 2:3, 4). Soon, however, other believers also were filled with the Holy Spirit (Acts 4:31; 9:17). Not everyone got filled at the same time; it took place in stages. But within a few years following the day of Pentecost, the Holy Spirit had swept through the world, filling all those who had put their faith in Christ. In fact, after Acts 13, we have no record of individuals being filled with or receiving the Holy Spirit, apart from salvation.

Today, the Holy Spirit indwells all believers in Christ. Paul wrote, "For by one Spirit we were all baptized into one body—whether Jews or Greeks, whether slaves or free—and have all been made to drink into one Spirit" (1 Cor. 12:13). The apostle John wrote, "By this we know that we abide in Him and He in us, because He has given us of His Spirit" (1 John 4:13). Christian believers everywhere are filled with the Spirit.

The presence of the Holy Spirit is a source of great assurance. In fact, "if anyone does not have the Spirit of Christ, he is not His" (Rom. 8:9). We know we belong to Christ because His Spirit dwells in us.

See the Life Principles Index for further study:
24. To live the Christian life is to allow Jesus to live His life in and through us.
4. The awareness of God's presence energizes us for our work.

23 And they proposed two: Joseph called Barsabas, who was surnamed Justus, and Matthias.
24 And they prayed and said, "You, O Lord, who know the hearts of all, show which of these two You have chosen
25 "to take part in this ministry and apostleship from which Judas by transgression fell, that he might go to his own place."
26 And they cast their lots, and the lot fell on Matthias. And he was numbered with the eleven apostles.

Coming of the Holy Spirit

2 When the Day of Pentecost had fully come, they were all with one accord[a] in one place.
2 And suddenly there came a sound from heaven, as of a rushing mighty wind, and it filled the whole house where they were sitting.
3 Then there appeared to them divided tongues, as of fire, and *one* sat upon each of them.
4 And they were all filled with the Holy Spirit and began to speak with other tongues, as the Spirit gave them utterance.

2:1 [a]NU-Text reads *together.*

LIFE LESSONS

➤ 2:4 — *And they were all filled with the Holy Spirit and began to speak with other tongues, as the Spirit gave them utterance.*

To demonstrate to the disciples and to the unbelieving world that the Spirit had come in power on the church in a new way, every believer in the Upper Room began to speak in languages he had never learned.

The Crowd's Response

5 And there were dwelling in Jerusalem
Jews, devout men, from every nation under
heaven.
6 And when this sound occurred, the multitude came together, and were confused, because everyone heard them speak in his own
language.
7 Then they were all amazed and marveled,
saying to one another, "Look, are not all these
who speak Galileans?
8 "And how *is it that* we hear, each in our
own language in which we were born?
9 "Parthians and Medes and Elamites, those
dwelling in Mesopotamia, Judea and Cappadocia, Pontus and Asia,
10 "Phrygia and Pamphylia, Egypt and the
parts of Libya adjoining Cyrene, visitors from
Rome, both Jews and proselytes,
11 "Cretans and Arabs—we hear them speaking in our own tongues the wonderful works
of God."
12 So they were all amazed and perplexed,
saying to one another, "Whatever could this
mean?"
13 Others mocking said, "They are full of
new wine."

Peter's Sermon

14 But Peter, standing up with the eleven,
raised his voice and said to them, "Men of
Judea and all who dwell in Jerusalem, let this
be known to you, and heed my words.
15 "For these are not drunk, as you suppose,
since it is *only* the third hour of the day.
16 "But this is what was spoken by the
prophet Joel:

17 '*And it shall come to pass in the last days, says God,*
That I will pour out of My Spirit on all flesh;
Your sons and your daughters shall prophesy,
Your young men shall see visions,
Your old men shall dream dreams.
18 *And on My menservants and on My maidservants*
I will pour out My Spirit in those days;
And they shall prophesy.
19 *I will show wonders in heaven above*
And signs in the earth beneath:
Blood and fire and vapor of smoke.
20 *The sun shall be turned into darkness,*
And the moon into blood,
Before the coming of the great and awesome day of the LORD.
21 *And it shall come to pass*
That whoever calls on the name of the LORD
Shall be saved.'[a]

22 "Men of Israel, hear these words: Jesus of
Nazareth, a Man attested by God to you by
miracles, wonders, and signs which God did
through Him in your midst, as you yourselves
also know—
23 "Him, being delivered by the determined
purpose and foreknowledge of God, you have
taken[a] by lawless hands, have crucified, and
put to death;
24 "whom God raised up, having loosed the
pains of death, because it was not possible
that He should be held by it.
25 "For David says concerning Him:

'*I foresaw the LORD always before my face,*
For He is at my right hand, that I may not be shaken.
26 *Therefore my heart rejoiced, and my tongue was glad;*
Moreover my flesh also will rest in hope.
27 *For You will not leave my soul in Hades,*
Nor will You allow Your Holy One to see corruption.
28 *You have made known to me the ways of life;*
You will make me full of joy in Your presence.'[a]

29 "Men *and* brethren, let *me* speak freely to
you of the patriarch David, that he is both
dead and buried, and his tomb is with us to
this day.
30 "Therefore, being a prophet, and knowing
that God had sworn with an oath to him that
of the fruit of his body, according to the flesh,
He would raise up the Christ to sit on his
throne,[a]
31 "he, foreseeing this, spoke concerning the
resurrection of the Christ, that His soul was
not left in Hades, nor did His flesh see corruption.
32 "This Jesus God has raised up, of which
we are all witnesses.
33 "Therefore being exalted to the right hand
of God, and having received from the Father
the promise of the Holy Spirit, He poured out
this which you now see and hear.

2:21 [a]Joel 2:28–32 **2:23** [a]NU-Text omits *have taken.*
2:28 [a]Psalm 16:8–11 **2:30** [a]NU-Text omits *according to the flesh, He would raise up the Christ* and completes the verse with *He would seat one on his throne.*

LIFE LESSONS

➤ 2:23 — *"Him, being delivered by the determined purpose and foreknowledge of God, you have taken by lawless hands, have crucified, and put to death . . . ."*

In a way none of us can fully understand, God orchestrated all the events of Jesus' arrest and death, and yet every individual who played a part in His execution remained personally responsible for his choices and actions.

34 "For David did not ascend into the heavens, but he says himself:

'The LORD said to my Lord,
"Sit at My right hand,
35 *Till I make Your enemies Your footstool."'*[a]

36 "Therefore let all the house of Israel know
assuredly that God has made this Jesus,
whom you crucified, both Lord and Christ."
37 Now when they heard *this*, they were cut
to the heart, and said to Peter and the rest of
the apostles, "Men *and* brethren, what shall
we do?"
✳ 38 Then Peter said to them, "Repent, and let
every one of you be baptized in the name of
Jesus Christ for the remission of sins; and you
shall receive the gift of the Holy Spirit.
39 "For the promise is to you and to your
children, and to all who are afar off, as many
as the Lord our God will call."

A Vital Church Grows

40 And with many other words he testified
and exhorted them, saying, "Be saved from
this perverse generation."
41 Then those who gladly[a] received his word
were baptized; and that day about three thousand souls were added *to them.*
➤ 42 And they continued steadfastly in the
apostles' doctrine and fellowship, in the
breaking of bread, and in prayers.
43 Then fear came upon every soul, and
many wonders and signs were done through
the apostles.
44 Now all who believed were together, and
had all things in common,
45 and sold their possessions and goods, and
divided them among all, as anyone had need.
46 So continuing daily with one accord in the
temple, and breaking bread from house to
house, they ate their food with gladness and
simplicity of heart,
47 praising God and having favor with all the
people. And the Lord added to the church[a]
daily those who were being saved.

A Lame Man Healed

3 Now Peter and John went up together to
the temple at the hour of prayer, the ninth
hour.
2 And a certain man lame from his mother's
womb was carried, whom they laid daily at
the gate of the temple which is called Beautiful, to ask alms from those who entered the
temple;
3 who, seeing Peter and John about to go
into the temple, asked for alms.
4 And fixing his eyes on him, with John, Peter said, "Look at us."
5 So he gave them his attention, expecting
to receive something from them.
6 Then Peter said, "Silver and gold I do not ◄
have, but what I do have I give you: In the
name of Jesus Christ of Nazareth, rise up and
walk."
7 And he took him by the right hand and
lifted *him* up, and immediately his feet and
ankle bones received strength.
8 So he, leaping up, stood and walked and
entered the temple with them—walking, leaping, and praising God.
9 And all the people saw him walking and
praising God.
10 Then they knew that it was he who sat
begging alms at the Beautiful Gate of the temple; and they were filled with wonder and
amazement at what had happened to him.

Preaching in Solomon's Portico

11 Now as the lame man who was healed
held on to Peter and John, all the people ran
together to them in the porch which is called
Solomon's, greatly amazed.
12 So when Peter saw *it*, he responded to the ◄
people: "Men of Israel, why do you marvel at
this? Or why look so intently at us, as though
by our own power or godliness we had made
this man walk?
13 "The God of Abraham, Isaac, and Jacob,
the God of our fathers, glorified His Servant
Jesus, whom you delivered up and denied in
the presence of Pilate, when he was determined to let *Him* go.
14 "But you denied the Holy One and the
Just, and asked for a murderer to be granted
to you,
15 "and killed the Prince of life, whom God

2:35 [a]Psalm 110:1 2:41 [a]NU-Text omits *gladly.* 2:47 [a]NU-Text omits *to the church.*

LIFE LESSONS

➤ 2:42 — *And they continued steadfastly in the apostles' doctrine and fellowship, in the breaking of bread, and in prayers.*

To grow in faith and to fulfill the mission Jesus has given to us, we must regularly gather together for instruction, worship, encouragement, and prayer. God never calls any Christian to a solitary life of faith.

➤ 3:6 — *Then Peter said, "Silver and gold I do not have, but what I do have I give you: In the name of Jesus Christ of Nazareth, rise up and walk."*

We may not have riches or political influence or many other things that the world craves, but we do have the Spirit of the Lord living within us—and we can always "give away" Jesus while still keeping Him.

➤ 3:12 — *"Men of Israel, why do you marvel at this? Or why look so intently at us, as though by our own power or godliness we had made this man walk?"*

No matter how greatly the Lord may choose to use us, we must be careful to let people know that God is the one at work within us; He accomplishes whatever good thing might occur through us.

raised from the dead, of which we are witnesses.
16 "And His name, through faith in His name, has made this man strong, whom you see and know. Yes, the faith which *comes* through Him has given him this perfect soundness in the presence of you all.
17 "Yet now, brethren, I know that you did *it* in ignorance, as *did* also your rulers.
18 "But those things which God foretold by the mouth of all His prophets, that the Christ would suffer, He has thus fulfilled.
➤ 19 "Repent therefore and be converted, that your sins may be blotted out, so that times of refreshing may come from the presence of the Lord,
20 "and that He may send Jesus Christ, who was preached to you before,[a]
21 "whom heaven must receive until the times of restoration of all things, which God has spoken by the mouth of all His holy prophets since the world began.
22 "For Moses truly said to the fathers, *'The LORD your God will raise up for you a Prophet like me from your brethren. Him you shall hear in all things, whatever He says to you.*
23 *'And it shall be that every soul who will not hear that Prophet shall be utterly destroyed from among the people.'*[a]
24 "Yes, and all the prophets, from Samuel and those who follow, as many as have spoken, have also foretold[a] these days.
25 "You are sons of the prophets, and of the covenant which God made with our fathers, saying to Abraham, *'And in your seed all the families of the earth shall be blessed.'*[a]
26 "To you first, God, having raised up His Servant Jesus, sent Him to bless you, in turning away every one of *you* from your iniquities."

Peter and John Arrested

4 Now as they spoke to the people, the priests, the captain of the temple, and the Sadducees came upon them,
2 being greatly disturbed that they taught the people and preached in Jesus the resurrection from the dead.
3 And they laid hands on them, and put *them* in custody until the next day, for it was already evening.
4 However, many of those who heard the word believed; and the number of the men came to be about five thousand.

Addressing the Sanhedrin

5 And it came to pass, on the next day, that their rulers, elders, and scribes,
6 as well as Annas the high priest, Caiaphas, John, and Alexander, and as many as were of the family of the high priest, were gathered together at Jerusalem.
7 And when they had set them in the midst, they asked, "By what power or by what name have you done this?"
8 Then Peter, filled with the Holy Spirit, said to them, "Rulers of the people and elders of Israel:
9 "If we this day are judged for a good deed *done* to a helpless man, by what means he has been made well,
10 "let it be known to you all, and to all the people of Israel, that by the name of Jesus Christ of Nazareth, whom you crucified, whom God raised from the dead, by Him this man stands here before you whole.
11 "This is the *'stone which was rejected by you builders, which has become the chief cornerstone.'*[a]
12 "Nor is there salvation in any other, for there is no other name under heaven given among men by which we must be saved." ➤

The Name of Jesus Forbidden

13 Now when they saw the boldness of Peter and John, and perceived that they were uneducated and untrained men, they marveled. And they realized that they had been with Jesus.
14 And seeing the man who had been healed standing with them, they could say nothing against it.
15 But when they had commanded them to go aside out of the council, they conferred among themselves,
16 saying, "What shall we do to these men? For, indeed, that a notable miracle has been done through them *is* evident to all who dwell in Jerusalem, and we cannot deny *it*.

3:20 [a]NU-Text and M-Text read *Christ Jesus, who was ordained for you before.* **3:23** [a]Deuteronomy 18:15, 18, 19 **3:24** [a]NU-Text and M-Text read *proclaimed.* **3:25** [a]Genesis 22:18; 26:4; 28:14 **4:11** [a]Psalm 118:22

LIFE LESSONS

➤ 3:19 — *"Repent therefore and be converted, that your sins may be blotted out, so that times of refreshing may come from the presence of the Lord . . . ."*

Who does not need "times of refreshing"? Who does not need a new start, a spiritual renewal, a fresh touch of God on their life? All these things come through an intimate relationship with the Lord.

➤ 4:12 — *"Nor is there salvation in any other, for there is no other name under heaven given among men by which we must be saved."*

If God knew that Jesus really did not have to die, then He is an uncaring monster for sending Him to the cross. And if He thought Jesus had to die when He really didn't, then He wouldn't be God.

17 "But so that it spreads no further among
the people, let us severely threaten them, that
from now on they speak to no man in this
name."
18 So they called them and commanded
them not to speak at all nor teach in the name
of Jesus.
➤ 19 But Peter and John answered and said to
them, "Whether it is right in the sight of God
to listen to you more than to God, you judge.
20 "For we cannot but speak the things which
we have seen and heard."
21 So when they had further threatened
them, they let them go, finding no way of punishing them, because of the people, since they
all glorified God for what had been done.
22 For the man was over forty years old on
whom this miracle of healing had been performed.

Prayer for Boldness

23 And being let go, they went to their own
companions and reported all that the chief
priests and elders had said to them.
24 So when they heard that, they raised their
voice to God with one accord and said: "Lord,
You *are* God, who made heaven and earth and
the sea, and all that is in them,
25 "who by the mouth of Your servant David[a]
have said:

'*Why did the nations rage,*
And the people plot vain things?
26 *The kings of the earth took their stand,*
And the rulers were gathered together
Against the LORD *and against His Christ.*'[a]

27 "For truly against Your holy Servant Jesus,
whom You anointed, both Herod and Pontius
Pilate, with the Gentiles and the people of Israel, were gathered together
28 "to do whatever Your hand and Your purpose determined before to be done.
➤ 29 "Now, Lord, look on their threats, and
grant to Your servants that with all boldness
they may speak Your word,
30 "by stretching out Your hand to heal, and
that signs and wonders may be done through
the name of Your holy Servant Jesus."
31 And when they had prayed, the place ➤
where they were assembled together was
shaken; and they were all filled with the Holy
Spirit, and they spoke the word of God with
boldness.

Sharing in All Things

32 Now the multitude of those who believed
were of one heart and one soul; neither did
anyone say that any of the things he possessed was his own, but they had all things in
common.
33 And with great power the apostles gave
witness to the resurrection of the Lord Jesus.
And great grace was upon them all.
34 Nor was there anyone among them who
lacked; for all who were possessors of lands
or houses sold them, and brought the proceeds of the things that were sold,
35 and laid *them* at the apostles' feet; and
they distributed to each as anyone had need.
36 And Joses,[a] who was also named Barnabas by the apostles (which is translated Son
of Encouragement), a Levite of the country of
Cyprus,
37 having land, sold *it*, and brought the
money and laid *it* at the apostles' feet.

Lying to the Holy Spirit

5 But a certain man named Ananias, with
Sapphira his wife, sold a possession.
2 And he kept back *part* of the proceeds, his
wife also being aware *of it*, and brought a certain part and laid *it* at the apostles' feet.
3 But Peter said, "Ananias, why has Satan
filled your heart to lie to the Holy Spirit and
keep back *part* of the price of the land for
yourself?
4 "While it remained, was it not your own?
And after it was sold, was it not in your own
control? Why have you conceived this thing in
your heart? You have not lied to men but to
God."
5 Then Ananias, hearing these words, fell

4:25 [a]NU-Text reads *who through the Holy Spirit, by the mouth of our father, Your servant David.* **4:26** [a]Psalm 2:1, 2
4:36 [a]NU-Text reads *Joseph.*

LIFE LESSONS

➤ **4:19 — *But Peter and John answered and said to them, "Whether it is right in the sight of God to listen to you more than to God, you judge."***

We are always to *respect* authority, even when it is in the wrong. But if some authority tells us to disobey God, we are to disobey that authority—and for Jesus' sake, gladly accept whatever punishment it metes out.

➤ **4:29 — *"Now, Lord, look on their threats, and grant to Your servants that with all boldness they may speak Your word . . . ."***

In a world that does not respect God or honor Jesus, we must pray for boldness and strength to represent Him well and by our words and actions draw some into a saving relationship with Christ.

➤ **4:31 — *And when they had prayed, the place where they were assembled together was shaken; and they were all filled with the Holy Spirit, and they spoke the word of God with boldness.***

There is no substitute for believers regularly coming together for earnest prayer. God does amazing things in response to the faith-filled, congregational prayers of His people.

down and breathed his last. So great fear
came upon all those who heard these things.
6 And the young men arose and wrapped
him up, carried *him* out, and buried *him.*
7 Now it was about three hours later when
his wife came in, not knowing what had happened.
8 And Peter answered her, "Tell me whether
you sold the land for so much?" She said,
"Yes, for so much."
9 Then Peter said to her, "How is it that you
have agreed together to test the Spirit of the
Lord? Look, the feet of those who have buried
your husband *are* at the door, and they will
carry you out."
10 Then immediately she fell down at his feet
and breathed her last. And the young men
came in and found her dead, and carrying *her*
out, buried *her* by her husband.
➤ 11 So great fear came upon all the church
and upon all who heard these things.

Continuing Power in the Church

12 And through the hands of the apostles
many signs and wonders were done among
the people. And they were all with one accord
in Solomon's Porch.
13 Yet none of the rest dared join them, but
the people esteemed them highly.
14 And believers were increasingly added to
the Lord, multitudes of both men and women,
15 so that they brought the sick out into the
streets and laid *them* on beds and couches,
that at least the shadow of Peter passing by
might fall on some of them.
16 Also a multitude gathered from the surrounding cities to Jerusalem, bringing sick
people and those who were tormented by unclean spirits, and they were all healed.

Imprisoned Apostles Freed

17 Then the high priest rose up, and all those
who *were* with him (which is the sect of the
Sadducees), and they were filled with indignation,
18 and laid their hands on the apostles and
put them in the common prison.
➤ 19 But at night an angel of the Lord opened
the prison doors and brought them out, and
said,
20 "Go, stand in the temple and speak to the
people all the words of this life."
21 And when they heard *that,* they entered
the temple early in the morning and taught.
But the high priest and those with him came
and called the council together, with all the elders of the children of Israel, and sent to the
prison to have them brought.

Apostles on Trial Again

22 But when the officers came and did not
find them in the prison, they returned and reported,
23 saying, "Indeed we found the prison shut
securely, and the guards standing outside[a] before the doors; but when we opened them, we
found no one inside!"
24 Now when the high priest,[a] the captain of
the temple, and the chief priests heard these
things, they wondered what the outcome
would be.
25 So one came and told them, saying,[a]
"Look, the men whom you put in prison are
standing in the temple and teaching the people!"
26 Then the captain went with the officers
and brought them without violence, for they
feared the people, lest they should be stoned.
27 And when they had brought them, they set
them before the council. And the high priest
asked them,
28 saying, "Did we not strictly command you
not to teach in this name? And look, you have
filled Jerusalem with your doctrine, and intend to bring this Man's blood on us!"
29 But Peter and the *other* apostles answered
and said: "We ought to obey God rather than
men.
30 "The God of our fathers raised up Jesus
whom you murdered by hanging on a tree.
31 "Him God has exalted to His right hand *to
be* Prince and Savior, to give repentance to Israel and forgiveness of sins.
32 "And we are His witnesses to these things,
and *so* also *is* the Holy Spirit whom God has
given to those who obey Him."

Gamaliel's Advice

33 When they heard *this,* they were furious
and plotted to kill them.
34 Then one in the council stood up, a Phar-

5:23 [a]NU-Text and M-Text omit *outside.* **5:24** [a]NU-Text omits *the high priest.* **5:25** [a]NU-Text and M-Text omit *saying.*

LIFE LESSONS

➤ 5:11 — *So great fear came upon all the church and upon all who heard these things.*

The fear of God purifies the church and puts it in a reverent frame of mind that encourages God to do amazing things through it. When we fear God, the fear of man will never dissuade us from doing God's will.

➤ 5:19, 20 — *But at night an angel of the Lord opened the prison doors and brought them out, and said, "Go, stand in the temple and speak to the people all the words of this life."*

God did not break the disciples out of prison so they could escape to safety; he freed them so they could go right back to where and what they had been doing. God wants His words of life to go forth!

isee named Gamaliel, a teacher of the law
held in respect by all the people, and commanded them to put the apostles outside for a
little while.
35 And he said to them: "Men of Israel, take
heed to yourselves what you intend to do regarding these men.
36 "For some time ago Theudas rose up,
claiming to be somebody. A number of men,
about four hundred, joined him. He was slain,
and all who obeyed him were scattered and
came to nothing.
37 "After this man, Judas of Galilee rose up in
the days of the census, and drew away many
people after him. He also perished, and all
who obeyed him were dispersed.
38 "And now I say to you, keep away from
these men and let them alone; for if this
plan or this work is of men, it will come to
nothing;
39 "but if it is of God, you cannot overthrow
it—lest you even be found to fight against
God."
40 And they agreed with him, and when they
had called for the apostles and beaten *them*,
they commanded that they should not speak
in the name of Jesus, and let them go.
➤ 41 So they departed from the presence of the
council, rejoicing that they were counted worthy to suffer shame for His[a] name.
42 And daily in the temple, and in every
house, they did not cease teaching and
preaching Jesus *as* the Christ.

Seven Chosen to Serve

6 Now in those days, when *the number of*
the disciples was multiplying, there arose
a complaint against the Hebrews by the Hellenists,[a] because their widows were neglected
in the daily distribution.
2 Then the twelve summoned the multitude
of the disciples and said, "It is not desirable
that we should leave the word of God and
serve tables.
3 "Therefore, brethren, seek out from
among you seven men of *good* reputation, full
of the Holy Spirit and wisdom, whom we may
appoint over this business;
4 "but we will give ourselves continually to ➤
prayer and to the ministry of the word."
5 And the saying pleased the whole multitude. And they chose Stephen, a man full of
faith and the Holy Spirit, and Philip, Prochorus, Nicanor, Timon, Parmenas, and Nicolas, a
proselyte from Antioch,
6 whom they set before the apostles; and
when they had prayed, they laid hands on
them.
7 Then the word of God spread, and the
number of the disciples multiplied greatly in
Jerusalem, and a great many of the priests
were obedient to the faith.

Stephen Accused of Blasphemy

8 And Stephen, full of faith[a] and power,
did great wonders and signs among the
people.
9 Then there arose some from what is called
the Synagogue of the Freedmen (Cyrenians,
Alexandrians, and those from Cilicia and
Asia), disputing with Stephen.
10 And they were not able to resist the wisdom and the Spirit by which he spoke.
11 Then they secretly induced men to say, ➤
"We have heard him speak blasphemous
words against Moses and God."
12 And they stirred up the people, the elders, and the scribes; and they came upon
him, seized him, and brought *him* to the
council.
13 They also set up false witnesses who said,
"This man does not cease to speak blasphemous[a] words against this holy place and the
law;
14 "for we have heard him say that this Jesus
of Nazareth will destroy this place and
change the customs which Moses delivered
to us."
15 And all who sat in the council, looking
steadfastly at him, saw his face as the face of
an angel.

5:41 [a]NU-Text reads *the name;* M-Text reads *the name of Jesus.*
6:1 [a]That is, Greek-speaking Jews **6:8** [a]NU-Text reads *grace.*
6:13 [a]NU-Text omits *blasphemous.*

LIFE LESSONS

➤ 5:41 — *So they departed from the presence of the council, rejoicing that they were counted worthy to suffer shame for His name.*

Our culture looks at shame as an almost entirely negative thing, but the Bible consistently recognizes the "shame" of being identified with Christ as one of the greatest possible blessings (see 1 Pet. 4:16).

➤ 6:4 — *". . . but we will give ourselves continually to prayer and to the ministry of the word."*

Church leaders and teachers, in particular, must never skimp on their time spent in prayer and in God's Word. Since they will "receive a stricter judgment" (James 3:1), they need to make sure they stay close to God.

➤ 6:11 — *Then they secretly induced men to say, "We have heard him speak blasphemous words against Moses and God."*

Just as the opponents of Jesus instructed witnesses to testify falsely against the Lord, so the opponents of Stephen followed the same strategy. Interestingly, neither man tried to refute the false charges.

Stephen's Address: The Call of Abraham

7 Then the high priest said, "Are these
things so?"
2 And he said, "Brethren and fathers, listen:
The God of glory appeared to our father
Abraham when he was in Mesopotamia, before he dwelt in Haran,
3 "and said to him, *'Get out of your country
and from your relatives, and come to a land
that I will show you.'*[a]
4 "Then he came out of the land of the
Chaldeans and dwelt in Haran. And from
there, when his father was dead, He moved
him to this land in which you now dwell.
5 "And *God* gave him no inheritance in it,
not even *enough* to set his foot on. But even
when *Abraham* had no child, He promised to
give it to him for a possession, and to his descendants after him.
6 "But God spoke in this way: that his descendants would dwell in a foreign land, and
that they would bring them into bondage and
oppress *them* four hundred years.
7 *'And the nation to whom they will be in
bondage I will judge,'*[a] said God, *'and after
that they shall come out and serve Me in this
place.'*[b]
8 "Then He gave him the covenant of circumcision; and so *Abraham* begot Isaac and
circumcised him on the eighth day; and Isaac
begot Jacob, and Jacob *begot* the twelve patriarchs.

The Patriarchs in Egypt

➢ 9 "And the patriarchs, becoming envious,
sold Joseph into Egypt. But God was with him
10 "and delivered him out of all his troubles,
and gave him favor and wisdom in the presence of Pharaoh, king of Egypt; and he made
him governor over Egypt and all his house.
11 "Now a famine and great trouble came
over all the land of Egypt and Canaan, and
our fathers found no sustenance.
12 "But when Jacob heard that there was
grain in Egypt, he sent out our fathers first.
13 "And the second *time* Joseph was made
known to his brothers, and Joseph's family
became known to the Pharaoh.
14 "Then Joseph sent and called his father
Jacob and all his relatives to *him*, seventy-
five[a] people.
15 "So Jacob went down to Egypt; and he
died, he and our fathers.
16 "And they were carried back to Shechem
and laid in the tomb that Abraham bought for
a sum of money from the sons of Hamor, *the
father* of Shechem.

God Delivers Israel by Moses

17 "But when the time of the promise drew
near which God had sworn to Abraham, the
people grew and multiplied in Egypt
18 "till another king arose who did not know
Joseph.
19 "This man dealt treacherously with our
people, and oppressed our forefathers, making them expose their babies, so that they
might not live.
20 "At this time Moses was born, and was
well pleasing to God; and he was brought up
in his father's house for three months.
21 "But when he was set out, Pharaoh's
daughter took him away and brought him up
as her own son.
22 "And Moses was learned in all the wisdom
of the Egyptians, and was mighty in words
and deeds.
23 "Now when he was forty years old, it came
into his heart to visit his brethren, the children of Israel.
24 "And seeing one of *them* suffer wrong, he
defended and avenged him who was oppressed, and struck down the Egyptian.
25 "For he supposed that his brethren would
have understood that God would deliver them
by his hand, but they did not understand.
26 "And the next day he appeared to *two of*
them as they were fighting, and *tried to* reconcile them, saying, 'Men, you are brethren;
why do you wrong one another?'
27 "But he who did his neighbor wrong
pushed him away, saying, *'Who made you a
ruler and a judge over us?*
28 *'Do you want to kill me as you did the
Egyptian yesterday?'*[a]
29 "Then, at this saying, Moses fled and became a dweller in the land of Midian, where
he had two sons.
30 "And when forty years had passed, an
Angel of the Lord[a] appeared to him in a flame
of fire in a bush, in the wilderness of Mount
Sinai.
31 "When Moses saw *it*, he marveled at the
sight; and as he drew near to observe, the
voice of the Lord came to him,
32 *"saying, 'I am the God of your fathers—the
God of Abraham, the God of Isaac, and the
God of Jacob.'*[a] And Moses trembled and
dared not look.
33 *'Then the* LORD *said to him, "Take your*

7:3 [a]Genesis 12:1 **7:7** [a]Genesis 15:14 [b]Exodus 3:12
7:14 [a]Or *seventy* (compare Exodus 1:5) **7:28** [a]Exodus 2:14
7:30 [a]NU-Text omits *of the Lord.* **7:32** [a]Exodus 3:6, 15

LIFE LESSONS

➢ **7:9, 10 — *"But God was with him and delivered him out of all his troubles, and gave him favor and wisdom in the presence of Pharaoh . . . ."***

Stephen reminded his audience that Joseph had been persecuted by his own brothers, but that God used even their evil deeds to bless him. God always blesses obedience—but note that while Joseph lived, Stephen died.

sandals off your feet, for the place where you stand is holy ground.
34 *"I have surely seen the oppression of My people who are in Egypt; I have heard their groaning and have come down to deliver them. And now come, I will send you to Egypt."'*[a]
35 "This Moses whom they rejected, saying, *'Who made you a ruler and a judge?'*[a] is the one God sent *to be* a ruler and a deliverer by the hand of the Angel who appeared to him in the bush.
36 "He brought them out, after he had shown wonders and signs in the land of Egypt, and in the Red Sea, and in the wilderness forty years.

Israel Rebels Against God

37 "This is that Moses who said to the children of Israel,[a] *'The LORD your God will raise up for you a Prophet like me from your brethren. Him you shall hear.'*[b]
38 "This is he who was in the congregation in the wilderness with the Angel who spoke to him on Mount Sinai, and *with* our fathers, the one who received the living oracles to give to us,
39 "whom our fathers would not obey, but rejected. And in their hearts they turned back to Egypt,
40 "saying to Aaron, *'Make us gods to go before us; as for this Moses who brought us out of the land of Egypt, we do not know what has become of him.'*[a]
41 "And they made a calf in those days, offered sacrifices to the idol, and rejoiced in the works of their own hands.
42 "Then God turned and gave them up to worship the host of heaven, as it is written in the book of the Prophets:

'Did you offer Me slaughtered animals
and sacrifices during forty years in
the wilderness,
O house of Israel?
43 *You also took up the tabernacle of Moloch,*
And the star of your god Remphan,
Images which you made to worship;
And I will carry you away beyond
Babylon.'[a]

God's True Tabernacle

44 "Our fathers had the tabernacle of witness in the wilderness, as He appointed, instructing Moses to make it according to the pattern that he had seen,
45 "which our fathers, having received it in turn, also brought with Joshua into the land possessed by the Gentiles, whom God drove out before the face of our fathers until the days of David,
46 "who found favor before God and asked to find a dwelling for the God of Jacob.
47 "But Solomon built Him a house.
48 "However, the Most High does not dwell in temples made with hands, as the prophet says:

49 *'Heaven is My throne,*
And earth is My footstool.
What house will you build for Me? says
the LORD,
Or what is the place of My rest?
50 *Has My hand not made all these*
things?'[a]

Israel Resists the Holy Spirit

51 "*You* stiff-necked and uncircumcised in heart and ears! You always resist the Holy Spirit; as your fathers *did,* so *do* you.
52 "Which of the prophets did your fathers not persecute? And they killed those who foretold the coming of the Just One, of whom you now have become the betrayers and murderers,
53 "who have received the law by the direction of angels and have not kept *it.*"

Stephen the Martyr

54 When they heard these things they were cut to the heart, and they gnashed at him with *their* teeth.
55 But he, being full of the Holy Spirit, gazed into heaven and saw the glory of God, and Jesus standing at the right hand of God,
56 and said, "Look! I see the heavens opened ➤
and the Son of Man standing at the right hand of God!"
57 Then they cried out with a loud voice, stopped their ears, and ran at him with one accord;
58 and they cast *him* out of the city and stoned *him.* And the witnesses laid down their clothes at the feet of a young man named Saul.
59 And they stoned Stephen as he was calling on *God* and saying, "Lord Jesus, receive my spirit."

7:34 [a]Exodus 3:5, 7, 8, 10 **7:35** [a]Exodus 2:14
7:37 [a]Deuteronomy 18:15 [b]NU-Text and M-Text omit *Him you shall hear.* **7:40** [a]Exodus 32:1, 23 **7:43** [a]Amos 5:25–27
7:50 [a]Isaiah 66:1, 2

LIFE LESSONS

➤ 7:56 — *"Look! I see the heavens opened and the Son of Man standing at the right hand of God!"*

We learn from several Bible passages that when Jesus ascended to heaven, He "sat down at the right hand of God" (Mark 16:19; Col. 3:1; Heb. 1:3; 10:12; 12:2). Yet to greet this first Christian martyr, the Lord stood!

➤ 60 Then he knelt down and cried out with a loud voice, "Lord, do not charge them with this sin." And when he had said this, he fell asleep.

Saul Persecutes the Church

8 Now Saul was consenting to his death. At that time a great persecution arose against the church which was at Jerusalem; and they were all scattered throughout the regions of Judea and Samaria, except the apostles.
2 And devout men carried Stephen *to his burial,* and made great lamentation over him.
➤ 3 As for Saul, he made havoc of the church, entering every house, and dragging off men and women, committing *them* to prison.

Christ Is Preached in Samaria

➤ 4 Therefore those who were scattered went everywhere preaching the word.
5 Then Philip went down to the[a] city of Samaria and preached Christ to them.
6 And the multitudes with one accord heeded the things spoken by Philip, hearing and seeing the miracles which he did.
7 For unclean spirits, crying with a loud voice, came out of many who were possessed; and many who were paralyzed and lame were healed.
8 And there was great joy in that city.

The Sorcerer's Profession of Faith

9 But there was a certain man called Simon, who previously practiced sorcery in the city and astonished the people of Samaria, claiming that he was someone great,
10 to whom they all gave heed, from the least to the greatest, saying, "This man is the great power of God."
11 And they heeded him because he had astonished them with his sorceries for a long time.
12 But when they believed Philip as he preached the things concerning the kingdom of God and the name of Jesus Christ, both men and women were baptized.
13 Then Simon himself also believed; and when he was baptized he continued with Philip, and was amazed, seeing the miracles and signs which were done.

Life Examples:

STEPHEN

Echoing His Savior

ACTS 7:59, 60

Stephen slumped to the ground as blood and forgiveness poured from his lips. Nearby, a young man watched, unaware that this death would bring life to worldwide evangelism. Years later, the young man who had supported the execution of Stephen for his "blasphemy" against Moses and the temple became the apostle Paul.

Stephen most revealed his Christlike qualities when under duress. As the stones pelted him, he cried, "Lord Jesus, receive my spirit!" And then, as death inched closer with every blow, he echoed his Savior by praying aloud, "Lord, do not hold this sin against them!"

The beauty of Stephen's final words can never be overstated. They most eloquently summarize the heart of the true Christian. They testify of the Lord of grace living inside him. They speak of ultimate love.

These words grab the attention of someone who is nearby . . . watching.

See the Life Principles Index for further study:

24. To live the Christian life is to allow Jesus to live His life in and through us.

1. Our intimacy with God—His highest priority for our lives—determines the impact of our lives.

17. We stand tallest and strongest on our knees.

8:5 [a]Or *a*

LIFE LESSONS

➤ 7:60 — *Then he knelt down and cried out with a loud voice, "Lord, do not charge them with this sin." And when he had said this, he fell asleep.*

Just as Jesus asked His Father to forgive those who crucified Him (Luke 23:34), so Stephen asked God to give his murderers a chance to repent. God's grace enables us to do what we would never do on our own.

➤ 8:3 — *As for Saul, he made havoc of the church, entering every house, and dragging off men and women, committing them to prison.*

Saul, who became the apostle Paul, could never forget that he had "persecuted the church of God beyond measure and tried to destroy it" (Gal. 1:13). Partly for this reason he called himself the "chief" of sinners (1 Tim. 1:15).

➤ 8:4 — *Therefore those who were scattered went everywhere preaching the word.*

God is an expert at using even hardship and suffering for His glory and our benefit. The opponents of Christ intended that their persecution wipe out the church; instead, it spread it rapidly.

The Sorcerer's Sin
14 Now when the apostles who were at Jerusalem heard that Samaria had received the
word of God, they sent Peter and John to
them,
15 who, when they had come down, prayed
for them that they might receive the Holy
Spirit.
16 For as yet He had fallen upon none of
them. They had only been baptized in the
name of the Lord Jesus.
17 Then they laid hands on them, and they
received the Holy Spirit.
18 And when Simon saw that through the
laying on of the apostles' hands the Holy
Spirit was given, he offered them money,
19 saying, "Give me this power also, that anyone on whom I lay hands may receive the
Holy Spirit."
20 But Peter said to him, "Your money perish
with you, because you thought that the gift of
God could be purchased with money!
21 "You have neither part nor portion in this
matter, for your heart is not right in the sight
of God.
22 "Repent therefore of this your wickedness, and pray God if perhaps the thought of
your heart may be forgiven you.
➤ 23 "For I see that you are poisoned by bitterness and bound by iniquity."
24 Then Simon answered and said, "Pray to
the Lord for me, that none of the things which
you have spoken may come upon me."
25 So when they had testified and preached
the word of the Lord, they returned to Jerusalem, preaching the gospel in many villages of
the Samaritans.

Christ Is Preached to an Ethiopian
26 Now an angel of the Lord spoke to Philip,
saying, "Arise and go toward the south along
the road which goes down from Jerusalem to
Gaza." This is desert.
27 So he arose and went. And behold, a man
of Ethiopia, a eunuch of great authority under
Candace the queen of the Ethiopians, who
had charge of all her treasury, and had come
to Jerusalem to worship,
28 was returning. And sitting in his chariot,
he was reading Isaiah the prophet.
29 Then the Spirit said to Philip, "Go near
and overtake this chariot."
30 So Philip ran to him, and heard him reading the prophet Isaiah, and said, "Do you understand what you are reading?"
31 And he said, "How can I, unless someone
guides me?" And he asked Philip to come up
and sit with him.
32 The place in the Scripture which he read
was this:

"He was led as a sheep to the slaughter;
And as a lamb before its shearer is silent,
So He opened not His mouth.
33 *In His humiliation His justice was taken*
away,
And who will declare His generation?
For His life is taken from the earth."[a]

34 So the eunuch answered Philip and said,
"I ask you, of whom does the prophet say this,
of himself or of some other man?"
35 Then Philip opened his mouth, and beginning at this Scripture, preached Jesus to him.
36 Now as they went down the road, they
came to some water. And the eunuch said,
"See, *here is* water. What hinders me from
being baptized?"
37 Then Philip said, "If you believe with all ◄
your heart, you may." And he answered and
said, "I believe that Jesus Christ is the Son of
God."[a]
38 So he commanded the chariot to stand
still. And both Philip and the eunuch went
down into the water, and he baptized him.
39 Now when they came up out of the water,
the Spirit of the Lord caught Philip away, so
that the eunuch saw him no more; and he
went on his way rejoicing.
40 But Philip was found at Azotus. And passing through, he preached in all the cities till
he came to Caesarea.

The Damascus Road: Saul Converted
9 Then Saul, still breathing threats and
murder against the disciples of the Lord,
went to the high priest
2 and asked letters from him to the synagogues of Damascus, so that if he found any
who were of the Way, whether men or women,
he might bring them bound to Jerusalem.
3 As he journeyed he came near Damascus,

8:33 [a]Isaiah 53:7, 8 **8:37** [a]NU-Text and M-Text omit this verse. It is found in Western texts, including the Latin tradition.

LIFE LESSONS

➤ 8:23 — *"For I see that you are poisoned by bitterness and bound by iniquity."*

We do not know if Simon the sorcerer made a big error as a baby Christian, or whether he had never truly come to faith, but in either case Peter rebuked him sharply—not to condemn him, but to rescue him.

➤ 8:37 — *Then Philip said, "If you believe with all your heart, you may." And he answered and said, "I believe that Jesus Christ is the Son of God."*

Philip made wholehearted belief in the resurrection of Christ a prerequisite for baptizing the Ethiopian eunuch. In baptism we identify with the death and resurrection of Christ and begin a new way of living in His name (Rom. 6:3–6).

WHAT THE BIBLE SAYS ABOUT HOW GOD USES ADVERSITY TO GET OUR ATTENTION

Acts 9:1–20

As any instructor can tell you, the first goal of a teacher is to get a student's attention. You can't teach someone who isn't paying attention.

Just so, the Lord sometimes uses adversity in our lives to cause us to pay attention to Him in a new way.

That's what happened to Saul of Tarsus as he traveled to Damascus, where he intended to bring great persecution upon the Christians in that city. The Scriptures tell us that Saul was "breathing threats and murder against the disciples of the Lord" (Acts 9:1). Saul's murderous intent nearly consumed him.

But God got Saul's attention in a way he never expected. He sent Paul crashing to the ground with a blazing light and instructed him to enter the city and there wait for instructions. When Paul opened his eyes, he found himself blind and had to ask others to lead him by the hand into the city.

Saul definitely received a wake-up call from the Lord that day. In one unforeseen moment, God gained Saul's undivided attention, striking him with the adversity of blindness and no doubt humiliating him in front of his traveling companions as he groveled in the dust.

But God had Saul exactly where He wanted him.

Saul felt more than ready to listen when the Lord asked, "Why are you persecuting Me?" Up to that point, Saul had no idea he was persecuting the Lord; he thought he was doing the Lord a favor by ridding the world of Christians. A period of intense adversity resulted in a complete turnaround for Saul. Within a matter of days, he was proclaiming Jesus in the synagogues (Acts 9:20).

If it took temporary blindness and humiliation to get Saul's attention, it was certainly worth it, for through Saul—known to us as Paul the apostle—the gospel expanded and churches grew across the Roman world.

Don't delay in responding to the Lord when He makes a move to get your attention. Respond quickly and humbly, and listen for what He has to say to you.

God had Saul exactly where He wanted him.

See the Life Principles Index for further study:
26. Adversity is a bridge to a deeper relationship with God.
15. Brokenness is God's requirement for maximum usefulness.

and suddenly a light shone around him from heaven.
➤ 4 Then he fell to the ground, and heard a voice saying to him, "Saul, Saul, why are you persecuting Me?"
5 And he said, "Who are You, Lord?" Then the Lord said, "I am Jesus, whom you are persecuting.[a] It *is* hard for you to kick against the goads."
6 So he, trembling and astonished, said, "Lord, what do You want me to do?" Then the Lord *said* to him, "Arise and go into the city, and you will be told what you must do."
7 And the men who journeyed with him stood speechless, hearing a voice but seeing no one.
8 Then Saul arose from the ground, and when his eyes were opened he saw no one. But they led him by the hand and brought *him* into Damascus.
9 And he was three days without sight, and neither ate nor drank.

Ananias Baptizes Saul

10 Now there was a certain disciple at Damascus named Ananias; and to him the Lord said in a vision, "Ananias." And he said, "Here I am, Lord."
➤ 11 So the Lord *said* to him, "Arise and go to the street called Straight, and inquire at the house of Judas for *one* called Saul of Tarsus, for behold, he is praying.
12 "And in a vision he has seen a man named Ananias coming in and putting *his* hand on him, so that he might receive his sight."
13 Then Ananias answered, "Lord, I have heard from many about this man, how much harm he has done to Your saints in Jerusalem.
14 "And here he has authority from the chief priests to bind all who call on Your name."
15 But the Lord said to him, "Go, for he is a chosen vessel of Mine to bear My name before Gentiles, kings, and the children of Israel.
16 "For I will show him how many things he must suffer for My name's sake."
17 And Ananias went his way and entered the house; and laying his hands on him he said, "Brother Saul, the Lord Jesus,[a] who appeared to you on the road as you came, has sent me that you may receive your sight and be filled with the Holy Spirit."
18 Immediately there fell from his eyes *something* like scales, and he received his sight at once; and he arose and was baptized.
19 So when he had received food, he was strengthened. Then Saul spent some days with the disciples at Damascus.

Saul Preaches Christ

20 Immediately he preached the Christ[a] in the synagogues, that He is the Son of God.
21 Then all who heard were amazed, and said, "Is this not he who destroyed those who called on this name in Jerusalem, and has come here for that purpose, so that he might bring them bound to the chief priests?"
22 But Saul increased all the more in strength, and confounded the Jews who dwelt in Damascus, proving that this *Jesus* is the Christ.

Saul Escapes Death

23 Now after many days were past, the Jews plotted to kill him.
24 But their plot became known to Saul. And they watched the gates day and night, to kill him.
25 Then the disciples took him by night and let *him* down through the wall in a large basket.

Saul at Jerusalem

26 And when Saul had come to Jerusalem, he tried to join the disciples; but they were all afraid of him, and did not believe that he was a disciple.
27 But Barnabas took him and brought *him* to the apostles. And he declared to them how he had seen the Lord on the road, and that He had spoken to him, and how he had preached boldly at Damascus in the name of Jesus. ➤

9:5 [a]NU-Text and M-Text omit the last sentence of verse 5 and begin verse 6 with *But arise and go.* **9:17** [a]M-Text omits *Jesus.* **9:20** [a]NU-Text reads *Jesus.*

LIFE LESSONS

➤ **9:4 — *Then he fell to the ground, and heard a voice saying to him, "Saul, Saul, why are you persecuting Me?"***

Saul thought he was arresting and imprisoning dangerous heretics; Jesus told him that he was persecuting the Christ Himself. When we bless other believers, we bless Christ; and when we wound other believers, we harm Christ (Matt. 25:40, 45).

➤ **9:11 — *So the Lord said to him, "Arise and go to the street called Straight, and inquire at the house of Judas for one called Saul of Tarsus . . . ."***

The Lord gave Ananias an assignment he did not particularly like. He objected that Saul was a dangerous man, but the Lord repeated His command to go. Unlike Jonah long before, Ananias obeyed—and the church got a new apostle.

➤ **9:27 — *But Barnabas took him and brought him to the apostles.***

The name Barnabas means "son of encouragement," and wherever we see him in the Book of Acts, he's encouraging someone. In this case he vouched for Saul when everyone else was afraid of him.

28 So he was with them at Jerusalem, coming in and going out.
29 And he spoke boldly in the name of the Lord Jesus and disputed against the Hellenists, but they attempted to kill him.
30 When the brethren found out, they brought him down to Caesarea and sent him out to Tarsus.

The Church Prospers

➤ **31** Then the churches[a] throughout all Judea, Galilee, and Samaria had peace and were edified. And walking in the fear of the Lord and in the comfort of the Holy Spirit, they were multiplied.

Aeneas Healed

32 Now it came to pass, as Peter went through all *parts of the country,* that he also came down to the saints who dwelt in Lydda.
33 There he found a certain man named Aeneas, who had been bedridden eight years and was paralyzed.
34 And Peter said to him, "Aeneas, Jesus the Christ heals you. Arise and make your bed." Then he arose immediately.
35 So all who dwelt at Lydda and Sharon saw him and turned to the Lord.

Dorcas Restored to Life

36 At Joppa there was a certain disciple named Tabitha, which is translated Dorcas. This woman was full of good works and charitable deeds which she did.
37 But it happened in those days that she became sick and died. When they had washed her, they laid *her* in an upper room.
38 And since Lydda was near Joppa, and the disciples had heard that Peter was there, they sent two men to him, imploring *him* not to delay in coming to them.
39 Then Peter arose and went with them. When he had come, they brought *him* to the upper room. And all the widows stood by him weeping, showing the tunics and garments which Dorcas had made while she was with them.
40 But Peter put them all out, and knelt down and prayed. And turning to the body he said, "Tabitha, arise." And she opened her eyes, and when she saw Peter she sat up.
41 Then he gave her *his* hand and lifted her up; and when he had called the saints and widows, he presented her alive.
42 And it became known throughout all Joppa, and many believed on the Lord.
43 So it was that he stayed many days in Joppa with Simon, a tanner.

Cornelius Sends a Delegation

10 There was a certain man in Caesarea called Cornelius, a centurion of what was called the Italian Regiment,
2 a devout *man* and one who feared God with all his household, who gave alms generously to the people, and prayed to God always.
3 About the ninth hour of the day he saw clearly in a vision an angel of God coming in and saying to him, "Cornelius!"
4 And when he observed him, he was afraid, and said, "What is it, lord?" So he said to him, "Your prayers and your alms have come up for a memorial before God.
5 "Now send men to Joppa, and send for Simon whose surname is Peter.
6 "He is lodging with Simon, a tanner, whose house is by the sea.[a] He will tell you what you must do."
7 And when the angel who spoke to him had departed, Cornelius called two of his household servants and a devout soldier from among those who waited on him continually.
8 So when he had explained all *these* things to them, he sent them to Joppa.

Peter's Vision

9 The next day, as they went on their journey and drew near the city, Peter went up on the housetop to pray, about the sixth hour.
10 Then he became very hungry and wanted to eat; but while they made ready, he fell into a trance
11 and saw heaven opened and an object like a great sheet bound at the four corners, descending to him and let down to the earth.
12 In it were all kinds of four-footed animals of the earth, wild beasts, creeping things, and birds of the air.
13 And a voice came to him, "Rise, Peter; kill and eat."
14 But Peter said, "Not so, Lord! For I have never eaten anything common or unclean."
15 And a voice *spoke* to him again the second time, "What God has cleansed you must not call common."
16 This was done three times. And the object was taken up into heaven again.

9:31 [a]NU-Text reads *church . . . was edified.* **10:6** [a]NU-Text and M-Text omit the last sentence of this verse.

LIFE LESSONS

➤ 9:31 — *Then the churches throughout all Judea, Galilee, and Samaria had peace and were edified. And walking in the fear of the Lord and in the comfort of the Holy Spirit, they were multiplied.*

"Peace" and "fear" and "comfort" may seem like unlikely partners, but the peace of Christ, combined with the fear of God, combined with the comfort of the Spirit, makes a powerful recipe for growth.

Summoned to Caesarea

17 Now while Peter wondered within himself
what this vision which he had seen meant, behold,
the men who had been sent from Cornelius
had made inquiry for Simon's house,
and stood before the gate.
18 And they called and asked whether Simon,
whose surname was Peter, was lodging there.
19 While Peter thought about the vision, the
Spirit said to him, "Behold, three men are
seeking you.
➤ 20 "Arise therefore, go down and go with
them, doubting nothing; for I have sent them."
21 Then Peter went down to the men who
had been sent to him from Cornelius,[a] and
said, "Yes, I am he whom you seek. For what
reason have you come?"
22 And they said, "Cornelius *the* centurion, a
just man, one who fears God and has a good
reputation among all the nation of the Jews,
was divinely instructed by a holy angel to
summon you to his house, and to hear words
from you."
23 Then he invited them in and lodged *them.*
On the next day Peter went away with them,
and some brethren from Joppa accompanied
him.

Peter Meets Cornelius

24 And the following day they entered Caesarea.
Now Cornelius was waiting for them,
and had called together his relatives and
close friends.
25 As Peter was coming in, Cornelius met
him and fell down at his feet and worshiped
him.
26 But Peter lifted him up, saying, "Stand up;
I myself am also a man."
27 And as he talked with him, he went in and
found many who had come together.
➤ 28 Then he said to them, "You know how unlawful
it is for a Jewish man to keep company
with or go to one of another nation. But God
has shown me that I should not call any man
common or unclean.
29 "Therefore I came without objection as
soon as I was sent for. I ask, then, for what
reason have you sent for me?"
30 So Cornelius said, "Four days ago I was
fasting until this hour; and at the ninth hour[a]
I prayed in my house, and behold, a man
stood before me in bright clothing,
31 "and said, 'Cornelius, your prayer has
been heard, and your alms are remembered
in the sight of God.
32 'Send therefore to Joppa and call Simon
here, whose surname is Peter. He is lodging in
the house of Simon, a tanner, by the sea.[a]
When he comes, he will speak to you.'
33 "So I sent to you immediately, and you
have done well to come. Now therefore, we
are all present before God, to hear all the
things commanded you by God."

Preaching to Cornelius' Household

34 Then Peter opened *his* mouth and said: "In
truth I perceive that God shows no partiality.
35 "But in every nation whoever fears Him ➤
and works righteousness is accepted by Him.
36 "The word which *God* sent to the children
of Israel, preaching peace through Jesus
Christ—He is Lord of all—
37 "that word you know, which was proclaimed
throughout all Judea, and began
from Galilee after the baptism which John
preached:
38 "how God anointed Jesus of Nazareth with
the Holy Spirit and with power, who went
about doing good and healing all who were oppressed
by the devil, for God was with Him.
39 "And we are witnesses of all things which
He did both in the land of the Jews and in Jerusalem,
whom they[a] killed by hanging on a
tree.
40 "Him God raised up on the third day, and ➤
showed Him openly,
41 "not to all the people, but to witnesses
chosen before by God, *even* to us who ate and
drank with Him after He arose from the dead.
42 "And He commanded us to preach to the
people, and to testify that it is He who was or-

10:21 [a]NU-Text and M-Text omit *who had been sent to him from Cornelius.* **10:30** [a]NU-Text reads *Four days ago to this hour, at the ninth hour.* **10:32** [a]NU-Text omits the last sentence of this verse. **10:39** [a]NU-Text and M-Text add *also.*

LIFE LESSONS

➤ 10:20 — *"Arise therefore, go down and go with them, doubting nothing; for I have sent them."*

Have you ever noticed that God tends to guide us in stages? He rarely, if ever, gives us a roadmap to follow; instead, He asks us to take His hand and go where He goes, without doubting our final destination.

➤ 10:28 — *"God has shown me that I should not call any man common or unclean."*

The Bible nowhere records that God told Peter, "don't call any man common or unclean." God showed Peter a vision of unclean animals made clean, and Peter reasoned out the rest. God's instruction never bypasses our minds.

➤ 10:35 — *"But in every nation whoever fears Him and works righteousness is accepted by Him."*

Cornelius feared God and performed "righteous" deeds before he heard a word about the risen Christ—but he still needed to come to faith in Jesus. Those who really seek God will find Him (Jer. 29:13).

➤ 10:40, 41 — *"Him God raised up on the third day, and showed Him openly, not to all the people, but to witnesses chosen before by God . . . ."*

After His resurrection, Jesus did not appear to Pilate, or to Herod, or to Annas, or to Caiaphas, or to those who crucified Him. He appeared only to those who loved Him. The rest will one day appear before *Him.*

dained by God *to be* Judge of the living and
the dead.
43 "To Him all the prophets witness that,
through His name, whoever believes in Him
will receive remission of sins."

The Holy Spirit Falls on the Gentiles

44 While Peter was still speaking these
words, the Holy Spirit fell upon all those who
heard the word.
45 And those of the circumcision who believed were astonished, as many as came with
Peter, because the gift of the Holy Spirit had
been poured out on the Gentiles also.
46 For they heard them speak with tongues
and magnify God. Then Peter answered,
47 "Can anyone forbid water, that these
should not be baptized who have received the
Holy Spirit just as we *have?*"
48 And he commanded them to be baptized
in the name of the Lord. Then they asked him
to stay a few days.

Peter Defends God's Grace

11 Now the apostles and brethren who
were in Judea heard that the Gentiles
had also received the word of God.
2 And when Peter came up to Jerusalem,
those of the circumcision contended with him,
3 saying, "You went in to uncircumcised
men and ate with them!"
4 But Peter explained *it* to them in order
from the beginning, saying:
5 "I was in the city of Joppa praying; and in
a trance I saw a vision, an object descending
like a great sheet, let down from heaven by
four corners; and it came to me.
6 "When I observed it intently and considered, I saw four-footed animals of the earth,
wild beasts, creeping things, and birds of the
air.
7 "And I heard a voice saying to me, 'Rise,
Peter; kill and eat.'
8 "But I said, 'Not so, Lord! For nothing
common or unclean has at any time entered
my mouth.'
9 "But the voice answered me again from
heaven, 'What God has cleansed you must not
call common.'
10 "Now this was done three times, and all
were drawn up again into heaven.
11 "At that very moment, three men stood before the house where I was, having been sent
to me from Caesarea.
12 "Then the Spirit told me to go with them,
doubting nothing. Moreover these six
brethren accompanied me, and we entered
the man's house.
13 "And he told us how he had seen an angel
standing in his house, who said to him, 'Send
men to Joppa, and call for Simon whose surname is Peter,
14 'who will tell you words by which you and
all your household will be saved.'
15 "And as I began to speak, the Holy Spirit
fell upon them, as upon us at the beginning.
16 "Then I remembered the word of the Lord,
how He said, 'John indeed baptized with
water, but you shall be baptized with the Holy
Spirit.'
17 "If therefore God gave them the same gift
as *He gave* us when we believed on the Lord
Jesus Christ, who was I that I could withstand
God?"
18 When they heard these things they became silent; and they glorified God, saying,
"Then God has also granted to the Gentiles
repentance to life."

Barnabas and Saul at Antioch

19 Now those who were scattered after the
persecution that arose over Stephen traveled as
far as Phoenicia, Cyprus, and Antioch, preaching the word to no one but the Jews only.
20 But some of them were men from Cyprus
and Cyrene, who, when they had come to Antioch, spoke to the Hellenists, preaching the
Lord Jesus.
21 And the hand of the Lord was with them,
and a great number believed and turned to
the Lord.
22 Then news of these things came to the
ears of the church in Jerusalem, and they sent
out Barnabas to go as far as Antioch.
23 When he came and had seen the grace of
God, he was glad, and encouraged them all
that with purpose of heart they should continue with the Lord.

LIFE LESSONS

➤ 11:17 — *"If therefore God gave them the same gift as He gave us when we believed on the Lord Jesus Christ, who was I that I could withstand God?"*

Once we recognize a clear move of God, we are wise to join it or stay out of the way. It may not be what we expected, or even what we hoped for, but He calls the shots, not us.

➤ 11:18 — *When they heard these things they became silent; and they glorified God, saying, "Then God has also granted to the Gentiles repentance to life."*

It had never occurred to the early Jewish believers that God might actually choose to put believing Gentiles on the same spiritual plane as believing Jews. But once they saw the truth, they responded correctly by praising God.

➤ 11:23 — *When he came and had seen the grace of God, he was glad, and encouraged them all that with purpose of heart they should continue with the Lord.*

How does one "see" the grace of God? By observing the fruit of genuine grace: dynamic worship, forgiving spirits, peace, joy, and so forth. We encourage such grace to flourish by exhorting each other to eagerly and tenaciously serve the living God.

LIFE PRINCIPLE 22

TO WALK IN THE SPIRIT IS TO OBEY THE INITIAL PROMPTINGS OF THE SPIRIT.

ACTS 10:19

To whom do you turn for daily guidance on how to live, what to do, where to go, whom to see, how to make decisions?

The Scriptures tell us that the only Guide worth trusting is the Holy Spirit. He is the only One who knows our past completely, from the moment we were conceived to the present, and who also knows our future, from this day to eternity. Only He fully knows God's plan and purpose for us, today and for each day of our lives. Only the Holy Spirit knows what is fully good and right for you. Any other opinion can reflect only part of the full truth, which the Holy Spirit knows completely.

Jesus repeatedly referred to the Holy Spirit as the Spirit of truth. Note what He said about the Holy Spirit's activity in your life: "He will guide you into all truth; for He will not speak on His own authority, but whatever He hears He will speak; and He will tell you things to come" (John 16:13).

The Spirit of truth is like an inner compass in our lives—always pointing us toward what Jesus would be, say, or do in any given moment.

God desires to make His will known to you. He wants you to know what to do and when to do it. Trust the Holy Spirit to be your daily Guide!

Throughout the Gospels, we see Jesus guided every day by the Holy Spirit. After God poured out the Holy Spirit on the disciples, they too found themselves led in profound ways by the Holy Spirit. The verses below give just a few examples of how the Holy Spirit dealt with His people in ways that provided very personal and specific guidance. What He did for them then, He desires to do for you today.

Then the Spirit told me to go with them, doubting nothing (Acts 11:12).

As they ministered to the Lord and fasted, the Holy Spirit said, "Now separate to Me Barnabas and Saul for the work to which I have called them" (Acts 13:2).

Now when they had gone through Phrygia and the region of Galatia, they were forbidden by the Holy Spirit to preach the word in Asia (Acts 16:6).

The leaders of the early church relied on the Holy Spirit to give them this kind of specific, personal guidance, and we are wise to do likewise. Both Romans 8:14

The Spirit of truth is like an inner compass in our lives.

and Galatians 5:18 refer to our being "led by the Spirit"—the norm of the Christian life.

You may ask, "Are there any conditions placed upon the guidance of the Holy Spirit in our lives?"

Yes.

First, we must stay yielded to the Spirit. We must say yes to the Spirit when He prompts us to take a certain action or say a certain word. We must give mental assent to the Spirit's direction, and then we must actually obey His prompting and follow through by doing or saying what He has called us to do or say.

The Spirit often speaks to us in the stillness of our hearts with a word of conviction or assurance. When the Holy Spirit is directing us away from something harmful, we very often have a heaviness or a feeling of trouble, foreboding, or uneasiness in our spirits. When the Holy Spirit is directing us toward helpful things we tend to feel a deep inner peace, an eagerness to see what God will do, and a feeling of joy.

The Holy Spirit has come to reveal the truth to us.

How can you know if you are yielded to the Holy Spirit? You are yielded to Him when you can say to Him, "Here is what I desire. But if Your answer to this is 'no,' it's all right. I'll do what You say."

Second, we must believe for His guidance. We are much more likely to hear what the Holy Spirit has to say to us if we are actively listening for Him to speak. We are much more likely to see the Holy Spirit's direction if we are looking for His signs. Hebrews 11:6 tells us that God is a "rewarder of those who diligently seek Him." We are to be diligent in seeking His guidance, asking for it, watching for it, anticipating it, and receiving it.

The Holy Spirit has come to reveal the truth to us. He has come in His all-knowing ability to impart to us what we need to know in order to live obedient and faithful lives. Trust Him to guide you, now and always!

See the Life Principles Index for further study.

24 For he was a good man, full of the Holy
Spirit and of faith. And a great many people
were added to the Lord.
25 Then Barnabas departed for Tarsus to
seek Saul.
26 And when he had found him, he brought
him to Antioch. So it was that for a whole
year they assembled with the church and
taught a great many people. And the disciples
were first called Christians in Antioch.

Relief to Judea

27 And in these days prophets came from Jerusalem to Antioch.
28 Then one of them, named Agabus, stood
up and showed by the Spirit that there was
going to be a great famine throughout all the
world, which also happened in the days of
Claudius Caesar.
➤ 29 Then the disciples, each according to his
ability, determined to send relief to the
brethren dwelling in Judea.
30 This they also did, and sent it to the elders
by the hands of Barnabas and Saul.

Herod's Violence to the Church

12 Now about that time Herod the king
stretched out *his* hand to harass some
from the church.
2 Then he killed James the brother of John
with the sword.
3 And because he saw that it pleased the
Jews, he proceeded further to seize Peter also.
Now it was *during* the Days of Unleavened
Bread.
4 So when he had arrested him, he put *him*
in prison, and delivered *him* to four squads of
soldiers to keep him, intending to bring him
before the people after Passover.

Peter Freed from Prison

➤ **5** Peter was therefore kept in prison, but
constant[a] prayer was offered to God for him
by the church.
6 And when Herod was about to bring him
out, that night Peter was sleeping, bound with
two chains between two soldiers; and the
guards before the door were keeping the
prison.
7 Now behold, an angel of the Lord stood by
him, and a light shone in the prison; and he
struck Peter on the side and raised him up,
saying, "Arise quickly!" And his chains fell off
his hands.
8 Then the angel said to him, "Gird yourself
and tie on your sandals"; and so he did. And
he said to him, "Put on your garment and follow me."
9 So he went out and followed him, and did ➤
not know that what was done by the angel
was real, but thought he was seeing a vision.
10 When they were past the first and the second guard posts, they came to the iron gate
that leads to the city, which opened to them of
its own accord; and they went out and went
down one street, and immediately the angel
departed from him.
11 And when Peter had come to himself, he
said, "Now I know for certain that the Lord
has sent His angel, and has delivered me from
the hand of Herod and *from* all the expectation of the Jewish people."
12 So, when he had considered *this*, he came
to the house of Mary, the mother of John
whose surname was Mark, where many were
gathered together praying.
13 And as Peter knocked at the door of the
gate, a girl named Rhoda came to answer.
14 When she recognized Peter's voice, because of *her* gladness she did not open the
gate, but ran in and announced that Peter
stood before the gate.
15 But they said to her, "You are beside yourself!" Yet she kept insisting that it was so. So
they said, "It is his angel."
16 Now Peter continued knocking; and when
they opened *the door* and saw him, they were
astonished.
17 But motioning to them with his hand to
keep silent, he declared to them how the Lord
had brought him out of the prison. And he
said, "Go, tell these things to James and to the
brethren." And he departed and went to another place.
18 Then, as soon as it was day, there was no

12:5 [a]NU-Text reads *constantly* (or *earnestly*).

LIFE LESSONS

➤ **11:29 — *Then the disciples, each according to his ability, determined to send relief to the brethren dwelling in Judea.***

A heart genuinely touched by the love of God desires to meet the needs of fellow believers in distress. God blesses us so that we might bless others. We all need each other.

➤ **12:5 — *Peter was therefore kept in prison, but constant prayer was offered to God for him by the church.***

The church had already lost one leader, James the brother of John, to the executioner (Acts 12:2). Now it appeared as though it would lose Peter, too. But God loves to perform miracles in response to corporate prayer!

➤ **12:9 — *So he went out and followed him, and did not know that what was done by the angel was real, but thought he was seeing a vision.***

Peter had seen visions from God before, and this scene looked so unusual that he thought it had to be another one. But it wasn't; it was actually happening, just as he saw it. Nothing is impossible for God!

small stir among the soldiers about what had
become of Peter.
19 But when Herod had searched for him and
not found him, he examined the guards and
commanded that *they* should be put to death.
And he went down from Judea to Caesarea,
and stayed *there*.

Herod's Violent Death

20 Now Herod had been very angry with the
people of Tyre and Sidon; but they came to
him with one accord, and having made Blas-
tus the king's personal aide their friend, they
asked for peace, because their country was
supplied with food by the king's *country*.
21 So on a set day Herod, arrayed in royal apparel, sat on his throne and gave an oration to
them.
22 And the people kept shouting, "The voice
of a god and not of a man!"
➤ 23 Then immediately an angel of the Lord
struck him, because he did not give glory to
God. And he was eaten by worms and died.
24 But the word of God grew and multiplied.

Barnabas and Saul Appointed

25 And Barnabas and Saul returned from[a] Jerusalem when they had fulfilled *their* ministry, and they also took with them John
whose surname was Mark.

13 Now in the church that was at Antioch
there were certain prophets and teachers: Barnabas, Simeon who was called Niger,
Lucius of Cyrene, Manaen who had been
brought up with Herod the tetrarch, and Saul.
➤ 2 As they ministered to the Lord and fasted,
the Holy Spirit said, "Now separate to Me
Barnabas and Saul for the work to which I
have called them."
3 Then, having fasted and prayed, and laid
hands on them, they sent *them* away.

Preaching in Cyprus

4 So, being sent out by the Holy Spirit, they
went down to Seleucia, and from there they
sailed to Cyprus.
5 And when they arrived in Salamis, they
preached the word of God in the synagogues
of the Jews. They also had John as *their* assistant.
6 Now when they had gone through the island[a] to Paphos, they found a certain sorcerer,
a false prophet, a Jew whose name *was* Bar-
Jesus,
7 who was with the proconsul, Sergius
Paulus, an intelligent man. This man called

Life Examples:

RHODA

Joy in Prayer

ACTS 12:12–17

Late into the night, the church pled for God's mercy on behalf of their imprisoned leader, Peter.

Rhoda, a household servant, knew well the believers who met in Mary's large house. But though they prayed earnestly for Peter, it seemed inevitable that he faced a morning execution.

Suddenly a sharp rap at the door interrupted their prayers. Rhoda approached the entrance, listened—and heard a familiar voice. At the gate stood Peter! In her excitement she forgot to let him in and instead ran to inform the praying church. "Peter is at the door!" she exclaimed. But not until Peter stood among them, recounting his deliverance, did they jubilantly acknowledge the Lord's provision.

Just as Rhoda's gladness sustained her heart when life became painful, so the joy of Christ sustains you when the future appears impossible. The delight of your salvation helps you endure when disappointments and difficult issues assail you.

See the Life Principles Index for further study:
8. Fight all your battles on your knees and you win every time.
18. As children of a sovereign God, we are never victims of our circumstances.

12:25 [a]NU-Text and M-Text read *to.* **13:6** [a]NU-Text reads *the whole island.*

LIFE LESSONS

➤ 12:23 — *Then immediately an angel of the Lord struck him, because he did not give glory to God. And he was eaten by worms and died.*

Herod persecuted the church; Herod exalted himself; Herod died a painful and ugly death. The impious king may have suffered from intestinal roundworms, which can block the intestines, causing severe pain, vomiting, and death.

➤ 13:2 — *As they ministered to the Lord and fasted, the Holy Spirit said, "Now separate to Me Barnabas and Saul for the work to which I have called them."*

Paul and Barnabas found their life calling in the midst of praying and worshiping among their fellow believers, not on their own. God calls us to serve Him together, to show the world how relationships are supposed to work.

for Barnabas and Saul and sought to hear the
word of God.
8 But Elymas the sorcerer (for so his name
is translated) withstood them, seeking to turn
the proconsul away from the faith.
9 Then Saul, who also *is called* Paul, filled
with the Holy Spirit, looked intently at him
10 and said, "O full of all deceit and all fraud,
you son of the devil, *you* enemy of all righteousness, will you not cease perverting the
straight ways of the Lord?
11 "And now, indeed, the hand of the Lord *is*
upon you, and you shall be blind, not seeing
the sun for a time." And immediately a dark
mist fell on him, and he went around seeking
someone to lead him by the hand.
12 Then the proconsul believed, when he saw
what had been done, being astonished at the
teaching of the Lord.

At Antioch in Pisidia

13 Now when Paul and his party set sail from
Paphos, they came to Perga in Pamphylia;
and John, departing from them, returned to
Jerusalem.
14 But when they departed from Perga, they
came to Antioch in Pisidia, and went into the
synagogue on the Sabbath day and sat down.
15 And after the reading of the Law and the
Prophets, the rulers of the synagogue sent to
them, saying, "Men *and* brethren, if you
have any word of exhortation for the people,
say on."
16 Then Paul stood up, and motioning with
his hand said, "Men of Israel, and you who
fear God, listen:
17 "The God of this people Israel[a] chose our
fathers, and exalted the people when they
dwelt as strangers in the land of Egypt, and
with an uplifted arm He brought them out of it.
18 "Now for a time of about forty years He
put up with their ways in the wilderness.
19 "And when He had destroyed seven nations in the land of Canaan, He distributed
their land to them by allotment.
20 "After that He gave *them* judges for about
four hundred and fifty years, until Samuel the
prophet.
21 "And afterward they asked for a king; so
God gave them Saul the son of Kish, a man of
the tribe of Benjamin, for forty years.
22 "And when He had removed him, He
raised up for them David as king, to whom
also He gave testimony and said, *'I have
found David*[a] the *son* of Jesse, *a man after My
own heart,* who will do all My will.'[b]
23 "From this man's seed, according to *the*
promise, God raised up for Israel a Savior—
Jesus—[a]
24 "after John had first preached, before His
coming, the baptism of repentance to all the
people of Israel.
25 "And as John was finishing his course, he
said, 'Who do you think I am? I am not *He.* But
behold, there comes One after me, the sandals
of whose feet I am not worthy to loose.'
26 "Men *and* brethren, sons of the family of
Abraham, and those among you who fear
God, to you the word of this salvation has
been sent.
27 "For those who dwell in Jerusalem, and
their rulers, because they did not know Him,
nor even the voices of the Prophets which are
read every Sabbath, have fulfilled *them* in
condemning *Him.*
28 "And though they found no cause for
death *in Him,* they asked Pilate that He
should be put to death.
29 "Now when they had fulfilled all that was
written concerning Him, they took *Him* down
from the tree and laid *Him* in a tomb.
30 "But God raised Him from the dead.
31 "He was seen for many days by those who
came up with Him from Galilee to Jerusalem,
who are His witnesses to the people.
32 "And we declare to you glad tidings—that
promise which was made to the fathers.
33 "God has fulfilled this for us their children, in that He has raised up Jesus. As it is
also written in the second Psalm:

*'You are My Son,
Today I have begotten You.'*[a]

34 "And that He raised Him from the dead, no
more to return to corruption, He has spoken
thus:

*'I will give you the sure mercies of
David.'*[a]

35 "Therefore He also says in another *Psalm:*

*'You will not allow Your Holy One to see
corruption.'*[a]

36 "For David, after he had served his own
generation by the will of God, fell asleep, was
buried with his fathers, and saw corruption;
37 "but He whom God raised up saw no corruption.
38 "Therefore let it be known to you,
brethren, that through this Man is preached
to you the forgiveness of sins;
39 "and by Him everyone who believes is justified from all things from which you could
not be justified by the law of Moses.
40 "Beware therefore, lest what has been spoken in the prophets come upon you:

41 *'Behold, you despisers,
Marvel and perish!
For I work a work in your days,
A work which you will by no means
believe,
Though one were to declare it to you.'"*[a]

13:17 [a]M-Text omits *Israel.* **13:22** [a]Psalm 89:20
[b]1 Samuel 13:14 **13:23** [a]M-Text reads *for Israel salvation.*
13:33 [a]Psalm 2:7 **13:34** [a]Isaiah 55:3 **13:35** [a]Psalm 16:10
13:41 [a]Habakkuk 1:5

Blessing and Conflict at Antioch

42 So when the Jews went out of the synagogue,[a] the Gentiles begged that these words
might be preached to them the next Sabbath.
43 Now when the congregation had broken
up, many of the Jews and devout proselytes
followed Paul and Barnabas, who, speaking
to them, persuaded them to continue in the
grace of God.
44 On the next Sabbath almost the whole city
came together to hear the word of God.
45 But when the Jews saw the multitudes,
they were filled with envy; and contradicting
and blaspheming, they opposed the things
spoken by Paul.
46 Then Paul and Barnabas grew bold and
said, "It was necessary that the word of God
should be spoken to you first; but since you
reject it, and judge yourselves unworthy of
everlasting life, behold, we turn to the Gentiles.
47 "For so the Lord has commanded us:

'I have set you as a light to the Gentiles,
That you should be for salvation to the
ends of the earth.'"[a]

➤ 48 Now when the Gentiles heard this, they
were glad and glorified the word of the Lord.
And as many as had been appointed to eternal life believed.
49 And the word of the Lord was being
spread throughout all the region.
50 But the Jews stirred up the devout and
prominent women and the chief men of
the city, raised up persecution against Paul
and Barnabas, and expelled them from their
region.
51 But they shook off the dust from their feet
against them, and came to Iconium.
➤ 52 And the disciples were filled with joy and
with the Holy Spirit.

At Iconium

14 Now it happened in Iconium that they
went together to the synagogue of the
Jews, and so spoke that a great multitude
both of the Jews and of the Greeks believed.
2 But the unbelieving Jews stirred up the
Gentiles and poisoned their minds against the
brethren.
3 Therefore they stayed there a long time,
speaking boldly in the Lord, who was bearing
witness to the word of His grace, granting
signs and wonders to be done by their hands.
4 But the multitude of the city was divided:
part sided with the Jews, and part with the
apostles.
5 And when a violent attempt was made by
both the Gentiles and Jews, with their rulers,
to abuse and stone them,
6 they became aware of it and fled to Lystra
and Derbe, cities of Lycaonia, and to the surrounding region.
7 And they were preaching the gospel there.

Idolatry at Lystra

8 And in Lystra a certain man without
strength in his feet was sitting, a cripple from
his mother's womb, who had never walked.
9 *This* man heard Paul speaking. Paul, observing him intently and seeing that he had
faith to be healed,
10 said with a loud voice, "Stand up straight
on your feet!" And he leaped and walked.
11 Now when the people saw what Paul had
done, they raised their voices, saying in the
Lycaonian *language*, "The gods have come
down to us in the likeness of men!"
12 And Barnabas they called Zeus, and Paul,
Hermes, because he was the chief speaker.
13 Then the priest of Zeus, whose temple was
in front of their city, brought oxen and gar-
lands to the gates, intending to sacrifice with
the multitudes.
14 But when the apostles Barnabas and Paul
heard this, they tore their clothes and ran in
among the multitude, crying out
15 and saying, "Men, why are you doing ➤
these things? We also are men with the same
nature as you, and preach to you that you
should turn from these useless things to the
living God, who made the heaven, the earth,
the sea, and all things that are in them,

13:42 [a]Or *And when they went out of the synagogue of the Jews;* NU-Text reads *And when they went out, they begged.*
13:47 [a]Isaiah 49:6

LIFE LESSONS

➤ **13:48 — *And as many as had been appointed to eternal life believed.***

We will never understand how the sovereignty of God works with the free choice of man to bring people to Christ, but both truths are clearly taught in Scripture. God chooses, and so must we.

➤ **13:52 — *And the disciples were filled with joy and with the Holy Spirit.***

God intends a life with His Spirit to be a life of joy. That doesn't mean that sorrow never intrudes on such a life, but that even in the midst of sorrow, the joy of the Spirit comes bubbling to the surface.

➤ **14:15 — *"We also are men with the same nature as you, and preach to you that you should turn from these useless things to the living God . . . ."***

God had performed such an astonishing miracle through Paul and Barnabas that the people of Lystra thought the pair must be Greek gods. Paul insisted that except for their faith they were no different from anyone else.

16 "who in bygone generations allowed all
nations to walk in their own ways.
17 "Nevertheless He did not leave Himself
without witness, in that He did good, gave us
rain from heaven and fruitful seasons, filling
our hearts with food and gladness."
18 And with these sayings they could
scarcely restrain the multitudes from sacrificing to them.

Stoning, Escape to Derbe

➤ **19** Then Jews from Antioch and Iconium
came there; and having persuaded the multitudes, they stoned Paul *and* dragged *him* out
of the city, supposing him to be dead.
20 However, when the disciples gathered
around him, he rose up and went into the city.
And the next day he departed with Barnabas
to Derbe.

Strengthening the Converts

21 And when they had preached the gospel
to that city and made many disciples, they returned to Lystra, Iconium, and Antioch,
➤ 22 strengthening the souls of the disciples,
exhorting *them* to continue in the faith, and
saying, "We must through many tribulations
enter the kingdom of God."
23 So when they had appointed elders in
every church, and prayed with fasting, they
commended them to the Lord in whom they
had believed.
24 And after they had passed through Pisidia, they came to Pamphylia.
25 Now when they had preached the word in
Perga, they went down to Attalia.
26 From there they sailed to Antioch, where
they had been commended to the grace of
God for the work which they had completed.
27 Now when they had come and gathered
the church together, they reported all that
God had done with them, and that He had
opened the door of faith to the Gentiles.
28 So they stayed there a long time with the
disciples.

Conflict over Circumcision

15 And certain *men* came down from
Judea and taught the brethren, "Unless
you are circumcised according to the custom
of Moses, you cannot be saved."
2 Therefore, when Paul and Barnabas had
no small dissension and dispute with them,
they determined that Paul and Barnabas and
certain others of them should go up to Jerusalem, to the apostles and elders, about this
question.
3 So, being sent on their way by the church,
they passed through Phoenicia and Samaria,
describing the conversion of the Gentiles; and
they caused great joy to all the brethren.
4 And when they had come to Jerusalem,
they were received by the church and the
apostles and the elders; and they reported all
things that God had done with them.
5 But some of the sect of the Pharisees who
believed rose up, saying, "It is necessary to
circumcise them, and to command *them* to
keep the law of Moses."

The Jerusalem Council

6 Now the apostles and elders came together to consider this matter.
7 And when there had been much dispute,
Peter rose up *and* said to them: "Men *and*
brethren, you know that a good while ago
God chose among us, that by my mouth the
Gentiles should hear the word of the gospel
and believe.
8 "So God, who knows the heart, acknowledged them by giving them the Holy Spirit,
just as *He did* to us,
9 "and made no distinction between us and
them, purifying their hearts by faith.
10 "Now therefore, why do you test God by
putting a yoke on the neck of the disciples
which neither our fathers nor we were able to
bear?
11 "But we believe that through the grace of ➤
the Lord Jesus Christ[a] we shall be saved in
the same manner as they."
12 Then all the multitude kept silent and listened to Barnabas and Paul declaring how
many miracles and wonders God had worked
through them among the Gentiles.

15:11 [a]NU-Text and M-Text omit *Christ.*

LIFE LESSONS

➤ **14:19, 20 —** ***. . . they stoned Paul and dragged him out of the city, supposing him to be dead. However, when the disciples gathered around him, he rose up and went into the city.***

Some believe that Paul really did die and "was caught up into Paradise and heard inexpressible words, which it is not lawful for a man to utter" (2 Cor. 12:4). Regardless, God preserved Paul's life until his time had come.

➤ **14:22 —** ***. . . strengthening the souls of the disciples, exhorting them to continue in the faith, and saying, "We must through many tribulations enter the kingdom of God."***

We find spiritual strength and encouragement not only in warm, tender words, but also in words that confront us with harsh realities. The Christian life is a war, and we must never forget it (Eph. 6:10–17).

➤ **15:11 —** ***"But we believe that through the grace of the Lord Jesus Christ we shall be saved in the same manner as they."***

A wealthy woman once objected to being saved in the same way as her poor servant. "You do not *have* to be saved at all," came the reply, "but if you ever are saved, it will be in the same way as anyone else."

13 And after they had become silent, James answered, saying, "Men *and* brethren, listen to me:
14 "Simon has declared how God at the first visited the Gentiles to take out of them a people for His name.
15 "And with this the words of the prophets agree, just as it is written:

16 '*After this I will return*
And will rebuild the tabernacle of David,
which has fallen down;
I will rebuild its ruins,
And I will set it up;
17 *So that the rest of mankind may seek the* LORD,
Even all the Gentiles who are called by My name,
Says the LORD *who does all these things.*'[a]

18 "Known to God from eternity are all His works.[a]
19 "Therefore I judge that we should not trouble those from among the Gentiles who are turning to God,
20 "but that we write to them to abstain from things polluted by idols, *from* sexual immorality,[a] *from* things strangled, and *from* blood.
21 "For Moses has had throughout many generations those who preach him in every city, being read in the synagogues every Sabbath."

The Jerusalem Decree

22 Then it pleased the apostles and elders, with the whole church, to send chosen men of their own company to Antioch with Paul and Barnabas, *namely,* Judas who was also named Barsabas,[a] and Silas, leading men among the brethren.
23 They wrote this *letter* by them:

The apostles, the elders, and the brethren,

To the brethren who are of the Gentiles in Antioch, Syria, and Cilicia:

Greetings.

24 Since we have heard that some who went out from us have troubled you with words, unsettling your souls, saying, "*You must* be circumcised and keep the law"[a]—to whom we gave no *such* commandment—
25 it seemed good to us, being assembled with one accord, to send chosen men to you with our beloved Barnabas and Paul,
26 men who have risked their lives for the name of our Lord Jesus Christ.
27 We have therefore sent Judas and Silas, who will also report the same things by word of mouth.
28 For it seemed good to the Holy Spirit, and to us, to lay upon you no greater burden than these necessary things:
29 that you abstain from things offered to idols, from blood, from things strangled, and from sexual immorality.[a] If you keep yourselves from these, you will do well.

Farewell.

Continuing Ministry in Syria

30 So when they were sent off, they came to Antioch; and when they had gathered the multitude together, they delivered the letter.
31 When they had read it, they rejoiced over its encouragement.
32 Now Judas and Silas, themselves being prophets also, exhorted and strengthened the brethren with many words.
33 And after they had stayed *there* for a time, they were sent back with greetings from the brethren to the apostles.[a]
34 However, it seemed good to Silas to remain there.[a]
35 Paul and Barnabas also remained in Antioch, teaching and preaching the word of the Lord, with many others also.

Division over John Mark

36 Then after some days Paul said to Barnabas, "Let us now go back and visit our brethren in every city where we have preached the word of the Lord, *and see* how they are doing."
37 Now Barnabas was determined to take with them John called Mark.
38 But Paul insisted that they should not take with them the one who had departed from them in Pamphylia, and had not gone with them to the work.

15:17 [a]Amos 9:11, 12 **15:18** [a]NU-Text (combining with verse 17) reads *Says the Lord, who makes these things known from eternity (of old).* **15:20** [a]Or *fornication* **15:22** [a]NU-Text and M-Text read *Barsabbas.* **15:24** [a]NU-Text omits *saying, "You must be circumcised and keep the law."* **15:29** [a]Or *fornication* **15:33** [a]NU-Text reads *to those who had sent them.* **15:34** [a]NU-Text and M-Text omit this verse.

LIFE LESSONS

➤ 15:28 — *"For it seemed good to the Holy Spirit, and to us . . ."*

The early church reached consensus on a crucial and sticky issue through respectful discussion, earnest prayer, careful listening, and Bible study. The same formula holds true today.

➤ 39 Then the contention became so sharp that
they parted from one another. And so Barnabas took Mark and sailed to Cyprus;
40 but Paul chose Silas and departed, being
commended by the brethren to the grace of
God.
41 And he went through Syria and Cilicia,
strengthening the churches.

Timothy Joins Paul and Silas

16 Then he came to Derbe and Lystra. And
behold, a certain disciple was there,
named Timothy, *the* son of a certain Jewish
woman who believed, but his father *was*
Greek.
2 He was well spoken of by the brethren
who were at Lystra and Iconium.
3 Paul wanted to have him go on with him.
And he took *him* and circumcised him because of the Jews who were in that region, for
they all knew that his father was Greek.
4 And as they went through the cities, they
delivered to them the decrees to keep, which
were determined by the apostles and elders at
Jerusalem.
5 So the churches were strengthened in the
faith, and increased in number daily.

The Macedonian Call

➤ **6** Now when they had gone through Phrygia
and the region of Galatia, they were forbidden by the Holy Spirit to preach the word in
Asia.
7 After they had come to Mysia, they tried
to go into Bithynia, but the Spirit[a] did not permit them.
8 So passing by Mysia, they came down to
Troas.
9 And a vision appeared to Paul in the night.
A man of Macedonia stood and pleaded with
him, saying, "Come over to Macedonia and
help us."
10 Now after he had seen the vision, immediately we sought to go to Macedonia, concluding that the Lord had called us to preach the
gospel to them.

Lydia Baptized at Philippi

11 Therefore, sailing from Troas, we ran a
straight course to Samothrace, and the next
day came to Neapolis,
12 and from there to Philippi, which is the
foremost city of that part of Macedonia, a
colony. And we were staying in that city for
some days.
13 And on the Sabbath day we went out of
the city to the riverside, where prayer was
customarily made; and we sat down and
spoke to the women who met *there.*
14 Now a certain woman named Lydia heard ◄
us. She was a seller of purple from the city of
Thyatira, who worshiped God. The Lord
opened her heart to heed the things spoken
by Paul.
15 And when she and her household were
baptized, she begged *us,* saying, "If you have
judged me to be faithful to the Lord, come to
my house and stay." So she persuaded us.

Paul and Silas Imprisoned

16 Now it happened, as we went to prayer,
that a certain slave girl possessed with a spirit
of divination met us, who brought her masters much profit by fortune-telling.
17 This girl followed Paul and us, and cried
out, saying, "These men are the servants of
the Most High God, who proclaim to us the
way of salvation."
18 And this she did for many days. But Paul,
greatly annoyed, turned and said to the spirit,
"I command you in the name of Jesus Christ
to come out of her." And he came out that very
hour.
19 But when her masters saw that their hope
of profit was gone, they seized Paul and Silas
and dragged *them* into the marketplace to the
authorities.
20 And they brought them to the magistrates,
and said, "These men, being Jews, exceedingly trouble our city;
21 "and they teach customs which are not
lawful for us, being Romans, to receive or observe."
22 Then the multitude rose up together
against them; and the magistrates tore off
their clothes and commanded *them* to be
beaten with rods.
23 And when they had laid many stripes on

16:7 [a]NU-Text adds *of Jesus.*

LIFE LESSONS

➤ 15:39 — *Then the contention became so sharp that they parted from one another.*

Even mature, godly believers can have big disagreements that lead to a parting of the ways. Yet God used the split between Paul and Barnabas to send out two missionary teams instead of one.

➤ 16:6, 7 — *. . . they were forbidden by the Holy Spirit to preach the word in Asia . . . they tried to go into Bithynia, but the Spirit did not permit them.*

Paul and his companions had developed a plan for evangelism that they tried to follow, but they never let their plans get in the way of the Spirit's leading. God wants our planning and His guidance to go hand-in-hand.

➤ 16:14 — *The Lord opened her heart to heed the things spoken by Paul.*

No one will respond to the gospel message unless God goes before us and sends His Spirit to do a work in human hearts. Jesus said, "no one can come to Me unless it has been granted to him by My Father" (John 6:65).

them, they threw *them* into prison, commanding the jailer to keep them securely.
24 Having received such a charge, he put them into the inner prison and fastened their feet in the stocks.

The Philippian Jailer Saved

➤ **25** But at midnight Paul and Silas were praying and singing hymns to God, and the prisoners were listening to them.
26 Suddenly there was a great earthquake, so that the foundations of the prison were shaken; and immediately all the doors were opened and everyone's chains were loosed.
27 And the keeper of the prison, awaking from sleep and seeing the prison doors open, supposing the prisoners had fled, drew his sword and was about to kill himself.
28 But Paul called with a loud voice, saying, "Do yourself no harm, for we are all here."
29 Then he called for a light, ran in, and fell down trembling before Paul and Silas.
30 And he brought them out and said, "Sirs, what must I do to be saved?"
31 So they said, "Believe on the Lord Jesus Christ, and you will be saved, you and your household."
32 Then they spoke the word of the Lord to him and to all who were in his house.
33 And he took them the same hour of the night and washed *their* stripes. And immediately he and all his *family* were baptized.
34 Now when he had brought them into his house, he set food before them; and he rejoiced, having believed in God with all his household.

Paul Refuses to Depart Secretly

35 And when it was day, the magistrates sent the officers, saying, "Let those men go."
36 So the keeper of the prison reported these words to Paul, saying, "The magistrates have sent to let you go. Now therefore depart, and go in peace."
37 But Paul said to them, "They have beaten us openly, uncondemned Romans, *and* have thrown *us* into prison. And now do they put us out secretly? No indeed! Let them come themselves and get us out."
38 And the officers told these words to the magistrates, and they were afraid when they heard that they were Romans.
39 Then they came and pleaded with them and brought *them* out, and asked *them* to depart from the city.

Life Examples:

SILAS

Singing for Victory

ACTS 16:24–34

As exhausted as he felt, Silas could not sleep. The stale air in the inner cell made breathing difficult, and the torment of his wounds kept him from getting much-needed sleep. Would he or Paul live to see another day? Silas did not know.

Yet Silas neither meditated on injustice nor despaired of his situation. Instead, faith filled his heart. When Silas and Paul lifted their voices in song, a violent earthquake shook the prison. Soon they led the jailer and his entire family to the Lord.

You have a song to sing as well. Though your situation may feel overwhelming, are you willing to trust God in your circumstances? Do you believe that no problem is beyond His power? As you allow God to conduct the symphony of your life, you will see Him shaking your own prisons. Will you, like Silas, lift up your voice to herald the coming victory?

See the Life Principles Index for further study:

9. Trusting God means looking beyond what we can see to what God sees.

17. We stand tallest and strongest on our knees.

40 So they went out of the prison and entered *the house* of Lydia; and when they had seen the brethren, they encouraged them and departed.

Preaching Christ at Thessalonica

17 Now when they had passed through Amphipolis and Apollonia, they came to Thessalonica, where there was a synagogue of the Jews.
2 Then Paul, as his custom was, went in to them, and for three Sabbaths reasoned with them from the Scriptures,

LIFE LESSONS

➤ **16:25 — *But at midnight Paul and Silas were praying and singing hymns to God, and the prisoners were listening to them.***

Paul and Silas had been attacked by a mob, beaten by soldiers, thrown in stocks and shoved into a dark, high-security prison cell. How did they react? With prayer and singing! Only the Spirit can produce such unexpected joy.

3 explaining and demonstrating that the
Christ had to suffer and rise again from the
dead, and *saying*, "This Jesus whom I preach
to you is the Christ."
4 And some of them were persuaded; and a
great multitude of the devout Greeks, and not
a few of the leading women, joined Paul and
Silas.

Assault on Jason's House

5 But the Jews who were not persuaded, becoming envious,[a] took some of the evil men
from the marketplace, and gathering a mob,
set all the city in an uproar and attacked the
house of Jason, and sought to bring them out
to the people.
6 But when they did not find them, they
dragged Jason and some brethren to the
rulers of the city, crying out, "These who have
turned the world upside down have come
here too.
7 "Jason has harbored them, and these are
all acting contrary to the decrees of Caesar,
saying there is another king—Jesus."
8 And they troubled the crowd and the
rulers of the city when they heard these
things.
9 So when they had taken security from Jason and the rest, they let them go.

Ministering at Berea

10 Then the brethren immediately sent Paul
and Silas away by night to Berea. When they
arrived, they went into the synagogue of the
Jews.
➤ 11 These were more fair-minded than those
in Thessalonica, in that they received the
word with all readiness, and searched the
Scriptures daily *to find out* whether these
things were so.
12 Therefore many of them believed, and
also not a few of the Greeks, prominent
women as well as men.
13 But when the Jews from Thessalonica
learned that the word of God was preached
by Paul at Berea, they came there also and
stirred up the crowds.
14 Then immediately the brethren sent Paul
away, to go to the sea; but both Silas and Timothy remained there.
15 So those who conducted Paul brought him
to Athens; and receiving a command for Silas
and Timothy to come to him with all speed,
they departed.

The Philosophers at Athens

16 Now while Paul waited for them at
Athens, his spirit was provoked within him
when he saw that the city was given over to
idols.
17 Therefore he reasoned in the synagogue
with the Jews and with the *Gentile* worshipers, and in the marketplace daily with
those who happened to be there.
18 Then[a] certain Epicurean and Stoic
philosophers encountered him. And some
said, "What does this babbler want to say?"
Others said, "He seems to be a proclaimer of
foreign gods," because he preached to them
Jesus and the resurrection.
19 And they took him and brought him to the
Areopagus, saying, "May we know what this
new doctrine *is* of which you speak?
20 "For you are bringing some strange things
to our ears. Therefore we want to know what
these things mean."
21 For all the Athenians and the foreigners
who were there spent their time in nothing
else but either to tell or to hear some new
thing.

Addressing the Areopagus

22 Then Paul stood in the midst of the Areopagus and said, "Men of Athens, I perceive
that in all things you are very religious;
23 "for as I was passing through and considering the objects of your worship, I even
found an altar with this inscription:

TO THE UNKNOWN GOD.

Therefore, the One whom you worship without knowing, Him I proclaim to you:
24 "God, who made the world and everything in it, since He is Lord of heaven and
earth, does not dwell in temples made with
hands.
25 "Nor is He worshiped with men's hands,
as though He needed anything, since He gives
to all life, breath, and all things.
26 "And He has made from one blood[a] every
nation of men to dwell on all the face of
the earth, and has determined their preappointed times and the boundaries of their
dwellings,

17:5 [a]NU-Text omits *who were not persuaded;* M-Text omits *becoming envious.* **17:18** [a]NU-Text and M-Text add *also.* **17:26** [a]NU-Text omits *blood.*

LIFE LESSONS

➤ **17:11 — . . . *they received the word with all readiness, and searched the Scriptures daily to find out whether these things were so.***

The Bereans didn't take Paul's word for it about how the Old Testament scriptures prophesied the ministry, sufferings, and resurrection of Christ. They looked for themselves—and God commended them for their diligence.

➤ 27 "so that they should seek the Lord, in the
hope that they might grope for Him and find
Him, though He is not far from each one of us;
28 "for in Him we live and move and have our
being, as also some of your own poets have
said, 'For we are also His offspring.'
29 "Therefore, since we are the offspring of
God, we ought not to think that the Divine
Nature is like gold or silver or stone, something shaped by art and man's devising.
30 "Truly, these times of ignorance God overlooked, but now commands all men everywhere to repent,
* 31 "because He has appointed a day on
which He will judge the world in righteousness by the Man whom He has ordained. He
has given assurance of this to all by raising
Him from the dead."
32 And when they heard of the resurrection
of the dead, some mocked, while others said,
"We will hear you again on this *matter*."
33 So Paul departed from among them.
34 However, some men joined him and believed, among them Dionysius the Are-
opagite, a woman named Damaris, and others
with them.

Ministering at Corinth

18 After these things Paul departed from
Athens and went to Corinth.
2 And he found a certain Jew named Aquila,
born in Pontus, who had recently come from
Italy with his wife Priscilla (because Claudius
had commanded all the Jews to depart from
Rome); and he came to them.
3 So, because he was of the same trade, he
stayed with them and worked; for by occupation they were tentmakers.
➤ 4 And he reasoned in the synagogue every
Sabbath, and persuaded both Jews and
Greeks.
5 When Silas and Timothy had come from
Macedonia, Paul was compelled by the Spirit,
and testified to the Jews *that* Jesus *is* the
Christ.
6 But when they opposed him and blasphemed, he shook *his* garments and said to
them, "Your blood *be* upon your *own* heads; I
am clean. From now on I will go to the Gentiles."
7 And he departed from there and entered
the house of a certain *man* named Justus,[a]
one who worshiped God, whose house was
next door to the synagogue.
8 Then Crispus, the ruler of the synagogue,
believed on the Lord with all his household.
And many of the Corinthians, hearing, believed and were baptized.
9 Now the Lord spoke to Paul in the night ➤
by a vision, "Do not be afraid, but speak, and
do not keep silent;
10 "for I am with you, and no one will attack
you to hurt you; for I have many people in this
city."
11 And he continued *there* a year and six
months, teaching the word of God among
them.
12 When Gallio was proconsul of Achaia, the
Jews with one accord rose up against Paul
and brought him to the judgment seat,
13 saying, "This *fellow* persuades men to
worship God contrary to the law."
14 And when Paul was about to open *his*
mouth, Gallio said to the Jews, "If it were a
matter of wrongdoing or wicked crimes, O
Jews, there would be reason why I should
bear with you.
15 "But if it is a question of words and names
and your own law, look *to it* yourselves; for I
do not want to be a judge of such *matters*."
16 And he drove them from the judgment
seat.
17 Then all the Greeks[a] took Sosthenes, the
ruler of the synagogue, and beat *him* before
the judgment seat. But Gallio took no notice
of these things.

Paul Returns to Antioch

18 So Paul still remained a good while. Then
he took leave of the brethren and sailed for
Syria, and Priscilla and Aquila *were* with
him. He had *his* hair cut off at Cenchrea, for
he had taken a vow.

18:7 [a]NU-Text reads *Titius Justus*. **18:17** [a]NU-Text reads *they all*.

LIFE LESSONS

➤ **17:27 — *". . . they should seek the Lord, in the hope that they might grope for Him and find Him, though He is not far from each one of us . . . ."***

When we seek the Lord, we do not go in search of a disinterested God who has better things to do five galaxies away. We seek a God already near to us who invites our search, and He promises to reward it.

➤ **18:4 — *And he reasoned in the synagogue every Sabbath, and persuaded both Jews and Greeks.***

Paul had a Bible-centered, thoughtful approach to evangelism. He *reasoned* and *persuaded* people of the truth of the gospel, working from the text of the Bible. He respected their intelligence and honored their questions.

➤ **18:9, 10 — *"Do not be afraid, but speak, and do not keep silent; for I am with you, and no one will attack you to hurt you; for I have many people in this city."***

Paul took courage in his evangelism efforts because: (1) Jesus told him to keep speaking; (2) Jesus promised to be with him; (3) Jesus promised to protect him; and (4) Jesus promised him success. We can take courage for identical reasons.

19 And he came to Ephesus, and left them
there; but he himself entered the synagogue
and reasoned with the Jews.
20 When they asked *him* to stay a longer time
with them, he did not consent,
21 but took leave of them, saying, "I must by
all means keep this coming feast in Jerusalem;[a] but I will return again to you, God willing." And he sailed from Ephesus.
22 And when he had landed at Caesarea, and
gone up and greeted the church, he went
down to Antioch.
23 After he had spent some time *there,* he
departed and went over the region of Galatia
and Phrygia in order, strengthening all the
disciples.

Ministry of Apollos

24 Now a certain Jew named Apollos, born at
Alexandria, an eloquent man *and* mighty in
the Scriptures, came to Ephesus.
25 This man had been instructed in the way
of the Lord; and being fervent in spirit, he
spoke and taught accurately the things of the
Lord, though he knew only the baptism of
John.
26 So he began to speak boldly in the synagogue. When Aquila and Priscilla heard him,
they took him aside and explained to him the
way of God more accurately.
➤ 27 And when he desired to cross to Achaia,
the brethren wrote, exhorting the disciples to
receive him; and when he arrived, he greatly
helped those who had believed through grace;
28 for he vigorously refuted the Jews publicly, showing from the Scriptures that Jesus
is the Christ.

Paul at Ephesus

19 And it happened, while Apollos was at
Corinth, that Paul, having passed
through the upper regions, came to Ephesus.
And finding some disciples
2 he said to them, "Did you receive the Holy
Spirit when you believed?" So they said to
him, "We have not so much as heard whether
there is a Holy Spirit."
3 And he said to them, "Into what then were
you baptized?" So they said, "Into John's baptism."
4 Then Paul said, "John indeed baptized
with a baptism of repentance, saying to the
people that they should believe on Him
who would come after him, that is, on Christ
Jesus."
5 When they heard *this,* they were baptized
in the name of the Lord Jesus.
6 And when Paul had laid hands on them,
the Holy Spirit came upon them, and they
spoke with tongues and prophesied.
7 Now the men were about twelve in all.
8 And he went into the synagogue and
spoke boldly for three months, reasoning and
persuading concerning the things of the kingdom of God.
9 But when some were hardened and did
not believe, but spoke evil of the Way before
the multitude, he departed from them and
withdrew the disciples, reasoning daily in the
school of Tyrannus.
10 And this continued for two years, so that
all who dwelt in Asia heard the word of the
Lord Jesus, both Jews and Greeks.

Miracles Glorify Christ

11 Now God worked unusual miracles by the ➤
hands of Paul,
12 so that even handkerchiefs or aprons were
brought from his body to the sick, and the diseases left them and the evil spirits went out of
them.
13 Then some of the itinerant Jewish exorcists took it upon themselves to call the name
of the Lord Jesus over those who had evil
spirits, saying, "We[a] exorcise you by the Jesus
whom Paul preaches."
14 Also there were seven sons of Sceva, a
Jewish chief priest, who did so.
15 And the evil spirit answered and said, "Jesus I know, and Paul I know; but who are you?"
16 Then the man in whom the evil spirit was
leaped on them, overpowered[a] them, and prevailed against them,[b] so that they fled out of
that house naked and wounded.
17 This became known both to all Jews and
Greeks dwelling in Ephesus; and fear fell on
them all, and the name of the Lord Jesus was
magnified.
18 And many who had believed came confessing and telling their deeds.

18:21 [a]NU-Text omits *I must* through *Jerusalem.* **19:13** [a]NU-Text reads *I.* **19:16** [a]M-Text reads *and they overpowered.* [b]NU-Text reads *both of them.*

LIFE LESSONS

➤ 18:27, 28 — *he greatly helped those who had believed through grace . . . showing from the Scriptures that Jesus is the Christ.*

Through grace people believe in Christ, and through grace they come to understand His will by grasping the instruction of the Bible. And through grace God gives us gifted teachers to help us understand.

➤ 19:11 — *Now God worked unusual miracles by the hands of Paul . . . .*

The same Spirit who worked miracles through Old Testament prophets such as Elijah and Elisha, and who performed great signs through Jesus and Peter, now worked similar miracles through Paul. Where faith meets God, extraordinary things happen.

19 Also, many of those who had practiced magic brought their books together and burned *them* in the sight of all. And they counted up the value of them, and *it* totaled fifty thousand *pieces* of silver.

➤ 20 So the word of the Lord grew mightily and prevailed.

The Riot at Ephesus

21 When these things were accomplished, Paul purposed in the Spirit, when he had passed through Macedonia and Achaia, to go to Jerusalem, saying, "After I have been there, I must also see Rome."

22 So he sent into Macedonia two of those who ministered to him, Timothy and Erastus, but he himself stayed in Asia for a time.

23 And about that time there arose a great commotion about the Way.

24 For a certain man named Demetrius, a silversmith, who made silver shrines of Diana,[a] brought no small profit to the craftsmen.

25 He called them together with the workers of similar occupation, and said: "Men, you know that we have our prosperity by this trade.

26 "Moreover you see and hear that not only at Ephesus, but throughout almost all Asia, this Paul has persuaded and turned away many people, saying that they are not gods which are made with hands.

27 "So not only is this trade of ours in danger of falling into disrepute, but also the temple of the great goddess Diana may be despised and her magnificence destroyed,[a] whom all Asia and the world worship."

28 Now when they heard *this*, they were full of wrath and cried out, saying, "Great *is* Diana of the Ephesians!"

29 So the whole city was filled with confusion, and rushed into the theater with one accord, having seized Gaius and Aristarchus, Macedonians, Paul's travel companions.

30 And when Paul wanted to go in to the people, the disciples would not allow him.

31 Then some of the officials of Asia, who were his friends, sent to him pleading that he would not venture into the theater.

➤ 32 Some therefore cried one thing and some another, for the assembly was confused, and most of them did not know why they had come together.

33 And they drew Alexander out of the multitude, the Jews putting him forward. And Alexander motioned with his hand, and wanted to make his defense to the people.

34 But when they found out that he was a Jew, all with one voice cried out for about two hours, "Great *is* Diana of the Ephesians!"

35 And when the city clerk had quieted the crowd, he said: "Men of Ephesus, what man is there who does not know that the city of the Ephesians is temple guardian of the great goddess Diana, and of the *image* which fell down from Zeus?

36 "Therefore, since these things cannot be denied, you ought to be quiet and do nothing rashly.

37 "For you have brought these men here who are neither robbers of temples nor blasphemers of your[a] goddess.

38 "Therefore, if Demetrius and his fellow craftsmen have a case against anyone, the courts are open and there are proconsuls. Let them bring charges against one another.

39 "But if you have any other inquiry to make, it shall be determined in the lawful assembly.

40 "For we are in danger of being called in question for today's uproar, there being no reason which we may give to account for this disorderly gathering."

41 And when he had said these things, he dismissed the assembly.

Journeys in Greece

20 After the uproar had ceased, Paul called the disciples to *himself*, embraced *them*, and departed to go to Macedonia.

2 Now when he had gone over that region and encouraged them with many words, he came to Greece

3 and stayed three months. And when the Jews plotted against him as he was about to sail to Syria, he decided to return through Macedonia.

4 And Sopater of Berea accompanied him to Asia—also Aristarchus and Secundus of the Thessalonians, and Gaius of Derbe, and Timothy, and Tychicus and Trophimus of Asia.

5 These men, going ahead, waited for us at Troas.

6 But we sailed away from Philippi after the

19:24 [a]Greek *Artemis* **19:27** [a]NU-Text reads *she be deposed from her magnificence.* **19:37** [a]NU-Text reads *our.*

LIFE LESSONS

➤ 19:20 — *So the word of the Lord grew mightily and prevailed.*

God loves to honor His Word so that it grows mightily and prevails. If we want to be connected with such a mighty move of God, we must faithfully proclaim His Word through the power of His Spirit.

➤ 19:32 — *Some therefore cried one thing and some another, for the assembly was confused, and most of them did not know why they had come together.*

Angry mobs are generally not good places to reason out disputes. When Paul wanted to speak to the volatile crowd—to reason and persuade, as was his custom—the disciples did not let him (Acts 19:30).

Days of Unleavened Bread, and in five days joined them at Troas, where we stayed seven days.

Ministering at Troas

7 Now on the first *day* of the week, when the disciples came together to break bread, Paul, ready to depart the next day, spoke to them and continued his message until midnight.
8 There were many lamps in the upper room where they[a] were gathered together.
9 And in a window sat a certain young man named Eutychus, who was sinking into a deep sleep. He was overcome by sleep; and as Paul continued speaking, he fell down from the third story and was taken up dead.
10 But Paul went down, fell on him, and embracing *him* said, "Do not trouble yourselves, for his life is in him."
11 Now when he had come up, had broken bread and eaten, and talked a long while, even till daybreak, he departed.
12 And they brought the young man in alive, and they were not a little comforted.

From Troas to Miletus

13 Then we went ahead to the ship and sailed to Assos, there intending to take Paul on board; for so he had given orders, intending himself to go on foot.
14 And when he met us at Assos, we took him on board and came to Mitylene.
15 We sailed from there, and the next *day* came opposite Chios. The following *day* we arrived at Samos and stayed at Trogyllium. The next *day* we came to Miletus.
16 For Paul had decided to sail past Ephesus, so that he would not have to spend time in Asia; for he was hurrying to be at Jerusalem, if possible, on the Day of Pentecost.

The Ephesian Elders Exhorted

17 From Miletus he sent to Ephesus and called for the elders of the church.
18 And when they had come to him, he said to them: "You know, from the first day that I came to Asia, in what manner I always lived among you,
19 "serving the Lord with all humility, with many tears and trials which happened to me by the plotting of the Jews;
20 "how I kept back nothing that was helpful, but proclaimed it to you, and taught you publicly and from house to house,
21 "testifying to Jews, and also to Greeks, repentance toward God and faith toward our Lord Jesus Christ.
22 "And see, now I go bound in the spirit to Jerusalem, not knowing the things that will happen to me there,
23 "except that the Holy Spirit testifies in every city, saying that chains and tribulations await me.
24 "But none of these things move me; nor do I count my life dear to myself,[a] so that I may finish my race with joy, and the ministry which I received from the Lord Jesus, to testify to the gospel of the grace of God.
25 "And indeed, now I know that you all, among whom I have gone preaching the kingdom of God, will see my face no more.
26 "Therefore I testify to you this day that I *am* innocent of the blood of all *men*.
27 "For I have not shunned to declare to you the whole counsel of God.
28 "Therefore take heed to yourselves and to all the flock, among which the Holy Spirit has made you overseers, to shepherd the church of God[a] which He purchased with His own blood.
29 "For I know this, that after my departure savage wolves will come in among you, not sparing the flock.
30 "Also from among yourselves men will rise up, speaking perverse things, to draw away the disciples after themselves.
31 "Therefore watch, and remember that for three years I did not cease to warn everyone night and day with tears.
32 "So now, brethren, I commend you to God and to the word of His grace, which is able to build you up and give you an inheritance among all those who are sanctified.
33 "I have coveted no one's silver or gold or apparel.
34 "Yes,[a] you yourselves know that these hands have provided for my necessities, and for those who were with me.

20:8 [a]NU-Text and M-Text read *we.* **20:24** [a]NU-Text reads *But I do not count my life of any value or dear to myself.* **20:28** [a]M-Text reads *of the Lord and God.* **20:34** [a]NU-Text and M-Text omit *Yes.*

LIFE LESSONS

➤ 20:24 — *". . . nor do I count my life dear to myself, so that I may finish my race with joy, and the ministry which I received from the Lord Jesus . . . ."*

Paul found his life by losing it, and loved his life by not counting it dear. He had learned from his Savior to love God's will over everything else, and he realized that obeying Him yielded the greatest joys.

➤ 20:27 — *"For I have not shunned to declare to you the whole counsel of God."*

Why would we ever hesitate to declare "the whole counsel of God"? Because some of it is not very popular. Some of it requires a change in behavior. Some of it is inconvenient—but to avoid it leads to destruction.

➤ 35 "I have shown you in every way, by laboring like this, that you must support the weak. And remember the words of the Lord Jesus, that He said, 'It is more blessed to give than to receive.'"
36 And when he had said these things, he knelt down and prayed with them all.
37 Then they all wept freely, and fell on Paul's neck and kissed him,
38 sorrowing most of all for the words which he spoke, that they would see his face no more. And they accompanied him to the ship.

Warnings on the Journey to Jerusalem

21 Now it came to pass, that when we had departed from them and set sail, running a straight course we came to Cos, the following *day* to Rhodes, and from there to Patara.
2 And finding a ship sailing over to Phoenicia, we went aboard and set sail.
3 When we had sighted Cyprus, we passed it on the left, sailed to Syria, and landed at Tyre; for there the ship was to unload her cargo.
4 And finding disciples,[a] we stayed there seven days. They told Paul through the Spirit not to go up to Jerusalem.
5 When we had come to the end of those days, we departed and went on our way; and they all accompanied us, with wives and children, till *we were* out of the city. And we knelt down on the shore and prayed.
6 When we had taken our leave of one another, we boarded the ship, and they returned home.
7 And when we had finished *our* voyage from Tyre, we came to Ptolemais, greeted the brethren, and stayed with them one day.
8 On the next *day* we who were Paul's companions[a] departed and came to Caesarea, and entered the house of Philip the evangelist, who was *one* of the seven, and stayed with him.
9 Now this man had four virgin daughters who prophesied.
10 And as we stayed many days, a certain prophet named Agabus came down from Judea.
11 When he had come to us, he took Paul's belt, bound his *own* hands and feet, and said, "Thus says the Holy Spirit, 'So shall the Jews at Jerusalem bind the man who owns this belt, and deliver *him* into the hands of the Gentiles.'"
12 Now when we heard these things, both we and those from that place pleaded with him not to go up to Jerusalem.
13 Then Paul answered, "What do you mean by weeping and breaking my heart? For I am ready not only to be bound, but also to die at Jerusalem for the name of the Lord Jesus." ◄
14 So when he would not be persuaded, we ceased, saying, "The will of the Lord be done." ◄

Paul Urged to Make Peace

15 And after those days we packed and went up to Jerusalem.
16 Also some of the disciples from Caesarea went with us and brought with them a certain Mnason of Cyprus, an early disciple, with whom we were to lodge.
17 And when we had come to Jerusalem, the brethren received us gladly.
18 On the following *day* Paul went in with us to James, and all the elders were present.
19 When he had greeted them, he told in detail those things which God had done among the Gentiles through his ministry.
20 And when they heard *it*, they glorified the Lord. And they said to him, "You see, brother, how many myriads of Jews there are who have believed, and they are all zealous for the law;
21 "but they have been informed about you that you teach all the Jews who are among the Gentiles to forsake Moses, saying that they ought not to circumcise *their* children nor to walk according to the customs.
22 "What then? The assembly must certainly meet, for they will[a] hear that you have come.
23 "Therefore do what we tell you: We have four men who have taken a vow.

21:4 [a]NU-Text reads *the disciples.* **21:8** [a]NU-Text omits *who were Paul's companions.* **21:22** [a]NU-Text reads *What then is to be done? They will certainly.*

LIFE LESSONS

➤ 20:35 — *"And remember the words of the Lord Jesus, that He said, 'It is more blessed to give than to receive.'"*

None of the four canonical Gospels record this saying of Jesus; apparently it circulated among the disciples and eventually made its way to Paul. But it carries just as much authority as the Lord's other sayings.

➤ 21:13 — *Then Paul answered, "What do you mean by weeping and breaking my heart? For I am ready not only to be bound, but also to die at Jerusalem for the name of the Lord Jesus."*

The potential loss of his life did not dissuade Paul from doing what he believed God had called him to do. He fit the mold of those described in Revelation 12:11 who "did not love their lives to the death."

➤ 21:14 — *So when he would not be persuaded, we ceased, saying, "The will of the Lord be done."*

Paul could not be talked out of his dangerous plan because he was convinced it was God's plan. Paul's friends had to end up where Jesus did in the garden: "Not My will, but Yours, be done" (Luke 22:42).

24 "Take them and be purified with them, and
pay their expenses so that they may shave
their heads, and that all may know that those
things of which they were informed concerning you are nothing, but *that* you yourself
also walk orderly and keep the law.
25 "But concerning the Gentiles who believe,
we have written *and* decided that they should
observe no such thing, except[a] that they
should keep themselves from *things* offered
to idols, from blood, from things strangled,
and from sexual immorality."

Arrested in the Temple

26 Then Paul took the men, and the next day,
having been purified with them, entered the
temple to announce the expiration of the days
of purification, at which time an offering
should be made for each one of them.
27 Now when the seven days were almost
ended, the Jews from Asia, seeing him in the
temple, stirred up the whole crowd and laid
hands on him,
28 crying out, "Men of Israel, help! This is the
man who teaches all *men* everywhere against
the people, the law, and this place; and furthermore he also brought Greeks into the
temple and has defiled this holy place."
29 (For they had previously[a] seen Trophimus
the Ephesian with him in the city, whom
they supposed that Paul had brought into the
temple.)
30 And all the city was disturbed; and the
people ran together, seized Paul, and dragged
him out of the temple; and immediately the
doors were shut.
31 Now as they were seeking to kill him,
news came to the commander of the garrison
that all Jerusalem was in an uproar.
➤ 32 He immediately took soldiers and centurions, and ran down to them. And when they
saw the commander and the soldiers, they
stopped beating Paul.
33 Then the commander came near and took
him, and commanded *him* to be bound with
two chains; and he asked who he was and
what he had done.
34 And some among the multitude cried one
thing and some another. So when he could not
ascertain the truth because of the tumult, he
commanded him to be taken into the barracks.
35 When he reached the stairs, he had to be
carried by the soldiers because of the violence of the mob.
36 For the multitude of the people followed
after, crying out, "Away with him!"

Addressing the Jerusalem Mob

37 Then as Paul was about to be led into the
barracks, he said to the commander, "May I
speak to you?" He replied, "Can you speak
Greek?
38 "Are you not the Egyptian who some time
ago stirred up a rebellion and led the four
thousand assassins out into the wilderness?"
39 But Paul said, "I am a Jew from Tarsus, in
Cilicia, a citizen of no mean city; and I implore you, permit me to speak to the people."
40 So when he had given him permission,
Paul stood on the stairs and motioned with
his hand to the people. And when there was a
great silence, he spoke to *them* in the Hebrew
language, saying,

22
"Brethren and fathers, hear my defense
before you now."
2 And when they heard that he spoke to
them in the Hebrew language, they kept all
the more silent. Then he said:
3 "I am indeed a Jew, born in Tarsus of Cilicia, but brought up in this city at the feet of
Gamaliel, taught according to the strictness
of our fathers' law, and was zealous toward
God as you all are today.
4 "I persecuted this Way to the death, binding and delivering into prisons both men and
women,
5 "as also the high priest bears me witness,
and all the council of the elders, from whom I
also received letters to the brethren, and went
to Damascus to bring in chains even those
who were there to Jerusalem to be punished.
6 "Now it happened, as I journeyed and
came near Damascus at about noon, suddenly
a great light from heaven shone around me.
7 "And I fell to the ground and heard a voice
saying to me, 'Saul, Saul, why are you persecuting Me?'
8 "So I answered, 'Who are You, Lord?' And
He said to me, 'I am Jesus of Nazareth, whom
you are persecuting.'
9 "And those who were with me indeed saw ➤
the light and were afraid,[a] but they did not
hear the voice of Him who spoke to me.

21:25 [a]NU-Text omits *that they should observe no such thing, except.* **21:29** [a]M-Text omits *previously.* **22:9** [a]NU-Text omits *and were afraid.*

LIFE LESSONS

➤ 21:32 — *And when they saw the commander and the soldiers, they stopped beating Paul.*

Even before Paul's conversion, Jesus told Ananias, "I will show him how many things he must suffer for My name's sake" (Acts 9:16). Paul did not like beatings, but he expected them and rejoiced in his identification with Christ.

➤ 22:9 — *"And those who were with me indeed saw the light and were afraid, but they did not hear the voice of Him who spoke to me."*

Acts 9:7 reports that the men "stood speechless, hearing a voice . . . ." So is this a contradiction? No. The Greek term translated "hear" can mean both "to perceive sound" and "to understand." The men heard, but did not understand.

10 "So I said, 'What shall I do, Lord?' And the
Lord said to me, 'Arise and go into Damascus,
and there you will be told all things which are
appointed for you to do.'
11 "And since I could not see for the glory of
that light, being led by the hand of those who
were with me, I came into Damascus.
12 "Then a certain Ananias, a devout man according to the law, having a good testimony
with all the Jews who dwelt *there*,
13 "came to me; and he stood and said to me,
'Brother Saul, receive your sight.' And at that
same hour I looked up at him.
➤ 14 "Then he said, 'The God of our fathers has
chosen you that you should know His will,
and see the Just One, and hear the voice of
His mouth.
15 'For you will be His witness to all men of
what you have seen and heard.
16 'And now why are you waiting? Arise and
be baptized, and wash away your sins, calling
on the name of the Lord.'
17 "Now it happened, when I returned to Jerusalem and was praying in the temple, that I
was in a trance
18 "and saw Him saying to me, 'Make haste
and get out of Jerusalem quickly, for they will
not receive your testimony concerning Me.'
19 "So I said, 'Lord, they know that in every
synagogue I imprisoned and beat those who
believe on You.
20 'And when the blood of Your martyr
Stephen was shed, I also was standing by consenting to his death,[a] and guarding the
clothes of those who were killing him.'
21 "Then He said to me, 'Depart, for I will
send you far from here to the Gentiles.'"

Paul's Roman Citizenship

22 And they listened to him until this word,
and *then* they raised their voices and said,
"Away with such a *fellow* from the earth, for
he is not fit to live!"
23 Then, as they cried out and tore off *their*
clothes and threw dust into the air,
24 the commander ordered him to be brought
into the barracks, and said that he should be
examined under scourging, so that he might
know why they shouted so against him.
25 And as they bound him with thongs, Paul
said to the centurion who stood by, "Is it lawful for you to scourge a man who is a Roman,
and uncondemned?"
26 When the centurion heard *that*, he went
and told the commander, saying, "Take care
what you do, for this man is a Roman."
27 Then the commander came and said to
him, "Tell me, are you a Roman?" He said,
"Yes."
28 The commander answered, "With a large
sum I obtained this citizenship." And Paul
said, "But I was born *a citizen*."
29 Then immediately those who were about ➤
to examine him withdrew from him; and the
commander was also afraid after he found
out that he was a Roman, and because he had
bound him.

The Sanhedrin Divided

30 The next day, because he wanted to know
for certain why he was accused by the Jews,
he released him from *his* bonds, and commanded the chief priests and all their council
to appear, and brought Paul down and set him
before them.

23 Then Paul, looking earnestly at the
council, said, "Men *and* brethren, I have
lived in all good conscience before God until
this day."
2 And the high priest Ananias commanded
those who stood by him to strike him on the
mouth.
3 Then Paul said to him, "God will strike
you, *you* whitewashed wall! For you sit to
judge me according to the law, and do you
command me to be struck contrary to the
law?"
4 And those who stood by said, "Do you revile God's high priest?"
5 Then Paul said, "I did not know, brethren,
that he was the high priest; for it is written,
*'You shall not speak evil of a ruler of your
people.'*"[a]
6 But when Paul perceived that one part ➤
were Sadducees and the other Pharisees, he

22:20 [a]NU-Text omits *to his death*. **23:5** [a]Exodus 22:28

LIFE LESSONS

➤ 22:14 — *"The God of our fathers has chosen you that you should know His will, and see the Just One, and hear the voice of His mouth."*

Paul never forgot the words of Ananias, that God had chosen him to both see and hear Jesus and to know His will. He never allowed affliction to shake him, for he wrote, "we are appointed to this" (1 Thess. 3:3).

➤ 22:29 — *Then immediately those who were about to examine him withdrew from him; and the commander was also afraid after he found out that he was a Roman, and because he had bound him.*

It was a serious offense to injure or harm a Roman citizen who had not been convicted of an offense in a Roman court of law. Paul did not hesitate to use the law when it helped his cause.

➤ 23:6 — *But when Paul perceived that one part were Sadducees and the other Pharisees, he cried out in the council, "Men and brethren, I am a Pharisee, the son of a Pharisee; concerning the hope and resurrection of the dead I am being judged!"*

Paul heeded the Lord's counsel to be "wise as serpents" (Matt. 10:16). When he saw that he could exploit the theological differences between the Pharisees and the Sadducees, he did so.

cried out in the council, "Men *and* brethren, I
am a Pharisee, the son of a Pharisee; concerning the hope and resurrection of the dead I
am being judged!"
7 And when he had said this, a dissension
arose between the Pharisees and the Sadducees; and the assembly was divided.
8 For Sadducees say that there is no resurrection—and no angel or spirit; but the Pharisees confess both.
9 Then there arose a loud outcry. And the
scribes of the Pharisees' party arose and
protested, saying, "We find no evil in this
man; but if a spirit or an angel has spoken to
him, let us not fight against God."[a]
10 Now when there arose a great dissension,
the commander, fearing lest Paul might be
pulled to pieces by them, commanded the soldiers to go down and take him by force from
among them, and bring *him* into the barracks.

The Plot Against Paul

➤ **11** But the following night the Lord stood by
him and said, "Be of good cheer, Paul; for as
you have testified for Me in Jerusalem, so you
must also bear witness at Rome."
12 And when it was day, some of the Jews
banded together and bound themselves under
an oath, saying that they would neither eat
nor drink till they had killed Paul.
13 Now there were more than forty who had
formed this conspiracy.
14 They came to the chief priests and elders,
and said, "We have bound ourselves under a
great oath that we will eat nothing until we
have killed Paul.
15 "Now you, therefore, together with the
council, suggest to the commander that he be
brought down to you tomorrow,[a] as though
you were going to make further inquiries concerning him; but we are ready to kill him before he comes near."
➤ 16 So when Paul's sister's son heard of their
ambush, he went and entered the barracks
and told Paul.
17 Then Paul called one of the centurions to
him and said, "Take this young man to the
commander, for he has something to tell
him."
18 So he took him and brought *him* to the
commander and said, "Paul the prisoner
called me to *him* and asked *me* to bring this
young man to you. He has something to say to
you."
19 Then the commander took him by the
hand, went aside, and asked privately, "What
is it that you have to tell me?"
20 And he said, "The Jews have agreed to ask
that you bring Paul down to the council tomorrow, as though they were going to inquire
more fully about him.
21 "But do not yield to them, for more than
forty of them lie in wait for him, men who
have bound themselves by an oath that they
will neither eat nor drink till they have killed
him; and now they are ready, waiting for the
promise from you."
22 So the commander let the young man depart, and commanded *him*, "Tell no one that
you have revealed these things to me."

Sent to Felix

23 And he called for two centurions, saying,
"Prepare two hundred soldiers, seventy
horsemen, and two hundred spearmen to go
to Caesarea at the third hour of the night;
24 "and provide mounts to set Paul on, and
bring *him* safely to Felix the governor."
25 He wrote a letter in the following manner:

26 Claudius Lysias,

To the most excellent governor Felix:

Greetings.

27 This man was seized by the Jews and was
about to be killed by them. Coming with
the troops I rescued him, having learned
that he was a Roman.
28 And when I wanted to know the reason
they accused him, I brought him before
their council.
29 I found out that he was accused concerning questions of their law, but had nothing
charged against him deserving of death or
chains.
30 And when it was told me that the Jews lay
in wait for the man,[a] I sent him immediately to you, and also commanded his ac-

23:9 [a]NU-Text omits last clause and reads *what if a spirit or an angel has spoken to him?* **23:15** [a]NU-Text omits *tomorrow.* **23:30** [a]NU-Text reads *there would be a plot against the man.*

LIFE LESSONS

➤ 23:11 — But the following night the Lord stood by him and said, "Be of good cheer, Paul; for as you have testified for Me in Jerusalem, so you must also bear witness at Rome."

Just before Paul's conversion, the Lord had told Ananias that Paul would bear His name "before Gentiles, kings, and the children of Israel" (Acts 9:15). This is the fulfillment of that promise.

➤ 23:16 — So when Paul's sister's son heard of their ambush, he went and entered the barracks and told Paul.

We must never imagine that God *must* work in a certain way. Here he rescued Paul, not through a miracle, but through the sharp ears of his nephew. God works in ways we cannot anticipate.

cusers to state before you the charges
against him.

Farewell.
31 Then the soldiers, as they were commanded, took Paul and brought *him* by night to Antipatris.
32 The next day they left the horsemen to go on with him, and returned to the barracks.
33 When they came to Caesarea and had delivered the letter to the governor, they also presented Paul to him.
34 And when the governor had read *it,* he asked what province he was from. And when he understood that *he was* from Cilicia,
35 he said, "I will hear you when your accusers also have come." And he commanded him to be kept in Herod's Praetorium.

Accused of Sedition

24 Now after five days Ananias the high priest came down with the elders and a certain orator *named* Tertullus. These gave evidence to the governor against Paul.
2 And when he was called upon, Tertullus began his accusation, saying: "Seeing that through you we enjoy great peace, and prosperity is being brought to this nation by your foresight,
3 "we accept *it* always and in all places, most noble Felix, with all thankfulness.
4 "Nevertheless, not to be tedious to you any further, I beg you to hear, by your courtesy, a few words from us.
5 "For we have found this man a plague, a creator of dissension among all the Jews throughout the world, and a ringleader of the sect of the Nazarenes.
6 "He even tried to profane the temple, and we seized him,[a] and wanted to judge him according to our law.
7 "But the commander Lysias came by and with great violence took *him* out of our hands,
8 "commanding his accusers to come to you. By examining him yourself you may ascertain all these things of which we accuse him."
9 And the Jews also assented,[a] maintaining that these things were so.

The Defense Before Felix

10 Then Paul, after the governor had nodded to him to speak, answered: "Inasmuch as I know that you have been for many years a judge of this nation, I do the more cheerfully answer for myself,
11 "because you may ascertain that it is no more than twelve days since I went up to Jerusalem to worship.
12 "And they neither found me in the temple disputing with anyone nor inciting the crowd, either in the synagogues or in the city.
13 "Nor can they prove the things of which they now accuse me.
14 "But this I confess to you, that according to the Way which they call a sect, so I worship the God of my fathers, believing all things which are written in the Law and in the Prophets.
15 "I have hope in God, which they themselves also accept, that there will be a resurrection of *the* dead,[a] both of *the* just and *the* unjust.
16 "This *being* so, I myself always strive to have a conscience without offense toward God and men.
17 "Now after many years I came to bring alms and offerings to my nation,
18 "in the midst of which some Jews from Asia found me purified in the temple, neither with a mob nor with tumult.
19 "They ought to have been here before you to object if they had anything against me.
20 "Or else let those who are *here* themselves say if they found any wrongdoing[a] in me while I stood before the council,
21 "unless *it is* for this one statement which I cried out, standing among them, 'Concerning the resurrection of the dead I am being judged by you this day.'"

Felix Procrastinates

22 But when Felix heard these things, having more accurate knowledge of *the* Way, he adjourned the proceedings and said, "When Lysias the commander comes down, I will make a decision on your case."
23 So he commanded the centurion to keep Paul and to let *him* have liberty, and told him not to forbid any of his friends to provide for or visit him.

24:6 [a]NU-Text ends the sentence here and omits the rest of verse 6, all of verse 7, and the first clause of verse 8.
24:9 [a]NU-Text and M-Text read *joined the attack.*
24:15 [a]NU-Text omits *of the dead.* **24:20** [a]NU-Text and M-Text read *say what wrongdoing they found.*

LIFE LESSONS

➤ 24:14 — *"I worship the God of my fathers, believing all things which are written in the Law and in the Prophets."*

Paul did not see the Christian faith as an alternative to his Jewish upbringing, but as the fulfillment of it. He worshiped the same God he always had, and had complete faith in the same Scriptures.

➤ 24:16 — *"I myself always strive to have a conscience without offense toward God and men."*

Paul never tried to earn right standing before God, but he did strive to live out the righteousness that God had credited to him through his faith in Jesus. Paul wanted his conduct to reflect well on his Savior.

24 And after some days, when Felix came
with his wife Drusilla, who was Jewish, he
sent for Paul and heard him concerning the
faith in Christ.
➤ 25 Now as he reasoned about righteousness,
self-control, and the judgment to come, Felix
was afraid and answered, "Go away for now;
when I have a convenient time I will call for
you."
26 Meanwhile he also hoped that money
would be given him by Paul, that he might release him.[a] Therefore he sent for him more
often and conversed with him.
27 But after two years Porcius Festus succeeded Felix; and Felix, wanting to do the
Jews a favor, left Paul bound.

Paul Appeals to Caesar

25 Now when Festus had come to the
province, after three days he went up
from Caesarea to Jerusalem.
2 Then the high priest[a] and the chief men of
the Jews informed him against Paul; and they
petitioned him,
3 asking a favor against him, that he would
summon him to Jerusalem—while *they* lay in
ambush along the road to kill him.
4 But Festus answered that Paul should be
kept at Caesarea, and that he himself was
going *there* shortly.
5 "Therefore," he said, "let those who have
authority among you go down with *me* and
accuse this man, to see if there is any fault in
him."
6 And when he had remained among them
more than ten days, he went down to Caesarea. And the next day, sitting on the judgment seat, he commanded Paul to be brought.
7 When he had come, the Jews who had
come down from Jerusalem stood about and
laid many serious complaints against Paul,
which they could not prove,
8 while he answered for himself, "Neither
against the law of the Jews, nor against the
temple, nor against Caesar have I offended in
anything at all."
9 But Festus, wanting to do the Jews a favor,
answered Paul and said, "Are you willing to
go up to Jerusalem and there be judged before me concerning these things?"
10 So Paul said, "I stand at Caesar's judgment seat, where I ought to be judged. To the
Jews I have done no wrong, as you very well
know.
11 "For if I am an offender, or have committed anything deserving of death, I do not object to dying; but if there is nothing in these
things of which these men accuse me, no one
can deliver me to them. I appeal to Caesar."
12 Then Festus, when he had conferred with
the council, answered, "You have appealed to
Caesar? To Caesar you shall go!"

Paul Before Agrippa

13 And after some days King Agrippa and
Bernice came to Caesarea to greet Festus.
14 When they had been there many days,
Festus laid Paul's case before the king, saying: "There is a certain man left a prisoner by
Felix,
15 "about whom the chief priests and the elders of the Jews informed *me*, when I was in
Jerusalem, asking for a judgment against
him.
16 "To them I answered, 'It is not the custom
of the Romans to deliver any man to destruction[a] before the accused meets the accusers
face to face, and has opportunity to answer
for himself concerning the charge against
him.'
17 "Therefore when they had come together,
without any delay, the next day I sat on the
judgment seat and commanded the man to be
brought in.
18 "When the accusers stood up, they
brought no accusation against him of such
things as I supposed,
19 "but had some questions against him ➤
about their own religion and about a certain
Jesus, who had died, whom Paul affirmed to
be alive.
20 "And because I was uncertain of such
questions, I asked whether he was willing to
go to Jerusalem and there be judged concerning these matters.
21 "But when Paul appealed to be reserved
for the decision of Augustus, I commanded
him to be kept till I could send him to Caesar."
22 Then Agrippa said to Festus, "I also would

24:26 [a]NU-Text omits *that he might release him.* **25:2** [a]NU-Text reads *chief priests.* **25:16** [a]NU-Text omits *to destruction,* although it is implied.

LIFE LESSONS

➤ 24:25 — *Now as he reasoned about righteousness, self-control, and the judgment to come, Felix was afraid . . . .*

It is one thing to discuss theology when it remains abstract, theoretical, and academic; it is quite another when it becomes concrete, close to home, and deeply personal.

➤ 25:19 — *". . . they . . . had some questions against him about their own religion and about a certain Jesus, who had died, whom Paul affirmed to be alive."*

To the Roman governor Festus, the gospel story was nothing but the religious fantasy of a superstitious and contentious people. We should not feel surprised or offended when secularized people treat it as myth.

like to hear the man myself." "Tomorrow," he
said, "you shall hear him."
23 So the next day, when Agrippa and Bernice had come with great pomp, and had entered the auditorium with the commanders and the prominent men of the city, at Festus' command Paul was brought in.
24 And Festus said: "King Agrippa and all the men who are here present with us, you see this man about whom the whole assembly of the Jews petitioned me, both at Jerusalem and here, crying out that he was not fit to live any longer.
25 "But when I found that he had committed nothing deserving of death, and that he himself had appealed to Augustus, I decided to send him.
26 "I have nothing certain to write to my lord concerning him. Therefore I have brought him out before you, and especially before you, King Agrippa, so that after the examination has taken place I may have something to write.
➤ 27 "For it seems to me unreasonable to send a prisoner and not to specify the charges against him."

Paul's Early Life

26 Then Agrippa said to Paul, "You are permitted to speak for yourself." So Paul stretched out his hand and answered for himself:
2 "I think myself happy, King Agrippa, because today I shall answer for myself before you concerning all the things of which I am accused by the Jews,
3 "especially because you are expert in all customs and questions which have to do with the Jews. Therefore I beg you to hear me patiently.
4 "My manner of life from my youth, which was spent from the beginning among my own nation at Jerusalem, all the Jews know.
5 "They knew me from the first, if they were willing to testify, that according to the strictest sect of our religion I lived a Pharisee.
6 "And now I stand and am judged for the hope of the promise made by God to our fathers.
7 "To this *promise* our twelve tribes, earnestly serving *God* night and day, hope to attain. For this hope's sake, King Agrippa, I am accused by the Jews.
8 "Why should it be thought incredible by you that God raises the dead?
9 "Indeed, I myself thought I must do many ➤
things contrary to the name of Jesus of Nazareth.
10 "This I also did in Jerusalem, and many of the saints I shut up in prison, having received authority from the chief priests; and when they were put to death, I cast my vote against *them*.
11 "And I punished them often in every synagogue and compelled *them* to blaspheme; and being exceedingly enraged against them, I persecuted *them* even to foreign cities.

Paul Recounts His Conversion

12 "While thus occupied, as I journeyed to Damascus with authority and commission from the chief priests,
13 "at midday, O king, along the road I saw a light from heaven, brighter than the sun, shining around me and those who journeyed with me.
14 "And when we all had fallen to the ground, I heard a voice speaking to me and saying in the Hebrew language, 'Saul, Saul, why are you persecuting Me? *It is* hard for you to kick against the goads.'
15 "So I said, 'Who are You, Lord?' And He said, 'I am Jesus, whom you are persecuting.
16 'But rise and stand on your feet; for I have appeared to you for this purpose, to make you a minister and a witness both of the things which you have seen and of the things which I will yet reveal to you.
17 'I will deliver you from the *Jewish* people, as well as *from* the Gentiles, to whom I now[a] send you, *
18 'to open their eyes, *in order* to turn *them* from darkness to light, and *from* the power of Satan to God, that they may receive forgiveness of sins and an inheritance among those who are sanctified by faith in Me.'

Paul's Post-Conversion Life

19 "Therefore, King Agrippa, I was not disobedient to the heavenly vision,

26:17 [a]NU-Text and M-Text omit *now*.

LIFE LESSONS

➤ **25:27 — *"For it seems to me unreasonable to send a prisoner and not to specify the charges against him."***

Festus had no interest in violations, real or imagined, concerning the Jewish law. He hoped that Agrippa, who knew the Jews well, could help him formulate some kind of legal charge against Paul that would make sense to the Romans.

➤ **26:9 — *"Indeed, I myself thought I must do many things contrary to the name of Jesus of Nazareth."***

Paul could understand the animosity of the Jewish leaders against him, because only a few short years before he had shared their fierce hatred of Christianity. He knew one could feel in the right while being deeply in the wrong.

➤ 20 "but declared first to those in Damascus
and in Jerusalem, and throughout all the region of Judea, and *then* to the Gentiles, that
they should repent, turn to God, and do works
befitting repentance.
21 "For these reasons the Jews seized me in
the temple and tried to kill *me*.
22 "Therefore, having obtained help from
God, to this day I stand, witnessing both to
small and great, saying no other things than
those which the prophets and Moses said
would come—
23 "that the Christ would suffer, that He
would be the first to rise from the dead, and
would proclaim light to the *Jewish* people and
to the Gentiles."

Agrippa Parries Paul's Challenge

24 Now as he thus made his defense, Festus
said with a loud voice, "Paul, you are beside
yourself! Much learning is driving you mad!"
25 But he said, "I am not mad, most noble
Festus, but speak the words of truth and
reason.
26 "For the king, before whom I also speak
freely, knows these things; for I am convinced
that none of these things escapes his attention, since this thing was not done in a corner.
27 "King Agrippa, do you believe the prophets? I know that you do believe."
28 Then Agrippa said to Paul, "You almost
persuade me to become a Christian."
29 And Paul said, "I would to God that not
only you, but also all who hear me today,
might become both almost and altogether
such as I am, except for these chains."
30 When he had said these things, the king
stood up, as well as the governor and Bernice
and those who sat with them;
31 and when they had gone aside, they talked
among themselves, saying, "This man is
doing nothing deserving of death or chains."
32 Then Agrippa said to Festus, "This man
might have been set free if he had not appealed to Caesar."

The Voyage to Rome Begins

27 And when it was decided that we
should sail to Italy, they delivered Paul
and some other prisoners to *one* named
Julius, a centurion of the Augustan Regiment.
2 So, entering a ship of Adramyttium, we
put to sea, meaning to sail along the coasts of
Asia. Aristarchus, a Macedonian of Thessalonica, was with us.
3 And the next *day* we landed at Sidon. And
Julius treated Paul kindly and gave *him* liberty to go to his friends and receive care.
4 When we had put to sea from there, we
sailed under *the shelter of* Cyprus, because
the winds were contrary.
5 And when we had sailed over the sea
which is off Cilicia and Pamphylia, we came
to Myra, *a city* of Lycia.
6 There the centurion found an Alexandrian
ship sailing to Italy, and he put us on board.
7 When we had sailed slowly many days,
and arrived with difficulty off Cnidus, the
wind not permitting us to proceed, we sailed
under *the shelter of* Crete off Salmone.
8 Passing it with difficulty, we came to a
place called Fair Havens, near the city of
Lasea.

Paul's Warning Ignored

9 Now when much time had been spent, and
sailing was now dangerous because the Fast
was already over, Paul advised them,
10 saying, "Men, I perceive that this voyage
will end with disaster and much loss, not only
of the cargo and ship, but also our lives."
11 Nevertheless the centurion was more persuaded by the helmsman and the owner of the
ship than by the things spoken by Paul.
12 And because the harbor was not suitable
to winter in, the majority advised to set sail
from there also, if by any means they could
reach Phoenix, a harbor of Crete opening toward the southwest and northwest, *and* winter *there*.

In the Tempest

13 When the south wind blew softly, supposing that they had obtained *their* desire, putting out to sea, they sailed close by Crete.
14 But not long after, a tempestuous head
wind arose, called Euroclydon.[a]
15 So when the ship was caught, and could
not head into the wind, we let *her* drive.
16 And running under *the shelter of* an island called Clauda,[a] we secured the skiff with
difficulty.
17 When they had taken it on board, they
used cables to undergird the ship; and fearing
lest they should run aground on the Syrtis[a]
Sands, they struck sail and so were driven.
18 And because we were exceedingly tem-

27:14 [a]NU-Text reads *Euraquilon*. **27:16** [a]NU-Text reads *Cauda*.
27:17 [a]M-Text reads *Syrtes*.

LIFE LESSONS

➤ 26:20 — *". . . that they should repent, turn to God, and do works befitting repentance."*

A gospel highlighting divine grace and faith in Jesus does not eliminate the need for repentance and godly behavior. Grace gives us the ability and the desire to obey, not the right and safety to disobey.

pest-tossed, the next *day* they lightened the
ship.
19 On the third *day* we threw the ship's
tackle overboard with our own hands.
➤ 20 Now when neither sun nor stars appeared
for many days, and no small tempest beat on
us, all hope that we would be saved was finally given up.
21 But after long abstinence from food, then
Paul stood in the midst of them and said,
"Men, you should have listened to me, and not
have sailed from Crete and incurred this disaster and loss.
22 "And now I urge you to take heart, for
there will be no loss of life among you, but
only of the ship.
23 "For there stood by me this night an angel
of the God to whom I belong and whom I
serve,
24 "saying, 'Do not be afraid, Paul; you must
be brought before Caesar; and indeed God
has granted you all those who sail with you.'
➤ 25 "Therefore take heart, men, for I believe
God that it will be just as it was told me.
26 "However, we must run aground on a certain island."
27 Now when the fourteenth night had come,
as we were driven up and down in the Adriatic *Sea*, about midnight the sailors sensed
that they were drawing near some land.
28 And they took soundings and found *it* to
be twenty fathoms; and when they had gone a
little farther, they took soundings again and
found *it* to be fifteen fathoms.
29 Then, fearing lest we should run aground
on the rocks, they dropped four anchors from
the stern, and prayed for day to come.
30 And as the sailors were seeking to escape
from the ship, when they had let down the
skiff into the sea, under pretense of putting
out anchors from the prow,
31 Paul said to the centurion and the soldiers,
"Unless these men stay in the ship, you cannot be saved."
32 Then the soldiers cut away the ropes of
the skiff and let it fall off.
33 And as day was about to dawn, Paul implored *them* all to take food, saying, "Today is
the fourteenth day you have waited and continued without food, and eaten nothing.
34 "Therefore I urge you to take nourishment, for this is for your survival, since not a
hair will fall from the head of any of you."
35 And when he had said these things, he
took bread and gave thanks to God in the
presence of them all; and when he had broken *it* he began to eat.
36 Then they were all encouraged, and also
took food themselves.
37 And in all we were two hundred and sev-
enty-six persons on the ship.
38 So when they had eaten enough, they
lightened the ship and threw out the wheat
into the sea.

Shipwrecked on Malta

39 When it was day, they did not recognize
the land; but they observed a bay with a
beach, onto which they planned to run the
ship if possible.
40 And they let go the anchors and left *them*
in the sea, meanwhile loosing the rudder
ropes; and they hoisted the mainsail to the
wind and made for shore.
41 But striking a place where two seas met,
they ran the ship aground; and the prow stuck
fast and remained immovable, but the stern
was being broken up by the violence of the
waves.
42 And the soldiers' plan was to kill the prisoners, lest any of them should swim away and
escape.
43 But the centurion, wanting to save Paul, ➤
kept them from *their* purpose, and commanded that those who could swim should
jump *overboard* first and get to land,
44 and the rest, some on boards and some on
parts of the ship. And so it was that they all
escaped safely to land.

Paul's Ministry on Malta

28 Now when they had escaped, they then
found out that the island was called
Malta.
2 And the natives showed us unusual kindness; for they kindled a fire and made us all

LIFE LESSONS

➤ 27:20 — *Now when neither sun nor stars appeared for many days, and no small tempest beat on us, all hope that we would be saved was finally given up.*

Hardships and trials can last for so long that we begin to despair that God will ever rescue us from our difficulties. Yet God remains faithful, and difficult circumstances never indicate that He has lost interest in us.

➤ 27:25 — *"Therefore take heart, men, for I believe God that it will be just as it was told me."*

When times get hard, those who do not have a relationship with God can take courage from those who do—if believers maintain and display their trust in the Lord. Paul's faith encouraged many unbelievers.

➤ 27:43, 44 — *But the centurion . . . commanded that those who could swim should jump overboard first and get to land . . . . And so it was that they all escaped safely to land.*

God had promised that everyone on board would be saved, and so it happened. Some swam, some floated on boards or pieces of the ship, but everyone made it to shore safely. We never go wrong by trusting God's Word!

welcome, because of the rain that was falling
and because of the cold.
➤ 3 But when Paul had gathered a bundle of
sticks and laid *them* on the fire, a viper came
out because of the heat, and fastened on his
hand.
4 So when the natives saw the creature
hanging from his hand, they said to one another, "No doubt this man is a murderer,
whom, though he has escaped the sea, yet justice does not allow to live."
5 But he shook off the creature into the fire
and suffered no harm.
6 However, they were expecting that he
would swell up or suddenly fall down dead.
But after they had looked for a long time and
saw no harm come to him, they changed their
minds and said that he was a god.
7 In that region there was an estate of the
leading citizen of the island, whose name was
Publius, who received us and entertained us
courteously for three days.
8 And it happened that the father of Publius
lay sick of a fever and dysentery. Paul went in
to him and prayed, and he laid his hands on
him and healed him.
9 So when this was done, the rest of those
on the island who had diseases also came and
were healed.
10 They also honored us in many ways; and
when we departed, they provided such things
as were necessary.

Arrival at Rome

11 After three months we sailed in an
Alexandrian ship whose figurehead was the
Twin Brothers, which had wintered at the
island.
12 And landing at Syracuse, we stayed three
days.
13 From there we circled round and reached
Rhegium. And after one day the south wind
blew; and the next day we came to Puteoli,
14 where we found brethren, and were invited to stay with them seven days. And so we
went toward Rome.
➤ 15 And from there, when the brethren heard
about us, they came to meet us as far as Appii
Forum and Three Inns. When Paul saw them,
he thanked God and took courage.
16 Now when we came to Rome, the centurion delivered the prisoners to the captain
of the guard; but Paul was permitted to
dwell by himself with the soldier who
guarded him.

Paul's Ministry at Rome

17 And it came to pass after three days that
Paul called the leaders of the Jews together.
So when they had come together, he said to
them: "Men *and* brethren, though I have done
nothing against our people or the customs of
our fathers, yet I was delivered as a prisoner
from Jerusalem into the hands of the Romans,
18 "who, when they had examined me,
wanted to let *me* go, because there was no
cause for putting me to death.
19 "But when the Jews[a] spoke against *it*, I
was compelled to appeal to Caesar, not that I
had anything of which to accuse my nation.
20 "For this reason therefore I have called for
you, to see *you* and speak with *you*, because
for the hope of Israel I am bound with this
chain."
21 Then they said to him, "We neither received letters from Judea concerning you, nor
have any of the brethren who came reported
or spoken any evil of you.
22 "But we desire to hear from you what you
think; for concerning this sect, we know that
it is spoken against everywhere."
23 So when they had appointed him a day,
many came to him at *his* lodging, to whom he
explained and solemnly testified of the kingdom of God, persuading them concerning Jesus from both the Law of Moses and the
Prophets, from morning till evening.
24 And some were persuaded by the things ➤
which were spoken, and some disbelieved.
25 So when they did not agree among themselves, they departed after Paul had said one
word: "The Holy Spirit spoke rightly through
Isaiah the prophet to our[a] fathers,

28:19 [a]That is, the ruling authorities **28:25** [a]NU-Text reads *your.*

LIFE LESSONS

➤ 28:3 — *But when Paul had gathered a bundle of sticks and laid them on the fire, a viper came out because of the heat, and fastened on his hand.*

God had just rescued Paul from drowning at sea, and immediately he suffered another kind of trouble. Yet God used both difficult incidents to showcase His power and love to those who did not yet believe in Him.

➤ 28:15 — *. . . when the brethren heard about us, they came to meet us as far as Appii Forum and Three Inns. When Paul saw them, he thanked God and took courage.*

Paul always traveled in ministry teams, and he always drew on the strength of his fellow believers. He knew that no Christian could grow in faith apart from connecting deeply with others in the body of Christ.

➤ 28:24 — *And some were persuaded by the things which were spoken, and some disbelieved.*

It is always this way when the gospel gets preached: some believe, and some don't. Paul said, "I have become all things to all men, that I might by all means save some" (1 Cor. 9:22).

26 "saying,

'*Go to this people and say:*
"*Hearing you will hear, and shall not understand;*
And seeing you will see, and not perceive;
27 *For the hearts of this people have grown dull.*
Their ears are hard of hearing,
And their eyes they have closed,
Lest they should see with their eyes and hear with their ears,
Lest they should understand with their hearts and turn,
So that I should heal them." '[a]

28 "Therefore let it be known to you that the salvation of God has been sent to the Gentiles, and they will hear it!"
29 And when he had said these words, the Jews departed and had a great dispute among themselves.[a]
30 Then Paul dwelt two whole years in his own rented house, and received all who came to him,
31 preaching the kingdom of God and teaching the things which concern the Lord Jesus Christ with all confidence, no one forbidding him.

28:27 [a]Isaiah 6:9, 10 **28:29** [a]NU-Text omits this verse.

THE BOOK OF

ROMANS

The epistle to the Romans, one of the apostle Paul's greatest works, is placed first among his thirteen epistles in the New Testament. While the four Gospels present the words and works of Jesus Christ, Romans explores the significance of His sacrificial death. Using a question-and-answer format, Paul offers us the most systematic presentation of doctrine in the Bible.

But Romans is much more than a book of theology; it is also a book of practical exhortation. The good news of Jesus Christ is more than facts to be believed; it is also a life to be lived—a life of righteousness befitting the person "justified freely by [God's] grace through the redemption that is in Christ Jesus" (3:24).

Romans is the preeminent book in the Bible on the crucial topics of grace and faith, but it is also a book about joyful obedience. Paul begins his letter talking about the necessity of obedience ("Through Him we have received grace and apostleship for obedience to the faith among all nations," 1:5) and he ends it in a similar way (" . . . according to the commandment of the everlasting God, for obedience to the faith," 16:26). Between those two points Paul explains how we obey God only by the power of divine grace through faith.

The title *Pros Romaious*, "To the Romans," has been associated with the epistle almost from the beginning.

Theme: People everywhere can enjoy peace and fellowship with God through faith in Jesus Christ, who gives them the desire and the strength to gladly obey the Lord.

Author: The apostle Paul.

Date: Most scholars believe Paul wrote Romans around A.D. 57.

Structure: The first section (chapters 1–8) expresses what has been called "the gospel according to Paul," meaning that the only way to fellowship with God is by grace through faith in the risen Jesus Christ. The second section (chapters 9–11) expounds Paul's expectation that the Jews, who have largely refused this teaching, will one day accept it. The final section (chapter 12–16) describes how people saved by grace through faith in Christ should live and behave.

As you read Romans, watch for some life principles that play an important part in this book:

9. Trusting God means looking beyond what we can see to what God sees. *See Romans 4:13–25; page 1314.*

12. Peace with God is the fruit of oneness with God. *See Romans 5:1; page 1314.*

18. As children of a sovereign God, we are never victims of our circumstances. *See Romans 8:18–25; page 1319.*

28. No Christian has ever been called to "go it alone" in his or her walk of faith. *See Romans 13:8–10; page 1325.*

Greeting

1 Paul, a bondservant of Jesus Christ, called
to be an apostle, separated to the gospel of
God
2 which He promised before through His
prophets in the Holy Scriptures,
3 concerning His Son Jesus Christ our Lord,
who was born of the seed of David according
to the flesh,
4 *and* declared *to be* the Son of God with
power according to the Spirit of holiness, by
the resurrection from the dead.
➤ 5 Through Him we have received grace and
apostleship for obedience to the faith among
all nations for His name,
6 among whom you also are the called of Jesus Christ;
7 To all who are in Rome, beloved of God,
called *to be* saints:

Grace to you and peace from God our Father and the Lord Jesus Christ.

Desire to Visit Rome

8 First, I thank my God through Jesus Christ
for you all, that your faith is spoken of
throughout the whole world.
9 For God is my witness, whom I serve with
my spirit in the gospel of His Son, that without ceasing I make mention of you always in
my prayers,
10 making request if, by some means, now at
last I may find a way in the will of God to
come to you.
11 For I long to see you, that I may impart to
you some spiritual gift, so that you may be established—
12 that is, that I may be encouraged together
with you by the mutual faith both of you and
me.
13 Now I do not want you to be unaware,
brethren, that I often planned to come to you
(but was hindered until now), that I might
have some fruit among you also, just as
among the other Gentiles.
14 I am a debtor both to Greeks and to barbarians, both to wise and to unwise.
15 So, as much as is in me, *I am* ready to
preach the gospel to you who are in Rome
also.

The Just Live by Faith

16 For I am not ashamed of the gospel of ➤
Christ,[a] for it is the power of God to salvation
for everyone who believes, for the Jew first
and also for the Greek.
17 For in it the righteousness of God is re- ➤
vealed from faith to faith; as it is written, *"The
just shall live by faith."*[a]

God's Wrath on Unrighteousness

18 For the wrath of God is revealed from
heaven against all ungodliness and unrighteousness of men, who suppress the truth in
unrighteousness,
19 because what may be known of God is
manifest in them, for God has shown *it* to
them.
20 For since the creation of the world His invisible *attributes* are clearly seen, being understood by the things that are made, *even*
His eternal power and Godhead, so that they
are without excuse,
21 because, although they knew God, they
did not glorify *Him* as God, nor were thankful, but became futile in their thoughts, and
their foolish hearts were darkened.
22 Professing to be wise, they became fools,
23 and changed the glory of the incorruptible
God into an image made like corruptible
man—and birds and four-footed animals and
creeping things.
24 Therefore God also gave them up to ➤
uncleanness, in the lusts of their hearts, to
dishonor their bodies among themselves,
25 who exchanged the truth of God for the
lie, and worshiped and served the creature

1:16 [a]NU-Text omits *of Christ*. 1:17 [a]Habakkuk 2:4

LIFE LESSONS

➤ 1:5 — *Through Him we have received grace and apostleship for obedience to the faith among all nations for His name . . . .*

Paul always connected grace and faith, not only to salvation, but also to obedience. Grace gives us the desire and the power to obey God, not the right and the safety to disobey.

➤ 1:16 — *For I am not ashamed of the gospel of Christ, for it is the power of God to salvation for everyone who believes . . .*

We must never feel ashamed of our connection to Christ or to the salvation which He freely offers to all. It is a high privilege to represent Him, and we must do so with boldness and enthusiasm.

➤ 1:17 — *For in it the righteousness of God is revealed from faith to faith; as it is written, "The just shall live by faith."*

We live the whole Christian life by faith. We take hold of grace for salvation by faith, and we take hold of grace for growing in godliness by faith. God loves to honor faith, because faith honors Him.

➤ 1:24 — *Therefore God also gave them up . . . .*

Romans 1 records how God will give people over to the sins they refuse to give up, so that those sins take over their lives and eventually destroy them. Three times Paul uses this or a related phrase (see also vv. 26, 28).

rather than the Creator, who is blessed forever. Amen.
26 For this reason God gave them up to vile passions. For even their women exchanged the natural use for what is against nature.
27 Likewise also the men, leaving the natural use of the woman, burned in their lust for one another, men with men committing what is shameful, and receiving in themselves the penalty of their error which was due.
28 And even as they did not like to retain God in *their* knowledge, God gave them over to a debased mind, to do those things which are not fitting;
29 being filled with all unrighteousness, sexual immorality,[a] wickedness, covetousness, maliciousness; full of envy, murder, strife, deceit, evil-mindedness; *they are* whisperers,
30 backbiters, haters of God, violent, proud, boasters, inventors of evil things, disobedient to parents,
31 undiscerning, untrustworthy, unloving, unforgiving,[a] unmerciful;
32 who, knowing the righteous judgment of God, that those who practice such things are deserving of death, not only do the same but also approve of those who practice them.

God's Righteous Judgment

2 Therefore you are inexcusable, O man, whoever you are who judge, for in whatever you judge another you condemn yourself; for you who judge practice the same things.
2 But we know that the judgment of God is according to truth against those who practice such things.
3 And do you think this, O man, you who judge those practicing such things, and doing the same, that you will escape the judgment of God?
➤ 4 Or do you despise the riches of His goodness, forbearance, and longsuffering, not knowing that the goodness of God leads you to repentance?
➤ 5 But in accordance with your hardness and your impenitent heart you are treasuring up for yourself wrath in the day of wrath and revelation of the righteous judgment of God,
6 who *"will render to each one according to his deeds"*:[a]
7 eternal life to those who by patient continuance in doing good seek for glory, honor, and immortality;
8 but to those who are self-seeking and do not obey the truth, but obey unrighteousness—indignation and wrath,
9 tribulation and anguish, on every soul of man who does evil, of the Jew first and also of the Greek;
10 but glory, honor, and peace to everyone who works what is good, to the Jew first and also to the Greek.
11 For there is no partiality with God.
12 For as many as have sinned without law will also perish without law, and as many as have sinned in the law will be judged by the law
13 (for not the hearers of the law *are* just in the sight of God, but the doers of the law will be justified;
14 for when Gentiles, who do not have the law, by nature do the things in the law, these, although not having the law, are a law to themselves,
15 who show the work of the law written in their hearts, their conscience also bearing witness, and between themselves *their* thoughts accusing or else excusing *them*)
16 in the day when God will judge the secrets of men by Jesus Christ, according to my gospel. ➤

The Jews Guilty as the Gentiles

17 Indeed[a] you are called a Jew, and rest on the law, and make your boast in God,
18 and know *His* will, and approve the things that are excellent, being instructed out of the law,
19 and are confident that you yourself are a guide to the blind, a light to those who are in darkness,
20 an instructor of the foolish, a teacher of babes, having the form of knowledge and truth in the law.

1:29 [a]NU-Text omits *sexual immorality.* **1:31** [a]NU-Text omits *unforgiving.* **2:6** [a]Psalm 62:12; Proverbs 24:12 **2:17** [a]NU-Text reads *But if.*

LIFE LESSONS

➤ 2:4 — *Or do you despise the riches of His goodness, forbearance, and longsuffering, not knowing that the goodness of God leads you to repentance?*

Salvation is a work of God from start to finish. Even our repentance demonstrates the Spirit of God at work in our hearts. We repent because of the goodness of God, not because of the goodness of our hearts.

➤ 2:5, 6 — *God . . . "will render to each one according to his deeds."*

Throughout the Bible we learn that God will reward believers for their Spirit-empowered good works and will punish unbelievers for their flesh-driven evil deeds. And God keeps accurate records!

➤ 2:16 — *. . . in the day when God will judge the secrets of men by Jesus Christ, according to my gospel.*

At the judgment, every "secret" motivation or desire or act will come out into the open. Jesus said, "For nothing is secret that will not be revealed, nor anything hidden that will not be known and come to light" (Luke 8:17).

ANSWERS TO LIFE'S QUESTIONS

How does my conscience differ from the guidance of the Holy Spirit?

ROM. 2:14, 15

The conscience functions something like a computer. A computer is programmed to respond in specific ways to specific information. Also, it responds to information based on the commands it has been programmed to follow.

When I click my word processing application, my computer knows to open my word processor. For the most part, computers are simply responders.

The conscience is a responder as well. It responds to certain input just as it has been programmed. Paul described it like this: "For when Gentiles, who do not have the law, by nature do the things in the law, these, although not having the law, are a law to themselves, who show the work of the law written in their hearts, their conscience also bearing witness, and between themselves their thoughts accusing or else excusing them" (Rom. 2:14, 15).

God has programmed His moral code into the heart of every man and woman. We are born with it. When a person's actions or thoughts violate that code, the conscience responds by sending a "NO" message to the brain. On the other hand, when the act or thought goes along with the preprogrammed moral code, the conscience says "GO."

Notice, Paul says our thoughts sometimes point out the legitimacy of certain actions. When that happens, if the actions line up with the law of God written in our hearts, the conscience gives us the go-ahead.

When you became a Christian, a change began to occur in your conscience. The basic moral code that everyone has at birth started to get overhauled. The Spirit of truth took up residency in your heart. Then, whether you were aware of it or not, He immediately set about to reprogram your conscience. Whereas before you had a general sense of right and wrong, the Holy Spirit began renewing your mind to more specific and complete truths (see 1 Cor. 2:10–13).

You participate in this renewal process every time you read your Bible, attend worship, memorize a verse, or pray. The Holy Spirit uses all this input to reprogram the database through which your conscience evaluates every opportunity, thought, invitation, word, and deed.

As this process continues, your conscience tunes in with the moral code of the Holy Spirit—a code reflecting the moral and ethical standards of God. This process sensitizes you not only to God's moral standards but also to the will of God.

See the Life Principles Index for further study:
22. *To walk in the Spirit is to obey the initial promptings of the Spirit.*
13. *Listening to God is essential to walking with God.*

21 You, therefore, who teach another, do you not teach yourself? You who preach that a man should not steal, do you steal?
22 You who say, "Do not commit adultery," do you commit adultery? You who abhor idols, do you rob temples?
23 You who make your boast in the law, do you dishonor God through breaking the law?
➤ 24 For *"the name of God is blasphemed among the Gentiles because of you,"*[a] as it is written.

Circumcision of No Avail

25 For circumcision is indeed profitable if you keep the law; but if you are a breaker of the law, your circumcision has become uncircumcision.
26 Therefore, if an uncircumcised man keeps the righteous requirements of the law, will not his uncircumcision be counted as circumcision?

2:24 [a]Isaiah 52:5; Ezekiel 36:22

LIFE LESSONS

➤ **2:24 — *For "the name of God is blasphemed among the Gentiles because of you," as it is written.***

Whether we realize it or not, unbelievers are watching both us and our conduct. God intends for what they see to attract them into His kingdom, but when we disobey the Lord and act foolishly, the opposite often happens.

27 And will not the physically uncircumcised, if he fulfills the law, judge you who,
even with *your* written *code* and circumcision, *are* a transgressor of the law?
28 For he is not a Jew who *is one* outwardly,
nor *is* circumcision that which *is* outward in
the flesh;
29 but *he is* a Jew who *is one* inwardly; and
circumcision *is that* of the heart, in the Spirit,
not in the letter; whose praise *is* not from men
but from God.

God's Judgment Defended

3 What advantage then has the Jew, or what
is the profit of circumcision?
2 Much in every way! Chiefly because to
them were committed the oracles of God.
3 For what if some did not believe? Will their
unbelief make the faithfulness of God without
effect?
4 Certainly not! Indeed, let God be true but
every man a liar. As it is written:

"That You may be justified in Your words,
And may overcome when You are
judged."[a]

5 But if our unrighteousness demonstrates
the righteousness of God, what shall we say?
Is God unjust who inflicts wrath? (I speak as
a man.)
6 Certainly not! For then how will God
judge the world?
7 For if the truth of God has increased
through my lie to His glory, why am I also still
judged as a sinner?
➤ 8 And *why* not *say*, "Let us do evil that good
may come"?—as we are slanderously reported and as some affirm that we say. Their
condemnation is just.

All Have Sinned

9 What then? Are we better *than they*? Not
at all. For we have previously charged both
Jews and Greeks that they are all under sin.
10 As it is written:

"There is none righteous, no, not one;
11 *There is none who understands;*
There is none who seeks after God.
12 *They have all turned aside;*
They have together become unprofitable;
There is none who does good, no, not
one."[a]
13 *"Their throat is an open tomb;*
With their tongues they have practiced
deceit";[a]
"The poison of asps is under their lips";[b]
14 *"Whose mouth is full of cursing and*
bitterness."[a]
15 *"Their feet are swift to shed blood;*
16 *Destruction and misery are in their ways;*
17 *And the way of peace they have not*
known."[a]
18 *"There is no fear of God before their eyes."*[a] ➤

19 Now we know that whatever the law says,
it says to those who are under the law, that
every mouth may be stopped, and all the
world may become guilty before God.
20 Therefore by the deeds of the law no flesh ➤
will be justified in His sight, for by the law *is*
the knowledge of sin.

God's Righteousness Through Faith

21 But now the righteousness of God apart
from the law is revealed, being witnessed by
the Law and the Prophets,
22 even the righteousness of God, through
faith in Jesus Christ, to all and on all[a] who believe. For there is no difference;
23 for all have sinned and fall short of the ➤
glory of God,
24 being justified freely by His grace through
the redemption that is in Christ Jesus,
25 whom God set forth *as* a propitiation by
His blood, through faith, to demonstrate His
righteousness, because in His forbearance
God had passed over the sins that were previously committed,

3:4 [a]Psalm 51:4 **3:12** [a]Psalms 14:1–3; 53:1–3; Ecclesiastes 7:20
3:13 [a]Psalm 5:9 [b]Psalm 140:3 **3:14** [a]Psalm 10:7
3:17 [a]Isaiah 59:7, 8 **3:18** [a]Psalm 36:1 **3:22** [a]NU-Text omits *and on all.*

LIFE LESSONS

➤ 3:8 — *And why not say, "Let us do evil that good may come"?—as we are slanderously reported and as some affirm that we say. Their condemnation is just.*

Some opponents of Paul claimed that the apostle's teaching on grace amounted to saying "I'm saved anyway, so I might as well sin. God's grace will take care of it." Paul condemned this distortion of grace.

➤ 3:18 — *"There is no fear of God before their eyes."*

All sin eventually comes down to the refusal to fear God. All of the heinous sins that Paul lists have their source in a rebellious attitude that will not honor God as God.

➤ 3:20 — *Therefore by the deeds of the law no flesh will be justified in His sight, for by the law is the knowledge of sin.*

God gave His people the law so they could understand their need for grace, not so that they could try to "earn" their way into His favor. The law shows us our sin; it doesn't empower us to follow it.

➤ 3:23 — *. . . for all have sinned and fall short of the glory of God . . . .*

Jesus alone, among all the billions of human beings ever born on this planet, lived His entire life by the power of the Spirit, always doing His Father's will and never committing a single sin (John 8:46; Heb. 4:15).

ANSWERS TO LIFE'S QUESTIONS

What Does God Really Think of Me?

ROM. 3:24

I never thought much about whether God liked me or approved of me when I was a young man. I knew that God *loved* me, but I never thought about whether He *liked* me. If someone had pressed me on that point, I probably would have concluded that God "somewhat" liked me. I don't think I would have said that He liked me through and through.

Only after I truly experienced God's love—His total, unconditional, overwhelming, abundant love—could I say with all honesty, "Yes, God likes me. He approves of me. He likes spending time with me. He likes being with me. He likes hearing me when I talk to Him, and He likes talking back to me through His Word. God thinks I'm okay."

I didn't come to that position on the basis of things I had accomplished or actions I had taken. Rather, I came to that position solely because I had a new appreciation for God's grace at work in my life. God certainly does expect obedience, but the fact is, I had done nothing and could do nothing to win God's approval. God likes me just the way I am because He created me to be just the way I am . . . . God's approval of me isn't based on anything I have accomplished or might accomplish in the future. He approves of me because I stand forgiven before Him, and I'm forgiven because I have accepted Jesus Christ as my Savior and have received God's forgiveness. That makes me *totally* acceptable to Him.

The first four chapters of Romans make it very clear that we can't save ourselves. We are all sinners and have fallen short of the glory of God (see Rom. 3:23). But because of what Jesus Christ did for us on the cross, by faith we are "justified freely by His grace" (Rom. 3:24).

Jesus has done for you what you cannot do. He won for you God's full approval. You cannot have grace without the cross. But because of the cross, you have full access to God's grace.

Grace is God's kindness and goodness toward you without regard to worth or merit. As a believer, you have a duty to obey God. But you can't earn grace, you can't buy grace, and you can't barter with God to receive grace. It is God's free gift to you. There is only one thing you can do in regard to grace: Receive it gladly!

See the Life Principles Index for further study:
12. Peace with God is the fruit of oneness with God.
3. God's Word is an immovable anchor in times of storm.

26 to demonstrate at the present time His
righteousness, that He might be just and the
justifier of the one who has faith in Jesus.

Boasting Excluded

27 Where *is* boasting then? It is excluded. By
what law? Of works? No, but by the law of faith.
28 Therefore we conclude that a man is justified by faith apart from the deeds of the law.
29 Or *is He* the God of the Jews only? *Is He*
not also the God of the Gentiles? Yes, of the
Gentiles also,
30 since *there is* one God who will justify the
circumcised by faith and the uncircumcised
through faith.
31 Do we then make void the law through
faith? Certainly not! On the contrary, we establish the law.

Abraham Justified by Faith

4 What then shall we say that Abraham our
father has found according to the flesh?[a]
2 For if Abraham was justified by works, he
has *something* to boast about, but not before
God.
3 For what does the Scripture say? *"Abraham believed God, and it was accounted to
him for righteousness."*[a]

4:1 [a]Or *Abraham our (fore)father according to the flesh has found?* **4:3** [a]Genesis 15:6

LIFE LESSONS

➤ **4:3 — *For what does the Scripture say? "Abraham believed God, and it was accounted to him for righteousness."***

Paul used the example of Abraham, who lived long before the Mosaic law, to show that the only way for any sinful person to come into a right relationship with God is by grace through faith.

4 Now to him who works, the wages are not
counted as grace but as debt.

David Celebrates the Same Truth

5 But to him who does not work but believes
on Him who justifies the ungodly, his faith is
accounted for righteousness,
6 just as David also describes the blessedness of the man to whom God imputes righteousness apart from works:
7 *"Blessed are those whose lawless deeds*
are forgiven,
And whose sins are covered;
8 *Blessed is the man to whom the* LORD
shall not impute sin."[a]

Abraham Justified Before Circumcision

9 *Does* this blessedness then *come* upon the
circumcised *only,* or upon the uncircumcised
also? For we say that faith was accounted to
Abraham for righteousness.
10 How then was it accounted? While he was
circumcised, or uncircumcised? Not while circumcised, but while uncircumcised.
11 And he received the sign of circumcision,
a seal of the righteousness of the faith which
he had while still uncircumcised, that he
might be the father of all those who believe,
though they are uncircumcised, that righteousness might be imputed to them also,
12 and the father of circumcision to those
who not only *are* of the circumcision, but who
also walk in the steps of the faith which our
father Abraham *had while still* uncircumcised.

The Promise Granted Through Faith

13 For the promise that he would be the heir
of the world *was* not to Abraham or to his
seed through the law, but through the righteousness of faith.
14 For if those who are of the law *are* heirs,
faith is made void and the promise made of
no effect,
15 because the law brings about wrath; for
where there is no law *there is* no transgression.
16 Therefore *it is* of faith that *it might be* according to grace, so that the promise might be
sure to all the seed, not only to those who are
of the law, but also to those who are of the
faith of Abraham, who is the father of us all
17 (as it is written, *"I have made you a father*
of many nations"[a]) in the presence of Him
whom he believed—God, who gives life to the
dead and calls those things which do not exist
as though they did;
18 who, contrary to hope, in hope believed, so
that he became the father of many nations,
according to what was spoken, *"So shall your*
descendants be."[a]
19 And not being weak in faith, he did not
consider his own body, already dead (since he
was about a hundred years old), and the dead-
ness of Sarah's womb.
20 He did not waver at the promise of God
through unbelief, but was strengthened in
faith, giving glory to God,
21 and being fully convinced that what He
had promised He was also able to perform.
22 And therefore *"it was accounted to him*
for righteousness."[a]
23 Now it was not written for his sake alone
that it was imputed to him,
24 but also for us. It shall be imputed to us
who believe in Him who raised up Jesus our
Lord from the dead,
25 who was delivered up because of our offenses, and was raised because of our justification.

Faith Triumphs in Trouble

5 Therefore, having been justified by faith,
we have[a] peace with God through our
Lord Jesus Christ,
2 through whom also we have access by
faith into this grace in which we stand, and
rejoice in hope of the glory of God.
3 And not only *that,* but we also glory in

4:8 [a]Psalm 32:1, 2 **4:17** [a]Genesis 17:5 **4:18** [a]Genesis 15:5
4:22 [a]Genesis 15:6 **5:1** [a]Another ancient reading is, *let us have peace.*

LIFE LESSONS

➤ 4:20 — *He did not waver at the promise of God through unbelief, but was strengthened in faith, giving glory to God.*

God promised Abraham that he and Sarah would have a son—and then made them wait a quarter century to fulfill His promise. He waited until Abraham was 100 years old and his wife was 90—yet Abraham continued to believe.

➤ 4:21 — *. . . being fully convinced that what He had promised He was also able to perform.*

God never promises us anything that He can't deliver. Do we believe that? If we do, then it only makes sense to put our complete trust in Him, regardless of how dark our circumstances might appear.

➤ 5:1 — *Therefore, having been justified by faith, we have peace with God through our Lord Jesus Christ . . . .*

For those who place their faith in the risen Christ, the war with heaven is over. We move from darkness to light, from enemies to beloved children, from death to life. God showers His peace on those who trust Him.

➤ 5:3, 4 — *And not only that, but we also glory in tribulations, knowing that tribulation produces perseverance; and perseverance, character; and character, hope.*

Trials, difficulties, and adversities are often God's way of maturing us into people who look more like His Son. No one likes trials, but by faith we can begin to understand how God may want to use them for our good.

WHAT THE BIBLE SAYS ABOUT THE GRACE IN WHICH WE STAND

Rom. 5:2

When we think of grace, we think of the favor of God. There is nothing you can do to earn God's grace. Salvation is His gift, given in love to you.

But does grace stop at the point when you receive Jesus as your Savior? No, His grace flows over your life each moment, bringing hope and an enormous sense of peace and security.

God's grace is founded in love, love that is not seasonal or temporary—the very love Jesus displayed at Calvary. In the Book of Romans, the apostle Paul wants us to have a firm mental picture of God's grace in our lives. To do this he uses the phrase "this grace in which we stand" (Rom. 5:2).

For the believer, living in God's grace is all-consuming. You can't walk away from it, because God thinks, responds, and views us through the eyes of grace. We live in a sphere of grace, surrounded by His goodness.

Even when disappointments come, they arrive wrapped in the grace of God. Through grace, you walk in God's favor, and through this gift of grace you have access to God the Father.

So when you think of your life before God, think of the way He wraps you in His loving care. Sure, at times you feel distracted from Him. Sin captures your attention or a sense of loneliness redirects your thoughts.

But there are no variables with God. He remains the same, just as His love toward you remains constant. Every good thing that comes your way is an act of His grace. Every answer to prayer is His personal response to your need.

His grace washes over your life like sunlight on a cloudless day. Hurt and pain, while they may invade, cannot change the presence of God's grace. Grace does not depend on circumstances. God's grace does not operate more or less in your life because you did or did not do a certain thing. Grace is a gift and always will be.

For now, we stand in the light of grace. One day we will walk its streets.

Living in God's grace is all-consuming.

See the Life Principles Index for further study:
9. Trusting God means looking beyond what we can see to what God sees.

tribulations, knowing that tribulation produces perseverance;
4 and perseverance, character; and character, hope.
5 Now hope does not disappoint, because
the love of God has been poured out in our
hearts by the Holy Spirit who was given to us.

Christ in Our Place

6 For when we were still without strength,
in due time Christ died for the ungodly.
7 For scarcely for a righteous man will one
die; yet perhaps for a good man someone
would even dare to die.
➤ 8 But God demonstrates His own love toward us, in that while we were still sinners,
Christ died for us.
9 Much more then, having now been justified by His blood, we shall be saved from
wrath through Him.
✳ 10 For if when we were enemies we were reconciled to God through the death of His Son,
much more, having been reconciled, we shall
be saved by His life.
11 And not only *that,* but we also rejoice in
God through our Lord Jesus Christ, through
whom we have now received the reconciliation.

Death in Adam, Life in Christ

12 Therefore, just as through one man sin entered the world, and death through sin, and
thus death spread to all men, because all
sinned—
13 (For until the law sin was in the world, but
sin is not imputed when there is no law.
14 Nevertheless death reigned from Adam to
Moses, even over those who had not sinned
according to the likeness of the transgression
of Adam, who is a type of Him who was to
come.
15 But the free gift *is* not like the offense. For
if by the one man's offense many died, much
more the grace of God and the gift by the
grace of the one Man, Jesus Christ, abounded
to many.
16 And the gift *is* not like *that which came*
through the one who sinned. For the judgment *which came* from one *offense resulted*
in condemnation, but the free gift *which came*
from many offenses *resulted* in justification.
17 For if by the one man's offense death
reigned through the one, much more those
who receive abundance of grace and of the
gift of righteousness will reign in life through
the One, Jesus Christ.)
18 Therefore, as through one man's offense
judgment came to all men, resulting in
condemnation, even so through one Man's
righteous act *the free gift came* to all men, resulting in justification of life.
19 For as by one man's disobedience many
were made sinners, so also by one Man's obedience many will be made righteous.
20 Moreover the law entered that the offense
might abound. But where sin abounded, grace
abounded much more,
21 so that as sin reigned in death, even so
grace might reign through righteousness to
eternal life through Jesus Christ our Lord.

Dead to Sin, Alive to God

6 What shall we say then? Shall we continue
in sin that grace may abound?
2 Certainly not! How shall we who died to ➤
sin live any longer in it?
3 Or do you not know that as many of us as
were baptized into Christ Jesus were baptized
into His death?
4 Therefore we were buried with Him
through baptism into death, that just as Christ
was raised from the dead by the glory of the
Father, even so we also should walk in newness of life.
5 For if we have been united together in the
likeness of His death, certainly we also shall
be *in the likeness* of *His* resurrection,
6 knowing this, that our old man was cruci- ➤
fied with *Him,* that the body of sin might be
done away with, that we should no longer be
slaves of sin.
7 For he who has died has been freed
from sin.
8 Now if we died with Christ, we believe
that we shall also live with Him,
9 knowing that Christ, having been raised
from the dead, dies no more. Death no longer
has dominion over Him.

LIFE LESSONS

➤ 5:8 — *But God demonstrates His own love toward us, in that while we were still sinners, Christ died for us.*

Jesus did not die only for "nice" people. He gave His God-honoring life for our God-dishonoring lives. He did this because of God's amazing love.

➤ 6:2 — *How shall we who died to sin live any longer in it?*

Paul cannot imagine why anyone who genuinely loves Christ would want to live for the very sins that cost Jesus His life. How could any real believer glory in what God abhors?

➤ 6:6 — *. . . our old man was crucified with Him, that the body of sin might be done away with, that we should no longer be slaves of sin.*

Before we came to Christ, sin had a chokehold on our lives, and we could do nothing but serve it as its obedient slaves. Through the death and resurrection of Christ, however, we gain the power to live for God.

10 For *the death* that He died, He died to sin
once for all; but *the life* that He lives, He lives
to God.
➤ 11 Likewise you also, reckon yourselves to be
dead indeed to sin, but alive to God in Christ
Jesus our Lord.
12 Therefore do not let sin reign in your mortal body, that you should obey it in its lusts.
13 And do not present your members *as* instruments of unrighteousness to sin, but
present yourselves to God as being alive from
the dead, and your members *as* instruments
of righteousness to God.
14 For sin shall not have dominion over you,
for you are not under law but under grace.

From Slaves of Sin to Slaves of God

15 What then? Shall we sin because we are
not under law but under grace? Certainly not!
16 Do you not know that to whom you present yourselves slaves to obey, you are that
one's slaves whom you obey, whether of sin
leading to death, or of obedience *leading* to
righteousness?
17 But God be thanked that *though* you were
slaves of sin, yet you obeyed from the heart
that form of doctrine to which you were delivered.
18 And having been set free from sin, you became slaves of righteousness.
19 I speak in human *terms* because of the
weakness of your flesh. For just as you presented your members *as* slaves of uncleanness, and of lawlessness *leading* to *more*
lawlessness, so now present your members *as*
slaves *of* righteousness for holiness.
20 For when you were slaves of sin, you were
free in regard to righteousness.
21 What fruit did you have then in the things
of which you are now ashamed? For the end
of those things *is* death.
22 But now having been set free from sin,
and having become slaves of God, you have
your fruit to holiness, and the end, everlasting
life.
✳ 23 For the wages of sin *is* death, but the gift
of God *is* eternal life in Christ Jesus our Lord.

Freed from the Law

7 Or do you not know, brethren (for I speak
to those who know the law), that the law
has dominion over a man as long as he lives?
2 For the woman who has a husband is
bound by the law to *her* husband as long as he
lives. But if the husband dies, she is released
from the law of *her* husband.
3 So then if, while *her* husband lives, she
marries another man, she will be called an
adulteress; but if her husband dies, she is free
from that law, so that she is no adulteress,
though she has married another man.
4 Therefore, my brethren, you also have become dead to the law through the body of
Christ, that you may be married to another—
to Him who was raised from the dead, that we
should bear fruit to God.
5 For when we were in the flesh, the sinful
passions which were aroused by the law were
at work in our members to bear fruit to death.
6 But now we have been delivered from the
law, having died to what we were held by, so
that we should serve in the newness of the
Spirit and not *in* the oldness of the letter.

Sin's Advantage in the Law

7 What shall we say then? *Is* the law sin?
Certainly not! On the contrary, I would not
have known sin except through the law. For I
would not have known covetousness unless
the law had said, *"You shall not covet."*[a]
8 But sin, taking opportunity by the commandment, produced in me all *manner of evil*
desire. For apart from the law sin *was* dead.
9 I was alive once without the law, but when
the commandment came, sin revived and I
died.
10 And the commandment, which *was* to
bring life, I found to *bring* death.
11 For sin, taking occasion by the commandment, deceived me, and by it killed *me*.
12 Therefore the law *is* holy, and the com- ➤
mandment holy and just and good.

Law Cannot Save from Sin

13 Has then what is good become death to
me? Certainly not! But sin, that it might appear sin, was producing death in me through
what is good, so that sin through the commandment might become exceedingly sinful.
14 For we know that the law is spiritual, but I
am carnal, sold under sin.

7:7 [a]Exodus 20:17; Deuteronomy 5:21

LIFE LESSONS

➤ 6:11 — *Likewise you also, reckon yourselves to be dead indeed to sin, but alive to God in Christ Jesus our Lord.*

One day, the sin that still dwells in our unredeemed bodies will be eradicated. Until then, we are to draw on the power of the Spirit to put to death the sin that still wants to express itself, and obey God for His glory.

➤ 7:12 — *Therefore the law is holy, and the commandment holy and just and good.*

The Word of God reveals to us the character of God—His holiness, righteousness, justice, goodness, kindness, and more. As a reflection of Him, the Word both celebrates His perfect nature and reveals to us our own fallen nature.

ANSWERS TO LIFE'S QUESTIONS

What does it mean to do spiritual battle?

ROM. 7:15–25

The conflict within you between the flesh and the Spirit is a form of spiritual warfare, and you win much of the battle just by realizing that the struggle exists.

Sin is still a powerful force, but it can no longer control you unless you allow it to do so. You are not doomed to failure, and to believe otherwise is to remain in needless, painful bondage. That breaks the heart of the Lord and grieves the Spirit (see Eph. 4:30).

The truth is, you cannot wander too far, fail too many times, or exceed Christ's forgiveness. When you repent and turn to Him, He restores you to fellowship as though nothing had ever happened.

Peter denied Jesus three times, despite his boasts to remain faithful; yet the Lord forgave him and made him a powerful leader in the early church. Peter had learned his lesson well. Though he surely experienced other failures and setbacks, he knew that his Savior remained forever at his side, ready to forgive.

Notice what an older and wiser Peter had to say about God's grace: "His divine power has given to us all things that pertain to life and godliness, through the knowledge of Him who called us by glory and virtue, by which have been given to us exceedingly great and precious promises, that through these you may be partakers of the divine nature, having escaped the corruption that is in the world through lust" (2 Pet. 1:3, 4).

You are on an ever-upward climb to holiness, set apart for God's purposes. As you learn to say no to the power of sin and to rest in His grace, you are made free to obey with renewed vigor and understanding. It is imperative to grasp that obedience is always a choice; you decide whether you will yield to God and so become more like Christ.

You have a great potential to live free and holy through Jesus Christ, but God will never force you to do what He desires. Yet He longs for you to turn to Him in every spiritual conflict, acknowledge your weakness, and ask for His power to say no.

Are you tired of fighting a losing battle? Do you secretly feel like a failure? It's not true! And the sooner you learn to rejoice and grow in the reality of your identity in Him, the sooner you will experience the thrill of victory.

See the Life Principles Index for further study:

24. To live the Christian life is to allow Jesus to live His life in and through us.

15. Brokenness is God's requirement for maximum usefulness.

➤ 15 For what I am doing, I do not understand.
For what I will to do, that I do not practice; but
what I hate, that I do.
16 If, then, I do what I will not to do, I agree
with the law that *it is* good.
17 But now, *it is* no longer I who do it, but sin
that dwells in me.
➤ 18 For I know that in me (that is, in my flesh)
nothing good dwells; for to will is present
with me, but *how* to perform what is good I do
not find.
19 For the good that I will *to do,* I do not
do; but the evil I will not *to do,* that I
practice.
20 Now if I do what I will not *to do,* it is no
longer I who do it, but sin that dwells in me.
21 I find then a law, that evil is present with
me, the one who wills to do good.
22 For I delight in the law of God according
to the inward man.
23 But I see another law in my members,
warring against the law of my mind, and

LIFE LESSONS

➤ 7:15 — *For what I am doing, I do not understand. For what I will to do, that I do not practice; but what I hate, that I do.*

All of us can relate to the fierce internal struggle that Paul describes. Until we stand in Jesus' presence, we will all experience this battle. The only way to win it is by joyfully tapping into the Spirit's overcoming power.

➤ 7:18 — *For I know that in me (that is, in my flesh) nothing good dwells; for to will is present with me, but how to perform what is good I do not find.*

We simply do not have the power by ourselves to do what pleases God. Even the "good things" we do in our own strength make us prideful and dishonoring to God (Is. 64:6).

bringing me into captivity to the law of sin
which is in my members.
24 O wretched man that I am! Who will deliver me from this body of death?
25 I thank God—through Jesus Christ our
Lord! So then, with the mind I myself serve the
law of God, but with the flesh the law of sin.

Free from Indwelling Sin

8 *There is* therefore now no condemnation
to those who are in Christ Jesus,[a] who do
not walk according to the flesh, but according
to the Spirit.
2 For the law of the Spirit of life in Christ Jesus has made me free from the law of sin and
death.
3 For what the law could not do in that it was
weak through the flesh, God *did* by sending
His own Son in the likeness of sinful flesh, on
account of sin: He condemned sin in the flesh,
4 that the righteous requirement of the law
might be fulfilled in us who do not walk according to the flesh but according to the Spirit.
5 For those who live according to the flesh
set their minds on the things of the flesh, but
those *who live* according to the Spirit, the
things of the Spirit.
6 For to be carnally minded *is* death, but to
be spiritually minded *is* life and peace.
7 Because the carnal mind *is* enmity against
God; for it is not subject to the law of God, nor
indeed can be.
8 So then, those who are in the flesh cannot
please God.
9 But you are not in the flesh but in the
Spirit, if indeed the Spirit of God dwells in
you. Now if anyone does not have the Spirit of
Christ, he is not His.
10 And if Christ *is* in you, the body *is* dead
because of sin, but the Spirit *is* life because of
righteousness.
11 But if the Spirit of Him who raised Jesus
from the dead dwells in you, He who raised
Christ from the dead will also give life to your
mortal bodies through His Spirit who dwells
in you.

Sonship Through the Spirit

12 Therefore, brethren, we are debtors—not
to the flesh, to live according to the flesh.
13 For if you live according to the flesh you
will die; but if by the Spirit you put to death
the deeds of the body, you will live.
14 For as many as are led by the Spirit of
God, these are sons of God.
15 For you did not receive the spirit of
bondage again to fear, but you received the
Spirit of adoption by whom we cry out,
"Abba, Father."
16 The Spirit Himself bears witness with our
spirit that we are children of God,
17 and if children, then heirs—heirs of God
and joint heirs with Christ, if indeed we suffer
with *Him*, that we may also be glorified together.

From Suffering to Glory

18 For I consider that the sufferings of this
present time are not worthy *to be compared*
with the glory which shall be revealed in us.
19 For the earnest expectation of the creation
eagerly waits for the revealing of the sons of
God.
20 For the creation was subjected to futility,
not willingly, but because of Him who subjected *it* in hope;
21 because the creation itself also will be delivered from the bondage of corruption into
the glorious liberty of the children of God.
22 For we know that the whole creation
groans and labors with birth pangs together
until now.
23 Not only *that*, but we also who have the
firstfruits of the Spirit, even we ourselves
groan within ourselves, eagerly waiting for
the adoption, the redemption of our body.
24 For we were saved in this hope, but hope
that is seen is not hope; for why does one still
hope for what he sees?
25 But if we hope for what we do not see, we
eagerly wait for *it* with perseverance.
26 Likewise the Spirit also helps in our
weaknesses. For we do not know what we
should pray for as we ought, but the Spirit
Himself makes intercession for us[a] with
groanings which cannot be uttered.

8:1 [a]NU-Text omits the rest of this verse. **8:26** [a]NU-Text omits *for us*.

LIFE LESSONS

➤ 8:8 — *So then, those who are in the flesh cannot please God.*

Since "the flesh" naturally puts itself first and does everything it can to honor itself, nothing done "in the flesh" can honor or please God. We please God only when we depend on Him to do through us what we cannot.

➤ 8:13 — *For if you live according to the flesh you will die; but if by the Spirit you put to death the deeds of the body, you will live.*

Grace does not change the nature of sin; sin leads to death, always. Grace never makes sin less deadly. Instead, grace enables us to rely on the power of the Spirit to put to death our sinful urges and desires.

➤ 8:18 — *For I consider that the sufferings of this present time are not worthy to be compared with the glory which shall be revealed in us.*

The Bible never minimizes our difficulties or sufferings; instead, it magnifies the rewards that accompany our faith. It doesn't say, "you don't really hurt," but instead declares, "you'll feel far better than you ever have."

ANSWERS TO LIFE'S QUESTIONS

What does it mean to be conformed to the truth?

ROM. 8:29

Paul wrote that the Lord has predestined us "to be conformed to the image of His Son" (Rom. 8:29)—but just *how* is God going to accomplish such a job?

Answer: by revealing the truth of His likeness.

As the truth confronts us, we can do one of two things: Either we can refuse to be pushed into God's mold, or we can yield to Him and be fashioned into His likeness.

I once preached a series of sermons, "How the Truth Can Set You Free." Week after week, people would say to me, "I want to tell you how the Lord has set me free. Last week's message changed my life." After they walked away, I would often think, *God, what about me? I'm the one who told them.* I knew I was not living as free as God wanted me to. After months of seeing other lives changed, God finally changed my own life in a remarkable way.

I learned that I had to *listen in order to comprehend* and to *comprehend in order to be conformed to His truth.* God never speaks in order to entertain us; God speaks that we may be made like Jesus. James says, "For if anyone is a hearer of the word and not a doer, he is like a man observing his natural face in a mirror; for he observes himself, goes away, and immediately forgets what kind of man he was" (1:23, 24). Obedience must accompany understanding. We are either in the process of resisting God's truth or in the process of being shaped by His truth.

After spending several years with Paul, Timothy, the apostle's protégé, began shepherding the work of the gospel in Ephesus and Asia Minor. As he labored there Paul wrote to him, "Let no one despise your youth, but be an example to the believers in word, in conduct, in love, in spirit, in faith, in purity" (1 Tim. 4:12).

In the Second Epistle to Timothy, Paul penned these words: "I call to remembrance the genuine faith that is in you, which dwelt first in your grandmother Lois and your mother Eunice, and I am persuaded is in you also" (2 Tim. 1:5).

Timothy didn't just *know* the truth; he allowed its power to transform him in such a way that his life became a constant example of godliness. How? Through the unfolding ministry of God's Word.

See the Life Principles Index for further study:
2. *Obey God and leave all the consequences to Him.*
3. *God's Word is an immovable anchor in times of storm.*

27 Now He who searches the hearts knows
what the mind of the Spirit *is,* because He
makes intercession for the saints according to
the will of God.
➤ 28 And we know that all things work together for good to those who love God, to
those who are the called according to *His*
purpose.
29 For whom He foreknew, He also predestined *to be* conformed to the image of His
Son, that He might be the firstborn among
many brethren.
30 Moreover whom He predestined, these He
also called; whom He called, these He also
justified; and whom He justified, these He
also glorified.

God's Everlasting Love

31 What then shall we say to these things? If ◄
God *is* for us, who *can be* against us?

LIFE LESSONS

➤ 8:28 — *And we know that all things work together for good to those who love God, to those who are the called according to His purpose.*

On this side of heaven we will never understand *how* "all things" can work together for good for God's children—certainly, not all things in themselves are good—but God knows how He'll do it. And in Him we trust.

➤ 8:31 — *If God is for us, who can be against us?*

All kinds of people can "be against us," causing us trouble and pain and sorrow. But nothing can ultimately triumph over us. God wins, and in Christ, we win with Him.

32 He who did not spare His own Son, but delivered Him up for us all, how shall He not
with Him also freely give us all things?
33 Who shall bring a charge against God's
elect? *It is* God who justifies.
34 Who *is* he who condemns? *It is* Christ who
died, and furthermore is also risen, who is
even at the right hand of God, who also
makes intercession for us.
35 Who shall separate us from the love of
Christ? *Shall* tribulation, or distress, or persecution, or famine, or nakedness, or peril, or
sword?
36 As it is written:

"For Your sake we are killed all day long;
We are accounted as sheep for the
slaughter."[a]

37 Yet in all these things we are more than
conquerors through Him who loved us.
38 For I am persuaded that neither death nor
life, nor angels nor principalities nor powers,
nor things present nor things to come,
39 nor height nor depth, nor any other created
thing, shall be able to separate us from the
love of God which is in Christ Jesus our Lord.

Israel's Rejection of Christ

9 I tell the truth in Christ, I am not lying, my
conscience also bearing me witness in the
Holy Spirit,
2 that I have great sorrow and continual
grief in my heart.
3 For I could wish that I myself were accursed from Christ for my brethren, my countrymen[a] according to the flesh,
4 who are Israelites, to whom *pertain* the
adoption, the glory, the covenants, the giving of
the law, the service *of God,* and the promises;
5 of whom *are* the fathers and from whom,
according to the flesh, Christ *came,* who is
over all, *the* eternally blessed God. Amen.

Israel's Rejection and God's Purpose

6 But it is not that the word of God has
taken no effect. For they *are* not all Israel who
are of Israel,
7 nor *are they* all children because they are
the seed of Abraham; but, *"In Isaac your seed
shall be called."*[a]
8 That is, those who *are* the children of the
flesh, these *are* not the children of God; but
the children of the promise are counted as the
seed.
9 For this *is* the word of promise: *"At this
time I will come and Sarah shall have a son."*[a]
10 And not only *this,* but when Rebecca also
had conceived by one man, *even* by our father
Isaac
11 (for *the children* not yet being born, nor
having done any good or evil, that the purpose of God according to election might
stand, not of works but of Him who calls),
12 it was said to her, *"The older shall serve
the younger."*[a]
13 As it is written, *"Jacob I have loved, but
Esau I have hated."*[a]

Israel's Rejection and God's Justice

14 What shall we say then? *Is there* unrighteousness with God? Certainly not!
15 For He says to Moses, *"I will have mercy
on whomever I will have mercy, and I will
have compassion on whomever I will have
compassion."*[a]
16 So then *it is* not of him who wills, nor of
him who runs, but of God who shows mercy.
17 For the Scripture says to the Pharaoh, *"For
this very purpose I have raised you up, that I
may show My power in you, and that My
name may be declared in all the earth."*[a]
18 Therefore He has mercy on whom He
wills, and whom He wills He hardens.
19 You will say to me then, "Why does He still
find fault? For who has resisted His will?"
20 But indeed, O man, who are you to reply
against God? Will the thing formed say to him
who formed *it,* "Why have you made me like
this?"
21 Does not the potter have power over the

8:36 [a]Psalm 44:22 **9:3** [a]Or *relatives* **9:7** [a]Genesis 21:12
9:9 [a]Genesis 18:10, 14 **9:12** [a]Genesis 25:23
9:13 [a]Malachi 1:2, 3 **9:15** [a]Exodus 33:19 **9:17** [a]Exodus 9:16

LIFE LESSONS

➤ 8:39 — *. . . nor height nor depth, nor any other created thing, shall be able to separate us from the love of God which is in Christ Jesus our Lord.*

Once God sets His love on us and we accept His love through faith in Jesus, *nothing* can ever break the bonds of love that He creates: ". . . no one is able to snatch them out of My Father's hand" (John 10:29).

➤ 9:3 — *For I could wish that I myself were accursed from Christ for my brethren, my countrymen according to the flesh . . . .*

Despite his frequent ill-treatment at the hands of his Jewish countrymen, Paul had an intense desire that they come to faith in Christ and so experience the new life available in Him. How badly do *we* want people to know Jesus?

➤ 9:15 — *For He says to Moses, "I will have mercy on whomever I will have mercy, and I will have compassion on whomever I will have compassion."*

God blesses people with His grace and mercy, not because they deserve it but because it is God's nature to give grace and mercy. Neither grace nor mercy can be demanded; they can only be gratefully accepted.

clay, from the same lump to make one vessel for honor and another for dishonor?
22 *What* if God, wanting to show *His* wrath and to make His power known, endured with much longsuffering the vessels of wrath prepared for destruction,
23 and that He might make known the riches of His glory on the vessels of mercy, which He had prepared beforehand for glory,
24 even us whom He called, not of the Jews only, but also of the Gentiles?
25 As He says also in Hosea:

"I will call them My people, who were not
My people,
And her beloved, who was not beloved."[a]
26*"And it shall come to pass in the place*
where it was said to them,
'You are not My people,'
There they shall be called sons of the
living God."[a]

➤ 27 Isaiah also cries out concerning Israel:[a]

"Though the number of the children of
Israel be as the sand of the sea,
The remnant will be saved.
28 *For He will finish the work and cut it*
short in righteousness,
Because the LORD will make a short work
upon the earth."[a]

29 And as Isaiah said before:

"Unless the LORD of Sabaoth[a] *had left us a*
seed,
We would have become like Sodom,
And we would have been made like
Gomorrah."[b]

Present Condition of Israel

30 What shall we say then? That Gentiles, who did not pursue righteousness, have attained to righteousness, even the righteousness of faith;
31 but Israel, pursuing the law of righteousness, has not attained to the law of righteousness.[a]
32 Why? Because *they did* not *seek it* by faith, but as it were, by the works of the law.[a] For they stumbled at that stumbling stone.
33 As it is written:

"Behold, I lay in Zion a stumbling stone
and rock of offense,
And whoever believes on Him will not be
put to shame."[a]

Israel Needs the Gospel

10 Brethren, my heart's desire and prayer to God for Israel[a] is that they may be saved.
2 For I bear them witness that they have a zeal for God, but not according to knowledge.
3 For they being ignorant of God's righteousness, and seeking to establish their own righteousness, have not submitted to the righteousness of God.
4 For Christ *is* the end of the law for righteousness to everyone who believes.
5 For Moses writes about the righteousness which is of the law, *"The man who does those things shall live by them."*[a]
6 But the righteousness of faith speaks in this way, *"Do not say in your heart, 'Who will ascend into heaven?'"*[a] (that is, to bring Christ down *from above*)
7 or, *"'Who will descend into the abyss?'"*[a] (that is, to bring Christ up from the dead).
8 But what does it say? *"The word is near you, in your mouth and in your heart"*[a] (that is, the word of faith which we preach):
9 that if you confess with your mouth the Lord Jesus and believe in your heart that God has raised Him from the dead, you will be saved.
10 For with the heart one believes unto righteousness, and with the mouth confession is made unto salvation.
11 For the Scripture says, *"Whoever believes on Him will not be put to shame."*[a]

9:25 [a]Hosea 2:23 **9:26** [a]Hosea 1:10 **9:27** [a]Isaiah 10:22, 23
9:28 [a]NU-Text reads *For the LORD will finish the work and cut it short upon the earth.* **9:29** [a]Literally, in Hebrew, *Hosts*
[b]Isaiah 1:9 **9:31** [a]NU-Text omits *of righteousness.*
9:32 [a]NU-Text reads *by works.* **9:33** [a]Isaiah 8:14; 28:16
10:1 [a]NU-Text reads *them.* **10:5** [a]Leviticus 18:5
10:6 [a]Deuteronomy 30:12 **10:7** [a]Deuteronomy 30:13
10:8 [a]Deuteronomy 30:14 **10:11** [a]Isaiah 28:16

LIFE LESSONS

➤ 9:27 — *Isaiah also cries out concerning Israel: "Though the number of the children of Israel be as the sand of the sea, the remnant will be saved."*

The idea of the remnant appears throughout Scripture (see 2 Kin. 19:30, 31; Ezra 9:8; Is.10:20, etc.). In His grace, God preserves a small portion of His people Israel until the day He rescues them all.

➤ 10:4 — *For Christ is the end of the law for righteousness to everyone who believes.*

When we place our faith in Christ, God looks at us just as He looks at Jesus, who completely obeyed the whole law, without exception and without fault. The perfect record of Christ becomes ours through faith.

➤ 10:11, 13 — *For the Scripture says, "Whoever believes on Him will not be put to shame." . . . For "whoever calls on the name of the LORD shall be saved."*

God never offers salvation to someone and then pulls the rug out from under him when he tries to accept the gracious offer. *Anyone* who puts their faith in Christ *will* be saved and *will* receive eternal life.

12 For there is no distinction between Jew
and Greek, for the same Lord over all is rich
to all who call upon Him.
13 For *"whoever calls on the name of the*
LORD shall be saved."[a]

Israel Rejects the Gospel

14 How then shall they call on Him in whom
they have not believed? And how shall they
believe in Him of whom they have not heard?
And how shall they hear without a preacher?
15 And how shall they preach unless they are
sent? As it is written:

"How beautiful are the feet of those who
preach the gospel of peace,[a]
Who bring glad tidings of good things!"[b]

16 But they have not all obeyed the gospel.
For Isaiah says, *"LORD, who has believed our*
report?"[a]
➤ 17 So then faith *comes* by hearing, and hearing by the word of God.
18 But I say, have they not heard? Yes indeed:

"Their sound has gone out to all the earth,
And their words to the ends of the
world."[a]

19 But I say, did Israel not know? First Moses
says:

"I will provoke you to jealousy by those
who are not a nation,
I will move you to anger by a foolish
nation."[a]

20 But Isaiah is very bold and says:

"I was found by those who did not seek
Me;
I was made manifest to those who did
not ask for Me."[a]

21 But to Israel he says:

"All day long I have stretched out My
hands
To a disobedient and contrary people."[a]

Israel's Rejection Not Total

11 I say then, has God cast away His
people? Certainly not! For I also am an
Israelite, of the seed of Abraham, *of* the tribe
of Benjamin.
2 God has not cast away His people whom
He foreknew. Or do you not know what the
Scripture says of Elijah, how he pleads with
God against Israel, saying,
3 *"LORD, they have killed Your prophets*
and torn down Your altars, and I alone am
left, and they seek my life"?[a]
4 But what does the divine response say to
him? *"I have reserved for Myself seven thou-*
sand men who have not bowed the knee to
Baal."[a]
5 Even so then, at this present time there is
a remnant according to the election of grace.
6 And if by grace, then *it is* no longer of
works; otherwise grace is no longer grace.[a]
But if *it is* of works, it is no longer grace; otherwise work is no longer work.
7 What then? Israel has not obtained what it
seeks; but the elect have obtained it, and the
rest were blinded.
8 Just as it is written:

"God has given them a spirit of stupor,
Eyes that they should not see
And ears that they should not hear,
To this very day."[a]

9 And David says:

"Let their table become a snare and a
trap,
A stumbling block and a recompense to
them.
10 *Let their eyes be darkened, so that they*
do not see,
And bow down their back always."[a]

Israel's Rejection Not Final

11 I say then, have they stumbled that they
should fall? Certainly not! But through their
fall, to provoke them to jealousy, salvation
has come to the Gentiles.
12 Now if their fall *is* riches for the world,
and their failure riches for the Gentiles, how
much more their fullness!
13 For I speak to you Gentiles; inasmuch as I
am an apostle to the Gentiles, I magnify my
ministry,
14 if by any means I may provoke to jealousy
those who are my flesh and save some of
them.
15 For if their being cast away *is* the reconciling of the world, what *will* their acceptance
be but life from the dead?
16 For if the firstfruit *is* holy, the lump *is* also

10:13 [a]Joel 2:32 **10:15** [a]NU-Text omits *preach the gospel of peace, Who.* [b]Isaiah 52:7; Nahum 1:15 **10:16** [a]Isaiah 53:1 **10:18** [a]Psalm 19:4 **10:19** [a]Deuteronomy 32:21 **10:20** [a]Isaiah 65:1 **10:21** [a]Isaiah 65:2 **11:3** [a]1 Kings 19:10, 14 **11:4** [a]1 Kings 19:18 **11:6** [a]NU-Text omits the rest of this verse. **11:8** [a]Deuteronomy 29:4; Isaiah 29:10 **11:10** [a]Psalm 69:22, 23

LIFE LESSONS

➤ ***10:17 — So then faith comes by hearing, and hearing by the word of God.***

Everything that we need to know in regard to salvation—what it is, why we need it, how we can receive it—can be found in God's Word. God blesses us when we hear His promises and respond in faith to them.

holy; and if the root *is* holy, so *are* the
branches.
17 And if some of the branches were broken
off, and you, being a wild olive tree, were
grafted in among them, and with them became a partaker of the root and fatness of the
olive tree,
18 do not boast against the branches. But if
you do boast, *remember that* you do not support the root, but the root *supports* you.
19 You will say then, "Branches were broken
off that I might be grafted in."
20 Well *said.* Because of unbelief they were
broken off, and you stand by faith. Do not be
haughty, but fear.
21 For if God did not spare the natural
branches, He may not spare you either.
22 Therefore consider the goodness and
severity of God: on those who fell, severity;
but toward you, goodness,[a] if you continue in
His goodness. Otherwise you also will be cut
off.
23 And they also, if they do not continue in
unbelief, will be grafted in, for God is able to
graft them in again.
24 For if you were cut out of the olive tree
which is wild by nature, and were grafted
contrary to nature into a cultivated olive tree,
how much more will these, who *are* natural
branches, be grafted into their own olive tree?
25 For I do not desire, brethren, that you
should be ignorant of this mystery, lest you
should be wise in your own opinion, that
blindness in part has happened to Israel until
the fullness of the Gentiles has come in.
26 And so all Israel will be saved,[a] as it is
written:

"The Deliverer will come out of Zion,
And He will turn away ungodliness from
Jacob;
27 *For this is My covenant with them,*
When I take away their sins."[a]

28 Concerning the gospel *they are* enemies
for your sake, but concerning the election
they are beloved for the sake of the fathers.
29 For the gifts and the calling of God *are* irrevocable.
30 For as you were once disobedient to God,
yet have now obtained mercy through their
disobedience,
31 even so these also have now been disobedient, that through the mercy shown you they
also may obtain mercy.
32 For God has committed them all to disobedience, that He might have mercy on all.
33 Oh, the depth of the riches both of the wisdom and knowledge of God! How unsearchable *are* His judgments and His ways past
finding out!

34 *"For who has known the mind of the*
LORD?
Or who has become His counselor?"[a]
35 *"Or who has first given to Him*
And it shall be repaid to him?"[a]

36 For of Him and through Him and to Him
are all things, to whom *be* glory forever.
Amen.

Living Sacrifices to God

12 I beseech you therefore, brethren, by
the mercies of God, that you present
your bodies a living sacrifice, holy, acceptable
to God, *which is* your reasonable service.
2 And do not be conformed to this world,
but be transformed by the renewing of your

11:22 [a]NU-Text adds *of God.* **11:26** [a]Or *delivered*
11:27 [a]Isaiah 59:20, 21 **11:34** [a]Isaiah 40:13; Jeremiah 23:18
11:35 [a]Job 41:11

LIFE LESSONS

➤ 11:22 — *Therefore consider the goodness and severity of God . . . .*

Paul urges us to remember that God is loving and holy, gracious and just, patient and faithful to *all* of His Word. "Knowing, therefore, the terror of the Lord, we persuade men . . . ." (2 Cor. 5:11).

➤ 11:29 — *For the gifts and the calling of God are irrevocable.*

Once you have placed your faith in Him, God will never cast you away. He will never abandon you, reject you, or turn you away. As a loving Father He will discipline you, but He will never throw you away.

➤ 11:33 — *Oh, the depth of the riches both of the wisdom and knowledge of God! How unsearchable are His judgments and His ways past finding out!*

We will never completely understand God's ways or grasp why He does what He does, but we *can* worship Him for the goodness and love and mercy that He has already shown us!

➤ 12:1 — *I beseech you therefore, brethren, by the mercies of God, that you present your bodies a living sacrifice, holy, acceptable to God, which is your reasonable service.*

Paul encourages us to imagine that we bring our bodies to God each day, lay them on the altar before His presence, and ask Him to use this "sacrifice" for His glory and the good of His people. It's only "reasonable"!

➤ 12:2 — *And do not be conformed to this world, but be transformed by the renewing of your mind, that you may prove what is that good and acceptable and perfect will of God.*

God does not want us to try hard to sin less, but to depend upon His Spirit to be transformed into people who love to please God through willing obedience. That transformation begins with the mind.

mind, that you may prove what *is* that good
and acceptable and perfect will of God.

Serve God with Spiritual Gifts

3 For I say, through the grace given to me, to
everyone who is among you, not to think *of
himself* more highly than he ought to think,
but to think soberly, as God has dealt to each
one a measure of faith.
4 For as we have many members in one
body, but all the members do not have the
same function,
➤ 5 so we, *being* many, are one body in Christ,
and individually members of one another.
6 Having then gifts differing according to
the grace that is given to us, *let us use them:*
if prophecy, *let us prophesy* in proportion to
our faith;
7 or ministry, *let us use it* in *our* ministering;
he who teaches, in teaching;
8 he who exhorts, in exhortation; he who
gives, with liberality; he who leads, with
diligence; he who shows mercy, with cheerfulness.

Behave Like a Christian

9 *Let* love *be* without hypocrisy. Abhor what
is evil. Cling to what is good.
10 *Be* kindly affectionate to one another with
brotherly love, in honor giving preference to
one another;
11 not lagging in diligence, fervent in spirit,
serving the Lord;
12 rejoicing in hope, patient in tribulation,
continuing steadfastly in prayer;
13 distributing to the needs of the saints,
given to hospitality.
14 Bless those who persecute you; bless and
do not curse.
➤ 15 Rejoice with those who rejoice, and weep
with those who weep.
16 Be of the same mind toward one another.
Do not set your mind on high things, but associate with the humble. Do not be wise in
your own opinion.
17 Repay no one evil for evil. Have regard for
good things in the sight of all men.
18 If it is possible, as much as depends on
you, live peaceably with all men.
19 Beloved, do not avenge yourselves, but
rather give place to wrath; for it is written,
"Vengeance is Mine, I will repay,"[a] says the
Lord.
20 Therefore

"If your enemy is hungry, feed him;
If he is thirsty, give him a drink;
For in so doing you will heap coals of
fire on his head."[a]

21 Do not be overcome by evil, but overcome
evil with good.

Submit to Government

13 Let every soul be subject to the govern- ➤
ing authorities. For there is no authority except from God, and the authorities that
exist are appointed by God.
2 Therefore whoever resists the authority
resists the ordinance of God, and those who
resist will bring judgment on themselves.
3 For rulers are not a terror to good works,
but to evil. Do you want to be unafraid of the
authority? Do what is good, and you will have
praise from the same.
4 For he is God's minister to you for good.
But if you do evil, be afraid; for he does not
bear the sword in vain; for he is God's minister, an avenger to *execute* wrath on him who
practices evil.
5 Therefore *you* must be subject, not only
because of wrath but also for conscience'
sake.
6 For because of this you also pay taxes, for
they are God's ministers attending continually to this very thing.
7 Render therefore to all their due: taxes to
whom taxes *are due,* customs to whom customs, fear to whom fear, honor to whom
honor.

Love Your Neighbor

8 Owe no one anything except to love one
another, for he who loves another has fulfilled
the law.
9 For the commandments, *"You shall not*

12:19 [a]Deuteronomy 32:35 **12:20** [a]Proverbs 25:21, 22

LIFE LESSONS

➤ 12:5 — *. . . so we, being many, are one body in Christ, and individually members of one another.*

God is never pleased when someone says, "I love Jesus, but I don't need the church." Jesus died to create the church, so to demean His beloved creation is to demean both Him and His work.

➤ 12:15 — *Rejoice with those who rejoice, and weep with those who weep.*

Both rejoicing and weeping imply genuine, heartfelt emotion. This kind of keenly felt connection happens only when we choose to get deeply involved in the lives of other believers.

➤ 13:1 — *Let every soul be subject to the governing authorities. For there is no authority except from God, and the authorities that exist are appointed by God.*

Joseph submitted to the Egyptian authorities; Daniel submitted to the Babylonian authorities; Mordecai submitted to the Persian authorities; Jesus submitted to the Roman authorities. While none of these regimes were godly, God had authorized them all.

commit adultery," "You shall not murder,"
"You shall not steal," "You shall not bear
false witness,"[a] *"You shall not covet,"*[b] and if
there is any other commandment, are *all*
summed up in this saying, namely, *"You shall*
love your neighbor as yourself."[c]
➤ 10 Love does no harm to a neighbor; therefore love *is* the fulfillment of the law.

Put on Christ

11 And *do* this, knowing the time, that now *it*
is high time to awake out of sleep; for now our
salvation *is* nearer than when we *first* believed.
12 The night is far spent, the day is at hand.
Therefore let us cast off the works of darkness, and let us put on the armor of light.
13 Let us walk properly, as in the day, not in
revelry and drunkenness, not in lewdness and
lust, not in strife and envy.
➤ 14 But put on the Lord Jesus Christ, and
make no provision for the flesh, to *fulfill its*
lusts.

The Law of Liberty

14 Receive one who is weak in the faith,
but not to disputes over doubtful
things.
2 For one believes he may eat all things, but
he who is weak eats *only* vegetables.
3 Let not him who eats despise him who
does not eat, and let not him who does not eat
judge him who eats; for God has received
him.
4 Who are you to judge another's servant?
To his own master he stands or falls. Indeed,
he will be made to stand, for God is able to
make him stand.
➤ 5 One person esteems *one* day above another; another esteems every day *alike.* Let
each be fully convinced in his own mind.
6 He who observes the day, observes *it* to
the Lord;[a] and he who does not observe the
day, to the Lord he does not observe *it.* He
who eats, eats to the Lord, for he gives God
thanks; and he who does not eat, to the Lord
he does not eat, and gives God thanks.
7 For none of us lives to himself, and no one
dies to himself.
8 For if we live, we live to the Lord; and if we ➤
die, we die to the Lord. Therefore, whether we
live or die, we are the Lord's.
9 For to this end Christ died and rose[a] and
lived again, that He might be Lord of both the
dead and the living.
10 But why do you judge your brother? Or
why do you show contempt for your brother?
For we shall all stand before the judgment
seat of Christ.[a]
11 For it is written:

> *"As I live, says the LORD,*
> *Every knee shall bow to Me,*
> *And every tongue shall confess to God."*[a]

12 So then each of us shall give account of ➤
himself to God.
13 Therefore let us not judge one another
anymore, but rather resolve this, not to put a
stumbling block or a cause to fall in *our*
brother's way.

The Law of Love

14 I know and am convinced by the Lord Jesus that *there is* nothing unclean of itself; but
to him who considers anything to be unclean,
to him *it is* unclean.
15 Yet if your brother is grieved because of
your food, you are no longer walking in love.
Do not destroy with your food the one for
whom Christ died.
16 Therefore do not let your good be spoken
of as evil;

13:9 [a]NU-Text omits *"You shall not bear false witness."* [b]*Exodus 20:13–15, 17; Deuteronomy 5:17–19, 21* [c]*Leviticus 19:18* **14:6** [a]NU-Text omits the rest of this sentence. **14:9** [a]NU-Text omits *and rose.* **14:10** [a]NU-Text reads *of God.* **14:11** [a]*Isaiah 45:23*

LIFE LESSONS

➤ 13:10 — *Love does no harm to a neighbor; therefore love is the fulfillment of the law.*

God is love, and the law reflects God's character; therefore love is the fulfillment of the law. Obedience is never about slavishly following rules, but always about eagerly pleasing a loving God.

➤ 13:14 — *But put on the Lord Jesus Christ, and make no provision for the flesh, to fulfill its lusts.*

We know we should avoid a certain place, but we go there anyway. We recognize a personal weakness for a particular activity, but we tempt ourselves anyway. How often do we fall into sin because we plan for it?

➤ 14:5 — *One person esteems one day above another; another esteems every day alike. Let each be fully convinced in his own mind.*

God wants us to learn how to live by faith, and that means He doesn't give us a thick rulebook that answers all our questions. He wants us to develop personal convictions based on our ongoing relationship with Him.

➤ 14:8 — *For if we live, we live to the Lord; and if we die, we die to the Lord. Therefore, whether we live or die, we are the Lord's.*

Everything we do should reflect well on the Savior who bought us with His own blood. Even the way we die should witness to the goodness of Jesus Christ. Every moment of every day we belong to Him.

➤ 14:12 — *So then each of us shall give account of himself to God.*

What sort of account would you have to give to Jesus of the way you lived this past week? What would you tell Him about the way you lived today? Would He be happy about your plans for tomorrow?

17 for the kingdom of God is not eating and
drinking, but righteousness and peace and
joy in the Holy Spirit.
18 For he who serves Christ in these things[a]
is acceptable to God and approved by men.
19 Therefore let us pursue the things *which*
make for peace and the things by which one
may edify another.
20 Do not destroy the work of God for the
sake of food. All things indeed *are* pure, but *it*
is evil for the man who eats with offense.
21 *It is* good neither to eat meat nor drink
wine nor *do anything* by which your brother
stumbles or is offended or is made weak.[a]
22 Do you have faith? Have[a] *it* to yourself before God. Happy *is* he who does not condemn
himself in what he approves.
➤ 23 But he who doubts is condemned if he
eats, because *he does* not *eat* from faith; for
whatever *is* not from faith is sin.[a]

Bearing Others' Burdens

15 We then who are strong ought to bear
with the scruples of the weak, and not
to please ourselves.
➤ 2 Let each of us please *his* neighbor for *his*
good, leading to edification.
3 For even Christ did not please Himself; but
as it is written, *"The reproaches of those who*
reproached You fell on Me."[a]
4 For whatever things were written before
were written for our learning, that we
through the patience and comfort of the
Scriptures might have hope.
5 Now may the God of patience and comfort
grant you to be like-minded toward one another, according to Christ Jesus,
6 that you may with one mind *and* one
mouth glorify the God and Father of our Lord
Jesus Christ.

Glorify God Together

7 Therefore receive one another, just as
Christ also received us,[a] to the glory of God.
8 Now I say that Jesus Christ has become a
servant to the circumcision for the truth of
God, to confirm the promises *made* to the fathers,
9 and that the Gentiles might glorify God
for *His* mercy, as it is written:

"For this reason I will confess to You
among the Gentiles,
And sing to Your name."[a]

10 And again he says:

"Rejoice, O Gentiles, with His people!"[a]

11 And again:

"Praise the LORD, all you Gentiles!
Laud Him, all you peoples!"[a]

12 And again, Isaiah says:

"There shall be a root of Jesse;
And He who shall rise to reign over the
Gentiles,
In Him the Gentiles shall hope."[a]

13 Now may the God of hope fill you with all ➤
joy and peace in believing, that you may
abound in hope by the power of the Holy Spirit.

From Jerusalem to Illyricum

14 Now I myself am confident concerning
you, my brethren, that you also are full of
goodness, filled with all knowledge, able also
to admonish one another.[a]
15 Nevertheless, brethren, I have written
more boldly to you on *some* points, as reminding you, because of the grace given to
me by God,
16 that I might be a minister of Jesus Christ
to the Gentiles, ministering the gospel of God,
that the offering of the Gentiles might be
acceptable, sanctified by the Holy Spirit.
17 Therefore I have reason to glory in Christ
Jesus in the things *which pertain* to God.
18 For I will not dare to speak of any of those
things which Christ has not accomplished
through me, in word and deed, to make the
Gentiles obedient—
19 in mighty signs and wonders, by the
power of the Spirit of God, so that from Jeru-

14:18 [a]NU-Text reads *this.* **14:21** [a]NU-Text omits *or is offended or is made weak.* **14:22** [a]NU-Text reads *The faith which you have—have.* **14:23** [a]M-Text puts Romans 16:25–27 here.
15:3 [a]Psalm 69:9 **15:7** [a]NU-Text and M-Text read *you.*
15:9 [a]2 Samuel 22:50; Psalm 18:49 **15:10** [a]Deuteronomy 32:43
15:11 [a]Psalm 117:1 **15:12** [a]Isaiah 11:10 **15:14** [a]M-Text reads *others.*

LIFE LESSONS

➤ 14:23 — *. . . for whatever is not from faith is sin.*

We are to live our whole lives relying on the power of grace as it comes to us through faith. If we are not sure that something we would like to do honors God—if we cannot do it in faith—then we should refrain.

➤ 15:2 — *Let each of us please his neighbor for his good, leading to edification.*

If we are serious about our Christian faith, we *have* to take into consideration how our actions affect others. We cannot grow in faith in isolation from others, and in our interactions with others we should have edification in mind.

➤ 15:13 — *Now may the God of hope fill you with all joy and peace in believing, that you may abound in hope by the power of the Holy Spirit.*

The normal Christian life is to be characterized by hope, joy, and peace. As we grow in grace, God wants us to experience more and more of each of them—and if they're lacking, something has gone wrong.

salem and round about to Illyricum I have
fully preached the gospel of Christ.
20 And so I have made it my aim to preach
the gospel, not where Christ was named, lest
I should build on another man's foundation,
21 but as it is written:

"To whom He was not announced, they
shall see;
And those who have not heard shall
understand."[a]

Plan to Visit Rome

22 For this reason I also have been much hindered from coming to you.
23 But now no longer having a place in these
parts, and having a great desire these many
years to come to you,
24 whenever I journey to Spain, I shall come
to you.[a] For I hope to see you on my journey,
and to be helped on my way there by you, if
first I may enjoy your *company* for a while.
25 But now I am going to Jerusalem to minister to the saints.
26 For it pleased those from Macedonia and
Achaia to make a certain contribution for the
poor among the saints who are in Jerusalem.
27 It pleased them indeed, and they are their
debtors. For if the Gentiles have been partakers of their spiritual things, their duty is also
to minister to them in material things.
28 Therefore, when I have performed this
and have sealed to them this fruit, I shall go
by way of you to Spain.
29 But I know that when I come to you, I shall
come in the fullness of the blessing of the
gospel[a] of Christ.
➤ 30 Now I beg you, brethren, through the Lord
Jesus Christ, and through the love of the
Spirit, that you strive together with me in
prayers to God for me,
31 that I may be delivered from those in
Judea who do not believe, and that my service
for Jerusalem may be acceptable to the saints,
32 that I may come to you with joy by the will
of God, and may be refreshed together with
you.
33 Now the God of peace *be* with you all.
Amen.

Sister Phoebe Commended

16 I commend to you Phoebe our sister,
who is a servant of the church in
Cenchrea,
2 that you may receive her in the Lord in a
manner worthy of the saints, and assist her in
whatever business she has need of you; for indeed she has been a helper of many and of
myself also.

Greeting Roman Saints

3 Greet Priscilla and Aquila, my fellow
workers in Christ Jesus,
4 who risked their own necks for my life, to
whom not only I give thanks, but also all the
churches of the Gentiles.
5 Likewise *greet* the church that is in their
house.Greet my beloved Epaenetus, who is
the firstfruits of Achaia[a] to Christ.
6 Greet Mary, who labored much for us.
7 Greet Andronicus and Junia, my countrymen and my fellow prisoners, who are of note
among the apostles, who also were in Christ
before me.
8 Greet Amplias, my beloved in the Lord.
9 Greet Urbanus, our fellow worker in
Christ, and Stachys, my beloved.
10 Greet Apelles, approved in Christ. Greet
those who are of the *household* of Aristo-
bulus.
11 Greet Herodion, my countryman.[a] Greet
those who are of the *household* of Narcissus
who are in the Lord.
12 Greet Tryphena and Tryphosa, who have
labored in the Lord. Greet the beloved Persis,
who labored much in the Lord.
13 Greet Rufus, chosen in the Lord, and his
mother and mine.
14 Greet Asyncritus, Phlegon, Hermas, Pa-
trobas, Hermes, and the brethren who are
with them.
15 Greet Philologus and Julia, Nereus and his
sister, and Olympas, and all the saints who
are with them.
16 Greet one another with a holy kiss. The[a]
churches of Christ greet you.

Avoid Divisive Persons

17 Now I urge you, brethren, note those who ➤
cause divisions and offenses, contrary to the
doctrine which you learned, and avoid them.

15:21 [a]Isaiah 52:15 **15:24** [a]NU-Text omits *I shall come to you* (and joins *Spain* with the next sentence). **15:29** [a]NU-Text omits *of the gospel.* **16:5** [a]NU-Text reads *Asia.* **16:11** [a]Or *relative* **16:16** [a]NU-Text reads *All the churches.*

LIFE LESSONS

➤ 15:30 — *Now I beg you, brethren, through the Lord Jesus Christ, and through the love of the Spirit, that you strive together with me in prayers to God for me . . . .*

God loves to answer the faithful prayers of believers that are offered on behalf of other believers. Paul, the great apostle, frequently asked others to pray for him. God wants us praying regularly for each other.

➤ 16:17 — *Now I urge you, brethren, note those who cause divisions and offenses, contrary to the doctrine which you learned, and avoid them.*

Division is a sure mark of the evil one. Factions and schisms and rancor and bitter interactions all point to the activity of Satan. God calls His people to unity to demonstrate His love to the world.

18 For those who are such do not serve our
Lord Jesus[a] Christ, but their own belly, and by
smooth words and flattering speech deceive
the hearts of the simple.
➤ 19 For your obedience has become known to
all. Therefore I am glad on your behalf; but I
want you to be wise in what is good, and simple concerning evil.
✳ 20 And the God of peace will crush Satan
under your feet shortly.The grace of our Lord
Jesus Christ *be* with you. Amen.

Greetings from Paul's Friends

21 Timothy, my fellow worker, and Lucius,
Jason, and Sosipater, my countrymen, greet
you.
22 I, Tertius, who wrote *this* epistle, greet you
in the Lord.
23 Gaius, my host and *the host* of the whole
church, greets you. Erastus, the treasurer
of the city, greets you, and Quartus, a
brother.
24 The grace of our Lord Jesus Christ *be* with
you all. Amen.[a]

Benediction

25 Now to Him who is able to establish you ➤
according to my gospel and the preaching of
Jesus Christ, according to the revelation of
the mystery kept secret since the world began
26 but now made manifest, and by the
prophetic Scriptures made known to all nations, according to the commandment of the
everlasting God, for obedience to the faith—
27 to God, alone wise, *be* glory through Jesus
Christ forever. Amen.[a]

16:18 [a]NU-Text and M-Text omit *Jesus.* **16:24** [a]NU-Text omits this verse. **16:27** [a]M-Text puts Romans 16:25–27 after Romans 14:23.

LIFE LESSONS

➤ 16:19 — *I want you to be wise in what is good, and simple concerning evil.*

We're on the wrong track if we're constantly asking ourselves, "What's wrong with it?" That's a question for immature believers, not growing ones. God wants us to focus on what's good, not on what might be bad.

➤ 16:25 — *Now to Him who is able to establish you according to my gospel . . . .*

All Christian growth ultimately comes down to our willing partnership with God, the only One who causes that growth. "So then neither he who plants is anything, nor he who waters, but God who gives the increase" (1 Cor. 3:7).

THE FIRST EPISTLE OF PAUL THE APOSTLE TO THE

CORINTHIANS

Corinth, perhaps the most important city in Greece during Paul's day, was a bustling hub of worldwide commerce, degraded culture, and idolatrous religion. Yet in that vibrant metropolis of perhaps 250,000 free persons and 400,000 slaves, Paul founded a church (Acts 18:1–17). He also addressed two of his letters "to the church of God which is at Corinth" (1 Cor. 1:2; 2 Cor. 1:1).

First Corinthians reveals the difficulties, pressures, and struggles of a young church called out of a pagan society. Paul addressed a variety of problems in the lifestyle of the Corinthian church: factions, lawsuits, immorality, questionable practices, and abuse of the Lord's Supper and spiritual gifts. In addition to words of discipline, Paul shared words of counsel in answer to questions raised by the Corinthian believers.

How did Paul learn of these problems? For one thing, he tells us that some members of "Chloe's household" had informed him about the divisiveness that existed in the church (1 Cor. 1:11). A few members of the Corinthian church itself had also visited Paul to deliver a letter asking about several areas of confusion (7:1; 8:1; 12:1; 16:1). Once before Paul had written to this church to warn its members against immorality (5:9, 10)—a letter no longer available—but he found it necessary to expand his counsel and try to get the church on a more solid spiritual footing. He also informed them that he planned to visit the church in person in order to straighten out any problems that persisted (4:19, 21; 16:5).

The oldest recorded title of this epistle is *Pros Korinthious A*—in effect, the "first to the Corinthians." The "A" was added later to distinguish this book from Second Corinthians.

Theme: How God wants believers in Christ to live in the midst of a corrupt culture.

Author: The apostle Paul.

Date: Paul probably wrote 1 Corinthians toward the end of his three-year stay in Ephesus, sometime around A.D. 55–56 (see 1 Cor. 16:5–9; Acts 20:31).

Structure: In the first section (chapters 1–11), Paul addresses various problems within the Corinthian church, including sectarianism (1–4), immorality (5), Christians taking one another to secular courts (6), marital questions (7), idolatry (8–10), and the improper administration of the Lord's Supper (11). The second section (chapters 12–14) offers instruction on the proper use of spiritual gifts. The final section (chapters 15, 16) reviews the doctrine of resurrection and includes Paul's parting comments.

As you read 1 Corinthians, watch for several life principles that play an important role in this book:

5. God does not require us to understand His will, just obey it, even if it seems unreasonable. *See 1 Corinthians 3:18–23; page 1334.*

15. Brokenness is God's requirement for maximum usefulness. *See 1 Corinthians 4:14–21; page 1334.*

6. You reap what you sow, more than you sow, and later than you sow. *See 1 Corinthians 10:1–11; page 1340.*

25. God blesses us so that we might bless others. *See 1 Corinthians 12:12–31; page 1343.*

Greeting

1 Paul, called *to be* an apostle of Jesus
Christ through the will of God, and Sosthenes *our* brother,

➤ 2 To the church of God which is at Corinth,
to those who are sanctified in Christ Jesus,
called *to be* saints, with all who in every place
call on the name of Jesus Christ our Lord,
both theirs and ours:

3 Grace to you and peace from God our Father and the Lord Jesus Christ.

Spiritual Gifts at Corinth

4 I thank my God always concerning you for
the grace of God which was given to you by
Christ Jesus,
5 that you were enriched in everything by
Him in all utterance and all knowledge,
6 even as the testimony of Christ was confirmed in you,
✳ 7 so that you come short in no gift, eagerly
waiting for the revelation of our Lord Jesus
Christ,
8 who will also confirm you to the end, *that
you may be* blameless in the day of our Lord
Jesus Christ.
9 God *is* faithful, by whom you were called
into the fellowship of His Son, Jesus Christ
our Lord.

Sectarianism Is Sin

➤ **10** Now I plead with you, brethren, by the
name of our Lord Jesus Christ, that you all
speak the same thing, and *that* there be no divisions among you, but *that* you be perfectly
joined together in the same mind and in the
same judgment.
11 For it has been declared to me concerning
you, my brethren, by those of Chloe's *household,* that there are contentions among you.
12 Now I say this, that each of you says, "I am
of Paul," or "I am of Apollos," or "I am of
Cephas," or "I am of Christ."
13 Is Christ divided? Was Paul crucified for
you? Or were you baptized in the name of Paul?
14 I thank God that I baptized none of you
except Crispus and Gaius,
15 lest anyone should say that I had baptized
in my own name.
16 Yes, I also baptized the household of
Stephanas. Besides, I do not know whether I
baptized any other.
17 For Christ did not send me to baptize, but
to preach the gospel, not with wisdom of
words, lest the cross of Christ should be made
of no effect.

Christ the Power and Wisdom of God

18 For the message of the cross is foolishness
to those who are perishing, but to us who are
being saved it is the power of God.
19 For it is written:

> *"I will destroy the wisdom of the wise,*
> *And bring to nothing the understanding*
> *of the prudent."*[a]

20 Where *is* the wise? Where *is* the scribe?
Where *is* the disputer of this age? Has not
God made foolish the wisdom of this world?
21 For since, in the wisdom of God, the world
through wisdom did not know God, it pleased
God through the foolishness of the message
preached to save those who believe.
22 For Jews request a sign, and Greeks seek
after wisdom;
23 but we preach Christ crucified, to the Jews
a stumbling block and to the Greeks[a] foolishness,
24 but to those who are called, both Jews and
Greeks, Christ the power of God and the wisdom of God.
25 Because the foolishness of God is wiser
than men, and the weakness of God is
stronger than men.

Glory Only in the Lord

26 For you see your calling, brethren, that not
many wise according to the flesh, not many
mighty, not many noble, *are called.*
27 But God has chosen the foolish things of ➤
the world to put to shame the wise, and God
has chosen the weak things of the world to
put to shame the things which are mighty;

1:19 [a]Isaiah 29:14 **1:23** [a]NU-Text reads *Gentiles.*

LIFE LESSONS

➤ 1:2 — *To the church of God which is at Corinth, to those who are sanctified in Christ Jesus, called to be saints . . . .*

Every believer in Jesus is "sanctified"—set apart to God and released from the power of sin—and can therefore be called a "saint"—a holy member of God's family, "zealous for good works" (Titus 2:14).

➤ 1:10 — *Now I plead with you, brethren, by the name of our Lord Jesus Christ, that you all speak the same thing, and that there be no divisions among you, but that you be perfectly joined together in the same mind and in the same judgment.*

Jesus had prayed for the unity of His followers before His arrest and crucifixion, and Paul also made frequent appeals to God's people, that they "may be one" (John 17:11, 22).

➤ 1:27 — *But God has chosen the foolish things of the world to put to shame the wise, and God has chosen the weak things of the world to put to shame the things which are mighty . . . .*

God loves to use weak, despised, and "inconsequential" things, people, and events to demonstrate His majesty, so "that the excellence of the power may be of God and not of us" (2 Cor. 4:7).

28 and the base things of the world and the
things which are despised God has chosen,
and the things which are not, to bring to nothing the things that are,
29 that no flesh should glory in His presence.
30 But of Him you are in Christ Jesus, who
became for us wisdom from God—and righteousness and sanctification and redemption—
31 that, as it is written, *"He who glories, let
him glory in the LORD."*[a]

Christ Crucified

2 And I, brethren, when I came to you, did
not come with excellence of speech or of
wisdom declaring to you the testimony[a] of
God.
➤ 2 For I determined not to know anything
among you except Jesus Christ and Him crucified.
3 I was with you in weakness, in fear, and in
much trembling.
4 And my speech and my preaching *were*
not with persuasive words of human[a] wisdom, but in demonstration of the Spirit and of
power,
➤ 5 that your faith should not be in the wisdom of men but in the power of God.

Spiritual Wisdom

6 However, we speak wisdom among those
who are mature, yet not the wisdom of this
age, nor of the rulers of this age, who are
coming to nothing.
7 But we speak the wisdom of God in a mystery, the hidden *wisdom* which God ordained
before the ages for our glory,
8 which none of the rulers of this age knew;
for had they known, they would not have crucified the Lord of glory.
9 But as it is written:

"Eye has not seen, nor ear heard,
Nor have entered into the heart of man
The things which God has prepared for
those who love Him."[a]

10 But God has revealed *them* to us through
His Spirit. For the Spirit searches all things,
yes, the deep things of God.
11 For what man knows the things of a man
except the spirit of the man which is in him?
Even so no one knows the things of God except the Spirit of God.
12 Now we have received, not the spirit of the ◄
world, but the Spirit who is from God, that we
might know the things that have been freely
given to us by God.
13 These things we also speak, not in words
which man's wisdom teaches but which the
Holy[a] Spirit teaches, comparing spiritual
things with spiritual.
14 But the natural man does not receive the
things of the Spirit of God, for they are foolishness to him; nor can he know *them,* because they are spiritually discerned.
15 But he who is spiritual judges all things,
yet he himself is *rightly* judged by no one.
16 For *"who has known the mind of the LORD
that he may instruct Him?"*[a] But we have the
mind of Christ.

Sectarianism Is Carnal

3 And I, brethren, could not speak to you as
to spiritual *people* but as to carnal, as to
babes in Christ.
2 I fed you with milk and not with solid
food; for until now you were not able *to receive it,* and even now you are still not able;
3 for you are still carnal. For where *there* ◄
are envy, strife, and divisions among you, are
you not carnal and behaving like *mere* men?
4 For when one says, "I am of Paul," and another, "I *am* of Apollos," are you not carnal?

Watering, Working, Warning

5 Who then is Paul, and who *is* Apollos, but
ministers through whom you believed, as the
Lord gave to each one?

1:31 [a]Jeremiah 9:24 **2:1** [a]NU-Text reads *mystery.* **2:4** [a]NU-Text omits *human.* **2:9** [a]Isaiah 64:4 **2:13** [a]NU-Text omits *Holy.* **2:16** [a]Isaiah 40:13

LIFE LESSONS

➤ 2:2 — *For I determined not to know anything among you except Jesus Christ and Him crucified.*

Paul could have preached about a thousand different topics, but he knew the Corinthians needed most to hear about how the death of Christ could free anyone from the power of sin.

➤ 2:5 — *. . . that your faith should not be in the wisdom of men but in the power of God.*

We ought to organize our thoughts about our faith and be able to explain it effectively to anyone who might ask, but the power of our faith comes not in our careful explanations but in the mighty resurrection of Christ.

➤ 2:12 — *Now we have received, not the spirit of the world, but the Spirit who is from God, that we might know the things that have been freely given to us by God.*

God does not want us to guess about what lies ahead for us; that's why He has told us a great deal in His Word about our future and why He has given us His Spirit, to help us understand what He has revealed.

➤ 3:3 — *For where there are envy, strife, and divisions among you, are you not carnal and behaving like mere men?*

No Christian should ever give the excuse, "I'm only human," when he or she succumbs to some temptation. Only carnal Christians could give such an excuse, for the Spirit gives us the ability to do what "mere men" cannot.

ANSWERS TO LIFE'S QUESTIONS

How can I rightly comprehend God's truth?

1 COR. 2:9, 10

Whenever God speaks to us, *His first goal is that we may comprehend the truth.* He desires that we fully understand His meaning.

God has given to all believers a divine Person who helps us to receive and understand the truth. The Holy Spirit, who perfectly knows the mind of God (1 Cor. 2:10) and who receives and communicates to our spirits the truth God wants us to hear, lives within all believers. God wants our understanding to grow in three primary areas.

❶ ***The truth about Himself.*** God wants us to grasp His majesty, His holiness, His power, His love, His grace, and His joy. When we begin to comprehend these mighty truths about the person of God, we find our lives enriched, enabled, and energized. Paul wrote that his ultimate aim in life was to know Christ (Phil. 3:10). Almost two thousand years later, can we think of anyone who has experienced a richer life?

❷ ***The truth about ourselves.*** God wants us to realize our importance in the scheme of His eternal plans; but most of all, God wants us to know our position and who we are in Christ. Since we are one with Christ, all His divine privileges become ours. His righteousness is ours because He abides in us. His wisdom and His sanctification we can now appropriate. Our enrollment in the Lamb's Book of Life carries all the glorious distinctions of our new status as God's children.

❸ ***The truth about other people.*** God wants us to view people as His chosen instruments and His creations. Some time ago God was sifting me, sanding me, pruning me, until I thought nothing would be left. A friend helped pull me through this deep valley. Sometimes I was harsh, even rude. He never reacted. He would just say, "I understand. What can I do to help?" He never rejected me or showed disappointment; he never angrily admonished me. When I poured out my insides to him, he just loved me. He wept with me, prayed with me, laughed with me, and patiently listened to me. Through his unwavering love we developed an unbreakable bond of deep friendship that strengthened my own intimacy with God.

When we begin to understand the truth of who God is and gain a better understanding of ourselves and others, we become thoroughly equipped to be fruitful, productive servants on earth.

See the Life Principles Index for further study:
10. If necessary, God will move heaven and earth to show us His will.
3. God's Word is an immovable anchor in times of storm.

6 I planted, Apollos watered, but God gave
the increase.
7 So then neither he who plants is anything,
nor he who waters, but God who gives the increase.
8 Now he who plants and he who waters are
one, and each one will receive his own reward
according to his own labor.
9 For we are God's fellow workers; you are
God's field, *you are* God's building.
10 According to the grace of God which was
given to me, as a wise master builder I have
laid the foundation, and another builds on it.
But let each one take heed how he builds on
it.
11 For no other foundation can anyone lay
than that which is laid, which is Jesus Christ.
12 Now if anyone builds on this foundation
with gold, silver, precious stones, wood, hay,
straw,
13 each one's work will become clear; for the ➤
Day will declare it, because it will be revealed
by fire; and the fire will test each one's work,
of what sort it is.

LIFE LESSONS

➤ 3:13 — *. . . each one's work will become clear; for the Day will declare it, because it will be revealed by fire . . . .*

One day when we stand before Christ, it will become absolutely clear what we accomplished for Him through the Spirit and what we did on our own power. No one will quibble with God's judgment.

14 If anyone's work which he has built on *it* endures, he will receive a reward.
15 If anyone's work is burned, he will suffer loss; but he himself will be saved, yet so as through fire.
16 Do you not know that you are the temple of God and *that* the Spirit of God dwells in you?
17 If anyone defiles the temple of God, God will destroy him. For the temple of God is holy, which *temple* you are.

Avoid Worldly Wisdom

18 Let no one deceive himself. If anyone among you seems to be wise in this age, let him become a fool that he may become wise.
19 For the wisdom of this world is foolishness with God. For it is written, *"He catches the wise in their own craftiness"*;[a]
20 and again, *"The LORD knows the thoughts of the wise, that they are futile."*[a]
21 Therefore let no one boast in men. For all things are yours:
22 whether Paul or Apollos or Cephas, or the world or life or death, or things present or things to come—all are yours.
23 And you *are* Christ's, and Christ *is* God's.

Stewards of the Mysteries of God

4 Let a man so consider us, as servants of Christ and stewards of the mysteries of God.
2 Moreover it is required in stewards that one be found faithful.
3 But with me it is a very small thing that I should be judged by you or by a human court.[a] In fact, I do not even judge myself.
4 For I know of nothing against myself, yet I am not justified by this; but He who judges me is the Lord.
5 Therefore judge nothing before the time, until the Lord comes, who will both bring to light the hidden things of darkness and reveal the counsels of the hearts. Then each one's praise will come from God.

Fools for Christ's Sake

6 Now these things, brethren, I have figuratively transferred to myself and Apollos for your sakes, that you may learn in us not to think beyond what is written, that none of you may be puffed up on behalf of one against the other.
7 For who makes you differ *from another?* And what do you have that you did not receive? Now if you did indeed receive *it*, why do you boast as if you had not received *it?*
8 You are already full! You are already rich! You have reigned as kings without us—and indeed I could wish you did reign, that we also might reign with you!
9 For I think that God has displayed us, the apostles, last, as men condemned to death; for we have been made a spectacle to the world, both to angels and to men.
10 We *are* fools for Christ's sake, but you *are* wise in Christ! We *are* weak, but you *are* strong! You *are* distinguished, but we *are* dishonored!
11 To the present hour we both hunger and thirst, and we are poorly clothed, and beaten, and homeless.
12 And we labor, working with our own hands. Being reviled, we bless; being persecuted, we endure;
13 being defamed, we entreat. We have been made as the filth of the world, the offscouring of all things until now.

Paul's Paternal Care

14 I do not write these things to shame you, but as my beloved children I warn *you*.
15 For though you might have ten thousand instructors in Christ, yet *you do* not *have* many fathers; for in Christ Jesus I have begotten you through the gospel.
16 Therefore I urge you, imitate me.
17 For this reason I have sent Timothy to you,

3:19 [a]Job 5:13 **3:20** [a]Psalm 94:11 **4:3** [a]Literally *day*

LIFE LESSONS

➤ 3:15 — *If anyone's work is burned, he will suffer loss; but he himself will be saved, yet so as through fire.*

Every believer in Christ already has eternal life; that question was settled forever at the cross. But rewards for service are another matter entirely. Some will receive many; others will get none.

➤ 4:5 — *Therefore judge nothing before the time, until the Lord comes, who will both bring to light the hidden things of darkness and reveal the counsels of the hearts.*

None of us are in a position to judge the motivations of the human heart. While the Bible does instruct us to react in certain ways to particular kinds of behavior (1 Cor. 5:2), we are never to judge anyone's intent.

➤ 4:7 — *For who makes you differ from another? And what do you have that you did not receive?*

In an ultimate sense, human arrogance makes very little sense, because we never accomplish *anything* except by using the gifts, talent, energy, inspiration—and even breath—that God gives to us.

➤ 4:14 — *I do not write these things to shame you, but as my beloved children I warn you.*

Paul learned such a loving attitude from Christ Himself. The Lord does not correct us in order to shame us, but because He loves us and wants to spare us the pain that our sinful actions always bring.

who is my beloved and faithful son in the Lord, who will remind you of my ways in Christ, as I teach everywhere in every church.
18 Now some are puffed up, as though I were not coming to you.
19 But I will come to you shortly, if the Lord wills, and I will know, not the word of those who are puffed up, but the power.
20 For the kingdom of God *is* not in word but in power.
21 What do you want? Shall I come to you with a rod, or in love and a spirit of gentleness?

Immorality Defiles the Church

5 It is actually reported *that there is* sexual immorality among you, and such sexual immorality as is not even named[a] among the Gentiles—that a man has his father's wife!
➤ 2 And you are puffed up, and have not rather mourned, that he who has done this deed might be taken away from among you.
3 For I indeed, as absent in body but present in spirit, have already judged (as though I were present) him who has so done this deed.
4 In the name of our Lord Jesus Christ, when you are gathered together, along with my spirit, with the power of our Lord Jesus Christ,
➤ 5 deliver such a one to Satan for the destruction of the flesh, that his spirit may be saved in the day of the Lord Jesus.[a]
6 Your glorying *is* not good. Do you not know that a little leaven leavens the whole lump?
7 Therefore purge out the old leaven, that you may be a new lump, since you truly are unleavened. For indeed Christ, our Passover, was sacrificed for us.[a]
8 Therefore let us keep the feast, not with old leaven, nor with the leaven of malice and wickedness, but with the unleavened *bread* of sincerity and truth.

Immorality Must Be Judged

9 I wrote to you in my epistle not to keep company with sexually immoral people.
10 Yet *I* certainly *did* not *mean* with the sexually immoral people of this world, or with the covetous, or extortioners, or idolaters, since then you would need to go out of the world.
11 But now I have written to you not to keep company with anyone named a brother, who is sexually immoral, or covetous, or an idolater, or a reviler, or a drunkard, or an extortioner—not even to eat with such a person. ➤
12 For what *have* I *to do* with judging those also who are outside? Do you not judge those who are inside?
13 But those who are outside God judges. Therefore *"put away from yourselves the evil person."*[a]

Do Not Sue the Brethren

6 Dare any of you, having a matter against another, go to law before the unrighteous, and not before the saints?
2 Do you not know that the saints will judge the world? And if the world will be judged by you, are you unworthy to judge the smallest matters?
3 Do you not know that we shall judge angels? How much more, things that pertain to this life?
4 If then you have judgments concerning things pertaining to this life, do you appoint those who are least esteemed by the church to judge?
5 I say this to your shame. Is it so, that there is not a wise man among you, not even one, who will be able to judge between his brethren?
6 But brother goes to law against brother, and that before unbelievers!
7 Now therefore, it is already an utter failure for you that you go to law against one another. Why do you not rather accept wrong? Why do you not rather *let yourselves* be cheated?

5:1 [a]NU-Text omits *named.* **5:5** [a]NU-Text omits *Jesus.* **5:7** [a]NU-Text omits *for us.* **5:13** [a]Deuteronomy 17:7; 19:19; 22:21, 24; 24:7

LIFE LESSONS

➤ **5:2 — *And you are puffed up, and have not rather mourned, that he who has done this deed might be taken away from among you.***

Apparently the Corinthians felt proud that they could tolerate such a shocking sin. Perhaps they congratulated themselves that their love could overlook the kind of behavior that ordinarily brought condemnation.

➤ **5:5 — *. . . deliver such a one to Satan for the destruction of the flesh, that his spirit may be saved in the day of the Lord Jesus.***

Blatant and persistent sin on the part of believers can have serious consequences, not only for the church in which the sin occurs but also for those involved. God's discipline can even lead to physical death (Acts 5:1–11).

➤ **5:11 — *But now I have written to you not to keep company with anyone named a brother, who is sexually immoral, or covetous, or an idolater, or a reviler, or a drunkard, or an extortioner—not even to eat with such a person.***

This kind of church discipline does not sound either loving or kind to many today, but it is much less loving and kind to tolerate a sin that can lead to serious personal and corporate injury.

ANSWERS TO LIFE'S QUESTIONS

Is there a limit to God's forgiveness?

1 COR. 6:9–11

Do you ever ask yourself:

- Have I committed the unpardonable sin?
- Can I ever be free of the weight of this guilt?
- Will God forgive *every* sin?

I have good news for you! Your loving heavenly Father will forgive you of *all* your sins. You can be released today from your sins if you will do what God says.

The apostle Paul dealt with an instance of gross sexual immorality in the Corinthian church: a man was sleeping with his stepmother. Against that backdrop, Paul wrote, "Do not be deceived. Neither fornicators, nor idolaters, nor adulterers, nor homosexuals, nor sodomites, nor thieves, nor covetous, nor drunkards, nor revilers, nor extortioners will inherit the kingdom of God. And such were some of you. But you were washed, but you were sanctified, but you were justified in the name of the Lord Jesus and by the Spirit of our God" (1 Cor. 6:9–11).

This passage holds three great messages for us.

First, it tells us that sin is sin. God doesn't differentiate between one type of sin and another. Most of us wouldn't consider slanderers in the same sin boat as thieves, but sin is sin.

Second, it tells us that sin is a lifestyle, a state of being. Paul declared that sin had been the identity of the Corinthians. Sin had been their all-consuming character. Paul called them former *thieves*—people who had stolen as a way of life. He didn't say, "Some of you had one too many drinks on occasion." He said some in the Corinthian church were *drunkards.* Sin isn't just something you *do.* Rather, sinful is something you *are* from birth.

Third, it tells us that all types of sin can be forgiven. Paul declared, "And such *were* some of you." And then Paul reminded them that they were no longer who they had been, but they had been washed, sanctified, and justified in the name of the Lord Jesus and by the Spirit of God. The Corinthians—as sorry a group of sinners as ever came together as a church—found a new life and a new identity in Christ Jesus.

Nothing is beyond God's forgiveness. No sin is too great or too awful for God to forgive. No person is so deep in sin, so ingrained in a wicked lifestyle, so steeped in evil, that he or she cannot be saved.

See the Life Principles Index for further study:

12. Peace with God is the fruit of oneness with God.

26. Adversity is a bridge to a deeper relationship with God.

8 No, you yourselves do wrong and cheat, and *you do* these things *to your* brethren!
9 Do you not know that the unrighteous will
not inherit the kingdom of God? Do not be deceived. Neither fornicators, nor idolaters, nor adulterers, nor homosexuals,[a] nor sodomites,
10 nor thieves, nor covetous, nor drunkards, nor revilers, nor extortioners will inherit the kingdom of God.
11 And such were some of you. But you were washed, but you were sanctified, but you were justified in the name of the Lord Jesus and by the Spirit of our God.

Glorify God in Body and Spirit

12 All things are lawful for me, but all things are not helpful. All things are lawful for me, but I will not be brought under the power of any.

6:9 [a]That is, catamites

LIFE LESSONS

➤ 6:9 — *Do you not know that the unrighteous will not inherit the kingdom of God? Do not be deceived.*

Something has gone dreadfully wrong when someone who professes faith in Christ continues to live according to the same sinful patterns exhibited before salvation (see 1 John 2:4).

➤ 6:12 — *All things are lawful for me, but all things are not helpful. All things are lawful for me, but I will not be brought under the power of any.*

Paul had no interest in allowing the sinful patterns from which he had escaped through God's grace to enslave him again. He didn't ask, "What's wrong with it?" as much as, "What's right with it?"

13 Foods for the stomach and the stomach for
foods, but God will destroy both it and them.
Now the body *is* not for sexual immorality but
for the Lord, and the Lord for the body.
14 And God both raised up the Lord and will
also raise us up by His power.
15 Do you not know that your bodies are
members of Christ? Shall I then take the
members of Christ and make *them* members
of a harlot? Certainly not!
16 Or do you not know that he who is joined
to a harlot is one body *with her*? For *"the*
two," He says, *"shall become one flesh."*[a]
17 But he who is joined to the Lord is one
spirit *with Him*.
18 Flee sexual immorality. Every sin that a
man does is outside the body, but he who
commits sexual immorality sins against his
own body.
19 Or do you not know that your body is the
temple of the Holy Spirit *who is* in you, whom
you have from God, and you are not your own?
20 For you were bought at a price; therefore
glorify God in your body[a] and in your spirit,
which are God's.

Principles of Marriage

7 Now concerning the things of which you
wrote to me: *It is* good for a man not to
touch a woman.
2 Nevertheless, because of sexual immorality, let each man have his own wife, and let
each woman have her own husband.
3 Let the husband render to his wife the affection due her, and likewise also the wife to
her husband.
4 The wife does not have authority over her
own body, but the husband *does*. And likewise the husband does not have authority
over his own body, but the wife *does*.
5 Do not deprive one another except with
consent for a time, that you may give yourselves to fasting and prayer; and come together again so that Satan does not tempt you
because of your lack of self-control.
6 But I say this as a concession, not as a
commandment.
7 For I wish that all men were even as I myself. But each one has his own gift from God,
one in this manner and another in that.
8 But I say to the unmarried and to the widows: It is good for them if they remain even as
I am;
9 but if they cannot exercise self-control, let
them marry. For it is better to marry than to
burn *with passion*.

Keep Your Marriage Vows

10 Now to the married I command, *yet* not I
but the Lord: A wife is not to depart from *her*
husband.
11 But even if she does depart, let her remain
unmarried or be reconciled to *her* husband.
And a husband is not to divorce *his* wife.
12 But to the rest I, not the Lord, say: If any
brother has a wife who does not believe, and
she is willing to live with him, let him not divorce her.
13 And a woman who has a husband who
does not believe, if he is willing to live with
her, let her not divorce him.
14 For the unbelieving husband is sanctified
by the wife, and the unbelieving wife is sanctified by the husband; otherwise your children would be unclean, but now they are holy.
15 But if the unbeliever departs, let him depart; a brother or a sister is not under
bondage in such *cases*. But God has called us
to peace.
16 For how do you know, O wife, whether you
will save *your* husband? Or how do you know,
O husband, whether you will save *your* wife?

Live as You Are Called

17 But as God has distributed to each one, as
the Lord has called each one, so let him walk.
And so I ordain in all the churches.

6:16 [a]Genesis 2:24 6:20 [a]NU-Text ends the verse at *body*.

LIFE LESSONS

6:18 — *Flee sexual immorality. Every sin that a man does is outside the body, but he who commits sexual immorality sins against his own body.*

All sin separates us from God, but sexual sin damages and sabotages the very physical processes that keep life going. It also tends to warp the human character at a very deep level.

6:20 — *For you were bought at a price; therefore glorify God in your body and in your spirit, which are God's.*

No Christian should ever say, "It's *my* body; I can do what I want with it!" No believer owns his or her body; Christ paid for it with His own blood on the cross. It belongs to Him.

7:5 — *Do not deprive one another except with consent for a time, that you may give yourselves to fasting and prayer; and come together again . . . .*

Sexual expression is a key and vital part of every Christian marriage. Believing couples should abstain from it only (1) by mutual consent, (2) for a limited time, and (3) for a specific prayer need.

7:11 — *But even if she does depart, let her remain unmarried or be reconciled to her husband. And a husband is not to divorce his wife.*

Paul follows the lead of the Old Testament and of Jesus on the topic of divorce. His teaching on grace does not mean that spouses can divorce at will; it means that God can give them the strength to persevere.

18 Was anyone called while circumcised? Let him not become uncircumcised. Was anyone called while uncircumcised? Let him not be circumcised.

19 Circumcision is nothing and uncircumcision is nothing, but keeping the commandments of God *is what matters.*

20 Let each one remain in the same calling in which he was called.

21 Were you called *while* a slave? Do not be concerned about it; but if you can be made free, rather use *it*.

22 For he who is called in the Lord *while* a slave is the Lord's freedman. Likewise he who is called *while* free is Christ's slave.

23 You were bought at a price; do not become slaves of men.

24 Brethren, let each one remain with God in that *state* in which he was called.

To the Unmarried and Widows

25 Now concerning virgins: I have no commandment from the Lord; yet I give judgment as one whom the Lord in His mercy has made trustworthy.

26 I suppose therefore that this is good because of the present distress—that *it is* good for a man to remain as he is:

27 Are you bound to a wife? Do not seek to be loosed. Are you loosed from a wife? Do not seek a wife.

28 But even if you do marry, you have not sinned; and if a virgin marries, she has not sinned. Nevertheless such will have trouble in the flesh, but I would spare you.

29 But this I say, brethren, the time *is* short, so that from now on even those who have wives should be as though they had none,

30 those who weep as though they did not weep, those who rejoice as though they did not rejoice, those who buy as though they did not possess,

31 and those who use this world as not misusing *it*. For the form of this world is passing away.

32 But I want you to be without care. He who is unmarried cares for the things of the Lord—how he may please the Lord.

33 But he who is married cares about the things of the world—how he may please *his* wife.

34 There is[a] a difference between a wife and a virgin. The unmarried woman cares about the things of the Lord, that she may be holy both in body and in spirit. But she who is married cares about the things of the world—how she may please *her* husband.

35 And this I say for your own profit, not that I may put a leash on you, but for what is proper, and that you may serve the Lord without distraction.

36 But if any man thinks he is behaving improperly toward his virgin, if she is past the flower of youth, and thus it must be, let him do what he wishes. He does not sin; let them marry.

37 Nevertheless he who stands steadfast in his heart, having no necessity, but has power over his own will, and has so determined in his heart that he will keep his virgin,[a] does well.

38 So then he who gives *her*[a] in marriage does well, but he who does not give *her* in marriage does better.

39 A wife is bound by law as long as her husband lives; but if her husband dies, she is at liberty to be married to whom she wishes, only in the Lord.

40 But she is happier if she remains as she is, according to my judgment—and I think I also have the Spirit of God.

Be Sensitive to Conscience

8 Now concerning things offered to idols: We know that we all have knowledge. Knowledge puffs up, but love edifies.

2 And if anyone thinks that he knows anything, he knows nothing yet as he ought to know.

3 But if anyone loves God, this one is known by Him.

4 Therefore concerning the eating of things offered to idols, we know that an idol *is* nothing in the world, and that *there is* no other God but one.

5 For even if there are so-called gods, whether in heaven or on earth (as there are many gods and many lords),

7:34 [a]M-Text adds *also.* **7:37** [a]Or *virgin daughter*
7:38 [a]NU-Text reads *his own virgin.*

LIFE LESSONS

➤ **7:19 — *Circumcision is nothing and uncircumcision is nothing, but keeping the commandments of God is what matters.***

Rituals help us only insofar as they move us toward God; in and of themselves, they have no intrinsic value. God values devoted obedience far more than adherence to religious ritual (see 1 Sam. 15:22).

➤ **7:20 — *Let each one remain in the same calling in which he was called.***

"I'd serve God if only I had a better job . . . a better home . . . a better spouse . . . a better position." Ever hear anything like this? Paul insists that we can serve God wherever we are when He first calls us.

➤ **8:1 — *Knowledge puffs up, but love edifies.***

God wants us to keep learning about Him and His ways, not merely to add to our storehouse of knowledge, but to better serve Him and His people. Knowledge plus love equals a powerful team!

➤ 6 yet for us *there is* one God, the Father, of
whom *are* all things, and we for Him; and one
Lord Jesus Christ, through whom *are* all
things, and through whom we *live*.
7 However, *there is* not in everyone that
knowledge; for some, with consciousness of
the idol, until now eat *it* as a thing offered to
an idol; and their conscience, being weak, is
defiled.
8 But food does not commend us to God; for
neither if we eat are we the better, nor if we
do not eat are we the worse.
9 But beware lest somehow this liberty of
yours become a stumbling block to those who
are weak.
10 For if anyone sees you who have knowledge eating in an idol's temple, will not the
conscience of him who is weak be emboldened to eat those things offered to idols?
➤ 11 And because of your knowledge shall the
weak brother perish, for whom Christ died?
12 But when you thus sin against the
brethren, and wound their weak conscience,
you sin against Christ.
13 Therefore, if food makes my brother
stumble, I will never again eat meat, lest I
make my brother stumble.

A Pattern of Self-Denial

9 Am I not an apostle? Am I not free? Have
I not seen Jesus Christ our Lord? Are you
not my work in the Lord?
2 If I am not an apostle to others, yet doubtless I am to you. For you are the seal of my
apostleship in the Lord.
3 My defense to those who examine me is
this:
4 Do we have no right to eat and drink?
5 Do we have no right to take along a believing wife, as *do* also the other apostles, the
brothers of the Lord, and Cephas?
6 Or *is it* only Barnabas and I *who* have no
right to refrain from working?
7 Who ever goes to war at his own expense?
Who plants a vineyard and does not eat of its
fruit? Or who tends a flock and does not drink
of the milk of the flock?
8 Do I say these things as a *mere* man? Or
does not the law say the same also?
9 For it is written in the law of Moses, *"You
shall not muzzle an ox while it treads out the
grain."*[a] Is it oxen God is concerned about?

Life Examples:

BARNABAS

Always an Encouraging Word

1 COR. 9:6

Wherever Barnabas went, people's faces lit up. They knew that his presence brought a kind word, a helpful suggestion, and a load of encouragement.

In fact, that's how he got his name. He was born Joses or Joseph, a Levite from Cyprus, but his reassuring and cheerful ways soon prompted the apostles to give him the nickname Barnabas, which means "son of encouragement" (Acts 4:36).

Without Barnabas, there might never have been an apostle Paul. It was Barnabas who introduced Saul to the church when everyone else was afraid of him (Acts 9:26–30). And when the apostles sent Barnabas to check up on a young church, he "encouraged them all that with purpose of heart they should continue with the Lord. For he was a good man, full of the Holy Spirit and of faith" (Acts 11:23, 24).

Don't you agree that we could use a few more believers like Barnabas?

See the Life Principles Index for further study:
25. God blesses us so that we might bless others.
28. No Christian has ever been called to "go it alone" in his or her walk of faith.

10 Or does He say *it* altogether for our sakes?
For our sakes, no doubt, *this* is written, that
he who plows should plow in hope, and he

9:9 [a]Deuteronomy 25:4

LIFE LESSONS

➤ **8:6 — *. . . for us there is one God, the Father, of whom are all things, and we for Him; and one Lord Jesus Christ, through whom are all things, and through whom we live.***

Paul often speaks of the Father and the Son in equal but complementary ways. We serve *one* God through *one* Lord by *one* Spirit.

➤ **8:11 — *And because of your knowledge shall the weak brother perish, for whom Christ died?***

Paul teaches us that love never insists on its own private convictions if the exercise of those convictions damages a fellow believer. Love always desires the best for those it loves, even if that means self-denial.

who threshes in hope should be partaker of
his hope.
11 If we have sown spiritual things for you, *is*
it a great thing if we reap your material
things?
12 If others are partakers of *this* right over
you, *are* we not even more? Nevertheless we
have not used this right, but endure all things
lest we hinder the gospel of Christ.
13 Do you not know that those who minister
the holy things eat *of the things* of the temple,
and those who serve at the altar partake of
the offerings of the altar?
14 Even so the Lord has commanded that
those who preach the gospel should live from
the gospel.
15 But I have used none of these things, nor
have I written these things that it should be
done so to me; for it *would be* better for me to
die than that anyone should make my boasting void.
16 For if I preach the gospel, I have nothing
to boast of, for necessity is laid upon me; yes,
woe is me if I do not preach the gospel!
➤ 17 For if I do this willingly, I have a reward;
but if against my will, I have been entrusted
with a stewardship.
18 What is my reward then? That when I
preach the gospel, I may present the gospel of
Christ[a] without charge, that I may not abuse
my authority in the gospel.

Serving All Men

19 For though I am free from all *men,* I have
made myself a servant to all, that I might win
the more;
20 and to the Jews I became as a Jew, that I
might win Jews; to those *who are* under the
law, as under the law,[a] that I might win those
who are under the law;
21 to those *who are* without law, as without
law (not being without law toward God,[a] but
under law toward Christ[b]), that I might win
those *who are* without law;
➤ 22 to the weak I became as[a] weak, that I
might win the weak. I have become all things
to all *men,* that I might by all means save
some.
23 Now this I do for the gospel's sake, that I
may be partaker of it with *you.*

Striving for a Crown

24 Do you not know that those who run in a ➤
race all run, but one receives the prize? Run
in such a way that you may obtain *it.*
25 And everyone who competes *for the prize* ✳
is temperate in all things. Now they *do it* to
obtain a perishable crown, but we *for* an
imperishable *crown.*
26 Therefore I run thus: not with uncertainty.
Thus I fight: not as *one who* beats the air.
27 But I discipline my body and bring *it* into
subjection, lest, when I have preached to others, I myself should become disqualified.

Old Testament Examples

10 Moreover, brethren, I do not want you
to be unaware that all our fathers were
under the cloud, all passed through the sea,
2 all were baptized into Moses in the cloud
and in the sea,
3 all ate the same spiritual food,
4 and all drank the same spiritual drink. For
they drank of that spiritual Rock that followed them, and that Rock was Christ.
5 But with most of them God was not well
pleased, for *their bodies* were scattered in the
wilderness.
6 Now these things became our examples, ➤
to the intent that we should not lust after evil
things as they also lusted.
7 And do not become idolaters as *were*
some of them. As it is written, *"The people sat*
down to eat and drink, and rose up to play."[a]
8 Nor let us commit sexual immorality, as

9:18 [a]NU-Text omits *of Christ.* **9:20** [a]NU-Text adds *though not being myself under the law.* **9:21** [a]NU-Text reads *God's law.* [b]NU-Text reads *Christ's law.* **9:22** [a]NU-Text omits *as.* **10:7** [a]Exodus 32:6

LIFE LESSONS

➤ 9:17 — *For if I do this willingly, I have a reward; but if against my will, I have been entrusted with a stewardship.*

It is a great privilege to serve the Lord, but it is also our solemn duty. The amazing thing is that God has promised to reward us richly for doing nothing but what we ought to do!

➤ 9:22 — *I have become all things to all men, that I might by all means save some.*

Paul never compromised his convictions or his calling, but he was more than willing to find common ground and meet his audience wherever they happened to be. More than anything, he wanted to lead people to life in Christ.

➤ 9:24 — *Do you not know that those who run in a race all run, but one receives the prize? Run in such a way that you may obtain it.*

We will not accomplish much in life if we do not have a clear purpose and mission in mind. The only way to consistently hit a target is to take careful aim. What is your own life mission?

➤ 10:6, 11 — *Now these things became our examples . . . . Now all these things happened to them as examples, and they were written for our admonition . . . .*

Everything in the Scripture exists for our example, warning, and admonition. We are to note what God's people did in the past and how God reacted to them in order to move ahead in our own walk of faith.

some of them did, and in one day twenty-
three thousand fell;
9 nor let us tempt Christ, as some of them
also tempted, and were destroyed by serpents;
10 nor complain, as some of them also complained, and were destroyed by the destroyer.
11 Now all[a] these things happened to them as
examples, and they were written for our admonition, upon whom the ends of the ages
have come.
12 Therefore let him who thinks he stands
take heed lest he fall.
✳ 13 No temptation has overtaken you except
such as is common to man; but God *is* faithful, who will not allow you to be tempted beyond what you are able, but with the
temptation will also make the way of escape,
that you may be able to bear *it.*

Flee from Idolatry

14 Therefore, my beloved, flee from idolatry.
15 I speak as to wise men; judge for yourselves what I say.
16 The cup of blessing which we bless, is it
not the communion of the blood of Christ?
The bread which we break, is it not the communion of the body of Christ?
17 For we, *though* many, are one bread *and*
one body; for we all partake of that one
bread.
18 Observe Israel after the flesh: Are not
those who eat of the sacrifices partakers of
the altar?
19 What am I saying then? That an idol is
anything, or what is offered to idols is anything?
20 Rather, that the things which the Gentiles
sacrifice they sacrifice to demons and not to
God, and I do not want you to have fellowship
with demons.
21 You cannot drink the cup of the Lord and
the cup of demons; you cannot partake of the
Lord's table and of the table of demons.
22 Or do we provoke the Lord to jealousy?
Are we stronger than He?

All to the Glory of God

➤ **23** All things are lawful for me,[a] but not all
things are helpful; all things are lawful for
me,[b] but not all things edify.
24 Let no one seek his own, but each one the
other's *well-being.*
25 Eat whatever is sold in the meat market,
asking no questions for conscience' sake;
26 for *"the earth is the* LORD*'s, and all its fullness."*[a]
27 If any of those who do not believe invites
you *to dinner,* and you desire to go, eat whatever is set before you, asking no question for
conscience' sake.
28 But if anyone says to you, "This was offered to idols," do not eat it for the sake of the
one who told you, and for conscience' sake;[a]
for *"the earth is the* LORD*'s, and all its fullness."*[b]
29 "Conscience," I say, not your own, but that
of the other. For why is my liberty judged by
another *man's* conscience?
30 But if I partake with thanks, why am I evil
spoken of for *the food* over which I give
thanks?
31 Therefore, whether you eat or drink, or ➤
whatever you do, do all to the glory of God.
32 Give no offense, either to the Jews or to
the Greeks or to the church of God,
33 just as I also please all *men* in all *things,*
not seeking my own profit, but the *profit* of
many, that they may be saved.
11 Imitate me, just as I also *imitate*
Christ.

Head Coverings

2 Now I praise you, brethren, that you remember me in all things and keep the traditions just as I delivered *them* to you.
3 But I want you to know that the head of
every man is Christ, the head of woman *is*
man, and the head of Christ *is* God.
4 Every man praying or prophesying, having *his* head covered, dishonors his head.
5 But every woman who prays or prophesies
with *her* head uncovered dishonors her head,
for that is one and the same as if her head
were shaved.
6 For if a woman is not covered, let her also
be shorn. But if it is shameful for a woman to
be shorn or shaved, let her be covered.
7 For a man indeed ought not to cover *his*
head, since he is the image and glory of God;
but woman is the glory of man.

10:11 [a]NU-Text omits *all.* **10:23** [a]NU-Text omits *for me.* [b]NU-Text omits *for me.* **10:26** [a]Psalm 24:1 **10:28** [a]NU-Text omits the rest of this verse. [b]Psalm 24:1

LIFE LESSONS

➤ 10:23 — *All things are lawful for me, but not all things are helpful; all things are lawful for me, but not all things edify.*

We are to ask not merely, "Is it okay?" but also, "Does this help?" God wants us to move beyond merely debating whether something is wrong or right, and instead choose actions that build up the faith of others.

➤ 10:31 — *Therefore, whether you eat or drink, or whatever you do, do all to the glory of God.*

There could hardly be a better standard of behavior than this. Before you commit to any action, ask yourself, "Can I do this to the glory of God? Would this action put God's reputation in a good light?"

8 For man is not from woman, but woman
from man.
9 Nor was man created for the woman, but
woman for the man.
10 For this reason the woman ought to have *a*
symbol of authority on *her* head, because of
the angels.
11 Nevertheless, neither *is* man independent
of woman, nor woman independent of man, in
the Lord.
12 For as woman *came* from man, even so
man also *comes* through woman; but all
things are from God.
13 Judge among yourselves. Is it proper for a
woman to pray to God with her head uncovered?
14 Does not even nature itself teach you that
if a man has long hair, it is a dishonor to him?
15 But if a woman has long hair, it is a glory
to her; for *her* hair is given to her[a] for a covering.
16 But if anyone seems to be contentious, we
have no such custom, nor *do* the churches of
God.

Conduct at the Lord's Supper

17 Now in giving these instructions I do not
praise *you,* since you come together not for
the better but for the worse.
18 For first of all, when you come together as
a church, I hear that there are divisions
among you, and in part I believe it.
19 For there must also be factions among
you, that those who are approved may be recognized among you.
20 Therefore when you come together in one
place, it is not to eat the Lord's Supper.
21 For in eating, each one takes his own supper ahead of *others;* and one is hungry and
another is drunk.
22 What! Do you not have houses to eat and
drink in? Or do you despise the church of God
and shame those who have nothing? What
shall I say to you? Shall I praise you in this? I
do not praise *you.*

Institution of the Lord's Supper

23 For I received from the Lord that which I
also delivered to you: that the Lord Jesus on
the *same* night in which He was betrayed
took bread;
24 and when He had given thanks, He broke
it and said, "Take, eat;[a] this is My body which
is broken[b] for you; do this in remembrance of
Me."
25 In the same manner *He* also *took* the cup
after supper, saying, "This cup is the new covenant in My blood. This do, as often as you
drink *it,* in remembrance of Me."
26 For as often as you eat this bread and
drink this cup, you proclaim the Lord's death
till He comes.

Examine Yourself

27 Therefore whoever eats this bread or
drinks *this* cup of the Lord in an unworthy
manner will be guilty of the body and blood[a]
of the Lord.
28 But let a man examine himself, and so let
him eat of the bread and drink of the cup.
29 For he who eats and drinks in an unworthy manner[a] eats and drinks judgment to himself, not discerning the Lord's[b] body.
30 For this reason many *are* weak and sick
among you, and many sleep.
31 For if we would judge ourselves, we would
not be judged.
32 But when we are judged, we are chastened
by the Lord, that we may not be condemned
with the world.
33 Therefore, my brethren, when you come
together to eat, wait for one another.
34 But if anyone is hungry, let him eat at
home, lest you come together for judgment.
And the rest I will set in order when I come.

Spiritual Gifts: Unity in Diversity

12 Now concerning spiritual *gifts,*
brethren, I do not want you to be ignorant:
2 You know that[a] you were Gentiles, carried
away to these dumb idols, however you were
led.

11:15 [a]M-Text omits *to her.* **11:24** [a]NU-Text omits *Take, eat.* [b]NU-Text omits *broken.* **11:27** [a]NU-Text and M-Text read *the blood.* **11:29** [a]NU-Text omits *in an unworthy manner.* [b]NU-Text omits *Lord's.* **12:2** [a]NU-Text and M-Text add *when.*

LIFE LESSONS

➤ 11:22 — *Do you not have houses to eat and drink in? Or do you despise the church of God and shame those who have nothing?*

While we all come to faith as individuals, God calls us to express our faith in community. When we act without consideration for other members of Christ's body, we "despise" the church He died for.

➤ 11:26 — *For as often as you eat this bread and drink this cup, you proclaim the Lord's death till He comes.*

The Lord's Supper not only looks back at Christ's sacrifice and gives Him praise for His willing obedience to the Father, but also looks ahead to that day when we will see Him again and reign with Him in power.

➤ 11:32 — *But when we are judged, we are chastened by the Lord, that we may not be condemned with the world.*

God does not discipline His erring children because He's disgusted with them, but because He wants to spare them the greater pain that comes because of persistent disobedience. His mercy prompts His discipline.

3 Therefore I make known to you that no one speaking by the Spirit of God calls Jesus accursed, and no one can say that Jesus is Lord except by the Holy Spirit.
4 There are diversities of gifts, but the same Spirit.
5 There are differences of ministries, but the same Lord.
6 And there are diversities of activities, but it is the same God who works all in all.
➤ 7 But the manifestation of the Spirit is given to each one for the profit *of all:*
8 for to one is given the word of wisdom through the Spirit, to another the word of knowledge through the same Spirit,
9 to another faith by the same Spirit, to another gifts of healings by the same[a] Spirit,
10 to another the working of miracles, to another prophecy, to another discerning of spirits, to another *different* kinds of tongues, to another the interpretation of tongues.
➤ 11 But one and the same Spirit works all these things, distributing to each one individually as He wills.

Unity and Diversity in One Body

12 For as the body is one and has many members, but all the members of that one body, being many, are one body, so also *is* Christ.
13 For by one Spirit we were all baptized into one body—whether Jews or Greeks, whether slaves or free—and have all been made to drink into[a] one Spirit.
14 For in fact the body is not one member but many.
15 If the foot should say, "Because I am not a hand, I am not of the body," is it therefore not of the body?
16 And if the ear should say, "Because I am not an eye, I am not of the body," is it therefore not of the body?
17 If the whole body *were* an eye, where *would be* the hearing? If the whole *were* hearing, where *would be* the smelling?
18 But now God has set the members, each one of them, in the body just as He pleased.
19 And if they were all one member, where *would* the body *be?*
20 But now indeed *there are* many members, yet one body.
21 And the eye cannot say to the hand, "I have no need of you"; nor again the head to the feet, "I have no need of you."
22 No, much rather, those members of the body which seem to be weaker are necessary.
23 And those *members* of the body which we think to be less honorable, on these we bestow greater honor; and our unpresentable *parts* have greater modesty,
24 but our presentable *parts* have no need. But God composed the body, having given greater honor to that *part* which lacks it,
25 that there should be no schism in the body, but *that* the members should have the same care for one another.
26 And if one member suffers, all the members suffer with *it;* or if one member is honored, all the members rejoice with *it.* ➤
27 Now you are the body of Christ, and members individually.
28 And God has appointed these in the church: first apostles, second prophets, third teachers, after that miracles, then gifts of healings, helps, administrations, varieties of tongues.
29 *Are* all apostles? *Are* all prophets? *Are* all teachers? *Are* all workers of miracles?
30 Do all have gifts of healings? Do all speak with tongues? Do all interpret?
31 But earnestly desire the best[a] gifts. And yet I show you a more excellent way.

The Greatest Gift

13 Though I speak with the tongues of men and of angels, but have not love, I have become sounding brass or a clanging cymbal.
2 And though I have *the gift of* prophecy, and understand all mysteries and all knowledge, and though I have all faith, so that I could remove mountains, but have not love, I am nothing.

12:9 [a]NU-Text reads *one.* **12:13** [a]NU-Text omits *into.*
12:31 [a]NU-Text reads *greater.*

LIFE LESSONS

➤ **12:7 — *But the manifestation of the Spirit is given to each one for the profit of all.***

At the time they come to faith in Christ, every believer receives at least one spiritual gift, not merely to encourage and build up their own life of faith, but more particularly to build up the faith of the whole church.

➤ **12:11 — *But one and the same Spirit works all these things, distributing to each one individually as He wills.***

God distributes spiritual gifts as He sees fit. While a church can and should pray that it be granted the greatest gifts (1 Cor. 14:1), individual believers are never encouraged to request specific gifts.

➤ **12:26 — *And if one member suffers, all the members suffer with it; or if one member is honored, all the members rejoice with it.***

This verse gives the reason for Paul's instruction to "rejoice with those who rejoice, and weep with those who weep" (Rom. 12:15). Since we all belong to each other, we should desire the welfare of each other.

WHAT THE BIBLE SAYS ABOUT GOD'S FOREVER LOVE

1 Cor. 13:1–13

First Corinthians 13 is probably the most widely quoted passage in the world on the subject of love. Verse 13 says, "And now abide faith, hope, love, these three; but the greatest of these is love."

We recognize that Jesus demonstrated sacrificial love for us by dying for our sins, making possible our forgiveness and restoring us to fellowship with the Father. Yet we often fail to realize that Christ's love goes even beyond the cross.

Everything we do, don't do, face, and don't face is touched by His continuing love. Everything about us hinges on love because God, who is love, created us in His image (1 John 4:8, 16). Because God loves us, He gives us blessings and lets us share them. When we pray and are told to wait, it is because He loves us and knows we need time to grow. When the overwhelming choices before us make it hard to know which way is up, our Lord and Savior shows us our need to depend on His guiding love.

Our most important dwelling place is God's love.

Jesus demonstrated this kind of amazing love to Mary and Martha upon Lazarus' death (John 11:6) says, "When He heard that he was sick, He stayed two more days in the place where he was." Jesus knew that Mary and Martha needed to grieve in order to grow. He allowed the sisters' pain *because* He loved them.

Until we come to understand and believe at our deepest, innermost level that God is love, we will struggle with trusting Him, yielding to Him, obeying Him, and serving Him wholeheartedly. One of the keys to our spiritual growth as Christians is believing in God's love even when we cannot see it.

While we are to live in faith and hope, our most important dwelling place is God's love. Without making His love our ultimate dwelling, we cannot fully live in faith and hope. We should refuse to take a step or a breath without remaining keenly sensitive to "the greatest of these"—our Father's love.

See the Life Principles Index for further study:

1. *Our intimacy with God—His highest priority for our lives—determines the impact of our lives.*

14. *God acts on behalf of those who wait for Him.*

➤ 3 And though I bestow all my goods to feed *the poor,* and though I give my body to be burned,[a] but have not love, it profits me nothing.
4 Love suffers long *and* is kind; love does not envy; love does not parade itself, is not puffed up;
5 does not behave rudely, does not seek its own, is not provoked, thinks no evil;
6 does not rejoice in iniquity, but rejoices in the truth;
7 bears all things, believes all things, hopes all things, endures all things.
8 Love never fails. But whether *there are* prophecies, they will fail; whether *there are* tongues, they will cease; whether *there is* knowledge, it will vanish away.
➤ 9 For we know in part and we prophesy in part.
10 But when that which is perfect has come, then that which is in part will be done away.
11 When I was a child, I spoke as a child, I understood as a child, I thought as a child; but when I became a man, I put away childish things.
✳ 12 For now we see in a mirror, dimly, but then face to face. Now I know in part, but then I shall know just as I also am known.
➤ 13 And now abide faith, hope, love, these three; but the greatest of these *is* love.

Prophecy and Tongues

14 Pursue love, and desire spiritual *gifts,* but especially that you may prophesy.
2 For he who speaks in a tongue does not speak to men but to God, for no one understands *him;* however, in the spirit he speaks mysteries.
3 But he who prophesies speaks edification and exhortation and comfort to men.
4 He who speaks in a tongue edifies himself, but he who prophesies edifies the church.
5 I wish you all spoke with tongues, but even more that you prophesied; for[a] he who prophesies *is* greater than he who speaks with tongues, unless indeed he interprets, that the church may receive edification.

Tongues Must Be Interpreted

6 But now, brethren, if I come to you speaking with tongues, what shall I profit you unless I speak to you either by revelation, by knowledge, by prophesying, or by teaching?
7 Even things without life, whether flute or harp, when they make a sound, unless they make a distinction in the sounds, how will it be known what is piped or played?
8 For if the trumpet makes an uncertain sound, who will prepare for battle?
9 So likewise you, unless you utter by the tongue words easy to understand, how will it be known what is spoken? For you will be speaking into the air.
10 There are, it may be, so many kinds of languages in the world, and none of them *is* without significance.
11 Therefore, if I do not know the meaning of the language, I shall be a foreigner to him who speaks, and he who speaks *will be* a foreigner to me.
12 Even so you, since you are zealous for spiritual *gifts, let it be* for the edification of the church *that* you seek to excel. ➤
13 Therefore let him who speaks in a tongue pray that he may interpret.
14 For if I pray in a tongue, my spirit prays, but my understanding is unfruitful.
15 What is *the conclusion* then? I will pray with the spirit, and I will also pray with the understanding. I will sing with the spirit, and I will also sing with the understanding.
16 Otherwise, if you bless with the spirit, how will he who occupies the place of the uninformed say "Amen" at your giving of thanks, since he does not understand what you say?
17 For you indeed give thanks well, but the other is not edified.
18 I thank my God I speak with tongues more than you all;
19 yet in the church I would rather speak five words with my understanding, that I may teach others also, than ten thousand words in a tongue.

13:3 [a]NU-Text reads *so I may boast.* **14:5** [a]NU-Text reads *and.*

LIFE LESSONS

➤ 13:3 — *And though I bestow all my goods to feed the poor, and though I give my body to be burned, but have not love, it profits me nothing.*

Love does mean action, but it means more than that. A person can literally give up his life for others—the supreme self-sacrifice—and yet do it without love. Love has a caring element that prompts its action.

➤ 13:9 — *For we know in part and we prophesy in part.*

God never gave any of His children a complete picture of what He was doing or what He planned to do. Can you imagine the arrogance that would result if He had? Instead, we need to depend upon each other.

➤ 13:13 — *And now abide faith, hope, love, these three; but the greatest of these is love.*

Hope will disappear in heaven, because we will already have everything we've ever hoped for. Faith will not be required, since we will see the King in His glory. But love will remain forever.

➤ 14:12 — *Even so you, since you are zealous for spiritual gifts, let it be for the edification of the church that you seek to excel.*

God intends that we grow in grace *together.* We are to learn about Him *together.* We are to serve others *together.* Why together? Because unity of heart and action best shows the power of God's love.

Tongues a Sign to Unbelievers
20 Brethren, do not be children in understanding; however, in malice be babes, but in
understanding be mature.
21 In the law it is written:

"With men of other tongues and other lips
I will speak to this people;
And yet, for all that, they will not hear
Me,"[a]

says the Lord.
22 Therefore tongues are for a sign, not to
those who believe but to unbelievers; but
prophesying is not for unbelievers but for
those who believe.
23 Therefore if the whole church comes together in one place, and all speak with
tongues, and there come in *those who are*
uninformed or unbelievers, will they not say
that you are out of your mind?
24 But if all prophesy, and an unbeliever or
an uninformed person comes in, he is convinced by all, he is convicted by all.
25 And thus[a] the secrets of his heart are revealed; and so, falling down on *his* face, he
will worship God and report that God is truly
among you.

Order in Church Meetings
26 How is it then, brethren? Whenever you
come together, each of you has a psalm, has a
teaching, has a tongue, has a revelation, has
an interpretation. Let all things be done for
edification.
27 If anyone speaks in a tongue, *let there be*
two or at the most three, *each* in turn, and let
one interpret.
28 But if there is no interpreter, let him keep
silent in church, and let him speak to himself
and to God.
29 Let two or three prophets speak, and let
the others judge.
30 But if *anything* is revealed to another who
sits by, let the first keep silent.
31 For you can all prophesy one by one, that
all may learn and all may be encouraged.
32 And the spirits of the prophets are subject
to the prophets.
➤ 33 For God is not *the author* of confusion but
of peace, as in all the churches of the saints.
34 Let your[a] women keep silent in the
churches, for they are not permitted to speak;
but *they are* to be submissive, as the law also
says.
35 And if they want to learn something, let
them ask their own husbands at home; for it
is shameful for women to speak in church.
36 Or did the word of God come *originally*
from you? Or *was it* you only that it reached?
37 If anyone thinks himself to be a prophet or
spiritual, let him acknowledge that the things
which I write to you are the commandments
of the Lord.
38 But if anyone is ignorant, let him be ignorant.[a]
39 Therefore, brethren, desire earnestly to
prophesy, and do not forbid to speak with
tongues.
40 Let all things be done decently and in ➤
order.

The Risen Christ, Faith's Reality
15 Moreover, brethren, I declare to you the
gospel which I preached to you, which
also you received and in which you stand,
2 by which also you are saved, if you hold
fast that word which I preached to you—unless you believed in vain.
3 For I delivered to you first of all that which
I also received: that Christ died for our sins
according to the Scriptures,
4 and that He was buried, and that He rose
again the third day according to the Scriptures,
5 and that He was seen by Cephas, then by
the twelve.
6 After that He was seen by over five hundred brethren at once, of whom the greater
part remain to the present, but some have
fallen asleep.
7 After that He was seen by James, then by
all the apostles.
8 Then last of all He was seen by me also, as
by one born out of due time.
9 For I am the least of the apostles, who am
not worthy to be called an apostle, because I
persecuted the church of God.
10 But by the grace of God I am what I am, ➤
and His grace toward me was not in vain; but
I labored more abundantly than they all, yet

14:21 [a]Isaiah 28:11, 12 **14:25** [a]NU-Text omits *And thus.* **14:34** [a]NU-Text omits *your.* **14:38** [a]NU-Text reads *if anyone does not recognize this, he is not recognized.*

LIFE LESSONS

➤ 14:33 — *For God is not the author of confusion but of peace . . . .*

God does not tell one person to do something that completely contradicts and invalidates what He told someone else to do. Nor does He ever lead in opposition to His eternal Word. He is a God of order (but also of surprises!).

➤ 14:40 — *Let all things be done decently and in order.*

Chaos is never a sign of God's leading. When something spirals out of control, you can be sure that God did not design it. He may lead in unusual ways, but He will never lead in inconsistent ways.

➤ 15:10 — *I labored more abundantly than they all, yet not I, but the grace of God which was with me.*

Anything worthwhile that we accomplish for God is done through the guidance and empowering of His Holy Spirit. His grace prompts us to get busy, not to get lazy.

not I, but the grace of God *which was* with me.
11 Therefore, whether *it was* I or they, so we preach and so you believed.

The Risen Christ, Our Hope

12 Now if Christ is preached that He has been raised from the dead, how do some among you say that there is no resurrection of the dead?
13 But if there is no resurrection of the dead, then Christ is not risen.
14 And if Christ is not risen, then our preaching *is* empty and your faith *is* also empty.
15 Yes, and we are found false witnesses of God, because we have testified of God that He raised up Christ, whom He did not raise up—if in fact the dead do not rise.
16 For if *the* dead do not rise, then Christ is not risen.
➤ 17 And if Christ is not risen, your faith *is* futile; you are still in your sins!
18 Then also those who have fallen asleep in Christ have perished.
19 If in this life only we have hope in Christ, we are of all men the most pitiable.

The Last Enemy Destroyed

20 But now Christ is risen from the dead, *and* has become the firstfruits of those who have fallen asleep.
21 For since by man *came* death, by Man also *came* the resurrection of the dead.
22 For as in Adam all die, even so in Christ all shall be made alive.
23 But each one in his own order: Christ the firstfruits, afterward those *who are* Christ's at His coming.
24 Then *comes* the end, when He delivers the kingdom to God the Father, when He puts an end to all rule and all authority and power.
25 For He must reign till He has put all enemies under His feet.
26 The last enemy *that* will be destroyed *is* death.
27 For *"He has put all things under His feet."*[a] But when He says "all things are put under *Him*," *it is* evident that He who put all things under Him is excepted.
28 Now when all things are made subject to Him, then the Son Himself will also be subject to Him who put all things under Him, that God may be all in all.

Effects of Denying the Resurrection

29 Otherwise, what will they do who are baptized for the dead, if the dead do not rise at all? Why then are they baptized for the dead?
30 And why do we stand in jeopardy every hour?
31 I affirm, by the boasting in you which I have in Christ Jesus our Lord, I die daily.
32 If, in the manner of men, I have fought with beasts at Ephesus, what advantage *is it* to me? If *the* dead do not rise, *"Let us eat and drink, for tomorrow we die!"*[a]
33 Do not be deceived: "Evil company corrupts good habits."
34 Awake to righteousness, and do not sin; for some do not have the knowledge of God. I speak *this* to your shame.

A Glorious Body

35 But someone will say, "How are the dead raised up? And with what body do they come?"
36 Foolish one, what you sow is not made alive unless it dies.
37 And what you sow, you do not sow that body that shall be, but mere grain—perhaps wheat or some other *grain*.
38 But God gives it a body as He pleases, and to each seed its own body.
39 All flesh *is* not the same flesh, but *there is* one *kind of* flesh[a] of men, another flesh of animals, another of fish, *and* another of birds.
40 *There are* also celestial bodies and terrestrial bodies; but the glory of the celestial *is* one, and the *glory* of the terrestrial *is* another.
41 *There is* one glory of the sun, another glory of the moon, and another glory of the stars; for *one* star differs from *another* star in glory.
42 So also *is* the resurrection of the dead. *The body* is sown in corruption, it is raised in incorruption.
43 It is sown in dishonor, it is raised in glory. It is sown in weakness, it is raised in power.
44 It is sown a natural body, it is raised a spiritual body. There is a natural body, and there is a spiritual body.
45 And so it is written, *"The first man Adam became a living being."*[a] The last Adam *became* a life-giving spirit.
46 However, the spiritual is not first, but the natural, and afterward the spiritual.

15:27 [a]Psalm 8:6 **15:32** [a]Isaiah 22:13 **15:39** [a]NU-Text and M-Text omit *of flesh*. **15:45** [a]Genesis 2:7

LIFE LESSONS

➤ 15:17 — *And if Christ is not risen, your faith is futile; you are still in your sins!*

The physical, bodily resurrection of Jesus Christ from the dead is essential to the truth and power of the gospel. There is no Christianity without His resurrection—at least, not one worthy of any followers.

47 The first man *was* of the earth, *made* of dust; the second Man *is* the Lord[a] from heaven.

48 As *was* the *man* of dust, so also *are* those *who are made* of dust; and as *is* the heavenly *Man,* so also *are* those *who are* heavenly.

✳ 49 And as we have borne the image of the *man* of dust, we shall also bear[a] the image of the heavenly *Man.*

Our Final Victory

50 Now this I say, brethren, that flesh and blood cannot inherit the kingdom of God; nor does corruption inherit incorruption.

51 Behold, I tell you a mystery: We shall not all sleep, but we shall all be changed—

52 in a moment, in the twinkling of an eye, at the last trumpet. For the trumpet will sound, and the dead will be raised incorruptible, and we shall be changed.

53 For this corruptible must put on incorruption, and this mortal *must* put on immortality.

54 So when this corruptible has put on incorruption, and this mortal has put on immortality, then shall be brought to pass the saying that is written: *"Death is swallowed up in victory."*[a]

55*"O Death, where is your sting?*[a]
O Hades, where is your victory?"[b]

56 The sting of death *is* sin, and the strength of sin *is* the law.

57 But thanks *be* to God, who gives us the victory through our Lord Jesus Christ.

➢ 58 Therefore, my beloved brethren, be steadfast, immovable, always abounding in the work of the Lord, knowing that your labor is not in vain in the Lord.

Collection for the Saints

16 Now concerning the collection for the saints, as I have given orders to the churches of Galatia, so you must do also:

➢ 2 On the first *day* of the week let each one of you lay something aside, storing up as he may prosper, that there be no collections when I come.

3 And when I come, whomever you approve by *your* letters I will send to bear your gift to Jerusalem.

4 But if it is fitting that I go also, they will go with me.

Personal Plans

5 Now I will come to you when I pass through Macedonia (for I am passing through Macedonia).

6 And it may be that I will remain, or even spend the winter with you, that you may send me on my journey, wherever I go.

7 For I do not wish to see you now on the way; but I hope to stay a while with you, if the Lord permits. ➢

8 But I will tarry in Ephesus until Pentecost.

9 For a great and effective door has opened to me, and *there are* many adversaries. ➢

10 And if Timothy comes, see that he may be with you without fear; for he does the work of the Lord, as I also *do.*

11 Therefore let no one despise him. But send him on his journey in peace, that he may come to me; for I am waiting for him with the brethren.

12 Now concerning *our* brother Apollos, I strongly urged him to come to you with the brethren, but he was quite unwilling to come at this time; however, he will come when he has a convenient time.

Final Exhortations

13 Watch, stand fast in the faith, be brave, be strong.

14 Let all *that* you *do* be done with love.

15 I urge you, brethren—you know the

15:47 [a]NU-Text omits *the Lord.* 15:49 [a]M-Text reads *let us also bear.* 15:54 [a]Isaiah 25:8 15:55 [a]Hosea 13:14 [b]NU-Text reads *O Death, where is your victory? O Death, where is your sting?*

LIFE LESSONS

➢ 15:58 — *Therefore, my beloved brethren, be steadfast, immovable, always abounding in the work of the Lord, knowing that your labor is not in vain in the Lord.*

Our work for God has value and meaning for at least two reasons: (1) God is the one behind it, empowering us through His Spirit; (2) He promises to reward us incredibly well for our faithful service.

➢ 16:2 — *On the first day of the week let each one of you lay something aside, storing up as he may prosper, that there be no collections when I come.*

Paul instructs believers to give to God on a regular, proportional basis—regular as opposed to sporadic, intermittent, or rarely; and proportional to income rather than based on a set or arbitrary amount.

➢ 16:7 — *For I do not wish to see you now on the way; but I hope to stay a while with you, if the Lord permits.*

Paul wisely made all kinds of plans for his travels and his evangelistic work, but he even more wisely left those plans in God's hands to fulfill, alter, or scrap, as the Lord deemed best.

➢ 16:9 — *For a great and effective door has opened to me, and there are many adversaries.*

The blessing of God—in this case, the opening of a "great and effective door"—often comes bundled with difficulties—in this case, "many adversaries." We should not grow discouraged by the difficulties or become presumptuous because of the blessings.

household of Stephanas, that it is the firstfruits of Achaia, and *that* they have devoted
themselves to the ministry of the saints—
16 that you also submit to such, and to everyone who works and labors with *us.*
17 I am glad about the coming of Stephanas,
Fortunatus, and Achaicus, for what was lacking on your part they supplied.
18 For they refreshed my spirit and yours.
Therefore acknowledge such men.

Greetings and a Solemn Farewell

19 The churches of Asia greet you. Aquila
and Priscilla greet you heartily in the Lord,
with the church that is in their house.
20 All the brethren greet you. Greet one another with a holy kiss.
21 The salutation with my own hand—
Paul's.
22 If anyone does not love the Lord Jesus
Christ, let him be accursed.[a] O Lord,
come![b]
23 The grace of our Lord Jesus Christ *be* with
you.
24 My love *be* with you all in Christ Jesus.
Amen.

16:22 [a]Greek *anathema* [b]Aramaic *Maranatha*

LIFE LESSONS

➤ ***16:22 — If anyone does not love the Lord Jesus Christ, let him be accursed. O Lord, come!***

After the Lord returns for His people, it will be too late for unbelievers to turn to Him in faith and so bask in His love. That is why the right time to "get right" with God is always *right now.*

THE SECOND EPISTLE OF PAUL THE APOSTLE TO THE

CORINTHIANS

Subsequent to Paul's first letter to the Corinthians, false teachers infiltrated the church there and stirred up the people against Paul. They claimed he was fickle, proud, unimpressive in appearance and speech, dishonest, and unqualified as an apostle of Jesus Christ.

Paul sent Titus to Corinth to deal with these difficulties, and upon his return, the apostle rejoiced to hear of the Corinthians' change of heart. Paul wrote this letter to express his thanksgiving for the repentant majority and to appeal to the rebellious minority to accept his authority. Throughout the book, he defends his conduct, character, and calling as an apostle of Jesus Christ.

Second Corinthians contains the longest sustained passage on giving found anywhere in the New Testament (chapters 8, 9). The apostle gives us not only the ground for generosity—"For you know the grace of our Lord Jesus Christ, that though He was rich, yet for your sakes He became poor, that you through His poverty might become rich" (8:9)—but also a basic principle regarding it—"He who sows sparingly will also reap sparingly, and he who sows bountifully will also reap bountifully. So let each one give as he purposes in his heart, not grudgingly or of necessity; for God loves a cheerful giver" (9:6, 7).

This letter also highlights some fascinating personal details regarding the apostle Paul. He catalogs the extent of his sufferings for Christ (11:22–33), gives a famous description of his mysterious visit to "the third heaven" (12:1–6), and offers an account of his "thorn in the flesh," from which the apostle learned to say, "when I am weak, then I am strong" (12:7, 10).

To distinguish this epistle from First Corinthians, it was given the title *Pros Korinthious B,* the "Second to the Corinthians."

Theme: Primarily a defense and vindication of Paul's apostolic ministry.

Author: The apostle Paul.

Date: Thought to have been written shortly after his first letter to the Corinthians, around A.D. 53–55.

Structure: The letter divides easily into three sections. In the first, Paul explains why he changed the timing of his third visit to Corinth (chapters 1–7). In the second, he urges the church to prepare for his arrival (chapters 8, 9). In the last, he defends his apostolic authority and warns that he will use it to discipline the church if necessary (chapters 10–13).

As you read 2 Corinthians, watch for several life principles that play an important role in this book:

25. God blesses us so that we might bless others. *See 2 Corinthians 1:3–7; page 1351.*

15. Brokenness is God's requirement for maximum usefulness. *See 2 Corinthians 2:3–11; page 1352.*

23. You can never outgive God. *See 2 Corinthians 8:1—9:15; pages 1357–1359.*

21. Obedience always brings blessing. *See 2 Corinthians 10:2–6; page 1359.*

Greeting

1 Paul, an apostle of Jesus Christ by the will
of God, and Timothy *our* brother,
To the church of God which is at Corinth,
with all the saints who are in all Achaia:
2 Grace to you and peace from God our Father and the Lord Jesus Christ.

Comfort in Suffering

➤ 3 Blessed *be* the God and Father of our Lord
Jesus Christ, the Father of mercies and God of
all comfort,
4 who comforts us in all our tribulation, that
we may be able to comfort those who are in
any trouble, with the comfort with which we
ourselves are comforted by God.
5 For as the sufferings of Christ abound in
us, so our consolation also abounds through
Christ.
6 Now if we are afflicted, *it is* for your consolation and salvation, which is effective for
enduring the same sufferings which we also
suffer. Or if we are comforted, *it is* for your
consolation and salvation.
7 And our hope for you *is* steadfast, because
we know that as you are partakers of the sufferings, so also *you will partake* of the consolation.

Delivered from Suffering

8 For we do not want you to be ignorant,
brethren, of our trouble which came to us in
Asia: that we were burdened beyond measure, above strength, so that we despaired even
of life.
➤ 9 Yes, we had the sentence of death in ourselves, that we should not trust in ourselves
but in God who raises the dead,
10 who delivered us from so great a death,
and does[a] deliver us; in whom we trust that
He will still deliver *us,*
11 you also helping together in prayer for us,
that thanks may be given by many persons on
our[a] behalf for the gift *granted* to us through
many.

Paul's Sincerity

12 For our boasting is this: the testimony of
our conscience that we conducted ourselves
in the world in simplicity and godly sincerity,
not with fleshly wisdom but by the grace of
God, and more abundantly toward you.
13 For we are not writing any other things
to you than what you read or understand.
Now I trust you will understand, even to the
end
14 (as also you have understood us in part),
that we are your boast as you also *are* ours, in
the day of the Lord Jesus.

Sparing the Church

15 And in this confidence I intended to come
to you before, that you might have a second
benefit—
16 to pass by way of you to Macedonia, to
come again from Macedonia to you, and be
helped by you on my way to Judea.
17 Therefore, when I was planning this, did I
do it lightly? Or the things I plan, do I plan according to the flesh, that with me there should
be Yes, Yes, and No, No?
18 But *as* God *is* faithful, our word to you was
not Yes and No.
19 For the Son of God, Jesus Christ, who was
preached among you by us—by me, Silvanus,
and Timothy—was not Yes and No, but in Him
was Yes.
20 For all the promises of God in Him *are*
Yes, and in Him Amen, to the glory of God
through us.
21 Now He who establishes us with you in
Christ and has anointed us *is* God,
22 who also has sealed us and given us the
Spirit in our hearts as a guarantee.
23 Moreover I call God as witness against my
soul, that to spare you I came no more to
Corinth.
24 Not that we have dominion over your
faith, but are fellow workers for your joy; for
by faith you stand.
2 But I determined this within myself, that I
would not come again to you in sorrow.
2 For if I make you sorrowful, then who
is he who makes me glad but the one who is
made sorrowful by me?

1:10 [a]NU-Text reads *shall.* **1:11** [a]M-Text reads *your behalf.*

LIFE LESSONS

➤ **1:3, 4 — *. . . the Father of mercies and God of all comfort . . . comforts us in all our tribulation, that we may be able to comfort those who are in any trouble . . . .***

When trials hit, we can always be sure that God will come to our aid. Why? (1) It's His nature—He is "the Father of mercies" and the "God of all comfort." (2) He's training us to comfort others.

➤ **1:9 — *Yes, we had the sentence of death in ourselves, that we should not trust in ourselves but in God who raises the dead . . . .***

Sometimes God allows us to fall into deep valleys and dark pits in order to show us that we are never really in control, but that He always is and that He knows how to rescue us from "impossible" situations.

➤ **1:21, 22 — *God . . . also has sealed us and given us the Spirit in our hearts as a guarantee.***

God has sent the Holy Spirit to live in our hearts as something of a down payment on the whole package of salvation. He is God's "earnest money" to remind us that He will certainly complete what He started.

Forgive the Offender

3 And I wrote this very thing to you, lest, when I came, I should have sorrow over those from whom I ought to have joy, having confidence in you all that my joy is *the joy* of you all.

➤ 4 For out of much affliction and anguish of heart I wrote to you, with many tears, not that you should be grieved, but that you might know the love which I have so abundantly for you.

5 But if anyone has caused grief, he has not grieved me, but all of you to some extent—not to be too severe.

➤ 6 This punishment which *was inflicted* by the majority *is* sufficient for such a man,

7 so that, on the contrary, you *ought* rather to forgive and comfort *him*, lest perhaps such a one be swallowed up with too much sorrow.

8 Therefore I urge you to reaffirm *your* love to him.

9 For to this end I also wrote, that I might put you to the test, whether you are obedient in all things.

10 Now whom you forgive anything, I also *forgive*. For if indeed I have forgiven anything, I have forgiven that one[a] for your sakes in the presence of Christ,

11 lest Satan should take advantage of us; for we are not ignorant of his devices.

Triumph in Christ

12 Furthermore, when I came to Troas to *preach* Christ's gospel, and a door was opened to me by the Lord,

13 I had no rest in my spirit, because I did not find Titus my brother; but taking my leave of them, I departed for Macedonia.

➤ 14 Now thanks *be* to God who always leads us in triumph in Christ, and through us diffuses the fragrance of His knowledge in every place.

15 For we are to God the fragrance of Christ among those who are being saved and among those who are perishing.

16 To the one *we are* the aroma of death *leading* to death, and to the other the aroma of life *leading* to life. And who *is* sufficient for these things?

17 For we are not, as so many,[a] peddling the word of God; but as of sincerity, but as from God, we speak in the sight of God in Christ.

Christ's Epistle

3 Do we begin again to commend ourselves? Or do we need, as some *others*, epistles of commendation to you or *letters* of commendation from you?

2 You are our epistle written in our hearts, known and read by all men;

3 clearly you are an epistle of Christ, ministered by us, written not with ink but by the Spirit of the living God, not on tablets of stone but on tablets of flesh, *that is*, of the heart.

The Spirit, Not the Letter

4 And we have such trust through Christ toward God.

5 Not that we are sufficient of ourselves to think of anything as *being* from ourselves, but our sufficiency *is* from God, ◄

6 who also made us sufficient as ministers of the new covenant, not of the letter but of the Spirit;[a] for the letter kills, but the Spirit gives life. ◄

Glory of the New Covenant

7 But if the ministry of death, written *and* engraved on stones, was glorious, so that the children of Israel could not look steadily at

---

2:10 [a]NU-Text reads *For indeed, what I have forgiven, if I have forgiven anything, I did it.* **2:17** [a]M-Text reads *the rest.*
3:6 [a]Or *spirit*

LIFE LESSONS

➤ 2:4 — *For out of much affliction and anguish of heart I wrote to you, with many tears, not that you should be grieved, but that you might know the love which I have so abundantly for you.*

We should never take God's discipline as a sign of His hostility toward us or disinterest in us, but rather as a sure token of His love. His goal is never to grieve us, but to get us back on a road to life.

➤ 2:6, 7 — *This punishment which was inflicted by the majority is sufficient for such a man, so that, on the contrary, you ought rather to forgive and comfort him, lest perhaps such a one be swallowed up with too much sorrow.*

The point of discipline—God's or the church's—is always restoration and renewal, not retribution and rejection. Sorrow has value only insofar as it moves someone to repentance and back into full fellowship.

➤ 2:14 — *Now thanks be to God who always leads us in triumph in Christ . . . .*

Paul does not mean that things always turn out the way we want, but that in Christ we are always on the road to victory. Setbacks happen, but they are never final or fatal.

➤ 3:5 — *Not that we are sufficient of ourselves to think of anything as being from ourselves, but our sufficiency is from God . . . .*

No one is so talented or capable that he or she can succeed in life or ministry without depending on God every step of the way. Jesus said, "without Me you can do nothing" (John 15:5).

➤ 3:6 — *. . . for the letter kills, but the Spirit gives life.*

The Old Covenant, the law, certainly expressed the divine will of God and accurately portrayed His holy and perfect nature, but it had no power to help us obey God's will. The Spirit does.

the face of Moses because of the glory of his countenance, which *glory* was passing away,
8 how will the ministry of the Spirit not be more glorious?
9 For if the ministry of condemnation *had* glory, the ministry of righteousness exceeds much more in glory.
10 For even what was made glorious had no glory in this respect, because of the glory that excels.
11 For if what is passing away *was* glorious, what remains *is* much more glorious.
12 Therefore, since we have such hope, we use great boldness of speech—
13 unlike Moses, *who* put a veil over his face so that the children of Israel could not look steadily at the end of what was passing away.
14 But their minds were blinded. For until this day the same veil remains unlifted in the reading of the Old Testament, because the *veil* is taken away in Christ.
15 But even to this day, when Moses is read, a veil lies on their heart.
16 Nevertheless when one turns to the Lord, the veil is taken away.
➤ 17 Now the Lord is the Spirit; and where the Spirit of the Lord *is,* there *is* liberty.
➤ 18 But we all, with unveiled face, beholding as in a mirror the glory of the Lord, are being transformed into the same image from glory to glory, just as by the Spirit of the Lord.

The Light of Christ's Gospel

4 Therefore, since we have this ministry, as we have received mercy, we do not lose heart.
2 But we have renounced the hidden things of shame, not walking in craftiness nor handling the word of God deceitfully, but by manifestation of the truth commending ourselves to every man's conscience in the sight of God.
3 But even if our gospel is veiled, it is veiled to those who are perishing,
➤ 4 whose minds the god of this age has blinded, who do not believe, lest the light of the gospel of the glory of Christ, who is the image of God, should shine on them.
5 For we do not preach ourselves, but Christ Jesus the Lord, and ourselves your bondservants for Jesus' sake.
6 For it is the God who commanded light to shine out of darkness, who has shone in our hearts to *give* the light of the knowledge of the glory of God in the face of Jesus Christ.

Cast Down but Unconquered

7 But we have this treasure in earthen vessels, that the excellence of the power may be of God and not of us.
8 *We are* hard-pressed on every side, yet not crushed; *we are* perplexed, but not in despair;
9 persecuted, but not forsaken; struck down, but not destroyed—
10 always carrying about in the body the dying of the Lord Jesus, that the life of Jesus also may be manifested in our body.
11 For we who live are always delivered to death for Jesus' sake, that the life of Jesus also may be manifested in our mortal flesh.
12 So then death is working in us, but life in you.
13 And since we have the same spirit of faith, according to what is written, *"I believed and therefore I spoke,"*[a] we also believe and therefore speak,
14 knowing that He who raised up the Lord Jesus will also raise us up with Jesus, and will present *us* with you.
15 For all things *are* for your sakes, that grace, having spread through the many, may cause thanksgiving to abound to the glory of God.

Seeing the Invisible

16 Therefore we do not lose heart. Even though our outward man is perishing, yet the inward *man* is being renewed day by day.

4:13 [a]Psalm 116:10

LIFE LESSONS

➤ 3:17 — *Now the Lord is the Spirit; and where the Spirit of the Lord is, there is liberty.*

When Jesus comes into a human heart by faith, through the Spirit He sets that person free from the bondage of sin, the chains of death, and the futile attempt of trying to become righteous through self-effort.

➤ 3:18 — *But we all, with unveiled face, beholding as in a mirror the glory of the Lord, are being transformed into the same image from glory to glory . . . .*

God is after transformed lives, not merely reformed ones. Part of that transformation happens as we train our minds to focus on the person of Jesus. As we meditate on Him, the Spirit begins molding us into His image.

➤ 4:4 — *. . . whose minds the god of this age has blinded, who do not believe, lest the light of the gospel of the glory of Christ . . . should shine on them.*

We could spare ourselves a lot of anxiety in our efforts at evangelism if we would remember that witnessing to others about Christ means serious spiritual warfare. Satan actively opposes our efforts (see Matt. 13:19).

➤ 4:7 — *But we have this treasure in earthen vessels, that the excellence of the power may be of God and not of us.*

We desire to be as strong as possible, and there's nothing wrong or unusual about that. But God often allows us to remain weak, at least in some areas, so that all can see *He* accomplishes the work, not us.

➤ 17 For our light affliction, which is but for a moment, is working for us a far more exceeding *and* eternal weight of glory,
18 while we do not look at the things which are seen, but at the things which are not seen. For the things which are seen *are* temporary, but the things which are not seen *are* eternal.

Assurance of the Resurrection

5 For we know that if our earthly house, *this* tent, is destroyed, we have a building from God, a house not made with hands, eternal in the heavens.
2 For in this we groan, earnestly desiring to be clothed with our habitation which is from heaven,
3 if indeed, having been clothed, we shall not be found naked.
4 For we who are in *this* tent groan, being burdened, not because we want to be unclothed, but further clothed, that mortality may be swallowed up by life.
5 Now He who has prepared us for this very thing *is* God, who also has given us the Spirit as a guarantee.
6 So *we are* always confident, knowing that while we are at home in the body we are absent from the Lord.
➤ 7 For we walk by faith, not by sight.
8 We are confident, yes, well pleased rather to be absent from the body and to be present with the Lord.

The Judgment Seat of Christ

➤ **9** Therefore we make it our aim, whether present or absent, to be well pleasing to Him.
10 For we must all appear before the judgment seat of Christ, that each one may receive the things *done* in the body, according to what he has done, whether good or bad.
11 Knowing, therefore, the terror of the Lord, we persuade men; but we are well known to God, and I also trust are well known in your consciences.

Be Reconciled to God

12 For we do not commend ourselves again to you, but give you opportunity to boast on our behalf, that you may have *an answer* for those who boast in appearance and not in heart.
13 For if we are beside ourselves, *it is* for God; or if we are of sound mind, *it is* for you.
14 For the love of Christ compels us, because we judge thus: that if One died for all, then all died;
15 and He died for all, that those who live should live no longer for themselves, but for Him who died for them and rose again.
16 Therefore, from now on, we regard no one according to the flesh. Even though we have known Christ according to the flesh, yet now we know *Him thus* no longer.
17 Therefore, if anyone *is* in Christ, *he is* a new creation; old things have passed away; behold, all things have become new. ✳
18 Now all things *are* of God, who has reconciled us to Himself through Jesus Christ, and has given us the ministry of reconciliation,
19 that is, that God was in Christ reconciling the world to Himself, not imputing their trespasses to them, and has committed to us the word of reconciliation. ➤
20 Now then, we are ambassadors for Christ, as though God were pleading through us: we implore *you* on Christ's behalf, be reconciled to God.
21 For He made Him who knew no sin *to be* sin for us, that we might become the righteousness of God in Him. ➤

LIFE LESSONS

➤ **4:17 — *For our light affliction, which is but for a moment, is working for us a far more exceeding and eternal weight of glory . . . .***

God will never be a debtor to anyone. That means that any "sacrifice" we make or hardship we endure for His sake and by His Spirit, He will amply reward out of all proportion to what we suffered.

➤ **5:7 — *For we walk by faith, not by sight.***

Paul writes this verse in the context of the resurrection of the body; we remain confident that we will live again in a new and glorified body, not because we see it, but because we trust the One who gave the promise.

➤ **5:9 — *Therefore we make it our aim, whether present or absent, to be well pleasing to Him.***

If we love the Lord, we will make it our aim and our delight to please Him by the way we live. We look for ways to make Him smile, rather than probing to see how close to the cliff's edge we can get without falling off.

➤ **5:19 — *God was in Christ reconciling the world to Himself, not imputing their trespasses to them, and has committed to us the word of reconciliation.***

God has given to us the task of letting the world know what Jesus has done to make it possible for everyone who has faith in Him to enjoy eternal life and an intimate relationship with the Father.

➤ **5:21 — *For He made Him who knew no sin to be sin for us, that we might become the righteousness of God in Him.***

God took the sins of the whole world and, on the cross, piled them on the back of Jesus Christ, the one person who had never committed a single sin. Jesus took our punishment so that we might receive His righteousness.

What the Bible Says About ACCOUNTABILITY RELATIONSHIPS

2 Cor. 5:10

In an age of individual rights, the principle of accountability runs strongly against the popular grain. Our pride, egotism, and self-sufficiency rebel against the concept of being accountable to one another for our conduct.

Yet accountability is a strong biblical teaching that greatly enhances our spiritual and vocational pursuits. Scripture tells us that God has made us accountable both to Him and to others.

Accountability provides a wise check and balance. Whether it be a supervisor at work or a personal friend, we all need someone who will be able both to admonish and encourage us. God allows others to observe and frankly discuss our areas of weakness, which otherwise could result in eventual ruin.

Let's face it: Nobody likes to admit his shortcomings. But in submitting to someone we hold in high esteem, or one in authority over us, we are winners. We stimulate our performance and help keep ourselves from turning freedom into license.

Even though he was the preeminent apostle of his day, Paul remained accountable to his home church at Antioch, returning there on occasion to report on his journeys. As a temperamental young preacher, Timothy was accountable to Paul. Jesus had sent out his disciples, not just for mutual support, but for accountability.

We are free in Christ, but we are also bondservants of Christ.

Rather than avoid or chafe in such relationships, we should thank God for very practical means of promoting our spiritual growth and developing our sense of responsibility.

Our ultimate accountability, of course, is to the Lord. "So then each of you shall give account of himself to God" (Rom. 14:12). Knowing that we must one day answer to a just God should be a powerful incentive for holiness and obedience. "For we must all appear before the judgment seat of Christ, that each may one day receive the things done in the body, according to what he has done, whether good or bad" (2 Cor. 5:10).

Becoming a Christian does not relieve us of personal responsibility. Although our sins have been forgiven through Christ's sacrifice, we still are responsible for our behavior. What we do on earth *matters.* We are free in Christ, but we are also bondservants of Christ.

God has so designed us that we need to remain continually aware of our accountability to an all-knowing Creator, as well as our accountability in personal relationships. "As iron sharpens iron, so a man sharpens the countenance of his friend" (Prov. 27:17).

See the Life Principles Index for further study:

28. No Christian has ever been called to "go it alone" in his or her walk of faith.

25. God blesses us so that we might bless others.

Marks of the Ministry

➤ **6** We then, *as* workers together *with Him*
also plead with *you* not to receive the
grace of God in vain.
➤ 2 For He says:

"In an acceptable time I have heard you,
And in the day of salvation I have helped
you."[a]

Behold, now *is* the accepted time; behold,
now *is* the day of salvation.
3 We give no offense in anything, that our
ministry may not be blamed.
4 But in all *things* we commend ourselves as
ministers of God: in much patience, in tribulations, in needs, in distresses,
5 in stripes, in imprisonments, in tumults, in
labors, in sleeplessness, in fastings;
6 by purity, by knowledge, by longsuffering,
by kindness, by the Holy Spirit, by sincere
love,
7 by the word of truth, by the power of God,
by the armor of righteousness on the right
hand and on the left,
8 by honor and dishonor, by evil report and
good report; as deceivers, and *yet* true;
9 as unknown, and *yet* well known; as
dying, and behold we live; as chastened, and
yet not killed;
10 as sorrowful, yet always rejoicing; as poor,
yet making many rich; as having nothing, and
yet possessing all things.

Be Holy

11 O Corinthians! We have spoken openly to
you, our heart is wide open.
12 You are not restricted by us, but you are
restricted by your *own* affections.
13 Now in return for the same (I speak as to
children), you also be open.
➤ 14 Do not be unequally yoked together with
unbelievers. For what fellowship has righteousness with lawlessness? And what communion has light with darkness?
15 And what accord has Christ with Belial?
Or what part has a believer with an unbeliever?
16 And what agreement has the temple of ✳
God with idols? For you[a] are the temple of the
living God. As God has said:

"I will dwell in them
And walk among them.
I will be their God,
And they shall be My people."[b]

17 Therefore

"Come out from among them
And be separate, says the Lord.
Do not touch what is unclean,
And I will receive you."[a]
18 *"I will be a Father to you,*
And you shall be My sons and
daughters,
Says the LORD Almighty."[a]

7 Therefore, having these promises, ◄
beloved, let us cleanse ourselves from all
filthiness of the flesh and spirit, perfecting
holiness in the fear of God.

The Corinthians' Repentance

2 Open *your hearts* to us. We have wronged
no one, we have corrupted no one, we have
cheated no one.
3 I do not say *this* to condemn; for I have
said before that you are in our hearts, to die
together and to live together.
4 Great *is* my boldness of speech toward
you, great *is* my boasting on your behalf. I am
filled with comfort. I am exceedingly joyful in
all our tribulation.
5 For indeed, when we came to Macedonia,
our bodies had no rest, but we were troubled
on every side. Outside *were* conflicts, inside
were fears.

6:2 [a]Isaiah 49:8 **6:16** [a]NU-Text reads *we.* [b]Leviticus 26:12; Jeremiah 32:38; Ezekiel 37:27 **6:17** [a]Isaiah 52:11; Ezekiel 20:34, 41 **6:18** [a]2 Samuel 7:14

LIFE LESSONS

➤ 6:1 — *We then, as workers together with Him also plead with you not to receive the grace of God in vain.*

We may "receive the grace of God in vain" in many ways: by failing to draw upon its power to live in a godly way; by hearing but never accepting the gospel; or by shifting allegiance to "another gospel" (2 Cor. 11:4).

➤ 6:2 — *For He says: "In an acceptable time I have heard you, and in the day of salvation I have helped you." Behold, now is the accepted time; behold, now is the day of salvation.*

It never makes sense to put off a decision to accept God's offer of salvation. How many have waited too long? And anyway, why would anyone want to delay the joy that comes through a vital relationship with God?

➤ 6:14 — *Do not be unequally yoked together with unbelievers. For what fellowship has righteousness with lawlessness? And what communion has light with darkness?*

This verse usually gets quoted in reference to choosing a marriage partner, and while that's certainly a legitimate application, marriage is not the context here. *All of life* is the context (see 1 Cor. 15:33).

➤ 7:1 — *Therefore, having these promises, beloved, let us cleanse ourselves from all filthiness of the flesh and spirit, perfecting holiness in the fear of God.*

The promises of God are meant to lead us to purity of life. But they do not do so automatically; *we* have to appropriate them and access their power by choosing to use them as God intended.

➤ 6 Nevertheless God, who comforts the
downcast, comforted us by the coming of Titus,
7 and not only by his coming, but also by
the consolation with which he was comforted
in you, when he told us of your earnest desire,
your mourning, your zeal for me, so that I rejoiced even more.
8 For even if I made you sorry with my letter, I do not regret it; though I did regret it. For
I perceive that the same epistle made you
sorry, though only for a while.
➤ 9 Now I rejoice, not that you were made
sorry, but that your sorrow led to repentance.
For you were made sorry in a godly manner,
that you might suffer loss from us in nothing.
➤ 10 For godly sorrow produces repentance
leading to salvation, not to be regretted; but
the sorrow of the world produces death.
11 For observe this very thing, that you sorrowed in a godly manner: What diligence it
produced in you, *what* clearing *of yourselves,*
what indignation, *what* fear, *what* vehement
desire, *what* zeal, *what* vindication! In all
things you proved yourselves to be clear in
this matter.
12 Therefore, although I wrote to you, *I did*
not *do it* for the sake of him who had done the
wrong, nor for the sake of him who suffered
wrong, but that our care for you in the sight of
God might appear to you.

The Joy of Titus

13 Therefore we have been comforted in your
comfort. And we rejoiced exceedingly more
for the joy of Titus, because his spirit has
been refreshed by you all.
14 For if in anything I have boasted to him
about you, I am not ashamed. But as we spoke
all things to you in truth, even so our boasting
to Titus was found true.
15 And his affections are greater for you as
he remembers the obedience of you all, how
with fear and trembling you received him.
16 Therefore I rejoice that I have confidence
in you in everything.

Excel in Giving

8 Moreover, brethren, we make known to
you the grace of God bestowed on the
churches of Macedonia:
2 that in a great trial of affliction the abundance of their joy and their deep poverty
abounded in the riches of their liberality.
3 For I bear witness that according to *their*
ability, yes, and beyond *their* ability, *they*
were freely willing,
4 imploring us with much urgency that we
would receive[a] the gift and the fellowship of
the ministering to the saints.
5 And not *only* as we had hoped, but they ➤
first gave themselves to the Lord, and *then* to
us by the will of God.
6 So we urged Titus, that as he had begun,
so he would also complete this grace in you as
well.
7 But as you abound in everything—in faith,
in speech, in knowledge, in all diligence, and
in your love for us—*see* that you abound in
this grace also.

Christ Our Pattern

8 I speak not by commandment, but I am
testing the sincerity of your love by the diligence of others.
9 For you know the grace of our Lord Jesus ➤
Christ, that though He was rich, yet for your
sakes He became poor, that you through His
poverty might become rich.

8:4 [a]NU-Text and M-Text omit *that we would receive,* thus changing text to *urgency for the favor and fellowship* . . . .

LIFE LESSONS

➤ 7:6 — *God, who comforts the downcast, comforted us by the coming of Titus . . . .*

How often do we miss God's answers to prayer because we don't recognize them when they come? We look for something miraculous, unusual, spectacular—and God sends us Titus.

➤ 7:9 — *Now I rejoice, not that you were made sorry, but that your sorrow led to repentance.*

God chastens us, not so that we will feel shamed, but so that our sorrow leads us to repentance and restored fellowship with God. The *result* makes Him happy, not the means He uses to achieve the result.

➤ 7:10 — *For godly sorrow produces repentance leading to salvation, not to be regretted; but the sorrow of the world produces death.*

Sorrow that doesn't lead anywhere has no value. Sorrow for the sake of sorrow comes from the devil's toolbox, not that of God. Godly sorrow leads to life; demonic sorrow leads to death.

➤ 8:5 — *And not only as we had hoped, but they first gave themselves to the Lord, and then to us by the will of God.*

God isn't after your time or your talents or your bank account; He desires *you*. He already owns the world and everything in it (Ex. 19:5), so the only thing you have that He wants is your heart.

➤ 8:9 — *For you know the grace of our Lord Jesus Christ, that though He was rich, yet for your sakes He became poor, that you through His poverty might become rich.*

In heaven, Jesus was rich through the love He shared with the Father and the Spirit. On earth, we were poor in our estrangement from God. Jesus emptied Himself on earth so that we might be full in heaven.

10 And in this I give advice: It is to your advantage not only to be doing what you began and were desiring to do a year ago;
11 but now you also must complete the doing *of it;* that as *there was* a readiness to desire *it,* so *there* also *may be* a completion out of what *you* have.
12 For if there is first a willing mind, *it is* accepted according to what one has, *and* not according to what he does not have.
13 For *I do* not *mean* that others should be eased and you burdened;
14 but by an equality, *that* now at this time your abundance *may supply* their lack, that their abundance also may *supply* your lack—that there may be equality.
15 As it is written, *"He who gathered much had nothing left over, and he who gathered little had no lack."*[a]

Collection for the Judean Saints

➤ **16** But thanks *be* to God who puts[a] the same earnest care for you into the heart of Titus.
17 For he not only accepted the exhortation, but being more diligent, he went to you of his own accord.
18 And we have sent with him the brother whose praise *is* in the gospel throughout all the churches,
19 and not only *that,* but who was also chosen by the churches to travel with us with this gift, which is administered by us to the glory of the Lord Himself and *to show* your ready mind,
20 avoiding this: that anyone should blame us in this lavish gift which is administered by us—
21 providing honorable things, not only in the sight of the Lord, but also in the sight of men.
22 And we have sent with them our brother whom we have often proved diligent in many things, but now much more diligent, because of the great confidence which *we have* in you.
23 If *anyone inquires* about Titus, *he is* my partner and fellow worker concerning you. Or if our brethren *are inquired about, they are* messengers of the churches, the glory of Christ.
24 Therefore show to them, and[a] before the churches, the proof of your love and of our boasting on your behalf.

Administering the Gift

9 Now concerning the ministering to the saints, it is superfluous for me to write to you;
2 for I know your willingness, about which I boast of you to the Macedonians, that Achaia was ready a year ago; and your zeal has stirred up the majority.
3 Yet I have sent the brethren, lest our boasting of you should be in vain in this respect, that, as I said, you may be ready;
4 lest if *some* Macedonians come with me and find you unprepared, we (not to mention you!) should be ashamed of this confident boasting.[a]
5 Therefore I thought it necessary to exhort the brethren to go to you ahead of time, and prepare your generous gift beforehand, which *you had* previously promised, that it may be ready as *a matter of* generosity and not as a grudging obligation.

The Cheerful Giver

6 But this *I say:* He who sows sparingly will also reap sparingly, and he who sows bountifully will also reap bountifully. ✳
7 *So let* each one *give* as he purposes in his heart, not grudgingly or of necessity; for God loves a cheerful giver. ≺
8 And God *is* able to make all grace abound toward you, that you, always having all sufficiency in all *things,* may have an abundance for every good work. ≺
9 As it is written:

"He has dispersed abroad,
He has given to the poor;
His righteousness endures forever."[a]

10 Now may[a] He who supplies seed to the sower, and bread for food, supply and multi-

8:15 [a]Exodus 16:18 **8:16** [a]NU-Text reads *has put.* **8:24** [a]NU-Text and M-Text omit *and.* **9:4** [a]NU-Text reads *this confidence.* **9:9** [a]Psalm 112:9 **9:10** [a]NU-Text reads *Now He who supplies . . . will supply . . .*

LIFE LESSONS

➤ ***8:16, 17 — But thanks be to God who puts the same earnest care for you into the heart of Titus. For . . . he went to you of his own accord.***

Here we see the sovereignty of God and the free will of man working hand-in-hand. God put a concern into the heart of Titus, but Titus acted on that concern "of his own accord."

➤ ***9:7 — So let each one give as he purposes in his heart, not grudgingly or of necessity; for God loves a cheerful giver.***

In giving, as in all other areas of Christian living, God wants our hearts. He wants willing, joyful, eager participation in His work, not grumbling, halfhearted compliance to a rule, as if we did God a favor by doing so.

➤ ***9:8 — And God is able to make all grace abound toward you, that you, always having all sufficiency in all things, may have an abundance for every good work.***

God's grace sustains us throughout our lives. His grace gives us our daily bread, supplies us with lungs full of air, and grants us the ability to make a living. God wants an *abundant* life for us; His grace makes it possible.

ply the seed you have *sown* and increase the fruits of your righteousness,
11 while *you are* enriched in everything for all liberality, which causes thanksgiving through us to God.
12 For the administration of this service not only supplies the needs of the saints, but also is abounding through many thanksgivings to God,
13 while, through the proof of this ministry, they glorify God for the obedience of your confession to the gospel of Christ, and for *your* liberal sharing with them and all *men,*
14 and by their prayer for you, who long for you because of the exceeding grace of God in you.
➤ 15 Thanks *be* to God for His indescribable gift!

The Spiritual War

10 Now I, Paul, myself am pleading with you by the meekness and gentleness of Christ—who in presence *am* lowly among you, but being absent am bold toward you.
2 But I beg *you* that when I am present I may not be bold with that confidence by which I intend to be bold against some, who think of us as if we walked according to the flesh.
➤ 3 For though we walk in the flesh, we do not war according to the flesh.
4 For the weapons of our warfare *are* not carnal but mighty in God for pulling down strongholds,
➤ 5 casting down arguments and every high thing that exalts itself against the knowledge of God, bringing every thought into captivity to the obedience of Christ,
6 and being ready to punish all disobedience when your obedience is fulfilled.

Reality of Paul's Authority

7 Do you look at things according to the outward appearance? If anyone is convinced in himself that he is Christ's, let him again consider this in himself, that just as he *is* Christ's, even so we *are* Christ's.[a]
8 For even if I should boast somewhat more about our authority, which the Lord gave us[a] for edification and not for your destruction, I shall not be ashamed—
9 lest I seem to terrify you by letters.
10 "For *his* letters," they say, "*are* weighty and powerful, but *his* bodily presence *is* weak, and *his* speech contemptible."
11 Let such a person consider this, that what we are in word by letters when we are absent, such *we will* also *be* in deed when we are present.

Limits of Paul's Authority

12 For we dare not class ourselves or compare ourselves with those who commend themselves. But they, measuring themselves by themselves, and comparing themselves among themselves, are not wise.
13 We, however, will not boast beyond measure, but within the limits of the sphere which God appointed us—a sphere which especially includes you.
14 For we are not overextending ourselves (as though *our authority* did not extend to you), for it was to you that we came with the gospel of Christ;
15 not boasting of things beyond measure, *that is,* in other men's labors, but having hope, *that* as your faith is increased, we shall be greatly enlarged by you in our sphere,
16 to preach the gospel in the *regions* beyond you, *and* not to boast in another man's sphere of accomplishment.
17 But *"he who glories, let him glory in the LORD."*[a]
18 For not he who commends himself is approved, but whom the Lord commends. ➤

Concern for Their Faithfulness

11 Oh, that you would bear with me in a little folly—and indeed you do bear with me.
2 For I am jealous for you with godly jealousy. For I have betrothed you to one husband,

10:7 [a]NU-Text reads *even as we are.* 10:8 [a]NU-Text omits *us.* 10:17 [a]Jeremiah 9:24 11:3 [a]NU-Text adds *and purity.*

LIFE LESSONS

➤ 9:15 — *Thanks be to God for His indescribable gift!*

The greatest gift we could ever receive is the marvelous grace of God, which hit its apex in the gift of God's Son, Jesus Christ. The only reason we have the privilege of giving is that God already gave far more.

➤ 10:3 — *For though we walk in the flesh, we do not war according to the flesh.*

We do not yet have our glorified bodies; we still live in tents of unredeemed flesh. Yet because the Spirit of the living God dwells within us, we serve God not in the flesh, but through faith, in the Spirit.

➤ 10:5 — *. . . bringing every thought into captivity to the obedience of Christ . . . .*

Paul speaks a great deal about training the mind to think in a way that honors God, because the mind is the primary battlefield for spiritual warfare on the personal level. Transformed minds lead to both joy and victory.

➤ 10:18 — *For not he who commends himself is approved, but whom the Lord commends.*

Self-congratulation is nothing but an expression of unredeemed flesh. Those who boast want to call attention to themselves, which has no value. So Paul says, "he who glories, let him glory in the Lord" (2 Cor. 10:17).

LIFE PRINCIPLE 23

YOU CAN NEVER OUTGIVE GOD.

2 COR. 9:8

King David knew that God had prospered him and given him rest from all his enemies. One day he looked around at his comfortable home and said to Nathan the prophet, "See now, I dwell in a house of cedar, but the ark of God dwells inside tent curtains" (2 Sam. 7:2). He wanted to build a temple for God—no small undertaking.

But God had a much bigger gift in mind for David. He said, "the LORD tells you that He will make you a house . . . . And your house and your kingdom shall be established forever" (2 Sam. 7:11, 16).

This story powerfully reminds us that you can *never* outgive God. While He invites your gifts and offerings, He will always give you far more than you could possibly give Him. He will never be a debtor to anyone.

Jesus declared that anybody who gave one of His followers even a cup of water in His name would be lavishly rewarded (Mark 9:41). He once illustrated God's generosity by describing how a wealthy "Lord" rewarded servants with multiple cities in return for their doubling the little bit of money he had given them. Peter once boasted to the Lord, "See, we have left all and followed you" (Luke 18:28). He probably expected a pat on the back. Instead Jesus told him, "Assuredly, I say to you, there is no one who has left house or parents or brothers or wife or children, for the sake of the kingdom of God, who shall not receive many times more in this present time, and in the age to come eternal life" (18:29, 30).

In one of the clearest examples of this principle in Scripture, Jesus tells us, "Give, and it will be given to you: good measure, pressed down, shaken together, and running over will be put into your bosom" (Luke 6:38).

It's just a fact: you can never outgive God.

The Old Testament prophet Malachi certainly believed this principle. Through him, God instructed the people to bring Him the full tithe and said, "'try Me now in this,' says the LORD of hosts, 'if I will not open for you the windows of heaven and pour out for you such blessing that there will not be room enough to receive it" (Mal. 3:10).

To tithe is to give ten percent of our income to God for His work. All that we have is a gift from God; therefore, a tithe is a mere portion of what He has already given to us. If we obey God's Word and cheerfully give the portion He has requested of us, He will bless us and the work of His kingdom.

All that we have is a gift from God.

Several years ago, God led us to purchase some property for the church. We knew that it was God's will for us, so we began to pray that He would provide the funds necessary. I began to pray about what the Lord would have me give. He began to impress upon me to sell my cameras. Photography is my hobby, and my cameras are obviously valuable to that pursuit. I felt convinced that was what God wanted me to do. So I sold my cameras and gave the money to the building fund. Many of the other members of our congregation also gave possessions and treasures. It was a great time in our fellowship for seeking His will in our finances and testing our willingness to obey the Lord.

Several months later I received a call from a woman who asked if I was the Charles Stanley who had owned a particular camera. When I said, "Yes," she replied, "I bought this and God told me I needed to give it to you." Her words took me by surprise, but I realized that because I was willing to part with that camera, God honored my obedience.

God's promises await the obedient. He challenges us to give Him the privilege to prove Himself and has promised to bless us in return (Prov. 3:9, 10). When we obey, He will protect our finances, just as He protected His obedient people in the Old Testament from the insects that otherwise would have devoured their crops.

The psalmist asked, "What shall I render to the LORD for all His benefits toward me?" (Ps. 116:12). The question could be translated, "How can I repay the Lord for all His goodness toward me?"

The answer is, he can't. No one can. Because nobody can outgive the Lord.

See the Life Principles Index for further study.

God's promises await the obedient.

that I may present *you as* a chaste virgin to Christ.

➤ 3 But I fear, lest somehow, as the serpent deceived Eve by his craftiness, so your minds may be corrupted from the simplicity[a] that is in Christ.

4 For if he who comes preaches another Jesus whom we have not preached, or *if* you receive a different spirit which you have not received, or a different gospel which you have not accepted—you may well put up with it!

Paul and False Apostles

5 For I consider that I am not at all inferior to the most eminent apostles.

6 Even though *I am* untrained in speech, yet *I am* not in knowledge. But we have been thoroughly manifested[a] among you in all things.

7 Did I commit sin in humbling myself that you might be exalted, because I preached the gospel of God to you free of charge?

8 I robbed other churches, taking wages *from them* to minister to you.

9 And when I was present with you, and in need, I was a burden to no one, for what I lacked the brethren who came from Macedonia supplied. And in everything I kept myself from being burdensome to you, and so I will keep *myself*.

10 As the truth of Christ is in me, no one shall stop me from this boasting in the regions of Achaia.

11 Why? Because I do not love you? God knows!

12 But what I do, I will also continue to do, that I may cut off the opportunity from those who desire an opportunity to be regarded just as we are in the things of which they boast.

13 For such *are* false apostles, deceitful workers, transforming themselves into apostles of Christ.

➤ 14 And no wonder! For Satan himself transforms himself into an angel of light.

15 Therefore *it is* no great thing if his ministers also transform themselves into ministers of righteousness, whose end will be according to their works.

Reluctant Boasting

16 I say again, let no one think me a fool. If otherwise, at least receive me as a fool, that I also may boast a little.

17 What I speak, I speak not according to the Lord, but as it were, foolishly, in this confidence of boasting.

18 Seeing that many boast according to the flesh, I also will boast.

19 For you put up with fools gladly, since you *yourselves* are wise!

20 For you put up with it if one brings you into bondage, if one devours *you*, if one takes *from you*, if one exalts himself, if one strikes you on the face.

21 To *our* shame I say that we were too weak for that! But in whatever anyone is bold—I speak foolishly—I am bold also.

Suffering for Christ

22 Are they Hebrews? So *am* I. Are they Israelites? So *am* I. Are they the seed of Abraham? So *am* I.

23 Are they ministers of Christ?—I speak as a fool—I *am* more: in labors more abundant, in stripes above measure, in prisons more frequently, in deaths often.

24 From the Jews five times I received forty *stripes* minus one.

25 Three times I was beaten with rods; once I was stoned; three times I was shipwrecked; a night and a day I have been in the deep;

26 *in* journeys often, *in* perils of waters, *in* perils of robbers, *in* perils of *my own* countrymen, *in* perils of the Gentiles, *in* perils in the city, *in* perils in the wilderness, *in* perils in the sea, *in* perils among false brethren;

27 in weariness and toil, in sleeplessness often, in hunger and thirst, in fastings often, in cold and nakedness—

28 besides the other things, what comes upon me daily: my deep concern for all the churches.

29 Who is weak, and I am not weak? Who is made to stumble, and I do not burn *with indignation?* ➤

30 If I must boast, I will boast in the things which concern my infirmity.

31 The God and Father of our Lord Jesus Christ, who is blessed forever, knows that I am not lying.

11:6 [a]NU-Text omits *been*.

LIFE LESSONS

➤ 11:3 — *But I fear, lest somehow, as the serpent deceived Eve by his craftiness, so your minds may be corrupted from the simplicity that is in Christ.*

God wants us to enjoy an intimate relationship with Him—that's the bottom line of our existence. He created us and redeemed us so that we might spend eternity with Him. When we forget that, we forget everything.

➤ 11:14 — *For Satan himself transforms himself into an angel of light.*

Cults and false religions through the ages have often begun out of interactions with beings who presented themselves as angels. Demonic double-agents can do a great deal of harm, and we must beware of them.

➤ 11:29 — *Who is weak, and I am not weak? Who is made to stumble, and I do not burn with indignation?*

Paul felt such a close connection with the churches he helped start that he took personally their troubles and challenges. Only through such close connections can we grow into the people God calls us to be.

32 In Damascus the governor, under Aretas
the king, was guarding the city of the Damascenes with a garrison, desiring to arrest me;
33 but I was let down in a basket through a
window in the wall, and escaped from his
hands.

The Vision of Paradise

12 It is doubtless[a] not profitable for me to
boast. I will come to visions and revelations of the Lord:
2 I know a man in Christ who fourteen
years ago—whether in the body I do not
know, or whether out of the body I do not
know, God knows—such a one was caught up
to the third heaven.
3 And I know such a man—whether in the
body or out of the body I do not know, God
knows—
4 how he was caught up into Paradise and
heard inexpressible words, which it is not
lawful for a man to utter.
5 Of such a one I will boast; yet of myself I
will not boast, except in my infirmities.
6 For though I might desire to boast, I will
not be a fool; for I will speak the truth. But I
refrain, lest anyone should think of me above
what he sees me *to be* or hears from me.

The Thorn in the Flesh

7 And lest I should be exalted above measure by the abundance of the revelations, a
thorn in the flesh was given to me, a messenger of Satan to buffet me, lest I be exalted
above measure.
8 Concerning this thing I pleaded with the
Lord three times that it might depart from me.
9 And He said to me, "My grace is sufficient
for you, for My strength is made perfect in
weakness." Therefore most gladly I will
rather boast in my infirmities, that the power
of Christ may rest upon me.
10 Therefore I take pleasure in infirmities, in
reproaches, in needs, in persecutions, in distresses, for Christ's sake. For when I am
weak, then I am strong.

Signs of an Apostle

11 I have become a fool in boasting;[a] you
have compelled me. For I ought to have been
commended by you; for in nothing was I behind the most eminent apostles, though I am
nothing.
12 Truly the signs of an apostle were accomplished among you with all perseverance, in
signs and wonders and mighty deeds.
13 For what is it in which you were inferior
to other churches, except that I myself was
not burdensome to you? Forgive me this
wrong!

Life Examples:

PAUL

Strength in Weakness

2 COR. 12:7

As a young man, Paul trained under one of the greatest Jewish scholars of his time. He understood the elements of the law and practiced them with great zeal. Yet when he came face-to-face with Jesus Christ, his life changed forever. He no longer viewed the world through merely human eyes. God gave him spiritual insight that far surpassed anything he had known.

Still, he had to be broken further so that he could be used in an even greater way. God allowed Paul to be buffeted by a severe trial in order to humble him and remove the potential for pride (2 Cor. 12:7). Through this time of weakness, Paul learned a new and unexpected principle: *Weakness is strength.*

When God humbles us before Him, He sees the meekness of our hearts and sends His strength and blessings into our lives. Frailty in a certain area should never bring embarrassment.

See the Life Principles Index for further study:

15. Brokenness is God's requirement for maximum usefulness.

26. Adversity is a bridge to a deeper relationship with God.

12:1 [a]NU-Text reads *necessary, though not profitable, to boast.*
12:11 [a]NU-Text omits *in boasting.*

LIFE LESSONS

➤ 12:9 — *Therefore most gladly I will rather boast in my infirmities, that the power of Christ may rest upon me.*

The gospel is full of seeming contradictions. If you want to be first, you must be last. If you want to save your life, you must lose it. And if you want to be strong, you must glory in your weakness.

ANSWERS TO LIFE'S QUESTIONS

What value could there possibly be in weakness?

2 COR. 12:9

None of us can escape the pressures of life. Most of us know what it feels like to be disappointed. We know the painfulness of embarrassment, the sting of rejection, and the sorrow of failure. There always comes a time when the lids come boiling off the pots and pans and crash to the floor.

What pots are boiling out of control in your life? Is there a financial need? Maybe you face a relationship crisis and are urgently praying for God's wisdom.

Regardless of your situation, you can trust this principle: *Whatever brings you to your knees in weakness carries the greatest potential for your personal success and spiritual victory.*

Even though Paul could have listed many personal accomplishments, he chose to tell his audience what he saw as the key to experiencing a victorious life: accepting his weakness so that the strength of Christ might live fully in him. "I will rather boast in my infirmities, that the power of Christ may rest upon me" (2 Cor. 12:9).

We do not know the trial that Paul faced; he called it a "thorn in the flesh" (v. 7). In the Greek, the word *thorn* means a stake used for torturing or impaling someone—no gentle affliction! He writes that it buffeted him, indicating that the trial was either ongoing or recurring. When Paul felt he could no longer withstand the blows, God reassured him that His grace was sufficient for anything he faced.

Strength that withstands the stresses and blows of this life comes from only one Source—the eternal, indwelling presence of God. What the world views as strong is really nothing more than weakness under wraps.

When we accept our weaknesses and the fact that we cannot handle life on our own, God goes to work. He sends encouragement and a sense of creativity, helping us to try new avenues that lead to hope and fresh beginnings.

Are you weary from trying? Has exhaustion left its mark? Are you afraid others will see your weaknesses and laugh? Could a thorn in your life expose your deepest fear? Let it go. Release your fears to Jesus who loves you. Let Him strengthen you. Nothing compares to the freedom that waits for you within His loving arms. Nothing will ever bring more completion to your heart and soul than knowing the unconditional love of God. It is yours today—if you choose it.

See the Life Principles Index for further study:
29. We learn more in our valley experiences than on our mountaintops.
24. To live the Christian life is to allow Jesus to live His life in and through us.

Love for the Church

➤ 14 Now *for* the third time I am ready to come to you. And I will not be burdensome to you; for I do not seek yours, but you. For the children ought not to lay up for the parents, but the parents for the children.
15 And I will very gladly spend and be spent for your souls; though the more abundantly I love you, the less I am loved.
16 But be that *as it may,* I did not burden you. Nevertheless, being crafty, I caught you by cunning!
17 Did I take advantage of you by any of those whom I sent to you?
18 I urged Titus, and sent our brother with *him.* Did Titus take advantage of you? Did we not walk in the same spirit? Did *we* not *walk* in the same steps?
19 Again, do you think[a] that we excuse ourselves to you? We speak before God in Christ. But *we do* all things, beloved, for your edification.

12:19 [a]NU-Text reads *You have been thinking for a long time. . . .*

LIFE LESSONS

➤ **12:14 — *And I will not be burdensome to you; for I do not seek yours, but you.***

Paul lived the way he did as a reflection of how God worked in his own life. Paul didn't want the material resources of his friends; he wanted *them.* Just so, God doesn't want our "stuff"; He wants *us.*

20 For I fear lest, when I come, I shall not find
you such as I wish, and *that* I shall be found
by you such as you do not wish; lest *there be*
contentions, jealousies, outbursts of wrath,
selfish ambitions, backbitings, whisperings,
conceits, tumults;
➤ 21 lest, when I come again, my God will humble me among you, and I shall mourn for
many who have sinned before and have not
repented of the uncleanness, fornication, and
lewdness which they have practiced.

Coming with Authority

13 This *will be* the third *time* I am coming
to you. *"By the mouth of two or three
witnesses every word shall be established."*[a]
2 I have told you before, and foretell as if I
were present the second time, and now being
absent I write[a] to those who have sinned before, and to all the rest, that if I come again I
will not spare—
➤ 3 since you seek a proof of Christ speaking
in me, who is not weak toward you, but
mighty in you.
4 For though He was crucified in weakness,
yet He lives by the power of God. For we also
are weak in Him, but we shall live with Him
by the power of God toward you.
➤ 5 Examine yourselves *as to* whether you are
in the faith. Test yourselves. Do you not know
yourselves, that Jesus Christ is in you?—unless indeed you are disqualified.
6 But I trust that you will know that we are
not disqualified.

Paul Prefers Gentleness

7 Now I[a] pray to God that you do no evil, not
that we should appear approved, but that you
should do what is honorable, though we may
seem disqualified.
8 For we can do nothing against the truth,
but for the truth.
9 For we are glad when we are weak and
you are strong. And this also we pray, that you
may be made complete.
10 Therefore I write these things being absent, lest being present I should use sharpness, according to the authority which the
Lord has given me for edification and not for
destruction.

Greetings and Benediction

11 Finally, brethren, farewell. Become complete. Be of good comfort, be of one mind, live
in peace; and the God of love and peace will
be with you.
12 Greet one another with a holy kiss.
13 All the saints greet you.
14 The grace of the Lord Jesus Christ, and ➤
the love of God, and the communion of the
Holy Spirit *be* with you all. Amen.

13:1 [a]Deuteronomy 19:15 13:2 [a]NU-Text omits *I write*.
13:7 [a]NU-Text reads *we*.

LIFE LESSONS

➤ 12:21 — . . . *I shall mourn for many who have sinned before and have not repented of the uncleanness, fornication, and lewdness which they have practiced.*

If God's Word condemns some practice, it's wrong, regardless of how we may feel about it. It is a serious thing to sin against the Lord, know it, and not repent of it. Unrepentant sin always brings the discipline of God.

➤ 13:3 — *Christ . . . is not weak toward you, but mighty in you.*

Some mistake the grace and love and patience of Jesus for weakness. When He does not immediately respond to rebellion with discipline, they feel encouraged to sin more boldly. But Paul warns us never to confuse God's love with weakness.

➤ 13:5 — *Examine yourselves as to whether you are in the faith. Test yourselves. Do you not know yourselves, that Jesus Christ is in you?*

Despite the Corinthians' problems, Paul does not believe that they have trusted Christ "in vain." He sees their genuine spiritual gifts, their repentance, their love for God, and he wants these things to encourage them to further growth.

➤ 13:14 — *The grace of the Lord Jesus Christ, and the love of God, and the communion of the Holy Spirit be with you all.*

In this simple but beautiful benediction Paul calls attention to all three Persons of the Trinity. As a single Godhead, they work together for our spiritual growth and joy in the Christian life.

THE EPISTLE OF PAUL THE APOSTLE TO THE

GALATIANS

Soon after the Galatians launched into their Christian life, they seemed content to leave their voyage of faith and chart a new course based on works—a course Paul found disturbing. His letter to the Galatians is a vigorous attack against the "gospel" of works and a defense of the gospel of grace.

Paul begins by setting forth his credentials as an apostle who received his message directly from God. Blessing comes from God on the basis of faith, not law. While the law declares men guilty and imprisons them, faith sets men free to enjoy liberty in Christ.

Liberty is not license to sin. Freedom in Christ means the freedom to produce the fruits of righteousness through a Spirit-led lifestyle (5:16–25). Grace does not encourage believers to sin, but rather bestows upon them the power to please the Lord by living a godly lifestyle (5:13, 14).

Paul urges the Galatians to consider the utter foolishness of trying to perfect through their own efforts what they had begun only by tapping into the power of God by faith (3:3). Only by following Jesus' example of depending upon the Holy Spirit for strength and direction can they hope to once more experience the sheer joy they felt at the beginning of the Christian life (4:15–20).

The book is called *Pros Galatas*, "To the Galatians," and it is the only letter of Paul specifically addressed to a group of churches ("to the churches of Galatia," 1:2). The name Galatians was given to this Celtic people because they originally lived in Gaul before their migration to Asia Minor.

Themes: A defense of the doctrine of justification by faith in Jesus Christ.

Authors: The apostle Paul.

Date: One theory holds that Paul wrote Galatians around A.D. 53–54 to churches in north-central Asia Minor. Another contends that he wrote the book to churches in southern Galatia around A.D. 48–49, which would make this Paul's first biblical letter.

Structure: After a short introduction, Paul denounces any divergence from a gospel of grace and sets up the rest of his letter (1:1–9). He then defends his apostleship and core doctrines (1:10—2:21). Next he develops the themes of justification by faith and the liberty Christians have in Christ (3:1—4:31). As he winds up his letter he gives some practical applications of his teachings (5:1—6:10) and then offers some concluding remarks (6:11–18).

As you read Galatians, watch for several life principles that play an important role in this book:

24. **To live the Christian life is to allow Jesus to live His life in and through us.** *See Galatians 2:20; 4:19; pages 1368, 1373.*

1. **Our intimacy with God—His highest priority for our lives—determines the impact of our lives.** *See Galatians 3:26–29; page 1372.*

22. **To walk in the Spirit is to obey the initial promptings of the Spirit.** *See Galatians 5:16, 25; pages 1374, 1376.*

6. **You reap what you sow, more than you sow, and later than you sow.** *See Galatians 6:7, 8; page 1376.*

Greeting

1 Paul, an apostle (not from men nor through man, but through Jesus Christ and God the Father who raised Him from the dead),

2 and all the brethren who are with me,

To the churches of Galatia:

➤ 3 Grace to you and peace from God the Father and our Lord Jesus Christ,

4 who gave Himself for our sins, that He might deliver us from this present evil age, according to the will of our God and Father,

5 to whom *be* glory forever and ever. Amen.

Only One Gospel

6 I marvel that you are turning away so soon from Him who called you in the grace of Christ, to a different gospel,

7 which is not another; but there are some who trouble you and want to pervert the gospel of Christ.

➤ 8 But even if we, or an angel from heaven, preach any other gospel to you than what we have preached to you, let him be accursed.

9 As we have said before, so now I say again, if anyone preaches any other gospel to you than what you have received, let him be accursed.

10 For do I now persuade men, or God? Or do I seek to please men? For if I still pleased men, I would not be a bondservant of Christ.

Call to Apostleship

➤ **11** But I make known to you, brethren, that the gospel which was preached by me is not according to man.

12 For I neither received it from man, nor was I taught *it*, but *it came* through the revelation of Jesus Christ.

13 For you have heard of my former conduct in Judaism, how I persecuted the church of God beyond measure and *tried to* destroy it.

14 And I advanced in Judaism beyond many of my contemporaries in my own nation, being more exceedingly zealous for the traditions of my fathers.

15 But when it pleased God, who separated me from my mother's womb and called *me* through His grace,

16 to reveal His Son in me, that I might preach Him among the Gentiles, I did not immediately confer with flesh and blood,

17 nor did I go up to Jerusalem to those *who were* apostles before me; but I went to Arabia, and returned again to Damascus.

Contacts at Jerusalem

18 Then after three years I went up to Jerusalem to see Peter,[a] and remained with him fifteen days.

19 But I saw none of the other apostles except James, the Lord's brother.

20 (Now *concerning* the things which I write to you, indeed, before God, I do not lie.)

21 Afterward I went into the regions of Syria and Cilicia.

22 And I was unknown by face to the churches of Judea which *were* in Christ.

23 But they were hearing only, "He who formerly persecuted us now preaches the faith which he once *tried to* destroy."

24 And they glorified God in me.

Defending the Gospel

2 Then after fourteen years I went up again to Jerusalem with Barnabas, and also took Titus with *me.*

2 And I went up by revelation, and communicated to them that gospel which I preach among the Gentiles, but privately to those who were of reputation, lest by any means I might run, or had run, in vain.

3 Yet not even Titus who *was* with me, being a Greek, was compelled to be circumcised.

4 And *this occurred* because of false brethren secretly brought in (who came in by stealth to spy out our liberty which we have in Christ Jesus, that they might bring us into bondage), ➤

1:18 [a]NU-Text reads *Cephas.*

LIFE LESSONS

➤ 1:3, 4 — *. . . our Lord Jesus Christ . . . gave Himself for our sins, that He might deliver us from this present evil age, according to the will of our God and Father . . . .*

Jesus saved us out of an "evil age" so that we might "become blameless and harmless, children of God without fault in the midst of a crooked and perverse generation, among whom you shine as lights" (Phil. 2:15).

➤ 1:8 — *But even if we, or an angel from heaven, preach any other gospel to you than what we have preached to you, let him be accursed.*

Whenever someone promotes a "restored" gospel or a "secret" gospel or a "fresh" gospel or any other "gospel" that deviates from what the Bible clearly teaches, run for your life. That person promotes death, not life.

➤ 1:11 — *But I make known to you, brethren, that the gospel which was preached by me is not according to man.*

The gospel of salvation by grace through faith—by which we receive new life through the risen Savior, Jesus Christ—is no human invention. Paul did not conceive it, nor did the other disciples. It comes directly from God.

➤ 2:4 — *. . . false brethren secretly . . . came in by stealth to spy out our liberty which we have in Christ Jesus, that they might bring us into bondage . . . .*

There is something about freedom that many people, even within the church, simply can't tolerate. They will try all sorts of tactics, both obvious and veiled, to bring you under their control. Don't let them.

5 to whom we did not yield submission even for an hour, that the truth of the gospel might continue with you.

6 But from those who seemed to be something—whatever they were, it makes no difference to me; God shows personal favoritism to no man—for those who seemed *to be something* added nothing to me.

7 But on the contrary, when they saw that the gospel for the uncircumcised had been committed to me, as *the gospel* for the circumcised *was* to Peter

8 (for He who worked effectively in Peter for the apostleship to the circumcised also worked effectively in me toward the Gentiles),

9 and when James, Cephas, and John, who seemed to be pillars, perceived the grace that had been given to me, they gave me and Barnabas the right hand of fellowship, that we *should go* to the Gentiles and they to the circumcised.

10 *They desired* only that we should remember the poor, the very thing which I also was eager to do.

No Return to the Law

11 Now when Peter[a] had come to Antioch, I withstood him to his face, because he was to be blamed;

12 for before certain men came from James, he would eat with the Gentiles; but when they came, he withdrew and separated himself, fearing those who were of the circumcision.

➤ 13 And the rest of the Jews also played the hypocrite with him, so that even Barnabas was carried away with their hypocrisy.

14 But when I saw that they were not straightforward about the truth of the gospel, I said to Peter before *them* all, "If you, being a Jew, live in the manner of Gentiles and not as the Jews, why do you[a] compel Gentiles to live as Jews?[b]

15 "We *who are* Jews by nature, and not sinners of the Gentiles,

16 "knowing that a man is not justified by the works of the law but by faith in Jesus Christ, even we have believed in Christ Jesus, that we might be justified by faith in Christ and not by the works of the law; for by the works of the law no flesh shall be justified.

17 "But if, while we seek to be justified by Christ, we ourselves also are found sinners, *is* Christ therefore a minister of sin? Certainly not!

18 "For if I build again those things which I destroyed, I make myself a transgressor.

19 "For I through the law died to the law that I might live to God.

20 "I have been crucified with Christ; it is no longer I who live, but Christ lives in me; and the *life* which I now live in the flesh I live by faith in the Son of God, who loved me and gave Himself for me.

21 "I do not set aside the grace of God; for if righteousness *comes* through the law, then Christ died in vain."

Justification by Faith

3 O foolish Galatians! Who has bewitched you that you should not obey the truth,[a] before whose eyes Jesus Christ was clearly portrayed among you[b] as crucified?

2 This only I want to learn from you: Did you receive the Spirit by the works of the law, or by the hearing of faith?

3 Are you so foolish? Having begun in the Spirit, are you now being made perfect by the flesh?

4 Have you suffered so many things in vain—if indeed *it was* in vain?

5 Therefore He who supplies the Spirit to you and works miracles among you, *does He do it* by the works of the law, or by the hearing of faith?—

6 just as Abraham *"believed God, and it was accounted to him for righteousness."*[a]

2:11 [a]NU-Text reads *Cephas.* **2:14** [a]NU-Text reads *how can you.* [b]Some interpreters stop the quotation here. **3:1** [a]NU-Text omits *that you should not obey the truth.* [b]NU-Text omits *among you.* **3:6** [a]Genesis 15:6

LIFE LESSONS

➤ **2:13 — *And the rest of the Jews also played the hypocrite with him, so that even Barnabas was carried away with their hypocrisy.***

We should never imagine that our sin affects only ourselves and no one else. Peter didn't mean for his sin to "infect" others, but it did. That's why we have to rely on God's Spirit to help us avoid spreading spiritual disease.

➤ **2:19 — *"For I through the law died to the law that I might live to God."***

When we trust in Jesus and so win an eternal place at God's side, we don't violate the law or somehow get around it. Jesus fulfilled the whole law, and by identifying with Him in His death and resurrection, we do too.

➤ **2:20 — *I have been crucified with Christ; it is no longer I who live, but Christ lives in me; and the life which I now live in the flesh I live by faith . . . .***

The secret to the Christian life is to allow Jesus Christ to live in and through you, by faith. When you invite and allow the Holy Spirit to work in your life, you become a vital representative of Christ.

➤ **3:3 — *Are you so foolish? Having begun in the Spirit, are you now being made perfect by the flesh?***

The entire Christian experience is to be lived by faith, from beginning to end. We are justified by grace through faith, we are sanctified by grace through faith, and we will be glorified by grace through faith.

ANSWERS TO LIFE'S QUESTIONS

Why do I still have the impulse to sin?

GAL. 2:20

One day the gospel made sense to you and you placed your faith in Jesus Christ to forgive you of all your sins. You felt thrilled with this new life and marveled that many of the ungodly things you once did had lost their attraction. Perhaps you even thought you had conquered every sinful impulse.

And then you stumbled . . . badly. A new temptation or a new set of trials brought to light some area of your life that you thought you had whipped. You felt confused, ashamed, maybe even alarmed. Perhaps you wondered, *How could this happen? I thought I was supposed to be free from sin!*

The truth is, Jesus has set us free from sin—but it is a kind of freedom that sets us free from ourselves. When Paul says, "I have been crucified with Christ," he means that God had broken his selfish individuality and united his spirit with his Lord. He truly became one with Jesus, and therefore he had many of the same resources available to him that Jesus enjoyed on this earth.

If you have accepted Christ as your Savior, then you are one with Him. His likeness and holiness are present within your life. The very power that enabled Jesus to resist all temptation dwells within you.

Still, there remains within your mortal body an impulse to sin, a "sinful nature" that must be surrendered to God. So Paul writes, "For I know that in me (that is, in my flesh) nothing good dwells" (Rom. 7:18). Yet we are not stranded in this barren place, for Paul also says, "the life which I now live in the flesh I live by faith in the Son of God, who loved me and gave Himself up for me" (Gal. 2:20). Through faith we access God's power to overcome our sinful impulses. A little later in Galatians, the apostle explains it in slightly different terms: "Walk in the Spirit, and you shall not fulfill the lust of the flesh" (Gal. 5:16).

We receive Jesus' gift of freedom only by exercising faith in God. We must believe that He can remove ungodly strongholds within our hearts and that He continuously works to make us free from *all* sin and bondage. Our responsibility is to say "no" to sin and "yes" to God as we trust Him to provide the all-encompassing liberty that our souls crave.

See the Life Principles Index for further study:

9. Trusting God means looking beyond what we can see to what God sees.

24. To live the Christian life is to allow Jesus to live His life in and through us.

7 Therefore know that *only* those who are of faith are sons of Abraham.
8 And the Scripture, foreseeing that God would justify the Gentiles by faith, preached the gospel to Abraham beforehand, *saying, "In you all the nations shall be blessed."*[a]
9 So then those who *are* of faith are blessed with believing Abraham.

The Law Brings a Curse

10 For as many as are of the works of the law are under the curse; for it is written, *"Cursed is everyone who does not continue in all things which are written in the book of the law, to do them."*[a]
11 But that no one is justified by the law in the sight of God *is* evident, for *"the just shall live by faith."*[a]
12 Yet the law is not of faith, but *"the man who does them shall live by them."*[a]
13 Christ has redeemed us from the curse of the law, having become a curse for us (for it is written, *"Cursed is everyone who hangs on a tree"*[a]),
14 that the blessing of Abraham might come upon the Gentiles in Christ Jesus, that we might receive the promise of the Spirit through faith.

3:8 [a]Genesis 12:3; 18:18; 22:18; 26:4; 28:14
3:10 [a]Deuteronomy 27:26 **3:11** [a]Habakkuk 2:4
3:12 [a]Leviticus 18:5 **3:13** [a]Deuteronomy 21:23

LIFE LESSONS

➤ 3:13 — *Christ has redeemed us from the curse of the law, having become a curse for us (for it is written, "Cursed is everyone who hangs on a tree")* . . . .

The law is a "curse" to us in that it condemns our sin and therefore condemns us. Jesus, the sinless Son of God, accepted our rightful condemnation and the punishment we deserved when He willingly went to the cross.

LIFE PRINCIPLE 24

TO LIVE THE CHRISTIAN LIFE IS TO ALLOW JESUS TO LIVE HIS LIFE IN AND THROUGH US.

GAL. 2:20

Many Christians today seem content to live an "adequate" Christian life. They believe that if they go to church, read their Bible occasionally, and say their prayers once in a while, they are all right with God. Occasionally, they may volunteer to serve others at church—perhaps as an usher, a member of a church committee, or a home visitor on an evangelism team—which they consider ministry "above the norm."

May I challenge you today? God doesn't call you or anyone to a merely "adequate" Christian life. He desires to have a daily, walking-and-talking relationship with you in which you experience His presence, trust Him for wisdom, courage, and strength, and rely on Him for remarkable results.

With every step you take, every decision you make, every conversation you have, and every thought you entertain, the Lord desires to live within you. He desires to communicate to you and through you. He desires to live out His life through your expression of it—a perfect blending of His perfection and your unique talents, traits, and personality.

To live the Christian life, in other words, is to allow Jesus to live in and through you. That is why Paul would write, "I will not dare to speak of any of those things which Christ has not accomplished through me" (Rom. 15:18). That is why the apostle told the Galatians that he labored "until Christ is formed in you" (Gal. 4:19). And that is why he said we are all "being transformed into the same image [of Christ] from glory to glory, just as by the Spirit of the Lord" (2 Cor. 3:18).

How do we get transformed into the image of Jesus? In what way does He live in and through us? This is where the Spirit-filled life comes in.

You may say, "I don't know what you're talking about." If that's your response, you aren't alone. Many people don't know much about the Holy Spirit, and they know less about how He works in the life of every Christian.

You may say, "I'm not sure I want anything to do with the Holy Spirit. Everything I've heard about Him seems divisive or too emotional for me." If that's your response, I have encouragement for you. If you are a genuine born-again Christian, you have a relationship with the Holy Spirit, whether you have

God desires to communicate to you and through you.

acknowledged Him or not. Furthermore, *He* is not divisive or invasive. People may be, but He is not.

You may say, "Oh, yes! The Spirit-filled life is the most wonderful life a person can know. I wouldn't trade it for all the riches in the world or for any other experience!" If that's your response, I say "amen."

In fact, the Spirit-filled life is the *only* way for a Christian to experience all that God has for us. It means life to the fullest, the abundant life that Jesus promised (see John 10:10).

The Spirit-filled life is not based on emotions, although you are likely to feel various emotions as the Spirit works in you and through you to produce the character of Christ Jesus and to replicate the ministry of Christ Jesus in your life and the world.

The Spirit-filled life also is not something that a person can study from afar. The Spirit-filled life must be experienced. It is lived out by real people in real life facing real, and sometimes difficult, circumstances.

The Spirit-filled life is marked by purpose, power, and effectiveness. It is not something that you do, but something that you are because of who lives and works inside you. God desires for each of His children to live a Spirit-filled life, and He expects you to be led by the Spirit every day.

There really is no such thing as an "average" Christian life. Either you are living a vibrant, Spirit-filled life, or you aren't. Either you are in forward motion or in a pause position. Either you are living in the fullness of the Holy Spirit, or you aren't.

Make a decision today to choose the Spirit-filled life. That's well within your prerogative and will to do. God will not force Himself on you or force Himself to operate within you. Since He works by invitation only, He won't overstep the boundaries of your will. But He does invite you to allow Jesus to live His life in and through you—and believe me, you won't find a better offer or a more exciting adventure anywhere else.

See the Life Principles Index for further study.

Make a decision today to choose the Spirit-filled life.

The Changeless Promise
15 Brethren, I speak in the manner of men:
Though *it is* only a man's covenant, yet *if it is*
confirmed, no one annuls or adds to it.
16 Now to Abraham and his Seed were the
promises made. He does not say, "And to
seeds," as of many, but as of one, *"And to your*
Seed,"[a] who is Christ.
17 And this I say, *that* the law, which was
four hundred and thirty years later, cannot
annul the covenant that was confirmed before
by God in Christ,[a] that it should make the
promise of no effect.
18 For if the inheritance *is* of the law, *it is* no
longer of promise; but God gave *it* to Abraham by promise.

Purpose of the Law
19 What purpose then *does* the law *serve*? It
was added because of transgressions, till the
Seed should come to whom the promise was
made; *and it was* appointed through angels
by the hand of a mediator.
20 Now a mediator does not *mediate* for one
only, but God is one.
21 *Is* the law then against the promises of
God? Certainly not! For if there had been a
law given which could have given life, truly
righteousness would have been by the law.
22 But the Scripture has confined all under
sin, that the promise by faith in Jesus Christ
might be given to those who believe.
23 But before faith came, we were kept under
guard by the law, kept for the faith which
would afterward be revealed.
24 Therefore the law was our tutor *to bring*
us to Christ, that we might be justified by
faith.
25 But after faith has come, we are no longer
under a tutor.

Sons and Heirs
26 For you are all sons of God through faith
in Christ Jesus.
27 For as many of you as were baptized into
Christ have put on Christ.
28 There is neither Jew nor Greek, there is
neither slave nor free, there is neither male
nor female; for you are all one in Christ Jesus.
29 And if you *are* Christ's, then you are Abraham's seed, and heirs according to the promise.

4 Now I say *that* the heir, as long as he is a
child, does not differ at all from a slave,
though he is master of all,
2 but is under guardians and stewards until
the time appointed by the father.
3 Even so we, when we were children, were
in bondage under the elements of the world.
4 But when the fullness of the time had
come, God sent forth His Son, born[a] of a
woman, born under the law,
5 to redeem those who were under the law,
that we might receive the adoption as sons.
6 And because you are sons, God has sent
forth the Spirit of His Son into your hearts,
crying out, "Abba, Father!"
7 Therefore you are no longer a slave but a
son, and if a son, then an heir of[a] God through
Christ.

Fears for the Church
8 But then, indeed, when you did not know
God, you served those which by nature are
not gods.
9 But now after you have known God, or
rather are known by God, how *is it that* you
turn again to the weak and beggarly elements, to which you desire again to be in
bondage?
10 You observe days and months and seasons
and years.
11 I am afraid for you, lest I have labored for
you in vain.

3:16 [a]Genesis 12:7; 13:15; 24:7 **3:17** [a]NU-Text omits *in Christ.*
4:4 [a]Or *made* **4:7** [a]NU-Text reads *through God* and omits *through Christ.*

LIFE LESSONS

➤ 3:24 — *Therefore the law was our tutor to bring us to Christ, that we might be justified by faith.*

God never intended that anyone try to "work" their way to heaven. Abraham couldn't, Moses couldn't, and neither could Paul. None of us can. The law shows us our need for a Savior, who rescues us by grace.

➤ 3:28 — *There is neither Jew nor Greek, there is neither slave nor free, there is neither male nor female; for you are all one in Christ Jesus.*

God does not play favorites (Acts 10:34; Rom. 2:11); He has no favorite sons or daughters. We all come to Him with exactly the same level of need, and He makes us into a single unit, the body of Christ.

➤ 4:4, 5 — *. . . God sent forth His Son, born of a woman, born under the law, to redeem those who were under the law, that we might receive the adoption as sons.*

God adopts us into His heavenly family the moment we place our faith in His Son, Jesus Christ. Because He accepts us just as He accepts His own Son, we are "joint heirs with Christ" (Rom. 8:17).

➤ 4:6 — *And because you are sons, God has sent forth the Spirit of His Son into your hearts, crying out, "Abba, Father!"*

Abba is an Aramaic term for "father" that suggests warmth, closeness, intimacy, and mutual delight. God did not bring us into His family to be our austere and stern Father, but to be our beloved and approachable Daddy.

12 Brethren, I urge you to become like me,
for I *became* like you. You have not injured
me at all.
13 You know that because of physical infirmity I preached the gospel to you at the first.
14 And my trial which was in my flesh you
did not despise or reject, but you received me
as an angel of God, *even* as Christ Jesus.
15 What[a] then was the blessing you *enjoyed?*
For I bear you witness that, if possible, you
would have plucked out your own eyes and
given them to me.
16 Have I therefore become your enemy because I tell you the truth?
17 They zealously court you, *but* for no good;
yes, they want to exclude you, that you may
be zealous for them.
18 But it is good to be zealous in a good thing
always, and not only when I am present with
you.
➤ 19 My little children, for whom I labor in
birth again until Christ is formed in you,
20 I would like to be present with you now and
to change my tone; for I have doubts about you.

Two Covenants

21 Tell me, you who desire to be under the
law, do you not hear the law?
22 For it is written that Abraham had two
sons: the one by a bondwoman, the other by a
freewoman.
23 But he *who was* of the bondwoman was
born according to the flesh, and he of the
freewoman through promise,
24 which things are symbolic. For these are
the[a] two covenants: the one from Mount Sinai
which gives birth to bondage, which is Hagar—
25 for this Hagar is Mount Sinai in Arabia,
and corresponds to Jerusalem which now is,
and is in bondage with her children—
26 but the Jerusalem above is free, which is
the mother of us all.
27 For it is written:

"Rejoice, O barren,
You who do not bear!
Break forth and shout,
You who are not in labor!
For the desolate has many more children
Than she who has a husband."[a]

28 Now we, brethren, as Isaac *was*, are children of promise.
29 But, as he who was born according to the
flesh then persecuted him *who was born* according to the Spirit, even so *it is* now.
30 Nevertheless what does the Scripture say?
"Cast out the bondwoman and her son, for
the son of the bondwoman shall not be heir
with the son of the freewoman."[a]
31 So then, brethren, we are not children of
the bondwoman but of the free.

Christian Liberty

5 Stand fast therefore in the liberty by ➤
which Christ has made us free,[a] and do not
be entangled again with a yoke of bondage.
2 Indeed I, Paul, say to you that if you become
circumcised, Christ will profit you nothing.
3 And I testify again to every man who becomes circumcised that he is a debtor to keep
the whole law.
4 You have become estranged from Christ,
you who *attempt to* be justified by law; you
have fallen from grace.
5 For we through the Spirit eagerly wait for
the hope of righteousness by faith.
6 For in Christ Jesus neither circumcision
nor uncircumcision avails anything, but faith
working through love.

Love Fulfills the Law

7 You ran well. Who hindered you from
obeying the truth?
8 This persuasion does not *come* from Him
who calls you.
9 A little leaven leavens the whole lump.
10 I have confidence in you, in the Lord, that
you will have no other mind; but he who troubles you shall bear his judgment, whoever he is.
11 And I, brethren, if I still preach circumcision, why do I still suffer persecution? Then
the offense of the cross has ceased.
12 I could wish that those who trouble you
would even cut themselves off!
13 For you, brethren, have been called to ➤

4:15 [a]NU-Text reads *Where.* **4:24** [a]NU-Text and M-Text omit *the.* **4:27** [a]Isaiah 54:1 **4:30** [a]Genesis 21:10 **5:1** [a]NU-Text reads *For freedom Christ has made us free; stand fast therefore.*

LIFE LESSONS

➤ 4:19 — *My little children, for whom I labor in birth again until Christ is formed in you . . . .*

The goal of Christian living is not to sin less, or to reform our manners, or to do better than we used to. The goal is total transformation, to see Jesus formed in us. God wants us to increasingly resemble His Son.

➤ 5:1 — *Stand fast therefore in the liberty by which Christ has made us free, and do not be entangled again with a yoke of bondage.*

In some ways, it's a lot easier to live by a set of rules. "Do this, don't do that; sit here, don't sit there." But while living by rules may seem easier, in fact it's not living at all: "the letter kills, but the Spirit gives life" (2 Cor. 3:6).

➤ 5:13 — *For you, brethren, have been called to liberty; only do not use liberty as an opportunity for the flesh, but through love serve one another.*

Grace gives us the freedom to explore creative and helpful ways to encourage and build up one another. Why would anyone who truly loves Jesus want to use their cross-bought freedom to do anything that disgraces His name?

ANSWERS TO LIFE'S QUESTIONS

What is the fruit of the Spirit and how does it grow in me?

GAL. 5:22, 23

The closer you get to believers who truly walk in the Spirit, the better they look. You don't get the impression that they're hiding something. They radiate integrity. You feel you could trust them with your most intimate secret. You may even find yourself opening up to them in a way quite uncharacteristic for you.

Of course, they're not perfect. You will likely hear more apologies from the lips of those who walk by the Spirit than from any other group. Their sensitivity to the Spirit provides them with an uncanny ability to know when they have offended or hurt someone, and their internal security allows them to respond quickly once they realize their sin or error in judgment. They never feel afraid to admit their faults, yet they always remember they have within them the power to rise above their fleshly appetites and desires.

Specifically, their lives exude nine virtues: love, joy, peace, longsuffering (patience), kindness, goodness, faithfulness, gentleness, and self-control. I won't give a blow-by-blow description of each quality, because I think such an elaboration creates a problem.

In preparing to write this, I read from several books that gave expanded definitions of each quality. When I read about kindness, I quickly became preoccupied with being more kind. I began thinking of all the unkind things I had done and said recently. Then I asked God to make me a kinder person. I found myself launching out on a mission of kindness.

When I read about gentleness, the same thing happened. I realized how abrupt and insensitive I can be. So I told God how much gentler I was going to be.

Do you see the problem?

- "I need to act more loving."
- "I need to be more patient."
- "I need to exercise more self-control."
- "I . . . I . . . I . . . I . . . I . . ."

I believe Paul listed these virtues and moved on for one simple reason. They aren't given to us as goals to pursue because *you and I cannot produce fruit.* The Holy Spirit is the producer; we are merely the bearers. The fruit of the Spirit was never intended to demonstrate our dedication and resolve. Rather, it reveals our dependency on and sensitivity to the promptings of the Spirit.

Fruit is not simply one mark of a Spirit-filled life; it is the preeminent mark.

See the Life Principles Index for further study:
24. To live the Christian life is to allow Jesus to live His life in and through us.

liberty; only do not *use* liberty as an opportunity for the flesh, but through love serve one
another.
14 For all the law is fulfilled in one word,
even in this: *"You shall love your neighbor as
yourself."*[a]
15 But if you bite and devour one another,
beware lest you be consumed by one another!

Walking in the Spirit
16 I say then: Walk in the Spirit, and you shall ✳
not fulfill the lust of the flesh.
17 For the flesh lusts against the Spirit, and
the Spirit against the flesh; and these are contrary to one another, so that you do not do the
things that you wish.
18 But if you are led by the Spirit, you are not
under the law.
19 Now the works of the flesh are evident,
which are: adultery,[a] fornication, uncleanness, lewdness,
20 idolatry, sorcery, hatred, contentions, jealousies, outbursts of wrath, selfish ambitions,
dissensions, heresies,
21 envy, murders,[a] drunkenness, revelries,
and the like; of which I tell you beforehand,
just as I also told *you* in time past, that those
who practice such things will not inherit the
kingdom of God.
22 But the fruit of the Spirit is love, joy,
peace, longsuffering, kindness, goodness,
faithfulness,
23 gentleness, self-control. Against such
there is no law.

5:14 [a]Leviticus 19:18 **5:19** [a]NU-Text omits *adultery.*
5:21 [a]NU-Text omits *murders.*

WHAT THE BIBLE SAYS ABOUT **BEARING ONE ANOTHER'S BURDENS**

Gal. 6:1–3

Many people object to the idea of accountability because they don't see how other people's actions are any of their business. But the Bible insists that we in the body of Christ all have a responsibility to one another.

Paul taught that if a believer is caught in sin, the strong members of the church are to help shoulder the responsibility of that person's sin. They are to work with the sinner to help him get back on track (Gal. 6:1–3). This implies that our sin *is* other people's business; and conversely, their sin becomes part of *our* responsibility. Nowhere in Scripture are we told that our sin is something just between us and God.

A woman in our church in Miami was married for only a short time when her husband revealed his homosexuality. Soon afterwards he left her to be with his lover. She told me something I shall never forget. "After I was divorced," he said, "several of my friends came to me and said they knew he was gay before we married. When I asked them why they didn't say anything, they replied, 'We didn't think it was any of our business.' "

We in the body of Christ all have a responsibility to one another.

After hearing her story, I made up my mind never to stand by quietly and watch a friend make what I felt sure was a mistake. This resolution occasionally makes me very unpopular. People have left the church over things I have confronted them about. But when I start thinking that maybe I should keep my mouth shut, I always remember Solomon's words: "He who rebukes a man will afterward find more favor than he who flatters with the tongue" (Prov. 28:23).

It amazes me how often people come back to me or write letters to apologize for their reaction to my warnings. More often than not, they admit that they should have listened.

Remember this, in an accountability relationship you are *not* responsible for how the other person responds to you. But you are responsible to tell the truth and then continue to love that person through the process.

See the Life Principles Index for further study:
28. No Christian has ever been called to "go it alone" in his or her walk of faith.
2. Obey God and leave all the consequences to Him.

➤ 24 And those *who are* Christ's have crucified
the flesh with its passions and desires.
25 If we live in the Spirit, let us also walk in
the Spirit.
26 Let us not become conceited, provoking
one another, envying one another.

Bear and Share the Burdens

6 Brethren, if a man is overtaken in any
trespass, you who *are* spiritual restore
such a one in a spirit of gentleness, considering yourself lest you also be tempted.
➤ 2 Bear one another's burdens, and so fulfill
the law of Christ.
3 For if anyone thinks himself to be something, when he is nothing, he deceives himself.
4 But let each one examine his own work,
and then he will have rejoicing in himself
alone, and not in another.
5 For each one shall bear his own load.

Be Generous and Do Good

6 Let him who is taught the word share in
all good things with him who teaches.
➤ 7 Do not be deceived, God is not mocked;
for whatever a man sows, that he will also
reap.
✳ 8 For he who sows to his flesh will of the
flesh reap corruption, but he who sows to the
Spirit will of the Spirit reap everlasting life.
✳ 9 And let us not grow weary while doing
good, for in due season we shall reap if we do
not lose heart.
10 Therefore, as we have opportunity, let us
do good to all, especially to those who are of
the household of faith.

Glory Only in the Cross

11 See with what large letters I have written
to you with my own hand!
12 As many as desire to make a good showing in the flesh, these *would* compel you to be
circumcised, only that they may not suffer
persecution for the cross of Christ.
13 For not even those who are circumcised
keep the law, but they desire to have you
circumcised that they may boast in your
flesh.
14 But God forbid that I should boast except
in the cross of our Lord Jesus Christ, by
whom[a] the world has been crucified to me,
and I to the world.
15 For in Christ Jesus neither circumcision
nor uncircumcision avails anything, but a
new creation.

Blessing and a Plea

16 And as many as walk according to this
rule, peace and mercy *be* upon them, and
upon the Israel of God.
17 From now on let no one trouble me, for I
bear in my body the marks of the Lord Jesus.
18 Brethren, the grace of our Lord Jesus
Christ *be* with your spirit. Amen.

6:14 [a]Or *by which* (the cross)

LIFE LESSONS

➤ 5:24 — *And those who are Christ's have crucified the flesh with its passions and desires.*

Everyone who is Christ's died with the Savior on the cross. But believers must also crucify the fleshly desires connected with their as yet unglorified bodies.

➤ 6:2 — *Bear one another's burdens, and so fulfill the law of Christ.*

No maturing Christian can ever say, "I don't need the church," because Jesus tells us that we all have work to do *in the church.* We cannot carry the burdens of those we have nothing to do with.

➤ 6:7 — *Do not be deceived, God is not mocked; for whatever a man sows, that he will also reap.*

Paul often uses the phrase, "do not be deceived," probably because so many of us are. Here he wants to remind us that our actions *always* have a consequence, either for good or for bad. To think otherwise is to be deceived.

➤ 6:15 — *For in Christ Jesus neither circumcision nor uncircumcision avails anything, but a new creation.*

God intends to make us into totally new people, not by tinkering with different kinds of religious rituals or by trying to reform our behavior, but by changing us through His Spirit into the likeness of Christ.

THE EPISTLE OF PAUL THE APOSTLE TO THE

EPHESIANS

Ephesians is addressed to a group of believers rich beyond measure in Jesus Christ, but who continue to live as beggars. Why do they remain in spiritual poverty? Because they remain ignorant of their true wealth.

No Christian has to live like a spiritual beggar when God offers riches beyond all imagining. To move from poverty to prosperity, however, believers must first listen to and meditate on what God's Word says about their true standing, and then access it and begin living it by faith. There is no other way.

The traditional title of this epistle is *Pros Ephesious*, "To the Ephesians." Many ancient manuscripts, however, omit *en Epheso*, "in Ephesus," in 1:1. This has led a number of scholars to challenge the traditional view that Paul directed this message specifically to the Ephesians.

The encyclical theory proposes that Ephesians was a circular letter sent by Paul to the churches in Asia. This viewpoint holds that the letter is really a Christian treatise designed for general use, since it involves no controversy and deals with no specific problems in any particular church. If Ephesians really did begin as a circular letter, however, eventually it became associated with Ephesus, the foremost of the Asian churches.

Another plausible option is that this epistle was directly addressed to the Ephesians, but written in such a way as to make it helpful for all the churches in Asia. Finally, some scholars accept the ancient tradition that Ephesians is Paul's letter to the Laodiceans (Col 4:16), but there is no way to be sure.

Themes: The spiritual bounty of the Christian and the unity of the church in Jesus Christ.

Author: The apostle Paul.

Time: Likely written from prison in Rome about A.D. 60–62.

Structure: The first half of the book (1–3) describes the content of the Christian's heavenly "bank account": adoption, acceptance, redemption, forgiveness, wisdom, inheritance, the seal of the Holy Spirit, life, grace, citizenship—in short, every spiritual blessing. The second half (4–6) lays out a spiritual walk rooted in that spiritual wealth. Ephesians 2:10 gives a good outline for the book: "For we are His workmanship, created in Christ Jesus [1–3] for good works, . . . that we should walk in them [4–6]."

As you read Ephesians, watch for several life principles that play an important role in this book:

- **Peace with God is the fruit of oneness with God.** *See Ephesians 1:3–12; page 1378.*
- **We stand tallest and strongest on our knees.** *See Ephesians 3:16–19; page 1380.*
- **Trusting God means looking beyond what we can see to what God sees.** *See Ephesians 3:20, 21; page 1381.*
- **God blesses us so that we might bless others.** *See Ephesians 4:28; page 1385.*
- **Fight all your battles on your knees and you win every time.** *See Ephesians 6:10–20; page 1387.*

Greeting
1 Paul, an apostle of Jesus Christ by the will
of God,

To the saints who are in Ephesus, and
faithful in Christ Jesus:

2 Grace to you and peace from God our Father and the Lord Jesus Christ.

Redemption in Christ
➤ **3** Blessed *be* the God and Father of our Lord
Jesus Christ, who has blessed us with every
spiritual blessing in the heavenly *places* in
Christ,
4 just as He chose us in Him before the
foundation of the world, that we should be
holy and without blame before Him in love,
5 having predestined us to adoption as sons
by Jesus Christ to Himself, according to the
good pleasure of His will,
6 to the praise of the glory of His grace, by
which He made us accepted in the Beloved.
7 In Him we have redemption through His
blood, the forgiveness of sins, according to
the riches of His grace
8 which He made to abound toward us in all
wisdom and prudence,
9 having made known to us the mystery of
His will, according to His good pleasure
which He purposed in Himself,
10 that in the dispensation of the fullness of
the times He might gather together in one all
things in Christ, both[a] which are in heaven
and which are on earth—in Him.
✳ 11 In Him also we have obtained an inheritance, being predestined according to the purpose of Him who works all things according
to the counsel of His will,
12 that we who first trusted in Christ should
be to the praise of His glory.
13 In Him you also *trusted,* after you heard
the word of truth, the gospel of your salvation; in whom also, having believed, you were
sealed with the Holy Spirit of promise,
14 who[a] is the guarantee of our inheritance
until the redemption of the purchased possession, to the praise of His glory.

Prayer for Spiritual Wisdom
15 Therefore I also, after I heard of your faith
in the Lord Jesus and your love for all the
saints,
16 do not cease to give thanks for you, making mention of you in my prayers:
17 that the God of our Lord Jesus Christ, the
Father of glory, may give to you the spirit of
wisdom and revelation in the knowledge of
Him,
18 the eyes of your understanding[a] being en- ➤
lightened; that you may know what is the
hope of His calling, what are the riches of the
glory of His inheritance in the saints,
19 and what *is* the exceeding greatness of His ➤
power toward us who believe, according to
the working of His mighty power
20 which He worked in Christ when He
raised Him from the dead and seated *Him* at
His right hand in the heavenly *places,*
21 far above all principality and power and
might and dominion, and every name that is
named, not only in this age but also in that
which is to come.
22 And He put all *things* under His feet, and
gave Him *to be* head over all *things* to the
church,
23 which is His body, the fullness of Him who
fills all in all.

By Grace Through Faith
2 And you *He made alive,* who were dead in
trespasses and sins,
2 in which you once walked according to ➤
the course of this world, according to the
prince of the power of the air, the spirit who
now works in the sons of disobedience,
3 among whom also we all once conducted
ourselves in the lusts of our flesh, fulfilling

1:10 [a]NU-Text and M-Text omit *both.* **1:14** [a]NU-Text reads *which.* **1:18** [a]NU-Text and M-Text read *hearts.*

LIFE LESSONS

➤ 1:3 — *Blessed be the God and Father of our Lord Jesus Christ, who has blessed us with every spiritual blessing in the heavenly places in Christ . . . .*

God is not stingy when it comes to bestowing His blessings on His much-loved children. He has already given us *every* spiritual blessing, securing them for us in heaven, where none can be stolen, damaged, or kept back.

➤ 1:18 — *. . . that you may know what is the hope of His calling, what are the riches of the glory of His inheritance in the saints . . . .*

There is a big difference between having the blessings of God and enjoying them; we move from the former to the latter by learning what those blessings are and then laying hold of them by faith.

➤ 1:19 — *. . . and what is the exceeding greatness of His power toward us who believe . . . .*

The disciples continually marveled at the overwhelmingly powerful miracles that the Lord performed (Matt. 9:33; 21:20; Mark 4:41, etc.). That same power is available to us by faith through the Spirit.

➤ 2:2 — *. . . according to the prince of the power of the air, the spirit who now works in the sons of disobedience . . . .*

As the "prince of the power of the air," Satan is not limited to the surface of the earth and so can move quickly to try to prevent unbelievers from coming to faith. Yet he is no match for the Holy Spirit.

ANSWERS TO LIFE'S QUESTIONS

How can I develop a better self-image?

EPH. 2:10

On April 12, 1945, U.S. President Franklin Delano Roosevelt was sitting for a portrait, when he died suddenly of a cerebral hemorrhage. The "Unfinished Portrait," as it is called, remains on its easel, looking out on the world much as it did when artist Elizabeth Shoumatoff laid her brush down at the sight of the president's collapse.

The watercolor likeness of the president shows a man of inner strength and calm. Photographs taken days before and placed alongside the artist's canvas for reference, however, reveal a much different view. In them we see a national leader worn emotionally and physically from the political load he bore.

Later, Madam Shoumatoff returned to her work on the president's portrait. She did not choose to complete the watercolor, however. She saw it as complete in its own right. Instead, she began and finished a new portrait, painted in oil. It is a handsome rendering of a strong and confident President Roosevelt, with no visible flaws.

Have you ever wondered how God views your life? Do you worry that He sees your flaws and mistakes and loves you less? Do not worry! God knows you perfectly and loves you completely just the way you are. You are His masterpiece—His workmanship of grace and love—His work of art. He continues to paint the colors of your life in such a way that you will glorify Him.

The apostle Paul tells us: "We are His workmanship, created in Christ Jesus for good works, which God prepared beforehand, that we should walk in them" (Eph. 2:10).

By God's loving grace we are created in the image of Christ. Though our lives remain on the canvas, God has seen the finished portrait. His eternal eyes know exactly where we need His greatest attention. Every frustration, every disappointment, and every joy has a purpose (Rom. 8:28).

Many find this a hard concept to grasp. They see their lives as incomplete, much like the unfinished portrait of President Roosevelt. But God views you from a totally different perspective. When He sees your life, He sees a person of worth and great promise.

God rejoices over you, though He knows you are not yet what you will be when you step into the eternal presence of God (1 Cor. 13:12). Until that time, God is patiently molding and shaping your life into the image of His Son.

See the Life Principles Index for further study:

3. God's Word is an immovable anchor in times of storm.

13. Listening to God is essential to walking with God.

the desires of the flesh and of the mind, and
were by nature children of wrath, just as the
others.
4 But God, who is rich in mercy, because of
His great love with which He loved us,
5 even when we were dead in trespasses,
made us alive together with Christ (by grace
you have been saved),
6 and raised *us* up together, and made *us* sit
together in the heavenly *places* in Christ Jesus,
7 that in the ages to come He might show
the exceeding riches of His grace in *His* kindness toward us in Christ Jesus.
8 For by grace you have been saved through ➤
faith, and that not of yourselves; *it is* the gift
of God,
9 not of works, lest anyone should boast.
10 For we are His workmanship, created in
Christ Jesus for good works, which God prepared beforehand that we should walk in
them.

Brought Near by His Blood

11 Therefore remember that you, once Gentiles in the flesh—who are called Uncircumci-

LIFE LESSONS

➤ 2:8, 9 — *For by grace you have been saved through faith, and that not of yourselves; it is the gift of God, not of works, lest anyone should boast.*

Salvation is a gift of God, presented free and not in exchange for anything when we place our faith in Christ. It therefore magnifies God alone, since He blesses us not because of our merit but because of His goodness.

sion by what is called the Circumcision made
in the flesh by hands—
12 that at that time you were without Christ,
being aliens from the commonwealth of Israel
and strangers from the covenants of promise,
having no hope and without God in the world.
➤ 13 But now in Christ Jesus you who once
were far off have been brought near by the
blood of Christ.

Christ Our Peace

14 For He Himself is our peace, who has
made both one, and has broken down the
middle wall of separation,
15 having abolished in His flesh the enmity,
that is, the law of commandments *contained*
in ordinances, so as to create in Himself one
new man *from* the two, *thus* making peace,
16 and that He might reconcile them both to
God in one body through the cross, thereby
putting to death the enmity.
17 And He came and preached peace to you
who were afar off and to those who were near.
18 For through Him we both have access by
one Spirit to the Father.

Christ Our Cornerstone

19 Now, therefore, you are no longer strangers and foreigners, but fellow citizens with
the saints and members of the household of
God,
20 having been built on the foundation of the
apostles and prophets, Jesus Christ Himself
being the chief corner*stone*,
21 in whom the whole building, being fitted
together, grows into a holy temple in the
Lord,
22 in whom you also are being built together
for a dwelling place of God in the Spirit.

The Mystery Revealed

3 For this reason I, Paul, the prisoner of
Christ Jesus for you Gentiles—
2 if indeed you have heard of the dispensation of the grace of God which was given to
me for you,
3 how that by revelation He made known to
me the mystery (as I have briefly written already,
4 by which, when you read, you may understand my knowledge in the mystery of Christ),
5 which in other ages was not made known
to the sons of men, as it has now been revealed by the Spirit to His holy apostles and
prophets:
6 that the Gentiles should be fellow heirs, of
the same body, and partakers of His promise
in Christ through the gospel,
7 of which I became a minister according to
the gift of the grace of God given to me by the
effective working of His power.

Purpose of the Mystery

8 To me, who am less than the least of all the ➤
saints, this grace was given, that I should
preach among the Gentiles the unsearchable
riches of Christ,
9 and to make all see what *is* the fellowship[a]
of the mystery, which from the beginning of
the ages has been hidden in God who created
all things through Jesus Christ;[b]
10 to the intent that now the manifold wis- ➤
dom of God might be made known by the
church to the principalities and powers in the
heavenly *places*,
11 according to the eternal purpose which He
accomplished in Christ Jesus our Lord,
12 in whom we have boldness and access
with confidence through faith in Him.
13 Therefore I ask that you do not lose heart
at my tribulations for you, which is your glory.

Appreciation of the Mystery

14 For this reason I bow my knees to the Father of our Lord Jesus Christ,[a]
15 from whom the whole family in heaven
and earth is named,
16 that He would grant you, according to the ➤
riches of His glory, to be strengthened with
might through His Spirit in the inner man,

3:9 [a]NU-Text and M-Text read *stewardship* (dispensation). [b]NU-Text omits *through Jesus Christ.* **3:14** [a]NU-Text omits *of our Lord Jesus Christ.*

LIFE LESSONS

➤ 2:13 — *But now in Christ Jesus you who once were far off have been brought near by the blood of Christ.*

God created you to enjoy an intimate relationship with Himself, and He redeemed you and saved you for the same reason. He yearns for close fellowship with you and makes that possible through the death of His Son.

➤ 3:8 — *To me, who am less than the least of all the saints, this grace was given, that I should preach among the Gentiles the unsearchable riches of Christ . . . .*

Paul never got over the fact that even though he once tried to destroy the church, the Lord gave him the task of helping to build that church worldwide—just one example of "the unsearchable riches of Christ."

➤ 3:10 — *. . . to the intent that now the manifold wisdom of God might be made known by the church to the principalities and powers in the heavenly places . . . .*

What happens in our lives of faith has implications far greater than what we can see. Powerful spiritual forces are watching us and stand amazed each time we glorify God through some unexpected act of faith, however small.

➤ 3:16 — *. . . that He would grant you, according to the riches of His glory, to be strengthened with might through His Spirit in the inner man . . . .*

If we feel weak, it is not because we suffer from a lack of available power. The might of God that created the universe and that raised Jesus from the dead is available to us at every moment through believing prayer.

17 that Christ may dwell in your hearts
through faith; that you, being rooted and
grounded in love,
18 may be able to comprehend with all the
saints what *is* the width and length and depth
and height—
19 to know the love of Christ which passes
knowledge; that you may be filled with all the
fullness of God.
➤ 20 Now to Him who is able to do exceedingly
abundantly above all that we ask or think, according to the power that works in us,
21 to Him *be* glory in the church by Christ Jesus to all generations, forever and ever.
Amen.

Walk in Unity

➤ 4 I, therefore, the prisoner of the Lord, beseech you to walk worthy of the calling
with which you were called,
2 with all lowliness and gentleness, with
longsuffering, bearing with one another in
love,
3 endeavoring to keep the unity of the Spirit
in the bond of peace.
4 *There is* one body and one Spirit, just as
you were called in one hope of your calling;
5 one Lord, one faith, one baptism;
6 one God and Father of all, who *is* above
all, and through all, and in you[a] all.

Spiritual Gifts

7 But to each one of us grace was given according to the measure of Christ's gift.
8 Therefore He says:

"When He ascended on high,
He led captivity captive,
And gave gifts to men."[a]

9 (Now this, *"He ascended"*—what does it
mean but that He also first[a] descended into
the lower parts of the earth?
10 He who descended is also the One who ascended far above all the heavens, that He
might fill all things.)
11 And He Himself gave some *to be* apostles,
some prophets, some evangelists, and some
pastors and teachers,
12 for the equipping of the saints for the
work of ministry, for the edifying of the body
of Christ,
13 till we all come to the unity of the faith ➤
and of the knowledge of the Son of God, to a
perfect man, to the measure of the stature of
the fullness of Christ;
14 that we should no longer be children,
tossed to and fro and carried about with every
wind of doctrine, by the trickery of men, in
the cunning craftiness of deceitful plotting,
15 but, speaking the truth in love, may grow
up in all things into Him who is the head—
Christ—
16 from whom the whole body, joined and
knit together by what every joint supplies, according to the effective working by which
every part does its share, causes growth of the
body for the edifying of itself in love.

The New Man

17 This I say, therefore, and testify in the Lord,
that you should no longer walk as the rest of[a]
the Gentiles walk, in the futility of their mind,
18 having their understanding darkened,
being alienated from the life of God, because
of the ignorance that is in them, because of
the blindness of their heart;
19 who, being past feeling, have given themselves over to lewdness, to work all uncleanness with greediness.
20 But you have not so learned Christ,
21 if indeed you have heard Him and have
been taught by Him, as the truth is in Jesus:
22 that you put off, concerning your former
conduct, the old man which grows corrupt according to the deceitful lusts,
23 and be renewed in the spirit of your mind,
24 and that you put on the new man which ➤
was created according to God, in true righteousness and holiness.

4:6 [a]NU-Text omits *you;* M-Text reads *us.* **4:8** [a]Psalm 68:18
4:9 [a]NU-Text omits *first.* **4:17** [a]NU-Text omits *the rest of.*

LIFE LESSONS

➤ 3:20 — *Now to Him who is able to do exceedingly abundantly above all that we ask or think, according to the power that works in us . . . .*

God loves to surprise His faithful people with answers to prayer far exceeding anything they had imagined (see Ex. 14:10, 13, 14; 2 Chr. 20:5–27; Acts 12:5–17). That power is as close as the Spirit within us.

➤ 4:1 — *I . . . beseech you to walk worthy of the calling with which you were called . . . .*

Our behavior in Christ is to match our profession of Christ. To "walk worthy" means that we are to live in a way that honors and pleases God; we were "created in Christ Jesus for good works" (Eph. 2:10).

➤ 4:13 — *. . . till we all come to the unity of the faith and of the knowledge of the Son of God, to a perfect man, to the measure of the stature of the fullness of Christ . . . .*

The Christian life is a life of growth. None of us has "arrived," none of us has already become all that God means for us to become; every day we are to be conformed a little more to the image of Christ.

➤ 4:24 — *. . . put on the new man which was created according to God, in true righteousness and holiness.*

When Paul tells us to "put on" the new man, he means that we have to make a conscious, moment-by-moment choice to depend upon the Spirit's power to transform us into the likeness of Christ.

LIFE PRINCIPLE 25

GOD BLESSES US SO THAT WE MIGHT BLESS OTHERS.

EPH. 4:28

How would you complete the following three statements?

1. God saved me because ____________________.

2. God's purpose for saving me was ____________________.

3. I am most like Jesus when I ____________________.

I give you this little quiz not to put you on the spot, but to set the proper framework for our discussion. I'm seeking the following answers to my questions:

1. God saved me because He loves me.

The sole reason that God sent His Son to this world to die for your sins and mine was because He loved us. God forgives us, grants us eternal life, and gives us the gift of His Holy Spirit out of His immeasurable love and grace. There is no other reason.

Many people seem to believe that God saves a man or woman because of the person's good works or service. Nothing could be further from the truth. No amount or type of service can earn salvation. The apostle Paul made this very clear when he wrote: "For by grace you have been saved through faith, and that not of yourselves; it is the gift of God, not of works, lest anyone should boast" (Eph. 2:8, 9). Even the faith by which we believe that God forgives us and saves us is a divine gift that flows from His love!

This point is critical to understand. Any good we do is in *response* to God's gifts of salvation, eternal life, and the Holy Spirit, never in order to earn, win, or warrant salvation.

2. God's purpose for saving me was to bring Him glory.

God saved you and me so that we might be His "trophies." We serve as examples to others of God's love and mercy at work in and through a human life.

Many people seem to think that the only reason for salvation is so that a person might go to heaven when he dies. Eternal life is part of God's plan of forgiveness, but that is not the sole reason for our salvation. God saved us so that we each might reflect His nature—that we might be His people on this earth, doing the kinds of works that Jesus Himself would do if He were walking in our shoes, through our world, during our lifetime. God desires to manifest His character through our personalities and giftedness.

When we allow His Holy Spirit to work in us and through us to others, we become vessels of His love in action. We

Any good we do is in *response* to God's gifts.

reflect His compassion, love, and mercy to others. And in so doing, we are His witnesses. We bring credit, honor, and glory to *Him*.

3. I am most like Jesus when I serve others.

The foremost characteristic of the life of Jesus Christ was and is *service*. We are most like Him when we serve as He served.

Many seem to think that a person is most like Jesus when he preaches like Jesus preached, teaches like Jesus taught, heals like Jesus healed, or performs miracles like Jesus performed miracles. They look only at the outward manifestation of a person's witness and ministry.

They need to look beyond the outer manifestation to the motivation for Jesus' life. That motivation was always service. Jesus preached, taught, healed, and performed miracles in order to help others, never to call attention to Himself. He poured out His very life so that others might be saved, never thinking for a moment to save Himself. Paul caught exactly the right tone when he wrote, "For you know the grace of our Lord Jesus Christ, that though He was rich, yet for your sakes He became poor, that you through His poverty might become rich" (2 Cor. 8:9).

Jesus poured out His very life so that others might be saved.

God has called you to serve others just as Jesus served others. He didn't save you or call you to service so that you might be exalted, praised, glorified, or put on a pedestal. He saved you so that you might serve others, and in so doing bring praise and honor to God's holy name. He blesses you so that you might bless others.

The good news is that any person who is saved *can* serve God and bring glory to Him. The nature of the ministry task or calling is not the important thing; what *is* important is the motivation behind our service.

God loved us so that we might love others. He blesses us so that we might bless others. In a nutshell, that's what the Christian life is all about.

See the Life Principles Index for further study.

WHAT THE BIBLE SAYS ABOUT GRIEVING THE HOLY SPIRIT

Eph. 4:30

Did you know that we can short-circuit the effective work of the Holy Spirit in our lives by grieving Him? Paul wrote, "Do not grieve the Holy Spirit of God" (Eph. 4:30).

How do we grieve the Holy Spirit? We grieve Him when we disobey God's commandments and when we choose to act in unrighteous ways. In other words, we displease the Lord when we know what to do and then choose to do the opposite.

The Ephesians knew very well that it was not godly to lie, steal, remain angry with one another, or speak cutting, hurting words to each other. They knew that such evil things "give place to the devil" (Eph. 4:27).

Paul lived and ministered among the Ephesians for two years, and his ministry had a powerful impact on the entire city of Ephesus. And yet, Paul had to remind the Christians not to do the things common among the non-Christians! It was as if he had to go back to square one with them. When the Ephesians broke the most obvious of God's commandments, they caused sorrow in the Holy Spirit. Paul said, in effect, "Your ungodly behavior breaks the heart of God."

"Your ungodly behavior breaks the heart of God."

The Holy Spirit is grieved not only because our conduct tarnishes God's good name, but also because He loves us and deeply desires to reward us, bless us, and see good fruit produced in and through us—not discipline us. He knows that sin injures us and saddles our lives with negative consequences. When we know that our loved ones do things that harm them, we feel grieved. So does He.

So how can we avoid grieving the Holy Spirit?

We can choose to keep God's commandments and to lead a disciplined life by depending on the power of the Spirit. When we sin, we confess the sin immediately and repent of it, changing our minds and our behavior to conform to God's Word.

As we ask the Holy Spirit to lead us and help us every day, we gain His help to enjoy a successful Christian walk. He keeps our footing sure.

See the Life Principles Index for further study:
21. Obedience always brings blessing.
22. To walk in the spirit is to obey the initial promptings of the Spirit.

ANSWERS TO LIFE'S QUESTIONS

Why is it so important to forgive others?

EPH. 4:31, 32

All of us, at some point, have to deal with the issue of unforgiveness. When we allow a bitter spirit to lodge in our souls, where it grows and festers, it becomes both painful and destructive. Unforgiveness lies at the root of many of the physical, emotional, psychological, and spiritual problems we see today.

The apostle Paul wrote, "Let all bitterness, wrath, anger, clamor, and evil speaking be put away from you, with all malice. And be kind to one another, tenderhearted, forgiving one another, even as God in Christ forgave you" (Eph. 4:31, 32). When Paul spoke of bitterness, wrath, anger, clamor, and evil speaking, he was describing the ugly manifestations of a "spirit of unforgiveness."

A spirit of unforgiveness goes beyond a temporary unwillingness to forgive, the period between the time a person gets hurt and the time he forgives the one who hurt him. A spirit of unforgiveness develops when the one hurt chooses to remain in that unforgiving state.

People who develop this nasty spirit often say, "I just don't think I could ever forgive *that.*" They make the statement when they feel they have been treated in such an unjust, unfair, harmful way that they simply can't let go of the pain.

We are all going to be hurt. Every one of us has been hurt, are hurting now, or are going to be hurt by somebody. The only way we can insulate ourselves against being hurt is to completely remove ourselves from the possibility of love. To risk love is to risk hurt.

Hurt is unavoidable, but we can deal with hurt. No pain is too deep or too widespread to lie beyond the power of God's forgiveness, working in and through us. Unforgiveness is a choice we make with the will—and it's a devastatingly bad choice, not only for the relationship, not only for the cause of Christ, but also for the one who refuses to forgive.

We shouldn't forget that it was our loving Savior, Jesus Christ, who ended a story on the necessity of forgiveness with these words: "And his master was angry, and delivered him to the torturers until he should pay all that was due to him. So My heavenly Father also will do to you if each of you, from his heart, does not forgive his brother his trespasses" (Matt. 18: 34, 35).

See the Life Principles Index for further study:

2. *Obey God and leave all the consequences to Him.*
5. *God does not require us to understand His will, just obey it, even if it seems unreasonable.*

Do Not Grieve the Spirit

25 Therefore, putting away lying, *"Let each one of you speak truth with his neighbor,"*[a]
for we are members of one another.
26 *"Be angry, and do not sin"*:[a] do not let the
sun go down on your wrath,
27 nor give place to the devil.
28 Let him who stole steal no longer, but
rather let him labor, working with *his* hands
what is good, that he may have something to
give him who has need.
29 Let no corrupt word proceed out of your
mouth, but what is good for necessary edification, that it may impart grace to the hearers.
30 And do not grieve the Holy Spirit of God,
by whom you were sealed for the day of redemption.
31 Let all bitterness, wrath, anger, clamor,
and evil speaking be put away from you, with
all malice.
32 And be kind to one another, tenderhearted, forgiving one another, even as God
in Christ forgave you.

Walk in Love

5 Therefore be imitators of God as dear children.

4:25 [a]Zechariah 8:16 **4:26** [a]Psalm 4:4

LIFE LESSONS

➤ 5:1 — *Therefore be imitators of God as dear children.*

If we are children of God, it only makes sense that we are to imitate our Father. And if we do not imitate our heavenly Father, there is biblical reason to wonder who our father really is (see 1 John 3:10).

2 And walk in love, as Christ also has loved
us and given Himself for us, an offering and a
sacrifice to God for a sweet-smelling aroma.
3 But fornication and all uncleanness or
covetousness, let it not even be named among
you, as is fitting for saints;
4 neither filthiness, nor foolish talking, nor
coarse jesting, which are not fitting, but
rather giving of thanks.
5 For this you know,[a] that no fornicator, unclean person, nor covetous man, who is an
idolater, has any inheritance in the kingdom
of Christ and God.
6 Let no one deceive you with empty words,
for because of these things the wrath of God
comes upon the sons of disobedience.
7 Therefore do not be partakers with them.

Walk in Light

➤ 8 For you were once darkness, but now *you
are* light in the Lord. Walk as children of light
9 (for the fruit of the Spirit[a] *is* in all goodness, righteousness, and truth),
10 finding out what is acceptable to the Lord.
11 And have no fellowship with the unfruitful
works of darkness, but rather expose *them.*
12 For it is shameful even to speak of those
things which are done by them in secret.
13 But all things that are exposed are made
manifest by the light, for whatever makes
manifest is light.
✳ 14 Therefore He says:

"Awake, you who sleep,
Arise from the dead,
And Christ will give you light."

Walk in Wisdom

15 See then that you walk circumspectly, not
as fools but as wise,
16 redeeming the time, because the days are
evil.
17 Therefore do not be unwise, but understand what the will of the Lord *is.*
➤ 18 And do not be drunk with wine, in which
is dissipation; but be filled with the Spirit,
19 speaking to one another in psalms and
hymns and spiritual songs, singing and making melody in your heart to the Lord,
20 giving thanks always for all things to God
the Father in the name of our Lord Jesus Christ,
21 submitting to one another in the fear of
God.[a]

Marriage—Christ and the Church

22 Wives, submit to your own husbands, as to
the Lord.
23 For the husband is head of the wife, as
also Christ is head of the church; and He is
the Savior of the body.
24 Therefore, just as the church is subject to
Christ, so *let* the wives *be* to their own husbands in everything.
25 Husbands, love your wives, just as Christ
also loved the church and gave Himself for her,
26 that He might sanctify and cleanse her
with the washing of water by the word,
27 that He might present her to Himself a
glorious church, not having spot or wrinkle or
any such thing, but that she should be holy
and without blemish.
28 So husbands ought to love their own
wives as their own bodies; he who loves his
wife loves himself.
29 For no one ever hated his own flesh, but
nourishes and cherishes it, just as the Lord
does the church.
30 For we are members of His body,[a] of His
flesh and of His bones.
31 *"For this reason a man shall leave his father and mother and be joined to his wife,
and the two shall become one flesh."*[a]
32 This is a great mystery, but I speak concerning Christ and the church.
33 Nevertheless let each one of you in particular so love his own wife as himself, and let
the wife *see* that she respects *her* husband.

Children and Parents

6 Children, obey your parents in the Lord,
for this is right.
2 *"Honor your father and mother,"* which is ✳
the first commandment with promise:
3 *"that it may be well with you and you may
live long on the earth."*[a]
4 And you, fathers, do not provoke your
children to wrath, but bring them up in the
training and admonition of the Lord.

Bondservants and Masters

5 Bondservants, be obedient to those who
are your masters according to the flesh, with
fear and trembling, in sincerity of heart, as to
Christ;
6 not with eyeservice, as men-pleasers, but
as bondservants of Christ, doing the will of
God from the heart,
7 with goodwill doing service, as to the
Lord, and not to men,

5:5 [a]NU-Text reads *For know this.* **5:9** [a]NU-Text reads *light.* **5:21** [a]NU-Text reads *Christ.* **5:30** [a]NU-Text omits the rest of this verse. **5:31** [a]Genesis 2:24 **6:3** [a]Deuteronomy 5:16

LIFE LESSONS

➤ 5:8 — *For you were once darkness, but now you are light in the Lord. Walk as children of light . . . .*

God intends that His children act as beacons of light in a dark world, as lighthouses showing the way to spiritual safety for those about to sink into the abyss.

➤ 5:18 — *And do not be drunk with wine, in which is dissipation; but be filled with the Spirit . . . .*

To get drunk you have to consume large quantities of alcohol, not just a little. In a similar way, to be filled with the Spirit we have to depend on Him every moment, not just once or twice every now and then.

8 knowing that whatever good anyone does,
he will receive the same from the Lord,
whether *he is* a slave or free.
9 And you, masters, do the same things to
them, giving up threatening, knowing that
your own Master also[a] is in heaven, and there
is no partiality with Him.

The Whole Armor of God

10 Finally, my brethren, be strong in the Lord
and in the power of His might.
11 Put on the whole armor of God, that you
may be able to stand against the wiles of the
devil.
12 For we do not wrestle against flesh and
blood, but against principalities, against powers, against the rulers of the darkness of this
age,[a] against spiritual *hosts* of wickedness in
the heavenly *places.*
13 Therefore take up the whole armor of
God, that you may be able to withstand in the
evil day, and having done all, to stand.
14 Stand therefore, having girded your waist
with truth, having put on the breastplate of
righteousness,
15 and having shod your feet with the preparation of the gospel of peace;
16 above all, taking the shield of faith with
which you will be able to quench all the fiery
darts of the wicked one.
17 And take the helmet of salvation, and the
sword of the Spirit, which is the word of God;
18 praying always with all prayer and supplication in the Spirit, being watchful to this end
with all perseverance and supplication for all
the saints—
19 and for me, that utterance may be given to
me, that I may open my mouth boldly to make
known the mystery of the gospel,
20 for which I am an ambassador in chains;
that in it I may speak boldly, as I ought to speak.

A Gracious Greeting

21 But that you also may know my affairs
and how I am doing, Tychicus, a beloved
brother and faithful minister in the Lord, will
make all things known to you;
22 whom I have sent to you for this very purpose, that you may know our affairs, and *that*
he may comfort your hearts.

Life Examples:

TYCHICUS

Beloved Messenger

EPH. 6:21

Each time Tychicus is mentioned in Scripture (Acts 20:4; Eph. 6:21; 2 Tim. 4:12; Titus 3:12), he is running errands for the apostle Paul, then a prisoner in Rome. In a sense, he is Paul's "messenger boy."

Paul himself wrote, "Tychicus, a beloved brother, faithful minister, and fellow servant in the Lord, will tell you all the news about me. I am sending him to you for this very purpose, that he may know your circumstances and comfort your hearts" (Col. 4:7, 8).

We might feel tempted to evaluate Tychicus's ministry as minor, especially when compared to Paul's. But do you realize that Tychicus delivered Paul's messages to several churches, and thus played a major part in distributing the Word of God? Is that unimportant? Absolutely not! Tychicus had a crucial ministry, and he fulfilled it.

Will you allow him to inspire you to fulfill your own crucial ministry, whatever it is?

See the Life Principles Index for further study:
6. *You reap what you sow, more than you sow, and later than you sow.*
22. *To walk in the Spirit is to obey the initial promptings of the Spirit.*

23 Peace to the brethren, and love with faith,
from God the Father and the Lord Jesus Christ.
24 Grace *be* with all those who love our Lord
Jesus Christ in sincerity. Amen.

6:9 aNU-Text reads *He who is both their Master and yours.*
6:12 aNU-Text reads *rulers of this darkness.*

LIFE LESSONS

➤ **6:8 — . . . *whatever good anyone does, he will receive the same from the Lord, whether he is a slave or free.***

Throughout the Bible the Lord promises that He will generously reward His children for "whatever good" they do, no matter how small or insignificant it may seem. Faithful service yields staggering blessing.

➤ **6:10 — *Finally, my brethren, be strong in the Lord and in the power of His might.***

The only way to really be strong is to depend upon the unlimited power of God. We draw on His strength by faith, asking Him to supply us with the resources we lack so that we might be strong for Him.

➤ **6:18 — . . . *praying always with all prayer and supplication in the Spirit, being watchful to this end with all perseverance and supplication for all the saints . . . .***

None of us can long survive, let alone prosper, without the sincere prayers of others offered on our behalf. God has designed the Christian life as a community event, not as a solo endeavor.

THE EPISTLE OF PAUL THE APOSTLE TO THE

PHILIPPIANS

Philippians is the apostle Paul's thank-you letter to the believers at Philippi for their help in his hour of need. Repeatedly he communicates one central thought: Only in Christ can we experience real unity and joy. With Christ as your model of humility and service, you too can enjoy a oneness of purpose, attitude, goal, and labor.

We sometimes think that joy can happen only in the presence of favorable circumstances, yet Paul showed the Philippians that we serve a God who can take even unexpected and unpleasant circumstances and use them for His glory and our good. Paul told his friends, "I want you to know, brethren, that the things which happened to me have actually turned out for the furtherance of the gospel, so that it has become evident to the whole palace guard, and to all the rest, that my chains are in Christ; and most of the brethren in the Lord, having become confident by my chains, are much more bold to speak the word without fear" (Phil. 1:12–14).

Paul stressed unity because within their own ranks, fellow workers in the Philippian church were at odds with one another, hindering the work of proclaiming new life in Christ. Because of this, Paul exhorts the church to "stand fast . . . be of the same mind . . . rejoice in the Lord always . . . in everything by prayer and supplication, with thanksgiving, let your requests be made known . . . and the peace of God, which surpasses all understanding, will guard your hearts and minds through Christ Jesus" (4:1, 2, 4, 6, 7).

This epistle is called *Pros Philippesious,* "To the Philippians." Paul founded the church at Philippi before any others in Macedonia. The apostle established this church during his second missionary journey (see Acts 16:6–40). Philippians is a very warm letter filled with much personal affection.

Themes: God intends the Christian life to be a joyful experience, made more so by the unity believers experience in community.

Author: The apostle Paul.

Time: Likely written from prison in Rome about A.D. 60–62.

Structure: After greeting his friends and describing his thankfulness and prayers for them (1:1–11), the apostle refers to his imprisonment and the benefit it has had in the preaching of the gospel (1:12–26). He then exhorts them to live worthy of the gospel (1:27—2:18), mentions his associates (2:19–30), issues some warnings (3:1—4:1), and concludes his letter (4:2–23).

As you read Philippians, watch for several life principles that play an important role in this book:

18. As children of a sovereign God, we are never victims of our circumstances. *See Philippians 1:12–18; page 1389.*

24. To live the Christian life is to allow Jesus to live His life in and through us. *See Philippians 1:20–26; page 1389.*

15. Brokenness is God's requirement for maximum usefulness. *See Philippians 2:1–4; page 1390.*

26. Adversity is a bridge to a deeper relationship with God. *See Philippians 3:10, 11; page 1391.*

17. We stand tallest and strongest on our knees. *See Philippians 4:6, 7; page 1394.*

Greeting

1 Paul and Timothy, bondservants of Jesus Christ,

To all the saints in Christ Jesus who are in Philippi, with the bishops[a] and deacons:

2 Grace to you and peace from God our Father and the Lord Jesus Christ.

Thankfulness and Prayer

3 I thank my God upon every remembrance of you,

4 always in every prayer of mine making request for you all with joy,

5 for your fellowship in the gospel from the first day until now,

6 being confident of this very thing, that He who has begun a good work in you will complete *it* until the day of Jesus Christ;

7 just as it is right for me to think this of you all, because I have you in my heart, inasmuch as both in my chains and in the defense and confirmation of the gospel, you all are partakers with me of grace.

8 For God is my witness, how greatly I long for you all with the affection of Jesus Christ.

9 And this I pray, that your love may abound still more and more in knowledge and all discernment,

10 that you may approve the things that are excellent, that you may be sincere and without offense till the day of Christ,

11 being filled with the fruits of righteousness which *are* by Jesus Christ, to the glory and praise of God.

Christ Is Preached

12 But I want you to know, brethren, that the things *which happened* to me have actually turned out for the furtherance of the gospel,

13 so that it has become evident to the whole palace guard, and to all the rest, that my chains are in Christ;

14 and most of the brethren in the Lord, having become confident by my chains, are much more bold to speak the word without fear.

15 Some indeed preach Christ even from envy and strife, and some also from goodwill:

16 The former[a] preach Christ from selfish ambition, not sincerely, supposing to add affliction to my chains;

17 but the latter out of love, knowing that I am appointed for the defense of the gospel.

18 What then? Only *that* in every way, whether in pretense or in truth, Christ is preached; and in this I rejoice, yes, and will rejoice.

To Live Is Christ

19 For I know that this will turn out for my deliverance through your prayer and the supply of the Spirit of Jesus Christ,

20 according to my earnest expectation and hope that in nothing I shall be ashamed, but with all boldness, as always, so now also Christ will be magnified in my body, whether by life or by death.

21 For to me, to live *is* Christ, and to die *is* gain.

22 But if *I* live on in the flesh, this *will mean* fruit from *my* labor; yet what I shall choose I cannot tell.

23 For[a] I am hard-pressed between the two, having a desire to depart and be with Christ, *which is* far better.

24 Nevertheless to remain in the flesh *is* more needful for you.

25 And being confident of this, I know that I shall remain and continue with you all for your progress and joy of faith,

26 that your rejoicing for me may be more abundant in Jesus Christ by my coming to you again.

Striving and Suffering for Christ

27 Only let your conduct be worthy of the gospel of Christ, so that whether I come and see you or am absent, I may hear of your affairs, that you stand fast in one spirit, with

1:1 [a]Literally *overseers* **1:16** [a]NU-Text reverses the contents of verses 16 and 17. **1:23** [a]NU-Text and M-Text read *But.*

LIFE LESSONS

➤ 1:6 — *. . . being confident of this very thing, that He who has begun a good work in you will complete it until the day of Jesus Christ . . . .*

God is faithful to finish what He starts. Once we accept Christ as our Savior, the work of sanctification begins. And it continues. There is always more to walking with God than what we've known, seen, learned, or experienced.

➤ 1:10 — *. . . that you may approve the things that are excellent, that you may be sincere and without offense till the day of Christ . . . .*

When you ponder whether to engage in some activity, it is a much better way to live to constantly ask yourself, "what is excellent about it?" rather than, "what's wrong with it?"

➤ 1:12 — *But I want you to know, brethren, that the things which happened to me have actually turned out for the furtherance of the gospel . . . .*

God has a delightful way of turning negatives into positives. He loves to take things that Satan means for our harm and use them instead for His glory and our benefit.

➤ 1:21 — *For to me, to live is Christ . . . .*

Paul did not want to do great things for God; He wanted God to do great things in and through him. His goal was to serve as the hands and feet and mouth of Christ, doing in Christ's power what Christ would do.

one mind striving together for the faith of the gospel,

28 and not in any way terrified by your adversaries, which is to them a proof of perdition, but to you of salvation,[a] and that from God.

➤ 29 For to you it has been granted on behalf of Christ, not only to believe in Him, but also to suffer for His sake,

30 having the same conflict which you saw in me and now hear *is* in me.

Unity Through Humility

2 Therefore if *there is* any consolation in Christ, if any comfort of love, if any fellowship of the Spirit, if any affection and mercy,

➤ 2 fulfill my joy by being like-minded, having the same love, *being* of one accord, of one mind.

3 *Let* nothing *be done* through selfish ambition or conceit, but in lowliness of mind let each esteem others better than himself.

4 Let each of you look out not only for his own interests, but also for the interests of others.

The Humbled and Exalted Christ

5 Let this mind be in you which was also in Christ Jesus,

6 who, being in the form of God, did not consider it robbery to be equal with God,

7 but made Himself of no reputation, taking the form of a bondservant, *and* coming in the likeness of men.

8 And being found in appearance as a man, He humbled Himself and became obedient to *the point of* death, even the death of the cross.

9 Therefore God also has highly exalted Him and given Him the name which is above every name,

10 that at the name of Jesus every knee should bow, of those in heaven, and of those on earth, and of those under the earth,

11 and *that* every tongue should confess that Jesus Christ *is* Lord, to the glory of God the Father.

Light Bearers

12 Therefore, my beloved, as you have always obeyed, not as in my presence only, but now much more in my absence, work out your own salvation with fear and trembling; ≺

13 for it is God who works in you both to will and to do for *His* good pleasure.

14 Do all things without complaining and disputing,

15 that you may become blameless and harmless, children of God without fault in the midst of a crooked and perverse generation, among whom you shine as lights in the world, ≺

16 holding fast the word of life, so that I may rejoice in the day of Christ that I have not run in vain or labored in vain.

17 Yes, and if I am being poured out *as a drink offering* on the sacrifice and service of your faith, I am glad and rejoice with you all.

18 For the same reason you also be glad and rejoice with me.

Timothy Commended

19 But I trust in the Lord Jesus to send Timothy to you shortly, that I also may be encouraged when I know your state.

20 For I have no one like-minded, who will sincerely care for your state.

21 For all seek their own, not the things which are of Christ Jesus.

22 But you know his proven character, that as a son with *his* father he served with me in the gospel.

23 Therefore I hope to send him at once, as soon as I see how it goes with me.

24 But I trust in the Lord that I myself shall also come shortly.

1:28 [a]NU-Text reads *of your salvation.*

LIFE LESSONS

➤ 1:29 — *For to you it has been granted on behalf of Christ, not only to believe in Him, but also to suffer for His sake . . . .*

The word "granted" comes from the Greek term *charis*, often translated "gift." Believing in Christ is a gift of God, but so is suffering for Christ. If we would not refuse the first, neither should we the second (Rom. 8:17).

➤ 2:2 — *. . . fulfill my joy by being like-minded, having the same love, being of one accord, of one mind.*

The joyful unity of believers in Christ offers a powerful testimony to the world that the God of love they preach is real, active, and eager to bring others into His loving family.

➤ 2:12 — *Therefore, my beloved, as you have always obeyed, not as in my presence only, but now much more in my absence, work out your own salvation with fear and trembling . . . .*

When Paul tells us to "work out" our own salvation "with fear and trembling," he means that we are to give careful attention to our actions and behavior, making sure that they well represent the One who saved us.

➤ 2:15 — *. . . that you may become blameless and harmless, children of God without fault in the midst of a crooked and perverse generation, among whom you shine as lights in the world . . . .*

If our behavior as God's children does not differ from that of unbelievers, then we look just as "crooked and perverse" as anyone else, and instead of shining "as lights," we leave the world as dark as we found it.

Epaphroditus Praised

25 Yet I considered it necessary to send to
you Epaphroditus, my brother, fellow worker,
and fellow soldier, but your messenger and
the one who ministered to my need;
26 since he was longing for you all, and was
distressed because you had heard that he was
sick.
27 For indeed he was sick almost unto death;
but God had mercy on him, and not only on
him but on me also, lest I should have sorrow
upon sorrow.
28 Therefore I sent him the more eagerly,
that when you see him again you may rejoice,
and I may be less sorrowful.
29 Receive him therefore in the Lord with all
gladness, and hold such men in esteem;
30 because for the work of Christ he came
close to death, not regarding his life, to supply
what was lacking in your service toward me.

All for Christ

3 Finally, my brethren, rejoice in the Lord.
For me to write the same things to you *is*
not tedious, but for you *it is* safe.
2 Beware of dogs, beware of evil workers,
beware of the mutilation!
3 For we are the circumcision, who worship
God in the Spirit,[a] rejoice in Christ Jesus, and
have no confidence in the flesh,
4 though I also might have confidence in the
flesh. If anyone else thinks he may have confidence in the flesh, I more so:
5 circumcised the eighth day, of the stock of
Israel, *of* the tribe of Benjamin, a Hebrew of
the Hebrews; concerning the law, a Pharisee;
6 concerning zeal, persecuting the church;
concerning the righteousness which is in the
law, blameless.
7 But what things were gain to me, these I
have counted loss for Christ.
8 Yet indeed I also count all things loss for
the excellence of the knowledge of Christ Jesus my Lord, for whom I have suffered the
loss of all things, and count them as rubbish,
that I may gain Christ
9 and be found in Him, not having my own
righteousness, which *is* from the law, but that
which *is* through faith in Christ, the righteousness which is from God by faith;
10 that I may know Him and the power of His
resurrection, and the fellowship of His sufferings, being conformed to His death,
11 if, by any means, I may attain to the resurrection from the dead.

Pressing Toward the Goal

12 Not that I have already attained, or am already perfected; but I press on, that I may lay
hold of that for which Christ Jesus has also
laid hold of me.
13 Brethren, I do not count myself to have apprehended; but one thing *I do*, forgetting
those things which are behind and reaching
forward to those things which are ahead,
14 I press toward the goal for the prize of the
upward call of God in Christ Jesus.
15 Therefore let us, as many as are mature,
have this mind; and if in anything you think
otherwise, God will reveal even this to you.
16 Nevertheless, to *the degree* that we have
already attained, let us walk by the same
rule,[a] let us be of the same mind.

Our Citizenship in Heaven

17 Brethren, join in following my example,
and note those who so walk, as you have us
for a pattern.
18 For many walk, of whom I have told
you often, and now tell you even weeping,
that they are the enemies of the cross of
Christ:
19 whose end *is* destruction, whose god *is*
their belly, and *whose* glory *is* in their
shame—who set their mind on earthly things.

3:3 [a]NU-Text and M-Text read *who worship in the Spirit of God.*
3:16 [a]NU-Text omits *rule* and the rest of the verse.

LIFE LESSONS

➤ 3:1 — *Finally, my brethren, rejoice in the Lord. For me to write the same things to you is not tedious, but for you it is safe.*

Because we so easily forget the lessons we've learned, the Bible often presents the same teaching in various forms. Peter wrote, "I will not be negligent to remind you always of these things, though you know" them (2 Pet. 1:12).

➤ 3:3 — *For we are the circumcision, who worship God in the Spirit, rejoice in Christ Jesus, and have no confidence in the flesh . . . .*

True religion is not a matter of carrying out traditions, rites and rituals, but always is based in a genuine and intimate relationship with God the Father made possible by faith in Christ and empowered by the Holy Spirit.

➤ 3:8 — *I also count all things loss for the excellence of the knowledge of Christ Jesus my Lord, for whom I have suffered the loss of all things, and count them as rubbish . . . .*

We never have to worry that we will "miss out" on the good things in life because of our Christian faith. *Nothing* we give up because of our connection to Christ has any lasting value.

➤ 3:13 — *Brethren, I do not count myself to have apprehended; but one thing I do, forgetting those things which are behind and reaching forward to those things which are ahead . . . .*

No matter what his circumstances, the apostle Paul never settled for the past. We, too, must "press on" with the mindset that there is always something more to be found in Christ.

LIFE PRINCIPLE 26

ADVERSITY IS A BRIDGE TO A DEEPER RELATIONSHIP WITH GOD.

PHIL. 3:10, 11

What is God's goal in adversity? His basic objective is to draw us closer to Himself. He does not glory in pain or sorrow, but He uses these things to teach us about His love and faithfulness.

The moment adversity comes, our vulnerability increases, and we wonder where God is. Pain, disappointment, and trial drive us to the Lord and to the cross, where we discover our personal need for a Savior, not just for our soul's salvation but for the entire span of life. We are struck with a defining thought: *I need God*. We need His fellowship and His presence, or we will collapse.

Later, there will be time enough to ask God to show you what you can learn from the pain you have suffered. God always has something in mind when He allows us to face difficulty. He has a plan, a purpose, and a goal, not just for this situation alone, but for your entire life. In times of difficulty, God is your immovable strength (Prov. 18:10).

What are you to do when adversity strikes? The Book of Hebrews encourages us by saying, "Do not cast away your confidence, which has great reward. For you have need of endurance, so that after you have done the will of God, you may receive the promise" (Heb. 10:35, 36).

When adversity strikes, the first thing we should do is turn to God. The second step is to affirm our commitment to Him that we will remain focused on Him and not on our circumstances. We see both of these portrayed in the lives of the men and women of the Bible.

Joseph's life is a study of faith, trust, and victory amid adversity. As a young man, he learned how God could take the cruelest act and turn it into a wondrous blessing. Sold into Egyptian bondage by his brothers, Joseph spent years bound and confined to a life of slavery. Even when it appeared that he would gain a reprieve from danger and heartache, adversity struck a second time as he was falsely accused of a crime. Back to the dungeon he went, only this time with a stiffer sentence.

We tend to think, "Poor Joseph!" But Joseph was rich in God's presence. He understood this principle about adversity and knew that God had something wonderful in mind for his life.

Adversity was a tool in Joseph's life. God used it to shape His servant for

We are struck with a defining thought: *I need God.*

service. Joseph landed in a key leadership role that ultimately led to the preservation of the nation of Israel. Had he escaped from prison and gone into hiding, the entire nation of Israel would have missed God's blessing. And without the training that came as a result of severe disappointment, Joseph may have become proud and self reliant. Instead, God used this young man's life to change the course of history.

People often ask, "What is the quickest way through seasons of adversity?" Many times there just is no quick solution to the trials we face. There is one sure way through the difficulties of life, however, and that is through obedience and surrender of selfish feelings and desires.

Adversity has a way of pushing us beyond ourselves where we find God waiting to gather us in His arms. It also stirs us to pray like nothing else can. And it is in prayer that we find shelter from the storms of life. Held under the canopy of God's presence, we discover a sense of security and hope that we thought had evaded us.

Even when life seems emotionally and spiritually dark, He will be your very light. You can be sure that God will use the trials you face to shape your life so that you reflect His love and care to others.

Never forget that God knows the future! He understands the advantage of adversity and how it can be used to strengthen your faith, refine your hope, and settle your heart into a place of contentment and trust. Without times of adversity, you would miss the powerful experience of God walking with you through the valley times of life.

Therefore, determine to keep the focus of your heart on Jesus. Don't let the negative talk of others sway you. Stay close to the Lord in devotion and prayer. Read His Word; He will guide you through the greatest difficulty, and then you will know what it means to live in a broad place of blessing.

See the Life Principles Index for further study.

Never forget that God knows the future!

ANSWERS TO LIFE'S QUESTIONS

How important is it to set goals?

PHIL. 3:11–14

Paul knew what it meant to set God-honoring goals. Philippians 3:8–11 describes not only where Paul had been, but also where he was going. Yes, he endured hardship. Yes, he experienced the joy of Christ. Yes, he had seen God use him, even from prison. Yet Paul understood that there was more of God to know, and so he set goals that would enable him and others to experience God at greater depths.

So how did Paul set these goals and move forward with such decisiveness, shrugging off passivity and complacency with every step? How can we follow his lead?

- *Believe and meditate on the promises of God.* Paul had full confidence that God's indwelling Spirit would give him the resurrection power to live up to his God-given potential in every area of life (Phil. 3:11).
- *Have a consuming desire to achieve a precise goal.* Paul had no foggy desires; he felt consumed by his desire to evangelize the lost (Phil. 3:13).
- *Have the courage to attempt, even at the risk of failure.* Paul didn't let his weaknesses or fears deter him; he understood that God used his weaknesses and fears to keep him dependent on and strengthened by Christ (Phil. 3:12).
- *Choose determination.* Paul faced more opposition than most of us can imagine. Yet he remained committed to whatever God told him was necessary to fulfill his goals (Phil. 3:14).
- *Be persistent.* Persistence means we're still going when everyone else has stopped. Paul had days, just like the rest of us, when he only inched forward. We won't always sprint toward our goal; some days it will be all we can do just to keep pressing on. Yet we must not give up.
- *Humble yourself.* Paul writes, "Not that I have already obtained it or have already become perfected . . ." (Phil. 3:12). Paul did not rest on his laurels because he knew he hadn't yet "arrived." Neither have we.
- *Let go of the past.* Clinging to bitterness, an unforgiving spirit, and old mistakes will always keep us from achieving our God-given potential (Phil. 3:13).

Evaluate your own goals and ask God how they fit into the greater goal of knowing Him. As He reveals His plans for you for this day, this year, this life on earth, don't let anything or anyone stamp out the zeal that rises in you.

See the Life Principles Index for further study:
13. *Listening to God is essential to walking with God.*
6. *You reap what you sow, more than you sow, and later than you sow.*

20 For our citizenship is in heaven, from ✳
which we also eagerly wait for the Savior, the
Lord Jesus Christ,
21 who will transform our lowly body that it
may be conformed to His glorious body, according to the working by which He is able
even to subdue all things to Himself.

4 Therefore, my beloved and longed-for brethren, my joy and crown, so stand fast in the Lord, beloved.

Be United, Joyful, and in Prayer

2 I implore Euodia and I implore Syntyche
to be of the same mind in the Lord.
3 And[a] I urge you also, true companion, help
these women who labored with me in the
gospel, with Clement also, and the rest of my
fellow workers, whose names *are* in the Book
of Life.
4 Rejoice in the Lord always. Again I will
say, rejoice!
5 Let your gentleness be known to all men.
The Lord *is* at hand.
6 Be anxious for nothing, but in everything ➤
by prayer and supplication, with thanksgiving, let your requests be made known to God;

4:3 [a]NU-Text and M-Text read *Yes.*

LIFE LESSONS

➤ **4:6 — *Be anxious for nothing, but in everything by prayer and supplication, with thanksgiving, let your requests be made known to God . . . .***

Anxiety wanes and eventually disappears when we take our concerns to the God who has the power and the wisdom to take care of them, believing that He always has our best interests at heart.

ANSWERS TO LIFE'S QUESTIONS

Will God really meet all my needs?

PHIL. 4:19

Have you ever pondered the real meaning of Philippians 4:19? If so, then you may also have encountered some frustration.

"What about this need I have had for years?" you wonder. "Doesn't God care about that aching hole in my heart? Why doesn't He just fill it?"

You may have attempted to meet the need yourself or to figure out why God hadn't responded. Sometimes you may even have felt faithless and thought that God did not hear you because of this "weakness" or a lack of consistent prayer. Deep inside, you know that only God can fill your need—which further frustrates matters and reveals your complete lack of control. You cannot successfully meet your own need *or* compel God to comply with your personal desires, time schedule, or concept of how it should be accomplished. So what are you to do?

Here's some good news—that is *exactly* the position God wants you in. No, God does not enjoy your pain or take delight in seeing you suffer or confused. He is a God of infinite love, gentleness, and compassion. Nothing He does (or does not do) comes from spite; even His discipline is perfectly administered out of love (Heb. 12:4–11). His purpose in allowing a delay to meet your need is to strengthen your faith and reliance on Him, and consequently to wean you of self-sufficiency.

In a very real sense, your unmet need is a form of trial and temptation. It's a trial because its lack of fulfillment can feel truly painful, and it's a temptation because it urges you to turn away from God to meet your own needs. But James says, "Blessed is the man who endures temptation; for when he has been approved, he will receive the crown of life which the Lord has promised to those who love him" (James 1:12).

So what are you to do when the delay goes on, the pressure to give up increases, and you feel weary of beating yourself up with false guilt? It may sound like a platitude, but keep your eyes on the Lord and follow Him, no matter what. James tells us that the testing of our faith leads to perseverance, which works to make us "perfect and complete, lacking nothing" (James 1:4).

Worked out on the journey of faith, such unwavering trust has profound results.

See the Life Principles Index for further study:
- *9. Trusting God means looking beyond what we can see to what God sees.*
- *6. You reap what you sow, more than you sow, and later than you sow.*
- *27. Prayer is life's greatest time saver.*

7 and the peace of God, which surpasses all understanding, will guard your hearts and minds through Christ Jesus.

Meditate on These Things

8 Finally, brethren, whatever things are
true, whatever things *are* noble, whatever things *are* just, whatever things *are* pure, whatever things *are* lovely, whatever things *are* of good report, if *there is* any virtue and if *there is* anything praiseworthy—meditate on these things.

9 The things which you learned and received and heard and saw in me, these do, and the God of peace will be with you.

Philippian Generosity

10 But I rejoiced in the Lord greatly that now at last your care for me has flourished again; though you surely did care, but you lacked opportunity.

11 Not that I speak in regard to need, for I have learned in whatever state I am, to be content:

12 I know how to be abased, and I know how to abound. Everywhere and in all things I have learned both to be full and to be hungry, both to abound and to suffer need.

LIFE LESSONS

➤ 4:8 — *. . . whatever things are true, whatever things are noble, whatever things are just, whatever things are pure . . . meditate on these things.*

If we ponder negative things, our frame of mind will soon turn sour, pessimistic and negative. If we fill our minds with the things of God, however, the opposite occurs, and we begin to see the world as God sees it.

➤ 13 I can do all things through Christ[a] who
strengthens me.
14 Nevertheless you have done well that you
shared in my distress.
15 Now you Philippians know also that in the
beginning of the gospel, when I departed
from Macedonia, no church shared with me
concerning giving and receiving but you only.
16 For even in Thessalonica you sent *aid* once
and again for my necessities.
17 Not that I seek the gift, but I seek the fruit
that abounds to your account.
18 Indeed I have all and abound. I am full,
having received from Epaphroditus the things
sent from you, a sweet-smelling aroma, an
acceptable sacrifice, well pleasing to God.
19 And my God shall supply all your need ✳
according to His riches in glory by Christ Jesus.
20 Now to our God and Father *be* glory forever and ever. Amen.

Greeting and Blessing

21 Greet every saint in Christ Jesus. The
brethren who are with me greet you.
22 All the saints greet you, but especially
those who are of Caesar's household.
23 The grace of our Lord Jesus Christ be with
you all.[a] Amen.

4:13 [a]NU-Text reads *Him who.* **4:23** [a]NU-Text reads *your spirit.*

LIFE LESSONS

➤ **4:13 — *I can do all things through Christ who strengthens me.***

While without Jesus we can do nothing (John 15:5), with Him nothing is impossible. The demands and stresses of life can easily overwhelm any of us, but they are no match for the risen Son of God.

THE EPISTLE OF PAUL THE APOSTLE TO THE

COLOSSIANS

If Ephesians portrays the "church of Christ," then Colossians must surely picture the "Christ of the church." While Ephesians focuses on the body, Colossians focuses on the Head.

Through everything he writes, Paul intends to show that Christ is preeminent—first and foremost in everything—and that the Christian's life should reflect that priority. In what ways is Christ unsurpassed? Paul does not give an exhaustive list, but he does give an impressive one. Jesus is: the exact image of almighty God; the Creator of all that exists; eternal; the glue that holds all things together; the first to rise from the dead, never to die again; the Savior of the world; the storehouse of all of God's wisdom and knowledge; victor over "principalities and powers"; Lord of life at His imminent return; generous rewarder for faithful service; and Master in heaven.

Because believers are rooted in this preeminent Jesus, alive in Him, hidden in Him, and complete in Him, it is utterly inconsistent for them to live without Him or as if He did not exist. Clothed in His love, with His peace ruling in their hearts, they are equipped to make Christ first in every area of life.

Paul's letter makes it clear that destructive teaching had crept its way into this young church. To counter it, Paul stresses the centrality of Jesus Christ to the gospel message.

This epistle became known as *Pros Kolossaeis*, "To the Colossians," because of 1:2. Paul also wanted it to be read in the neighboring church of Laodicea (4:16). One of Paul's converts, a man named Epaphras (1:7; 4:12), had a hand in founding the church in Colosse.

Theme: The centrality of Jesus Christ.

Author: The apostle Paul.

Time: Likely written from prison in Rome about A.D. 60–62.

Structure: Like Ephesians, the little book of Colossians divides neatly in half, with the first part doctrinal (1–2) and the second part practical (3–4). Chapter 1 looks at the identity of Jesus and what He means to believers. Chapter 2 describes a growing relationship with God through Christ. Chapters 3 and 4 apply the doctrines surveyed in the first two chapters, covering the various functions of the members of a Christian household.

As you read Colossians, watch for several life principles that play an important role in this book:

24. To live the Christian life is to allow Jesus to live His life in and through us. *See Colossians 1:26–28; page 1398.*

21. Obedience always brings blessing. *See Colossians 3:5–10; page 1401.*

28. No Christian has ever been called to "go it alone" in his or her walk of faith. *See Colossians 3:12–16; page 1402.*

8. Fight all your battles on your knees and you win every time. *See Colossians 4:2–4; page 1402.*

Greeting

1 Paul, an apostle of Jesus Christ by the will of God, and Timothy our brother,

2 To the saints and faithful brethren in Christ *who are* in Colosse:

Grace to you and peace from God our Father and the Lord Jesus Christ.[a]

Their Faith in Christ

3 We give thanks to the God and Father of our Lord Jesus Christ, praying always for you,
4 since we heard of your faith in Christ Jesus and of your love for all the saints;
5 because of the hope which is laid up for you in heaven, of which you heard before in the word of the truth of the gospel,
6 which has come to you, as *it has* also in all the world, and is bringing forth fruit,[a] as *it is* also among you since the day you heard and knew the grace of God in truth;
7 as you also learned from Epaphras, our dear fellow servant, who is a faithful minister of Christ on your behalf,
8 who also declared to us your love in the Spirit.

Preeminence of Christ

9 For this reason we also, since the day we heard it, do not cease to pray for you, and to ask that you may be filled with the knowledge of His will in all wisdom and spiritual understanding;
➤ 10 that you may walk worthy of the Lord, fully pleasing *Him,* being fruitful in every good work and increasing in the knowledge of God;
11 strengthened with all might, according to His glorious power, for all patience and longsuffering with joy;
12 giving thanks to the Father who has qualified us to be partakers of the inheritance of the saints in the light.
➤ 13 He has delivered us from the power of darkness and conveyed *us* into the kingdom of the Son of His love,
14 in whom we have redemption through His blood,[a] the forgiveness of sins.
15 He is the image of the invisible God, the firstborn over all creation.
16 For by Him all things were created that are in heaven and that are on earth, visible and invisible, whether thrones or dominions or principalities or powers. All things were created through Him and for Him.
17 And He is before all things, and in Him all things consist.
18 And He is the head of the body, the church, who is the beginning, the firstborn from the dead, that in all things He may have the preeminence.

Reconciled in Christ

19 For it pleased *the Father that* in Him all the fullness should dwell,
20 and by Him to reconcile all things to Himself, by Him, whether things on earth or things in heaven, having made peace through the blood of His cross.
21 And you, who once were alienated and enemies in your mind by wicked works, yet now ✳
He has reconciled
22 in the body of His flesh through death, to present you holy, and blameless, and above reproach in His sight—
23 if indeed you continue in the faith, grounded and steadfast, and are not moved away from the hope of the gospel which you heard, which was preached to every creature under heaven, of which I, Paul, became a minister.

Sacrificial Service for Christ

24 I now rejoice in my sufferings for you, and fill up in my flesh what is lacking in the afflictions of Christ, for the sake of His body, which is the church,
25 of which I became a minister according to the stewardship from God which was given to me for you, to fulfill the word of God,
26 the mystery which has been hidden from ages and from generations, but now has been revealed to His saints.
27 To them God willed to make known what ➤
are the riches of the glory of this mystery among the Gentiles: which[a] is Christ in you, the hope of glory.

1:2 [a]NU-Text omits *and the Lord Jesus Christ.* **1:6** [a]NU-Text and M-Text add *and growing.* **1:14** [a]NU-Text and M-Text omit *through His blood.* **1:27** [a]M-Text reads *who.*

LIFE LESSONS

➤ **1:10 — *. . . walk worthy of the Lord, fully pleasing Him, being fruitful in every good work and increasing in the knowledge of God . . . .***

It pleases God when we depend upon His Spirit to do "good works." It also pleases Him when we spend time in His Word, learning more about Him. This is what it means to "walk worthy" of Jesus.

➤ **1:13 — *He has delivered us from the power of darkness and conveyed us into the kingdom of the Son of His love . . . .***

We do not have the power to escape our slavery in the eternally dark kingdom of Satan, but God does, and He exercised that power to bring us into the light and into the life of freedom provided by Jesus.

➤ **1:27 — *. . . the riches of the glory of this mystery among the Gentiles: which is Christ in you, the hope of glory.***

In Old Testament times, the Holy Spirit came upon chosen men and women of God to enable them to accomplish God's will—but no one ever imagined that God would actually take up residence in believers, as He does today.

WHAT THE BIBLE SAYS ABOUT THE MANY FACES OF PRAYER

Col. 1:9–12

Charles Finney, a nineteenth century American evangelist, sometimes wrestled with what to say in prayer. One day a woman acquaintance fell deathly ill. She did not know Christ, but her husband asked Finney to pray for her.

Finney immediately became burdened for the woman, but he didn't know how to pray. Finally, after grasping for the right words, Finney received a breakthrough. He said he "was enabled to roll the burden upon" God and that he immediately felt sure the woman would not die.

Not long afterwards, the woman made a full recovery and committed her life to Christ.

There's much more to prayer, however, than a passionate plea for God to intervene. Paul often sprinkled his letters with intriguing prayers. We find one of them in Colossians 1:9–12. In seven requests, Paul covers every area of our lives that needs the daily touch of God:

Paul often sprinkled his letters with intriguing prayers.

1. *May we be filled with the knowledge of His will in all wisdom and spiritual understanding* (v. 9). Ask God to fill you with the spiritual understanding you need as you walk in His will and study His Word.

2. *May we walk in a manner worthy of the Lord Jesus Christ* (v. 10). Jesus lived a blameless life, exactly what we should pursue.

3. *May we please God in all respects* (v. 10). Paul encourages believers to live a life pleasing to God and to excel in their Christian walk.

4. *May we bear fruit in every good work* (v. 10). We prove we are Jesus' disciples when we bear fruit.

5. *May we increasingly grow in the knowledge of God* (v. 10). We should ask for more and more knowledge from His tremendous resources.

6. *May we be strengthened with all might, according to His glorious power* (v. 11). Ask God to strengthen you to do His will for His glory—and He will do it.

7. *May our lives express joyous thanks to the Father for His grace to us* (v. 12). Our love for Him should run so deep that we can't help but give glory and honor to Him.

See the Life Principles Index for further study:
8. Fight all your battles on your knees and you win every time.
17. We stand tallest and strongest on our knees.
27. Prayer is life's greatest time saver.

ANSWERS TO LIFE'S QUESTIONS

How can I partner with the Holy Spirit in my life?

COL. 2:6, 7

Before I answer, let me ask a question. What allowed you to begin a relationship with God? How did you—a sinner—enter into a friendship with a holy God? What brought the two of you together? Was it dedication on your part? Was it a result of your unceasing effort? Of course not! You entered it by faith. And nothing has changed.

"As you therefore have received Christ Jesus the Lord, so walk in Him, rooted and built up in Him and established in the faith, as you have been taught" (Col. 2:6, 7).

We are not the first generation of Christians who have tried to take matters into our own hands; the early church had the same problem. It's part of fallen human nature to want to maintain control, to do things ourselves. When it comes to righteousness, whether for salvation or for living, we must allow God to do the work.

The Spirit-filled life is a life of faith. It started by faith and it runs on faith. It is faith from start to finish.

Then we believed that Jesus saved us from the guilt of sin; now we must believe that He saves us from the power of sin. Then we trusted Him for forgiveness and it became ours; now we must trust Him for righteousness and it shall become ours also. Then we took Him as a Savior from the penalties of our sins; now we must take Him as a Savior from the bondage of our sins. Then He lifted us out of the pit; now He seats us in heavenly places with Himself.

The Bible never makes a distinction between the faith that saved us from the penalty of sin, once and for all, and the faith that saves us from the power of sin, every day. It is all the same.

So what is faith? Faith is believing that God will do as He has promised. Faith is not a power or something we're supposed to drum up inside ourselves. Faith is trusting that God will honor His promises. That's all there is to it. We are to go about our lives, making decisions, handling crises, raising our families, and so on, as if God will really do what He said He would do. That is what it means to partner with the Spirit.

See the Life Principles Index for further study:

22. *To walk in the Spirit is to obey the initial promptings of the Spirit.*
9. *Trusting God means looking beyond what you can see to what God sees.*

28 Him we preach, warning every man and
teaching every man in all wisdom, that we may
present every man perfect in Christ Jesus.
29 To this *end* I also labor, striving according
to His working which works in me mightily.

Not Philosophy but Christ

2 For I want you to know what a great conflict I have for you and those in Laodicea,
and *for* as many as have not seen my face in
the flesh,
2 that their hearts may be encouraged,
being knit together in love, and *attaining* to
all riches of the full assurance of understanding, to the knowledge of the mystery of God,
both of the Father and[a] of Christ,
3 in whom are hidden all the treasures of
wisdom and knowledge.
4 Now this I say lest anyone should deceive
you with persuasive words.
5 For though I am absent in the flesh, yet I
am with you in spirit, rejoicing to see your
good order and the steadfastness of your faith
in Christ.
6 As you therefore have received Christ Jesus the Lord, so walk in Him,
7 rooted and built up in Him and established in the faith, as you have been taught,
abounding in it[a] with thanksgiving.

2:2 [a]NU-Text omits *both of the Father and.* **2:7** [a]NU-Text omits *in it.*

LIFE LESSONS

➤ 2:6 — *As you have therefore received Christ Jesus the Lord, so walk in Him . . . .*

How did you receive Jesus as your Lord and Savior? By faith. And that is exactly how you grow into maturity—by faith. Through faith you depend upon God's Spirit to mold you into the image of Christ.

8 Beware lest anyone cheat you through philosophy and empty deceit, according to the tradition of men, according to the basic principles
of the world, and not according to Christ.
➤ 9 For in Him dwells all the fullness of the
Godhead bodily;
➤ 10 and you are complete in Him, who is the
head of all principality and power.

Not Legalism but Christ

11 In Him you were also circumcised with the
circumcision made without hands, by putting
off the body of the sins[a] of the flesh, by the
circumcision of Christ,
12 buried with Him in baptism, in which you
also were raised with *Him* through faith in the
working of God, who raised Him from the
dead.
13 And you, being dead in your trespasses
and the uncircumcision of your flesh, He has
made alive together with Him, having forgiven you all trespasses,
14 having wiped out the handwriting of requirements that was against us, which was
contrary to us. And He has taken it out of the
way, having nailed it to the cross.
15 Having disarmed principalities and powers, He made a public spectacle of them, triumphing over them in it.
16 So let no one judge you in food or in drink,
or regarding a festival or a new moon or sabbaths,
17 which are a shadow of things to come, but
the substance is of Christ.
18 Let no one cheat you of your reward, taking delight in *false* humility and worship of
angels, intruding into those things which he
has not[a] seen, vainly puffed up by his fleshly
mind,
19 and not holding fast to the Head, from
whom all the body, nourished and knit together by joints and ligaments, grows with
the increase *that is* from God.
20 Therefore,[a] if you died with Christ from
the basic principles of the world, why, as
though living in the world, do you subject
yourselves to regulations—
21 "Do not touch, do not taste, do not handle,"
22 which all concern things which perish
with the using—according to the commandments and doctrines of men?
23 These things indeed have an appearance ➤
of wisdom in self-imposed religion, *false* humility, and neglect of the body, *but are* of no
value against the indulgence of the flesh.

Not Carnality but Christ

3 If then you were raised with Christ, seek
those things which are above, where
Christ is, sitting at the right hand of God.
2 Set your mind on things above, not on ➤
things on the earth.
3 For you died, and your life is hidden with
Christ in God.
4 When Christ *who is* our life appears, then ✳
you also will appear with Him in glory.
5 Therefore put to death your members
which are on the earth: fornication, uncleanness, passion, evil desire, and covetousness,
which is idolatry.
6 Because of these things the wrath of God
is coming upon the sons of disobedience,
7 in which you yourselves once walked
when you lived in them.
8 But now you yourselves are to put off all
these: anger, wrath, malice, blasphemy, filthy
language out of your mouth.
9 Do not lie to one another, since you have
put off the old man with his deeds,
10 and have put on the new *man* who is renewed in knowledge according to the image
of Him who created him,
11 where there is neither Greek nor Jew, circumcised nor uncircumcised, barbarian,
Scythian, slave *nor* free, but Christ *is* all and
in all.

2:11 [a]NU-Text omits *of the sins.* **2:18** [a]NU-Text omits *not.*
2:20 [a]NU-Text and M-Text omit *Therefore.*

LIFE LESSONS

➤ **2:9 — *For in Him dwells all the fullness of the Godhead bodily . . . .***

It may be impossible for us to understand how Jesus could be totally human and totally divine, but that is the clear teaching of Scripture. "He who has seen me has seen the Father," Jesus said (John 14:9).

➤ **2:10 — *. . . and you are complete in Him, who is the head of all principality and power.***

Since "all the fullness of the Godhead" dwells in Jesus, and Jesus dwells in you through the Spirit, then it only makes sense that in Him you are complete. What could be lacking in "all the fullness of the Godhead"?

➤ **2:23 — *These things indeed have an appearance of wisdom in self-imposed religion, false humility, and neglect of the body, but are of no value against the indulgence of the flesh.***

Spiritual problems need spiritual answers. We cannot train the flesh to act more godly, because even when it "behaves," it sins by congratulating itself for its "success." The flesh needs to be crucified, not retrained.

➤ **3:2 — *Set your mind on things above, not on things on the earth.***

Transformation is God's goal for us, and we cooperate with His plan of spiritual metamorphosis when we train our minds to dwell on the things of God rather than on the things of the flesh.

Life Examples:

JOHN MARK

Learning to End Well

COL. 4:10

John Mark had gotten off to a great start. He accompanied Barnabas and Paul on an exciting missionary journey and saw God do amazing things. For whatever reason, however, he left them in the middle of their work, and Paul refused to team up with the young man again (Acts 13:13; 15:36–40).

Paul's jaded opinion of Mark eventually changed, however (Col. 4:10; 2 Tim. 4:11). Mark went on to minister once more with Barnabas, his cousin, and eventually wrote the Gospel of Mark. He accepted the challenge of ministry—difficulties and all—and ended up a winner.

Many believers fail to end well because they mistakenly think that God's call to personal ministry depends on their skill level. None of us are adequate in ourselves, any more than any of us can save ourselves. Throughout our lives we must glorify God, and that means depending on Him from beginning to end.

See the Life Principles Index for further study:
4. The awareness of God's presence energizes us for our work.
15. Brokenness is God's requirement for maximum usefulness.

Character of the New Man
12 Therefore, as *the* elect of God, holy and
beloved, put on tender mercies, kindness, humility, meekness, longsuffering;
13 bearing with one another, and forgiving
one another, if anyone has a complaint
against another; even as Christ forgave you,
so you also *must do.*
14 But above all these things put on love,
which is the bond of perfection.
15 And let the peace of God rule in your
hearts, to which also you were called in one
body; and be thankful.
16 Let the word of Christ dwell in you richly in
all wisdom, teaching and admonishing one another in psalms and hymns and spiritual songs,
singing with grace in your hearts to the Lord.
17 And whatever you do in word or deed, *do*
all in the name of the Lord Jesus, giving
thanks to God the Father through Him.

The Christian Home
18 Wives, submit to your own husbands, as is
fitting in the Lord.
19 Husbands, love your wives and do not be
bitter toward them.
20 Children, obey your parents in all things,
for this is well pleasing to the Lord.
21 Fathers, do not provoke your children, lest
they become discouraged.
22 Bondservants, obey in all things your masters according to the flesh, not with eyeservice, as men-pleasers, but in sincerity of
heart, fearing God.
23 And whatever you do, do it heartily, as to
the Lord and not to men,
24 knowing that from the Lord you will receive the reward of the inheritance; for[a] you
serve the Lord Christ.
25 But he who does wrong will be repaid for
what he has done, and there is no partiality.
4 Masters, give your bondservants what is
just and fair, knowing that you also have a
Master in heaven.

Christian Graces
2 Continue earnestly in prayer, being vigilant in it with thanksgiving;
3 meanwhile praying also for us, that God
would open to us a door for the word, to
speak the mystery of Christ, for which I am
also in chains,
4 that I may make it manifest, as I ought to
speak.
5 Walk in wisdom toward those *who are*
outside, redeeming the time.

3:24 [a]NU-Text omits *for.*

LIFE LESSONS

➤ 3:16 — *Let the word of Christ dwell in you richly in all wisdom, teaching and admonishing one another in psalms and hymns and spiritual songs . . . .*

The "you" Paul has in mind here is plural—"you" as in "all of you in the church of Jesus." We cannot grow into maturity in Christ Jesus without the encouragement, help, and even the needs of others.

➤ 3:23 — *And whatever you do, do it heartily, as to the Lord and not to men . . . .*

In a very real sense, everything we do, we do for Jesus. We can do our jobs for Christ, or we can do them for a cranky supervisor. We can grocery shop for Jesus, or we can do it for whining kids. It's our choice.

➤ 4:5 — *Walk in wisdom toward those who are outside, redeeming the time.*

Unbelievers are watching us, whether we know it or not. We never know when it might be the Lord's timing for one of them to ask us about heaven, eternal life, or God. Therefore we must always be ready.

6 *Let* your speech always *be* with grace,
seasoned with salt, that you may know how
you ought to answer each one.

Final Greetings

7 Tychicus, a beloved brother, faithful minister, and fellow servant in the Lord, will tell
you all the news about me.
8 I am sending him to you for this very purpose, that he[a] may know your circumstances
and comfort your hearts,
9 with Onesimus, a faithful and beloved
brother, who is *one* of you. They will make
known to you all things which *are happening*
here.
10 Aristarchus my fellow prisoner greets
you, with Mark the cousin of Barnabas (about
whom you received instructions: if he comes
to you, welcome him),
11 and Jesus who is called Justus. These *are*
my only fellow workers for the kingdom of
God who are of the circumcision; they have
proved to be a comfort to me.
12 Epaphras, who is *one* of you, a bondservant of Christ, greets you, always laboring
fervently for you in prayers, that you may
stand perfect and complete[a] in all the will of
God.
13 For I bear him witness that he has a great
zeal[a] for you, and those who are in Laodicea,
and those in Hierapolis.
14 Luke the beloved physician and Demas
greet you.
15 Greet the brethren who are in Laodicea,
and Nymphas and the church that *is* in his[a]
house.

Closing Exhortations and Blessing

16 Now when this epistle is read among you,
see that it is read also in the church of the
Laodiceans, and that you likewise read the
epistle from Laodicea.
17 And say to Archippus, "Take heed to the
ministry which you have received in the Lord,
that you may fulfill it."
18 This salutation by my own hand—Paul.
Remember my chains. Grace *be* with you.
Amen.

4:8 [a]NU-Text reads *you may know our circumstances and he may.*
4:12 [a]NU-Text reads *fully assured.* **4:13** [a]NU-Text reads *concern.*
4:15 [a]NU-Text reads *Nympha . . . her house.*

LIFE LESSONS

➤ 4:14 — *Luke the beloved physician and Demas greet you.*

While at this point Demas is Paul's faithful companion, some time later he would turn his back on his apostolic friend because he "loved this present world" (2 Tim. 4:10). Finishing well does not happen by accident.

➤ 4:17 — *And say to Archippus, "Take heed to the ministry which you have received in the Lord, that you may fulfill it."*

Each of us has some special work or ministry to which the Lord has assigned us. To what has God called you? Do you know the particular mission He has carved out for you? How are you working to fulfill it?

THE FIRST EPISTLE OF PAUL THE APOSTLE TO THE

THESSALONIANS

Paul had many pleasant memories of the days he spent with the infant Thessalonian church. The faith, hope, love, and perseverance that its members displayed in the face of severe persecution deeply encouraged him. Paul's labors as a spiritual parent to the fledgling church were richly rewarded, and we see his obvious affection for his friends in every line of this letter.

Paul founded the Thessalonian church during his second missionary journey (Acts 17:1–9), in the face of intense opposition from the Jews. He did not stay there long—most estimates range from a few weeks to a few months—and then he was forced to leave. The apostle made his way to Athens, but could not get the young church out of his mind. He worried that the antagonism they faced might damage and even destroy the church. So the apostle sent Timothy to encourage and strengthen his Thessalonian brothers and sisters in Christ. When Timothy returned, his positive report, mixed with a few lingering concerns, apparently inspired the apostle to write this letter.

Paul encouraged his friends to excel in their newfound faith, to increase in their love for one another, and to rejoice, pray, and give thanks always. He closes every chapter with a reminder that the Lord is coming back; Jesus' advent signals hope and comfort for all believers, living and dead. The fact that Paul emphasizes the Lord's return to a young church just getting started should perhaps suggest to us the importance of teaching the doctrine in a practical way so as to lay a foundation for a mature Christian faith.

Because this is the first of Paul's two known letters to the church at Thessalonica, it received the title *Pros Thessalonikeis A*, the "First to the Thessalonians."

Themes: The certain return of Christ should fill believers with unquenchable hope and help them to find strength when they come under attack for their faith.

Author: The apostle Paul.

Date: Probably written around A.D. 51–52. This is among Paul's earliest letters.

Structure: Paul begins by giving thanks for the Thessalonians and their testimony (1:1–10). He then defends his conduct and absence (2:1—3:13) and exhorts them to godly conduct, reminds them of the Lord's coming, and gives direction for church life (4:1—5:22). He ends with a prayer, greetings, and conclusion (5:23–28).

As you read 1 Thessalonians, watch for several life principles that play an important role in this book:

17. We stand tallest and strongest on our knees. *See 1 Thessalonians 1:2; 2:13; 3:9–13; 5:17, 25; pages 1405, 1406, 1409, 1410.*

26. Adversity is a bridge to a deeper relationship with God. *See 1 Thessalonians 1:6–9; 3:1–5; pages 1405, 1406.*

30. An eager anticipation of the Lord's return keeps us living productively. *See 1 Thessalonians 1:10; 2:19; 3:13; 4:13—5:11, 23; pages 1405, 1406, 1408, 1410.*

28. No Christian has ever been called to "go it alone" in his or her walk of faith. *See 1 Thessalonians 3:12, 13; page 1406.*

Greeting

1 Paul, Silvanus, and Timothy,

To the church of the Thessalonians in God
the Father and the Lord Jesus Christ:

Grace to you and peace from God our Father and the Lord Jesus Christ.[a]

Their Good Example

2 We give thanks to God always for you all,
making mention of you in our prayers,
3 remembering without ceasing your work
of faith, labor of love, and patience of hope in
our Lord Jesus Christ in the sight of our God
and Father,
4 knowing, beloved brethren, your election
by God.
5 For our gospel did not come to you in
word only, but also in power, and in the Holy
Spirit and in much assurance, as you know
what kind of men we were among you for
your sake.
6 And you became followers of us and of the
Lord, having received the word in much affliction, with joy of the Holy Spirit,
7 so that you became examples to all in
Macedonia and Achaia who believe.
8 For from you the word of the Lord has
sounded forth, not only in Macedonia and
Achaia, but also in every place. Your faith toward God has gone out, so that we do not
need to say anything.
9 For they themselves declare concerning us
what manner of entry we had to you, and how
you turned to God from idols to serve the living and true God,
10 and to wait for His Son from heaven,
whom He raised from the dead, *even* Jesus
who delivers us from the wrath to come.

Paul's Conduct

2 For you yourselves know, brethren, that
our coming to you was not in vain.
2 But even[a] after we had suffered before and
were spitefully treated at Philippi, as you
know, we were bold in our God to speak to
you the gospel of God in much conflict.
3 For our exhortation *did* not *come* from
error or uncleanness, nor *was it* in deceit.
4 But as we have been approved by God to
be entrusted with the gospel, even so we
speak, not as pleasing men, but God who tests
our hearts.
5 For neither at any time did we use flattering words, as you know, nor a cloak for
covetousness—God *is* witness.
6 Nor did we seek glory from men, either
from you or from others, when we might have
made demands as apostles of Christ.
7 But we were gentle among you, just as a
nursing *mother* cherishes her own children.
8 So, affectionately longing for you, we
were well pleased to impart to you not only
the gospel of God, but also our own lives, because you had become dear to us.
9 For you remember, brethren, our labor
and toil; for laboring night and day, that we
might not be a burden to any of you, we
preached to you the gospel of God.
10 You *are* witnesses, and God *also*, how devoutly and justly and blamelessly we behaved
ourselves among you who believe;
11 as you know how we exhorted, and comforted, and charged[a] every one of you, as a father *does* his own children,

1:1 [a]NU-Text omits *from God our Father and the Lord Jesus Christ.* **2:2** [a]NU-Text and M-Text omit *even.* **2:11** [a]NU-Text and M-Text read *implored.*

LIFE LESSONS

➤ 1:3 — *. . . your work of faith, labor of love, and patience of hope in our Lord Jesus Christ . . . .*

Faith gets to work, love has its labors, and hope requires patience. A balanced and effective Christian life features all three—faith, hope, and love—working together to prepare us for the return of Christ.

➤ 1:6 — *And you became followers of us and of the Lord, having received the word in much affliction, with joy of the Holy Spirit . . . .*

The world does not see how "joy" and "affliction" can possibly go together, but throughout the Bible we see the two of them paired up. A life of faith may entail suffering, but it also comes with joy.

➤ 1:7 — *. . . so that you became examples to all in Macedonia and Achaia who believe.*

The believers in Thessalonica were very young in the faith, and yet Paul claims that they had already greatly inspired other believers who heard of their experience. The Holy Spirit, not age, is what makes someone a good example.

➤ 2:2 — *But even after we had suffered before and were spitefully treated at Philippi, as you know, we were bold in our God to speak to you the gospel of God in much conflict.*

The best place to find boldness—really, the only reliable place—is "in God." Boldness inspired by the Spirit cannot be quenched by suffering or conflict.

➤ 2:7 — *But we were gentle among you, just as a nursing mother cherishes her own children.*

It may startle us to picture the apostle Paul with the surprising image he uses here, as a gentle nursing mother tenderly doting on her children. Yet it is an accurate picture of the way God wants to deal with us.

➤ 2:11 — *. . . as you know how we exhorted, and comforted, and charged every one of you, as a father does his own children . . . .*

To his young Christian friends, Paul could not only act with the tenderness of a loving mother, but he could also act with the stronger and sterner attitude of a loving father. God acts in both ways toward us.

12 that you would walk worthy of God who
calls you into His own kingdom and glory.

Their Conversion

13 For this reason we also thank God without
ceasing, because when you received the word
of God which you heard from us, you welcomed *it* not *as* the word of men, but as it is in
truth, the word of God, which also effectively
works in you who believe.
14 For you, brethren, became imitators of the
churches of God which are in Judea in Christ
Jesus. For you also suffered the same things
from your own countrymen, just as they *did*
from the Judeans,
15 who killed both the Lord Jesus and their
own prophets, and have persecuted us; and
they do not please God and are contrary to all
men,
16 forbidding us to speak to the Gentiles that
they may be saved, so as always to fill up *the*
measure of their sins; but wrath has come
upon them to the uttermost.

Longing to See Them

17 But we, brethren, having been taken away
from you for a short time in presence, not in
heart, endeavored more eagerly to see your
face with great desire.
➤ 18 Therefore we wanted to come to you—
even I, Paul, time and again—but Satan hindered us.
19 For what *is* our hope, or joy, or crown of
rejoicing? *Is it* not even you in the presence of
our Lord Jesus Christ at His coming?
20 For you are our glory and joy.

Concern for Their Faith

3 Therefore, when we could no longer endure it, we thought it good to be left in
Athens alone,
2 and sent Timothy, our brother and minister of God, and our fellow laborer in the
gospel of Christ, to establish you and encourage you concerning your faith,
➤ 3 that no one should be shaken by these afflictions; for you yourselves know that we are
appointed to this.
4 For, in fact, we told you before when we
were with you that we would suffer tribulation, just as it happened, and you know.
5 For this reason, when I could no longer
endure it, I sent to know your faith, lest by
some means the tempter had tempted you,
and our labor might be in vain.

Encouraged by Timothy

6 But now that Timothy has come to us from
you, and brought us good news of your faith
and love, and that you always have good remembrance of us, greatly desiring to see us,
as we also *to see* you—
7 therefore, brethren, in all our affliction ➤
and distress we were comforted concerning
you by your faith.
8 For now we live, if you stand fast in the
Lord.
9 For what thanks can we render to God for
you, for all the joy with which we rejoice for
your sake before our God,
10 night and day praying exceedingly that we
may see your face and perfect what is lacking
in your faith?

Prayer for the Church

11 Now may our God and Father Himself, and
our Lord Jesus Christ, direct our way to you.
12 And may the Lord make you increase and
abound in love to one another and to all, just
as we *do* to you,
13 so that He may establish your hearts ➤
blameless in holiness before our God and Father at the coming of our Lord Jesus Christ
with all His saints.

Plea for Purity

4 Finally then, brethren, we urge and exhort
in the Lord Jesus that you should abound
more and more, just as you received from us
how you ought to walk and to please God;
2 for you know what commandments we
gave you through the Lord Jesus.

LIFE LESSONS

➤ 2:18 — *Therefore we wanted to come to you—even I, Paul, time and again—but Satan hindered us.*

The opposition of Satan is real and can cause definite problems. Yet Paul knew that the might of Satan is no match for the great power of God. God can turn even Satan's "victories" into blessings for His people.

➤ 3:3 — *. . . no one should be shaken by these afflictions; for you yourselves know that we are appointed to this.*

It might be natural to assume that if God loves us, He will keep us from suffering. But "natural" does not mean "right." In fact, "all who desire to live godly in Christ Jesus *will* suffer persecution" (2 Tim. 3:12).

➤ 3:7 — *. . . in all our affliction and distress we were comforted concerning you by your faith.*

There is little so comforting as seeing your believing friends and loved ones growing closer to the Lord. Who might you be able to encourage right now through your own growing faith?

➤ 3:13 — *. . . so that He may establish your hearts blameless in holiness before our God and Father at the coming of our Lord Jesus Christ with all His saints.*

The Bible very often connects holy living with the return of Christ. The Second Coming is not a doctrine to satisfy our curiosity, but a truth meant to inspire us to living wholeheartedly for God.

WHAT THE BIBLE SAYS ABOUT THE MAKING OF AN ENCOURAGER

1 Thess. 3:1–10

Sometimes it takes only one little word, or a smile, or a grasp of the hand. Sometimes it means standing by someone during a particularly hard time, and helping him or her not give in to despair.

What does encouragement mean to you? Can you recall a time when someone came alongside you for the sole purpose of lifting your spirits or making you smile?

Have you ever done that for a hurting person? It feels good to know you're loved. It feels especially good in those low moments when you can't see ahead clearly, when you don't grasp God's perspective and vision for your life.

God has given each of us special tasks within the body of Christ, and those with the gift of exhortation or encouragement (Rom. 12:8) can rejoice in their unique and tender ministries. But encouragement isn't strictly the domain of those to whom the Lord has given a special gift; it's not an activity exclusively for those with naturally "bubbly" or "warm" personalities. Encouragement is the wonderful, God-given function of everyone who belongs to Jesus Christ.

It feels good to know you're loved.

In the early days of the church, new believers badly needed encouragement. Societal pressures mounted, persecution multiplied, and few had access to the apostle's teaching (1 Thess. 3:1–10).

Very often, encouragement for the early church came in the form of a person, as it does today. Sometimes just the sight of a certain loved one can reinvigorate your spirits and remove your focus from yourself. Sometimes Paul sent Timothy. More than once, he sent his associate, Tychicus, as a special envoy of joy.

The ministry of encouragement is indispensable, both to yourself and to the body of Christ. There's no such thing as a person who doesn't need encouragement.

By seeking ways to daily build up those with whom you interact, you further the potential for meaningful, Christ-centered relationships. As Paul told the persecuted Thessalonians, "Comfort each other and edify one another, just as you also are doing . . . . Warn those who are unruly, comfort the fainthearted, uphold the weak, be patient with all" (1 Thess. 5:11, 14).

See the Life Principles Index for further study:
28. No Christian has ever been called to "go it alone" in his or her walk of faith.

3 For this is the will of God, your sanctification: that you should abstain from sexual immorality;
4 that each of you should know how to possess his own vessel in sanctification and honor,
5 not in passion of lust, like the Gentiles who do not know God;
6 that no one should take advantage of and defraud his brother in this matter, because the Lord *is* the avenger of all such, as we also forewarned you and testified.
7 For God did not call us to uncleanness, but in holiness.
8 Therefore he who rejects *this* does not reject man, but God, who has also given[a] us His Holy Spirit.

A Brotherly and Orderly Life

9 But concerning brotherly love you have no need that I should write to you, for you yourselves are taught by God to love one another;
10 and indeed you do so toward all the brethren who are in all Macedonia. But we urge you, brethren, that you increase more and more;
11 that you also aspire to lead a quiet life, to mind your own business, and to work with your own hands, as we commanded you,
12 that you may walk properly toward those who are outside, and *that* you may lack nothing.

The Comfort of Christ's Coming

13 But I do not want you to be ignorant, brethren, concerning those who have fallen asleep, lest you sorrow as others who have no hope.
14 For if we believe that Jesus died and rose again, even so God will bring with Him those who sleep in Jesus.[a]
15 For this we say to you by the word of the Lord, that we who are alive *and* remain until the coming of the Lord will by no means precede those who are asleep.
16 For the Lord Himself will descend from heaven with a shout, with the voice of an archangel, and with the trumpet of God. And the dead in Christ will rise first.
17 Then we who are alive *and* remain shall be caught up together with them in the clouds to meet the Lord in the air. And thus we shall always be with the Lord.
18 Therefore comfort one another with these words.

The Day of the Lord

5 But concerning the times and the seasons, brethren, you have no need that I should write to you.
2 For you yourselves know perfectly that the day of the Lord so comes as a thief in the night.
3 For when they say, "Peace and safety!" then sudden destruction comes upon them, as labor pains upon a pregnant woman. And they shall not escape.
4 But you, brethren, are not in darkness, so that this Day should overtake you as a thief.
5 You are all sons of light and sons of the day. We are not of the night nor of darkness.
6 Therefore let us not sleep, as others *do*, but let us watch and be sober.
7 For those who sleep, sleep at night, and those who get drunk are drunk at night.
8 But let us who are of the day be sober, putting on the breastplate of faith and love, and *as* a helmet the hope of salvation.
9 For God did not appoint us to wrath, but to obtain salvation through our Lord Jesus Christ,

4:8 [a]NU-Text reads *who also gives.* **4:14** [a]Or *those who through Jesus sleep*

LIFE LESSONS

➤ 4:3 — *For this is the will of God, your sanctification: that you should abstain from sexual immorality . . . .*

We do not have to pray about whether it is God's will for us to get sexually involved with anyone who is not our spouse. Sexual intercourse outside of marriage always grieves the Holy Spirit.

➤ 4:11 — *. . . that you also aspire to lead a quiet life, to mind your own business, and to work with your own hands . . . .*

The Christian life is not a nonstop parade of miracles and astonishing answers to prayer and extraordinary visions and angelic visitations. Much of it is low-key, tame, and ordinary. Yet a godly life will always be celebrated in heaven.

➤ 4:16 — *For the Lord Himself will descend from heaven with a shout, with the voice of an archangel, and with the trumpet of God. And the dead in Christ will rise first.*

This amazing passage describes the moment when the Lord returns for His church, when those who are alive will go directly into His presence and the dead in Christ will receive their glorified bodies.

➤ 5:2 — *For you yourselves know perfectly that the day of the Lord so comes as a thief in the night.*

When does a thief hit his target? No one knows. So it is with the return of Christ. No one knows when He might return, and there are no clues hidden in the Bible that can help anyone figure it out.

➤ 5:6 — *Therefore let us not sleep, as others do, but let us watch and be sober.*

Jesus told us to watch for Him and keep at His business until He comes, and Paul merely elaborated on the same message. The prospect of Jesus' return should inspire us to keep working, not to get lazy.

ANSWERS TO LIFE'S QUESTIONS

What does it mean to "pray without ceasing"?

1 THESS. 5:17

What did the apostle Paul mean by "pray without ceasing" (1 Thess. 5:17)? How is it possible to carry on with normal life while praying without a break?

First, the apostle did not mean that we should walk around all day mumbling prayers to God. Rather, he taught that we can live in a constant attitude of prayer, even as we go about our daily routines. Of course, on some days we'll pray much more than on others. But regardless of the particular items on our "to do" list for that day, we can maintain a natural attitude of prayer that encompasses our whole lives.

When we develop such a prayerful outlook, prayer becomes our first instinct any time we face a challenge or encounter a difficulty. When we maintain an attitude of prayer, we don't even have to think about moving from first gear to second, from an attitude of prayer to the practice of prayer. It never occurs to us that we should *not* pray.

Should you pray about trivial matters? Yes! God listens to every prayer. Since He is interested in every aspect of your life, He invites you to pray about whatever concerns you, interests you, confuses you, frightens you, or in any way touches or challenges your life. Prayers to find lost glasses or to mentally retrieve forgotten information are both worthy requests.

God has called us to be people of prayer. Regular communication on this level creates intimate fellowship with the Savior. Through prayer we discover the goodness and faithfulness of God. But while taking time to get alone with God is the ideal, we don't have to limit ourselves to such times. God hears our prayers no matter where we pray.

The devotional writer Oswald Chambers encourages us to put "reckless" confidence in God. He says that too often we limit our praying precisely because we do not cast ourselves on His grace and mercy. Will outsiders consider such wild trust in God foolhardy, even madness? Probably. But so what? Only through prayer can we tap into the limitless resources of God. Only by praying can we test the Lord's promise: "If you ask anything in My name, I will do it" (John 14:14).

Prayer is one of the best ways we have to remind ourselves that God is our gracious heavenly Father and that we are His much-loved children.

See the Life Principles Index for further study:

8. *Fight all your battles on your knees and you win every time.*
17. *We stand tallest and strongest on our knees.*
27. *Prayer is life's greatest time saver.*

10 who died for us, that whether we wake or
sleep, we should live together with Him.
11 Therefore comfort each other and edify
one another, just as you also are doing.

Various Exhortations

12 And we urge you, brethren, to recognize
those who labor among you, and are over you
in the Lord and admonish you,
13 and to esteem them very highly in love for
their work's sake. Be at peace among yourselves.
14 Now we exhort you, brethren, warn those ➤
who are unruly, comfort the fainthearted, uphold the weak, be patient with all.
15 See that no one renders evil for evil to
anyone, but always pursue what is good both
for yourselves and for all.
16 Rejoice always,
17 pray without ceasing,
18 in everything give thanks; for this is the
will of God in Christ Jesus for you.
19 Do not quench the Spirit.
20 Do not despise prophecies.

LIFE LESSONS

➤ **5:14 — *Now we exhort you, brethren, warn those who are unruly, comfort the fainthearted, uphold the weak, be patient with all.***

Grace ministers to different people in different ways, depending upon what they most need at the time. Some need stern warnings; others need comfort; some need help. But everyone needs patience, for we all fall short in many ways.

21 Test all things; hold fast what is good.
22 Abstain from every form of evil.

Blessing and Admonition
23 Now may the God of peace Himself sanctify you completely; and may your whole spirit, soul, and body be preserved blameless at the coming of our Lord Jesus Christ.
24 He who calls you *is* faithful, who also will do *it*.

25 Brethren, pray for us.
26 Greet all the brethren with a holy kiss.
27 I charge you by the Lord that this epistle be read to all the holy[a] brethren.
28 The grace of our Lord Jesus Christ *be* with you. Amen.

5:27 [a]NU-Text omits *holy*.

THE SECOND EPISTLE OF PAUL THE APOSTLE TO THE

THESSALONIANS

Paul's first letter encouraged the Thessalonians, but after its arrival, additional seeds of false doctrine were sown among the Thessalonians, causing them to waver in their faith. Paul responded by writing this letter, trying to remove those destructive seeds and again plant the seeds of truth.

The apostle begins by commending the believers on their faithfulness in the midst of persecution, and encouraging them that their present suffering will be repaid in far greater measure with future glory. Therefore, even in the midst of persecution, they can live confidently and with high expectations of a bright future.

Paul then deals with the central matter of his letter: a misunderstanding regarding the coming of the Lord, an error spawned by false teachers. Despite reports to the contrary, the apostle insists that day has not yet come. To prove his contention, the apostle recounts the extraordinary events that must take place before the great day of the Lord arrives. Paul says several things must happen first:

- *The "falling away" must occur* (2:3). Most Bible scholars believe this refers to a "great apostasy" of the church, when a large portion of the church descends into heresy and ungodly living.
- *The "man of sin" must be revealed* (2:3, 4). This extraordinarily wicked leader is known by several names in Scripture: the antichrist, the beast, the son of perdition, the lawless one, etc.
- *The "restrainer" must be removed from the earth* (2:6, 7). Many have suggested who this "restrainer" might be, but the most likely suggestion seems to be the Holy Spirit at work in the church.

So how should the Thessalonians respond to this kind of prophecy? Should they forget about living wisely in the here and now in order to get ready for life in the hereafter? Hardly. Paul insists that rather than lazy resignation, laboring for the gospel is the proper response to the fact of the Lord's return.

As the second letter in Paul's Thessalonian correspondence, this was entitled *Pros Thessalonikeis B*, the "Second to the Thessalonians."

Theme: The return of Jesus Christ.

Author: The apostle Paul.

Time: Written perhaps six months after his first letter to the Thessalonians, A.D. 51–52.

Structure: After an introduction (chapter 1), Paul gives instructions regarding the Second Coming (chapter 2) and then suggests some practical applications of his teaching (chapter 3).

As you read 2 Thessalonians, watch for several life principles that play an important role in this book:

28. No Christian has ever been called to "go it alone" in his or her walk of faith. *See 2 Thessalonians 1:3–5; page 1412.*

30. An eager anticipation of the Lord's return keeps us living productively. *See 2 Thessalonians 1:6–2:12; page 1412.*

27. Prayer is life's greatest time saver. *See 2 Thessalonians 3:1; page 1413.*

11. God assumes full responsibility for our needs when we obey Him. *See 2 Thessalonians 3:6–12; page 1413.*

12. Peace with God is the fruit of oneness with God. *See 2 Thessalonians 3:16; page 1416.*

Greeting

1 Paul, Silvanus, and Timothy,

To the church of the Thessalonians in God
our Father and the Lord Jesus Christ:
2 Grace to you and peace from God our Father and the Lord Jesus Christ.

God's Final Judgment and Glory

➤ **3** We are bound to thank God always for
you, brethren, as it is fitting, because your
faith grows exceedingly, and the love of every
one of you all abounds toward each other,
4 so that we ourselves boast of you among
the churches of God for your patience and
faith in all your persecutions and tribulations
that you endure,
5 *which is* manifest evidence of the righteous judgment of God, that you may be
counted worthy of the kingdom of God, for
which you also suffer;
✳ 6 since *it is* a righteous thing with God to
repay with tribulation those who trouble you,
7 and to *give* you who are troubled rest with
us when the Lord Jesus is revealed from
heaven with His mighty angels,
8 in flaming fire taking vengeance on those
who do not know God, and on those who do
not obey the gospel of our Lord Jesus Christ.
➤ 9 These shall be punished with everlasting
destruction from the presence of the Lord and
from the glory of His power,
10 when He comes, in that Day, to be glorified in His saints and to be admired among all
those who believe,[a] because our testimony
among you was believed.
11 Therefore we also pray always for you
that our God would count you worthy of *this*
calling, and fulfill all the good pleasure of *His*
goodness and the work of faith with power,
12 that the name of our Lord Jesus Christ ◄
may be glorified in you, and you in Him, according to the grace of our God and the Lord
Jesus Christ.

The Great Apostasy

2 Now, brethren, concerning the coming of
our Lord Jesus Christ and our gathering
together to Him, we ask you,
2 not to be soon shaken in mind or troubled,
either by spirit or by word or by letter, as if
from us, as though the day of Christ[a] had come.
3 Let no one deceive you by any means; for ◄
that Day will not come unless the falling
away comes first, and the man of sin[a] is revealed, the son of perdition,
4 who opposes and exalts himself above all
that is called God or that is worshiped, so that
he sits as God[a] in the temple of God, showing
himself that he is God.
5 Do you not remember that when I was still
with you I told you these things?
6 And now you know what is restraining,
that he may be revealed in his own time.
7 For the mystery of lawlessness is already ◄
at work; only He[a] who now restrains *will do*
so until He[b] is taken out of the way.
8 And then the lawless one will be revealed,
whom the Lord will consume with the breath
of His mouth and destroy with the brightness
of His coming.
9 The coming of the *lawless one* is accord- ◄

1:10 [a]NU-Text and M-Text read *have believed.* **2:2** [a]NU-Text reads *the Lord.* **2:3** [a]NU-Text reads *lawlessness.* **2:4** [a]NU-Text omits *as God.* **2:7** [a]Or *he* [b]Or *he*

LIFE LESSONS

➤ 1:3 — *We are bound to thank God always for you, brethren, as it is fitting, because your faith grows exceedingly, and the love of every one of you all abounds toward each other . . . .*

One good way to tell if you are growing in your faith is to notice how you react toward your brothers and sisters in the faith. Does your love abound toward them? Do you feel a greater urgency to pray for them?

➤ 1:9 — *These shall be punished with everlasting destruction from the presence of the Lord and from the glory of His power . . . .*

The worst thing about hell is not any physical suffering that may be involved, but the intense loneliness of absolute separation from the Creator, the Giver of life. Those who want no part of God will get their way in hell.

➤ 1:12 — *. . . that the name of our Lord Jesus Christ may be glorified in you, and you in Him, according to the grace of our God and the Lord Jesus Christ.*

How is Jesus glorified in us? When we strive to please God and eagerly do His will by tapping into the Spirit's power, Jesus is revealed as a Lord infinitely worthy of our service—and He gets the glory.

➤ 2:3 — *Let no one deceive you by any means; for that Day will not come unless the falling away comes first . . . .*

The time is coming when the majority of the church will abandon sound doctrine and will instead endorse whatever teaching seems popular at the moment. The way to combat such an error now is to stick close to Jesus.

➤ 2:7 — *For the mystery of lawlessness is already at work . . . .*

Paul taught that the evil world system that would culminate in the antichrist was active in the world even in his time. While no genuine believer would endorse the antichrist, we help his side every time we choose "lawlessness."

➤ 2:9 — *The coming of the lawless one is according to the working of Satan, with all power, signs, and lying wonders . . . .*

We must anchor our faith in the Word of God, not in miraculous signs and wonders. Satan can counterfeit many of God's works, and if we do not know God's Word, we may be duped by them.

ing to the working of Satan, with all power,
signs, and lying wonders,
10 and with all unrighteous deception among
those who perish, because they did not receive the love of the truth, that they might be
saved.
11 And for this reason God will send them
strong delusion, that they should believe the
lie,
12 that they all may be condemned who did
not believe the truth but had pleasure in unrighteousness.

Stand Fast

13 But we are bound to give thanks to God
always for you, brethren beloved by the Lord,
because God from the beginning chose you
for salvation through sanctification by the
Spirit and belief in the truth,
14 to which He called you by our gospel, for
the obtaining of the glory of our Lord Jesus
Christ.
15 Therefore, brethren, stand fast and hold
the traditions which you were taught,
whether by word or our epistle.
16 Now may our Lord Jesus Christ Himself,
and our God and Father, who has loved us
and given *us* everlasting consolation and
good hope by grace,
➤ 17 comfort your hearts and establish you in
every good word and work.

Pray for Us

3 Finally, brethren, pray for us, that the
word of the Lord may run *swiftly* and be
glorified, just as *it is* with you,
➤ 2 and that we may be delivered from unreasonable and wicked men; for not all have
faith.
✳ 3 But the Lord is faithful, who will establish
you and guard *you* from the evil one.
4 And we have confidence in the Lord concerning you, both that you do and will do the
things we command you.
5 Now may the Lord direct your hearts into ➤
the love of God and into the patience of
Christ.

Warning Against Idleness

6 But we command you, brethren, in the
name of our Lord Jesus Christ, that you withdraw from every brother who walks disorderly and not according to the tradition which
he[a] received from us.
7 For you yourselves know how you ought
to follow us, for we were not disorderly
among you;
8 nor did we eat anyone's bread free of
charge, but worked with labor and toil night
and day, that we might not be a burden to any
of you,
9 not because we do not have authority, but
to make ourselves an example of how you
should follow us.
10 For even when we were with you, we com- ➤
manded you this: If anyone will not work, neither shall he eat.
11 For we hear that there are some who walk
among you in a disorderly manner, not working at all, but are busybodies.
12 Now those who are such we command
and exhort through our Lord Jesus Christ
that they work in quietness and eat their own
bread.
13 But *as for* you, brethren, do not grow
weary *in* doing good.
14 And if anyone does not obey our word in
this epistle, note that person and do not keep
company with him, that he may be ashamed.
15 Yet do not count *him* as an enemy, but ad- ➤
monish *him* as a brother.

3:6 [a]NU-Text and M-Text read *they.*

LIFE LESSONS

➤ 2:17 — *. . . comfort your hearts and establish you in every good word and work.*

God comforts us in our distress, not merely so that we can feel comfortable, but so that we will find the strength and encouragement to minister once more to others through "every good word and work."

➤ 3:2 — *. . . and that we may be delivered from unreasonable and wicked men; for not all have faith.*

When the Word of God is preached, some accept it and some don't. It's always been that way, and it will be that way right up to the end. It is perfectly legitimate to pray for protection against those who reject God's Word.

➤ 3:5 — *Now may the Lord direct your hearts into the love of God and into the patience of Christ.*

This verse notes two crucial items necessary for spiritual growth. First, we must meditate on God's love for us and become increasingly convinced of it. Second, we must focus on Christ's return and wait patiently for it.

➤ 3:10 — *If anyone will not work, neither shall he eat.*

Paul does not give this instruction out of anger, but because this guideline—even though it may sound harsh to some—stands the best chance of moving lazy Christians to a place of God's blessing.

➤ 3:15 — *Yet do not count him as an enemy, but admonish him as a brother.*

The goal of all discipline ought to be restoration. God wants to bless us, not judge us, and sometimes the best way to move us into a place fit for blessing is to make us uncomfortable for a while.

LIFE PRINCIPLE 27

PRAYER IS LIFE'S GREATEST TIME SAVER.

2 THESS. 3:1

When my family and I first moved to Atlanta, Georgia, we couldn't seem to find the right house. It took us more than a month before we found a house we felt good about. In the meantime, we had been living with friends. As you can imagine, we were ready for a place of our own.

We prayed and applied for a loan. We asked God every day to get the loan approved. We really believed He would; we thanked Him in advance.

One week later, the banker turned down our loan request. What a shock! I just couldn't imagine why. And we couldn't understand what God was up to. "Why didn't He answer our prayer?" we asked.

God answered our question the next day by sending a tremendous rainstorm. The basement of the house we almost bought flooded with a foot of water. We had planned to use it for a study and for storage. But God was watching out for us. One week later we found the right house, and we enjoyed living there for eight years.

Prayer not only spared us a lot of trouble, it saved us a lot of time. God's answer seemed like a delay to us, but in fact it kept us from wasting countless hours trying to fix a defective house. Prayer really is life's greatest time saver.

Jesus spoke of this relationship between an apparent delay in God's answers to our prayers, and the fact of how it actually saves us time. In Luke 18 He told a parable to teach us "that men always ought to pray and not lose heart" (v. 1). That doesn't sound like a passage on how prayer saves time, does it? Yet by the end of His story, Jesus explained His point like this: "And shall God not avenge His own elect who cry out day and night to Him, though He bears long with them? I tell you that He will avenge them speedily" (Luke 18:7, 8).

Did you catch it? God may "bear long" with us in our prayers, and yet He is committed to acting on our behalf "speedily." That means that prayer really is life's greatest time saver, for God will answer our prayers as soon as it is best for us—not one moment sooner, not one second later. What may feel like a delay to us is actually God sparing us tremendous amounts of wasted time.

In 1971, our church's television broadcast was taken off the air because of conflict within the church. After we resolved the conflict, we asked the same station if we could be rescheduled at our prior broadcast time. It refused. We offered to buy time on the station, but it refused that request as well.

We believed God wanted us on television, so we prayed that He would once

God will answer our prayers as soon as it is best for us.

again allow us to begin a television ministry. When we started praying, we thought something would open up soon. But it took a year before anything happened.

Eventually two stations offered us a spot in their weekly programming. One opportunity led to another, till today our service is broadcast by In Touch Ministries throughout the world. God didn't answer our prayer to be put right back on the air for a reason. He waited and provided us with something much better than we asked for.

Many young people pray and pray that the Lord will send a marriage partner. As they enter their late twenties, many question God's interest. They wonder, "What is God waiting for?" He may be waiting till He knows they are ready. What seems like a delay to them is actually sparing them countless hours, days, months, even years of heartache.

As I reflect on my life, I realize that if God had answered certain prayers according to my timing, I would have missed His best in every case.

Imagine for a moment a five-year-old who wants a pocketknife and a flashlight. A good father might not mind giving the knife to him, but the boy needs to grow up a little before he can be trusted with it. In the same way, God waits for us to grow spiritually in some areas before He gives us all the spiritual and material blessings He has in store (Eph. 1:3).

God will answer our prayers as soon it is best, not one moment sooner or one second later. This is why prayer really is life's greatest time saver.

See the Life Principles Index for further study.

God waited and provided us with something much better.

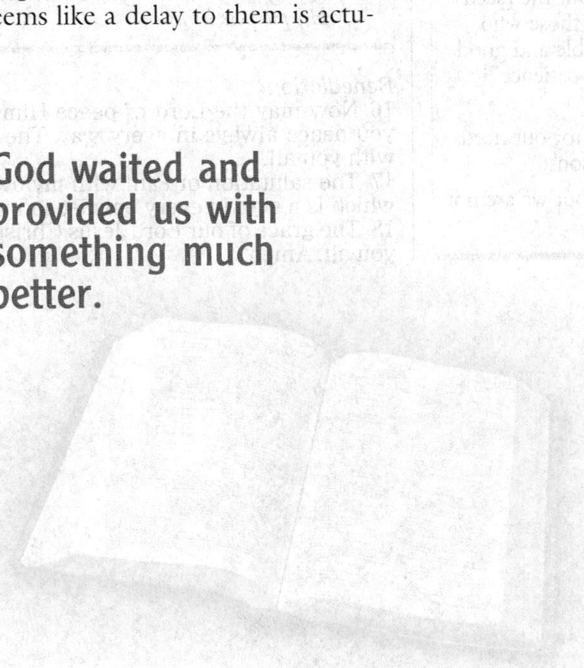

ANSWERS TO LIFE'S QUESTIONS

How does God teach me patience?

2 THESS. 3:5

Patience has been defined as learning to accept difficult situations as from God without giving Him a deadline for their removal. We know we need it, but we generally shun the process by which we learn it.

Ours is the "now" generation. We want it *now*! We cannot wait for God's direction; so we move ahead on our own initiative. We cannot wait for sex in marriage, so we damage the relationship by demanding immediate gratification. We cannot wait for our wealth to grow, so we prefer get-rich-quick schemes.

Striving to have it all "now" is a costly and disappointing approach to life.

The Old Testament admonishes us, "Wait on the LORD; be of good courage, and He shall strengthen your heart; wait, I say, on the LORD" (Ps. 27:14). And it promises, "Those who wait on the LORD . . . shall inherit the earth" (Ps. 37:9). In the New Testament parable of the sower, we read, "But the [seed] that fell on the good ground are those who, having heard the word with a noble and good heart, keep it and bear fruit with patience" (Luke 8:15).

God may require us to wait for our needs and desires for any of several reasons:

- What we want is right for us, but we are not yet ready for it.
- Our motivation for having it opposes God's purpose for us.
- God is trying to get our attention about some hidden sin in our lives.
- God wants to teach us discipline through waiting.
- Getting what we want would have a negative effect on someone else.
- God wants to teach us to depend on Him, not on ourselves or others.
- God wants to teach us to trust His ways and timing, and to learn that they are best.

How do we learn patience? Through trials and tribulations! The Bible encourages us to "count it all joy" when we face trying times. But why? Not because it is pleasant, but because it is profitable. Trials produce patience (James 1:2, 3). Tribulations produce patience (Rom. 5:3). In times of difficulty, we learn to endure, to bear up, to persevere, to keep holding on with no help in sight.

When we can do so without setting a deadline for surrender, then we have developed one of life's greatest qualities—patience.

See the Life Principles Index for further study:
14. God acts on behalf of those who wait for Him.
7. The dark moments of our life will last only so long as is necessary for God to accomplish His purpose in us.

Benediction
16 Now may the Lord of peace Himself give
you peace always in every way. The Lord *be*
with you all.
17 The salutation of Paul with my own hand,
which is a sign in every epistle; so I write.
18 The grace of our Lord Jesus Christ *be* with
you all. Amen.

THE FIRST EPISTLE OF PAUL THE APOSTLE TO

TIMOTHY

Paul, the aged and experienced apostle, writes to his young and inexperienced protégé, Timothy, who faces a heavy burden of responsibility as pastor of the church at Ephesus. Paul originally met Timothy during his second missionary journey (Acts 16:1–3), and shortly afterwards Timothy began working with him. Now the young man must deal with several formidable challenges: He must correct false doctrine, safeguard public worship, and develop mature leadership.

In addition to the conduct of the church, Paul talks pointedly about the conduct of the minister. Timothy must be on his guard, lest his youthfulness become a liability rather than an asset to the gospel. He must carefully avoid false teachers and greedy motives and instead pursue righteousness, godliness, faith, love, perseverance, and the gentleness that befits a man of God.

The apostle especially emphasizes the dangers of materialism. He decries the idea that "godliness is a means of gain" (6:5) and tells Timothy that he should feel content with "having food and clothing" (6:8). The apostle warns that "those who desire to be rich fall into temptation and a snare, and into many foolish and harmful lusts which drown men in destruction" (6:9). And then he writes what has become one of the most famous lines in history: "For the love of money is a root of all kinds of evil . . . ." Greed can cause men to stray from the faith, Paul warns, and before they know it, they have "pierced themselves through with many sorrows" (6:10).

This letter also features two of the most magnificent short descriptions of God anywhere in Scripture. Paul calls God, "the King eternal, immortal, invisible . . . God who alone is wise" (1:17) and "the blessed and only Potentate, the King of kings and Lord of lords, who alone has immortality, dwelling in unapproachable light, whom no man has seen or can see, to whom be honor and everlasting power" (6:15, 16).

The Greek title for this letter is *Pros Timotheon A*, the "First to Timothy." Timothy means "honoring God" or "honored by God."

Theme: The exhortation of a young pastor by a man seasoned in the faith.

Author: The apostle Paul.

Date: Written probably between A.D. 62–67.

Structure: After a brief greeting (1:1, 2), Paul warns against false teachers (1:3–11), gives thanks for God's grace (1:12–17), instructs Timothy in the administration of the church (1:18—6:2), offers some miscellaneous suggestions (6:3–19), and finally urges his young friend to guard the faith (6:20, 21).

As you read 1 Timothy, watch for several life principles that play an important role in this book:

4. The awareness of God's presence energizes us for our work. *See 1 Timothy 1:17, 18; page 1419.*

8. Fight all your battles on your knees and you win every time. *See 1 Timothy 2:1–4; page 1419.*

21. Obedience always brings blessing. *See 1 Timothy 3:1–13; page 1419.*

19. Anything you hold too tightly you will lose. *See 1 Timothy 6:6–10; page 1423.*

Life Examples:

TIMOTHY

A Man Who Honored God

1 TIM. 1:2, 18

Timothy, born half Greek and half Jew, probably accepted Christ in his hometown, Lystra, during Paul's first missionary journey. Paul learned of Timothy's growth in his walk with Christ and made the young man his aide during his second missionary journey.

The name Timothy means "one who honors God," and Paul entrusted him with the toughest of assignments in Ephesus, Corinth, Macedonia, and Thessalonica. In an ultimate show of commitment, Timothy as an adult submitted to the painful procedure of circumcision to accommodate Paul's preaching to Jews (Acts 16:3). The writer of Hebrews reports that at some point Timothy also was imprisoned (Heb. 13:23).

Scripture reveals Timothy as a sometimes timid man who, early in life, devoted himself to the Lord, and then spent his young adult years traversing the world to share the gospel. He continues to inspire us toward courage and boldness, even when we feel we naturally lack those qualities.

See the Life Principles Index for further study:

1. *Our intimacy with God—His highest priority for our lives—determines the impact of our lives.*

Greeting

1 Paul, an apostle of Jesus Christ, by the
commandment of God our Savior and the
Lord Jesus Christ, our hope,
2 To Timothy, a true son in the faith:

Grace, mercy, *and* peace from God our Father and Jesus Christ our Lord.

No Other Doctrine

3 As I urged you when I went into Macedonia—remain in Ephesus that you may charge
some that they teach no other doctrine,
4 nor give heed to fables and endless genealogies, which cause disputes rather than
godly edification which is in faith.
5 Now the purpose of the commandment is
love from a pure heart, *from* a good conscience, and *from* sincere faith,
6 from which some, having strayed, have
turned aside to idle talk,
7 desiring to be teachers of the law, understanding neither what they say nor the things
which they affirm.
8 But we know that the law *is* good if one
uses it lawfully,
9 knowing this: that the law is not made for
a righteous person, but for *the* lawless and insubordinate, for *the* ungodly and for sinners,
for *the* unholy and profane, for murderers of
fathers and murderers of mothers, for
manslayers,
10 for fornicators, for sodomites, for kidnap-
pers, for liars, for perjurers, and if there is any
other thing that is contrary to sound doctrine,
11 according to the glorious gospel of the
blessed God which was committed to my
trust.

Glory to God for His Grace

12 And I thank Christ Jesus our Lord who
has enabled me, because He counted me
faithful, putting *me* into the ministry,
13 although I was formerly a blasphemer, a
persecutor, and an insolent man; but I obtained mercy because I did *it* ignorantly in
unbelief.
14 And the grace of our Lord was exceedingly abundant, with faith and love which are
in Christ Jesus.
15 This *is* a faithful saying and worthy of
all acceptance, that Christ Jesus came into the world to save sinners, of whom I am
chief.
16 However, for this reason I obtained
mercy, that in me first Jesus Christ might
show all longsuffering, as a pattern to those

LIFE LESSONS

➤ 1:4 — *. . . nor give heed to fables and endless genealogies, which cause disputes rather than godly edification which is in faith.*

The goal of all Christian instruction ought to be "godly edification," which does not merely fuel speculation or cause useless arguments, but which helps people in practical ways to grow closer to God and each other.

➤ 1:15 — *This is a faithful saying and worthy of all acceptance, that Christ Jesus came into the world to save sinners, of whom I am chief.*

No one persecuted the early Christian church more zealously than did Saul, and nobody preached forgiveness more than Paul. Yet he received God's *complete* forgiveness—and so can you.

who are going to believe on Him for everlasting life.
17 Now to the King eternal, immortal, invisible, to God who alone is wise,[a] *be* honor and
glory forever and ever. Amen.

Fight the Good Fight

18 This charge I commit to you, son Timothy,
according to the prophecies previously made
concerning you, that by them you may wage
the good warfare,
19 having faith and a good conscience, which
some having rejected, concerning the faith
have suffered shipwreck,
➤ 20 of whom are Hymenaeus and Alexander,
whom I delivered to Satan that they may
learn not to blaspheme.

Pray for All Men

2 Therefore I exhort first of all that supplications, prayers, intercessions, *and* giving
of thanks be made for all men,
2 for kings and all who are in authority, that
we may lead a quiet and peaceable life in all
godliness and reverence.
➤ 3 For this *is* good and acceptable in the sight
of God our Savior,
4 who desires all men to be saved and to
come to the knowledge of the truth.
➤ 5 For *there is* one God and one Mediator between God and men, *the* Man Christ Jesus,
6 who gave Himself a ransom for all, to be
testified in due time,
7 for which I was appointed a preacher and
an apostle—I am speaking the truth in Christ[a]
and not lying—a teacher of the Gentiles in
faith and truth.

Men and Women in the Church

➤ **8** I desire therefore that the men pray everywhere, lifting up holy hands, without wrath
and doubting;
9 in like manner also, that the women adorn
themselves in modest apparel, with propriety
and moderation, not with braided hair or gold
or pearls or costly clothing,
10 but, which is proper for women professing
godliness, with good works.
11 Let a woman learn in silence with all submission.
12 And I do not permit a woman to teach or
to have authority over a man, but to be in silence.
13 For Adam was formed first, then Eve.
14 And Adam was not deceived, but the
woman being deceived, fell into transgression.
15 Nevertheless she will be saved in child- ✳
bearing if they continue in faith, love, and
holiness, with self-control.

Qualifications of Overseers

3 This *is* a faithful saying: If a man desires
the position of a bishop,[a] he desires a good
work.
2 A bishop then must be blameless, the husband of one wife, temperate, sober-minded, of
good behavior, hospitable, able to teach;
3 not given to wine, not violent, not greedy
for money,[a] but gentle, not quarrelsome, not
covetous;
4 one who rules his own house well, having
his children in submission with all reverence
5 (for if a man does not know how to rule ➤
his own house, how will he take care of the
church of God?);

1:17 [a]NU-Text reads *to the only God.* **2:7** [a]NU-Text omits *in Christ.* **3:1** [a]Literally *overseer* **3:3** [a]NU-Text omits *not greedy for money.*

LIFE LESSONS

➤ 1:16 — . . . *for this reason I obtained mercy, that in me first Jesus Christ might show all longsuffering, as a pattern to those who are going to believe on Him . . . .*

What "pattern" did Paul establish in his salvation? Certainly not in how he was saved, with a blinding light and a vision of Christ. But if God saved him who tried to destroy the church, then he can save anyone.

➤ 1:20 — . . . *of whom are Hymenaeus and Alexander, whom I delivered to Satan that they may learn not to blaspheme.*

Paul did not want God to destroy these men, but to do whatever was necessary in their lives—even severe things—to jolt them back into a solid faith.

➤ 2:3, 4 — *God our Savior . . . desires all men to be saved and to come to the knowledge of the truth.*

The Lord does not celebrate the need to judge wicked people and send them to hell, but the opportunity to redeem repentant people and bring them to heaven. He opens wide the doors to His home.

➤ 2:5 — *For there is one God and one Mediator between God and men, the Man Christ Jesus . . . .*

There are not five mediators between God and man, or three, or even two. There is only *one*, and His name is Jesus Christ. No one else qualifies, and God accepts no one else. Only Jesus has the necessary credentials.

➤ 2:8 — *I desire therefore that the men pray everywhere, lifting up holy hands, without wrath and doubting . . . .*

In our day, many men have left the church largely in the hands of women, perhaps thinking to focus their energies on more "manly" tasks. But God desires men to partner with Him in the greatest task ever—the church.

➤ 3:5 — . . . *for if a man does not know how to rule his own house, how will he take care of the church of God?*

Before God gives us greater responsibilities in a larger sphere of influence, He requires us to demonstrate our faithfulness with a lesser responsibility in a smaller sphere of influence.

6 not a novice, lest being puffed up with
pride he fall into the *same* condemnation as
the devil.
7 Moreover he must have a good testimony
among those who are outside, lest he fall into
reproach and the snare of the devil.

Qualifications of Deacons

8 Likewise deacons *must be* reverent, not
double-tongued, not given to much wine, not
greedy for money,
9 holding the mystery of the faith with a
pure conscience.
10 But let these also first be tested; then let
them serve as deacons, being *found* blameless.
11 Likewise, *their* wives *must be* reverent,
not slanderers, temperate, faithful in all
things.
12 Let deacons be the husbands of one wife,
ruling *their* children and their own houses
well.
13 For those who have served well as deacons obtain for themselves a good standing
and great boldness in the faith which is in
Christ Jesus.

The Great Mystery

14 These things I write to you, though I hope
to come to you shortly;
15 but if I am delayed, *I write* so that you may
know how you ought to conduct yourself in
the house of God, which is the church of the
living God, the pillar and ground of the truth.
16 And without controversy great is the mystery of godliness:

God[a] was manifested in the flesh,
Justified in the Spirit,
Seen by angels,
Preached among the Gentiles,
Believed on in the world,
Received up in glory.

The Great Apostasy

4 Now the Spirit expressly says that in latter
times some will depart from the faith, giving heed to deceiving spirits and doctrines of
demons,
2 speaking lies in hypocrisy, having their
own conscience seared with a hot iron,
3 forbidding to marry, *and commanding* to
abstain from foods which God created to be
received with thanksgiving by those who believe and know the truth.
4 For every creature of God *is* good, and
nothing is to be refused if it is received with
thanksgiving;
5 for it is sanctified by the word of God and
prayer.

A Good Servant of Jesus Christ

6 If you instruct the brethren in these
things, you will be a good minister of Jesus
Christ, nourished in the words of faith and of
the good doctrine which you have carefully
followed.
7 But reject profane and old wives' fables,
and exercise yourself toward godliness.
8 For bodily exercise profits a little, but godliness is profitable for all things, having
promise of the life that now is and of that
which is to come.
9 This *is* a faithful saying and worthy of all
acceptance.
10 For to this *end* we both labor and suffer reproach,[a] because we trust in the living God,
who is *the* Savior of all men, especially of
those who believe.
11 These things command and teach.

Take Heed to Your Ministry

12 Let no one despise your youth, but be an

3:16 [a]NU-Text reads *Who.* **4:10** [a]NU-Text reads *we labor and strive.*

LIFE LESSONS

➤ 3:6 — *. . . not a novice, lest being puffed up with pride he fall into the same condemnation as the devil.*

Satan became the devil through his pride. Once he was an honored and holy angel, created to glorify God; he became "the evil one" when he became so impressed with himself that he tried to take God's place.

➤ 3:10 — *But let these also first be tested; then let them serve as deacons, being found blameless.*

What kind of tests does Paul have in mind? What could show a person's readiness for a leadership role? You give them a smaller task, and if they do well and inspire others, they're probably ready for something bigger.

➤ 3:15 — *I write so that you may know how you ought to conduct yourself in the house of God . . . .*

Every believer is to bring honor to God, but it is especially important for church leaders to provide a stellar example of faith in action. "If anyone defiles the temple of God, God will destroy him" (1 Cor. 3:17).

➤ 4:1 — *Now the Spirit expressly says that in latter times some will depart from the faith, giving heed to deceiving spirits and doctrines of demons . . . .*

False teaching and deceptive doctrines have always plagued the church, but the closer we get to the return of Christ, the more prevalent these challenges will become. That is why we must remain vigilant.

➤ 4:12 — *Let no one despise your youth, but be an example to the believers in word, in conduct, in love, in spirit, in faith, in purity.*

Regardless of how old you are or how long you have followed Christ, you can become an excellent example to others by submitting your life to Christ and learning how to rely upon the power and leading of the Spirit.

example to the believers in word, in conduct,
in love, in spirit,[a] in faith, in purity.
13 Till I come, give attention to reading, to
exhortation, to doctrine.
14 Do not neglect the gift that is in you,
which was given to you by prophecy with the
laying on of the hands of the eldership.
➤ 15 Meditate on these things; give yourself entirely to them, that your progress may be evident to all.
16 Take heed to yourself and to the doctrine.
Continue in them, for in doing this you will
save both yourself and those who hear you.

Treatment of Church Members

5 Do not rebuke an older man, but exhort
him as a father, younger men as brothers,
2 older women as mothers, younger women
as sisters, with all purity.

Honor True Widows

3 Honor widows who are really widows.
4 But if any widow has children or
grandchildren, let them first learn to show
piety at home and to repay their parents; for
this is good and[a] acceptable before God.
5 Now she who is really a widow, and left
alone, trusts in God and continues in supplications and prayers night and day.
6 But she who lives in pleasure is dead
while she lives.
7 And these things command, that they may
be blameless.
➤ 8 But if anyone does not provide for his
own, and especially for those of his household, he has denied the faith and is worse
than an unbeliever.
9 Do not let a widow under sixty years old
be taken into the number, *and not unless* she
has been the wife of one man,
10 well reported for good works: if she has
brought up children, if she has lodged strangers, if she has washed the saints' feet, if she
has relieved the afflicted, if she has diligently
followed every good work.
11 But refuse *the* younger widows; for when
they have begun to grow wanton against
Christ, they desire to marry,
12 having condemnation because they have
cast off their first faith.
13 And besides they learn *to be* idle, wandering about from house to house, and not only
idle but also gossips and busybodies, saying
things which they ought not.
14 Therefore I desire that *the* younger *widows* marry, bear children, manage the house,
give no opportunity to the adversary to speak
reproachfully.
15 For some have already turned aside after
Satan.
16 If any believing man or[a] woman has widows, let them relieve them, and do not let the
church be burdened, that it may relieve those
who are really widows.

Honor the Elders

17 Let the elders who rule well be counted
worthy of double honor, especially those who
labor in the word and doctrine.
18 For the Scripture says, *"You shall not
muzzle an ox while it treads out the grain,"*[a]
and, "The laborer *is* worthy of his wages."[b]
19 Do not receive an accusation against an
elder except from two or three witnesses.
20 Those who are sinning rebuke in the pres- ➤
ence of all, that the rest also may fear.
21 I charge *you* before God and the Lord Jesus Christ and the elect angels that you observe these things without prejudice, doing
nothing with partiality.
22 Do not lay hands on anyone hastily, nor
share in other people's sins; keep yourself
pure.
23 No longer drink only water, but use a little ➤
wine for your stomach's sake and your frequent infirmities.

4:12 [a]NU-Text omits *in spirit.* **5:4** [a]NU-Text and M-Text omit *good and.* **5:16** [a]NU-Text omits *man or.*
5:18 [a]Deuteronomy 25:4 [b]Luke 10:7

LIFE LESSONS

➤ 4:15 — *Meditate on these things; give yourself entirely to them, that your progress may be evident to all.*

The modern church has largely lost the art of pondering God's Word, mulling it over, letting it simmer, and focusing prolonged attention on it. But hard thinking remains a crucial piece in becoming more like Christ.

➤ 5:8 — *But if anyone does not provide for his own, and especially for those of his household, he has denied the faith and is worse than an unbeliever.*

Many unbelievers fall into gross sin because they don't know any better. Before his conversion, Paul fell into this category (1 Tim. 1:13). But someone who knows the truth and refuses to act on it has no excuse.

➤ 5:20 — *Those who are sinning rebuke in the presence of all, that the rest also may fear.*

Paul is speaking here of church leaders. If they abuse their positions and sin publicly, he instructs Timothy to rebuke them publicly—not to shame them, but to let everyone know that God does not play favorites.

➤ 5:23 — *No longer drink only water, but use a little wine for your stomach's sake and your frequent infirmities.*

God is interested in the whole person, not merely the "spiritual" side. Paul knows that if Timothy does not take care of his body, neither can he take care of the souls of those whom God has entrusted to him.

ANSWERS TO LIFE'S QUESTIONS

How can I learn to feel content?

1 TIM. 6:7, 8

Many in today's workforce feel deeply discontented. "If only I had a better boss . . . . If only I could make more money . . . . If I could just work for *that* company . . . ." And so it goes.

Two thousand years ago, John the Baptist exhorted disgruntled Roman soldiers to be content with their wages (Luke 3:14). It's still good advice.

We can grow content when we see God as our sole provider: "Give me neither poverty nor riches—feed me with the food allotted to me; lest I be full and deny You, and say, 'Who is the LORD?' or lest I be poor and steal, and profane the name of my God" (Prov. 30:8, 9).

We can also grow content as we focus on the necessities of life: "For we brought nothing into this world, and it is certain that we can carry nothing out. And having food and clothing, with these we shall be content" (1 Tim. 6:7, 8).

Much of our restlessness comes from desiring the many perks our affluent culture offers. But do we really need them? Can we get along without designer jeans? God will often supply our wants out of His goodness and grace, but He promises to supply only our needs.

We can grow content as we learn to express gratitude for what we have, rather than complain about what we're missing: "Let your conduct be without covetousness; be content for such things as you have" (Heb. 13:5). Solomon said, "Better is the sight of the eyes than the wandering of desire" (Eccl. 6:9).

God already has blessed us with so much. Satan schemes to redirect our focus to what eludes us, thus fostering a malignant virus of discontent. Instead, why not take inventory of all that God has blessed you with and thank Him for each and every blessing you note?

We find our greatest source of contentment, of course, in a delightful relationship with Jesus Christ: "Not that I speak in regard to need, for I have learned in whatever state I am to be content . . . . I can do all things through Christ who strengthens me" (Phil. 4:11, 13). Paul could feel satisfied with his often harsh lot in life because his communion with the Savior filled his heart to overflowing.

"Delight yourself also in the LORD, and He shall give you the desires of your heart" (Ps. 37:4).

See the Life Principles Index for further study:

11. God assumes full responsibility for our needs when we obey Him.

16. Whatever you acquire outside of God's will eventually turns to ashes.

➤ 24 Some men's sins are clearly evident, preceding *them* to judgment, but those of some *men* follow later.
25 Likewise, the good works *of some* are clearly evident, and those that are otherwise cannot be hidden.

Honor Masters

6 Let as many bondservants as are under the yoke count their own masters worthy of all honor, so that the name of God and *His* doctrine may not be blasphemed.
2 And those who have believing masters, let them not despise *them* because they are brethren, but rather serve *them* because those who are benefited are believers and beloved. Teach and exhort these things.

Error and Greed

3 If anyone teaches otherwise and does not consent to wholesome words, *even* the words of our Lord Jesus Christ, and to the doctrine which accords with godliness,
4 he is proud, knowing nothing, but is obsessed with disputes and arguments over words, from which come envy, strife, reviling, evil suspicions,

LIFE LESSONS

➤ 5:24 — *Some men's sins are clearly evident, preceding them to judgment, but those of some men follow later.*

Some crimes escape the judgment of human beings, but no sin escapes the judgment of God. Nobody ultimately "gets away with" anything. If we do not allow Jesus to take away our sins, we will have to bear them ourselves.

5 useless wranglings[a] of men of corrupt
minds and destitute of the truth, who suppose
that godliness is a *means of* gain. From such
withdraw yourself.[b]
6 Now godliness with contentment is great
gain.
7 For we brought nothing into *this* world,
and it is certain[a] we can carry nothing out.
8 And having food and clothing, with these
we shall be content.
➤ 9 But those who desire to be rich fall into
temptation and a snare, and *into* many foolish and harmful lusts which drown men in destruction and perdition.
10 For the love of money is a root of all *kinds*
of evil, for which some have strayed from the
faith in their greediness, and pierced themselves through with many sorrows.

The Good Confession

11 But you, O man of God, flee these things
and pursue righteousness, godliness, faith,
love, patience, gentleness.
➤ 12 Fight the good fight of faith, lay hold on
eternal life, to which you were also called and
have confessed the good confession in the
presence of many witnesses.
13 I urge you in the sight of God who gives
life to all things, and *before* Christ Jesus who
witnessed the good confession before Pontius
Pilate,
14 that you keep *this* commandment without
spot, blameless until our Lord Jesus Christ's
appearing,
15 which He will manifest in His own time,
He who is the blessed and only Potentate, the
King of kings and Lord of lords,
16 who alone has immortality, dwelling in
unapproachable light, whom no man has seen
or can see, to whom *be* honor and everlasting
power. Amen.

Instructions to the Rich

17 Command those who are rich in this present age not to be haughty, nor to trust in
uncertain riches but in the living God, who
gives us richly all things to enjoy.
18 *Let them* do good, that they be rich in ➤
good works, ready to give, willing to share,
19 storing up for themselves a good foundation for the time to come, that they may lay
hold on eternal life.

Guard the Faith

20 O Timothy! Guard what was committed to
your trust, avoiding the profane *and* idle babblings and contradictions of what is falsely
called knowledge—
21 by professing it some have strayed concerning the faith. Grace *be* with you. Amen.

6:5 [a]NU-Text and M-Text read *constant friction.* [b]NU-Text omits this sentence. **6:7** [a]NU-Text omits *and it is certain.*

LIFE LESSONS

➤ **6:9 — *But those who desire to be rich fall into temptation and a snare, and into many foolish and harmful lusts which drown men in destruction and perdition.***

The Bible condemns the desire to get rich, not because having money is a sin, but because money makes a terrible master. People who make it their goal to get rich *do* serve money—and therefore can't serve God (Matt. 6:24).

➤ **6:12 — *Fight the good fight of faith . . . .***

Faith is a fight because many obstacles and challenges stand in the way of its development and advance. That fight is good because it leads to eternal life and an everlasting home with God.

➤ **6:18 — *Let them do good, that they be rich in good works, ready to give, willing to share . . . .***

God blesses us financially not simply so that we can spend His blessings on ourselves, but so that we can use the resources He gives us to help others and to expand the kingdom of God.

THE SECOND EPISTLE OF PAUL THE APOSTLE TO TIMOTHY

Prison is the last place from which to expect a letter of encouragement, but that is where Paul's second letter to Timothy originated.

The apostle begins by assuring Timothy of his continuing love and prayers, and then reminds him of his spiritual heritage and responsibilities. Only the one who perseveres—whether as a soldier, athlete, farmer, or minister of Jesus Christ—will reap the reward.

Paul warns Timothy that his teaching will come under attack as faithless men desert the truth in favor of words for itching ears (4:3). But Timothy has Paul's example to guide him and God's Word to fortify him as he faces both growing opposition and glowing opportunities.

This letter may be one of the most personal letters we have from the apostle Paul. He knows he faces his final days, yet he finds himself increasingly alone. He tells Timothy, "all those in Asia have turned away from me" (1:15) and "Demas has forsaken me, having loved this present world, and has departed for Thessalonica—Crescens for Galatia, Titus for Dalmatia . . . Tychicus I have sent to Ephesus . . . At my first defense no one stood with me, but all forsook me . . . Erastus stayed in Corinth, but Trophimus I have left in Miletus sick" (4:9, 12, 16, 20). So he tells his young protégé, "Be diligent to come to me quickly . . . . Get Mark and bring him with you . . . . Do your utmost to come before winter" (4:9, 11, 21). The apostle's reports and requests remind us that God designed the Christian life to occur within community and that everyone—even revered apostles—needs the fellowship of other believers.

Paul's last epistle received the title *Pros Timotheon B*, the "Second to Timothy."

Theme: Be on the alert for wrong teachings and cling to the truth.

Author: The apostle Paul.

Date: Written not later than A.D. 68, when the Roman emperor Nero committed suicide. Before Nero died, he had Paul executed.

Structure: After a short introduction (1:1–2), Paul expresses his love for Timothy (1:3–7), encourages him to remain true to the faith (1:8—2:13), warns him of several dangers (2:14—3:9), instructs him in his work (3:10—4:5), informs him of his dire situation (4:6–18), and finally concludes his letter and makes some last requests (4:19–22).

As you read 2 Timothy, watch for several life principles that play an important role in this book:

4. The awareness of God's presence energizes us for our work. *See 2 Timothy 2:8–13); page 1426.*

3. God's Word is an immovable anchor in times of storm. *See 2 Timothy 3:16, 17; page 1427.*

28. No Christian has ever been called to "go it alone" in his or her walk of faith. *See 2 Timothy 4:9–13; page 1429.*

26. Adversity is a bridge to a deeper relationship with God. *See 2 Timothy 4:17, 18; page 1430.*

ANSWERS TO LIFE'S QUESTIONS

How can I combat my fears?

2 TIM. 1:7

Paul's words to Timothy are equally God's words to you. God gives you "a spirit of power and of love and of a sound mind" (2 Tim. 1:7). Respond to every person or situation that you fear with God's power, God's love, and God's mind.

1. Ask for God's help.

When fear strikes you, immediately ask for God's help. Tap into the power of God. Remember when Peter tried to walk on the water to Jesus, but his fear overcame him (Matt. 14:30)? When he found himself in trouble and fear—sinking in the sea—he had the right response. He asked for God's help. "Lord, save me!" is your best first response any time you feel fear.

2. Ask for God's love to fill your heart.

Love is a potent antidote to fear. I recall the first time I preached in my home church. I had a "fear attack." I felt they expected more from me than a group of strangers might expect. So what helped me? I read the words of the Lord to Joshua in Joshua 1:5–9, and then turned my focus on the people of my home church. I felt overwhelmed by how much I loved them and how they had loved me through the years. By the time I stood in the pulpit, the fear had completely drained out of me. John tells us, "There is no fear in love; but perfect love casts out fear" (1 John 4:18). Ask your heavenly Father to impart to you more of Christ's love and to take away any torment you feel. As you do, fear will lose its grip on you.

3. Ask God to give you a sound mind, filled with and operating according to God's Word.

The basis for a sound mind is the Word of God. The more you know of God's promises and the more you live according to His commandments, the greater your strength to withstand fear. Use Scripture to speak directly to the source of your fear, just as Jesus quoted Scripture to Satan during His time of temptation in the wilderness (Luke 4:1–13).

When you feel gripped by fear, turn your gaze upon God, redirect your heart to love, speak to your fear from the Word of God, and then respond boldly to the situation. The Lord desires that you "be strong and of good courage" today.

See the Life Principles Index for further study:

8. Fight all your battles on your knees and you win every time.

3. God's Word is an immovable anchor in times of storm.

Greeting

1 Paul, an apostle of Jesus Christ[a] by the
will of God, according to the promise of
life which is in Christ Jesus,

2 To Timothy, a beloved son:

Grace, mercy, *and* peace from God the Father and Christ Jesus our Lord.

Timothy's Faith and Heritage

3 I thank God, whom I serve with a pure
conscience, as *my* forefathers *did*, as without
ceasing I remember you in my prayers night
and day,
4 greatly desiring to see you, being mindful
of your tears, that I may be filled with joy,
5 when I call to remembrance the genuine
faith that is in you, which dwelt first in your
grandmother Lois and your mother Eunice,
and I am persuaded is in you also.
6 Therefore I remind you to stir up the gift
of God which is in you through the laying on
of my hands.
7 For God has not given us a spirit of fear,
but of power and of love and of a sound mind.

1:1 [a]NU-Text and M-Text read *Christ Jesus.*

LIFE LESSONS

➤ 1:3 — *. . . without ceasing I remember you in my prayers night and day . . . .*

We learn from Paul's letters that he had an extremely active prayer life. Did he keep a list? A prayer journal? We don't know, but he must have developed some kind of system to help direct his many prayers.

➤ 1:6 — *Therefore I remind you to stir up the gift of God which is in you . . . .*

God never takes away the spiritual gifts He bestows upon us (Rom. 11:29), but they can lose their sharp edge of effectiveness through our neglect. God instructs us to use our gifts for the benefit of His people (1 Pet. 4:10)

Not Ashamed of the Gospel

➤ 8 Therefore do not be ashamed of the testimony of our Lord, nor of me His prisoner, but
share with me in the sufferings for the gospel
according to the power of God,
9 who has saved us and called *us* with a
holy calling, not according to our works, but
according to His own purpose and grace
which was given to us in Christ Jesus before
time began,
10 but has now been revealed by the appearing of our Savior Jesus Christ, *who* has abolished death and brought life and immortality
to light through the gospel,
11 to which I was appointed a preacher, an
apostle, and a teacher of the Gentiles.[a]
✳ 12 For this reason I also suffer these things;
nevertheless I am not ashamed, for I know
whom I have believed and am persuaded that
He is able to keep what I have committed to
Him until that Day.

Be Loyal to the Faith

13 Hold fast the pattern of sound words
which you have heard from me, in faith and
love which are in Christ Jesus.
14 That good thing which was committed to
you, keep by the Holy Spirit who dwells in us.
15 This you know, that all those in Asia have
turned away from me, among whom are
Phygellus and Hermogenes.
16 The Lord grant mercy to the household of
Onesiphorus, for he often refreshed me, and
was not ashamed of my chain;
17 but when he arrived in Rome, he sought
me out very zealously and found *me.*
18 The Lord grant to him that he may find
mercy from the Lord in that Day—and you
know very well how many ways he ministered *to me*[a] at Ephesus.

Be Strong in Grace

➤ **2** You therefore, my son, be strong in the
grace that is in Christ Jesus.
2 And the things that you have heard from
me among many witnesses, commit these to
faithful men who will be able to teach others
also.
3 You therefore must endure[a] hardship as a ➤
good soldier of Jesus Christ.
4 No one engaged in warfare entangles
himself with the affairs of *this* life, that
he may please him who enlisted him as a
soldier.
5 And also if anyone competes in athletics,
he is not crowned unless he competes according to the rules.
6 The hardworking farmer must be first to
partake of the crops.
7 Consider what I say, and may[a] the Lord ➤
give you understanding in all things.
8 Remember that Jesus Christ, of the seed of
David, was raised from the dead according to
my gospel,
9 for which I suffer trouble as an evildoer,
even to the point of chains; but the word of
God is not chained.
10 Therefore I endure all things for the sake
of the elect, that they also may obtain the salvation which is in Christ Jesus with eternal
glory.
11 *This is* a faithful saying: ✳

For if we died with *Him,*
We shall also live with *Him.*
12 If we endure,
We shall also reign with *Him.*
If we deny *Him,*
He also will deny us.
13 If we are faithless,
He remains faithful;
He cannot deny Himself.

Approved and Disapproved Workers

14 Remind *them* of these things, charging
them before the Lord not to strive about
words to no profit, to the ruin of the hearers.
15 Be diligent to present yourself approved to

1:11 [a]NU-Text omits *of the Gentiles.* **1:18** [a]*To me* is from the Vulgate and a few Greek manuscripts. **2:3** [a]NU-Text reads *You must share.* **2:7** [a]NU-Text reads *the Lord will give you.*

LIFE LESSONS

➤ 1:8 — *. . . do not be ashamed of the testimony of our Lord, nor of me His prisoner, but share with me in the sufferings for the gospel according to the power of God.*

As human beings, we have a natural tendency to feel ashamed of beliefs or individuals that get ridiculed by the majority. God calls us to draw upon His power to identify courageously with His Son.

➤ 2:1 — *You therefore, my son, be strong in the grace that is in Christ Jesus.*

Paul doesn't encourage Timothy merely to "be strong"—any pagan can do that (1 Sam. 4:9). He encourages him to be strong in the grace of Jesus. Only in God's strength can we become strong.

➤ 2:3 — *You therefore must endure hardship as a good soldier of Jesus Christ.*

If we are in a spiritual war, then we must be soldiers in God's army—and that's exactly what Paul tells Timothy. Soldiers are called on to endure hardship in order to win their wars; so are we.

➤ 2:7 — *Consider what I say, and may the Lord give you understanding in all things.*

How do we gain spiritual understanding? First, we have to "consider" what God says in His Word—ponder it, turn it over in our minds. Then we have to pray that He enlightens our quest for understanding. Both work together.

God, a worker who does not need to be
ashamed, rightly dividing the word of truth.
16 But shun profane *and* idle babblings, for
they will increase to more ungodliness.
17 And their message will spread like cancer.
Hymenaeus and Philetus are of this sort,
18 who have strayed concerning the truth,
saying that the resurrection is already past;
and they overthrow the faith of some.
19 Nevertheless the solid foundation of God
stands, having this seal: "The Lord knows those
who are His," and, "Let everyone who names
the name of Christ[a] depart from iniquity."
20 But in a great house there are not only vessels of gold and silver, but also of wood and
clay, some for honor and some for dishonor.
21 Therefore if anyone cleanses himself from
the latter, he will be a vessel for honor, sanctified and useful for the Master, prepared for
every good work.
22 Flee also youthful lusts; but pursue righteousness, faith, love, peace with those who
call on the Lord out of a pure heart.
23 But avoid foolish and ignorant disputes,
knowing that they generate strife.
24 And a servant of the Lord must not quarrel but be gentle to all, able to teach, patient,
25 in humility correcting those who are in
opposition, if God perhaps will grant them repentance, so that they may know the truth,
26 and *that* they may come to their senses
and escape the snare of the devil, having been
taken captive by him to *do* his will.

Perilous Times and Perilous Men

3 But know this, that in the last days perilous times will come:
2 For men will be lovers of themselves, lovers
of money, boasters, proud, blasphemers,
disobedient to parents, unthankful, unholy,
3 unloving, unforgiving, slanderers, without
self-control, brutal, despisers of good,
4 traitors, headstrong, haughty, lovers of
pleasure rather than lovers of God,
5 having a form of godliness but denying its
power. And from such people turn away!
6 For of this sort are those who creep into
households and make captives of gullible
women loaded down with sins, led away by
various lusts,
7 always learning and never able to come to
the knowledge of the truth.
8 Now as Jannes and Jambres resisted Moses, so do these also resist the truth: men of corrupt minds, disapproved concerning the faith;
9 but they will progress no further, for their
folly will be manifest to all, as theirs also was.

The Man of God and the Word of God

10 But you have carefully followed my doctrine, manner of life, purpose, faith, longsuffering, love, perseverance,
11 persecutions, afflictions, which happened
to me at Antioch, at Iconium, at Lystra—what
persecutions I endured. And out of *them* all
the Lord delivered me.
12 Yes, and all who desire to live godly in
Christ Jesus will suffer persecution.
13 But evil men and impostors will grow worse
and worse, deceiving and being deceived.
14 But you must continue in the things which
you have learned and been assured of, knowing from whom you have learned *them*,
15 and that from childhood you have known
the Holy Scriptures, which are able to make
you wise for salvation through faith which is
in Christ Jesus.
16 All Scripture *is* given by inspiration of God,
and *is* profitable for doctrine, for reproof, for
correction, for instruction in righteousness,
17 that the man of God may be complete,
thoroughly equipped for every good work.

2:19 [a]NU-Text and M-Text read *the Lord.*

LIFE LESSONS

➤ 2:19 — *"Let everyone who names the name of Christ depart from iniquity."*

If we claim to be Christians, then we must live for God as Jesus did. The love and grace of God does not free us to sin; it gives us the strength and the desire to gladly discover and do His will.

➤ 3:5 — *. . . having a form of godliness but denying its power.*

Human beings love the trappings of religion: special costumes, mysterious rituals, revered traditions, solemn atmosphere. It soothes and reassures them, so long as they can control it and a sovereign God never insists on His way.

➤ 3:7 — *. . . always learning and never able to come to the knowledge of the truth.*

Does it ever strike you as odd that some of the most learned men in history have spent their lives poring over the Bible—and yet never come to faith in Christ? Salvation is not about learning, but about submission.

➤ 3:12 — *Yes, and all who desire to live godly in Christ Jesus will suffer persecution.*

This is one of those promises of God that we'd really rather do without. God tells us this, not to discourage us, but to prepare us for the inevitable so that we can shine for Him when the time comes.

➤ 3:16, 17 — *All Scripture is given by inspiration of God, and is profitable for doctrine, for reproof, for correction, for instruction in righteousness, that the man of God may be complete, thoroughly equipped for every good work.*

God gave us Scriptures for a particular reason: our growth in grace. It teaches us the truth about God, corrects us when we're wrong, and explains how to grow so that we can become effective ambassadors for Jesus.

WHAT THE BIBLE SAYS ABOUT **THE IMPORTANCE OF THE SCRIPTURES**

2 Tim. 3:16, 17

The Bible applies to all men and women in every culture, in every age, in every walk of life. It is God's supernatural manual that alone reveals the mind and ways of God so that humankind may know and experience His blessings.

The Bible is God's written record of His works through the ages. It provides substantial evidence of His nature, plan, and purposes so that we can confidently place our faith in Him. Because of the Bible, we are not left to archaeological, historical, or theological guesswork. We can know, for "it is written."

Because the Bible is inspired (God-breathed) it is life's final and ultimate authority. The Bible is the "last word" on issues pertaining to God and His ways. No individual, institution, or organization can supersede the authority of Scripture.

That is exactly why we are admonished not to add to or take away from the Scriptures (Rev. 22:18, 19). They perfectly express the decrees and judgments of almighty God. The Bible is authoritative because it is the truth: "The entirety of Your word is truth" (Ps. 119:160). The Bible is also God's guide to salvation and wise living: "Your word is a lamp to my feet and a light to my path" (Ps. 119:105).

The Bible is authoritative because it is the truth.

Through the ministry of the Holy Spirit, the Bible enlightens each individual to recognize personal sin, the need for salvation, and the best possible life course. Without the Bible informing and illumining us, we would be hopelessly unable to know and follow the true and living God.

When we say, "Oh, I just wish I could hear God speak to me!" we have forgotten that He *has* spoken and *still* speaks through His Word. God is not silent. He has spoken, and He has done so in the Bible, the "oracles of God" (Rom. 3:2; Heb. 5:12).

The Bible is also profitable and nourishing. It provides us with an advantage in every department of life—family, business, and social relationships. It is profitable because it reflects the wisdom of God; when we abide by its teachings, we are blessed. As we meditate and consider its truth, our spirits and souls find nourishment; we become established and enriched in every experience of life by living according to God's perspective.

The Bible is the book for everyone. It is revelation, inspiration, and communication of the Person and plan of the eternal, living, and powerful God.

See the Life Principles Index for further study:
3. God's Word is an immovable anchor in times of storm.

Preach the Word

4 I charge *you* therefore before God and the
Lord Jesus Christ, who will judge the living and the dead at[a] His appearing and His
kingdom:
2 Preach the word! Be ready in season *and*
out of season. Convince, rebuke, exhort, with
all longsuffering and teaching.
➤ 3 For the time will come when they will not
endure sound doctrine, but according to their
own desires, *because* they have itching ears,
they will heap up for themselves teachers;
4 and they will turn *their* ears away from
the truth, and be turned aside to fables.
5 But you be watchful in all things, endure
afflictions, do the work of an evangelist, fulfill
your ministry.

Paul's Valedictory

6 For I am already being poured out as a
drink offering, and the time of my departure
is at hand.
➤ 7 I have fought the good fight, I have finished the race, I have kept the faith.
8 Finally, there is laid up for me the crown
of righteousness, which the Lord, the righteous Judge, will give to me on that Day, and
not to me only but also to all who have loved
His appearing.

The Abandoned Apostle

9 Be diligent to come to me quickly;
10 for Demas has forsaken me, having loved
this present world, and has departed for
Thessalonica—Crescens for Galatia, Titus for
Dalmatia.
11 Only Luke is with me. Get Mark and bring
him with you, for he is useful to me for ministry.
12 And Tychicus I have sent to Ephesus.
13 Bring the cloak that I left with Carpus at
Troas when you come—and the books, especially the parchments.
14 Alexander the coppersmith did me much
harm. May the Lord repay him according to
his works.
15 You also must beware of him, for he has
greatly resisted our words.
16 At my first defense no one stood with me,
but all forsook me. May it not be charged
against them.

Life Examples:

LUKE

Laboring in the Background

2 TIM. 4:11

We know so little about Luke. The Bible contains only three references to him (Col. 4:14; 2 Tim. 4:11; Philem. 24), but we can sketch a glimpse of the man whom God used to write more words of the New Testament than anyone else.

Luke was probably a Greek physician and often traveled with Paul (Col. 4:14). Tradition calls him a native of Antioch and says he died unmarried and childless at the age of eighty-four. He wrote Luke and Acts to fellow Gentiles, reassuring them that Christ came for all mankind. Luke's Gospel emphasizes the manhood of Jesus in all its perfection and stresses the plight of women, children, and the poor, sick, and outcast.

Luke labored without regard to himself or the persecution that raged around him. He did so by dying to self and living for the Lord, whom he came to love more and more through his careful interviews.

See the Life Principles Index for further study:

4. The awareness of God's presence energizes us for our work.

1. Our intimacy with God—His highest priority for our lives—determines the impact of our lives.

4:1 [a]NU-Text omits *therefore* and reads *and by* for *at.*

LIFE LESSONS

➤ 4:3 — For the time will come when they will not endure sound doctrine, but according to their own desires, because they have itching ears, they will heap up for themselves teachers . . . .

This verse sounds a great deal like our own age, doesn't it? We live in a time of "designer doctrine," when people pick and choose what to believe, based on their desires and preferences. But it's a worthless pursuit.

➤ 4:7 — I have fought the good fight, I have finished the race, I have kept the faith.

Paul faced many adversaries in his fruitful ministry—and successfully opposed them. He kept to the same path of Christian discipleship for a long time—and successfully completed his course. So can we.

ANSWERS TO LIFE'S QUESTIONS

How can I cope with feelings of loneliness?

2 TIM. 4:13, 17, 21

Paul endured prison alone, where he felt deeply isolated. In the last months of his life, he gave us the wonderful secret of what to do in times of intense loneliness.

First, he recognized the presence of God. He wrote that the Lord stood with him (2 Tim. 4:17). Paul couldn't change his situation, but in that lonely, damp prison cell, he called to mind that One remained with him.

Second, Paul dealt with loneliness by recalling how God faithfully strengthened him (2 Tim. 4:17). The Lord supported Paul, infusing him with strength. The apostle knew that no one could take his life without God's permission. We often quote Philippians 4:13: "I can do all things through Christ who strengthens me." Paul sat in jail when he wrote that verse also.

Third, Paul combated his feelings of loneliness by reminding himself that he had the awesome privilege of fulfilling God's purpose for his life. What incredible encouragement that is—to know we are part of God's providential plan!

Still, in his loneliness, Paul treasured his friends. He wrote that only Luke remained with him and that he wanted Timothy and Mark to join him. He mentioned four people by name who comforted him: Eubulus, Pudens, Linus, and Claudia (2 Tim. 4:21). We know nothing about those four people, other than they stuck with the apostle Paul. That has to be one of the greatest compliments they could have been paid.

Finally, Paul asked Timothy to bring some books with him, "especially the parchments" (2 Tim. 4:13). The books may have been the Gospels, and the parchments may have been the Hebrew Scriptures. Knowing the apostle Paul, we may assume that he hungered for copies of the Scriptures. In an hour of great loneliness, the Word of God brings great comfort.

The Lord Jesus Christ felt totally alone as He faced his own death. The Bible says that "all the disciples forsook Him and fled" (Matt. 26:56). And on the cross, He cried out, "My God, My God, why have You forsaken Me?" (Matt. 27:46). Jesus knows all about loneliness. Yet He also knows the joy of being carried through the loneliest of times on the wings of faith, confident that the Father will never abandon one He loves. Jesus stands as the ultimate example of One who faced the perils of loneliness without losing heart.

See the Life Principles Index for further study:

4. The awareness of God's presence energizes us for our work.

24. To live the Christian life is to allow Jesus to live His life in and through us.

The Lord Is Faithful

17 But the Lord stood with me and strengthened me, so that the message might be
preached fully through me, and *that* all the
Gentiles might hear. Also I was delivered out
of the mouth of the lion.
18 And the Lord will deliver me from every
evil work and preserve *me* for His heavenly
kingdom. To Him *be* glory forever and ever.
Amen!

Come Before Winter

19 Greet Prisca and Aquila, and the household of Onesiphorus.
20 Erastus stayed in Corinth, but Trophimus I
have left in Miletus sick.
21 Do your utmost to come before winter.
Eubulus greets you, as well as Pudens, Linus,
Claudia, and all the brethren.

Farewell

22 The Lord Jesus Christ[a] be with your spirit.
Grace be with you. Amen.

4:22 [a]NU-Text omits *Jesus Christ.*

LIFE LESSONS

➤ ***4:17 — But the Lord stood with me and strengthened me, so that the message might be preached fully through me . . . .***

When everyone else abandons us, the Lord stands solidly at our side. When we feel absolutely spent, He gives us strength. When failure appears inevitable, He steps in and helps us to finish what He gave us to do.

THE EPISTLE OF PAUL THE APOSTLE TO TITUS

Titus, a young pastor, faced the unenviable assignment of setting in order the church at Crete. Paul advised him to appoint elders, men of proven spiritual character, to oversee the work of the church.

But elders are not the only individuals in the church required to excel spiritually. Men and women, young and old, each have their vital functions to fulfill if they are to become living examples of the doctrine they profess. Throughout his letter, Paul stresses the necessary, practical working out of salvation in the daily lives of both elders and the congregations they serve. Good works are desirable and profitable for *all* believers.

This emphasis had special importance to Titus, for he had been assigned a very difficult ministry on the island of Crete. Paul cited a local commentary about the Cretans that called them, "always liars, evil beasts, lazy gluttons," and warned Titus, "This testimony is true. Therefore rebuke them sharply, that they may be sound in the faith . . . ." (1:12, 13). He also warned Titus about those who "profess to know God, but in works they deny Him, being abominable, disobedient, and disqualified for every good work" (1:16).

Yet how was Titus to help these struggling believers to obey the righteous commands of God? Should he condemn them? Threaten them? Force them to obey through coercion or some other harsh means? No. Paul knows only one force that could turn the tide: grace. It is only "the grace of God that brings salvation," Paul insists, that teaches us to deny "ungodliness and worldly lusts" and to "live soberly, righteously, and godly in the present age" (2:11, 12). Our Savior Jesus Christ died on the cross "that He might redeem us from every lawless deed and purify for Himself His own special people, zealous for good works" (2:14).

This third pastoral epistle is simply titled *Pros Titon*, "To Titus." Ironically, this was also the name of the Roman general who destroyed Jerusalem in A.D. 70; later he succeeded his father, Vespasian, as emperor.

Themes: God saves us by His grace to live in a way that honors and pleases Him.

Authors: The apostle Paul.

Date: Probably written around A.D. 63–65.

Structure: After a brief greeting (1:1–4), Paul gives instructions about church leadership (1:5–9), gives a warning about false teachers (1:10–16), describes a healthy church (2:1—3:11), and finishes with some miscellaneous instructions and a farewell (3:12–15).

As you read Titus, watch for several life principles that play an important part in this book:

15. Brokenness is God's requirement for maximum usefulness. *See Titus 1:13–16; page 1432.*

2. Obey God and leave all the consequences to Him. *See Titus 2:9, 10; page 1433.*

1. Our intimacy with God—His highest priority for our lives—determines the impact of our lives. *See Titus 3:4–8; page 1433.*

28. No Christian has ever been called to "go it alone" in his or her walk of faith. *See Titus 3:12–15; page 1434.*

Greeting

1 Paul, a bondservant of God and an apostle
of Jesus Christ, according to the faith of
God's elect and the acknowledgment of the
truth which accords with godliness,
2 in hope of eternal life which God, who
cannot lie, promised before time began,
3 but has in due time manifested His word
through preaching, which was committed to
me according to the commandment of God
our Savior;

4 To Titus, a true son in *our* common faith:

Grace, mercy, *and* peace from God the Father and the Lord Jesus Christ[a] our Savior.

Qualified Elders

5 For this reason I left you in Crete, that you
should set in order the things that are lacking,
and appoint elders in every city as I commanded you—
6 if a man is blameless, the husband of one
wife, having faithful children not accused of
dissipation or insubordination.
7 For a bishop[a] must be blameless, as a
steward of God, not self-willed, not quick-tempered, not given to wine, not violent, not
greedy for money,
8 but hospitable, a lover of what is good,
sober-minded, just, holy, self-controlled,
➤ 9 holding fast the faithful word as he has
been taught, that he may be able, by sound
doctrine, both to exhort and convict those
who contradict.

The Elders' Task

10 For there are many insubordinate, both
idle talkers and deceivers, especially those of
the circumcision,
11 whose mouths must be stopped, who subvert whole households, teaching things which
they ought not, for the sake of dishonest gain.
12 One of them, a prophet of their own, said,
"Cretans *are* always liars, evil beasts, lazy
gluttons."
➤ 13 This testimony is true. Therefore rebuke
them sharply, that they may be sound in the
faith,
14 not giving heed to Jewish fables and commandments of men who turn from the truth.
15 To the pure all things are pure, but to
those who are defiled and unbelieving nothing is pure; but even their mind and conscience are defiled.
16 They profess to know God, but in works ➤

Life Examples:

TITUS

Serving God with Abandon

TITUS 1:4

In the days following Titus' conversion, a deep love and mutual respect grew between him and the apostle Paul, a bond that lasted throughout their days. So strong was their connection that Paul said of Titus, "He is my true child in common faith" (Titus 1:4).

Paul saw in this new believer a rare and refreshing quality. Trustworthy and dependable as he was, it is no surprise that Paul would write of Titus, "He is my partner and fellow worker" (2 Cor. 8:23). Consequently, Titus began traveling with Paul to places such as Corinth and Jerusalem.

Titus is a picture of God's grace. As a redeemed Gentile, he experienced intimate fellowship with God. And because he willingly served unselfishly in places of obscurity, he became a treasured instrument for God's own glory.

What could God do with us if we served Him with the same abandon as did Titus?

See the Life Principles Index for further study:
1. *Our intimacy with God—His highest priority for our lives—determines the impact of our lives.*

1:4 [a]NU-Text reads *and Christ Jesus.* **1:7** [a]Literally *overseer*

LIFE LESSONS

➤ 1:9 — *. . . holding fast the faithful word as he has been taught, that he may be able, by sound doctrine, both to exhort and convict those who contradict.*

"Sound doctrine" does not refer merely to an accurate presentation of biblical data. Sound doctrine always has a practical application to godly living, with either a positive emphasis ("exhort") or a negative one ("convict").

➤ 1:13 — *. . . Therefore rebuke them sharply, that they may be sound in the faith . . . .*

It's no fun to "rebuke" someone "sharply"—at least, it shouldn't be; the apostle Paul often did it "with tears" (Phil. 3:18)—but sometimes it's necessary. When it becomes necessary, it's the most loving thing you can do.

➤ 1:16 — *They profess to know God, but in works they deny Him . . . .*

This verse almost sounds as if it could have been written by James, who wrote the famous biblical line, "be doers of the word, and not hearers only, deceiving yourselves" (James 1:22).

they deny *Him,* being abominable, disobedient, and disqualified for every good
work.

Qualities of a Sound Church

2 But as for you, speak the things which are
proper for sound doctrine:
2 that the older men be sober, reverent,
temperate, sound in faith, in love, in patience;
3 the older women likewise, that they be
reverent in behavior, not slanderers, not given
to much wine, teachers of good things—
4 that they admonish the young women to
love their husbands, to love their children,
5 *to be* discreet, chaste, homemakers, good,
obedient to their own husbands, that the word
of God may not be blasphemed.
6 Likewise, exhort the young men to be
sober-minded,
➤ 7 in all things showing yourself *to be* a pattern of good works; in doctrine *showing* integrity, reverence, incorruptibility,[a]
8 sound speech that cannot be condemned,
that one who is an opponent may be
ashamed, having nothing evil to say of you.[a]
9 *Exhort* bondservants to be obedient to
their own masters, to be well pleasing in all
things, not answering back,
10 not pilfering, but showing all good fidelity,
that they may adorn the doctrine of God our
Savior in all things.

Trained by Saving Grace

➤ **11** For the grace of God that brings salvation
has appeared to all men,
12 teaching us that, denying ungodliness and
worldly lusts, we should live soberly, righteously, and godly in the present age,
13 looking for the blessed hope and glorious ◄
appearing of our great God and Savior Jesus
Christ,
14 who gave Himself for us, that He might
redeem us from every lawless deed and purify
for Himself *His* own special people, zealous
for good works.
15 Speak these things, exhort, and rebuke
with all authority. Let no one despise you.

Graces of the Heirs of Grace

3 Remind them to be subject to rulers and
authorities, to obey, to be ready for every
good work,
2 to speak evil of no one, to be peaceable, ◄
gentle, showing all humility to all men.
3 For we ourselves were also once foolish,
disobedient, deceived, serving various lusts
and pleasures, living in malice and envy, hateful and hating one another.
4 But when the kindness and the love of
God our Savior toward man appeared,
5 not by works of righteousness which we
have done, but according to His mercy He
saved us, through the washing of regeneration and renewing of the Holy Spirit,
6 whom He poured out on us abundantly
through Jesus Christ our Savior,
7 that having been justified by His grace we
should become heirs according to the hope of
eternal life.
8 This is a faithful saying, and these things I ◄
want you to affirm constantly, that those who
have believed in God should be careful to
maintain good works. These things are good
and profitable to men.

2:7 [a]NU-Text omits *incorruptibility.* **2:8** [a]NU-Text and M-Text read *us.*

LIFE LESSONS

➤ **2:7 — . . . *in all things showing yourself to be a pattern of good works; in doctrine showing integrity, reverence, incorruptibility . . . .***

Leaders must make sure they're worth following, in both conduct and in what they teach. Character and competence are both necessary if the church of God is to successfully fulfill its mission.

➤ **2:11, 12 — *For the grace of God . . . has appeared . . . , teaching us that, denying ungodliness and worldly lusts, we should live soberly, righteously, and godly . . . .***

Just as we laid hold of salvation by grace through faith, so we lay hold of sanctification by grace through faith. By the power of grace we daily crucify our flesh in order to live for God.

➤ **2:13, 14 — . . . *our great God and Savior Jesus Christ . . . gave Himself for us, that He might . . . purify for Himself His own special people, zealous for good works.***

The object of Christianity is not to sin less, but to glorify God more. It is not to somehow stop ourselves from doing the bad things we really want to do, but to find ourselves craving to do what pleases God.

➤ **3:2 — . . . *to speak evil of no one, to be peaceable, gentle, showing all humility to all men.***

The way of the cross is the way of potent tenderness. Jesus had all power, yet He came to serve, not to be served. Paul says that "in lowliness of mind" one should "esteem others better than himself" (Phil. 2:3).

➤ **3:8 — . . . *those who have believed in God should be careful to maintain good works . . . .***

"Good works" become bad only when we try to use them to earn the favor of God. In their proper place, however—as evidence of the salvation God provided us through grace—they remain crucial.

Avoid Dissension

➤ **9** But avoid foolish disputes, genealogies, contentions, and strivings about the law; for they are unprofitable and useless.
10 Reject a divisive man after the first and second admonition,
11 knowing that such a person is warped and sinning, being self-condemned.

Final Messages

12 When I send Artemas to you, or Tychicus, be diligent to come to me at Nicopolis, for I have decided to spend the winter there.
13 Send Zenas the lawyer and Apollos on their journey with haste, that they may lack nothing.
14 And let our *people* also learn to maintain good works, to *meet* urgent needs, that they may not be unfruitful.

Farewell

15 All who *are* with me greet you. Greet those who love us in the faith. Grace *be* with you all. Amen.

LIFE LESSONS

➤ **3:9 — *But avoid foolish disputes, genealogies, contentions, and strivings about the law; for they are unprofitable and useless.***

How do you know when a dispute, a discussion, an argument, or a fight becomes "foolish"? When God is in these things, even the interaction itself tends to reflect God's love and truth. When He isn't, it's just plain nasty.

THE EPISTLE OF PAUL THE APOSTLE TO

PHILEMON

Does Christian brotherly love really work, even in situations of extraordinary tension and difficulty? Will it work, for example, between a prominent slave owner and one of his runaway slaves?

Paul had no doubt.

The apostle writes a "postcard" to Philemon, his beloved brother and fellow worker, on behalf of Onesimus—a deserter, thief, and formerly worthless slave, but after his conversion in Rome, now Philemon's brother in Christ. With much tact and tenderness, Paul asks Philemon to receive Onesimus back with the same gentleness with which he would receive Paul himself. Ordinarily, a runaway slave would be treated harshly; but Paul carefully reminds Philemon that, in Christ, he is now a fellow heir to the grace of God. Any debt Onesimus owes, Paul promises to make good. Knowing Philemon well, Paul feels confident that brotherly love and forgiveness will carry the day.

Philemon was likely one of Paul's converts and had become a church worker. Onesimus had met Paul in Rome and became a Christian, so Paul writes to Philemon on Onesimus's behalf to ask Philemon to forgive and reinstate Onesimus.

Since this letter is addressed to Philemon in verse 1, it became known as *Pros Philemona*, "To Philemon." Like 1 and 2 Timothy and Titus, it is addressed to an individual; but unlike the Pastoral Epistles, Philemon is also addressed to a family and a church (vs. 2).

Themes: We are to forgive and restore, as Christ has forgiven and restored us.

Authors: The apostle Paul.

Time: Likely written from prison in Rome about A.D. 60–62.

Structure: Paul greets his old friend (1–3), gives thanks for him and describes his prayers for him (4–7), makes his plea for Onesimus (8–21), and closes his short letter (22–25).

As you read Philemon, watch for several life principles that play an important role in this book:

17. We stand tallest and strongest on our knees. *See Philemon 4, 5; page 1436.*

28. No Christian has ever been called to "go it alone" in his or her walk of faith. *See Philemon 7; page 1436.*

25. God blesses us so that we might bless others. *See Philemon 10–16; page 1436.*

Life Examples:

O N E S I M U S

Doing the Hard Thing

PHILEM. 13

By the grace of God, Onesimus, a runaway slave, crossed Paul's path and became a follower of Jesus Christ. Paul then urged him to return to his master, who "just happened" to be an old friend of Paul and a fellow believer.

Paul wrote to Philemon, the owner of Onesimus, that he really wished to keep the new convert with him, "that on your behalf he might minister to me in my chains for the gospel" (Philem. 13). Paul also mentions Onesimus in the book of Colossians: "Onesimus, a faithful and beloved brother, who is one of you" (4:9).

Although Onesimus stood condemned by Roman law because he had run away, he had become a close personal friend of Paul, ministering to his personal needs as a prisoner. No doubt Onesimus feared to return home—but he did so out of respect for Paul and love for God.

See the Life Principles Index for further study:
2. Obey God and leave all the consequences to Him.

Greeting
Paul, a prisoner of Christ Jesus, and Timothy
our brother,

To Philemon our beloved *friend* and fellow
laborer,
2 to the beloved[a] Apphia, Archippus our fellow soldier, and to the church in your house:
3 Grace to you and peace from God our Father and the Lord Jesus Christ.

Philemon's Love and Faith
4 I thank my God, making mention of you
always in my prayers,
5 hearing of your love and faith which you
have toward the Lord Jesus and toward all the
saints,
6 that the sharing of your faith may become
effective by the acknowledgment of every
good thing which is in you[a] in Christ Jesus.
7 For we have[a] great joy[b] and consolation in
your love, because the hearts of the saints
have been refreshed by you, brother.

The Plea for Onesimus
8 Therefore, though I might be very bold in
Christ to command you what is fitting,
9 *yet* for love's sake I rather appeal *to you*—
being such a one as Paul, the aged, and now
also a prisoner of Jesus Christ—
10 I appeal to you for my son Onesimus,
whom I have begotten *while* in my chains,
11 who once was unprofitable to you, but
now is profitable to you and to me.
12 I am sending him back.[a] You therefore receive him, that is, my own heart,
13 whom I wished to keep with me, that on
your behalf he might minister to me in my
chains for the gospel.
14 But without your consent I wanted to do
nothing, that your good deed might not be by
compulsion, as it were, but voluntary.
15 For perhaps he departed for a while for
this *purpose*, that you might receive him forever,
16 no longer as a slave but more than a
slave—a beloved brother, especially to me but
how much more to you, both in the flesh and
in the Lord.

Philemon's Obedience Encouraged
17 If then you count me as a partner, receive
him as *you would* me.

---

2 [a]NU-Text reads *to our sister Apphia.* **6** [a]NU-Text and M-Text read *us.* **7** [a]NU-Text reads *had.* [b]M-Text reads *thanksgiving.* **12** [a]NU-Text reads *back to you in person, that is, my own heart.*

LIFE LESSONS

➤ 6 — *. . . that the sharing of your faith may become effective by the acknowledgment of every good thing which is in you in Christ Jesus.*

Paul wants his friend Philemon to know that his testimony to outsiders about the glories of Jesus will become strong and powerful as he meditates on how much Christ has already done for him.

➤ 14 — *But without your consent I wanted to do nothing, that your good deed might not be by compulsion, as it were, but voluntary.*

God has the power to compel us to do anything He wants, but He does not normally choose to use that power. Why not? Because He wants willing and joyful hearts, not grudging and sour ones.

➤ 15 — *For perhaps he departed for a while for this purpose, that you might receive him forever . . . .*

Paul does not know why God allowed the slave, Onesimus, to run away from his Christian master—the escape probably caused some economic damage—but he conjectures an answer based on the grace of God.

18 But if he has wronged you or owes anything, put that on my account.
19 I, Paul, am writing with my own hand. I
will repay—not to mention to you that you
owe me even your own self besides.
➤ 20 Yes, brother, let me have joy from you in
the Lord; refresh my heart in the Lord.
21 Having confidence in your obedience, I
write to you, knowing that you will do even
more than I say.
22 But, meanwhile, also prepare a guest
room for me, for I trust that through your
prayers I shall be granted to you.

Farewell

23 Epaphras, my fellow prisoner in Christ Jesus, greets you,
24 *as do* Mark, Aristarchus, Demas, Luke, my
fellow laborers.
25 The grace of our Lord Jesus Christ *be* with
your spirit. Amen.

LIFE LESSONS

➤ 20 — *Yes, brother, let me have joy from you in the Lord; refresh my heart in the Lord.*

We have the power to give others "joy in the Lord." We have the ability to "refresh their heart" in Jesus. But we must choose to use this power. We can "let" ourselves do the gracious thing, or not.

THE EPISTLE TO THE

HEBREWS

Many Jewish believers who moved from Judaism into Christianity soon found themselves persecuted by their countrymen. Some of them wanted to reverse course in order to escape suffering for their identification with Christ. The writer of Hebrews responds by declaring, "let us hold fast our confession" (4:14) and exhorts his readers to "go on to perfection" (6:1).

The writer makes his appeal based on the superiority of Christ over the old Judaic system. Christ is better than the angels, for they worship Him. He is better than Moses, for He built the house in which Moses served. He is better than the Aaronic priesthood, for He ministers forever, and He once for all offered the infinitely valuable sacrifice of Himself. He is better than the law, for He mediates a better covenant. In short, there is far more to be gained by embracing Christ than might be lost by holding on to Judaism. Pressing on in Christ produces tested faith, self-discipline, visible love seen in good works, and divine rewards worth far more than the effort required to receive them.

The book reminds us of the best way to persevere in the faith: "looking unto Jesus, the author and finisher of our faith . . . . For consider Him who endured such hostility from sinners against Himself, lest you become weary and discouraged in your souls" (Heb. 12:2, 3).

No early manuscript evidence names the author in the title, although tradition assigns authorship to the apostle Paul. The oldest and most reliable title is simply, *Pros Ebraious*, "To the Hebrews."

Theme: Since Jesus Christ is superior in every way to the old covenant, it only makes sense to persevere in Him and so reap the amazing rewards God offers faithful believers.

Authors: Unknown. Some say that significant stylistic and thematic differences with the known letters of the apostle Paul make it unlikely that he wrote the book. Many scholars believe Luke, Barnabas, and Apollos are the leading candidates.

Date: Likely sometime before A.D. 70, since if the temple had been destroyed by the time of its writing, it seems the author would surely have noted this (see 8:3, 4).

Structure: The book has three primary sections. In the first section (chapters 1–10), Christ is portrayed as better than the elements of the old covenant. The second section (chapters 11, 12) features a plea for believers to persevere in their Christian faith. The final section (chapter 13) concludes the book and gives some final exhortations.

As you read Hebrews, watch for several life principles that play an important role in this book:

3. God's Word is an immovable anchor in times of storm. *See Hebrews 4:12, 13; pages 1442, 1443*

6. You reap what you sow, more than you sow, and later than you sow. *See Hebrews 6:12; 10:35; pages 1444, 1452.*

28. No Christian has ever been called to "go it alone" in his or her walk of faith. *See Hebrews 10:24, 25; page 1449.*

9. Trusting God means looking beyond what we can see to what God sees. *See Hebrews 11:8–16; pages 1452–1453.*

26. Adversity is a bridge to a deeper relationship with God. *See Hebrews 12:12–28; pages 1454–1455.*

God's Supreme Revelation

1 God, who at various times and in various
ways spoke in time past to the fathers by
the prophets,
2 has in these last days spoken to us by
His Son, whom He has appointed heir of all
things, through whom also He made the
worlds;
➤ 3 who being the brightness of *His* glory and
the express image of His person, and upholding
all things by the word of His power, when
He had by Himself[a] purged our[b] sins, sat
down at the right hand of the Majesty on high,
4 having become so much better than the
angels, as He has by inheritance obtained a
more excellent name than they.

The Son Exalted Above Angels

5 For to which of the angels did He ever say:

"You are My Son,
Today I have begotten You"?[a]

And again:

"I will be to Him a Father,
And He shall be to Me a Son"?[b]

6 But when He again brings the firstborn
into the world, He says:

"Let all the angels of God worship Him."[a]

7 And of the angels He says:

"Who makes His angels spirits
And His ministers a flame of fire."[a]

➤ 8 But to the Son *He says:*

"Your throne, O God, is forever and ever;
A scepter of righteousness is the scepter
of Your kingdom.
9 *You have loved righteousness and hated*
lawlessness;
Therefore God, Your God, has anointed
You
With the oil of gladness more than Your
companions."[a]

10 And:

"You, LORD, in the beginning laid the
foundation of the earth,
And the heavens are the work of Your
hands.
11 *They will perish, but You remain;*
And they will all grow old like a
garment;
12 *Like a cloak You will fold them up,*
And they will be changed.
But You are the same,
And Your years will not fail."[a]

13 But to which of the angels has He ever
said:

"Sit at My right hand,
Till I make Your enemies Your
footstool"?[a]

14 Are they not all ministering spirits sent ➤
forth to minister for those who will inherit
salvation?

Do Not Neglect Salvation

2 Therefore we must give the more earnest
heed to the things we have heard, lest we
drift away.
2 For if the word spoken through angels
proved steadfast, and every transgression and
disobedience received a just reward,
3 how shall we escape if we neglect so great ➤
a salvation, which at the first began to be spoken
by the Lord, and was confirmed to us by
those who heard *Him,*
4 God also bearing witness both with signs
and wonders, with various miracles, and gifts
of the Holy Spirit, according to His own will?

The Son Made Lower than Angels

5 For He has not put the world to come, of
which we speak, in subjection to angels.
6 But one testified in a certain place, saying:

1:3 [a]NU-Text omits *by Himself.* [b]NU-Text omits *our.*
1:5 [a]Psalm 2:7 [b]2 Samuel 7:14 **1:6** [a]Deuteronomy 32:43 (Septuagint, Dead Sea Scrolls); Psalm 97:7 **1:7** [a]Psalm 104:4
1:9 [a]Psalm 45:6, 7 **1:12** [a]Psalm 102:25–27 **1:13** [a]Psalm 110:1

LIFE LESSONS

➤ **1:3 — *. . . who being the brightness of His glory and the express image of His person . . . .***

When we hear Jesus we hear God. When we observe Jesus we observe God. If we ever want to know what God is like or how He might act or where He might go, all we have to do is watch Jesus.

➤ **1:8 — *But to the Son He says: "Your throne, O God, is forever and ever; a scepter of righteousness is the scepter of Your Kingdom."***

Repeatedly the Book of Hebrews tells us that Jesus is God in the flesh. Jesus is to be worshiped as God, praised as the Creator, recognized as Ruler, and glorified as God's only Son.

➤ **1:14 — *Are they not all ministering spirits sent forth to minister for those who will inherit salvation?***

We may not see most of their activity, but God has given His angels the job of "ministering" to us. We may never know how often an angel spared us from injury, guided us to safety, or engineered some success.

➤ **2:3 — *. . . how shall we escape if we neglect so great a salvation . . . ?***

The writer does not worry in this verse that we might "reject" or "disdain" the salvation Christ won for us, but that we might do ourselves harm by "neglecting" it. We are to meditate on what God has accomplished for us.

"What is man that You are mindful of
him,
Or the son of man that You take care of
him?
7 *You have made him a little lower than*
the angels;
You have crowned him with glory and
honor,[a]
And set him over the works of Your
hands.
8 *You have put all things in subjection*
under his feet."[a]

For in that He put all in subjection under him, He left nothing *that is* not put under him. But now we do not yet see all things put under him.
9 But we see Jesus, who was made a little lower than the angels, for the suffering of death crowned with glory and honor, that He, by the grace of God, might taste death for everyone.

Bringing Many Sons to Glory

10 For it was fitting for Him, for whom *are* all things and by whom *are* all things, in bringing many sons to glory, to make the captain of their salvation perfect through sufferings.
11 For both He who sanctifies and those who are being sanctified *are* all of one, for which reason He is not ashamed to call them brethren,
12 saying:

"I will declare Your name to My brethren;
In the midst of the assembly I will sing
praise to You."[a]

13 And again:

"I will put My trust in Him."[a]

And again:

"Here am I and the children whom God
has given Me."[b]

14 Inasmuch then as the children have partaken of flesh and blood, He Himself likewise shared in the same, that through death He might destroy him who had the power of death, that is, the devil,
15 and release those who through fear of death were all their lifetime subject to bondage.
16 For indeed He does not give aid to angels, but He does give aid to the seed of Abraham.
17 Therefore, in all things He had to be made like *His* brethren, that He might be a merciful and faithful High Priest in things *pertaining* to God, to make propitiation for the sins of the people.
18 For in that He Himself has suffered, being tempted, He is able to aid those who are tempted.

The Son Was Faithful

3 Therefore, holy brethren, partakers of the heavenly calling, consider the Apostle and High Priest of our confession, Christ Jesus,
2 who was faithful to Him who appointed Him, as Moses also *was faithful* in all His house.
3 For this One has been counted worthy of more glory than Moses, inasmuch as He who built the house has more honor than the house.
4 For every house is built by someone, but He who built all things *is* God.
5 And Moses indeed *was* faithful in all His house as a servant, for a testimony of those things which would be spoken *afterward,*
6 but Christ as a Son over His own house, whose house we are if we hold fast the confidence and the rejoicing of the hope firm to the end.[a]

2:7 [a]NU-Text and M-Text omit the rest of verse 7.
2:8 [a]Psalm 8:4–6 **2:12** [a]Psalm 22:22 **2:13** [a]2 Samuel 22:3; Isaiah 8:17 [b]Isaiah 8:18 **3:6** [a]NU-Text omits *firm to the end.*

LIFE LESSONS

➤ ***2:14 — . . . that through death He might destroy him who had the power of death, that is, the devil . . . .***

The Bible gives many reasons for Christ's coming to earth. One of them was to defeat Satan and forever take away his weapon of death, so that God's people might say goodbye to fear and hello to life.

➤ ***2:17 — Therefore, in all things He had to be made like His brethren, that He might be a merciful and faithful High Priest . . . .***

Jesus had to leave heaven and take on human flesh, not only to become our sacrifice, but also so He would know experientially exactly what it's like to be one of us. That's what makes Him a great advocate.

➤ ***2:18 — For in that He Himself has suffered, being tempted, He is able to aid those who are tempted.***

Jesus knows what it feels like to be tempted. We can never say to Him, "You don't know what it's like," because He does. In fact, we know less of the pain of temptation than He does, since He never gave in to it.

➤ ***3:3 — For this One has been counted worthy of more glory than Moses, inasmuch as He who built the house has more honor than the house.***

The writer here claims that Jesus existed before Moses, much as Jesus claimed to have existed before Abraham (John 8:58). Long before His birth at Bethlehem, Jesus existed as the Creator God.

➤ ***3:6 — . . . Christ as a Son over His own house, whose house we are if we hold fast the confidence and the rejoicing of the hope firm to the end.***

Those who truly accept Jesus Christ as Savior and Lord will persevere in their faith until the end. One of the hallmarks of a genuine relationship with God is the commitment to stick with Him through everything.

WHAT THE BIBLE SAYS ABOUT YOUR IDENTITY IN CHRIST

Heb. 3:1

Hebrews 3:1 tells us, "Therefore, holy brethren, partakers of a heavenly calling, consider the Apostle and High Priest of our confession Christ Jesus." This single verse overflows with assurance for the believer.

First, note that it's addressed to the "holy brethren." This refers to anyone who has trusted Jesus Christ as Lord and Savior. The word *holy* signifies that believers have been set apart for God. Because of who you are in Christ, God sees you as unique. Neither your profession, your salary, your appearance, or your nationality defines you. Only your status as a child of God gives you the special identity you enjoy.

As one of the "partakers of a heavenly calling," your destination is heaven. Your heart resides with Christ, where your home is. Knowing where your home is means you aren't searching for this temporary dwelling—earth—to satisfy you. Regardless of what happens around you, you can rejoice, because this life does not hold you; God does.

Your heart resides with Christ, where your home is.

By knowing who you are in Christ, you can deny all the false messages of the world. Many strident voices will try to convince you that you're not pretty enough, not smart enough, and not successful enough. But your identity in Christ alone completes you! You can add nothing to it, and this world's detractors can take nothing from it.

The final phrase of Hebrews 3:1 reminds us that Jesus is our "Apostle" and "High Priest." The first title signifies that Jesus represents God to us. When we want to know what God is like or how God would act in a given situation, we look to Jesus. The second title signifies that Jesus represents us to God. God looks at His children through the eyes of His blameless and holy Son.

The command in this verse tells believers to "consider Christ Jesus." The word "consider" means to observe or think. We are to observe Christ, meditate on His Word, and imitate what we see.

Let the assurance of your identity, home, and Lord inspire you to explore new depths of God and serve Him with all your heart. You won't be disappointed!

See the Life Principles Index for further study:

12. Peace with God is the fruit of oneness with God.

20. Disappointments are inevitable; discouragement is a choice.

Be Faithful

7 Therefore, as the Holy Spirit says:

"Today, if you will hear His voice,
8 *Do not harden your hearts as in the rebellion,*
In the day of trial in the wilderness,
9 *Where your fathers tested Me, tried Me,*
And saw My works forty years.
10 *Therefore I was angry with that generation,*
And said, 'They always go astray in their heart,
And they have not known My ways.'
11 *So I swore in My wrath,*
'They shall not enter My rest.'"[a]

12 Beware, brethren, lest there be in any of you an evil heart of unbelief in departing from the living God;
➤ 13 but exhort one another daily, while it is called *"Today,"* lest any of you be hardened through the deceitfulness of sin.
14 For we have become partakers of Christ if we hold the beginning of our confidence steadfast to the end,
15 while it is said:

"Today, if you will hear His voice,
Do not harden your hearts as in the rebellion."[a]

Failure of the Wilderness Wanderers

16 For who, having heard, rebelled? Indeed, *was it* not all who came out of Egypt, *led* by Moses?
17 Now with whom was He angry forty years? *Was it* not with those who sinned, whose corpses fell in the wilderness?
➤ 18 And to whom did He swear that they would not enter His rest, but to those who did not obey?
19 So we see that they could not enter in because of unbelief.

The Promise of Rest

4 Therefore, since a promise remains of entering His rest, let us fear lest any of you seem to have come short of it.
2 For indeed the gospel was preached to us
as well as to them; but the word which they heard did not profit them,[a] not being mixed with faith in those who heard *it.*
3 For we who have believed do enter that rest, as He has said:

"So I swore in My wrath,
'They shall not enter My rest,'"[a]

although the works were finished from the foundation of the world.
4 For He has spoken in a certain place of the seventh *day* in this way: *"And God rested on the seventh day from all His works"*;[a]
5 and again in this *place: "They shall not enter My rest."*[a]
6 Since therefore it remains that some *must* enter it, and those to whom it was first preached did not enter because of disobedience,
7 again He designates a certain day, saying in David, *"Today,"* after such a long time, as it has been said:

"Today, if you will hear His voice,
Do not harden your hearts."[a]

8 For if Joshua had given them rest, then He would not afterward have spoken of another day.
9 There remains therefore a rest for the people of God. ✳
10 For he who has entered His rest has himself also ceased from his works as God *did* from His.

The Word Discovers Our Condition

11 Let us therefore be diligent to enter that rest, lest anyone fall according to the same example of disobedience.
12 For the word of God *is* living and powerful, and sharper than any two-edged sword, piercing even to the division of soul and spirit, and of joints and marrow, and is a discerner of the thoughts and intents of the heart. ➤

3:11 [a]Psalm 95:7–11 **3:15** [a]Psalm 95:7, 8 **4:2** [a]NU-Text and M-Text read *profit them, since they were not united by faith with those who heeded it.* **4:3** [a]Psalm 95:11 **4:4** [a]Genesis 2:2 **4:5** [a]Psalm 95:11 **4:7** [a]Psalm 95:7, 8

LIFE LESSONS

➤ 3:13 — *. . . exhort one another daily, while it is called "Today," lest any of you be hardened through the deceitfulness of sin.*

None of us can progress in our faith or stay true to our Lord without the help and encouragement of fellow believers. In fact, we need this kind of healthy interaction every day, not merely one day out of seven.

➤ 3:18, 19 — *And to whom did He swear that they would not enter His rest, but to those who did not obey? So we see that they could not enter in because of unbelief.*

There is a direct and clear connection between unbelief and disobedience. When we disobey, it is always because we do not believe either God's promises of blessing or His warnings against rebellion.

➤ 4:12 — *For the word of God is living and powerful, and sharper than any two-edged sword . . . and is a discerner of the thoughts and intents of the heart.*

The Bible is not dead but living. It lives both because God brought it into existence and because the Spirit of God brings its message to life in our hearts. It has God's power to provoke change in our lives.

13 And there is no creature hidden from
His sight, but all things *are* naked and open to
the eyes of Him to whom we *must give* account.

Our Compassionate High Priest

14 Seeing then that we have a great High
Priest who has passed through the heavens,
Jesus the Son of God, let us hold fast *our* confession.
➤ 15 For we do not have a High Priest who cannot sympathize with our weaknesses, but was
in all *points* tempted as *we are, yet* without
sin.
➤ 16 Let us therefore come boldly to the throne
of grace, that we may obtain mercy and find
grace to help in time of need.

Qualifications for High Priesthood

5 For every high priest taken from among
men is appointed for men in things *pertaining* to God, that he may offer both gifts
and sacrifices for sins.
2 He can have compassion on those who are
ignorant and going astray, since he himself is
also subject to weakness.
3 Because of this he is required as for the
people, so also for himself, to offer *sacrifices*
for sins.
4 And no man takes this honor to himself,
but he who is called by God, just as Aaron
was.

A Priest Forever

5 So also Christ did not glorify Himself to
become High Priest, but *it was* He who said to
Him:

"You are My Son,
Today I have begotten You."[a]

6 As *He* also says in another *place:*

"You are a priest forever
According to the order of Melchizedek";[a]

7 who, in the days of His flesh, when He had ➤
offered up prayers and supplications, with vehement cries and tears to Him who was able
to save Him from death, and was heard because of His godly fear,
8 though He was a Son, *yet* He learned obe- ➤
dience by the things which He suffered.
9 And having been perfected, He became ➤
the author of eternal salvation to all who obey
Him,
10 called by God as High Priest *"according to
the order of Melchizedek,"*
11 of whom we have much to say, and hard to
explain, since you have become dull of hearing.

Spiritual Immaturity

12 For though by this time you ought to be
teachers, you need *someone* to teach you
again the first principles of the oracles of
God; and you have come to need milk and not
solid food.
13 For everyone who partakes *only* of milk *is*
unskilled in the word of righteousness, for he
is a babe.
14 But solid food belongs to those who are of ➤
full age, *that is,* those who by reason of use

5:5 [a]Psalm 2:7 5:6 [a]Psalm 110:4

LIFE LESSONS

➤ 4:15 — *For we do not have a High Priest who cannot sympathize with our weaknesses, but was in all points tempted as we are, yet without sin.*

Because Jesus knows what it feels like to be tempted, He is sympathetic toward us—that is, He does not feel annoyed at our failures or exasperated with our struggles. He knows just how to move us on to maturity.

➤ 4:16 — *Let us therefore come boldly to the throne of grace, that we may obtain mercy and find grace to help in time of need.*

God wants us to come "boldly" into His presence, not timidly or anxiously or in fear of how He might respond. He wants to help us, and He has all the grace we need to confront any challenge we might face.

➤ 5:7 — *. . . when He had offered up prayers and supplications, with vehement cries and tears to Him who was able to save Him from death, and was heard . . . .*

This verse immediately recalls Jesus' petition in the Garden of Gethsemane that God might find a way to spare Him the "cup" of crucifixion. God did not spare Him that bitter cup—and yet God heard Him.

➤ 5:8 — *. . . though He was a Son, yet He learned obedience by the things which He suffered.*

Jesus had to learn obedience, just as we do. What teacher did God use? Suffering—just as He does with us. God intends to use our suffering to teach us the value and the power of obedience.

➤ 5:9 — *And having been perfected, He became the author of eternal salvation to all who obey Him . . . .*

Does our obedience gain us a Savior? No. *Nothing* we do can ever earn our salvation. And yet, all those who truly believe *will* obey. If we habitually disobey Him, we should re-examine our connection to Him.

➤ 5:14 — *But solid food belongs to those who are of full age, that is, those who by reason of use have their senses exercised to discern both good and evil.*

Spiritual maturity comes not merely by hearing God's Word, but by making it a habit to put it into practice. Only "by reason of use" do we become proficient at discerning good and evil.

have their senses exercised to discern both
good and evil.

The Peril of Not Progressing

6 Therefore, leaving the discussion of the
elementary *principles* of Christ, let us go
on to perfection, not laying again the foundation of repentance from dead works and of
faith toward God,
2 of the doctrine of baptisms, of laying on of
hands, of resurrection of the dead, and of
eternal judgment.
3 And this we will[a] do if God permits.
4 For *it is* impossible for those who were
once enlightened, and have tasted the heavenly gift, and have become partakers of the
Holy Spirit,
5 and have tasted the good word of God and
the powers of the age to come,
6 if they fall away,[a] to renew them again to
repentance, since they crucify again for themselves the Son of God, and put *Him* to an open
shame.
7 For the earth which drinks in the rain that
often comes upon it, and bears herbs useful
for those by whom it is cultivated, receives
blessing from God;
8 but if it bears thorns and briers, *it is* rejected and near to being cursed, whose end *is*
to be burned.

A Better Estimate

9 But, beloved, we are confident of better
things concerning you, yes, things that
accompany salvation, though we speak in this
manner.
✳ 10 For God *is* not unjust to forget your work
and labor of[a] love which you have shown toward His name, *in that* you have ministered
to the saints, and do minister.
11 And we desire that each one of you show
the same diligence to the full assurance of
hope until the end,
➤ 12 that you do not become sluggish, but imitate those who through faith and patience inherit the promises.

God's Infallible Purpose in Christ

13 For when God made a promise to Abraham, because He could swear by no one
greater, He swore by Himself,
14 saying, *"Surely blessing I will bless you,
and multiplying I will multiply you."*[a]
15 And so, after he had patiently endured, he
obtained the promise.
16 For men indeed swear by the greater, and
an oath for confirmation *is* for them an end of
all dispute.
17 Thus God, determining to show more
abundantly to the heirs of promise the immutability of His counsel, confirmed *it* by an
oath,
18 that by two immutable things, in which it
is impossible for God to lie, we might[a] have
strong consolation, who have fled for refuge
to lay hold of the hope set before *us*.
19 This *hope* we have as an anchor of the ➤
soul, both sure and steadfast, and which enters the *Presence* behind the veil,
20 where the forerunner has entered for us,
even Jesus, having become High Priest forever according to the order of Melchizedek.

The King of Righteousness

7 For this Melchizedek, king of Salem,
priest of the Most High God, who met
Abraham returning from the slaughter of the
kings and blessed him,
2 to whom also Abraham gave a tenth part
of all, first being translated "king of righteousness," and then also king of Salem,
meaning "king of peace,"
3 without father, without mother, without
genealogy, having neither beginning of days
nor end of life, but made like the Son of God,
remains a priest continually.
4 Now consider how great this man *was*, to
whom even the patriarch Abraham gave a
tenth of the spoils.
5 And indeed those who are of the sons of
Levi, who receive the priesthood, have a commandment to receive tithes from the people
according to the law, that is, from their
brethren, though they have come from the
loins of Abraham;
6 but he whose genealogy is not derived
from them received tithes from Abraham and
blessed him who had the promises.
7 Now beyond all contradiction the lesser is
blessed by the better.
8 Here mortal men receive tithes, but there

6:3 [a]M-Text reads *let us do.* **6:6** [a]Or *and have fallen away*
6:10 [a]NU-Text omits *labor of.* **6:14** [a]Genesis 22:17
6:18 [a]M-Text omits *might.*

LIFE LESSONS

➤ 6:12 — *. . . do not become sluggish, but imitate those who through faith and patience inherit the promises.*

Everyone wants to enjoy the blessings of God's promises, but not everyone will. Lazy believers who exercise neither their faith nor their patience should expect to receive few to none of the benefits of God's promises.

➤ 6:19 — *This hope we have as an anchor of the soul, both sure and steadfast, and which enters the Presence . . . .*

Our hope in Christ gives us a firm and rock-solid confidence that nothing life throws at us can ultimately move us. This hope reaches to the very throne of God Himself to bring us comfort and assurance.

ANSWERS TO LIFE'S QUESTIONS

How can I be the kind of faithful person God honors?

Do you want to see the favor of God blossom in your life? If you do, the writer of Hebrews has some advice for you: "show the same diligence to the full assurance of hope until the end, that you do not become sluggish, but imitate those who faith and patience inherit the promises" (Heb. 6:11, 12).

The writer has in mind someone like the Old Testament saint Abraham, who displayed great faith and patience. Remember when God called Abraham to leave his homeland for a place unknown? Genesis 12:4 displays Abraham's (Abram's) diligence: "So Abram went forth as the LORD had spoken to him."

Remember when God told Abraham that he would have a son, even though his wife Sarah was already 90 years old? (Gen. 17:17–19). God displayed His faithfulness a year later by giving Isaac to Abraham and Sarah.

Remember when Abraham heard God tell him to sacrifice the son for whom he had waited 100 years? Abraham faithfully obeyed God—and was blessed for his devotion (Gen. 22:1–18).

We are to mirror Abraham's faithfulness. In our attempts to pursue God with diligence, we need to take stock of *everything* we do:

- *Set clear goals.* Olympic athletes don't begin with a vague notion of becoming an Olympian. Each step of the way requires them to work for a faster time, a higher jump, or an improved technique.
- *Be patient.* When Pablo Casals reached age 95, a young reporter asked him, "Mr. Casals, you are 95 and the greatest cellist that ever lived. Why do you still practice six hours a day?" Casals answered, "Because I think I'm making progress."
- *Be willing to take risks.* God asks that we trust Him despite our limited understanding. As the saying goes, a turtle makes progress only when he sticks his neck out.
- *Be persistent.* If God has given you a clearly defined goal and you sincerely believe it to be His will, don't let doubt or discouragement defeat you. Keep at it and don't give up.
- *Be flexible.* Remember that the process is the greatest learning experience we have. Learn from your mistakes and move on. Flexibility enables you to change as God changes you.

If you want God to honor you, then be the kind of person who honors Him by consistently acting on your faith.

See the Life Principles Index for further study:
21. Obedience always brings blessing.
9. Trusting God means looking beyond what we can see to what God sees.

he *receives them,* of whom it is witnessed that he lives.
9 Even Levi, who receives tithes, paid tithes through Abraham, so to speak,
10 for he was still in the loins of his father when Melchizedek met him.

Need for a New Priesthood

11 Therefore, if perfection were through the Levitical priesthood (for under it the people received the law), what further need *was there* that another priest should rise according to the order of Melchizedek, and not be called according to the order of Aaron?
12 For the priesthood being changed, of necessity there is also a change of the law.
13 For He of whom these things are spoken belongs to another tribe, from which no man has officiated at the altar.
14 For *it is* evident that our Lord arose from Judah, of which tribe Moses spoke nothing concerning priesthood.[a]
15 And it is yet far more evident if, in the likeness of Melchizedek, there arises another priest
16 who has come, not according to the law of a fleshly commandment, but according to the power of an endless life.
17 For He testifies:[a]

"You are a priest forever
According to the order of Melchizedek."[b]

18 For on the one hand there is an annulling of the former commandment because of its weakness and unprofitableness,

7:14 [a]NU-Text reads *priests.* **7:17** [a]NU-Text reads *it is testified.* [b]Psalm 110:4

➤ 19 for the law made nothing perfect; on the
other hand, *there is the* bringing in of a better
hope, through which we draw near to God.

Greatness of the New Priest

20 And inasmuch as *He was* not *made priest*
without an oath
➤ 21 (for they have become priests without an
oath, but He with an oath by Him who said to
Him:

> *"The LORD has sworn*
> *And will not relent,*
> *'You are a priest forever*[a]
> *According to the order of*
> *Melchizedek'"*),[b]

22 by so much more Jesus has become a
surety of a better covenant.
23 Also there were many priests, because they
were prevented by death from continuing.
24 But He, because He continues forever, has
an unchangeable priesthood.
✳ 25 Therefore He is also able to save to the uttermost those who come to God through Him,
since He always lives to make intercession for
them.
➤ 26 For such a High Priest was fitting for
us, *who is* holy, harmless, undefiled, separate from sinners, and has become higher
than the heavens;
27 who does not need daily, as those high
priests, to offer up sacrifices, first for His own
sins and then for the people's, for this He did
once for all when He offered up Himself.
28 For the law appoints as high priests men
who have weakness, but the word of the oath,
which came after the law, *appoints* the Son
who has been perfected forever.

The New Priestly Service

➤ **8** Now *this is* the main point of the things
we are saying: We have such a High Priest,
who is seated at the right hand of the throne
of the Majesty in the heavens,
2 a Minister of the sanctuary and of the true
tabernacle which the Lord erected, and not
man.
3 For every high priest is appointed to offer
both gifts and sacrifices. Therefore *it is* necessary that this One also have something to
offer.
4 For if He were on earth, He would not be a
priest, since there are priests who offer the
gifts according to the law;
5 who serve the copy and shadow of the
heavenly things, as Moses was divinely instructed when he was about to make the tabernacle. For He said, *"See that you make all*
things according to the pattern shown you on
the mountain."[a]
6 But now He has obtained a more excellent ➤
ministry, inasmuch as He is also Mediator of
a better covenant, which was established on
better promises.

A New Covenant

7 For if that first *covenant* had been faultless, then no place would have been sought
for a second.
8 Because finding fault with them, He says:
"Behold, the days are coming, says the LORD,
when I will make a new covenant with the
house of Israel and with the house of Judah—
9 *"not according to the covenant that I*
made with their fathers in the day when I
took them by the hand to lead them out of the
land of Egypt; because they did not continue
in My covenant, and I disregarded them, says
the LORD.
10 *"For this is the covenant that I will make*
with the house of Israel after those days, says

7:21 [a]NU-Text ends the quotation here. [b]Psalm 110:4
8:5 [a]Exodus 25:40

LIFE LESSONS

➤ 7:19 — *. . . the law made nothing perfect; on the other hand, there is the bringing in of a better hope, through which we draw near to God.*

The law can show us God's righteous demands, but it has no power to help us comply with those demands. Our "better hope" of salvation through faith in Christ, however, enables us to please God and grow close to Him.

➤ 7:21 — *"The LORD has sworn and will not relent, 'You are a priest forever according to the order of Melchizedek.'"*

The priesthood of Jesus supersedes that of Aaron's line for several reasons: (1) it has a longer history, dating to Abraham's day; (2) it boasts a greater heritage, since even Abraham paid it homage; (3) it lasts forever.

➤ 7:26 — *For such a High Priest was fitting for us, who is holy, harmless, undefiled, separate from sinners, and has become higher than the heavens . . . .*

As our perfect High Priest, Jesus knows exactly how to minister to us in the way that will most benefit us and that will best bring us to maturity in Him. He makes no mistakes and always has our best interests at heart.

➤ 8:1 — *We have such a High Priest, who is seated at the right hand of the throne of the Majesty in the heavens . . . .*

To be seated at "the right hand of the throne of the Majesty in the heavens" is to occupy the most influential seat anywhere. Jesus intercedes for us with His Father as our Friend, Savior, Lord, Brother, and fellow heir.

➤ 8:6 — *But now He has obtained a more excellent ministry, inasmuch as He is also Mediator of a better covenant, which was established on better promises.*

The Old Covenant depended upon divine words written in stone; in the New Covenant, God writes His thoughts upon the hearts of His redeemed children through the ministry of Christ's living Spirit.

the LORD: I will put My laws in their mind and
write them on their hearts; and I will be their
God, and they shall be My people.
11 *"None of them shall teach his neighbor,*
and none his brother, saying, 'Know the
LORD,' for all shall know Me, from the least of
them to the greatest of them.
12 *"For I will be merciful to their unright-*
eousness, and their sins and their lawless
deeds[a] *I will remember no more."*[b]
➤ 13 In that He says, *"A new covenant,"* He has
made the first obsolete. Now what is becoming obsolete and growing old is ready to vanish away.

The Earthly Sanctuary

9 Then indeed, even the first *covenant* had
ordinances of divine service and the
earthly sanctuary.
2 For a tabernacle was prepared: the first
part, in which *was* the lampstand, the table,
and the showbread, which is called the sanctuary;
3 and behind the second veil, the part of the
tabernacle which is called the Holiest of All,
4 which had the golden censer and the ark
of the covenant overlaid on all sides with
gold, in which *were* the golden pot that had
the manna, Aaron's rod that budded, and the
tablets of the covenant;
5 and above it were the cherubim of glory
overshadowing the mercy seat. Of these
things we cannot now speak in detail.

Limitations of the Earthly Service

6 Now when these things had been thus prepared, the priests always went into the first
part of the tabernacle, performing the services.
7 But into the second part the high priest
went alone once a year, not without blood,
which he offered for himself and *for* the people's sins *committed* in ignorance;
8 the Holy Spirit indicating this, that the
way into the Holiest of All was not yet made
manifest while the first tabernacle was still
standing.
9 It *was* symbolic for the present time in
which both gifts and sacrifices are offered
which cannot make him who performed the
service perfect in regard to the conscience—
10 *concerned* only with foods and drinks,
various washings, and fleshly ordinances imposed until the time of reformation.

The Heavenly Sanctuary

11 But Christ came *as* High Priest of the good
things to come,[a] with the greater and more
perfect tabernacle not made with hands, that
is, not of this creation.
12 Not with the blood of goats and calves, but
with His own blood He entered the Most Holy
Place once for all, having obtained eternal redemption.
13 For if the blood of bulls and goats and the
ashes of a heifer, sprinkling the unclean, sanctifies for the purifying of the flesh,
14 how much more shall the blood of Christ, ➤
who through the eternal Spirit offered Himself without spot to God, cleanse your conscience from dead works to serve the living
God?
15 And for this reason He is the Mediator of
the new covenant, by means of death, for the
redemption of the transgressions under the
first covenant, that those who are called may
receive the promise of the eternal inheritance.

The Mediator's Death Necessary

16 For where there *is* a testament, there must
also of necessity be the death of the testator.
17 For a testament *is* in force after men are
dead, since it has no power at all while the
testator lives.
18 Therefore not even the first *covenant* was
dedicated without blood.
19 For when Moses had spoken every precept
to all the people according to the law, he took
the blood of calves and goats, with water,
scarlet wool, and hyssop, and sprinkled both
the book itself and all the people,
20 saying, *"This is the blood of the covenant*
which God has commanded you."[a]
21 Then likewise he sprinkled with blood
both the tabernacle and all the vessels of the
ministry.
22 And according to the law almost all things
are purified with blood, and without shedding
of blood there is no remission.

8:12 [a]NU-Text omits *and their lawless deeds.* [b]Jeremiah 31:31–34 **9:11** [a]NU-Text reads *that have come.* **9:20** [a]Exodus 24:8

LIFE LESSONS

➤ 8:13 — *In that He says, "A new covenant," He has made the first obsolete. Now what is becoming obsolete and growing old is ready to vanish away.*

At the time Hebrews was written, the Jerusalem temple apparently still existed. In A.D. 70, however, the Romans destroyed Jerusalem and the temple, and the old system in fact "vanished away."

➤ 9:14 — *. . . how much more shall the blood of Christ, who through the eternal Spirit offered Himself without spot to God, cleanse your conscience from dead works to serve the living God?*

None of us have to live with unresolved guilt. Jesus wants to take our accusing consciences and wipe them clean with His blood, enabling us to serve Him with joy and without the slightest bit of shame.

Greatness of Christ's Sacrifice
23 Therefore *it was* necessary that the copies
of the things in the heavens should be purified with these, but the heavenly things themselves with better sacrifices than these.
24 For Christ has not entered the holy places
made with hands, *which are* copies of the
true, but into heaven itself, now to appear in
the presence of God for us;
25 not that He should offer Himself often, as
the high priest enters the Most Holy Place
every year with blood of another—
➤ 26 He then would have had to suffer often
since the foundation of the world; but now,
once at the end of the ages, He has appeared
to put away sin by the sacrifice of Himself.
➤ 27 And as it is appointed for men to die once,
but after this the judgment,
✳ 28 so Christ was offered once to bear the sins
of many. To those who eagerly wait for Him
He will appear a second time, apart from sin,
for salvation.

Animal Sacrifices Insufficient
10 For the law, having a shadow of the
good things to come, *and* not the very
image of the things, can never with these
same sacrifices, which they offer continually
year by year, make those who approach perfect.
2 For then would they not have ceased to
be offered? For the worshipers, once purified, would have had no more consciousness
of sins.
3 But in those *sacrifices there is* a reminder
of sins every year.
➤ 4 For *it is* not possible that the blood of bulls
and goats could take away sins.

Christ's Death Fulfills God's Will
5 Therefore, when He came into the world,
He said:

"Sacrifice and offering You did not desire,
But a body You have prepared for Me.
6 *In burnt offerings and sacrifices for sin*
You had no pleasure.
7 *Then I said, 'Behold, I have come—*
In the volume of the book it is written of
Me—
To do Your will, O God.'"[a]
8 Previously saying, *"Sacrifice and offering,*
burnt offerings, and offerings for sin You did
not desire, nor had pleasure in them" (which
are offered according to the law),
9 then He said, *"Behold, I have come to do*
Your will, O God."[a] He takes away the first
that He may establish the second.
10 By that will we have been sanctified
through the offering of the body of Jesus
Christ once *for all.*

Christ's Death Perfects the Sanctified
11 And every priest stands ministering daily
and offering repeatedly the same sacrifices,
which can never take away sins.
12 But this Man, after He had offered one
sacrifice for sins forever, sat down at the right
hand of God,
13 from that time waiting till His enemies are
made His footstool.
14 For by one offering He has perfected for- ➤
ever those who are being sanctified.
15 But the Holy Spirit also witnesses to us;
for after He had said before,
16 *"This is the covenant that I will make with*
them after those days, says the LORD: *I will*
put My laws into their hearts, and in their
minds I will write them,"[a]
17 *then He adds, "Their sins and their law-*
less deeds I will remember no more."[a]
18 Now where there is remission of these,
there is no longer an offering for sin.

Hold Fast Your Confession
19 Therefore, brethren, having boldness to
enter the Holiest by the blood of Jesus,
20 by a new and living way which He consecrated for us, through the veil, that is, His flesh,
21 and *having* a High Priest over the house of
God,

10:7 [a]Psalm 40:6–8 **10:9** [a]NU-Text and M-Text omit *O God.*
10:16 [a]Jeremiah 31:33 **10:17** [a]Jeremiah 31:34

LIFE LESSONS

➤ **9:26 — *. . . but now, once at the end of the ages, He has appeared to put away sin by the sacrifice of Himself.***

As God in the flesh, Jesus presented God with a sacrifice both infinite in value and eternal in duration. Jesus' purity made His sacrifice valid, and His divine nature made it sufficient for all who believe.

➤ **9:27 — *. . . it is appointed for men to die once, but after this the judgment . . . .***

Few can avoid death and taxes, but none of us can avoid death and judgment. Unless we're alive when the Lord returns, all of us will die; and every person in history will answer to God for how they lived.

➤ **10:4 — *For it is not possible that the blood of bulls and goats could take away sins.***

The shed blood of animals provided only a temporary "covering" of human sin; it could never fully and finally pay the penalty for that sin. Only the blood of the God-Man, Jesus Christ, has the power to take away sin.

➤ **10:14 — *For by one offering He has perfected forever those who are being sanctified.***

Our salvation is both a finished project and an ongoing process. Through faith in Jesus, God made us right with Him; and by the power of His Spirit, He enables us to become more like the Jesus whose righteousness we received.

ANSWERS TO LIFE'S QUESTIONS

How can I claim God's promises?

HEB. 10:23

By some counts, God has issued more than 40 thousand promises in the Bible. That's *a lot* of promises! But sometimes it can be difficult to determine how to properly respond to God's awesome assurances.

The first thing to keep in mind is that the Bible contains two kinds of divine promises.

❶ ***Limited promises***

God has made many promises to specific people living in particular circumstances for explicit purposes. These promises are definitely *not* "one size fits all." If you try to "claim" these promises for yourself, you're headed for trouble.

For example, the resurrected Jesus told His disciples to wait in Jerusalem "for the Promise of the Father" and that as they did, they would "be baptized with the Holy Spirit" (Acts 1:4, 5). It would be foolish for you to travel to Jerusalem and wait there to receive this promise, since Jesus already fulfilled it that first Pentecost. Today, the Spirit baptizes every believer into the body of Christ and takes up residence within at the very moment that person trusts in Christ. Jesus gave this promise to a specific group of people at a particular time for an explicit purpose; it isn't for anyone else to "claim."

❷ ***General promises***

God has made many universal promises, applicable to all His children throughout all of history. For example, He has promised to never leave or forsake us (Heb. 13:5). He also promised many times to return for us (John 14:3). These promises pertain to all believers across all of time. Yet general promises can also be of two types.

(a) *Conditional promises.* Texts like Philippians 4:19, Psalm 37:4, and others contain conditional promises; to receive the benefit offered, we have to meet some condition. Conditional promises require something of the believer.

In Philippians 4:19 the condition is that we be in Christ; the believer must be living for Him and in total submission to His will. The same holds true for "delighting" in the Lord, as stated in Psalm 37:4. Clearly a relationship comes before a request.

(b) *Unconditional promises.* Unconditional promises require nothing of the believer. The promises mentioned above in Hebrews 13:5 and John 14:3 are of this type. God will fulfill these promises because He has pledged to fulfill them. Nothing anyone does can alter His commitment or change His plans. He will keep these promises, not because of anything we do, but because of His own faithfulness.

See the Life Principles Index for further study:
21. Obedience always brings blessing.
3. God's Word is an immovable anchor in times of storm.

22 let us draw near with a true heart in full
assurance of faith, having our hearts sprinkled from an evil conscience and our bodies
washed with pure water.
23 Let us hold fast the confession of *our* hope
without wavering, for He who promised *is*
faithful.
24 And let us consider one another in order
to stir up love and good works,
25 not forsaking the assembling of ourselves
together, as *is* the manner of some, but exhorting *one another,* and so much the more as
you see the Day approaching.

The Just Live by Faith

26 For if we sin willfully after we have received the knowledge of the truth, there no
longer remains a sacrifice for sins,

LIFE LESSONS

➤ ***10:24, 25 — And let us consider one another in order to stir up love and good works, not forsaking the assembling of ourselves together . . . .***

This is the most explicit text in the New Testament about the necessity of believers gathering for corporate worship, instruction, encouragement, and "good works." God simply did not design us to grow in isolation.

LIFE PRINCIPLE 28

NO CHRISTIAN HAS EVER BEEN CALLED TO "GO IT ALONE" IN HIS OR HER WALK OF FAITH.

HEB. 10:24, 25

The writer of Hebrews knew that his audience, Jewish Christians who had just come to faith, were struggling with how to incorporate their Jewish heritage into their walk with Christ. The author therefore spends a great deal of time explaining that Jesus Christ prepared the way for uninterrupted fellowship with the Father. He is the new High Priest. His death provided the way for individuals to have personal access to God without a series of complicated steps.

That was difficult for the Jewish Christians to accept. They were accustomed to participating in a variety of ceremonial washings and offerings to be cleansed from their sins; immediate access to God apart from those things was something new. But the writer insisted they could go directly to the Father through Christ. The author also knew the challenge facing these recent converts to remain faithful to their newly formed faith. So he exhorted them to "hold fast."

Then he took it one step farther. He instructed his readers to *help one another* "hold fast." He knew they would tend to drift from the truth. He anticipated their need for other believers to help them stay on track. So he said, "Let us consider one another in order to stir up love and good works" (Heb. 10:24). The Greek term translated "stir up" literally means "to irritate." In essence he was instructing them to spur one another along, watch out for one another, take responsibility for one another.

With that backdrop, he instructed them not to stop meeting together (10:25). They needed one another. To give up meeting together would spell disaster. In meeting together they found the mutual encouragement to keep going.

God wants His children to regularly meet with other believers. He wants His people in church! Many believers don't take this admonition seriously because they don't know the reason behind it. How often I have heard this refrain: "I can worship God at home. I don't need to go to church." Many believers believe the sole reason we meet together is to worship—and understandably so. After all, we call it a worship service.

If worship were the only reason we are commanded to meet, then those who claim they can worship at home would have a strong argument. But worship is

Christ prepared the way for uninterrupted fellowship with the Father.

not the sole reason we are commanded to meet together. Nor is it so that we can be taught the Word. We can turn on our radios and televisions and hear good Bible teaching. On the surface, it would seem that anything we can do at church, we can do just as well at home, alone.

So why are we commanded to meet? Why go to church?

The writer of Hebrews says it is to safeguard against drifting.

Forces around us work to blow us off course. Sheer individual commitment is not enough to keep us in line. At times we feel as if our faith makes no difference. We see no fruit in our lives and we don't seem to be making any difference in anyone else's life, either. During those times, we feel tempted to pull up anchor and drift. After all, isn't everybody else?

Then we drag ourselves to church and discover that we are not alone. We hear others testify how God came through for them in a tight spot. Someone else describes the pain suffered when he left the faith. A new believer tells her story and rejoices in God's grace. And then something begins to happen inside us. We are spurred on to faithfulness!

The accountability and encouragement found in church anchor us against the tides that work to sweep us away. To neglect the regular assembly of fellow Christians is to miss out on this essential element in the development of our faith.

God desires a close relationship with His children. By becoming active in a local church, you safeguard yourself against missing out on all that God has for you. Your participation in a local church protects your personal fellowship with God. When you drift away from the family of God, it is only a matter of time until you drift away from fellowship with God.

Church should encourage you to cling to the hope that is in you. If yours doesn't, then I recommend you visit another church. Keep in mind, however, that there is no perfect church. Find one that accurately presents Scripture and practically demonstrates God's love. And remember that you too have a responsibility to actively use your spiritual gifts for the benefit of other believers.

See the Life Principles Index for further study.

Your participation in a local church protects your personal fellowship with God.

27 but a certain fearful expectation of judgment, and fiery indignation which will devour the adversaries.
28 Anyone who has rejected Moses' law dies without mercy on *the testimony of* two or three witnesses.
29 Of how much worse punishment, do you suppose, will he be thought worthy who has trampled the Son of God underfoot, counted the blood of the covenant by which he was sanctified a common thing, and insulted the Spirit of grace?
30 For we know Him who said, *"Vengeance is Mine, I will repay,"*[a] says the Lord.[b] And again, *"The LORD will judge His people."*[c]
➤ 31 It is a fearful thing to fall into the hands of the living God.
32 But recall the former days in which, after you were illuminated, you endured a great struggle with sufferings:
33 partly while you were made a spectacle both by reproaches and tribulations, and partly while you became companions of those who were so treated;
34 for you had compassion on me[a] in my chains, and joyfully accepted the plundering of your goods, knowing that you have a better and an enduring possession for yourselves in heaven.[b]
35 Therefore do not cast away your confidence, which has great reward.
36 For you have need of endurance, so that after you have done the will of God, you may receive the promise:

37 *"For yet a little while,*
And He[a] *who is coming will come and*
will not tarry.
38 *Now the*[a] *just shall live by faith;*
But if anyone draws back,
My soul has no pleasure in him."[b]

39 But we are not of those who draw back to perdition, but of those who believe to the saving of the soul.

By Faith We Understand

➤ **11** Now faith is the substance of things hoped for, the evidence of things not seen.
2 For by it the elders obtained a *good* testimony.
3 By faith we understand that the worlds were framed by the word of God, so that the things which are seen were not made of things which are visible.

Faith at the Dawn of History

4 By faith Abel offered to God a more excellent sacrifice than Cain, through which he obtained witness that he was righteous, God testifying of his gifts; and through it he being dead still speaks.
5 By faith Enoch was taken away so that he did not see death, *"and was not found, because God had taken him"*;[a] for before he was taken he had this testimony, that he pleased God.
6 But without faith *it is* impossible to please *Him,* for he who comes to God must believe that He is, and *that* He is a rewarder of those who diligently seek Him. ✳ ◂
7 By faith Noah, being divinely warned of things not yet seen, moved with godly fear, prepared an ark for the saving of his household, by which he condemned the world and became heir of the righteousness which is according to faith.

Faithful Abraham

8 By faith Abraham obeyed when he was called to go out to the place which he would receive as an inheritance. And he went out, not knowing where he was going.
9 By faith he dwelt in the land of promise as *in* a foreign country, dwelling in tents with Isaac and Jacob, the heirs with him of the same promise;
10 for he waited for the city which has foundations, whose builder and maker *is* God.
11 By faith Sarah herself also received strength to conceive seed, and she bore a child[a] when she was past the age, because she judged Him faithful who had promised.

10:30 [a]Deuteronomy 32:35 [b]NU-Text omits *says the Lord.* [c]Deuteronomy 32:36 **10:34** [a]NU-Text reads *the prisoners* instead of *me in my chains.* [b]NU-Text omits *in heaven.* **10:37** [a]Or *that which* **10:38** [a]NU-Text reads *My just one.* [b]Habakkuk 2:3, 4 **11:5** [a]Genesis 5:24 **11:11** [a]NU-Text omits *she bore a child.*

LIFE LESSONS

➤ 10:31 — *It is a fearful thing to fall into the hands of the living God.*

The "hands" the writer has in mind here are not the hands of divine grace but those of divine judgment. Can a gracious God also dispense "fearful" discipline? The writer of Hebrews thought so.

➤ 11:1 — *Now faith is the substance of things hoped for, the evidence of things not seen.*

Faith is not wishful thinking or "believing what you know isn't true," to paraphrase Mark Twain. Instead it is the conviction that God will always do what He promises to do, regardless of the circumstances.

➤ 11:6 — *But without faith it is impossible to please Him . . . .*

Faith declares our weakness while it proclaims the trustworthiness of God and His complete and willing ability to do what we cannot. A lack of faith insults God even as it puts foolish confidence in ourselves.

12 Therefore from one man, and him as good
as dead, were born *as many* as the stars of the
sky in multitude—innumerable as the sand
which is by the seashore.

The Heavenly Hope

➤ **13** These all died in faith, not having received
the promises, but having seen them afar off
were assured of them,[a] embraced *them* and
confessed that they were strangers and pilgrims on the earth.
14 For those who say such things declare
plainly that they seek a homeland.
15 And truly if they had called to mind that
country from which they had come out, they
would have had opportunity to return.
✳ 16 But now they desire a better, that is, a
heavenly *country.* Therefore God is not
ashamed to be called their God, for He has
prepared a city for them.

The Faith of the Patriarchs

17 By faith Abraham, when he was tested, offered up Isaac, and he who had received the
promises offered up his only begotten *son,*
18 of whom it was said, *"In Isaac your seed
shall be called,"*[a]
19 concluding that God *was* able to raise *him*
up, even from the dead, from which he also
received him in a figurative sense.
20 By faith Isaac blessed Jacob and Esau
concerning things to come.
21 By faith Jacob, when he was dying,
blessed each of the sons of Joseph, and worshiped, *leaning* on the top of his staff.
22 By faith Joseph, when he was dying, made
mention of the departure of the children of Israel, and gave instructions concerning his
bones.

The Faith of Moses

23 By faith Moses, when he was born, was
hidden three months by his parents, because
they saw *he was* a beautiful child; and they
were not afraid of the king's command.
24 By faith Moses, when he became of age,
refused to be called the son of Pharaoh's
daughter,
➤ 25 choosing rather to suffer affliction with
the people of God than to enjoy the passing
pleasures of sin,
26 esteeming the reproach of Christ greater
riches than the treasures in[a] Egypt; for he
looked to the reward.
27 By faith he forsook Egypt, not fearing the
wrath of the king; for he endured as seeing
Him who is invisible.
28 By faith he kept the Passover and the
sprinkling of blood, lest he who destroyed the
firstborn should touch them.
29 By faith they passed through the Red Sea
as by dry *land, whereas* the Egyptians, attempting to do so, were drowned.

By Faith They Overcame

30 By faith the walls of Jericho fell down
after they were encircled for seven days.
31 By faith the harlot Rahab did not perish
with those who did not believe, when she had
received the spies with peace.
32 And what more shall I say? For the time
would fail me to tell of Gideon and Barak and
Samson and Jephthah, also *of* David and
Samuel and the prophets:
33 who through faith subdued kingdoms,
worked righteousness, obtained promises,
stopped the mouths of lions,
34 quenched the violence of fire, escaped the
edge of the sword, out of weakness were
made strong, became valiant in battle, turned
to flight the armies of the aliens.
35 Women received their dead raised to life
again. Others were tortured, not accepting deliverance, that they might obtain a better resurrection.
36 Still others had trial of mockings and
scourgings, yes, and of chains and imprisonment.
37 They were stoned, they were sawn in
two, were tempted,[a] were slain with the
sword. They wandered about in sheepskins
and goatskins, being destitute, afflicted, tormented—
38 of whom the world was not worthy. They
wandered in deserts and mountains, *in* dens
and caves of the earth.
39 And all these, having obtained a good testimony through faith, did not receive the
promise,
40 God having provided something better for
us, that they should not be made perfect apart
from us.

11:13 [a]NU-Text and M-Text omit *were assured of them.*
11:18 [a]Genesis 21:12 **11:26** [a]NU-Text and M-Text read *of.*
11:37 [a]NU-Text omits *were tempted.*

LIFE LESSONS

➤ 11:13 — *These all died in faith, not having received the promises, but having seen them afar off were assured of them . . . .*

Abraham died having seen some, but not all, of God's promises fulfilled. We stand in precisely the same situation. God will certainly fulfill *all* His promises, but the greatest of them await the next life. Do we believe?

➤ 11:25, 26 — *. . . choosing rather to suffer affliction with the people of God than to enjoy the passing pleasures of sin . . . for he looked to the reward.*

The Bible tries to fool nobody. There *is* some pleasure in sin, even though it quickly passes. And there *is* some affliction in godliness, even though that quickly passes too. Yet the reward for godliness far outstrips any pleasure in sin.

The Race of Faith

12 Therefore we also, since we are surrounded by so great a cloud of witnesses, let us lay aside every weight, and the sin which so easily ensnares *us,* and let us run with endurance the race that is set before us,

➤ 2 looking unto Jesus, the author and finisher of *our* faith, who for the joy that was set before Him endured the cross, despising the shame, and has sat down at the right hand of the throne of God.

The Discipline of God

3 For consider Him who endured such hostility from sinners against Himself, lest you become weary and discouraged in your souls.

4 You have not yet resisted to bloodshed, striving against sin.

5 And you have forgotten the exhortation which speaks to you as to sons:

"My son, do not despise the chastening of the LORD,
Nor be discouraged when you are rebuked by Him;
6 *For whom the LORD loves He chastens,*
And scourges every son whom He receives."[a]

7 If[a] you endure chastening, God deals with you as with sons; for what son is there whom a father does not chasten?

8 But if you are without chastening, of which all have become partakers, then you are illegitimate and not sons.

9 Furthermore, we have had human fathers who corrected *us,* and we paid *them* respect. Shall we not much more readily be in subjection to the Father of spirits and live?

✳ 10 For they indeed for a few days chastened *us* as seemed *best* to them, but He for *our* profit, that *we* may be partakers of His holiness.

➤ 11 Now no chastening seems to be joyful for the present, but painful; nevertheless, afterward it yields the peaceable fruit of righteousness to those who have been trained by it.

Renew Your Spiritual Vitality

12 Therefore strengthen the hands which hang down, and the feeble knees,

13 and make straight paths for your feet, so that what is lame may not be dislocated, but rather be healed.

14 Pursue peace with all *people,* and holiness, without which no one will see the Lord:

15 looking carefully lest anyone fall short of the grace of God; lest any root of bitterness springing up cause trouble, and by this many become defiled;

16 lest there *be* any fornicator or profane person like Esau, who for one morsel of food sold his birthright.

17 For you know that afterward, when he wanted to inherit the blessing, he was rejected, for he found no place for repentance, though he sought it diligently with tears.

The Glorious Company

18 For you have not come to the mountain that[a] may be touched and that burned with fire, and to blackness and darkness[b] and tempest,

19 and the sound of a trumpet and the voice of words, so that those who heard *it* begged that the word should not be spoken to them anymore.

20 (For they could not endure what was commanded: *"And if so much as a beast touches the mountain, it shall be stoned*[a] *or shot with an arrow."*[b]

21 And so terrifying was the sight *that* Moses said, *"I am exceedingly afraid* and trembling."[a])

22 But you have come to Mount Zion and to the city of the living God, the heavenly Jerusalem, to an innumerable company of angels,

23 to the general assembly and church of the firstborn *who are* registered in heaven, to God the Judge of all, to the spirits of just men made perfect,

24 to Jesus the Mediator of the new covenant, and to the blood of sprinkling that speaks better things than *that of* Abel.

Hear the Heavenly Voice

25 See that you do not refuse Him who speaks. For if they did not escape who refused

---

12:6 [a]Proverbs 3:11, 12 **12:7** [a]NU-Text and M-Text read *It is for discipline that you endure; God . . . .* **12:18** [a]NU-Text reads *to that which.* [b]NU-Text reads *gloom.* **12:20** [a]NU-Text and M-Text omit the rest of this verse. [b]Exodus 19:12, 13 **12:21** [a]Deuteronomy 9:19

LIFE LESSONS

➤ 12:2 — *. . . looking unto Jesus, the author and finisher of our faith, who for the joy that was set before Him endured the cross, despising the shame . . . .*

Just as Abraham kept on his course of faith by trusting in God's promise to reward his obedience, so Jesus kept on His infinitely tougher course by looking toward God's promise to reward Him for His obedience.

➤ 12:11 — *Now no chastening seems to be joyful for the present, but painful; nevertheless, afterward it yields the peaceable fruit of righteousness to those who have been trained by it.*

Nobody likes to be disciplined. It never feels good. It never puts a smile on your face or a spring in your step—at least not initially. But if we cooperate with God when He corrects us, blessing always results.

Him who spoke on earth, much more *shall we not escape* if we turn away from Him who *speaks* from heaven,
26 whose voice then shook the earth; but now He has promised, saying, *"Yet once more I shake*[a] *not only the earth, but also heaven."*[b]
27 Now this, *"Yet once more,"* indicates the removal of those things that are being shaken, as of things that are made, that the things which cannot be shaken may remain.
28 Therefore, since we are receiving a kingdom which cannot be shaken, let us have grace, by which we may[a] serve God acceptably with reverence and godly fear.
29 For our God *is* a consuming fire.

Concluding Moral Directions

13 Let brotherly love continue.
2 Do not forget to entertain strangers, for by so *doing* some have unwittingly entertained angels.
3 Remember the prisoners as if chained with them—those who are mistreated—since you yourselves are in the body also.
4 Marriage *is* honorable among all, and the bed undefiled; but fornicators and adulterers God will judge.
5 *Let your* conduct *be* without covetousness; *be* content with such things as you have. For He Himself has said, *"I will never leave you nor forsake you."*[a]
6 So we may boldly say:

"The LORD is my helper;
I will not fear.
What can man do to me?"[a]

Concluding Religious Directions

7 Remember those who rule over you, who have spoken the word of God to you, whose faith follow, considering the outcome of *their* conduct.
8 Jesus Christ *is* the same yesterday, today, and forever.
9 Do not be carried about[a] with various and strange doctrines. For *it is* good that the heart be established by grace, not with foods which have not profited those who have been occupied with them.
10 We have an altar from which those who serve the tabernacle have no right to eat.
11 For the bodies of those animals, whose blood is brought into the sanctuary by the high priest for sin, are burned outside the camp.
12 Therefore Jesus also, that He might sanctify the people with His own blood, suffered outside the gate.
13 Therefore let us go forth to Him, outside the camp, bearing His reproach.
14 For here we have no continuing city, but we seek the one to come.
15 Therefore by Him let us continually offer the sacrifice of praise to God, that is, the fruit of *our* lips, giving thanks to His name.
16 But do not forget to do good and to share, for with such sacrifices God is well pleased.
17 Obey those who rule over you, and be submissive, for they watch out for your souls, as those who must give account. Let them do so with joy and not with grief, for that would be unprofitable for you.

Prayer Requested

18 Pray for us; for we are confident that we have a good conscience, in all things desiring to live honorably.
19 But I especially urge *you* to do this, that I may be restored to you the sooner.

Benediction, Final Exhortation, Farewell

20 Now may the God of peace who brought up our Lord Jesus from the dead, that great Shepherd of the sheep, through the blood of the everlasting covenant,

12:26 [a]NU-Text reads *will shake.* [b]Haggai 2:6 **12:28** [a]M-Text omits *may.* **13:5** [a]Deuteronomy 31:6, 8; Joshua 1:5 **13:6** [a]Psalm 118:6 **13:9** [a]NU-Text and M-Text read *away.*

LIFE LESSONS

➤ 12:28 — *Therefore, since we are receiving a kingdom which cannot be shaken, let us have grace, by which we may serve God acceptably with reverence and godly fear.*

Divine grace never encourages us to live in ungodly ways, but instead motivates us to fear and obey God in a healthy and reverent way. Grace enables us to serve, not to sin.

➤ 13:8 — *Jesus Christ is the same yesterday, today, and forever.*

Just like His Father, "the Everlasting God" (Gen. 21:33), whose "ways are everlasting" (Hab. 3:6) and who says, "I do not change" (Mal. 3:6), so Jesus remains the same forever.

➤ 13:13 — *Therefore let us go forth to Him, outside the camp, bearing His reproach.*

Identification with Jesus brings undeniable blessings, but it can also bring reproach and persecution. This is not something to be avoided at all costs, but rather is something to be embraced when it occurs.

➤ 13:20, 21 — *Now may the God of peace . . . make you complete in every good work to do His will, working in you what is well pleasing in His sight . . . .*

It is *God* working *in us* that enables us to do anything worthwhile for His kingdom. We obey God, do His will, and please Him only by relying on the Holy Spirit who dwells within us.

21 make you complete in every good work to
do His will, working in you[a] what is well
pleasing in His sight, through Jesus Christ, to
whom *be* glory forever and ever. Amen.
22 And I appeal to you, brethren, bear with
the word of exhortation, for I have written to
you in few words.
23 Know that *our* brother Timothy has been
set free, with whom I shall see you if he comes
shortly.
24 Greet all those who rule over you, and all
the saints. Those from Italy greet you.
25 Grace *be* with you all. Amen.

13:21 [a]NU-Text and M-Text read *us.*

THE EPISTLE OF

JAMES

Faith without works cannot be called faith. "Faith without works is dead" (2:26), James insists; and a dead faith is worse than no faith at all.

Faith must work; it must produce; it must make itself visible. Verbal faith is not enough and mental faith is insufficient. Genuine faith inspires and empowers godly action. Throughout his letter, James integrates true faith and everyday practical experience by stressing that true faith must manifest itself in works of faith—otherwise, it is not real faith at all.

Genuine faith endures trials. Trials are bound to come, but a strong faith will face them head-on and develop endurance.

Genuine faith understands temptations. It will never consent to our lusts and thereby slide into sin.

Genuine faith harbors no prejudice. For James, faith and favoritism cannot coexist.

Genuine faith has the power to control the tongue. This small but immensely powerful part of the body must be held in check—and only grace, working through faith, can manage it.

Genuine faith acts wisely. It gives us the ability to choose heavenly wisdom that brings life and to shun earthly wisdom that brings death.

Genuine faith produces separation from the world and submission to God. It provides us with the ability to resist the devil and humbly draw near to God.

Finally, genuine faith waits patiently for the coming of the Lord. Although troubles and trials cause us grief, faith in the return of Christ stifles complaining.

The name *Iakobos* (James) in 1:1 is the basis for the early title, *Iakobou Epistole*, "Epistle of James." *Iakobos* is the Greek form of the common Hebrew name Jacob.

Theme: Genuine faith gets to work on a daily basis by depending on the power of God.

Author: Generally agreed that James "the Lord's brother" (Gal. 1:19) wrote this letter.

Date: Probably written before A.D. 50, making it perhaps the earliest book in the New Testament, with the possible exception of Galatians.

Structure: James briefly greets his audience (1:1); then instructs them about trials (1:2–20), the nature of true faith (1:21—2:26), the untamable tongue (3:1–12), heavenly wisdom (3:13–18), pride versus humility (4:1–17), warnings to the rich (5:1–6), persevering patience (5:7–12), and miscellaneous matters (5:13–18); and then gives a brief conclusion (5:19, 20).

As you read James, watch for several life principles that play an important role in this book:

29. **We learn more in our valley experiences than on our mountaintops.** *See James 1:2–4; 5:10; pages 1458, 1462.*

22. **To walk in the Spirit is to obey the initial promptings of the Spirit.** *See James 1:22–27; page 1459.*

15. **Brokenness is God's requirement for maximum usefulness.** *See James 5:1–6; page 1461.*

14. **God acts on behalf of those who wait for Him.** *See James 5:7–11; page 1462.*

Greeting to the Twelve Tribes

1 James, a bondservant of God and of the
Lord Jesus Christ,

To the twelve tribes which are scattered abroad:

Greetings.

Profiting from Trials

➤ **2** My brethren, count it all joy when you fall
into various trials,
3 knowing that the testing of your faith produces patience.
4 But let patience have *its* perfect work, that
you may be perfect and complete, lacking
nothing.
✳ 5 If any of you lacks wisdom, let him ask of
God, who gives to all liberally and without reproach, and it will be given to him.
6 But let him ask in faith, with no doubting,
for he who doubts is like a wave of the sea
driven and tossed by the wind.
7 For let not that man suppose that he will
receive anything from the Lord;
8 *he is* a double-minded man, unstable in all
his ways.

The Perspective of Rich and Poor

9 Let the lowly brother glory in his exaltation,
10 but the rich in his humiliation, because as
a flower of the field he will pass away.
11 For no sooner has the sun risen with a
burning heat than it withers the grass; its
flower falls, and its beautiful appearance perishes. So the rich man also will fade away in
his pursuits.

Loving God Under Trials

✳ **12** Blessed *is* the man who endures temptation; for when he has been approved, he will
receive the crown of life which the Lord has
promised to those who love Him.
➤ 13 Let no one say when he is tempted, "I am
tempted by God"; for God cannot be tempted
by evil, nor does He Himself tempt anyone.
14 But each one is tempted when he is drawn
away by his own desires and enticed.
15 Then, when desire has conceived, it gives
birth to sin; and sin, when it is full-grown,
brings forth death.
16 Do not be deceived, my beloved brethren.
17 Every good gift and every perfect gift is ◄
from above, and comes down from the Father
of lights, with whom there is no variation or
shadow of turning.

Life Examples:

JAMES

A Changed Man

JAMES 1:1

At the beginning, James refused to believe in either the ministry or the deity of Jesus, his brother (Mark 3:32–35; John 7:5). James' disbelief remained steadfast throughout Jesus' earthly life. Only after the Resurrection did James finally realize the truth.

In 1 Corinthians 15:5–8, Paul lists those to whom the risen Christ appeared. There, along with the disciples, James is singled out. Soon after the Resurrection, James and his brothers joined the disciples in devoting themselves to prayer as they awaited the Holy Spirit (Acts 1:14).

James—not Peter or one of the other disciples—led the Jerusalem church through its early days. The missionaries who informed this church of their activities reported to James, its leader (Acts 15:12–21; 21:18).

James proves that even when you feel the most comfortable with the Lord—even when you believe you have Him figured out—He can still surprise you and change your world.

See the Life Principles Index for further study:

1. *Our intimacy with God—His highest priority for our lives—determines the impact of our lives.*

LIFE LESSONS

➤ ***1:2, 3 — My brethren, count it all joy when you fall into various trials, knowing that the testing of your faith produces patience.***

There is nothing joyful about trials, in and of themselves. There is no value in suffering for its own sake. God uses both trials and suffering to test our faith, so that we may learn to patiently endure.

➤ ***1:13 — Let no one say when he is tempted, "I am tempted by God"; for God cannot be tempted by evil, nor does He Himself tempt anyone.***

To say that God tempts anyone to sin is to confuse the Lord with the devil. The whole satanic purpose of temptation is to entice people away from God and His best for them.

➤ ***1:17 — Every good gift and every perfect gift is from above, and comes down from the Father of lights, with whom there is no variation or shadow of turning.***

Do you enjoy good health and a roof over your head? If so, that's God's gift. Do you have enough to eat, a solid church home, some faithful friends, a source of income? A generous God bestows them all.

18 Of His own will He brought us forth by the
word of truth, that we might be a kind of firstfruits of His creatures.

Qualities Needed in Trials

19 So then,[a] my beloved brethren, let every
man be swift to hear, slow to speak, slow to
wrath;
20 for the wrath of man does not produce the
righteousness of God.

Doers—Not Hearers Only

21 Therefore lay aside all filthiness and overflow of wickedness, and receive with meekness the implanted word, which is able to
save your souls.
➤ 22 But be doers of the word, and not hearers
only, deceiving yourselves.
23 For if anyone is a hearer of the word and
not a doer, he is like a man observing his natural face in a mirror;
24 for he observes himself, goes away, and
immediately forgets what kind of man he
was.
25 But he who looks into the perfect law of
liberty and continues *in it*, and is not a forgetful hearer but a doer of the work, this one
will be blessed in what he does.
26 If anyone among you[a] thinks he is religious, and does not bridle his tongue but deceives his own heart, this one's religion *is*
useless.
27 Pure and undefiled religion before God
and the Father is this: to visit orphans and
widows in their trouble, *and* to keep oneself
unspotted from the world.

Beware of Personal Favoritism

2 My brethren, do not hold the faith of our
Lord Jesus Christ, *the Lord* of glory, with
partiality.
2 For if there should come into your assembly a man with gold rings, in fine apparel, and
there should also come in a poor man in filthy
clothes,
3 and you pay attention to the one wearing
the fine clothes and say to him, "You sit here
in a good place," and say to the poor man,
"You stand there," or, "Sit here at my footstool,"
4 have you not shown partiality among
yourselves, and become judges with evil
thoughts?
5 Listen, my beloved brethren: Has God not ➤
chosen the poor of this world *to be* rich in
faith and heirs of the kingdom which He
promised to those who love Him?
6 But you have dishonored the poor man.
Do not the rich oppress you and drag you into
the courts?
7 Do they not blaspheme that noble name
by which you are called?
8 If you really fulfill *the* royal law according
to the Scripture, *"You shall love your neighbor as yourself,"*[a] you do well;
9 but if you show partiality, you commit sin,
and are convicted by the law as transgressors.
10 For whoever shall keep the whole law, ➤
and yet stumble in one *point*, he is guilty of
all.
11 For He who said, *"Do not commit adultery,"*[a] also said, *"Do not murder."*[b] Now if
you do not commit adultery, but you do murder, you have become a transgressor of the
law.
12 So speak and so do as those who will be
judged by the law of liberty.
13 For judgment is without mercy to the one
who has shown no mercy. Mercy triumphs
over judgment.

Faith Without Works Is Dead

14 What *does it* profit, my brethren, if someone says he has faith but does not have
works? Can faith save him?
15 If a brother or sister is naked and destitute
of daily food,
16 and one of you says to them, "Depart in
peace, be warmed and filled," but you do not
give them the things which are needed for the
body, what *does it* profit?

1:19 [a]NU-Text reads *Know this* or *This you know.* **1:26** [a]NU-Text omits *among you.* **2:8** [a]Leviticus 19:18 **2:11** [a]Exodus 20:14; Deuteronomy 5:18 [b]Exodus 20:13; Deuteronomy 5:17

LIFE LESSONS

➤ 1:22 — *But be doers of the word, and not hearers only, deceiving yourselves.*

Our culture tends to consider people "spiritual" merely if they have an interest in spiritual things. That is not the biblical perspective. Only those who hear God's voice and obey it are spiritual.

➤ 2:5 — *Has God not chosen the poor of this world to be rich in faith and heirs of the kingdom which He promised to those who love Him?*

Earthly riches do not equal spiritual wealth, anymore than economic destitution indicates spiritual poverty. Those who love God, regardless of their earthly financial position, are "rich in faith" and "heirs of the kingdom."

➤ 2:10 — *For whoever shall keep the whole law, and yet stumble in one point, he is guilty of all.*

James does not mean that if you steal a pretzel you are guilty of murder. He means that all sin is a violation of God's holy character, and therefore you oppose not only His commandment but Him (see Ps. 51:4).

17 Thus also faith by itself, if it does not have works, is dead.
➤ 18 But someone will say, "You have faith, and I have works." Show me your faith without your[a] works, and I will show you my faith by my[b] works.
➤ 19 You believe that there is one God. You do well. Even the demons believe—and tremble!
20 But do you want to know, O foolish man, that faith without works is dead?[a]
21 Was not Abraham our father justified by works when he offered Isaac his son on the altar?
22 Do you see that faith was working together with his works, and by works faith was made perfect?
23 And the Scripture was fulfilled which says, *"Abraham believed God, and it was accounted to him for righteousness."*[a] And he was called the friend of God.
24 You see then that a man is justified by works, and not by faith only.
25 Likewise, was not Rahab the harlot also justified by works when she received the messengers and sent *them* out another way?
26 For as the body without the spirit is dead, so faith without works is dead also.

The Untamable Tongue

3 My brethren, let not many of you become teachers, knowing that we shall receive a stricter judgment.
➤ 2 For we all stumble in many things. If anyone does not stumble in word, he *is* a perfect man, able also to bridle the whole body.
3 Indeed,[a] we put bits in horses' mouths that they may obey us, and we turn their whole body.
4 Look also at ships: although they are so large and are driven by fierce winds, they are turned by a very small rudder wherever the pilot desires.
➤ 5 Even so the tongue is a little member and boasts great things. See how great a forest a little fire kindles!
6 And the tongue *is* a fire, a world of iniquity. The tongue is so set among our members that it defiles the whole body, and sets on fire the course of nature; and it is set on fire by hell.
7 For every kind of beast and bird, of reptile and creature of the sea, is tamed and has been tamed by mankind.
8 But no man can tame the tongue. *It is* an unruly evil, full of deadly poison.
9 With it we bless our God and Father, and with it we curse men, who have been made in the similitude of God.
10 Out of the same mouth proceed blessing and cursing. My brethren, these things ought not to be so.
11 Does a spring send forth fresh *water* and bitter from the same opening?
12 Can a fig tree, my brethren, bear olives, or a grapevine bear figs? Thus no spring yields both salt water and fresh.[a]

Heavenly Versus Demonic Wisdom

13 Who *is* wise and understanding among you? Let him show by good conduct *that* his works *are done* in the meekness of wisdom.
14 But if you have bitter envy and self-seeking in your hearts, do not boast and lie against the truth.
15 This wisdom does not descend from above, but *is* earthly, sensual, demonic.
16 For where envy and self-seeking *exist*, confusion and every evil thing *are* there.
17 But the wisdom that is from above is first pure, then peaceable, gentle, willing to yield, full of mercy and good fruits, without partiality and without hypocrisy. ◄

2:18 [a]NU-Text omits *your.* [b]NU-Text omits *my.* **2:20** [a]NU-Text reads *useless.* **2:23** [a]Genesis 15:6 **3:3** [a]NU-Text reads *Now if.* **3:12** [a]NU-Text reads *Neither can a salty spring produce fresh water.*

LIFE LESSONS

➤ **2:18 — *But someone will say, "You have faith, and I have works." Show me your faith without your works, and I will show you my faith by my works.***

James has no quarrel with faith. He understands that faith alone can save someone. What he opposes is a phony faith, the kind that supposedly exists without giving any practical confirmation of its existence.

➤ **2:19 — *You believe that there is one God. You do well. Even the demons believe—and tremble!***

Belief in God is not the same as faith in God. Demons believe that God exists. They also believe that Christ rose from the grave. But they do not willingly submit to His will or eagerly put their destiny in His hands.

➤ **3:2 — *For we all stumble in many things.***

None of us has become perfect (see Phil. 3:12). None of us does everything right. None of us is so wise that we always speak the right word or so strong that we always do the right thing. Remembering this keeps us humble.

➤ **3:5 — *Even so the tongue is a little member and boasts great things. See how great a forest a little fire kindles!***

James does not mean to glorify the power of the tongue, but rather he wants to show how even a very small part of our body remains out of our control, so long as we try to control it in our own strength.

➤ **3:17 — *But the wisdom that is from above is first pure, then peaceable, gentle, willing to yield, full of mercy and good fruits, without partiality and without hypocrisy.***

God's wisdom leads to harmony and peace, while human wisdom leads to arrogance and dissension. What kind of wisdom do you tend to rely on? You can answer that question by evaluating your relationships.

18 Now the fruit of righteousness is sown in peace by those who make peace.

Pride Promotes Strife

4 Where do wars and fights *come* from among you? Do *they* not *come* from your *desires for* pleasure that war in your members?
➤ 2 You lust and do not have. You murder and covet and cannot obtain. You fight and war. Yet[a] you do not have because you do not ask.
➤ 3 You ask and do not receive, because you ask amiss, that you may spend *it* on your pleasures.
4 Adulterers and[a] adulteresses! Do you not know that friendship with the world is enmity with God? Whoever therefore wants to be a friend of the world makes himself an enemy of God.
5 Or do you think that the Scripture says in vain, "The Spirit who dwells in us yearns jealously"?
6 But He gives more grace. Therefore He says:

"God resists the proud,
But gives grace to the humble."[a]

Humility Cures Worldliness

✳ **7** Therefore submit to God. Resist the devil and he will flee from you.
✳ 8 Draw near to God and He will draw near to you. Cleanse *your* hands, *you* sinners; and purify *your* hearts, *you* double-minded.
9 Lament and mourn and weep! Let your laughter be turned to mourning and *your* joy to gloom.
➤ 10 Humble yourselves in the sight of the Lord, and He will lift you up.

Do Not Judge a Brother

11 Do not speak evil of one another, brethren. He who speaks evil of a brother and judges his brother, speaks evil of the law and judges the law. But if you judge the law, you are not a doer of the law but a judge.
12 There is one Lawgiver,[a] who is able to save and to destroy. Who[b] are you to judge another?[c]

Do Not Boast About Tomorrow

13 Come now, you who say, "Today or tomorrow we will[a] go to such and such a city, spend a year there, buy and sell, and make a profit";
14 whereas you do not know what *will happen* tomorrow. For what *is* your life? It is even a vapor that appears for a little time and then vanishes away.
15 Instead you *ought* to say, "If the Lord wills, we shall live and do this or that."
16 But now you boast in your arrogance. All such boasting is evil.
17 Therefore, to him who knows to do good and does not do *it*, to him it is sin. ➤

Rich Oppressors Will Be Judged

5 Come now, *you* rich, weep and howl for your miseries that are coming upon *you!*
2 Your riches are corrupted, and your garments are moth-eaten.
3 Your gold and silver are corroded, and their corrosion will be a witness against you and will eat your flesh like fire. You have heaped up treasure in the last days.
4 Indeed the wages of the laborers who mowed your fields, which you kept back by fraud, cry out; and the cries of the reapers have reached the ears of the Lord of Sabaoth.[a]
5 You have lived on the earth in pleasure and luxury; you have fattened your hearts as[a] in a day of slaughter.
6 You have condemned, you have murdered the just; he does not resist you.

4:2 [a]NU-Text and M-Text omit *Yet.* 4:4 [a]NU-Text omits *Adulterers and.* 4:6 [a]Proverbs 3:34 4:12 [a]NU-Text adds *and Judge.* [b]NU-Text and M-Text read *But who.* [c]NU-Text reads *a neighbor.* 4:13 [a]M-Text reads *let us.* 5:4 [a]Literally, in Hebrew, *Hosts* 5:5 [a]NU-Text omits *as.*

LIFE LESSONS

➤ 4:2 — *. . . you do not have because you do not ask.*

Why does God make us ask Him for what we need and want, rather than just giving it to us without asking? For one thing, He knows that if He did not set it up this way, He might never get to fellowship with us.

➤ 4:3 — *You ask and do not receive, because you ask amiss, that you may spend it on your pleasures.*

By "pleasures," James means "ungodly pleasures." He does not mean, as some think, that they can ask God only for those things that will give them no pleasure. God wants us to enjoy that which honors Him.

➤ 4:10 — *Humble yourselves in the sight of the Lord, and He will lift you up.*

This is another way of saying, as God spoke through Samuel the prophet, "those who honor Me I will honor, and those who despise Me shall be lightly esteemed" (1 Sam. 2:30).

➤ 4:17 — *Therefore, to him who knows to do good and does not do it, to him it is sin.*

When God puts a burden on our hearts for someone, we dare not shove the inclination to the back of our minds. If we do such a wicked thing, John asks, "how does the love of God abide in" us (1 John 3:17)?

ANSWERS TO LIFE'S QUESTIONS

How can I enrich my time alone with God?

JAMES 4:8

Have you ever sat down in a quiet place with your Bible, ready to have a devotional time with the Lord—but you felt aimless? Maybe you flipped through the pages and finally settled on a psalm. But then you remembered another appointment, so you said a quick prayer and told yourself you would pray more later—but it never happens.

You're not alone if you feel frustrated with the quality of your quiet times. As much as you may desire real intimacy with your personal Savior, however, remember that He longs for it even more. James 4:8 promises, "Draw near to God and He will draw near to you."

It helps many people to get some direction on how to develop a close walk with Christ. Specific goals can help you to focus on His Word daily.

First, select a plan that fits your lifestyle and level of understanding. Remember, spending time with God will almost never just "fit in" to your daily routine. You must schedule and then jealously guard your time with God. The more you honor that appointment, the greater you will desire to protect it—and the greater your enrichment.

Have you ever run across puzzling words or passages? Instead of waiting until later to consider the issues, sit down with a Bible dictionary and concordance or other study aids. You may not resolve your question completely, but seeking His truth on your own can spur amazing growth.

Maybe you cannot afford to purchase your own Bible study tools. Never give up! Seek other options. A lot of good Bible reference material is available free on the Internet. Some churches have libraries where you can borrow what you need, as do selected public libraries. Ask your pastor or church associate if they have materials you may use. Most people find the body of Christ eager to help in this pursuit.

As you read the Bible, have a notebook and pen ready to write a spiritual journal. Some people record their daily prayers, leaving a space to describe how God answered them. You may prefer a format in which you write down a special verse and describe why it impacted you. If you have kept a journal before, you know what a treat it is to see a reminder of your spiritual journey.

Are you ready for a relationship with Jesus that knows no boundaries? Then open your time, your life, your heart—and expect the Lord's involvement.

See the Life Principles Index for further study:
13. Listening to God is essential to walking with God.
3. God's Word is an immovable anchor in times of storm.

Be Patient and Persevering

7 Therefore be patient, brethren, until the
coming of the Lord. See *how* the farmer
waits for the precious fruit of the earth,
waiting patiently for it until it receives the
early and latter rain.
8 You also be patient. Establish your hearts,
for the coming of the Lord is at hand.
9 Do not grumble against one another,
brethren, lest you be condemned.[a] Behold,
the Judge is standing at the door!
10 My brethren, take the prophets, who
spoke in the name of the Lord, as an example of suffering and patience.
11 Indeed we count them blessed who endure. You have heard of the perseverance of
Job and seen the end *intended by* the Lord—

5:9 [a]NU-Text and M-Text read *judged.*

LIFE LESSONS

➤ 5:7 — *Therefore be patient, brethren, until the coming of the Lord.*

We do not know when the Lord will return to reward His faithful people and to set right the world, but we know that He will. His promise gives us hope—but we must remain patient until He fulfills it.

➤ 5:11 — *You have heard of the perseverance of Job and seen the end intended by the Lord—that the Lord is very compassionate and merciful.*

Job had to go through some very dark, excruciating days, but never once during his trials did the Lord ever leave him. It helps to remember God's unchanging compassion and mercy when we suffer.

WHAT THE BIBLE SAYS ABOUT PRINCIPLES FOR EFFECTIVE INTERCESSION

James 5:15, 16

Each of us has prayed for others without seeing results. When that happens, it's easy to get discouraged. Rather than give up, we should review our lives to see if we need to alter something.

1. Our prayers must flow from a heart filled with love, compassion, and forgiveness.

Our prayers will fail if our hearts fill up with bitterness, resentment, or anger. Pray first that you might have God's love and compassion for others, and then that you might forgive them fully.

2. We must recognize that our prayers are the link between another person's need and God's inexhaustible resources.

Ask the Lord to reveal to you the true needs of a person, not just the superficial or symptomatic needs. Ask Him also to reveal to you the greatness of His love and power and to help you desire to meet those needs.

3. We must identify with the need of the other person.

Compassion feels the full depth of another's need. When we see people as truly hurting, bleeding, and agonizing on the inside—when we see them with the eyes of Jesus—our compassion gets released and we pray with a new degree of understanding and depth of emotion.

Compassion feels the full depth of another's need.

4. We must desire the highest good in the person's life.

God may not reveal to us His highest good for another person, but we can make it our prayer nonetheless. We do not need to know exactly what God wants to bring to pass. Ultimately, God's highest good is *wholeness.* Wholeness includes vibrancy and life in every domain: spirit, mind, body, emotions, relationships, and finances.

5. We must be willing to be part of the answer in meeting the person's need.

If you pray for another but remain unwilling for God to use you to meet that person's need, God will not hear your prayer. Jesus touched lepers, the unclean, the desperately sick, and the dead. He never backed away from people in need, nor did He pass them on to someone else. We are to follow His example.

6. We must be willing to persevere.

We must keep on praying, regardless of whether we see immediate results. The longer we pray for a person, the more tightly our hearts will be knit to him or her. Prayer binds us together with a spiritual glue far stronger than anything man can create. Such a bond lasts into eternity.

See the Life Principles Index for further study:
8. Fight all your battles on your knees and you win every time.
13. Listening to God is essential to walking with God.

LIFE PRINCIPLE 29

WE LEARN MORE IN OUR VALLEY EXPERIENCES THAN ON OUR MOUNTAINTOPS.

JAMES 5:10

Adversity, anguish, trials, tribulations, and heartaches operate as lessons in the school of experience. They bring us to a place of new insight and understanding; they can alter our perception of the world and of God, and lead us to change our behavior. The Lord, of course, is the ultimate Teacher. He is the One to whom we must look for the meaning of any lesson related to adversity.

God allows adversity for at least three reasons:

1. God uses adversity to get our attention

The Lord uses a wide variety of methods to gain our attention when necessary; adversity is one of them. One of the best responses I know to adversity that strikes us suddenly—and yet obviously—with a God-intended message is to turn to Psalm 25 and make it our personal prayer:

> To You, O LORD, I lift up my soul. O my God, I trust in You; let me not be ashamed; let not my enemies triumph over me. Indeed, let no one who waits on You be ashamed; let those be ashamed who deal treacherously without cause. Show me Your ways, O LORD; teach me Your paths. Lead me in Your truth and teach me, for You are the God of my salvation; on You I wait all the day. Remember, O LORD, Your tender mercies and Your lovingkindnesses, for they are from of old. Do not remember the sins of my youth, nor my transgressions; according to Your mercy remember me, for Your goodness' sake, O LORD (vv. 1–7).

Don't delay in responding to the Lord when He moves to get your attention. Respond quickly and humbly. Hear what He has to say to you.

2. Adversity leads to examination

At times God sees fit to allow adversity into our lives to motivate us to self-examination. The winds of adversity blow away the surface issues and force us to cope with things on a deeper level. Adversity removes the cloak of what we are *supposed* to be to reveal the truth of who we *are*. The "real us" shows through.

We are to regularly examine both our faith and ourselves. Paul encouraged the

Don't delay in responding to the Lord when He moves to get your attention.

Corinthians, "Let a man examine himself" (1 Cor. 11:28). In other words, "Take an inquisitive look inside and discover what is driving you, motivating you, and enticing you."

God does not want negative elements from the past to lie around our lives and cause us trouble. Each of us is the temple of the Holy Spirit, and He wants us to be clean and usable vessels. We have no reason to allow the rubbish of the past to remain in our lives for years—old memories, haunting temptations, the baggage of unresolved hurts and unreconciled relationships. The Lord desires that we free ourselves of anything that might keep us in inner bondage, whether mentally, emotionally, psychologically, or spiritually. When we become complacent in accepting the hurts of the past as part of who we are, the Lord may bring a little adversity to lead us to pursue instead who we might be in Christ Jesus.

Allow God to surface the inner rubbish of your life.

3. The effective lesson leads to change in behavior

Teachers often prepare behavioral objectives for their classroom lectures. These objectives list in concrete and measurable form the behaviors that the teacher desires for a student to display as proof that the student has learned the lesson. The lessons that the Lord teaches us through adversity are ultimately for that very purpose: a change in behavior, including a change in the belief that prompted the behavior.

It isn't enough that the Lord gets our attention or that we engage in self-examination. We can see a problem and know ourselves thoroughly, but unless we change our response to God in some way, we will never benefit fully from adversity or grow as a result of it.

Self-examination may feel painful. But remember, whatever you find within yourself, Jesus Himself came to help you carry that burden to the cross and deal with it there, once and for all. He has your best interest in mind. He knows that pain sometimes paves the path to complete healing and restoration.

If you are willing to allow God to surface the inner rubbish of your life, and if you are willing to change what needs to be changed, you will emerge from adversity closer to Christ, more mature as His child, and with far greater potential to reflect the love of God to the world around you.

See the Life Principles Index for further study.

that the Lord is very compassionate and merciful.
12 But above all, my brethren, do not swear,
either by heaven or by earth or with any other
oath. But let your "Yes" be "Yes," and *your*
"No," "No," lest you fall into judgment.[a]

Meeting Specific Needs
13 Is anyone among you suffering? Let him
pray. Is anyone cheerful? Let him sing psalms.
14 Is anyone among you sick? Let him call
for the elders of the church, and let them pray
over him, anointing him with oil in the name
of the Lord.
✳ 15 And the prayer of faith will save the sick,
and the Lord will raise him up. And if he has
committed sins, he will be forgiven.
➤ 16 Confess *your* trespasses[a] to one another,
and pray for one another, that you may be
healed. The effective, fervent prayer of a righteous man avails much.
17 Elijah was a man with a nature like ours,
and he prayed earnestly that it would not
rain; and it did not rain on the land for three
years and six months.
18 And he prayed again, and the heaven gave
rain, and the earth produced its fruit.

Bring Back the Erring One
19 Brethren, if anyone among you wanders
from the truth, and someone turns him back,
20 let him know that he who turns a sinner
from the error of his way will save a soul[a]
from death and cover a multitude of sins.

5:12 [a]M-Text reads *hypocrisy.* 5:16 [a]NU-Text reads *Therefore confess your sins.* 5:20 [a]NU-Text reads *his soul.*

LIFE LESSONS

➤ 5:16 — *Confess your trespasses to one another, and pray for one another, that you may be healed.*

We cannot obey a multitude of God's commands without being in regular, close fellowship with other believers. He has designed this world so that many of our needs get met only through mutual interdependence.

THE FIRST EPISTLE OF

PETER

Persecution can cause either growth or bitterness in the Christian life. It's our response that determines the result.

In his first letter, Peter encourages believers struggling with persecution to conduct themselves courageously for the Person and program of Christ. They must keep both their character and conduct above reproach. Having been born again to a living hope, they are to imitate the Holy One who has called them. The fruit of that character will result in conduct rooted in honor and submission: citizens toward government; servants toward masters; wives toward husbands; husbands toward wives; and Christians toward one another.

Only after Peter explains the meaning of submission does he deal with the difficult area of suffering. Persecuted Christians are not to "think it strange concerning the fiery trial which is to try you, as though some strange thing happened to you" (4:12). Instead they are to rejoice as partakers of the suffering of Christ. In fact, "let those who suffer according to the will of God commit their souls to Him in doing good, as to a faithful Creator" (4:19). Only those who joyfully submit their lives to the good hand of God can manage such a supernatural response to a sometimes painful life.

Peter wrote his letter to Christians in the Black Sea coastal area. Evidently they were facing severe suffering and persecution because of their faith. Peter wanted them to know that they shouldn't be surprised or dismayed if they faced opposition and persecution, for Jesus Himself certainly faced both. Indeed, believers should feel hope and joy whenever God asks them to share with Jesus in His suffering: "rejoice to the extent that you partake of Christ's sufferings, that when His glory is revealed, you may also be glad with exceeding joy" (4:13).

This epistle begins with the phrase *Petros apostolos Jesou Christou*, "Peter, the apostle of Jesus Christ." This is the basis of the early title *Petrou A*, the "First of Peter."

Theme: Suffering is part of walking with and serving Jesus Christ, and it is not to be feared, but to be embraced.

Author: The apostle Peter.

Date: Probably in the early A.D. 60s, but certainly before the death of emperor Nero in A.D. 68. Nero had Peter executed.

Structure: Peter greets the recipients (1:1, 2), praises God for His salvation (1:3–12), then encourages his readers to honor God by living in a godly way (1:13—5:12). He ends his letter with a brief final greeting (5:13, 14).

As you read 1 Peter, watch for several life principles that play an important role in this book:

23. You can never outgive God. *See 1 Peter 1:3–5; page 1468.*

2. Obey God and leave all the consequences to Him. *See 1 Peter 2:8–12; page 1470.*

27. Prayer is life's greatest time saver. *See 1 Peter 3:7; page 1471.*

7. The dark moments of our life will last only so long as is necessary for God to accomplish His purpose in us. *See 1 Peter 3:13–17; page 1471.*

ANSWERS TO LIFE'S QUESTIONS

How do I handle a difficult trial not of my own doing?

1 PET. 1:6, 7

God knows when we face horrendous situations. He hears our cries. Even those who maintain the closest fellowship with Him are not immune to feelings of hopelessness.

Many times God allows us to face hopeless circumstances in order to test and try our faith; it is the hopelessness that forces us to seek God, and it is there that we find strength and refreshment.

Does God care that your trials make you weary? Yes, and He knows every emotion, need, and desire you have. He also knows exactly what it will take to bring you into a more intimate relationship with Him.

The apostle Peter addressed his two letters to "those who reside as aliens, scattered throughout Pontus, Galatia, Cappadocia, Asia, and Bithynia" (1 Pet. 1:1; 2 Pet. 3:1). If he were choosing a modern title for his letters, he might consider "Encouragement For Times of Hopelessness," or "Hope For The Hurting," because encouragement and hope is exactly what Peter conveyed to these hurting believers.

These believers faced all kinds of persecution. They were beaten, slandered, assaulted, and in some cases would lose their lives for their faith in Jesus Christ. Peter called them "aliens" because they held a citizenship not of this world but of the kingdom of God. Still, they faced times of discouragement and needed hope. Peter explained that they could rejoice even in times of trial because of Jesus Christ, the living hope within them—their risen Savior and Lord (1 Pet. 1:3). Jesus protected them by the power of God (v. 5).

So long as we have Jesus, no situation is hopeless.

Would you like to enjoy an eternal hope? Then focus your heart on Jesus (1 Tim. 4:6). Remember, He is working to bring His will and good pleasure to the forefront of your life.

Even if you find yourself in a seemingly hopeless situation, know that God has an entirely different view of the details. If you will let Him, He will take your life, no matter how bruised and broken, and make something beautiful out of it.

Isn't this what hope is all about—beauty for ashes, gladness instead of sorrow, and a coat of praise instead of fainting (see Is. 61:1-3)? *This* is the ongoing ministry of Jesus Christ in your life. Therefore bring to Him your afflictions and disappointments. Tell Him your sorrows, and He will restore your hope.

See the Life Principles Index for further study:

26. Adversity is a bridge to a deeper relationship with God.

7. The dark moments in our life will last only so long as is necessary for God to accomplish His purpose in us.

Greeting to the Elect Pilgrims

1 Peter, an apostle of Jesus Christ,
To the pilgrims of the Dispersion in Pontus, Galatia, Cappadocia, Asia, and Bithynia,
2 elect according to the foreknowledge of God the Father, in sanctification of the Spirit, for obedience and sprinkling of the blood of Jesus Christ:

Grace to you and peace be multiplied.

A Heavenly Inheritance

3 Blessed *be* the God and Father of our Lord Jesus Christ, who according to His abundant mercy has begotten us again to a living hope through the resurrection of Jesus Christ from the dead,
4 to an inheritance incorruptible and undefiled and that does not fade away, reserved in heaven for you,
5 who are kept by the power of God through faith for salvation ready to be revealed in the last time.
6 In this you greatly rejoice, though now for

LIFE LESSONS

➤ 1:3 — *. . . according to His abundant mercy has begotten us again to a living hope through the resurrection of Jesus Christ from the dead . . . .*

Because we do not have a dead Savior, we have a living hope. The resurrection of Jesus guarantees that God will honor all His promises to His faithful children. That hope keeps us going in the darkest of times.

a little while, if need be, you have been
grieved by various trials,
7 that the genuineness of your faith, *being*
much more precious than gold that perishes,
though it is tested by fire, may be found to
praise, honor, and glory at the revelation of
Jesus Christ,
➤ 8 whom having not seen[a] you love. Though
now you do not see *Him*, yet believing, you
rejoice with joy inexpressible and full of glory,
9 receiving the end of your faith—the salvation of *your* souls.
10 Of this salvation the prophets have inquired and searched carefully, who prophesied of the grace *that would come* to you,
11 searching what, or what manner of time,
the Spirit of Christ who was in them was
indicating when He testified beforehand the
sufferings of Christ and the glories that would
follow.
12 To them it was revealed that, not to themselves, but to us[a] they were ministering
the things which now have been reported
to you through those who have preached
the gospel to you by the Holy Spirit sent
from heaven—things which angels desire to
look into.

Living Before God Our Father

➤ **13** Therefore gird up the loins of your mind,
be sober, and rest *your* hope fully upon the
grace that is to be brought to you at the revelation of Jesus Christ;
14 as obedient children, not conforming yourselves to the former lusts, *as* in your ignorance;
➤ 15 but as He who called you *is* holy, you also
be holy in all *your* conduct,
16 because it is written, *"Be holy, for I am*
holy."[a]
17 And if you call on the Father, who without partiality judges according to each one's
work, conduct yourselves throughout the time
of your stay *here* in fear;
18 knowing that you were not redeemed with
corruptible things, *like* silver or gold, from
your aimless conduct *received* by tradition
from your fathers,
19 but with the precious blood of Christ, as of
a lamb without blemish and without spot.
20 He indeed was foreordained before the
foundation of the world, but was manifest in
these last times for you
21 who through Him believe in God, who
raised Him from the dead and gave Him glory,
so that your faith and hope are in God.

The Enduring Word

22 Since you have purified your souls in obeying the truth through the Spirit[a] in sincere love
of the brethren, love one another fervently
with a pure heart,
23 having been born again, not of corruptible
seed but incorruptible, through the word of
God which lives and abides forever,[a]
24 because

"All flesh is as grass,
And all the glory of man[a] *as the flower of*
the grass.
The grass withers,
And its flower falls away,
25 *But the word of the* LORD *endures*
forever."[a]

Now this is the word which by the gospel was
preached to you.

2 Therefore, laying aside all malice, all deceit, hypocrisy, envy, and all evil speaking,
2 as newborn babes, desire the pure milk of ➤
the word, that you may grow thereby,[a]
3 if indeed you have tasted that the Lord *is*
gracious.

1:8 [a]M-Text reads *known*. **1:12** [a]NU-Text and M-Text read *you*. **1:16** [a]Leviticus 11:44, 45; 19:2; 20:7 **1:22** [a]NU-Text omits *through the Spirit*. **1:23** [a]NU-Text omits *forever*. **1:24** [a]NU-Text reads *all its glory*. **1:25** [a]Isaiah 40:6–8 **2:2** [a]NU-Text adds *up to salvation*.

LIFE LESSONS

➤ 1:8 — *. . . Though now you do not see Him, yet believing, you rejoice with joy inexpressible and full of glory . . . .*

A Christian life devoid of joy is not only unbiblical, it's not much worth having. How could we not have joy in our hearts when we know that God loves us, is with us, promises to help us, and wants to bless us forever?

➤ 1:13 — *Therefore gird up the loins of your mind, be sober, and rest your hope fully upon the grace that is to be brought to you at the revelation of Jesus Christ . . . .*

The Christian life is both a joyful experience and a serious business. It takes conscious, deliberate, Spirit-filled action to ponder God's grace and Jesus' return in such a way that it positively shapes how we live.

➤ 1:15 — *. . . as He who called you is holy, you also be holy in all your conduct . . . .*

Holiness is not a dour, grim-faced determination to do the religious things that drain all enjoyment out of life. God is a delightfully joyful God, and He invites us to join in His joy by imitating His ways.

➤ 2:2 — *. . . as newborn babes, desire the pure milk of the word, that you may grow thereby . . . .*

As infants have a taste and a craving for their mothers' nutritious milk, so we are to develop a taste and a craving for the life-giving Word of God. Growing in Christ requires that we spend time in His Word.

The Chosen Stone and His Chosen People
4 Coming to Him *as to* a living stone, rejected indeed by men, but chosen by God *and*
precious,
5 you also, as living stones, are being built
up a spiritual house, a holy priesthood, to
offer up spiritual sacrifices acceptable to God
through Jesus Christ.
✳6 Therefore it is also contained in the Scripture,

"Behold, I lay in Zion
A chief cornerstone, elect, precious,
And he who believes on Him will by no
means be put to shame."[a]

7 Therefore, to you who believe, *He is* precious; but to those who are disobedient,[a]

"The stone which the builders rejected
Has become the chief cornerstone,"[b]

8 and

"A stone of stumbling
And a rock of offense."[a]

They stumble, being disobedient to the word,
to which they also were appointed.
➤9 But you *are* a chosen generation, a royal
priesthood, a holy nation, His own special people, that you may proclaim the praises of Him
who called you out of darkness into His marvelous light;
10 who once *were* not a people but *are* now
the people of God, who had not obtained
mercy but now have obtained mercy.

Living Before the World
➤**11** Beloved, I beg *you* as sojourners and pilgrims, abstain from fleshly lusts which war
against the soul,
12 having your conduct honorable among the
Gentiles, that when they speak against you as
evildoers, they may, by *your* good works
which they observe, glorify God in the day of
visitation.

Submission to Government
13 Therefore submit yourselves to every ordinance of man for the Lord's sake, whether to
the king as supreme,
14 or to governors, as to those who are sent
by him for the punishment of evildoers and
for the praise of those who do good.
15 For this is the will of God, that by doing
good you may put to silence the ignorance of
foolish men—
16 as free, yet not using liberty as a cloak for
vice, but as bondservants of God.
17 Honor all *people.* Love the brotherhood.
Fear God. Honor the king.

Submission to Masters
18 Servants, *be* submissive to *your* masters
with all fear, not only to the good and gentle,
but also to the harsh.
19 For this *is* commendable, if because of
conscience toward God one endures grief,
suffering wrongfully.
20 For what credit *is it* if, when you are
beaten for your faults, you take it patiently?
But when you do good and suffer, if you take
it patiently, this *is* commendable before God.
21 For to this you were called, because Christ ◄
also suffered for us,[a] leaving us[b] an example,
that you should follow His steps:

22"*Who committed no sin,*
Nor was deceit found in His mouth";[a]

23 who, when He was reviled, did not revile
in return; when He suffered, He did not
threaten, but committed *Himself* to Him who
judges righteously;
24 who Himself bore our sins in His own
body on the tree, that we, having died to sins,
might live for righteousness—by whose
stripes you were healed.
25 For you were like sheep going astray, but
have now returned to the Shepherd and Overseer[a] of your souls.

Submission to Husbands
3 Wives, likewise, *be* submissive to your own
husbands, that even if some do not obey
the word, they, without a word, may be won
by the conduct of their wives,
2 when they observe your chaste conduct
accompanied by fear.

2:6 [a]Isaiah 28:16 **2:7** [a]NU-Text reads *to those who disbelieve.* [b]Psalm 118:22 **2:8** [a]Isaiah 8:14 **2:21** [a]NU-Text reads *you.* [b]NU-Text and M-Text read *you.* **2:22** [a]Isaiah 53:9 **2:25** [a]Greek *Episkopos*

LIFE LESSONS

➤ **2:9 — *But you are a chosen generation, a royal priesthood, a holy nation, His own special people . . . .***

Peter uses a flurry of wonderful descriptions to portray the exalted position we enjoy as believers "in Christ." God calls us "chosen" and "royal" and "holy" and "special" so that we might begin to act like who we really are.

➤ **2:11 — *Beloved, I beg you as sojourners and pilgrims, abstain from fleshly lusts which war against the soul . . . .***

We get ourselves into trouble when we forget that this world is not our home. If we would remember we are only aliens and strangers here, we would not feel tempted to put down roots that can never take root.

➤ **2:21 — *. . . Christ also suffered for us, leaving us an example, that you should follow His steps . . . .***

Jesus is our example in all things, even in suffering. He did not willingly suffer merely for suffering's sake (see John 18:23), but He eagerly accepted it when He saw it as God's will for Him (see Luke 22:42).

3 Do not let your adornment be *merely* outward—arranging the hair, wearing gold, or
putting on *fine* apparel—
➤ 4 rather *let it be* the hidden person of the
heart, with the incorruptible *beauty* of a gentle and quiet spirit, which is very precious in
the sight of God.
5 For in this manner, in former times,
the holy women who trusted in God also
adorned themselves, being submissive to
their own husbands,
6 as Sarah obeyed Abraham, calling him
lord, whose daughters you are if you do good
and are not afraid with any terror.

A Word to Husbands

➤ **7** Husbands, likewise, dwell with *them* with
understanding, giving honor to the wife, as to
the weaker vessel, and as *being* heirs together
of the grace of life, that your prayers may not
be hindered.

Called to Blessing

8 Finally, all *of you be* of one mind, having
compassion for one another; love as brothers,
be tenderhearted, *be* courteous;[a]
9 not returning evil for evil or reviling for
reviling, but on the contrary blessing, knowing that you were called to this, that you may
inherit a blessing.
10 For

"He who would love life
And see good days,
Let him refrain his tongue from evil,
And his lips from speaking deceit.
11 *Let him turn away from evil and do good;*
Let him seek peace and pursue it.
12 *For the eyes of the* L*ORD are on the*
righteous,
And His ears are open to their prayers;
But the face of the L*ORD is against those*
who do evil."[a]

Suffering for Right and Wrong

13 And who *is* he who will harm you if you
become followers of what is good?
14 But even if you should suffer for righteousness' sake, *you are* blessed. *"And do not*
be afraid of their threats, nor be troubled."[a]
15 But sanctify the Lord God[a] in your hearts, ➤
and always *be* ready to *give* a defense to
everyone who asks you a reason for the
hope that is in you, with meekness and fear;
16 having a good conscience, that when they
defame you as evildoers, those who revile
your good conduct in Christ may be ashamed.
17 For *it is* better, if it is the will of God, to
suffer for doing good than for doing evil.

Christ's Suffering and Ours

18 For Christ also suffered once for sins, the
just for the unjust, that He might bring us[a] to
God, being put to death in the flesh but made
alive by the Spirit,
19 by whom also He went and preached to
the spirits in prison,
20 who formerly were disobedient, when once
the Divine longsuffering waited[a] in the days
of Noah, while *the* ark was being prepared,
in which a few, that is, eight souls, were saved
through water.
21 There is also an antitype which now saves
us—baptism (not the removal of the filth of
the flesh, but the answer of a good conscience
toward God), through the resurrection of Jesus Christ,
22 who has gone into heaven and is at the
right hand of God, angels and authorities and
powers having been made subject to Him.

4 Therefore, since Christ suffered for us[a] in
the flesh, arm yourselves also with the
same mind, for he who has suffered in the
flesh has ceased from sin,
2 that he no longer should live the rest of *his* ➤
time in the flesh for the lusts of men, but for
the will of God.

3:8 [a]NU-Text reads *humble.* **3:12** [a]Psalm 34:12–16
3:14 [a]Isaiah 8:12 **3:15** [a]NU-Text reads *Christ as Lord.*
3:18 [a]NU-Text and M-Text read *you.* **3:20** [a]NU-Text and M-Text read *when the longsuffering of God waited patiently.*
4:1 [a]NU-Text omits *for us.*

LIFE LESSONS

➤ 3:4 — *. . . let it be the hidden person of the heart, with the incorruptible beauty of a gentle and quiet spirit, which is very precious in the sight of God.*

What would happen in our spiritual lives if we spent as much time working on our souls as we do on our bodies? Our bodies are not unimportant, but they will die; our spirits, however, will live forever.

➤ 3:7 — *Husbands, likewise, dwell with them with understanding, giving honor to the wife . . . that your prayers may not be hindered.*

Why would failing to make the effort to understand and honor his wife hinder a husband's prayers? All believers, men and women, are co-heirs of God's promises, and He wants us to treat each other as we would treat Him.

➤ 3:15 — *. . . always be ready to give a defense to everyone who asks you a reason for the hope that is in you, with meekness and fear . . . .*

If someone were to ask you today why you are a Christian, what would you say? How would you answer someone who said there are many ways to God? How would you defend your belief in the resurrection of Christ?

➤ 4:2 — *. . . that he no longer should live the rest of his time in the flesh for the lusts of men, but for the will of God.*

Had He chosen to do so, God could have taken us immediately to heaven when we placed our faith in Christ. But He didn't. Why not? He wants us reach others for Him by showing them how His power changes our lives.

3 For we *have spent* enough of our past lifetime[a] in doing the will of the Gentiles—when
we walked in lewdness, lusts, drunkenness,
revelries, drinking parties, and abominable
idolatries.
4 In regard to these, they think it strange that
you do not run with *them* in the same flood of
dissipation, speaking evil of *you.*
5 They will give an account to Him who is
ready to judge the living and the dead.
6 For this reason the gospel was preached
also to those who are dead, that they might be
judged according to men in the flesh, but live
according to God in the spirit.

Serving for God's Glory

7 But the end of all things is at hand; therefore be serious and watchful in your prayers.
8 And above all things have fervent love for
one another, for *"love will cover a multitude
of sins."*[a]
9 *Be* hospitable to one another without
grumbling.
10 As each one has received a gift, minister it
to one another, as good stewards of the manifold grace of God.
11 If anyone speaks, *let him speak* as the oracles of God. If anyone ministers, *let him do it*
as with the ability which God supplies, that in
all things God may be glorified through Jesus
Christ, to whom belong the glory and the dominion forever and ever. Amen.

Suffering for God's Glory

12 Beloved, do not think it strange concerning the fiery trial which is to try you, as though
some strange thing happened to you;
13 but rejoice to the extent that you partake
of Christ's sufferings, that when His glory is
revealed, you may also be glad with exceeding joy.
14 If you are reproached for the name of
Christ, blessed *are you,* for the Spirit of glory
and of God rests upon you.[a] On their part He
is blasphemed, but on your part He is glorified.
15 But let none of you suffer as a murderer, a
thief, an evildoer, or as a busybody in other
people's matters.
16 Yet if *anyone suffers* as a Christian, let him
not be ashamed, but let him glorify God in
this matter.[a]
17 For the time *has come* for judgment to
begin at the house of God; and if *it begins* with
us first, what will *be* the end of those who do
not obey the gospel of God?
18 Now

"If the righteous one is scarcely saved,
Where will the ungodly and the sinner
appear?"[a]

19 Therefore let those who suffer according
to the will of God commit their souls *to Him*
in doing good, as to a faithful Creator.

Shepherd the Flock

5 The elders who are among you I exhort, I
who am a fellow elder and a witness of the
sufferings of Christ, and also a partaker of the
glory that will be revealed:
2 Shepherd the flock of God which is among
you, serving as overseers, not by compulsion
but willingly,[a] not for dishonest gain but eagerly;
3 nor as being lords over those entrusted to
you, but being examples to the flock;
4 and when the Chief Shepherd appears,
you will receive the crown of glory that does
not fade away.

Submit to God, Resist the Devil

5 Likewise you younger people, submit
yourselves to *your* elders. Yes, all of *you* be
submissive to one another, and be clothed
with humility, for

"God resists the proud,
But gives grace to the humble."[a]

4:3 [a]NU-Text reads *time.* **4:8** [a]Proverbs 10:12 **4:14** [a]NU-Text omits the rest of this verse. **4:16** [a]NU-Text reads *name.* **4:18** [a]Proverbs 11:31 **5:2** [a]NU-Text adds *according to God.* **5:5** [a]Proverbs 3:34

LIFE LESSONS

➤ 4:4 — *. . . they think it strange that you do not run with them in the same flood of dissipation, speaking evil of you.*

People who knew us before we placed our faith in Christ simply will not understand why we no longer want to participate in some of the ungodly things we did before we found God's love. Don't listen to their taunts.

➤ 4:8 — *And above all things have fervent love for one another, for "love will cover a multitude of sins."*

Even in the best of churches and the most godly of homes, things go wrong. What do we do then? The place to start (and end) is to choose to imitate God's love to us, and bear with one another (Col. 3:13).

➤ 4:19 — *Therefore let those who suffer according to the will of God commit their souls to Him in doing good, as to a faithful Creator.*

Did you realize that it is God's will for us to suffer at some points along the way of life's journey? We are "appointed" to it (1 Thess. 3:3) and are to "glory" in it (Rom. 5:3). Only trust in God enables us to endure.

➤ 5:2 — *Shepherd the flock of God which is among you, serving as overseers, not by compulsion but willingly . . . .*

God delights in willing service, not in grudging obedience—as if we were doing Him a favor by complying with His instructions. Eager obedience reveals a heart in love with the One who gave the command.

✳ 6 Therefore humble yourselves under the
mighty hand of God, that He may exalt you in
due time,
➢ 7 casting all your care upon Him, for He cares
for you.
➢ 8 Be sober, be vigilant; because[a] your adversary the devil walks about like a roaring lion,
seeking whom he may devour.
9 Resist him, steadfast in the faith, knowing
that the same sufferings are experienced by
your brotherhood in the world.
10 But may[a] the God of all grace, who called
us[b] to His eternal glory by Christ Jesus, after
you have suffered a while, perfect, establish,
strengthen, and settle *you*.
11 To Him *be* the glory and the dominion forever and ever. Amen.

Farewell and Peace

12 By Silvanus, our faithful brother as I
consider him, I have written to you briefly,
exhorting and testifying that this is the true
grace of God in which you stand.
13 She who is in Babylon, elect together
with *you*, greets you; and *so does* Mark my
son.
14 Greet one another with a kiss of love.
Peace to you all who are in Christ Jesus.
Amen.

5:8 [a]NU-Text and M-Text omit *because.* **5:10** [a]NU-Text reads *But the God of all grace . . . will perfect, establish, strengthen, and settle you.* [b]NU-Text and M-Text read *you.*

LIFE LESSONS

➢ 5:7 — *. . . casting all your care upon Him, for He cares for you.*

Regardless of the concern or worry, God wants us to bring everything to Him. He always has our best interests at heart and will rouse all His infinite power to help us become the people we are meant to be.

➢ 5:8 — *Be sober, be vigilant; because your adversary the devil walks about like a roaring lion, seeking whom he may devour.*

We must never forget that we are in a spiritual war. Regardless of how well things may seem to be going for us, we live in a perpetual war zone. How many casualties occur because we think we live in a time of peace?

THE SECOND EPISTLE OF PETER

First Peter deals with problems from the outside; Second Peter deals with problems from the inside. Peter writes in his second letter to warn believers about false teachers who promote damaging doctrine.

He begins by urging his friends in Christ to keep close watch on their personal lives. The Christian life demands diligence in pursuing moral excellence, knowledge, self-control, perseverance, godliness, brotherly kindness, and selfless love. Such careful attention to godliness pays huge dividends, "For if these things are yours and abound, you will be neither barren nor unfruitful in the knowledge of our Lord Jesus Christ" (1:8).

By contrast, the false teachers trying to seduce unsuspecting believers are sensual, arrogant, greedy, and covetous. They scoff at the thought of future judgment and live as if their current prosperity would remain the unalterable pattern for the future. Peter reminds his readers that although God's longsuffering nature may prompt Him to delay in sending judgment, ultimately that judgment will come; and these false teacher "will utterly perish in their own corruption, and will receive the wages of unrighteousness" (2:12, 13), and so for them "is reserved the blackness of darkness forever" (2:17).

Peter does not want his Christian friends to forget that the Lord Jesus is most certainly coming back to earth in power and great glory, bringing both His judgment and His rewards with Him. In view of that awesome fact, believers should live in a godly, blameless, and steadfast manner (3:11–15).

To distinguish this epistle from the first by Peter, it was given the Greek title *Petrou B*, the "Second of Peter."

Themes: False teachers may spread doctrine that appeals to the flesh, but they face the awesome judgment of God—and so will all those who embrace their teaching.

Author: The apostle Peter.

Time: Probably written around A.D. 65–67.

Structure: Peter introduces himself (1:1, 2), encourages his friends to grow in godliness (1:3–11), explains his purpose for and authority in writing (1:12–21), warns against false teachers (2:1–22), reminds them of the return of Jesus (3:1–16), and makes a few closing remarks (3:17, 18).

As you read 2 Peter, watch for several life principles that play an important role in this book:

9. Trusting God means looking beyond what we can see to what God sees. *See 2 Peter 1:2–4; page 1475.*

3. God's Word is an immovable anchor in times of storm. *See 2 Peter 1:19–21; page 1475.*

14. God acts on behalf of those who wait for Him. *See 2 Peter 3:1–9; pages 1476, 1478.*

30. An eager anticipation of the Lord's return keeps us living productively. *See 2 Peter 3:10–13; page 1478.*

Greeting the Faithful

1 Simon Peter, a bondservant and apostle of
Jesus Christ,

To those who have obtained like precious
faith with us by the righteousness of our God
and Savior Jesus Christ:

2 Grace and peace be multiplied to you in
the knowledge of God and of Jesus our Lord,
➤ 3 as His divine power has given to us all
things that *pertain* to life and godliness,
through the knowledge of Him who called
us by glory and virtue,
✳ 4 by which have been given to us exceedingly great and precious promises, that
through these you may be partakers of the
divine nature, having escaped the corruption
that is in the world through lust.

Fruitful Growth in the Faith

5 But also for this very reason, giving all
diligence, add to your faith virtue, to virtue
knowledge,
6 to knowledge self-control, to self-control
perseverance, to perseverance godliness,
7 to godliness brotherly kindness, and to
brotherly kindness love.
➤ 8 For if these things are yours and abound,
you will be neither barren nor unfruitful in
the knowledge of our Lord Jesus Christ.
9 For he who lacks these things is shortsighted, even to blindness, and has forgotten
that he was cleansed from his old sins.
✳ 10 Therefore, brethren, be even more diligent
to make your call and election sure, for if you
do these things you will never stumble;
11 for so an entrance will be supplied to you
abundantly into the everlasting kingdom of
our Lord and Savior Jesus Christ.

Peter's Approaching Death

12 For this reason I will not be negligent to
remind you always of these things, though
you know and are established in the present
truth.
13 Yes, I think it is right, as long as I am in
this tent, to stir you up by reminding *you,*
14 knowing that shortly I *must* put off my
tent, just as our Lord Jesus Christ showed me.
15 Moreover I will be careful to ensure that
you always have a reminder of these things
after my decease.

The Trustworthy Prophetic Word

16 For we did not follow cunningly devised
fables when we made known to you the
power and coming of our Lord Jesus Christ,
but were eyewitnesses of His majesty.
17 For He received from God the Father honor
and glory when such a voice came to Him
from the Excellent Glory: "This is My beloved
Son, in whom I am well pleased."
18 And we heard this voice which came from
heaven when we were with Him on the holy
mountain.
19 And so we have the prophetic word confirmed,[a] which you do well to heed as a light
that shines in a dark place, until the day
dawns and the morning star rises in your
hearts;
20 knowing this first, that no prophecy of
Scripture is of any private interpretation,[a]
21 for prophecy never came by the will of ◄
man, but holy men of God[a] spoke *as they
were* moved by the Holy Spirit.

Destructive Doctrines

2 But there were also false prophets among ◄
the people, even as there will be false
teachers among you, who will secretly bring
in destructive heresies, even denying the Lord
who bought them, *and* bring on themselves
swift destruction.
2 And many will follow their destructive
ways, because of whom the way of truth will
be blasphemed.

1:19 [a]Or *We also have the more sure prophetic word.* **1:20** [a]Or *origin* **1:21** [a]NU-Text reads *but men spoke from God.*

LIFE LESSONS

➤ 1:3 — . . . *His divine power has given to us all things that pertain to life and godliness, through the knowledge of Him who called us . . . .*

Everything we need to become more like Christ, God has already given us. We do not need some new experience or fresh revelation to help us draw close to God; we simply have to appropriate what He's already given.

➤ 1:8 — *For if these things are yours and abound, you will be neither barren nor unfruitful in the knowledge of our Lord Jesus Christ.*

Jesus wants our spiritual lives to become both lush and fruitful, for He knows that such a fertile life greatly pleases God and gives us enormous satisfaction. How do we become fruitful? By abiding in Christ.

➤ 1:21 — . . . *prophecy never came by the will of man, but holy men of God spoke as they were moved by the Holy Spirit.*

Although the Bible came to us through redeemed men, and therefore displays many of their traits and unique ways of communicating, yet the message is directly from God and relays exactly what He wanted to say.

➤ 2:1 — *But there were also false prophets among the people, even as there will be false teachers among you, who will secretly bring in destructive heresies . . . .*

The best way to recognize counterfeit doctrine is to become thoroughly familiar with the truth. Someone whose mind has been trained to know and love the truth will not easily be led astray by false teaching.

3 By covetousness they will exploit you with
deceptive words; for a long time their judgment has not been idle, and their destruction
does[a] not slumber.

Doom of False Teachers

4 For if God did not spare the angels who
sinned, but cast *them* down to hell and delivered *them* into chains of darkness, to be reserved for judgment;
5 and did not spare the ancient world, but
saved Noah, *one of* eight *people*, a preacher of
righteousness, bringing in the flood on the
world of the ungodly;
6 and turning the cities of Sodom and Gomorrah into ashes, condemned *them* to destruction, making *them* an example to those
who afterward would live ungodly;
7 and delivered righteous Lot, *who was* oppressed by the filthy conduct of the wicked
8 (for that righteous man, dwelling among
them, tormented *his* righteous soul from day
to day by seeing and hearing *their* lawless
deeds)—
9 *then* the Lord knows how to deliver the
godly out of temptations and to reserve the
unjust under punishment for the day of judgment,
10 and especially those who walk according
to the flesh in the lust of uncleanness and despise authority. [R]*They are* presumptuous, self-
willed. They are not afraid to speak evil of
dignitaries,
11 whereas angels, who are greater in power
and might, do not bring a reviling accusation
against them before the Lord.

Depravity of False Teachers

12 But these, like natural brute beasts made
to be caught and destroyed, speak evil of the
things they do not understand, and will utterly perish in their own corruption,
13 *and* will receive the wages of unrighteousness, *as* those who count it pleasure to ca-
rouse in the daytime. *They are* spots and
blemishes, carousing in their own deceptions
while they feast with you,
14 having eyes full of adultery and that cannot cease from sin, enticing unstable souls.
They have a heart trained in covetous practices, *and are* accursed children.
15 They have forsaken the right way and
gone astray, following the way of Balaam the
son of Beor, who loved the wages of unrighteousness;
16 but he was rebuked for his iniquity: a
dumb donkey speaking with a man's voice restrained the madness of the prophet.
17 These are wells without water, clouds[a] carried by a tempest, for whom is reserved the
blackness of darkness forever.[b]

Deceptions of False Teachers

18 For when they speak great swelling *words*
of emptiness, they allure through the lusts
of the flesh, through lewdness, the ones who
have actually escaped[a] from those who live in
error.
19 While they promise them liberty, they
themselves are slaves of corruption; for by
whom a person is overcome, by him also he
is brought into bondage.
20 For if, after they have escaped the pollutions of the world through the knowledge of
the Lord and Savior Jesus Christ, they are
again entangled in them and overcome, the
latter end is worse for them than the beginning.
21 For it would have been better for them not
to have known the way of righteousness, than
having known *it*, to turn from the holy commandment delivered to them.
22 But it has happened to them according to
the true proverb: *"A dog returns to his own
vomit,"*[a] and, "a sow, having washed, to her
wallowing in the mire."

God's Promise Is Not Slack

3 Beloved, I now write to you this second
epistle (in *both of* which I stir up your
pure minds by way of reminder),
2 that you may be mindful of the words
which were spoken before by the holy prophets, and of the commandment of us,[a] the apostles of the Lord and Savior,

2:3 [a]M-Text reads *will not.* **2:17** [a]NU-Text reads *and mists.* [b]NU-Text omits *forever.* **2:18** [a]NU-Text reads *are barely escaping.* **2:22** [a]Proverbs 26:11 **3:2** [a]NU-Text and M-Text read *commandment of the apostles of your Lord and Savior* or *commandment of your apostles of the Lord and Savior.*

LIFE LESSONS

➤ 2:19 — *While they promise them liberty, they themselves are slaves of corruption; for by whom a person is overcome, by him also he is brought into bondage.*

People who encourage us to join them in their sin are like junkies who encourage people to join them in their drug habit. They promise a good time and a real high, but in fact they are trapped in a destructive lifestyle.

➤ 2:21 — *For it would have been better for them not to have known the way of righteousness, than having known it, to turn from the holy commandment delivered to them.*

When Jesus asked Peter and the other disciples if they would leave Him, as others had, the burly fisherman replied, "Lord, to whom shall we go? You have the words of eternal life" (John 6:68). No one else does.

WHAT THE BIBLE SAYS ABOUT SPIRITUAL GROWTH

2 Pet.3:18

Not many people can say that on the day they were saved, someone explained to them the steps to spiritual growth. Unfortunately, some believers *never* hear how to grow in grace. Since none of us grows as a Christian without taking action, Peter instructs believers to "grow in the grace and knowledge of our Lord and Savior Jesus Christ" (2 Pet. 3:18).

Then how are we to grow? The Bible gives us some powerful guidelines.

First, we are responsible for renewing our mind (Rom. 12:2). Though God saves us and gives us a new spirit, He does not give us a new brain. Disobedience and rebellion have dug or worn many ugly trenches in our minds. So we must meditate on the Bible, which expresses the thoughts of God. Meditation is more than reading—it involves thinking about what the words mean and then applying the truth we discover. When we meditate on His Word and depend upon the Spirit's power to help us put it into practice, our minds undergo the wonderful process of transformation. That is how we obtain "the mind of Christ" (1 Cor. 2:16).

Some believers never hear how to grow in grace.

Second, we must be ready to admit our failures and assume responsibility for them. When we deny our sins, we delay our spiritual growth; but when we confess our failures, the opposite happens—growth becomes inevitable. James tells us, "Confess your trespasses to one another, and pray for one another, that you may be healed" (James 5:16).

The third step naturally follows the second: After confession should come repentance. This is more than acknowledging wrongdoing or promising to try harder. Repentance means that we commit to make an about-face and head in the opposite direction from our sin. Paul taught new converts "that they should repent, turn to God, and do works befitting repentance" (Acts 26:20).

God's ultimate goal is for all believers to become more Christlike. That happens only when, through faith, we tap into the power of God. With these steps, we will begin to move in that direction. And soon our relationship with God begins to deepen.

See the Life Principles Index for further study:

2. Obey God and leave all the consequences to Him.
24. To live the Christian life is to allow Jesus to live His life in and through us.
1. Our intimacy with God—His highest priority for our lives—determines the impact of our lives.

➤ 3 knowing this first: that scoffers will come
in the last days, walking according to their
own lusts,
4 and saying, "Where is the promise of His
coming? For since the fathers fell asleep, all
things continue as *they were* from the beginning of creation."
5 For this they willfully forget: that by the
word of God the heavens were of old, and the
earth standing out of water and in the water,
6 by which the world *that* then existed perished, being flooded with water.
7 But the heavens and the earth *which*
are now preserved by the same word, are reserved for fire until the day of judgment and
perdition of ungodly men.
➤ 8 But, beloved, do not forget this one thing,
that with the Lord one day *is* as a thousand
years, and a thousand years as one day.
✳ 9 The Lord is not slack concerning *His*
promise, as some count slackness, but is longsuffering toward us,[a] not willing that any
should perish but that all should come to repentance.

The Day of the Lord

10 But the day of the Lord will come as a
thief in the night, in which the heavens will
pass away with a great noise, and the elements will melt with fervent heat; both the
earth and the works that are in it will be
burned up.[a]
11 Therefore, since all these things will be
dissolved, what manner *of persons* ought you
to be in holy conduct and godliness,
12 looking for and hastening the coming of ➤
the day of God, because of which the heavens
will be dissolved, being on fire, and the elements will melt with fervent heat?
13 Nevertheless we, according to His prom- ✳
ise, look for new heavens and a new earth in
which righteousness dwells.

Be Steadfast

14 Therefore, beloved, looking forward to
these things, be diligent to be found by Him
in peace, without spot and blameless;
15 and consider *that* the longsuffering of our
Lord *is* salvation—as also our beloved brother
Paul, according to the wisdom given to him,
has written to you,
16 as also in all his epistles, speaking in them ➤
of these things, in which are some things hard
to understand, which untaught and unstable
people twist to their own destruction, as *they*
do also the rest of the Scriptures.
17 You therefore, beloved, since you know
this beforehand, beware lest you also fall from
your own steadfastness, being led away with
the error of the wicked;
18 but grow in the grace and knowledge of
our Lord and Savior Jesus Christ. To Him *be*
the glory both now and forever. Amen.

3:9 [a]NU-Text reads *you.* **3:10** [a]NU-Text reads *laid bare* (literally *found*).

LIFE LESSONS

➤ 3:3 — *. . . knowing this first: that scoffers will come in the last days, walking according to their own lusts . . . .*

Why does Peter want us to know "first" that scoffers will come? Unless we are ready for it, scoffing can accomplish what reasoned debate cannot. Ridicule can prompt those who are unaware to unwisely conform.

➤ 3:8 — *But, beloved, do not forget this one thing, that with the Lord one day is as a thousand years, and a thousand years as one day.*

God simply does not run this world by our timetable. What feels like a delay to us is right on schedule by His calendar. He often makes us wait, not to frustrate us, but to deepen our trust in Him.

➤ 3:12 — *. . . looking for and hastening the coming of the day of God . . . .*

While we often turn biblical prophecy into a forum for debate, the Scripture uses prophecy for far more practical purposes. Knowing what lies ahead should move us to please the God before whom we will soon stand for judgment.

➤ 3:16 — *. . . in which are some things hard to understand, which untaught and unstable people twist to their own destruction, as they do also the rest of the Scriptures.*

We should be neither discouraged nor surprised when we come upon Bible passages that we have a hard time understanding. Peter had the same difficulty—and God used him to help *write* Scripture!

THE FIRST EPISTLE OF

JOHN

God is light; God is love; and God is life. John enjoyed a delightful fellowship with that God and desperately wanted his spiritual children to enjoy the same thing.

God is light. To enjoy fellowship with the Lord we must walk in light. As we do so, we will regularly confess our sins, allowing the blood of Christ to continually cleanse us. We must avoid falling in love with the world and falling for the alluring lies of false teachers.

God is love. Since we are God's children, we must walk in love. In fact, John says that if we do not love, we do not know God. Love is more than just words; it requires action. Biblical love is unconditional, and when that brand of love characterizes us, we free ourselves of self-condemnation and increase our confidence before God.

God is life. Those who fellowship with God must possess His quality of life. Faith in Jesus Christ infuses us with God's life—eternal life.

John's second epistle reminds "the elect lady and her children" to love one another, but indicates that this love must be discerning. False teachers abound who do not acknowledge Christ as having come in the flesh—and it is false charity to open the door to false teaching.

In Third John, the apostle encourages a man named Gaius to foster Christian fellowship by hosting and supporting visiting missionaries. He also warns against the "me first" attitude of a church leader who left the way of love.

Although the apostle John's name is not found any of these books, they were given the titles *Ioannou A*, *B*, and *C*, the "First of John," the "Second of John," and the "Third of John."

Themes: By His very character, God is love, and to know Him is to extend that love to those around us.

Author: The apostle John.

Date: Believed to have been written from Ephesus near the end of the first century.

Structure: First John begins with a reminder of Christ's incarnation (1:1–4), followed by instruction on what it means to have fellowship with God (1:5—2:28) and further teaching on how a child of God should live (2:29—5:17). The book ends with how to identify the true and reject the false (5:18–21). 2 John encourages believers to walk in Christ's commandments and beware of deceivers, while 3 John commends hospitality and godly living.

As you read John's epistles, watch for several life principles that play an important role in these books:

15. Brokenness is God's requirement for maximum usefulness. *See 1 John 1:6–10; page 1480.*

30. An eager anticipation of the Lord's return keeps us living productively. *See 1 John 2:28, 29; page 1482.*

2. Obey God and leave all the consequences to Him. *See 1 John 3:22–24; 5:2, 3; pages 1483, 1484.*

28. No Christian has ever been called to "go it alone" in his or her walk of faith. *See 2 John 5; 3 John 5–8; pages 1486, 1487.*

What Was Heard, Seen, and Touched

1 That which was from the beginning, which we have heard, which we have seen with our eyes, which we have looked upon, and our hands have handled, concerning the Word of life—
2 the life was manifested, and we have seen, and bear witness, and declare to you that eternal life which was with the Father and was manifested to us—
3 that which we have seen and heard we declare to you, that you also may have fellowship with us; and truly our fellowship *is* with the Father and with His Son Jesus Christ.
4 And these things we write to you that your[a] joy may be full.

Fellowship with Him and One Another

5 This is the message which we have heard from Him and declare to you, that God is light and in Him is no darkness at all.
6 If we say that we have fellowship with Him, and walk in darkness, we lie and do not practice the truth.
7 But if we walk in the light as He is in the light, we have fellowship with one another, and the blood of Jesus Christ His Son cleanses us from all sin.
8 If we say that we have no sin, we deceive ourselves, and the truth is not in us.
9 If we confess our sins, He is faithful and just to forgive us *our* sins and to cleanse us from all unrighteousness.
10 If we say that we have not sinned, we make Him a liar, and His word is not in us.

2 My little children, these things I write to you, so that you may not sin. And if anyone sins, we have an Advocate with the Father, Jesus Christ the righteous.
2 And He Himself is the propitiation for our sins, and not for ours only but also for the whole world.

The Test of Knowing Him

3 Now by this we know that we know Him, if we keep His commandments.
4 He who says, "I know Him," and does not keep His commandments, is a liar, and the truth is not in him.
5 But whoever keeps His word, truly the love of God is perfected in him. By this we know that we are in Him.
6 He who says he abides in Him ought himself also to walk just as He walked.
7 Brethren,[a] I write no new commandment to you, but an old commandment which you have had from the beginning. The old commandment is the word which you heard from the beginning.[b]
8 Again, a new commandment I write to you, which thing is true in Him and in you, because the darkness is passing away, and the true light is already shining.
9 He who says he is in the light, and hates his brother, is in darkness until now.
10 He who loves his brother abides in the light, and there is no cause for stumbling in him.
11 But he who hates his brother is in darkness and walks in darkness, and does not

1:4 [a]NU-Text and M-Text read *our.* 2:7 [a]NU-Text reads *Beloved.* [b]NU-Text omits *from the beginning.*

LIFE LESSONS

➤ 1:3 — *. . . that which we have seen and heard we declare to you, that you also may have fellowship with us; and truly our fellowship is with the Father and with His Son Jesus Christ.*

Everything in the Bible has been given to us to help us and enable us to enjoy an intimate relationship with God. God's top priority for your life is to walk in close fellowship with Him.

➤ 1:4 — *And these things we write to you that your joy may be full.*

Believers sometimes excuse some very foolish behavior with the statement, "But God wants me to be happy!" The truth is, God wants something much better for us than happiness—He wants joy. But that comes only in obedience to Him.

➤ 1:6 — *If we say that we have fellowship with Him, and walk in darkness, we lie and do not practice the truth.*

John, "the apostle of love," tends to be very uncompromising in his perspective on the Christian walk. Obedience to God is necessary, He says, not optional; and those who habitually disobey do not know God.

➤ 2:1 — *My little children, these things I write to you, so that you may not sin. And if anyone sins, we have an Advocate with the Father, Jesus Christ the righteous.*

There is no divine commandment to sin. Therefore, when we rely on the indwelling Spirit, we do not *have* to sin (see Gal. 5:16). Yet when we do occasionally sin by relying on ourselves, Jesus helps us get back on track.

➤ 2:3 — *Now by this we know that we know Him, if we keep His commandments.*

When we obey God by the power of His Spirit, we not only please God and make it possible for us to enjoy close fellowship with Him, we also build confidence in our hearts that we truly belong to Him.

➤ 2:6 — *He who says he abides in Him ought himself also to walk just as He walked.*

An intimate relationship with Christ makes it both possible and appealing for us to obey God, just as Jesus did. If we think of salvation as an invitation to sin—"He'll forgive me anyway"—we're on the wrong track.

ANSWERS TO LIFE'S QUESTIONS

How can God use an imperfect person like me?

1 JOHN 1:9

Once you have accepted Jesus Christ, God's Holy Spirit lives in you. Through Him, God enables you to do everything He asks, making the possibilities for service limitless.

Have you been sitting on the sidelines because you have let sin and shame discourage you? Perhaps you feel as though God can't use your broken vessel.

Don't let your feelings overshadow the truth! God is big enough to forgive you, restore you, and use you to restore others. First John 1:9 says, "If we confess our sins, He is faithful and just to forgive us our sins and to cleanse us from all unrighteousness."

Once you have confessed and turned from your sins, you are cleansed—but God does not purify you and empower you with His Spirit merely to make you feel good. God's purification process fulfills the Scriptures and equips His children for service. The question is not, "Do I have the power?" It is, "How will I use that power?" Once you're asking the right question, consider a few prerequisites to answering it:

- *Conviction of inadequacy.* This is more than merely feeling as though God can't use you if you walk in the flesh; and it's not simply knowing that God alone is sovereign. It is knowing and acknowledging that without the Holy Spirit, you are incapable, unwilling, and too weak to do what He asks of you.
- *Purity of life.* Don't confuse purity with perfection. Purity is continual, immediate confession of and repentance from sin.
- *Prayer.* When you willingly and genuinely acknowledge your inadequacy, you will consistently reach up to God through prayer. You know that He is your lifeline and that you cannot live without Him.
- *Belief.* Jesus tells us, "And all things you ask in prayer, believing, you will receive" (Matt. 21:22). When you ask according to God's will, He answers. You must believe that He will do what He says.
- *Engaged in service.* God has given you the power of the Holy Spirit, and He wants you to be eager to use it.

Whether for ministry to one person or to many, the power of God's Spirit changes lives. God was big enough to transform your heart and save you from bondage to sin. He is also big enough to cleanse you, help you rise above discouragement, and use you to influence the lives of others—all for His glory.

See the Life Principles Index for further study:
9. Trusting God means looking beyond what we can see to what God sees.
4. The awareness of God's presence energizes us for our work.
1. Our intimacy with God—His highest priority for our lives—determines the impact of our lives.

know where he is going, because the darkness has blinded his eyes.

Their Spiritual State

12 I write to you, little children,
Because your sins are forgiven you for His name's sake.
13 I write to you, fathers,
Because you have known Him *who is* from the beginning.
I write to you, young men,
Because you have overcome the wicked one.
I write to you, little children,
Because you have known the Father.
14 I have written to you, fathers,
Because you have known Him *who is* from the beginning.
I have written to you, young men,
Because you are strong, and the word of God abides in you,
And you have overcome the wicked one.

Do Not Love the World

15 Do not love the world or the things in the world. If anyone loves the world, the love of the Father is not in him.
16 For all that *is* in the world—the lust of the flesh, the lust of the eyes, and the pride of life—is not of the Father but is of the world.
17 And the world is passing away, and the *

lust of it; but he who does the will of God
abides forever.

Deceptions of the Last Hour

18 Little children, it is the last hour; and as
you have heard that the[a] Antichrist is coming,
even now many antichrists have come, by
which we know that it is the last hour.
19 They went out from us, but they were not
of us; for if they had been of us, they would
have continued with us; but *they went out*
that they might be made manifest, that none
of them were of us.
20 But you have an anointing from the Holy
One, and you know all things.[a]
21 I have not written to you because you do
not know the truth, but because you know it,
and that no lie is of the truth.
22 Who is a liar but he who denies that Jesus
is the Christ? He is antichrist who denies the
Father and the Son.
23 Whoever denies the Son does not have the
Father either; he who acknowledges the Son
has the Father also.

Let Truth Abide in You

24 Therefore let that abide in you which you
heard from the beginning. If what you heard
from the beginning abides in you, you also
will abide in the Son and in the Father.
25 And this is the promise that He has promised us—eternal life.
26 These things I have written to you concerning those who *try to* deceive you.
27 But the anointing which you have received
from Him abides in you, and you do not need
that anyone teach you; but as the same
anointing teaches you concerning all things,
and is true, and is not a lie, and just as it has
taught you, you will[a] abide in Him.

The Children of God

28 And now, little children, abide in Him, that
when[a] He appears, we may have confidence
and not be ashamed before Him at His coming.
29 If you know that He is righteous, you
know that everyone who practices righteousness is born of Him.

3 Behold what manner of love the Father
has bestowed on us, that we should be
called children of God![a] Therefore the world
does not know us,[b] because it did not know
Him.
2 Beloved, now we are children of God; and
it has not yet been revealed what we shall be,
but we know that when He is revealed, we
shall be like Him, for we shall see Him as He
is.
3 And everyone who has this hope in Him
purifies himself, just as He is pure.

Sin and the Child of God

4 Whoever commits sin also commits lawlessness, and sin is lawlessness.
5 And you know that He was manifested to
take away our sins, and in Him there is no sin.
6 Whoever abides in Him does not sin.
Whoever sins has neither seen Him nor
known Him.
7 Little children, let no one deceive you. He
who practices righteousness is righteous, just
as He is righteous.
8 He who sins is of the devil, for the devil
has sinned from the beginning. For this purpose the Son of God was manifested, that He
might destroy the works of the devil.
9 Whoever has been born of God does not
sin, for His seed remains in him; and he cannot sin, because he has been born of God.

The Imperative of Love

10 In this the children of God and the children of the devil are manifest: Whoever does
not practice righteousness is not of God, nor
is he who does not love his brother.
11 For this is the message that you heard
from the beginning, that we should love one
another,
12 not as Cain *who* was of the wicked one

2:18 [a]NU-Text omits *the*. **2:20** [a]NU-Text reads *you all know*.
2:27 [a]NU-Text reads *you abide*. **2:28** [a]NU-Text reads *if*.
3:1 [a]NU-Text adds *And we are*. [b]M-Text reads *you*.

LIFE LESSONS

➤ 2:19 — *They went out from us, but they were not of us; for if they had been of us, they would have continued with us . . . .*

Not even John the apostle knew what was in the hearts of those who made up his local church. He did not know that some members of his congregation did not truly know Jesus, until they abandoned the faith.

➤ 3:2 — *. . . we know that when He is revealed, we shall be like Him, for we shall see Him as He is.*

One day we will exchange our worn-out, sin-prone, weak bodies for new models patterned after Jesus' resurrection body—strong, ageless, free of all sin and completely at home in the holy presence of God.

➤ 3:6 — *Whoever abides in Him does not sin. Whoever sins has neither seen Him nor known Him.*

Jesus said that those who "abide" in Him—draw near to Him, listen to His words and obey them—would bear "much fruit," something that glorifies the Father (John 15:5, 8). Fruitful believers have the power to avoid sin.

and murdered his brother. And why did he
murder him? Because his works were evil and
his brother's righteous.
13 Do not marvel, my brethren, if the world
hates you.
14 We know that we have passed from death
to life, because we love the brethren. He who
does not love *his* brother[a] abides in death.
15 Whoever hates his brother is a murderer,
and you know that no murderer has eternal
life abiding in him.

The Outworking of Love

16 By this we know love, because He laid
down His life for us. And we also ought to lay
down *our* lives for the brethren.
17 But whoever has this world's goods, and
sees his brother in need, and shuts up his
heart from him, how does the love of God
abide in him?
18 My little children, let us not love in word
or in tongue, but in deed and in truth.
19 And by this we know[a] that we are of the
truth, and shall assure our hearts before Him.
20 For if our heart condemns us, God is
greater than our heart, and knows all things.
21 Beloved, if our heart does not condemn us,
we have confidence toward God.
22 And whatever we ask we receive from
Him, because we keep His commandments
and do those things that are pleasing in His
sight.
23 And this is His commandment: that we
should believe on the name of His Son Jesus
Christ and love one another, as He gave us[a]
commandment.

The Spirit of Truth and the Spirit of Error

24 Now he who keeps His commandments
abides in Him, and He in him. And by this we
know that He abides in us, by the Spirit whom
He has given us.

4 Beloved, do not believe every spirit, but
test the spirits, whether they are of God;
because many false prophets have gone out
into the world.
2 By this you know the Spirit of God: Every
spirit that confesses that Jesus Christ has
come in the flesh is of God,
3 and every spirit that does not confess that[a]
Jesus Christ has come in the flesh is not of
God. And this is the *spirit* of the Antichrist,
which you have heard was coming, and is
now already in the world.
4 You are of God, little children, and have
overcome them, because He who is in you is
greater than he who is in the world.
5 They are of the world. Therefore they speak
as of the world, and the world hears them.
6 We are of God. He who knows God hears
us; he who is not of God does not hear us. By
this we know the spirit of truth and the spirit
of error.

Knowing God Through Love

7 Beloved, let us love one another, for love is
of God; and everyone who loves is born of
God and knows God.
8 He who does not love does not know God,
for God is love.
9 In this the love of God was manifested toward us, that God has sent His only begotten
Son into the world, that we might live through
Him.
10 In this is love, not that we loved God, but
that He loved us and sent His Son *to be* the
propitiation for our sins.
11 Beloved, if God so loved us, we also ought
to love one another.

Seeing God Through Love

12 No one has seen God at any time. If we
love one another, God abides in us, and His
love has been perfected in us.

3:14 [a]NU-Text omits *his brother.* **3:19** [a]NU-Text reads *we shall know.* **3:23** [a]M-Text omits *us.* **4:3** [a]NU-Text omits *that* and *Christ has come in the flesh.*

LIFE LESSONS

➤ 3:20 — *For if our heart condemns us, God is greater than our heart, and knows all things.*

Believers who, more than anything else, want to obey and please God usually have tender consciences. Sometimes those consciences can condemn us—but "The Spirit Himself bears witness . . . that we are children of God" (Rom. 8:16).

➤ 4:1 — *Beloved, do not believe every spirit, but test the spirits, whether they are of God; because many false prophets have gone out into the world.*

Luke called the Berean Jews "fair-minded" because after Paul preached to them, they "searched the Scriptures daily to find out whether these things were so" (Acts 17:11). We are to "Test all things; hold fast what is good" (1 Thess. 5:21).

➤ 4:4 — *You are of God, little children, and have overcome them, because He who is in you is greater than he who is in the world.*

Anytime we resist some temptation, overcome some spiritual challenge, or triumph in a contest of faith, we do so because God's Spirit lives in us. We move ahead in a walk with God by relying on His power, not ours.

➤ 4:8 — *He who does not love does not know God, for God is love.*

To be transformed into the image of Christ—God's ultimate goal for us—means to increasingly reflect His loving character in our behavior and attitudes. Therefore if we are not becoming more loving, we have taken a wrong turn somewhere.

13 By this we know that we abide in Him, and He in us, because He has given us of His Spirit.
14 And we have seen and testify that the Father has sent the Son *as* Savior of the world.
15 Whoever confesses that Jesus is the Son of God, God abides in him, and he in God.
16 And we have known and believed the love that God has for us. God is love, and he who abides in love abides in God, and God in him.

The Consummation of Love

17 Love has been perfected among us in this: that we may have boldness in the day of judgment; because as He is, so are we in this world.
18 There is no fear in love; but perfect love casts out fear, because fear involves torment. But he who fears has not been made perfect in love.
19 We love Him[a] because He first loved us.

Obedience by Faith

➤ **20** If someone says, "I love God," and hates his brother, he is a liar; for he who does not love his brother whom he has seen, how can[a] he love God whom he has not seen?
21 And this commandment we have from Him: that he who loves God *must* love his brother also.

5 Whoever believes that Jesus is the Christ is born of God, and everyone who loves Him who begot also loves him who is begotten of Him.
2 By this we know that we love the children of God, when we love God and keep His commandments.
➤ 3 For this is the love of God, that we keep His commandments. And His commandments are not burdensome.
✳ 4 For whatever is born of God overcomes the world. And this is the victory that has overcome the world—our[a] faith.
5 Who is he who overcomes the world, but he who believes that Jesus is the Son of God?

The Certainty of God's Witness

6 This is He who came by water and blood—Jesus Christ; not only by water, but by water and blood. And it is the Spirit who bears witness, because the Spirit is truth.
7 For there are three that bear witness in heaven: the Father, the Word, and the Holy Spirit; and these three are one.
8 And there are three that bear witness on earth:[a] the Spirit, the water, and the blood; and these three agree as one.
9 If we receive the witness of men, the witness of God is greater; for this is the witness of God which[a] He has testified of His Son.
10 He who believes in the Son of God has the witness in himself; he who does not believe God has made Him a liar, because he has not believed the testimony that God has given of His Son.
11 And this is the testimony: that God has given us eternal life, and this life is in His Son.
12 He who has the Son has life; he who does not have the Son of God does not have life. ➤
13 These things I have written to you who believe in the name of the Son of God, that you may know that you have eternal life,[a] and that you may *continue to* believe in the name of the Son of God.

Confidence and Compassion in Prayer

14 Now this is the confidence that we have in Him, that if we ask anything according to His will, He hears us.
15 And if we know that He hears us, whatever we ask, we know that we have the petitions that we have asked of Him. ✳
16 If anyone sees his brother sinning a sin *which does* not *lead* to death, he will ask, and He will give him life for those who commit sin not *leading* to death. There is sin *leading* to death. I do not say that he should pray about that.
17 All unrighteousness is sin, and there is sin not *leading* to death.

4:19 [a]NU-Text omits *Him*. **4:20** [a]NU-Text reads *he cannot*.
5:4 [a]M-Text reads *your*. **5:8** [a]NU-Text and M-Text omit the words from *in heaven* (verse 7) through *on earth* (verse 8). Only four or five very late manuscripts contain these words in Greek.
5:9 [a]NU-Text reads *God, that*. **5:13** [a]NU-Text omits the rest of this verse.

LIFE LESSONS

➤ 4:20 — *If someone says, "I love God," and hates his brother, he is a liar . . . .*

Love for God is not merely a warm sentiment or a pleasant feeling; it is a living, active force that changes who we are. Jesus Himself forever connected love for God with love for people (Mat. 22:37–40).

➤ 5:3 — *For this is the love of God, that we keep His commandments. And His commandments are not burdensome.*

Only when we try to obey God through our own power do His commandments feel burdensome. When we rely on His Spirit to enable us to do what we can't, we find great joy in obedience.

➤ 5:12 — *He who has the Son has life; he who does not have the Son of God does not have life.*

Have you asked the Lord Jesus Christ to come into your heart through faith, forgive you of your sins and give you an eternal home in heaven? If you have, you have life; if you haven't, you don't.

Knowing the True—Rejecting the False
18 We know that whoever is born of God
does not sin; but he who has been born of
God keeps himself,[a] and the wicked one does
not touch him.
19 We know that we are of God, and the
whole world lies *under the sway of* the
wicked one.
➤ 20 And we know that the Son of God has
come and has given us an understanding, that
we may know Him who is true; and we are in
Him who is true, in His Son Jesus Christ. This
is the true God and eternal life.
21 Little children, keep yourselves from idols.
Amen.

5:18 [a]NU-Text reads *him.*

LIFE LESSONS

➤ 5:20 — *And we know that the Son of God has come and has given us an understanding, that we may know Him who is true . . . .*

God helps us to grasp His Word, not merely so we can amass an impressive body of religious knowledge, but so that we can come to know, love, obey, and enjoy the God of the universe.

THE SECOND EPISTLE OF JOHN

Greeting the Elect Lady
The Elder,

To the elect lady and her children, whom I
love in truth, and not only I, but also all those
who have known the truth,
➤ 2 because of the truth which abides in us
and will be with us forever:

3 Grace, mercy, *and* peace will be with you[a]
from God the Father and from the Lord Jesus
Christ, the Son of the Father, in truth and love.

Walk in Christ's Commandments
4 I rejoiced greatly that I have found *some*
of your children walking in truth, as we received commandment from the Father.
➤ 5 And now I plead with you, lady, not as
though I wrote a new commandment to you,
but that which we have had from the beginning: that we love one another.
6 This is love, that we walk according to His
commandments. This is the commandment,
that as you have heard from the beginning,
you should walk in it.

Beware of Antichrist Deceivers
7 For many deceivers have gone out into the
world who do not confess Jesus Christ *as*
coming in the flesh. This is a deceiver and an
antichrist.
8 Look to yourselves, that we[a] do not lose ➤
those things we worked for, but *that* we[b] may
receive a full reward.
9 Whoever transgresses[a] and does not abide
in the doctrine of Christ does not have God.
He who abides in the doctrine of Christ has
both the Father and the Son.
10 If anyone comes to you and does not bring
this doctrine, do not receive him into your
house nor greet him;
11 for he who greets him shares in his evil
deeds.

John's Farewell Greeting
12 Having many things to write to you, I did
not wish *to do so* with paper and ink; but I
hope to come to you and speak face to face,
that our joy may be full.
13 The children of your elect sister greet you.
Amen.

3 [a]NU-Text and M-Text read *us.* **8** [a]NU-Text reads *you.* [b]NU-Text reads *you.* **9** [a]NU-Text reads *goes ahead.*

LIFE LESSONS

➤ 2 — . . . *because of the truth which abides in us and will be with us forever . . . .*

Neither the Word of God which we have received, nor the Savior and Lord who inspired it and lives in us, will ever change or abandon us. God's truth does not alter from age to age, nor does He.

➤ 5 — *And now I plead with you, lady, not as though I wrote a new commandment to you, but that which we have had from the beginning: that we love one another.*

To love God and to love others as we love ourselves—the core requirement of heaven has remained the same from Old Testament times, to the days of the New Testament, and on to today.

➤ 8 — *Look to yourselves, that we do not lose those things we worked for, but that we may receive a full reward.*

God desires to fully bless us by giving us the maximum number and quality of rewards possible—but *we* determine what kind of reward we will receive, based on how closely we walk with Him and thereby obey His voice.

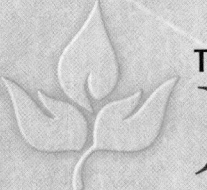

THE THIRD EPISTLE OF

JOHN

Greeting to Gaius
The Elder,

To the beloved Gaius, whom I love in truth:

➤ 2 Beloved, I pray that you may prosper in all
things and be in health, just as your soul prospers.
3 For I rejoiced greatly when brethren came
and testified of the truth *that is* in you, just as
you walk in the truth.
➤ 4 I have no greater joy than to hear that my
children walk in truth.[a]

Gaius Commended for Generosity
5 Beloved, you do faithfully whatever you
do for the brethren and[a] for strangers,
6 who have borne witness of your love before the church. *If* you send them forward on
their journey in a manner worthy of God, you
will do well,
7 because they went forth for His name's
sake, taking nothing from the Gentiles.
8 We therefore ought to receive[a] such, that
we may become fellow workers for the
truth.

Diotrephes and Demetrius
9 I wrote to the church, but Diotrephes, who ➤
loves to have the preeminence among them,
does not receive us.
10 Therefore, if I come, I will call to mind his
deeds which he does, prating against us with
malicious words. And not content with that,
he himself does not receive the brethren, and
forbids those who wish to, putting *them* out
of the church.
11 Beloved, do not imitate what is evil, but
what is good. He who does good is of God,
but[a] he who does evil has not seen God.
12 Demetrius has a *good* testimony from all,
and from the truth itself. And we also bear witness, and you know that our testimony is true.

Farewell Greeting
13 I had many things to write, but I do not
wish to write to you with pen and ink;
14 but I hope to see you shortly, and we shall
speak face to face. Peace to you. Our friends
greet you. Greet the friends by name.

4 [a]NU-Text reads *the truth.* **5** [a]NU-Text adds *especially.*
8 [a]NU-Text reads *support.* **11** [a]NU-Text and M-Text omit *but.*

LIFE LESSONS

➤ 2 — *Beloved, I pray that you may prosper in all things and be in health, just as your soul prospers.*

Prayers for our physical well-being are just as legitimate as prayers for our spiritual health. God wants us to prosper in all ways that will draw our hearts closer to Him and to our fellow believers in Christ.

➤ 4 — *I have no greater joy than to hear that my children walk in truth.*

To "walk in truth" means to believe the Word of God and to gladly obey its instruction by drawing on the power of the Spirit. This kind of life brings great joy both to us and to our spiritual forebears.

➤ 9 — *I wrote to the church, but Diotrephes, who loves to have the preeminence among them, does not receive us.*

A "me first" attitude is the polar opposite of what Jesus promised would bring health and joy to His children: "If anyone desires to be first, he shall be last of all and servant of all" (Mark 9:35).

THE EPISTLE OF

JUDE

Fight! Contend! Do battle! When apostasy arises, when false teachers emerge, when the truth of God is attacked, the time has come to fight for the faith—and only believers who are spiritually "in shape" can answer the summons.

At the beginning of his brief letter, Jude focus on the believers' common salvation. Almost immediately he feels compelled to switch themes, however, and instead challenges them to contend for the faith "which was once for all delivered to the saints" (3). Why the abrupt change? The danger was real. False teachers had crept into the church, turning God's grace into an invitation to sin and denying "the only Lord God and our Lord Jesus Christ" (4).

Jude reminds his readers of God's holy judgments on unbelieving Israel, disobedient angels, and wicked Sodom and Gomorrah. A gracious God will give sinners plenty of time to repent; but if they refuse, even in His grace they will suffer a decisive and devastating judgment.

In the face of such danger from false leaders and such divine judgment on unrepentant sinners, Christians should not be caught off guard. Not only must they keep themselves "in the love of God" (21), but they must also make it their business to rescue fellow believers from the deception and devastation of sin. Yes, the challenge may be great—but even greater is the God who is able to keep His children from stumbling.

The Greek title, "Of Jude," comes from the name *Ioudas*, which appears in verse 1. This name, which is Judah in Hebrew and can be translated Jude or Judas, was popular in the first century because of Judas Maccabaeus (died 160 B.C.), a leader of the Jewish resistance against Syria during the Maccabean revolt.

Themes: Beware of false teachers, live for God, and depend on the grace of God to "keep you from stumbling, and to present you faultless before the presence of His glory with exceeding joy" (24).

Author: Probably Jude, the brother of James.

Time: Likely between A.D. 65-80.

Structure: Jude greets his readers (1, 2), urges them to contend for the faith (3, 4), warns of false teachers (5–19), encourages them to live for God (20–23), and concludes his letter with a beautiful benediction (24, 25).

As you read Jude, watch for a few life principles that play an important part in this book:

2. Obey God and leave all the consequences to Him. *See Jude 4–11; page 1489.*

30. An eager anticipation of the Lord's return keeps us living productively. *See Jude 14, 15; page 1489.*

17. We stand tallest and strongest on our knees. *See Jude 20; page 1489.*

Greeting to the Called
Jude, a bondservant of Jesus Christ, and
brother of James,

To those who are called, sanctified[a] by
God the Father, and preserved in Jesus Christ:

2 Mercy, peace, and love be multiplied to you.

Contend for the Faith
➤ **3** Beloved, while I was very diligent to write
to you concerning our common salvation, I
found it necessary to write to you exhorting
you to contend earnestly for the faith which
was once for all delivered to the saints.
4 For certain men have crept in unnoticed,
who long ago were marked out for this
condemnation, ungodly men, who turn the
grace of our God into lewdness and deny the
only Lord God[a] and our Lord Jesus Christ.

Old and New Apostates
➤ **5** But I want to remind you, though you once
knew this, that the Lord, having saved the
people out of the land of Egypt, afterward destroyed those who did not believe.
6 And the angels who did not keep their
proper domain, but left their own abode, He
has reserved in everlasting chains under
darkness for the judgment of the great day;
7 as Sodom and Gomorrah, and the cities
around them in a similar manner to these,
having given themselves over to sexual immorality and gone after strange flesh, are set
forth as an example, suffering the vengeance
of eternal fire.
8 Likewise also these dreamers defile the
flesh, reject authority, and speak evil of dignitaries.
9 Yet Michael the archangel, in contending
with the devil, when he disputed about the
body of Moses, dared not bring against him a
reviling accusation, but said, "The Lord rebuke you!"
10 But these speak evil of whatever they do
not know; and whatever they know naturally,
like brute beasts, in these things they corrupt
themselves.
11 Woe to them! For they have gone in the
way of Cain, have run greedily in the error of
Balaam for profit, and perished in the rebellion of Korah.

Apostates Depraved and Doomed
12 These are spots in your love feasts, while
they feast with you without fear, serving *only*
themselves. *They are* clouds without water,
carried about[a] by the winds; late autumn trees
without fruit, twice dead, pulled up by the roots;
13 raging waves of the sea, foaming up their
own shame; wandering stars for whom is reserved the blackness of darkness forever.
14 Now Enoch, the seventh from Adam,
prophesied about these men also, saying, "Behold, the Lord comes with ten thousands of
His saints,
15 "to execute judgment on all, to convict
all who are ungodly among them of all their
ungodly deeds which they have committed in
an ungodly way, and of all the harsh things
which ungodly sinners have spoken against
Him."

Apostates Predicted
16 These are grumblers, complainers, walking according to their own lusts; and they
mouth great swelling *words,* flattering people
to gain advantage.
17 But you, beloved, remember the words
which were spoken before by the apostles of
our Lord Jesus Christ:
18 how they told you that there would be ➤
mockers in the last time who would walk according to their own ungodly lusts.
19 These are sensual persons, who cause
divisions, not having the Spirit.

Maintain Your Life with God
20 But you, beloved, building yourselves up
on your most holy faith, praying in the Holy
Spirit,
21 keep yourselves in the love of God, looking for the mercy of our Lord Jesus Christ
unto eternal life.

1 [a]NU-Text reads *beloved.* **4** [a]NU-Text omits *God.*
12 [a]NU-Text and M-Text read *along.*

LIFE LESSONS

➤ 3 — *. . . contend earnestly for the faith which was once for all delivered to the saints.*

The gospel of Jesus Christ does not change. Since He is the same yesterday, today, and forever (Heb. 13:8), so His gospel remains eternally the same. And it is worth fighting for, since through it alone we find eternal life.

➤ 5 — *I want to remind you, though you once knew this, that the Lord, having saved the people out of the land of Egypt, afterward destroyed those who did not believe.*

Here we see both the goodness and severity of God, side-by-side. The Lord showed His goodness in rescuing the Israelites from Egyptian slavery, but His severity in punishing their stubborn disobedience and rebellion.

➤ 18 — *. . . they told you that there would be mockers in the last time who would walk according to their own ungodly lusts.*

As the return of Jesus draws nearer, we will see an increase in those who mock genuine faith in Jesus. They will make vicious fun of believers and hold them up to ridicule—just as Jesus' enemies mocked Him.

22 And on some have compassion, making a distinction;[a]
23 but others save with fear, pulling *them* out of the fire,[a] hating even the garment defiled by the flesh.

Glory to God

➤ 24 Now to Him who is able to keep you[a]
from stumbling,
And to present *you* faultless
Before the presence of His glory with
exceeding joy,
25 To God our Savior,[a]
Who alone is wise,[b]
Be glory and majesty,
Dominion and power,[c]
Both now and forever.
Amen.

22 [a]NU-Text reads *who are doubting* (or *making distinctions*). **23** [a]NU-Text adds *and on some have mercy with fear* and omits *with fear* in first clause. **24** [a]M-Text reads *them.* **25** [a]NU-Text reads *To the only God our Savior.* [b]NU-Text omits *Who . . . is wise* and adds *Through Jesus Christ our Lord.* [c]NU-Text adds *Before all time.*

LIFE LESSONS

➤ 24 — Now to Him who is able to keep you from stumbling, and to present you faultless before the presence of His glory with exceeding joy . . . .

While God asks us to cooperate with Him in the process of sanctification, it is He who conforms us to the image of Jesus by His power and infinite wisdom. That is why we can joyfully anticipate our total transformation.

THE REVELATION

OF JESUS CHRIST

Just as Genesis is the book of beginnings, so Revelation is the book of completion. In it, we see how God finalizes the divine program of redemption and vindicates His holy name before all creation.

Although the Gospels and Epistles contain numerous prophecies, only Revelation among all the New Testament books focuses primarily on prophetic events. It borrows heavily from Old Testament symbols and passages, and seems to have a special connection to the Book of Daniel. Because of this potent imagery, it is often difficult to know in Revelation when the author is speaking literally and when he is speaking symbolically.

Revelation also features several high moments of worship in which the residents of heaven and the saints of God praise the Lord for His holy character and righteous judgments. These extraordinary times of worship are usually presented as joyful songs of praise (see Rev. 4:8–11; 5:8–14; 7:9–12; 11:15–18; 15:2–4; 16:5–7; 19:1–7).

The title of this book in the Greek text is *Apokalypsis Ioannou*, "Revelation of John." It is also known as the Apocalypse, a transliteration of the word *apokalypsis*, meaning "unveiling," "disclosure," or "revelation." Thus the book unveils what otherwise could not be known. A better title comes from the first verse, the "Revelation of Jesus Christ." This could be taken as a revelation that came from Christ, or as a revelation about Christ; both are appropriate.

Revelation was originally written to seven local churches in Asia Minor (modern Turkey), but its message applies to all Christians everywhere. Jesus is coming again in great power and glory, and His certain return should motivate us every day to Spirit-filled, loving action on His behalf.

Theme: Revelation centers around awesome visions and extraordinary symbols of the resurrected Christ, who alone has authority to judge the earth, to remake it, and to rule it in righteousness.

Author: The apostle John wrote Revelation during his exile on the island of Patmos.

Date: Most scholars believe the book was written around A.D. 90–95.

Structure: Revelation starts out with a vision of Jesus Christ (chapter 1), followed by a message from Him to the seven churches in Asia Minor (chapters 2, 3), followed by another vision of Jesus (chapters 4, 5). The rest of the book employs difficult symbolism and startling imagery to picture the final triumph of good over evil.

As you read Revelation, watch for several life principles that play an important role in this book:

30. An eager anticipation of the Lord's return keeps us living productively. *See Revelation 1:3; 21:6–8; 22:7, 12–14; pages 1492, 1510–1511, 1513.*

21. Obedience always brings blessing. *See Revelation 3:3; 12:17; 14:12; pages 1494, 1502, 1504.*

7. The dark moments of our life will last only so long as is necessary for God to accomplish His purpose in us. *See Revelation 6:9–11; page 1497.*

6. You reap what you sow, more than you sow, and later than you sow. *See Revelation 16:6; 22:12; pages 1505, 1513.*

Introduction and Benediction

1 The Revelation of Jesus Christ, which
God gave Him to show His servants—
things which must shortly take place. And
He sent and signified *it* by His angel to His
servant John,
2 who bore witness to the word of God, and
to the testimony of Jesus Christ, to all things
that he saw.
✳ 3 Blessed *is* he who reads and those who
hear the words of this prophecy, and keep
those things which are written in it; for the
time *is* near.

Greeting the Seven Churches

➤ 4 John, to the seven churches which are in
Asia:

Grace to you and peace from Him who is
and who was and who is to come, and from
the seven Spirits who are before His throne,
➤ 5 and from Jesus Christ, the faithful witness, the firstborn from the dead, and the
ruler over the kings of the earth. To Him
who loved us and washed[a] us from our sins
in His own blood,
6 and has made us kings[a] and priests to His
God and Father, to Him *be* glory and dominion forever and ever. Amen.
7 Behold, He is coming with clouds, and
every eye will see Him, even they who pierced
Him. And all the tribes of the earth will mourn
because of Him. Even so, Amen.
8 "I am the Alpha and the Omega, *the* Beginning and *the* End,"[a] says the Lord,[b] "who
is and who was and who is to come, the Almighty."

Vision of the Son of Man

9 I, John, both[a] your brother and companion
in the tribulation and kingdom and patience
of Jesus Christ, was on the island that is called
Patmos for the word of God and for the testimony of Jesus Christ.
10 I was in the Spirit on the Lord's Day, and I
heard behind me a loud voice, as of a trumpet,
11 saying, "I am the Alpha and the Omega, the
First and the Last,"[a] and, "What you see, write
in a book and send *it* to the seven churches
which are in Asia:[b] to Ephesus, to Smyrna, to
Pergamos, to Thyatira, to Sardis, to Philadelphia, and to Laodicea."
12 Then I turned to see the voice that spoke
with me. And having turned I saw seven
golden lampstands,
13 and in the midst of the seven lampstands
One like the Son of Man, clothed with a garment down to the feet and girded about the
chest with a golden band.
14 His head and hair *were* white like wool, as
white as snow, and His eyes like a flame of
fire;
15 His feet *were* like fine brass, as if refined
in a furnace, and His voice as the sound of
many waters;
16 He had in His right hand seven stars, out
of His mouth went a sharp two-edged sword,
and His countenance *was* like the sun shining
in its strength.
17 And when I saw Him, I fell at His feet as ➤
dead. But He laid His right hand on me, saying to me,[a] "Do not be afraid; I am the First
and the Last.
18 "I *am* He who lives, and was dead, and behold, I am alive forevermore. Amen. And I
have the keys of Hades and of Death.
19 "Write[a] the things which you have seen,
and the things which are, and the things
which will take place after this.
20 "The mystery of the seven stars which you
saw in My right hand, and the seven golden
lampstands: The seven stars are the angels of
the seven churches, and the seven lampstands
which you saw[a] are the seven churches.

The Loveless Church

2 "To the angel of the church of Ephesus
write,

'These things says He who holds the seven
stars in His right hand, who walks in the
midst of the seven golden lampstands:

1:5 [a]NU-Text reads *loves us and freed;* M-Text reads *loves us and washed.* **1:6** [a]NU-Text and M-Text read *a kingdom.* **1:8** [a]NU-Text and M-Text omit *the Beginning and the End.* [b]NU-Text and M-Text add *God.* **1:9** [a]NU-Text and M-Text omit *both.* **1:11** [a]NU-Text and M-Text omit *I am* through third *and.* [b]NU-Text and M-Text omit *which are in Asia.* **1:17** [a]NU-Text and M-Text omit *to me.* **1:19** [a]NU-Text and M-Text read *Therefore, write.* **1:20** [a]NU-Text and M-Text omit *which you saw.*

LIFE LESSONS

➤ 1:4 — *. . . Grace to you and peace . . . .*

"Grace" was a typical Greek greeting of the first century, while "peace" served as the typical Hebrew greeting. The author thus lets his readers know that this book is for everyone, Jew and Gentile alike.

➤ 1:5 — *. . . Jesus Christ . . . the firstborn from the dead . . . .*

Several individuals in the Bible, before Jesus, had been raised from the dead. But all of them—the Shunammite's son (2 Kin. 4:35), Jairus' daughter (Mark 5:42), Lazarus (John 11:44)—died later. Jesus conquered death, never to die again.

➤ 1:17 — *And when I saw Him, I fell at His feet as dead.*

The majestic, glorious appearance of the unveiled Christ so overwhelmed John that he fainted. We must never forget that our Savior and Friend is also our Lord, Master, King, and Sovereign.

2 "I know your works, your labor, your patience, and that you cannot bear those who
are evil. And you have tested those who say
they are apostles and are not, and have found
them liars;
3 "and you have persevered and have patience, and have labored for My name's sake
and have not become weary.
4 "Nevertheless I have *this* against you, that
you have left your first love.
5 "Remember therefore from where you
have fallen; repent and do the first works, or
else I will come to you quickly and remove
your lampstand from its place—unless you repent.
6 "But this you have, that you hate the deeds
of the Nicolaitans, which I also hate.
7 "He who has an ear, let him hear what
the Spirit says to the churches. To him who
overcomes I will give to eat from the tree of
life, which is in the midst of the Paradise of
God."'

The Persecuted Church

8 "And to the angel of the church in Smyrna
write,
'These things says the First and the Last,
who was dead, and came to life:
9 "I know your works, tribulation, and
poverty (but you are rich); and *I know* the
blasphemy of those who say they are Jews
and are not, but *are* a synagogue of Satan.
10 "Do not fear any of those things which
you are about to suffer. Indeed, the devil is
about to throw *some* of you into prison, that
you may be tested, and you will have tribulation ten days. Be faithful until death, and I
will give you the crown of life.
11 "He who has an ear, let him hear what the
Spirit says to the churches. He who overcomes shall not be hurt by the second death."'

The Compromising Church

12 "And to the angel of the church in Pergamos write,
'These things says He who has the sharp
two-edged sword:
13 "I know your works, and where you dwell,
where Satan's throne *is*. And you hold fast to
My name, and did not deny My faith even in
the days in which Antipas *was* My faithful
martyr, who was killed among you, where Satan dwells.
14 "But I have a few things against you, because you have there those who hold the doctrine of Balaam, who taught Balak to put a
stumbling block before the children of Israel,
to eat things sacrificed to idols, and to commit
sexual immorality.
15 "Thus you also have those who hold the
doctrine of the Nicolaitans, which thing I hate.[a]
16 "Repent, or else I will come to you quickly
and will fight against them with the sword of
My mouth.
17 "He who has an ear, let him hear what the
Spirit says to the churches. To him who overcomes I will give some of the hidden manna
to eat. And I will give him a white stone, and
on the stone a new name written which no
one knows except him who receives *it*."'

The Corrupt Church

18 "And to the angel of the church in Thyatira
write,
'These things says the Son of God, who
has eyes like a flame of fire, and His feet like
fine brass:
19 "I know your works, love, service, faith,[a]
and your patience; and *as* for your works, the
last *are* more than the first.

2:15 [a]NU-Text and M-Text read *likewise* for *which thing I hate.*
2:19 [a]NU-Text and M-Text read *faith, service.*

LIFE LESSONS

2:2 — *"I know your works, your labor, your patience . . . ."*

We may sometimes feel as though we toil in anonymity and that our labors go unnoticed and unappreciated. Remember, Jesus notices everything. He sees both our work and our attitude as we work. And He remembers.

2:3 — *" . . . you have persevered and have patience, and have labored for My name's sake and have not become weary."*

The work Jesus gives every one of us to do can feel taxing and almost unending. To complete our assignment takes both perseverance and patience. Only when we labor in His strength can we avoid complete weariness.

2:4 — *"Nevertheless I have this against you, that you have left your first love."*

God created us for an intimate relationship with Himself, and developing that relationship must always remain our top priority. Working for God must never replace loving God.

2:10 — *"Do not fear any of those things which you are about to suffer. Indeed, the devil is about to throw some of you into prison, that you may be tested . . . ."*

Obedience always brings blessing, but it may first bring suffering. God allows Satan to persecute some believers in order to test them and refine them. Satan means it for evil, but God means it for good.

2:16 — *"Repent, or else I will come to you quickly and will fight against them with the sword of My mouth."*

No one should ever imagine that the unconditional love of God means that He will never discipline His unrepentant children. Jesus uses strong language here to remind us that He expects us to represent Him well.

20 "Nevertheless I have a few things against
you, because you allow[a] that woman[b] Jezebel,
who calls herself a prophetess, to teach and
seduce[c] My servants to commit sexual immorality and eat things sacrificed to idols.
21 "And I gave her time to repent of her sexual immorality, and she did not repent.[a]
22 "Indeed I will cast her into a sickbed,
and those who commit adultery with her into
great tribulation, unless they repent of their[a]
deeds.
➤ 23 "I will kill her children with death, and
all the churches shall know that I am He
who searches the minds and hearts. And I
will give to each one of you according to your
works.
24 "Now to you I say, and[a] to the rest in Thyatira, as many as do not have this doctrine,
who have not known the depths of Satan, as
they say, I will[b] put on you no other burden.
25 "But hold fast what you have till I come.
26 "And he who overcomes, and keeps My
works until the end, to him I will give power
over the nations—

27 '*He shall rule them with a rod of iron;*
They shall be dashed to pieces like the
potter's vessels'[a]—

as I also have received from My Father;
28 "and I will give him the morning star.
29 "He who has an ear, let him hear what the
Spirit says to the churches."'

The Dead Church

3 "And to the angel of the church in Sardis
write,
'These things says He who has the seven
Spirits of God and the seven stars: "I know
your works, that you have a name that you
are alive, but you are dead.
2 "Be watchful, and strengthen the things
which remain, that are ready to die, for I have
not found your works perfect before God.[a]
3 "Remember therefore how you have received and heard; hold fast and repent. Therefore if you will not watch, I will come upon
you as a thief, and you will not know what
hour I will come upon you.
4 "You[a] have a few names even in Sardis
who have not defiled their garments; and they
shall walk with Me in white, for they are worthy.
5 "He who overcomes shall be clothed in ✱
white garments, and I will not blot out his
name from the Book of Life; but I will confess
his name before My Father and before His angels.
6 "He who has an ear, let him hear what the
Spirit says to the churches."'

The Faithful Church

7 "And to the angel of the church in
Philadelphia write,
'These things says He who is holy, He who
is true, *"He who has the key of David, He who*
opens and no one shuts, and shuts and no
one opens":[a]
8 "I know your works. See, I have set before ◄
you an open door, and no one can shut it;[a] for
you have a little strength, have kept My word,
and have not denied My name.
9 "Indeed I will make *those* of the synagogue of Satan, who say they are Jews and
are not, but lie—indeed I will make them
come and worship before your feet, and to
know that I have loved you.
10 "Because you have kept My command to
persevere, I also will keep you from the hour
of trial which shall come upon the whole
world, to test those who dwell on the earth.
11 "Behold,[a] I am coming quickly! Hold fast
what you have, that no one may take your
crown.
12 "He who overcomes, I will make him a pillar in the temple of My God, and he shall go
out no more. I will write on him the name of
My God and the name of the city of My God,
the New Jerusalem, which comes down out of
heaven from My God. And *I will write on him*
My new name.
13 "He who has an ear, let him hear what the
Spirit says to the churches."'

2:20 [a]NU-Text and M-Text read *I have against you that you tolerate.* [b]M-Text reads *your wife Jezebel.* [c]NU-Text and M-Text read *and teaches and seduces.* **2:21** [a]NU-Text and M-Text read *time to repent, and she does not want to repent of her sexual immorality.* **2:22** [a]NU-Text and M-Text read *her.* **2:24** [a]NU-Text and M-Text omit *and.* [b]NU-Text and M-Text omit *will.* **2:27** [a]Psalm 2:9 **3:2** [a]NU-Text and M-Text read *My God.* **3:4** [a]NU-Text and M-Text read *Nevertheless you have a few names in Sardis.* **3:7** [a]Isaiah 22:22 **3:8** [a]NU-Text and M-Text read *which no one can shut.* **3:11** [a]NU-Text and M-Text omit *Behold.*

LIFE LESSONS

➤ 2:23 — *"I will kill her children with death, and all the churches shall know that I am He who searches the minds and hearts."*

We reap what we sow. Paul says that if we sow to the flesh, we will from the flesh reap "corruption" (Gal. 6:8). Jesus knows exactly what thoughts we harbor in our minds and hearts, and He responds accordingly.

➤ 3:8 — *"See, I have set before you an open door, and no one can shut it; for you have a little strength, have kept My word, and have not denied My name."*

We do not have to be mighty conquerors or giant-killers to take advantage of the open doors of opportunity that God sets before us; a "little strength" is plenty when we obey His Word and honor His Son.

The Lukewarm Church

14 "And to the angel of the church of the Laodiceans[a] write,

'These things says the Amen, the Faithful
and True Witness, the Beginning of the creation of God:

➤ 15 "I know your works, that you are neither
cold nor hot. I could wish you were cold or
hot.
16 "So then, because you are lukewarm, and
neither cold nor hot,[a] I will vomit you out of
My mouth.
17 "Because you say, 'I am rich, have become
wealthy, and have need of nothing'—and do
not know that you are wretched, miserable,
poor, blind, and naked—
18 "I counsel you to buy from Me gold refined in the fire, that you may be rich; and
white garments, that you may be clothed, *that*
the shame of your nakedness may not be revealed; and anoint your eyes with eye salve,
that you may see.
➤ 19 "As many as I love, I rebuke and chasten.
Therefore be zealous and repent.
20 "Behold, I stand at the door and knock. If
anyone hears My voice and opens the door, I
will come in to him and dine with him, and he
with Me.
21 "To him who overcomes I will grant to sit
with Me on My throne, as I also overcame and
sat down with My Father on His throne.
22 "He who has an ear, let him hear what the
Spirit says to the churches."'"

The Throne Room of Heaven

4 After these things I looked, and behold, a
door *standing* open in heaven. And the
first voice which I heard *was* like a trumpet
speaking with me, saying, "Come up here,
and I will show you things which must take
place after this."
2 Immediately I was in the Spirit; and behold, a throne set in heaven, and *One* sat on
the throne.
3 And He who sat there was[a] like a jasper
and a sardius stone in appearance; and *there*
was a rainbow around the throne, in appearance like an emerald.
4 Around the throne *were* twenty-four
thrones, and on the thrones I saw twenty-four
elders sitting, clothed in white robes; and they
had crowns[a] of gold on their heads.
5 And from the throne proceeded lightnings, thunderings, and voices.[a] Seven lamps
of fire *were* burning before the throne, which
are the[b] seven Spirits of God.
6 Before the throne *there was*[a] a sea of
glass, like crystal. And in the midst of the
throne, and around the throne, *were* four living creatures full of eyes in front and in back.
7 The first living creature *was* like a lion,
the second living creature like a calf, the third
living creature had a face like a man, and the
fourth living creature *was* like a flying eagle.
8 *The* four living creatures, each having six ➤
wings, were full of eyes around and within.
And they do not rest day or night, saying:

"Holy, holy, holy,[a]
Lord God Almighty,
Who was and is and is to come!"

9 Whenever the living creatures give glory
and honor and thanks to Him who sits on the
throne, who lives forever and ever,
10 the twenty-four elders fall down before
Him who sits on the throne and worship Him
who lives forever and ever, and cast their
crowns before the throne, saying:

11 "You are worthy, O Lord,[a] ➤
To receive glory and honor and power;
For You created all things,
And by Your will they exist[b] and were
created."

3:14 [a]NU-Text and M-Text read *in Laodicea.* **3:16** [a]NU-Text and M-Text read *hot nor cold.* **4:3** [a]M-Text omits *And He who sat there was* (which makes the description in verse 3 modify the throne rather than God). **4:4** [a]NU-Text and M-Text read *robes, with crowns.* **4:5** [a]NU-Text and M-Text read *voices, and thunderings.* [b]M-Text omits *the.* **4:6** [a]NU-Text and M-Text add *something like.* **4:8** [a]M-Text has *holy* nine times. **4:11** [a]NU-Text and M-Text read *our Lord and God.* [b]NU-Text and M-Text read *existed.*

LIFE LESSONS

➤ 3:15 — *"I know your works, that you are neither cold nor hot. I could wish you were cold or hot."*

Jesus tells the smug and self-satisfied members of the Laodicean church that they are essentially useless to Him. They had chosen comfort over spiritual combat, and their complacency nauseated Jesus.

➤ 3:19 — *"As many as I love, I rebuke and chasten."*

Nobody likes to be rebuked or chastened; but the presence of these things, when necessary, indicates not a lack of love, but its fullness. Jesus rebukes us because it "yields the peaceable fruit of righteousness" (Heb. 12:11).

➤ 4:8 — *And they do not rest day or night, saying: "Holy, holy, holy, Lord God Almighty, who was and is and is to come!"*

In a sense, the whole Book of Revelation proceeds out of this verse. God judges the earth and every individual in it on the basis of His holiness, and He can tell us what is coming because He inhabits eternity.

➤ 4:11 — *"You are worthy, O Lord, to receive glory and honor and power; for You created all things, and by Your will they exist and were created."*

As the Creator, God is worthy of all praise and adoration. He has a special concern for judging those who destroy His creation (Rev. 11:18), for that creation was meant to display His glory.

The Lamb Takes the Scroll

5 And I saw in the right *hand* of Him who
sat on the throne a scroll written inside
and on the back, sealed with seven seals.
2 Then I saw a strong angel proclaiming
with a loud voice, "Who is worthy to open the
scroll and to loose its seals?"
3 And no one in heaven or on the earth or
under the earth was able to open the scroll, or
to look at it.
➤4 So I wept much, because no one was
found worthy to open and read[a] the scroll, or
to look at it.
➤5 But one of the elders said to me, "Do not
weep. Behold, the Lion of the tribe of Judah,
the Root of David, has prevailed to open the
scroll and to loose[a] its seven seals."
6 And I looked, and behold,[a] in the midst of
the throne and of the four living creatures, and
in the midst of the elders, stood a Lamb as
though it had been slain, having seven horns
and seven eyes, which are the seven Spirits of
God sent out into all the earth.
7 Then He came and took the scroll out of
the right hand of Him who sat on the throne.

Worthy Is the Lamb

8 Now when He had taken the scroll, the
four living creatures and the twenty-four elders fell down before the Lamb, each having a
harp, and golden bowls full of incense, which
are the prayers of the saints.
➤9 And they sang a new song, saying:

"You are worthy to take the scroll,
And to open its seals;
For You were slain,
And have redeemed us to God by Your
blood
Out of every tribe and tongue and people
and nation,
10 And have made us[a] kings[b] and priests to
our God;
And we[c] shall reign on the earth."

11 Then I looked, and I heard the voice of
many angels around the throne, the living
creatures, and the elders; and the number of
them was ten thousand times ten thousand,
and thousands of thousands,
12 saying with a loud voice:

"Worthy is the Lamb who was slain
To receive power and riches and
wisdom,
And strength and honor and glory and
blessing!"

13 And every creature which is in heaven and
on the earth and under the earth and such as
are in the sea, and all that are in them, I heard
saying:

"Blessing and honor and glory and power
Be to Him who sits on the throne,
And to the Lamb, forever and ever!"[a]

14 Then the four living creatures said,
"Amen!" And the twenty-four[a] elders fell
down and worshiped Him who lives forever
and ever.[b]

First Seal: The Conqueror

6 Now I saw when the Lamb opened one of
the seals;[a] and I heard one of the four living creatures saying with a voice like thunder,
"Come and see."
2 And I looked, and behold, a white horse.
He who sat on it had a bow; and a crown was
given to him, and he went out conquering and
to conquer.

5:4 [a]NU-Text and M-Text omit *and read.* **5:5** [a]NU-Text and M-Text omit *to loose.* **5:6** [a]NU-Text and M-Text read *I saw in the midst . . . a Lamb standing.* **5:10** [a]NU-Text and M-Text read *them.* [b]NU-Text reads *a kingdom.* [c]NU-Text and M-Text read *they.* **5:13** [a]M-Text adds *Amen.* **5:14** [a]NU-Text and M-Text omit *twenty-four.* [b]NU-Text and M-Text omit *Him who lives forever and ever.* **6:1** [a]NU-Text and M-Text read *seven seals.*

LIFE LESSONS

➤ 5:4 — *So I wept much, because no one was found worthy to open and read the scroll, or to look at it.*

Buddha could not open the scroll. Socrates could not open the scroll. Confucius could not open the scroll. Only one person, the risen Son of God, could open the scroll. Jesus is unique and superior to all.

➤ 5:5 — *"Do not weep. Behold, the Lion of the tribe of Judah, the Root of David, has prevailed . . . ."*

Jesus prevails when no one else can. As a Lamb He took our sins upon Himself, but as a Lion He triumphs over all opposition. Therefore we do not have to weep, for ultimate victory is assured.

➤ 5:9, 10 — *"You were slain, and have redeemed us to God by Your blood out of every tribe and tongue and people and nation . . . ."*

God does not play favorites. He searches for men and women, boys and girls, to redeem from every ethnic group, race, and language subculture from throughout the world. He is truly the God of all the earth.

➤ 5:13 — *"Blessing and honor and glory and power be to Him who sits on the throne, and to the Lamb, forever and ever!"*

Throughout the Book of Revelation we see the Son and the Father honored and worshiped side-by-side. We see this even with titles; "the Alpha and the Omega" can refer to the Father (1:8) and to the Son (22:13).

Second Seal: Conflict on Earth

3 When He opened the second seal, I heard the second living creature saying, "Come and see."[a]

4 Another horse, fiery red, went out. And it was granted to the one who sat on it to take peace from the earth, and that *people* should kill one another; and there was given to him a great sword.

Third Seal: Scarcity on Earth

5 When He opened the third seal, I heard the third living creature say, "Come and see." So I looked, and behold, a black horse, and he who sat on it had a pair of scales in his hand.
6 And I heard a voice in the midst of the four living creatures saying, "A quart[a] of wheat for a denarius,[b] and three quarts of barley for a denarius; and do not harm the oil and the wine."

Fourth Seal: Widespread Death on Earth

7 When He opened the fourth seal, I heard the voice of the fourth living creature saying, "Come and see."
8 So I looked, and behold, a pale horse. And the name of him who sat on it was Death, and Hades followed with him. And power was given to them over a fourth of the earth, to kill with sword, with hunger, with death, and by the beasts of the earth.

Fifth Seal: The Cry of the Martyrs

9 When He opened the fifth seal, I saw under the altar the souls of those who had been slain for the word of God and for the testimony which they held.
10 And they cried with a loud voice, saying, "How long, O Lord, holy and true, until You judge and avenge our blood on those who dwell on the earth?"
11 Then a white robe was given to each of them; and it was said to them that they should rest a little while longer, until both *the number* of their fellow servants and their brethren, who would be killed as they *were*, was completed.

Sixth Seal: Cosmic Disturbances

12 I looked when He opened the sixth seal, and behold,[a] there was a great earthquake; and the sun became black as sackcloth of hair, and the moon[b] became like blood.
13 And the stars of heaven fell to the earth, as a fig tree drops its late figs when it is shaken by a mighty wind.
14 Then the sky receded as a scroll when it is rolled up, and every mountain and island was moved out of its place.
15 And the kings of the earth, the great men, the rich men, the commanders,[a] the mighty men, every slave and every free man, hid themselves in the caves and in the rocks of the mountains,
16 and said to the mountains and rocks, "Fall on us and hide us from the face of Him who sits on the throne and from the wrath of the Lamb!
17 "For the great day of His wrath has come, and who is able to stand?"

The Sealed of Israel

7 After these things I saw four angels standing at the four corners of the earth, holding the four winds of the earth, that the wind should not blow on the earth, on the sea, or on any tree.
2 Then I saw another angel ascending from the east, having the seal of the living God. And he cried with a loud voice to the four angels to whom it was granted to harm the earth and the sea,
3 saying, "Do not harm the earth, the sea, or the trees till we have sealed the servants of our God on their foreheads."

6:3 [a]NU-Text and M-Text omit *and see.* **6:6** [a]Greek *choinix;* that is, approximately one quart [b]This was approximately one day's wage for a worker. **6:12** [a]NU-Text and M-Text omit *behold.* [b]NU-Text and M-Text read *the whole moon.* **6:15** [a]NU-Text and M-Text read *the commanders, the rich men.*

LIFE LESSONS

➤ 6:4 — *And it was granted to the one who sat on it to take peace from the earth, and that people should kill one another; and there was given to him a great sword.*

The staggering violence that "the beast" unleashes on the earth may make it seem as though God has lost control, but in fact, God is the one who "grants" him the power to do his wicked work. God still rules.

➤ 6:9 — *I saw under the altar the souls of those who had been slain for the word of God and for the testimony which they held.*

Godly people have always died for the faith. From Abel (Gen. 4:8) at the beginning to Antipas (Rev. 2:13) and these unnamed martyrs at the end of time, God sometimes requires that His people sacrifice their lives for Him.

➤ 6:17 — *"For the great day of His wrath has come, and who is able to stand?"*

Judgment finally comes when repentance doesn't. Note that it is the ungodly who make this statement—they recognize God's hand—and yet they refuse to repent. Better to kneel in repentance than fall in judgment!

➤ 7:3 — *"Do not harm the earth, the sea, or the trees till we have sealed the servants of our God on their foreheads."*

God knows how to protect His children even in the most catastrophic of times. The servants who are "sealed" here are all safe and well at the end (Rev. 14:1–5; see also Ezek. 9:4–6).

4 And I heard the number of those who were sealed. One hundred *and* forty-four thousand of all the tribes of the children of Israel *were* sealed:

5 of the tribe of Judah
twelve thousand *were* sealed;[a]
of the tribe of Reuben
twelve thousand *were* sealed;
of the tribe of Gad
twelve thousand *were* sealed;
6 of the tribe of Asher
twelve thousand *were* sealed;
of the tribe of Naphtali
twelve thousand *were* sealed;
of the tribe of Manasseh
twelve thousand *were* sealed;
7 of the tribe of Simeon
twelve thousand *were* sealed;
of the tribe of Levi
twelve thousand *were* sealed;
of the tribe of Issachar
twelve thousand *were* sealed;
8 of the tribe of Zebulun
twelve thousand *were* sealed;
of the tribe of Joseph
twelve thousand *were* sealed;
of the tribe of Benjamin
twelve thousand *were* sealed.

A Multitude from the Great Tribulation

➢ 9 After these things I looked, and behold, a great multitude which no one could number, of all nations, tribes, peoples, and tongues, standing before the throne and before the Lamb, clothed with white robes, with palm branches in their hands,
10 and crying out with a loud voice, saying, "Salvation *belongs* to our God who sits on the throne, and to the Lamb!"
11 All the angels stood around the throne and the elders and the four living creatures, and fell on their faces before the throne and worshiped God,
12 saying:

"Amen! Blessing and glory and wisdom,
Thanksgiving and honor and power and might,
Be to our God forever and ever.
Amen."

13 Then one of the elders answered, saying to me, "Who are these arrayed in white robes, and where did they come from?"
14 And I said to him, "Sir,[a] you know." So he said to me, "These are the ones who come out of the great tribulation, and washed their robes and made them white in the blood of the Lamb.
15 "Therefore they are before the throne of God, and serve Him day and night in His temple. And He who sits on the throne will dwell among them.
16 "They shall neither hunger anymore nor thirst anymore; the sun shall not strike them, nor any heat; ✳
17 "for the Lamb who is in the midst of the throne will shepherd them and lead them to living fountains of waters.[a] And God will wipe away every tear from their eyes." ➤

Seventh Seal: Prelude to the Seven Trumpets

8 When He opened the seventh seal, there was silence in heaven for about half an hour. ➤
2 And I saw the seven angels who stand before God, and to them were given seven trumpets.
3 Then another angel, having a golden censer, came and stood at the altar. He was given much incense, that he should offer *it* with the prayers of all the saints upon the golden altar which was before the throne.
4 And the smoke of the incense, with the prayers of the saints, ascended before God from the angel's hand. ➤

7:5 [a]In NU-Text and M-Text *were sealed* is stated only in verses 5a and 8c; the words are understood in the remainder of the passage. **7:14** [a]NU-Text and M-Text read *My lord.*
7:17 [a]NU-Text and M-Text read *to fountains of the waters of life.*

LIFE LESSONS

➢ 7:9 — *. . . a great multitude which no one could number, of all nations, tribes, peoples, and tongues, standing before the throne and before the Lamb, clothed with white robes . . . .*

God not only redeems people from every imaginable point of origin and background, He also redeems multitudes beyond count. His grace reaches into every corner of the world.

➢ 7:17 — *". . . And God will wipe away every tear from their eyes."*

This line is repeated later in Revelation (see also Rev. 21:4). It is as if God wants us to remember that though our tears will flow, yet He will personally comfort us. He will delegate this task to no one else.

➢ 8:1 — *When He opened the seventh seal, there was silence in heaven for about half an hour.*

Some of God's judgments and works are so awesome that the only appropriate response is reverent silence. "But the LORD is in His holy temple. Let all the earth keep silence fore Him" (Hab. 2:20).

➢ 8:4 — *And the smoke of the incense, with the prayers of the saints, ascended before God from the angel's hand.*

God accepts the prayers of His faithful people and treats them like sacrifices—offerings to Him that cost the giver something and which honor Him. In prayer, we admit our weakness and declare God's strength.

5 Then the angel took the censer, filled it with
fire from the altar, and threw *it* to the earth.
And there were noises, thunderings, lightnings, and an earthquake.
6 So the seven angels who had the seven
trumpets prepared themselves to sound.

First Trumpet: Vegetation Struck

7 The first angel sounded: And hail and fire
followed, mingled with blood, and they were
thrown to the earth.[a] And a third of the trees
were burned up, and all green grass was
burned up.

Second Trumpet: The Seas Struck

8 Then the second angel sounded: And
something like a great mountain burning
with fire was thrown into the sea, and a third
of the sea became blood.
9 And a third of the living creatures in the
sea died, and a third of the ships were destroyed.

Third Trumpet: The Waters Struck

10 Then the third angel sounded: And a great
star fell from heaven, burning like a torch,
and it fell on a third of the rivers and on the
springs of water.
11 The name of the star is Wormwood. A third
of the waters became wormwood, and many
men died from the water, because it was made
bitter.

Fourth Trumpet: The Heavens Struck

12 Then the fourth angel sounded: And a
third of the sun was struck, a third of the
moon, and a third of the stars, so that a third
of them were darkened. A third of the day did
not shine, and likewise the night.
➤ 13 And I looked, and I heard an angel[a] flying
through the midst of heaven, saying with a
loud voice, "Woe, woe, woe to the inhabitants
of the earth, because of the remaining blasts
of the trumpet of the three angels who are
about to sound!"

Fifth Trumpet: The Locusts from the Bottomless Pit

9 Then the fifth angel sounded: And I saw a
star fallen from heaven to the earth. To
him was given the key to the bottomless pit.
2 And he opened the bottomless pit, and
smoke arose out of the pit like the smoke of a
great furnace. So the sun and the air were
darkened because of the smoke of the pit.
3 Then out of the smoke locusts came upon
the earth. And to them was given power, as
the scorpions of the earth have power.
4 They were commanded not to harm the
grass of the earth, or any green thing, or any
tree, but only those men who do not have the
seal of God on their foreheads.
5 And they were not given *authority* to kill
them, but to torment them *for* five months.
Their torment *was* like the torment of a scorpion when it strikes a man.
6 In those days men will seek death and will ➤
not find it; they will desire to die, and death
will flee from them.
7 The shape of the locusts was like horses
prepared for battle. On their heads were
crowns of something like gold, and their faces
were like the faces of men.
8 They had hair like women's hair, and their
teeth were like lions' *teeth*.
9 And they had breastplates like breastplates of iron, and the sound of their wings
was like the sound of chariots with many
horses running into battle.
10 They had tails like scorpions, and there
were stings in their tails. Their power *was* to
hurt men five months.
11 And they had as king over them the angel
of the bottomless pit, whose name in Hebrew
is Abaddon, but in Greek he has the name
Apollyon.
12 One woe is past. Behold, still two more
woes are coming after these things.

Sixth Trumpet: The Angels from the Euphrates

13 Then the sixth angel sounded: And I heard
a voice from the four horns of the golden altar
which is before God,
14 saying to the sixth angel who had the
trumpet, "Release the four angels who are
bound at the great river Euphrates."
15 So the four angels, who had been prepared ➤

8:7 [a]NU-Text and M-Text add *and a third of the earth was burned up.* **8:13** [a]NU-Text and M-Text read *eagle.*

LIFE LESSONS

➤ 8:13 — *"Woe, woe, woe to the inhabitants of the earth, because of the remaining blasts of the trumpet of the three angels who are about to sound!"*

The judgments described in Revelation grow in intensity and scale as the book progresses. God typically employs escalating judgments to prompt repentance, until the wicked reach the point of no return.

➤ 9:6 — *In those days men will seek death and will not find it; they will desire to die, and death will flee from them.*

Since God does not desire the death of anyone, when necessary He will use "severe mercies" to get our attention and urge us back to Him. Even severe pain is a good thing if it keeps someone from eternal death.

➤ 9:15 — *So the four angels, who had been prepared for the hour and day and month and year, were released . . . .*

Despite the chaos on earth that the Book of Revelation describes, we still get indications throughout the book that God remains completely in charge. God has prepared these angels for a specific work at a specific time.

for the hour and day and month and year, were released to kill a third of mankind.
16 Now the number of the army of the horsemen *was* two hundred million; I heard the number of them.
17 And thus I saw the horses in the vision: those who sat on them had breastplates of fiery red, hyacinth blue, and sulfur yellow; and the heads of the horses *were* like the heads of lions; and out of their mouths came fire, smoke, and brimstone.
18 By these three *plagues* a third of mankind was killed—by the fire and the smoke and the brimstone which came out of their mouths.
19 For their power[a] is in their mouth and in their tails; for their tails *are* like serpents, having heads; and with them they do harm.
➤ 20 But the rest of mankind, who were not killed by these plagues, did not repent of the works of their hands, that they should not worship demons, and idols of gold, silver, brass, stone, and wood, which can neither see nor hear nor walk.
21 And they did not repent of their murders or their sorceries[a] or their sexual immorality or their thefts.

The Mighty Angel with the Little Book

10 I saw still another mighty angel coming down from heaven, clothed with a cloud. And a rainbow *was* on his head, his face *was* like the sun, and his feet like pillars of fire.
2 He had a little book open in his hand. And he set his right foot on the sea and *his* left *foot* on the land,
3 and cried with a loud voice, as *when* a lion roars. When he cried out, seven thunders uttered their voices.
➤ 4 Now when the seven thunders uttered their voices,[a] I was about to write; but I heard a voice from heaven saying to me,[b] "Seal up the things which the seven thunders uttered, and do not write them."
5 The angel whom I saw standing on the sea and on the land raised up his hand[a] to heaven
6 and swore by Him who lives forever and ever, who created heaven and the things that are in it, the earth and the things that are in it, and the sea and the things that are in it, that there should be delay no longer,
7 but in the days of the sounding of the seventh angel, when he is about to sound, the mystery of God would be finished, as He declared to His servants the prophets. ➤

John Eats the Little Book

8 Then the voice which I heard from heaven spoke to me again and said, "Go, take the little book which is open in the hand of the angel who stands on the sea and on the earth."
9 So I went to the angel and said to him, "Give me the little book." And he said to me, "Take and eat it; and it will make your stomach bitter, but it will be as sweet as honey in your mouth." ➤
10 Then I took the little book out of the angel's hand and ate it, and it was as sweet as honey in my mouth. But when I had eaten it, my stomach became bitter.
11 And he[a] said to me, "You must prophesy again about many peoples, nations, tongues, and kings."

The Two Witnesses

11 Then I was given a reed like a measuring rod. And the angel stood,[a] saying, "Rise and measure the temple of God, the altar, and those who worship there.
2 "But leave out the court which is outside the temple, and do not measure it, for it has been given to the Gentiles. And they will tread the holy city underfoot *for* forty-two months.

9:19 [a]NU-Text and M-Text read *the power of the horses.*
9:21 [a]NU-Text and M-Text read *drugs.* **10:4** [a]NU-Text and M-Text read *sounded.* [b]NU-Text and M-Text omit *to me.*
10:5 [a]NU-Text and M-Text read *right hand.* **10:11** [a]NU-Text and M-Text read *they.* **11:1** [a]NU-Text and M-Text omit *And the angel stood.*

LIFE LESSONS

➤ 9:20 — *But the rest of mankind, who were not killed by these plagues, did not repent of the works of their hands . . . .*

Why does the Book of Revelation repeatedly tell us that the wicked did not repent? First, because it shows the necessity of God's judgment. Second, because it shows God's desire that they repent and live.

➤ 10:4 — *I was about to write; but I heard a voice from heaven saying to me, "Seal up the things which the seven thunders uttered, and do not write them."*

God reveals to us the things He wants us to know. He does not reveal details about the future to satisfy our curiosity, but to motivate and equip us to live for Him today with passion, holiness, and joy.

➤ 10:7 — *. . . the mystery of God would be finished, as He declared to His servants the prophets.*

History is moving relentlessly to a predetermined conclusion. We may not know what will happen from day to day, but we already know how everything will turn out. God triumphs, and we triumph with Him.

➤ 10:9 — *And he said to me, "Take and eat it; and it will make your stomach bitter, but it will be as sweet as honey in your mouth."*

It is always a joy to read and proclaim the Word of God, but some of that Word—like the passages describing catastrophic divine judgment—give no pleasure either to the prophets or to the Lord.

3 "And I will give *power* to my two witnesses, and they will prophesy one thousand two hundred and sixty days, clothed in sackcloth."

4 These are the two olive trees and the two lampstands standing before the God[a] of the earth.

5 And if anyone wants to harm them, fire proceeds from their mouth and devours their enemies. And if anyone wants to harm them, he must be killed in this manner.

➤ 6 These have power to shut heaven, so that no rain falls in the days of their prophecy; and they have power over waters to turn them to blood, and to strike the earth with all plagues, as often as they desire.

The Witnesses Killed

➤ **7** When they finish their testimony, the beast that ascends out of the bottomless pit will make war against them, overcome them, and kill them.

8 And their dead bodies *will lie* in the street of the great city which spiritually is called Sodom and Egypt, where also our[a] Lord was crucified.

9 Then *those* from the peoples, tribes, tongues, and nations will see their dead bodies three-and-a-half days, and not allow[a] their dead bodies to be put into graves.

10 And those who dwell on the earth will rejoice over them, make merry, and send gifts to one another, because these two prophets tormented those who dwell on the earth.

The Witnesses Resurrected

11 Now after the three-and-a-half days the breath of life from God entered them, and they stood on their feet, and great fear fell on those who saw them.

12 And they[a] heard a loud voice from heaven saying to them, "Come up here." And they ascended to heaven in a cloud, and their enemies saw them.

➤ 13 In the same hour there was a great earthquake, and a tenth of the city fell. In the earthquake seven thousand people were killed, and the rest were afraid and gave glory to the God of heaven.

14 The second woe is past. Behold, the third woe is coming quickly.

Seventh Trumpet: The Kingdom Proclaimed

15 Then the seventh angel sounded: And there were loud voices in heaven, saying, "The kingdoms[a] of this world have become *the kingdoms* of our Lord and of His Christ, and He shall reign forever and ever!" ➤

16 And the twenty-four elders who sat before God on their thrones fell on their faces and worshiped God,

17 saying:

"We give You thanks, O Lord God
Almighty,
The One who is and who was and who is
to come,[a]
Because You have taken Your great
power and reigned.
18 The nations were angry, and Your wrath
has come,
And the time of the dead, that they
should be judged,
And that You should reward Your
servants the prophets and the saints,
And those who fear Your name, small
and great,
And should destroy those who destroy
the earth."

19 Then the temple of God was opened in heaven, and the ark of His covenant[a] was seen in His temple. And there were lightnings, noises, thunderings, an earthquake, and great hail.

11:4 [a]NU-Text and M-Text read *Lord.* **11:8** [a]NU-Text and M-Text read *their.* **11:9** [a]NU-Text and M-Text read *nations see . . . and will not allow.* **11:12** [a]M-Text reads *I.* **11:15** [a]NU-Text and M-Text read *kingdom . . . has become.* **11:17** [a]NU-Text and M-Text omit *and who is to come.* **11:19** [a]M-Text reads *the covenant of the Lord.*

LIFE LESSONS

➤ 11:6 — *These have power to shut heaven . . . and they have power over waters to turn them to blood, and to strike the earth with all plagues, as often as they desire.*

The miracles described here inescapably remind us of the wonders performed through Elijah (1 Kin. 17:1) and Moses (Ex. 9:14). The same God who empowered them will demonstrate His power once again.

➤ 11:7 — *When they finish their testimony, the beast that ascends out of the bottomless pit will make war against them, overcome them, and kill them.*

We are immortal until our time comes to go to the Father. The "two witnesses" described here cannot be touched by their enemies until they have completed every task assigned to them by God.

➤ 11:13 — *In the earthquake seven thousand people were killed, and the rest were afraid and gave glory to the God of heaven.*

This is the only time in Revelation that a tragedy prompts those who survive to give "glory" to God. Tragedies are terrible things, but God wants to use even them to rescue people from a far worse spiritual catastrophe.

➤ 11:15 — *"The kingdoms of this world have become the kingdoms of our Lord and of His Christ, and He shall reign forever and ever!"*

The time is coming when every square inch of this planet will be illuminated by the glory of Christ's everlasting rule. "For the earth shall be full of the knowledge of the Lord as the waters cover the sea" (Is. 11:9).

The Woman, the Child, and the Dragon

12 Now a great sign appeared in heaven: a
woman clothed with the sun, with the
moon under her feet, and on her head a garland of twelve stars.
2 Then being with child, she cried out in
labor and in pain to give birth.
3 And another sign appeared in heaven: behold, a great, fiery red dragon having seven
heads and ten horns, and seven diadems on
his heads.
➤ 4 His tail drew a third of the stars of heaven
and threw them to the earth. And the dragon
stood before the woman who was ready to
give birth, to devour her Child as soon as it
was born.
5 She bore a male Child who was to rule all
nations with a rod of iron. And her Child was
caught up to God and His throne.
6 Then the woman fled into the wilderness,
where she has a place prepared by God, that
they should feed her there one thousand two
hundred and sixty days.

Satan Thrown Out of Heaven

7 And war broke out in heaven: Michael and
his angels fought with the dragon; and the
dragon and his angels fought,
8 but they did not prevail, nor was a place
found for them[a] in heaven any longer.
➤ 9 So the great dragon was cast out, that serpent of old, called the Devil and Satan, who
deceives the whole world; he was cast to the
earth, and his angels were cast out with him.
10 Then I heard a loud voice saying in
heaven, "Now salvation, and strength, and
the kingdom of our God, and the power of
His Christ have come, for the accuser of our
brethren, who accused them before our God
day and night, has been cast down.
➤ 11 "And they overcame him by the blood of
the Lamb and by the word of their testimony,
and they did not love their lives to the death.
12 "Therefore rejoice, O heavens, and you
who dwell in them! Woe to the inhabitants of
the earth and the sea! For the devil has come
down to you, having great wrath, because he
knows that he has a short time."

The Woman Persecuted

13 Now when the dragon saw that he had
been cast to the earth, he persecuted the
woman who gave birth to the male *Child.*
14 But the woman was given two wings of a
great eagle, that she might fly into the wilderness to her place, where she is nourished for
a time and times and half a time, from the
presence of the serpent.
15 So the serpent spewed water out of his
mouth like a flood after the woman, that he
might cause her to be carried away by the flood.
16 But the earth helped the woman, and the
earth opened its mouth and swallowed up the
flood which the dragon had spewed out of his
mouth.
17 And the dragon was enraged with the ➤
woman, and he went to make war with the
rest of her offspring, who keep the commandments of God and have the testimony of Jesus
Christ.[a]

The Beast from the Sea

13 Then I[a] stood on the sand of the sea.
And I saw a beast rising up out of the
sea, having seven heads and ten horns,[b] and
on his horns ten crowns, and on his heads a
blasphemous name.
2 Now the beast which I saw was like a ➤
leopard, his feet were like *the feet of* a bear,
and his mouth like the mouth of a lion. The
dragon gave him his power, his throne, and
great authority.

12:8 [a]M-Text reads *him.* **12:17** [a]NU-Text and M-Text omit *Christ.*
13:1 [a]NU-Text reads *he.* [b]NU-Text and M-Text read *ten horns and seven heads.*

LIFE LESSONS

➤ 12:4 — *His tail drew a third of the stars of heaven and threw them to the earth.*

Some commentators believe the "stars" represent angels and that Satan convinced a third of all the angels God had created to rebel against Him. In any case, the devil has great power to do evil, and we must resist him (1 Pet. 5:9).

➤ 12:9 — *So the great dragon was cast out, that serpent of old, called the Devil and Satan, who deceives the whole world; he was cast to the earth, and his angels were cast out with him.*

Some interpreters believe this text describes a future time; others believe it describes something that has already happened. In either case, it points to the superior power of God and His ultimate triumph over evil.

➤ 12:11 — *"And they overcame him by the blood of the Lamb and by the word of their testimony . . . ."*

We cannot win our battles against Satan with bombs and swords and bullets; our invincible weapons are the death of Christ and the Word of God. These weapons are "mighty in God for pulling down strongholds" (2 Cor. 10:4).

➤ 12:17 — *And the dragon was enraged with the woman, and he went to make war with the rest of her offspring, who keep the commandments of God and have the testimony of Jesus Christ.*

Satan has a particular hatred for Christians who obey God and who work to represent Jesus to the best of their ability, for they are the only ones who really make a difference for good in the world.

➤ 13:2 — *The dragon gave him his power, his throne, and great authority.*

The "antichrist," the "beast," the "man of sin," the "son of perdition"—whatever we call this coming figure, he will get his power and authority directly from the devil. That means he will be cunning as well as evil.

3 And I saw one of his heads as if it had
been mortally wounded, and his deadly
wound was healed. And all the world marveled and followed the beast.
4 So they worshiped the dragon who gave
authority to the beast; and they worshiped the
beast, saying, "Who *is* like the beast? Who is
able to make war with him?"
➤ 5 And he was given a mouth speaking great
things and blasphemies, and he was given authority to continue[a] for forty-two months.
6 Then he opened his mouth in blasphemy
against God, to blaspheme His name, His tabernacle, and those who dwell in heaven.
7 It was granted to him to make war with
the saints and to overcome them. And authority was given him over every tribe,[a] tongue,
and nation.
➤ 8 All who dwell on the earth will worship
him, whose names have not been written in
the Book of Life of the Lamb slain from the
foundation of the world.
9 If anyone has an ear, let him hear.
10 He who leads into captivity shall go into
captivity; he who kills with the sword must be
killed with the sword. Here is the patience
and the faith of the saints.

The Beast from the Earth

11 Then I saw another beast coming up out of
the earth, and he had two horns like a lamb
and spoke like a dragon.
12 And he exercises all the authority of the
first beast in his presence, and causes the
earth and those who dwell in it to worship the
first beast, whose deadly wound was healed.
➤ 13 He performs great signs, so that he even
makes fire come down from heaven on the
earth in the sight of men.
14 And he deceives those[a] who dwell on the
earth by those signs which he was granted to do
in the sight of the beast, telling those who dwell
on the earth to make an image to the beast who
was wounded by the sword and lived.
15 He was granted *power* to give breath to
the image of the beast, that the image of the
beast should both speak and cause as many
as would not worship the image of the beast
to be killed.
16 He causes all, both small and great, rich
and poor, free and slave, to receive a mark on
their right hand or on their foreheads,
17 and that no one may buy or sell except
one who has the mark or[a] the name of the
beast, or the number of his name.
18 Here is wisdom. Let him who has understanding calculate the number of the beast, for
it is the number of a man: His number *is* 666.

The Lamb and the 144,000

14 Then I looked, and behold, a[a] Lamb
standing on Mount Zion, and with Him
one hundred *and* forty-four thousand, having[b]
His Father's name written on their foreheads.
2 And I heard a voice from heaven, like the
voice of many waters, and like the voice of
loud thunder. And I heard the sound of harpists playing their harps.
3 They sang as it were a new song before
the throne, before the four living creatures,
and the elders; and no one could learn that
song except the hundred *and* forty-four thousand who were redeemed from the earth.
4 These are the ones who were not defiled
with women, for they are virgins. These are
the ones who follow the Lamb wherever He
goes. These were redeemed[a] from *among*
men, *being* firstfruits to God and to the Lamb.
5 And in their mouth was found no deceit,[a]
for they are without fault before the throne of
God.[b]

The Proclamations of Three Angels

6 Then I saw another angel flying in the
midst of heaven, having the everlasting gospel
to preach to those who dwell on the earth—to
every nation, tribe, tongue, and people—
7 saying with a loud voice, "Fear God and ◄

13:5 [a]M-Text reads *make war.* **13:7** [a]NU-Text and M-Text add *and people.* **13:14** [a]M-Text reads *my own people.* **13:17** [a]NU-Text and M-Text omit *or.* **14:1** [a]NU-Text and M-Text read *the.* [b]NU-Text and M-Text add *His name and.* **14:4** [a]M-Text adds *by Jesus.* **14:5** [a]NU-Text and M-Text read *falsehood.* [b]NU-Text and M-Text omit *before the throne of God.*

LIFE LESSONS

➤ 13:5 — *And he was given a mouth speaking great things and blasphemies, and he was given authority to continue for forty-two months.*

No horror of history will compare with the antichrist's reign of terror, but the God of heaven will strictly control even the length of his rule. God remains sovereign, even when it appears He doesn't.

➤ 13:8 — *. . . the Lamb slain from the foundation of the world.*

Even before He created Adam and Eve, God knew that they would sin and that He would respond by sending His Son to die on the cross to atone for their sin. "Known to God from eternity are all His works" (Acts 15:18).

➤ 13:13 — *He performs great signs, so that he even makes fire come down from heaven on the earth in the sight of men.*

Satan cannot counterfeit all of God's miracles, but he can certainly fabricate a few. "The coming of the lawless one is according to the working of Satan, with all power, signs, and lying wonders" (2 Thess. 2:9).

➤ 14:7 — *"Fear God and give glory to Him, for the hour of His judgment has come . . . ."*

Modern believers do not often connect divine judgment with glory, but the Bible does (Ex. 14:4, 17, 18; Ezek. 28:22; 39:21; John 8:50). God reveals His majesty not only in loving acts of mercy, but also in holy acts of vengeance.

give glory to Him, for the hour of His judgment
has come; and worship Him who made heaven
and earth, the sea and springs of water."
8 And another angel followed, saying,
"Babylon[a] is fallen, is fallen, that great city,
because she has made all nations drink of the
wine of the wrath of her fornication."
9 Then a third angel followed them, saying
with a loud voice, "If anyone worships the
beast and his image, and receives *his* mark on
his forehead or on his hand,
10 "he himself shall also drink of the wine of
the wrath of God, which is poured out full
strength into the cup of His indignation. He
shall be tormented with fire and brimstone in
the presence of the holy angels and in the
presence of the Lamb.
➤ 11 "And the smoke of their torment ascends
forever and ever; and they have no rest day or
night, who worship the beast and his image,
and whoever receives the mark of his name."
12 Here is the patience of the saints; here *are*
those[a] who keep the commandments of God
and the faith of Jesus.
✳ 13 Then I heard a voice from heaven saying
to me,[a] "Write: 'Blessed *are* the dead who die
in the Lord from now on.'" "Yes," says the
Spirit, "that they may rest from their labors,
and their works follow them."

Reaping the Earth's Harvest

14 Then I looked, and behold, a white cloud,
and on the cloud sat *One* like the Son of Man,
having on His head a golden crown, and in
His hand a sharp sickle.
15 And another angel came out of the temple,
crying with a loud voice to Him who sat on
the cloud, "Thrust in Your sickle and reap, for
the time has come for You[a] to reap, for the
harvest of the earth is ripe."
16 So He who sat on the cloud thrust in His
sickle on the earth, and the earth was reaped.

Reaping the Grapes of Wrath

17 Then another angel came out of the temple which is in heaven, he also having a sharp
sickle.
18 And another angel came out from the
altar, who had power over fire, and he cried
with a loud cry to him who had the sharp
sickle, saying, "Thrust in your sharp sickle
and gather the clusters of the vine of the
earth, for her grapes are fully ripe."
19 So the angel thrust his sickle into the
earth and gathered the vine of the earth, and
threw *it* into the great winepress of the wrath
of God.
20 And the winepress was trampled outside
the city, and blood came out of the winepress,
up to the horses' bridles, for one thousand six
hundred furlongs.

Prelude to the Bowl Judgments

15 Then I saw another sign in heaven,
great and marvelous: seven angels having the seven last plagues, for in them the
wrath of God is complete.
2 And I saw *something* like a sea of glass
mingled with fire, and those who have the victory over the beast, over his image and over
his mark[a] *and* over the number of his name,
standing on the sea of glass, having harps of
God.
3 They sing the song of Moses, the servant
of God, and the song of the Lamb, saying:

"Great and marvelous *are* Your works,
Lord God Almighty!
Just and true *are* Your ways,
O King of the saints![a]
4 Who shall not fear You, O Lord, and
glorify Your name? ➤
For *You* alone *are* holy.
For all nations shall come and worship
before You,
For Your judgments have been
manifested."

5 After these things I looked, and behold,[a]
the temple of the tabernacle of the testimony
in heaven was opened.
6 And out of the temple came the seven angels having the seven plagues, clothed in pure
bright linen, and having their chests girded
with golden bands.

14:8 [a]NU-Text reads *Babylon the great is fallen, is fallen, which has made;* M-Text reads *Babylon the great is fallen. She has made.* **14:12** [a]NU-Text and M-Text omit *here are those.* **14:13** [a]NU-Text and M-Text omit *to me.* **14:15** [a]NU-Text and M-Text omit *for You.* **15:2** [a]NU-Text and M-Text omit *over his mark.* **15:3** [a]NU-Text and M-Text read *nations.* **15:5** [a]NU-Text and M-Text omit *behold.*

LIFE LESSONS

➤ 14:11 — *"And the smoke of their torment ascends ɔrever and ever; and they have no rest day or ˈght . . . ."*

Hell is a place of eternal suffering and restlessness, because its doomed souls are forever separated from the only One who could have made them ꞉. "There is no peace for the wicked," says the Lord :22).

➤ 15:4 — *"Who shall not fear You, O Lord, and glorify Your name? For You alone are holy . . . ."*

One day, every knee shall bow to God and every tongue confess that Jesus is Lord (Rom. 14:11; Phil. 2:10)—but some will bow willingly and joyfully, while others will bow grudgingly and in dread. But everyone *will* bow.

7 Then one of the four living creatures gave
to the seven angels seven golden bowls full of
the wrath of God who lives forever and ever.
➤ 8 The temple was filled with smoke from the
glory of God and from His power, and no one
was able to enter the temple till the seven
plagues of the seven angels were completed.

16 Then I heard a loud voice from the temple saying to the seven angels, "Go and
pour out the bowls[a] of the wrath of God on
the earth."

First Bowl: Loathsome Sores

2 So the first went and poured out his bowl
upon the earth, and a foul and loathsome sore
came upon the men who had the mark of the
beast and those who worshiped his image.

Second Bowl: The Sea Turns to Blood

3 Then the second angel poured out his
bowl on the sea, and it became blood as of a
dead *man;* and every living creature in the sea
died.

Third Bowl: The Waters Turn to Blood

4 Then the third angel poured out his bowl
on the rivers and springs of water, and they
became blood.
5 And I heard the angel of the waters saying:

"You are righteous, O Lord,[a]
The One who is and who was and who is to be,[b]
Because You have judged these things.
6 For they have shed the blood of saints and prophets,
And You have given them blood to drink.
For[b] it is their just due."

7 And I heard another from[a] the altar saying, "Even so, Lord God Almighty, true and
righteous *are* Your judgments."

Fourth Bowl: Men Are Scorched

8 Then the fourth angel poured out his bowl
on the sun, and power was given to him to
scorch men with fire.
9 And men were scorched with great heat, ➤
and they blasphemed the name of God who
has power over these plagues; and they did
not repent and give Him glory.

Fifth Bowl: Darkness and Pain

10 Then the fifth angel poured out his bowl
on the throne of the beast, and his kingdom
became full of darkness; and they gnawed
their tongues because of the pain.
11 They blasphemed the God of heaven because of their pains and their sores, and did ➤
not repent of their deeds.

Sixth Bowl: Euphrates Dried Up

12 Then the sixth angel poured out his bowl
on the great river Euphrates, and its water
was dried up, so that the way of the kings
from the east might be prepared.
13 And I saw three unclean spirits like frogs
coming out of the mouth of the dragon, out of
the mouth of the beast, and out of the mouth
of the false prophet.
14 For they are spirits of demons, performing
signs, *which* go out to the kings of the earth
and[a] of the whole world, to gather them to the
battle of that great day of God Almighty.
15 "Behold, I am coming as a thief. Blessed *is* ➤
he who watches, and keeps his garments, lest
he walk naked and they see his shame."
16 And they gathered them together to the
place called in Hebrew, Armageddon.[a]

Seventh Bowl: The Earth Utterly Shaken

17 Then the seventh angel poured out his
bowl into the air, and a loud voice came out of
the temple of heaven, from the throne, saying,
"It is done!"
18 And there were noises and thunderings

16:1 [a]NU-Text and M-Text read *seven bowls.* **16:5** [a]NU-Text and M-Text omit *O Lord.* [b]NU-Text and M-Text read *who was, the Holy One.* **16:6** [a]NU-Text and M-Text omit *For.* **16:7** [a]NU-Text and M-Text omit *another from.* **16:14** [a]NU-Text and M-Text omit *of the earth and.* **16:16** [a]M-Text reads *Megiddo.*

LIFE LESSONS

➤ **15:8 — *The temple was filled with smoke from the glory of God and from His power, and no one was able to enter the temple . . . .***

Whenever God unveils His full majesty, His splendor overwhelms the stoutest heart and forces it into worshipful retreat. This happened with Isaiah (Is. 6:4, 5) and at the dedication of the Jerusalem temple (1 Kin. 8:10, 11).

➤ **16:9 — *And men were scorched with great heat, and they blasphemed the name of God who has power over these plagues; and they did not repent and give Him glory.***

Even today God has power over natural calamities that we commonly call "acts of God," but merely recognizing that power often does not prompt repentance. Just as often it sparks the complaint, "Why didn't He prevent it?"

➤ **16:11 — *They blasphemed the God of heaven because of their pains and their sores, and did not repent of their deeds.***

It is a curious fact that the more ungodly a culture becomes, the more "spiritual" it considers itself and the more likely its members will say things like, "I can't believe in a God who would allow such suffering."

➤ **16:15 — *"Behold, I am coming as a thief. Blessed is he who watches, and keeps his garments, lest he walk naked and they see his shame."***

We must remain ready for Christ's return, *whenever* He comes back. We are to keep at whatever tasks He gives us, so that "we may have confidence and not be ashamed before Him at His coming" (1 John 2:28).

and lightnings; and there was a great earthquake, such a mighty and great earthquake
as had not occurred since men were on the
earth.
19 Now the great city was divided into three
parts, and the cities of the nations fell. And
great Babylon was remembered before God,
to give her the cup of the wine of the fierceness of His wrath.
20 Then every island fled away, and the
mountains were not found.
21 And great hail from heaven fell upon men,
each hailstone about the weight of a talent.
Men blasphemed God because of the plague
of the hail, since that plague was exceedingly
great.

The Scarlet Woman and the Scarlet Beast

17 Then one of the seven angels who had
the seven bowls came and talked with
me, saying to me,[a] "Come, I will show you the
judgment of the great harlot who sits on
many waters,
2 "with whom the kings of the earth committed fornication, and the inhabitants of the
earth were made drunk with the wine of her
fornication."
3 So he carried me away in the Spirit into
the wilderness. And I saw a woman sitting on
a scarlet beast *which was* full of names of
blasphemy, having seven heads and ten
horns.
4 The woman was arrayed in purple and
scarlet, and adorned with gold and precious
stones and pearls, having in her hand a
golden cup full of abominations and the filthiness of her fornication.[a]
5 And on her forehead a name *was* written:

MYSTERY,
BABYLON THE GREAT,
THE MOTHER OF HARLOTS AND OF THE
ABOMINATIONS OF THE EARTH.

➤ 6 I saw the woman, drunk with the blood of
the saints and with the blood of the martyrs
of Jesus. And when I saw her, I marveled with
great amazement.

The Meaning of the Woman and the Beast

7 But the angel said to me, "Why did you
marvel? I will tell you the mystery of the
woman and of the beast that carries her,
which has the seven heads and the ten horns.
8 "The beast that you saw was, and is not,
and will ascend out of the bottomless pit and
go to perdition. And those who dwell on the
earth will marvel, whose names are not written in the Book of Life from the foundation of
the world, when they see the beast that was,
and is not, and yet is.[a]
9 "Here *is* the mind which has wisdom: The
seven heads are seven mountains on which
the woman sits.
10 "There are also seven kings. Five have
fallen, one is, *and* the other has not yet come.
And when he comes, he must continue a short
time.
11 "The beast that was, and is not, is himself
also the eighth, and is of the seven, and is
going to perdition.
12 "The ten horns which you saw are ten
kings who have received no kingdom as yet,
but they receive authority for one hour as
kings with the beast.
13 "These are of one mind, and they will give
their power and authority to the beast.
14 "These will make war with the Lamb, and ➤
the Lamb will overcome them, for He is Lord
of lords and King of kings; and those *who are*
with Him *are* called, chosen, and faithful."
15 Then he said to me, "The waters which
you saw, where the harlot sits, are peoples,
multitudes, nations, and tongues.
16 "And the ten horns which you saw on[a] the
beast, these will hate the harlot, make her
desolate and naked, eat her flesh and burn
her with fire.
17 "For God has put it into their hearts to ful- ➤
fill His purpose, to be of one mind, and to give
their kingdom to the beast, until the words of
God are fulfilled.

17:1 [a]NU-Text and M-Text omit *to me.* **17:4** [a]M-Text reads *the filthiness of the fornication of the earth.* **17:8** [a]NU-Text and M-Text read *and shall be present.* **17:16** [a]NU-Text and M-Text read *saw, and the beast.*

LIFE LESSONS

➤ 17:6 — *I saw the woman, drunk with the blood of the saints and with the blood of the martyrs of Jesus. And when I saw her, I marveled with great amazement.*

It still shocks us today when we hear of Christians being murdered for their faith. We rightly grieve at the loss of life—but God also delights in their faithfulness and willing sacrifice.

➤ 17:14 — *"These will make war with the Lamb, and the Lamb will overcome them, for He is Lord of lords and King of kings . . . ."*

It doesn't make much sense to us as we read that *anyone* would so foolishly attack the Lord. Yet every time we sin, in a sense we make war against Jesus. How much more sense is there in that?

➤ 17:17 — *"For God has put it into their hearts to fulfill His purpose, to be of one mind, and to give their kingdom to the beast, until the words of God are fulfilled."*

The sovereignty of God extends so far that even the willing alliance of evil rulers against the Lord, actually serves God's purposes and plays right into His hand! He uses their best weapons against them.

18 "And the woman whom you saw is that great city which reigns over the kings of the earth."

The Fall of Babylon the Great

18 After these things I saw another angel coming down from heaven, having great authority, and the earth was illuminated with his glory.

2 And he cried mightily[a] with a loud voice, saying, "Babylon the great is fallen, is fallen, and has become a dwelling place of demons, a prison for every foul spirit, and a cage for every unclean and hated bird!

3 "For all the nations have drunk of the wine of the wrath of her fornication, the kings of the earth have committed fornication with her, and the merchants of the earth have become rich through the abundance of her luxury."

➤ 4 And I heard another voice from heaven saying, "Come out of her, my people, lest you share in her sins, and lest you receive of her plagues.

5 "For her sins have reached[a] to heaven, and God has remembered her iniquities.

6 "Render to her just as she rendered to you,[a] and repay her double according to her works; in the cup which she has mixed, mix double for her.

7 "In the measure that she glorified herself and lived luxuriously, in the same measure give her torment and sorrow; for she says in her heart, 'I sit *as* queen, and am no widow, and will not see sorrow.'

➤ 8 "Therefore her plagues will come in one day—death and mourning and famine. And she will be utterly burned with fire, for strong *is* the Lord God who judges[a] her.

The World Mourns Babylon's Fall

9 "The kings of the earth who committed fornication and lived luxuriously with her will weep and lament for her, when they see the smoke of her burning,

10 "standing at a distance for fear of her torment, saying, 'Alas, alas, that great city Babylon, that mighty city! For in one hour your judgment has come.'

11 "And the merchants of the earth will weep and mourn over her, for no one buys their merchandise anymore:

12 "merchandise of gold and silver, precious stones and pearls, fine linen and purple, silk and scarlet, every kind of citron wood, every kind of object of ivory, every kind of object of most precious wood, bronze, iron, and marble;

13 "and cinnamon and incense, fragrant oil and frankincense, wine and oil, fine flour and wheat, cattle and sheep, horses and chariots, and bodies and souls of men.

14 "The fruit that your soul longed for has gone from you, and all the things which are rich and splendid have gone from you,[a] and you shall find them no more at all.

15 "The merchants of these things, who became rich by her, will stand at a distance for fear of her torment, weeping and wailing,

16 "and saying, 'Alas, alas, that great city that was clothed in fine linen, purple, and scarlet, and adorned with gold and precious stones and pearls!

17 'For in one hour such great riches came to nothing.' Every shipmaster, all who travel by ship, sailors, and as many as trade on the sea, stood at a distance

18 "and cried out when they saw the smoke of her burning, saying, 'What *is* like this great city?'

19 "They threw dust on their heads and cried out, weeping and wailing, and saying, 'Alas, alas, that great city, in which all who had ships on the sea became rich by her wealth! For in one hour she is made desolate.'

20 "Rejoice over her, O heaven, and *you* holy apostles[a] and prophets, for God has avenged you on her!"

Finality of Babylon's Fall

21 Then a mighty angel took up a stone like a great millstone and threw *it* into the sea, saying, "Thus with violence the great city Babylon shall be thrown down, and shall not be found anymore.

22 "The sound of harpists, musicians, flutists, and trumpeters shall not be heard in you anymore. No craftsman of any craft shall be found in you anymore, and the sound of a millstone shall not be heard in you anymore.

18:2 [a]NU-Text and M-Text omit *mightily.* **18:5** [a]NU-Text and M-Text read *have been heaped up.* **18:6** [a]NU-Text and M-Text omit *to you.* **18:8** [a]NU-Text and M-Text read *has judged.* **18:14** [a]NU-Text and M-Text read *been lost to you.* **18:20** [a]NU-Text and M-Text read *saints and apostles.*

LIFE LESSONS

➤ 18:4 — *And I heard another voice from heaven saying, "Come out of her, my people, lest you share in her sins, and lest you receive of her plagues."*

God does not want His people entwined with evil because He wants to bless them, not judge them. "Come out from among them and be separate, says the Lord. Do not touch what is unclean" (2 Cor. 6:17).

➤ 18:8 — *". . . she will be utterly burned with fire, for strong is the Lord God who judges her."*

Just as God wiped out Sodom and Gomorrah with a hail of fire, so He promises to destroy the evil world system, "Babylon the great," at the time of the end. No one can restrain the Lord's hand of judgment.

ANSWERS TO LIFE'S QUESTIONS

Can the devil really make me do it?

REV. 18:23

The late comedian Flip Wilson may have popularized the catchphrase, "The devil made me do it," but this excuse has always been around. We blame Satan since we know he has something to do with the temptation process.

But in fact, the devil cannot *make* us do anything. The Bible calls Satan a deceiver (Gen. 3:13; 2 Cor. 11:3; Rev. 18:23) and the "father of lies" (John 8:44). Satan's only power over us is through manipulation and deceit.

If the devil could actually *make* us do things, then he wouldn't need to go to all the trouble of deceiving us. When he dangles the right bait in front of us at the right time, our fleshly desires make it seem as though something is relentlessly drawing us toward sin; but this power does not control us. In each case we *choose* to disobey.

Think of it this way. Imagine yourself standing at the edge of a cliff that drops off into a deep, rocky gorge. Now suppose I walked up to you and said, "We have kidnapped a member of your family. If you refuse to jump, your relative will be brutally beaten and then killed." Have I made you jump? If you believed my story and you believed that by jumping you could save your family member, I may have made you *willing* to jump or even *anxious* to jump. But I have not *made* you jump. Even if you jumped and you found out on the way to the bottom that I had lied about the whole thing, I still did not *make* you jump. I simply tricked you into jumping. On the other hand, if I walked up behind you and pushed you, then I made you do something contrary to what you wanted to do, felt like doing, or even thought about doing.

Now think about the last time you felt tempted to sin. Did you suddenly discover that you were sinning or had sinned? Were you in the process before you ever thought about it? Or did it begin with a thought; then a feeling; then maybe a little struggle; then the actual sin?

Just as no one held Eve and forced her to bite the fruit, so no one holds you down and forces you to sin. Satan cannot *make* you do anything, but he will do all he can to deceive you into dishonoring God.

See the Life Principles Index for further study:
2. Obey God and leave all the consequences to Him.

23 "The light of a lamp shall not shine in you anymore, and the voice of bridegroom and bride shall not be heard in you anymore. For your merchants were the great men of the earth, for by your sorcery all the nations were deceived.
24 "And in her was found the blood of prophets and saints, and of all who were slain on the earth."

Heaven Exults over Babylon

19 After these things I heard[a] a loud voice of a great multitude in heaven, saying, "Alleluia! Salvation and glory and honor and power *belong* to the Lord[b] our God!
2 "For true and righteous *are* His judgments, because He has judged the great harlot who corrupted the earth with her fornication; and He has avenged on her the blood of His servants *shed* by her."
3 Again they said, "Alleluia! Her smoke rises up forever and ever!"
4 And the twenty-four elders and the four living creatures fell down and worshiped God who sat on the throne, saying, "Amen! Alleluia!"
5 Then a voice came from the throne, saying, "Praise our God, all you His servants and those who fear Him, both[a] small and great!"
6 And I heard, as it were, the voice of a great multitude, as the sound of many waters and as the sound of mighty thunderings, saying, "Alleluia! For the[a] Lord God Omnipotent reigns!

19:1 [a]NU-Text and M-Text add *something like.* [b]NU-Text and M-Text omit *the Lord.* **19:5** [a]NU-Text and M-Text omit *both.* **19:6** [a]NU-Text and M-Text read *our.*

LIFE LESSONS

➤ 19:5 — *Then a voice came from the throne, saying, "Praise our God, all you His servants and those who fear Him, both small and great!"*

Many differences separate us during most of the week—height, weight, color, social status, financial situation, intelligence, background—and yet in worship, both "small and great" approach God on the same level.

7 "Let us be glad and rejoice and give Him
glory, for the marriage of the Lamb has come,
and His wife has made herself ready."
8 And to her it was granted to be arrayed in
fine linen, clean and bright, for the fine linen
is the righteous acts of the saints.
9 Then he said to me, "Write: 'Blessed *are*
those who are called to the marriage supper
of the Lamb!'" And he said to me, "These are
the true sayings of God."
➤ 10 And I fell at his feet to worship him. But he
said to me, "See *that you do* not *do that!* I am
your fellow servant, and of your brethren who
have the testimony of Jesus. Worship God!
For the testimony of Jesus is the spirit of
prophecy."

Christ on a White Horse

➤ **11** Now I saw heaven opened, and behold, a
white horse. And He who sat on him *was*
called Faithful and True, and in righteousness
He judges and makes war.
12 His eyes *were* like a flame of fire, and on
His head *were* many crowns. He had[a] a name
written that no one knew except Himself.
13 He *was* clothed with a robe dipped in
blood, and His name is called The Word of God.
14 And the armies in heaven, clothed in fine
linen, white and clean,[a] followed Him on
white horses.
15 Now out of His mouth goes a sharp[a]
sword, that with it He should strike the nations. And He Himself will rule them with a
rod of iron. He Himself treads the winepress
of the fierceness and wrath of Almighty God.
➤ 16 And He has on *His* robe and on His thigh
a name written:

KING OF KINGS AND
LORD OF LORDS.

The Beast and His Armies Defeated

17 Then I saw an angel standing in the sun;
and he cried with a loud voice, saying to all
the birds that fly in the midst of heaven,
"Come and gather together for the supper of
the great God,[a]
18 "that you may eat the flesh of kings, the
flesh of captains, the flesh of mighty men, the
flesh of horses and of those who sit on them,
and the flesh of all *people*, free[a] and slave,
both small and great."
19 And I saw the beast, the kings of the earth,
and their armies, gathered together to make
war against Him who sat on the horse and
against His army.
20 Then the beast was captured, and with ➤
him the false prophet who worked signs in his
presence, by which he deceived those who received the mark of the beast and those who
worshiped his image. These two were cast
alive into the lake of fire burning with brimstone.
21 And the rest were killed with the sword
which proceeded from the mouth of Him who
sat on the horse. And all the birds were filled
with their flesh.

Satan Bound 1000 Years

20 Then I saw an angel coming down from
heaven, having the key to the bottomless pit and a great chain in his hand.
2 He laid hold of the dragon, that serpent of
old, who is *the* Devil and Satan, and bound
him for a thousand years;
3 and he cast him into the bottomless pit, ➤
and shut him up, and set a seal on him, so
that he should deceive the nations no more till
the thousand years were finished. But after
these things he must be released for a little
while.

19:12 [a]M-Text adds *names written, and.* **19:14** [a]NU-Text and M-Text read *pure white linen.* **19:15** [a]M-Text adds *two-edged.*
19:17 [a]NU-Text and M-Text read *the great supper of God.*
19:18 [a]NU-Text and M-Text read *both free.*

LIFE LESSONS

➤ 19:10 — *I fell at his feet to worship him. But he said to me, "See that you do not do that! I am your fellow servant . . . . Worship God!"*

Angels have such majesty and power that human beings always feel tempted to worship them—even someone as mature and godly as John. But angels know their place. God alone deserves our worship!

➤ 19:11 — *He . . . was called Faithful and True, and in righteousness He judges and makes war.*

Jesus told His disciples that His Father had committed all judgment to Him (John 5:22). He is perfectly suited for the role, as He not only knows us thoroughly, but also is flawlessly just, honest, and trustworthy.

➤ 19:16 — *And He has on His robe and on His thigh a name written: KING OF KINGS AND LORD OF LORDS.*

The Lord veiled his royal majesty during His years of earthly ministry, but God will spotlight His glory upon His return so that no one could possibly miss it: "He is coming with clouds, and every eye will see Him" (Rev. 1:7).

➤ 19:20 — *These two were cast alive into the lake of fire burning with brimstone.*

Some teach that those who wind up in hell are annihilated, but the "beast" and "false prophet" who get thrown into the lake of fire are still there one thousand years later when Satan is judged (Rev. 20:10).

➤ 20:3 — *. . . But after these things he must be released for a little while.*

Why "must" Satan be released after his long imprisonment? Why doesn't God judge him immediately? God uses Satan to reveal the unconverted hearts of those who pretend to love God (Rev. 20:7–9). And then Satan meets his final judgment.

The Saints Reign with Christ 1000 Years
4 And I saw thrones, and they sat on them,
and judgment was committed to them. Then *I*
saw the souls of those who had been beheaded for their witness to Jesus and for the
word of God, who had not worshiped the
beast or his image, and had not received *his*
mark on their foreheads or on their hands.
And they lived and reigned with Christ for a[a]
thousand years.
5 But the rest of the dead did not live again
until the thousand years were finished. This *is*
the first resurrection.
6 Blessed and holy *is* he who has part in the
first resurrection. Over such the second death
has no power, but they shall be priests of God
and of Christ, and shall reign with Him a
thousand years.

Satanic Rebellion Crushed
7 Now when the thousand years have expired, Satan will be released from his prison
8 and will go out to deceive the nations
which are in the four corners of the earth,
Gog and Magog, to gather them together to
battle, whose number *is* as the sand of the
sea.
9 They went up on the breadth of the earth
and surrounded the camp of the saints and the
beloved city. And fire came down from God
out of heaven and devoured them.
10 The devil, who deceived them, was cast
into the lake of fire and brimstone where[a]
the beast and the false prophet *are*. And they
will be tormented day and night forever and
ever.

The Great White Throne Judgment
11 Then I saw a great white throne and Him
who sat on it, from whose face the earth and
the heaven fled away. And there was found no
place for them.
12 And I saw the dead, small and great,
standing before God,[a] and books were
opened. And another book was opened,
which is *the Book* of Life. And the dead were
judged according to their works, by the things
which were written in the books.
13 The sea gave up the dead who were in it,
and Death and Hades delivered up the dead
who were in them. And they were judged,
each one according to his works.
14 Then Death and Hades were cast into the
lake of fire. This is the second death.[a]
15 And anyone not found written in the Book
of Life was cast into the lake of fire.

All Things Made New
21 Now I saw a new heaven and a new
earth, for the first heaven and the first
earth had passed away. Also there was no
more sea.
2 Then I, John,[a] saw the holy city, New Jerusalem, coming down out of heaven from
God, prepared as a bride adorned for her
husband.
3 And I heard a loud voice from heaven saying, "Behold, the tabernacle of God *is* with
men, and He will dwell with them, and they
shall be His people. God Himself will be with
them *and be* their God.
4 "And God will wipe away every tear from
their eyes; there shall be no more death, nor
sorrow, nor crying. There shall be no more
pain, for the former things have passed
away."
5 Then He who sat on the throne said, "Behold, I make all things new." And He said to
me,[a] "Write, for these words are true and
faithful."
6 And He said to me, "It is done![a] I am the
Alpha and the Omega, the Beginning and the
End. I will give of the fountain of the water of
life freely to him who thirsts.

20:4 [a]M-Text reads *the*. **20:10** [a]NU-Text and M-Text add *also*. **20:12** [a]NU-Text and M-Text read *the throne*. **20:14** [a]NU-Text and M-Text add *the lake of fire*. **21:2** [a]NU-Text and M-Text omit *John*. **21:5** [a]NU-Text and M-Text omit *to me*. **21:6** [a]M-Text omits *It is done*.

LIFE LESSONS

➤ 20:12 — *And I saw the dead, small and great, standing before God, and books were opened . . . . And the dead were judged according to their works . . . .*

Those who do not depend on Christ for their salvation will be judged "according to their works." Since all have sinned, and the wages of sin is death, they will all receive the wages they earned: the second death.

➤ 20:15 — *And anyone not found written in the Book of Life was cast into the lake of fire.*

Those who place their faith in Jesus Christ have their names permanently written in the Lamb's Book of Life (Rev. 21:27). Those who depend on their own efforts to reach heaven will instead find themselves in the lake of fire.

➤ 21:3 — *"Behold, the tabernacle of God is with men, and He will dwell with them, and they shall be His people."*

The best part of heaven will not be the streets of gold, or the pearly gates, or even the happy reunions we will enjoy with believing loved ones. The best thing about heaven is the loving presence of God Himself.

➤ 21:5 — *Then He who sat on the throne said, "Behold, I make all things new."*

Our eternal home will never grow old, because God promises to make *all* things new. The Eternal One loves new things: new hearts (Ezek. 36:26), new songs (Is. 42:10), new heavens and a new earth (2 Pet. 3:13), new life (Rom. 6:4).

7 "He who overcomes shall inherit all things,[a] and I will be his God and he shall be My son.
8 "But the cowardly, unbelieving,[a] abominable, murderers, sexually immoral, sorcerers, idolaters, and all liars shall have their part in the lake which burns with fire and brimstone, which is the second death."

The New Jerusalem

9 Then one of the seven angels who had the seven bowls filled with the seven last plagues came to me[a] and talked with me, saying, "Come, I will show you the bride, the Lamb's wife."[b]
10 And he carried me away in the Spirit to a great and high mountain, and showed me the great city, the holy[a] Jerusalem, descending out of heaven from God,
11 having the glory of God. Her light *was* like a most precious stone, like a jasper stone, clear as crystal.
12 Also she had a great and high wall with twelve gates, and twelve angels at the gates, and names written on them, which are *the names* of the twelve tribes of the children of Israel:
13 three gates on the east, three gates on the north, three gates on the south, and three gates on the west.
14 Now the wall of the city had twelve foundations, and on them were the names[a] of the twelve apostles of the Lamb.
15 And he who talked with me had a gold reed to measure the city, its gates, and its wall.
16 The city is laid out as a square; its length is as great as its breadth. And he measured the city with the reed: twelve thousand furlongs. Its length, breadth, and height are equal.
17 Then he measured its wall: one hundred *and* forty-four cubits, *according* to the measure of a man, that is, of an angel.
18 The construction of its wall was *of* jasper; and the city *was* pure gold, like clear glass.
19 The foundations of the wall of the city *were* adorned with all kinds of precious stones: the first foundation *was* jasper, the second sapphire, the third chalcedony, the fourth emerald,
20 the fifth sardonyx, the sixth sardius, the seventh chrysolite, the eighth beryl, the ninth topaz, the tenth chrysoprase, the eleventh jacinth, and the twelfth amethyst.
21 The twelve gates *were* twelve pearls: each individual gate was of one pearl. And the street of the city *was* pure gold, like transparent glass.

The Glory of the New Jerusalem

22 But I saw no temple in it, for the Lord God Almighty and the Lamb are its temple.
23 The city had no need of the sun or of the moon to shine in it,[a] for the glory[b] of God illuminated it. The Lamb *is* its light.
24 And the nations of those who are saved[a] shall walk in its light, and the kings of the earth bring their glory and honor into it.[b]
25 Its gates shall not be shut at all by day (there shall be no night there).
26 And they shall bring the glory and the honor of the nations into it.[a]
27 But there shall by no means enter it anything that defiles, or causes[a] an abomination or a lie, but only those who are written in the Lamb's Book of Life.

The River of Life

22 And he showed me a pure[a] river of water of life, clear as crystal, proceeding from the throne of God and of the Lamb.
2 In the middle of its street, and on either side of the river, *was* the tree of life, which bore twelve fruits, each *tree* yielding its fruit every month. The leaves of the tree *were* for the healing of the nations.

21:7 [a]M-Text reads *overcomes, I shall give him these things.* **21:8** [a]M-Text adds *and sinners.* **21:9** [a]NU-Text and M-Text omit *to me.* [b]M-Text reads *I will show you the woman, the Lamb's bride.* **21:10** [a]NU-Text and M-Text omit *the great* and read *the holy city, Jerusalem.* **21:14** [a]NU-Text and M-Text read *twelve names.* **21:23** [a]NU-Text and M-Text omit *in it.* [b]M-Text reads *the very glory.* **21:24** [a]NU-Text and M-Text omit *of those who are saved.* [b]M-Text reads *the glory and honor of the nations to Him.* **21:26** [a]M-Text adds *that they may enter in.* **21:27** [a]NU-Text and M-Text read *anything profane, nor one who causes.* **22:1** [a]NU-Text and M-Text omit *pure.*

LIFE LESSONS

➤ 21:7 — *"He who overcomes shall inherit all things, and I will be his God and he shall be My son."*

As the adopted children of God (Eph. 1:5), we are "heirs—heirs of God and joint heirs with Christ;" and we overcome when we "suffer with Him, that we may also be glorified together" (Rom. 8:17).

➤ 21:23 — *The city had no need of the sun or of the moon to shine in it, for the glory of God illuminated it. The Lamb is its light.*

We got a small hint of coming attractions when Jesus displayed a little of His glory at the Transfiguration. There, "His face shone like the sun, and His clothes became as white as the light" (Matt. 17:2).

➤ 21:27 — *. . . there shall by no means enter it anything that defiles, or causes an abomination or a lie . . . .*

Sin will have no place in our eternal home. Nothing evil or wicked or immoral or foul or depraved or fiendish will ever cast a shadow there. Purity will reign and spread its ecstasies of joy everywhere.

WHAT THE BIBLE SAYS ABOUT HOW GOD JUDGES AND REWARDS OUR WORK

Rev. 22:12

Though we consider the apostle Paul the greatest missionary in history, he received more lashes and stones than honorary banquets, and spent more time in jail than in mansions. How did he continue under such duress? He looked ahead to God's reward: "Finally, there is laid up for me the crown of righteousness, which the Lord, the righteous Judge, will give to me on that Day" (2 Tim. 4:8).

Why would Moses leave the luxury of Pharaoh's palace for the harshness of the desert? Because he considered the "reproach of Christ greater riches than the treasures in Egypt; for he looked to the reward" (Heb. 11:26). Serving God yielded Moses a vast storehouse of heavenly reward, though it meant a lifetime of struggle.

Every act, word, and thought will be credited by Christ: "Each one will receive his own reward according to his own labor" (1 Cor. 3:8). If we seek to glorify God with a diligent and humble spirit, our laurels will multiply. If we seek merely to please others and reap their praise, then our rewards will shrink.

Rewards are not limited to the hereafter. Whenever we follow the principles of Scripture, we enjoy the blessings of obedience: "He who fears the commandment will be rewarded" (Prov. 13:13).

When Peter reminded Jesus that he had left everything behind to follow the Messiah, Christ responded, "There is no one who has left house or parents or brothers or wife or children, for the sake of the kingdom of God, who shall not receive many times more in this present time, and in the age to come eternal life" (Luke 18:29, 30).

When one knows and serves God, every product of his or her life will be rewarded, either in this life or in heaven. God watches over all our ways, and He has promised to perfectly reward us. All those who "serve the Lord Christ" (Col. 3:24) will be rewarded, either positively or negatively, on the day of judgment of believers. The Christian who seeks to please God lays up treasures that can never be devalued or depleted.

God watches over all our ways.

See the Life Principles Index for further study:
21. Obedience always brings blessing.
6. You reap what you sow, more than you sow, and later than you sow.

➢ 3 And there shall be no more curse, but the
throne of God and of the Lamb shall be in it,
and His servants shall serve Him.
4 They shall see His face, and His name *shall*
be on their foreheads.
5 There shall be no night there: They need
no lamp nor light of the sun, for the Lord God
gives them light. And they shall reign forever
and ever.

The Time Is Near

6 Then he said to me, "These words *are*
faithful and true." And the Lord God of the
holy[a] prophets sent His angel to show His
servants the things which must shortly take
place.
➢ 7 "Behold, I am coming quickly! Blessed *is*
he who keeps the words of the prophecy of
this book."
8 Now I, John, saw and heard[a] these things.
And when I heard and saw, I fell down to
worship before the feet of the angel who
showed me these things.
9 Then he said to me, "See *that you do* not
do that. For[a] I am your fellow servant, and of
your brethren the prophets, and of those who
keep the words of this book. Worship God."
10 And he said to me, "Do not seal the words
of the prophecy of this book, for the time is at
hand.
11 "He who is unjust, let him be unjust still;
he who is filthy, let him be filthy still; he who
is righteous, let him be righteous[a] still; he who
is holy, let him be holy still."

Jesus Testifies to the Churches

✳ **12** "And behold, I am coming quickly, and My
reward *is* with Me, to give to every one according to his work.
13 "I am the Alpha and the Omega, *the* Beginning and *the* End, the First and the Last."[a]
➢ 14 Blessed *are* those who do His commandments,[a] that they may have the right to the
tree of life, and may enter through the gates
into the city.
15 But[a] outside *are* dogs and sorcerers and
sexually immoral and murderers and idolaters, and whoever loves and practices a lie.
16 "I, Jesus, have sent My angel to testify to
you these things in the churches. I am the
Root and the Offspring of David, the Bright
and Morning Star."
17 And the Spirit and the bride say, "Come!" ➣
And let him who hears say, "Come!" And let
him who thirsts come. Whoever desires, let
him take the water of life freely.

A Warning

18 For[a] I testify to everyone who hears the
words of the prophecy of this book: If anyone
adds to these things, God will add[b] to him the
plagues that are written in this book;
19 and if anyone takes away from the words
of the book of this prophecy, God shall take
away[a] his part from the Book[b] of Life, from
the holy city, and *from* the things which are
written in this book.

I Am Coming Quickly

20 He who testifies to these things says, ➣
"Surely I am coming quickly." Amen. Even so,
come, Lord Jesus!
21 The grace of our Lord Jesus Christ *be* with
you all.[a] Amen.

22:6 [a]NU-Text and M-Text read *spirits of the prophets.*
22:8 [a]NU-Text and M-Text read *am the one who heard and saw.*
22:9 [a]NU-Text and M-Text omit *For.* **22:11** [a]NU-Text and M-Text read *do right.* **22:13** [a]NU-Text and M-Text read *the First and the Last, the Beginning and the End.* **22:14** [a]NU-Text reads *wash their robes.* **22:15** [a]NU-Text and M-Text omit *But.*
22:18 [a]NU-Text and M-Text omit *For.* [b]M-Text reads *may God add.* **22:19** [a]M-Text reads *may God take away.* [b]NU-Text and M-Text read *tree of life.* **22:21** [a]NU-Text reads *with all;* M-Text reads *with all the saints.*

LIFE LESSONS

➢ ***22:3 — And there shall be no more curse . . . .***

We can hardly imagine life without the curse. No more pain or broken relationships. No more frustration or regret or exhaustion. And most of all, no death. "The last enemy that will be destroyed is death" (1 Cor. 15:26).

➢ ***22:7 — "Behold, I am coming quickly! Blessed is he who keeps the words of the prophecy of this book."***

Revelation concludes with a reminder that Jesus may return at any moment, and repeats a blessing on those who not only hear its words, but who commit themselves to Spirit-empowered, godly obedience (see Rev. 1:3).

➢ ***22:14 — Blessed are those who do His commandments, that they may have the right to the tree of life, and may enter through the gates into the city.***

All the way through the Bible, from Genesis to Revelation, God insists that obedience to His commands brings astonishing blessing. Obedient Christians delight in God, and God delights in obedient Christians.

➢ ***22:17 — And the Spirit and the bride say, "Come!" And let him who hears say, "Come!" And let him who thirsts come.***

God is always inviting people to come to Him. He is not trying to keep men and women out of heaven, but is doing everything He can to bring as many as possible into His dearly loved family.

➢ ***22:20 — "Surely I am coming quickly." Amen. Even so, come, Lord Jesus!***

When will Jesus return? No one can say. Maybe today. Maybe tonight. Maybe tomorrow. Maybe next century. No one knows the hour he will descend from the clouds in great glory. But make no mistake: He *is* coming!

LIFE PRINCIPLE 30

AN EAGER ANTICIPATION OF THE LORD'S RETURN KEEPS US LIVING PRODUCTIVELY.

REV. 22:12

Throughout Scripture we find three admonitions given to us about the Lord's return:

1. Watch faithfully.
2. Work diligently.
3. Wait peacefully.

1. We are to watch. The Lord said repeatedly that we are to watch for His coming because we do not know the day or hour of His return (Matt. 24:42; 25:13). In Luke 21:36 Jesus gave this specific instruction: "Watch, therefore, and pray always that you may be counted worthy to escape all these things that will come to pass, and to stand before the Son of Man."

We are to do more than pray as we watch. We are to stand fast in the faith, with courage and strength (see 1 Cor. 16:13). We are to watch soberly, arming ourselves with faith and love and salvation (see 1 Thess. 5:8). As we watch, we are to remain especially aware of false prophets; we are to discern the spirits and to reject soundly all who do not confess that Jesus Christ is God in the flesh (see 1 John 4:1–2; 2 Peter 2:1).

Jesus spoke to John in a vision and gave this great promise to those who remain watchful: "Behold, I am coming as a thief. Blessed is he who watches . . ." (Rev. 16:15).

2. We are to work. Why does Jesus leave us here on earth after He saves us? Why aren't we born again, and then immediately taken into the Lord's presence? Because we still have work to do!

First, God calls us to win souls. We are to be the Lord's witnesses—telling of the love of God and the atoning death of Jesus Christ for sin. We are to testify about what He has done in our own lives, both with our words and by our example. So long as there remains a soul on earth who hasn't heard the gospel of our Lord Jesus Christ, we have work to do!

Second, we are to grow spiritually, developing an ever-increasing intimacy with the Lord. None of us fully lives up to our spiritual potential. We *all* have room to grow. In those areas where we discover we are unlike Christ, we must work with the Spirit to become conformed to His likeness. Our minds must be renewed (see Rom. 12:1). Our inner hurts and emotions must be healed. We must grow in spiritual discernment and in the wisdom of God. Our faith must be

We do not know the day or hour of His return.

strengthened and used so that our prayers and our actions more effectively build up the Lord's kingdom.

3. We are to wait. Waiting isn't easy. Impatience often leads to frustration. Waiting can also cause a buildup of fear; the longer something anticipated doesn't happen, the greater our concern with what will happen, which can degenerate into worry over what might happen—and fear is only a step away.

The angels spoke peace to the earth at Jesus' first coming (see Luke 2:14). More than four hundred times in the Scriptures, the Lord says that we are not to fear, but to enjoy peace. The prophet Isaiah referred to Jesus as the Prince of Peace (Is. 9:6). Throughout His ministry, the Lord Jesus spoke peace: to the woman with an issue of blood He said, "Go in peace"; to a stormy sea He said, "Peace be still"; and to His disciples He said, "My peace I give you." The Lord calls us to peace as we await His return.

When the Lord comes, will He find you eager to see Him?

Apart from Jesus, there is no peace—not within a human heart, and not among human beings or nations. With Jesus, we can experience peace that passes our rational minds and settles deep within (Phil. 4:7). We are to seek and find this peace as we await the Lord's return.

When the Lord comes, will He find you among those who love Him and call Him Savior and Lord?

When the Lord comes, will He find you doing what He has command you to do?

When the Lord comes, will He find you eager to see Him?

When the Lord comes, will He find you ready for His appearing?

When the Lord calls with a shout from heaven, will you instantly rise to be with Him?

When the Lord appears in the clouds, will your heart rejoice with exceedingly great joy?

You have it within your grasp to positively answer these questions. How will you choose to respond to the Lord's challenges upon your life?

The fact is: He is coming again!

See the Life Principles Index for further study.

CONCORDANCE

This Concordance is designed to help you locate important occurrences of significant words, phrases, and proper names found in the Bible. Words and phrases are referenced with Scripture quotations, in which the first letter of the word or phrase, italicized, stands for the entire word or phrase. Phrases are cross-referenced under every major word of the phrase except the first. When looking up a word, be sure to check for related forms of the word and for phrases beginning with that word.

Proper names are defined by descriptive phrases and Scripture references. If a name applies to more than one person, place, or group (see ABIJAH, below), the different identities are distinguished by the dash ("———").

Rebuked by David, 2 Sam 16:9–12; 19:21–23
His exploits, 2 Sam 21:16, 17; 23:18; 1 Chr 18:12, 13

ABLE
you are *a* to number .... Gen 15:5
the LORD was not *a* .... Num 14:16
shall give as he is *a* .... Deut 16:17
For who is *a* to judge .... 1 Kin 3:9
should be *a* to offer ...... 1 Chr 29:14
who is *a* to build Him ...... 2 Chr 2:6
"The LORD is *a*. .... 2 Chr 25:9
Who then is *a* to stand ..... Job 41:10
gold will not be *a* to .... Ezek 7:19
God whom we serve is *a* .... Dan 3:17
in pride He is *a* to abase .... Dan 4:37
God is *a* to raise up .... Matt 3:9
believe that I am *a* .... Matt 9:28
fear Him who is *a* .... Matt 10:28
Are you *a* to drink the .... Matt 20:22
enter and will not be *a* ... Luke 13:24
was not *a* to finish .... Luke 14:30
be *a* to contradict or ...... Luke 21:15
shall be *a* to separate ...... Rom 8:39
God is *a* to make him ...... Rom 14:4
Now to Him who is *a* ..... Rom 16:25
beyond what you are *a* ... 1 Cor 10:13
And God is *a* to make ...... 2 Cor 9:8
may be *a* to comprehend .... Eph 3:18
that you may be *a* to .... Eph 6:13
hospitable, *a* to teach ...... 1 Tim 3:2
persuaded that He is *a* .... 2 Tim 1:12
learning and never *a* .... 2 Tim 3:7
being tempted, He is *a* ...... Heb 2:18
Therefore He is also *a* to .... Heb 7:25
that God was *a* to .... Heb 11:19
a also to bridle the .... James 3:2
to Him who is *a* .... Jude 24
was *a* to open the scroll, ... Rev 5:3
has come, and who is *a* ..... Rev 6:17

ABNER
Saul's cousin; commander of his army, 1 Sam 14:50, 51
Rebuked by David, 1 Sam 26:5, 14–16
Supports Ishbosheth; defeated by David's men; kills Asahel, 2 Sam 2:8–32
Makes covenant with David, 2 Sam 3:6–21
Killed by Joab; mourned by David, 2 Sam 3:22–39

ABODE
but left their own *a* .... Jude 6

ABOLISHED
your works may be *a* .... Ezek 6:6
having *a* in His flesh .... Eph 2:15
Christ, who has *a* .... 2 Tim 1:10

ABOMINABLE
not make yourselves *a* ..... Lev 11:43
They have done *a* .... Ps 14:1
your grave like an *a* .... Is 14:19
Oh, do not do this *a* .... Jer 44:4
they deny Him, being *a* ... Titus 1:16
and *a* idolatries .... 1 Pet 4:3
unbelieving, *a*, murderers ... Rev 21:8

ABOMINATION
every shepherd is an *a* .... Gen 46:34
If we sacrifice the *a* .... Ex 8:26
You have made me an *a* ...... Ps 88:8
yes, seven are an *a* .... Prov 6:16
wickedness is an *a* .... Prov 8:7
Dishonest scales are an *a* .. Prov 11:1
the scoffer is an *a* .... Prov 24:9
even his prayer is an *a* ..... Prov 28:9
An unjust man is an *a* .... Prov 29:27
incense is an *a* to Me .... Is 1:13
and place there the *a* ...... Dan 11:31
the *a* of desolation .... Dan 12:11
the '*a* of desolation,' ...... Matt 24:15
among men is an *a* .... Luke 16:15

ABOMINATIONS
to follow the *a* .... Deut 18:9
delights in their *a* .... Is 66:3
will put away your *a* .... Jer 4:1
your harlotry, your *a* .... Jer 13:27
will see greater *a* .... Ezek 8:6
a which they commit ...... Ezek 8:17
you, throw away the *a* .... Ezek 20:7
show her all her *a* .... Ezek 22:2
a golden cup full of *a* .... Rev 17:4
of the *a* of the earth .... Rev 17:5

ABOUND
lawlessness will *a* .... Matt 24:12
the offense might *a* .... Rom 5:20
sin that grace may *a* .... Rom 6:1
thanksgiving to *a* .... 2 Cor 4:15
to make all grace *a* .... 2 Cor 9:8
and I know how to *a* .... Phil 4:12
that you should *a* .... 1 Thess 4:1
things are yours and *a* ...... 2 Pet 1:8

ABOUNDED
But where sin *a* .... Rom 5:20

ABOUNDING
and *a* in goodness and .... Ex 34:6
and *a* in mercy .... Ps 103:8
immovable, always *a* ..... 1 Cor 15:58
a in it with thanksgiving ...... Col 2:7

ABOVE
that is in heaven *a* .... Ex 20:4
"He sent from *a* .... 2 Sam 22:17
A it stood seraphim .... Is 6:2
nor a servant *a* his .... Matt 10:24
He who comes from *a* ..... John 3:31
beneath; I am from *a* ...... John 8:23
been given you from *a* .... John 19:11
of all, who is *a* all .... Eph 4:6
the name which is *a* .... Phil 2:9
things which are *a* .... Col 3:1
perfect gift is from *a* ...... James 1:17

ABRAHAM
Ancestry and family, Gen 11:26–31
Receives God's call; enters Canaan, Gen 12:1–6
Promised Canaan by God; pitches tent near Bethel, Gen 12:7, 8
Deceives Egyptians concerning Sarai, Gen 12:11–20
Separates from Lot; inherits Canaan, Gen 13
Rescues Lot from captivity, Gen 14:11–16
Gives a tithe to Melchizedek; refuses spoil, Gen 14:18–24
Covenant renewed; promised a son, Gen 15
Takes Hagar as concubine; Ishmael born, Gen 16
Name changed from Abram; circumcision commanded, Gen 17
Entertains Lord and angels, Gen 18:1–15
Intercedes for Sodom, Gen 18:16–33
Deceives Abimelech concerning Sarah, Gen 20
Birth of Isaac, Gen 21:1–7
Sends Hagar and Ishmael away, Gen 21:9–14
Offers Isaac in obedience to God, Gen 22:1–19
Finds wife for Isaac, Gen 24
Marries Keturah; fathers other children; dies, Gen 25:1–10
Friend of God, 2 Chr 20:7
Justified by faith, Rom 4:1–12
Father of true believers, Rom 4:11–25
In the line of faith, Heb 11:8–10
Eternal home of, in heaven, Luke 16:19–25
A was circumcised .... Gen 17:26
bore *A* a son in his .... Gen 21:2
A circumcised his son ...... Gen 21:4
A was one hundred .... Gen 21:5
God tested *A*, and .... Gen 22:1
A said, "My son, God .... Gen 22:8
A begot Isaac .... Gen 25:19
His covenant with *A* .... Ex 2:24
I swore to give to *A* .... Ex 6:8
which I swore to *A* .... Num 32:11
which He made with *A* .. 1 Chr 16:16
O seed of *A* His servant ..... Ps 105:6
LORD, who redeemed *A* ..... Is 29:22
descendants of *A* My .... Is 41:8
David, the Son of *A* .... Matt 1:1
to you, before *A* was .... John 8:58
For if *A* was justified .... Rom 4:2
A believed God, and .... Rom 4:3
are of the faith of *A* .... Rom 4:16
of *A* might come upon .... Gal 3:14
Now to *A* and his Seed ...... Gal 3:16
that *A* had two sons .... Gal 4:22
also *A* gave a tenth .... Heb 7:2
By faith *A* obeyed when ... Heb 11:8
By faith *A*, when he .... Heb 11:17
A believed God, and ...... James 2:23
as Sarah obeyed *A*, ... 1 Pet 3:6

ABRAM
See ABRAHAM

ABRONAH
Israelite encampment, Num 33:34

ABSALOM
Son of David, 2 Sam 3:3
Kills Amnon for raping Tamar; flees from David, 2 Sam 13:20–39
Returns through Joab's intrigue; reconciled to David, 2 Sam 14
Attempts to usurp throne, 2 Sam 15:1—18:8
Caught and killed by Joab, 2 Sam 18:9–18
Mourned by David, 2 Sam 18:19—19:8

ABSENT
For I indeed, as *a* .... 1 Cor 5:3
in the body we are *a* ...... 2 Cor 5:6

ABSTAIN
we write to them to *a* ..... Acts 15:20
A from every form ..... 1 Thess 5:22
and commanding to *a* ...... 1 Tim 4:3
a from fleshly lusts .... 1 Pet 2:11

ABUNDANCE
is the sound of *a* .... 1 Kin 18:41
workmen with you in *a* .. 1 Chr 22:15
flourish, and *a* of peace ...... Ps 72:7
eyes bulge with *a* .... Ps 73:7
nor he who loves *a* .... Eccl 5:10
delight itself in *a* .... Is 55:2
out of the *a* of the heart ... Matt 12:34
put in out of their *a* ...... Mark 12:44
not consist in the *a* .... Luke 12:15
of affliction the *a* .... 2 Cor 8:2
above measure by the *a* ... 2 Cor 12:7
rich through the *a* .... Rev 18:3

ABUNDANT
in judgment and *a* .... Job 37:23
a in mercy to all those .... Ps 86:5
Longsuffering and *a* .... Ps 86:15
Him is *a* redemption .... Ps 130:7
placed it by *a* waters .... Ezek 17:5
lovely and its fruit *a* .... Dan 4:21
slow to anger and *a* .... Jon 4:2
in labors more *a* .... 2 Cor 11:23
may be more *a* in Jesus ...... Phil 1:26
Lord was exceedingly *a* ... 1 Tim 1:14
a mercy has begotten .... 1 Pet 1:3

ABUNDANTLY
a satisfied with the .... Ps 36:8
may have it more *a* .... John 10:10
to do exceedingly *a* .... Eph 3:20
to show more *a* to the ...... Heb 6:17

ACACIA
make an ark of *a* wood . . . . . Ex 25:10
make a table of *a* wood . . . . . Ex 25:23

ACACIA GROVE
Spies sent from, Josh 2:1
Israel's last camp before crossing the Jordan, Josh 3:1

ACCEPT
For I will *a* him . . . . Job 42:8
a your burnt sacrifice . . . . Ps 20:3
offering, I will not *a* . . . . Jer 14:12
Should I *a* this from . . . . Mal 1:13

ACCEPTABLE
sought to find *a* . . . . Eccl 12:10
a time I have heard . . . . Is 49:8
proclaim the *a* year . . . . Is 61:2
proclaim the *a* year . . . . Luke 4:19
is that good and *a* . . . . Rom 12:2
finding out what is *a* . . . . Eph 5:10
For this is good and *a* . . . . . . 1 Tim 2:3
spiritual sacrifices *a* . . . . 1 Pet 2:5

ACCEPTABLY
we may serve God *a* . . . . Heb 12:28

ACCEPTED
Behold, now is the *a* . . . . 2 Cor 6:2
by which He made us *a* . . . . . . Eph 1:6

ACCESS
we have *a* by faith . . . . Rom 5:2
we have boldness and *a* . . . . Eph 3:12

ACCOMPLISHED
today the LORD has *a* . . . . 1 Sam 11:13
A desire *a* is sweet to . . . . . Prov 13:19
must still be *a* in Me . . . . . Luke 22:37
all things were now *a* . . . . . John 19:28

ACCORD
See WITH ONE ACCORD
and Israel with one *a* . . . . Josh 9:2
serve Him with one *a* . . . . Zeph 3:9
continued with one *a* . . . . Acts 1:14
daily with one *a* . . . . Acts 2:46
what *a* has Christ with . . . . 2 Cor 6:15
love, being of one *a* . . . . Phil 2:2

ACCORDING TO THE FLESH
You judge *a*; I judge . . . . John 8:15
of the seed of David *a* . . . . Rom 1:3
who do not walk *a* . . . . Rom 8:1
not many wise *a* . . . . 1 Cor 1:26
do I plan *a*, that with . . . . . . 2 Cor 1:17
we regard no one *a* . . . . 2 Cor 5:16
we do not war *a* . . . . 2 Cor 10:3
that many boast *a* . . . . 2 Cor 11:18
as he who was born *a* . . . . Gal 4:29
those who walk *a* . . . . 2 Pet 2:10

ACCORDING TO THE LAW
a of his separation . . . . Num 6:21
let it be done *a* . . . . Ezra 10:3
a of the Medes . . . . Dan 6:8
of her purification *a* . . . . Luke 2:22
performed all things *a* . . . . . Luke 2:39
Ananias, a devout man *a* . . Acts 22:12
you sit to judge me *a* . . . . Acts 23:3
who has come, not *a* . . . . Heb 7:16
a almost all things are . . . . . . Heb 9:22
(which are offered *a* . . . . Heb 10:8

ACCORDING TO THE WORD OF THE LORD
Moses numbered them *a* . . . Num 3:16
in the land of Moab, *a* . . . . . Deut 34:5
booty for themselves, *a* . . . . Josh 8:27
they had obtained *a* . . . . Josh 22:9
him and killed him, *a* . . . . . 1 Kin 13:26
he had destroyed him, *a* . . 1 Kin 15:29
he set up its gates, *a* . . . . . 1 Kin 16:34
jar of oil run dry, *a* . . . . . . 1 Kin 17:16
a which he had spoken . . . 1 Kin 22:38
barley for a shekel, *a* . . . . . 2 Kin 7:16
David king over Israel, *a* . . 1 Chr 11:3
So I got a sash *a* . . . . Jer 13:2

arose and went to Nineveh, *a* . Jon 3:3

ACCOUNT
they will give *a* of it . . . . . . Matt 12:36
The former *a* I made . . . . Acts 1:1
each of us shall give *a* . . . . Rom 14:12
put that on my *a* . . . . Philem 18
those who must give *a* . . . . . Heb 13:17

ACCOUNTED
and He *a* it to him . . . . Gen 15:6
And that was *a* to him . . . . . Ps 106:31
his faith is *a* for . . . . Rom 4:5
a as sheep for the . . . . Rom 8:36
and it was *a* to him . . . . Gal 3:6
and it was *a* to him . . . . James 2:23

ACCURSED
he who is hanged is *a* . . . . . Deut 21:23
regarding the *a* things . . . . Josh 7:1
years old shall be *a* . . . . Is 65:20
not know the law is *a* . . . . John 7:49
that I myself were *a* . . . . Rom 9:3
calls Jesus *a*, and no . . . . . . 1 Cor 12:3
let him be *a* . . . . Gal 1:8

ACCUSATION
they wrote an *a* against . . . . . Ezra 4:6
over His head the *a* . . . . Matt 27:37
they might find an *a* . . . . Luke 6:7
Do not receive an *a* . . . . 1 Tim 5:19
not bring a reviling *a* . . . . . . 2 Pet 2:11

ACCUSE
anyone or *a* falsely . . . . Luke 3:14
they began to *a* Him . . . . Luke 23:2
think that I shall *a* . . . . John 5:45

ACCUSED
forward and *a* the Jews . . . . . . Dan 3:8
while He was being *a* . . . . . Matt 27:12

ACCUSER
a of our brethren . . . . Rev 12:10

ACCUSERS
Let my *a* be clothed . . . . Ps 109:29
meets the *a* face to . . . . Acts 25:16

ACCUSING
their thoughts *a* or else . . . . Rom 2:15

ACHAIA
Visited by Paul, Acts 18:1, 12
Apollos preaches in, Acts 18:24–28
Gospel proclaimed throughout, 1 Thess 1:7, 8

ACHAN (or Achar)
Sin of, caused Israel's defeat, Josh 7:1–15
Stoned to death, Josh 7:16–25
Sin of, recalled, Josh 22:20
Also called Achar, 1 Chr 2:7

ACHISH
A king of Gath, 1 Sam 21:10–15
David seeks refuge with, 1 Sam 27:1–12
Forced by Philistine lords to expel David, 1 Sam 29:1–11
Receives Shimei's servants, 1 Kin 2:39, 40

ACHOR, VALLEY OF
Site of Achan's stoning, Josh 7:24–26
On Judah's boundary, Josh 15:7
Promises concerning, Is 65:10

ACHSAH
A daughter of Caleb, 1 Chr 2:49
Given to Othniel, Josh 15:16–19
Given springs of water, Judg 1:12–15

ACKNOWLEDGE
did he *a* his brothers . . . . Deut 33:9
a my transgressions . . . . Ps 51:3
in all your ways *a* . . . . Prov 3:6
and Israel does not *a* . . . . Is 63:16
Only *a* your iniquity . . . . Jer 3:13
let him *a* that the . . . . 1 Cor 14:37

ACKNOWLEDGED
of Israel, and God *a* them . . . . Ex 2:25
a my sin to You . . . . Ps 32:5

ACKNOWLEDGES
there is no one who *a* . . . . Ps 142:4
he who *a* the Son has . . . . 1 John 2:23

ACQUAINT
a yourself with Him . . . . Job 22:21

ACQUAINTANCES
You have put away my *a* . . . . . Ps 88:8
All my *a* watched for . . . . Jer 20:10
all His *a*, and the women . Luke 23:49

ACQUAINTED
a with all my ways . . . . Ps 139:3
a Man of sorrows and *a* . . . . Is 53:3

ACQUIRE
a possessions for . . . . Gen 34:10

ACQUIRED
he has *a* all this wealth . . . . . Gen 31:1
I have *a* as my wife . . . . Ruth 4:10
I *a* male and female . . . . Eccl 2:7

ACQUIT
at all *a* the wicked . . . . Nah 1:3

ACQUITTED
struck him shall be *a* . . . . Ex 21:19
of the ox shall be *a* . . . . Ex 21:28
that you may be *a* . . . . Is 43:26
whom I had not *a* . . . . Joel 3:21

ACT
a corruptly and make . . . . Deut 4:25
seen every great *a* . . . . Deut 11:7
hear in heaven, and *a* . . . . . 1 Kin 8:32
hear from heaven, and *a* . . 2 Chr 6:23
Thus you shall *a* in . . . . 2 Chr 19:9
is time for You to *a* . . . . Ps 119:126
His *a*, His unusual *a* . . . . Is 28:21
O Lord, listen and *a* . . . . Dan 9:19
adultery, in the very *a* . . . . John 8:4

ACTED
if you have *a* in truth . . . . . . Judg 9:16
But Jehu *a* deceptively, . . 2 Kin 10:19
a more wickedly than . . . . . 2 Kin 21:11

ACTIONS
by Him *a* are weighed . . . . . 1 Sam 2:3

ACTS
LORD, the righteous *a* . . . . . . Judg 5:11
His *a* to the children . . . . Ps 103:7
declare Your mighty *a* . . . . Ps 145:4
of Your awesome *a* . . . . Ps 145:6

ADAM
Creation of, Gen 1:26, 27; 2:7
Given dominion over the earth, Gen 1:28–30
Given a wife, Gen 2:18–25
Temptation, fall, and exile from Eden, Gen 3
Children of, Gen 4:1, 2; 5:3, 4
Transgression results in sin and death, Rom 5:12–14
——— Last or second Adam, an appellation of Christ, Rom 5:14, 15; 1 Cor 15:20–24, 45–48

ADD
The LORD shall *a* to me . . . . Gen 30:24
You shall not *a* . . . . Deut 4:2
you shall not *a* to it . . . . Deut 12:32
A iniquity to their . . . . Ps 69:27
Do not *a* to His words . . . . . . Prov 30:6
by worrying can *a* one . . . . . . Matt 6:27
by worrying can *a* one . . . . Luke 12:25
a to your faith virtue, to . . . . 2 Pet 1:5
Gold will *a* to him the . . . . . Rev 22:18

ADDED
things shall be *a* . . . . Matt 6:33
And the Lord *a* to the . . . . Acts 2:47
many people were *a* . . . . . . Acts 11:24

It was *a* because of .... Gal 3:19

ADDS
and He *a* no sorrow ...... Prov 10:22
no one annuls or *a* to it ...... Gal 3:15
If anyone *a* to these .... Rev 22:18

ADMINISTERS
a justice for the .... Deut 10:18

ADMONISH
also to *a* one another ..... Rom 15:14
a him as a brother .... 2 Thess 3:15

ADMONISHED
further, my son, be *a* ...... Eccl 12:12
Angel of the LORD *a* .... Zech 3:6

ADMONISHING
a one another in .... Col 3:16

ADMONITION
were written for our *a* ... 1 Cor 10:11
in the training and *a* .... Eph 6:4

ADONI-ZEDEK
An Amorite king of Jerusalem, Josh 10:1–5
Defeated and slain by Joshua, Josh 10:6–27

ADONIJAH
David's fourth son, 2 Sam 3:2, 4
Attempts to usurp throne, 1 Kin 1:5–53
Desires Abishag as wife, 1 Kin 2:13–18
Executed by Solomon, 1 Kin 2:19–25

ADONIRAM (or Adoram)
Official under David, Solomon, and Rehoboam, 2 Sam 20:24; 1 Kin 5:14; 12:18
Stoned by angry Israelites, 1 Kin 12:18
Called Hadoram, 2 Chr 10:18

ADOPTION
received the Spirit of *a* ..... Rom 8:15
waiting for the *a* .... Rom 8:23
to whom pertain the *a* ...... Rom 9:4
we might receive the *a* .... Gal 4:5
a as sons by Jesus .... Eph 1:5

ADORN
a the monuments .... Matt 23:29
also, that the women *a* ..... 1 Tim 2:9

ADORNED
By His Spirit He *a* .... Job 26:13
You shall again be *a* .... Jer 31:4
temple, how it was *a* ...... Luke 21:5
also *a* themselves .... 1 Pet 3:5
prepared as a bride *a* .... Rev 21:2

ADRIFT
A among the dead .... Ps 88:5

ADULLAM
A town of Canaan, Gen 38:1, 12, 20; Josh 12:7, 15; 15:20, 35
David seeks refuge in caves of, 1 Sam 23:13–17

ADULTERER
the *a* and the adulteress .... Lev 20:10
The eye of the *a* .... Job 24:15

ADULTERERS
the land is full of *a* .... Jer 23:10
nor idolaters, nor *a* .... 1 Cor 6:9
a God will judge .... Heb 13:4
A and adulteresses .... James 4:4

ADULTERIES
I have seen your *a* .... Jer 13:27
her sight, and her *a* .... Hos 2:2
evil thoughts, *a* .... Mark 7:21

ADULTEROUS
evil and *a* generation ..... Matt 12:39

ADULTERY
You shall not commit *a* .... Ex 20:14
You shall not commit *a* .... Deut 5:18
Whoever commits *a* ...... Prov 6:32
Israel had committed *a* .... Jer 3:8
have committed *a* with ...... Jer 29:23
a with their idols .... Ezek 23:37
and is committing *a* .... Hos 3:1
already committed *a* .... Matt 5:28
is divorced commits *a* ...... Matt 5:32
You shall not commit *a* ... Matt 19:18
another commits *a* .... Mark 10:11
husband commits *a* .... Luke 16:18
a woman caught in *a* .... John 8:3
which are: *a*, fornication, ... Gal 5:19
having eyes full of *a* .... 2 Pet 2:14
those who commit *a* .... Rev 2:22

ADVANCED
Joshua was old, *a* in .... Josh 13:1
I am old, *a* in age .... Josh 23:2
David was old, *a* in years ... 1 Kin 1:1
were both well *a* in years ... Luke 1:7
wife is well *a* in years ..... Luke 1:18
I *a* in Judaism beyond .... Gal 1:14

ADVANTAGE
a will it be to You .... Job 35:3
man has no *a* over .... Eccl 3:19
a that I go away .... John 16:7
What *a* then has the .... Rom 3:1
Satan should take *a* .... 2 Cor 2:11
no one should take *a* ..... 1 Thess 4:6
people to gain *a* .... Jude 16

ADVERSARIES
The *a* of the LORD .... 1 Sam 2:10
rid Myself of My *a* .... Is 1:24
a will not be able .... Luke 21:15
and there are many *a* ..... 1 Cor 16:9
terrified by your *a* .... Phil 1:28
will devour the *a* .... Heb 10:27

ADVERSARY
in the way as an *a* .... Num 22:22
battle he become our *a* ... 1 Sam 29:4
how long will the *a* .... Ps 74:10
a has spread his hand .... Lam 1:10
Agree with your *a* .... Matt 5:25
for me from my *a* .... Luke 18:3
opportunity to the *a* .... 1 Tim 5:14
your *a* the devil walks .... 1 Pet 5:8

ADVERSITIES
you from all your *a* ...... 1 Sam 10:19
known my soul in *a* .... Ps 31:7

ADVERSITY
them with every *a* .... 2 Chr 15:6
I shall never be in *a* .... Ps 10:6
from the days of *a* .... Ps 94:13
brother is born for *a* ..... Prov 17:17
faint in the day of *a* .... Prov 24:10
the day of *a* consider .... Eccl 7:14
you the bread of *a* .... Is 30:20

ADVICE
And blessed is your *a* .... 1 Sam 25:33
in this I give my *a* .... 2 Cor 8:10

ADVOCATE
we have an *A* with the ..... 1 John 2:1

AENON
A place near Salim where John the Baptist baptized, John 3:22, 23

AFAR
and worship from *a* .... Ex 24:1
sons shall come from *a* .... Is 60:4
and not a God *a* .... Jer 23:23
and saw Abraham *a* ...... Luke 16:23
to all who are *a* .... Acts 2:39
to you who were *a* .... Eph 2:17
but having seen them *a* .... Heb 11:13

AFFAIRS
he will guide his *a* .... Ps 112:5
I may hear of your *a* .... Phil 1:27
himself with the *a* .... 2 Tim 2:4

AFFECTION
to his wife the *a* .... 1 Cor 7:3
for you all with the *a* .... Phil 1:8
if any *a* and mercy .... Phil 2:1

AFFECTIONATE
Be kindly *a* to one .... Rom 12:10

AFFIRM
you to *a* constantly .... Titus 3:8

AFFLICT
a them with their .... Ex 1:11
oath to *a* her soul .... Num 30:13
may be bound to *a* you .... Judg 16:6
a the descendants .... 1 Kin 11:39
will hear, and *a* them .... Ps 55:19
a Your heritage .... Ps 94:5
a man to *a* his soul .... Is 58:5
to destroy, and to *a* .... Jer 31:28
For He does not *a* .... Lam 3:33
deal with all who *a* .... Zeph 3:19

AFFLICT YOUR SOULS
shall *a*, and do no work .... Lev 16:29
you shall *a*, and offer ...... Lev 23:27
You shall *a*; you shall not .. Num 29:7

AFFLICTED
"Why have You *a* .... Num 11:11
and the Almighty has *a* .... Ruth 1:21
To him who is *a* .... Job 6:14
hears the cry of the *a* ...... Job 34:28
You *a* the peoples .... Ps 44:2
Before I was *a* .... Ps 119:67
I am *a* very much .... Ps 119:107
Many a time they have *a* .... Ps 129:1
the cause of the *a* .... Ps 140:12
days of the *a* are evil ..... Prov 15:15
Smitten by God, and *a* .... Is 53:4
oppressed and He was *a* ...... Is 53:7
"O you *a* one, tossed .... Is 54:11
Why have we *a* our .... Is 58:3
and satisfy the *a* .... Is 58:10
her virgins are *a* .... Lam 1:4
she has relieved the *a* ...... 1 Tim 5:10
being destitute, *a* .... Heb 11:37

AFFLICTING
A the just and taking ...... Amos 5:12

AFFLICTION
in the land of my *a* .... Gen 41:52
the bread of *a* .... Deut 16:3
indeed look on the *a* ...... 1 Sam 1:11
LORD saw that the *a* ...... 2 Kin 14:26
a take hold of me .... Job 30:16
days of *a* confront me ..... Job 30:27
held in the cords of *a* .... Job 36:8
of death, bound in *a* .... Ps 107:10
is my comfort in my *a* ...... Ps 119:50
and it is an evil *a* .... Eccl 6:2
a He was afflicted .... Is 63:9
refuge in the day of *a* ...... Jer 16:19
"O LORD, behold my *a* .... Lam 1:9
not grieved for the *a* .... Amos 6:6
For our light *a* .... 2 Cor 4:17
supposing to add *a* .... Phil 1:16
the word in much *a* ...... 1 Thess 1:6

AFFLICTIONS
Many are the *a* of the .... Ps 34:19
in the *a* of Christ .... Col 1:24
shaken by these *a* .... 1 Thess 3:3
persecutions, *a*, which .... 2 Tim 3:11
in all things, endure *a*, ... 2 Tim 4:5

AFFORD
poor and cannot *a* it .... Lev 14:21
such as he can *a* .... Lev 14:30

AFRAID
See DO NOT BE AFRAID
garden, and I was *a* .... Gen 3:10
saying, "Do not be *a* .... Gen 15:1
his face, for he was *a* .... Ex 3:6
none will make you *a* .... Lev 26:6
you shall not be *a* in .... Deut 1:17
of whom you are *a* .... Deut 7:19
do not be *a* of them .... Deut 20:1
Do not be *a* of the .... 2 Kin 25:24

David was *a* of God . . . . . . 1 Chr 13:12
I will not be *a* of ten . . . . Ps 3:6
ungodliness made me *a* . . . . . . Ps 18:4
Of whom shall I be *a* . . . . Ps 27:1
Do not be *a* when one . . . . Ps 49:16
Whenever I am *a* . . . . Ps 56:3
farthest parts are *a* . . . . Ps 65:8
you will not be *a* . . . . Prov 3:24
nor be *a* of their threats . . . . Is 8:12
be *a* of the Assyrian . . . . Is 10:24
I will trust and not be *a* . . . . Is 12:2
no one will make them *a* . . . . . . Is 17:2
Do not fear, nor be *a* . . . . Is 44:8
that you should be *a* . . . . Is 51:12
Do not be *a* of their faces, ... Jer 1:8
dream which made me *a* . . . . . Dan 4:5
Then the mariners were *a* . . . . Jon 1:5
It is I; do not be *a* . . . . Matt 14:27
Do not be *a*; only believe . . Mark 5:36
Do not be *a*, Zacharias, ... Luke 1:13
Do not be *a*, Mary, for . . . . . Luke 1:30
not be *a* of those who . . . . . Luke 12:4
neither let it be *a* . . . . John 14:27
"Do not be *a*, Paul . . . . Acts 27:24
if you do evil, be *a* . . . . Rom 13:4
do good and are not *a* . . . . 1 Pet 3:6

AFTERWARD
A he will let you go . . . . Ex 11:1
a we will speak . . . . Job 18:2
a receive me to glory . . . . Ps 73:24
you shall follow Me *a* . . . . . John 13:36
the firstfruits, *a* . . . . 1 Cor 15:23

AGAG
A king of Amalek in Balaam's prophecy, Num 24:7
—— Amalekite king spared by Saul, but slain by Samuel, 1 Sam 15:8, 9, 20–24, 32, 33

AGAIN
See BORN AGAIN
day He will rise *a* . . . . Matt 20:19
'You must be born *a* . . . . John 3:7
to renew them *a* . . . . Heb 6:6
having been born *a* . . . . 1 Pet 1:23

AGAINST
See SINNED AGAINST THE LORD; SINNED AGAINST YOU
his hand shall be *a* . . . . Gen 16:12
I will set My face *a* . . . . Lev 20:3
come to 'set a man *a* . . . . . . Matt 10:35
or house divided *a* . . . . Matt 12:25
not with Me is *a* Me . . . . . . Matt 12:30
blasphemy *a* the Spirit . . . . Matt 12:31
For nation will rise *a* . . . . Matt 24:7
out, as *a* a robber . . . . Matt 26:55
I have sinned *a* . . . . Luke 15:18
lifted up his heel *a* . . . . John 13:18
LORD and *a* His Christ . . . . . . Acts 4:26
to kick *a* the goads . . . . Acts 9:5
all men everywhere *a* . . . . . Acts 21:28
let us not fight *a* . . . . Acts 23:9
a the promises of God . . . . Gal 3:21
we do not wrestle *a* . . . . Eph 6:12
I have a few things *a* . . . . Rev 2:20

AGE
well advanced in *a* . . . . Gen 18:11
Israel were dim with *a* . . . . Gen 48:10
the flower of their *a* . . . . . . 1 Sam 2:33
the grave at a full *a* . . . . Job 5:26
a is as nothing . . . . Ps 39:5
and in the *a* to come . . . . . . Mark 10:30
"The sons of this *a* . . . . Luke 20:34
He is of *a*; ask him . . . . John 9:21
who are of full *a* . . . . Heb 5:14
the powers of the *a* . . . . Heb 6:5

AGE TO COME
in this age or in the *a* . . . . . Matt 12:32
in the *a*, eternal life . . . . . . Mark 10:30
in the *a* eternal life . . . . Luke 18:30
the powers of the *a* . . . . Heb 6:5

AGED
Wisdom is with *a* . . . . Job 12:12
a one as Paul, the *a* . . . . Philem 9

AGES
ordained before the *a* . . . . 1 Cor 2:7
in other *a* was not . . . . Eph 3:5
at the end of the *a* . . . . Heb 9:26

AGONY
And being in *a* . . . . Luke 22:44

AGREE
A with your adversary . . . . . Matt 5:25
that if two of you *a* . . . . Matt 18:19
testimonies did not *a* . . . . . Mark 14:56
and these three *a* . . . . 1 John 5:8

AGREED
unless they are *a* . . . . Amos 3:3
they were glad, and *a* . . . . . Luke 22:5

AGREEMENT
with Sheol we are in *a* . . . . Is 28:15
the North to make an *a* . . . . . . Dan 11:6
what *a* has the temple . . . . . . 2 Cor 6:16

AHAB
A wicked king of Israel, 1 Kin 16:29
Marries Jezebel; promotes Baal worship, 1 Kin 16:31–33; 18:17–46
Denounced by Elijah, 1 Kin 17:1
Wars against Ben-Hadad, 1 Kin 20:1–43
Covets Naboth's vineyard, 1 Kin 21:1–16
Death predicted; repentance delays judgment, 1 Kin 21:17–29
Goes to war in spite of Micaiah's warning; killed in battle, 1 Kin. 22:1–37
Prophecy concerning, fulfilled, 1 Kin 22:38
—— Lying prophet, Jer 29:21–23

AHASUERUS
The father of Darius the Mede, Dan 9:1
—— Persian king, probably Xerxes I, 486–465 B.C., Ezra 4:6; Esth 1:1
Makes Esther queen, Esth 2:16, 17
Orders Jews annihilated, by Haman's advice, Esth 3:8–15
Reverses decree at Esther's request, Esth 7; 8
Exalts Mordecai, Esth 10:1–3

AHAZ
King of Judah; pursues idolatry; submits to Assyrian rule; desecrates the temple, 2 Kin 16
Defeated by Syria and Israel, 2 Chr 28:5–15
Comforted by Isaiah; refuses to ask a sign, Is 7:1–17

AHAZIAH
King of Israel; son of Ahab and Jezebel; worships Baal, 1 Kin 22:51–53
Falls through lattice; calls on Baal-Zebub; dies according to Elijah's word, 2 Kin 1:2–18
—— King of Judah; Ahab's son-in-law; reigns wickedly, 2 Kin 8:25–29; 2 Chr 22:1–6
Killed by Jehu, 2 Kin 9:27–29; 2 Chr 22:7–9

AHIJAH
A prophet of Shiloh who foretells division of Solomon's kingdom, 1 Kin 11:29–39
Foretells elimination of Jeroboam's line, 1 Kin 14:1–18
A writer of prophecy, 2 Chr 9:29

AHIKAM
Sent in Josiah's mission to Huldah, 2 Kin 22:12–14
Protects Jeremiah, Jer 26:24
The father of Gedaliah, governor under Nebuchadnezzar, 2 Kin 25:22; Jer 39:14

AHIMAAZ
A son of Zadok the high priest, 1 Chr 6:8, 9
Warns David of Absalom's plans, 2 Sam 15:27, 36
First to tell David of Absalom's defeat, 2 Sam 18:19–30

AHIMELECH
High priest in Saul's reign; helps David, 1 Sam 21:1–9
Betrayed and killed by Doeg; son Abiathar escapes, 1 Sam 22:9–20
David writes concerning, Ps 52:title

AHINOAM
Wife of David, 1 Sam 25:43; 27:3; 30:5, 18
Mother of Amnon, 2 Sam 3:2

AHITHOPHEL
David's counselor, 2 Sam 15:12
Joins Absalom's insurrection; counsels him, 2 Sam 15:31; 16:20–23
His counsel rejected; commits suicide, 2 Sam 17:1–23

AI
Israel defeated at, Josh 7:2–5
Israel destroys completely, Josh 8:1–28

AIDE
the king's personal *a* . . . . . . Acts 12:20

AIJALON
Amorites not driven from, Judg 1:35
Miracle there, Josh 10:12, 13
City of refuge, 1 Chr 6:66–69
Fortified by Rehoboam, 2 Chr 11:5, 10
Captured by Philistines, 2 Chr 28:18

AIR
the birds of the *a* . . . . Gen 1:26
of the *a* have nests . . . . Luke 9:58
as one who beats the *a* . . . . 1 Cor 9:26
be speaking into the *a* . . . . . . 1 Cor 14:9
of the power of the *a* . . . . Eph 2:2
the Lord in the *a* . . . . 1 Thess 4:17
his bowl into the *a* . . . . Rev 16:17

AKEL DAMA
Field called "Field of Blood," Acts 1:19

AKRABBIM
An "ascent" on the south of the Dead Sea, Num 34:4
One border of Judah, Josh 15:3

ALABASTER
mosaic pavement of *a* . . . . Esth 1:6
an *a* flask of very costly . . . . Matt 26:7
woman came having an *a* . Mark 14:3
brought an *a* flask of . . . . Luke 7:37

ALARM
to sound the *a* against . . . . 2 Chr 13:12
A day of trumpet and *a* . . . . Zeph 1:16

ALEXANDER
A member of the high-priestly family, Acts 4:6
—— A Jew in Ephesus, Acts 19:33, 34
—— An apostate condemned by Paul, 1 Tim 1:19, 20

ALEXANDRIA
Men of, persecute Stephen, Acts 6:9
Paul sails in ship of, Acts 27:6

ALGUM
a logs from Lebanon, ... 2 Chr 2:8
Ophir, brought *a* wood . . . . 2 Chr 9:10
a wood for the house . . . . . 2 Chr 9:11

ALIEN
because you were an *a* . . . . . Deut 23:7
I am an *a* in their . . . . Job 19:15
who turn away an *a* . . . . Mal 3:5

ALIENATED
a herself from them .... Ezek 23:17
darkened, being *a* .... Eph 4:18
you, who once were *a* .... Col 1:21

ALIENS
For we are *a* and .... 1 Chr 29:15
For I have loved *a* .... Jer 2:25
A have devoured his .... Hos 7:9
without Christ, being *a* ..... Eph 2:12
the armies of the *a* .... Heb 11:34

ALIGHTING
dove and *a* upon Him ...... Matt 3:16

ALIKE
All things come *a* .... Eccl 9:2
esteems every day *a* .... Rom 14:5

ALIVE
in the ark remained *a* .... Gen 7:23
with them went down *a* ... Num 16:33
LORD your God are *a* .... Deut 4:4
I kill and I make *a* .... Deut 32:39
Let them go down *a* .... Ps 55:15
he preserves himself *a* .... Ezek 18:27
heard that He was *a* ..... Mark 16:11
son was dead and is *a* .... Luke 15:24
presented Himself *a* .... Acts 1:3
dead indeed to sin, but *a* ... Rom 6:11
I was *a* once without .... Rom 7:9
all shall be made *a* .... 1 Cor 15:22
trespasses, made us *a* .... Eph 2:5
flesh, He has made *a* .... Col 2:13
that we who are *a* .... 1 Thess 4:15
the flesh but made *a* .... 1 Pet 3:18
and behold, I am *a* .... Rev 1:18
a name that you are *a* .... Rev 3:1
These two were cast *a* ...... Rev 19:20

ALL
See WITH ALL YOUR HEART
for this is man's *a* .... Eccl 12:13

ALL THE DAYS OF HIS LIFE
he shall read it *a* .... Deut 17:19
give him to the LORD *a* .... 1 Sam 1:11
I have made him ruler *a* .. 1 Kin 11:34
He commanded him *a* ..... 1 Kin 15:5
toils under the sun *a* .... Eccl 5:18
before the king *a* .... Jer 52:33

ALL THE EARTH
over the cattle, over *a* ...... Gen 1:26
alive on the face of *a* .... Gen 7:3
confused the language of *a* . Gen 11:9
Shall not the Judge of *a* ... Gen 18:25
there is none like Me in *a* .... Ex 9:14
going the way of *a* .... Josh 23:14
I go the way of *a*; .... 1 Kin 2:2
a sought the presence .... 1 Kin 10:24
Sing to the LORD, *a*; .... 1 Chr 16:23
Let *a* fear the LORD; .... Ps 33:8
A shall worship You .... Ps 66:4
I have gathered *a* .... Is 10:14
that made *a* drunk .... Jer 51:7
which shall rule over *a* ..... Dan 2:39
Let *a* keep silence .... Hab 2:20
was darkness over *a* ...... Luke 23:44
sound has gone out to *a* ... Rom 10:18
of God sent out into *a* .... Rev 5:6

ALL THE SAINTS
God will come, and *a* ...... Zech 14:5
your love for *a* .... Eph 1:15
less than the least of *a* ...... Eph 3:8
able to comprehend with *a* .. Eph 3:18
and supplication for *a* ...... Eph 6:18
your love for *a* .... Col 1:4
with the prayers of *a* .... Rev 8:3

ALLELUIA
Again they said, "*A* .... Rev 19:3

ALLOW
a Your Holy One .... Ps 16:10
a My faithfulness .... Ps 89:33
nor do you *a* those .... Matt 23:13
a Your Holy One .... Acts 2:27
who will not *a* you to be .. 1 Cor 10:13

ALLOWED
bygone generations *a* ..... Acts 14:16

ALLURE
behold, I will *a* .... Hos 2:14
they *a* through the lusts .... 2 Pet 2:18

ALMIGHTY
I am *A* God; walk before .... Gen 17:1
May God *A* bless you, and .. Gen 28:3
and to Jacob, as God *A* .... Ex 6:3
for the *A* has dealt very .... Ruth 1:20
does the *A* pervert justice .... Job 8:3
find out the limits of the *A* .. Job 11:7
of the wrath of the *A* ...... Job 21:20
your delight in the *A* .... Job 22:26
breath of the *A* gives me ..... Job 33:4
under the shadow of the *A* ... Ps 91:1
as destruction from the *A* ...... Is 13:6
as destruction from the *A* .... Joel 1:15
and who is to come, the *A* .... Rev 1:8
holy, holy, Lord God *A* ...... Rev 4:8
Even so, Lord God *A* .... Rev 16:7
fierceness and wrath of *A* .. Rev 19:15

ALMOND
a blossoms on one .... Ex 25:33
a tree blossoms .... Eccl 12:5
branch of an *a* tree .... Jer 1:11

ALMOST
for me, my feet had *a* .... Ps 73:2
a persuade me to .... Acts 26:28
a all things are .... Heb 9:22

ALMS
But rather give *a* .... Luke 11:41
you have and give *a* ..... Luke 12:33
I came to bring *a* .... Acts 24:17

ALOES
with myrrh and *a* .... Ps 45:8
my bed with myrrh, *a* ...... Prov 7:17
mixture of myrrh and *a* ... John 19:39

ALOUD
And he wept *a*, and the ..... Gen 45:2
many shouted *a* for joy .... Ezra 3:12
them sing *a* on their beds .... Ps 149:5
Wisdom calls *a* outside .... Prov 1:20
Cry *a* at Beth Aven .... Hos 5:8

ALPHA
I am the *A* and the .... Rev 1:8
I am the *A* and the .... Rev 22:13

ALTAR
Then Noah built an *a* .... Gen 8:20
he built an *a* to the LORD .... Gen 12:7
built an *a* there .... Gen 13:18
Abraham built an *a* .... Gen 22:9
son and laid him on the *a* ... Gen 22:9
So he built an *a* there ..... Gen 26:25
make an *a* there to God ...... Gen 35:1
And Moses built an *a* .... Ex 17:15
An *a* of earth you .... Ex 20:24
two sides of the *a* .... Ex 27:7
incense *a* of acacia wood .... Ex 37:25
a shall be kept .... Lev 6:9
it to you upon the *a* .... Lev 17:11
offering for the *a* .... Num 7:84
a to the LORD your God .... Deut 27:5
Joshua built an *a* .... Josh 8:30
a great, impressive *a* ...... Josh 22:10
called the *a* Witness ...... Josh 22:34
and tear down the *a* .... Judg 6:25
early and built an *a* .... Judg 21:4
built an *a* to the LORD ..... 1 Sam 7:17
Saul built an *a* .... 1 Sam 14:35
"Go up, erect an *a* .... 2 Sam 24:18
built there an *a* .... 2 Sam 24:25
a which he had made .... 1 Kin 12:33
cried out against the *a* .... 1 Kin 13:2
set up an *a* for Baal ...... 1 Kin 16:32
he repaired the *a* .... 1 Kin 18:30
a according to all that .... 2 Kin 16:11
built there an *a* .... 1 Chr 21:26
made a bronze *a* .... 2 Chr 4:1
a of gold and the tables .... 2 Chr 4:19
he restored the *a* .... 2 Chr 15:8
worship before one *a* .... 2 Chr 32:12
repaired the *a* of the ..... 2 Chr 33:16
the *a* of the God of .... Ezra 3:2
I will go to the *a* .... Ps 43:4
tongs from the *a* .... Is 6:6
there will be an *a* .... Is 19:19
Lord has spurned His *a* ..... Lam 2:7
The *a* was in front .... Ezek 40:47
you cover the *a* .... Mal 2:13
your gift to the *a* .... Matt 5:23
swears by the *a* .... Matt 23:18
I even found an *a* .... Acts 17:23
the offerings of the *a* ...... 1 Cor 9:13
partakers of the *a* .... 1 Cor 10:18
We have an *a* from .... Heb 13:10
Isaac his son on the *a* .... James 2:21
under the *a* the souls .... Rev 6:9
and stood at the *a* .... Rev 8:3
horns of the golden *a* .... Rev 9:13
angel came out from the *a* . Rev 14:18

ALTARS
a Hezekiah has taken .... 2 Kin 18:22
Even Your *a*, O LORD .... Ps 84:3
on the horns of your *a* .... Jer 17:1
a shall be broken .... Ezek 6:4
has made many *a* .... Hos 8:11
a shall be heaps .... Hos 12:11
destruction on the *a* .... Amos 3:14
and torn down Your *a* ..... Rom 11:3

ALTER
put their hand to *a* it .... Ezra 6:12
Nor *a* the word .... Ps 89:34
Persians, which does not *a* ... Dan 6:8
Persians, which does not *a* .. Dan 6:12

ALTERED
of His face was *a* .... Luke 9:29

ALWAYS
delight, rejoicing *a* .... Prov 8:30
the poor with you *a* .... Matt 26:11
Me you do not have *a* ..... Matt 26:11
lo, I am with you *a* .... Matt 28:20
'Son, you are *a* .... Luke 15:31
men *a* ought to pray .... Luke 18:1
immovable, *a* abounding . 1 Cor 15:58
Rejoice in the Lord *a* .... Phil 4:4
thus we shall *a* .... 1 Thess 4:17
a be ready to give a .... 1 Pet 3:15

AM
See HERE I AM; I AM WITH YOU
to Moses, "I *A* WHO I *A* ...... Ex 3:14
First and I *a* the Last .... Is 44:6
in My name, I *a* there ..... Matt 18:20
I *a* the bread of life .... John 6:35
I *a* the light of the .... John 8:12
I *a* from above .... John 8:23
Abraham was, I *A* .... John 8:58
I *a* the door .... John 10:9
I *a* the good shepherd .... John 10:11
I *a* the resurrection .... John 11:25
to him, "I *a* the way .... John 14:6
of God I *a* what I *a* .... 1 Cor 15:10

AMALEK
Grandson of Esau, Gen 36:11, 12
A chief of Edom, Gen 36:16
First among nations, Num 24:20

AMALEKITES
Destruction predicted, Ex 17:14; Deut 25:17–19
Defeated by Israel, Ex 17:8–13; Judg 7:12–25; 1 Sam 14:47, 48; 27:8, 9; 1 Chr 4:42, 43
Overcome Israel, Num 14:39–45; Judg 3:13

AMASA
Commands Absalom's rebels, 2 Sam 17:25

Made David's commander, 2 Sam 19:13
Treacherously killed by Joab, 2 Sam 20:9–12
Death avenged, 1 Kin 2:28–34

AMAZED
the multitudes were *a* ..... Matt 12:23
trembled and were *a* ...... Mark 16:8
saw Him, they were *a* ..... Luke 2:48
Then they were all *a* and .... Acts 2:7
with Philip, and was *a* ..... Acts 8:13

AMAZIAH
King of Judah; kills his father's assassinators, 2 Kin 14:1–6; 2 Chr 25:1–4
Hires troops from Israel; is rebuked by a man of God; sends troops home, 2 Chr 25:5–10
Defeats Edomites; worships their gods, 2 Chr 25:11–16
Wars with Israel, 2 Kin 14:8–14; 2 Chr 25:17–24
Killed by conspirators, 2 Chr 25:25–28

AMBASSADOR
but a faithful *a* .... Prov 13:17
for which I am an *a* .... Eph 6:20

AMBASSADORS
which sends *a* by sea .... Is 18:2
cry outside, the *a* .... Is 33:7
we are *a* for Christ .... 2 Cor 5:20

AMBITION
Christ from selfish *a* .... Phil 1:16
through selfish *a* .... Phil 2:3

AMBUSH
Lay an *a* for the city .... Josh 8:2
a all around Gibeah ...... Judg 20:29
son heard of their *a* .... Acts 23:16
they lay in *a* along .... Acts 25:3

AMEN
shall say, "*A*, so be it ...... Num 5:22
answer and say, '*A* .... Deut 27:15
the people said, "*A!*" ..... 1 Chr 16:36
all the people say, "*A!*" .... Ps 106:48
and the glory forever. *A*. ... Matt 6:13
to the end of the age." *A*. . Matt 28:20
accompanying signs. *A*. .. Mark 16:20
and blessing God. *A*. ..... Luke 24:53
that would be written. *A*. . John 21:25
uninformed say "*A* .... 1 Cor 14:16
are Yes, and in Him *A* ..... 2 Cor 1:20
These things says the *A* ..... Rev 3:14
creatures said, "*A* .... Rev 5:14
I am coming quickly." *A*. . Rev 22:20

AMEND
A your ways and your .... Jer 7:3
from his evil way, *a* .... Jer 35:15

AMETHYST
an agate, and an *a* .... Ex 28:19
the twelfth *a* .... Rev 21:20

AMMON
A nation fathered by Lot, Gen 19:36, 38

AMMONITES
Excluded from assembly for hostility to Israel, Deut 23:3–6
Propose cruel treaty; conquered by Saul, 1 Sam 11:1–3, 11
Abuse David's ambassadors; conquered by his army, 2 Sam 10:1–14
Harass postexilic Jews, Neh 4:3, 7, 8
Defeated by Israel and Judah, Judg 11:4–33; 2 Chr 20:1–25; 27:5, 6
Prophecies concerning, Ps 83:1–18; Jer 25:9–21; Ezek 25:1–7; Amos 1:13–15; Zeph 2:9–11

AMNON
A son of David, 2 Sam 3:2
Rapes his half sister, 2 Sam 13:1–18
Killed by Absalom, 2 Sam 13:19–29

AMON
King of Judah, 2 Kin 21:18, 19
Follows evil, 2 Chr 33:22, 23
Killed by conspiracy, 2 Kin 21:23, 24
—— A governor of Samaria, 1 Kin 22:10, 26

AMORITES
Defeated by Joshua, Josh 10:1–43
Not driven out of Canaan, Judg 1:34–36
Put to forced labor under Solomon, 1 Kin 9:20, 21

AMOS
A prophet of Israel, Amos 1:1
Pronounces judgment against nations, Amos 1:1–3, 15
Denounces Israel's sins, Amos 4:1—7:9
Condemns Amaziah, the priest of Bethel, Amos 7:10–17
Predicts Israel's downfall, Amos 9:1–10
Foretells great blessings, Amos 9:11–15

AMPHIPOLIS
A city in Macedonia visited by Paul, Acts 17:1

AMRAM
Son of Kohath, Num 3:17–19
The father of Aaron, Moses and Miriam, Ex 6:18–20; 1 Chr 6:3

ANAKIM
A race of giants; very strong, Num 13:28–33; Deut 2:10, 11, 21
Defeated:
by Joshua, Josh 10:36–39; 11:21
by Caleb, Josh 14:6–15

ANANIAS
Disciple at Jerusalem; slain for lying to God, Acts 5:1–11
—— A Christian disciple at Damascus, Acts 9:10–19; 22:12–16
—— A Jewish high priest, Acts 23:1–5

ANATHOTH
A Levitical city in Benjamin, Josh 21:18
Jeremiah's birthplace; he buys property there, Jer 1:1; 32:6–15
To be invaded by Assyria, Is 10:30

ANCHOR
hope we have as an *a* .... Heb 6:19

ANCIENT
Do not remove the *a* ...... Prov 23:10
a times that I .... Is 37:26
until the *A* of Days .... Dan 7:22

ANDREW
A disciple of John the Baptist, then of Christ, Matt 4:18, 19; John 1:40–42
Enrolled among the Twelve, Matt 10:2
Mentioned, Mark 13:3, 4; John 6:8, 9; 12:20–22; Acts 1:13

ANGEL
Now the *A* of the LORD ..... Gen 16:7
A who has redeemed me .. Gen 48:16
"Behold, I send an *A* .... Ex 23:20
the donkey saw the *A* ..... Num 22:23
For I have seen the *A* ...... Judg 6:22
Manoah said to the *A* ..... Judg 13:17
in my sight as an *a* .... 1 Sam 29:9
a who was destroying .... 2 Sam 24:16
night that the *a* .... 2 Kin 19:35
the *A* of His Presence .... Is 63:9
struggled with the *A* .... Hos 12:4
standing before the *A* ...... Zech 3:3
like God, like the *A* .... Zech 12:8
things, behold, an *a* .... Matt 1:20
for an *a* of the Lord .... Matt 28:2
Then an *a* of the Lord ..... Luke 1:11
And behold, an *a* .... Luke 2:9
a appeared to Him from .. Luke 22:43
For an *a* went down at ...... John 5:4
a has spoken to Him ..... John 12:29
But at night an *a* .... Acts 5:19
A who appeared to him .... Acts 7:35
Then immediately an *a* .. Acts 12:23
and no *a* or spirit .... Acts 23:8
a has spoken to him ...... Acts 23:9
by me this night an *a* ..... Acts 27:23
himself into an *a* .... 2 Cor 11:14
even if we, or an *a* .... Gal 1:8
Then I saw a strong *a* .... Rev 5:2
over them the *a* .... Rev 9:11
Then I saw an *a* .... Rev 19:17
Jesus, have sent My *a* ..... Rev 22:16

ANGEL OF GOD
the *a* called to Hagar ...... Gen 21:17
Then the *A* spoke to me ... Gen 31:11
A, who went before the ..... Ex 14:19
the *A* came to the woman .. Judg 13:9
the king is like the *a* ..... 2 Sam 19:27
in a vision an *a* coming .... Acts 10:3
you received me as an *a*, ... Gal 4:14

ANGEL OF THE LORD
A found her by a spring .... Gen 16:7
the *A* called to Abraham .. Gen 22:15
A appeared to him in a flame .. Ex 3:2
the donkey saw the *A* .... Num 22:23
the *A* came up from Gilgal .. Judg 2:1
the *A* appeared to him ..... Judg 6:12
A appeared to the woman .. Judg 13:3
A was by the threshing .. 2 Sam 24:16
a said to Elijah .... 2 Kin 1:3
a went out, and killed .... 2 Kin 19:35
in the land, with the *a* .... 1 Chr 21:12
The *a* encamps all around .... Ps 34:7
let the *a* pursue them .... Ps 35:6
A, who stood among the ... Zech 1:11
priest standing before the *A* . Zech 3:1
like the *A* before them ..... Zech 12:8
a appeared to him in a ..... Matt 1:20
an *a* appeared to Joseph ... Matt 2:13
a descended from heaven, .. Matt 28:2
an *a* appeared to him, ... Luke 1:11
an *a* opened the prison ..... Acts 5:19
a spoke to Philip, saying ... Acts 8:26
an *a* stood by him, ... Acts 12:7
an *a* struck him, ... Acts 12:23

ANGELS
If He charges His *a* .... Job 4:18
lower than the *a* .... Ps 8:5
He shall give His *a* .... Ps 91:11
Praise Him, all His *a* .... Ps 148:2
He shall give His *a* .... Matt 4:6
a will come forth .... Matt 13:49
a always see the face ..... Matt 18:10
but are like *a* of God ...... Matt 22:30
not even the *a* of heaven .. Matt 24:36
and all the holy *a* .... Matt 25:31
twelve legions of *a* .... Matt 26:53
the presence of the *a* ..... Luke 15:10
was carried by the *a* ..... Luke 16:22
are equal to the *a* .... Luke 20:36
And she saw two *a* .... John 20:12
that we shall judge *a* .... 1 Cor 6:3
head, because of the *a* .... 1 Cor 11:10
and worship of *a* .... Col 2:18
with His mighty *a* .... 2 Thess 1:7
the Spirit, seen by *a* ...... 1 Tim 3:16
much better than the *a* .... Heb 1:4
does not give aid to *a* .... Heb 2:16
company of *a*, to the ...... Heb 12:22
unwittingly entertained *a* ... Heb 13:2
things which *a* desire ...... 1 Pet 1:12
did not spare the *a* .... 2 Pet 2:4
a who did not keep .... Jude 6
Michael and his *a* .... Rev 12:7

ANGER
See SLOW TO ANGER
Cursed be their *a* .... Gen 49:7

sun, that the fierce *a* .... Num 25:4
fierceness of His *a* .... Deut 13:17
heat of this great *a* .... Deut 29:24
So the *a* of the LORD .... Judg 10:7
to provoke Me to *a* .... 1 Kin 16:2
For His *a* is but for a .... Ps 30:5
let Your wrathful *a* .... Ps 69:24
a time He turned His *a* ...... Ps 78:38
made a path for His *a* .... Ps 78:50
You prolong Your *a* .... Ps 85:5
the power of Your *a* .... Ps 90:11
gracious, slow to *a* .... Ps 103:8
Nor will He keep His *a* ...... Ps 103:9
harsh word stirs up *a* ...... Prov 15:1
a sins against his own ...... Prov 20:2
a rests in the bosom .... Eccl 7:9
a the Holy One of .... Is 1:4
a is not turned away .... Is 5:25
a is turned away .... Is 12:1
'I will not cause My *a* .... Jer 3:12
For great is the *a* .... Jer 36:7
and I will send My *a* .... Ezek 7:3
does not retain His *a* .... Mic 7:18
fierceness of His *a* .... Nah 1:6
a is kindled against .... Zech 10:3
around at them with *a* ...... Mark 3:5
bitterness, wrath, *a* .... Eph 4:31

ANGER OF THE LORD

a was kindled against Moses, . Ex 4:14
a was aroused against ..... Num 25:3
a burned against the .... Josh 7:1
a was hot against Israel .... Judg 2:14
a was aroused against ..... 2 Sam 6:7
a was aroused against ..... 2 Kin 13:3
a is aroused against His .... Is 5:25
a will not turn back .... Jer 23:20
because of the *a* this .... Jer 52:3

ANGRY

Cain, "Why are you *a* .... Gen 4:6
"Let not the Lord be *a* ..... Gen 18:30
the Son, lest He be *a* .... Ps 2:12
judge, and God is *a* .... Ps 7:11
When once You are *a* .... Ps 76:7
Will you be *a* forever .... Ps 79:5
friendship with an *a* ...... Prov 22:24
backbiting tongue an *a* .... Prov 25:23
a man stirs up strife ...... Prov 29:22
in your spirit to be *a* .... Eccl 7:9
I was *a* with My people .... Is 47:6
nor will I always be *a* .... Is 57:16
covetousness I was *a* .... Is 57:17
right for you to be *a* .... Jon 4:4
LORD has been very *a* .... Zech 1:2
I am exceedingly *a* .... Zech 1:15
you that whoever is *a* ...... Matt 5:22
"Be *a*, and do not sin" ...... Eph 4:26
Therefore I was *a* .... Heb 3:10
with whom was He *a* .... Heb 3:17
The nations were *a* .... Rev 11:18

ANGUISH

a has come upon me .... 2 Sam 1:9
a make him afraid .... Job 15:24
I will be in *a* over my .... Ps 38:18
and *a* have overtaken ..... Ps 119:143
longer remembers the *a* .. John 16:21
tribulation and *a* .... Rom 2:9
much affliction and *a* .... 2 Cor 2:4

ANIMAL

of every clean *a* .... Gen 7:2
Whoever kills an *a* .... Lev 24:18
the life of his *a* .... Prov 12:10
set him on his own *a* ..... Luke 10:34

ANIMALS

of *a* after their kind .... Gen 6:20
sacrifices of fat *a* .... Ps 66:15
of four-footed *a* .... Acts 10:12
and four-footed *a* .... Rom 1:23

ANISE

tithe of mint and *a* .... Matt 23:23

ANNA

Aged prophetess, Luke 2:36–38

ANNAS

A Jewish high priest, Luke 3:2
Christ appeared before, John 18:12–24
Peter and John appeared before, Acts 4:6

ANNUL

and who will *a* .... Is 14:27
years later, cannot *a* .... Gal 3:17

ANNULLING

one hand there is an *a* ...... Heb 7:18

ANNULS

is confirmed, no one *a* .... Gal 3:15

ANOINT

You shall *a* them .... Ex 28:41
but you shall not *a* .... Deut 28:40
you shall *a* for Me the .... 1 Sam 16:3
a yourself with oil .... 2 Sam 14:2
a my head with oil .... Ps 23:5
Arise, you princes, *a* .... Is 21:5
a the Most Holy .... Dan 9:24
when you fast, *a* .... Matt 6:17
a My body for burial ...... Mark 14:8
they might come and *a* .... Mark 16:1
a your eyes with eye .... Rev 3:18

ANOINTED

See LORD'S ANOINTED
the priest, who is *a* .... Lev 16:32
"Surely the LORD'S *a* ..... 1 Sam 16:6
destroy the LORD'S *a* ...... 2 Sam 1:14
he cursed the LORD'S *a* .. 2 Sam 19:21
shows mercy to His *a* .... 2 Sam 22:51
"Do not touch My *a* .... 1 Chr 16:22
the LORD saves His *a* .... Ps 20:6
because the LORD has *a* .... Is 61:1
"These are the two *a* .... Zech 4:14
Because He has *a* .... Luke 4:18
but this woman has *a* ..... Luke 7:46
a the eyes of the .... John 9:6
It was that Mary who *a* .... John 11:2
Jesus, whom You *a* .... Acts 4:27
and has *a* us is God .... 2 Cor 1:21

ANOINTING

also made the holy *a* .... Ex 37:29
pray over him, *a* him ..... James 5:14
But you have an *a* .... 1 John 2:20
but as the same *a* .... 1 John 2:27

ANOTHER

See LOVE ONE ANOTHER
that you love one *a* .... John 13:34
and He will give you *a* .... John 14:16
'Let *a* take his office .... Acts 1:20

ANSWER

will give Pharaoh an *a* .... Gen 41:16
a I should take back ..... 2 Sam 24:13
Him, he could not *a* .... Job 9:3
Call, and I will *a* .... Job 13:22
how shall I *a* Him .... Job 31:14
and you shall *a* .... Job 40:7
the day that I call, *a* .... Ps 102:2
In Your faithfulness *a* .... Ps 143:1
a turns away wrath .... Prov 15:1
A man has joy by the *a* ... Prov 15:23
He who gives a right *a* ... Prov 24:26
a a fool according .... Prov 26:4
was there none to *a* .... Is 50:2
for there is no *a* .... Mic 3:7
or what you should *a* ..... Luke 12:11
you may have an *a* .... 2 Cor 5:12
ought to *a* each one .... Col 4:6

ANSWERS

a a matter before he ...... Prov 18:13
but the rich *a* roughly ..... Prov 18:23
money *a* everything .... Eccl 10:19

ANT

Go to the *a*, you sluggard ... Prov 6:6

ANTICHRIST

heard that the *A* .... 1 John 2:18
a who denies the .... 1 John 2:22
is the spirit of the *A* .... 1 John 4:3
is a deceiver and an *a* .... 2 John 7

ANTIOCH

——— In Syria:
First Gentile church established, Acts 11:19–21
Disciples first called "Christians" in, Acts 11:26
Church commissions Paul, Acts 13:1–4; 15:35–41
Church troubled by Judaizers, Acts 15:1–4; Gal 2:11–21
——— In Pisidia:
Paul visits; Jews reject the gospel, Acts 13:14, 42–51

ANTIPATRIS

A city between Jerusalem and Caesarea, Acts 23:31

ANTITYPE

a which now saves us ..... 1 Pet 3:21

ANXIETIES

the multitude of my *a* .... Ps 94:19
Try me, and know my *a* .... Ps 139:23

ANXIETY

A in the heart of man ..... Prov 12:25
eat their bread with *a* ..... Ezek 12:19

ANXIOUS

drink, nor have an *a* ...... Luke 12:29
Be *a* for nothing .... Phil 4:6

APART

See SET APART
that you shall set *a* .... Ex 13:12
she shall be set *a* .... Lev 15:19
the LORD has set *a* .... Ps 4:3
justified by faith *a* .... Rom 3:28

APHEK

A town in the Plain of Sharon, Josh 12:18
Site of Philistine camp, 1 Sam 4:1; 29:1
——— A city in Jezreel, 1 Kin 20:26–30
Syria's defeat prophesied here, 2 Kin 13:14–19

APOLLOS

An Alexandrian Jew; instructed by Aquila and Priscilla and sent to Achaia, Acts 18:24–28
Referred to as having ministered in Corinth, 1 Cor 1:12; 3:4, 22; 4:6; 16:12

APOLLONIA

A town between Amphipolis and Thessalonica, Acts 17:1

APOLLYON

Angel of the bottomless pit, Rev 9:11

APOSTLE

called to be an *a* .... Rom 1:1
inasmuch as I am an *a* .... Rom 11:13
Am I not an *a* .... 1 Cor 9:1
the signs of an *a* were .... 2 Cor 12:12
a preacher and an *a* .... 1 Tim 2:7
consider the *A* and High ..... Heb 3:1

APOSTLES

See TWELVE APOSTLES
names of the twelve *a* ...... Matt 10:2
whom He also named *a* .... Luke 6:13
displayed us, the *a* .... 1 Cor 4:9
am the least of the *a* ...... 1 Cor 15:9
to the most eminent *a* ...... 2 Cor 11:5
themselves into *a* .... 2 Cor 11:13
none of the other *a* .... Gal 1:19
gave some to be *a* .... Eph 4:11
who say they are *a* .... Rev 2:2
heaven, and you holy *a* .... Rev 18:20

APOSTLESHIP

in this ministry and *a* ...... Acts 1:25

received grace and *a* .... Rom 1:5
are the seal of my *a* .... 1 Cor 9:2
in Peter for the *a* .... Gal 2:8

APPAREL
is glorious in His *a* .... Is 63:1
clothed with foreign *a* .... Zeph 1:8
by them in white *a* .... Acts 1:10
themselves in modest *a* .... 1 Tim 2:9
gold rings, in fine *a* .... James 2:2
or putting on fine *a* .... 1 Pet 3:3

APPEAL
I *a* to Caesar .... Acts 25:11
love's sake I rather *a* .... Philem 9

APPEAR
and let the dry land *a* .... Gen 1:9
all your males shall *a* .... Ex 23:17
all Israel comes to *a* .... Deut 31:11
shall I come and *a* .... Ps 42:2
Let Your work *a* .... Ps 90:16
He shall *a* in His .... Ps 102:16
doings your sins *a* .... Ezek 21:24
faces that they may *a* .... Matt 6:16
also outwardly *a* .... Matt 23:28
kingdom of God would *a* . Luke 19:11
For we must all *a* .... 2 Cor 5:10
for Him He will *a* .... Heb 9:28
and the sinner *a* .... 1 Pet 4:18

APPEARANCE
Do not look at his *a* .... 1 Sam 16:7
a is blacker than soot .... Lam 4:8
As He prayed, the *a* .... Luke 9:29
judge according to *a* .... John 7:24
those who boast in *a* .... 2 Cor 5:12
to the outward *a* .... 2 Cor 10:7
found in *a* as a man .... Phil 2:8
indeed have an *a* .... Col 2:23

APPEARED
See LORD APPEARED TO
an angel of the Lord *a* .... Luke 1:11
who *a* in glory and .... Luke 9:31
brings salvation has *a* .... Titus 2:11
of the ages, He has *a* .... Heb 9:26

APPEARING
Lord Jesus Christ's *a* .... 1 Tim 6:14
been revealed by the *a* .... 2 Tim 1:10
and the dead at His *a* .... 2 Tim 4:1
who have loved His *a* .... 2 Tim 4:8
hope and glorious *a* .... Titus 2:13

APPEARS
can stand when He *a* .... Mal 3:2
who is our life *a* .... Col 3:4
the Chief Shepherd *a* .... 1 Pet 5:4
in Him, that when He *a* ... 1 John 2:28

APPETITE
or satisfy the *a* .... Job 38:39
are a man given to *a* .... Prov 23:2

APPII FORUM
A town about 40 miles south of Rome where Christians came to meet Paul, Acts 28:15

APPLE
He kept him as the *a* .... Deut 32:10
And my law as the *a* .... Prov 7:2
Like an *a* tree among .... Song 2:3
touches the *a* of His eye .... Zech 2:8

APPLES
fitly spoken is like *a* .... Prov 25:11
refresh me with *a* .... Song 2:5

APPLIED
a my heart to know .... Eccl 7:25

APPOINT
I will even *a* terror .... Lev 26:16
a each of them to his .... Num 4:19
a me ruler over the .... 2 Sam 6:21
a salvation for walls .... Is 26:1
For God did not *a* .... 1 Thess 5:9
a elders in every city .... Titus 1:5

APPOINTED
You have *a* his limits .... Job 14:5
To release those *a* .... Ps 102:20
And as it is *a* for men .... Heb 9:27

APPOINTED FEASTS
to the LORD at your *a* .... Num 29:39
your *a* my soul hates .... Is 1:14
her Sabbaths, all her *a* .... Hos 2:11
O Judah, keep your *a* .... Nah 1:15

APPOINTED TIME
At the *a* I will return to .... Gen 18:14
keep the Passover at its *a* ... Num 9:2
the morning till the *a* ... 2 Sam 24:15
at the *a* the end shall be .... Dan 8:19
end will still be at the *a* .... Dan 11:27
vision is yet for an *a* .... Hab 2:3

APPROACH
a anyone who is near .... Lev 18:6
And cause to *a* You .... Ps 65:4
year, make those who *a* .... Heb 10:1

APPROACHING
take delight in *a* God .... Is 58:2
as you see the Day *a* .... Heb 10:25

APPROVE
their posterity who *a* .... Ps 49:13
do the same but also *a* .... Rom 1:32
a the things that .... Rom 2:18
a the things that are .... Phil 1:10

APPROVED
to God and *a* by men .... Rom 14:18
to present yourself *a* .... 2 Tim 2:15
when he has been *a* .... James 1:12

APRONS
a were brought from his .. Acts 19:12

AQUEDUCT
stood by the *a* .... 2 Kin 18:17
at the end of the *a* .... Is 7:3
he stood by the *a* .... Is 36:2

AQUILA
Paul's host in Corinth, Acts 18:2, 3
Travels to Syria and Ephesus with Paul, Acts 18:18, 19
Instructs Apollos, Acts 18:24–26
Esteemed by Paul, Rom 16:3, 4

AR
A chief Moabite city, Num 21:15
On Israel's route, Deut 2:18
Destroyed by Sihon, Num 21:28
Destroyed by God, Is 15:1

ARABIA
Pays tribute to Solomon, 1 Kin 10:14, 15
Plunders Jerusalem, 2 Chr 21:16, 17
Defeated by Uzziah, 2 Chr 26:1, 7
Denounced by prophets, Is 21:13–17

ARARAT
Site of ark's landing, Gen 8:4
Assassins flee to, 2 Kin 19:37; Is 37:38

ARAUNAH (or Ornan)
A Jebusite, 2 Sam 24:15–25
His threshing floor bought by David, 2 Sam 24:18–25
becomes site of temple, 2 Chr 3:1
Also called Ornan, 1 Chr 21:18–28

ARBITRATOR
a judge or an *a* over .... Luke 12:14

ARCHANGEL
with the voice of an *a* ... 1 Thess 4:16
Yet Michael the *a* .... Jude 9

ARCHELAUS
Son of Herod the Great, Matt 2:22

AREOPAGUS
Paul preaches at, Acts 17:18–34

ARGUMENTS
fill my mouth with *a* .... Job 23:4
casting down *a* and .... 2 Cor 10:5

ARIEL
Ezra's friend, Ezra 8:15–17
——— Name applied to Jerusalem, Is 29:1, 2, 7

ARISE
needy, now I will *a* .... Ps 12:5
A for our help .... Ps 44:26
Let God *a* .... Ps 68:1
A, shine; for your light .... Is 60:1
But the LORD will *a* .... Is 60:2
Righteousness shall *a* .... Mal 4:2
I will *a* and go to .... Luke 15:18
you who sleep, *a* .... Eph 5:14

ARISTARCHUS
A Macedonian Christian, Acts 19:29
Accompanies Paul, Acts 20:1, 4
Imprisoned with Paul, Col 4:10

ARK
Make yourself an *a* .... Gen 6:14
two of every sort into the *a* . Gen 6:19
Then the *a* rested .... Gen 8:4
she took an *a* of bulrushes .... Ex 2:3
in the *a* you shall put .... Ex 25:21
Bezalel made the *a* .... Ex 37:1
seat which is on the *a* .... Lev 16:2
the *a* which I had made .... Deut 10:5
"Cross over before the *a* .... Josh 4:5
"Take up the *a* .... Josh 6:6
Let us bring the *a* .... 1 Sam 4:3
Also the *a* of God .... 1 Sam 4:11
a of God was captured .... 1 Sam 4:19
Philistines took the *a* .... 1 Sam 5:1
the *a* remained in Kirjath .. 1 Sam 7:2
out his hand to the *a* .... 2 Sam 6:6
brought the *a* of the .... 2 Sam 6:17
Nothing was in the *a* .... 1 Kin 8:9
his hand to hold the *a* .... 1 Chr 13:9
the holy *a* in the house .... 2 Chr 35:3
golden censer and the *a* .... Heb 9:4
prepared an *a* for the .... Heb 11:7
of Noah, while the *a* .... 1 Pet 3:20
in heaven, and the *a* .... Rev 11:19

ARM
with an outstretched *a* .... Ex 6:6
"Has the LORD's *a* .... Num 11:23
With him is an *a* .... 2 Chr 32:8
a that has no strength .... Job 26:2
Have you an *a* like God .... Job 40:9
Break the *a* of the .... Ps 10:15
You have a mighty *a* .... Ps 89:13
a have gained Him the .... Ps 98:1
a shall rule for Him .... Is 40:10
therefore His own *a* .... Is 59:16
strength with His *a* .... Luke 1:51
with an uplifted *a* .... Acts 13:17
a yourselves also with .... 1 Pet 4:1

ARMAGEDDON
See MEGIDDO
Possible site of final battle, Rev 16:16

ARMED
You have *a* me with .... 2 Sam 22:40
a strong man, fully *a* .... Luke 11:21

ARMIES
make captains of the *a* .... Deut 20:9
"I defy the *a* of Israel .... 1 Sam 17:10
any number to His *a* .... Job 25:3
not go out with our *a* .... Ps 60:10
And he sent out his *a* .... Matt 22:7
surrounded by *a* .... Luke 21:20
And the *a* in heaven .... Rev 19:14
the earth, and their *a* .... Rev 19:19

ARMOR
but he put his *a* .... 1 Sam 17:54
spears, put on the *a* .... Jer 46:4
let us put on the *a* .... Rom 13:12
Put on the whole *a* .... Eph 6:11

ARMORBEARER
to the young man, his *a* ... Judg 9:54

Jonathan said to his *a* . . . 1 Sam 14:12
he became his *a* . . . . 1 Sam 16:21
Saul said to his *a* . . . . 1 Sam 31:4
his *a* would not, for he . . . . 1 Chr 10:4
when his *a* saw that Saul . . 1 Chr 10:5

ARMS

are the everlasting *a* . . . . . . Deut 33:27
into the clash of *a* . . . . Job 39:21
It is God who *a* . . . . Ps 18:32
My *a* will judge the . . . . Is 51:5
wounds between your *a* . . . . Zech 13:6
took them up in His *a* . . . . Mark 10:16
took Him up in his *a* . . . . Luke 2:28

ARMY

the multitude of an *a* . . . . Ps 33:16
an exceedingly great *a* . . . . Ezek 37:10
the number of the *a* . . . . Rev 9:16

ARNON

Boundary between Moab and Ammon, Num 21:13, 26
Border of Reuben, Deut 3:12, 16
Ammonites reminded of, Judg 11:18–26

AROER

A town in east Jordan; rebuilt by Gadites, Num 32:34; Deut 2:36
Assigned to Reuben, Deut 3:12
Ruled by Amorites, Josh 12:2; 13:9, 10, 16

AROMA

smelled a soothing *a* . . . . Gen 8:21
To the one we are the *a* . . . 2 Cor 2:16
for a sweet-smelling *a* . . . . Eph 5:2
a sweet-smelling *a* . . . . Phil 4:18

AROSE

younger *a* and lay with . . . . Gen 19:35
a and crossed the river . . . . Gen 31:21
behold, my sheaf *a* . . . . Gen 37:7
there *a* a new king . . . . Ex 1:8
Deborah *a* and went . . . . Judg 4:9
until I, Deborah, *a* . . . . Judg 5:7
a a mother in Israel . . . . Judg 5:7
Samuel *a* and went to Eli, . . 1 Sam 3:6
David *a* and fled . . . . 1 Sam 21:10
LORD *a* against His . . . . 2 Chr 36:16
Then I *a* in the night . . . . Neh 2:12
Esther *a* and stood before . . . Esth 8:4
I *a* to open for my beloved . . Song 5:5
the king *a* very early . . . . . . Dan 6:19
afterward I *a* and went . . . . . Dan 8:27
Jonah *a* to flee to . . . . Jon 1:3
And she *a* and served . . . . . Matt 8:15
tempest *a* on the sea . . . . Matt 8:24
He *a* and rebuked . . . . Matt 8:26
all those virgins *a* and . . . . . Matt 25:7
a great windstorm *a* . . . . Mark 4:37
a and rebuked the wind . . . Mark 4:39
a against the church . . . . Acts 8:1
he *a* and was baptized . . . . . Acts 9:18
with Him after He *a* . . . . Acts 10:41
a dissension *a* between . . . . . Acts 23:7
smoke *a* out of the pit . . . . Rev 9:2

AROUSED

the LORD was greatly *a* . . . Num 11:10
his wrath was *a* because . . . . Job 32:2
Then Joseph, being *a* . . . . . . Matt 1:24

ARPHAXAD

A son of Shem, Gen 10:22, 24
Born two years after the flood, Gen 11:10–13
An ancestor of Christ, Luke 3:36

ARRAY

a against Gibeah . . . . Judg 20:30
battle *a* against Israel . . . . . . 1 Sam 4:2
drew up in battle *a* . . . . 1 Sam 17:2
a yourself with glory . . . . Job 40:10

ARRAYED

his glory was not *a* . . . . Matt 6:29
"Who are these *a* . . . . Rev 7:13
The woman was *a* . . . . Rev 17:4

ARREST

come up to *a* Samson . . . . . Judg 15:10
the altar, saying, "A him . . 1 Kin 13:4
when they *a* you . . . . Mark 13:11

ARROGANCE

Pride and *a* and the . . . . Prov 8:13
I will halt the *a* . . . . Is 13:11

ARROGANT

the fruit of the *a* . . . . Is 10:12
sanctuary, your *a* boast . . . Ezek 24:21

ARROW

deliverance and the *a* . . . . 2 Kin 13:17
a cannot make him flee . . . . Job 41:28
make ready their *a* . . . . Ps 11:2
a that flies by day . . . . Ps 91:5
a sword, and a sharp *a* . . . . Prov 25:18
Their tongue is an *a* . . . . Jer 9:8
as a target for the *a* . . . . Lam 3:12

ARROWS

He sent out *a* and . . . . 2 Sam 22:15
a pierce me deeply . . . . Ps 38:2
There He broke the *a* . . . . Ps 76:3
Like *a* in the hand of . . . . Ps 127:4
He has caused the *a* . . . . Lam 3:13
were sworn over Your *a* . . . . Hab 3:9

ARTAXERXES

Artaxerxes I, king of Persia (465–425 B.C.), authorizes Ezra's mission to Jerusalem, Ezra 7:1–28
Temporarily halts rebuilding program at Jerusalem, Ezra 4:7–23
Authorizes Nehemiah's mission, Neh 2:1–10
Permits Nehemiah to return, Neh 13:6

ARTISAN

gifted *a* in whom . . . . Ex 36:1
the skillful *a*, and the expert . . . Is 3:3

ARTISTIC

a designs of cherubim . . . . Ex 26:1
to design *a* works . . . . Ex 31:4
a designs of cherubim . . . . Ex 36:8
linen, into *a* designs . . . . Ex 39:3

AS IT IS WRITTEN

A in the Law of Moses, ... Dan 9:13
of Man indeed goes just *a* . Matt 26:24
A in the Prophets: "Behold, . Mark 1:2
of you hypocrites, *a* . . . . Mark 7:6
whatever they wished, *a* . . Mark 9:13
a, 'He gave them bread . . . . John 6:31
donkey, sat on it; *a* . . . . John 12:14
a, "The just shall live . . . . . . Rom 1:17
Israel will be saved, *a* . . . . . Rom 11:26
but *a*, "The reproaches of . . Rom 15:3

ASA

Third king of Judah; restores true worship, 1 Kin 15:8–15; 2 Chr 14; 15
Hires Ben-Hadad against Baasha; rebuked by a prophet, 1 Kin 15:16–22; 2 Chr 16:1–10
Diseased, seeks physicians rather than the Lord, 2 Chr 16:12
Death and burial, 2 Chr 16:13, 14

ASAHEL

David's nephew; captain in his army; noted for valor, 2 Sam 2:18; 23:24; 1 Chr 2:16; 27:7
Killed by Abner, 2 Sam 2:19–23
Avenged by Joab, 2 Sam 3:27, 30

ASAPH

A Levite choir leader under David and Solomon, 1 Chr 15:16–19; 16:1–7; 2 Chr 5:6, 12
Twelve psalms assigned to, 2 Chr 29:30; Ps 50; 73—83

ASCEND

Who may *a* into the . . . . Ps 24:3
If I *a* into heaven . . . . Ps 139:8
'I will *a* into heaven . . . . Is 14:13
a as high as the eagle . . . . Obad 4
see the Son of Man *a* . . . . . . John 6:62

ASCENDED

You have *a* on high . . . . Ps 68:18
Who has *a* into heaven . . . . Prov 30:4
No one has *a* to heaven . . . . John 3:13
"When He *a* on high . . . . Eph 4:8
also the One who *a* . . . . Eph 4:10
And they *a* to heaven . . . . . . Rev 11:12

ASCENDING

angels of God were *a* . . . . . Gen 28:12
the angels of God *a* . . . . John 1:51

ASCRIBE

a greatness to our God . . . . . Deut 32:3
I will *a* righteousness to . . . . . Job 36:3
A strength to God . . . . Ps 68:34

ASENATH

Daughter of Poti-Pherah and wife of Joseph, Gen 41:45
Mother of Manasseh and Ephraim, Gen 41:50–52; 46:20

ASHAMED

O my God, I am too *a* and . . . Ezra 9:6
all my enemies be *a* . . . . Ps 6:10
Let me not be *a* . . . . Ps 25:2
who waits on You be *a* . . . . Ps 25:3
The wise men are *a* . . . . Jer 8:9
forsake You shall be *a* . . . . . Jer 17:13
And Israel shall be *a* . . . . Hos 10:6
For whoever is *a* . . . . Mark 8:38
am not *a* of the gospel . . . . . Rom 1:16
nothing I shall be *a* . . . . Phil 1:20
Therefore God is not *a* . . . . Heb 11:16
in Christ may be *a* . . . . 1 Pet 3:16
let him not be *a* . . . . 1 Pet 4:16
and not be *a* before . . . . . . 1 John 2:28

ASHDOD

One of five Philistine cities, Josh 13:3
Seat of Dagon worship, 1 Sam 5:1–8
Opposes Nehemiah, Neh 4:7
Women of, marry Jews, Neh 13:23, 24
Called Azotus, Acts 8:40

ASHER

Jacob's second son by Zilpah, Gen 30:12, 13
Goes to Egypt with Jacob, Gen 46:8, 17
Blessed by Jacob, Gen 49:20
——— Tribe of:
Census of, Num 1:41; 26:47
Slow to fight against Canaanites, Judg 1:31, 32; 5:17
Among Gideon's army, Judg 6:35; 7:23
A godly remnant among, 2 Chr 30:11

ASHERAH

The female counterpart of Baal, Judg 3:7; 1 Kin 18:19
Image of, erected by Manasseh in the temple, 2 Kin 21:7
Vessels of, destroyed by Josiah, 2 Kin 23:4
——— Translated "wooden images," idols used in the worship of Asherah, Ex 34:13; Deut 12:3; 16:21; 1 Kin 16:32, 33; 2 Kin 23:6, 7

ASHES

are proverbs of *a* . . . . Job 13:12
become like dust and *a* . . . . Job 30:19
For I have eaten *a* . . . . Ps 102:9
He feeds on *a*; a deceived . . . . Is 44:20
sackcloth and sat in *a* . . . . Jon 3:6
in sackcloth and *a* . . . . Luke 10:13
and the *a* of a heifer . . . . Heb 9:13

ASHKELON

One of five Philistine cities, Josh 13:3; Jer 47:5, 7

Captured by Judah, Judg 1:18
Men of, killed by Samson, Judg 14:19, 20
Repossessed by Philistines, 1 Sam 6:17; 2 Sam 1:20
Doom of, pronounced by the prophets, Jer 47:5, 7; Amos 1:8; Zeph 2:4, 7; Zech 9:5

ASHTAROTH
A city in Bashan; residence of King Og, Deut 1:4; Josh 12:4
Captured by Israel, Josh 9:10
——— A general designation of the Canaanite female deities, 1 Sam 7:3, 4; 31:10

ASHTORETH
A mother-goddess worshiped by the Philistines, 1 Sam 31:10
Israel ensnared by, Judg 2:13; 10:6
Worshiped by Solomon, 1 Kin 11:5, 33
Destroyed by Josiah, 2 Kin 23:13

ASIA
Paul forbidden to preach in, Acts 16:6
Paul's later ministry in, Acts 19:1–26
Seven churches of, Rev 1:4, 11

ASIDE
See TURN ASIDE
lay something *a*, storing . . . 1 Cor 16:2
lay *a* all filthiness . . . . James 1:21
Therefore, laying *a* . . . . 1 Pet 2:1

ASK
"Why is it that you *a* . . . . . . Gen 32:29
when your children *a* . . . . Josh 4:6
"*A* a sign for yourself . . . . Is 7:11
They shall *a* the way . . . . Jer 50:5
the young children *a* . . . . Lam 4:4
A the LORD for rain in . . . . . Zech 10:1
whatever things you *a* . . . . Matt 21:22
a, and it will be . . . . Luke 11:9
that whatever You *a* . . . . . . John 11:22
a anything in My . . . . John 14:14
in that day you will *a* . . . . . . John 16:23
something, let them *a* . . . . 1 Cor 14:35
above all that we *a* . . . . Eph 3:20
wisdom, let him *a* . . . . James 1:5
But let him *a* in faith . . . . . . James 1:6
because you do not *a* . . . . . . James 4:2
hears us, whatever we *a* . . 1 John 5:15

ASKS
For everyone who *a* . . . . Matt 7:8
if his son *a* for bread . . . . Matt 7:9
Or if he *a* for a fish . . . . Luke 11:11

ASLEEP
down, and was fast *a* . . . . Jon 1:5
But He was *a* . . . . Matt 8:24
but some have fallen *a* . . . . 1 Cor 15:6
those who are *a* . . . . 1 Thess 4:15
the fathers fell *a* . . . . 2 Pet 3:4

ASSEMBLE
A the men of Judah . . . . . . 2 Sam 20:4
a the outcasts of Israel . . . . Is 11:12
A yourselves, and let . . . . Jer 4:5
I will *a* them in the midst . . . . Jer 21:4
A yourselves and come . . . Ezek 39:17
a a multitude of great . . . . . Dan 11:10
A and come, all you . . . . Joel 3:11
I will surely *a* all of you . . . . . Mic 2:12

ASSEMBLED
a all the congregation . . . . . Num 1:18
Israel *a* together at Shiloh . . Josh 18:1
Solomon *a* the elders . . . . 1 Kin 8:1
David *a* the children of . . . . 1 Chr 15:4
of the God of Israel *a* . . . . Ezra 9:4
Israel were *a* with fasting . . . . Neh 9:1
who were at Shushan *a* . . . . Esth 9:18
behold, the kings *a* . . . . Ps 48:4
elders of the people *a* at . . . . Matt 26:3
with him were *a* all the . . Mark 14:53
the disciples were *a* . . . . . . John 20:19
a together was shaken . . . . . . Acts 4:31
being *a* with one accord, . . Acts 15:25

ASSEMBLING
not forsaking the *a* . . . . Heb 10:25

ASSEMBLY
to kill this whole *a* . . . . Ex 16:3
It is a sacred *a* . . . . Lev 23:36
a I will praise You . . . . Ps 22:22
I have hated the *a* . . . . Ps 26:5
also in the *a* of the . . . . Ps 89:5
to be feared in the *a* . . . . Ps 89:7
will rest in the *a* of the . . . . Prov 21:16
fast, call a sacred *a* . . . . Joel 1:14
people, sanctify the *a* . . . . Joel 2:15
a I will sing praise . . . . Heb 2:12
to the general *a* . . . . Heb 12:23
come into your *a* . . . . James 2:2

ASSHUR
One of the sons of Shem; progenitor of the Assyrians, Gen 10:22; 1 Chr 1:17
——— The chief god of the Assyrians; seen in names like Ashurbanipal (Osnapper), Ezra 4:10
——— A city in Assyria or the nation of Assyria, Num 24:22, 24

ASSOS
A seaport of Mysia in Asia to which Paul walked, Acts 20:13

ASSURANCE
night, and have no *a* . . . . . . Deut 28:66
riches of the full *a* . . . . Col 2:2
Spirit and in much *a* . . . . . . 1 Thess 1:5
to the full *a* of hope . . . . Heb 6:11
a true heart in full *a* . . . . Heb 10:22

ASSURE
a our hearts before . . . . 1 John 3:19

ASSURED
I will give you *a* peace . . . . . Jer 14:13
learned and been *a* . . . . 2 Tim 3:14

ASSUREDLY, I SAY TO YOU
"For *a*, till heaven and . . . . . Matt 5:18
"*A*, you will by no means . . Matt 5:26
A, they have their reward. . . . Matt 6:2
"*A*, I have not found such . . Matt 8:10
"*A*, it will be more . . . . Matt 10:15
For *a*, you will not have . . . Matt 10:23
a, he shall by no means . . . Matt 10:42
"*A*, among those born of . . Matt 11:11
"*a* that many prophets . . . . Matt 13:17
"*A*, there are some . . . . Matt 16:28
for *a*, if you have faith . . . . Matt 17:20
"*A*, unless you are . . . . Matt 18:3
a, he rejoices more over . . . Matt 18:13
"*A*, whatever you bind . . . . Matt 18:18
"*A* that it is hard for a . . . . . Matt 19:23
"*A*, that in the . . . . Matt 19:28
"*A*, if you have faith and . . Matt 21:21
"*A* that tax collectors . . . . . Matt 21:31
"*A*, all these things will . . . Matt 23:36
A, not one stone shall be . . . Matt 24:2
"*A*, this generation will . . . Matt 24:34
"*A* that he will make . . . . . Matt 24:47
'*A*, I do not know you.' . . . . Matt 25:12
'*A*, inasmuch as you did . . Matt 25:40
'*A*, inasmuch as you did . . Matt 25:45
A, wherever this gospel . . . Matt 26:13
"*A*, one of you will betray . Matt 26:21
"*A* that this night, before . Matt 26:34
"*A*, all sins will be . . . . Mark 3:28
A, no sign shall be given . . Mark 8:12
A, whoever does not . . . . . Mark 10:15
"*A*, there is no one who . . Mark 10:29
a, whoever says to this . . . Mark 11:23
"*A* that this poor widow . . Mark 12:43
"*A*, I will no longer . . . . . . Mark 14:25
"*A*, no prophet is accepted . Luke 4:24
A that he will gird . . . . Luke 12:37
a, you shall not see Me . . . Luke 13:35
"*A*, today you will be . . . . . Luke 23:43
"Most *a*, hereafter you . . . . . . John 1:51
"Most *a*, unless one is born . John 3:3
"Most *a*, We speak what . . . John 3:11
"Most *a*, the Son can do . . . John 5:19
"Most *a*, he who hears . . . . . John 5:24
"Most *a*, the hour is . . . . John 5:25
"Most *a*, you seek Me, not . John 6:26
"Most *a*, Moses did not . . . . John 6:32
"Most *a*, he who believes . . . John 6:47
"Most *a*, unless you eat . . . . John 6:53
"Most *a*, whoever commits . John 8:34
"Most *a*, if anyone keeps . . John 8:51
"Most *a*, before Abraham . . John 8:58
"Most *a*, he who does not . . John 10:1
"Most *a*, I am the door of . . John 10:7
"Most *a*, unless a grain . . . John 12:24
Most *a*, he who receives . . . John 13:20
"Most *a*, he who believes . John 14:12
"Most *a* that you will . . . . . John 16:20
Most *a*, whatever you ask . John 16:23
"Most *a*, when you were . . John 21:18

ASSYRIA (or Asshur)
Founded by Nimrod, Gen 10:8–12; Mic 5:6
Agent of God's purposes, Is 7:17–20; 10:5, 6
Attacks and finally conquers Israel, 2 Kin 15:19, 20, 29; 17:3–41
Invades and threatens Judah, 2 Kin 18:13–37
Hezekiah prays for help against; army miraculously slain, 2 Kin 19:1–35
Prophecies concerning, Num 24:22–24; Is 10:12–19; 14:24, 25; 19:23–25; Hos 10:6; 11:5; Nah 3:1–19

ASTONISHED
dwell in it shall be *a* . . . . Lev 26:32
who passes by it will be *a* . . 1 Kin 9:8
I sat *a* until the evening . . . . . Ezra 9:4
are *a* at His rebuke . . . . Job 26:11
Just as many were *a* . . . . Is 52:14
Be *a*, O heavens, at . . . . Jer 2:12
remained there *a* . . . . Ezek 3:15
was *a* for a time, and his . . . Dan 4:19
that the people were *a* . . . . . . Matt 7:28
so that they were *a* . . . . Matt 13:54
disciples were *a* at His . . . . Mark 10:24
who heard Him were *a* . . . . . Luke 2:47
a at the catch of fish . . . . Luke 5:9
her parents were *a*, ... Luke 8:56
at the tomb early, *a* us . . . . Luke 24:22
So he, trembling and *a*, ... Acts 9:6
who believed were *a*, ... Acts 10:45
saw him, they were *a* . . . . . Acts 12:16
being *a* at the teaching . . . . Acts 13:12

ASTONISHMENT
you shall become an *a* . . . . Deut 28:37
a has taken hold . . . . Jer 8:21

ASTRAY
is a people who go *a* . . . . Ps 95:10
a fool, shall not go *a* . . . . Is 35:8
Their lies lead them *a* . . . . . . Amos 2:4
and one of them goes *a* . . . Matt 18:12
'They always go *a* . . . . Heb 3:10
like sheep going *a* . . . . 1 Pet 2:25

ASTROLOGERS
the *a*, the stargazers . . . . Is 47:13
the magicians, the *a* . . . . Dan 2:2
bring in the *a* . . . . Dan 5:7

AT THE RIGHT HAND
Son of Man sitting *a* . . . . . . Matt 26:64
heaven, and sat down *a* . . Mark 16:19
Jesus standing *a* of God . . . . Acts 7:55
who is even *a* of God, ... Rom 8:34
sat down *a* of the Majesty . . . . Heb 1:3
Priest, who is seated *a* . . . . Heb 8:1
heaven and is *a* of God, ... 1 Pet 3:22

ATE
she took of its fruit and *a* .... Gen 3:6
near to him, and he *a* ..... Gen 27:25
I *a* all of it before .... Gen 27:33
gaunt cows *a* up the seven .. Gen 41:4
a manna forty years .... Ex 16:35
died, you arose and *a* .... 2 Sam 12:21
Men *a* angels' food .... Ps 78:25
I *a* them, and Your word ... Jer 15:16
I *a* it, and it was in my ..... Ezek 3:3
all *a* and were filled ...... Matt 14:20
all *a* and were filled ...... Matt 15:37
he *a* locusts and wild .... Mark 1:6
a the showbread .... Mark 2:26
all *a* and were filled .... Mark 6:42
they *a* and were filled ...... Mark 8:8
all *a* and were filled .... Luke 9:17
Our fathers *a* the manna .... John 6:31
men and *a* with them .... Acts 11:3
a the same spiritual .... 1 Cor 10:3
a it, and it was as sweet ... Rev 10:10

ATHALIAH
Daughter of Ahab and Jezebel, 2 Kin 8:18, 26; 2 Chr 22:2, 3
Kills royal children; usurps throne, 2 Kin 11:1–3; 2 Chr 22:10, 11
Killed in priestly uprising, 2 Kin 11:4–16; 2 Chr 23:1–21

ATHENS
Paul preaches in, Acts 17:15–34
Paul resides in, 1 Thess 3:1

ATONEMENT
a year he shall make *a* ...... Ex 30:10
priest shall make *a* .... Lev 16:30
the blood that makes *a* .... Lev 17:11
for it is the Day of *A* .... Lev 23:28
what shall I make *a* ...... 2 Sam 21:3
offerings to make *a* .... Neh 10:33
a is provided for .... Prov 16:6
there will be no *a* .... Is 22:14
I provide you an *a* .... Ezek 16:63

ATTACK
the Midianites, and *a* ..... Num 25:17
men go up and *a* Ai .... Josh 7:3
a Amalek, and utterly .... 1 Sam 15:3
got ready to *a* the city .... 1 Kin 20:12
a Jerusalem and create .... Neh 4:8
king of the South shall *a* .. Dan 11:40
no one will *a* you to hurt .. Acts 18:10

ATTACKED
a the Rephaim in .... Gen 14:5
who *a* Midian in the .... Gen 36:35
they *a* them until they left .. Josh 11:8
he *a* the army while the .... Judg 8:11
Jonathan *a* the garrison ... 1 Sam 13:3
a Ziklag and burned it .... 1 Sam 30:1
David *a* the Philistines ..... 2 Sam 8:1
a Judah, and carried ..... 2 Chr 28:17
a the ram, and broke .... Dan 8:7
a the house of Jason .... Acts 17:5

ATTAIN
It is high, I cannot *a* .... Ps 139:6
understanding will *a* .... Prov 1:5
How long until they *a* .... Hos 8:5
worthy to *a* that age ...... Luke 20:35
by any means, I may *a* ..... Phil 3:11

ATTALIA
A seaport of Pamphylia from which Paul sailed to Antioch, Acts 14:25

ATTEND
just cause, O LORD, *a* .... Ps 17:1
And *a* to the voice of .... Ps 86:6
behold, I will *a* .... Jer 23:2

ATTENTION
My son, give *a* to my ...... Prov 4:20
Till I come, give *a* .... 1 Tim 4:13
and you pay *a* to the ...... James 2:3

ATTENTIVE
Let Your ears be *a* .... Ps 130:2

the people were very *a* ... Luke 19:48

ATTESTED
a Man *a* by God to you ..... Acts 2:22

AUSTERE
because you are an *a* ...... Luke 19:21

AUTHOR
For God is not the *a* ...... 1 Cor 14:33
He became the *a* .... Heb 5:9
unto Jesus, the *a* .... Heb 12:2

AUTHORITIES
magistrates and *a* .... Luke 12:11
a that exist are .... Rom 13:1
subject to rulers and *a* ...... Titus 3:1
of God, angels and *a* .... 1 Pet 3:22

AUTHORITY
Jew, wrote with full *a* ...... Esth 9:29
the righteous are in *a* ...... Prov 29:2
them as one having *a* ...... Matt 7:29
a man under *a* .... Matt 8:9
who are great exercise *a* .. Matt 20:25
"All *a* has been given ..... Matt 28:18
ones exercise *a* over ...... Mark 10:42
By what *a* are You .... Mark 11:28
a I will give You .... Luke 4:6
His word was with *a* ...... Luke 4:32
a over all demons .... Luke 9:1
and has given Him *a* .... John 5:27
You have given Him *a* .... John 17:2
has put in His own *a* .... Acts 1:7
For there is no *a* .... Rom 13:1
a over her own body .... 1 Cor 7:4
to have a symbol of *a* .... 1 Cor 11:10
end to all rule and all *a* ... 1 Cor 15:24
and all who are in *a* .... 1 Tim 2:2
have *a* over a man .... 1 Tim 2:12
and rebuke with all *a* ...... Titus 2:15
defile the flesh, reject *a* ...... Jude 8
his throne, and great *a* ...... Rev 13:2
they receive *a* for one ..... Rev 17:12

AUTUMN
a trees without fruit .... Jude 12

AVAILS
nor uncircumcision *a* .... Gal 5:6
of a righteous man *a* ..... James 5:16

AVEN
The city of On in Egypt near Cairo; known as Heliopolis, Gen 41:45; Ezek 30:17
—— A name contemptuously applied to Bethel, Hos 10:5, 8
—— Valley in Syria, Amos 1:5

AVENGE
for He will *a* the .... Deut 32:43
you that He will *a* .... Luke 18:8
Beloved, do not *a* .... Rom 12:19
a our blood on those .... Rev 6:10

AVENGER
The *a* of blood .... Num 35:19
the enemy and the *a* .... Ps 8:2
God's minister, an *a* .... Rom 13:4
the Lord is the *a* .... 1 Thess 4:6

AVENGES
It is God who *a* .... 2 Sam 22:48
When He *a* blood .... Ps 9:12

AVOID
a foolish and ignorant .... 2 Tim 2:23
a foolish disputes .... Titus 3:9

AWAKE
be satisfied when I *a* .... Ps 17:15
I lie *a* and am like .... Ps 102:7
A, lute and harp .... Ps 108:2
My eyes are *a* through .... Ps 119:148
A, O north wind .... Song 4:16
but my heart is *a* .... Song 5:2
of the earth shall *a* .... Dan 12:2
it is high time to *a* .... Rom 13:11
A to righteousness .... 1 Cor 15:34

"*A*, you who sleep .... Eph 5:14

AWARE
Before I was even *a* .... Song 6:12
hour that he is not *a* of ... Matt 24:50
But Jesus, being *a* of it .... Mark 8:17
hour when he is not *a* .... Luke 12:46
his wife also being *a* .... Acts 5:2

AWAY
the wind drives *a* .... Ps 1:4
Do not cast me *a* .... Ps 51:11
A time to cast *a* .... Eccl 3:5
fair one, and come *a* .... Song 2:10
and the shadows flee *a* .... Song 2:17
minded to put her *a* .... Matt 1:19
and earth will pass *a* ..... Matt 24:35
and steal Him *a* .... Matt 27:64
the rich He has sent *a* ..... Luke 1:53
of God who takes *a* .... John 1:29
"I am going *a*, and you .... John 8:21
they cried out, "*A* .... John 19:15
"They have taken *a* .... John 20:2
crying out, "*A* with him ... Acts 21:36
the veil is taken *a* .... 2 Cor 3:14
Barnabas was carried *a* ..... Gal 2:13
unless the falling *a* .... 2 Thess 2:3
in Asia have turned *a* ..... 2 Tim 1:15
heard, lest we drift *a* .... Heb 2:1
if they fall *a*, to renew .... Heb 6:6
which can never take *a* .... Heb 10:11
that does not fade *a* .... 1 Pet 5:4
the world is passing *a* .... 1 John 2:17
and the heaven fled *a* ...... Rev 20:11
if anyone takes *a* .... Rev 22:19

AWE
the world stand in *a* .... Ps 33:8
my heart stands in *a* ...... Ps 119:161

AWESOME
How *a* is this place .... Gen 28:17
a thing that I will do .... Ex 34:10
God, the great and *a* .... Deut 7:21
God, mighty and *a* .... Deut 10:17
a things which your eyes .. Deut 10:21
a name, THE LORD .... Deut 28:58
Angel of God, very *a* .... Judg 13:6
a deeds for Your land .... 2 Sam 7:23
a deeds, by driving out ... 1 Chr 17:21
heaven, O great and *a* .... Neh 1:5
the Lord, great and *a* .... Neh 4:14
a God, Who keeps .... Neh 9:32
show Yourself *a* .... Job 10:16
with God is *a* majesty ...... Job 37:22
hand shall teach You *a* ...... Ps 45:4
LORD Most High is *a* .... Ps 47:2
By *a* deeds in .... Ps 65:5
a are Your works .... Ps 66:3
He is *a* in His doing .... Ps 66:5
O God, You are more *a* ..... Ps 68:35
He is *a* to the kings .... Ps 76:12
Your great and *a* name .... Ps 99:3
a things by the Red Sea .... Ps 106:22
Holy and *a* is His name ...... Ps 111:9
of the might of Your *a* ...... Ps 145:6
When You did *a* things .... Is 64:3
with me as a mighty, *a* ..... Jer 20:11
her collapse was *a* .... Lam 1:9
so high they were *a* .... Ezek 1:18
color of an *a* crystal .... Ezek 1:22
its form was *a* .... Dan 2:31
"O Lord, great and *a* .... Dan 9:4
The LORD will be *a* .... Zeph 2:11

AWL
his ear with an *a* .... Ex 21:6
you shall take an *a* .... Deut 15:17

AWOKE
Noah *a* from his wine, ... Gen 9:24
Jacob *a* from his sleep ..... Gen 28:16
I *a*, for the LORD sustained ..... Ps 3:5
Then the Lord *a* as .... Ps 78:65
came to Him and *a* Him, ... Matt 8:25
they *a* Him and said to .... Mark 4:38

came to Him and *a* Him, . . . Luke 8:24

AX
a stroke with the *a* . . . . Deut 19:5
Abimelech took an *a* . . . . Judg 9:48
a tree, the iron *a* . . . . 2 Kin 6:5
If the *a* is dull, and one . . . . Eccl 10:10
a boast itself against . . . . Is 10:15
And even now the *a* . . . . Matt 3:10

AZARIAH
A prophet who encourages King Asa, 2 Chr 15:1–8
——— Son of King Jehoshaphat, 2 Chr 21:2
——— King of Judah, 2 Kin 15:1
——— A high priest who rebukes King Uzziah, 2 Chr 26:16–20
——— Chief priest in the time of Hezekiah, 2 Chr 31:9, 10
——— The Hebrew name of Abed-Nego, Dan 1:7

AZEKAH
Camp of Goliath, 1 Sam 17:1, 4, 17
Besieged by Nebuchadnezzar, Jer 34:7

AZMAVETH
A village near Jerusalem, Neh 12:29
Also called Beth Azmaveth, Neh 7:28

AZOTUS
A city which Philip the evangelist visited, Acts 8:40

BAAL (or Baals)
Deities of Canaanite polytheism, Judg 10:10–14
The male god of the Phoenicians and Canaanites; the counterpart of the female Ashtaroth, 2 Kin 23:5
Nature of the worship of, 1 Kin 18:26, 28; 19:18; Ps 106:28; Jer 7:9; 19:5; Hos 9:10; 13:1, 2
Worshiped by Israelites, Num 25:1–5; Judg 2:11–14; 3:7; 6:28–32; 1 Kin 16:31, 32; 2 Kin 21:3; Jer 11:13; Hos 2:8
Ahaz makes images to, 2 Chr 28:1–4
Overthrown by Elijah, 1 Kin 18:17–40 by Josiah, 2 Kin 23:4, 5
Denounced by prophets, Jer 19:4–6; Ezek 16:1, 2, 20, 21
Historic retrospect, Rom 11:4

BAAL PEOR (or Baal of Peor)
A Moabite god; worshiped by Israelites, Num 25:1–9

BAAL PERAZIM
Site of David's victory over the Philistines, 2 Sam 5:18–20
Same as Perazim, Is 28:21

BAAL-ZEBUB
A Philistine god at Ekron, 2 Kin 1:2
Ahaziah inquires of, 2 Kin 1:2, 6, 16
Also called Beelzebub, Matt 10:25; 12:24

BAALAH
A town also known as Kirjath Jearim, Josh 15:9, 10

BAALS
Deities of Canaanite polytheism, Judg 10:10–14
Ensnare Israelites, Judg 2:11–14; 3:7
Ahaz makes images to, 2 Chr 28:1–4

BAANAH
A murderer of Ishbosheth, 2 Sam 4:1–12

BAASHA
Usurps throne of Israel; his evil reign; wars with Judah, 1 Kin 15:16—16:7

BABBLER
b is no different . . . . Eccl 10:11
"What does this *b* . . . . Acts 17:18

BABBLINGS
the profane and idle *b* . . . . 1 Tim 6:20

BABE
the *b* leaped in my . . . . Luke 1:44
You will find a *B* . . . . Luke 2:12
righteousness, for he is a *b* . Heb 5:13

BABEL, TOWER OF
A huge brick structure intended to magnify man and preserve the unity of the race, Gen 11:1–4
Objectives of, thwarted by God, Gen 11:5–9

BABES
Out of the mouth of *b* . . . . Ps 8:2
b shall rule over them . . . . Is 3:4
revealed them to *b* . . . . Matt 11:25
'Out of the mouth of *b* . . . . Matt 21:16
foolish, a teacher of *b* . . . . . . Rom 2:20
as to carnal, as to *b* . . . . 1 Cor 3:1
as newborn *b*, desire . . . . 1 Pet 2:2

BABYLON
Built by Nimrod; Tower of Babel, Gen 10:8–10; 11:1–9
Descriptions of, Is 13:19; 14:4; Jer 51:44; Dan 4:30
Jews carried captive to, 2 Kin 25:1–21; 2 Chr 36:5–21
Inhabitants of, described, Is 47:1, 9–13; Jer 50:35–38; Dan 5:1–3
Prophecies concerning, Is 13:1–22; Jer 21:1–7; 25:9–12; 27:5–8; 29:10; Jer 50:1–46; Dan 2:31–38; 7:2–4
The prophetic city, Rev 14:8; 16:19; 17:1—18:24

BACK
Jordan turned *b* . . . . Ps 114:3
but a rod is for the *b* . . . . . . Prov 10:13
a rod for the fool's *b* . . . . Prov 26:3
I gave My *b* to those . . . . Is 50:6
cast Me behind your *b* . . . . Ezek 23:35
found Him, bring *b* word . . . . Matt 2:8
plow, and looking *b* . . . . Luke 9:62
they drew *b* and fell . . . . John 18:6
I am sending him *b* . . . . Philem 12
of those who draw *b* . . . . . . Heb 10:39
someone turns him *b* . . . . . James 5:19
inside and on the *b* . . . . Rev 5:1

BACKBITERS
b, haters of God . . . . Rom 1:30

BACKBITING
b tongue an angry . . . . Prov 25:23

BACKSLIDER
The *b* in heart will be . . . . . Prov 14:14

BACKSLIDINGS
b will rebuke you . . . . Jer 2:19
And I will heal your *b* . . . . Jer 3:22
b have increased . . . . Jer 5:6
for our *b* are many . . . . Jer 14:7

BACKWARD
fell off the seat *b* . . . . 1 Sam 4:18
shadow ten degrees *b* . . . . . 2 Kin 20:11

BAD
speak to you either *b* . . . . . Gen 24:50
good for *b* or *b* for good . . . Lev 27:10
trouble is like a *b* tooth . . . Prov 25:19
as the *b* figs which cannot . . . Jer 24:8
if your eye is *b*, your . . . . . . Matt 6:23
b tree bears *b* fruit . . . . Matt 7:17
a *b* tree bear good . . . . Luke 6:43
whether good or *b* . . . . 2 Cor 5:10

BADGER
covering of *b* skins . . . . Ex 26:14
sandals of *b* skin . . . . Ezek 16:10

BAG
is sealed up in a *b* . . . . Job 14:17
wages to put into a *b* . . . . Hag 1:6
nor *b* for your journey . . . . . . Matt 10:10

BAKE
b twelve cakes with it . . . . Lev 24:5

BAKED
b unleavened cakes . . . . Ex 12:39
b unleavened bread . . . . . 1 Sam 28:24

BAKER
the butler and the *b* . . . . Gen 40:1
an oven heated by a *b* . . . . . . Hos 7:4

BAKERS
of bread from the *b* . . . . Jer 37:21

BAKES
kindles it and *b* bread . . . . Is 44:15

BALAAM
Sent by Balak to curse Israel, Num 22:5–7; Josh 24:9
Hindered by talking donkey, Num 22:22–35; 2 Pet 2:16
Curse becomes a blessing, Deut 23:4, 5; Josh 24:10
Prophecies of, Num 23:7–10, 18–24; 24:3–9, 15–24
N.T. references to, 2 Pet 2:15, 16; Jude 11; Rev 2:14

BALAK
A Moabite king, Num 22:4
Hires Balaam to curse Israel, Num 22—24

BALANCE
and the hills in a *b* . . . . Is 40:12

BALANCES
weighed in the *b* . . . . Dan 5:27

BALD
shall not make any *b* . . . . Lev 21:5
every head shall be *b* . . . . Jer 48:37
completely *b* because . . . . . Ezek 27:31

BALDHEAD
Go up, you *b* . . . . 2 Kin 2:23

BALM
a little *b* and a little . . . . Gen 43:11
Is there no *b* in Gilead . . . . Jer 8:22

BAN
No person under the *b* . . . . . . Lev 27:29

BAND
A *b* of robbers takes . . . . Hos 7:1
with a golden *b* . . . . Rev 1:13

BANDS
their *b* shall be silver . . . . Ex 27:10
broken the *b* of your yoke . Lev 26:13
broken the *b* of their . . . . . Ezek 34:27
with *b* of love, and I was . . . . Hos 11:4
girded with golden *b* . . . . Rev 15:6

BANDAGED
him, and *b* his wounds . . . Luke 10:34

BANISHED
bring his *b* one home . . . . . 2 Sam 14:13
he *b* the perverted . . . . 1 Kin 15:12

BANK
cows on the *b* of the river . . . Gen 41:3
the reeds by the river's *b* . . . . . . Ex 2:3
along the *b* of the river, ... Ezek 47:7
put my money in the *b* . . . Luke 19:23

BANKERS
my money with the *b* . . . . . Matt 25:27

BANKS
the *b* of the Jordan . . . . Num 13:29
overflows all its *b* . . . . Josh 3:15
overflowed all its *b* . . . . . . 1 Chr 12:15
b of scented herbs . . . . Song 5:13
the *b* of the Ulai . . . . Dan 8:16

BANNER
his *b* over me was love . . . . . Song 2:4
a *b* to the people . . . . Is 11:10

a *b* for the nations .... Is 11:12
lift up a *b* for the peoples .... Is 62:10
Set up a *b* in the land ...... Jer 51:27
a *b* over His land .... Zech 9:16

BANNERS
we will set up our *b* .... Ps 20:5
They set up their *b* .... Ps 74:4
as an army with *b* .... Song 6:4

BANQUET
b that I have prepared .... Esth 5:4
companions make a *b* .... Job 41:6
lords, came to the *b* .... Dan 5:10

BANQUETING
He brought me to the *b* ..... Song 2:4

BANQUETS
b shall be removed .... Amos 6:7

BAPTISM
coming to his *b* .... Matt 3:7
b that I am baptized ...... Matt 20:22
The *b* of John—where .... Matt 21:25
a *b* of repentance .... Mark 1:4
baptized with the *b* that .. Mark 10:38
The *b* of John—was it ... Mark 11:30
a *b* of repentance .... Luke 3:3
But I have a *b* to be ...... Luke 12:50
The *b* of John—was it ..... Luke 20:4
from the *b* of John .... Acts 1:22
b which John preached ... Acts 10:37
b of repentance to all ..... Acts 13:24
only the *b* of John .... Acts 18:25
said, "Into John's *b* .... Acts 19:3
a *b* of repentance, ... Acts 19:4
with Him through *b* .... Rom 6:4
Lord, one faith, one *b* .... Eph 4:5
buried with Him in *b* .... Col 2:12
now saves us—*b* .... 1 Pet 3:21

BAPTISMS
of the doctrine of *b* .... Heb 6:2

BAPTIZE
I indeed *b* you with .... Matt 3:11
He will *b* you with .... Mark 1:8
b you with the Holy .... Luke 3:16
"Why then do you *b* .... John 1:25
me to *b* with water .... John 1:33
Himself did not *b* .... John 4:2
did not send me to *b* ...... 1 Cor 1:17

BAPTIZED
b by him in the Jordan, ... Matt 3:6
at the Jordan to be *b* by .... Matt 3:13
"I need to be *b* by You ..... Matt 3:14
When He had been *b* .... Matt 3:16
were all *b* by him .... Mark 1:5
was *b* by John .... Mark 1:9
b with the baptism that ... Mark 10:38
b with you will be *b* ..... Mark 10:39
and is *b* will be saved .... Mark 16:16
came out to be *b* .... Luke 3:7
also came to be *b* .... Luke 3:12
Jesus also was *b* .... Luke 3:21
not having been *b* .... Luke 7:30
with them and *b* .... John 3:22
b more disciples .... John 4:1
for John truly *b* with water .. Acts 1:5
every one of you be *b* ...... Acts 2:38
received his word were *b* ... Acts 2:41
men and women were *b* ...... Acts 8:12
he was *b* he continued ..... Acts 8:13
only been *b* in the name .... Acts 8:16
hinders me from being *b* ... Acts 8:36
water, and he *b* him .... Acts 8:38
he arose and was *b* .... Acts 9:18
these should not be *b* ..... Acts 10:47
be *b* in the name .... Acts 10:48
you shall be *b* with .... Acts 11:16
her household were *b* ...... Acts 16:15
all his family were *b* ...... Acts 16:33
believed and were *b* .... Acts 18:8
Into what then were you *b* .. Acts 19:3
Arise and be *b*, and wash . Acts 22:16
were *b* into Christ .... Rom 6:3
I thank God that I *b* .... 1 Cor 1:14
b the household .... 1 Cor 1:16
all were *b* into Moses ...... 1 Cor 10:2
Spirit we were all *b* ...... 1 Cor 12:13
who are *b* for the dead ... 1 Cor 15:29
as many of you as were *b* ... Gal 3:27

BAPTIZING
b them in the name of ..... Matt 28:19
b in the wilderness .... Mark 1:4
where John was *b* .... John 1:28
therefore I came *b* .... John 1:31
John also was *b* in Aenon .. John 3:23
behold, He is *b* .... John 3:26
where John was *b* .... John 10:40

BAR-JESUS (or Elymas)
A Jewish false prophet, Acts 13:6–12

BAR-JONAH
Surname of Simon (Peter), Matt 16:17

BARABBAS
A murderer released in place of Jesus, Matt 27:16–26; Acts 3:14, 15

BARAK
Defeats Jabin, Judg 4:1–24
A man of faith, Heb 11:32

BARBARIAN
nor uncircumcised, *b* .... Col 3:11

BARBARIANS
to Greeks and to *b* .... Rom 1:14

BARE
make yourselves *b* .... Is 32:11
The LORD has made *b* .... Is 52:10

BAREFOOT
covered and went *b* ..... 2 Sam 15:30
walking naked and *b* .... Is 20:2

BARLEY
a land of wheat and *b* .... Deut 8:8
loaf of *b* bread tumbled .... Judg 7:13
beginning of *b* harvest ..... Ruth 1:22
who has five *b* loaves .... John 6:9
and three quarts of *b* .... Rev 6:6

BARN
seed still in the *b* .... Hag 2:19
the wheat into my *b* ...... Matt 13:30
storehouse nor *b* .... Luke 12:24

BARNABAS
A disciple from Cyprus; gives property, Acts 4:36, 37
Supports Paul, Acts 9:27
Ministers in Antioch, Acts 11:22–30
Travels with Paul, Acts 12:25; 13—15
Breaks with Paul over John Mark, Acts 15:36–39

BARNS
so your *b* will be filled ..... Prov 3:10
b are broken down .... Joel 1:17
reap nor gather into *b* ...... Matt 6:26
I will pull down my *b* ..... Luke 12:18

BARREN
But Sarai was *b* .... Gen 11:30
b has borne seven .... 1 Sam 2:5
He grants the *b* .... Ps 113:9
"Sing, O *b*, you who have ...... Is 54:1
'Blessed are the *b* .... Luke 23:29
"Rejoice, O *b*, you who do ... Gal 4:27
you will be neither *b* .... 2 Pet 1:8

BARRENNESS
A fruitful land into *b* .... Ps 107:34

BARS
has strengthened the *b* ..... Ps 147:13
bronze and cut the *b* .... Is 45:2
the earth with its *b* .... Jon 2:6

BARSABAS
Nominated to replace Judas, Acts 1:23
Sent to Antioch, Acts 15:22

BARTHOLOMEW
Called Nathanael, John 1:45, 46
One of the twelve apostles, Matt 10:3; Acts 1:13

BARTIMAEUS
Blind beggar healed by Jesus, Mark 10:46–52

BARUCH
Son of Neriah, Jer 32:12, 13
Jeremiah's faithful friend and scribe, Jer 36:4–32

BARZILLAI
Supplies David with food, 2 Sam 17:27–29
Age restrains him from following David, 2 Sam 19:31–39

BASE
the elder, and the *b* .... Is 3:5
and the *b* things of .... 1 Cor 1:28

BASHAN
Conquered by Israel, Num 21:33–35
Assigned to Manasseh, Deut 3:13
Conquered by Hazael, king of Syria, 2 Kin 10:32, 33

BASIC
to the *b* principles .... Col 2:8
b principles of the world .... Col 2:20

BASIN
poured water into a *b* ..... John 13:5

BASINS
its shovels and its *b* .... Ex 27:3
b of silver, trimmers ..... 2 Kin 12:13
gold for the forks, the *b* .. 1 Chr 28:17
filled with blood like *b* ..... Zech 9:15

BASKET
the *b* on my head .... Gen 40:17
the *b* out of your hand ..... Deut 26:4
Blessed shall be your *b* .... Deut 28:5
Cursed shall be your *b* .... Deut 28:17
b had very good figs .... Jer 24:2
"A *b* of summer fruit .... Amos 8:2
lifted up the *b* between ..... Zech 5:9
and put it under a *b* .... Matt 5:15
under a *b*, but on a .... Luke 11:33
I was let down in a *b* ..... 2 Cor 11:33

BASKETS
there were three white *b* .. Gen 40:16
and there were two *b* .... Jer 24:1
they took up twelve *b* ..... Matt 14:20
took up seven large *b* ..... Matt 15:37

BATHED
My sword shall be *b* .... Is 34:5
to him, "He who is *b* ..... John 13:10

BATHSHEBA
Wife of Uriah, taken by David, 2 Sam 11
Her first child dies, 2 Sam 12:14–19
Bears Solomon, 2 Sam 12:24
Secures throne for Solomon, 1 Kin 1:15–31
Deceived by Adonijah, 1 Kin 2:13–25

BATS
To the moles and *b* .... Is 2:20

BATTLE
b is the LORD's .... 1 Sam 17:47
out to God in the *b* .... 1 Chr 5:20
strength for the *b* .... Ps 18:39
shield and sword of *b* .... Ps 76:3
for the day of *b* .... Prov 21:31
the *b* to the strong .... Eccl 9:11
who turn back the *b* .... Is 28:6
A sound of *b* is in the ...... Jer 50:22
who will prepare for *b*? ..... 1 Cor 14:8
became valiant in *b* .... Heb 11:34
gather them to the *b* .... Rev 16:14

BATTLE-AX
You are My *b* .... Jer 51:20

each with his *b* in his hand . . Ezek 9:2

BATTLEMENT
upon her a *b* of silver . . . . Song 8:9

BATTLES
before us and fight our *b* . . 1 Sam 8:20
to fight our *b* . . . . 2 Chr 32:8

BDELLIUM
B and the onyx stone . . . . Gen 2:12
like the color of *b* . . . . Num 11:7

BE FRUITFUL AND MULTIPLY
blessed them, saying, "*B* . . . . Gen 1:22
on the earth, and *b* . . . . Gen 8:17
"*B*, and fill the earth . . . . Gen 9:1
B; a nation and a . . . . Gen 35:11

BE GLAD AND REJOICE
I will *b* in You; I will . . . . Ps 9:2
I will *b* in Your mercy, ... Ps 31:7
We will *b* in you . . . . Song 1:4
we will *b* in His salvation . . . . . Is 25:9
you also *b* with me . . . . Phil 2:18
us *b* and give Him glory, ... Rev 19:7

BE OF GOOD CHEER
to the paralytic, "Son, *b* . . . . . Matt 9:2
her He said, "*B*, daughter . . . Matt 9:22
to them, saying, "*B* . . . . Matt 14:27
man, saying to him, "*B* . . . Mark 10:49
b, I have overcome . . . . John 16:33
by him and said, "*B* . . . . . . Acts 23:11

BEAM
on a carrying *b* . . . . Num 4:10
like a weaver's *b* . . . . 1 Sam 17:7
the *b* from the timbers . . . . . . Hab 2:11

BEAMS
paneled the temple with *b* . . 1 Kin 6:9
cedar *b* on the pillars . . . . 1 Kin 7:2
the *b* and doorposts . . . . 2 Chr 3:7
make *b* for the gates . . . . Neh 2:8
bones are like *b* . . . . Job 40:18
He lays the *b* of His . . . . Ps 104:3
b of our houses are cedar . . Song 1:17

BEAR
greater than I can *b* . . . . Gen 4:13
whom Sarah shall *b* . . . . Gen 17:21
not *b* false witness . . . . Ex 20:16
from the paw of the *b* . . . 1 Sam 17:37
they shall *b* you up in . . . . Ps 91:12
b a broken spirit . . . . Prov 18:14
be clean, you who *b* . . . . Is 52:11
b their iniquities . . . . Is 53:11
LORD could no longer *b* . . . . . Jer 44:22
b deprived of her cubs . . . . . . Hos 13:8
lion, and a *b* met him . . . . . Amos 5:19
He shall *b* the glory . . . . Zech 6:13
child, and *b* a Son . . . . Matt 1:23
A good tree cannot *b* . . . . Matt 7:18
how long shall I *b* . . . . Matt 17:17
by, to *b* His cross . . . . Mark 15:21
wife Elizabeth will *b* . . . . Luke 1:13
And whoever does not *b* . . Luke 14:27
in Me that does not *b* . . . . . . John 15:2
for he does not *b* . . . . Rom 13:4
are strong ought to *b* . . . . Rom 15:1
you may be able to *b* . . . . . 1 Cor 10:13
B one another's . . . . Gal 6:2
I *b* in my body the . . . . Gal 6:17
b the sins of many . . . . Heb 9:28
like the feet of a *b* . . . . Rev 13:2

BEAR FRUIT
take root downward, and *b* . . Is 37:31
bring forth branches, *b*, ... Ezek 17:8
shall the vine fail to *b* . . . . . . Mal 3:11
the word, accept it, and *b* . . Mark 4:20
it and *b* with patience . . . . . Luke 8:15
does not *b* He takes away . . John 15:2
branch cannot *b* of itself, . . John 15:4
that we should *b* to God . . . . . Rom 7:4
our members to *b* to death . . . Rom 7:5

BEAR WITNESS
you *b* that you approve . . . Luke 11:48
to *b* of the Light, ... John 1:7
If I *b* of Myself, ... John 5:31
"You *b* of Yourself . . . . John 8:13
Father's name, they *b* . . . . . John 10:25
And you also will *b* . . . . John 15:27
I should *b* to the truth . . . . John 18:37
must also *b* at Rome . . . . . . Acts 23:11
we have seen, and *b*, and . . . 1 John 1:2
three who *b* in heaven . . . . . 1 John 5:7
three that *b* on earth: . . . . . . 1 John 5:8

BEARD
the edges of your *b* . . . . Lev 19:27
I caught it by its *b* . . . . . . 1 Sam 17:35
took Amasa by the *b* . . . . . . 2 Sam 20:9
Running down on the *b* . . . . . Ps 133:2

BEARING
goes forth weeping, *b* . . . . Ps 126:6
And He, *b* His cross . . . . . . John 19:17
b with one another . . . . Col 3:13
the camp, *b* His reproach . . Heb 13:13

BEARS
Every branch that *b* . . . . John 15:2
b all things, believes . . . . . . 1 Cor 13:7
it is the Spirit who *b* . . . . . . 1 John 5:6

BEAST
b has devoured him . . . . Gen 37:20
You preserve man and *b* . . . . . Ps 36:6
I was like a *b* before . . . . Ps 73:22
to the *b* its food . . . . Ps 147:9
b touches the mountain . . . . Heb 12:20
And I saw a *b* rising . . . . Rev 13:1
Then I saw another *b* . . . . . . Rev 13:11
the mark of the *b* . . . . Rev 19:20

BEASTS
are we counted as *b* . . . . Job 18:3
The *b* go into dens . . . . Job 37:8
like the *b* that perish . . . . Ps 49:12
I have fought with *b* . . . . . 1 Cor 15:32
naturally, like brute *b* . . . . Jude 10

BEAT
I will *b* down his foes . . . . Ps 89:23
You shall *b* him with a . . . . Prov 23:14
b their swords into . . . . Is 2:4
you shall *b* in pieces . . . . Mic 4:13
spat in His face and *b* . . . . Matt 26:67
but *b* his breast . . . . Luke 18:13

BEATEN
and you will be *b* . . . . Mark 13:9
his will, shall be *b* . . . . Luke 12:47
Three times I was *b* . . . . . . 2 Cor 11:25
when you are *b* for your . . . 1 Pet 2:20

BEATS
one who *b* the air . . . . 1 Cor 9:26

BEAUTIFUL
of men, that they were *b* . . . . Gen 6:2
woman of *b* countenance . . Gen 12:11
that she was very *b* . . . . Gen 12:14
woman was very *b* . . . . Gen 24:16
she is *b* to behold . . . . Gen 26:7
but Rachel was *b* . . . . Gen 29:17
he was a *b* child . . . . Ex 2:2
the captives a *b* woman . . . Deut 21:11
a *b* Babylonian garment . . . . Josh 7:21
and *b* appearance . . . . 1 Sam 25:3
woman was very *b* . . . . 2 Sam 11:2
a woman of *b* . . . . 2 Sam 14:27
she was *b* to behold . . . . Esth 1:11
woman was lovely and *b* . . . . . Esth 2:7
b as the daughters of Job . . Job 42:15
B in elevation, the joy . . . . Ps 48:2
has made everything *b* . . . . . Eccl 3:11
my love, you are as *b* . . . . Song 6:4
How *b* are your feet . . . . Song 7:1
of the LORD shall be *b* . . . . Is 4:2
How *b* upon the . . . . Is 52:7
a *b* heritage of the hosts . . . . . . Jer 3:19
became very *b* . . . . Ezek 16:7
a *b* crown on your head . . Ezek 16:12
You were exceedingly *b* . . Ezek 16:13
b crowns on their heads . . Ezek 23:42
b with a multitude . . . . Ezek 31:9
indeed appear *b* . . . . Matt 23:27
adorned with *b* stones . . . . . Luke 21:5
temple which is called *B* . . . . . Acts 3:2
begging alms at the *B* . . . . . . Acts 3:10
How *b* are the feet . . . . Rom 10:15
they saw he was a *b* . . . . Heb 11:23
b appearance perishes . . . . James 1:11

BEAUTIFY
b the humble with . . . . Ps 149:4
b the place of My . . . . Is 60:13

BEAUTY
for glory and for *b* . . . . Ex 28:2
"The *b* of Israel is . . . . 2 Sam 1:19
in the *b* of holiness . . . . 1 Chr 16:29
show her *b* to the people . . . Esth 1:11
let *b* preparations be given . . . Esth 2:3
yourself with glory and *b* . . Job 40:10
To behold the *b* . . . . Ps 27:4
greatly desire your *b* . . . . Ps 45:11
Zion, the perfection of *b* . . . . . Ps 50:2
b of the LORD our God . . . . . . Ps 90:17
do not lust after her *b* . . . . . . Prov 6:25
and *b* is passing . . . . Prov 31:30
branding instead of *b* . . . . Is 3:24
glorious *b* is a fading . . . . Is 28:1
see the King in His *b* . . . . Is 33:17
no *b* that we should . . . . Is 53:2
to give them *b* for ashes . . . . . . Is 61:3
'the perfection of *b* . . . . Lam 2:15
b to be abhorred . . . . Ezek 16:25
said, 'I am perfect in *b* . . . . . Ezek 27:3
wisdom and perfect in *b* . . . Ezek 28:12
of God was like it in *b* . . . . . Ezek 31:8
the one I called *B* . . . . Zech 11:7
the incorruptible *b* . . . . 1 Pet 3:4

BECAME
man *b* a living being . . . . Gen 2:7
to the Jews I *b* as a Jew . . . 1 Cor 9:20
like me, for I *b* like you . . . . . . Gal 4:12

BED
house, if I make my *b* . . . . . . Job 17:13
I remember You on my *b* . . . . . Ps 63:6
if I make my *b* in hell . . . . Ps 139:8
Also our *b* is green . . . . Song 1:16
b is too short to stretch . . . . . . Is 28:20
you have set your *b* . . . . Is 57:7
"Arise, take up your *b* . . . . Matt 9:6
be two men in one *b* . . . . . . Luke 17:34
and the *b* undefiled . . . . Heb 13:4

BEDRIDDEN
had been *b* eight years . . . . . Acts 9:33

BEDROOM
lying on his bed in his *b* . . . 2 Sam 4:7
her brother in the *b* . . . . . . 2 Sam 13:10
and his nurse in the *b* . . . . . . 2 Kin 11:2

BEDS
sing aloud on their *b* . . . . Ps 149:5
shall rest in their *b* . . . . Is 57:2
who lie on *b* of ivory . . . . Amos 6:4

BEDSTEAD
his *b* was an iron *b* . . . . Deut 3:11

BEE
Egypt, and for the *b* . . . . Is 7:18

BEELZEBUB
Jesus accused of serving, Matt 10:25; 12:24–27

BEER LAHAI ROI
Angel meets Hagar there, Gen 16:7–14
Isaac dwells in, Gen 24:62

BEERSHEBA
God appears there to Hagar, Gen 21:14–19

to Isaac, Gen 26:23–25
to Jacob, Gen 46:1–5
to Elijah, 1 Kin 19:3–7
Oaths sworn there by Abraham, Gen 21:31–33
by Isaac, Gen 26:26–33

BEFALL
calamity *b* him .... Gen 42:4
b you in the last days .... Gen 49:1
No evil shall *b* you .... Ps 91:10

BEFOREHAND
do not worry *b* .... Mark 13:11
told you all things *b* ..... Mark 13:23
not to meditate *b* .... Luke 21:14
when He testified *b* .... 1 Pet 1:11

BEG
I would *b* mercy of my ...... Job 9:15
I am ashamed to *b* .... Luke 16:3
b you as sojourners .... 1 Pet 2:11

BEGAN
Then men *b* to call on ...... Gen 4:26
since the world *b* .... Luke 1:70

BEGETS
b a scoffer does .... Prov 17:21
b a wise child will .... Prov 23:24
b a hundred children .... Eccl 6:3

BEGGAR
lifts the *b* from the ash ...... 1 Sam 2:8
there was a certain *b* ..... Luke 16:20

BEGGARLY
weak and *b* elements .... Gal 4:9

BEGGED
So the demons *b* Him, ... Matt 8:31
they *b* Him to depart .... Matt 8:34
b him, saying, 'Have .... Matt 18:29
b Him to put His hand .... Mark 7:32
b Him earnestly, saying ..... Luke 7:4
b Him to come to his ...... Luke 8:41
not this he who sat and *b* ... John 9:8
the Gentiles *b* that these ... Acts 13:42
those who heard it *b* ...... Heb 12:19

BEGINNING
b God created the .... Gen 1:1
Though your *b* was .... Job 8:7
of the LORD is the *b* .... Ps 111:10
that God does from *b* .... Eccl 3:11
who made them at the *b* .... Matt 19:4
In the *b* was the Word .... John 1:1
This *b* of signs Jesus .... John 2:11
a murderer from the *b* ..... John 8:44
with Me from the *b* .... John 15:27
the *b*, the firstborn .... Col 1:18
having neither *b* .... Heb 7:3
True Witness, the *B* .... Rev 3:14
and the Omega, the *B* .... Rev 21:6

BEGOTTEN
See ONLY BEGOTTEN SON
today I have *b* You .... Ps 2:7
heart, 'Who has *b* .... Is 49:21
glory as of the only *b* ...... John 1:14
Christ Jesus I have *b* ...... 1 Cor 4:15
abundant mercy has *b* .... 1 Pet 1:3
loves him who is *b* .... 1 John 5:1

BEGUN
Having *b* in the Spirit .... Gal 3:3
that He who has *b* .... Phil 1:6

BEHALF
to speak on God's *b* .... Job 36:2
you on Christ's *b* .... 2 Cor 5:20
has been granted on *b* .... Phil 1:29

BEHAVE
I will *b* wisely in a .... Ps 101:2
does not *b* rudely .... 1 Cor 13:5

BEHAVED
sent him, and *b* wisely .... 1 Sam 18:5
and blamelessly we *b* .... 1 Thess 2:10

BEHAVIOR
of good *b*, hospitable .... 1 Tim 3:2
they be reverent in *b* .... Titus 2:3

BEHEADED
he sent and had John *b* ... Matt 14:10
those who had been *b* .... Rev 20:4

BEHEMOTH
Described, Job 40:15–24

BEHOLD
the eyes to *b* the sun .... Eccl 11:7
B, you are fair .... Song 1:15
B, the virgin shall .... Is 7:14
Judah, "*B* your God .... Is 40:9
B the Lamb of God .... John 1:36
I am, that they may *b* ..... John 17:24
to them, "*B* the Man .... John 19:5
B what manner of love .... 1 John 3:1

BEHOLDING
with unveiled face, *b* ..... 2 Cor 3:18

BEING
man became a living *b* .... Gen 2:7
God while I have my *b* ..... Ps 104:33
move and have our *b* ..... Acts 17:28
who, *b* in the form of .... Phil 2:6

BEL
Patron god of Babylon, Is 46:1; Jer 50:2; 51:44

BELIEF
by the Spirit and *b* ...... 2 Thess 2:13

BELIEVE
b me or listen to my voice ...... Ex 4:1
will they not *b* Me .... Num 14:11
did not *b* the LORD .... Deut 1:32
I did not *b* the words ...... 1 Kin 10:7
B in the LORD your God .. 2 Chr 20:20
did not *b* in His wondrous ... Ps 78:32
which you would not *b* .... Hab 1:5
ones who *b* in Me to sin .... Matt 18:6
'Why then did you not *b* .. Matt 21:25
cross, and we will *b* Him .. Matt 27:42
Repent, and *b* .... Mark 1:15
Do not be afraid; only *b* ... Mark 5:36
tears, "Lord, I *b* .... Mark 9:24
b in Me to stumble .... Mark 9:42
b that you receive .... Mark 11:24
that we may see and *b* ... Mark 15:32
because they did not *b* .. Mark 16:14
have no root, who *b* .... Luke 8:13
only *b*, and she will .... Luke 8:50
will by no means *b* .... Luke 22:67
and slow of heart to *b* .... Luke 24:25
all through him might *b* ...... John 1:7
to those who *b* .... John 1:12
how will you *b* .... John 3:12
Now we *b*, not because .... John 4:42
sent, Him you do not *b* .... John 5:38
we may see it and *b* .... John 6:30
we have come to *b* .... John 6:69
brothers did not *b* in Him ... John 7:5
not *b* that I am He .... John 8:24
to him, "Do you *b* .... John 9:35
not *b*, because you .... John 10:26
b that the Father is in Me . John 10:38
b that You are the Christ . John 11:27
this, that they may *b* ...... John 11:42
they did not *b* in Him ..... John 12:37
may *b* that I am He .... John 13:19
you *b* in God, *b* also in ..... John 14:1
B Me that I am in .... John 14:11
we *b* that You came .... John 16:30
b that You sent Me .... John 17:21
truth, so that you may *b* .. John 19:35
into His side, I will not *b* .. John 20:25
written that you may *b* ... John 20:31
word of the gospel and *b* ... Acts 15:7
"*B* on the Lord Jesus ..... Acts 16:31
b on Him who would .... Acts 19:4
King Agrippa, do you *b* ... Acts 26:27
to all and on all who *b* ...... Rom 3:22

father of all those who *b* ... Rom 4:11
the Lord Jesus and *b* .... Rom 10:9
And how shall they *b* ..... Rom 10:14
to save those who *b* .... 1 Cor 1:21
a wife who does not *b* ..... 1 Cor 7:12
I spoke," we also *b* .... 2 Cor 4:13
given to those who *b* .... Gal 3:22
Christ, not only to *b* .... Phil 1:29
if we *b* that Jesus died ... 1 Thess 4:14
should *b* the lie .... 2 Thess 2:11
of those who *b* .... 1 Tim 4:10
comes to God must *b* .... Heb 11:6
Even the demons *b* .... James 2:19
to you who *b*, He .... 1 Pet 2:7
should *b* on the name .... 1 John 3:23
Beloved, do not *b* .... 1 John 4:1
written to you who *b* ..... 1 John 5:13

BELIEVED
And he *b* in the LORD ...... Gen 15:6
So the people *b* .... Ex 4:31
b that I would see the .... Ps 27:13
Who has *b* our report .... Is 53:1
people of Nineveh *b* .... Jon 3:5
Blessed is she who *b* .... Luke 1:45
they *b* the Scripture .... John 2:22
because he has not *b* ...... John 3:18
of that city *b* in Him .... John 4:39
you *b* Moses, you would ... John 5:46
Jesus did, *b* in Him .... John 11:45
who has *b* our report ..... John 12:38
and he saw and *b* .... John 20:8
seen Me, you have *b* ..... John 20:29
who heard the word *b* .... Acts 4:4
of those who *b* were of ..... Acts 4:32
appointed to eternal life *b* . Acts 13:48
Holy Spirit when you *b* ..... Acts 19:2
"Abraham *b* God .... Rom 4:3
in whom they have not *b* .. Rom 10:14
than when we first *b* ...... Rom 13:11
unless you *b* in vain .... 1 Cor 15:2
'I *b* and therefore I spoke .. 2 Cor 4:13
b God, and it was accounted .. Gal 3:6
b on in the world .... 1 Tim 3:16
I know whom I have *b* .... 2 Tim 1:12
b the love that God has .. 1 John 4:16

BELIEVERS
be an example to the *b* .... 1 Tim 4:12
are benefited are *b* .... 1 Tim 6:2

BELIEVES
See HE WHO BELIEVES
The simple *b* every .... Prov 14:15
possible to him who *b* ...... Mark 9:23
b that those things he .... Mark 11:23
He who *b* and is .... Mark 16:16
that whoever *b* in Him ..... John 3:16
He who *b* in the Son .... John 3:36
b in Him who sent Me ...... John 5:24
who *b* in Me shall never ... John 6:35
b in Him may have .... John 6:40
he who *b* in Me has .... John 6:47
He who *b* in Me, as the .... John 7:38
He who *b* in Me, though .. John 11:25
He who *b* in Me .... John 12:44
whoever *b* in Him .... Acts 10:43
Him everyone who *b* is .... Acts 13:39
for everyone who *b* .... Rom 1:16
to everyone who *b* .... Rom 10:4
with the heart one *b* .... Rom 10:10
b all things, hopes all ..... 1 Cor 13:7
Whoever *b* that Jesus is ... 1 John 5:1
he who *b* that Jesus is ..... 1 John 5:5
b in the Son of God ...... 1 John 5:10

BELIEVING
you ask in prayer, *b* ...... Matt 21:22
b you may have life ...... John 20:31
take along a *b* wife .... 1 Cor 9:5
blessed with *b* Abraham .... Gal 3:9
those who have *b* masters ... 1 Tim 6:2

BELLY
On your *b* you shall go ...... Gen 3:14

And Jonah was in the *b* . . . . Jon 1:17
three nights in the *b* . . . . . Matt 12:40
whose god is their *b* . . . . Phil 3:19

BELONG

interpretations *b* to God . . . . Gen 40:8
highest heavens *b* to . . . . . . Deut 10:14
secret things *b* to . . . . Deut 29:29
"Dominion and fear *b* . . . . Job 25:2
shields of the earth *b* . . . . Ps 47:9
things also *b* to the wise . . Prov 24:23
To the Lord our God *b* . . . . Dan 9:9
My name, because you *b* . . Mark 9:41
to whom *b* the glory . . . . 1 Pet 4:11

BELONGS

offering that *b* to the LORD . . Lev 7:20
Salvation *b* to the LORD . . . . Ps 3:8
that power *b* to God . . . . Ps 62:11
to You, O Lord, *b* mercy . . . . Ps 62:12
shield *b* to the LORD . . . . Ps 89:18
to whom vengeance *b* . . . . Ps 94:1
righteousness *b* to You . . . . . . Dan 9:7
solid food *b* to those . . . . Heb 5:14
b to another tribe . . . . Heb 7:13
"Salvation *b* to our God . . . . . Rev 7:10

BELOVED

"The *b* of the Lord . . . . Deut 33:12
so He gives His *b* . . . . Ps 127:2
of myrrh is my *b* . . . . Song 1:13
My *b* is mine, and I am . . . . Song 2:16
b more than another . . . . Song 5:9
Where has your *b* . . . . Song 6:1
leaning upon her *b* . . . . Song 8:5
a song of my *B* . . . . Is 5:1
for you are greatly *b* . . . . Dan 9:23
"This is My *b* Son . . . . Matt 3:17
election they are *b* . . . . Rom 11:28
us accepted in the *B* . . . . Eph 1:6
Luke the *b* physician . . . . Col 4:14
than a slave as a *b* . . . . Philem 16
"This is My *b* Son . . . . 2 Pet 1:17
our *b* brother Paul . . . . 2 Pet 3:15
the saints and the *b* . . . . Rev 20:9

BELOVED SON

saying, "This is My *b*. . . . . . . Matt 3:17
"This is My *b*, in whom . . . . Matt 17:5
I will send my *b*. . . . . Luke 20:13
To Timothy, a *b*: . . . . 2 Tim 1:2

BELSHAZZAR

King of Babylon; Daniel interprets his dream, Dan 5

BELT

with a leather *b* . . . . Matt 3:4
us, he took Paul's *b* . . . . . . Acts 21:11

BELTESHAZZAR

Daniel's Babylonian name, Dan 1:7

BEMOAN

Or who will *b* you . . . . Jer 15:5
for the dead, nor *b* . . . . Jer 22:10

BEN-AMMI

Son of Lot; father of the Ammonites, Gen 19:38

BEN-HADAD

Ben-Hadad I, king of Damascus; hired by Asa, king of Judah, to attack Baasha, king of Israel, 1 Kin 15:18–21
——— Ben-Hadad II, king of Damascus; makes war on Ahab, king of Israel, 1 Kin 20
Falls in siege against Samaria, 2 Kin 6:24–33; 7:6–20
Killed by Hazael, 2 Kin 8:7–15
——— Ben-Hadad III, king of Damascus; loses all Israelite conquests made by Hazael, his father, 2 Kin 13:3–25

BEN-ONI

Rachel's name for Benjamin, Gen 35:16–18

BENAIAH

The son of Jehoiada; a mighty man, 2 Sam 23:20–23
Faithful to David, 2 Sam 15:18; 20:23
Escorts Solomon to the throne, 1 Kin 1:38–40
Executes Adonijah, Joab and Shimei, 1 Kin 2:25, 29–34, 46
——— A Pirathonite; another of David's mighty men, 2 Sam 23:30
Divisional commander, 1 Chr 27:14

BEND

The wicked *b* their bow . . . . . . Ps 11:2

BENEATH

and on the earth *b* . . . . Deut 4:39
"You are from *b* . . . . John 8:23

BENEFACTORS

them are called '*b* . . . . Luke 22:25

BENEFIT

That I may see the *b* . . . . Ps 106:5
people who could not *b* . . . . Is 30:5
might have a second *b* . . . . 2 Cor 1:15

BENEFITS

daily loads us with *b* . . . . Ps 68:19
forget not all His *b* . . . . Ps 103:2
for all His *b* toward me . . . . . Ps 116:12

BENJAMIN

Jacob's youngest son, Gen 35:16–20
Taken to Egypt against Jacob's wishes, Gen 42—45
Jacob's prophecy concerning, Gen 49:27
——— Tribe of:
Families of, Num 26:38–41
Territory allotted to, Josh 18:11–28
Attacked by remaining tribes for condoning sin of Gibeah, Judg 20:12–48
Wives provided for remnant of, Judg 21:1–23
Tribe of Saul, 1 Sam 9:1, 2
of Paul, Phil 3:5

BENT

have *b* their bow, ... Ps 37:14
and all their bows *b* . . . . Is 5:28
behold, this vine *b* . . . . Ezek 17:7
hearts shall be *b* on evil . . . Dan 11:27
I have *b* Judah, My bow, . . . Zech 9:13
was *b* over and could . . . . Luke 13:11

BEREA

A city of Macedonia; visited by Paul, Acts 17:10–15

BEREAVE

I will *b* them of . . . . Jer 15:7
no more shall you *b* . . . . . . Ezek 36:12
children, yet I will *b* . . . . Hos 9:12

BERNICE

Sister of Herod Agrippa II, Acts 25:13, 23
Hears Paul's defense, Acts 26:1–30

BERODACH-BALADAN

See MERODACH-BALADAN
A king of Babylon, 2 Kin 20:12–19

BERYL

fourth row, a *b* . . . . Ex 28:20
a *b*, an onyx . . . . Ex 39:13
rods of gold set with *b* . . . . . Song 5:14
was like the color of *b* . . . . . Ezek 1:16
the color of a *b* . . . . Ezek 10:9
topaz, and diamond, *b* . . . . . Ezek 28:13
His body was like *b* . . . . Dan 10:6
chrysolite, the eighth *b* . . . . Rev 21:20

BESEECH

Return, we *b* You . . . . Ps 80:14
b you therefore . . . . Rom 12:1
of the LORD, *b* you to . . . . Eph 4:1

BESIDE

He leads me *b* the . . . . Ps 23:2

"Paul, you are *b* . . . . Acts 26:24
For if we are *b* . . . . 2 Cor 5:13

BESIEGED

Joab *b* the city . . . . 2 Sam 11:16
went up and *b* Samaria . . . . 2 Kin 6:24
and the city was *b* . . . . 2 Kin 24:10
of cucumbers, as a *b* city . . . . Is 1:8
army *b* Jerusalem . . . . Jer 32:2
to Jerusalem and *b* it . . . . Dan 1:1

BEST

with the *b* ointments . . . . Amos 6:6
b seats in the synagogues . . Matt 23:6
b places at feasts . . . . Mark 12:39
sit down in the *b* place . . . . Luke 14:8
'Bring out the *b* . . . . Luke 15:22
earnestly desire the *b* . . . . 1 Cor 12:31

BESTOW

LORD, that He may *b*. . . . . Ex 32:29
b greater honor . . . . 1 Cor 12:23

BESTOWED

love the Father has *b* . . . . . . 1 John 3:1

BETH HORON

Twin towns of Ephraim, Josh 16:3, 5
Fortified by Solomon, 2 Chr 8:3–5
Prominent in battles, Josh 10:10–14; 1 Sam 13:18

BETH PEOR

Town near Pisgah, Deut 3:29
Moses buried near, Deut 34:6
Assigned to Reubenites, Josh 13:15, 20

BETH SHAN (or Beth Shean)

A town in Issachar, Josh 17:11–16
Saul's corpse hung up at, 1 Sam 31:10–13; 2 Sam 21:12–14

BETH SHEMESH

Ark brought to, 1 Sam 6:12–19
Joash defeats Amaziah at, 2 Kin 14:11
Taken by Philistines, 2 Chr 28:18

BETHABARA

A place beyond the Jordan where John baptized, John 1:28

BETHANY

A town on the Mt. of Olives, Luke 19:29
Home of Lazarus, John 11:1
Home of Simon, the leper, Matt 26:6
Jesus visits there, Mark 11:1, 11, 12
Scene of the ascension, Luke 24:50, 51

BETHEL

Abram settles near, Gen 12:7, 8
Site of Abram's altar, Gen 13:3, 4
Site of Jacob's vision of the ladder, Gen 28:10–19
Jacob returns to, Gen 35:1–15
Samuel judges there, 1 Sam 7:15, 16
Site of worship and sacrifice, 1 Sam 10:3
Center of idolatry, 1 Kin 12:28–33
Josiah destroys altars of, 2 Kin 23:4, 15–20
Denounced by prophets, 1 Kin 13:1–10; Amos 7:10–13; Jer 48:13; Hos 10:15

BETHESDA

Jerusalem pool, John 5:2–4

BETHLEHEM

Originally called Ephrath, Gen 35:16
Rachel buried there, Gen 35:19
Home of Naomi and Boaz, Ruth 1:1, 19; 4:9–11
Home of David, 1 Sam 16:1–18
Predicted place of Messiah's birth, Mic 5:2
Christ born there, Matt 2:1; Luke 2:4–7; John 7:42
Infants of, killed by Herod, Matt 2:16–18

BETHPHAGE

Village near Bethany, Mark 11:1

Near Mt. of Olives, Matt 21:1

BETHSAIDA
A city of Galilee, Mark 6:45
Home of Andrew, Peter and Philip, John 1:44; 12:21
Blind man healed there, Mark 8:22, 23
5,000 fed nearby, Luke 9:10–17
Unbelief of, denounced, Matt 11:21; Luke 10:13

BETRAY
the outcasts, do not *b* ... Is 16:3
you, one of you will *b* ... Matt 26:21
Now brother will *b* ... Mark 13:12

BETRAYED
Man is about to be *b* ... Matt 17:22
in which He was *b* ... 1 Cor 11:23

BETRAYER
See, My *b* is at hand ... Matt 26:46

BETRAYING
"Judas, are you *b* ... Luke 22:48

BETRAYS
who is the one who *b* ... John 21:20

BETROTH
"You shall *b* a wife ... Deut 28:30
"I will *b* you to Me ... Hos 2:19

BETROTHED
a virgin who is not *b* ... Ex 22:16
finds a *b* young woman ... Deut 22:25
I *b* to myself for a ... 2 Sam 3:14
mother Mary was *b* to ... Matt 1:18
to a virgin *b* to a man ... Luke 1:27
For I have *b* you to ... 2 Cor 11:2

BETTER
obey is *b* than sacrifice ... 1 Sam 15:22
It is *b* to trust in ... Ps 118:8
B is a little with the ... Prov 15:16
B is a dry morsel ... Prov 17:1
B is the poor who ... Prov 19:1
B to dwell in ... Prov 21:19
b is a neighbor ... Prov 27:10
B a handful with ... Eccl 4:6
Two are *b* than one ... Eccl 4:9
B a poor and wise ... Eccl 4:13
were the former days *b* ... Eccl 7:10
features appeared *b* ... Dan 1:15
For it is *b* to marry ... 1 Cor 7:9
Christ, which is far *b* ... Phil 1:23
b than the angels ... Heb 1:4
b things concerning ... Heb 6:9
b things than that ... Heb 12:24

BEULAH
A symbol of true Israel, Is 62:4, 5

BEVERAGE
lacks no blended *b* ... Song 7:2

BEWAIL
Israel, *b* the burning ... Lev 10:6
b my virginity ... Judg 11:37
I will *b* the vine ... Is 16:9

BEWARE
"*B* of false prophets ... Matt 7:15
b of evil workers ... Phil 3:2
B lest anyone cheat ... Col 2:8

BEWILDERED
"They are *b* by the land ... Ex 14:3

BEWITCHED
b you that you should ... Gal 3:1

BEYOND
b what is written ... 1 Cor 4:6
yes, and *b* their ability ... 2 Cor 8:3
advanced in Judaism *b* ... Gal 1:14

BEZALEL
Hur's grandson, 1 Chr 2:20
Tabernacle builder, Ex 31:1–11; 35:30–35

BEZER
A city of refuge in the territory of Reuben, Deut 4:43; John 20:8

BILDAD
One of Job's friends, Job 2:11
Makes three speeches, Job 8:1–22; 18:1–21; 25:1–6

BILHAH
Rachel's maid, Gen 29:29
The mother of Dan and Naphtali, Gen 30:1–8
Commits incest with Reuben, Gen 35:22

BILLOWS
b have gone over me ... Ps 42:7
all Your *b* and Your ... Jon 2:3

BIND
b them as a sign ... Deut 6:8
b this line of scarlet ... Josh 2:18
b the cluster of the ... Job 38:31
b the wild ox in the ... Job 39:10
b the sacrifice with cords ... Ps 118:27
b them around your ... Prov 3:3
B them continually upon ... Prov 6:21
B them on your fingers ... Prov 7:3
B up the testimony ... Is 8:16
but He will *b* us up ... Hos 6:1
and whatever you *b* ... Matt 16:19
'*B* him hand and foot ... Matt 22:13
b heavy burdens ... Matt 23:4
b the man who owns this ... Acts 21:11

BINDS
first *b* the strong man ... Matt 12:29

BIRD
the blood of the *b* ... Lev 14:52
with him as with a *b* ... Job 41:5
soul, "Flee as a *b* ... Ps 11:1
has escaped as a *b* ... Ps 124:7
b hastens to the snare ... Prov 7:23
for a *b* of the air may ... Eccl 10:20
fly away like a *b* ... Hos 9:11
unclean and hated *b* ... Rev 18:2

BIRDS
b will eat your flesh ... Gen 40:19
b make their nests ... Ps 104:17
b caught in a snare ... Eccl 9:12
Look at the *b* of the air ... Matt 6:26
"Foxes have holes and *b* ... Matt 8:20

BIRTH
cursed the day of his *b* ... Job 3:1
heaven, who gives it *b* ... Job 38:29
makes the deer give *b* ... Ps 29:9
the day of one's *b* ... Eccl 7:1
bring to the time of *b* ... Is 66:9
the deer also gave *b* ... Jer 14:5
no *b*, no pregnancy ... Hos 9:11
Now the *b* of Jesus ... Matt 1:18
will rejoice at his *b* ... Luke 1:14
who was blind from *b* ... John 9:1
labors with *b* pangs ... Rom 8:22
conceived, it gives *b* ... James 1:15

BIRTHDAY
which was Pharaoh's *b* ... Gen 40:20
b gave a feast for his ... Mark 6:21

BIRTHRIGHT
"Sell me your *b* ... Gen 25:31
Esau despised his *b* ... Gen 25:34
according to his *b* ... Gen 43:33
of food sold his *b* ... Heb 12:16

BIRTHSTOOLS
see them on the *b* ... Ex 1:16

BISHOP
the position of a *b* ... 1 Tim 3:1
b must be blameless ... Titus 1:7

BIT
and they *b* the people ... Num 21:6
be harnessed with *b* ... Ps 32:9

BITE
A serpent may *b* ... Eccl 10:11
But if you *b* and ... Gal 5:15

BITHYNIA
The Spirit keeps Paul from, Acts 16:7
Peter writes to Christians of, 1 Pet 1:1

BITS
the great house into *b* ... Amos 6:11
Indeed, we put *b* ... James 3:3

BITTER
made their lives *b* ... Ex 1:14
b herbs they shall eat it ... Ex 12:8
to those who are *b* ... Prov 31:6
who put *b* for sweet ... Is 5:20
and do not be *b* ... Col 3:19
But if you have *b* ... James 3:14
make your stomach *b* ... Rev 10:9

BITTERLY
has dealt very *b* ... Ruth 1:20
And Hezekiah wept *b* ... 2 Kin 20:3
he went out and wept *b* ... Matt 26:75

BITTERNESS
man dies in the *b* ... Job 21:25
heart knows its own *b* ... Prov 14:10
all my years in the *b* ... Is 38:15
you are poisoned by *b* ... Acts 8:23
b springing up cause ... Heb 12:15

BLACK
My skin grows *b* ... Job 30:30
wavy, and *b* as a raven ... Song 5:11
one hair white or *b* ... Matt 5:36
a *b* horse and he who sat ... Rev 6:5
and the sun became *b* ... Rev 6:12

BLACKNESS
the heavens with *b* ... Is 50:3
whom is reserved the *b* ... Jude 13

BLACKSMITH
no *b* to be found ... 1 Sam 13:19
The *b* with the tongs ... Is 44:12
I have created the *b* ... Is 54:16

BLADE
went in after the *b* ... Judg 3:22
first the *b*, then the head ... Mark 4:28

BLAME
that anyone should *b* ... 2 Cor 8:20
be holy and without *b* ... Eph 1:4

BLAMELESS
walk before Me and be *b* ... Gen 17:1
You shall be *b* ... Deut 18:13
b before Him, and I ... 2 Sam 22:24
and that man was *b* ... Job 1:1
a *b* and upright man ... Job 1:8
a *b* and upright man ... Job 2:3
will not cast away the *b* ... Job 8:20
though I were *b* ... Job 9:20
b who is ridiculed ... Job 12:4
make your ways *b* ... Job 22:3
I was also *b* before Him ... Ps 18:23
Then I shall be *b* ... Ps 19:13
Mark the *b* man ... Ps 37:37
when You speak, and *b* ... Ps 51:4
Let my heart be *b* ... Ps 119:80
the *b* will remain ... Prov 2:21
righteousness of the *b* ... Prov 11:5
the *b* in their ways ... Prov 11:20
the *b* will inherit good ... Prov 28:10
Sabbath, and are *b* ... Matt 12:5
end, that you may be *b* ... 1 Cor 1:8
that you may become *b* ... Phil 2:15
which is in the law, *b* ... Phil 3:6
you holy, and *b* ... Col 1:22
your hearts *b* in ... 1 Thess 3:13
body be preserved *b* ... 1 Thess 5:23
bishop then must be *b* ... 1 Tim 3:2
deacons, being found *b* ... 1 Tim 3:10
man is *b*, the husband ... Titus 1:6
a bishop must be *b* ... Titus 1:7
without spot and *b* ... 2 Pet 3:14

BLAMELESSLY
b we behaved ... 1 Thess 2:10

BLANKET
covered him with a *b* ... Judg 4:18

BLASPHEME
b Your name forever ... Ps 74:10
compelled them to *b* ... Acts 26:11
may learn not to *b* ... 1 Tim 1:20
b that noble name ... James 2:7
God, to *b* His name ... Rev 13:6

BLASPHEMED
a foolish people has *b* ... Ps 74:18
b continually every ... Is 52:5
who passed by *b* Him ... Matt 27:39
who were hanged *b* ... Luke 23:39
The name of God is *b* ... Rom 2:24
doctrine may not be *b* ... 1 Tim 6:1
On their part He is *b* ... 1 Pet 4:14
great heat, and they *b* ... Rev 16:9

BLASPHEMER
I was formerly a *b* ... 1 Tim 1:13

BLASPHEMERS
boasters, proud, *b* ... 2 Tim 3:2

BLASPHEMES
b the name of the LORD ... Lev 24:16
"This Man *b*!" ... Matt 9:3
who *b* against the Holy ... Mark 3:29
to him who *b* against ... Luke 12:10

BLASPHEMIES
false witness, *b* ... Matt 15:19
is this who speaks *b* ... Luke 5:21
great things and *b* ... Rev 13:5

BLASPHEMY
trouble and rebuke and *b* ... Is 37:3
but the *b* against ... Matt 12:31
"He has spoken *b* ... Matt 26:65
You have heard the *b* ... Mark 14:64
not stone You, but for *b* ... John 10:33
mouth in *b* against God ... Rev 13:6
was full of names of *b* ... Rev 17:3

BLAST
By the *b* of God they ... Job 4:9
for the *b* of the terrible ... Is 25:4

BLASTED
"I *b* you with blight ... Amos 4:9

BLEATING
"What then is this *b* ... 1 Sam 15:14

BLEMISH
shall be without *b* ... Ex 12:5
LORD, a ram without *b* ... Lev 6:6
be holy and without *b* ... Eph 5:27
as of a lamb without *b* ... 1 Pet 1:19

BLEMISHED
to the Lord what is *b* ... Mal 1:14

BLESS
I will *b* you and make ... Gen 12:2
b those who *b* you ... Gen 12:3
blessing I will *b* you ... Gen 22:17
I will *b* you and multiply ... Gen 26:24
b you before I die ... Gen 27:4
"*B* me—me also ... Gen 27:34
You go unless You *b* ... Gen 32:26
He will *b* your bread ... Ex 23:25
"The LORD *b* you and ... Num 6:24
whom you *b* is blessed ... Num 22:6
Gerizim to *b* the people ... Deut 27:12
returned to *b* his house ... 1 Chr 16:43
b the LORD at all ... Ps 34:1
b with their mouth ... Ps 62:4
b You while I live ... Ps 63:4
b His holy name ... Ps 103:1
b the house of Israel ... Ps 115:12
b those who fear the ... Ps 115:13
b you in the name of ... Ps 129:8
I will abundantly *b* ... Ps 132:15
this day forward I will *b* ... Hag 2:19
b those who curse ... Luke 6:28
B those who persecute ... Rom 12:14
Being reviled, we *b* ... 1 Cor 4:12
of blessing which we *b* ... 1 Cor 10:16
"blessing I will *b* you ... Heb 6:14
With it we *b* our God ... James 3:9

BLESS THE LORD
then you shall *b* your God ... Deut 8:10
the assembly, "Now *b* ... 1 Chr 29:20
Stand up and *b* ... Neh 9:5
I will *b* who has given ... Ps 16:7
the congregations I will *b* ... Ps 26:12
I will *b* at all times; ... Ps 34:1
B, O my soul; and all ... Ps 103:1
B, O my soul! O LORD ... Ps 104:1
we will *b* from this time ... Ps 115:18
b, all you servants ... Ps 134:1
B, O house of Israel! ... Ps 135:19

BLESSED
And God *b* them ... Gen 1:22
God *b* the seventh day ... Gen 2:3
God *b* Noah and his sons ... Gen 9:1
the earth shall be *b* ... Gen 12:3
b be those who ... Gen 27:29
indeed he shall be *b* ... Gen 27:33
b the Sabbath day ... Ex 20:11
he whom you bless is *b* ... Num 22:6
b, and I cannot reverse ... Num 23:20
B is he who blesses ... Num 24:9
B shall you be in the city ... Deut 28:3
b among women is Jael ... Judg 5:24
grew, and the LORD *b* ... Judg 13:24
the LORD *b* Obed-Edom ... 2 Sam 6:11
You have *b* the work of ... Job 1:10
B is the man who walks ... Ps 1:1
B is the man to whom ... Ps 32:2
B is the nation whose ... Ps 33:12
B is he who considers ... Ps 41:1
B are those who keep ... Ps 106:3
B is he who comes ... Ps 118:26
b who fears the LORD ... Ps 128:4
rise up and call her *b* ... Prov 31:28
nations will call you *b* ... Mal 3:12
B are the poor in ... Matt 5:3
B are those who mourn ... Matt 5:4
B are the meek ... Matt 5:5
B are those who hunger ... Matt 5:6
B are the merciful ... Matt 5:7
B are the pure in ... Matt 5:8
B are the peacemakers ... Matt 5:9
B are those who are ... Matt 5:10
B are you when they ... Matt 5:11
b is he who is not ... Matt 11:6
b are your eyes ... Matt 13:16
B is He who comes ... Matt 21:9
hand, 'Come, you *b* ... Matt 25:34
Jesus took bread, *b* ... Matt 26:26
b are you among women ... Luke 1:28
'*B* is He who comes ... Luke 13:35
know these things, *b* ... John 13:17
B are those who have ... John 20:29
'It is more *b* to give ... Acts 20:35
the Creator, who is *b* ... Rom 1:25
all, the eternally *b* ... Rom 9:5
B be the God and Father ... 2 Cor 1:3
b with believing Abraham ... Gal 3:9
B be the God and ... Eph 1:3
b God which was ... 1 Tim 1:11
the lesser is *b* by the better ... Heb 7:7
this one will be *b* ... James 1:25
B is he who reads ... Rev 1:3
'*B* are the dead who ... Rev 14:13
B is he who watches ... Rev 16:15
B are those who are ... Rev 19:9
B and holy is he who ... Rev 20:6
B is he who keeps the ... Rev 22:7
B are those who do His ... Rev 22:14

BLESSED BE THE LORD
B God of my master ... Gen 24:27
"*B*, who has delivered you ... Ex 18:10
"*B*, who has not left you ... Ruth 4:14
"*B*, who has pleaded ... 1 Sam 25:39
'*B* God of Israel, who ... 1 Kin 1:48
B God of Israel from ... 1 Chr 16:36
B God of our fathers, ... Ezra 7:27
B, because He has heard ... Ps 28:6
B, for he has shown me ... Ps 31:21
B, who daily loads us ... Ps 68:19
B, who has not given us ... Ps 124:6
B my Rock, who trains ... Ps 144:1

BLESSING
and you shall be a *b* ... Gen 12:2
the *b* of Abraham ... Gen 28:4
I will command My *b* ... Lev 25:21
before you today a *b* ... Deut 11:26
LORD will command the *b* ... Deut 28:8
life and death, *b* ... Deut 30:19
exalted above all *b* ... Neh 9:5
The *b* of a perishing ... Job 29:13
Your *b* is upon Your ... Ps 3:8
did not delight in *b* ... Ps 109:17
The *b* of the LORD ... Prov 10:22
My *b* on your offspring ... Is 44:3
shall be showers of *b* ... Ezek 34:26
relent, and leave a *b* ... Joel 2:14
and you shall be a *b* ... Zech 8:13
pour out for you such *b* ... Mal 3:10
the fullness of the *b* ... Rom 15:29
b which we bless ... 1 Cor 10:16
that the *b* of Abraham ... Gal 3:14
with every spiritual *b* ... Eph 1:3
cultivated, receives *b* ... Heb 6:7
"Surely *b* I will bless you ... Heb 6:14
to inherit the *b* ... Heb 12:17
same mouth proceed *b* ... James 3:10
honor and glory and *b* ... Rev 5:12

BLESSINGS
of the law, the *b* ... Josh 8:34
B are on the head of ... Prov 10:6

BLEW
b them into the Red Sea ... Ex 10:19
b the trumpets, and the ... Josh 6:8
Then Saul *b* the trumpet ... 1 Sam 13:3
the priests regularly *b* ... 1 Chr 16:6
came, and the winds *b* ... Matt 7:25

BLIGHT
"I blasted you with *b* ... Amos 4:9
I struck you with *b* ... Hag 2:17

BLIND
I was eyes to the *b* ... Job 29:15
B yourselves and be ... Is 29:9
To open *b* eyes ... Is 42:7
I will bring the *b* ... Is 42:16
b people who have eyes ... Is 43:8
His watchmen are *b* ... Is 56:10
They wandered *b* ... Lam 4:14
when you offer the *b* ... Mal 1:8
The *b* see and the lame ... Matt 11:5
if the *b* leads the *b* ... Matt 15:14
of sight to the *b* ... Luke 4:18
to Him, "Are we *b* ... John 9:40
miserable, poor, *b* ... Rev 3:17

BLINDED
b their eyes and ... John 12:40
and the rest were *b* ... Rom 11:7
of this age has *b* ... 2 Cor 4:4
the darkness has *b* ... 1 John 2:11

BLINDFOLD
to *b* Him, and to beat ... Mark 14:65

BLINDS
a bribe, for a bribe *b* ... Deut 16:19

BLOCK
See STUMBLING BLOCK
not to put a stumbling *b* ... Rom 14:13
the Jews a stumbling *b* ... 1 Cor 1:23

BLOOD
See FLESH AND BLOOD; INNOCENT BLOOD
of your brother's *b* ... Gen 4:10
life, that is, its *b* ... Gen 9:4
b shall be shed ... Gen 9:6
the tunic in the *b* ... Gen 37:31

you are a husband of *b* .... Ex 4:25
river were turned to *b* .... Ex 7:20
when I see the *b*, I will .... Ex 12:13
the *b* of the covenant .... Ex 24:8
b that makes atonement .... Lev 17:11
b sustains its life .... Lev 17:14
do not cover my *b* .... Job 16:18
is there in my *b* .... Ps 30:9
And condemn innocent *b* .... Ps 94:21
hands are full of *b* .... Is 1:15
also disclose her *b* .... Is 26:21
to you in your *b* .... Ezek 16:6
And the moon into *b* .... Joel 2:31
to the *b* of Zechariah ...... Matt 23:35
For this is My *b* .... Matt 26:28
betraying innocent *b* .... Matt 27:4
called the Field of *B* .... Matt 27:8
b of this just Person .... Matt 27:24
"His *b* be on us and ...... Matt 27:25
new covenant in My *b* .... Luke 22:20
b falling down .... Luke 22:44
were born, not of *b* .... John 1:13
b has eternal life .... John 6:54
that is, Field of *B* .... Acts 1:19
the moon into *b* .... Acts 2:20
b every nation of men ..... Acts 17:26
with His own *b* .... Acts 20:28
propitiation by His *b* .... Rom 3:25
justified by His *b* .... Rom 5:9
communion of the *b* ..... 1 Cor 10:16
b cannot inherit .... 1 Cor 15:50
confer with flesh and *b* .... Gal 1:16
redemption through His *b* .... Eph 1:7
brought near by the *b* .... Eph 2:13
against flesh and *b* .... Eph 6:12
peace through the *b* .... Col 1:20
His own *b* He entered .... Heb 9:12
"This is the *b* of the .... Heb 9:20
are purified with *b* .... Heb 9:22
the Holiest by the *b* .... Heb 10:19
sprinkling of the *b* .... 1 Pet 1:2
with the precious *b* .... 1 Pet 1:19
b of Jesus Christ His ...... 1 John 1:7
the water, and the *b* .... 1 John 5:8
our sins in His own *b* .... Rev 1:5
us to God by Your *b* .... Rev 5:9
moon became like *b* .... Rev 6:12
them white in the *b* .... Rev 7:14
the sea became *b* .... Rev 8:8
overcame him by the *b* .... Rev 12:11
with the *b* of the martyrs .... Rev 17:6
a robe dipped in *b* .... Rev 19:13

BLOODSHED
me from the guilt of *b* .... Ps 51:14
the land is full of *b* .... Ezek 9:9
build up Zion with *b* .... Mic 3:10

BLOODTHIRSTY
The LORD abhors the *b* .... Ps 5:6
B and deceitful men .... Ps 55:23

BLOSSOM
Israel shall *b* and bud .... Is 27:6
and *b* as the rose .... Is 35:1
the fig tree may not *b* ...... Hab 3:17

BLOT
b me out of Your book ...... Ex 32:32
say that He would *b* ...... 2 Kin 14:27
from my sins, and *b* .... Ps 51:9
and I will not *b* .... Rev 3:5

BLOTTED
Let them be *b* out of .... Ps 69:28
I have *b* out, like a thick ..... Is 44:22
your sins may be *b* .... Acts 3:19

BLOW
b the trumpets over .... Num 10:10
priests shall *b* the .... Josh 6:4
When I *b* the trumpet ...... Judg 7:18
an east wind to *b* .... Ps 78:26
B upon my garden .... Song 4:16
with a very severe *b* .... Jer 14:17
B the trumpet in Zion .... Joel 2:1

Lord GOD will *b* the .... Zech 9:14

BLOWS
B that hurt cleanse .... Prov 20:30
breath of the LORD *b* .... Is 40:7
The wind *b* where it .... John 3:8

BLUE
b, purple, and scarlet .... Ex 25:4
pomegranates of *b* .... Ex 28:33
tabernacle door, of *b* .... Ex 36:37
spread a *b* cloth .... Num 4:7
put a *b* thread in the ...... Num 15:38
made the veil of *b* .... 2 Chr 3:14
royal apparel of *b* .... Esth 8:15
of fiery red, hyacinth *b* ...... Rev 9:17

BLUSH
did they know how to *b* ..... Jer 6:15

BOANERGES
Surname of James and John, Mark 3:17

BOAST
puts on his armor *b* ...... 1 Kin 20:11
soul shall make its *b* .... Ps 34:2
God we *b* all day long .... Ps 44:8
and make your *b* .... Rom 2:17
that we are your *b* .... 2 Cor 1:14
you, and not to *b* .... 2 Cor 10:16
that I also may *b* .... 2 Cor 11:16
lest anyone should *b* .... Eph 2:9
your hearts, do not *b* .... James 3:14

BOASTERS
God, violent, proud, *b* .... Rom 1:30
lovers of money, *b* .... 2 Tim 3:2

BOASTFUL
b shall not stand .... Ps 5:5
I was envious of the *b* .... Ps 73:3

BOASTING
Where is *b* then .... Rom 3:27
should make my *b* .... 1 Cor 9:15
you, great is my *b* .... 2 Cor 7:4
All such *b* is evil .... James 4:16

BOASTS
Whoever falsely *b* .... Prov 25:14

BOAT
in the *b* with Zebedee .... Matt 4:21
So He got into a *b* .... Matt 9:1
disciples get into the *b* .... Matt 14:22
by *b* to the other side ...... Mark 5:21
in the *b* by themselves ..... Mark 6:32
b was in the middle .... Mark 6:47
b with His disciples .... Luke 8:22
immediately the *b* was ...... John 6:21

BOAZ
A wealthy Bethlehemite, Ruth 2:1, 4–18
Husband of Ruth, Ruth 4:10–13
Ancestor of Christ, Matt 1:5
—— Pillar of the temple, 1 Kin 7:21

BODIES
valley of the dead *b* .... Jer 31:40
b a living sacrifice .... Rom 12:1
not know that your *b* ...... 1 Cor 6:15
also celestial *b* .... 1 Cor 15:40
wives as their own *b* .... Eph 5:28
and chariots, and *b* .... Rev 18:13

BODILY
b form like a dove .... Luke 3:22
b presence is weak ...... 2 Cor 10:10
of the Godhead *b* .... Col 2:9
b exercise profits .... 1 Tim 4:8

BODY
b clings to the ground .... Ps 44:25
b is carved ivory .... Song 5:14
b was wet with the dew ..... Dan 4:33
of the *b* is the eye .... Matt 6:22
those who kill the *b* .... Matt 10:28
Take, eat; this is My *b* .... Matt 26:26
and asked for the *b* .... Matt 27:58

around his naked *b* .... Mark 14:51
of the temple of His *b* .... John 2:21
deliver me from this *b* .... Rom 7:24
redemption of our *b* .... Rom 8:23
members in one *b* .... Rom 12:4
and the Lord for the *b* ..... 1 Cor 6:13
against his own *b* .... 1 Cor 6:18
not know that your *b* ...... 1 Cor 6:19
glorify God in your *b* ...... 1 Cor 6:20
But I discipline my *b* .... 1 Cor 9:27
one bread and one *b* ...... 1 Cor 10:17
b which is broken .... 1 Cor 11:24
be guilty of the *b* .... 1 Cor 11:27
For as the *b* is one .... 1 Cor 12:12
baptized into one *b* .... 1 Cor 12:13
b is not one member ...... 1 Cor 12:14
are the *b* of Christ .... 1 Cor 12:27
though I give my *b* .... 1 Cor 13:3
It is sown a natural *b* ..... 1 Cor 15:44
both to God in one *b* .... Eph 2:16
be magnified in my *b* .... Phil 1:20
in the *b* of His flesh .... Col 1:22
by putting off the *b* .... Col 2:11
and neglect of the *b* .... Col 2:23
were called in one *b* .... Col 3:15
b You have prepared .... Heb 10:5
the offering of the *b* .... Heb 10:10
For as the *b* without ...... James 2:26
our sins in His own *b* .... 1 Pet 2:24

BOILS
Job with painful *b* .... Job 2:7

BOISTEROUS
that the wind was *b* .... Matt 14:30

BOLD
the righteous are *b* .... Prov 28:1
whatever anyone is *b* .... 2 Cor 11:21
are much more *b* .... Phil 1:14

BOLDLY
I may open my mouth *b* .... Eph 6:19
therefore come *b* .... Heb 4:16
So we may *b* say .... Heb 13:6

BOLDNESS
Great is my *b* of .... 2 Cor 7:4
in whom we have *b* .... Eph 3:12
but with all *b* .... Phil 1:20
standing and great *b* ...... 1 Tim 3:13
brethren, having *b* .... Heb 10:19
that we may have *b* ...... 1 John 4:17

BOND
bring you into the *b* ..... Ezek 20:37
of the Spirit in the *b* .... Eph 4:3
love, which is the *b* .... Col 3:14

BONDAGE
because of the *b* .... Ex 2:23
out of the house of *b* .... Ex 13:14
receive the spirit of *b* ...... Rom 8:15
might bring us into *b* .... Gal 2:4
which gives birth to *b* .... Gal 4:24
again with a yoke of *b* .... Gal 5:1
lifetime subject to *b* .... Heb 2:15
he is brought into *b* .... 2 Pet 2:19

BONDS
"Let us break Their *b* .... Ps 2:3
the other I called *B* .... Zech 11:7

BONDSERVANT
Paul, a *b* of Jesus Christ, ... Rom 1:1
would not be a *b* of Christ ... Gal 1:10
who is one of you, a *b* .... Col 4:12
Paul, a *b* of God and an ..... Titus 1:1
James, a *b* of God and of .. James 1:1
Simon Peter, a *b* and .... 2 Pet 1:1
Jude, a *b* of Jesus Christ, ... Jude 1

BONDSERVANTS
your *b* for Jesus' sake .... 2 Cor 4:5
B, be obedient to .... Eph 6:5
as men-pleasers, but as *b* .... Eph 6:6
Paul and Timothy, *b* of ...... Phil 1:1
B, obey in all things .... Col 3:22

Masters, give your *b* .... Col 4:1
Exhort *b* to be obedient ..... Titus 2:9
for vice, but as *b* .... 1 Pet 2:16

BONDWOMAN
"Cast out this *b* .... Gen 21:10
the one by a *b* .... Gal 4:22

BONE
"This is now *b* of my .... Gen 2:23
b clings to my skin .... Job 19:20
bonds came together, *b* .... Ezek 37:7

BONES
shall carry up my *b* .... Gen 50:25
which made all my *b* .... Job 4:14
His *b* are like beams .... Job 40:18
I can count all My *b* .... Ps 22:17
and my *b* waste away .... Ps 31:10
I kept silent, my *b* .... Ps 32:3
the wind, or how the *b* ..... Eccl 11:5
say to them, 'O dry *b* ...... Ezek 37:4
b are the whole house .... Ezek 37:11
of dead men's *b* .... Matt 23:27
b shall be broken .... John 19:36
concerning his *b* .... Heb 11:22

BOOK
you will find in the *b* .... Ezra 4:15
distinctly from the *b* .... Neh 8:8
were inscribed in a *b* ...... Job 19:23
"Search from the *b* .... Is 34:16
'Write in a *b* for .... Jer 30:2
found written in the *b* ...... Dan 12:1
so a *b* of remembrance .... Mal 3:16
are written in the *b* .... Gal 3:10
sprinkled both the *b* .... Heb 9:19
in the Lamb's *B* .... Rev 21:27
the prophecy of this *b* ..... Rev 22:18
the words of the *b* .... Rev 22:19

BOOK OF LIFE
whose names are in the *B* .... Phil 4:3
out his name from the *B* ..... Rev 3:5
written in the *B* of the ...... Rev 13:8
not written in the *B* .... Rev 17:8
opened, which is the *B* ..... Rev 20:12
found written in the *B* ..... Rev 20:15
written in the Lamb's *B* .... Rev 21:27
away his part from the *B* .. Rev 22:19

BOOK OF THE LAW
are written in this *B*, ... Deut 30:10
Take this *B*, and put it ..... Deut 31:26
This *B* shall not depart .... Josh 1:8
that is written in the *B* ..... Josh 8:34
that is written in the *B* ..... Josh 23:6
"I have found the *B* .... 2 Kin 22:8
the words of the *B* .... 2 Kin 22:11
in Judah, and had the *B* ... 2 Chr 17:9
the scribe to bring the *B* ..... Neh 8:1
written in the *b* .... Gal 3:10

BOOKS
b there is no end .... Eccl 12:12
not contain the *b* .... John 21:25
magic brought their *b* ..... Acts 19:19
God, and *b* were opened ... Rev 20:12

BOOTH
b which a watchman .... Job 27:18
of Zion is left as a *b* .... Is 1:8

BOOTHS
dwell in *b* for seven .... Lev 23:42
in *b* during the feast .... Neh 8:14

BORDER
pillar to the LORD at its *b* .... Is 19:19

BORDERS
and enlarge your *b* .... Ex 34:24
makes peace in your *b* ..... Ps 147:14
and enlarge the *b* .... Matt 23:5

BORE
conceived and *b* Cain .... Gen 4:1
And to Sarah who *b* .... Is 51:2
b the sin of many .... Is 53:12

and He *b* them and .... Is 63:9
b our sicknesses .... Matt 8:17
who Himself *b* our sins ..... 1 Pet 2:24
b a male Child who was ..... Rev 12:5

BORN
"Every son who is *b* .... Ex 1:22
yet man is *b* to trouble .... Job 5:7
"Man who is *b* .... Job 14:1
'This one was *b* .... Ps 87:4
A time to be *b* .... Eccl 3:2
unto us a Child is *b* .... Is 9:6
Or shall a nation be *b* .... Is 66:8
b Jesus who is called .... Matt 1:16
For there is *b* to you .... Luke 2:11
unless one is *b* again .... John 3:3
That which is *b* .... John 3:6
For this cause I was *b* .... John 18:37
me also, as by one *b* ...... 1 Cor 15:8
of the bondwoman was *b* .... Gal 4:23
having been *b* again .... 1 Pet 1:23
who loves is *b* of God ..... 1 John 4:7
is the Christ is *b* .... 1 John 5:1
know that whoever is *b* .. 1 John 5:18

BORN AGAIN
unless one is *b*, ... John 3:3
'You must be *b* .... John 3:7
having been *b*, not of ...... 1 Pet 1:23

BORNE
had *b* him no children ...... Gen 16:1
the barren has *b* seven .... 1 Sam 2:5
not my son whom I had *b* . 1 Kin 3:21
'I have *b* chastening .... Job 34:31
Surely He has *b* our griefs .... Is 53:4
you who have not *b* .... Is 54:1
you have *b* the shame ...... Ezek 36:6
who have *b* the burden .... Matt 20:12
And as we have *b* .... 1 Cor 15:49

BORROWER
b is servant to the .... Prov 22:7
lender, so with the *b* .... Is 24:2

BORROWS
The wicked *b* and does ...... Ps 37:21

BOSOM
man take fire to his *b* ...... Prov 6:27
consolation of her *b* .... Is 66:11
angels to Abraham's *b* .... Luke 16:22
Son, who is in the *b* .... John 1:18
leaning on Jesus' *b* .... John 13:23

BOTTLE
tears into Your *b* .... Ps 56:8
b shall be filled .... Jer 13:12

BOTTOM
they sank to the *b* .... Ex 15:5
in two from top to *b* .... Matt 27:51
in two from top to *b* ..... Mark 15:38

BOTTOMLESS
given the key to the *b* .... Rev 9:1
ascend out of the *b* .... Rev 17:8
the key to the *b* .... Rev 20:1

BOTTOMLESS PIT
given the key to the *b* .... Rev 9:1
the angel of the *b*, ... Rev 9:11
ascends out of the *b* .... Rev 11:7
ascend out of the *b* .... Rev 17:8
having the key to the *b* ..... Rev 20:1
cast him into the *b* .... Rev 20:3

BOUGH
Joseph is a fruitful *b* ...... Gen 49:22
cut down a *b* from the ..... Judg 9:48
lop off the *b* with terror ...... Is 10:33
will be as a forsaken *b* .... Is 17:9

BOUGHS
cedars with its *b* .... Ps 80:10
She sent out her *b* .... Ps 80:11

BOUGHT
the hand of him who *b* ..... Lev 25:28
not your Father, who *b* ..... Deut 32:6

b the threshing floor ..... 2 Sam 24:24
b the field from .... Jer 32:9
all that he had and *b* ..... Matt 13:46
For you were *b* at a .... 1 Cor 6:20
denying the Lord who *b* ..... 2 Pet 2:1

BOUND
he *b* Isaac his son .... Gen 22:9
she *b* the scarlet cord ...... Josh 2:21
b him with two new ...... Judg 15:13
b him with bronze .... Judg 16:21
of the wicked have *b* .... Ps 119:61
cast three men *b* .... Dan 3:24
b the waters in a .... Prov 30:4
not been closed or *b* .... Is 1:6
on earth will be *b* .... Matt 16:19
b hand and foot with ..... John 11:44
b at the four corners ...... Acts 10:11
And see, now I go *b* .... Acts 20:22
of Israel I am *b* .... Acts 28:20
who has a husband is *b* ..... Rom 7:2
Are you *b* to a wife .... 1 Cor 7:27
Devil and Satan, and *b* ..... Rev 20:2

BOUNDARY
b that they may not .... Ps 104:9

BOUNDS
You shall set *b* .... Ex 19:12
I will set your *b* .... Ex 23:31

BOUNTIFUL
the miser said to be *b* .... Is 32:5
you into a *b* country .... Jer 2:7

BOUNTIFULLY
Because He has dealt *b* .... Ps 13:6
and he who sows *b* .... 2 Cor 9:6

BOW
sons *b* down to you .... Gen 27:29
brothers indeed come to *b* . Gen 37:10
b remained in strength ..... Gen 49:24
You shall not *b* .... Ex 23:24
to serve them and *b* .... Judg 2:19
b is renewed in my .... Job 29:20
Judah the Song of the *B* .. 2 Sam 1:18
will not trust in my *b* .... Ps 44:6
He breaks the *b* .... Ps 46:9
like a deceitful *b* .... Ps 78:57
let us worship and *b* .... Ps 95:6
B down Your heavens .... Ps 144:5
Me every knee shall *b* .... Is 45:23
not save them by *b* .... Hos 1:7
knee shall *b* to Me .... Rom 14:11
For this reason I *b* .... Eph 3:14
Jesus every knee should *b* .. Phil 2:10
who sat on it had a *b* .... Rev 6:2

BOWED
stood all around and *b* ...... Gen 37:7
b the heavens also .... 2 Sam 22:10
whose knees have not *b* .. 1 Kin 19:18
They have *b* down and .... Ps 20:8
And they *b* the knee ...... Matt 27:29
men who have not *b* .... Rom 11:4

BOWED THEIR HEADS
then they *b* and worshiped ..... Ex 4:31
So the people *b* .... Ex 12:27
b and prostrated .... 1 Chr 29:20
b and worshiped the Lord ... Neh 8:6

BOWL
his hand in the *b* .... Prov 19:24
or the golden *b* .... Eccl 12:6
and poured out his *b* .... Rev 16:2

BOWLS
who drink wine from *b* ..... Amos 6:6
a harp, and golden *b* .... Rev 5:8
Go and pour out the *b* ...... Rev 16:1
who had the seven *b* .... Rev 21:9

BOWS
"The *b* of the mighty .... 1 Sam 2:4

BOWSTRING
He has loosed my *b* .... Job 30:11

BOX
Judas had the money *b* ... John 13:29

BOY
b to Hagar, and sent her ... Gen 21:14
Do not sin against the *b*' .. Gen 42:22
the *b* Samuel ministered ... 1 Sam 3:1
B Jesus lingered behind ... Luke 2:43

BOYS
Shall be full of *b* .... Zech 8:5

BOZRAH
City of Edom, Gen 36:33
Destruction of, foretold, Amos 1:12
Figurative of Messiah's victory, Is 63:1

BRACELET
b that was on his arm, ... 2 Sam 1:10

BRACELETS
two *b* for her wrists .... Gen 24:22
of gold: armlets and *b* .... Num 31:50
b on their wrists .... Ezek 23:42

BRAIDED
not with *b* hair or .... 1 Tim 2:9

BRAMBLE
gather grapes from a *b* .... Luke 6:44

BRANCH
blossoms on one *b* .... Ex 25:33
b will not be green .... Job 15:32
from Israel, palm *b* .... Is 9:14
B shall grow out of .... Is 11:1
raise to David a *B* .... Jer 23:5
grow up to David a *B* ...... Jer 33:15
forth My Servant the *B* ..... Zech 3:8
whose name is the *B* ...... Zech 6:12
b has already become ..... Matt 24:32
b that bears fruit He .... John 15:2
b cannot bear fruit .... John 15:4
he is cast out as a *b* .... John 15:6

BRANCHES
in the sun, and his *b* .... Job 8:16
and bring forth *b* .... Job 14:9
and cut down the *b* .... Is 18:5
and its *b* are broken .... Jer 11:16
His *b* shall spread .... Hos 14:6
of the air nested in its *b* .. Luke 13:19
vine, you are the *b* .... John 15:5
root is holy, so are the *b* .. Rom 11:16
b were broken off .... Rom 11:17

BRAND
Is this not a *b* plucked .... Zech 3:2

BRASS
become sounding *b* .... 1 Cor 13:1
feet were like fine *b* .... Rev 1:15

BRAVE
in the faith, be *b* .... 1 Cor 16:13

BREACH
before Him in the *b* .... Ps 106:23
the Repairer of the *B* ...... Is 58:12

BREACHES
Heal its *b*, for it is .... Ps 60:2

BREAD
See FEAST OF UNLEAVENED BREAD; UNLEAVENED BREAD
face you shall eat *b* .... Gen 3:19
of Salem brought out *b* .... Gen 14:18
"Behold, I will rain *b* .... Ex 16:4
shall eat unleavened *b* ..... Ex 23:15
not live by *b* alone .... Deut 8:3
lives, I do not have *b* ..... 1 Kin 17:12
new wine, a land of *b* .... 2 Kin 18:32
that his life abhors *b* .... Job 33:20
people as they eat *b* .... Ps 14:4
Can He give *b* also .... Ps 78:20
up late, to eat the *b* .... Ps 127:2
her poor with *b* .... Ps 132:15
For they eat the *b* .... Prov 4:17
b eaten in secret is .... Prov 9:17
B gained by deceit is ..... Prov 20:17
Go, eat your *b* with .... Eccl 9:7
Cast your *b* upon the .... Eccl 11:1
b will be given him .... Is 33:16
for what is not *b* .... Is 55:2
to share your *b* .... Is 58:7
We get our *b* at the .... Lam 5:9
who give me my *b* .... Hos 2:5
For their *b* shall be .... Hos 9:4
And lack of *b* in all .... Amos 4:6
these stones become *b* ...... Matt 4:3
not live by *b* alone .... Matt 4:4
this day our daily *b* .... Matt 6:11
eating, Jesus took *b* .... Matt 26:26
no bag, no *b*, no copper .... Mark 6:8
is he who shall eat *b* ..... Luke 14:15
gives you the true *b* .... John 6:32
I am the *b* of life .... John 6:48
having dipped the *b* ...... John 13:26
b which we break .... 1 Cor 10:16
He was betrayed took *b* .. 1 Cor 11:23
as you eat this *b* .... 1 Cor 11:26
did we eat anyone's *b* .... 2 Thess 3:8
and eat their own *b* ..... 2 Thess 3:12

BREADTH
is as great as its *b* .... Rev 21:16

BREAK
that you shall *b* his yoke .. Gen 27:40
nor shall you *b* one of its .... Ex 12:46
lest the LORD *b* out against .. Ex 19:22
B off the golden earrings ..... Ex 32:2
b their bones and .... Num 24:8
never *b* My covenant .... Judg 2:1
torment my soul, and *b* ...... Job 19:2
They *b* up my path .... Job 30:13
B their teeth in their .... Ps 58:6
And now they *b* down .... Ps 74:6
b My statutes and do .... Ps 89:31
covenant I will not *b* .... Ps 89:34
reed He will not *b* .... Is 42:3
and that you *b* every yoke .... Is 58:6
your light shall *b* forth .... Is 58:8
Remember, do not *b* .... Jer 14:21
b your fallow ground, ... Hos 10:12
and where thieves *b* in ..... Matt 6:19
reed He will not *b* .... Matt 12:20
they did not *b* His legs .... John 19:33
together to *b* bread .... Acts 20:7
bread which we *b*, ... 1 Cor 10:16
B forth and shout, ... Gal 4:27

BREAKING
in the *b* of bread .... Acts 2:42
b bread from house to ...... Acts 2:46
weeping and *b* my heart .. Acts 21:13
dishonor God through *b* .... Rom 2:23

BREAKS
He *b* in pieces mighty .... Job 34:24
My soul *b* with longing ..... Ps 119:20
Until the day *b* .... Song 2:17
Whoever therefore *b* .... Matt 5:19

BREAST
back on Jesus' *b* .... John 13:25

BREASTPLATE
a *b*, an ephod .... Ex 28:4
righteousness as a *b* .... Is 59:17
having put on the *b* .... Eph 6:14

BREASTS
blessings of the *b* .... Gen 49:25
on My mother's *b* .... Ps 22:9
doe, let her *b* satisfy .... Prov 5:19
Your two *b* are like .... Song 4:5
b which nursed You .... Luke 11:27
done, beat their *b* .... Luke 23:48

BREATH
nostrils the *b* of life .... Gen 2:7
at the blast of the *b* ...... 2 Sam 22:16
that there was no *b* ...... 1 Kin 17:17
perish, and by the *b* .... Job 4:9
as long as my *b* .... Job 27:3
has made me, and the *b* ..... Job 33:4
You take away their *b* ..... Ps 104:29
Man is like a *b* .... Ps 144:4
everything that has *b* .... Ps 150:6
they all have one *b* .... Eccl 3:19
from it, who gives *b* .... Is 42:5
"Surely I will cause *b* ...... Ezek 37:5
God who holds your *b* .... Dan 5:23
gives to all life, *b* .... Acts 17:25
consume with the *b* ...... 2 Thess 2:8
power to give *b* .... Rev 13:15

BREATH OF LIFE
into his nostrils the *b* .... Gen 2:7
flesh in which is the *b* ...... Gen 6:17
flesh in which is the *b* ...... Gen 7:15
b from God entered them ... Rev 11:11

BREATHE
me, and such as *b* .... Ps 27:12
winds, O breath, and *b* ...... Ezek 37:9

BREATHED
and *b* into his nostrils the .... Gen 2:7
a loud voice, and *b* His .... Mark 15:37
He *b* on them, and said .... John 20:22
fell down and *b* his last ...... Acts 5:5
at his feet and *b* her last .... Acts 5:10

BREATHES
indeed he *b* his last .... Job 14:10

BRETHREN
presence of all his *b* .... Gen 16:12
be lifted above his *b* ...... Deut 17:20
how good it is for *b* to .... Ps 133:1
and you are all *b* .... Matt 23:8
least of these My *b* .... Matt 25:40
Go and tell My *b* .... Matt 28:10
Men and *b*, this Scripture .. Acts 1:16
six *b* accompanied me ..... Acts 11:12
firstborn among many *b* .... Rom 8:29
to judge between his *b* ...... 1 Cor 6:5
thus sin against the *b* ...... 1 Cor 8:12
over five hundred *b* .... 1 Cor 15:6
perils among false *b* ..... 2 Cor 11:26
b secretly brought .... Gal 2:4
Finally, my *b*, be strong ..... Eph 6:10
Greet all the *b* with ..... 1 Thess 5:26
to be made like His *b* .... Heb 2:17
sincere love of the *b* .... 1 Pet 1:22
because we love the *b* .... 1 John 3:14
our lives for the *b* .... 1 John 3:16
does not receive the *b* .... 3 John 10
for the accuser of our *b* .... Rev 12:10
of your *b* the prophets ...... Rev 22:9

BRIBE
you shall take no *b* .... Ex 23:8
b blinds the eyes .... Deut 16:19
b debases the heart .... Eccl 7:7

BRIBERY
consume the tents of *b* ..... Job 15:34

BRIBES
hand is full of *b* .... Ps 26:10
but he who hates *b* .... Prov 15:27
but he who receives *b* .... Prov 29:4
everyone loves *b* .... Is 1:23
the just and taking *b* ...... Amos 5:12

BRICK
people straw to make *b* .... Ex 5:7
incense on altars of *b* .... Is 65:3
Make strong the *b* .... Nah 3:14

BRICKS
"Come, let us make *b* .... Gen 11:3
b which they made .... Ex 5:8
deliver the quota of *b* .... Ex 5:18
b have fallen down .... Is 9:10

BRIDE
them on you as a *b* .... Is 49:18
He who has the *b* .... John 3:29
I will show you the *b* .... Rev 21:9
the Spirit and the *b* .... Rev 22:17

BRIDEGROOM
righteousness, as a *b* .... Is 61:10

and as the *b* rejoices .... Is 62:5
mourn as long as the *b* ..... Matt 9:15
b will be taken away .... Matt 9:15
went out to meet the *b* ..... Matt 25:1
b fast while the .... Mark 2:19
the friend of the *b* .... John 3:29

BRIDLE
harnessed with bit and *b* ..... Ps 32:9
b the whole body .... James 3:2

BRIER
b shall come up the .... Is 55:13
longer be a pricking *b* .... Ezek 28:24
of them is like a *b* .... Mic 7:4

BRIERS
there shall come up *b* .... Is 5:6
their words, though *b* .... Ezek 2:6

BRIGHTER
Her Nazirites were *b* .... Lam 4:7
a light from heaven, *b* ..... Acts 26:13

BRIGHTNESS
From the *b* before Him .. 2 Sam 22:13
and kings to the *b* .... Is 60:3
goes forth as *b* .... Is 62:1
very dark, with no *b* ...... Amos 5:20
who being the *b* .... Heb 1:3

BRIMSTONE
Then the LORD rained *b*.... Gen 19:24
b is scattered on his .... Job 18:15
fire, smoke, and *b* .... Rev 9:17
the lake of fire and *b* ...... Rev 20:10

BRING
LORD your God will *b* ...... Deut 30:3
b back his soul .... Job 33:30
for they *b* down .... Ps 55:3
Lord said, "I will *b* .... Ps 68:22
B forth your strong .... Is 41:21
He will *b* forth justice .... Is 42:3
b My righteousness .... Is 46:13
Though they *b* up their ..... Hos 9:12
she will *b* forth a Son ...... Matt 1:21
b no fruit to maturity ...... Luke 8:14
b this Man's blood .... Acts 5:28
Who shall *b* a charge ...... Rom 8:33
b Christ down from .... Rom 10:6
b Christ up from the .... Rom 10:7
even so God will *b* ...... 1 Thess 4:14

BROAD
set me in a *b* place .... Ps 118:5
b is the way that .... Matt 7:13
their phylacteries *b* .... Matt 23:5

BROKE
b them at the foot of .... Ex 32:19
b open the fountain .... Ps 74:15
covenant which they *b* ..... Jer 31:32
He blessed and *b* .... Matt 14:19
b the flask and poured ...... Mark 14:3
b the legs of the .... John 19:32

BROKEN
he has *b* My covenant ..... Gen 17:14
I am like a *b* vessel .... Ps 31:12
their bows shall be *b* .... Ps 37:15
He has *b* his covenant .... Ps 55:20
heart the spirit is *b* .... Prov 15:13
b spirit dries the .... Prov 17:22
but who can bear a *b* ..... Prov 18:14
in the staff of this *b* .... Is 36:6
heart within me is *b* .... Jer 23:9
is oppressed and *b* .... Hos 5:11
this stone will be *b* .... Matt 21:44
Scripture cannot be *b* ..... John 10:35
is My body which is *b* .... 1 Cor 11:24

BROKENHEARTED
He heals the *b* and .... Ps 147:3
sent Me to heal the *b* .... Is 61:1
sent Me to heal the *b* ...... Luke 4:18

BRONZE
So Moses made a *b* .... Num 21:9
your head shall be *b* ...... Deut 28:23
b serpent that Moses ...... 2 Kin 18:4
Or is my flesh *b* .... Job 6:12
b as rotten wood .... Job 41:27
broken the gates of *b* .... Ps 107:16
b I will bring .... Is 60:17
b walls against the .... Jer 1:18
people a fortified *b* .... Jer 15:20
a third kingdom of *b* .... Dan 2:39
make your hooves *b* .... Mic 4:13
were mountains of *b* .... Zech 6:1

BROOD
The *b* of evildoers .... Is 14:20
B of vipers .... Matt 12:34
hen gathers her *b* .... Luke 13:34

BROOD OF VIPERS
he said to them, "*B* .... Matt 3:7
B! How can you, being .... Matt 12:34
Serpents, *b*! How can ...... Matt 23:33
baptized by him, "*B* .... Luke 3:7

BROOK
stones from the *b* .... 1 Sam 17:40
shall drink of the *b* .... Ps 110:7
disciples over the *B* .... John 18:1

BROOK CHERITH
God hides Elijah here and the ravens feed him, 1 Kin 17:3–6

BROOKS
good land, a land of *b* .... Deut 8:7
b that pass away .... Job 6:15
for the water *b* .... Ps 42:1

BROTHER
"Where is Abel your *b* .... Gen 4:9
he were my friend or *b* ...... Ps 35:14
speak against your *b* .... Ps 50:20
and a *b* is born for .... Prov 17:17
b offended is harder ...... Prov 18:19
has neither son nor *b* .... Eccl 4:8
and do not trust any *b* .... Jer 9:4
he pursued his *b* .... Amos 1:11
Was not Esau Jacob's *b* ...... Mal 1:2
b will deliver up .... Matt 10:21
how often shall my *b* ..... Matt 18:21
"Teacher, tell my *b* .... Luke 12:13
b will rise again .... John 11:23
do you judge your *b* .... Rom 14:10
b goes to law against .... 1 Cor 6:6
shall the weak *b* .... 1 Cor 8:11
slave—a beloved *b* .... Philem 16
He who loves his *b* .... 1 John 2:10
and murdered his *b* .... 1 John 3:12
Whoever hates his *b* ..... 1 John 3:15
b sinning a sin which ..... 1 John 5:16
I, John, both your *b* .... Rev 1:9

BROTHERHOOD
the covenant of *b* .... Amos 1:9
I might break the *b* .... Zech 11:14
Love the *b* .... 1 Pet 2:17
experienced by your *b* ...... 1 Pet 5:9

BROTHERLY
to one another with *b* ..... Rom 12:10
b love continue .... Heb 13:1

BROTHER'S
Am I my *b* keeper .... Gen 4:9
at the speck in your *b* .... Matt 7:3

BROTHERS
My *b* have dealt .... Job 6:15
a stranger to my *b* .... Ps 69:8
is My mother, or My *b* .... Mark 3:33
b are these who hear ...... Luke 8:21
b did not believe .... John 7:5
love as *b*, be tenderhearted .. 1 Pet 3:8

BROUGHT
He *b* out His people .... Ps 105:43
The king has *b* me into ..... Song 1:4
to heaven, will be *b* ...... Luke 10:15

BRUISE
He shall *b* your head .... Gen 3:15
LORD binds up the *b* .... Is 30:26
the LORD to *b* Him .... Is 53:10

BRUISED
b reed He will not .... Is 42:3
He was *b* for our .... Is 53:5
b reed He will not .... Matt 12:20

BRUTAL
b men who are .... Ezek 21:31

BUCKET
are as a drop in a *b* .... Is 40:15

BUCKLER
be your shield and *b* .... Ps 91:4

BUD
it bring forth and *b* .... Is 55:10

BUFFET
of Satan to *b* me .... 2 Cor 12:7

BUILD
b ourselves a city .... Gen 11:4
cities which you did not *b* .. Deut 6:10
shall *b* with whole stones .. Deut 27:6
b an altar to the LORD...... Judg 6:26
will *b* him a sure house ... 1 Sam 2:35
"Would you *b* a house ..... 2 Sam 7:5
b a temple for the name ..... 1 Kin 8:17
that the LORD will *b* ...... 1 Chr 17:10
Solomon who shall *b* .... 1 Chr 28:6
able to *b* Him a temple ..... 2 Chr 2:6
b the house of the LORD ..... Ezra 1:5
and let us *b* the wall of .... Neh 2:17
B the walls of Jerusalem ..... Ps 51:18
labor in vain who *b* .... Ps 127:1
afterward *b* your house .... Prov 24:27
down, and a time to *b* .... Eccl 3:3
house that you will *b* .... Is 66:1
I will *b* them and not .... Jer 24:6
Who *b* up Zion with .... Mic 3:10
b the desolate places .... Mal 1:4
'This man began to *b* ..... Luke 14:30
What house will you *b* ...... Acts 7:49
b you up and give you .... Acts 20:32
named, lest I should *b* .... Rom 15:20
For if I *b* again .... Gal 2:18

BUILDER
me, as a wise master *b* .... 1 Cor 3:10
foundations, whose *b* ...... Heb 11:10

BUILDERS
The stone which the *b* ..... Ps 118:22
The stone which the *b* ..... Matt 21:42
The stone which the *b* .... Mark 12:10
The stone which the *b* .... Luke 20:17
was rejected by you *b* ...... Acts 4:11
The stone which the *b* ...... 1 Pet 2:7

BUILDING
field, you are God's *b* .... 1 Cor 3:9
destroyed, we have a *b* ..... 2 Cor 5:1
in whom the whole *b* .... Eph 2:21
But you, beloved, *b* .... Jude 20

BUILDS
The LORD *b* up .... Ps 147:2
The wise woman *b* .... Prov 14:1
one take heed how he *b* ... 1 Cor 3:10

BUILT
Wisdom has *b* her house .... Prov 9:1
my works great, I *b* .... Eccl 2:4
Babylon, that I have *b* ...... Dan 4:30
to a wise man who *b* .... Matt 7:24
a foolish man who *b* .... Matt 7:26
work which he has *b* ...... 1 Cor 3:14
having been *b* on the .... Eph 2:20
rooted and *b* up in Him .... Col 2:7
For every house is *b* .... Heb 3:4
stones, are being *b* .... 1 Pet 2:5

BULL
I will not take a *b* .... Ps 50:9
like an untrained *b* .... Jer 31:18

BULLS
in the blood of *b* .... Is 1:11

For if the blood of *b* … Heb 9:13

BULRUSHES
she took an ark of *b* … Ex 2:3

BULWARKS
Mark well her *b* … Ps 48:13
for walls and *b* … Is 26:1

BUNDLE
each man's *b* of money … Gen 42:35
A *b* of myrrh is my … Song 1:13

BURDEN
You have laid the *b* … Num 11:11
one knows his own *b* … 2 Chr 6:29
so that I am a *b* … Job 7:20
Cast your *b* on the … Ps 55:22
the grasshopper is a *b* … Eccl 12:5
in that day that his *b* … Is 10:27
its reproach is a *b* … Zeph 3:18
easy and My *b* is light … Matt 11:30
upon you no greater *b* … Acts 15:28
as it may, I did not *b* … 2 Cor 12:16
we might not be a *b* … 1 Thess 2:9
on you no other *b* … Rev 2:24

BURDENED
but you have *b* Me with … Is 43:24
were *b* beyond measure … 2 Cor 1:8
this tent groan, being *b* … 2 Cor 5:4
be eased and you *b* … 2 Cor 8:13
not let the church be *b* … 1 Tim 5:16

BURDENS
and looked at their *b* … Ex 2:11
For they bind heavy *b* … Matt 23:4
Bear one another's *b* … Gal 6:2

BURDENSOME
b task God has given … Eccl 1:13
his life will be *b* … Is 15:4
I myself was not *b* … 2 Cor 12:13
commandments are not *b* … 1 John 5:3

BURIAL
as property for a *b* place … Gen 23:20
indeed he has no *b* … Eccl 6:3
she did it for My *b* … Matt 26:12
to anoint My body for *b* … Mark 14:8
for the day of My *b* … John 12:7
Stephen to his *b* … Acts 8:2

BURIED
and there will I be *b* … Ruth 1:17
I saw the wicked *b* … Eccl 8:10
away the body and *b* … Matt 14:12
also died and was *b* … Luke 16:22
Therefore we were *b* … Rom 6:4
and that He was *b* … 1 Cor 15:4
b with Him in baptism … Col 2:12

BURN
the bush does not *b* … Ex 3:3
that My wrath may *b* … Ex 32:10
b their chariots … Josh 11:6
both will *b* together … Is 1:31
"Did not our heart *b* … Luke 24:32
eat her flesh and *b* … Rev 17:16

BURNED
If anyone's work is *b* … 1 Cor 3:15
my body to be *b* … 1 Cor 13:3
whose end is to be *b* … Heb 6:8
be touched and that *b* … Heb 12:18
are *b* outside the camp … Heb 13:11
in it will be *b* … 2 Pet 3:10
all green grass was *b* … Rev 8:7

BURNING
b torch that passed … Gen 15:17
with severe *b* fever … Deut 28:22
on his lips like a *b* … Prov 16:27
b fire shut up in my … Jer 20:9
b jealousy against the … Ezek 36:5
plucked from the *b* … Amos 4:11
a great mountain *b* … Rev 8:8
fell from heaven, *b* … Rev 8:10

BURNT
offered *b* offerings … Gen 8:20
lamb for a *b* offering … Gen 22:7
and *b* offerings, that … Ex 10:25
took a *b* offering and … Ex 18:12
shall set the altar of the *b* … Ex 40:6
is a *b* sacrifice of the herd … Lev 1:3
And they offered on it *b* … Josh 8:31
offer a *b* sacrifice with … Judg 6:26
if you offer a *b* offering … Judg 13:16
accepted a *b* offering … Judg 13:23
b offerings on that altar … 1 Kin 3:4
offered *b* offerings … 1 Kin 9:25
offer *b* offerings on it, … Ezra 3:2
delight in *b* offering … Ps 51:16
b offerings are not … Jer 6:20
sacrificing *b* offerings … Ezek 43:18
Though you offer Me *b* … Amos 5:22

BURST
it is ready to *b* … Job 32:19
with doors, when it *b* … Job 38:8
the new wine will *b* … Luke 5:37
falling headlong, he *b* … Acts 1:18

BURY
b your dead in the … Gen 23:6
was no one to *b* them … Ps 79:3
go and *b* my father … Matt 8:21
and let the dead *b* … Matt 8:22

BUSH
from the midst of a *b* … Ex 3:2
Him who dwelt in the *b* … Deut 33:16
to him in the *b* … Acts 7:35

BUSINESS
in ships, who do *b* … Ps 107:23
farm, another to his *b* … Matt 22:5
about My Father's *b* … Luke 2:49

BUSYBODIES
at all, but are *b* … 2 Thess 3:11
but also gossips and *b* … 1 Tim 5:13

BUT I SAY TO YOU
B that whoever is angry … Matt 5:22
B that whoever looks … Matt 5:28
B that whoever divorces … Matt 5:32
B, do not swear at all … Matt 5:34
B, love your enemies, … Matt 5:44
B, it will be more … Matt 11:22
B that for every idle … Matt 12:36
B that Elijah has come … Matt 17:12
B, I will not drink of … Matt 26:29
B that Elijah has also … Mark 9:13
B who hear: Love … Luke 6:27
B that it will be more … Luke 10:12

BUTLER
b did not remember … Gen 40:23

BUTTER
So he took *b* and milk … Gen 18:8
were smoother than *b* … Ps 55:21
of milk produces *b* … Prov 30:33

BUY
in Egypt to *b* grain … Gen 41:57
B it back in the presence … Ruth 4:4
b the threshing floor … 2 Sam 24:21
B the truth, and do not … Prov 23:23
Yes, come, *b* wine and … Is 55:1
B the field for money, and … Jer 32:25
will *b* fields for money … Jer 32:44
that we may *b* the poor … Amos 8:6
b food for all these … Luke 9:13
"*B* those things we … John 13:29
rejoice, those who *b* … 1 Cor 7:30
spend a year there, *b* … James 4:13
I counsel you to *b* … Rev 3:18
and that no one may *b* … Rev 13:17

BUYER
nothing," cries the *b* … Prov 20:14
as with the *b*, so with … Is 24:2
'Let not the *b* rejoice … Ezek 7:12

BUYS
a field and *b* it … Prov 31:16
has and *b* that field … Matt 13:44
b their merchandise … Rev 18:11

BYGONE
b generations … Acts 14:16

BYWORD
But He has made me a *b* … Job 17:6
You made us a *b* … Ps 44:14

CAESAR
—— Augustus Caesar (31 B.C.–A.D. 14):
Decree of brings Joseph and Mary to Bethlehem, Luke 2:1
—— Tiberius Caesar (A.D. 14–37):
Christ's ministry dated by, Luke 3:1–23
Tribute paid to, Matt 22:17–21
Jews side with, John 19:12
—— Claudius Caesar (A.D. 41–54):
Famine in time of, Acts 11:28
Banished Jews from Rome, Acts 18:2
—— Nero Caesar (A.D. 54–68):
Paul appealed to, Acts 25:8–12
Christian converts in household of, Phil 4:22
Paul tried before, 2 Tim 4:16–18
Called Augustus, Acts 25:21

CAESAREA
Roman capital of Palestine, Acts 12:19; 23:33
Paul escorted to, Acts 23:23–33
Paul imprisoned at; appeals to Caesar, Acts 25:4, 8–13
Peter preaches at, Acts 10:34–43
Paul preaches at, Acts 9:26–30; 18:22; 21:8

CAESAREA PHILIPPI
A city in northern Palestine; scene of Peter's great confession, Matt 16:13–20
Probable site of the transfiguration, Matt 17:1–3

CAGE
c is full of birds … Jer 5:27
foul spirit, and a *c* … Rev 18:2

CAIAPHAS
Son-in-law of Annas; high priest, John 18:13
Makes prophecy, John 11:49–52
Jesus appears before, John 18:23, 24
Apostles appear before, Acts 4:1–22

CAIN
Adam's first son, Gen 4:1
His offering rejected, Gen 4:2–7; Heb 11:4
Murders Abel; is exiled; settles in Nod, Gen 4:8–17
A type of evil, Jude 11

CAKE
Ephraim is a *c* … Hos 7:8

CAKES
Sustain me with *c* … Song 2:5
and love the raisin *c* … Hos 3:1

CALAMITIES
refuge, until these *c* … Ps 57:1

CALAMITY
for the day of their *c* … Deut 32:35
will laugh at your *c* … Prov 1:26
c shall come suddenly … Prov 6:15
If there is *c* in a … Amos 3:6

CALCULATED
c the dust of the … Is 40:12

CALDRON
this city is the *c* … Ezek 11:3

CALEB
Sent as spy; gives good report; rewarded, Num 13:2, 6, 27, 30; 14:5–9, 24–38

Inherits Hebron, Josh 14:6–15
Conquers his territory with Othniel's help, Josh 15:13–19

CALF
and made a molded c .... Ex 32:4
They made a c in Horeb .... Ps 106:19
is, than a fatted c .... Prov 15:17
like a stubborn c .... Hos 4:16
Your c is rejected .... Hos 8:5
And bring the fatted c ..... Luke 15:23
creature like a c .... Rev 4:7

CALL
Then men began to c .... Gen 4:26
I c heaven and earth .... Deut 4:26
I did not c, my son .... 1 Sam 3:6
I will c to the LORD ...... 1 Sam 12:17
c their lands after .... Ps 49:11
To you, O men, I c .... Prov 8:4
c upon Him while He .... Is 55:6
c the Sabbath a delight, ... Is 58:13
'C to Me, and I will .... Jer 33:3
Arise, c on your God .... Jon 1:6
They will c on My name .... Zech 13:9
c His name JESUS .... Matt 1:21
c the righteous .... Matt 9:13
Why do you c Me good .. Mark 10:18
shall c his name John ..... Luke 1:13
shall c His name JESUS .... Luke 1:31
Lord our God will c .... Acts 2:39
you must not c common ... Acts 10:15
c them My people .... Rom 9:25
then shall they c .... Rom 10:14
For God did not c .... 1 Thess 4:7
Let him c for the elders ... James 5:14
c and election sure .... 2 Pet 1:10

CALLED
c the light Day .... Gen 1:5
c his wife's name Eve .... Gen 3:20
"I, the LORD, have c .... Is 42:6
I have c you by your .... Is 43:1
The LORD has c Me from ...... Is 49:1
and out of Egypt I c .... Hos 11:1
"Out of Egypt I c .... Matt 2:15
a city c Nazareth .... Matt 2:23
For many are c .... Matt 20:16
to those who are the c ...... Rom 8:28
these He also c .... Rom 8:30
But God has c us to .... 1 Cor 7:15
praises of Him who c .... 1 Pet 2:9
knowledge of Him who c .... 2 Pet 1:3
c children of God .... 1 John 3:1

CALLED BY MY NAME
if My people who are c .... 2 Chr 7:14
everyone who is c, ... Is 43:7
a nation that was not c .... Is 65:1
this house which is c .... Jer 7:10
the city which is c .... Jer 25:29
house which is c .... Jer 32:34
the Gentiles who are c ..... Amos 9:12
the Gentiles who are c ... Acts 15:17

CALLING
the gifts and the c .... Rom 11:29
For you see your c .... 1 Cor 1:26
remain in the same c .... 1 Cor 7:20
to walk worthy of the c ...... Eph 4:1
in one hope of your c .... Eph 4:4
us with a holy c .... 2 Tim 1:9
of the heavenly c .... Heb 3:1

CALLS
c them all by name .... Ps 147:4
there is no one who c .... Is 64:7
David himself c .... Mark 12:37
c his own sheep .... John 10:3
For "whoever c .... Rom 10:13

CALM
the sea will become c .... Jon 1:12
there was a great c .... Matt 8:26

CALMED
Surely I have c .... Ps 131:2

CALVARY
Christ crucified there, Luke 23:33
Same as "Golgotha" in Hebrew, John 19:17

CALVES
made two c of gold .... 1 Kin 12:28
their cow c without .... Job 21:10
like stall-fed c .... Mal 4:2
blood of goats and c .... Heb 9:12
he took the blood of c ...... Heb 9:19

CAMEL
it is easier for a c .... Matt 19:24
and swallow a c .... Matt 23:24

CAMEL'S
John was clothed with c .... Mark 1:6

CAMP
"This is God's c .... Gen 32:2
who went before the c ...... Ex 14:19
to Him, outside the c ...... Heb 13:13

CAN
I c do all things .... Phil 4:13

CANA
A village of upper Galilee; home of Nathanael, John 21:2
Site of Christ's first miracle, John 2:1–11
Healing at, John 4:46–54

CANAAN
A son of Ham, Gen 10:6
Cursed by Noah, Gen 9:20–25
—— Promised Land, Gen 12:5
Boundaries of, Gen 10:19
God's promises concerning, given to
Abraham, Gen 12:1–3
to Isaac, Gen 26:2, 3
to Jacob, Gen 28:10–13
to Israel, Ex 3:8
Conquest of, announced, Gen 15:7–21
preceded by spying expedition, Num 13:1–33
delayed by unbelief, Num 14:1–35
accomplished by the Lord, Josh 23:1–16
achieved only in part, Judg 1:21, 27–36

CANAANITES
Israelites commanded to:
drive them out; not serve their gods, Ex 23:23–33
shun their abominations, Lev 18:24–30
not make covenants or intermarry with them, Deut 7:1–3

CANCER
will spread like c .... 2 Tim 2:17

CANE
bought Me no sweet c .... Is 43:24
Sheba, and sweet c .... Jer 6:20

CANOPIES
He made darkness c ..... 2 Sam 22:12

CANOPY
His c around Him was ...... Ps 18:11

CAPERNAUM
Simon Peter's home, Mark 1:21, 29
Christ performs healings there, Matt 8:5–17; 9:1–8; Mark 1:21–28; John 4:46–54
preaches there, Mark 9:33–50; John 6:24–71
uses as headquarters, Matt 4:13–17
pronounces judgment upon, Matt 11:23, 24

CAPPADOCIA
Jews from, at Pentecost, Acts 2:1, 9
Christians of, addressed by Peter, 1 Pet 1:1

CAPSTONE
bring forth the c .... Zech 4:7

CAPTAIN
c of the guard, an .... Gen 39:1
made Amasa c of the .... 2 Sam 17:25
Nebuzaradan the c .... 2 Kin 25:11
which, having no c .... Prov 6:7
of troops and the c .... John 18:12
to the c of the guard ...... Acts 28:16

CAPTIVE
have led captivity c .... Ps 68:18
of your neck, O c .... Is 52:2
they shall now go c .... Amos 6:7
and be led away c .... Luke 21:24
He led captivity c .... Eph 4:8

CAPTIVES
will bring back the c .... Amos 9:14
and return their c .... Zeph 2:7
make c of gullible women .. 2 Tim 3:6

CAPTIVITY
bring you back from c ..... Deut 30:3
high, You have led c .... Ps 68:18
Judah has gone into c .... Lam 1:3
from David until the c .... Matt 1:17
and bringing me into c ..... Rom 7:23
every thought into c .... 2 Cor 10:5
on high, He led c .... Eph 4:8
shall go into c .... Rev 13:10

CARCASS
honey were in the c .... Judg 14:8
For wherever the c .... Matt 24:28

CARE
and let her c for him .... 1 Kin 1:2
into the c of Hegai the .... Esth 2:8
Your c has preserved my .. Job 10:12
the LORD will take c of me ... Ps 27:10
do You c about anyone, ... Matt 22:16
to an inn, and took c of ... Luke 10:34
"Lord, do You not c ...... Luke 10:40
not c about the sheep ...... John 10:13
you to be without c .... 1 Cor 7:32
same c for one another ... 1 Cor 12:25
but that our c for you ..... 2 Cor 7:12
who will sincerely c .... Phil 2:20
that now at last your c for .. Phil 4:10
how will he take c .... 1 Tim 3:5
that You take c of him .... Heb 2:6
casting all your c .... 1 Pet 5:7

CARED
he said, not that he c .... John 12:6

CAREFUL
c to observe all the .... Deut 17:19
shall be c to observe ..... 2 Kin 17:37
c to maintain good works ... Titus 3:8

CAREFULLY
c keep all these .... Deut 11:22
choose his friends c .... Prov 12:26
than love c concealed .... Prov 27:5
I shall walk c all my .... Is 38:15
you have c followed .... 1 Tim 4:6

CARELESS
but he who is c .... Prov 19:16

CARES
no one c for my soul .... Ps 142:4
and are choked with c ..... Luke 8:14
He who is unmarried c ..... 1 Cor 7:32
for He c for you .... 1 Pet 5:7

CARMEL
City of Judah, Josh 15:55
Site of Saul's victory, 1 Sam 15:12
—— A mountain of Palestine, Josh 19:26
Scene of Elijah's triumph, 1 Kin 18:19–45
Elisha visits, 2 Kin 2:25

CARNAL
spiritual, but I am c .... Rom 7:14

c mind is enmity . . . . Rom 8:7
for you are still *c* . . . . 1 Cor 3:3
our warfare are not *c* . . . . . . 2 Cor 10:4

CARNALLY
we may know them *c* . . . . . . Gen 19:5
that we may know him *c* . . Judg 19:22
c minded is death . . . . Rom 8:6

CAROUSE
count it pleasure to *c* . . . . . . 2 Pet 2:13

CAROUSING
be weighed down with *c* . . Luke 21:34

CARPENTER
Is this not the *c* . . . . Mark 6:3

CARRIED
the LORD your God *c* . . . . . . Deut 1:31
and *c* our sorrows . . . . Is 53:4
parted from them and *c* . . Luke 24:51
c me away in the . . . . Rev 17:3

CARRY
shall *c* me out of Egypt . . . . Gen 47:30
you shall *c* up my bones . . . . Ex 13:19
longer *c* the tabernacle . . . 1 Chr 23:26
their hands cannot *c* . . . . Job 5:12
c them away like a . . . . Ps 90:5
to gray hairs I will *c* you . . . . . . Is 46:4
and *c* out great exploits . . . Dan 11:32
I am not worthy to *c* . . . . Matt 3:11
C neither money bag . . . . . . Luke 10:4
for you to *c* your bed . . . . . . John 5:10
c you where you do not . . . John 21:18
it is certain we can *c* . . . . 1 Tim 6:7

CARRYING
a man will meet you *c* . . . . Mark 14:13
always *c* about in the . . . . . 2 Cor 4:10

CART
ark of the LORD on the *c* . . 1 Sam 6:11
ark of God on a new *c* . . . . . 2 Sam 6:3
Every *c* had four bronze . . 1 Kin 7:30
and sin as if with a *c* rope . . . . Is 5:18
as a *c* is weighed down . . . Amos 2:13

CARTS
and Joseph gave them *c*, . . Gen 45:21
made ten *c* of bronze . . . . . . 1 Kin 7:27
the ten *c*, and ten lavers . . . 1 Kin 7:43
one Sea, and the *c* . . . . . . 2 Kin 25:16

CARVE
that its maker should *c* it . . . Hab 2:18

CARVED
for yourself a *c* image . . . . Ex 20:4
shall burn the *c* images . . . . Deut 7:25
the *c* images of their gods . . Deut 12:3
son, to make a *c* image . . . . Judg 17:3
Micah's *c* image which . . . . Judg 18:31
Then he *c* cherubim . . . . 1 Kin 6:35
He even set a *c* image, ... 2 Chr 33:7
to shame who serve *c* . . . . Ps 97:7
workman to prepare a *c* . . . . . Is 40:20
the *c* images of Babylon . . . . Jer 51:47
I will cut off the *c* image . . . . Nah 1:14

CASE
God has judged my *c* . . . . Gen 30:6
c that is too hard . . . . Deut 1:17
I have prepared my *c* . . . . Job 13:18
I would present my *c* . . . . . . Job 23:4
"Present your *c* . . . . Is 41:21
plead His *c* with all flesh . . . Jer 25:31
My *c* with you face to . . . . Ezek 20:35
plead your *c* before the . . . . . . Mic 6:1
Him, until He pleads my *c* . . . . Mic 7:9
Festus laid Paul's *c* . . . . Acts 25:14

CASSIA
myrrh and aloes and *c* . . . . Ps 45:8

CAST
C out this bondwoman . . . . Gen 21:10
c him into this pit which . . . Gen 37:22
c longing eyes on Joseph . . . Gen 39:7
c it before Pharaoh, ... Ex 7:9
army He has *c* into the sea . . . Ex 15:4
that I may *c* lots for you . . . . Josh 18:6
c two pillars of bronze . . . . . 1 Kin 7:15
they *c* lots for their duty, . . 1 Chr 25:8
they *c* Pur (that is, the lot) . . . Esth 3:7
had *c* Pur (that is, the lot), . . Esth 9:24
When they *c* you down . . . . Job 22:29
c away Their cords from . . . . . . Ps 2:3
c upon You from birth . . . . . . Ps 22:10
for My clothing they *c* lots . . . Ps 22:18
Why are you *c* down . . . . Ps 42:5
But You have *c* us off . . . . Ps 44:9
c me away from Your . . . . Ps 51:11
C your burden on the . . . . Ps 55:22
He *c* on them the . . . . Ps 78:49
the LORD will not *c* . . . . Ps 94:14
me up and *c* me away . . . . . . Ps 102:10
The lot is *c* into the lap, . . . Prov 16:33
the people *c* off restraint . . Prov 29:18
and the earth shall *c* . . . . Is 26:19
My sight, as I have *c* . . . . Jer 7:15
C away from you all . . . . . . Ezek 18:31
Did we not *c* three men . . . . . Dan 3:24
brought Daniel and *c* . . . . Dan 6:16
c all our sins into . . . . Mic 7:19
whole body to be *c* . . . . Matt 5:29
c out demons in Your . . . . . . Matt 7:22
the kingdom will be *c* . . . . . . Matt 8:12
spirits, to *c* them out . . . . Matt 10:1
And if I *c* out demons by . . Matt 12:27
My clothing they *c* lots . . . . Matt 27:35
can Satan *c* out Satan . . . . . . Mark 3:23
In My name they will *c* . . . Mark 16:17
do your sons *c* them out . . Luke 11:19
has power to *c* into hell . . . Luke 12:5
His garments and *c* lots . . . Luke 23:34
by no means *c* out . . . . John 6:37
C the net on the right . . . . . John 21:6
c away His people . . . . Rom 11:1
C out the bondwoman . . . . Gal 4:30
c away your confidence . . . . Heb 10:35
c their crowns before . . . . Rev 4:10
the great dragon was *c* . . . . . Rev 12:9
c him into the bottomless . . . Rev 20:3
was *c* into the lake of fire . . Rev 20:15

CAST OUT DEMONS
c in Your name, ... Matt 7:22
raise the dead, *c* . . . . Matt 10:8
"This fellow does not *c* . . . Matt 12:24
heal sicknesses and to *c* . . . Mark 3:15
In My name they will *c* . . . Mark 16:17
And if I *c* by Beelzebub, . . Luke 11:19
that fox, 'Behold, I *c* . . . . . Luke 13:32

CASTING
nation which I am *c* . . . . Lev 20:23
Andrew his brother, *c* . . . . . . Matt 4:18
c down arguments . . . . 2 Cor 10:5
c all your care . . . . 1 Pet 5:7

CASTING OUT DEMONS
all Galilee, and *c* . . . . Mark 1:39
who does not follow us *c* . . Mark 9:38
someone *c* in Your name, . . . Luke 9:49

CASTLE
are like the bars of a *c* . . . . Prov 18:19

CASTS
If Satan *c* out Satan . . . . . . Matt 12:26
perfect love *c* out . . . . 1 John 4:18

CATASTROPHE
bring such a *c* on this place . . Jer 19:3
not rise from the *c* that I . . . . Jer 51:64

CATCH
in wait to *c* the poor . . . . Ps 10:9
c Him in His words . . . . Mark 12:13
down your nets for a *c* . . . . . Luke 5:4
From now on you will *c* . . Luke 5:10
seeking to *c* Him in . . . . Luke 11:54
they could not *c* Him in . . . Luke 20:26

CATCHES
and the wolf *c* the . . . . John 10:12
c the wise in their . . . . 1 Cor 3:19

CATERPILLAR
their crops to the *c* . . . . Ps 78:46

CATTLE
c you shall take as . . . . Josh 8:2
does not let their *c* . . . . Ps 107:38

CAUGHT
behind him was a ram *c* . . . Gen 22:13
and that night they *c* . . . . . . John 21:3
Spirit of the Lord *c* . . . . Acts 8:39
her Child was *c* up . . . . Rev 12:5

CAUSE
I would commit my *c* . . . . Job 5:8
my enemy without *c* . . . . Ps 7:4
hate me without a *c* . . . . Ps 35:19
c His face to shine . . . . Ps 67:1
C me to know the way . . . . . . Ps 143:8
one to plead his *c* . . . . Prov 18:17
God, Who pleads the *c* . . . . Is 51:22
He judged the *c* . . . . Jer 22:16
brother without a *c* . . . . Matt 5:22
hated Me without a *c* . . . . . John 15:25
For this *c* I was born . . . . . . John 18:37

CAUSED
not *c* it to rain on the earth . . Gen 2:5
LORD God *c* a deep sleep . . . . Gen 2:21
LORD *c* the sea to go back . . Ex 14:21
Jonathan again *c* . . . . 1 Sam 20:17
pagan women *c* even him . . Neh 13:26
c the dawn to know its . . . . . Job 38:12
which You have *c* me . . . . . . Ps 119:49
I have *c* to be carried . . . . Jer 29:4
the LORD has *c* the . . . . Lam 2:6
He *c* me to eat that scroll . . . Ezek 3:2

CAVALRY
and cities for his *c* . . . . 1 Kin 9:19
on a horse with the *c* . . . . 1 Kin 20:20
their *c* comes from afar . . . . . . Hab 1:8

CAVE
daughters dwelt in a *c* . . . . . Gen 19:30
field and the *c* that is in . . . . Gen 23:11
him in the *c* of Machpelah . . Gen 25:9
in a *c* at Makkedah . . . . Josh 10:16
escaped to the *c* of . . . . 1 Sam 22:1
hidden them, fifty to a *c* . . . 1 Kin 18:4
It was a *c*, and a stone . . . . . John 11:38

CAVES
the people hid in *c* . . . . 1 Sam 13:6
rocks, and into the *c* . . . . Is 2:19
in dens and *c* of the . . . . Heb 11:38

CEASE
and night shall not *c* . . . . Gen 8:22
Why should the work *c* . . . . Neh 6:3
There the wicked *c* . . . . Job 3:17
He makes wars *c* . . . . Ps 46:9
C listening to . . . . Prov 19:27
when the grinders *c* . . . . Eccl 12:3
C to do evil . . . . Is 1:16
eyes flow and do not *c*, ... Lam 3:49
cause all her mirth to *c* . . . . . . Hos 2:11
they did not *c* teaching . . . . . . Acts 5:42
tongues, they will *c* . . . . 1 Cor 13:8
do not *c* to give . . . . Eph 1:16
do not *c* to pray for . . . . Col 1:9

CEASED
c building the city . . . . Gen 11:8
the sea, and the sea *c* . . . . Jon 1:15
this woman has not *c* to . . . Luke 7:45
offense of the cross has *c* . . . . Gal 5:11

CEASES
for the godly man *c* . . . . Ps 12:1

CEASING
c your work of faith . . . . . . 1 Thess 1:3
thank God without *c* . . . . . 1 Thess 2:13
pray without *c* . . . . 1 Thess 5:17

CEDAR
dwell in a house of *c* . . . . 2 Sam 7:2

He shall grow like a *c* . . . . Ps 92:12
of our houses are *c* . . . . Song 1:17
it, paneling it with *c* . . . . Jer 22:14
Indeed Assyria was a *c* . . . . Ezek 31:3

CEDARS
the LORD breaks the *c* . . . . Ps 29:5
c of Lebanon which He . . . . Ps 104:16

CELEBRATE
you shall *c* your sabbath . . . Lev 23:32
You shall *c* it in the . . . . Lev 23:41
to *c* the dedication with . . . . Neh 12:27
c yearly the fourteenth . . . . . Esth 9:21

CELEBRATED
Herod's birthday was *c* . . . . . Matt 14:6

CELESTIAL
but the glory of the *c* . . . . . 1 Cor 15:40

CENCHREA
A harbor of Corinth, Acts 18:18
Home of Phoebe, Rom 16:1

CENSER
Aaron, each took his *c* . . . . . . Lev 10:1
Each man had a *c* . . . . Ezek 8:11
which had the golden *c* . . . . . . Heb 9:4
the angel took the *c* . . . . Rev 8:5

CENSUS
When you take the *c* of . . . . . . Ex 30:12
"Take a *c* of all the . . . . Num 1:2
Take a *c* of the people . . . . . Num 26:4
Israel because of this *c* . . . 1 Chr 27:24
the *c* in which David . . . . 2 Chr 2:17
c first took place while . . . . . . Luke 2:2
in the days of the *c* . . . . Acts 5:37

CENTER
the sanctuary in the *c* . . . . . . Ezek 48:8
side, and Jesus in the *c* . . . John 19:18

CENTURION
c came to Him, pleading . . . . Matt 8:5
when the *c*, who stood . . . Mark 15:39
when the *c* saw what . . . . . Luke 23:47
Cornelius the *c*, a just . . . . . Acts 10:22
said to the *c* who stood . . . . Acts 22:25
a *c* of the Augustan . . . . Acts 27:1

CENTURION'S
a certain *c* servant, who . . . . Luke 7:2

CEPHAS
Aramaic for Peter, John 1:42

CERAMIC
the iron mixed with *c* clay . . Dan 2:41

CEREMONIALLY
Israel and cleanse them *c* . . . Num 8:6

CEREMONIES
rites and *c* you shall keep . . . Num 9:3
as in the *c* of your fathers, . . . Jer 34:5

CERTAIN
a *c* man of Bethlehem, ... Ruth 1:1
Know for *c* that on the . . . . 1 Kin 2:42
a *c* man clothed in linen, . . . Dan 10:5
was a *c* landowner . . . . Matt 21:33
into the city to a *c* man . . . Matt 26:18
But a *c* Samaritan, as he . . Luke 10:33
A *c* man had a fig tree . . . . . Luke 13:6
A *c* man gave a great . . . . . Luke 14:16
A *c* man had two sons . . . . Luke 15:11
There was a *c* rich man . . . . Luke 16:1
there was a *c* beggar . . . . . . Luke 16:20
there was a *c* nobleman . . . . John 4:46
c we can carry nothing . . . . . 1 Tim 6:7
He designates a *c* day . . . . Heb 4:7
a *c* fearful expectation . . . . . Heb 10:27

CERTAINLY NOT
C! Indeed, let God be true . . . Rom 3:4
C! For then how will God . . . Rom 3:6
the law through faith? *C*! . . . . Rom 3:31
C! How shall we who died . . . Rom 6:2
law but under grace? *C* . . . . . Rom 6:15
Is the law sin? *C* . . . . Rom 7:7
C! But sin, that it might . . . . . Rom 7:13
with God? *C* . . . . Rom 9:14
cast away His people? *C* . . . Rom 11:1
C! But through their fall, . . Rom 11:11
members of a harlot? *C* . . . 1 Cor 6:15
a minister of sin? *C* . . . . Gal 2:17
C! For if there had been . . . . Gal 3:21

CERTAINTY
make you know the *c* . . . . . Prov 22:21
you may know the *c* . . . . Luke 1:4

CERTIFICATE
writes her a *c* of divorce . . . Deut 24:1
Where is the *c* of your . . . . Is 50:1
given her a *c* of divorce . . . . . . Jer 3:8
a man to write a *c* . . . . Mark 10:4

CERTIFIED
His testimony has *c* . . . . John 3:33

CHAFF
c that a storm . . . . Job 21:18
c which the wind . . . . Ps 1:4
Let them be like *c* . . . . Ps 35:5
be chased like the *c* . . . . Is 17:13
You shall conceive *c* . . . . Is 33:11
the day passes like *c* . . . . Zeph 2:2
He will burn up the *c* . . . . . . Matt 3:12

CHAIN
He has made my *c* . . . . Lam 3:7
pit and a great *c* . . . . Rev 20:1

CHAINED
of God is not *c* . . . . 2 Tim 2:9
the prisoners as if *c* . . . . Heb 13:3

CHAINS
their kings with *c* . . . . Ps 149:8
your neck with *c* . . . . Song 1:10
And his *c* fell off . . . . Acts 12:7
am, except for these *c* . . . . Acts 26:29
Remember my *c* . . . . Col 4:18
minister to me in my *c* . . . . . Philem 13
delivered them into *c* . . . . 2 Pet 2:4

CHAINWORK
with wreaths of *c* . . . . 1 Kin 7:17
carved palm trees and *c* . . . . 2 Chr 3:5

CHAIR
and a table and a *c* . . . . 2 Kin 4:10

CHALCEDONY
sapphire, the third *c* . . . . . . Rev 21:19

CHALDEA
Originally, the southern portion of Babylonia, Gen 11:31
Applied later to all Babylonia, Dan 3:8
Abram came from, Gen 11:28–31

CHALDEANS
Attack Job, Job 1:17
Nebuchadnezzar, king of, 2 Kin 24:1
Jerusalem defeated by, 2 Kin 25:1–21
Babylon, "the glory of," Is 13:19
Predicted captivity of Jews among, Jer 25:1–26
God's agent, Hab 1:6

CHALK
he marks one out with *c* . . . . . Is 44:13

CHALKSTONES
c that are beaten to dust . . . . . Is 27:9

CHAMBER
went into his *c* and wept . . Gen 43:30
in his cool private *c*) . . . . Judg 3:20
into an inner *c* to hide . . . . 2 Chr 18:24
go out from his *c* . . . . Joel 2:16

CHAMBERS
and the *c* of the south . . . . . . Job 9:9
brought me into his *c* . . . . Song 1:4
and his *c* by injustice . . . . Jer 22:13

CHAMPION
And a *c* went out from . . . . 1 Sam 17:4

CHANCE
time and *c* happen to . . . . Eccl 9:11

CHANGE
c his countenance . . . . Job 14:20
c the night into day . . . . Job 17:12
and who can make Him *c* . . Job 23:13
Because they do not *c* . . . . Ps 55:19
a cloak You will *c* . . . . Ps 102:26
with those given to *c* . . . . . Prov 24:21
Can the Ethiopian *c* . . . . Jer 13:23
c times and law . . . . Dan 7:25
c their glory into . . . . Hos 4:7
the LORD, I do not *c* . . . . Mal 3:6
now and to *c* my tone . . . . Gal 4:20
there is also a *c* . . . . Heb 7:12

CHANGED
c my wages ten times, ... Gen 31:7
c his clothing, and came . . . Gen 41:14
them, and they will be *c* . . . Ps 102:26
But My people have *c* . . . . Jer 2:11
his countenance was *c*, ... Dan 5:9
c the glory of the . . . . Rom 1:23
but we shall all be *c* . . . . . . 1 Cor 15:51
up, and they will be *c* . . . . Heb 1:12
the priesthood being *c* . . . . Heb 7:12

CHANGERS'
and poured out the *c* . . . . John 2:15

CHANGES
c the times and the . . . . Dan 2:21

CHANNELS
c of the sea were seen . . . . Ps 18:15

CHANT
who *c* "Peace" while . . . . Mic 3:5

CHARACTER
and *c*, hope . . . . Rom 5:4
you know his proven *c* . . . . Phil 2:22

CHARCOAL
As *c* is to burning coals, . . . Prov 26:21

CHARGE
My voice and kept My *c* . . . . Gen 26:5
shall not *c* him interest . . . . . Ex 22:25
You shall not *c* interest . . . . Deut 23:19
in *c* of the music . . . . 1 Chr 15:22
kept the *c* of their God . . . . Neh 12:45
not sin nor *c* God with . . . . Job 1:22
His angels *c* over you . . . . Ps 91:11
His angels *c* over you . . . . Matt 4:6
His angels *c* over You . . . . . . Luke 4:10
not *c* them with this sin . . . . Acts 7:60
shall bring a *c* against . . . . . Rom 8:33
of Christ without *c* . . . . 1 Cor 9:18
of God to you free of *c* . . . . 2 Cor 11:7
anyone's bread free of *c* . . 2 Thess 3:8
This *c* I commit to you, ... 1 Tim 1:18

CHARGED
May it not be *c* . . . . 2 Tim 4:16

CHARIOT
He took off their *c* . . . . Ex 14:25
that suddenly a *c* . . . . 2 Kin 2:11
makes the clouds His *c* . . . . . . Ps 104:3
and overtake this *c* . . . . Acts 8:29

CHARIOTEERS
killed seven hundred *c* . . 2 Sam 10:18

CHARIOTS
the clatter of his *c* . . . . Judg 5:28
Some trust in *c* . . . . Ps 20:7
The *c* of God are . . . . Ps 68:17

CHARITABLE
you do not do your *c* . . . . Matt 6:1
that your *c* deed . . . . Matt 6:4
c deeds which she . . . . Acts 9:36

CHARM
C is deceitful and . . . . Prov 31:30

CHARMED
may bite when it is not *c* . . Eccl 10:11
vipers which cannot be *c* . . . . Jer 8:17

CHARMERS
heed the voice of *c* . . . . Ps 58:5

CHARMS
the perfume boxes, the *c*. ... Is 3:20
have scattered your *c* to ... Jer 3:13
who sew magic *c* ... Ezek 13:18

CHASE
Five of you shall *c* ... Lev 26:8
How could one *c* ... Deut 32:30
angel of the LORD *c* ... Ps 35:5

CHASTE
may present you as a *c* ... 2 Cor 11:2
to be discreet, *c* ... Titus 2:5
c conduct accompanied ... 1 Pet 3:2

CHASTEN
C your son while there ... Prov 19:18
is My desire, I will *c* ... Hos 10:10
a father does not *c* ... Heb 12:7
I love, I rebuke and *c* ... Rev 3:19

CHASTENED
c my soul with fasting ... Ps 69:10
c every morning ... Ps 73:14
The LORD has *c* me ... Ps 118:18
In vain I have *c* ... Jer 2:30
c us as seemed best ... Heb 12:10

CHASTENING
have not seen the *c* ... Deut 11:2
do not despise the *c* ... Job 5:17
'I have borne *c* ... Job 34:31
a prayer when Your *c* ... Is 26:16
if you are without *c* ... Heb 12:8
Now no *c* seems to be ... Heb 12:11

CHASTENS
the LORD your God *c* you ... Deut 8:5
the LORD loves He *c* ... Heb 12:6

CHASTISE
and I, even I, will *c* ... Lev 26:28
c them according ... Hos 7:12
I will therefore *c* ... Luke 23:22

CHASTISED
father *c* you with whips, .. 1 Kin 12:11
have *c* me, and I was *c* ... Jer 31:18

CHASTISEMENT
the *c* for our peace ... Is 53:5

CHATTER
c leads only to poverty ... Prov 14:23

CHEAT
'You shall not *c* ... Lev 19:13
Beware lest anyone *c* ... Col 2:8

CHEATED
let yourselves be *c* ... 1 Cor 6:7
we have *c* no one ... 2 Cor 7:2

CHEBAR
River in Babylonia, Ezek 1:3
Site of Ezekiel's visions, Ezek 10:15, 20

CHEDORLAOMER
A king of Elam; invaded Canaan, Gen 14:1–16

CHEEK
Let him give his *c* ... Lam 3:30
with a rod on the *c* ... Mic 5:1
on your right *c* ... Matt 5:39

CHEEKBONE
my enemies on the *c* ... Ps 3:7

CHEEKS
c are lovely with ... Song 1:10
His *c* are like a bed ... Song 5:13
struck Me, and My *c* ... Is 50:6

CHEER
See BE OF GOOD CHEER
and let your heart *c* ... Eccl 11:9
"Son, be of good *c* ... Matt 9:2

CHEERFUL
makes a *c* countenance ... Prov 15:13
for God loves a *c* ... 2 Cor 9:7
Is anyone *c*? Let him ... James 5:13

CHEERFULNESS
shows mercy, with *c* ... Rom 12:8

CHEESE
and curdle me like *c* ... Job 10:10

CHEMOSH
The god of the Moabites, Num 21:29
Children sacrificed to, 2 Kin 3:26, 27
Solomon builds altars to, 1 Kin 11:7
Josiah destroys altars of, 2 Kin 23:13

CHERISHES
but nourishes and *c* ... Eph 5:29
as a nursing mother *c* ... 1 Thess 2:7

CHERUB
Make one *c* at one end, ... Ex 25:19
c at one end on this side ... Ex 37:8
He rode upon a *c* ... 2 Sam 22:11
other *c* was ten cubits ... 1 Kin 6:25
And He rode upon a *c*, ... Ps 18:10
the wheels, under the *c* ... Ezek 10:2
anointed *c* who covers ... Ezek 28:14
tree between *c* and *c* ... Ezek 41:18

CHERUBIM
and He placed *c* ... Gen 3:24
shall make two *c* of gold ... Ex 25:18
an artistic design of *c* ... Ex 26:31
dwells between the *c* ... 2 Sam 6:2
two *c* of olive wood ... 1 Kin 6:23
out the wings of the *c* so .. 1 Kin 6:27
were lions, oxen, and *c* ... 1 Kin 7:29
its panels he engraved *c* ... 1 Kin 7:36
under the wings of the *c* ... 1 Kin 8:6
c overshadowed the ark ... 2 Chr 5:8
dwell between the *c* ... Ps 80:1
who dwells between the *c* ... Is 37:16
fire from among the *c* ... Ezek 10:2
above it were the *c* ... Heb 9:5

CHEST
offering in a *c* by its side .. 1 Sam 6:8
the *c* with the gold rats ... 1 Sam 6:11
the priest took a *c* ... 2 Kin 12:9
came and emptied the *c* .. 2 Chr 24:11

CHESTNUT
c trees, peeled white ... Gen 30:37

CHEW
or does not *c* the cud, is ... Lev 11:26

CHEWING
What the *c* locust left, the ... Joel 1:4
the *c* locust, my great ... Joel 2:25

CHICKS
gathers her *c* under her ... Matt 23:37

CHIEF
is white and ruddy, *c* ... Song 5:10
of whom I am *c* ... 1 Tim 1:15
Zion a *c* cornerstone ... 1 Pet 2:6
has become the *c* ... 1 Pet 2:7
C Shepherd appears ... 1 Pet 5:4

CHILD
See WITH CHILD
she is with *c* by harlotry ... Gen 38:24
that he was a beautiful *c* ... Ex 2:2
c grew, and she brought ... Ex 2:10
the *c* shall be a Nazirite ... Judg 13:5
the *c* ministered to the ... 1 Sam 2:11
c Samuel grew in stature .. 1 Sam 2:26
named the *c* Ichabod ... 1 Sam 4:21
her dead *c* in my bosom ... 1 Kin 3:20
Divide the living *c* in two ... 1 Kin 3:25
soul of the *c* came back .. 1 Kin 17:22
flesh of the *c* became ... 2 Kin 4:34
Like a weaned *c* ... Ps 131:2
c is known by his ... Prov 20:11
Train up a *c* in the ... Prov 22:6
before the *C* shall know ... Is 7:16
For unto us a *C* ... Is 9:6
c shall lead them ... Is 11:6
When Israel was a *c* ... Hos 11:1
with *c* of the Holy Spirit ... Matt 1:18
virgin shall be with *c* ... Matt 1:23
He took a little *c* ... Mark 9:36
of God as a little *c* ... Mark 10:15
kind of *c* will this be ... Luke 1:66
So the *c* grew and ... Luke 1:80
the circumcision of the *C* .. Luke 2:21
When I was a *c* ... 1 Cor 13:11
She bore a male *C* ... Rev 12:5

CHILDBEARING
she will be saved in *c* ... 1 Tim 2:15

CHILDBIRTH
pain as a woman in *c* ... Is 13:8

CHILDHOOD
from your flesh, for *c* ... Eccl 11:10
And he said, "From *c* ... Mark 9:21
c you have known ... 2 Tim 3:15

CHILDISH
I put away *c* things ... 1 Cor 13:11

CHILDLESS
give me, seeing I go *c* ... Gen 15:2
this man down as *c* ... Jer 22:30

CHILDREN
See LITTLE CHILDREN
she bore Jacob no *c* ... Gen 30:1
and all of you are *c* ... Ps 82:6
c are a heritage ... Ps 127:3
He has blessed your *c* ... Ps 147:13
let the *c* of Zion be ... Ps 149:2
c are blessed after ... Prov 20:7
c rise up and call her ... Prov 31:28
c are their oppressors ... Is 3:12
c whom the LORD has ... Is 8:18
be the peace of your *c* ... Is 54:13
they are My people, *c* ... Is 63:8
the hearts of the *c* ... Mal 4:6
c will rise up against ... Matt 10:21
and become as little *c* ... Matt 18:3
c were brought to Him ... Matt 19:13
"Let the little *c* ... Matt 19:14
the right to become *c* ... John 1:12
you were Abraham's *c* ... John 8:39
spirit that we are *c* ... Rom 8:16
but as my beloved *c* ... 1 Cor 4:14
Brethren, do not be *c* ... 1 Cor 14:20
c ought not to lay up ... 2 Cor 12:14
and were by nature *c* ... Eph 2:3
should no longer be *c* ... Eph 4:14
Walk as *c* of light ... Eph 5:8
and harmless, *c* of God ... Phil 2:15
now we are *c* of God ... 1 John 3:2
that we love the *c* ... 1 John 5:2
to hear that my *c* ... 3 John 4

CHILDREN'S
are really ours and our *c* .. Gen 31:16
the *c* children to the third ... Ex 34:7
His righteousness to *c* ... Ps 103:17
you see your *c* children ... Ps 128:6
inheritance to his *c* ... Prov 13:22
C children are the crown ... Prov 17:6
the *c* teeth are set on edge .. Jer 31:29
good to take the *c* bread .. Matt 15:26
eat from the *c* crumbs ... Mark 7:28

CHILION
Elimelech's son, Ruth 1:2
Orpah's deceased husband, Ruth 1:4, 5
Boaz redeems his estate, Ruth 4:9

CHINNERETH (or Chinneroth)
Fortified city in Naphtali, Deut 3:17
A region bordering the Sea of Galilee, 1 Kin 15:20
Same as the plain of Gennesaret, Matt 14:34
——— The O.T. name for the Sea of Galilee, Num 34:11
Also called Lake of Gennesaret, Luke 5:1

CHOICE
rather than *c* gold ... Prov 8:10

CHOIR
c went the opposite way, . . Neh 12:38

CHOKE
things entering in c the . . . . Mark 4:19

CHOKED
thorns sprang up and c . . . . Matt 13:7
are c with cares, riches, ... Luke 8:14

CHOOSE
therefore c life . . . . Deut 30:19
c none of his ways . . . . Prov 3:31
evil and c the good . . . . Is 7:15
will still c Israel . . . . Is 14:1
will again c Jerusalem . . . . . Zech 1:17
You did not c Me, but I . . . John 15:16
yet what I shall c . . . . Phil 1:22

CHOOSES
in the way He c . . . . Ps 25:12

CHOSE
a good while ago God c . . . . Acts 15:7
just as He c us in Him . . . . Eph 1:4
from the beginning c . . . . 2 Thess 2:13

CHOSEN
the LORD has c you to be . . . Deut 14:2
has c them to minister to . . . Deut 21:5
c the son of Jesse to . . . . . 1 Sam 20:30
of Jacob, His c . . . . 1 Chr 16:13
I have c Jerusalem, that . . . . 2 Chr 6:6
I have c David to be over . . . 2 Chr 6:6
people He has c . . . . Ps 33:12
a covenant with My c . . . . Ps 89:3
c the way of truth . . . . Ps 119:30
A good name is to be c . . . Prov 22:1
servant whom I have c . . . . Is 43:10
Is it a fast that I have c . . . . Is 58:5
c that good part . . . . Luke 10:42
I know whom I have c . . . . John 13:18
c you that you should . . . . . Acts 22:14
c the foolish things . . . . 1 Cor 1:27
Has God not c the poor . . . . James 2:5
But you are a c . . . . 1 Pet 2:9

CHRIST
See JESUS; LORD JESUS CHRIST; LOVE OF CHRIST; YOU ARE THE CHRIST
Preexistence of, Ps 2:7; John 8:58; Col 1:15–18
Birth of, from a virgin, Is 7:14; Matt 1:18–25
Deity of, Is 9:6; John 1:1, 14, 18; 20:28, 29; Rom 9:5; Heb 1:8
Humanity of, Gen 3:15; Matt 22:45; Luke 3:38; John 1:14; 1 Cor 15:45–47; Gal 4:4; Phil 2:5–11; 1 Tim 2:5
Character of:
omnipotent, Matt 28:18
omniscient, Col 2:3
omnipresent, Matt 18:20
eternal, John 1:1, 2, 15
holy, Luke 1:35
righteous, Is 53:11
just, Zech 9:9
guileless, 1 Pet 2:22
sinless, 2 Cor 5:21
spotless, 1 Pet 1:19
innocent, Matt 27:4
gentle, Matt 11:29
merciful, Heb 2:17
humble, Phil 2:8
forgiving, Luke 23:34
Mission of:
do God's will, John 6:38
save sinners, Luke 19:10
destroy Satan's works, Heb 2:14; 1 John 3:8
fulfill the O.T., Matt 5:17
give life, John 10:10, 28
complete revelation, Heb 1:1
Worshiped by:
O.T. saints, Josh 5:13–15
demons, Mark 5:2, 6
men, John 9:38
angels, Heb 1:6
disciples, Luke 24:52
saints in glory, Rev 7:9, 10
all, Phil 2:10, 11
O.T. types of:
Adam, Rom 5:14
Abel, Heb 12:24
Moses, Deut 18:15
Passover, 1 Cor 5:7
manna, John 6:32
bronze serpent, John 3:14
genealogy of Jesus C . . . . Matt 1:1
Jesus who is called C . . . . . . Matt 1:16
"You are the C . . . . Matt 16:16
do you think about the C . . Matt 22:42
if You are the C . . . . Matt 26:63
of the gospel of Jesus C, ... Mark 1:1
You are the C . . . . Mark 8:29
Are You the C, the Son . . Mark 14:61
a Savior, who is C . . . . Luke 2:11
and said, "The C of God . . . Luke 9:20
that He Himself is C . . . . Luke 23:2
is translated, the C) . . . . John 1:41
the law that the C . . . . John 12:34
believe that Jesus is the C . John 20:31
crucified, both Lord and C . . Acts 2:36
preaching Jesus as the C . . . . Acts 5:42
he preached the C . . . . Acts 9:20
that this Jesus is the C . . . . . Acts 9:22
Jesus the C heals . . . . Acts 9:34
the C had to suffer and . . . . . Acts 17:3
that Jesus is the C . . . . Acts 18:28
that the C would suffer, . . . Acts 26:23
His Son Jesus C our Lord . . . Rom 1:3
faith in Jesus C to all and . . Rom 3:22
through our Lord Jesus C . . . Rom 5:1
in due time C died for the . . . Rom 5:6
through our Lord Jesus C . . Rom 5:11
through the One, Jesus C . . Rom 5:17
that just as C was raised . . . . Rom 6:4
life in C Jesus our Lord . . . . Rom 6:23
law through the body of C . . Rom 7:4
those who are in C Jesus . . . . Rom 8:1
have the Spirit of C . . . . Rom 8:9
and joint heirs with C . . . . . . Rom 8:17
It is C who died . . . . Rom 8:34
C came, who is over all . . . . . Rom 9:5
C is the end of the law . . . . . Rom 10:4
many, are one body in C . . . . Rom 12:5
put on the Lord Jesus C . . . Rom 13:14
For to this end C died . . . . . . Rom 14:9
C did not please . . . . Rom 15:3
just as C also received us, . . Rom 15:7
serve our Lord Jesus C . . . Rom 16:18
are sanctified in C Jesus . . . . 1 Cor 1:2
Is C divided . . . . 1 Cor 1:13
For C did not send me to . . 1 Cor 1:17
we preach C crucified . . . . . . 1 Cor 1:23
Him you are in C Jesus . . . . 1 Cor 1:30
among you except Jesus C . 1 Cor 2:2
is laid, which is Jesus C . . . 1 Cor 3:11
indeed C, our Passover, ... 1 Cor 5:7
bodies are members of C . . 1 Cor 6:15
Lord Jesus C, through . . . . . 1 Cor 8:6
you sin against C . . . . 1 Cor 8:12
and that Rock was C . . . . . . 1 Cor 10:4
just as I also imitate C . . . . 1 Cor 11:1
head of every man is C . . . . 1 Cor 11:3
you are the body of C . . . . 1 Cor 12:27
that C died for our sins . . . . 1 Cor 15:3
if C is not risen, then . . . . . 1 Cor 15:14
even so in C all shall be . . 1 Cor 15:22
our Lord Jesus C . . . . 1 Cor 15:57
sufferings of C abound . . . . . 2 Cor 1:5
leads us in triumph in C, . . . 2 Cor 2:14
you are an epistle of C . . . . . 2 Cor 3:3
veil is taken away in C . . . . 2 Cor 3:14
gospel of the glory of C . . . . . 2 Cor 4:4
the judgment seat of C . . . . 2 Cor 5:10
if anyone is in C . . . . 2 Cor 5:17
accord has C with Belial . . 2 Cor 6:15
and gentleness of C . . . . 2 Cor 10:1
as a chaste virgin to C . . . . 2 Cor 11:2
to pervert the gospel of C . . . . Gal 1:7
which we have in C Jesus, ... Gal 2:4
to be justified by C . . . . Gal 2:17
been crucified with C . . . . . . Gal 2:20
your Seed," who is C . . . . Gal 3:16
before by God in C . . . . Gal 3:17
through faith in C Jesus . . . . . Gal 3:26
until C is formed in you, ... Gal 4:19
which C has made us free . . . . Gal 5:1
become estranged from C . . . . Gal 5:4
cross of our Lord Jesus C . . . Gal 6:14
the heavenly places in C . . . . . Eph 1:3
in one all things in C, ... Eph 1:10
which He worked in C . . . . . . Eph 1:20
C (by grace you have been . . . Eph 2:5
time you were without C . . . . Eph 2:12
Jesus C Himself being . . . . . . Eph 2:20
unsearchable riches of C . . . . . Eph 3:8
C may dwell in your . . . . Eph 3:17
stature of the fullness of C . . Eph 4:13
Him who is the head—C . . . . Eph 4:15
even as God in C forgave . . . Eph 4:32
C will give you light . . . . Eph 5:14
C is head of the church . . . . . Eph 5:23
just as C also loved the . . . . . Eph 5:25
or in truth, C is preached . . . Phil 1:18
to me, to live is C . . . . Phil 1:21
to depart and be with C . . . . . Phil 1:23
worthy of the gospel of C . . . Phil 1:27
which was also in C Jesus . . . Phil 2:5
confess that Jesus C . . . . Phil 2:11
I have counted loss for C . . . . Phil 3:7
enemies of the cross of C . . . Phil 3:18
C who strengthens . . . . Phil 4:13
riches in glory by C Jesus . . Phil 4:19
of your faith in C Jesus . . . . . . Col 1:4
which is C in you . . . . Col 1:27
every man perfect in C . . . . . . Col 1:28
of the Father and of C . . . . Col 2:2
received C Jesus the Lord . . . . Col 2:6
but the substance is of C . . . . Col 2:17
you were raised with C . . . . Col 3:1
hidden with C in God . . . . Col 3:3
C who is our life . . . . Col 3:4
C is all and in all . . . . Col 3:11
Let the word of C dwell . . . . . Col 3:16
dead in C will rise first . . 1 Thess 4:16
our Lord Jesus C, ... 1 Thess 5:9
and the Lord Jesus C . . . . . 2 Thess 1:2
of our Lord Jesus C . . . . . . 2 Thess 2:1
of our Lord Jesus C . . . . . 2 Thess 2:14
I thank C Jesus our Lord . . 1 Tim 1:12
that C Jesus came into . . . . 1 Tim 1:15
first Jesus C might show . . . 1 Tim 1:16
and men, the Man C . . . . 1 Tim 2:5
in C Jesus before time . . . . . 2 Tim 1:9
good soldier of Jesus C . . . . 2 Tim 2:3
in C Jesus with eternal . . . 2 Tim 2:10
in C Jesus will suffer . . . . . 2 Tim 3:12
faith which is in C Jesus . . 2 Tim 3:15
and the Lord Jesus C, ... 2 Tim 4:1
God and Savior Jesus C . . . . Titus 2:13
of our confession, C Jesus, . . . Heb 3:1
C as a Son over His own . . . . . Heb 3:6
C if we hold the beginning . . Heb 3:14
So also C did not glorify . . . . . Heb 5:5
elementary principles of C . . . Heb 6:1
But C came as High Priest . . Heb 9:11
more shall the blood of C . . . Heb 9:14
For C has not entered the . . . Heb 9:24
C was offered once to bear . . Heb 9:28
body of Jesus C once for . . Heb 10:10
Jesus C is the same . . . . Heb 13:8
of the blood of Jesus C . . . . . 1 Pet 1:2
Spirit of C who was in . . . . . 1 Pet 1:11
the precious blood of C . . . . 1 Pet 1:19
because C also suffered . . . . 1 Pet 2:21
For C also suffered once . . . 1 Pet 3:18
resurrection of Jesus C . . . . 1 Pet 3:21

for the name of C . . . . 1 Pet 4:14
God and Savior Jesus C . . . . 2 Pet 1:1
of our Lord Jesus C . . . . 2 Pet 1:16
C His Son cleanses us . . . . . 1 John 1:7
Jesus C the righteous . . . . . 1 John 2:1
denies that Jesus is the C . 1 John 2:22
name of His Son Jesus C . 1 John 3:23
confesses that Jesus C . . . . 1 John 4:2
that Jesus is the C . . . . 1 John 5:1
true, in His Son Jesus C . . 1 John 5:20
of C does not have God . . . . . 2 John 9
and our Lord Jesus C . . . . Jude 4
The Revelation of Jesus C . . . . Rev 1:1
from Jesus C, the faithful . . . . Rev 1:5
the testimony of Jesus C . . . . . Rev 1:9
of our Lord and of His C, . . Rev 11:15
of His C have come . . . . Rev 12:10
and reigned with C . . . . Rev 20:4
be priests of God and of C . . Rev 20:6

CHRISTIAN
me to become a C . . . . Acts 26:28
anyone suffers as a C . . . . . . 1 Pet 4:16

CHRISTIANS
were first called C . . . . Acts 11:26

CHRIST'S
you are C, and Christ is . . . 1 Cor 3:23
We are fools for C sake, . . . 1 Cor 4:10
are C at His coming . . . . . 1 Cor 15:23
in himself that he is C, ... 2 Cor 10:7
if you are C, then you are . . . Gal 3:29
partake of C sufferings . . . . . 1 Pet 4:13

CHRISTS
For false c and . . . . Matt 24:24

CHRYSOLITE
sardius, the seventh c . . . . . . Rev 21:20

CHRYSOPRASE
ninth topaz, the tenth c . . . . Rev 21:20

CHURCH
rock I will build My c . . . . . Matt 16:18
them, tell it to the c . . . . . . Matt 18:17
c daily those who were . . . . . Acts 2:47
elders in every c . . . . Acts 14:23
do you despise the c . . . . . 1 Cor 11:22
persecuted the c of God . . . 1 Cor 15:9
over all things to the c . . . . . Eph 1:22
be made known by the c . . . . Eph 3:10
also loved the c . . . . Eph 5:25
Himself a glorious c . . . . Eph 5:27
as the Lord does the c . . . . . . Eph 5:29
no c shared with me . . . . Phil 4:15
body, which is the c . . . . Col 1:24
is the c of the living . . . . . . 1 Tim 3:15
and do not let the c . . . . 1 Tim 5:16
general assembly and c . . . . Heb 12:23
To the angel of the c . . . . Rev 2:1

CHURCHES
strengthening the c . . . . Acts 15:41
The c of Christ greet . . . . . . Rom 16:16
imitators of the c . . . . 1 Thess 2:14
John, to the seven c . . . . Rev 1:4
angels of the seven c . . . . Rev 1:20
these things in the c . . . . Rev 22:16

CHURNING
For as the c of milk . . . . Prov 30:33

CHURNS
My heart c within Me . . . . Hos 11:8

CILICIA
Paul's homeland, Acts 21:39
Students from, argued with Stephen, Acts 6:9
Paul labors in, Gal 1:21

CINNAMON
sweet-smelling c . . . . Ex 30:23
saffron, calamus and c, ... Song 4:14
c and incense, fragrant . . . . . Rev 18:13

CIRCLE
He walks above the c . . . . Job 22:14
when He drew a c . . . . Prov 8:27
who sits above the c . . . . Is 40:22

CIRCUIT
of heaven, and its c . . . . Ps 19:6
comes again on its c . . . . Eccl 1:6

CIRCUMCISE
c the foreskin of your . . . . . Deut 10:16
LORD your God will c . . . . . . Deut 30:6
C yourselves to the . . . . Jer 4:4
is necessary to c them . . . . Acts 15:5

CIRCUMCISED
among you shall be c . . . . . . Gen 17:10
day Abraham was c . . . . Gen 17:26
Abraham c his son Isaac . . . . Gen 21:4
every male was c, all . . . . . . Gen 34:24
let all his males be c . . . . Ex 12:48
of Egypt, had not been c . . . . . Josh 5:5
c him on the eighth day . . . . . . Acts 7:8
who will justify the c . . . . Rom 3:30
While he was c . . . . Rom 4:10
the gospel for the c . . . . Gal 2:7
if you become c . . . . Gal 5:2
c the eighth day . . . . Phil 3:5
In Him you were also c . . . . . . Col 2:11

CIRCUMCISION
him the covenant of c . . . . Acts 7:8
c that which is outward . . . . . Rom 2:28
c is that of the heart . . . . Rom 2:29
a servant to the c . . . . Rom 15:8
C is nothing and . . . . 1 Cor 7:19
Christ Jesus neither c . . . . Gal 5:6
For we are the c . . . . Phil 3:3
circumcised with the c . . . . Col 2:11
those of the c . . . . Titus 1:10

CIRCUMSPECTLY
then that you walk c . . . . Eph 5:15

CISTERN
waters of his own c . . . . 2 Kin 18:31
from your own c . . . . Prov 5:15

CISTERNS
and hewn themselves c . . . . Jer 2:13
went to the c and found . . . . . . Jer 14:3

CITIES
He overthrew those c . . . . . . Gen 19:25
repair the ruined c . . . . Is 61:4
c are a wilderness . . . . Is 64:10
c will be laid waste . . . . Jer 4:7
three parts, and the c . . . . Rev 16:19

CITIZEN
But I was born a c . . . . Acts 22:28

CITIZENS
But his c hated him . . . . Luke 19:14
but fellow c with the . . . . Eph 2:19

CITIZENSHIP
sum I obtained this c . . . . . . Acts 22:28
For our c is in heaven . . . . Phil 3:20

CITY
See HOLY CITY
And he built a c . . . . Gen 4:17
shall make glad the c . . . . Ps 46:4
c shall flourish . . . . Ps 72:16
They found no c . . . . Ps 107:4
c that is compact . . . . Ps 122:3
the LORD guards the c . . . . Ps 127:1
at the entry of the c . . . . Prov 8:3
c has become a harlot . . . . Is 1:21
upon Zion, the c . . . . Is 33:20
after the holy c . . . . Is 48:2
How lonely sits the c . . . . Lam 1:1
Nineveh, that great c . . . . Jon 4:11
c that dwelt securely . . . . Zeph 2:15
to the oppressing c . . . . Zeph 3:1
c called Nazareth . . . . Matt 2:23
c that is set on a . . . . Matt 5:14
He has prepared a c . . . . Heb 11:16
Zion and to the c . . . . Heb 12:22
have no continuing c . . . . Heb 13:14
will tread the holy c . . . . Rev 11:2
fallen, that great c . . . . Rev 14:8
and the beloved c . . . . Rev 20:9
John, saw the holy c . . . . Rev 21:2
c was pure gold . . . . Rev 21:18
c had no need of the . . . . Rev 21:23
the gates into the c . . . . Rev 22:14

CITY OF DAVID
of Zion (that is, the C . . . . . . 2 Sam 5:7
with him into the C . . . . 2 Sam 6:10
was buried in the C . . . . 1 Kin 2:10
of the Lord from the C . . . . . . 1 Kin 8:1
was buried in the C . . . . 1 Kin 11:43
for himself in the C . . . . 1 Chr 15:1
the Millo in the C . . . . 2 Chr 32:5
the west side of the C . . . . 2 Chr 32:30
that go down from the C . . . . Neh 3:15
up the stairs of the C, ... Neh 12:37
the damage to the c, ... Is 22:9
into Judea, to the c, ... Luke 2:4
this day in the c a Savior, . . Luke 2:11

CLAD
was c with zeal as a cloak . . . Is 59:17

CLAMOROUS
A foolish woman is c . . . . Prov 9:13

CLANGING
brass or a c cymbal . . . . 1 Cor 13:1

CLAP
c their hands at him . . . . Job 27:23
Oh, c your hands . . . . Ps 47:1
let the rivers c . . . . Ps 98:8
of the field shall c . . . . Is 55:12

CLAUDIUS LYSIAS
Roman commander who protected Paul, Acts 24:22–24, 26

CLAY
dwell in houses of c . . . . Job 4:19
have made me like c . . . . Job 10:9
are defenses of c . . . . Job 13:12
been formed out of c . . . . Job 33:6
takes on form like c . . . . Job 38:14
pit, out of the miry c . . . . Ps 40:2
be esteemed as the c . . . . Is 29:16
Shall the c say to him . . . . Is 45:9
We are the c, and You . . . . Is 64:8
"Look, as the c . . . . Jer 18:6
iron and partly of c . . . . Dan 2:33
blind man with the c . . . . John 9:6
have power over the c . . . . . . Rom 9:21
but also of wood and c . . . . 2 Tim 2:20

CLEAN
seven each of every c . . . . Gen 7:2
outside the camp to a c . . . . Lev 4:12
all who are c may eat of it . . . . Lev 7:19
between unclean and c . . . . . . Lev 10:10
shall be c from the flow . . . . . . Lev 12:7
shall pronounce him c . . . . . . Lev 13:23
wash his clothes and be c . . Lev 13:34
wash in them and be c . . . . . 2 Kin 5:12
all of them were ritually c . . Ezra 6:20
pure, and I am c in your . . . . . Job 11:4
Who can bring a c . . . . Job 14:4
He who has c hands and . . . . Ps 24:4
hyssop, and I shall be c . . . . Ps 51:7
Create in me a c heart, ... Ps 51:10
I have made my heart c, ... Prov 20:9
make yourselves c . . . . Is 1:16
the midst of her, be c . . . . Is 52:11
Then I will sprinkle c . . . . . Ezek 36:25
c out His threshing . . . . Matt 3:12
You can make me c . . . . Matt 8:2
outside of them may be c . Matt 23:26
wrapped it in a c linen . . . . . Matt 27:59
all things are c . . . . Luke 11:41
but is completely c . . . . John 13:10
"You are not all c . . . . John 13:11
You are already c . . . . John 15:3
your own heads; I am c . . . . . Acts 18:6

in fine linen, *c* .... Rev 19:8

CLEANNESS

according to the *c* of .... 2 Sam 22:21
According to the *c* of my .... Ps 18:20
Also I gave you *c* of teeth .. Amos 4:6

CLEANSE

You shall *c* the altar .... Ex 29:36
and *c* them ceremonially .... Num 8:6
and *c* my hands with soap, .. Job 9:30
C me from secret .... Ps 19:12
and *c* me from my sin .... Ps 51:2
How can a young man *c* .... Ps 119:9
I will *c* you from all ...... Ezek 36:25
they shall *c* the altar ...... Ezek 43:22
c the lepers, raise .... Matt 10:8
For you *c* the outside ..... Matt 23:25
let us *c* ourselves from all .. 2 Cor 7:1
might sanctify and *c* .... Eph 5:26
c your conscience .... Heb 9:14
C your hands .... James 4:8
us our sins and to *c* .... 1 John 1:9

CLEANSED

He who is to be *c* shall ...... Lev 14:8
Surely I have *c* .... Ps 73:13
and you were not *c* .... Ezek 24:13
the sanctuary shall be *c* .... Dan 8:14
I am willing; be *c*." .... Matt 8:3
the lepers are *c* .... Matt 11:5
they went, they were *c* ... Luke 17:14
"Were there not ten *c* .... Luke 17:17
God has *c* you must .... Acts 10:15

CLEANSES

Therefore if anyone *c* ..... 2 Tim 2:21
Jesus Christ His Son *c* .... 1 John 1:7

CLEAR

c shining after rain .... 2 Sam 23:4
fair as the moon, *c* .... Song 6:10
yourselves to be *c* .... 2 Cor 7:11
like a jasper stone, *c* ...... Rev 21:11
of life, *c* as crystal .... Rev 22:1

CLEARLY

I not *c* reveal Myself ..... 1 Sam 2:27
you will see *c* to remove .... Matt 7:5
hour of the day he saw *c* ... Acts 10:3
c portrayed among you .... Gal 3:1
men's sins are *c* evident .. 1 Tim 5:24

CLEARS

by no means *c* the guilty .. Num 14:18

CLEFTS

to go into the *c* .... Is 2:21
valleys and in the *c* .... Is 7:19
you who dwell in the *c* ..... Jer 49:16

CLERK

c had quieted the .... Acts 19:35

CLIFF

secret places of the *c* ...... Song 2:14

CLIMB

go into thickets and *c* .... Jer 4:29
mighty men, they *c* .... Joel 2:7
though they *c* up to .... Amos 9:2

CLIMBED

c up into a sycamore tree .. Luke 19:4

CLIMBS

c up some other way ...... John 10:1

CLING

and that you may *c* .... Deut 30:20
to her, "Do not *c* .... John 20:17
C to what is good .... Rom 12:9

CLINGS

and My tongue *c* .... Ps 22:15
My soul *c* to the dust .... Ps 119:25

CLOAK

c You will change them .... Ps 102:26
let him have your *c* .... Matt 5:40
c You will fold them .... Heb 1:12
using liberty as a *c* .... 1 Pet 2:16

CLODS

The *c* of the valley .... Job 21:33

CLOSE

c friends abhor me .... Job 19:19
of Christ he came *c* .... Phil 2:30

CLOSED

c up the flesh in its place ... Gen 2:21
LORD had *c* her womb ...... 1 Sam 1:5
and has *c* your eyes .... Is 29:10
for the words are *c* .... Dan 12:9
the deep *c* around me .... Jon 2:5
Then He *c* the book, and .. Luke 4:20
their eyes they have *c* ...... Acts 28:27

CLOSER

sticks *c* than a brother .... Prov 18:24

CLOTH

a piece of unshrunk *c* ...... Matt 9:16
in a clean linen *c* .... Matt 27:59

CLOTHE

c them with tunics .... Ex 40:14
c me with skin and .... Job 10:11
c her priests with .... Ps 132:16
His enemies I will *c* .... Ps 132:18
Though you *c* yourself .... Jer 4:30
He not much more *c* .... Matt 6:30

CLOTHED

of skin, and *c* them .... Gen 3:21
Have you *c* his neck .... Job 39:19
off my sackcloth and *c* ...... Ps 30:11
The pastures are *c* .... Ps 65:13
the LORD is *c* .... Ps 93:1
You are *c* with honor .... Ps 104:1
c himself with cursing ...... Ps 109:18
Let Your priests be *c* .... Ps 132:9
all her household is *c* ..... Prov 31:21
c you with fine linen ...... Ezek 16:10
A man *c* in soft .... Matt 11:8
I was naked and you *c* .... Matt 25:36
legion, sitting and *c* .... Mark 5:15
And they *c* Him with ..... Mark 15:17
rich man who was *c* ...... Luke 16:19
desiring to be *c* .... 2 Cor 5:2
that you may be *c* .... Rev 3:18
a woman *c* with the sun .... Rev 12:1
He was *c* with a robe ...... Rev 19:13

CLOTHES

See TORE HIS CLOTHES
c will abhor me .... Job 9:31
c became shining .... Mark 9:3
many spread their *c* ...... Luke 19:36
laid down their *c* .... Acts 7:58
and tore off their *c* .... Acts 22:23
a poor man in filthy *c* ..... James 2:2

CLOTHING

c they cast lots .... Ps 22:18
c is woven with gold .... Ps 45:13
will provide your *c* .... Prov 27:26
and honor are her *c* ...... Prov 31:25
of vengeance for *c* .... Is 59:17
the body more than *c* ...... Matt 6:25
do you worry about *c* ...... Matt 6:28
to you in sheep's *c* .... Matt 7:15
those who wear soft *c* ..... Matt 11:8
c as white as snow .... Matt 28:3
c they cast lots .... John 19:24
before me in bright *c* ..... Acts 10:30

CLOTHS

wrapped in swaddling *c* ..... Luke 2:12
in, saw the linen *c* .... John 20:5

CLOUD

My rainbow in the *c* .... Gen 9:13
rainbow shall be in the *c* .... Gen 9:16
day in a pillar of *c* .... Ex 13:21
c covered the mountain ..... Ex 24:15
c descended and stood .... Ex 33:9
the *c* above the mercy seat .. Lev 16:2
that the *c* of incense may .. Lev 16:13
that the *c* filled the house .. 1 Kin 8:10
LORD, was filled with a *c* .. 2 Chr 5:13
would dwell in the dark *c* .. 2 Chr 6:1
c did not depart .... Neh 9:19
He led them with the *c* ...... Ps 78:14
his favor is like a *c* ...... Prov 16:15
like a *c* of dew in the heat ..... Is 18:4
these who fly like a *c* .... Is 60:8
rainbow in a *c* on a .... Ezek 1:28
like a morning *c* .... Hos 6:4
behold, a bright *c* .... Matt 17:5
c came and overshadowed . Luke 9:34
of Man coming in a *c* ..... Luke 21:27
c received Him out of .... Acts 1:9
were under the *c* .... 1 Cor 10:1
by so great a *c* .... Heb 12:1
ascended to heaven in a *c* .. Rev 11:12

CLOUDS

a morning without *c* ...... 2 Sam 23:4
c poured out water .... Ps 77:17
and hail, snow and *c* .... Ps 148:8
c drop down the dew ...... Prov 3:20
he who regards the *c* .... Eccl 11:4
of Man coming on the *c* ... Matt 24:30
with them in the *c* ...... 1 Thess 4:17
are *c* without water .... Jude 12
He is coming with *c* .... Rev 1:7

CLOUDY

them by day with a *c* .... Neh 9:12
spoke to them in the *c* .... Ps 99:7

CLOVEN

the hoof, having *c* .... Lev 11:3
chew the cud or have *c* .... Deut 14:7

CLUNG

but Ruth *c* to her .... Ruth 1:14
Solomon *c* to these in ...... 1 Kin 11:2

CLUSTER

beloved is to me a *c* .... Song 1:14
wine is found in the *c* .... Is 65:8

CNIDUS

City of Asia Minor on Paul's voyage, Acts 27:7

COAL

in his hand a live *c* .... Is 6:6
it shall not be a *c* .... Is 47:14

COALS

wicked He will rain *c* .... Ps 11:6
c were kindled by it .... Ps 18:8
let burning *c* fall .... Ps 140:10
Can one walk on hot *c* ..... Prov 6:28
so you will heap *c* .... Prov 25:22
doing you will heap *c* ..... Rom 12:20

COARSE

robe of *c* hair to deceive ... Zech 13:4
nor *c* jesting, which are ...... Eph 5:4

COBRA

it becomes *c* venom .... Job 20:14
c that stops its ear .... Ps 58:4
the lion and the *c* .... Ps 91:13

COBRA'S

shall play by the *c* .... Is 11:8

CODE

even with your written *c* ... Rom 2:27

COFFIN

and he was put in a *c* ..... Gen 50:26
David followed the *c* ..... 2 Sam 3:31
touched the open *c* .... Luke 7:14

COIN

sold for a copper *c* .... Matt 10:29
if she loses one *c* .... Luke 15:8

COLD

and harvest, *c* and .... Gen 8:22
can stand before His *c* ..... Ps 147:17
Like the *c* of snow in ..... Prov 25:13
c water to a weary .... Prov 25:25
c water in the name of .... Matt 10:42
of many will grow *c* ...... Matt 24:12

that you are neither *c* . . . . . . Rev 3:15

COLLECTED
coming I might have *c* . . . . Luke 19:23

COLLECTION
from Jerusalem the *c* . . . . . . 2 Chr 24:6
concerning the *c* . . . . 1 Cor 16:1

COLLECTOR
See TAX COLLECTOR; TAX COLLECTORS AND SINNERS

COLOR
c like the *c* of bdellium . . . . Num 11:7
the *c* of burnished bronze . . . Ezek 1:7
c of an awesome crystal . . . Ezek 1:22
the *c* of a beryl stone . . . . . Ezek 10:9
all faces are drained of *c* . . . . . Joel 2:6

COLORS
him a tunic of many *c* . . . . . . Gen 37:3
on a robe of many *c* . . . . . 2 Sam 13:18
stones of various *c*, all . . . . 1 Chr 29:2

COLOSSE
A city in Asia Minor, Col 1:2
Evangelized by Epaphras, Col 1:7
Not visited by Paul, Col 2:1
Paul writes against errors of, Col 2:16–23

COLT
and his donkey's *c* . . . . Gen 49:11
on a donkey, a *c* . . . . Zech 9:9
on a donkey, a *c* . . . . Matt 21:5
own clothes on the *c* . . . . . Luke 19:35

COME
then does wisdom *c* . . . . Job 28:20
of glory shall *c* . . . . Ps 24:7
Our God shall *c* . . . . Ps 50:3
You all flesh will *c* . . . . Ps 65:2
C with me from Lebanon . . . Song 4:8
He will *c* and save you . . . . Is 35:4
who have no money, *C* . . . . Is 55:1
Your kingdom *c* . . . . Matt 6:10
C to Me . . . . Matt 11:28
For many will *c* . . . . Matt 24:5
Israel, let Him now *c* . . . . . Matt 27:42
If anyone desires to *c* . . . . . . Luke 9:23
kingdom of God has *c* . . . . . Luke 10:9
I have *c* in My . . . . John 5:43
and I have not *c* . . . . John 7:28
thirsts, let him *c* . . . . John 7:37
c that they may have . . . . . John 10:10
c as a light into the . . . . John 12:46
I will *c* to you . . . . John 14:18
If I had not *c* . . . . John 15:22
savage wolves will *c* . . . . . . Acts 20:29
O Lord, *c* . . . . 1 Cor 16:22
the door, I will *c* . . . . Rev 3:20
the bride say, "*C* . . . . Rev 22:17

COMELINESS
He has no form or *c* . . . . Is 53:2

COMES
Who is this who *c* . . . . Is 63:1
'Come,' and he *c* . . . . Matt 8:9
Lord's death till He *c* . . . . . 1 Cor 11:26
Then *c* the end . . . . 1 Cor 15:24

COMFORT
one will *c* us concerning . . . . Gen 5:29
daughters arose to *c* him . . Gen 37:35
speak *c* to your servants . . 2 Sam 19:7
with him, and to *c* him . . . . . . Job 2:11
and Your staff, they *c* . . . . Ps 23:4
And *c* me on every side . . . . . Ps 71:21
is my *c* in my affliction . . . . Ps 119:50
kindness be for my *c* . . . . Ps 119:76
When will you *c* . . . . Ps 119:82
go up to the *c* of my bed . . . Ps 132:3
yes, *c* My people . . . . Is 40:1
For the LORD will *c* . . . . Is 51:3
c all who mourn . . . . Is 61:2
comforts, so I will *c* you . . . . . Is 66:13
she has none to *c* her . . . . Lam 1:2

wilderness, and speak *c* to . . Hos 2:14
the LORD will again *c* . . . . . . Zech 1:17
c them concerning their . . John 11:19
in the *c* of the Holy Spirit, . . Acts 9:31
c of the Scriptures might . . . Rom 15:4
and exhortation and *c* to . . . 1 Cor 14:3
and God of all *c* . . . . 2 Cor 1:3
trouble, with the *c* . . . . 2 Cor 1:4
that he may *c* your hearts . . . Eph 6:22
in Christ, if any *c* . . . . Phil 2:1
and *c* your hearts, ... Col 4:8
c one another . . . . 1 Thess 4:18
c each other and edify . . . 1 Thess 5:11
c your hearts and . . . . 2 Thess 2:17

COMFORTED
So Isaac was *c* after . . . . . . Gen 24:67
c them and spoke kindly . . Gen 50:21
David *c* Bathsheba . . . . 2 Sam 12:24
soul refused to be *c* . . . . Ps 77:2
For the LORD has *c* . . . . Is 49:13
refusing to be *c* . . . . Jer 31:15
children, refusing to be *c* . . . Matt 2:18
mourn, for they shall be *c* . . . Matt 5:4
but now he is *c* . . . . Luke 16:25
they were not a little *c* . . . Acts 20:12
ourselves are *c* by God . . . . . 2 Cor 1:4

COMFORTER
but they have no *c* . . . . Eccl 4:1
She had no *c* . . . . Lam 1:9

COMFORTERS
because he has sent *c* to . . 2 Sam 10:3
miserable *c* are you all . . . . . . Job 16:2
for *c*, but I found none . . . . . . Ps 69:20

COMFORTS
the army, as one who *c* . . . . Job 29:25
I, even I, am He who *c* . . . . Is 51:12
him, and restore *c* . . . . Is 57:18
one whom his mother *c* . . . . . . Is 66:13
who *c* us in all our . . . . 2 Cor 1:4
who *c* the downcast . . . . 2 Cor 7:6

COMING
your salvation is *c* . . . . Is 62:11
behold, the day is *c* . . . . Mal 4:1
but He who is *c* . . . . Matt 3:11
"Are You the *C* . . . . Matt 11:3
be the sign of Your *c* . . . . Matt 24:3
is delaying his *c* . . . . Matt 24:48
see the Son of Man *c* . . . . . Mark 13:26
mightier than I is *c* . . . . Luke 3:16
are Christ's at His *c* . . . . . . 1 Cor 15:23
to you the power and *c* . . . . . 2 Pet 1:16
the promise of His *c* . . . . 2 Pet 3:4
Behold, I am *c* . . . . Rev 3:11
"Behold, I am *c* . . . . Rev 22:7
"Surely I am *c* . . . . Rev 22:20

COMMAND
in order that he may *c* . . . . . Gen 18:19
shall speak all that I *c* you . . . . . Ex 7:2
transgress the *c* of the . . . . Num 14:41
add to the word which I *c* . . . Deut 4:2
I *c* you today you must be . . . Deut 8:1
Whatever I *c* you, be . . . . . . Deut 12:32
therefore I *c* you, saying . . Deut 15:11
"The LORD will *c* . . . . Deut 28:8
in that I *c* you . . . . Deut 30:16
today, which you shall *c* . . Deut 32:46
c His lovingkindness . . . . Ps 42:8
c victories for Jacob . . . . Ps 44:4
you, and whatever I *c* you . . . . Jer 1:7
to them all that I *c* you . . . . . . Jer 1:17
to all that I *c* . . . . Jer 11:4
that I *c* you to speak to . . . . . . Jer 26:2
c that these stones . . . . Matt 4:3
if it is You, *c* . . . . Matt 14:28
c fire to come down . . . . Luke 9:54
c I have received . . . . John 10:18
And I know that His *c* . . . . John 12:50
if you do whatever I *c* . . . . John 15:14
These things I *c* you, ... John 15:17
do the things we *c* . . . . 2 Thess 3:4

C those who are rich in . . . . 1 Tim 6:17
kept My *c* to persevere . . . . . . Rev 3:10

COMMANDED
See LORD COMMANDED
the LORD God *c* the man . . . . Gen 2:16
to all that the LORD *c* him . . . . Gen 7:5
Joseph *c* his servants the . . . . Gen 50:2
just as the LORD *c* them, ... Ex 7:6
which the LORD *c* him . . . . Ex 19:7
just as the LORD my God *c* . . Deut 4:5
LORD *c* us to observe all . . . . Deut 6:24
Have I not *c* you . . . . Josh 1:9
did so, as the LORD *c* . . . . . 2 Sam 5:25
which I *c* your fathers . . . . 2 Kin 17:13
to all that I have *c* them . . . 2 Kin 21:8
do all that I have *c* them . . 2 Chr 33:8
"Have you *c* the . . . . Job 38:12
He *c*, and it stood fast . . . . Ps 33:9
Which He *c* our fathers, ... Ps 78:5
c His covenant forever . . . . . . Ps 111:9
For there the LORD *c* . . . . Ps 133:3
of the LORD, for He *c* . . . . Ps 148:5
things that I have *c* you . . . Matt 28:20
Even so the Lord has *c* . . . . 1 Cor 9:14
it is the God who *c* . . . . 2 Cor 4:6
not endure what was *c* . . . . Heb 12:20

COMMANDER
the *c* of his army, spoke . . . Gen 21:22
but as *C* of the army of . . . . Josh 5:14
c of his army was Sisera, ... Judg 4:2
c over His inheritance . . . . . 1 Sam 10:1
Abner, the *c* of the . . . . . . 1 Sam 17:55
Joab the *c* of the army . . . . 1 Kin 1:19
have a message for you, *C* . . 2 Kin 9:5
Rehum the *c* and Shimshai . . Ezra 4:8
news came to the *c* of . . . . . Acts 21:31
But the *c* Lysias came by . . . Acts 24:7

COMMANDMENT
to the *c* of the LORD, ... Ex 17:1
numbered at the *c* of the . . . Num 3:39
shall keep every *c* which . . . Deut 11:8
heed to do the *c* . . . . Josh 22:5
observe the law and the *c* . 2 Chr 14:4
according to the *c* of . . . . . 2 Chr 29:25
c of the LORD is pure . . . . Ps 19:8
c is exceedingly broad . . . . . Ps 119:96
For the *c* is a lamp . . . . Prov 6:23
Me is taught by the *c* . . . . Is 29:13
which is the great *c* . . . . . . Matt 22:36
is the first and great *c* . . . . Matt 22:38
no other *c* greater than . . . Mark 12:31
according to the *c* . . . . Luke 23:56
A new *c* I give to . . . . John 13:34
the Father gave Me *c* . . . . . John 14:31
is My *c*, that you love . . . . . John 15:12
whom we gave no such *c* . . Acts 15:24
law, but when the *c* . . . . Rom 7:9
the *c* might become . . . . Rom 7:13
and if there is any other *c* . . Rom 13:9
as a concession, not as a *c* . . 1 Cor 7:6
I speak not by *c*, but . . . . 2 Cor 8:8
which is the first *c* . . . . Eph 6:2
have a *c* to receive tithes . . . . . Heb 7:5
the holy *c* delivered to . . . . . 2 Pet 2:21
of the *c* of us, the apostles . . 2 Pet 3:2
c is the word which . . . . 1 John 2:7
And this is His *c* . . . . 1 John 3:23
as we received *c* . . . . 2 John 4
I wrote a new *c* to you . . . . . . 2 John 5
This is the *c* that as you . . . . . 2 John 6

COMMANDMENTS
love Me and keep My *c* . . . . . . Ex 20:6
c which I have written, ... Ex 24:12
covenant, the Ten *C* . . . . Ex 34:28
he gave them as *c* all that . . . Ex 34:32
you shall keep My *c* . . . . Lev 22:31
all the *c* of the LORD and . . Num 15:39
perform the Ten *C* . . . . Deut 4:13
love Me and keep My *c* . . . . Deut 5:10
to observe all these *c* . . . . . . Deut 6:25

filthiness *c* from you .... Ezek 22:15
I made a man *c* well .... John 7:23
You were *c* born in sins, ... John 9:34
his feet, but is *c* clean ..... John 13:10
Himself sanctify you *c* ... 1 Thess 5:23

COMPOSED
But God *c* the body ...... 1 Cor 12:24

COMPREHEND
which we cannot *c* .... Job 37:5
c my path and my lying ..... Ps 139:3
the darkness did not *c* .... John 1:5
may be able to *c* .... Eph 3:18

CONCEAL
Almighty I will not *c* .... Job 27:11
c pride from man .... Job 33:17
of God to *c* a matter .... Prov 25:2

CONCEALED
c Your lovingkindness ...... Ps 40:10
than love carefully *c* .... Prov 27:5

CONCEIT
selfish ambition or *c* .... Phil 2:3

CONCEITED
Let us not become *c* .... Gal 5:26

CONCEIVE
the virgin shall *c* .... Is 7:14
And behold, you will *c* .... Luke 1:31

CONCEIVED
in sin my mother *c* .... Ps 51:5
when desire has *c* .... James 1:15

CONCERN
Neither do I *c* myself .... Ps 131:1
c for My holy name, ... Ezek 36:21
may the dream *c* those ..... Dan 4:19
the things which *c* .... Acts 28:31
my deep *c* for all the ..... 2 Cor 11:28

CONCERNED
Is it oxen God is *c* .... 1 Cor 9:9
c only with foods and .... Heb 9:10

CONCESSION
But I say this as a *c* .... 1 Cor 7:6

CONCILIATION
c pacifies great .... Eccl 10:4

CONCLUSION
Let us hear the *c* .... Eccl 12:13

CONCUBINE
with Bilhah his father's *c* .. Gen 35:22
c who was in Shechem ..... Judg 8:31
He took for himself a *c* .... Judg 19:1
Saul had a *c*, whose .... 2 Sam 3:7
to Keturah, Abraham's *c* .. 1 Chr 1:32

CONCUBINES
And David took more *c* ... 2 Sam 5:13
Go in to your father's *c* .. 2 Sam 16:21
and three hundred *c* .... 1 Kin 11:3
eunuch who kept the *c* ..... Esth 2:14
sixty queens and eighty *c* ... Song 6:8

CONDEMN
say to God, 'Do not *c* .... Job 10:2
Would you *c* Me that you ... Job 40:8
who is he who will *c* Me ...... Is 50:9
they will *c* Him to death, .. Matt 20:18
C not, and you shall not ... Luke 6:37
world to *c* the world .... John 3:17
her, "Neither do I *c* .... John 8:11
judge another you *c* .... Rom 2:1
is he who does not *c* ...... Rom 14:22
I do not say this to *c* .... 2 Cor 7:3
our heart does not *c* ...... 1 John 3:21

CONDEMNATION
will receive greater *c* ..... Matt 23:14
can you escape the *c* ...... Matt 23:33
subject to eternal *c* .... Mark 3:29
And this is the *c* .... John 3:19
the resurrection of *c* .... John 5:29
Their *c* is just .... Rom 3:8
therefore now no *c* .... Rom 8:1
of *c* had glory .... 2 Cor 3:9
having *c* because they .... 1 Tim 5:12
marked out for this *c* .... Jude 4

CONDEMNED
David's heart *c* him ..... 2 Sam 24:10
words you will be *c* .... Matt 12:37
and you shall not be *c* ..... Luke 6:37
does not believe is *c* .... John 3:18
Has no one *c* you .... John 8:10
c sin in the flesh .... Rom 8:3
he who doubts is *c* if he ... Rom 14:23
last, as men *c* to death ..... 1 Cor 4:9
by which he *c* the world .... Heb 11:7
brethren, lest you be *c* .... James 5:9
c them to destruction, ... 2 Pet 2:6

CONDEMNS
Who is he who *c* .... Rom 8:34
For if our heart *c* .... 1 John 3:20

CONDUCT
c yourselves like men ...... 1 Sam 4:9
who are of upright *c* .... Ps 37:14
c yourself in the .... 1 Tim 3:15
c that his works are ...... James 3:13
to each one's work, *c* ...... 1 Pet 1:17
from your aimless *c* .... 1 Pet 1:18
may be won by the *c* .... 1 Pet 3:1

CONFERRED
c with the chief priests .... Luke 22:4
they *c* among themselves, .. Acts 4:15
when he had *c* with the ... Acts 25:12

CONFESS
c my transgressions .... Ps 32:5
that if you *c* with .... Rom 10:9
every tongue shall *c* ..... Rom 14:11
C your trespasses .... James 5:16
If we *c* our sins .... 1 John 1:9
but I will *c* his name .... Rev 3:5

CONFESSED
stood and *c* their sins .... Neh 9:2
did not deny, but *c*, "I ..... John 1:20
c that He was Christ .... John 9:22
c the good confession ..... 1 Tim 6:12

CONFESSES
prosper, but whoever *c* ... Prov 28:13
Every spirit that *c* that .... 1 John 4:2
c that Jesus is the .... 1 John 4:15

CONFESSION
of Israel, and make *c* .... Josh 7:19
with the mouth *c* .... Rom 10:10
c to the gospel of Christ ... 2 Cor 9:13
confessed the good *c* ...... 1 Tim 6:12
witnessed the good *c* ...... 1 Tim 6:13
High Priest of our *c* .... Heb 3:1
let us hold fast our *c* .... Heb 4:14

CONFIDENCE
fine gold, 'You are my *c*' ... Job 31:24
You who are the *c* .... Ps 65:5
the LORD than to put *c* .... Ps 118:8
the LORD will be your *c* .... Prov 3:26
c shall be your .... Is 30:15
Jesus Christ with all *c* .... Acts 28:31
having *c* in you all that ..... 2 Cor 2:3
Jesus, and have no *c* .... Phil 3:3
we have *c* in the Lord .... 2 Thess 3:4
if we hold fast the *c* .... Heb 3:6
do not cast away your *c*, ... Heb 10:35
appears, we may have *c* .. 1 John 2:28
Now this is the *c* that .... 1 John 5:14

CONFIDENT
me, in this I will be *c* .... Ps 27:3
I myself am *c* .... Rom 15:14
so we are always *c* .... 2 Cor 5:6
become *c* by my chains ..... Phil 1:14
we are *c* that we have a ... Heb 13:18

CONFINED
saying, "I am *c* .... Jer 36:5
the Scripture has *c* .... Gal 3:22

CONFIRM
c the promises .... Rom 15:8
who will also *c* .... 1 Cor 1:8

CONFIRMATION
c of the gospel, you all .... Phil 1:7
an oath for *c* is for them .... Heb 6:16

CONFIRMED
covenant that was *c* .... Gal 3:17
by the Lord, and was *c* ...... Heb 2:3
c it by an oath .... Heb 6:17
prophetic word *c* .... 2 Pet 1:19

CONFIRMING
c the word through the ... Mark 16:20

CONFLICT
having the same *c* .... Phil 1:30
to know what a great *c* .... Col 2:1

CONFLICTS
Outside were *c* .... 2 Cor 7:5

CONFORMED
predestined to be *c* .... Rom 8:29
And do not be *c* .... Rom 12:2
sufferings, being *c* .... Phil 3:10
body that it may be *c* .... Phil 3:21

CONFOUNDED
who seek You be *c* .... Ps 69:6
ashamed and *c* who seek ..... Ps 70:2
c the Jews who dwelt in .... Acts 9:22

CONFRONTED
They *c* me in the day .... 2 Sam 22:19
The snares of death *c* me ..... Ps 18:5
c Him as He was .... Matt 21:23
with the elders, *c* Him ..... Luke 20:1

CONFUSE
c their language .... Gen 11:7

CONFUSED
there the LORD *c* .... Gen 11:9
the assembly was *c* .... Acts 19:32

CONFUSION
I will cause *c* among all ..... Ex 23:27
blindness and *c* of heart ... Deut 28:28
c who plot my hurt .... Ps 35:4
us drink the wine of *c* .... Ps 60:3
strike every horse with *c* ... Zech 12:4
city was filled with *c* ...... Acts 19:29
author of *c* but of peace .. 1 Cor 14:33
and self-seeking exist, *c* .. James 3:16

CONGREGATION
Nor sinners in the *c* .... Ps 1:5
the *c* of the wicked .... Ps 22:16
God stands in the *c* .... Ps 82:1
is he who was in the *c* ..... Acts 7:38
the *c* had broken up, ... Acts 13:43

CONIAH
King of Judah, Jer 22:24, 28
Same as Jehoiachin, 2 Kin 24:8

CONJURES
or one who *c* spells, or a .. Deut 18:11

CONQUER
conquering and to *c* .... Rev 6:2

CONQUERORS
we are more than *c* .... Rom 8:37

CONSCIENCE
convicted by their *c* .... John 8:9
strive to have a *c* .... Acts 24:16
c also bearing witness, ... Rom 2:15
I am not lying, my *c* .... Rom 9:1
wrath but also for *c* .... Rom 13:5
and their *c*, being weak, is .. 1 Cor 8:7
no questions for *c* .... 1 Cor 10:25
by another man's *c* .... 1 Cor 10:29
c in the sight of God .... 2 Cor 4:2
faith with a pure *c* .... 1 Tim 3:9
having their own *c* .... 1 Tim 4:2
mind and *c* are defiled ...... Titus 1:15
to God, cleanse your *c* .... Heb 9:14
from an evil *c* and our ..... Heb 10:22
having a good *c* .... 1 Pet 3:16

CONVULSED
unclean spirit had *c* him . . . Mark 1:26
immediately the spirit *c* . . . Mark 9:20

COOKED
c their own children . . . . Lam 4:10

COOL
in the garden in the *c* . . . . Gen 3:8
and *c* my tongue . . . . Luke 16:24

COPIES
necessary that the *c* . . . . Heb 9:23
hands, which are *c* . . . . Heb 9:24

COPPER
hills you can dig *c* . . . . Deut 8:9
c in your money belts . . . . . . Matt 10:9
of cups, pitchers, *c* . . . . Mark 7:4
sold for two *c* coins . . . . Luke 12:6

COPPERSMITH
c did me much harm . . . . . . 2 Tim 4:14

COPY
who serve the *c* . . . . Heb 8:5

CORBAN
from me is C (that is, ... Mark 7:11

CORD
this line of scarlet *c* . . . . Josh 2:18
And a threefold *c* . . . . Eccl 4:12
before the silver *c* . . . . Eccl 12:6

CORDS
cut in pieces the *c* . . . . Ps 129:4
he is caught in the *c* . . . . Prov 5:22
draw iniquity with *c* . . . . Is 5:18
them with gentle *c* . . . . Hos 11:4
had made a whip of *c* . . . . . . John 2:15

CORIANDER
it was like white *c* seed . . . . . Ex 16:31
manna was like *c* seed . . . . . Num 11:7

CORINTH
Paul labors at, Acts 18:1–18
Site of church, 1 Cor 1:2
Visited by Apollos, Acts 19:1

CORNELIUS
A religious Gentile, Acts 10:1–48

CORNER
cut off a *c* of Saul's robe . . 1 Sam 24:4
Jerusalem at the C Gate . . . 2 Chr 26:9
dwell in a *c* of a housetop . . Prov 21:9
in the *c* of a bed and on . . . Amos 3:12
was not done in a *c* . . . . Acts 26:26

CORNERS
its horns on its four *c* . . . . Ex 27:2
in the tassels of the *c* . . . . . Num 15:38
sheet bound at the four *c* . . Acts 10:11
at the four *c* of the earth . . . . . Rev 7:1

CORNERSTONE
Or who laid its *c* . . . . Job 38:6
has become the chief *c* . . . . . Ps 118:22
stone, a precious *c* . . . . Is 28:16
become the chief *c* . . . . Matt 21:42
has become the chief *c* . . . . . . Acts 4:11
Himself being the chief *c* . . . . Eph 2:20
in Zion a chief *c* . . . . 1 Pet 2:6

CORPSE
c was thrown on the . . . . . 1 Kin 13:24
c trodden underfoot . . . . Is 14:19

CORRECT
with rebukes You *c* . . . . Ps 39:11
C your son, and he will . . . Prov 29:17
But I will *c* you in . . . . Jer 30:11

CORRECTED
human fathers who *c* . . . . Heb 12:9

CORRECTION
nor detest His *c* . . . . Prov 3:11
but he who refuses *c* . . . . . . Prov 10:17
but he who hates *c* . . . . Prov 12:1
rod of *c* will drive it . . . . Prov 22:15
Do not withhold *c* . . . . Prov 23:13
they received no *c* . . . . Jer 2:30
for reproof, for *c* . . . . 2 Tim 3:16

CORRECTS
is the man whom God *c* . . . . . Job 5:17
the LORD loves He *c* . . . . Prov 3:12

CORRODED
and silver are *c* . . . . James 5:3

CORRUPT
earth also was *c* before . . . . . Gen 6:11
the sons of Eli were *c* . . . . . 1 Sam 2:12
have together become *c* . . . . . . Ps 14:3
have together become *c* . . . . . . Ps 53:3
old man which grows *c* . . . . . Eph 4:22
Let no *c* word . . . . Eph 4:29
men of *c* minds . . . . 2 Tim 3:8
in these things they *c* . . . . Jude 10

CORRUPTED
for all flesh had *c* . . . . Gen 6:12
we have *c* no one . . . . 2 Cor 7:2
so your minds may be *c* . . . 2 Cor 11:3
Your riches are *c* . . . . James 5:2
the great harlot who *c* . . . . . . Rev 19:2

CORRUPTIBLE
For this *c* must put on . . . . 1 Cor 15:53
redeemed with *c* things . . . . 1 Pet 1:18

CORRUPTION
Your Holy One to see *c* . . . . . Ps 16:10
God raised up saw no *c* . . . Acts 13:37
from the bondage of *c* . . . . . Rom 8:21
The body is sown in *c* . . . . 1 Cor 15:42
c inherit incorruption . . . . 1 Cor 15:50
of the flesh reap *c* . . . . Gal 6:8
having escaped the *c* . . . . 2 Pet 1:4
perish in their own *c* . . . . . . 2 Pet 2:12

COST
and count the *c* . . . . Luke 14:28

COSTLY
foundation was of *c* . . . . 1 Kin 7:10
of very *c* oil of spikenard . . Mark 14:3
or pearls or *c* clothing . . . . . . 1 Tim 2:9

COSTS
which *c* me nothing . . . . . 2 Sam 24:24

COUCH
He went up to my *c* . . . . Gen 49:4
I drench my *c* with my . . . . Ps 6:6
Behold, it is Solomon's *c* . . . . Song 3:7

COULD
has done what she *c* . . . . . . Mark 14:8
c remove mountains . . . . 1 Cor 13:2
which no one *c* number . . . . . . Rev 7:9

COUNCIL
shall be in danger of the *c* . . Matt 5:22
all the *c* sought false . . . . . . Matt 26:59
a prominent *c* member, . . . Mark 15:43
Pharisees gathered a *c* . . . . John 11:47
and called the *c* together . . . Acts 5:21
all the *c* of the elders, ... Acts 22:5

COUNCILS
deliver you up to *c* . . . . Mark 13:9

COUNSEL
and strength, He has *c* . . . . . . Job 12:13
the *c* of the wicked is . . . . . . Job 21:16
when the friendly *c* . . . . Job 29:4
is this who darkens *c* . . . . Job 38:2
who walks not in the *c* . . . . Ps 1:1
We took sweet *c* . . . . Ps 55:14
guide me with Your *c* . . . . Ps 73:24
you disdained all my *c* . . . . . Prov 1:25
have none of my *c* . . . . Prov 1:30
Where there is no *c* . . . . Prov 11:14
C in the heart of man . . . . . . Prov 20:5
by wise *c* wage war . . . . Prov 20:18
whom did He take *c* . . . . Is 40:14
You are great in *c* . . . . Jer 32:19
according to the *c* . . . . Eph 1:11
immutability of His *c* . . . . Heb 6:17
I *c* you to buy from . . . . Rev 3:18

COUNSELOR
be called Wonderful, C . . . . Is 9:6
but there was no *c* . . . . Is 41:28
Has your *c* perished . . . . Mic 4:9
who has become His *c* . . . Rom 11:34

COUNSELORS
c there is safety . . . . Prov 11:14

COUNT
c the people of Israel . . . . 2 Sam 24:4
I can *c* all My bones . . . . Ps 22:17
all *c* John as a prophet . . . . Matt 21:26
c my life dear to . . . . Acts 20:24
c me as a partner . . . . Philem 17
c it all joy when you fall . . . James 1:2
His promise, as some *c* . . . . . 2 Pet 3:9

COUNTED
Even a fool is *c* . . . . Prov 17:28
c as the small dust . . . . Is 40:15
the wages are not *c* . . . . Rom 4:4
me, these I have *c* loss for . . . Phil 3:7
He *c* me faithful . . . . 1 Tim 1:12
who rule well be *c* . . . . 1 Tim 5:17
c the blood of the . . . . Heb 10:29

COUNTENANCE
The LORD lift up His *c* . . . . . Num 6:26
c they did not cast . . . . Job 29:24
up the light of Your *c* . . . . Ps 4:6
His *c* is like Lebanon . . . . Song 5:15
hypocrites, with a sad *c* . . . . Matt 6:16
His *c* was like . . . . Matt 28:3
of the glory of his *c* . . . . 2 Cor 3:7
sword, and His *c* . . . . Rev 1:16

COUNTRY
See FAR COUNTRY
"Get out of your *c* . . . . Gen 12:1
but you shall go to my *c* . . . . Gen 24:4
us pass through your *c* . . . Num 20:17
Israel to search out the *c* . . . . Josh 2:2
an end of dividing the *c* . . . Josh 19:51
the *c* was quiet for forty . . . . Judg 8:28
dwell in the *c* of Moab . . . . Ruth 1:1
the *c* of the Philistines . . . 1 Sam 27:11
good news from a far *c* . . . Prov 25:25
you into a bountiful *c*, ... Jer 2:7
their own *c* another way . . . Matt 2:12
honor except in his own *c* . Matt 13:57
and went into a far *c* . . . . . Matt 21:33
the *c* of the Gadarenes . . . . . Mark 5:1
go into the surrounding *c* . . Mark 6:36
and went into a far *c* . . . . . . Mark 12:1
there were in the same *c* . . . . Luke 2:8
journeyed to a far *c*, ... Luke 15:13
as in a foreign *c* . . . . Heb 11:9
that is, a heavenly *c* . . . . Heb 11:16

COUNTRYMEN
for my brethren, my *c* . . . . Rom 9:3

COUNTS
c the number of the stars . . . . Ps 147:4

COURAGE
strong and of good *c* . . . . Deut 31:6
c in anyone because of . . . . . Josh 2:11
the prophet, he took *c* . . . . . 2 Chr 15:8
Be of good *c*, and do it . . . . . Ezra 10:4
his *c* against the king of . . . Dan 11:25
thanked God and took *c* . . Acts 28:15

COURAGEOUS
Only be strong and very *c*. . . Josh 1:7
Be strong and *c* . . . . 2 Chr 32:7

COURSE
and sets on fire the *c* . . . . . . James 3:6

COURT
the *c* of the tabernacle . . . . Ex 27:9
men, and they come to *c*, . . Deut 25:1
made the *c* of the priests . . . . 2 Chr 4:9
the inner *c* to the king . . . . . . Esth 4:11
appoint my day in *c* . . . . Job 9:19
many would *c* your favor . . . Job 11:19
Do not go hastily to *c* . . . . . . Prov 25:8

sort are those who *c* . . . . 2 Tim 3:6

CREEPING
c thing and beast of . . . . Gen 1:24
every sort of *c* thing . . . . Ezek 8:10
animals and *c* things . . . . Rom 1:23

CREPT
For certain men have *c* . . . . Jude 4

CRETE
Paul visits, Acts 27:7–21
Titus dispatched to, Titus 1:5
Inhabitants of, evil and lazy, Titus 1:12

CRIB
donkey its master's *c* . . . . Is 1:3

CRIED
he *c* with an exceedingly . . Gen 27:34
the poor who *c* out . . . . Job 29:12
They *c* to You . . . . Ps 22:5
of the depths I have *c* . . . . Ps 130:1
of the belly of Sheol I *c* . . . . . Jon 2:2
beginning to sink he *c* . . . . Matt 14:30
Jesus *c* out and said . . . . . . John 12:44
they *c* out, "Away with . . . John 19:15

CRIES
your brother's blood *c* . . . . . . Gen 4:10
with vehement *c* . . . . Heb 5:7

CRIMES
land is filled with *c* . . . . Ezek 7:23

CRIMINALS
also two others, *c* . . . . Luke 23:32

CRIMSON
blue, and purple, and *c* . . . . 2 Chr 3:14
though they are red like *c* . . . . . Is 1:18

CRIPPLE
c from his mother's womb . . Acts 14:8

CRISPUS
Chief ruler of synagogue of Corinth, Acts 18:8
Baptized by Paul, 1 Cor 1:14

CROOKED
perverse and *c* generation . . Deut 32:5
turn aside to their *c* . . . . Ps 125:5
whose ways are *c* . . . . Prov 2:15
What is *c* cannot be made . . Eccl 1:15
what He has made *c* . . . . Eccl 7:13
c places shall be made . . . . Is 40:4
c places straight . . . . Is 45:2
c places shall be made . . . . . . Luke 3:5
in the midst of a *c* . . . . Phil 2:15

CROSS
I would not *c* over the . . . . . Deut 4:21
But when you *c* over the . . Deut 12:10
does not take his *c* . . . . Matt 10:38
and take up his *c* . . . . Matt 16:24
compelled to bear His *c* . . . Matt 27:32
down from the *c* . . . . Matt 27:40
and take up his *c* . . . . Mark 8:34
and take up his *c* daily, ... Luke 9:23
does not bear his *c* . . . . Luke 14:27
And He, bearing His *c*, . . . John 19:17
lest the *c* of Christ . . . . 1 Cor 1:17
offense of the *c* has ceased . . Gal 5:11
persecution for the *c* . . . . Gal 6:12
boast except in the *c* . . . . Gal 6:14
one body through the *c* . . . . . Eph 2:16
even the death of the *c* . . . . . . Phil 2:8
the enemies of the *c* . . . . Phil 3:18
through the blood of His *c* . . . Col 1:20
having nailed it to the *c* . . . . . Col 2:14
Him endured the *c* . . . . Heb 12:2

CROW
rooster will not *c* this . . . . Luke 22:34

CROWD
shall not follow a *c* . . . . Ex 23:2

CROWN
the holy *c* on the turban . . . . . Ex 29:6
You set a *c* of pure . . . . Ps 21:3
c the year with Your . . . . Ps 65:11
have profaned his *c* . . . . Ps 89:39
upon Himself His *c* . . . . Ps 132:18
The *c* of the wise is . . . . Prov 14:24
head is a *c* of glory . . . . Prov 16:31
Woe to the *c* of pride . . . . Is 28:1
hosts will be for a *c* . . . . Is 28:5
c has fallen from our . . . . Lam 5:16
they had twisted a *c* . . . . . . Matt 27:29
wearing the *c* of thorns . . . . John 19:5
obtain a perishable *c* . . . . . . 1 Cor 9:25
brethren, my joy and *c* . . . . Phil 4:1
or joy, or *c* of rejoicing . . 1 Thess 2:19
laid up for me the *c* . . . . 2 Tim 4:8
he will receive the *c* . . . . . . James 1:12
you will receive the *c* of . . . . . 1 Pet 5:4
I will give you the *c* of life . . Rev 2:10
no one may take your *c* . . . . . Rev 3:11
on His head a golden *c* . . . . Rev 14:14

CROWNED
angels, and You have *c* . . . . Ps 8:5
but the prudent are *c* . . . . . Prov 14:18
athletics, he is not *c* . . . . 2 Tim 2:5
You have *c* him with glory . . . Heb 2:7

CROWNS
and they had *c* of gold . . . . Rev 4:4
on his horns ten *c* . . . . Rev 13:1
His head were many *c* . . . . . Rev 19:12

CRUCIFIED
be delivered up to be *c* . . . . . Matt 26:2
"Let Him be *c* . . . . Matt 27:22
robbers were *c* with Him . . Matt 27:38
you seek Jesus who was *c* . . Matt 28:5
scourged Him, to be *c* . . . . Mark 15:15
third hour, and they *c* . . . . Mark 15:25
of Nazareth, who was *c* . . . Mark 16:6
Calvary, there they *c* . . . . . Luke 23:33
of sinful men, and be *c* . . . . Luke 24:7
to death, and *c* Him . . . . . . Luke 24:20
Him to them to be *c* . . . . . . John 19:16
c there was a garden . . . . . John 19:41
lawless hands, have *c* . . . . . . Acts 2:23
of Nazareth, whom you *c*, . . . Acts 4:10
that our old man was *c* . . . . Rom 6:6
Was Paul *c* for you . . . . 1 Cor 1:13
but we preach Christ *c*, ... 1 Cor 1:23
Jesus Christ and Him *c* . . . . . . 1 Cor 2:2
they would not have *c* . . . . . . 1 Cor 2:8
though He was *c* . . . . 2 Cor 13:4
I have been *c* with Christ . . . . Gal 2:20
portrayed among you as *c* . . . . Gal 3:1
c the flesh with its passions . . Gal 5:24
the world has been *c* to me . . Gal 6:14
where also our Lord was *c* . . Rev 11:8

CRUCIFY
and to scourge and to *c* . . . Matt 20:19
them you will kill and *c* . . . Matt 23:34
out again, "*C* Him . . . . Mark 15:13
saying, "*C* Him, *c* Him . . . . Luke 23:21
I have power to *c* You . . . . John 19:10
"Shall I *c* your King . . . . . . John 19:15
since they *c* again . . . . Heb 6:6

CRUEL
wrath, for it is *c* . . . . Gen 49:7
spirit and *c* bondage . . . . Ex 6:9
hate me with *c* hatred . . . . Ps 25:19
of the wicked are *c* . . . . Prov 12:10

CRUELTY
of *c* are in their . . . . Gen 49:5
the haunts of *c* . . . . Ps 74:20
c you have ruled . . . . Ezek 34:4

CRUMBS
eat from the children's *c* . . Mark 7:28
c which fell from the . . . . . Luke 16:21

CRUSH
that a foot may *c* . . . . Job 39:15
that your foot may *c* . . . . Ps 68:23
the poor, who *c* . . . . Amos 4:1
of peace will *c* . . . . Rom 16:20

CRUSHED
in the dust, who are *c* . . . . Job 4:19
c my life to the . . . . Ps 143:3
every side, yet not *c* . . . . 2 Cor 4:8

CRUST
man is reduced to a *c* . . . . . . Prov 6:26

CRY
and their *c* came up to . . . . Ex 2:23
of oppressions they *c* . . . . Job 35:9
heart and my flesh *c* . . . . Ps 84:2
I *c* out with my whole . . . . . Ps 119:145
Does not wisdom *c* . . . . Prov 8:1
"What shall I *c* . . . . Is 40:6
nor lift up a *c* . . . . Jer 7:16
c mightily to God . . . . Jon 3:8
at midnight a *c* . . . . Matt 25:6
His own elect who *c* . . . . Luke 18:7

CRYING
"The voice of one *c* . . . . Matt 3:3
nor sorrow, nor *c* . . . . Rev 21:4

CRYSTAL
nor *c* can equal it . . . . Job 28:17
your gates of *c* . . . . Is 54:12
of an awesome *c* . . . . Ezek 1:22
a sea of glass, like *c* . . . . Rev 4:6

CUBIT
shall finish it to a *c* . . . . Gen 6:16
can add one *c* . . . . Matt 6:27

CUCUMBERS
in Egypt, the *c* . . . . Num 11:5
a hut in a garden of *c* . . . . Is 1:8

CUD
c or those that have cloven . . Lev 11:4
the *c* or have cloven . . . . Deut 14:7

CUMI
Talitha, *c*," which is . . . . Mark 5:41

CUNNING
the serpent was more *c* . . . . . . Gen 3:1
c comes quickly . . . . Job 5:13
c craftiness of deceitful . . . . . Eph 4:14

CUP
My *c* runs over . . . . Ps 23:5
waters of a full *c* are . . . . Ps 73:10
the LORD there is a *c* . . . . Ps 75:8
I will take up the *c* . . . . Ps 116:13
the dregs of the *c* . . . . Is 51:17
men give them the *c* . . . . Jer 16:7
"Take this wine *c* . . . . Jer 25:15
The *c* of the LORD's . . . . Hab 2:16
make Jerusalem a *c* . . . . Zech 12:2
little ones only a *c* . . . . Matt 10:42
will indeed drink My *c* . . . . Matt 20:23
cleanse the inside of the *c* . Matt 23:26
Then He took the *c* . . . . Matt 26:27
possible, let this *c* . . . . Matt 26:39
c of water to drink in My . . Mark 9:41
the outside of the *c* . . . . Luke 11:39
c is the new covenant . . . . Luke 22:20
this *c* away from Me . . . . . . Luke 22:42
cannot drink the *c* . . . . 1 Cor 10:21
c is the new covenant . . . . . 1 Cor 11:25
the *c* of His indignation . . . . Rev 14:10
to give her the *c* . . . . Rev 16:19
c full of abominations . . . . Rev 17:4

CURE
but they could not *c* . . . . . . Matt 17:16
and to *c* diseases . . . . Luke 9:1

CURES
and perform *c* . . . . Luke 13:32

CURSE
c the ground for man's . . . . . Gen 8:21
will *c* him who curses you . . . Gen 12:3
your *c* be on me, my son . . Gen 27:13
c a ruler of your . . . . Ex 22:28
You shall not *c* the deaf . . . . Lev 19:14
c this people for me . . . . Num 22:6
Balaam, "Neither *c* . . . . Num 23:25

your God turned the *c* ..... Deut 23:5
on Mount Ebal to *c* .... Deut 27:13
c which I have set before .. Deut 30:1
said to him, '*C* David ..... 2 Sam 16:10
the *c* into a blessing .... Neh 13:2
C God and die .... Job 2:9
mouth, but they *c* .... Ps 62:4
Let them *c*, but You bless .. Ps 109:28
The *c* of the LORD is .... Prov 3:33
So a *c* without cause shall .. Prov 26:2
Do not *c* the king .... Eccl 10:20
the *c* has devoured .... Is 24:6
a byword, a taunt and a *c* .... Jer 24:9
This is the *c* that goes out ... Zech 5:3
a *c* among the nations ..... Zech 8:13
"I will send a *c* .... Mal 2:2
are cursed with a *c* .... Mal 3:9
bless those who *c* you, ... Luke 6:28
bless and do not *c* .... Rom 12:14
law are under the *c* .... Gal 3:10
us from the *c* of the law, ... Gal 3:13
Father, and with it we *c* ... James 3:9
there shall be no more *c* .... Rev 22:3

CURSED
c more than all cattle .... Gen 3:14
C is the man who .... Jer 17:5
c is he who keeps .... Jer 48:10
'Depart from Me, you *c* ... Matt 25:41
C is everyone who hangs .... Gal 3:13
and near to being *c* .... Heb 6:8

CURSES
I will curse him who *c* ..... Gen 12:3
'For everyone who *c* .... Lev 20:9
write these *c* in a book .... Num 5:23
c his father or his .... Prov 20:20
'He who *c* father or .... Mark 7:10

CURSINGS
by the sword for the *c* ...... Hos 7:16

CURTAIN
of each *c* shall be .... Ex 26:2
the heavens like a *c* .... Ps 104:2

CUSH
Ham's oldest son, 1 Chr 1:8–10
——— Another name for Ethiopia, Is 18:1

CUSHAN-RISHATHAIM
Mesopotamian king; oppresses Israel, Judg 3:8
Othniel delivers Israel from, Judg 3:9, 10

CUSTOM
to me, as Your *c* .... Ps 119:132
according to the *c* .... Acts 15:1
we have no such *c* .... 1 Cor 11:16

CUT
confidence shall be *c* .... Job 8:14
evildoers shall be *c* .... Ps 37:9
the wicked will be *c* .... Prov 2:22
c off your supply of bread .. Ezek 5:16
your navel cord was not *c* .. Ezek 16:4
stone was *c* out without .... Dan 2:34
that I will *c* off the names .. Zech 13:2
not bear good fruit is *c* ..... Matt 3:10
causes you to sin, *c* .... Matt 5:30
and will *c* him in .... Matt 24:51
him whose ear Peter *c* ..... John 18:26
He had his hair *c* .... Acts 18:18

CYMBAL
or a clanging *c* .... 1 Cor 13:1

CYPRUS
Mentioned in prophecies, Num 24:24; Is 23:1–12; Jer 2:10
Christians preach to Jews of, Acts 11:19, 20
Paul and Barnabas visit, Acts 13:4–13; 15:39

CYRENE
A Greek colonial city in North Africa; home of Simon the cross-bearer, Matt 27:32

Synagogue of, Acts 6:9
Christians from, become missionaries, Acts 11:20

CYRUS
King of Persia, referred to as God's anointed, Is 44:28—45:1

DAGON
The national god of the Philistines, Judg 16:23
Falls before ark, 1 Sam 5:1–5

DAILY
much as they gather *d* .... Ex 16:5
d He shall be praised .... Ps 72:15
to me, watching *d* .... Prov 8:34
Yet they seek Me *d* .... Is 58:2
Give us this day our *d* ...... Matt 6:11
I sat *d* with you .... Matt 26:55
take up his cross *d* .... Luke 9:23
the Scriptures *d* .... Acts 17:11
our Lord, I die *d* .... 1 Cor 15:31
stands ministering *d* .... Heb 10:11

DALMATIA
A region east of the Adriatic Sea; Titus departs for, 2 Tim 4:10

DAMASCUS
Capital of Syria; captured by David; ruled by enemy kings, 2 Sam 8:5, 6; 1 Kin 11:23, 24; 15:18
Elisha's prophecy in, 2 Kin 8:7–15
Taken by Assyrians, 2 Kin 16:9
Prophecy concerning, Is 8:3, 4
Paul converted on road to; first preaches there, Acts 9:1–22
escapes from, 2 Cor 11:32, 33
revisits, Gal 1:17

DAN
Jacob's son by Bilhah, Gen 30:5, 6
Prophecy concerning, Gen 49:16, 17
——— Tribe of:
Numbered, Num 1:38, 39
Blessed, Deut 33:22
Receive their inheritance, Josh 19:40–47
Fall into idolatry, Judg 18:1–31
——— Town, northern boundary of Israel, Judg 20:1
Called Leshem; captured by Danites, Josh 19:47
Center of idolatry, 1 Kin 12:28–30
Destroyed by Ben-Hadad, 1 Kin 15:20

DANCE
and their children *d* .... Job 21:11
His name with the *d* .... Ps 149:3
mourn, and a time to *d* ...... Eccl 3:4
d has turned into .... Lam 5:15
and you did not *d* .... Matt 11:17

DANCED
Then David *d* before ...... 2 Sam 6:14
daughter of Herodias *d* ..... Matt 14:6

DANCING
saw the calf and the *d* ...... Ex 32:19
me my mourning into *d* ..... Ps 30:11
he heard music and *d* .... Luke 15:25

DANIEL
Taken to Babylon; refuses Nebuchadnezzar's foods, Dan 1
Interprets dreams; honored by king, Dan 2
Interprets handwriting on wall; honored by Belshazzar, Dan 5:10–29
Appointed to high office; conspired against and thrown to lions, Dan 6:1–23
Visions of four beasts, ram and goat, Dan 7; 8
Intercedes for Israel, Dan 9:1–19
Further visions, Dan 9:20—12:13

DARE
someone would even *d* ...... Rom 5:7
D any of you .... 1 Cor 6:1

DARIUS
Darius the Mede, son of Ahasuerus; made king of the Chaldeans, Dan 9:1
Succeeds Belshazzar, Dan 5:30, 31
Co-ruler with Cyrus, Dan 6:28
——— Darius Hystaspis (522–486 B.C.), king of all Persia; temple work dated by his reign, Ezra 4:5, 24
Confirms Cyrus's royal edict, Ezra 6:1–14
——— Darius the Persian (423–404 B.C.); priestly records kept during his reign, Neh 12:22

DARK
dwell in the *d* cloud .... 1 Kin 8:12
I am *d*, but lovely .... Song 1:5
d place of the earth .... Is 45:19
d places like the dead .... Lam 3:6
and makes the day *d* .... Amos 5:8
and the day shall be *d* .... Mic 3:6
I tell you in the *d* .... Matt 10:27
while it was still *d* .... John 20:1
shines in a *d* place .... 2 Pet 1:19

DARKENED
so that the land was *d* .... Ex 10:15
Let their eyes be *d* .... Ps 69:23
their understanding *d* ...... Eph 4:18

DARKNESS
d He called Night .... Gen 1:5
shall enlighten my *d* ..... 2 Sam 22:29
through the deep *d* .... Job 22:13
Those who sat in *d* .... Ps 107:10
d shall not hide .... Ps 139:12
d have seen a great light .... Is 9:2
I will make *d* light .... Is 42:16
and deep *d* the people .... Is 60:2
Israel, or a land of *d* .... Jer 2:31
body will be full of *d* .... Matt 6:23
cast out into outer *d* .... Matt 8:12
and the power of *d* .... Luke 22:53
d rather than light .... John 3:19
d does not know .... John 12:35
For you were once *d* .... Eph 5:8
the rulers of the *d* .... Eph 6:12
us from the power of *d* ...... Col 1:13
of the night nor of *d* ...... 1 Thess 5:5
and to blackness and *d* .... Heb 12:18
called you out of *d* .... 1 Pet 2:9
blackness of *d* forever ..... 2 Pet 2:17
and in Him is no *d* .... 1 John 1:5
Him, and walk in *d* .... 1 John 1:6
d is passing away .... 1 John 2:8
blackness of *d* forever .... Jude 13

DARTS
quench all the fiery *d* .... Eph 6:16

DASH
You shall *d* them to .... Ps 2:9
lest you *d* your foot .... Matt 4:6

DASHED
hand, O LORD, has *d* .... Ex 15:6
also will be *d* to .... Is 13:16
infants shall be *d* .... Hos 13:16

DATHAN
Joins Korah's rebellion, Num 16:1–35
Swallowed up by the earth, Ps 106:17

DAUGHTER
I am the *d* of Bethuel, ... Gen 24:24
Dinah the *d* of Leah .... Gen 34:1
Jochebed the *d* of Levi .... Num 26:59
had neither son nor *d* ..... Judg 11:34
cry of the *d* of my people ..... Jer 8:19
the virgin *d* of my people ... Jer 14:17

O virgin, the *d* of Egypt . . . . Jer 46:11
"Rejoice greatly, O *d* . . . . Zech 9:9
My *d* has just died, ... Matt 9:18
Be of good cheer, *d* . . . . Matt 9:22
being a *d* of Abraham, ... Luke 13:16
"Fear not, *d* of Zion . . . . . . John 12:15
the son of Pharaoh's *d* . . . . . Heb 11:24

DAUGHTER-IN-LAW

Judah said to Tamar his *d* . Gen 38:11
the Moabitess her *d* with . . . Ruth 1:22
lewdly defiles his *d* . . . . Ezek 22:11
d against her . . . . Mic 7:6
a *d* against her . . . . Matt 10:35

DAUGHTERS

he had sons and *d* . . . . Gen 5:4
of God saw the *d* . . . . Gen 6:2
Thus both the *d* of Lot . . . . . Gen 19:36
years for your two *d* . . . . . . Gen 31:41
the *d* of Zelophehad . . . . Num 27:1
not give them our *d* as . . . . . Judg 21:7
Turn back, my *d* . . . . Ruth 1:11
O *d* of Israel, weep over . . 2 Sam 1:24
d wore such apparel . . . . . 2 Sam 13:18
beautiful as the *d* of Job . . . Job 42:15
Kings' *d* are among Your . . . . . Ps 45:9
Let the *d* of Judah be glad, . . Ps 48:11
The leech has two *d* . . . . Prov 30:15
"Many *d* have done well . . . Prov 31:29
a bird, and all the *d* . . . . Eccl 12:4
O *d* of Jerusalem, like the . . . Song 1:5
"Because the *d* of Zion are . . . . . Is 3:16
d shall go into captivity . . . Ezek 30:18
your *d* shall prophesy . . . . . . Joel 2:28
D of Jerusalem, do not . . . Luke 23:28
d shall prophesy . . . . Acts 2:17
man had four virgin *d* . . . . . Acts 21:9
shall be My sons and *d* . . . . 2 Cor 6:18
whose *d* you are if you . . . . . . 1 Pet 3:6

DAVID

See CITY OF DAVID; HOUSE OF DAVID; SEED OF DAVID; SON OF DAVID; THRONE OF DAVID

Anointed by Samuel, 1 Sam 16:1–13
Becomes royal harpist, 1 Sam 16:14–23
Defeats Goliath, 1 Sam 17
Makes covenant with Jonathan, 1 Sam 18:1–4
Honored by Saul; loved by the people; Saul becomes jealous, 1 Sam 18:5–16
Wins Michal as wife, 1 Sam 18:17–30
Flees from Saul, 1 Sam 19; 20; 21:10—22:5; 23:14–29
Eats the holy bread, 1 Sam 21:1–6; Matt 12:3, 4
Saves Keilah from Philistines, 1 Sam 23:1–13
Twice spares Saul's life, 1 Sam 24:1–22; 26:1–25
Anger at Nabal appeased by Abigail; marries her, 1 Sam 25:2–42
Allies with the Philistines, 1 Sam 27:1—28:2
Rejected by them, 1 Sam 29
Avenges destruction of Ziklag, 1 Sam 30
Mourns death of Saul and Jonathan, 2 Sam 1
Anointed king of Judah, 2 Sam 2:1–7
War with Saul's house; Abner defects to David, 2 Sam 3:1, 6–21
Mourns Abner's death, 2 Sam 3:28–39
Punishes Ishbosheth's murderers, 2 Sam 4
Anointed king of all Israel, 2 Sam 5:1–5
Conquers Jerusalem; makes it his capital, 2 Sam 5:6–16
Defeats Philistines, 2 Sam 5:17–25
Brings ark to Jerusalem, 2 Sam 6
Receives eternal covenant, 2 Sam 7
Further conquests, 2 Sam 8; 10
Shows mercy to Mephibosheth, 2 Sam 9
Commits adultery and murder, 2 Sam 11
Rebuked by Nathan; repents, 2 Sam 12:1–23; Ps 32; 51
Absalom's rebellion, 2 Sam 15—18
Mourns Absalom's death, 2 Sam 18:33—19:8
Shows himself merciful, 2 Sam 19:18–39
Sheba's rebellion, 2 Sam 19:40—20:22
Avenges the Gibeonites, 2 Sam 21:1–14
Song of deliverance, 2 Sam 22
Sins by numbering the people, 2 Sam 24:1–17
Buys threshing floor to build altar, 2 Sam 24:18–25
Secures Solomon's succession, 1 Kin 1:5–53
Instructions to Solomon, 1 Kin 2:1–11
Last words, 2 Sam 23:1–7
Inspired by Spirit, Matt 22:43
As prophet, Acts 2:29–34
Faith of, Heb 11:32–34

DAY

See LAST DAY; THIRD DAY

God called the light *D* . . . . Gen 1:5
blessed the seventh *d* . . . . Gen 2:3
garden in the cool of the *d* . . . Gen 3:8
on that *d* all the fountains . . Gen 7:11
and *d* and night . . . . Gen 8:22
"Swear to me as of this *d* . . Gen 25:33
shall observe this *d* . . . . Ex 12:17
a certain quota every *d* . . . . Ex 16:4
sixth *d* bread for two days . . Ex 16:29
rested on the seventh *d* . . . . . Ex 16:30
Remember the Sabbath *d* . . . . Ex 20:8
eaten the same *d* . . . . Lev 19:6
seventh *d* shall be a holy . . . . Lev 23:8
be the *D* of Atonement . . . . . Lev 23:27
clothes on the seventh *d* . . Num 31:24
and in the cloud by *d* . . . . . . Deut 1:33
This *d* you are to cross . . . . Deut 2:18
witness against you this *d* . . . Deut 4:26
the *d* of their calamity . . . . Deut 32:35
you shall meditate in it *d* . . . . Josh 1:8
"This *d* I have rolled away . . Josh 5:9
grain, on the very same *d* . . . Josh 5:11
has been no *d* like that . . . . Josh 10:14
rebel this *d* against the . . . . Josh 22:16
You are witnesses this *d* . . . Ruth 4:10
on the *d* of battle, that . . . 1 Sam 13:22
the victory that *d* was . . . . . 2 Sam 19:2
This *d* is a *d* of good news, . . 2 Kin 7:9
This *d* is a *d* of trouble, ... 2 Kin 19:3
of a pit on a snowy *d* . . . . . 1 Chr 11:22
d of the foundation of . . . . . 2 Chr 8:16
Be still, for the *d* is holy . . . . Neh 8:11
made it a *d* of feasting . . . . . Esth 9:18
and cursed the *d* . . . . Job 3:1
for the *d* of battle and . . . . . . Job 38:23
d utters speech . . . . Ps 19:2
For a *d* in Your courts . . . . Ps 84:10
In the *d* of my trouble . . . . Ps 86:7
d the LORD has made . . . . Ps 118:24
not strike you by *d* . . . . Ps 121:6
night shines as the *d* . . . . Ps 139:12
unto the perfect *d* . . . . Prov 4:18
do not know what a *d* . . . . . . Prov 27:1
the *d* when the keepers . . . . . Eccl 12:3
Until the *d* breaks and . . . . . . Song 4:6
In that *d* the Branch of the . . . . . Is 4:2
in the *d* of your fast you . . . . . . Is 58:3
tears, that I might weep *d* . . . . . Jer 9:1
My covenant with the *d* . . . . . Jer 33:20
a cloud on a rainy *d*, so . . . . . Ezek 1:28
Behold, the *d* . . . . Ezek 7:10
on the *d* of the LORD . . . . Ezek 13:5
the *d* you were created . . . Ezek 28:15
life, in the *d* of your fall . . Ezek 32:10
knees three times that *d* . . . . Dan 6:10
you shall stumble in the *d* . . . . Hos 4:5
a *d* of clouds and thick . . . . . . Joel 2:2
For the *d* of the LORD . . . . Joel 2:11
who put far off the *d* . . . . Amos 6:3
next *d* God prepared a . . . . Jon 4:7
the *d* of your watchman . . . . . . Mic 7:4
for the *d* of the LORD . . . . Zeph 1:7
who has despised the *d* . . . . . Zech 4:10
neither *d* nor night . . . . Zech 14:7
who can endure the *d* . . . . Mal 3:2
d our daily bread . . . . Matt 6:11
and Gomorrah in the *d* . . . . Matt 10:15
d when I drink it new . . . . . Matt 26:29
this *d* in the city of David . . Luke 2:11
you seven times in a *d* . . . . . Luke 17:4
and the third *d* rise again . . . Luke 24:7
sent Me while it is *d* . . . . John 9:4
great and awesome *d* . . . . Acts 2:20
person esteems one *d* . . . . . . Rom 14:5
D will declare it . . . . 1 Cor 3:13
again the third *d* . . . . 1 Cor 15:4
d I have been in the . . . . . . 2 Cor 11:25
perfectly that the *d* . . . . 1 Thess 5:2
and sons of the *d* . . . . 1 Thess 5:5
He designates a certain *d* . . . . Heb 4:7
God in the *d* of visitation . . . 1 Pet 2:12
with the Lord one *d* . . . . 2 Pet 3:8
great *d* of God Almighty . . . Rev 16:14

DAY OF THE LORD

For the *d* of hosts shall . . . . Is 2:12
Wail, for the *d* is at hand . . . . . Is 13:6
the holy *d* honorable, ... Is 58:13
is the *d* God of hosts, ... Jer 46:10
stand in battle on the *d* . . . . Ezek 13:5
is near, even the *d* . . . . Ezek 30:3
For the *d* is at hand; . . . . Joel 1:15
the great and awesome *d* . . . Joel 2:31
For what good is the *d* . . . . . Amos 5:18
d upon all the nations . . . . Obad 15
for the *d* is at hand, ... Zeph 1:7
the great and dreadful *d* . . . . . . Mal 4:5
the great and awesome *d* . . . Acts 2:20
may be saved in the *d* . . . . . . 1 Cor 5:5
also are ours, in the *d* . . . . . 2 Cor 1:14
d will come as a thief . . . . . . 2 Pet 3:10

DAYS

See ALL THE DAYS OF HIS LIFE; LAST DAYS

seasons, and for *d* . . . . Gen 1:14
rain on the earth forty *d* . . . . . Gen 7:4
He who is eight *d* old . . . . . . Gen 17:12
Seven *d* you shall eat . . . . Ex 12:15
Six *d* you shall gather it, ... Ex 16:26
Six *d* you shall labor . . . . Ex 20:9
that your *d* may be long . . . . Deut 5:16
d are swifter than a . . . . Job 7:6
Let me alone, for my *d* . . . . . . Job 7:16
of woman is of few *d* . . . . Job 14:1
blessed the latter *d* . . . . Job 42:12
me all the *d* of my life . . . . Ps 23:6
The *d* of our lives are . . . . Ps 90:10
teach us to number our *d* . . . . Ps 90:12
For my *d* are consumed . . . . . . Ps 102:3
I remember the *d* of old . . . . . Ps 143:5
for length of *d* and long . . . . . Prov 3:2
of the LORD prolongs *d* . . . . Prov 10:27
evil all the *d* of her life . . . . Prov 31:12
"Why were the former *d* . . . . Eccl 7:10
Before the difficult *d* . . . . Eccl 12:1
and tested them ten *d* . . . . . . Dan 1:14
He had fasted forty *d* . . . . Matt 4:2
But the *d* will come when . . Matt 9:15
those *d* were shortened . . . Matt 24:22
had shortened those *d* . . . . Mark 13:20
the *d* were completed . . . . Luke 2:6
But the *d* will come when . . Luke 5:35
raise it up in three *d* . . . . John 2:20
he has been dead four *d* . . John 11:39
by them during forty *d* . . . . Acts 1:3

let a *d* be written that they ... Esth 3:9
"I will declare the *d* ... Ps 2:7
d which shall not pass ... Ps 148:6
Woe to those who *d* ... Is 10:1
by a perpetual *d* ... Jer 5:22
is by the *d* of the watchers .. Dan 4:17
Nineveh by the *d* of the ... Jon 3:7
in those days that a *d* ... Luke 2:1

DEDICATED
house and has not *d* ... Deut 20:5
every *d* thing in ... Ezek 44:29
first covenant was *d* ... Heb 9:18

DEDICATION
sacrifices at the *d* ... Ezra 6:17
it was the Feast of *D* ... John 10:22

DEED
What *d* is this you have ... Gen 44:15
d has been done ... Judg 19:30
So I took the purchase *d*, ... Jer 32:11
you do a charitable *d* ... Matt 6:2
a Prophet mighty in *d* ... Luke 24:19
you do in word or *d* ... Col 3:17
us from every lawless *d* ... Titus 2:14
your good *d* might not ... Philem 14
or in tongue, but in *d* ... 1 John 3:18

DEEDS
works and Your mighty *d* .. Deut 3:24
make known His *d* ... 1 Chr 16:8
Declare His *d* among ... Ps 9:11
them according to their *d* ... Ps 28:4
d You did in their days, ... Ps 44:1
awesome *d* in righteousness .. Ps 65:5
vengeance on their *d* ... Ps 99:8
Make known His *d* ... Ps 105:1
harlot by their own *d* ... Ps 106:39
against the *d* of the wicked .. Ps 141:5
man according to his *d* ... Prov 24:12
declare His *d* among ... Is 12:4
they surpass the *d* ... Jer 5:28
their *d* on their own head .. Ezek 9:10
charitable *d* before men ... Matt 6:1
the *d* of your fathers ... Luke 11:48
because their *d* ... John 3:19
You do the *d* of your ... John 8:41
mighty in words and *d* ... Acts 7:22
one according to his *d* ... Rom 2:6
apart from the *d* of the law . Rom 3:28
you put to death the *d* ... Rom 8:13
off the old man with his *d* ... Col 3:9
shares in his evil *d* ... 2 John 11
that you hate the *d* of the ... Rev 2:6
did not repent of their *d* ... Rev 16:11

DEEP
LORD God caused a *d* ... Gen 2:21
He lays up the *d* ... Ps 33:7
D calls unto *d* ... Ps 42:7
In His hand are the *d* ... Ps 95:4
His wonders in the *d* ... Ps 107:24
put out in *d* darkness ... Prov 20:20
led them through the *d* ... Is 63:13
d closed around me ... Jon 2:5
d uttered its voice ... Hab 3:10
"Launch out into the *d* ... Luke 5:4
I have been in the *d* ... 2 Cor 11:25

DEEPER
D than Sheol ... Job 11:8

DEEPLY
Drink, yes, drink *d* ... Song 5:1
But He sighed *d* ... Mark 8:12

DEER
"Naphtali is a *d* ... Gen 49:21
my feet like the feet of *d* ... Ps 18:33
As the *d* pants for the ... Ps 42:1
shall leap like a *d* ... Is 35:6

DEER'S
will make my feet like *d* ... Hab 3:19

DEFEATED
and Israel was *d* ... 1 Sam 4:10

DEFECT
who has any *d* ... Lev 21:17

DEFEND
'For I will *d* this ... 2 Kin 19:34
d my own ways before ... Job 13:15
for joy, because You *d* ... Ps 5:11
of the God of Jacob *d* you ... Ps 20:1
D the poor and ... Ps 82:3
d the fatherless ... Is 1:17
of hosts *d* Jerusalem ... Is 31:5
The LORD of hosts will *d* ... Zech 9:15

DEFENDER
a *d* of widows ... Ps 68:5

DEFENSE
For wisdom is a *d* ... Eccl 7:12
d will be the fortress ... Is 33:16
am appointed for the *d* ... Phil 1:17
d no one stood with me ... 2 Tim 4:16
be ready to give a *d* ... 1 Pet 3:15

DEFERRED
Hope *d* makes the heart ... Prov 13:12

DEFILE
the heart, and they *d* ... Matt 15:18
also these dreamers *d* ... Jude 8

DEFILED
had *d* Dinah his daughter ... Gen 34:5
d the dwelling place ... Ps 74:7
For your hands are *d* ... Is 59:3
lest they should be *d* ... John 18:28
and has *d* this holy place .. Acts 21:28
being weak, is *d* ... 1 Cor 8:7
and conscience are *d* ... Titus 1:15
even the garment *d* ... Jude 23
have not *d* their garments ... Rev 3:4

DEFILES
mouth, this *d* a man ... Matt 15:11
d the temple of God ... 1 Cor 3:17
it anything that *d* ... Rev 21:27

DEFRAUD
d his brother in this ... 1 Thess 4:6

DEGENERATE
before Me into the *d* ... Jer 2:21
d is your heart ... Ezek 16:30

DEGREES
go forward ten *d* ... 2 Kin 20:9

DELAIAH
Son of Shemaiah; urges Jehoiakim not to burn Jeremiah's scroll, Jer 36:12, 25

DELICACIES
let me eat of their *d* ... Ps 141:4
Do not desire his *d* ... Prov 23:3
of the king's *d* ... Dan 1:5

DELICATE
Leah's eyes were *d*, but ... Gen 29:17
be called tender and *d* ... Is 47:1
a lovely and *d* woman ... Jer 6:2

DELIGHT
the LORD as great *d* ... 1 Sam 15:22
And his heart took *d* ... 2 Chr 17:6
your *d* in the Almighty ... Job 22:26
Will he *d* himself in ... Job 27:10
But his *d* is in the ... Ps 1:2
ones, in whom is all my *d* ... Ps 16:3
D yourself also in the ... Ps 37:4
I *d* to do Your will ... Ps 40:8
You do not *d* in burnt ... Ps 51:16
They *d* in lies ... Ps 62:4
the peoples who *d* in war ... Ps 68:30
I will *d* myself in Your ... Ps 119:16
commandments, For I *d* ... Ps 119:35
For Your law is my *d* ... Ps 119:77
Your law had been my *d* ... Ps 119:92
And Your law is my *d* ... Ps 119:174
does not *d* in the strength .. Ps 147:10
For scorners *d* in their ... Prov 1:22
d in the perversity of the ... Prov 2:14
d ourselves with love ... Prov 7:18
And I was daily His *d* ... Prov 8:30
but a just weight is His *d* ... Prov 11:1
truthfully are His *d* ... Prov 12:22
will give *d* to your soul ... Prov 29:17
in his shade with great *d* ... Song 2:3
His *d* is in the fear of the ... Is 11:3
gold, they will not *d* in it ... Is 13:17
And let your soul *d* ... Is 55:2
call the Sabbath a *d* ... Is 58:13
that in which I do not *d* ... Is 65:12
For in these I *d*," says the ... Jer 9:24
eyes, the *d* of your soul ... Ezek 24:21
For I *d* in the law of ... Rom 7:22
taking *d* in false humility ... Col 2:18

DELIGHTED
The LORD *d* only in ... Deut 10:15
d greatly in David ... 1 Sam 19:1
because He *d* in me ... 2 Sam 22:20
who *d* in you, setting you ... 2 Chr 9:8
me because He *d* in me ... Ps 18:19

DELIGHTS
whom the king *d* to honor ... Esth 6:6
Him, since He *d* in Him ... Ps 22:8
the LORD, and He *d* in his ... Ps 37:23
the son in whom he *d* ... Prov 3:12
O love, with your *d* ... Song 7:6
For the LORD *d* in you ... Is 62:4
forever, because He *d* ... Mic 7:18

DELILAH
Deceives Samson, Judg 16:4–22

DELIVER
d them out of the hand ... Ex 3:8
will *d* him into your hand' ... Judg 4:7
The LORD will *d* us ... 2 Kin 18:32
He shall *d* you in six ... Job 5:19
is no one who can *d* ... Job 10:7
'*D* him from going down ... Job 33:24
Let Him *d* Him ... Ps 22:8
d their soul from ... Ps 33:19
I will *d* him and honor ... Ps 91:15
d you from the immoral ... Prov 2:16
wickedness will not *d* ... Eccl 8:8
have I no power to *d* ... Is 50:2
we serve is able to *d* ... Dan 3:17
into temptation, but *d* ... Matt 6:13
let Him *d* Him now if ... Matt 27:43
d such a one to Satan ... 1 Cor 5:5
And the Lord will *d* ... 2 Tim 4:18
d the godly out of ... 2 Pet 2:9

DELIVERANCE
d He gives to His king ... Ps 18:50
but *d* is of the LORD ... Prov 21:31
not accepting *d* ... Heb 11:35

DELIVERED
d the poor who cried ... Job 29:12
for You have *d* my soul ... Ps 56:13
For He has *d* the life ... Jer 20:13
All things have been *d* ... Matt 11:27
who was *d* up because ... Rom 4:25
But now we have been *d* ... Rom 7:6
who *d* us from so great ... 2 Cor 1:10
was once for all *d* ... Jude 3

DELIVERER
the LORD raised up a *d* ... Judg 3:9
LORD raised up a *d* for ... Judg 3:15
my fortress and my *d* ... 2 Sam 22:2
LORD gave Israel a *d* ... 2 Kin 13:5
You are my help and my *d* .. Ps 40:17
My high tower and my *d* ... Ps 144:2
d by the hand of the Angel . Acts 7:35
D will come out of ... Rom 11:26

DELIVERERS
d who saved them ... Neh 9:27

DELIVERS
d the kingdom to God ... 1 Cor 15:24
even Jesus who *d* ... 1 Thess 1:10

DELUSION
send them strong *d* ... 2 Thess 2:11

DEMAS
Follows Paul, Col 4:14
Forsakes Paul, 2 Tim 4:10

DEMETRIUS
A silversmith at Ephesus, Acts 19:24–31
—— A good Christian, 3 John 12

DEMON
when the *d* was cast out ... Matt 9:33
they say, 'He has a *d* ... Matt 11:18
Jesus rebuked the *d* ... Matt 17:18
the *d* out of her daughter .. Mark 7:26
a spirit of an unclean *d* ... Luke 4:33
you say, 'He has a *d* ... Luke 7:33
was driven by the *d* into ... Luke 8:29
d threw him down and ... Luke 9:42
He was casting out a *d* ... Luke 11:14
You have a *d* ... John 7:20
and have a *d* ... John 8:48
He has a *d* and is mad ... John 10:20

DEMON-POSSESSED
and those who were *d* ... Matt 4:24
to Him many who were *d* .. Matt 8:16
there met Him two *d* men, .. Matt 8:28
Him a man, mute and *d* ... Matt 9:32
to Him who was *d* ... Matt 12:22
daughter is severely *d* ... Matt 15:22
and those who were *d* ... Mark 1:32
one who had been *d* ... Mark 5:15
had been *d* was healed ... Luke 8:36

DEMONIC
is earthly, sensual, *d* ... James 3:15

DEMONS
See CAST OUT DEMONS; CASTING OUT DEMONS
They sacrificed to *d* ... Deut 32:17
their daughters to *d* ... Ps 106:37
cast out *d* in Your name ... Matt 7:22
d begged Him, saying, ... Matt 8:31
He casts out *d* ... Matt 9:34
raise the dead, cast out *d* .. Matt 10:8
except by Beelzebub ... Matt 12:24
and cast out many *d* ... Mark 1:34
and to cast out *d* ... Mark 3:15
d begged Him, saying, ... Mark 5:12
they cast out many *d* ... Mark 6:13
out *d* in Your name ... Mark 9:38
He had cast seven *d* ... Mark 16:9
name they will cast out *d* . Mark 16:17
And *d* also came out of ... Luke 4:41
whom had come seven *d* ... Luke 8:2
many *d* had entered ... Luke 8:30
authority over all *d* ... Luke 9:1
casting out *d* in Your ... Luke 9:49
the *d* are subject ... Luke 10:17
casts out *d* by Beelzebub . Luke 11:15
fox, 'Behold, I cast out *d* . Luke 13:32
Lord and the cup of *d* ... 1 Cor 10:21
spirits and doctrines of *d* ... 1 Tim 4:1
Even the *d* believe ... James 2:19
they should not worship *d* .. Rev 9:20
For they are spirits of *d* ... Rev 16:14
a dwelling place of *d* ... Rev 18:2

DEMONSTRATE
faith, to *d* His ... Rom 3:25

DEMONSTRATES
d His own love toward ... Rom 5:8

DEMONSTRATION
but in *d* of the Spirit and ... 1 Cor 2:4

DEN
in the viper's *d* ... Is 11:8
by My name, become a *d* ... Jer 7:11
cast him into the *d* ... Dan 6:16
it a '*d* of thieves ... Matt 21:13

DENARIUS
the laborers for a *d* ... Matt 20:2
they brought Him a *d* ... Matt 22:19
quart of wheat for a *d* ... Rev 6:6

DENIED
before men will be *d* ... Luke 12:9
Peter then *d* again ... John 18:27
d the Holy One and the ... Acts 3:14
things cannot be *d* ... Acts 19:36
household, he has *d* ... 1 Tim 5:8
word, and have not *d* ... Rev 3:8

DENIES
But whoever *d* Me ... Matt 10:33
d that Jesus is the ... 1 John 2:22

DENS
lie down in their *d* ... Ps 104:22
and mountains, in *d* ... Heb 11:38

DENY
lest you *d* your God ... Josh 24:27
place, then it will *d* him ... Job 8:18
lest I be full and *d* ... Prov 30:9
him I will also *d* before ... Matt 10:33
let him *d* himself ... Matt 16:24
will *d* Me three times ... Matt 26:34
who *d* that there is a ... Luke 20:27
confessed, and did not *d* ... John 1:20
He cannot *d* Himself ... 2 Tim 2:13
in works they *d* ... Titus 1:16
d the only Lord ... Jude 4
d My faith even ... Rev 2:13

DENYING
but *d* its power ... 2 Tim 3:5
d ungodliness and ... Titus 2:12
d the Lord who bought ... 2 Pet 2:1

DEPART
scepter shall not *d* ... Gen 49:10
they say to God, '*D* ... Job 21:14
D from evil and do good ... Ps 34:14
fear the LORD and *d* ... Prov 3:7
the mountains, shall *d* ... Is 54:10
on the left hand, '*D* ... Matt 25:41
will *d* from the faith ... 1 Tim 4:1

DEPARTED
the day that you *d* ... Deut 9:7

DEPARTING
heart of unbelief in *d* ... Heb 3:12

DEPARTS
His spirit *d*, he returns to ... Ps 146:4
But if the unbeliever *d* ... 1 Cor 7:15

DEPARTURE
d savage wolves will ... Acts 20:29
and the time of my *d* ... 2 Tim 4:6

DEPRESSION
of man causes *d* ... Prov 12:25

DEPRIVE
d myself of good ... Eccl 4:8
d one another except ... 1 Cor 7:5

DEPRIVED
like a bear *d* of her cubs ... Hos 13:8

DEPTH
because they had no *d* ... Matt 13:5
nor height nor *d* ... Rom 8:39
Oh, the *d* of the ... Rom 11:33
width and length and *d* ... Eph 3:18

DEPTHS
d have covered them ... Ex 15:5
The *d* also trembled ... Ps 77:16
my soul from the *d* ... Ps 86:13
led them through the *d* ... Ps 106:9
go down again to the *d* ... Ps 107:26
d I was brought forth ... Prov 8:24
our sins into the *d* ... Mic 7:19
have not known the *d* ... Rev 2:24

DERANGED
the nations are *d* ... Jer 51:7

DERBE
Paul visits, Acts 14:6, 20
Paul meets Timothy at, Acts 16:1

DERISION
shall hold them in *d* ... Ps 2:4
I am in *d* daily ... Jer 20:7

DESCEND
His glory shall not *d* ... Ps 49:17
d now from the cross ... Mark 15:32
Lord Himself will *d* ... 1 Thess 4:16
This wisdom does not *d* .. James 3:15

DESCENDANTS
All you *d* of Jacob ... Ps 22:23
d shall inherit the ... Ps 25:13
pour My Spirit on your *d* ... Is 44:3
In the LORD all the *d* ... Is 45:25
none of his *d* shall prosper . Jer 22:30
"We are Abraham's *d* ... John 8:33
So shall your *d* be ... Rom 4:18

DESCENDED
because the LORD *d* ... Ex 19:18
that He also first *d* ... Eph 4:9
He who *d* is also the ... Eph 4:10

DESCENDING
were ascending and *d* ... Gen 28:12
"I saw the Spirit *d* ... John 1:32
God ascending and *d* ... John 1:51
the holy Jerusalem, *d* ... Rev 21:10

DESERT
And tested God in the *d* ... Ps 106:14
d shall rejoice and blossom ... Is 35:1
and rivers in the *d* ... Is 43:19
her *d* like the garden of ... Is 51:3
'Look, He is in the *d* ... Matt 24:26
ate the manna in the *d* ... John 6:31

DESERTED
d place by Himself ... Matt 14:13

DESERTS
led them through the *d* ... Is 48:21
They wandered in *d* ... Heb 11:38

DESERVE
to them what they *d* ... Ps 28:4
d I will judge them ... Ezek 7:27

DESIGN
with an artistic *d* ... Ex 26:31
may keep its whole *d* ... Ezek 43:11

DESIRABLE
the eyes, and a tree *d* ... Gen 3:6
d that we should leave ... Acts 6:2

DESIRE
d shall be for your ... Gen 3:16
and you shall not *d* your ... Deut 5:21
is all the *d* of Israel ... 1 Sam 9:20
salvation and all my *d* ... 2 Sam 23:5
I *d* to reason with God ... Job 13:3
for we do not *d* ... Job 21:14
boasts of his heart's *d* ... Ps 10:3
heard the *d* of the humble ... Ps 10:17
him his heart's *d* ... Ps 21:2
and offering You did not *d* ... Ps 40:6
Behold, You *d* truth in ... Ps 51:6
confused Who *d* my hurt ... Ps 70:2
upon earth that I *d* ... Ps 73:25
the *d* of the wicked ... Ps 112:10
and satisfy the *d* ... Ps 145:16
all the things you may *d* ... Prov 3:15
all the things one may *d* ... Prov 8:11
d of the righteous will ... Prov 10:24
The *d* of the righteous is .. Prov 11:23
The *d* of the lazy ... Prov 21:25
nor *d* to be with them ... Prov 24:1
a burden, and *d* fails ... Eccl 12:5
and his *d* is toward me ... Song 7:10
the *d* of our soul is ... Is 26:8
beauty that we should *d* ... Is 53:2
the *d* of their eyes, and ... Ezek 24:25
For I *d* mercy and not ... Hos 6:6
great man utters his evil *d* ... Mic 7:3
d mercy and not sacrifice .. Matt 9:13
d I have desired ... Luke 22:15
"Father, I *d* that ... John 17:24
all manner of evil *d* ... Rom 7:8
Brethren, my heart's *d* ... Rom 10:1

d the best gifts .... 1 Cor 12:31
d spiritual gifts .... 1 Cor 14:1
was a readiness to *d* .... 2 Cor 8:11
the two, having a *d* .... Phil 1:23
passion, evil *d* .... Col 3:5
offering You did not *d* ...... Heb 10:5
But now they *d* a better .... Heb 11:16
d has conceived .... James 1:15
angels *d* to look into .... 1 Pet 1:12
d the pure milk of the .... 1 Pet 2:2

DESIRED
d are they than gold .... Ps 19:10
One thing I have *d* .... Ps 27:4
guides them to their *d* ...... Ps 107:30
What is *d* in a man is ..... Prov 19:22
Whatever my eyes *d* .... Eccl 2:10
desire I have *d* .... Luke 22:15

DESIRES
all that your heart *d* ...... 2 Sam 3:21
Who is the man who *d* .... Ps 34:12
shall give you the *d* .... Ps 37:4
the *d* of the wicked .... Ps 140:8
soul of a lazy man *d* .... Prov 13:4
for himself of all he *d* .... Eccl 6:2
d to come after Me, ... Matt 16:24
d to become great .... Matt 20:26
the *d* for other things ..... Mark 4:19
wine, immediately *d* new .. Luke 5:39
the devil, and the *d* .... John 8:44
with its passions and *d* ...... Gal 5:24
fulfilling the *d* of the flesh ... Eph 2:3
If a man *d* the position ... 1 Tim 3:1
according to their own *d* ... 2 Tim 4:3
away by his own *d* .... James 1:14
not come from your *d* ..... James 4:1
Whoever *d*, let him take ... Rev 22:17

DESIRING
earnestly *d* to be clothed .... 2 Cor 5:2
d to be teachers of the .... 1 Tim 1:7
in all things *d* to live ...... Heb 13:18

DESOLATE
on me, for I am *d* .... Ps 25:16
the wilderness in a *d* .... Ps 107:4
my children and am *d* .... Is 49:21
any more be termed *D* .... Is 62:4
to make your land *d* .... Jer 4:7
house is left to you *d* ..... Matt 23:38
one hour she is made *d* .... Rev 18:19

DESOLATION
the 'abomination of *d* ..... Matt 24:15
then know that its *d* ...... Luke 21:20

DESOLATIONS
LORD, who has made *d* .... Ps 46:8

DESPAIRED
turned my heart and *d* ...... Eccl 2:20
strength, so that we *d* ...... 2 Cor 1:8

DESPERATELY
he flees *d* from its .... Job 27:22

DESPISE
if you *d* My statutes .... Lev 26:15
d Me shall be lightly ...... 1 Sam 2:30
I *d* my life .... Job 9:21
but fools *d* wisdom .... Prov 1:7
People do not *d* a thief if ... Prov 6:30
d your mother when she .. Prov 23:22
Because you *d* this word ..... Is 30:12
d your feast days .... Amos 5:21
to you priests who *d* .... Mal 1:6
one and *d* the other .... Matt 6:24
d one of these little ones .. Matt 18:10
d the riches of His .... Rom 2:4
d the church of God ...... 1 Cor 11:22
Therefore let no one *d* .... 1 Cor 16:11
Do not *d* prophecies ..... 1 Thess 5:20
Let no one *d* your youth .. 1 Tim 4:12
do not *d* the chastening of .. Heb 12:5
and *d* authority .... 2 Pet 2:10

DESPISED
mistress became *d* in her ... Gen 16:4
Esau *d* his birthright ...... Gen 25:34
you have *d* the LORD ...... Num 11:20
she *d* him in her heart .... 2 Sam 6:16
men, and *d* by the people ..... Ps 22:6
d the counsel of the Most ... Ps 107:11
perverse heart will be *d* ... Prov 12:8
poor man's wisdom is *d* .... Eccl 9:16
it would be utterly *d* .... Song 8:7
d the word of the Holy .... Is 5:24
He is *d* and rejected .... Is 53:3
have *d* My holy things ..... Ezek 22:8
For who has *d* the day of .. Zech 4:10
righteous, and *d* others .... Luke 18:9
the things which are *d* ..... 1 Cor 1:28

DESPISES
wisdom *d* his neighbor .... Prov 11:12
d the word will be .... Prov 13:13
d his neighbor sins .... Prov 14:21
but a foolish man *d* .... Prov 15:20
d the scepter of My .... Ezek 21:10

DESPISING
the cross, *d* the shame ...... Heb 12:2

DESTINED
this Child is *d* for the fall .. Luke 2:34

DESTINY
did not consider her *d* .... Lam 1:9

DESTITUTE
the prayer of the *d* .... Ps 102:17
of corrupt minds and *d* ..... 1 Tim 6:5
sister is naked and *d* ..... James 2:15

DESTROY
d the righteous .... Gen 18:23
d all the wicked .... Ps 101:8
of the LORD I will *d* .... Ps 118:10
the wicked He will *d* .... Ps 145:20
Why should you *d* .... Eccl 7:16
shall not hurt nor *d* .... Is 11:9
have mercy, but will *d* ...... Jer 13:14
d them with double .... Jer 17:18
I did not come to *d* .... Matt 5:17
where moth and rust *d* ..... Matt 6:19
Him who is able to *d* ..... Matt 10:28
I am able to *d* the temple .. Matt 26:61
Barabbas and *d* Jesus ..... Matt 27:20
You who *d* the temple .... Matt 27:40
'I will *d* this temple ...... Mark 14:58
to save life or to *d* .... Luke 6:9
d men's lives but to .... Luke 9:56
D this temple, and in ...... John 2:19
and to kill, and to *d* .... John 10:10
d the work of God for ..... Rom 14:20
d the wisdom of the .... 1 Cor 1:19
God will *d* him .... 1 Cor 3:17
foods, but God will *d* ...... 1 Cor 6:13
d with the brightness of .. 2 Thess 2:8
able to save and to *d* ..... James 4:12
He might *d* the works ..... 1 John 3:8

DESTROYED
d all living things .... Gen 7:23
d those who hated me ... 2 Sam 22:41
My people are *d* .... Hos 4:6
"O Israel, you are *d* .... Hos 13:9
house, this tent, is *d* .... 2 Cor 5:1

DESTROYER
the paths of the *d* .... Ps 17:4
him who is a great *d* .... Prov 18:9
destroyed by the *d* .... 1 Cor 10:10

DESTRUCTION
not be afraid of *d* .... Job 5:21
D has no covering .... Job 26:6
d come upon him .... Ps 35:8
cast them down to *d* .... Ps 73:18
You turn man to *d* .... Ps 90:3
d that lays waste .... Ps 91:6
your life from *d* .... Ps 103:4
d will come to the .... Prov 10:29
Pride goes before *d* .... Prov 16:18
d the heart of a man ...... Prov 18:12
called the City of *D* .... Is 19:18
neither wasting nor *d* .... Is 60:18
heifer, but *d* comes .... Jer 46:20
wrath prepared for *d* .... Rom 9:22
one to Satan for the *d* ...... 1 Cor 5:5
whose end is *d* .... Phil 3:19
then sudden *d* .... 1 Thess 5:3
with everlasting *d* .... 2 Thess 1:9
which drown men in *d* ..... 1 Tim 6:9
twist to their own *d* .... 2 Pet 3:16

DESTRUCTIVE
bring in *d* heresies .... 2 Pet 2:1

DETERMINED
Since his days are *d* .... Job 14:5
of hosts will make a *d* .... Is 10:23
"Seventy weeks are *d* ...... Dan 9:24
d their preappointed ...... Acts 17:26
For I *d* not to know .... 1 Cor 2:2

DETESTABLE
shall not eat any *d* .... Deut 14:3

DEVICE
there is no work or *d* .... Eccl 9:10

DEVICES
not ignorant of his *d* ...... 2 Cor 2:11

DEVIL
See SATAN
Titles of:
Abaddon, Apollyon, angel of the bottomless pit, Rev 9:11
accuser, Rev 12:10
adversary, 1 Pet 5:8
Beelzebub, prince of demons, Matt 12:24
Belial, 2 Cor 6:15
evil one, Matt 6:13; Luke 11:4
god of this age, 2 Cor 4:4
murderer, father of lies, John 8:44
prince of the power of the air, Eph 2:2
ruler of darkness, Eph 6:12
ruler of this world, John 14:30
Satan, Luke 10:18
serpent, Gen 3:4
serpent of old, Rev 20:2
wicked one, Matt 13:19
Origin of, in heaven, Is 14:12–20; Rev 12:7–9
Power and activities of:
tempted Eve, Gen 3:1
tempted David, 1 Chr 21:1
accused and tormented Job, Job 1:6–2:10
opposed Joshua the high priest, Zech 3:1
tempted Jesus, Matt 4:1–11; Mark 3:22–28; Luke 22:31
entered Judas at betrayal, Luke 22:3; John 13:27
deceives and ensnares, 2 Cor 11:3–15; 1 Tim 3:6, 7; Rev 20:7, 8
works in evildoers, Acts 13:8–10; Eph 2:2
accuses believers before God, Rev 12:10
Believers must resist, 2 Cor 2:10, 11; Eph 6:11–16; James 4:7; 1 Pet 5:8, 9; 1 John 2:13
His defeat by Christ, Gen 3:15; Rev 12:10–12; 20:7–10

to be tempted by the *d* ...... Matt 4:1
who sowed them is the *d* .. Matt 13:39
prepared for the *d* .... Matt 25:41
forty days by the *d* .... Luke 4:2
then the *d* comes and ...... Luke 8:12
and one of you is a *d* ...... John 6:70
of your father the *d* .... John 8:44
d having already put .... John 13:2
oppressed by the *d* .... Acts 10:38
fraud, you son of the *d* .... Acts 13:10

give place to the *d* .... Eph 4:27
the wiles of the *d* .... Eph 6:11
condemnation as the *d* ..... 1 Tim 3:6
the snare of the *d* .... 2 Tim 2:26
of death, that is, the *d* ...... Heb 2:14
Resist the *d* and he .... James 4:7
d walks about like a .... 1 Pet 5:8
the works of the *d* .... 1 John 3:8
contending with the *d* .... Jude 9
Indeed, the *d* is about .... Rev 2:10
serpent of old, called the *D* .. Rev 12:9
the *d* has come down to .... Rev 12:12
serpent of old, who is the *D* . Rev 20:2
d, who deceived them ...... Rev 20:10

DEVIOUS
crooked, and who are *d* .... Prov 2:15

DEVISE
Do not *d* evil against .... Prov 3:29
Woe to those who *d* .... Mic 2:1

DEVISES
d wickedness on his .... Ps 36:4
he *d* evil continually .... Prov 6:14
d wicked plans to .... Is 32:7
But a generous man *d* .... Is 32:8

DEVOID
He who is *d* of wisdom .... Prov 11:12

DEVOTE
d rashly something as .... Prov 20:25

DEVOTED
d offering is most .... Lev 27:28
"Every *d* thing in .... Num 18:14
Your servant, who is *d* ..... Ps 119:38

DEVOUR
A fire shall *d* before .... Ps 50:3
For you *d* widows' .... Matt 23:14
bite and *d* one another ...... Gal 5:15
seeking whom he may *d* .... 1 Pet 5:8
d her Child as .... Rev 12:4

DEVOURED
Some wild beast has *d* ..... Gen 37:20
rebel, you shall be *d* .... Is 1:20
the curse has *d* .... Is 24:6
Your sword has *d* .... Jer 2:30
For shame has *d* .... Jer 3:24
have *d* their judges .... Hos 7:7
trees, the locust *d* .... Amos 4:9
birds came and *d* them ..... Matt 13:4
of heaven and *d* them .... Rev 20:9

DEVOURER
I will rebuke the *d* .... Mal 3:11

DEVOURING
You love all *d* words .... Ps 52:4
the flame of *d* fire .... Is 29:6

DEVOUT
man was just and *d* .... Luke 2:25
d men carried Stephen ...... Acts 8:2
d soldier from among .... Acts 10:7
d proselytes followed Paul . Acts 13:43

DEW
God give you of the *d* ..... Gen 27:28
shall also drop *d* .... Deut 33:28
have the *d* of Your youth .... Ps 110:3
his favor is like *d* .... Prov 19:12
a cloud of *d* in the heat .... Is 18:4
your *d* is like the *d* .... Is 26:19
like the early *d* .... Hos 6:4
many peoples, like *d* .... Mic 5:7

DIADEM
LORD, and a royal *d* .... Is 62:3

DIADEMS
ten horns, and seven *d* ...... Rev 12:3

DIAL
d by which it had gone .... Is 38:8

DIAMOND
a sapphire, and a *d* .... Ex 28:18
d it is engraved .... Jer 17:1

the sardius, topaz, and *d* .. Ezek 28:13

DIANA
Worship of at Ephesus creates uproar, Acts 19:23–41

DIBON
Amorite town, Num 21:30
Taken by Israel, Num 32:2–5
Destruction of, foretold, Jer 48:18, 22

DICTATES
according to the *d* .... Jer 23:17

DIE
it you shall surely *d* .... Gen 2:17
you touch it, lest you *d* .... Gen 3:3
the land of Egypt shall *d* ..... Ex 11:5
Where you *d*, I will *d*, ... Ruth 1:17
but a person shall *d* .... 2 Chr 25:4
Curse God and *d* .... Job 2:9
sees wise men *d* .... Ps 49:10
I shall not *d*, but live .... Ps 118:17
He shall *d* for lack of .... Prov 5:23
but fools *d* for lack of ..... Prov 10:21
hates correction will *d* .... Prov 15:10
with a rod, he will not *d* .. Prov 23:13
who are appointed to *d* .... Prov 31:8
how does a wise man *d* ..... Eccl 2:16
born, and a time to *d* .... Eccl 3:2
why should you *d* .... Eccl 7:17
drink, for tomorrow we *d* .... Is 22:13
their worm does not *d* .... Is 66:24
every one shall *d* for his ..... Jer 31:30
wicked way, he shall *d* ..... Ezek 3:19
the soul who sins shall *d* ... Ezek 18:4
man, you shall surely *d* .... Ezek 33:8
"Even if I have to *d* .... Matt 26:35
'their worm does not *d* ...... Mark 9:44
nor can they *d* .... Luke 20:36
eat of it and not *d* .... John 6:50
to you that you will *d* .... John 8:24
though he may *d* .... John 11:25
that one man should *d* .... John 11:50
that Jesus would *d* .... John 11:51
our law He ought to *d* ...... John 19:7
righteous man will one *d* .... Rom 5:7
the flesh you will *d* .... Rom 8:13
if we *d*, we *d* to the Lord ... Rom 14:8
For as in Adam all *d* ..... 1 Cor 15:22
Jesus our Lord, I *d* daily .. 1 Cor 15:31
and to *d* is gain .... Phil 1:21
for men to *d* once .... Heb 9:27
are the dead who *d* .... Rev 14:13

DIED
And all flesh *d* .... Gen 7:21
"Oh, that we had *d* .... Ex 16:3
himself with fire, and *d* .. 1 Kin 16:18
Hadad *d* also .... 1 Chr 1:51
So Saul *d* for his .... 1 Chr 10:13
was that the beggar *d* ...... Luke 16:22
in due time Christ *d* .... Rom 5:6
Christ *d* for us .... Rom 5:8
For he who has *d* .... Rom 6:7
Now if we *d* with .... Rom 6:8
sin revived and I *d* .... Rom 7:9
For to this end Christ *d* .... Rom 14:9
perish, for whom Christ *d* . 1 Cor 8:11
that Christ *d* for our sins .. 1 Cor 15:3
that if One *d* for all .... 2 Cor 5:14
and He *d* for all .... 2 Cor 5:15
through the law *d* .... Gal 2:19
if you *d* with Christ from .... Col 2:20
For you *d*, and your life is .... Col 3:3
believe that Jesus *d* ..... 1 Thess 4:14
who *d* for us .... 1 Thess 5:10
for if we *d* with Him .... 2 Tim 2:11
These all *d* in faith .... Heb 11:13
having *d* to sins .... 1 Pet 2:24

DIES
If a man *d*, shall he live .... Job 14:14
When a wicked man *d* ..... Prov 11:7
into the ground and *d* ..... John 12:24
if the husband *d*, she is ..... Rom 7:2

and no one *d* to himself .... Rom 14:7
made alive unless it *d* .... 1 Cor 15:36

DIFFERENCE
the LORD will make a *d* .... Ex 9:4
d between the unclean .... Ezek 22:26
the *d* between the holy .... Ezek 44:23
For there is no *d* .... Rom 3:22
were, it makes no *d* to me .... Gal 2:6

DIFFERENCES
There are *d* of ministries, .. 1 Cor 12:5

DIFFERENT
he has a *d* spirit in him ... Num 14:24
with *d* kinds of seed .... Deut 22:9
each *d* from the other .... Dan 7:3
d kinds of tongues .... 1 Cor 12:10
if you receive a *d* spirit .... 2 Cor 11:4
of Christ, to a *d* gospel, ... Gal 1:6

DIFFERING
Having then gifts *d* .... Rom 12:6

DIFFERS
for one star *d* from ...... 1 Cor 15:41

DIFFICULT
d is the way which leads ... Matt 7:14

DIFFUSED
By what way is light *d* ..... Job 38:24

DIFFUSES
us *d* the fragrance .... 2 Cor 2:14

DIG
wells which you did not *d* .. Deut 6:11
Son of man, *d* into the ...... Ezek 8:8
Though they *d* into hell ..... Amos 9:2
I cannot *d*; I am ashamed .. Luke 16:3

DIGNITARIES
afraid to speak evil of *d* .... 2 Pet 2:10
and speak evil of *d* .... Jude 8

DILIGENCE
your heart with all *d* .... Prov 4:23
d is man's precious .... Prov 12:27
he who leads, with *d* .... Rom 12:8
not lagging in *d*, fervent .. Rom 12:11
d it produced in you .... 2 Cor 7:11
of your love by the *d* .... 2 Cor 8:8
giving all *d*, add to your ...... 2 Pet 1:5

DILIGENT
d in sanctifying .... 2 Chr 29:34
and my spirit makes *d* .... Ps 77:6
hand of the *d* makes rich ... Prov 10:4
of the *d* will rule .... Prov 12:24
d shall be made rich .... Prov 13:4
proved *d* in many things ... 2 Cor 8:22
d to come to me quickly ..... 2 Tim 4:9
Let us therefore be *d* .... Heb 4:11
be *d* to be found by Him ... 2 Pet 3:14

DILIGENTLY
if you *d* obey the voice of .. Deut 28:1
seek me *d* will find me ..... Prov 8:17
d followed every good .... 1 Tim 5:10
he sought it *d* with tears ... Heb 12:17

DIM
His eyes were not *d* .... Deut 34:7
the windows grow *d* .... Eccl 12:3
the gold has become *d* ...... Lam 4:1

DIMINISH
stars *d* their brightness ...... Joel 2:10
the lights will *d* .... Zech 14:6

DIMLY
we see in a mirror, *d* ..... 1 Cor 13:12

DINAH
Daughter of Leah, Gen 30:20, 21
Defiled by Shechem, Gen 34:1–24
Avenged by brothers, Gen 34:25–31

DINE
asked Him to *d* with ...... Luke 11:37
come in to him and *d* .... Rev 3:20

DINNER
Better is a *d* of herbs ..... Prov 15:17

I have prepared my *d* ...... Matt 22:4
invites you to *d* .... 1 Cor 10:27

DIOTREPHES
Unruly church member, 3 John 9, 10

DIP
d them in the blood .... Lev 14:51
d it in the water, ... Num 19:18
let him *d* his foot in oil .... Deut 33:24
d your piece of bread ...... Ruth 2:14
d the tip of his finger in .. Luke 16:24

DIPPED
d the tunic in the blood .... Gen 37:31
d his finger in the .... Lev 9:9
d seven times in the ...... 2 Kin 5:14
of bread when I have *d* ... John 13:26
clothed with a robe *d* ...... Rev 19:13

DIRECT
the morning I will *d* .... Ps 5:3
and He shall *d* your paths ... Prov 3:6
d their work in truth .... Is 61:8
Now may the Lord *d* ..... 2 Thess 3:5

DIRT
I cast them out like *d* .... Ps 18:42
cast up mire and *d* .... Is 57:20

DISAPPEARS
As water *d* from the .... Job 14:11

DISARMED
d principalities .... Col 2:15

DISARMS
and *d* the mighty .... Job 12:21

DISASTER
bring *d* on the house ..... 1 Kin 14:10
I am fashioning a *d* .... Jer 18:11
war and *d* and pestilence .... Jer 28:8
D will come upon .... Ezek 7:26
you shall see *d* .... Zeph 3:15
voyage will end with *d* .... Acts 27:10

DISCERN
Can I *d* between the ..... 2 Sam 19:35
Then you shall again *d* ...... Mal 3:18
d the face of the sky .... Matt 16:3
senses exercised to *d* .... Heb 5:14

DISCERNED
they are spiritually *d* ..... 1 Cor 2:14

DISCERNER
d of the thoughts .... Heb 4:12

DISCERNING
not *d* the Lord's body .... 1 Cor 11:29
another *d* of spirits, to .... 1 Cor 12:10

DISCERNMENT
and takes away the *d* ...... Job 12:20

DISCERNS
a wise man's heart *d* .... Eccl 8:5

DISCIPLE
d is not above his .... Matt 10:24
in the name of a *d* .... Matt 10:42
he cannot be My *d* .... Luke 14:26
the *d* whom He loved ..... John 19:26
d whom Jesus loved .... John 21:7
the *d* whom Jesus loved .. John 21:20

DISCIPLES
See TWELVE DISCIPLES
but Your *d* do not fast ..... Matt 9:14
called His twelve *d* to ...... Matt 10:1
d transgress the .... Matt 15:2
took the twelve *d* .... Matt 20:17
all the *d* forsook Him ..... Matt 26:56
make *d* of all the nations, . Matt 28:19
with His *d* to the sea .... Mark 3:7
called His *d* to Himself ..... Luke 6:13
His *d* believed in Him ...... John 2:11
many of His *d* went back .. John 6:66
My word, you are My *d* .... John 8:31
to become His *d* .... John 9:27
but we are Moses' *d* .... John 9:28
His *d* did not understand .. John 12:16
know that you are My *d* .. John 13:35
so you will be My *d* .... John 15:8
Then the *d* were glad ..... John 20:20
of the *d* was multiplying, ... Acts 6:1
the *d* were first called ..... Acts 11:26
souls of the *d*, exhorting .. Acts 14:22
strengthening all the *d* .... Acts 18:23

DISCIPLES'
began to wash the *d* feet ... John 13:5

DISCIPLINE
Harsh *d* is for him who ... Prov 15:10
I *d* my body and bring ..... 1 Cor 9:27

DISCIPLINES
but he who loves him *d* ... Prov 13:24

DISCLOSE
d my dark saying .... Ps 49:4

DISCORD
and one who sows *d* .... Prov 6:19

DISCOURAGE
why will you *d* the heart ... Num 32:7

DISCOURAGED
do not fear or be *d* .... Deut 1:21
will not fail nor be *d* .... Is 42:4
lest they become *d* .... Col 3:21
you become weary and *d* ... Heb 12:3
d when you are rebuked .... Heb 12:5

DISCREET
d, chaste, homemakers, ... Titus 2:5

DISCRETION
D will preserve you .... Prov 2:11
out knowledge and *d* .... Prov 8:12
woman who lacks *d* ...... Prov 11:22
The *d* of a man makes .... Prov 19:11
the heavens at His *d* .... Jer 10:12

DISEASE
Shall I recover from this *d* .. 2 Kin 8:8
in his *d* he did not seek .. 2 Chr 16:12
all kinds of *d* among the ... Matt 4:23
every *d* among the people .. Matt 9:35
well of whatever *d* he had ... John 5:4

DISEASES
Who heals all your *d*, ... Ps 103:3
afflicted with various *d* ..... Matt 4:24
various *d* brought them .... Luke 4:40
all demons, and to cure *d* ... Luke 9:1
d left them and the evil ..... Acts 19:12

DISFIGURE
nor shall you *d* the edges .. Lev 19:27
d their faces that .... Matt 6:16

DISGRACE
plead my *d* against me, ... Job 19:5
do not *d* the throne of .... Jer 14:21

DISGRACEFUL
he had done a *d* thing ...... Gen 34:7
done a *d* thing in Israel ..... Josh 7:15
Do not do this *d* thing ... 2 Sam 13:12

DISGUISES
and he *d* his face .... Job 24:15
He who hates, *d* .... Prov 26:24

DISHONEST GAIN
turned aside after *d* .... 1 Sam 8:3
for the sake of *d* .... Titus 1:11
not for *d* but eagerly .... 1 Pet 5:2

DISHONESTY
Wealth gained by *d* will ... Prov 13:11

DISHONOR
d who wish me evil .... Ps 40:14
with *d* comes reproach ..... Prov 18:3
d the pride of all .... Is 23:9
Her rulers dearly love *d* .... Hos 4:18
My Father, and you *d* Me ... John 8:49
d their bodies among ...... Rom 1:24
and another for *d* .... Rom 9:21
long hair, it is a *d* to ...... 1 Cor 11:14
It is sown in *d* .... 1 Cor 15:43
by honor and *d* .... 2 Cor 6:8
honor and some for *d* ..... 2 Tim 2:20

DISHONORED
but we are *d* .... 1 Cor 4:10
But you have *d* the .... James 2:6

DISHONORS
For son *d* father .... Mic 7:6
covered, *d* his head .... 1 Cor 11:4

DISOBEDIENCE
d many were made .... Rom 5:19
works in the sons of *d* .... Eph 2:2
d received a just .... Heb 2:2

DISOBEDIENT
Nevertheless they were *d* ... Neh 9:26
the *d* to the wisdom of ..... Luke 1:17
out My hands to a *d* ...... Rom 10:21
you were once *d* to God .... Rom 11:30
d to parents, unthankful, ... 2 Tim 3:2
d, deceived, serving .... Titus 3:3
They stumble, being *d* ...... 1 Pet 2:8
who formerly were *d* ...... 1 Pet 3:20

DISORDERLY
for this *d* gathering .... Acts 19:40
brother who walks *d* ..... 2 Thess 3:6

DISPENSATION
d of the fullness of .... Eph 1:10
d of the grace of God .... Eph 3:2

DISPERSE
d them throughout the .... Ezek 20:23

DISPERSION
intend to go to the *D* .... John 7:35
the pilgrims of the *D* .... 1 Pet 1:1

DISPLEASE
LORD see it, and it *d*....... Prov 24:18

DISPLEASED
that David had done *d* ... 2 Sam 11:27
You have been *d* .... Ps 60:1
they were greatly *d* .... Matt 20:24
it, He was greatly *d* .... Mark 10:14

DISPUTE
Now there was also a *d* ... Luke 22:24

DISPUTED
when he *d* about the body .... Jude 9

DISPUTER
Where is the *d* of this ..... 1 Cor 1:20

DISPUTES
d rather than godly .... 1 Tim 1:4
but is obsessed with *d* ...... 1 Tim 6:4
foolish and ignorant *d* ..... 2 Tim 2:23
But avoid foolish *d* .... Titus 3:9

DISQUALIFIED
myself should become *d* ... 1 Cor 9:27
indeed you are *d* .... 2 Cor 13:5
though we may seem *d* .... 2 Cor 13:7

DISQUIETED
And why are you *d* .... Ps 42:5

DISSENSION
had no small *d* and .... Acts 15:2
this, a *d* arose between ..... Acts 23:7
a creator of *d* among all .... Acts 24:5

DISSENSIONS
selfish ambitions, *d* .... Gal 5:20

DISSIPATION
not accused of *d* .... Titus 1:6
in the same flood of *d* .... 1 Pet 4:4

DISSOLVED
of heaven shall be *d* .... Is 34:4
the heavens will be *d* ...... 2 Pet 3:12

DISTINCTION
and made no *d* .... Acts 15:9
For there is no *d* .... Rom 10:12
compassion, making a *d* .... Jude 22

DISTRACTED
But Martha was *d* with ... Luke 10:40

DISTRESS
me in the day of my *d* ...... Gen 35:3
When you are in *d* ...... Deut 4:30
my life from every *d* ...... 1 Kin 1:29
you out of dire *d* ...... Job 36:16
keep you from *d* ...... Job 36:19
d them in His deep ...... Ps 2:5
on the LORD in *d* ...... Ps 118:5
a whirlwind, when *d* ...... Prov 1:27
and on the earth *d* ...... Luke 21:25
tribulation, or *d* ...... Rom 8:35
of the present *d* ...... 1 Cor 7:26

DISTRESSED
was greatly afraid and *d* ... Gen 32:7
Israel was severely *d* ...... Judg 10:9
David was greatly *d* ...... 1 Sam 30:6
the queen was deeply *d* ...... Esth 4:4
heart within me is *d* ...... Ps 143:4
not be upon her who is *d* ...... Is 9:1
troubled and deeply *d* .... Mark 14:33
and how *d* I am till it is ... Luke 12:50

DISTRESSES
bring me out of my *d* ...... Ps 25:17

DISTRESSING
d spirit from the LORD ... 1 Sam 16:14
Now the *d* spirit from ...... 1 Sam 19:9

DISTRIBUTE
that you have and *d* ...... Luke 18:22

DISTRIBUTED
and they *d* to each as ...... Acts 4:35
But as God has *d* ...... 1 Cor 7:17

DISTRIBUTING
d to the needs of the ...... Rom 12:13

DITCH
will fall into a *d* ...... Matt 15:14

DIVERSE
D weights are an ...... Prov 20:23

DIVERSITIES
There are *d* of gifts ...... 1 Cor 12:4
there are *d* of activities ...... 1 Cor 12:6

DIVIDE
D the living child ...... 1 Kin 3:25
d My garments among ...... Ps 22:18
d their tongues ...... Ps 55:9
d the spoil with the ...... Prov 16:19
d the inheritance ...... Luke 12:13
"Take this and *d* ...... Luke 22:17

DIVIDED
and the waters were *d* ...... Ex 14:21
death they were not *d* ...... 2 Sam 1:23
And You *d* the sea ...... Neh 9:11
"Who has *d* a channel ...... Job 38:25
shall they ever be *d* ...... Ezek 37:22
kingdom has been *d* ...... Dan 5:28
your land shall be *d* ...... Amos 7:17
"Every kingdom *d* ...... Matt 12:25
and a house *d* against ...... Luke 11:17
in one house will be *d* ...... Luke 12:52
So he *d* to them his ...... Luke 15:12
they *d* His garments and ... Luke 23:34
d My garments among .... John 19:24
appeared to them *d* ...... Acts 2:3
d them among all ...... Acts 2:45
Is Christ *d*? Was Paul ...... 1 Cor 1:13
the great city was *d* ...... Rev 16:19

DIVIDES
at home *d* the spoil ...... Ps 68:12

DIVIDING
rightly *d* the word of ...... 2 Tim 2:15

DIVINATION
shall you practice *d* ...... Lev 19:26
D is on the lips of ...... Prov 16:10
darkness without *d* ...... Mic 3:6
a spirit of *d* met us ...... Acts 16:16

DIVINE
futility and who *d* ...... Ezek 13:9
and her prophets *d* ...... Mic 3:11
d service and the ...... Heb 9:1
d power has given ...... 2 Pet 1:3

DIVINERS
your prophets, your *d* ...... Jer 27:9

DIVISION
So there was a *d* ...... John 7:43
piercing even to the *d* ...... Heb 4:12

DIVISIONS
note those who cause *d* ... Rom 16:17
and that there be no *d* ...... 1 Cor 1:10
envy, strife, and *d* ...... 1 Cor 3:3
hear that there are *d* ...... 1 Cor 11:18
persons, who cause *d* ...... Jude 19

DIVISIVE
Reject a *d* man after ...... Titus 3:10

DIVORCE
cannot *d* her all his days .. Deut 22:19
her a certificate of *d* ...... Deut 24:1
of your mother's *d* ...... Is 50:1
given her a certificate of *d* .... Jer 3:8
Israel says that He hates *d* .. Mal 2:16
give her a certificate of *d* ... Matt 5:31
to *d* his wife for just any .... Matt 19:3
a certificate of *d* ...... Mark 10:4
husband is not to *d* his ...... 1 Cor 7:11

DIVORCED
d from her husband ...... Lev 21:7
A widow or a *d* woman ...... Lev 21:14
daughter is a widow or *d* ... Lev 22:13
vow of a widow or a *d* ...... Num 30:9
d her must not take her ...... Deut 24:4
a widow or a *d* woman ...... Ezek 44:22
is *d* commits adultery ...... Matt 5:32
is *d* from her husband .... Luke 16:18

DIVORCES
say, 'If a man *d* his wife ...... Jer 3:1
said, 'Whoever *d* his wife .. Matt 5:31
whoever *d* his wife ...... Matt 19:9
Whoever *d* his wife ...... Mark 10:11
Whoever *d* his wife ...... Luke 16:18

DO
set in them to *d* evil ...... Eccl 8:11
I will also *d* it ...... Is 46:11
men to *d* to you, *d* ...... Matt 7:12
d this and you will ...... Luke 10:28
He sees the Father *d* ...... John 5:19
without Me you can *d* ...... John 15:5
"Sirs, what must I *d* ...... Acts 16:30
d evil that good may ...... Rom 3:8
For what I will to *d* ...... Rom 7:15
good that I will to *d* ...... Rom 7:19
or whatever you *d*, *d* ...... 1 Cor 10:31
d all things through ...... Phil 4:13
d in word or deed, *d* ...... Col 3:17
d good and to share ...... Heb 13:16
and *d* this or that ...... James 4:15

DO NOT BE AFRAID
vision, saying, "*D*, Abram .. Gen 15:1
said to the people, "*D* ...... Ex 14:13
d, and do not tremble ...... Deut 20:3
Lord said to Joshua, "*D* ...... Josh 11:6
d of him." So he arose ...... 2 Kin 1:15
D of the words ...... 2 Kin 19:6
D of sudden terror ...... Prov 3:25
D of their faces, for ...... Jer 1:8
"*D* to serve the Chaldeans .... Jer 40:9
And you, son of man, *d* ...... Ezek 2:6
D, you beasts of the ...... Joel 2:22
"Joseph, son of David, *d* ... Matt 1:20
It is I; *d* ...... Matt 14:27
"Arise, and *d* ...... Matt 17:7
said to the women, "*D* ...... Matt 28:5
of the synagogue, "*D* ...... Mark 5:36
angel said to him, "*D* ...... Luke 1:13
"*D*, Mary, for you have .... Luke 1:30
angel said to them, "*D*, ... Luke 2:10
Jesus said to Simon, "*D* ...... Luke 5:10
d of those who kill the ...... Luke 12:4
"*D*, but speak ...... Acts 18:9
"*D*, Paul; you must ...... Acts 27:24
saying to me, "*D* ...... Rev 1:17

DO NOT FEAR
d, for I am with you ...... Gen 26:24
d to go down to Egypt ...... Gen 46:3
D; for God has come ...... Ex 20:20
d or be discouraged ...... Deut 1:21
d the gods of the ...... Judg 6:10
d, you shall not die ...... Judg 6:23
D. You have done all .... 1 Sam 12:20
D, for I will surely ...... 2 Sam 9:7
Elijah said to her, "*D*; .... 1 Kin 17:13
D, for those who are with .. 2 Kin 6:16
d or be fainthearted ...... Is 7:4
fearful-hearted, "Be strong, *d* .. Is 35:4
d the reproach of men ...... Is 51:7
d, O My servant Jacob,' ...... Jer 30:10
said to me, "*D*, Daniel ...... Dan 10:12
remains among you; *d* ...... Hag 2:5
D, let your hands be ...... Zech 8:13
d them. For there is ...... Matt 10:26
D therefore; you are of .... Luke 12:7
D any of those things ...... Rev 2:10

DOCTRINE
said, 'My *d* is pure ...... Job 11:4
for I give you good *d* ...... Prov 4:2
idol is a worthless *d* ...... Jer 10:8
of bread, but of the *d* ...... Matt 16:12
What new *d* is this ...... Mark 1:27
"My *d* is not Mine ...... John 7:16
Jerusalem with your *d* ...... Acts 5:28
heart that form of *d* ...... Rom 6:17
with every wind of *d* ...... Eph 4:14
is contrary to sound *d* ...... 1 Tim 1:10
followed my *d* ...... 2 Tim 3:10
is profitable for *d* ...... 2 Tim 3:16
not endure sound *d* ...... 2 Tim 4:3
in *d* showing integrity ...... Titus 2:7
they may adorn the *d* ...... Titus 2:10
not abide in the *d* ...... 2 John 9

DOCTRINES
the commandments and *d* ... Col 2:22
spirits and *d* of demons .... 1 Tim 4:1
various and strange *d* ...... Heb 13:9

DOEG
An Edomite; chief of Saul's herdsmen, 1 Sam 21:7
Betrays David, 1 Sam 22:9, 10
Kills 85 priests, 1 Sam 22:18, 19

DOERS
of God, but the *d* ...... Rom 2:13
But be *d* of the word ...... James 1:22

DOG
to David, "Am I a *d* ...... 1 Sam 17:43
they growl like a *d* ...... Ps 59:6
d returns to his own ...... Prov 26:11
d is better than a ...... Eccl 9:4
d returns to his own ...... 2 Pet 2:22

DOGS
you shall throw it to the *d* ... Ex 22:31
The *d* shall eat whoever ... 1 Kin 14:11
The *d* shall eat Jezebel .... 2 Kin 9:10
Yes, they are greedy *d* ...... Is 56:11
what is holy to the *d* ...... Matt 7:6
d eat the crumbs which ... Matt 15:27
Moreover the *d* came ...... Luke 16:21
But outside are *d* ...... Rev 22:15

DOMINION
let them have *d* ...... Gen 1:26
"*D* and fear belong ...... Job 25:2
made him to have *d* ...... Ps 8:6
let them not have *d* ...... Ps 19:13
besides You have had *d* ...... Is 26:13
d is an everlasting ...... Dan 4:34
sin shall not have *d* ...... Rom 6:14
Not that we have *d* ...... 2 Cor 1:24
glory and majesty, *d* ...... Jude 25

DONKEY
d saw the Angel . . . . Num 22:23
Does the wild *d* . . . . Job 6:5
d its master's crib . . . . Is 1:3
and riding on a *d* . . . . Zech 9:9
colt, the foal of a *d* . . . . Matt 21:5
He had found a young *d* . . John 12:14
d speaking with a . . . . 2 Pet 2:16

DONKEY'S
d colt is born a man . . . . . . Job 11:12

DONKEYS
d quench their thirst . . . . . . Ps 104:11
a chariot of *d* . . . . Is 21:7
And the wild *d* stood . . . . Jer 14:6

DOOM
for the day of *d* . . . . Prov 16:4

DOOR
sin lies at the *d* . . . . Gen 4:7
keep watch over the *d* . . . . . . Ps 141:3
d turns on its hinges . . . . . . Prov 26:14
stone against the *d* . . . . Matt 27:60
to you, I am the *d* . . . . John 10:7
and effective *d* . . . . 1 Cor 16:9
d was opened to me by . . . . 2 Cor 2:12
would open to us a *d* . . . . Col 4:3
is standing at the *d* . . . . James 5:9
before you an open *d* . . . . Rev 3:8
I stand at the *d* . . . . Rev 3:20
and behold, a *d* . . . . Rev 4:1

DOORKEEPER
I would rather be a *d* . . . . Ps 84:10
To him the *d* . . . . John 10:3

DOORPOSTS
write them on the *d* . . . . Deut 6:9
"Strike the *d* . . . . Amos 9:1

DOORS
up, you everlasting *d* . . . . Ps 24:7
the entrance of the *d* . . . . Prov 8:3
when the *d* are shut in . . . . . Eccl 12:4
who would shut the *d* . . . . Mal 1:10

DOR
City captured by Joshua and assigned to Manasseh, Josh 12:23; 17:11; Judg 1:27

DORCAS
Disciple at Joppa, also called Tabitha; raised to life, Acts 9:36–42

DOTHAN
Ancient town where Joseph was sold, Gen 37:14–25
Elisha strikes Syrians at, 2 Kin 6:8–23

DOUBLE
Please let a *d* portion of . . . . 2 Kin 2:9
from the LORD's hand *d* . . . . Is 40:2
first I will repay *d* . . . . Jer 16:18
worthy of *d* honor . . . . 1 Tim 5:17
and repay her *d* . . . . Rev 18:6

DOUBLE-MINDED
I hate the *d* . . . . Ps 119:113
he is a *d* man . . . . James 1:8
your hearts, you *d* . . . . James 4:8

DOUBT
life shall hang in *d* . . . . Deut 28:66
faith, why did you *d* . . . . Matt 14:31
does not *d* in his heart . . . . Mark 11:23
No *d* this man is a . . . . Acts 28:4

DOUBTING
without wrath and *d* . . . . 1 Tim 2:8
in faith, with no *d* . . . . James 1:6

DOUBTS
And why do *d* arise in . . . . Luke 24:38
for I have *d* about you . . . . Gal 4:20
doubting, for he who *d* . . . . James 1:6

DOUGH
d before it was leavened, ... Ex 12:34

DOVE
d found no resting . . . . Gen 8:9
I had wings like a *d* . . . . Ps 55:6
I mourned like a *d* . . . . Is 38:14
also is like a silly *d* . . . . Hos 7:11
descending like a *d* . . . . Matt 3:16

DOVES
and moan sadly like *d* . . . . Is 59:11
and harmless as *d* . . . . Matt 10:16
of those who sold *d* . . . . Matt 21:12

DOWNCAST
who comforts the *d* . . . . 2 Cor 7:6

DRAGNET
gather them in their *d* . . . . . . Hab 1:15
d that was cast . . . . Matt 13:47

DRAGON
a great, fiery red *d* . . . . Rev 12:3
fought with the *d* . . . . Rev 12:7
they worshiped the *d* . . . . Rev 13:4
He laid hold of the *d* . . . . Rev 20:2

DRAIN
wicked of the earth *d* . . . . Ps 75:8

DRAINED
all faces are *d* . . . . Joel 2:6

DRANK
them, and they all *d* . . . . . . Mark 14:23
d with Him after He . . . . Acts 10:41
d the same spiritual . . . . 1 Cor 10:4

DRAW
d honey from the rock . . . . Deut 32:13
me to *d* near to God . . . . Ps 73:28
and the years *d* . . . . Eccl 12:1
D me away . . . . Song 1:4
Woe to those who *d* . . . . Is 5:18
with joy you will *d* . . . . Is 12:3
"*D* some out now . . . . John 2:8
You have nothing to *d* . . . . . . John 4:11
will *d* all peoples . . . . John 12:32
let us *d* near with a . . . . Heb 10:22
who *d* back to perdition . . . . Heb 10:39
D near to God and He . . . . . . James 4:8

DRAWN
The wicked have *d* . . . . Ps 37:14
tempted when he is *d* . . . . . . James 1:14

DRAWS
and my life *d* near to . . . . Ps 88:3
your redemption *d* . . . . Luke 21:28
the Father who sent Me *d* . . John 6:44
but if anyone *d* back . . . . Heb 10:38

DREAD
fear of you and the *d* . . . . Gen 9:2
begin to put the *d* . . . . Deut 2:25

DREADFUL
of the great and *d* . . . . Mal 4:5

DREAM
Now Joseph had a *d* . . . . Gen 37:5
We each have had a *d* . . . . Gen 40:8
I speak to him in a *d* . . . . Num 12:6
will fly away like a *d* . . . . Job 20:8
As a *d* when one awakes . . . . . . Ps 73:20
like those who *d* . . . . Ps 126:1
For a *d* comes through . . . . Eccl 5:3
her, shall be as a *d* . . . . Is 29:7
prophet who has a *d* . . . . Jer 23:28
do not let the *d* . . . . Dan 4:19
your old men shall *d* . . . . Joel 2:28
to Joseph in a *d* . . . . Matt 2:13
things today in a *d* . . . . Matt 27:19
your old men shall *d* . . . . Acts 2:17

DREAMERS
d defile the flesh . . . . Jude 8

DREAMS
in the multitude of *d* . . . . Eccl 5:7
when a hungry man *d* . . . . Is 29:8
Nebuchadnezzar had *d* . . . . Dan 2:1

DREGS
d shall all the wicked . . . . Ps 75:8
has settled on his *d* . . . . Jer 48:11

DREW
and *d* for all his camels . . . . Gen 24:20
Because I *d* him out of . . . . Ex 2:10
d me out of many waters . . . . . Ps 18:16
and *d* his sword, struck . . . Matt 26:51

DRIED
My strength is *d* . . . . Ps 22:15
of her blood was *d* . . . . Mark 5:29
saw the fig tree *d* . . . . Mark 11:20
and its water was *d* . . . . Rev 16:12

DRIFT
have heard, lest we *d* . . . . Heb 2:1

DRINK
"What shall we *d* . . . . Ex 15:24
"Do not *d* wine or . . . . Lev 10:9
and let him *d* of the . . . . Job 21:20
gave me vinegar to *d* . . . . Ps 69:21
D water from your own . . . . Prov 5:15
mocker, strong *d* . . . . Prov 20:1
lest they *d* and forget . . . . Prov 31:5
Give strong *d* to him . . . . Prov 31:6
Let him *d* and forget . . . . Prov 31:7
d your wine with a . . . . Eccl 9:7
follow intoxicating *d* . . . . Is 5:11
mixing intoxicating *d* . . . . Is 5:22
d the milk of the . . . . Is 60:16
My servants shall *d* . . . . Is 65:13
bosom, that you may *d* . . . . Is 66:11
d water by measure . . . . Ezek 4:11
"Bring wine, let us *d* . . . . Amos 4:1
to you of wine and *d* . . . . Mic 2:11
and you gave Me no *d* . . . . Matt 25:42
that day when I *d* . . . . Matt 26:29
mingled with gall to *d* . . . . . Matt 27:34
with myrrh to *d* . . . . Mark 15:23
to her, "Give Me a *d* . . . . John 4:7
him come to Me and *d* . . . . . . John 7:37
d wine nor do anything . . . Rom 14:21
do, as often as you *d* . . . . . . 1 Cor 11:25
all been made to *d* . . . . 1 Cor 12:13
No longer *d* only water . . . . . 1 Tim 5:23
has made all nations *d* . . . . Rev 14:8

DRINKS
to her, "Whoever *d* . . . . John 4:13
d My blood has eternal . . . . . John 6:54
For he who eats and *d* . . . . . 1 Cor 11:29
For the earth which *d* . . . . Heb 6:7

DRIP
immoral woman *d* honey . . . . Prov 5:3
d as the honeycomb . . . . Song 4:11
shall *d* with new wine, the . . . . . Joel 3:18

DRIPPED
my hands *d* with myrrh, ... Song 5:5

DRIPPING
wife are a continual *d* . . . . . Prov 19:13
His lips are lilies, *d* . . . . Song 5:13

DRIVE
Little by little I will *d* . . . . Ex 23:30
then you shall *d* out all . . . . . Num 33:52
not utterly *d* them out . . . . . . Josh 17:13
but they could not *d* out . . . . . . Judg 1:19
of the wicked *d* . . . . Ps 36:11
so *d* them away . . . . Ps 68:2
will *d* it far from him . . . . Prov 22:15
They shall *d* you from . . . . Dan 4:25
I will *d* them from My . . . . Hos 9:15
temple and began to *d* . . . Mark 11:15

DRIVEN
They were *d* out from . . . . Job 30:5
Let them be *d* backward . . . . . . Ps 40:14
sail and so were *d* . . . . Acts 27:17
a wave of the sea *d* . . . . James 1:6

DROP
They *d* on the pastures . . . . . . Ps 65:12
the nations are as a *d* . . . . Is 40:15

DROSS
of the earth like *d* . . . . Ps 119:119
Take away the *d* . . . . Prov 25:4
purge away your *d* . . . . Is 1:25
of Israel has become *d* . . . . Ezek 22:18

DROUGHT
through a land of d … Jer 2:6
in the year of d … Jer 17:8
For I called for a d … Hag 1:11

DROVE
So He d out the man … Gen 3:24
temple of God and d … Matt 21:12
a whip of cords, He d … John 2:15

DROWN
nor can the floods d … Song 8:7
harmful lusts which d … 1 Tim 6:9

DROWSINESS
d will clothe a … Prov 23:21

DRUNK
of the wine and was d … Gen 9:21
d my wine with my milk … Song 5:1
you afflicted, and d … Is 51:21
My anger, made them d … Is 63:6
be satiated and made d … Jer 46:10
the guests have well d … John 2:10
For these are not d … Acts 2:15
and another is d … 1 Cor 11:21
And do not be d … Eph 5:18
and those who get d … 1 Thess 5:7
the earth were made d … Rev 17:2
I saw the woman, d … Rev 17:6

DRUNKARD
d could be included … Deut 29:19
d is a proverb in the … Prov 26:9
to and fro like a d … Is 24:20
or a reviler, or a d … 1 Cor 5:11

DRUNKEN
I am like a d man … Jer 23:9

DRUNKENNESS
will be filled with d … Ezek 23:33
Jerusalem a cup of d … Zech 12:2
with carousing, d … Luke 21:34
not in revelry and d … Rom 13:13
envy, murders, d … Gal 5:21
lusts, d, revelries … 1 Pet 4:3

DRUSILLA
Wife of Felix; hears Paul, Acts 24:24, 25

DRY
place, and let the d … Gen 1:9
made the sea into d … Ex 14:21
It was d on the fleece … Judg 6:40
I will d up her sea … Jer 51:36
d tree flourish … Ezek 17:24
will make the rivers d … Ezek 30:12
will be done in the d … Luke 23:31

DUE
because it is your d … Lev 10:13
their food in d season … Ps 104:27
pay all that was d … Matt 18:34
d time Christ died … Rom 5:6
to whom taxes are d … Rom 13:7
d season we shall … Gal 6:9
exalt you in d time … 1 Pet 5:6

DUG
that I have d this well … Gen 21:30
father's servants had d … Gen 26:15
in my grave which I d for … Gen 50:5
They have d a pit before … Ps 57:6
the pit is d for the wicked … Ps 94:13
proud have d pits for me … Ps 119:85
He d it up and cleared out … Is 5:2
to the Euphrates and d … Jer 13:7
d a winepress in it and … Matt 21:33
d in the ground, and hid … Matt 25:18
who d deep and laid … Luke 6:48

DULL
heart of this people d … Is 6:10
people have grown d … Matt 13:15
you have become d … Heb 5:11

DUMB
the tongue of the d … Is 35:6
"Deaf and d spirit … Mark 9:25

DUNGHILL
the land nor for the d … Luke 14:35

DUST
formed man of the d … Gen 2:7
d you shall return … Gen 3:19
descendants as the d … Gen 13:16
now, I who am but d … Gen 18:27
"Who can count the d … Num 23:10
lay your gold in the d … Job 22:24
and repent in d … Job 42:6
Will the d praise You … Ps 30:9
like the whirling d … Ps 83:13
show favor to her d … Ps 102:14
remembers that we are d … Ps 103:14
or the primal d … Prov 8:26
all are from the d … Eccl 3:20
counted as the small d … Is 40:15
They shall lick the d … Mic 7:17
city, shake off the d … Matt 10:14
image of the man of d … 1 Cor 15:49

DUTY
the d of a husband's … Deut 25:5
d of a close relative … Ruth 3:13
done what was our d … Luke 17:10

DWELL
O LORD, make me d … Ps 4:8
Who may d in Your holy … Ps 15:1
He himself shall d … Ps 25:13
d in the land, and feed on … Ps 37:3
the LORD God might d … Ps 68:18
of my God than d … Ps 84:10
Him, that glory may d … Ps 85:9
Woe is me, that I d … Ps 120:5
better to d in a corner … Prov 25:24
he will d on high … Is 33:16
into Egypt to d there … Is 52:4
"I d in the high and … Is 57:15
Restorer of Streets to D In … Is 58:12
"They shall no longer d … Lam 4:15
they enter and d there … Matt 12:45
of Judea and all who d … Acts 2:14
"I will d in them … 2 Cor 6:16
that Christ may d … Eph 3:17
the fullness should d … Col 1:19
the word of Christ d … Col 3:16
men, and He will d … Rev 21:3

DWELLER
fled and became a d … Acts 7:29

DWELLING
A people d alone … Num 23:9
is the way to the d … Job 38:19
built together for a d … Eph 2:22
a foreign country, d … Heb 11:9

DWELLS
He who d in the secret … Ps 91:1
but the Father who d … John 14:10
do it, but sin that d … Rom 7:17
the Spirit of God d … Rom 8:9
from the dead d … Rom 8:11
the Spirit of God d … 1 Cor 3:16
d all the fullness … Col 2:9
which righteousness d … 2 Pet 3:13
you, where Satan d … Rev 2:13

DWELT
Egypt, and Jacob d … Ps 105:23
became flesh and d … John 1:14
By faith he d in the … Heb 11:9

DYING
I do not object to d … Acts 25:11
in the body the d … 2 Cor 4:10
Jacob, when he was d … Heb 11:21

EAGLE
As an e stirs up its … Deut 32:11
e swooping on its prey … Job 9:26
fly away like an e … Prov 23:5
The way of an e … Prov 30:19
nest as high as the e … Jer 49:16
had the face of an e … Ezek 1:10
like a flying e … Rev 4:7
two wings of a great e … Rev 12:14

EAGLES
up with wings like e … Is 40:31
are swifter than e … Jer 4:13
e will be gathered … Matt 24:28

EAGLES'
how I bore you on e … Ex 19:4

EAR
shall pierce his e … Ex 21:6
Does not the e test … Job 12:11
Bow down Your e … Ps 31:2
And the e of the wise … Prov 18:15
He awakens My e … Is 50:4
e is uncircumcised … Jer 6:10
what you hear in the e … Matt 10:27
cut off his right e … John 18:10
not seen, nor e heard … 1 Cor 2:9
if the e should say … 1 Cor 12:16
He who has an e … Rev 2:7

EARLY
Very e in the morning … Mark 16:2
arrived at the tomb e … Luke 24:22

EARNEST
must give the more e … Heb 2:1

EARNESTLY
if you e obey My … Deut 11:13
He prayed more e … Luke 22:44
in this we groan, e … 2 Cor 5:2
e that it would not … James 5:17
you to contend e … Jude 3

EARS
both his e will tingle … 2 Kin 21:12
Whoever shuts his e … Prov 21:13
And hear with their e … Is 6:10
He who has e … Matt 11:15
e are hard of hearing … Matt 13:15
they have itching e … 2 Tim 4:3
e are open to their … 1 Pet 3:12

EARS TO HEAR
eyes to see and e … Deut 29:4
e but does not hear … Ezek 12:2
He who has e, … Matt 11:15
He who has e … Matt 13:9
He who has e, … Matt 13:43
"He who has e, … Mark 4:9
If anyone has e, … Mark 4:23
If anyone has e, … Mark 7:16
"He who has e, … Luke 8:8
He who has e, … Luke 14:35

EARTH
See ALL THE EARTH; HEAVEN AND EARTH
The e was without form … Gen 1:2
God called the dry land E … Gen 1:10
caused it to rain on the e … Gen 2:5
The e also was corrupt … Gen 6:11
a wind to pass over the e … Gen 8:1
and multiply, and fill the e … Gen 9:1
the whole e was populated … Gen 9:19
and struck the dust of the e … Ex 8:17
the e is the LORD's … Ex 9:29
the e swallowed them … Ex 15:12
"Lest the e swallow us … Num 16:34
or that is in the e beneath … Deut 5:8
e which is under you … Deut 28:23
e to witness against … Deut 31:28
fell to the e on his face … Josh 7:6
the e trembled … Judg 5:4
e are the LORD's … 1 Sam 2:8
the e quaked … 1 Sam 14:15
"I go the way of all the e … 1 Kin 2:2
the e was divided … 1 Chr 1:19
to the LORD, all the e … 1 Chr 16:23
coming to judge the e … 1 Chr 16:33

service for man on *e* ... Job 7:1
He hangs the *e* on ... Job 26:7
foundations of the *e* ... Job 38:4
tried in a furnace of *e* ... Ps 12:6
e is the LORD's ... Ps 24:1
the shields of the *e* ... Ps 47:9
You visit the *e* ... Ps 65:9
You had formed the *e* ... Ps 90:2
let the *e* be moved ... Ps 99:1
glory is above the *e* ... Ps 148:13
wisdom founded the *e* ... Prov 3:19
there was ever an *e* ... Prov 8:23
For three things the *e* ... Prov 30:21
e abides forever ... Eccl 1:4
heaven, and you on *e* ... Eccl 5:2
the fruit of the *e* ... Is 4:2
for the meek of the *e* ... Is 11:4
the *e* shall be full of ... Is 11:9
curse has devoured the *e* ... Is 24:6
a dark place of the *e* ... Is 45:19
the foundations of the *e* ... Is 51:16
are higher than the *e* ... Is 55:9
e is My footstool ... Is 66:1
new *e* which I will make ... Is 66:22
O *e*, *e*, *e*, hear the word ... Jer 22:29
lifted me up between *e* ... Ezek 8:3
and the *e* shone with ... Ezek 43:2
a tree in the midst of the *e* .. Dan 4:10
in heaven and on *e* ... Dan 6:27
The *e* shall answer ... Hos 2:22
I will darken the *e* ... Amos 8:9
e will be filled ... Hab 2:14
Let all the *e* keep silence ... Hab 2:20
shall inherit the *e* ... Matt 5:5
heaven and *e* pass away ... Matt 5:18
e as it is in heaven ... Matt 6:10
treasures on *e*, where ... Matt 6:19
whatever you bind on *e* ... Matt 18:18
of the *e* will mourn ... Matt 24:30
Me in heaven and on *e* ... Matt 28:18
all the seeds on *e* ... Mark 4:31
and *e* will pass away ... Mark 13:31
on *e* peace, goodwill ... Luke 2:14
power on *e* to forgive ... Luke 5:24
find faith on the *e* ... Luke 18:8
e is My footstool ... Acts 7:49
then shook the *e* ... Heb 12:26
e which are now ... 2 Pet 3:7
heavens and a new *e* ... 2 Pet 3:13
all the tribes of the *e* ... Rev 1:7
"Do not harm the *e* ... Rev 7:3
he was cast to the *e* ... Rev 12:9
the *e* helped the woman ... Rev 12:16
on the *e* will worship him ... Rev 13:8
and the *e* was reaped ... Rev 14:16
the *e* was illuminated ... Rev 18:1
from whose face the *e* ... Rev 20:11
new heaven and a new *e* ... Rev 21:1

EARTHEN
holy water in an *e* vessel ... Num 5:17
a potter's *e* flask ... Jer 19:1
treasure in *e* vessels ... 2 Cor 4:7

EARTHLY
If I have told you *e* ... John 3:12
that if our *e* house ... 2 Cor 5:1
their mind on *e* things ... Phil 3:19
from above, but is *e* ... James 3:15

EARTHQUAKE
LORD was not in the *e* ... 1 Kin 19:11
as you fled from the *e* ... Zech 14:5
there was a great *e* ... Matt 28:2
there was a great *e* ... Acts 16:26
there was a great *e* ... Rev 6:12
e as had not occurred ... Rev 16:18

EARTHQUAKES
And there will be *e* ... Mark 13:8

EASE
I was at *e*, but He has ... Job 16:12
you women who are at *e* ... Is 32:9
to you who are at *e* ... Amos 6:1

take your *e*; eat, drink ... Luke 12:19

EASIER
Which is *e*, to say ... Mark 2:9
It is *e* for a camel ... Mark 10:25
e for heaven and earth ... Luke 16:17

EAST
goes toward the *e* ... Gen 2:14
e of the garden of Eden ... Gen 3:24
the LORD brought an *e* ... Ex 10:13
e wind scattered ... Job 38:24
As far as the *e* ... Ps 103:12
descendants from the *e* ... Is 43:5
wise men from the *E* ... Matt 2:1
many will come from *e* ... Matt 8:11
will come from the *e* ... Luke 13:29
e might be prepared ... Rev 16:12

EASTWARD
planted a garden *e* in Eden ... Gen 2:8

EASY
My yoke is *e* and My ... Matt 11:30

EAT
you may freely *e* ... Gen 2:16
e dust all the days ... Gen 3:14
'You shall not *e* ... Gen 3:17
you shall *e* the herb ... Gen 3:18
e of my game ... Gen 27:19
brethren to *e* bread ... Gen 31:54
you shall *e* it in haste ... Ex 12:11
No foreigner shall *e* it ... Ex 12:43
may not *e* the life ... Deut 12:23
dogs shall *e* Jezebel ... 2 Kin 9:10
my people as they *e* ... Ps 53:4
love it will *e* its fruit ... Prov 18:21
E only as much as you ... Prov 25:16
good to *e* much honey ... Prov 25:27
e your bread with joy ... Eccl 9:7
Curds and honey He shall *e* ... Is 7:15
You shall *e* this year such ... Is 37:30
lion shall *e* straw ... Is 65:25
e this scroll ... Ezek 3:1
on your couches, *e* ... Amos 6:4
e the flesh of My ... Mic 3:3
life, what you will *e* ... Matt 6:25
even the little dogs *e* ... Matt 15:27
You to *e* the Passover ... Matt 26:17
I may *e* the Passover ... Mark 14:14
e; this is My body ... Mark 14:22
what you will *e* ... Luke 12:22
food to *e* of which you ... John 4:32
give us His flesh to *e* ... John 6:52
"Rise, Peter; kill and *e*." ... Acts 10:13
e nor drink till they have .. Acts 23:21
one believes he may *e* ... Rom 14:2
e meat nor drink wine ... Rom 14:21
I will never again *e* ... 1 Cor 8:13
e whatever is set ... 1 Cor 10:27
e; this is My body ... 1 Cor 11:24
neither shall he *e* ... 2 Thess 3:10
have no right to *e* ... Heb 13:10
e your flesh like fire ... James 5:3
"Take and *e* it ... Rev 10:9

EATEN
Have you *e* from the ... Gen 3:11
It shall be *e* the same day ... Lev 19:6
Your house has *e* me up ... Ps 69:9
e my honeycomb with my ... Song 5:1
bad figs which cannot be *e* ... Jer 24:8
e the fruit of lies ... Hos 10:13
And he was *e* by worms .. Acts 12:23

EATING
by *e* with the blood ... 1 Sam 14:33
sons and daughters were *e* .. Job 1:13
e swine's flesh ... Is 66:17
neither *e* nor drinking ... Matt 11:18
the flood, they were *e* ... Matt 24:38
as they were *e*, He said ... Matt 26:21
Pharisees saw Him *e* ... Mark 2:16
in the same house, *e* ... Luke 10:7
e in an idol's temple ... 1 Cor 8:10

in *e*, each one takes ... 1 Cor 11:21

EATS
The righteous *e* ... Prov 13:25
receives sinners and *e* ... Luke 15:2
Whoever *e* My flesh ... John 6:54
e this bread will live ... John 6:58
e despise him who does ... Rom 14:3
He who *e*, *e* to the ... Rom 14:6
an unworthy manner *e* ... 1 Cor 11:29

EBAL
Mountain in Samaria, Deut 27:12, 13
Stones of the Law erected upon, Deut 27:1–8; Josh 8:30–35

EBED-MELECH
Ethiopian eunuch; rescues Jeremiah, Jer 38:7–13
Promised divine protection, Jer 39:15–18

EBENEZER
Site of Israel's defeat, 1 Sam 4:1–10
Ark transferred from, 1 Sam 5:1
Site of memorial stone, 1 Sam 7:10, 12

EBER
Great-grandson of Shem, Gen 10:21–24; 1 Chr 1:25
Progenitor of the:
Hebrews, Gen 11:16–26
Arabians and Arameans, Gen 10:25–30
Ancestor of Christ, Luke 3:35

EDEN
First home of mankind, Gen 2:8–15
Zion becomes like, Is 51:3
Called the "garden of God," Ezek 28:13

EDIFICATION
his good, leading to *e* ... Rom 15:2
prophesies speaks *e* ... 1 Cor 14:3
things be done for *e* ... 1 Cor 14:26
the Lord gave us for *e* ... 2 Cor 10:8
has given me for *e* ... 2 Cor 13:10
rather than godly *e* ... 1 Tim 1:4

EDIFIES
puffs up, but love *e* ... 1 Cor 8:1
he who prophesies *e* ... 1 Cor 14:4

EDIFY
but not all things *e* ... 1 Cor 10:23
and *e* one another ... 1 Thess 5:11

EDIFYING
of the body for the *e* ... Eph 4:16

EDOM
Name given to Esau, Gen 25:30
——— Land of Esau; called Seir, Gen 32:3
Called Edom and Idumea, Mark 3:8
People of, cursed, Is 34:5, 6

EDOMITES
Descendants of Esau, Gen 36:9
Refuse passage to Israel, Num 20:18–20
Hostile to Israel, Gen 27:40; 1 Sam 14:47; 2 Chr 20:10; Ps 137:7
Prophecies concerning, Gen 27:37; Is 34:5–17; Ezek 25:12–14; 35:5–7; Amos 9:11, 12

EDREI
Capital of Bashan, Deut 3:10
Site of Og's defeat, Num 21:33–35

EFFECT
of the peoples of no *e* ... Ps 33:10
of no *e* by your tradition ... Matt 15:6
promise made of no *e* ... Rom 4:14
make the promise of no *e* ... Gal 3:17

EFFECTIVELY
for He who worked *e* ... Gal 2:8
e works in you who ... 1 Thess 2:13

EGG
in the white of an *e* ... Job 6:6

Or if he asks for an *e* ..... Luke 11:12

EGLON
City of Judah, Josh 15:39

EGYPT
Abram visits, Gen 12:10
Joseph sold into, Gen 37:28, 36
Joseph becomes leader in, Gen 39:1–4
Hebrews move to, Gen 46:5–7
Hebrews persecuted in, Ex 1:15–22
Plagues on, Ex 7—11
Israel leaves, Ex 12:31–33
Army of, perishes, Ex 14:26–28
Prophecies concerning, Gen 15:13; Is 19:18–25; Ezek 29:14, 15; 30:24, 25; Matt 2:15

EHUD
Son of Gera, Judg 3:15
Slays Eglon, Judg 3:16–26

EIGHT
Isaac when he was *e* days .. Gen 21:4
Jesse, and who had *e* .... 1 Sam 17:12
Josiah was *e* years old .... 2 Kin 22:1
e days were completed .... Luke 2:21
about *e* days after these ... Luke 9:28
bedridden *e* years .... Acts 9:33
a few, that is, *e* .... 1 Pet 3:20
saved Noah, one of *e* .... 2 Pet 2:5

EIGHTH
shall sow in the *e* year ..... Lev 25:22
So it was, on the *e* day ..... Luke 1:59
circumcised the *e* day, of .... Phil 3:5

EIGHTY
Moses was *e* years old .... Ex 7:7
land had rest for *e* years ... Judg 3:30
I am today *e* years old ... 2 Sam 19:35
with him were *e* priests .. 2 Chr 26:17
strength they are *e* years .... Ps 90:10
your bill, and write *e* ...... Luke 16:7

EKRON
Philistine city, Josh 13:3
Captured by Judah, Judg 1:18
Assigned to Dan, Josh 19:40, 43
Ark sent to, 1 Sam 5:10
Denounced by the prophets, Jer 25:9, 20

EL BETHEL
Site of Jacob's altar, Gen 35:6, 7

ELAH
King of Israel, 1 Kin 16:6, 8–10

ELAMITES
Descendants of Shem, Gen 10:22
Destruction of, Jer 49:34–39
In Persian Empire, Ezra 4:9
Jews from, at Pentecost, Acts 2:9

ELATH
Seaport on Red Sea, 1 Kin 9:26
Built by Azariah, 2 Kin 14:21, 22
Captured by Syrians, 2 Kin 16:6
Same as Ezion Geber, 2 Chr 8:17

ELDER
clothes of her *e* son Esau .. Gen 27:15
The *e* and honorable .... Is 9:15
against an *e* except .... 1 Tim 5:19
I who am a fellow *e* .... 1 Pet 5:1
The *E*, To the elect lady ...... 2 John 1
The *E*, To the beloved .... 3 John 1

ELDERS
See TWENTY-FOUR ELDERS
and seventy of the *e* .... Ex 24:1
called for the *e* of Israel .... Josh 24:1
the advice of the *e* .... 2 Chr 10:13
And teach his *e* .... Ps 105:22
in the company of the *e* .... Ps 107:32
and counsel from the *e* .... Ezek 7:26
the tradition of the *e* ...... Matt 15:2
many things from the *e* ... Matt 16:21
e of the people plotted ..... Matt 27:1
be rejected by the *e* .... Luke 9:22
e who had come to Him .. Luke 22:52
the people, the *e* .... Acts 6:12
they had appointed *e* ...... Acts 14:23
e came together to .... Acts 15:6
and called for the *e* .... Acts 20:17
e who rule well be .... 1 Tim 5:17
lacking, and appoint *e* .... Titus 1:5
e obtained a good .... Heb 11:2
Let him call for the *e* ..... James 5:14
e who are among you I .... 1 Pet 5:1
I saw twenty-four *e* .... Rev 4:4
twenty-four *e* fall down ..... Rev 4:10
the twenty-four *e* fell down ... Rev 5:8

ELDERSHIP
of the hands of the *e* .... 1 Tim 4:14

ELEAZAR
Son of Aaron; succeeds him as high priest, Ex 6:23, 25; 28:1; Lev 10:6, 7; Num 3:32; 20:25–28; Josh 14:1; 24:33

ELECT
whom I uphold, My *E* .... Is 42:1
and Israel My *e* .... Is 45:4
e shall long enjoy the .... Is 65:22
gather together His *e* ..... Matt 24:31
e have obtained it .... Rom 11:7
e according to the .... 1 Pet 1:2
a chief cornerstone, *e* .... 1 Pet 2:6
e sister greet you .... 2 John 13

ELECTION
e they are beloved .... Rom 11:28
call and *e* sure .... 2 Pet 1:10

ELEMENTS
weak and beggarly *e* .... Gal 4:9
e will melt with .... 2 Pet 3:10

ELEVEN
and his *e* sons .... Gen 32:22
the *e* stars bowed down ..... Gen 37:9
e disciples went away ..... Matt 28:16
and found the *e* .... Luke 24:33
numbered with the *e* .... Acts 1:26

ELI
Officiates in Shiloh, 1 Sam 1:3
Blesses Hannah, 1 Sam 1:12–19
Becomes Samuel's guardian, 1 Sam 1:20–28
Samuel ministers before, 1 Sam 2:11
Sons of, 1 Sam 2:12–17
Rebukes sons, 1 Sam 2:22–25
Rebuked by a man of God, 1 Sam 2:27–36
Instructs Samuel, 1 Sam 3:1–18
Death of, 1 Sam 4:15–18

ELIAB
Brother of David, 1 Sam 16:5–13
Fights in Saul's army, 1 Sam 17:13
Discounts David's worth, 1 Sam 17:28, 29

ELIAKIM
Son of Hilkiah, 2 Kin 18:18
Confers with Rabshakeh, Is 36:4, 11–22
Sent to Isaiah, Is 37:2–5
Becomes type of the Messiah, Is 22:20–25
——— Son of King Josiah, 2 Kin 23:34
Name changed to Jehoiakim, 2 Chr 36:4

ELIASHIB
High priest, Neh 12:10
Rebuilds Sheep Gate, Neh 3:1, 20, 21
Allies with foreigners, Neh 13:4, 5, 28

ELIHU
David's brother, 1 Chr 27:18
Called Eliab, 1 Sam 16:6
——— One who reproved Job and his friends, Job 32:2, 4–6

ELIJAH
Denounces Ahab; goes into hiding; fed by ravens, 1 Kin 17:1–7
Dwells with widow; performs miracles for her, 1 Kin 17:8–24
Sends message to Ahab; overthrows prophets of Baal, 1 Kin 18:1–40
Brings rain, 1 Kin 18:41–45
Flees from Jezebel; fed by angels, 1 Kin 19:1–8
Receives revelation from God, 1 Kin 19:9–18
Condemns Ahab, 1 Kin 21:15–29
Condemns Ahaziah; fire consumes troops sent against him, 2 Kin 1:1–16
Taken up to heaven, 2 Kin 2:1–15
Appears with Christ in transfiguration, Matt 17:1–4
Type of John the Baptist, Mal 4:5, 6; Luke 1:17

ELIMELECH
Naomi's husband, Ruth 1:1–3; 2:1, 3; 4:3–9

ELIPHAZ
One of Job's friends, Job 2:11
Rebukes Job, Job 4:1, 5
Is forgiven, Job 42:7–9

ELISHA
Chosen as Elijah's successor; follows him, 1 Kin 19:16–21
Witnesses Elijah's translation; receives his spirit and mantle, 2 Kin 2:1–18
Performs miracles, 2 Kin 2:19–25; 4:1—6:23
Prophesies victory over Moab; fulfilled, 2 Kin 3:11–27
Prophesies end of siege; fulfilled, 2 Kin 7
Prophesies death of Ben-Hadad, 2 Kin 8:7–15
Sends servant to anoint Jehu, 2 Kin 9:1–3
Last words and death; miracle performed by his bones, 2 Kin 13:14–21

ELIZABETH
Barren wife of Zacharias, Luke 1:5–7
Conceives a son, Luke 1:13, 24, 25
Salutation to Mary, Luke 1:36–45
Mother of John the Baptist, Luke 1:57–60

ELIZAPHAN
Chief of Kohathites, Num 3:30
Heads family, 1 Chr 15:5, 8
Family consecrated, 2 Chr 29:12–16

ELKANAH
Father of Samuel, 1 Sam 1:1–23
——— Son of Korah, Ex 6:24
Escapes judgment, Num 26:11

ELNATHAN
Father of Nehushta, 2 Kin 24:8
Goes to Egypt, Jer 26:22
Entreats with king, Jer 36:25

ELOQUENT
"O my Lord, I am not *e* ...... Ex 4:10
an *e* man and mighty ..... Acts 18:24

ELYMAS
Arabic name of Bar-Jesus, a false prophet, Acts 13:6–12

EMBALM
to *e* his father .... Gen 50:2

EMBANKMENT
will build an *e* .... Luke 19:43

EMBRACE
you shall *e* a son .... 2 Kin 4:
a time to *e*, and a time .... Ec

EMBRACED
and have *e* other gods ...

be *e* in the arms of .... Prov 5:20
e them, and departed to .... Acts 20:1
e them, and confessed ...... Heb 11:13

EMBRACES
his right hand *e* me .... Song 2:6

EMERALD
sardius, a topaz, and an *e* ... Ex 28:17
turquoise, and *e* with ..... Ezek 28:13
chalcedony, the fourth *e* ... Rev 21:19

EMERALDS
for your wares *e* .... Ezek 27:16

EMMAUS
Town near Jerusalem, Luke 24:13–18

EMPTY
And the pit was *e* .... Gen 37:24
appear before Me *e* .... Ex 23:15
e pitchers, and torches ..... Judg 7:16
after *e* things which ...... 1 Sam 12:21
comfort me with *e* words ... Job 21:34
not listen to *e* talk .... Job 35:13
LORD makes the earth *e* .... Is 24:1
trust in *e* words .... Is 59:4
comes, he finds it *e* .... Matt 12:44
He has sent away *e* .... Luke 1:53
you with *e* words .... Eph 5:6

EMPTY-HANDED
sent me away *e* .... Gen 31:42
appear before Me *e* .... Ex 34:20
'Do not go *e* to your .... Ruth 3:17
and sent him away *e* ...... Mark 12:3

EMPTY-HEADED
e man will be wise .... Job 11:12

EN DOR
Town of Manasseh which was the home of the witch whom Saul consulted, Josh 17:11; 1 Sam 28:1–10; Ps 83:9, 10

EN GEDI
Occupied by the Amorites, Gen 14:7
Assigned to Judah, Josh 15:62, 63
David's hiding place, 1 Sam 23:29
Noted for vineyards, Song 1:14

EN HAKKORE
Miraculous spring, Judg 15:14–19

EN ROGEL
Fountain outside Jerusalem, 2 Sam 17:17
Seat of Adonijah's plot, 1 Kin 1:5–9

ENABLED
our Lord who has *e* .... 1 Tim 1:12

ENCHANTER
and the expert *e* .... Is 3:3

ENCOURAGE
e him and strengthen him .. Deut 3:28
e you concerning your .... 1 Thess 3:2

ENCOURAGED
is, that I may be *e* .... Rom 1:12
and all may be *e* .... 1 Cor 14:31
their hearts may be *e* .... Col 2:2

ENCOURAGEMENT
Hezekiah gave *e* to .... 2 Chr 30:22
translated Son of *E*) .... Acts 4:36
they rejoiced over its *e* ..... Acts 15:31

END
at the *e* of forty days .... Gen 8:6
one cherub at one *e* .... Ex 25:19
at the *e* of forty days .... Deut 9:11
the *e* of every seven years .. Deut 15:1
made an *e* of dividing ..... Josh 19:51
yet your latter *e* .... Job 8:7
Man puts an *e* to darkness .. Job 28:3
from one *e* of heaven .... Ps 19:6
make me to know my *e* ...... Ps 39:4
Your years will have no *e* .. Ps 102:27
shall keep it to the *e* .... Ps 119:33
e is the way of death ...... Prov 14:12
not be blessed at the *e* .... Prov 20:21
There was no *e* of all .... Eccl 4:16
The *e* of a thing is better ..... Eccl 7:8
and peace there will be no *e* .... Is 9:7
Declaring the *e* .... Is 46:10
Our *e* was near .... Lam 4:18
whose iniquity shall *e* ..... Ezek 21:25
shall endure to the *e* .... Dan 6:26
the time of the *e* .... Dan 8:17
until the time of the *e* ..... Dan 11:35
what shall be the *e* .... Dan 12:8
e has come upon my .... Amos 8:2
to the *e* will be saved ...... Matt 10:22
the harvest is the *e* .... Matt 13:39
to pass, but the *e* .... Matt 24:6
always, even to the *e* ...... Matt 28:20
there will be no *e* .... Luke 1:33
He loved them to the *e* ..... John 13:1
to the *e* of the earth .... Acts 1:8
the *e* of those things is ..... Rom 6:21
For Christ is the *e* .... Rom 10:4
the hope firm to the *e* .... Heb 3:6
steadfast to the *e* .... Heb 3:14
but now, once at the *e* ...... Heb 9:26
of Job and seen the *e* ..... James 5:11
the *e* of your faith .... 1 Pet 1:9
But the *e* of all .... 1 Pet 4:7
what will be the *e* .... 1 Pet 4:17
the latter *e* is worse .... 2 Pet 2:20
My works until the *e* .... Rev 2:26
Beginning and the *E* .... Rev 22:13

ENDEAVORING
e to keep the unity .... Eph 4:3

ENDED
the seventh day God *e* His ... Gen 2:2
that her warfare is *e* .... Is 40:2
is past, the summer is *e* ...... Jer 8:20
Jesus had *e* these sayings ... Matt 7:28
had *e* every temptation ..... Luke 4:13
supper being *e*, the devil ..... John 13:2

ENDLESS
and *e* genealogies .... 1 Tim 1:4
to the power of an *e* .... Heb 7:16

ENDS
cherubim at the two *e* of .... Ex 25:19
judge the *e* of the earth .... 1 Sam 2:10
looks to the *e* of the earth .. Job 28:24
All the *e* of the world .... Ps 22:27
all the *e* of the earth have .... Ps 98:3
established all the *e* .... Prov 30:4
Creator of the *e* of the .... Is 40:28
from the *e* of the earth .... Is 42:10
she came from the *e* ...... Matt 12:42
salvation to the *e* .... Acts 13:47
their words to the *e* .... Rom 10:18

ENDURANCE
For you have need of *e* .... Heb 10:36
run with *e* the race that ..... Heb 12:1

ENDURE
But the LORD shall *e* .... Ps 9:7
weeping may *e* for a night .... Ps 30:5
as the sun and moon *e* .... Ps 72:5
His name shall *e* .... Ps 72:17
heart, Him I will not *e* .... Ps 101:5
glory of the LORD *e* .... Ps 104:31
nor does a crown *e* .... Prov 27:24
Can your heart *e* .... Ezek 22:14
e only for a time .... Mark 4:17
persecuted, we *e* .... 1 Cor 4:12
must *e* hardship .... 2 Tim 2:3
Therefore I *e* all .... 2 Tim 2:10
If you *e* chastening .... Heb 12:7
them blessed who *e* .... James 5:11

ENDURED
what persecutions I *e* ..... 2 Tim 3:11
he had patiently *e* .... Heb 6:15
e as seeing Him who .... Heb 11:27
For consider Him who *e* .... Heb 12:3

ENDURES
See HIS MERCY ENDURES FOREVER
goodness of God *e* .... Ps 52:1
And His truth *e* .... Ps 100:5
his righteousness *e* forever .. Ps 112:3
truth of the LORD *e* forever .. Ps 117:2
For His mercy *e* .... Ps 136:1
But he who *e* to the .... Matt 10:22
e only for a while .... Matt 13:21
for the food which *e* .... John 6:27
he has built on it *e* .... 1 Cor 3:14
hopes all things, *e* .... 1 Cor 13:7
is the man who *e* .... James 1:12
word of the LORD *e* .... 1 Pet 1:25

ENDURING
the LORD is clean, *e* .... Ps 19:9
e possession for .... Heb 10:34

ENEMIES
See LOVE YOUR ENEMIES
an enemy to your *e* .... Ex 23:22
Your *e* be scattered .... Num 10:35
I took you to curse my *e* .. Num 23:11
LORD will cause your *e* ..... Deut 28:7
from the hand of our *e* .. 1 Sam 12:10
your *e* from before you .... 2 Sam 7:9
be saved from my *e* ...... 2 Sam 22:4
Let all my *e* be ashamed ...... Ps 6:10
be saved from my *e* .... Ps 18:3
delivers me from my *e* .... Ps 18:48
the presence of my *e* .... Ps 23:5
Let not my *e* triumph .... Ps 25:2
But my *e* are vigorous .... Ps 38:19
arise, let His *e* be scattered ... Ps 68:1
e will lick the dust .... Ps 72:9
Your *e* with Your mighty ... Ps 89:10
Your *e* Your footstool .... Ps 110:1
me wiser than my *e* .... Ps 119:98
rescued us from our *e*, ... Ps 136:24
I count them my *e* .... Ps 139:22
makes even his *e* to be ..... Prov 16:7
e are the men of his .... Mic 7:6
darkness will pursue His *e* ... Nah 1:8
to you, love your *e* .... Matt 5:44
a man's *e* will be those .... Matt 10:36
be saved from our *e* .... Luke 1:71
Your *e* Your footstool ..... Luke 20:43
e we were reconciled ...... Rom 5:10
the gospel they are *e* ...... Rom 11:28
till He has put all *e* .... 1 Cor 15:25
were alienated and *e* .... Col 1:21
His *e* are made His .... Heb 10:13
and devours their *e* .... Rev 11:5

ENEMY
then I will be an *e* .... Ex 23:22
out the *e* from before ..... Deut 33:27
David's *e* continually .... 1 Sam 18:29
delivered your *e* into ..... 1 Sam 26:8
Haman, the *e* of the Jews .... Esth 8:1
regard me as Your *e* .... Job 13:24
He counts me as His *e* ..... Job 33:10
or have plundered my *e* .... Ps 7:4
You may silence the *e* .... Ps 8:2
e does not triumph .... Ps 41:11
e who reproaches me .... Ps 55:12
a strong tower from the *e* .... Ps 61:3
e has persecuted my .... Ps 143:3
If your *e* is hungry .... Prov 25:21
kisses of an *e* are .... Prov 27:6
the *e* comes in like .... Is 59:19
with the wound of an *e* ...... Jer 30:14
rejoice over me, my *e* .... Mic 7:8
and hate your *e* .... Matt 5:43
The *e* who sowed them ... Matt 13:39
all the power of the *e* ..... Luke 10:19
"If your *e* hungers .... Rom 12:20
last *e* that will be .... 1 Cor 15:26
become your *e* because ...... Gal 4:16
not count him as an *e* ... 2 Thess 3:15
makes himself an *e* .... James 4:4

ENGRAVE
two onyx stones and *e* ..... Ex 28:9
e its inscription .... Zech 3:9

ENJOY
e its sabbaths as long ... Lev 26:34
therefore *e* pleasure ... Eccl 2:1
e the good of all his labor ... Eccl 3:13
richly all things to *e* ... 1 Tim 6:17
than to *e* the passing ... Heb 11:25

ENJOYMENT
So I commended *e* ... Eccl 8:15

ENLARGES
He *e* nations ... Job 12:23
e his desire as hell ... Hab 2:5

ENLIGHTEN
E my eyes, lest I sleep ... Ps 13:3
the LORD my God will *e* ... Ps 18:28

ENLIGHTENED
those who were once *e* ... Heb 6:4

ENMITY
And I will put *e* ... Gen 3:15
the carnal mind is *e* ... Rom 8:7
in His flesh the *e* ... Eph 2:15
putting to death the *e* ... Eph 2:16
with the world is *e* ... James 4:4

ENOCH
Father of Methuselah, Gen 5:21
Walks with God, Gen 5:22
Taken up to heaven, Gen 5:24
Prophecy of, cited, Jude 14, 15

ENOUGH
four never say, "*E* ... Prov 30:15
It is *e*! The hour has ... Mark 14:41
servants have bread *e* ... Luke 15:17

ENRAGED
being exceedingly *e* ... Acts 26:11
And the dragon was *e* ... Rev 12:17

ENRAPTURED
And always be *e* ... Prov 5:19

ENRICHED
that you were *e* ... 1 Cor 1:5
while you are *e* ... 2 Cor 9:11

ENSNARED
The wicked is *e* ... Prov 12:13

ENSNARES
sin which so easily *e* ... Heb 12:1

ENTANGLE
how they might *e* ... Matt 22:15

ENTANGLES
engaged in warfare *e* ... 2 Tim 2:4

ENTER
'They shall not *e* My rest ... Ps 95:11
E into His gates ... Ps 100:4
Do not *e* into judgment ... Ps 143:2
E into the rock ... Is 2:10
He shall *e* into peace ... Is 57:2
Jonah began to *e* the city on ... Jon 3:4
you will by no means *e* ... Matt 5:20
"*E* by the narrow ... Matt 7:13
Lord,' shall *e* the kingdom ... Matt 7:21
city or town you *e* ... Matt 10:11
e into life with one eye ... Matt 18:9
e the kingdom of God ... Matt 19:24
E into the joy of your ... Matt 25:21
and pray, lest you *e* ... Matt 26:41
e a strong man's ... Mark 3:27
child will by no means *e* ... Mark 10:15
e the kingdom of God ... Mark 10:24
Whatever house you *e* ... Luke 9:4
"Strive to *e* through ... Luke 13:24
Can he *e* a second time ... John 3:4
cannot *e* the kingdom ... John 3:5
you, he who does not *e* ... John 10:1
who have believed do *e* ... Heb 4:3
e the Holiest by the ... Heb 10:19
e the temple till the ... Rev 15:8
e through the gates ... Rev 22:14

ENTERED
day that Noah *e* the ark ... Matt 24:38
went out and *e* the swine ... Mark 5:13
as they *e* the cloud ... Luke 9:34
day that Noah *e* the ark ... Luke 17:27
Then Satan *e* Judas ... Luke 22:3
through one man sin *e* ... Rom 5:12
ear heard, nor have *e* ... 1 Cor 2:9
he who has *e* His rest ... Heb 4:10
the forerunner has *e* ... Heb 6:20
e the Most Holy Place ... Heb 9:12

ENTERS
If anyone *e* by Me ... John 10:9
e the Presence behind ... Heb 6:19

ENTHRONED
You are holy, *e* in ... Ps 22:3
LORD sat *e* at the Flood ... Ps 29:10

ENTICED
his own desires and *e* ... James 1:14

ENTICING
e speech she caused ... Prov 7:21
e unstable souls ... 2 Pet 2:14

ENTIRELY
give yourself *e* to them ... 1 Tim 4:15

ENTRANCE
The *e* of Your words ... Ps 119:130
e will be supplied ... 2 Pet 1:11

ENTREAT
"*E* me not to leave you ... Ruth 1:16
"But now *e* God's favor ... Mal 1:9
being defamed, we *e* ... 1 Cor 4:13

ENTREATED
man of God *e* the LORD ... 1 Kin 13:6
e our God for this ... Ezra 8:23

ENTRUSTED
e with a stewardship ... 1 Cor 9:17
e with the gospel ... 1 Thess 2:4

ENVIOUS
For I was *e* of the ... Ps 73:3
Do not be *e* of evil ... Prov 24:1
patriarchs, becoming *e* ... Acts 7:9

ENVY
e slays a simple ... Job 5:2
e the oppressor ... Prov 3:31
e is rottenness ... Prov 14:30
not let your heart *e* ... Prov 23:17
e have now perished ... Eccl 9:6
Him over because of *e* ... Matt 27:18
full of *e*, murder ... Rom 1:29
not in strife and *e* ... Rom 13:13
where there are *e*, strife ... 1 Cor 3:3
love does not *e* ... 1 Cor 13:4
e, murders, drunkenness ... Gal 5:21
preach Christ even from *e* ... Phil 1:15
living in malice and *e* ... Titus 3:3
For where *e* and ... James 3:16
deceit, hypocrisy, *e* ... 1 Pet 2:1

EPAPHRAS
Leader of the Colossian church, Col 1:7, 8
Suffers as a prisoner in Rome, Philem 23

EPAPHRODITUS
Messenger from Philippi, Phil 2:25–27
Brings a gift to Paul, Phil 4:18

EPHES DAMMIM
Philistine encampment, 1 Sam 17:1
Called Pasdammim, 1 Chr 11:13

EPHESUS
Paul visits, Acts 18:18–21
Miracles done here, Acts 19:11–21
Demetrius stirs up riot in, Acts 19:24–29
Elders of, addressed by Paul at Miletus, Acts 20:17–38
Letter sent to, Eph 1:1
Site of one of seven churches, Rev 1:11

EPHOD
stones to be set in the *e* ... Ex 25:7
a breastplate, an *e* ... Ex 28:4
made the *e* of gold, blue ... Ex 39:2
and put the *e* on him ... Lev 8:7
Gideon made it into an *e* ... Judg 8:27
a shrine, and made an *e* ... Judg 17:5
a child, wearing a linen *e* ... 1 Sam 2:18
was wearing an *e* ... 1 Sam 14:3
"Bring the *e* here ... 1 Sam 23:9
brought the *e* to David ... 1 Sam 30:7
was wearing a linen *e* ... 2 Sam 6:14

EPHRAIM
Joseph's younger son, Gen 41:52
Obtains Jacob's blessing, Gen 48:8–20
—— Tribe of:
Predictions concerning, Gen 48:20
Territory assigned to, Josh 16:1–10
Assist Deborah, Judg 5:14, 15
Assist Gideon, Judg 7:24, 25
Quarrel with Gideon, Judg 8:1–3
Quarrel with Jephthah, Judg 12:1–4
Leading tribe of kingdom of Israel, Is 7:2–17
Provoke God by sin, Hos 12:7–14
Many of, join Judah, 2 Chr 15:8, 9
Captivity of, predicted, Hos 9:3–17
Messiah promised to, Zech 9:9–13

EPHRATHAH
Ancient name of Bethlehem, Ruth 4:11
Prophecy concerning, Mic 5:2

EPHRON
Hittite who sold Machpelah to Abraham, Gen 23:8–20

EPICUREANS
Sect of pleasure-loving philosophers, Acts 17:18

EPISTLE
You are our *e* written ... 2 Cor 3:2
you are an *e* ... 2 Cor 3:3
by word or our *e* ... 2 Thess 2:15
our word in this *e* ... 2 Thess 3:14
is a sign in every *e* ... 2 Thess 3:17

EPISTLES
e of commendation to ... 2 Cor 3:1
as also in all his *e* ... 2 Pet 3:16

EQUAL
it was you, a man my *e* ... Ps 55:13
and you made them *e* ... Matt 20:12
they are *e* to the angels ... Luke 20:36
making Himself *e* ... John 5:18
it robbery to be *e* ... Phil 2:6

EQUALITY
that there may be *e* ... 2 Cor 8:14

EQUITY
You have established *e* ... Ps 99:4
judgment, and *e* ... Prov 1:3
and *e* cannot enter ... Is 59:14
and pervert all *e* ... Mic 3:9
with Me in peace and *e* ... Mal 2:6

ER
Son of Judah, Gen 38:1–7; 46:12

ERASTUS
Paul's friend at Ephesus, Acts 19:21, 22; 2 Tim 4:20
Treasurer of Corinth, Rom 16:23

ERR
you cause you to *e* ... Is 3:12
My people Israel to *e* ... Jer 23:13

ERROR
God that it was an *e* ... Eccl 5:6
utter *e* against the LORD ... Is 32:6
nor was there any *e* ... Dan 6:4
e which was due ... Rom 1:27
a sinner from the *e* ... James 5:20
led away with the *e* ... 2 Pet 3:17
and the spirit of *e* ... 1 John 4:6
run greedily in the *e* ... Jude 11

ERRORS
can understand his *e* ... Ps 19:12

ESARHADDON
Son of Sennacherib; king of Assyria (681–669 B.C.), 2 Kin 19:36, 37

ESAU
Isaac's favorite son, Gen 25:25–28
Sells his birthright, Gen 25:29–34
Deprived of blessing; seeks to kill Jacob, Gen 27
Reconciled to Jacob, Gen 33:1–17
Descendants of, Gen 36

ESCAPE
E to the mountains ... Gen 19:17
Do not let one of them *e* .. 1 Kin 18:40
and they shall not *e* ... Job 11:20
Shall they *e* by ... Ps 56:7
speaks lies will not *e* ... Prov 19:5
who fears God will *e* ... Eccl 7:18
and how shall we *e* ... Is 20:6
who does such things *e* ... Ezek 17:15
nothing shall *e* them ... Joel 2:3
How can you *e* the ... Matt 23:33
e all these things ... Luke 21:36
same, that you will *e* ... Rom 2:3
also make the way of *e* ... 1 Cor 10:13
And they shall not *e* ... 1 Thess 5:3
e the snare of the devil ... 2 Tim 2:26
how shall we *e* if we ... Heb 2:3
e who refused Him who ... Heb 12:25

ESCAPED
I alone have *e* to tell ... Job 1:15
my flesh, and I have *e* ... Job 19:20
Our soul has *e* as a ... Ps 124:7
all *e* safely to land ... Acts 27:44
having *e* the corruption ... 2 Pet 1:4
after they have *e* ... 2 Pet 2:20

ESH-BAAL
Son of Saul, 1 Chr 8:33

ESHCOL
Valley near Hebron, Num 13:22–27; Deut 1:24

ESTABLISH
But I will *e* My covenant ... Gen 6:18
I will *e* the throne of his .. 2 Sam 7:13
to *e* them forever ... 2 Chr 9:8
'Your seed I will *e* ... Ps 89:4
e the work of our ... Ps 90:17
E Your word to Your ... Ps 119:38
e an everlasting ... Ezek 16:60
e justice in the gate ... Amos 5:15
seeking to *e* their own ... Rom 10:3
to Him who is able to *e* ... Rom 16:25
He may *e* your hearts ... 1 Thess 3:13
e you in every good ... 2 Thess 2:17
faithful, who will *e* ... 2 Thess 3:3
that He may *e* the second ... Heb 10:9
E your hearts ... James 5:8
a while, perfect, *e* ... 1 Pet 5:10

ESTABLISHED
He not made you and *e* ... Deut 32:6
also is firmly *e* ... 1 Chr 16:30
David my father be *e* ... 2 Chr 1:9
e it upon the waters ... Ps 24:2
a rock, and *e* my steps ... Ps 40:2
e a testimony in Jacob ... Ps 78:5
It shall be *e* forever ... Ps 89:37
Your throne is *e* ... Ps 93:2
LORD has *e* His throne ... Ps 103:19
let all your ways be *e* ... Prov 4:26
e the clouds above ... Prov 8:28
lip shall be *e* forever ... Prov 12:19
your thoughts will be *e* ... Prov 16:3
by understanding it is *e* ... Prov 24:3
house shall be *e* ... Is 2:2
In mercy the throne will be *e* .. Is 16:5
by His power, He has *e* ... Jer 10:12
every word may be *e* ... Matt 18:16
built up in Him and *e* ... Col 2:7
covenant, which was *e* ... Heb 8:6
that the heart be *e* ... Heb 13:9

ESTABLISHES
The king *e* the land by ... Prov 29:4
Now He who *e* us with ... 2 Cor 1:21

ESTEEM
high wall in his own *e* ... Prov 18:11
and we did not *e* ... Is 53:3
e others better than ... Phil 2:3
and hold such men in *e* ... Phil 2:29
e them very highly ... 1 Thess 5:13

ESTEEMED
For what is highly *e* ... Luke 16:15
those who are least *e* ... 1 Cor 6:4

ESTEEMS
One person *e* one day ... Rom 14:5

ESTHER
Selected for harem, Esth 2:7–16
Chosen to be queen, Esth 2:17, 18
Agrees to intercede for her people, Esth 4
Invites king to banquet, Esth 5:1–8
Denounces Haman; obtains reversal of decree, Esth 7:1—8:8
Establishes Purim, Esth 9:29–32

ESTRANGED
The wicked are *e* ... Ps 58:3
because they are all *e* ... Ezek 14:5
You have become *e* ... Gal 5:4

ETAM
Rock where Samson took refuge, Judg 15:8–19

ETERNAL
e God is your refuge ... Deut 33:27
For man goes to his *e* ... Eccl 12:5
I do that I may have *e* ... Matt 19:16
and inherit *e* life ... Matt 19:29
the righteous into *e* life ... Matt 25:46
that I may inherit *e* life ... Mark 10:17
in the age to come, *e* ... Mark 10:30
not perish but have *e* ... John 3:15
gathers fruit for *e* life ... John 4:36
you think you have *e* ... John 5:39
drinks My blood has *e* life . John 6:54
the words of *e* life ... John 6:68
And I give them *e* life ... John 10:28
that He should give *e* ... John 17:2
And this is *e* life ... John 17:3
e life to those who by ... Rom 2:7
righteousness to *e* ... Rom 5:21
the gift of God is *e* ... Rom 6:23
e weight of glory ... 2 Cor 4:17
are not seen are *e* ... 2 Cor 4:18
not made with hands, *e* ... 2 Cor 5:1
to the King *e*, immortal ... 1 Tim 1:17
lay hold on *e* life ... 1 Tim 6:12
e life which God ... Titus 1:2
to the hope of *e* life ... Titus 3:7
and of *e* judgment ... Heb 6:2
obtained *e* redemption ... Heb 9:12
e life which was ... 1 John 1:2
has promised us—*e* life ... 1 John 2:25
that no murderer has *e* ... 1 John 3:15
God has given us *e* ... 1 John 5:11
that you have *e* life ... 1 John 5:13
the true God and *e* life ... 1 John 5:20
Jesus Christ unto *e* ... Jude 21

ETERNAL LIFE
that I may have *e* ... Matt 19:16
the righteous into *e* ... Matt 25:46
in the age to come, *e* ... Mark 10:30
I do to inherit *e* ... Luke 10:25
not perish but have *e* ... John 3:15
and gathers fruit for *e* ... John 4:36
you think you have *e* ... John 5:39
You have the words of *e* ... John 6:68
will keep it for *e* ... John 12:25
is *e*, that they may know ... John 17:3
had been appointed to *e* ... Acts 13:48
e to those who by patient ... Rom 2:7
righteousness to *e* ... Rom 5:21
the gift of God is *e* ... Rom 6:23
lay hold on *e* ... 1 Tim 6:12
in hope of *e* which God ... Titus 1:2
declare to you that *e* ... 1 John 1:2
He has promised us *e* ... 1 John 2:25
no murderer has *e* ... 1 John 3:15
that God has given us *e* .. 1 John 5:11
Lord Jesus Christ unto *e* ... Jude 21

ETERNITY
Also He has put *e* ... Eccl 3:11
One who inhabits *e* ... Is 57:15

ETHAM
Israel's encampment, Ex 13:20

ETHIOPIA
See CUSH
Hostile to Israel and Judah, 2 Chr 12:2, 3; 14:9–15; Is 43:3; Dan 11:43
Prophecies against, Is 20:1–6; Ezek 30:4–9

ETHIOPIANS
Skin of, unchangeable, Jer 13:23

EUNICE
Mother of Timothy, 2 Tim 1:5

EUNUCH
eczema or scab, or is a *e* ... Lev 21:20
Hegai the king's *e* ... Esth 2:3
of Ethiopia, a *e* ... Acts 8:27

EUNUCHS
seven *e* who served ... Esth 1:10
be *e* in the palace ... Is 39:7
Ethiopian, one of the *e* ... Jer 38:7
the master of his *e* ... Dan 1:3
have made themselves *e* .. Matt 19:12

EUPHRATES
River of Eden, Gen 2:14
Boundary of Promised Land, Gen 15:18; 1 Kin 4:21, 24
Scene of battle, Jer 46:2, 6, 10
Angels bound there, Rev 9:14

EUTYCHUS
Sleeps during Paul's sermon, Acts 20:9
Restored to life, Acts 20:12

EVANGELIST
house of Philip the *e* ... Acts 21:8
do the work of an *e* ... 2 Tim 4:5

EVANGELISTS
some prophets, some *e* ... Eph 4:11

EVEN
E in laughter the heart ... Prov 14:13
E a child is known ... Prov 20:11
e nature itself teach ... 1 Cor 11:14
e denying the Lord who ... 2 Pet 2:1

EVENING
the *e* and the morning were .. Gen 1:5
quails came up at *e* ... Ex 16:13
At *e* they return ... Ps 59:6
e it is cut down and ... Ps 90:6
of my hands as the *e* ... Ps 141:2
e do not withhold your ... Eccl 11:6
and more fierce than *e* ... Hab 1:8
When it is *e* you say, 'It ... Matt 16:2
when *e* came, the boat ... Mark 6:47
in the *e*, at midnight ... Mark 13:35
it is toward *e* ... Luke 24:29

EVER
shall reign forever and *e* ... Ex 15:18
No razor has *e* come ... Judg 16:17
were the upright *e* cut off ... Job 4:7
Let them *e* shout for joy ... Ps 5:11
eyes are *e* toward the LORD .. Ps 25:15
He is *e* merciful ... Ps 37:26
Or *e* You had formed ... Ps 90:2
Your name forever and *e* ... Ps 145:1
shines *e* brighter unto ... Prov 4:18
there was *e* an earth ... Prov 8:23
even forever and *e* ... Dan 7:18
time, no, nor *e* shall be ... Matt 24:21
eat fruit from you *e* ... Mark 11:14

EXAMPLE
to make her a public *e* . . . . . Matt 1:19
I have given you an *e* . . . . . John 13:15
in following my *e* . . . . . Phil 3:17
to make ourselves an *e* . . . 2 Thess 3:9
youth, but be an *e* . . . . . 1 Tim 4:12
us, leaving us an *e* . . . . . 1 Pet 2:21
making them an *e* . . . . . 2 Pet 2:6
are set forth as an *e* . . . . . Jude 7

EXAMPLES
happened to them as *e* . . . 1 Cor 10:11
so that you became *e* . . . 1 Thess 1:7
to you, but being *e* . . . . . 1 Pet 5:3

EXCEEDING
for us a far more *e* . . . . . 2 Cor 4:17
the *e* greatness of . . . . . Eph 1:19
He might show the *e* . . . . . Eph 2:7
also be glad with *e* joy . . . . 1 Pet 4:13

EXCEEDINGLY
prevailed *e* on the earth . . . . Gen 7:19
your *e* great reward . . . . . Gen 15:1
your descendants *e* . . . . . Gen 16:10
and grew *e* mighty . . . . . Ex 1:7
for the LORD must be *e* . . . 1 Chr 22:5
You have made him *e* . . . . . Ps 21:6
let them rejoice *e* . . . . . Ps 68:3
and I love them *e* . . . . . Ps 119:167
is far off and *e* deep . . . . . Eccl 7:24
it displeased Jonah *e* . . . . . Jon 4:1
rejoiced with *e* great joy . . . . Matt 2:10
e high mountain . . . . . Matt 4:8
Rejoice and be *e* . . . . . Matt 5:12
they were *e* sorrowful . . . . . Matt 26:22
e white, like snow . . . . . Mark 9:3
"My soul is *e* sorrowful . . Mark 14:34
Him who is able to do *e* . . . . Eph 3:20
our Lord was *e* abundant . . 1 Tim 1:14
given to us *e* great . . . . . 2 Pet 1:4

EXCEEDS
your righteousness *e* . . . . . Matt 5:20

EXCEL
you His angels, who *e* . . . . . Ps 103:20
but you *e* them all . . . . . Prov 31:29
that you seek to *e* . . . . . 1 Cor 14:12

EXCELLENCE
e You have overthrown . . . . . Ex 15:7
did not come with *e* . . . . . 1 Cor 2:1
the *e* of the power . . . . . 2 Cor 4:7
things loss for the *e* . . . . . Phil 3:8

EXCELLENT
He is *e* in power . . . . . Job 37:23
How *e* is Your name in all . . . . Ps 8:1
It shall be as *e* oil . . . . . Ps 141:5
to His *e* greatness . . . . . Ps 150:2
will speak of *e* things . . . . . Prov 8:6
An *e* wife is the crown of . . . Prov 12:4
like Lebanon, *e* . . . . . Song 5:15
for He has done *e* . . . . . Is 12:5
in counsel and *e* . . . . . Is 28:29
Inasmuch as an *e* . . . . . Dan 5:12
the things that are *e* . . . . . Rom 2:18
show you a more *e* way . . 1 Cor 12:31
the things that are *e* . . . . . Phil 1:10
a more *e* name . . . . . Heb 1:4
e sacrifice than Cain . . . . . Heb 11:4
came to Him from the *E* . . . 2 Pet 1:17

EXCELS
Do you see a man who *e* . . Prov 22:29
I saw that wisdom *e* . . . . . Eccl 2:13
of the glory that *e* . . . . . 2 Cor 3:10

EXCHANGE
give in *e* for his soul . . . . . Matt 16:26

EXCHANGED
Nor can it be *e* . . . . . Job 28:17
e the truth of God for . . . . . Rom 1:25
For even their women *e* . . . . Rom 1:26

EXCLUDE
you, and when they *e* . . . . . Luke 6:22

they want to *e* you . . . . . Gal 4:17

EXCUSE
God be angry at your *e* . . . . . Eccl 5:6
but now they have no *e* . . . John 15:22
they are without *e* . . . . . Rom 1:20
do you think that we *e* . . . 2 Cor 12:19

EXCUSES
began to make *e* . . . . . Luke 14:18

EXECUTE
nor *e* His fierce wrath . . . 1 Sam 28:18
e vengeance on the . . . . . Ps 149:7
if you thoroughly *e* . . . . . Jer 7:5
E judgment and . . . . . Jer 22:3
e the fierceness . . . . . Hos 11:9
'*E* true justice . . . . . Zech 7:9
e judgment also . . . . . John 5:27
e wrath on him who . . . . . Rom 13:4

EXECUTES
by the judgment He *e* . . . . . Ps 9:16
e righteousness . . . . . Ps 103:6
e justice for the . . . . . Ps 146:7
One whose *e* His word . . . . . Joel 2:11
e justice for me . . . . . Mic 7:9

EXERCISE
those who are great *e* . . . . Matt 20:25
e yourself toward . . . . . 1 Tim 4:7
e profits a little . . . . . 1 Tim 4:8

EXERCISED
have their senses *e* . . . . . Heb 5:14

EXHORT
we command and *e* . . . . 2 Thess 3:12
I *e* first of all . . . . . 1 Tim 2:1
e him as a father . . . . . 1 Tim 5:1
and *e* these things . . . . . 1 Tim 6:2
Convince, rebuke, *e* . . . . . 2 Tim 4:2
doctrine, both to *e* . . . . . Titus 1:9
e the young men . . . . . Titus 2:6
Speak these things, *e* . . . . . Titus 2:15
e one another . . . . . Heb 3:13

EXHORTATION
you have any word of *e* . . . Acts 13:15
he who exhorts, in *e* . . . . . Rom 12:8
to reading, to *e* . . . . . 1 Tim 4:13
with the word of *e* . . . . . Heb 13:22

EXHORTED
For I earnestly *e* . . . . . Jer 11:7
e and strengthened . . . . . Acts 15:32
as you know how we *e* . . 1 Thess 2:11

EXILE
and also an *e* from . . . . . 2 Sam 15:19
The captive *e* hastens . . . . . Is 51:14

EXIST
things which do not *e* . . . . . Rom 4:17
by Your will they *e* . . . . . Rev 4:11

EXPECT
an hour you do not *e* . . . . . Luke 12:40

EXPECTATION
The *e* of the poor . . . . . Ps 9:18
God alone, for my *e* . . . . . Ps 62:5
the people were in *e* . . . . . Luke 3:15
For the earnest *e* . . . . . Rom 8:19
a certain fearful *e* . . . . . Heb 10:27

EXPECTING
e to receive something . . . . . Acts 3:5

EXPEDIENT
e for us that one man . . . . . John 11:50

EXPERT
and the *e* enchanter . . . . . Is 3:3
those of an *e* warrior . . . . . Jer 50:9
because you are *e* . . . . . Acts 26:3

EXPLAIN
was no one who could *e* . . . Gen 41:24
days they could not *e* . . . . . Judg 14:14
"*E* this parable to us . . . . . Matt 15:15
to say, and hard to *e* . . . . . Heb 5:11

EXPLAINED
He *e* all things to His . . . . . Mark 4:34
e to him the way of God . . . Acts 18:26

EXPLOIT
e all your laborers . . . . . Is 58:3
against those who *e* . . . . . Mal 3:5
they will *e* you with . . . . . 2 Pet 2:3

EXPOSED
his deeds should be *e* . . . . . John 3:20
all things that are *e* . . . . . Eph 5:13

EXPOUNDED
He *e* to them in all . . . . . Luke 24:27

EXPRESS
man cannot *e* it . . . . . Eccl 1:8
of His glory and the *e* . . . . . Heb 1:3

EXPRESSLY
of the LORD came *e* . . . . . Ezek 1:3
Now the Spirit *e* . . . . . 1 Tim 4:1

EXTEND
none to *e* mercy to him . . . . Ps 109:12
"Behold, I will *e* . . . . . Is 66:12
did not *e* to you . . . . . 2 Cor 10:14

EXTINGUISHED
broken, my days are *e* . . . . . Job 17:1
They are *e*, they are . . . . . Is 43:17

EXTOL
I will *e* You . . . . . Ps 30:1
e Him who rides . . . . . Ps 68:4

EXTOLLED
e with my tongue . . . . . Ps 66:17
shall be exalted and *e* . . . . . Is 52:13

EXTORTION
e gathers it for him . . . . . Prov 28:8
your neighbors by *e* . . . . . Ezek 22:12
they are full of *e* . . . . . Matt 23:25

EXTORTIONERS
nor *e* will inherit . . . . . 1 Cor 6:10

EXULT
in anguish I would *e* . . . . . Job 6:10

EYE
e for *e*, tooth for tooth . . . . . Ex 21:24
your *e* be evil against . . . . . Deut 15:9
the ear, but now my *e* . . . . . Job 42:5
me as the apple of Your *e* . . . . Ps 17:8
guide you with My *e* . . . . . Ps 32:8
Behold, the *e* of the . . . . . Ps 33:18
He who formed the *e* . . . . . Ps 94:9
with the *e* causes trouble . . Prov 10:10
and the seeing *e* . . . . . Prov 20:12
who has a generous *e* . . . . . Prov 22:9
A man with an evil *e* . . . . . Prov 28:22
e that mocks his . . . . . Prov 30:17
e is not satisfied . . . . . Eccl 1:8
labors, nor is his *e* . . . . . Eccl 4:8
for they shall see *e* . . . . . Is 52:8
e seen any God besides . . . . . Is 64:4
the apple of His *e* . . . . . Zech 2:8
If your right *e* causes . . . . . Matt 5:29
it was said, 'An *e* . . . . . Matt 5:38
lamp of the body is the *e* . . . Matt 6:22
plank in your own *e* . . . . . Matt 7:3
e causes you to sin . . . . . Matt 18:9
Or is your *e* evil . . . . . Matt 20:15
e causes you to sin . . . . . Mark 9:47
when your *e* is good . . . . . Luke 11:34
the *e* of a needle . . . . . Luke 18:25
"*E* has not seen . . . . . 1 Cor 2:9
"Because I am not an *e* . . . 1 Cor 12:16
whole body were an *e* . . . . 1 Cor 12:17
the twinkling of an *e* . . . . . 1 Cor 15:52
every *e* will see Him . . . . . Rev 1:7
your eyes with *e* salve . . . . . Rev 3:18

EYELIDS
His eyes behold, His *e* . . . . . Ps 11:4
e look right before . . . . . Prov 4:25
slumber to your *e* . . . . . Prov 6:4

EYES

e will be opened ... Gen 3:5
"Lift your *e* now and ... Gen 13:14
Abraham lifted his *e* ... Gen 22:13
the *e* of Israel were dim ... Gen 48:10
and you can be our *e* ... Num 10:31
hallow Me in the *e* of ... Num 20:12
Your *e* have seen what the ... Deut 4:3
frontlets between your *e* ... Deut 6:8
right in his own *e* ... Deut 12:8
in the *e* of the LORD ... Deut 13:18
e to see and ears to hear ... Deut 29:4
thorns in your *e* ... Josh 23:13
found favor in your *e* ... Ruth 2:10
open his *e* that he may ... 2 Kin 6:17
she put paint on her *e* ... 2 Kin 9:30
My *e* will be open ... 2 Chr 7:15
For the *e* of the LORD ... 2 Chr 16:9
God may enlighten our *e* ... Ezra 9:8
Do You have *e* of flesh ... Job 10:4
And my *e* shall behold ... Job 19:27
His *e* are on their ways ... Job 24:23
I was *e* to the blind ... Job 29:15
e observe from afar ... Job 39:29
e are secretly fixed ... Ps 10:8
His *e* behold, His eyelids ... Ps 11:4
enlightening the *e* ... Ps 19:8
e are ever toward the ... Ps 25:15
is before my *e* ... Ps 26:3
The *e* of the LORD are ... Ps 34:15
His *e* observe the nations ... Ps 66:7
e fail while I wait ... Ps 69:3
e shall you look ... Ps 91:8
E they have, but they ... Ps 115:5
marvelous in our *e* ... Ps 118:23
Open my *e*, that I may see ... Ps 119:18
I will lift up my *e* ... Ps 121:1
our *e* look to the LORD ... Ps 123:2
not give sleep to my *e* ... Ps 132:4
e saw my substance ... Ps 139:16
wise in your own *e* ... Prov 3:7
not depart from your *e* ... Prov 3:21
e look straight ahead ... Prov 4:25
is right in his own *e* ... Prov 12:15
The *e* of the LORD are ... Prov 15:3
but the *e* of a fool ... Prov 17:24
Will you set your *e* ... Prov 23:5
Who has redness of *e* ... Prov 23:29
be wise in his own *e* ... Prov 26:5
so the *e* of man are ... Prov 27:20
pure in its own *e* ... Prov 30:12
The wise man's *e* ... Eccl 2:14
e than the wandering ... Eccl 6:9
You have dove's *e* ... Song 1:15
the *e* of the lofty ... Is 5:15
e have seen the King ... Is 6:5
lest they see with their *e* ... Is 6:10
of the book, and the *e* ... Is 29:18
open Your *e*, O LORD ... Is 37:17
e fail from looking ... Is 38:14
O LORD, are not Your *e* ... Jer 5:3
Who have *e* and see ... Jer 5:21
e will weep bitterly ... Jer 13:17
For I will set My *e* ... Jer 24:6
your *e* from tears ... Jer 31:16
rims were full of *e* ... Ezek 1:18
full of *e* all around ... Ezek 10:12
e to see but does ... Ezek 12:2
that horn which had *e* ... Dan 7:20
horn between his *e* ... Dan 8:5
e like torches of fire, ... Dan 10:6
the *e* of the Lord GOD ... Amos 9:8
You are of purer *e* ... Hab 1:13
their *e* were opened ... Matt 9:30
But blessed are your *e* ... Matt 13:16
their *e* were heavy ... Matt 26:43
it is marvelous in our *e* ... Mark 12:11
Hades, he lifted up his *e* ... Luke 16:23
raise his *e* to heaven ... Luke 18:13
lift up your *e* and look ... John 4:35
"He put clay on my *e* ... John 9:15
e of one who was born ... John 9:32
fixing his *e* on him ... Acts 3:4
e they have closed ... Acts 28:27
e that they should not ... Rom 11:8
plucked out your own *e* ... Gal 4:15
e of your understanding ... Eph 1:18
have seen with our *e* ... 1 John 1:1
the lust of the *e* ... 1 John 2:16
as snow, and His *e* ... Rev 1:14
and anoint your *e* ... Rev 3:18
creatures full of *e* ... Rev 4:6
horns and seven *e* ... Rev 5:6
tear from their *e* ... Rev 21:4

EYESERVICE

not with *e*, as ... Eph 6:6
the flesh, not with *e* ... Col 3:22

EYEWITNESSES

the beginning were *e* ... Luke 1:2
e of His majesty ... 2 Pet 1:16

EZEKIEL

Sent to rebellious Israel, Ezek 2; 3
Prophesies by symbolic action:
siege of Jerusalem, Ezek 4
destruction of Jerusalem, Ezek 5
captivity of Judah, Ezek 12:1–20
destruction of the temple, Ezek 24:15–27
Visions of:
God's glory, Ezek 1:4–28
abominations, Ezek 8:5–18
valley of dry bones, Ezek 37:1–14
messianic times, Ezek 40—48
river of life, Ezek 47:1–5
Parables, allegories, dirges of, Ezek 15; 16; 17; 19; 23; 24

EZION GEBER

See ELATH
Town on the Red Sea, 1 Kin 9:26
Israelite encampment, Num 33:35
Seaport of Israel's navy, 1 Kin 22:48

EZRA

Scribe, priest and reformer of post-exilic times; commissioned by Artaxerxes, Ezra 7
Returns with exiles to Jerusalem, Ezra 8
Institutes reforms, Ezra 9
Reads the Law, Neh 8
Assists in dedication of wall, Neh 12:27–43

FABLES

nor give heed to *f* ... 1 Tim 1:4
be turned aside to *f* ... 2 Tim 4:4
cunningly devised *f* ... 2 Pet 1:16

FACE

was on the *f* of the deep ... Gen 1:2
In the sweat of your *f* you ... Gen 3:19
"For I have seen God *f* ... Gen 32:30
shall see my *f* no more ... Gen 44:23
Joseph fell on his father's *f* ... Gen 50:1
LORD spoke to Moses *f* to *f* ... Ex 33:11
f shone while he ... Ex 34:29
he put a veil on his *f* ... Ex 34:33
the LORD make His *f* ... Num 6:25
I will hide My *f* from ... Deut 31:17
his *f* in his mantle ... 1 Kin 19:13
Then he turned his *f* ... 2 Kin 20:2
seek His *f* evermore ... 1 Chr 16:11
and pray and seek My *f* ... 2 Chr 7:14
not turn His *f* from you ... 2 Chr 30:9
Why is your *f* sad, since ... Neh 2:2
curse You to Your *f* ... Job 1:11
I will put off my sad *f* and ... Job 9:27
and lift up your *f* to God ... Job 22:26
He shall see His *f* with joy ... Job 33:26
me, I will see Your *f* ... Ps 17:15
"Your *f*, LORD, I will seek ... Ps 27:8
Do not hide Your *f* from ... Ps 27:9
Why do You hide Your *f* ... Ps 44:24
and cause His *f* to shine ... Ps 67:1
Do not hide Your *f* from ... Ps 102:2
Make Your *f* shine upon ... Ps 119:135
As in water *f* reflects ... Prov 27:19
of his *f* is changed ... Eccl 8:1
I have set My *f* like a flint ... Is 50:7
sins have hidden His *f* ... Is 59:2
I have made your *f* ... Ezek 3:8
set your *f* against Gog, of ... Ezek 38:2
but to us shame of *f* ... Dan 9:7
before Your *f* who ... Matt 11:10
to discern the *f* of the sky ... Matt 16:3
f shone like the sun ... Matt 17:2
of His *f* was altered ... Luke 9:29
His *f* to go to Jerusalem ... Luke 9:51
they struck Him on the *f* ... Luke 22:64
always before my *f* ... Acts 2:25
his *f* as the *f* of an angel ... Acts 6:15
dimly, but then *f* ... 1 Cor 13:12
look steadily at the *f* ... 2 Cor 3:7
with unveiled *f* ... 2 Cor 3:18
one strikes you on the *f* ... 2 Cor 11:20
withstood him to his *f* ... Gal 2:11
that we may see your *f* ... 1 Thess 3:10
his natural *f* in a ... James 1:23
but the *f* of the LORD ... 1 Pet 3:12
creature had a *f* like a man ... Rev 4:7
They shall see His *f* ... Rev 22:4

FACE TO FACE

For I have seen God *f*, ... Gen 32:30
the Lord spoke to Moses *f* ... Ex 33:11
I speak with him *f* ... Num 12:8
the LORD talked with you *f* ... Deut 5:4
whom the LORD knew *f* ... Deut 34:10
Angel of the LORD *f* ... Judg 6:22
My case with you *f* ... Ezek 20:35
mirror, dimly, but then *f* ... 1 Cor 13:12

FACES

f were not ashamed ... Ps 34:5
wipe away tears from all *f* ... Is 25:8
hid, as it were, our *f* ... Is 53:3
be afraid of their *f* ... Jer 1:8
and all *f* turned pale ... Jer 30:6
Each one had four *f* ... Ezek 1:6
the gate that *f* toward the ... Ezek 43:1
your *f* looking worse than ... Dan 1:10
all *f* are drained of color ... Joel 2:6
they disfigure their *f* ... Matt 6:16
fell on their *f* before the ... Rev 7:11

FACTIONS

there must also be *f* ... 1 Cor 11:19

FADE

we all *f* as a leaf ... Is 64:6
and the leaf shall *f* ... Jer 8:13
rich man also will *f* ... James 1:11
and that does not *f* ... 1 Pet 1:4
of glory that does not *f* ... 1 Pet 5:4

FADES

withers, the flower *f* ... Is 40:7

FAIL

eyes shall look and *f* ... Deut 28:32
man's heart *f* because ... 1 Sam 17:32
You shall not *f* to have a ... 1 Kin 8:25
eyes of the wicked will *f* ... Job 11:20
flesh and my heart *f* ... Ps 73:26
of the thirsty to *f* ... Is 32:6
not one of these shall *f* ... Is 34:16
their tongues *f* ... Is 41:17
whose waters do not *f* ... Is 58:11
have caused wine to *f* ... Jer 48:33
His compassions *f* not ... Lam 3:22
of the olive may *f* ... Hab 3:17
nor shall the vine *f* ... Mal 3:11
heavens that does not *f* ... Luke 12:33
that when you *f* ... Luke 16:9
tittle of the law to *f* ... Luke 16:17
faith should not *f* ... Luke 22:32
prophecies, they will *f* ... 1 Cor 13:8

Your years will not *f* . . . . Heb 1:12
For the time would *f* . . . . Heb 11:32

FAILED
Not a word *f* of any . . . . Josh 21:45
My relatives have *f* . . . . Job 19:14
Has His promise *f* . . . . Ps 77:8
refuge has *f* me . . . . Ps 142:4

FAILING
men's hearts *f* . . . . Luke 21:26

FAILS
my strength *f* because . . . . Ps 31:10
Therefore my heart *f* me . . . . Ps 40:12
my spirit *f* . . . . Ps 143:7
and every vision *f* . . . . Ezek 12:22
wine is dried up, the oil *f* . . . Joel 1:10
He never *f*, but the unjust . . . Zeph 3:5
Love never *f* . . . . 1 Cor 13:8

FAINT
If you *f* in the day of . . . . . . Prov 24:10
the youths shall *f* . . . . Is 40:30
shall walk and not *f* . . . . Is 40:31
my heart is *f* in me . . . . Jer 8:18
and the infants *f* . . . . Lam 2:11

FAINTED
thirsty, their soul *f* . . . . Ps 107:5

FAINTHEARTED
unruly, comfort the *f* . . . . 1 Thess 5:14

FAINTS
longs, yes, even *f* . . . . Ps 84:2
My soul *f* for Your . . . . Ps 119:81
And the whole heart *f* . . . . Is 1:5
the earth, neither *f* . . . . Is 40:28

FAIR
Behold, you are *f* . . . . Song 1:15
How *f* and how pleasant . . . . Song 7:6
of the Lord is not *f* . . . . Ezek 18:25
My ways which are *f* . . . . . Ezek 18:29
say, 'It will be *f* weather . . . . Matt 16:2
to a place called *F* . . . . Acts 27:8
what is just and *f* . . . . Col 4:1

FAIR HAVENS
Harbor of Crete at which Paul landed, Acts 27:8

FAIR-MINDED
These were more *f* . . . . Acts 17:11

FAIRER
f than the sons . . . . Ps 45:2

FAIREST
another beloved, O *f* . . . . Song 5:9
your beloved gone, O *f* . . . . . Song 6:1

FAITH
in whom is no *f* . . . . Deut 32:20
shall live by his *f* . . . . Hab 2:4
you, O you of little *f* . . . . . . Matt 6:30
not found such great *f* . . . . . . Matt 8:10
your *f* has made you well . . Matt 9:22
"O you of little *f* . . . . Matt 14:31
woman, great is your *f* . . . . Matt 15:28
f as a mustard seed . . . . Matt 17:20
that you have no *f* . . . . Mark 4:40
to them, "Have *f* . . . . Mark 11:22
not found such great *f* . . . . . . Luke 7:9
you, O you of little *f* . . . . . . Luke 12:28
"Increase our *f* . . . . Luke 17:5
will He really find *f* . . . . Luke 18:8
through *f* in His name . . . . . . Acts 3:16
a man full of *f* . . . . Acts 6:5
the Holy Spirit and of *f* . . . . Acts 11:24
that he had *f* to be healed . . . Acts 14:9
were strengthened in the *f* . . Acts 16:5
are sanctified by *f* . . . . Acts 26:18
for obedience to the *f* . . . . Rom 1:5
that your *f* is spoken of . . . . . Rom 1:8
God is revealed from *f* . . . . . . Rom 1:17
God, through *f* . . . . Rom 3:22
f apart from the deeds . . . . . Rom 3:28
his *f* is accounted for . . . . Rom 4:5
f which he had while still . . . Rom 4:11
f is made void and the . . . . . . Rom 4:14
those who are of the *f* . . . . . . Rom 4:16
And not being weak in *f* . . . Rom 4:19
having been justified by *f* . . . Rom 5:1
of *f* speaks in this way . . . . . Rom 10:6
f which we preach . . . . Rom 10:8
f comes by hearing . . . . Rom 10:17
and you stand by *f* . . . . Rom 11:20
each one a measure of *f* . . . . Rom 12:3
in proportion to our *f* . . . . . . Rom 12:6
Do you have *f* . . . . Rom 14:22
whatever is not from *f* . . . . Rom 14:23
that your *f* should not be . . . 1 Cor 2:5
though I have all *f* . . . . 1 Cor 13:2
And now abide *f* . . . . 1 Cor 13:13
your *f* is also empty . . . . . . 1 Cor 15:14
stand fast in the *f* . . . . 1 Cor 16:13
For we walk by *f* . . . . 2 Cor 5:7
as your *f* is increased . . . . . 2 Cor 10:15
now preaches the *f* which . . . Gal 1:23
law but by *f* in Jesus Christ . . Gal 2:16
the flesh I live by *f* . . . . Gal 2:20
or by the hearing of *f* . . . . Gal 3:2
f are sons of Abraham . . . . Gal 3:7
the just shall live by *f* . . . . Gal 3:11
the law is not of *f* . . . . Gal 3:12
of the Spirit through *f* . . . . Gal 3:14
But before *f* came . . . . Gal 3:23
But after *f* has come . . . . Gal 3:25
f working through love . . . . Gal 5:6
of the household of *f* . . . . Gal 6:10
been saved through *f* . . . . Eph 2:8
one Lord, one *f* . . . . Eph 4:5
to the unity of the *f* . . . . Eph 4:13
taking the shield of *f* . . . . Eph 6:16
for the *f* of the gospel . . . . Phil 1:27
established in the *f* . . . . Col 2:7
your work of *f* . . . . 1 Thess 1:3
on the breastplate of *f* . . . . . 1 Thess 5:8
work of *f* with power . . . . . 2 Thess 1:11
for not all have *f* . . . . 2 Thess 3:2
a true son in the *f* . . . . 1 Tim 1:2
edification which is in *f* . . . . . 1 Tim 1:4
having *f* and a good . . . . 1 Tim 1:19
if they continue in *f*, love . . 1 Tim 2:15
the mystery of the *f* . . . . 1 Tim 3:9
great boldness in the *f* . . . . . 1 Tim 3:13
in love, in spirit, in *f* . . . . . . 1 Tim 4:12
he has denied the *f* . . . . 1 Tim 5:8
righteousness, godliness, *f* . 1 Tim 6:11
Fight the good fight of *f* . . . 1 Tim 6:12
I have kept the *f* . . . . 2 Tim 4:7
in our common *f* . . . . Titus 1:4
temperate, sound in *f* . . . . Titus 2:2
not being mixed with *f* . . . . Heb 4:2
of *f* toward God, ... Heb 6:1
those who through *f* . . . . Heb 6:12
in full assurance of *f* . . . . . . Heb 10:22
the just shall live by *f* . . . . . Heb 10:38
f is the substance . . . . Heb 11:1
without *f* it is . . . . Heb 11:6
These all died in *f* . . . . Heb 11:13
good testimony through *f* . . Heb 11:39
author and finisher of our *f* . Heb 12:2
whose *f* follow . . . . Heb 13:7
your *f* produces patience . . . James 1:3
But let him ask in *f* . . . . James 1:6
someone says he has *f* . . . . James 2:14
Show me your *f* . . . . James 2:18
f without works is dead . . . . James 2:20
and not by *f* only . . . . James 2:24
f will save the sick . . . . James 5:15
the genuineness of your *f* . . . . 1 Pet 1:7
receiving the end of your *f* . . . 1 Pet 1:9
him, steadfast in the *f* . . . . 1 Pet 5:9
add to your *f* virtue . . . . 2 Pet 1:5
on your most holy *f* . . . . Jude 20
works, love, service, *f* . . . . Rev 2:19
the patience and the *f* . . . . . . Rev 13:10
of God and the *f* . . . . Rev 14:12

FAITHFUL
he is *f* in all My house . . . . . Num 12:7
God, He is God, the *f* . . . . Deut 7:9
found his heart *f* . . . . Neh 9:8
f disappear from among . . . . . Ps 12:1
LORD preserves the *f* . . . . Ps 31:23
whose spirit was not *f* . . . . Ps 78:8
eyes shall be on the *f* . . . . . . Ps 101:6
commandments are *f* . . . . . . Ps 119:86
are righteous and very *f* . . Ps 119:138
f spirit conceals a . . . . Prov 11:13
A *f* witness does not lie . . . . Prov 14:5
But who can find a *f* . . . . Prov 20:6
A *f* man will abound . . . . . . Prov 28:20
the LORD who is *f* . . . . Is 49:7
f witness between us . . . . Jer 42:5
or fault, because he was *f* . . . Dan 6:4
the Holy One who is *f* . . . . . . Hos 11:12
"Who then is a *f* . . . . Matt 24:45
good and *f* servant . . . . Matt 25:23
"Who then is that *f* . . . . Luke 12:42
He who is *f* in what . . . . . . Luke 16:10
if you have not been *f* . . . . Luke 16:12
have judged me to be *f* . . . . . Acts 16:15
God is *f*, by whom . . . . 1 Cor 1:9
that one be found *f* . . . . 1 Cor 4:2
is my beloved and *f* . . . . 1 Cor 4:17
God is *f*, who will not . . . . . 1 Cor 10:13
But as God is *f* . . . . 2 Cor 1:18
f minister in the LORD. . . . . . . Eph 6:21
f brethren in Christ . . . . Col 1:2
He who calls you is *f* . . . . 1 Thess 5:24
because He counted me *f* . . 1 Tim 1:12
This is a *f* saying and . . . . . 1 Tim 1:15
temperate, *f* in all things . . . 1 Tim 3:11
commit these to *f* men . . . . . . 2 Tim 2:2
f High Priest in . . . . Heb 2:17
as Moses also was *f* . . . . Heb 3:2
Moses indeed was *f* . . . . Heb 3:5
He who promised is *f* . . . . . . Heb 10:23
judged Him *f* who had . . . . . Heb 11:11
He is *f* and just to . . . . 1 John 1:9
Be *f* until death . . . . Rev 2:10
words are true and *f* . . . . Rev 21:5

FAITHFULNESS
righteousness and his *f* . . 1 Sam 26:23
for in their *f* they . . . . 2 Chr 31:18
f reaches to the clouds . . . . Ps 36:5
I have declared Your *f* . . . . . . Ps 40:10
Your *f* to all generations . . . . . . Ps 89:1
f You shall establish . . . . Ps 89:2
Your *f* also surrounds . . . . Ps 89:8
allow My *f* to fail . . . . Ps 89:33
and Your *f* every night . . . . Ps 92:2
f endures to all . . . . Ps 119:90
In Your *f* answer me . . . . Ps 143:1
counsels of old are *f* . . . . Is 25:1
great is Your *f* . . . . Lam 3:23
your *f* is like a morning . . . . . . Hos 6:4
unbelief make the *f* . . . . Rom 3:3
kindness, goodness, *f* . . . . Gal 5:22

FAITHLESS
the words of the *f* . . . . Prov 22:12
"O *f* and perverse . . . . Matt 17:17
"O *f* generation . . . . Mark 9:19
If we are *f*, He remains . . . . . 2 Tim 2:13

FALL
a deep sleep to *f* . . . . Gen 2:21
but do not let me *f* . . . . 2 Sam 24:14
Let them *f* by their . . . . Ps 5:10
Though he *f*, he shall not . . . . Ps 37:24
For I am ready to *f* . . . . Ps 38:17
Yes, all kings shall *f* . . . . Ps 72:11
A thousand may *f* at your . . . . Ps 91:7
Let the wicked *f* into their . . Ps 141:10
LORD upholds all who *f* . . . . . Ps 145:14
but a prating fool will *f* . . . . Prov 10:8
the wicked will *f* by his . . . . . Prov 11:5
no counsel, the people *f* . . . Prov 11:14
trusts in his riches will *f* . . . Prov 11:28
haughty spirit before a *f* . . Prov 16:18

but the wicked shall *f* ... Prov 24:16
digs a pit will *f* ... Prov 26:27
For if they *f*, one will lift ... Eccl 4:10
both he who helps will *f* ... Is 31:3
all their host shall *f* ... Is 34:4
men shall utterly *f* ... Is 40:30
"Will they *f* and not rise ... Jer 8:4
F and rise no more ... Jer 25:27
proud shall stumble and *f* ... Jer 50:32
of music, you shall *f* ... Dan 3:5
if You will *f* down ... Matt 4:9
And great was its *f* ... Matt 7:27
the blind, both will *f* ... Matt 15:14
f from their masters' ... Matt 15:27
the stars will *f* ... Matt 24:29
Child is destined for the *f* .. Luke 2:34
"I saw Satan *f* ... Luke 10:18
they will *f* by the edge ... Luke 21:24
might *f* on some ... Acts 5:15
f short of the glory of ... Rom 3:23
that they should *f* ... Rom 11:11
block or a cause to *f* in ... Rom 14:13
take heed lest he *f* ... 1 Cor 10:12
with pride he *f* ... 1 Tim 3:6
be rich *f* into temptation ... 1 Tim 6:9
if they *f* away ... Heb 6:6
to *f* into the hands of the .. Heb 10:31
lest anyone *f* short of ... Heb 12:15
it all joy when you *f* ... James 1:2
and rocks, "*F* on us ... Rev 6:16

FALLEN
has your countenance *f* ... Gen 4:6
terror of you has *f* on us ... Josh 2:9
f on its face to the earth ... 1 Sam 5:3
who reproach You have *f* ... Ps 69:9
you are *f* from heaven ... Is 14:12
"Babylon is *f* ... Is 21:9
Babylon has suddenly *f* ... Jer 51:8
you have *f* from grace ... Gal 5:4
who have *f* asleep ... 1 Thess 4:13
And I saw a star *f* ... Rev 9:1
"Babylon is *f* ... Rev 14:8

FALLING
and my feet from *f* ... Ps 116:8
and *f* down before Him ... Luke 8:47
great drops of blood *f* ... Luke 22:44
f away comes first ... 2 Thess 2:3

FALLS
when your enemy *f* ... Prov 24:17
who is alone when he *f* ... Eccl 4:10
not one of them *f* to the ... Matt 10:29
And whoever *f* ... Matt 21:44
divided against a house *f* . Luke 11:17
wheat *f* into the ground .. John 12:24
master he stands or *f* ... Rom 14:4
grass; its flower *f* ... James 1:11
withers, and its flower *f* ... 1 Pet 1:24
so that no rain *f* ... Rev 11:6

FALSE
"You shall not bear *f* ... Ex 20:16
shall not bear *f* witness ... Deut 5:20
I hate every *f* way ... Ps 119:104
f witness who speaks lies .. Prov 6:19
gives heed to *f* lips ... Prov 17:4
f witness shall perish ... Prov 21:28
the *f* pen of the scribe ... Jer 8:8
walk in a *f* spirit ... Mic 2:11
and do not love a *f* ... Zech 8:17
"Beware of *f* prophets ... Matt 7:15
shall not bear *f* witness ... Matt 19:18
f christs and *f* ... Matt 24:24
at last two *f* witnesses ... Matt 26:60
f prophets will rise ... Mark 13:22
and we are found *f* ... 1 Cor 15:15
among *f* brethren ... 2 Cor 11:26
of *f* brethren secretly ... Gal 2:4
taking delight in *f* humility .. Col 2:18
f prophets have gone ... 1 John 4:1
f teachers among you ... 2 Pet 2:1
mouth of the *f* prophet ... Rev 16:13

FALSE PROPHETS
Beware of *f*, who come to .. Matt 7:15
many *f* will rise up ... Matt 24:11
false christs and *f* ... Matt 24:24
f will rise and show ... Mark 13:22
their fathers to the *f* ... Luke 6:26
But there were also *f* ... 2 Pet 2:1
many *f* have gone out ... 1 John 4:1

FALSE WITNESS
You shall not bear *f* ... Ex 20:16
a *f* who speaks lies, ... Prov 6:19
But a *f*, deceit ... Prov 12:17
f will not go unpunished ... Prov 19:5
A man who bears *f* ... Prov 25:18
thefts, *f*, blasphemies ... Matt 15:19
bore *f* against Him ... Mark 14:56

FALSEHOOD
since *f* remains in your ... Job 21:34
If I have walked with *f* ... Job 31:5
those who speak *f* ... Ps 5:6
and brings forth *f* ... Ps 7:14
For their deceit is *f* ... Ps 119:118
remove *f* and lies far ... Prov 30:8
under *f* we have hidden ... Is 28:15
offspring of *f* ... Is 57:4
and trusted in *f* ... Jer 13:25

FALSELY
it, and swears *f* ... Lev 6:3
shall not steal, nor deal *f* ... Lev 19:11
nor have we dealt *f* ... Ps 44:17
Whoever *f* boasts of ... Prov 25:14
surely they swear *f* ... Jer 5:2
prophesy *f* to you ... Jer 29:9
words, swearing *f* ... Hos 10:4
of evil against you *f* ... Matt 5:11
anyone or accuse *f* ... Luke 3:14
f called knowledge ... 1 Tim 6:20

FAME
his *f* spread throughout ... Josh 6:27
Sheba heard of the *f* ... 1 Kin 10:1
exceed the *f* of which ... 1 Kin 10:7
his *f* spread throughout all ... Esth 9:4
endures forever, Your *f* ... Ps 135:13
heard My *f* nor seen ... Is 66:19
Your *f* went out ... Ezek 16:14
them for praise and *f* ... Zeph 3:19
Then His *f* went ... Matt 4:24

FAMILIAR
to mediums and *f* spirits ... Lev 19:31
and *f* spirits, to prostitute ... Lev 20:6
Even my own *f* friend ... Ps 41:9

FAMILIES
in you all the *f* ... Gen 12:3
in your seed all the *f* of ... Gen 28:14
and all the *f* of the nations .. Ps 22:27
God sets the solitary in *f* ... Ps 68:6
and makes their *f* ... Ps 107:41
the God of all the *f* ... Jer 31:1
f which the LORD has ... Jer 33:24
of all the *f* of the earth ... Amos 3:2
in your seed all the *f* ... Acts 3:25

FAMILY
that man and against his *f* ... Lev 20:5
against the whole *f* ... Amos 3:1
shall mourn, every *f* ... Zech 12:12
Joseph's *f* became known .. Acts 7:13
sons of the *f* of Abraham .. Acts 13:26
f were baptized ... Acts 16:33
from whom the whole *f* ... Eph 3:15

FAMINE
Now there was a *f* ... Gen 12:10
besides the first *f* that was .. Gen 26:1
seven years of *f* will arise .. Gen 41:30
the *f* was severe in the ... Gen 43:1
the LORD has called for a *f* .. 2 Kin 8:1
In *f* He shall redeem you ... Job 5:20
keep them alive in *f* ... Ps 33:19
He called for a *f* ... Ps 105:16
and destruction, *f* ... Is 51:19
shall die by the sword, by *f* .. Jer 21:9
send the sword, the *f* ... Jer 24:10
of the fever of *f* ... Lam 5:10
I will increase the *f* ... Ezek 5:16
there arose a severe *f* ... Luke 15:14
a *f* and great trouble came .. Acts 7:11
or persecution, or *f*, or ... Rom 8:35

FAMINES
And there will be *f* ... Matt 24:7

FAMISH
righteous soul to *f* ... Prov 10:3

FAMISHED
honorable men are *f* ... Is 5:13

FAMOUS
and may his name be *f* ... Ruth 4:14

FAN
not to *f* or to cleanse ... Jer 4:11
His winnowing *f* ... Matt 3:12

FANCIES
with their own *f* ... Prov 1:31

FAR
removed my brothers *f* ... Job 19:13
Your judgments are *f* ... Ps 10:5
Be not *f* from Me ... Ps 22:11
those who are *f* ... Ps 73:27
The LORD is *f* from the ... Prov 15:29
but it was *f* from me ... Eccl 7:23
removed their hearts *f* ... Is 29:13
Those near and those *f* ... Ezek 22:5
their heart is *f* from ... Matt 15:8
going to a *f* country ... Mark 13:34
though He is not *f* ... Acts 17:27
you who once were *f* ... Eph 2:13

FAR BE IT FROM ME
"*F* that I should do so ... Gen 44:17
'*F*; for those who honor ... 1 Sam 2:30
f that I should sin ... 1 Sam 12:23
F! Let not the king ... 1 Sam 22:15
f, that I should swallow .. 2 Sam 20:20
"*F*, O LORD, that ... 2 Sam 23:17
"*F*, O my God, that ... 1 Chr 11:19
F that I should say ... Job 27:5

FAR COUNTRY
"We have come from a *f* ... Josh 9:6
good news from a *f* ... Prov 25:25
f, from the end of heaven ... Is 13:5
from a *f*, from Babylon ... Is 39:3
and went into a *f* ... Matt 21:33
man traveling to a *f* ... Matt 25:14
a *f*, and there wasted ... Luke 15:13
nobleman went into a *f* ... Luke 19:12
and went into a *f* ... Luke 20:9

FARMER
The hard-working *f* ... 2 Tim 2:6
See how the *f* waits ... James 5:7

FASHIONED
have made me and *f* ... Job 10:8

FASHIONS
He *f* their hearts ... Ps 33:15

FAST
"But you who held *f* to the .. Deut 4:4
serve Him and hold *f* to ... Deut 13:4
For he held *f* to the LORD ... 2 Kin 18:6
My maids and I will *f* ... Esth 4:16
commanded, and it stood *f* ... Ps 33:9
of your *f* you find pleasure ... Is 58:3
f that I have chosen ... Is 58:5
they *f*, I will not hear ... Jer 14:12
Consecrate a *f*, call a ... Joel 1:14
believed God, proclaimed a *f* .. Jon 3:5
"Moreover, when you *f* ... Matt 6:16
disciples do not *f* ... Matt 9:14
f while the bridegroom is .. Mark 2:19
I *f* twice a week ... Luke 18:12
if you hold *f* that word ... 1 Cor 15:2
stand *f* in the faith, be ... 1 Cor 16:13
holding *f* the word of life ... Phil 2:16
you stand *f* in the Lord ... 1 Thess 3:8

holding *f* the faithful word .. Titus 1:9
hold *f* our confession .... Heb 4:14
hold *f* the confession ...... Heb 10:23
Hold *f* what you have .... Rev 3:11

FASTED

and *f* seven days .... 1 Sam 31:13
the child, and David *f* .... 2 Sam 12:16
f and entreated our God .... Ezra 8:23
'Why have we *f* .... Is 58:3
'When you *f* and .... Zech 7:5
And when He had *f* .... Matt 4:2
Then, having *f* and prayed .. Acts 13:3

FASTENED

were its foundations *f* .... Job 38:6
'the peg that is *f* .... Is 22:25

FASTING

I was *f* and praying before ... Neh 1:4
humbled myself with *f* .... Ps 35:13
are weak through *f* .... Ps 109:24
house on the day of *f* .... Jer 36:6
and spent the night *f* .... Dan 6:18
with all your heart, with *f* ... Joel 2:12
not appear to men to be *f* ... Matt 6:18
except by prayer and *f* .... Matt 17:21
I was *f* until this hour ..... Acts 10:30
give yourselves to *f* .... 1 Cor 7:5

FASTINGS

but served God with *f* ..... Luke 2:37
in sleeplessness, in *f* .... 2 Cor 6:5

FAT

the first seven, the *f* cows .. Gen 41:20
and you will eat the *f* ...... Gen 45:18
f is the LORD's .... Lev 3:16
Now Eglon was a very *f* .... Judg 3:17
have closed up their *f* .... Ps 17:10

FATHER

See GOD THE FATHER; HEAVENLY FATHER

man shall leave his *f* .... Gen 2:24
saw the nakedness of his *f* .. Gen 9:22
and you shall be a *f* .... Gen 17:4
the lineage of our *f* .... Gen 19:32
his *f* blessed him .... Gen 27:41
God of my *f* has been with .. Gen 31:5
Esau was the *f* of the ...... Gen 36:43
f loved him more than all ... Gen 37:4
Thus his *f* wept for him .... Gen 37:35
'Is your *f* still alive .... Gen 43:7
bring my *f* down here ..... Gen 45:13
God, the God of your *f* ...... Gen 46:3
to meet his *f* Israel .... Gen 46:29
went up to bury his *f* .... Gen 50:7
Honor your *f* and your ...... Ex 20:12
Honor your *f* and your .... Deut 5:16
obey the voice of his *f* .. Deut 21:18
of Jesse, the *f* of David .... Ruth 4:17
son, and I will be his *F* ... 1 Chr 22:10
son, and I will be his *F* .... 1 Chr 28:6
'You are my *f* .... Job 17:14
I was a *f* to the poor .... Job 29:16
When my *f* and my mother .. Ps 27:10
A *f* of the fatherless .... Ps 68:5
f pities his children .... Ps 103:13
the instruction of a *f* .... Prov 4:1
wise son makes a glad *f* .... Prov 10:1
wise son makes a *f* glad ... Prov 15:20
glory of children is their *f* .. Prov 17:6
the *f* of a fool has no joy .. Prov 17:21
son is a grief to his *f* ...... Prov 17:25
curses his *f* or his .... Prov 20:20
f of the righteous will ..... Prov 23:24
makes his *f* rejoice .... Prov 29:3
that curses its *f* .... Prov 30:11
God, Everlasting *F* .... Is 9:6
Your first *f* sinned .... Is 43:27
You, O LORD, are our *F* ...... Is 63:16
time cry to Me, My *F* .... Jer 3:4
for I am a *F* to Israel .... Jer 31:9
for the iniquity of his *f* ..... Ezek 18:17
not bear the guilt of the *f* . Ezek 18:20
"A son honors his *f* .... Mal 1:6
Have we not all one *F* .... Mal 2:10
your *F* who sees in secret ... Matt 6:4
your heavenly *F* will also .. Matt 6:14
neither will your *F* forgive .. Matt 6:15
your heavenly *F* knows .... Matt 6:32
much more will your *F* ..... Matt 7:11
He who loves *f* .... Matt 10:37
does anyone know the *F* .. Matt 11:27
'He who curses *f* .... Matt 15:4
My *F* who is in heaven .... Matt 18:10
a man shall leave his *f* ..... Matt 19:5
for One is your *F* .... Matt 23:9
you blessed of My *F* ...... Matt 25:34
"O My *F*, if this cup ...... Matt 26:42
in the name of the *F* ...... Matt 28:19
F with the holy angels ..... Mark 8:38
a man shall leave his *f* .... Mark 10:7
the Son, but only the *F* ... Mark 13:32
"Abba, *F*, all things are .. Mark 14:36
Your *f* and I have sought .. Luke 2:48
just as your *F* also is ...... Luke 6:36
first go and bury my *f* ...... Luke 9:59
who the Son is but the *F* .. Luke 10:22
bread from any *f* among .. Luke 11:11
F give the Holy Spirit to .. Luke 11:13
F will be divided .... Luke 12:53
does not hate his *f* .... Luke 14:26
arise and go to my *f* ...... Luke 15:18
'I beg you therefore, *f* .... Luke 16:27
"*F*, if it is Your will .... Luke 22:42
"*F*, forgive them, for ..... Luke 23:34
only begotten of the *F* ..... John 1:14
F loves the Son .... John 3:35
worship the *F* in spirit ..... John 4:23
F has been working .... John 5:17
what He sees the *F* do ..... John 5:19
F raises the dead .... John 5:21
F judges no one .... John 5:22
not honor the *F* who sent .. John 5:23
All that the *F* gives Me .... John 6:37
He has seen the *F* .... John 6:46
F who sent Me bears ...... John 8:18
but as My *F* taught Me, I ... John 8:28
we have one *F* .... John 8:41
he is a liar and the *f* of it ... John 8:44
I and My *F* are one .... John 10:30
and believe that the *F* .... John 10:38
"*F*, I thank You that ..... John 11:41
F, glorify Your name ...... John 12:28
"Lord, show us the *F* ...... John 14:8
seen Me has seen the *F* .... John 14:9
believe that I am in the *F* . John 14:10
because I go to My *F* ..... John 14:12
And I will pray the *F* ..... John 14:16
will be loved by My *F* .... John 14:21
'I am going to the *F* ...... John 14:28
F is the vinedresser .... John 15:1
whatever you ask the *F* ... John 15:16
you ask the *F* in My ...... John 16:23
came forth from the *F* ..... John 16:28
And now, O *F*, glorify Me .. John 17:5
yet ascended to My *F* ..... John 20:17
F the promise of the Holy .. Acts 2:33
that he might be the *f* ...... Rom 4:11
"I have made you a *f* .... Rom 4:17
we cry out, "Abba, *F*." ...... Rom 8:15
F of our Lord Jesus .... Rom 15:6
F of mercies and God of .... 2 Cor 1:3
"I will be a *F* to you .... 2 Cor 6:18
by one Spirit to the *F* ...... Eph 2:18
I bow my knees to the *F* of .. Eph 3:14
one God and *F* of all .... Eph 4:6
a man shall leave his *f* and .. Eph 5:31
F be glory forever and ...... Phil 4:20
For it pleased the *F* that in .. Col 1:19
f does his own children .. 1 Thess 2:11
but exhort him as a *f* .... 1 Tim 5:1
"I will be to Him a *F* .... Heb 1:5
without *f*, without mother .... Heb 7:3
whom a *f* does not chasten .. Heb 12:7
comes down from the *F* .. James 1:17
we bless our God and *F* .... James 3:9
if you call on the *F* .... 1 Pet 1:17
an Advocate with the *F* .... 1 John 2:1
love of the *F* is not in .... 1 John 2:15
love the *F* has bestowed ... 1 John 3:1
and testify that the *F* ..... 1 John 4:14
F, the Word, and the .... 1 John 5:7
his name before My *F* .... Rev 3:5

FATHER IN HEAVEN

and glorify your *F* .... Matt 5:16
may be sons of your *F* ..... Matt 5:45
just as your *F* is perfect .... Matt 5:48
no reward from your *F* ...... Matt 6:1
Our *F*, hallowed be Your .... Matt 6:9
who does the will of My *F* .. Matt 7:21
does the will of My *F* .... Matt 12:50
done for them by My *F* ... Matt 18:19
F may also forgive you ... Mark 11:25
Our *F*, hallowed be .... Luke 11:2

FATHER'S

Joseph fell on his *f* face ..... Gen 50:1
he and his *f* household .... Gen 50:22
my *f* God, and I will exalt .... Ex 15:2
When I was my *f* son .... Prov 4:3
keep your *f* command ...... Prov 6:20
heeds his *f* instruction ..... Prov 13:1
you in My *F* kingdom ..... Matt 26:29
I must be about My *F* ...... Luke 2:49
many of my *f* hired .... Luke 15:17
Do not make My *F* house .. John 2:16
works that I do in My *F* .. John 10:25
F house are many .... John 14:2
the *F* who sent Me .... John 14:24
that a man has his *f* .... 1 Cor 5:1

FATHERLESS

afflict any widow or *f* child .. Ex 22:22
and your children *f* .... Ex 22:24
justice for the *f* .... Deut 10:18
my hand against the *f* ...... Job 31:21
the helper of the *f* .... Ps 10:14
to do justice to the *f* .... Ps 10:18
father of the *f*, a defender ...... Ps 68:5
Let his children be *f* .... Ps 109:9
He relieves the *f* .... Ps 146:9
the fields of the *f* .... Prov 23:10
do not defend the *f* .... Is 1:23
they may rob the *f* .... Is 10:2
You the *f* finds mercy .... Hos 14:3
the widow or the *f* .... Zech 7:10

FATHERS

bury me with my *f* .... Gen 49:29
swore to your *f* to give you ... Ex 13:5
the iniquity of the *f* .... Ex 20:5
the LORD swore to your *f* .... Deut 1:8
f make you a thousand ...... Deut 1:11
the iniquity of the *f* upon .... Deut 5:9
the LORD God of our *f* ...... Ezra 7:27
f trusted in You .... Ps 22:4
sojourner, as all my *f* were .. Ps 39:12
our ears, O God, our *f* .... Ps 44:1
He commanded our *f* .... Ps 78:5
did in the sight of their *f* .... Ps 78:12
have sinned with our *f* ...... Ps 106:6
that I gave to your *f* forever ... Jer 7:7
f have eaten sour grapes .... Jer 31:29
f have eaten sour grapes ... Ezek 18:2
for the iniquities of our *f* .... Dan 9:16
f provoked Me to wrath ..... Zech 8:14
For so did their *f* to the .... Luke 6:26
Our *f* worshiped on this .... John 4:20
f ate the manna .... John 6:31
f nor we were able to ..... Acts 15:10
of whom are the *f* .... Rom 9:5
you do not have many *f* ... 1 Cor 4:15
unaware that all our *f* ..... 1 Cor 10:1
f, do not provoke .... Eph 6:4
F, do not provoke your ...... Col 3:21
where your *f* tested Me .... Heb 3:9

FATLING

and the *f* together .... Is 11:6

FEAST OF INGATHERING
F at the end of the year, ... Ex 23:16
and the *F* at the year's end . . Ex 34:22

FEAST OF TABERNACLES
the *F* for seven days . . . . Lev 23:34
observe the *F* seven . . . . . . Deut 16:13
year of release, at the *F* . . . Deut 31:10
They also kept the *F*, ... Ezra 3:4
and to keep the *F* . . . . Zech 14:16
Now the Jews' *F* . . . . John 7:2

FEAST OF UNLEAVENED BREAD
you shall observe the *F* . . . . . Ex 12:17
You shall keep the *F* . . . . Ex 23:15
F you shall keep. Seven . . . . . Ex 34:18
Jerusalem to keep the *F* . . 2 Chr 30:13
And they kept the *F* . . . . Ezra 6:22
on the first day of the *F* . . . Matt 26:17
the Passover and the *F* . . . . Mark 14:1
Now the *F* drew near, ... Luke 22:1

FEAST OF WEEKS
you shall observe the *F* . . . . . Ex 34:22
at your *f*, you shall have . . Num 28:26
you shall keep the *F* . . . . . . Deut 16:10

FEASTING
house full of *f* with strife . . . Prov 17:1
go to the house of *f* . . . . Eccl 7:2

FEASTS
See APPOINTED FEASTS
These are the *f* of the LORD . . Lev 23:4
in your appointed *f* . . . . Num 10:10
Moons and on the set *f* . . . 1 Chr 23:31
I will turn your *f* . . . . Amos 8:10
the best places at *f* . . . . . . Luke 20:46
spots in your love *f* . . . . Jude 12

FEATHERS
shall cover you with His *f* . . . . Ps 91:4

FED
f me all my life long . . . . Gen 48:15
and *f* you with manna . . . . Deut 8:3
but the shepherds *f* . . . . Ezek 34:8
They *f* him with grass like . . Dan 5:21
So those who *f* the swine . . Mark 5:14
desiring to be *f* with the . . Luke 16:21
f you with milk and . . . . 1 Cor 3:2

FEEBLE
strengthened the *f* . . . . Job 4:4
And there was none *f* . . . . . . Ps 105:37
And my flesh is *f* . . . . Ps 109:24
and make firm the *f* knees . . . . Is 35:3
Every hand will be *f* . . . . Ezek 7:17
hang down, and the *f* . . . . Heb 12:12

FEED
ravens to *f* you there . . . . . . 1 Kin 17:4
and *f* on His faithfulness . . . . . Ps 37:3
death shall *f* on them . . . . Ps 49:14
of the righteous *f* . . . . Prov 10:21
He will *f* His flock like a . . . . . Is 40:11
and *f* your flocks . . . . Is 61:5
f you with knowledge . . . . Jer 3:15
over them who will *f* them . . . Jer 23:4
I will *f* My flock, and I . . . Ezek 34:15
to him, "*F* My lambs . . . . . John 21:15
to him, "*F* My sheep . . . . . . John 21:17
your enemy hungers, *f* . . . . Rom 12:20
my goods to *f* the poor . . . . 1 Cor 13:3

FEEDS
"Ephraim *f* on the wind . . . . . . Hos 12:1
your heavenly Father *f* . . . . . Matt 6:26
he who *f* on Me will live . . . John 6:57

FEET
See UNDER HIS FEET
your sandals off your *f* . . . . Ex 3:5
not worn out on your *f* . . . . . Deut 29:5
f touched the dry land . . . . . Josh 4:18
So she lay at his *f* . . . . Ruth 3:14
was lame in both his *f* . . . . 2 Sam 9:13
so my *f* did not slip . . . . . . 2 Sam 22:37
in places forgotten by *f* . . . . . Job 28:4
I was *f* to the lame . . . . Job 29:15
all things under his *f* . . . . Ps 8:6
He makes my *f* like the . . . . Ps 18:33
pierced My hands and My *f* . . Ps 22:16
You have set my *f* . . . . Ps 31:8
and set my *f* upon a rock . . . . . . Ps 40:2
does not allow our *f* . . . . Ps 66:9
f had almost stumbled . . . . Ps 73:2
and my *f* from falling . . . . Ps 116:8
f from every evil way . . . . . . Ps 119:101
word is a lamp to my *f* . . . . Ps 119:105
f have been standing . . . . Ps 122:2
For their *f* run to . . . . Prov 1:16
Her *f* go down to death . . . . . . Prov 5:5
f that are swift in running . . Prov 6:18
spreads a net for his *f* . . . . . . Prov 29:5
with two he covered his *f* . . . . . . Is 6:2
sandals off your *f* . . . . Is 20:2
called him to His *f* . . . . Is 41:2
up the dust of your *f* . . . . Is 49:23
mountains are the *f* . . . . Is 52:7
place of My *f* glorious . . . . Is 60:13
have not restrained their *f* . . Jer 14:10
its *f* partly of iron and . . . . Dan 2:33
f like burnished bronze in . . Dan 10:6
are the dust of His *f* . . . . Nah 1:3
on the mountains the *f* of . . . Nah 1:15
make my *f* like deer's *f* . . . . . . Hab 3:19
in that day His *f* . . . . Zech 14:4
off the dust from your *f* . . . Matt 10:14
two hands or two *f* . . . . Matt 18:8
saw Him, he fell at His *f* . . . Mark 5:22
she came and fell at His *f* . . . Mark 7:25
rather than having two *f* . . . Mark 9:45
began to wash His *f* . . . . Luke 7:38
sitting at the *f* of Jesus . . . . . Luke 8:35
also sat at Jesus' *f* . . . . Luke 10:39
and sandals on his *f* . . . . Luke 15:22
My hands and My *f* . . . . Luke 24:39
wash the disciples' *f* . . . . John 13:5
wash one another's *f* . . . . . . John 13:14
and the other at the *f* . . . . . John 20:12
up, and immediately his *f* . . . . . Acts 3:7
at the apostles' *f* . . . . Acts 4:35
your sandals off your *f* . . . . . . Acts 7:33
his own hands and *f* . . . . Acts 21:11
f are swift to shed . . . . Rom 3:15
beautiful are the *f* . . . . Rom 10:15
all things under His *f* . . . . . . 1 Cor 15:27
put all things under His *f* . . . . Eph 1:22
and having shod your *f* . . . . Eph 6:15
straight paths for your *f* . . . . Heb 12:13
fell at His *f* as dead . . . . Rev 1:17
And I fell at his *f* . . . . Rev 19:10

FELIX
Governor of Judea; letter addressed to, Acts 23:24–30
Paul's defense before, Acts 24:1–27

FELL
f on his neck and kissed . . . . Gen 33:4
Joseph *f* on his father's . . . . . . Gen 50:1
Saul took a sword and *f* . . . 1 Sam 31:4
ax head *f* into the water . . . . 2 Kin 6:5
Saul took a sword and *f* . . . 1 Chr 10:4
fear of the Jews *f* upon . . . . . Esth 8:17
fire of God *f* from heaven . . . . Job 1:16
foes, they stumbled and *f* . . . . . Ps 27:2
f on my face, and I heard . . . Ezek 1:28
Spirit of the LORD *f* upon . . . Ezek 11:5
f down bound into the . . . . Dan 3:23
lots, and the lot *f* on Jonah . . . Jon 1:7
on that house; and it *f* . . . . . . Matt 7:27
seed *f* by the wayside . . . . Matt 13:4
others *f* on good ground . . . . . Matt 13:8
saw Him, he *f* at His feet . . Mark 5:22
as they sailed He *f* asleep . . Luke 8:23
f among thieves . . . . Luke 10:30
the tower in Siloam *f* . . . . Luke 13:4
f from the rich man's . . . . . . Luke 16:21
she *f* down at His feet . . . . John 11:32
and the lot *f* on Matthias . . . . Acts 1:26
f down and breathed his . . . . . . Acts 5:5
had said this, he *f* asleep . . . . Acts 7:60
ready, he *f* into a trance . . . . Acts 10:10
the Holy Spirit *f* upon all . . . Acts 10:44
his chains *f* off his hands . . . . Acts 12:7
he *f* down from the third . . . . Acts 20:9
who reproached You *f* on . . . Rom 15:3
f down after they were . . . . . Heb 11:30
elders *f* down before . . . . Rev 5:8
of heaven *f* to the earth . . . . . . Rev 6:13
a great star *f* from heaven . . . Rev 8:10
four living creatures *f* . . . . Rev 19:4

FELLOW
f servants who owed . . . . . . Matt 18:28
begins to beat his *f* . . . . Matt 24:49
f worker concerning . . . . 2 Cor 8:23
f citizens with the . . . . Eph 2:19
Gentiles should be *f* . . . . Eph 3:6
rest of my *f* workers . . . . Phil 4:3
These are my only *f* . . . . Col 4:11
that we may become *f* . . . . 3 John 8
I am your *f* servant . . . . Rev 19:10

FELLOWSHIP
doctrine and *f* . . . . Acts 2:42
were called into the *f* . . . . 1 Cor 1:9
not want you to have *f* . . . . 1 Cor 10:20
f has righteousness . . . . 2 Cor 6:14
the right hand of *f* . . . . Gal 2:9
And have no *f* with the . . . . Eph 5:11
for your *f* in the . . . . Phil 1:5
of love, if any *f* . . . . Phil 2:1
and the *f* of His . . . . Phil 3:10
also may have *f* . . . . 1 John 1:3
we say that we have *f* . . . . . . 1 John 1:6
the light, we have *f* . . . . 1 John 1:7

FEMALE
male and *f* He created . . . . Gen 1:27
they shall be male and *f* . . . . Gen 6:19
ark to Noah, male and *f* . . . . . . Gen 7:9
has borne a male or a *f* . . . . . . Lev 12:7
made them male and *f* . . . . Matt 19:4
there is neither male nor *f* . . . Gal 3:28

FENCE
and a tottering *f* . . . . Ps 62:3

FENCED
He has *f* up my way . . . . Job 19:8

FERTILIZE
I dig around it and *f* . . . . Luke 13:8

FERVENT
f desire I have desired . . . . Luke 22:15
and being *f* in spirit . . . . Acts 18:25
f in spirit, serving the . . . . . Rom 12:11
f prayer of a . . . . James 5:16
all things have *f* . . . . 1 Pet 4:8
will melt with *f* . . . . 2 Pet 3:10

FERVENTLY
you, always laboring *f* . . . . Col 4:12
love one another *f* . . . . 1 Pet 1:22

FESTIVAL
night when a holy *f* . . . . Is 30:29
or regarding a *f* . . . . Col 2:16

FESTUS
Governor of Judea, Acts 24:27
Paul's defense made to, Acts 25:1–22

FETCH
f my knowledge from . . . . Job 36:3

FETTERS
hurt his feet with *f* . . . . Ps 105:18
their nobles with *f* . . . . Ps 149:8

FEVER
f which shall consume . . . . . Lev 26:16
my bones burn with *f* . . . . Job 30:30
mother lying sick with a *f* . . Matt 8:14
immediately the *f* left her . . Mark 1:31
and rebuked the *f* . . . . Luke 4:39
of Publius lay sick of a *f* . . . . Acts 28:8

FEW
f and evil have been . . . . Gen 47:9
f days and full of . . . . Job 14:1
Let his days be *f* . . . . Ps 109:8
let your words be *f* . . . . Eccl 5:2
there are *f* who find it . . . . . . Matt 7:14
but the laborers are *f* . . . . Matt 9:37
called, but *f* chosen . . . . Matt 20:16
"Lord, are there *f* . . . . Luke 13:23
prepared, in which a *f* . . . . . . 1 Pet 3:20
I have a *f* things . . . . Rev 2:20

FIDELITY
but showing all good *f* . . . . . Titus 2:10

FIELD
and to every beast of the *f* . . Gen 2:20
f which the LORD has . . . . Gen 27:27
gleaned in the *f* after the . . . . Ruth 2:3
even the beasts of the *f* . . . . Ps 8:7
Let the *f* be joyful . . . . Ps 96:12
as a flower of the *f*, so he . . Ps 103:15
went by the *f* of the lazy . . Prov 24:30
She considers a *f* and . . . . . Prov 31:16
to house; they add *f* . . . . Is 5:8
becomes a fruitful *f* . . . . Is 32:15
is like the flower of the *f* . . . . . . Is 40:6
beast of the *f* will honor . . . . . Is 43:20
all the trees of the *f* shall . . . . Is 55:12
"Buy the *f* for money . . . . Jer 32:25
thrive like a plant in the *f* . . Ezek 16:5
shall be plowed like a *f* . . . . . Mic 3:12
Consider the lilies of the *f* . . Matt 6:28
clothes the grass of the *f* . . . Matt 6:30
The *f* is the world . . . . Matt 13:38
and buys that *f* . . . . Matt 13:44
let him who is in the *f* . . . . Matt 24:18
f has been called the . . . . Matt 27:8
which today is in the *f* . . . . Luke 12:28
Two men will be in the *f* . . Luke 17:36
you are God's *f* . . . . 1 Cor 3:9
the *f* he will pass away . . . James 1:10

FIELD OF BLOOD
A field bought as a cemetery for Judas's burial, Matt 27:1–10
Predicted in the O.T., Zech 11:12, 13

FIELDS
and sends waters on the *f* . . . Job 5:10
nor enter the *f* of the . . . . . . Prov 23:10
f yield no food . . . . Hab 3:17
living out in the *f* . . . . Luke 2:8
eyes and look at the *f* . . . . . . John 4:35

FIERCE
the *f* wrath of our God . . . . Ezra 10:14
f wrath has gone over me . . . Ps 88:16
A *f* lion is in the streets . . . Prov 26:13
the *f* anger of the LORD . . . . Jer 4:8
in the day of His *f* anger . . . Lam 1:12
turn away from His *f* anger . . Jon 3:9
the tombs, exceedingly *f* . . . . Matt 8:28
are driven by *f* winds . . . . . . James 3:4

FIERCENESS
f has deceived you . . . . Jer 49:16
the winepress of the *f* . . . . . . Rev 19:15

FIERY
the LORD sent *f* serpents . . . . Num 21:6
right hand came a *f* . . . . Deut 33:2
shall make them as a *f* . . . . Ps 21:9
their flocks to *f* lightning . . . . Ps 78:48
offspring will be a *f* . . . . Is 14:29
burning *f* furnace . . . . Dan 3:6
from the burning *f* furnace . . Dan 3:17
f darts of the wicked one . . . . Eph 6:16
concerning the *f* trial . . . . . . 1 Pet 4:12
horse, *f* red, went out . . . . Rev 6:4
f red dragon having . . . . Rev 12:3

FIFTEEN
about *f* thousand all who . . . Judg 8:10
add to your days *f* years . . . 2 Kin 20:6
remained with him *f* days . . . Gal 1:18

FIFTH
morning were the *f* day . . . . . Gen 1:23
He opened the *f* seal . . . . Rev 6:9
the *f* angel poured out . . . . . Rev 16:10

FIFTY
nine hundred and *f* years . . . Gen 9:29
Suppose there were *f* . . . . . . Gen 18:24
f prophets of Baal, and . . . 1 Kin 18:19
denarii, and the other *f* . . . . Luke 7:41
sit down in groups of *f* . . . . . Luke 9:14
down quickly and write *f* . . Luke 16:6
"You are not yet *f* years . . . John 8:57

FIG
f leaves together . . . . Gen 3:7
f trees and pomegranates . . . . Deut 8:8
his vine and his *f* . . . . 1 Kin 4:25
from his own *f* tree . . . . . . 2 Kin 18:31
fruit falling from a *f* . . . . Is 34:4
and the *f* tree has withered . . Joel 1:12
f tree and the vine yield . . . . . Joel 2:22
f tree may not blossom . . . . . Hab 3:17
immediately the *f* tree . . . . . Matt 21:19
parable from the *f* tree . . . . Matt 24:32
saw the *f* tree dried up . . . Mark 11:20
fruit on this *f* . . . . Luke 13:7
"Look at the *f* . . . . Luke 21:29
'I saw you under the *f* . . . . . John 1:50
Can a *f* tree . . . . James 3:12
f tree drops its late . . . . Rev 6:13

FIGHT
The LORD will *f* for you . . . . . Ex 14:14
like men, and *f* . . . . 1 Sam 4:9
you go with me to *f* . . . . 1 Kin 22:4
Our God will *f* for us . . . . Neh 4:20
My servants would *f* . . . . . . John 18:36
to him, let us not *f* . . . . Acts 23:9
Thus I *f*: not as one who . . . 1 Cor 9:26
F the good *f* . . . . 1 Tim 6:12
have fought the good *f* . . . . . 2 Tim 4:7
You *f* and war . . . . James 4:2

FIGHTS
your God is He who *f* . . . . . Josh 23:10
because my lord *f* . . . . 1 Sam 25:28
f come from among . . . . James 4:1

FIGS
puts forth her green *f* . . . . . . Song 2:13
f set before the . . . . Jer 24:1
from thornbushes or *f* . . . . . . Matt 7:16
men do not gather *f* . . . . Luke 6:44
or a grapevine bear *f* . . . . . James 3:12

FIGURATIVELY
brethren, I have *f* . . . . 1 Cor 4:6

FIGURE
using no *f* of speech . . . . . . John 16:29

FILL
f the earth and subdue . . . . . . Gen 1:28
multiply, and *f* the earth . . . . . Gen 9:1
f their sacks with grain . . . . Gen 42:25
"*F* four waterpots . . . . 1 Kin 18:33
He will yet *f* your mouth . . . . . Job 8:21
f my mouth with . . . . Job 23:4
wealth, that I may *f* . . . . Prov 8:21
out of his wings will *f* the . . . . . . Is 8:8
"Do I not *f* heaven . . . . Jer 23:24
f this temple with . . . . Hag 2:7
f such a great multitude . . . Matt 15:33
"*F* the waterpots . . . . John 2:7
hope *f* you with all joy . . . . Rom 15:13
that He might *f* . . . . Eph 4:10
so as always to *f* . . . . 1 Thess 2:16

FILLED
f her pitcher, and came . . . . Gen 24:16
you shall be *f* with bread . . . . Ex 16:12
the LORD *f* the tabernacle . . . Ex 40:34
all the earth shall be *f* . . . . Num 14:21
f the house of the LORD . . . . 1 Kin 8:11
So they ate and were *f* . . . . . Neh 9:25
the whole earth be *f* . . . . Ps 72:19
they are *f* with good . . . . Ps 104:28
Then our mouth was *f* . . . . Ps 126:2
barns will be *f* with . . . . Prov 3:10
of his lips he shall be *f* . . . . Prov 18:20
for they shall be *f* . . . . Matt 5:6
they all ate and were *f* . . . . Matt 14:20
"Let the children be *f* . . . . . Mark 7:27
in spirit, *f* with wisdom . . . . . Luke 2:40
f with the Holy Spirit . . . . Luke 4:1
were *f* with fear, saying . . . . Luke 5:26
he would gladly have *f* . . . Luke 15:16
they *f* them up to the brim . . John 2:7
f twelve baskets with the . . . John 6:13
sorrow has *f* your heart . . . . John 16:6
were all *f* with the Holy . . . . . Acts 2:4
why has Satan *f* your heart . . Acts 5:3
being *f* with all . . . . Rom 1:29
full of goodness, *f* . . . . Rom 15:14
that you may be *f* . . . . Eph 3:19
but be *f* with the Spirit . . . . . Eph 5:18
being *f* with the fruits . . . . Phil 1:11
peace, be warmed and *f* . . James 2:16

FILLED WITH THE HOLY SPIRIT
He will also be *f* . . . . Luke 1:15
and Elizabeth was *f* . . . . Luke 1:41
father Zacharias was *f* . . . . . Luke 1:67
Then Jesus, being *f* . . . . Luke 4:1
And they were all *f* . . . . Acts 2:4
Peter, *f*, said to them . . . . Acts 4:8
and they were all *f*, ... Acts 4:31
your sight and be *f* . . . . Acts 9:17
who also is called Paul, *f*, . . . Acts 13:9

FILTH
has washed away the *f* . . . . Is 4:4
been made as the *f* . . . . 1 Cor 4:13
the removal of the *f* . . . . 1 Pet 3:21

FILTHINESS
from all your *f* . . . . Ezek 36:25
ourselves from all *f* . . . . 2 Cor 7:1
lay aside all *f* . . . . James 1:21
abominations and the *f* . . . . . Rev 17:4

FILTHY
is abominable and *f* . . . . Job 15:16
with *f* garments . . . . Zech 3:3
malice, blasphemy, *f* . . . . Col 3:8
poor man in *f* clothes . . . . . . James 2:2
oppressed by the *f* . . . . 2 Pet 2:7
let him be *f* . . . . Rev 22:11

FIND
"If I *f* in Sodom fifty . . . . Gen 18:26
not *f* the household idols . . Gen 31:35
Can we *f* such a one as . . . . Gen 41:38
straw where you can *f* it . . . . . Ex 5:11
that I may *f* grace in Your . . Ex 33:13
sure your sin will *f* . . . . Num 32:23
you will *f* Him if you seek . . Deut 4:29
"Let me *f* favor in your . . . . Ruth 2:13
f the arrows which I . . . . . 1 Sam 20:36
f in the book of the . . . . Ezra 4:15
Can you *f* out the limits of . . . Job 11:7
knew where I might *f* Him . . Job 23:3
Almighty, we cannot *f* . . . . . Job 37:23
but they will not *f* me . . . . . . Prov 1:28
life to those who *f* . . . . Prov 4:22
seek me diligently will *f* . . . . Prov 8:17
word wisely will *f* good . . . Prov 16:20
can *f* a virtuous wife . . . . . . Prov 31:10
that no one can *f* . . . . Eccl 3:11
waters, for you will *f* . . . . Eccl 11:1
if you *f* my beloved . . . . Song 5:8
f Me, when you search for . . Jer 29:13
seek, and you will *f* . . . . Matt 7:7
and there are few who *f* it . . . Matt 7:14
for My sake will *f* . . . . Matt 10:39
will *f* a piece of money . . . . Matt 17:27
when he comes, will *f* . . . . . Matt 24:46
you will *f* a colt tied . . . . Mark 11:2
he *f* you sleeping . . . . Mark 13:36
f a Babe wrapped . . . . Luke 2:12
seek, and you will *f* . . . . Luke 11:9
you will *f* a colt tied . . . . . . Luke 19:30

f no fault in this Man ...... Luke 23:4
seek Me and not *f* Me ...... John 7:34
not *f* them in the prison .... Acts 5:22
I *f* then a law .... Rom 7:21
f grace to help in .... Heb 4:16
seek death and will not *f* it ... Rev 9:6

FINDING
great things past *f* .... Job 9:10
rest; and *f* none .... Luke 11:24
and His ways past *f* .... Rom 11:33

FINDS
one who *f* great treasure .. Ps 119:162
the man who *f* wisdom ..... Prov 3:13
whoever *f* me *f* life .... Prov 8:35
f a wife *f* a good .... Prov 18:22
Whatever your hand *f* ...... Eccl 9:10
You the fatherless *f* mercy .. Hos 14:3
and he who seeks *f* .... Matt 7:8
f his life will lose .... Matt 10:39
he *f* it empty, swept, and .. Matt 12:44
and he who seeks *f* .... Luke 11:10
carefully until she *f* it ...... Luke 15:8

FINE
ate up the seven *f* looking ... Gen 41:4
Then I beat them as *f* .... 2 Sam 22:43
gold, yea, than much *f* ...... Ps 19:10
than gold, yes, than *f* gold .. Prov 8:19
f gold is a wise .... Prov 25:12
her clothing is *f* linen ..... Prov 31:22
set on bases of *f* gold ...... Song 5:15
more rare than *f* .... Is 13:12
and for *f* clothing .... Is 23:18
how changed the *f* .... Lam 4:1
Then he bought *f* linen ... Mark 15:46
rings, in *f* apparel .... James 2:2
His feet were like *f* brass .... Rev 1:15
for the *f* linen is the .... Rev 19:8

FINGER
written with the *f* .... Ex 31:18
written with the *f* of God ... Deut 9:10
f shall be thicker .... 1 Kin 12:10
the pointing of the *f* .... Is 58:9
demons with the *f* of ..... Luke 11:20
dip the tip of his *f* .... Luke 16:24
the ground with His *f* .... John 8:6
"Reach your *f* .... John 20:27

FINGERS
the work of Your *f* .... Ps 8:3
he points with his *f* .... Prov 6:13
Bind them on your *f* .... Prov 7:3
that which their own *f* .... Is 2:8
In the same hour the *f* of a ... Dan 5:5
with one of their *f* .... Matt 23:4
put His *f* in his ears .... Mark 7:33

FINISH
We *f* our years like a sigh .... Ps 90:9
to *f* the transgression .... Dan 9:24
he has enough to *f* .... Luke 14:28
has given Me to *f* .... John 5:36
so that I may *f* .... Acts 20:24

FINISHED
house of the LORD was *f* ... 1 Kin 7:51
f the work which You ..... John 17:4
He said, "It is *f* .... John 19:30
I have *f* the race .... 2 Tim 4:7
thousand years were *f* ...... Rev 20:3

FIRE
rained brimstone and *f* .... Gen 19:24
to him in a flame of *f* .... Ex 3:2
the pillar of *f* by night ...... Ex 13:22
descended upon it in *f* ...... Ex 19:18
made, burned it in the *f* ...... Ex 32:20
by day, and *f* was over ...... Ex 40:38
profane *f* before the LORD ... Lev 10:1
through the *f* to Molech .... Lev 18:21
like the appearance of *f* .... Num 9:15
the *f* was quenched .... Num 11:2
from the midst of the *f* ..... Deut 5:24
God, who answers by *f* ... 1 Kin 18:24
the *f* of the LORD fell ...... 1 Kin 18:38
LORD was not in the *f* ..... 1 Kin 19:12
of *f* appeared with horses .. 2 Kin 2:11
I was musing, the *f* .... Ps 39:3
we went through *f* .... Ps 66:12
they have set *f* .... Ps 74:7
f goes before Him .... Ps 97:3
His ministers a flame of *f* .... Ps 104:4
f and hail, snow and .... Ps 148:8
burns as the *f* .... Is 9:18
says the LORD, whose *f* .... Is 31:9
you walk through the *f* .... Is 43:2
f that burns all the .... Is 65:5
My fury come forth like *f* ..... Jer 4:4
their daughters in the *f* ...... Jer 7:31
His waist and downward, *f* .. Ezek 8:2
in the midst of the *f* .... Dan 3:25
the smell of *f* was not on ... Dan 3:27
He break out like *f* .... Amos 5:6
for conflict by *f* .... Amos 7:4
a brand plucked from the *f* .. Zech 3:2
like a refiner's *f* .... Mal 3:2
the Holy Spirit and *f* .... Matt 3:11
chaff with unquenchable *f* .. Matt 3:12
shall be in danger of hell *f* .. Matt 5:22
he often falls into the *f* ... Matt 17:15
into the everlasting *f* ..... Matt 25:41
f is not quenched .... Mark 9:44
"I came to send *f* .... Luke 12:49
tongues, as of *f* .... Acts 2:3
off the creature into the *f* ... Acts 28:5
coals of *f* on his head ..... Rom 12:20
f taking vengeance .... 2 Thess 1:8
His ministers a flame of *f* .... Heb 1:7
and that burned with *f* ..... Heb 12:18
our God is a consuming *f* .. Heb 12:29
And the tongue is a *f* ...... James 3:6
vengeance of eternal *f* .... Jude 7
His eyes like a flame of *f* .... Rev 1:14
f came down from God ..... Rev 20:9
into the lake of *f* .... Rev 20:14

FIREBRAND
f plucked from the .... Amos 4:11

FIREBRANDS
a madman who throws *f* .. Prov 26:18
two stubs of smoking *f* .... Is 7:4

FIRM
their strength is *f* .... Ps 73:4
shall stand *f* with him .... Ps 89:28
Take *f* hold of instruction .. Prov 4:13
f the feeble knees .... Is 35:3
of the hope *f* to the .... Heb 3:6

FIRMAMENT
Thus God made the *f* .... Gen 1:7
f shows His handiwork .... Ps 19:1
in His mighty *f* .... Ps 150:1
brightness of the *f* .... Dan 12:3

FIRST
the morning were the *f* day .. Gen 1:5
cows ate up the *f* seven ... Gen 41:20
The *f* of the firstfruits of .... Ex 23:19
"Give the *f* woman the .... 1 Kin 3:27
The *f* one to plead his ..... Prov 18:17
f father sinned .... Is 43:27
the *F* and I am the Last ..... Is 44:6
f was like a lion, and had ..... Dan 7:4
F be reconciled to your ..... Matt 5:24
seek *f* the kingdom of ...... Matt 6:33
F remove the plank from .... Matt 7:5
unless he *f* binds the ...... Matt 12:29
man is worse than the *f* ... Matt 12:45
who are *f* will be last ..... Matt 19:30
desires to be *f* .... Matt 20:27
This is the *f* and great .... Matt 22:38
f the blade, then the .... Mark 4:28
that Elijah must come *f* .... Mark 9:11
f shall be slave .... Mark 10:44
the *f* commandment ...... Mark 12:30
And the gospel must *f* .... Mark 13:10
He appeared *f* to Mary .... Mark 16:9
let me *f* go and bury my ... Luke 9:59
f He must suffer many .... Luke 17:25
f took a wife, and died .... Luke 20:29
f found his own brother .... John 1:41
him throw a stone at her *f* .. John 8:7
disciples were *f* called ..... Acts 11:26
evil, of the Jew *f* .... Rom 2:9
"Or who has *f* given ...... Rom 11:35
f apostles, second .... 1 Cor 12:28
f man Adam became a ... 1 Cor 15:45
f a willing mind .... 2 Cor 8:12
that we who *f* trusted .... Eph 1:12
the *f* commandment with .... Eph 6:2
in Christ will rise *f* .... 1 Thess 4:16
the falling away comes *f* .. 2 Thess 2:3
Therefore I exhort *f* of all .. 1 Tim 2:1
For Adam was formed *f* ... 1 Tim 2:13
let them *f* learn to show .... 1 Tim 5:4
to teach you again the *f* ..... Heb 5:12
f covenant had been .... Heb 8:7
from above is *f* pure ...... James 3:17
knowing this *f*, that no .... 2 Pet 1:20
this *f*: that scoffers will ..... 2 Pet 3:3
love Him because He *f* ... 1 John 4:19
I am the *F* and the .... Rev 1:17
you have left your *f* .... Rev 2:4
The *f* angel sounded .... Rev 8:7
is the *f* resurrection .... Rev 20:5
f earth had passed away .... Rev 21:1

FIRST AND THE LAST
and the Omega, the *F* .... Rev 1:11
not be afraid; I am the *F* .... Rev 1:17
'These things says the *F*, ... Rev 2:8
and the End, the *F* .... Rev 22:13

FIRST-RIPE
f fruit which my soul .... Mic 7:1

FIRSTBORN
"I am Esau your *f* .... Gen 27:19
"Israel is My son, My *f* .... Ex 4:22
LORD struck all the *f* .... Ex 12:29
"Consecrate to Me all the *f* ... Ex 13:2
was the *f* of Israel .... Num 26:5
destroyed all the *f* in Egypt .. Ps 78:51
I will make him My *f* .... Ps 89:27
Shall I give my *f* .... Mic 6:7
as one grieves for a *f* ..... Zech 12:10
brought forth her *f* .... Matt 1:25
brought forth her *f* Son ..... Luke 2:7
that He might be the *f* ..... Rom 8:29
invisible God, the *f* .... Col 1:15
the beginning, the *f* .... Col 1:18
witness, the *f* from .... Rev 1:5

FIRSTFRUIT
For if the *f* is holy .... Rom 11:16

FIRSTFRUITS
the *f* of your harvest to .... Lev 23:10
bring the *f* of our ground .. Neh 10:35
with the *f* of all your .... Prov 3:9
also who have the *f* .... Rom 8:23
and has become the *f* ..... 1 Cor 15:20
order: Christ the *f* .... 1 Cor 15:23
might be a kind of *f* ...... James 1:18
among men, being *f* .... Rev 14:4

FISH
over the *f* of the sea .... Gen 1:28
f taken in a cruel net .... Eccl 9:12
had prepared a great *f* ...... Jon 1:17
do You make men like *f* .... Hab 1:14
Or if he asks for a *f* .... Matt 7:10
belly of the great *f* .... Matt 12:40
five loaves and two *f* ...... Matt 14:17
and likewise the *f* .... John 21:13

FISHERMEN
The *f* also will mourn .... Is 19:8
I will send for many *f* ...... Jer 16:16

FISHERS
and I will make you *f* ...... Matt 4:19

FIT
and looking back, is *f* ..... Luke 9:62

FITTING
Therefore it is not *f* for the .. Esth 3:8
Is it *f* to say to a .... Job 34:18
Luxury is not *f* .... Prov 19:10
so honor is not *f* .... Prov 26:1
things which are not *f* ..... Rom 1:28
husbands, as is *f* in the ...... Col 3:18
a High Priest was *f* .... Heb 7:26

FIVE
bring out those *f* kings .... Josh 10:22
f smooth stones .... 1 Sam 17:40
about *f* thousand men ..... Matt 14:21
and *f* were foolish .... Matt 25:2
to one he gave *f* talents ... Matt 25:15
Are not *f* sparrows sold .... Luke 12:6
bought *f* yoke of oxen .... Luke 14:19
you have had *f* husbands .. John 4:18
speak *f* words with my ... 1 Cor 14:19

FIXED
f My limit for it .... Job 38:10
is a great gulf *f* .... Luke 16:26

FLAME
appeared to him in a *f* .... Ex 3:2
f will dry out his .... Job 15:30
His ministers a *f* of fire ...... Ps 104:4
f consumes the chaff .... Is 5:24
and his Holy One for a *f* ..... Is 10:17
and tempest and the *f* .... Is 29:6
nor shall the *f* scorch you ..... Is 43:2
hot, the *f* of the fire killed .. Dan 3:22
behind them a *f* .... Joel 2:3
am tormented in this *f* .... Luke 16:24
and His ministers a *f* .... Heb 1:7
and His eyes like a *f* .... Rev 1:14

FLAMES
the LORD divides the *f* .... Ps 29:7

FLAMING
f sword which turned .... Gen 3:24
f fire in their land .... Ps 105:32
in *f* fire taking .... 2 Thess 1:8

FLANKS
Strengthen your *f* .... Nah 2:1

FLASK
alabaster *f* of fragrant oil .. Luke 7:37

FLATTER
I do not know how to *f* ..... Job 32:22
They *f* with their .... Ps 5:9

FLATTERED
Nevertheless they *f* .... Ps 78:36

FLATTERING
f mouth works ruin .... Prov 26:28
f speech deceive .... Rom 16:18
any time did we use *f* ..... 1 Thess 2:5
swelling words, *f* .... Jude 16

FLATTERS
with one who *f* with ...... Prov 20:19
f his neighbor spreads ..... Prov 29:5

FLATTERY
shall corrupt with *f* .... Dan 11:32

FLAVOR
the salt loses its *f* .... Matt 5:13

FLAVORLESS
f food be eaten .... Job 6:6

FLAX
f He will not quench .... Is 42:3
f He will not quench ...... Matt 12:20

FLED
Moses *f* from the face of ..... Ex 2:15
f before the men of Ai .... Josh 7:4
The sea saw it and *f* .... Ps 114:3
who have *f* for refuge .... Heb 6:18

FLEE
f away secretly .... Gen 31:27
those who hate You *f* ..... Num 10:35
such a man as I *f* .... Neh 6:11
who see me outside *f* .... Ps 31:11
Or where can I *f* .... Ps 139:7
wicked *f* when no one ..... Prov 28:1
And the shadows *f* .... Song 2:17
f to Egypt, and stay there .. Matt 2:13
who are in Judea *f* .... Matt 24:16
F sexual immorality .... 1 Cor 6:18
f these things and .... 1 Tim 6:11
F also youthful lusts ...... 2 Tim 2:22
devil and he will *f* .... James 4:7

FLEECE
there is dew on the *f* only .. Judg 6:37

FLESH
See ACCORDING TO THE FLESH
bone of my bones and *f* ..... Gen 2:23
shall become one *f* .... Gen 2:24
f had corrupted their .... Gen 6:12
f I shall see God .... Job 19:26
My *f* also will rest in .... Ps 16:9
What can *f* do to me .... Ps 56:4
f longs for You in a dry ...... Ps 63:1
that they were but *f* .... Ps 78:39
my heart and my *f* .... Ps 84:2
Who gives food to all *f* ..... Ps 136:25
f shall bless His holy .... Ps 145:21
It will be health to your *f* .... Prov 3:8
and health to all their *f* .... Prov 4:22
mouth cause your *f* to sin .... Eccl 5:6
is wearisome to the *f* ...... Eccl 12:12
And all *f* shall see it .... Is 40:5
"All *f* is grass .... Is 40:6
give them a heart of *f* ..... Ezek 11:19
of stone out of your *f* ..... Ezek 36:26
out My Spirit on all *f* .... Joel 2:28
Be silent, all *f*, before the .. Zech 2:13
two shall become one *f* ..... Matt 19:5
were shortened, no *f* ...... Matt 24:22
is willing, but the *f* is ..... Matt 26:41
shall become one *f* .... Mark 10:8
but the *f* is weak .... Mark 14:38
f shall see the salvation ...... Luke 3:6
And the Word became *f* .... John 1:14
is born of the *f* is *f* .... John 3:6
I shall give is My *f* .... John 6:51
unless you eat the *f* .... John 6:53
Whoever eats My *f* and .... John 6:54
For My *f* is food indeed .... John 6:55
f profits nothing .... John 6:63
according to the *f* .... John 8:15
Him authority over all *f* .... John 17:2
out of My Spirit on all *f* .... Acts 2:17
did His *f* see corruption .... Acts 2:31
no *f* will be justified in ..... Rom 3:20
when we were in the *f* ...... Rom 7:5
in my *f*) nothing good ...... Rom 7:18
of God, but with the *f* ...... Rom 7:25
not walk according to the *f* .. Rom 8:1
on the things of the *f* .... Rom 8:5
in the *f* cannot please God .. Rom 8:8
you are not in the *f* .... Rom 8:9
to the *f* you will die .... Rom 8:13
no provision for the *f* ..... Rom 13:14
f should glory in His .... 1 Cor 1:29
for the destruction of the *f* .. 1 Cor 5:5
"shall become one *f* .... 1 Cor 6:16
there is one kind of *f* ..... 1 Cor 15:39
no one according to the *f* .. 2 Cor 5:16
from all filthiness of the *f* ... 2 Cor 7:1
war according to the *f* ..... 2 Cor 10:3
immediately confer with *f* ... Gal 1:16
law no *f* shall be justified .... Gal 2:16
which I now live in the *f* .... Gal 2:20
not fulfill the lust of the *f* .... Gal 5:16
For the *f* lusts .... Gal 5:17
have crucified the *f* .... Gal 5:24
his *f* will of the *f* reap .... Gal 6:8
good showing in the *f* .... Gal 6:12
may boast in your *f* .... Gal 6:13
one ever hated his own *f* .... Eph 5:29
two shall become one *f* ..... Eph 5:31
have no confidence in the *f* .. Phil 3:3
of His *f* through death .... Col 1:22
was manifested in the *f* ... 1 Tim 3:16
the veil, that is, His *f* ...... Heb 10:20
f has ceased from sin .... 1 Pet 4:1
of his time in the *f* .... 1 Pet 4:2
the lust of the *f* .... 1 John 2:16
has come in the *f* .... 1 John 4:2
dreamers defile the *f* .... Jude 8

FLESH AND BLOOD
f has not revealed this .... Matt 16:17
f cannot inherit the ...... 1 Cor 15:50
do not wrestle against *f* ..... Eph 6:12
have partaken of *f* .... Heb 2:14

FLESHLY
f wisdom but by the .... 2 Cor 1:12
law of a *f* commandment .... Heb 7:16
f lusts which war against .. 1 Pet 2:11

FLIES
will send swarms of *f* .... Ex 8:21
He sent swarms of *f* .... Ps 78:45
of the arrow that *f* by day .... Ps 91:5
Dead *f* putrefy the .... Eccl 10:1

FLIGHT
put ten thousand to *f* ..... Deut 32:30
f shall perish from .... Amos 2:14
And pray that your *f* .... Matt 24:20
turned to *f* the armies of ... Heb 11:34

FLINT
will seem like *f* .... Is 5:28
set My face like a *f* .... Is 50:7

FLINTY
out of the *f* rock .... Deut 8:15
oil from the *f* rock .... Deut 32:13

FLOAT
and he made the iron *f* ..... 2 Kin 6:6

FLOCK
of the firstborn of his *f* .... Gen 4:4
Go now to the *f* and bring .. Gen 27:9
pass through all your *f* .... Gen 30:32
put them with Laban's *f* .... Gen 30:40
Moses was tending the *f* .... Ex 3:1
Your people like a *f* .... Ps 77:20
wilderness like a *f* .... Ps 78:52
lead Joseph like a *f* .... Ps 80:1
their families like a *f* .... Ps 107:41
the footsteps of the *f* .... Song 1:8
He will feed His *f* .... Is 40:11
with the shepherd of His *f* ... Is 63:11
"You have scattered My *f* .... Jer 23:2
gather the remnant of My *f* .. Jer 23:3
oil, for the young of the *f* ... Jer 31:12
you do not feed the *f* .... Ezek 34:3
are My *f*, the *f* .... Ezek 34:31
though the *f* be cut .... Hab 3:17
my God, "Feed the *f* .... Zech 11:4
sheep of the *f* will be ..... Matt 26:31
watch over their *f* by night .. Luke 2:8
"Do not fear, little *f* ...... Luke 12:32
there will be one *f* .... John 10:16
and to all the *f* .... Acts 20:28
not sparing the *f* .... Acts 20:29
of the milk of the *f* .... 1 Cor 9:7
Shepherd the *f* of God ...... 1 Pet 5:2
examples to the *f* .... 1 Pet 5:3

FLOCKS
fed the rest of Laban's *f* ... Gen 30:36
their little ones, their *f* ..... Gen 50:8
Also take your *f* and your ... Ex 12:32
are clothed with *f* .... Ps 65:13
the *f* of your companions ... Song 1:7
lion among *f* of sheep .... Mic 5:8
for they shall feed their *f* .. Zeph 3:13

FLOOD
the waters of the *f* .... Gen 7:10
a *f* to destroy all flesh ...... Gen 9:15
on the earth after the *f* .... Gen 10:32
sat enthroned at the *F* .... Ps 29:10
them away like a *f* .... Ps 90:5
enemy comes in like a *f* ...... Is 59:19

the days before the *f* . . . . . . Matt 24:38
when the *f* arose, the . . . . . . Luke 6:48
bringing in the *f* . . . . 2 Pet 2:5
of his mouth like a *f* . . . . Rev 12:15

FLOODS
me, and the *f* of . . . . Ps 18:4
f on the dry ground . . . . Is 44:3
and the *f* surrounded me . . . . . . Jon 2:3
rain descended, the *f* . . . . Matt 7:25

FLOOR
down to the threshing *f* . . . . . Ruth 3:6
came to the threshing *f* . . . . Ruth 3:14
bought the threshing *f* . . . 2 Sam 24:24
clean out His threshing *f* . . . Matt 3:12
clean out His threshing *f* . . . Luke 3:17

FLOUR
a handful of *f* in a bin . . . . 1 Kin 17:12
bin of *f* was not used up . . 1 Kin 17:16
"Then bring some *f* . . . . 2 Kin 4:41

FLOURISH
the righteous shall *f* . . . . Ps 72:7
f in the courts of our God . . . . Ps 92:13
tent of the upright will *f* . . . Prov 14:11

FLOURISHED
your care for me has *f* . . . . . . Phil 4:10

FLOURISHES
In the morning it *f* . . . . Ps 90:6

FLOW
f away as waters which . . . . . . Ps 58:7
and the waters *f* . . . . Ps 147:18
that its spices may *f* . . . . Song 4:16
all nations shall *f* . . . . Is 2:2
and peoples shall *f* to it . . . . . . Mic 4:1
who had a *f* of blood . . . . . . Matt 9:20
f of blood for twelve . . . . . . Mark 5:25
immediately her *f* of . . . . Luke 8:44
of his heart will *f* . . . . John 7:38

FLOWER
comes forth like a *f* . . . . Job 14:2
as a *f* of the field . . . . Ps 103:15
beauty is a fading *f* . . . . Is 28:4
is like the *f* of the . . . . Is 40:6
grass withers, the *f* . . . . Is 40:7
if she is past the *f* . . . . 1 Cor 7:36
of man as the *f* . . . . 1 Pet 1:24

FLOWERS
f appear on the earth . . . . . . Song 2:12

FLOWING
'a land *f* with milk . . . . Deut 6:3
of wisdom is a *f* . . . . Prov 18:4
the Gentiles like a *f* . . . . Is 66:12

FLUTE
play the harp and *f* . . . . Gen 4:21
sound of the horn, *f* . . . . Dan 3:5
saw the *f* players . . . . Matt 9:23
"We played the *f* for you . . Luke 7:32

FLUTES
instruments and *f* . . . . Ps 150:4

FLUTISTS
harpists, musicians, *f* . . . . . . Rev 18:22

FLY
let birds *f* above the earth . . . Gen 1:20
I would *f* away and be . . . . Ps 55:6
soon cut off, and we *f* . . . . Ps 90:10
they *f* away like an . . . . Prov 23:5
being caused to *f* swiftly . . . . Dan 9:21

FLYING
a *f* swallow, so a curse . . . . . Prov 26:2

FOAL
a colt, the *f* of a donkey . . . . . Zech 9:9
a colt, the *f* of a donkey . . . . Matt 21:5

FOAMS
so that he *f* at the mouth . . . Luke 9:39

FOE
and scattered the *f* . . . . Ps 18:14

FOES
my enemies and *f* . . . . Ps 27:2
I will beat down his *f* . . . . Ps 89:23

FOLD
are not of this *f* . . . . John 10:16
a cloak You will *f* . . . . Heb 1:12

FOLDING
slumber, a little *f* . . . . Prov 6:10
f of the hands to sleep . . . . Prov 24:33

FOLLOW
willing to *f* me to this land . . Gen 24:5
f what is altogether . . . . Deut 16:20
If the LORD is God, *f* . . . . . . 1 Kin 18:21
shall *f* me all the days . . . . Ps 23:6
to Me, you who *f* . . . . Is 51:1
"*F* Me, and I will make . . . . . Matt 4:19
f You wherever You go . . . . Matt 8:19
"*F* Me, and let the dead . . . . Matt 8:22
He said to him, "*F* . . . . Matt 9:9
f after Me is not worthy . . . Matt 10:38
his cross, and *f* Me . . . . Matt 16:24
up his cross, and *f* . . . . Mark 8:34
someone who does not *f* . . . Mark 9:38
the cross, and *f* Me . . . . Mark 10:21
signs will *f* those who . . . . Mark 16:17
he does not *f* with us . . . . . . Luke 9:49
I will *f* You wherever . . . . . . Luke 9:57
said to another, "*F* Me . . . . . Luke 9:59
not go after them or *f* . . . . . Luke 17:23
and come, *f* Me . . . . Luke 18:22
f him into the house . . . . . . Luke 22:10
the sheep *f* him, for they . . . John 10:4
will by no means *f* . . . . John 10:5
serves Me, let him *f* . . . . John 12:26
on your garment and *f* . . . . . Acts 12:8
those of some men *f* . . . . . . 1 Tim 5:24
God to you, whose faith *f* . . . Heb 13:7
that you should *f* . . . . 1 Pet 2:21
f the Lamb wherever He . . . . Rev 14:4
and their works *f* . . . . Rev 14:13

FOLLOWED
f the LORD my God . . . . Josh 14:8
LORD took me as I *f* . . . . Amos 7:15
left their nets and *f* Him . . . . Matt 4:20
great multitudes *f* Him . . . . . . Matt 8:1
Peter *f* Him at a distance . . Matt 26:58
women who *f* Jesus . . . . Matt 27:55
we have left all and *f* . . . . . Mark 10:28
sight and *f* Jesus . . . . Mark 10:52
This girl *f* Paul and us . . . . Acts 16:17
spiritual Rock that *f* . . . . 1 Cor 10:4
diligently *f* every good . . . . 1 Tim 5:10
carefully *f* my doctrine . . . . 2 Tim 3:10

FOLLOWING
if you turn away from *f* . . . Num 32:15
away this day from *f* the . . Josh 22:16
back from *f* after you . . . . . . Ruth 1:16
continue *f* the LORD . . . . . 1 Sam 12:14
f the sheep, to be ruler . . . . 2 Sam 7:8
away from *f* the LORD . . . . 2 Chr 25:27
turned, and seeing them *f* . . John 1:38
whom Jesus loved *f* . . . . John 21:20
join in *f* my example . . . . Phil 3:17
f the way of Balaam . . . . 2 Pet 2:15

FOLLOWS
My soul *f* close behind . . . . Ps 63:8
but he who *f* frivolity is . . . Prov 12:11
loves him who *f* . . . . Prov 15:9
f Me shall not walk . . . . John 8:12

FOLLY
taken much notice of *f* . . . . . Job 35:15
not turn back to *f* . . . . Ps 85:8
F is joy to him who is . . . . . Prov 15:21
correction of fools is *f* . . . . . Prov 16:22
F is set in great . . . . Eccl 10:6

FOOD
you it shall be for *f* . . . . Gen 1:29
that lives shall be *f* . . . . Gen 9:3
stranger, giving him *f* . . . . . Deut 10:18
He gives *f* in abundance . . . . Job 36:31
he may bring forth *f* . . . . Ps 104:14
Who gives *f* to all . . . . Ps 136:25
Much *f* is in the . . . . Prov 13:23
feed me with the *f* . . . . Prov 30:8
their *f* in the summer . . . . . Prov 30:25
night, and provides *f* . . . . . . Prov 31:15
f which you eat shall . . . . . . Ezek 4:10
I ate no pleasant *f* . . . . Dan 10:3
the fields yield no *f* . . . . Hab 3:17
that there may be *f* . . . . Mal 3:10
is worthy of his *f* . . . . Matt 10:10
to give them *f* in due . . . . . . Matt 24:45
and you gave Me *f* . . . . Matt 25:35
and he who has *f* . . . . Luke 3:11
Life is more than *f* . . . . Luke 12:23
I have *f* to eat of which . . . . John 4:32
f is to do the will of Him . . . John 4:34
for the *f* which perishes . . . . John 6:27
have you any *f* . . . . John 21:5
they ate their *f* . . . . Acts 2:46
our hearts with *f* . . . . Acts 14:17
destroy with your *f* . . . . Rom 14:15
f makes my brother . . . . 1 Cor 8:13
the same spiritual *f* . . . . 1 Cor 10:3
sower, and bread for *f* . . . . . 2 Cor 9:10
And having *f* and . . . . 1 Tim 6:8
and not solid *f* . . . . Heb 5:12
But solid *f* belongs to . . . . Heb 5:14
of *f* sold his birthright . . . . . Heb 12:16
destitute of daily *f* . . . . James 2:15

FOODS
F for the stomach . . . . 1 Cor 6:13
f which God created . . . . 1 Tim 4:3

FOOL
I have played the *f* . . . . . . 1 Sam 26:21
Should Abner die as a *f* . . 2 Sam 3:33
f has said in his . . . . Ps 14:1
or as a *f* to the correction . . Prov 7:22
is like sport to a *f* . . . . Prov 10:23
f will be servant . . . . Prov 11:29
f is right in his own . . . . Prov 12:15
f lays open his folly . . . . Prov 13:16
A *f* despises his father's . . . . Prov 15:5
a hundred blows on a *f* . . . Prov 17:10
is too lofty for a *f* . . . . Prov 24:7
Do not answer a *f* . . . . Prov 26:4
"As it happens to the *f*, it . . . Eccl 2:15
A *f* also multiplies words . . Eccl 10:14
whoever says, 'You *f* . . . . Matt 5:22
But God said to him, '*F* . . . Luke 12:20
let him become a *f* that . . . . 1 Cor 3:18
I speak as a *f* . . . . 2 Cor 11:23
I have become a *f* . . . . 2 Cor 12:11

FOOLISH
of the *f* women speaks . . . . . . Job 2:10
I was so *f* and . . . . Ps 73:22
f pulls it down with . . . . Prov 14:1
f man squanders it . . . . Prov 21:20
"For My people are *f* . . . . Jer 4:22
f hearts were darkened . . . . Rom 1:21
Has not God made *f* . . . . 1 Cor 1:20
But God has chosen the *f* . . 1 Cor 1:27
O *f* Galatians . . . . Gal 3:1
nor *f* talking, nor coarse . . . . . Eph 5:4
But avoid *f* and ignorant . . 2 Tim 2:23
were also once *f* . . . . Titus 3:3
But avoid *f* disputes . . . . Titus 3:9

FOOLISHLY
man acts *f*, and a man . . . . Prov 14:17
I speak *f*—I am bold . . . . . . 2 Cor 11:21

FOOLISHNESS
O God, You know my *f* . . . . . . Ps 69:5
Forsake *f* and live . . . . Prov 9:6
of fools proclaims *f* . . . . Prov 12:23
The *f* of a man twists . . . . . . Prov 19:3
F is bound up in the . . . . . . Prov 22:15
devising of *f* is sin . . . . Prov 24:9
person will speak *f* . . . . Is 32:6
of the cross is *f* . . . . 1 Cor 1:18

Because the *f* of God ...... 1 Cor 1:25
this world is *f* with God ... 1 Cor 3:19

FOOLS
f despise wisdom .... Prov 1:7
folly of *f* is deceit .... Prov 14:8
F mock at sin .... Prov 14:9
has no pleasure in *f* .... Eccl 5:4
F and blind! .... Matt 23:17
to be wise, they became *f* .. Rom 1:22
We are *f* for Christ's ...... 1 Cor 4:10
not as *f* but as wise .... Eph 5:15

FOOT
your *f* will tread upon .... Josh 1:3
your sandal off your *f* ...... Josh 5:15
f has trodden shall be ...... Josh 14:9
dash your *f* against a stone .. Ps 91:12
will not allow your *f* .... Ps 121:3
f will not stumble .... Prov 3:23
From the sole of the *f* .... Is 1:6
you turn away your *f* .... Is 58:13
dash your *f* against a stone .. Matt 4:6
f causes you to sin .... Matt 18:8
you dash your *f* .... Luke 4:11
If the *f* should say .... 1 Cor 12:15

FOOTMEN
have run with the *f* .... Jer 12:5

FOOTSTEPS
f were not known .... Ps 77:19
and shall make His *f* .... Ps 85:13

FOOTSTOOL
God, and worship at His *f* .... Ps 99:5
Your enemies Your *f* .... Ps 110:1
throne, and earth is My *f* ..... Is 66:1
by the earth, for it is His *f* .. Matt 5:35
Your enemies Your *f* ..... Matt 22:44
throne, and earth is My *f* ... Acts 7:49
"Sit here at my *f* .... James 2:3

FORBID
come to Me, and do not *f* .. Matt 19:14
said, "Do not *f* him .... Mark 9:39
"Can anyone *f* water ...... Acts 10:47
prophesy, and do not *f* ... 1 Cor 14:39
f that I should boast .... Gal 6:14

FORBIDDEN
LORD your God has *f* you ... Deut 4:23
they were *f* by the Holy .... Acts 16:6

FORBIDDING
confidence, no one *f* ...... Acts 28:31
f us to speak to the ...... 1 Thess 2:16
f to marry .... 1 Tim 4:3

FORCE
violent take it by *f* .... Matt 11:12
come and take Him by *f* ... John 6:15
a testament is in *f* .... Heb 9:17

FORCEFUL
f are right words .... Job 6:25

FORCES
Though they join *f* .... Prov 11:21

FOREFATHERS
f who refused to hear .... Jer 11:10
and oppressed our *f* .... Acts 7:19
conscience, as my *f* .... 2 Tim 1:3

FOREHEADS
strong against their *f* .... Ezek 3:8
put a mark on the *f* .... Ezek 9:4
seal of God on their *f* .... Rev 9:4
his mark on their *f* .... Rev 20:4

FOREIGN
been a stranger in a *f* land ... Ex 2:22
put away the *f* gods .... Josh 24:23
loved many *f* women ...... 1 Kin 11:1
the LORD's song in a *f* land .. Ps 137:4
set out *f* seedlings .... Is 17:10
promise as in a *f* country ... Heb 11:9

FOREIGN GODS
"put away the *f* .... Gen 35:2
to jealousy with *f*; .... Deut 32:16
the LORD and serve *f* ...... Josh 24:20
So they put away the *f* .... Judg 10:16
then put away the *f* .... 1 Sam 7:3
the altars of the *f* .... 2 Chr 14:3
He took away the *f* .... 2 Chr 33:15
forsaken Me and served *f* .... Jer 5:19
to be a proclaimer of *f* .... Acts 17:18

FOREIGNER
"I am a *f* and a .... Gen 23:4
of me, since I am a *f* .... Ruth 2:10
to God except this *f* ...... Luke 17:18
who speaks will be a *f* ... 1 Cor 14:11

FOREIGNERS
from the hand of *f* .... Ps 144:11
with the children of *f* .... Is 2:6
f shall build up your .... Is 60:10
f who were there .... Acts 17:21
longer strangers and *f* ...... Eph 2:19

FOREKNEW
For whom He *f* .... Rom 8:29
His people whom He *f* ..... Rom 11:2

FOREKNOWLEDGE
purpose and *f* of God ...... Acts 2:23
according to the *f* .... 1 Pet 1:2

FOREORDAINED
He indeed was *f* .... 1 Pet 1:20

FORERUNNER
f has entered for us .... Heb 6:20

FORESAW
'I *f* the LORD .... Acts 2:25

FORESEEING
f that God would .... Gal 3:8

FORESEES
A prudent man *f* .... Prov 22:3

FORESKINS
in the flesh of your *f* .... Gen 17:11
f of the Philistines .... 1 Sam 18:25

FOREST
beast of the *f* is Mine .... Ps 50:10
See how great a *f* .... James 3:5

FORESTS
and strips the *f* .... Ps 29:9

FORETOLD
have also *f* these days ...... Acts 3:24
killed those who *f* .... Acts 7:52

FOREVER
See HIS MERCY ENDURES FOREVER
and eat, and live *f* .... Gen 3:22
shall not strive with man *f* ... Gen 6:3
This is My name *f* .... Ex 3:15
and they shall inherit it *f* .... Ex 32:13
to our children *f* .... Deut 29:29
has loved Israel *f* .... 1 Kin 10:9
for His mercy endures *f* ... 2 Chr 5:13
for His mercy endures *f* ... 2 Chr 7:3
I would not live *f* .... Job 7:16
from this generation *f* .... Ps 12:7
LORD sits as King *f* .... Ps 29:10
Do not cast us off *f* .... Ps 44:23
throne, O God, is *f* .... Ps 45:6
"You are a priest *f* .... Ps 110:4
His mercy endures *f* .... Ps 118:1
F, O LORD, Your word is.... Ps 119:89
be moved, but abides *f* ...... Ps 125:1
From this time forth and *f* ... Ps 125:2
This is My resting place *f* .. Ps 132:14
name, O LORD, endures *f* ... Ps 135:13
His mercy endures *f* .... Ps 136:1
will bless Your name *f* .... Ps 145:1
bless His holy name *f* ...... Ps 145:21
who keeps truth *f* .... Ps 146:6
The LORD shall reign *f* ..... Ps 146:10
also established them *f* ...... Ps 148:6
lip shall be established *f* .. Prov 12:19
for riches are not *f* .... Prov 27:24
Trust in the LORD *f* .... Is 26:4
of our God stands *f* .... Is 40:8
My salvation will be *f* .... Is 51:6
will not cast off *f* .... Lam 3:31
be the name of God *f* .... Dan 2:20
Like the stars *f* .... Dan 12:3
of the LORD our God *f* .... Mic 4:5
and the glory *f* .... Matt 6:13
eats this bread will live *f* ... John 6:58
the Christ remains *f* .... John 12:34
He may abide with you *f* .. John 14:16
righteousness endures *f* .... 2 Cor 9:9
who is blessed *f* .... 2 Cor 11:31
to whom be glory *f* .... Gal 1:5
generation, *f* and ever .... Eph 3:21
and Father be glory *f* .... Phil 4:20
throne, O God, is *f* .... Heb 1:8
"You are a priest *f* .... Heb 5:6
f according to the order of .. Heb 6:20
has been perfected *f* .... Heb 7:28
one sacrifice for sins *f* ..... Heb 10:12
yesterday, today, and *f* ..... Heb 13:8
lives and abides *f* .... 1 Pet 1:23
of the LORD endures *f* .... 1 Pet 1:25
blackness of darkness *f* ...... Jude 13
power, both now and *f* .... Jude 25
throne, and to the Lamb, *f* .. Rev 5:13
And they shall reign *f* .... Rev 22:5

FOREVERMORE
Blessed be the LORD *f* .... Ps 89:52
this time forth and *f* .... Ps 113:2
behold, I am alive *f* .... Rev 1:18

FOREWARNED
all such, as we also *f* ..... 1 Thess 4:6

FORGAVE
f the iniquity of my .... Ps 32:5
and *f* him the debt .... Matt 18:27
I *f* you all that debt .... Matt 18:32
to repay, he freely *f* .... Luke 7:42
the one whom he *f* more ... Luke 7:43
God in Christ *f* .... Eph 4:32
even as Christ *f* .... Col 3:13

FORGED
The proud have *f* .... Ps 119:69

FORGERS
But you *f* of lies .... Job 13:4

FORGET
"For God has made me *f* .. Gen 41:51
yourselves, lest you *f* .... Deut 4:23
f the covenant of your ..... Deut 4:31
f the LORD who brought ..... Deut 6:12
the paths of all who *f* .... Job 8:13
all the nations that *f* .... Ps 9:17
this, you who *f* God .... Ps 50:22
f the works of God .... Ps 78:7
I will not *f* Your word ...... Ps 119:16
If I *f* you, O Jerusalem ...... Ps 137:5
My son, do not *f* .... Prov 3:1
f her nursing child .... Is 49:15
f the LORD your Maker .... Is 51:13
virgin *f* her ornaments .... Jer 2:32
f your work and labor ...... Heb 6:10
Do not *f* to entertain .... Heb 13:2
But do not *f* to do good .... Heb 13:16
do not *f* this one thing ...... 2 Pet 3:8

FORGETFUL
not a *f* hearer but a doer .. James 1:25

FORGETFULNESS
in the land of *f* .... Ps 88:12

FORGETS
f the covenant of her .... Prov 2:17
and immediately *f* .... James 1:24

FORGETTING
f those things which .... Phil 3:13

FORGIVE
please *f* my sin only this .... Ex 10:17
if You will *f* their sin .... Ex 32:32
dwelling place, and *f* ...... 1 Kin 8:39
f their sin and heal .... 2 Chr 7:14

good, and ready to *f* . . . . Ps 86:5
For I will *f* their iniquity . . . . Jer 31:34
O Lord, hear! O Lord, *f* . . . . Dan 9:19
And *f* us our debts . . . . Matt 6:12
Father will also *f* . . . . Matt 6:14
f men their trespasses . . . . . . Matt 6:15
sin against me, and I *f* . . . . Matt 18:21
his heart, does not *f* . . . . . . Matt 18:35
Who can *f* sins but God . . . . . Mark 2:7
f him, that your Father . . . Mark 11:25
if you do not *f*, neither . . . Mark 11:26
power on earth to *f* sins . . . Luke 5:24
F, and you will be . . . . Luke 6:37
f us our sins, for we also . . . Luke 11:4
and if he repents, *f* him . . . Luke 17:3
'I repent,' you shall *f* him . . Luke 17:4
f them, for they do not . . . . Luke 23:34
f the sins of any . . . . John 20:23
you ought rather to *f* . . . . . . 2 Cor 2:7
anything, I also *f* . . . . 2 Cor 2:10
F me this wrong . . . . 2 Cor 12:13
f us our sins and to . . . . 1 John 1:9

FORGIVEN
transgression is *f* . . . . Ps 32:1
sins be *f* them . . . . Mark 4:12
to whom little is *f* . . . . Luke 7:47
of your heart may be *f* . . . . . . Acts 8:22
indeed I have *f* . . . . 2 Cor 2:10
f you all trespasses . . . . Col 2:13
sins, he will be *f* . . . . James 5:15
your sins are *f* . . . . 1 John 2:12

FORGIVENESS
But there is *f* with . . . . Ps 130:4
God belong mercy and *f* . . . . . Dan 9:9
never has *f*, but is subject . Mark 3:29
preached to you the *f* . . . . . Acts 13:38
they may receive *f* . . . . Acts 26:18
His blood, the *f* . . . . Eph 1:7
His blood, the *f* of sins . . . . . . Col 1:14

FORGIVES
f all your iniquities . . . . Ps 103:3
"Who is this who even *f* . . . Luke 7:49

FORGIVING
tenderhearted, *f* . . . . Eph 4:32
and *f* one another . . . . Col 3:13

FORGOT
remember Joseph, but *f* . . . . Gen 40:23
f the LORD their God . . . . Judg 3:7
f His works and His . . . . Ps 78:11
They soon *f* His works . . . . . Ps 106:13

FORGOTTEN
f the God who fathered . . . Deut 32:18
needy shall not always be *f* . . . Ps 9:18
"Why have You *f* . . . . Ps 42:9
If we had *f* the name . . . . Ps 44:20
memory of them is *f* . . . . Eccl 9:5
you will not be *f* . . . . Is 44:21
And my Lord has *f* . . . . Is 49:14
I have *f* prosperity . . . . Lam 3:17
not one of them is *f* . . . . Luke 12:6
f the exhortation . . . . Heb 12:5
f that he was cleansed . . . . 2 Pet 1:9

FORM
earth was without *f* . . . . Gen 1:2
he sees the *f* of the LORD . . . . . Num 12:8
of the words, but saw no *f* . . Deut 4:12
Who would *f* a god or . . . . Is 44:10
f the light and create . . . . Is 45:7
He has no *f* or comeliness . . . . . Is 53:2
descended in bodily *f* . . . . . . Luke 3:22
time, nor seen His *f* . . . . John 5:37
having the *f* of knowledge . . Rom 2:20
For the *f* of this . . . . 1 Cor 7:31
who, being in the *f* . . . . Phil 2:6
the *f* of a bondservant . . . . Phil 2:7
Abstain from every *f* . . . . 1 Thess 5:22
having a *f* of godliness . . . . . 2 Tim 3:5

FORMED
And the LORD God *f* . . . . Gen 2:7
And His hands *f* . . . . Ps 95:5
f my inward parts . . . . Ps 139:13
f everything gives the . . . . . Prov 26:10
say of him who *f* . . . . Is 29:16
Me there was no God *f* . . . . Is 43:10
This people I have *f* . . . . Is 43:21
No weapon *f* against you . . . . Is 54:17
"Before I *f* you in . . . . Jer 1:5
Will the thing *f* say to . . . . . . Rom 9:20
until Christ is *f* . . . . Gal 4:19
For Adam was *f* first . . . . . . 1 Tim 2:13

FORMER
according to the *f* . . . . Gen 40:13
not remember *f* inquiries . . . . . . Ps 79:8
f lovingkindness . . . . Ps 89:49
f days better than . . . . Eccl 7:10
Who gives rain, both the *f* . . . Jer 5:24
f rain to the earth . . . . Hos 6:3
the *f* rain, and the latter . . . . Joel 2:23
f prophets preached . . . . Zech 1:4
through the *f* prophets . . . . . Zech 7:12
The *f* account I made, O . . . . . Acts 1:1
f conduct in Judaism . . . . Gal 1:13
your *f* conduct, the old . . . . . . Eph 4:22
yourselves to the *f* lusts . . . . 1 Pet 1:14
in *f* times, the holy women . . . 1 Pet 3:5
f things have passed . . . . Rev 21:4

FORMS
clay say to him who *f* . . . . Is 45:9
f the spirit of man . . . . Zech 12:1

FORNICATION
"We were not born of *f* . . . . John 8:41
adultery, *f*, uncleanness . . . . . Gal 5:19
of the wrath of her *f* . . . . Rev 14:8

FORNICATOR
you know, that no *f* . . . . Eph 5:5
lest there be any *f* . . . . Heb 12:16

FORNICATORS
but *f* and adulterers . . . . Heb 13:4

FORSAKE
but if you *f* Him . . . . 2 Chr 15:2
and did not *f* them . . . . Neh 9:17
mercies You did not *f* . . . . Neh 9:19
Do not leave me nor *f* me . . . . . Ps 27:9
father and my mother *f* me . . Ps 27:10
Cease from anger, and *f* . . . . . . Ps 37:8
And does not *f* His saints . . . . . Ps 37:28
"If his sons *f* My law . . . . Ps 89:30
f His inheritance . . . . Ps 94:14
But I did not *f* Your . . . . Ps 119:87
father, and do not *f* . . . . Prov 1:8
Let not mercy and truth *f* . . . Prov 3:3
worthless idols *f* . . . . Jon 2:8
of you does not *f* . . . . Luke 14:33
never leave you nor *f* . . . . Heb 13:5

FORSAKEN
My God, why have You *f* . . . . . Ps 22:1
seen the righteous *f* . . . . Ps 37:25
you dread will be *f* . . . . Is 7:16
cities will be as a *f* . . . . Is 17:9
a mere moment I have *f* . . . . Is 54:7
no longer be termed *F* . . . . Is 62:4
they have *f* Me . . . . Jer 2:13
My God, why have You *f* . . Matt 27:46
persecuted, but not *f* . . . . 2 Cor 4:9
for Demas has *f* . . . . 2 Tim 4:10
f the right way . . . . 2 Pet 2:15

FORSAKES
f the companion of her . . . . . Prov 2:17
and *f* them will have . . . . . . Prov 28:13

FORSAKING
f the assembling . . . . Heb 10:25

FORSOOK
f God who made him . . . . . Deut 32:15
all the disciples *f* . . . . Matt 26:56
with me, but all *f* . . . . 2 Tim 4:16
By faith he *f* Egypt . . . . Heb 11:27

FORT
Man the *f*! . . . . Nah 2:1

FORTRESS
LORD is my rock, my *f* . . . . 2 Sam 22:2
my rock of refuge, a *f* . . . . Ps 31:2
He is my refuge and my *f* . . . . Ps 91:2

FORTUNE-TELLING
masters much profit by *f* . . Acts 16:16

FORTY
to rain on the earth *f* days . . . Gen 7:4
to pass, at the end of *f* days . . Gen 8:6
not do it for the sake of *f* . . Gen 18:29
Isaac was *f* years old . . . . . . Gen 25:20
Esau was *f* years old . . . . . . Gen 26:34
F days were required . . . . Gen 50:3
Israel ate manna *f* years . . . . . Ex 16:35
mountain *f* days and *f* . . . . . . Ex 24:18
LORD *f* days and *f* nights . . . . Ex 34:28
out the land after *f* days . . . Num 13:25
in the wilderness *f* years . . Num 14:33
f days, for each day you . . Num 14:34
in the wilderness *f* years . . Num 32:13
These *f* years the LORD . . . . . . Deut 2:7
f years in the wilderness . . . . Deut 8:2
foot swell these *f* years . . . . . . Deut 8:4
first, *f* days and *f* nights . . . . Deut 9:18
f nights I kept prostrating . . Deut 9:25
mountain *f* days and *f* . . . . . Deut 10:10
F blows he may give him . . Deut 25:3
f years old when Moses . . . . Josh 14:7
land had rest for *f* years . . . . Judg 5:31
the Philistines for *f* years . . . Judg 13:1
judged Israel *f* years . . . . . . 1 Sam 4:18
presented himself *f* . . . . . . 1 Sam 17:16
f nights as far as Horeb . . . 1 Kin 19:8
For *f* years I was grieved . . . . Ps 95:10
f days, and Nineveh shall . . . . Jon 3:4
when He had fasted *f* days . . . Matt 4:2
for *f* days by the devil . . . . . . Luke 4:2
seen by them during *f* days . . Acts 1:3
when he was *f* years old . . . . Acts 7:23
when *f* years had passed . . . Acts 7:30
f who had formed this . . . . Acts 23:13
more than *f* of them lie . . . . Acts 23:21
f stripes minus one . . . . 2 Cor 11:24
and saw My works *f* years . . . Heb 3:9
was He angry *f* years . . . . Heb 3:17

FORWARD
David from that day *f* . . . 1 Sam 16:13
David from that day *f* . . . 1 Sam 18:9

FOUGHT
f against me without . . . . Ps 109:3
I have *f* the good fight, I . . . . 2 Tim 4:7

FOUL
My wounds are *f* . . . . Ps 38:5
f weather today . . . . Matt 16:3
a prison for every *f* . . . . Rev 18:2

FOUND
f a helper comparable . . . . . . Gen 2:20
Why have I *f* favor in . . . . . . Ruth 2:10
where can wisdom be *f* . . . . Job 28:12
when You may be *f* . . . . Ps 32:6
f My servant David . . . . Ps 89:20
a thousand I have *f* . . . . Eccl 7:28
this only I have *f* . . . . Eccl 7:29
f the one I love . . . . Song 3:4
LORD while He may be *f* . . . . Is 55:6
none was *f* like Daniel . . . . . . Dan 1:19
he *f* them ten times better . . Dan 1:20
balances, and *f* wanting . . . . . Dan 5:27
any error or fault *f* in him . . . Dan 6:4
f Daniel praying and . . . . Dan 6:11
your fruit is *f* . . . . Hos 14:8
and when you have *f* Him . . . Matt 2:8
not *f* such great faith . . . . Matt 8:10
when he had *f* one pearl . . Matt 13:46
f nothing on it but leaves . . Matt 21:19
f them sleeping, and said . . Matt 26:40
have *f* favor with God . . . . . Luke 1:30
they *f* Him in the temple . . . Luke 2:46
fruit on it and *f* none . . . . . . Luke 13:6

he was lost and is *f* . . . . . . Luke 15:24
they *f* the stone rolled . . . . . Luke 24:2
f the Messiah" (which . . . . . John 1:41
we *f* the prison shut . . . . Acts 5:23
I even *f* an altar with . . . . . . Acts 17:23
I *f* to bring death . . . . Rom 7:10
that one be *f* faithful . . . . 1 Cor 4:2
and be *f* in Him . . . . Phil 3:9
being *f* blameless . . . . 1 Tim 3:10
be diligent to be *f* . . . . 2 Pet 3:14
anyone not *f* written in . . . . Rev 20:15

FOUNDATION
he shall lay its *f* . . . . Josh 6:26
His *f* is in the holy . . . . Ps 87:1
and justice are the *f* . . . . Ps 89:14
Of old You laid the *f* . . . . Ps 102:25
has an everlasting *f* . . . . Prov 10:25
deep and laid the *f* . . . . Luke 6:48
the earth without a *f* . . . . Luke 6:49
loved Me before the *f* . . . . . John 17:24
I have laid the *f* . . . . 1 Cor 3:10
f can anyone lay than . . . . . 1 Cor 3:11
us in Him before the *f* . . . . Eph 1:4
the solid *f* of God . . . . 2 Tim 2:19
not laying again the *f* . . . . Heb 6:1
Lamb slain from the *f* . . . . Rev 13:8
the first *f* was jasper . . . . . . Rev 21:19

FOUNDATIONS
when I laid the *f* . . . . Job 38:4
f are destroyed . . . . Ps 11:3
You who laid the *f* . . . . Ps 104:5
shall raise up the *f* . . . . Is 58:12
that the *f* of the prison . . . . Acts 16:26
The *f* of the wall . . . . Rev 21:19

FOUNDED
For He has *f* it upon . . . . Ps 24:2
by wisdom *f* the earth . . . . Prov 3:19
shake it, for it was *f* . . . . Luke 6:48

FOUNTAIN
Let your *f* be blessed . . . . Prov 5:18
Immediately the *f* of her . . . Mark 5:29
will become in him a *f* . . . . . John 4:14
I will give of the *f* of the . . . . Rev 21:6

FOUNTAINS
on that day all the *f* . . . . Gen 7:11
f be dispersed abroad . . . . . . Prov 5:16
when there were no *f* . . . . Prov 8:24
lead them to living *f* . . . . Rev 7:17

FOUR
became *f* riverheads . . . . Gen 2:10
prophets are *f* hundred . . . 1 Kin 18:22
Each one had *f* faces . . . . . Ezek 10:14
and each one *f* wings . . . . . Ezek 10:21
I see *f* men loose, walking . . Dan 3:25
f great beasts came up . . . . Dan 7:3
f kingdoms shall arise . . . . . . Dan 8:22
are *f* spirits of heaven . . . . Zech 6:5
ate were *f* thousand . . . . Matt 15:38
been in the tomb *f* days . . . John 11:17
sheet bound at the *f* . . . . Acts 10:11
Now this man had *f* virgin . . Acts 21:9
were *f* living creatures full . . . Rev 4:6
the *f* angels to whom it was . . Rev 7:2

FOWLER
you from the snare of the *f* . . . Ps 91:3
bird from the hand of the *f* . . Prov 6:5

FOX
build, if even a *f* . . . . Neh 4:3
"Go, tell that *f* . . . . Luke 13:32

FOXES
caught three hundred *f* . . . . . Judg 15:4
f that spoil the vines . . . . Song 2:15
F have holes and birds . . . . Luke 9:58

FRAGMENTS
f that remained . . . . Matt 14:20
of the leftover *f* . . . . Luke 9:17
baskets with the *f* . . . . John 6:13

FRAGRANCE
garments is like the *f* . . . . . . Song 4:11
was filled with the *f* . . . . John 12:3
we are to God the *f* . . . . 2 Cor 2:15

FRAGRANT
the merchant's *f* powders . . . Song 3:6
flask of very costly *f* oil . . . . Matt 26:7
an alabaster flask of *f* oil . . Luke 7:37
prepared spices and *f* . . . . . Luke 23:56
was this *f* oil not sold . . . . . . John 12:5
f oil and frankincense . . . . . Rev 18:13

FRAIL
that I may know how *f* . . . . Ps 39:4

FRAME
For He knows our *f* . . . . Ps 103:14
f was not hidden . . . . Ps 139:15

FRAMED
that the worlds were *f* . . . . . . Heb 11:3

FRANKINCENSE
oil on it, and put *f* on it . . . . . . Lev 2:1
with myrrh and *f* . . . . Song 3:6
gold, *f*, and myrrh . . . . Matt 2:11
incense, fragrant oil and *f* . . Rev 18:13

FREE
and the servant is *f* . . . . Job 3:19
let the oppressed go *f* . . . . Is 58:6
'You will be made *f* . . . . John 8:33
if the Son makes you *f* . . . . . John 8:36
And having been set *f* . . . . . . Rom 6:18
now having been set *f* . . . . . . Rom 6:22
Jesus has made me *f* . . . . Rom 8:2
Am I not *f* . . . . 1 Cor 9:1
is neither slave nor *f* . . . . Gal 3:28
Jerusalem above is *f* . . . . Gal 4:26
Christ has made us *f* . . . . Gal 5:1
he is a slave or *f* . . . . Eph 6:8
poor, *f* and slave . . . . Rev 13:16

FREED
has died has been *f* . . . . Rom 6:7

FREEDMAN
slave is the Lord's *f* . . . . 1 Cor 7:22

FREEDOM
The LORD gives *f* to the . . . . . . Ps 146:7

FREELY
the garden you may *f* . . . . Gen 2:16
I will love them *f* . . . . Hos 14:4
F you have received . . . . Matt 10:8
f give us all things . . . . Rom 8:32
that have been *f* . . . . 1 Cor 2:12
the water of life *f* . . . . Rev 22:17

FREEWOMAN
the other by a *f* . . . . Gal 4:22
with the son of the *f* . . . . Gal 4:30

FRESH
My glory is *f* within . . . . Job 29:20
they shall be *f* . . . . Ps 92:14
both salt water and *f* . . . . . James 3:12

FRETS
and his heart *f* . . . . Prov 19:3

FRIEND
a man speaks to his *f* . . . . Ex 33:11
of Abraham Your *f* . . . . 2 Chr 20:7
though he were my *f* . . . . Ps 35:14
f You have put far from me . . Ps 88:18
f loves at all times . . . . Prov 17:17
f who sticks closer . . . . Prov 18:24
not forsake your own *f* . . . . . Prov 27:10
a *f* of tax collectors . . . . Matt 11:19
of you shall have a *f* . . . . Luke 11:5
f Lazarus sleeps . . . . John 11:11
you are not Caesar's *f* . . . . John 19:12
Philemon our beloved *f* . . . . . Philem 1
he was called the *f* . . . . James 2:23
wants to be a *f* . . . . James 4:4

FRIENDLY
friends must himself be *f* . . Prov 18:24

FRIENDS
and hate your *f* . . . . 2 Sam 19:6
My *f* scorn me . . . . Job 16:20
f have forgotten me . . . . Job 19:14
the rich has many *f* . . . . Prov 14:20
one's life for his *f* . . . . John 15:13
You are My *f* . . . . John 15:14
I have called you *f* . . . . John 15:15
to forbid any of his *f* . . . . Acts 24:23

FRIENDSHIP
no *f* with an angry man . . . Prov 22:24
that *f* with the world . . . . James 4:4

FROGS
your territory with *f* . . . . Ex 8:2
f coming out of the . . . . Rev 16:13

FRONTLETS
on your hand and as *f* . . . . Ex 13:16
and they shall be as *f* . . . . Deut 6:8

FROZEN
the broad waters are *f* . . . . . Job 37:10

FRUIT
See BEAR FRUIT
and showed them the *f* . . . . Num 13:26
Blessed shall be the *f* . . . . . . Deut 28:4
brings forth its *f* . . . . Ps 1:3
f is better than gold . . . . Prov 8:19
The *f* of the righteous . . . . . Prov 11:30
with good by the *f* . . . . Prov 12:14
f was sweet to my . . . . Song 2:3
they shall eat the *f* . . . . Is 3:10
like the first *f* . . . . Is 28:4
"I create the *f* . . . . Is 57:19
f is found in Me . . . . Hos 14:8
does not bear good *f* . . . . Matt 3:10
good tree bears good *f* . . . . . Matt 7:17
not drink of this *f* . . . . Matt 26:29
and blessed is the *f* . . . . Luke 1:42
life, and bring no *f* . . . . Luke 8:14
and he came seeking *f* . . . . . Luke 13:6
And if it bears *f* . . . . Luke 13:9
branch that bears *f* . . . . John 15:2
that you bear much *f* . . . . John 15:8
should go and bear *f* . . . . . . John 15:16
f did you have then in . . . . . Rom 6:21
God, you have your *f* . . . . . . Rom 6:22
that we should bear *f* . . . . Rom 7:4
But the *f* of the Spirit is . . . . . Gal 5:22
(for the *f* of the Spirit is . . . . . . Eph 5:9
but I seek the *f* . . . . Phil 4:17
yields the peaceable *f* . . . . . . Heb 12:11
the *f* of our lips, giving . . . . Heb 13:15
Now the *f* of . . . . James 3:18
precious *f* of the earth . . . . . James 5:7
autumn trees without *f* . . . . Jude 12
tree yielding its *f* . . . . Rev 22:2

FRUITFUL
See BE FRUITFUL AND MULTIPLY
them, saying, "Be *f* . . . . Gen 1:22
a *f* bough, a *f* . . . . Gen 49:22
wife shall be like a *f* . . . . Ps 128:3
heaven and *f* seasons . . . . . Acts 14:17
pleasing Him, being *f* . . . . Col 1:10

FRUITS
Therefore bear *f* . . . . Matt 3:8
know them by their *f* . . . . Matt 7:16
and increase the *f* . . . . 2 Cor 9:10
being filled with the *f* of . . . . Phil 1:11
of mercy and good *f* . . . . James 3:17
which bore twelve *f* . . . . Rev 22:2

FUEL
people shall be as *f* . . . . Is 9:19
into the fire for *f* . . . . Ezek 15:4

FUGITIVE
A *f* and a vagabond . . . . Gen 4:12

FULFILL
the LORD, to *f* his vow . . . . . Lev 22:21
And you shall *f* . . . . 1 Kin 5:9
f all your petitions . . . . Ps 20:5

f the desire of those . . . . Ps 145:19
for us to *f* all . . . . Matt 3:15
come to destroy but to *f* . . . . Matt 5:17
for the flesh, to *f* its lusts . . Rom 13:14
f the law of Christ . . . . Gal 6:2
f my joy by being . . . . Phil 2:2
and *f* all the good . . . . 2 Thess 1:11
evangelist, *f* your ministry . . 2 Tim 4:5
If you really *f* . . . . James 2:8

FULFILLED
be *f* which was spoken by . . Matt 1:22
the law till all is *f* . . . . Matt 5:18
could the Scriptures be *f* . . Matt 26:54
is *f*, and the kingdom . . . . . Mark 1:15
is *f* in your hearing . . . . Luke 4:21
of the Gentiles are *f* . . . . . . Luke 21:24
all things must be *f* . . . . . . Luke 24:44
this joy of mine is *f* . . . . John 3:29
the Scripture may be *f* . . . . John 13:18
My joy *f* in themselves . . . . John 17:13
this Scripture had to be *f* . . . Acts 1:16
they had *f* their ministry . . Acts 12:25
of the law might be *f* . . . . Rom 8:4
loves another has *f* . . . . Rom 13:8
For all the law is *f* . . . . Gal 5:14
the words of God are *f* . . . . . Rev 17:17

FULFILLMENT
for there will be a *f* . . . . Luke 1:45
love is the *f* of the . . . . Rom 13:10

FULL
I went out *f* . . . . Ruth 1:21
For I am *f* of words . . . . Job 32:18
of the LORD is *f* . . . . Ps 29:4
who has his quiver *f* . . . . Ps 127:5
Lest I be *f* and deny . . . . Prov 30:9
yet the sea is not *f* . . . . Eccl 1:7
the whole earth is *f* . . . . Is 6:3
and it was *f* of bones . . . . . . Ezek 37:1
But truly I am *f* . . . . Mic 3:8
whole body will be *f* . . . . Matt 6:22
of the Father, *f* of grace . . . . John 1:14
your joy may be *f* . . . . John 15:11
chose Stephen, a man *f* . . . . . . Acts 6:5
You are already *f* . . . . 1 Cor 4:8
learned both to be *f* . . . . Phil 4:12
I am *f*, having received . . . . . . Phil 4:18
in *f* assurance of faith . . . . . Heb 10:22
that your joy may be *f* . . . . . 1 John 1:4
we may receive a *f* reward . . 2 John 8

FULL-GROWN
and sin, when it is *f* . . . . . . James 1:15

FULLNESS
satisfied with the *f* . . . . Ps 36:8
f we have all received . . . . . John 1:16
to Israel until the *f* . . . . Rom 11:25
But when the *f* of the . . . . Gal 4:4
dispensation of the *f* . . . . Eph 1:10
filled with all the *f* . . . . Eph 3:19
Him dwells all the *f* . . . . Col 2:9

FULLY
did not *f* follow the LORD . . 1 Kin 11:6
time has not yet *f* come . . . . John 7:8
Pentecost had *f* come . . . . Acts 2:1
being *f* convinced that . . . . . Rom 4:21
f preached the gospel . . . . . Rom 15:19
f pleasing Him, being . . . . Col 1:10
preached *f* through me . . . . 2 Tim 4:17
rest your hope *f* upon the . . 1 Pet 1:13

FUME
Why do you *f* with envy . . . . . Ps 68:16

FUNCTION
do not have the same *f* . . . . . Rom 12:4

FURIOUS
You have been *f* . . . . Ps 89:38
f man do not go . . . . Prov 22:24
fury and in *f* rebukes . . . . Ezek 5:15
LORD avenges and is *f* . . . . Nah 1:2
this, they were *f* . . . . Acts 5:33

FURIOUSLY
for he drives *f* . . . . 2 Kin 9:20

FURNACE
you out of the iron *f* . . . . Deut 4:20
tested you in the *f* . . . . Is 48:10
of a burning fiery *f* . . . . Dan 3:6
cast them into the *f* . . . . Matt 13:42
the smoke of a great *f* . . . . Rev 9:2

FURNISHED
also *f* her table . . . . Prov 9:2
a large upper room, *f* . . . . . Mark 14:15

FURNISHINGS
and the pattern of all its *f* . . . . Ex 25:9
tabernacle and all its *f* . . . . . Num 1:50
Solomon had all the *f* . . . . . 1 Kin 7:48
all the holy *f* that were in . . . 2 Chr 5:5

FURY
F is not in Me . . . . Is 27:4
they are full of the *f* . . . . Is 51:20
f to His adversaries . . . . Is 59:18
My own *f*, it sustained . . . . Is 63:5
even in anger and *f* . . . . Jer 21:5
and I will cause My *f* . . . . . . Ezek 5:13
Thus will I spend My *f* . . . . . Ezek 6:12
in anger and *f* on the . . . . Mic 5:15

FUTILE
For it is not a *f* thing . . . . . . Deut 32:47
of the peoples are *f* . . . . Jer 10:3
wise, that they are *f* . . . . 1 Cor 3:20
risen, your faith is *f* . . . . . . 1 Cor 15:17

FUTILITY
allotted months of *f* . . . . Job 7:3
f have You created all . . . . Ps 89:47
was subjected to *f* . . . . Rom 8:20

FUTURE
for the *f* of that man . . . . Ps 37:37
the *f* of the wicked . . . . Ps 37:38
to give you a *f* and a hope . . Jer 29:11
to many days in the *f* . . . . Dan 8:26

GAAL
Son of Ebed; vilifies Abimelech, Judg 9:26–41

GAASH
Hill of Ephraim, Judg 2:9
Joshua buried near, Josh 24:30

GABBATHA
Place of Pilate's court, John 19:13

GABRIEL
Messenger archangel; interprets Daniel's vision, Dan 8:16–27
Reveals the prophecy of 70 weeks, Dan 9:21–27
Announces John's birth, Luke 1:11–22
Announces Christ's birth, Luke 1:26–38
Stands in God's presence, Luke 1:19

GAD
Son of Jacob by Zilpah, Gen 30:10, 11
Blessed by Jacob, Gen 49:19
——— Tribe of:
Census of, Num 1:24, 25
Territory of, Num 32:20–36
Captivity of, 1 Chr 5:26
Later references to, Rev 7:5
——— Prophet in David's reign, 1 Sam 22:5
Message of, to David, 2 Sam 24:10–16

GADARENES (or Gergesenes)
People east of the Sea of Galilee, Mark 5:1
Healing of demon-possessed in territory of, Matt 8:28–34

GAIN
See DISHONEST GAIN

aside after dishonest *g* . . . . . 1 Sam 8:3
they did not *g* possession . . . . . Ps 44:3
That we may *g* a heart of . . . . Ps 90:12
g than fine gold . . . . Prov 3:14
He who is greedy for *g* . . . . Prov 15:27
will have no lack of *g* . . . . . Prov 31:11
a time to *g* . . . . Eccl 3:6
to get dishonest *g* . . . . Ezek 22:27
him who covets evil *g* . . . . Hab 2:9
and to die is *g* . . . . Phil 1:21
what things were *g* to me . . . . Phil 3:7
rubbish, that I may *g* . . . . Phil 3:8
is a means of *g* . . . . 1 Tim 6:5
contentment is great *g* . . . . . . 1 Tim 6:6
the sake of dishonest *g* . . . . . Titus 1:11
for dishonest *g* . . . . 1 Pet 5:2
people to *g* advantage . . . . Jude 16

GAINED
which he had *g* . . . . Gen 31:18
g in the land of Canaan . . . . . Gen 36:6
have *g* Him the victory . . . . Ps 98:1
Wealth *g* by dishonesty . . Prov 13:11
Bread *g* by deceit is . . . . Prov 20:17
An inheritance *g* hastily . . Prov 20:21
g more wisdom than all . . . . Eccl 1:16
you have *g* your brother . . . Matt 18:15
received two *g* two more . . Matt 25:17
g five more talents . . . . Matt 25:20

GAINS
understanding *g* favor . . . . Prov 13:15
g the whole world . . . . Matt 16:26

GAIUS
Companion of Paul, Acts 19:29
——— Convert at Derbe, Acts 20:4
——— Paul's host at Corinth, Rom 16:23; 1 Cor 1:14

GALATIA
Paul visits, Acts 16:6; 18:23
Paul writes to Christians in, Gal 1:1
Peter writes to Christians in, 1 Pet 1:1

GALILEANS
Speech of, Mark 14:70
Faith of, John 4:45
Pilate's cruelty toward, Luke 13:1, 2

GALILEE
Prophecies concerning, Deut 33:18–23; Is 9:1, 2
Dialect of, distinctive, Matt 26:73
Herod's jurisdiction over, Luke 3:1
Christ's contacts with, Matt 2:22; 4:12–25; 26:32; 27:55; John 4:1, 3

GALILEE, SEA OF
Scene of many events in Christ's life, Mark 7:31
Called Chinnereth, Num 34:11
Later called Gennesaret, Luke 5:1

GALL
grapes are grapes of *g* . . . . Deut 32:32
They also gave me *g* . . . . Ps 69:21
the wormwood and the *g* . . . Lam 3:19
turned justice into *g* . . . . Amos 6:12
wine mingled with *g* . . . . Matt 27:34

GALLIO
Roman proconsul of Achaia, dismisses charges against Paul, Acts 18:12–17

GALLONS
twenty or thirty *g* apiece . . . . John 2:6

GALLOWS
both were hanged on a *g* . . . Esth 2:23
should be hanged on the *g* . . Esth 9:25

GAMALIEL
Famous Jewish teacher, Acts 22:3
Respected by people, Acts 5:34–39

GAME
because he ate of his *g* . . . . . Gen 25:28
Bring me *g* and make . . . . Gen 27:7

GAP
and stand in the *g* . . . . Ezek 22:30

GARDEN
LORD God planted a *g* .... Gen 2:8
g enclosed is my .... Song 4:12
like a watered *g* .... Is 58:11
Eden, the *g* of God .... Ezek 28:13
raise up for them a *g* ..... Ezek 34:29
where there was a *g* .... John 18:1
in the *g* a new tomb ...... John 19:41

GARDENER
Him to be the *g* .... John 20:15

GARDENS
I made myself *g* .... Eccl 2:5
plant *g* and eat their .... Jer 29:5

GARLANDS
brought oxen and *g* .... Acts 14:13

GARLIC
the onions, and the *g* ...... Num 11:5

GARMENT
and Japheth took a *g* ...... Gen 9:23
like a hairy *g* all over ..... Gen 25:25
she caught him by his *g* ... Gen 39:12
she kept his *g* with her .... Gen 39:16
beautiful Babylonian *g* ..... Josh 7:21
put on your best *g* .... Ruth 3:3
g that is moth-eaten .... Job 13:28
made sackcloth my *g* .... Ps 69:11
with light as with a *g* ...... Ps 104:2
one who takes away a *g* .. Prov 25:20
the *g* of praise for the .... Is 61:3
the hem of His *g* .... Matt 9:20
have on a wedding *g* ..... Matt 22:11
cloth on an old *g* .... Mark 2:21
throwing aside his *g* ..... Mark 10:50
all grow old like a *g* .... Heb 1:11
hating even the *g* .... Jude 23

GARMENTS
took off her widow's *g* ..... Gen 38:14
the *g* of her widowhood ... Gen 38:19
g did not wear out on .... Deut 8:4
and old *g* on themselves ..... Josh 9:5
our *g* and our sandals ...... Josh 9:13
cut off their *g* in the ...... 2 Sam 10:4
Why are your *g* hot .... Job 37:17
They divide My *g* .... Ps 22:18
She makes linen *g* and .... Prov 31:24
g always be white .... Eccl 9:8
g rolled in blood .... Is 9:5
from Edom, with dyed *g* ...... Is 63:1
nor were their *g* affected .... Dan 3:27
your heart, and not your *g* .. Joel 2:13
Take away the filthy *g* ...... Zech 3:4
man clothed in soft *g* .... Matt 11:8
and divided His *g* .... Matt 27:35
by them in shining *g* .... Luke 24:4
and laid aside His *g* .... John 13:4
divided My *g* among ...... John 19:24
g which Dorcas had made .. Acts 9:39
g are moth-eaten .... James 5:2
be clothed in white *g* .... Rev 3:5

GARRISON
gathered the whole *g* ..... Matt 27:27
Damascenes with a *g* ..... 2 Cor 11:32

GATE
sitting in the *g* of Sodom .... Gen 19:1
Boaz went up to the *g* .... Ruth 4:1
people who were at the *g* .. Ruth 4:11
This is the *g* of the .... Ps 118:20
by the narrow *g* .... Matt 7:13
Because narrow is the *g* .... Matt 7:14
by the Sheep *G* a pool ...... John 5:2
laid daily at the *g* .... Acts 3:2
she did not open the *g* .... Acts 12:14
suffered outside the *g* ..... Heb 13:12
each individual *g* .... Rev 21:21

GATES
possess the *g* of those ..... Gen 24:60
g are burned with fire .... Neh 1:3
I commanded the *g* to be .. Neh 13:19
they go down to the *g* ...... Job 17:16
up your heads, O you *g* .... Ps 24:7
The LORD loves the *g* .... Ps 87:2
Enter into His *g* with .... Ps 100:4
Open to me the *g* .... Ps 118:19
watching daily at my *g* ..... Prov 8:34
is known in the *g* .... Prov 31:23
praise her in the *g* .... Prov 31:31
go through the *g* .... Is 62:10
and the *g* of Hades .... Matt 16:18
wall with twelve *g* .... Rev 21:12
g were twelve pearls .... Rev 21:21
g shall not be shut .... Rev 21:25

GATH
Philistine city, 1 Sam 6:17
Ark carried to, 1 Sam 5:8
David takes refuge in, 1 Sam 21:10–15
David's second flight to, 1 Sam 27:3–12
Captured by David, 1 Chr 18:1
Destruction of, prophetic, Amos 6:1–3
Name becomes proverbial, Mic 1:10

GATH HEPHER
Birthplace of Jonah, 2 Kin 14:25

GATHER
g my soul with sinners .... Ps 26:9
G My saints together .... Ps 50:5
and a time to *g* stones .... Eccl 3:5
g the lambs with His .... Is 40:11
g His wheat into the .... Matt 3:12
sow nor reap nor *g* .... Matt 6:26
Do men *g* grapes from ..... Matt 7:16
g where I have not .... Matt 25:26
g together His elect ...... Mark 13:27
who does not *g* with Me .. Luke 11:23
often I wanted to *g* your .. Luke 13:34
G up the fragments that .... John 6:12
of the times He might *g* .... Eph 1:10

GATHERED
g little had no lack .... Ex 16:18
And *g* out of the lands .... Ps 107:3
g some of every kind ..... Matt 13:47
g together in My name .... Matt 18:20
the nations will be *g* ..... Matt 25:32
many were *g* together ..... Acts 12:12
g the church together ..... Acts 14:27
when Paul had *g* a bundle .. Acts 28:3
when you are *g* together .... 1 Cor 5:4
who *g* much had nothing .. 2 Cor 8:15
they *g* them together ...... Rev 16:16

GATHERING
g together of the waters .... Gen 1:10
widow was there *g* .... 1 Kin 17:10
I am *g* a couple of sticks .. 1 Kin 17:12
they were three days *g* ... 2 Chr 20:25
He gives the work of *g* ...... Eccl 2:26
g where you have not ..... Matt 25:24
g a mob, set all the city in .. Acts 17:5
for this disorderly *g* .... Acts 19:40
g together to Him .... 2 Thess 2:1

GATHERS
g the waters of the .... Ps 33:7
His heart *g* iniquity .... Ps 41:6
He *g* together the outcasts ... Ps 147:2
g her food in the .... Prov 6:8
He who *g* in summer is a .. Prov 10:5
he who *g* by labor will .... Prov 13:11
extortion *g* it for him who .. Prov 28:8
The Lord GOD, who *g* .... Is 56:8
together, as a hen *g* .... Matt 23:37

GAUNT
out of the river, ugly and *g* .. Gen 41:3
g and ugly cows ate up .... Gen 41:20

GAVE
So Adam *g* names to all .... Gen 2:20
She also *g* to her husband ... Gen 3:6
to be with me, she *g* .... Gen 3:12
he *g* him a tithe of all ..... Gen 14:20
g her to her husband .... Gen 16:3
and *g* the lad a drink ...... Gen 21:19
hand, and *g* him a drink ... Gen 24:18
Abraham *g* all that he had .. Gen 25:5
Jacob *g* Esau bread and .... Gen 25:34
which God *g* to Abraham ... Gen 28:4
g him favor in the sight .... Gen 39:21
Joseph *g* a command ...... Gen 42:25
it *g* light by night to the ..... Ex 14:20
He *g* Moses two tablets of ... Ex 31:18
So they *g* it to me, and I .... Ex 32:24
g the children of Israel .... Num 13:32
stone and *g* them to me .... Deut 5:22
the LORD *g* me the two ..... Deut 9:11
g you on this side of the .... Josh 1:14
g it as an inheritance ..... Josh 11:23
So he *g* her the upper ..... Josh 15:19
The LORD *g* them rest all .. Josh 21:44
Samson *g* a feast there ...... Judg 14:10
g the changes of clothing .Judg 14:19
therefore I *g* her to your ... Judg 15:2
LORD *g* her conception ..... Ruth 4:13
g birth, for her labor ..... 1 Sam 4:19
God *g* him another heart .. 1 Sam 10:9
g it to David, with his ..... 1 Sam 18:4
Saul *g* him Michal .... 1 Sam 18:27
So the priest *g* him holy .. 1 Sam 21:6
g him the sword of .... 1 Sam 22:10
this woman also *g* birth ... 1 Kin 3:18
God *g* Solomon wisdom ... 1 Kin 4:29
Hiram *g* Solomon cedar ... 1 Kin 5:10
g to King Solomon .... 1 Kin 10:10
g a commandment .... 1 Chr 14:12
David *g* his son .... 1 Chr 28:11
g it to the workmen ...... 2 Chr 34:10
Hilkiah *g* the book to .... 2 Chr 34:15
Josiah *g* the lay people .... 2 Chr 35:7
so he readily *g* beauty .... Esth 2:9
g gifts according to the ..... Esth 2:18
He also *g* him a copy of ..... Esth 4:8
and *g* it to Mordecai .... Esth 8:2
return to God who *g* it ...... Eccl 12:7
of the eunuchs *g* names ..... Dan 1:7
and *g* them vegetables .... Dan 1:16
God *g* them knowledge ..... Dan 1:17
g him many great gifts ..... Dan 2:48
Belshazzar *g* the command .. Dan 5:2
g thanks before his God .... Dan 6:10
He *g* them power over ..... Matt 10:1
g You this authority ...... Matt 21:23
hungry and you *g* Me ..... Matt 25:35
g thanks, and *g* it to ...... Matt 26:27
g Him sour wine .... Matt 27:34
platter, and *g* it to .... Mark 6:28
To many blind He *g* sight .. Luke 7:21
g Me no water for My ..... Luke 7:44
g them to the innkeeper .. Luke 10:35
no one *g* him anything .... Luke 15:16
saw it, *g* praise to God .... Luke 18:43
to them He *g* the right to ... John 1:12
that He *g* His only .... John 3:16
Those whom You *g* .... John 17:12
glory which You *g* Me .... John 17:22
head, He *g* up His spirit ... John 19:30
tongues, as the Spirit *g* .... Acts 2:4
great power the apostles *g* .. Acts 4:33
who *g* alms generously to .. Acts 10:2
g us rain from heaven ..... Acts 14:17
God also *g* them up .... Rom 1:24
but God *g* the increase ...... 1 Cor 3:6
but first *g* themselves to .... 2 Cor 8:5
but God *g* it to Abraham .... Gal 3:18
g Him to be head over all ... Eph 1:22
captive, and *g* gifts to men ... Eph 4:8
He Himself *g* some to be .... Eph 4:11
Abraham *g* a tenth part of ... Heb 7:2
and the heaven *g* rain .... James 5:18
g Him glory, so that your ... 1 Pet 1:21
He *g* us commandment ... 1 John 3:23
which God *g* Him to show .... Rev 1:1
g to the seven angels .... Rev 15:7
The sea *g* up the dead ..... Rev 20:13

"If you knew the *g* .... John 4:10
the *g* of the Holy Spirit ..... Acts 2:38
thought that the *g* of God ... Acts 8:20
the *g* of the Holy .... Acts 10:45
same *g* as He gave us ..... Acts 11:17
to you some spiritual *g* ..... Rom 1:11
But the free *g* is not .... Rom 5:15
of the *g* of righteousness ... Rom 5:17
but the *g* of God is .... Rom 6:23
each one has his own *g* ..... 1 Cor 7:7
though I have the *g* .... 1 Cor 13:2
it is the *g* of God .... Eph 2:8
Not that I seek the *g* .... Phil 4:17
Do not neglect the *g* ...... 1 Tim 4:14
you to stir up the *g* .... 2 Tim 1:6
tasted the heavenly *g* .... Heb 6:4
Every good *g* and every .. James 1:17
one has received a *g* .... 1 Pet 4:10

GIFTED
the women who were *g* ..... Ex 35:25
but good-looking, *g* .... Dan 1:4

GIFTS
g you shall offer .... Num 18:29
You have received *g* .... Ps 68:18
and Seba will offer *g* .... Ps 72:10
though you give many *g* ... Prov 6:35
to one who gives *g* .... Prov 19:6
how to give good *g* .... Matt 7:11
rich putting their *g* .... Luke 21:1
Having then *g* differing .... Rom 12:6
are diversities of *g* .... 1 Cor 12:4
and desire spiritual *g* ...... 1 Cor 14:1
captive, and gave *g* .... Eph 4:8

GIHON
River of Eden, Gen 2:13
—— Spring outside Jerusalem, 1 Kin 1:33–45
Source of water supply, 2 Chr 32:30

GILBOA
Range of limestone hills in Issachar, 1 Sam 28:4
Scene of Saul's death, 1 Sam 31:1–9
Under David's curse, 2 Sam 1:17, 21

GILEAD
Plain east of the Jordan; taken from the Amorites and assigned to Gad, Reuben, and Manasseh, Num 21:21–31; 32:33–40; Deut 3:12, 13; Josh 13:24–31
Ishbosheth rules over, 2 Sam 2:8, 9
David takes refuge in, 2 Sam 17:21–26
Conquered by Hazael, 2 Kin 10:32, 33
Balm of, figurative of national healing, Jer 8:22

GILGAL
Site of memorial stones, circumcision, first Passover in the Promised Land, Josh 4:19—5:12
Site of Gibeonite covenant, Josh 9:3–15
One location on Samuel's circuit, 1 Sam 7:15, 16
Saul made king and later rejected, 1 Sam 11:15; 13:4–15
Denounced for idolatry, Hos 9:15

GIRD
G Your sword upon Your .... Ps 45:3
of wrath You shall *g* .... Ps 76:10
I will *g* you, though you .... Is 45:5
and another will *g* .... John 21:18
Therefore *g* up the .... 1 Pet 1:13

GIRDED
a towel and *g* Himself ..... John 13:4
down to the feet and *g* ...... Rev 1:13

GIRGASHITES
Descendants of Canaan, Gen 10:15, 16
Land of, given to Abraham's descendants, Gen 15:18, 21
Delivered to Israel, Josh 24:11

GITTITES
600 follow David, 2 Sam 15:18–23

GIVE
g thanks to the LORD ...... 1 Chr 16:8
g me wisdom and .... 2 Chr 1:10
G ear to my prayer .... Ps 17:1
G to them according .... Ps 28:4
g you the desires .... Ps 37:4
Yes, the LORD will *g* .... Ps 85:12
G me understanding .... Ps 119:34
g me your heart .... Prov 23:26
You will *g* truth to .... Mic 7:20
G to him who asks .... Matt 5:42
G us this day our .... Matt 6:11
what you have and *g* ..... Matt 19:21
authority I will *g* .... Luke 4:6
g them eternal life .... John 10:28
new commandment I *g* ... John 13:34
but what I do have I *g* .... Acts 3:6
g us all things .... Rom 8:32
G no offense .... 1 Cor 10:32
So let each one *g* .... 2 Cor 9:7
nor *g* place to the devil ...... Eph 4:27
g him who has need .... Eph 4:28
g thanks to God .... 2 Thess 2:13
g yourself entirely .... 1 Tim 4:15
good works, ready to *g* ... 1 Tim 6:18
and always be ready to *g* .. 1 Pet 3:15
They will *g* an account to ... 1 Pet 4:5
I will *g* you the crown of .... Rev 2:10
I will *g* him a white stone, .. Rev 2:17
I will *g* him the morning .... Rev 2:28
"*G* me the little book .... Rev 10:9
I will *g* of the fountain of ... Rev 21:6
g to every one according ... Rev 22:12

GIVEN
I have *g* every green herb ... Gen 1:30
land which He has *g* you ... Deut 8:10
will tread upon I have *g* ..... Josh 1:3
I had *g* rest to Israel from .. Josh 23:1
see, I have *g* you a wise ... 1 Kin 3:12
He has *g* us rest on .... 2 Chr 14:7
she was *g* whatever she .... Esth 2:13
You have *g* me wisdom ..... Dan 2:23
Ask and it will be *g* to you .. Matt 7:7
to him more will be *g* ..... Matt 13:12
nor are *g* in marriage ..... Matt 22:30
has, more will be *g* .... Matt 25:29
to whom much is *g* .... Luke 12:48
and are *g* in marriage .... Luke 20:34
My body which is *g* for .... Luke 22:19
law was *g* through Moses ... John 1:17
has *g* Him authority to ...... John 5:27
g Me I should lose .... John 6:39
Spirit was not yet *g* .... John 7:39
have been freely *g* .... 1 Cor 2:12
g us the Spirit in our ...... 2 Cor 1:22
g according to the .... Eph 4:7
utterance may be *g* to me ... Eph 6:19
not *g* to wine .... 1 Tim 3:3
God has not *g* us a spirit ... 2 Tim 1:7
All Scripture is *g* by ...... 2 Tim 3:16
robe was *g* to each of .... Rev 6:11

GIVES
He who *g* to the poor ..... Prov 28:27
For God *g* wisdom and ..... Eccl 2:26
g life to the world .... John 6:33
All that the Father *g* .... John 6:37
The good shepherd *g* ..... John 10:11
not as the world *g* .... John 14:27
g us richly all things ...... 1 Tim 6:17
who *g* to all liberally ...... James 1:5
g grace to the humble ..... James 4:6

GLAD
See BE GLAD AND REJOICE
g of heart for the good ..... 2 Chr 7:10
I will be *g* and .... Ps 9:2
my heart is *g* .... Ps 16:9
Be *g* in the LORD and .... Ps 32:11
streams shall make *g* .... Ps 46:4
And wine that makes *g* .... Ps 104:15
I will be *g* in the LORD ..... Ps 104:34
I was *g* when they said ...... Ps 122:1
son makes a *g* father .... Prov 10:1
We will be *g* and rejoice .... Song 1:4
Be *g* and rejoice with all ... Zeph 3:14
shall see it and be *g* .... Zech 10:7
and be exceedingly *g* .... Matt 5:12
bring you these *g* tidings .... Luke 1:19
bringing the *g* tidings of .... Luke 8:1
make merry and be *g* ..... Luke 15:32
he saw it and was *g* .... John 8:56
Let us be *g* and rejoice ...... Rev 19:7

GLADNESS
in the day of your *g* ...... Num 10:10
day of feasting and *g* .... Esth 9:17
You have put *g* in my .... Ps 4:7
me hear joy and *g* .... Ps 51:8
Serve the LORD with *g* ...... Ps 100:2
shall obtain joy and *g* .... Is 35:10
They shall obtain joy and *g* .. Is 51:11
over you with *g* .... Zeph 3:17
receive it with *g* .... Mark 4:16
they ate their food with *g* ... Acts 2:46
You with the oil of *g* more ... Heb 1:9

GLASS
there was a sea of *g* .... Rev 4:6
like transparent *g* .... Rev 21:21

GLORIFIED
the people I must be *g* ...... Lev 10:3
and they *g* the God of ..... Matt 15:31
Jesus was not yet *g* .... John 7:39
when Jesus was *g* .... John 12:16
By this My Father is *g* ..... John 15:8
I have *g* You on the .... John 17:4
g His Servant Jesus .... Acts 3:13
these He also *g* .... Rom 8:30
things God may be *g* ...... 1 Pet 4:11

GLORIFY
My altar, and I will *g* .... Is 60:7
g your Father in .... Matt 5:16
"Father, *g* Your name .... John 12:28
He will *g* Me .... John 16:14
And now, O Father, *g* ...... John 17:5
what death he would *g* ... John 21:19
God, they did not *g* .... Rom 1:21
therefore *g* God in .... 1 Cor 6:20
also Christ did not *g* .... Heb 5:5
ashamed, but let him *g* .... 1 Pet 4:16

GLORIOUS
g in holiness, fearful in ..... Ex 15:11
daughter is all *g* .... Ps 45:13
And blessed be His *g* .... Ps 72:19
G things are spoken .... Ps 87:3
is honorable and *g* .... Ps 111:3
g splendor of Your .... Ps 145:5
habitation, holy and *g* .... Is 63:15
also enter the *G* Land ..... Dan 11:41
engraved on stones, was *g* .. 2 Cor 3:7
it to Himself a *g* .... Eph 5:27
be conformed to His *g* ...... Phil 3:21
g appearing of our .... Titus 2:13

GLORY
"Please, show me Your *g* ... Ex 33:18
filled with the *g* of the .... Num 14:21
g has departed from ...... 1 Sam 4:21
G in His holy name ...... 1 Chr 16:10
a shield for me, my *g* .... Ps 3:3
who have set Your *g* .... Ps 8:1
Who is this King of *g* .... Ps 24:8
the place where Your *g* .... Ps 26:8
Your power and Your *g* ...... Ps 63:2
shall speak of the *g* .... Ps 145:11
wise shall inherit *g* .... Prov 3:35
head is a crown of *g*, if ... Prov 16:31
The *g* of young men is .... Prov 20:29
It is the *g* of God to .... Prov 25:2
"*G* to the righteous .... Is 24:16
g I will not give .... Is 42:8
g will be seen upon .... Is 60:2

brightness of the LORD's *g*. . Ezek 10:4
then be likened in *g* . . . . . Ezek 31:18
I will set My *g* among . . . . Ezek 39:21
I will change their *g* . . . . Hos 4:7
and I will be the *g* . . . . Zech 2:5
He shall bear the *g* . . . . Zech 6:13
that they may have *g* . . . . Matt 6:2
the power and the *g* . . . . Matt 6:13
g was not arrayed . . . . Matt 6:29
Man will come in the *g* . . . Matt 16:27
with power and great *g* . . . Matt 24:30
"*G* to God in the . . . . Luke 2:14
and we beheld His *g* . . . . . . John 1:14
and manifested His *g* . . . . . . John 2:11
I do not seek My own *g* . . . . John 8:50
"Give God the *g* . . . . John 9:24
g which I had with You . . . . . John 17:5
g which You gave Me I . . . John 17:22
he did not give *g* . . . . Acts 12:23
doing good seek for *g* . . . . Rom 2:7
in faith, giving *g* . . . . Rom 4:20
the adoption, the *g* . . . . Rom 9:4
the riches of His *g* . . . . Rom 9:23
God, alone wise, be *g* . . . . . Rom 16:27
who glories, let him *g* . . . . . 1 Cor 1:31
but woman is the *g* . . . . 1 Cor 11:7
of the *g* that excels . . . . 2 Cor 3:10
of the gospel of the *g* . . . . 2 Cor 4:4
eternal weight of *g* . . . . 2 Cor 4:17
who glories, let him *g* . . . . 2 Cor 10:17
to His riches in *g* . . . . Phil 4:19
appear with Him in *g* . . . . Col 3:4
For you are our *g* . . . . 1 Thess 2:20
You crowned him with *g* . . . . . Heb 2:7
many sons to *g* . . . . Heb 2:10
grass, and all the *g* . . . . 1 Pet 1:24
to whom belong the *g* . . . . 1 Pet 4:11
for the Spirit of *g* . . . . 1 Pet 4:14
To Him be the *g* and the . . . . 1 Pet 5:11
the presence of His *g* . . . . Jude 24
O Lord, to receive *g* . . . . Rev 4:11

GLORY OF GOD

The heavens declare the *g* . . . . Ps 19:1
unto death, but for the *g* . . . John 11:4
into heaven and saw the *g* . . Acts 7:55
fall short of the *g* . . . . Rom 3:23
do all to the *g* . . . . 1 Cor 10:31
he is the image and *g* . . . . . 1 Cor 11:7
g in the face of Jesus . . . . 2 Cor 4:6
with smoke from the *g* . . . . . . Rev 15:8
having the *g*. . . . . Rev 21:11
for the *g* illuminated it . . . . . Rev 21:23

GLORY OF THE LORD

g appeared in the cloud . . . . . Ex 16:10
g rested on Mount Sinai, ... Ex 24:16
g filled the tabernacle . . . . Ex 40:34
the *g* will appear to you . . . . . . Lev 9:6
g appeared in the . . . . Num 14:10
the *g* appeared to all . . . . . Num 16:19
and the *g* appeared . . . . Num 16:42
the *g* appeared to them . . . . Num 20:6
the *g* filled the house . . . . . . 1 Kin 8:11
the *g* filled the temple . . . . . . 2 Chr 7:1
May the *g* endure forever . . Ps 104:31
They shall see the *g* . . . . Is 35:2
the *g* shall be revealed, ... Is 40:5
the *g* is risen upon you . . . . Is 60:1
of the likeness of the *g* . . . . . Ezek 1:28
behold, the *g* stood there . . . Ezek 3:23
the *g* went up . . . . Ezek 10:4
the *g* came into the . . . . Ezek 43:4
g filled the house of the . . . . Ezek 44:4
the knowledge of the *g* . . . . . Hab 2:14
the *g* shone around them, . . . Luke 2:9
as in a mirror the *g*, ... 2 Cor 3:18
by us to the *g* . . . . 2 Cor 8:19

GLORYING

Your *g* is not good . . . . 1 Cor 5:6

GLUTTON

g will come to poverty . . . . Prov 23:21
you say, 'Look, a *g* . . . . Luke 7:34

GLUTTONS

companion of *g* shames . . . . Prov 28:7
evil beasts, lazy *g* . . . . Titus 1:12

GNASHING

will be weeping and *g* . . . . . . Matt 8:12

GO

He said, "Let Me *g* . . . . Gen 32:26
'Let My people *g* . . . . Ex 5:1
Presence does not *g* . . . . Ex 33:15
for wherever you *g* . . . . Ruth 1:16
"Look, I *g* forward . . . . Job 23:8
For I used to *g* with the . . . . . . Ps 42:4
g astray as soon as . . . . Ps 58:3
I will *g* in the strength of . . . . Ps 71:16
Those who *g* down to . . . . . . Ps 107:23
Where can I *g* from . . . . Ps 139:7
G to the ant . . . . Prov 6:6
All *g* to one place . . . . Eccl 3:20
of mourning than to *g* . . . . Eccl 7:2
out of Zion shall *g* forth . . . . Is 2:3
You wherever You *g* . . . . Matt 8:19
do not *g* out . . . . Matt 24:26
He said to them, "*G* . . . . . . Mark 16:15
And I say to one, '*G* . . . . Luke 7:8
also want to *g* away . . . . John 6:67
to whom shall we *g* . . . . John 6:68
g you cannot come . . . . John 8:21
I *g* to prepare a place . . . . . John 14:2
will do, because I *g* . . . . John 14:12
seek Me, let these *g* . . . . John 18:8
and he shall *g* out no more . . Rev 3:12

GOADS

of the wise are like *g* . . . . . . Eccl 12:11
to kick against the *g* . . . . Acts 9:5

GOAL

I press toward the *g* . . . . Phil 3:14

GOATS

drink the blood of *g* . . . . Ps 50:13
his sheep from the *g* . . . . . . Matt 25:32
with the blood of *g* . . . . Heb 9:12
g could take away . . . . Heb 10:4

GOD

See ANGEL OF GOD; GLORY OF GOD; HAND OF GOD; HOUSE OF GOD; KINGDOM OF GOD; LORD GOD OF HOSTS; LORD GOD OF ISRAEL; LOVE OF GOD; LOVE THE LORD YOUR GOD; MAN OF GOD; PEOPLE OF GOD; POWER OF GOD; RIGHTEOUSNESS OF GOD; SON OF GOD; SONS OF GOD; SPIRIT OF GOD; THINGS OF GOD; THRONE OF GOD; WILL OF GOD; WORD OF GOD; WRATH OF GOD

Names of:
God, Gen 1:1
LORD God, Gen 2:4
God Most High, Gen 14:18–22
Lord GOD, Gen 15:2, 8
Almighty God, Gen 17:1, 2
I AM, Ex 3:14
Jealous, Ex 34:14
Eternal God, Deut 33:27
Living God, Josh 3:10
God of hosts, Ps 80:7
LORD of hosts, Is 1:24
Holy One of Israel, Is 43:3, 14, 15
Mighty God, Jer 32:18
God of heaven, Jon 1:9
Heavenly Father, Matt 6:26
King eternal, 1 Tim 1:17
only Potentate, 1 Tim 6:15
Father of lights, James 1:17

Manifestations of:
face of, Gen 32:30
voice of, Deut 5:22–26
glory of, Ex 40:34, 35
Angel of, Gen 16:7–13
name of, Ex 34:5–7
form of, Num 12:6–8

Nature of:
spirit, John 4:24
one, Deut 6:4
personal, John 17:1–3
trinitarian, 2 Cor 13:14

Attributes of:
incomparable, 2 Sam 7:22
invisible, John 1:18
inscrutable, Is 40:28
unchangeable, Num 23:19
unequaled, Is 40:13–25
unsearchable, Rom 11:33, 34
infinite, 1 King 8:27
eternal, Is 57:15
omnipotent, Jer 32:17, 27
omnipresent, Ps 139:7–12
omniscient, 1 John 3:20
foreknowing, Is 48:3, 5
wise, Acts 15:18
holy, Rev 4:8
impartial, 1 Pet 1:17
just, Ps 89:14
longsuffering, Ex 34:6, 7
love, 1 John 4:8, 16
mercy, Lam 3:22, 23
truth, Ps 117:2
vengeance, Deut 32:34–41
wrath, Deut 32:22

G created the heavens . . . . Gen 1:1
Abram of *G* Most High . . . . Gen 14:19
and I will be their *G* . . . . Gen 17:8
hands of the Mighty *G* . . . . Gen 49:24
the *G* of Abraham . . . . Ex 3:6
He is my *G* . . . . Ex 15:2
Stand before *G* for the . . . . . . Ex 18:19
"I am the LORD your *G* . . . . Ex 20:2
"This is your *g* . . . . Ex 32:4
G is not a man . . . . Num 23:19
G is a consuming fire . . . . . . Deut 4:24
great and awesome *G* . . . . . . Deut 7:21
my people, and your *G* . . . . . Ruth 1:16
know that there is a *G* . . . 1 Sam 17:46
a rock, except our *G* . . . . . 2 Sam 22:32
If the LORD is *G* . . . . 1 Kin 18:21
G is greater than all . . . . 2 Chr 2:5
G is greater than . . . . Job 33:12
"Behold, *G* is mighty . . . . Job 36:5
"Behold, *G* is great . . . . Job 36:26
You have been My *G* . . . . Ps 22:10
"Where is your *G* . . . . Ps 42:3
G is our refuge . . . . Ps 46:1
G is in the midst of . . . . Ps 46:5
G is the King of all . . . . Ps 47:7
The Mighty One, *G* . . . . Ps 50:1
I am *G*, your *G* . . . . Ps 50:7
me a clean heart, O *G* . . . . Ps 51:10
Our *G* is the *G* . . . . Ps 68:20
Who is so great a *G* . . . . Ps 77:13
Restore us, O *G* . . . . Ps 80:7
You alone are *G* . . . . Ps 86:10
Exalt the LORD our *G* . . . . Ps 99:9
Yes, our *G* is merciful . . . . Ps 116:5
give thanks to the *G* . . . . Ps 136:26
For *G* is in heaven . . . . Eccl 5:2
Counselor, Mighty *G* . . . . Is 9:6
G is my salvation . . . . Is 12:2
Behold, this is our *G* . . . . Is 25:9
"Behold your *G* . . . . Is 40:9
Is there a *G* besides . . . . Is 44:8
to Zion, "Your *G* . . . . Is 52:7
stricken, smitten by *G* . . . . Is 53:4
and I will be their *G* . . . . Jer 31:33
and I saw visions of *G* . . . . . . Ezek 1:1
Who is a *G* like You . . . . Mic 7:18
translated, "*G* with us." . . . . Matt 1:23
in *G* my Savior . . . . Luke 1:47
the Word was with *G* . . . . John 1:1
enter the kingdom of *G* . . . . . John 3:5
For *G* so loved the . . . . John 3:16
has certified that *G* . . . . John 3:33
G is Spirit, and those . . . . . . John 4:24

"My Lord and my G ...... John 20:28
Christ is the Son of G ...... Acts 8:37
To the Unknown G .... Acts 17:23
Indeed, let G be true .... Rom 3:4
If G is for us .... Rom 8:31
G is faithful .... 1 Cor 1:9
us there is one G .... 1 Cor 8:6
G shall supply all .... Phil 4:19
and I will be their G .... Heb 8:10
G is a consuming fire ..... Heb 12:29
G is greater than our ..... 1 John 3:20
for G is love .... 1 John 4:8
No one has seen G .... 1 John 4:12
in the temple of My G ...... Rev 3:12
gave glory to the G .... Rev 11:13
G Himself will be .... Rev 21:3
and I will be his G .... Rev 21:7

GOD THE FATHER
G has set His seal on Him .. John 6:27
the kingdom to G .... 1 Cor 15:24
through Jesus Christ and G ... Gal 1:1
G and our Lord Jesus Christ .. Gal 1:3
for all things to G .... Eph 5:20
love with faith, from G ..... Eph 6:23
to the glory of G .... Phil 2:11
giving thanks to G .... Col 3:17
in G and the Lord Jesus .. 1 Thess 1:1
mercy, and peace from G ... 2 Tim 1:2
mercy, and peace from G ... Titus 1:4
the foreknowledge of G ...... 1 Pet 1:2
For He received from G .... 2 Pet 1:17
G and from the Lord Jesus .. 2 John 3
sanctified by G, and .... Jude 1

GODDESS
after Ashtoreth the g ...... 1 Kin 11:5
of the great g Diana ...... Acts 19:35

GODHEAD
eternal power and G .... Rom 1:20
the fullness of the G .... Col 2:9

GODLINESS
is the mystery of g .... 1 Tim 3:16
g is profitable .... 1 Tim 4:8
Now g with contentment ... 1 Tim 6:6
having a form of g .... 2 Tim 3:5
pertain to life and g .... 2 Pet 1:3
to perseverance g .... 2 Pet 1:6

GODLY
Himself him who is g .... Ps 4:3
everyone who is g .... Ps 32:6
who desire to live g .... 2 Tim 3:12
righteously, and g .... Titus 2:12
reverence and g fear ...... Heb 12:28
to deliver the g .... 2 Pet 2:9

GODS
See FOREIGN GODS
your God is God of g ..... Deut 10:17
the household g .... 2 Kin 23:24
He judges among the g .... Ps 82:1
I said, "You are g .... Ps 82:6
yourselves with g .... Is 57:5
If He called them g .... John 10:35
g have come down to ..... Acts 14:11

GOG
Prince of Rosh, Meshech, and Tubal, Ezek 38:2, 3
—— Leader of the final battle, Rev 20:8–15

GOLAN
City of refuge, Josh 20:8, 21:27

GOLD
And the g of that land ...... Gen 2:12
a mercy seat of pure g ...... Ex 25:17
multiply silver and g ...... Deut 17:17
"If I have made g .... Job 31:24
yea, than much fine g .... Ps 19:10
is like apples of g .... Prov 25:11
is Mine, and the g .... Hag 2:8
g I do not have .... Acts 3:6
with braided hair or g ...... 1 Tim 2:9
a man with g rings .... James 2:2
Your g and silver are ...... James 5:3
more precious than g .... 1 Pet 1:7
like silver or g .... 1 Pet 1:18
of the city was pure g ...... Rev 21:21

GOLDEN
g bell and a pomegranate ... Ex 28:34
g tumors and five g rats .... 1 Sam 6:4
from the g calves that .... 2 Kin 10:29
or the g bowl is broken, or .. Eccl 12:6
the seven g lampstands ..... Rev 1:20
and g bowls full of incense, .. Rev 5:8
g altar which is before ...... Rev 9:13
having in her hand a g cup .. Rev 17:4

GOLGOTHA
Where Jesus died, Matt 27:33–35

GOLIATH
Giant of Gath, 1 Sam 17:4
Killed by David, 1 Sam 17:50
—— Brother of above; killed by Elhanan, 2 Sam 21:19

GOMER
Son of Japheth, Gen 10:2, 3; 1 Chr 1:5, 6
Northern nation, Ezek 38:6
—— Wife of Hosea, Hos 1:2, 3

GOMORRAH
See SODOM AND GOMORRAH
With Sodom, defeated by Chedorlaomer; Lot captured, Gen 14:8–12
Destroyed by God, Gen 19:23–29
Later references to, Is 1:10; Amos 4:11; Matt 10:15

GONE
I am g like a shadow .... Ps 109:23
I have g astray like a ..... Ps 119:176
the word has g out of .... Is 45:23
like sheep have g .... Is 53:6

GOOD
See BE OF GOOD CHEER; LORD IS GOOD
God saw that it was g ...... Gen 1:10
but God meant it for g .... Gen 50:20
LORD has promised g ..... Num 10:29
you have spoken is g ..... 2 Kin 20:19
seeking the g of his .... Esth 10:3
Shall we indeed accept g .... Job 2:10
"Who will show us any g ...... Ps 4:6
is none who does g .... Ps 14:1
G and upright is the .... Ps 25:8
that he may see g .... Ps 34:12
Truly God is g to .... Ps 73:1
g man deals graciously ...... Ps 112:5
Your Spirit is g .... Ps 143:10
g man obtains favor .... Prov 12:2
g word makes it glad ..... Prov 12:25
on the evil and the g .... Prov 15:3
A merry heart does g ..... Prov 17:22
who knows what is g .... Eccl 6:12
learn to do g .... Is 1:17
Zion, you who bring g .... Is 40:9
tidings of g things .... Is 52:7
talked to me, with g .... Zech 1:13
said, "Be of g cheer .... Matt 9:22
A g man out of the .... Matt 12:35
"G Teacher, what g .... Matt 19:16
No one is g but One ...... Matt 19:17
For she has done a g ..... Matt 26:10
behold, I bring you g ...... Luke 2:10
love your enemies, do g ... Luke 6:35
"Can anything g come ..... John 1:46
Some said, "He is g .... John 7:12
who went about doing g .. Acts 10:38
For he was a g man .... Acts 11:24
in that He did g .... Acts 14:17
g man someone would ...... Rom 5:7
in my flesh) nothing g ..... Rom 7:18
overcome evil with g ...... Rom 12:21
according to the g pleasure .. Eph 1:5
fruitful in every g .... Col 1:10
know that the law is g ..... 1 Tim 1:8
may wage the g warfare .. 1 Tim 1:18
For this is g and .... 1 Tim 2:3
bishop, he desires a g ...... 1 Tim 3:1
for this is g and .... 1 Tim 5:4
a g soldier of Jesus Christ .. 2 Tim 2:3
prepared for every g ...... 2 Tim 2:21
I have fought the g fight ... 2 Tim 4:7
and have tasted the g .... Heb 6:5
obtained a g testimony ..... Heb 11:2
Every g gift and every .... James 1:17
g days, let him refrain ..... 1 Pet 3:10
to suffer for doing g .... 1 Pet 3:17
g stewards of the .... 1 Pet 4:10

GOOD WORKS
that they may see your g ... Matt 5:16
"Many g I have shown .... John 10:32
woman was full of g .... Acts 9:36
in Christ Jesus for g, ... Eph 2:10
godliness, with g .... 1 Tim 2:10
well reported for g; .... 1 Tim 5:10
g of some are clearly, ... 1 Tim 5:25
that they be rich in g ..... 1 Tim 6:18
to be a pattern of g .... Titus 2:7
stir up love and g .... Heb 10:24
by your g which they ...... 1 Pet 2:12

GOODNESS
"I will make all My g .... Ex 33:19
and abounding in g .... Ex 34:6
"You are my Lord, my g ..... Ps 16:2
Surely g and mercy .... Ps 23:6
that I would see the g .... Ps 27:13
how great is Your g .... Ps 31:19
The g of God endures .... Ps 52:1
how great is its g .... Zech 9:17
the riches of His g .... Rom 2:4
consider the g and .... Rom 11:22
kindness, g .... Gal 5:22

GOODS
When g increase .... Eccl 5:11
and plunder his g .... Matt 12:29
ruler over all his g .... Matt 24:47
"Soul, you have many g .. Luke 12:19
man was wasting his g .... Luke 16:1
I give half of my g .... Luke 19:8
has this world's g .... 1 John 3:17

GOSHEN
District of Egypt where Israel lived; the best of the land, Gen 45:10; 46:28, 29; 47:1–11

GOSPEL
See PREACH THE GOSPEL
The beginning of the g ..... Mark 1:1
and believe in the g .... Mark 1:15
g must first be preached .. Mark 13:10
to testify to the g .... Acts 20:24
separated to the g .... Rom 1:1
not ashamed of the g ...... Rom 1:16
should live from the g ..... 1 Cor 9:14
if our g is veiled .... 2 Cor 4:3
to a different g .... Gal 1:6
of truth, the g .... Eph 1:13
the mystery of the g .... Eph 6:19
g which you heard .... Col 1:23
the everlasting g .... Rev 14:6

GOSSIPS
only idle but also g .... 1 Tim 5:13

GOVERNMENT
and the g will be upon .... Is 9:6

GRACE
But Noah found g .... Gen 6:8
G is poured upon Your .... Ps 45:2
The LORD will give g .... Ps 84:11
the Spirit of g .... Zech 12:10
and the g of God was ...... Luke 2:40
g and truth came .... John 1:17
And great g was upon ...... Acts 4:33
G to you and peace .... Rom 1:7

But the word of God *g* .... Acts 12:24
the word of the Lord *g* .... Acts 19:20

GRIEF
burden and his own *g* ..... 2 Chr 6:29
g were fully weighed .... Job 6:2
Though I speak, my *g* .... Job 16:6
observe trouble and *g* .... Ps 10:14
of mirth may be *g* .... Prov 14:13
much wisdom is much *g* .... Eccl 1:18
and acquainted with *g* .... Is 53:3
joy and not with *g* .... Heb 13:17

GRIEVE
g the children of men ...... Lam 3:33
g the Holy Spirit .... Eph 4:30

GRIEVED
earth, and He was *g* .... Gen 6:6
Has not my soul *g* .... Job 30:25
forty years I was *g* .... Ps 95:10
a woman forsaken and *g* ...... Is 54:6
g His Holy Spirit .... Is 63:10
with anger, being *g* .... Mark 3:5
Peter was *g* because ...... John 21:17

GRINDERS
when the *g* cease .... Eccl 12:3

GRINDING
the sound of *g* is low .... Eccl 12:4
g the faces of the poor .... Is 3:15
Two women will be *g* ..... Matt 24:41

GROAN
The dying *g* in the .... Job 24:12
even we ourselves *g* .... Rom 8:23
who are in this tent *g* .... 2 Cor 5:4

GROANED
He *g* in the spirit and ...... John 11:33

GROANING
So God heard their *g* .... Ex 2:24
I am weary with my *g* .... Ps 6:6
Then Jesus, again *g* ...... John 11:38

GROANINGS
g which cannot .... Rom 8:26

GROPE
And you shall *g* .... Deut 28:29
They *g* in the dark .... Job 12:25
We *g* for the wall like .... Is 59:10
hope that they might *g* .... Acts 17:27

GROUND
"Cursed is the *g* .... Gen 3:17
you stand is holy *g* .... Ex 3:5
up your fallow *g* .... Jer 4:3
give its fruit, the *g* .... Zech 8:12
others fell on good *g* .... Matt 13:8
bought a piece of *g* .... Luke 14:18
God, the pillar and *g* ...... 1 Tim 3:15

GROUNDED
being rooted and *g* .... Eph 3:17

GROUPS
sit down in *g* of fifty .... Luke 9:14

GROW
they will all *g* old like ...... Ps 102:26
the horn of David *g* .... Ps 132:17
the earth will *g* old like .... Is 51:6
you shall go out and *g* .... Mal 4:2
truth in love, may *g* .... Eph 4:15
and they will all *g* .... Heb 1:11
but *g* in the grace and ..... 2 Pet 3:18

GROWN
plants *g* up in their youth .. Ps 144:12
They have *g* fat, they are ..... Jer 5:28
this people have *g* dull .... Matt 13:15
this people have *g* dull .... Acts 28:27

GROWS
shall eat every tree which *g* .. Ex 10:5
what *g* of its own accord ... Lev 25:11
It *g* old because of all my ...... Ps 6:7
when it is sown, it *g* up ..... Mark 4:32
g into a holy temple in the .. Eph 2:21

your faith *g* exceedingly .. 2 Thess 1:3

GROWTH
causes *g* of the body for .... Eph 4:16

GRUDGINGLY
in his heart, not *g* .... 2 Cor 9:7

GRUMBLERS
These are *g* .... Jude 16

GUARANTEE
in our hearts as a *g* .... 2 Cor 1:22
us the Spirit as a *g* .... 2 Cor 5:5
who is the *g* of our .... Eph 1:14

GUARD
g the way to the tree .... Gen 3:24
I will *g* my ways, lest I sin .... Ps 39:1
will be your rear *g* .... Is 52:12
g the doors of your .... Mic 7:5
we were kept under *g* .... Gal 3:23
to the whole palace *g* .... Phil 1:13
g your hearts and minds ...... Phil 4:7
g you from the evil one ... 2 Thess 3:3
G what was committed ..... 1 Tim 6:20

GUARDIANS
but is under *g* and .... Gal 4:2

GUARDS
Unless the LORD *g* .... Ps 127:1
And the *g* shook for .... Matt 28:4

GUIDANCE
and excellent in *g* .... Is 28:29

GUIDE
I will *g* you with My eye ..... Ps 32:8
He will be our *g* .... Ps 48:14
Father, You are the *g* .... Jer 3:4
g our feet into the .... Luke 1:79
has come, He will *g* ...... John 16:13
Judas, who became a *g* .... Acts 1:16
you yourself are a *g* .... Rom 2:19

GUIDES
Woe to you, blind *g* .... Matt 23:16
unless someone *g* .... Acts 8:31

GUILT
they accept their *g* .... Lev 26:41
g has grown up to the .... Ezra 9:6
of your fathers' *g* .... Matt 23:32

GUILTLESS
g who takes His name .... Ex 20:7
have condemned the *g* ..... Matt 12:7

GUILTY
"We are truly *g* .... Gen 42:21
we have been very *g* .... Ezra 9:7
the world may become *g* ... Rom 3:19
in one point, he is *g* ...... James 2:10

GULF
you there is a great *g* ..... Luke 16:26

HABAKKUK
Prophet in Judah just prior to Babylonian invasion, Hab 1:1
Prayer of, in praise of God, Hab 3:1–19

HABITATION
to Your holy *h* .... Ex 15:13
Is God in His holy *h* .... Ps 68:5
in a peaceful *h* .... Is 32:18
from His holy *h* .... Zech 2:13
be clothed with our *h* .... 2 Cor 5:2

HACHILAH
Hill in the Wilderness of Ziph where David hid, 1 Sam 23:19–26

HADADEZER
King of Zobah, 2 Sam 8:3–13
Defeated by David, 2 Sam 10:6–19

HADASSAH
Esther's Jewish name, Esth 2:7

HADES
be brought down to *H* .... Matt 11:23
H shall not prevail .... Matt 16:18
being in torments in *H* .... Luke 16:23
not leave my soul in *H* ..... Acts 2:27
I have the keys of *H* .... Rev 1:18
H were cast into the .... Rev 20:14

HAGAR
Sarah's servant; bears Ishmael to Abraham, Gen 16
Abraham sends her away; God comforts her, Gen 21:9–21
Paul explains symbolic meaning of, Gal 4:22–31

HAGGAI
Postexilic prophet; contemporary of Zechariah, Ezra 5:1, 2; 6:14; Hag 1:1

HAGGITH
One of David's wives, 2 Sam 3:4
Mother of Adonijah, 1 Kin 1:5

HAIL
cause very heavy *h* .... Ex 9:18
seen the treasury of *h* ..... Job 38:22
He casts out His *h* .... Ps 147:17
h will sweep away the .... Is 28:17
of the plague of the *h* ...... Rev 16:21

HAILSTONES
clouds passed with *h* .... Ps 18:12

HAIR
bring down my gray *h* ..... Gen 42:38
shaved his consecrated *h* .. Num 6:19
h of his head began to ..... Judg 16:22
he cut the *h* of his .... 2 Sam 14:26
the *h* on my body stood ..... Job 4:15
Your *h* is like a flock .... Song 4:1
h had grown like eagles' .... Dan 4:33
you cannot make one *h* .... Matt 5:36
clothed with camel's *h* ..... Mark 1:6
But not a *h* of your .... Luke 21:18
wiped His feet with her *h* .. John 11:2
He had his *h* cut off at ... Acts 18:18
since not a *h* will fall ..... Acts 27:34
if a woman has long *h* .... 1 Cor 11:15
not with braided *h* .... 1 Tim 2:9
arranging the *h* .... 1 Pet 3:3
h were white like wool, ... Rev 1:14
black as sackcloth of *h*, ... Rev 6:12
h like women's *h* .... Rev 9:8

HAIRS
are more than the *h* .... Ps 40:12
h I will carry you .... Is 46:4
yes, gray *h* are here .... Hos 7:9
But the very *h* .... Matt 10:30

HAIRY
h garment all over .... Gen 25:25
A *h* man wearing a leather .. 2 Kin 1:8

HAKKOZ
Descendant of Aaron, 1 Chr 24:1, 10
Called Koz, Ezra 2:61, 62
Descendants of, kept from priesthood, Neh 7:63, 64

HALF
h of it in the morning and ... Lev 6:20
h the tribe of Manasseh ..... Josh 22:9
h of the people followed .. 1 Kin 16:21
up to *h* the kingdom .... Esth 5:6
you, up to *h* my kingdom .. Mark 6:23
I give *h* of my goods to ..... Luke 19:8
h a time, from the .... Rev 12:14

HALLOW
hosts, Him you shall *h* .... Is 8:13
h the Holy One of .... Is 29:23
h the Sabbath day .... Jer 17:24

HALLOWED
the Sabbath day and *h* .... Ex 20:11
but I will be *h* .... Lev 22:32
who is holy shall be *h* .... Is 5:16

heaven, *h* be Your name .... Matt 6:9

HAM
Noah's youngest son, Gen 5:32
Enters ark, Gen 7:7
His immoral behavior merits Noah's curse, Gen 9:22–25
Father of descendants of repopulated earth, Gen 10:6–20

HAMAN
Plots to destroy Jews, Esth 3:3–15
Invited to Esther's banquet, Esth 5:1–14
Forced to honor Mordecai, Esth 6:5–14
Hanged on his own gallows, Esth 7:1–10

HAMATH
Israel's northern boundary, Num 34:8; 1 Kin 8:65; Ezek 47:16–20
Conquered, 2 Kin 18:34; Jer 49:23
Israelites exiled there, Is 11:11

HAMMER
h that breaks the rock ...... Jer 23:29
How the *h* of the whole ..... Jer 50:23

HAMOR
Sells land to Jacob, Gen 33:18–20; Acts 7:16
Killed by Jacob's sons, Gen 34:1–31

HAMSTRUNG
their self-will they *h* an ox .. Gen 49:6
David *h* all the chariot ..... 2 Sam 8:4

HANANI
Father of Jehu the prophet, 1 Kin 16:1, 7
Rebukes Asa; confined to prison, 2 Chr 16:7–10
—— Nehemiah's brother; brings news concerning the Jews, Neh 1:2
Becomes a governor of Jerusalem, Neh 7:2

HANANIAH
False prophet who contradicts Jeremiah, Jer 28:1–17
—— Hebrew name of Shadrach, Dan 1:6, 7, 11

HAND
See AT THE RIGHT HAND; HIS RIGHT HAND; MY RIGHT HAND; STRETCH OUT MY HAND; STRETCHED OUT HIS HAND
lest he put out his *h* .... Gen 3:22
h shall be against .... Gen 16:12
your *h* under my thigh .... Gen 24:2
h toward Israel's right *h* ... Gen 48:13
What is that in your *h* .... Ex 4:2
took the rod of God in his *h* .. Ex 4:20
tooth for tooth, *h* .... Ex 21:24
lay his *h* on the bull's head ... Lev 4:4
Egypt with a mighty *h* ..... Deut 9:26
and strengthened his *h* .. 1 Sam 23:16
Uzzah put out his *h* .... 2 Sam 6:6
let us fall into the *h* ...... 2 Sam 24:14
Then, by the good *h* .... Ezra 8:18
He would loose His *h* .... Job 6:9
he stretches out his *h* ...... Job 15:25
that your own right *h* ...... Job 40:14
h has held me up .... Ps 18:35
My times are in Your *h* ..... Ps 31:15
and night Your *h* .... Ps 32:4
Your right *h* is full .... Ps 48:10
Let Your *h* be upon the ..... Ps 80:17
h shall be established .... Ps 89:21
"Sit at My right *h* .... Ps 110:1
days is in her right *h* .... Prov 3:16
heart is in the *h* .... Prov 21:1
Whatever your *h* finds ...... Eccl 9:10
is at his right *h* .... Eccl 10:2
do not withhold your *h* ..... Eccl 11:6
His left *h* is under my .... Song 8:3
My *h* has laid the .... Is 48:13
Behold, the LORD's *h* .... Is 59:1
are the work of Your *h* .... Is 64:8
the clay is in the potter's *h* ... Jer 18:6
Am I a God near at *h* .... Jer 23:23
and incense in their *h*, to .... Jer 41:5
h under their wings .... Ezek 10:8
a measuring rod in his *h* ... Ezek 40:3
of a man's *h* appeared .... Dan 5:5
a *h* touched me, which .... Dan 10:10
of heaven is at *h* .... Matt 3:2
if your right *h* causes ...... Matt 5:30
do not let your left *h* .... Matt 6:3
h causes you to sin .... Mark 9:43
sitting at the right *h* ..... Mark 14:62
delivered from the *h* .... Luke 1:74
Sit at My right *h*. .... Acts 2:34
at the right *h* of God .... Acts 7:55
is even at the right *h* .... Rom 8:34
Because I am not a *h* ..... 1 Cor 12:15
with my own *h* .... 1 Cor 16:21
the right *h* of fellowship ..... Gal 2:9
by the *h* of a mediator .... Gal 3:19
to you with my own *h* .... Gal 6:11
The Lord is at *h* .... Phil 4:5
sitting at the right *h* of God ... Col 3:1
"Sit at My right *h* .... Heb 1:13
right *h* of the throne of the ... Heb 8:1
down at the right *h* .... Heb 10:12
of the Lord is at *h* .... James 5:8
in His right *h* seven stars .... Rev 1:16
stars in His right *h* .... Rev 2:1

HAND OF GOD
the *h* was very heavy ..... 1 Sam 5:11
the *h* was on Judah ..... 2 Chr 30:12
the *h* has struck me .... Job 19:21
was from the *h* .... Eccl 2:24
their works are in the *h* ..... Eccl 9:1
under the mighty *h*, ... 1 Pet 5:6

HAND OF THE LORD
the *h* was against them, ... Deut 2:15
earth may know the *h*, ... Josh 4:24
of Israel out of the *h* ...... Josh 22:31
h has gone out against ..... Ruth 1:13
h was heavy on the .... 1 Sam 5:6
h was against the .... 1 Sam 7:13
let us fall into the *h* ...... 2 Sam 24:14
h came upon Elijah; ..... 1 Kin 18:46
the *h* came upon him ...... 2 Kin 3:15
according to the *h* .... Ezra 7:6
h my God was upon me .... Ezra 7:28
the *h* has done this .... Job 12:9
the right *h* does valiantly ... Ps 118:15
king's heart is in the *h* ..... Prov 21:1
crown of glory in the *h* .... Is 62:3
the *h* shall be known .... Is 66:14
the *h* was strong upon me .. Ezek 3:14
the *h* came upon me .... Ezek 37:1
And the *h* was with him ... Luke 1:66
And the *h* was with them .. Acts 11:21
the *h* is upon you, ... Acts 13:11

HANDIWORK
firmament shows His *h* .... Ps 19:1

HANDKERCHIEFS
so that even *h* or aprons .. Acts 19:12

HANDLE
h the law did not know .... Jer 2:8
H Me and see .... Luke 24:39
do not taste, do not *h* .... Col 2:21

HANDLED
and our hands have *h* ...... 1 John 1:1

HANDS
the *h* are the *h* .... Gen 27:22
and Hur supported his *h* .... Ex 17:12
Moses had laid his *h* on ... Deut 34:9
here we are, in your *h* ..... Josh 9:25
took his life in his *h* ...... 1 Sam 19:5
put my life in my *h* ...... 1 Sam 28:21
but His *h* make whole .... Job 5:18
and cleanse my *h* .... Job 9:30
h have made me and .... Job 10:8
They pierced My *h* .... Ps 22:16
washed my *h* in innocence .. Ps 73:13
establish the work of our *h* .. Ps 90:17
In their *h* they shall bear .... Ps 91:12
h formed the dry land .... Ps 95:5
stretches out her *h* .... Prov 31:19
say, 'He has no *h* .... Is 45:9
strike your *h* together .... Ezek 21:14
was cut out without *h* ...... Dan 2:34
on the palms of my *h* ...... Dan 10:10
The *h* of Zerubbabel have .... Zech 4:9
than having two *h* .... Matt 18:8
will lay *h* on the sick ..... Mark 16:18
into Your *h* I commit ..... Luke 23:46
Behold My *h* and My ..... Luke 24:39
only, but also my *h* .... John 13:9
h the print of the .... John 20:25
his chains fell off his *h* ..... Acts 12:7
know that these *h* .... Acts 20:34
and he laid his *h* on him .... Acts 28:8
a house not made with *h* .... 2 Cor 5:1
his *h* what is good .... Eph 4:28
made without *h* .... Col 2:11
lifting up holy *h* .... 1 Tim 2:8
the laying on of the *h* ..... 1 Tim 4:14
Do not lay *h* on anyone ... 1 Tim 5:22
the laying on of my *h* ...... 2 Tim 1:6
baptisms, of laying on of *h* ... Heb 6:2
not made with *h* .... Heb 9:11
to fall into the *h* .... Heb 10:31
Cleanse your *h*, you .... James 4:8
and our *h* have handled, ... 1 John 1:1
foreheads or on their *h* ..... Rev 20:4

HANDWRITING
having wiped out the *h* ...... Col 2:14

HANG
They will *h* on him all the .... Is 22:24
commandments *h* all the .. Matt 22:40
the hands which *h* down .. Heb 12:12

HANGED
for he who is *h* .... Deut 21:23
went and *h* himself .... Matt 27:5

HANGS
h the earth on nothing .... Job 26:7
is everyone who *h* .... Gal 3:13

HANNAH
Barren wife of Elkanah; prays for a son, 1 Sam 1:1–18
Bears Samuel and dedicates him to the Lord, 1 Sam 1:19–28
Magnifies God, 1 Sam 2:1–10

HANUN
King of Ammon; disgraces David's ambassadors and is defeated by him, 2 Sam 10:1–14

HAPPEN
show us what will *h* .... Is 41:22
understand what will *h* .... Dan 10:14
not know what will *h* ..... James 4:14

HAPPINESS
one year, and bring *h* ...... Deut 24:5

HAPPY
h are these your servants ... 2 Chr 9:7
H is the man who has .... Ps 127:5
H are the people who ...... Ps 144:15
H is the man who finds .... Prov 3:13
mercy on the poor, *h* ..... Prov 14:21
trusts in the LORD, *h* ...... Prov 16:20
h is he who keeps .... Prov 29:18
H is he who does not ..... Rom 14:22

HARAN
Abraham's younger brother, Gen 11:26–31
—— City of Mesopotamia, Gen 11:31
Abraham leaves, Gen 12:4, 5
Jacob dwells at, Gen 29:4–35

HARASS
and Judah shall not *h* . . . . Is 11:13
h some from the church . . . . Acts 12:1

HARD
Is anything too *h* . . . . Gen 18:14
Pharaoh's heart is *h* . . . . Ex 7:14
test him with *h* questions . . 1 Kin 10:1
His heart is as *h* . . . . Job 41:24
shown Your people *h* . . . . Ps 60:3
of the unfaithful is *h* . . . . . . Prov 13:15
h to bear, and lay them . . . . Matt 23:4
I knew you to be a *h* . . . . . . Matt 25:24
"This is a *h* saying . . . . John 6:60
It is *h* for you to kick . . . . Acts 9:5
are some things *h* . . . . 2 Pet 3:16

HARDEN
But I will *h* his heart . . . . Ex 4:21
Do not *h* your hearts . . . . Ps 95:8
h your hearts as . . . . Heb 3:8

HARDENED
But Pharaoh *h* his . . . . Ex 8:32
Who has *h* himself . . . . Job 9:4
their heart was *h* . . . . Mark 6:52
eyes and *h* their hearts . . . John 12:40
lest any of you be *h* . . . . Heb 3:13

HARDENS
A wicked man *h* his . . . . . . Prov 21:29
h his heart will fall . . . . Prov 28:14
whom He wills He *h* . . . . Rom 9:18

HARDER
brother offended is *h* to . . . Prov 18:19
their faces *h* than rock . . . . Jer 5:3
h than flint, I have made . . . . Ezek 3:9

HARDSHIP
h that has befallen us . . . . . Num 20:14
h as a good soldier . . . . 2 Tim 2:3

HARLOT
play the *h* with their gods . . . Ex 34:16
shall be no ritual *h* . . . . Deut 23:17
of a *h* named Rahab . . . . Josh 2:1
h is a deep pit . . . . Prov 23:27
the deeds of a brazen *h* . . . Ezek 16:30
Oholah played the *h* . . . . Ezek 23:5
you, Israel, play the *h*, let . . . Hos 4:15
h is one body with . . . . 1 Cor 6:16
h Rahab did not perish . . . . Heb 11:31
of the great *h* who . . . . Rev 17:1

HARLOTRIES
the land with your *h* . . . . Jer 3:2
Let her put away her *h* . . . . . . Hos 2:2

HARLOTRY
through her casual *h* . . . . Jer 3:9
the lewdness of your *h* . . . . . Jer 13:27
let them put their *h* . . . . Ezek 43:9
are the children of *h* . . . . Hos 2:4
Ephraim, you commit *h* . . . . . . Hos 5:3
for the spirit of *h* . . . . Hos 5:4

HARLOTS
his blood while the *h* . . . . . 1 Kin 22:38
h enter the kingdom . . . . . . Matt 21:31
Great, The Mother of *H* . . . . . Rev 17:5

HARM
do My prophets no *h* . . . . . 1 Chr 16:22
they thought to do me *h* . . . . . Neh 6:2
those who sought their *h* . . . . Esth 9:2
it only causes *h* . . . . Ps 37:8
and do My prophets no *h* . . . Ps 105:15
and I will not *h* you . . . . Jer 25:6
Do yourself no *h*, for we . . Acts 16:28
Love does no *h* to a . . . . Rom 13:10
and do not *h* the oil . . . . Rev 6:6
Do not *h* the earth, the . . . . Rev 7:3

HARMLESS
become blameless and *h* . . . . Phil 2:15
for us, who is holy, *h* . . . . Heb 7:26

HARMONIOUS
the harp, with *h* sound . . . . Ps 92:3

HAROD
Well near Gideon's camp, Judg 7:1

HARP
those who play the *h* . . . . Gen 4:21
skillful player on the *h* . . 1 Sam 16:16
Praise the LORD with the *h*. . . . Ps 33:2
Sing to the LORD with the *h*. . . Ps 98:5
On a *h* of ten strings I will . . Ps 144:9
with the lute and *h* . . . . Ps 150:3
Lamb, each having a *h* . . . . Rev 5:8

HARPS
to direct with *h* on the . . . . 1 Chr 15:21
We hung our *h* upon the . . . . Ps 137:2
playing their *h* . . . . Rev 14:2
of glass, having *h* of God . . . . Rev 15:2

HARSH
a *h* word stirs up anger . . . . Prov 15:1
"Your words have been *h* . . . Mal 3:13
but also to the *h* . . . . 1 Pet 2:18

HARVEST
See FEAST OF HARVEST
seedtime and *h* . . . . Gen 8:22
to death in the days of *h* . . 2 Sam 21:9
He who sleeps in *h* is a . . . . Prov 10:5
to the joy of *h* . . . . Is 9:3
cloud of dew in the heat of *h* . . Is 18:4
shall eat up your *h* . . . . Jer 5:17
"The *h* is past . . . . Jer 8:20
of her *h* will come . . . . Jer 51:33
the sickle, for the *h* is ripe . . Joel 3:13
h truly is plentiful . . . . Matt 9:37
pray the Lord of the *h* . . . . . Matt 9:38
sickle, because the *h* . . . . . . Mark 4:29
pray the Lord of the *h* to . . . Luke 10:2
already white for *h* . . . . John 4:35
the *h* of the earth is . . . . Rev 14:15

HASTE
you shall eat it in *h* . . . . Ex 12:11
For I said in my *h* . . . . Ps 31:22
And they came with *h* . . . . . Luke 2:16
"Zacchaeus, make *h* . . . . Luke 19:5

HASTEN
be multiplied who *h* . . . . Ps 16:4
Do not *h* in your . . . . Eccl 7:9
I, the LORD, will *h* . . . . Is 60:22

HASTENING
h the coming of the . . . . 2 Pet 3:12

HASTENS
and he sins who *h* . . . . Prov 19:2
with an evil eye *h* . . . . Prov 28:22
is near and *h* quickly . . . . . . Zeph 1:14

HASTILY
utter anything *h* . . . . Eccl 5:2
lay hands on anyone *h* . . . . 1 Tim 5:22

HASTY
Do you see a man *h* . . . . Prov 29:20

HATE
'You shall not *h* . . . . Lev 19:17
h all workers of . . . . Ps 5:5
h the righteous shall . . . . Ps 34:21
love the LORD, *h* evil . . . . Ps 97:10
h every false way . . . . Ps 119:104
h the double-minded . . . . . . Ps 119:113
I *h* and abhor lying . . . . Ps 119:163
love, and a time to *h* . . . . Eccl 3:8
h robbery for burnt . . . . Is 61:8
H evil, love good . . . . Amos 5:15
I *h*, I despise your feast . . . Amos 5:21
You who *h* good and . . . . Mic 3:2
either he will *h* the one . . . . . Matt 6:24
but what I *h*, that I do . . . . . . Rom 7:15
Nicolaitans, which I also *h* . . . Rev 2:6
these will *h* the harlot, ... Rev 17:16

HATED
So Esau *h* Jacob because . . Gen 27:41
they *h* knowledge . . . . Prov 1:29
Therefore I *h* life . . . . Eccl 2:17
h all my labor in . . . . Eccl 2:18
but Esau I have *h* . . . . Mal 1:3
And you will be *h* . . . . Matt 10:22
have seen and also *h* . . . . . John 15:24
h Me without a cause . . . . . . John 15:25
world has *h* them . . . . John 17:14
but Esau I have *h* . . . . Rom 9:13
For no one ever *h* . . . . Eph 5:29
and *h* lawlessness . . . . Heb 1:9

HATEFUL
h woman when she is . . . . . Prov 30:23
in malice and envy, *h* . . . . Titus 3:3

HATERS
The *h* of the LORD . . . . Ps 81:15
backbiters, *h* of God . . . . Rom 1:30

HATES
six things the LORD *h* . . . . . . Prov 6:16
lose it, and he who *h* . . . . . . John 12:25
"If the world *h* . . . . John 15:18
h his brother is . . . . 1 John 2:11

HATING
h even the garment defiled . . . Jude 23

HATRED
I hate them with perfect *h* . . Ps 139:22

HAUGHTY
Your eyes are on the *h* . . 2 Sam 22:28
bring down *h* looks . . . . Ps 18:27
my heart is not *h* . . . . Ps 131:1
h spirit before a fall . . . . . . Prov 16:18
A proud and *h* man . . . . Prov 21:24
Do not be *h*, but fear . . . . . . Rom 11:20
age not to be *h* . . . . 1 Tim 6:17

HAUNTS
are full of the *h* . . . . Ps 74:20

HAURAN
District southeast of Mt. Hermon, Ezek 47:16

HAVE MERCY
h on me, and hear my prayer . . Ps 4:1
h on me, for I am . . . . Ps 25:16
H upon me, O God, ... Ps 51:1
arise and *h* on Zion; . . . . Ps 102:13
and forsakes them will *h* . . Prov 28:13
nor *h* on their fatherless . . . . . . Is 9:17
the Lord will *h* . . . . Is 14:1
will *h* on His afflicted . . . . Is 49:13
not pity nor spare nor *h* . . . . Jer 13:14
I will surely *h* on him," . . . . . Jer 31:20
captives of Jacob, and *h* . . Ezek 39:25
I will no longer *h* . . . . Hos 1:6
how long will You not *h* . . . Zech 1:12
"Son of David, *h* on us . . . . . Matt 9:27
"*H* on me, O Lord . . . . Matt 15:22
Lord, *h* on my son, ... Matt 17:15
"*H* on us, O Lord, ... Matt 20:30
"Jesus, Son of David, *h* . . Mark 10:47
'Father Abraham, *h* . . . . Luke 16:24
"Jesus, Master, *h* on us . . . Luke 17:13
"Jesus, Son of David, *h* . . . Luke 18:38
"I will *h* on whomever . . . . . Rom 9:15
that He might *h* on all . . . . . Rom 11:32

HAVEN
shall dwell by the *h* . . . . Gen 49:13
to their desired *h* . . . . Ps 107:30

HAVOC
for Saul, he made *h* . . . . Acts 8:3

HAY
precious stones, wood, *h* . . 1 Cor 3:12

HAZAEL
Anointed king of Syria by Elijah, 1 Kin 19:15–17
Elisha predicts his taking the throne, 2 Kin 8:7–15
Oppresses Israel, 2 Kin 8:28, 29; 10:32, 33; 12:17, 18; 13:3–7, 22

HAZAR ENAN
Village of north Palestine, Num 34:9, 10

HAZEROTH
Scene of sedition of Miriam and Aaron, Num 11:35—12:16

HAZOR
Royal Canaanite city destroyed by Joshua, Josh 11:1–13
Rebuilt and assigned to Naphtali, Josh 19:32, 36
Army of, defeated by Deborah and Barak, Judg 4:1–24

HE WHO BELIEVES
H and is baptized . . . . Mark 16:16
H in Him is not . . . . John 3:18
H in the Son has . . . . John 3:36
h in Me shall never thirst . . John 6:35
h in Me has everlasting . . . . John 6:47
H in Me, as the Scripture . . John 7:38
H, though he may die, ... John 11:25
and said, "*H* in Me, ... John 12:44
h in Me, the works that . . . John 14:12
precious, and *h* on Him . . . . . 1 Pet 2:6
the world, but *h* . . . . 1 John 5:5
H in the Son of God . . . . . . 1 John 5:10

HEAD
He shall bruise your *h* . . . . . . Gen 3:15
white baskets on my *h* . . . . Gen 40:16
on the *h* of the bed . . . . Gen 47:31
your right hand on his *h* . . . Gen 48:18
shall come upon his *h* . . . . 1 Sam 1:11
a bronze helmet on his *h* . . 1 Sam 17:5
and cut off his *h* with . . . . 1 Sam 17:51
crown from his *h* . . . . 2 Sam 12:30
put ashes on her *h* . . . . 2 Sam 13:19
and dust on his *h* . . . . 2 Sam 15:32
My *h*, my *h*!" . . . . 2 Kin 4:19
is with us as our *h* . . . . 2 Chr 13:12
my skin, and laid my *h* . . . . Job 16:15
return upon his own *h* . . . . Ps 7:16
of pure gold upon his *h* . . . . Ps 21:3
the lip, they shake the *h* . . . . . . Ps 22:7
You anoint my *h* with oil . . . . . Ps 23:5
than the hairs of my *h* . . . . . . Ps 40:12
the precious oil upon the *h* . . Ps 133:2
The silver-haired *h* is a . . . Prov 16:31
old men is their gray *h* . . . . Prov 20:29
coals of fire on his *h* . . . . . Prov 25:22
h is covered with dew . . . . . . Song 5:2
The whole *h* is sick . . . . Is 1:5
it to bow down his *h* . . . . Is 58:5
For every *h* shall be bald . . . Jer 48:37
visions of my *h* troubled . . . . . Dan 4:5
could lift up his *h* . . . . Zech 1:21
you swear by your *h* . . . . Matt 5:36
you fast, anoint your *h* . . . . . Matt 6:17
Baptist's *h* here on a . . . . Matt 14:8
first the blade, then the *h* . . Mark 4:28
and poured it on His *h* . . . . . Mark 14:3
thorns, put it on His *h* . . . . Mark 15:17
did not anoint My *h* with . . Luke 7:46
has nowhere to lay His *h* . . Luke 9:58
bowing His *h*, He gave . . . . John 19:30
coals of fire on his *h* . . . . . . Rom 12:20
having his *h* covered . . . . . . 1 Cor 11:4
or prophesies with her *h* . . . 1 Cor 11:5
and gave Him to be *h* . . . . Eph 1:22
For the husband is *h* . . . . Eph 5:23
His *h* and his hair . . . . Rev 1:14
having on His *h* a golden . . Rev 14:14
His *h* were many crowns . . Rev 19:12

HEADS
See BOWED THEIR HEADS
men to ride over our *h* . . . . . . Ps 66:12
Him, wagging their *h* . . . . . Matt 27:39
dragon having seven *h* . . . . . . Rev 12:3

HEAL
I wound and I *h* . . . . Deut 32:39
surely I will *h* you . . . . 2 Kin 20:5
O LORD, *h* me . . . . Ps 6:2
H my soul, for I have . . . . Ps 41:4
time to kill, and a time to *h* . . Eccl 3:3
sent Me to *h* the . . . . Is 61:1
h your backslidings . . . . Jer 3:22
who can *h* you . . . . Lam 2:13
torn, but He will *h* . . . . Hos 6:1
h all kinds of sickness . . . . . Matt 10:1
H the sick, cleanse . . . . Matt 10:8
to *h* on the Sabbath . . . . Matt 12:10
so that I should *h* . . . . Matt 13:15
power to *h* sicknesses . . . . . Mark 3:15
sent Me to *h* the . . . . Luke 4:18
Physician, *h* yourself . . . . . . Luke 4:23

HEALED
I have *h* this water . . . . 2 Kin 2:21
His word and *h* them . . . . Ps 107:20
And return and be *h* . . . . Is 6:10
His stripes we are *h* . . . . Is 53:5
h the hurt of My . . . . Jer 6:14
When I would have *h* . . . . Hos 7:1
and He *h* them . . . . Matt 4:24
and my servant will be *h* . . . . Matt 8:8
and *h* all who were sick, . . . Matt 8:16
Jesus' feet, and He *h* . . . . . . Matt 15:30
be *h* of their diseases, ... Luke 6:17
demon-possessed was *h* . . . Luke 8:36
h the child, and gave him . . Luke 9:42
touched his ear and *h* . . . . Luke 22:51
and they were all *h* . . . . Acts 5:16
he had faith to be *h* . . . . Acts 14:9
but rather be *h* . . . . Heb 12:13
that you may be *h* . . . . James 5:16
whose stripes you were *h* . . 1 Pet 2:24
his deadly wound was *h* . . . . Rev 13:3

HEALING
h shall spring forth . . . . Is 58:8
so that there is no *h* . . . . Jer 14:19
Your injury has no *h* . . . . Nah 3:19
shall arise with *h* . . . . Mal 4:2
and *h* all kinds of . . . . Matt 4:23
h all who were oppressed . Acts 10:38
tree were for the *h* . . . . Rev 22:2

HEALINGS
to another gifts of *h* . . . . 1 Cor 12:9
Do all have gifts of *h* . . . . . 1 Cor 12:30

HEALS
h all your diseases . . . . Ps 103:3
He *h* the broken-hearted . . . . Ps 147:3
h the stroke of their . . . . Is 30:26
Jesus the Christ *h* . . . . Acts 9:34

HEALTH
It will be *h* to your flesh, ... Prov 3:8
and *h* to all their flesh . . . . . Prov 4:22
of the wise promotes *h* . . . . Prov 12:18
to the soul and *h* . . . . Prov 16:24
and for a time of *h* . . . . Jer 8:15
no recovery for the *h* . . . . Jer 8:22
For I will restore *h* to you . . Jer 30:17
all things and be in *h* . . . . 3 John 2

HEAP
This *h* is a witness . . . . Gen 31:48
I could *h* up words . . . . Job 16:4
sea together as a *h* . . . . Ps 33:7
so you will *h* coals of . . . . . . Prov 25:22
ears, they will *h* . . . . 2 Tim 4:3

HEAPS
Though he *h* up silver . . . . . Job 27:16

HEAR
See EARS TO HEAR
with us, and we will *h* . . . . . Ex 20:19
Me, I will surely *h* their . . . . . Ex 22:23
"*H*, O Israel: The LORD . . . . . . Deut 6:4
Him you shall *h* . . . . Deut 18:15
of the oxen which I *h* . . . . 1 Sam 15:14
You *h* the supplication of . . 1 Kin 8:30
h in heaven Your . . . . 1 Kin 8:43
H me when I call . . . . Ps 4:1
O You who *h* prayer . . . . Ps 65:2
h what God the LORD . . . . Ps 85:8
ear, shall He not *h* . . . . Ps 94:9
h the words of the . . . . Prov 22:17
h rather than to give . . . . Eccl 5:1
H, O heavens, and give ear . . . . . Is 1:2
H, you who are afar . . . . Is 33:13
Let the earth *h* . . . . Is 34:1
I have made you *h* new . . . . Is 48:6
I spoke, you did not *h* . . . . Is 65:12
cleansed and the deaf *h* . . . . Matt 11:5
'Hearing you will *h* . . . . Matt 13:14
if he will not *h* . . . . Matt 18:16
"Take heed what you *h* . . . . Mark 4:24
ears, do you not *h* . . . . Mark 8:18
h the sound of it . . . . John 3:8
that God does not *h* . . . . John 9:31
My sheep *h* My voice . . . . . John 10:27
And how shall they *h* . . . . . Rom 10:14
man be swift to *h* . . . . James 1:19
those who *h* the words of . . . . Rev 1:3
h what the Spirit says . . . . Rev 2:7
has an ear, let him *h* . . . . Rev 13:9

HEARD
h the sound of the . . . . Gen 3:8
h their cry because of . . . . Ex 3:7
you only *h* a voice . . . . Deut 4:12
certainly God has *h* . . . . Ps 66:19
quietly, should be *h* . . . . Eccl 9:17
Have you not *h* . . . . Is 40:21
world men have not *h* . . . . Is 64:4
Who has *h* such a thing . . . . Is 66:8
h Ephraim bemoaning . . . . . . Jer 31:18
that they will be *h* . . . . Matt 6:7
h the word believed . . . . Acts 4:4
I say, have they not *h* . . . . . Rom 10:18
not seen, nor ear *h* . . . . 1 Cor 2:9
h inexpressible words . . . . . 2 Cor 12:4
things that you have *h* . . . . . 2 Tim 2:2
the things we have *h* . . . . Heb 2:1
the word which they *h* . . . . Heb 4:2
from death, and was *h* . . . . Heb 5:7
which we have *h* . . . . 1 John 1:1
Lord's Day, and I *h* . . . . Rev 1:10

HEARER
if anyone is a *h* . . . . James 1:23
is not a forgetful *h* . . . . James 1:25

HEARERS
for not the *h* of the . . . . Rom 2:13
impart grace to the *h* . . . . Eph 4:29
of the word, and not *h* . . . . James 1:22

HEARING
and read in the *h* . . . . Ex 24:7
Book of Moses in the *h* . . . . . Neh 13:1
Do not speak in the *h* . . . . . . Prov 23:9
'Keep on *h*, but do not . . . . Is 6:9
h they do not . . . . Matt 13:13
h they may hear . . . . Mark 4:12
If the whole were *h* . . . . . . 1 Cor 12:17
or by the *h* of faith . . . . Gal 3:2
have become dull of *h* . . . . . . Heb 5:11

HEARS
for Your servant *h* . . . . 1 Sam 3:9
out, and the LORD *h* . . . . Ps 34:17
He who *h* you *h* Me . . . . . . Luke 10:16
of God *h* God's words . . . . . . John 8:47
And if anyone *h* . . . . John 12:47
who is of the truth *h* . . . . . . John 18:37
He who knows God *h* . . . . . 1 John 4:6
And let him who *h* . . . . Rev 22:17

HEART
See UPRIGHT IN HEART; WITH ALL YOUR HEART
h was only evil . . . . Gen 6:5
for you know the *h* . . . . Ex 23:9
as many as had a willing *h* . . Ex 35:22
h the LORD had put . . . . Ex 36:2
seek Him with all your *h* . . . Deut 4:29
the foreskin of your *h* . . . . . Deut 10:16
whatever your *h* desires . . Deut 14:26
and confusion of *h* . . . . Deut 28:28
will circumcise your *h* . . . . . Deut 30:6
incline your *h* to the . . . . . . Josh 24:23
great searchings of *h* . . . . . . Judg 5:16

HEARTILY

HEARTS

HEAT

HEATHEN

HEAVEN

HEAVEN AND EARTH

HEAVENLY

HEAVENLY FATHER

HEAVENS

HEAVINESS

HEAVY

HEBREW

HEBRON

HEDGE

HEDGED

HEED

and let us not give *h* ... Jer 18:18
Take *h*, watch and pray ... Mark 13:33
stands take *h* lest he ... 1 Cor 10:12
nor give *h* to fables ... 1 Tim 1:4
giving *h* to deceiving ... 1 Tim 4:1
the more earnest *h* ... Heb 2:1

HEEDS
h counsel is wise ... Prov 12:15

HEEL
you shall bruise His *h* ... Gen 3:15
took hold of Esau's *h* ... Gen 25:26
has lifted up his *h* ... Ps 41:9
Me has lifted up his *h* ... John 13:18

HEIFER
a red *h* without blemish ... Num 19:2
not plowed with my *h* ... Judg 14:18
goats and the ashes of a *h* ... Heb 9:13

HEIGHT
"Is not God in the *h* ... Job 22:12
looked down from the *h* ... Ps 102:19
nor *h* nor depth ... Rom 8:39
length and depth and *h* ... Eph 3:18

HEIR
own body shall be your *h* ... Gen 15:4
Has he no *h* ... Jer 49:1
Now I say that the *h* ... Gal 4:1
if a son, then an *h* ... Gal 4:7
He has appointed *h* ... Heb 1:2
the world and became *h* ... Heb 11:7

HEIRS
of God and joint *h* ... Rom 8:17
should be fellow *h* ... Eph 3:6
be rich in faith and *h* ... James 2:5
vessel, and as being *h* ... 1 Pet 3:7

HELAM
Place between Damascus and Hamath where David defeated Syrians, 2 Sam 10:16–19

HELL
shall be turned into *h* ... Ps 9:17
go down alive into *h* ... Ps 55:15
house is the way to *h* ... Prov 7:27
his soul from *h* ... Prov 23:14
H and Destruction are ... Prov 27:20
"*H* from beneath is ... Is 14:9
be in danger of *h* fire ... Matt 5:22
to be cast into *h* ... Matt 18:9
the condemnation of *h* ... Matt 23:33
power to cast into *h* ... Luke 12:5
it is set on fire by *h* ... James 3:6

HELLENISTS
Greek-speaking Jews, Acts 6:1
Hostile to Paul, Acts 9:29
Gospel preached to, Acts 11:20

HELMET
a breastplate, and a *h* ... Is 59:17
And take the *h* of ... Eph 6:17
and love, and as a *h* ... 1 Thess 5:8

HELP
the shield of your *h* ... Deut 33:29
Is my *h* not within me ... Job 6:13
"There is no *h* for him ... Ps 3:2
May He send you *h* ... Ps 20:2
He is our *h* and our ... Ps 33:20
yet praise Him, the *h* ... Ps 42:11
A very present *h* ... Ps 46:1
Give us *h* from trouble ... Ps 60:11
God, make haste to *h* ... Ps 71:12
"I have given *h* ... Ps 89:19
the LORD had been my *h* ... Ps 94:17
there was none to *h* ... Ps 107:12
He is their *h* and ... Ps 115:9
Our *h* is in the name ... Ps 124:8
let no one *h* him ... Prov 28:17
h my unbelief ... Mark 9:24
tell her to *h* me ... Luke 10:40
and find grace to *h* ... Heb 4:16

HELPED
far the LORD has *h* ... 1 Sam 7:12
h the people to ... Neh 8:7
fall, but the LORD *h* ... Ps 118:13
of salvation I have *h* ... Is 49:8
h His servant Israel ... Luke 1:54

HELPER
I will make him a *h* ... Gen 2:18
Behold, God is my *h* ... Ps 54:4
give you another *H* ... John 14:16
"But when the *H* ... John 15:26
she has been a *h* ... Rom 16:2
"The LORD is my *h* ... Heb 13:6

HELPFUL
all things are not *h* ... 1 Cor 6:12

HELPS
the Spirit also *h* ... Rom 8:26
gifts of healings, *h* ... 1 Cor 12:28

HEM
and touched the *h* ... Matt 9:20
might only touch the *h* ... Matt 14:36

HEMAN
Composer of a psalm, Ps 88:title

HEMLOCK
judgment springs up like *h* ... Hos 10:4

HEN
as a *h* gathers her chicks ... Matt 23:37
as a *h* gathers her brood ... Luke 13:34

HENNA
is to me a cluster of *h* ... Song 1:14
fragrant *h* with spikenard ... Song 4:13

HERB
the *h* that yields seed, and ... Gen 1:11
every green *h* for food ... Gen 1:30
struck every *h* of the field ... Ex 9:25
ate every *h* of the land ... Ex 10:15
raindrops on the tender *h* ... Deut 32:2
field and the green *h* ... 2 Kin 19:26
And wither as the green *h* ... Ps 37:2
the field and the green *h* ... Is 37:27

HERBS
with bitter *h* they shall eat ... Ex 12:8
bread and bitter *h* ... Num 9:11
a dinner of *h* where love ... Prov 15:17

HERD
And Abraham ran to the *h* ... Gen 18:7
a burnt sacrifice of the *h* ... Lev 1:3
tithe of the *h* or the flock ... Lev 27:32
there be no *h* in the stalls ... Hab 3:17
into the *h* of swine ... Matt 8:31

HERE
Then I said, "*H* am I ... Is 6:8

HERE I AM
And he said, "*H* ... Gen 22:1
And he answered him, "*H* ... Gen 27:1
'Jacob.' And I said, '*H* ... Gen 31:11
So he said to him, "*H* ... Gen 37:13
Jacob!" And he said, "*H* ... Gen 46:2
Moses!" And he said, "*H* ... Ex 3:4
And he answered, "*H* ... 1 Sam 3:4
"*H*. Witness against me ... 1 Sam 12:3
h, let Him do to me as ... 2 Sam 15:26
h, the first to come ... 2 Sam 19:20
nor let the eunuch say, "*H* ... Is 56:3
cry, and He will say, '*H* ... Is 58:9
I said, '*H*, *h*,' to a nation ... Is 65:1
h, in your hand; do with ... Jer 26:14
And he said, "*H* ... Acts 9:10

HERESIES
dissensions, *h* ... Gal 5:20
in destructive *h* ... 2 Pet 2:1

HERITAGE
give it to you as a *h* ... Ex 6:8
have given me the *h* ... Ps 61:5
for that is his *h* ... Eccl 3:22
for it is his *h* ... Eccl 5:18
This is the *h* of the ... Is 54:17
of My people, My *h* ... Joel 3:2
The flock of Your *h* ... Mic 7:14

HERMES
Paul acclaimed as, Acts 14:12

HERMON
Highest mountain (9,166 ft.) in Syria; also called Sirion, Shenir, Deut 3:8, 9

HEROD
——— Herod the Great, procurator of Judea (37–4 B.C.), Luke 1:5
Inquires about Jesus' birth, Matt 2:3–8
Slays infants of Bethlehem, Matt 2:12–18
——— Herod Antipas, the tetrarch, ruler of Galilee and Perea (4 B.C.–A.D. 39), Luke 3:1
Imprisons John the Baptist, Luke 3:18–21
Has John the Baptist beheaded, Matt 14:1–12
Disturbed about Jesus, Luke 9:7–9
Jesus sent to him, Luke 23:7–11
——— Herod Agrippa I (A.D. 37–44), Acts 12:1, 19
Kills James, Acts 12:1, 2
Imprisons Peter, Acts 12:3–11, 19
Slain by an angel, Acts 12:20–23
——— Herod Agrippa II (A.D. 53–70); called Agrippa and King Agrippa, Acts 25:22–24, 26
Festus tells him about Paul, Acts 25:13–27
Paul makes a defense before, Acts 26:1–32

HERODIANS
Join Pharisees against Jesus, Mark 3:6
Seek to trap Jesus, Matt 22:15–22
Jesus warns against, Mark 8:15

HERODIAS
Granddaughter of Herod the Great; plots John's death, Matt 14:3–12
Married her uncle, Mark 6:17, 18

HESHBON
Ancient Moabite city; taken by Moses, Num 21:23–34
Assigned to Reubenites, Num 32:1–37
Prophecies concerning, Is 15:1–4; 16:8–14; Jer 48:2, 34, 35

HETH
Son of Canaan, Gen 10:15
Abraham buys field from sons of, Gen 23:3–20
Esau marries daughters of, Gen 27:46

HEW
H for yourself two tablets ... Deut 10:1

HEWN
she has *h* out her seven ... Prov 9:1
in a tomb that was *h* ... Luke 23:53

HEZEKIAH
Righteous king of Judah; reforms temple and worship, 2 Chr 29—31
Wars with Assyria; prayer for deliverance is answered, 2 Kin 18:7—19:37
His sickness and recovery; thanksgiving, 2 Kin 20:1–11; Is 38:9–22
Boasts to Babylonian ambassadors, 2 Kin 20:12–19
Death, 2 Kin 20:20, 21

HID
naked; and I *h* myself ... Gen 3:10
child, she *h* him three ... Ex 2:2
Egyptian and *h* him in the ... Ex 2:12
she *h* the messengers ... Josh 6:25
David *h* in the field ... 1 Sam 20:24
they *h* him and his nurse ... 2 Kin 11:2
And we *h*, as it were, our ... Is 53:3
and *h* his lord's money ... Matt 25:18

she *h* herself five months. . . Luke 1:24
h in three measures of . . . . Luke 13:21
but Jesus *h* Himself and . . . John 8:59
h themselves in the caves . . . Rev 6:15

HIDDEKEL
Hebrew name of the river Tigris, Gen 2:14; Dan 10:4

HIDDEN
and the LORD has *h*. . . . . 2 Kin 4:27
It is *h* from the eyes . . . . Job 28:21
h Your righteousness . . . . Ps 40:10
and my sins are not *h* . . . . Ps 69:5
Your word I have *h* . . . . Ps 119:11
h riches of secret places . . . . . . Is 45:3
there His power was *h* . . . . Hab 3:4
h that will not . . . . Matt 10:26
the *h* wisdom which God . . . 1 Cor 2:7
bring to light the *h* . . . . 1 Cor 4:5
have renounced the *h* . . . . . . 2 Cor 4:2
rather let it be the *h* . . . . 1 Pet 3:4
give some of the *h* . . . . Rev 2:17

HIDE
h by the Brook Cherith, . . . 1 Kin 17:3
H me under the shadow . . . . . . Ps 17:8
tabernacle He shall *h* me . . . . . Ps 27:5
You shall *h* them in . . . . Ps 31:20
O God, and do not *h* . . . . Ps 55:1
You *h* Your face . . . . Ps 104:29
darkness shall not *h* . . . . Ps 139:12
You are God, who *h* . . . . Is 45:15
h yourself from your . . . . Is 58:7
"Fall on us and *h* . . . . Rev 6:16

HIDES
He *h* His face . . . . Ps 10:11

HIDING
You are my *h* place . . . . Ps 32:7
A man will be as a *h* . . . . Is 32:2

HIEL
Native of Bethel; rebuilds Jericho, 1 Kin 16:34
Fulfills Joshua's curse, Josh 6:26

HIGH
See MOST HIGH
priest of God Most *H* . . . . . . Gen 14:18
For the LORD Most *H* . . . . Ps 47:2
h is Your right hand . . . . Ps 89:13
are on *h* forevermore . . . . Ps 92:8
the LORD is on *h* . . . . Ps 138:6
"I dwell in the *h* . . . . Is 57:15
know that the Most *H* . . . . . . Dan 4:17
whose habitation is *h* . . . . Obad 3
up on a *h* mountain by . . . . . . Matt 17:1
your mind on *h* things . . . . Rom 12:16
h thing that exalts . . . . 2 Cor 10:5
and faithful *H* Priest . . . . Heb 2:17

HIGH PLACE
people today on the *h* . . . . . 1 Sam 9:12
coming down from the *h* . . 1 Sam 10:5
great *h*: Solomon offered . . . . 1 Kin 3:4
Solomon built a *h* for . . . . 1 Kin 11:7
h which Jeroboam the . . . . 2 Kin 23:15
h that was at Gibeon . . . . . 1 Chr 16:39
Moab is weary on the *h* . . . . . . Is 16:12
made a *h* for yourself in . . . Ezek 16:24
this *h* to which you go?' . . . Ezek 20:29

HIGH PLACES
I will destroy your *h* . . . . Lev 26:30
him up to the *h* of Baal . . . Num 22:41
demolish all their *h* . . . . Num 33:52
shall tread down their *h* . . Deut 33:29
Israel is slain on your *h* . . . 2 Sam 1:19
and sets me on my *h* . . . . 2 Sam 22:34
people sacrificed at the *h* . . . 1 Kin 3:2
made shrines on the *h* . . . . 1 Kin 12:31
the *h* were not removed . . 1 Kin 15:14
He removed the *h* and . . . . . 2 Kin 18:4
to burn incense on the *h* . . . 2 Kin 23:5
He also removed the *h* . . . . 2 Chr 14:5
threw down the *h* and . . . . . 2 Chr 31:1
taken away His *h* . . . . 2 Chr 32:12
h, the wooden images . . . . . . 2 Chr 34:3
He makes peace in His *h* . . . . Job 25:2
deer, and sets me on my *h* . . . Ps 18:33
Him to anger with their *h* . . . Ps 78:58
to the *h* to weep. Moab will . . . Is 15:2
have built the *h* of Tophet . . . . Jer 7:31
your *h* of sin within all . . . . Jer 17:3
I will destroy your *h* . . . . Ezek 6:3
adorned multicolored *h* . . . Ezek 16:16
of their kings on their *h* . . . . Ezek 43:7
Also the *h* of Aven, the sin . . Hos 10:8
who treads the *h* of the . . . Amos 4:13

HIGH PRIEST
'And he who is the *h* . . . . Lev 21:10
until the death of the *h* . . . . Num 35:25
"Go up to Hilkiah the *h* . . . . 2 Kin 22:4
h, was a son-in-law of . . . . . Neh 13:28
son of Jehozadak, the *h* . . . . . Hag 1:1
showed me Joshua the *h* . . . . Zech 3:1
at the palace of the *h* . . . . Matt 26:3
days of Abiathar the *h* . . . . Mark 2:26
servant of the *h*, and . . . . . Mark 14:47
Caiaphas, being *h* that . . . . John 11:49
the courtyard of the *h* . . . . John 18:15
Annas the *h*, Caiaphas, ... Acts 4:6
of the Lord, went to the *h* . . . . Acts 9:1
h Ananias commanded . . . . . Acts 23:2
a merciful and faithful *H* . . . . Heb 2:17
we have a great *H* who . . . . . Heb 4:14
we do not have a *H* who . . . . Heb 4:15
called by God as *H* . . . . Heb 5:10
H forever according to the . . Heb 6:20
We have such a *H*, who is . . . Heb 8:1
h went alone once a year . . . . Heb 9:7
H over the house of God . . . Heb 10:21

HIGHER
They are *h* than heaven . . . . . Job 11:8
you, 'Friend, go up *h* . . . . . Luke 14:10
h than the heavens . . . . Heb 7:26

HIGHEST
the *h* heavens belong to . . . Deut 10:14
Hosanna in the *h*! . . . . Matt 21:9
the power of the *H* will . . . . Luke 1:35
Glory to God in the *h* . . . . . . Luke 2:14
and glory in the *h* . . . . Luke 19:38

HIGHLY
Rejoice, *h* favored one . . . . . Luke 1:28
also has *h* exalted Him . . . . . . Phil 2:9

HIGHWAY
of the upright is a *h* . . . . Prov 15:19
in the desert a *h* . . . . Is 40:3
up, build up the *h* . . . . Is 62:10

HIGHWAYS
h shall be elevated . . . . Is 49:11
go into the *h* . . . . Matt 22:9

HILKIAH
Shallum's son, 1 Chr 6:13
High priest in Josiah's reign, 2 Chr 34:9–22
Oversees temple work, 2 Kin 22:4–7
Finds the Book of the Law, 2 Kin 22:8–14
Aids in reformation, 2 Kin 23:4

HILL
My King on My holy *h* . . . . Ps 2:6
h cannot be hidden . . . . Matt 5:14
and *h* brought low . . . . Luke 3:5
to the brow of the *h* . . . . Luke 4:29

HILLS
of the everlasting *h* . . . . Gen 49:26
possess is a land of *h* . . . . . Deut 11:11
of the *h* are His also . . . . Ps 95:4
up my eyes to the *h* . . . . Ps 121:1
settled, before the *h* . . . . Prov 8:25

HINDER
takes away, who can *h* . . . . . . Job 9:12
all things lest we *h* . . . . 1 Cor 9:12

HINDERED
come to you (but was *h* . . . . Rom 1:13
Who *h* you from obeying . . . . . Gal 5:7
prayers may not be *h* . . . . 1 Pet 3:7

HINDERS
h me from being baptized . . Acts 8:36

HINNOM, VALLEY OF THE SON OF
See TOPHET
Place near Jerusalem used for human sacrifice, 2 Kin 23:10; 2 Chr 28:3; Jer 7:31, 32; 19:1–15

HIP
socket of Jacob's *h* . . . . Gen 32:25

HIRAM
King of Tyre; provided materials for David's palace and Solomon's temple, 2 Sam 5:11; 1 Kin 5:1–12; 9:10–14, 26–28; 10:11; 1 Chr 14:1

HIRE
h laborers for his . . . . Matt 20:1

HIRED
h man who eagerly . . . . Job 7:2
as the years of a *h* man . . . . . . Is 16:14
h about the eleventh hour . . Matt 20:9
h servants have bread . . . . Luke 15:17

HIRELING
The *h* flees because . . . . John 10:13

HIS MERCY ENDURES FOREVER
for He is good! For *H* . . . . 1 Chr 16:34
"For He is good, for *H* . . . . 2 Chr 5:13
"Praise the LORD, for *H* . . 2 Chr 20:21
For *H* toward Israel." . . . . . . Ezra 3:11
for He is good! For *H* . . . . Ps 106:1
for He is good! For *H* . . . . Ps 107:1
for He is good! For *H* . . . . Ps 118:1
for He is good! For *H* . . . . Ps 136:1
the LORD is good, for *H* . . . . . Jer 33:11

HIS RIGHT HAND
Ephraim with *h* toward . . . . Gen 48:13
on the thumb of *h*, and on . . . Lev 8:23
on *H* and on His left . . . . . 1 Kin 22:19
the saving strength of *H* . . . . . . Ps 20:6
H and His holy arm have . . . . . Ps 98:1
A wise man's heart is at *h* . . Eccl 10:2
is under my head, and *h* . . . . Song 2:6
The LORD has sworn by *H* . . . . . Is 62:8
He has drawn back *H* from . . . Lam 2:3
when he held up *h* and his . . Dan 12:7
Satan standing at *h* to . . . . . . Zech 3:1
will set the sheep on *H* . . . . Matt 25:33
a reed in *H*. And they . . . . . Matt 27:29
God has exalted to *H* . . . . Acts 5:31
seated Him at *H* in . . . . Eph 1:20
He had in *H* seven stars . . . . . Rev 1:16
holds the seven stars in *H* . . . . Rev 2:1

HITTITES
One of seven Canaanite nations, Deut 7:1
Israelites intermarry with, Judg 3:5, 6; 1 Kin 11:1; Ezra 9:1, 2

HIVITES
One of seven Canaanite nations, Deut 7:1
Esau intermarries with, Gen 36:2
Gibeonites belong to, Josh 9:3, 7

HOLD
he took *h* of his father's . . . Gen 48:17
for we must *h* a feast to the . . . Ex 10:9
sorrow will take *h* of the . . . . Ex 15:14
trembling will take *h* of . . . . . Ex 15:15
took *h* of the doors of the . . Judg 16:3
took *h* of the horns of the . . 1 Kin 1:50
enough to *h* two seahs . . . . 1 Kin 18:32

out his hand to *h* the ark . . 1 Chr 13:9
Take *h* of shield and . . . . Ps 35:2
h my eyelids open . . . . Ps 77:4
right hand shall *h* . . . . Ps 139:10
LORD your God, will *h* . . . . Is 41:13
cisterns that can *h* no . . . . Jer 2:13
I cannot *h* my peace . . . . Jer 4:19
Herod had laid *h* of John . . . Matt 14:3
who had laid *h* of Jesus . . . Matt 26:57
you *h* the tradition of men . . Mark 7:8
h fast that word . . . . 1 Cor 15:2
h fast our confession . . . . Heb 4:14
h fast and repent . . . . Rev 3:3
H fast what you have, that . . Rev 3:11

HOLES

"Foxes have *h* . . . . Matt 8:20

HOLIER

near me, for I am *h* . . . . Is 65:5

HOLIEST

the way into the *H* . . . . Heb 9:8
to enter the *H* by the . . . . . . Heb 10:19

HOLINESS

You, glorious in *h* . . . . Ex 15:11
H to the LORD . . . . Ex 28:36
LORD in the beauty of *h* . . 1 Chr 16:29
has spoken in His *h* . . . . Ps 60:6
I have sworn by My *h* . . . . Ps 89:35
h adorns Your house . . . . Ps 93:5
the Highway of *H* . . . . Is 35:8
to the Spirit of *h* . . . . Rom 1:4
spirit, perfecting *h* . . . . 2 Cor 7:1
uncleanness, but in *h* . . . . . 1 Thess 4:7
be partakers of His *h* . . . . . . Heb 12:10

HOLY

See MOST HOLY PLACE
where you stand is *h* . . . . Ex 3:5
rest, a *h* Sabbath to the . . . . . Ex 16:23
priests and a *h* nation . . . . Ex 19:6
day, to keep it *h* . . . . Ex 20:8
put the *h* crown on the . . . . Ex 29:6
the altar shall be most *h* . . . . Ex 29:37
It shall be a *h* anointing oil . . Ex 30:25
distinguish between *h* . . . . . Lev 10:10
the LORD your God am *h* . . . . Lev 19:2
the priest is *h* to his God . . . Lev 21:7
all the congregation is *h* . . . Num 16:3
"No one is *h* like the . . . . . . 1 Sam 2:2
priest gave him *h* bread . . . 1 Sam 21:6
the *h* ark in the house . . . . . 2 Chr 35:3
h seed is mixed . . . . Ezra 9:2
This day is *h* to the LORD . . . . Neh 8:9
h ones will you turn . . . . Job 5:1
LORD is in His *h* temple . . . . Ps 11:4
may dwell in Your *h* hill . . . . . Ps 15:1
H One to see corruption . . . . . Ps 16:10
God sits on His *h* . . . . Ps 47:8
God, in His *h* mountain . . . . Ps 48:1
my life, for I am *h* . . . . Ps 86:2
"*H*, *h*, *h* is the LORD . . . . Is 6:3
H One of Israel, in truth . . . . . Is 10:20
destroy in all My *h* . . . . Is 11:9
hallow the *H* One of Jacob . . . Is 29:23
Redeemer, the *H* One of . . . . . Is 41:14
call them The *H* People . . . . . . Is 62:12
It shall be the *h* district . . . Ezek 48:21
Spirit of the *H* God is in . . . . . Dan 4:9
I heard a *h* one speaking . . . Dan 8:13
the *h* angels with Him . . . . Matt 25:31
name of Your *h* Servant . . . . Acts 4:30
if the firstfruit is *h* . . . . Rom 11:16
bodies a living sacrifice, *h* . . Rom 12:1
one another with a *h* . . . . . Rom 16:16
that we should be *h* . . . . Eph 1:4
lifting up *h* hands, without . . 1 Tim 2:8
called us with a *h* calling . . . 2 Tim 1:9
has not entered the *h* . . . . Heb 9:24
He who called you is *h* . . . . 1 Pet 1:15
it is written, "Be *h* . . . . 1 Pet 1:16
a *h* priesthood, to offer up . . . 1 Pet 2:5
a *h* nation, His own special . . 1 Pet 2:9
you to be in *h* conduct . . . . . 2 Pet 3:11
says He who is *h* . . . . Rev 3:7
H, *h*, *h*, Lord God . . . . Rev 4:8
For You alone are *h* . . . . Rev 15:4
is *h*, let him be *h* . . . . Rev 22:11

HOLY CITY

dwell in Jerusalem, the *h* . . . Neh 11:1
call themselves after the *h* . . . . Is 48:2
O Jerusalem, the *h* . . . . Is 52:1
people and for your *h* . . . . . . Dan 9:24
took Him up into the *h* . . . . . . Matt 4:5
they went into the *h* and . . Matt 27:53
they will tread the *h* under . . Rev 11:2
Then I, John, saw the *h* . . . . . . Rev 21:2
Book of Life, from the *h* . . . Rev 22:19

HOLY NAME

and profane My *h* . . . . Lev 20:3
Glory in His *h*; let . . . . 1 Chr 16:10
You a house for Your *h* . . 1 Chr 29:16
remembrance of His *h* . . . . Ps 30:4
we have trusted in His *h* . . . . Ps 33:21
remembrance of His *h* . . . . Ps 97:12
is within me, bless His *h* . . . . Ps 103:1
Glory in His *h*; let the . . . . Ps 105:3
to give thanks to Your *h* . . . Ps 106:47
all flesh shall bless His *h* . . . Ps 145:21
profane My *h* no more . . . . Ezek 20:39
I had concern for My *h* . . . Ezek 36:21
be jealous for My *h* . . . . Ezek 39:25
same girl, to defile My *h* . . . Amos 2:7

HOLY ONE OF ISRAEL

on high? Against the *H* . . . 2 Kin 19:22
sing with the harp, O *H* . . . . . Ps 71:22
And our king to the *H* . . . . Ps 89:18
have provoked to anger the *H* . . Is 1:4
depend on the LORD, the *H* . . . Is 10:20
great is the *H* in your midst . . . Is 12:6
and your Redeemer, the *H* . . . Is 41:14
LORD who is faithful, the *H* . . . . Is 49:7
of the LORD, Zion of the *H* . . . Is 60:14
the LORD, against the *H* . . . . . Jer 50:29

HOLY PLACE

between the *h* and the . . . . . . Ex 26:33
when he goes into the *h* . . . . . Ex 28:29
sweet incense for the *h* . . . . . Ex 31:11
it shall be eaten in a *h* . . . . Lev 6:16
any time into the *H* inside . . . . Lev 16:2
most *h* you shall eat . . . . . . Num 18:10
sanctuary, as the Most *H* . . 1 Kin 6:16
the needs of the *h*, and . . . 1 Chr 23:32
And he made the Most *H* . . . 2 Chr 3:8
H, under the wings of the . . . 2 Chr 5:7
the rubbish from the *h* . . . . 2 Chr 29:5
stand in the *h* according . . . 2 Chr 35:5
to give us a peg in His *h* . . . . Ezra 9:8
who may stand in His *h*? . . . . . Ps 24:3
the *h* of the tabernacle of . . . . . Ps 46:4
as in Sinai, in the *H* . . . . Ps 68:17
"I dwell in the high and *h* . . . . Is 57:15
"This is the Most *H* . . . . Ezek 41:4
standing in the *h* . . . . Matt 24:15
words against this *h* and . . . Acts 6:13
and has defiled this *h* . . . . . Acts 21:28
He entered the Most *H* . . . . . Heb 9:12
priest enters the Most *H* . . . . Heb 9:25

HOLY SPIRIT

See FILLED WITH THE HOLY SPIRIT
Affirmed as divine:
called God, Acts 5:3, 4
joined with the Father and the Son, Matt 28:19; 2 Cor 13:14
eternal, Heb 9:14
omnipotent, Luke 1:35
omniscient, 1 Cor 2:10, 11
omnipresent, Ps 139:7–13
Creator, Gen 1:2
sovereign, 1 Cor 12:6, 11
new creation, John 3:3, 8
sin against, unforgiveable, Matt 12:31, 32
Work of:
speaks in Scripture, Acts 1:16, 17; 28:25; 2 Tim 3:16
role in Christ's ministry, Matt 3:16; 12:28; Luke 1:35; 4:1, 17, 18; Rom 1:4; 1 Tim 3:16; Heb 9:14
regenerates, John 3:3, 5
indwells, Rom 8:11
anoints, 1 John 2:20, 27
baptizes, Acts 2:17–41
guides, John 16:13
empowers, Mic 3:8
sanctifies, Rom 15:16; 2 Thess 2:13
bears witness, Rom 8:16; Heb 10:15
helps, John 14:16–26
gives joy, Rom 14:17
gives discernment, 1 Cor 2:10–16; 1 John 4:1–6
bears fruit, Gal 5:22, 23
gives gifts, 1 Cor 12:3–11
comforts, Acts 9:31
illuminates the mind, 1 Cor 2:12, 13; Eph 1:16, 17
reveals things of God, Is 40:13, 14; 1 Cor 2:10, 13
Promised, Joel 2:28–32
Received by disciples, Acts 2:1–21
Received by Gentiles, Acts 10:45
Persons filled by:
Bezalel, Ex 31:2
Jesus, Luke 4:1
John the Baptist, Luke 1:15, 60
Elizabeth, Luke 1:41
Zacharias, Luke 1:67
Pentecost Christians, Acts 2:1–4
Peter, Acts 4:8
seven deacons, Acts 6:3–5
Stephen, Acts 7:55
Barnabas, Acts 11:22, 24
Paul, Acts 13:9
certain disciples, Acts 13:52

not take Your *H* from me . . . Ps 51:11
rebelled and grieved His *H* . . . Is 63:10
found with child of the *H* . . . Matt 1:18
baptize you with the *H* . . . . . Matt 3:11
speaks against the *H*, it . . . Matt 12:32
of the Son and of the *H* . . . Matt 28:19
himself said by the *H* . . . . Mark 12:36
who speak, but the *H* . . . . Mark 13:11
filled with the *H*, even . . . . . Luke 1:15
was filled with the *H* . . . . . . Luke 1:41
the *H*, and prophesied . . . . . Luke 1:67
and the *H* was upon him . . . Luke 2:25
And the *H* descended in . . . Luke 3:22
being filled with the *H* . . . . . . Luke 4:1
Father give the *H* . . . . Luke 11:13
the *H* was not yet given . . . . John 7:39
"But the Helper, the *H* . . . John 14:26
to them, "Receive the *H* . . John 20:22
be baptized with the *H* . . . . . . Acts 1:5
receive power when the *H* . . . Acts 1:8
were all filled with the *H* . . . Acts 2:4
the promise of the *H* . . . . Acts 2:33
receive the gift of the *H* . . . . Acts 2:38
Peter, filled with the *H* . . . . . . Acts 4:8
were all filled with the *H* . . . Acts 4:31
to lie to the *H* and keep . . . . . Acts 5:3
full of the *H* and wisdom . . . . Acts 6:3
You always resist the *H* . . . . Acts 7:51
they might receive the *H* . . . . Acts 8:15
and be filled with the *H* . . . . Acts 9:17
in the comfort of the *H* . . . . . Acts 9:31
the *H* fell upon all those . . . Acts 10:44
the *H* fell upon them, as . . . Acts 11:15
the *H* said, "Now separate . . Acts 13:2
with joy and with the *H* . . . Acts 13:52
by giving them the *H* just . . . Acts 15:8
it seemed good to the *H* . . . Acts 15:28
were forbidden by the *H* . . . . Acts 16:6
the *H* testifies in every . . . . Acts 20:23
H has made you . . . . Acts 20:28

says the *H*, "So shall the . . Acts 21:11
out in our hearts by the *H* . . . Rom 5:5
me witness in the *H* . . . . Rom 9:1
peace and joy in the *H* . . . . Rom 14:17
sanctified by the *H* . . . . Rom 15:16
but which the *H* teaches . . . 1 Cor 2:13
is the temple of the *H* . . . . . 1 Cor 6:19
is Lord except by the *H* . . . . 1 Cor 12:3
by kindness, by the *H* . . . . . . 2 Cor 6:6
were sealed with the *H* of . . . Eph 1:13
And do not grieve the *H* . . . . Eph 4:30
by the *H* who dwells . . . . . . 2 Tim 1:14
and renewing of the *H* . . . . . . Titus 3:5
miracles, and gifts of the *H* . . Heb 2:4
become partakers of the *H* . . . Heb 6:4
were moved by the *H* . . . . . . 2 Pet 1:21
the Word, and the *H* . . . . . . 1 John 5:7

HOME
LORD has brought me *h* . . . . Ruth 1:21
sparrow has found a *h* . . . . Ps 84:3
the stork has her *h* . . . . Ps 104:17
to his eternal *h* . . . . Eccl 12:5
said to him, "Go *h* . . . . Mark 5:19
into an everlasting *h* . . . . Luke 16:9
to him and make Our *h* . . . John 14:23
took her to his own *h* . . . . . John 19:27
let him eat at *h* . . . . 1 Cor 11:34
own husbands at *h* . . . . 1 Cor 14:35
that while we are at *h* . . . . . . 2 Cor 5:6
to show piety at *h* . . . . 1 Tim 5:4

HOMELESS
and beaten, and *h* . . . . 1 Cor 4:11

HOMEMAKERS
be discreet, chaste, *h* . . . . Titus 2:5

HOMOSEXUALS
nor adulterers, nor *h*, nor . . . 1 Cor 6:9

HONEST
we are *h* men . . . . Gen 42:11

HONEY
See MILK AND HONEY
flowing with milk and *h* . . Num 16:13
"What is sweeter than *h* . . Judg 14:18
I tasted a little of this *h* . . 1 Sam 14:29
Sweeter also than *h* and . . . . . Ps 19:10
and with *h* from the . . . . Ps 81:16
sweeter than *h* to my . . . . . Ps 119:103
My son, eat *h* because . . . . Prov 24:13
not good to eat much *h* . . . Prov 25:27
h and milk are under . . . . . . Song 4:11
was locusts and wild *h* . . . . . . Matt 3:4
sweet as *h* in my mouth . . . . Rev 10:10

HONEYCOMB
than honey and the *h* . . . . Ps 19:10
words are like a *h* . . . . Prov 16:24
fish and some *h* . . . . Luke 24:42

HONOR
H your father and your . . . . . Ex 20:12
both riches and *h* . . . . 1 Kin 3:13
the king delights to *h* . . . . Esth 6:6
earth, and lay my *h* . . . . Ps 7:5
A man who is in *h* . . . . Ps 49:20
Sing out the *h* of His . . . . Ps 66:2
will deliver him and *h* . . . . Ps 91:15
H and majesty are . . . . Ps 96:6
h have all His saints . . . . Ps 149:9
H the LORD with your . . . . Prov 3:9
before *h* is humility . . . . Prov 15:33
h is not fitting . . . . Prov 26:1
spirit will retain *h* . . . . Prov 29:23
Father, where is My *h* . . . . Mal 1:6
is not without *h* . . . . Matt 13:57
'*H* your father and your . . . . Matt 15:4
h the Son just as they . . . . . . John 5:23
"I do not receive *h* . . . . John 5:41
but I *h* My Father . . . . John 8:49
"If I *h* Myself . . . . John 8:54
him My Father will *h* . . . . . John 12:26
make one vessel for *h* . . . . . . Rom 9:21
to whom fear, *h* . . . . Rom 13:7
we bestow greater *h* . . . . . 1 Cor 12:23
sanctification and *h* . . . . . . 1 Thess 4:4
alone is wise, be *h* . . . . 1 Tim 1:17
worthy of double *h* . . . . 1 Tim 5:17
and clay, some for *h* . . . . . . 2 Tim 2:20
no man takes this *h* . . . . Heb 5:4
H the king . . . . 1 Pet 2:17
from God the Father *h* . . . . . 2 Pet 1:17
give glory and *h* . . . . Rev 4:9

HONORABLE
of God, and he is an *h* . . . . . 1 Sam 9:6
His work is *h* and . . . . Ps 111:3
It is *h* for a man to . . . . Prov 20:3
traders are the *h* . . . . Is 23:8
holy day of the LORD *h* . . . . Is 58:13
providing *h* things . . . . 2 Cor 8:21
Marriage is *h* among . . . . Heb 13:4
having your conduct *h* . . . . . 1 Pet 2:12

HONORABLY
desiring to live *h* . . . . Heb 13:18

HONORS
h those who fear the . . . . Ps 15:4
'This people *h* Me . . . . Mark 7:6
It is My Father who *h* . . . . . . John 8:54

HOOKS
will lament who cast *h* . . . . Is 19:8
spears into pruning *h* . . . . Mic 4:3

HOOVES
those that have cloven *h* . . . . Lev 11:4
I will make your *h* bronze . . . Mic 4:13

HOPE
I should say I have *h* . . . . . . Ruth 1:12
are spent without *h* . . . . Job 7:6
so You destroy the *h* . . . . Job 14:19
where then is my *h* . . . . Job 17:15
h He has uprooted . . . . Job 19:10
also will rest in *h* . . . . Ps 16:9
heart, all you who *h* . . . . Ps 31:24
My *h* is in You . . . . Ps 39:7
For You are my *h* . . . . Ps 71:5
I *h* in Your word . . . . Ps 119:147
O Israel, *h* in the . . . . Ps 130:7
h will not be cut . . . . Prov 23:18
There is more *h* . . . . Prov 26:12
the living there is *h* . . . . Eccl 9:4
O the *H* of Israel . . . . Jer 14:8
good that one should *h* . . . . . Lam 3:26
Achor as a door of *h* . . . . Hos 2:15
you prisoners of *h* . . . . Zech 9:12
I have *h* in God . . . . Acts 24:15
to *h*, in *h* believed . . . . Rom 4:18
and rejoice in *h* . . . . Rom 5:2
h does not disappoint . . . . Rom 5:5
h that is seen is . . . . Rom 8:24
But if we *h* for what . . . . Rom 8:25
And now abide faith, *h* . . . 1 Cor 13:13
life only we have *h* . . . . 1 Cor 15:19
may know what is the *h* . . . . Eph 1:18
were called in one *h* . . . . Eph 4:4
h which is laid . . . . Col 1:5
Christ in you, the *h* . . . . Col 1:27
For what is our *h* . . . . 1 Thess 2:19
others who have no *h* . . . 1 Thess 4:13
and as a helmet the *h* . . . . . 1 Thess 5:8
Jesus Christ, our *h* . . . . 1 Tim 1:1
in *h* of eternal life . . . . Titus 1:2
for the blessed *h* . . . . Titus 2:13
to lay hold of the *h* . . . . Heb 6:18
of a better *h* . . . . Heb 7:19
us again to a living *h* . . . . 1 Pet 1:3
you a reason for the *h* . . . . . 1 Pet 3:15
who has this *h* in Him . . . . . 1 John 3:3

HOPED
substance of things *h* . . . . Heb 11:1

HOPHNI
Wicked son of Eli, 1 Sam 1:3; 2:12–17, 22–25
Prophecy against, 1 Sam 2:27–36; 3:11–14
Carries ark into battle; killed, 1 Sam 4:1–11

HOR
Mountain of Edom; scene of Aaron's death, Num 20:22–29; 33:37–39

HOREB
See SINAI
God appears to Moses at, Ex 3:1–22
Water flows from, Ex 17:6
Elijah lodged here 40 days, 1 Kin 19:8, 9

HORITES
Inhabitants of Mt. Seir, Gen 36:20
Defeated by Chedorlaomer, Gen 14:5, 6
Driven out by Esau's descendants, Gen 36:20–29; Deut 2:12, 22

HORMAH
Destroyed by Israel, Num 21:1–3

HORN
my shield and the *h* . . . . Ps 18:2
h will be exalted . . . . Ps 112:9
goat had a notable *h* . . . . Dan 8:5
and has raised up a *h* . . . . . . Luke 1:69

HORRIBLE
h thing has been . . . . Jer 5:30
I have seen a *h* . . . . Hos 6:10

HORROR
and behold, *h* and . . . . Gen 15:12
sorrow, the cup of *h* . . . . . . Ezek 23:33
you will become a *h* . . . . . . Ezek 27:36

HORSE
The *h* and its rider He . . . . Ex 15:1
Have you given the *h* . . . . . . Job 39:19
h is a vain hope . . . . Ps 33:17
the strength of the *h* . . . . Ps 147:10
h is prepared for the . . . . . . Prov 21:31
and behold, a white *h* . . . . Rev 6:2
and behold, a black *h* . . . . Rev 6:5
and behold, a pale *h* . . . . Rev 6:8
and behold, a white *h* . . . . Rev 19:11

HORSES
seen servants on *h* . . . . Eccl 10:7
h are swifter than . . . . Jer 4:13
Do *h* run on rocks . . . . Amos 6:12
we put bits in *h* . . . . James 3:3

HOSANNA
H in the highest . . . . Matt 21:9

HOSEA
Son of Beeri, prophet of the northern kingdom, Hos 1:1

HOSHEA
Original name of Joshua, the son of Nun, Deut 32:44; Num 13:8, 16
——— Israel's last king; usurps throne, 2 Kin 15:30
Reigns wickedly; Israel taken to Assyria during his reign, 2 Kin 17:1–23

HOSPITABLE
of good behavior, *h* . . . . 1 Tim 3:2
Be *h* to one another . . . . 1 Pet 4:9

HOST
who brings out their *h* . . . . Is 40:26
of the heavenly *h* . . . . Luke 2:13

HOST OF HEAVEN
all the *h*, you feel driven . . . Deut 4:19
throne, and all the *h* . . . . . 1 Kin 22:19
worshiped all the *h* . . . . 2 Kin 17:16
and for all the *h* . . . . 2 Kin 23:4
The *h* worships You . . . . Neh 9:6
All the *h* shall be dissolved . . . . Is 34:4
the moon and all the *h* . . . . Jer 8:2
burned incense to all the *h* . . Jer 19:13
the *h* cannot be numbered . . Jer 33:22
And it grew up to the *h* . . . . . Dan 8:10
them up to worship the *h* . . . Acts 7:42

HOSTILITY
Him who endured such *h* . . . Heb 12:3

HOSTS
See LORD GOD OF HOSTS; LORD OF HOSTS
name of the LORD of *h* . . . 1 Sam 17:45
As the LORD of *h* lives . . . . 1 Kin 18:15
The LORD of *h* is with . . . . Ps 46:7
LORD, all you His *h* . . . . Ps 103:21
praise Him, all His *h* . . . . Ps 148:2
word of the LORD of *h* . . . . Is 39:5
LORD of *h* is His name . . . . Is 47:4
against spiritual *h* . . . . Eph 6:12

HOT
of the LORD was *h* . . . . Judg 2:14
My heart was *h* within . . . . Ps 39:3
are neither cold nor *h* . . . . Rev 3:15

HOUND
My enemies would *h* . . . . Ps 56:2

HOUR
h what you should . . . . Matt 10:19
day and *h* no one knows . . Matt 24:36
Man is coming at an *h* . . . . Matt 24:44
Behold, the *h* is at . . . . Matt 26:45
But this is your *h* . . . . Luke 22:53
h has not yet come . . . . John 2:4
But the *h* is coming . . . . John 4:23
h has come that the . . . . John 12:23
save Me from this *h* . . . . . . John 12:27
"Father, the *h* has come . . . . John 17:1
will not know what *h* . . . . Rev 3:3
keep you from the *h* . . . . Rev 3:10

HOURS
Are there not twelve *h* . . . . . John 11:9

HOUSE
from your father's *h* . . . . Gen 12:1
But as for me and my *h* . . . . Josh 24:15
h appointed for all . . . . Job 30:23
with them to the *h* . . . . Ps 42:4
the goodness of Your *h* . . . . Ps 65:4
For her *h* leads down . . . . . . Prov 2:18
Through wisdom a *h* . . . . . . Prov 24:3
better to go to the *h* . . . . Eccl 7:2
of the *h* tremble . . . . Eccl 12:3
to the *h* of the God of . . . . Is 2:3
to those who join *h* . . . . Is 5:8
h was filled with . . . . Is 6:4
'Set your *h* in order . . . . Is 38:1
h shall be called a . . . . Is 56:7
built his *h* on the rock . . . . . Matt 7:24
and beat on that *h* . . . . Matt 7:25
blew and beat on that *h* . . . . Matt 7:27
had come into Peter's *h* . . . . Matt 8:14
came into the ruler's *h* . . . . . Matt 9:23
sheep of the *h* of Israel . . . . . Matt 10:6
h divided against . . . . Matt 12:25
enter a strong man's *h* . . . . Matt 12:29
h shall be called a . . . . Matt 21:13
Your *h* is left to you . . . . . . Matt 23:38
the *h* of Simon the leper . . . . Matt 26:6
no one who has left *h* . . . . Mark 10:29
My *h* shall be called a *h* . . Mark 11:17
the *h* of Zacharias . . . . Luke 1:40
bed, and go to your *h* . . . . . . Luke 5:24
ruin of that *h* was great . . . . Luke 6:49
Whatever *h* you enter . . . . . . Luke 9:4
h may be filled . . . . Luke 14:23
light a lamp, sweep the *h* . . Luke 15:8
has come to this *h* . . . . Luke 19:9
make My Father's *h* . . . . John 2:16
for Your *h* has eaten Me . . . John 2:17
the *h* was filled with the . . . John 12:3
h are many mansions . . . . . . John 14:2
bread from *h* to *h*, they . . . . . Acts 2:46
hour I prayed in my *h* . . . . . Acts 10:30
in the *h* of Simon . . . . Acts 10:32
publicly and from *h* . . . . Acts 20:20
in his own rented *h* . . . . Acts 28:30
church that is in their *h* . . . . Rom 16:5
a *h* not made with hands, . . . 2 Cor 5:1
who rules his own *h* . . . . 1 Tim 3:4
children, manage the *h* . . . . 1 Tim 5:14
in a great *h* there are . . . . . 2 Tim 2:20
the church in your *h* . . . . Philem 2
has more honor than the *h* . . . Heb 3:3
For every *h* is built . . . . Heb 3:4
His own *h*, whose *h* . . . . Heb 3:6
Priest over the *h* of God . . . Heb 10:21
being built up a spiritual *h* . . 1 Pet 2:5
to begin at the *h* of God . . . . 1 Pet 4:17
him into your *h* . . . . 2 John 1:10

HOUSE OF DAVID
a covenant with the *h* . . . . 1 Sam 20:16
house of Saul and the *h* . . . . 2 Sam 3:1
rebellion against the *h* . . . . 1 Kin 12:19
may return to the *h* . . . . . . 1 Kin 12:26
shall be born to the *h* . . . . . . 1 Kin 13:2
away from the *h* . . . . 1 Kin 14:8
shall not dwell in the *h* . . . . 2 Chr 8:11
would not destroy the *h* . . . 2 Chr 21:7
the wall, beyond the *h* . . . . . Neh 12:37
the thrones of the *h* . . . . Ps 122:5
And it was told to the *h* . . . . Is 7:2
The key of the *h* I will lay . . . . Is 22:22
'O *h!* Thus says the LORD: . . . Jer 21:12
h shall be like God . . . . Zech 12:8
was Joseph, of the *h* . . . . Luke 1:27

HOUSE OF GOD
none other than the *h* . . . . . Gen 28:17
the *h* was in Shiloh . . . . Judg 18:31
of the tabernacle of the *h* . . 1 Chr 6:48
stones to build the *h* . . . . . . 1 Chr 22:2
all the service of the *h* . . . . 1 Chr 28:21
King Solomon for the *h* . . . 2 Chr 4:11
of the LORD filled the *h* . . . . 2 Chr 5:14
people dedicated the *h* . . . . . 2 Chr 7:5
also brought into the *h* . . . 2 Chr 15:18
with them in the *h* . . . . 2 Chr 22:12
articles from the *h* . . . . 2 Chr 36:18
freewill offerings for the *h* . . . Ezra 1:4
oversee the work of the *h* . . . Ezra 3:8
or the courts of the *h* . . . . Neh 8:16
"Why is the *h* forsaken?" . . . Neh 13:11
I went with them to the *h* . . . . . Ps 42:4
a green olive tree in the *h* . . . . Ps 52:8
walked to the *h* in the . . . . Ps 55:14
when you go to the *h* . . . . Eccl 5:1
the articles of the *h* . . . . Dan 1:2
from the temple of the *h* . . . . . Dan 5:3
how he entered the *h* and . . Matt 12:4
conduct yourself in the *h* . . 1 Tim 3:15
High Priest over the *h* . . . . . Heb 10:21
to begin at the *h* . . . . 1 Pet 4:17

HOUSE OF THE LORD
you shall bring into the *h* . . . Ex 23:19
price of a dog to the *h* . . . . Deut 23:18
into the treasury of the *h* . . . Josh 6:24
she went up to the *h* . . . . 1 Sam 1:7
brought him to the *h* . . . . . . 1 Sam 1:24
he went into the *h* and . . . 2 Sam 12:20
his own house, and the *h* . . . 1 Kin 3:1
he began to build the *h* . . . . . . 1 Kin 6:1
the cloud filled the *h* . . . . 1 Kin 8:10
hidden with her in the *h* . . . 2 Kin 11:3
the damage of the *h* . . . . . . 2 Kin 12:12
service of song in the *h* . . . . 1 Chr 6:31
David said, "This is the *h* . . 1 Chr 22:1
began to build the *h* . . . . 2 Chr 3:1
for the *h* was finished . . . . . . 2 Chr 5:1
So the *h* was completed. . . . 2 Chr 8:16
heart on repairing the *h* . . . 2 Chr 24:4
cut off from the *h* . . . . 2 Chr 26:21
of the *h* to cleanse it . . . . . 2 Chr 29:16
built altars in the *h* . . . . 2 Chr 33:4
of the Law in the *h* . . . . 2 Chr 34:15
from the *h* to Babylon . . . . . 2 Chr 36:7
build the *h* God of Israel . . . . Ezra 1:3
heart, to beautify the *h* . . . . . Ezra 7:27
I will dwell in the *h* forever . . . Ps 23:6
that I may dwell in the *h* . . . . . Ps 27:4
who are planted in the *h* . . . . Ps 92:13
"Let us go into the *h* . . . . Ps 122:1
Hezekiah went up to the *h* . . . Is 37:14
these words in the *h* . . . . Jer 26:7
of praise into the *h*. For I . . . . Jer 33:11
He burned the *h* and the . . . . Jer 52:13
noise in the *h* as on the . . . . . . Lam 2:7
LORD filled the *h*; and I . . . . Ezek 44:4
it shall not come into the *h* . . . Hos 9:4
shall flow from the *h* . . . . Joel 3:18
came and worked on the *h* . . Hag 1:14
priests who were in the *h* . . . Zech 7:3

HOUSEHOLD
over the ways of her *h* . . . . Prov 31:27
If the *h* is worthy . . . . Matt 10:13
be those of his own *h* . . . . . Matt 10:36
make ruler over his *h* . . . . . Luke 12:42
h were baptized . . . . Acts 16:15
saved, you and your *h* . . . . Acts 16:31
also baptized the *h* . . . . 1 Cor 1:16
the *h* of Stephanas . . . . 1 Cor 16:15
those who are of the *h* . . . . Gal 6:10
who are of Caesar's *h* . . . . . . Phil 4:22
mercy to the *h* of . . . . 2 Tim 1:16
ark for the saving of his *h* . . Heb 11:7

HOUSEHOLDER
h who brings out of . . . . Matt 13:52

HOUSEHOLDS
that He provided *h* for . . . . Ex 1:21
heads of the fathers' *h* . . . . Ezra 10:16
those who creep into *h* . . . . . 2 Tim 3:6
who subvert whole *h* . . . . Titus 1:11

HOUSES
h are safe from fear . . . . Job 21:9
Yet He filled their *h* . . . . Job 22:18
is that their *h* will last . . . . Ps 49:11
H and riches are an . . . . Prov 19:14
who has left *h* or . . . . Matt 19:29
you devour widows' *h* . . . . . Matt 23:14
Do you not have *h* . . . . 1 Cor 11:22

HOUSETOP
dwell in a corner of a *h* . . . Prov 25:24
they went up on the *h* . . . . . Luke 5:19
went up on the *h* to pray, . . . Acts 10:9

HOUSETOPS
herb, as the grass on the *h* . . . Is 37:27
ear, preach on the *h* . . . . . . Matt 10:27
be proclaimed on the *h* . . . . . Luke 12:3

HOVERING
Spirit of God was *h* . . . . Gen 1:2

HOW
"*H* can this be . . . . Luke 1:34
H long do You keep . . . . John 10:24
h you turned to God . . . . . . 1 Thess 1:9

HULDAH
Wife of Shallum, 2 Kin 22:14
Foretells Jerusalem's ruin, 2 Kin 22:15–17; 2 Chr 34:22–25
Exempts Josiah from trouble, 2 Kin 22:18–20

HUMAN
broken without *h* means . . . . Dan 8:25
for joy that a *h* being . . . . . John 16:21
I speak in *h* terms . . . . Rom 6:19
words of *h* wisdom . . . . 1 Cor 2:4
we have had *h* fathers . . . . Heb 12:9

HUMBLE
man Moses was very *h* . . . . Num 12:3
h you and test you . . . . Deut 8:2
who is proud, and *h* . . . . Job 40:11
the cry of the *h* . . . . Ps 9:12
Do not forget the *h* . . . . Ps 10:12
the desire of the *h* . . . . Ps 10:17
h He guides in justice . . . . Ps 25:9
h shall hear of it and . . . . Ps 34:2
LORD lifts up the *h* . . . . Ps 147:6
h spirit with the . . . . Prov 16:19
contrite and *h* spirit . . . . Is 57:15
a meek and *h* people . . . . . . Zeph 3:12
associate with the *h* . . . . Rom 12:16
gives grace to the *h* . . . . James 4:6

H yourselves in the . . . . James 4:10
gives grace to the *h* . . . . 1 Pet 5:5
h yourselves under the . . . . . . 1 Pet 5:6

HUMBLED
h himself greatly . . . . 2 Chr 33:12
as a man, He *h* Himself . . . . . . Phil 2:8

HUMBLES
h Himself to behold . . . . Ps 113:6

HUMILIATION
to plunder, and to *h* . . . . Ezra 9:7
h His justice was . . . . Acts 8:33
but the rich in his *h* . . . . . . James 1:10

HUMILITY
By *h* and the fear of . . . . Prov 22:4
righteousness, seek *h* . . . . Zeph 2:3
the Lord with all *h* . . . . Acts 20:19
delight in false *h* . . . . Col 2:18
mercies, kindness, *h* . . . . Col 3:12
h correcting those . . . . 2 Tim 2:25
gentle, showing all *h* . . . . Titus 3:2
and be clothed with *h* . . . . 1 Pet 5:5

HUNDRED
Adam lived were nine *h* . . . . . Gen 5:5
of Lamech were seven *h* . . . . Gen 5:31
of Jacob's life was one *h* . . . Gen 47:28
Joseph lived one *h* and . . . . . Gen 50:22
one *h* cubits long for one . . . . . Ex 27:9
of which was one *h* . . . . Num 7:13
for a *h* foreskins of the . . . . 2 Sam 3:14
one *h* summer fruits . . . . . . 2 Sam 16:1
had taken one *h* prophets . . 1 Kin 18:4

HUNDREDFOLD
in the same year a *h* . . . . . . Gen 26:12
some a *h*, some sixty . . . . Matt 13:8
receive a *h* now in this . . . Mark 10:30
up, and yielded a crop a *h* . . Luke 8:8

HUNGER
you, allowed you to *h* . . . . Deut 8:3
lack and suffer *h* . . . . Ps 34:10
They shall neither *h* . . . . Is 49:10
likely to die from *h* . . . . Jer 38:9
are those who *h* . . . . Matt 5:6
for you shall *h* . . . . Luke 6:25
to Me shall never *h* . . . . John 6:35
present hour we both *h* . . . . 1 Cor 4:11
They shall neither *h* . . . . Rev 7:16

HUNGRY
bread from the *h* . . . . Job 22:7
and fills the *h* . . . . Ps 107:9
gives food to the *h* . . . . Ps 146:7
h soul every bitter . . . . Prov 27:7
your soul to the *h* . . . . Is 58:10
for I was *h* and you . . . . Matt 25:35
when did we see You *h* . . . Matt 25:37
and one is *h* and . . . . 1 Cor 11:21
But if anyone is *h* . . . . 1 Cor 11:34
to be full and to be *h* . . . . Phil 4:12

HUNT
Yet you *h* my life to . . . . . 1 Sam 24:11
h the violent man . . . . Ps 140:11
h the souls of My . . . . Ezek 13:18

HUNTER
Nimrod the mighty *h* . . . . Gen 10:9
Esau was a skillful *h* . . . . Gen 25:27

HUR
Man of Judah; of Caleb's house, 1 Chr 2:18–20
Supports Moses' hands, Ex 17:10–12
Aids Aaron, Ex 24:14

HURAM
Master craftsman of Solomon's temple, 1 Kin 7:13–40, 45; 2 Chr 2:13, 14

HURT
h a woman with child . . . . Ex 21:22
who plot my *h* . . . . Ps 35:4
but I was not *h* . . . . Prov 23:35
another to his own *h* . . . . Eccl 8:9

They shall not *h* . . . . Is 11:9
of my people I am *h* . . . . Jer 8:21
Woe is me for my *h* . . . . Jer 10:19
it will by no means *h* . . . . . Mark 16:18
shall not be *h* by the . . . . Rev 2:11

HUSBAND
She also gave to her *h* . . . . Gen 3:6
desire shall be for your *h* . . . . Gen 3:16
"Surely you are a *h* . . . . Ex 4:25
Uriah her *h* was dead . . . . 2 Sam 11:26
h safely trusts her . . . . Prov 31:11
Her *h* is known in the . . . . . Prov 31:23
your Maker is your *h* . . . . Is 54:5
though I was a *h* . . . . Jer 31:32
you will call Me "My *H* . . . . . Hos 2:16
I have no *h* . . . . John 4:17
now have is not your *h* . . . . John 4:18
But if the *h* dies, she is . . . . . . Rom 7:2
woman have her own *h* . . . . . . 1 Cor 7:2
For the unbelieving *h* . . . . . . 1 Cor 7:14
you will save your *h* . . . . 1 Cor 7:16
betrothed you to one *h* . . . . 2 Cor 11:2
For the *h* is head of . . . . Eph 5:23
the *h* of one wife . . . . 1 Tim 3:2
a bride adorned for her *h* . . . Rev 21:2

HUSBANDS
them ask their own *h* . . . . . 1 Cor 14:35
H, love your wives . . . . Eph 5:25
H, love your wives and do . . . . Col 3:19
Let deacons be the *h* . . . . . . 1 Tim 3:12
women to love their *h* . . . . Titus 2:4
submissive to your own *h* . . . 1 Pet 3:1

HUSHAI
Archite; David's friend, 2 Sam 15:32–37
Feigns sympathy with Absalom, 2 Sam 16:16–19
Defeats Ahithophel's advice, 2 Sam 17:5–23

HYACINTH
h blue, and sulfur yellow . . . . Rev 9:17

HYMENAEUS
False teacher excommunicated by Paul, 1 Tim 1:19, 20

HYMN
they had sung a *h* . . . . Matt 26:30

HYMNS
praying and singing *h* . . . . . Acts 16:25
in psalms and *h* . . . . Eph 5:19

HYPOCRISY
you are full of *h* . . . . Matt 23:28
Pharisees, which is *h* . . . . Luke 12:1
Let love be without *h* . . . . . . Rom 12:9
away with their *h* . . . . Gal 2:13
and without *h* . . . . James 3:17
malice, all deceit, *h* . . . . 1 Pet 2:1

HYPOCRITE
of the *h* shall perish . . . . Job 8:13
and the joy of the *h* . . . . Job 20:5
is the hope of the *h* . . . . Job 27:8
for everyone is a *h* . . . . Is 9:17
also played the *h* . . . . Gal 2:13

HYPOCRITES
"But the *h* in heart . . . . Job 36:13
will I go in with *h* . . . . Ps 26:4
For you were *h* . . . . Jer 42:20
not be like the *h* . . . . Matt 6:5
do you test Me, you *h* . . . . . . Matt 22:18
and Pharisees, *h* . . . . Matt 23:13

HYSSOP
Purge me with *h* . . . . Ps 51:7
sour wine, put it on *h* . . . . . John 19:29

I AM WITH YOU
do not fear, for *I*. I will . . . . Gen 26:24
"Behold, *I* and will keep . . . Gen 28:15

Fear not, for *I*; be not . . . . Is 41:10
I to deliver you," says the . . . . . Jer 1:8
prevail against you; for *I* . . . . Jer 15:20
For *I*,' says the LORD, 'to . . . . Jer 30:11
I, to save you and deliver . . . . Jer 42:11
saying, "*I*, says the LORD." . . Hag 1:13
and lo, *I* always, even to . . Matt 28:20
I, and no one will attack . . Acts 18:10
absent in the flesh, yet *I* in . . . Col 2:5

I WILL BE WITH YOU
"Dwell in this land, and *I* . . . Gen 26:3
to your family, and *I* . . . . Gen 31:3
I swore to them, and *I* . . . . . Deut 31:23
as I was with Moses, so *I* . . . . Josh 1:5
"Surely *I*, and you shall . . . . . Judg 6:16
David did, then *I* . . . . 1 Kin 11:38
pass through the waters, *I* . . . . Is 43:2

IBZAN
Judge of Israel; father of 60 children, Judg 12:8, 9

ICE
dark because of the *i* . . . . Job 6:16

ICHABOD
Son of Phinehas, 1 Sam 4:19–22

ICONIUM
City of Asia Minor; visited by Paul, Acts 13:51
Many converts in, Acts 14:1–6

IDDO
Leader of Jews at Casiphia, Ezra 8:17–20
——— Seer whose writings are cited, 2 Chr 9:29

IDLE
For they are *i* . . . . Ex 5:8
i person will suffer . . . . Prov 19:15
i word men may speak . . . . Matt 12:36
saw others standing *i* . . . . . . Matt 20:3
they learn to be *i* . . . . 1 Tim 5:13
both *i* talkers and . . . . Titus 1:10

IDLENESS
not eat the bread of *i* . . . . . Prov 31:27
through *i* of hands the . . . . . . Eccl 10:18
food, and abundance of *i* . . Ezek 16:49

IDLY
They speak *i* everyone with . . Ps 12:2

IDOL
lifted up his soul to an *i* . . . . . . Ps 24:4
if he blesses an *i* . . . . Is 66:3
a wooden *i* is a worthless . . . . Jer 10:8
that an *i* is nothing . . . . 1 Cor 8:4
thing offered to an *i* . . . . 1 Cor 8:7
That an *i* is anything . . . . . . 1 Cor 10:19

IDOLATER
or covetous, or an *i* . . . . 1 Cor 5:11
man, who is an *i* . . . . Eph 5:5

IDOLATERS
fornicators, nor *i* . . . . 1 Cor 6:9
immoral, sorcerers, *i* . . . . Rev 21:8
and murderers and *i* . . . . Rev 22:15

IDOLATRIES
and abominable *i* . . . . 1 Pet 4:3

IDOLATROUS
he removed the *i* priests . . . 2 Kin 23:5
I have not sat with *i* mortals . . Ps 26:4
pay for your *i* sins . . . . Ezek 23:49
the names of the *i* priests . . . Zeph 1:4

IDOLATRY
beloved, flee from *i* . . . . 1 Cor 10:14
i, sorcery, hatred . . . . Gal 5:20
covetousness, which is *i* . . . . . . Col 3:5

IDOLS
stolen the household *i* . . . . . Gen 31:19
of the peoples are *i* . . . . Ps 96:5
i are silver and gold . . . . Ps 115:4
land is also full of *i* . . . . Is 2:8

insane with their *i* .... Jer 50:38
in the room of his *i* .... Ezek 8:12
from their wooden *i* .... Hos 4:12
who regard worthless *i* .... Jon 2:8
i speak delusion .... Zech 10:2
things polluted by *i* .... Acts 15:20
You who abhor *i* .... Rom 2:22
This was offered to *i* ..... 1 Cor 10:28
keep yourselves from *i* ... 1 John 5:21
worship demons, and *i* .... Rev 9:20

IDUMEA
Name used by Greeks and Romans to designate Edom, Mark 3:8

IGNORANCE
unintentionally or in *i* .... Ezek 45:20
that you did it in *i* .... Acts 3:17
i God overlooked .... Acts 17:30
sins committed in *i* .... Heb 9:7
to silence the *i* .... 1 Pet 2:15

IGNORANT
I was so foolish and *i* .... Ps 73:22
though Abraham was *i* .... Is 63:16
For they being *i* of God's ... Rom 10:3
be *i* of this mystery .... Rom 11:25
not want you to be *i* .... 1 Cor 12:1
But if anyone is *i* .... 1 Cor 14:38
i disputes, knowing that ... 2 Tim 2:23
on those who are *i* .... Heb 5:2

IGNORANTLY
because I did it *i* .... 1 Tim 1:13

IJON
Town of Naphtali; captured by Ben-Hadad, 1 Kin 15:20
Captured by Tiglath-Pileser, 2 Kin 15:29

ILL
God sent a spirit of *i* will ... Judg 9:23
David, and it became *i* ... 2 Sam 12:15
bed and pretend to be *i* ... 2 Sam 13:5
go *i* with him who is .... Job 20:26

ILLEGITIMATE
then you are *i* .... Heb 12:8

ILLUMINATED
after you were *i* .... Heb 10:32
and the earth was *i* .... Rev 18:1
for the glory of God *i* ...... Rev 21:23

ILLYRICUM
Paul preaches in, Rom 15:19

IMAGE
See WOODEN IMAGE; WOODEN IMAGES
Us make man in Our *i* ...... Gen 1:26
yourselves a carved *i* ...... Deut 4:16
shall despise their *i* .... Ps 73:20
the king made an *i* .... Dan 3:1
to them, "Whose *i* .... Matt 22:20
since he is the *i* .... 1 Cor 11:7
He is the *i* of the .... Col 1:15
and not the very *i* .... Heb 10:1
the beast and his *i* .... Rev 14:9
who worshiped his *i* .... Rev 19:20

IMAGINATION
although the *i* of man's .... Gen 8:21
the proud in the *i* .... Luke 1:51

IMITATE
I urge you, *i* me .... 1 Cor 4:16
as I also *i* Christ .... 1 Cor 11:1
i those who through .... Heb 6:12

IMMANUEL
shall call His name *I* .... Is 7:14
shall call His name *I* .... Matt 1:23

IMMEDIATELY
I the fig tree withered ..... Matt 21:19
i the Spirit drove Him ..... Mark 1:12
i they left their nets and ... Mark 1:18
hear, Satan comes *i* .... Mark 4:15
i he puts in the sickle, ... Mark 4:29
I his mouth was opened ... Luke 1:64
i her flow of blood .... Luke 8:44
stones would *i* cry out .... Luke 19:40
I sent to you *i*, and you .... Acts 10:33
i an angel of the Lord ..... Acts 12:23
I did not *i* confer with flesh .. Gal 1:16
i forgets what kind of ..... James 1:24
I I was in the Spirit .... Rev 4:2

IMMORAL
lips of an *i* woman drip ..... Prov 5:3
i woman is a deep pit ..... Prov 22:14
with sexually *i* people .... 1 Cor 5:9
murderers, sexually *i* .... Rev 21:8

IMMORALITY
except sexual *i* .... Matt 5:32
wife, except for sexual *i* .... Matt 19:9
and from sexual *i* .... Acts 15:29
unrighteousness, sexual *i* .. Rom 1:29
i as is not even named .... 1 Cor 5:1
Flee sexual *i* .... 1 Cor 6:18
abstain from sexual *i* ..... 1 Thess 4:3
themselves over to sexual *i* .... Jude 7
to repent of her sexual *i* ..... Rev 2:21

IMMORTAL
to the King eternal, *i* .... 1 Tim 1:17

IMMORTALITY
glory, honor, and *i* .... Rom 2:7
mortal must put on *i* ...... 1 Cor 15:53
who alone has *i* .... 1 Tim 6:16
and brought life and *i* ..... 2 Tim 1:10

IMMOVABLE
be steadfast, *i* .... 1 Cor 15:58

IMMUTABLE
that by two *i* things .... Heb 6:18

IMPART
see you, that I may *i* .... Rom 1:11
that it may *i* grace .... Eph 4:29

IMPENITENT
i heart you are .... Rom 2:5

IMPERISHABLE
but we for an *i* crown .... 1 Cor 9:25

IMPLANTED
with meekness the *i* ...... James 1:21

IMPORTED
had horses *i* from Egypt .. 1 Kin 10:28
i from Egypt a chariot ..... 2 Chr 1:17

IMPOSSIBLE
and nothing will be *i* ...... Matt 17:20
"With men this is *i* .... Matt 19:26
God nothing will be *i* ...... Luke 1:37
It is *i* that no offenses ..... Luke 17:1
For it is *i* for those who .... Heb 6:4
which it is *i* for God to lie ... Heb 6:18
without faith it is *i* .... Heb 11:6

IMPOSTORS
i will grow worse .... 2 Tim 3:13

IMPRISONMENT
and of chains and *i* .... Heb 11:36

IMPRISONMENTS
in stripes, in *i* .... 2 Cor 6:5

IMPULSIVE
but he who is *i* .... Prov 14:29

IMPURITY
during her *i* shall be .... Lev 15:20
cleansed from her *i* .... 2 Sam 11:4
end to another with their *i* . Ezra 9:11
a woman during her *i* .... Ezek 18:6

IMPUTE
"Do not let my lord *i* .... 2 Sam 19:19
the LORD does not *i* .... Ps 32:2
the LORD shall not *i* .... Rom 4:8

IMPUTED
bloodshed shall be *i* .... Lev 17:4
might be *i* to them .... Rom 4:11
alone that it was *i* .... Rom 4:23
but sin is not *i* .... Rom 5:13

IMPUTES
i righteousness apart .... Rom 4:6

IN MY NAME
which He speaks *i* .... Deut 18:19
to speak a word *i* .... Deut 18:20
i his horn shall be exalted. .. Ps 89:24
prophets prophesy lies *i* .... Jer 14:14
prophesy falsely to you *i* ..... Jer 29:9
little child like this *i* .... Matt 18:5
are gathered together *i* .... Matt 18:20
many will come *i*, saying ... Matt 24:5
who works a miracle *i* ..... Mark 9:39
cup of water to drink *i* .... Mark 9:41
I they will cast out .... Mark 16:17
whatever you ask *i* .... John 14:13
the Father will send *i* ..... John 14:26
you ask the Father *i* ...... John 15:16
day you will ask *i* .... John 16:26

IN THE WORLD
He was *i*, and the world .... John 1:10
"As long as I am *i*, I am ..... John 9:5
His own who were *i* .... John 13:1
I you will have .... John 16:33
"Now I am no longer *i* ... John 17:11
I was with them *i* .... John 17:12
until the law sin was *i* ...... Rom 5:13
an idol is nothing *i* .... 1 Cor 8:4
we conducted ourselves *i* .. 2 Cor 1:12
no hope and without God *i* .. Eph 2:12
you shine as lights *i* .... Phil 2:15
why, as though living *i* .... Col 2:20
believed on *i*, received ..... 1 Tim 3:16
the corruption that is *i* .... 2 Pet 1:4
the world or the things *i* .. 1 John 2:15
greater than he who is *i* ... 1 John 4:4

INCENSE
oil and for the sweet *i* .... Ex 25:6
lamps, he shall burn *i* on it ... Ex 30:7
perpetual *i* before the LORD .. Ex 30:8
the pure *i* of sweet spices, ... Ex 37:29
the cloud of *i* may cover ... Lev 16:13
put *i* in it, and each of .... Num 16:17
burned *i* at the high places .. 1 Kin 3:3
be set before You as *i* .... Ps 141:2
i is an abomination to Me ..... Is 1:13
i to the queen of heaven .... Jer 44:18
oil and My *i* before them .. Ezek 16:18
In every place *i* shall be ..... Mal 1:11
his lot fell to burn *i* when ... Luke 1:9
right side of the altar of *i* .. Luke 1:11
golden bowls full of *i* .... Rev 5:8
the smoke of the *i*, with .... Rev 8:4
cinnamon and *i*, fragrant .. Rev 18:13

INCLINE
i your heart to the .... Josh 24:23
I Your ear to me, and hear ... Ps 17:6
I Your ear to my cry .... Ps 88:2
I my heart to Your .... Ps 119:36
i my heart to any evil .... Ps 141:4
i your ear to my sayings ... Prov 4:20
not obey Me or *i* their ear ..... Jer 7:26
O my God, *i* Your ear and ... Dan 9:18

INCORRUPTIBLE
the glory of the *i* .... Rom 1:23
dead will be raised *i* ...... 1 Cor 15:52
to an inheritance *i* .... 1 Pet 1:4
corruptible seed but *i* ...... 1 Pet 1:23
i beauty of a gentle .... 1 Pet 3:4

INCORRUPTION
it is raised in *i* .... 1 Cor 15:42
corruption inherit *i* .... 1 Cor 15:50
must put on *i* .... 1 Cor 15:53

INCREASE
if riches *i*, do not set .... Ps 62:10
the LORD give you *i* .... Ps 115:14
hear and *i* learning .... Prov 1:5
When goods *i*, they .... Eccl 5:11
Of the *i* of His .... Is 9:7
and knowledge shall *i* ...... Dan 12:4

Lord, "*I* our faith . . . . Luke 17:5
He must *i*, but I must . . . . . . John 3:30
but God gave the *i* . . . . 1 Cor 3:6
grows with the *i* . . . . Col 2:19
for they will *i* . . . . 2 Tim 2:16

INCREASED
The waters *i* and . . . . Gen 7:17
i your mercy which you . . . Gen 19:19
nation and *i* its joy . . . . Is 9:3
And Jesus *i* in wisdom . . . . . Luke 2:52

INCREASES
i knowledge *i* sorrow . . . . Eccl 1:18
who have no might He *i* . . . . . Is 40:29

INCREDIBLE
should it be thought *i* . . . . Acts 26:8

INCURABLE
My wound is *i* . . . . Job 34:6
'Your affliction is *i* . . . . Jer 30:12
Your sorrow is *i* . . . . Jer 30:15

INDEBTED
everyone who is *i* . . . . Luke 11:4

INDEED
i it was very good . . . . Gen 1:31
"But will God *i* . . . . 1 Kin 8:27
"Behold, an Israelite *i* . . . . . . John 1:47

INDIA
Eastern limit of Persian Empire, Esth 1:1

INDICATING
the Holy Spirit *i* . . . . Heb 9:8
who was in them was *i* . . . . . 1 Pet 1:11

INDIGNANT
saw it, they were *i* . . . . Matt 26:8

INDIGNATION
of His anger, wrath, *i* . . . . Ps 78:49
I has taken hold . . . . Ps 119:53
in whose hand is My *i* . . . . Is 10:5
For the *i* of the LORD . . . . Is 34:2
have filled me with *i* . . . . Jer 15:17
can stand before His *i* . . . . Nah 1:6
i which will devour . . . . Heb 10:27
into the cup of His *i* . . . . Rev 14:10

INDIVIDUALLY
He fashions their hearts *i* . . . . Ps 33:15
i members of one another . . . Rom 12:5
Christ, and members *i* . . . . 1 Cor 12:27

INDUCED
O LORD, You *i* me . . . . Jer 20:7
if the prophet is *i* . . . . Ezek 14:9

INDULGENCE
no value against the *i* . . . . Col 2:23

INEXCUSABLE
Therefore you are *i* . . . . Rom 2:1

INEXPRESSIBLE
Paradise and heard *i* . . . . . . 2 Cor 12:4
you rejoice with joy *i* . . . . 1 Pet 1:8

INFALLIBLE
suffering by many *i* . . . . Acts 1:3

INFANTS
i who never saw . . . . Job 3:16
i You have ordained . . . . Ps 8:2
i You have perfected . . . . . . Matt 21:16
they also brought *i* . . . . Luke 18:15

INFERIOR
another kingdom *i* . . . . Dan 2:39
that I am not at all *i* . . . . 2 Cor 11:5

INFIRMITIES
"He Himself took our *i* . . . . . Matt 8:17
boast, except in my *i* . . . . . . 2 Cor 12:5
and your frequent *i* . . . . 1 Tim 5:23

INFIRMITY
a spirit of *i* eighteen . . . . . . Luke 13:11
had an *i* thirty-eight years . . John 5:5
i I preached the gospel to . . . . Gal 4:13

INFLAMING
i yourselves with gods . . . . Is 57:5

INGATHERING
the Feast of *I* at the year's . . Ex 34:22

INHABIT
the wicked will not *i* . . . . . . Prov 10:30
cities and *i* them . . . . Amos 9:14

INHABITANT
Cry out and shout, O *i* . . . . Is 12:6
And the *i* will not say . . . . Is 33:24

INHABITANTS
He looks on all the *i* . . . . Ps 33:14
give ear, all *i* . . . . Ps 49:1
Let the *i* of Sela sing . . . . Is 42:11
Woe to the *i* of the . . . . Rev 12:12

INHABITED
rejoicing in His *i* . . . . Prov 8:31
'You shall be *i* . . . . Is 44:26
who formed it to be *i* . . . . Is 45:18

INHERIT
i the iniquities . . . . Job 13:26
descendants shall *i* . . . . Ps 25:13
The righteous shall *i* . . . . Ps 37:29
The wise shall *i* . . . . Prov 3:35
love me to *i* wealth . . . . Prov 8:21
The simple *i* folly . . . . Prov 14:18
the blameless will *i* . . . . Prov 28:10
i the kingdom prepared . . . Matt 25:34
I do that I may *i* . . . . Mark 10:17
unrighteous will not *i* . . . . 1 Cor 6:9
you may *i* a blessing . . . . 1 Pet 3:9
who overcomes shall *i* . . . . . . Rev 21:7

INHERITANCE
"You shall have no *i* . . . . . . Num 18:20
is the place of His *i* . . . . Deut 32:9
the portion of my *i* . . . . Ps 16:5
yes, I have a good *i* . . . . Ps 16:6
i shall be forever . . . . Ps 37:18
He will choose our *i* . . . . Ps 47:4
You confirmed Your *i* . . . . Ps 68:9
the tribe of Your *i* . . . . Ps 74:2
i gained hastily . . . . Prov 20:21
right of *i* is yours . . . . Jer 32:8
i has been turned . . . . Lam 5:2
will arise to your *i* . . . . Dan 12:13
And God gave him no *i* . . . . . . Acts 7:5
and give you an *i* . . . . Acts 20:32
For if the *i* is of the . . . . Gal 3:18
we have obtained an *i* . . . . . . Eph 1:11
be partakers of the *i* . . . . Col 1:12
receive as an *i* . . . . Heb 11:8
to an *i* incorruptible . . . . 1 Pet 1:4

INIQUITIES
How many are my *i* . . . . Job 13:23
i have overtaken me . . . . Ps 40:12
I prevail against me . . . . Ps 65:3
forgives all your *i* . . . . Ps 103:3
LORD, should mark *i* . . . . Ps 130:3
was bruised for our *i* . . . . Is 53:5
He shall bear their *i* . . . . Is 53:11
i have separated you . . . . Is 59:2

INIQUITY
See WORKERS OF INIQUITY
God, visiting the *i* of the . . . . Ex 20:5
He has not observed *i* . . . . Num 23:21
wicked brings forth *i* . . . . Ps 7:14
O LORD, pardon my *i* . . . . Ps 25:11
i I have not hidden . . . . Ps 32:5
was brought forth in *i* . . . . Ps 51:5
If I regard *i* in my . . . . Ps 66:18
Add *i* to their *i* . . . . Ps 69:27
workers of *i* flourish . . . . Ps 92:7
i boast in themselves . . . . Ps 94:4
Shall the throne of *i* . . . . Ps 94:20
let no *i* have dominion . . . . Ps 119:133
i will reap sorrow . . . . Prov 22:8
a people laden with *i* . . . . Is 1:4
i is taken away . . . . Is 6:7
has laid on Him the *i* . . . . Is 53:6
will remember their *i* . . . . Hos 9:9
to those who devise *i* . . . . Mic 2:1
like You, pardoning *i* . . . . Mic 7:18
all you workers of *i* . . . . Luke 13:27
a fire, a world of *i* . . . . James 3:6

INJUSTICE
of truth and without *i* . . . . . . Deut 32:4
i shuts her mouth . . . . Job 5:16
i have your fathers . . . . Jer 2:5

INK
us, written not with *i* . . . . 2 Cor 3:3
do so with paper and *i* . . . . . 2 John 12

INN
room for them in the *i* . . . . . . Luke 2:7
brought him to an *i* . . . . Luke 10:34

INNOCENCE
of my heart and *i* . . . . Gen 20:5
washed my hands in *i* . . . . Ps 73:13

INNOCENT
do not kill the *i* . . . . Ex 23:7
a bribe to slay an *i* . . . . Deut 27:25
i will divide the . . . . Job 27:17
a bribe against the *i* . . . . Ps 15:5
because I was found *i* . . . . Dan 6:22
by betraying *i* blood . . . . Matt 27:4
saying, "I am *i* . . . . Matt 27:24
this day that I am *i* . . . . Acts 20:26

INNOCENT BLOOD
"lest *i* be shed in the . . . . . . Deut 19:10
against *i*, to kill David . . . . 1 Sam 19:5
the *i* which Joab shed . . . . . . 1 Kin 2:31
shed very much *i* . . . . 2 Kin 21:16
righteous, and condemn *i* . . . . Ps 94:21
And shed *i*, the blood . . . . . . Ps 106:38
tongue, hands that shed *i* . . . Prov 6:17
they make haste to shed *i* . . . . . Is 59:7
do not shed *i* in this place . . . . . Jer 7:6
you will surely bring *i* . . . . . . Jer 26:15
for they have shed *i* . . . . Joel 3:19
do not charge us with *i* . . . . . Jon 1:14
sinned by betraying *i* . . . . Matt 27:4

INNUMERABLE
i as the sand which is . . . . . Heb 11:12
i company of angels . . . . Heb 12:22

INQUIRE
went to *i* of the LORD . . . . . . Gen 25:22
a man went to *i* of God . . . . . 1 Sam 9:9
I may go to her and *i* . . . . . 1 Sam 28:7
sent you to Me to *i* of Me . . . . Jer 37:7
i who in it is worthy . . . . . . Matt 10:11
to *i* more fully about him . . Acts 23:20

INQUIRED
children of Israel *i* . . . . Judg 20:27
Therefore David *i* . . . . 1 Sam 23:2
the LORD, nor *i* of Him . . . . . . Zeph 1:6
the prophets have *i* . . . . 1 Pet 1:10

INQUIRY
shall make careful *i* . . . . Deut 19:18

INSANE
images, and they are *i* . . . . . . Jer 50:38
the spiritual man is *i* . . . . Hos 9:7

INSCRIBED
Oh, that they were *i* . . . . Job 19:23
See, I have *i* you on . . . . Is 49:16

INSCRIPTION
wrote on it an *i* like the . . . . . Ex 39:30
image and *i* is this . . . . Matt 22:20
the *i* of His accusation . . . Mark 15:26
found an altar with this *i* . . Acts 17:23

INSPIRATION
is given by *i* of God . . . . 2 Tim 3:16

INSTRUCT
good Spirit to *i* them . . . . Neh 9:20
I will *i* you and teach . . . . Ps 32:8
is the man whom You *i* . . . . . Ps 94:12

the LORD that he may *i* .... 1 Cor 2:16
If you *i* the brethren in ..... 1 Tim 4:6

INSTRUCTED
Surely you have *i* .... Job 4:3
counsel, and who *i* .... Is 40:14
This man had been *i* ...... Acts 18:25
are excellent, being *i* .... Rom 2:18
Moses was divinely *i* .... Heb 8:5

INSTRUCTION
also opens their ear to *i* .... Job 36:10
seeing you hate *i* .... Ps 50:17
despise wisdom and *i* .... Prov 1:7
Take firm hold of *i* .... Prov 4:13
He shall die for lack of *i* ... Prov 5:23
Hear *i* and be wise .... Prov 8:33
Give *i* to a wise man .... Prov 9:9
i loves knowledge .... Prov 12:1
fool despises his father's *i* .. Prov 15:5
Cease listening to *i* .... Prov 19:27
Apply your heart to *i* ..... Prov 23:12
you have written at my *i*, ... Jer 36:6
for correction, for *i* .... 2 Tim 3:16

INSTRUCTORS
have ten thousand *i* .... 1 Cor 4:15

INSTRUCTS
My heart also *i* .... Ps 16:7
He who *i* the nations .... Ps 94:10

INSTRUMENT
to Him with an *i* .... Ps 33:2
on an *i* of ten strings .... Ps 92:3

INSTRUMENTS
i of cruelty are in .... Gen 49:5
on harps, on stringed *i* ..... 2 Sam 6:5
by *i* of music .... 1 Chr 15:16
with stringed *i* .... 2 Chr 20:28
cymbals and stringed *i* .... Neh 12:27
for Himself *i* of death .... Ps 7:13
with stringed *i* .... Ps 150:4
and musical *i* of all kinds .... Eccl 2:8
i of unrighteousness .... Rom 6:13

INSUBORDINATE
for the lawless and *i* .... 1 Tim 1:9
For there are many *i* .... Titus 1:10

INSUBORDINATION
of dissipation or *i* .... Titus 1:6

INSULT
shall not return *i* for *i* .... Mic 2:6

INSULTED
will be mocked and *i* ..... Luke 18:32
i the Spirit of grace .... Heb 10:29

INSULTS
nor be afraid of their *i* .... Is 51:7

INTEGRITY
In the *i* of my heart .... Gen 20:5
walked, in *i* of heart and .... 1 Kin 9:4
he holds fast to his *i* .... Job 2:3
that God may know my *i* .... Job 31:6
Let *i* and uprightness .... Ps 25:21
I have walked in my *i* .... Ps 26:1
You uphold me in my *i* .... Ps 41:12
with *i* walks securely ...... Prov 10:9
The *i* of the upright .... Prov 11:3
poor who walks in his *i* .... Prov 19:1
man walks in his *i* .... Prov 20:7
i than one perverse in his .. Prov 28:6
in doctrine showing *i* .... Titus 2:7

INTELLIGENT
Sergius Paulus, an *i* .... Acts 13:7

INTENT
that every *i* of the thoughts .. Gen 6:5
all the *i* of the thoughts .... 1 Chr 28:9
brings it with wicked *i* .... Prov 21:27
to the *i* that we should ..... 1 Cor 10:6

INTERCEDE
the LORD, who will *i* ...... 1 Sam 2:25

INTERCESSION
of many, and made *i* .... Is 53:12
Spirit Himself makes *i* ...... Rom 8:26
always lives to make *i* ...... Heb 7:25

INTERCESSOR
that there was no *i* .... Is 59:16

INTEREST
shall not charge him *i* .... Ex 22:25
men lent to me for *i* .... Jer 15:10
collected it with *i* .... Luke 19:23

INTERPRET
could *i* them for Pharaoh ... Gen 41:8
Do all *i* .... 1 Cor 12:30
pray that he may *i* .... 1 Cor 14:13
in turn, and let one *i* ..... 1 Cor 14:27

INTERPRETATION
"This is the *i* .... Gen 40:12
who knows the *i* of a thing .. Eccl 8:1
you tell the dream and its *i* .. Dan 2:6
to another the *i* .... 1 Cor 12:10
a revelation, has an *i* ..... 1 Cor 14:26
of any private *i* .... 2 Pet 1:20

INTERPRETATIONS
Do not *i* belong to God ..... Gen 40:8
that you can give *i* .... Dan 5:16

INTOXICATING
not drink wine or *i* drink .... Lev 10:9

INTRIGUE
seize the kingdom by *i* .... Dan 11:21
join with them by *i* .... Dan 11:34

INTRUDING
i into those things which .... Col 2:18

INVENT
but you *i* them in your own .. Neh 6:8
i for yourselves musical .... Amos 6:5

INVISIBLE
of the world His *i* .... Rom 1:20
is the image of the *i* .... Col 1:15
eternal, immortal, *i* .... 1 Tim 1:17
as seeing Him who is *i* .... Heb 11:27

INVITE
i Jesse to the sacrifice ..... 1 Sam 16:3
he did not *i* Nathan the .... 1 Kin 1:10
you find, *i* to the wedding .. Matt 22:9
lest they also *i* you back .. Luke 14:12

INVITED
so Absalom *i* all the ..... 2 Sam 13:23
has *i* all the sons of the .... 1 Kin 1:19
Queen Esther *i* no one but .. Esth 5:12
were *i* to the wedding ...... Matt 22:3
who had *i* Him saw this .... Luke 7:39
to those who were *i* .... Luke 14:7
were *i* to the wedding .... John 2:2
he *i* them in and lodged .... Acts 10:23
were *i* to stay with them .. Acts 28:14

INWARD
i part is destruction .... Ps 5:9
Both the *i* thought .... Ps 64:6
You have formed my *i* ..... Ps 139:13
God according to the *i* ..... Rom 7:22
i man is being renewed .... 2 Cor 4:16

INWARDLY
i they are ravenous .... Matt 7:15
is a Jew who is one *i* .... Rom 2:29

IRON
make your heavens like *i* .. Lev 26:19
was an *i* bedstead .... Deut 3:11
He will put a yoke of *i* .... Deut 28:48
i picks and *i* axes, and ... 2 Sam 12:31
He regards *i* as straw ...... Job 41:27
i sharpens *i* .... Prov 27:17
and your neck was an *i* .... Is 48:4
its feet partly of *i* .... Dan 2:33
seared with a hot *i*, ... 1 Tim 4:2
all nations with a rod of *i* ... Rev 12:5

IRREVOCABLE
calling of God are *i* .... Rom 11:29

ISAAC
Promised heir of the covenant, Gen 17:16–21
Born and circumcised, Gen 21:1–7
Offered up as a sacrifice, Gen 22:1–19
Marries Rebekah, Gen 24:62–67
Prays for children; prefers Esau, Gen 25:21–28
Dealings with Abimelech, king of Gerar, Gen 26:1–31
Mistakenly blesses Jacob, Gen 27:1—28:5
Dies in his old age, Gen 35:28, 29
N.T. references to, Luke 3:34; Gal 4:21–31; Heb 11:9, 20

ISAIAH
Prophet during reigns of Uzziah, Jotham, Ahaz, and Hezekiah, Is 1:1
Responds to prophetic call, Is 6:1–13
Prophesies to Hezekiah, 2 Kin 19; 20
Writes Uzziah's biography, 2 Chr 26:22
Writes Hezekiah's biography, 2 Chr 32:32
Quoted in N.T., Matt 1:22, 23; 3:3; 8:17; 12:17–21; Luke 4:17–19; Acts 13:34; Rom 9:27, 29; 10:16, 20, 21; 11:26, 27; 15:12; 1 Pet 2:22

ISCARIOT, JUDAS
Listed among the Twelve, Mark 3:14, 19; Luke 6:16
Criticizes Mary, John 12:3–6
Identified as betrayer, John 13:21–30
Takes money to betray Christ, Matt 26:14–16
Betrays Christ with a kiss, Mark 14:43–45
Repents and commits suicide, Matt 27:3–10
His place filled, Acts 1:15–26

ISHBOSHETH
One of Saul's sons; made king, 2 Sam 2:8–10
Offends Abner, 2 Sam 3:7–11
Slain; his assassins executed, 2 Sam 4:1–12

ISHMAEL
Abram's son by Hagar, Gen 16:3, 4, 11–16
Circumcised, Gen 17:25
Scoffs at Isaac's feast; exiled with his mother, Gen 21:8–21
His sons; his death, Gen 25:12–18
—— Son of Nethaniah; kills Gedaliah, 2 Kin 25:22–26

ISHMAELITES
Settle at Havilah, Gen 25:17, 18
Joseph sold to, Gen 37:25–28
Sell Joseph to Potiphar, Gen 39:1

ISLAND
aground on a certain *i* .... Acts 27:26
the leading citizen of the *i* .. Acts 28:7
i was moved out of its ...... Rev 6:14
Then every *i* fled away ..... Rev 16:20

ISLES
the multitude of *i* be glad ..... Ps 97:1
declare it in the *i* afar off ... Jer 31:10
many *i* were the market .. Ezek 27:15
i will be astonished at .... Ezek 27:35

ISRAEL
See HOLY ONE OF ISRAEL; LORD GOD OF ISRAEL
Used to refer to:
Jacob, Gen 32:28
descendants of Jacob, Gen 49:16, 28
ten northern tribes (in contrast to Judah), 1 Sam 11:8
restored nation after exile, Ezra 9:1
true church, Gal 6:16

be called Jacob, but *I* ...... Gen 32:28
"Hear, O *I*: The LORD .... Deut 6:4
shepherd My people *I* ...... 2 Sam 7:7

Jacob rejoice and *I* be glad . . . Ps 14:7
Redeem *I*, O God, out of . . . . . Ps 25:22
Truly God is good to *I* . . . . Ps 73:1
O *I*, if you will listen to Me . . . Ps 81:8
When *I* went out of Egypt, . . Ps 114:1
Let *I* now say, "His mercy . . . Ps 118:2
O *I*, hope in the LORD . . . . Ps 130:7
Let *I* rejoice in their Maker . . Ps 149:2
will shepherd My people *I* . . . Matt 2:6
great faith, not even in *I* . . . . Matt 8:10
sheep of the house of *I* . . . . . Matt 10:6
the twelve tribes of *I* . . . . . . Matt 19:28
If He is the King of *I*, let . . Matt 27:42
helped His servant *I* . . . . Luke 1:54
of his manifestation to *I* . . . Luke 1:80
Are you the teacher of *I*, ... John 3:10
restore the kingdom to *I* . . . . . Acts 1:6
God raised up for *I* a . . . . . . Acts 13:23
because for the hope of *I* . . Acts 28:20
For they are not all *I* . . . . Rom 9:6
so all *I* will be saved . . . . . . Rom 11:26
Observe *I* after the flesh . . 1 Cor 10:18
and upon the *I* of God . . . . Gal 6:16
eighth day, of the stock of *I* . . Phil 3:5
with the house of *I* . . . . Heb 8:8
children of *I* were sealed . . . . . Rev 7:4
tribes of the children of *I* . . Rev 21:12

ISRAELITES
Afflicted in Egypt, Ex 1:12–22
Escape from Egypt, Ex 12:29–42, 50; 13:17–22
Receive law at Sinai, Ex 19
Idolatry and rebellion of, Ex 32; Num 13; 14
Wander in the wilderness, Num 14:26–39
Cross Jordan; conquer Canaan, Josh 4; 12
Ruled by judges, Judg 2
Saul chosen as king, 1 Sam 10
Kingdom divided, 1 Kin 12
Northern kingdom carried captive, 2 Kin 17
Southern kingdom carried captive, 2 Kin 24
70 years in exile, 2 Chr 36:20, 21
Return after exile, Ezra 1:1–5
Nation rejects Christ, Matt 27:20–27
Nation destroyed, Luke 21:20–24

ISSACHAR
Jacob's fifth son, Gen 30:17, 18
——— Tribe of:
Genealogy of, 1 Chr 7:1–5
Prophecy concerning, Gen 49:14, 15
Census at Sinai, Num 1:28, 29
Inheritance of, Josh 19:17–23

ISSUED
King Darius *i* a decree . . . . . . Ezra 6:1
be *i* as law in every . . . . Esth 3:14
i as a decree in every . . . . Esth 8:13
A fiery stream *i* and came . . Dan 7:10
before the decree is *i*, ... Zeph 2:2

IT IS WRITTEN
as *i* in the Law of Moses . . . . 1 Kin 2:3
as *i* in this Book of . . . . 2 Kin 23:21
Feast of Tabernacles, as *i* . . . . Ezra 3:4
trees, to make booths, as *i* . . Neh 8:15
in the scroll of the Book *i* . . . . . Ps 40:7
"Behold, *i* before Me: I will . . . . Is 65:6
"As *i* in the Law of Moses . . . Dan 9:13
for thus *i* by the prophet: . . . . Matt 2:5
"*I*, 'Man shall not live by . . . . Matt 4:4
throw Yourself down. For *i* . . Matt 4:6
"*I* again, 'You shall not . . . . . Matt 4:7
i, 'You shall worship . . . . Matt 4:10
"For this is he of whom *i* . . Matt 11:10
"*I*, 'My house shall be . . . . . Matt 21:13
i: 'I will strike the . . . . Matt 26:31
"Thus *i*, and thus it was . . . Luke 24:46
"*I* in the prophets, 'And . . . . John 6:45
i in the book of Psalms . . . . . Acts 1:20
i, 'You shall not speak . . . . . Acts 23:5
volume of the book *i* . . . . Heb 10:7
because *i*, "Be holy, for . . . . 1 Pet 1:16

ITALIAN
was called the *I* Regiment . . Acts 10:1

ITALY
Jews expelled from, Acts 18:2
Paul sails for, Acts 27:1, 6
Christians in, Acts 28:14

ITCHING
they have *i* ears . . . . 2 Tim 4:3

ITHAMAR
Youngest son of Aaron, Ex 6:23
Consecrated as priest, Ex 28:1
Duty entrusted to, Ex 38:21
Jurisdiction over Gershonites and Merarites, Num 4:21–33

ITINERANT
i Jewish exorcists . . . . Acts 19:13

ITUREA
Region ruled by Herod Philip, Luke 3:1

IVORY
made a great throne of *i* . . 1 Kin 10:18
Out of the *i* palaces . . . . Ps 45:8
neck is like an *i* tower . . . . . . Song 7:4
lie on beds of *i*, stretch . . . . . Amos 6:4

JABBOK
River entering the Jordan about 20 miles north of the Dead Sea, Num 21:24
Scene of Jacob's conflict, Gen 32:22–32
Boundary marker, Deut 3:16

JABESH GILEAD
Consigned to destruction, Judg 21:8–15
Saul defeats the Ammonites at, 1 Sam 11:1–11
Citizens of, rescue Saul's body, 1 Sam 31:11–13
David thanks citizens of, 2 Sam 2:4–7

JABIN
Canaanite king of Hazor; leads confederacy against Joshua, Josh 11:1–14
——— Another king of Hazor; oppresses Israelites, Judg 4:2
Defeated by Deborah and Barak, Judg 4:3–24
Immortalized in poetry, Judg 5:1–31

JACHIN
One of two pillars in front of Solomon's temple, 1 Kin 7:21, 22

JACINTH
third row, a *j*, an agate, ... Ex 28:19
the eleventh *j* . . . . Rev 21:20

JACKALS
it shall be a habitation of *j* . . . Is 34:13
make a wailing like the *j* . . . . . Mic 1:8

JACOB
Son of Isaac and Rebekah; Rebekah's favorite, Gen 25:21–28
Obtains birthright, Gen 25:29–34
Obtains blessing meant for Esau; flees, Gen 27:1—28:5
Sees vision of ladder, Gen 28:10–22
Serves Laban for Rachel and Leah, Gen 29:1–30
Fathers children, Gen 29:31—30:24
Flees from, makes covenant with Laban, Gen 30:25—31:55
Makes peace with Esau, Gen 32:1–21; 33:1–17
Wrestles with God, Gen 32:22–32
Returns to Bethel; renamed Israel, Gen 35:1–15
Shows preference for Joseph, Gen 37:3
Mourns Joseph's disappearance, Gen 37:32–35
Sends sons to Egypt for food, Gen 42:1–5
Reluctantly allows Benjamin to go, Gen 43:1–15
Moves his household to Egypt, Gen 45:25—47:12
Blesses his sons and grandsons; dies, Gen 48; 49
Buried in Canaan, Gen 50:1–14

JACOB'S WELL
Christ teaches a Samaritan woman at, John 4:5–26

JAEL
Wife of Heber the Kenite; kills Sisera, Judg 4:17–22
Praised by Deborah, Judg 5:24–27

JAIR
Manassite warrior; conquers towns in Gilead, Num 32:41; Deut 3:14
——— Eighth judge of Israel, Judg 10:3–5

JAIRUS
Ruler of the synagogue; Jesus raises his daughter, Mark 5:22–24, 35–43

JAMES
Son of Zebedee, called as disciple, Matt 4:21, 22; Luke 5:10, 11
One of the Twelve, Matt 10:2; Mark 3:17
Zealous for the Lord, Luke 9:52–54
Ambitious for honor, Mark 10:35–45
Witnesses transfiguration, Matt 17:1–9
Martyred by Herod Agrippa, Acts 12:2
——— Son of Alphaeus; one of the Twelve, Matt 10:3, 4
Called "the Less," Mark 15:40
——— Jesus' half brother, Matt 13:55, 56; Gal 1:19
Becomes leader of Jerusalem Council and Jerusalem church, Acts 15:13–22; Gal 2:9
Author of an epistle, James 1:1

JANNES AND JAMBRES
Two Egyptian magicians; oppose Moses, Ex 7:11–22; 2 Tim 3:8

JANOAH
Town of Naphtali, 2 Kin 15:29

JAPHETH
One of Noah's three sons, Gen 5:32
Receives blessing, Gen 9:20–27
His descendants occupy Asia Minor and Europe, Gen 10:2–5

JARED
Father of Enoch, Gen 5:15–20
Ancestor of Noah, 1 Chr 1:2
Ancestor of Christ, Luke 3:37

JASHER
Book of, quoted, Josh 10:13

JASON
Welcomes Paul at Thessalonica, Acts 17:5–9
Described as Paul's kinsman, Rom 16:21

JASPER
a beryl, an onyx, and a *j* . . . . Ex 28:20
beryl, onyx, and *j* . . . . Ezek 28:13
stone, like a *j* stone, clear . . Rev 21:11

JAVAN
Son of Japheth, Gen 10:2, 4
Descendants of, to receive good news, Is 66:19, 20

JAVELINS
bows and arrows, the *j* . . . . . Ezek 39:9

JAW
or pierce his *j* with a hook . . Job 41:2

JAWBONE
a fresh *j* of a donkey . . . . . . Judg 15:15

JAWS
My tongue clings to My *j* . . . . Ps 22:15
bridle in the *j* of the people . . Is 30:28
I will put hooks in your *j* . . . Ezek 29:4
put hooks into your *j* . . . . . . Ezek 38:4

JEALOUS
your God, am a *j* God . . . . Ex 20:5
LORD, whose name is *J* . . . . . . Ex 34:14
he becomes *j* of his wife, . . . Num 5:14
a consuming fire, a *j* . . . . Deut 4:24
I will be *j* for My holy . . . . Ezek 39:25
For I am *j* for you . . . . 2 Cor 11:2

JEALOUSY
They provoked Him to *j* . . . Deut 32:16
Will Your *j* burn like . . . . Ps 79:5
j is a husband's . . . . Prov 6:34
as strong as death, *j* . . . . Song 8:6
will provoke you to *j* . . . . . . Rom 10:19
fall, to provoke them to *j* . . Rom 11:11
provoke the Lord to *j* . . . . 1 Cor 10:22
for you with godly *j* . . . . 2 Cor 11:2

JEBUS
Canaanite name of Jerusalem before captured by David, 1 Chr 11:4–8

JEBUSITES
Descendants of Canaan, Gen 15:18–21; Num 13:29
Defeated by Joshua, Josh 11:1–12
Not driven from Jerusalem; later conquered by David, Judg 1:21; 2 Sam 5:6–8
Put to forced labor under Solomon, 1 Kin 9:20, 21

JECONIAH
See JEHOIACHIN
Variant form of Jehoiachin, 1 Chr 3:16, 17
Abbreviated to Coniah, Jer 22:24, 28

JEDIDIAH
Name given to Solomon by Nathan, 2 Sam 12:24, 25

JEDUTHUN
Levite musician appointed by David, 1 Chr 16:41, 42
Heads a family of musicians, 2 Chr 5:12
Name appears in psalm titles, Ps 39; 62; 77

JEGAR SAHADUTHA
Name given by Laban to memorial stones, Gen 31:46, 47

JEHOAHAZ
Son and successor of Jehu, king of Israel, 2 Kin 10:35
Seeks the Lord in defeat, 2 Kin 13:2–9
——— Son and successor of Josiah, king of Judah, 2 Kin 23:30–34
Called Shallum, 1 Chr 3:15
——— Another form of Ahaziah, youngest son of King Joram, 2 Chr 21:17

JEHOASH
See JOASH

JEHOIACHIN
Son of Jehoiakim; next to the last king of Judah, 2 Kin 24:8
Deported to Babylon, 2 Kin 24:8–16
Liberated by Evil-Merodach, Jer 52:31–34

JEHOIADA
High priest during reign of Joash, 2 Kin 11:4—12:16
Instructs Joash, 2 Kin 12:2

JEHOIAKIM
Wicked king of Judah; son of Josiah; serves Pharaoh and Nebuchadnezzar, 2 Kin 23:34—24:7
Taken captive to Babylon, 2 Chr 36:6–8
Kills prophet Urijah, Jer 26:20–23
Destroys Jeremiah's scroll; cursed by God, Jer 36

JEHORAM (or Joram)
Wicked king of Judah; son of Jehoshaphat, 2 Kin 8:16–24
Marries Athaliah, 2 Kin 8:18, 19
Kills his brothers, 2 Chr 21:2, 4
Elijah prophesies against him; prophecy fulfilled, 2 Chr 21:12–20
——— Wicked king of Israel; son of Ahab, 2 Kin 3:1–3
Counseled by Elisha, 2 Kin 3; 5:8; 6:8–12
Wounded in battle, 2 Kin 8:28, 29
Killed by Jehu, 2 Kin 9:14–26

JEHOSHAPHAT
Righteous king of Judah; son of Asa, 1 Kin 22:41–50
Goes to war with Ahab against Syria, 1 Kin 22:1–36
Institutes reforms; sends out teachers of the Law, 2 Chr 17:6–9; 19
His enemies defeated through his faith, 2 Chr 20:1–30

JEHOZABAD
Son of a Moabitess; assassinates Joash, 2 Kin 12:20, 21
Put to death, 2 Chr 25:3

JEHU
Prophet; denounces Baasha, 1 Kin 16:1–7
Rebukes Jehoshaphat, 2 Chr 19:2, 3
——— Commander under Ahab; anointed king, 1 Kin 19:16; 2 Kin 9:1–13
Destroys the house of Ahab, 2 Kin 9:14—10:30
Turns away from the Lord; dies, 2 Kin 10:31–36

JEHUDI
Reads Jeremiah's scroll, Jer 36:14, 21, 23

JEOPARDY
stand in *j* every hour . . . . . 1 Cor 15:30

JEPHTHAH
Gilead's son by a harlot, Judg 11:1
Driven out, then brought back to command army against Ammonites, Judg 11:2–28
Sacrifices his daughter to fulfill a vow, Judg 11:29–40
Chastises Ephraim, Judg 12:1–7

JEREMIAH
Prophet under Josiah, Jehoiakim, and Zedekiah, Jer 1:1–3
Called by God, Jer 1:4–9
Forbidden to marry, Jer 16:2
Imprisoned by Pashhur, Jer 20:1–6
Prophecy written, destroyed, rewritten, Jer 36
Accused of defection and imprisoned; released by Zedekiah, Jer 37
Cast into dungeon; rescued; prophesies to Zedekiah, Jer 38
Set free by Nebuchadnezzar, Jer 39:11—40:6
Forcibly taken to Egypt, Jer 43:5–7

JERICHO
City near the Jordan, Num 22:1
Called the city of palm trees, Deut 34:3; 2 Chr 28:15
Miraculously defeated by Joshua, Josh 6
Rebuilt by Hiel, 1 Kin 16:34
Visited by Jesus, Matt 20:29–34; Luke 19:1–10

JEROBOAM
Son of Nebat; receives prophecy that he will be king, 1 Kin 11:26–40
Made king; leads revolt against Rehoboam, 1 Kin 12:1–24
Sets up idols, 1 Kin 12:25–33
Rebuked by a man of God, 1 Kin 13:1–10
Judgment on house of, 1 Kin 13:33—14:20
——— Wicked king of Israel; son of Joash; successful in war, 2 Kin 14:23–29
Prophecy concerning, Amos 7:7–13

JERUBBAAL
Name given to Gideon for destroying Baal's altar, Judg 6:32

JERUSALEM
Originally called Salem, Gen 14:18
Jebusite city, Josh 15:8; Judg 1:8, 21
King of, defeated by Joshua, Josh 10:5–23
Conquered by David; made capital, 2 Sam 5:6–9
Ark brought to, 2 Sam 6:12–17; 1 Kin 8:1–13
Saved from plague, 2 Sam 24:16
Temple built and dedicated here, 1 Kin 6; 8:14–66
Suffers in war, 1 Kin 14:25–27; 2 Kin 14:13, 14; Is 7:1
Miraculously saved, 2 Kin 19:31–36
Captured by Babylon, 2 Kin 24:10—25:21; Jer 39:1–8
Exiles return and rebuild temple, Ezra 1:1–4; 2:1
Walls of, dedicated, Neh 12:27–47
Christ enters as King, Matt 21:4–11
Christ laments for, Matt 23:37; Luke 19:41–44
Church born in, Acts 2
Christians of, persecuted, Acts 4

Jebusite city (which is *J*) . . . Josh 15:8
in *J* he reigned . . . . 2 Sam 5:5
were born to him in *J* . . . . . 2 Sam 5:14
ark of God back to *J* . . . . 2 Sam 15:29
yourself a house in *J* . . . . . . 1 Kin 2:36
a lamp before Me in *J* . . . . 1 Kin 11:36
Solomon reigned in *J* . . . . 1 Kin 11:42
Rehoboam came to *J* . . . . . 1 Kin 12:21
gave him a lamp in *J* . . . . . . 1 Kin 15:4
down the wall of *J* from . . . . 2 Kin 14:13
up to *J* to make war . . . . 2 Kin 16:5
before this altar in *J*' . . . . . 2 Kin 18:22
should deliver *J* from . . . . . 2 Kin 18:35
J shall not be given into . . 2 Kin 19:10
daughter of *J* has . . . . 2 Kin 19:21
I will stretch over *J* the . . . 2 Kin 21:13
(She dwelt in *J* in the . . . . 2 Kin 22:14
elders of Judah and *J* to . . . . 2 Kin 23:1
burned them outside *J* . . . . . 2 Kin 23:4
from *J* to Babylon . . . . 2 Kin 24:15
his army came against *J* . . . . 2 Kin 25:1
the walls of *J* all around . . 2 Kin 25:10
J into captivity by the . . . . . 1 Chr 6:15
house of the LORD in *J* . . . . 1 Chr 6:32
Now in *J* the children of . . . . 1 Chr 9:3
and all Israel went to *J* . . . . 1 Chr 11:4
took more wives in *J* . . . . . . 1 Chr 14:3

all Israel together at *J*, to . . 1 Chr 15:3
angel to *J* to destroy it . . . 1 Chr 21:15
they may dwell in *J* . . . . . . 1 Chr 23:25
David assembled at *J* all . . 1 Chr 28:1
gold as common in *J* as . . . 2 Chr 1:15
the LORD at *J* on Mount . . . . . 2 Chr 3:1
Solomon reigned in *J* . . . . . 2 Chr 9:30
So Rehoboam dwelt in *J*, . . 2 Chr 11:5
of Judah and came to *J* . . . . 2 Chr 12:4
him in the city, in *J* . . . . . . 2 Chr 28:27
the altars that were in *J* . . 2 Chr 30:14
against the God of *J* . . . . . 2 Chr 32:19
the inhabitants of *J* . . . . . . 2 Chr 32:26
to *J* into his kingdom . . . . 2 Chr 33:13
and the inhabitants of *J* . . 2 Chr 35:18
of the LORD which is in *J* . . . Ezra 2:68
together as one man to *J* . . . . Ezra 3:1
out of the captivity to *J* . . . . . . Ezra 3:8
the temple which is in *J* . . . . . Ezra 6:5
to bring them to *J* to the . . . . Ezra 8:30
a wall in Judah and *J* . . . . Ezra 9:9
that they must gather at *J* . . Ezra 10:7
I came to *J* and was there . . Neh 2:11
let us build the wall of *J* . . . . Neh 2:17
to come and attack *J* . . . . Neh 4:8
it was, at the gates of *J* . . . . Neh 13:19
build the walls of *J* . . . . Ps 51:18
In the midst of you, O *J* . . . . Ps 116:19
J is built as a city that is . . . . Ps 122:3
If I forget you, O *J*, let my . . . Ps 137:5
The LORD builds up *J* . . . . Ps 147:2
was king over Israel in *J* . . . . Eccl 1:12
you, O daughters of *J* . . . . Song 5:8
as Tirzah, lovely as *J*, ... Song 6:4
snare to the inhabitants of *J* . . . Is 8:14
of Zion, the hill of *J* . . . . Is 10:32
numbered the houses of *J* . . . . Is 22:10
watchmen on your walls, O *J* . . Is 62:6
a wilderness, *J* a desolation . . Is 64:10
yes, proclaim against *J*, ... Jer 4:16
Be instructed, O *J*, lest My . . . . Jer 6:8
will make *J* a heap of ruins . . Jer 9:11
the cry of *J* has gone up . . . . . Jer 14:2
reigned eleven years in *J* . . . . Jer 52:1
J has become an unclean . . . Lam 1:17
and portray on it a city, *J* . . . Ezek 4:1
me in visions of God to *J* . . . . Ezek 8:3
Oholah, and *J* is Oholibah . . Ezek 23:4
build *J* until Messiah the . . . . Dan 9:25
then *J* shall be holy, and . . . . Joel 3:17
utters His voice from *J* . . . . . Amos 1:2
The captives of *J* who are . . . Obad 20
You not have mercy on *J* . . Zech 1:12
To measure *J*, to see what . . . Zech 2:2
again in her own place—*J*. . Zech 12:6
to *J* to worship the King . . Zech 14:17
from the East came to *J* . . . . Matt 2:1
that He must go to *J* . . . . . . Matt 16:21
O *J*, *J*, the one who . . . . Matt 23:37
we are going up to *J* . . . . . Mark 10:33
Jesus lingered behind in *J* . Luke 2:43
you see *J* surrounded . . . . . Luke 21:20
Daughters of *J*, do not . . . . Luke 23:28
but tarry in the city of *J* . . Luke 24:49
J before the Passover . . . . . John 11:55
be witnesses to Me in *J* . . . . . . Acts 1:8
were gathered together at *J* . . Acts 4:6
you have filled *J* with . . . . . . Acts 5:28
Lord, they returned to *J* . . . . Acts 8:25
bring them bound to *J* . . . . Acts 9:2
when Saul had come to *J* . . . Acts 9:26
when Peter came up to *J* . . . Acts 11:2
came from *J* to Antioch . . . Acts 11:27
bound in the spirit to *J* . . . . Acts 20:22
shall the Jews at *J* bind . . . Acts 21:11
I went up to *J* to worship . . Acts 24:11
he was willing to go to *J* . . Acts 25:20
the saints who are in *J* . . . . Rom 15:26
to bear your gift to *J* . . . . . . 1 Cor 16:3
corresponds to *J* which . . . . . . Gal 4:25
city of My God, the New *J* . . Rev 3:12
saw the holy city, New *J* . . . . Rev 21:2

JESHIMON
Wilderness west of the Dead Sea, 1 Sam 23:19, 24

JESHUA (or Joshua)
Postexilic high priest; returns with Zerubbabel, Ezra 2:2
Aids in rebuilding temple, Ezra 3:2–8
Also called Joshua; seen in vision, Zech 3:1–10

JESHURUN
Poetic name of endearment for Israel, Deut 32:15

JESSE
Grandson of Ruth and Boaz, Ruth 4:17–22
Father of David, 1 Sam 16:1–13
Mentioned in prophecy, Is 11:1, 10

JESTING
talking, nor coarse *j* . . . . Eph 5:4

JESUS
See CHRIST; LORD JESUS CHRIST
birth of *J* Christ was as . . . . Matt 1:18
shall call His name *J* . . . . Matt 1:21
J was led up by the . . . . Matt 4:1
These twelve *J* sent . . . . Matt 10:5
and laid hands on *J* . . . . Matt 26:50
Barabbas and destroy *J* . . . Matt 27:20
we to do with You, *J* . . . . . . Mark 1:24
J withdrew with His . . . . Mark 3:7
J said, "Do not forbid . . . . . Mark 9:39
J went into Jerusalem . . . . Mark 11:11
as they were eating, *J* . . . . Mark 14:22
and he delivered *J* . . . . Mark 15:15
J increased in wisdom . . . . . Luke 2:52
J said, "Who touched . . . . . . Luke 8:45
J rebuked the unclean . . . . . Luke 9:42
J said to him, "Foxes . . . . . . Luke 9:58
sought to see who *J* was . . . Luke 19:3
near to *J* to kiss Him . . . . . Luke 22:47
J Himself stood in the . . . . Luke 24:36
truth came through *J* . . . . . . John 1:17
J said to him, "Rise, take . . . . John 5:8
J lifted up His eyes . . . . John 6:5
they saw *J* walking on . . . . . John 6:19
But *J* stooped down and . . . . John 8:6
J wept . . . . John 11:35
anointed the feet of *J* . . . . . . John 12:3
J was crucified . . . . John 19:20
other things that *J* did . . . . John 21:25
This *J* God has raised . . . . Acts 2:32
of Your holy Servant *J* . . . . . Acts 4:30
believed on the Lord *J* . . . . Acts 11:17
baptized into Christ *J* . . . . Rom 6:3
Spirit of life in Christ *J* . . . . . . Rom 8:2
your mouth the Lord *J* . . . . . Rom 10:9
among you except *J* . . . . 1 Cor 2:2
the day of the Lord *J* . . . . 1 Cor 5:5
heavenly places in Christ *J* . . . Eph 2:6
that at the name of *J* every . . Phil 2:10
perfect in Christ *J* . . . . Col 1:28
exhort in the Lord *J* . . . . 1 Thess 4:1
But we see *J*, who was . . . . Heb 2:9
J the Son of God, let us . . . . . Heb 4:14
looking unto *J*, the author . . Heb 12:2
J Christ the righteous . . . . . 1 John 2:1
that *J* is the Son of God . . . 1 John 5:5
Revelation of *J* Christ . . . . Rev 1:1
Even so, come, Lord *J* . . . . . Rev 22:20

JETHER
Gideon's oldest son, Judg 8:20, 21

JETHRO
Priest of Midian; becomes Moses' father-in-law, Ex 2:16–22
Blesses Moses' departure, Ex 4:18
Visits and counsels Moses, Ex 18
Also called Reuel, Num 10:29

JEW
J whose name was . . . . Esth 2:5
is it that You, being a *J* . . . . . John 4:9
Am I a *J*? . . . . John 18:35
found out that he was a *J* . Acts 19:34
I am indeed a *J*, born in . . . . Acts 22:3
believes, for the *J* first . . . . . Rom 1:16
who does evil, of the *J* first . . Rom 2:9
he is not a *J* who is one . . . . Rom 2:28
advantage then has the *J* . . . . Rom 3:1
no distinction between *J* . . Rom 10:12
Jews I became as a *J* . . . . . . 1 Cor 9:20
If you, being a *J*, live in . . . . . Gal 2:14
is neither *J* nor Greek . . . . Gal 3:28
is neither Greek nor *J* . . . . Col 3:11

JEWELS
your thighs are like *j* . . . . . . Songs 7:1
that I make them My *j* . . . . . . Mal 3:17

JEWISH
against their *J* brethren . . . . . . Neh 5:1
J descent, you will not . . . . . Esth 6:13
a *J* brother in bondage . . . . Jer 34:9
expectation of the *J* . . . . Acts 12:11
J exorcists took it upon . . . Acts 19:13
light to the *J* people and . . Acts 26:23
giving heed to *J* fables . . . . . Titus 1:14

JEWS
See KING OF THE JEWS
Jesus born King of the, Matt 2:2
Salvation comes through the, John 4:22; Acts 11:19; Rom 1:16; 2:9, 10
Reject Christ, Matt 27:21–25
Reject the gospel, Acts 13:42–46

the elders of the *J* build . . . . . Ezra 6:7
are these feeble *J* doing . . . . . . Neh 4:2
J who were at Shushan . . . . . Esth 9:18
sent letters to all the *J* . . . . . . Esth 9:30
I am afraid of the *J* who . . . . Jer 38:19
of the *J* seven hundred . . . . . Jer 52:30
There are certain *J* whom . . Dan 3:12
You the King of the *J* . . . . . Matt 27:11
of purification of the *J*, ... John 2:6
for salvation is of the *J* . . . . John 4:22
those *J* who believed Him . . John 8:31
the *J* took up stones . . . . . . John 10:31
The King of the *J* . . . . John 19:19
dwelling in Jerusalem *J* . . . . . Acts 2:5
confounded the *J* who . . . . . . Acts 9:22
in the land of the *J* . . . . Acts 10:39
in the synagogues of the *J* . . Acts 13:5
But the *J* stirred up the . . . . Acts 13:50
refuted the *J* publicly, ... Acts 18:28
the God of the *J* only . . . . . . Rom 3:29
J a stumbling block . . . . 1 Cor 1:23
whether *J* or Greeks, ... 1 Cor 12:13
From the *J* five times I . . . . 2 Cor 11:24
compel Gentiles to live as *J* . . Gal 2:14
of those who say they are *J* . . Rev 2:9
Satan, who say they are *J* . . . . Rev 3:9

JEZEBEL
Ahab's idolatrous wife, 1 Kin 16:31
Her abominable acts, 1 Kin 18:4, 13; 19:1, 2; 21:1–16
Death prophesied; prophecy fulfilled, 1 Kin 21:23; 2 Kin 9:7, 30–37
—— Type of paganism in the church, Rev 2:20

JEZREEL
Ahab's capital, 1 Kin 18:45; 21:1
Ahab's family destroyed at, 1 Kin 21:23; 2 Kin 9:30–37; 10:1–11

JOAB
David's nephew; commands his army, 2 Sam 2:10–32; 8:16; 10:1–14; 11:1, 14–25; 20:1–23
Kills Abner, 2 Sam 3:26, 27
Intercedes for Absalom, 2 Sam 14:1–33
Remains loyal to David; kills Absalom, 2 Sam 18:1–5, 9–17
Demoted; kills Amasa, 2 Sam 19:13; 20:8–10

Opposes census, 2 Sam 24:1–9; 1 Chr 21:1–6
Supports Adonijah, 1 Kin 1:7
Solomon orders his death in obedience to David's command, 1 Kin 2:1–6, 28–34

JOANNA
Wife of Chuza, Herod's steward, Luke 8:1–3
With others, heralds Christ's resurrection, Luke 23:55, 56

JOASH (or Jehoash)
Son of Ahaziah; saved from Athaliah's massacre and crowned by Jehoiada, 2 Kin 11:1–12
Repairs the temple, 2 Kin 12:1–16
Turns away from the Lord and is killed, 2 Chr 24:17–25
—— Wicked king of Israel; son of Jehoahaz, 2 Kin 13:10–25
Defeats Amaziah in battle, 2 Kin 14:8–15; 2 Chr 25:17–24

JOB
Model of righteousness, Job 1:1–5
His faith tested, Job 1:6—2:10
Debates with his three friends; complains to God, Job 3—33
Elihu intervenes, Job 34—37
God's answer, Job 38—41
Humbles himself and repents, Job 42:1–6
Restored to prosperity, Job 42:10–17

JOCHEBED
Daughter of Levi; mother of Miriam, Aaron, and Moses, Ex 6:20

JOEL
Preexilic prophet, Joel 1:1
Quoted in N.T., Acts 2:16

JOGBEHAH
Town in Gilead, Judg 8:11

JOHANAN
Military leader of Judah; warns Gedaliah of Ishmael's plot, Jer 40:13–16
Avenges Gedaliah; takes the people to Egypt, Jer 41:11–18

JOHN
The apostle, son of Zebedee; called as disciple, Matt 4:21, 22; Luke 5:1–11
Chosen as one of the Twelve, Matt 10:2
Especially close to Christ, Matt 17:1–9; Mark 13:3; John 13:23–25; 19:26, 27; 20:2–8; 21:7, 20
Ambitious and overzealous, Mark 10:35–41; Luke 9:54–56
Sent to prepare the Passover, Luke 22:8–13
With Peter, heals a man and is arrested, Acts 3:1—4:22
Goes on missionary trip with Peter, Acts 8:14–25
Exiled on Patmos, Rev 1:9
Author of Gospel, three epistles, and the Revelation, John 21:23–25; 1 John; 2 John; 3 John; Rev 1:1
—— The Baptist; O.T. prophecy concerning, Is 40:3–5; Mal 4:5
His birth announced and accomplished, Luke 1:11–20, 57–80
Preaches repentance, Luke 3:1–20
Bears witness to Christ, John 1:19–36; 3:25–36
Baptizes Jesus, Matt 3:13–17
Jesus speaks about, Matt 11:7–19
Identified with Elijah, Matt 11:13, 14
Herod imprisons and kills, Matt 14:3–12
—— Surnamed Mark: *see* MARK

JOIN
Woe to those who *j* . . . . Is 5:8
'Come and let us *j* . . . . Jer 50:5
of the rest dared *j* . . . . Acts 5:13

JOINED
and mother and be *j* . . . . Gen 2:24
for him who is *j* . . . . Eccl 9:4
"Ephraim is *j* . . . . Hos 4:17
what God has *j* . . . . Matt 19:6
you be perfectly *j* . . . . 1 Cor 1:10
But he who is *j* . . . . 1 Cor 6:17
the whole body, *j* . . . . Eph 4:16

JOINT
j as He wrestled . . . . Gen 32:25
My bones are out of *j* . . . . Ps 22:14
j heirs with Christ . . . . Rom 8:17
by what every *j* . . . . Eph 4:16

JOINTS
and knit together by *j* . . . . Col 2:19
and spirit, and of *j* . . . . Heb 4:12

JOKTAN
See ARABIA
Descendants of Shem, Gen. 10:21, 25

JONADAB (or Jehonadab)
David's nephew; encourages Amnon in sin, 2 Sam 13:3–5, 32–36
—— Son of Rechab; father of the Rechabites, Jer 35:5–19
Helps Jehu overthrow Baal, 2 Kin 10:15–28

JONAH
Prophet sent to Nineveh; rebels and is punished, Jon 1
Repents and is saved, Jon 2
Preaches in Nineveh, Jon 3
Becomes angry at God's mercy, Jon 4
Type of Christ's resurrection, Matt 12:39, 40

JONATHAN
King Saul's eldest son; his exploits in battle, 1 Sam 13:2, 3; 14:1–14, 49
Saved from his father's wrath, 1 Sam 14:24–45
Makes covenant with David; protects him from Saul, 1 Sam 18:1–4; 19:1–7; 20:1–42; 23:15–18
Killed by Philistines, 1 Sam 31:2, 8
Mourned by David; his son provided for, 2 Sam 1:17–27; 9:1–8
—— Son of high priest Abiathar; faithful to David, 2 Sam 15:26–36; 17:15–22
Informs Adonijah of Solomon's coronation, 1 Kin 1:41–49

JOPPA
Scene of Peter's vision, Acts 10:5–23, 32

JORAM
See JEHORAM

JORDAN RIVER
Lot dwells near, Gen 13:8–13
Canaan's eastern boundary, Num 34:12
Moses forbidden to cross, Deut 3:27
Miraculous dividing of, for Israel, Josh 3:1–17
by Elijah, 2 Kin 2:5–8
by Elisha, 2 Kin 2:13,14
Naaman healed in, 2 Kin 5:10–14
John baptizes in, Matt 3:6, 13–17

JOSEPH
Son of Jacob by Rachel, Gen 30:22–24
Loved by Jacob; hated by his brothers, Gen 37:3–11
Sold into slavery, Gen 37:12–36
Unjustly imprisoned in Egypt, Gen 39:1–23
Interprets dreams in prison, Gen 40:1–23
Wins Pharaoh's favor, Gen 41:1–44
Prepares Egypt for famine, Gen 41:45–57
Sells grain to his brothers, Gen 42—44
Reveals identity and reconciles with brothers; sends for Jacob, Gen 45:1–28
Settles family in Egypt, Gen 47:1–12
His sons blessed by Jacob, Gen 48:1–22
Blessed by Jacob, Gen 49:22–26
Buries his father; reassures his brothers, Gen 50:1–21
His death, Gen 50:22–26
—— Husband of Mary, Jesus' mother, Matt 1:16
Visited by angel, Matt 1:19–25
Takes Mary to Bethlehem, Luke 2:3–7
Protects Jesus from Herod, Matt 2:13–23
Jesus subject to, Luke 2:51
—— Secret disciple from Arimathea; donates tomb and assists in Christ's burial, Mark 15:42–46; Luke 23:50–53; John 19:38–42

JOSES
One of Jesus' half brothers, Matt 13:55
—— The name of Barnabas, Acts 4:36

JOSHUA
See JESHUA
—— Leader of Israel succeeding Moses, Num 27:18–23
Leads battle against Amalek, Ex 17:8–16
Sent as spy into Canaan; reports favorably, Num 13:16–25; 14:6–9
Assumes command, Josh 1:1–18
Sends spies to Jericho, Josh 2:1
Leads Israel across Jordan, Josh 3:1–17
Sets up commemorative stones, Josh 4:1–24
Circumcises the people, Josh 5:2–9
Conquers Jericho, Josh 5:13—6:27
Punishes Achan, Josh 7:10–26
Conquers Canaan, Josh 8—12
Divides the land, Josh 13—19
Addresses rulers, Josh 23:1–16
Addresses the people, Josh 24:1–28
His death, Josh 24:29, 30

JOSIAH
Righteous king of Judah; son of Amon, 2 Kin 22:1, 2
Repairs the temple, 2 Kin 22:3–9
Hears the Law; spared for his humility, 2 Kin 22:10–20
Institutes reforms, 2 Kin 23:1–25
Killed in battle, 2 Chr 35:20–25

JOT
one *j* or one tittle . . . . Matt 5:18

JOTHAM
Gideon's youngest son; escapes Abimelech's massacre, Judg 9:5
Utters prophetic parable, Judg 9:7–21
—— Righteous king of Judah; son of Azariah, 2 Kin 15:32–38; 2 Chr 27:1–9

JOURNEY
us go three days' *j* . . . . Ex 3:18
busy, or he is on a *j* . . . . . . 1 Kin 18:27
he has gone on a long *j* . . . . Prov 7:19
city, a three-day *j* in extent . . . Jon 3:3
nor bag for your *j*, nor . . . . Matt 10:10
he went on a *j* . . . . Matt 25:15
Nevertheless I must *j* . . . . . Luke 13:33
wearied from His *j* . . . . John 4:6
may send me on my *j* . . . . . 1 Cor 16:6
j in a manner worthy of . . . . . 3 John 6

j as my strength was . . . . . Josh 14:11
Hear a *j* cause . . . . . Ps 17:1
the path of the *j* is like . . . . . Prov 4:18
j weight is His delight . . . . . Prov 11:1
It is a joy for the *j* . . . . . Prov 21:15
j man who perishes . . . . . Eccl 7:15
For there is not a *j* . . . . . Eccl 7:20
way of the *j* is uprightness . . . . . Is 26:7
the blood of the *j* . . . . . Lam 4:13
j shall live by his . . . . . Hab 2:4
He is *j* and having . . . . . Zech 9:9
her husband, being a *j* . . . . . Matt 1:19
resurrection of the *j* . . . . . Luke 14:14
j persons who need no . . . . . Luke 15:7
the Holy One and the *J* . . . . . Acts 3:14
dead, both of the *j* . . . . . Acts 24:15
j shall live by faith . . . . . Rom 1:17
that He might be *j* . . . . . Rom 3:26
the *j* shall live by faith . . . . . Gal 3:11
j as you were called in one . . . Eph 4:4
j as Christ also loved the . . . . . Eph 5:25
whatever things are *j* . . . . . Phil 4:8
received a *j* reward . . . . . Heb 2:2
j men made perfect . . . . . Heb 12:23
have murdered the *j* . . . . . James 5:6
He is faithful and *j* . . . . . 1 John 1:9
J and true are Your . . . . . Rev 15:3

JUSTICE
to do righteousness and *j* . . Gen 18:19
after many to pervert *j* . . . . . Ex 23:2
for all His ways are *j* . . . . . Deut 32:4
bribes, and perverted *j* . . . . . 1 Sam 8:3
to discern *j* . . . . . 1 Kin 3:11
the Almighty pervert *j* . . . . . Job 8:3
gives *j* to the oppressed . . . . . Job 36:6
j as the noonday . . . . . Ps 37:6
and Your poor with *j* . . . . . Ps 72:2
Do *j* to the afflicted . . . . . Ps 82:3
and *j* are the . . . . . Ps 89:14
j for all who are oppressed . . Ps 103:6
He guards the paths of *j* . . . . . Prov 2:8
revenues without *j* . . . . . Prov 16:8
do not understand *j* . . . . . Prov 28:5
j the measuring line . . . . . Is 28:17
the LORD is a God of *j* . . . . . Is 30:18
He will bring forth *j* . . . . . Is 42:1
No one calls for *j* . . . . . Is 59:4
J is turned back . . . . . Is 59:14
I, the LORD, love *j* . . . . . Is 61:8
you, O home of *j* . . . . . Jer 31:23
plundering, execute *j* . . . . . Ezek 45:9
truth, and His ways *j* . . . . . Dan 4:37
observe mercy and *j* . . . . . Hos 12:6
who turn *j* to wormwood . . . Amos 5:7
'Execute true *j* . . . . . Zech 7:9
"Where is the God of *j* . . . . . Mal 2:17
And He will declare *j* . . . . . Matt 12:18
of herbs, and pass by *j* . . . . . Luke 11:42
His humiliation His *j* . . . . . Acts 8:33

JUSTIFICATION
because of our *j* . . . . . Rom 4:25
offenses resulted in *j* . . . . . Rom 5:16
men, resulting in *j* . . . . . Rom 5:18

JUSTIFIED
Me that you may be *j* . . . . . Job 40:8
of Israel shall be *j* . . . . . Is 45:25
words you will be *j* . . . . . Matt 12:37
But wisdom is *j* . . . . . Luke 7:35
j rather than the . . . . . Luke 18:14
who believes is *j* . . . . . Acts 13:39
"That You may be *j* . . . . . Rom 3:4
law no flesh will be *j* . . . . . Rom 3:20
j freely by His grace . . . . . Rom 3:24
having been *j* by . . . . . Rom 5:1
these He also *j* . . . . . Rom 8:30
but you were *j* . . . . . 1 Cor 6:11
that we might be *j* . . . . . Gal 2:16
who attempt to be *j* . . . . . Gal 5:4
j in the Spirit . . . . . 1 Tim 3:16
then that a man is *j* . . . . . James 2:24
the harlot also *j* . . . . . James 2:25

JUSTIFIER
be just and the *j* . . . . . Rom 3:26

JUSTIFIES
He who *j* the wicked . . . . . Prov 17:15
It is God who *j* . . . . . Rom 8:33

JUSTIFY
j the wicked for a . . . . . Is 5:23
wanting to *j* himself . . . . . Luke 10:29
"You are those who *j* . . . . . Luke 16:15
is one God who will *j* . . . . . Rom 3:30
that God would *j* . . . . . Gal 3:8

JUSTLY
of you but to do *j* . . . . . Mic 6:8
And we indeed *j* . . . . . Luke 23:41
how devoutly and *j* . . . . . 1 Thess 2:10

JUSTUS
Surname of Joseph, a disciple, Acts 1:23
——— Man of Corinth; befriends Paul, Acts 18:7
——— Fellow worker of Paul, also called Jesus, Col 4:11

KADESH
Spies sent from, Num 13:3, 26
Moses strikes rock at, Num 20:1–13
Boundary in the new Israel, Ezek 47:19

KADESH BARNEA
Boundary of Promised Land, Num 34:1–4
Limit of Joshua's military campaign, Josh 10:41

KARNAIM
Conquered region, Amos 6:13

KEDESH
Town in south Judah, Josh 15:23
——— Levite city in Issachar, 1 Chr 6:72

KEDESH NAPHTALI
City of refuge, Josh 21:27, 32
Home of Barak, Judg 4:6

KEEP
k you wherever you . . . . . Gen 28:15
day, to *k* it holy . . . . . Ex 20:8
and *k* My judgments . . . . . Lev 25:18
k all My commandments . . . 1 Kin 6:12
and that You would *k* . . . . . 1 Chr 4:10
Even he who cannot *k* . . . . . Ps 22:29
K my soul, and deliver me . . . Ps 25:20
do not *k* silence . . . . . Ps 35:22
k Your righteous . . . . . Ps 119:106
k them in the midst of . . . . . Prov 4:21
K your heart with all . . . . . Prov 4:23
a time to *k* silence . . . . . Eccl 3:7
k your appointed feasts . . . . . Nah 1:15
Let all the earth *k* . . . . . Hab 2:20
k the commandments . . . . . Matt 19:17
charge over you, to *k* . . . . . Luke 4:10
If you love Me, *k* . . . . . John 14:15
k through Your name . . . . . John 17:11
orderly and *k* the law . . . . . Acts 21:24
and *k* the traditions . . . . . 1 Cor 11:2
Let your women *k* . . . . . 1 Cor 14:34
a debtor to *k* the whole law . . . Gal 5:3
k the unity of the . . . . . Eph 4:3
k yourself pure . . . . . 1 Tim 5:22
He is able to *k* what I . . . . . 2 Tim 1:12
to *k* oneself unspotted . . . . . James 1:27
k His commandments . . . . . 1 John 2:3
k His commandments . . . . . 1 John 3:22
k yourselves from idols . . . 1 John 5:21
k yourselves in the . . . . . Jude 21
k you from stumbling . . . . . Jude 24
k those things . . . . . Rev 1:3
I also will *k* you from the . . . Rev 3:10
of those who *k* the words . . . Rev 22:9

KEEPER
Am I my brother's *k* . . . . . Gen 4:9
of the *k* of the prison . . . . . Gen 39:21
The LORD is your *k* . . . . . Ps 121:5
me the *k* of the vineyards . . . Song 1:6
to the *k* of his vineyard . . . . . Luke 13:7
of the prison, awaking . . . . . Acts 16:27

KEEPERS
in the day when the *k* . . . . . Eccl 12:3

KEEPS
the faithful God who *k* . . . . . Deut 7:9
God, Who *k* covenant and . . Neh 9:32
who *k* you will not slumber . . Ps 121:3
k truth forever . . . . . Ps 146:6
k his way preserves . . . . . Prov 16:17
k the commandment . . . . . Prov 19:16
Whoever *k* the law is a . . . Prov 28:7
none of you *k* the law . . . . . John 7:19
born of God *k* himself . . . 1 John 5:18
and *k* his garments . . . . . Rev 16:15

KEILAH
Town of Judah; rescued from Philistines by David, 1 Sam 23:1–5
Prepares to betray David; he escapes, 1 Sam 23:6–13

KENITES
Canaanite tribe whose land is promised to Abraham's seed, Gen 15:19
Subjects of Balaam's prophecy, Num 24:20–22
Settle with Judahites, Judg 1:16
Spared by Saul in war with Amalekites, 1 Sam 15:6

KEPT
shall be *k* burning on it . . . . . Lev 6:9
be *k* as a sign against . . . . . Num 17:10
He *k* him as the apple of . . Deut 32:10
For I have *k* the ways . . . . 2 Sam 22:22
k what You promised . . . . . 2 Chr 6:15
Now Josiah *k* a Passover . . 2 Chr 35:1
desolate she *k* Sabbath . . 2 Chr 36:21
brethren who *k* the gates . . . Neh 11:19
gatekeepers *k* the charge . . Neh 12:45
that *k* a pilgrim feast . . . . . Ps 42:4
vineyard I have not *k* . . . . . Song 1:6
when a holy festival is *k* . . . . . Is 30:29
k charge of My . . . . . Ezek 44:15
we have *k* His ordinance . . . . Mal 3:14
these things I have *k* . . . . . Matt 19:20
But Jesus *k* silent . . . . . Matt 26:63
she *k* asking Him to cast . . . . . Mark 7:26
all these things I have *k* . . Mark 10:20
k all these things . . . . . Luke 2:19
love, just as I have *k* . . . . . John 15:10
If they *k* My word, they . . . . John 15:20
You gave Me I have *k* . . . John 17:12
k back part of the . . . . . Acts 5:2
k secret since the world . . . Rom 16:25
I have *k* the faith . . . . . 2 Tim 4:7
who are *k* by the power . . . . . 1 Pet 1:5
Because you have *k* My . . . . Rev 3:10

KETURAH
Abraham's second wife, Gen 25:1
Sons of:
listed, Gen 25:1, 2
given gifts and sent away, Gen 25:6

KEY
The *k* of the house of . . . . . Is 22:22
have taken away the *k* . . . Luke 11:52
"He who has the *k* . . . . . Rev 3:7
heaven, having the *k* . . . . . Rev 20:1

KEYS
I will give you the *k* . . . . . Matt 16:19
And I have the *k* . . . . . Rev 1:18

KIBROTH HATTAAVAH
Burial site of Israelites slain by God, Num 11:33–35

KICK
is hard for you to *k* . . . . . Acts 9:5

KIDNAPPERS
for sodomites, for *k* . . . . . 1 Tim 1:10

KIRJATH ARBA
- Ancient name of Hebron, Gen 23:2
- Possessed by Judah, Judg 1:10

KIRJATH JEARIM
- Gibeonite town, Josh 9:17
- Ark taken from, 1 Chr 13:5

KISH
- Benjamite of Gibeah; father of King Saul, 1 Sam 9:1–3

KISHON
- River of north Palestine; Sisera's army swept away by, Judg 4:7, 13
- Elijah executes prophets of Baal at, 1 Kin 18:40

KISS
- *K* the Son, lest He be . . . Ps 2:12
- Let him *k* me with the . . . Song 1:2
- who sacrifice *k* the calves . . . Hos 13:2
- Whomever I *k*, He is . . . Mark 14:44
- You gave Me no *k* . . . Luke 7:45
- drew near to Jesus to *k* . . . Luke 22:47
- another with a holy *k* . . . Rom 16:16
- another with a holy *k* . . . 2 Cor 13:12
- with a holy *k* . . . 1 Thess 5:26
- one another with a *k* . . . 1 Pet 5:14

KISSED
- they *k* one another . . . 1 Sam 20:41
- and peace have *k* each. . . . Ps 85:10
- Rabbi!" and *k* Him . . . Matt 26:49
- and she *k* His feet and . . . Luke 7:38

KITTIM
- *See* CYPRUS
- Descendants of Javan, Gen 10:4

KNEE
- that to Me every *k* . . . Is 45:23
- And they bowed the *k* . . . Matt 27:29
- have not bowed the *k* . . . Rom 11:4
- every *k* shall bow to . . . Rom 14:11
- of Jesus every *k* . . . Phil 2:10

KNEES
- make firm the feeble *k* . . . Is 35:3
- be dandled on her *k* . . . Is 66:12
- this reason I bow my *k* . . . Eph 3:14
- and the feeble *k* . . . Heb 12:12

KNEW
- *k* that they were naked . . . Gen 3:7
- Adam *k* Eve his wife . . . Gen 4:1
- in the womb I *k* . . . Jer 1:5
- to them, 'I never *k* . . . Matt 7:23
- *k* what was in man . . . John 2:25
- For He made Him who *k* . . . 2 Cor 5:21

KNIFE
- fire in his hand, and a *k* . . . Gen 22:6
- his house he took a *k* . . . Judg 19:29
- put a *k* to your throat if . . . Prov 23:2
- cut it with the scribe's *k* . . . Jer 36:23

KNIT
- of Jonathan was *k* . . . 1 Sam 18:1
- *k* me together with . . . Job 10:11
- be encouraged, being *k* . . . Col 2:2

KNOCK
- *k*, and it will be . . . Matt 7:7
- at the door and *k* . . . Rev 3:20

KNOW
- *k* good and evil . . . Gen 3:22
- and I did not *k* . . . Gen 28:16
- Egypt, who did not *k* Joseph . . . Ex 1:8
- *k* that I am the LORD . . . Ex 6:7
- 'I *k* you by name, and you . . . Ex 33:12
- way, that I may *k* You . . . Ex 33:13
- to *k* how to do all manner . . . Ex 36:1
- Therefore *k* that the LORD . . . Deut 7:9
- *k* what was in your heart . . . Deut 8:2
- You should *k* in your heart . . . Deut 8:5
- that you may *k* the way by . . . Josh 3:4
- might be taught to *k* war, . . . Judg 3:2
- Samuel did not yet *k* the . . . 1 Sam 3:7
- *k* that there is a God . . . 1 Sam 17:46
- I *k* that this is a holy man . . . 2 Kin 4:9
- *k* that there is no God . . . 2 Kin 5:15
- you, my son Solomon, *k* . . . 1 Chr 28:9
- Hear it, and *k* for . . . Job 5:27
- and *k* nothing, because . . . Job 8:9
- *k* that my Redeemer . . . Job 19:25
- 'What does God *k* . . . Job 22:13
- *k* Your name will put . . . Ps 9:10
- Now I *k* that the LORD saves . . . Ps 20:6
- *k* that I am God . . . Ps 46:10
- make me to *k* wisdom . . . Ps 51:6
- O God, and *k* my heart . . . Ps 139:23
- *k* wisdom and instruction, . . . Prov 1:2
- to *k* understanding . . . Prov 4:1
- set my heart to *k* wisdom . . . Eccl 1:17
- that He may *k* to refuse the . . . Is 7:15
- Egyptians will *k* the LORD . . . Is 19:21
- But I *k* your dwelling place, . . . Is 37:28
- do not *k* nor understand . . . Is 44:18
- All flesh shall *k* that I, the . . . Is 49:26
- My people shall *k* My name . . . Is 52:6
- call a nation you do not *k* . . . Is 55:5
- language you do not *k* . . . Jer 5:15
- nor did they *k* how to blush . . . Jer 6:15
- Who can *k* it . . . Jer 17:9
- saying, '*K* the LORD . . . Jer 31:34
- you shall *k* that I am . . . Ezek 6:13
- of the field shall *k* that I . . . Ezek 17:24
- Gentiles shall *k* that . . . Ezek 39:23
- is anxious to *k* the dream . . . Dan 2:3
- you may *k* the thoughts . . . Dan 2:30
- I wished to *k* the truth . . . Dan 7:19
- you shall *k* no God but Me . . . Hos 13:4
- For I *k* your manifold . . . Amos 5:12
- for you to *k* justice . . . Mic 3:1
- did not *k* her till she had . . . Matt 1:25
- You *k* how to discern the . . . Matt 16:3
- *k* that summer is near . . . Matt 24:32
- *k* what hour your Lord . . . Matt 24:42
- an oath, "I do not *k* . . . Matt 26:72
- I do not *k* the Man . . . Matt 26:74
- *k* the mystery of the . . . Mark 4:11
- *k* the commandments . . . Mark 10:19
- do not *k* what you ask . . . Mark 10:38
- do not *k* what manner of . . . Luke 9:55
- *k* how to give good gifts . . . Luke 11:13
- *k* that its desolation is . . . Luke 21:20
- the world did not *k* . . . John 1:10
- We speak what We *k* . . . John 3:11
- *k* what we worship . . . John 4:22
- *k* that You are the Christ . . . John 6:69
- *k* that you are Abraham's . . . John 8:37
- we *k* that God does not . . . John 9:31
- hear My voice, and I *k* . . . John 10:27
- If you *k* these things . . . John 13:17
- *k* whom I have chosen . . . John 13:18
- we are sure that You *k* . . . John 16:30
- *k* that I love You . . . John 21:15
- *k* times or seasons . . . Acts 1:7
- and said, "Jesus I *k* . . . Acts 19:15
- we *k* that all things work . . . Rom 8:28
- wisdom did not *k* . . . 1 Cor 1:21
- nor can he *k* them . . . 1 Cor 2:14
- For we *k* in part and . . . 1 Cor 13:9
- *k* a man in Christ who . . . 2 Cor 12:2
- when you did not *k* God, . . . Gal 4:8
- *k* the love of Christ . . . Eph 3:19
- *k* Him and the power . . . Phil 3:10
- abased, and I *k* how to . . . Phil 4:12
- *k* how to possess his . . . 1 Thess 4:4
- *k* what is restraining . . . 2 Thess 2:6
- *k* whom I have believed . . . 2 Tim 1:12
- so that they may *k* . . . 2 Tim 2:25
- this we *k* that we *k* Him . . . 1 John 2:3
- He who says, "I *k* . . . 1 John 2:4
- and you *k* all things . . . 1 John 2:20
- By this we *k* love . . . 1 John 3:16
- *k* that we are of the . . . 1 John 3:19
- *k* that He abides . . . 1 John 3:24
- *k* that we are of God . . . 1 John 5:19
- "I *k* your works . . . Rev 2:2

KNOWING
- like God, *k* good and evil . . . Gen 3:5
- *k* their thoughts, said, . . . Matt 9:4
- not *k* the Scriptures nor . . . Matt 22:29
- *k* all things that would . . . John 18:4
- *k* that tribulation produces . . . Rom 5:3
- *k* that your labor is not . . . 1 Cor 15:58
- *k* that He who raised up . . . 2 Cor 4:14
- *k* that while we are at . . . 2 Cor 5:6
- *k* that I am appointed for . . . Phil 1:17
- *k* that you also have a . . . Col 4:1
- *k* that you have a better . . . Heb 10:34
- not *k* where he was going . . . Heb 11:8
- *k* that the testing of your . . . James 1:3
- *k* that the same sufferings . . . 1 Pet 5:9

KNOWLEDGE
- and the tree of the *k* . . . Gen 2:9
- and understanding, in *k* . . . Ex 35:31
- LORD is the God of *k* . . . 1 Sam 2:3
- give me wisdom and *k*, . . . 2 Chr 1:10
- Can anyone teach God *k* . . . Job 21:22
- who is perfect in *k* . . . Job 36:4
- unto night reveals *k* . . . Ps 19:2
- me good judgment and *k* . . . Ps 119:66
- *k* is too wonderful . . . Ps 139:6
- LORD is the beginning of *k* . . . Prov 1:7
- *k* the depths were . . . Prov 3:20
- *k* rather than choice . . . Prov 8:10
- Wise people store up *k* . . . Prov 10:14
- prudent man conceals *k* . . . Prov 12:23
- *k* is easy to him who . . . Prov 14:6
- *k* spares his words . . . Prov 17:27
- a soul to be without *k* . . . Prov 19:2
- by *k* the rooms are filled . . . Prov 24:4
- of *k* increases strength . . . Prov 24:5
- and he who increases *k* . . . Eccl 1:18
- *k* is that wisdom . . . Eccl 7:12
- no work or device or *k* . . . Eccl 9:10
- Whom will he teach *k* . . . Is 28:9
- His *k* My righteous Servant . . . Is 53:11
- *k* shall increase . . . Dan 12:4
- you have rejected *k* . . . Hos 4:6
- taken away the key of *k* . . . Luke 11:52
- having more accurate *k* . . . Acts 24:22
- to retain God in their *k* . . . Rom 1:28
- having the form of *k* . . . Rom 2:20
- by the law is the *k* of sin . . . Rom 3:20
- *K* puffs up, but love . . . 1 Cor 8:1
- to another the word of *k* . . . 1 Cor 12:8
- all mysteries and all *k* . . . 1 Cor 13:2
- whether there is *k* . . . 1 Cor 13:8
- of His *k* in every place . . . 2 Cor 2:14
- to give the light of the *k* . . . 2 Cor 4:6
- by purity, by *k*, by . . . 2 Cor 6:6
- against the *k* of God . . . 2 Cor 10:5
- Christ which passes *k* . . . Eph 3:19
- *k* of His will in all wisdom . . . Col 1:9
- treasures of wisdom and *k* . . . Col 2:3
- is falsely called *k* . . . 1 Tim 6:20
- faith virtue, to virtue *k* . . . 2 Pet 1:5
- in the grace and *k* . . . 2 Pet 3:18

KNOWN
- In Judah God is *k* . . . Ps 76:1
- my mouth will I make *k* . . . Ps 89:1
- If you had *k* Me . . . John 8:19
- My sheep, and am *k* . . . John 10:14
- The world has not *k* . . . John 17:25
- peace they have not *k* . . . Rom 3:17
- I would not have *k* . . . Rom 7:7
- "For who has *k* . . . Rom 11:34
- after you have *k* . . . Gal 4:9
- requests be made *k* . . . Phil 4:6
- *k* the Holy Scriptures . . . 2 Tim 3:15
- have not *k* the depths of . . . Rev 2:24

KNOWS
- For God *k* that in . . . Gen 3:5
- *k* the secrets of the . . . Ps 44:21
- he understands and *k* . . . Jer 9:24
- *k* what is in the . . . Dan 2:22
- *k* those who trust . . . Nah 1:7
- *k* the things you have . . . Matt 6:8

and hour no one *k* ... Matt 24:36
k who the Son is ... Luke 10:22
but God *k* your hearts ... Luke 16:15
searches the hearts *k* ... Rom 8:27
k the things of God ... 1 Cor 2:11
The LORD *k* the thoughts ... 1 Cor 3:20
k those who are His ... 2 Tim 2:19
to him who *k* to do ... James 4:17
and *k* all things ... 1 John 3:20
written which no one *k* ... Rev 2:17

KOHATH
Second son of Levi, Gen 46:8, 11
Brother of Jochebed, mother of Aaron and Moses, Ex 6:16–20

KOHATHITES
Numbered, Num 3:27, 28
Duties assigned to, Num 4:15–20
Leaders of temple music, 1 Chr 6:31–38; 2 Chr 20:19

KORAH
Leads rebellion against Moses and Aaron; supernaturally destroyed, Num 16:1–35
Sons of, not destroyed, Num 26:9–11

LABAN
Son of Bethuel; brother of Rebekah; father of Leah and Rachel, Gen 24:15, 24, 29; 29:16
Agrees to Rebekah's marriage to Isaac, Gen 24:50, 51
Entertains Jacob, Gen 29:1–14
Substitutes Leah for Rachel, Gen 29:15–30
Agrees to division of cattle; grows resentful of Jacob, Gen 30:25—31:2
Pursues Jacob and makes covenant with him, Gen 31:21–55

LABOR
Six days you shall *l* ... Ex 20:9
why then do I *l* ... Job 9:29
their boast is only *l* ... Ps 90:10
The *l* of the righteous ... Prov 10:16
l will increase ... Prov 13:11
l there is profit ... Prov 14:23
things are full of *l* ... Eccl 1:8
has man for all his *l* ... Eccl 2:22
He shall see the *l* ... Is 53:11
"Before she was in *l* ... Is 66:7
from the womb to see *l* ... Jer 20:18
to Me, all you who *l* ... Matt 11:28
Do not *l* for the ... John 6:27
knowing that your *l* ... 1 Cor 15:58
but rather let him *l* ... Eph 4:28
mean fruit from my *l* ... Phil 1:22
your work of faith, *l* ... 1 Thess 1:3
forget your work and *l* ... Heb 6:10
your works, your *l* ... Rev 2:2

LABORED
l more abundantly than ... 1 Cor 15:10
for you, lest I have *l* ... Gal 4:11

LABORERS
but the *l* are few ... Matt 9:37

LABORING
of a *l* man is sweet ... Eccl 5:12
l night and day ... 1 Thess 2:9

LABORS
The person who *l* ... Prov 16:26
is no end to all his *l* ... Eccl 4:8
entered into their *l* ... John 4:38
creation groans and *l* ... Rom 8:22
l more abundant ... 2 Cor 11:23
may rest from their *l* ... Rev 14:13

LACHISH
Defeated by Joshua, Josh 10:3–33
Taken by Sennacherib, 2 Kin 18:13–17; Is 36:1, 2; 37:8

LACK
the city for *l* of five ... Gen 18:28
gathered little had no *l* ... Ex 16:18
'you shall not *l* a man on ... 1 Kin 2:4
anyone perish for *l* ... Job 31:19
the LORD shall not *l* ... Ps 34:10
fools die for *l* of wisdom ... Prov 10:21
for *l* of justice there is ... Prov 13:23
to the poor will not *l* ... Prov 28:27
l a man to stand before ... Jer 35:19
for *l* of knowledge ... Hos 4:6
What do I still *l* ... Matt 19:20
"One thing you *l* ... Mark 10:21
did you *l* anything ... Luke 22:35
of your *l* of self-control ... 1 Cor 7:5
may supply their *l* ... 2 Cor 8:14
gathered little had no *l* ... 2 Cor 8:15

LACKED
among them who *l* ... Acts 4:34

LACKING
is *l* cannot be numbered ... Eccl 1:15
to supply what was *l* in ... Phil 2:30
the things that are *l* ... Titus 1:5
and complete, *l* nothing ... James 1:4

LACKS
woman who *l* discretion ... Prov 11:22
who *l* understanding ... Prov 28:16
to that part which *l* ... 1 Cor 12:24
If any of you *l* wisdom ... James 1:5
he who *l* these things is ... 2 Pet 1:9

LAD
and gave the *l* a drink ... Gen 21:19
lay your hand on the *l* ... Gen 22:12
said, "The *l* is no more ... Gen 37:30
'The *l* cannot leave his ... Gen 44:30
As the *l* ran, he shot an ... 1 Sam 20:36
"There is a *l* here who has ... John 6:9

LADDER
and behold, a *l* ... Gen 28:12

LADEN
nation, a people *l* ... Is 1:4
and are heavy *l* ... Matt 11:28

LADIES
wisest *l* answered her ... Judg 5:29
very day the noble *l* ... Esth 1:18

LADY
'I shall be a *l* ... Is 47:7
To the elect *l* ... 2 John 1

LAGGING
not *l* in diligence ... Rom 12:11

LAHAI ROI
Name of a well, Gen 16:7, 14
Same as Beer Lahai Roi, Gen 24:62

LAID
l him on the altar ... Gen 22:9
l up the food in the cities ... Gen 41:48
and *l* it in the reeds by the ... Ex 2:3
l the staff on the face of ... 2 Kin 4:31
l the foundation of the ... Ezra 5:16
But man dies and is *l* ... Job 14:10
You *l* the foundation ... Ps 102:25
He has *l* waste My vine ... Joel 1:7
have *l* the foundation of ... Zech 4:9
even now the ax is *l* to ... Matt 3:10
the place where they *l* ... Mark 16:6
l Him in a manger ... Luke 2:7
l the foundation on the ... Luke 6:48
"Where have you *l* ... John 11:34
l aside His garments ... John 13:4
where You have *l* Him ... John 20:15
l it at the apostles' feet ... Acts 4:37
and he *l* his hands on him ... Acts 28:8
I have *l* the foundation ... 1 Cor 3:10
He *l* down His life ... 1 John 3:16
He *l* His right hand on me ... Rev 1:17

LAISH
Called Leshem, Josh 19:47; Judg 18:29
Taken by Danites, Judg 18:7, 14, 27

LAKE
by the *L* of Gennesaret ... Luke 5:1
to the other side of the *l* ... Luke 8:22
cast alive into the *l* ... Rev 19:20

LAMB
but where is the *l* ... Gen 22:7
a *l* for a household ... Ex 12:3
and kill the Passover *l* ... Ex 12:21
took the poor man's *l* ... 2 Sam 12:4
shall dwell with the *l* ... Is 11:6
He was led as a *l* ... Is 53:7
l shall feed together ... Is 65:25
The *L* of God who takes ... John 1:29
as a *l* before its shearer ... Acts 8:32
of Christ, as of a *l* ... 1 Pet 1:19
the elders, stood a *L* ... Rev 5:6
"Worthy is the *L* ... Rev 5:12
by the blood of the *L* ... Rev 12:11
Book of Life of the *L* ... Rev 13:8
supper of the *L* ... Rev 19:9

LAMB'S
the bride, the *L* wife ... Rev 21:9
in the *L* Book of Life ... Rev 21:27

LAMBS
slaughtered the Passover *l* ... Ezra 6:20
O little hills, like *l* ... Ps 114:6
with the blood of *l* and ... Is 34:6
gather the *l* with His arm ... Is 40:11
out as *l* among wolves ... Luke 10:3
"Feed My *l* ... John 21:15

LAME
l take the prey ... Is 33:23
l shall leap like a ... Is 35:6
when you offer the *l* ... Mal 1:8
blind see and the *l* ... Matt 11:5
And a certain man *l* ... Acts 3:2
so that what is *l* ... Heb 12:13

LAMECH
Son of Methushael, of Cain's race, Gen 4:17, 18
——Son of Methuselah; father of Noah, Gen 5:25–31

LAMENT
l the daughter of ... Judg 11:40
king sang a *l* over Abner ... 2 Sam 3:33
Her gates shall *l* and mourn ... Is 3:26
"They shall not *l* for him, ... Jer 22:18
they shall *l* for her ... Ezek 32:16
to you, and you did not *l* ... Matt 11:17
that you will weep and *l* ... John 16:20
L and mourn and weep ... James 4:9
l for her, when they see ... Rev 18:9

LAMENTATION
a great and very solemn *l* ... Gen 50:10
with this *l* over Saul and ... 2 Sam 1:17
was heard in Ramah, *l* ... Jer 31:15
l in the daughter of Judah ... Lam 2:5
was heard in Ramah, *l* ... Matt 2:18
and made great *l* ... Acts 8:2

LAMP
For You are my *l* ... 2 Sam 22:29
"How often is the *l* ... Job 21:17
You will light my *l* ... Ps 18:28
Your word is a *l* ... Ps 119:105
the *l* of the wicked ... Prov 13:9
his *l* will be put out ... Prov 20:20
Nor do they light a *l* ... Matt 5:15
"The *l* of the body ... Matt 6:22
when he has lit a *l* ... Luke 8:16
l gives you light ... Luke 11:36
does not light a *l* ... Luke 15:8
burning and shining *l* ... John 5:35
l shall not shine ... Rev 18:23
They need no *l* nor ... Rev 22:5

LAMPS
he made its seven *l* ... Ex 37:23
Jerusalem with *l* ... Zeph 1:12

and trimmed their *l* ... Matt 25:7
Seven *l* of fire ... Rev 4:5

LAMPSTAND
branches of the *l* ... Ex 25:32
and there is a *l* ... Zech 4:2
a basket, but on a *l* ... Matt 5:15
in which was the *l* ... Heb 9:2
and remove your *l* ... Rev 2:5

LAND
and let the dry *l* appear ... Gen 1:9
God called the dry *l* Earth ... Gen 1:10
dwelt in the *l* of Nod ... Gen 4:16
l that I will show you ... Gen 12:1
I will give this *l* ... Gen 12:7
was a famine in the *l* ... Gen 12:10
Is not the whole *l* before ... Gen 13:9
walk in the *l* through its ... Gen 13:17
I have given this *l* ... Gen 15:18
arise, get out of this *l* ... Gen 31:13
the best of the *l* of Egypt ... Gen 45:18
dwell in the *l* of Goshen ... Gen 46:34
a stranger in a foreign *l* ... Ex 2:22
l flowing with milk ... Ex 3:8
to a *l* flowing with milk and ... Ex 3:17
the *l* of their pilgrimage ... Ex 6:4
firstborn in the *l* of Egypt ... Ex 12:12
and the *l* vomits out its ... Lev 18:25
for the *l* is Mine ... Lev 25:23
I will give peace in the *l* ... Lev 26:6
And all the tithe of the *l* ... Lev 27:30
spy out the *l* of Canaan ... Num 13:17
evil report about the *l* ... Num 14:37
l is subdued before the ... Num 32:22
possess the good *l* ... Deut 6:18
a *l* of wheat and barley ... Deut 8:8
He will bless you in the *l* ... Deut 28:8
the produce of your *l* ... Deut 28:51
l which I am giving ... Josh 1:2
to go in to possess the *l* ... Josh 1:11
Joshua took the whole *l* ... Josh 11:23
Joshua divided the *l* ... Josh 18:10
to return to the *l* of Judah ... Ruth 1:7
sold the piece of *l* which ... Ruth 4:3
spiritists from the *l* ... 1 Sam 28:9
In the *l* of the living ... Ps 27:13
dwell in the *l*, and feed on ... Ps 37:3
turned the sea into dry *l* ... Ps 66:6
in the *l* of forgetfulness ... Ps 88:12
l was polluted with blood ... Ps 106:38
dry *l* into watersprings ... Ps 107:35
for You like a thirsty *l* ... Ps 143:6
is heard in our *l* ... Song 2:12
they will see the *l* ... Is 33:17
a *l* of grain and new wine ... Is 36:17
and your *l* shall be married ... Is 62:4
Bethlehem, in the *l* ... Matt 2:6
put out a little from the *l* ... Luke 5:3
price of the *l* for yourself ... Acts 5:3
and his left foot on the *l* ... Rev 10:2

LAND OF THE LIVING
nor is it found in the *l* ... Job 28:13
of the LORD in the *l* ... Ps 27:13
uproot you from the *l* ... Ps 52:5
before the LORD in the *l* ... Ps 116:9
my portion in the *l* ... Ps 142:5
the LORD in the *l* ... Is 38:11
cut off from the *l* ... Is 53:8
establish glory in the *l* ... Ezek 26:20

LANDMARK
your neighbor's *l* ... Deut 19:14
remove the ancient *l* ... Prov 22:28
those who remove a *l* ... Hos 5:10

LANDS
We have mortgaged our *l* ... Neh 5:3
to scatter them in the *l* ... Ps 106:27
or wife or children or *l* ... Matt 19:29
of *l* or houses sold them ... Acts 4:34

LANGUAGE
whole earth had one *l* ... Gen 11:1
there confuse their *l* ... Gen 11:7
is no speech nor *l* ... Ps 19:3
a people of strange *l* ... Ps 114:1
the peoples a pure *l* ... Zeph 3:9
speak in his own *l* ... Acts 2:6
blasphemy, filthy *l* ... Col 3:8

LANGUAGES
according to their *l* ... Gen 10:20
be, so many kinds of *l* ... 1 Cor 14:10

LAODICEA
Paul's concern for, Col 2:1; 4:12–16
Letter to church of, Rev 3:14–22

LAST
See FIRST AND THE LAST
He shall stand at *l* ... Job 19:25
First and I am the *L* ... Is 44:6
l man the same as ... Matt 20:14
l will be first ... Matt 20:16
are first who will be *l* ... Luke 13:30
raise him up at the *l* day ... John 6:40
On the *l* day, that great ... John 7:37
come to pass in the *l* days ... Acts 2:17
The *l* enemy that will be ... 1 Cor 15:26
eye, at the *l* trumpet ... 1 Cor 15:52
has in these *l* days spoken ... Heb 1:2
children, it is the *l* ... 1 John 2:18
the First and the *L* ... Rev 1:11
l are more than the first ... Rev 2:19

LAST DAY
raise it up at the *l* ... John 6:39
the resurrection at the *l* ... John 11:24
will judge him in the *l* ... John 12:48

LAST DAYS
shall befall you in the *l* ... Gen 49:1
come to pass in the *l* ... Acts 2:17
in the *l* perilous times ... 2 Tim 3:1
these *l* spoken to us ... Heb 1:2
up treasure in the *l* ... James 5:3
will come in the *l* ... 2 Pet 3:3

LATE
to rise up early, to sit up *l* ... Ps 127:2
and already the hour is *l* ... Mark 6:35
l autumn trees without ... Jude 12
as a fig tree drops its *l* ... Rev 6:13

LATIN
in Hebrew, Greek, and *L* ... John 19:20

LATTER
people in the *l* days ... Dan 10:14
former rain, and the *l* ... Joel 2:23
The glory of this *l* temple ... Hag 2:9
l times some will ... 1 Tim 4:1
the early and *l* rain ... James 5:7
l end is worse for them ... 2 Pet 2:20

LATTICE
I looked through my *l* ... Prov 7:6
gazing through the *l* ... Song 2:9

LAUGH
Why did Sarah *l* ... Gen 18:13
"God has made me *l* ... Gen 21:6
sits in the heavens shall *l* ... Ps 2:4
You, O LORD, shall *l* ... Ps 59:8
to weep, and a time to *l* ... Eccl 3:4
Woe to you who *l* ... Luke 6:25

LAUGHS
he *l* at the threat of ... Job 41:29
The Lord *l* at him ... Ps 37:13

LAUGHTER
was filled with *l* ... Ps 126:2
your *l* be turned to ... James 4:9

LAUNDERER
such as no *l* on earth can ... Mark 9:3

LAVER
also make a *l* of bronze ... Ex 30:18
l contained forty baths ... 1 Kin 7:38

LAW
See ACCORDING TO THE LAW; BOOK OF THE LAW; UNDER THE LAW; WORKS OF THE LAW
stones a copy of the *l* ... Josh 8:32
When He made a *l* ... Job 28:26
The *l* of the LORD is ... Ps 19:7
The *l* of his God is in ... Ps 37:31
I delight in Your *l* ... Ps 119:70
The *l* of Your mouth is ... Ps 119:72
l is my delight ... Ps 119:77
Oh, how I love Your *l* ... Ps 119:97
And Your *l* is truth ... Ps 119:142
and the *l* a light ... Prov 6:23
is he who keeps the *l* ... Prov 29:18
shall go forth the *l* ... Is 2:3
l will proceed from Me ... Is 51:4
in whose heart is My *l* ... Is 51:7
the *L* is no more ... Lam 2:9
The *l* of truth was in ... Mal 2:6
to destroy the *L* ... Matt 5:17
for this is the *L* ... Matt 7:12
l prophesied until John ... Matt 11:13
hang all the *L* and the ... Matt 22:40
one tittle of the *l* to fail ... Luke 16:17
l was given through ... John 1:17
"Does our *l* judge a ... John 7:51
a teacher of the *l* held in ... Acts 5:34
and keep the *l* ... Acts 15:24
are all zealous for the *l* ... Acts 21:20
man according to the *l* ... Acts 22:12
l is the knowledge ... Rom 3:20
By what *l*? Of works? ... Rom 3:27
because the *l* brings ... Rom 4:15
when there is no *l* ... Rom 5:13
you are not under *l* ... Rom 6:14
have become dead to the *l* ... Rom 7:4
Is the *l* sin ... Rom 7:7
For we know that the *l* ... Rom 7:14
warring against the *l* ... Rom 7:23
For the *l* of the Spirit of ... Rom 8:2
For what the *l* could ... Rom 8:3
A wife is bound by *l* as ... 1 Cor 7:39
who are without *l* ... 1 Cor 9:21
strength of sin is the *l* ... 1 Cor 15:56
l that I might live ... Gal 2:19
Spirit by the works of the *l* ... Gal 3:2
under guard by the *l* ... Gal 3:23
the *l* was our tutor ... Gal 3:24
born under the *l* ... Gal 4:4
l is fulfilled in one ... Gal 5:14
and so fulfill the *l* of Christ ... Gal 6:2
concerning the *l*, a Pharisee ... Phil 3:5
to be teachers of the *l* ... 1 Tim 1:7
l is not made for a ... 1 Tim 1:9
and strivings about the *l* ... Titus 3:9
into the perfect *l* ... James 1:25
fulfill the royal *l* ... James 2:8

LAW AND THE PROPHETS
them, for this is the *L* ... Matt 7:12
hang all the *L* ... Matt 22:40
The *l* were until John ... Luke 16:16
being witnessed by the *L* ... Rom 3:21

LAW OF MOSES
the stones a copy of the *l* ... Josh 8:32
a skilled scribe in the *L* ... Ezra 7:6
bring the Book of the *L* ... Neh 8:1
oath written in the *L* ... Dan 9:11
the *L*, My servant ... Mal 4:4
according to the *l* ... Luke 2:22
were written in the *L* ... Luke 24:44
Sabbath, so that the *l* ... John 7:23
not be justified by the *l* ... Acts 13:39
them to keep the *l* ... Acts 15:5

LAW OF THE LORD
that you may keep the *l* ... 1 Chr 22:12
that he forsook the *l* ... 2 Chr 12:1
themselves to the *L* ... 2 Chr 31:4
his heart to seek the *L* ... Ezra 7:10
his delight is in the *l* ... Ps 1:2
l is perfect, converting ... Ps 19:7
way, who walk in the *l* ... Ps 119:1
they have rejected the *l* ... Is 5:24
who will not hear the *l* ... Is 30:9
'We are wise, and the *l* ... Jer 8:8

they have despised the *l*, . . . Amos 2:4
things according to the *l* . . . Luke 2:39

LAWFUL
doing what is not *l* . . . . Matt 12:2
Is it *l* to pay taxes . . . . Matt 22:17
All things are *l* . . . . 1 Cor 6:12

LAWGIVER
Judah is My *l* . . . . Ps 60:7
the LORD is our *L* . . . . Is 33:22
There is one *L* . . . . James 4:12

LAWLESS
l one will be revealed . . . . . 2 Thess 2:8
and hearing their *l* . . . . 2 Pet 2:8

LAWLESSNESS
Me, you who practice *l* . . . . . Matt 7:23
l is already at work . . . . 2 Thess 2:7
and hated *l* . . . . Heb 1:9
and sin is *l* . . . . 1 John 3:4

LAWYERS
l rejected the will of . . . . Luke 7:30
Woe to you also, *l* . . . . Luke 11:46

LAY
l it on the wood, but put . . 1 Kin 18:23
I *l* down and slept . . . . Ps 3:5
I will *l* your stones with . . . . . . Is 54:11
Do not *l* up for yourselves . . Matt 6:19
nowhere to *l* His head . . . . Matt 8:20
I have power to *l* it down . John 10:18
Will you *l* down your life . John 13:38
l hands may receive . . . . Acts 8:19
Do not *l* hands on . . . . 1 Tim 5:22
let us *l* aside every weight, . . Heb 12:1
l aside all filthiness . . . . James 1:21
"Behold, I *l* in Zion a chief . . 1 Pet 2:6

LAYING
l on of the apostles' hands . . Acts 8:18
the *l* on of my hands . . . . 2 Tim 1:6
not *l* again the foundation . . . . . Heb 6:1
of *l* on of hands, of . . . . Heb 6:2
l aside all malice, all deceit . . 1 Pet 2:1

LAYS
'God *l* up one's iniquity . . . . Job 21:19
He *l* up the deep in . . . . Ps 33:7
He *l* the beams of His . . . . Ps 104:3
which the LORD *l* on him . . . . . Is 30:32
l the foundation of the . . . . . Zech 12:1
he who *l* up treasure . . . . . Luke 12:21
he *l* it on his shoulders, ... Luke 15:5

LAZARUS
Beggar described in a parable, Luke 16:20–25
—— Brother of Mary and Martha; raised from the dead, John 11:1–44
Attends a supper, John 12:1, 2
Jews seek to kill, John 12:9–11

LAZINESS
L casts one into a . . . . Prov 19:15
l the building decays . . . . . . Eccl 10:18

LAZY
l man will be put to . . . . Prov 12:24
l man does not roast . . . . . . Prov 12:27
soul of a *l* man desires . . . . . Prov 13:4
l man buries his hand . . . . . Prov 19:24
by the field of the *l* . . . . Prov 24:30
l man is wiser in his . . . . . . Prov 26:16
wicked and *l* servant . . . . . . Matt 25:26
liars, evil beasts, *l* . . . . Titus 1:12

LEAD
pillar of cloud to *l* the way . . Ex 13:21
they sank like *l* . . . . Ex 15:10
L me in Your truth and . . . . Ps 25:5
And *l* me in a smooth path . . Ps 27:11
L me and guide me . . . . Ps 31:3
L me to the rock that is . . . . . . Ps 61:2
Your hand shall *l* . . . . Ps 139:10
a little child shall *l* them . . . . . . Is 11:6
I will *l* them in paths they . . . . Is 42:16
l is consumed by the fire . . . . . Jer 6:29
bronze, tin, iron, and *l* . . . . Ezek 22:18
tin, and *l* for your goods . . Ezek 27:12
threw the *l* cover over its . . . . Zech 5:8
And do not *l* us into . . . . Matt 6:13
"Can the blind *l* . . . . Luke 6:39
not *l* us into temptation . . . . . Luke 11:4
someone to *l* him by the . . . Acts 13:11
aspire to *l* a quiet life . . . . 1 Thess 4:11
that we may *l* a quiet and . . 1 Tim 2:2
to *l* them out of the land of . . . Heb 8:9
sin which does not *l* to . . . 1 John 5:16
l them to living fountains . . . Rev 7:17

LEADING
l men among the . . . . Acts 15:22
not a few of the *l* women . . . Acts 17:4
of lawlessness *l* to more . . . . Rom 6:19
his good, *l* to edification . . . . Rom 15:2
sin not *l* to death . . . . 1 John 5:16

LEADS
He *l* me beside the . . . . Ps 23:2
He *l* me in the paths . . . . Ps 23:3
And if the blind *l* . . . . Matt 15:14
by name and *l* them out . . . . John 10:3
the goodness of God *l* . . . . Rom 2:4

LEAF
plucked olive *l* . . . . Gen 8:11
Will You frighten a *l* . . . . Job 13:25
l will be green . . . . Jer 17:8

LEAH
Laban's eldest daughter; given to Jacob deceitfully, Gen 29:16–27
Unloved by Jacob, but bears children, Gen 29:30–35; 30:16–21

LEAN
all your heart, and *l* . . . . Prov 3:5
Yet they *l* on the LORD . . . . . . Mic 3:11

LEANING
Then, *l* back on Jesus' . . . . John 13:25
l on the top of his . . . . Heb 11:21

LEANNESS
request, but sent *l* . . . . Ps 106:15
of hosts, will send *l* . . . . Is 10:16

LEAP
by my God I can *l* . . . . Ps 18:29
Then the lame shall *l* . . . . Is 35:6

LEAPED
the rams which *l* upon . . . . . Gen 31:10
they *l* about the altar . . . . . 1 Kin 18:26
the babe *l* in her womb . . . . Luke 1:41
and he *l* and walked . . . . . . Acts 14:10

LEAPING
saw King David *l* . . . . 2 Sam 6:16
walking, *l*, and praising . . . . . Acts 3:8

LEARN
it, may hear and *l* . . . . Deut 31:13
l Your statutes . . . . Ps 119:71
lest you *l* his ways . . . . Prov 22:25
l to do good . . . . Is 1:17
neither shall they *l* . . . . Is 2:4
My yoke upon you and *l* . . Matt 11:29
Let a woman *l* in . . . . 1 Tim 2:11
let our people also *l* . . . . Titus 3:14
no one could *l* that song . . . . Rev 14:3

LEARNED
Me the tongue of the *l* . . . . Is 50:4
who has heard and *l* . . . . John 6:45
have not so *l* Christ . . . . Eph 4:20
in all things I have *l* . . . . Phil 4:12
l obedience by the . . . . Heb 5:8

LEARNING
hear and increase *l* . . . . Prov 1:5
l is driving you mad . . . . . . Acts 26:24
were written for our *l* . . . . . . Rom 15:4

LEAST
Judah, are not the *l* . . . . Matt 2:6
so, shall be called *l* . . . . Matt 5:19
For I am the *l* of the . . . . 1 Cor 15:9

LEATHER
everything made of *l* . . . . . Num 31:20
wearing a *l* belt around . . . . . . 2 Kin 1:8
with a *l* belt around his . . . . . Mark 1:6

LEAVE
a man shall *l* his . . . . Gen 2:24
He will not *l* you nor . . . . Deut 31:6
For You will not *l* . . . . Ps 16:10
do not *l* me nor . . . . Ps 27:9
"I will never *l* . . . . Heb 13:5

LEAVEN
day you shall remove *l* . . . . . . Ex 12:15
of heaven is like *l* . . . . Matt 13:33
and beware of the *l* . . . . Matt 16:6
know that a little *l* . . . . 1 Cor 5:6
l leavens the whole . . . . Gal 5:9

LEAVENED
For whoever eats *l* bread . . . . Ex 12:15
shall eat no *l* bread with . . . Deut 16:3
of meal till it was all *l* . . . . . Matt 13:33

LEAVES
and they sewed fig *l* . . . . Gen 3:7
nothing on it but *l* . . . . Matt 21:19
l the sheep and flees . . . . . . John 10:12
The *l* of the tree . . . . Rev 22:2

LEBANON
Part of Israel's inheritance, Josh 13:5–7
Not completely conquered, Judg 3:1–3
Source of materials for temple, 1 Kin 5:2–18; Ezra 3:7
Mentioned in prophecy, Is 10:34; 29:17; 35:2; Ezek 17:3; Hos 14:5–7

LEBBAEUS
See JUDAS
Surname of Judas (Jude), Matt 10:3

LEBONAH
Town north of Shiloh, Judg 21:19

LED
l the people around by . . . . . . Ex 13:18
I have *l* you forty years in . . Deut 29:5
so the LORD alone *l* . . . . Deut 32:12
have *l* captivity captive . . . . . . Ps 68:18
l them forth by the . . . . Ps 107:7
He was *l* as a lamb to the . . . . . Is 53:7
and be *l* out with peace . . . . . . Is 55:12
l them by the right . . . . Is 63:12
have *l* them astray . . . . Jer 50:6
Then Jesus was *l* up by the . . Matt 4:1
l Him out to crucify . . . . . . Mark 15:20
"He was *l* as a sheep to . . . . Acts 8:32
For as many as are *l* . . . . Rom 8:14
sorrow *l* to repentance . . . . . 2 Cor 7:9
if you are *l* by the Spirit . . . . . Gal 5:18
l captivity captive . . . . Eph 4:8
l away by various . . . . 2 Tim 3:6

LEFT
Lie also on your *l* side . . . . . . Ezek 4:4
l hand know what your . . . . . Matt 6:3
"See, we have *l* . . . . Matt 19:27
And everyone who has *l* . . Matt 19:29
on My *l* is not Mine to . . . . . Mark 10:40
right hand and on the *l* . . . . . 2 Cor 6:7

LEGACY
shame shall be the *l* . . . . Prov 3:35

LEGION
"My name is *L* . . . . Mark 5:9
"*L*," because many . . . . Luke 8:30

LEGIONS
twelve *l* of angels . . . . Matt 26:53

LEGS
Like the *l* of the lame . . . . . . Prov 26:7
l are pillars of . . . . Song 5:15
did not break His *l* . . . . John 19:33

LEHI
Samson kills Philistines at, Judg 15:9–19

LEMUEL
King taught by his mother, Prov 31:1–31

LEND
"If you *l* money to .... Ex 22:25
l him sufficient .... Deut 15:8
And if you *l* to those .... Luke 6:34
l me three loaves .... Luke 11:5

LENDER
is servant to the *l* .... Prov 22:7
as with the *l* .... Is 24:2

LENDING
and my servants, am *l* ...... Neh 5:10

LENDS
ever merciful, and *l* .... Ps 37:26
deals graciously and *l* .... Ps 112:5
has pity on the poor *l* .... Prov 19:17

LENGTH
The *l* of the ark shall .... Gen 6:15
is your life and the *l* .... Deut 30:20
L of days is in her .... Prov 3:16
l is as great as its .... Rev 21:16

LENGTHENS
a shadow when it *l* .... Ps 109:23

LEOPARD
the *l* shall lie down .... Is 11:6
or the *l* its spots .... Jer 13:23

LEPER
put out of the camp every *l* .. Num 5:2
and there she was, a *l* .... Num 12:10
King Uzziah was a *l* ...... 2 Chr 26:21
l came and worshiped .... Matt 8:2
house of Simon the *l* ...... Mark 14:3

LEPERS
And when these *l* .... 2 Kin 7:8
the sick, cleanse the *l* ...... Matt 10:8
And many *l* were in .... Luke 4:27
ten men who were *l* ...... Luke 17:12

LEPROSY
This is the law of *l* .... Lev 14:57
he would heal him of his *l* .. 2 Kin 5:3
l broke out on his .... 2 Chr 26:19
immediately the *l* left him .. Luke 5:13

LEPROUS
out, behold, his hand was *l* .... Ex 4:6
Miriam became *l* .... Num 12:10
out from his presence *l* .... 2 Kin 5:27
his forehead, he was *l* .... 2 Chr 26:20

LET
"*L* there be light" .... Gen 1:3
L the little children .... Matt 19:14

LETTER
they delivered the *l* .... Acts 15:30
the Spirit, and not in the *l* .. Rom 2:29
the oldness of the *l* .... Rom 7:6
for the *l* kills .... 2 Cor 3:6
you sorry with my *l* .... 2 Cor 7:8
or by word or by *l* .... 2 Thess 2:2

LETTERS
does this Man know *l* ...... John 7:15
or *l* of commendation .... 2 Cor 3:1
"For his *l*," they say ...... 2 Cor 10:10
with what large *l* .... Gal 6:11

LEVI
Third son of Jacob and Leah, Gen 29:34
Avenges rape of Dinah, Gen 34:25–31
Jacob's prophecy concerning, Gen 49:5–7
Ancestor of Moses and Aaron, Ex 6:16–27

LEVIATHAN
"Can you draw out *L* .... Job 41:1
L which You have made ... Ps 104:26

LEVITE
"Is not Aaron the *L* .... Ex 4:14
Likewise a *L*, when he .... Luke 10:32
a *L* of the country of .... Acts 4:36

LEVITES
Rewarded for dedication, Ex 32:26–29
Appointed over tabernacle, Num 1:47–54
Substituted for Israel's firstborn, Num 3:12–45
Consecrated to the Lord's service, Num 8:5–26
Cities assigned to, Num 35:2–8; Josh 14:3, 4; 1 Chr 6:54–81
Organized for temple service, 1 Chr 9:14–34; 23:1—26:28

LEVITICAL
were through the *L* .... Heb 7:11

LEWDNESS
wickedness, deceit, *l* ...... Mark 7:22
drunkenness, not in *l* ..... Rom 13:13
themselves over to *l* .... Eph 4:19
when we walked in *l* .... 1 Pet 4:3

LIAR
a *l* listens eagerly to a ..... Prov 17:4
for he is a *l* and the .... John 8:44
but every man a *l* .... Rom 3:4
we make Him a *l* .... 1 John 1:10
Who is a *l* but he who .... 1 John 2:22
his brother, he is a *l* ...... 1 John 4:20
God has made Him a *l* .... 1 John 5:10

LIARS
"All men are *l* .... Ps 116:11
Cretans are always *l* .... Titus 1:12
and have found them *l* .... Rev 2:2
l shall have their .... Rev 21:8

LIBERALITY
he who gives, with *l* .... Rom 12:8
the riches of their *l* .... 2 Cor 8:2

LIBERALLY
who gives to all *l* .... James 1:5

LIBERTY
year, and proclaim *l* ...... Lev 25:10
And I will walk at *l* .... Ps 119:45
to proclaim *l* to the .... Is 61:1
to proclaim *l* to the .... Luke 4:18
into the glorious *l* .... Rom 8:21
For why is my *l* .... 1 Cor 10:29
Lord is, there is *l* .... 2 Cor 3:17
therefore in the *l* .... Gal 5:1
l as an opportunity .... Gal 5:13
the perfect law of *l* ...... James 1:25
yet not using *l* .... 1 Pet 2:16

LIBNAH
Canaanite city, captured by Joshua, Josh 10:29, 30
Given to Aaron's descendants, Josh 21:13

LIBYA
Mentioned in prophecy, Ezek 30:5; Dan 11:43
Jews from, present at Pentecost, Acts 2:1–10

LICE
so that it may become *l* ...... Ex 8:16
and *l* in all their territory ... Ps 105:31

LIE
man, that He should *l* ..... Num 23:19
to Samuel, "Go, *l* down .... 1 Sam 3:9
For now I will *l* .... Job 7:21
I will not *l* to David .... Ps 89:35
forged a *l* against me .... Ps 119:69
leopard shall *l* down with ..... Is 11:6
prophesy a *l* to you in My .. Jer 29:21
heart to *l* to the Holy Spirit .. Acts 5:3
Do not *l* to one .... Col 3:9
God, who cannot *l* .... Titus 1:2
do not boast and *l* .... James 3:14
know it, and that no *l* ..... 1 John 2:21
an abomination or a *l* ...... Rev 21:27

LIED
They have *l* about the .... Jer 5:12
You have not *l* to men .... Acts 5:4

LIES
sin *l* at the door .... Gen 4:7
not say, "Here *l* Jezebel ... 2 Kin 9:37
He *l* in wait secretly .... Ps 10:9
speak *l* shall be stopped ...... Ps 63:11
and he who speaks *l* .... Prov 19:5
She also *l* in wait as for ... Prov 23:28
prophesy *l* in My name ...... Jer 14:14
they shall speak *l* at the .... Dan 11:27
l in the name of the LORD .. Zech 13:3
speaking *l* in hypocrisy ..... 1 Tim 4:2
and the whole world *l* .... 1 John 5:19

LIFE
See ALL THE DAYS OF HIS LIFE; BOOK OF LIFE; BREATH OF LIFE; ETERNAL LIFE; EVERLASTING LIFE; TREE OF LIFE; WATER OF LIFE
the breath of *l* .... Gen 2:7
l was also in the .... Gen 2:9
I will require the *l* of man .... Gen 9:5
then you shall give *l* .... Ex 21:23
For the *l* of the .... Lev 17:11
before you today *l* .... Deut 30:15
You have granted me *l* ...... Job 10:12
in whose hand is the *l* ...... Job 12:10
God takes away his *l* .... Job 27:8
with the light of *l* .... Job 33:30
He will redeem their *l* .... Ps 72:14
word has given me *l* .... Ps 119:50
blessing—*L* forevermore .... Ps 133:3
regain the paths of *l* .... Prov 2:19
She is a tree of *l* .... Prov 3:18
so they will be *l* .... Prov 3:22
finds me finds *l* .... Prov 8:35
the *l* of his animal .... Prov 12:10
LORD is a fountain of *l* .... Prov 14:27
l winds upward for the .... Prov 15:24
thief hates his own *l* .... Prov 29:24
is that wisdom gives *l* .... Eccl 7:12
I have cut off my *l* .... Is 38:12
you the way of *l* .... Jer 21:8
l shall be as a prize .... Jer 39:18
not worry about your *l* ..... Matt 6:25
l does not consist .... Luke 12:15
L is more than food ...... Luke 12:23
l was the light .... John 1:4
so the Son gives *l* .... John 5:21
as the Father has *l* .... John 5:26
spirit, and they are *l* .... John 6:63
have the light of *l* .... John 8:12
and I lay down My *l* ...... John 10:15
resurrection and the *l* ..... John 11:25
you lay down your *l* ...... John 13:38
God, who gives *l* .... Rom 4:17
that pertain to this *l* .... 1 Cor 6:3
Lord Jesus, that the *l* ...... 2 Cor 4:10
l which I now live .... Gal 2:20
l is hidden with .... Col 3:3
of God who gives *l* .... 1 Tim 6:13
For what is your *l* .... James 4:14
that pertain to *l* .... 2 Pet 1:3
l was manifested .... 1 John 1:2
and the pride of *l* .... 1 John 2:16
has given us eternal *l* .... 1 John 5:11
who has the Son has *l* .... 1 John 5:12
the Lamb's Book of *L* ...... Rev 21:27
right to the tree of *l* .... Rev 22:14
the water of *l* freely .... Rev 22:17
from the Book of *L* .... Rev 22:19

LIFT
"*L* your eyes now and ..... Gen 13:14
l up His countenance ...... Num 6:26
L up your heads .... Ps 24:7
I will *l* up my hands .... Ps 63:4

angels desire to *l* into ...... 1 Pet 1:12
l for new heavens and a ... 2 Pet 3:13
L to yourselves .... 2 John 8
open the scroll, or to *l* at it ... Rev 5:3

LOOKED
But when I *l* for good ...... Job 30:26
They *l* to Him and were ...... Ps 34:5
For He *l* down from the .... Ps 102:19
He *l* for justice .... Is 5:7
"We *l* for peace .... Jer 8:15
"You *l* for much .... Hag 1:9
the Lord turned and *l* ..... Luke 22:61
for he *l* to the reward ..... Heb 11:26

LOOKING
the plow, and *l* back .... Luke 9:62
l for the blessed hope ...... Titus 2:13
l unto Jesus, the author ..... Heb 12:2
l carefully lest .... Heb 12:15
l for the mercy of .... Jude 21

LOOKS
Absalom for his good *l* .. 2 Sam 14:25
Then he *l* at men and ...... Job 33:27
God *l* down from heaven ..... Ps 53:2
The lofty *l* of man .... Is 2:11
to you that whoever *l* ...... Matt 5:28

LOOM
and the web from the *l* .... Judg 16:14
cuts me off from the *l* .... Is 38:12

LOOSE
l the armor of kings .... Is 45:1
and whatever you *l* .... Matt 16:19
said to them, "*L* him ...... John 11:44

LOOSED
You have *l* my bonds ...... Ps 116:16
the silver cord is *l* .... Eccl 12:6
on earth will be *l* in .... Matt 16:19
his tongue was *l*, and he ... Mark 7:35
l from your infirmity ..... Luke 13:12
be *l* from this bond .... Luke 13:16
l the pains of death .... Acts 2:24
everyone's chains were *l* .. Acts 16:26
Do not seek to be *l* .... 1 Cor 7:27

LORD
See ANGEL OF THE LORD; ANGER OF THE LORD; BLESS THE LORD; BLESSED BE THE LORD; DAY OF THE LORD; FEAR OF THE LORD; FEAR THE LORD; GLORY OF THE LORD; HAND OF THE LORD; HOUSE OF THE LORD; LAW OF THE LORD; LOVE THE LORD YOUR GOD; PRAISE THE LORD; REJOICE IN THE LORD; SEEK THE LORD; SERVE THE LORD; SINNED AGAINST THE LORD; SPIRIT OF THE LORD; VOICE OF THE LORD; VOW TO THE LORD; WAIT ON THE LORD; WAY OF THE LORD; WRATH OF THE LORD
L is my strength .... Ex 15:2
L is a man of war .... Ex 15:3
L our God, the *L* .... Deut 6:4
sacrifice to the *L* your ..... Deut 17:1
may know that the *L* ...... 1 Kin 8:60
If the *L* is God .... 1 Kin 18:21
You alone are the *L* .... Neh 9:6
The *L* of hosts .... Ps 24:10
belongs to the *L* .... Ps 89:18
let us sing to the *L* .... Ps 95:1
L is the great God .... Ps 95:3
Gracious is the *L* .... Ps 116:5
L surrounds His people ...... Ps 125:2
The *L* is righteous .... Ps 129:4
L is near to all who .... Ps 145:18
L is a God of justice .... Is 30:18
L Our Righteousness .... Jer 23:6
L has done marvelous ...... Joel 2:21
L God is my strength .... Hab 3:19
"The *L* is one .... Zech 14:9
shall not tempt the *L* .... Matt 4:7
shall worship the *L* .... Matt 4:10
Son of Man is also *L* ...... Mark 2:28
who is Christ the *L* .... Luke 2:11
why do you call Me '*L* ...... Luke 6:46
L is risen indeed .... Luke 24:34
call Me Teacher and *L* .... John 13:13
He is *L* of all .... Acts 10:36
'Who are You, *L* .... Acts 26:15
with your mouth the *L* ..... Rom 10:9
Greek, for the same *L* ..... Rom 10:12
say that Jesus is *L* .... 1 Cor 12:3
second Man is the *L* ...... 1 Cor 15:47
the Spirit of the *L* .... 2 Cor 3:17
that Jesus Christ is *L* .... Phil 2:11
and deny the only *L* .... Jude 4
L God Omnipotent .... Rev 19:6

LORD APPEARED TO
Then the *L* Abram and ..... Gen 12:7
the *L* Abram and said to .... Gen 17:1
L him by the terebinth ...... Gen 18:1
Then the *L* him and said .... Gen 26:2
Then the glory of the *L* ..... Lev 9:23
glory of the *L* them .... Num 20:6
L Solomon in a dream ...... 1 Kin 3:5
L Solomon the second ...... 1 Kin 9:2

LORD COMMANDED
all that the *L* him .... Gen 7:5
L Moses and Aaron, ... Ex 12:50
words which the *L* him ...... Ex 19:7
the thing which the *L*, ... Ex 35:4
The *L* this to be given .... Lev 7:36
which the *L* Moses .... Lev 27:34
As the *L* Moses, so he ..... Num 1:19
as the *L* Moses, all .... Num 15:36
Moses did as the *L* .... Num 27:22
statutes which the *L* ...... Num 30:16
the *L* us to observe .... Deut 6:24
not kept what the *L* ..... 1 Sam 13:14
David did so, as the *L* .... 2 Sam 5:25
So the *L* the angel, ... 1 Chr 21:27
there the *L* the blessing ..... Ps 133:3
the Euphrates, as the *L* ...... Jer 13:5
did as the angel of the *L* ... Matt 1:24

LORD GOD OF HOSTS
the *L* was with him .... 2 Sam 5:10
very zealous for the *L* .... 1 Kin 19:10
who wait for You, O *L*, ... Ps 69:6
Restore us, O *L*; .... Ps 80:19
O *L*, hear my prayer; .... Ps 84:8
Therefore thus says the *L*: ... Is 10:24
L in the Valley of Vision ...... Is 22:5
I have heard from the *L*, ... Is 28:22
called by Your name, O *L* .. Jer 15:16
this is the day of the *L* ..... Jer 46:10
the work of the *L* .... Jer 50:25
the *L* is his name .... Amos 4:13
The *L*, he who touches .... Amos 9:5

LORD GOD OF ISRAEL
Pharaoh, "Thus says the *L* .... Ex 5:1
before the Lord, the *L* ...... Ex 34:23
give glory to the *L*, ... Josh 7:19
built an altar to the *L* .... Josh 8:30
sworn to them by the *L* .... Josh 9:19
the *L* fought for Israel ..... Josh 10:42
L was their inheritance .... Josh 13:33
your heart to the *L* .... Josh 24:23
will sing praise to the *L* ..... Judg 5:3
"O *L*, why has this come ... Judg 21:3
be given you by the *L*, ... Ruth 2:12
Saul said to the *L* .... 1 Sam 14:41
"O *L*, Your servant ...... 1 Sam 23:10
Blessed is the *L* .... 1 Sam 25:32
L: 'I anointed you .... 2 Sam 12:7
'Blessed be the *L* .... 1 Kin 1:48
for the name of the *L* ...... 1 Kin 8:17
turned away from the *L* ... 1 Kin 11:9
provoked the *L* to anger .. 1 Kin 15:30
O *L*, the One who .... 2 Kin 19:15
the ark of the *L* .... 1 Chr 15:12
build a house for the *L* ... 1 Chr 22:6
"The *L* has given rest .... 1 Chr 23:25
their heart to seek the *L* .. 2 Chr 11:16
they turned to the *L* .... 2 Chr 15:4
the Passover to the *L* ...... 2 Chr 30:1
build the house of the *L* ..... Ezra 1:3
in order to seek the *L* .... Exra 6:21
Blessed be the *L*, from ...... Ps 41:13
Blessed is the *L*, for he .... Luke 1:68

LORD HAS SPOKEN
son's wife, as the *L* .... Gen 24:51
that the *L* we will do .... Ex 19:8
the statutes which the *L* .... Lev 10:11
which the *L* to Moses ..... Num 15:22
For the *L* of David .... 2 Sam 3:18
the sign which the *L* ...... 1 Kin 13:3
the mouth of the *L* .... Is 1:20
for the mouth of the *L* .... Is 40:5
not be proud, for the *L* ..... Jer 13:15
Hear this word that the *L* .. Amos 3:1

LORD IS GOOD
taste and see that the *L* .... Ps 34:8
For the *L*; His mercy .... Ps 100:5
Praise the Lord, for the *L* .... Ps 135:3
L to all, and His .... Ps 145:9
Lord of hosts, for the *L* ..... Jer 33:11
The *L* to those who wait .... Lam 3:25
The *L*, a stronghold .... Nah 1:7

LORD JESUS CHRIST
we believed on the *L* ...... Acts 11:17
the grace of the *L* .... Acts 15:11
for the name of our *L* ..... Acts 15:26
"Believe on the *L* .... Acts 16:31
with God through our *L* ..... Rom 5:1
in God through our *L* ...... Rom 5:11
But put on the *L* .... Rom 13:14
do not serve our *L* .... Rom 16:18
the revelation of our *L* ..... 1 Cor 1:7
in the day of our *L* .... 1 Cor 1:8
victory through our *L* .... 1 Cor 15:57
does not love the *L* .... 1 Cor 16:22
know the grace of our *L* .... 2 Cor 8:9
in the cross of our *L* .... Gal 6:14
in the name of our *L* .... Eph 5:20
for the Savior, the *L* .... Phil 3:20
presence of our *L* .... 1 Thess 2:19
salvation through our *L* ... 1 Thess 5:9
at the coming of our *L* ... 1 Thess 5:23
obey the gospel of our *L* .. 2 Thess 1:8
the coming of our *L* ...... 2 Thess 2:1
hold the faith of our *L* ..... James 2:1
in the knowledge of *L* ...... 2 Pet 1:8
just as our *L* showed me ... 2 Pet 1:14
Lord God and our *L* .... Jude 4
by the apostles of our *L* ...... Jude 17
The grace of our *L* .... Rev 22:21

LORD OF HOSTS
to the *L* in Shiloh .... 1 Sam 1:3
"O *L*, if You will indeed .. 1 Sam 1:11
L, who dwells between ..... 1 Sam 4:4
in the name of the *L* ..... 1 Sam 17:45
'*L* is the God over Israel .. 2 Sam 7:26
The zeal of the *L* .... 2 Kin 19:31
the *L* was with him .... 1 Chr 11:9
The *L*, He is the King .... Ps 24:10
The *L* is with us; .... Ps 46:7
Your tabernacle, O *L* .... Ps 84:1
Unless the *L* had left to .... Is 1:9
For the day of the *L* .... Is 2:12
vineyard of the *L* .... Is 5:7
Holy, holy, holy is the *L* .... Is 6:3
The *L*, Him you shall .... Is 8:13
The zeal of the *L* .... Is 9:7
Through the wrath of the *L* ... Is 9:19
in the wrath of the *L* .... Is 13:13
L will reign on Mount Zion .. Is 24:23
In that day the *L* .... Is 28:5
O *L*, God of Israel .... Is 37:16
his Redeemer, the *L* .... Is 44:6
is your husband, the *L* .... Is 54:5
But, O *L*, You who test ...... Jer 20:12
of the living God, the *L* ..... Jer 23:36

intercession to the *L* ... Jer 27:18
the *L* is His name ... Jer 31:35
Praise the *L*, for the Lord ... Jer 33:11
by his God, the *L* ... Jer 51:5
The *L* has sworn ... Jer 51:14
the people of the *L* ... Zeph 2:10
on the house of the *L* ... Hag 1:14
with glory,' says the *L* ... Hag 2:7
"Return to me," says the *L* .. Zech 1:3
"O *L*, how long will You ... Zech 1:12
L has sent me ... Zech 2:9
My Spirit,' says the *L* ... Zech 4:6
wrath came from the *L* ... Zech 7:12
the Mountain of the *L* ... Zech 8:3
shall come to seek the *L* ... Zech 8:22
The *L* will defend them ... Zech 9:15
worship the King, the *L* ... Zech 14:16
a great King," says the *L* ... Mal 1:14
is the messenger of the *L* ... Mal 2:7
return to you, says the *L* ... Mal 3:7

LORD OF LORDS
God of gods and *L* ... Deut 10:17
give thanks to the *L* ... Ps 136:3
King of kings and *L* ... 1 Tim 6:15
He is *L* and King of kings .. Rev 17:14
King of kings and *L* ... Rev 19:16

LORD WAS WITH HIM
master saw that the *L* ... Gen 39:3
Samuel grew, and the *L* ... 1 Sam 3:19
David, because the *L* ... 1 Sam 18:12
ways, and the *L* ... 1 Sam 18:14
The *L*; he prospered ... 2 Kin 18:7
And the hand of the *L* ... Luke 1:66

LORD'S ANOINTED
"Surely the *L* is before ... 1 Sam 16:6
to my master, the *L* ... 1 Sam 24:6
his hand against the *L* ... 1 Sam 26:9
hand to destroy the *L* ... 2 Sam 1:14
he cursed the *L* ... 2 Sam 19:21

LORDS
many gods and many *l* ... 1 Cor 8:5
nor as being *l* over ... 1 Pet 5:3
for He is Lord of *l* ... Rev 17:14

LORDSHIP
Gentiles exercise *l* ... Luke 22:25

LOSE
gain, and a time to *l* ... Eccl 3:6
save his life will *l* ... Matt 16:25
reap if we do not *l* ... Gal 6:9
that we do not *l* ... 2 John 8

LOSES
but if the salt *l* ... Matt 5:13
and *l* his own soul ... Matt 16:26
if she *l* one coin ... Luke 15:8
l his life will preserve ... Luke 17:33

LOSS
he will suffer *l* ... 1 Cor 3:15
count all things *l* ... Phil 3:8

LOST
are dry, our hope is *l* ... Ezek 37:11
save that which was *l* ... Matt 18:11
the one which is *l* ... Luke 15:4
my sheep which was *l* ... Luke 15:6
the piece which I *l* ... Luke 15:9
and none of them is *l* ... John 17:12
You gave Me I have *l* ... John 18:9

LOT
Abram's nephew; accompanies him, Gen 11:27—12:5; 13:1
Separates from Abram, Gen 13:5–12
Rescued by Abram, Gen 14:12–16
Saved from Sodom for his hospitality, Gen 19:1–29
Tricked into committing incest, Gen 19:30–38

LOT
shall be divided by *l* ... Num 26:55
You maintain my *l* ... Ps 16:5
cast in your *l* among ... Prov 1:14
l is cast into the lap ... Prov 16:33

LOT'S WIFE
Disobedient, becomes pillar of salt, Gen 19:26
Event to be remembered, Luke 17:32

LOTS
l causes contentions ... Prov 18:18
garments, casting *l* ... Mark 15:24
And they cast their *l* ... Acts 1:26

LOUD
I cried out with a *l* ... Gen 39:14
Him with *l* cymbals ... Ps 150:5
cried out with a *l* ... Matt 27:46
I heard behind me a *l* ... Rev 1:10

LOVE
l your neighbor as ... Lev 19:18
l the LORD your God ... Deut 6:5
your *l* to me was ... 2 Sam 1:26
How long will you *l* ... Ps 4:2
Oh, *l* the LORD ... Ps 31:23
l righteousness ... Ps 45:7
he has set his *l* ... Ps 91:14
Oh, how I *l* Your law ... Ps 119:97
peace have those who *l* ... Ps 119:165
preserves all who *l* ... Ps 145:20
us take our fill of *l* ... Prov 7:18
l covers all sins ... Prov 10:12
a time to *l* ... Eccl 3:8
People know neither *l* ... Eccl 9:1
l is better than wine ... Song 1:2
banner over me was *l* ... Song 2:4
stir up nor awaken *l* ... Song 3:5
I will give you my *l* ... Song 7:12
l is as strong as death ... Song 8:6
waters cannot quench *l* ... Song 8:7
time was the time of *l* ... Ezek 16:8
backsliding, I will *l* ... Hos 14:4
do justly, to *l* mercy ... Mic 6:8
to you, *l* your enemies ... Matt 5:44
l those who *l* you ... Matt 5:46
which of them will *l* ... Luke 7:42
you do not have the *l* ... John 5:42
if you have *l* for one ... John 13:35
"If you *l* Me, keep My ... John 14:15
and My Father will *l* ... John 14:23
l one another as I ... John 15:12
l has no one than this ... John 15:13
l Me more than these ... John 21:15
of Jonah, do you *l* ... John 21:16
because the *l* of God ... Rom 5:5
Let *l* be without ... Rom 12:9
to *l* one another ... Rom 13:8
L does no harm to a ... Rom 13:10
up, but *l* edifies ... 1 Cor 8:1
L suffers long and is ... 1 Cor 13:4
L never fails ... 1 Cor 13:8
greatest of these is *l* ... 1 Cor 13:13
For the *l* of Christ ... 2 Cor 5:14
and the God of *l* ... 2 Cor 13:11
of the Spirit is *l* ... Gal 5:22
rooted and grounded in *l* ... Eph 3:17
the edifying of itself in *l* ... Eph 4:16
Husbands, *l* your wives ... Eph 5:25
if any comfort of *l* ... Phil 2:1
of the Son of His *l* ... Col 1:13
being knit together in *l* ... Col 2:2
l your wives and do ... Col 3:19
breastplate of faith and *l* .. 1 Thess 5:8
the commandment is *l* ... 1 Tim 1:5
continue in faith, *l* ... 1 Tim 2:15
word, in conduct, in *l* ... 1 Tim 4:12
For the *l* of money is ... 1 Tim 6:10
l their husbands ... Titus 2:4
Let brotherly *l* ... Heb 13:1
having not seen you *l* ... 1 Pet 1:8
L the brotherhood ... 1 Pet 2:17
for "*l* will cover a ... 1 Pet 4:8
with a kiss of *l* ... 1 Pet 5:14
brotherly kindness *l* ... 2 Pet 1:7
loves the world, the *l* ... 1 John 2:15
we *l* the brethren ... 1 John 3:14
By this we know *l* ... 1 John 3:16
him, how does the *l* ... 1 John 3:17
Beloved, let us *l* ... 1 John 4:7
know God, for God is *l* ... 1 John 4:8
In this is *l* ... 1 John 4:10
If we *l* one another ... 1 John 4:12
L has been perfected ... 1 John 4:17
There is no fear in *l* ... 1 John 4:18
l Him because He first ... 1 John 4:19
who loves God must *l* ... 1 John 4:21
For this is the *l* ... 1 John 5:3
and *l* be multiplied to you ... Jude 2
are spots in your *l* feasts ... Jude 12
have left your first *l* ... Rev 2:4
your works, *l*, service ... Rev 2:19
and they did not *l* ... Rev 12:11

LOVE OF CHRIST
separate us from the *l* ... Rom 8:35
For the *l* compels us ... 2 Cor 5:14
l which passes knowledge .. Eph 3:19

LOVE OF GOD
pass by justice and the *l* .. Luke 11:42
you do not have the *l* ... John 5:42
the *l* has been poured ... Rom 5:5
separate us from the *l* ... Rom 8:39
l is perfected in him ... 1 John 2:5
the *l* abide in him ... 1 John 3:17
In this the *l* ... 1 John 4:9
For this is the *l* ... 1 John 5:3
keep yourselves in the *l* ... Jude 21

LOVE ONE ANOTHER
l; as I have loved you ... John 13:34
that you *l* as I have ... John 15:12
anything except to *l* ... Rom 13:8
are taught by God to *l* ... 1 Thess 4:9
l fervently with a pure ... 1 Pet 1:22
that we should *l* ... 1 John 3:11
Beloved, let us *l* ... 1 John 4:7
the beginning: that we *l* ... 2 John 5

LOVE THE LORD YOUR GOD
You shall *l* with all your ... Deut 6:5
to *l* with all your heart ... Deut 30:6
l, to walk in all His ways ... Josh 22:5
"You shall *l* with ... Matt 22:37
l with all your heart ... Mark 12:30
l with all your heart ... Luke 10:27

LOVE YOUR ENEMIES
in that you *l* ... 2 Sam 19:6
But I say to you, *l* ... Matt 5:44
L, do good to those ... Luke 6:27

LOVE YOUR NEIGHBOR
you shall *l* as yourself ... Lev 19:18
l and hate your enemy ... Matt 5:43
'You shall *l* as yourself ... Matt 19:19
l as yourself ... Gal 5:14
"You shall *l* as yourself ... James 2:8

LOVED
Because the LORD has *l* ... 1 Kin 10:9
L one and friend You ... Ps 88:18
Yet Jacob I have *l* ... Mal 1:2
forgiven, for she *l* ... Luke 7:47
so *l* the world that ... John 3:16
"See how He *l* ... John 11:36
whom Jesus *l* ... John 13:23
"As the Father *l* ... John 15:9
l them as You have ... John 17:23
"Jacob I have *l* ... Rom 9:13
the Son of God, who *l* ... Gal 2:20
l the church and gave ... Eph 5:25
l righteousness ... Heb 1:9
God, but that He *l* ... 1 John 4:10
Beloved, if God so *l* ... 1 John 4:11
To Him who *l* us and ... Rev 1:5

LOVELY
l are your tents, O Jacob ... Num 24:5
of David had a *l* sister ... 2 Sam 13:1
The young woman was *l* ... Esth 2:7
l is Your tabernacle ... Ps 84:1

l woman who lacks ...... Prov 11:22
I am dark, but *l* .... Song 1:5
he is altogether *l* .... Song 5:16
whatever things are *l* .... Phil 4:8

LOVER
a *l* of what is good .... Titus 1:8

LOVERS
the harlot with many *l* .... Jer 3:1
your *l* have forgotten you ... Jer 30:14
"I will go after my *l* .... Hos 2:5
Ephraim has hired *l* .... Hos 8:9
who were *l* of money ..... Luke 16:14
For men will be *l* .... 2 Tim 3:2

LOVES
l righteousness .... Ps 33:5
life, and *l* many days .... Ps 34:12
A friend *l* at all .... Prov 17:17
He who *l* father or .... Matt 10:37
l his life will lose .... John 12:25
l Me will be loved .... John 14:21
l a cheerful giver .... 2 Cor 9:7
who *l* his wife *l* .... Eph 5:28
If anyone *l* the world ..... 1 John 2:15
l God must love his ...... 1 John 4:21
l him who is .... 1 John 5:1

LOVESICK
apples, for I am *l* .... Song 2:5
you tell him I am *l* .... Song 5:8

LOVINGKINDNESS
not concealed Your *l* .... Ps 40:10
l is better than life .... Ps 63:3
to declare Your *l* .... Ps 92:2
Who crowns you with *l* ...... Ps 103:4
l I have drawn .... Jer 31:3
You show *l* to thousands .... Jer 32:18
justice, in *l* and mercy ...... Hos 2:19
abundant in *l* .... Jon 4:2

LOVINGKINDNESSES
mercies and Your *l* .... Ps 25:6
where are Your former *l* .... Ps 89:49
the multitude of His *l* .... Is 63:7

LOW
He brings *l* and lifts .... 1 Sam 2:7
both *l* and high .... Ps 49:2
it *l*, He lays it *l* .... Is 26:5
and hill brought *l* .... Luke 3:5

LOWER
made him a little *l* .... Ps 8:5
shall go into the *l* .... Ps 63:9
made him a little *l* .... Heb 2:7

LOWEST
and sets over it the *l* .... Dan 4:17

LOWLINESS
with all *l* and .... Eph 4:2
or conceit, but in *l* .... Phil 2:3

LOWLY
yet He regards the *l* .... Ps 138:6
for I am gentle and *l* .... Matt 11:29
He has regarded the *l* ...... Luke 1:48
and exalted the *l* .... Luke 1:52
in presence am *l* .... 2 Cor 10:1
l body that it may be .... Phil 3:21
l brother glory .... James 1:9

LOYAL
be *l* to the LORD our God .. 1 Kin 8:61
truth and with a *l* heart .... 2 Kin 20:3
with a *l* heart they .... 1 Chr 29:9
faithfully and with a *l* ..... 2 Chr 19:9
or else he will be *l* .... Matt 6:24

LUCIFER
Name applied to Satan, Is 14:12

LUD
See LYDIA
A people descended from Shem, 1 Chr 1:17

LUKE
"The beloved physician," Col 4:14
Paul's last companion, 2 Tim 4:11
Author of third Gospel, Luke (title)

LUKEWARM
because you are *l* .... Rev 3:16

LUMP
from the same *l* .... Rom 9:21
you may be a new *l* .... 1 Cor 5:7

LUST
Do not *l* after her .... Prov 6:25
caught by their *l* .... Prov 11:6
looks at a woman to *l* ...... Matt 5:28
not fulfill the *l* .... Gal 5:16
not in passion of *l* .... 1 Thess 4:5
You *l* and do not have ..... James 4:2
the *l* of the flesh .... 1 John 2:16

LUSTS
to fulfill its *l* .... Rom 13:14
l which drown men .... 1 Tim 6:9
also youthful *l* .... 2 Tim 2:22
and worldly *l* .... Titus 2:12
to the former *l* .... 1 Pet 1:14
abstain from fleshly *l* ...... 1 Pet 2:11
to their own ungodly *l* .... Jude 18

LUTE
Awake, *l* and harp .... Ps 57:8
l I will praise You .... Ps 71:22
harp with the *l* .... Ps 81:2
ten strings, on the *l* .... Ps 92:3
Awake, *l* and harp .... Ps 108:2
Praise Him with the *l* .... Ps 150:3

LUXURY
L is not fitting .... Prov 19:10
l are in kings' courts .... Luke 7:25
in pleasure and *l* .... James 5:5
the abundance of her *l* ...... Rev 18:3

LYCAONIA
District of Asia Minor where Paul preached, Acts 14:6, 11

LYCIA
Province of Asia Minor visited by Paul, Acts 21:1, 2; 27:5, 6

LYDDA
Aeneas healed at, Acts 9:32–35

LYDIA
Woman of Thyatira; Paul's first European convert, Acts 16:14, 15, 40
——— District of Asia Minor containing Ephesus, Smyrna, Thyatira, and Sardis, Rev 1:11

LYING
has put a *l* spirit .... 1 Kin 22:23
I hate and abhor *l* .... Ps 119:163
proud look, a *l* tongue ..... Prov 6:17
L lips are an .... Prov 12:22
righteous man hates *l* ...... Prov 13:5
not trust in these *l* .... Jer 7:4
a paralytic *l* on a bed .... Matt 9:2
in swaddling cloths, *l* .... Luke 2:12
the Babe *l* in a manger .... Luke 2:16
cloths *l* by themselves .... Luke 24:12
saw the linen cloths *l* ...... John 20:5
putting away *l* .... Eph 4:25
signs, and *l* wonders ..... 2 Thess 2:9

LYRE
the horn, flute, harp, *l* ...... Dan 3:15

LYSIAS, CLAUDIUS
See CLAUDIUS LYSIAS

LYSTRA
Paul visits; is worshiped by people of and stoned by Jews, Acts 14:6–20
Home of Timothy, Acts 16:1, 2

MAACAH (or Maachah)
Small Syrian kingdom near Mt. Hermon, Deut 3:14
Not possessed by Israel, Josh 13:13
——— David's wife; mother of Absalom, 2 Sam 3:3
——— Wife of Rehoboam; mother of King Abijah, 2 Chr 11:18–21
Makes idol; is deposed as queen mother, 1 Kin 15:13

MACEDONIA
Paul preaches in, Acts 16:9—17:14
Paul's troubles in, 2 Cor 7:5
Churches of, generous, Rom 15:26; 2 Cor 8:1–5

MACHIR
Manasseh's only son, Gen 50:23
Founder of the family of Machirites, Num 26:29
Conqueror of Gilead, Num 32:39, 40

MACHPELAH
Field containing a cave; bought by Abraham, Gen 23:9–18
Sarah and Abraham buried here, Gen 23:19; 25:9, 10
Isaac, Rebekah, Leah, and Jacob buried here, Gen 49:29–31

MAD
has a demon and is *m* .... John 10:20
he said, "I am not *m* ...... Acts 26:25

MADE
m the stars also .... Gen 1:16
everything that He had *m* ... Gen 1:31
wife the LORD God *m* .... Gen 3:21
God *m* a wind to pass over ... Gen 8:1
'I have *m* Abram rich' ..... Gen 14:23
LORD *m* a covenant with ... Gen 15:18
I have *m* you a father of .... Gen 17:5
he *m* him a tunic of many ... Gen 37:3
Joseph *m* himself known ..... Gen 45:1
they *m* their lives bitter ...... Ex 1:14
m the sea into dry land ...... Ex 14:21
tool, and *m* a molded calf .... Ex 32:4
He also *m* the mercy seat .... Ex 37:6
LORD *m* between Himself .. Lev 26:46
Moses *m* a bronze serpent . Num 21:9
m a covenant .... 1 Sam 20:16
has *m* Solomon king ...... 1 Kin 1:43
he *m* the Most Holy Place .. 2 Chr 3:8
had *m* to praise the LORD, .. 2 Chr 7:6
Have You not *m* a hedge ...... Job 1:10
You have *m* me like clay ... Job 10:9
He has *m* me a byword of ... Job 17:6
For You have *m* him a little .... Ps 8:5
You have *m* him to have ...... Ps 8:6
You *m* Me trust while on ..... Ps 22:9
by which they have *m* You ... Ps 45:8
have *m* summer and winter .. Ps 74:17
you have *m* the LORD......... Ps 91:9
It is He who has *m* us, and .. Ps 100:3
m known His ways to .... Ps 103:7
LORD, who *m* heaven and .. Ps 115:15
the day the LORD has *m* .... Ps 118:24
by wisdom *m* the heavens ... Ps 136:5
and wonderfully *m* .... Ps 139:14
generous soul will be *m* ... Prov 11:25
m everything beautiful ..... Eccl 3:11
A feast is *m* for laughter ... Eccl 10:19
hear long ago how I *m* .... Is 37:26
I have *m* the earth, and ...... Is 45:12
things My hand has *m* .... Is 66:2
He has *m* the earth by His .. Jer 10:12
I have *m* you a watchman .. Ezek 3:17
king *m* a great feast for a .... Dan 5:1
your faith has *m* you well .. Matt 9:22
you have *m* it a den of .... Matt 21:13
m another five talents ..... Matt 25:16
God '*m* them male and .... Mark 10:6
temple *m* with hands ..... Mark 14:58
places shall be *m* straight ... Luke 3:5
she was *m* straight, and ... Luke 13:13
All things were *m* .... John 1:3
the water that was *m* wine .. John 2:9

in temples *m* with hands ... Acts 7:48
he *m* havoc of the church, ... Acts 8:3
are heirs, faith is *m* void ... Rom 4:14
m me free from the law of ... Rom 8:2
confession is *m* unto ... Rom 10:10
Has not God *m* foolish ... 1 Cor 1:20
all shall be *m* alive ... 1 Cor 15:22
m Him who knew no ... 2 Cor 5:21
strength is *m* perfect ... 2 Cor 12:9
Seed were the promises *m* ... Gal 3:16
And you He *m* alive, who ... Eph 2:1
and *m* us sit together in ... Eph 2:6
of God might be *m* ... Eph 3:10
but *m* Himself of no ... Phil 2:7
requests be *m* known to ... Phil 4:6
He has *m* alive together ... Col 2:13
m him a little lower than ... Heb 2:7
are *m* His footstool ... Heb 10:13
but *m* alive by the Spirit ... 1 Pet 3:18
not been *m* perfect in ... 1 John 4:18
has *m* us kings and priests ... Rev 1:6
m them white in the blood ... Rev 7:14
worship Him who *m* ... Rev 14:7
of the earth were *m* drunk ... Rev 17:2

MADNESS
pretended *m* in ... 1 Sam 21:13
wisdom and to know *m* ... Eccl 1:17
m is in their hearts ... Eccl 9:3

MAGDALA
City of Galilee, Matt 15:39

MAGDALENE
See MARY

MAGIC
women who sew *m* ... Ezek 13:18
m brought their books ... Acts 19:19

MAGNIFICENCE
m I cannot endure ... Job 31:23

MAGNIFIED
So let Your name be *m* ... 2 Sam 7:26
"Let the LORD be *m* ... Ps 35:27
The LORD be *m* ... Ps 40:16
for You have *m* Your ... Ps 138:2
The LORD is *m* beyond the ... Mal 1:5
the Lord Jesus was *m* ... Acts 19:17
also Christ will be *m* ... Phil 1:20

MAGNIFIES
"My soul *m* the Lord ... Luke 1:46

MAGNIFY
m the LORD with me ... Ps 34:3
m himself above every ... Dan 11:36

MAGOG
People among Japheth's descendants, Gen 10:2
Associated with Gog, Ezek 38:2
Representatives of final enemies, Rev 20:8

MAHANAIM
Name given by Jacob to a sacred site, Gen 32:2
Becomes Ishbosheth's capital, 2 Sam 2:8–29
David flees to, during Absalom's rebellion, 2 Sam 17:24, 27

MAHER-SHALAL-HASH-BAZ
Symbolic name of Isaiah's second son; prophetic of the fall of Damascus and Samaria, Is 8:1–4

MAHLON
Husband of Ruth; without child, Ruth 1:2–5

MAIDENS
Both young men and *m* ... Ps 148:12
She has sent out her *m* ... Prov 9:3

MAIDSERVANT
"I am Ruth, your *m* ... Ruth 3:9
save the son of Your *m* ... Ps 86:16
"Behold the *m* ... Luke 1:38
lowly state of His *m* ... Luke 1:48

MAIDSERVANTS
m shall lead her as ... Nah 2:7
m I will pour out My ... Acts 2:18

MAIMED
to enter into life *m* ... Mark 9:43
the poor and the *m* ... Luke 14:21

MAINTAIN
and *m* their cause ... 1 Kin 8:45
careful to *m* good works ... Titus 3:8

MAINTAINED
For You have *m* my ... Ps 9:4

MAJESTIC
thunders with His *m* voice ... Job 37:4
which are *m* in pace ... Prov 30:29
But there the *m* LORD will ... Is 33:21

MAJESTY
Honor and *m* are before ... 1 Chr 16:27
the victory and the *m* ... 1 Chr 29:11
with God is awesome *m* ... Job 37:22
of the LORD is full of *m* ... Ps 29:4
He is clothed with *m* ... Ps 93:1
Honor and *m* are before ... Ps 96:6
splendor of Your *m* ... Ps 145:5
LORD and the glory of His *m* ... Is 2:10
in the *m* of the name of the ... Mic 5:4
right hand of the *M* ... Heb 1:3
eyewitnesses of His *m* ... 2 Pet 1:16
wise, be glory and *m* ... Jude 25

MAKE
"Let Us *m* man in Our ... Gen 1:26
desirable to *m* one wise ... Gen 3:6
let us *m* a name for ... Gen 11:4
m you a great nation ... Gen 12:2
m My covenant between ... Gen 17:2
"You shall not *m* ... Ex 20:4
I will *m* of you a great ... Ex 32:10
m your belly swell and ... Num 5:22
LORD *m* His face shine ... Num 6:25
M a fiery serpent, and ... Num 21:8
husband may *m* it void ... Num 30:13
m yourself an ark of ... Deut 10:1
Now *m* us a king to judge ... 1 Sam 8:5
m me a small cake from ... 1 Kin 17:13
m confession to the ... Ezra 10:11
I *m* my bed in the ... Job 17:13
LORD, *m* me dwell in safety ... Ps 4:8
M Your face shine upon ... Ps 31:16
My soul shall *m* its boast in ... Ps 34:2
shall *m* glad the city of God ... Ps 46:4
wings I will *m* my refuge ... Ps 57:1
m His praise glorious ... Ps 66:2
my mouth will I *m* known ... Ps 89:1
M a joyful shout to the ... Ps 100:1
I *m* my bed in hell, behold ... Ps 139:8
M haste, my beloved, and ... Song 8:14
m mention that His name ... Is 12:4
m the crooked places ... Is 45:2
I will *m* an everlasting ... Jer 32:40
writing and *m* known to ... Dan 5:15
m it plain on tablets, that ... Hab 2:2
m me walk on my high ... Hab 3:19
no one shall *m* them ... Zeph 3:13
m you fishers of men ... Matt 4:19
till I *m* Your enemies ... Matt 22:44
let us *m* three tabernacles ... Mark 9:5
there *m* ready for us ... Mark 14:15
M them sit down in ... Luke 9:14
M me like one of your ... Luke 15:19
m haste and come down, ... Luke 19:5
not *m* My Father's house ... John 2:16
the truth shall *m* you free ... John 8:32
m Our home with him ... John 14:23
we then *m* void the law ... Rom 3:31
m no provision for the ... Rom 13:14
m my brother stumble ... 1 Cor 8:13
m the way of escape ... 1 Cor 10:13
God is able to *m* all grace ... 2 Cor 9:8
to *m* known the mystery ... Eph 6:19
Lord *m* you increase ... 1 Thess 3:12
till I *m* Your enemies Your ... Heb 1:13
m you complete in every ... Heb 13:21
diligent to *m* your call ... 2 Pet 1:10
we *m* Him a liar, and ... 1 John 1:10
will *m* your stomach bitter ... Rev 10:9
Behold, I *m* all things new ... Rev 21:5

MAKER
where is God my *M* ... Job 35:10
before the LORD our *M* ... Ps 95:6
the LORD is the *m* of them ... Prov 22:2
man will look to his *M* ... Is 17:7
who strives with his *M* ... Is 45:9
M is your husband ... Is 54:5
has forgotten his *M* ... Hos 8:14
builder and *m* is God ... Heb 11:10

MAKES
He *m* nations great, and ... Job 12:23
He *m* my feet like the feet ... Ps 18:33
He *m* me to lie down in ... Ps 23:2
He *m* wars cease to the end ... Ps 46:9
Who *m* His angels spirits, ... Ps 104:4
son *m* a glad father, ... Prov 10:1
Hope deferred *m* the ... Prov 13:12
he *m* even his enemies to ... Prov 16:7
He *m* lightnings for the ... Jer 51:16
for He *m* His sun rise on ... Matt 5:45
m both the deaf to hear ... Mark 7:37
He *m* intercession ... Rom 8:27
m himself an enemy of ... James 4:4

MAKING
is sure, *m* wise the simple ... Ps 19:7
m the word of God of no ... Mark 7:13
m mention of you in my ... Eph 1:16
m melody in your heart to ... Eph 5:19

MAKKEDAH
Canaanite town assigned to Judah, Josh 15:20, 41

MALACHI
Prophet and writer, Mal 1:1

MALCHISHUA
Son of King Saul, 1 Sam 14:49
Killed at Gilboa, 1 Sam 31:2

MALCHUS
Servant of the high priest, John 18:10

MALE
He created them *m* and ... Gen 5:2
into the ark to Noah, *m* ... Gen 7:9
every *m* child in your ... Gen 17:12
who has borne a *m* or a ... Lev 12:7
lie with a *m* as with a ... Lev 18:22
utterly destroy every *m* ... Judg 21:11
came, she delivered a *m* ... Is 66:7
beginning 'made them *m* ... Matt 19:4
is neither *m* nor female ... Gal 3:28
gave birth to the *m* Child ... Rev 12:13

MALICE
in *m* be babes ... 1 Cor 14:20
away from you, with all *m* ... Eph 4:31
wrath, *m*, blasphemy, ... Col 3:8
pleasures, living in *m* ... Titus 3:3
laying aside all *m* ... 1 Pet 2:1

MALICIOUSNESS
covetousness, *m* ... Rom 1:29

MALIGN
m a servant to his ... Prov 30:10

MALTA
Site of Paul's shipwreck, Acts 28:1–8

MAMMON
cannot serve God and *m* ... Matt 6:24
by unrighteous *m* ... Luke 16:9

MAMRE
Town or district near Hebron, Gen 23:19
Abram dwells by the oaks of, Gen 13:18

MAN
See NEW MAN; OLD MAN; RIGHTEOUS MAN; SON OF MAN; WISE MAN

"Let Us make *m* . . . . Gen 1:26
she was taken out of *M* . . . . . Gen 2:23
Therefore a *m* shall leave . . . Gen 2:24
were both naked, the *m* . . . . . Gen 2:25
I will destroy *m* whom I . . . . . Gen 6:7
M wrestled with him . . . . . . Gen 32:24
God is not a *m*, that He . . . Num 23:19
but *m* lives by every word . . . Deut 8:3
No *m* shall be able to . . . . . Deut 11:25
m looks at the outward . . . 1 Sam 16:7
"You are the *m* . . . . 2 Sam 12:7
and prove yourself a *m* . . . . . 1 Kin 2:2
"What is *m* . . . . Job 7:17
For an empty-headed *m* . . . . Job 11:12
"Are you the first *m* . . . . Job 15:7
Blessed is the *m* who . . . . Ps 1:1
m that You are mindful . . . . Ps 8:4
The steps of a good *m* are . . . Ps 37:23
Blessed is that *m* who . . . . . . Ps 40:4
What can *m* do to me . . . . Ps 118:6
Happy is the *m* who finds . . Prov 3:13
rebuke a wise *m*, and he . . . . Prov 9:8
A good *m* obtains favor . . . . Prov 12:2
that seems right to a *m* . . . Prov 16:25
The spirit of a *m* is the . . . . Prov 20:27
Let another *m* praise you, . . Prov 27:2
shall take hold of one *m*, ... Is 4:1
Because I am a *m* of unclean . . . Is 6:5
marred more than any *m* . . . . . Is 52:14
M of sorrows and . . . . Is 53:3
mighty *m* glory in his . . . . Jer 9:23
Blessed is the *m* who trusts . . Jer 17:7
Son of *m*, can these . . . . Ezek 37:3
He has shown you, O *m*, ... Mic 6:8
Will a *m* rob God . . . . Mal 3:8
M shall not live by bread . . . . Matt 4:4
A good *m* out of the . . . . Matt 12:35
the mouth defiles a *m* . . . . . Matt 15:11
For this reason a *m* shall . . . Matt 19:5
coming of the Son of *M* . . . Matt 24:27
first binds the strong *m* . . . Mark 3:27
within and defile a *m* . . . . . Mark 7:23
what will it profit a *m* . . . . . Mark 8:36
m had two sons . . . . Luke 15:11
a certain rich *m* . . . . Luke 16:19
a *m* named Zacchaeus . . . . . Luke 19:2
can a *m* be born when he . . . John 3:4
blind *m* with the clay . . . . John 9:6
m should die for the . . . . . . John 11:50
"Behold the *M* . . . . John 19:5
name, has made this *m* . . . . . Acts 3:16
a *m* full of faith and the . . . . . Acts 6:5
you are inexcusable, O *m*, . . . Rom 2:1
blessed is the *m* to whom . . . . Rom 4:8
m is not from woman . . . . . 1 Cor 11:8
I became a *m*, I put . . . . . . 1 Cor 13:11
since by *m* came death . . . . 1 Cor 15:21
though our outward *m* . . . 2 Cor 4:16
for whatever a *m* sows, that . . Gal 6:7
in Himself one new *m* . . . . . . Eph 2:15
that the *m* of God may . . . . 2 Tim 3:17
m can tame the tongue . . . . James 3:8
a righteous *m* avails . . . . . James 5:16
is the number of a *m* . . . . . . Rev 13:18

MAN OF GOD

Moses the *m* blessed . . . . Deut 33:1
"A *m* came to me, and . . . . . Judg 13:6
a *m* came to Eli and said . . 1 Sam 2:27
there is in this city a *m* . . . . 1 Sam 9:6
to Shemaiah the *m* . . . . 1 Kin 12:22
a *m* went from Judah to . . . 1 Kin 13:1
m who was disobedient . . 1 Kin 13:26
I to do with you, O *m* . . . . 1 Kin 17:18
a *m* came and spoke to . . . 1 Kin 20:28
"*M*, the king has said . . . . 2 Kin 1:9
this a holy *m* . . . . 2 Kin 4:9
M, there is death . . . . 2 Kin 4:40
m sent to the king . . . . 2 Kin 6:9
he died, just as the *m* . . . . . . 2 Kin 7:17
the *m* was angry with . . . . 2 Kin 13:19
"It is the tomb of the *m* . . 2 Kin 23:17
for so David the *m* . . . . 2 Chr 8:14
But a *m* came to him . . . . . . 2 Chr 25:7
Law of Moses the *m* . . . . Ezra 3:2
command of David the *m* . . Neh 12:24
son of Igdaliah, a *m* . . . . Jer 35:4
But you, O *m*, flee these . . . 1 Tim 6:11
m may be complete . . . . 2 Tim 3:17

MAN'S

curse the ground for *m* . . . . . Gen 8:21
every *m* hand against . . . . . Gen 16:12
We are all one *m* sons . . . . . Gen 42:11
each *m* money was in the . . Gen 43:21
The rich *m* wealth is his . . Prov 10:15
When a *m* ways please . . . . Prov 16:7
A *m* heart plans his way . . . Prov 16:9
The rich *m* wealth is his . . Prov 18:11
A *m* gift makes room for . . Prov 18:16
m steps are of the LORD . . . Prov 20:24
A *m* pride will bring him . . Prov 29:23
a righteous *m* reward . . . . Matt 10:41
enter a strong *m* house . . . . Mark 3:27
from the rich *m* table . . . . . Luke 16:21
one *m* offense many died . . Rom 5:15
on another *m* foundation . . Rom 15:20

MANASSEH

Joseph's firstborn son, Gen 41:50, 51
Adopted by Jacob, Gen 48:5, 6
Loses his birthright to Ephraim, Gen 48:13–20
——— Tribe of:
Numbered, Num 1:34, 35
Half-tribe of, settle east of Jordan, Num 32:33–42; Deut 3:12–15
Help Joshua against Canaanites, Josh 1:12–18
Land assigned to western half-tribe, Josh 17:1–13
Eastern half-tribe builds altar, Josh 22:9–34
Some of, help David, 1 Chr 12:19–31
——— Wicked king of Judah; son of Hezekiah, 2 Kin 21:1–18; 2 Chr 33:1–9
Captured and taken to Babylon; repents and is restored, 2 Chr 33:10–13
Removes idols and altars, 2 Chr 33:14–20

MANGER

Will he bed by your *m* . . . . . . Job 39:9
and laid Him in a *m* . . . . Luke 2:7
the Babe lying in a *m* . . . . . . Luke 2:16

MANIFEST

m Myself to him . . . . John 14:21
is it that You will *m* . . . . . . John 14:22
be known of God is *m* in . . . . Rom 1:19
but now made *m*, and . . . . . Rom 16:26
that I may make it *m*, as I . . . . Col 4:4
was *m* in these last times . . 1 Pet 1:20

MANIFESTATION

But the *m* of the . . . . 1 Cor 12:7
deceitfully, but by *m* . . . . 2 Cor 4:2

MANIFESTED

Galilee, and *m* His glory . . . John 2:11
"I have *m* Your name . . . . . . John 17:6
God was *m* in the flesh . . . . 1 Tim 3:16
the life was *m* . . . . 1 John 1:2
the Son of God was *m* . . . . . 1 John 3:8
the love of God was *m* . . . . 1 John 4:9

MANIFOLD

m are Your works . . . . Ps 104:24
the *m* wisdom of God . . . . . . Eph 3:10
good stewards of the *m* . . . . 1 Pet 4:10

MANKIND

called them *M* in the day . . . . Gen 5:2
of *m* may seek the LORD . . Acts 15:17
to kill a third of *m* . . . . Rev 9:15
But the rest of *m*, who . . . . . . Rev 9:20

MANNA

of Israel ate *m* . . . . Ex 16:35
the *m* was like coriander . . . Num 11:7
the *m* ceased on the day . . . . Josh 5:12
Your *m* from their mouth . . . . Neh 9:20
had rained down *m* . . . . Ps 78:24
Our fathers ate the *m* . . . . . . John 6:31
golden pot that had the *m* . . . . Heb 9:4
of the hidden *m* . . . . Rev 2:17

MANNER

in all *m* of workmanship, ... Ex 31:3
Is this the *m* of man . . . . . . 2 Sam 7:19
In this *m*, therefore, pray . . . . Matt 6:9
m of life from my youth, . . . Acts 26:4
same *m* He also took . . . . . 1 Cor 11:25
in an unworthy *m* . . . . 1 Cor 11:27
sorrowed in a godly *m* . . . . 2 Cor 7:11
m of life, purpose, faith, . . . 2 Tim 3:10
as is the *m* of some . . . . Heb 10:25
what *m* of persons . . . . 2 Pet 3:11
Behold what *m* of love . . . . . 1 John 3:1
m worthy of God . . . . 3 John 6

MANOAH

Danite; father of Samson, Judg 13:1–25

MANSIONS

house are many *m* . . . . John 14:2

MANTLE

Then he took the *m* . . . . 2 Kin 2:14

MAON

Village in Judah, Josh 15:55
David stays at, 1 Sam 23:24, 25
Nabal's house here, 1 Sam 25:2

MARA

Name chosen by Naomi, Ruth 1:20

MARAH

First Israelite camp after passing through the Red Sea, Num 33:8, 9

MARCHED

people, when You *m* . . . . Ps 68:7

MARK (John)

Son of Mary of Jerusalem; travels with Barnabas and Saul, Acts 12:12, 25
Leaves Paul at Perga, Acts 13:13
Barnabas and Paul separate because of him, Acts 15:37–40
Later approved by Paul, Col 4:10; 2 Tim 4:11
Companion of Peter, 1 Pet 5:13
Author of the second Gospel, Mark 1:1

MARK

And the LORD set a *m* . . . . Gen 4:15
M the blameless man . . . . Ps 37:37
slave, to receive a *m* . . . . . . Rev 13:16
whoever receives the *m* . . . . Rev 14:11

MARKET

is sold in the meat *m* . . . . . 1 Cor 10:25

MARRED

so His visage was *m* . . . . Is 52:14
he made of clay was *m* . . . . Jer 18:4

MARRIAGE

join in *m* with the people . . . Ezra 9:14
were not given in *m* . . . . Ps 78:63
nor are given in *m* . . . . Matt 22:30
they were given in *m* . . . . . Luke 17:27
her in *m* does well . . . . 1 Cor 7:38
M is honorable among . . . . . . Heb 13:4
the *m* of the Lamb has . . . . . . Rev 19:7

MARRIED

and *m* Pharaoh's daughter . . . 1 Kin 3:1
woman when she is *m* . . . . Prov 30:23
"for I am *m* to you . . . . Jer 3:14
first died after he had *m* . . Matt 22:25
said, 'I have *m* a wife . . . . . Luke 14:20
m wives, they were . . . . Luke 17:27
But he who is *m* . . . . 1 Cor 7:33
But she who is *m* . . . . 1 Cor 7:34

MARRIES

If a man *m* a woman and . . Lev 20:14

by the hand of a *m* .... Gal 3:19
is one God and one *M* ...... 1 Tim 2:5
as He is also *M* .... Heb 8:6
to Jesus the *M* of the .... Heb 12:24

MEDICINE
does good, like *m* .... Prov 17:22

MEDICINES
you will use many *m* .... Jer 46:11

MEDITATE
Isaac went out to *m* .... Gen 24:63
but you shall *m* .... Josh 1:8
M within your heart on .... Ps 4:4
I *m* within my heart .... Ps 77:6
I will *m* on Your .... Ps 119:15
Your heart will *m* .... Is 33:18
m beforehand on what ... Luke 21:14
m on these things .... Phil 4:8

MEDITATES
in His law he *m* .... Ps 1:2

MEDITATION
O LORD, consider my *m* .... Ps 5:1
of my mouth and the *m* ..... Ps 19:14
the *m* of my heart shall .... Ps 49:3
m be sweet to Him .... Ps 104:34
It is my *m* all the day ...... Ps 119:97

MEDITERRANEAN SEA
Described as:
Sea, Gen 49:13
Great Sea, Josh 1:4; 9:1
Sea of the Philistines, Ex 23:31
Western Sea, Deut 11:24; Joel 2:20; Zech 14:8

MEDIUM
a woman who is a *m* ...... Lev 20:27
a woman who is a *m* ...... 1 Sam 28:7

MEDIUM'S
shall be like a *m* .... Is 29:4

MEDIUMS
"Seek those who are *m* .... Is 8:19

MEEK
But the *m* shall inherit the ... Ps 37:11
with equity for the *m* .... Is 11:4
all you *m* of the earth .... Zeph 2:3
Blessed are the *m* .... Matt 5:5

MEEKNESS
with you by the *m* .... 2 Cor 10:1
are done in the *m* .... James 3:13
that is in you, with *m* ...... 1 Pet 3:15

MEET
from the tent door to *m* ...... Gen 18:2
For You *m* him with the .... Ps 21:3
mercies come speedily to *m* .. Ps 79:8
prepare to *m* your God .... Amos 4:12
out to *m* the bridegroom ... Matt 25:1
go out to *m* him .... Matt 25:6
a man will *m* you .... Luke 22:10
m the Lord in the air .... 1 Thess 4:17

MEETING
In the tabernacle of *m* ...... Ex 27:21
burned up all the *m* .... Ps 74:8

MEGIDDO
City of Canaan; scene of battles, Judg 5:19–21; 2 Kin 23:29, 30
Fortified by Solomon, 1 Kin 9:15
Possible site of Armageddon, Rev 16:16

MELCHIZEDEK
Priest and king of Salem, Gen 14:18–20
Type of Christ's eternal priesthood, Heb 7:1–22

MELODY
make sweet *m* .... Is 23:16
singing and making *m* ...... Eph 5:19

MELT
You make his beauty *m* ..... Ps 39:11
The mountains *m* like wax ... Ps 97:5
man's heart will *m* .... Is 13:7
mountains will *m* under ...... Mic 1:4
the elements will *m* .... 2 Pet 3:10

MEMBER
body is not one *m* .... 1 Cor 12:14
if they were all one *m* ..... 1 Cor 12:19
if one *m* suffers, all the ... 1 Cor 12:26
tongue is a little *m* .... James 3:5

MEMBERS
you that one of your *m* ..... Matt 5:29
do not present your *m* ..... Rom 6:13
have many *m* in one body .. Rom 12:4
that your bodies are *m* .... 1 Cor 6:15
there are many *m* .... 1 Cor 12:20
neighbor, for we are *m* ..... Eph 4:25
m that it defiles the .... James 3:6

MEMORIAL
and this is My *m* .... Ex 3:15
day shall be to you a *m* ..... Ex 12:14
as a *m* between your eyes, ... Ex 13:9
also be told as a *m* .... Matt 26:13
be told of as a *m* .... Mark 14:9
come up for a *m* before .... Acts 10:4

MEMORY
The *m* of him perishes ..... Job 18:17
He may cut off the *m* .... Ps 109:15
The *m* of the righteous ..... Prov 10:7

MEMPHIS (or Noph)
Ancient capital of Egypt, Hos 9:6
Prophesied against by Isaiah, Is 19:13
Jews flee to, Jer 44:1
Denounced by the prophets, Jer 46:19

MEN
See WISE MEN
m began to call on the ...... Gen 4:26
saw the daughters of *m* ...... Gen 6:2
But the *m* of Sodom were .. Gen 13:13
Hebrew *m* were fighting ..... Ex 2:13
Send *m* to spy out the ..... Num 13:2
So Gideon took ten *m* ...... Judg 6:27
with the LORD and *m* ..... 1 Sam 2:26
reproach of *m*, and despised .. Ps 22:6
All *m* shall fear, and shall .... Ps 64:9
received gifts among *m* ..... Ps 68:18
you shall die like *m* .... Ps 82:7
with wise *m* will be wise .. Prov 13:20
are the crown of old *m* ..... Prov 17:6
not be envious of evil *m* .... Prov 24:1
m should fear before Him .. Eccl 3:14
the Egyptians are *m* .... Is 31:3
despised and rejected by *m* ... Is 53:3
I see four *m* loose .... Dan 3:25
make you fishers of *m* ..... Matt 4:19
light so shine before *m* ..... Matt 5:16
forgive *m* their trespasses .. Matt 6:14
confesses Me before *m* .... Matt 10:32
will not be forgiven *m* .... Matt 12:31
every idle word *m* may ... Matt 12:36
was carried by four *m* ...... Mark 2:3
Who do *m* say that I am ... Mark 8:27
With *m* it is impossible ... Mark 10:27
goodwill toward *m* .... Luke 2:14
when all *m* speak well of .. Luke 6:26
m always ought to pray .... Luke 18:1
from heaven or from *m* .... Luke 20:4
the life was the light of *m* ... John 1:4
loved the praise of *m* ..... John 12:43
old *m* shall dream dreams .. Acts 2:17
have not lied to *m* but to .... Acts 5:4
m everywhere to repent ... Acts 17:30
Likewise also the *m* ...... Rom 1:27
in the sight of all *m* .... Rom 12:17
let no one boast in *m* ...... 1 Cor 3:21
all things to all *m* .... 1 Cor 9:22
with the tongues of *m* ..... 1 Cor 13:1
speak to *m* but to God ..... 1 Cor 14:2
the Lord, and not to *m* .... Eph 6:7
to the tradition of *m*, ... Col 2:8
between God and *m* .... 1 Tim 2:5
rejected indeed by *m* .... 1 Pet 2:4
In those days *m* will seek .... Rev 9:6
to scorch *m* with fire .... Rev 16:8

MENAHEM
Cruel king of Israel, 2 Kin 15:14–18

MENSERVANTS
And also on My *m* .... Joel 2:29
And on My *m* and on My ... Acts 2:18

MENTION
I will make *m* of Your ...... Ps 71:16
make *m* that His name is ..... Is 12:4
by You only we make *m* ..... Is 26:13
He has made *m* of My name ...... Is 49:1
You who make *m* of the ...... Is 62:6
will *m* the lovingkindnesses ... Is 63:7
Make *m* to the nations, ... Jer 4:16
m of you always in my ...... Rom 1:9
he was dying, made *m* ...... Heb 11:22

MEPHIBOSHETH
Son of King Saul, 2 Sam 21:8
——— Grandson of King Saul; crippled son of Jonathan, 2 Sam 4:4–6
Sought out and honored by David, 2 Sam 9:1–13
Accused by Ziba, 2 Sam 16:1–4
Later explains himself to David, 2 Sam 19:24–30
Spared by David, 2 Sam 21:7

MERAB
King Saul's eldest daughter, 1 Sam 14:49
Saul promises her to David, but gives her to Adriel, 1 Sam 18:17–19

MERARI
Third son of Levi, Gen 46:11
——— Descendants of, called Merarites:
Duties in the tabernacle, Num 3:35–37
Cities assigned to, Josh 21:7, 34–40
Duties in the temple, 1 Chr 26:10–19
Assist Ezra after Exile, Ezra 8:18, 19

MERCHANDISE
perceives that her *m* ...... Prov 31:18
house a house of *m* .... John 2:16

MERCHANTS
set it in a city of *m* .... Ezek 17:4
have multiplied your *m* ..... Nah 3:16
m were the great men ...... Rev 18:23

MERCIES
for His *m* are great .... 2 Sam 24:14
in Your manifold *m* You .... Neh 9:19
multitude of Your tender *m* ... Ps 51:1
I will sing of the *m* of the ..... Ps 89:1
and His tender *m* .... Ps 145:9
give you the sure *m* .... Acts 13:34
brethren, by the *m* of God ... Rom 12:1
the Father of *m* .... 2 Cor 1:3
beloved, put on tender *m* .... Col 3:12

MERCIFUL
LORD, the LORD God, *m* .... Ex 34:6
your God is a *m* God .... Deut 4:31
With the *m* You will show .... Ps 18:25
He is ever *m* .... Ps 37:26
God be *m* to us and .... Ps 67:1
for He is gracious and *m* .... Joel 2:13
Blessed are the *m* .... Matt 5:7
Therefore be *m*, just as .... Luke 6:36
saying, 'God be *m* .... Luke 18:13
For I will be *m* .... Heb 8:12
compassionate and *m* .... James 5:11

MERCY
See HAVE MERCY; HIS MERCY ENDURES FOREVER
but showing *m* to .... Ex 20:6
You shall put the *m* seat .... Ex 26:34
and abundant in *m* .... Num 14:18
m endures forever .... 1 Chr 16:34
I have trusted in Your *m* ...... Ps 13:5
to Your *m* remember me ...... Ps 25:7
I trust in the *m* .... Ps 52:8

shall send forth His *m* .... Ps 57:3
You, O Lord, belongs *m* ..... Ps 62:12
m ceased forever .... Ps 77:8
M and truth have met .... Ps 85:10
M shall be built .... Ps 89:2
m and truth go before .... Ps 89:14
m is everlasting .... Ps 100:5
I will sing of *m* .... Ps 101:1
For Your *m* is great .... Ps 108:4
is full of Your *m* .... Ps 119:64
the LORD there is *m* .... Ps 130:7
to anger and great in *m* ..... Ps 145:8
Let not *m* and truth .... Prov 3:3
who honors Him has *m* ... Prov 14:31
cruel and have no *m* .... Jer 6:23
Lord our God belong *m* ...... Dan 9:9
For I desire *m* and not .... Hos 6:6
do justly, to love *m* .... Mic 6:8
'I desire *m* and not .... Matt 9:13
And His *m* is on those ..... Luke 1:50
"I will have *m*, ... Rom 9:15
of God who shows *m* ...... Rom 9:16
that He might have *m* ..... Rom 11:32
m has made trustworthy ... 1 Cor 7:25
as we have received *m* ..... 2 Cor 4:1
God, who is rich in *m* .... Eph 2:4
but I obtained *m* .... 1 Tim 1:13
that he may find *m* .... 2 Tim 1:18
to His *m* He saved us .... Titus 3:5
that we may obtain *m* ...... Heb 4:16
judgment is without *m* .... James 2:13
God, looking for the *m* .... Jude 21

MERCY SEAT
make a *m* .... Ex 25:17
put the *m* on top of the ..... Ex 40:20
the veil, before the *m* .... Lev 16:2
incense may cover the *m* .. Lev 16:13
to him from above the *m* ... Num 7:89
and the place of the *m* ... 1 Chr 28:11
glory overshadowing the *m* .. Heb 9:5

MERIB-BAAL
Another name for Mephibosheth, 1 Chr 8:34

MERODACH
Supreme deity of the Babylonians, Jer 50:2
Otherwise called Bel, Is 46:1

MERODACH-BALADAN
Sends ambassadors to Hezekiah, Is 39:1–8
Also called Berodach-Baladan, 2 Kin 20:12

MEROM
Lake on Jordan, Josh 11:5, 7

MEROZ
Town cursed for failing to help the Lord, Judg 5:23

MERRY
m heart makes a .... Prov 15:13
A *m* heart does good ..... Prov 17:22
eat, drink, and be *m* .... Eccl 8:15
eat, drink, and be *m* ...... Luke 12:19
we should make *m* .... Luke 15:32

MESHACH
Babylonian name given to Mishael, Dan 1:7
Advanced to high position, Dan 2:49
Remains faithful in testing, Dan 3:13–30

MESHECH
Son of Japheth, Gen 10:2
His descendants, mentioned in prophecy, Ezek 27:13; 32:26; 38:2, 3

MESOPOTAMIA
Home of Abraham's relatives, Gen 24:4, 10, 15
Called Padan Aram and Syria, Gen 25:20; 31:20, 24
Israel enslaved to, Judg 3:8–10
Jews from, present at Pentecost, Acts 2:9

MESSAGE
He who sends a *m* by the .. Prov 26:6
I have heard a *m* .... Jer 49:14
m was revealed to Daniel ...... Dan 10:1
to it the *m* that I tell you ..... Jon 3:2
For the *m* of the cross ..... 1 Cor 1:18
is the *m* which we have .... 1 John 1:5

MESSENGER
Jezebel sent a *m* to Elijah . 1 Kin 19:2
a *m* came to Job and said, ... Job 1:14
is a faithful *m* .... Prov 25:13
"Behold, I send My *m* .... Mal 3:1
'Behold, I send My *m* ..... Matt 11:10
a *m* of Satan to buffet me .. 2 Cor 12:7

MESSIAH
until *M* the Prince .... Dan 9:25
"We have found the *M* ..... John 1:41

MET
the angels of God *m* him .... Gen 32:1
and truth have *m* together ... Ps 85:10
there *m* Him ten men ..... Luke 17:12
m Him, but Mary was ..... John 11:20
coming in, Cornelius *m* ... Acts 10:25
spirit of divination *m* us ... Acts 16:16
who *m* Abraham returning ... Heb 7:1

METHUSELAH
Oldest man on record, Gen 5:27

MICAH
Prophet, contemporary of Isaiah, Is 1:1; Mic 1:1

MICAIAH (or Michaiah)
Prophet who predicts Ahab's death, 1 Kin 22:8–28
——— Contemporary of Jeremiah, Jer 36:11–13

MICHAEL
Chief prince, Dan 10:13, 21
Disputes with Satan, Jude 9
Fights the dragon, Rev 12:7–9

MICHAL
Daughter of King Saul, 1 Sam 14:49
Loves and marries David, 1 Sam 18:20–28
Saves David from Saul, 1 Sam 19:9–17
Given to Palti, 1 Sam 25:44
David demands her from Abner, 2 Sam 3:13–16
Ridicules David; becomes barren, 2 Sam 6:16–23

MICHMASH
Site of battle with Philistines, 1 Sam 13:5, 11, 16, 23
Scene of Jonathan's victory, 1 Sam 14:1–16

MIDDLE
in the *m* of a wheel .... Ezek 10:10
boat was in the *m* of the .. Mark 6:47
about the *m* of the feast .... John 7:14
broken down the *m* wall .... Eph 2:14

MIDIAN
Son of Abraham by Keturah, Gen 25:1–4
——— Region in the Arabian desert occupied by the Midianites, Gen 25:6; Ex 2:15

MIDIANITES
Descendants of Abraham by Keturah, Gen 25:1, 2
Moses flees to, Ex 2:15
Join Moab in cursing Israel, Num 22:4–7
Intermarriage with incurs God's wrath, Num 25:1–18
Defeated by Israel, Num 31:1–10
Oppress Israel; defeated by Gideon, Judg 6; 7

MIDST
God is in the *m* .... Ps 46:5
that I am in the *m* .... Joel 2:27
I am there in the *m* .... Matt 18:20

MIGDOL
Israelite encampment, Ex 14:2
Place Jews flee to in Egypt, Jer 44:1

MIGHT
'My power and the *m* ...... Deut 8:17
hand is power and *m* ..... 1 Chr 29:12
shall speak of the *m* .... Ps 145:6
to do, do it with your *m* .... Eccl 9:10
the Spirit of counsel and *m* ... Is 11:2
the greatness of His *m* .... Is 40:26
man glory in his *m* .... Jer 9:23
their *m* has failed .... Jer 51:30
'Not by *m* nor by .... Zech 4:6
and power and *m* .... Eph 1:21
in the power of His *m* ...... Eph 6:10
greater in power and *m* .... 2 Pet 2:11
honor and power and *m* .... Rev 7:12

MIGHTIER
The LORD on high is *m* .... Ps 93:4
coming after me is *m* ...... Matt 3:11

MIGHTILY
to shake the earth *m* .... Is 2:19
sackcloth, and cry *m* to God .. Jon 3:8
word of the Lord grew *m* .. Acts 19:20
which works in me *m* .... Col 1:29
cried *m* with a loud voice, ... Rev 18:2

MIGHTY
Those were the *m* men who .. Gen 6:4
He was a *m* hunter .... Gen 10:9
and grew exceedingly *m* ...... Ex 1:7
son's son the *m* things I ...... Ex 10:2
for they are too *m* .... Num 22:6
with His *m* power .... Deut 4:37
How the *m* have fallen .... 2 Sam 1:19
is wise in heart and *m* .... Job 9:4
The LORD *m* in battle .... Ps 24:8
m man is not delivered by ... Ps 33:16
The *M* One, God the LORD, ... Ps 50:1
the *m* acts of the LORD ...... Ps 106:2
Praise Him for His *m* acts ... Ps 150:2
their Redeemer is *m* ...... Prov 23:11
Woe to men *m* at .... Is 5:22
M God, Everlasting Father, ... Is 9:6
Redeemer, the *M* One of ..... Is 49:26
in righteousness, *m* to save ... Is 63:1
great in counsel and *m* ...... Jer 32:19
righteousness like a *m* ..... Amos 5:24
m men are made red .... Nah 2:3
For if the *m* works .... Matt 11:21
not do many *m* works .... Matt 13:58
m has done great .... Luke 1:49
He has put down the *m* .... Luke 1:52
as of a rushing *m* wind ...... Acts 2:2
the flesh, not many *m* ..... 1 Cor 1:26
m in God for pulling .... 2 Cor 10:4
the working of His *m* .... Eph 1:19
from heaven with His *m* .. 2 Thess 1:7
city Babylon, that *m* city ... Rev 18:10

MILCOM
Ammonite god worshiped by Solomon, 1 Kin 11:5
Altar of, destroyed by Josiah, 2 Kin 23:12, 13

MILETUS
Paul meets Ephesian elders here, Acts 20:15–38
Paul leaves Trophimus here, 2 Tim 4:20

MILK
to a land flowing with *m* ...... Ex 3:8
for water, she gave *m* ...... Judg 5:25
not pour me out like *m* ..... Job 10:10
honey and *m* are under .... Song 4:11

come, buy wine and *m* . . . . Is 55:1
and whiter than *m* . . . . Lam 4:7
shall flow with *m* . . . . Joel 3:18
have come to need *m* . . . . Heb 5:12
m is unskilled in the . . . . Heb 5:13
desire the pure *m* . . . . 1 Pet 2:2

MILK AND HONEY
to a land flowing with *m* . . . . . . Ex 3:8
It truly flows with *m* . . . . . . Num 13:27
land flowing with *m* . . . . Deut 6:3
land flowing with *m* . . . . Josh 5:6
land flowing with *m* . . . . Jer 11:5
m, the glory of all . . . . Ezek 20:6

MILL
be grinding at the *m* . . . . . . Matt 24:41

MILLO
Fort at Jerusalem, 2 Sam 5:9
Prepared by Solomon, 1 Kin 9:15
Strengthened by Hezekiah, 2 Chr 32:5
Scene of Joash's death, 2 Kin 12:20, 21

MILLSTONE
m were hung around his . . . Matt 18:6
a stone like a great *m* . . . . . . Rev 18:21

MIND
the people had a *m* to work . . Neh 4:6
put wisdom in the *m* . . . . . . Job 38:36
perfect peace, whose *m* . . . . Is 26:3
and with all your *m* . . . . . . Matt 22:37
and in his right *m* . . . . Mark 5:15
nor have an anxious *m* . . . Luke 12:29
m I myself serve the . . . . Rom 7:25
Because the carnal *m* is . . . . . Rom 8:7
the *m* of the Spirit is . . . . Rom 8:27
who has known the *m* . . . . Rom 11:34
renewing of your *m* . . . . Rom 12:2
Be of the same *m* . . . . Rom 12:16
convinced in his own *m* . . . . Rom 14:5
have the *m* of Christ . . . . . . 1 Cor 2:16
you are out of your *m* . . . . 1 Cor 14:23
Let this *m* be in you . . . . Phil 2:5
Set your *m* on things above, . . Col 3:2
to *m* your own . . . . 1 Thess 4:11
love and of a sound *m* . . . . . . 2 Tim 1:7
put My laws in their *m* . . . . . Heb 8:10
the loins of your *m* . . . . 1 Pet 1:13

MINDFUL
is man that You are *m* . . . . Ps 8:4
The LORD has been *m* . . . . . . Ps 115:12
for you are not *m* . . . . Matt 16:23
is man that You are *m* . . . . Heb 2:6

MINDS
people change their *m* . . . . . . Ex 13:17
put My law in their *m* . . . . . . Jer 31:33
I stir up your pure *m* . . . . 2 Pet 3:1
He who searches the *m* . . . . . Rev 2:23

MINISTER
to make you a *m* . . . . Acts 26:16
for he is God's *m* . . . . Rom 13:4
you will be a good *m* . . . . 1 Tim 4:6
spirits sent forth to *m* for . . . Heb 1:14
a *M* of the sanctuary . . . . Heb 8:2

MINISTERED
But the child *m* . . . . 1 Sam 2:11
a thousand thousands *m* . . . . Dan 7:10
angels came and *m* to . . . . Matt 4:11
As they *m* to the Lord . . . . . . Acts 13:2

MINISTERS
angels spirits, His *m* . . . . Ps 104:4
for they are God's *m* . . . . Rom 13:6
commend ourselves as *m* . . . 2 Cor 6:4
Are they *m* of Christ . . . . . 2 Cor 11:23
If anyone *m* . . . . 1 Pet 4:11

MINISTRIES
are differences of *m* . . . . 1 Cor 12:5

MINISTRY
I magnify my *m* . . . . Rom 11:13
But if the *m* of death . . . . 2 Cor 3:7
since we have this *m* . . . . 2 Cor 4:1
and has given us the *m* . . . . 2 Cor 5:18
for the work of *m* . . . . Eph 4:12
m which you have . . . . Col 4:17
fulfill your *m* . . . . 2 Tim 4:5
a more excellent *m* . . . . Heb 8:6

MINT
For you pay tithe of *m* . . . . Matt 23:23

MIRACLE
saying, 'Show a *m* . . . . Ex 7:9
no one who works a *m* . . . . Mark 9:39
see some *m* done by Him . . Luke 23:8
that a notable *m* . . . . Acts 4:16

MIRACLES
God worked unusual *m* . . . Acts 19:11
the working of *m* . . . . 1 Cor 12:10
Are all workers of *m* . . . . . 1 Cor 12:29
with various *m* . . . . Heb 2:4

MIRIAM
Sister of Aaron and Moses, Num 26:59
Chosen by God; called a prophetess, Ex 15:20
Punished for rebellion, Num 12:1–16
Buried at Kadesh, Num 20:1

MIRTH
I will test you with *m* . . . . Eccl 2:1
is in the house of *m* . . . . Eccl 7:4
joy is darkened, the *m* . . . . Is 24:11

MISER
eat the bread of a *m* . . . . Prov 23:6

MISERIES
m that are coming . . . . James 5:1

MISERY
would forget your *m* . . . . Job 11:16
and remember his *m* . . . . Prov 31:7

MISTREATED
But the Egyptians *m* . . . . Deut 26:6
those who are *m* . . . . Heb 13:3

MISTREATS
m his father and . . . . Prov 19:26

MITES
widow putting in two *m* . . . Luke 21:2

MITYLENE
Visited by Paul, Acts 20:13–15

MIZPAH
Site of covenant between Jacob and Laban, Gen 31:44–53
—— Town of Benjamin; outraged Israelites gather here, Josh 18:21, 26; Judg 20:1, 3
Samuel gathers Israel, 1 Sam 7:5–16; 10:17–25
Residence of Gedaliah, 2 Kin 25:23, 25

MOAB
Son of Lot, Gen 19:33–37
—— Country of the Moabites, Deut 1:5

MOABITES
Descendants of Lot, Gen 19:36, 37
Join Midian in cursing Israel, Num 22:4
Excluded from Israel, Deut 23:3–6
Kindred of Ruth, Ruth 1:4
Subdued by Israel, 1 Sam 14:47; 2 Sam 8:2; 2 Kin 3:4–27
Women of, lead Solomon astray, 1 Kin 11:1–8
Prophecies concerning, Is 11:14; 15:1–9; Jer 48:1–47; Amos 2:1–3

MOAN
m sadly like doves . . . . Is 59:11

MOCK
I will *m* when your . . . . Prov 1:26
Fools *m* at sin . . . . Prov 14:9
to the Gentiles to *m* . . . . Matt 20:19

MOCKED
at noon, that Elijah *m* . . . . 1 Kin 18:27
"I am one *m* by his . . . . Job 12:4
knee before Him and *m* . . . Matt 27:29
deceived, God is not *m* . . . . Gal 6:7

MOCKER
Wine is a *m* . . . . Prov 20:1

MOCKERS
that there would be *m* . . . . Jude 18

MOCKINGS
others had trial of *m* . . . . . . Heb 11:36

MOCKS
He who *m* the poor . . . . Prov 17:5

MODERATION
with propriety and *m* . . . . 1 Tim 2:9

MOLECH
God of the Ammonites; worshiped by Solomon, 1 Kin 11:7
Human sacrifice made to, Lev 18:21; 2 Kin 23:10

MOMENT
consume them in a *m* . . . . . Num 16:21
In a *m* they die . . . . Job 34:20
For His anger is but for a *m* . . Ps 30:5
face from you for a *m* . . . . Is 54:8
of the world in a *m* of time . . Luke 4:5
m, in the twinkling . . . . 1 Cor 15:52
which is but for a *m* . . . . 2 Cor 4:17

MONEY
man's *m* to his sack . . . . Gen 42:25
does not put out his *m* . . . . Ps 15:5
m answers every . . . . Eccl 10:19
be redeemed without *m* . . . . Is 52:3
and you who have no *m* . . . . . . Is 55:1
of the *m* changers . . . . Matt 21:12
and hid his lord's *m* . . . . . . Matt 25:18
put *m* into the treasury . . . Mark 12:41
promised to give him *m* . . Mark 14:11
Carry neither *m* . . . . Luke 10:4
I sent you without *m* . . . . . Luke 22:35
the *m* changers doing . . . . . . John 2:14
a thief, and had the *m* . . . . . John 12:6
be purchased with *m* . . . . Acts 8:20
not greedy for *m* . . . . 1 Tim 3:3
m is a root of all . . . . 1 Tim 6:10
not greedy for *m* . . . . Titus 1:7

MONSTER
me up like a *m* . . . . Jer 51:34
of Egypt, O great *m* . . . . Ezek 29:3

MONTH
ark rested in the seventh *m* . . Gen 8:4
first *m* of the year to you . . . Ex 12:2
will bear fruit every *m* . . . . . Ezek 47:12
latter rain in the first *m* . . . . . Joel 2:23
in the sixth *m* the angel . . . . Luke 1:26
this is now the sixth *m* . . . . . Luke 1:36
yielding its fruit every *m* . . . . Rev 22:2

MONTHS
child, she hid him three *m* . . . . Ex 2:2
with her about three *m* . . . . . Luke 1:56
up three years and six *m* . . . Luke 4:25
You observe days and *m* . . . . . . Gal 4:10
to torment them for five *m* . . . Rev 9:5
continue for forty-two *m* . . . . Rev 13:5

MOON
this time, the sun, the *m* . . . Gen 37:9
and the *m* stopped, till . . . . Josh 10:13
of Your fingers, the *m* . . . . Ps 8:3
until the *m* is no more . . . . Ps 72:7
the *m* for seasons . . . . Ps 104:19
by day, nor the *m* by night . . Ps 121:6
morning, fair as the *m* . . . . . . Song 6:10
sun and *m* grow dark . . . . Joel 2:10
the *m* into blood, before . . . . . Joel 2:31
and *m* will grow dark, and . . . Joel 3:15
sun and *m* stood still in . . . . . . Hab 3:11
m will not give its . . . . Mark 13:24
in the sun, in the *m* . . . . Luke 21:25
or a new *m* or sabbaths, ... Col 2:16

the *m* became like blood .... Rev 6:12
or of the *m* to shine in it ... Rev 21:23

MORDECAI
Esther's guardian; advises her, Esth 2:5–20
Reveals plot to kill the king, Esth 2:21–23
Refuses homage to Haman, Esth 3:1–6
Honored by the king, Esth 6:1–12
Exalted highly, Esth 8:15; 9:4
Institutes feast of Purim, Esth 9:20–31

MORESHETH GATH
Birthplace of Micah the prophet, Mic 1:14

MORIAH
See MOUNT MORIAH

MORNING
the *m* were the first day ..... Gen 1:5
none of it remain until *m* .... Ex 12:10
they gathered it every *m* .... Ex 16:21
up in the *m* to Mount Sinai ... Ex 34:2
she lay at his feet until *m* .. Ruth 3:14
the eyelids of the *m* .... Job 41:18
You shall hear in the *m* .... Ps 5:3
but joy comes in the *m* .... Ps 30:5
Evening and *m* and at .... Ps 55:17
in the *m* my prayer comes ... Ps 88:13
lovingkindness in the *m* ...... Ps 92:2
the wings of the *m* .... Ps 139:9
looks forth as the *m* .... Song 6:10
Lucifer, son of the *m* .... Is 14:12
shall break forth like the *m* ... Is 58:8
They are new every *m* ..... Lam 3:23
established as the *m* .... Hos 6:3
in the *m*, 'It will be foul .... Matt 16:3
rooster, or in the *m* ...... Mark 13:35
very early in the *m* .... Luke 24:1
the *m* star rises in your .... 2 Pet 1:19
the Bright and *M* Star ..... Rev 22:16

MORSEL
or eaten my *m* by .... Job 31:17
Better is a dry *m* .... Prov 17:1
Esau, who for one *m* ...... Heb 12:16

MORTAL
sin reign in your *m* .... Rom 6:12
m bodies through His ...... Rom 8:11
and this *m* must put ...... 1 Cor 15:53
Here *m* men receive tithes, ... Heb 7:8

MORTALITY
m may be swallowed .... 2 Cor 5:4

MORTALS
with idolatrous *m* .... Ps 26:4

MOSES
See LAW OF MOSES
Born; hidden by mother; adopted by Pharaoh's daughter, Ex 2:1–10
Kills Egyptian and flees to Midian, Ex 2:11–22
Receives call from God, Ex 3:1—4:17
Returns to Israelites in Egypt, Ex 4:18–31
Wins Israel's deliverance with plagues, Ex 5:1—6:13; 6:28—11:10; 12:29–42
Leads Israel out of Egypt and through the Red Sea, Ex 13:17—14:31
His song of praise, Ex 15:1–18
Provides miraculously for the people, Ex 15:22—17:7
Appoints judges, Ex 18
Receives the law on Mount Sinai, Ex 19—23
Receives instructions for tabernacle, Ex 25—31
Intercedes for Israel's sin, Ex 32
Recommissioned and encouraged, Ex 33; 34
Further instructions and building of the tabernacle, Ex 35—40
Consecrates Aaron, Lev 8:1–36
Takes census, Num 1:1–54
Resumes journey to Canaan, Num 10:11–36
Complains; 70 elders appointed, Num 11:1–35
Intercedes for people when they refuse to enter Canaan, Num 14:11–25
Puts down Korah's rebellion, Num 16
Sins in anger, Num 20:1–13
Makes bronze serpent, Num 21:4–9
Travels toward Canaan, Num 21:10–20
Takes second census, Num 26
Commissions Joshua as his successor, Num 27:12–23
Receives further laws, Num 28—30
Commands conquest of Midian, Num 31
Final instructions, Num 32—36
Forbidden to enter Promised Land, Deut 3:23–28
Gives farewell messages, Deut 32; 33
Sees Promised Land; dies, Deut 34:1–7
Is mourned and extolled, Deut 34:8–12
Appears with Christ at transfiguration, Matt 17:1–3

MOST
His mouth is *m* sweet ..... Song 5:16
on your *m* holy faith .... Jude 20

MOST HIGH
be Abram of God *M* .... Gen 14:19
the knowledge of the *M* ... Num 24:16
the *M* uttered His voice .. 2 Sam 22:14
praise to Your name, O *M* ..... Ps 9:2
through the mercy of the *M* .. Ps 21:7
the Lord *M* is awesome .... Ps 47:2
I will cry out to God *M* .... Ps 57:2
M God their Redeemer ...... Ps 78:35
you are children of the *M* ..... Ps 82:6
secret place of the *M* .... Ps 91:1
the counsel of the *M* .... Ps 107:11
I will be like the *M* .... Is 14:14
from the mouth of the *M* ... Lam 3:38
servants of the *M* God ...... Dan 3:26
M rules in the kingdom of .. Dan 4:17
But the saints of the *M* ...... Dan 7:18
Though they call to the *M* .. Hos 11:7
Jesus, Son of the *M* .... Mark 5:7
M does not dwell in .... Acts 7:48
are the servants of the *M* .. Acts 16:17
Salem, priest of the *M* .... Heb 7:1

MOST HOLY PLACE
m you shall eat it .... Num 18:10
sanctuary, as the *M* ...... 1 Kin 6:16
And he made the *M* .... 2 Chr 3:8
to me, "This is the *M* ...... Ezek 41:4
blood He entered the *M* ..... Heb 9:12
high priest enters the *M* .... Heb 9:25

MOTH
m will eat them .... Is 50:9
where *m* and rust .... Matt 6:19

MOTHER
because she was the *m* ...... Gen 3:20
your father and your *m* ..... Ex 20:12
your father and your *m* .... Deut 5:16
like a joyful *m* .... Ps 113:9
son is the grief of his *m* .... Prov 10:1
the only one of her *m* .... Song 6:9
m might have been my ...... Jer 20:17
Like *m*, like dauther ...... Ezek 16:44
Child with Mary His *m* ..... Matt 2:11
who loves father or *m* ..... Matt 10:37
leave his father and *m* ..... Matt 19:5
Who is My *m*, or My ...... Mark 3:33
His *m* marveled at those ... Luke 2:33
but His *m* kept all these ... Luke 2:51
wife's *m* was sick .... Luke 4:38
out, the only son of his *m* .. Luke 7:12
m against daughter .... Luke 12:53
hate his father and *m* ..... Luke 14:26
"Behold your *m* .... John 19:27
free, which is the *m* .... Gal 4:26
without father, without *m* .... Heb 7:3
The *M* of Harlots .... Rev 17:5

MOTHER'S
return each to her *m* house .. Ruth 1:8
Naked I came from my *m* ... Job 1:21
while on My *m* breasts .... Ps 22:9
who took me out of my *m* .... Ps 71:6
Spirit, even from his *m* ..... Luke 1:15
his *m* womb was carried .... Acts 3:2

MOUNT
the *M* of the LORD it shall .. Gen 22:14
come up to *M* Sinai .... Ex 19:23
came down from *M* Sinai ... Ex 34:29
M Zion on the sides of the .... Ps 48:2
Let *M* Zion rejoice, let the ... Ps 48:11
the LORD are like *M* Zion .... Ps 125:1
you like *M* Carmel .... Song 7:5
they shall *m* up with .... Is 40:31
stand on the *M* of Olives ... Zech 14:4
He sat on the *M* of Olives .. Matt 24:3
to the *M* of Olives .... Mark 14:26
for this Hagar is *M* .... Gal 4:25

MOUNT CARMEL
Prophets gather at, 1 Kin 18:19, 20
Elisha journeys to, 2 Kin 2:25
Shunammite woman comes to Elisha at, 2 Kin 4:25

MOUNT EBAL
Cursed by God, Deut 11:29
Joshua builds an altar on, Josh 8:30

MOUNT GERIZIM
Mount of blessing, Deut 11:29; 27:12
Jotham speaks to people of Shechem here, Judg 9:7
Samaritans' sacred mountain, John 4:20, 21

MOUNT GILBOA
Men of Israel slain at, 1 Sam 31:1
Saul and his sons slain at, 1 Sam 31:8

MOUNT GILEAD
Gideon divides the people for battle at, Judg 7:3

MOUNT HOR
Lord speaks to Moses and Aaron on, Num 20:23
Aaron dies on, Num 20:25–28

MOUNT HOREB
Sons of Israel stripped of ornaments at, Ex 33:6
The same as Sinai, Ex 3:1

MOUNT MORIAH
Place where Abraham offered Isaac, Gen 22:2
Elevation where Solomon built the temple, 1 Chr 3:1

MOUNT NEBO
Place where Moses viewed the Promised Land, Deut 32:49

MOUNT OF OLIVES
See OLIVES, MOUNT OF

MOUNT SINAI
Lord descends upon, in fire, Ex 19:18
Lord calls Moses to the top of, Ex 19:20
The glory of the Lord rests on, for six days, Ex 24:16

MOUNT TABOR
Deborah sends Barak there to defeat Canaanites, Judg 4:6–14

MOUNT ZION
Survivors shall go out from, 2 Kin 19:31

MOUNTAIN
to Horeb, the *m* .... Ex 3:1
Whoever touches the *m* ..... Ex 19:12

and a thick cloud on the *m* . . Ex 19:16
Moses was on the *m* forty . . . Ex 24:18
"But as a *m* falls . . . . Job 14:18
You have made my *m* . . . . Ps 30:7
of many peaks is the *m* . . . . . Ps 68:15
let us go up to the *m* . . . . Is 2:3
be exalted, and every *m* . . . . . . Is 40:4
image became a great *m* . . . . Dan 2:35
an alarm in My holy *m* . . . . . . Joel 2:1
Who are you, O great *m* . . . . Zech 4:7
on an exceedingly high *m* . . . Matt 4:8
He went up on a *m* . . . . Matt 5:1
you will say to this *m* . . . . . Matt 17:20
came down from the *m* . . . . . . Mark 9:9
whoever says to this *m* . . . Mark 11:23
shall be filled and every *m* . . Luke 3:5
feeding there on the *m* . . . . Luke 8:32
worshiped on this *m* . . . . John 4:20
with Him on the holy *m* . . . . 2 Pet 1:18
it is rolled up, and every *m* . . Rev 6:14
to a great and high *m* . . . . . . Rev 21:10

MOUNTAINS

tops of the *m* were seen . . . . . Gen 8:5
He removes the *m* . . . . Job 9:5
Surely the *m* yield . . . . Job 40:20
though the *m* be carried . . . . . . Ps 46:2
m will bring peace . . . . Ps 72:3
excellent than the *m* . . . . Ps 76:4
m were brought forth . . . . Ps 90:2
m melt like wax at the . . . . Ps 97:5
m skipped like rams . . . . Ps 114:4
m surround Jerusalem . . . . . . Ps 125:2
forth into singing, you *m* . . . . . Is 44:23
How beautiful upon the *m* . . . . Is 52:7
m shall depart and the . . . . Is 54:10
m shook at Your presence . . . . Is 64:3
m shall be thrown down . . Ezek 38:20
in Judea flee to the *m* . . . . Matt 24:16
and day, he was in the *m* . . . Mark 5:5
begin 'to say to the *m*' . . . Luke 23:30
that I could remove *m* . . . . . 1 Cor 13:2
in deserts and *m* . . . . Heb 11:38
m were not found . . . . Rev 16:20

MOURN

and you *m* at last . . . . Prov 5:11
a time to *m* . . . . Eccl 3:4
to comfort all who *m*, ... Is 61:2
will *m* for Him as one . . . . Zech 12:10
are those who *m* . . . . Matt 5:4
m as long as the . . . . Matt 9:15
Lament and *m* and weep . . . James 4:9
of the earth will *m* . . . . Rev 1:7

MOURNED

we *m* to you . . . . Matt 11:17
and have not rather *m* . . . . 1 Cor 5:2

MOURNING

This is a deep *m* . . . . Gen 50:11
for me my *m* into dancing . . . Ps 30:11
m all the day long . . . . Ps 38:6
m shall be ended . . . . Is 60:20
ashes, the oil of joy for *m* . . . . . Is 61:3
men break bread in *m* . . . . Jer 16:7
I will turn their *m* . . . . Jer 31:13
shall be a great *m* . . . . Zech 12:11
be turned to *m* and . . . . James 4:9

MOURNS

heavily, as one who *m* . . . . . . Ps 35:14
The earth *m* and fades . . . . Is 24:4
for Him as one *m* . . . . Zech 12:10

MOUTH

"Who has made man's *m* . . . . Ex 4:11
and put the words in his *m* . . . Ex 4:15
the earth opened its *m* . . . . Num 16:32
the *m* of the donkey . . . . . . Num 22:28
from the *m* of the LORD . . . . . Deut 8:3
near you, in your *m* . . . . Deut 30:14
not depart from your *m* . . . . . Josh 1:8
Out of the *m* of babes . . . . Ps 8:2
Let the words of my *m* and . . Ps 19:14
shall continually be in my *m* . . Ps 34:1
The *m* of the righteous . . . . . . Ps 37:30
m shall speak wisdom . . . . Ps 49:3
my *m* shall show forth . . . . . . Ps 51:15
with my *m* will I make . . . . Ps 89:1
iniquity stops its *m* . . . . Ps 107:42
Then our *m* was filled with . . Ps 126:2
by the words of your *m* . . . . . Prov 6:2
knowledge, but the *m* . . . . . Prov 10:14
by the fruit of his *m* . . . . . . Prov 12:14
m preserves his life . . . . Prov 13:3
The *m* of an immoral . . . . . Prov 22:14
and a flattering *m* . . . . Prov 26:28
her *m* with wisdom . . . . Prov 31:26
And he touched my *m* with . . . . Is 6:7
yet He opened not His *m* . . . . . . Is 53:7
not depart from your *m* . . . . . . Is 59:21
put My words in your *m* . . . . . . Jer 1:9
it was in my *m* like honey . . . Ezek 3:3
m speaking pompous . . . . Dan 7:8
the doors of your *m* . . . . Mic 7:5
from the *m* of God . . . . Matt 4:4
near to Me with their *m* . . . . Matt 15:8
m defiles a man . . . . Matt 15:11
that 'by the *m* of two or . . . Matt 18:16
'Out of the *m* of babes . . . . . Matt 21:16
m I will judge you . . . . Luke 19:22
I will give you a *m* . . . . Luke 21:15
so He opened not His *m* . . . . Acts 8:32
is near you, in your *m* . . . . . . Rom 10:8
with your *m* the Lord . . . . . . Rom 10:9
m confession is made . . . . . Rom 10:10
proceed out of your *m*, but . . Eph 4:29
the same *m* proceed . . . . . . James 3:10
m great swelling words . . . . . . Jude 16
vomit you out of My *m* . . . . . Rev 3:16
sweet as honey in your *m* . . . Rev 10:9
m was found no deceit . . . . . . Rev 14:5

MOUTHS

gape at Me with their *m* . . . . . Ps 22:13
food was still in their *m* . . . . . Ps 78:30
have *m*, but they do not . . . . . Ps 115:5
near to Me with their *m* . . . . . Is 29:13
and shut the lions' *m* . . . . Dan 6:22

MOVE

and the earth will *m* . . . . Is 13:13
the mountain shall *m* . . . . . . Zech 14:4
M from here to there,' . . . . Matt 17:20
m them with one of their . . . Matt 23:4
in Him we live and *m* . . . . . Acts 17:28

MOVED

shall never be *m* . . . . Ps 15:5
right hand I shall not be *m* . . . Ps 16:8
she shall not be *m* . . . . Ps 46:5
I shall not be greatly *m* . . . . Ps 62:2
m Him to jealousy with . . . . . Ps 78:58
m with compassion . . . . Matt 14:14
all the city was *m* . . . . Matt 21:10
spoke as they were *m* . . . . . . 2 Pet 1:21

MUCH

m study is wearisome . . . . . . Eccl 12:12
m better than wine is . . . . . . Song 4:10
to whom *m* is given . . . . . . Luke 12:48
M more then . . . . Rom 5:9

MULTIPLIED

the more they *m* and grew . . . Ex 1:12
sorrows shall be *m* . . . . Ps 16:4
your days will be *m* . . . . Prov 9:11
When the wicked are *m*, . . Prov 29:16
m before You, and our sins . . Is 59:12
of the disciples *m* . . . . Acts 6:7
Holy Spirit, they were *m* . . . Acts 9:31
word of God grew and *m* . . Acts 12:24
peace, and love be *m* to you . . . Jude 2

MULTIPLY

See BE FRUITFUL AND MULTIPLY
"Be fruitful and *m* . . . . Gen 1:22
will greatly *m* your sorrow . . Gen 3:16
m your descendants . . . . Gen 16:10
multiplying I will *m* your . . . Gen 22:17
m my days as the . . . . Job 29:18
m the descendants . . . . Jer 33:22
m the seed you have . . . . . . 2 Cor 9:10

MULTITUDE

stars of heaven in *m* . . . . Deut 1:10
m of years should teach . . . . . Job 32:7
Your house in the *m* . . . . Ps 5:7
m that kept a pilgrim . . . . Ps 42:4
in the *m* of Your mercy, ... Ps 69:13
In the *m* of words sin . . . . . Prov 10:19
In a *m* of people is a . . . . . . Prov 14:28
bury Gog and all his *m* . . . Ezek 39:11
to the *m* in parables . . . . Matt 13:34
compassion on the *m* . . . . . Matt 15:32
commanded the *m* to sit . . Matt 15:35
a great *m* followed Him . . . Matt 20:29
with the angel a *m* . . . . Luke 2:13
whole *m* sought to touch . . Luke 6:19
because of the *m* of fish . . . . John 21:6
stars of the sky in *m* . . . . Heb 11:12
"love will cover a *m* . . . . 1 Pet 4:8
and behold, a great *m* . . . . Rev 7:9
voice of a great *m* in . . . . Rev 19:1

MULTITUDES

M, *m* in the valley of . . . . Joel 3:14
when the *m* saw it, they . . . . . Matt 9:8
all the *m* were amazed . . . . Matt 12:23
He commanded the *m* to . . Matt 14:19
taught the *m* from the . . . . . . Luke 5:3
m throng and press You . . . Luke 8:45
m from sacrificing to . . . . . . Acts 14:18

MURDER

"You shall not *m* . . . . Ex 20:13
Will you steal, *m*, commit . . . . . Jer 7:9
'You shall not *m* . . . . Matt 5:21
they had committed *m* in . . Mark 15:7
threats and *m* against . . . . Acts 9:1
full of envy, *m*, strife . . . . Rom 1:29
You *m* and covet and . . . . . . James 4:2

MURDERED

sons of those who *m* . . . . . . Matt 23:31
Jesus whom you *m* . . . . Acts 5:30
one and *m* his brother . . . . 1 John 3:12

MURDERER

He was a *m* from the . . . . . . John 8:44
and asked for a *m* . . . . Acts 3:14
of you suffer as a *m* . . . . 1 Pet 4:15
his brother is a *m* . . . . 1 John 3:15

MURDERERS

in it, but now *m* . . . . Is 1:21
and profane, for *m* . . . . 1 Tim 1:9
abominable, *m* . . . . Rev 21:8

MURDERS

whoever *m* will be in . . . . Matt 5:21
evil thoughts, *m* . . . . Matt 15:19
envy, *m*, drunkenness . . . . Gal 5:21
did not repent of their *m* . . . . Rev 9:21

MUSIC

So David played *m* . . . . . . 1 Sam 18:10
I will play *m* before the . . . 2 Sam 6:21
Israel played *m* before . . . . 1 Chr 13:8
whirling and playing *m* . . 1 Chr 15:29
but Asaph made *m* with . . . 1 Chr 16:5
the *m* of the LORD, which . . . 2 Chr 7:6
m are brought low . . . . Eccl 12:4
the house, he heard *m* . . . . Luke 15:25

MUSING

while I was *m*, the fire . . . . Ps 39:3

MUST

touches the altar *m* be . . . . . . Ex 29:37
I *m* be regarded as holy . . . . . Lev 10:3
m be careful to observe . . . . . Deut 8:1
is sleeping and *m* be . . . . . 1 Kin 18:27
Him, and you *m* wait for . . . Job 35:14
he *m* restore sevenfold . . . . . Prov 6:31
precept *m* be upon precept . . . Is 28:10
that Elijah *m* come first . . . Matt 17:10
offenses *m* come, but woe . . Matt 18:7
Man *m* suffer many . . . . Mark 8:31

such things *m* happen ..... Mark 13:7
And the gospel *m* first ... Mark 13:10
m be about My Father's .... Luke 2:49
you, 'You *m* be born again .. John 3:7
He *m* increase, but I .... John 3:30
Him *m* worship in spirit .... John 4:24
I *m* work the works of ...... John 9:4
that He *m* rise again from .. John 20:9
by which we *m* be saved ... Acts 4:12
m suffer for My name's ..... Acts 9:16
you *m* not call common ..... Acts 10:15
m put on incorruption, ... 1 Cor 15:53
If I *m* boast, I will .... 2 Cor 11:30
bishop then *m* be .... 1 Tim 3:2
deacons *m* be reverent ..... 1 Tim 3:8
servant of the Lord *m* ..... 2 Tim 2:24
to God *m* believe that He ... Heb 11:6
m love his brother also ... 1 John 4:21
things which *m* shortly ...... Rev 1:1
m be released for a little .... Rev 20:3
m shortly take place .... Rev 22:6

MUSTARD
heaven is like a *m* seed ... Matt 13:31
have faith as a *m* seed .... Matt 17:20

MUTE
Or who makes the *m* .... Ex 4:11
m who does not open .... Ps 38:13
I was *m* with silence .... Ps 39:2
was cast out, the *m* spoke .. Matt 9:33
who has a *m* spirit .... Mark 9:17
But behold, you will be *m* .. Luke 1:20
demon, and it was *m* ..... Luke 11:14

MUTILATION
beware of the *m* .... Phil 3:2

MUTUAL
by the *m* faith both .... Rom 1:12

MUZZLE
"You shall not *m* .... Deut 25:4
"You shall not *m* .... 1 Tim 5:18

MY RIGHT HAND
Because He is at *m* .... Ps 16:8
You hold me by *m* .... Ps 73:23
my Lord, "Sit at *M* .... Ps 110:1
let *m* forget its skill .... Ps 137:5
Look on *m* and see .... Ps 142:4
and *M* has stretched out ..... Is 48:13
but to sit on *M* .... Matt 20:23
to my Lord, "Sit at *M* ..... Matt 22:44
for He is at *m* .... Acts 2:25
Sit at *M*, till I make .... Heb 1:13
stars which you saw in *M* ... Rev 1:20

MYRA
Paul changes ships here, Acts 27:5, 6

MYRRH
perfumed my bed with *m* .. Prov 7:17
my hands dripped with *m* .. Song 5:5
gold, frankincense, and *m* .. Matt 2:11
wine mingled with *m* to .. Mark 15:23

MYSIA
Paul and Silas pass through here, Acts 16:7, 8

MYSTERIES
to you to know the *m* ..... Matt 13:11
and understand all *m* ...... 1 Cor 13:2
the spirit he speaks *m* ..... 1 Cor 14:2

MYSTERIOUS
today is not too *m* .... Deut 30:11

MYSTERY
given to know the *m* .... Mark 4:11
wisdom of God in a *m* .... 1 Cor 2:7
Behold, I tell you a *m* ..... 1 Cor 15:51
made known to us the *m* ..... Eph 1:9
This is a great *m* .... Eph 5:32
m which has been .... Col 1:26
the *m* of godliness .... 1 Tim 3:16

NAAMAN
Captain in the Syrian army, 2 Kin 5:1–11
Healed of his leprosy, 2 Kin 5:14–17
Referred to by Christ, Luke 4:27

NABAL
Refuses David's request, 1 Sam 25:2–12
Escapes David's wrath but dies of a stroke, 1 Sam 25:13–39

NABOTH
Murdered for his vineyard by King Ahab, 1 Kin 21:1–16
His murder avenged, 1 Kin 21:17–25

NADAB
Eldest of Aaron's four sons, Ex 6:23
Takes part in affirming covenant, Ex 24:1, 9–12
Becomes priest, Ex 28:1
Consumed by fire, Lev 10:1–7
——— King of Israel, 1 Kin 14:20
Killed by Baasha, 1 Kin 15:25–31

NAHASH
King of Ammon; makes impossible demands, 1 Sam 11:1–15

NAHOR
Grandfather of Abraham, Gen 11:24–26
——— Son of Terah, brother of Abraham, Gen 11:17

NAHUM
Prophet to Judah concerning Nineveh, Nah 1:1

NAILED
n it to the cross .... Col 2:14

NAIN
Village south of Nazareth; Jesus raises widow's son here, Luke 7:11–17

NAIOTH
Prophets' school in Ramah, 1 Sam 19:18, 19, 22, 23

NAKED
And they were both *n* ...... Gen 2:25
knew that they were *n* .... Gen 3:7
told you that you were *n* ..... Gen 3:11
"*N* I came from my .... Job 1:21
Sheol is *n* before Him, and .. Job 26:6
Isaiah has walked *n* .... Is 20:3
I was *n* and you .... Matt 25:36
and fled from them *n* ..... Mark 14:52
shall not be found *n* .... 2 Cor 5:3
but all things are *n* .... Heb 4:13
brother or sister is *n* ..... James 2:15
poor, blind, and *n* .... Rev 3:17

NAKEDNESS
of Canaan, saw the *n* .... Gen 9:22
The *n* of your father's wife .. Lev 18:8
in hunger, in thirst, in *n* ... Deut 28:48
or famine, or *n* .... Rom 8:35
often, in cold and *n* ...... 2 Cor 11:27
n may not be revealed .... Rev 3:18

NAME
See CALLED BY MY NAME; HOLY NAME; IN MY NAME
creature, that was its *n* ..... Gen 2:19
called his wife's *n* Eve ...... Gen 3:20
and make your *n* great .... Gen 12:2
Abram called on the *n* ...... Gen 13:4
your *n* shall be Abraham ... Gen 17:5
but Sarah shall be her *n* ... Gen 17:15
Israel shall be your *n* ...... Gen 35:10
So she called his *n* Moses .... Ex 2:10
This is My *n* forever .... Ex 3:15
My *n* may be declared in ...... Ex 9:16
the LORD is His *n* .... Ex 15:3
Israel called its *n* Manna .... Ex 16:31
shall not take the *n* .... Ex 20:7
whose *n* is Jealous, is a .... Ex 34:14
are called by the *n* .... Deut 28:10
glorious and awesome *n* .. Deut 28:58
by My *n* will humble .... 2 Chr 7:14
and he has no *n* .... Job 18:17
excellent is Your *n* .... Ps 8:1
n will put their trust .... Ps 9:10
LORD the glory due to His *n* .. Ps 29:2
let us exalt His *n* together .... Ps 34:3
lift up my hands in Your *n* ... Ps 63:4
the clouds, by His *n* YAH ..... Ps 68:4
be His glorious *n* .... Ps 72:19
n is great in Israel .... Ps 76:1
do not call on Your *n* .... Ps 79:6
whose *n* alone is the LORD ... Ps 83:18
to Him, and bless His *n* ..... Ps 100:4
to Your *n* give glory .... Ps 115:1
above all Your *n* .... Ps 138:2
He calls them all by *n* .... Ps 147:4
The *n* of the LORD is a ..... Prov 18:10
A good *n* is to be .... Prov 22:1
what is His Son's *n* .... Prov 30:4
And His *n* will be called .... Is 9:6
mention that His *n* is exalted .. Is 12:4
make mention of Your *n* ..... Is 26:13
the LORD, that is My *n* .... Is 42:8
be to the LORD for a *n* .... Is 55:13
be called by a new *n* .... Is 62:2
Everlasting is Your *n* .... Is 63:16
who calls on Your *n* .... Is 64:7
it shall be to Me a *n* .... Jer 33:9
and made Yourself a *n* ...... Dan 9:15
we will walk in the *n* .... Mic 4:5
They will call on My *n* ...... Zech 13:9
n shall be great .... Mal 1:11
to you who fear My *n* .... Mal 4:2
you shall call His *n* .... Matt 1:21
hallowed be Your *n* .... Matt 6:9
prophesied in Your *n* .... Matt 7:22
righteous man in the *n* .... Matt 10:41
n Gentiles will trust .... Matt 12:21
together in My *n* .... Matt 18:20
will come in My *n* .... Matt 24:5
"My *n* is Legion .... Mark 5:9
children in My *n* receives .. Mark 9:37
In My *n* they will cast .... Mark 16:17
The virgin's *n* was .... Luke 1:27
for me, and holy is His *n* .. Luke 1:49
"His *n* is John .... Luke 1:63
and cast out your *n* .... Luke 6:22
who believe in His *n* .... John 1:12
comes in his own *n* .... John 5:43
his own sheep by *n* .... John 10:3
you ask in My *n* .... John 14:13
Father will send in My *n* .. John 14:26
keep through Your *n* ..... John 17:11
whoever calls on the *n* ..... Acts 2:21
through faith in His *n* ...... Acts 3:16
there is no other *n* .... Acts 4:12
suffer shame for His *n* ...... Acts 5:41
baptized in the *n* of .... Acts 10:48
whoever calls on the *n* .... Rom 10:13
every *n* that is named, not .. Eph 1:21
which is above every *n* ...... Phil 2:9
at the *n* of Jesus every ..... Phil 2:10
deed, do all in the *n* .... Col 3:17
a more excellent *n* .... Heb 1:4
giving thanks to His *n* ..... Heb 13:15
blaspheme that noble *n* .... James 2:7
with oil in the *n* of the .... James 5:14
reproached for the *n* .... 1 Pet 4:14
n of the Son of God ...... 1 John 5:13
you hold fast to My *n* .... Rev 2:13
n that you are alive .... Rev 3:1
and have not denied My *n* .... Rev 3:8
or the *n* of the beast .... Rev 13:17
having His Father's *n* .... Rev 14:1
and glorify Your *n* .... Rev 15:4
n written that no one ...... Rev 19:12

NAME'S
by all for My *n* sake ...... Matt 10:22

or lands, for My *n* sake, . . . Matt 19:29
saved them for His *n* . . . . Ps 106:8
forgiven you for His *n* . . . . 1 John 2:12

NAMED
let my name be *n* . . . . Gen 48:16
I have *n* you . . . . Is 45:4
of a young man *n* Saul . . . . . Acts 7:58
not even *n* among the . . . . . . 1 Cor 5:1
and every name that is *n* . . . . Eph 1:21

NAMES
So Adam gave *n* to all . . . . . . Gen 2:20
lands after their own *n* . . . . . . Ps 49:11
Now the *n* of the twelve . . . . Matt 10:2
n are written in heaven . . . Luke 10:20
whose *n* are in the Book of . . Phil 4:3
Let everyone who *n* the . . . 2 Tim 2:19
whose *n* are not written in . . Rev 17:8
the *n* of the twelve . . . . Rev 21:12
on them were the *n* of the . . Rev 21:14

NAOMI
Widow of Elimelech, Ruth 1:1–3
Returns to Bethlehem with Ruth, Ruth 1:14–19
Arranges Ruth's marriage to Boaz, Ruth 3; 4

NAPHTALI
Son of Jacob by Bilhah, Gen 30:1–8
Receives Jacob's blessing, Gen 49:21, 28
——— Tribe of:
Numbered, Num 1:42, 43
Territory assigned to, Josh 19:32–39
Joins Gideon's army, Judg 7:23
Attacked by Ben-Hadad and Tiglath-Pileser, 1 Kin 15:20; 2 Kin 15:29
Prophecy of great light in; fulfilled in Christ's ministry, Is 9:1–7; Matt 4:12–16

NARROW
"Enter by the *n* gate . . . . Matt 7:13
n is the gate and . . . . Matt 7:14

NATHAN
Son of David, 2 Sam 5:14
Mary's lineage traced through, Zech 12:12
——— Prophet under David and Solomon, 1 Chr 29:29
Reveals God's plan to David, 2 Sam 7:2–29
Rebukes David's sin, 2 Sam 12:1–15
Reveals Adonijah's plot, 1 Kin 1:10–46

NATHANAEL
One of Christ's disciples, John 1:45–51

NATION
make you a great *n* . . . . Gen 12:2
You slay a righteous *n* . . . . . . Gen 20:4
priests and a holy *n* . . . . Ex 19:6
Blessed is the *n* whose . . . . . . Ps 33:12
dealt thus with any *n* . . . . Ps 147:20
Righteousness exalts a *n* . . Prov 14:34
lift up sword against *n* . . . . Is 2:4
that the righteous *n* . . . . Is 26:2
call a *n* you do not know . . . . . Is 55:5
a small one a strong *n* . . . . Is 60:22
n that was not called . . . . Is 65:1
Or shall a *n* be born at once . . . Is 66:8
n changed its gods . . . . Jer 2:11
I will make them one *n* . . . Ezek 37:22
since there was a *n* . . . . Dan 12:1
N shall not lift up sword . . . . . Mic 4:3
Me, even this whole *n* . . . . Mal 3:9
n will rise against . . . . Matt 24:7
for he loves our *n* . . . . Luke 7:5
N will rise against *n*, ... Luke 21:10
whole *n* should perish . . . . John 11:50
those who are not a *n* . . . . . Rom 10:19
royal priesthood, a holy *n* . . . 1 Pet 2:9
tribe, tongue, and *n* . . . . Rev 13:7

NATIONS
Two *n* are in your womb . . Gen 25:23
itself among the *n* . . . . Num 23:9
shall lend to many *n* . . . . . . Deut 28:12
Why do the *n* rage . . . . Ps 2:1
I will give You the *n* . . . . Ps 2:8
be exalted among the *n* . . . . . Ps 46:10
n shall serve Him . . . . Ps 72:11
n shall call Him . . . . Ps 72:17
n shall fear the name . . . . . . Ps 102:15
is high above all *n* . . . . Ps 113:4
All *n* before Him are . . . . Is 40:17
n who do not know . . . . Is 55:5
a house of prayer for all *n* . . . . Is 56:7
the wise men of the *n* . . . . Jer 10:7
a reproach to the *n* . . . . Ezek 22:4
come to the Desire of All *N* . . Hag 2:7
n shall be joined . . . . Zech 2:11
speak peace to the *n* . . . . Zech 9:10
For I will gather all the *n* . . Zech 14:2
disciples of all the *n* . . . . . . Matt 28:19
in His name to all *n* . . . . . . Luke 24:47
the father of many *n* . . . . Rom 4:18
In you all the *n* shall be . . . . . Gal 3:8
who was to rule all *n* . . . . Rev 12:5
For all the *n* have drunk of . . Rev 18:3
the healing of the *n* . . . . Rev 22:2

NATURAL
nor his *n* vigor abated . . . . . . Deut 34:7
women exchanged the *n* . . . Rom 1:26
the men, leaving the *n* . . . . Rom 1:27
did not spare the *n* . . . . Rom 11:21
n man does not receive . . . . 1 Cor 2:14
It is sown a *n* body . . . . 1 Cor 15:44
not first, but the *n* . . . . 1 Cor 15:46
his *n* face in a mirror . . . . . James 1:23

NATURE
men with the same *n* . . . . . . Acts 14:15
that the Divine *N* is . . . . Acts 17:29
for what is against *n* . . . . Rom 1:26
by *n* do the things in . . . . Rom 2:14
n itself teach you . . . . 1 Cor 11:14
We who are Jews by *n* . . . . Gal 2:15
by *n* children of wrath . . . . Eph 2:3
on fire the course of *n* . . . . . James 3:6
man with a *n* like ours . . . . James 5:17
of the divine *n* . . . . 2 Pet 1:4

NAZARENE
Jesus to be called, Matt 2:23
Descriptive of Jesus' followers, Acts 24:5

NAZARETH
Town in Galilee; considered obscure, John 1:46
City of Jesus' parents, Matt 2:23
Early home of Jesus, Luke 2:39–51
Jesus rejected by, Luke 4:16–30

NEAPOLIS
Seaport of Philippi, Acts 16:11

NEAR
that has God so *n* to it . . . . . . Deut 4:7
But the word is very *n* . . . . Deut 30:14
The LORD is *n* to all . . . . Ps 145:18
upon Him while He is *n* . . . . Is 55:6
know that it is *n* . . . . Matt 24:33
kingdom of God is *n* . . . . . Luke 21:31
"The word is *n* . . . . Rom 10:8
to those who were *n* . . . . Eph 2:17
for the time is *n* . . . . Rev 1:3

NEARER
now our salvation is *n* . . . . Rom 13:11

NEBO
Babylonian god, Is 46:1
——— Summit of Pisgah; Moses dies here, Deut 32:49; 34:1, 5

NEBUCHADNEZZAR
Monarch of the Neo-Babylonian Empire (605–562 B.C.); carries Jews captive to Babylon, Dan 1:1–3
Crushes Jehoiachin's revolt, 2 Kin 24:10–17
Destroys Jerusalem; captures Zedekiah, Jer 39:5–8
Prophecies concerning, Is 14:4–27; Jer 21:7–10; 25:8, 9; 27:4–11; 32:28–36; 43:10–13; Ezek 26:7–12

NEBUZARADAN
Nebuchadnezzar's captain at siege of Jerusalem, 2 Kin 25:8–20
Protects Jeremiah, Jer 39:11–14

NECESSARY
mouth more than my *n* . . . . . Job 23:12
and thus it was *n* . . . . Luke 24:46
n that the word of God . . . . Acts 13:46
It is *n* to circumcise them, . . Acts 15:5
burden than these *n* . . . . Acts 15:28
to be weaker are *n* . . . . 1 Cor 12:22
Therefore it is *n* that this . . . . Heb 8:3
Therefore it was *n* that the . . Heb 9:23
I found it *n* to write . . . . Jude 3

NECESSITIES
have provided for my *n* . . . Acts 20:34
and again for my *n* . . . . Phil 4:16

NECESSITY
n is laid upon me . . . . 1 Cor 9:16
not grudgingly or of *n* . . . . . . 2 Cor 9:7
there must also of *n* be the . . Heb 9:16

NECK
smooth part of his *n* . . . . Gen 27:16
wept on his *n* a good . . . . Gen 46:29
bind them around your *n*, . . . Prov 3:3
and grace to your *n* . . . . Prov 3:22
and hardens his *n* . . . . Prov 29:1
Your *n* is like an ivory . . . . . . Song 7:4
and his yoke from your *n* . . . . Is 10:27
n was an iron sinew . . . . Is 48:4
were hung around his *n* . . . . Matt 18:6
ran and fell on his *n* . . . . . . Luke 15:20

NECKS
stiffened their *n* . . . . Neh 9:29
with outstretched *n* . . . . Is 3:16
who risked their own *n* . . . . . Rom 16:4

NEED
in nakedness, and in *n* . . . . Deut 28:48
a prowler, and your *n* . . . . . Prov 24:34
the things you have *n* . . . . Matt 6:8
no *n* of a physician . . . . Matt 9:12
'The Lord has *n* . . . . Matt 21:3
did when he was in *n* . . . . . . Mark 2:25
say, 'The Lord has *n* of it . . Mark 11:3
testimony do we *n* . . . . Luke 22:71
all, as anyone had *n* . . . . Acts 2:45
each as anyone had *n* . . . . . . Acts 4:35
hand, "I have no *n* . . . . 1 Cor 12:21
who ministered to my *n* . . . . . Phil 2:25
to abound and to suffer *n* . . . Phil 4:12
supply all your *n* . . . . Phil 4:19
not *n* to be ashamed . . . . . . 2 Tim 2:15
to help in time of *n* . . . . Heb 4:16
you *n* someone to teach . . . . . Heb 5:12
do not *n* that anyone . . . . . 1 John 2:27
sees his brother in *n* . . . . . 1 John 3:17
The city had no *n* . . . . Rev 21:23

NEEDY
your poor and your *n* . . . . . Deut 15:11
They push the *n* . . . . Job 24:4
n shall not always be . . . . Ps 9:18
He will deliver the *n* . . . . Ps 72:12
and lifts the *n* . . . . Ps 113:7
Him has mercy on the *n* . . Prov 14:31
out her hands to the *n* . . . . Prov 31:20
to rob the *n* of . . . . Is 10:2
n will lie down in . . . . Is 14:30
a strength to the *n* . . . . Is 25:4

NEGLECT
n the gift that is . . . . 1 Tim 4:14
if we *n* so great a . . . . Heb 2:3

NEGLECTED
n the weightier . . . . Matt 23:23
their widows were *n* . . . . Acts 6:1

NEHEMIAH
Jewish cupbearer to King Artaxerxes; prays for restoration of Jerusalem, Neh 1:4–11
King commissions him to rebuild walls, Neh 2:1–8
Overcomes opposition and accomplishes rebuilding, Neh 4—6
Appointed governor, Neh 5:14
Participates with Ezra in restored worship, Neh 8—10
Registers the people and the priests and Levites, Neh 11:1—12:26
Dedicates the wall, Neh 12:27–43
Returns to Jerusalem after absence and institutes reforms, Neh 13:4–31

NEIGHBOR
See LOVE YOUR NEIGHBOR
every man ask from his *n* .... Ex 11:2
witness against your *n* ...... Ex 20:16
you shall love your *n* ...... Lev 19:18
witness against your *n* ..... Deut 5:20
secretly slanders his *n* .... Ps 101:5
Do not say to your *n*, "Go .. Prov 3:28
He who despises his *n* .... Prov 14:21
against your *n* without .... Prov 24:28
for better is a *n* .... Prov 27:10
every man teach his *n* ...... Jer 31:34
gives drink to his *n* .... Hab 2:15
man the truth to his *n* ...... Zech 8:16
'You shall love your *n* ...... Matt 5:43
love your *n* as yourself .... Matt 22:39
"And who is my *n* .... Luke 10:29
do you think was *n* .... Luke 10:36
"You shall love your *n* ..... Rom 13:9
love your *n* as yourself ...... Gal 5:14
of them shall teach his *n* .... Heb 8:11

NEIGHBOR'S
shall not covet your *n* wife .. Ex 20:17
n garment as a pledge .... Ex 22:26
or anything that is your *n* .. Deut 5:21
remove your *n* landmark .. Deut 19:14
goes in to his *n* wife .... Prov 6:29

NEIGHBORS
from all your *n* .... 2 Kin 4:3
Who speak peace to their *n* ... Ps 28:3
a reproach to our *n* .... Ps 44:13
return to our *n* sevenfold .... Ps 79:12
nor your rich *n* .... Luke 14:12
Therefore the *n* and those ... John 9:8

NEST
As an eagle stirs up its *n* .. Deut 32:11
and make its *n* .... Job 39:27
n is a man who wanders ... Prov 27:8
though you set your *n* .... Obad 4
that he may set his *n* .... Hab 2:9
and *n* in its branches ..... Matt 13:32

NET
me with His *n* .... Job 19:6
pluck my feet out of the *n* ... Ps 25:15
have hidden their *n* .... Ps 35:7
They have prepared a *n* ...... Ps 57:6
an antelope in a *n* .... Is 51:20
catch in their *n* .... Hab 1:15
casting a *n* into the sea ..... Matt 4:18
I will let down the *n* .... Luke 5:5
to them, "Cast the *n* .... John 21:6
so many, the *n* was not ... John 21:11

NETHINIM
Servants of the Levites, Ezra 8:20
Possible origins of:
Gibeonites, Josh 9:23–27
Solomon's forced laborers, 1 Kin 9:20, 21
Mentioned, 1 Chr 9:2; Ezra 2:43–54; 7:24; 8:17; Neh 3:31; 7:46–60, 73; 10:28, 29; 11:21

NETS
fall into their own *n* .... Ps 141:10
immediately left their *n* ..... Matt 4:20
down your *n* for a catch ..... Luke 5:4

NEVER
in Me shall *n* thirst .... John 6:35
in Me shall *n* die .... John 11:26
Love *n* fails .... 1 Cor 13:8
n take away sins .... Heb 10:11
"I will *n* leave you .... Heb 13:5
prophecy *n* came by .... 2 Pet 1:21

NEW
Now there arose a *n* .... Ex 1:8
the LORD creates a *n* ...... Num 16:30
man has taken a *n* wife .... Deut 24:5
They chose *n* gods .... Judg 5:8
him with two *n* ropes ..... Judg 15:13
ark of God on a *n* cart ..... 2 Sam 6:3
He has put a *n* song in my .... Ps 40:3
sing to the LORD a *n* song ..... Ps 96:1
will overflow with *n* wine .. Prov 3:10
and there is nothing *n* .... Eccl 1:9
Behold, I will do a *n* .... Is 43:19
shall be called by a *n* name ... Is 62:2
For behold, I create *n* .... Is 65:17
when I will make a *n* .... Jer 31:31
n every morning .... Lam 3:23
I will give you a *n* heart .. Ezek 36:26
shall overflow with *n* wine .. Joel 2:24
wine into *n* wineskins ...... Matt 9:17
of the *n* covenant .... Matt 26:28
laid it in his *n* tomb ...... Matt 27:60
speak with *n* tongues .... Mark 16:17
n commandment I give ... John 13:34
tell or to hear some *n* .... Acts 17:21
he is a *n* creation .... 2 Cor 5:17
n man who is renewed ...... Col 3:10
when I will make a *n* .... Heb 8:8
Mediator of the *n* covenant . Heb 9:15
n heavens and a *n* .... 2 Pet 3:13
n commandment I write ... 1 John 2:8
n name written which .... Rev 2:17
the *N* Jerusalem, which ...... Rev 3:12
And they sang a *n* .... Rev 5:9
And I saw a *n* heaven .... Rev 21:1
I make all things *n* .... Rev 21:5

NEW COVENANT
I will make a *n* with .... Jer 31:31
this is My blood of the *n* .. Matt 26:28
"This cup is the *n* in ..... Luke 22:20
"This cup is the *n* .... 1 Cor 11:25
as ministers of the *n* ..... 2 Cor 3:6
"when I will make a *n* .... Heb 8:8
Mediator of the *n* .... Heb 9:15
the Mediator of the *n* ...... Heb 12:24

NEW MAN
create in Himself one *n* ..... Eph 2:15
that you put on the *n* .... Eph 4:24
and have put on the *n* ...... Col 3:10

NEWNESS
also should walk in *n* .... Rom 6:4
should serve in the *n* .... Rom 7:6

NEWS
heard this bad *n* .... Ex 33:4
Proclaim the good *n* of His ... Ps 96:2
soul, so is good *n* .... Prov 25:25
him who brings good *n* .... Is 52:7
n of Him went out .... Luke 4:14
good *n* of your faith ...... 1 Thess 3:6

NICANOR
One of the first seven deacons, Acts 6:1–5

NICODEMUS
Pharisee; converses with Jesus, John 3:1–12
Protests unfairness of Christ's trial, John 7:50–52
Brings gifts to anoint Christ's body, John 19:39, 40

NICOLAITANS
Group teaching moral laxity, Rev 2:6–15

NICOLAS
One of the first seven deacons, Acts 6:5

NIGHT
darkness He called *N* .... Gen 1:5
day and *n* shall not cease ... Gen 8:22
father drink wine that *n* ... Gen 19:33
It is a *n* of solemn .... Ex 12:42
pillar of fire by *n* .... Ex 13:22
strong east wind all that *n* .. Ex 14:21
came to Balaam at *n* ..... Num 22:20
meditate in it day and *n* ..... Josh 1:8
and the *n* be ended .... Job 7:4
gives songs in the *n* .... Job 35:10
law he meditates day and *n* .... Ps 1:2
instructs me in the *n* seasons . Ps 16:7
n reveals knowledge .... Ps 19:2
Weeping may endure for a *n* . Ps 30:5
be afraid of the terror by *n* ... Ps 91:5
Your faithfulness every *n* ..... Ps 92:2
awake through the *n* ...... Ps 119:148
and stars to rule by *n* .... Ps 136:9
the *n* shines as the day ..... Ps 139:12
rises while it is yet *n* ...... Prov 31:15
Watchman, what of the *n* .... Is 21:11
desired You in the *n* .... Is 26:9
and perished in a *n* .... Jon 4:10
Child and His mother by *n* . Matt 2:14
His disciples come by *n* ... Matt 27:64
over their flock by *n* .... Luke 2:8
and continued all *n* .... Luke 6:12
man came to Jesus by *n* ..... John 3:2
n is coming when no .... John 9:4
came to Jesus by *n* .... John 19:39
that *n* Peter was sleeping, .. Acts 12:6
stood by me this *n* .... Acts 27:23
The *n* is far spent .... Rom 13:12
as a thief in the *n* .... 1 Thess 5:2
We are not of the *n* .... 1 Thess 5:5
they do not rest day or *n* ...... Rev 4:8
before our God day and *n* .. Rev 12:10
there shall be no *n* .... Rev 21:25
there shall be no *n* .... Rev 22:5

NIGHTS
earth forty days and forty *n* .. Gen 7:4
forty days and forty *n* .... Ex 24:18
forty days and forty *n* .... Matt 4:2
three *n* in the belly of ..... Matt 12:40

NILE
Hebrew children drowned in, Ex 1:22
Moses hidden in, Ex 2:3–10
Water of, turned to blood, Ex 7:14–21
Mentioned in prophecies, Is 19:5–8; 23:3; 27:12; Jer 46:7–9; Amos 9:5

NIMROD
Ham's grandson, Gen 10:6–12

NINE
Adam lived were *n* hundred .. Gen 5:5
of Methuselah were *n* .... Gen 5:27
where are the *n* .... Luke 17:17

NINETY-NINE
he not leave the *n* .... Matt 18:12
n just persons .... Luke 15:7

NINEVEH
Capital of Assyria, 2 Kin 19:36
Jonah preaches to; people repent, Jon 3:1–10; Matt 12:41
Prophecy against, Nah 2:13—3:19; Zeph 2:13–15

NOAH
Son of Lamech, Gen 5:28–32
Finds favor with God; commissioned to build the ark, Gen 6:8–22
Fills ark and survives flood, Gen 7
Leaves ark; builds altar; receives God's promise, Gen 8
God's covenant with, Gen 9:1–17
Blesses and curses his sons; dies, Gen 9:18–29

NO AMON (or Thebes)
Nineveh compared to, Nah 3:8

NOB
City of priests; David flees to, 1 Sam 21:1–9
Priests of, killed by Saul, 1 Sam 22:9–23

NOBLE
of the king's most *n* princes . Esth 6:9
I had planted you a *n* vine . . . Jer 2:21
heard the word with a *n* . . . Luke 8:15
most *n* Festus, but speak . . Acts 26:25
mighty, not many *n* . . . . 1 Cor 1:26
whatever things are *n* . . . . . . Phil 4:8
not blaspheme that *n* . . . . . James 2:7

NOBLES
voice of *n* was hushed . . . . . Job 29:10
king is the son of *n* . . . . Eccl 10:17
n have sent their lads . . . . Jer 14:3
your *n* rest in the . . . . Nah 3:18

NOD
Place (east of Eden) of Cain's exile, Gen 4:16, 17

NOISE
There is a *n* of war in the . . . Ex 32:17
any *n* with your voice . . . . . . Josh 6:10
the *n* of a great army . . . . 2 Kin 7:6
Than the *n* of many waters . . . . Ps 93:4
The *n* of a multitude . . . . Is 13:4
people who make a *n* . . . . Is 17:12
of Egypt, is but a *n* . . . . Jer 46:17
They have made a *n* . . . . Lam 2:7
the *n* of many waters . . . . Ezek 1:24
the *n* of the wheels beside . . Ezek 3:13
the *n* of your songs . . . . Amos 5:23
n of the day of the . . . . Zeph 1:14
away with a great *n* . . . . 2 Pet 3:10

NORTH
Zion on the sides of the *n* . . . . Ps 48:2
O *n* wind, and come . . . . Song 4:16
I will say to the *n*, 'Give . . . . . . Is 43:6
Israel from the land of . . . . . Jer 16:15
Togarmah from the far *n* . . Ezek 38:6
place out of the far *n* . . . . . Ezek 38:15
the west, from the *n* . . . . . . Luke 13:29

NOSTRILS
n the breath of life . . . . Gen 2:7
breath of God in my *n* . . . . Job 27:3
breath is in his *n* . . . . Is 2:22

NOTE
urge you, brethren, *n* . . . . . Rom 16:17
n those who so walk . . . . Phil 3:17

NOTHING
For now you are *n* . . . . Job 6:21
rich, yet has *n* . . . . Prov 13:7
"It is good for *n* . . . . Prov 20:14
before Him are as *n* . . . . Is 40:17
their works are *n* . . . . Is 41:29
I can of Myself do *n* . . . . John 5:30
Me you can do *n* . . . . John 15:5
men, it will come to *n* . . . . . . Acts 5:38
bring to *n* the things . . . . . . 1 Cor 1:28
For I know of *n* against . . . . . 1 Cor 4:4
have not love, I am *n* . . . . . . 1 Cor 13:2
love, it profits me *n* . . . . 1 Cor 13:3
Be anxious for *n* . . . . Phil 4:6
For we brought *n* . . . . 1 Tim 6:7
complete, lacking *n* . . . . James 1:4
name's sake, taking *n* . . . . 3 John 7

NOTORIOUS
n prisoner called . . . . Matt 27:16

NOURISHED
"I have *n* and . . . . Is 1:2
n and knit together . . . . Col 2:19
n in the words of . . . . 1 Tim 4:6

NOURISHES
n and cherishes it . . . . Eph 5:29

NOVICE
not a *n*, lest being . . . . 1 Tim 3:6

NUMBER
if a man could *n* . . . . Gen 13:16
fulfill the *n* of your days . . . . Ex 23:26
that I may know the *n* . . . . 2 Sam 24:2
and moved David to *n* . . . . 1 Chr 21:1
things without *n* . . . . Job 5:9
For now You *n* my steps . . . Job 14:16
n the clouds by wisdom . . . . Job 38:37
teach us to *n* our days . . . . Ps 90:12
He counts the *n* . . . . Ps 147:4
Me days without *n* . . . . Jer 2:32
in *n* about five thousand . . . John 6:10
a great *n* believed and . . . . Acts 11:21
and increased in *n* daily . . . . Acts 16:5
which no one could *n* . . . . Rev 7:9
His *n* is 666 . . . . Rev 13:18

NUMBERED
David *n* the people . . . . 2 Sam 18:1
he had *n* the people . . . . . 2 Sam 24:10
are more than can be *n* . . . . Ps 40:5
death, and He was *n* with . . . . Is 53:12
God has *n* your kingdom . . . Dan 5:26
of your head are all *n* . . . . . Matt 10:30
n among the twelve . . . . Luke 22:3
'And He was *n* with . . . . . . Luke 22:37
was *n* with the eleven . . . . . . Acts 1:26

OAKS
Wail, O *o* of Bashan . . . . Zech 11:2

OARSMEN
o brought you into . . . . . . Ezek 27:26

OATH
two of them swore an *o* . . . Gen 21:31
the *o* which He swore to . . . . Deut 7:8
people feared the *o* . . . . . 1 Sam 14:26
Judah rejoiced at the *o* . . . 2 Chr 15:15
o to walk in God's Law . . . . Neh 10:29
for the sake of your *o* . . . . Eccl 8:2
I may establish the *o* . . . . Jer 11:5
And you shall be an *o* . . . . Jer 42:18
raised My hand in an *o* . . . . Ezek 20:5
the *o* written in the Law . . . . Dan 9:11
he denied with an *o* . . . . Matt 26:72
o which He swore . . . . Luke 1:73
themselves under an *o* . . . . . Acts 23:12
made priest without an *o* . . . Heb 7:20
or with any other *o* . . . . James 5:12

OATHS
shall perform your *o* . . . . . . Matt 5:33
because of the *o* . . . . Matt 14:9

OBADIAH
King Ahab's steward, 1 Kin 18:3–16
—— Prophet of Judah, Obad 1

OBED
Son of Boaz and Ruth, Ruth 4:17–22

OBED-EDOM
Philistine from Gath; ark of the Lord left in his house, 2 Sam 6:10–12; 1 Chr 13:13, 14

OBEDIENCE
scorns *o* to his mother . . . . Prov 30:17
and apostleship for *o* . . . . Rom 1:5
o many will be made . . . . Rom 5:19
For your *o* has become . . . . Rom 16:19
glorify God for the *o* of . . . . 2 Cor 9:13
captivity to the *o* . . . . 2 Cor 10:5
confidence in your *o* . . . . Philem 21
yet He learned *o* . . . . Heb 5:8
for *o* and sprinkling . . . . 1 Pet 1:2

OBEDIENT
said we will do, and be *o* . . . . . Ex 24:7
you are willing and *o* . . . . Is 1:19
of the priests were *o* . . . . Acts 6:7
make the Gentiles *o* . . . . . . Rom 15:18
bondservants, be *o* to . . . . Eph 6:5
Himself and became *o* . . . . Phil 2:8
homemakers, good, *o* . . . . Titus 2:5
as *o* children . . . . 1 Pet 1:14

OBEY
LORD, that I should *o* . . . . Ex 5:2
God and *o* His voice . . . . Deut 4:30
o the commandments . . . . . Deut 11:27
if you diligently *o* the . . . . . . Deut 28:1
if you do not *o* the voice . . Deut 28:15
His voice we will *o* . . . . Josh 24:24
o is better than . . . . 1 Sam 15:22
they hear of me they *o* . . . . . . Ps 18:44
O My voice, and I will be . . . . Jer 7:23
O My voice, and do . . . . Jer 11:4
we will *o* the voice of the . . . . . Jer 42:6
shall serve and *o* Him . . . . . . Dan 7:27
if you diligently *o* . . . . Zech 6:15
winds and the sea *o* Him . . . Matt 8:27
spirits, and they *o* Him . . . . Mark 1:27
o God rather than men . . . . . Acts 5:29
and do not *o* the truth . . . . Rom 2:8
yourselves slaves to *o* . . . . . . Rom 6:16
o your parents in all . . . . Col 3:20
Bondservants, *o* in all . . . . Col 3:22
on those who do not *o* . . . . . . 2 Thess 1:8
salvation to all who *o* Him . . . Heb 5:9
O those who rule . . . . Heb 13:17
mouths that they may *o* . . . . James 3:3
if some do not *o* . . . . 1 Pet 3:1

OBEYED
Abraham *o* My voice . . . . Gen 26:5
you have not *o* My voice . . . . Judg 2:2
bondage anymore, they *o* . . . Jer 34:10
of sin, yet you *o* . . . . Rom 6:17
they have not all *o* . . . . Rom 10:16
By faith Abraham *o* . . . . Heb 11:8
as Sarah *o* Abraham . . . . 1 Pet 3:6

OBEYING
o the truth through . . . . 1 Pet 1:22

OBSCURITY
shall see out of *o* . . . . Is 29:18

OBSERVANCE
the LORD, a solemn *o* . . . . Ex 12:42

OBSERVATION
does not come with *o* . . . . . Luke 17:20

OBSERVE
So you shall *o* the Feast of . . Ex 12:17
to *o* the Sabbath . . . . Ex 31:16
which I teach you to *o* . . . . . . Deut 4:1
night, that you may *o* to do . . Josh 1:8
man, and *o* the upright . . . . Ps 37:37
is wise will *o* these things . . Ps 107:43
and let your eyes *o* . . . . Prov 23:26
o mercy and justice . . . . Hos 12:6
teaching them to *o* all . . . . . Matt 28:20
who does not *o* the day . . . . . Rom 14:6
o days and months and . . . . . Gal 4:10
o your chaste conduct . . . . 1 Pet 3:2

OBSERVES
o the wind will not . . . . Eccl 11:4
He who *o* the day . . . . Rom 14:6

OBSERVING
o his natural face . . . . James 1:23

OBSESSED
nothing, but is *o* . . . . 1 Tim 6:4

OBSOLETE
Now what is becoming *o* . . . . Heb 8:13

OBSTINATE
and made his heart *o* . . . . Deut 2:30
I knew that you were *o* . . . . Is 48:4

OBTAIN
They shall *o* joy and . . . . Is 35:10
for they shall *o* mercy . . . . Matt 5:7
they also may *o* mercy . . . . Rom 11:31
way that you may *o* it . . . . . 1 Cor 9:24
o salvation through . . . . 1 Thess 5:9

o for themselves a good ... 1 Tim 3:13
that they might o a better .. Heb 11:35
and covet and cannot o ... James 4:2

OBTAINED
Esther o favor in the sight .. Esth 2:15
o a part in this ... Acts 1:17
yet have now o mercy ... Rom 11:30
have o an inheritance ... Eph 1:11
He has by inheritance o ... Heb 1:4
endured, he o the ... Heb 6:15
o eternal redemption ... Heb 9:12
o promises, stopped the ... Heb 11:33
To those who have o ... 2 Pet 1:1

OBTAINS
o favor from the LORD ... Prov 8:35

ODED
Prophet of Samaria, 2 Chr 28:9–15

OF THE WORLD
men o who have ... Ps 17:14
their words to the end o ... Ps 19:4
the ends o shall remember .. Ps 22:27
all inhabitants o ... Ps 49:1
All inhabitants o ... Is 18:3
proclaimed to the end o ... Is 62:11
all the kingdoms o ... Matt 4:8
You are the light o ... Matt 5:14
from the foundation o ... Matt 13:35
since the beginning o ... Matt 24:21
nations o seek after ... Luke 12:30
takes away the sin o ... John 1:29
The Christ, the Savior o ... John 4:42
give for the life o ... John 6:51
"I am the light o ... John 8:12
If you were o ... John 15:19
have given Me out o ... John 17:6
he would be the heir o ... Rom 4:13
is the reconciling o ... Rom 11:15
foolish things o to put ... 1 Cor 1:27
not the spirit o ... 1 Cor 2:12
made as the filth o ... 1 Cor 4:13
cares about the things o ... 1 Cor 7:33
sorrow o produces death .. 2 Cor 7:10
under the elements o ... Gal 4:3
before the foundation o ... Eph 1:4
basic principles o ... Col 2:8
wants to be a friend o ... James 4:4
escaped the pollutions o ... 2 Pet 2:20
of the Father but is o ... 1 John 2:16
sent the Son as Savior o .. 1 John 4:14
from the foundation o ... Rev 17:8

OF THIS WORLD
word, and the cares o ... Matt 13:22
o, the deceitfulness ... Mark 4:19
sons o are more shrewd ... Luke 16:8
You are o; I am not o ... John 8:23
he sees the light o ... John 11:9
Now is the judgment o ... John 12:31
for the ruler o is coming .. John 14:30
the ruler o is judged ... John 16:11
"My kingdom is not o ... John 18:36
foolish the wisdom o ... 1 Cor 1:20
wisdom o is foolishness ... 1 Cor 3:19
immoral people o ... 1 Cor 5:10
form o is passing away ... 1 Cor 7:31
according to the course o ... Eph 2:2
not chosen the poor o ... James 2:5
kingdoms o have become .. Rev 11:15

OFFEND
I will o no more ... Job 34:31
that devour him will o ... Jer 2:3
lest we o them ... Matt 17:27
than that he should o ... Luke 17:2
them, "Does this o ... John 6:61

OFFENDED
How have I o you, that ... Gen 20:9
A brother o is harder ... Prov 18:19
is not o because of Me ... Matt 11:6
So they were o at Him ... Matt 13:57
And then many will be o .. Matt 24:10

have I o in anything at all .. Acts 25:8
stumbles or is o ... Rom 14:21

OFFENDER
who make a man an o ... Is 29:21
For if I am an o ... Acts 25:11

OFFENSE
and a rock of o ... Is 8:14
You are an o to Me ... Matt 16:23
by whom the o comes ... Matt 18:7
one man's o many died ... Rom 5:15
by the one man's o ... Rom 5:17
stone and rock of o ... Rom 9:33
Give no o, either to ... 1 Cor 10:32
the o of the cross ... Gal 5:11
sincere and without o ... Phil 1:10
and a rock of o ... 1 Pet 2:8

OFFENSES
For o must come ... Matt 18:7
impossible that no o ... Luke 17:1
up because of our o ... Rom 4:25

OFFER
and o him there as a burnt .. Gen 22:2
You shall not o strange ... Ex 30:9
o for a sweet aroma to the .. Lev 6:21
to o willingly to You ... 1 Chr 29:17
o up for yourselves a burnt .. Job 42:8
Therefore I will o sacrifices ... Ps 27:6
o to You the sacrifice ... Ps 116:17
o the blind as a ... Mal 1:8
come and o your gift ... Matt 5:24
one cheek, o the other ... Luke 6:29
egg, will he o him a ... Luke 11:12
to o up sacrifices, first for ... Heb 7:27
which they o continually ... Heb 10:1
let us continually o ... Heb 13:15
to o up spiritual sacrifices ... 1 Pet 2:5

OFFERED
Jacob o a sacrifice on ... Gen 31:54
eaten the same day it is o ... Lev 7:15
o profane fire before the ... Lev 10:1
Solomon o a thousand ... 1 Kin 3:4
who willingly o a ... Ezra 3:5
he o them money, ... Acts 8:18
from things o to idols ... Acts 15:29
to eat those things o ... 1 Cor 8:10
"This was o to idols," ... 1 Cor 10:28
when He o up Himself ... Heb 7:27
the eternal Spirit o ... Heb 9:14
so Christ was o ... Heb 9:28
in them" (which are o ... Heb 10:8
o one sacrifice ... Heb 10:12
By faith Abel o ... Heb 11:4

OFFERING
not respect Cain and his o ... Gen 4:5
poured a drink o on it ... Gen 35:14
a freewill o to the LORD, all .. Ex 35:29
you shall bring your o ... Lev 1:2
This is the law of the sin o .. Lev 6:25
Do not respect their o ... Num 16:15
fifty men who were o ... Num 16:35
he offered the burnt o ... 1 Sam 13:9
at the time of the o of ... 1 Kin 18:36
the o for the house of our ... Ezra 8:25
of God, with the grain o ... Neh 13:9
o You did not require ... Ps 40:6
You make His soul an o ... Is 53:10
they should present an o ... Dan 2:46
drink o have been cut off ... Joel 1:9
I accept an o from your ... Mal 1:10
to the LORD an o ... Mal 3:3
an o for your cleansing, ... Luke 5:14
Himself for us, an o ... Eph 5:2
out as a drink o ... Phil 2:17
o You did not ... Heb 10:5
o of the body of Jesus ... Heb 10:10
o He has perfected ... Heb 10:14
is no longer an o ... Heb 10:18

OFFERINGS
and offered burnt o ... Gen 8:20
It is most holy of the o ... Lev 2:3

My food for My o made ... Num 28:2
on it burnt o to the LORD ... Josh 8:31
delight in burnt o ... 1 Sam 15:22
burnt o and peace o ... 2 Sam 24:25
heart brought burnt o ... 2 Chr 29:31
He remember all your o ... Ps 20:3
freewill o of my mouth ... Ps 119:108
enough of burnt o of rams ... Is 1:11
In burnt o and ... Heb 10:6

OFFERS
Whoever o praise glorifies .. Ps 50:23
o sacrifices in the high ... Jer 48:35
that he o God service ... John 16:2

OFFICE
He restored me to my o ... Gen 41:13
let another take his o ... Ps 109:8
sitting at the tax o ... Matt 9:9
Levi, sitting at the tax o ... Luke 5:27
'Let another take his o ... Acts 1:20

OFFICERS
appoint o over the land ... Gen 41:34
also make your o ... Is 60:17
the o struck Him with ... Mark 14:65
o answered, "No man ... John 7:46
o saw Him, they cried ... John 19:6

OFFSCOURING
You have made us an o ... Lam 3:45
the o of all things ... 1 Cor 4:13

OFFSPRING
You have given me no o ... Gen 15:3
also shown me your o ... Gen 48:11
because of the o which ... Ruth 4:12
your o like the grass of the .. Job 5:25
My blessing on your o ... Is 44:3
He seeks godly o ... Mal 2:15
wife and raise up o ... Matt 22:24
had her and left no o ... Mark 12:22
For we are also His o ... Acts 17:28
we are the o of God ... Acts 17:29
am the Root and the O ... Rev 22:16

OFTEN
o I wanted to gather ... Luke 13:34
as o as you eat this ... 1 Cor 11:26
in sleeplessness o ... 2 Cor 11:27
should offer Himself o ... Heb 9:25

OG
Amorite king of Bashan, Deut 3:1–13
Defeated and killed by Israel, Num 21:32–35

OHOLAH
Symbolic name of Samaria, Ezek 23:4, 5, 36

OIL
for the anointing o ... Ex 25:6
o to Me throughout your ... Ex 30:31
shall take the anointing o ... Ex 40:9
anointing o on Aaron's ... Lev 8:12
land of olive o and honey ... Deut 8:8
I cease giving my o ... Judg 9:9
a bin, and a little o ... 1 Kin 17:12
the jar of o run dry ... 1 Kin 17:16
So the o ceased ... 2 Kin 4:6
o to the storehouse ... Neh 13:12
poured out rivers of o ... Job 29:6
You anoint my head with o ... Ps 23:5
anointed with fresh o ... Ps 92:10
the heart of man, o ... Ps 104:15
like the precious o ... Ps 133:2
be as excellent o ... Ps 141:5
the o of joy for mourning, ... Is 61:3
and I anointed you with o .. Ezek 16:9
with new wine and o ... Joel 2:24
thousand rivers of o ... Mic 6:7
and took no o with them, ... Matt 25:3
the wise took o in their ... Matt 25:4
'Give us some of your o ... Matt 25:8
very costly fragrant o ... Matt 26:7
o might have been sold ... Matt 26:9

costly *o* of spikenard . . . . . . Mark 14:3
anoint My head with *o* . . . . Luke 7:46
wounds, pouring on *o* . . . . Luke 10:34
Why was this fragrant *o* . . . John 12:5
anointing him with *o* . . . . . James 5:14
and do not harm the *o* . . . . Rev 6:6

OINTMENT
O and perfume delight . . . . . Prov 27:9
your name is *o* . . . . Song 1:3

OLD
was five hundred years *o* . . . Gen 5:32
was ninety-nine years *o* . . . . Gen 17:1
who is ninety years *o* . . . . . Gen 17:17
Remember the days of *o*, . . . Deut 32:7
o lion perishes for lack . . . . . . Job 4:11
So Job died, *o* and full of . . Job 42:17
young, and now am *o* . . . . Ps 37:25
me off in the time of *o* age . . . . Ps 71:9
will utter dark sayings of *o* . . . Ps 78:2
still bear fruit in *o* age . . . . . . Ps 92:14
are the crown of *o* men . . . . . Prov 17:6
and when he is *o* he will . . . Prov 22:6
all manner, new and *o* . . . . . Song 7:13
die one hundred years *o* . . . . . Is 65:20
o men shall dream dreams . . Joel 2:28
was said to those of *o* . . . . . . Matt 5:21
wine into *o* wineskins . . . . . . Matt 9:17
He was twelve years *o* . . . . . Luke 2:42
man be born when he is *o* . . John 3:4
yet fifty years *o* . . . . John 8:57
but when you are *o* . . . . John 21:18
Your *o* men shall dream . . . . Acts 2:17
o man was crucified . . . . Rom 6:6
of the *O* Testament . . . . 2 Cor 3:14
o things have passed . . . . . . 2 Cor 5:17
have put off the *o* man . . . . Col 3:9
o wives' fables, and . . . . 1 Tim 4:7
obsolete and growing *o* . . . . . Heb 8:13
that serpent of *o* . . . . Rev 20:2

OLD MAN
the presence of an *o* . . . . Lev 19:32
there will not be an *o* . . . . . 1 Sam 2:31
nor an *o* who has not . . . . Is 65:20
I am an *o*, and my wife . . . . Luke 1:18
our *o* was crucified . . . . Rom 6:6
the *o* which grows corrupt . . Eph 4:22
put off the *o* with his . . . . Col 3:9

OLDER
o shall serve the . . . . Gen 25:23
o than your father . . . . Job 15:10
"Now his *o* son was . . . . . . Luke 15:25
not rebuke an *o* man . . . . 1 Tim 5:1
o women as mothers . . . . 1 Tim 5:2
that the *o* men be sober, ... Titus 2:2
the *o* women likewise, that . . Titus 2:3

OLDEST
beginning with the *o* . . . . John 8:9

OLIVE
a freshly plucked *o* . . . . Gen 8:11
o trees which you did not . . Deut 6:11
a land of *o* groves . . . . 2 Kin 18:32
I am like a green *o* . . . . Ps 52:8
Your children like *o* plants . . Ps 128:3
of the *o* may fail . . . . Hab 3:17
the *o* tree have not yielded . . Hag 2:19
and you, being a wild *o* . . . Rom 11:17
o tree which is wild . . . . Rom 11:24
These are the two *o* trees . . . Rev 11:4

OLIVES, MOUNT OF
David flees to, 2 Sam 15:30
Prophecy concerning, Zech 14:4
Christ's triumphal entry from, Matt 21:1
Prophetic discourse delivered from, Matt 24:3
Christ's ascension from, Acts 1:9–12

OMNIPOTENT
For the Lord God *O* . . . . Rev 19:6

OMRI
Made king of Israel by army, 1 Kin 16:16, 21, 22
Builds Samaria; reigns wickedly, 1 Kin 16:23–27

ON
City of Lower Egypt; center of sun worship, Gen 41:45, 50
Called Beth Shemesh, Jer 43:13

ONAN
Second son of Judah; slain for failure to give his brother an heir, Gen 38:8–10

ONCE
please come at *o* . . . . Num 22:6
marched around the city *o* . . Josh 6:14
o more with the fleece . . . . . . Judg 6:39
God has spoken *o*, twice I . . . Ps 62:11
shall a nation be born at *o* . . . . Is 66:8
died, He died to sin *o* . . . . . . Rom 6:10
alive *o* without the law . . . . . . Rom 7:9
o I was stoned . . . . 2 Cor 11:25
o were far off have been . . . . Eph 2:13
who *o* was unprofitable . . . . . Philem 11
for this He did *o* for all . . . . . Heb 7:27
Most Holy Place *o* for all . . . . Heb 9:12
for men to die *o* . . . . Heb 9:27
so Christ was offered *o* to . . . Heb 9:28
who *o* were not a people . . . 1 Pet 2:10
also suffered *o* . . . . 1 Pet 3:18

ONE
See EVIL ONE; HOLY ONE OF ISRAEL; LOVE ONE ANOTHER; WITH ONE ACCORD
He took *o* of his ribs, and . . . Gen 2:21
they shall become *o* flesh . . . Gen 2:24
desirable to make *o* wise . . . . . Gen 3:6
o language and *o* speech . . . . Gen 11:1
our God, the LORD is *o* . . . . . . Deut 6:4
Blessed be the *o* who . . . . . . Ruth 2:19
on a mountain on *o* side . . 1 Sam 17:3
kissed *o* another . . . . 1 Sam 20:41
in two, and give half to *o* . . 1 Kin 3:25
failed *o* word of all His . . . . 1 Kin 8:56
I told no *o* what my God . . . . Neh 2:12
no *o* could withstand them, . . Esth 9:2
o who feared God and . . . . Job 1:1
o mocked by his friends, ... Job 12:4
find *o* wise man among . . . . Job 17:10
God may speak in *o* way . . . Job 33:14
who does good, no, not *o* . . . . . Ps 53:3
limited the Holy *O* of Israel . . Ps 78:41
Blessed is every *o* who . . . . . . Ps 128:1
there is *o* who withholds . . Prov 11:24
flee when no *o* pursues . . . . Prov 28:1
Two are better than *o* . . . . Eccl 4:9
up, my love, my fair *o* . . . . . Song 2:10
I will seek the *o* I love . . . . . . Song 3:2
shall take hold of *o* man, ... Is 4:1
open, and no *o* shall shut . . . . . Is 22:22
you will be gathered *o* . . . . Is 27:12
Return now every *o* from . . . Jer 18:11
wings touched *o* another . . . . Ezek 1:9
Each *o* had four faces . . . . . Ezek 10:21
o who is found written . . . . . Dan 12:1
Holy *O* who is faithful . . . . . Hos 11:12
Has not *o* God created us . . . Mal 2:10
deliver us from the evil *o* . . . Matt 6:13
whoever causes *o* of . . . . Matt 18:6
two shall become *o* flesh' . . . Matt 19:5
and hour no *o* knows . . . . . . Matt 24:36
watch with Me *o* hour . . . . . Matt 26:40
receives *o* of these . . . . Mark 9:37
"*O* thing you lack . . . . Mark 10:21
o on Your right hand . . . . . Mark 10:37
Surely you are *o* of . . . . Mark 14:70
The voice of *o* crying in . . . . Luke 3:4
No *o*, when he has lit a . . . . Luke 8:16
o thing is needed . . . . Luke 10:42
o sinner who repents . . . . . . Luke 15:10
You still lack *o* thing . . . . . Luke 18:22
O sows and another . . . . John 4:37
Has no *o* condemned you . . John 8:10
I and My Father are *o* . . . . John 10:30
you love *o* another . . . . John 13:34
Me, that they may be *o* . . . John 17:11
Not *o* of His bones . . . . John 19:36
Holy *O* to see corruption . . . Acts 2:27
o accord in the temple . . . . . Acts 2:46
none righteous, no, not *o* . . . Rom 3:10
each *o* a measure of faith . . Rom 12:3
Repay no *o* evil for evil . . . Rom 12:17
Owe no *o* anything except . Rom 13:8
that *o* be found faithful . . . . . 1 Cor 4:2
to *o* is given the word . . . . . 1 Cor 12:8
body is not *o* member . . . . 1 Cor 12:14
if *o* strikes you on the . . . . 2 Cor 11:20
for you are all *o* . . . . Gal 3:28
love serve *o* another . . . . Gal 5:13
Bear *o* another's burdens, ... Gal 6:2
to create in Himself *o* . . . . Eph 2:15
o body and *o* Spirit . . . . Eph 4:4
o Lord, *o* faith, *o* . . . . Eph 4:5
o God and Father of . . . . Eph 4:6
but *o* thing I do, forgetting . . Phil 3:13
o Mediator between God . . . 1 Tim 2:5
the husband of *o* wife . . . . . . 1 Tim 3:2
Let no *o* despise your . . . . . 1 Tim 4:12
But each *o* is tempted . . . . James 1:14
love *o* another fervently . . . 1 Pet 1:22
Be hospitable to *o* another . . . 1 Pet 4:9
a thousand years as *o* . . . . . . 2 Pet 3:8
and these three are *o* . . . . . 1 John 5:7
I will give to each *o* of you . . Rev 2:23
Lamb opened *o* of the seals . . Rev 6:1
on the cloud sat *O* like . . . . . Rev 14:14

ONESIMUS
Slave of Philemon converted by Paul in Rome, Philem 10–17
With Tychicus, carries Paul's letters to Colosse and to Philemon, Col 4:7–9

ONESIPHORUS
Ephesian Christian commended for his service, 2 Tim 1:16–18

ONLY BEGOTTEN SON
The *o*, who is in . . . . John 1:18
world that He gave His *o* . . John 3:16
offered up his *o* . . . . Heb 11:17
God has sent His *o* . . . . 1 John 4:9

OPEN
o his eyes that he may . . . . 2 Kin 6:17
o the eyes of these men . . . 2 Kin 6:20
o His lips against you . . . . Job 11:5
His ears are *o* to their cry . . . Ps 34:15
You *o* Your hand . . . . Ps 104:28
O my eyes, that I may see . . Ps 119:18
O rebuke is better than . . . . Prov 27:5
O your mouth for the . . . . . . Prov 31:8
and no one shall *o* . . . . Is 22:22
I will *o* your mouth to . . . . Ezek 29:21
o toward Jerusalem . . . . Dan 6:10
a lamb in *o* country . . . . Hos 4:16
o My mouth in parables . . . Matt 13:35
Can a demon *o* the eyes . . John 10:21
she did not *o* the gate . . . . . Acts 12:14
our heart is wide *o* . . . . 2 Cor 6:11
things are naked and *o* . . . . . Heb 4:13
set before you an *o* door . . . . . Rev 3:8
o the scroll and to . . . . Rev 5:2

OPENED
eat of it your eyes will be *o* . . Gen 3:5
the earth *o* its mouth . . . . . Num 16:32
the LORD *o* the mouth . . . . . Num 22:28
the LORD *o* the eyes . . . . 2 Kin 6:17
Ezra *o* the book in the sight . . Neh 8:5
o not His mouth . . . . Is 53:7
that the heavens were *o* . . . . . Ezek 1:1
knock, and it will be *o* to . . . . Matt 7:7
our eyes may be *o* . . . . Matt 20:33
his ears were *o* . . . . Mark 7:35

when He had *o* the book . . . Luke 4:17
Then their eyes were *o* . . . Luke 24:31
o the Scriptures . . . . Luke 24:32
o their understanding . . . . Luke 24:45
clay and *o* his eyes . . . . John 9:14
Lord *o* the prison doors . . . . Acts 5:19
I see the heavens *o* and . . . . Acts 7:56
effective door has *o* . . . . 1 Cor 16:9
when the Lamb *o* . . . . Rev 6:1
he *o* the bottomless pit, and . . Rev 9:2
Now I saw heaven *o* . . . . Rev 19:11
God, and books were *o* . . . . Rev 20:12

OPENLY
will Himself reward you *o* . . . Matt 6:4
to the feast, not *o* . . . . John 7:10
o among the Jews, ... John 11:54
and showed Him *o* . . . . Acts 10:40
They have beaten us *o*, ... Acts 16:37

OPENS
o the ears of men . . . . Job 33:16
The LORD *o* the eyes of . . . . . . Ps 146:8
him the doorkeeper *o* . . . . . . John 10:3
and shuts and no one *o* . . . . . . Rev 3:7
o the door, I will come in . . . Rev 3:20

OPHEL
Hill, southeast of Jerusalem, Neh 3:15–27
Fortified by Manasseh, 2 Chr 27:3
Residence of Nethinim, Neh 3:26

OPHIR
Famous for gold, 1 Chr 29:4

OPHRAH
Town in Manasseh; home of Gideon, Judg 6:11, 15
Site of Gideon's burial, Judg 8:32

OPINION
dared not declare my *o* . . . . . Job 32:6
be wise in your own *o* . . . . Rom 11:25

OPINIONS
falter between two *o* . . . . . 1 Kin 18:21

OPPORTUNITY
sought *o* to betray Him . . . Matt 26:16
o to answer for himself . . . Acts 25:16
But sin, taking *o* . . . . Rom 7:8
but give you *o* to boast . . . . . 2 Cor 5:12
that I may cut off the *o* . . . 2 Cor 11:12
liberty as an *o* for the flesh . . Gal 5:13
as we have *o* . . . . Gal 6:10
but you lacked *o* . . . . Phil 4:10
no *o* to the adversary . . . . . 1 Tim 5:14
they would have had *o* . . . . Heb 11:15

OPPOSES
who *o* and exalts . . . . 2 Thess 2:4

OPPOSITE
wrote *o* the lampstand on . . . . Dan 5:5
Go into the village *o* you . . . Matt 21:2
Mary, sitting *o* the tomb . . Matt 27:61
Jesus sat *o* the treasury . . Mark 12:41
Gadarenes, which is *o* . . . . . Luke 8:26

OPPRESS
mistreat a stranger nor *o* . . . . Ex 22:21
you shall not *o* . . . . Lev 25:17
You that You should *o* . . . . . . Job 10:3
He does not *o* . . . . Job 37:23
no more *o* My people . . . . . . Ezek 45:8
he loves to *o* . . . . Hos 12:7
they *o* a man and his house, . . . Mic 2:2
o the widow or the . . . . Zech 7:10
o them four hundred years . . Acts 7:6
Do not the rich *o* . . . . James 2:6

OPPRESSED
Whom have I *o* . . . . 1 Sam 12:3
For he has *o* and . . . . Job 20:19
fatherless and the *o* . . . . Ps 10:18
for all who are *o* . . . . Ps 103:6
The tears of the *o* . . . . Eccl 4:1
He was *o* and He was . . . . Is 53:7

her midst, and the *o* . . . . Amos 3:9
at liberty those who are *o* . . Luke 4:18
healing all who were *o* . . . . . Acts 10:38
Lot, who was *o* by . . . . 2 Pet 2:7

OPPRESSES
o the poor reproaches . . . . . Prov 14:31
o the poor to increase . . . . . Prov 22:16
A poor man who *o* . . . . Prov 28:3

OPPRESSION
have surely seen the *o* . . . . Ex 3:7
"For the *o* of the . . . . Ps 12:5
Do not trust in *o* . . . . Ps 62:10
their life from *o* . . . . Ps 72:14
brought low through *o* . . . . . Ps 107:39
Redeem me from the *o* . . . . Ps 119:134
considered all the *o* . . . . Eccl 4:1
o destroys a wise . . . . Eccl 7:7
justice, but behold, *o* . . . . Is 5:7
surely seen the *o* . . . . Acts 7:34

OPPRESSIONS
of *o* they cry out . . . . Job 35:9

OPPRESSOR
the voice of the *o* . . . . Job 3:18
Do not envy the *o* . . . . Prov 3:31
is a great *o* . . . . Prov 28:16
of the fury of the *o* . . . . Is 51:13
No more shall an *o* . . . . Zech 9:8

OPPRESSORS
me from the hand of *o* . . . . Job 6:23
not leave me to my *o* . . . . . Ps 119:121
o there is power . . . . Eccl 4:1
LORD because of the *o* . . . . Is 19:20

ORACLES
received the living *o* . . . . Acts 7:38
were committed the *o* . . . . Rom 3:2
principles of the *o* . . . . Heb 5:12
let him speak as the *o* . . . . . 1 Pet 4:11

ORDAINED
infants You have *o* . . . . Ps 8:2
the stars, which You have *o* . . . . Ps 8:3
o you a prophet . . . . Jer 1:5
the Man whom He has *o* . . Acts 17:31
God *o* before the ages . . . . . . 1 Cor 2:7

ORDER
in *o* that you may know . . . . . . Ex 8:22
'Set your house in *o* . . . . 2 Kin 20:1
of the LORD was set in *o* . . 2 Chr 29:35
in *o* to seek the LORD . . . . Ezra 6:21
set your words in *o* . . . . Job 33:5
you, and set them in *o* . . . . Ps 50:21
to the *o* of Melchizedek . . . . . Ps 110:4
in *o* to cleanse the land . . . Ezek 39:12
swept, and put in *o* . . . . Matt 12:44
it swept and put in *o* . . . . . . Luke 11:25
done decently and in *o* . . . . 1 Cor 14:40
each one in his own *o* . . . . 1 Cor 15:23
to see your good *o* . . . . Col 2:5
according to the *o* . . . . Heb 5:6
in *o* to stir up love . . . . Heb 10:24

ORDERED
man did as Joseph *o* . . . . . . Gen 43:17
for so the LORD has *o* . . . . 2 Sam 16:11
for so the king had *o* all . . . . . Esth 1:8
a good man are *o* by the . . . . Ps 37:23

ORDERS
o his conduct aright I . . . . Ps 50:23
as I have given *o* to the . . . . 1 Cor 16:1

ORDINANCE
the *o* of the Passover . . . . Ex 12:43
you shall keep My *o* . . . . Lev 18:30
an *o* forever throughout . . . . Num 10:8
o for Israel to this day . . . 1 Sam 30:25
required by *o* for each day . . Ezra 3:4
forsake the *o* of their God . . . . . Is 58:2
that we have kept His *o* . . . . . Mal 3:14
resists the *o* of God . . . . Rom 13:2
yourselves to every *o* . . . . . . 1 Pet 2:13

ORDINANCES
shall you walk in their *o* . . . . Lev 18:3

o by the hand of Moses . . . 2 Chr 33:8
and gave them just *o* . . . . Neh 9:13
Do you know the *o* . . . . Job 38:33
according to Your *o* . . . . Ps 119:91
"If those *o* depart . . . . Jer 31:36
not appointed the *o* . . . . Jer 33:25
gone away from My *o* . . . . Mal 3:7
contained in *o* . . . . Eph 2:15
and fleshly *o* imposed . . . . . . Heb 9:10

ORION
Brilliant constellation, Job 9:9

ORNAMENT
will be a graceful *o* . . . . Prov 1:9
of gold and an *o* . . . . Prov 25:12
with them all as an *o* . . . . Is 49:18

ORNAMENTS
cheeks are lovely with *o* . . . . Song 1:10
a virgin forget her *o* . . . . Jer 2:32
I adorned you with *o*, put . Ezek 16:11

ORPAH
Ruth's sister-in-law, Ruth 1:4, 14

ORPHANS
We have become *o* . . . . Lam 5:3
I will not leave you *o* . . . . . John 14:18
to visit *o* and widows . . . . . James 1:27

OSNAPPER
Called "the great and noble," Ezra 4:10

OSTRICHES
o will dwell there . . . . Is 13:21
is cruel, like *o* . . . . Lam 4:3
a mourning like the *o* . . . . Mic 1:8

OTHNIEL
Son of Kenaz, Caleb's youngest brother, Judg 1:13
Captures Kirjath Sepher; receives Caleb's daughter as wife, Josh 15:15–17
First judge of Israel, Judg 3:9–11

OUGHT
what Israel *o* to do . . . . 1 Chr 12:32
These you *o* to have . . . . . . Matt 23:23
pray for as we *o* . . . . Rom 8:26
how you *o* to conduct . . . . . . 1 Tim 3:15
which they *o* not . . . . 1 Tim 5:13
persons *o* you to be . . . . 2 Pet 3:11

OUTCAST
they called you an *o* . . . . Jer 30:17
the lame, I will gather the *o* . . Mic 4:6
and the *o* a strong nation . . . . . Mic 4:7

OUTCASTS
gathers together the *o* . . . . Ps 147:2
will assemble the *o* . . . . Is 11:12
hide the *o*, do not betray . . . . . . Is 16:3
Let My *o* dwell with . . . . Is 16:4

OUTCRY
because the *o* against . . . . . . Gen 19:13
that there be no *o* . . . . Ps 144:14
Then there arose a loud *o* . . . Acts 23:9

OUTGOINGS
You make the *o* of the . . . . Ps 65:8

OUTRAGE
lewdness and *o* in . . . . Judg 20:6

OUTRAN
the other disciple *o* . . . . John 20:4

OUTSIDE
and dish, that the *o* . . . . Matt 23:26
Pharisees make the *o* . . . . . Luke 11:39
toward those who are *o* . . . . Col 4:5
to Him, *o* the camp . . . . Heb 13:13
But *o* are dogs and . . . . Rev 22:15

OUTSTRETCHED
power and by Your *o* arm . . Deut 9:29
and with an *o* arm . . . . Deut 26:8
an *o* arm, Him you shall . . 2 Kin 17:36
against you with an *o* . . . . Jer 21:5

OUTWARD
at the *o* appearance ...... 1 Sam 16:7
Even though our *o* man ... 2 Cor 4:16
to the *o* appearance .... 2 Cor 10:7
adornment be merely *o* ..... 1 Pet 3:3

OUTWARDLY
appear beautiful *o* .... Matt 23:27
not a Jew who is one *o* .... Rom 2:28

OUTWIT
The enemy shall not *o* .... Ps 89:22

OVEN
make them as a fiery *o* .... Ps 21:9
burning like an *o* .... Mal 4:1
is thrown into the *o* .... Matt 6:30

OVERCAME
My throne, as I also *o* .... Rev 3:21
And they *o* him by .... Rev 12:11

OVERCOME
we are well able to *o* it ... Num 13:30
for they have *o* me .... Song 6:5
to those who are *o* with wine .. Is 28:1
good cheer, I have *o* ...... John 16:33
o when You are judged ...... Rom 3:4
o evil with good .... Rom 12:21
entangled in them and *o* ... 2 Pet 2:20
because you have *o* ...... 1 John 2:13
and have *o* them, ... 1 John 4:4
that has *o* the world .... 1 John 5:4
and the Lamb will *o* .... Rev 17:14

OVERCOMES
of God *o* the world .... 1 John 5:4
he who *o* the world .... 1 John 5:5
o I will give to eat .... Rev 2:7
o shall not be hurt .... Rev 2:11
To him who *o* I will give .... Rev 2:17
He who *o* shall be clothed ...... Rev 3:5
To him who *o* I will grant ... Rev 3:21
o shall inherit all .... Rev 21:7

OVERFLOW
Let not the floodwater *o* ..... Ps 69:15
vats will *o* with new wine .. Prov 3:10
shall *o* with righteousness ... Is 10:22
rivers, they shall not *o* you .... Is 43:2
vats shall *o* with new wine .. Joel 2:24

OVERFLOWING
My heart is *o* with a .... Ps 45:1
a flood of mighty waters *o* ..... Is 28:2
and shall be an *o* flood ...... Jer 47:2
But with an *o* flood He will ... Nah 1:8

OVERSEER
Then he made him *o* .... Gen 39:4
having no captain, *o* .... Prov 6:7
to the Shepherd and O ..... 1 Pet 2:25

OVERSEERS
Spirit has made you *o* ..... Acts 20:28
you, serving as *o* .... 1 Pet 5:2

OVERSHADOW
of the Highest will *o* .... Luke 1:35

OVERTAKE
some evil *o* me and I die ... Gen 19:19
o you, because you obey ... Deut 28:2
upon you and *o* you ...... Deut 28:15
and *o* you, until you are ... Deut 28:45
lest he *o* us suddenly .... 2 Sam 15:14
does righteousness *o* .... Is 59:9
you feared shall *o* .... Jer 42:16
lest darkness *o* you .... John 12:35
and *o* this chariot .... Acts 8:29
that this Day should *o* .... 1 Thess 5:4

OVERTAKEN
and anguish have *o* me ... Ps 119:143
No temptation has *o* ..... 1 Cor 10:13
if a man is *o* in any .... Gal 6:1

OVERTHREW
So He *o* those cities .... Gen 19:25
will be as when God *o* .... Is 13:19
As God *o* Sodom and .... Jer 50:40
"I *o* some of you .... Amos 4:11

OVERTHROW
you shall utterly *o* .... Ex 23:24
o them in the wilderness ... Ps 106:26
o their descendants .... Ps 106:27
o the righteous in .... Prov 18:5
As in the *o* of Sodom and ... Jer 49:18
o the throne of .... Hag 2:22
of God, you cannot *o* it ..... Acts 5:39
o the faith of some .... 2 Tim 2:18

OVERTHROWN
Their judges are *o* .... Ps 141:6
but it is *o* by the mouth ... Prov 11:11
The wicked are *o* and are .. Prov 12:7
desolate, as *o* by strangers ..... Is 1:7
of Sodom, which was *o* ..... Lam 4:6
I will make it *o* .... Ezek 21:27
and Nineveh shall be *o* ...... Jon 3:4

OVERTHROWS
and *o* the mighty .... Job 12:19
o them in the night .... Job 34:25
o the words of the .... Prov 22:12

OVERTURNED
my heart is *o* within .... Lam 1:20
o the tables of the .... Matt 21:12
money and *o* the tables ..... John 2:15

OVERWHELM
o the fatherless .... Job 6:27
sends them out, they *o* .... Job 12:15

OVERWHELMED
when my heart is *o* .... Ps 61:2
and my spirit was *o* .... Ps 77:3
o their enemies .... Ps 78:53
waters would have *o* .... Ps 124:4
my spirit is *o* within .... Ps 143:4

OVERWORK
Do not *o* to be rich .... Prov 23:4

OWE
Pay me what you *o* ...... Matt 18:28
'How much do you *o* ...... Luke 16:5
O no one anything .... Rom 13:8
o me even your own .... Philem 19

OWED
o him ten thousand .... Matt 18:24
fellow servants who *o* ..... Matt 18:28
o five hundred denarii ..... Luke 7:41

OWN
created man in His *o* .... Gen 1:27
interpretation of his *o* ..... Gen 41:11
of his *o* people as wife ..... Lev 21:14
grasshoppers in our *o* .... Num 13:33
is right in his *o* eyes ...... Deut 12:8
each to his *o* inheritance .. Josh 24:28
a man after His *o* heart .. 1 Sam 13:14
loved him as his *o* soul ... 1 Sam 18:1
Your very *o* people .... 2 Sam 7:24
Your *o* we have given .... 1 Chr 29:14
everyone to his *o* city .... Ezra 2:1
reproach on their *o* heads .... Neh 4:4
wise in their *o* craftiness .... Job 5:13
He who swears to his *o* hurt .. Ps 15:4
Even my *o* familiar friend in .. Ps 41:9
on your *o* understanding .... Prov 3:5
not be wise in your *o* eyes .. Prov 3:7
troubles his *o* house ..... Prov 11:29
a fool is right in his *o* ..... Prov 12:15
a man are pure in his *o* .... Prov 16:2
wisdom loves his *o* soul .... Prov 19:8
no rule over his *o* spirit ... Prov 25:28
forsake your *o* friend ..... Prov 27:10
her *o* works praise her .... Prov 31:31
over another to his *o* hurt .... Eccl 8:9
the work of their *o* hands ...... Is 2:8
every one from his *o* fig ..... Is 36:16
dictates of their *o* heart ...... Jer 9:14
return upon your *o* head .... Obad 15
idols forsake their *o* Mercy ... Jon 2:8
men of his *o* household .... Mic 7:6
the plank in your *o* eye ..... Matt 7:3
dead bury their *o* dead ..... Matt 8:22
and loses his *o* soul .... Matt 16:26
honor except in his *o* .... Mark 6:4
is known by its *o* fruit ..... Luke 6:44
He came to His *o* .... John 1:11
not to do My *o* will .... John 6:38
I do not seek My *o* glory ... John 8:50
and am known by My *o* .. John 10:14
having loved His *o* .... John 13:1
world would love its *o* .... John 15:19
took her to his *o* home .... John 19:27
speak in his *o* language ..... Acts 2:6
by our *o* power or .... Acts 3:12
His *o* love toward us .... Rom 5:8
did not spare His *o* Son .... Rom 8:32
and you are not your *o* .... 1 Cor 6:19
But each one has his *o* ..... 1 Cor 7:7
ask their *o* husbands at .. 1 Cor 14:35
plucked out your *o* eyes ..... Gal 4:15
submit to your *o* husbands .. Eph 5:22
ought to love their *o* wives .. Eph 5:28
work out your *o* salvation .. Phil 2:12
For all seek their *o* .... Phil 2:21
who rules his *o* house ...... 1 Tim 3:4
but with His *o* blood He .... Heb 9:12
in His *o* body on the tree .. 1 Pet 2:24
but left their *o* abode .... Jude 6
from our sins in His *o* .... Rev 1:5

OX
shall not muzzle an *o* ...... Deut 25:4
"Will the wild *o* .... Job 39:9
you bind the wild *o* .... Job 39:10
like a young wild *o* .... Ps 29:6
exalted like a wild *o* .... Ps 92:10
o knows its owner .... Is 1:3
had the face of an *o* .... Ezek 1:10
Sabbath loose his *o* ...... Luke 13:15
shall not muzzle an *o* .... 1 Cor 9:9

PACE
are majestic in *p* .... Prov 30:29

PACIFIES
A gift in secret *p* .... Prov 21:14
for conciliation *p* .... Eccl 10:4

PADAN ARAM
Same as Mesopotamia, Gen 24:10; *see* MESOPOTAMIA
Home of Isaac's wife, Gen 25:20
Jacob flees to, Gen 28:2–7
Jacob returns from, Gen 31:17, 18
People of, called Syrians, Gen 31:24
Language of, called Aramaic, 2 Kin 18:26

PAGAN
have taken *p* wives from ... Ezra 10:2
by marrying *p* women ..... Neh 13:27
have begotten *p* children ..... Hos 5:7
priests with the *p* priests .... Zeph 1:4

PAID
today I have *p* my vows .... Prov 7:14
p the very last mite .... Luke 12:59
p tithes through Abraham .... Heb 7:9

PAILS
p are full of milk .... Job 21:24

PAIN
p you shall bring .... Gen 3:16
Because I bore him in *p* .... 1 Chr 4:9
on my affliction and my *p* ... Ps 25:18
p as a woman in .... Is 13:8
are filled with *p* .... Is 21:3
before her *p* came .... Is 66:7
Why is my *p* perpetual ..... Jer 15:18
labor and in *p* to give birth .. Rev 12:2
shall be no more *p* .... Rev 21:4

PAINED
My heart is severely *p* .... Ps 55:4
I am *p* in my very .... Jer 4:19

PAINFUL
this, it was too *p* .... Ps 73:16
for the present, but *p* ...... Heb 12:11

PAINS
The *p* of death .... Ps 116:3
having loosed the *p* .... Acts 2:24
upon them, as labor *p* .... 1 Thess 5:3

PAINT
and she put *p* on her ...... 2 Kin 9:30
your eyes with *p* .... Jer 4:30

PAINTING
it with cedar and *p* .... Jer 22:14

PALACE
support from the *p* .... Ezra 4:14
was taken to the king's *p* .... Esth 2:8
was great in the king's *p* .... Esth 9:4
enter the King's *p* .... Ps 45:15
a *p* of foreigners .... Is 25:2
to serve in the king's *p* .... Dan 1:4
the king went to his *p* ...... Dan 6:18
at the *p* of the high priest .. Matt 26:3
guards his own *p* .... Luke 11:21
evident to the whole *p* ...... Phil 1:13

PALACES
out of the ivory *p* .... Ps 45:8
God is in her *p* .... Ps 48:3
has entered our *p* .... Jer 9:21
has swallowed up all her *p* .. Lam 2:5
in the *p* at Ashdod .... Amos 3:9

PALANQUIN
the King made himself a *p* .. Song 3:9

PALE
his face now grow *p* .... Is 29:22
and all faces turned *p* .... Jer 30:6
behold, a *p* horse .... Rev 6:8

PALM
of water and seventy *p* ..... Ex 15:27
p trees, and open flowers .. 1 Kin 6:29
of yours is like a *p* tree ..... Song 7:7
p branch and bulrush in .... Is 9:14
p branch or bulrush, may .... Is 19:15
and *p* trees were carved .. Ezek 41:20
p trees and went out ...... John 12:13
p branches in their .... Rev 7:9

PALMS
you on the *p* of My hands .... Is 49:16
struck Him with the *p* ..... Matt 26:67

PALTI (or Paltiel)
Man to whom Saul gives Michal, David's wife, in marriage, 1 Sam 25:44; 2 Sam 3:15

PAMPERS
p his servant from .... Prov 29:21

PAMPHYLIA
People from, at Pentecost, Acts 2:10
Paul visits; John Mark returns home from, Acts 13:13; 15:38
Paul preaches in cities of, Acts 14:24, 25

PANGS
The *p* of death .... Ps 18:4
P and sorrows will .... Is 13:8
labors with birth *p* .... Rom 8:22

PANICKED
the men of Benjamin *p* .... Judg 20:41

PANT
They *p* after the dust .... Amos 2:7

PANTS
As the deer *p* for the .... Ps 42:1

PAPHOS
Paul blinds Elymas at, Acts 13:6–13

PAPYRUS
"Can the *p* grow up .... Job 8:11

PARABLE
open my mouth in a *p* .... Ps 78:2
speak a *p* to the house of .. Ezek 17:2
utter a *p* to the rebellious .. Ezek 24:3
p He did not speak .... Matt 13:34
learn this *p* from the fig ... Matt 24:32
spoken the *p* against ..... Mark 12:12
do You speak this *p* .... Luke 12:41

PARABLES
'Does he not speak *p* ..... Ezek 20:49
understand all the *p* .... Mark 4:13
rest it is given in *p* .... Luke 8:10

PARADE
love does not *p* .... 1 Cor 13:4

PARADISE
will be with Me in *P* ...... Luke 23:43
was caught up into *P* ...... 2 Cor 12:4
in the midst of the *P* .... Rev 2:7

PARALYTIC
then He said to the *p* .... Matt 9:6
on which the *p* was lying .... Mark 2:4

PARALYZED
servant is lying at home *p* ... Matt 8:6
sick people, blind, lame, *p* .. John 5:3
who were *p* and lame .... Acts 8:7

PARAN
Residence of exiled Ishmael, Gen 21:21
Israelites camp in, Num 10:12
Headquarters of spies, Num 13:3, 26
Site of David's refuge, 1 Sam 25:1

PARCHMENTS
especially the *p* .... 2 Tim 4:13

PARDON
p your transgressions ...... Ex 23:21
You are God, ready to *p* .... Neh 9:17
not *p* my transgression .... Job 7:21
O LORD, *p* my iniquity .... Ps 25:11
He will abundantly *p* .... Is 55:7
p all their iniquities .... Jer 33:8

PARDONED
ended, that her iniquity is *p* ... Is 40:2

PARDONING
is a God like You, *p* .... Mic 7:18

PARENTS
will rise up against *p* ..... Matt 10:21
His *p* went to Jerusalem ... Luke 2:41
has left house or *p* .... Luke 18:29
sinned, this man or his *p* .... John 9:2
disobedient to *p* .... Rom 1:30
to lay up for the *p* .... 2 Cor 12:14
obey your *p* in all things, ... Col 3:20
disobedient to *p* .... 2 Tim 3:2

PARMENAS
One of the first seven deacons, Acts 6:5

PART
You have no *p* in the ..... Josh 22:25
has chosen that good *p* ... Luke 10:42
you, you have no *p* .... John 13:8
And he kept back *p* of the .... Acts 5:2
that blindness in *p* has .... Rom 11:25
to that *p* which lacks it, .. 1 Cor 12:24
For we know in *p* .... 1 Cor 13:9
p has a believer .... 2 Cor 6:15
Abraham gave a tenth *p* ..... Heb 7:2
shall take away his *p* ...... Rev 22:19

PARTAKE
for we all *p* of that .... 1 Cor 10:17
you cannot *p* of the ...... 1 Cor 10:21

PARTAKER
and have been a *p* .... Ps 50:18
in hope should be *p* .... 1 Cor 9:10
Christ, and also a *p* .... 1 Pet 5:1

PARTAKERS
Gentiles have been *p* ..... Rom 15:27
of the sacrifices *p* .... 1 Cor 10:18
know that as you are *p* ..... 2 Cor 1:7
gospel, you all are *p* .... Phil 1:7
qualified us to be *p* .... Col 1:12
For we have become *p* ...... Heb 3:14

PARTED
them, that He was *p* ...... Luke 24:51
so sharp that they *p* .... Acts 15:39

PARTIAL
You shall not be *p* .... Lev 19:15

PARTIALITY
You shall not show *p* ...... Deut 1:17
unjustly, and show *p* .... Ps 82:2
is not good to show *p* ...... Prov 18:5
but have shown *p* .... Mal 2:9
that God shows no *p* ...... Acts 10:34
For there is no *p* .... Rom 2:11
doing nothing with *p* .... 1 Tim 5:21
but if you show *p* .... James 2:9
good fruits, without *p* .... James 3:17

PARTIES
revelries, drinking *p* .... 1 Pet 4:3

PARTING
at the *p* of the road .... Ezek 21:21

PARTITION
the Testimony, and *p* .... Ex 40:3

PARTNER
Whoever is a *p* with a .... Prov 29:24
you count me as a *p* .... Philem 17

PARTRIDGE
when one hunts a *p* ..... 1 Sam 26:20

PARTS
anything but death *p* ...... Ruth 1:17
in the inward *p* .... Ps 51:6
uttermost *p* of the sea .... Ps 139:9
Shout, you lower *p* .... Is 44:23
and made four *p* .... John 19:23
but our presentable *p* .... 1 Cor 12:24
into the lower *p* .... Eph 4:9

PASHHUR
Official opposing Jeremiah, Jer 21:1; 38:1–13
——— Priest who puts Jeremiah in jail, Jer 20:1–6

PASS
I will *p* over you .... Ex 12:13
of the sea that *p* .... Ps 8:8
When you *p* through the ...... Is 43:2
"I will make you *p* .... Ezek 20:37
seven times shall *p* over .... Dan 4:32
I will not *p* by them .... Amos 7:8
and earth will *p* .... Matt 24:35
let this cup *p* from Me .... Matt 26:39
will by no means *p* .... Mark 13:31
p away with a great noise .. 2 Pet 3:10

PASSED
And behold, the LORD *p* .. 1 Kin 19:11
and Your waves *p* over me ... Jon 2:3
p by on the other side .... Luke 10:31
forbearance God had *p* .... Rom 3:25
all *p* through the sea ...... 1 Cor 10:1
old things have *p* away .... 2 Cor 5:17
High Priest who has *p* ...... Heb 4:14
By faith they *p* through .... Heb 11:29
know that we have *p* ..... 1 John 3:14
former things have *p* away .. Rev 21:4

PASSES
For the wind *p* over it ...... Ps 103:16
of Christ which *p* .... Eph 3:19

PASSING
days are like a *p* shadow .... Ps 144:4
and *p* by, to bear His ..... Mark 15:21
Jesus of Nazareth was *p* .. Luke 18:37
which glory was *p* away, ... 2 Cor 3:7
the *p* pleasures of sin ...... Heb 11:25
the darkness is *p* away ..... 1 John 2:8

PASSION
than to burn with *p* .... 1 Cor 7:9
uncleanness, *p*, evil .... Col 3:5

PASSIONS
gave them up to vile *p* ..... Rom 1:26

PASSOVER
It is the LORD's *P* ..... Ex 12:11
of the Feast of the *P* be left .. Ex 34:25
at twilight is the LORD's *P* ... Lev 23:5
the *P* at its appointed time .. Num 9:2
to the rite of the *P* and ..... Num 9:14
sacrifice the *P* at twilight ... Deut 16:6
the *P* on the fourteenth ..... Josh 5:10
of King Josiah this *P* ..... 2 Kin 23:23
P in the second month .... 2 Chr 30:2
of the slaughter of the *P* .. 2 Chr 30:17
Now Josiah kept a *P* to .... 2 Chr 35:1
the *P* lambs for all the ..... Ezra 6:20
you shall observe the *P* ... Ezek 45:21
I will keep the *P* .... Matt 26:18
P with My disciples ...... Mark 14:14
the *P* must be killed .... Luke 22:7
Now the *P* of the Jews ..... John 2:13
Now the *P*, a feast of the .... John 6:4
P of the Jews was near ... John 11:55
six days before the *P* ...... John 12:1
that they might eat the *P* .. John 18:28
Preparation Day of the *P* . John 19:14
indeed Christ, our *P* .... 1 Cor 5:7
By faith he kept the *P* ..... Heb 11:28

PAST
My days are *p* .... Job 17:11
lo, the winter is *p* .... Song 2:11
harvest is *p*, the summer ..... Jer 8:20
and His ways *p* finding ... Rom 11:33
resurrection is already *p* .. 2 Tim 2:18
ways spoke in time *p* .... Heb 1:1
p lifetime in doing .... 1 Pet 4:3

PASTORS
and some *p* and .... Eph 4:11

PASTURE
the sheep of Your *p* .... Ps 74:1
the people of His *p* .... Ps 95:7
feed them in good *p* ...... Ezek 34:14
in and out and find *p* ...... John 10:9

PASTURES
to lie down in green *p* .... Ps 23:2

PATARA
Port of Lycia where Paul changes ships, Acts 21:1, 2

PATH
You enlarged my *p* ...... 2 Sam 22:37
p no bird knows .... Job 28:7
You will show me the *p* ..... Ps 16:11
lead me in a smooth *p* ...... Ps 27:11
comprehend my *p* and my ... Ps 139:3
But the *p* of the just .... Prov 4:18
You weigh the *p* of the just ... Is 26:7
Him in the *p* of justice .... Is 40:14
way in the sea and a *p* .... Is 43:16

PATHROS
Described as a lowly kingdom, Ezek 29:14–16
Refuge for dispersed Jews, Jer 44:1–15
Jews to be regathered from, Is 11:11

PATHS
He leads me in the *p* .... Ps 23:3
Teach me Your *p* .... Ps 25:4
and all her *p* are .... Prov 3:17
p they have not .... Is 42:16
themselves crooked *p* .... Is 59:8
Make His *p* straight .... Matt 3:3
and make straight *p* .... Heb 12:13

PATIENCE
'Master, have *p* .... Matt 18:26
and bear fruit with *p* ...... Luke 8:15
p possess your souls ..... Luke 21:19
Now may the God of *p* ..... Rom 15:5
labor of love, and *p* ...... 1 Thess 1:3
faith, love, *p* .... 1 Tim 6:11
and *p* inherit the promises .. Heb 6:12
your faith produces *p* ...... James 1:3
p have its perfect .... James 1:4
of suffering and *p* .... James 5:10
in the kingdom and *p* .... Rev 1:9
Here is the *p* and the ...... Rev 13:10

PATIENT
rejoicing in hope, *p* .... Rom 12:12
uphold the weak, be *p* ... 1 Thess 5:14

PATIENTLY
the LORD, and wait *p* .... Ps 37:7
if you take it *p* .... 1 Pet 2:20

PATMOS
John, banished here, receives the Revelation, Rev 1:9

PATRIARCHS
begot the twelve *p* .... Acts 7:8

PATTERN
p which you were .... Ex 26:30
as you have us for a *p* ...... Phil 3:17
Hold fast the *p* .... 2 Tim 1:13
p shown you on the .... Heb 8:5

PAUL
Roman citizen from Tarsus; studied under Gamaliel, Acts 22:3, 25–28
Originally called Saul; persecutes the church, Acts 7:58; 8:1, 3; 9:1, 2
Converted on road to Damascus, Acts 9:3–19
Preaches in Damascus; escapes to Jerusalem and then to Tarsus, Acts 9:20–30
Ministers in Antioch; sent to Jerusalem, Acts 11:25–30
First missionary journey, Acts 13; 14
Speaks for Gentiles at Jerusalem Council, Acts 15:1–5, 12
Second missionary journey, Acts 15:36—18:22
Third missionary journey, Acts 18:23—21:14
Arrested in Jerusalem; defense before Roman authorities, Acts 21:15—26:32
Sent to Rome, Acts 27:1—28:31
His epistles, Rom; 1 and 2 Cor; Gal; Eph; Phil; Col; 1 and 2 Thess; 1 and 2 Tim; Titus; Philem

PAULUS, SERGIUS
Roman proconsul of Cyprus, Acts 13:4, 7

PAVED
a *p* work of sapphire stone .. Ex 24:10

PAVEMENT
that is called The *P* .... John 19:13

PAVILION
shall hide me in His *p* .... Ps 27:5
them secretly in a *p* .... Ps 31:20

PAW
from the *p* of the lion .... 1 Sam 17:37

PAWS
He *p* in the valley .... Job 39:21

PAY
sell the oil and *p* your debt .. 2 Kin 4:7
p attention to my wisdom ... Prov 5:1
with which to *p* .... Prov 22:27
priests teach for *p* .... Mic 3:11
with me, and I will *p* ..... Matt 18:26
p taxes to Caesar .... Matt 22:17
For you *p* tithe of .... Matt 23:23
to *p* taxes to Caesar ...... Mark 12:14

PEACE
"These men are at *p* .... Gen 34:21
sacrifice of the *p* offering .... Lev 3:9
I will give *p* in the .... Lev 26:6
you, and give you *p* .... Num 6:26
Joshua made *p* with them .. Josh 9:15
had made *p* with Israel ..... Josh 10:1
'Make *p* with me by a ..... 2 Kin 18:31
If you ever return in *p* .... 2 Chr 18:27
field shall be at *p* .... Job 5:23
both lie down in *p* .... Ps 4:8
seek *p* and pursue it .... Ps 34:14
for He will speak *p* .... Ps 85:8
p have those who .... Ps 119:165
I am for *p* .... Ps 120:7
for the *p* of Jerusalem .... Ps 122:6
P be within your walls .... Ps 122:7
P be upon Israel .... Ps 125:5
war, and a time of *p* .... Eccl 3:8
Father, Prince of *P* .... Is 9:6
keep him in perfect *p* .... Is 26:3
p they have not .... Is 59:8
slightly, saying, '*P* .... Jer 6:14
"We looked for *p* .... Jer 8:15
give you assured *p* .... Jer 14:13
they will seek *p* .... Ezek 7:25
My people, saying, '*P* ..... Ezek 13:10
P be multiplied .... Dan 4:1
this One shall be *p* .... Mic 5:5
place I will give *p* .... Hag 2:9
speak *p* to the nations ..... Zech 9:10
is worthy, let your *p* ...... Matt 10:13
that I came to bring *p* ..... Matt 10:34
and on earth *p* .... Luke 2:14
if a son of *p* is there .... Luke 10:6
that make for your *p* ...... Luke 19:42
I leave with you, My *p* .... John 14:27
in Me you may have *p* .... John 16:33
Grace to you and *p* .... Rom 1:7
by faith, we have *p* .... Rom 5:1
minded is life and *p* .... Rom 8:6
of *p* will crush Satan ..... Rom 16:20
God has called us to *p* ..... 1 Cor 7:15
p will be with you .... 2 Cor 13:11
Spirit is love, joy, *p* .... Gal 5:22
He Himself is our *p* .... Eph 2:14
the Spirit in the bond of *p* .... Eph 4:3
of the gospel of *p* .... Eph 6:15
and the *p* of God .... Phil 4:7
heaven, having made *p* ...... Col 1:20
And let the *p* of God .... Col 3:15
Be at *p* among .... 1 Thess 5:13
faith, love, *p* .... 2 Tim 2:22
meaning "king of *p*," .... Heb 7:2
Pursue *p* with all people ... Heb 12:14
is sown in *p* by those ..... James 3:18
p be multiplied .... 2 Pet 1:2
it to take *p* from the earth .... Rev 6:4

PEACEABLE
and *p* life in all .... 1 Tim 2:2
is first pure, then *p* .... James 3:17

PEACEABLY
Do you come *p* .... 1 Sam 16:4
p?" And he said, "*P*." ..... 1 Kin 2:13
speaks *p* to his neighbor ...... Jer 9:8
He shall enter *p*, even ..... Dan 11:24
on you, live *p* .... Rom 12:18

PEACEFUL
in a *p* habitation .... Is 32:18

PEACEMAKERS
Blessed are the *p* .... Matt 5:9

PEARL
had found one *p* .... Matt 13:46
gate was of one *p* .... Rev 21:21

PEARLS
nor cast your *p* .... Matt 7:6
hair or gold or *p* .... 1 Tim 2:9
gates were twelve *p* .... Rev 21:21

PEG
wife, took a tent *p* .... Judg 4:21
will fasten him as a *p* .... Is 22:23

PEKAH
Son of Remaliah; usurps Israel's throne, 2 Kin 15:25–28
Forms alliance with Rezin of Syria against Ahaz, Is 7:1–9

Alliance defeated; captives returned, 2 Kin 16:5–9
Territory of, overrun by Tiglath-Pileser, 2 Kin 15:29
Assassinated by Hoshea, 2 Kin 15:30

PEKAHIAH
Son of Menahem; king of Israel, 2 Kin 15:22–26
Assassinated by Pekah, 2 Kin 15:23–25

PEN
My tongue is the *p* .... Ps 45:1
on it with a man's *p* .... Is 8:1
to write to you with *p* ...... 3 John 13

PENNY
have paid the last *p* .... Matt 5:26

PENTECOST
P had fully come .... Acts 2:1
on the Day of *P* .... Acts 20:16
tarry in Ephesus until *P* ... 1 Cor 16:8

PENUEL
Place east of Jordan; site of Jacob's wrestling with angel, Gen 32:24–31
Inhabitants of, slain by Gideon, Judg 8:8, 9, 17

PEOPLE
will take you as My *p* .... Ex 6:7
Who is like you, a *p* ...... Deut 33:29
p shall be my *p* .... Ruth 1:16
p who know the joyful ...... Ps 89:15
We are His *p* and the .... Ps 100:3
Happy are the *p* .... Ps 144:15
"Blessed is Egypt My *p* ...... Is 19:25
this is a rebellious *p* .... Is 30:9
p who provoke Me .... Is 65:3
and they shall be My *p* ...... Jer 24:7
Then they shall be My *p* .. Ezek 37:23
for you are not My *p* .... Hos 1:9
like *p*, like priest .... Hos 4:9
to make ready a *p* .... Luke 1:17
taught the *p* in the .... Luke 20:1
Unless you *p* see signs ...... John 4:48
a great multitude of sick *p* .. John 5:3
all the *p* came to Him .... John 8:2
man should die for the *p* .. John 11:50
favor with all the *p* .... Acts 2:47
were done among the *p* ... Acts 5:12
for they feared the *p*, lest ... Acts 5:26
and signs among the *p* ...... Acts 6:8
the *p* grew and multiplied .. Acts 7:17
of My *p* who are in Egypt .. Acts 7:34
astonished the *p* of .... Acts 8:9
a great many *p* were .... Acts 11:24
take out of them a *p* ...... Acts 15:14
his defense to the *p* .... Acts 19:33
of this *p* has grown dull ... Acts 28:27
who were not My *p* .... Rom 9:25
and contrary *p* .... Rom 10:21
His *p* whom He foreknew .. Rom 11:2
and they shall be My *p* .... 2 Cor 6:16
His own special *p* .... Titus 2:14
and they shall be My *p* ..... Heb 8:10
LORD will judge His *p* ..... Heb 10:30
His own special *p* .... 1 Pet 2:9
but are now the *p* .... 1 Pet 2:10
tribe and tongue and *p* .... Rev 5:9
tribe, tongue, and *p* .... Rev 14:6
they shall be His *p* .... Rev 21:3

PEOPLE OF GOD
in the assembly of the *p* .... Judg 20:2
a thing against the *p* ..... 2 Sam 14:13
a rest for the *p* .... Heb 4:9
affliction with the *p* .... Heb 11:25
people but are now the *p* .. 1 Pet 2:10

PEOPLES
Let *p* serve you .... Gen 27:29
separated you from the *p* .. Lev 20:26
scatter you among all *p* ... Deut 28:64
His deeds among the *p* .... 1 Chr 16:8
The LORD shall judge the *p* .... Ps 7:8
clap your hands, all you *p* .... Ps 47:1
Let all the *p* praise You .... Ps 67:5
of the earth and all *p* .... Ps 148:11
lift up a banner for the *p* ..... Is 62:10
customs of the *p* are futile ... Jer 10:3
to the *p* a pure language, ... Zeph 3:9
sow them among the *p* ..... Zech 10:9
heavy stone for all *p* .... Zech 12:3
will draw all *p* to Myself .. John 12:32

PEOR
Mountain of Moab opposite Jericho, Num 23:28
Israel's camp seen from, Num 24:2
——— Moabite god called Baal of Peor, Num 25:3, 5, 18
Israelites punished for worship of, Num 31:16

PERCEIVE
given you a heart to *p* ..... Deut 29:4
but I cannot *p* .... Job 23:8
seeing, but do not *p* .... Is 6:9
may see and not *p* .... Mark 4:12
not yet *p* nor understand .. Mark 8:17
In truth I *p* that God ...... Acts 10:34

PERCEIVED
not heard nor *p* by the ear .... Is 64:4
Jesus *p* their wickedness .. Matt 22:18
when Jesus *p* in His spirit .. Mark 2:8
Jesus *p* their thoughts ..... Luke 5:22
for I *p* power going out ..... Luke 8:46
p the grace that had been .... Gal 2:9

PERDITION
except the son of *p* .... John 17:12
to them a proof of *p* .... Phil 1:28
revealed, the son of *p* ..... 2 Thess 2:3
who draw back to *p* .... Heb 10:39
day of judgment and *p* ...... 2 Pet 3:7

PEREZ
One of Judah's twin sons by Tamar, Gen 38:24–30

PERFECT
Noah was a just man, *p* ...... Gen 6:9
His work is *p* .... Deut 32:4
Give a *p* lot .... 1 Sam 14:41
one who is *p* in .... Job 36:4
for God, His way is *p* .... Ps 18:30
The law of the LORD is *p*, ... Ps 19:7
I hate them with *p* hatred .. Ps 139:22
will keep him in *p* peace ...... Is 26:3
You were *p* in your .... Ezek 28:15
Father in heaven is *p* .... Matt 5:48
"If you want to be *p* ...... Matt 19:21
they may be made *p* ...... John 17:23
and *p* will of God .... Rom 12:2
when that which is *p* ..... 1 Cor 13:10
is made *p* in weakness ..... 2 Cor 12:9
present every man *p* .... Col 1:28
the law made nothing *p* ..... Heb 7:19
more *p* tabernacle .... Heb 9:11
of just men made *p* .... Heb 12:23
patience have its *p* work ... James 1:4
good gift and every *p* ..... James 1:17
in word, he is a *p* .... James 3:2
p love casts out fear .... 1 John 4:18

PERFECTED
third day I shall be *p* ..... Luke 13:32
or am already *p* .... Phil 3:12
the Son who has been *p* .... Heb 7:28
the love of God is *p* .... 1 John 2:5

PERFECTION
the *p* of beauty .... Ps 50:2
consummation of all *p* ..... Ps 119:96
You were the seal of *p* .... Ezek 28:12
let us go on to *p* .... Heb 6:1

PERFORM
p the duty .... Ruth 3:13
p Your statutes .... Ps 119:112
am ready to *p* My word ..... Jer 1:12
he is obliged to *p* it .... Matt 23:16
What sign will You *p* .... John 6:30
how to *p* what is good .... Rom 7:18

PERFORMED
They *p* His signs .... Ps 105:27
works are *p* by His hands .. Mark 6:2
John *p* no sign .... John 10:41
who *p* the service perfect in .. Heb 9:9

PERFUMER'S
putrefy the *p* ointment ...... Eccl 10:1

PERGA
Visited by Paul, Acts 13:13, 14; 14:25

PERGAMOS
Site of one of the seven churches, Rev 1:11
Special message to, Rev 2:12–17

PERIL
or nakedness, or *p* .... Rom 8:35

PERILOUS
from the *p* pestilence .... Ps 91:3
in the last days *p* .... 2 Tim 3:1

PERILS
journeys often, in *p* ...... 2 Cor 11:26

PERISH
"Surely we die, we *p* ..... Num 17:12
until you *p* from this ...... Josh 23:13
and if I *p*, I *p* .... Esth 4:16
Why did I not *p* .... Job 3:11
All flesh would *p* .... Job 34:15
way of the ungodly shall *p* .... Ps 1:6
He is like the beasts that *p* .. Ps 49:12
they *p* at the rebuke .... Ps 80:16
very day his plans *p* .... Ps 146:4
he who speaks lies shall *p* .. Prov 19:9
But those riches *p* through .. Eccl 5:14
they all will *p* together .... Is 31:3
the remnant in Judah *p* ..... Jer 40:15
so that we may not *p* .... Jon 1:6
one of your members *p* .... Matt 5:29
little ones should *p* ...... Matt 18:14
will *p* by the sword .... Matt 26:52
will all likewise *p* .... Luke 13:3
in Him should not *p* .... John 3:16
they shall never *p* .... John 10:28
whole nation should *p* .... John 11:50
Your money *p* with you, ... Acts 8:20
will also *p* without law ..... Rom 2:12
shall the weak brother *p* ... 1 Cor 8:11
concern things which *p* ..... Col 2:22
among those who *p* ...... 2 Thess 2:10
They will *p*, ... Heb 1:11
that any should *p* .... 2 Pet 3:9

PERISHABLE
do it to obtain a *p* .... 1 Cor 9:25

PERISHED
p being innocent .... Job 4:7
Truth has *p* and has .... Jer 7:28
The faithful man has *p* .... Mic 7:2

PERISHES
The old lion *p* for lack of .... Job 4:11
The righteous *p*, ... Is 57:1
for the food which *p* .... John 6:27
precious than gold that *p* .... 1 Pet 1:7

PERISHING
We are *p* .... Matt 8:25
to those who are *p* .... 2 Cor 4:3

PERIZZITES
One of seven Canaanite nations, Deut 7:1
Possessed Palestine in Abraham's time, Gen 13:7
Jacob's fear of, Gen 34:30
Many of, slain by Judah, Judg 1:4, 5

PERJURER
p shall be expelled .... Zech 5:3

PERMIT
the Spirit did not *p* .... Acts 16:7
I do not *p* a woman .... 1 Tim 2:12

PERMITS
you, if the Lord *p* ... 1 Cor 16:7
we will do if God *p* ... Heb 6:3

PERMITTED
p no one to do them ... Ps 105:14

PERPETUAL
p incense before the LORD ... Ex 30:8
It shall be a *p* statute for .. Num 19:21
Why is my pain *p* ... Jer 15:18
make it a *p* desolation ... Jer 25:12
saltpits, and a *p* desolation .. Zeph 2:9

PERPETUATED
Your name shall be *p* ... Nah 1:14

PERPLEXED
at one another, *p* ... John 13:22
we are *p* ... 2 Cor 4:8

PERSECUTE
p me as God does ... Job 19:22
p me wrongfully ... Ps 119:86
when they revile and *p* ... Matt 5:11
Bless those who *p* ... Rom 12:14

PERSECUTED
p the poor and needy ... Ps 109:16
p the prophets who ... Matt 5:12
If they *p* Me ... John 15:20
p the church of God ... 1 Cor 15:9
p, but not forsaken ... 2 Cor 4:9
p us now preaches the ... Gal 1:23

PERSECUTES
wicked in his pride *p* ... Ps 10:2

PERSECUTION
p arises because of ... Matt 13:21
At that time a great *p* ... Acts 8:1
do I still suffer *p* ... Gal 5:11

PERSECUTIONS
and lands, with *p* ... Mark 10:30
in needs, in *p* ... 2 Cor 12:10
p, afflictions, which ... 2 Tim 3:11

PERSECUTOR
a blasphemer, a *p* ... 1 Tim 1:13

PERSECUTORS
Deliver me from my *p*, for ... Ps 142:6
vengeance for me on my *p* .. Jer 15:15
all her *p* overtake her in ... Lam 1:3

PERSEVERANCE
tribulation produces *p* ... Rom 5:3
to this end will all *p* ... Eph 6:18
longsuffering, love, *p* ... 2 Tim 3:10
heard of the *p* of Job ... James 5:11
to self-control *p* ... 2 Pet 1:6

PERSEVERE
kept My command to *p* ... Rev 3:10

PERSISTENCE
p he will rise and ... Luke 11:8

PERSON
In whose eyes a vile *p* ... Ps 15:4
p will suffer hunger ... Prov 19:15
do not regard the *p* ... Matt 22:16
One *p* esteems one day ... Rom 14:5
to eat with such a *p* ... 1 Cor 5:11
no fornicator, unclean *p* ... Eph 5:5
that such a *p* is warped ... Titus 3:11
express image of His *p* ... Heb 1:3
let it be the hidden *p* ... 1 Pet 3:4
by whom a *p* is overcome .. 2 Pet 2:19

PERSUADE
Who will *p* Ahab to ... 1 Kin 22:20
"You almost *p* me ... Acts 26:28
the Lord, we *p* men ... 2 Cor 5:11
For do I now *p* men ... Gal 1:10

PERSUADED
a ruler is *p* ... Prov 25:15
neither will they be *p* ... Luke 16:31
p that He is able ... 2 Tim 1:12

PERSUASIVE
p words of human ... 1 Cor 2:4
you with *p* words ... Col 2:4

PERTAINING
Priest in things *p* ... Heb 2:17
for men in things *p* ... Heb 5:1

PERTURBED
things the earth is *p* ... Prov 30:21

PERVERSE
your way is *p* ... Num 22:32
for the *p* person is an ... Prov 3:32
p lips far from you ... Prov 4:24
p heart will be ... Prov 12:8
p man sows strife ... Prov 16:28
but he who is *p* ... Prov 28:18
from this *p* generation ... Acts 2:40

PERVERSITY
in oppression and *p* ... Is 30:12

PERVERT
You shall not *p* ... Deut 16:19
and *p* all equity ... Mic 3:9
p the gospel of Christ ... Gal 1:7

PERVERTING
We found this fellow *p* ... Luke 23:2
will you not cease *p* ... Acts 13:10

PERVERTS
p the words of the ... Ex 23:8
p his ways will become ... Prov 10:9

PESTILENCE
from the perilous *p* ... Ps 91:3
p that walks in ... Ps 91:6
Before Him went *p* ... Hab 3:5

PESTILENCES
will be famines, *p* ... Matt 24:7

PETER
Fisherman; called to discipleship, Matt 4:18–20; John 1:40–42
Called as apostle, Matt 10:2–4
Walks on water, Matt 14:28–33
Confesses Christ's deity, Matt 16:13–19
Rebuked by Christ, Matt 16:21–23
Witnesses transfiguration, Matt 17:1–8; 2 Pet 1:16–18
Denies Christ three times, Matt 26:69–75
Commissioned to feed Christ's sheep, John 21:15–17
Leads disciples, Acts 1:15–26
Preaches at Pentecost, Acts 2:1–41
Performs miracles, Acts 3:1–11; 5:14–16; 9:32–43
Called to minister to Gentiles, Acts 10
Defends his visit to Gentiles, Acts 11:1–18
Imprisoned and delivered, Acts 12:3–19
Speaks at Jerusalem Council, Acts 15:7–14
Writes epistles, 1 Pet 1:1; 2 Pet 1:1

PETITION
of Israel grant your *p* ... 1 Sam 1:17
What is your *p* ... Esth 5:6
present your *p* before Him ... Jer 42:9
makes his *p* three times ... Dan 6:13

PETITIONS
fulfill all your *p* ... Ps 20:5
p that we have asked ... 1 John 5:15

PHARAOH
Kings of Egypt, contemporaries of:
Abraham, Gen 12:15–20
Joseph, Gen 40; 41
Moses in youth, Ex 1:8–11
the Exodus, Ex 5—14
Solomon, 1 Kin 3:1; 11:17–20
Other Pharaohs, 1 Kin 14:25, 26; 2 Kin 17:4; 18:21; 19:9; 23:29; Jer 44:30

PHARISEE
"Blind *P*, first cleanse ... Matt 23:26
P who had invited Him ... Luke 7:39
P asked Him to dine ... Luke 11:37
temple to pray, one a *P* ... Luke 18:10
P named Gamaliel ... Acts 5:34
I am a *P*, the son of a *P* ... Acts 23:6
our religion I lived a *P* ... Acts 26:5
concerning the law, a *P* ... Phil 3:5

PHARISEES
See SCRIBES AND PHARISEES
when he saw many of the *P* . Matt 3:7
when the *P* saw it, they ... Matt 9:11
we and the *P* fast often ... Matt 9:14
P said, "He casts out ... Matt 9:34
P saw it, they said to ... Matt 12:2
P were offended when ... Matt 15:12
of the leaven of the *P* ... Matt 16:6
P also came to Him ... Matt 19:3
P heard His parables ... Matt 21:45
P went and plotted how ... Matt 22:15
P heard that He had ... Matt 22:34
P gathered together to ... Matt 27:62
P came out and began to ... Mark 8:11
P and teachers of the law .. Luke 5:17
P and lawyers rejected ... Luke 7:30
you *P* make the outside ... Luke 11:39
"But woe to you *P*! For ... Luke 11:42
of the leaven of the *P* ... Luke 12:1
P came, saying to Him ... Luke 13:31
to the lawyers and *P* ... Luke 14:3
P and scribes murmured ... Luke 15:2
P, who were lovers of ... Luke 16:14
P when the kingdom of ... Luke 17:20
of the *P* named Nicodemus .. John 3:1
P heard the crowd ... John 7:32
P therefore said to Him ... John 8:13
P also asked him again ... John 9:15
went away to the *P* ... John 11:46
P had given a command .. John 11:57
because of the *P* they ... John 12:42
of the *P* who believed ... Acts 15:5
Sadducees and the other *P* . Acts 23:6

PHILADELPHIA
City of Lydia in Asia Minor; church established here, Rev 1:11

PHILEMON
Christian at Colosse to whom Paul writes, Philem 1
Paul appeals to him to receive Onesimus, Philem 9–21

PHILETUS
False teacher, 2 Tim 2:17, 18

PHILIP
Son of Herod the Great, Matt 14:3
——— One of the twelve apostles, Matt 10:3
Brings Nathanael to Christ, John 1:43–48
Tested by Christ, John 6:5–7
Introduces Greeks to Christ, John 12:20–22
Gently rebuked by Christ, John 14:8–12
——— One of the first seven deacons, Acts 6:5
Called an evangelist, Acts 21:8
Preaches in Samaria, Acts 8:5–13
Leads the Ethiopian eunuch to Christ, Acts 8:26–40

PHILIPPI
City of Macedonia (named after Philip of Macedon); visited by Paul, Acts 16:12; 20:6
Paul writes letter to church of, Phil 1:1

PHILISTIA
The land of the Philistines, Gen 21:32, 34; Josh 13:2; Ps 60:8

PHILISTINES
Not attacked by Joshua, Josh 13:1–3

Left to test Israel, Judg 3:1–4
God delivers Israel to, as punishment, Judg 10:6, 7
Israel delivered from, by Samson, Judg 13—16
Capture, then return the ark of the Lord, 1 Sam 4—6
Wars and dealings with Saul and David, 1 Sam 13:15—14:23; 17:1–52; 18:25–27; 21:10–15; 27:1—28:6; 29:1–11; 31:1–13; 2 Sam 5:17–25
Originally on the island of Caphtor, Jer 47:4
Prophecies concerning, Is 9:11, 12; Jer 25:15–20; 47:1–7; Ezek 25:15–17; Zeph 2:4–6

PHILOSOPHERS
p encountered him . . . . Acts 17:18

PHILOSOPHY
cheat you through *p* . . . . Col 2:8

PHINEHAS
Aaron's grandson; executes God's judgment, Num 25:1–18; Ps 106:30, 31
Settles dispute over memorial altar, Josh 22:11–32
——— Younger son of Eli; abuses his office, 1 Sam 1:3; 2:12–17, 22–36
Killed by Philistines, 1 Sam 4:11, 17

PHOENICIA
Mediterranean coastal region including the cities of Ptolemais, Tyre, Zarephath and Sidon; evangelized by early Christians, Acts 11:19
Jesus preaches here, Matt 15:21

PHRYGIA
Jews from, at Pentecost, Acts 2:1, 10
Visited twice by Paul, Acts 16:6

PHYLACTERIES
They make their *p* . . . . Matt 23:5

PHYSICIAN
Gilead, is there no *p* . . . . Jer 8:22
have no need of a *p* . . . . Matt 9:12
Luke the beloved *p* . . . . Col 4:14

PHYSICIANS
are all worthless *p* . . . . Job 13:4
her livelihood on *p* . . . . Luke 8:43

PI HAHIROTH
Israel camps there before crossing the Red Sea, Ex 14:2, 9; Num 33:7, 8

PICTURE
what parable shall we *p* . . . Mark 4:30

PIECE
placed each *p* opposite . . . . Gen 15:10
hammered *p* of pure gold . . . Ex 25:36
one *p* with the mercy seat . . . . Ex 37:8
two legs or a *p* of an ear . . Amos 3:12
No one puts a *p* . . . . Matt 9:16
bought a *p* of ground . . . . . Luke 14:18
Him a *p* of a broiled fish . . Luke 24:42
from the top in one *p* . . . . . John 19:23

PIECES
for my wages thirty *p* . . . . . Zech 11:12
they took the thirty *p* . . . . Matt 27:9
shall be dashed to *p* . . . . Rev 2:27

PIERCE
and his master shall *p* . . . . Ex 21:6
a sword will *p* . . . . Luke 2:35

PIERCED
p My hands and My feet . . . . Ps 22:16
Me whom they have *p* . . . . Zech 12:10
of the soldiers *p* . . . . John 19:34
p themselves through . . . . . 1 Tim 6:10
and they also who *p* . . . . Rev 1:7

PIERCING
p even to the division . . . . Heb 4:12

PIETY
first learn to show *p* . . . . 1 Tim 5:4

PILATE, PONTIUS
Governor of Judea (A.D. 26–36), Luke 3:1
Questions Jesus and delivers Him to Jews, Matt 27:2, 11–26; John 18:28—19:16

PILGRIMAGE
heart is set on *p* . . . . Ps 84:5
In the house of my *p* . . . . Ps 119:54

PILGRIMS
we are aliens and *p* . . . . . . 1 Chr 29:15
were strangers and *p* . . . . . . Heb 11:13

PILLAR
and she became a *p* . . . . Gen 19:26
where you anointed the *p* . . Gen 31:13
and by night in a *p* . . . . Ex 13:21
standing by a *p* . . . . 2 Kin 11:14
a *p* to the LORD. . . . . Is 19:19
the living God, the *p* . . . . . . 1 Tim 3:15
I will make him a *p* in the . . . Rev 3:12

PILLARS
break their sacred *p* . . . . Ex 34:13
between the *p* . . . . Judg 16:25
And he cast two *p* . . . . 1 Kin 7:15
bronze *p* that were in . . . . 2 Kin 25:13
I set up its *p* firmly . . . . Ps 75:3
out her seven *p* . . . . Prov 9:1
blood and fire and *p* . . . . Joel 2:30
who seemed to be *p* . . . . Gal 2:9
and his feet like *p* . . . . Rev 10:1

PILOT
rudder wherever the *p* . . . . . James 3:4

PIM
p for the plowshares . . . . . 1 Sam 13:21

PINE
cypress tree and the *p* . . . . Is 41:19
for these *p* away . . . . Lam 4:9

PINNACLE
set Him on the *p* . . . . Luke 4:9

PISGAH
Mountain in Moab where Balaam offers sacrifice, Num 23:14
Moses views Promised Land from, Deut 3:27
Site of Moses' death, Deut 34:1–7

PISHON
One of Eden's four rivers, Gen 2:10, 11

PISIDIA
Twice visited by Paul, Acts 13:13, 14; 14:24

PIT
See BOTTOMLESS PIT
cast him into some *p* . . . . . . Gen 37:20
soul draws near the *P* . . . . . . Job 33:22
who go down to the *p* . . . . Ps 28:1
woman is a deep *p* . . . . Prov 22:14
a harlot is a deep *p* . . . . Prov 23:27
fall into his own *p* . . . . Prov 28:10
my life in the *p* . . . . Lam 3:53
who descend into the *P* . . . Ezek 31:16
up my life from the *p* . . . . Jon 2:6
from the waterless *p* . . . . Zech 9:11
if it falls into a *p* . . . . Matt 12:11
ox that has fallen into a *p* . . Luke 14:5
the key to the bottomless *p* . . . Rev 9:1
into the bottomless *p* . . . . Rev 20:3

PITCH
inside and outside with *p* . . . Gen 6:14
Israel would *p* their tents . . . Num 9:17

PITCHER
her *p* on her shoulder . . . . Gen 24:15
or the *p* shattered at the . . . . Eccl 12:6
carrying a *p* of water . . . . . Luke 22:10

PITCHERS
and torches inside the *p* . . . . Judg 7:16
the *p* of pure gold . . . . 1 Chr 28:17
the washing of cups, *p* . . . . . Mark 7:4

PITHOM
Egyptian city built by Hebrew slaves, Ex 1:11

PITIABLE
of all men the most *p* . . . . . 1 Cor 15:19

PITS
The proud have dug *p* . . . . . . Ps 119:85

PITY
eye shall have no *p* . . . . Deut 7:16
"Have *p* on me . . . . Job 19:21
for someone to take *p* . . . . Ps 69:20
He who has *p* on the . . . . . . Prov 19:17
p He redeemed them . . . . Is 63:9
land, and *p* His people . . . . Joel 2:18
And should I not *p* . . . . Jon 4:11
just as I had *p* . . . . Matt 18:33

PLACE
See HIGH PLACE; HOLY PLACE; MOST HOLY PLACE
p know him anymore . . . . Job 7:10
All go to one *p* . . . . Eccl 3:20
return again to My *p* . . . . Hos 5:15
Come, see the *p* . . . . Matt 28:6
My word has no *p* . . . . John 8:37
I go to prepare a *p* . . . . John 14:2
might go to his own *p* . . . . . . Acts 1:25

PLACES
See HIGH PLACES
set them in slippery *p* . . . . Ps 73:18
dark *p* of the earth . . . . Ps 74:20
and the rough *p* . . . . Is 40:4
They love the best *p* . . . . Matt 23:6
in the heavenly *p* . . . . Eph 1:3

PLAGUE
bring yet one more *p* . . . . Ex 11:1
with a very great *p* . . . . Num 11:33
those who died in the *p* . . . . Num 25:9
three days' *p* in your . . . . . 2 Sam 24:13
p come near your . . . . Ps 91:10
and the *p* was stopped . . . . . . Ps 106:30
And this shall be the *p* . . . . Zech 14:12
because of the *p* of the . . . . . Rev 16:21

PLAGUES
I will send all My *p* . . . . Ex 9:14
I will be your *p* . . . . Hos 13:14
p that are written . . . . Rev 22:18

PLAINLY
the Christ, tell us *p* . . . . John 10:24
now You are speaking *p* . . John 16:29
such things declare *p* . . . . Heb 11:14

PLAN
p evil things in their . . . . Ps 140:2
Let none of you *p* . . . . Zech 7:10
p according to the flesh . . . . 2 Cor 1:17

PLANK
First remove the *p* . . . . Matt 7:5

PLANS
He makes the *p* of the . . . . Ps 33:10
in that very day his *p* . . . . Ps 146:4
that devises wicked *p* . . . . Prov 6:18
A man's heart *p* . . . . Prov 16:9
P are established . . . . Prov 20:18

PLANT
A time to *p* . . . . Eccl 3:2
Him as a tender *p* . . . . Is 53:2
they shall *p* vineyards . . . . Is 65:21
p of an alien vine . . . . Jer 2:21
the LORD God prepared a *p* . . . Jon 4:6
p which My heavenly . . . . . Matt 15:13

PLANTED
The LORD God *p* a garden . . . . Gen 2:8
and he *p* a vineyard . . . . Gen 9:20
Abraham *p* a tamarisk . . . . Gen 21:33

shall be like a tree *p* .... Ps 1:3
Your right hand has *p* .... Ps 80:15
p it with the choicest vine .... Is 5:2
shall they be *p* .... Is 40:24
like a tree *p* by the waters .... Jer 17:8
by the roots and be *p* .... Luke 17:6
I *p*, Apollos watered .... 1 Cor 3:6

PLANTS
our sons may be as *p* .... Ps 144:12
down its choice *p* .... Is 16:8
neither he who *p* .... 1 Cor 3:7

PLASTERED
p with untempered .... Ezek 13:14
Her prophets *p* them ..... Ezek 22:28

PLATFORM
scribe stood on a *p* .... Neh 8:4

PLATTER
head here on a *p* .... Matt 14:8

PLAY
and rose up to *p* .... Ex 32:6
p skillfully with a .... Ps 33:3
nursing child shall *p* .... Is 11:8
and rose up to *p* .... 1 Cor 10:7

PLAYED
So David *p* music with .. 1 Sam 18:10
We *p* the flute for you .... Matt 11:17

PLEAD
the one who would *p* ...... Judg 6:31
Oh, that one might *p* .... Job 16:21
p my cause against an .... Ps 43:1
p with your friend .... Prov 6:3
Behold, I will *p* .... Jer 2:35
p His case with all .... Jer 25:31

PLEADED
Then Moses *p* with the ...... Ex 32:11
this thing I *p* with .... 2 Cor 12:8

PLEADING
though God were *p* .... 2 Cor 5:20

PLEASANT
food, that it was *p* .... Gen 3:6
fallen to me in *p* places .... Ps 16:6
they despised the *p* .... Ps 106:24
how good and how *p* .... Ps 133:1
and knowledge is *p* .... Prov 2:10
words of the pure are *p* ... Prov 15:26
P words are like a .... Prov 16:24
p places of the .... Jer 23:10
Is he a *p* child .... Jer 31:20
I ate no *p* food .... Dan 10:3

PLEASANTNESS
Her ways are ways of *p* .... Prov 3:17

PLEASE
P say you are my sister, ... Gen 12:13
P, go in to my maid .... Gen 16:2
p let me escape there ...... Gen 19:20
P come near, ... Gen 27:21
P hear this dream which I .. Gen 37:6
Now, *p*, forgive the .... Gen 50:17
P, let us go three days' .... Ex 5:3
P inquire of God, ... Judg 18:5
p pardon my sin, ... 1 Sam 15:25
yet honor me now, *p*, ... 1 Sam 15:30
P bring the ephod here .... 1 Sam 30:7
P let my sister Tamar ..... 2 Sam 13:5
p let my brother .... 2 Sam 13:26
When a man's ways *p* ...... Prov 16:7
do those things that *p* ...... John 8:29
in the flesh cannot *p* .... Rom 8:8
p his neighbor for his .... Rom 15:2
how he may *p* the Lord .... 1 Cor 7:32
how he may *p* his wife .... 1 Cor 7:33
may *p* her husband .... 1 Cor 7:34
Or do I seek to *p* men .... Gal 1:10
is impossible to *p* Him ...... Heb 11:6

PLEASED
and she *p* Samson well .... Judg 14:7
Then You shall be *p* .... Ps 51:19
The LORD is well *p* .... Is 42:21
Yet it *p* the LORD to bruise .... Is 53:10
Would he be *p* with you ...... Mal 1:8
in whom I am well *p* .... Matt 3:17
danced before them and *p* .. Matt 14:6
God was not well *p* .... 1 Cor 10:5
But when it *p* God, who ...... Gal 1:15
testimony, that he *p* .... Heb 11:5
in whom I am well *p* .... 2 Pet 1:17

PLEASES
dwell where it *p* you ...... Gen 20:15
He does whatever He *p* ...... Ps 115:3
Whatever the LORD *p* .... Ps 135:6
who *p* God shall escape .... Eccl 7:26
nor awaken love until it *p* .. Song 2:7

PLEASING
sacrifice, well *p* .... Phil 4:18
for this is well *p* .... Col 3:20
in you what is well *p* .... Heb 13:21

PLEASURE
grown old, shall I have *p* .. Gen 18:12
not a God who takes *p* .... Ps 5:4
has *p* in the prosperity .... Ps 35:27
Do good in Your good *p* ..... Ps 51:18
Your servants take *p* .... Ps 102:14
The LORD takes *p* in those .. Ps 147:11
p will be a poor man ...... Prov 21:17
for He has no *p* .... Eccl 5:4
shall perform all My *p* .... Is 44:28
your fast you find *p* .... Is 58:3
nor finding your own *p* ...... Is 58:13
Do I have any *p* .... Ezek 18:23
I have no *p* in you .... Mal 1:10
your Father's good *p* ..... Luke 12:32
to the good *p* of His .... Eph 1:5
to do for His good *p* .... Phil 2:13
fulfill all the good *p* ..... 2 Thess 1:11
p is dead while .... 1 Tim 5:6
for sin You had no *p* .... Heb 10:6
back, My soul has no *p* ... Heb 10:38
p that war in your .... James 4:1
on the earth in *p* .... James 5:5

PLEASURES
Your right hand are *p* .... Ps 16:11
cares, riches, and *p* .... Luke 8:14
to enjoy the passing *p* ..... Heb 11:25
may spend it on your *p* .... James 4:3

PLEDGE
give me a *p* till you send .. Gen 38:17
hands in *p* for a stranger .... Prov 6:1
shakes hands in a *p*, and .. Prov 17:18
who shakes hands in a *p* .. Prov 22:26

PLEIADES
Part of God's creation, Job 9:9; Amos 5:8

PLENTIFUL
You, O God, sent a *p* .... Ps 68:9
The harvest truly is *p* .... Matt 9:37

PLENTIFULLY
rich man yielded *p* .... Luke 12:16

PLENTY
p which were in the .... Gen 41:53
LORD will grant you *p* ..... Deut 28:11
barns will be filled with *p* .. Prov 3:10
diligent lead surely to *p* .... Prov 21:5
his land will have *p* .... Prov 28:19

PLIGHT
He laughs at the *p* .... Job 9:23

PLOT
in the *p* at Jezreel, so that . 2 Kin 9:37
and the people *p* .... Ps 2:1
near the *p* of ground that ... John 4:5
p became known to Saul ... Acts 9:24

PLOTS
The wicked *p* against .... Ps 37:12

PLOTTED
and *p* to take Jesus by ..... Matt 26:4
chief priests *p* .... John 12:10

PLOW
lazy man will not *p* .... Prov 20:4
Does one *p* there with ..... Amos 6:12
put his hand to the *p* .... Luke 9:62
he who plows should *p* .... 1 Cor 9:10

PLOWED
"Zion shall be *p* .... Jer 26:18
You have *p* wickedness .... Hos 10:13
of you Zion shall be *p* ...... Mic 3:12

PLOWMAN
p shall overtake the .... Amos 9:13

PLOWSHARES
beat their swords into *p* .... Is 2:4
Beat your *p* into swords ...... Joel 3:10
beat their swords into *p* ...... Mic 4:3

PLUCK
grain, you may *p* .... Deut 23:25
who pass by the way *p* ...... Ps 80:12
obey, I will utterly *p* .... Jer 12:17
p the heads of grain .... Mark 2:23

PLUCKED
p the victim from his .... Job 29:17
cheeks to those who *p* .... Is 50:6
And His disciples *p* .... Luke 6:1
you would have *p* .... Gal 4:15

PLUMB
a *p* line, with a *p* .... Amos 7:7
rejoice to see the *p* .... Zech 4:10

PLUNDER
p the Egyptians .... Ex 3:22
who pass by the way *p* ...... Ps 89:41
The *p* of the poor is .... Is 3:14
p you shall become .... Jer 30:16
house and *p* his goods .... Matt 12:29

PLUNDERED
stouthearted were *p* .... Ps 76:5
a people robbed and *p* .... Is 42:22
"And when you are *p* .... Jer 4:30
Because you have *p* .... Hab 2:8

PLUNDERING
me because of the *p* .... Is 22:4
accepted the *p* of your ...... Heb 10:34

POETS
some of your own *p* .... Acts 17:28

POINT
obedient to the *p* of death .... Phil 2:8
even to the *p* of chains ..... 2 Tim 2:9
Now this is the main *p* .... Heb 8:1
yet stumble in one *p* ...... James 2:10

POINTS
but was in all *p* tempted .... Heb 4:15

POISON
the *p* of asps is under ...... Ps 140:3
"The *p* of asps is .... Rom 3:13
evil, full of deadly *p* .... James 3:8

POISONED
p by bitterness .... Acts 8:23
p their minds against .... Acts 14:2

POLLUTIONS
have escaped the *p* .... 2 Pet 2:20

POMEGRANATE
a golden bell and a *p*, a ..... Ex 28:34
the *p* tree, the palm tree ..... Joel 1:12

POMEGRANATES
you shall make *p* of blue .... Ex 28:33
brought some of the *p* .... Num 13:23
grain or figs or vines or *p* .. Num 20:5
of vines and fig trees and *p* .. Deut 8:8

POMP
multitude and their *p* .... Is 5:14
p is brought down to .... Is 14:11
had come with great *p* .... Acts 25:23

POMPOUS
and a mouth speaking *p* ..... Dan 7:8

PONDER
P the path of your . . . . Prov 4:26

PONDERED
p them in her heart . . . . Luke 2:19

PONDERS
p all his paths . . . . Prov 5:21

PONTUS
Jews from, at Pentecost, Acts 2:5, 9
Home of Aquila, Acts 18:2
Christians of, addressed by Peter, 1 Pet 1:1

POOL
the rock into a *p* of water . . . Ps 114:8
the wilderness a *p* . . . . Is 41:18
by the Sheep Gate a *p* . . . . . . John 5:2
at a certain time into the *p* . . John 5:4
wash in the *p* of Siloam . . . . . . John 9:7
'Go to the *p* of Siloam . . . . . John 9:11

POOLS
also covers it with *p* . . . . Ps 84:6
a wilderness into *p* . . . . Ps 107:35
your eyes like the *p* . . . . Song 7:4

POOR
p shall not give less . . . . Ex 30:15
be partial to the *p* . . . . Lev 19:15
p will never cease . . . . Deut 15:11
whether *p* or rich . . . . Ruth 3:10
raises the *p* from the dust . . 1 Sam 2:8
seeing I am a *p* . . . . 1 Sam 18:23
one rich and the other *p* . . 2 Sam 12:1
left some of the *p* . . . . 2 Kin 25:12
and gifts to the *p* . . . . Esth 9:22
So the *p* have hope . . . . Job 5:16
and forsaken the *p* . . . . Job 20:19
I delivered the *p* . . . . Job 29:12
soul grieved for the *p* . . . . . . Job 30:25
The expectation of the *p* . . . . . Ps 9:18
p shall eat and be . . . . Ps 22:26
p man cried out . . . . Ps 34:6
delivering the *p* from him . . . Ps 35:10
to cast down the *p* . . . . Ps 37:14
But I am *p* and needy . . . . Ps 40:17
is he who considers the *p* . . . . . Ps 41:1
goodness for the *p* . . . . Ps 68:10
For the LORD hears the *p*, ... Ps 69:33
and Your *p* with justice . . . . . . Ps 72:2
Let the *p* and needy . . . . Ps 74:21
Defend the *p* and fatherless . . Ps 82:3
yet He sets the *p* . . . . Ps 107:41
at the right hand of the *p* . . . Ps 109:31
He has given to the *p* . . . . Ps 112:9
He raises the *p* . . . . Ps 113:7
satisfy her *p* with bread . . . . Ps 132:15
and justice for the *p* . . . . Ps 140:12
a slack hand becomes *p* . . . . Prov 10:4
one who makes himself *p* . . Prov 13:7
p man is hated even . . . . . . Prov 14:20
p reproaches his Maker . . . . Prov 17:5
p man uses entreaties . . . . . Prov 18:23
Better is the *p* who . . . . Prov 19:1
p will also cry himself . . . . Prov 21:13
p have this in common . . . . . Prov 22:2
p man who oppresses . . . . . . Prov 28:3
Better is the *p* who . . . . Prov 28:6
the cause of the *p* . . . . Prov 29:7
Or lest I be *p* and steal . . . . . Prov 30:9
to devour the *p* from . . . . . . Prov 30:14
plead the cause of the *p* . . . . Prov 31:9
her hand to the *p* . . . . Prov 31:20
remembered that same *p* . . . Eccl 9:15
He shall judge the *p*, and . . . . . Is 11:4
the *p* of His people shall . . . . . Is 14:32
a strength to the *p* . . . . Is 25:4
The *p* and needy seek . . . . Is 41:17
preach good tidings to the *p* . . Is 61:1
on him who is *p* and of a . . . . . Is 66:2
delivered the life of the *p* . . . Jer 20:13
land of Judah the *p* people . . Jer 39:10
the hand of the *p* . . . . Ezek 16:49
and mistreated the *p* . . . . . . Ezek 22:29
by showing mercy to the *p* . . Dan 4:27
for silver, and the *p* . . . . Amos 2:6
you tread down the *p* . . . . . . Amos 5:11
the alien or the *p* . . . . Zech 7:10
in particular the *p* . . . . Zech 11:7
"Blessed are the *p* . . . . Matt 5:3
p have the gospel . . . . Matt 11:5
have and give to the *p* . . . . Matt 19:21
For you have the *p* . . . . Matt 26:11
one *p* widow came . . . . Mark 12:42
the gospel to the *p* . . . . Luke 4:18
Blessed are you *p*, ... Luke 6:20
the *p* have the gospel . . . . Luke 7:22
give a feast, invite the *p* . . Luke 14:13
half of my goods to the *p* . . Luke 19:8
contribution for the *p* . . . . . Rom 15:26
my goods to feed the *p* . . . . 1 Cor 13:3
as *p*, yet making many . . . . 2 Cor 6:10
your sakes He became *p* . . . . 2 Cor 8:9
He has given to the *p* . . . . . . 2 Cor 9:9
should remember the *p* . . . . . Gal 2:10
and say to the *p* man . . . . . . James 2:3
God not chosen the *p* . . . . . . James 2:5
wretched, miserable, *p* . . . . . . Rev 3:17
and great, rich and *p* . . . . . . Rev 13:16

POORLY
we are *p* clothed, ... 1 Cor 4:11

POPLAR
himself rods of green *p* . . . . Gen 30:37

POPULATED
the whole earth was *p* . . . . . . Gen 9:19

POPULOUS
great, mighty, and *p* . . . . . . Deut 26:5

PORCH
p which is called . . . . Acts 3:11

PORCHES
Bethesda, having five *p* . . . . . John 5:2

PORCIUS FESTUS
Paul stands trial before, Acts 25:1–22

PORCUPINE
the *p* shall possess it, also . . . . Is 34:11

PORTION
For the LORD's *p* . . . . Deut 32:9
This is the *p* from God . . . . . Job 20:29
O LORD, You are the *p* . . . . Ps 16:5
heart and my *p* forever . . . . . . Ps 73:26
You are my *p* . . . . Ps 119:57
p for her maidservants . . . . Prov 31:15
I will divide Him a *p* . . . . Is 53:12
rejoice in their *p* . . . . Is 61:7
The *P* of Jacob is not . . . . Jer 10:16
they have trodden My *p* . . . . Jer 12:10
"The LORD is my *p* . . . . Lam 3:24
p of the king's delicacies . . . . . Dan 1:8
and appoint him his *p* . . . . Matt 24:51
to give them their *p* . . . . . . Luke 12:42
give me the *p* . . . . Luke 15:12
part nor *p* in this matter . . . . Acts 8:21

PORTRAYED
Christ was clearly *p* . . . . Gal 3:1

POSITION
If a man desires the *p* . . . . . . 1 Tim 3:1

POSSESS
descendants shall *p* . . . . Gen 22:17
which you are going to *p* . . Deut 28:21
land which you go to *p* . . . Deut 28:63
p the land which . . . . Josh 1:11
told them to go in to *p* the . . Neh 9:15
fathers to go in and *p* . . . . . . Neh 9:23
may dwell there and *p* it . . . . Ps 69:35
tithes of all that I *p* . . . . Luke 18:12
By your patience *p* . . . . Luke 21:19
as though they did not *p* . . 1 Cor 7:30
p his own vessel . . . . 1 Thess 4:4

POSSESSED
much land yet to be *p* . . . . . . Josh 13:1
"The LORD *p* me at . . . . Prov 8:22
of the things he *p* . . . . Acts 4:32
that a certain slave girl *p* . . Acts 16:16

POSSESSING
p knowledge and quick to . . . Dan 1:4
and yet *p* all things . . . . 2 Cor 6:10

POSSESSION
as an everlasting *p* . . . . Gen 17:8
ends of the earth for Your *p* . . . Ps 2:8
the rest of their *p* . . . . Ps 17:14
they did not gain *p* . . . . Ps 44:3
is man's precious *p* . . . . Prov 12:27
Sapphira his wife, sold a *p* . . Acts 5:1
to give it to him for a *p* . . . . . . Acts 7:5
of the purchased *p* . . . . Eph 1:14
and an enduring *p* . . . . Heb 10:34

POSSESSIONS
is full of Your *p* . . . . Ps 104:24
kinds of precious *p* . . . . Prov 1:13
the LORD with your *p* . . . . Prov 3:9
Yes, I had greater *p* . . . . Eccl 2:7
for he had great *p* . . . . Mark 10:22
and there wasted his *p* . . . . Luke 15:13
and sold their *p* . . . . Acts 2:45

POSSESSOR
P of heaven and earth . . . . . Gen 14:19

POSSESSORS
all who were *p* of lands . . . . Acts 4:34

POSSIBLE
God all things are *p* . . . . . . Matt 19:26
O My Father, if it is *p* . . . . Matt 26:39
all things are *p* to him . . . . . Mark 9:23
God all things are *p* . . . . . . Mark 10:27
men are *p* with God . . . . Luke 18:27
If it is *p*, as much as . . . . Rom 12:18
bear you witness that, if *p* . . . Gal 4:15
p that the blood . . . . Heb 10:4

POSTERITY
to preserve a *p* . . . . Gen 45:7
p shall serve Him . . . . Ps 22:30
p who approve their . . . . Ps 49:13
the *p* of the righteous . . . . . . Prov 11:21

POSTPONED
it will no more be *p* . . . . Ezek 12:25

POT
to Aaron, "Take a *p* . . . . Ex 16:33
from a boiling *p* . . . . Job 41:20
The refining *p* is for . . . . Prov 17:3
p that had the manna . . . . Heb 9:4

POTENTATE
the blessed and only *P* . . . . . 1 Tim 6:15

POTI-PHERAH
Egyptian priest of On (Heliopolis), Gen 41:45–50
Father of Asenath, Joseph's wife, Gen 46:20

POTIPHAR
High Egyptian officer, Gen 39:1
Puts Joseph in jail, Gen 39:20

POTS
when we sat by the *p* . . . . Ex 16:3
also took away the *p* . . . . Jer 52:18
are regarded as clay *p* . . . . . . Lam 4:2

POTSHERD
for himself a *p* . . . . Job 2:8
is dried up like a *p* . . . . Ps 22:15
Let the *p* strive with . . . . Is 45:9

POTTER
Shall the *p* be esteemed as . . . Is 29:16
the clay, and You our *p* . . . . Is 64:8
seemed good to the *p* . . . . Jer 18:4
Does not the *p* have . . . . Rom 9:21

POTTER'S FIELD
Judas's money used for purchase of, Matt 27:7, 8

POUND
Mary took a *p* of very . . . . . . John 12:3

POUNDS
about a hundred *p* .... John 19:39

POUR
p out your heart .... Ps 62:8
P out Your wrath .... Ps 79:6
p My Spirit on your .... Is 44:3
and let the skies *p* .... Is 45:8
P out Your fury .... Jer 10:25
that I will *p* out My .... Joel 2:28
"And I will *p* .... Zech 12:10
p out for you such blessing .. Mal 3:10
that I will *p* out of My ...... Acts 2:17
My maidservants I will *p* ... Acts 2:18
angels, "Go and *p* .... Rev 16:1

POURED
And now my soul is *p* ...... Job 30:16
I am *p* out like water .... Ps 22:14
grace is *p* upon Your .... Ps 45:2
name is ointment *p* .... Song 1:3
visited You, they *p* .... Is 26:16
strong, because He *p* .... Is 53:12
and My fury will be *p* .... Jer 7:20
His fury is *p* out like .... Nah 1:6
broke the flask and *p* ..... Mark 14:3
of God has been *p* .... Rom 5:5
if I am being *p* .... Phil 2:17
I am already being *p* .... 2 Tim 4:6
whom He *p* out on us .... Titus 3:6

POVERTY
of the poor is their *p* ...... Prov 10:15
but it leads to *p* .... Prov 11:24
P and shame will come .... Prov 13:18
leads only to *p* .... Prov 14:23
lest you come to *p* .... Prov 20:13
give me neither *p* .... Prov 30:8
p put in all the .... Luke 21:4
and their deep *p* .... 2 Cor 8:2
p might become rich .... 2 Cor 8:9
tribulation, and *p* .... Rev 2:9

POWER
that I may show My *p* .... Ex 9:16
become glorious in *p* .... Ex 15:6
for God has *p* to help ..... 2 Chr 25:8
him who is without *p* .... Job 26:2
p who can understand ..... Job 26:14
p belongs to God .... Ps 62:11
p Your enemies shall .... Ps 66:3
gives strength and *p* .... Ps 68:35
when it is in the *p* of your .. Prov 3:27
in the *p* of the tongue ..... Prov 18:21
a king is, there is *p* .... Eccl 8:4
No one has *p* over the .... Eccl 8:8
the strength of His *p* .... Is 40:26
bodies the fire had no *p* .... Dan 3:27
truly I am full of *p* .... Mic 3:8
anger and great in *p* .... Nah 1:3
'Not by might nor by *p* ..... Zech 4:6
the kingdom and the *p* ..... Matt 6:13
the Son of Man has *p* .... Matt 9:6
who had given such *p* .... Matt 9:8
gave them *p* over unclean .. Matt 10:1
Scriptures nor the *p* ...... Matt 22:29
the Son of Man has *p* ..... Mark 2:10
p to heal sicknesses .... Mark 3:15
that *p* had gone out .... Mark 5:30
Scriptures nor the *p* of ... Mark 12:24
p of the Spirit to Galilee ... Luke 4:14
And the *p* of the Lord ..... Luke 5:17
the Son of Man has *p* ...... Luke 5:24
p went out from Him .... Luke 6:19
I perceived *p* going out .... Luke 8:46
and gave them *p* .... Luke 9:1
all the *p* of the enemy .... Luke 10:19
and the *p* of darkness .... Luke 22:53
you are endued with *p* .... Luke 24:49
I have *p* to lay it .... John 10:18
not know that I have *p* .... John 19:10
"You could have no *p* .... John 19:11
you shall receive *p* .... Acts 1:8
as though by our own *p* .... Acts 3:12
Stephen, full of faith and *p* .. Acts 6:8
man is the great *p* .... Acts 8:10
"Give me this *p* .... Acts 8:19
Holy Spirit and with *p* .... Acts 10:38
the *p* of Satan to God, ... Acts 26:18
the Son of God with *p* ...... Rom 1:4
for it is the *p* .... Rom 1:16
even His eternal *p* .... Rom 1:20
My *p* in you .... Rom 9:17
potter have *p* over the ..... Rom 9:21
the *p* of the Holy Spirit ... Rom 15:13
by the *p* of the Spirit of ... Rom 15:19
saved it is the *p* .... 1 Cor 1:18
Greeks, Christ the *p* .... 1 Cor 1:24
of the Spirit and of *p*, ... 1 Cor 2:4
men but in the *p* of God .... 1 Cor 2:5
is not in word but in *p* .... 1 Cor 4:20
be brought under the *p* .... 1 Cor 6:12
and all authority and *p* ... 1 Cor 15:24
it is raised in *p* .... 1 Cor 15:43
of the *p* may be of God ..... 2 Cor 4:7
of truth, by the *p* of God .... 2 Cor 6:7
that the *p* of Christ .... 2 Cor 12:9
He lives by the *p* of God .. 2 Cor 13:4
greatness of His *p* .... Eph 1:19
all principality and *p* .... Eph 1:21
prince of the *p* of the air ..... Eph 2:2
working of His *p* .... Eph 3:7
to the *p* that works in us .... Eph 3:20
the Lord and in the *p* .... Eph 6:10
the *p* of His resurrection .... Phil 3:10
to His glorious *p* .... Col 1:11
us from the *p* of darkness ... Col 1:13
of all principality and *p* ..... Col 2:10
only, but also in *p* .... 1 Thess 1:5
the glory of His *p* .... 2 Thess 1:9
work of faith with *p* ..... 2 Thess 1:11
of Satan, with all *p* .... 2 Thess 2:9
of fear, but of *p* .... 2 Tim 1:7
according to the *p* of God .. 2 Tim 1:8
godliness but denying its *p* . 2 Tim 3:5
by the word of His *p* .... Heb 1:3
p of death, that .... Heb 2:14
but according to the *p* ...... Heb 7:16
since it has no *p* at all ...... Heb 9:17
are kept by the *p* of God ... 1 Pet 1:5
as His divine *p* .... 2 Pet 1:3
made known to you the *p* .. 2 Pet 1:16
who are greater in *p* ...... 2 Pet 2:11
dominion and *p* .... Jude 25
to him I will give *p* .... Rev 2:26
glory and honor and *p* ...... Rev 4:11
honor and glory and *p* ...... Rev 5:13
and honor and *p* .... Rev 7:12
and *p* belong to the Lord .... Rev 19:1
the second death has no *p* .. Rev 20:6

POWER OF GOD
the Scriptures nor the *p* ... Matt 22:29
the right hand of the *p* .... Luke 22:69
"This man is the great *p* .... Acts 8:10
it is the *p* to salvation ...... Rom 1:16
being saved it is the *p* ..... 1 Cor 1:18
Christ the *p* and the .... 1 Cor 1:24
word of truth, by the *p* ..... 2 Cor 6:7
yet He lives by the *p* ...... 2 Cor 13:4
gospel according to the *p* ... 2 Tim 1:8
who are kept by the *p* ...... 1 Pet 1:5

POWERFUL
of the LORD is *p* .... Ps 29:4
of God is living and *p* .... Heb 4:12

POWERS
the *p* of the heavens ...... Matt 24:29
nor principalities nor *p*, ... Rom 8:38
p in the heavenly places, ... Eph 3:10
principalities, against *p* ..... Eph 6:12
or principalities or *p* .... Col 1:16
principalities and *p* .... Col 2:15
word of God and the *p* .... Heb 6:5
p having been made .... 1 Pet 3:22

PRACTICE
to do, that I do not *p* .... Rom 7:15
I will not to do, that I *p* .... Rom 7:19
those who *p* such things ..... Gal 5:21
and do not *p* the truth ..... 1 John 1:6
Whoever does not *p* ..... 1 John 3:10

PRACTICED
p witchcraft and .... 2 Kin 17:17
previously *p* sorcery in ...... Acts 8:9
those who had *p* magic .... Acts 19:19
they have *p* deceit .... Rom 3:13
which they have *p* .... 2 Cor 12:21

PRACTICES
wrath on him who *p* evil ... Rom 13:4
trained in covetous *p* ...... 2 Pet 2:14
p righteousness is born .. 1 John 2:29
whoever loves and *p* a lie .. Rev 22:15

PRACTICING
For everyone *p* evil hates .. John 3:20
judge those *p* such things ... Rom 2:3

PRAETORIUM
Pilate's palace in Jerusalem, Mark 15:16; John 18:28; Matt 27:27
——— Herod's palace at Caesarea, Acts 23:35

PRAISE
Now I will *p* the LORD ..... Gen 29:35
your brothers shall *p* .... Gen 49:8
He is my God, and I will *p* ... Ex 15:2
He is your *p* .... Deut 10:21
which He has made, in *p* .. Deut 26:19
I will sing *p* to the .... Judg 5:3
to *p* the LORD God of ...... 1 Chr 16:4
to triumph in Your *p* ..... 1 Chr 16:35
David, "for giving *p*." ..... 1 Chr 23:5
p the LORD, and .... 1 Chr 23:30
and to *p* the LORD .... 1 Chr 25:3
p Your glorious name .... 1 Chr 29:13
offered *p* by their ministry .. 2 Chr 7:6
for their duties (to *p* and .. 2 Chr 8:14
"*P* the LORD, for His ..... 2 Chr 20:21
began to sing and to *p* ... 2 Chr 20:22
the Levites to sing *p* ..... 2 Chr 29:30
to *p* in the gates of the .... 2 Chr 31:2
to *p* the LORD, according ... Ezra 3:10
above all blessing and *p* ..... Neh 9:5
singers, and songs of *p* .... Neh 12:46
I will *p* You, O LORD .... Ps 9:1
p shall be of You in .... Ps 22:25
For *p* from the upright .... Ps 33:1
p shall continually be .... Ps 34:1
of Your *p* all the day long .... Ps 35:28
the people shall *p* .... Ps 45:17
Whoever offers *p* .... Ps 50:23
P is awaiting You .... Ps 65:1
make His *p* glorious .... Ps 66:2
let all the peoples *p* .... Ps 67:3
Let heaven and earth *p* ...... Ps 69:34
p shall be continually .... Ps 71:6
And the heavens will *p* .... Ps 89:5
and into His courts with *p* ... Ps 100:4
silent, O God of my *p* .... Ps 109:1
Seven times a day I *p* ..... Ps 119:164
All Your works shall *p* ..... Ps 145:10
shall speak the *p* .... Ps 145:21
P the LORD .... Ps 148:1
P Him with high sounding ... Ps 150:5
that has breath *p* .... Ps 150:6
Let another man *p* .... Prov 27:2
let her own works *p* ...... Prov 31:31
And your gates *P* .... Is 60:18
the garment of *p* for the ...... Is 61:3
He makes Jerusalem a *p* ...... Is 62:7
For You are my *p* .... Jer 17:14
Me a name of joy, a *p* .... Jer 33:9
p You, O God of my .... Dan 2:23
Nebuchadnezzar, *p* and .... Dan 4:37
p the name of the LORD ..... Joel 2:26
give you fame and *p* .... Zeph 3:20
You have perfected *p* ..... Matt 21:16
saw it, gave *p* to God ..... Luke 18:43
p God with a loud voice .. Luke 19:37

of men more than the *p* . . . John 12:43
p is not from men but . . . . . . Rom 2:29
will have *p* from the same . . Rom 13:3
"*P* the LORD, ... Rom 15:11
Then each one's *p* . . . . 1 Cor 4:5
Now I *p* you, brethren . . . . . 1 Cor 11:2
I do not *p* you . . . . 1 Cor 11:22
the brother whose *p* . . . . 2 Cor 8:18
to the *p* of the glory of His . . . Eph 1:6
should be to the *p* . . . . Eph 1:12
to the *p* of His glory . . . . Eph 1:14
to the glory and *p* . . . . Phil 1:11
I will sing *p* to You . . . . Heb 2:12
the sacrifice of *p* . . . . Heb 13:15
and for the *p* of those . . . . . . 1 Pet 2:14
saying, "*P* our God . . . . Rev 19:5

PRAISE THE LORD

and said, "Now I will *p* . . . . Gen 29:35
to thank, and to *p* . . . . 1 Chr 16:4
King David had made to *p* . . 2 Chr 7:6
"*P*, for His mercy . . . . 2 Chr 20:21
with cymbals, to *p* . . . . Ezra 3:10
Those who seek Him will *p* . . Ps 22:26
P with the harp . . . . Ps 33:2
yet to be created may *p* . . . . Ps 102:18
the Lord, O my soul! *P* . . . . . Ps 104:35
P! Oh, give thanks . . . . Ps 106:1
The dead do not *p* . . . . Ps 115:17
p, all you Gentiles . . . . Ps 117:1
while I live I will *p* . . . . Ps 146:2
P! P from the heavens . . . . Ps 148:1
that has breath *p* . . . . Ps 150:6
P, call upon His name . . . . Is 12:4
shall eat it, and *p* . . . . Is 62:9
P! For He has delivered . . . . . Jer 20:13
P, all you Gentiles . . . . Rom 15:11

PRAISED

who is worthy to be *p* . . . . 2 Sam 22:4
and greatly to be *p* . . . . . 1 Chr 16:25
and *p* the LORD . . . . 1 Chr 16:36
thousand *p* the LORD . . . . . . 1 Chr 23:5
music, and *p* the LORD, ... 2 Chr 5:13
and *p* the LORD, saying . . . . . 2 Chr 7:3
the priests *p* the LORD . . . . 2 Chr 30:21
when they *p* the LORD . . . . . . Ezra 3:11
and *p* the LORD . . . . Neh 5:13
daily He shall be *p* . . . . Ps 72:15
LORD's name is to be *p* . . . . . . Ps 113:3
and greatly to be *p* . . . . Ps 145:3
the LORD, she shall be *p* . . . Prov 31:30
where our fathers *p* . . . . Is 64:11
the Most High and *p* . . . . Dan 4:34

PRAISES

in holiness, fearful in *p* . . . . . Ex 15:11
sang *p* with gladness, ... 2 Chr 29:30
enthroned in the *p* . . . . Ps 22:3
O LORD, I will sing *p* . . . . Ps 101:1
it is good to sing *p* . . . . Ps 147:1
and he *p* her . . . . Prov 31:28
shall proclaim the *p* . . . . Is 60:6
you may proclaim the *p* . . . . . 1 Pet 2:9

PRAISEWORTHY

if there is anything *p* . . . . Phil 4:8

PRAISING

they sang responsively, *p* . . Ezra 3:11
they will still be *p* . . . . Ps 84:4
of the heavenly host *p* . . . . . Luke 2:13
p God for all the things . . . . Luke 2:20
in the temple *p* . . . . Luke 24:53
p God and having favor . . . . Acts 2:47
leaping, and *p* God . . . . Acts 3:8

PRATING

p fool will fall . . . . Prov 10:8
p against us with . . . . 3 John 10

PRAY

heal her, O God, I *p* . . . . . . Num 12:13
of this people, I *p* . . . . Num 14:19
p to the LORD that He . . . . . Num 21:7
Strengthen me, I *p*. . . . . Judg 16:28
LORD in ceasing to *p* . . . . . 1 Sam 12:23
my God, for to You I will *p* . . . Ps 5:2
p to You in a time when . . . . . . Ps 32:6
at noon I will *p* . . . . Ps 55:17
I *p*, send now prosperity. . . . Ps 118:25
who hate you, and *p* . . . . Matt 5:44
"And when you *p* . . . . Matt 6:5
But you, when you *p* . . . . Matt 6:6
when you *p*, do not use . . . . . Matt 6:7
manner, therefore, *p* . . . . Matt 6:9
Therefore *p* the LORD of . . . . Matt 9:38
by Himself to *p* . . . . Matt 14:23
hands on them and *p* . . . . . Matt 19:13
while I go and *p* over . . . . . Matt 26:36
Watch and *p* . . . . Matt 26:41
I cannot now *p* . . . . Matt 26:53
to the mountain to *p* . . . . . . Mark 6:46
you ask when you *p* . . . . . Mark 11:24
Take heed, watch and *p* . . Mark 13:33
Sit here while I *p* . . . . Mark 14:32
"Watch and *p*, lest you . . . Mark 14:38
out to the mountain to *p* . . . Luke 6:12
p for those who spitefully . . Luke 6:28
up on the mountain to *p* . . . Luke 9:28
"Lord, teach us to *p* . . . . Luke 11:1
men always ought to *p* . . . . . Luke 18:1
up to the temple to *p* . . . . . Luke 18:10
P that you may not . . . . Luke 22:40
Rise and *p*, lest you . . . . . . Luke 22:46
And I will *p* . . . . John 14:16
I shall *p* the Father for . . . . John 16:26
I do not *p* for the . . . . John 17:9
I do not *p* that You . . . . John 17:15
"I do not *p* for . . . . John 17:20
p God if perhaps the . . . . Acts 8:22
P to the Lord for me, that . . . Acts 8:24
up on the housetop to *p* . . . . Acts 10:9
know what we should *p* . . . . Rom 8:26
to *p* to God with her . . . . . 1 Cor 11:13
p that he may interpret . . . 1 Cor 14:13
For if I *p* in a tongue . . . . 1 Cor 14:14
I will *p* with the . . . . 1 Cor 14:15
Now I *p* to God . . . . 2 Cor 13:7
And this also we *p* . . . . 2 Cor 13:9
And this I *p*, that your love . . Phil 1:9
do not cease to *p* for you . . . . Col 1:9
p without ceasing . . . . 1 Thess 5:17
Brethren, *p* for us . . . . 1 Thess 5:25
we also *p* always . . . . 2 Thess 1:11
p for us, that the word . . . . 2 Thess 3:1
therefore that the men *p* . . . . 1 Tim 2:8
P for us, for we are . . . . Heb 13:18
Let him *p* . . . . James 5:13
to one another, and *p* . . . . . . James 5:16
say that he should *p* . . . . . . 1 John 5:16
p that you may prosper . . . . . . 3 John 2

PRAYED

So Abraham *p* to God . . . . . Gen 20:17
So Moses *p* for the people . . Num 21:7
Manoah *p* to the LORD . . . . Judg 13:8
For this child I *p*, and . . . . 1 Sam 1:27
Then Hezekiah *p* before . . 2 Kin 19:15
times that day, and *p* . . . . Dan 6:10
Then Jonah *p* to the LORD . . . . Jon 2:1
So he *p* to the LORD, ... Jon 4:2
into the wilderness and *p* . . Luke 5:16
Pharisee stood and *p* . . . . . Luke 18:11
p more earnestly . . . . Luke 22:44
p earnestly that it . . . . James 5:17

PRAYER

God heeded the *p* . . . . 2 Sam 21:14
in heaven their *p* . . . . 1 Kin 8:45
p made in this place . . . . . . 2 Chr 7:15
the thanksgiving with *p* . . . . Neh 11:17
fear, and restrain *p* . . . . Job 15:4
And my *p* is pure . . . . Job 16:17
p would return to my . . . . Ps 35:13
A *p* to the God of my . . . . Ps 42:8
P also will be made . . . . Ps 72:15
Let my *p* come before . . . . Ps 88:2
He shall regard the *p* . . . . Ps 102:17
but I give myself to *p* . . . . Ps 109:4
to the LORD, but the *p* . . . . . . Prov 15:8
hears the *p* of the . . . . Prov 15:29
hear the *p* of Your servant . . Dan 9:17
while I was speaking in *p* . . . Dan 9:21
not go out except by *p* . . . . Matt 17:21
things you ask in *p* . . . . Matt 21:22
out by nothing but *p* . . . . . . Mark 9:29
a house of *p* for all . . . . Mark 11:17
all night in *p* to God . . . . Luke 6:12
My house is a house of *p* . Luke 19:46
with one accord in *p* and . . . Acts 1:14
the temple at the hour of *p* . . . Acts 3:1
continually to *p* . . . . Acts 6:4
your *p* has been heard . . . . Acts 10:31
where *p* was . . . . Acts 16:13
as we went up to *p* . . . . Acts 16:16
p to God for Israel is that . . . Rom 10:1
steadfastly in *p* . . . . Rom 12:12
to fasting and *p* . . . . 1 Cor 7:5
always with all *p* . . . . Eph 6:18
always in every *p* of mine . . . . Phil 1:4
deliverance through your *p* . Phil 1:19
but in everything by *p* . . . . Phil 4:6
Continue earnestly in *p*, ... Col 4:2
the word of God and *p* . . . . . . 1 Tim 4:5
And the *p* of faith . . . . James 5:15

PRAYERS

though you make many *p* . . . . . Is 1:15
pretense make long *p* . . . . . Matt 23:14
fastings and *p* night and . . . . Luke 2:37
pretense make long *p* . . . . . Luke 20:47
of bread, and in *p* . . . . Acts 2:42
Your *p* and your alms . . . . Acts 10:4
always in my *p* . . . . Rom 1:9
me in *p* to God for me . . . . . . Rom 15:30
fervently for you in *p* . . . . Col 4:12
that supplications, *p* . . . . 1 Tim 2:1
and *p* night and day . . . . 1 Tim 5:5
always in my *p* . . . . Philem 4
when He had offered up *p* . . . Heb 5:7
p may not be hindered . . . . . . 1 Pet 3:7
are open to their *p* . . . . 1 Pet 3:12
and watchful in your *p* . . . . . . 1 Pet 4:7
which are the *p* . . . . Rev 5:8

PRAYING

and found Daniel *p* . . . . Dan 6:11
whenever you stand *p* . . . . Mark 11:25
Paul and Silas were *p* . . . . . Acts 16:25
p always with all prayer . . . . Eph 6:18
faith, *p* in the Holy Spirit, ... Jude 20

PRAYS

every woman who *p* or . . . . 1 Cor 11:5
tongue, my spirit *p* . . . . 1 Cor 14:14

PREACH

to *p* good tidings . . . . Is 61:1
that great city, and *p* . . . . Jon 3:2
time Jesus began to *p* . . . . Matt 4:17
you hear in the ear, *p* . . . . . Matt 10:27
p the gospel to every . . . . . . Mark 16:15
P the gospel to the . . . . Luke 4:18
p the kingdom of God . . . . . . Luke 9:60
to *p* the word in Asia . . . . Acts 16:6
ready to *p* the gospel . . . . Rom 1:15
word of faith which we *p*) . . Rom 10:8
And how shall they *p* . . . . . . Rom 10:15
it my aim to *p* the gospel . . Rom 15:20
p Christ crucified . . . . 1 Cor 1:23
is me if I do not *p* . . . . 1 Cor 9:16
I or they, so we *p* . . . . 1 Cor 15:11
For we do not *p* . . . . 2 Cor 4:5
p any other gospel to you . . . . Gal 1:8
that I might *p* Him among . . . Gal 1:16
gospel which I *p* . . . . Gal 2:2
p Christ even from . . . . Phil 1:15
The former *p* Christ from . . . Phil 1:16
P the word . . . . 2 Tim 4:2

PREACH THE GOSPEL

into all the world and *p* . . Mark 16:15
He has anointed Me to *p* . . . Luke 4:18

the LORD *p* David ... 2 Sam 8:6
Your care has *p* my spirit ... Job 10:12
soul, and body be *p* ... 1 Thess 5:23

PRESERVES
For the LORD *p* the ... Ps 31:23
p the souls of His ... Ps 97:10
The LORD *p* the simple ... Ps 116:6
p the way of His saints ... Prov 2:8
who guards his mouth *p* ... Prov 13:3
he who keeps his way *p* ... Prov 16:17

PRESS
but I *p* on, that I may lay ... Phil 3:12
I *p* toward the goal ... Phil 3:14

PRESSED
p her virgin bosom ... Ezek 23:8
p about Him to touch ... Mark 3:10
the multitude *p* about Him ... Luke 5:1
p down, shaken together, ... Luke 6:38
We are hard *p* on every ... 2 Cor 4:8
For I am hard *p* ... Phil 1:23

PRESUMPTUOUS
servant also from *p* ... Ps 19:13
They are *p*, self-willed ... 2 Pet 2:10

PRETENDED
them, *p* madness ... 1 Sam 21:13

PRETENSE
whole heart, but in *p* ... Jer 3:10
p make long prayers ... Matt 23:14

PREVAIL
He did not *p* against him ... Gen 32:25
no man shall *p* ... 1 Sam 2:9
do not let man *p* ... 2 Chr 14:11
our tongue we will *p* ... Ps 12:4
He shall *p* against His ... Is 42:13
but they shall not *p* ... Jer 1:19
but he will not *p* ... Dan 11:12
of Hades shall not *p* ... Matt 16:18
but they did not *p*, ... Rev 12:8

PREVAILED
The waters *p* and greatly ... Gen 7:18
hand, that Israel *p* ... Ex 17:11
Judah *p* over his brothers ... 1 Chr 5:2
with the Angel and *p* ... Hos 12:4
grew mightily and *p* ... Acts 19:20
has *p* to open the scroll and ... Rev 5:5

PREVIOUSLY
who *p* practiced sorcery in ... Acts 8:9

PREY
the mountains of *p* ... Ps 76:4
has not given us as *p* ... Ps 124:6
Shall the *p* be taken ... Is 49:24
evil makes himself a *p* ... Is 59:15
shall no longer be a *p* ... Ezek 34:22
when he has no *p* ... Amos 3:4

PRICE
be weighed for its *p* ... Job 28:15
a fool the purchase *p* ... Prov 17:16
one pearl of great *p* ... Matt 13:46
back part of the *p* ... Acts 5:3
you were bought at a *p* ... 1 Cor 6:20
You were bought at a *p* ... 1 Cor 7:23

PRIDE
p come against me ... Ps 36:11
p serves as their necklace ... Ps 73:6
p and arrogance and ... Prov 8:13
By *p* comes nothing ... Prov 13:10
P goes before ... Prov 16:18
p will bring him low ... Prov 29:23
and her daughter had *p* ... Ezek 16:49
p He is able to put down ... Dan 4:37
was hardened in *p* ... Dan 5:20
has sworn by the *p* ... Amos 8:7
For the *p* of the ... Zech 11:3
evil eye, blasphemy, *p* ... Mark 7:22
p he fall into the ... 1 Tim 3:6
eyes, and the *p* of life ... 1 John 2:16

PRIEST
See HIGH PRIEST
he was the *p* of God ... Gen 14:18
That son who becomes *p* ... Ex 29:30
The sons of Aaron the *p* ... Lev 1:7
the *p* shall burn all on the ... Lev 1:9
p shall lay them in order ... Lev 1:12
p shall make atonement ... Lev 19:22
for the *p* is holy to his God ... Lev 21:7
Eleazar the *p* spoke ... Num 26:3
and Eleazar the *p* ... Num 26:63
Eleazar the *p*, Joshua ... Josh 19:51
when Phinehas the *p* ... Josh 22:30
The *p* stood at the ... Judg 18:17
Eli the *p* was sitting ... 1 Sam 1:9
Myself a faithful *p* ... 1 Sam 2:35
Eli, the LORD's *p* in ... 1 Sam 14:3
Saul talked to the *p* ... 1 Sam 14:19
to Ahimelech the *p* ... 1 Sam 21:2
p gave him holy bread ... 1 Sam 21:6
Urijah the *p* built an ... 2 Kin 16:11
Jehoiada the *p* brought ... 2 Chr 23:14
the *p* found the Book ... 2 Chr 34:14
gave Ezra the *p* ... Ezra 7:11
p could consult ... Neh 7:65
p forever according ... Ps 110:4
the *p* and the prophet ... Is 28:7
So He shall be a *p* ... Zech 6:13
of a *p* should keep ... Mal 2:7
show yourself to the *p* ... Matt 8:4
to Caiaphas the high *p* ... Matt 26:57
And the high *p* arose ... Matt 26:62
away to the high *p* ... Mark 14:53
well as Annas the high *p* ... Acts 4:6
and faithful High *P* ... Heb 2:17
High *P* of our confession, ... Heb 3:1
we have a great High *P* ... Heb 4:14
we do not have a High *P* ... Heb 4:15
p forever according ... Heb 5:6
We have such a High *P*, ... Heb 8:1
high *p* went alone ... Heb 9:7
Christ came as High *P* ... Heb 9:11

PRIEST'S
the high *p* servant ... John 18:10

PRIESTHOOD
be an everlasting *p* ... Ex 40:15
have defiled the *p* ... Neh 13:29
p being changed ... Heb 7:12
has an unchangeable *p* ... Heb 7:24
house, a holy *p* ... 1 Pet 2:5
generation, a royal *p* ... 1 Pet 2:9

PRIESTS
to Me a kingdom of *p* ... Ex 19:6
may minister to Me as *p* ... Ex 28:41
and the *p*, Aaron's sons, ... Lev 1:5
"Command the *p* ... Josh 4:16
and let seven *p* bear seven ... Josh 6:6
the *p* blew the trumpets ... Josh 6:20
had killed the LORD's *p* ... 1 Sam 22:21
removed the idolatrous *p* ... 2 Kin 23:5
Jahaziel the *p* ... 1 Chr 16:6
and Benjamin, and the *p* ... Ezra 1:5
yet told the Jews, the *p* ... Neh 2:16
Their *p* fell by the sword, ... Ps 78:64
Aaron were among His *p* ... Ps 99:6
Let Your *p* be clothed with ... Ps 132:9
her *p* with salvation ... Ps 132:16
named the *p* of the LORD ... Is 61:6
which the *p* ministered ... Jer 52:18
and the iniquities of her *p* ... Lam 4:13
p have violated My law ... Ezek 22:26
the *p* shall throw salt on ... Ezek 43:24
"Hear this, O *p!* ... Hos 5:1
the *p* mourn, who minister ... Joel 1:9
her *p* teach for pay ... Mic 3:11
p in the temple profane ... Matt 12:5
But when the chief *p* ... Matt 21:15
went to the chief *p* ... Matt 26:14
of silver to the chief *p* and ... Matt 27:3
the chief *p* stirred up ... Mark 15:11
Caiaphas being high *p* ... Luke 3:2
show yourselves to the *p* ... Luke 17:14
Jesus said to the chief *p* ... Luke 22:52
Pilate said to the chief *p* ... Luke 23:4
But the chief *p* plotted ... John 12:10
become *p* without an oath ... Heb 7:21
need daily, as those high *p* ... Heb 7:27
high *p* men who have ... Heb 7:28
since there are *p* who offer ... Heb 8:4
made us kings and *p* ... Rev 1:6
but they shall be *p* ... Rev 20:6

PRIESTS'
where the *p* feet stood firm ... Josh 4:3
and the soles of the *p* feet ... Josh 4:18

PRINCE
"Who made you a *p* ... Ex 2:14
is the house of the *p* ... Job 21:28
is the downfall of a *p* ... Prov 14:28
Everlasting Father, *P* ... Is 9:6
against the *P* of princes ... Dan 8:25
until Messiah the *P* ... Dan 9:25
with the *p* of Persia ... Dan 10:20
except Michael your *p* ... Dan 10:21
days without king or *p* ... Hos 3:4
p asks for gifts ... Mic 7:3
and killed the *P* ... Acts 3:15
His right hand to be *P* ... Acts 5:31
the *p* of the power ... Eph 2:2

PRINCES
He is not partial to *p* ... Job 34:19
to bind his *p* at his ... Ps 105:22
He may seat him with *p* ... Ps 113:8
to put confidence in *p* ... Ps 118:9
P also sit and speak ... Ps 119:23
p and all judges of ... Ps 148:11
good, nor to strike *p* ... Prov 17:26
is a child, and your *p* ... Eccl 10:16
of nobles, and your *p* ... Eccl 10:17
children to be their *p* ... Is 3:4
p will rule with ... Is 32:1
He brings the *p* ... Is 40:23

PRINCIPAL
Wisdom is the *p* ... Prov 4:7

PRINCIPALITIES
nor *p* nor powers ... Rom 8:38
and blood, but against *p* ... Eph 6:12
dominions or *p* or powers ... Col 1:16
disarmed *p* and powers, ... Col 2:15

PRINCIPALITY
far above all *p* ... Eph 1:21
is the head of all *p* ... Col 2:10

PRINCIPLES
from the basic *p* ... Col 2:20
again the first *p* ... Heb 5:12

PRINT
hands the *p* of the nails ... John 20:25

PRISCILLA (or Prisca)
Wife of Aquila, Acts 18:1–3
With Aquila, instructs Apollos, Acts 18:26
Mentioned by Paul, Rom 16:3; 1 Cor 16:19; 2 Tim 4:19

PRISON
and put him into the *p* ... Gen 39:20
Bring my soul out of *p* ... Ps 142:7
in darkness from the *p* ... Is 42:7
the opening of the *p* ... Is 61:1
should put him in *p* ... Jer 29:26
John had been put in *p* ... Matt 4:12
John had heard in *p* ... Matt 11:2
had John beheaded in *p* ... Matt 14:10
I was in *p* and you ... Matt 25:36
we see You sick, or in *p* ... Matt 25:39
or naked or sick or in *p* ... Matt 25:44
after John was put in *p* ... Mark 1:14
put them in the common *p* ... Acts 5:18
Lord opened the *p* doors ... Acts 5:19
did not find them in the *p* ... Acts 5:22
was therefore kept in *p* ... Acts 12:5
of the *p* were shaken ... Acts 16:26
seeing the *p* doors open ... Acts 16:27

So the keeper of the *p* .... Acts 16:36
to the spirits in *p* .... 1 Pet 3:19
a *p* for every foul spirit, ... Rev 18:2
will be released from his *p* .. Rev 20:7

PRISONER
the groaning of the *p* .... Ps 79:11
p called Barabbas .... Matt 27:16
releasing one *p* to them .... Mark 15:6
reason I, Paul, the *p* .... Eph 3:1
the *p* of the Lord, beseech .... Eph 4:1
Lord, nor of me His *p* ...... 2 Tim 1:8
Paul, a *p* of Christ Jesus, ... Philem 1

PRISONERS
p rest together .... Job 3:18
does not despise His *p* ...... Ps 69:33
gives freedom to the *p* ...... Ps 146:7
the stronghold, you *p* ...... Zech 9:12
the *p* were listening to .... Acts 16:25
and my fellow *p* .... Rom 16:7
Remember the *p* as if ...... Heb 13:3

PRISONS
the synagogues and *p* .... Luke 21:12
p more frequently .... 2 Cor 11:23

PRIVATE
is of any *p* interpretation .. 2 Pet 1:20

PRIVATELY
disciples came to Jesus *p* .. Matt 17:19
Andrew asked Him *p* ..... Mark 13:3
aside *p* into a deserted ..... Luke 9:10

PRIZE
life shall be as a *p* .... Jer 21:9
but one receives the *p* ...... 1 Cor 9:24
the goal for the *p* .... Phil 3:14

PROCEED
For they *p* from evil .... Jer 9:3
heart *p* evil thoughts ...... Matt 15:19
p evil thoughts, adulteries . Mark 7:21
not permitting us to *p* ...... Acts 27:7
p out of your mouth, ... Eph 4:29
of the same mouth *p* ..... James 3:10

PROCEEDED
for I *p* forth .... John 8:42
p from the mouth of Him .. Rev 19:21

PROCEEDINGS
he adjourned the *p* .... Acts 24:22

PROCEEDS
by every word that *p* .... Deut 8:3
by every word that *p* .... Matt 4:4
Spirit of truth who *p* ...... John 15:26
back part of the *p* .... Acts 5:2

PROCESS
in the *p* of time .... 1 Sam 1:20

PROCESSION
They have seen Your *p* ...... Ps 68:24

PROCHORUS
One of the first seven deacons, Acts 6:5

PROCLAIM
you, and I will *p* .... Ex 33:19
p the name of the LORD .... Deut 32:3
p it not in the .... 2 Sam 1:20
and they shall *p* .... Is 60:6
to *p* liberty to the captives, ... Is 61:1
to *p* the acceptable year of .... Is 61:2
began to *p* it freely .... Mark 1:45
knowing, Him I *p* .... Acts 17:23
drink this cup, you *p* ..... 1 Cor 11:26
that you may *p* the praises .. 1 Pet 2:9

PROCLAIMED
p the good news .... Ps 40:9
company of those who *p* .... Ps 68:11
p a fast, and put on .... Jon 3:5
he went his way and *p* ..... Luke 8:39
inner rooms will be *p* ...... Luke 12:3

PROCLAIMER
"He seems to be a *p* ...... Acts 17:18

PROCLAIMS
good news, who *p* .... Is 52:7

PROCONSUL
seeking to turn the *p* ...... Acts 13:8
When Gallio was *p* ...... Acts 18:12

PRODIGAL
with *p* living .... Luke 15:13

PRODUCE
land shall yield its *p* .... Lev 26:4
all kinds of *p* .... Ps 144:13
p the righteousness of .... James 1:20

PRODUCED
p in me all manner of evil ... Rom 7:8
What diligence it *p* in ..... 2 Cor 7:11

PRODUCES
forcing of wrath *p* strife ... Prov 30:33
indeed bears fruit and *p* .. Matt 13:23
if it dies, it *p* much grain .. John 12:24
tribulation *p* perseverance .. Rom 5:3
sorrow *p* repentance ...... 2 Cor 7:10
of your faith *p* patience .... James 1:3

PRODUCING
p death in me through ..... Rom 7:13

PROFANE
and offered *p* fire .... Lev 10:1
and priest are *p* .... Jer 23:11
"But you *p* it .... Mal 1:12
tried to *p* the temple .... Acts 24:6
But reject *p* and old .... 1 Tim 4:7
p person like Esau .... Heb 12:16

PROFANED
p his crown by casting ...... Ps 89:39
and *p* My Sabbaths .... Ezek 22:8
p the LORD's holy .... Mal 2:11

PROFANENESS
of Jerusalem *p* has .... Jer 23:15

PROFANING
p the covenant of the .... Mal 2:10

PROFESS
They *p* to know God .... Titus 1:16

PROFESSING
P to be wise .... Rom 1:22
is proper for women *p* .... 1 Tim 2:10

PROFIT
p is there in my blood .... Ps 30:9
p has a man from all .... Eccl 1:3
There was no *p* under ...... Eccl 2:11
for they will not *p* .... Is 57:12
words that cannot *p* .... Jer 7:8
p which you have made .. Ezek 22:13
p is it that we have .... Mal 3:14
For what *p* is it to .... Matt 16:26
For what will it *p* .... Mark 8:36
For what *p* is it to .... Luke 9:25
her masters much *p* ...... Acts 16:16
hope of *p* was gone .... Acts 16:19
brought no small *p* .... Acts 19:24
what is the *p* of .... Rom 3:1
not seeking my own *p* .... 1 Cor 10:33
Christ will *p* you .... Gal 5:2
about words to no *p* ...... 2 Tim 2:14
them, but He for our *p* .... Heb 12:10
What does it *p* .... James 2:14
and sell, and make a *p* .... James 4:13

PROFITABLE
"Can a man be *p* .... Job 22:2
It is doubtless not *p* ...... 2 Cor 12:1
godliness is *p* for all ...... 1 Tim 4:8
of God, and is *p* .... 2 Tim 3:16
things are good and *p* .... Titus 3:8
to you, but now is *p* .... Philem 11

PROFITS
p a man nothing that .... Job 34:9
from her *p* she plants a .... Prov 31:16
the flesh *p* nothing .... John 6:63
have not love, it *p* .... 1 Cor 13:3
exercise *p* a little .... 1 Tim 4:8

PROFOUND
with things too *p* .... Ps 131:1

PROGRESS
your *p* may be evident ...... 1 Tim 4:15

PROLONG
you will not *p* your .... Deut 4:26
p Your anger to all .... Ps 85:5
nor will he *p* his days .... Eccl 8:13

PROLONGED
and his days are *p* .... Eccl 8:12

PROLONGS
The fear of the LORD *p* .... Prov 10:27

PROMISE
of all His good *p* .... 1 Kin 8:56
Has His *p* failed .... Ps 77:8
remembered His holy *p* .... Ps 105:42
Behold, I send the *P* ...... Luke 24:49
but to wait for the *P* .... Acts 1:4
p of the Holy Spirit, He .... Acts 2:33
For the *p* is to you .... Acts 2:39
p drew near which God ...... Acts 7:17
for the hope of the *p* .... Acts 26:6
is made void and the *p* ..... Rom 4:14
p might be sure .... Rom 4:16
p of God through unbelief .. Rom 4:20
For this is the word of *p* ..... Rom 9:9
make the *p* of no effect ...... Gal 3:17
it is no longer of *p* .... Gal 3:18
heirs according to the *p* ..... Gal 3:29
Isaac was, are children of *p* . Gal 4:28
first commandment with *p* ... Eph 6:2
having *p* of the life that .... 1 Tim 4:8
Therefore, since a *p* .... Heb 4:1
endured, he obtained the *p* .. Heb 6:15
to the heirs of *p* .... Heb 6:17
did not receive the *p* ...... Heb 11:39
they *p* them liberty .... 2 Pet 2:19
not slack concerning His *p* .. 2 Pet 3:9
p that He has promised .... 1 John 2:25

PROMISED
bless you as He has *p* ...... Deut 1:11
that what He had *p* .... Rom 4:21
Him faithful who had *p* .... Heb 11:11

PROMISES
For all the *p* of God .... 2 Cor 1:20
his Seed were the *p* .... Gal 3:16
patience inherit the *p* .... Heb 6:12
having received the *p* ...... Heb 11:13
great and precious *p* .... 2 Pet 1:4

PROMOTE
Exalt her, and she will *p* .... Prov 4:8

PROMOTED
Then the king *p* Daniel ..... Dan 2:48
Then the king *p* Shadrach, .. Dan 3:30

PROMOTES
tongue of the wise *p* ...... Prov 12:18

PROMPTLY
him disciplines him *p* ..... Prov 13:24

PRONOUNCE
for he could not *p* it right .. Judg 12:6
P them guilty, O God .... Ps 5:10

PROOF
which is to them a *p* .... Phil 1:28

PROOFS
by many infallible *p* .... Acts 1:3

PROPER
you, but for what is *p* ..... 1 Cor 7:35
Is it *p* for a woman to .... 1 Cor 11:13
but, which is *p* .... 1 Tim 2:10
are *p* for sound doctrine .... Titus 2:1

PROPERLY
Let us walk *p* .... Rom 13:13
that you may walk *p* ..... 1 Thess 4:12

PROPHECIES
Do not despise *p* .... 1 Thess 5:20

PROPHECY
if *p*, let us prophesy in ..... Rom 12:6
miracles, to another *p* .... 1 Cor 12:10
I have the gift of *p* .... 1 Cor 13:2
p with the laying on of .... 1 Tim 4:14
for *p* never came by .... 2 Pet 1:21
is the spirit of *p* .... Rev 19:10
of the book of this *p* .... Rev 22:19

PROPHESIED
upon them, that they *p* .... Num 11:25
to them, yet they *p* .... Jer 23:21
Lord, have we not *p* .... Matt 7:22
prophets and the law *p* ... Matt 11:13
virgin daughters who *p* ..... Acts 21:9
even more that you *p* ...... 1 Cor 14:5

PROPHESIES
for the prophet who *p* .... Jer 28:9
woman who prays or *p* .... 1 Cor 11:5
p edifies the church .... 1 Cor 14:4

PROPHESY
prophets, "Do not *p* .... Is 30:10
The prophets *p* falsely .... Jer 5:31
your daughters shall *p* ...... Joel 2:28
Who can but *p* .... Amos 3:8
saying, "*P* to us .... Matt 26:68
and to say to Him, "*P*!" ... Mark 14:65
your daughters shall *p* .... Acts 2:17
if prophecy, let us *p* .... Rom 12:6
know in part and we *p* .... 1 Cor 13:9
that you may *p* .... 1 Cor 14:1
For you can all *p* one ..... 1 Cor 14:31
desire earnestly to *p* ..... 1 Cor 14:39

PROPHESYING
he had finished *p* .... 1 Sam 10:13
Every man praying or *p*, .. 1 Cor 11:4
p is not for unbelievers ... 1 Cor 14:22

PROPHET
shall be your *p* .... Ex 7:1
raise up for you a *P* .... Deut 18:15
arisen in Israel a *p* .... Deut 34:10
"I alone am left a *p* ...... 1 Kin 18:22
is no longer any *p* .... Ps 74:9
I ordained you a *p* .... Jer 1:5
p is induced to speak ...... Ezek 14:9
The *p* is a fool .... Hos 9:7
nor was I a son of a *p* ..... Amos 7:14
send you Elijah the *p* .... Mal 4:5
p shall receive a .... Matt 10:41
the sign of the *p* Jonah .... Matt 12:39
p is not without honor .... Matt 13:57
by Daniel the *p* .... Mark 13:14
no *p* is accepted in his ..... Luke 4:24
is not a greater *p* .... Luke 7:28
it cannot be that a *p* ...... Luke 13:33
Nazareth, who was a *P* ... Luke 24:19
"Are you the *P* .... John 1:21
"This is truly the *P* .... John 6:14
for no *p* has arisen out of .. John 7:52
p named Agabus .... Acts 21:10
with him the false *p* .... Rev 19:20

PROPHET'S
shall receive a *p* reward .. Matt 10:41

PROPHETESS
Then Miriam the *p*, ... Ex 15:20
Now Deborah, a *p*, ... Judg 4:4
there was one, Anna, a *p* .. Luke 2:36

PROPHETIC
by the *p* Scriptures .... Rom 16:26
p word confirmed .... 2 Pet 1:19

PROPHETS
See FALSE PROPHETS; LAW AND THE PROPHETS
LORD's people were *p* .... Num 11:29
Saul also among the *p* ... 1 Sam 10:12
the mouth of all his *p* .... 1 Kin 22:22
Where now are your *p* ...... Jer 37:19
prophesy against the *p* .... Ezek 13:2
Her *p* are insolent .... Zeph 3:4
the Law or the *P* .... Matt 5:17
is the Law and the *P* .... Matt 7:12
or one of the *p* .... Matt 16:14
the tombs of the *p* .... Matt 23:29
indeed, I send you *p* ...... Matt 23:34
one who kills the *p* .... Matt 23:37
Then many false *p* .... Matt 24:11
have Moses and the *p* .... Luke 16:29
You are sons of the *p* ...... Acts 3:25
p did your fathers not ...... Acts 7:52
To Him all the *p* .... Acts 10:43
do you believe the *p* ...... Acts 26:27
before through His *p* .... Rom 1:2
by the Law and the *P* ...... Rom 3:21
have killed Your *p* .... Rom 11:3
p are subject to the ...... 1 Cor 14:32
to be apostles, some *p* ...... Eph 4:11
brethren, take the *p* ...... James 5:10
this salvation the *p* .... 1 Pet 1:10
were also false *p* .... 2 Pet 2:1
because many false *p* ..... 1 John 4:1
blood of saints and *p* .... Rev 16:6
found the blood of *p* .... Rev 18:24
of your brethren the *p* ...... Rev 22:9

PROPITIATION
set forth as a *p* .... Rom 3:25
to God, to make *p* .... Heb 2:17
He Himself is the *p* .... 1 John 2:2
His Son to be the *p* ...... 1 John 4:10

PROPORTION
let us prophesy in *p* .... Rom 12:6

PROPOSED
And they *p* two .... Acts 1:23

PROPRIETY
modest apparel, with *p* ...... 1 Tim 2:9

PROSECUTOR
answer me, that my *P* ...... Job 31:35

PROSELYTE
and sea to win one *p* ...... Matt 23:15
Nicolas, a *p* from Antioch, ... Acts 6:5

PROSELYTES
Rome, both Jews and *p* .... Acts 2:10

PROSPER
made all he did to *p* .... Gen 39:3
you shall not *p* .... Deut 28:29
LORD, God made him *p* .... 2 Chr 26:5
they *p* who love you .... Ps 122:6
his sins will not *p* .... Prov 28:13
of the LORD shall *p* .... Is 53:10
against you shall *p* .... Is 54:17
please, and it shall *p* .... Is 55:11
of the wicked *p* .... Jer 12:1
King shall reign and *p* .... Jer 23:5
storing up as he may *p* ... 1 Cor 16:2
I pray that you may *p* .... 3 John 2

PROSPERED
since the LORD has *p* .... Gen 24:56
he *p* wherever he went .... 2 Kin 18:7
David his father, and *p* .. 1 Chr 29:23
all his heart. So he *p* .... 2 Chr 31:21
Hezekiah *p* in all his ..... 2 Chr 32:30
and they *p* through the .... Ezra 6:14
in the LORD will be *p* ..... Prov 28:25
Daniel *p* in the reign .... Dan 6:28
He did all this and *p* .... Dan 8:12

PROSPERING
His ways are always *p* .... Ps 10:5

PROSPERITY
p all your days .... Deut 23:6
p exceed the fame .... 1 Kin 10:7
p the destroyer .... Job 15:21
spend their days in *p* ...... Job 36:11
Now in my *p* I said .... Ps 30:6
has pleasure in the *p* .... Ps 35:27
When I saw the *p* .... Ps 73:3
I pray, send now *p* .... Ps 118:25
the day of *p* be joyful .... Eccl 7:14
that we have our *p* .... Acts 19:25

PROSPEROUS
had made his journey *p* ... Gen 24:21
will make your way *p* .... Josh 1:8

PROSPERS
he turns, he *p* .... Prov 17:8
just as your soul *p* .... 3 John 2

PROSTRATE
of the proud lie *p* .... Job 9:13

PROTECTED
holy man, and he *p* him ... Mark 6:20

PROUD
p waves must stop .... Job 38:11
tongue that speaks *p* .... Ps 12:3
and fully repays the *p* .... Ps 31:23
does not respect the *p* .... Ps 40:4
a haughty look and a *p* ...... Ps 101:5
p He knows from afar ...... Ps 138:6
the house of the *p* .... Prov 15:25
Everyone *p* in heart .... Prov 16:5
p heart stirs up .... Prov 28:25
is better than the *p* .... Eccl 7:8
by wine, he is a *p* .... Hab 2:5
He has scattered the *p* ..... Luke 1:51
boasters, *p* .... 2 Tim 3:2
"God resists the *p*, but ..... James 4:6
"God resists the *p* .... 1 Pet 5:5

PROVE
p yourself a man .... 1 Kin 2:2
does your arguing *p* .... Job 6:25
mind, that you may *p* ...... Rom 12:2

PROVERB
an astonishment, a *p* ..... Deut 28:37
incline my ear to a *p* .... Ps 49:4
that hang limp is a *p* .... Prov 26:7
of a drunkard is a *p* .... Prov 26:9
one shall take up a *p* .... Mic 2:4
to the true *p* .... 2 Pet 2:22

PROVERBS
spoke three thousand *p* .... 1 Kin 4:32
The *p* of Solomon the .... Prov 1:1
are *p* of Solomon .... Prov 25:1
in order many *p* .... Eccl 12:9

PROVIDE
"My son, God will *p* .... Gen 22:8
Can He *p* meat for His ...... Ps 78:20
lambs will *p* your .... Prov 27:26
prosperity that I *p* .... Jer 33:9
P neither gold nor .... Matt 10:9
if anyone does not *p* .... 1 Tim 5:8

PROVIDED
I have *p* Myself a king .... 1 Sam 16:1
p for her from the king's ...... Esth 2:9
p from Your godness .... Ps 68:10
atonement is *p* for iniquity . Prov 16:6
these hands have *p* .... Acts 20:34
p something better .... Heb 11:40

PROVIDES
p food for the raven .... Job 38:41
p her supplies in the .... Prov 6:8
p food for her household .. Prov 31:15

PROVIDING
p honorable things, ... 2 Cor 8:21

PROVISION
bread of their *p* was dry .... Josh 9:5
Now Solomon's *p* .... 1 Kin 4:22
abundantly bless her *p* ..... Ps 132:15
p of the king's delicacies ..... Dan 1:5
no *p* for the flesh .... Rom 13:14

PROVOKE
do not *p* Him .... Ex 23:21
p God are secure .... Job 12:6
Do they *p* Me to .... Jer 7:19
p them to jealousy .... Rom 11:11
you, fathers, do not *p* .... Eph 6:4
do not *p* your children, lest .. Col 3:21

PROVOKED
How often they *p* .... Ps 78:40

p the Most High .... Ps 78:56
Thus they *p* Him to .... Ps 106:29
his spirit was *p* .... Acts 17:16
seek its own, is not *p* .... 1 Cor 13:5

PROVOKING
p one another, envying one .. Gal 5:26

PROWLER
poverty come like a *p* ..... Prov 24:34

PRUDENCE
son, endowed with *p* ...... 2 Chr 2:12
To give *p* to the .... Prov 1:4
wisdom, dwell with *p* ...... Prov 8:12
us in all wisdom and *p* .... Eph 1:8

PRUDENT
p man covers shame ...... Prov 12:16
A *p* man conceals .... Prov 12:23
The wisdom of the *p* .... Prov 14:8
p considers well .... Prov 14:15
receives correction is *p* .... Prov 15:5
heart will be called *p* ..... Prov 16:21
p acquires knowledge ..... Prov 18:15
p wife is from the .... Prov 19:14
p man foresees evil .... Prov 22:3
perished from the *p* .... Jer 49:7
Therefore the *p* .... Amos 5:13
from the wise and *p* ...... Matt 11:25

PRUDENTLY
Servant shall deal *p* .... Is 52:13

PRUNES
that bears fruit He *p* .... John 15:2

PSALM
and the sound of a *p* .... Ps 98:5
in the second *P* .... Acts 13:33
each of you has a *p* ..... 1 Cor 14:26

PSALMIST
And the sweet *p* .... 2 Sam 23:1

PSALMS
Sing to Him, sing *p* .... 1 Chr 16:9
to one another in *p* .... Eph 5:19
one another in *p* .... Col 3:16
Let him sing *p* .... James 5:13

PSALTERY
harp, lyre, and *p* .... Dan 3:10

PTOLEMAIS
Seaport city south of Tyre; Paul lands at, Acts 21:7

PUBLIC
to make her a *p* example ... Matt 1:19

PUBLISHED
to be proclaimed and *p* .... Jon 3:7

PUBLIUS
Roman official; entertains Paul, Acts 28:7, 8

PUFFED
Now some are *p* up .... 1 Cor 4:18
itself, is not *p* .... 1 Cor 13:4
a novice, lest being *p* .... 1 Tim 3:6

PUFFS
Knowledge *p* up .... 1 Cor 8:1

PUL
King of Assyria; same as Tiglath-Pileser, 2 Kin 15:19
——— Country and people in Africa, Is 66:19

PULL
P me out of the net .... Ps 31:4
I will *p* down my barns ... Luke 12:18

PULLING
for *p* down strongholds .... 2 Cor 10:4

PUNISH
take that man and *p* ...... Deut 22:18
p the righteous is .... Prov 17:26
"I will *p* the world .... Is 13:11
Shall I not *p* them for .... Jer 5:9
p all who oppress them ..... Jer 30:20

p your iniquity .... Lam 4:22
So I will *p* them for .... Hos 4:9

PUNISHED
You our God have *p* .... Ezra 9:13
because He has not *p* ...... Job 35:15
p them often in every ...... Acts 26:11
These shall be *p* .... 2 Thess 1:9

PUNISHES
will you say when He *p* ...... Jer 13:21

PUNISHMENT
p is greater than I .... Gen 4:13
you do in the day of *p* .... Is 10:3
p they shall be cast .... Jer 8:12
p they shall perish .... Jer 10:15
a man for the *p* .... Lam 3:39
The *p* of the iniquity .... Lam 4:6
days of *p* have come .... Hos 9:7
not turn away its *p* .... Amos 1:3
into everlasting *p* .... Matt 25:46
p which was inflicted .... 2 Cor 2:6
Of how much worse *p* ...... Heb 10:29
sent by him for the *p* .... 1 Pet 2:14
the unjust under *p* .... 2 Pet 2:9

PUNON
Israelite camp, Num 33:42, 43

PURCHASED
(Now this man *p* a field .... Acts 1:18
of God could be *p* .... Acts 8:20
of the *p* possession .... Eph 1:14

PURE
a mercy seat of *p* gold ...... Ex 25:17
Can a man be more *p* .... Job 4:17
if you were *p* and .... Job 8:6
'My doctrine is *p* .... Job 11:4
that he could be *p* .... Job 15:14
the heavens are not *p* ...... Job 15:15
the stars are not *p* .... Job 25:5
of the LORD are *p* .... Ps 12:6
will show Yourself *p* .... Ps 18:26
To such as are *p* .... Ps 73:1
of the *p* are pleasant ...... Prov 15:26
ways of a man are *p* .... Prov 16:2
my heart clean, I am *p* ..... Prov 20:9
but as for the *p* .... Prov 21:8
a generation that is *p* ..... Prov 30:12
Shall I count *p* .... Mic 6:11
Blessed are the *p* in heart ... Matt 5:8
things indeed are *p* .... Rom 14:20
whatever things are *p* .... Phil 4:8
with a *p* conscience .... 1 Tim 3:9
keep yourself *p* .... 1 Tim 5:22
serve with a *p* conscience ... 2 Tim 1:3
p all things are *p* .... Titus 1:15
bodies washed with *p* ...... Heb 10:22
P and undefiled religion .. James 1:27
above is first *p* .... James 3:17
babes, desire the *p* .... 1 Pet 2:2
just as He is *p* .... 1 John 3:3

PURER
p eyes than to behold .... Hab 1:13

PURGE
P me with hyssop .... Ps 51:7
p them as gold and .... Mal 3:3

PURGED
away, and your sin *p* .... Is 6:7
He had by Himself *p* .... Heb 1:3

PURIFICATION
for the water of *p* .... Num 19:9
with the water of *p* .... Num 31:23

PURIFIED
earth, *p* seven times .... Ps 12:6
all things are *p* .... Heb 9:22
Since you have *p* .... 1 Pet 1:22

PURIFIES
hope in Him *p* himself ..... 1 John 3:3

PURIFY
p the sons of Levi .... Mal 3:3
and *p* your hearts .... James 4:8

PURIFYING
thus *p* all foods .... Mark 7:19
p their hearts by .... Acts 15:9
sanctifies for the *p* .... Heb 9:13

PURIM
called these days *P* .... Esth 9:26

PURITY
be delivered by the *p* ...... Job 22:30
He who loves *p* of .... Prov 22:11
by *p*, by knowledge .... 2 Cor 6:6
spirit, in faith, in *p* .... 1 Tim 4:12

PURPLE
who was clothed in *p* ..... Luke 16:19
they put on Him a *p* .... John 19:2
She was a seller of *p* ..... Acts 16:14

PURPOSE
and fulfill all your *p* .... Ps 20:4
A time for every *p* .... Eccl 3:1
p that is purposed .... Is 14:26
But for this *p* I came ...... John 12:27
by the determined *p* .... Acts 2:23
them all that with *p* .... Acts 11:23
called according to His *p* ... Rom 8:28
to the eternal *p* .... Eph 3:11
sent to you for this very *p* ... Eph 6:22
Now the *p* of the .... 1 Tim 1:5
manner of life, *p* .... 2 Tim 3:10
For this *p* the Son of God .. 1 John 3:8
to fulfill His *p* .... Rev 17:17

PURPOSED
For the LORD had *p* ...... 2 Sam 17:14
LORD of hosts has *p* .... Is 23:9
But Daniel *p* in his .... Dan 1:8
Paul *p* in the Spirit .... Acts 19:21
pleasure which He *p* .... Eph 1:9

PURPOSELY
the bundles fall *p* for her .. Ruth 2:16

PURPOSES
each one give as he *p* .... 2 Cor 9:7

PURSE
let us all have one *p* .... Prov 1:14

PURSES
p his lips and brings ...... Prov 16:30

PURSUE
And will You *p* dry .... Job 13:25
p my honor as the wind .... Job 30:15
The sword shall *p* .... Jer 48:2
but their hearts *p* .... Ezek 33:31
Let us know, let us *p* .... Hos 6:3
p righteousness .... Rom 9:30
P love, and desire .... 1 Cor 14:1
p what is good .... 1 Thess 5:15
p righteousness .... 1 Tim 6:11
p righteousness, faith ..... 2 Tim 2:22
P peace with all people .... Heb 12:14
him seek peace and *p* ...... 1 Pet 3:11

PURSUES
Evil *p* sinners .... Prov 13:21
flee when no one *p* .... Prov 28:1

PURSUING
but Israel, *p* the law .... Rom 9:31

PUT
Also He has *p* eternity .... Eccl 3:11
pride He is able to *p* down .. Dan 4:37
what you will *p* on .... Matt 6:25
p my hand into His .... John 20:25
But *p* on the Lord .... Rom 13:14

PUT OFF
I will *p* my sad face .... Job 9:27
You have *p* my sackcloth ...... Ps 30:11
you *p*, concerning your ...... Eph 4:22
you yourselves are to *p* all .... Col 3:8
shortly I must *p* my tent ... 2 Pet 1:14

PUT ON
I *p* righteousness .... Job 29:14

awake, *p* strength, O arm . . . . . Is 51:9
For He *p* righteousness . . . . . . Is 59:17
body, what you will *p* . . . . . . Matt 6:25
they *p* Him a purple robe . . John 19:2
p the armor of light . . . . Rom 13:12
p the Lord Jesus Christ . . . Rom 13:14
must *p* incorruption . . . . . . 1 Cor 15:53
into Christ have *p* Christ . . . . Gal 3:27
you *p* the new man . . . . Eph 4:24
P the whole armor of God . . Eph 6:11
having *p* the breastplate . . . . Eph 6:14
have *p* the new man . . . . Col 3:10
p tender mercies . . . . Col 3:12
all these things *p* love . . . . Col 3:14
I will *p* you no other . . . . Rev 2:24

PUTEOLI
Seaport of Italy, Acts 28:13

PUTREFYING
bruises and *p* sores . . . . Is 1:6

QUAIL
and it brought *q* . . . . Num 11:31
and He brought *q* . . . . Ps 105:40

QUAKED
the whole mountain *q* . . . . Ex 19:18
and the earth *q* . . . . Matt 27:51

QUAKES
The earth *q* before . . . . Joel 2:10

QUALIFIED
the Father who has *q* . . . . Col 1:12

QUARREL
see how he seeks a *q* . . . . 2 Kin 5:7
any fool can start a *q* . . . . . . Prov 20:3
He will not *q* nor cry . . . . . Matt 12:19
of the Lord must not *q* . . . . 2 Tim 2:24

QUARRELSOME
but gentle, not *q* . . . . 1 Tim 3:3

QUARTER
in the Second *Q* . . . . 2 Kin 22:14
from the Second *Q* . . . . Zeph 1:10

QUARTZ
be made of coral or *q* . . . . . . Job 28:18

QUEEN
Q Vashti also made a . . . . Esth 1:9
stands the *q* in gold . . . . Ps 45:9
burn incense to the *q* . . . . Jer 44:17
The *q* of the South . . . . Matt 12:42
under Candace the *q* . . . . Acts 8:27
heart, 'I sit as *q* . . . . Rev 18:7

QUEENS
There are sixty *q* . . . . Song 6:8
q your nursing mothers . . . . . . Is 49:23

QUENCH
Many waters cannot *q* . . . . Song 8:7
so that no one can *q* . . . . Jer 4:4
flax He will not *q* . . . . Matt 12:20
q all the fiery . . . . Eph 6:16
Do not *q* the Spirit . . . . . . 1 Thess 5:19

QUENCHED
LORD, the fire was *q* . . . . Num 11:2
they were *q* like a . . . . Ps 118:12
their fire is not *q* . . . . Is 66:24
that shall never be *q* . . . . . . Mark 9:43
and the fire is not *q* . . . . Mark 9:44
q the violence of fire . . . . . . Heb 11:34

QUESTIONS
test him with hard *q* . . . . 1 Kin 10:1
and asking them *q* . . . . Luke 2:46
market, asking no *q* . . . . . . 1 Cor 10:25

QUICK-TEMPERED
q man acts foolishly . . . . Prov 14:17
not self-willed, not *q* . . . . Titus 1:7

QUICKLY
have turned aside *q* . . . . Ex 32:8
with your adversary *q* . . . . . . Matt 5:25
"What you do, do *q* . . . . John 13:27
Behold, I am coming *q* . . . . Rev 3:11
"Surely I am coming *q* . . . . . . Rev 22:20

QUIET
lain still and been *q* . . . . Job 3:13
'Take heed, and be *q* . . . . Is 7:4
earth is at rest and *q* . . . . Is 14:7
gladness, He will *q* . . . . Zeph 3:17
warned him to be *q* . . . . . . Mark 10:48
aspire to lead a *q* . . . . 1 Thess 4:11
we may lead a *q* and . . . . 1 Tim 2:2
a gentle and *q* spirit . . . . 1 Pet 3:4

QUIETED
calmed and *q* my soul . . . . Ps 131:2
the city clerk had *q* . . . . Acts 19:35

QUIETNESS
will give peace and *q* . . . . . . 1 Chr 22:9
When He gives *q* . . . . Job 34:29
a handful with *q* . . . . Eccl 4:6
in *q* and confidence . . . . Is 30:15
of righteousness, *q* . . . . Is 32:17
that they work in *q* . . . . . . 2 Thess 3:12

QUIETS
q the earth by the . . . . Job 37:17

QUIVER
q rattles against him . . . . Job 39:23
the man who has his *q* . . . . . . Ps 127:5
q He has hidden Me . . . . Is 49:2
Their *q* is like an . . . . Jer 5:16

RAAMSES
Treasure city built by Hebrew slaves, Ex 1:11

RABBAH
Capital of Ammon, Amos 1:14
Besieged by Joab; defeated and enslaved by David, 2 Sam 12:26–31
Destruction of, foretold, Jer 49:2, 3

RABBI
be called by men, '*R* . . . . Matt 23:7
do not be called '*R* . . . . Matt 23:8

RABBONI
Mary addresses Christ as, John 20:16

RABMAG
Title applied to Babylonian prince, Jer 39:3, 13

RABSARIS
Title applied to:
Assyrian officials sent by Sennacherib, 2 Kin 18:17
Babylonian prince, Jer 39:3, 13

RABSHAKEH
Sent by king of Assyria to threaten Hezekiah, 2 Kin 18:17–37; Is 36:2–22
The Lord sends rumor to take him away, 2 Kin 19:6–8; Is 37:6–8

RACA
to his brother, '*R* . . . . Matt 5:22

RACE
man to run its *r* . . . . Ps 19:5
r is not to the swift . . . . Eccl 9:11
who run in a *r* all run . . . . . 1 Cor 9:24
I have finished the *r* . . . . 2 Tim 4:7
with endurance the *r* . . . . Heb 12:1

RACHEL
Laban's younger daughter; Jacob's favorite wife, Gen 29:28–30
Supports her husband's position, Gen 31:14–16
Mother of Joseph and Benjamin, Gen 30:22–25
Prophecy concerning; quoted, Jer 31:15; Matt 2:18

RADIANT
to Him and were *r* . . . . Ps 34:5

RAGE
Disperse the *r* of your . . . . . Job 40:11
Why do the nations *r* . . . . Ps 2:1
'Why did the nations *r* . . . . . Acts 4:25

RAGES
he *r* against all wise . . . . Prov 18:1

RAGS
clothe a man with *r* . . . . Prov 23:21
are like filthy *r* . . . . Is 64:6

RAHAB
Prostitute in Jericho; helps Joshua's spies, Josh 2:1–21
Spared in battle, Josh 6:17–25
Mentioned in the N.T., Matt 1:5; Heb 11:31; James 2:25
——— Used figuratively of Egypt, Ps 87:4

RAIN
had not caused it to *r* . . . . Gen 2:5
And the *r* was on the . . . . Gen 7:12
I will *r* bread from heaven . . . . Ex 16:4
early *r* and the latter *r* . . . . . Deut 11:14
my teaching drop as the *r* . . Deut 32:2
be dew nor *r* these years . . . 1 Kin 17:1
sound of abundance of *r* . . 1 Kin 18:41
He gives *r* on the . . . . Job 5:10
to the gentle *r* . . . . Job 37:6
sent a plentiful *r* . . . . Ps 68:9
clouds, who prepares *r* . . . . . . Ps 147:8
snow in summer and *r* . . . . . Prov 26:1
r which leaves no food . . . . . Prov 28:3
not return after the *r* . . . . Eccl 12:2
the *r* is over and gone . . . . . . Song 2:11
our God, who gives *r* . . . . Jer 5:24
I will *r* down on him . . . . . . Ezek 38:22
given you the former *r* . . . . Joel 2:23
there will be no *r* . . . . Zech 14:17
the good, and sends *r* . . . . . . Matt 5:45
and the *r* descended . . . . Matt 7:25
He did good, gave us *r* . . . . Acts 14:17
r that often comes . . . . Heb 6:7
the early and latter *r* . . . . James 5:7
that it would not *r* . . . . James 5:17
and the heaven gave *r* . . . . James 5:18

RAINBOW
I set My *r* in the . . . . Gen 9:13
the appearance of a *r* . . . . . . Ezek 1:28
and there was a *r* . . . . Rev 4:3

RAINED
had *r* down manna on . . . . Ps 78:24
r fire and brimstone . . . . Luke 17:29

RAINS
r righteousness . . . . Hos 10:12

RAISE
shall *r* up the tabernacle . . . . Ex 26:30
that I will *r* to David a . . . . Jer 23:5
third day He will *r* . . . . Hos 6:2
that God is able to *r* . . . . Matt 3:9
in three days I will *r* . . . . John 2:19
and I will *r* him up at . . . . . . John 6:40
Lord and will also *r* . . . . 1 Cor 6:14
will also *r* us up with . . . . . . 2 Cor 4:14
and the Lord will *r* . . . . James 5:15

RAISED
this purpose I have *r* . . . . Ex 9:16
the LORD *r* up judges . . . . Judg 2:16
LORD has *r* up prophets . . . . . Jer 29:15
be killed, and be *r* . . . . Matt 16:21
whom God *r* up . . . . Acts 2:24
just as Christ was *r* . . . . Rom 6:4
Spirit of Him who *r* . . . . Rom 8:11
And God both *r* up the . . . . 1 Cor 6:14
"How are the dead *r* . . . . . 1 Cor 15:35
and the dead will be *r* . . . . 1 Cor 15:52
and *r* us up together . . . . Eph 2:6
then you were *r* . . . . Col 3:1

RAISED FROM THE DEAD
beheaded; he has been *r* . . . Mark 6:16

whom He had *r* ... John 12:1
disciples after He was *r* ... John 21:14
Prince of life, whom God *r* . Acts 3:15
Christ was *r* by the glory ... Rom 6:4
been *r*, dies no more ... Rom 6:9
that He has been *r* ... 1 Cor 15:12
heaven, whom He *r* ... 1 Thess 1:10
r according to my gospel ... 2 Tim 2:8

RAISED HIM FROM THE DEAD
out of his tomb and *r* ... John 12:17
But God *r* ... Acts 13:30
your heart that God has *r* ... Rom 10:9
God the Father who *r* ... Gal 1:1
in Christ when He *r* ... Eph 1:20
the working of God, who *r* .. Col 2:12
believe in God, who *r* ... 1 Pet 1:21

RAISES
r the poor out of the ... Ps 113:7
r those who are bowed ... Ps 146:8
For as the Father *r* ... John 5:21
but in God who *r* ... 2 Cor 1:9

RAM
r which had two horns ... Dan 8:3

RAMAH
Fortress built, 1 Kin 15:17–22
Samuel's headquarters, 1 Sam 7:15, 17
David flees to, 1 Sam 19:18–23

RAMOTH GILEAD
City of refuge east of Jordan, Deut 4:43; Josh 20:8; 1 Chr 6:80
Site of Ahab's fatal conflict with Syrians, 1 Kin 22:1–39

RAMPART
and it stood by the *r* ... 2 Sam 20:15
whose *r* was like the sea, ... Nah 3:8
and set myself on the *r* ... Hab 2:1

RAMS
the sweet aroma of *r* ... Ps 66:15
r of Nebaioth shall ... Is 60:7

RAN
they both *r* together ... John 20:4
You *r* well ... Gal 5:7

RANKS
r out of the land of Egypt ... Ex 13:18
war, who could keep *r* ... 1 Chr 12:38
and they do not break *r* ... Joel 2:7

RANSOM
r would not help you ... Job 36:18
nor give to God a *r* ... Ps 49:7
The *r* of a man's life ... Prov 13:8
"I will *r* them from ... Hos 13:14
to give His life a *r* ... Mark 10:45
who gave Himself a *r* ... 1 Tim 2:6

RANSOMED
and the *r* of the LORD ... Is 35:10
redeemed Jacob, and *r* ... Jer 31:11

RARE
of the LORD was *r* ... 1 Sam 3:1
make a mortal more *r* ... Is 13:12

RASH
Do not be *r* with your ... Eccl 5:2

RASHLY
so that he spoke *r* ... Ps 106:33
and do nothing *r* ... Acts 19:36

RATS
tumors and five golden *r* ... 1 Sam 6:4

RAVEN
Then he sent out a *r*, ... Gen 8:7
food for the *r* ... Job 38:41
and black as a *r* ... Song 5:11
and the *r* shall dwell in it ... Is 34:11

RAVENOUS
inwardly they are *r* ... Matt 7:15

RAVENS
and to the young *r* ... Ps 147:9
Consider the *r* ... Luke 12:24

RAVISHED
You have *r* my heart ... Song 4:9
r the women in Zion ... Lam 5:11

RAYS
He had *r* flashing from His ... Hab 3:4

RAZOR
no *r* shall come upon his ... Num 6:5
no *r* shall come upon his ... Judg 13:5
r has ever come upon ... Judg 16:17
like a sharp *r* ... Ps 52:2
will shave with a hired *r* ... Is 7:20

REACHED
earth, and its top *r* ... Gen 28:12
For her sins have *r* ... Rev 18:5

REACHING
r forward to those ... Phil 3:13

READ
saying, "*R* this, please" ... Is 29:11
if you can *r* the writing ... Dan 5:16
"Have you never *r* ... Matt 21:42
day, and stood up to *r* ... Luke 4:16
hearts, known and *r* ... 2 Cor 3:2
when Moses is *r* ... 2 Cor 3:15
when this epistle is *r* ... Col 4:16
r the scroll, or to look at ... Rev 5:4

READER
let the *r* understand ... Mark 13:14

READINESS
the word with all *r* ... Acts 17:11
that as there was a *r* ... 2 Cor 8:11

READING
r the prophet Isaiah ... Acts 8:30
give attention to *r* ... 1 Tim 4:13

READS
that he may run who *r* ... Hab 2:2
Blessed is he who *r* ... Rev 1:3

READY
"The LORD was *r* ... Is 38:20
and those who were *r* ... Matt 25:10
"Lord, I am *r* ... Luke 22:33
and being *r* to punish ... 2 Cor 10:6
Be *r* in season and out ... 2 Tim 4:2
and always be *r* ... 1 Pet 3:15

REAFFIRM
r your love to him ... 2 Cor 2:8

REAP
in tears shall *r* ... Ps 126:5
the clouds will not *r* ... Eccl 11:4
r the whirlwind ... Hos 8:7
r in mercy ... Hos 10:12
You shall sow, but not *r* ... Mic 6:15
they neither sow nor *r* ... Matt 6:26
you knew that I *r* ... Matt 25:26
if we *r* your material ... 1 Cor 9:11
that he will also *r* ... Gal 6:7
due season we shall *r* ... Gal 6:9
in Your sickle and *r* ... Rev 14:15

REAPED
wheat but *r* thorns ... Jer 12:13
you have *r* iniquity ... Hos 10:13
earth, and the earth was *r* .. Rev 14:16

REAPER
r does not fill his ... Ps 129:7
shall overtake the *r* ... Amos 9:13

REAPERS
I will say to the *r* ... Matt 13:30
r are the angels ... Matt 13:39

REAPING
r what I did not ... Luke 19:22

REAPS
One sows and another *r* ... John 4:37

REASON
out wisdom and the *r* ... Eccl 7:25
Come now, and let us *r* ... Is 1:18

faith, why do you *r* ... Matt 16:8
words of truth and *r* ... Acts 26:25
who asks you a *r* ... 1 Pet 3:15

REASONED
for three Sabbaths *r* ... Acts 17:2
r about righteousness ... Acts 24:25

REBEKAH
Great-niece of Abraham, Gen 22:20–23
Becomes Isaac's wife, Gen 24:15–67
Mother of Esau and Jacob, Gen 25:21–28
Encourages Jacob to deceive Isaac, then to flee, Gen 27:1–29, 42–46

REBEL
Only do not *r* ... Num 14:9
Will you *r* against the ... Neh 2:19
There are those who *r* ... Job 24:13
and they did not *r* ... Ps 105:28
if you refuse and *r* ... Is 1:20

REBELLED
r against You, cast Your ... Neh 9:26
for they have *r* against You ... Ps 5:10
and they have *r* against Me ... Is 1:2
nation that has *r* against ... Ezek 2:3
have done wickedly and *r* ... Dan 9:5
For who, having heard, *r* ... Heb 3:16

REBELLING
more against Him by *r* ... Ps 78:17

REBELLION
r is as the sin ... 1 Sam 15:23
For he adds *r* to his ... Job 34:37
evil man seeks only *r* ... Prov 17:11
you have taught *r* ... Jer 28:16
hearts as in the *r* ... Heb 3:8
and perished in the *r* ... Jude 11

REBELLIOUS
r exalt themselves ... Ps 66:7
but the *r* dwell in a ... Ps 68:6
day long to a *r* people ... Is 65:2
a defiant and *r* heart ... Jer 5:23
their princes are *r* ... Hos 9:15

REBELS
are all stubborn *r* ... Jer 6:28

REBUILD
God, to *r* its ruins ... Ezra 9:9
tombs, that I may *r* ... Neh 2:5
they shall *r* the old ruins ... Is 61:4
r it as in the days of ... Amos 9:11
will *r* the tabernacle of ... Acts 15:16

REBUILDING
we are *r* the temple that ... Ezra 5:11
heard that we were *r* the ... Neh 4:1

REBUILT
be *r* on its former site ... Ezra 5:15
heard that I had *r* the wall ... Neh 6:1
and the ruins shall be *r* ... Ezek 36:33

REBUKE
He will surely *r* ... Job 13:10
astonished at His *r* ... Job 26:11
they perish at the *r* ... Ps 80:16
At Your *r* they fled ... Ps 104:7
And let him *r* me ... Ps 141:5
Turn at my *r* ... Prov 1:23
r a wise man ... Prov 9:8
R is more effective ... Prov 17:10
r is better than love ... Prov 27:5
better to hear the *r* ... Eccl 7:5
r the oppressor ... Is 1:17
sake I have suffered *r* ... Jer 15:15
r strong nations ... Mic 4:3
sins against you, *r* ... Luke 17:3
r Your disciples ... Luke 19:39
Do not *r* an older man ... 1 Tim 5:1
who are sinning *r* ... 1 Tim 5:20
r them sharply ... Titus 1:13
"The Lord *r* you ... Jude 9
As many as I love, I *r* ... Rev 3:19

REFUSES
My soul *r* to touch ... Job 6:7
he who *r* correction goes .. Prov 10:17
he who *r*, let him refuse .... Ezek 3:27
And if he *r* to hear ... Matt 18:17

REGARD
Yet *r* the prayer of Your ... 1 Kin 8:28
r the rich more than ... Job 34:19
r iniquity in my heart ... Ps 66:18
r the prayer of the ... Ps 102:17
You do not *r* the person ... Matt 22:16
did not fear God nor *r* ... Luke 18:2
we *r* no one according to .. 2 Cor 5:16

REGARDED
I must be *r* as holy ... Lev 10:3
my hand and no one *r* ... Prov 1:24
r the lowly state ... Luke 1:48

REGARDS
on high, yet He *r* the lowly .. Ps 138:6
r a rebuke will be ... Prov 13:18
He no longer *r* them ... Lam 4:16

REGENERATION
to you, that in the *r* ... Matt 19:28
the washing of *r* ... Titus 3:5

REGISTERED
So all went to be *r* ... Luke 2:3
firstborn who are *r* ... Heb 12:23

REGRETTED
but afterward he *r* ... Matt 21:29

REGULATIONS
yourselves to *r* ... Col 2:20

REHOBOAM
Son and successor of Solomon; refuses reform, 1 Kin 11:43—12:15
Ten tribes revolt against, 1 Kin 12:16–24
Reigns over Judah 17 years, 1 Kin 14:21–31; 2 Chr 11:5–23
Apostasizes, then repents, 2 Chr 12:1–16

REHOBOTH
Name of a well dug by Isaac, Gen 26:22

REIGN
The LORD shall *r* forever ... Ex 15:18
but a king shall *r* ... 1 Sam 12:12
hypocrite should not *r* ... Job 34:30
so the LORD will *r* ... Mic 4:7
And He will *r* ... Luke 1:33
not have this man to *r* ... Luke 19:14
righteousness will *r* ... Rom 5:17
so grace might *r* ... Rom 5:21
do not let sin *r* ... Rom 6:12
to *r* over the Gentiles ... Rom 15:12
For He must *r* till He ... 1 Cor 15:25
and we shall *r* on the ... Rev 5:10
and He shall *r* forever ... Rev 11:15
of Christ, and shall *r* ... Rev 20:6

REIGNED
death *r* from Adam to ... Rom 5:14
so that as sin *r* ... Rom 5:21
You have *r* as kings ... 1 Cor 4:8
And they lived and *r* ... Rev 20:4

REIGNS
God *r* over the nations ... Ps 47:8
The LORD *r* ... Ps 93:1
to Zion, "Your God *r* ... Is 52:7
Lord God Omnipotent *r* ... Rev 19:6

REJECT
will these people *r* ... Num 14:11
r all those who stray ... Ps 119:118
"All too well you *r* ... Mark 7:9
R a divisive man ... Titus 3:10

REJECTED
r has become the chief ... Ps 118:22
He is despised and *r* ... Is 53:3
Israel has *r* the ... Hos 8:3
r has become the chief ... Matt 21:42
many things and be *r* ... Luke 17:25
This Moses whom they *r* ... Acts 7:35
to a living stone, *r* ... 1 Pet 2:4
r has become the chief ... 1 Pet 2:7

REJECTION
you shall know My *r* ... Num 14:34

REJECTS
he who *r* Me *r* ... Luke 10:16
r this does not reject ... 1 Thess 4:8

REJOICE
See BE GLAD AND REJOICE
so the LORD will *r* ... Deut 28:63
let the field *r* ... 1 Chr 16:32
and let Your saints *r* ... 2 Chr 6:41
r who put their trust ... Ps 5:11
people, let Jacob *r* ... Ps 14:7
R in the LORD ... Ps 33:1
mutual confusion who *r* ... Ps 35:26
The righteous shall *r* ... Ps 58:10
of Your wings I will *r* ... Ps 63:7
But the king shall *r* ... Ps 63:11
Let them *r* before God ... Ps 68:3
In Your name they *r* ... Ps 89:16
Let the heavens *r* ... Ps 96:11
Let the earth *r* ... Ps 97:1
righteous see it and *r* ... Ps 107:42
we will *r* and be glad ... Ps 118:24
who *r* in doing evil ... Prov 2:14
be blessed, and *r* ... Prov 5:18
she shall *r* in time to ... Prov 31:25
R, O young man ... Eccl 11:9
We will be glad and *r* ... Song 1:4
among men shall *r* ... Is 29:19
I will greatly *r* ... Is 61:10
My servants shall *r* ... Is 65:13
your heart shall *r* ... Is 66:14
Yes, I will *r* ... Jer 32:41
Do not *r* over me ... Mic 7:8
He will *r* over you ... Zeph 3:17
do not *r* in this ... Luke 10:20
loved Me, you would *r* ... John 14:28
but the world will *r* ... John 16:20
and your heart will *r* ... John 16:22
R with those who ... Rom 12:15
and in this I *r* ... Phil 1:18
faith, I am glad and *r* ... Phil 2:17
R in the Lord always ... Phil 4:4
R always ... 1 Thess 5:16
yet believing, you *r* ... 1 Pet 1:8

REJOICE IN THE LORD
R, O you righteous ... Ps 33:1
R, you righteous ... Ps 97:12
you shall *r*, and glory in ... Is 41:16
I will greatly *r* ... Is 61:10
you children of Zion and *r* .. Joel 2:23
Yet I will *r*, I will joy ... Hab 3:18
their heart shall *r* ... Zech 10:7
Finally, my brethren, *r* ... Phil 3:1
R always. Again I will say ... Phil 4:4

REJOICED
for good as He *r* ... Deut 30:9
for my heart *r* ... Eccl 2:10
and my spirit has *r* ... Luke 1:47
In that hour Jesus *r* ... Luke 10:21
Your father Abraham *r* ... John 8:56
But I *r* in the Lord ... Phil 4:10

REJOICES
My heart *r* in the LORD ... 1 Sam 2:1
glad, and my glory *r* ... Ps 16:9
bridegroom *r* over the bride .. Is 62:5
r more over that sheep ... Matt 18:13
but *r* in the truth ... 1 Cor 13:6

REJOICING
His works with *r* ... Ps 107:22
The voice of *r* and ... Ps 118:15
for they are the *r* ... Ps 119:111
come again with *r* ... Ps 126:6
r in His inhabited ... Prov 8:31
he went on his way *r* ... Acts 8:39
yet always *r* ... 2 Cor 6:10
or joy, or crown of *r* ... 1 Thess 2:19
confidence and the *r* ... Heb 3:6

RELATIVES
r stand afar off ... Ps 38:11

RELEASE
shall grant a *r* of debts ... Deut 15:1
time in the year of *r*, at ... Deut 31:10
do you want me to *r* ... Matt 27:17
and power to *r* You ... John 19:10
"*R* the four angels ... Rev 9:14

RELEASED
r him, and forgave him ... Matt 18:27
he *r* Barabbas to them ... Matt 27:26
she is *r* from the law of ... Rom 7:2
Satan will be *r* from his ... Rev 20:7

RELEASING
of strife is like *r* water ... Prov 17:14
to *r* one prisoner to them .. Mark 15:6

RELENT
sworn and will not *r* ... Ps 110:4
and will not *r* ... Jer 4:28
then the LORD will *r* ... Jer 26:13
if He will turn and *r* ... Joel 2:14
sworn and will not *r* ... Heb 7:21

RELENTED
So the LORD *r* from the ... Ex 32:14
the LORD looked and *r* ... 1 Chr 21:15
and God *r* from the ... Jon 3:10

RELENTING
I am weary of *r* ... Jer 15:6

RELIEF
saw that there was *r* ... Ex 8:15
that I may find *r* ... Job 32:20

RELIEVE
of my lips would *r* ... Job 16:5
r those who are really ... 1 Tim 5:16

RELIEVED
You have *r* me when I ... Ps 4:1

RELIEVES
r the fatherless ... Ps 146:9

RELIGION
about their own *r* ... Acts 25:19
in self-imposed *r* ... Col 2:23
heart, this one's *r* ... James 1:26
and undefiled *r* ... James 1:27

RELIGIOUS
things you are very *r* ... Acts 17:22
you thinks he is *r* ... James 1:26

RELY
name of the LORD and *r* ... Is 50:10
You *r* on your sword ... Ezek 33:26

REMAIN
shall let none of it *r* ... Ex 12:10
r angry forever ... Jer 3:5
and this city shall *r* ... Jer 17:25
that if ten men *r* ... Amos 6:9
you, that My joy may *r* ... John 15:11
your fruit should *r* ... John 15:16
"If I will that he *r* ... John 21:22
the greater part *r* ... 1 Cor 15:6
Nevertheless to *r* ... Phil 1:24
we who are alive and *r* .. 1 Thess 4:15
the things which *r* ... Rev 3:2

REMAINDER
with the *r* of wrath ... Ps 76:10
I am deprived of the *r* ... Is 38:10

REMAINED
Also my wisdom *r* ... Eccl 2:9
And Mary *r* with her ... Luke 1:56
like a dove, and He *r* ... John 1:32

REMAINS
"While the earth *r* ... Gen 8:22
Therefore your sin *r* ... John 9:41

There *r* therefore a .... Heb 4:9
sin, for His seed *r* .... 1 John 3:9

REMEMBER
But *r* me when it is .... Gen 40:14
R the Sabbath day .... Ex 20:8
r that you were a .... Deut 15:15
R His marvelous works .. 1 Chr 16:12
but we will *r* the name .... Ps 20:7
r the sins of my youth .... Ps 25:7
r Your name in the .... Ps 119:55
R now your Creator .... Eccl 12:1
r your love more than ...... Song 1:4
r the former things .... Is 43:18
"I *r* you, the kindness .... Jer 2:2
and their sin I will *r* .... Jer 31:34
r the covenant of .... Amos 1:9
in wrath *r* mercy .... Hab 3:2
or *r* the five loaves of the ... Matt 16:9
and to *r* His holy .... Luke 1:72
R Lot's wife .... Luke 17:32
r me when You come ..... Luke 23:42
r the words of the .... Acts 20:35
that we should *r* the poor ..... Gal 2:10
R my chains .... Col 4:18
R that Jesus Christ .... 2 Tim 2:8
deeds I will *r* no more ...... Heb 8:12
R those who rule .... Heb 13:7
R therefore from where you .. Rev 2:5

REMEMBERED
Then God *r* Noah .... Gen 8:1
r His covenant with .... Ex 2:24
I *r* God, and was .... Ps 77:3
r Your judgments .... Ps 119:52
Who *r* us in our lowly ..... Ps 136:23
yea, we wept when we *r* ..... Ps 137:1
r that same poor man .... Eccl 9:15
r the days of old .... Is 63:11
And Peter *r* the word ..... Matt 26:75
r the word of the Lord .... Acts 11:16

REMEMBERS
r His covenant forever ...... Ps 105:8
My soul still *r* .... Lam 3:20

REMEMBRANCE
in death there is no *r* .... Ps 6:5
I call to *r* my song .... Ps 77:6
There is no *r* of .... Eccl 1:11
Put Me in *r* .... Is 43:26
do this in *r* of Me .... Luke 22:19
do this in *r* of Me .... 1 Cor 11:24

REMIND
r you always of these ...... 2 Pet 1:12
But I want to *r* you .... Jude 5

REMINDER
there is a *r* of sins .... Heb 10:3
you always have a *r* .... 2 Pet 1:15
pure minds by way of *r* ..... 2 Pet 3:1

REMISSION
repentance for the *r* .... Mark 1:4
Jesus Christ for the *r* .... Acts 2:38
where there is *r* .... Heb 10:18

REMNANT
Jerusalem shall go a *r* .... 2 Kin 19:31
r of you who have .... 2 Chr 30:6
would be no *r* or survivor .. Ezra 9:14
to us a very small *r* .... Is 1:9
The *r* will return .... Is 10:21
be well with your *r* .... Jer 15:11
I will gather the *r* .... Jer 23:3
and all the *r* of Judah .... Jer 44:28
Yet I will leave a *r* .... Ezek 6:8
r whom the LORD calls ...... Joel 2:32
I will not treat the *r* .... Zech 8:11
time there is a *r* .... Rom 11:5

REMORSEFUL
been condemned, was *r* .... Matt 27:3

REMOVE
I will also *r* Judah from .. 2 Kin 23:27
R Your plague from me ..... Ps 39:10
R Your gaze from me .... Ps 39:13
r your foot from evil .... Prov 4:27
r falsehood and lies .... Prov 30:8
Therefore *r* sorrow .... Eccl 11:10
R violence and .... Ezek 45:9
I will *r* the iniquity of that ... Zech 3:9
let me *r* the speck that ..... Luke 6:42
r your lampstand .... Rev 2:5

REMOVED
Though the earth be *r* .... Ps 46:2
r our transgressions .... Ps 103:12
will never be *r* .... Prov 10:30
and the hills be *r* .... Is 54:10
this mountain, 'Be *r* .... Matt 21:21

REMOVES
r the mountains .... Job 9:5

REND
So *r* your heart .... Joel 2:13

RENDER
What shall I *r* to the .... Ps 116:12
who will *r* to him the ...... Matt 21:41
"*R* therefore to Caesar .... Matt 22:21
r to each one according ..... Rom 2:6
R to her just as she .... Rev 18:6

RENDERS
See that no one *r* evil ... 1 Thess 5:15

RENEW
r a steadfast spirit .... Ps 51:10
r the face of the .... Ps 104:30
on the LORD shall *r* .... Is 40:31

RENEWED
that your youth is *r* .... Ps 103:5
inward man is being *r* ..... 2 Cor 4:16
and be *r* in the spirit .... Eph 4:23
the new man who is *r* .... Col 3:10

RENEWING
transformed by the *r* .... Rom 12:2
of regeneration and *r* .... Titus 3:5

RENOUNCE
Why do the wicked *r* .... Ps 10:13

RENOUNCED
r the covenant of Your ...... Ps 89:39
r the hidden things .... 2 Cor 4:2

RENOUNCES
greedy and *r* the LORD .... Ps 10:3

RENOWN
were of old, men of *r* .... Gen 6:4

RENTED
years in his own *r* house .. Acts 28:30

REPAID
done, so God has *r* .... Judg 1:7
And he has *r* me evil .... 1 Sam 25:21
good shall be *r* .... Prov 13:21
Shall evil be *r* .... Jer 18:20

REPAIR
r the house of your .... 2 Chr 24:5
r the ruined cities .... Is 61:4

REPAY
He will *r* him to his .... Deut 7:10
silence, but will *r* .... Is 65:6
He will surely *r* .... Jer 51:56
again, I will *r* .... Luke 10:35
because they cannot *r* ..... Luke 14:14
R no one evil for evil .... Rom 12:17
is Mine, I will *r* .... Rom 12:19
r their parents .... 1 Tim 5:4
I will *r* .... Philem 19

REPAYS
and who *r* him for what .... Job 21:31
r the proud person .... Ps 31:23
shall he be who *r* .... Ps 137:8
the LORD, who fully *r* .... Is 66:6

REPEATS
r a matter separates .... Prov 17:9

REPENT
of man, that He should *r* .. Num 23:19
I abhor myself, and *r* .... Job 42:6
R now everyone of his evil ... Jer 25:5
R, turn away from your ..... Ezek 14:6
because they refused to *r* .... Hos 11:5
"*R*, for the kingdom .... Matt 3:2
R, and believe in the ...... Mark 1:15
you *r* you will all .... Luke 13:3
said to them, "*R* .... Acts 2:38
R therefore and be .... Acts 3:19
men everywhere to *r* .... Acts 17:30
and do the first works, or .... Rev 2:5
be zealous and *r* .... Rev 3:19

REPENTANCE
bear fruits worthy of *r* .... Matt 3:8
you with water unto *r* ...... Matt 3:11
a baptism of *r* for the .... Mark 1:4
but sinners, to *r* .... Mark 2:17
persons who need no *r* .... Luke 15:7
to the Gentiles *r* to life .... Acts 11:18
of God leads you to *r* .... Rom 2:4
sorrow produces *r* .... 2 Cor 7:10
will grant them *r* .... 2 Tim 2:25
of *r* from dead works and .... Heb 6:1
renew them again to *r* .... Heb 6:6
found no place for *r* .... Heb 12:17
all should come to *r* .... 2 Pet 3:9

REPENTED
No man *r* of his .... Jer 8:6
after my turning, I *r* .... Jer 31:19
it, because they *r* .... Matt 12:41

REPETITIONS
r as the heathen do .... Matt 6:7

REPHAIM
Valley near Jerusalem, 2 Sam 23:13, 14
Scene of Philistine defeats, 2 Sam 5:18–22

REPHIDIM
Israelite camp, Num 33:12–15
Moses strikes rock at, Ex 17:1–7
Amalek defeated at, Ex 17:8–16

REPORT
circulate a false *r* .... Ex 23:1
For it is not a good *r* ...... 1 Sam 2:24
r makes the bones .... Prov 15:30
Who has believed our *r* .... Is 53:1
who has believed our *r* .... Rom 10:16
things are of good *r* .... Phil 4:8

REPRIMANDED
And they *r* him sharply .... Judg 8:1

REPROACH
has taken away my *r* ...... Gen 30:23
away the *r* of Egypt from .... Josh 5:9
and bring *r* on all Israel .. 1 Sam 11:2
we may no longer be a *r* .... Neh 2:17
r me as long as I live .... Job 27:6
does he take up a *r* .... Ps 15:3
You make us a *r* .... Ps 44:13
sake I have borne *r* .... Ps 69:7
R has broken my heart ...... Ps 69:20
Remove from me *r* and .... Ps 119:22
nation, but sin is a *r* .... Prov 14:34
with dishonor comes *r* ..... Prov 18:3
do not fear the *r* .... Is 51:7
not remember the *r* .... Is 54:4
bring an everlasting *r* ...... Jer 23:40
because I bore the *r* .... Jer 31:19
become a desolation, a *r* ..... Jer 49:13
you shall bear the *r* .... Mic 6:16
to take away my *r* among .. Luke 1:25
these things You *r* .... Luke 11:45
lest he fall into *r* .... 1 Tim 3:7
esteeming the *r* .... Heb 11:26
the camp, bearing His *r* .... Heb 13:13
and without *r* .... James 1:5

REPROACHED
of those who *r* You fell ..... Rom 15:3
If you are *r* for the .... 1 Pet 4:14

REPROACHES
is not an enemy who *r* ...... Ps 55:12

oppresses the poor *r* ...... Prov 14:31
curse, and Israel to *r* .... Is 43:28
in infirmities, in *r* .... 2 Cor 12:10

REPROACHFULLY
they strike me *r* .... Job 16:10

REPROOF
for doctrine, for *r* .... 2 Tim 3:16

REPROOFS
R of instruction are .... Prov 6:23

REPUTATION
seven men of good *r* .... Acts 6:3
to those who were of *r* .... Gal 2:2
made Himself of no *r* .... Phil 2:7

REQUEST
not withheld the *r* .... Ps 21:2
He gave them their *r* .... Ps 106:15
the Lord God to make *r* ...... Dan 9:3
For Jews *r* a sign .... 1 Cor 1:22
of mine making *r* .... Phil 1:4

REQUESTS
r be made known .... Phil 4:6

REQUIRE
the LORD your God *r* ...... Deut 10:12
a foreigner you may *r* ...... Deut 15:3
"You will not *r* .... Ps 10:13
offering You did not *r* .... Ps 40:6
what does the LORD *r* .... Mic 6:8

REQUIRED
of the world may be *r* .... Luke 11:50
your soul will be *r* .... Luke 12:20
him much will be *r* .... Luke 12:48
Moreover it is *r* .... 1 Cor 4:2

REQUIREMENTS
keeps the righteous *r* ...... Rom 2:26
r that was against us .... Col 2:14

RESCUE
R me from their .... Ps 35:17
and no one shall *r* .... Hos 5:14

RESERVE
r the unjust under .... 2 Pet 2:9

RESERVED
Have you not *r* a blessing .. Gen 27:36
I have *r* seven thousand .. 1 Kin 19:18
which I have *r* for the ...... Job 38:23
"I have *r* for Myself .... Rom 11:4
r in heaven for you .... 1 Pet 1:4
of darkness, to be *r* .... 2 Pet 2:4
habitation, He has *r* .... Jude 6

RESERVES
He *r* wrath for His enemies .. Nah 1:2

RESIDUE
The *r* of My people .... Zeph 2:9

RESIST
r an evil person .... Matt 5:39
not able to *r* the wisdom .... Acts 6:10
r the Holy Spirit .... Acts 7:51
these also *r* the truth .... 2 Tim 3:8
R the devil and he .... James 4:7
R him, steadfast in the ...... 1 Pet 5:9

RESISTED
For who has *r* His will ..... Rom 9:19
Jannes and Jambres *r* ...... 2 Tim 3:8
for he has greatly *r* .... 2 Tim 4:15
You have not yet *r* .... Heb 12:4

RESISTS
"God *r* the proud .... James 4:6
for "God *r* the proud .... 1 Pet 5:5

RESOLVED
I have *r* what to do .... Luke 16:4

RESORT
to which I may *r* .... Ps 71:3

RESOUND
my heart shall *r* .... Is 16:11

RESPECT
Have *r* to the covenant ...... Ps 74:20
his eyes will have *r* .... Is 17:7
saying, 'They will *r* ...... Matt 21:37
of the law held in *r* .... Acts 5:34
and we paid them *r* .... Heb 12:9

RESPECTED
And the LORD *r* Abel .... Gen 4:4
little folly to one *r* .... Eccl 10:1

RESPONSE
in whose mouth is no *r* ...... Ps 38:14

REST
is the Sabbath of *r* .... Ex 31:15
you shall find no *r* .... Deut 28:65
to build a house of *r* .... 1 Chr 28:2
I would have been at *r* .... Job 3:13
the weary are at *r* .... Job 3:17
My flesh also will *r* in hope ... Ps 16:9
R in the LORD .... Ps 37:7
fly away and be at *r* .... Ps 55:6
of the LORD shall *r* .... Is 11:2
whole earth is at *r* .... Is 14:7
"This is the *r* .... Is 28:12
sake I will not *r* .... Is 62:1
is the place of My *r* .... Is 66:1
then you will find *r* .... Jer 6:16
and I will give you *r* ...... Matt 11:28
and you will find *r* .... Matt 11:29
you who are troubled *r* ... 2 Thess 1:7
shall not enter My *r* .... Heb 3:11
remains therefore a *r* .... Heb 4:9
to enter that *r* .... Heb 4:11
And they do not *r* .... Rev 4:8
that they should *r* .... Rev 6:11
"that they may *r* .... Rev 14:13
But the *r* of the dead .... Rev 20:5

RESTED
He had done, and He *r* .... Gen 2:2
glory of the LORD *r* .... Ex 24:16
when the Spirit *r* .... Num 11:25
"And God *r* on the .... Heb 4:4

RESTING
the dove found no *r* place .... Gen 8:9
foot have a *r* place .... Deut 28:65
do not plunder his *r* .... Prov 24:15
r place shall be .... Is 11:10
all the earth is *r* .... Zech 1:11
still sleeping and *r* .... Matt 26:45

RESTLESS
I am *r* in my complaint ...... Ps 55:2

RESTORATION
until the times of *r* .... Acts 3:21

RESTORE
R to me the joy .... Ps 51:12
I still must *r* .... Ps 69:4
r your judges as .... Is 1:26
r them to this place .... Jer 27:22
For I will *r* health to .... Jer 30:17
"So I will *r* to you .... Joel 2:25
declare that I will *r* .... Zech 9:12
and will *r* all things ...... Matt 17:11
I *r* fourfold .... Luke 19:8
You at this time *r* .... Acts 1:6
who are spiritual *r* .... Gal 6:1

RESTORED
it was *r* like his other flesh .... Ex 4:7
whose son he had *r* to life ... 2 Kin 8:1
LORD *r* Job's losses when ... Job 42:10
hand was *r* as whole as ..... Mark 3:5
that I may be *r* to you the .. Heb 13:19

RESTORER
may he be to you a *r* .... Ruth 4:15

RESTORES
with joy, for He *r* .... Job 33:26
He *r* my soul .... Ps 23:3

RESTRAIN
now *r* Your hand .... 2 Sam 24:16
Therefore I will not *r* .... Job 7:11
Will You *r* Yourself .... Is 64:12
no one can *r* His hand ...... Dan 4:35

RESTRAINED
r my feet from every .... Ps 119:101
Are they *r* .... Is 63:15

RESTRAINS
For nothing *r* the LORD .... 1 Sam 14:6
r his lips is wise .... Prov 10:19
only He who now *r* .... 2 Thess 2:7

RESTRAINT
they have cast off *r* .... Job 30:11
they break all *r* .... Hos 4:2

RESTS
r quietly in the heart ...... Prov 14:33

RESURRECTION
who say there is no *r* ..... Matt 22:23
Therefore, in the *r* .... Matt 22:28
of the graves after His *r* ... Matt 27:53
Therefore, in the *r* ...... Mark 12:23
repaid at the *r* of the ..... Luke 14:14
being sons of the *r* .... Luke 20:36
done good, to the *r* .... John 5:29
to her, "I am the *r* .... John 11:25
a witness with us of His *r* ... Acts 1:22
them Jesus and the *r* ...... Acts 17:18
heard of the *r* of the ...... Acts 17:32
that there will be a *r* ...... Acts 24:15
the likeness of His *r* .... Rom 6:5
say that there is no *r* ..... 1 Cor 15:12
and the power of His *r* .... Phil 3:10
that the *r* is already .... 2 Tim 2:18
obtain a better *r* .... Heb 11:35
the *r* of Jesus Christ .... 1 Pet 3:21
This is the first *r* .... Rev 20:5

RETAIN
happy are all who *r* .... Prov 3:18
spirit to *r* the spirit .... Eccl 8:8
r the sins of any .... John 20:23
like to *r* God in their .... Rom 1:28

RETURN
So the LORD will *r* .... 1 Kin 2:32
and *r* to our neighbors ...... Ps 79:12
R, O LORD .... Ps 90:13
none who go to her *r* ...... Prov 2:19
womb, naked shall he *r* ..... Eccl 5:15
the clouds do not *r* .... Eccl 12:2
let him *r* to the LORD .... Is 55:7
it shall not *r* to Me .... Is 55:11
"If you will *r* .... Jer 4:1
for they shall *r* .... Jer 24:7
me, and I will *r* .... Jer 31:18
say, 'I will go and *r* .... Hos 2:7
help of your God, *r* .... Hos 12:6
"*R* to Me," says the LORD ... Zech 1:3
R to Me, and I will *r* to .... Mal 3:7
he says, 'I will *r* .... Matt 12:44
if not, it will *r* to you ...... Luke 10:6
reviled, did not revile in *r* .. 1 Pet 2:23

RETURNED
and they *r* and sought .... Ps 78:34
yet you have not *r* .... Amos 4:6
astray, but have now *r* ..... 1 Pet 2:25

RETURNING
"I am *r* to Jerusalem .... Zech 1:16
r evil for evil or .... 1 Pet 3:9

RETURNS
spirit departs, he *r* .... Ps 146:4
As a dog *r* to his own ..... Prov 26:11
"A dog *r* to his own .... 2 Pet 2:22

REUBEN
Jacob's eldest son, Gen 29:31, 32
Lies with Bilhah; loses preeminence, Gen 35:22; 49:3, 4
Plots to save Joseph, Gen 37:21–30
Offers sons as pledge for Benjamin, Gen 42:37
——— Tribe of:
Numbered, Num 1:20, 21; 26:5–11
Settle east of Jordan, Num 32:1–42

Join in war against Canaanites, Josh 1:12–18
Erect memorial altar, Josh 22:10–34

REVEAL
The heavens will *r* ....Job 20:27
I will heal them and *r* ....Jer 33:6
the Son wills to *r* Him ....Matt 11:27
r His Son in me ....Gal 1:16
otherwise, God will *r* ....Phil 3:15

REVEALED
things which are *r* ....Deut 29:29
of the LORD shall be *r* ....Is 40:5
righteousness to be *r* ....Is 56:1
Then the secret was *r* ....Dan 2:19
blood has not *r* this to .....Matt 16:17
which will not be *r* ....Mark 4:22
covered that will not be *r* ..Luke 12:2
the Son of Man is *r* ....Luke 17:30
the wrath of God is *r* ....Rom 1:18
glory which shall be *r* ......Rom 8:18
But God has *r* them to .....1 Cor 2:10
secrets of his heart are *r* ..1 Cor 14:25
as it has now been *r* ....Eph 3:5
but now has been *r* ....Col 1:26
the Lord Jesus is *r* ....2 Thess 1:7
lawless one will be *r* .....2 Thess 2:8
ready to be *r* in the ....1 Pet 1:5
when His glory is *r* ....1 Pet 4:13
r what we shall be ....1 John 3:2

REVEALER
Lord of kings, and a *r* ......Dan 2:47

REVEALING
waits for the *r* ....Rom 8:19

REVEALS
as a talebearer *r* ....Prov 20:19
r deep and secret ....Dan 2:22
r secrets has made ....Dan 2:29
r His secret to His ....Amos 3:7

REVELATION
was no widespread *r* ......1 Sam 3:1
Where there is no *r* ....Prov 29:18
to bring *r* to the Gentiles ...Luke 2:32
the day of wrath and *r* ....Rom 2:5
eagerly waiting for the *r* ....1 Cor 1:7
has a tongue, has a *r* .....1 Cor 14:26
it came through the *r* ....Gal 1:12
And I went up by *r*, and ....Gal 2:2
spirit of wisdom and *r* ......Eph 1:17
r He made known to ....Eph 3:3
and glory at the *r* ....1 Pet 1:7
The *R* of Jesus Christ ....Rev 1:1

REVELATIONS
come to visions and *r* .....2 Cor 12:1

REVELRIES
drunkenness, *r* ....Gal 5:21
lusts, drunkenness, *r* ....1 Pet 4:3

REVENGE
and we will take our *r* ......Jer 20:10

REVENUES
than vast *r* without ....Prov 16:8

REVERENCE
and *r* My sanctuary ....Lev 19:30
and to be held in *r* ....Ps 89:7
Master, where is My *r* ....Mal 1:6
submission with all *r* ....1 Tim 3:4
God acceptably with *r* .....Heb 12:28

REVERENT
man who is always *r* ......Prov 28:14
their wives must be *r* .....1 Tim 3:11
older men be sober, *r* ....Titus 2:2

REVILE
are you when they *r* ....Matt 5:11
r God's high priest ....Acts 23:4
evildoers, those who *r* ......1 Pet 3:16

REVILED
crucified with Him *r* .....Mark 15:32
who, when He was *r* ....1 Pet 2:23

REVILER
or an idolater, or a *r* ....1 Cor 5:11

REVILERS
nor drunkards, nor *r* ......1 Cor 6:10

REVILING
come envy, strife, *r* ....1 Tim 6:4

REVIVAL
give us a measure of *r* ....Ezra 9:8

REVIVE
troubles, shall *r* ....Ps 71:20
Will You not *r* us ....Ps 85:6
r me according to Your ....Ps 119:25
r the spirit of the ....Is 57:15
two days He will *r* ....Hos 6:2
r Your work in the ....Hab 3:2

REVIVED
they shall be *r* ....Hos 14:7
came, sin *r* and I died ....Rom 7:9

REVOLT
You will *r* more and ....Is 1:5

REVOLTED
Israel have deeply *r* ....Is 31:6
they have *r* and ....Jer 5:23

REVOLTERS
r are deeply involved ....Hos 5:2

REWARD
exceedingly great *r* ....Gen 15:1
them there is great *r* ....Ps 19:11
r me evil for good ....Ps 35:12
"Surely there is a *r* ....Ps 58:11
look, and see the *r* ....Ps 91:8
will a sure *r* ....Prov 11:18
and the LORD will *r* ....Prov 25:22
and this was my *r* ....Eccl 2:10
behold, His *r* is with ....Is 40:10
r them for their deeds ....Hos 4:9
for great is your *r* ....Matt 5:12
you have no *r* from ....Matt 6:1
you, they have their *r* ....Matt 6:2
receive a prophet's *r* ......Matt 10:41
by no means lose his *r* .....Matt 10:42
r will be great ....Luke 6:35
we receive the due *r* ......Luke 23:41
will receive his own *r* ....1 Cor 3:8
cheat you of your *r* ....Col 2:18
for he looked to the *r* ......Heb 11:26
may receive a full *r* ....2 John 8
quickly, and My *r* ....Rev 22:12

REWARDED
Thus they have *r* ....Ps 109:5

REWARDER
and that He is a *r* ....Heb 11:6

REWARDS
Whoever *r* evil for ....Prov 17:13
and follows after *r* ....Is 1:23
and give your *r* ....Dan 5:17

REZIN
King of Damascus; joins Pekah against Ahaz, 2 Kin 15:37
Confederacy of, inspires Isaiah's great messianic prophecy, Is 7:1—9:12

REZON
Son of Eliadah; establishes Syrian kingdom, 1 Kin 11:23–25

RHEGIUM
City in Italy where Paul visits, Acts 28:13

RHODA
Servant girl, Acts 12:13–16

RHODES
Island off coast of Asia Minor which Paul passes, Acts 21:1

RIBLAH
Headquarters of:
Pharaoh Necho, 2 Kin 23:31–35
Nebuchadnezzar, 2 Kin 25:6, 20, 21
Zedekiah blinded here, Jer 39:5–7

RICH
Abram was very *r* ....Gen 13:2
makes poor and makes *r* ....1 Sam 2:7
r man will lie down ....Job 27:19
the *r* among the people ......Ps 45:12
when one becomes *r* ....Ps 49:16
soul will be made *r* ....Prov 11:25
who makes himself *r* ....Prov 13:7
r has many friends ....Prov 14:20
The *r* and the poor ....Prov 22:2
r rules over the poor ....Prov 22:7
r man is wise in his ....Prov 28:11
do not curse the *r* ....Eccl 10:20
it is hard for a *r* ....Matt 19:23
to you who are *r* ....Luke 6:24
from the *r* man's table ....Luke 16:21
for he was very *r* ....Luke 18:23
Lord over all is *r* ....Rom 10:12
You are already *r* ....1 Cor 4:8
though He was *r* ....2 Cor 8:9
who desire to be *r* ....1 Tim 6:9
but the *r* in his ....James 1:10
So the *r* man also will ....James 1:11
of this world to be *r* ....James 2:5
you say, 'I am *r* ....Rev 3:17

RICHES
Both *r* and honor come ...1 Chr 29:12
He swallows down *r* ....Job 20:15
he heaps up *r* ....Ps 39:6
the abundance of his *r* ....Ps 52:7
if *r* increase ....Ps 62:10
r will be in his house ....Ps 112:3
in her left hand *r* ....Prov 3:16
R and honor are ....Prov 8:18
R do not profit ....Prov 11:4
in his *r* will fall ....Prov 11:28
yet has great *r* ....Prov 13:7
of the wise is their *r* ....Prov 14:24
Houses and *r* are an ....Prov 19:14
of the LORD are *r* ....Prov 22:4
r are not forever ....Prov 27:24
r kept for their owner ......Eccl 5:13
darkness and hidden *r* ....Is 45:3
you shall eat the *r* ....Is 61:6
so is he who gets *r* ....Jer 17:11
have increased your *r* ......Ezek 28:5
for those who have *r* .....Mark 10:23
do you despise the *r* ....Rom 2:4
might make known the *r* ....Rom 9:23
what are the *r* ....Eph 1:18
show the exceeding *r* ....Eph 2:7
the unsearchable *r* ....Eph 3:8
trust in uncertain *r* ....1 Tim 6:17
r than the treasures ....Heb 11:26
r are corrupted ....James 5:2
to receive power and *r* ....Rev 5:12

RICHLY
Christ dwell in you *r* ....Col 3:16
God, who gives us *r* ....1 Tim 6:17

RIDDLE
"Let me pose a *r* ....Judg 14:12

RIDDLES
the wise and their *r* ....Prov 1:6

RIDE
wind and cause me to *r* ....Job 30:22
in Your majesty *r* ....Ps 45:4
have caused men to *r* ....Ps 66:12

RIDER
r He has thrown ....Ex 15:1
the horse and its *r* ....Job 39:18

RIDES
Behold, the LORD *r* ....Is 19:1

RIDGES
You water its *r* ....Ps 65:10

RIDICULE
those who see Me *r* Me ....Ps 22:7
Whom do you *r* ....Is 57:4

RIDICULED
they *r* Him ... Matt 9:24

RIGHT
See AT THE RIGHT HAND; HIS RIGHT HAND; MY RIGHT HAND
then I will go to the *r* ... Gen 13:9
of all the earth do *r* ... Gen 18:25
tip of the *r* ear of Aaron ... Ex 29:20
on the thumb of his *r* hand ... Lev 8:23
you shall do what is *r* ... Deut 6:18
the *r* of the firstborn ... Deut 21:17
did what was *r* in his ... Judg 21:25
my *r* of redemption ... Ruth 4:6
"Is your heart *r* ... 2 Kin 10:15
them forth by the *r* ... Ps 107:7
Lord, "Sit at My *r* ... Ps 110:1
is a way which seems *r* ... Prov 14:12
way of a man is *r* ... Prov 21:2
things that are *r* ... Is 45:19
until He comes whose *r* ... Ezek 21:27
of the LORD are *r* ... Hos 14:9
do not know to do *r* ... Amos 3:10
If your *r* eye causes you ... Matt 5:29
slaps you on your *r* cheek ... Matt 5:39
and whatever is *r* ... Matt 20:4
Sit at My *r* hand, till I ... Matt 22:44
sheep on His *r* hand ... Matt 25:33
clothed and in his *r* ... Mark 5:15
r hand of the Power ... Mark 14:62
clothed and in his *r* mind ... Luke 8:35
not judge what is *r* ... Luke 12:57
to them He gave the *r* ... John 1:12
standing at the *r* hand of ... Acts 7:55
your heart is not *r* ... Acts 8:21
Do we have no *r* ... 1 Cor 9:4
in the Lord, for this is *r* ... Eph 6:1
sat down at the *r* hand of ... Heb 10:12
tabernacle have no *r* to ... Heb 13:10
seven stars in His *r* ... Rev 2:1
I saw in the *r* hand of Him ... Rev 5:1
r hand or on their ... Rev 13:16
the *r* to the tree of life ... Rev 22:14

RIGHTEOUS
also destroy the *r* ... Gen 18:23
Sodom fifty *r* within the ... Gen 18:26
has been more *r* than I ... Gen 38:26
not kill the innocent and *r* ... Ex 23:7
me die the death of the *r* ... Num 23;10
and they justify the *r* ... Deut 25:1
"You are more *r* ... 1 Sam 24:17
down two men more *r* ... 1 Kin 2:32
that he could be *r* ... Job 15:14
r will hold to his way ... Job 17:9
"The *r* see it and ... Job 22:19
knows the way of the *r* ... Ps 1:6
LORD, will bless the *r* ... Ps 5:12
r God tests the hearts ... Ps 7:9
what can the *r* ... Ps 11:3
The *r* cry out ... Ps 34:17
the LORD upholds the *r* ... Ps 37:17
r shows mercy and ... Ps 37:21
I have not seen the *r* ... Ps 37:25
the *r* will be in ... Ps 112:6
The LORD is *r* in all ... Ps 145:17
the LORD loves the *r* ... Ps 146:8
will not allow the *r* ... Prov 10:3
r is a well of life ... Prov 10:11
The labor of the *r* ... Prov 10:16
r will be gladness ... Prov 10:28
r is delivered from ... Prov 11:8
r will be delivered ... Prov 11:21
r will flourish ... Prov 11:28
r will be recompensed ... Prov 11:31
r man regards the life ... Prov 12:10
r should choose his ... Prov 12:26
r there is much ... Prov 15:6
the prayer of the *r* ... Prov 15:29
the *r* run to it and ... Prov 18:10
r are bold as a lion ... Prov 28:1
When the *r* are in ... Prov 29:2
r considers the cause ... Prov 29:7
Do not be overly *r* ... Eccl 7:16
event happens to the *r* ... Eccl 9:2
r that it shall be ... Is 3:10
the gates, that the *r* ... Is 26:2
with My *r* right hand ... Is 41:10
By His knowledge My *r* ... Is 53:11
The *r* perishes ... Is 57:1
people shall all be *r* ... Is 60:21
R are You ... Jer 12:1
your sins by being *r* ... Dan 4:27
they sell the *r* ... Amos 2:6
not come to call the *r* ... Matt 9:13
receive a *r* man's reward ... Matt 10:41
r men desired to see ... Matt 13:17
r will shine forth as ... Matt 13:43
the blood of *r* Abel to ... Matt 23:35
And they were both *r* ... Luke 1:6
that they were *r* ... Luke 18:9
"Certainly this was a *r* ... Luke 23:47
"There is none *r* ... Rom 3:10
r man will one die ... Rom 5:7
witness that he was *r* ... Heb 11:4
prayer of a *r* man avails ... James 5:16
If the *r* one is scarcely ... 1 Pet 4:18
Jesus Christ the *r* ... 1 John 2:1
just as He is *r* ... 1 John 3:7
r are Your judgments ... Rev 16:7
fine linen is the *r* ... Rev 19:8
who is *r*, let him be *r* still ... Rev 22:11

RIGHTEOUS MAN
A little that a *r* ... Ps 37:16
r walks in his integrity ... Prov 20:7
away justice from the *r* ... Is 5:23
if you warn the *r* ... Ezek 3:21
when a *r* turns away ... Ezek 18:24
And he who receives a *r* ... Matt 10:41
"Certainly this was a *r* ... Luke 23:47
For scarcely for a *r* ... Rom 5:7
fervent prayer of a *r* ... James 5:16
r, dwelling among them ... 2 Pet 2:8

RIGHTEOUSLY
judge the people *r* ... Ps 67:4
He who walks *r* and ... Is 33:15
should live soberly, *r* ... Titus 2:12
to Him who judges *r* ... 1 Pet 2:23

RIGHTEOUSNESS
it to him for *r* ... Gen 15:6
In *r* you shall judge your ... Lev 19:15
Because of my *r* the LORD ... Deut 9:4
every man for his *r* ... 1 Sam 26:23
me according to my *r* ... 2 Sam 22:21
My *r* I hold fast ... Job 27:6
I put on *r* ... Job 29:14
I will ascribe *r* ... Job 36:3
I call, O God of my *r* ... Ps 4:1
righteous, He loves *r* ... Ps 11:7
from the LORD, and *r* ... Ps 24:5
shall speak of Your *r* ... Ps 35:28
the good news of *r* ... Ps 40:9
You love *r* and hate ... Ps 45:7
heavens declare His *r* ... Ps 50:6
sing aloud of Your *r* ... Ps 51:14
r and peace have ... Ps 85:10
R will go before Him ... Ps 85:13
r they are exalted ... Ps 89:16
will return to *r* ... Ps 94:15
r and justice are the ... Ps 97:2
and he who does *r* ... Ps 106:3
r endures forever ... Ps 111:3
r is an everlasting ... Ps 119:142
r delivers from death ... Prov 10:2
The *r* of the blameless ... Prov 11:5
The *r* of the upright ... Prov 11:6
r leads to life ... Prov 11:19
the way of *r* is life ... Prov 12:28
R guards him whose way ... Prov 13:6
R exalts a nation ... Prov 14:34
found in the way of *r* ... Prov 16:31
He who follows *r* ... Prov 21:21
r lodged in it ... Is 1:21
r He shall judge ... Is 11:4
R shall be the belt ... Is 11:5
he will not learn *r* ... Is 26:10
and *r* the plummet ... Is 28:17
r will be peace ... Is 32:17
in the LORD I have *r* ... Is 45:24
who are far from *r* ... Is 46:12
r will be forever ... Is 51:8
I will declare your *r* ... Is 57:12
and His own *r* ... Is 59:16
r as a breastplate ... Is 59:17
be called trees of *r* ... Is 61:3
r goes forth as ... Is 62:1
The LORD Our *R* ... Jer 23:6
to David a Branch of *r* ... Jer 33:15
The Lord Our *R* ... Jer 33:16
has revealed our *r* ... Jer 51:10
The *r* of the righteous ... Ezek 18:20
O Lord, *r* belongs ... Dan 9:7
in everlasting *r* ... Dan 9:24
who turn many to *r* ... Dan 12:3
for yourselves *r* ... Hos 10:12
Seek *r*, seek humility ... Zeph 2:3
to fulfill all *r* ... Matt 3:15
exceeds the *r* of the ... Matt 5:20
to you in the way of *r* ... Matt 21:32
in holiness and *r* ... Luke 1:75
For in it the *r* ... Rom 1:17
even the *r* of God ... Rom 3:22
a seal of the *r* ... Rom 4:11
accounted to him for *r* ... Rom 4:22
r will reign in life ... Rom 5:17
might reign through *r* ... Rom 5:21
is life because of *r* ... Rom 8:10
who did not pursue *r* ... Rom 9:30
pursuing the law of *r* ... Rom 9:31
ignorant of God's *r* ... Rom 10:3
we might become the *r* ... 2 Cor 5:21
the fruits of your *r* ... 2 Cor 9:10
r comes through the ... Gal 2:21
was accounted to him for *r* ... Gal 3:6
the breastplate of *r* ... Eph 6:14
not having my own *r* ... Phil 3:9
things and pursue *r* ... 1 Tim 6:11
r which we have ... Titus 3:5
r which is according ... Heb 11:7
does not produce the *r* ... James 1:20
Now the fruit of *r* is ... James 3:18
should suffer for *r* ... 1 Pet 3:14
a preacher of *r* ... 2 Pet 2:5
a new earth in which *r* ... 2 Pet 3:13
who practices *r* ... 1 John 2:29
He who practices *r* ... 1 John 3:7
does not practice *r* ... 1 John 3:10

RIGHTEOUSNESS OF GOD
r is revealed from faith ... Rom 1:17
demonstrates the *r* ... Rom 3:5
r through faith ... Rom 3:22
not submitted to the *r* ... Rom 10:3
we might become the *r* ... 2 Cor 5:21
does not produce the *r* ... James 1:20

RIGHTEOUSNESS'
are persecuted for *r* sake ... Matt 5:10
should suffer for *r* sake ... 1 Pet 3:14

RIGHTEOUSNESSES
all our *r* are like filthy ... Is 64:6

RIGHTLY
wise uses knowledge *r* ... Prov 15:2
R do they love you ... Song 1:4
"You have answered *r* ... Luke 10:28
r dividing the word ... 2 Tim 2:15

RIGHTS
and her marriage *r* ... Ex 21:10

RING
his signet *r* from his hand ... Esth 3:10
a *r* of gold in a swine's ... Prov 11:22
it with his own signet *r* ... Dan 6:17
and put a *r* on his hand ... Luke 15:22

RINGLEADER
the world, and a *r* ... Acts 24:5

RINGS
a man with gold *r* ... James 2:2

RIPE
figs that are first *r* ... Jer 24:2

RISE
is vain for you to *r* ... Ps 127:2
"Now I will *r* ... Is 33:10
for He makes His sun *r* ... Matt 5:45
of Nineveh will *r* ... Matt 12:41
third day He will *r* ... Matt 20:19
false prophets will *r* ... Matt 24:24
persuaded though one *r* ... Luke 16:31
third day He will *r* ... Luke 18:33
had to suffer and *r* ... Acts 17:3
be the first to *r* ... Acts 26:23
fact the dead do not *r* ... 1 Cor 15:15
in Christ will *r* ... 1 Thess 4:16

RISEN
of the LORD is *r* ... Is 60:1
women there has not *r* ... Matt 11:11
disciples that He is *r* ... Matt 28:7
"The Lord is *r* ... Luke 24:34
furthermore is also *r* ... Rom 8:34
then Christ is not *r* ... 1 Cor 15:13
if Christ is not *r* ... 1 Cor 15:17
But now Christ is *r* ... 1 Cor 15:20

RISES
shall I do when God *r* ... Job 31:14
every tongue which *r* ... Is 54:17

RISING
may know from the *r* ... Is 45:6
questioning what the *r* ... Mark 9:10
for the fall and *r* ... Luke 2:34

RIVER
Indeed the *r* may rage ... Job 40:23
them drink from the *r* ... Ps 36:8
r whose streams shall ... Ps 46:4
the *r* of God is full ... Ps 65:9
went through the *r* ... Ps 66:6
peace to her like a *r* ... Is 66:12
in the Jordan *R* ... Mark 1:5
he showed me a pure *r* ... Rev 22:1

RIVERS
He turns *r* into a ... Ps 107:33
R of water run down ... Ps 119:136
By the *r* of Babylon ... Ps 137:1
All the *r* run into the ... Eccl 1:7
us a place of broad *r* ... Is 33:21
the wilderness and *r* ... Is 43:19
the sea, I make the *r* ... Is 50:2
his heart will flow *r* ... John 7:38

RIZPAH
Saul's concubine taken by Abner, 2 Sam 3:6–8
Sons of, killed, 2 Sam 21:8, 9
Grief-stricken, cares for corpses, 2 Sam 21:10–14

ROAD
I will even make a *r* ... Is 43:19
depths of the sea a *r* ... Is 51:10
seen the Lord on the *r* ... Acts 9:27

ROAR
Let the sea *r* ... 1 Chr 16:32
though its waters *r* ... Ps 46:3
The young lions *r* ... Ps 104:21
'The LORD will *r* ... Jer 25:30
He will *r* like a lion ... Hos 11:10
The LORD also will *r* ... Joel 3:16
Will a lion *r* in the ... Amos 3:4

ROARING
wrath is like the *r* ... Prov 19:12
Like a *r* lion and a ... Prov 28:15
and the waves *r* ... Luke 21:25
walks about like a *r* ... 1 Pet 5:8

ROARS
their voice *r* like the ... Jer 6:23
"The LORD *r* from ... Amos 1:2
as when a lion *r* ... Rev 10:3

ROB
r the poor because he ... Prov 22:22
r the needy of justice ... Is 10:2
"Will a man *r* God ... Mal 3:8
do you *r* temples ... Rom 2:22

ROBBED
r their treasuries ... Is 10:13
But this is a people *r* ... Is 42:22
Yet you have *r* Me ... Mal 3:8
r other churches ... 2 Cor 11:8

ROBBER
a son who is a *r* ... Ezek 18:10
is a thief and a *r* ... John 10:1
Barabbas was a *r* ... John 18:40

ROBBERS
and Israel to the *r* ... Is 42:24
also crucified two *r* ... Mark 15:27
Me are thieves and *r* ... John 10:8
here who are neither *r* ... Acts 19:37
waters, in perils of *r* ... 2 Cor 11:26

ROBBERY
nor vainly hope in *r* ... Ps 62:10
I hate *r* for burnt ... Is 61:8
did not consider it *r* ... Phil 2:6

ROBE
r of the ephod, the ephod ... Ex 29:5
off a corner of Saul's *r* ... 1 Sam 24:4
her *r* of many colors ... 2 Sam 13:19
with a *r* of fine linen, ... 1 Chr 15:27
let a royal *r* be brought ... Esth 6:8
justice was like a *r* ... Job 29:14
instead of a rich *r* ... Is 3:24
covered me with the *r* ... Is 61:10
His *r* became white and ... Luke 9:29
'Bring out the best *r* ... Luke 15:22
on Him a purple *r* ... John 19:2
Then a white *r* was ... Rev 6:11
with a *r* dipped in blood, ... Rev 19:13

ROBES
to the King in *r* ... Ps 45:14
have stained all My *r* ... Is 63:3
clothe you with rich *r* ... Zech 3:4
go around in long *r* ... Luke 20:46
clothed with white *r* ... Rev 7:9

ROCK
you shall strike the *r* ... Ex 17:6
put you in the cleft of the *r* ... Ex 33:22
and struck the *r* ... Num 20:11
R who begot you ... Deut 32:18
For their *r* is not ... Deut 32:31
and fire rose out of the *r* ... Judg 6:21
nor is there any *r* ... 1 Sam 2:2
"The LORD is my *r* ... 2 Sam 22:2
And who is a *r* ... 2 Sam 22:32
Blessed be my *R* ... 2 Sam 22:47
away, and as a *r* ... Job 14:18
set me high upon a *r* ... Ps 27:5
For You are my *r* ... Ps 31:3
r that is higher than ... Ps 61:2
and my God the *r* ... Ps 94:22
who turned the *r* ... Ps 114:8
been mindful of the *R* ... Is 17:10
shadow of a great *r* ... Is 32:2
look to the *r* from which ... Is 51:1
that breaks the *r* in pieces ... Jer 23:29
dwell in the clefts of the *r* ... Obad 3
his house on the *r* ... Matt 7:24
r I will build My ... Matt 16:18
Some fell on *r* ... Luke 8:6
stumbling stone and *r* ... Rom 9:33
R that followed them ... 1 Cor 10:4
and a *r* of offense ... 1 Pet 2:8

ROCKS
and the *r* were split ... Matt 27:51
to the mountains and *r* ... Rev 6:16

ROD
And Moses took the *r* ... Ex 4:20
man threw down his *r* ... Ex 7:12
passes under the *r* ... Lev 27:32
the rock twice with his *r* ... Num 20:11
chasten him with the *r* ... 2 Sam 7:14
break them with a *r* of iron ... Ps 2:9
Your *r* and Your staff ... Ps 23:4
The *r* and rebuke give ... Prov 29:15
shall come forth a *R* ... Is 11:1
you pass under the *r* ... Ezek 20:37
measuring *r* six cubits ... Ezek 40:5
I come to you with a *r* ... 1 Cor 4:21
Aaron's *r* that budded, ... Heb 9:4
rule them with a *r* ... Rev 2:27
rule them with a *r* of iron ... Rev 19:15

ROLL
ruinous storm they *r* ... Job 30:14
r away the stone ... Mark 16:3

ROLLED
the heavens shall be *r* ... Is 34:4
the stone had been *r* ... Mark 16:4

ROMAN
Tell me, are you a *R* ... Acts 22:27
learned that he was a *R* ... Acts 23:27

ROME
Jews expelled from, Acts 18:2
Paul:
writes to Christians of, Rom 1:7
desires to go to, Acts 19:21
comes to, Acts 28:14
imprisoned in, Acts 28:16

ROOF
the *r* he saw a woman ... 2 Sam 11:2
stuck the the *r* of their ... Job 29:10
cling to the *r* of my mouth ... Ps 137:6
uncovered the *r* where He ... Mark 2:4

ROOM
See UPPER ROOM
You prepared *r* for it ... Ps 80:9
until no more *r* ... Zech 10:10
you a large upper *r* ... Mark 14:15
no *r* for them in the ... Luke 2:7
still there is *r* ... Luke 14:22
into the upper *r* ... Acts 1:13

ROOMS
make *r* in the ark ... Gen 6:14
He is in the inner *r* ... Matt 24:26

ROOSTER
him, "Before the *r* ... Matt 26:75

ROOT
r bearing bitterness ... Deut 29:18
the foolish taking *r* ... Job 5:3
r may grow old in the ... Job 14:8
day there shall be a *R* ... Is 11:10
shall again take *r* ... Is 37:31
because they had no *r* ... Matt 13:6
and if the *r* is holy ... Rom 11:16
of money is a *r* ... 1 Tim 6:10
lest any *r* of ... Heb 12:15
I am the *R* and the ... Rev 22:16

ROOTED
that you, being *r* ... Eph 3:17
r and built up in Him ... Col 2:7

ROOTS
because its *r* reached ... Ezek 31:7
and lengthen his *r* ... Hos 14:5
dried up from the *r* ... Mark 11:20
pulled up by the *r* ... Jude 12

ROSE
I am the *r* of Sharon ... Song 2:1
and blossom as the *r* ... Is 35:1
end Christ died and *r* ... Rom 14:9
buried, and that He *r* ... 1 Cor 15:4
that Jesus died and *r* ... 1 Thess 4:14

ROTTENNESS
is like *r* in his bones ... Prov 12:4

ROUGH
and the *r* places smooth ... Is 40:4
and the *r* ways smooth ... Luke 3:5

ROUGHLY
answered the people *r* ... 1 Kin 12:13

ROYAL
dwell in the *r* city with ... 1 Sam 27:5
son was over the *r* house .. 2 Kin 15:5
and a *r* house for himself ... 2 Chr 2:1
destroyed all the *r* heirs .. 2 Chr 22:10
so he set the *r* crown ... Esth 2:17
a *r* diadem in the hand of ... Is 62:3
to establish a *r* statute and ... Dan 6:7
the *r* law according to the .. James 2:8
r priesthood, a holy nation .. 1 Pet 2:9

RUBBISH
things, and count them as *r* .. Phil 3:8

RUBIES
of wisdom is above *r* ... Job 28:18
more precious than *r* ... Prov 3:15
is better than *r* ... Prov 8:11
worth is far above *r* ... Prov 31:10
your pinnacles of *r* ... Is 54:12
ruddy in body than *r* ... Lam 4:7

RUDDY
Now he was *r* ... 1 Sam 16:12
beloved is white and *r* ... Song 5:10

RUIN
r those two can bring ... Prov 24:22
flattering mouth works *r* .. Prov 26:28
have made a city a *r* ... Is 25:2
I will *r* the pride of Judah ... Jer 13:9
will not be your *r* ... Ezek 18:30
And the *r* of that ... Luke 6:49
to no profit, to the *r* ... 2 Tim 2:14

RUINED
shall be utterly *r* ... Is 60:12
the mighty trees are *r* ... Zech 11:2
wineskins will be *r* ... Luke 5:37

RUINS
rebuild the old *r* ... Is 61:4
of My house that is in *r*, ... Hag 1:9
I will rebuild its *r*, and I ... Acts 15:16

RULE
greater light to *r* the day ... Gen 1:16
and he shall *r* ... Gen 3:16
r the raging of the ... Ps 89:9
R in the midst of Your ... Ps 110:2
A wise servant will *r* ... Prov 17:2
Whoever has no *r* over ... Prov 25:28
Yet he will *r* over all ... Eccl 2:19
sit and *r* on His throne ... Zech 6:13
puts an end to all *r* ... 1 Cor 15:24
us walk by the same *r* ... Phil 3:16
let the peace of God *r* ... Col 3:15
Let the elders who *r* ... 1 Tim 5:17
Remember those who *r* ... Heb 13:7
He shall *r* them with a rod .. Rev 2:27
He Himself will *r* them ... Rev 19:15

RULER
the sheep, to be *r* ... 2 Sam 7:8
down to eat with a *r* ... Prov 23:1
bear is a wicked *r* ... Prov 28:15
r pays attention ... Prov 29:12
to Me the One to be *r* ... Mic 5:2
by Beelzebub, the *r* ... Matt 12:24
I will make you *r* ... Matt 25:21
the *r* of this world ... John 12:31
because the *r* of this ... John 16:11
'Who made you a *r* ... Acts 7:27
speak evil of a *r* ... Acts 23:5

RULER OF THE SYNAGOGUE
He said to the *r* ... Mark 5:36
Jairus, and he was a *r* ... Luke 8:41
r answered with ... Luke 13:14
r, believed on the Lord ... Acts 18:8
took Sosthenes, the *r* ... Acts 18:17

RULERS
and the *r* take counsel ... Ps 2:2
r decree justice ... Prov 8:15
"You know that the *r* ... Matt 20:25
Have any of the *r* ... John 7:48
r are not a terror ... Rom 13:3
which none of the *r* ... 1 Cor 2:8
powers, against the *r* ... Eph 6:12
to be subject to *r* ... Titus 3:1

RULES
'He who *r* over men ... 2 Sam 23:3
them know that God *r* ... Ps 59:13
He *r* by His power ... Ps 66:7
r his spirit than he ... Prov 16:32
that the Most High *r* ... Dan 4:17
that the Most High *r* ... Dan 4:32
r his own house well ... 1 Tim 3:4
according to the *r* ... 2 Tim 2:5

RULING
r their children ... 1 Tim 3:12

RUMOR
r will be upon *r* ... Ezek 7:26

RUMORS
hear of wars and *r* ... Matt 24:6
you hear of wars and *r* ... Mark 13:7

RUN
I will *r* the course of ... Ps 119:32
r and not be weary ... Is 40:31
many shall *r* to and ... Dan 12:4
Therefore I *r* thus ... 1 Cor 9:26
I might *r*, or had *r* ... Gal 2:2
that I have not *r* ... Phil 2:16
us, and let us *r* ... Heb 12:1
that you do not *r* ... 1 Pet 4:4

RUNNER
are swifter than a *r* ... Job 9:25
r will run to meet ... Jer 51:31

RUNS
word *r* very swiftly ... Ps 147:15
nor of him who *r* ... Rom 9:16

RUSH
The nations will *r* ... Is 17:13

RUSHING
like the *r* of the seas ... Is 17:12
as of a *r* mighty wind, and ... Acts 2:2

RUST
r destroy and where ... Matt 6:19

RUTH
Moabitess, Ruth 1:4
Follows Naomi, Ruth 1:6–18
Marries Boaz, Ruth 4:9–13
Ancestress of Christ, Ruth 4:13, 21, 22

SABAOTH
S had left us a ... Rom 9:29
ears of the Lord of *S* ... James 5:4

SABBATH
'Tomorrow is a *S* ... Ex 16:23
"Remember the *S* ... Ex 20:8
You shall keep the *S* ... Ex 31:14
a *S* of rest to the LORD ... Ex 35:2
day is a *S* of solemn rest ... Lev 23:3
shall keep a *s* to the LORD ... Lev 25:2
Observe the *S* day, to ... Deut 5:12
bear no burden on the *S* ... Jer 17:21
the grainfields on the *S* ... Matt 12:1
S was made for man ... Mark 2:27
is also Lord of the *S* ... Mark 2:28
"Is it lawful on the *S* to do .. Mark 3:4
Is it lawful on the *S* to do ... Luke 6:9
It is the *S*; it is not lawful .. John 5:10
not only broke the *S* ... John 5:18
circumcise a man on the *S* . John 7:22
the synagogues every *S* ... Acts 15:21

SABBATHS
S you shall keep ... Ex 31:13
You shall keep My *S* ... Lev 26:2
The New Moons, the *S* ... Is 1:13
also gave them My *S* ... Ezek 20:12
for three *S* reasoned with ... Acts 17:2
festival or a new moon or *s* .. Col 2:16

SACKCLOTH
I have sewn *s* over my ... Job 16:15
You have put off my *s* ... Ps 30:11
and remove the *s* ... Is 20:2
with fasting, *s*, and ashes ... Dan 9:3
a fast, and put on *s* ... Jon 3:5
repented long ago in *s* ... Matt 11:21

SACRED
have a *s* assembly ... Num 29:35
iniquity and the *s* ... Is 1:13
call a *s* assembly ... Joel 1:14

SACRIFICE
I *s* to the LORD all males ... Ex 13:15
is a burnt *s* of the herd ... Lev 1:3
is a *s* of peace offering ... Lev 3:1
the law of the *s* of peace ... Lev 7:11
a *s* of a peace offering to ... Num 6:17
you shall *s* the Passover ... Deut 16:2
s to the LORD of hosts ... 1 Sam 1:3
do you kick at My *s* ... 1 Sam 2:29
to *s* to the LORD your ... 1 Sam 15:15
S and offering You did ... Ps 40:6
offer to You the *s* ... Ps 116:17
to the LORD than *s* ... Prov 21:3
The *s* of the wicked is ... Prov 21:27
than to give the *s* of fools ... Eccl 5:1
in that day, and will make *s* . Is 19:21
For the LORD has a *s* ... Is 34:6
who will bring the *s* ... Jer 33:11
I desire mercy and not *s* ... Hos 6:6
of My offerings they *s* ... Hos 8:13
But I will *s* to You ... Jon 2:9
LORD has prepared a *s* ... Zeph 1:7
offer the blind as a *s* ... Mal 1:8
desire mercy and not *s* ... Matt 9:13
'I desire mercy and not *s* ... Matt 12:7
s will be seasoned ... Mark 9:49
your bodies a living *s* ... Rom 12:1
an offering and a *s* ... Eph 5:2
aroma, an acceptable *s* ... Phil 4:18
put away sin by the *s* ... Heb 9:26
He had offered one *s* ... Heb 10:12
no longer remains a *s* ... Heb 10:26
God a more excellent *s* ... Heb 11:4
offer the *s* of praise ... Heb 13:15

SACRIFICED
s their sons and their ... Ps 106:37
They *s* to the Baals ... Hos 11:2
our Passover, was *s* for us .. 1 Cor 5:7
to eat things *s* ... Rev 2:14

SACRIFICES
He who *s* to any god ... Ex 22:20
burnt offerings, your *s* ... Deut 12:6
The *s* of God are a ... Ps 51:17
the *s* of thanksgiving ... Ps 107:22
multitude of your *s* ... Is 1:11
Bring no more futile *s* ... Is 1:13
he who *s* a lamb ... Is 66:3
acceptable, nor your *s* ... Jer 6:20
bringing *s* of praise to the .. Jer 17:26
by him the daily *s* ... Dan 8:11
burnt offerings and *s* ... Mark 12:33
priests, to offer up *s* ... Heb 7:27
with better *s* than these ... Heb 9:23
s for sin you had no ... Heb 10:6
s God is well pleased ... Heb 13:16
offer up spiritual *s* ... 1 Pet 2:5

SAD
"Why is your face *s* ... Neh 2:2
s countenance the ... Eccl 7:3
whom I have not made *s* .. Ezek 13:22
as you walk and are *s* ... Luke 24:17

SADDUCEES
Rejected by John, Matt 3:7
Test Jesus, Matt 16:1–12

Silenced by Jesus, Matt 22:23–34
Disturbed by teaching of resurrection, Acts 4:1, 2
Oppose apostles, Acts 5:17–40

SAFE
and I shall be *s* . . . . Ps 119:117
in the LORD shall be *s* . . . . . Prov 29:25
he has received him *s* . . . . Luke 15:27

SAFELY
And He led them on *s* . . . . . . Ps 78:53
make them lie down *s* . . . . . . Hos 2:18

SAFETY
sons are far from *s* . . . . Job 5:4
take your rest in *s* . . . . Job 11:18
will set him in the *s* . . . . Ps 12:5
the needy will lie down in *s* . . Is 14:30
say, "Peace and *s* . . . . 1 Thess 5:3

SAFETY'S
by you for *s* sake . . . . Prov 3:29

SAINTS
See ALL THE SAINTS
ten thousands of *s* . . . . Deut 33:2
the feet of His *s* . . . . 1 Sam 2:9
puts no trust in His *s* . . . . . . Job 15:15
s who are on the earth . . . . . . Ps 16:3
does not forsake His *s* . . . . . . Ps 37:28
"Gather My *s* . . . . Ps 50:5
the souls of His *s* . . . . Ps 97:10
is the death of His *s* . . . . . . Ps 116:15
the way of His *s* . . . . Prov 2:8
war against the *s* . . . . Dan 7:21
shall persecute the *s* . . . . Dan 7:25
Jesus, called to be *s* . . . . 1 Cor 1:2
the least of all the *s* . . . . Eph 3:8
Christ with all His *s* . . . . . 1 Thess 3:13
be glorified in His *s* . . . . . 2 Thess 1:10
all delivered to the *s* . . . . Jude 3
ways, O King of the *s* . . . . Rev 15:3
shed the blood of *s* . . . . Rev 16:6
the camp of the *s* . . . . Rev 20:9

SAKE
My servant Abraham's *s* . . . Gen 26:24
has blessed me for your *s* . . Gen 30:27
the Egyptians for Israel's *s* . . . Ex 18:8
for His great name's *s* . . . 1 Sam 12:22
kindness for Jonathan's *s* . . 2 Sam 9:1
for the *s* of your father . . . 1 Kin 11:12
the *s* of Your great name . . 2 Chr 6:32
save me for Your mercies' *s* . . . Ps 6:4
For His name's *s* . . . . Ps 23:3
Your name's *s*, O LORD . . . . Ps 25:11
for Your name's *s* . . . . Ps 31:3
sins, for Your name's *s* . . . . Ps 79:9
for His name's *s* . . . . Ps 106:8
me for Your name's *s* . . . . Ps 109:21
LORD, for Your name's *s* . . . . Ps 143:11
for Your *s* I have . . . . Jer 15:15
for righteousness' *s* . . . . Matt 5:10
you falsely for My *s* . . . . Matt 5:11
and kings for My *s* . . . . Matt 10:18
by all for My name's *s* . . . . Matt 10:22
life for My *s* will find it . . . Matt 10:39
life for My *s* will find it . . . Matt 16:25
kingdom of heaven's *s* . . . . Matt 19:12
lands, for My name's *s* . . . . Matt 19:29
nations for My name's *s* . . . . Matt 24:9
elect's *s* those days will . . . Matt 24:22
loses his life for My *s* . . . . . . Mark 8:35
rulers and kings for My *s* . . Mark 13:9
men for My name's *s* . . . . . Mark 13:13
but for the elect's *s* . . . . . . Mark 13:20
life for My *s* will save it . . . . Luke 9:24
s of the kingdom of . . . . . . Luke 18:29
rulers for My name's *s* . . . . Luke 21:12
by all for My name's *s* . . . . Luke 21:17
my life for Your *s* . . . . John 13:37
down your life for My *s* . . . John 13:38
to you for My name's *s* . . . John 15:21
suffer for My name's *s* . . . . . . Acts 9:16
are fools for Christ's *s* . . . . . 1 Cor 4:10
I do for the gospel's *s* . . . . . 1 Cor 9:23
s of him who had done . . . . 2 Cor 7:12
for your stomach's *s* . . . . . . 1 Tim 5:23
suffer for righteousness' *s* . . 1 Pet 3:14
for His name's *s* . . . . 1 John 2:12
labored for My name's *s* . . . . . Rev 2:3

SAKES
for their *s* I sanctify . . . . . . John 17:19
your *s* He became poor . . . . . 2 Cor 8:9

SALAMIS
Paul preaches here, Acts 13:4, 5

SALEM
Jerusalem's original name, Gen 14:18
Used poetically, Ps 76:2

SALIM
Place near Aenon, John 3:23

SALOME
One of the ministering women, Mark 15:40, 41
Visits empty tomb, Mark 16:1
——— Herodias' daughter (not named in the Bible), Matt 14:6–11

SALT
she became a pillar of *s* . . . Gen 19:26
shall season with *s* . . . . Lev 2:13
covenant of *s* forever . . . . . . Num 18:19
city and sowed it with *s* . . . . Judg 9:45
s nor wrapped in . . . . Ezek 16:4
"You are the *s* . . . . Matt 5:13
s loses its flavor . . . . Mark 9:50
with grace, seasoned with *s* . . . Col 4:6

SALT SEA
O.T. name for the Dead Sea, Gen 14:3; Num 34:3, 12

SALVATION
still, and see the *s* . . . . Ex 14:13
the Rock of my *s* . . . . 2 Sam 22:47
For this is all my *s* . . . . 2 Sam 23:5
the good news of His *s* . . . 1 Chr 16:23
S belongs to the LORD . . . . Ps 3:8
I will rejoice in Your *s* . . . . Ps 9:14
shield and the horn of my *s* . . . Ps 18:2
We will rejoice in your *s* . . . . . Ps 20:5
You are the God of my *s* . . . . . Ps 25:5
is my light and my *s* . . . . Ps 27:1
to me the joy of Your *s* . . . . . Ps 51:12
From Him comes my *s* . . . . Ps 62:1
on earth, Your *s* . . . . Ps 67:2
God is the God of *s* . . . . Ps 68:20
and Your *s* all the day . . . . . . Ps 71:15
Restore us, O God of our *s* . . . Ps 85:4
Surely His *s* is near . . . . Ps 85:9
and He has become my *s* . . . Ps 118:14
S is far from the . . . . Ps 119:155
LORD, I hope for Your *s* . . . Ps 119:166
forgotten the God of your *s* . . Is 17:10
God will appoint *s* . . . . Is 26:1
with an everlasting *s* . . . . Is 45:17
for My *s* is about to . . . . Is 56:1
call your walls *S* . . . . Is 60:18
s as a lamp that burns . . . . Is 62:1
LORD our God is the *s* . . . . Jer 3:23
joy in the God of my *s* . . . . . . Hab 3:18
is just and having *s* . . . . Zech 9:9
raised up a horn of *s* . . . . . . Luke 1:69
eyes have seen Your *s* . . . . . Luke 2:30
to him, "Today *s* . . . . Luke 19:9
what we worship, for *s* . . . . John 4:22
Nor is there *s* in any . . . . Acts 4:12
you should be for *s* . . . . Acts 13:47
the power of God to *s* . . . . Rom 1:16
is made unto *s* . . . . Rom 10:10
s has come to the . . . . Rom 11:11
s is nearer than . . . . Rom 13:11
now is the day of *s* . . . . 2 Cor 6:2
And take the helmet of *s* . . . . Eph 6:17
work out your own *s* . . . . Phil 2:12
wrath, but to obtain *s* . . . . . 1 Thess 5:9
chose you for *s* . . . . 2 Thess 2:13
also may obtain the *s* . . . . . 2 Tim 2:10
of God that brings *s* . . . . Titus 2:11
neglect so great a *s* . . . . Heb 2:3
s perfect through . . . . Heb 2:10
s the prophets have . . . . 1 Pet 1:10
"*S* belongs to our God . . . . . . Rev 7:10
S and glory and honor . . . . . . Rev 19:1

SAMARIA
Capital of Israel, 1 Kin 16:24–29
Besieged by Ben-Hadad, 1 Kin 20:1–21
Besieged again; miraculously delivered, 2 Kin 6:24—7:20
Inhabitants deported by Assyria; repopulated with foreigners, 2 Kin 17:5, 6, 24–41
——— District of Palestine in Christ's time, Luke 17:11–19
Disciples forbidden to preach in, Matt 10:5
Gospel preached there after the ascension, Acts 1:8; 9:31; 15:3

SAMARITAN
But a certain *S* . . . . Luke 10:33
a drink from me, a *S* . . . . John 4:9

SAMARITANS
People of mixed heredity, 2 Kin 17:24–41
Christ preaches to, John 4:5–42
Story of "the good Samaritan," Luke 10:30–37
Converts among, Acts 8:5–25

SAMOS
Paul visits, Acts 20:15

SAMSON
Birth predicted and accomplished, Judg 13:2–25
Marries Philistine; avenges betrayal, Judg 14
Defeats Philistines singlehandedly, Judg 15
Betrayed by Delilah; loses strength, Judg 16:4–22
Destroys many in his death, Judg 16:23–31

SAMUEL
Born in answer to prayer; dedicated to God, 1 Sam 1:1–28
Receives revelation; recognized as prophet, 1 Sam 3:1–21
Judges Israel, 1 Sam 7:15–17
Warns Israel against a king, 1 Sam 8:10–18
Anoints Saul, 1 Sam 9:15—10:1
Rebukes Saul, 1 Sam 15:10–35
Anoints David, 1 Sam 16:1–13
Death of, 1 Sam 25:1

SANBALLAT
Influential Samaritan; attempts to thwart Nehemiah's plans, Neh 2:10; 4:7, 8; 6:1–14

SANCTIFICATION
righteousness and *s* . . . . 1 Cor 1:30
will of God, your *s* . . . . 1 Thess 4:3
salvation through *s* . . . . . . 2 Thess 2:13

SANCTIFIED
s it, because in it He rested . . Gen 2:3
s the people, and they . . . . . . Ex 19:14
I *s* to Myself all the . . . . Num 3:13
s this house, that My . . . . . . 2 Chr 7:16
I have commanded My *s* . . . . . . Is 13:3
you were born I *s* . . . . Jer 1:5
Him whom the Father *s* . . . John 10:36
they also may be *s* . . . . John 17:19
might be acceptable, *s* . . . . Rom 15:16
to those who are *s* . . . . 1 Cor 1:2
washed, but you were *s* . . . . 1 Cor 6:11
husband is *s* by the . . . . 1 Cor 7:14
for it is *s* by the . . . . 1 Tim 4:5
those who are being *s* . . . . . . Heb 2:11

will we have been *s* .... Heb 10:10
who are called, *s* .... Jude 1

SANCTIFIES
or the temple that *s* .... Matt 23:17
For both He who *s* .... Heb 2:11

SANCTIFY
"*S* yourselves .... Josh 3:5
would send and *s* them .... Job 1:5
s My great name .... Ezek 36:23
that I, the LORD, *s* .... Ezek 37:28
Myself and *s* Myself ...... Ezek 38:23
S them by Your .... John 17:17
for their sakes I *s* .... John 17:19
that He might *s* .... Eph 5:26
s you completely .... 1 Thess 5:23

SANCTUARY
let them make Me a *s* .... Ex 25:8
I went into the *s* .... Ps 73:17
set fire to Your *s* .... Ps 74:7
O God, is in the *s* .... Ps 77:13
He will be as a *s* .... Is 8:14
He has abandoned His *s* ..... Lam 2:7
I shall be a little *s* ...... Ezek 11:16
to shine on Your *s* .... Dan 9:17
and the earthly *s* .... Heb 9:1
is brought into the *s* ..... Heb 13:11

SAND
descendants as the *s* ...... Gen 32:12
be heavier than the *s* .... Job 6:3
in number than the *s* .... Ps 139:18
O Israel, be as the *s* .... Is 10:22
innumerable as the *s* ...... Heb 11:12

SANDAL
remove his *s* from his ...... Deut 25:9
So he took off his *s* .... Ruth 4:8
s strap I am not worthy ..... Mark 1:7

SANDALS
Take your *s* off your feet ...... Ex 3:5
beautiful are your feet in *s* .. Song 7:1
whose *s* I am not worthy ... Matt 3:11
bag, knapsack, nor *s* ...... Luke 10:4
tie on your *s* .... Acts 12:8

SANG
s this song to the LORD .... Ex 15:1
worshiped, the singers *s* . 2 Chr 29:28
The singers *s* loudly .... Neh 12:42
morning stars *s* together .... Job 38:7
They *s* His praise .... Ps 106:12
they *s* a new song, saying .... Rev 5:9
s as it were a new song ..... Rev 14:3

SAPPHIRA
Wife of Ananias; struck dead for lying, Acts 5:1–11

SAPPHIRE
shall be a turquoise, a *s* ..... Ex 28:18
was jasper, the second *s* ... Rev 21:19

SAPPHIRES
are the source of *s* .... Job 28:6

SARAH (or Sarai)
Barren wife of Abram, Gen 11:29–31
Represented as Abram's sister, Gen 12:10–20
Gives Abram her maid, Gen 16:1–3
Receives promise of a son, Gen 17:15–21
Gives birth to Isaac, Gen 21:1–8

SARDIS
Site of one of the seven churches, Rev 1:11

SARDONYX
the fifth *s*, the sixth .... Rev 21:20

SASH
tunic, a turban, and a *s* ...... Ex 28:4
get yourself a linen *s* .... Jer 13:1

SASHES
girded them with *s* .... Lev 8:13
s for the merchants .... Prov 31:24

SAT
of Babylon, there we *s* ...... Ps 137:1
I *s* down in his shade .... Song 2:3
s alone because of .... Jer 15:17
people who *s* in darkness .. Matt 4:16
Now Peter *s* outside in .... Matt 26:69
into heaven, and *s* .... Mark 16:19
s down again, He said .... John 13:12
s down at the right hand ..... Heb 1:3
And He who *s* there was ..... Rev 4:3
Him who *s* on the horse .... Rev 19:19

SATAN
See DEVIL
S stood up against .... 1 Chr 21:1
before the LORD, and *S* .... Job 1:6
And the LORD said to *S* ..... Zech 3:2
"Away with you, *S* .... Matt 4:10
"Get behind Me, *S* .... Matt 16:23
forty days, tempted by *S* .. Mark 1:13
"How can *S* cast out .... Mark 3:23
to them, "I saw *S* .... Luke 10:18
Then *S* entered Judas ..... Luke 22:3
S has asked for you ...... Luke 22:31
S filled your heart .... Acts 5:3
S under your feet shortly .. Rom 16:20
such a one to *S* .... 1 Cor 5:5
For *S* himself .... 2 Cor 11:14
messenger of *S* to buffet ... 2 Cor 12:7
to the working of *S* .... 2 Thess 2:9
whom I delivered to *S* .... 1 Tim 1:20
are a synagogue of *S* .... Rev 2:9
you, where *S* dwells .... Rev 2:13
known the depths of *S* ...... Rev 2:24
called the Devil and *S* ...... Rev 12:9
years have expired, *S* .... Rev 20:7

SATIATED
s the weary soul .... Jer 31:25
It shall be *s* and made ...... Jer 46:10

SATISFIED
I shall be *s* when I .... Ps 17:15
his land will be *s* .... Prov 12:11
a good man will be *s* ..... Prov 14:14
s soul loathes the .... Prov 27:7
that are never *s* .... Prov 30:15
silver will not be *s* .... Eccl 5:10
left hand and not be *s* .... Is 9:20
of His soul, and be *s* .... Is 53:11
My people shall be *s* .... Jer 31:14
still were not *s* .... Ezek 16:28
but they were not *s* .... Amos 4:8
and cannot be *s* .... Hab 2:5

SATISFIES
s your mouth with good ..... Ps 103:5
s the longing soul .... Ps 107:9

SATISFY
s us early with Your .... Ps 90:14
long life I will *s* .... Ps 91:16
s her poor with bread .... Ps 132:15
for what does not *s* .... Is 55:2

SATISFYING
eats to the *s* of his .... Prov 13:25

SAUL
Becomes first king of Israel, 1 Sam 9—11
Sacrifices unlawfully, 1 Sam 13:1–14
Wars with Philistines, 1 Sam 13:15—14:52
Disregards the Lord's command; rejected by God, 1 Sam 15
Suffers from distressing spirits, 1 Sam 16:14–23
Becomes jealous of David; attempts to kill him, 1 Sam 18:5—19:22
Pursues David; twice spared by him, 1 Sam 22—24; 26
Consults medium, 1 Sam 28:7–25
Defeated, commits suicide; buried, 1 Sam 31

—— of Tarsus, apostle to the Gentiles: *see* PAUL

SAVE
will *s* Israel by my hand ... Judg 6:37
the LORD does not *s* ..... 1 Sam 17:47
there was none to *s* .... 2 Sam 22:42
s the humble person .... Job 22:29
Oh, *s* me for Your .... Ps 6:4
s me from all those who .... Ps 7:1
S Your people, and bless ..... Ps 28:9
send from heaven and *s* ...... Ps 57:3
Your ear to me, and *s* me ..... Ps 71:2
s the children of the .... Ps 72:4
s the souls of the .... Ps 72:13
s me, and I will keep ..... Ps 119:146
LORD, and He will *s* .... Prov 20:22
He will come and *s* .... Is 35:4
LORD was ready to *s* .... Is 38:20
s your children .... Is 49:25
that it cannot *s* .... Is 59:1
mighty to *s* .... Is 63:1
one who cannot *s* .... Jer 14:9
s you and deliver you .... Jer 15:20
s me, and I shall be .... Jer 17:14
O LORD, *s* Your people .... Jer 31:7
other, That he may *s* ...... Hos 13:10
Assyria shall not *s* .... Hos 14:3
the Mighty One, will *s* ..... Zeph 3:17
JESUS, for He will *s* .... Matt 1:21
Him, saying, "Lord, *s* us .... Matt 8:25
s his life will lose it .... Matt 16:25
s that which was .... Matt 18:11
three days, *s* Yourself ..... Matt 27:40
s life or to kill .... Mark 3:4
to *s* his life will lose it ..... Mark 8:35
s Yourself, and come ..... Mark 15:30
to *s* life or to destroy .... Luke 6:9
life for My sake will *s* it ... Luke 9:24
seeks to *s* his life .... Luke 17:33
let Him *s* Himself if ...... Luke 23:35
You are the Christ, *s* ..... Luke 23:39
'Father, *s* Me from .... John 12:27
but to *s* the world .... John 12:47
and *s* some of them .... Rom 11:14
to *s* those who believe ..... 1 Cor 1:21
by all means *s* some .... 1 Cor 9:22
the world to *s* sinners .... 1 Tim 1:15
doing this you will *s* ...... 1 Tim 4:16
able to *s* Him from death .... Heb 5:7
able to *s* your souls ...... James 1:21
Can faith *s* him .... James 2:14
who is able to *s* .... James 4:12
will *s* a soul from death .. James 5:20

SAVED
See WILL BE SAVED
the LORD *s* Israel that day ... Ex 14:30
you will be *s* from your .... Num 10:9
like you, a people *s* .... Deut 33:29
But You have *s* us from ...... Ps 44:7
blamelessly will be *s* ...... Prov 28:18
Look to Me, and be *s* .... Is 45:22
and we are not *s* .... Jer 8:20
"Who then can be *s* .... Matt 19:25
to the end shall be *s* ...... Matt 24:13
"He *s* others .... Matt 27:42
"Who then can be *s* .... Mark 10:26
to the end shall be *s* ..... Mark 13:13
no flesh would be *s* ...... Mark 13:20
"He *s* others .... Mark 15:31
and is baptized will be *s* .. Mark 16:16
That we should be *s* .... Luke 1:71
"Your faith has *s* .... Luke 7:50
through Him might be *s* .... John 3:17
enters by Me, he will be *s* .. John 10:9
of the LORD shall be *s* ...... Acts 2:21
them, saying, "Be *s* .... Acts 2:40
of Moses, you cannot be *s* .. Acts 15:1
what must I do to be *s* .... Acts 16:30
For we were *s* in this ...... Rom 8:24
is that they may be *s* .... Rom 10:1
all Israel will be *s* .... Rom 11:26

SEAM
tunic was without *s* . . . . John 19:23

SÉANCE
"Please conduct a *s* . . . . 1 Sam 28:8

SEARCH
"Can you *s* out the . . . . Job 11:7
would not God *s* . . . . Ps 44:21
glory of kings is to *s* . . . . Prov 25:2
found it by secret *s* . . . . Jer 2:34
I, the LORD, *s* the . . . . Jer 17:10
s the Scriptures . . . . John 5:39
S and look, for no . . . . John 7:52

SEARCHED
O LORD, You have *s* . . . . Ps 139:1
s the Scriptures . . . . Acts 17:11
and *s* carefully . . . . 1 Pet 1:10

SEARCHES
for the LORD *s* all . . . . 1 Chr 28:9
s the hearts knows . . . . Rom 8:27
For the Spirit *s* . . . . 1 Cor 2:10
that I am He who *s* . . . . Rev 2:23

SEASON
I will give you rain in its *s* . . Lev 26:4
bring forth its fruit in its *s* . . . . . Ps 1:3
their food in due *s* . . . . Ps 104:27
a word spoken in due *s* . . . Prov 15:23
To everything there is a *s* . . . . Eccl 3:1
word in *s* to him who is . . . . Is 50:4
give them food in due *s* . . . Matt 24:45
flavor, how will you *s* it . . . Mark 9:50
for in due *s* we shall reap . . . . . Gal 6:9
Be ready in *s* and out . . . . . . 2 Tim 4:2

SEASONED
how shall it be *s* . . . . Matt 5:13
"For everyone will be *s* . . . . Mark 9:49

SEASONS
let them be for signs and *s* . . Gen 1:14
appointed the moon for *s* . . . Ps 104:19
the times and the *s* . . . . Dan 2:21
for you to know times or *s* . . . Acts 1:7
days and months and *s* . . . . . . Gal 4:10
the times and the *s* . . . . 1 Thess 5:1

SEAT
See MERCY SEAT
shall make a mercy *s* . . . . Ex 25:17
I might come to His *s* . . . . Job 23:3
that He may *s* him with . . . . . Ps 113:8
sit in Moses' *s* . . . . Matt 23:2
before the judgment *s* . . . . . 2 Cor 5:10
the mercy *s* . . . . Heb 9:5

SEATED
the Ancient of Days was *s* . . . Dan 7:9
s Him at His right hand . . . . . Eph 1:20
who is *s* at the right hand . . . . Heb 8:1

SEATS
at feasts, the best *s* . . . . Matt 23:6
you love the best *s* . . . . Luke 11:43

SECOND
morning were the *s* day . . . . . . Gen 1:8
And the *s* is like it . . . . Matt 22:39
Can he enter a *s* time into . . . John 3:4
the *s* Man is the Lord . . . . 1 Cor 15:47
and behind the *s* veil, the . . . . Heb 9:3
He will appear a *s* time . . . . . Heb 9:28
the *s* living creature like a . . . . Rev 4:7
Then the *s* angel sounded . . . . . Rev 8:8

SECOND DEATH
not be hurt by the *s* . . . . Rev 2:11
Over such the *s* has no . . . . . Rev 20:6
of fire. This is the *s* . . . . Rev 20:14
brimstone, which is the *s* . . . . Rev 21:8

SECRET
s things belong . . . . Deut 29:29
The *s* of the LORD is . . . . Ps 25:14
in the *s* place of His . . . . Ps 27:5
when I was made in *s* . . . . . . Ps 139:15
do not disclose the *s* . . . . Prov 25:9
I have not spoken in *s* . . . . Is 45:19
Father who is in the *s* . . . . Matt 6:6
s from the foundation of . . Matt 13:35
For nothing is *s* that will . . . Luke 8:17
in *s* I have said nothing . . . John 18:20
s since the world began . . . Rom 16:25
are done by them in *s* . . . . . . Eph 5:12

SECRETLY
"Now a word was *s* . . . . Job 4:12
He lies in wait *s* . . . . Ps 10:9
minded to put her away *s* . . Matt 1:19
a disciple of Jesus, but *s* . . John 19:38

SECRETS
would show you the *s* . . . . Job 11:6
For He knows the *s* . . . . Ps 44:21
A talebearer reveals *s* . . . . . Prov 11:13
heaven who reveals *s* . . . . Dan 2:28
God will judge the *s* . . . . Rom 2:16
And thus the *s* of his . . . . . 1 Cor 14:25

SECT
him (which is the *s* . . . . Acts 5:17
to the strictest *s* . . . . Acts 26:5

SECURE
while the camp felt *s* . . . . Judg 8:11
dwell safely, and will be *s* . . Prov 1:33
him as a peg in a *s* place . . . . Is 22:23
made *s* until the third . . . . . Matt 27:64

SECURELY
pleasures, who dwell *s* . . . . Is 47:8
nation that dwells *s* . . . . Jer 49:31

SECURES
he *s* it for himself among . . . . Is 44:14

SECURITY
gives them *s*, and they . . . . . Job 24:23

SEDUCED
flattering lips she *s* . . . . Prov 7:21
because they have *s* . . . . . . Ezek 13:10

SEE
for no man shall *s* . . . . Ex 33:20
the LORD does not *s*. . . . . . . 1 Sam 16:7
in my flesh I shall *s* . . . . Job 19:26
s the works of God . . . . Ps 66:5
lest they *s* with their . . . . Is 6:10
for sin, He shall *s* . . . . Is 53:10
for they shall *s* God . . . . Matt 5:8
seeing they do not *s* . . . . Matt 13:13
s greater things than . . . . John 1:50
rejoiced to *s* My day . . . . John 8:56
we wish to *s* Jesus . . . . John 12:21
and the world will *s* . . . . John 14:19
Him, for we shall *s* . . . . 1 John 3:2
They shall *s* His face . . . . Rev 22:4

SEED
s shall be called . . . . Gen 21:12
s shall be its stump . . . . Is 6:13
He shall see His *s* . . . . Is 53:10
you a noble vine, a *s* . . . . Jer 2:21
s is the word of God . . . . Luke 8:11
had left us a *s* . . . . Rom 9:29
to each *s* its own body . . . . 1 Cor 15:38
S were the promises . . . . Gal 3:16
you are Abraham's *s* . . . . Gal 3:29
of corruptible *s* . . . . 1 Pet 1:23
not sin, for His *s* . . . . 1 John 3:9

SEED OF DAVID
Christ comes from the *s* . . . . John 7:42
who was born of the *s* . . . . . . Rom 1:3
Jesus Christ, of the *s* . . . . 2 Tim 2:8

SEEDS
the good *s* are the . . . . Matt 13:38
not say, "And to *s* . . . . Gal 3:16

SEEK
will find Him if you *s* . . . . . . Deut 4:29
pray and *s* My face . . . . 2 Chr 7:14
your heart to *s* God . . . . 2 Chr 19:3
s your God as you do . . . . Ezra 4:2
may God above not *s* . . . . Job 3:4
countenance does not *s* . . . . Ps 10:4
LORD, that will I *s* . . . . Ps 27:4
You said, "*S* My face . . . . Ps 27:8
early will I *s* You . . . . Ps 63:1
s me diligently will . . . . Prov 8:17
s one's own glory . . . . Prov 25:27
s justice, rebuke . . . . Is 1:17
Should they *s* the dead . . . . Is 8:19
the Gentiles shall *s* . . . . Is 11:10
Jacob, '*S* Me in vain . . . . Is 45:19
Yet they *s* Me daily . . . . Is 58:2
s great things for . . . . Jer 45:5
s what was lost . . . . Ezek 34:16
"*S* Me and live . . . . Amos 5:4
and people should *s* . . . . Mal 2:7
things the Gentiles *s* . . . . Matt 6:32
s, and you will find . . . . Matt 7:7
of Man has come to *s* . . . . . Luke 19:10
because I do not *s* . . . . John 5:30
You will *s* Me and . . . . John 7:34
in doing good *s* . . . . Rom 2:7
Because they did not *s* . . . . . . Rom 9:32
Let no one *s* his own . . . . . . 1 Cor 10:24
for I do not *s* yours . . . . 2 Cor 12:14
For all *s* their own . . . . Phil 2:21
s those things which . . . . Col 3:1
s the one to come . . . . Heb 13:14

SEEK THE LORD
from there you will *s* . . . . Deut 4:29
of those rejoice who *s* . . . . 1 Chr 16:10
heart and your soul to *s* . . 1 Chr 22:19
set their heart to *s* . . . . 2 Chr 11:16
disease he did not *s* . . . . . . 2 Chr 16:12
set himself to *s* . . . . 2 Chr 20:3
of the land in order to *s* . . . . Ezra 6:21
who *s* shall not lack . . . . Ps 34:10
S and His strength . . . . Ps 105:4
those who *s* understand . . . . Prov 28:5
righteousness, you who *s* . . . . . Is 51:1
S while He may be found . . . . . Is 55:6
Israel shall return and *s* . . . . . Hos 3:5
S and live, lest He . . . . Amos 5:6
S, all you meek . . . . Zeph 2:3
nations shall come to *s* . . . . Zech 8:22
rest of mankind may *s* . . . . Acts 15:17
so that they should *s* . . . . . . Acts 17:27

SEEKING
run to and fro, *s* . . . . Amos 8:12
and he came *s* fruit . . . . Luke 13:6
for the Father is *s* . . . . John 4:23
like a roaring lion, *s* . . . . 1 Pet 5:8

SEEKS
Zion; no one *s* her . . . . Jer 30:17
receives, and he who *s* . . . . . . Matt 7:8
There is none who *s* . . . . Rom 3:11

SEEMS
There is a way which *s* . . . . Prov 14:12
have, even what he *s* . . . . Luke 8:18
If anyone among you *s* . . . . . 1 Cor 3:18

SEEN
s God face to face . . . . Gen 32:30
All this I have *s* . . . . Eccl 8:9
s the one I love . . . . Song 3:3
Who has *s* such things . . . . Is 66:8
s strange things today . . . . . Luke 5:26
No one has *s* God at . . . . John 1:18
time, nor *s* His form . . . . John 5:37
I speak what I have *s* . . . . . . John 8:38
s Me has *s* the . . . . John 14:9
things which we have *s* . . . . Acts 4:20
s Jesus Christ our . . . . 1 Cor 9:1
things which are not *s* . . . . . 2 Cor 4:18
whom no man has *s* . . . . 1 Tim 6:16
heard, which we have *s* . . . . 1 John 1:1

SEES
here seen Him who *s* . . . . Gen 16:13
s all the sons of men . . . . Ps 33:13
s his brother in need . . . . . 1 John 3:17
s his brother sinning . . . . . . 1 John 5:16

SEIR
Home of Esau, Gen 32:3
Horites of, dispossessed by Esau's descendants, Deut 2:12
Desolation of, Ezek 35:15

SEIZE
s the city, for the LORD ...... Josh 8:7
Will not pangs *s* you, like ... Jer 13:21
also houses, and *s* them ...... Mic 2:2
s his inheritance .... Matt 21:38
you did not *s* Me .... Matt 26:55
further to *s* Peter also ...... Acts 12:3

SEIZED
pangs have *s* you like a ...... Mic 4:9
For it had often *s* him ..... Luke 8:29
profit was gone, they *s* ..... Acts 16:19
Jews *s* me in the temple ... Acts 26:21

SELF-CONFIDENT
a fool rages and is *s* ...... Prov 14:16

SELF-CONTROL
about righteousness, *s* .... Acts 24:25
because of your lack of *s* ... 1 Cor 7:5
they cannot exercise *s* ...... 1 Cor 7:9
gentleness, *s* .... Gal 5:23
love, and holiness, with *s* . 1 Tim 2:15
slanderers, without *s* .... 2 Tim 3:3
to knowledge *s* .... 2 Pet 1:6

SELF-CONTROLLED
just, holy, *s* .... Titus 1:8

SELF-SEEKING
envy and *s* exist .... James 3:16

SELFISH
s ambitions, backbitings .. 2 Cor 12:20
s ambitions, dissensions ..... Gal 5:20
preach Christ from *s* .... Phil 1:16
s ambition or conceit .... Phil 2:3

SELL
said, "*S* me your .... Gen 25:31
s Your people for .... Ps 44:12
s the righteous .... Amos 2:6
s whatever you have ..... Mark 10:21
no sword, let him *s* .... Luke 22:36
no one may buy or *s* .... Rev 13:17

SEND
He shall *s* from heaven .... Ps 57:3
"Whom shall I *s* .... Is 6:8
s them a Savior .... Is 19:20
"Behold, I *s* you out ...... Matt 10:16
The Son of Man will *s* .... Matt 13:41
S the multitudes away .... Matt 14:15
He will *s* His angels ...... Matt 24:31
"*S* us to the swine, that .... Mark 5:12
s them out two by two ...... Mark 6:7
S them away, that they .... Mark 6:36
I *s* you out as lambs .... Luke 10:3
I will *s* them prophets .... Luke 11:49
s Lazarus that he .... Luke 16:24
s the Promise of My ...... Luke 24:49
God did not *s* His Son ..... John 3:17
whom the Father will *s* .... John 14:26
has sent Me, I also *s* ...... John 20:21

SENDING
I am *s* you to Jesse .... 1 Sam 16:1
God did by *s* His own Son .. Rom 8:3

SENDS
s rain on the just and ...... Matt 5:45
till He *s* forth justice to .... Matt 12:20

SENNACHERIB
Assyrian king (705–681 B.C.); son and successor of Sargon II, 2 Kin 18:13
Death of, by assassination, 2 Kin 19:36, 37

SENSELESS
Understand, you *s* .... Ps 94:8

SENSES
of use have their *s* .... Heb 5:14

SENSIBLY
who can answer *s* .... Prov 26:16

SENSUAL
but is earthly, *s* .... James 3:15
These are *s* persons .... Jude 19

SENT
s out the dove .... Gen 8:12
'I AM has *s* me to you .... Ex 3:14
s to spy out the land ...... Num 13:16
LORD *s* me to anoint you .. 1 Sam 15:1
and His Spirit have *s* .... Is 48:16
s these prophets .... Jer 23:21
s this commandment .... Mal 2:4
receives Him who *s* Me .... Matt 10:40
not Me but Him who *s* .... Mark 9:37
he *s* a servant to the .... Mark 12:2
He has *s* Me to heal the .... Luke 4:18
Baptist has *s* us to You .... Luke 7:20
receives Him who *s* Me .... Luke 9:48
rejects Him who *s* Me .... Luke 10:16
a man *s* from God .... John 1:6
the will of Him who *s* Me .. John 6:38
Father who *s* Me bears .... John 8:18
is he who is *s* greater ..... John 13:16
You *s* Me into the world .. John 17:18
As the Father has *s* .... John 20:21
unless they are *s* .... Rom 10:15
Spirit *s* from heaven .... 1 Pet 1:12
s His Son to be the ...... 1 John 4:10
s His angel to show His ..... Rev 22:6

SEPARATE
he shall *s* himself .... Num 6:3
s yourselves from the ..... Ezra 10:11
let not man *s* .... Matt 19:6
Who shall *s* us from .... Rom 8:35
harmless, undefiled, *s* .... Heb 7:26

SEPARATED
but the poor is *s* .... Prov 19:4
"The LORD has utterly *s* .... Is 56:3
to be an apostle, *s* .... Rom 1:1
it pleased God, who *s* .... Gal 1:15

SEPARATES
who repeats a matter *s* ..... Prov 17:9

SEPARATION
the middle wall of *s* .... Eph 2:14

SERAPHIM
Above it stood *s* .... Is 6:2

SERGIUS PAULUS
Roman proconsul of Cyprus, converted by Paul, Acts 13:7–12

SERIOUS
therefore be *s* and .... 1 Pet 4:7

SERPENT
s was more cunning .... Gen 3:1
"The *s* deceived me .... Gen 3:13
"Make a fiery *s* .... Num 21:8
like the poison of a *s* .... Ps 58:4
s you shall trample .... Ps 91:13
their tongues like a *s* .... Ps 140:3
air, the way of a *s* .... Prov 30:19
s may bite when it is .... Eccl 10:11
be a fiery flying *s* .... Is 14:29
and wounded the *s* .... Is 51:9
will he give him a *s* .... Matt 7:10
Moses lifted up the *s* .... John 3:14
was cast out, that *s* .... Rev 12:9

SERPENTS
is the poison of *s* .... Deut 32:33
be wise as *s* .... Matt 10:16
to trample on *s* .... Luke 10:19

SERVANT
a *s* of servants he .... Gen 9:25
take a gift from your *s* .... 2 Kin 5:15
the *s* of the man of God .... 2 Kin 8:4
s who earnestly .... Job 7:2
bountifully with Your *s* .... Ps 119:17
and the fool will be *s* ..... Prov 11:29
s will rule over a son ...... Prov 17:2
A *s* will not be .... Prov 29:19
Who is blind but My *s* .... Is 42:19
"Is Israel a *s* .... Jer 2:14
and a *s* his master .... Mal 1:6
nor a *s* above his master .. Matt 10:24
My *S* whom I have .... Matt 12:18
you, let him be your *s* ..... Matt 20:26
good and faithful *s* .... Matt 25:21
'You wicked and lazy *s* ... Matt 25:26
the unprofitable *s* .... Matt 25:30
be last of all and *s* of all ... Mark 9:35
you shall be your *s* .... Mark 10:43
a *s* to the vinedressers .... Mark 12:2
to my *s*, 'Do this,' .... Luke 7:8
that *s* who knew his ...... Luke 12:47
I am, there My *s* will be .. John 12:26
s does not know what .... John 15:15
'A *s* is not greater than ... John 15:20
struck the high priest's *s* .. John 18:10
against Your holy *S* .... Acts 4:27
Christ has become a *s* ..... Rom 15:8

SERVANTS
puts no trust in His *s* .... Job 4:18
for all your *s* .... Ps 119:91
on the ground like *s* .... Eccl 10:7
shall call you the *s* .... Is 61:6
S rule over us .... Lam 5:8
Again he sent other *s* ..... Matt 21:36
the king said to the *s* ..... Matt 22:13
s whom the master .... Luke 12:37
are unprofitable *s* .... Luke 17:10
longer do I call you *s* ..... John 15:15
My *s* would fight, so ...... John 18:36
so consider us, as *s* .... 1 Cor 4:1

SERVE
people go, that they may *s* .... Ex 8:1
s you until the Year of ..... Lev 25:40
LORD your God and *s* .... Deut 6:13
S the LORD .... Josh 24:14
land, so you shall *s* aliens .... Jer 5:19
s Him with one accord .... Zeph 3:9
You cannot *s* God and ..... Matt 6:24
to be served, but to *s* ..... Matt 20:28
to be served, but to *s* ..... Mark 10:45
the mind I myself *s* .... Rom 7:25
but through love *s* .... Gal 5:13
s the living God .... Heb 9:14
s Him day and night in ...... Rev 7:15

SERVE THE LORD
men go, that they may *s* ..... Ex 10:7
go, *s* as you have said ...... Ex 12:31
So you shall *s* .... Ex 23:25
to *s* your God with all ..... Deut 10:12
Because you did not *s* ..... Deut 28:47
and my house, we will *s* ... Josh 24:15
s with all your heart ..... 1 Sam 12:20
commanded Judah to *s* .. 2 Chr 33:16
S with fear, and rejoice .... Ps 2:11
S with gladness .... Ps 100:2
the kingdoms, to *s* .... Ps 102:22
But they shall *s* their God .... Jer 30:9
s without distraction ...... 1 Cor 7:35
inheritance, for you *s* .... Col 3:24

SERVED
did not come to be *s* .... Matt 20:28
did not come to be *s* .... Mark 10:45
s the creature rather than .. Rom 1:25

SERVES
If anyone *s* Me .... John 12:26

SERVICE
do you mean by this *s* ..... Ex 12:26
that he offers God *s* .... John 16:2
is your reasonable *s* .... Rom 12:1
with goodwill doing *s* .... Eph 6:7
your works, love, *s* .... Rev 2:19

SERVING
years I have been *s* .... Luke 15:29
s the Lord with all .... Acts 20:19

fervent in spirit, *s* .... Rom 12:11
you, *s* as overseers .... 1 Pet 5:2

SET
"See, I have *s* .... Deut 30:15
s the LORD always .... Ps 16:8
I will *s* him on high .... Ps 91:14
s aside the grace .... Gal 2:21

SET APART
will *s* the land of Goshen ..... Ex 8:22
s to the Lord all that .... Ex 13:12
she shall be *s* seven days .. Lev 15:19
Then Moses *s* three cities .. Deut 4:41
as a dog laps, you shall *s* .... Judg 7:5
It was *s* for you .... 1 Sam 9:24
Aaron was *s*, he and his .. 1 Chr 23:13
the Lord has *s* for Himself ..... Ps 4:3
s a district for the Lord .... Ezek 45:1

SETH
Third son of Adam, Gen 4:25
In Christ's ancestry, Luke 3:38

SETTLE
Therefore *s* it in .... Luke 21:14

SETTLED
and my speech *s* .... Job 29:22
O LORD, Your word is *s* .... Ps 119:89
the mountains were *s* ...... Prov 8:25
s accounts with them ..... Matt 25:19

SEVEN
Then *s* priests bearing ..... Josh 6:13
he had *s* hundred wives ... 1 Kin 11:3
the child sneezed *s* times .. 2 Kin 4:35
Joash was *s* years old ..... 2 Chr 24:1
S times a day I praise .... Ps 119:164
may fall *s* times and rise .. Prov 24:16
there are *s* abominations .. Prov 26:25
in that day *s* women shall ...... Is 4:1
Passover, a feast of *s* ..... Ezek 45:21
s times more than it was .... Dan 3:19
let *s* times pass over him .... Dan 4:16
there shall be *s* weeks and .. Dan 9:25
He took the *s* loaves ...... Matt 15:36
forgive him? Up to *s* .... Matt 18:21
wife of the *s* will she be ... Matt 22:28
had come *s* demons .... Luke 8:2
s other spirits more .... Luke 11:26
s times in a day .... Luke 17:4
out from among you *s* .... Acts 6:3
s churches which are .... Rev 1:4
I saw *s* golden lampstands .. Rev 1:12
The mystery of the *s* stars .. Rev 1:20
He who holds the *s* stars ..... Rev 2:1
has the *s* Spirits of God ...... Rev 3:1
S lamps of fire were .... Rev 4:5
sealed with *s* seals .... Rev 5:1
saw the *s* angels who stand .. Rev 8:2
s thunders uttered their ..... Rev 10:3
earthquake *s* thousand ..... Rev 11:13
red dragon having *s* heads .. Rev 12:3
of the sea, having *s* heads ... Rev 13:1
s angels having the *s* last ... Rev 15:1
who had the *s* bowls .... Rev 17:1
s last plagues came to me ... Rev 21:9

SEVENFOLD
light of the sun will be *s* ..... Is 30:26

SEVENTH
the *s* day God ended His ..... Gen 2:2
ark rested in the *s* month .... Gen 8:4
on the *s* day there shall ..... Ex 12:16
gather it, but on the *s* day ... Ex 16:26
When He opened the *s* seal ... Rev 8:1
the sounding of the *s* angel .. Rev 10:7
Then the *s* angel sounded .. Rev 11:15
the *s* angel poured out ...... Rev 16:17
s chrysolite, the eighth ..... Rev 21:20

SEVENTY
S weeks are .... Dan 9:24
up to *s* times seven .... Matt 18:22
Then the *s* returned ...... Luke 10:17

SEVERE
My wound is *s* .... Jer 10:19
not to be too *s* .... 2 Cor 2:5

SEVERITY
the goodness and *s* ...... Rom 11:22

SEWS
s a piece of unshrunk ..... Mark 2:21

SEXUAL
s immorality causes her .... Matt 5:32
except for *s* immorality .... Matt 19:9
from *s* immorality, from ... Acts 15:20
s immorality, wickedness .. Rom 1:29
s immorality among you .... 1 Cor 5:1
the body is not for *s* .... 1 Cor 6:13
Flee *s* immorality .... 1 Cor 6:18
commit *s* immorality ...... 1 Cor 10:8
abstain from *s* .... 1 Thess 4:3
to commit *s* immorality ...... Rev 2:14
repent of her *s* immorality .. Rev 2:21

SEXUALLY
company with *s* immoral ... 1 Cor 5:9
s immoral, sorcerers .... Rev 21:8

SHADE
I sat down in his *s* .... Song 2:3
be a tabernacle for *s* .... Is 4:6
may nest under its *s* .... Mark 4:32

SHADOW
May darkness and the *s* .... Job 3:5
He flees like a *s* .... Job 14:2
hide me under the *s* .... Ps 17:8
walks about like a *s* .... Ps 39:6
like a passing *s* .... Ps 144:4
he passes like a *s* .... Eccl 6:12
and to trust in the *s* .... Is 30:2
In the *s* of His hand .... Is 49:2
which are a *s* of .... Col 2:17
the law, having a *s* .... Heb 10:1
is no variation or *s* .... James 1:17

SHADOW OF DEATH
of darkness and the *s* ...... Job 10:21
my eyelids is the *s* .... Job 16:16
seen the doors of the *s* ..... Job 38:17
the valley of the *s* .... Ps 23:4
out of darkness and the *s* .. Ps 107:14
s, upon them a light .... Is 9:2
turns the *s* into morning ..... Amos 5:8
s light has dawned .... Matt 4:16
in darkness and the *s* ...... Luke 1:79

SHADOWS
my members are like *s* ...... Job 17:7
and the *s* flee away .... Song 2:17

SHADRACH
Hananiah's Babylonian name, Dan 1:3, 7
Cast into the fiery furnace, Dan 3:1–28

SHAKE
Who is he who will *s* .... Job 17:3
their loins *s* continually ..... Ps 69:23
s the earth .... Is 2:19
S yourself from the .... Is 52:2
you *s* your head in scorn ... Jer 48:27
s their heads at the .... Lam 2:15
that the thresholds may *s* .. Amos 9:1
and the knees *s* .... Nah 2:10
hiss and *s* his fist .... Zeph 2:15
little while) I will *s* heaven ... Hag 2:6
I will *s* all nations .... Hag 2:7
s off the dust from your ... Matt 10:14
s off the dust under your .. Mark 6:11
house, and could not *s* it ... Luke 6:48
s not only the earth .... Heb 12:26

SHAKEN
reed is *s* in the water ..... 1 Kin 14:15
quaked and were *s* .... Ps 18:7
he will never be *s* .... Ps 112:6
A reed *s* by the wind .... Matt 11:7
of the heavens will be *s* ... Matt 24:29
the heavens will be *s* ..... Mark 13:25
s together, and running .... Luke 6:38
together was *s* .... Acts 4:31
of the prison were *s* .... Acts 16:26
not to be soon *s* .... 2 Thess 2:2
which cannot be *s* .... Heb 12:28

SHAKES
s the earth out of its .... Job 9:6
s the Wilderness .... Ps 29:8
The earth *s* at the noise ..... Jer 49:21

SHALLUM
King of Israel, 2 Kin 15:10–15

SHALMANESER
Assyrian king, 2 Kin 17:3

SHAME
you turn my glory to *s* .... Ps 4:2
let them be put to *s* .... Ps 83:17
s who serve carved .... Ps 97:7
hate Zion be put to *s* .... Ps 129:5
s shall be the .... Prov 3:35
is a son who causes *s* ...... Prov 10:5
hide My face from *s* .... Is 50:6
S has covered our .... Jer 51:51
their glory into *s* .... Hos 4:7
never be put to *s* .... Joel 2:26
Pass by in naked *s*, you ..... Mic 1:11
the unjust knows no *s* ...... Zeph 3:5
worthy to suffer *s* .... Acts 5:41
will not be put to *s* .... Rom 9:33
to put to *s* the wise .... 1 Cor 1:27
I say this to your *s* .... 1 Cor 6:5
glory is in their *s* .... Phil 3:19
put Him to an open *s* .... Heb 6:6
the cross, despising the *s* ... Heb 12:2

SHAMEFUL
committing what is *s* .... Rom 1:27
for it is *s* for women ..... 1 Cor 14:35
For it is *s* even to .... Eph 5:12

SHAMGAR
Judge of Israel; strikes down 600 Philistines, Judg 3:31

SHAMMAH
Son of Jesse, 1 Sam 16:9
Called Shimea, 1 Chr 2:13
——— One of David's mighty men, 2 Sam 23:11
Also called Shammoth the Harorite, 1 Chr 11:27

SHAPHAN
Scribe under Josiah, 2 Kin 22:3–14

SHARE
a stranger does not *s* ..... Prov 14:10
s in anything done under .... Eccl 9:6
s your bread with the .... Is 58:7
is taught the word *s* .... Gal 6:6
to give, willing to *s* .... 1 Tim 6:18
to do good and to *s* .... Heb 13:16
lest you *s* in her sins, and .... Rev 18:4

SHARING
for your liberal *s* .... 2 Cor 9:13

SHARON
Coastal plain between Joppa and Mt. Carmel, 1 Chr 27:29
Famed for roses, Song 2:1
Inhabitants of, turn to the Lord, Acts 9:35

SHARP
destruction, like a *s* razor .... Ps 52:2
S as a two-edged sword ..... Prov 5:4
sledge with *s* teeth .... Is 41:15
My mouth like a *s* sword .... Is 49:2
son of man, take a *s* sword .. Ezek 5:1
went a *s* two-edged sword .. Rev 1:16
who has the *s* two-edged .... Rev 2:12
and in His hand a *s* sickle .. Rev 14:14

SHARPEN
s their tongue like a .... Ps 64:3
and one does not *s* .... Eccl 10:10

SHARPENS
My adversary *s* His . . . . Job 16:9

SHARPNESS
I should use *s* . . . . 2 Cor 13:10

SHATTERED
at ease, but He has *s* . . . . . Job 16:12

SHAVE
Then the Nazirite shall *s* . . . Num 6:18
s off the seven locks . . . . . . Judg 16:19
will *s* with a hired razor . . . . . . Is 7:20
they may *s* their heads . . . . Acts 21:24

SHAVED
s off half of their beards . . 2 Sam 10:4
as if her head were *s* . . . . . . 1 Cor 11:5

SHEALTIEL
Son of King Jeconiah and father of Zerubbabel, 1 Chr 3:17

SHEAR-JASHUB
Symbolic name given to Isaiah's son, Is 7:3

SHEATH
'Return it to its *s* . . . . Ezek 21:30
your sword into the *s* . . . . . John 18:11

SHEAVES
bringing his *s* . . . . Ps 126:6
nor he who binds *s* . . . . Ps 129:7
gather them like *s* . . . . Mic 4:12

SHEBA
Land of, occupied by Sabeans, famous traders, Job 1:15; Ps 72:10
Queen of, visits Solomon; marvels at his wisdom, 1 Kin 10:1–13
Mentioned by Christ, Matt 12:42

SHEBAH
Name given to a well and town (Beersheba), Gen 26:31–33

SHEBNA
Treasurer under Hezekiah, Is 22:15
Demoted to position of scribe, 2 Kin 19:2
Man of pride and luxury, replaced by Eliakim, Is 22:19–21

SHECHEM
Son of Hamor; rapes Dinah, Jacob's daughter, Gen 34:1–31
——— Ancient city of Ephraim, Gen 33:18
Joshua's farewell address delivered at, Josh 24:1–25
Supports Abimelech; destroyed, Judg 9
Rebuilt by Jeroboam I, 1 Kin 12:25

SHED
s blood without cause . . . 1 Sam 25:31
s innocent blood . . . . Ps 106:38
which is *s* for many . . . . . . Matt 26:28
which is *s* for many . . . . . . Mark 14:24
s from the foundation of . . Luke 11:50
blood, which is *s* for . . . . . . Luke 22:20
martyr Stephen was *s* . . . . . Acts 22:20
feet are swift to *s* blood . . . . Rom 3:15
they have *s* the blood of . . . . Rev 16:6
of His servants *s* by her . . . . . Rev 19:2

SHEDDING
blood, and without *s* . . . . Heb 9:22

SHEEP
spared the best of the *s* . . 1 Sam 15:15
as *s* that have no . . . . 2 Chr 18:16
like *s* intended for food . . . . . Ps 44:11
as *s* for the slaughter . . . . Ps 44:22
s of Your pasture . . . . Ps 79:13
and the *s* of His hand . . . . Ps 95:7
and the *s* of His pasture . . . . . Ps 100:3
astray like a lost *s* . . . . Ps 119:176
All we like *s* have gone . . . . Is 53:6
slaughter, and as a *s* . . . . Is 53:7
Pull them out like *s* . . . . Jer 12:3
scatter the *s* of My pasture . . . Jer 23:1
have been lost *s* . . . . Jer 50:6
My *s* wandered through . . . . Ezek 34:6
will search for My *s* . . . . Ezek 34:11
shall judge between *s* . . . . . Ezek 34:17
lion among flocks of *s* . . . . Mic 5:8
s will be scattered . . . . Zech 13:7
like *s* having no shepherd . . Matt 9:36
rather to the lost *s* . . . . Matt 10:6
I send you out as *s* . . . . Matt 10:16
lost *s* of the house of . . . . . . Matt 15:24
If a man has a hundred *s* . . Matt 18:12
his *s* from the goats . . . . Matt 25:32
And He will set the *s* . . . . . . Matt 25:33
s not having a shepherd . . . . Mark 6:34
s will be scattered . . . . Mark 14:27
having a hundred *s* . . . . Luke 15:4
plowing or tending *s* . . . . Luke 17:7
the shepherd of the *s* . . . . . . John 10:2
and he calls his own *s* . . . . . John 10:3
and I know My *s* . . . . John 10:14
s I have which are not . . . . John 10:16
you are not of My *s* . . . . John 10:26
said to him, "Tend My *s* . . John 21:16
said to him, "Feed My *s*. . . John 21:17
"He was led as a *s* . . . . Acts 8:32
as *s* for the slaughter . . . . . . Rom 8:36
great Shepherd of the *s* . . . . Heb 13:20
like *s* going astray . . . . 1 Pet 2:25

SHEEPFOLDS
lie down among the *s* . . . . Ps 68:13

SHEET
object like a great *s* . . . . Acts 10:11

SHELTER
I will trust in the *s* . . . . Ps 61:4
in You I take *s* . . . . Ps 143:9
the LORD will be a *s* . . . . Joel 3:16

SHELTERS
s him all the day long . . . . . Deut 33:12
be pastures, with *s* . . . . Zeph 2:6

SHEM
Oldest son of Noah, Gen 5:32
Escapes the flood, Gen 7:13
Receives a blessing, Gen 9:23, 26
Ancestor of Semitic people, Gen 10:22–32

SHEMAIAH
Prophet of Judah, 1 Kin 12:22–24
Explains Shishak's invasion as divine punishment, 2 Chr 12:5–8
Records Rehoboam's reign, 2 Chr 12:15

SHEMER
Sells Omri the hill on which Samaria is built, 1 Kin 16:23, 24

SHEOL
down to the gates of *S* . . . . . Job 17:16
not leave my soul in *S* . . . . Ps 16:10
S laid hold of me . . . . Ps 116:3
S cannot thank . . . . Is 38:18
the belly of *S* I cried . . . . Jon 2:2

SHEPHERD
s is an abomination . . . . Gen 46:34
s My people Israel . . . . 2 Sam 5:2
The LORD is my *s* . . . . Ps 23:1
s Jacob His people . . . . Ps 78:71
His flock like a *s* . . . . Is 40:11
of Cyrus, 'He is My *s* . . . . Is 44:28
s who follows You . . . . Jer 17:16
because there was no *s* . . . . Ezek 34:5
I will establish one *s* . . . . . . Ezek 34:23
"As a *s* takes from . . . . Amos 3:12
to the worthless *s* . . . . Zech 11:17
'I will strike the *S* . . . . Matt 26:31
"I am the good *s* . . . . John 10:11
s the church of God . . . . Acts 20:28
the dead, that great *S* . . . . . . Heb 13:20
S the flock of God . . . . 1 Pet 5:2
when the Chief *S* . . . . 1 Pet 5:4
of the throne will *s* . . . . Rev 7:17

SHEPHERDS
your sons shall be *s* . . . . . Num 14:33
And they are *s* who . . . . Is 56:11
And I will give you *s* . . . . Jer 3:15
s who destroy and . . . . Jer 23:1
s who feed My people . . . . Jer 23:2
s have led them astray . . . . Jer 50:6
s fed themselves . . . . Ezek 34:8
in the same country *s* . . . . Luke 2:8

SHESHACH
Symbolic of Babylon, Jer 25:26

SHESHBAZZAR
Prince of Judah, Ezra 1:8, 11

SHETHAR-BOZNAI
Official of Persia, Ezra 5:3, 6

SHIELD
I am your *s* . . . . Gen 15:1
the *s* of your help and . . . . Deut 33:29
s of Saul, not anointed . . . . 2 Sam 1:21
whom I will trust: my *s* . . . 2 Sam 22:3
He is a *s* to all who . . . . . . 2 Sam 22:31
gold went into each *s* . . . . . 2 Chr 9:15
are a *s* for me, my glory . . . . Ps 3:3
surround him as with a *s* . . . . . Ps 5:12
my *s* and the horn of . . . . Ps 18:2
He is a *s* to all who trust in . . Ps 18:30
me the *s* of Your salvation . . Ps 18:35
my strength and my *s* . . . . Ps 28:7
He is our help and our *s* . . . . . Ps 33:20
God is a sun and *s* . . . . Ps 84:11
truth shall be your *s* . . . . Ps 91:4
He is their help and their *s* . . Ps 115:9
hiding place and my *s* . . . . Ps 119:114
all, taking the *s* . . . . Eph 6:16

SHIHOR
Name given to the Nile, Is 23:3
Israel's southwestern border, Josh 13:3

SHILOH
Center of worship, Judg 18:31
Headquarters for division of Promised Land, Josh 18:1, 10
Benjamites seize women of, Judg 21:19–23
Ark of the covenant taken from, 1 Sam 4:3–11
Punishment given to, Jer 7:12–15
——— Messianic title, Gen 49:10

SHIMEI
Benjamite; insults David, 2 Sam 16:5–13
Pardoned, but confined, 2 Sam 19:16–23
Breaks agreement; executed by Solomon, 1 Kin 2:39–46

SHIMSHAI
Scribe opposing the Jews, Ezra 4:8–24

SHINAR
Tower built at, Gen 11:2–9

SHINE
LORD make His face *s* . . . . . . Num 6:25
even the moon does not *s* . . . Job 25:5
Make Your face *s* upon . . . . . Ps 31:16
cause His face to *s* . . . . Ps 67:1
the cherubim, *s* . . . . Ps 80:1
Make Your face *s* . . . . Ps 119:135
will not cause its light to *s* . . . Is 13:10
Arise, *s*; for your light . . . . Is 60:1
who are wise shall *s* . . . . Dan 12:3
your light so *s* before men . . Matt 5:16
the righteous will *s* . . . . Matt 13:43
among whom you *s* . . . . Phil 2:15
a third of the day did not *s* . . Rev 8:12
sun or of the moon to *s* . . . Rev 21:23

SHINED
them a light has *s* . . . . Is 9:2

SHINES
But the night *s* as the day . . Ps 139:12
that *s* ever brighter unto . . . Prov 4:18
And the light *s* . . . . John 1:5
light that *s* in a dark . . . . 2 Pet 1:19

SHINING
the earth, by clear *s* . . . . . . 2 Sam 23:4
the just is like the *s* sun . . . . Prov 4:18
His clothes became *s* . . . . Mark 9:3
by them in *s* garments . . . . . Luke 24:4
light is already *s* . . . . 1 John 2:8
was like the sun *s* . . . . Rev 1:16

SHIP
the way of a *s* in the . . . . . . Prov 30:19
found a *s* going to Tarshish . . Jon 1:3
finding a *s* sailing over to . . Acts 21:2
some on parts of the *s* . . . . Acts 27:44

SHIPHRAH
Hebrew midwife, Ex 1:15

SHIPS
pass by like swift *s* . . . . Job 9:26
down to the sea in *s* . . . . Ps 107:23
like the merchant *s* . . . . Prov 31:14
Look also at *s* . . . . James 3:4

SHIPWRECK
faith have suffered *s* . . . . . . 1 Tim 1:19

SHONE
the skin of Moses' face *s* . . . . Ex 34:35
His face *s* like the sun . . . . . Matt 17:2
of the Lord *s* around them . . Luke 2:9
a light *s* around him . . . . Acts 9:3
and a light *s* in the prison . . Acts 12:7

SHOOK
so loudly that the earth *s* . . 1 Sam 4:5
the earth *s* and trembled . . 2 Sam 22:8
earth *s*; the heavens also . . . . . Ps 68:8
The earth trembled and *s* . . . . Ps 77:18
guards *s* for fear of him . . . . Matt 28:4
they *s* off the dust from . . . . Acts 13:51

SHOOT
they *s* out the lip . . . . Ps 22:7
But God shall *s* . . . . Ps 64:7

SHORT
of the wicked is *s* . . . . Job 20:5
Remember how *s* my time . . . Ps 89:47
for he was of *s* stature . . . . . Luke 19:3
have sinned and fall *s* . . . . . . Rom 3:23
the work and cut it *s* . . . . Rom 9:28
fall *s* of the grace of God . . Heb 12:15
knows that he has a *s* . . . . . . Rev 12:12

SHORTENED
his youth You have *s* . . . . Ps 89:45
the wicked will be *s* . . . . Prov 10:27
those days were *s* . . . . Matt 24:22
Lord had *s* those days . . . . Mark 13:20

SHORTLY
which must *s* take place . . . . . Rev 1:1
which must *s* take place . . . . Rev 22:6

SHOT
shall be stoned or *s* . . . . Heb 12:20

SHOULDER
will be upon His *s* . . . . Is 9:6

SHOUT
shall *s* with a great *s* . . . . Josh 6:5
s for joy, all you upright in . . Ps 32:11
skillfully with a *s* of joy . . . . . . Ps 33:3
s for joy and be glad . . . . Ps 35:27
S to God with the voice of . . . . Ps 47:1
Make a joyful *s* to God, all . . . Ps 66:1
Make a joyful *s* to the God . . . Ps 81:1
s joyfully to the Rock . . . . Ps 95:1
S joyfully to the LORD . . . . Ps 98:4
Make a joyful *s* . . . . Ps 100:1
from heaven with a *s* . . . . 1 Thess 4:16

SHOUTED
So the people *s* when the . . . Josh 6:20
they *s*, saying, "Crucify . . . Luke 23:21

SHOW
a land that I will *s* . . . . Gen 12:1
will *s* Yourself merciful . . 2 Sam 22:26
will *s* Yourself merciful . . . . . . Ps 18:25
S me Your ways . . . . Ps 25:4
I will *s* the salvation of . . . . . . Ps 50:23
mouth shall *s* forth Your . . . . . Ps 51:15
S us Your mercy, LORD . . . . Ps 85:7
and *s* us what will happen . . . Is 41:22
s yourselves men . . . . Is 46:8
s mercy and compassion . . . . Zech 7:9
s them a sign from . . . . Matt 16:1
S Me the tax money . . . . . . Matt 22:19
s great signs and . . . . Matt 24:24
s signs and wonders to . . . Mark 13:22
s Him greater works . . . . John 5:20
s Yourself to the world . . . . . . John 7:4
s us the Father . . . . John 14:8
you say, '*S* us the Father . . . John 14:9
I *s* you a more excellent . . 1 Cor 12:31
S me your faith without . . James 2:18
I will *s* you things which . . . . . Rev 4:1

SHOWBREAD
you shall set the *s* . . . . Ex 25:30
s which had been taken . . . 1 Sam 21:6
s which was not lawful . . . . . Matt 12:4

SHOWED
s him mercy, and He . . . . . . Gen 39:21
and the LORD *s* him a tree . . . Ex 15:25
s Him all the kingdoms . . . . . Matt 4:8
s Him all the kingdoms . . . . . Luke 4:5
But even Moses *s* in the . . . Luke 20:37
s them His hands and . . . . Luke 24:40
s them His hands and . . . . . John 20:20
Jesus *s* Himself again to . . . John 21:1
third day, and *s* Him . . . . . . Acts 10:40
s me the great city, the . . . . Rev 21:10

SHOWERS
make it soft with *s* . . . . Ps 65:10
s have been withheld . . . . Jer 3:3
can the heavens give *s* . . . . . Jer 14:22
from the LORD, like *s* . . . . Mic 5:7

SHOWN
You have *s* Your servant . . Gen 32:10
have *s* more kindness . . . . . . Ruth 3:10
grace be *s* to the wicked . . . . . Is 26:10
s you from My Father . . . . John 10:32

SHOWS
firmament *s* His handiwork . . . Ps 19:1
that God *s* no partiality . . . . Acts 10:34
God *s* personal favoritism . . . . . Gal 2:6

SHREWDLY
because he had dealt *s* . . . . . Luke 16:8

SHRINES
who made silver *s* . . . . Acts 19:24

SHRIVELED
You have *s* me up . . . . Job 16:8

SHUFFLES
with his eyes, he *s* . . . . Prov 6:13

SHULAMITE
Beloved of the bridegroom king, Song 6:13

SHUNAMMITE
Abishag, David's nurse, 1 Kin 1:3, 15
—— Woman who cared for Elisha, 2 Kin 4:8–12

SHUNEM
Town of Issachar, Josh 19:18

SHUNNED
feared God and *s* evil . . . . Job 1:1

SHUR
Wilderness in south Palestine, Gen 16:7
Israel went from Red Sea to, Ex 15:22
Hagar fled here, Gen 16:7

SHUSHAN
Residence of Persian monarchs, Esth 1:2

SHUT
s the door behind him . . . . . . Gen 19:6
Let her be *s* out of the . . . . Num 12:14
"Or who *s* in the sea . . . . Job 38:8
Has He in anger *s* . . . . Ps 77:9
For you *s* up the . . . . Matt 23:13
came, the doors being *s* . . . John 20:26
door, and no one can *s* it . . . . . Rev 3:8
have power to *s* heaven . . . . . Rev 11:6

SHUTS
s his ears to the cry . . . . Prov 21:13
s his eyes from seeing . . . . Is 33:15
brother in need, and *s* . . . . 1 John 3:17
who opens and no one *s* . . . . . Rev 3:7

SICK
have made him *s* . . . . Hos 7:5
I was *s* and you . . . . Matt 25:36
he whom You love is *s* . . . . . John 11:3
many are weak and *s* . . . . 1 Cor 11:30
have left in Miletus *s* . . . . . . 2 Tim 4:20
faith will save the *s* . . . . James 5:15

SICKLE
Put in the *s* . . . . Joel 3:13
"Thrust in Your *s* . . . . Rev 14:15

SICKNESS
will sustain him in *s* . . . . . . Prov 18:14
"This *s* is not unto . . . . John 11:4

SICKNESSES
And bore our *s* . . . . Matt 8:17

SIDE
two rings shall be on one *s* . . Ex 25:12
And a cubit on one *s* . . . . Ex 26:13
For the south *s* there shall . . . Ex 27:9
this *s* of the Jordan in the . . . Deut 1:1
on this *s* of the Jordan . . . . . Josh 1:14
me down on every *s* . . . . Job 19:10
wicked prowl on every *s* . . . . . . Ps 12:8
Fear is on every *s* . . . . Ps 31:13
hills rejoice on every *s* . . . . . . Ps 65:12
comfort me on every *s* . . . . . . Ps 71:21
The LORD is on my *s* . . . . Ps 118:6
Lie also on your left *s* . . . . Ezek 4:4
gate chambers on one *s* . . . Ezek 40:10
robe sitting on the right *s* . . Mark 16:5
pierced His *s* with a . . . . . . John 19:34
His hands and His *s* . . . . . . John 20:20
put my hand into His *s* . . . John 20:25
the net on the right *s* . . . . . . John 21:6

SIDON
See TYRE AND SIDON
Canaanite city; inhabitants not expelled, Judg 1:31
Hostile relations with Israel, Judg 10:12; Is 23:12; Joel 3:4–6
Jesus preaches to, Matt 15:21; Luke 6:17

SIFT
s the nations with the . . . . Is 30:28
s the house of Israel . . . . Amos 9:9
for you, that he may *s* . . . . Luke 22:31

SIFTS
A wise king *s* out the . . . . . Prov 20:26

SIGH
our years like a *s* . . . . Ps 90:9
the merry-hearted *s* . . . . Is 24:7
of the men who *s* . . . . Ezek 9:4

SIGHING
For my *s* comes before . . . . . . Job 3:24
s is not hidden . . . . Ps 38:9

SIGHT
and see this great *s* . . . . Ex 3:3
evil in the *s* of the LORD . . . Judg 2:11
as stupid in your *s* . . . . Job 18:3
of human waste in their *s* . . Ezek 4:12
seemed good in Your *s* . . . . Matt 11:26
he received his *s* . . . . Mark 10:52
abomination in the *s* of . . . . Luke 16:15

washed, and I received *s* ... John 9:11
he marveled at the *s* ... Acts 7:31
three days without *s* ... Acts 9:9
are just in the *s* of God ... Rom 2:13
will be justified in His *s* ... Rom 3:20
by faith, not by *s* ... 2 Cor 5:7
precious in the *s* of God ... 1 Pet 3:4

SIGN
Show me a *s* for good ... Ps 86:17
will give you a *s* ... Is 7:14
for an everlasting *s* ... Is 55:13
we want to see a *s* ... Matt 12:38
seeks after a *s* ... Matt 12:39
And what will be the *s* ... Matt 24:3
s which will be spoken ... Luke 2:34
again is the second *s* ... John 4:54
For Jews request a *s* ... 1 Cor 1:22
Now a great *s* appeared ... Rev 12:1

SIGNS
and let them be for *s* ... Gen 1:14
you not know their *s* ... Job 21:29
They performed His *s* ... Ps 105:27
We are for *s* and ... Is 8:18
How great are His *s* ... Dan 4:3
cannot discern the *s* ... Matt 16:3
the accompanying *s* ... Mark 16:20
s Jesus did in Cana of ... John 2:11
no one can do these *s* ... John 3:2
because you saw the *s* ... John 6:26
is a sinner do such *s* ... John 9:16
this Man works many *s* ... John 11:47
Jesus did many other *s* ... John 20:30
demons, performing *s* ... Rev 16:14

SIGNS AND WONDERS
Lord showed *s* ... Deut 6:22
great terror and with *s* ... Deut 26:8
s against Pharaoh ... Neh 9:10
He sent *s* ... Ps 135:9
We are for *s* in Israel ... Is 8:18
good to declare the *s* ... Dan 4:2
He works *s* in heaven ... Dan 6:27
rise and show great *s* ... Matt 24:24
"Unless you people see *s* ... John 4:48
s may be done through ... Acts 4:30
of the apostles many *s* ... Acts 5:12
His grace, granting *s* ... Acts 14:3
mighty *s*, by the power ... Rom 15:19
in *s* and mighty deeds ... 2 Cor 12:12
bearing witness both with *s* ... Heb 2:4

SIHON
Amorite king; defeated by Israel, Num 21:21–32
Territory of, assigned to Reuben and Gad, Num 32:1–38

SILAS (or Silvanus)
Leader in Jerusalem church; sent to Antioch, Acts 15:22–35
Travels with Paul, Acts 15:40, 41
Jailed and released, Acts 16:25–40
Mentioned in epistles, 2 Cor 1:19; 1 Thess 1:1; 2 Thess 1:1; 1 Pet 5:12

SILENCE
that You may *s* ... Ps 8:2
I was mute with *s* ... Ps 39:2
soon have settled in *s* ... Ps 94:17
"Sit in *s* ... Is 47:5
I will not keep *s*, but will ... Is 65:6
in *s* with all submission ... 1 Tim 2:11
s the ignorance of foolish ... 1 Pet 2:15
seal, there was *s* ... Rev 8:1

SILENT
the wicked shall be *s* ... 1 Sam 2:9
Oh, that you would be *s* ... Job 13:5
season, and am not *s* ... Ps 22:2
Do not be *s* to me ... Ps 28:1
praise to You and not be *s* ... Ps 30:12
Let them be *s* in the ... Ps 31:17
come, and shall not keep *s* ... Ps 50:3
before its shearers is *s* ... Is 53:7
Be *s* in the presence ... Zeph 1:7
But Jesus kept *s* ... Matt 26:63
His answer and kept *s* ... Luke 20:26
before its shearer is *s* ... Acts 8:32
Let your women keep *s* ... 1 Cor 14:34

SILK
and covered you with *s* ... Ezek 16:10

SILLY
They are *s* children ... Jer 4:22

SILOAM
Tower of, falls and kills 18 people, Luke 13:4
Blind man washes in pool of, John 9:1–11

SILVER
and your precious *s* ... Job 22:25
Though he heaps up *s* ... Job 27:16
s tried in a furnace ... Ps 12:6
have refined us as *s* ... Ps 66:10
than the profits of *s* ... Prov 3:14
chosen rather than *s* ... Prov 16:16
refining pot is for *s* ... Prov 17:3
He who loves *s* will ... Eccl 5:10
s has become dross ... Is 1:22
call them rejected *s* ... Jer 6:30
may buy the poor for *s* ... Amos 8:6
him thirty pieces of *s* ... Matt 26:15

SIMEON
Son of Jacob by Leah, Gen 29:32, 33
Avenges his sister's dishonor, Gen 34:25–31
Held hostage by Joseph, Gen 42:18–20, 24
Rebuked by Jacob, Gen 49:5–7
—— Tribe of:
Numbered, Num 1:23; 26:12–14
Receive inheritance, Josh 19:1–9
Fight Canaanites with Judah, Judg 1:1–3, 17–20
—— Just man; blesses infant Jesus, Luke 2:25–35

SIMILITUDE
been made in the *s* ... James 3:9

SIMON
Simon Peter: *see* PETER
—— One of the Twelve; called "the Cananite," Matt 10:4
—— One of Jesus' half brothers, Matt 13:55
—— Pharisee, Luke 7:36–40
—— Man of Cyrene, bears Jesus' cross, Matt 27:32
—— Sorcerer, Acts 8:9–24
—— Tanner in Joppa, Acts 9:43

SIMPLE
making wise the *s* ... Ps 19:7
LORD preserves the *s* ... Ps 116:6
understanding to the *s* ... Ps 119:130
s believes every word ... Prov 14:15
the hearts of the *s* ... Rom 16:18

SIMPLICITY
ones, will you love *s* ... Prov 1:22
in the world in *s* ... 2 Cor 1:12
corrupted from the *s* ... 2 Cor 11:3

SIN
not well, *s* lies at the door ... Gen 4:7
because their *s* is very ... Gen 18:20
brothers and their *s* ... Gen 50:17
It is a *s* offering ... Ex 29:14
committed a great *s* ... Ex 32:30
offer to the LORD for his *s* ... Lev 4:3
the *s* which they have ... Lev 4:14
a lamb as his *s* offering ... Lev 4:32
of the goats as a *s* offering ... Lev 5:6
is the law of the *s* offering ... Lev 6:25
They shall bear their *s* ... Lev 20:20
his God shall bear his *s* ... Lev 24:15
any *s* that men commit in ... Num 5:6
If you *s* unintentionally ... Num 15:22
flesh, shall one man *s* ... Num 16:22
he died in his own *s* ... Num 27:3
goats as a *s* offering ... Num 29:5
and be sure your *s* ... Num 32:23
because of all your *s* ... Deut 9:18
it become *s* among you ... Deut 15:9
or any *s* that he commits ... Deut 19:15
you *s* against the LORD ... Deut 20:18
a *s* deserving of death ... Deut 21:22
no *s* deserving of death ... Deut 22:26
to death for his own *s* ... Deut 24:16
forgive the *s* of Your ... 1 Kin 8:34
When they *s* against You ... 1 Kin 8:46
this thing became a *s* ... 1 Kin 12:30
in his *s* by which ... 1 Kin 15:26
and made Israel *s* ... 1 Kin 21:22
to death for his own *s* ... 2 Kin 14:6
made Judah *s* with his ... 2 Kin 21:11
forgive the *s* of Your ... 2 Chr 6:25
and will forgive their *s* ... 2 Chr 7:14
shall die for his own *s* ... 2 Chr 25:4
do not let their *s* be blotted ... Neh 4:5
In all this Job did not *s* nor ... Job 1:22
all this Job did not *s* ... Job 2:10
and search out my *s* ... Job 10:6
he adds rebellion to his *s* ... Job 34:37
Be angry, and do not *s* ... Ps 4:4
whose *s* is covered ... Ps 32:1
I acknowledged my *s* ... Ps 32:5
my bones because of my *s* ... Ps 38:3
my ways, lest I *s* ... Ps 39:1
And cleanse me from my *s* ... Ps 51:2
s is always before me ... Ps 51:3
in *s* my mother ... Ps 51:5
the *s* of their mouth ... Ps 59:12
I might not *s* against You ... Ps 119:11
of the wicked to *s* ... Prov 10:16
Fools mock at *s* ... Prov 14:9
s is a reproach ... Prov 14:34
I am pure from my *s* ... Prov 20:9
mouth cause your flesh to *s* ... Eccl 5:6
good and does not *s* ... Eccl 7:20
away, and your *s* purged ... Is 6:7
soul an offering for *s* ... Is 53:10
And He bore the *s* ... Is 53:12
what is our *s* that we have ... Jer 16:10
your high places of *s* ... Jer 17:3
s I will remember no ... Jer 31:34
he shall die in his *s* ... Ezek 3:20
and confessing my *s* ... Dan 9:20
They eat up the *s* ... Hos 4:8
Now they *s* more and ... Hos 13:2
right eye causes you to *s* ... Matt 5:29
I say to you, every *s* and ... Matt 12:31
who believe in Me to *s* ... Matt 18:6
hand causes you to *s* ... Mark 9:43
who takes away the *s* ... John 1:29
S no more ... John 5:14
"He who is without *s* ... John 8:7
go and *s* no more ... John 8:11
Me, and will die in your *s* ... John 8:21
commits *s* is a slave of *s* ... John 8:34
of you convicts Me of *s* ... John 8:46
you would have no *s* ... John 9:41
convict the world of *s* ... John 16:8
they are all under *s* ... Rom 3:9
law is the knowledge of *s* ... Rom 3:20
LORD shall not impute *s* ... Rom 4:8
s entered the world ... Rom 5:12
s is not imputed ... Rom 5:13
where *s* abounded, grace ... Rom 5:20
s that grace may ... Rom 6:1
that the body of *s* might be ... Rom 6:6
died to *s* once for all ... Rom 6:10
s shall not have ... Rom 6:14
Shall we *s* because we ... Rom 6:15
you were slaves of *s* ... Rom 6:17
been set free from *s* ... Rom 6:22
the wages of *s* is death ... Rom 6:23
Is the law *s*? ... Rom 7:7
s revived and I died ... Rom 7:9

s that dwells in me . . . . Rom 7:17
me free from the law of s . . . Rom 8:2
body is dead because of s . . Rom 8:10
Every s that a man does . . . 1 Cor 6:18
you s against Christ . . . . 1 Cor 8:12
The sting of death is s . . . . 1 Cor 15:56
Him who knew no s . . . . 2 Cor 5:21
man of s is revealed . . . . . . 2 Thess 2:3
we are, yet without s . . . . Heb 4:15
appeared to put away s . . . . . Heb 9:26
longer an offering for s . . . . Heb 10:18
s willfully after we . . . . Heb 10:26
it gives birth to s . . . . James 1:15
partiality, you commit s . . . . James 2:9
do it, to him it is s . . . . James 4:17
"Who committed no s . . . . . . 1 Pet 2:22
the flesh has ceased from s . . 1 Pet 4:1
that cannot cease from s . . 2 Pet 2:14
cleanses us from all s . . . . . 1 John 1:7
say that we have no s . . . . . 1 John 1:8
that you may not s . . . . 1 John 2:1
s is lawlessness . . . . 1 John 3:4
in Him there is no s . . . . 1 John 3:5
and he cannot s . . . . 1 John 3:9
s which does not lead . . . . 1 John 5:16
there is s not leading to . . 1 John 5:17

SINAI

Mountain (same as Horeb) where the law was given, Ex 19:1–25
Used allegorically by Paul, Gal 4:24, 25

SINCERE

Holy Spirit, by s love . . . . 2 Cor 6:6
that you may be s . . . . Phil 1:10
and from s faith . . . . 1 Tim 1:5
s love of the brethren . . . . . . 1 Pet 1:22

SINCERITY

LORD, serve Him in s . . . . . . Josh 24:14
unleavened bread of s . . . . . . 1 Cor 5:8
simplicity and godly s . . . . . 2 Cor 1:12
as of s, but as from God, . . 2 Cor 2:17
testing the s of your love . . . 2 Cor 8:8
in s of heart, as to Christ . . . . Eph 6:5
our Lord Jesus Christ in s . . Eph 6:24
men-pleasers, but in s . . . . Col 3:22

SINFUL

place, a brood of s men . . . Num 32:14
Alas, s nation . . . . Is 1:4
and s generation . . . . Mark 8:38
from me, for I am a s . . . . Luke 5:8
the hands of s men . . . . Luke 24:7
become exceedingly s . . . . . . Rom 7:13
likeness of s flesh . . . . Rom 8:3

SING

"S to the LORD . . . . Ex 15:21
Awake, awake, s a song . . . Judg 5:12
s praises to Your name . . 2 Sam 22:50
S to the LORD, all the . . . . . 1 Chr 16:23
when they began to s . . . . 2 Chr 20:22
the widow's heart to s . . . . . Job 29:13
S praises to the LORD, who . . . Ps 9:11
I will s to the LORD . . . . Ps 13:6
S to Him a new song . . . . Ps 33:3
my tongue shall s aloud of . . Ps 51:14
shout for joy, they also s . . . . Ps 65:13
S out the honor . . . . Ps 66:2
nations be glad and s for . . . . . Ps 67:4
You I will s with the harp . . . Ps 71:22
I will s of the mercies of . . . . . . Ps 89:1
s to the LORD a new song . . . . . Ps 98:1
I will s of mercy and . . . . Ps 101:1
I will s to the LORD as . . . . . . Ps 104:33
S praises to His name . . . . Ps 135:3
"S us one of the songs . . . . Ps 137:3
they shall s of the ways of . . . Ps 138:5
S to the LORD a new song . . . Ps 149:1
S to the LORD, for He has . . . . . Is 12:5
up their voice, they shall s . . . Is 24:14
S to the LORD a new song . . . . Is 42:10
My servants shall s . . . . Is 65:14
she shall s there, as in the . . Hos 2:15
S and rejoice, O daughter . . Zech 2:10
I will s with the . . . . 1 Cor 14:15
assembly I will s . . . . Heb 2:12
Let him s psalms . . . . James 5:13
They s the song of Moses . . . Rev 15:3

SINGERS

instruments for s . . . . 1 Kin 10:12
who bore the ark, the s . . 1 Chr 15:27
instruments for s . . . . 2 Chr 9:11
s with musical . . . . 2 Chr 23:13
s sang, and the . . . . 2 Chr 29:28
The s sang loudly with . . . . Neh 12:42
The s went before . . . . Ps 68:25
male and female s . . . . Eccl 2:8

SINGING

rejoicing and with s . . . . . . 2 Chr 23:18
s to the LORD . . . . 2 Chr 30:21
with thanksgivings and s . . Neh 12:27
His presence with s . . . . Ps 100:2
and our tongue with s . . . . . . Ps 126:2
the time of s has come . . . . . Song 2:12
break forth into s . . . . Is 14:7
even with joy and s . . . . Is 35:2
come to Zion with s . . . . Is 35:10
With a voice of s, declare . . . . Is 48:20
and come to Zion with s . . . . . Is 51:11
and s hymns to God . . . . . . Acts 16:25
and spiritual songs, s . . . . Eph 5:19
s with grace in your hearts . . Col 3:16

SINGLENESS

them s of heart to obey . . 2 Chr 30:12

SINISTER

who understands s . . . . Dan 8:23

SINK

I s in deep mire . . . . Ps 69:2
to s he cried out . . . . Matt 14:30

SINNED

had ceased, he s yet more . . . . Ex 9:34
has s a young bull without . . . Lev 4:3
promised, for we have s . . Num 14:40
s against their own souls . . Num 16:38
to the LORD, "We have s . . Judg 10:15
Saul said, "I have s . . . . . 1 Sam 26:21
may be that my sons have s . . Job 1:5
Have I s? What have I . . . . . . Job 7:20
those who have s . . . . Job 24:19
for I have s against You . . . . . . Ps 41:4
You only, have I s . . . . Ps 51:4
you say, 'I have not s . . . . Jer 2:35
Jerusalem has s . . . . Lam 1:8
Our fathers s and are . . . . Lam 5:7
we have s and committed . . . . Dan 9:5
the more they s against Me . . Hos 4:7
you have s from the days . . . Hos 10:9
"I have s by betraying . . . . . Matt 27:4
"Father, I have s . . . . Luke 15:18
"Rabbi, who s . . . . John 9:2
For as many as have s . . . . . Rom 2:12
for all have s and . . . . Rom 3:23
marries, she has not s . . . . . 1 Cor 7:28
not spare the angels who s . . 2 Pet 2:4
say that we have not s . . . . 1 John 1:10
for the devil has s . . . . 1 John 3:8

SINNED AGAINST THE LORD

"I have s your God . . . . Ex 10:16
s your God—had made . . . . . Deut 9:16
"Indeed I have s . . . . Josh 7:20
said there, "We have s . . . . 1 Sam 7:6
to Nathan, "I have s . . . . . 2 Sam 12:13
For we have s . . . . Jer 3:25
because we have s . . . . Jer 8:14
because you have s . . . . Jer 44:23
because they have s . . . . Zeph 1:17

SINNED AGAINST YOU

saying, "We have s . . . . Judg 10:10
I have not s, but you . . . . . . Judg 11:27
I have not s . . . . 1 Sam 24:11
because they have s . . . . 1 Kin 8:33
Your people who have s . . 2 Chr 6:39
Israel which we have s . . . . Neh 1:6
heal my soul, for I have s . . . . . Ps 41:4
many, we have s . . . . Jer 14:7
fathers, because we have s . . . Dan 9:8

SINNER

the ungodly and the s . . . . . Prov 11:31
overthrows the s . . . . Prov 13:6
of the s is stored up for . . . Prov 13:22
s He gives the work . . . . Eccl 2:26
s shall be trapped by her . . . Eccl 7:26
s does evil a hundred . . . . Eccl 8:12
As is the good, so is the s . . . . Eccl 9:2
s destroys much good . . . . . . Eccl 9:18
the city who was a s . . . . Luke 7:37
s who repents than . . . . Luke 15:7
be merciful to me a s . . . . . Luke 18:13
can a man who is a s . . . . John 9:16
know that this Man is a s . . John 9:24
the ungodly and the s . . . . . . 1 Pet 4:18

SINNERS

See TAX COLLECTORS AND SINNERS
utterly destroy the s . . . . . 1 Sam 15:18
in the path of s . . . . Ps 1:1
nor s in the congregation . . . . . . Ps 1:5
therefore He teaches s . . . . Ps 25:8
soul with s . . . . Ps 26:9
s be consumed from the . . . . Ps 104:35
son, if s entice you . . . . Prov 1:10
Evil pursues s, but to the . . Prov 13:21
not let your heart envy s . . Prov 23:17
The s in Zion are . . . . Is 33:14
All the s of My people . . . . Amos 9:10
s came and sat down with . . Matt 9:10
the righteous, but s . . . . Matt 9:13
tax collectors and s . . . . Matt 11:19
into the hands of s . . . . Matt 26:45
and s also sat together . . . . Mark 2:15
into the hands of s . . . . Mark 14:41
call the righteous, but s . . . . Luke 5:32
s love those who love . . . . . . Luke 6:32
of tax collectors and s . . . . . Luke 7:34
Galileans were worse s . . . . Luke 13:2
man receives s and eats . . . Luke 15:2
God does not hear s . . . . John 9:31
while we were still s . . . . Rom 5:8
many were made s . . . . Rom 5:19
the ungodly and for s . . . . 1 Tim 1:9
the world to save s . . . . 1 Tim 1:15
separate from s . . . . Heb 7:26
such hostility from s . . . . Heb 12:3
things which ungodly s . . . . . . Jude 15

SINS

'If a person s . . . . Lev 4:2
s unintentionally in regard . . Lev 5:15
of the s of Jeroboam . . . . . 1 Kin 14:16
my iniquities and s . . . . Job 13:23
from presumptuous s . . . . Ps 19:13
the s of my youth . . . . Ps 25:7
pain, and forgive all my s . . . Ps 25:18
Hide Your face from my s . . . . Ps 51:9
s are not hidden from You . . . . Ps 69:5
atonement for our s . . . . Ps 79:9
You, our secret s . . . . Ps 90:8
but he who s against . . . . Prov 8:36
but love covers all s . . . . . . Prov 10:12
despises his neighbor s . . . Prov 14:21
s against his own life . . . . . . Prov 20:2
s have hidden His face . . . . Is 59:2
your s have withheld good . . . Jer 5:25
He will uncover your s . . . . . Lam 4:22
the soul who s shall . . . . Ezek 18:4
to make an end of s . . . . Dan 9:24
His people from their s . . . . . Matt 1:21
Jordan, confessing their s . . . Matt 3:6
power on earth to forgive s . . Matt 9:6
if your brother s . . . . Matt 18:15
for the remission of s . . . . . Matt 26:28
for the remission of s . . . . Mark 1:4
forgive s but God alone . . . . . Mark 2:7
for the remission of s . . . . Luke 3:3

on earth to forgive *s* .... Luke 5:24
brother *s* against you ...... Luke 17:3
that you will die in your *s* .. John 8:24
I take away their *s* .... Rom 11:27
s according to the .... 1 Cor 15:3
are still in your *s* .... 1 Cor 15:17
who gave Himself for our *s* ... Gal 1:4
the forgiveness of *s* .... Eph 1:7
blood, the forgiveness of *s* ... Col 1:14
s are clearly evident ...... 1 Tim 5:24
by Himself purged our *s* ..... Heb 1:3
once to bear the *s* .... Heb 9:28
one sacrifice for *s* forever .. Heb 10:12
cover a multitude of *s* .... James 5:20
that we, having died to *s* ... 1 Pet 2:24
If we confess our *s* .... 1 John 1:9
propitiation for our *s* ...... 1 John 2:2
s are forgiven you .... 1 John 2:12
Whoever *s* has neither ..... 1 John 3:6
He who *s* is of the devil .... 1 John 3:8
propitiation for our *s* ..... 1 John 4:10
you share in her *s* .... Rev 18:4

SION
See ZION
Name given to all or part of Mt. Hermon, Deut 4:48

SISERA
Canaanite commander of Jabin's army; slain by Jael, Judg 4:2–22

SISTER
Please say you are my *s* ... Gen 12:13
And he said, "She is my *s* .. Gen 26:7
of David had a lovely *s* ... 2 Sam 13:1
are my mother and my *s* ... Job 17:14
fair is your love, my *s* ..... Song 4:10
We have a little *s* .... Song 8:8
treacherous *s* Judah saw it .... Jer 3:7
Your elder *s* is Samaria ... Ezek 16:46
is My brother and *s* .... Matt 12:50
You not care that my *s* ... Luke 10:40
loved Martha and her *s* .... John 11:5
to you Phoebe our *s* .... Rom 16:1
s is not under bondage .... 1 Cor 7:15

SIT
he shall *s* on my throne .... 1 Kin 1:13
Those who *s* in the .... Ps 69:12
"Come down and *s* .... Is 47:1
"Why do we *s* still .... Jer 8:14
but to *s* on My right ...... Matt 20:23
and the Pharisees *s* .... Matt 23:2
Grant us that we may *s* .. Mark 10:37
"*S* at My right hand ..... Mark 12:36
those who *s* in darkness ... Luke 1:79
s down in the lowest ..... Luke 14:10
"*S* at My right hand .... Heb 1:13
say to him, "You *s* .... James 2:3
I will grant to *s* .... Rev 3:21
heart, 'I *s* as queen .... Rev 18:7

SITS
God *s* on His holy .... Ps 47:8
It is He who *s* above .... Is 40:22
so that he *s* as God .... 2 Thess 2:4
Him who *s* on the throne ..... Rev 4:9
harlot who *s* on many ...... Rev 17:1
where the harlot *s* .... Rev 17:15

SITTING
Eli the priest was *s* on .... 1 Sam 1:9
LORD *s* on His throne ..... 1 Kin 22:19
LORD *s* on His throne .... 2 Chr 18:18
You know my *s* down and ... Ps 139:2
s on a donkey, a colt, the ... Matt 21:5
see the Son of Man *s* .... Mark 14:62
s on a donkey's colt ...... John 12:15
two angels in white *s* ..... John 20:12
where Christ is, *s* .... Col 3:1
I saw twenty-four elders *s* .... Rev 4:4
a woman *s* on a scarlet ..... Rev 17:3

SIX
S days you shall gather it, .. Ex 16:26
S days you shall labor .... Ex 20:9

SKIES
thick clouds of the *s* ..... 2 Sam 22:12
have you spread out the *s* .. Job 37:18
the *s* sent out a sound .... Ps 77:17
and is lifted up to the *s* .... Jer 51:9

SKILL
hand forget its *s* .... Ps 137:5
nor favor to men of *s* .... Eccl 9:11
them knowledge and *s* .... Dan 1:17
forth to give you *s* .... Dan 9:22

SKILLFUL
Esau was a *s* hunter, a .... Gen 25:27
a *s* player on the harp ... 1 Sam 16:16
all types of *s* men for .... 1 Chr 22:15
s work a man is envied ...... Eccl 4:4
the hands of a *s* workman .. Song 7:1
send for *s* wailing women .... Jer 9:17
who are *s* to destroy .... Ezek 21:31

SKILLFULNESS
guided them by the *s* .... Ps 78:72

SKIN
God made tunics of *s* .... Gen 3:21
s of his face shone while .... Ex 34:29
LORD and said, "*S* .... Job 2:4
sewn sackcloth over my *s* .. Job 16:15
have escaped by the *s* ...... Job 19:20
My bones cling to my *s* ..... Ps 102:5
nation tall and smooth of *s* .... Is 18:2
Ethiopian change his *s* ..... Jer 13:23
s is hot as an oven .... Lam 5:10
who strip the *s* from My .... Mic 3:2

SKINS
she put the *s* of the kids ... Gen 27:16

SKIP
He makes them also *s* .... Ps 29:6

SKIPPING
upon the mountains, *s* ...... Song 2:8

SKULL
to say, Place of a *S* .... Matt 27:33

SKY
the faithful witness in the *s* .. Ps 89:37
weather, for the *s* is red .... Matt 16:2
stars of the *s* in multitude .. Heb 11:12
s receded as a scroll .... Rev 6:14

SLACK
He will not be *s* .... Deut 7:10
s hand becomes poor ...... Prov 10:4
The Lord is not *s* .... 2 Pet 3:9

SLAIN
s his thousands .... 1 Sam 18:7
beauty of Israel is *s* .... 2 Sam 1:19
the dead, like the *s* .... Ps 88:5
and all who were *s* .... Prov 7:26
I shall be *s* in the .... Prov 22:13
s men are not *s* .... Is 22:2
no more cover her *s* .... Is 26:21
and the *s* of the LORD .... Is 66:16
and night for the *s* .... Jer 9:1
Those *s* by the sword .... Lam 4:9
the prophets, I have *s* .... Hos 6:5
is the Lamb who was *s* ..... Rev 5:12

SLANDER
s your own mother's .... Ps 50:20
and whoever spreads *s* .... Prov 10:18

SLANDERERS
be reverent, not *s* .... 1 Tim 3:11
unforgiving, *s* .... 2 Tim 3:3
in behavior, not *s* .... Titus 2:3

SLANDEROUSLY
as we are *s* reported .... Rom 3:8

SLAUGHTER
as sheep for the *s* .... Ps 44:22
led as a lamb to the *s* .... Is 53:7
but the Valley of *S* .... Jer 7:32
lamb brought to the *s* .... Jer 11:19
"Feed the flock for *s* .... Zech 11:4
led as a sheep to the *s* ...... Acts 8:32
as sheep for the *s* .... Rom 8:36

SLAVE
that you were a *s* .... Deut 15:15
first shall be *s* of all ...... Mark 10:44
commits sin is a *s* .... John 8:34
you called while a *s* .... 1 Cor 7:21
there is neither *s* nor free .... Gal 3:28
you are no longer a *s* .... Gal 4:7
s nor free, but Christ is all ... Col 3:11

SLAVES
here we are, my lord's *s* ... Gen 44:16
they shall not be sold as *s* .. Lev 25:42
free his male and female *s* .. Jer 34:10
should no longer be *s* .... Rom 6:6
though you were *s* .... Rom 6:17
your members as *s* .... Rom 6:19
having become *s* of God ... Rom 6:22
do not become *s* .... 1 Cor 7:23
whether *s* or free .... 1 Cor 12:13
are *s* of corruption .... 2 Pet 2:19

SLAY
s the righteous .... Gen 18:25
s a righteous nation .... Gen 20:4
Evil shall *s* the .... Ps 34:21
Oh, that You would *s* .... Ps 139:19
s them before me .... Luke 19:27

SLEEP
God caused a deep *s* .... Gen 2:21
Jacob awoke from his *s* ... Gen 28:16
him to *s* on her knees ..... Judg 16:19
the night, when deep *s* ...... Job 4:13
my eyes, lest I *s* .... Ps 13:3
Why do You *s* .... Ps 44:23
have sunk into their *s* .... Ps 76:5
they are like a *s* .... Ps 90:5
neither slumber nor *s* .... Ps 121:4
He gives His beloved *s* ...... Ps 127:2
I will not give *s* .... Ps 132:4
s will be sweet .... Prov 3:24
For they do not *s* .... Prov 4:16
A little *s* .... Prov 6:10
Do not love *s* .... Prov 20:13
a little *s*, a little slumber .. Prov 24:33
The *s* of a laboring .... Eccl 5:12
I *s*, but my heart is awake .. Song 5:2
the spirit of deep *s* .... Is 29:10
Also his *s* went from .... Dan 6:18
I was in a deep *s* .... Dan 8:18
him were heavy with *s* .... Luke 9:32
them, "Why do you *s* ..... Luke 22:46
He was overcome by *s* .... Acts 20:9
time to awake out of *s* .... Rom 13:11
among you, and many *s* .. 1 Cor 11:30
We shall not all *s* .... 1 Cor 15:51
"Awake, you who *s* .... Eph 5:14
with Him those who *s* ... 1 Thess 4:14
Therefore let us not *s* ..... 1 Thess 5:6

SLEEPERS
gently the lips of *s* .... Song 7:9

SLEEPING
or perhaps he is *s* .... 1 Kin 18:27
is not dead, but *s* .... Matt 9:24
"Are you still *s* .... Matt 26:45
suddenly, he find you *s* ... Mark 13:36
that night Peter was *s* ...... Acts 12:6

SLEEPLESSNESS
in labors, in *s* .... 2 Cor 6:5
and toil, in *s* often .... 2 Cor 11:27

SLEEPS
wise son; he who *s* .... Prov 10:5
"Our friend Lazarus *s* .... John 11:11

SLEPT
I lay down and *s* .... Ps 3:5
but while men *s* .... Matt 13:25

SLIGHTED
is the one who is *s* .... Prov 12:9

s shall come from afar .... Is 60:4
"Has Israel no s .... Jer 49:1
The precious s of Zion ...... Lam 4:2
eat their s in your midst .... Ezek 5:10
'You are the s .... Hos 1:10
He will purify the s .... Mal 3:3
to him, "Then the s .... Matt 17:26
A man had two s, and ..... Matt 21:28
be forgiven the s of men .. Mark 3:28
and you will be s .... Luke 6:35
that you may become s ... John 12:36
You are s of the .... Acts 3:25
called s of the living God ... Rom 9:26
and you shall be My s ..... 2 Cor 6:18
who are of faith are s .... Gal 3:7
the adoption as s .... Gal 4:5
because you are s .... Gal 4:6
us to adoption as s by Jesus .. Eph 1:5
You are all s of light ..... 1 Thess 5:5
in bringing many s .... Heb 2:10
speaks to you as to s .... Heb 12:5
illegitimate and not s .... Heb 12:8

SONS OF GOD
s saw the daughters of men .. Gen 6:2
s came to present .... Job 1:6
all the s shouted for .... Job 38:7
for they shall be called s ..... Matt 5:9
to the angels and are s .... Luke 20:36
Spirit of God, these are s ... Rom 8:14
for the revealing of the s .... Rom 8:19
For you are all s .... Gal 3:26

SOON
for it is s cut off .... Ps 90:10
s forgot His works .... Ps 106:13

SOOTHED
or bound up, or s .... Is 1:6

SOOTHSAYERS
your dreamers, your s, or .... Jer 27:9
A sword is against the s .... Jer 50:36
the s cannot declare to the .. Dan 2:27

SORCERER
omens, or a s .... Deut 18:10
But Elymas the s .... Acts 13:8

SORCERERS
soothsayers, or your s .... Jer 27:9
outside are dogs and s ..... Rev 22:15

SORCERESS
shall not permit a s .... Ex 22:18

SORCERY
For there is no s .... Num 23:23
idolatry, s .... Gal 5:20

SORES
and putrefying s .... Is 1:6
Lazarus, full of s .... Luke 16:20

SORROW
multiply your s .... Gen 3:16
s dances before him .... Job 41:22
in my soul, having s .... Ps 13:2
s is continually .... Ps 38:17
I found trouble and s .... Ps 116:3
And He adds no s .... Prov 10:22
the heart may s .... Prov 14:13
S is better than .... Eccl 7:3
Therefore remove s .... Eccl 11:10
and desperate s .... Is 17:11
you shall cry for s .... Is 65:14
to see labor and s .... Jer 20:18
Your s is incurable .... Jer 30:15
added grief to my s .... Jer 45:3
gather those who s .... Zeph 3:18
them sleeping from s ..... Luke 22:45
s has filled your .... John 16:6
s will be turned .... John 16:20
that I have great s .... Rom 9:2
s produces repentance ..... 2 Cor 7:10
lest I should have s .... Phil 2:27
s as others who have .... 1 Thess 4:13
no more death, nor s .... Rev 21:4

SORROWFUL
am a woman of s spirit ... 1 Sam 1:15
But I am poor and s .... Ps 69:29
For all his days are s .... Eccl 2:23
replenished every s .... Jer 31:25
were exceedingly s .... Matt 17:23
saying, he went away s ... Matt 19:22
soul is exceedingly s .... Matt 26:38
and went away s .... Mark 10:22
and you will be s .... John 16:20
if I make you s .... 2 Cor 2:2
and I may be less s .... Phil 2:28

SORROWS
the s of Sheol .... 2 Sam 22:6
s God distributes .... Job 21:17
s shall be multiplied .... Ps 16:4
by men, a Man of s .... Is 53:3
are the beginning of s ..... Matt 24:8
through with many s .... 1 Tim 6:10

SORRY
s that He had made man ..... Gen 6:6
who will be s for you .... Is 51:19
And the king was s .... Matt 14:9
For you were made s .... 2 Cor 7:9

SOSTHENES
Ruler of the synagogue at Corinth, Acts 18:17
—— Paul's Christian brother, 1 Cor 1:1

SOUGHT
I s the LORD .... Ps 34:4
whole heart I have s .... Ps 119:10
s the one I love .... Song 3:1
shall be called S Out .... Is 62:12
So I s for a man .... Ezek 22:30
s what was lost .... Ezek 34:4
s favor from Him .... Hos 12:4
LORD, and have not s .... Zeph 1:6
s it diligently .... Heb 12:17

SOUL
s enter their council .... Gen 49:6
with all your s .... Deut 6:5
was knit to the s .... 1 Sam 18:1
your heart and your s .... 1 Chr 22:19
"My s loathes my life .... Job 10:1
as you do, if your s .... Job 16:4
s draws near the Pit .... Job 33:22
will not leave my s .... Ps 16:10
converting the s .... Ps 19:7
He restores my s .... Ps 23:3
s shall make its boast .... Ps 34:2
s shall be joyful .... Ps 35:9
you cast down, O my s .... Ps 42:5
s silently waits .... Ps 62:1
He has done for my s .... Ps 66:16
Let my s live .... Ps 119:175
s knows very well .... Ps 139:14
No one cares for my s .... Ps 142:4
so destroys his own s ...... Prov 6:32
me wrongs his own s ...... Prov 8:36
it is not good for a s .... Prov 19:2
A satisfied s loathes .... Prov 27:7
When You make His s .... Is 53:10
s delight itself .... Is 55:2
and your s shall live .... Is 55:3
you have heard, O my s ...... Jer 4:19
the s of the father as .... Ezek 18:4
the proud, his s .... Hab 2:4
able to destroy both s ..... Matt 10:28
and loses his own s .... Matt 16:26
with all your s .... Matt 22:37
"My s magnifies the Lord .. Luke 1:46
through your own s also ... Luke 2:35
And I will say to my s .... Luke 12:19
Now My s is troubled ..... John 12:27
not leave my s in Hades .... Acts 2:27
of one heart and one s ...... Acts 4:32
your whole spirit, s ...... 1 Thess 5:23
to the saving of the s ...... Heb 10:39
his way will save a s .... James 5:20
which war against the s .... 1 Pet 2:11
his righteous s .... 2 Pet 2:8
health, just as your s .... 3 John 2

SOULS
See AFFLICT YOUR SOULS
and will save the s .... Ps 72:13
and he who wins s .... Prov 11:30
s shall be like a .... Jer 31:12
who made our very s .... Jer 38:16
will find rest for your s ... Matt 11:29
patience possess your s ... Luke 21:19
unsettling your s .... Acts 15:24
is able to save your s ..... James 1:21
the salvation of your s ...... 1 Pet 1:9
and bodies and s of men .... Rev 18:13
I saw the s of those who .... Rev 20:4

SOUND
He stores up s wisdom ...... Prov 2:7
s heart is life .... Prov 14:30
one rises up at the s .... Eccl 12:4
to you at the s of your cry ... Is 30:19
voice was like the s .... Ezek 43:2
s an alarm in My holy .... Joel 2:1
do not s a trumpet .... Matt 6:2
For the trumpet will s .... 1 Cor 15:52
is contrary to s doctrine ... 1 Tim 1:10
s words which you .... 2 Tim 1:13
that they may be s .... Titus 1:13
as the s of many waters .... Rev 1:15
s of their wings was like ..... Rev 9:9

SOUNDED
The first angel s .... Rev 8:7

SOUNDNESS
There is no s in my .... Ps 38:3
him this perfect s .... Acts 3:16

SOUNDS
Dreadful s are in his .... Job 15:21
a distinction in the s .... 1 Cor 14:7

SOUTH
s comes the whirlwind ...... Job 37:9
as the streams in the S ...... Ps 126:4
And to the s, 'Do not keep .... Is 43:6
the S shall become strong .. Dan 11:5
The queen of the S will ... Matt 12:42

SOW
s trouble reap .... Job 4:8
then let me s .... Job 31:8
s fields and plant .... Ps 107:37
Those who s in tears .... Ps 126:5
the wind will not s .... Eccl 11:4
Blessed are you who s .... Is 32:20
ground, and do not s .... Jer 4:3
"They s the wind .... Hos 8:7
S for yourselves .... Hos 10:12
You shall s, but not reap .... Mic 6:15
s is not made alive .... 1 Cor 15:36
they neither s nor reap ... Luke 12:24

SOWED
s tares among the wheat .. Matt 13:25

SOWER
may give seed to the s .... Is 55:10
"Behold, a s went .... Matt 13:3
a s went out to sow .... Mark 4:3
The s sows the word ...... Mark 4:14
A s went out to sow .... Luke 8:5

SOWN
shall they be s .... Is 40:24
a land not s .... Jer 2:2
"You have s much .... Hag 1:6
where you have not s ..... Matt 25:24
that was s in their hearts .. Mark 4:15
s spiritual things .... 1 Cor 9:11
It is s in weakness .... 1 Cor 15:43
of righteousness is s ...... James 3:18

SOWS
s righteousness will .... Prov 11:18
s the good seed is the ..... Matt 13:37
'One s and another .... John 4:37

s sparingly will ....2 Cor 9:6
for whatever a man *s* ....Gal 6:7

SPAN
My life *s* is gone, taken ......Is 38:12
measured heaven with a *s* ...Is 40:12

SPARE
The LORD would not *s*.....Deut 29:20
hand, but *s* his life ....Job 2:6
S the poor and needy ....Ps 72:13
I will not pity nor *s*.........Jer 13:14
say, "*S* Your people ....Joel 2:17
s them as a man spares .....Mal 3:17
He who did not *s* ....Rom 8:32
s the natural branches ....Rom 11:21
flesh, but I would *s*........1 Cor 7:28
if God did not *s*.............2 Pet 2:4

SPARES
s his rod hates his ....Prov 13:24

SPARK
the work of it as a *s* ....Is 1:31

SPARKLES
it is red, when it *s* ....Prov 23:31

SPARKS
to trouble, as the *s* ....Job 5:7
s you have kindled ....Is 50:11

SPARROW
s has found a home ....Ps 84:3
awake, and am like a *s*......Ps 102:7

SPARROWS
more value than many *s* ..Matt 10:31

SPAT
Then they *s* on Him.......Matt 27:30
in his ears, and He *s* ......Mark 7:33

SPEAK
only the word that I *s*.....Num 22:35
s just once more ....Judg 6:39
s good words to them ......1 Kin 12:7
oh, that God would *s*.........Job 11:5
Will you *s* wickedly ....Job 13:7
For God may *s* in one ......Job 33:14
Will he *s* softly to ....Job 41:3
Do not *s* in the ....Prov 23:9
and a time to *s* ....Eccl 3:7
If they do not *s*................Is 8:20
tongue He will *s*.............Is 28:11
s anymore in His name ......Jer 20:9
and *s* comfort to her ....Hos 2:14
at the end it will *s*............Hab 2:3
s each man the truth........Zech 8:16
But only *s* a word, and my ..Matt 8:8
or what you should *s*......Matt 10:19
it is not you who *s* ....Matt 10:20
to you when all men *s* .....Luke 6:26
s what We know and ......John 3:11
"I who *s* to you am He .....John 4:26
s what I have seen ....John 8:38
The words that I *s* to .....John 14:10
He hears He will *s*.........John 16:13
Spirit and began to *s* ....Acts 2:4
Do all *s* with tongues.....1 Cor 12:30
I *s* with the tongues ....1 Cor 13:1
I would rather *s* ....1 Cor 14:19
So *s* and so do as ....James 2:12

SPEAKING
s your own words ....Is 58:13
while they are still *s* ....Is 65:24
a proof of Christ *s* ....2 Cor 13:3
envy, and all evil *s* ....1 Pet 2:1

SPEAKS
to face, as a man *s* ....Ex 33:11
this day that God *s* ....Deut 5:24
day that I am He who *s* ....Is 52:6
the one who *s* uprightly ...Amos 5:10
He whom God has sent *s* ..John 3:34
When he *s* a lie ....John 8:44
he who *s* with tongues ....1 Cor 14:5
If anyone *s* in a tongue ...1 Cor 14:27
he being dead still *s*........Heb 11:4

of sprinkling that *s*........Heb 12:24
s evil of a brother ....James 4:11

SPEAR
lay hold on bow and *s*.........Jer 6:23
His side with a *s* ....John 19:34

SPEARS
whose teeth are *s* ....Ps 57:4
and their *s* into ....Is 2:4
pruning hooks into *s* ....Joel 3:10

SPECIAL
you shall be a *s* treasure .....Ex 19:5
you to be His *s* people .....Deut 26:18
Israel for His *s* treasure ......Ps 135:4
His own *s* people ....Titus 2:14
nation, His own *s* people ....1 Pet 2:9

SPECK
do you look at the *s*..........Matt 7:3

SPECTACLE
and make you a *s* ....Nah 3:6
we have been made a *s*.....1 Cor 4:9
He made a public *s* ....Col 2:15
you were made a *s* ....Heb 10:33

SPEECH
one language and one *s*.....Gen 11:1
drop as the rain, my *s* .....Deut 32:2
s settled on them as........Job 29:22
There is no *s* nor ....Ps 19:3
s is not becoming ....Prov 17:7
your *s* shall be low ....Is 29:4
a people of obscure *s* ....Is 33:19
not understand My *s*.......John 8:43
s deceive the hearts ....Rom 16:18
and his *s* contemptible ...2 Cor 10:10
I am untrained in *s*........2 Cor 11:6
s always be with grace ....Col 4:6

SPEECHLESS
your mouth for the *s*.......Prov 31:8
And he was *s* ....Matt 22:12

SPEED
they shall come with *s* ....Is 5:26

SPEEDILY
judgment be executed *s* ....Ezra 7:26
to me, deliver me *s*...........Ps 31:2
I call, answer me *s* ....Ps 102:2

SPEND
Why do you *s* money for......Is 55:2
whatever more you *s* .....Luke 10:35
I will very gladly *s*........2 Cor 12:15
amiss, that you may *s* .....James 4:3

SPENT
strength shall be *s* ....Lev 26:20
For my life is *s* ....Ps 31:10
in vain, I have *s* ....Is 49:4
"But when he had *s* ......Luke 15:14

SPICES
s for the anointing oil ....Ex 25:6
s in great quantity ....1 Kin 10:10
that its *s* may flow out .....Song 4:16
and Salome bought *s*.......Mark 16:1
s which they had ....Luke 24:1
strips of linen with the *s* ..John 19:40

SPIDER
s skillfully grasps ....Prov 30:28

SPIES
to them, "You are *s* ....Gen 42:9
men who had been *s* ....Josh 6:23
s who pretended ....Luke 20:20

SPIKENARD
fragrant henna with *s* ......Song 4:13
of very costly oil of *s*.......Mark 14:3

SPIN
neither toil nor *s*............Matt 6:28

SPINDLE
her hand holds the *s*.......Prov 31:19

SPIRIT
See HOLY SPIRIT; FILLED WITH THE HOLY SPIRIT; UNCLEAN SPIRIT

S shall not strive ....Gen 6:3
the breath of the *s* of life ....Gen 7:22
filled with the *s* of wisdom ...Ex 28:3
and everyone whose *s* ....Ex 35:21
S that is upon you ....Num 11:17
And the *S* rested upon .....Num 11:26
LORD would put His *S*......Num 11:29
he has a different *s* ....Num 14:24
in whom is the *S* ....Num 27:18
God sent a *s* of ill will ......Judg 9:23
portion of your *s* ....2 Kin 2:9
I will send a *s* upon him ...2 Kin 19:7
there was no more *s*..........2 Chr 9:4
s came forward and ....2 Chr 18:20
also gave Your good *S* ....Neh 9:20
against them by Your *S* .....Neh 9:30
Then a *s* passed before ....Job 4:15
care has preserved my *s* ...Job 10:12
And whose *s* came from .....Job 26:4
hand I commit my *s*............Ps 31:5
Your Holy *S* from me ....Ps 51:11
s was not faithful ....Ps 78:8
You send forth Your *S* ....Ps 104:30
Your *S* is good ....Ps 143:10
I will pour out my *s* on ....Prov 1:23
The *s* of a man is the ....Prov 20:27
Who knows the *s* ....Eccl 3:21
s will return to God ....Eccl 12:7
night, yes, by my *s* ....Is 26:9
out on you the *s*...................Is 29:10
are flesh, and not *s* ....Is 31:3
S has gathered them ....Is 34:16
is the life of my *s* ....Is 38:16
I have put My *S* ....Is 42:1
and His *S* have sent Me ....Is 48:16
s would fail before Me ....Is 57:16
S entered me when He ....Ezek 2:2
the *S* lifted me up ....Ezek 3:12
who follow their own *s* ....Ezek 13:3
new heart and a new *s*......Ezek 18:31
be feeble, every *s* ....Ezek 21:7
I will put My *S* ....Ezek 36:27
in him is the *S* ....Dan 4:8
as an excellent *s* ....Dan 5:12
walk in a false *s* ....Mic 2:11
and forms the *s* ....Zech 12:1
with child of the Holy *S*.......Matt 1:18
"Blessed are the poor in *s* ...Matt 5:3
I will put My *S* ....Matt 12:18
S descending upon Him ....Mark 1:10
Immediately the *S* ....Mark 1:12
s indeed is willing ....Mark 14:38
go before Him in the *s*..........Luke 1:17
in the power of the *S* ....Luke 4:14
manner of *s* you are of ....Luke 9:55
When an unclean *s* goes ..Luke 11:24
against the Holy *S* ....Luke 12:10
hands I commit My *s* ....Luke 23:46
they had seen a *s* ....Luke 24:37
s does not have flesh ....Luke 24:39
I saw the *S* descending ......John 1:32
born of water and the *S* ....John 3:5
God is *S* ....John 4:24
I speak to you are *s* ....John 6:63
He groaned in the *s*.............John 11:33
He was troubled in *s* ....John 13:21
all filled with the Holy *S*.........Acts 2:4
but if a *s* or an angel ....Acts 23:9
to the *S* of holiness, by the ..Rom 1:4
whom I serve with my *s* ....Rom 1:9
but according to the *S* ....Rom 8:1
according to the *S* ....Rom 8:5
the flesh but in the *S* ....Rom 8:9
s that we are children ....Rom 8:16
what the mind of the *S*.........Rom 8:27
to us through His *S* ....1 Cor 2:10
gifts, but the same *S*.............1 Cor 12:4
in a tongue, my *s* ....1 Cor 14:14
but the *S* gives life ....2 Cor 3:6
Now the Lord is the *S*..........2 Cor 3:17
we have the same *s* ....2 Cor 4:13
Having begun in the *S* ....Gal 3:3

STAGGER
and He makes them *s* ...... Job 12:25
they will drink and *s* .... Jer 25:16

STAGGERS
as a drunken man *s* .... Is 19:14

STAKES
s will ever be removed .... Is 33:20

STALLS
be no herd in the *s* .... Hab 3:17

STAMMERERS
s will be ready .... Is 32:4

STAMMERING
For with *s* lips and .... Is 28:11
s tongue that you .... Is 33:19

STAMPING
At the noise of the *s* .... Jer 47:3

STAND
where you *s* is holy ground .... Ex 3:5
S still, and see the .... Ex 14:13
one shall be able to *s* .... Deut 7:24
"Who is able to *s* .... 1 Sam 6:20
took a *s* for the covenant .. 2 Kin 23:3
we are not able to *s* .... Ezra 10:13
but it does not *s* .... Job 8:15
lives, and He shall *s* .... Job 19:25
ungodly shall not *s* .... Ps 1:5
Why do You *s* afar off .... Ps 10:1
Or who may *s* in His .... Ps 24:3
the world *s* in awe of Him .... Ps 33:8
Who will *s* up for me .... Ps 94:16
and let an accuser *s* .... Ps 109:6
They *s* fast forever .... Ps 111:8
he will not *s* before .... Prov 22:29
Do not take your *s* .... Eccl 8:3
"It shall not *s* .... Is 7:7
"*S* in the ways and .... Jer 6:16
not lack a man to *s* .... Jer 35:19
whose words will *s* .... Jer 44:28
s in the gap before Me .... Ezek 22:30
and it shall *s* .... Dan 2:44
but she shall not *s* .... Dan 11:17
Who can *s* before His .... Nah 1:6
s on the Mount of Olives ... Zech 14:4
And who can *s* when He ...... Mal 3:2
against itself will not *s* .... Matt 12:25
that kingdom cannot *s* ..... Mark 3:24
how will his kingdom *s* ... Luke 11:18
why do you *s* gazing up ..... Acts 1:11
you *s* is holy ground .... Acts 7:33
this grace in which we *s* .... Rom 5:2
he will be made to *s* .... Rom 14:4
Watch, *s* fast in the ...... 1 Cor 16:13
for by faith you *s* .... 2 Cor 1:24
S fast therefore in the .... Gal 5:1
having done all, to *s* .... Eph 6:13
S therefore .... Eph 6:14
s fast in the Lord .... Phil 4:1
now we live, if you *s* ..... 1 Thess 3:8
of God in which you *s* ..... 1 Pet 5:12
Behold, I *s* at the .... Rev 3:20

STANDARD
LORD will lift up a *s* .... Is 59:19
Set up the *s* toward .... Jer 4:6

STANDING
the Lord *s* by the altar ..... Amos 9:1
the LORD, and Satan *s* .... Zech 3:1
they love to pray *s* .... Matt 6:5
and saw others *s* idle .... Matt 20:3
s here who will not taste .... Mark 9:1
the woman *s* in the midst .... John 8:9
and the Son of Man *s* .... Acts 7:56
the Judge is *s* at the door .. James 5:9
Then I saw an angel *s* ..... Rev 19:17

STANDS
Nor *s* in the path of sinners .... Ps 1:1
counsel of the LORD *s* .... Ps 33:11
my heart *s* in awe of ...... Ps 119:161
The LORD *s* up to plead .... Is 3:13

there *s* One among you ..... John 1:26
him who thinks he *s* ...... 1 Cor 10:12
foundation of God *s* .... 2 Tim 2:19

STAR
S shall come out of .... Num 24:17
For we have seen His *s* ...... Matt 2:2
for one *s* differs from ..... 1 Cor 15:41
give him the morning *s* ...... Rev 2:28
And a great *s* fell .... Rev 8:10
Bright and Morning *S* ...... Rev 22:16

STARS
He made the *s* also .... Gen 1:16
as the *s* of the heaven .... Gen 22:17
s bowed down to me .... Gen 37:9
s are not pure in His .... Job 25:5
when the morning *s* .... Job 38:7
the moon and the *s* .... Ps 8:3
s to rule by night, for His .... Ps 136:9
praise Him, all you *s* .... Ps 148:3
the *s* will diminish their ..... Joel 3:15
the *s* of heaven will fall .. Mark 13:25
born as many as the *s* ..... Heb 11:12
wandering *s* for whom .... Jude 13
in His right hand seven *s* .... Rev 1:16
a garland of twelve *s* .... Rev 12:1

STARVED
His strength is *s* .... Job 18:12

STATE
man at his best *s* .... Ps 39:5
us in our lowly *s* .... Ps 136:23
and the last *s* of that ...... Matt 12:45
learned in whatever *s* .... Phil 4:11

STATURE
add one cubit to his *s* ...... Matt 6:27
in wisdom and *s* .... Luke 2:52
add one cubit to his *s* ..... Luke 12:25
for he was of short *s* ...... Luke 19:3
the measure of the *s* .... Eph 4:13

STATUTE
It shall be a *s* forever to .... Ex 27:21
be theirs for a perpetual *s* .... Ex 29:9
shall be a perpetual *s* .... Lev 3:17
it shall be a *s* forever ...... Lev 23:14
For this is a *s* for Israel .... Ps 81:4
to establish a royal *s* .... Dan 6:7

STATUTES
shall therefore keep My *s* .... Lev 18:5
My ways, to keep My *s* .... 1 Kin 3:14
not put away His *s* from ...... Ps 18:22
the *s* of the LORD are .... Ps 19:8
Teach me Your *s* .... Ps 119:12
s have been my songs ...... Ps 119:54
observe Your *s* .... Ps 119:117
not walked in My *s* .... Ezek 5:6
did not walk in My *s* ...... Ezek 20:21

STAY
her feet would not *s* .... Prov 7:11
S here and watch with .... Matt 26:38
for today I must *s* .... Luke 19:5
the time of your *s* .... 1 Pet 1:17

STEADFAST
yes, you could be *s* .... Job 11:15
O God, my heart is *s* .... Ps 57:7
their heart was not *s* .... Ps 78:37
his heart is *s* .... Ps 112:7
God, and *s* forever .... Dan 6:26
brethren, be *s* .... 1 Cor 15:58
faith, grounded and *s* .... Col 1:23
angels proved *s* .... Heb 2:2
of our confidence *s* .... Heb 3:14
soul, both sure and *s* ...... Heb 6:19
Resist him, *s* in the .... 1 Pet 5:9

STEADFASTLY
s set His face to go .... Luke 9:51
And they continued *s* .... Acts 2:42
continuing *s* in .... Rom 12:12

STEADFASTNESS
good order and the *s* .... Col 2:5
from your own *s* .... 2 Pet 3:17

STEADILY
could not look *s* .... 2 Cor 3:13

STEADY
and his hands were *s* .... Ex 17:12

STEAL
"You shall not *s* .... Ex 20:15
Will you *s* .... Jer 7:9
s My words every one .... Jer 23:30
thieves break in and *s* .... Matt 6:19
night and *s* Him away .... Matt 27:64
murder, 'Do not *s* .... Mark 10:19
not come except to *s* ...... John 10:10
a man should not *s* .... Rom 2:21
Let him who stole *s* .... Eph 4:28

STEEP
s places shall fall .... Ezek 38:20
waters poured down a *s* ...... Mic 1:4
violently down the *s* .... Matt 8:32

STEM
forth a Rod from the *s* .... Is 11:1

STENCH
there will be a *s* .... Is 3:24
this time there is a *s* .... John 11:39

STEP
there is but a *s* .... 1 Sam 20:3
s has turned from the .... Job 31:7

STEPHEN
One of the first seven deacons, Acts 6:1–8
Falsely accused by Jews; gives defense, Acts 6:9—7:53
Becomes first Christian martyr, Acts 7:54–60

STEPS
has held fast to His *s* ...... Job 23:11
and count all my *s* .... Job 31:4
and He sees all his *s* .... Job 34:21
Uphold my *s* in Your .... Ps 17:5
The *s* of a good man .... Ps 37:23
of his *s* shall slide .... Ps 37:31
and established my *s* .... Ps 40:2
hide, they mark my *s* .... Ps 56:6
s had nearly slipped .... Ps 73:2
Direct my *s* by Your .... Ps 119:133
s will not be hindered .... Prov 4:12
the LORD directs his *s* ...... Prov 16:9
A man's *s* are of the .... Prov 20:24
to direct his own *s* .... Jer 10:23
should follow His *s* .... 1 Pet 2:21

STEWARD
faithful and wise *s* .... Luke 12:42
you can no longer be *s* .... Luke 16:2
commended the unjust *s* ... Luke 16:8
be blameless, as a *s* .... Titus 1:7

STEWARDS
of Christ and *s* .... 1 Cor 4:1
one another, as good *s* ..... 1 Pet 4:10

STEWARDSHIP
entrusted with a *s* .... 1 Cor 9:17

STICK
and his bones *s* .... Job 33:21
and *s* out the tongue .... Is 57:4
'For Joseph, the *s* ...... Ezek 37:16

STICKS
a man gathering *s* .... Num 15:32
was there gathering *s* .... 1 Kin 17:10
And the *s* on which ...... Ezek 37:20

STIFF
rebellion and your *s* ...... Deut 31:27
do not speak with a *s* .... Ps 75:5

STIFF-NECKED
Now do not be *s* .... 2 Chr 30:8
"You *s* and uncircumcised .. Acts 7:51

STILL
on your bed, and be *s* .... Ps 4:4

SURE
s your sin will find .... Num 32:23
build Him a *s* house .... 1 Sam 2:35
but no man is *s* .... Job 24:22
testimony of the LORD is *s* .... Ps 19:7
all His precepts are *s* .... Ps 111:7
call and election *s* .... 2 Pet 1:10

SURETY
Be *s* for Your servant ..... Ps 119:122
one who hates being *s* .... Prov 11:15
Jesus has become a *s* .... Heb 7:22

SURROUND
But you shall *s* .... 2 Kin 11:8
LORD, mercy shall *s* .... Ps 32:10

SURROUNDED
the waves of death *s* ...... 2 Sam 22:5
The pangs of death *s* .... Ps 18:4
The pains of death *s* .... Ps 116:3
All nations *s* me .... Ps 118:10
their own deeds have *s* ...... Hos 7:2
and the floods *s* .... Jon 2:3
also, since we are *s* .... Heb 12:1

SURVIVOR
was no refugee or *s* .... Lam 2:22

SUSANNA
Believing woman ministering to Christ, Luke 8:2, 3

SUSPICIONS
reviling, evil *s* .... 1 Tim 6:4

SUSTAIN
You will *s* him on his .... Ps 41:3
of a man will *s* .... Prov 18:14
S me with cakes of .... Song 2:5

SUSTAINED
Forty years You *s* them ..... Neh 9:21
I awoke, for the LORD *s* me ...... Ps 3:5
and My own fury, it *s* Me ..... Is 63:5

SWADDLING
thick darkness its *s* .... Job 38:9
Him in *s* cloths .... Luke 2:7

SWALLOW
like a flying *s* .... Prov 26:2
Like a crane or a *s* .... Is 38:14
s observe the time .... Jer 8:7
great fish to *s* Jonah .... Jon 1:17
a gnat and *s* a camel ...... Matt 23:24

SWALLOWED
Aaron's rod *s* up their rods ... Ex 7:12
the earth *s* them .... Ex 15:12
s me up like a monster ..... Jer 51:34
He has *s* up Israel .... Lam 2:5
"Death is *s* up in victory .. 1 Cor 15:54
s up with too much sorrow .. 2 Cor 2:7

SWEAR
shall I make you *s* .... 1 Kin 22:16
in the earth shall *s* .... Is 65:16
s oaths by the LORD .... Zeph 1:5
'You shall not *s* .... Matt 5:33
began to curse and *s* ...... Matt 26:74
because He could *s* .... Heb 6:13
my brethren, do not *s* ..... James 5:12

SWEARING
By *s* and lying .... Hos 4:2

SWEARS
he who *s* to his own .... Ps 15:4
everyone who *s* by Him ..... Ps 63:11
but whoever *s* by the ..... Matt 23:18

SWEAT
In the *s* of your face .... Gen 3:19
Then His *s* became like ... Luke 22:44

SWEET
it is a *s* aroma, an offering .. Ex 29:18
a *s* aroma to the LORD .... Lev 1:9
by fire as a *s* aroma to ..... Num 28:2
Though evil is *s* .... Job 20:12
valley shall be *s* to him .... Job 21:33
s are Your words .... Ps 119:103
my words, for they are *s* .... Ps 141:6
his fruit was *s* to my taste .. Song 2:3
for your voice is *s* .... Song 2:14
His mouth is most *s* .... Song 5:16
shall drip with *s* wine ..... Amos 9:13
but it will be as *s* .... Rev 10:9

SWEETER
"What is *s* than honey .... Judg 14:18
S also than honey and the ... Ps 19:10
s than honey to my .... Ps 119:103

SWEETNESS
'Should I cease my *s* .... Judg 9:11
called prudent, and *s* .... Prov 16:21
s of a man's friend gives ... Prov 27:9
mouth like honey in *s* .... Ezek 3:3

SWELL
thigh rot and your belly *s* .. Num 5:21
their feet did not *s* .... Neh 9:21
your heart shall *s* with joy .... Is 60:5

SWELLING
they speak great *s* .... 2 Pet 2:18

SWEPT
his army shall be *s* away .. Dan 11:26
he finds it empty, *s* .... Matt 12:44

SWIFT
s as the eagle flies .... Deut 28:49
pass by like *s* ships .... Job 9:26
handles the bow, the *s* .... Amos 2:15
let every man be *s* .... James 1:19

SWIFTLY
His word runs very *s* .... Ps 147:15

SWIM
night I make my bed *s* .... Ps 6:6

SWINE
the *s*, though it divides ...... Lev 11:7
cast your pearls before *s* .... Matt 7:6
went into the herd of *s* ..... Matt 8:32
the pods that the *s* ate .... Luke 15:16

SWINE'S
ring of gold in a *s* snout ... Prov 11:22
in the midst, eating *s* flesh ... Is 66:17

SWOON
as they *s* like the .... Lam 2:12

SWORD
See TWO-EDGED SWORD
s which turned every .... Gen 3:24
but not with your *s* .... Josh 24:12
the wicked with Your *s* ...... Ps 17:13
land by their own *s* .... Ps 44:3
my bow, nor shall my *s* .... Ps 44:6
their tongue a sharp *s* .... Ps 57:4
shall not lift up *s* .... Is 2:4
But he shall flee from the *s* .... Is 31:8
s shall be bathed .... Is 34:5
The *s* of the LORD is .... Is 34:6
And I will send a *s* .... Jer 9:16
will die by the *s* .... Ezek 7:15
'A *s*, a *s* is sharpened ...... Ezek 21:9
'A *s*, a *s* is drawn .... Ezek 21:28
Bow and *s* of battle I .... Hos 2:18
people shall die by the *s* .. Amos 9:10
not lift up *s* against nation ... Mic 4:3
"Awake, O *s* .... Zech 13:7
to bring peace but a *s* ..... Matt 10:34
for all who take the *s* ..... Matt 26:52
s will pierce through .... Luke 2:35
he does not bear the *s* ..... Rom 13:4
the *s* of the Spirit .... Eph 6:17
than any two-edged *s* .... Heb 4:12
a sharp two-edged *s* .... Rev 1:16
mouth goes a sharp *s* ...... Rev 19:15

SWORDS
yet they were drawn *s* ...... Ps 55:21
shall beat their *s* .... Is 2:4
beat their *s* into plowshares .. Mic 4:3
look, here are two *s* ...... Luke 22:38

SWORE
So I *s* in My wrath .... Ps 95:11
So I *s* in My wrath .... Heb 3:11
and *s* by Him who lives ...... Rev 10:6

SWORN
"By Myself I have *s* .... Gen 22:16
The LORD has *s* in .... Ps 132:11
I have *s* by Myself .... Is 45:23
"The LORD has *s* .... Heb 7:21

SYCAMORE
into a *s* tree to see Him .... Luke 19:4

SYCHAR
Town of Samaria; Jesus talks to woman at well here, John 4:5–39

SYMBOLIC
which things are *s* .... Gal 4:24
It was *s* for the .... Heb 9:9

SYMBOLS
I have given *s* through ..... Hos 12:10

SYMPATHIZE
Priest who cannot *s* .... Heb 4:15

SYMPATHY
My *s* is stirred .... Hos 11:8

SYNAGOGUE
See RULER OF THE SYNAGOGUE
He went into the *s* .... Luke 4:16
he was a ruler of the *s* ..... Luke 8:41
in the *s* every Sabbath ..... Acts 18:4
but are a *s* of Satan .... Rev 2:9

SYRACUSE
City visited by Paul, Acts 28:12

SYRIANS
Abraham's kindred, Gen 22:20–23; 25:20
Hostile to Israel, 2 Sam 8:11–13; 10:6–19; 1 Kin 20:1–34; 22:1–38; 2 Kin 6:8—7:7
Defeated by Assyria, 2 Kin 16:9
Destruction of, foretold, Is 17:1–3
Gospel preached to, Acts 15:23, 41

SYRO-PHOENICIAN
Daughter of, freed of demon, Mark 7:25–31

TABERAH
Israelite camp; fire destroys many there, Num 11:1–3

TABERNACLE
that is, the pattern of the *t* ... Ex 25:9
you shall make the *t* .... Ex 26:1
called it the *t* of meeting ...... Ex 33:7
did not depart from the *t* .... Ex 33:11
covered the *t* of meeting ..... Ex 40:34
t He shall hide me .... Ps 27:5
I will abide in Your *t* .... Ps 61:4
In Salem also is His *t* .... Ps 76.2
How lovely is Your *t* .... Ps 84:1
Let us go into His *t* .... Ps 132:7
quiet home, a *t* .... Is 33:20
has done violence to His *t* ... Lam 2:6
My *t* also shall be with ... Ezek 37:27
You also took up the *t* ..... Acts 7:43
and will rebuild the *t* ..... Acts 15:16
the true *t* which the Lord .... Heb 8:2
and more perfect *t* .... Heb 9:11
the temple of the *t* of the .... Rev 15:5
Behold, the *t* .... Rev 21:3

TABERNACLES
See FEAST OF TABERNACLES
T for seven days to the ...... Lev 23:34
Feast of *T* seven days ..... Deut 16:13
us make here three *t* .... Matt 17:4
Feast of *T* was at hand ...... John 7:2

TABITHA
See DORCAS

TABLE
shall also make a *t* .... Ex 25:23
prepare a *t* before me .... Ps 23:5
t become a snare .... Ps 69:22
a *t* in the wilderness .... Ps 78:19
head as He sat at the *t* ..... Matt 26:7
dogs under the *t* .... Mark 7:28
t in the Pharisee's house ... Luke 7:37
t become a snare .... Rom 11:9
of the Lord's *t* .... 1 Cor 10:21

TABLES
t are full of vomit .... Is 28:8
and overturned the *t* ...... Matt 21:12
of God and serve *t* .... Acts 6:2

TABLET
write them on the *t* .... Prov 3:3
is engraved on the *t* .... Jer 17:1

TABLETS
I will give you *t* of stone .... Ex 24:12
Cut two *t* of stone like the .... Ex 34:1
wrote on the *t* the words .... Ex 34:28
the two *t* of the Testimony .. Ex 34:29
wrote them on two *t* of .... Deut 4:13
God, not on *t* of stone ...... 2 Cor 3:3
and the *t* of the covenant .... Heb 9:4

TABOR
Scene of rally against Sisera, Judg 4:6, 12, 14

TADMOR
Trading center near Damascus, 2 Chr 8:4

TAHPANHES (or Tehaphnehes)
City of Egypt; refuge of fleeing Jews, Jer 2:16; 44:1; Ezek 30:18

TAIL
hand and take it by the *t*" ...... Ex 4:4
the head and not the *t* .... Deut 28:13
turned the foxes *t* to *t* ...... Judg 15:4
He moves his *t* like a ...... Job 40:17
t drew a third of the .... Rev 12:4

TAILS
They had *t* like scorpions, .. Rev 9:10
for their *t* are like serpents .. Rev 9:19

TAKE
You shall *t* with you seven ... Gen 7:2
T now your son, your only .. Gen 22:2
I will *t* you as My people, ... Ex 6:7
You shall not *t* the name of .. Ex 20:7
I will *t* sickness away .... Ex 23:25
t off your ornaments, that .... Ex 33:5
I will *t* away My hand ...... Ex 33:23
t us as Your inheritance ..... Ex 34:9
T heed to yourself, lest ..... Ex 34:12
shall not *t* vengeance .... Lev 19:18
to *t* the vow of a Nazirite ... Num 6:2
T heed to yourselves, lest .. Deut 4:23
You shall not *t* the name ... Deut 5:11
shall *t* oaths in His name .. Deut 6:13
add to it nor *t* away ...... Deut 12:32
T your sandal off your ..... Josh 5:15
God does not *t* away .... 2 Sam 14:14
How long shall I *t* counsel .... Ps 13:2
t Your Holy Spirit .... Ps 51:11
I will not utterly *t* from ..... Ps 89:33
His wings you shall *t* refuge .. Ps 91:4
I will *t* up the cup of .... Ps 116:13
t not the word of .... Ps 119:43
In You I *t* refuge .... Ps 141:8
in You I *t* shelter .... Ps 143:9
T firm hold of instruction, .. Prov 4:13
and *t* away all your alloy ..... Is 1:25
will *t* the heart of stone ... Ezek 36:26
t words with you .... Hos 14:2
t away your tunic, let him .. Matt 5:40
does not *t* his cross .... Matt 10:38
T My yoke upon .... Matt 11:29
t up his cross, and .... Matt 16:24
T what is yours and ...... Matt 20:14
t You in, or naked and .... Matt 25:38
and you did not *t* Me in ... Matt 25:43
T, eat; this is My body .... Matt 26:26
and *t* up his cross .... Mark 8:34
t up the cross, and .... Mark 10:21
T, eat; this is My body ... Mark 14:22
T this cup away .... Mark 14:36
t up his cross daily, and ... Luke 9:23
My life that I may *t* .... John 10:17
I urge you to *t* heart ...... Acts 27:22
T, eat; this is My body .... 1 Cor 11:24
Therefore *t* up the whole ... Eph 6:13

TAKE HEED
T to yourself and see .... Ex 10:28
'*T* to yourselves that .... Ex 19:12
T to yourself, lest you .... Ex 34:12
t to speak what the Lord .. Num 23:12
t, lest you lift your eyes .... Deut 4:19
your sons *t* to their way .... 1 Kin 2:4
T, do not turn to iniquity ... Job 36:21
T, and be quiet .... Is 7:4
t, you peoples from afar ...... Is 49:1
Everyone *t* to his neighbor ... Jer 9:4
t to your spirit .... Mal 2:15
T that you do not do .... Matt 6:1
"*T* and beware of the ...... Matt 16:6
T that you do not .... Matt 18:10
"*T* that no one deceives .... Matt 24:4
"*T* what you hear .... Mark 4:24
t; see, I have told you .... Mark 13:23
T, watch and pray .... Mark 13:33
t that the light .... Luke 11:35
"*T* and beware .... Luke 12:15
t to yourselves, lest ...... Luke 21:34
t how he builds on it ...... 1 Cor 3:10
stands *t* lest he fall .... 1 Cor 10:12
"*T* to the ministry .... Col 4:17
T to yourself and to .... 1 Tim 4:16

TAKEN
t from man He made into ... Gen 2:22
because she was *t* out of .... Gen 2:23
for out of it you were *t* ..... Gen 3:19
have you *t* us away to die ... Ex 14:11
But the LORD has *t* you .... Deut 4:20
t the wife of Uriah .... 2 Sam 12:10
and the LORD has *t* away .... Job 1:21
God has *t* away my justice .. Job 34:5
you are *t* by the words ...... Prov 6:2
He was *t* from prison .... Is 53:8
righteous is *t* away from ...... Is 57:1
of God will be *t* from ..... Matt 21:43
one will be *t* and the ...... Matt 24:40
what he has will be *t* ...... Mark 4:25
He was *t* up .... Acts 1:9
veil is *t* away in Christ ..... 2 Cor 3:14
until He is *t* out of .... 2 Thess 2:7
By faith Enoch was *t* .... Heb 11:5

TAKES
who *t* His name in vain ...... Ex 20:7
LORD *t* pleasure in those.... Ps 147:11
For the LORD *t* pleasure in ... Ps 149:4
than he who *t* a city ...... Prov 16:32
does not bear fruit He *t* .... John 15:2

TAKING
the fruit of *t* away his sin .... Is 27:9
t Him up on a high .... Luke 4:5
t the shield of faith with .... Eph 6:16
t the form of a bondservant .. Phil 2:7

TALEBEARER
not go about as a *t* .... Lev 19:16
t reveals secrets .... Prov 11:13

TALENT
went and hid your *t* ...... Matt 25:25

TALENTS
owed him ten thousand *t* .. Matt 18:24
to one he gave five *t* ...... Matt 25:15

TALITHA
T, cumi," which is .... Mark 5:41

TALK
shall *t* of them when .... Deut 6:7
t be vindicated .... Job 11:2
with unprofitable *t* .... Job 15:3
My tongue also shall *t* ...... Ps 71:24
entangle Him in His *t* ..... Matt 22:15
I will no longer *t* .... John 14:30
turned aside to idle *t* .... 1 Tim 1:6

TALKED
within us while He *t* ...... Luke 24:32

TALKERS
both idle *t* and .... Titus 1:10

TALL
and *t* as the Anakim .... Deut 2:10
to a nation *t* and .... Is 18:2

TAMAR
Wife of Er and mother of Perez and Zerah, Gen 38:6–30
——— Absalom's sister, 2 Sam 13:1–32

TAMBOURINE
They sing to the *t* .... Job 21:12
The mirth of the *t* .... Is 24:8

TAME
no man can *t* the tongue ... James 3:8

TANNER
in Joppa with Simon, a *t* ... Acts 9:43

TAPESTRY
She makes *t* for herself ... Prov 31:22

TARES
the *t* also appeared .... Matt 13:26

TARGET
You set me as Your *t* .... Job 7:20
and set me up as a *t* .... Lam 3:12

TARRY
who turns aside to *t* .... Jer 14:8
come and will not *t* .... Heb 10:37

TARSHISH
City at a great distance from Palestine, Jon 1:3
Ships of, noted in commerce, Ps 48:7

TARSUS
Paul's birthplace, Acts 21:39
Saul sent to, Acts 9:30
Visited by Barnabas, Acts 11:25

TARTAN
Sent to fight against Jerusalem, 2 Kin 18:17

TASK
your *t* in making brick both .. Ex 5:14
this burdensome *t* .... Eccl 1:13

TASKMASTERS
Therefore they set *t* over ...... Ex 1:11

TASSELS
Tell them to make *t* on ... Num 15:38
shall make *t* on the four .. Deut 22:12

TASTE
the *t* of it was like wafers ... Ex 16:31
and its *t* was like the ...... Num 11:8
Oh, *t* and see that the .... Ps 34:8
are Your words to my *t* ... Ps 119:103
was sweet to my *t* .... Song 2:3
not *t* death till they see ..... Mark 9:1
shall *t* my supper .... Luke 14:24
Do not touch, do not *t* .... Col 2:21
might *t* death for .... Heb 2:9

TASTED
But when He had *t* .... Matt 27:34
t the heavenly gift .... Heb 6:4
t the good word .... Heb 6:5
t that the Lord is .... 1 Pet 2:3

TATTENAI
Persian governor opposing the Jews, Ezra 5:3, 6

TAUGHT
O God, You have *t* .... Ps 71:17
as His counselor has *t* .... Is 40:13

the synagogue and *t* . . . . . . Mark 1:21
He *t* them many things by . . Mark 4:2
presence, and You *t* . . . . . Luke 13:26
they shall all be *t* . . . . John 6:45
but as My Father *t* . . . . John 8:28
that they *t* the people and . . . Acts 4:2
t accurately the things of . . Acts 18:25
from man, nor was I *t* . . . . Gal 1:12
and have been *t* by Him . . . . Eph 4:21
the faith, as you have been *t* . . Col 2:7
which you were *t* . . . . 2 Thess 2:15

TAUNT
and a byword, a *t* . . . . Jer 24:9

TAX
t collectors do the . . . . Matt 5:46
received the temple *t* . . . . . . Matt 17:24
I say to you that *t* . . . . Matt 21:31
Show Me the *t* . . . . Matt 22:19

TAX COLLECTOR
Matthew the *t* . . . . Matt 10:3
like heathen and a *t* . . . . . . Matt 18:17
a *t* named Levi . . . . Luke 5:27
and the other a *t* . . . . Luke 18:10
who was a chief *t* . . . . Luke 19:2

TAX COLLECTORS AND SINNERS
your Teacher eat with *t* . . . . Matt 9:11
He eats and drinks with *t* . Mark 2:16
winebibber, a friend of *t* . . . Luke 7:34

TAXES
take customs or *t* . . . . Matt 17:25
Is it lawful to pay *t* . . . . Matt 22:17
forbidding to pay *t* . . . . Luke 23:2
t to whom *t* . . . . Rom 13:7

TEACH
t them to your children . . . . . Deut 4:9
t them diligently . . . . Deut 6:7
t Jacob Your judgments . . . . Deut 33:10
t you the good and the . . 1 Sam 12:23
"Can anyone *t* . . . . Job 21:22
"I will *t* you about . . . . Job 27:11
t me what I do not see . . . . . Job 34:32
t me Your paths . . . . Ps 25:4
T me Your way . . . . Ps 27:11
t you the fear of the . . . . Ps 34:11
t You awesome things . . . . Ps 45:4
t transgressors Your . . . . Ps 51:13
So *t* us to number our . . . . Ps 90:12
T me Your statutes . . . . Ps 119:12
He will *t* us His ways . . . . Is 2:3
"Whom will he *t* . . . . Is 28:9
every man *t* his neighbor . . . Jer 31:34
a bribe, her priests *t* . . . . Mic 3:11
t the way of God in . . . . Matt 22:16
He began to *t* them . . . . Mark 6:34
t us to pray, as John also . . Luke 11:1
the Holy Spirit will *t* . . . . . . Luke 12:12
in My name, He will *t* . . . . John 14:26
you not to *t* in this name . . . Acts 5:28
therefore, who *t* another . . . Rom 2:21
even nature itself *t* . . . . 1 Cor 11:14
permit a woman to *t* . . . . 1 Tim 2:12
things command and *t* . . . . 1 Tim 4:11
T and exhort these . . . . 1 Tim 6:2
t you again the first . . . . Heb 5:12
not need that anyone *t* . . . 1 John 2:27

TEACHER
for One is your *T* . . . . Matt 23:8
T, do You not care that . . . . Mark 4:38
asked Him, "Good *T* . . . . . Mark 10:17
know that You are a *t* . . . . . . John 3:2
T, this woman was caught . . John 8:4
T has come and is . . . . John 11:28
You call Me *T* . . . . John 13:13
named Gamaliel, a *t* . . . . Acts 5:34
a *t* of babes, having . . . . Rom 2:20
a *t* of the Gentiles in . . . . 1 Tim 2:7

TEACHERS
than all my *t* . . . . Ps 119:99
t will not be moved . . . . Is 30:20
prophets, third *t* . . . . 1 Cor 12:28
and some pastors and *t* . . . . . Eph 4:11
desiring to be *t* . . . . 1 Tim 1:7
time you ought to be *t* . . . . . . Heb 5:12
of you become *t* . . . . James 3:1
there will be false *t* . . . . 2 Pet 2:1

TEACHES
therefore He *t* sinners . . . . Ps 25:8
He who *t* man knowledge . . . Ps 94:10
t men so, shall be called . . . . Matt 5:19
the Holy Spirit *t* . . . . 1 Cor 2:13
If anyone *t* otherwise . . . . . . 1 Tim 6:3
the same anointing *t* . . . . . 1 John 2:27

TEACHING
t them to observe all . . . . . . Matt 28:20
were astonished at His *t* . . Mark 1:22
Me, *t* as doctrines the . . . . . . Mark 7:7
they did not cease *t* . . . . Acts 5:42
he who teaches, in *t* . . . . Rom 12:7
by prophesying, or by *t* . . . . 1 Cor 14:6
t every man in all . . . . Col 1:28
t things which they . . . . Titus 1:11
t us that . . . . Titus 2:12

TEAR
t yourself in anger . . . . Job 18:4
lest they *t* me like a . . . . Ps 7:2
I, even I, will *t* . . . . Hos 5:14
feet, and turn and *t* . . . . Matt 7:6
will wipe away every *t* . . . . Rev 21:4

TEARS
I have seen your *t* . . . . 2 Kin 20:5
my couch with my *t* . . . . Ps 6:6
t have been my food . . . . Ps 42:3
with the bread of *t* . . . . Ps 80:5
drench you with my *t* . . . . Is 16:9
GOD will wipe away *t* . . . . Is 25:8
eyes may run with *t* . . . . Jer 9:18
My eyes fail with *t* . . . . Lam 2:11
His feet with her *t* . . . . Luke 7:38
night and day with *t* . . . . . . Acts 20:31
mindful of your *t* . . . . 2 Tim 1:4
vehement cries and *t* . . . . Heb 5:7
it diligently with *t* . . . . Heb 12:17

TEETH
t whiter than milk . . . . Gen 49:12
by the skin of my *t* . . . . Job 19:20
You have broken the *t* . . . . Ps 3:7
As vinegar to the *t* . . . . Prov 10:26
you cleanness of *t* . . . . Amos 4:6
and gnashing of *t* . . . . Matt 8:12

TEKOA
Home of a wise woman, 2 Sam 14:2, 4, 9
Home of Amos, Amos 1:1

TELL
that you may *t* it to . . . . Ps 48:13
the message that I *t* . . . . Jon 3:2
Who can *t* if God . . . . Jon 3:9
t him his fault . . . . Matt 18:15
whatever they *t* . . . . Matt 23:3
He comes, He will *t* . . . . John 4:25

TEMAN
Tribe in northeast Edom, Gen 36:34
Judgment pronounced against, Amos 1:12
God appears from, Hab 3:3

TEMPERATE
for the prize is *t* in all . . . . . 1 Cor 9:25
husband of one wife, *t* . . . . . . 1 Tim 3:2

TEMPEST
the windy storm and *t* . . . . Ps 55:8
one, tossed with *t* . . . . Is 54:11
And suddenly a great *t* . . . . . Matt 8:24

TEMPLE
So Solomon built the *t* . . . . 1 Kin 6:14
build a *t* for the LORD . . . . . 2 Chr 2:12
t for the name of the LORD . . 2 Chr 6:7
of the LORD filled the *t* . . . . . 2 Chr 7:1
LORD is in His holy *t* . . . . Ps 11:4
to inquire in His *t* . . . . Ps 27:4
The *t* of the LORD . . . . Jer 7:4
suddenly come to His *t* . . . . Mal 3:1
One greater than the *t* . . . . . Matt 12:6
murdered between the *t* . . Matt 23:35
veil of the *t* was torn . . . . . Matt 27:51
found Him in the *t* . . . . Luke 2:46
"Destroy this *t* . . . . John 2:19
was speaking of the *t* . . . . . . John 2:21
one accord in the *t* . . . . Acts 2:46
the Beautiful Gate of the *t* . . Acts 3:10
that you are the *t* . . . . 1 Cor 3:16
your body is the *t* . . . . 1 Cor 6:19
grows into a holy *t* . . . . Eph 2:21
sits as God in the *t* . . . . 2 Thess 2:4
Then the *t* of God was . . . . . Rev 11:19
But I saw no *t* in it . . . . Rev 21:22
and the Lamb are its *t* . . . . . Rev 21:22

TEMPLES
t made with hands . . . . Acts 7:48

TEMPORARY
which are seen are *t* . . . . . . 2 Cor 4:18

TEMPT
Why do you *t* the LORD . . . . . . Ex 17:2
You shall not *t* the LORD . . . Deut 6:16
they even *t* God . . . . Mal 3:15
t the LORD your God . . . . Matt 4:7
that Satan does not *t* . . . . 1 Cor 7:5
nor let us *t* Christ . . . . 1 Cor 10:9
nor does He Himself *t* . . . . James 1:13

TEMPTATION
do not lead us into *t* . . . . Matt 6:13
lest you enter into *t* . . . . Matt 26:41
in time of *t* fall away . . . . . . Luke 8:13
And do not lead us into *t* . . . Luke 11:4
t has overtaken you . . . . . . 1 Cor 10:13
to be rich fall into *t* . . . . 1 Tim 6:9
the man who endures *t* . . . James 1:12

TEMPTED
because they *t* the LORD . . . . . Ex 17:7
again and again they *t* God . . Ps 78:41
forty days, *t* by Satan . . . . . . Mark 1:13
being *t* for forty days by . . . . Luke 4:2
not allow you to be *t* . . . . . 1 Cor 10:13
lest you also be *t* . . . . Gal 6:1
has suffered, being *t* . . . . Heb 2:18
in all points *t* . . . . Heb 4:15
he is *t*, "I am *t* by God" . . James 1:13
But each one is *t* . . . . James 1:14

TEMPTER
Now when the *t* came . . . . Matt 4:3

TEN
t should be found . . . . Gen 18:32
the *T* Commandments . . . . . . Ex 34:28
David his *t* thousands . . . . 1 Sam 18:7
or go backward *t* . . . . 2 Kin 20:9
an instrument of *t* strings . . . . Ps 92:3
test your servants for *t* . . . . . Dan 1:12
before it, and it had *t* horns . . Dan 7:7
The *t* horns are *t* kings . . . . . Dan 7:24
owed him *t* thousand . . . . . . Matt 18:24
him who has *t* talents . . . . . Matt 25:28
there met Him *t* men . . . . . Luke 17:12
t horns, and seven . . . . Rev 12:3
seven heads and *t* horns . . . . Rev 13:1
The *t* horns which you . . . . . Rev 17:12

TEND
to him, "*T* My sheep . . . . . . John 21:16

TENDER
your heart was *t* . . . . 2 Kin 22:19
t shoots will not . . . . Job 14:7
Let Your *t* mercies come . . . . . Ps 79:8
Your *t* mercies come to . . . Ps 119:77
no more be called *t* . . . . Is 47:1
through the *t* mercy of . . . . . Luke 1:78
put on *t* mercies . . . . Col 3:12

hundred and forty-four *t* .... Rev 14:1
bound him for a *t* years ..... Rev 20:2

THREAT
shall flee at the *t* .... Is 30:17

THREATEN
suffered, He did not *t* ...... 1 Pet 2:23

THREATENING
to them, giving up *t* .... Eph 6:9

THREATS
Lord, look on their *t* .... Acts 4:29
still breathing *t* .... Acts 9:1

THREE
the vine were *t* branches .. Gen 40:10
were *t* white baskets ..... Gen 40:16
child, she hid him *t* months ... Ex 2:2
T times you shall keep a .... Ex 23:14
T times in the year all ...... Ex 34:23
T times a year all your .... Deut 16:16
t hundred concubines ...... 1 Kin 11:3
on the child *t* times, and ... 1 Kin 17:21
so he struck *t* times ...... 2 Kin 13:18
either *t* years of famine .. 1 Chr 21:12
Now when Job's *t* friends ... Job 2:11
There are *t* things that .... Prov 30:15
Did we not cast *t* men .... Dan 3:24
his petition *t* times a day .... Dan 6:13
came up, before which *t* ...... Dan 7:20
t more kings will arise in .... Dan 11:2
For *t* transgressions of ...... Amos 1:3
Son of Man be *t* days ..... Matt 12:40
make here *t* tabernacles .... Matt 17:4
For where two or *t* are .... Matt 18:20
you will deny Me *t* .... Matt 26:34
temple and build it in *t* .... Matt 27:40
After *t* days I will rise .... Matt 27:63
after *t* days rise again ...... Mark 8:31
will deny Me *t* times ...... Mark 14:30
and build it in *t* days ...... Mark 15:29
will deny Me *t* times ...... Luke 22:61
that day about *t* thousand .. Acts 2:41
was *t* days without sight .... Acts 9:9
This was done *t* times ..... Acts 10:16
spoke boldly for *t* months .. Acts 19:8
hope, love, these *t* .... 1 Cor 13:13
and these *t* are one .... 1 John 5:7
By these *t* plagues a third ... Rev 9:18
I saw *t* unclean spirits ...... Rev 16:13

THRESH
he does not *t* it .... Is 28:28
t the mountains .... Is 41:15
it is time to *t* her .... Jer 51:33
"Arise and *t* .... Mic 4:13

THRESHING
t shall last till the .... Lev 26:5
fleece of wool on the *t* ..... Judg 6:37
went down to the *t* floor .... Ruth 3:6
David bought the *t* floor . 2 Sam 24:24
like the dust at *t* .... 2 Kin 13:7
t floor of Ornan the ...... 1 Chr 21:18
Oh, my *t* and the grain .... Is 21:10
clean out His *t* floor .... Matt 3:12

THRESHOLD
with her hands on the *t* ... Judg 19:27
were broken off on the *t* ... 1 Sam 5:4
been, to the *t* of the temple .. Ezek 9:3

THREW
every man *t* down his rod ..... Ex 7:12
he *t* stones at David ...... 2 Sam 16:6
t him into the sea, and the ... Jon 1:15
t him into prison till he ... Matt 18:30
he *t* down the pieces .... Matt 27:5
t their own clothes on .... Luke 19:35
they *t* them into prison, ... Acts 16:23
t it into the great .... Rev 14:19
t it into the sea, saying, ... Rev 18:21

THROAT
t is an open tomb .... Ps 5:9
put a knife to your *t* .... Prov 23:2
unshod, and your *t* .... Jer 2:25
t is an open tomb .... Rom 3:13

THRONE
LORD sitting on His *t* ..... 1 Kin 22:19
He has prepared His *t* .... Ps 9:7
temple, the LORD's *t* .... Ps 11:4
Your *t*, O God, is .... Ps 45:6
has established His *t* .... Ps 103:19
he upholds his *t* .... Prov 20:28
Lord sitting on a *t* .... Is 6:1
"Heaven is My *t* .... Is 66:1
shall be called The *T* .... Jer 3:17
do not disgrace the *t* .... Jer 14:21
A glorious high *t* .... Jer 17:12
t was a fiery flame .... Dan 7:9
sit and rule on His *t* .... Zech 6:13
for it is God's *t* .... Matt 5:34
will give Him the *t* .... Luke 1:32
"Your *t*, O God, is .... Heb 1:8
come boldly to the *t* .... Heb 4:16
where Satan's *t* .... Rev 2:13
My Father on His *t* .... Rev 3:21
I saw a great white *t* .... Rev 20:11

THRONE OF DAVID
set up the *t* over Israel .... 2 Sam 3:10
and set me on the *t* .... 1 Kin 2:24
t shall be established ...... 1 Kin 2:45
t and over His kingdom .... Is 9:7
princes sitting on the *t* ...... Jer 17:25
you who sit on the *t* .... Jer 22:2
king who sits on the *t* ...... Jer 29:16
no one to sit on the *t* .... Jer 36:30

THRONE OF GOD
swears by the *t* .... Matt 23:22
right hand of the *t* .... Heb 12:2
they are before the *t* .... Rev 7:15
without fault before the *t* ... Rev 14:5
proceeding from the *t* .... Rev 22:1

THRONES
t are set there .... Ps 122:5
also sit on twelve *t* .... Matt 19:28
mighty from their *t* .... Luke 1:52
invisible, whether *t* .... Col 1:16
t I saw twenty-four .... Rev 4:4

THRONG
house of God in the *t* .... Ps 55:14

THROW
he said, "*T* her down ...... 2 Kin 9:33
keep, and a time to *t* away .. Eccl 3:6
the LORD will *t* you away .... Is 22:17
of your land and *t* .... Mic 5:11
me, "*T* it to the potter" ... Zech 11:13
may build, but I will *t* down .. Mal 1:4
t Yourself down .... Matt 4:6
children's bread and *t* .... Matt 15:26
let him *t* a stone at her ...... John 8:7
t them into the fire, and .... John 15:6

THROWN
rider He has *t* into the sea .... Ex 15:1
their slain shall be *t* .... Is 34:3
mountains shall be *t* ...... Ezek 38:20
down and *t* into the fire .... Matt 3:10
neck, and he were *t* .... Mark 9:42
down and *t* into the fire .... Luke 3:9

THRUST
and rose up and *t* .... Luke 4:29
T in Your sickle and reap .. Rev 14:15

THUMMIM
the Urim and the *T* .... Ex 28:30
Your *T* and Your Urim ...... Deut 33:8
with the Urim and *T* .... Ezra 2:63
with the Urim and *T* .... Neh 7:65

THUNDER
But the *t* of His power ...... Job 26:14
The voice of Your *t* .... Ps 77:18
the secret place of *t* .... Ps 81:7
t they hastened away .... Ps 104:7
that is, "Sons of *T*" .... Mark 3:17
the voice of loud *t* .... Rev 14:2

THUNDERED
"The LORD *t* from .... 2 Sam 22:14
The LORD *t* .... Ps 18:13

THUNDERINGS
people witnessed the *t* ...... Ex 20:18
the sound of mighty *t* .... Rev 19:6

THUNDERS
t marvelously with His ...... Job 37:5
The God of glory *t* .... Ps 29:3

THYATIRA
Residence of Lydia, Acts 16:14
Site of one of the seven churches, Rev 2:18–24

TIBERIAS
Sea of Galilee called, John 6:1, 23

TIDINGS
be afraid of evil *t* .... Ps 112:7
you who bring good *t*, lift ...... Is 40:9
brings glad *t* of good things ... Is 52:7
preach good *t* to the poor ..... Is 61:1
of him who brings good *t* ... Nah 1:15
I bring you good *t* .... Luke 2:10
who bring glad *t* .... Rom 10:15

TIGLATH-PILESER
Powerful Assyrian king who invades Samaria, 2 Kin 15:29

TILL
no man to *t* the ground ...... Gen 2:5

TILLER
but Cain was a *t* .... Gen 4:2

TILLS
t his land will be .... Prov 12:11
t his land will have .... Prov 28:19

TIMBREL
took the *t* in her hand ...... Ex 15:20
Praise Him with the *t* and .... Ps 150:4

TIMBRELS
out to meet him with *t* .... Judg 11:34

TIME
See APPOINTED TIME
in the appointed *t* of the .... Ex 34:18
LORD at its appointed *t* ..... Num 9:13
children ask in *t* to come .... Josh 4:6
t I shall be blameless ...... Judg 15:3
For in the *t* of trouble He ...... Ps 27:5
pray to You in a *t* .... Ps 32:6
ashamed in the evil *t* .... Ps 37:19
strength in the *t* of trouble .. Ps 37:39
how short my *t* is .... Ps 89:47
t for every purpose under ..... Eccl 3:1
A *t* to be born .... Eccl 3:2
but *t* and chance .... Eccl 9:11
LORD, will hasten it in its *t* ... Is 60:22
But in the *t* of their trouble .. Jer 2:27
the *t* of their punishment .... Jer 8:12
you in the *t* of adversity .... Jer 15:11
in the *t* of Your anger .... Jer 18:23
your *t* was the *t* .... Ezek 16:8
a *t* and times and half a *t* .. Dan 7:25
at that *t* your people shall .. Dan 12:1
The *t* has not come .... Hag 1:2
says, "My *t* is at hand .... Matt 26:18
A second *t* the rooster ... Mark 14:72
t of temptation fall away .. Luke 8:13
you did not know the *t* ... Luke 19:44
has seen God at any *t* .... John 1:18
Can he enter a second *t* ..... John 3:4
t has not yet come .... John 7:6
the *t* is coming when I .... John 16:25
to him again a second *t* ... John 21:16
I have a convenient *t* ...... Acts 24:25
be revealed in his own *t* .. 2 Thess 2:6
Jesus before *t* began .... 2 Tim 1:9
for the *t* is near .... Rev 1:3
that he has a short *t* .... Rev 12:12
a *t* and times and half a *t* .. Rev 12:14

Then He *t* the cup, and ... Matt 26:27
Peter *t* Him aside and ... Mark 8:32
Then He *t* a little child ... Mark 9:36
He *t* the cup, and gave ... Luke 22:17

TOOTH
eye for eye, *t* ... Ex 21:24
eye for eye, *t* for *t* ... Lev 24:20
t for *t*, hand for hand, ... Deut 19:21
is like a bad *t* ... Prov 25:19
eye for an eye and a *t* ... Matt 5:38

TOP
a tower whose *t* is in the ... Gen 11:4
consuming fire on the *t* of ... Ex 24:17
mercy seat on *t* of the ark ... Ex 25:21
in two from *t* to bottom ... Matt 27:51
torn in two from *t* to ... Mark 15:38

TOPHET
See HINNOM, VALLEY OF THE SON OF
T was established ... Is 30:33
the high places of *T* ... Jer 7:31
make this city like *T* ... Jer 19:12
like the place of *T* ... Jer 19:13

TORCH
and a burning *t* that ... Gen 15:17
and like a fiery *t* ... Zech 12:6

TORCHES
When he had set the *t* ... Judg 15:5
his eyes like *t* ... Dan 10:6
come with flaming *t* ... Nah 2:3

TORE
that he *t* his clothes, and ... Judg 11:35
t his garments and lay ... 2 Sam 13:31
t it into twelve pieces ... 1 Kin 11:30
t down the temple of ... 2 Kin 10:27
temple of Baal, and *t* it ... 2 Chr 23:17
t his robe, and shaved his ... Job 1:20
and each one *t* his robe ... Job 2:12

TORE HIS CLOTHES
in the pit, and he *t* ... Gen 37:29
Then Jacob *t*, put ... Gen 37:34
Then Joshua *t*, and fell ... Josh 7:6
he *t* and put sackcloth ... 1 Kin 21:27
the letter, that he *t* ... 2 Kin 5:7
of the Law, that he *t* ... 2 Kin 22:11
of the Law, that he *t* ... 2 Chr 34:19
he *t* and put on sackcloth ... Esth 4:1
heard it, that he *t* ... Is 37:1
Then the high priest *t* ... Matt 26:65
Then the high priest *t* ... Mark 14:63

TORMENT
"How long will you *t* ... Job 19:2
shall lie down in *t* ... Is 50:11
You come here to *t* ... Matt 8:29
to this place of *t* ... Luke 16:28
fear involves *t* ... 1 John 4:18
to *t* them for five months ... Rev 9:5
t ascends forever ... Rev 14:11

TORMENTED
t with unclean spirits ... Luke 6:18
for I am *t* in this ... Luke 16:24
He shall be *t* with fire ... Rev 14:10
And they will be *t* ... Rev 20:10

TORMENTS
And being in *t* ... Luke 16:23

TORN
Joseph is *t* to pieces ... Gen 37:33
the altar of Baal, *t* down ... Judg 6:28
has *t* the kingdom ... 1 Sam 15:28
lion, which has *t* him ... 1 Kin 13:26
aside my ways and *t* ... Lam 3:11
for He has *t* ... Hos 6:1
of the temple was *t* ... Matt 27:51
t in two from top to ... Mark 15:38

TORTURED
Others were *t* ... Heb 11:35

TOSSED
t with tempest ... Is 54:11
t to and fro and ... Eph 4:14

TOTTER
drunkard, and shall *t* ... Is 24:20

TOUCH
eat it, nor shall you *t* it ... Gen 3:3
the mountain or *t* its base ... Ex 19:12
carcasses you shall not *t* ... Lev 11:8
seven no evil shall *t* ... Job 5:19
t no unclean thing ... Is 52:11
"If only I may *t* ... Matt 9:21
that they might only *t* ... Matt 14:36
If only I may *t* His ... Mark 5:28
and begged Him to *t* him ... Mark 8:22
that He might *t* them ... Luke 18:15
a man not to *t* a woman ... 1 Cor 7:1
Do not *t* what is unclean, ... 2 Cor 6:17
wicked one does not *t* ... 1 John 5:18

TOUCHED
whoever has *t* any slain ... Num 31:19
whose hearts God had *t* ... 1 Sam 10:26
t my mouth with it ... Is 6:7
hand and *t* my mouth ... Jer 1:9
but he *t* me, and stood me ... Dan 8:18
said, "Who *t* My clothes ... Mark 5:30
t the open coffin, and ... Luke 7:14
Jesus said, "Who *t* Me? ... Luke 8:45
mountain that may be *t* ... Heb 12:18

TOUCHES
if a person *t* any unclean ... Lev 5:2
whoever *t* the carcass of ... Lev 11:24
Whoever *t* those things ... Lev 15:27
whoever *t* anything made ... Lev 22:4
He *t* the hills ... Ps 104:32
t you *t* the ... Zech 2:8

TOWEL
His garments, took a *t* ... John 13:4

TOWER
t whose top is in the ... Gen 11:4
t which the sons of men ... Gen 11:5
the *t* of salvation to ... 2 Sam 22:51
for me, a strong *t* ... Ps 61:3
my fortress, my high *t* ... Ps 144:2
like an ivory *t* ... Song 7:4
a watchman in the *t* ... Is 21:5
in it and built a *t* ... Matt 21:33
whom the *t* in Siloam fell ... Luke 13:4
intending to build a *t* ... Luke 14:28

TOWN
Neither go into the *t* ... Mark 8:26
from the *t* of Bethlehem, ... John 7:42

TOWNS
of Megiddo and its *t* ... Josh 17:11
as *t* without walls ... Zech 2:4

TRACE
no *t* of them was found ... Dan 2:35

TRACKED
t our steps so that we ... Lam 4:18

TRADERS
Then Midianite *t* passed ... Gen 37:28
are princes, whose *t* ... Is 23:8

TRADITION
transgress the *t* ... Matt 15:2
of no effect by your *t* ... Matt 15:6
holding the *t* of the elders ... Mark 7:3
according to the *t* ... Col 2:8
t which he received ... 2 Thess 3:6
conduct received by *t* ... 1 Pet 1:18

TRADITIONS
zealous for the *t* ... Gal 1:14
t which you were ... 2 Thess 2:15

TRAIN
T up a child in the ... Prov 22:6
t of His robe filled ... Is 6:1

TRAINED
who is perfectly *t* ... Luke 6:40
those who have been *t* ... Heb 12:11

TRAINING
bring them up in the *t* ... Eph 6:4

TRAITOR
also became a *t* ... Luke 6:16

TRAITORS
t, headstrong ... 2 Tim 3:4

TRAMPLE
Your name we will *t* ... Ps 44:5
serpent you shall *t* ... Ps 91:13
hand, to *t* My courts ... Is 1:12
You shall *t* the wicked ... Mal 4:3
swine, lest they *t* ... Matt 7:6
you the authority to *t* ... Lk 10:19

TRAMPLED
wall, and it shall be *t* down ... Is 5:5
as straw is *t* down for the ... Is 25:10
t them in My fury ... Is 63:3
The Lord has *t* underfoot ... Lam 1:15
now she will be *t* ... Mic 7:10
t the nations in anger ... Hab 3:12
Jerusalem will be *t* ... Luke 21:24
t the Son of God ... Heb 10:29
the winepress was *t* ... Rev 14:20

TRANCE
he fell into a *t* ... Acts 10:10
t I saw a vision ... Acts 11:5

TRANSFIGURED
and was *t* before them ... Matt 17:2

TRANSFORMED
this world, but be *t* ... Rom 12:2
the Lord, are being *t* ... 2 Cor 3:18

TRANSFORMING
t themselves into ... 2 Cor 11:13

TRANSFORMS
Satan himself *t* himself ... 2 Cor 11:14

TRANSGRESS
t the command of the ... Num 14:41
the LORD's people *t* ... 1 Sam 2:24
my mouth shall not *t* ... Ps 17:3
his mouth must not *t* ... Prov 16:10
of bread a man will *t* ... Prov 28:21
those who *t* against Me ... Ezek 20:38
in which you *t* against ... Zeph 3:11
do Your disciples *t* ... Matt 15:2

TRANSGRESSED
t My covenant ... Josh 7:11
they had *t* against the ... 2 Chr 12:2
your mediators have *t* ... Is 43:27
the rulers also *t* ... Jer 2:8
who have *t* My covenant ... Jer 34:18
their fathers have *t* ... Ezek 2:3
Yes, all Israel has *t* ... Dan 9:11
t your commandment ... Luke 15:29

TRANSGRESSES
"Indeed, because he *t* ... Hab 2:5
Whoever *t* and does not ... 2 John 9

TRANSGRESSING
God, in *t* His covenant, ... Deut 17:2
t against our God by ... Neh 13:27

TRANSGRESSION
iniquity and *t* and sin ... Ex 34:7
Make me know my *t* ... Job 13:23
t is sealed up in a ... Job 14:17
I am pure, without *t* ... Job 33:9
though I am without *t* ... Job 34:6
be innocent of great *t* ... Ps 19:13
is he whose *t* is forgiven ... Ps 32:1
their *t* with the rod ... Ps 89:32
because of their *t* ... Ps 107:17
He who covers a *t* ... Prov 17:9
He who loves *t* loves ... Prov 17:19
By *t* an evil man is ... Prov 29:6
man abounds in *t* ... Prov 29:22
tell My people their *t* ... Is 58:1
and the *t* of desolation ... Dan 8:13
at Gilgal multiply *t* ... Amos 4:4
my firstborn for my *t* ... Mic 6:7

and passing over the *t* ...... Mic 7:18
no law there is no *t* .... Rom 4:15
deceived, fell into *t* .... 1 Tim 2:14
steadfast, and every *t* .... Heb 2:2

TRANSGRESSIONS
He will not pardon your *t* ... Ex 23:21
forgive your *t* nor your .... Josh 24:19
if I have covered my *t* ..... Job 31:33
"I will confess my *t* .... Ps 32:5
me from all my *t* .... Ps 39:8
mercies, blot out my *t* .... Ps 51:1
For I acknowledge my *t* .... Ps 51:3
has He removed our *t* ...... Ps 103:12
who blots out your *t* .... Is 43:25
was wounded for our *t* .... Is 53:5
for the *t* of My people .... Is 53:8
for our *t* are with us, and .... Is 59:12
yoke of my *t* was bound ..... Lam 1:14
from you all the *t* .... Ezek 18:31
I punish Israel for their *t* .. Amos 3:14
was added because of *t* ...... Gal 3:19
redemption of the *t* .... Heb 9:15

TRANSGRESSOR
and were called a *t* .... Is 48:8
are a *t* of the law .... Rom 2:27
I make myself a *t* .... Gal 2:18
become a *t* of the law .... James 2:11

TRANSGRESSORS
the *t* shall be destroyed ..... Ps 37:38
Then I will teach *t* .... Ps 51:13
to any wicked *t* .... Ps 59:5
The destruction of *t* and of .... Is 1:28
numbered with the *t* .... Is 53:12
when the *t* have reached ... Dan 8:23
numbered with the *t* ..... Mark 15:28
numbered with the *t* ..... Luke 22:37
convicted by the law as *t* .. James 2:9

TRANSLATED
Immanuel," which is *t* ...... Matt 1:23
cumi," which is *t* .... Mark 5:41
Golgotha, which is *t* ..... Mark 15:22
which is *t*, "My God .... Mark 15:34
the Messiah" (which is *t* ... John 1:41
Cephas" (which is *t* .... John 1:42

TRAP
of Israel, as a *t* .... Is 8:14
where there is no *t* .... Amos 3:5
become a snare and a *t* .... Rom 11:9

TRAPS
they have set *t* .... Ps 140:5
for me, and from the *t* ...... Ps 141:9

TRAVEL
For you *t* land and sea .... Matt 23:15
Paul's *t* companions ...... Acts 19:29

TRAVELER
t who turns aside .... Jer 14:8

TRAVELING
lodge, O you *t* companies .... Is 21:13
lie waste, the *t* .... Is 33:8
t in the greatness of His ...... Is 63:1
a man *t* to a far country .. Matt 25:14
two of them were *t* that .. Luke 24:13

TRAVERSE
t the way of .... Prov 8:20

TREACHEROUS
the *t* dealer deals .... Is 21:2
The *t* dealers have dealt ..... Is 24:16
yet her *t* sister Judah did ..... Jer 3:8
an assembly of *t* men .... Jer 9:2
are insolent, *t* .... Zeph 3:4

TREACHEROUSLY
and you who deal *t* .... Is 33:1
have you dealt *t* with Me .... Jer 3:20
happy who deal so *t* .... Jer 12:1
even they have dealt *t* .... Jer 12:6
They have dealt *t* .... Hos 5:7
Why do we deal *t* .... Mal 2:10

that you do not deal *t* .... Mal 2:16
This man dealt *t* .... Acts 7:19

TREAD
t down the wicked in ...... Job 40:12
it is He who shall *t* .... Ps 60:12
You shall *t* upon the .... Ps 91:13
shout, as those who *t* .... Jer 25:30
because you *t* down the ... Amos 5:11
will come down and *t* .... Mic 1:3
And they will *t* .... Rev 11:2

TREADS
like one who *t* in the .... Is 63:2
t the high places .... Amos 4:13
an ox while it *t* .... 1 Tim 5:18
t the winepress .... Rev 19:15

TREASURE
a special *t* above all the ..... Deut 7:6
to you His good *t* .... Deut 28:12
one who finds great *t* ..... Ps 119:162
for His special *t* .... Ps 135:4
t my commands within .... Prov 2:1
there is much *t* .... Prov 15:6
There is desirable *t* .... Prov 21:20
of the LORD is His *t* .... Is 33:6
For where your *t* .... Matt 6:21
t brings forth evil .... Matt 12:35
is like *t* hidden in a field .. Matt 13:44
t things new and old ...... Matt 13:52
and you will have *t* .... Matt 19:21
will have *t* in heaven ..... Mark 10:21
So is he who lays up *t* .... Luke 12:21
t in the heavens that ..... Luke 12:33
For where your *t* is .... Luke 12:34
will have *t* in heaven ..... Luke 18:22
But we have this *t* .... 2 Cor 4:7
You have heaped up *t* ..... James 5:3

TREASURED
t the words of His .... Job 23:12

TREASURER
Erastus, the *t* of the .... Rom 16:23

TREASURES
sealed up among My *t* .... Deut 32:34
t hidden in the sand ...... Deut 33:19
it more than hidden *t* .... Job 3:21
her as for hidden *t* .... Prov 2:4
t of wickedness profit ...... Prov 10:2
Getting *t* by a lying .... Prov 21:6
is no end to their *t* .... Is 2:7
I will give you the *t* .... Is 45:3
in your works and your *t*, ... Jer 48:7
Are there yet the *t* .... Mic 6:10
for yourselves *t* .... Matt 6:19
are hidden all the *t* .... Col 2:3
riches than the *t* .... Heb 11:26

TREASURIES
that I may fill their *t* .... Prov 8:21

TREASURING
t up for yourself wrath in ... Rom 2:5

TREASURY
you entered the *t* of snow .. Job 38:22
who have given to the *t* .. Mark 12:43
their gifts into the *t* .... Luke 21:1

TREAT
Should he *t* our sister ..... Gen 34:31
not *t* her brutally .... Deut 21:14

TREATED
He *t* Abram well for her ... Gen 12:16
t them spitefully, and ...... Matt 22:6
and be *t* with contempt .... Mark 9:12
were spitefully *t* at ...... 1 Thess 2:2

TREATS
Cursed is the one who *t* ... Deut 27:16

TREATY
Now Solomon made a *t* .... 1 Kin 3:1
Let there be a *t* between .. 1 Kin 15:19
So he made a *t* with ...... 1 Kin 20:34
Let there be a *t* between .. 2 Chr 16:3

TREE
LORD God made every *t* ...... Gen 2:9
but of the *t* .... Gen 2:17
you eaten from the *t* .... Gen 3:11
tamarisk *t* in Beersheba ... Gen 21:33
for the *t* of the field is .... Deut 20:19
they said to the olive *t* ...... Judg 9:8
the Diviners' Terebinth *T* ... Judg 9:37
the cedar *t* of Lebanon .... 1 Kin 4:33
down under a broom *t* .... 1 Kin 19:4
there is hope for a *t* .... Job 14:7
t planted by the .... Ps 1:3
like a native green *t* .... Ps 37:35
shall flourish like a palm *t* .. Ps 92:12
t falls to the south .... Eccl 11:3
Like an apple *t* .... Song 2:3
the cedar and the acacia *t* .... Is 41:19
for as the days of a *t* .... Is 65:22
are upright, like a palm *t* .... Jer 10:5
your name, Green Olive *T*, .. Jer 11:16
t planted by the .... Jer 17:8
and set it like a willow *t* ... Ezek 17:5
brought down the high *t* .. Ezek 17:24
The *t* that you saw, which .. Dan 4:20
and the fig *t* has withered ..... Joel 1:12
t bears good fruit .... Matt 7:17
t is known by its fruit ..... Matt 12:33
And seeing a fig *t* by the .. Matt 21:19
fig *t* which You cursed .... Mark 11:21
For every *t* is known by ... Luke 6:44
a sycamore *t* to see Him ... Luke 19:4
everyone who hangs on a *t* .. Gal 3:13
His own body on the *t* ..... 1 Pet 2:24
as a fig *t* drops its late ...... Rev 6:13

TREE OF LIFE
The *t* was also in the midst .. Gen 2:9
and take also of the *t* .... Gen 3:22
guard the way to the *t* ...... Gen 3:24
She is a *t* to those .... Prov 3:18
of the righteous is a *t* ..... Prov 11:30
desire comes, it is a *t* ..... Prov 13:12
wholesome tongue is a *t* .... Prov 15:4
to eat from the *t* .... Rev 2:7
t, which bore twelve fruits .. Rev 22:2
have the right to the *t* ..... Rev 22:14

TREES
and the *t* of the field shall ... Lev 26:4
t once went forth .... Judg 9:8
Then all the *t* said to the ... Judg 9:14
Also he spoke of *t* .... 1 Kin 4:33
Then all the *t* of the .... Ps 96:12
The *t* of the LORD are ...... Ps 104:16
all kinds of fruit *t* .... Eccl 2:5
all the *t* of the field shall ..... Is 55:12
they may be called *t* .... Is 61:3
and on beast, on the *t* .... Jer 7:20
all the *t* of the field shall .. Ezek 17:24
so that all the *t* .... Ezek 31:9
"I see men like *t* .... Mark 8:24
took branches of palm *t* .. John 12:13
late autumn *t* without .... Jude 12
the sea, or the *t* .... Rev 7:3
third of the *t* were burned .... Rev 8:7

TREMBLE
T before Him .... 1 Chr 16:30
The dead *t*, those under ..... Job 26:5
have made the earth *t* .... Ps 60:2
T before Him, all the earth ... Ps 96:9
let the peoples *t* .... Ps 99:1
T, O earth, at the presence .. Ps 114:7
who made the earth *t* .... Is 14:16
That the nations may *t* .... Is 64:2
LORD, you who *t* at His .... Is 66:5
'Will you not *t* .... Jer 5:22
wrath the earth will *t* .... Jer 10:10
they shall fear and *t* .... Jer 33:9
my kingdom men must *t* .... Dan 6:26
the inhabitants of the land *t* .. Joel 2:1
before them, the heavens *t* .. Joel 2:10
demons believe—and *t*! ... James 2:19

TREMBLED
the people saw it, they *t* .... Ex 20:18
of Edom, the earth *t* .... Judg 5:4
for his heart *t* .... 1 Sam 4:13
Then everyone who *t* .... Ezra 9:4
the earth shook and *t* .... Ps 18:7
and indeed they *t* .... Jer 4:24
whole land *t* at the sound .... Jer 8:16
mountains saw You and *t* .. Hab 3:10
When I heard, my body *t* ... Hab 3:16

TREMBLES
the earth sees and *t* .... Ps 97:4
flesh *t* for fear of You ..... Ps 119:120

TREMBLING
t will take hold of them ..... Ex 15:15
will give you a *t* heart .... Deut 28:65
it was a very great *t* ..... 1 Sam 14:15
your water with *t* .... Ezek 12:18
in fear, and in much *t* ...... 1 Cor 2:3
t you received .... 2 Cor 7:15
flesh, with fear and *t* .... Eph 6:5
with fear and *t* .... Phil 2:12

TRENCH
and he made a *t* .... 1 Kin 18:32

TRESPASS
he shall bring his *t* offering .. Lev 5:6
If a person commits a *t*, ... Lev 5:15
commits a *t* against the .... Lev 6:2
this is the law of the *t* .... Lev 7:1
and offer it as a *t* offering .. Lev 14:12
bring his *t* offering .... Lev 19:21
to *t* against the LORD in ... Num 31:16
forgive the *t* of your ..... 1 Sam 25:28
a man is overtaken in any *t* .. Gal 6:1

TRESPASSED
t against the LORD God .... 2 Chr 30:7
We have *t* against our ..... Ezra 10:2

TRESPASSES
still goes on in his *t* .... Ps 68:21
forgive men their *t* .... Matt 6:14
forgive his brother his *t* ... Matt 18:35
forgive you your *t* .... Mark 11:25
not imputing their *t* .... 2 Cor 5:19
who were dead in *t* .... Eph 2:1
forgiven you all *t* .... Col 2:13
Confess your *t* to one .... James 5:16

TRIAL
as in the day of *t* .... Ps 95:8
in the day of *t* .... Heb 3:8
concerning the fiery *t* ...... 1 Pet 4:12
t which shall come .... Rev 3:10

TRIALS
with Me in My *t* .... Luke 22:28
fall into various *t* .... James 1:2

TRIBE
a man from every *t* .... Num 1:4
Only the *t* of Levi you ..... Num 1:49
Do not cut off the *t* of the .. Num 4:18
one thousand from each *t* .. Num 31:6
one leader of every *t* ..... Num 34:18
One *t* is cut off from .... Judg 21:6
of old, the *t* of Your .... Ps 74:2
belongs to another *t* .... Heb 7:13
the Lion of the *t* .... Rev 5:5
blood out of every *t* .... Rev 5:9
given him over every *t* ...... Rev 13:7

TRIBES
See TWELVE TRIBES
are the twelve *t* of Israel .. Gen 49:28
where the *t* go up .... Ps 122:4
to raise up the *t* .... Is 49:6
the *t* of Your inheritance .... Is 63:17
promise our twelve *t* .... Acts 26:7
t which are scattered ...... James 1:1

TRIBULATION
when *t* or persecution .... Matt 13:21
there will be great *t* .... Matt 24:21
t or persecution arises .... Mark 4:17
world you will have *t* ..... John 16:33
Shall *t*, or distress, or ...... Rom 8:35
in hope, patient in *t* .... Rom 12:12
comforts us in all our *t* ..... 2 Cor 1:4
joyful in all our *t* .... 2 Cor 7:4
that we would suffer *t* .... 1 Thess 3:4
t those who .... 2 Thess 1:6
and you will have *t* .... Rev 2:10
with her into great *t* .... Rev 2:22
out of the great *t* .... Rev 7:14

TRIBULATIONS
t enter the kingdom .... Acts 14:22
but we also glory in *t* .... Rom 5:3
in much patience, in *t*, in ... 2 Cor 6:4
not lose heart at my *t* .... Eph 3:13
t that you endure .... 2 Thess 1:4

TRICKERY
plotted to take Jesus by *t* ... Matt 26:4
they might take Him by *t* .. Mark 14:1
doctrine, by the *t* of men .... Eph 4:14

TRIED
like silver *t* in a furnace of ... Ps 12:6
You have *t* me and have ..... Ps 17:3
a *t* stone, a precious .... Is 28:16

TRIMMED
and *t* their lamps .... Matt 25:7

TRIUMPH
Let not my enemies *t* .... Ps 25:2
I will *t* in the works .... Ps 92:4
how long will the wicked *t* .... Ps 94:3
always leads us in *t* .... 2 Cor 2:14

TRIUMPHED
the LORD, for He has *t* .... Ex 15:1

TRIUMPHING
that the *t* of the wicked is ... Job 20:5
of them, *t* over them in it .... Col 2:15

TRIUMPHS
Mercy *t* over judgment ... James 2:13

TROAS
Paul receives vision at, Acts 16:8–11

TRODDEN
t the winepress alone .... Is 63:3

TROOP
Then Leah said, "A *t* ...... Gen 30:11
a *t* shall tramp upon him, .. Gen 49:19
I can run against a *t* ..... 2 Sam 22:30

TROUBLE
See TIME OF TROUBLE
that they were in *t* .... Ex 5:19
The LORD will *t* you this .... Josh 7:25
This day is a day of *t* ...... 2 Kin 19:3
no rest, for *t* comes .... Job 3:26
yet man is born to *t*, as the ... Job 5:7
few days and full of *t* .... Job 14:1
for the time of *t* .... Job 38:23
have increased who *t* .... Ps 3:1
a refuge in times of *t* .... Ps 9:9
under his tongue is *t* .... Ps 10:7
from Me, for *t* is near .... Ps 22:11
t He shall hide me .... Ps 27:5
You have considered my *t* .... Ps 31:7
O LORD, for I am in *t* .... Ps 31:9
shall preserve me from *t* ..... Ps 32:7
strength in the time of *t* ..... Ps 37:39
Your servant, for I am in *t* .. Ps 69:17
not in *t* as other men .... Ps 73:5
will be with him in *t* .... Ps 91:15
walk in the midst of *t* .... Ps 138:7
is delivered from *t* .... Prov 11:8
but *t* will come to him .... Prov 11:27
of the wicked is *t* .... Prov 15:6
t is like a bad tooth .... Prov 25:19
they are a *t* to Me, I am .... Is 1:14
t they have .... Is 26:16
also in the time of *t* .... Is 33:2
and there was *t* .... Jer 8:15
Savior in time of *t* .... Jer 14:8
I will hand them over to *t* .... Jer 15:4
I will deliver them to *t* ...... Jer 29:18
there shall be a time of ..... Dan 12:1
for the day is its own *t* ..... Matt 6:34
do not *t* Yourself, for I am .. Luke 7:6
such will have *t* .... 1 Cor 7:28
there are some who *t* .... Gal 1:7
and widows in their *t* ..... James 1:27

TROUBLED
Your face, and I was *t* .... Ps 30:7
God, and was *t* .... Ps 77:3
Your face, they are *t* .... Ps 104:29
wicked are like the *t* .... Is 57:20
in distress; my soul is *t* .... Lam 1:20
with tears, my heart is *t* .... Lam 2:11
heard this, he was *t* .... Matt 2:3
on the sea, they were *t*, ... Matt 14:26
You are worried and *t* .... Luke 10:41
to give you who are *t* ... 2 Thess 1:7
shaken in mind or *t* ...... 2 Thess 2:2

TROUBLES
t shall befall them, so ..... Deut 31:17
"What *t* the people .... 1 Sam 11:5
deliver you in six *t* .... Job 5:19
The *t* of my heart have ...... Ps 25:17
out of all their *t* .... Ps 25:22
my soul is full of *t* .... Ps 88:3
He who *t* his own house .. Prov 11:29
for gain *t* his own house, .. Prov 15:27
keeps his soul from *t* ..... Prov 21:23
because the former *t* .... Is 65:16
will be famines and *t* ...... Mark 13:8
him out of all his *t* .... Acts 7:10
but he who *t* you shall ...... Gal 5:10

TROUBLING
spirit from God is *t* ...... 1 Sam 16:15
wicked cease from *t* .... Job 3:17

TRUE
and Your words are *t* ..... 2 Sam 7:28
let Your word come *t* ..... 1 Kin 8:26
been without the *t* God .... 2 Chr 15:3
t before the LORD his ..... 2 Chr 31:20
and *t* laws, good statutes ... Neh 9:13
it is *t*. Hear it, and know .... Job 5:27
judgments of the LORD are *t* .. Ps 19:9
A *t* witness delivers .... Prov 14:25
But the LORD is the *t* .... Jer 10:10
"Let the LORD be a *t* .... Jer 42:5
executed *t* judgment .... Ezek 18:8
Execute *t* justice, show ..... Zech 7:9
we know that You are *t* ... Matt 22:16
That was the *t* Light .... John 1:9
He witnesses of Me is *t* .... John 5:32
the *t* bread from heaven ... John 6:32
One who sent Him is *t* ..... John 7:18
He who sent Me is *t* .... John 7:28
judge, My judgment is *t* .... John 8:16
testimony of two men is *t* .. John 8:17
about this Man were *t* .... John 10:41
I am the *t* vine, and My .... John 15:1
You, the only *t* God .... John 17:3
Indeed, let God be *t* .... Rom 3:4
whatever things are *t* .... Phil 4:8
which are copies of the *t* .... Heb 9:24
let us draw near with a *t* .. Heb 10:22
which thing is *t* in Him .... 1 John 2:8
may know Him who is *t* .. 1 John 5:20
is holy, He who is *t* .... Rev 3:7
t are Your ways, O King .... Rev 15:3
For *t* and righteous are ..... Rev 19:2
"These are the *t* .... Rev 19:9
was called Faithful and *T* .. Rev 19:11
for these words are *t* .... Rev 21:5

TRULY
It *t* flows with milk and ... Num 13:27
You shall *t* tithe all the ... Deut 14:22
t my words are not false .... Job 36:4
T God is good to Israel, to .... Ps 73:1
LORD, *t* I am Your servant .. Ps 116:16
T You are God, who hide .... Is 45:15

T You are the Son of . . . . . Matt 14:33
T this was the Son of . . . . . Matt 27:54
T this Man was the Son . . Mark 15:39
T, I say to you that he . . . . Luke 12:44
t the Son of Man goes . . . . Luke 22:22
that this is *t* the Christ . . . . . John 7:26
"*T* this is the Prophet . . . . . . John 7:40
that God is *t* among you . . 1 Cor 14:25
T the signs of an . . . . 2 Cor 12:12
t righteousness would have . . Gal 3:21
t the love of God is . . . . 1 John 2:5

TRUMPET
When the *t* sounds long, ... Ex 19:13
you hear the sound of the *t* . . Josh 6:5
LORD with the sound of a *t* . . . Ps 47:5
Blow the *t* at the time . . . . Ps 81:3
and when he blows a *t*, you . . . Is 18:3
"Blow the *t* in the . . . . Jer 4:5
Lord GOD will blow the *t* . . . Zech 9:14
deed, do not sound a *t* . . . . . . Matt 6:2
t makes an uncertain . . . . . . 1 Cor 14:8
For the *t* will sound . . . . . . 1 Cor 15:52
and with the *t* of God . . . 1 Thess 4:16
loud voice, as of a *t* . . . . Rev 1:10
t of the three angels who . . . Rev 8:13
sixth angel who had the *t* . . . Rev 9:14

TRUMPETS
the priests shall blow the *t* . . Josh 6:4
and their *t* in their hands . . . . Judg 7:8
With *t* and the sound of a . . . . Ps 98:6
to them were given seven *t* . . Rev 8:2

TRUST
in whom I will *t* . . . . 2 Sam 22:3
a shield to all who *t* in . . . 2 Sam 22:31
We *t* in the LORD our . . . . . 2 Kin 18:22
they put their *t* in Him . . . . 1 Chr 5:20
t is a spider's web . . . . Job 8:14
He slay me, yet will I *t* . . . . . Job 13:15
If God puts no *t* . . . . Job 15:15
and put your *t* in the LORD . . . . Ps 4:5
who put their *t* in You . . . . Ps 5:11
strength, in whom I will *t* . . . . Ps 18:2
shield to all who *t* in Him . . . Ps 18:30
you made Me *t* . . . . Ps 22:9
as for me, I *t* in You, O . . . . . . Ps 31:14
T in the LORD . . . . Ps 37:3
t also in Him, and He shall . . . Ps 37:5
I *t* in the mercy of God . . . . Ps 52:8
In You, O LORD, I put my *t* . . . Ps 71:1
You are my *t* from my . . . . Ps 71:5
my God, in Him I will *t* . . . . Ps 91:2
It is better to *t* in the LORD . . Ps 118:8
T in the LORD with all . . . . Prov 3:5
that your *t* may be in . . . . . Prov 22:19
who put their *t* in Him . . . . . Prov 30:5
my salvation, I will *t* . . . . Is 12:2
T in the LORD forever, for in . . Is 26:4
We *t* in the LORD our God,' . . . . Is 36:7
Let him *t* in the name . . . . Is 50:10
But he who puts his *t* in Me . . Is 57:13
Do not *t* in these . . . . Jer 7:4
My name, in which you *t* . . . . Jer 7:14
you have put your *t* in Me . . Jer 39:18
Do not *t* in a friend . . . . Mic 7:5
He knows those who *t* in . . . . . Nah 1:7
name Gentiles will *t* . . . . . . Matt 12:21
those who *t* in riches . . . . . Mark 10:24
such *t* through Christ . . . . 2 Cor 3:4
committed to your *t* . . . . 1 Tim 6:20
I will put My *t* in Him . . . . . . Heb 2:13

TRUSTED
He *t* in the LORD God of . . . 2 Kin 18:5
"He *t* in the LORD . . . . Ps 22:8
Because we have *t* in His . . . . Ps 33:21
t in the abundance of his . . . . . Ps 52:7
He *t* in God . . . . Matt 27:43
that we who first *t* . . . . Eph 1:12
the holy women who *t* . . . . . . 1 Pet 3:5

TRUSTS
But he who *t* in the . . . . Ps 32:10
is the man who *t* in Him . . . . . . Ps 34:8
whoever *t* in the LORD, ... Prov 16:20
he who *t* in the LORD . . . . . Prov 28:25
He who *t* in his own . . . . . . Prov 28:26
whoever *t* in the LORD . . . . . Prov 29:25
the man who *t* in the LORD . . Jer 17:7

TRUTH
See SPIRIT OF TRUTH; WORD OF TRUTH
led me in the way of *t* . . . . . Gen 24:48
justice, a God of *t* . . . . Deut 32:4
Him in sincerity and in *t*, . . Josh 24:14
serve Him in *t* with all . . . 1 Sam 12:24
the *t* in the name of the . . . 2 Chr 18:15
and speaks the *t* . . . . Ps 15:2
me in Your *t* and teach me . . . Ps 25:5
all His work is done in *t* . . . . . Ps 33:4
t continually preserve . . . . Ps 40:11
Behold, You desire *t* . . . . Ps 51:6
T shall spring out of . . . . Ps 85:11
t shall be your shield . . . . Ps 91:4
And His *t* endures to all . . . . . Ps 100:5
the *t* of the LORD endures . . . . Ps 117:2
t utterly out of my . . . . Ps 119:43
and Your law is *t* . . . . Ps 119:142
commandments are *t* . . . . Ps 119:151
of Your word is *t* . . . . Ps 119:160
who speaks *t* declares . . . . . Prov 12:17
t belong to those who . . . . . Prov 14:22
t atonement is provided . . . . . Prov 16:6
walked before You in *t* . . . . Is 38:3
t is fallen in the . . . . Is 59:14
not valiant for the *t* . . . . Jer 9:3
cast *t* down to the ground . . Dan 8:12
in the Scripture of *T* . . . . Dan 10:21
"There is no *t* . . . . Hos 4:1
called the City of *T* . . . . Zech 8:3
speak each man the *t* . . . . . . Zech 8:16
love *t* and peace . . . . Zech 8:19
t was in his mouth . . . . Mal 2:6
t came through Jesus . . . . John 1:17
worship in spirit and *t* . . . . . . John 4:24
you shall know the *t* . . . . John 8:32
"I am the way, the *t* . . . . John 14:6
He, the Spirit of *t* . . . . John 16:13
Your word is *t* . . . . John 17:17
be sanctified by the *t* . . . . . John 17:19
to Him, "What is *t* . . . . John 18:38
speak the words of *t* . . . . . . Acts 26:25
who suppress the *t* . . . . Rom 1:18
of sincerity and *t* . . . . 1 Cor 5:8
but rejoices in the *t* . . . . 1 Cor 13:6
but, speaking the *t* . . . . Eph 4:15
each one speak *t* with his . . . Eph 4:25
your waist with *t* . . . . Eph 6:14
in the word of the *t* . . . . Col 1:5
the love of the *t* . . . . 2 Thess 2:10
I am speaking the *t* . . . . 1 Tim 2:7
they may know the *t* . . . . . . 2 Tim 2:25
the knowledge of the *t* . . . . . . 2 Tim 3:7
in the present *t* . . . . 2 Pet 1:12
way of *t* will be . . . . 2 Pet 2:2
but in deed and in *t* . . . . . . 1 John 3:18
that we are of the *t* . . . . 1 John 3:19
we know the spirit of *t* . . . . 1 John 4:6
the Spirit is *t* . . . . 1 John 5:6
t that is in you . . . . 3 John 3

TRUTHFUL
The *t* lip shall be . . . . Prov 12:19

TRUTHFULLY
deal *t* are His delight . . . . . Prov 12:22

TRY
t my mind and my heart . . . . . Ps 26:2
t me, and know my . . . . Ps 139:23
refine them and *t* them . . . . Jer 9:7
t Me now in this . . . . Mal 3:10
which is to *t* you . . . . 1 Pet 4:12

TUBAL
Son of Japheth, Gen 10:2
——Tribe associated with Javan and Meshech, Is 66:19
In Gog's army, Ezek 38:2, 3
Punishment of, Ezek 32:26, 27

TUBAL-CAIN
Son of Lamech, Gen 4:19–22

TUMORS
the boils of Egypt, with *t* . . Deut 28:27
and struck them with *t* . . . . . 1 Sam 5:6
Five golden *t* and five . . . . . 1 Sam 6:4

TUMULT
their waves, and the *t* . . . . Ps 65:7
Your enemies make a *t* . . . . Ps 83:2

TUNIC
Also he made him a *t* . . . . Gen 37:3
and take away your *t* . . . . . . Matt 5:40
not withhold your *t* . . . . Luke 6:29
the *t* was without seam, . . . John 19:23

TUNICS
the LORD God made *t* . . . . Gen 3:21
not to put on two *t* . . . . Mark 6:9
He who has two *t*, let him . Luke 3:11
weeping, showing the *t* . . . . . Acts 9:39

TURBAN
like a robe and a *t* . . . . Job 29:14
"Remove the *t* . . . . Ezek 21:26

TURN
T from Your fierce wrath, . . . Ex 32:12
Do not *t* to idols, nor make . . Lev 19:4
you shall not *t* . . . . Deut 17:11
LORD may *t* away from . . . . Num 25:4
do not *t* from it to the right . . Josh 1:7
t from their sin because . . . 1 Kin 8:35
T from your evil ways, . . . 2 Kin 17:13
do not *t* to iniquity, for . . . . . Job 36:21
t to the LORD, and all the . . . . Ps 22:27
T Yourself to me, and have . . Ps 25:16
do not *t* Your servant away . . Ps 27:9
Then we will not *t* . . . . Ps 80:18
but let them not *t* . . . . Ps 85:8
t to me, and have mercy . . . . Ps 86:16
yet I do not *t* . . . . Ps 119:51
T at my rebuke . . . . Prov 1:23
Do not *t* to the right or . . . . Prov 4:27
not let your heart *t* . . . . Prov 7:25
I will *t* My hand against you, . . Is 1:25
every man will *t* to his own . . Is 13:14
'*T* now everyone from . . . . . . Jer 35:15
T us back to You, O . . . . Lam 5:21
"Repent, *t* away from . . . . . . Ezek 14:6
Repent, and *t* from all . . . . Ezek 18:30
T, *t* from your evil ways . . Ezek 33:11
T to me with all your . . . . Joel 2:12
yes, let every one *t* . . . . Jon 3:8
"*T* now from your evil . . . . . . Zech 1:4
those who *t* away an alien . . . . Mal 3:5
he will *t* the hearts of the . . . . Mal 4:6
on your right cheek, *t* . . . . . . Matt 5:39
t the hearts of the . . . . Luke 1:17
you that you should *t* . . . . . Acts 14:15
t them from darkness . . . . . Acts 26:18
repent, *t* to God, and do . . . Acts 26:20
Let him *t* away from . . . . 1 Pet 3:11
waters to *t* them to blood . . . Rev 11:6

TURN ASIDE
t and see this great . . . . Ex 3:3
t after many to pervert . . . . Ex 23:2
t and serve other gods . . . . Deut 11:16
So you shall not *t* . . . . Deut 28:14
Law of Moses, lest you *t* . . . Josh 23:6
they went, and did not *t* . . . 1 Sam 6:12
t from following the . . . . . . 1 Sam 12:20
He did not *t* from them . . . . 1 Kin 22:43
did not *t* from it . . . . 2 Chr 20:32
The paths of their way *t* . . . . Job 6:18
nor such as *t* to lies . . . . Ps 40:4
I do not *t* from Your law . . . Ps 119:51
such as *t* to their crooked . . . Ps 125:5
Do not let your heart *t* . . . . . Prov 7:25
to *t* the justice due . . . . Lam 3:35

did not *t* when they went .. Ezek 1:17
did not *t* when they ...... Ezek 10:11

TURNED
in the river were *t* to blood ... Ex 7:20
who *t* to the LORD with ... 2 Kin 23:25
t to the LORD God of ...... 2 Chr 15:4
and *t* their backs on ...... 2 Chr 29:6
t me over to the hands of .. Job 16:11
I love have *t* against .... Job 19:19
kept His way and not *t* .... Job 23:11
The wicked shall be *t* .... Ps 9:17
let them be *t* back and .... Ps 70:2
t my feet to Your .... Ps 119:59
of Israel, they have *t* .... Is 1:4
LORD has not *t* back from ..... Jer 4:8
shall be *t* into darkness ..... Joel 2:31
that they *t* from their evil ... Jon 3:10
Then He *t* to the woman ... Luke 7:44
sorrow will be *t* into joy .. John 16:20
sun shall be *t* into .... Acts 2:20
saw him and *t* to the Lord .. Acts 9:35
number believed and *t* .... Acts 11:21
and how you *t* to God .... 1 Thess 1:9

TURNING
Gentiles who are *t* to ..... Acts 15:19
marvel that you are *t* .... Gal 1:6
or shadow of *t* .... James 1:17
and *t* the cities of Sodom .... 2 Pet 2:6

TURNS
of the wicked He *t* .... Ps 146:9
A soft answer *t* .... Prov 15:1
he *t*, he prospers .... Prov 17:8
One who *t* away his ear .... Prov 28:9
when a righteous man *t* .... Ezek 3:20
But if a wicked man *t* .... Ezek 18:21
a wicked man *t* away ..... Ezek 18:27
he *t* from his sin and ..... Ezek 33:14
t from his wickedness ..... Ezek 33:19
but no one *t* back .... Nah 2:8
that he who *t* .... James 5:20

TURTLEDOVE
the life of Your *t* .... Ps 74:19
t is heard in our land ...... Song 2:12

TURTLEDOVES
of *t* or young pigeons .... Lev 1:14
A pair of *t* or two young ... Luke 2:24

TUTOR
the law was our *t* .... Gal 3:24
no longer under a *t* .... Gal 3:25

TWELVE
the sons of Jacob were *t* ... Gen 35:22
are the *t* tribes of Israel ... Gen 49:28
were *t* stones according ..... Ex 39:14
t men, each one .... Num 1:44
Joshua set up *t* stones .... Josh 4:9
Solomon had *t* governors ... 1 Kin 4:7
Elijah took *t* stones, ... 1 Kin 18:31
Manasseh was *t* years ..... 2 Kin 21:1
called His *t* disciples to .... Matt 10:1
These *t* Jesus sent out ..... Matt 10:5
they took up *t* baskets .... Matt 14:20
more than *t* legions of .... Matt 26:53
Then He appointed *t* ...... Mark 3:14
of blood for *t* years .... Mark 5:25
took up *t* baskets full ..... Mark 6:43
when He was *t* years old .. Luke 2:42
He chose *t* whom He .... Luke 6:13
a flow of blood for *t* .... Luke 8:43
t baskets of the leftover ... Luke 9:17
filled *t* baskets with the .... John 6:13
I not choose you, the *t* ..... John 6:70
head a garland of *t* stars ... Rev 12:1
t gates were *t* pearls .... Rev 21:21

TWELVE APOSTLES
Now the names of the *t* .... Matt 10:2
and the *t* with Him ...... Luke 22:14
the names of the *t* .... Rev 21:14

TWELVE DISCIPLES
when He had called His *t* .. Matt 10:1
commanding His *t* .... Matt 11:1
took the *t* aside on the .... Matt 20:17
Then He called His *t* .... Luke 9:1

TWELVE TRIBES
these are the *t* of Israel .... Gen 49:28
pillars according to the *t* ..... Ex 24:4
name according to the *t* ..... Ex 39:14
inheritance among the *t* .. Ezek 47:13
judging the *t* .... Matt 19:28
To this promise our *t* ...... Acts 26:7
the *t* which are scattered .. James 1:1
the names of the *t* .... Rev 21:12

TWENTY-FOUR ELDERS
on the thrones I saw *t* .... Rev 4:4
t fall down before Him ...... Rev 4:10
t fell down before the .... Rev 5:8
t fell down and worshiped .. Rev 5:14
t who sat before God ...... Rev 11:16
t and the four living .... Rev 19:4

TWICE
the rock *t* with his rod .... Num 20:11
t as much as he had .... Job 42:10
the rooster crows *t* .... Mark 14:30
the rooster crows *t* .... Mark 14:72

TWILIGHT
at *t* is the LORD's Passover .. Lev 23:5
sacrifice the Passover at *t* .. Deut 16:6

TWIN
figurehead was the *T* ..... Acts 28:11

TWINS
there were *t* in her womb .. Gen 25:24
behold, *t* were in her ...... Gen 38:27
two fawns, *t* of a gazelle .... Song 7:3

TWIST
All day they *t* my .... Ps 56:5
unstable people *t* to .... 2 Pet 3:16

TWO
God made *t* great lights ..... Gen 1:16
t each of animals that are .... Gen 7:2
the ark to Noah, *t* .... Gen 7:15
T nations are in your ...... Gen 25:23
t rams without blemish, ... Ex 29:1
He gave Moses *t* tablets of .. Ex 31:18
shall be unclean *t* weeks .... Lev 12:5
t young pigeons .... Lev 12:8
t tablets of the covenant ... Deut 9:15
hewed *t* tablets of stone .... Deut 10:3
by the mouth of *t* or ...... Deut 19:15
the *t* middle pillars .... Judg 16:29
divided the Red Sea in *t* .... Ps 136:13
T are better than one .... Eccl 4:9
t he covered his .... Is 6:2
a ram which had *t* horns .... Dan 8:3
saw, having the *t* horns .... Dan 8:20
there stood *t* others, one .... Dan 12:5
one mile, go with him *t* .... Matt 5:41
five loaves and *t* fish ..... Matt 14:17
'by the mouth of *t* or ..... Matt 18:16
For where *t* or three are .. Matt 18:20
t shall become one .... Matt 19:5
A man had *t* sons, and .... Matt 21:28
five talents, to another *t* .. Matt 25:15
t robbers were crucified .. Matt 27:38
in *t* from top to bottom ... Matt 27:51
said, "Five, and *t* fish ..... Mark 6:38
t shall become one flesh' .. Mark 10:8
and threw in *t* mites, ... Mark 12:42
also crucified *t* robbers ... Mark 15:27
in *t* from top to bottom ... Mark 15:38
t young pigeons .... Luke 2:24
t fish, unless we go and .... Luke 9:13
certain man had *t* sons ... Luke 15:11
servant can serve *t* .... Luke 16:13
widow putting in *t* mites ... Luke 21:2
were also *t* others, ... Luke 23:32
temple was torn in *t* .... Luke 23:45
t of them were traveling .. Luke 24:13
T hundred denarii worth .... John 6:7
t small fish, but what are ... John 6:9
these are the *t* covenants .... Gal 4:24
new man from the *t* .... Eph 2:15
t shall become one flesh .... Eph 5:31
from *t* or three witnesses .. 1 Tim 5:19
was *t* hundred million; I .... Rev 9:16
power to my *t* witnesses .... Rev 11:3
had *t* horns like a lamb .... Rev 13:11

TWO-EDGED SWORD
and a *t* in their hand .... Ps 149:6
as wormwood, sharp as a *t* .. Prov 5:4
sharper than any *t* .... Heb 4:12
His mouth went a sharp *t* ... Rev 1:16
He who has the sharp *t* ..... Rev 2:12

TYCHICUS
Paul's companion, Acts 20:1, 4
Paul's messenger, Eph 6:21, 22; Col 4:7–9; 2 Tim 4:12

TYPE
of Adam, who is a *t* .... Rom 5:14

TYRE
City of Phoenicia noted for its commerce, Josh 19:29; 2 Sam 5:11; Jer 25:22

TYRE AND SIDON
cut off from *T* every helper .. Jer 47:4
you to do with Me, O *T* ...... Joel 3:4
had been done in *T* .... Matt 11:21
to the region of *T* .... Matt 15:21
more tolerable for *T* at ... Luke 10:14
with the people of *T* ...... Acts 12:20

UGLY
And the *u* and gaunt cows .. Gen 41:4

ULAI
Scene of Daniel's visions, Dan 8:2–16

UNAFRAID
Do you want to be *u* ...... Rom 13:3

UNAWARE
I do not want you to be *u* .. Rom 1:13
not want you to be *u* ..... 1 Cor 10:11

UNBELIEF
because of their *u* .... Matt 13:58
Because of your *u* .... Matt 17:20
help my *u* .... Mark 9:24
and He rebuked their *u* .. Mark 16:14
promise of God through *u* .. Rom 4:20
did it ignorantly in *u* ...... 1 Tim 1:13
you an evil heart of *u* ...... Heb 3:12
enter in because of *u* .... Heb 3:19

UNBELIEVER
But if the *u* departs, let .... 1 Cor 7:15
has a believer with an *u* ... 2 Cor 6:15
and is worse than an *u* ..... 1 Tim 5:8

UNBELIEVERS
his portion with the *u* .... Luke 12:46
who believe but to *u* ...... 1 Cor 14:22
are uninformed or *u* ...... 1 Cor 14:23
yoked together with *u* ..... 2 Cor 6:14

UNBELIEVING
Do not be *u* .... John 20:27
u Jews stirred up the .... Acts 14:2
For the *u* husband is ...... 1 Cor 7:14
u nothing is pure .... Titus 1:15
But the cowardly, *u* .... Rev 21:8

UNCIRCUMCISED
heed me, for I am of *u* lips ... Ex 6:12
Behold, I am of *u* lips, and ... Ex 6:30
For no *u* person shall eat it .. Ex 12:48
u hearts are humbled ...... Lev 26:41
is this *u* Philistine .... 1 Sam 17:26
of Israel are *u* in the heart ... Jer 9:26
u in heart and *u* in flesh ... Ezek 44:7
You stiff-necked and *u* ..... Acts 7:51
not the physically *u* .... Rom 2:27
by faith and the *u* .... Rom 3:30
only, or upon the *u* also ..... Rom 4:9

u had been committed ... Gal 2:7
nor Jew, circumcised nor *u* .. Col 3:11

UNCIRCUMCISION
has become *u* ... Rom 2:25
u is nothing, but keeping .. 1 Cor 7:19
who are called *U* by ... Eph 2:11

UNCLEAN
of animals that are *u* ... Gen 7:2
person touches any *u* thing ... Lev 5:2
u thing shall not be eaten ... Lev 7:19
to the LORD, while he is *u* ... Lev 7:20
who touches any *u* ... Lev 7:21
They are *u* to you ... Lev 11:8
these you shall become *u* .. Lev 11:24
I am a man of *u* lips ... Is 6:5
u shall no longer come ... Is 52:1
we are all like an *u* thing ... Is 64:6
I pronounced them *u* ... Ezek 20:26
He commands even the *u* .. Mark 1:27
commands the *u* spirits ... Luke 4:36
any man common or *u* ... Acts 10:28
there is nothing *u* ... Rom 14:14
your children would be *u* .. 1 Cor 7:14
Do not touch what is *u* ... 2 Cor 6:17
that no fornicator, *u* ... Eph 5:5

UNCLEAN SPIRIT
u to depart from the land .. Zech 13:2
u goes out of a man ... Matt 12:43
synagogue with an *u* ... Mark 1:23
u had convulsed him ... Mark 1:26
"He has an *u* ... Mark 3:30
a man with an *u* ... Mark 5:2
daughter had an *u* ... Mark 7:25
He rebuked the *u* ... Mark 9:25
He had commanded the *u* .. Luke 8:29
Jesus rebuked the *u* ... Luke 9:42
u goes out of a man ... Luke 11:24

UNCLEAN SPIRITS
them power over *u* ... Matt 10:1
He commands even the *u* .. Mark 1:27
u, whenever they saw ... Mark 3:11
u went out and entered ... Mark 5:13
tormented with *u* ... Luke 6:18
who were tormented by *u* .. Acts 5:16
u, crying with a loud ... Acts 8:7
three *u* like frogs ... Rev 16:13

UNCLEANNESS
of Israel from their *u*, lest .. Lev 15:31
for sin and for *u* ... Zech 13:1
men's bones and all *u* ... Matt 23:27
also gave them up to *u* ... Rom 1:24
members as slaves of *u* ... Rom 6:19
adultery, fornication, *u*, ... Gal 5:19
fornication, *u*, passion, evil ... Col 3:5
did not call us to *u* ... 1 Thess 4:7
flesh in the lust of *u* ... 2 Pet 2:10

UNCLEANNESSES
from all your *u* ... Ezek 36:29

UNCLOTHED
we want to be *u* ... 2 Cor 5:4

UNCOVER
Do not *u* your heads nor ... Lev 10:6
shall not *u* her nakedness ... Lev 18:7
u the woman's head, and ... Num 5:18
the LORD will *u* their secret ... Is 3:17
skirt, *u* the thigh ... Is 47:2
he will *u* your sins ... Lam 4:22

UNCOVERED
and became *u* in his tent ... Gen 9:21
of the world were *u* ... 2 Sam 22:16
I have *u* his secret places, .. Jer 49:10
its foundation will be *u* ... Ezek 13:14
transgressions are *u* ... Ezek 21:24
they *u* the roof where He ... Mark 2:4
head *u* dishonors her ... 1 Cor 11:5
to God with her head *u* ... 1 Cor 11:13

UNCOVERS
u her nakedness, he has ... Lev 20:18
u deep things out of ... Job 12:22

UNDEFILED
Blessed are the *u* ... Ps 119:1
all, and the bed *u* ... Heb 13:4
u religion before God ... James 1:27
incorruptible and *u* ... 1 Pet 1:4

UNDER HIS FEET
And there was *u* ... Ex 24:10
down with darkness *u* ... 2 Sam 22:10
You have put all things *u* ... Ps 8:6
has put all enemies *u* ... 1 Cor 15:25
And He put all things *u* ... Eph 1:22
things in subjection *u* ... Heb 2:8

UNDER THE LAW
to those who are *u* ... Rom 3:19
to those who are *u* ... 1 Cor 9:20
of a woman, born *u* ... Gal 4:4
you who desire to be *u* ... Gal 4:21
Spirit, you are not *u* ... Gal 5:18

UNDERFOOT
Lord has trampled *u* all ... Lam 1:15
the Son of God *u* ... Heb 10:29

UNDERMINE
And you *u* your friend ... Job 6:27

UNDERSTAND
u one another's speech ... Gen 11:7
cause me to *u* wherein I ... Job 6:24
of His power who can *u* ... Job 26:14
can anyone *u* the ... Job 36:29
uttered what I did not *u* ... Job 42:3
if there are any who *u* ... Ps 14:2
Who can *u* his errors ... Ps 19:12
in Egypt did not *u* ... Ps 106:7
Make me *u* the way of ... Ps 119:27
then you will *u* the fear of ... Prov 2:5
you will *u* righteousness ... Prov 2:9
is to *u* his way ... Prov 14:8
Evil men do not *u* ... Prov 28:5
hearing, but do not *u* ... Is 6:9
so that they cannot *u* ... Is 44:18
and quick to *u* ... Dan 1:4
set your heart to *u* ... Dan 10:12
u shall instruct many ... Dan 11:33
of the wicked shall *u* ... Dan 12:10
people who do not *u* ... Hos 4:14
Let him *u* these things ... Hos 14:9
nor do they *u* His counsel ... Mic 4:12
will hear and shall not *u* .. Matt 13:14
should *u* with their heart .. Matt 13:15
they may hear and not *u* .. Mark 4:12
hearing they may not *u* ... Luke 8:10
Why do you not *u* ... John 8:43
u with their hearts and ... John 12:40
I am doing you do not *u* ... John 13:7
u what you are reading ... Acts 8:30
lest they should *u* ... Acts 28:27
I am doing, I do not *u* ... Rom 7:15
have not heard shall *u* ... Rom 15:21
u all mysteries ... 1 Cor 13:2
some things hard to *u* ... 2 Pet 3:16

UNDERSTANDING
of God, in wisdom, in *u*, in ... Ex 31:3
a woman of good *u* ... 1 Sam 25:3
asked for yourself *u* ... 1 Kin 3:11
and exceedingly great *u* ... 1 Kin 4:29
filled with wisdom and *u* .. 1 Kin 7:14
He has counsel and *u* ... Job 12:13
He takes away the *u* of ... Job 12:24
by His *u* He breaks up ... Job 26:12
is the place of *u* ... Job 28:12
depart from evil is *u* ... Job 28:28
Almighty gives him *u* ... Job 32:8
If you have *u*, hear this ... Job 34:16
has given *u* to the heart ... Job 38:36
not endow her with *u* ... Job 39:17
my heart shall give *u* ... Ps 49:3
a good *u* have all those ... Ps 111:10
Give me *u* ... Ps 119:34
give me *u*, that I may ... Ps 119:73
Your precepts I get *u* ... Ps 119:104
give me *u*, that I may ... Ps 119:125
give me *u*, and I shall ... Ps 119:144
give me *u* according to ... Ps 119:169
His *u* is infinite ... Ps 147:5
a man of *u* will attain wise .. Prov 1:5
apply your heart to *u* ... Prov 2:2
u will keep you ... Prov 2:11
lean not on your own *u* ... Prov 3:5
u He established ... Prov 3:19
with a woman lacks *u* ... Prov 6:32
As for him who lacks *u*, ... Prov 9:4
and go in the way of *u* ... Prov 9:6
of the Holy One is *u* ... Prov 9:10
a man of *u* has wisdom ... Prov 10:23
but a man of *u* holds his .. Prov 11:12
frivolity is devoid of *u* ... Prov 12:11
Good *u* gains favor, but ... Prov 13:15
to wrath has great *u* ... Prov 14:29
him who has *u* seeks ... Prov 15:14
but a man of *u* walks ... Prov 15:21
who heeds rebuke gets *u* .. Prov 15:32
And to get *u* is to be ... Prov 16:16
U is a wellspring ... Prov 16:22
A man devoid of *u* ... Prov 17:18
A fool has no delight in *u* .. Prov 18:2
u will find good ... Prov 19:8
the way of *u* will rest in ... Prov 21:16
and instruction and *u* ... Prov 23:23
but the poor who has *u* ... Prov 28:11
A ruler who lacks *u* is a .. Prov 28:16
Spirit of wisdom and *u* ... Is 11:2
For it is a people of no *u* ... Is 27:11
His *u* is unsearchable ... Is 40:28
the heaven by His *u* ... Jer 51:15
also still without *u* ... Matt 15:16
heart, with all the *u* ... Mark 12:33
And He opened their *u* ... Luke 24:45
also pray with the *u* ... 1 Cor 14:15
five words with my *u* ... 1 Cor 14:19
but in *u* be mature ... 1 Cor 14:20
having their *u* darkened, ... Eph 4:18
God, which surpasses all *u* ... Phil 4:7
and spiritual *u* ... Col 1:9
the Lord give you *u* ... 2 Tim 2:7
Who is wise and *u* ... James 3:13
and has given us an *u* ... 1 John 5:20
him who has *u* calculate ... Rev 13:18

UNDERSTANDS
God *u* its way, and He ... Job 28:23
all plain to him who *u* ... Prov 8:9
is easy to him who *u* ... Prov 14:6
there is none who *u* ... Rom 3:11

UNDERSTOOD
all Israel *u* that day ... 2 Sam 3:37
my ear has heard and *u* it ... Job 13:1
Then I *u* their end ... Ps 73:17
My heart has *u* great ... Eccl 1:16
Have you not *u* from ... Is 40:21
u all these things ... Matt 13:51
clearly seen, being *u* ... Rom 1:20
I *u* as a child, I thought .. 1 Cor 13:11

UNDESIRABLE
gather together, O *u* ... Zeph 2:1

UNDIGNIFIED
I will be even more *u* ... 2 Sam 6:22

UNDISCERNING
u, untrustworthy ... Rom 1:31

UNDONE
He left nothing *u* of all ... Josh 11:15
"Woe is me, for I am *u* ... Is 6:5
leaving the others *u* ... Matt 23:23

UNEDUCATED
that they were *u* ... Acts 4:13

UNEQUALLY
Do not be *u* yoked ... 2 Cor 6:14

UNEXPECTEDLY
that Day come on you *u* .. Luke 21:34

u will be blessed .... Ps 112:2
u there arises light .... Ps 112:4
For the *u* will dwell in the .. Prov 2:21
is strength for the *u* .... Prov 10:29
u will guide them .... Prov 11:3
u will deliver them .... Prov 11:6
u will flourish .... Prov 14:11
u is His delight .... Prov 15:8
of the *u* is a highway ..... Prov 15:19
Whoever causes the *u* to .. Prov 28:10
that God made man *u* ...... Eccl 7:29
and there is no one *u* .... Mic 7:2
his soul is not *u* .... Hab 2:4

UPRIGHT IN HEART
God, Who saves the *u* .... Ps 7:10
shoot secretly at the *u* .... Ps 11:2
shout for joy, all you *u* ...... Ps 32:11
righteousness to the *u* .... Ps 36:10
all the *u* shall glory .... Ps 64:10
all the *u* will follow it .... Ps 94:15
gladness for the *u* .... Ps 97:11

UPRIGHTLY
He who walks *u*, and works .. Ps 15:2
from those who walk *u* ...... Ps 84:11
shield to those who walk *u* .. Prov 2:7
understanding walks *u* .... Prov 15:21
good to him who walks *u* .... Mic 2:7

UPRIGHTNESS
to show man His *u* .... Job 33:23
praise You with *u* of heart ... Ps 119:7
me in the land of *u* .... Ps 143:10
of *u* to walk in the ways ... Prov 2:13
walks in his *u* fears the .... Prov 14:2
princes for their *u* .... Prov 17:26
of the just is *u* .... Is 26:7
land of *u* he will deal .... Is 26:10

UPROAR
so that the city is in an *u* .. 1 Kin 1:45
be an *u* of the people ...... Mark 14:2
After the *u* had ceased, ... Acts 20:1

UPROOT
He will *u* Israel from ..... 1 Kin 14:15
then I will *u* .... 2 Chr 7:20
u you from the land .... Ps 52:5
u the wheat with .... Matt 13:29

UPROOTED
LORD *u* them from their ... Deut 29:28
my hope He has *u* like a ... Job 19:10
unfaithful will be *u* from ... Prov 2:22

UPWARD
prevailed fifteen cubits *u* .... Gen 7:20
trouble, as the sparks fly *u* .... Job 5:7
winds *u* for the wise ...... Prov 15:24
downward, and bear fruit *u* .. Is 37:31
my eyes fail from looking *u* .. Is 38:14

UR OF THE CHALDEANS
City of Abram's early life, Gen 11:28–31; 15:7
Located in Mesopotamia by Stephen, Acts 7:2, 4

URGE
I *u* you to take heart, ... Acts 27:22
I *u* you, imitate .... 1 Cor 4:16
Therefore I *u* you to .... 2 Cor 2:8
I *u* you to become like me .... Gal 4:12
I *u* you in the sight of ..... 1 Tim 6:13

URGED
the angels *u* Lot to hurry, .. Gen 19:15
His disciples *u* Him .... John 4:31
I strongly *u* him to .... 1 Cor 16:12

URIAH
Hittite; one of David's warriors, 2 Sam 23:39
Husband of Bathsheba; condemned to death by David, 2 Sam 11:1–27

URIJAH
High priest in Ahaz's time, 2 Kin 16:10–16
—— Prophet in Jeremiah's time, Jer 26:20–23

URIM
of judgment of *U* .... Ex 28:30
the judgment of the *U* ..... Num 27:21
Thummim and Your *U* .... Deut 33:8
could consult with the *U* .... Ezra 2:63
could consult with the *U* .... Neh 7:65

US
"God with *u* .... Matt 1:23
who is not against *u* .... Mark 9:40
If God is for *u* .... Rom 8:31
They went out from *u* .... 1 John 2:19

USE
who spitefully *u* you .... Matt 5:44
leaving the natural *u* .... Rom 1:27
u this world as not .... 1 Cor 7:31
u liberty as an .... Gal 5:13
u a little wine .... 1 Tim 5:23
reason of *u* have their ...... Heb 5:14

USEFUL
Is it *u* for any work .... Ezek 15:4
u for the Master .... 2 Tim 2:21
you, for he is *u* to me for ... 2 Tim 4:11

USELESS
all of them are *u* .... Is 44:9
are unprofitable and *u* ...... Titus 3:9
one's religion is *u* .... James 1:26

USES
if one *u* it lawfully .... 1 Tim 1:8

USING
u no figure of speech ..... John 16:29
perish with the *u* .... Col 2:22
u liberty as a .... 1 Pet 2:16

USURY
Take no *u* or .... Lev 25:36
exacting *u* from his brother .. Neh 5:7
put out his money at *u* .... Ps 15:5

UTTER
u words from their heart .... Job 8:10
nor my tongue *u* deceit ..... Job 27:4
u pure knowledge .... Job 33:3
u dark sayings of old .... Ps 78:2
My lips shall *u* praise ..... Ps 119:171
a false witness will *u* lies ... Prov 14:5
heart will *u* perverse ...... Prov 23:33
let not your heart *u* .... Eccl 5:2
I will *u* My judgments .... Jer 1:16
lawful for a man to *u* ...... 2 Cor 12:4

UTTERANCE
the Spirit gave them *u* .... Acts 2:4
u may be given to me .... Eph 6:19

UTTERED
The deep *u* its voice .... Hab 3:10
which cannot be *u* .... Rom 8:26
the seven thunders *u* .... Rev 10:4

UTTERLY
that I will *u* blot out the ..... Ex 17:14
they *u* destroyed all that .... Josh 6:21
lands by *u* destroying .... 2 Kin 19:11
he shall not be *u* cast down .. Ps 37:24
Oh, do not forsake me *u* ..... Ps 119:8
it would be *u* despised ...... Song 8:7
You have *u* rejected .... Lam 5:22
u destroyed from among ..... Acts 3:23
she will be *u* burned with .... Rev 18:8

UTTERMOST
upon them to the *u* .... 1 Thess 2:16
u those who come .... Heb 7:25

UTTERS
Day unto day *u* speech .... Ps 19:2
u His voice from .... Amos 1:2
and the great man *u* .... Mic 7:3

UZZAH
Son of Abinadab, struck down for touching the ark of the covenant, 2 Sam 6:3–11

UZZIAH
King of Judah, called Azariah, 2 Kin 14:21; 15:1–7
Reigns righteously, 2 Chr 26:1–15
Usurps priestly function; stricken with leprosy, 2 Chr 26:16–21
Life of, written by Isaiah, 2 Chr 26:22, 23

VAGABOND
v you shall be on the .... Gen 4:12

VAIN
of the LORD your God in *v* .... Ex 20:7
of the LORD your God in *v* .. Deut 5:11
the people plot a *v* .... Ps 2:1
they labor in *v* who build it .. Ps 127:1
v life which he passes ...... Eccl 6:12
'I have labored in *v* .... Is 49:4
And in *v* they worship Me .. Matt 15:9
And in *v* they worship Me, .. Mark 7:7
you believed in *v* .... 1 Cor 15:2
labor is not in *v* in the .... 1 Cor 15:58
law, then Christ died in *v* .... Gal 2:21
run in *v* or labored in *v* ..... Phil 2:16

VALIANT
Only be *v* for me .... 1 Sam 18:17
They are not *v* for the .... Jer 9:3
v men swept away .... Jer 46:15

VALIANTLY
while Israel does *v* .... Num 24:18
God we will do *v* .... Ps 60:12
of the LORD does *v* .... Ps 118:15

VALLEY
in the *V* of Megiddo ..... 2 Chr 35:22
I walk through the *v* .... Ps 23:4
pass through the *V* .... Ps 84:6
the verdure of the *v* .... Song 6:11
v shall be exalted .... Is 40:4
in the midst of the *v* .... Ezek 37:1
in the *v* of decision .... Joel 3:14
v shall be filled .... Luke 3:5

VALLEYS
He is not God of the *v* .... 1 Kin 20:28
and the lily of the *v* .... Song 2:1
the *v* will split like wax .... Mic 1:4

VALOR
a mighty man of *v* .... 1 Sam 16:18

VALUE
does not know its *v* .... Job 28:13
of more *v* than they .... Matt 6:26
you are of more *v* than .... Matt 10:31
Of how much more *v* .... Matt 12:12
you are of more *v* than .... Luke 12:7
Of how much more *v* ..... Luke 12:24
they counted up the *v* ..... Acts 19:19
but are of no *v* against the .. Col 2:23

VALUED
It cannot be *v* in the .... Job 28:16
is *v* by what others say ... Prov 27:21

VANISH
when it is hot, they *v* .... Job 6:17
For the heavens will *v* .... Is 51:6
knowledge, it will *v* .... 1 Cor 13:8
old is ready to *v* away ...... Heb 8:13

VANISHED
Has their wisdom *v* .... Jer 49:7
and He *v* from their ...... Luke 24:31

VANITY
of vanities, all is *v* .... Eccl 1:2
This also is *v* and grasping .. Eccl 6:9
iniquity with cords of *v* .... Is 5:18

VANQUISH
God will *v* him, not man ... Job 32:13

VAPOR
best state is but *v* .... Ps 39:5

surely every man is *v* .... Ps 39:11
It is even a *v* that .... James 4:14

VARIATION
whom there is no *v* .... James 1:17

VARIETIES
v of tongues .... 1 Cor 12:28

VARIOUS
glistening stones of *v* ..... 1 Chr 29:2
earthquakes in *v* places .... Matt 24:7
were sick with *v* diseases .. Mark 1:34
sins, led away by *v* lusts ... 2 Tim 3:6
God, who at *v* times and in .. Heb 1:1
when you fall into *v* trials .. James 1:2

VASHTI
Queen of Ahasuerus, deposed and divorced, Esth 1:9–22

VEGETABLES
and let them give us *v* ...... Dan 1:12
is weak eats only *v* .... Rom 14:2

VEHEMENT
of fire, a most *v* .... Song 8:6

VEIL
she took a *v* and covered .. Gen 24:65
The *v* shall be a divider for .. Ex 26:33
he put a *v* on his face .... Ex 34:33
temples behind your *v* ...... Song 6:7
v of the temple was .... Matt 27:51
Moses, who put a *v* .... 2 Cor 3:13
because the *v* is taken ..... 2 Cor 3:14
the *v* is taken away .... 2 Cor 3:16
Presence behind the *v* ...... Heb 6:19

VEILED
Give them a *v* heart .... Lam 3:65
it is *v* to those who are ..... 2 Cor 4:3

VEILS
v herself by the flocks of .... Song 1:7
I will also tear off your *v* .. Ezek 13:21

VENGEANCE
You shall not take *v* .... Lev 19:18
V is Mine .... Deut 32:35
spare in the day of *v* .... Prov 6:34
it is the day of the LORD's *v* ... Is 34:8
God will come with *v* .... Is 35:4
on the garments of *v* .... Is 59:17
and the day of *v* of our God ... Is 61:2
let me see Your *v* .... Jer 11:20
for it is the *v* of the LORD ... Jer 50:15
are the days of *v* .... Luke 21:22
written, "*V* is Mine .... Rom 12:19
flaming fire taking *v* .... 2 Thess 1:8
who said, "*V* is Mine ...... Heb 10:30
suffering the *v* .... Jude 7

VENOM
It becomes cobra *v* .... Job 20:14

VESSEL
like a potter's *v* .... Ps 2:9
v that he made of clay .... Jer 18:4
like a precious *v* .... Jer 25:34
been emptied from *v* .... Jer 48:11
for he is a chosen *v* .... Acts 9:15
lump to make one *v* .... Rom 9:21
to possess his own *v* ...... 1 Thess 4:4
to the weaker *v* .... 1 Pet 3:7

VESSELS
longsuffering the *v* .... Rom 9:22
treasure in earthen *v* .... 2 Cor 4:7
like the potter's *v* .... Rev 2:27

VEXED
grieved, and I was *v* .... Ps 73:21

VICE
as a cloak for *v* .... 1 Pet 2:16

VICTIM
and plucked the *v* .... Job 29:17

VICTORY
brought about a great *v* .. 2 Sam 23:12
is swallowed up in *v* ..... 1 Cor 15:54
Hades, where is your *v* ... 1 Cor 15:55
who gives us the *v* .... 1 Cor 15:57
v that has overcome .... 1 John 5:4
have the *v* over the beast ... Rev 15:2

VIEW
"Go, *v* the land .... Josh 2:1

VIGILANT
in prayer, being *v* .... Col 4:2
Be sober, be *v* .... 1 Pet 5:8

VIGOR
nor his natural *v* .... Deut 34:7

VILE
sons made themselves *v* .. 1 Sam 3:13
"Behold, I am *v* .... Job 40:4
them up to *v* passions ...... Rom 1:26

VILLAGES
of Megiddo and its *v* .... Judg 1:27
they may go into the *v* .... Matt 14:15
many *v* of the Samaritans .. Acts 8:25

VINDICATE
V me, O LORD, for I have ..... Ps 26:1
V me, O LORD my God, ... Ps 35:24
V me, O God, And plead ..... Ps 43:1
And *v* me by Your strength ... Ps 54:1

VINDICATED
know that I shall be *v* ...... Job 13:18

VINDICATES
indeed this *v* you before .... Gen 20:16

VINDICATION
Let my *v* come from .... Ps 17:2

VINE
in my dream a *v* was .... Gen 40:9
to the choice *v* .... Gen 49:11
their *v* is of the *v* .... Deut 32:32
You have brought a *v* .... Ps 80:8
planted you a noble *v* .... Jer 2:21
as a *v* the remnant of Israel ... Jer 6:9
grapes shall be on the *v* ...... Jer 8:13
Israel empties his *v* .... Hos 10:1
shall sit under his *v* .... Mic 4:4
the *v* shall give its fruit, ... Zech 8:12
of this fruit of the *v* .... Matt 26:29
of the fruit of the *v* .... Mark 14:25
"I am the true *v* .... John 15:1
unless it abides in the *v* .... John 15:4
I am the *v*, you are the ...... John 15:5

VINEDRESSER
and My Father is the *v* ..... John 15:1

VINEDRESSERS
he leased it to *v* and ...... Matt 21:33
leased it to *v* and went .... Mark 12:1
a vineyard, leased it to *v* ... Luke 20:9

VINEGAR
they gave me *v* to drink ..... Ps 69:21
As *v* to the teeth and ...... Prov 10:26
weather, and like *v* .... Prov 25:20

VINES
foxes that spoil the *v* ...... Song 2:15
nor fruit be on the *v* .... Hab 3:17

VINEYARD
and the best of his own *v* .... Ex 22:5
shall not glean your *v* ..... Lev 19:10
field nor prune your *v* .... Lev 25:4
v which Your right .... Ps 80:15
For the *v* of the LORD of .... Is 5:7
laborers for his *v* .... Matt 20:1
go, work today in my *v* .. Matt 21:28
owner of the *v* comes ..... Matt 21:40
A man planted a *v* and .... Mark 12:1
certain man planted a *v* .... Luke 20:9
Who plants a *v* and .... 1 Cor 9:7

VINEYARDS
which you did not dig, *v* ... Deut 6:11
in the *v* there will be no ..... Is 16:10
wine, a land of bread and *v* .. Is 36:17
nothing, and gave them *v* ... Jer 39:10
they shall plant *v* and ..... Amos 9:14

VIOLENCE
was filled with *v* .... Gen 6:11
You save me from *v* .. 2 Sam 22:3
the one who loves *v* .... Ps 11:5
such as breathe out *v* .... Ps 27:12
from oppression and *v* ...... Ps 72:14
v covers the .... Prov 10:6
The *v* of the wicked will ... Prov 21:7
He had done no *v* .... Is 53:9
and *v* in the land .... Jer 51:46
filled the land with *v* ...... Ezek 8:17
LORD, 'Who store up *v* .... Amos 3:10
cause the seat of *v* .... Amos 6:3
For *v* against your .... Obad 10
way and from the *v* .... Jon 3:8
rich men are full of *v* .... Mic 6:12
For plundering and *v* .... Hab 1:3
have done *v* to the law ..... Zeph 3:4
one's garment with *v* .... Mal 2:16
of heaven suffers *v* .... Matt 11:12

VIOLENT
me from the *v* man .... Ps 18:48
let evil hunt the *v* .... Ps 140:11
A *v* man entices his .... Prov 16:29
violence, and the *v* .... Matt 11:12
haters of God, *v* .... Rom 1:30
given to wine, not *v* .... 1 Tim 3:3

VIOLENTLY
The earth is *v* broken, the .... Is 24:19
It will fall *v* on the head of ... Jer 23:19
herd ran *v* down the .... Mark 5:13

VIPER
and stings like a *v* .... Prov 23:32
will come forth a *v* .... Is 14:29
which is crushed a *v* .... Is 59:5

VIPERS
See BROOD OF VIPERS

VIRGIN
v shall conceive .... Is 7:14
O you oppressed *v* .... Is 23:12
v daughter of my .... Jer 14:17
the *v* daughter of Judah ..... Lam 1:15
you, O *v* daughter of Zion .. Lam 2:13
The *v* of Israel has .... Amos 5:2
"Behold, the *v* shall .... Matt 1:23
if a *v* marries, she has ..... 1 Cor 7:28
between a wife and a *v* ..... 1 Cor 7:34
you as a chaste *v* .... 2 Cor 11:2

VIRGINITY
take a wife in her *v* .... Lev 21:13
and bewail my *v* .... Judg 11:37

VIRGINS
v who took their lamps ..... Matt 25:1
Now concerning *v*; I ...... 1 Cor 7:25
women, for they are *v* ...... Rev 14:4

VIRTUE
if there is any *v* .... Phil 4:8
us by glory and *v* .... 2 Pet 1:3
to your faith *v* .... 2 Pet 1:5

VIRTUOUS
that you are a *v* woman .... Ruth 3:11
Who can find a *v* wife .... Prov 31:10

VISAGE
v was marred more than ...... Is 52:14

VISIBLE
that are on earth, *v* .... Col 1:16
of things which are *v* .... Heb 11:3

VISION
came to Abram in a *v* .... Gen 15:1
chased away like a *v* .... Job 20:8
Then You spoke in a *v* ...... Ps 89:19
the Valley of *V* .... Is 22:1
a dream of a night *v* .... Is 29:7
her prophets find no *v* .... Lam 2:9
the fulfillment of every *v* .. Ezek 12:23
v which I saw by the ...... Ezek 43:3

have night without *v* .... Mic 3:6
they had also seen a *v* .... Luke 24:23
in a *v* he has seen a man ... Acts 9:12
in a trance I saw a *v* .... Acts 11:5
v appeared to Paul in .... Acts 16:9
to the heavenly *v* .... Acts 26:19

VISIONS
thoughts from the *v* .... Job 4:13
opened and I saw *v* of God .. Ezek 1:1
These were the *v* of my ...... Dan 4:10
young men shall see *v* .... Joel 2:28
young men shall see *v* ...... Acts 2:17
I will come to *v* .... 2 Cor 12:1

VISIT
but God will surely *v* ...... Gen 50:24
in the day when I *v* .... Ex 32:34
v the earth and water .... Ps 65:9
Oh, *v* me with Your .... Ps 106:4
and you did not *v* Me ..... Matt 25:43
v orphans and widows .... James 1:27

VISITATION
the time of your *v* .... Luke 19:44
God in the day of *v* .... 1 Pet 2:12

VISITED
he will not be *v* .... Prov 19:23
many days you will be *v* .... Ezek 38:8
I was sick and you *v* Me .. Matt 25:36
Israel, for He has *v* .... Luke 1:68
"God has *v* His people ...... Luke 7:16
how God at the first *v* ..... Acts 15:14

VISITING
v the iniquity of the fathers .. Ex 20:5

VISITOR
am a foreigner and a *v* ..... Gen 23:4

VITALITY
v was turned into the .... Ps 32:4

VOICE
"I heard Your *v* .... Gen 3:10
God heard the *v* of the ..... Gen 21:17
you have obeyed My *v* ..... Gen 22:18
only obey my *v*, and go, ... Gen 27:13
v is Jacob's *v* .... Gen 27:22
I should obey His *v* .... Ex 5:2
God answered him by *v* ..... Ex 19:19
your God and obey His *v* ... Deut 4:30
obey the *v* of the LORD .... Deut 30:10
wept with a loud *v* .... 2 Sam 15:23
heard the *v* of Elijah ...... 1 Kin 17:22
fire a still small *v* .... 1 Kin 19:12
and my flute to the *v* .... Job 30:31
you thunder with a *v* .... Job 40:9
cried to the LORD with my *v* ... Ps 3:4
with the *v* of thanksgiving .... Ps 26:7
the *v* of my supplications ...... Ps 28:6
He uttered His *v* .... Ps 46:6
Hear my *v*, O God, in my ...... Ps 64:1
He sends out His *v* .... Ps 68:33
cried out to God with my *v* ... Ps 77:1
have lifted up their *v* .... Ps 93:3
if you will hear His *v* .... Ps 95:7
word, heeding the *v* .... Ps 103:20
for your *v* is sweet .... Song 2:14
their *v* shall be heard as far ... Is 15:4
The *v* of one crying in .... Is 40:3
the *v* of weeping shall .... Is 65:19
A *v* from the temple .... Is 66:6
the *v* of the LORD our God ... Jer 3:25
that does not obey the *v* of ... Jer 7:28
v was heard in Ramah ...... Jer 31:15
the *v* of joy and .... Jer 33:11
I heard a *v* of One .... Ezek 1:28
who has a pleasant *v* ...... Ezek 33:32
like the *v* of a multitude .... Dan 10:6
with the *v* of thanksgiving .... Jon 2:9
v was heard in Ramah ...... Matt 2:18
"The *v* of one crying .... Matt 3:3
And suddenly a *v* .... Matt 3:17
will anyone hear His *v* .... Matt 12:19
and suddenly a *v* .... Matt 17:5
cried out with a loud *v* .... Matt 27:46
a loud *v* glorified God, ... Luke 17:15
hear the *v* of the Son of .... John 5:25
for they know his *v* .... John 10:4
v did not come because .... John 12:30
the truth hears My *v* ...... John 18:37
the *v* of an archangel .... 1 Thess 4:16
whose *v* then shook the .... Heb 12:26
glory when such a *v* .... 2 Pet 1:17
If anyone hears My *v* .... Rev 3:20
I heard a *v* from heaven, ... Rev 14:2

VOICE OF THE LORD
diligently heed the *v* .... Ex 15:26
if we hear the *v* .... Deut 5:25
they did not obey the *v* .... Josh 5:6
as in obeying the *v* ...... 1 Sam 15:22
you did not obey the *v* ... 1 Sam 28:18
v is over the waters .... Ps 29:3
did not heed the *v* .... Ps 106:25
Also I heard the *v* .... Is 6:8
v, who fully repays .... Is 66:6
they did not obey the *v* .... Jer 43:7
We have not obeyed the *v* .. Dan 9:10
people, obeyed the *v* .... Hag 1:12
diligently obey the *v* ...... Zech 6:15
the *v* came to him .... Acts 7:31

VOICES
God of Israel with *v* ..... 2 Chr 20:19
shall lift up their *v* .... Is 52:8
demanding with loud *v* ... Luke 23:23
And there were loud *v* ..... Rev 11:15

VOID
was without form, and *v* ..... Gen 1:2
they are a nation *v* .... Deut 32:28
the LORD had made a *v* .... Judg 21:15
regarded Your law as *v* .... Ps 119:126
it shall not return to Me *v* .... Is 55:11
Do we then make *v* .... Rom 3:31
heirs, faith is made *v* .... Rom 4:14
make my boasting *v* .... 1 Cor 9:15

VOLUME
in the *v* of the book .... Heb 10:7

VOLUNTEERS
Your people shall be *v* ...... Ps 110:3

VOMIT
lest the land *v* .... Lev 18:28
dog returns to his own *v* .. Prov 26:11
man staggers in his *v* .... Is 19:14
returns to his own *v* .... 2 Pet 2:22
cold nor hot, I will *v* .... Rev 3:16

VOW
Then Jacob made a *v* ...... Gen 28:20
to take the *v* of a Nazirite ... Num 6:2
he carried out his *v* .... Judg 11:39
v shall be performed .... Ps 65:1
When you make a *v* .... Eccl 5:4
not to *v* than to *v* .... Eccl 5:5
for he had taken a *v* .... Acts 18:18
men who have taken a *v* .. Acts 21:23

VOW TO THE LORD
So Israel made a *v* .... Num 21:2
Or if a woman makes a *v* .. Num 30:3
When you make a *v* ...... Deut 23:21
And Jephthah made a *v* ... Judg 11:30
yes, they will make a *v* ...... Is 19:21

VOWED
If she *v* in her husband's .. Num 30:10
v to the Mighty One of ...... Ps 132:2
Pay what you have *v* .... Eccl 5:4
I will pay what I have *v* ...... Jon 2:9

VOWS
v to the LORD the offering .. Num 6:21
you will pay your *v* .... Job 22:27
I will pay My *v* .... Ps 22:25
V made to You are .... Ps 56:12
Make *v* to the LORD .... Ps 76:11
today I have paid my *v* ..... Prov 7:14
to reconsider his *v* .... Prov 20:25
And what, son of my *v* ..... Prov 31:2
to the LORD and took *v* .... Jon 1:16

WAFERS
like *w* made with honey .... Ex 16:31

WAGE
those who exploit *w* .... Mal 3:5
w the good warfare .... 1 Tim 1:18

WAGES
I will give you your *w* .... Ex 2:9
the *w* of the wicked .... Prov 10:16
the transgressor his *w* .... Prov 26:10
w will be troubled .... Is 19:10
and he who earns *w* .... Hag 1:6
to you, give me my *w* ..... Zech 11:12
and give them their *w* ...... Matt 20:8
be content with your *w* .... Luke 3:14
is worthy of his *w* .... Luke 10:7
him who works, the *w* .... Rom 4:4
For the *w* of sin is .... Rom 6:23
is worthy of his *w* .... 1 Tim 5:18
Indeed the *w* of the .... James 5:4
and will receive the *w* of ... 2 Pet 2:13

WAIL
streets everyone will *w* .... Is 15:3
everyone shall *w* .... Is 16:7
My heart shall *w* .... Jer 48:36
"Son of man, *w* .... Ezek 32:18

WAILING
w is heard from Zion .... Jer 9:19
shall be *w* in all streets ... Amos 5:16
of heart and bitter *w* ..... Ezek 27:31
There will be *w* .... Matt 13:42
cried out, weeping and *w* .. Rev 18:19

WAIST
than my father's *w* ...... 1 Kin 12:10
Your *w* is a heap of wheat ... Song 7:2
put it around your *w* .... Jer 13:1
the appearance of His *w* .... Ezek 1:27
w was girded with gold ..... Dan 10:5
Let your *w* be girded ...... Luke 12:35
girded your *w* with truth .... Eph 6:14

WAIT
if he did not lie in *w* .... Ex 21:13
would you *w* for them till .. Ruth 1:13
w until you have .... 1 Sam 1:23
hard service I will *w* .... Job 14:14
If I *w* for the grave .... Job 17:13
w patiently for Him .... Ps 37:7
my eyes fail while I *w* .... Ps 69:3
These all *w* for You .... Ps 104:27
let us lie in *w* to shed ...... Prov 1:11
And I will *w* on the .... Is 8:17
the LORD will *w* .... Is 30:18
not be ashamed who *w* ...... Is 49:23
w quietly for the .... Lam 3:26
I will *w* for the God .... Mic 7:7
Though it tarries, *w* for it .... Hab 2:3
be like men who *w* .... Luke 12:36
but to *w* for the Promise ..... Acts 1:4
see, we eagerly *w* .... Rom 8:25
w for one another .... 1 Cor 11:33
the Spirit eagerly *w* .... Gal 5:5
we also eagerly *w* .... Phil 3:20
and to *w* for His Son ..... 1 Thess 1:10
To those who eagerly *w* ..... Heb 9:28

WAIT ON THE LORD
W, be of good courage ...... Ps 27:14
But those who *w* .... Ps 37:9
W, and keep His way .... Ps 37:34
And I will *w* .... Is 8:17
w shall renew their .... Is 40:31

WAITED
w for your salvation .... Gen 49:18
and when I *w* for light ..... Job 30:26
w patiently for the .... Ps 40:1
we have *w* for Him .... Is 25:9

And the people *w* .... Luke 1:21
day you have *w* and ...... Acts 27:33
for he *w* for the city ...... Heb 11:10
Divine longsuffering *w* ..... 1 Pet 3:20

WAITING
w at the posts of my .... Prov 8:34
who was himself *w* for ... Mark 15:43
w for the Consolation ...... Luke 2:25
who himself was also *w* .. Luke 23:51
ourselves, eagerly *w* .... Rom 8:23
w for the revelation .... 1 Cor 1:7
from that time *w* .... Heb 10:13

WAITS
of the adulterer *w* .... Job 24:15
my soul silently *w* .... Ps 62:1
My soul *w* for the Lord ...... Ps 130:6
for the one who *w* .... Is 64:4
the creation eagerly *w* ..... Rom 8:19

WAKE
us, that whether we *w* ... 1 Thess 5:10

WALK
w before Me and be .... Gen 17:1
in which they must *w* ...... Ex 18:20
You shall *w* in all .... Deut 5:33
Yea, though I *w* .... Ps 23:4
W about Zion .... Ps 48:12
that Israel would *w* .... Ps 81:13
I will *w* within my .... Ps 101:2
I will *w* before the .... Ps 116:9
Though I *w* in the .... Ps 138:7
W prudently when you ...... Eccl 5:1
w in the ways of your ...... Eccl 11:9
come and let us *w* .... Is 2:5
"This is the way, *w* .... Is 30:21
be weary, they shall *w* ...... Is 40:31
w in the light of your .... Is 50:11
people, who *w* in a way .... Is 65:2
commit adultery and *w* ...... Jer 23:14
the righteous *w* .... Hos 14:9
w humbly with your God ..... Mic 6:8
take up your bed and *w* ..... John 5:8
W while you have the .... John 12:35
so we also should *w* .... Rom 6:4
Let us *w* properly .... Rom 13:13
For we *w* by faith .... 2 Cor 5:7
W in the Spirit .... Gal 5:16
that we should *w* .... Eph 2:10
And *w* in love .... Eph 5:2
W as children of light .... Eph 5:8
attained, let us *w* .... Phil 3:16
note those who so *w* .... Phil 3:17
that you may *w* worthy ...... Col 1:10
Jesus the Lord, so *w* .... Col 2:6
us how you ought to *w* .... 1 Thess 4:1
w just as He .... 1 John 2:6
and they shall *w* .... Rev 3:4

WALKED
Enoch *w* with God .... Gen 5:22
by His light I *w* .... Job 29:3
The people who *w* .... Is 9:2
He *w* with Me in peace ...... Mal 2:6
Jesus no longer *w* .... John 11:54
w according to the .... 2 Cor 10:2
in which you once *w* .... Eph 2:2
to walk just as He *w* ...... 1 John 2:6

WALKING
of the LORD God *w* .... Gen 3:8
see four men loose, *w* ...... Dan 3:25
before God, *w* in all .... Luke 1:6
they saw Jesus *w* .... John 6:19
And *w* in the fear of .... Acts 9:31
you are no longer *w* .... Rom 14:15
not *w* in craftiness .... 2 Cor 4:2
of your children *w* .... 2 John 4

WALKS
the LORD your God *w* ..... Deut 23:14
is the man who *w* .... Ps 1:1
He who *w* uprightly .... Ps 15:2
He who *w* with .... Prov 10:9
He who *w* with wise ...... Prov 13:20
w blamelessly will be ..... Prov 28:18
w wisely will be .... Prov 28:26
Whoever *w* the road .... Is 35:8
Who *w* in darkness and ..... Is 50:10
it is not in man who *w* ..... Jer 10:23
do good to him who *w* .... Mic 2:7
If anyone *w* in the day ..... John 11:9
he who *w* in darkness .... John 12:35
adversary the devil *w* .... 1 Pet 5:8
is in darkness and *w* ..... 1 John 2:11

WALL
then the *w* of the city ...... Josh 6:5
his face toward the *w* .... 2 Kin 20:2
like a leaning *w* .... Ps 62:3
and like a high *w* .... Prov 18:11
If she is a *w* .... Song 8:9
We grope for the *w* .... Is 59:10
you, you whitewashed *w* ... Acts 23:3
a window in the *w* .... 2 Cor 11:33
down the middle *w* .... Eph 2:14
Now the *w* of the city ...... Rev 21:14

WALLS
broken down, without *w* .. Prov 25:28
salvation for *w* .... Is 26:1
you shall call your *w* .... Is 60:18
By faith the *w* of .... Heb 11:30

WANDER
and makes them *w* .... Job 12:24
ones cry to God, and *w* ... Job 38:41
Indeed, I would *w* .... Ps 55:7
Oh, let me not *w* .... Ps 119:10
they have loved to *w* .... Jer 14:10

WANDERED
w blind in the streets .... Lam 4:14
My sheep *w* through .... Ezek 34:6
They *w* in deserts and .... Heb 11:38

WANDERERS
And they shall be *w* .... Hos 9:17

WANDERING
learn to be idle, *w* .... 1 Tim 5:13
w stars for whom is .... Jude 13

WANDERS
He *w* about for bread ...... Job 15:23
Like a bird that *w* .... Prov 27:8
if anyone among you *w* ... James 5:19

WANT
I shall not *w* .... Ps 23:1
he began to be in *w* .... Luke 15:14

WANTING
balances, and found *w* ..... Dan 5:27

WANTON
necks and *w* eyes .... Is 3:16
have begun to grow *w* .... 1 Tim 5:11

WAR
"There is a noise of *w* ...... Ex 32:17
the LORD for the *w* .... Num 32:20
my hands to make *w* .... 2 Sam 22:35
day of battle and *w* .... Job 38:23
w may rise against .... Ps 27:3
speak, they are for *w* .... Ps 120:7
by wise counsel wage *w* .. Prov 20:18
will wage your own *w* ...... Prov 24:6
shall they learn *w* .... Is 2:4
from the distress of *w* .... Is 21:15
we shall see no *w* .... Jer 42:14
same horn was making *w* .. Dan 7:21
men returned from *w* .... Mic 2:8
king, going to make *w* .... Luke 14:31
Who ever goes to *w* .... 1 Cor 9:7
for pleasure that *w* .... James 4:1
You fight and *w* .... James 4:2
fleshly lusts which *w* ...... 1 Pet 2:11
w broke out in heaven ...... Rev 12:7
He judges and makes *w* .... Rev 19:11

WARFARE
to her, that her *w* .... Is 40:2
w are not carnal .... 2 Cor 10:4
may wage the good *w* ..... 1 Tim 1:18
w entangles .... 2 Tim 2:4

WARM
but he could not get *w* ...... 1 Kin 1:1
of the child became *w* ..... 2 Kin 4:34
they will keep *w* .... Eccl 4:11
but no one is *w* .... Hag 1:6

WARMED
w himself at the fire ..... Mark 14:54
Depart in peace, be *w* ... James 2:16

WARMING
when she saw Peter *w* ... Mark 14:67

WARMS
w them in the dust .... Job 39:14
He even *w* himself and ...... Is 44:16

WARN
w the people, lest they ...... Ex 19:21
w the wicked from his ..... Ezek 3:18
w everyone night .... Acts 20:31
beloved children I *w* .... 1 Cor 4:14
w those who are .... 1 Thess 5:14

WARNED
"The man solemnly *w* ...... Gen 43:3
them Your servant is *w* ..... Ps 19:11
Then, being divinely *w* ..... Matt 2:12
Who *w* you to flee .... Matt 3:7
Noah, being divinely *w* ..... Heb 11:7

WARNING
he who takes *w* will save .. Ezek 33:5
w every man and .... Col 1:28

WARPED
such a person is *w* .... Titus 3:11

WARRING
w against the law of .... Rom 7:23

WARRIOR
He runs at me like a *w* ..... Job 16:14

WARS
He makes *w* cease to .... Ps 46:9
And you will hear of *w* ..... Matt 24:6
Where do *w* and fights ..... James 4:1

WASH
w myself with snow .... Job 9:30
I will *w* my hands in .... Ps 26:6
W me thoroughly .... Ps 51:2
he shall *w* his feet in .... Ps 58:10
"*W* yourselves .... Is 1:16
O Jerusalem, *w* your .... Jer 4:14
head and *w* your face ...... Matt 6:17
For they do not *w* .... Matt 15:2
not eat unless they *w* .... Mark 7:3
w His feet with her .... Luke 7:38
said to him, "Go, *w* .... John 9:7
w the disciples' .... John 13:5
"You shall never *w* .... John 13:8
w one another's .... John 13:14
w away your sins .... Acts 22:16

WASHED
and *w* my hands in .... Ps 73:13
When the Lord has *w* .... Is 4:4
cut, nor were you *w* .... Ezek 16:4
w his hands before the .... Matt 27:24
My feet, but she has *w* ..... Luke 7:44
So when He had *w* .... John 13:12
w their stripes .... Acts 16:33
But you were *w* .... 1 Cor 6:11
if she has *w* the .... 1 Tim 5:10
Him who loved us and *w* ..... Rev 1:5
w their robes and made ..... Rev 7:14

WASHING
have come up from the *w* ... Song 4:2
hold, like the *w* of cups ...... Mark 7:4
cleanse her with the *w* ..... Eph 5:26
us, through the *w* .... Titus 3:5

WASHINGS
and drinks, various *w* ...... Heb 9:10

WASTE
who are left shall *w* ... Lev 26:39
the cities are laid *w* ... Is 6:11
empty and makes it *w* ... Is 24:1
w the mountains ... Is 42:15
"Why this *w* ... Matt 26:8

WASTED
The field is *w* ... Joel 1:10
this fragrant oil *w* ... Mark 14:4
w his possessions ... Luke 15:13

WASTELAND
w shall be glad ... Is 35:1

WASTES
His flesh *w* away from ... Job 33:21
My eye *w* away because of ... Ps 6:7
cities shall be perpetual *w* ... Jer 49:13

WASTING
w and destruction are ... Is 59:7
that this man was *w* ... Luke 16:1

WATCH
Therefore *w* yourselves ... Deut 2:4
of them we set a *w* ... Neh 4:9
my steps, but do not *w* ... Job 14:16
is past, and like a *w* ... Ps 90:4
keep *w* over the door ... Ps 141:3
and all who *w* for ... Is 29:20
W the road ... Nah 2:1
W therefore, for you ... Matt 24:42
"What! Could you not *w* ... Matt 26:40
W and pray, lest you ... Matt 26:41
W therefore, for you do ... Mark 13:35
Could you not *w* one ... Mark 14:37
W and pray, lest you ... Mark 14:38
keeping *w* over their flock ... Luke 2:8
W therefore, and pray ... Luke 21:36
W, stand fast in the ... 1 Cor 16:13
submissive, for they *w* ... Heb 13:17

WATCHED
in the days when God *w* ... Job 29:2
w while a stone was cut ... Dan 2:34
come, he would have *w* ... Matt 24:43
Pharisees *w* Him closely ... Luke 6:7

WATCHER
I done to You, O *w* of men ... Job 7:20

WATCHES
w the righteous ... Ps 37:32
LORD *w* over the strangers ... Ps 146:9
She *w* over the ways of ... Prov 31:27
Blessed is he who *w* ... Rev 16:15

WATCHFUL
But you be *w* in all ... 2 Tim 4:5
be serious and *w* ... 1 Pet 4:7
Be *w*, and strengthen the ... Rev 3:2

WATCHING
who listens to me, *w* ... Prov 8:34
the flock, who were *w* ... Zech 11:11
he comes, will find *w* ... Luke 12:37

WATCHMAN
guards the city, the *w* ... Ps 127:1
W, what of the night ... Is 21:11
I have made you a *w* ... Ezek 3:17
the day of your *w* ... Mic 7:4

WATCHMEN
w who go about the ... Song 3:3
w shall lift up their ... Is 52:8
His *w* are blind ... Is 56:10
I have set *w* on your ... Is 62:6
Also, I set *w* over you ... Jer 6:17
strong, set up the *w* ... Jer 51:12

WATER
Eden to *w* the garden ... Gen 2:10
Unstable as *w* ... Gen 49:4
your bread and your *w* ... Ex 23:25
of affliction and *w* ... 1 Kin 22:27
w disappears from the ... Job 14:11
w wears away stones ... Job 14:19
drinks iniquity like *w* ... Job 15:16
not given the weary *w* ... Job 22:7
He binds up the *w* ... Job 26:8
I am poured out like *w* ... Ps 22:14
where there is no *w* ... Ps 63:1
they have shed like *w* ... Ps 79:3
Drink *w* from your own ... Prov 5:15
"Stolen *w* is sweet ... Prov 9:17
the whole supply of *w* ... Is 3:1
and needy seek *w* ... Is 41:17
For I will pour *w* ... Is 44:3
silence and given us *w* ... Jer 8:14
eye overflows with *w* ... Lam 1:16
will be as weak as *w* ... Ezek 7:17
w the land with the ... Ezek 32:6
you gave Me no *w* ... Luke 7:44
there was much *w* ... John 3:23
given you living *w* ... John 4:10
rivers of living *w* ... John 7:38
blood and *w* came out ... John 19:34
"Can anyone forbid *w* ... Acts 10:47
with the washing of *w* ... Eph 5:26
can yield both salt *w* ... James 3:12
were saved through *w* ... 1 Pet 3:20
is He who came by *w* ... 1 John 5:6
the Spirit, the *w* ... 1 John 5:8
are clouds without *w* ... Jude 12

WATER OF LIFE
w freely to him who ... Rev 21:6
a pure river of *w* ... Rev 22:1
let him take the *w* ... Rev 22:17

WATERED
w the whole face ... Gen 2:6
that it was well *w* ... Gen 13:10
I planted, Apollos *w* ... 1 Cor 3:6

WATERPOTS
"Fill four *w* with water ... 1 Kin 18:33
"Fill the *w* with water ... John 2:7

WATERS
and struck the *w* ... Ex 7:20
If He withholds the *w* ... Job 12:15
me beside the still *w* ... Ps 23:2
though its *w* roar and ... Ps 46:3
w have come up to my ... Ps 69:1
then the *w* would have ... Ps 124:4
rich, and he who *w* ... Prov 11:25
Who has bound the *w* ... Prov 30:4
your bread upon the *w* ... Eccl 11:1
a well of living *w* ... Song 4:15
w cannot quench love ... Song 8:7
of the LORD as the *w* ... Is 11:9
w will fail from the ... Is 19:5
because I give *w* ... Is 43:20
have sworn that the *w* ... Is 54:9
thirsts, come to the *w* ... Is 55:1
fountain of living *w* ... Jer 2:13
w flowed over my head ... Lam 3:54
the sound of many *w* ... Ezek 43:2
w surrounded me ... Jon 2:5
shall be that living *w* ... Zech 14:8
often, in perils of *w* ... 2 Cor 11:26
living fountains of *w* ... Rev 7:17
w became wormwood ... Rev 8:11

WAVE
you shall *w* them as a *w* ... Ex 29:24
w offering before the LORD ... Lev 7:30
the priest shall *w* them ... Num 6:20
Its fruit shall *w* ... Ps 72:16
is like a *w* of the sea ... James 1:6

WAVER
He did not *w* at the ... Rom 4:20

WAVERING
of our hope without *w* ... Heb 10:23

WAVES
and here your proud *w* ... Job 38:11
all Your *w* and billows ... Ps 42:7
the noise of their *w* ... Ps 65:7
the multitude of its *w* ... Jer 51:42
was covered with the *w* ... Matt 8:24
sea, tossed by the *w* ... Matt 14:24
raging *w* of the sea ... Jude 13

WAX
My heart is like *w* ... Ps 22:14
w melts before the ... Ps 68:2
mountains melt like *w* ... Ps 97:5

WAY
and show them the *w* ... Ex 18:20
day I am going the *w* ... Josh 23:14
and the right *w* ... 1 Sam 12:23
As for God, His *w* ... 2 Sam 22:31
to a man whose *w* ... Job 3:23
But He knows the *w* ... Job 23:10
"Where is the *w* ... Job 38:19
the LORD knows the *w* ... Ps 1:6
you perish in the *w* ... Ps 2:12
Teach me Your *w* ... Ps 27:11
This is the *w* of those ... Ps 49:13
w may be known on ... Ps 67:2
Your *w* was in the sea ... Ps 77:19
where there is no *w* ... Ps 107:40
I have chosen the *w* ... Ps 119:30
I hate every false *w* ... Ps 119:104
in the *w* everlasting ... Ps 139:24
and preserves the *w* ... Prov 2:8
The *w* of the wicked is ... Prov 4:19
instruction are the *w* ... Prov 6:23
w that seems right ... Prov 14:12
not know what is the *w* ... Eccl 11:5
of terrors in the *w* ... Eccl 12:5
The *w* of the just is ... Is 26:7
"This is the *w* ... Is 30:21
LORD, who makes a *w* ... Is 43:16
wicked forsake his *w* ... Is 55:7
O LORD, I know the *w* ... Jer 10:23
one heart and one *w* ... Jer 32:39
Israel, is it not My *w* ... Ezek 18:25
w which is not fair ... Ezek 33:17
and pervert the *w* ... Amos 2:7
the LORD has His *w* ... Nah 1:3
he will prepare the *w* ... Mal 3:1
and broad is the *w* ... Matt 7:13
and difficult is the *w* ... Matt 7:14
will prepare Your *w* ... Matt 11:10
and teach the *w* ... Matt 22:16
and the *w* you know ... John 14:4
to him, "I am the *w* ... John 14:6
proclaim to us the *w* ... Acts 16:17
explained to him the *w* ... Acts 18:26
you a more excellent *w* ... 1 Cor 12:31
w which He consecrated ... Heb 10:20
forsaken the right *w* ... 2 Pet 2:15
to have known the *w* ... 2 Pet 2:21
have gone in the *w* ... Jude 11

WAY OF THE LORD
that they keep the *w* ... Gen 18:19
did not walk in the *w* ... 2 Kin 21:22
w is strength for the ... Prov 10:29
Prepare the *w*, make ... Is 40:3
for they do not know the *w* ... Jer 5:4
"The *w* is not fair ... Ezek 18:25
Prepare the *w*, make His ... Matt 3:3
Prepare the *w*, make His ... Mark 1:3
Prepare the *w*, make His ... Luke 3:4
Make straight the *w* ... John 1:23
instructed in the *w* ... Acts 18:25

WAYS
for all His *w* are ... Deut 32:4
they do not know its *w* ... Job 24:13
is the first of the *w* ... Job 40:19
Show me Your *w* ... Ps 25:4
transgressors Your *w* ... Ps 51:13
would walk in My *w* ... Ps 81:13
w were directed ... Ps 119:5
I thought about my *w* ... Ps 119:59
righteous in all His *w* ... Ps 145:17
For the *w* of man are ... Prov 5:21
w please the LORD ... Prov 16:7
He will teach us His *w* ... Is 2:3
nor are your *w* ... Is 55:8
"Stand in the *w* ... Jer 6:16

"Amend your *w* . . . . Jer 7:3
and examine our *w* . . . . Lam 3:40
and owns all your *w* . . . . Dan 5:23
w are everlasting . . . . Hab 3:6
misery are in their *w* . . . . Rom 3:16
judgments and His *w* . . . . . Rom 11:33
unstable in all his *w* . . . . . . James 1:8
their destructive *w* . . . . 2 Pet 2:2
and true are Your *w* . . . . Rev 15:3

WEAK
then I shall become *w* . . . . . Judg 16:7
And I am *w* today . . . . 2 Sam 3:39
me, O LORD, for I am *w* . . . . Ps 6:2
gives power to the *w* . . . . Is 40:29
knee will be as *w* . . . . Ezek 7:17
let the *w* say . . . . Joel 3:10
not your hands be *w* . . . . Zeph 3:16
but the flesh is *w* . . . . Matt 26:41
And not being *w* . . . . Rom 4:19
Receive one who is *w* . . . . . . Rom 14:1
God has chosen the *w* . . . . . 1 Cor 1:27
We are *w*, but you are . . . . . 1 Cor 4:10
to the *w* I became as *w* . . . . 1 Cor 9:22
this reason many are *w* . . 1 Cor 11:30
For when I am *w* . . . . 2 Cor 12:10

WEAKENED
w my strength in the . . . . Ps 102:23
the ground, you who *w* . . . . . . Is 14:12

WEAKENS
w the hands of the men . . . . . . Jer 38:4

WEAKER
house of Saul grew *w* . . . . . . 2 Sam 3:1
the wife, as to the *w* . . . . 1 Pet 3:7

WEAKNESS
than men, and the *w* . . . . . . 1 Cor 1:25
I was with you in *w* . . . . 1 Cor 2:3
It is sown in *w* . . . . 1 Cor 15:43
is also subject to *w* . . . . Heb 5:2
w were made strong . . . . Heb 11:34

WEAKNESSES
also helps in our *w* . . . . Rom 8:26
sympathize with our *w* . . . . . . Heb 4:15

WEALTH
have gained me this *w* . . . . . Deut 8:17
a man of great *w* . . . . Ruth 2:1
not asked riches or *w* . . . . . 2 Chr 1:11
who trust in their *w* . . . . Ps 49:6
W and riches will be in his . . Ps 112:3
w is his strong city . . . . Prov 10:15
W gained by dishonesty . . . . Prov 13:11
but the *w* of the sinner is . . Prov 13:22
The rich man's *w* is his . . . . Prov 18:11
W makes many friends . . . . . Prov 19:4
love all the *w* of his house . . Song 8:7
may bring to you the *w* . . . . Is 60:11
shall take away her *w* . . . . Ezek 29:19
sea became rich by her *w* . . Rev 18:19

WEALTHY
w nation that dwells . . . . Jer 49:31
rich, have become *w* . . . . Rev 3:17

WEANED
wait until you have *w* . . . . 1 Sam 1:23
w child shall put his . . . . Is 11:8
Those just *w* from milk . . . . Is 28:9

WEAPON
w formed against you . . . . Is 54:17
with a deadly *w* . . . . Ezek 9:1

WEAPONS
is better than *w* . . . . Eccl 9:18
the LORD and His *w* . . . . Is 13:5
For the *w* of our . . . . 2 Cor 10:4

WEAR
garments did not *w* out . . . . . Deut 8:4
A woman shall not *w* . . . . Deut 22:5
w an ephod before Me . . . . 1 Sam 2:28
but the just will *w* . . . . Job 27:17
they will not *w* a robe of . . . Zech 13:4
'What shall we *w* . . . . Matt 6:31
those who *w* soft clothing . . Matt 11:8

WEARIED
you have *w* Me with . . . . Is 43:24
You are *w* in the . . . . Is 57:10
and they have *w* . . . . Jer 12:5
You have *w* the LORD . . . . Mal 2:17
therefore, being *w* . . . . John 4:6

WEARINESS
say, 'Oh, what a *w* . . . . Mal 1:13
in *w* and toil . . . . 2 Cor 11:27

WEARING
child, *w* a linen ephod . . . . 1 Sam 2:18
David was *w* a linen . . . . . 2 Sam 6:14
w the crown of thorns . . . . . John 19:5
w gold, or putting on . . . . 1 Pet 3:3

WEARISOME
and much study is *w* . . . . . . Eccl 12:12

WEARS
As water *w* away stones . . . . Job 14:19

WEARY
to Isaac, "I am *w* . . . . Gen 27:46
lest he become *w* . . . . Prov 25:17
As cold water to a *w* . . . . . . Prov 25:25
No one will be *w* . . . . Is 5:27
you may cause the *w* . . . . Is 28:12
shall run and not be *w* . . . . Is 40:31
to him who is *w* . . . . Is 50:4
I am *w* of holding it . . . . Jer 6:11
w themselves to commit . . . . . . Jer 9:5
I was *w* of holding it . . . . Jer 20:9
continual coming she *w* . . . Luke 18:5
And let us not grow *w* . . . . Gal 6:9
do not grow *w* in . . . . 2 Thess 3:13
lest you become *w* . . . . Heb 12:3

WEATHER
a garment in cold *w* . . . . . . Prov 25:20
'It will be fair *w* . . . . Matt 16:2

WEAVE
You shall skillfully *w* the . . . Ex 28:39
w the seven locks . . . . Judg 16:13

WEAVER'S
spear was like a *w* . . . . 1 Sam 17:7
are swifter than a *w* shuttle . . Job 7:6

WEDDING
were invited to the *w* . . . . . . Matt 22:3
Come to the *w* . . . . Matt 22:4
find, invite to the *w* . . . . Matt 22:9
in with him to the *w* . . . . . . Matt 25:10
day there was a *w* . . . . John 2:1

WEEK
Fulfill her *w*, and we . . . . . . Gen 29:27
with many for one *w* . . . . Dan 9:27
the first day of the *w* . . . . Matt 28:1
I fast twice a *w* . . . . Luke 18:12
the first day of the *w* . . . . Acts 20:7
the first day of the *w* . . . . 1 Cor 16:2

WEEKS
See FEAST OF WEEKS
observe the Feast of *W* . . . . . Ex 34:22
w are determined . . . . Dan 9:24
w Messiah shall be cut . . . . . Dan 9:26

WEEP
"Hannah, why do you *w* . . . 1 Sam 1:8
a time to *w* . . . . Eccl 3:4
you shall *w* no more . . . . Is 30:19
it, my soul will *w* . . . . Jer 13:17
W not for the dead . . . . Jer 22:10
to the LORD, *w* between . . . . . Joel 2:17
this commotion and *w* . . . . Mark 5:39
Blessed are you who *w* . . . . Luke 6:21
to her, "Do not *w* . . . . Luke 7:13
and you did not *w* . . . . Luke 7:32
of Jerusalem, do not *w* . . . Luke 23:28
to the tomb to *w* there . . . . John 11:31
w with those who *w* . . . . . . Rom 12:15
those who *w* as though . . . . 1 Cor 7:30

WEEPING
of Israel, who were *w* . . . . . . Num 25:6
w as they went up . . . . 2 Sam 15:30
the noise of the *w* . . . . Ezra 3:13
face is flushed from *w* . . . . . Job 16:16
the voice of my *w* . . . . Ps 6:8
my drink with *w* . . . . Ps 102:9
of hosts called for *w* . . . . Is 22:12
w shall no longer . . . . Is 65:19
They shall come with *w* . . . . . Jer 31:9
w they shall come . . . . Jer 50:4
were sitting there *w* . . . . Ezek 8:14
with fasting, with *w* . . . . Joel 2:12
with tears, with *w* . . . . Mal 2:13
There will be *w* . . . . Matt 8:12
outside by the tomb *w* . . . . John 20:11
why are you *w* . . . . John 20:13
do you mean by *w* . . . . Acts 21:13

WEIGH
You *w* out the violence . . . . Ps 58:2
O Most Upright, You *w* . . . . Is 26:7

WEIGHED
nor can silver be *w* . . . . Job 28:15
W the mountains . . . . Is 40:12
You have been *w* . . . . Dan 5:27
lest your hearts be *w* . . . . . Luke 21:34

WEIGHS
eyes, but the LORD *w* . . . . Prov 16:2
Where is he who *w* . . . . Is 33:18

WEIGHT
a perfect and just *w* . . . . Deut 25:15
a just *w* is His delight . . . . . . Prov 11:1
and eternal *w* of glory . . . . . 2 Cor 4:17
us lay aside every *w* . . . . Heb 12:1

WEIGHTIER
have neglected the *w* . . . . . . Matt 23:23

WELFARE
does not seek the *w* . . . . Jer 38:4

WELL
If you do *w* . . . . Gen 4:7
that it may go *w* . . . . Deut 4:40
you when you do *w* . . . . Ps 49:18
daughters have done *w* . . . Prov 31:29
know that it will be *w* . . . . Eccl 8:12
wheel broken at the *w* . . . . . . Eccl 12:6
that it shall be *w* . . . . Is 3:10
"Those who are *w* . . . . Matt 9:12
said to him, '*W* done . . . . . . Matt 25:21
faith has made you *w* . . . . . Mark 5:34
Now Jacob's *w* was . . . . John 4:6
the elders who rule *w* . . . . . . 1 Tim 5:17

WELL-BEING
them, and their *w* . . . . Ps 69:22
each one the other's *w* . . . 1 Cor 10:24

WELL-BELOVED
sing to my *W* a song . . . . Is 5:1

WELL KNOWN
we are *w* to God, and I . . . . 2 Cor 5:11
as unknown, and yet *w* . . . . . 2 Cor 6:9

WELLS
draw water from the *w* . . . . Is 12:3
These are *w* without . . . . 2 Pet 2:17

WELLSPRING
w of wisdom is a flowing . . Prov 18:4

WENT
They *w* out from us . . . . . . 1 John 2:19

WEPT
away from them and *w* . . . . Gen 42:24
Joseph *w* when they . . . . Gen 50:17
and behold, the baby *w* . . . . Ex 2:6
voices and *w* bitterly . . . . Judg 21:2
she *w* and did not . . . . 1 Sam 1:7
w together, but David . . . 1 Sam 20:41
w for the child while . . . . 2 Sam 12:21
and the man of God *w* . . . . . . 2 Kin 8:11
And Hezekiah *w* bitterly . . 2 Kin 20:3
for the people *w* . . . . Ezra 10:1

that I sat down and *w* .... Neh 1:4
Have I not *w* for him .... Job 30:25
I *w* and chastened my soul .. Ps 69:10
down, yea, we *w* .... Ps 137:1
out and *w* bitterly .... Matt 26:75
He saw the city and *w* .... Luke 19:41
Jesus *w* .... John 11:35
as she *w* she stooped ..... John 20:11
So I *w* much .... Rev 5:4

WEST
in the *w* are astonished .... Job 18:20
as the east is from the *w* ... Ps 103:12
of the LORD from the *w* ...... Is 59:19
male goat came from the *w* .. Dan 8:5
in two, from east to *w* ..... Zech 14:4
east and flashes to the *w* .. Matt 24:27
rising out of the *w* .... Luke 12:54

WET
They are *w* with the .... Job 24:8
his body was *w* with .... Dan 4:33

WHEAT
with the finest of *w* .... Ps 81:16
we may trade *w* .... Amos 8:5
even sell the bad *w* .... Amos 8:6
but gather the *w* .... Matt 13:30
w falls into the .... John 12:24
perhaps *w* or some .... 1 Cor 15:37
oil, fine flour and *w* .... Rev 18:13

WHEEL
brings the threshing *w* .... Prov 20:26
the fountain, or the *w* .... Eccl 12:6
in the middle of a *w* .... Ezek 1:16

WHEELS
off their chariot *w* .... Ex 14:25
the rumbling of his *w* .... Jer 47:3
appearance of the *w* .... Ezek 1:16
noise of rattling *w* .... Nah 3:2

WHERE
not knowing *w* he was ...... Heb 11:8

WHIP
A *w* for the horse .... Prov 26:3
The noise of a *w* .... Nah 3:2

WHIPS
chastised you with *w* ..... 1 Kin 12:11

WHIRLING
saw King David *w* .... 1 Chr 15:29

WHIRLWIND
Elijah went up by a *w* ..... 2 Kin 2:11
Job out of the *w* .... Job 38:1
them away as with a *w* .... Ps 58:9
w will take them away .... Is 40:24
w shall scatter them .... Is 41:16
w shall be raised .... Jer 25:32
has His way in the *w* .... Nah 1:3

WHISPER
my ear received a *w* .... Job 4:12
and wizards, who *w* .... Is 8:19

WHISPERER
w separates the best ...... Prov 16:28

WHISPERERS
they are *w* .... Rom 1:29

WHISPERINGS
backbitings, *w* .... 2 Cor 12:20

WHISTLE
w for the fly that is in the ..... Is 7:18

WHITE
like *w* coriander seed .... Ex 16:31
leprous, as *w* as snow .... Num 12:10
My beloved is *w* .... Song 5:10
they shall be as *w* as snow .... Is 1:18
and make them *w* .... Dan 11:35
be purified, made *w* .... Dan 12:10
red, sorrel, and *w* .... Zech 1:8
make one hair *w* or black .. Matt 5:36
his clothing as *w* as snow .. Matt 28:3
shining, exceedingly *w* ..... Mark 9:3
for they are already *w* ..... John 4:35
saw two angels in *w* ...... John 20:12
by them in *w* apparel .... Acts 1:10
and hair were *w* like wool ... Rev 1:14
walk with Me in *w* .... Rev 3:4
clothed in *w* garments .... Rev 3:5
behold, a *w* horse .... Rev 6:2
and made them *w* .... Rev 7:14
Then I saw a great *w* .... Rev 20:11

WHITE AS SNOW
became leprous, as *w* ..... Num 12:10
presence leprous, as *w* ..... 2 Kin 5:27
they shall be as *w* .... Is 1:18
His garment was *w* .... Dan 7:9
his clothing as *w* .... Matt 28:3
white like wool, as *w* .... Rev 1:14

WHITEN
launderer on earth can *w* ... Mark 9:3

WHITER
and I shall be *w* than snow ... Ps 51:7

WHITEWASHED
you are like *w* tombs ..... Matt 23:27
strike you, you *w* wall ..... Acts 23:3

WHOLE
the face of the *w* earth ...... Gen 11:4
Is not the *w* land before .... Gen 13:9
w house of Israel, bewail .... Lev 10:6
shall build with *w* stones ... Deut 27:6
down for about a *w* day ... Josh 10:13
let the *w* earth be filled .... Ps 72:19
Who seek Him with the *w* ... Ps 119:2
my *w* heart I have sought .. Ps 119:10
observe it with my *w* .... Ps 119:34
You with my *w* heart .... Ps 138:1
the *w* earth is full of His .... Is 6:3
to Me with her *w* heart ...... Jer 3:10
The *w* earth will rejoice ... Ezek 35:14
on the *w* house of Israel .. Ezek 39:25
than for your *w* body to .... Matt 5:29
your *w* body will be full .... Matt 6:22
if he gains the *w* world .... Matt 16:26
if he gains the *w* world .... Mark 8:36
if he gains the *w* world .... Luke 9:25
the *w* body will be full .... Luke 11:36
the *w* creation groans .... Rom 8:22
w body were an eye ...... 1 Cor 12:17
a debtor to keep the *w* law .... Gal 5:3
on the *w* armor of God ...... Eph 6:11
may your *w* spirit, soul .. 1 Thess 5:23
also to bridle the *w* body .... James 3:2
that it defiles the *w* body .... James 3:6
who deceives the *w* world ... Rev 12:9

WHOLESOME
w tongue is a tree .... Prov 15:4
not consent to *w* words ...... 1 Tim 6:3

WHOLLY
w followed the LORD .... Deut 1:36
I will not leave you *w* .... Jer 46:28

WICKED
were exceedingly *w* .... Gen 13:13
the righteous with the *w* ... Gen 18:25
For I will not justify the *w* ... Ex 23:7
a *w* thought in your heart ... Deut 15:9
from every *w* thing .... Deut 23:9
and condemn the *w* .... Deut 25:1
w shall be silent .... 1 Sam 2:9
proceeds from the *w* .... 1 Sam 24:13
was *w* in the sight of the ... 1 Chr 2:3
turn from their *w* ways .... 2 Chr 7:14
Should you help the *w* .... 2 Chr 19:2
turn from their *w* works .... Neh 9:35
on the counsel of the *w* ...... Job 10:3
You know that I am not *w* .. Job 10:7
w man writhes with pain ... Job 15:20
triumphing of the *w* is .... Job 20:5
Why do the *w* live and ...... Job 21:7
w are reserved for the ...... Job 21:30
to nobles, 'You are *w* ...... Job 34:18
of the *w* come to an end .... Ps 7:9
with the *w* every day .... Ps 7:11
You have destroyed the *w* ...... Ps 9:5
w is snared in the .... Ps 9:16
w shall be turned .... Ps 9:17
do the *w* renounce God ..... Ps 10:13
w bend their bow .... Ps 11:2
w He will rain coals .... Ps 11:6
the *w* who oppress me .... Ps 17:9
Evil shall slay the *w* .... Ps 34:21
w shall be no more .... Ps 37:10
The *w* watches the .... Ps 37:32
But to the *w* God says .... Ps 50:16
So let the *w* perish at the ..... Ps 68:2
of the *w* I will also cut off ... Ps 75:10
how long will the *w* .... Ps 94:3
nothing *w* before my eyes ... Ps 101:3
and the *w* be no more ...... Ps 104:35
of the *w* shall perish .... Ps 112:10
is far from the *w* .... Ps 119:155
if there is any *w* .... Ps 139:24
the way of the *w* He turns ... Ps 146:9
w will be cut off from ...... Prov 2:22
The way of the *w* is like .... Prov 4:19
heart that devises *w* plans .. Prov 6:18
he who rebukes a *w* man .... Prov 9:7
the wages of the *w* to sin .. Prov 10:16
of the *w* will perish .... Prov 10:28
w will fall by his own ...... Prov 11:5
w man does deceptive ..... Prov 11:18
w will not go .... Prov 11:21
expectation of the *w* is .... Prov 11:23
words of the *w* are, "Lie .... Prov 12:6
mercies of the *w* are ...... Prov 12:10
w covet the catch of evil .. Prov 12:12
The way of the *w* is an ..... Prov 15:9
thoughts of the *w* are an .. Prov 15:26
LORD is far from the *w* .... Prov 15:29
He who says to the *w* ..... Prov 24:24
w flee when no one .... Prov 28:1
the righteous and the *w* ..... Eccl 3:17
Do not be overly *w* .... Eccl 7:17
not be well with the *w* ...... Eccl 8:13
Woe to the *w*! It shall be ill .... Is 3:11
w forsake his way .... Is 55:7
But the *w* are like the .... Is 57:20
the way of the *w* prosper ..... Jer 12:1
from the hand of the *w* .... Jer 15:21
and desperately *w* .... Jer 17:9
if a *w* man turns from ..... Ezek 18:21
a *w* man turns away ...... Ezek 18:27
if you warn the *w* to turn .. Ezek 33:9
when the *w* turns from .... Ezek 33:19
w shall do wickedly .... Dan 12:10
at all acquit the *w* .... Nah 1:3
the righteous and the *w* ...... Mal 3:18
You shall trample the *w* ...... Mal 4:3
with this *w* generation .... Matt 12:45
separate the *w* from .... Matt 13:49
A *w* and adulterous .... Matt 16:4
fiery darts of the *w* one ..... Eph 6:16
have overcome the *w* ..... 1 John 2:14
w one does not touch ..... 1 John 5:18
the sway of the *w* .... 1 John 5:19

WICKEDLY
brethren, do not do so *w* .... Gen 19:7
beg you, do not act so *w* .. Judg 19:23
and I have done *w* .... 2 Sam 24:17
Will you speak *w* .... Job 13:7
God will never do *w* .... Job 34:12
iniquity, we have done *w* .... Ps 106:6
Those who do *w* .... Dan 11:32
yes, all who do *w* .... Mal 4:1

WICKEDNESS
LORD saw that the *w* .... Gen 6:5
can I do this great *w* .... Gen 39:9
the land become full of *w* .. Lev 19:29
may be no *w* among .... Lev 20:14
'*W* proceeds from the .... 1 Sam 24:13
w oppress them .... 2 Sam 7:10
if *w* is found in him, he .... 1 Kin 1:52
do *w* in the sight of the .. 1 Kin 21:25

be, that even the *w* ... Matt 8:27
holding the four *w* ... Rev 7:1

WINDSTORM

And a great *w* arose ... Mark 4:37

WINE

Noah awoke from his *w* ... Gen 9:24
Do not drink *w* or ... Lev 10:9
Nazirite may drink *w* ... Num 6:20
drink *w* or similar drink ... Judg 13:4
I have drunk neither *w* ... 1 Sam 1:15
w for those who are ... 2 Sam 16:2
king was merry with *w* ... Esth 1:10
drinking *w* in their oldest ... Job 1:13
drink the *w* of confusion ... Ps 60:3
w that makes glad ... Ps 104:15
W is a mocker ... Prov 20:1
Do not look on the *w* ... Prov 23:31
w makes merry ... Eccl 10:19
love is better than *w* ... Song 1:2
w goes down smoothly ... Song 7:9
w inflames them ... Is 5:11
are drunk, but not with *w* ... Is 29:9
Yes, come, buy *w* ... Is 55:1
Take this *w* cup of fury ... Jer 25:15
We will drink no *w*, for ... Jer 35:6
new *w* into old wineskins ... Matt 9:17
they gave Him sour *w* ... Matt 27:34
w nor strong drink ... Luke 1:15
pouring on oil and *w* ... Luke 10:34
when they ran out of *w* ... John 2:3
"They are full of new *w* ... Acts 2:13
do not be drunk with *w* ... Eph 5:18
given to *w*, nor violent ... 1 Tim 3:3
but use a little *w* ... 1 Tim 5:23
not given to much *w* ... Titus 2:3
not harm the oil and the *w* ... Rev 6:6
the *w* of the wrath of her ... Rev 14:8
her the cup of the *w* ... Rev 16:19

WINEBIBBER

'Look, a glutton and a *w* ... Luke 7:34

WINEBIBBERS

Do not mix with *w* ... Prov 23:20

WINEPRESS

"I have trodden the *w* ... Is 63:3
for the *w* is full ... Joel 3:13
into the great *w* ... Rev 14:19
Himself treads the *w* ... Rev 19:15

WINESKIN

I have become like a *w* ... Ps 119:83

WINESKINS

new wine into old *w* ... Matt 9:17

WING

maidservant under your *w* ... Ruth 3:9
One *w* of the cherub ... 1 Kin 6:24
so I spread My *w* ... Ezek 16:8

WINGS

I bore you on eagles' *w* ... Ex 19:4
w you have come ... Ruth 2:12
the shadow of Your *w* ... Ps 17:8
He flew upon the *w* ... Ps 18:10
the shadow of Your *w* ... Ps 36:7
w I will make my refuge ... Ps 57:1
If I take the *w* ... Ps 139:9
each one had six *w* ... Is 6:2
up with *w* like eagles ... Is 40:31
a lion, and had eagle's *w* ... Dan 7:4
with healing in His *w* ... Mal 4:2
her chicks under her *w* ... Matt 23:37
each having six *w* ... Rev 4:8
woman was given two *w* ... Rev 12:14

WINNOW

You shall *w* them ... Is 41:16

WINNOWING

His *w* fan is in His hand ... Luke 3:17

WINS

w souls is wise ... Prov 11:30

WINTER

have made summer and *w* ... Ps 74:17
For lo, the *w* is past ... Song 2:11
w it shall occur ... Zech 14:8
flight may not be in *w* ... Matt 24:20

WIPE

the Lord GOD will *w* ... Is 25:8
w them with the towel ... John 13:5
w away every tear ... Rev 21:4

WIPED

reproach will not be *w* ... Prov 6:33
w them with the hair of ... Luke 7:38
w out the handwriting ... Col 2:14

WIPES

eats and *w* her mouth ... Prov 30:20

WISDOM

for this is your *w* ... Deut 4:6
God gave Solomon *w* ... 1 Kin 4:29
w will die with you ... Job 12:2
where can *w* be found ... Job 28:12
fear of the Lord, that is *w* ... Job 28:28
Who has put *w* in the ... Job 38:36
of the righteous speaks *w* ... Ps 37:30
will make me to know *w* ... Ps 51:6
is the beginning of *w* ... Ps 111:10
but fools despise *w* and ... Prov 1:7
For the LORD gives *w* ... Prov 2:6
is the man who finds *w* ... Prov 3:13
Get *w*! Get understanding! ... Prov 4:5
W is the principal ... Prov 4:7
is the beginning of *w* ... Prov 9:10
W rests in the heart ... Prov 14:33
to get *w* than gold ... Prov 16:16
W is in the sight of him ... Prov 17:24
w loves his own soul ... Prov 19:8
W is too lofty for a ... Prov 24:7
w is much grief ... Eccl 1:18
gives *w* and knowledge ... Eccl 2:26
W is better than ... Eccl 9:16
W is better than weapons ... Eccl 9:18
He gives *w* to the wise ... Dan 2:21
w is justified by her ... Matt 11:19
Jesus increased in *w* ... Luke 2:52
the *w* of God also ... Luke 11:49
riches both of the *w* ... Rom 11:33
the gospel, not with *w* ... 1 Cor 1:17
Greeks seek after *w* ... 1 Cor 1:22
For the *w* of this world ... 1 Cor 3:19
not with fleshly *w* ... 2 Cor 1:12
now the manifold *w* ... Eph 3:10
all the treasures of *w* ... Col 2:3
Walk in *w* toward those ... Col 4:5
If any of you lacks *w* ... James 1:5
power and riches and *w* ... Rev 5:12
and glory and *w* ... Rev 7:12

WISE

great nation is a *w* ... Deut 4:6
He catches the *w* ... Job 5:13
God is *w* in heart and ... Job 9:4
not find one *w* man ... Job 17:10
men are not always *w* ... Job 32:9
when will you be *w* ... Ps 94:8
w will observe these ... Ps 107:43
Do not be *w* in your ... Prov 3:7
The *w* in heart will ... Prov 10:8
W people store up ... Prov 10:14
he who wins souls is *w* ... Prov 11:30
w son heeds his father's ... Prov 13:1
The *w* woman builds her ... Prov 14:1
w man fears and departs ... Prov 14:16
The *w* in heart will be ... Prov 16:21
folly, lest he be *w* ... Prov 26:5
w men turn away wrath ... Prov 29:8
they are exceedingly *w* ... Prov 30:24
The words of the *w* ... Eccl 12:11
They are *w* to do evil ... Jer 4:22
is *w*? Let him understand ... Hos 14:9
Therefore be *w* as ... Matt 10:16
five of them were *w* ... Matt 25:2
barbarians, both to *w* ... Rom 1:14
to God, alone *w* ... Rom 16:27
Where is the *w* ... 1 Cor 1:20
sake, but you are *w* ... 1 Cor 4:10
not as fools but as *w* ... Eph 5:15
to God who alone is *w* ... 1 Tim 1:17
are able to make you *w* ... 2 Tim 3:15

WISE MAN

select a discerning and *w* ... Gen 41:33
w answer with empty ... Job 15:2
I shall not find one *w* ... Job 17:10
A *w* will hear and ... Prov 1:5
rebuke a *w*, and he will ... Prov 9:8
w fears and departs ... Prov 14:16
w will appease it ... Prov 16:14
w holds them back ... Prov 29:11
what more has the *w* ... Eccl 6:8
found in it a poor *w* ... Eccl 9:15
Let not the *w* glory ... Jer 9:23
w who built his house ... Matt 7:24
that there is not a *w* ... 1 Cor 6:5

WISE MEN

Egypt and all its *w* ... Gen 41:8
Pharaoh also called the *w* ... Ex 7:11
the king said to the *w* ... Esth 1:13
For he sees *w* die ... Ps 49:10
Where are your *w* ... Is 19:12
the wisdom of their *w* ... Is 29:14
all the *w* of the nations ... Jer 10:7
to destroy all the *w* ... Dan 2:12
all the *w* of Babylon ... Dan 2:48
Now all the king's *w* ... Dan 5:8
w from the East came ... Matt 2:1
secretly called the *w* ... Matt 2:7
he was deceived by the *w* ... Matt 2:16
prophets, *w*, and scribes ... Matt 23:34
I speak as to *w* ... 1 Cor 10:15

WISELY

I will behave *w* ... Ps 101:2
who heeds the word *w* ... Prov 16:20
you do not inquire *w* ... Eccl 7:10
saw that he answered *w* ... Mark 12:34

WISER

he was *w* than all men ... 1 Kin 4:31
w than the birds ... Job 35:11
w than my enemies ... Ps 119:98
of God is *w* than men ... 1 Cor 1:25

WISH

for me to do what I *w* ... Matt 20:15
w it were already ... Luke 12:49
where you do not *w* ... John 21:18
For I *w* that all men were ... 1 Cor 7:7
I could *w* you were cold or ... Rev 3:15

WISHED

Then he *w* death for ... Jon 4:8
him whatever they *w* ... Mark 9:13

WISHES

turns it wherever He *w* ... Prov 21:1
wind blows where it *w* ... John 3:8

WITCHCRAFT

is as the sin of *w* ... 1 Sam 15:23

WITH ALL YOUR HEART

if you seek Him *w* ... Deut 4:29
love the Lord your God *w* ... Deut 6:5
the Lord your God *w* ... Deut 10:12
and to serve Him *w* ... Josh 22:5
but serve the Lord *w* ... 1 Sam 12:20
Trust in the Lord *w* ... Prov 3:5
you search for Me *w* ... Jer 29:13
Lord, "Turn to me *w* ... Joel 2:12
Be glad and rejoice *w* ... Zeph 3:14
the Lord your God *w* ... Matt 22:37
the Lord your God *w* ... Mark 12:30
the Lord your God *w* ... Luke 10:27
"If you believe *w* ... Acts 8:37

WITH CHILD

you are *w*, and you shall ... Gen 16:11
daughters of Lot were *w* ... Gen 19:36
she is *w* by harlotry." So ... Gen 38:24
fight, and hurt a woman *w* ... Ex 21:22
David, and said, "I am *w* ... 2 Sam 11:5

womb of her who is *w* ...... Eccl 11:5
As a woman *w* is in pain ..... Is 26:17
who have not travailed *w!* ..... Is 54:1
a man is ever in labor *w* ...... Jer 30:6
women *w* ripped open ..... Hos 13:16
found *w* of the Holy Spirit .. Matt 1:18
a virgin shall be *w* .... Matt 1:23
betrothed wife, who was *w* .. Luke 2:5
being *w*, she cried out ...... Rev 12:2

WITH ONE ACCORD
words of the prophets *w* .. 1 Kin 22:13
the Lord, to serve Him *w* ... Zeph 3:9
w began to make .... Luke 14:18
continued *w* in prayer ...... Acts 1:14
with *w* in one place .... Acts 2:1
So continuing daily *w* ...... Acts 2:46
their voice to God *w* .... Acts 4:24
w in Solomon's Porch ...... Acts 5:12
multitudes *w* heeded .... Acts 8:6
being assembled *w* .... Acts 15:25

WITHDRAW
God will not *w* His .... Job 9:13
He does not *w* His eyes ..... Job 36:7
From such *w* yourself ...... 1 Tim 6:5

WITHER
also shall not *w* .... Ps 1:3
w as the green .... Ps 37:2
leaves will not *w* .... Ezek 47:12
How did the fig tree *w* .... Matt 21:20

WITHERED
behold, seven heads, *w* .... Gen 41:23
stricken and *w* like grass .... Ps 102:4
surely joy has *w* away .... Joel 1:12
the plant that it *w* .... Jon 4:7
man who had a *w* hand ... Matt 12:10
had no root they *w* away ... Matt 13:6
the fig tree *w* away .... Matt 21:19
out as a branch and is *w* ... John 15:6

WITHERS
The grass *w* .... Is 40:7
burning heat than it *w* .... James 1:11
The grass *w* .... 1 Pet 1:24

WITHHELD
and your sins have *w* .... Jer 5:25

WITHHOLD
w Your tender mercies ...... Ps 40:11
good thing will He *w* .... Ps 84:11
Do not *w* good from .... Prov 3:27
your cloak, do not *w* ...... Luke 6:29

WITHOUT
having no hope and *w* ...... Eph 2:12
pray *w* ceasing .... 1 Thess 5:17
w controversy .... 1 Tim 3:16
w works is dead .... James 2:26

WITHSTAND
no one is able to *w* You ... 2 Chr 20:6
no animal could *w* him ...... Dan 8:4
was I that I could *w* .... Acts 11:17
you may be able to *w* .... Eph 6:13

WITHSTOOD
Persia *w* me twenty-one ... Dan 10:13
I *w* him to his face .... Gal 2:11

WITNESS
See BEAR WITNESS; FALSE WITNESS
see, God is *w* between ..... Gen 31:50
Surely even now my *w* ..... Job 16:19
like the faithful *w* .... Ps 89:37
w does not lie .... Prov 14:5
have given him as a *w* .... Is 55:4
a true and faithful *w* .... Jer 42:5
I will be a swift *w* .... Mal 3:5
all the world as a *w* .... Matt 24:14
This man came for a *w* ..... John 1:7
do not receive Our *w* .... John 3:11
"If I bear *w* of .... John 5:31
is another who bears *w* .... John 5:32
But I have a greater *w* ..... John 5:36
who was bearing *w* .... Acts 14:3
For you will be His *w* ..... Acts 22:15
For God is my *w* .... Phil 1:8
are three who bear *w* ...... 1 John 5:7
If we receive the *w* .... 1 John 5:9
who bore *w* to the word ...... Rev 1:2
Christ, the faithful *w* .... Rev 1:5
beheaded for their *w* .... Rev 20:4

WITNESSED
is revealed, being *w* .... Rom 3:21
w the good confession .... 1 Tim 6:13

WITNESSES
of two or three *w* .... Deut 17:6
for Myself faithful *w* .... Is 8:2
"You are My *w* .... Is 43:10
the presence of many *w* ... 1 Tim 6:12
the Holy Spirit also *w* ..... Heb 10:15
so great a cloud of *w* .... Heb 12:1
give power to my two *w* ..... Rev 11:3

WIVES
two *w*, one loved .... Deut 21:15
he had seven hundred *w* .. 1 Kin 11:3
daughters as *w* for .... Ezra 9:2
you to divorce your *w* ...... Matt 19:8
W, submit to your own ...... Eph 5:22
Husbands, love your *w* ...... Eph 5:25
Husbands, love your *w* .... Col 3:19
w must be reverent .... 1 Tim 3:11
by the conduct of their *w* .... 1 Pet 3:1

WIZARDS
who are mediums and *w* ...... Is 8:19

WOE
W is me, that I dwell in ..... Ps 120:5
Who has *w*? .... Prov 23:29
W to the wicked .... Is 3:11
W to those who call evil ...... Is 5:20
W to you, O Jerusalem ...... Jer 13:27
"*W* to the bloody city ...... Ezek 24:9
'*W* to him who increases ..... Hab 2:6
"*W* to you, Chorazin ...... Matt 11:21
w to that man by whom .... Matt 18:7
But *w* to you, scribes ...... Matt 23:13
But *w* to those who are .. Mark 13:17
W to you who are full ..... Luke 6:25
w is me if I do not .... 1 Cor 9:16
W, *w*, *w* to the inhabitants .. Rev 8:13
One *w* is past .... Rev 9:12

WOLF
The *w* and the lamb .... Is 65:25
the sheep, sees the *w* ..... John 10:12

WOLVES
they are ravenous *w* .... Matt 7:15
out as lambs among *w* ...... Luke 10:3
savage *w* will come in ..... Acts 20:29

WOMAN
she shall be called *W* .... Gen 2:23
every *w* shall ask of her .... Ex 3:22
A widow or a divorced *w* .. Lev 21:14
stand the *w* before the .... Num 5:18
w shall not wear anything .. Deut 22:5
the *w* took the two men ..... Josh 2:4
that you are a virtuous *w* .. Ruth 3:11
keep you from the evil *w* ... Prov 6:24
adultery with a *w* lacks .... Prov 6:32
A foolish *w* is clamorous ... Prov 9:13
A gracious *w* retains ...... Prov 11:16
w builds her house .... Prov 14:1
w who fears the LORD ..... Prov 31:30
Can a *w* forget her nursing .. Is 49:15
w shall encompass a .... Jer 31:22
whoever looks at a *w* ...... Matt 5:28
a *w* of Canaan came ...... Matt 15:22
"O *w*, great is your faith .. Matt 15:28
if a *w* divorces .... Mark 10:12
w came having an .... Mark 14:3
"Do you see this *w* .... Luke 7:44
Then the *w* of Samaria ..... John 4:9
brought to Him a *w* .... John 8:3
"*W*, behold your .... John 19:26
w was full of good .... Acts 9:36
Jewish *w* who believed ..... Acts 16:1
natural use of the *w* .... Rom 1:27
a man not to touch a *w* ..... 1 Cor 7:1
the head of *w* is man ...... 1 Cor 11:3
For if a *w* is not covered .... 1 Cor 11:6
w is the glory of man ...... 1 Cor 11:7
but *w* from man .... 1 Cor 11:8
but *w* for the man .... 1 Cor 11:9
this reason the *w* ought .. 1 Cor 11:10
His Son, born of a *w* .... Gal 4:4
Let a *w* learn in .... 1 Tim 2:11
I do not permit a *w* .... 1 Tim 2:12
w being deceived .... 1 Tim 2:14
you allow that *w* Jezebel ..... Rev 2:20
w clothed with the sun .... Rev 12:1
the earth helped the *w* ..... Rev 12:16
And I saw a *w* sitting on a .. Rev 17:3
the *w* whom you saw is ..... Rev 17:18

WOMB
nations are in your *w* ..... Gen 25:23
LORD had closed her *w* ..... 1 Sam 1:5
took Me out of the *w* .... Ps 22:9
formed you from the *w* .... Is 44:2
called Me from the *w* .... Is 49:1
in the *w* I knew you .... Jer 1:5
is the fruit of your *w* ...... Luke 1:42
"Blessed is the *w* .... Luke 11:27

WOMEN
the Hebrew *w* are not .... Ex 1:19
All the *w* who were gifted .... Ex 35:25
ten *w* shall bake your ...... Lev 26:26
blessed is she among *w* .... Judg 5:24
loved many foreign *w* ..... 1 Kin 11:1
pagan *w* caused .... Neh 13:26
among Your honorable *w* .... Ps 45:9
O fairest among *w* .... Song 1:8
w rule over them .... Is 3:12
new wine the young *w* ...... Zech 9:17
thousand men, besides *w* .. Matt 14:21
thousand men, besides *w* .. Matt 15:38
w will be grinding .... Matt 24:41
w who followed Jesus .... Matt 27:55
are you among *w* .... Luke 1:28
it just as the *w* had said .. Luke 24:24
devout and prominent *w* .. Acts 13:50
not a few of the leading *w* .. Acts 17:4
w keep silent in the ..... 1 Cor 14:34
the *w* adorn themselves .... 1 Tim 2:9
which is proper for *w* ..... 1 Tim 2:10
admonish the young *w* ...... Titus 2:4
times, the holy *w* .... 1 Pet 3:5
not defiled with *w* .... Rev 14:4

WONDER
gives you a sign or a *w* .... Deut 13:1
I have become as a *w* .... Ps 71:7
marvelous work and a *w* ..... Is 29:14
they were filled with *w* ..... Acts 3:10

WONDERFUL
name, seeing it is *w* .... Judg 13:18
Your love to me was *w* ... 2 Sam 1:26
things too *w* for me .... Job 42:3
Your *w* works Which You ...... Ps 40:5
He has made His *w* works ... Ps 111:4
Your testimonies are *w* ... Ps 119:129
things which are too *w* ... Prov 30:18
name will be called *W* .... Is 9:6
of hosts, who is *w* .... Is 28:29
all His *w* works .... Jer 21:2
and scribes saw the *w* .... Matt 21:15
our own tongues the *w* ..... Acts 2:11

WONDERFULLY
fearfully and *w* made ...... Ps 139:14

WONDERS
See SIGNS AND WONDERS
w which I will do .... Ex 3:20
LORD will do *w* among you .. Josh 3:5
are the God who does *w* .... Ps 77:14
Shall Your *w* be known ..... Ps 88:12
heavens will praise Your *w* ... Ps 89:5
who alone does great *w* ..... Ps 136:4

for the *w* of man does .... James 1:20
throne and from the *w* ...... Rev 6:16
to you, having great *w* ..... Rev 12:12
of the wine of the *w* .... Rev 14:8
winepress of the *w* .... Rev 14:19
for in them the *w* .... Rev 15:1
fierceness of His *w* .... Rev 16:19

WRATH OF GOD
w abides on him .... John 3:36
w is revealed from .... Rom 1:18
w comes upon the sons of .... Eph 5:6
of the wine of the *w* ...... Rev 14:10
great winepress of the *w* .. Rev 14:19
the *w* is complete .... Rev 15:1
the bowls of the *w* .... Rev 16:1

WRATH OF THE LORD
w was aroused against .... Num 11:33
for great is the *w* .... 2 Kin 22:13
w turned from him .... 2 Chr 12:12
fierce *w* is upon you ..... 2 Chr 28:11
w fell upon Judah .... 2 Chr 29:8
w did not come upon ...... 2 Chr 32:26
w arose against His ...... 2 Chr 36:16
w was kindled against ..... Ps 106:40
w of hosts the land .... Is 9:19
w of hosts and in the day ..... Is 13:13
in the day of the *w* .... Ezek 7:19

WRATHFUL
w man stirs up strife ...... Prov 15:18

WRESTLE
For we do not *w* .... Eph 6:12

WRESTLED
I have *w* with my sister ..... Gen 30:8
a Man *w* with him until .... Gen 32:24

WRETCHED
w man that I am .... Rom 7:24
know that you are *w* .... Rev 3:17

WRETCHEDNESS
do not let me see my *w* ... Num 11:15

WRINGING
w the nose produces ...... Prov 30:33

WRINKLE
not having spot or *w* .... Eph 5:27

WRITE
I will *w* on these tablets ...... Ex 34:1
"*W* these words .... Ex 34:27
w bitter things .... Job 13:26
w them on the tablet of .... Prov 3:3
w them on the tablet .... Prov 7:3
"*W* this man down as .... Jer 22:30
and *w* it on their hearts ...... Jer 31:33
w them on their hearts ..... Heb 8:10
their minds I will *w* .... Heb 10:16
w no new commandment .. 1 John 2:7
a new commandment I *w* .. 1 John 2:8
I had many things to *w* .... 3 John 13
W the things which you ...... Rev 1:19
w on him My new name .... Rev 3:12

WRITER
is the pen of a ready *w* .... Ps 45:1

WRITING
the *w* was the *w* .... Ex 32:16
read the *w* to the king ...... Dan 5:17
And the *w* was: Jesus ..... John 19:19

WRITINGS
do not believe his *w* .... John 5:47

WRITTEN
See AS IT IS WRITTEN; IT IS WRITTEN
which I have *w* .... Ex 24:12
tablets of stone, *w* .... Ex 31:18
tablets were *w* on both .... Ex 32:15
book which You have *w* .... Ex 32:32
w with the finger of God ... Deut 9:10
law that are *w* in this ..... Deut 28:58
w in this Book of the ...... Deut 29:21
as it is *w* in the Book of .... Josh 8:31
w in the Law of the ...... 1 Chr 16:40
scroll of the Book it is *w* ..... Ps 40:7
be *w* with the righteous ...... Ps 69:28
book they all were *w* .... Ps 139:16
Have I not *w* to you .... Prov 22:20
is found *w* in the book ...... Dan 12:1
thus it is *w* by the prophet ... Matt 2:5
your names are *w* .... Luke 10:20
are *w* may be fulfilled .... Luke 21:22
"What I have *w* .... John 19:22
as it is *w*, "The just shall ... Rom 1:17
law *w* in their hearts .... Rom 2:15
it is *w*, "Vengeance is ...... Rom 12:19
our epistle *w* in our hearts .. 2 Cor 3:2
ministered by us, *w* .... 2 Cor 3:3
for it is *w*, "Cursed is .... Gal 3:10
because it is *w*, "Be holy ... 1 Pet 1:16
the stone a new name *w* .... Rev 2:17
names have not been *w* ..... Rev 13:8
name *w* on their foreheads . Rev 14:1
forehead a name was *w* .... Rev 17:5
the plagues that are *w* ...... Rev 22:18

WRONG
sinned, we have done *w* ... 2 Chr 6:37
sin nor charge God with *w* .. Job 1:22
I cry out concerning *w* ...... Job 19:7
not charge them with *w* .... Job 24:12
no one to do them *w* ...... Ps 105:14
Do no *w* and do no .... Jer 22:3
I am doing you no *w* ...... Matt 20:13
has done nothing *w* ...... Luke 23:41
of them suffer *w* .... Acts 7:24
Jews I have done no *w* .... Acts 25:10
Forgive me this *w* .... 2 Cor 12:13
But he who does *w* .... Col 3:25

WRONGDOING
say if they found any *w* ... Acts 24:20

WRONGED
give it to the one he has *w* .. Num 5:7
have seen how I am *w* ..... Lam 3:59
then that God has *w* .... Job 19:6
We have *w* no one .... 2 Cor 7:2
But if he has *w* .... Philem 18

WRONGFULLY
hate me *w* have multiplied .. Ps 38:19
endures grief, suffering *w* .. 1 Pet 2:19

WRONGS
me *w* his own soul .... Prov 8:36

WROTE
w on the tablets the words .. Ex 34:28
of the hand that *w* .... Dan 5:5
stooped down and *w* .... John 8:6

WROUGHT
And skillfully *w* .... Ps 139:15

YEAR
first month of the *y* .... Ex 12:2
That fiftieth *y* shall be a .... Lev 25:11
In this *Y* of Jubilee, each ... Lev 25:13
we eat in the seventh *y* .... Lev 25:20
In the *Y* of Jubilee .... Lev 27:24
crown the *y* with Your .... Ps 65:11
the acceptable *y* .... Is 61:2
be his until the *y* .... Ezek 46:17
to Jerusalem every *y* ...... Luke 2:41
went alone once a *y* .... Heb 9:7
of sins every *y* .... Heb 10:3

YEARS
and for days and *y* .... Gen 1:14
Are Your *y* like the .... Job 10:5
y should teach .... Job 32:7
I will remember the *y* .... Ps 77:10
For a thousand *y* .... Ps 90:4
lives are seventy *y* .... Ps 90:10
Your *y* are throughout ..... Ps 102:24
y will have no end .... Ps 102:27
when He was twelve *y* ..... Luke 2:42
are not yet fifty *y* .... John 8:57
y will not fail .... Heb 1:12
for a thousand *y* .... Rev 20:2
with Him a thousand *y* ...... Rev 20:6

YES
let your '*Y*' be '*Y*,' .... Matt 5:37
No, but in Him was *Y* ..... 2 Cor 1:19

YESTERDAY
For we were born *y* .... Job 8:9
Are like *y* when it is past ..... Ps 90:4
Jesus Christ is the same *y* ... Heb 13:8

YIELD
the land will *y* its fruit ...... Lev 25:19
y yourselves to the LORD .. 2 Chr 30:8
That they may *y* a fruitful .. Ps 107:37
shall *y* her increase .... Ezek 34:27
But do not *y* to them ...... Acts 23:21
gentle, willing to *y*, full ... James 3:17

YIELDED
y to intense craving .... Num 11:4
y their bodies, that they .... Dan 3:28
good ground and *y* a crop .. Matt 13:8
voice, *y* up His spirit ...... Matt 27:50
rich man *y* plentifully .... Luke 12:16

YIELDS
the herb that *y* seed .... Gen 1:11
of the righteous *y* fruit .... Prov 12:12
it *y* the peaceable .... Heb 12:11

YOKE
you shall break his *y* .... Gen 27:40
and He will put a *y* .... Deut 28:48
Your father made our *y* .... 1 Kin 12:4
You have broken the *y* .... Is 9:4
a man to bear the *y* .... Lam 3:27
Take My *y* upon you ..... Matt 11:29
as are under the *y* .... 1 Tim 6:1

YOKED
Do not be unequally *y* ..... 2 Cor 6:14

YOU ARE THE CHRIST
answered and said, "*Y* .... Matt 16:16
God: Tell us if *Y* .... Matt 26:63
and said to Him, "*Y* ...... Mark 8:29
crying out and saying, "*Y* .. Luke 4:41
If *Y*, tell us .... Luke 22:67
"If *Y*, save Yourself ...... Luke 23:39
believe and know that *Y* ... John 6:69
If *Y*, tell us plainly .... John 10:24
Lord I believe that *Y* ..... John 11:27

YOUNG
His flesh shall be *y* .... Job 33:25
I have been *y* .... Ps 37:25
she may lay her *y* .... Ps 84:3
How can a *y* man cleanse ... Ps 119:9
The glory of *y* men is ..... Prov 20:29
y ones shall lie .... Is 11:7
dream dreams, your *y* ...... Joel 2:28
y man followed Him ..... Mark 14:51
they admonish the *y* .... Titus 2:4
I write to you, *y* .... 1 John 2:13

YOUNGER
they mock at me, men *y* .... Job 30:1
y son gathered all .... Luke 15:13
let him be as the *y* .... Luke 22:26
y women as sisters .... 1 Tim 5:2
Likewise you *y* people ...... 1 Pet 5:5

YOURS
all that I have are *y* .... 1 Kin 20:4
the battle is not *y* .... 2 Chr 20:15
I am *Y*, save me .... Ps 119:94
Y is the kingdom .... Matt 6:13
Take what is *y* .... Matt 20:14
y is the kingdom .... Luke 6:20
And all Mine are *Y* .... John 17:10
For all things are *y* .... 1 Cor 3:21
for I do not seek *y* .... 2 Cor 12:14

YOUTH
for he was only a *y* . . . . . . 1 Sam 17:42
the LORD from my *y* . . . . . . 1 Kin 18:12
the sins of my *y* . . . . Ps 25:7
the companion of her *y* . . . . Prov 2:17
with the wife of your *y* . . . . . Prov 5:18
in the days of your *y* . . . . Eccl 11:9
and *y* are vanity . . . . Eccl 11:10
in the days of your *y* . . . . Eccl 12:1
the shame of your *y* . . . . Is 54:4
speak, for I am a *y* . . . . Jer 1:6
Do not say, 'I am a *y*,' for . . . . . Jer 1:7
the kindness of your *y* . . . . Jer 2:2
the days of your *y* . . . . Ezek 16:22
with the wife of his *y* . . . . Mal 2:15
I have kept from my *y* . . . . Matt 19:20
I have kept from my *y* . . . . Mark 10:20
I have kept from my *y* . . . . Luke 18:21
the flower of her *y* . . . . 1 Cor 7:36
no one despise your *y* . . . . . 1 Tim 4:12

YOUTHFUL
Flee also *y* lusts . . . . 2 Tim 2:22

YOUTHS
perceived among the *y* . . . . . . Prov 7:7
y shall faint and be . . . . Is 40:30

ZACCHAEUS
Wealthy tax collector converted to Christ, Luke 19:1–10

ZACHARIAS
Father of John the Baptist, Luke 1:5–17

ZADOK
Co-priest with Abiathar; remains loyal to David, 2 Sam 15:24–29; 20:25
Rebuked by David, 2 Sam 19:11, 12
Does not follow Adonijah; anoints Solomon, 1 Kin 1:8–45
Takes Abiathar's place, 1 Kin 2:35

ZALMUNNA
Midianite king, Judg 8:4–21

ZAREPHATH
Town of Sidon where Elijah revives widow's son, 1 Kin 17:8–24; Luke 4:26

ZEAL
The *z* of the LORD of . . . . . 2 Kin 19:31
z has consumed me . . . . Ps 119:139
He shall stir up His *z* . . . . Is 42:13
have spoken it in My *z* . . . . Ezek 5:13
for Zion with great *z* . . . . . . Zech 8:2
"*Z* for Your house has . . . . . John 2:17
that they have a *z* . . . . Rom 10:2
z has stirred up the . . . . 2 Cor 9:2

ZEALOUS
he was *z* for his God . . . . . Num 25:13
"I have been very *z* . . . . . . 1 Kin 19:10
'I am *z* for Zion with . . . . Zech 8:2
they are all *z* for the law . . Acts 21:20
since you are *z* . . . . 1 Cor 14:12
But it is good to be *z* . . . . Gal 4:18
z for good works . . . . Titus 2:14
Therefore be *z* and repent . . Rev 3:19

ZEBAH
King of Midian killed by Gideon, Judg 8:4–28

ZEBEDEE
Galilean fisherman; father of James and John, Matt 4:21, 22

ZEBULUN
Sixth son of Jacob and Leah, Gen 30:19, 20
Prophecy concerning, Gen 49:13
——— Tribe of:
Numbered, Num 1:30, 31; 26:27
Territory assigned to, Josh 19:10–16
Joins Gideon in battle, Judg 6:34, 35
Some respond to Hezekiah's reforms, 2 Chr 30:10–18
Christ visits territory of, Matt 4:13–16

ZECHARIAH
King of Israel; last ruler of Jehu's dynasty, 2 Kin 15:8–12
——— Postexilic prophet and priest, Ezra 5:1; Zech 1:1, 7

ZEDEKIAH
Last king of Judah; uncle and successor of Jehoiachin; reigns wickedly, 2 Kin 24:17–19; 2 Chr 36:10
Rebels against Nebuchadnezzar, 2 Chr 36:11–13
Denounced by Jeremiah, Jer 34:1–22
Consults Jeremiah, Jer 37; 38
Captured and taken to Babylon, 2 Kin 25:1–7; Jer 39:1–7

ZELOPHEHAD
Manassite whose five daughters secure female rights, Num 27:1–7

ZEPHANIAH
Author of Zephaniah, Zeph 1:1
——— Priest and friend of Jeremiah during Zedekiah's reign, Jer 21:1

ZERUBBABEL
Descendant of David, 1 Chr 3:1–19
Leader of Jewish exiles, Neh 7:6, 7; Hag 2:21–23
Rebuilds the temple, Ezra 3:1–10; Zech 4:1–14

ZIBA
Saul's servant, 2 Sam 9:9
Befriends David, 2 Sam 16:1–4
Accused of deception by Mephibosheth, 2 Sam 19:17–30

ZIKLAG
City on the border of Judah, Josh 15:1, 31
Held by David, 1 Sam 27:6
Overthrown by Amalekites, 1 Sam 30:1–31

ZILPAH
Leah's maid, Gen 29:24
Mother of Gad and Asher, Gen 30:9–13

ZIMRI
Simeonite prince slain by Phinehas, Num 25:6–14
——— King of Israel for seven days, 1 Kin 16:8–20

ZIN
Wilderness through which the Israelites passed, Num 20:1
Border between Judah and Edom, Josh 15:1–3

ZION
Literally, an area in Jerusalem; called the City of David, 2 Sam 5:6–9; 2 Chr 5:2
Used figuratively of God's kingdom, Ps 125:1; Heb 12:22; Rev 14:1
City of David, which is *Z* . . . 1 Kin 8:1
City of David, which is *Z* . . . 2 Chr 5:2
the LORD, who dwells in *Z* . . . . Ps 9:11
Is Mount *Z* on the sides of . . . . Ps 48:2
in Your good pleasure to *Z* . . Ps 51:18
God will save *Z* and build . . . Ps 69:35
And of *Z* it will be said . . . . Ps 87:5
the LORD shall build up *Z* . . Ps 102:16
the name of the LORD in *Z* . . Ps 102:21
back the captivity of *Z* . . . . . . Ps 126:1
the LORD has chosen *Z* . . . . . Ps 132:13
when we remembered *Z* . . . . . Ps 137:1
Z shall be redeemed with . . . . . Is 1:27
For out of *Z* shall go forth . . . . . Is 2:3
My people, who dwell in *Z* . . . Is 10:24
shout, O Inhabitant of *Z* . . . . . . Is 12:6
hosts will reign on Mount *Z* . . Is 24:23
I lay in *Z* a stone for a . . . . Is 28:16
down to fight for Mount *Z* . . . . Is 31:4
come to *Z* with singing . . . . . . Is 35:10
virgin, the daughter of *Z* . . . . . Is 37:22
I will place salvation in *Z* . . . . Is 46:13
the LORD will comfort *Z* . . . . Is 51:3
come to *Z* with singing . . . . . . Is 51:11
Redeemer will come to *Z* . . . . Is 59:20
Z of the Holy One of Israel . . Is 60:14
Arise, and let us go up to *Z* . . Jer 31:6
to be forgotten in *Z* . . . . Lam 2:6
Blow the trumpet in *Z* . . . . Joel 2:1
for the LORD dwells in *Z* . . . . Joel 3:21
on Mount *Z* there shall be . . . Obad 17
For out of *Z* the law shall . . . . Mic 4:2
Sing, O daughter of *Z* . . . . . Zeph 3:14
LORD will gain comfort *Z* . . Zech 1:17
rejoice, O daughter of *Z* . . . . Zech 2:10
Fear not, daughter of *Z* . . . John 12:15
in *Z* a stumbling stone . . . . . Rom 9:33
will come out of *Z* . . . . Rom 11:26
Behold, I lay in *Z* a chief . . . . 1 Pet 2:6

ZIPPORAH
Daughter of Jethro; wife of Moses, Ex 18:1, 2

ZOAR
Ancient city of Canaan originally named Bela, Gen 14:2, 8
Spared destruction at Lot's request, Gen 19:20–23

ZOPHAR
Naamathite; friend of Job, Job 2:11

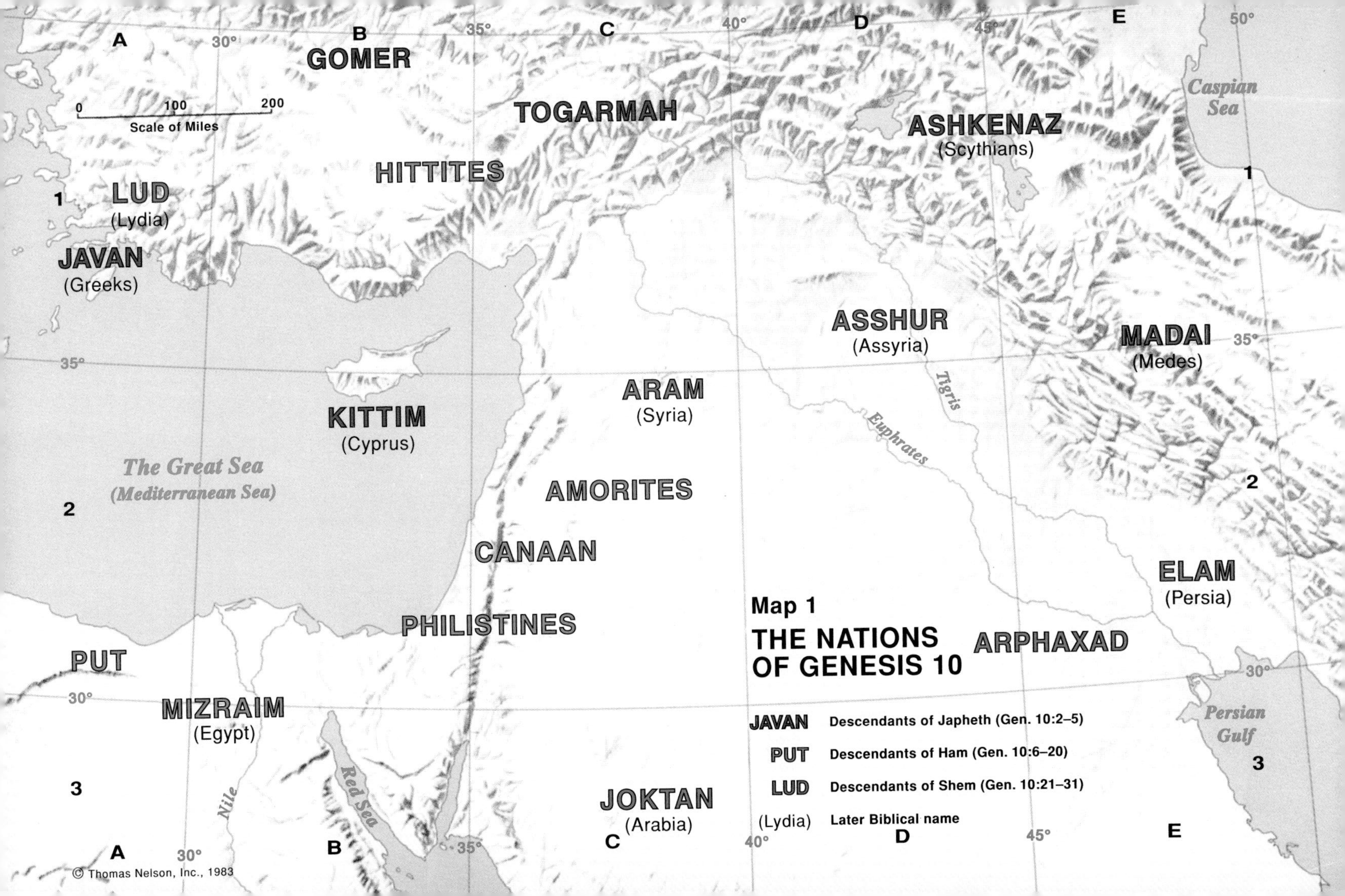
Map 1
THE NATIONS OF GENESIS 10
JAVAN Descendants of Japheth (Gen. 10:2–5)
PUT Descendants of Ham (Gen. 10:6–20)
LUD Descendants of Shem (Gen. 10:21–31)
(Lydia) Later Biblical name
GOMER
TOGARMAH
ASHKENAZ
(Scythians)
HITTITES
LUD
(Lydia)
JAVAN
(Greeks)
ASSHUR
(Assyria)
MADAI
(Medes)
ARAM
(Syria)
KITTIM
(Cyprus)
AMORITES
CANAAN
PHILISTINES
ELAM
(Persia)
ARPHAXAD
PUT
MIZRAIM
(Egypt)
JOKTAN
(Arabia)
The Great Sea
(Mediterranean Sea)
Caspian Sea
Persian Gulf
Red Sea
Nile
Tigris
Euphrates
0 100 200
Scale of Miles
© Thomas Nelson, Inc., 1983

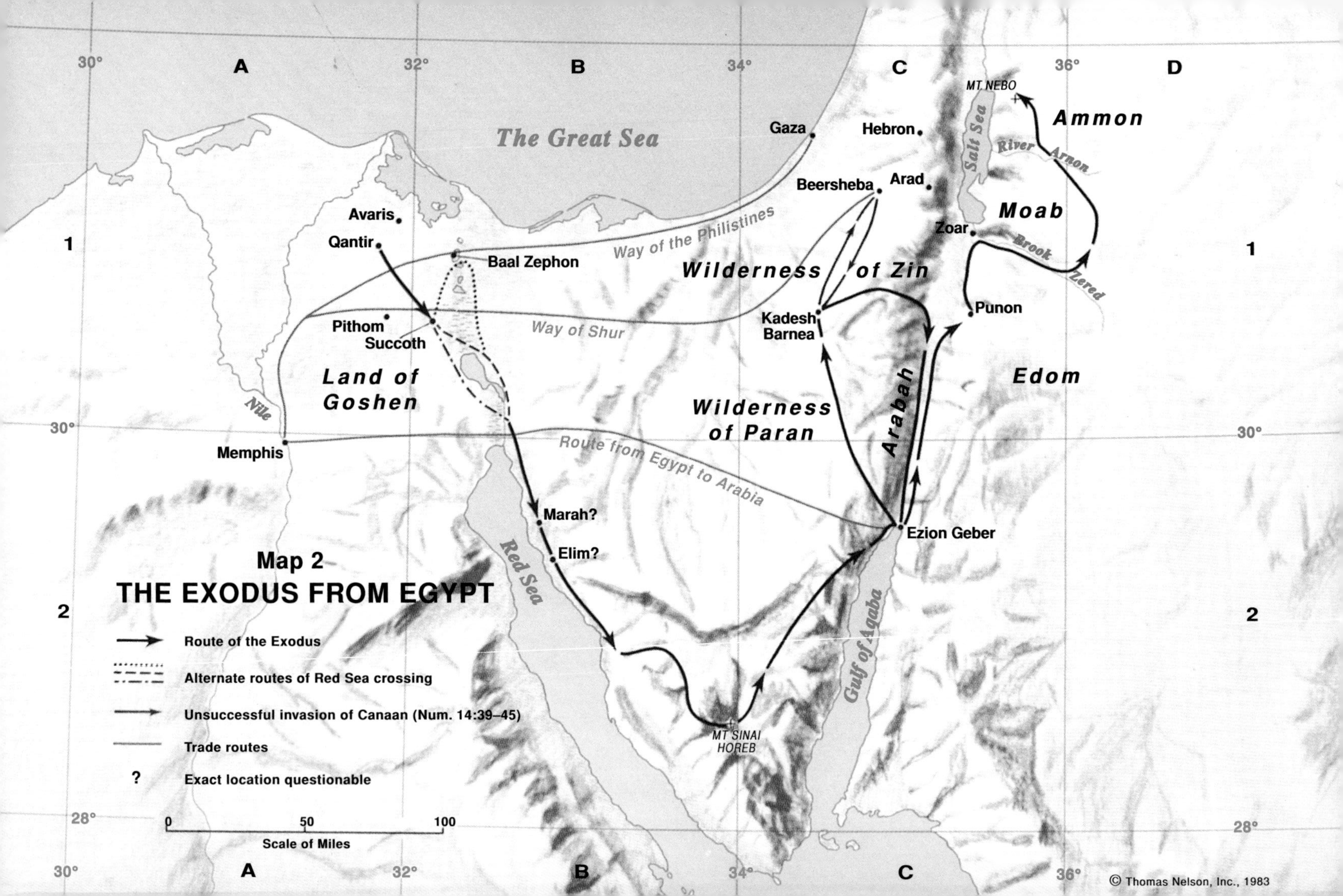
Map 2
THE EXODUS FROM EGYPT
Route of the Exodus
Alternate routes of Red Sea crossing
Unsuccessful invasion of Canaan (Num. 14:39–45)
Trade routes
? Exact location questionable
0 50 100
Scale of Miles
The Great Sea
Gaza
Hebron
Beersheba
Arad
Avaris
Qantir
Baal Zephon
Way of the Philistines
Wilderness of Zin
Pithom
Succoth
Way of Shur
Kadesh Barnea
Land of Goshen
Nile
Memphis
Route from Egypt to Arabia
Wilderness of Paran
Arabah
Marah?
Elim?
Red Sea
MT SINAI HOREB
Gulf of Aqaba
Ezion Geber
MT. NEBO
Salt Sea
Ammon
River Arnon
Moab
Zoar
Brook Zered
Punon
Edom
A B C D
1 2
30° 32° 34° 36° 28°

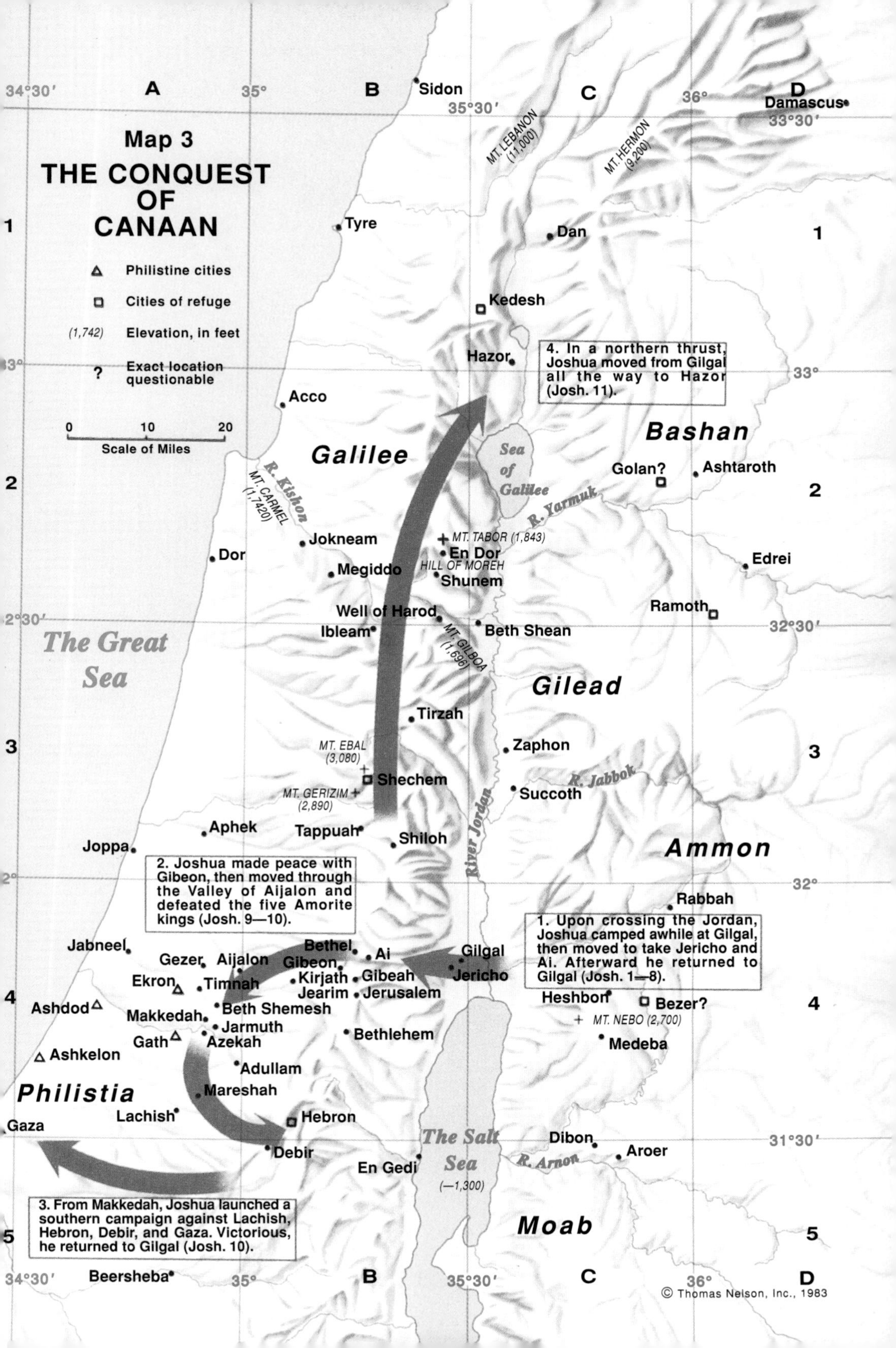
Map 3
THE CONQUEST OF CANAAN
Philistine cities
Cities of refuge
(1,742) Elevation, in feet
? Exact location questionable
0 10 20
Scale of Miles
A
B
C
D
1
2
3
4
5
34°30′
35°
35°30′
36°
33°30′
33°
32°30′
32°
31°30′
Sidon
Damascus
MT. LEBANON (11,000)
MT. HERMON (9,200)
Tyre
Dan
Kedesh
Hazor
4. In a northern thrust, Joshua moved from Gilgal all the way to Hazor (Josh. 11).
Acco
Galilee
Sea of Galilee
Bashan
Golan?
Ashtaroth
R. Kishon
MT. CARMEL (1,7420)
R. Yarmuk
MT. TABOR (1,843)
Jokneam
En Dor
HILL OF MOREH
Dor
Megiddo
Shunem
Edrei
Well of Harod
Ramoth
Ibleam
MT. GILBOA (1,696)
Beth Shean
The Great Sea
Gilead
Tirzah
MT. EBAL (3,080)
Zaphon
Shechem
R. Jabbok
MT. GERIZIM (2,890)
Succoth
River Jordan
Aphek
Tappuah
Shiloh
Joppa
Ammon
2. Joshua made peace with Gibeon, then moved through the Valley of Aijalon and defeated the five Amorite kings (Josh. 9—10).
Rabbah
1. Upon crossing the Jordan, Joshua camped awhile at Gilgal, then moved to take Jericho and Ai. Afterward he returned to Gilgal (Josh. 1—8).
Jabneel
Bethel
Ai
Gilgal
Gezer
Aijalon
Gibeon
Kirjath Jearim
Gibeah
Jericho
Ekron
Timnah
Jerusalem
Heshbon
Bezer?
Ashdod
Beth Shemesh
Makkedah
Jarmuth
MT. NEBO (2,700)
Gath
Azekah
Bethlehem
Medeba
Ashkelon
Adullam
Philistia
Mareshah
Lachish
Hebron
Gaza
The Salt Sea
(—1,300)
Dibon
Debir
En Gedi
R. Arnon
Aroer
3. From Makkedah, Joshua launched a southern campaign against Lachish, Hebron, Debir, and Gaza. Victorious, he returned to Gilgal (Josh. 10).
Moab
Beersheba

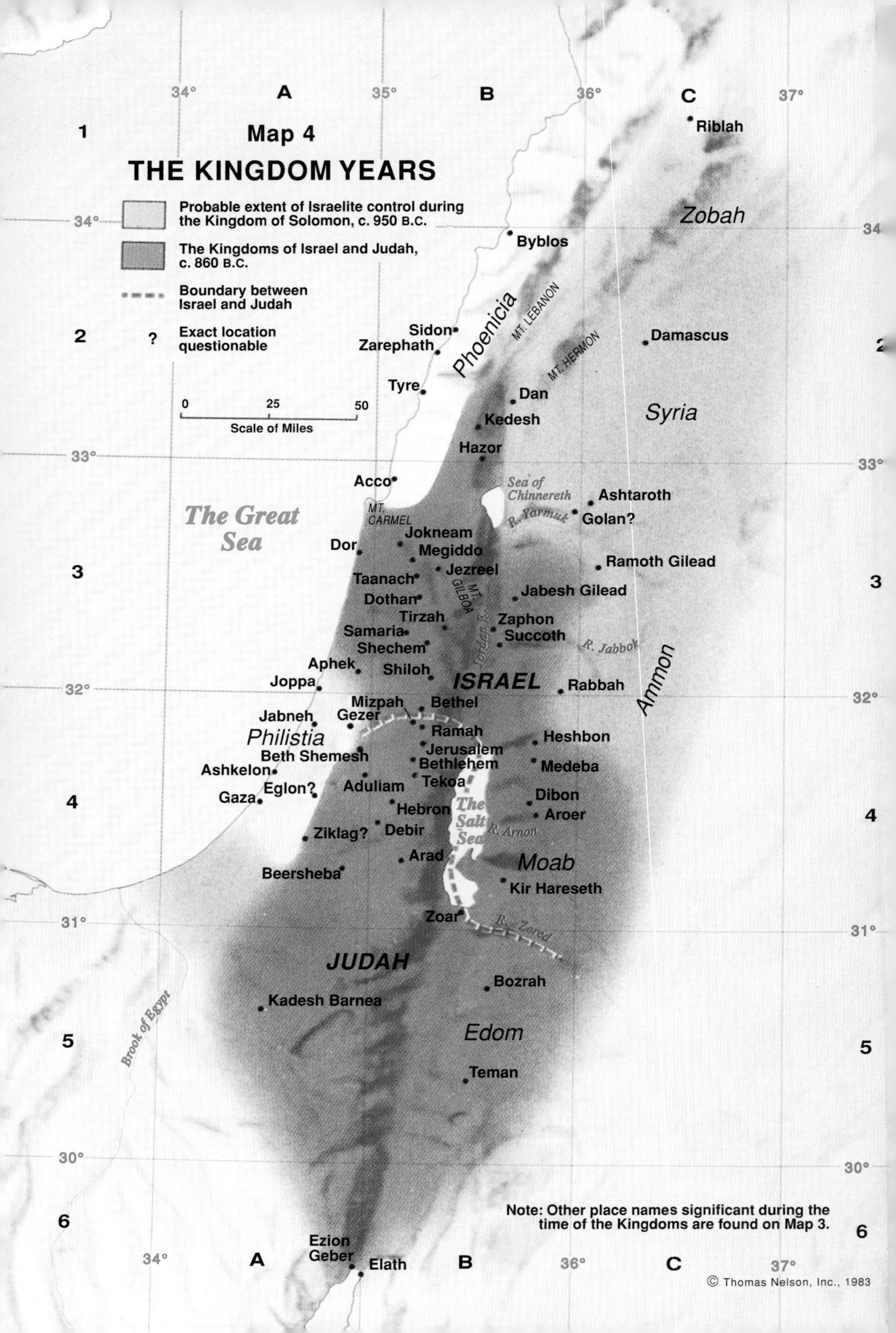
Map 4
THE KINGDOM YEARS
Probable extent of Israelite control during the Kingdom of Solomon, c. 950 B.C.
The Kingdoms of Israel and Judah, c. 860 B.C.
Boundary between Israel and Judah
? Exact location questionable
0 25 50
Scale of Miles
A B C
34° 35° 36° 37°
1 2 3 4 5 6
33° 32° 31° 30°
Riblah
Zobah
Byblos
Phoenicia
MT. LEBANON
MT. HERMON
Sidon
Zarephath
Damascus
Tyre
Dan
Kedesh
Syria
Hazor
Acco
Sea of Chinnereth
Ashtaroth
MT. CARMEL
R. Yarmuk
Golan?
The Great Sea
Jokneam
Dor
Megiddo
Ramoth Gilead
Jezreel
Taanach
MT. GILBOA
Jabesh Gilead
Dothan
Tirzah
Zaphon
Samaria
Jordan R.
Succoth
Shechem
R. Jabbok
Aphek
Shiloh
Ammon
Joppa
ISRAEL
Rabbah
Mizpah
Bethel
Jabneh
Gezer
Ramah
Philistia
Heshbon
Jerusalem
Beth Shemesh
Bethlehem
Medeba
Ashkelon
Tekoa
Eglon?
Aduliam
Dibon
Gaza
Hebron
The Salt Sea
Aroer
R. Arnon
Ziklag?
Debir
Arad
Moab
Beersheba
Kir Hareseth
Zoar
R. Zered
JUDAH
Bozrah
Kadesh Barnea
Edom
Brook of Egypt
Teman
Note: Other place names significant during the time of the Kingdoms are found on Map 3.
Ezion Geber
Elath
© Thomas Nelson, Inc., 1983

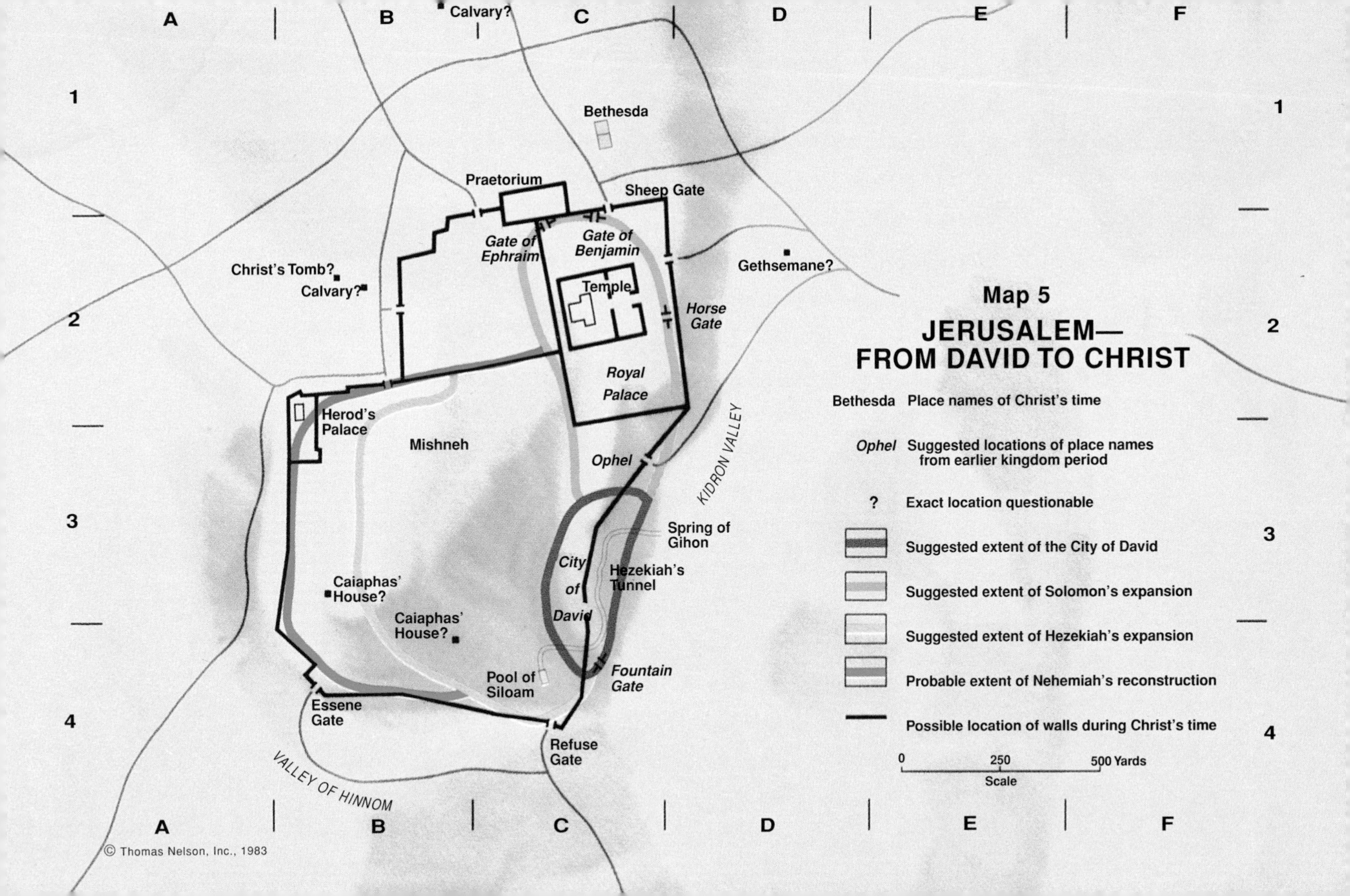
Map 5
JERUSALEM—
FROM DAVID TO CHRIST
Bethesda Place names of Christ's time
Ophel Suggested locations of place names from earlier kingdom period
? Exact location questionable
Suggested extent of the City of David
Suggested extent of Solomon's expansion
Suggested extent of Hezekiah's expansion
Probable extent of Nehemiah's reconstruction
Possible location of walls during Christ's time
0
250
500 Yards
Scale
A
B
C
D
E
F
1
2
3
4
Calvary?
Bethesda
Praetorium
Sheep Gate
Gate of Ephraim
Gate of Benjamin
Gethsemane?
Christ's Tomb?
Calvary?
Temple
Horse Gate
Royal Palace
Herod's Palace
Mishneh
Ophel
KIDRON VALLEY
Spring of Gihon
City of David
Hezekiah's Tunnel
Caiaphas' House?
Caiaphas' House?
Pool of Siloam
Fountain Gate
Essene Gate
Refuse Gate
VALLEY OF HINNOM

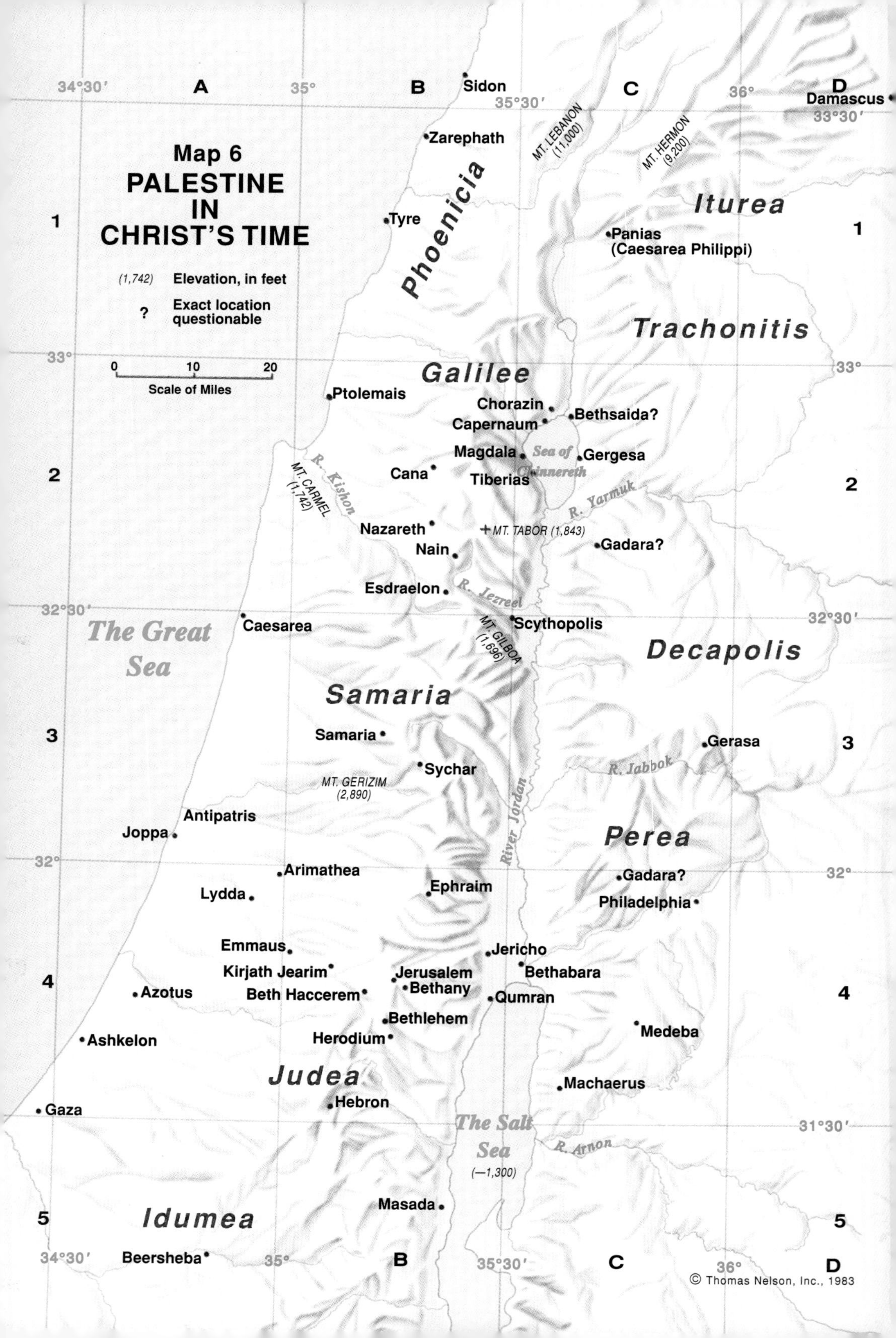
Map 6
PALESTINE IN CHRIST'S TIME
(1,742) Elevation, in feet
? Exact location questionable
0 10 20
Scale of Miles
A
B
C
D
1
2
3
4
5
34°30′
35°
35°30′
36°
33°30′
33°
32°30′
32°
31°30′
Sidon
Damascus
Zarephath
MT. LEBANON (11,000)
MT. HERMON (9,200)
Phoenicia
Tyre
Iturea
Panias (Caesarea Philippi)
Trachonitis
Galilee
Ptolemais
Chorazin
Bethsaida?
Capernaum
Magdala
Sea of Chinnereth
Gergesa
Cana
Tiberias
R. Kishon
MT. CARMEL (1,742)
R. Yarmuk
Nazareth
MT. TABOR (1,843)
Gadara?
Nain
Esdraelon
R. Jezreel
The Great Sea
Caesarea
Scythopolis
MT. GILBOA (1,696)
Decapolis
Samaria
Samaria
Gerasa
Sychar
R. Jabbok
MT. GERIZIM (2,890)
River Jordan
Antipatris
Joppa
Perea
Arimathea
Gadara?
Lydda
Ephraim
Philadelphia
Emmaus
Jericho
Kirjath Jearim
Jerusalem
Bethabara
Bethany
Azotus
Beth Haccerem
Qumran
Bethlehem
Medeba
Ashkelon
Herodium
Judea
Machaerus
Hebron
Gaza
The Salt Sea
(—1,300)
R. Arnon
Masada
Idumea
Beersheba
© Thomas Nelson, Inc., 1983

Map 7

PAUL'S FIRST AND SECOND JOURNEYS
(Acts 13–14; 15:39–18:22)

First missionary journey, with Barnabas and Mark (c. A.D. 46–48)

Second missionary journey, with Silas (c. A.D. 49–52)

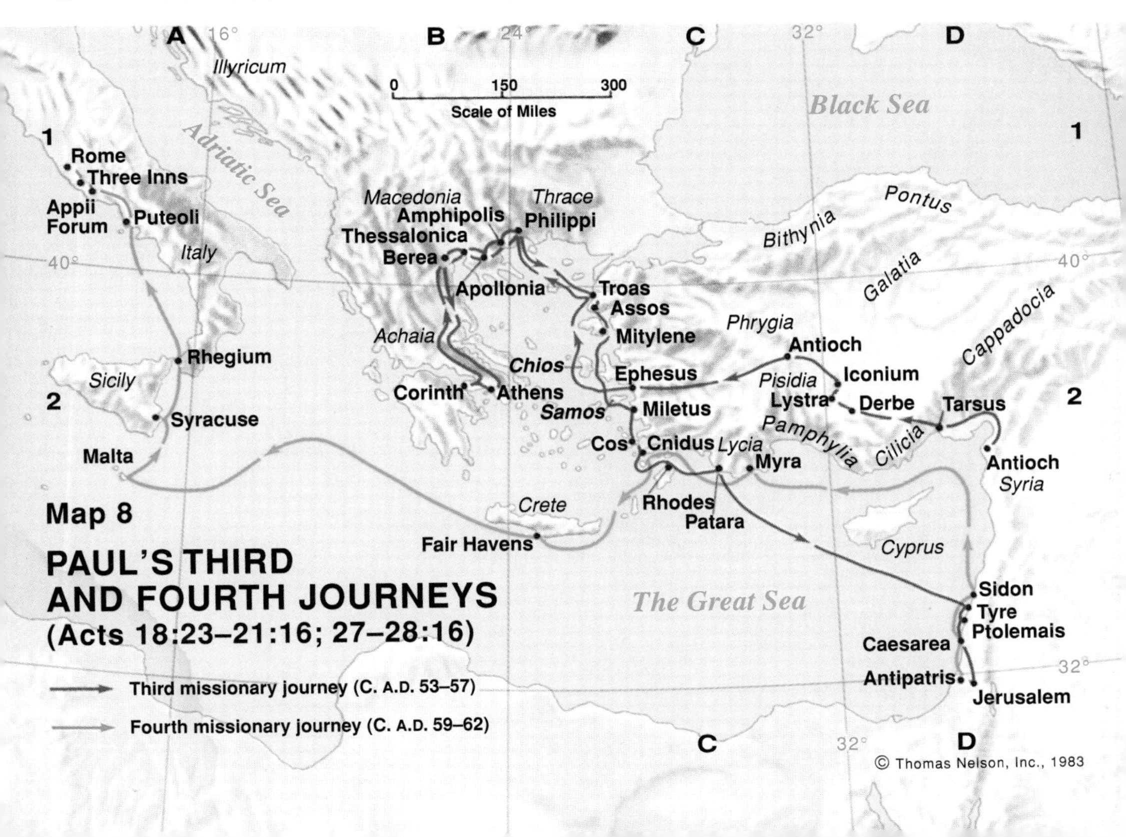

Map 8

PAUL'S THIRD AND FOURTH JOURNEYS
(Acts 18:23–21:16; 27–28:16)

Third missionary journey (C. A.D. 53–57)

Fourth missionary journey (C. A.D. 59–62)

Map 9
THE HOLY LAND
IN MODERN TIMES
Area occupied by Israel since June, 1967
0 25 50
Scale of Miles
A
B
C
D
E
1
2
3
4
5
6
34°
35°
36°
37°
33°
32°
31°
30°
LEBANON
SYRIA
JORDAN
ISRAEL
EGYPT
Tripoli
Beirut
Sidon
Tyre
Damascus
BEKAA VALLEY
LEBANON MTS.
ANTI-LEBANON MTS.
Dan
Qiryat Shemona
U.N. Buffer Zone
1973 Line
Quneitra
1967 Cease-Fire Line
Golan Heights
Nahariyya
Akko
Haifa
Safad
Sea of Galilee
Tiberias
Nazareth
Afula
Dera
Ramtha
Mediterranean Sea
Beth Shean
Hadera
Netanya
Tulkarm
Nablus
Jarash
Herzliyya
Tel Aviv
Yafo
Petah Tiqwa
West Bank
Jordan River
Rishon le Zion
Lod
Ramla
Ramalah
Amman
Ashdod
Jericho
Jerusalem
Bethlehem
Madaba
Ashqelon
Gaza
Qiryat Gat
Hebron
Dead Sea
En Gedi
Dhiban
Beersheba
Al-Arish
Karak
Negev
Arabah
Sinai
Elat
Aqaba
© Thomas Nelson, Inc., 1983